ARCO

# THE RIGHT COLLEGE

## 7TH EDITION

*College Research Group of Concord, Massachusetts*

MACMILLAN
U.S.A.

Seventh Edition

Macmillan General Reference
A Prentice Hall/Macmillan Company
15 Columbus Circle
New York, NY 10023



Manufactured in the United States of America

ISBN 0-671-89030-1

10 9 8 7 6 5 4 3 2 1

# Contents

# Preface

Arco's *The Right College* was developed to help students, parents, and counselors arrive at the "right" choice of a college by furnishing them the "right" information with which to make their choice. Although there is a great deal of published information for college-bound students today, much of it is outdated, or not relevant for those needing accurate, timely, and complete answers to their questions regarding their choice of the "right" college.

Arco has selected College Research Group (CRG) to compile the information presented in this book. Since 1938, CRG and its predecessor, Educational Research Corporation, a nonprofit organization established by members of the faculty of Harvard University's Graduate School of Education, have been conducting research in the area of college admissions. For over fifty years, both groups have been supplying college data on an annual basis to major book publishers, computer software developers, industrial firms, and educational organizations.

CRG's database is the most complete and up-to-date information source on American colleges available today. All college data stored in CRG's computer system has been furnished by the colleges' admissions, financial aid, and athletic staffs and supplemented with information supplied by representative students.

The CRG data-gathering and analysis cycle is extensive and thorough. Each year every accredited four-year college in the U.S. receives a comprehensive questionnaire as soon as the college's programs and activities for the coming year are finalized, and in the spring of each year, tuition update forms are sent to every college for reporting of tuition, room, board, and fees for the coming fall semester as soon as they are established; colleges that do not respond by mail are telephoned by an editor before *The Right College* goes to press. All data is then checked by CRG's research and editorial staff and entered in CRG's state-of-the-art computer database.

Once the database updating has been completed, the data is sorted, analyzed, and transferred to a computer publishing system that quickly generates the completed book in a form ready for printing. With this advanced publishing system, it is possible to provide finished books to college-bound students within weeks of the receipt of data from the colleges, thus assuring students, parents, counselors, and librarians of having the very latest and most complete information available on four-year colleges.

It is due to the many advantages of CRG's electronic publishing system over conventional publishing procedures that Arco selected it to produce the college entries and indexes included in this book. The reader will quickly discover the value of this in-depth and relevant information in seeking out the "right" college for his or her education.

We are grateful for the diligent efforts of editors Amanda Hawxhurst, Mary Goodhue Lynch, Ellen Randall, Hillary Foote Schwartz, Cynthia Talbot, and Susan Weddle and of database applications developer and systems administrator Don Beattie.

Allan B. Corderman
*Publisher*

Patrick Files
*Project Editor*

College Research Group
A Division of Wintergreen/Orchard House, Inc.
P.O. Box 15899, New Orleans, LA 70175-5899
(504) 866-8658

# Choosing and Applying to College

*by Karen Clagett, College Guidance Counselor, Winnacut High School, Hampton, New Hampshire*

## Selecting a College

"How can I possibly choose?" you probably ask despairingly when you realize that there are over 1,500 four-year colleges and universities in the U.S., each with its own individual character. Yet your counselor has told you by the fall of your senior year that you will need a list of between one and six colleges to which you will apply.

"How can I make such a list?" First, it helps to remember that high school students tackle this challenge every year, that many people experienced in college admissions stand ready to help you, and that most students are successful in gaining admission to their favorite college and are very happy with the choices they do make. Even many of the top-ranked, selective colleges admit 40 percent or more of those who apply. Second, remember that every seemingly complicated process can be broken down into smaller steps you can take on one at a time—that's what this section is all about. It will show you what to do and when, and tell you why you should do it.

The most important piece of advice: *No one college is the only one for you.* Think of what you want from "ideal" colleges; don't have one or two real institutions in mind. You have to be open to the exploration of lots of possibilities and you have to be willing to make compromises and set priorities. Please remember that what is an excellent choice for you may be a poor choice for your closest friend, or may have been a poor choice for a parent or older sibling. You've got to begin by considering yourself.

By all means, listen to what people have to say about colleges and collect information on colleges throughout high school. Early groundwork avoids later panic. But, before you can make a good match between you and one of those schools, you must consider what kind of person you are and what you would like to be and do in the future. *Throughout this whole process, it is essential to be honest with yourself and others.*

To ponder in all those spare moments between science tests and basketball games:

1. *What do I like to do? What am I good at?*

Do you like to work with people, ideas, machines, your hands, facts and figures? Do you want to be involved with the arts? business? law? medicine? selling? What do you like best in school? least? Why? What do you do best at school? Why? Do you enjoy being out-of-doors? What extracurricular interests do you wish to continue? to begin? What frustrates you? worries you? What do you look forward to?

2. *What are the strengths and weaknesses of my character and personality and how might they affect my choices?*

Are you organized, impulsive, aggressive, reserved, a leader, a follower? Are you a self-starter or do you need structure? Are you comfortable with new people and tasks or do you enjoy routine? Are you a perfectionist? Do you need some control over your environment?

3. *Why do I want to go to college? What might be alternatives?*

Do you want to go to college because you want to learn to think critically and to analyze, to gain cultural perspective and historical information, to get a good job (personally satisfying, well-paying or both), to have fun, to meet new people and make contacts, to participate in extracurricular activities, to please your parents, to do what everybody else is doing?

4. *What kind of environment do I wish to live in for the next few years?*

Are you comfortable in a small or large area? Do you think that students should be culturally, religiously, and economically homogenous? heterogeneous? Do you want to be near a city? in the country? near home? far away?

5. *What are my goals? And (realistically) what careers will be best suited to them?*

6. *How will I be seen by colleges?* What is your grade point average, class rank? What positions of leadership have you held? What long-term interests have you maintained?

How highly do you value fame, fortune, creativity, intellectual challenge, security, helping others? How well do you know what kind of preparation leads to various careers? Which careers interest you now? How can you find out more about what careers mean in terms of lifestyle?

Answering these questions isn't easy. Your answers will change over the next few years and probably throughout your life. Many answers will involve a combination of ideas and reactions, but you might want to try to list your strengths and weaknesses and ask others to make a list for you and compare. Discuss these ideas with parents, teachers, peers. Think about the people you admire. Why do you respect them?

This self-assessment will help you decide such specific questions as whether you wish to attend a small, liberal arts college or a large, research-oriented university. You will need to match what you learn about yourself with what you discover about the environment of the institutions you consider attending. You might learn that you would benefit from a year off to study abroad or work before college. You might want to explore vocational schools or the military. Almost anything you might choose to do, from applying to college to filling out job applications, will require that you present yourself, and to do that you have to have a sense of who you are. The grappling you do with these admittedly difficult questions will help you in such specific tasks as interviewing and essay writing where a good knowledge of yourself is invaluable.

Of course, you know that you can't spend your four years of high school solely on philosophical considerations. What else should you do to prepare for application to college? Other things you need to do—and the earlier in high school you start the better—fall into two areas. One specifically concerns research on colleges and universities, taking standardized tests, and writing applications; the other is what you can do as a student to enlarge your options by becoming the strongest possible candidate.

Let's take the second first. What can you do *right now* to make yourself a better applicant and your application a successful one?

1. *Make certain that your high school courses are challenging and appropriate.*

Sample a variety of courses, but be sure that reading and writing courses are an important part of your curriculum. Colleges know that success in further education requires good skills in these areas. And, don't forget math. Lots of career possibilities depend on confidence and ability in mathematics. Remember you will need to show to admissions officers that you are willing to take academic chances and to stretch your mind. A "B" grade in a demanding honors course, if you have been working hard, is better than an "A" in a less challenging class. If your interest and talent lie in one area—say the sciences or foreign languages—take additional courses. Work for a balanced program, however, that involves you in most disciplines. Be sure to follow through; don't stop a sequence of courses in a discipline you may later continue. Be aware, too, that colleges have minimum requirements. Your counselor and college catalogues can help you discover what they are. When you do well in a course for which there is an SAT II test or an advanced placement examination, arrange to take that test as near as possible to completion of the course. Check with your college counselor for the best date and to learn what tests and examinations are available to you.

2. *Keep your best work—whether done in or out of the classroom.*

Fantastic photographs, scorching editorials, prize-winning flower collections should all be documented. Some college applications will offer you a chance to submit supplementary material that demonstrates your achievement, and almost all admissions interviewers will be happy to discuss areas of real interest to you. Some colleges are now even requiring you to submit an essay you have written for a high school course. Be prepared.

3. *Read.*

If you like reading—you're off to a great start. Try to expand areas of knowledge by consciously making the effort to read about ideas and subjects that are new to you. Stay in touch with current events through newspapers and magazines. Take out and read a 19th-century British novel or two; there is no better way of enlarging your vocabulary to prepare for the rigors of college reading or for the vocabulary sections of the SAT.

If you think you don't like to read, don't despair. Reading is habit-forming. You need only the discipline to set up a reading plan. Start small. Begin by reading for fifteen or twenty minutes *every day* something that really interests you. There are magazines for almost every hobby and talent. Whether it is fashion or sports, photography or romance that interests you, with a little effort you can find reading material. As soon as you feel that you've established a pattern of reading, move to new fields. Weekly news magazines offer a variety of articles, have good vocabulary, and allow you to improve your general knowledge while you work on reading skills.

4. *Establish good study habits now.*

If you find it is difficult to get homework done with Mom supervising and daily quizzes threatening, imagine how tough it will be when your only check on you is yourself and that one exam at the end of the semester. If you are not an organized person, begin to use lists and assignment books to get on top of things. Look ahead a week or more to prepare for tests and papers, keep neat and informative notebooks, and go to teachers for help before they come after you. *Ask questions.* You are responsible for your education. Asking good questions involves you in the class, makes it more interesting, helps you understand and remember what is going on, and impresses teachers favorably.

5. *Find time (somehow) for that one thing you do well or like best and pursue it.*

Colleges often have tons of "well-rounded" applicants, but someone who can play the French horn in the orchestra, direct a student performance, run for a touchdown, or organize campus events really adds to the college community—and admissions officers know it. Devotion to and achievement in one special activity demonstrate your self-discipline and your ability for sustained effort.

What is great about this list is that following it pays off twice. You'll get a better education *and* be a stronger applicant. Now, what do you need to do about that college list?

## A Plan for Selecting and Applying to College

### Freshman and sophomore years (and beyond)

1. *Begin by getting to know your teachers and counselors well.*

You needn't be teacher's pet or loiter around the Guidance Office, but, let's face it, teachers and counselors are busy people. You need to make the effort so that communication is easier, so you'll be able to ask for help easily. The better others know you, the more they can help you, and, it must be remembered, the more fully they can write about you on recommendation forms. Always ask questions about anything that confuses you in the process of applying to college and try to anticipate problems. For example, an important question would be "Can I take every subject test every time the tests are offered?" The answer is "No." If you want to take an achievement test in German or Hebrew or in a number of other subjects, you need to know on which of the testing dates it will be offered.

2. *Be a collector of all information about colleges.*

Talk with relatives, friends, alums of your school. Attend college nights and college fairs. Use football games or art shows or plays as an excuse to get on local campuses. Even if you want to attend college far away from home, a visit to a nearby campus can bring such issues as the best campus size, location, and curriculum offerings into perspective for you. Always keep in mind the source of your information; not everyone is objective or shares your concerns. Read newspaper and magazine articles on issues of higher education. Look at campus publications. Learn what resources your guidance office offers—computer software, catalogues, videos, viewbooks. Begin flipping through the pages on specific colleges and universities in this guide.

## Junior year

If you're reading this as a junior, you just have to work a little harder and more quickly. Don't neglect the suggestions made for the freshman and sophomore years.

1. *Make an appointment with your guidance counselor for your parents and you.*

You will want to discuss what you must do to improve your preparation for both college and college selection.

2. *Get a social security number.*

You'll need it to apply for college, financial aid, and jobs.

3. *Work conscientiously on your self-assessment.*

4. *List the college features you value.* Consider:

A. In what kind of *environment* are you comfortable, challenged?

- *Size* (small – under 2,500; medium – 2,500 to 8,000; large – 8,000 to 15,000; jumbo – over 15,000). Do you value individual attention or do you want a vast menu of course offerings? How important is it to you to know many of your fellow students? to have access to faculty? to have a sense of control over your environment? Do you enjoy working with vastly different kinds of people? Is it important to keep an almost family-like atmosphere in your dorm or do you long for autonomy?

- What about *location*? Is this your chance for the big city? Big cities mean excitement, lots of cultural and sports events, job opportunities. They also mean distractions from study and campus life (if indeed there is a campus), noise, and dirt. Do you long for green pastures? Rural environments make outing clubs, ski trips, agricultural study easier. It may also be a long drive to another college for a date. Does suburbia appeal to you? Does being just outside a big city offer the best of both urban and rural environments or not enough of either for you? How close do you want to be to home?

B. Do you want to attend a liberal arts college, a business college, a university, a college for the performing arts, etc.? Might a two-year college be a good match for you? (About half of all entering freshmen begin with this choice.) Have you chosen what you wish to study or do you need the more exploratory approach of liberal arts colleges? Does a core curriculum with course requirements make sense to you or do you want free choice of all classes?

C. Will you consider a *single-sex institution*? What are the advantages and disadvantages of such schools? Because not every student will consider a single-sex college and because about 50% of the student population is ineligible, you may find that you can be a successful applicant at a college with high selectivity. (You might wish to talk with alumni/ae here.)

D. What *sports and other extracurricular activities* do you want to find? At what competitive level are various sports played? Will you be able to compete successfully? Will you be so outstanding that your skills will help your admission's chances? What special programs (such as junior year abroad) are attractive? Do you wish to participate in co-op education where you work and study at the same time? Do internships in government or business interest you?

E. How important is *financial aid*? Are the colleges you are interested in "need-blind"? In other words, can they fund the students they want? How many students receive some kind of aid? Would you like to be involved in a Cooperative Education program that would allow you to work while you attend college? Do the institutions you are considering have such coop programs in your field of interest?

F. How *selective* a college do you want and are you qualified to attend? Be both frank and realistic with yourself here and encourage counselors, teachers, and admissions officers to be the same. Read "How Competitive Colleges Select From Among Applicants" to help you here. Make lists and take notes.

5. *Make a note of the tests you should take (PSAT [Preliminary SAT], SAT I, SAT II, ACT, etc.). Note when they will be given so family activities may be planned accordingly.*

Your counselor may have this information and registration details and deadlines already gathered together for you. Be certain to find out from teachers and counselors when it would be best for you to take specific achievement tests. Remember that if you are considering applying for Early Decision or Early Action, you will need to take tests early. Fill out the Student Descriptive Questionnaire on the SAT form so that you'll be able to receive information from colleges and so that searches by colleges interested in you will find you.

6. *Write away for college catalogues and viewbooks when you become interested in an institution.*

A simple postcard is fine. This is the time to ask for specifics on financial aid or on majors and programs that are of interest to you. Clear out a box or a drawer of your desk and buy file folders for it. Use a folder for each college and for special topics such as "Deadlines" or "Financial Aid."

7. *In the spring develop a preliminary list of colleges.*

Write or call for information from any that are new to your list. *Think about visiting colleges for viewing and interviewing in the summer*—especially if you are considering colleges that are far from home. Write ahead to schedule interviews—popular colleges become booked early. You won't have much time to spare next year and high schools frown on absences due to college visiting. Visit and interview during the summer between your junior and senior year even if you later decide not to apply.

8. *Consider participation in one of the many summer study programs and locate a summer job if you need to make money to help with college costs.*

Try to make the most of your summer through an interesting job, travel with an academic program, or summer study. This is a chance for you to do something that will distinguish you from the rest.

9. *If you think you may be an Early Decision or Early Action candidate, or if you are graduating early, you must have all required tests completed by the July following your junior year.*

10. *Know your grade point average and class rank.*

Try to get a realistic picture of yourself as a candidate. Have a good talk about this with your college counselor.

### Senior year

Let's assume you've followed the calendar to this point. (If not, you need to review the suggestions for earlier years and do some *quick* catching up.)

1. Remember that the first semester of your senior year is seen by many colleges as the most current and best indicator of the type of student you will be in college. You will be busy this semester, *but do not neglect your school work.*

2. In early fall, narrow your list of colleges to between five and ten. One way of narrowing your list is to think about applying to one college that is a "reach" for you in its selectivity but that offers what you really want, one or two colleges at which you have a 50-50 chance of acceptance, and one "safety." Remember that one way you can "stretch" your options is to consider institutions outside of your geographical area. You will be a more attractive candidate to institutions that are far away from your home because you will represent "diversity" to them. *You should be happy to attend every college to which you apply, including your "safety."* Your counselor can help here. Be sure you have application forms and all other materials for each. If you have not visited colleges on the list and it is at all possible to do so without missing too much school, call and make appointments. Call early.

3. Familiarize yourself with all applications and forms. Make a note of all important deadlines (for tests, registrations, applications, interviews, etc.).You will probably have to write at least one essay for each application. Jot down topics and begin to think about ideas. Separate school report forms and teacher recommendation forms from the pile of material you will keep. Give school report forms to your counselor when you have your final list. (Occasionally a university may ask for the whole application to be submitted together, and you will need to take your part to school to be sent with your transcript and recommendations.) Select those teachers who know you and your work best and for whom you have done well, and ask them to complete teacher recommendation forms. Supply teachers with a list of your interests, activities, and accomplishments. Give teachers addressed, stamped envelopes for recommendations. Keep track of who is writing where, and be sure to note deadlines on the recommendations. Send thank-you notes to teachers.

4. Keep track of which colleges will be sending representatives to your school and make arrangements to meet with those from institutions in which you are interested.

5. Through your own thoughts, and discussion with counselors, parents, and others, get your list into final form and begin filling out applications.

# How to Complete the Application Process

## Standardized Tests You Will Take

The words "SAT scores" loom large in the world of high school juniors and seniors. To a student, the idea of being compared with thousands of others, ranked and "quantified" is more than scary. The scores sometimes seem a measure of personal worth. Parents can do a great deal to alleviate the counterproductive anxiety that surrounds these tests by understanding this and by refraining from adding, however subtly, to the already considerable pressure.

It may help to know that while standardized tests are taken into account by most admissions offices, they can be low on the list of factors that determine admission. What they do is provide a measure of a student's ability and achievement, but that reading must be given greater dimension by a knowledge of the student's environment and school record. Usually tests are used in conjunction with a student's transcript to determine whether he is an overachiever (low scores, high grades—often good) or an underachiever (high scores, low grades—generally bad). An 800 score on a Math SAT I can be damning if you are receiving a D in mathematics. A 500 in the verbal SAT I coupled with a teacher recommendation that points to significant accomplishment and improvement, can demonstrate your motivation and grit. This does not mean that a student should not try to do his very best on the exam, for it should be obvious that the best combination is high scores *and* high grades!

You do need to know what tests you will take, when you will take them, and how to prepare for them.

Students are given standardized tests throughout their school careers, but the following tests are specifically related to the college admissions process. For all tests mentioned below, registration materials and sample test questions are available through high school counselors. The tests are listed in the order in which most students will take them.

1. *PSAT/NMSQT* (Preliminary SAT/National Merit Scholarship Qualifying Test). This test is given in October of each year. Some students take the test only as juniors. Other students take the test for practice as sophomores. The test functions as a trial run for the SAT I, and junior-year PSAT scores are used as qualification for National Merit Scholarships. Black and Hispanic students can use the test to qualify for other scholarships. The test

has verbal and mathematical sections and is largely multiple-choice. There are a few questions in the math section that require students to grid in their own answers. A score page that gives test results helps students interpret their scores and plan for the SAT I.

2. *SAT I:* If you are using this book well ahead of applying to college, you should be aware that the formats of both the PSAT and the SAT I have changed. The PSAT and SAT I are tests which measure verbal and mathematical reasoning. The tests are not greatly changed, but the differences are that there is more emphasis on reading comprehension, the reading passages are longer, and there are no antonym questions. Comparisons of several selected reading passages will also be required. The math sections of the tests will have a few questions that do not offer multiple-choice answers but instead require students to grid in their own answers. You should be sure to carefully read the PSAT and SAT information booklets that you receive when you register so that you are familiar with the format of the questions.

You will be given an opportunity to fill out the Student Descriptive Questionnaire when you take the SAT I. Completing this will ensure that you receive mail from colleges.

*The SAT I.* This is given a number of times throughout the year. Your counselor will let you know the dates it will be given at your school or in your area. Most students take the examination in late spring of their junior year and in autumn of their senior year. Some students also take the test early in the junior year for additional preparation. The SAT I is a two-and-one-half-hour, largely multiple-choice exam measuring verbal and mathematical reasoning abilities. Students have to grid in their own answers to a few of the questions in the math section. Vocabulary, verbal reasoning, and comprehension of reading material are tested in the English sections; arithmetic, elementary algebra, and geometry are covered in the math sections. The test is scored on a scale of 200 to 800, and a booklet useful in score interpretation accompanies the results.

*The ACT.* This test combines the ability orientation of the SAT with the accomplishment orientation of the achievement tests. The ACT measures educational development in English and mathematics. The ACT tests a student's ability to reason and solve problems. It is a multiple-choice examination, and scores are reported on a scale of 1 to 36, 36 being the highest.

3. *SAT II.* If you take the SAT I, you will probably have to take several SAT II subject tests. SAT II tests are given in many disciplines. Some achievement tests evaluate disciplines not generally taught in high schools, e.g., Hebrew. If you have a special area of academic achievement, check for an examination covering it. The tests are one-hour, multiple-choice exams that measure knowledge in such areas as English, foreign languages, the sciences, history, and mathematics. A new opportunity is an SAT II foreign language test given in the fall only. To determine which and how many tests to take, you should consult the catalogues of the colleges in which you are interested for their specific requirements. You should also check with your subject teachers especially in foreign languages and mathematics to be certain you are making the best decision. You will need, for example, to decide whether to take Mathematics Level One or Level Two and whether the number of years you have studied a foreign language makes the SAT II test in that discipline a good choice for you. Your guidance or college counselor can also help here. SAT II tests are given more than once a year, and your counselor can advise you as to the appropriate date. However, some tests on certain subject areas are given only *once* a year. Plan ahead. You may wish to take a test in one discipline twice for practice. Often a series of SAT II tests are taken twice. *If you complete a course for which there is an SAT II test—say biology in the 10th grade—you should arrange to take the test as near as possible to the date you completed the course.*

Scores for these tests are reported on the same 200 to 800 scale as the SAT I.

4. *AP* (Advanced Placement). The AP examinations given each year in May allow able students who do well on the tests to receive college credit and/or advanced standing for work done while in high school. The examinations are given in many fields, and a student's school does not have to have an established AP course for students to take the test. While the exams vary from discipline to discipline, most involve both objective and essay sections and are several hours long. The test is scored from 1 to 5, with 5 the highest. Each institution treats the examinations differently, but many will grant college credit for scores from 3 to 5.

5. *TOEFL* (Test of English as a Foreign Language). You will need to take this test if you have been in the U.S. only a few years and if English is not your native language. Consult your counselor for dates and information about this test.

6. *CLEP* (College-Level Exam Program). This series of examinations is designed to test knowledge gained by students through life experience as well as academic study. It involves a series of five examinations on general topics and several on specific subjects. Students and nonstudents interested in finding out more about these tests which allow college credit to those with demonstrated competency should check with the counselor at the nearest high school.

Students are given sample test questions with registration for all of these tests. Don't forget to read through them carefully.

## "Can I Prepare for Standardized Tests?"

A conscientious, sustained effort through your school years supplemented by extensive reading is the most effective preparation for a test designed, like the SAT, to gauge general abilities. Many evaluators of the scores of standardized tests say that the test separates readers from nonreaders, with the scores of readers *significantly* higher.

There are many prep courses for takers of the SAT. These courses can alleviate the anxiety and uncertainty centering around the test. By introducing you to the format of the test, giving you the basic strategies involved in analyzing and answering the different types of questions, they help to allay fears of the unknown. The drill offered in such courses can increase your speed and facility in dealing with the test through creating a familiarity with its structure and limits.

You can also improve your own skills by a self- directed

program of drill, study, and practice testing. The College Board publishes *Taking the SAT*, given to you when you register for the test. Arco's Test Preparation books provide a complete course of review and reinforcement for all facets of standardized test taking. Learning analytical and study techniques may sharpen your awareness and understanding of the nature and structure of the tests. Sample exams allow you to develop reflexive, automatic skills through repetition and to analyze your strengths and weaknesses through explained answers. See reading list below for relevant titles.

Whether to take a preparation course is a purely personal decision. Do *not*, however, take an SAT course in place of a school English or other academic course. College admissions officers frown on such tactics.

For the SAT II tests, the ACT, the AP, and the CLEP (all of which examine knowledge rather than ability), methodical, structured review will be very helpful. You will do best by planning out your review over a period of time. This will permit you to cover each phase of the material in some depth. For help in implementing your own study program, see the list below, and don't forget to use the samples given out when you register for the tests.

### Reading List:

Following are a number of books published by Arco that cover all facets of the standardized tests taken by college-bound students. They may be ordered from Simon & Schuster, Inc., 200 Old Tappan Road, Old Tappan, New Jersey 07675.

*Preparation for the SAT—Scholastic Assessment Test*, Eleventh Edition, Deptula. *Verbal Workbook for the SAT*, Miller, Morse-Cluley, Freedman, Haller. *Mathematics Workbook for the ACT*, Saunders, et al. *American College Testing Program (ACT)*, Twelfth Edition, Levy & Levy. *Verbal Workbook for the ACT*, Lakritz. *Mathematics Workbook for the ACT*, Saunders, et al. *CLEP College-Level Examination Program*, Third Edition, Lieberman, Ph.D., et al, Third Edition. *Advanced Placement Examination in English: Composition and Literature*, Second Edition, Rozakis. *Advanced Placement Examination in Biology*, Heller. *Advanced Placement Examination in Mathematics*, Smith, Griffin. *Advanced Placement Examination in American History*, Second Edition, Crum. *Advanced Placement Examination in Computer Science*, Schulman, Austin, Page. *Advanced Placement Examination in European History*, Levy & Levy.

## The Campus Visit and Personal Interview

The interview seems like one of the scariest aspects of the college process. Many students feel shy speaking about themselves or unsure about what questions they should ask. The interview may even come relatively early in the selection process, before you are really set to think about college. It doesn't have to be horrific, however, and may be useful and fun if you follow a few suggestions.

As is said about so much in the college selection process, start early. Otherwise, if you are interested in highly competitive colleges, you may not even obtain an interview. Whenever possible, make arrangements by letter or phone *several months* before you plan to visit. Ask for written confirmation of the arrangements you make. Many colleges will arrange for you to spend a night in the dorms and attend classes if you ask well ahead of your visit. You might wish to ask to speak with a professor in your field of interest or with a coach. Try to get as much as possible of your campus visiting and interviewing done in the summer between junior and senior year. Senior year is a hectic round of academic responsibilities, extracurricular activities, and college application duties. It is hard to do much traveling then. You must also learn your school's policy about absence from classes for visiting colleges. Many schools discourage such absences during the fall of your important senior year. Abide by the rules; adhering to policy will save you and everyone else a lot of hassle. If you visit in the summer and a campus doesn't seem very lively or if you simply want to check it out again, there is the possibility of a return visit. Get started early.

Some colleges seem too far away for a visit. This may be true, but there are a few points you should consider before you give up the idea of a campus visit. First, would you buy a $80,000 car without a test drive? That's what many four-year colleges will cost. Maybe you should get on that campus, somehow. It is extremely difficult to discover the character and personality of an institution without a visit. Second, if it is really impossible to visit, at least arrange for an alumni/ae interview. Most colleges and universities have alums in all areas of the country and will set up an interview for you. Second-hand information is better than none, but do consider whether the alumnus attended the institution recently or is up-to-date about it.

When you make your appointment, find out if the interview will be *evaluative* or *informative*. The first is a part of the admissions selection process and will be used to help determine how good a candidate you are. The second provides an opportunity for you to learn about the institution and is *not* a part of the selection process. You should know how the interview will be used before it begins.

*How important is the interview?* Well, as you can see, interviews are used differently by different colleges. In general, however, an evaluative interview that goes well will help keep you in the mind of the interviewer when decisions are made in the spring. Often interviews that do not go well are not held against students. Admissions officers are aware of the pressures involved and the natural tendency to be nervous. Still, it is obviously to your advantage to do as well as you can.

*How can you have a good interview?* Know something about yourself and about the institution before you arrive. Think about your strengths and weaknesses, your accomplishments and interests. Try to present yourself as confident, but not overly aggressive. Ask interesting questions (questions that do not cover material answered in the college's catalogue!). Dress neatly, but don't overdress. Sit up, show you are interested and interesting, and look your interviewer in the eye. This is not the time to hold back; you want to show who you are. Take some initiative. Be sure you mention aspects of yourself and your life you wish to emphasize. Do not try to "psych out" the interviewer and give him what he wants to hear. He is a professional who interviews many students a day during the interview season. He will quickly see through any facade you present. Instead, try to encourage a real conversation. Colleges are looking for students who have a sense of themselves and where they may be heading. Through their selections, college admissions officers must create the community for the college. They need to feel you will contribute to and benefit from their institution so you should consider what makes each college and university you visit unique.

*Questions you may encounter at an interview.* You might like to practice answering some of these in a mock interview with a friend or parent who can offer an evaluation of the clarity, enthusiasm, and substance of your response.

*1.* Describe yourself. Do you think others see you as different from the way you see yourself? Why?

*2.* If you could change something about yourself, what would you change? Why?

*3.* How would you like to be remembered after you leave your college campus? at the end of your life?

*4.* What is your most important characteristic? Why?

*5.* Tell about a book, movie, television program, experience you have read, seen, had recently. Why did it have an impact on you?

*6.* Whom do you admire? Why?

*7.* Tell about your family and describe your relationships with family members.

*8.* What new areas of interest do you want to explore in college?

*9.* What especially attracts you to this institution?

*10.* What will you miss most when you leave your home and community?

*When you go for your visit*—Take a tour *before* your interview so that you'll be in a better position to ask questions and understand your interviewer's comments. Try to see as much as possible. Check out student facilities such as sports arenas, dining halls, bookstores, and pubs. Can you imagine yourself in these places? Does the size of the campus seem comfortable? Are the facilities appropriate for pursuing your major interests? Eavesdrop on student conversations, and don't be shy about asking students questions. Most students will be flattered to be asked their opinions. They've been through the visiting process, too. Visit classes if possible. Try to evaluate the atmosphere of the campus. Friendly? Sophisticated? Hard-working? Fun-loving? Use your notebook or folders on colleges in which to record impressions. If your parents and friends are along, discuss impressions but try to do so after you have formed your own.

Other considerations in evaluating a college or university include the availability of internships, foreign study, intercampus exchanges, and independent study. How many students opt for these and how difficult are they to incorporate into a required program? How much flexibility in your choice of curriculum is there? Will you be required to take core courses or are you free to elect all courses? When do you need to decide on a major? Are double majors possible? Interdisciplinary, self-constructed majors? How many classes are you likely to have with under 20 students? over 50 or 75? What is the mix of commuter and residential students? Is the academic year based on semesters? trimesters? What is the geographical and socioeconomic diversity of the student body? What kind of access will you have to computers? labs? studios? Many of these questions will be answered in catalogues. If they are not, they are good questions to ask as part of your visit.

*Arrive on time* for your interview and take, if possible, a copy of your school transcript, or at least, a record of the courses you have taken. You may also want to provide a list of your activities and interests. While colleges and universities are academic institutions, don't think everything you say has to involve school, reading, or academic achievements. Try to leave a sense of the total you. Record the name of your interviewer. You may wish to follow up with a thank-you note. And, if you have any questions later, or if something special, such as an award, happens to you between application time and when you are notified of the admissions decision, you may want to contact him. Your interviewer of the summer may also arrive at your high school in the fall as the visiting representative from his college, and it would be nice to remember who he is!

Near the end of your interview, it is entirely appropriate for you to ask the interviewer how he sees you as a candidate for admission to his institution. His answer will help you plan more successfully as you make the many decisions ahead.

## The Application

Before you actually write your application, you should read carefully "How Competitive Colleges Select from Among Applicants." It will give you an understanding of why colleges ask what they do and how best to complete the application.

Although applications differ from college to college, most consist of: 1) your part (data to be supplied, a personal essay, and the application fee); 2) your high school's part (a secondary report form for grades and information about the school and a mid-year report form to keep you honest and keep you from coasting); 3) a part for teachers' recommendations.

The first section of your part of the application usually asks for specific information on your personal and school life. You may need to include your social security number, your class rank, and your school's College Board Code number. Often you must state whether you plan to live on campus, whether you are applying for financial aid, and what your tentative plans for a major and an occupation are. (Colleges don't require you to have your life completely planned, but want to have a sense of how many English majors or pre-med students they may have on campus. Don't feel you have to commit yourself to an area but do indicate any genuine interests.) There is a place to list the names of your parents and siblings. A request is often made for the names of colleges and universities they have attended.

Colleges want the names of all the schools you have attended during your high school years, including summer school. Besides providing a place for the schools' names and addresses, colleges may want you to arrange for a copy of your transcript from *each* institution to be forwarded. Colleges often ask for the names of the teachers who will submit a teacher's recommendation for you, so that if a recommendation is delayed, you and the teacher can be easily notified. There is usually a place for SAT I, ACT, SAT II tests, Advanced Placement Tests, and the Test of English as a Foreign Language (TOEFL) scores. Some colleges will ask whether you have ever been suspended or expelled and provide an opportunity for you to explain the circumstances.

You may often have a chance to list academic and nonacademic honors and to record extracurricular, summer, and employment experiences in this part of the application. The application may ask questions about community service, your travel experience, and your foreign language abilities. Remember, when you have been given the opportunity to include lists of honors, sports teams, or countries visited, do not repeat your lists as part of your essay. Instead, treat one experience or activity in detail.

Institutions are, of course, interested in what you have learned. You may be asked to list books you have read, or to comment on your reading, and/or to evaluate an important educational experience. Colleges want to see that you are an interested and receptive student. Take care with such questions. Think and plan before you answer them.

Finally, you may be asked whether you wish to waive your right under the Family Educational Rights and Privacy Act of 1974 to see interview notes and recommendations should you matriculate.

Each application is somewhat different from all others. The information above should, however, give you an idea of an application's basic elements and prepare the way for the first time you stare at that formal application. The second part of the application you must complete is the personal essay. Not all institutions require an essay, but most do, and it is a very important way of presenting yourself. Because it is so important and because it is often the most intimidating task for students, there is a special article devoted to suggestions on how to write it. See page *xvii.*

A few, simple suggestions concerning the whole application procedure are in order here:

*1.* Apply early. Many colleges and universities make their decisions as student applications are received. You don't want to risk having the freshman class filled when your application is received. Even at institutions that do not use a kind of rolling admission, applications are often read in the order in which they are completed. It is better to be early than late or even just on time!

*2.* Write your application yourself or type it yourself. Do *not* have it professionally typed. Colleges want to feel that students are willing to take the time and care to do their own applications. The typing skills of your father's secretary do not impress them. Your application should present *you* as clearly and as *personally* as possible. Be certain, of course, that all information is clear, accurate, and complete.

*3.* Keep standardized test scores. These are often requested. It is also your responsibility to have official scores sent to each college. You can do this when you take the tests or later. It is best to use the spaces provided on the tests and to obtain Additional Report Forms from your counselor only when needed. Remember, you must write your name and address exactly the same way each time you take a test, or your scores will not be combined.

*4.* Ask teachers well in advance for recommendations. They are time-consuming and a labor of love. Appreciate the work done. Teachers may certainly write one letter of recommendation that is appropriate for a number of colleges and that can be xeroxed and sent to each. It is better to ask the one teacher who knows you best to send off six copies than to ask six different teachers. Supply stamped, addressed envelopes for each recommendation. A list of your activities, accomplishments, and interests is often helpful to the teacher. Be sure to underline or point out the deadline for the submission of each recommendation. Keep a record of who writes which recommendations and send thank-you notes to teachers.

*5.* You may want to send supporting material—photographs, drawings, tapes—if you are especially talented in one area. Be honest, but not too critical when you assess how helpful these materials may be.

*6.* Additional recommendations from others, outside of school, who know *you* (not your mom or dad) well may be included, but don't overload.

*7.* You may be able to use your essay for several applications, but be certain that it is well-suited to each.

*8.* There is a Common Application that many colleges accept that allows you to take a shortcut and avoid so many different applications. If the colleges to which you are applying also have their own applications, you may want, however, to use the individual applications which are tailored to the institution.

*9.* If a college to which you are applying does not provide a school report form, you should ask your counselor to send a transcript, school profile, and school letter of recommendation anyway. If a college does not require a teacher recommendation, but you feel that you will have a good one, arrange for a copy to be sent to the college.

A short glossary of terms that pertain to the applications process follows. There is a more extensive glossary for other college terms located on page *xxxvii* of this book.

### *Application Glossary*

**Deferred Admission.** This is a term used to indicate that many colleges will allow an admitted student to postpone matriculation for a year for a number of reasons (financial, to be a foreign exchange student, etc.).

**Early Action, Early Notification.** The name of an admissions program that allows a candidate who applies by a certain date, usually in the autumn, to receive early notification of the admissions decision. If a student is accepted under an Early Action Program, the student *is not obligated* to attend that institution.

**Early Admission.** A policy that allows extremely well-qualified students to enter college before graduation from high school.

**Early Decision.** The name of an admissions program that allows a candidate who applies by a certain date, no later than November 15, to receive notification of the admissions decision soon after December 15. Unlike Early Action, acceptance under Early Decision obligates a student to attend only that institution. Colleges may offer either of two plans: 1) Early Decision, First Choice (EDP–F). Students must withdraw applications from all other colleges as soon as they receive acceptance. 2) Early Decision, Single Choice Plan (EDP–S). Students may not apply to other colleges unless they are rejected.

**Early Entrance.** This is similar to Early Admission. A student matriculates at an institution before having graduated from high school. This type of admission is reserved for very few, extremely well-qualified students.

**Early Evaluation.** This provides an opportunity for students who apply by a specified date to be told whether their admission to a particular college is "likely," "not likely," or "possible." Knowing your chances helps in planning whether you will apply to other colleges, to how many others you will apply, and of what degree of selectivity they should be.

**Rolling Admission.** Under this type of admissions system, colleges and universities admit students at various times in the year depending on the date of application and the qualifications of the student. *When the upcoming freshman class is filled, admissions close.* It is naturally to your advantage to apply early to such institutions.

## The Essay

Just how do you show your talent, intelligence, humor, creativity, and writing ability in one short essay? Well, no one will say that it's easy. But college isn't easy either and that is where a good essay will get you. The answer, though not easy, is simple: *You must be courageous enough to be you.*

Why courageous? Most of us feel our lives are too insignificant to appeal to someone else without window dressing. We're tempted to incorporate the thoughts of others, to take on earth-shattering issues—to do anything in short to make us seem better than we think we are. Unfortunately (fortunately?) a college admissions officer isn't interested in the ideas of your parents, counselors, or friends. Nor is he interested in what you think he will want to hear; don't second-guess. He does not need to read another seventeen-year-old's solution to nuclear war. *He wants to get to know the student whose essay is in front of him—you.*

Everyone has in his life the stuff of excellent college essays; the trick is to find it. And, how do you locate this "stuff" and use it to show your best self? By thinking about the specific essay questions posed, by studying all other directions carefully, by reflecting on your own experiences, and by responding in clear, honest, and direct prose.

*Essays too often sound exactly the same.* Think of your reader. An admissions officer may be faced with fifty application folders to read in a day; certainly he will read thousands before the end of the admissions season. Stay away from traditional treatments of traditional topics; it's hard to grab an admissions officer's attention and interest with the twentieth travelogue of his day, a biography that begins, "I was born . . . ," or the hundredth piece he has read in a week on "Why I would like to attend your college."

Instead of listing the countries you visited on a trip abroad or the pavilions at the World's Fair, select one experience that really had an impact on you and explore that experience in depth. Explain how it changed you and why. Don't try to impress, but do try to interest. And one of the best ways of interesting someone else is to be interested in what you are writing yourself.

*Your essay is your chance to show who you are.* Try to be spontaneous and imaginative. Look for original approaches or viewpoints. For example, a failure that is well-described, has clearly shown your ability to cope, and pinpoints what you have learned from it is really more impressive than a list of ten accomplishments. In fact, problems, difficulties, or fears can often lead to interesting discussions. Think about all that has happened to you in your family, with friends, at school, in activities. Locate turning points in your life, analyze important relationships, consider family crises. Remember your subject should be a vehicle for showing your values and beliefs. Don't be afraid to be personal—that's what it's all about. You want to remain in the mind of your reader as a distinctive individual.

To find the best topic for you and to write well about it you will need time. Some can be gained by planning ahead. Some by disciplining yourself to cut out the agony; many students spend hours on the telephone commiserating with friends who are also struggling. This is counterproductive; it wastes valuable time and postpones your thinking about your purpose. To keep the bother to a minimum, start small. Jot down a few possible topics. Try to develop each. Look for the connections and conclusions that can be made. Try out a few paragraphs on what seem the likeliest topics. Remember, with enough time you can scrap one idea for another. Explore. When you are satisfied that your topic is personal, character-revealing, and interesting, write your rough draft. Let it sit for awhile and then try to revise it objectively, but don't water it down to rob it of spontaneity. Be sure to check for spelling errors and other problems with "mechanics." Colleges are not interested in sloppy efforts. Be certain you have followed all directions.

Here is a checklist that you can use to evaluate your essay. You may also want to ask someone else to check your essay against it after reading what you have written.

*1.* Is this interesting? *Will it stand out because it shows who I really am?* Is it about something that is important to me?

*2.* Do I analyze, conclude, offer observations, present theories? In other words, *do I show I can think?* Do I get every bit that is possible out of my issue, experience, story?

*3.* Is my presentation logical? Do I support my contentions?

*4.* Is there good transition between ideas?

*5.* Do I have a conclusion rather than a summary at the end?

*6.* Is all the information relevant? Is everything stated as clearly and effectively as possible?

If you ask for the opinions of others, be certain it is you who do the rewriting and devise solutions to problems. You are ultimately responsible for your essay's vision and revision. Decide whether you will type or write out the final copy. Be as neat as possible. Mail your essay off on time. Take a deep breath and give yourself a hand.

## Applying for Financial Aid

When financial aid is an important consideration in your acceptance of a college—and these days it is for just about everyone—please remember to consider that the "award package" (which consists of loans, student work, and scholarships) can vary greatly from college to college. This means that you must consider the award in relation to the cost of each college. You may find that the small expensive college you thought you could never afford is well endowed and can offer you far more aid than a state university, making the smaller college actually cheaper! This is one of the reasons why, though aid or the lack of it may determine your final college decision, you shouldn't allow concerns over money issues to keep you from considering colleges in the beginning. You just have no way of knowing what may happen; hence, work to keep money worries apart from the initial decisions.

*Federal Financial Aid*—Most federal financial aid is based on your financial need as determined by subtracting what you (and your parents, if you are dependent) can reasonably be expected to contribute toward your educational costs (known as the Expected Family Contribution, or EFC) from the cost of attendance at a specific school. Probably the most important part of this simple-looking formula is the calculation of your EFC. This is done by completing one of several need-analysis forms. The most common are the Free Application for Federal Student Aid (FAFSA) and the Financial Aid Form (FAF). To find out which one you should use, contact the financial aid office at the school or schools you are considering attending. A college may ask for both the FAFSA and the FAF, and may also ask for its own form to be completed as well. (The FAFSA and FAF forms are available at your high school.) Once you have the right form(s), fill it (them) out completely and carefully. Errors can cause delays in the financial aid process.

Although these forms ask many different questions, the most important ones relate to income, and require specific information directly from your or your parents' federal tax returns. After you have completed the form, mail it as soon as possible—deadlines are important throughout the entire financial aid process! You should try to apply for financial aid in January or February preceding the academic year you plan to enter college, but you may apply at any time. Be sure to make a photocopy of your application and have copies ready of any of the documents you used to complete your application, in the event your financial aid administrator requests them. Do *not* send them with your application.

If you or your family have special circumstances that are not covered by the questions on the form, be sure to explain those circumstances fully and clearly in the appropriate section and provide a separate statement directly to the financial aid administrator of each college. He or she will then be able to make a much more accurate assessment of your need for financial aid. Note that all information used in determining need will be kept confidential by the financial aid office.

While all the details of applying for student financial aid seem to be a bother, the rewards—in terms of the assistance you receive—can be great. If you read and follow all application instructions, meet deadlines, and provide additional documentation when necessary, the application process is easier than it may first appear. However, don't get lazy and assume that your financial aid is taking care of itself. The result can be disastrous. When you have any doubts or questions, contact a professional financial aid administrator at any college for assistance. He or she will be happy to help you.

If you do not think you will be eligible for aid, you might still want to fill out the FAFSA. Now there are federal, low-interest loans available to *all* families *regardless* of income.

*State Financial Aid*—After federal aid, the second most commonly known type of assistance comes from your state. Generally, you must be a resident of the state in which you are enrolled in school to qualify for these funds; however, some states have reciprocal agreements which allow you to use the funds outside your home state. To inquire about this, as well as how to apply, you need to contact the appropriate agency for your state.

*Merit Scholarships*—While many colleges do earmark the largest percentage of scholarship money to needy students, merit scholarships are having a resurgence. Greater competition among colleges means that some are trying to attract good candidates through financial incentives. If you are a good student, be sure to inquire about the possibility of merit scholarships at each of the institutions to which you apply.

*Co-op Education*—Check out the possibility of entering a co-op (cooperative education) program. Schools that have such programs, and there are many, allow you to work while you study. The financial and career benefits are great, though you may need some extra time to earn your degree. Read the section on Cooperative Education below.

*Local and Employment-Related Awards*—Almost every community, service organization, and large company has special scholarships available. Check with your school counselor, employers (yours, your parents'), personnel offices, churches, etc. Look in your local newspapers for announcements of application dates for community scholarships and competitions.

*Private Sources of Financial Aid*—The merit, local, and employment-related awards mentioned above are really a part of this broader category of student financial aid. Because individual programs are too numerous to mention, we will simply point you in the right direction so that you may research these alternative sources of assistance if you wish. While there are firms that will do this type of research for you (for a fee), you will generally have as great a success or better by going to the public library and doing the work yourself. You will find many reference books that list these private sources. You need to determine the specific programs for which you may qualify, request any application materials, and complete them accurately within required deadlines. Funds from these sources may generally be used in combination with any aid you receive from state or federal sources, or may be an alternative if you do not qualify for need-based financial aid. Like any research project, searching for these funds is time-consuming, but the payoff can be just what it takes to cover any remaining need you have that is not met by aid from another source.

While financial aid is intended to help you cover your educational costs, remember that the government still maintains that the primary responsibility to pay for an education lies with the student and family. If you find that all of your need has not been met, review what you feel you and your family can contribute to be certain you have planned to contribute your full share. Check with banks and other financial institutions to see if they offer plans for borrowing for college. If a gap still exists, contact the college of your choice. Some help may be available. Once you matriculate, changing financial situations can usually be accommodated; once an institution has invested time and money in you, it wants to keep you. Help may involve a regular payment plan, or counseling to take fewer courses to reduce your costs. After all, "sticking it out" is better than wasting the time you've already invested. So, be a good student aid consumer, seek help when you have problems, and financial aid will help you achieve your educational goals.

Additional Reading: *College Financial Aid*, John Schwartz and College Reasearch Group (ARCO).

## Cooperative Education: Financial Aid Alternative

When financial aid is not enough to pay spiraling college costs, an important option you should consider is using a cooperative education program. In fact, because the advantages of "co-op education" go well beyond allowing you to finance your college education while receiving it, students for whom financial considerations are not a factor might also do well participating in a co-op.

Cooperative education is the name given to a variety of plans in 900 colleges and universities in the United States and Canada which allow students to integrate academic study with work experience. Students have the opportunity while still in college to earn money, test career options, gain work experience, and participate fully in the "working world." Institutions offering co-op plans vary in admissions selectivity and include both four-year and two-year colleges. Cooperative programs can be found in the fields of agriculture, arts, business, computer sciences, education, engineering, health professions, home economics, humanities, natural sciences, social and behavioral sciences, technologies, and vocational arts. Not all participating colleges and universities offer co-op in all fields, however, so you should ask about the possibility of combining work and study in your areas of interest when you make preliminary inquiries.

Some institutions offer parallel study and work programs while others alternate several months of classes with work opportunities. Student commitments to athletics and other interests can often be accommodated by local placements. There is usually a chance for several different placements during your college career should you wish to experiment with career possibilities. Campus Cooperative Education Coordinators help locate positions, provide counseling, and monitor student performance.

The National Commission for Cooperative Education offers a sampling of previous co-op assignments: library assistant at the Library of Congress, copy person at the *New York Times*, shuttle resources assistant for NASA, physical therapy aid at a Denver hospital, assistant to the General Director of Banque Franco-Portugaise in Paris, accounting assistant for Arthur Andersen & Company, traffic analyst for Continental Forest Industries, programmer for an observatory in Northern Ireland, nursing assistant at Johns Hopkins, and industrial engineering analyst. Even such a short list suggests the great variety of opportunities, here and abroad, and the potential for valuable entrees into professional fields.

Some 200,000 students are now a part of cooperative education programs with a combined wage of one billion dollars a year. Statistics on career decisions and job placement for co-op students are impressive. According to the Commission for Co-op Education, 40 percent of students continue to work for their co-op employers after graduation, 40 percent upon graduation find work in their field of interest, and 15 percent decide to remain in school to earn professional degrees.

For free information concerning co-op education and a comprehensive list of participating colleges and universities including the areas in which each institution participates in co-op, write The National Commission for Cooperative Education, 360 Huntington Avenue, Boston, Massachusetts 02115.

## After Acceptance

Notices of acceptance may arrive as early as the autumn of your senior year if you apply to some colleges with rolling admissions or as late as the summer after graduation if you are admitted from a college's wait list. A few extremely well-qualified and mature students may even be admitted a year early (Early Acceptance). In general, however, here's what to expect.

If you are an Early Decision (E.D.) candidate or an Early Action (E.A.) candidate who has submitted an application by December 1, you should hear from the college in the third or fourth week of December. (A few colleges have a second, slightly later E.D. date. If you apply later, of course, you will be notified of the admissions decision later.) If you are admitted as an E.D. candidate, you are obligated to attend that college unless financial aid is insufficient and may wish to send your deposit as soon as possible so you can sit back and relax (about admission, not about school, for your record throughout your senior year will be reported to the college and should be consistent with your earlier record). If you are accepted as an E.A. candidate, you are free to apply to other colleges and are under no obligation to make an immediate response in order to save your place. You may find that your application has been deferred for consideration with the regular admissions pool later in the spring. While this is disappointing, be assured that your desire to attend that college has been made clear by your choice to apply E.D. or E.A., and that knowledge of this desire will certainly not hurt you.

A rolling admissions candidate may hear almost anytime during the senior year, depending on the date of the submission of the application. A few colleges even offer the option of immediate acceptance based on interview or audition. Most candidates for regular admissions, however, will receive notification from colleges in March and April.

Whenever you are accepted, you need to know that *colleges have agreed to abide by the Candidates Reply Date of May 1*. This means that you should not have to respond to an offer of admission until you have heard from all colleges or universities to which you have applied or by May 1, whichever comes earlier. *Important*: If you receive pressure from colleges for a decision before you have heard from all of those to which you applied, tactfully remind them of this policy. Athletes and other students whose abilities and talents make them prime candidates may receive this kind of pressure from coaches or admissions offices. If the college or university is unwilling to cooperate, contact your school counselor for help and ask him to notify the president of your state or regional Association of College Admissions Counselors.

*Wait lists*. You may find that a college is not able immediately to offer you a place, but puts your name on a "wait list." These lists are used when students who have received an offer of admission decline that offer and a position in the freshman class is thus open. If you are "wait listed" and do not hear from that college by May 1, you must accept another offer and send a deposit. If you are then notified of an opening from the wait list, you may change your mind, but will have to forfeit your deposit.

*Be considerate*. Once you have made your decision, notify all colleges and universities *immediately*. If you accept one offer and turn down four, four places at colleges will be available to others. If someone else is considerate, you may get a place from a wait list even before May 1.

*Visits*. In the period between mailing out decisions and May 1, many colleges sponsor days on campus to bring students to the college for one final look. If you are at all undecided, take advantage of this opportunity, and if no formal visiting day exists, ask to visit on your own. Making your final decision is obviously important; go about it wisely.

*Financial aid*. Occasionally you will be notified of acceptance before the financial aid packages are finished. If you do not have all the financial aid information that you need in order to make a decision, notify those colleges in which you are most interested that you need more time. Getting more time is usually not a problem. If the financial aid offer from the college you are most interested in is not what you feel you need, it might be worth asking for a reconsideration. You may not get it, but if you do and it enables you to attend that college, the letter will be worth it.

*All acceptances are conditional*. They depend on your continuing to produce the work and show the maturity that earned you that acceptance. Your high school will be asked to make reports during your senior year and is under a moral obligation to report any serious problems that arise. Forewarned is forearmed.

---

*Karen Clagett has taught English at public and private secondary schools in the U.S. and abroad. She is a former Lecturer in English at Boston College. Now a college counselor in New Hampshire, she has written on various issues related to college admissions.*

# Financial Aid

*By Andre L. Bell, Dean for Enrollment Management, Bentley College*

## An Overview

Financing the cost of higher education in the United States has been viewed as a financial partnership comprised of students, parents, government, private donors, and colleges and universities. During the 1992-93 academic year, over $34.6 billion in student assistance was received nationwide. Financial aid is most often direct financial support, or a reduction in the cost of attendance received either in cash or in kind. In this category, we find traditional scholarships, grants, and tuition waivers. However, financial aid should be thought of as any programmatic means to reduce the burden of meeting the cost of higher education. This broader view of financial aid encompasses student loans, parent loans, employment, and deferred or extended payment plans. As the cost of higher education continues to rise, many more institutions are providing extended or installment payment options which may ease a family's burden of meeting that cost.

Student assistance programs generally fall into one of two categories. The first, commonly known as need-based, may include gifts (grants and scholarships), student loans (deferred payments), and employment. In need-based programs, an analysis of financial circumstances results in an estimate of the family's ability to meet the cost of higher education and, consequently, determines its eligibility for financial assistance. The following formula summarizes the need-based aid approach:

| | |
|---|---|
| $$$ | (College Cost) |
| –$$ | (Student/Family Resources) |
| $$$ | (Financial Need/Elgibility) |

The need-based approach determines eligibility for the vast majority of student assistance funding available nationally. Recent college and university surveys indicate that more than 80 percent of student aid awards are need-based. The second category of student assistance programs comes under the heading "merit or performance-based programs." This category also includes gifts (grants and scholarships), loans, and employment. Assistance in this category is generally offered to a student who presents a record of high achievement. In a real sense, this category of assistance is best labeled "talent recognition." Traditionally, assistance available in this category has recognized athletic ability, performance in the fine arts, or academic achievement. When compared to need-based programs, funding available in the performance or merit category of student assistance is limited.

In addition to need-based and performance-based programs, a third category of student assistance should not be overlooked—assistance based primarily on group affiliation. Again, this type of assistance may include all forms of aid, but eligibility is primarily based on association or group ties, such as fraternal or civic organizations, parents' employers, or religious or professional associations. Also included in this category is financial assistance available as a result of a current or future employment or a service commitment on the part of the student. Examples include military service, teaching or nursing scholarships or loans, and of course, financial assistance provided by an employer directly to an employee.

A growing category of assistance programs falls under the heading of "financial management programs." These programs, administered by post–secondary institutions, government agencies, or financial institutions, usually offer assistance to families who do not qualify or who have exceeded eligibility guidelines for need-based financial assistance. These programs generally assist families by making payments of higher education expenses more manageable. In this arena we find installment payment plans, extended payment plans (loans), and plans that guarantee or limit the cost of education over the period of study. The primary goal of this last type of assistance program is to enhance a family's ability to choose high-cost programs or schools without sacrificing the family's financial reserves or lifestyle.

A student or family who plans to invest in post–secondary education should consider the appropriateness of the types of assistance mentioned above. A family should first take an inventory of its financial resources, any unusual characteristics that the student may have relative to performance-based assistance, and association ties. In addition, families should be sure to inquire among the schools being considered about the availability of "payment plans." Application procedures will vary among the different sources and types of assistance options mentioned previously. Secondary school guidance departments and school admission and financial aid offices are good sources of information and insight. In addition, students may obtain information from the higher education assistance agency in their home state.

As mentioned earlier, the majority of student assistance funding is available on the basis of financial need. The first step in establishing the student's ability to meet the cost of higher education is an analysis of the family's financial resources. The analysis uses standardized documents and formulas used by government agencies as well as colleges and universities. The primary document used for need-based financial assistance programs is the Free Application for Federal Student Aid (FAFSA), which is generally available in high schools or from post–secondary education institutions. The FAFSA provides a financial profile of the student's family. A national formula establishes an estimate of a family's ability to contribute toward educational expenses. The estimate of a family's ability to pay remains constant as the student considers institutions with different costs of attendance and establishes the student's eligibility for federal, most state, private agency, and institutional assistance programs. The goal of the national form and formula is to establish a single estimate of ability to pay so that when a student considers an institution with a high cost of attendance, the estimated ability to pay remains the same as it would be at a school of lower cost. As a consequence, the student's remaining financial need, or eligibility for need-based student assistance, is generally greater at a high-cost school than it would be at a less expensive institution.

However, some agencies and schools will request additional or supplemental information to establish a separate expectation of the family's ability to pay or to assist in establishing a rank ordering among applicants for their own funds. The existence of supplemental need analysis documents may be confusing on the surface, but the process always starts with the Free Application for Federal Student Assistance (FAFSA). The federal form and analysis establish the foundation for all other financial assistance programs. Consequently, families should keep copies of the financial information reported as it will, most likely, be the same for other need-analysis documents required to apply to other sources for student assistance. One of the most common supplemental need analysis documents is the Financial Aid Form (FAF) of the College Scholarship Service, which is also available in most secondary schools.

Often when considering need-based financial aid programs, families find themselves asking "Should I apply?" The answer is simple—if in doubt as to whether or not your family's resources are adequate to meet the cost of attendance at a school you are considering, apply.

The goal of the college selection process, as well as the student selection process on the part of schools, is to achieve the best match between the student's academic preparation, academic, career, and social interests and personal objectives. Similarly, the goal of most student aid programs is to facilitate the achievement of the best match between the student and the educational institution. Thus, student assistance programs should play a secondary role in the student and school matching process. Students should base their primary selection of potential schools on factors other than the cost of attendance and then be advised to pursue financial assistance aggressively to minimize considerations of cost. Such an approach will maximize choice and attainment of the ultimate goal, achieving the best match between the student and school.

---

*Andre L. Bell, Dean for Enrollment Management at Bentley College in Waltham Massachusetts, is a former Vice President for Admission Practices of the National Association of College Admission Counselors and a Past President of the Illinois Association of Student Financial Administrators.*

# Sources of Information on Financial Aid: U.S. Dept. of Education Regional Offices

**Region I**
**Connecticut, Maine, Massachusetts, New Hampshire, Rhode Island, Vermont**

U.S. Dept. of Education
Office of Student Financial Assistance
J.W. McCormack Post Office and Courthouse Bldg., Room 502
Boston, MA 02109
(617) 223-9338

**Region II**
**New Jersey, New York, Puerto Rico, Virgin Islands, Panama Canal Zone**

U.S. Dept. of Education
Office of Student Financial Assistance
26 Federal Plaza, Room 3954
New York, NY 10278
(212) 264-4426

**Region III**
**Delaware, District of Columbia, Maryland, Pennsylvania, Virginia, West Virginia**

U.S. Dept. of Education
Office of Student Financial Assistance
3535 Market Street, Room 16200
Philadelphia, PA 19104
(215) 596-0247

**Region IV**
**Alabama, Florida, Georgia, Kentucky, Mississippi, North Carolina, South Carolina, Tennessee**

U.S. Dept. of Education
Office of Student Financial Assistance
101 Marietta Tower, Suite 323
Atlanta, GA 30323
(404) 331–2502

**Region V**
**Illinois, Indiana, Michigan, Minnesota, Ohio, Wisconsin**

U.S. Dept. of Education
Office of Student Financial Assistance
401 South State Street, 12th Floor, Room 700D
Chicago, IL 60605
(312) 353-8103

**Region VI**
**Arkansas, Louisiana, New Mexico, Oklahoma, Texas**

U.S. Dept. of Education
Office of Student Financial Assistance
1200 Main Tower, Room 2150
Dallas, TX 75202
(214) 767-3811

**Region VII**
**Iowa, Kansas, Missouri, Nebraska**

U.S. Dept. of Education
Office of Student Financial Assistance
10220 N. Executive Hills Blvd., 9th Floor
Kansas City, MO 64153
(816) 891-8055

**Region VIII**
**Colorado, Montana, North Dakota, South Dakota, Utah, Wyoming**

U.S. Dept. of Education
Office of Student Financial Assistance
1244 Speer Blvd., Suite 310
Denver, CO 80204
(303) 844-3676

**Region IX**
**Arizona, California, Hawaii, Nevada, American Samoa, Guam, Federated States of Micronesia, Marshall Islands, Republic of Palau, Wake Island**

U.S. Dept. of Education
Office of Student Financial Assistance
50 United Nations Plaza
San Francisco, CA 94102
(415) 556-1630

**Region X**
**Alaska, Idaho, Oregon, Washington**

U.S. Dept. of Education
Office of Student Financial Assistance
915 Second Avenue, Room 3388
Seattle, WA 98174
(206) 220–7813

# Competitive College Data

## How Competitive Colleges Select from Among Applicants

*By Karen Clagett, College Guidance Counselor*

No single factor is likely to determine whether or not you are granted admission by a college or university. At competitive institutions, more attention than you probably think possible is given to your achievements, background, interests, and personality. In spite of the vast numbers of applicants at some institutions and the increasing use of computers to aid admissions offices, the process is still largely a personal one. And the more competitive the college or university, the more care is taken to decide which will be best suited to it among the many applicants. This is important to remember because though there are some factors over which you have little control, the fact that such attention is paid to what you say and write and who you are means that you have more control than you think over this seemingly complex process. The amount of care you take with essays, interviews, applications, and general organization, is, after all, up to you, and it can make the difference.

Factors in the admissions decision can be divided into those over which you have a great deal of control (academic and personal) and those over which you have little control, but may still make work for you.

### Factors Over Which You Have Control

*Academic* —

*1.* **Your school record and program.** Any competitive college wants and will attract students who are serious. *Without a doubt the single most important document you present to such a college is your high school transcript.* Your transcript is considered by many college admissions officers to be the best predictor of your future college performance. You should take the most demanding program you can and do as well as you can. Never coast. Junior and first-semester senior year grades and courses are most important. (See page *x* for suggestions on course selections.)

*2.* **Your school letter of recommendation.** A headmaster, principal, or counselor will write a letter of recommendation for you. You want him to be able to say you are responsible, mature, involved. Be a contributor to your community. Try to get to know the person who will write this letter. Better, let him get to know you.

*3.* **Your teacher recommendations.** Choose your recommending teachers wisely. They should be those who know you best inside, and, if possible, outside the classroom. If you have a special relationship with a publications adviser or coach who has seen you confront difficulties and achieve goals, be sure that that teacher is the one you select. (Teachers do not have to fill out different forms for each college. One letter that is specific, informative, anecdotal, and well-written can be photocopied by the teacher and a copy can be sent to each college.) Choose teachers who are best qualified to write your recommendation and have them do all of your recommendations. Some colleges may request a recommendation from an English teacher or two from teachers in different disciplines, but if there is no requirement, get the best. Be certain you keep a record of which teachers write what recommendations so that should one be missing, you will know whom to contact.

*4.* **Your standardized test scores.** You need to take these seriously and do as well as you can on the tests. See the section on standardized tests on page *xii*. Many students feel the tests are all-important. They are not. Scores are used differently by different institutions, but generally they are used as a barometer of your academic promise *in conjunction with grades and your socioeconomic background.* For example, high scores coupled with the possibility of taking lots of advanced classes at your school show there is potential for high achievement. If your grades show mediocre effort and achievement, then you are not a promising candidate.

*Personal* (here is where you have the most control) —

*1.* **Application and application essays.** Special articles in other sections of this book are devoted to these important factors (see pages *xvi-xix*), but a few words here. You can make these work for you. Your application should be complete, accurate, neat. This sounds like common sense, but the number of spelling errors that make their way to admissions desks is appalling. *Whenever possible, submit your application earlier than its deadline.* Colleges often see late submission as evidence of disorganization and procrastination and early submission as evidence of active interest in their institutions. Get your applications in well ahead; this is especially important if you apply for Rolling Admissions, for if you are too late, the class may be filled. Early submission is also important at large universities. Would you like your application to be the tenth or the eight-hundredth read? Show through your good organization and early submission that you know what you want and can "get it all together." Your essay is the only opportunity to show your ability to communicate ideas in writing. It should be clear and technically flawless. Most important, your essay should convey your values, concerns, and education; it should present you as an individual. Support all ideas and concentrate on depth rather than breadth. (Be sure to read the section with suggestions on essay writing.)

*2.* **Interviews.** Colleges want to admit intelligent, articulate, confident students. We can't always be as relaxed in interview situations as we'd like, but do your best through preparation to present yourself as mature and intelligent. Admissions officers often have a way of remembering who is organized and who takes charge. Make your appointments early and make them yourself. Read the section that is devoted to the campus visit and interview.

*3.* **Special talents.** A college community is just that—a community. It requires diversity and talent. Colleges must look for orchestra players, quarterbacks, yearbook editors, peer counselors. Be sure your special talents are made known. Colleges are interested in a few talents pursued fully rather than a long list of memberships in organizations whose meetings you only attend. Sending prints of artwork and tapes of musical performances or having coaches make contact can help you. Colleges appreciate the stamina and discipline necessary to become really good at something.

*4.* **Involvement in school and local community.** Genuine and sustained service to others and effective, long-term leadership are of great interest to admissions officers. Colleges are more than classrooms; a concerned, good citizen is a valuable asset to the college community.

*5.* **Recommendations from outside your school community.** Be careful here. There is a saying in some admissions offices that goes, "The thicker the file, the thicker the candidate." Admissions officers don't want to read twenty testimonials by your parents' best friends. On the other hand, a Scout leader, a community sports coach, or a nursing home director may provide really important information about *you* that distinguishes you from others.

*6.* **First-choice college.** Colleges, no matter how selective, want to know you will accept if admitted. This increases their "yield," helps in their planning, and makes your eventual satisfaction with the college more likely. This is one reason why applying Early Decision is a good strategy if you are sure of your first choice. If you apply to more than one college and you have a first choice, inform the college. *Play fair. You can have only one first choice.*

## Factors Largely Outside Your Control

(That you may still be able to use to your advantage)

*1.* **Alumni/ae connections.** You can't change where your parents went to college, but if a parent or sibling attended a college you are really interested in, chances are that you'll have a better chance for admission. If you feel you are a "borderline" candidate for a certain level of selectivity, you might wish to consider a school in that category where you have a good "connection," e.g., because of parents, primarily. Remember, though, the college must be a good one for *you.*

*2.* **Geographical distribution.** Because colleges and universities want to have a varied student body, they are interested in attracting students from areas far from their campus. If you live in New England, you will be a more attractive candidate to a western or midwestern college than you will be to one in Boston. There are many advantages to using the college years as a time to discover another part of the country, so why not put geographical distribution to work for you? Don't feel your area has the corner on the best colleges; there are excellent institutions throughout the country. (Remember that financial aid usually takes into account travel costs between home and college if money is a worry.)

*3.* **Your family and socioeconomic background.** Again, institutions want diversity. They don't want all rich kids or all poor ones. They don't want members of only one race or religion. They also know that, for example, standardized test scores are related to family background and neighborhood income levels. Suffice it to say, you will be seen in the context of the opportunities you have had or made. You will not be penalized for never having been abroad, or for not having taken AP courses if your high school is unable to offer them.

As we've said before, competitive colleges want contributors. There are many ways you can add to a college community, and you should realistically take stock of what you offer so that you can be sure to present your assets. You can also do a great deal to improve your ability to contribute by working on talents and academics, by becoming involved, and by documenting what you do. Substance and presentation are both important, and you have a large amount of control over both. Remember, too, that there is a human dimension to the process, i.e., a person will be reading your application and committees of individuals will discuss you as a candidate. Don't lose sight of that as you write essays, sit in interviews, and fill out applications.

This human dimension may mean that from colleges of roughly equal selectivity you might receive some acceptances and some rejections. You may "connect" with some interviewers more than with others. The needs and interests of relatively similar colleges differ as do the needs and interests of even the very same college from year to year. Consequently it isn't really helpful to compare decisions you receive with those of friends, even if their records *seem* similar to yours. *If you find you are not admitted by a particular institution, it may mean not that you were an unacceptable candidate, but only that you were one of too many good candidates.* The more selective the college, the more likely this is to be true, and this is one of the reasons for applying to more than one college with the same degree of selectivity.

# Criteria Used in Rating College Competitiveness

## The Criteria

The following three factors were used to determine the rating describing the competitiveness of each college and university:

- The average combined SAT and/or ACT composite scores of 1993-94 (or 1992-93) entering freshmen.
- The relative secondary school class ranking of 1993-94 (or 1992-93) entering freshmen.
- The percentage of applicants who were offered admission for 1993-94 (or 1992-93).

Because certain institutions with high standards often recruit only among students likely to gain acceptance, they may accept a high percentage of applicants while being quite competitive. Therefore, in determining the competitiveness ratings, SAT/ACT scores and secondary school class rank are weighted more heavily than the percentage of applicants offered admission.

Since each college and university has developed its own admissions policies, giving varying priority to these criteria and often including other factors, the competitiveness rating must serve only as a guideline. The rating is intended simply to give the student a perspective on admissions conditions at colleges where he or she is considering applying. Under the *Basis for Candidate Selection* heading in each institution's description is listed the total number of factors used in making admissions decisions, presented in order of priority as supplied by the admissions offices.

The following classifications show the ranges of test scores, class rankings, and percentages of accepted applicants used to determine each category:

**Most Competitive**

This category includes colleges and universities to which it is considered most difficult to gain admission. Admitted students generally have combined SAT scores above 1200 or composite ACT scores above 27, and students usually ranked in the top 15% of their secondary school class. The schools in this category accept 11% to 55% of all applicants, with the majority accepting under 28%.

**Highly Competitive**

This rating indicates institutions that generally accept students with combined SAT scores above 1100 or composite ACT scores above 25 and secondary school rank in the top third of their class. The schools in this category generally accept approximately 36% to 69% of all applicants.

**More Competitive**

This rating indicates institutions that generally accept students with combined SAT scores above 1000 or composite ACT scores above 23 and secondary school rank in the top half of their class. The schools in this category generally accept approximately 32% to 66% of all applicants.

**Competitive**

This rating indicates institutions that generally accept students with combined SAT scores above 800 or composite ACT scores above 21 and secondary school rank in the top half of their class. The schools in this category generally accept approximately 49% to 80% of all applicants.

**Less Competitive**

This rating indicates institutions that generally accept students with combined SAT scores below 900 or composite ACT scores of less than 21. Secondary school class rank is not considered in this ranking calculation. The schools in this category generally accept approximately 45% to 98% of all applicants.

**Noncompetitive**

This rating indicates institutions that generally accept students with combined SAT scores below 800 or composite ACT scores of less than 20. The schools in this category generally accept more than 90% of all applicants. Also rated noncompetitive are those public institutions which admit all state residents even though they may have requirements for out-of-state candidates.

**Not Available (N/A)**

Not available is used for colleges and institutions that have not supplied sufficient information (SAT or ACT test scores, secondary school rankings, and/or acceptance rate) to allow a ranking to be determined.

**Not Applicable**

Institutions in this category include those for which test scores and secondary school rankings are of little consequence in the admissions process. These are generally art or music schools at which a portfolio or audition is the major factor in determining a student's acceptability.

## How to Use the Data

The following lists, categorizing colleges and universities by selectivity, are in alphabetical order; no relative ranking within groupings is intended.

In choosing the right college for you, the competitive ranking should be used only in establishing the overall parameters for your search. The standards listed under the ratings for SAT/ACT scores and class rank may be compared with your own, but you should not neglect to refer to the detailed descriptions of the colleges, where you will find the other factors that may weigh significantly with admissions committees and make your candidacy more or less likely.

It is important to examine the Admissions section for academic and other factors considered as a basis for selection, as well as to read the rest of the description as you determine how a particular school provides what you want and need in a college.

# Listing of Colleges by Competitive Ranking

## Most competitive

Amherst Coll, MA
Bowdoin Coll, ME
Brandeis U, MA
Brown U, RI
California Inst of Tech, CA
Chicago, U of, IL
Claremont McKenna Coll, CA
Columbia U, Columbia Coll, NY
Columbia U, Sch of Engineering and Applied Science, NY
Cooper Union, NY
Cornell U, NY
Dartmouth Coll, NH
Davidson Coll, NC
Duke U, NC
Georgetown U, DC
Harvard U, MA
Harvey Mudd Coll, CA
Haverford Coll, PA
Holy Cross, Coll of the, MA
Johns Hopkins U, MD
Massachusetts Inst of Tech, MA
Middlebury Coll, VT
Northwestern U, IL
Notre Dame, U of, IN
Pennsylvania, U of, PA
Pomona Coll, CA
Princeton U, NJ
Rice U, TX
Stanford U, CA
Swarthmore Coll, PA
U.S. Air Force Acad, CO
Virginia, U of, VA
Washington & Lee U, VA
Webb Inst of Naval Architecture, NY
Wellesley Coll, MA
William & Mary, Coll of, VA
Williams Coll, MA
Yale U, CT

## Highly competitive

Alma Coll, MI
Bard Coll, NY
Barnard Coll, NY
Bates Coll, ME
Beloit Coll, WI
Benedict Coll, SC
Boston Coll, MA
Boston U, MA
Brigham Young U, UT
Bryn Mawr Coll, PA
Bucknell U, PA
California, U of, Berkeley, CA
California, U of, Santa Cruz, CA
Carleton Coll, MN
Carnegie Mellon U, PA
Case Western Reserve U, OH
Centre Coll, KY
Clarkson U, NY
Colby Coll, ME
Colgate U, NY
Colorado Coll, CO
Colorado Sch of Mines, CO
Connecticut Coll, CT
Dallas, U of, TX
Drew U, NJ
Emory U, GA
Florida, U of, FL
Franklin & Marshall Coll, PA
Furman U, SC
Georgia Inst of Tech, GA
Gettysburg Coll, PA
GMI Engineering & Management Inst, MI
Grinnell Coll, IA
Grove City Coll, PA
Hamilton Coll, NY
Hendrix Coll, AR
Illinois Wesleyan U, IL
Illinois, U of, Urbana-Champaign, IL
James Madison U, VA
Kalamazoo Coll, MI
Kenyon Coll, OH
Lafayette Coll, PA
Lawrence U, WI
Lehigh U, PA
Macalester Coll, MN
Mary Washington Coll, VA
Miami U, OH
Michigan Tech U, MI
Michigan, U of, Ann Arbor, MI
Minnesota, U of, Morris, MN
Missouri, U of, Rolla, MO
Mount Holyoke Coll, MA
New Coll of the U of South Florida, FL
New Mexico Inst of Mining & Tech, NM
New York U, NY
North Carolina, U of, Chapel Hill, NC
Northeast Missouri St U, MO
Oberlin Coll, OH
Occidental Coll, CA
Oglethorpe U, GA
Pitzer Coll, CA
Polytechnic U, NY
Presbyterian Coll, SC
Puget Sound, U of, WA
Reed Coll, OR
Rensselaer Polytechnic Inst, NY
Rhodes Coll, TN
Richmond, U of, VA
Rochester, U of, NY
Rose-Hulman Inst of Tech, IN
Rutgers U, Coll of Engineering, NJ
Rutgers U, Coll of Pharmacy, NJ
Rutgers U, Rutgers Coll, NJ
Sarah Lawrence Coll, NY
Scripps Coll, CA
Smith Coll, MA
South, U of the, TN
Southern California, U of, CA
Southwestern U, TX
St. John's Coll, MD
St. Mary's Coll of Maryland, MD
Stevens Inst of Tech, NJ
SUNY at Binghamton, NY
SUNY Coll at Geneseo, NY
SUNY Coll of Environmental Science & Forestry, NY
Taylor U, IN
Texas, U of, Austin, TX
Texas, U of, Dallas, TX
Transylvania U, KY
Trenton St Coll, NJ
Trinity Coll, CT
Trinity U, TX
Tufts U, MA
Tulane U, LA
U.S. Coast Guard Acad, CT
U.S. Merchant Marine Acad, NY
U.S. Military Acad, NY
U.S. Naval Acad, MD
Union Coll, NY
Valparaiso U, IN
Vanderbilt U, TN
Vassar Coll, NY
Wabash Coll, IN
Wake Forest U, NC
Washington U, MO
Wesleyan U, CT
Wheaton Coll, IL
Whitman Coll, WA
Willamette U, OR
Wisconsin, U of, Madison, WI
Worcester Polytechnic Inst, MA

## More competitive

Agnes Scott Coll, GA
Allegheny Coll, PA
American U, DC
Atlantic, Coll of the, ME
Babson Coll, MA
Baylor U, TX
Bennington Coll, VT
Birmingham-Southern Coll, AL
California, U of, Davis, CA
California, U of, Los Angeles, CA
California, U of, San Diego, CA
Canisius Coll, NY
Clemson U, SC
Colorado Tech, CO
CUNY, New York City Tech Coll, NY
DePauw U, IN
Dickinson Coll, PA
Erskine Coll, SC
Florida Inst of Tech, FL
Florida International U, FL
Fresno Pacific Coll, CA
George Washington U, DC
Georgia, U of, GA
Goucher Coll, MD
Gustavus Adolphus Coll, MN
Harding U, AR
Hillsdale Coll, MI
Hofstra U, NY
Illinois Inst of Tech, IL
Insurance, Coll of, NY
Judaism, U of, Lee Coll, CA
Juniata Coll, PA
Knox Coll, IL
Kutztown U of Pennsylvania, PA
Lake Forest Coll, IL
Lewis & Clark Coll, OR
Linfield Coll, OR
Luther Coll, IA
Lyon Coll, AR
Marietta Coll, OH
Messiah Coll, PA
Millersville U of Pennsylvania, PA
Mills Coll, CA
Millsaps Coll, MS
Milwaukee Sch of Engineering, WI
Missouri, U of, Columbia, MO
Morehouse Coll, GA
North Carolina St U, NC
North Carolina, U of, Asheville, NC
Ohio Northern U, OH
Ohio Wesleyan U, OH
Pennsylvania St U, PA
Pepperdine U, CA
Philadelphia Coll of Pharmacy & Science, PA
Quinnipiac Coll, CT
Redlands, U of, CA
Rhode Island Sch of Design, RI
Rutgers U, Camden Coll of Arts & Sciences, NJ
Rutgers U, Coll of Nursing, NJ
Rutgers U, Cook Coll, NJ
Rutgers U, Mason Gross Sch of the Arts, NJ
Salisbury St U, MD
Samford U, AL
Siena Coll, NY
Simon's Rock Coll of Bard, MA
Spelman Coll, GA
St. John's Coll, NM
St. Mary's Coll, CA
St. Olaf Coll, MN
St. Thomas, U of, TX
Stockton Coll of New Jersey, NJ
SUNY at Albany, NY
SUNY at Stony Brook, NY
SUNY Coll at New Paltz, NY
SUNY Coll at Oswego, NY
Texas A&M U, College Station, TX
Thomas Aquinas Coll, CA
Trinity Coll, DC
Ursinus Coll, PA
Villanova U, PA
Virginia Polytechnic Inst & St U, VA
Washington, U of, WA
Whitworth Coll, WA
William Jewell Coll, MO

Wittenberg U, OH
Wofford Coll, SC
Yeshiva U, NY

## Competitive

Adams St Coll, CO
Alaska Pacific U, AK
Albertson Coll, ID
Albion Coll, MI
Albright Coll, PA
Alderson-Broaddus Coll, WV
Alfred U, NY
Alverno Coll, WI
Anderson U, IN
Angelo St U, TX
Antioch Coll of Antioch U, OH
Appalachian St U, NC
Art Center Coll of Design, CA
Auburn U, AL
Augustana Coll, IL
Avila Coll, MO
Bartlesville Wesleyan Coll, OK
Berea Coll, KY
Blackburn Coll, IL
Bloomsburg U of Pennsylvania, PA
Bluefield Coll, VA
Bradley U, IL
Brigham Young U, Hawaii Campus, HI
Buena Vista Coll, IA
Butler U, IN
California Baptist Coll, CA
California Maritime Acad, CA
California Polytechnic St U, San Luis Obispo, CA
California St Polytechnic U, Pomona, CA
California St U, Bakersfield, CA
California St U, Fresno, CA
California St U, Stanislaus, CA
California U of Pennsylvania, PA
California, U of, Irvine, CA
California, U of, Santa Barbara, CA
Calvin Coll, MI
Campbell U, NC
Campbellsville Coll, KY
Catholic U of America, DC
Cedarville Coll, OH
Centenary Coll of Louisiana, LA
Central Coll, IA
Central Florida, U of, FL
Central Washington U, WA
Central Wesleyan C, SC
Charleston, Coll of, SC
Charleston, U of, WV
Christendom Coll, VA
Christopher Newport U, VA
Clark U, MA
Clarkson Coll, NE
Coe Coll, IA
College Misericordia, PA
Colorado St U, CO
Colorado, U of, Boulder, CO
Colorado, U of, Denver, CO
Concordia Coll, Moorhead, MN
Connecticut, U of, CT
Converse Coll, SC
Corcoran Sch of Art, DC
Cornell Coll, IA
Covenant Coll, GA
Creighton U, NE
Cumberland Coll, KY
CUNY, Lehman Coll, NY
Dakota Wesleyan U, SD
Dayton, U of, OH
Delaware, U of, DE
Denison U, OH
Denver, U of, CO
DePaul U, IL
Drake U, IA
Drexel U, PA
Drury Coll, MO
Earlham Coll, IN
East Central U, OK
East Stroudsburg U of Pennsylvania, PA
East Tennessee St U, TN
East Texas Baptist U, TX
Eckerd Coll, FL
Elizabethtown Coll, PA
Elmhurst Coll, IL
Elms Coll, MA
Embry-Riddle Aeronautical U, FL
Emerson Coll, MA
Eugene Lang Coll of the New Sch for Social Research, NY
Evansville, U of, IN
Evergreen St Coll, WA
Fairfield U, CT
Fairleigh Dickinson U, NJ
Fashion Inst of Tech, NY
Findlay, U of, OH
Flagler Coll, FL
Florida Southern Coll, FL
Florida St U, FL
Fordham U, NY
Fort Lewis Coll, CO
Franciscan U of Steubenville, OH
Georgia St U, GA
Georgian Court Coll, NJ
Gonzaga U, WA
Gordon Coll, MA
Goshen Coll, IN
Greenville Coll, IL
Guilford Coll, NC
Gwynedd-Mercy Coll, PA
Hamline U, MN
Hampden-Sydney Coll, VA
Hanover Coll, IN
Hartwick Coll, NY
Hawaii Pacific U, HI
Hawaii, U of, Hilo, HI
Heidelberg Coll, OH
Hiram Coll, OH
Hobart and William Smith Coll, NY
Hollins Coll, VA
Holy Family Coll, PA
Hood Coll, MD
Hope Coll, MI
Houghton Coll, NY
Houston, U of, TX
Illinois, U of, Chicago, IL
Indiana U of Pennsylvania, PA
Iowa St U, IA
Iowa Wesleyan Coll, IA
Iowa, U of, IA
Ithaca Coll, NY
Jersey City St Coll, NJ
Judson Coll, IL
Kansas, U of, KS
Kentucky Christian C, KY
Kentucky, U of, KY
LaSalle U, PA
LaVerne, U of, CA
LeMoyne Coll, NY
LeTourneau U, TX
Lindenwood Coll, MO
Lock Haven U of Pennsylvania, PA
Long Island U, C.W. Post Campus, NY
Louisiana Coll, LA
Loyola Coll, MD
Loyola Marymount U, CA
Loyola U, LA
Loyola U, Chicago, IL
Maine, U of, Fort Kent, ME
Malone Coll, OH
Manhattan Coll, NY
Manhattanville Coll, NY
Mansfield U of Pennsylvania, PA
Marian Coll, IN
Marist Coll, NY
Marlboro Coll, VT
Marquette U, WI
Maryland, U of, Baltimore County, MD
Maryland, U of, College Park, MD
Maryville U of St. Louis, MO
Massachusetts Coll of Art, MA
McKendree Coll, IL
McMurry U, TX
McPherson Coll, KS
Mercer U, GA
Miami, U of, FL
Midwestern St U, TX
Milligan Coll, TN
Millikin U, IL
Minnesota, U of, Twin Cities, MN
Missouri Southern St Coll, MO
Missouri, U of, Kansas City, MO
Mobile, U of, AL
Montana, U of, MT
Montclair St Coll, NJ
Montevallo, U of, AL
Moravian Coll, PA
Mt Mary Coll, WI
Mt Union Coll, OH
Muhlenberg Coll, PA
Nazareth Coll of Rochester, NY
Nebraska, U of, Kearney, NE
New England, U of, ME
New Hampshire, U of, NH
New Jersey Inst of Tech, NJ
New Rochelle, Coll of, NY
North Alabama, U of, AL
North Carolina Sch of the Arts, NC
North Carolina, U of, Wilmington, NC
North Central Coll, IL
Northern Arizona U, AZ
Northwestern Coll, MN
Northwestern Coll, WI
Notre Dame Coll of Ohio, OH
Notre Dame, Coll of, CA
Ohio U, OH
Oklahoma St U, OK
Oklahoma, U of, OK
Oral Roberts U, OK
Oregon, U of, OR
Otis Coll of Art & Design, CA
Ottawa U, KS
Ozarks, Coll of the, MO
Pacific U, OR
Palm Beach Atlantic Coll, FL
Philadelphia Coll of Bible, PA
Pittsburgh, U of, Pittsburgh, PA
Portland, U of, OR
Principia Coll, IL
Providence Coll, RI
Queens Coll, NC
Radford U, VA
Ramapo Coll of New Jersey, NJ
Randolph-Macon Coll, VA
Randolph-Macon Woman's Coll, VA
Rhode Island Coll, RI
Ripon Coll, WI
Roanoke Coll, VA
Rochester Inst of Tech, NY
Rockford Coll, IL
Rockhurst Coll, MO
Roger Williams U, RI
Rollins Coll, FL
Rosemont C, PA
Rowan Coll of New Jersey, NJ
Rutgers U, Douglass Coll, NJ
Rutgers U, Livingston Coll, NJ
Rutgers U, Newark Coll of Arts & Sciences, NJ
Salem Coll, NC
Samuel Merritt Coll, CA
Santa Clara U, CA
Savannah Coll of Art & Design, GA
Schreiner Coll, TX
Scranton, U of, PA
Seattle Pacific U, WA
Seton Hill Coll, PA
Shepherd Coll, WV
Shippensburg U of Pennsylvania, PA
Simpson Coll, IA
Sioux Falls Coll, SD
Skidmore Coll, NY
Slippery Rock U of Pennsylvania, PA
South Carolina, U of, Spartanburg, SC
South Dakota Sch of Mines & Tech, SD
South Florida, U of, FL
Southeast Missouri St U, MO
Southern California Coll, CA
Southern Illinois U, Carbondale, IL
Southern Illinois U, Edwardsville, IL
Southern Indiana, U of, IN
Southern Methodist U, TX
Southern Vermont Coll, VT
Southwest Texas St U, TX
Southwestern Coll, KS

Spalding U, KY
Spring Hill Coll, AL
Springfield Coll, MA
St. Bonaventure U, NY
St. Francis C, IN
St. John's U, NY
St. Joseph Coll, CT
St. Joseph's U, PA
St. Lawrence U, NY
St. Louis Coll of Pharmacy, MO
St. Louis U, MO
St. Mary Coll, KS
St. Mary's Coll, IN
St. Mary, Coll of, NE
St. Michael's Coll, VT
St. Norbert Coll, WI
Stetson U, FL
Stonehill Coll, MA
SUNY at Buffalo, NY
SUNY Coll at Brockport, NY
SUNY Coll at Cortland, NY
SUNY Coll at Fredonia, NY
SUNY Coll at Potsdam, NY
SUNY Coll at Purchase, NY
SUNY Maritime Coll, NY
Susquehanna U, PA
Sweet Briar Coll, VA
Syracuse U, NY
Tabor Coll, KS
Temple U, PA
Texas Christian U, TX
Texas Wesleyan U, TX
Texas, U of, San Antonio, TX
Thomas Coll, ME
Thomas More Coll, KY
Tulsa, U of, OK
Utica Coll of Syracuse U, NY
Vermont, U of, VT
Virginia Commonwealth U, VA
Virginia Wesleyan Coll, VA
Viterbo Coll, WI
Warren Wilson Coll, NC
Wartburg Coll, IA
Washburn U of Topeka, KS
Washington & Jefferson Coll, PA
Wells Coll, NY
West Chester U of Pennsylvania, PA
Westbrook Coll, ME
Western Baptist Coll, OR
Western Illinois U, IL
Western Maryland Coll, MD
Westfield St Coll, MA
Westminster Choir Coll, The Sch of Music of Rider Coll, NJ
Westminster Coll, MO
Westmont Coll, CA
Wheaton Coll, MA
Whittier Coll, CA
Widener U, PA
William Paterson Coll of New Jersey, NJ
William Tyndale Coll, MI
Winona St U, MN
Wisconsin, U of, LaCrosse, WI
Wisconsin, U of, Oshkosh, WI
Wisconsin, U of, Platteville, WI
Wisconsin, U of, River Falls, WI
Wisconsin, U of, Stevens Point, WI
Wisconsin, U of, Whitewater, WI
Wooster, The Coll of, OH
Xavier U, OH
Xavier U of Louisiana, LA
York Coll of Pennsylvania, PA

## Less competitive

Abilene Christian U, TX
Acad of the New Church Coll, PA
Adelphi U, NY
Adrian Coll, MI
Alabama A&M U, AL
Alabama, U of, Birmingham, AL
Alabama, U of, Huntsville, AL
Alabama, U of, Tuscaloosa, AL
Alaska, U of, Fairbanks, AK
Albany Coll of Pharmacy, NY
Albany St Coll, GA
Albertus Magnus Coll, CT
Alcorn St U, MS
Allentown Coll of St. Francis de Sales, PA
Alvernia Coll, PA
American International Coll, MA
Anderson Coll, SC
Andrews U, MI
Anna Maria Coll, MA
Aquinas Coll, MI
Arizona Coll of the Bible, AZ
Arizona St U - Main Campus, AZ
Arizona, U of, AZ
Arkansas, U of, Fayetteville, AR
Arkansas, U of, Little Rock, AR
Arkansas, U of, Monticello, AR
Art Acad of Cincinnati, OH
Arts, U of the, PA
Asbury Coll, KY
Assumption Coll, MA
Atlanta Coll of Art, GA
Atlantic Union Coll, MA
Augsburg Coll, MN
Augusta Coll, GA
Augustana Coll, SD
Aurora U, IL
Austin Coll, TX
Austin Peay St U, TN
Averett Coll, VA
Azusa Pacific U, CA
Baker U, KS
Baldwin-Wallace Coll, OH
Ball St U, IN
Baptist Bible Coll & Theological Sem, PA
Barry U, FL
Barton Coll, NC
Bay Path Coll, MA
Beaver Coll, PA
Belhaven Coll, MS
Bellarmine Coll, KY
Belmont Abbey Coll, NC
Belmont U, TN
Bemidji St U, MN
Benedictine Coll, KS
Bennett Coll, NC
Bentley Coll, MA
Bethany Coll, WV
Bethany Coll, KS
Bethel Coll, KS
Bethel Coll, IN
Bethune-Cookman Coll, FL
Biola U, CA
Bluefield St Coll, WV
Bluffton Coll, OH
Boise St U, ID
Boston Conservatory, MA
Bowie St U, MD
Bowling Green St U, OH
Brenau U, GA
Brescia Coll, KY
Brewton-Parker Coll, GA
Briar Cliff Coll, IA
Bridgeport, U of, CT
Bryan Coll, TN
Bryant Coll, RI
Cabrini Coll, PA
Caldwell Coll, NJ
California Coll of Arts & Crafts, CA
California Lutheran U, CA
California St U, Chico, CA
California St U, Fullerton, CA
California St U, Long Beach, CA
California St U, Northridge, CA
California St U, Sacramento, CA
California, U of, Riverside, CA
Calumet Coll of St. Joseph, IN
Capital U, OH
Capitol Coll, MD
Cardinal Stritch Coll, WI
Carroll Coll, WI
Carroll Coll, MT
Carson-Newman Coll, TN
Carthage Coll, WI
Castleton St Coll, VT
Catawba Coll, NC
Cazenovia Coll, NY
Cedar Crest Coll, PA
Centenary Coll, NJ
Center for Creative Studies - Coll of Art & Design, MI
Central Arkansas, U of, AR
Central Bible Coll, MO
Central Connecticut St U, CT
Central Methodist Coll, MO
Central Michigan U, MI
Central Missouri St U, MO
Central Oklahoma, U of, OK
Chadron St Coll, NE
Chaminade U of Honolulu, HI
Champlain Coll, VT
Chapman U, CA
Chatham Coll, PA
Chestnut Hill Coll, PA
Chicago St U, IL
Chowan Coll, NC
Christian Brothers U, TN
Cincinnati, U of, OH
Citadel, The, SC
Clarion U of Pennsylvania, PA
Clarke Coll, IA
Clayton St Coll, GA
Cleveland Inst of Art, OH
Cleveland St U, OH
Coastal Carolina U, SC
Coker Coll, SC
Colby-Sawyer Coll, NH
Colorado, U of, Colorado Springs, CO
Columbia Bible Coll, SC
Columbia Coll, SC
Columbia Coll, MO
Columbus Coll of Art & Design, OH
Conception Seminary Coll, MO
Concordia Coll, MI
Concordia Coll, NE
Concordia Coll, OR
Concordia Coll, St. Paul, MN
Concordia Lutheran Coll, TX
Concordia U, IL
Concordia U, CA
Concordia U Wisconsin, WI
Coppin St Coll, MD
Crown Coll, MN
Culver-Stockton Coll, MO
Curry Coll, MA
D'Youville Coll, NY
Dakota St U, SD
Dallas Baptist U, TX
Dana Coll, NE
Daniel Webster Coll, NH
David Lipscomb U, TN
Davis & Elkins Coll, WV
Defiance Coll, OH
Delaware Valley Coll, PA
Delta St U, MS
Detroit Mercy, U of, MI
Dillard U, LA
Doane Coll, NE
Dominican Coll of San Rafael, CA
Dordt Coll, IA
Dowling Coll, NY
Dr. Martin Luther Coll, MN
Dubuque, U of, IA
Duquesne U, PA
East Carolina U, NC
East Texas St U, TX
Eastern Coll, PA
Eastern Connecticut St U, CT
Eastern Illinois U, IL
Eastern Mennonite Coll, VA
Eastern Michigan U, MI
Eastern Montana Coll, MT
Eastern Nazarene Coll, MA
Eastern Washington U, WA
Edgewood Coll, WI
Elmira Coll, NY
Elon Coll, NC
Embry-Riddle Aeronautical U, AZ
Emory & Henry Coll, VA
Endicott Coll, MA
Eureka Coll, IL
Fairmont St Coll, WV
Faith Baptist Bible Coll & Sem, IA
Faulkner U, AL
Felician Coll, NJ
Ferrum Coll, VA
Fitchburg St Coll, MA

Five Towns Coll, NY
Florida A&M U, FL
Florida Atlantic U, FL
Fontbonne Coll, MO
Framingham St Coll, MA
Franklin Coll, IN
Franklin Pierce Coll, NH
Free Will Baptist Bible Coll, TN
Freed-Hardeman U, TN
Frostburg St U, MD
Gannon U, PA
Gardner-Webb Coll, NC
Geneva Coll, PA
George Fox Coll, OR
George Mason U, VA
Georgetown Coll, KY
Georgia Coll, GA
Georgia Southern U, GA
Goddard Coll, VT
Goldey-Beacom Coll, DE
Grace Coll, IN
Graceland Coll, IA
Grambling St U, LA
Grand Rapids Baptist Coll & Sem, MI
Grand Valley St U, MI
Grand View Coll, IA
Green Mountain Coll, VT
Greensboro Coll, NC
Hahnemann U, Sch of Health Sciences & Humanities, PA
Hampton U, VA
Hardin-Simmons U, TX
Hartford, U of, CT
Hastings Coll, NE
Hawaii, U of, Manoa, HI
Henderson St U, AR
High Point U, NC
Hilbert Coll, NY
Holy Names Coll, CA
Houston Baptist U, TX
Howard Payne U, TX
Howard U, DC
Huntingdon Coll, AL
Huntington Coll, IN
Husson Coll, ME
Huston-Tillotson Coll, TX
Idaho St U, ID
Idaho, U of, ID
Illinois Benedictine Coll, IL
Illinois Coll, IL
Illinois St U, IL
Immaculata Coll, PA
Incarnate Word Coll, TX
Indiana Inst of Tech, IN
Indiana St U, IN
Indiana U Bloomington, IN
Indiana U Kokomo, IN
Indiana U Purdue U, Indianapolis, IN
Indiana U South Bend, IN
Indiana U-Purdue U, Fort Wayne, IN
Indianapolis, U of, IN
Iona Coll, NY
Jackson St U, MS
Jacksonville St U, AL
Jacksonville U, FL
Jamestown Coll, ND

John Brown U, AR
John Carroll U, OH
Johnson & Wales U, RI
Johnson Bible Coll, TN
Johnson C. Smith U, NC
Johnson St Coll, VT
Judson Coll, AL
Kansas Newman Coll, KS
Kansas St U, KS
Kansas Wesleyan U, KS
Kean Coll of New Jersey, NJ
Keene St Coll, NH
Kendall Coll, IL
Kennesaw St Coll, GA
Kent St U, OH
Kentucky Wesleyan Coll, KY
Keuka Coll, NY
King Coll, TN
King's Coll, NY
King's Coll, PA
LaGrange Coll, GA
Lake Erie Coll, OH
Lake Superior St U, MI
Lakeland Coll, WI
Lamar U, TX
Lancaster Bible Coll, PA
LaRoche Coll, PA
Lasell Coll, MA
LaSierra U, CA
Lawrence Tech U, MI
Lebanon Valley Coll, PA
Lees-McRae Coll, NC
Lenoir-Rhyne Coll, NC
Lesley Coll, MA
Lewis U, IL
Limestone Coll, SC
Lincoln Memorial U, TN
Lindsey Wilson Coll, KY
Livingston U, AL
Livingstone Coll, NC
Long Island U, Southampton Campus, NY
Longwood Coll, VA
Loras Coll, IA
Louisiana St U & A&M Coll, LA
Louisiana Tech U, LA
Louisville, U of, KY
Lycoming Coll, PA
Lynchburg Coll, VA
Lyndon St Coll, VT
Lynn U, FL
MacMurray Coll, IL
Maharishi International U, IA
Maine Coll of Art, ME
Maine, U of, ME
Maine, U of, Augusta, ME
Maine, U of, Farmington, ME
Maine, U of, Machias, ME
Maine, U of, Presque Isle, ME
Manchester Coll, IN
Manhattan Christian Coll, KS
Mankato St U, MN
Marian Coll of Fond du Lac, WI
Mars Hill Coll, NC
Mary Baldwin Coll, VA
Mary, U of, ND

Maryland, U of, Eastern Shore, MD
Marymount Coll, NY
Marymount U, VA
Maryville Coll, TN
Marywood Coll, PA
Massachusetts, U of, Amherst, MA
Massachusetts, U of, Boston, MA
Massachusetts, U of, Dartmouth, MA
Massachusetts, U of, Lowell, MA
Master's Coll, CA
Memphis, U of, TN
Mercyhurst Coll, PA
Meredith Coll, NC
Merrimack Coll, MA
Methodist Coll, NC
Metropolitan St Coll of Denver, CO
Michigan Christian Coll, MI
Michigan St U, MI
Michigan, U of, Dearborn, MI
Michigan, U of, Flint, MI
Middle Tennessee St U, TN
Midland Lutheran Coll, NE
Midway Coll, KY
Minneapolis Coll of Art & Design, MN
Minnesota, U of, Duluth, MN
Mississippi Coll, MS
Mississippi St U, MS
Mississippi U for Women, MS
Mississippi Valley St U, MS
Mississippi, U of, MS
Missouri Baptist Coll, MO
Missouri Valley Coll, MO
Missouri, U of, St. Louis, MO
Molloy Coll, NY
Monmouth Coll, NJ
Monmouth Coll, IL
Montana Coll of Mineral Science & Tech, MT
Montana St U, MT
Moody Bible Inst, IL
Moore Coll of Art & Design, PA
Moorhead St U, MN
Morehead St U, KY
Morgan St U, MD
Morningside Coll, IA
Mount Aloysius Coll, PA
Mt Marty Coll, SD
Mt Mercy Coll, IA
Mt Olive Coll, NC
Mt Senario Coll, WI
Mt St. Joseph, Coll of, OH
Mt St. Mary Coll, NY
Mt St. Mary's Coll, CA
Mt St. Mary's Coll, MD
Mt St. Vincent, Coll of, NY
Mt Vernon Nazarene Coll, OH
Murray St U, KY
Muskingum Coll, OH
National-Louis U, IL
Nebraska Wesleyan U, NE
Nebraska, U of, Lincoln, NE
Nebraska, U of, Omaha, NE
Nevada, U of, Las Vegas, NV
Nevada, U of, Reno, NV
New England Coll, NH

New Hampshire Coll, NH
New Haven, U of, CT
New Mexico Highlands U, NM
New Mexico, U of, NM
New Orleans, U of, LA
New York Inst of Tech, NY
Newberry C, SC
Niagara U, NY
North Adams St Coll, MA
North Carolina A&T St U, NC
North Carolina Wesleyan Coll, NC
North Carolina, U of, Charlotte, NC
North Carolina, U of, Greensboro, NC
North Dakota St U, ND
North Dakota, U of, ND
North Georgia Coll, GA
North Park Coll, IL
North Texas, U of, TX
Northeastern Illinois U, IL
Northeastern St U, OK
Northeastern U, MA
Northern Colorado, U of, CO
Northern Illinois U, IL
Northern Iowa, U of, IA
Northern Michigan U, MI
Northern Montana Coll, MT
Northland Coll, WI
Northwest Christian Coll, OR
Northwest Coll, WA
Northwest Missouri St U, MO
Northwestern Coll, IA
Northwestern St U of Louisiana, LA
Northwood U - Texas Campus, TX
Norwich U, VT
Notre Dame of Maryland, Coll of, MD
Nova Southeastern U, FL
Oakland U, MI
Oakwood Coll, AL
Ohio St U, Columbus, OH
Ohio St U, Lima, OH
Ohio St U, Mansfield, OH
Ohio St U, Newark, OH
Oklahoma Baptist U, OK
Oklahoma Christian U of Science & Arts, OK
Oklahoma City U, OK
Old Dominion U, VA
Olivet Coll, MI
Olivet Nazarene U, IL
Oregon Inst of Tech, OR
Otterbein Coll, OH
Ouachita Baptist U, AR
Pace U, New York City, NY
Pace U, Pleasantville/Briarcliff, NY
Pace U, White Plains, NY
Pacific Christian Coll, CA
Pacific Lutheran U, WA
Pacific Northwest C of Art, OR
Pacific Union Coll, CA
Pacific, U of the, CA
Paine Coll, GA
Panhandle St U, OK
Park Coll, MO
Parks Coll of St. Louis U, IL
Pembroke St U, NC

Pennsylvania St U, Erie, Behrend Coll, PA
Pfeiffer Coll, NC
Philadelphia Coll of Textiles & Science, PA
Phillips U, OK
Piedmont Coll, GA
Pikeville Coll, KY
Pittsburg St U, KS
Pittsburgh, U of, Bradford, PA
Pittsburgh, U of, Greensburg, PA
Pittsburgh, U of, Johnstown, PA
Plymouth St Coll, NH
Point Loma Nazarene Coll, CA
Point Park Coll, PA
Prairie View A&M U, TX
Pratt Inst, NY
Purdue U, IN
Purdue U - North Central, IN
Purdue U, Calumet, IN
Quincy U, IL
Regis Coll, MA
Regis U, CO
Rhode Island, U of, RI
Rider Coll, NJ
Rivier Coll, NH
Robert Morris Coll, PA
Roberts Wesleyan Coll, NY
Rocky Mountain Coll, MT
Roosevelt U, IL
Rosary Coll, IL
Russell Sage Coll, NY
Rust Coll, MS
Saginaw Valley St U, MI
Salem St Coll, MA
Salem-Teikyo U, WV
Sam Houston St U, TX
San Diego St U, CA
San Diego, U of, CA
San Francisco St U, CA
San Francisco, U of, CA
Santa Fe, Coll of, NM
Seattle U, WA
Seton Hall U, NJ
Shenandoah U, VA
Silver Lake Coll, WI
Simmons Coll, MA
Sonoma St U, CA
South Alabama, U of, AL
South Carolina, U of (Columbia), SC
South Carolina, U of, Aiken, SC
South Dakota St U, SD
South Dakota, U of, Vermillion, SD
Southeastern Bible Coll, AL
Southeastern Oklahoma St U, OK
Southern Arkansas U - Magnolia, AR
Southern C of Seventh-day Adventists, TN
Southern Coll of Tech, GA
Southern Connecticut St U, CT
Southern Maine, U of, ME
Southern Mississippi, U of, MS
Southern Oregon St Coll, OR
Southwest Baptist U, MO
Southwest Missouri St U, MO
Southwest, C of the, NM
Southwestern Adventist Coll, TX
Spring Arbor C, MI
St. Ambrose U, IA
St. Andrews Presbyterian Coll, NC
St. Anselm Coll, NH
St. Benedict, Coll of, MN
St. Catherine, The Coll of, MN
St. Cloud St U, MN
St. Edward's U, TX
St. Elizabeth, Coll of, NJ
St. Francis Coll, PA
St. Francis, Coll of, IL
St. John Fisher Coll, NY
St. John's U, MN
St. Joseph Seminary Coll, LA
St. Joseph's Coll, ME
St. Joseph's Coll, IN
St. Joseph's Coll (Brooklyn), NY
St. Joseph's Coll (Patchogue), NY
St. Leo Coll, FL
St. Mary's Coll of Minnesota, MN
St. Mary's U, TX
St. Mary-of-the-Woods Coll, IN
St. Paul's Coll, VA
St. Peter's Coll, NJ
St. Rose, The Coll of, NY
St. Scholastica, Coll of, MN
St. Thomas Aquinas Coll, NY
St. Thomas U, FL
St. Thomas, U of, MN
St. Vincent Coll, PA
St. Xavier U, IL
Stephen F. Austin St U, TX
Stephens Coll, MO
Stillman Coll, AL
Suffolk U, MA
SUNY Coll at Oneonta, NY
SUNY Coll at Plattsburgh, NY
Talladega Coll, AL
Tampa, U of, FL
Tarleton St U, TX
Taylor U, Fort Wayne Campus, IN
Teikyo Westmar U, IA
Tennessee St U, TN
Tennessee Tech U, TN
Tennessee, U of, Chattanooga, TN
Tennessee, U of, Knoxville, TN
Tennessee, U of, Martin, TN
Texas A&M U - Kingsville, TX
Texas A&M U, Galveston, TX
Texas Lutheran Coll, TX
Texas Tech U, TX
Texas Woman's U, TX
Texas, U of, Arlington, TX
Texas, U of, El Paso, TX
Texas, U of, Permian Basin, TX
Thiel Coll, PA
Toccoa Falls Coll, GA
Tougaloo Coll, MS
Towson St U, MD
Tri-State U, IN
Trinity Christian Coll, IL
Trinity Coll, IL
Trinity Coll, VT
Troy St U, AL
Tusculum Coll, TN
Tuskegee U, AL
U.S. International U, CA
Union Coll, KY
Union U, TN
Unity Coll, ME
Upsala Coll, NJ
Urbana U, OH
Ursuline Coll, OH
Utah St U, UT
Utah, U of, UT
Valdosta St Coll, GA
VanderCook Coll of Music, IL
Vennard Coll, IA
Virginia Intermont Coll, VA
Virginia Military Inst, VA
Virginia, U of, Clinch Valley Coll, VA
Voorhees Coll, SC
Wagner Coll, NY
Walla Walla Coll, WA
Walsh U, OH
Warner Pacific Coll, OR
Warner Southern Coll, FL
Washington Coll, MD
Washington St U, WA
Wayland Baptist U, TX
Wayne St Coll, NE
Wayne St U, MI
Webber Coll, FL
Webster U, MO
Wentworth Inst of Tech, MA
Wesley Coll, DE
Wesleyan Coll, GA
West Florida, U of, FL
West Georgia Coll, GA
West Liberty St Coll, WV
West Virginia St Coll, WV
West Virginia U, WV
West Virginia Wesleyan Coll, WV
Western Carolina U, NC
Western Kentucky U, KY
Western Michigan U, MI
Western New England Coll, MA
Western Oregon St Coll, OR
Western St Coll of Colorado, CO
Western Washington U, WA
Westminster Coll, PA
Westminster Coll of Salt Lake City, UT
Wheeling Jesuit Coll, WV
Wheelock Coll, MA
Wichita St U, KS
William Penn Coll, IA
William Woods U, MO
Williams Baptist Coll, AR
Wilmington Coll, OH
Wilson Coll, PA
Wingate Coll, NC
Winston-Salem St U, NC
Winthrop U, SC
Wisconsin Lutheran Coll, WI
Wisconsin, U of, Eau Claire, WI
Wisconsin, U of, Green Bay, WI
Wisconsin, U of, Milwaukee, WI
Wisconsin, U of, Stout, WI
Wisconsin, U of, Superior, WI
Woodbury U, CA
Wright St U, OH
Wyoming, U of, WY
Youngstown St U, OH

## Noncompetitive

Akron, The U of, OH
Alabama St U, AL
Alice Lloyd Coll, KY
Arkansas St U, AR
Arkansas Tech U, AR
Ashland U, OH
Barat Coll, IL
Barber-Scotia Coll, NC
Bellevue Coll, NE
Bethel Coll, TN
Black Hills St U, SD
Calvary Bible Coll, MO
Cameron U, OK
Colorado Christian U, CO
Columbus Coll, GA
Concord Coll, WV
CUNY, Staten Island, Coll of, NY
DeVry Inst of Tech, TX
DeVry Inst of Tech, MO
DeVry Inst of Tech, CA
DeVry Inst of Tech, OH
DeVry Inst of Tech, AZ
DeVry Inst of Tech, GA
DeVry Inst of Tech (Addison), IL
DeVry Inst of Tech (Chicago), IL
Dickinson St U, ND
Eastern Kentucky U, KY
Eastern New Mexico U, NM
Emporia St U, KS
Evangel Coll, MO
Fayetteville St U, NC
Ferris St U, MI
Fort Hays St U, KS
Georgia Southwestern Coll, GA
Glenville St Coll, WV
Hannibal-LaGrange Coll, MO
Indiana U East, IN
Jarvis Christian Coll, TX
Lane Coll, TN
Lincoln U, MO
Louisiana St U, Shreveport, LA
Lubbock Christian U, TX
Marshall U, WV
Mary Hardin-Baylor, U of, TX
McNeese St U, LA
Menlo Coll, CA
Mesa St Coll, CO
Missouri Western St Coll, MO
Morris Brown Coll, GA
Mt St. Clare Coll, IA
Mt Vernon C, DC
National Coll, SD
New Mexico St U, NM
Nicholls St U, LA
Nichols Coll, MA
North Central Bible Coll, MN
Northeast Louisiana U, LA
Northern Kentucky U, KY
Northern St U, SD
Northwestern Oklahoma St U, OK

Nyack Coll, NY
Oakland City Coll, IN
Ohio St U, Marion, OH
Our Lady of the Lake U, TX
Ozarks, U of the, AR
Pine Manor Coll, MA
Pontifical Coll Josephinum, OH
Portland St U, OR
Rio Grande, U of, OH
San Jose St U, CA
Savannah St Coll, GA
Sheldon Jackson Coll, AK
Siena Heights Coll, MI
Southeastern Louisiana U, LA
Southern Colorado, U of, CO
Southern Nazarene U, OK
Southern Utah U, UT
Southwestern Assemblies of God Coll, TX
Southwestern Oklahoma St U, OK
St. Joseph, Coll of, VT
St. Martin's Coll, WA
St. Mary's Coll, MI
Sul Ross St U, TX
Teikyo Marycrest U, IA
Tennessee Wesleyan Coll, TN
Tiffin U, OH
Toledo, The U of, OH
Trevecca Nazarene Coll, TN
Trinity C at Miami, FL
Valley City St U, ND
Virginia Union U, VA
Visual Arts, Sch of, NY
Weber St U, UT
West Virginia Inst of Tech, WV
Western New Mexico U, NM
Wiley Coll, TX

## N/A

Alaska Southeast, U of, Juneau Campus, AK
Alaska, U of, Anchorage, AK
Arkansas, U of, Pine Bluff, AR
Armstrong St Coll, GA
Auburn U, Montgomery, AL
Audrey Cohen Coll, NY
Baker Coll, MI
Baker Coll of Muskegon, MI
Baptist Bible Coll, MO
Boricua Coll, NY
Bradford Coll, MA
Bridgewater Coll, VA
Burlington Coll, VT
California St U, Dominguez Hills, CA
California St U, Hayward, CA
California St U, San Bernardino, CA
Carlow Coll, PA
Central St U, OH
Cheyney U of Pennsylvania, PA
Christian Heritage Coll, CA
Cincinnati Bible Coll, OH
City U, WA
Clark Atlanta U, GA
Cleary Coll, MI
Cogswell Polytechnical Coll, CA
Columbia Coll, IL
Cumberland U, TN
CUNY, Baruch Coll, NY
CUNY, Brooklyn Coll, NY
CUNY, City Coll, NY
CUNY, Hunter Coll, NY
CUNY, John Jay Coll of Criminal Justice, NY
CUNY, Medgar Evers Coll, NY
CUNY, Queens Coll, NY
CUNY, York Coll, NY
Daemen Coll, NY
Delaware St Coll, DE
District of Columbia, U of the, DC
Dominican Coll of Blauvelt, NY
Dyke Coll, OH
East-West U, IL
Eastern Oregon St Coll, OR
Edinboro U of Pennsylvania, PA
Emmanuel Coll, MA
Fisk U, TN
Florida Baptist Theological Coll, FL
Francis Marion U, SC
Franklin U, OH
Gallaudet U, DC
Golden Gate U, CA
Grand Canyon U, AZ
Great Falls, Coll of, MT
Hampshire Coll, MA
Hellenic Coll, MA
Heritage Coll, WA
Houston, U of, Downtown, TX
Humphreys Coll, CA
Indiana U Northwest, IN
John F. Kennedy U, CA
Kendall Coll of Art & Design, MI
Kentucky St U, KY
Laboratory Inst of Merchandising, NY
Lander U, SC
Langston U, OK
Lee Coll, TN
LeMoyne-Owen Coll, TN
Lewis-Clark St Coll, ID
Liberty U, VA
Life Coll, GA
Loma Linda U, CA
Long Island U, Brooklyn Campus, NY
Lourdes Coll, OH
Maine Maritime Acad, ME
Marygrove Coll, MI
Marylhurst Coll, OR
Massachusetts Maritime Acad, MA
Medaille Coll, NY
Medical Coll of Georgia, GA
Memphis Coll of Art, TN
Mercy Coll, NY
MidAmerica Nazarene Coll, KS
Minot St U, ND
Morris Coll, SC
Mt Ida Coll, MA
Multnomah Bible Coll & Biblical Seminary, OR
New Coll of California, CA
Norfolk St U, VA
Northrop-Rice Aviation Inst of Tech, CA
Northwood U, Midland Campus, MI
Oglala Lakota Coll, SD
Ohio Dominican Coll, OH
Our Lady of Holy Cross Coll, LA
Parsons Sch of Design, NY
Patten Coll, CA
Peru St Coll, NE
Prescott Coll, AZ
Salve Regina U, RI
San Francisco Conservatory of Music, CA
Shawnee St U, OH
Sierra Nevada Coll, NV
Simpson Coll, CA
Southeastern Coll of the Assemblies of God, FL
Southern U at New Orleans, LA
Southwest St U, MN
St. Francis Coll, NY
SUNY Coll at Buffalo, NY
SUNY Coll of Tech at Farmingdale, NY
Teikyo Post U, CT
Texas Coll, TX
Texas Southern U, TX
Thomas A. Edison St Coll, NJ
Union Coll, NE
Virginia St U, VA
Washington Bible Coll, MD
Waynesburg Coll, PA
West Coast U, CA
West Texas St U, TX
Western International U, AZ
Wilmington Coll, DE

## Not applicable

Acad of Art Coll, CA
American Coll for the Applied Arts, GA
American Cons of Music, IL
Art Inst of Chicago, Sch of the, IL
Bassist Coll, OR
Berklee Coll of Music, MA
Boston Architectural Center, MA
California Inst of the Arts, CA
Cleveland Inst of Music, OH
Cornish Coll of the Arts, WA
International Acad for Merchandising and Design, IL
Juilliard Sch, NY
Lifelong Learning, Sch for, NH
Manhattan Sch of Music, NY
Mannes Coll of Music, NY
Maryland Institute, Coll of Art, MD
Milwaukee Inst of Art & Design, WI
Museum of Fine Arts, Sch of the, MA
New England Conservatory of Music, MA
Ringling Sch of Art and Design, FL
San Francisco Art Inst, CA
Science & Arts of Oklahoma, U of, OK
Southern California Inst of Architecture, CA

# How to Use This Book

## Organization of This Book

For high school students looking toward college, the process of getting there can seem overwhelming. From choosing and applying to a college, to investigating and securing financial aid and keeping track of all the available options and opportunities, the scope of the undertaking can make students and their parents feel they are maneuvering through a maze of unmarked passageways.

Arco's *The Right College* is organized to help keep that complexity navigable. It is comprised of several useful sections, each dealing with a primary issue. One section covers choosing a college and the step-by-step procedure for applying, including advice concerning the application, the essay, and the personal interview. Another is devoted to an overview of the financial aid process describing the sources of financial aid, how and when to apply for aid, and how much a family or individual should be expected to contribute beyond the aid received. Still another describes the admissions process, particularly as it relates to selectivity, with a list of American colleges grouped by their relative competitiveness.

Also in *The Right College* are indexes showing the ranges of costs, enrollments, and test scores at each college, along with its religious affiliation, and whether it has a Phi Beta Kappa chapter and/or ROTC military training. To help with the specialized terminology of higher education, *The Right College* has included a Glossary and a list of Abbreviations.

The heart of the book is the college entries, which cover more than 1,400 accredited four-year, bachelor's degree-granting colleges and universities in the United States. Information provided in each entry is described in the sections titled "The Capsule" and "The Entry."

## The Capsule

The capsule (sample on following page) is both a preview of what is developed more fully in the entry and a compilation of all the essential data the reader is likely to want at a glance.

### School Name, Address, Telephone Number

The school name, address, and general telephone number are prominently displayed in the shaded region for easy reference.

### Costs

First, the tuition for the upcoming academic year is given. For institutions that charge tuition by the credit hour rather than for the year or semester, the cost has been calculated at 30 credit hours per year to reflect the average full-time course load. For institutions that have different tuition rates for state residents and out-of-state students, both figures are provided. For those that had not determined their tuition for the 1994-95 academic year by the deadline of this book, tuition for 1993-94 is given.

Second, housing costs are given. At institutions where housing costs vary, the figures appear as a range.

Next are board costs. As with housing, the figure given is sometimes a range of costs.

Last are fees, books, and miscellaneous academic expenses. This figure comprises such costs as activities and library fees and charges for use of athletic and other facilities. Travel costs are not included.

### Enrollment

The number of full-time undergraduates is listed. These numbers are also broken down by gender to indicate whether the institution is coeducational or a women's or men's college.

This section also provides statistics on 1993-94 freshman enrollment, listing the number of applicants for admission, the number accepted, and the number who chose to enroll. These statistics are useful not only in determining how selective the institution is, but also as an indicator of whether the institution is a "first choice" or "alternative choice" college.

### Test Scores

For institutions that use SAT scores in their admissions process, average scores for the verbal and math sections and/or a range of scores for the middle 50% of freshmen are provided. For those that request ACT scores, averages are given for the English and math components and a composite score is generally provided; as in the case of SAT scores, the range of scores for the middle 50% of freshmen is sometimes provided. Some institutions accept, and provide data for, both SAT and ACT scores. Other institutions, including those that do not rely on SAT or ACT scores in making admissions determinations, do not provide any information; these are designated as *N/A*.

### Faculty

This entry lists the numbers of both full-time and part-time faculty members employed by the institution. The percentage of faculty members who have earned doctorates follows; some institutions choose to provide the percentage of faculty who have earned the highest degree in their field as an alternative. The current student/faculty ratio is then listed.

### Selectivity Rating

Each institution is categorized according to the selectivity of its admissions process. Ratings include *Most competitive, Highly competitive, More competitive, Competitive, Less competitive*, and *Noncompetitive*; other entries may be *N/A* or *Not applicable*. The selectivity process is discussed in greater detail in the section titled "Criteria Used in Rating College Competitiveness."

| Name of School | |
|---|---|
| **City, State, Zip Code** | **Telephone Number** |

**1994–95 Costs.** The full-time tuition (for in-state and out-of-state students, if applicable); the room and board costs; and fees, books, and miscellaneous academic expenses.

**Enrollment.** The number of full-time undergraduates; the size of the freshman class, with the number of applicants, the number accepted, and the number who chose to attend; and the number of graduate students enrolled.

**Test score averages/ranges.** Average SAT scores, SAT scores of the middle 50%, average ACT scores, and/or ACT scores of the middle 50% of 1993–94 (or 1992–93) enrolled freshmen.

**Faculty.** The number of full-time and part-time faculty members; the percentage of faculty who hold a doctoral degree or the highest degree in their field; and the student/faculty ratio.

**Selectivity rating.** Rated as Most competitive, Highly competitive, More competitive, Competitive, Less competitive, Noncompetitive, N/A, and Not Applicable.

# The Entry

The entry for each institution is written in a standardized format for the reader's convenience in locating data and comparing colleges. Each entry begins with a ***Profile*** and continues with major sections entitled ***Student Body***, ***Programs of Study***, ***Student Life***, ***Athletics***, ***Admissions***, ***Financial Aid***, ***Student Employment***, ***Computer Facilities***, ***Graduate Career Data***, and ***Prominent Alumni/ae***. If an institution has supplied no information for a particular subsection of these sections, that subsection heading has been omitted. For colleges and universities with enrollments under 1,000, entries include the following sections: ***Profile, Student Body, Programs of Study, Admissions,*** and ***Financial Aid***.

### *PROFILE*

Each profile provides an overview of the college or university, including such information as background on the founding and history of the institution, its academic organization and religious orientation, and relevant name changes. The profile also contains information on whether an institution is single-sex or not, whether control is public or private, and whether the institution emphasizes the liberal arts and sciences, business, or finearts; and it may provide additional information, including campus size and a description of its architecture, its prominent buildings, the type of neighborhood in which it is located, and its proximity to landmarks and large cities.

**Accreditation.** Each of the colleges and universities described in the book has been granted accreditation by one of the following national and/or regional accreditation agencies, all members of the American Council on Education for the Council on Postsecondary Accreditation (COPA):

Assn. of Independent Schools and Colleges
Middle States Assn. of Colleges and Schools
New England Assn. of Schools and Colleges
North Central Assn. of Colleges and Schools
Northwest Assn. of Schools and Colleges
Southern Assn. of Colleges and Schools
Western Assn. of Schools and Colleges

**Religious orientation.** If a college is sponsored or controlled by a religious organization, its affiliation is described here. Institutions that are nondenominational are listed as such.

**Library.** This section indicates the number of volumes, periodical subscriptions, and microform items in the institution's library.

**Special facilities/museums.** Noteworthy scientific, educational, cultural, and entertainment facilities operated by the institution are listed here.

**Athletic facilities.** This section lists both intercollegiate and intramural sports and recreation facilities, from bowling alleys to football fields.

### *STUDENT BODY*

The Student Body section's undergraduate and freshman profiles and the academic achievement and foreign student subsections describes the students enrolled at an institution.

**Undergraduate profile.** Listed here are the percentages of students who are state residents, transfers, and members of minority groups, as well as the average age of undergraduates.

**Freshman profile.** This lists the percentages and scores of freshmen who took SAT or ACT tests and the percentage of freshmen from public schools.

**Undergraduate achievement.** This section gives the percentage of freshmen who returned for the fall semester following their freshman year, the percentage of the entering class who graduated, and the percentage of graduates who went on to graduate study.

**Foreign students.** Here the number of students from outside the U.S. is given; a list or number of countries represented by the foreign student body also may be given.

### *PROGRAMS OF STUDY*

The Programs of Study section describes an institution's academic offerings by listing its undergraduate degrees and majors, most popular programs, academic requirements and regulations, special programs, honor societies, and remedial services.

**Degrees.** Bachelor's degrees granted by the institution are listed.

**Majors.** This is a complete list of the institution's undergraduate majors. Majors are presented in alphabetical order and are listed as closely as possible to the way they are named by the colleges.

**Distribution of degrees.** The majors with the highest enrollments are listed in descending order; when available, the programs with the lowest enrollments are also listed.

**Academic regulations.** If an institution has established a minimum academic performance level, it is described in this subsection. This generally includes the minimum GPA required to remain in good standing.

**Special.** Since the range of special programs available through American institutions of higher education is extremely broad, this is the most inclusive subsection in most entries.

Minors are often noted, as well as many courses of study offered in areas other than those of major programs. The availability of associate's degrees, self-designed majors, double majors, dual degrees, independent and accelerated study, pass/fail grading option, internships, and cooperative education programs is also noted.

Preprofessional programs, programs of cooperative study (programs wherein course work is taken at two institutions for completion of degree study) and dual-degree programs are listed in this subsection. Also noted is the availability of teacher certification in early childhood, elementary, secondary, vo-tech, bilingual/ bicultural, and special education and in special subject areas.

Also listed are semester-away and study-abroad programs, as well as cooperative programs with foreign institutions. ROTC, AFROTC, and NROTC programs are noted as well.

**Honors.** The availability of Phi Beta Kappa, honors programs, and academic honor societies appears.

**Academic assistance.** The availability of academic assistance services such as tutoring and learning centers is listed.

### *STUDENT LIFE*

The Student Life section surveys a college's social and extracurricular activities through descriptions of its housing, social atmosphere, student services programs, campus organizations, religious organizations, and minority/foreign student organizations.

**Housing.** The housing subsection describes the type of facilities available and specifies any rules concerning who must live on campus. Also included is the percentage of the student population who live in college housing.

**Social atmosphere.** To sample the social atmosphere of colleges, a student representative from each institution was asked to describe campus social life. These comments mention on-campus and off-campus student gathering spots, the groups and organizations that have widespread influence on social life, and the popular sports and entertainment events on campus. General comments on the college's social and cultural life are also given.

**Services and counseling/handicapped student services.** Listed here are psychological, career, and academic counseling services; testing services; reader services for the blind; hearing-impaired student services; and many other student services.

**Campus organizations.** This subsection lists extracurricular activities, including newspapers and literary magazines, musical groups and ensembles, departmental and special-interest groups, and student government. Also noted is the availability of national fraternities and sororities and the percentage of students who join a Greek organization.

**Religious organizations.** Lists the religious organizations operating on campus.

**Minority/foreign student organizations.** Organizations on campus serving minority students and foreign students are listed.

### *ATHLETICS*

This section lists the intercollegiate, intramural, and club sports available to students and indicates whether intercollegiate and club sports are offered to men and/or women. Also listed are percentages of students participating in intercollegiate and intramural sports, as well as intercollegiate sports associations. In addition, any physical education requirements are described.

### *ADMISSIONS*

This section describes basic admissions information, such as deadlines and criteria for filing, special admissions programs, admissions procedures for transfer students, and specific requirements for admission.

**Academic basis for candidate selection.** Presented in order of priority are specific indicators of academic performance that each college uses to judge its applicants. Such indicators generally include the student's secondary school record; class rank; the secondary school's recommendation; SAT, ACT, or ACH scores; and the essay.

**Nonacademic basis for candidate selection.** Listed here are the often intangible elements a college considers in its admissions process. These elements normally include qualities such as character and personality, extracurricular participation, alumni/ae relationship, geographical distribution, and talent and ability.

**Requirements.** This section describes specific requirements for admission, including the number of units the secondary school student must present as well as the distribution by subject, if applicable. Also included are the standardized tests a student must take to be considered for admission.

**Procedure.** This entry details when a student should submit the appropriate paperwork and fees to be considered for admission and notes the dates by which admission notices are sent and by which students must reply. The availability of admissions for terms other than fall is also mentioned.

**Special programs.** Listed here are such options as admission deferral, advanced placement and credit programs, and the college's participation in early decision, early admissions, and concurrent enrollment programs.

**Transfer students.** Information provided for transfer students includes the academic terms during which transfers may be accepted and the percentage of new students who were transfers in the most recent year of recorded figures. Also listed are the number of transfer applications received and accepted, the minimum GPA, the lowest course grade accepted for credit, the maximum allowable number of transferable credits, and the minimum number of new credits required to graduate.

**Admissions Contact.** This is the name and phone number of the person applicants must contact for admissions information.

### *FINANCIAL AID*

The statistical picture of an institution's financial aid is presented in this section.

**Available aid.** The types of scholarships, grants and loans, and payment plans available to students are listed.

**Financial aid statistics.** Noted are the percentages of freshmen and of all undergraduates who received aid in the most recent year of recorded statistics. The range of aid available and the average amount awarded also may be listed.

**Supporting data/closing dates.** Any forms needed to apply for financial aid (such as FAFSA) are listed here, as well as priority and deadline dates.

**Financial aid contact.** The chief financial aid officer of the institution is listed as the contact person.

### *STUDENT EMPLOYMENT*

This section includes such information as the availability of College Work/Study and institutional employment, the average amount a student may expect to earn through on-campus employment, the percentage of full-time undergraduates who work during the school year, and a rating of the off-campus employment opportunities ("excellent," "good," "fair," "poor").

### *COMPUTER FACILITIES*

This section describes the primary types of computer equipment available to students, along with types of local and wide area networks students may access. Also listed are availability of computer facilities in residence halls, any restrictions imposed on student access to computers, languages and applications available, hours computers may be used, and any fees charged for computer use.

### *GRADUATE CAREER DATA*

Information included in the graduate career section may include the percentage of graduates who enter graduate school, the percentages who enter various types of graduate schools (e.g., law, medicine, business), and a list of the graduate schools that have enrolled the highest numbers of the college's graduates.

### *PROMINENT ALUMNI/AE*

Listed here are both contemporary and historically significant persons, along with their fields of endeavor.

# Glossary

**AABC (American Association of Bible Colleges).** National accrediting agency and member of the American Council on Education for the Council on Postsecondary Accreditation (COPA).

**Academic unit.** One year of study of one academic subject in secondary school.

**Accelerated study.** Completion of a college program of study in fewer than the usual number of years, most often by attending summer sessions and carrying extra courses during regular academic terms.

**Accreditation.** Formal approval granted for meeting certain standards of quality. Colleges and universities listed in this book are accredited by one of six regional accrediting boards. In addition, specific academic programs may be accredited by a professional association.

**ACH (Achievement Tests; see SAT II: Subject Tests).** Subject exams administered by the CEEB, used in measuring academic achievement and for student placement purposes.

**ACT (American College Testing Program).** The American College Testing Program's standardized test battery for secondary school students, used by colleges and universities for admissions and placement purposes.

**Advanced Placement.** Waiver of introductory courses and placement in higher-level courses for students who demonstrate knowledge in a given subject. Some colleges administer their own placement exams to entering freshmen, and many evaluate the CEEB Advanced Placement exams, the CLEP exams, and other standardized tests for placement purposes.

**AFROTC (Air Force Reserve Officers' Training Corps).** The United States Air Force's college-based training program.

**AICS (Association of Independent Colleges and Schools).** A national accrediting agency and member of the American Council on Education for COPA.

**Associate's degree.** A degree granted upon completion of a two-year program of study.

**Baccalaureate/bachelor's degree.** A degree granted upon completion of a four-year program of study.

**Calendar.** The system an institution uses to organize its academic year.

**CEEB (College Entrance Examination Board).** The agency that administers the SAT, ACH (SAT II), and CEEB Advanced Placement exams. Also referred to as the College Board.

**Class rank.** The relative position of a student in his or her graduating class, calculated according to grade point average.

**CLEP (College-Level Examination Program).** General and subject exams administered by the CEEB, for students with nontraditional learning such as work experience, independent reading, or correspondence courses. Many colleges award advanced placement and/or degree credit based on CLEP results.

**College Work/Study Program.** A federally subsidized part-time employment program. Students work on or off campus throughout the academic year, frequently in positions relating to their educational goals.

**Common Application Form.** A standardized admission application form to ease the workload of students and high school guidance personnel, accepted by approximately 120 private colleges.

**Concurrent enrollment.** A program enabling secondary school students to attend a nearby college part-time while completing secondary school.

**Consortium.** An arrangement between colleges for the sharing of faculties, facilities, and programs.

**Cooperative education.** A program in which a student alternates terms of academic study with terms of employment, often in a job related to the student's major field. Most cooperative education programs take five years to complete a bachelor's degree. Also called "Cooperative Work/Study."

**Cross-registration.** A system whereby students enrolled at one institution may take courses at another institution without having to apply to the second institution.

**DANTES (Defense Activity for Non-Traditional Educational Support).** A test used to grant college-level credit or advanced placement.

**Deferred admission.** A practice of allowing an accepted candidate to postpone enrollment in a college, generally for a period of an academic term or year.

**Double major.** A program of study in which a student completes the requirements of two majors at the same time.

**Dual degree.** A program of study in which a student receives two degrees from the same institution.

**Early admission.** A program allowing well-qualified high school students to enter college full-time before completing secondary school.

**Early decision.** Notification of acceptance into college early in the applicant's 12th year of secondary school. Some colleges stipulate that a student must withdraw all other college applications if accepted under early decision. Others require that the student apply only to that institution.

**Eligibility index.** A number calculated from secondary school GPA and SAT or ACT scores; used by California state colleges and universities for admissions purposes.

**EOP (Educational Opportunity Program).** An academic and economic support program.

**ESL (English as a Second Language).** A course of study designed specifically for students whose native language is not English. Also see TESOL.

**FAF (Financial Aid Form).** The CEEB College Scholarship Service form assessing and informing specified colleges of the financial situation of a student's family. It is generally available from high school guidance offices.

**FAFSA (Free Application for Federal Student Aid).** The federal form used to determine eligibility for federal aid, including Pell Grants and student loans. It establishes a single estimate of a student's or family's ability to pay and is generally available from high school guidance offices.

**FFS (Family Financial Statement).** The American College Testing Program Financial Aid Services form assessing and informing specified colleges of the financial situation of a student's family. It is generally available from high school guidance offices.

**4-1-4.** An academic calendar consisting of two long semesters separated by a short (generally month-long) intersession for nontraditional study programs.

**GED (General Educational Development Test).** A high school equivalency exam accepted by many colleges in lieu of a secondary school diploma.

**General education requirements.** The group of courses required of all students regardless of their particular majors. General education courses usually include a range of arts and sciences.

**GPA (Grade Point Average).** The translation of a student's letter grades into a numeric system reflecting academic performance. The most common system counts four points for an "A," three points for a "B," two points for a "C," one point for a "D," and no points for an "F."

**GRE (Graduate Record Examination).** A standardized test battery of general and subject exams designed for college graduates interested in applying to graduate school. Administered by the Educational Testing Service.

**Guaranteed Tuition Rate.** An agreement by a college to charge the student the same tuition each year of attendance as was charged during the student's freshman year.

**HEOP (Higher Education Opportunity Program).** A New York State admissions program for applicants not normally admissible due to economic or academic disadvantages.

**Honors program.** An enriched academic program for students of high ability and motivation, often leading to a degree granted with honors.

**HPL (Health Professions Loan).** A loan program for undergraduates planning to pursue degrees in the health professions.

**Independent study.** Academic work earning college credit that is undertaken outside the regular class structure.

**Interdisciplinary study.** Study in a combination of academic disciplines rather than within one discipline.

**Internships.** Short-term, supervised work experiences, generally relating to the student's field of interest and receiving degree credit.

**January interim.** The short, usually month-long, session of a 4-1-4 calendar during which one course of study is pursued intensively.

**MEChA (Movimiento Estudiantil Chicano de Aztlan).** A national ethnic student organization.

**Michigan Test.** A test of English usage including grammar and vocabulary, devised by the University of Michigan English Language Institute. Some colleges may accept the Michigan Test in lieu of TOEFL (see TOEFL).

**MSACS (Middle States Association of Colleges and Schools).** One of six regional accrediting agencies and a member of the American Council on Education for COPA.

**NASC (Northwest Association of Schools and Colleges).** One of six regional accrediting agencies and a member of the American Council on Education for COPA.

**NATTS (National Association of Trade and Technical Schools).** A national accrediting agency of vocational-technical institutions.

**NEASC (New England Association of Schools and Colleges).** One of six regional accrediting agencies and a member of the American Council on Education for COPA.

**NCACS (North Central Association of Colleges and Schools).** One of six regional accrediting agencies and a member of the American Council on Education for COPA.

**New England Regional Student Program.** A cooperative program through which a student may enroll in another state university offering a program not offered at the home state university and pay the same costs as at the home state university.

**NROTC (Naval Reserve Officers' Training Corps).** The United States Navy's college-based training program.

**NSL (Nursing Student Loan).** A program of federally funded, college-administered loans for nursing students.

**NSS (Nursing Student Scholarship).** A program of federally funded, college-administered scholarships for nursing students.

**Open admissions.** An admissions policy granting acceptance to all secondary school graduates without regard to additional qualifications.

**Pass-fail grading option (or credit/no credit grading option).** A simplified grading method whereby a student receives a 'pass' or 'fail' notation in a course rather than a letter grade.

**Pell Grant.** A gift-aid program sponsored by the federal government, available to undergraduates who are pursuing their first bachelor's degree.

**Perkins Loan (formerly NDSL).** A program of federally funded, college-administered loans available to students from low-income families.

**PHEAA (Pennsylvania Higher Education Assistance Agency Document).** A form used by Pennsylvania colleges and universities to establish eligibility for state aid. It can sometimes be used to apply for a Pell Grant.

**Phi Beta Kappa.** A national honor society recognizing outstanding collegiate academic achievement.

**PLUS (Parent Loan for Undergraduate Students).** A loan program that is not need-based; available to the parents of dependent students.

**PSAT/NMSQT (Preliminary Scholastic Assessment Test/National Merit Scholarship Qualifying Test).** A CEEB standardized test usually taken by secondary school students in their sophomore or junior year. The test functions as a trial run for the SAT; junior-year PSAT scores are used as qualification for National Merit Scholarship and the National Hispanic Scholar Awards Programs.

**Quarter system.** A calendar in which the academic year is broken into four units of roughly 11 weeks each. Under a quarter system, students normally enroll in three of the four quarters per year.

**R.N. (Registered Nurse).** Nursing certification.

**Rolling admissions.** A policy in which colleges without a specific date for notification of admission inform the applicant as soon as the admissions decision is made.

**ROTC (Reserve Officers' Training Corps).** The United States Army's two- and four-year college-based training program leading to an officer's commission upon graduation and generally including liberal financial aid.

**SAAC (Student Aid Application of California).** California's state aid application form.

**SACS (Southern Association of Colleges and Schools).** One of six regional accrediting agencies and a member of the American Council on Education for COPA.

**SAT I (Scholastic Assessment Test).** The College Entrance Examination Board's standardized test battery for secondary school students, used by colleges and universities for admissions and placement purposes.

**SAT II: Subject Tests (see ACH).** Subject exams administered by the CEEB, used in measuring academic achievement and for student placement purposes.

**SEEK (Search for Education, Elevation, and Knowledge).** A support program for economically disadvantaged residents of New York City who have graduated from secondary school or hold equivalency diplomas.

**Semester system.** A calendar in which the academic year is broken into two units of roughly 18 weeks each.

**SEOG (Supplemental Educational Opportunity Grant).** Federally funded gift aid for students with extreme financial need.

**SLS (Supplemental Loans for Students).** A college-administered loan program.

**SSIG (State Student Incentive Grant).** A state-funded, college-administered loan program.

**Stafford Loan.** A student loan administered and guaranteed by a nonprofit, private institution.

**State high school equivalency certificate.** A certificate granted after successful completion of a secondary school equivalency exam; accepted by many colleges in lieu of a secondary school diploma. Also see GED.

**TAP (New York Tuition Assistance Program).** A state-funded aid program.

**TEG (Tuition Equalization Grant).** A Texas grant program.

**TESOL (Teaching of English to Speakers of Other Languages).** A program designed specifically for the training of educators of English as a Second Language. Also see ESL.

**3-2 program.** A cooperative academic program involving three years attendance at one institution and two years at another, upon completion of which two degrees are generally granted. 2-2 and 3-1 programs are also available.

**TOEFL (Test of English as a Foreign Language).** An exam designed to evaluate the English proficiency of students whose native language is not English.

**Trimester system.** A calendar in which the academic year is broken down into three units. Sometimes called a "quarter" or "three term" system.

**Upper-division college or university.** An institution offering only the last two years of a bachelor's degree program. Students must have completed their freshman and sophomore years at other colleges.

**WASC (Western Association of Schools and Colleges).** One of six regional accrediting agencies and a member of the American Council on Education for COPA.

# Abbreviations

**The following are some standard usages and abbreviations for degrees that may be listed in this book:**

**A.B.** Bachelor of Arts
**B.A.** Bachelor of Arts
**B.A./B.F.A.** Bachelor of Arts/Bachelor of Fine Arts
**B.A.Classics** Bachelor of Arts in Classics
**B.A.Ed.** Bachelor of Arts in Education
**B.A.Interdis.Studies** Bachelor of Arts in Interdisciplinary Studies
**B.A.Internat.Studies** Bachelor of Arts in International Studies
**B.A.Journ.** Bachelor of Arts in Journalism
**B.A.Lib.Arts** Bachelor of Arts in Liberal Arts
**B.A.Lib.Studies** Bachelor of Arts in Liberal Studies
**B.A.Mus.** Bachelor of Arts in Music
**B.A.Soc.Work** Bachelor of Arts in Social Work
**B.A.Teach.** Bachelor of Arts in Teaching
**B.Acct.** Bachelor of Accounting
**B.Aero.Eng.** Bachelor of Aeronautical Engineering
**B.Appl.Arts** Bachelor of Applied Arts
**B.Appl.Arts/Sci.** Bachelor of Applied Arts and Sciences
**B.Appl.Sci.** Bachelor of Applied Science
**B.Arch.** Bachelor of Architecture
**B.Arch.Eng.** Bachelor of Architectural Engineering
**B.Art** Bachelor of Art
**B.Art Ed.** Bachelor of Art Education
**B.Arts/Sci.** Bachelor of Arts and Sciences
**B.Avia.Mgmt.** Bachelor of Aviation Management
**B.Bus.Admin.** Bachelor of Business Administration
**B.Bus.Ed.** Bachelor of Business Education
**B.Chem.Eng.** Bachelor of Chemical Engineering
**B.Church Mus.** Bachelor of Church Music
**B.Civil Eng.** Bachelor of Civil Engineering
**B.Comp.Eng.** Bachelor of Computer Engineering
**B.Comp.Sci.** Bachelor of Computer Science
**B.Crim.Just.** Bachelor of Criminal Justice
**B.Dent.Hyg.Ed.** Bachelor of Dental Hygiene Education
**B.Ed.** Bachelor of Education
**B.Elec.Eng.** Bachelor of Electrical Engineering
**B.Elect.Studies** Bachelor of Elective Studies
**B.Eng.** Bachelor of Engineering
**B.Eng.Tech.** Bachelor of Engineering Technology
**B.Env.Design** Bachelor of Environmental Design
**B.F.A.** Bachelor of Fine Arts
**B.Gen.Studies** Bachelor of General Studies
**B.Gen.Tech.** Bachelor of General Technology
**B.Hlth.Info.Mgmt.** Bachelor of Health Information Management
**B.Hlth.Sci.** Bachelor of Health Science
**B.Human.** Bachelor of Humanities
**B.Indiv.Studies** Bachelor of Individual Studies
**B.Indust.Design** Bachelor of Industrial Design
**B.Indust.Eng.** Bachelor of Industrial Engineering
**B.Indust.Mgmt.** Bachelor of Industrial Management
**B.Info.Sys.** Bachelor of Information Systems
**B.Inter.Arch.** Bachelor of Interior Architecture
**B.Inter.Design** Bachelor of Interior Design
**B.Interdis.Studies** Bachelor of Interdisciplinary Studies
**B.Internat.Studies** Bachelor of International Studies
**B.Journ.** Bachelor of Journalism
**B.Land.Arch.** Bachelor of Landscape Architecture
**B.Lib.Arts** Bachelor of Liberal Arts
**B.Lib.Studies** Bachelor of Liberal Studies
**B.Mech.Eng.** Bachelor of Mechanical Engineering
**B.Med.Tech.** Bachelor of Medical Technology
**B.Minis.** Bachelor of Ministry
**B.Mus.** Bachelor of Music
**B.Mus.Arts** Bachelor of Musical Arts
**B.Mus.Ed.** Bachelor of Music Education
**B.Mus.Perf.** Bachelor of Music Performance
**B.Mus.Ther.** Bachelor of Music Therapy
**B.Phil.** Bachelor of Philosophy
**B.Phys.Ed.** Bachelor of Physical Education
**B.Prof.Studies** Bachelor of Professional Studies
**B.Pub.Admin.** Bachelor of Public Administration
**B.Relig.Ed.** Bachelor of Religious Education
**B.S.** Bachelor of Science
**B.S./B.A.** Bachelor of Science/Bachelor of Arts
**B.S.Acct.** Bachelor of Science in Accounting
**B.S.Admin.** Bachelor of Science in Administration
**B.S.Aero.Eng.** Bachelor of Science in Aeronautical Engineering
**B.S.Agri.** Bachelor of Science in Agriculture
**B.S.Agri.Eng.** Bachelor of Science in Agricultural Engineering
**B.S.Appl.Sci.** Bachelor of Science in Applied Science
**B.S.Arch.** Bachelor of Science in Architecture
**B.S.Art Ed.** Bachelor of Science in Art Education
**B.S.Bus.** Bachelor of Science in Business
**B.S.Bus.Admin.** Bachelor of Science in Business Administration
**B.S.Chem.** Bachelor of Science in Chemistry
**B.S.Chem.Eng.** Bachelor of Science in Chemical Engineering
**B.S.Civil Eng.** Bachelor of Science in Civil Engineering
**B.S.Comm.Disorders** Bachelor of Science in Communication Disorders
**B.S.Commerce** Bachelor of Science in Commerce
**B.S.Comp.Eng.** Bachelor of Science in Computer Engineering
**B.S.Comp.Sci.** Bachelor of Science in Computer Science
**B.S.Comp.Sys.Eng.** Bachelor of Science in Computer Systems Engineering
**B.S.Constr.** Bachelor of Science in Construction
**B.S.Crim.Just.** Bachelor of Science in Criminal Justice
**B.S.Dent.** Bachelor of Science in Dentistry
**B.S.Dent.Hyg.** Bachelor of Science in Dental Hygiene
**B.S.Design** Bachelor of Science in Design
**B.S.Diet.** Bachelor of Science in Dietetics
**B.S.Econ.** Bachelor of Science in Economics

**B.S.Ed.** Bachelor of Science in Education
**B.S.Elec.Eng.** Bachelor of Science in Electrical Engineering
**B.S.Elec.Eng.Tech.** Bachelor of Science in Electrical Engineering Technology
**B.S.Elem.Ed.** Bachelor of Science in Elementary Education
**B.S.Eng.** Bachelor of Science in Engineering
**B.S.Eng.Sci.** Bachelor of Science in Engineering Science
**B.S.Eng.Tech.** Bachelor of Science in Engineering Technology
**B.S.Env.Hlth.** Bachelor of Science in Environmental Health
**B.S.Fam./Cons.Sci.** Bachelor of Science in Family and Consumer Science
**B.S.Forestry** Bachelor of Science in Forestry
**B.S.Gen.Studies** Bachelor of Science in General Studies
**B.S.Geol.** Bachelor of Science in Geology
**B.S.Hlth.Care Admin.** Bachelor of Science in Health Care Admin.
**B.S.Hlth.Sci.** Bachelor of Science in Health Science
**B.S.Home Econ.** Bachelor of Science in Home Economics
**B.S.Human Sci.** Bachelor of Science in Human Science
**B.S.Indust.Eng.** Bachelor of Science in Industrial Engineering
**B.S.Indust.Mgmt.** Bachelor of Science in Industrial Management
**B.S.Indust.Tech.** Bachelor of Science in Industrial Technology
**B.S.Info.Sci.** Bachelor of Science in Information Science
**B.S.Interdis.Studies** Bachelor of Science in Interdisciplinary Studies
**B.S.Journ.** Bachelor of Science Journalism
**B.S.Land.Arch.** Bachelor of Science in Landscape Architecture
**B.S.Mat.Eng.** Bachelor of Science in Materials Engineering
**B.S.Math.** Bachelor of Science in Mathematics
**B.S.Mech.Eng.** Bachelor of Science in Mechanical Engineering
**B.S.Med.** Bachelor of Science in Medicine
**B.S.Med.Rec.Admin.** Bachelor of Science in Medical Records Administration
**B.S.Med.Tech.** Bachelor of Science in Medical Technology
**B.S.Mgmt.** Bachelor of Science in Management
**B.S.Mus.** Bachelor of Science in Music
**B.S.Mus.Ed.** Bachelor of Science in Music Education
**B.S.Nat.Res.** Bachelor of Science in Natural Resources
**B.S.Nurs.** Bachelor of Science in Nursing
**B.S.Occup.Ther.** Bachelor of Science in Occupational Therapy
**B.S.Petrol.Eng.** Bachelor of Science in Petroleum Engineering
**B.S.Pharm.** Bachelor of Science in Pharmacy
**B.S.Phys.Ed.** Bachelor of Science in Physical Education
**B.S.Phys.Ther.** Bachelor of Science in Physical Therapy
**B.S.Physics** Bachelor of Science in Physics
**B.S.Pub.Admin.** Bachelor of Science in Public Administration
**B.S.Pub.Aff.** Bachelor of Science in Public Affairs
**B.S.Radiol.Tech.** Bachelor of Science in Radiology Technology
**B.S.Recr.** Bachelor of Science in Recreation
**B.S.Sec.Ed.** Bachelor of Science in Secondary Education
**B.S.Soc.Work** Bachelor of Science in Social Work
**B.S.Speech/Hear.Sci.** Bachelor of Science in Speech and Hearing Science
**B.S.Tech.** Bachelor of Science in Technology
**B.S.Textile Eng.** Bachelor of Science in Textile Engineering
**B.S.Voc.Tech.Ed.** Bachelor of Science in Vocational Technology Education
**B.Sacred Mus.** Bachelor of Sacred Music
**B.Soc.Work** Bachelor of Social Work
**B.Spec.Studies** Bachelor of Special Studies
**B.Tech.** Bachelor of Technology
**B.Theol.** Bachelor of Theology
**B.Univ.Studies** Bachelor of University Studies
**B.Voc.Ed.** Bachelor of Vocational Education
**Regents B.A.** Regents Bachelor of Arts
**S.B.** Bachelor of Science
**Theol.B.** Bachelor of Theology

# Alabama

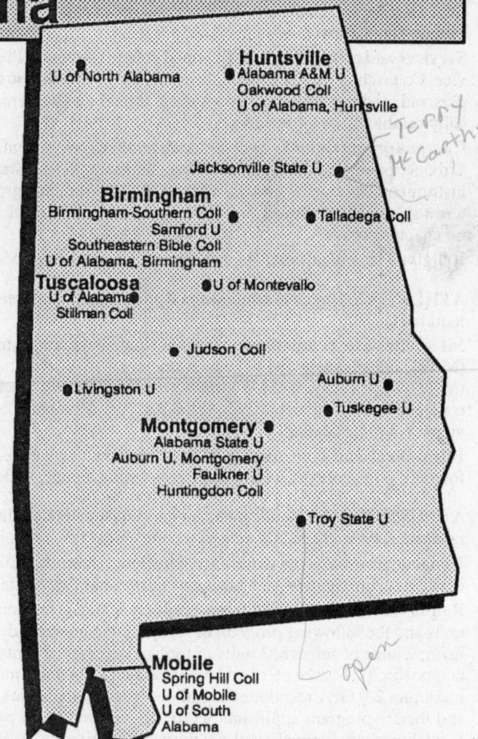


## Alabama Agricultural and Mechanical University

**Normal, AL 35762** **205 851-5000**

**1993-94 Costs.** Tuition: $1,600 (state residents), $3,150 (out-of-state). Room & board: $2,550. Fees, books, misc. academic expenses (school's estimate): $571.
**Enrollment.** Undergraduates: 1,889 men, 2,069 women (full-time). Freshman class: 2,830 applicants, 1,929 accepted, 985 enrolled. Graduate enrollment: 547 men, 783 women.
**Test score averages/ranges.** Average ACT scores: 16 English, 17 math, 17 composite. Range of ACT scores of middle 50%: 12-17 English, 12-17 math.
**Faculty.** 311 full-time. 59% of faculty holds doctoral degree. Student/faculty ratio: 18 to 1.
**Selectivity rating.** Less competitive.

**PROFILE.** Alabama A&M, founded in 1875, is a public, land-grant university. Undergraduate courses are offered through the Schools of Agriculture, Environmental Science, and Home Economics; Arts and Sciences; Business; Education; and Technology. Its 1,700-acre campus (200-acre main campus) is located in northern Alabama.

**Accreditation:** SACS. Professionally accredited by the Accreditation Board for Engineering and Technology, the Council on Social Work Education, the National Council for Accreditation of Teacher Education.
**Religious orientation:** Alabama Agricultural and Mechanical University is nonsectarian; no religious requirements.
**Library:** Collections totaling over 339,272 volumes, 1,606 periodical subscriptions, and 488,759 microform items.
**Athletic facilities:** Gymnasiums, tennis courts, football, soccer fields, track, swimming pool, weight room.

**STUDENT BODY. Undergraduate profile:** 72% are state residents; 20% are transfers. .5% Asian-American, 92% Black, .5% Hispanic, .5% Native American, 2% White, 4.5% Other. Average age of undergraduates is 19.
**Freshman profile:** 79% of accepted applicants took ACT.
**Undergraduate achievement:** 90% of fall 1992 freshmen returned for fall 1993 term.
**Foreign students:** 223 students are from out of the country. Countries represented include Bermuda, China, India, Jamaica, Kuwait, and Nigeria; 41 in all.

**PROGRAMS OF STUDY. Degrees:** B.A., B.S.
**Majors:** Academy of Freedom, Accounting, Agribusiness, Agribusiness Management, Agricultural Economics, Agriculture, Animal Science, Apparel Merchandising/Design, Applied Physics, Art Education, Biology, Business Administration, Chemistry, Civil Engineering, Civil Engineering Technology, Commercial/Advertising Art, Computer Science, Crop Science, Early Childhood Education, Economics, Electrical Engineering Technology, Elementary Education, English, Environmental Science, Finance, Food Sciences, Forest Management, French, General Business, History, Home Economics, Horticulture, Human Development/Family Studies, Industrial Arts Education, Industrial Technology, Management, Marketing, Mathematics, Mechanical Drafting/Design Technology, Middle School/Junior High School Principal, Music Education/Choral, Music Education/Instrumental, Music Education/Vocal, Nutrition/Hospitality Management, Office Administration, Physical Education, Physical Education/Non-teaching, Physics, Plant/Soil Science, Political Science, Pre-Nursing, Pre-Veterinary, Printing Production/Management, Psychology, Reading, Secondary Education, Social Work, Sociology, Soil Science, Special Education, Speech Pathology, Systems Management, Telecommunications, Trade/Industrial Education, Urban/Regional Planning, Urban Studies.
**Distribution of degrees:** The majors with the highest enrollment are business administration, education, and computer science; social work, engineering technology, and urban studies have the lowest.
**Requirements:** General education requirement.
**Academic regulations:** Freshmen must maintain minimum 1.6 GPA; sophomores, 1.8 GPA; juniors, 2.0 GPA; seniors, 2.2 GPA.
**Special:** Minors offered in most majors. Associate's degrees offered. Double majors. Dual degrees. Accelerated study. Internships. Cooperative education programs. Graduate school at which undergraduates may take graduate-level courses. Preprofessional programs in law, medicine, veterinary science, and dentistry. 2-2 nursing program with Emory U. 3-2 engineering program with Georgia Tech. Other programs with Alabama State U, Miles Coll, Oakwood Coll, Stillman Coll, and Talladega Coll. Cross-registration with Athens State Coll, John C. Calhoun State Comm Coll, Oakwood Coll, and U of Alabama at Huntsville. Teacher certification in early childhood, elementary, secondary, and special education. Certification in specific subject areas. ROTC.
**Honors:** Honors program. Honor societies.
**Academic Assistance:** Remedial reading, writing, math, and study skills. Nonremedial tutoring.

**STUDENT LIFE. Housing:** Students may live on or off campus. Women's dorms. School-owned/operated apartments. 38% of students live in college housing.
**Services and counseling/handicapped student services:** Placement services. Health service. Counseling services for veteran students. Personal counseling. Career and academic guidance services. Religious counseling. Physically disabled student services. Learning disabled services. Tutors. Reader services for the blind.
**Campus organizations:** Undergraduate student government. Student newspaper (Maroon and White). Yearbook. Radio and TV stations. Choir, concert and marching bands, jazz band, modern dance group, radio club, cheerleaders, service and special-interest groups, 40 organizations in all. Four fraternities, no chapter houses; three sororities, no chapter houses. 23% of men join a fraternity. 25% of women join a sorority.
**Religious organizations:** Angelic Voices of Faith, Bahai Faith Club, Baptist Student Union, Christian Student Organization, YWCA.
**Minority/foreign student organizations:** NAACP. International Student Organization, Caribbean Student Club, Nigerian Student Organization.

**ATHLETICS. Physical education requirements:** None.
**Intercollegiate competition:** 6% of students participate. Baseball (M), basketball (M,W), cheerleading (W), cross-country (M,W), football (M), soccer (M), tennis (M), track (indoor) (M,W), track (outdoor) (M,W), track and field (indoor) (M,W), track and field (outdoor) (M,W), volleyball (W). Member of NCAA Division I for soccer, NCAA Division II, SIAC.
**Intramural and club sports:** 6% of students participate. Intramural basketball, football, swimming, volleyball.

**ADMISSIONS. Academic basis for candidate selection** (in order of priority): Secondary school record, standardized test scores, class rank, school's recommendation, essay.
**Nonacademic basis for candidate selection:** Particular talent or ability is important. Character and personality and extracurricular participation are considered.
**Requirements:** Graduation from secondary school is required; GED is accepted. 22 units and the following program of study are required: 4 units of English, 2 units of math, 2 units of science, 3 units of social studies, 11 units of electives. Minimum "C" average required. Conditional admission possible for applicants not meeting standard requirements. ACT is required; SAT may be substituted. Campus visit recommended. Off-campus interviews available with admissions and alumni representatives.
**Procedure:** Take SAT or ACT by February 1 of 12th year. Visit college for interview by January of 12th year. Suggest filing application by April 1; no deadline. Notification of admission on rolling basis. $100 nonrefundable room deposit. Freshmen accepted for terms other than fall.
**Special programs:** Admission may be deferred one year. Credit and/or placement may be granted through CEEB Advanced Placement exams for scores of 3 or higher. Credit and/or placement may be granted through CLEP general and subject exams. Credit may be granted through DANTES exams and military experience. Early entrance/early admission program. Concurrent enrollment program.
**Transfer students:** Transfer students accepted for terms other than fall. In fall 1993, 20% of all new students were transfers into all classes. 469 transfer applications were received, 303 were accepted. Minimum 2.0 GPA required. Lowest course grade accepted is "C." At least 30 semester hours must be completed at the university to receive degree.
**Admissions contact:** James Heyward, M.Ed., Director of Admissions. 205 851-5245.

**FINANCIAL AID. Available aid:** Pell grants, SEOG, state grants, school scholarships and grants, private scholarships, ROTC scholarships, academic merit scholarships, and athletic scholarships. Tuition waivers. Perkins Loans (NDSL), PLUS, Stafford Loans (GSL), state loans, private loans, and SLS.
**Financial aid statistics:** 27% of aid is not need-based. In 1993-94, 85% of all undergraduate applicants received aid. Average amounts of aid awarded freshmen: Scholarships and grants, $1,838.
**Supporting data/closing dates:** FAFSA/FAF/FFS: Accepted on rolling basis. School's own aid application: Deadline is April 1. Notification of awards on rolling basis.
**Financial aid contact:** Percy N. Lanier, Director of Financial Aid. 205 851-5400.

**STUDENT EMPLOYMENT.** College Work/Study Program. Institutional employment. 32% of full-time undergraduates work on campus during school year. Students may expect to earn an average of $1,954 during school year. Freshmen are discouraged from working during their first term. Off-campus part-time employment opportunities rated "excellent."

**COMPUTER FACILITIES.** 850 IBM/IBM-compatible and Macintosh/Apple microcomputers. Students may access IBM minicomputer/mainframe systems. Client/LAN operating systems include Apple/Macintosh, DOS. Computer languages and software packages include Assembly, BASIC, COBOL, FORTRAN, Pascal, RPG, SAS, SPSS. Computer facilities are available to all students.
**Fees:** None.
**Hours:** 8:30 AM-9:30 PM (M-F); 8:30 AM-4:30 PM (Sa).

**GRADUATE CAREER DATA.** Companies and businesses that hire graduates: IBM, government agencies, education boards/systems.

**PROMINENT ALUMNI/AE.** James A. Chapman, corporate manager; John Stallworth, professional athlete, Pittsburgh Steelers; D.B. Robinson, owner, D.B. Robinson Corp., trustee, AAMU; Marilyn Gurley Foreman, doctor; Frankie F. Smith, judge; William Cox, publisher.

# Alabama State University

**Montgomery, AL 36101-0271 205 293-4200**

**1993-94 Costs.** Tuition: $1,500 (state residents), $3,000 (out-of-state). Room & board: $2,550. Fees, books, misc. academic expenses (school's estimate): $808.
**Enrollment.** Undergraduates: 2,125 men, 2,572 women (full-time). Freshman class: 3,825 applicants, 3,825 accepted, 1,512 enrolled. Graduate enrollment: 100 men, 373 women.
**Test score averages/ranges.** Average SAT scores: 310 verbal, 342 math. Average ACT scores: 16 composite.
**Faculty.** 219 full-time; 90 part-time. 46% of faculty holds highest degree in specific field. Student/faculty ratio: 20 to 1.
**Selectivity rating.** Noncompetitive.

**PROFILE.** Alabama State is a historically black, public university. It was founded as a Normal school in 1866, joined the state university system in 1887, and gained university status in 1969. Programs are offered through the Colleges of Arts and Sciences, Business Administration, Education, and Music; University College; Division of Aerospace Studies; and the School of Graduate Studies. Its 83-acre campus is located near downtown Montgomery.

**Accreditation:** SACS. Professionally accredited by the National Association of Schools of Music, the National Council for Accreditation of Teacher Education.
**Religious orientation:** Alabama State University is nonsectarian; no religious requirements.
**Library:** Collections totaling over 204,118 volumes, 755 periodical subscriptions, and 10,490 microform items.
**Special facilities/museums:** Early childhood center.
**Athletic facilities:** Baseball, football, and track stadiums, gymnasium, swimming pool, basketball, tennis, and volleyball courts, sports arena, weight room, baseball and football fields.

**STUDENT BODY. Undergraduate profile:** 63% are state residents; 4% are transfers. 99% Black, 1% Other. Average age of undergraduates is 19.
**Freshman profile:** 1% of freshmen who took SAT scored 600 or over on math; 1% scored 500 or over on verbal, 3% scored 500 or over on math; 13% scored 400 or over on verbal, 23% scored 400 or over on math; 54% scored 300 or over on verbal, 72% scored 300 or over on math. 25% of accepted applicants took SAT; 85% took ACT.
**Undergraduate achievement:** 63% of fall 1991 freshmen returned for fall 1992 term.
**Foreign students:** 23 students are from out of the country. Countries represented include Bangladesh, Bermuda, Canada, Nigeria, the Bahamas, and Trinidad; 11 in all.

**PROGRAMS OF STUDY. Degrees:** B.A., B.F.A., B.Mus.Ed., B.S., B.Soc.Work.
**Majors:** Accounting, Art, Biology, Business Education, Chemistry, Communications Media, Computer Information Systems, Computer Science, Criminal Justice, Early Childhood Education, Economics, Elementary Education, English, Finance, French, Graphic Arts, History, Human Services, Laboratory Technology, Management, Management/Technology, Marine Biology, Marketing, Mathematics, Music, Office Administration, Physics, Political Science, Psychology, Secondary Education, Social Work, Sociology, Spanish, Special Education, Speech Communication, Theatre Arts.
**Distribution of degrees:** The majors with the highest enrollment are accounting, criminal justice, and computer information systems; business education and sociology have the lowest.
**Requirements:** General education requirement.
**Academic regulations:** Minimum 2.0 GPA must be maintained.
**Special:** Minors offered in most majors and in anthropology, library science, and philosophy. Associate's degrees offered. Double majors. Dual degrees. Independent study. Internships. Cooperative education programs. Graduate school at which undergraduates may take graduate-level courses. Combined-degree medical lab technology program with U of Alabama. 3-2 engineering program with Auburn U. Member of Alabama Marine Environmental Sciences Consortium; off-campus study possible at Dauphin Island Sea Lab. Teacher certification in early childhood, elementary, secondary, and special education. Certification in specific subject areas. AFROTC. ROTC at Auburn U.
**Honors:** Honors program.
**Academic Assistance:** Nonremedial tutoring.

**STUDENT LIFE. Housing:** Students may live on or off campus. Women's and men's dorms. School-owned/operated apartments. 41% of students live in college housing.
**Social atmosphere:** According to the editor of the student newspaper, "Because ASU is a historically black institution, cultural life is very important. Cultural awareness is very obvious." On campus, students gather at the Student University Center and the library. Students hang out at Philly's Steak and Grill and the Hornet Grill when off campus. Greeks, Baptist Student Union, Student Orientation Services, and the Student Government Association are influential groups on campus. Popular campus events include the Miss ASU Coronation, Homecoming Week, Martin Luther King Convocation, and the Annual Turkey Day Classic.
**Services and counseling/handicapped student services:** Placement services. Health service. Counseling services for minority, military, veteran, and older students. Birth control, personal, and psychological counseling. Career and academic guidance services. Physically disabled student services.
**Campus organizations:** Undergraduate student government. Student newspaper (Hornet Tribune, published once/two months). Yearbook. Radio station. Marching band, choir, instrumental and vocal groups, athletic and departmental groups, service and special-interest groups, 14 organizations in all. Five fraternities, no chapter houses; four sororities, no chapter houses.
**Religious organizations:** Baptist Student Union, United Methodist group.

**ATHLETICS. Physical education requirements:** Two semesters of physical education required.
**Intercollegiate competition:** 10% of students participate. Baseball (M), basketball (M,W), cheerleading (M,W), cross-country (M,W), football (M), golf (M,W), tennis (M,W), track (indoor) (M,W), track (outdoor) (M,W), track and field (indoor) (M,W), track and field (outdoor) (M,W), volleyball (W). Member of NCAA Division I, NCAA Division I-AA for football, SWAC.
**Intramural and club sports:** 25% of students participate. Intramural basketball, flag football, pool, softball, swimming, table tennis, tennis, volleyball.

**ADMISSIONS. Academic basis for candidate selection** (in order of priority): Standardized test scores, secondary school record, class rank, school's recommendation, essay.
**Nonacademic basis for candidate selection:** Alumni/ae relationship is important. Extracurricular participation and particular talent or ability are considered.
**Requirements:** Graduation from secondary school is recommended; GED is accepted. 12 units and the following program of study are recommended: 4 units of English, 2 units of math, 2 units of science, 2 units of foreign language, 2 units of social studies. Minimum composite ACT score of 15 and minimum 1.5 GPA recommended of in-state applicants; minimum 2.0 GPA recommended of out-of-state applicants. Audition required of music and theatre program applicants. Portfolio required of art program applicants. Developmental program for applicants not normally admissible. ACT is recommended; SAT may be substituted. Campus visit and interview recommended. Off-campus interviews available with admissions and alumni representatives.
**Procedure:** Take SAT or ACT by October of 12th year. Visit college for interview by November of 12th year. Suggest filing application by November. Application deadline is June 30. Notification of admission on rolling basis. $75 room deposit, refundable until August 1. Freshmen accepted for terms other than fall.
**Special programs:** Admission may be deferred one year. Credit and/or placement may be granted through CEEB Advanced Placement exams for scores of 4 or higher. Credit may be granted through CLEP general and subject exams, challenge exams, and military experience. Credit and placement may be granted through life experience. Early decision program. Early entrance/early admission program. Concurrent enrollment program.
**Transfer students:** Transfer students accepted for terms other than fall. In fall 1992, 4% of all new students were transfers into all classes. 321 transfer applications were received, 321 were accepted. Application deadline is June 30. Minimum 2.0 GPA required. Lowest course grade accepted is "C." Maximum number of transferable credits is 64 semester hours. At least 30 semester hours must be completed at the university to receive degree.
**Admissions contact:** Debbie Moore, Admissions Staff Associate. 205 293-4291.

**FINANCIAL AID. Available aid:** Pell grants, SEOG, state scholarships and grants, school scholarships and grants, private scholarships and grants, ROTC scholarships, academic merit scholarships, and athletic scholarships. Perkins Loans (NDSL), PLUS, and Stafford Loans (GSL). Deferred payment plan.
**Financial aid statistics:** In 1992-93, 84% of all undergraduate applicants received aid; 80% of freshman applicants. Average amounts of aid awarded freshmen: Scholarships and grants, $1,500; loans, $1,500.
**Supporting data/closing dates:** FAFSA: Accepted on rolling basis. FAF/FFS: Priority filing date is May 1; accepted on rolling basis. School's own aid application: Priority filing date is May 1; accepted on rolling basis. Notification of awards on rolling basis.
**Financial aid contact:** Billy Brooks, M.Ed., Director of Financial Aid. 205 293-4323.

**STUDENT EMPLOYMENT.** College Work/Study Program. Institutional employment. 45% of full-time undergraduates work on campus during school year. Students may expect to earn an average of $1,591 during school year. Freshmen are discouraged from working during their first term. Off-campus part-time employment opportunities rated "excellent."

**COMPUTER FACILITIES.** 259 IBM/IBM-compatible microcomputers. Students may access IBM minicomputer/mainframe systems. Client/LAN operating systems include Novell. Computer languages and software packages include Assembly, BASIC, COBOL, dBASE, FORTRAN, Pascal, RPG, SPSS-X, WordStar; 300 in all. Computer facilities are available to all students.
**Fees:** None.
**Hours:** 8 AM-10 PM (M-F); variable hours on weekends.

**GRADUATE CAREER DATA.** Highest graduate school enrollments: Alabama State U, Atlanta U, Auburn U at Montgomery, Howard U, U of Alabama. Companies and businesses that hire graduates: AFB, IBM, NCR, Warren Robins.

**PROMINENT ALUMNI/AE.** Eugene Sawyer, former mayor of Chicago; Yvonne Kennedy, president, Bishop College; James E. Walker, president, Middle Tennessee State U.

## Auburn University

**Auburn University, AL 36849 205 844-4000**

**1994-95 Costs.** Tuition: $2,100 (state residents), $6,300 (out-of-state). Room: $1,719. Fees, books, misc. academic expenses (school's estimate): $600.
**Enrollment.** Undergraduates: 8,911 men, 7,720 women (full-time). Freshman class: 7,548 applicants, 6,791 accepted, 3,070 enrolled. Graduate enrollment: 1,795 men, 1,219 women.
**Test score averages/ranges.** Average SAT scores: 501 verbal, 575 math. Range of SAT scores of middle 50%: 453-559 verbal, 520-638 math. Average ACT scores: 23 English, 23 math, 24 composite. Range of ACT scores of middle 50%: 21-27 English, 20-26 math.
**Faculty.** 1,109 full-time; 107 part-time. 90% of faculty holds highest degree in specific field. Student/faculty ratio: 16 to 1.
**Selectivity rating.** Competitive.

**PROFILE.** Auburn is a public, multipurpose, land-grant university. It was founded as a private, liberal arts institution in 1858, came under state control in 1872, and began admitting women in 1872. Its 1,871-acre campus is located in Auburn.

**Accreditation:** SACS. Professionally accredited by the Accreditation Board for Engineering and Technology, the American Assembly of Collegiate Schools of Business, the American Council for Construction Education, the American Council on Pharmaceutical Education, the American Dietetic Association, the American Home Economics Association, the American Psychological Association, the American Society of Landscape Architects, the American Speech-Language-Hearing Association, the Council on Education American Veterinary Medical Association, the Council on Rehabilitation Education, the Council on Social Work Education, the Foundation for Interior Design Education Research, the National Architecture Accrediting Board, the National Association of Schools of Art and Design, the National Association of Schools of Music, the National Association of Schools of Public Affairs and Administration, the National Council for Accreditation of Teacher Education, the National League for Nursing, the Society of American Foresters.
**Religious orientation:** Auburn University is nonsectarian; no religious requirements.
**Library:** Collections totaling over 2,140,856 volumes, 21,611 periodical subscriptions, and 2,811,499 microform items.
**Special facilities/museums:** Speech and hearing clinic, center for arts and humanities, TV studio, electron microscopes, nuclear science center, torsatron.
**Athletic facilities:** Gymnasium, field house, swimming pools, tracks, basketball, handball, racquetball, tennis, and volleyball courts, stadium, weight rooms, baseball, football, and intramural fields, coliseum, soccer field.

**STUDENT BODY. Undergraduate profile:** 64% are state residents; 38% are transfers. 1% Asian-American, 6% Black, 1% Hispanic, 91% White, 1% Other. Average age of undergraduates is 21.
**Freshman profile:** 1% of freshmen who took SAT scored 700 or over on verbal, 8% scored 700 or over on math; 13% scored 600 or over on verbal, 42% scored 600 or over on math; 51% scored 500 or over on verbal, 83% scored 500 or over on math; 93% scored 400 or over on verbal, 99% scored 400 or over on math; 100% scored 300 or over on verbal, 100% scored 300 or over on math. 8% of freshmen who took ACT scored 30 or over on English, 8% scored 30 or over on math, 8% scored 30 or over on composite; 48% scored 24 or over on English, 41% scored 24 or over on math, 49% scored 24 or over on composite; 92% scored 18 or over on English, 90% scored 18 or over on math, 98% scored 18 or over on composite; 100% scored 12 or over on English, 100% scored 12 or over on math, 100% scored 12 or over on composite. 36% of accepted applicants took SAT; 81% took ACT. 82% of freshmen come from public schools.
**Undergraduate achievement:** 84% of fall 1992 freshmen returned for fall 1993 term. 3% of entering class graduated. 20% of students who completed a degree program immediately went on to graduate study.
**Foreign students:** 110 students are from out of the country. Countries represented include Canada, Germany, India, Korea, the former Soviet Union, and the United Kingdom; 50 in all.

**PROGRAMS OF STUDY. Degrees:** B.A., B.Arch., B.Avia.Mgmt., B.Eng., B.F.A., B.Indust.Design, B.Inter.Design, B.Land.Arch., B.Mus., B.S., B.Textile Chem., B.Textile Mgmt.Tech.
**Majors:** Accounting, Adult Education, Aerospace Engineering, Agricultural Business/Economics, Agricultural Education, Agricultural Engineering, Agricultural Journalism, Agricultural Sciences, Agronomy/Soils, Animal/Dairy Science, Anthropology, Apparel/Textiles, Applied Discrete Mathematics, Applied Mathematics, Applied Physics, Architecture, Art, Aviation Management, Behavior Disturbance Education, Biochemistry, Biological Sciences, Botany, Building Science, Business Education, Chemical Engineering, Chemistry, Child Care Social Work, Civil Engineering, Communication, Communications Disorders, Computer Engineering, Computer Science, Corporate Journalism, Criminal Justice, Criminology, Distributive Education, Early Childhood Education, Early Childhood Education/Handicapped, Earth Sciences, Economics, Electrical Engineering, Elementary Education, English, Entomology, Family/Child Development, Fashion Merchandising, Finance, Fisheries/Allied Aquaculture, Foreign Language/International Trade, Foreign Languages, Forest Engineering, Forest Resources, Forestry Operations, Geography, Geological Engineering, Geology, Health Education, Health Occupations Education, Health/Physical Education, Health/Physical Education/Recreation, Health Services Administration, Health Systems Administration, History, Home Economics Education, Horticulture, Hotel/Restaurant Management, Housing/Interiors, Human Movement Studies, Human Resource Management, Industrial Arts Education, Industrial Design, Industrial Engineering, Integrated Pest Management, Interior Design, International Business, Journalism, Laboratory Technology, Landscape Architecture, Landscape/Ornamental Horticulture, Management, Management Information Systems, Marine Biology, Marketing, Materials Engineering, Mathematics, Mechanical Engineering, Medical Technology, Mental Retardation Education, Microbiology, Middle School Education, Molecular Biology, Music, Music Education, Nursing, Nutrition/Food Science, Operations Management, Pharmacy, Philosophy, Physics, Plant Protection, Political Science, Poultry Science, Pre-Dentistry, Pre-Medicine, Pre-Optometry, Pre-Physical Therapy, Pre-Veterinary Medicine, Psychology, Public Administration, Public Relations, Recreation Administration, Recreation/Sports Management, Rehabilitation Services, Rehabilitation/Special Education, Religion, Rural Sociology, Russian Studies, Secondary Education, Social Work, Sociology, Speech Pathology Education, Textile Chemistry, Textile Engineering, Textile Management/Technology, Theatre, Trade/Industrial Education, Transportation, Vocational/Adult Education, Wildlife Science, Zoology.
**Distribution of degrees:** The majors with the highest enrollment are marketing, accounting, and psychology.
**Requirements:** General education requirement.
**Academic regulations:** Freshmen must maintain minimum 1.5 GPA; sophomores, 1.7 GPA; juniors, 1.8 GPA; seniors, 1.9 GPA.
**Special:** Minors offered in most majors. Interdepartmental program offered in environmental science. Undecided students register in the School of Arts and Sciences and take courses in any of the other schools. Honors program for highly qualified freshmen. Concentration available in aviation management. Double majors. Internships. Cooperative education programs. Graduate school at which undergraduates may take graduate-level courses. Preprofessional programs in medicine, veterinary science, pharmacy, dentistry, and optometry. Host university for 3-2 engineering program. Member of Mississippi/Alabama Sea Grant, NASULG, and Oak Ridge Associated Universities. Teacher certification in early childhood, elementary, secondary, special education, and vo-tech education. Certification in specific subject areas. Study abroad in Argentina, Australia, Austria, Brazil, Chile, China, Costa Rica, the Czech Republic, Dominican Republic, England, France, Germany, Guatemala, Hungary, Indonesia, Italy, Japan, Kenya, Mexico, the Netherlands, New Zealand, Poland, Slovakia, the former Soviet Republics, and Spain. ROTC, NROTC, and AFROTC.
**Honors:** Honors program. Honor societies.
**Academic Assistance:** Nonremedial tutoring.

**STUDENT LIFE. Housing:** Students may live on or off campus. Women's and men's dorms. Fraternity housing. School-owned/operated apartments. Off-campus privately-owned housing. On-campus married-student housing. 16% of students live in college housing.
**Social atmosphere:** The student newspaper reports, "Many comments have been made on campus that if you're not Greek then you can't have a good time–this is not true. If you have enough gumption, then you can have a good time. Sports–football especially–dominate the social scene during fall, and one of the most awaited social events of the year is the Homecoming concert. We've had Tina Turner, Chicago, and in previous years, Elvis, the Eagles, and the Doobie Brothers." Off campus, students gather at Harry's Bar and Sani-Freeze, an outdoor dairy dip that is "an Auburn tradition."
**Services and counseling/handicapped student services:** Placement services. Health service. Counseling services for minority, military, veteran, and older students. Birth control, personal, and psychological counseling. Career and academic guidance services. Physically disabled student services. Learning disabled program/services. Notetaking services. Tape recorders. Tutors. Reader services for the blind.
**Campus organizations:** Undergraduate student government. Student newspaper (Auburn Plainsman, published once/week). Literary magazine. Yearbook. Radio station. Music, debating, and theatre groups, opera workshop, dance and jazz bands, cultural organizations, community service groups, student government groups, sports club, academic, departmental, and special-interest groups, 300 organizations in all. 31 fraternities, all with chapter houses; 17 sororities, no chapter houses. 20% of men join a fraternity. 28% of women join a sorority.
**Religious organizations:** Campus Crusade for Christ, Christian Fellowship, B'nai B'rith, Hillel, Chi Alpha, Wesley Foundation.
**Minority/foreign student organizations:** Black Student Union, Latin American Society. International Student Organization, Chinese, Indian, Korean, and other foreign student groups.

**ATHLETICS. Physical education requirements:** None.
**Intercollegiate competition:** 8% of students participate. Baseball (M), basketball (M,W), cross-country (M,W), diving (M,W), football (M), golf (M,W), gymnastics (W), soccer (W), swimming (M,W), tennis (M,W), track and field (indoor) (M,W), track and field (outdoor) (M,W), volleyball (W). Member of NCAA Division I, Southeastern Conference.
**Intramural and club sports:** 60% of students participate. Intramural badminton, basketball, billiards, bowling, flag football, golf, horseshoes, racquetball, soccer, softball, swimming, table tennis, tennis, track and field, volleyball, wrestling. Men's club aikido, badminton, bowling, cycling, fencing, horsemanship, judo, karate, lacrosse, outing, racquetball, rowing, rugby, sailing, scuba, table tennis, tennis triathlon, volleyball, water skiing. Women's club aikido, badminton, bowling, cycling, fencing, horsemanship, judo, karate, lacrosse, outing, racquetball, rowing, rugby, sailing, scuba, table tennis, tennis, triathlon, volleyball, water skiing.

**ADMISSIONS. Academic basis for candidate selection** (in order of priority): Standardized test scores, secondary school record.
**Nonacademic basis for candidate selection:** Geographical distribution and alumni/ae relationship are emphasized. Particular talent or ability is considered.
**Requirements:** Graduation from secondary school is required; GED is accepted. 12 units and the following program of study are required: 4 units of English, 3 units of math, 2 units of lab science, 3 units of social studies. Minimum composite ACT score of 18 required of in-state applicants; minimum composite ACT score of 22 required of out-of-state applicants. Minimum 2.5 GPA required of all applicants. Slightly lower test scores may be offset by higher GPA and vice versa. Auditions required of music program applicants. Auditions or portfolios required of theatre program applicants. Higher standards may be required of architecture and engineering program applicants. SAT or ACT is required. Off-campus interviews available with an admissions representative.
**Procedure:** Take SAT/ACT by spring of 11th year. Suggest filing application by September 1. Application deadline is September 1. Notification of admission on rolling basis. $100 room deposit, refundable until six weeks prior to beginning of term. Freshmen accepted for terms other than fall.

**Special programs:** Admission may be deferred one year. Credit and/or placement may be granted through CEEB Advanced Placement exams and CLEP general and subject exams. Credit and placement may be granted through challenge exams, and military and life experience. Early entrance/early admission program. Concurrent enrollment program.
**Transfer students:** Transfer students accepted for terms other than fall. In fall 1993, 38% of all new students were transfers into all classes. 2,676 transfer applications were received, 2,372 were accepted. Application deadline is September 1 for fall; March 1 for spring. Minimum 2.5 GPA required. Lowest course grade accepted is "C." At least 45 quarter hours must be completed at the university to receive degree.
**Admissions contact:** Charles E. Reeder, Ed.D., Director of Admissions. 205 844-4080.

**FINANCIAL AID. Available aid:** Pell grants, SEOG, state grants, school scholarships, private scholarships, ROTC scholarships, academic merit scholarships, and athletic scholarships. Perkins Loans (NDSL), PLUS, Stafford Loans (GSL), Health Professions Loans, school loans, private loans, and SLS.
**Financial aid statistics:** In 1993-94, 54% of all undergraduate applicants received aid; 46% of freshman applicants. Average amounts of aid awarded freshmen: Scholarships and grants, $1,448; loans, $2,775.
**Supporting data/closing dates:** FAFSA: Priority filing date is April 15. School's own aid application: Priority filing date is April 15. Notification of awards begins June 1.
**Financial aid contact:** Clark Aldridge, M.Ed., Director of Financial Aid. 205 844-4723.

**STUDENT EMPLOYMENT.** College Work/Study Program. Institutional employment. 15% of full-time undergraduates work on campus during school year. Students may expect to earn an average of $1,800 during school year. Off-campus part-time employment opportunities rated "good."

**COMPUTER FACILITIES.** 300 IBM/IBM-compatible and Macintosh/Apple microcomputers; all are networked. Students may access Digital, IBM, SUN minicomputer/mainframe systems, BITNET, Internet. Residence halls may be equipped with networked microcomputers. Client/LAN operating systems include Apple/Macintosh, DOS, UNIX/XENIX/AIX. Computer languages and software packages include Assembler H, C/370, COBOL, Easytrieve, EXCEL, VS FORTRAN, Lotus 1-2-3, Mantis, PageMaker, VS Pascal, PL/1 Optimizer, SAS, SPSS, WordPerfect; 105 in all. Access to some facilities must be granted by department.
**Fees:** None.
**Hours:** 24 hours.

**GRADUATE CAREER DATA.** Graduate school percentages: 3% enter law school. 1% enter medical school. 1% enter dental school. 10% enter graduate business programs. 6% enter graduate arts and sciences programs. 1% enter theological school/seminary. Highest graduate school enrollments: Auburn U, Florida State U, Georgia Tech, U of Alabama, U of Georgia, U of North Carolina. 55% of graduates choose careers in business and industry. Companies and businesses that hire graduates: Alabama Power, Big Six accounting firms, Chevron, Dow Chemical, DuPont, Exxon, South Central Bell, Texas Instruments, Westinghouse.

**PROMINENT ALUMNI/AE.** Henry Hartsfield, Ken Mattingsly, and Kathryn Thornton, astronauts; Bill Fickling, president and CEO, Charter Medical Corp.; John Thomas Hartley, president and CEO, Harris Corp.; Jack Mosley, chairperson, USF&G Corp.; Jean Woodham, sculptor; Anne Rivers Siddons, novelist; Bo Jackson, professional athlete; John Harbert, president and CEO, Harbert Corp.

## Auburn University at Montgomery

**Montgomery, AL 36117-3596 — 205 244-3000**

**1994-95 Costs.** Tuition: $1,905 (state residents), $3,810 (out-of-state). Room: $1,650. Fees, books, misc. academic expenses (school's estimate): $600.
**Enrollment.** Undergraduates: 1,384 men, 2,035 women (full-time). Freshman class: 985 applicants, 868 accepted, 645 enrolled. Graduate enrollment: 351 men, 514 women.
**Test score averages/ranges.** N/A.
**Faculty.** 201 full-time; 155 part-time. 74% of faculty holds doctoral degree. Student/faculty ratio: 20 to 1.
**Selectivity rating.** N/A.

**PROFILE.** Auburn University at Montgomery, founded in 1967, is a public institution. Programs are offered through the Schools of Liberal Arts, Sciences, Education, Nursing, and Business and the Air University Graduate Division, which operates in cooperation with Maxwell Air Force Base in Montgomery. Its 500-acre campus is located near downtown Montgomery.

**Accreditation:** SACS. Professionally accredited by the American Assembly of Collegiate Schools of Business, the American Bar Association, the American Medical Association (CAHEA), the National Association of Schools of Public Affairs and Administration, the National Council for Accreditation of Teacher Education, the National League for Nursing.
**Religious orientation:** Auburn University at Montgomery is nonsectarian; no religious requirements.
**Library:** Collections totaling over 235,258 volumes, 1,537 periodical subscriptions, and 1,005,525 microform items.
**Athletic facilities:** Gymnasium, soccer field.

**STUDENT BODY. Undergraduate profile:** 99% are state residents. 2% Asian-American, 20% Black, 77% White, 1% Other. Average age of undergraduates is 24.
**Foreign students:** 80 students are from out of the country. Countries represented include Bahamas, China, Korea, Malaysia, South Africa, and Taiwan; 15 in all.

**PROGRAMS OF STUDY. Degrees:** B.A., B.S.
**Majors:** Accounting, Art Education, Biology, Communication, Counseling, Decision Science, Early Childhood Education, Economics, Elementary Education, English, Finance, Fine Arts, General Business, General Studies, History, Human Resource Management, Information Systems, International Studies, Justice/Public Safety, Management, Marketing, Mathematics, Medical Technology, Nursing, Physical Education, Physical Science, Political Science, Psychology, Reading, Secondary Education, Sociology, Special Education, Speech/Theatre Education, Urban Studies.
**Distribution of degrees:** The majors with the highest enrollment are education, business, and sciences; nursing and liberal arts have the lowest.
**Requirements:** General education requirement.
**Academic regulations:** Minimum 2.0 GPA required for graduation.
**Special:** Minor required in some majors for graduation. Each student must complete component of general studies in addition to requirements of school or major. This component is divided into foundation year of course work in English composition, world history, natural or physical sciences, and math, taken primarily in freshman year; some courses must also be completed outside student's major during upper-division years. Double majors. Independent study. Accelerated study. Pass/fail grading option. Internships. Cooperative education programs. Graduate school at which undergraduates may take graduate-level courses. Preprofessional programs in law, medicine, veterinary science, pharmacy, dentistry, and optometry. Member of Alabama Marine Environmental Sciences Consortium; off-campus study possible at Dauphin Island Sea Lab. Cross-registration with Auburn U at Auburn and Huntingdon Coll. Teacher certification in early childhood, elementary, secondary, and special education. Certification in specific subject areas. Study abroad through American Institute for Foreign Studies. ROTC. AFROTC at Alabama State U.
**Honors:** Honors program. Honor societies.
**Academic Assistance:** Remedial writing, math, and study skills.

**STUDENT LIFE. Housing:** Students may live on or off campus. School-owned/operated apartments. No meal plan. On-campus married-student housing. 6% of students live in college housing.
**Social atmosphere:** The Greek community has a strong influence on campus life, as do the numerous religious organizations. Most functions revolve around fraternity and sorority get-togethers. Students hang-out at the mall and the movie houses. Popular annual events include the Reggae Fest and the Fall Event. Once a month there are comedians at lunchtime, performing on an outside stage. Despite the increased racial diversity of students, AUM still experiences its share of racial discontent. According to the editor of the school newspaper, a large percentage of the student body is not as open-minded as it might be, making the campus a difficult environment for gay, liberal, feminist, or minority students. There are, however, "those who are committed to being open-minded, and they help to balance the campus."
**Services and counseling/handicapped student services:** Placement services. Health service. Day care. Counseling services for veteran and older students. Birth control, personal, and psychological counseling. Career and academic guidance services. Physically disabled student services. Learning disabled services. Notetaking services. Tape recorders. Tutors. Reader services for the blind.
**Campus organizations:** Undergraduate student government. Student newspaper (Aumnibus, published once/week). Literary magazine. Chorus, gospel choir, student host group, theatre, social, curriculum, and special-interest groups, 35 organizations in all. Five fraternities, one chapter house; six sororities, no chapter houses. 3% of men join a fraternity. 4% of women join a sorority.
**Religious organizations:** Baptist Campus Ministry, Newman Club.
**Minority/foreign student organizations:** Students in Action, Black Student Union. International Student Association.

**ATHLETICS. Physical education requirements:** None.
**Intercollegiate competition:** 3% of students participate. Baseball (M), basketball (M,W), cheerleading (M,W), soccer (M), tennis (M,W). Member of NAIA.
**Intramural and club sports:** 2% of students participate.

**ADMISSIONS. Academic basis for candidate selection** (in order of priority): Secondary school record, standardized test scores.
**Requirements:** Graduation from secondary school is required; GED is accepted. No specific distribution of secondary school units required. Minimum composite ACT score of 19, rank in top half of secondary school class, and minimum 2.0 GPA recommended. Conditional admission possible for applicants not meeting standard requirements. ACT is required; SAT may be substituted. Campus visit and interview recommended. No off-campus interviews.
**Procedure:** Take SAT or ACT by June of 12th year. Application deadline is September 1. Notification of admission on rolling basis. No set date by which applicants must accept offer. $100 refundable room deposit. Freshmen accepted for terms other than fall.
**Special programs:** Credit and/or placement may be granted through CEEB Advanced Placement exams for scores of 3 or higher. Credit may be granted through CLEP subject exams, DANTES exams, and military experience. Credit and placement may be granted through challenge exams. Early decision program. Early entrance/early admission program. Concurrent enrollment program.
**Transfer students:** Transfer students accepted for terms other than fall. Application deadline is September 1 for fall; March 15 for spring. Minimum 2.0 GPA required. Lowest course grade accepted is "D." Maximum number of transferable credits is 100 quarter hours from a two-year school and 155 quarter hours from a four-year school. At least 45 quarter hours must be completed at the university to receive degree.
**Admissions contact:** Lee Davis, M.Ed., Director of Admissions. 205 244-3611.

**FINANCIAL AID. Available aid:** Pell grants, SEOG, state scholarships and grants, school scholarships, private scholarships, ROTC scholarships, academic merit scholarships, and athletic scholarships. Perkins Loans (NDSL), PLUS, Stafford Loans (GSL), and SLS. Deferred payment plan.
**Financial aid statistics:** 10% of aid is not need-based. Average amounts of aid awarded freshmen: Scholarships and grants, $1,800.
**Supporting data/closing dates:** FAFSA: Priority filing date is April 15. School's own aid application: Priority filing date is April 15. Notification of awards on rolling basis.
**Financial aid contact:** James Berry, M.S., Director of Financial Aid. 205 244-3571.

**STUDENT EMPLOYMENT.** College Work/Study Program. Institutional employment. 7% of full-time undergraduates work on campus during school year. Students may expect to earn an average of $4,420 during school year. Off-campus part-time employment opportunities rated "good."

**COMPUTER FACILITIES.** 70 IBM/IBM-compatible and Macintosh/Apple microcomputers. Students may access Digital, IBM minicomputer/mainframe systems. 50 major computer languages and software packages available. Computer facilities are available to all students.
**Fees:** None.
**Hours:** 8 AM-11:30 PM (M-Th); 8 AM-10 PM (Fri); 8 AM-5 PM (Sa); 1:30 PM-10:30 PM (Su).

**GRADUATE CAREER DATA.** 48% of graduates choose careers in business and industry. Companies and businesses that hire graduates: Federal/state agencies, health care facilities, public/private schools, local and area businesses.

**PROMINENT ALUMNI/AE.** Gen. Prince Kahled Bin Sultan Abdulaziz (Ret.), Commander, Saudi Forces; Elmer Harris, president and CEO, Alabama Power; Johnny Ford, mayor of Tuskegee.

# Birmingham-Southern College

**Birmingham, AL 35254** **205 226-4600**

**1993-94 Costs.** Tuition: $11,000. Room: $2,300. Board: $2,100. Fees, books, misc. academic expenses (school's estimate): $600.
**Enrollment.** Undergraduates: 627 men, 749 women (full-time). Freshman class: 805 applicants, 588 accepted, 287 enrolled. Graduate enrollment: 50 men, 41 women.
**Test score averages/ranges.** Average SAT scores: 525 verbal, 545 math. Average ACT scores: 26 composite. Range of ACT scores of middle 50%: 24-28 composite.
**Faculty.** 98 full-time; 46 part-time. 71% of faculty holds doctoral degree. Student/faculty ratio: 14 to 1.
**Selectivity rating.** More competitive.

**PROFILE.** Birmingham-Southern, founded in 1856, is a church-affiliated, liberal arts college. Programs are offered through the Divisions of Adult Studies, Behavioral and Social Sciences, Economics and Business Administration, Education, Fine and Performing Arts, Humanities, Library Services, Nursing, and Science and Mathematics. Its 185-acre campus is in the western section of Birmingham.

**Accreditation:** SACS. Professionally accredited by the National Association of Schools of Music, the National Council for Accreditation of Teacher Education.
**Religious orientation:** Birmingham-Southern College is affiliated with the United Methodist Church; no religious requirements.
**Library:** Collections totaling over 190,922 volumes, 849 periodical subscriptions, and 29,961 microform items.
**Special facilities/museums:** Theatre, planetarium.
**Athletic facilities:** Gymnasium, swimming pool, racquetball and tennis courts, track, baseball, intramural, and soccer fields, weight room, billiards and table tennis facilities.

**STUDENT BODY. Undergraduate profile:** 73% are state residents; 18% are transfers. 2% Asian-American, 12% Black, 84% White, 2% Other. Average age of undergraduates is 20.
**Freshman profile:** 3% of freshmen who took SAT scored 700 or over on verbal, 8% scored 700 or over on math; 21% scored 600 or over on verbal, 33% scored 600 or over on math; 55% scored 500 or over on verbal, 71% scored 500 or over on math; 100% scored 400 or over on verbal, 100% scored 400 or over on math. 19% of freshmen who took ACT scored 30 or over on composite; 73% scored 24 or over on composite; 100% scored 18 or over on composite. 57% of accepted applicants took SAT; 94% took ACT. 73% of freshmen come from public schools.
**Undergraduate achievement:** 92% of fall 1992 freshmen returned for fall 1993 term. 71% of entering class graduated. 42% of students who completed a degree program immediately went on to graduate study.
**Foreign students:** Eight students are from out of the country. Countries represented include Japan; six in all.

**PROGRAMS OF STUDY. Degrees:** B.A., B.F.A., B.Mus., B.Mus.Ed., B.S.
**Majors:** Accounting, Art, Art Education, Biology, Business Administration, Chemistry, Dance, Early Childhood Education, Economics, Elementary Education, English, French, German, History, Individualized Majors, Interdisciplinary Majors, Mathematics, Music, Music Education, Philosophy, Physics, Political Science, Psychology, Religion, Secondary Education, Sociology, Spanish, Theatre Arts.
**Distribution of degrees:** The majors with the highest enrollment are business administration, biology, and English; physics, German, and dance have the lowest.
**Requirements:** General education requirement.
**Academic regulations:** Freshmen must maintain minimum 1.5 GPA; sophomores, 1.8 GPA; juniors, 2.0 GPA; seniors, 2.0 GPA.
**Special:** Minors offered in most majors. Courses offered in astronomy. Self-designed majors. Double majors. Dual degrees. Independent study. Accelerated study. Pass/fail grading option. Internships. Graduate school at which undergraduates may take graduate-level courses. Preprofessional programs in law, medicine, pharmacy, dentistry, theology, and optometry. 3-2 engineering programs with Auburn U, Columbia U, U of Alabama at Birmingham, and Washington U. 3-2 nursing program with Vanderbilt U. Member of Associated Colleges of the South; exchange possible. Washington Semester and Sea Semester. Alabama Capitol Program. Oak Ridge Science Semester (Tennessee). Public Service Intern Program. Exchange programs with U of Alabama at Birmingham and Samford U. Teacher certification in early childhood, elementary, and secondary education. Certification in specific subject areas. Study abroad in England, France, Germany, Italy, and other countries. ROTC at U of Alabama at Birmingham. AFROTC at Samford U.
**Honors:** Phi Beta Kappa. Honors program. Honor societies.
**Academic Assistance:** Remedial writing, math, and study skills.

**STUDENT LIFE. Housing:** All unmarried students under age 21 must live on campus unless living near campus with relatives. Women's and men's dorms. Sorority and fraternity housing. School-owned/operated apartments. 85% of students live in college housing.
**Social atmosphere:** Students gather in the many Birmingham nightclubs for jazz, new age, and alternative music. "Greek life is strong but not omnipresent. There are many strong smaller organizations and societies, such as the Student Government Association, the student newspaper, and the Environmental Conservancy," reports the student newspaper. Among the most popular events of the year are Bives on the Quad, the Entertainment Festival, Octoberfest, Southern Comfort, and City Stages. "BSC is a small college, but there is a creative, highly motivated student body that always finds something to do. Unbelievably, Birmingham has grown to be one of the most entertaining cities in the South. Students really take advantage of Birmingham's new museum, zoo, botanical gardens, and state park, as well as the Cahaba River and the outstanding civic center."
**Services and counseling/handicapped student services:** Placement services. Health service. Counseling services for minority, veteran, and older students. Personal and psychological counseling. Career and academic guidance services. Religious counseling. Learning disabled services.
**Campus organizations:** Undergraduate student government. Student newspaper (Hilltop News, published once/week). Literary magazine. Yearbook. Musical groups, concert choir, chorale bands, dance groups, theatre, political, service, and special-interest groups, 74 organizations in all. Six fraternities, all with chapter houses; seven sororities, all with chapter houses. 62% of men join a fraternity. 70% of women join a sorority.
**Religious organizations:** Baptist Student Movement, Catholic, Episcopal, Methodist, and Presbyterian groups.
**Minority/foreign student organizations:** Black Student Union. International Student Association.

**ATHLETICS. Physical education requirements:** None.
**Intercollegiate competition:** 8% of students participate. Baseball (M), basketball (M), cheerleading (M,W), soccer (M), tennis (M,W). Member of NAIA, Southern States Conference.
**Intramural and club sports:** 38% of students participate. Intramural basketball, billiards, flag football, indoor soccer, racquetball, softball, table tennis, tennis, volleyball. Men's club rugby, soccer, volleyball. Women's club volleyball.

**ADMISSIONS. Academic basis for candidate selection** (in order of priority): Secondary school record, class rank, standardized test scores, school's recommendation, essay.
**Nonacademic basis for candidate selection:** Character and personality are emphasized. Particular talent or ability is important. Extracurricular participation, geographical distribution, and alumni/ae relationship are considered.
**Requirements:** Graduation from secondary school is required; GED is accepted. 12 units and the following program of study are required: 4 units of English, 2 units of math, 2 units of science including 1 unit of lab, 2 units of social studies, 2 units of history. Minimum composite ACT score of 21 (SAT scores of 400 in both verbal and math) and minimum 2.0 GPA required. Portfolio required of art program applicants. Audition required of music program applicants. SAT or ACT is required. Campus visit and interview recommended. Off-campus interviews available with admissions and alumni representatives.
**Procedure:** Take SAT or ACT by November of 12th year. Visit college for interview by December of 12th year. Suggest filing application by December 15. Application deadline is March 1. Acceptance notification by March 1; rolling admissions after March 1 if space is available. Reply is required by May 1. $100 nonrefundable room deposit. Freshmen accepted for terms other than fall.
**Special programs:** Admission may be deferred one year. Credit and/or placement may be granted through CEEB Advanced Placement exams. Credit may be granted through CLEP general exams, challenge exams, and life experience. Credit and/or placement may be granted through CLEP subject exams. Early entrance/early admission program. Concurrent enrollment program.
**Transfer students:** Transfer students accepted for terms other than fall. In fall 1993, 18% of all new students were transfers into all classes. 86 transfer applications were received, 57 were accepted. Application deadline is March 1 for fall; December 1 for spring. Minimum 2.0 GPA required. Lowest course grade accepted is "C." Maximum number of transferable credits is 64 semester hours. At least 64 semester hours must be completed at the college to receive degree.
**Admissions contact:** Bobby Johnson, Ed.D., Director of Admissions. 205 226-4686.

**FINANCIAL AID. Available aid:** Pell grants, SEOG, state scholarships and grants, school scholarships and grants, private scholarships, ROTC scholarships, academic merit scholarships, and athletic scholarships. Perkins Loans (NDSL), PLUS, Stafford Loans (GSL), school loans, private loans, and SLS. Tuition Plan Inc., AMS, and deferred payment plan. Monthly payment plan.
**Financial aid statistics:** 55% of aid is not need-based. In 1993-94, 92% of all undergraduate applicants received aid; 99% of freshman applicants. Average amounts of aid awarded freshmen: Scholarships and grants, $1,500; loans, $2,500.
**Supporting data/closing dates:** FAFSA: Priority filing date is March 31. School's own aid application: Priority filing date is March 31; accepted on rolling basis. Income tax forms: Priority filing date is March 31. Verification documents: Priority filing date is March 31. Notification of awards on rolling basis.
**Financial aid contact:** Ron Elmore, M.A., Director of Financial Aid. 205 226-4688.

**STUDENT EMPLOYMENT.** College Work/Study Program. Institutional employment. 22% of full-time undergraduates work on campus during school year. Students may expect to earn an average of $1,000 during school year. Off-campus part-time employment opportunities rated "good."

**COMPUTER FACILITIES.** 114 IBM/IBM-compatible microcomputers; all are networked. Students may access Hewlett-Packard minicomputer/mainframe systems. Residence halls may be equipped with networked microcomputers. Client/LAN operating systems include DOS. Computer languages and software packages include Ada, Aldus PageMaker, Assembler, BASIC, C, COBOL, Corel Draw, dBASE, Excel, FORTRAN, Informix, LISP, Lotus 1-2-3, MINITAB, Pascal, Prolog, SNOBOL, SPSS, Visual Basic, WordPerfect. Computer facilities are available to all students.
**Fees:** None.
**Hours:** 8 AM-2 AM.

**GRADUATE CAREER DATA.** Graduate school percentages: 8% enter law school. 6% enter medical school. 2% enter dental school. 6% enter graduate business programs. 21% enter graduate arts and sciences programs. 1% enter theological school/seminary. Highest graduate school enrollments: Duke U, Emory U, U of Alabama, U of Virginia, Vanderbilt U. 40% of graduates choose careers in business and industry. Companies and businesses that hire graduates: Big Six accounting firms, Blue Cross/Blue Shield of Alabama, Federal Reserve Bank of Atlanta.

**PROMINENT ALUMNI/AE.** Howell Heflin, U.S. senator; Robert Morgan, bishop, United Methodist Church; Howell H. Raines, Washington editor, *New York Times;* James W. Walker, executive vice-president, CIGNA; G. Thomas Patton, executive vice-president, General Motors.

# Faulkner University

**Montgomery, AL 36109 — 205 272-5820**

**1994-95 Costs.** Tuition: $5,600. Room & board: $3,200. Fees, books, misc. academic expenses (school's estimate): $600.
**Enrollment.** Undergraduates: 256 men, 230 women (full-time). Freshman class: 287 applicants, 146 accepted, 171 enrolled. Graduate enrollment: 180.
**Test score averages/ranges.** Average ACT scores: 16 composite.
**Faculty.** 26 full-time; 11 part-time. 28% of faculty holds doctoral degree. Student/faculty ratio: 15 to 1.
**Selectivity rating.** Less competitive.

**PROFILE.** Faulkner, founded in 1942, is a church-affiliated university. Its 92-acre campus is located in Montgomery.

**Accreditation:** SACS.
**Religious orientation:** Faulkner University is affiliated with the Church of Christ; eight semesters of religion required.
**Library:** Collections totaling over 40,000 volumes, 300 periodical subscriptions and 500 microform items.
**Athletic facilities:** Gymnasium, field house, weight room, basketball, tennis, and volleyball courts, baseball, softball, and soccer fields.

**STUDENT BODY. Undergraduate profile:** 75% are state residents. 1% Asian-American, 24% Black, 1% Hispanic, 74% White. Average age of undergraduates is 21.
**Freshman profile:** 19% of accepted applicants took ACT. 90% of freshmen come from public schools.
**Undergraduate achievement:** 74% of fall 1992 freshmen returned for fall 1993 term.
**Foreign students:** 10 students are from out of the country. Countries represented include Cayman Islands, India, Indonesia, Korea, Malaysia, and Scotland.

**PROGRAMS OF STUDY. Degrees:** B.A., B.Bus.Admin., B.S.
**Majors:** Accounting, Bible, Biology, Business Administration, Computer Business Applications, Elementary Education, English, Liberal Arts, Management of Human Resources, Physical Education, Political Science, Psychology, Secondary Education, Social Science, Sports Management.
**Distribution of degrees:** The majors with the highest enrollment are business administration, education, and computer business applications; English and biology have the lowest.
**Requirements:** General education requirement.
**Special:** Minors offered in most majors and in history, humanities, and math. Associate's degrees offered. Self-designed majors. Double majors. Dual degrees. Accelerated study. Internships. Preprofessional programs in law, medicine, and dentistry. Cross-registration with Auburn U at Montgomery, Huntingdon Coll, and U of Alabama at Birmingham. Teacher certification in elementary and secondary education.
**Academic Assistance:** Nonremedial tutoring.

**ADMISSIONS. Academic basis for candidate selection** (in order of priority): Secondary school record, standardized test scores, school's recommendation, class rank.
**Nonacademic basis for candidate selection:** Character and personality are emphasized. Extracurricular participation and particular talent or ability are considered.
**Requirements:** Graduation from secondary school is required; GED is accepted. 16 secondary school units recommended, including 3 units of English, 9 units selected from math, science, foreign language, and social studies, and 3 units of electives. Student Support Services for applicants not normally admissible. ACT is required; SAT may be substituted. Campus visit and interview recommended. Off-campus interviews available with an admissions representative.
**Procedure:** Take SAT or ACT by April of 12th year. Suggest filing application by March 1. Application deadline is August 1. Notification of admission on rolling basis. $250 nonrefundable tuition deposit. $25 nonrefundable room deposit. Freshmen accepted for terms other than fall.
**Special programs:** Admission may be deferred. Credit may be granted through CLEP subject exams, challenge exams, and military experience. Early entrance/early admission program. Concurrent enrollment program.
**Transfer students:** Transfer students accepted for terms other than fall. Application deadline is August 1 for fall; December 1 for spring. Lowest course grade accepted is "C." Maximum number of transferable credits is 98 semester hours. At least 30 semester hours must be completed at the university to receive degree.
**Admissions contact:** Joey Wiginton, Director of Admissions. 205 260-6200, extension 189.

**FINANCIAL AID. Available aid:** Pell grants, SEOG, state grants, school grants, private scholarships, academic merit scholarships, and athletic scholarships. Perkins Loans (NDSL), PLUS, Stafford Loans (GSL), school loans, and SLS. Deferred payment plan.
**Financial aid statistics:** Average amounts of aid awarded freshmen: Loans, $2,000.
**Supporting data/closing dates:** FAFSA: Priority filing date is April 15. School's own aid application: Priority filing date is April 15. State aid form: Priority filing date is September 1. Notification of awards begins June 15.
**Financial aid contact:** Ann Chaffin, Director of Financial Aid. 205 260-6195, extension 116.

# Huntingdon College

**Montgomery, AL 36106-2148 — 205 265-0511**

**1994-95 Costs.** Tuition: $8,080. Room: $1,380. Board: $2,540. Fees, books, misc. academic expenses (school's estimate): $600.
**Enrollment.** Undergraduates: 282 men, 382 women (full-time). Freshman class: 473 applicants, 406 accepted, 130 enrolled.
**Test score averages/ranges.** Average SAT scores: 470 verbal, 517 math. Average ACT scores: 23 composite. Range of ACT scores of middle 50%: 21-22 composite.
**Faculty.** 43 full-time; 22 part-time. 70% of faculty holds highest degree in specific field. Student/faculty ratio: 13 to 1.
**Selectivity rating.** Less competitive.

**PROFILE.** Huntingdon, founded in 1854, is a church-affiliated, liberal arts college. Its 58-acre campus is located near the Old Cloverdale section of Montgomery. Campus architecture includes Gothic style buildings.

**Accreditation:** SACS. Professionally accredited by the National Association of Schools of Music.
**Religious orientation:** Huntingdon College is affiliated with the United Methodist Church; two semesters of religion required.
**Library:** Collections totaling over 95,000 volumes, 318 periodical subscriptions, and 6,000 microform items.
**Special facilities/museums:** Art gallery.
**Athletic facilities:** Gymnasium, baseball, football, soccer, and softball fields, swimming pool, weight room, tennis and volleyball courts.

**STUDENT BODY. Undergraduate profile:** 68% are state residents; 26% are transfers. 1% Asian-American, 8% Black, 1% Hispanic, 1% Native American, 82% White, 7% Other. Average age of undergraduates is 20.
**Freshman profile:** 2% of freshmen who took SAT scored 700 or over on math; 12% scored 600 or over on verbal, 33% scored 600 or over on math; 37% scored 500 or over on verbal, 68% scored 500 or over on math; 82% scored 400 or over on verbal, 90% scored 400 or over on math; 100% scored 300 or over on verbal, 96% scored 300 or over on math. 5% of freshmen who took ACT scored 30 or over on composite; 39% scored 24 or over on composite; 89% scored 18 or over on composite; 100% scored 12 or over on composite. 40% of accepted applicants took SAT; 84% took ACT. 83% of freshmen come from public schools.
**Undergraduate achievement:** 67% of fall 1992 freshmen returned for fall 1993 term. 45% of entering class graduated. 32% of students who completed a degree program immediately went on to graduate study.
**Foreign students:** Countries represented include Canada, Iceland, Jamaica, Japan, and Trinidad; 11 in all.

**PROGRAMS OF STUDY. Degrees:** B.A.
**Majors:** Accounting, Applied Music, Art, Biology, Business Administration, Chemistry, Christian Education, Church Music, Computer Information Systems, Computer Science, Dance, Drama, Elementary Education, English, History, International Business, Mathematics, Music, Music Theory/Literature, Physical Education, Pre-Law, Pre-Medicine, Pre-Physical Therapy, Pre-Theology, Psychology, Religion/Philosophy.
**Distribution of degrees:** The majors with the highest enrollment are business administration, English, and history; art, computer information systems, and social work have the lowest.
**Requirements:** General education requirement.
**Academic regulations:** Freshmen must maintain minimum 1.50 GPA; sophomores, 1.80 GPA; juniors, 2.00 GPA; seniors, 2.00 GPA.
**Special:** Minors offered. Courses offered in French, geography, German, health, physical science, physics, political science, sociology, and speech. Self-designed majors. Double majors. Dual degrees. Independent study. Pass/fail grading option. Internships. Cooperative education programs. Preprofessional programs in law, medicine, dentistry, theology, and physical therapy. 3-2 engineering program with Auburn U. Member of Alabama Consortium for the Development of Higher Education and Alabama Marine Environmental Sciences Consortium; off-campus study possible at Dauphin Island Sea Lab. Cross-registration with Auburn U. Teacher certification in early childhood, elementary, and secondary education. Certification in specific subject areas. ROTC at Auburn U at Montgomery, AFROTC at Alabama State U.
**Honors:** Honors program.
**Academic Assistance:** Nonremedial tutoring.

**ADMISSIONS. Academic basis for candidate selection** (in order of priority): Secondary school record, standardized test scores, class rank, school's recommendation, essay.
**Nonacademic basis for candidate selection:** Character and personality and extracurricular participation are emphasized. Particular talent or ability is important. Alumni/ae relationship is considered.
**Requirements:** Graduation from secondary school is required; GED is accepted. 15 units and the following program of study are recommended: 4 units of English, 3 units of math, 3 units of science, 3 units of social studies, 2 units of history. Minimum composite ACT score of 20 and minimum 2.3 GPA required. Portfolio required of art program applicants. Audition required of music program applicants. SAT or ACT is required. Campus visit and interview recommended.
**Procedure:** Take SAT or ACT by January of 12th year. Visit college for interview by March of 12th year. Suggest filing application by January. Application deadline is June. Notification of admission on rolling basis. Reply is required within 30 days of acceptance. $75 nonrefundable tuition deposit. $50 nonrefundable room deposit. Freshmen accepted for terms other than fall.

**Special programs:** Admission may be deferred one year. Credit and/or placement may be granted through CEEB Advanced Placement exams for scores of 3 or higher. Credit and/or placement may be granted through CLEP general and subject exams. Credit may be granted through life experience. Early entrance/early admission program.
**Transfer students:** Transfer students accepted for terms other than fall. In fall 1993, 26% of all new students were transfers into all classes. 80 transfer applications were received, 68 were accepted. Application deadline is August 15 for fall; January 10 for spring. Minimum 2.0 GPA required. Lowest course grade accepted is "D." Maximum number of transferable credits is 64 semester hours. At least 30 semester hours must be completed at the college to receive degree.
**Admissions contact:** Paul Mittelhammer, M.B.A., Dean of Enrollment Management. 205 834-3300.

**FINANCIAL AID. Available aid:** Pell grants, SEOG, state scholarships and grants, school scholarships, ROTC scholarships, academic merit scholarships, and athletic scholarships. Perkins Loans (NDSL), PLUS, Stafford Loans (GSL), and SLS. AMS and deferred payment plan.
**Financial aid statistics:** Average amounts of aid awarded freshmen: Scholarships and grants, $3,791; loans, $2,878.
**Supporting data/closing dates:** FAFSA/FAF/FFS: Priority filing date is April 1; deadline is August 1. School's own aid application: Priority filing date is April 1; deadline is June 1. State aid form: Deadline is September 15. Notification of awards on rolling basis.
**Financial aid contact:** Thomas G. Dismukes, Director of Financial Aid. 205 265-0511.

## Jacksonville State University

**Jacksonville, AL 36265** — **205 782-5781**

**1994-95 Costs.** Tuition: $1,680 (state residents), $2,520 (out-of-state). Room & board: $2,520.
**Enrollment.** Undergraduates: 2,390 men, 2,770 women (full-time). Freshman class: 1,621 applicants, 1,413 accepted, 887 enrolled. Graduate enrollment: 356 men, 515 women.
**Test score averages/ranges.** Average ACT scores: 19 English, 17 math, 18 composite.
**Faculty.** 272 full-time; 80 part-time. 66% of faculty holds doctoral degree. Student/faculty ratio: 23 to 1.
**Selectivity rating.** Less competitive.

**PROFILE.** Jacksonville State, founded in 1883, is a public, multipurpose university. Programs are offered through the Colleges of Commerce and Business Administration, Education, Library Science, Communications and Instructional Media, Criminal Justice, Nursing, Humanities and Social Sciences, Music and Fine Arts, and Science and Mathematics. Its 345-acre campus is located in Jacksonville, 75 miles east of Birmingham.

**Accreditation:** SACS. Professionally accredited by the Council on Social Work Education, the National Association of Schools of Art and Design, the National Association of Schools of Music, the National Council for Accreditation of Teacher Education, the National League for Nursing.
**Religious orientation:** Jacksonville State University is nonsectarian; no religious requirements.
**Library:** Collections totaling over 593,034 volumes, 2,035 periodical subscriptions, and 550 microform items.
**Special facilities/museums:** Observatory.
**Athletic facilities:** Indoor swimming pool, basketball, racquetball, tennis, and volleyball courts, playing fields, weight rooms.

**STUDENT BODY. Undergraduate profile:** 82% are state residents; 43% are transfers. 1% Asian-American, 17% Black, 1% Hispanic, 1% Native American, 80% White.
**Freshman profile:** Majority of accepted applicants took ACT.
**Undergraduate achievement:** 62% of fall 1992 freshmen returned for fall 1993 term.
**Foreign students:** 158 students are from out of the country. Countries represented include Canada, Japan, Jordan, Malaysia, Mexico, and the Netherlands; 65 in all.

**PROGRAMS OF STUDY. Degrees:** B.A., B.F.A., B.Mus., B.S., B.Soc.Work.
**Majors:** Accounting, Art, Biology, Chemistry, Communication, Computer Information Systems, Computer Science, Dietetics, Drama, Early Childhood Education, Economics, Education, Electronic Technology, Elementary Education, English, Exercise Science/Wellness, Finance, French, General Science Education, General Studies, Geography, German, Health Education, History, Home Economics, Language Arts Education, Law Enforcement, Management, Marketing, Mathematics, Merchandising, Music, Music Education, Music Performance, Nursing, Nutrition/Food Service, Physical Education, Physics, Political Science, Psychology, Recreation, Secondary Education, Social Science Education, Social Work, Sociology, Spanish, Special Education, Technology.
**Distribution of degrees:** The majors with the highest enrollment are education, management/marketing, and criminal justice; physics, economics, and music have the lowest.
**Requirements:** General education requirement.
**Academic regulations:** Minimum 2.0 GPA must be maintained.
**Special:** Minors offered in most majors and in approximately 20 other fields. Courses offered in journalism, philosophy, and religion. Double majors. Independent study. Accelerated study. Pass/fail grading option. Internships. Cooperative education programs. Graduate school at which undergraduates may take graduate-level courses. Preprofessional programs in law, medicine, veterinary science, pharmacy, and dentistry. Member of Alabama Marine Environmental Sciences Consortium; off-campus study possible at Dauphin Island Sea Lab. Teacher certification in early childhood, elementary, secondary, and special education. Certification in specific subject areas. ROTC.
**Honors:** Honors program.
**Academic Assistance:** Remedial reading, writing, math, and study skills. Nonremedial tutoring.

**STUDENT LIFE. Housing:** Students may live on or off campus. Coed, women's, and men's dorms. School-owned/operated apartments. 40% of students live in college housing.
**Social atmosphere:** The student newspaper reports, "Greeks make up less than 10 percent of our enrollment, but they get 90 percent of things done. For the most part, however, we are such a 'suitcase' college that no group has much influence on the majority. Social life in this area is always there; sometimes it just takes longer to find." On campus, favorite student gathering spots include the Roost, the Game Room, and the Coliseum; Katz, Sports Nut, and the Pub are among favorite off-campus haunts. Social events which draw the most enthusiasm include Homecoming, Whup Troy Week, Spring Cotillion, Greek Week, and J-Day.
**Services and counseling/handicapped student services:** Placement services. Health service. Day care. Counseling services for military, veteran, and older students. Birth control, personal, and psychological counseling. Career and academic guidance services. Physically disabled student services. Notetaking services. Tutors. Reader services for the blind.
**Campus organizations:** Undergraduate student government. Student newspaper (Chanticleer, published once/week). Yearbook. Radio station. Concert and marching bands, Masque and Wig Guild, ballet group, service groups. 10 fraternities, six chapter houses; eight sororities, no chapter houses. 12% of men join a fraternity. 10% of women join a sorority.
**Religious organizations:** Baptist Campus Ministry, Catholic Student Union, Charismatic Christian Fellowship, Episcopal College Community, Faith Outreach for Christ, Fellowship of Christian Athletes, University Christian Fellowship, Wesleyan-Westminster Foundation.
**Minority/foreign student organizations:** Afro-American Club. International Club.

**ATHLETICS. Physical education requirements:** None.
**Intercollegiate competition:** 4% of students participate. Baseball (M), basketball (M,W), cheerleading (M,W), football (M), golf (M), riflery (M,W), softball (W), tennis (M,W), volleyball (W). Member of NCAA Division II.
**Intramural and club sports:** 20% of students participate. Intramural basketball, golf, soccer, softball, tennis, volleyball. Men's club soccer.

**ADMISSIONS. Academic basis for candidate selection** (in order of priority): Standardized test scores, secondary school record.
**Requirements:** Graduation from secondary school is required; GED is accepted. No specific distribution of secondary school units required. Portfolios required of B.F.A. applicants. SAT or ACT is required. Off-campus interviews available with an admissions representative.
**Procedure:** Notification of admission on rolling basis. No set date by which applicants must accept offer. $100 room deposit, refundable until beginning of semester. Freshmen accepted for terms other than fall.
**Special programs:** Admission may be deferred one year. Credit and/or placement may be granted through CEEB Advanced Placement exams for scores of 3 or higher. Credit and/or placement may be granted through CLEP general and subject exams. Credit may be granted through military experience. Credit and placement may be granted through DANTES and challenge exams. Early entrance/early admission program. Concurrent enrollment program.
**Transfer students:** Transfer students accepted for terms other than fall. In fall 1993, 43% of all new students were transfers into all classes. 945 transfer applications were received, 935 were accepted. Application deadline is by start of classes for fall; by start of classes for spring. Minimum 2.0 GPA recommended. Lowest course grade accepted is "C." At least 32 semester hours must be completed at the university to receive degree.
**Admissions contact:** Jerry D. Smith, Ed.D., Dean of Admissions and Records. 205 782-5400.

**FINANCIAL AID. Available aid:** Pell grants, SEOG, state scholarships and grants, school scholarships, private scholarships, ROTC scholarships, academic merit scholarships, athletic scholarships, and aid for undergraduate foreign students. Disadvantaged Students in Nursing Program Perkins Loans (NDSL), PLUS, Stafford Loans (GSL), state loans, school loans, private loans, and SLS.
**Financial aid statistics:** 20% of aid is not need-based. In 1993-94, 50% of all undergraduate applicants received aid; 50% of freshman applicants. Average amounts of aid awarded freshmen: Scholarships and grants, $1,000; loans, $1,500.
**Supporting data/closing dates:** FAFSA/FAF/FFS: Priority filing date is April 1; accepted on rolling basis. School's own aid application: Priority filing date is April 1; accepted on rolling basis. Notification of awards on rolling basis.
**Financial aid contact:** Larry J. Smith, Director of Financial Aid. 205 782-5006.

**STUDENT EMPLOYMENT.** College Work/Study Program. Institutional employment. 5% of full-time undergraduates work on campus during school year. Students may expect to earn an average of $2,100 during school year. Off-campus part-time employment opportunities rated "fair."

**COMPUTER FACILITIES.** 300 IBM/IBM-compatible and Macintosh/Apple microcomputers; 100 are networked. Students may access IBM minicomputer/mainframe systems, BITNET, Internet. Client/LAN operating systems include Apple/Macintosh, DOS. Computer languages and software packages include Assembler, C, COBOL, dBASE, FORTRAN, Lotus 1-2-3, Pascal, PL/1, R:BASE, SPSS, WordPerfect; 16 in all. Computer facilities are available to all students.
**Fees:** $10 computer fee per course.
**Hours:** 8 AM-9 PM.

**GRADUATE CAREER DATA.** Highest graduate school enrollments: Auburn U, U of Alabama.

**PROMINENT ALUMNI/AE.** Dr. Wayne H. Finley, genetic researcher; Randy Owen, musician, the band Alabama; James E. Folsom, Jr., governor of Alabama.

# Judson College

**Marion, AL 36756** **205 683-6161**

**1994-95 Costs.** Tuition: $5,782. Room & board: $3,600. Fees, books, misc. academic expenses (school's estimate): $550.
**Enrollment.** Undergraduates: 1 man, 359 women (full-time). Freshman class: 299 applicants, 222 accepted, 112 enrolled.
**Test score averages/ranges.** N/A.
**Faculty.** 29 full-time; 14 part-time. 67% of faculty holds doctoral degree. Student/faculty ratio: 12 to 1.
**Selectivity rating.** Less competitive.

**PROFILE.** Judson, founded in 1838, is a private, church-affiliated college. Its 103-acre campus is in Marion, 75 miles from Birmingham.

**Accreditation:** SACS.
**Religious orientation:** Judson College is affiliated with the Alabama Baptist Church; no religious requirements.
**Athletic facilities:** Gymnasium, indoor pool, weight room, tennis courts.
**STUDENT BODY. Undergraduate profile:** 75% are state residents; 5% are transfers. 5% Black, 95% White. Average age of undergraduates is 20.
**Freshman profile:** 2% of freshmen who took ACT scored 30 or over on composite; 30% scored 24 or over on composite; 88% scored 18 or over on composite; 100% scored 12 or over on composite. 75% of accepted applicants took ACT.
**Undergraduate achievement:** 19% of students who completed a degree program immediately went on to graduate study.
**Foreign students:** Three students are from out of the country. Countries represented include China and Russia; two in all.
**PROGRAMS OF STUDY. Degrees:** B.A., B.S.
**Majors:** Art History/Appreciation, Biology, Business/Management, Chemistry, Computer/Information Sciences, Criminal Justice Studies, Economics, Elementary Education, English, English Education, Fine Arts, History, Interior Design, Junior High Education, Mathematics, Mathematics Education, Music, Music Education, Physical Sciences, Pre-Dentistry, Pre-Law, Pre-Medicine, Pre-Pharmacy, Pre-Veterinary, Psychology, Religion, Science Education, Secondary Education, Social Science Education, Social Sciences, Sociology, Spanish, Textiles/Clothing.
**Special:** Double majors. Internships. Preprofessional programs in law, medicine, veterinary science, pharmacy, dentistry, and optometry. Teacher certification in elementary and secondary education. ROTC at Marion Military Inst.
**ADMISSIONS. Academic basis for candidate selection** (in order of priority): Standardized test scores, secondary school record, school's recommendation, class rank.
**Nonacademic basis for candidate selection:** Character and personality are important. Extracurricular participation and particular talent or ability are considered.
**Requirements:** Graduation from secondary school is required; GED is accepted. 15 units and the following program of study are required: 4 units of English, 2 units of math, 2 units of science, 2 units of social studies, 5 units of electives. Units in social studies may include history. Minimum 2.0 GPA required. Conditional admission possible for applicants not meeting standard requirements. SAT or ACT is required. Campus visit recommended. Off-campus interviews available with an admissions representative.
**Procedure:** Take SAT or ACT by August of 12th year. Notification of admission on rolling basis. Reply is required by August 25. $60 nonrefundable tuition deposit. $60 nonrefundable room deposit.
**Special programs:** Credit and/or placement may be granted through CEEB Advanced Placement exams for scores of 3 or higher.
**Transfer students:** Transfer students accepted for terms other than fall. In fall 1993, 5% of all new students were transfers into all classes. 12 transfer applications were received, 12 were accepted. Minimum 2.0 GPA required. Lowest course grade accepted is "C." Maximum number of transferable credits is 64 semester hours from a two-year school and 98 from a four-year school.
**Admissions contact:** Ginger L. Bagby, Director of Admissions. 800 447-9472.
**FINANCIAL AID. Available aid:** Pell grants, SEOG, Federal Nursing Student Scholarships, state scholarships and grants, school scholarships, and athletic scholarships. SLS.
**Financial aid statistics:** 44% of aid is not need-based. In 1993-94, 95% of all undergraduate applicants received aid; 97% of freshman applicants. Average amounts of aid awarded freshmen: Scholarships and grants, $3,821; loans, $2,625.
**Supporting data/closing dates:** FAFSA: Priority filing date is April 1. FFS: Priority filing date is April 1; accepted on rolling basis. School's own aid application: Priority filing date is April 1. Notification of awards on rolling basis.
**Financial aid contact:** Doris Wilson, Director of Financial Aid. 205 683-6161.

# Livingston University

**Livingston, AL 35470** **205 652-9661**

**1994-95 Costs.** Tuition: $1,590. Room: $975. Board: $1,236. Fees, books, misc. academic expenses (school's estimate): $630.
**Enrollment.** Undergraduates: 744 men, 883 women (full-time). Freshman class: 1,206 applicants, 957 accepted, 444 enrolled. Graduate enrollment: 61 men, 165 women.
**Test score averages/ranges.** Average ACT scores: 19 English, 18 math, 19 composite. Range of ACT scores of middle 50%: 23-23 English, 23-27 math.
**Faculty.** 90 full-time; 15 part-time. 59% of faculty holds doctoral degree. Student/faculty ratio: 18 to 1.
**Selectivity rating.** Less competitive.

**PROFILE.** Livingston is a public university. It was founded as a church-affiliated academy for women in 1835, served as a teachers college for much of its history, and gained university status in 1967. Programs are offered through the Colleges of General Studies, Business and Commerce, Education, and Graduate Studies. Its 600-acre campus is located in Livingston, 60 miles southwest of Tuscaloosa.

**Accreditation:** SACS. Professionally accredited by the National League for Nursing.
**Religious orientation:** Livingston University is nonsectarian; no religious requirements.
**Library:** Collections totaling over 118,000 volumes, 882 periodical subscriptions, and 485,657 microform items.
**Athletic facilities:** Gymnasiums, field house, basketball, tennis, and volleyball courts, swimming pool, lake, baseball, football, intramural, and softball fields, stadium, weight rooms.
**STUDENT BODY. Undergraduate profile:** 69% are state residents; 28% are transfers. 1% Asian-American, 32% Black, 1% Native American, 65% White, 1% Other. Average age of undergraduates is 24.
**Freshman profile:** 2% of freshmen who took ACT scored 30 or over on English, 2% scored 30 or over on math; 15% scored 24 or over on English, 9% scored 24 or over on math, 12% scored 24 or over on composite; 56% scored 18 or over on English, 45% scored 18 or over on math, 57% scored 18 or over on composite; 95% scored 12 or over on English, 96% scored 12 or over on math, 96% scored 12 or over on composite; 97% scored 6 or over on English. 1% of accepted applicants took SAT; 99% took ACT. 88% of freshmen come from public schools.
**Undergraduate achievement:** 59% of fall 1992 freshmen returned for fall 1993 term. 20% of students who completed a degree program went on to graduate study within five years.
**Foreign students:** 32 students are from out of the country. Countries represented include Bahamas, Canada, Cyprus, Egypt, Japan, and Malaysia; 13 in all.
**PROGRAMS OF STUDY. Degrees:** B.A., B.Mus.Ed., B.S., B.Tech.
**Majors:** Accounting, Athletic Training, Biology, Business Administration, Business Education, Chemistry, Computer Information Processing, Early Childhood Education, Elementary Education, English, Environmental Science, General Business, History, Industrial Arts Education, Management, Marine Biology, Mathematics, Medical Technology, Music, Music Education, Natural Science, Physical Education, Secondary Education, Secretarial Education, Social Science, Sociology, Special Education.
**Distribution of degrees:** The majors with the highest enrollment are elementary education, business administration, and physical education; music, chemistry, and English have the lowest.
**Requirements:** General education requirement.
**Academic regulations:** Minimum 2.0 GPA required for graduation.
**Special:** Minors offered in many majors and in approximately 20 other fields. Courses offered in French, geography, physics, Spanish, and speech. Freshmen Studies Program. Associate's degrees offered. Dual degrees. Preprofessional programs in law, medicine, veterinary science, pharmacy, and dentistry. Two-year transfer programs in fisheries and wildlife management. 3-2 engineering program with Auburn U. Member of Alabama Marine Environmental Sciences Consortium; off-campus study possible at Dauphin Island Sea Lab. Teacher certification in early childhood, elementary, and secondary education. Certification in specific subject areas.
**Honors:** Honors program. Honor societies.
**Academic Assistance:** Remedial reading, writing, math, and study skills. Nonremedial tutoring.
**STUDENT LIFE. Housing:** All unmarried students under age 21 must live on campus unless living near campus with relatives. Coed, women's, and men's dorms. On-campus married-student housing. 41% of students live in college housing.
**Social atmosphere:** "The campus is relatively isolated; therefore, most social and campus events are campus-based. Student activity programming is large-scale and active," reports the student newspaper. Among the most popular student events are Homecoming, Springfest, the movie series, concerts, Tiger Tail Productions, and athletic events. Influential student groups include the various Greek organizations and a Christian group called Main Event. Favorite student destinations include the Brass Monkey, the Best Western, and Travel Time Restaurant.
**Services and counseling/handicapped student services:** Placement services. Health service. Counseling services for veteran students. Personal counseling. Career and academic guidance services. Learning disabled services.
**Campus organizations:** Undergraduate student government. Student newspaper (Livingston Life, published once/week). Yearbook. Band, choir, stage band, Collegiate Journalist Association, Owen Love Business Association, Student Nurses Association, Association for Women Students, departmental groups, special-interest groups, 37 organizations in all. Six fraternities, three chapter houses; five sororities, no chapter houses. 20% of men join a fraternity. 15% of women join a sorority.
**Religious organizations:** Baptist Student Union, Fellowship of Christian Athletes, Wesley Foundation.
**Minority/foreign student organizations:** Afro-American Cultural Association.
**ATHLETICS. Physical education requirements:** Three quarters of physical education required.
**Intercollegiate competition:** 11% of students participate. Baseball (M), basketball (M,W), cheerleading (M,W), football (M), softball (W), tennis (M,W), volleyball (W). Member of Gulf South Conference, NCAA Division II.
**Intramural and club sports:** 55% of students participate. Intramural basketball, cross-country, flag football, golf, handball, softball, swimming, table tennis, tennis, ultimate frisbee, volleyball, weight lifting. Men's club soccer.
**ADMISSIONS. Academic basis for candidate selection** (in order of priority): Secondary school record, standardized test scores, class rank, school's recommendation.
**Requirements:** Graduation from secondary school is required; GED is accepted. 15 units and the following program of study are required: 4 units of English. Minimum 2.0 GPA required. ACT is required; SAT may be substituted. Campus visit recommended. No off-campus interviews.
**Procedure:** Take SAT or ACT by April of 12th year. Suggest filing application by May 1; no deadline. Notification of admission on rolling basis. No set date by which applicants

must accept offer. $50 refundable room deposit. Freshmen accepted for terms other than fall.

**Special programs:** Admission may be deferred two years. Credit and/or placement may be granted through CEEB Advanced Placement exams for scores of 3 or higher. Credit and/or placement may be granted through CLEP general and subject exams. Credit and placement may be granted through Regents College, ACT PEP, DANTES, and challenge exams and military experience. Early entrance/early admission program. Concurrent enrollment program.

**Transfer students:** Transfer students accepted for terms other than fall. In fall 1993, 28% of all new students were transfers into all classes. 339 transfer applications were received, 214 were accepted. Application deadline is rolling for fall; rolling for spring. Minimum 2.0 GPA required. Lowest course grade accepted is "C." At least 48 quarter hours must be completed at the university to receive degree.

**Admissions contact:** Ervin L. Wood, Director of Admissions. 205 652-9661, extension 352.

**FINANCIAL AID. Available aid:** Pell grants, SEOG, state scholarships and grants, school scholarships, private scholarships, academic merit scholarships, and athletic scholarships. Perkins Loans (NDSL), PLUS, Stafford Loans (GSL), state loans, and SLS. Deferred payment plan.

**Financial aid statistics:** 10% of aid is not need-based. In 1993-94, 96% of all undergraduate applicants received aid; 94% of freshman applicants. Average amounts of aid awarded freshmen: Scholarships and grants, $750; loans, $2,504.

**Supporting data/closing dates:** FAFSA/FAF/FFS: Priority filing date is April 20. Notification of awards on rolling basis.

**Financial aid contact:** Patsy Reedy, Director of Financial Aid. 205 652-9661, extension 350.

**STUDENT EMPLOYMENT.** College Work/Study Program. 20% of full-time undergraduates work on campus during school year. Students may expect to earn an average of $1,500 during school year. Off-campus part-time employment opportunities rated "fair."

**COMPUTER FACILITIES.** IBM/IBM-compatible and Macintosh/Apple microcomputers. Students may access IBM minicomputer/mainframe systems. Client/LAN operating systems include Apple/Macintosh, DOS, OS/2. Computer facilities are available to all students.

**Fees:** Computer fee is included in tuition/fees.

**GRADUATE CAREER DATA.** Graduate school percentages: 1% enter law school. 1% enter medical school. 1% enter dental school. 1% enter graduate business programs. 55% of graduates choose careers in business and industry.

# Oakwood College

**Huntsville, AL 35896** **205 726-7000**

**1993-94 Costs.** Tuition: $6,639. Room & board: $3,999. Fees, books, misc. academic expenses (school's estimate): $848.

**Enrollment.** Undergraduates: 547 men, 769 women (full-time). Freshman class: 949 applicants, 605 accepted, 385 enrolled.

**Test score averages/ranges.** Average SAT scores: 378 verbal, 382 math. Range of SAT scores of middle 50%: 360-370 verbal, 340-350 math. Average ACT scores: 16 English, 16 math, 17 composite. Range of ACT scores of middle 50%: 16-17 English, 15-16 math.

**Faculty.** 77 full-time; 45 part-time. 52% of faculty holds doctoral degree. Student/faculty ratio: 12 to 1.

**Selectivity rating.** Less competitive.

**PROFILE.** Oakwood, founded in 1896, is a private, church-affiliated, liberal arts college. Its 105-acre campus is located five miles from downtown Huntsville.

**Accreditation:** SACS. Professionally accredited by the American Dietetic Association, the Council on Social Work Education, the National Council for Accreditation of Teacher Education.

**Religious orientation:** Oakwood College is affiliated with the General Conference of Seventh-day Adventists; 8-16 quarter hours of religion/theology required.

**Library:** Collections totaling over 96,000 volumes, 587 periodical subscriptions, and 3,376 microform items.

**Special facilities/museums:** On-campus elementary and secondary school, child development lab.

**Athletic facilities:** Tennis and racquetball courts, ball fields, gymnasium.

**STUDENT BODY. Undergraduate profile:** 30% are state residents; 19% are transfers. 87.3% Black, .4% Hispanic, .1% Native American, .2% White, 12% Other. Average age of undergraduates is 22.

**Freshman profile:** 1% of freshmen who took SAT scored 700 or over on verbal; 5% scored 600 or over on verbal, 4% scored 600 or over on math; 10% scored 500 or over on verbal, 17% scored 500 or over on math; 43% scored 400 or over on verbal, 40% scored 400 or over on math; 77% scored 300 or over on verbal, 76% scored 300 or over on math. 1% of freshmen who took ACT scored 30 or over on composite; 14% scored 24 or over on English, 4% scored 24 or over on math, 6% scored 24 or over on composite; 45% scored 18 or over on English, 31% scored 18 or over on math, 45% scored 18 or over on composite; 90% scored 12 or over on English, 95% scored 12 or over on math, 97% scored 12 or over on composite; 100% scored 6 or over on English, 100% scored 6 or over on math, 100% scored 6 or over on composite. 45% of accepted applicants took SAT; 67% took ACT. 61% of freshmen come from public schools.

**Undergraduate achievement:** 66% of fall 1992 freshmen returned for fall 1993 term.

**Foreign students:** 169 students are from out of the country. Countries represented include Barbados, Bermuda, Canada, Jamaica, the Bahamas, and Trinidad and Tobago; 31 in all.

**PROGRAMS OF STUDY. Degrees:** B.A., B.S., B.Soc.Work.

**Majors:** Accounting, Biochemistry, Biology, Biology Education, Business Education, Chemical Engineering, Chemistry, Chemistry Education, Communications, Computer Science, Dietetics, Economics, Elementary Education, English, English Education, History, History Education, Home Economics, Home Economics Education, Human Development/Family Studies, Interdisciplinary Studies, Language Arts Education, Management, Mathematics, Mathematics/Computer Science, Mathematics Education, Ministerial Theology, Music, Music Education, Natural Science, Office Systems Management, Physical Education, Psychology, Religion, Religious Education, Social Science Education, Social Work.

**Distribution of degrees:** The majors with the highest enrollment are biology, ministerial theology, and psychology; chemistry, music, and mathematics have the lowest.

**Requirements:** General education requirement.

**Academic regulations:** Minimum 2.0 GPA must be maintained.

**Special:** Minors offered in some majors and in art, child development, correctional science, gerontology, office administration, physics, political science, sociology, and theology. Student missionary program. Associate's degrees offered. Double majors. Dual degrees. Pass/fail grading option. Internships. Preprofessional programs in law, medicine, veterinary science, pharmacy, dentistry, allied health sciences, and engineering. 2-2 occupational therapy program with U of Alabama at Birmingham. 2-2 natural science program. Two-year transfer programs in anesthesia, dental hygiene, occupational therapy, physical therapy, and public health with Loma Linda U. Two-year transfer program in engineering with Walla Walla Coll. Two-year transfer programs in medical technology, occupational therapy, and physical therapy with Andrews U, Florida Hospital, Howard U, Meharry Medical Coll, Tennessee State U, and U of Alabama at Birmingham. 3-1 medical technology program. 3-2 engineering program with Alabama A&M U. B.S. in natural science awarded for successful completion of three years of undergraduate work and one year of professional study in dentistry, medicine, or allied health sciences. Member of Alabama Center for Higher Education. Cross-registration with Alabama A&M U, U of Alabama at Huntsville, Athens State Coll, and John C. Calhoun State Community Coll. Teacher certification in early childhood, elementary, secondary, and special education. Study abroad in France.

**Academic Assistance:** Remedial reading, writing, math, and study skills. Nonremedial tutoring.

**STUDENT LIFE. Housing:** All unmarried students under age 21 must live on campus unless living near campus with relatives. Women's and men's dorms. On-campus married-student housing. 69% of students live in college housing.

**Services and counseling/handicapped student services:** Placement services. Health service. Counseling services for minority, veteran, and older students. Personal and psychological counseling. Career and academic guidance services. Religious counseling.

**Campus organizations:** Undergraduate student government. Student newspaper (Spreading Oak, published once/month). Yearbook. Radio station. Choir, band, other music groups, dormitory clubs, United Student Movement.

**Religious organizations:** Adventist Youth Society, Religion and Theology Forum, Outreach.

**Minority/foreign student organizations:** International Student Club.

**ATHLETICS. Physical education requirements:** Six quarter hours of physical education required.

**Intramural and club sports:** 65% of students participate. Intramural basketball, flagball, soccer, volleyball.

**ADMISSIONS. Academic basis for candidate selection** (in order of priority): Secondary school record, standardized test scores, school's recommendation, class rank.

**Nonacademic basis for candidate selection:** Character and personality are important. Extracurricular participation is considered.

**Requirements:** Graduation from secondary school is required; GED is accepted. 18 units and the following program of study are required: 4 units of English, 2 units of math, 2 units of science, 2 units of social studies, 6 units of electives. Minimum 2.0 GPA required. Minimum composite ACT score of 16 (combined SAT score of 745), minimum 2.5 GPA, and satisfactory performance on Alabama English Proficiency Test required of teacher education program applicants (entered after sophomore year). Minimum ACT scores of 21 in English and 17 in both math and social science, minimum 2.5 GPA, and minimum grade of "C" in secondary school chemistry and U.S. history required of nursing program applicants. SAT or ACT is required. Campus visit recommended. Off-campus interviews available with an alumni representative.

**Procedure:** Take SAT or ACT by spring of 12th year. ACT may be taken at Oakwood during freshman orientation if not taken prior to entrance. Notification of admission on rolling basis. $150 refundable room deposit. Freshmen accepted for terms other than fall.

**Special programs:** Admission may be deferred one year. Credit may be granted through CLEP subject exams. Credit may be granted through life experience.

**Transfer students:** Transfer students accepted for terms other than fall. In fall 1993, 19% of all new students were transfers into all classes. 139 transfer applications were received, 126 were accepted. Minimum 2.0 GPA recommended. Lowest course grade accepted is "C." Maximum number of transferable credits is 96 quarter hours. At least 36 quarter hours must be completed at the college to receive degree.

**Admissions contact:** Trevor Fraser, M.Div., Enrollment Management. 205 726-7030.

**FINANCIAL AID. Available aid:** Pell grants, SEOG, Federal Nursing Student Scholarships, state grants, school scholarships, private scholarships, academic merit scholarships, aid for undergraduate foreign students, and United Negro College Fund. PLUS, Stafford Loans (GSL), and SLS. AMS, deferred payment plan, and family tuition reduction.

**Financial aid statistics:** Average amounts of aid awarded freshmen: Scholarships and grants, $2,018; loans, $2,625.

**Supporting data/closing dates:** FAFSA/FAF: Priority filing date is April 15; accepted on rolling basis. Income tax forms: Priority filing date is April 15; accepted on rolling basis. Notification of awards on rolling basis.

**Financial aid contact:** Charlotte Smith, Acting Director of Financial Aid. 205 726-7208.

**STUDENT EMPLOYMENT.** College Work/Study Program. Institutional employment. 65% of full-time undergraduates work on campus during school year. Students may expect to earn an average of $1,800 during school year. Off-campus part-time employment opportunities rated "fair."

**COMPUTER FACILITIES.** 177 IBM/IBM-compatible and Macintosh/Apple microcomputers; 112 are networked. Students may access AT&T minicomputer/mainframe systems. Residence halls may be equipped with stand-alone microcomputers. Client/LAN operating systems include Apple/Macintosh, DOS, UNIX/XENIX/AIX, Novell. Computer languages and software packages include BASIC, COBOL, FORTRAN, Lotus 1-2-3, Pascal, Turbo C, WordPerfect. Computer facilities are available to all students.
**Fees:** $10 computer fee per class.
**Hours:** 8 AM-10 PM (M,T,Th); 8 AM-7 PM (W); 9 AM-10 PM (Su).

# Samford University

**Birmingham, AL 35229** **205 870-2011**

**1994-95 Costs.** Tuition: $8,236. Room & board: $3,650. Fees, books, misc. academic expenses (school's estimate): $450.
**Enrollment.** Undergraduates: 1,155 men, 1,802 women (full-time). Freshman class: 1,511 applicants, 1,396 accepted, 692 enrolled. Graduate enrollment: 689 men, 395 women.
**Test score averages/ranges.** Range of SAT scores of middle 50%: 920-1120 combined. Average ACT scores: 24 composite. Range of ACT scores of middle 50%: 22-26 composite.
**Faculty.** 203 full-time; 181 part-time. 83% of faculty holds highest degree in specific field. Student/faculty ratio: 15 to 1.
**Selectivity rating.** More competitive.

**PROFILE.** Samford, founded in 1841, is a private, church-affiliated university. Programs are offered through the Schools of Business, Education, Law, Music, Nursing, and Pharmacy; the Howard College of Arts and Sciences; and the Graduate School. Its 280-acre campus, of Georgian Colonial architectural style, is located in Shades Valley, five miles from Birmingham.

**Accreditation:** SACS. Professionally accredited by the American Bar Association, the American Council on Pharmaceutical Education, the American Dietetic Association, the National Association of Schools of Music, the National Association of Schools of Public Affairs and Administration, the National Council for Accreditation of Teacher Education, the National League for Nursing.
**Religious orientation:** Samford University is affiliated with the Southern Baptist Church; two semesters of religion required.
**Library:** Collections totaling over 523,183 volumes, 1,600 periodical subscriptions, and 272,940 microform items.
**Special facilities/museums:** Language lab, observatory, reflective telescope.
**Athletic facilities:** Gymnasium, field house, basketball, racquetball, tennis, and volleyball courts, weight room, tracks, swimming pool, baseball, football, intramural, and softball fields, stadium.

**STUDENT BODY. Undergraduate profile:** 45% are state residents; 28% are transfers. 1% Asian-American, 7% Black, 1% Hispanic, 91% White. Average age of undergraduates is 21.
**Freshman profile:** 7% of freshmen who took ACT scored 30 or over on composite; 53% scored 24 or over on composite; 96% scored 18 or over on composite. 30% of accepted applicants took SAT; 70% took ACT. 75% of freshmen come from public schools.
**Undergraduate achievement:** 93% of fall 1992 freshmen returned for fall 1993 term. 17% of students who completed a degree program immediately went on to graduate study.
**Foreign students:** Countries represented include Canada, China, England, India, Jordan, and South Korea; 13 in all.

**PROGRAMS OF STUDY. Degrees:** B.A., B.Gen.Studies, B.Mus., B.S.
**Majors:** Accounting, Art, Art Education, Athletic Training, Biology, Business, Chemistry, Church Music, Church Recreation, Communications, Computer Science, Drama, Early Childhood Education, Economics, Elementary Education, Engineering Physics, English, Environmental Science, Exercise Science, Fashion Merchandising, French, General Business, General Science, German, Graphic Design, Health Education, History, Home Economics, Home Economics Education, Human Development/Family Studies, Human Relations, Instrumental Music, Interior Design, International Business, International Relations, Journalism/Mass Communication, Language/World Culture, Management, Management Information Systems, Marine Science, Marketing, Mathematics, Merchandising, Music, Music Education, Nursing, Nutrition/Dietetics, Organ, Paralegal Studies, Pharmacy, Philosophy, Physical Education, Physics, Piano, Political Science, Psychology, Public Administration, Religion, Religious Education, School Psychology, Secondary Education, Social Studies, Sociology, Spanish, Speech/Communication/Theatre, Sports Medicine, Theory/Composition, Voice.
**Distribution of degrees:** The majors with the highest enrollment are pharmacy, management, and elementary education; art and physics have the lowest.
**Requirements:** General education requirement.
**Academic regulations:** Minimum 2.0 GPA must be maintained.
**Special:** Minors offered in all liberal arts majors. Associate's degrees offered. Double majors. Dual degrees. Accelerated study. Internships. Cooperative education programs. Graduate school at which undergraduates may take graduate-level courses. Preprofessional programs in law, medicine, pharmacy, dentistry, theology, optometry, cytotechnology, engineering, medical records, medical technology, nuclear medicine technology, occupational therapy, radiologic technology, and surgeon's assistant. 3-2 engineering programs with Auburn U, Georgia Tech, Mercer U, U of Southern California, and Washington U. 3-2 forestry and environmental studies program with Duke U. 1-3 health science program with U of Alabama at Birmingham. Member of Alabama Marine Environmental Sciences Consortium; off-campus study possible at Dauphin Island Sea Lab. Exchange program with Birmingham-Southern Coll and U of Alabama at Birmingham. Teacher certification in early childhood, elementary, and secondary education. Certification in specific subject areas. Study abroad in China, England, Germany, Latin American countries, and other European countries. AFROTC. ROTC at U of Alabama at Birmingham.
**Honors:** Honors program. Honor societies.
**Academic Assistance:** Remedial reading, writing, and math. Nonremedial tutoring.

**STUDENT LIFE. Housing:** All unmarried students under age 21 must live on campus unless living near campus with relatives. Women's and men's dorms. Sorority and fraternity housing. On-campus married-student housing. 58% of students live in college housing.
**Social atmosphere:** The student newspaper reports, "There is not much of a social life on campus except for within the Greek system. Most people find entertainment off campus." Off-campus spots include the Galleria and the Southside, a popular area downtown. On campus, students like to congregate at the Student Center and at Howards, the snack bar. Groups important to Samford social life include the Greeks, the football team, and the Baptist Student Union. Among favorite campus events are the Step Sing, Homecoming, the Fall Carnival and the Spring Fling.
**Services and counseling/handicapped student services:** Placement services. Psychological counseling. Career and academic guidance services. Religious counseling. Physically disabled student services. Learning disabled services.
**Campus organizations:** Undergraduate student government. Student newspaper (Crimson, published once/week). Literary magazine. Yearbook. Radio station. A cappella choir, chorale, band, chamber music ensemble, debating, Koinonia, publications, Circle K, Readers Theatre, Samford Masquers, Student Activities Council, departmental, professional, and service groups, 110 organizations in all. Four fraternities, five chapter houses; six sororities, five chapter houses. 30% of men join a fraternity. 30% of women join a sorority.
**Religious organizations:** Campus Ministries, Ministerial Association, Baptist Pharmacy Fellowship, Fellowship of Christian Athletes.
**Minority/foreign student organizations:** Black Student Organization, Missionary Student Organization.

**ATHLETICS. Physical education requirements:** Four semesters of physical education required.
**Intercollegiate competition:** 6% of students participate. Baseball (M), basketball (M), cheerleading (M,W), cross-country (M,W), football (M), golf (M,W), softball (W), tennis (M,W), track (indoor) (M,W), track (outdoor) (M,W), track and field (indoor) (M,W), track and field (outdoor) (M,W), volleyball (W). Member of NCAA Division I, NCAA Division I-AA for football, Trans America Athletic Conference.
**Intramural and club sports:** 36% of students participate. Intramural badminton, basketball, bowling, flag football, golf, racquetball, softball, table tennis, tennis, volleyball, walleyball, water polo, weight lifting. Men's club soccer.

**ADMISSIONS. Academic basis for candidate selection** (in order of priority): Secondary school record, standardized test scores, class rank, school's recommendation, essay.
**Nonacademic basis for candidate selection:** Character and personality and extracurricular participation are emphasized. Particular talent or ability and alumni/ae relationship are considered.
**Requirements:** Graduation from secondary school is required; GED is accepted. 18 units (including 4 units of English) required and the following program of study recommended: 3 units of math, 3 units of science, 2 units of foreign language, 3 units of social studies. Minimum combined SAT score of 900 and minimum 3.0 GPA required. Audition required of music program applicants. SAT is required; ACT may be substituted. ACH recommended. Campus visit and interview recommended. Off-campus interviews available with an admissions representative.
**Procedure:** Take SAT or ACT by October of 12th year. Visit college for interview by March of 12th year. Suggest filing application by December 15. Application deadline is June 1. Notification of admission on rolling basis. Reply is required by May 1. $200 nonrefundable tuition deposit. $200 combined tuition and room deposit, refundable until May 30. Freshmen accepted for terms other than fall.
**Special programs:** Admission may be deferred one year. Credit and/or placement may be granted through CEEB Advanced Placement exams for scores of 3 or higher. Credit may be granted through CLEP general and subject exams. Credit may be granted through military and life experience. Early decision program. In fall 1992, 620 applied for early decision and 320 were accepted. Deadline for applying for early decision is December 1. Early entrance/early admission program. Concurrent enrollment program.
**Transfer students:** Transfer students accepted for terms other than fall. In fall 1993, 28% of all new students were transfers into all classes. 759 transfer applications were received, 667 were accepted. Application deadline is June 1 for fall; December 30 for spring. Minimum 2.5 GPA required. Lowest course grade accepted is "D." Maximum number of transferable credits is 64 semester hours from a two-year school and 96 semester hours from a four-year school. At least 32 semester hours must be completed at the university to receive degree.
**Admissions contact:** Don Belcher, Ed.D., Dean of Admissions and Financial Aid. 800 888-7218.

**FINANCIAL AID. Available aid:** Pell grants, SEOG, state scholarships and grants, school scholarships, private scholarships, ROTC scholarships, academic merit scholarships, and athletic scholarships. Perkins Loans (NDSL), PLUS, Stafford Loans (GSL), NSL, Health Professions Loans, private loans, and SLS.
**Financial aid statistics:** In 1993-94, 85% of all undergraduate applicants received aid; 85% of freshman applicants. Average amounts of aid awarded freshmen: Scholarships and grants, $1,500; loans, $2,625.
**Supporting data/closing dates:** FAFSA/FAF/FFS: Priority filing date is March 1; accepted on rolling basis. Notification of awards begins March 1.
**Financial aid contact:** Joseph Clyde Walker, M.S., Director of Financial Aid. 800 888-7245.

**STUDENT EMPLOYMENT.** College Work/Study Program. Institutional employment. 25% of full-time undergraduates work on campus during school year. Students may expect to earn an average of $934 during school year. Off-campus part-time employment opportunities rated "excellent."

**COMPUTER FACILITIES.** 230 IBM/IBM-compatible and Macintosh/Apple microcomputers. Students may access IBM minicomputer/mainframe systems, BITNET. Computer languages and software packages include SAS, SASS, UNITAE; 7 in all. Computer facilities are available to all students.
**Fees:** None.
**Hours:** 24 hours (one lab); 10 AM-midn. (three labs).

**GRADUATE CAREER DATA.** Graduate school percentages: 10% enter law school. 1% enter graduate business programs. 16% enter graduate arts and sciences programs. 14% enter theological school/seminary. Highest graduate school enrollments: U of Alabama at Birmingham Sch of Medicine, U of Alabama at Tuscaloosa, Southern Seminary. 70% of graduates choose careers in business and industry. Companies and businesses that hire graduates: Alabama Power, Clayton McWhorter, Dow Chemical, IBM, Presidential Health Trust, SONAT, Southern Bell, U.S. Steel.

**PROMINENT ALUMNI/AE.** Edward W. May, chairperson, CIT Financial Corp. (N.J.); Ralph C. McWhorter, president, Hospital Corp. of America; Jack F. Mayer, president of Texize Division, Morton Thiokol; Marvin L. Mann, president of Information Products Division, IBM.

## Southeastern Bible College

**Birmingham, AL 35243** — **205 969-0880**

**1994-95 Costs.** Tuition: $4,000. Room & board: $2,700. Fees, books, misc. academic expenses (school's estimate): $620.
**Enrollment.** Undergraduates: 79 men, 33 women (full-time). Freshman class: 90 applicants, 89 accepted, 75 enrolled.
**Test score averages/ranges.** Average ACT scores: 22 English, 18 math, 20 composite.
**Faculty.** 12 full-time; 6 part-time. 64% of faculty holds doctoral degree. Student/faculty ratio: 10 to 1.
**Selectivity rating.** Less competitive.

**PROFILE.** Southeastern Bible, founded in 1935, is a private college with religious orientation. Its 10-acre campus is located in Birmingham.

**Accreditation:** AABC.
**Religious orientation:** Southeastern Bible College is an interdenominational Christian school; eight semesters of religion/theology required.
**Library:** Collections totaling over 30,000 volumes and 250 periodical subscriptions.
**Athletic facilities:** Gymnasium, softball and soccer fields. Access to YMCA swimming pool, racquetball courts, weight room.

**STUDENT BODY. Undergraduate profile:** 70% are state residents; 30% are transfers. 6% Black, 93% White, 1% Other. Average age of undergraduates is 24.
**Freshman profile:** 1% of freshmen who took ACT scored 30 or over on English, 3% scored 30 or over on math, 4% scored 30 or over on composite; 33% scored 24 or over on English, 24% scored 24 or over on math, 34% scored 24 or over on composite; 78% scored 18 or over on English, 45% scored 18 or over on math, 69% scored 18 or over on composite; 92% scored 12 or over on English, 74% scored 12 or over on math, 99% scored 12 or over on composite; 100% scored 6 or over on English, 92% scored 6 or over on math, 100% scored 6 or over on composite. 2% of accepted applicants took SAT; 98% took ACT. 75% of freshmen come from public schools.
**Undergraduate achievement:** 50% of fall 1992 freshmen returned for fall 1993 term. 23% of entering class graduated.
**Foreign students:** Seven students are from out of the country. Countries represented include Germany, Japan, Kenya, Korea, Mexico, and Tanzania; six in all.

**PROGRAMS OF STUDY. Degrees:** B.A., B.S.
**Majors:** Church Education, Church Education Counseling, Church Education/Music, Elementary Education, Missions/Evangelism, Pastoral Theology, Pre-Seminary.
**Distribution of degrees:** The majors with the highest enrollment are pastoral theology, elementary education, and church education; missions has the lowest.
**Requirements:** General education requirement.
**Academic regulations:** Freshmen must maintain minimum 1.75 GPA; sophomores, juniors, seniors 2.0 GPA.
**Special:** Minors offered in all majors. Associate's degrees offered. Double majors. Independent study. Preprofessional programs in theology. Teacher certification in elementary education. Certification in specific subject areas.

**ADMISSIONS. Academic basis for candidate selection** (in order of priority): Secondary school record, school's recommendation, essay, standardized test scores, class rank.
**Nonacademic basis for candidate selection:** Character and personality are emphasized. Extracurricular participation is considered.
**Requirements:** Graduation from secondary school is required; GED is accepted. No specific distribution of secondary school units required. Minimum composite ACT score of 18, rank in top quarter of secondary school class, and minimum 1.5 GPA required. Conditional admission possible for applicants not meeting standard requirements. ACT is required; SAT may be substituted. Campus visit and interview recommended. Off-campus interviews available with an admissions representative.
**Procedure:** Take SAT or ACT by April of 12th year. Visit college for interview by June of 12th year. Suggest filing application by March 1. Application deadline is August 15. Notification of admission on rolling basis. Reply is required within two weeks of notification. $100 tuition deposit, refundable until August 1. $50 room deposit, refundable until August 1. Freshmen accepted for terms other than fall.
**Special programs:** Admission may be deferred one year. Credit may be granted through CEEB Advanced Placement for scores of 3 or higher. Credit may be granted through CLEP general and subject exams and ACT PEP exams. Placement may be granted through challenge exams. Credit and placement may be granted through life experience.
**Transfer students:** Transfer students accepted for terms other than fall. In fall 1993, 30% of all new students were transfers into all classes. 30 transfer applications were received, 25 were accepted. Application deadline is August 15 for fall; December 15 for spring. Minimum 2.0 GPA recommended. Lowest course grade accepted is "C." At least 96 semester hours must be completed at the college to receive degree.
**Admissions contact:** Shane Hudman, M.A., Director of Admissions. 800 749-8878.

**FINANCIAL AID. Available aid:** Pell grants, SEOG, state grants, school scholarships and grants, and private grants. PLUS, Stafford Loans (GSL), and SLS. Monthly payment plan.
**Financial aid statistics:** 15% of aid is not need-based. In 1993-94, 72% of all undergraduate applicants received aid; 79% of freshman applicants. Average amounts of aid awarded freshmen: Scholarships and grants, $1,500; loans, $2,625.
**Supporting data/closing dates:** FAFSA/FAF: Priority filing date is May 1; accepted on rolling basis. School's own aid application: Priority filing date is May 1; accepted on rolling basis. State aid form: Priority filing date is May 1; deadline is September 15. Income tax forms: Accepted on rolling basis. Notification of awards on rolling basis.
**Financial aid contact:** Joanne Belin, Director of Financial Aid. 205 970-9215.

## Spring Hill College

**Mobile, AL 36608** — **205 460-2130**

**1994-95 Costs.** Tuition: $11,478. Room: $2,450. Board: $2,338. Fees, books, misc. academic expenses (school's estimate): $1,145.
**Enrollment.** Undergraduates: 415 men, 518 women (full-time). Freshman class: 773 applicants, 694 accepted, 230 enrolled. Graduate enrollment: 39 men, 28 women.
**Test score averages/ranges.** Average SAT scores: 480 verbal, 525 math. Range of SAT scores of middle 50%: 430-520 verbal, 470-580 math. Average ACT scores: 24 composite. Range of ACT scores of middle 50%: 21-26 composite.
**Faculty.** 64 full-time; 20 part-time. 90% of faculty holds highest degree in specific field. Student/faculty ratio: 15 to 1.
**Selectivity rating.** Competitive.

**PROFILE.** Spring Hill, founded in 1830, is a church-affiliated, liberal arts college. Its 500-acre campus, located in a residential section of Mobile, includes several 19th-and early 20th-century buildings.

**Accreditation:** SACS.
**Religious orientation:** Spring Hill College is affiliated with the Roman Catholic Church (Society of Jesus); four semesters of theology required.
**Library:** Collections totaling over 150,000 volumes, 725 periodical subscriptions and 165 microform items.
**Special facilities/museums:** Human relations center, U.S. seismographic station, language lab.
**Athletic facilities:** Golf course, tennis courts, baseball, football, intramural, and soccer fields.

**STUDENT BODY. Undergraduate profile:** 30% are state residents; 16% are transfers. 1% Asian-American, 7% Black, 4% Hispanic, 1% Native American, 86% White, 1% Other. Average age of undergraduates is 20.
**Freshman profile:** 8% of freshmen who took ACT scored 30 or over on composite; 46% scored 24 or over on composite; 100% scored 18 or over on composite. 50% of accepted applicants took SAT; 50% took ACT. 32% of freshmen come from public schools.
**Undergraduate achievement:** 77% of fall 1992 freshmen returned for fall 1993 term. 67% of entering class graduated. 35% of students who completed a degree program immediately went on to graduate study.
**Foreign students:** Countries represented include Belize, El Salvador, Guatemala, and Panama.

**PROGRAMS OF STUDY. Degrees:** B.A., B.Gen.Studies, B.S.
**Majors:** Accounting, Advertising, Art/Business, Art Therapy, Biology, Business/Chemistry, Business/Management, Chemistry, Communication Arts, Computer Information Systems, Computer Science, Early Childhood Education, Economics, Elementary Education, English, Environmental Science, Finance, Fine Arts, General Studies, History, Humanities, Interdisciplinary Humanities, International Business, International Studies, Journalism, Management Sociology, Marine Biology, Marketing, Mathematics, Philosophy, Political Science, Pre-Dentistry, Pre-Engineering, Pre-Law, Pre-Medicine, Pre-Optometry, Psychology, Public Relations, Radio/Television, Studio Art, Theology.
**Distribution of degrees:** The majors with the highest enrollment are psychology, biology, and political science; mathematics, interdisciplinary humanities, and art therapy have the lowest.
**Requirements:** General education requirement.
**Academic regulations:** Minimum 2.0 GPA must be maintained.
**Special:** Minors offered. Courses offered in French, German, music, physics, and Spanish. GRE, departmental comprehensive exam, position paper, senior project, or special seminar required of seniors. Associate's degrees offered. Self-designed majors. Double majors. Independent study. Accelerated study. Pass/fail grading option. Internships. Preprofessional programs in law, medicine, veterinary science, dentistry, and optometry. 3-1 and 4-1 medical technology programs. 3-1 respiratory therapy program offered in cooperation with Ochsner Memorial Hospital, New Orleans. 3-2 engineering programs with Auburn U and Georgia Tech. 5-year accounting/M.B.A. program. Member of Alabama Marine Environmental Sciences Consortium; off-campus study possible at Dauphin Island sea lab. Washington Semester. Teacher certification in early childhood, elementary, and secondary education. Study abroad in Italy, Latin America, Mexico, and Spain. ROTC and AFROTC.
**Honors:** Honors program. Honor societies.

**ADMISSIONS. Academic basis for candidate selection** (in order of priority): Secondary school record, standardized test scores, class rank, school's recommendation, essay.
**Nonacademic basis for candidate selection:** Character and personality and extracurricular participation are emphasized. Particular talent or ability, geographical distribution, and alumni/ae relationship are considered.
**Requirements:** Graduation from secondary school is required; GED is accepted. 16 units and the following program of study are required: 4 units of English, 2 units of math, 2 units of lab science, 2 units of social studies, 2 units of history, 4 units of electives. Additional secondary units in math, science, and history recommended. Minimum combined SAT score of 850 (composite ACT score of 20), rank in top half of secondary school class, and minimum 2.5 GPA required. Conditional admission possible for applicants not meeting standard requirements. SAT or ACT is required. Campus visit and interview recommended. Off-campus interviews available with admissions and alumni representatives.

**Procedure:** Take SAT or ACT by February of 12th year. Visit college for interview by May 1 of 12th year. Notification of admission on rolling basis. Reply is required by May 1. $50 tuition deposit, refundable until May 1. $100 room deposit, refundable until May 1. Freshmen accepted for terms other than fall.
**Special programs:** Admission may be deferred one year. Credit may be granted through CEEB Advanced Placement for scores of 3 or higher. Credit may be granted through CLEP general and subject exams, challenge exams, and military and life experience. Early entrance/early admission program.
**Transfer students:** Transfer students accepted for terms other than fall. In fall 1993, 16% of all new students were transfers into all classes. 95 transfer applications were received, 76 were accepted. Application deadline is rolling for fall; rolling for spring. Minimum 2.0 GPA required. Lowest course grade accepted is "C."
**Admissions contact:** Timothy S. Williams, Director of Admissions.

**FINANCIAL AID. Available aid:** Pell grants, SEOG, state grants, school scholarships and grants, private scholarships, ROTC scholarships, academic merit scholarships, athletic scholarships, and aid for undergraduate foreign students. Perkins Loans (NDSL), PLUS, Stafford Loans (GSL), state loans, school loans, private loans, and SLS. AMS, deferred payment plan, and family tuition reduction.
**Financial aid statistics:** 28% of aid is not need-based. In 1993-94, 62% of all undergraduate applicants received aid; 66% of freshman applicants. Average amounts of aid awarded freshmen: Scholarships and grants, $7,026; loans, $2,570.
**Supporting data/closing dates:** FAFSA. School's own aid application: Priority filing date is March 1; accepted on rolling basis. Notification of awards on rolling basis.
**Financial aid contact:** Betty H. Harlan, Director of Financial Aid. 205 460-2140.

## Stillman College

**Tuscaloosa, AL 35403** — **205 349-4240**

**1992-93 Costs.** Tuition: $4,460. Room: $1,071. Board: $1,713. Fees, books, misc. academic expenses (school's estimate): $500.
**Enrollment.** Undergraduates: 286 men, 646 women (full-time). Freshman class: 726 applicants, 593 accepted, 240 enrolled.
**Test score averages/ranges.** Average ACT scores: 17 composite.
**Faculty.** 59 full-time; 17 part-time. 41% of faculty holds doctoral degree. Student/faculty ratio: 13 to 1.
**Selectivity rating.** Less competitive.

**PROFILE.** Stillman is a church-affiliated, predominantly black, liberal arts college. Founded in 1876, it adopted coeducation in 1899. Its 100-acre campus is located in Tuscaloosa, 60 miles from Birmingham.

**Accreditation:** SACS.
**Religious orientation:** Stillman College is affiliated with the Presbyterian Church; five semesters of religion required. Regular attendance required at chapel, assemblies, and convocations.
**Library:** Collections totaling over 103,530 volumes and 350 periodical subscriptions.
**Special facilities/museums:** Electron microscope.
**Athletic facilities:** Gymnasium, softball field, tennis courts.

**STUDENT BODY. Undergraduate profile:** 73% are state residents; 4% are transfers. 97% Black, 2% White, 1% Other. Average age of undergraduates is 20.
**Freshman profile:** 3% of freshmen who took ACT scored 24 or over on composite; 39% scored 18 or over on composite; 100% scored 12 or over on composite. 65% of accepted applicants took ACT. 99% of freshmen come from public schools.
**Undergraduate achievement:** 58% of fall 1992 freshmen returned for fall 1993 term. 23% of entering class graduated. 16% of students who completed a degree program immediately went on to graduate study.
**Foreign students:** Seven students are from out of the country. Countries represented include Nigeria and St. Kitts-Nevis; two in all.

**PROGRAMS OF STUDY. Degrees:** B.A., B.S.
**Majors:** Biology, Business, Chemistry, Communications, Computer Science, Elementary Education, English, Health/Physical Education, History, Interdisciplinary Studies, International Studies, Mathematics, Music, Physics, Religion/Philosophy, Sociology.
**Distribution of degrees:** The majors with the highest enrollment are business, computer science, and biology; education, English, and physics have the lowest.
**Requirements:** General education requirement.
**Academic regulations:** Minimum 2.0 GPA required for graduation.
**Special:** Minors offered in all majors except elementary education and in art, foreign languages, political science, and psychology. Certificate program in gerontology. Double majors. Dual degrees. Independent study. Internships. Graduate school at which undergraduates may take graduate-level courses. Member of Alabama Center for Higher Education. Exchange program with Alma Coll, Marietta Coll, U of Alabama at Birmingham, Whitworth Coll. Teacher certification in elementary and secondary education. ROTC at U of Alabama.
**Honors:** Honors program.

**STUDENT LIFE. Housing:** Students may live on or off campus. Women's and men's dorms. School-owned/operated apartments. Cooperative dorms. 68% of students live in college housing.
**Social atmosphere:** Some popular gathering spots for students include the College Student Center and the Greek Square. The Student Government Association, Delta Sigma Theta, and the basketball team are influential groups on campus. Among the popular events of the year are Founder's Day, Homecoming, Black History Month, Martin Luther King Convocation, Matriculation Convocation, basketball games and social forums. According to the student newspaper, "most students on campus enjoy recreational activities such as basketball, playing cards, video games, and other sports. They also spend a good deal of time in the various computer centers. Activities such as Homecoming and Founder's Day get the most student support."
**Services and counseling/handicapped student services:** Placement services. Health service. Counseling services for minority and older students. Birth control and personal counseling. Career and academic guidance services. Religious counseling. Physically disabled student services. Tape recorders. Tutors. Reader services for the blind.
**Campus organizations:** Undergraduate student government. Student newspaper (Tiger's Paw, published once/month). Yearbook. Radio station. Band, choir, veterans club, women's social club, academic clubs. Five fraternities, no chapter houses; four sororities, no chapter houses.
**Religious organizations:** Christian Student Association.
**Minority/foreign student organizations:** Intercultural Club.

**ATHLETICS. Physical education requirements:** Two semesters of physical education required. ROTC fulfills requirement.
**Intercollegiate competition:** 4% of students participate. Basketball (M,W), cross-country (M), tennis (M,W), track and field (outdoor) (M,W), volleyball (W). Member of NCAA Division III.
**Intramural and club sports:** 10% of students participate. Intramural basketball, billiards, bowling, softball, swimming, tennis, touch football.

**ADMISSIONS. Academic basis for candidate selection** (in order of priority): Secondary school record, standardized test scores, class rank, school's recommendation.
**Nonacademic basis for candidate selection:** Character and personality and geographical distribution are emphasized. Extracurricular participation and alumni/ae relationship are important.
**Requirements:** Graduation from secondary school is required; GED is accepted. 16 units and the following program of study are required: 4 units of English, 4 units of math, 4 units of science, 4 units of social studies. Minimum 2.0 GPA recommended. Conditional admission for applicants with minimum 1.6 GPA. SAT or ACT is recommended.
**Procedure:** Take SAT or ACT by December of 12th year. Notification of admission on rolling basis. $25 nonrefundable tuition deposit. $50 nonrefundable room deposit. Freshmen accepted for terms other than fall.
**Special programs:** Admission may be deferred. Credit and/or placement may be granted through CEEB Advanced Placement exams.
**Transfer students:** Transfer students accepted for terms other than fall. In fall 1993, 4% of all new students were transfers into all classes. 80 transfer applications were received, 69 were accepted. Lowest course grade accepted is "C."
**Admissions contact:** Barbara K. Smith, M.A., Director of Admissions. 205 349-4240.

**FINANCIAL AID. Available aid:** Pell grants, SEOG, state grants, school scholarships and grants, and private scholarships and grants. Perkins Loans (NDSL), PLUS, Stafford Loans (GSL), state loans, school loans, private loans, and SLS.
**Financial aid statistics:** 15% of aid is not need-based. In 1993-94, 90% of all undergraduate applicants received aid; 90% of freshman applicants. Average amounts of aid awarded freshmen: Scholarships and grants, $3,031; loans, $2,100.
**Supporting data/closing dates:** FAFSA: Priority filing date is June 15. School's own aid application: Priority filing date is June 15. State aid form: Deadline is September 15. Income tax forms: Priority filing date is June 15.
**Financial aid contact:** Joseph Davis, M.A., Director of Financial Aid. 205 349-4240.

**STUDENT EMPLOYMENT.** College Work/Study Program. Institutional employment. 35% of full-time undergraduates work on campus during school year. Students may expect to earn an average of $700 during school year. Off-campus part-time employment opportunities rated "fair."

**COMPUTER FACILITIES.** 80 IBM/IBM-compatible and Macintosh/Apple microcomputers; 50 are networked. Students may access Digital minicomputer/mainframe systems. Client/LAN operating systems include Apple/Macintosh, DOS, Novell. Computer languages and software packages include BASIC, C, COBOL, FORTRAN, Pascal, VMS. Computer facilities are available to all students.
**Fees:** $20 computer fee per course.
**Hours:** Micros: 8 AM-5 PM (daily); minicomputers: 8 AM-8 PM (M-Sa), 4 PM-8 PM (Su).

**GRADUATE CAREER DATA.** Highest graduate school enrollments: U of Alabama, U of Alabama at Birmingham, Alabama State U.

**PROMINENT ALUMNI/AE.** Dr. Haywood Strickland, director of grant management, United Negro College Fund; Bryant Melton, state representative; Betty B. Williamson, entrepreneur, health care services.

## Talladega College

**Talladega, AL 35160** — **205 362-0206**

**1993-94 Costs.** Tuition: $5,166. Room: $1,324. Board: $1,340. Fees, books, misc. academic expenses (school's estimate): $983.
**Enrollment.** Undergraduates: 321 men, 587 women (full-time). Freshman class: 4,243 applicants, 1,455 accepted, 374 enrolled.
**Test score averages/ranges.** Average SAT scores: 770 combined. Average ACT scores: 17 composite.
**Faculty.** 45 full-time; 17 part-time. 64% of faculty holds highest degree in specific field. Student/faculty ratio: 13 to 1.
**Selectivity rating.** Less competitive.

**PROFILE.** Talladega is a private, historically black, liberal arts college. Founded in 1867, it adopted coeducation in 1880. Its 130-acre campus is located in Talladega, 50 miles east of Birmingham.

**Accreditation:** SACS. Professionally accredited by the Council on Social Work Education.
**Religious orientation:** Talladega College is affiliated with the United Church of Christ; no religious requirements.
**Library:** Collections totaling over 92,500 volumes, 501 periodical subscriptions, and 1,250 microform items.

**Special facilities/museums:** Art gallery.
**Athletic facilities:** Gymnasium, baseball field, basketball and tennis courts, swimming pool.

**STUDENT BODY. Undergraduate profile:** 52% are state residents. 97% Black, 3% White. Average age of undergraduates is 20.
**Freshman profile:** 11% of accepted applicants took SAT; 62% took ACT. 86% of freshmen come from public schools.

**PROGRAMS OF STUDY. Degrees:** B.A., B.Mus.
**Majors:** Biology, Business Administration, Chemistry, Computer/Information Sciences, Economics, English, History, Mathematics, Music, Music Education, Music Performance, Physics, Psychology, Public Administration, Rehabilitation Education Services, Social Work, Sociology.
**Distribution of degrees:** The majors with the highest enrollment are business, biology, and English; physics, mathematics, and chemistry have the lowest.
**Requirements:** General education requirement.
**Academic regulations:** Minimum 2.0 GPA must be maintained.
**Special:** Courses offered in art, communications, criminal justice, French, German, journalism, marine sciences, philosophy, political science, religion, secondary education, and Spanish. Students admitted to General Division and after two years of basic study move into concentrated major field. Double majors. Dual degrees. Internships. Preprofessional programs in law, medicine, dentistry, allied health fields, and nursing. ROTC at Jacksonville State U.
**Honors:** Honors program.
**Academic Assistance:** Remedial reading, writing, math, and study skills. Nonremedial tutoring.

**ADMISSIONS. Academic basis for candidate selection** (in order of priority): Secondary school record, standardized test scores, class rank, school's recommendation, essay.
**Nonacademic basis for candidate selection:** Character and personality and alumni/ae relationship are emphasized. Particular talent or ability is considered.
**Requirements:** Graduation from secondary school is required; GED is not accepted. 13 units and the following program of study are required: 4 units of English, 2 units of math, 2 units of science, 3 units of social studies, 2 units of academic electives. Minimum composite ACT score of 18 and minimum 2.5 GPA required. Audition required of music program applicants. ACT is required; SAT may be substituted. Campus visit and interview recommended. Off-campus interviews available with an admissions representative.
**Procedure:** Take SAT or ACT by March of 12th year. Suggest filing application by June 15; no deadline. Notification of admission by June 1. Reply is required by August 1. Nonrefundable deposit of one-third of tuition. $15 nonrefundable room deposit. Freshmen accepted for terms other than fall.
**Special programs:** Admission may be deferred. Credit and/or placement may be granted through CEEB Advanced Placement exams for scores of 3 or higher. Credit and/or placement may be granted through CLEP general and subject exams. Placement may be granted through challenge exams. Credit and placement may be granted through Regents College and ACT PEP exams. Early decision program. Early entrance/early admission program.
**Transfer students:** Transfer students accepted for terms other than fall. Application deadline is rolling for fall; rolling for spring. Minimum 2.0 GPA required. Lowest course grade accepted is "C." Maximum number of transferable credits is 90 semester hours. At least 60 semester hours must be completed at the college to receive degree.
**Admissions contact:** Monroe Thornton, M.B.A., Director of Admissions. 800 633-2440, (out-of-state), 800 762-2468, (in-state).

**FINANCIAL AID. Available aid:** Pell grants, SEOG, state grants, school scholarships and grants, private scholarships and grants, academic merit scholarships, athletic scholarships, and aid for undergraduate foreign students. Perkins Loans (NDSL) and Stafford Loans (GSL). AMS and Tuition Management Systems.
**Financial aid statistics:** 20% of aid is not need-based. In 1993-94, 89% of all undergraduate applicants received aid; 86% of freshman applicants. Average amounts of aid awarded freshmen: Scholarships and grants, $3,886; loans, $2,225.
**Supporting data/closing dates:** FAFSA/FAF/FFS. School's own aid application: Priority filing date is May 1. Income tax forms: Priority filing date is May 1. Notification of awards on rolling basis.
**Financial aid contact:** Johnny Byrd, Director of Financial Aid. 205 362-0206, extension 236.

# Troy State University

**Troy, AL 36082** — **205 670-3175**

**1993-94 Costs.** Tuition: $1,617 (state residents), $2,517 (out-of-state). Room & board: $2,368. Fees, books, misc. academic expenses (school's estimate): $350.
**Enrollment.** Undergraduates: 2,300 men, 2,120 women (full-time). Freshman class: 2,487 applicants, 1,692 accepted, 1,175 enrolled. Graduate enrollment: 97 men, 123 women.
**Test score averages/ranges.** Average SAT scores: 430 verbal, 470 math. Average ACT scores: 21 composite.
**Faculty.** 155 full-time; 1 part-time. 53% of faculty holds highest degree in specific field. Student/faculty ratio: 32 to 1.
**Selectivity rating.** Less competitive.

**PROFILE.** Troy State, founded in 1887, is a public university. Programs are offered through the Colleges of Arts and Sciences; Applied Science Programs; the Schools of Business and Commerce, Education, Fine Arts, Journalism, and Nursing; and the Graduate School. Its 433-acre campus is located in Troy, 48 miles southeast of Montgomery.
**Accreditation:** SACS. Professionally accredited by the National Council for Accreditation of Teacher Education, the National League for Nursing.
**Religious orientation:** Troy State University is nonsectarian; no religious requirements.
**Library:** Collections totaling over 201,200 volumes, 1,500 periodical subscriptions, and 50,000 microform items.
**Special facilities/museums:** Art museum, recording studio.
**Athletic facilities:** Gymnasiums, field house, baseball, football, intramural, and softball fields, golf course, track, basketball, tennis, and volleyball courts, bowling lanes, swimming pool, weight rooms.

**STUDENT BODY. Undergraduate profile:** 72% are state residents; 35% are transfers. 1% Asian-American, 18% Black, 81% White. Average age of undergraduates is 20.
**Freshman profile:** 25% of accepted applicants took SAT; 75% took ACT. 76% of freshmen come from public schools.
**Undergraduate achievement:** 72% of fall 1991 freshmen returned for fall 1992 term. 61% of entering class graduated.
**Foreign students:** 62 students are from out of the country. Countries represented include China, India, and Malaysia; 18 in all.

**PROGRAMS OF STUDY. Degrees:** B.A., B.Appl.Sci., B.Mus.Ed., B.S.
**Majors:** Accounting, American History, Art, Art Education, Art History, Biology, Broadcast Journalism, Business Administration, Business Education, Chemistry, Computer/Information Sciences, Corrections, Criminal Justice, Dramatic Arts, Early Childhood Education, Economics, Elementary Education, English, English Education, Environmental Science, European/Asian History, Finance, General Science, History, Journalism, Management, Marine Biology, Marketing, Mathematics, Medical Technology, Music Education, Nursing, Physical Education, Physical Sciences, Psychology, Resource Management, Secondary Education, Secretarial, Social/Rehabilitation Services, Social Sciences, Social Work, Sociology, Special Education, Special/Elementary Education, Speech Communication, Speech Education, Writing Arts.
**Distribution of degrees:** The majors with the highest enrollment are business administration, health-related fields, and education.
**Requirements:** General education requirement.
**Special:** Minors offered in most majors and in classics, French, geography, German, philosophy/religion, physics, political science, and Spanish. Associate's degrees offered. Double majors. Independent study. Internships. Preprofessional programs in law, medicine, dentistry, and optometry. Teacher certification in early childhood, elementary, secondary, and special education. Exchange program abroad in Japan. Study abroad also in England (Oxford U) and the Netherlands. AFROTC.
**Honors:** Honors program.
**Academic Assistance:** Remedial reading, writing, math, and study skills. Nonremedial tutoring.

**STUDENT LIFE. Housing:** Freshmen under age 19 must live on campus unless living with family. Coed, women's, and men's dorms. Sorority and fraternity housing. School-owned/operated apartments. 40% of students live in college housing.
**Social atmosphere:** The student newspaper reports, "The Greek system here offers the most activities. Independents get organized and involved only in intramural sports. Greeks pretty much dominate socially." Campus Outreach and Baptist Campus Ministries also influence student life. While on campus, students gather at the fraternity houses, sorority dorms, and Adams Center. Off-campus hangouts include the local bars: Front Porch and Cheers. Popular campus events include Homecoming, Greek formals, concerts (two each year), drama performances, and guest lecturers.
**Services and counseling/handicapped student services:** Placement services. Health service. Day care. Counseling services for minority, military, veteran, and older students. Birth control, personal, and psychological counseling. Career and academic guidance services. Physically disabled student services. Learning disabled services. Notetaking services.
**Campus organizations:** Undergraduate student government. Student newspaper (Tropolitan, published once/week). Literary magazine. Yearbook. Radio and TV stations. Band, choir, Pied Pipers, Collegiate Singers, dance group, debating, Playmakers, Young Democrats, Young Republicans, departmental, professional, and service groups, 168 organizations in all. Eight fraternities, seven chapter houses; eight sororities, no chapter houses. 26% of men join a fraternity. 28% of women join a sorority.
**Religious organizations:** Baptist Student Union, Christian Student Center, Campus Outreach, Wesley Foundation.
**Minority/foreign student organizations:** African-American Association. International Student Organization.

**ATHLETICS. Physical education requirements:** Two semesters of physical education required.
**Intercollegiate competition:** 8% of students participate. Baseball (M), basketball (M,W), cheerleading (M,W), cross-country (M,W), football (M), golf (M,W), softball (W), tennis (M,W), track (outdoor) (M,W), volleyball (W).
**Intramural and club sports:** 30% of students participate. Intramural basketball, football, golf, softball, tennis, track and field, volleyball. Men's club bowling, soccer. Women's club bowling.

**ADMISSIONS. Academic basis for candidate selection** (in order of priority): Secondary school record, standardized test scores, school's recommendation.
**Nonacademic basis for candidate selection:** Character and personality are emphasized. Extracurricular participation is important.
**Requirements:** Graduation from secondary school is required; GED is accepted. 15 secondary school units required, including 3 units of English and 12 other academic units. Minimum combined SAT score of 740 (composite ACT score of 18) and minimum 2.0 GPA required. SAT or ACT is required. Campus visit and interview recommended. Off-campus interviews available with an admissions representative.
**Procedure:** Take SAT or ACT by February of 12th year. Visit college for interview by May of 12th year. Suggest filing application by May 1. Application deadline is August 1. Notification of admission on rolling basis. Reply is required by term registration date. $35 room deposit, refundable until August 1. Freshmen accepted for terms other than fall.
**Special programs:** Admission may be deferred one year. Credit and/or placement may be granted through CEEB Advanced Placement exams for scores of 3 or higher. Credit may be granted through CLEP general and subject exams, ACT PEP and DANTES exams, and military experience. Concurrent enrollment program.

**Transfer students:** Transfer students accepted for terms other than fall. In fall 1992, 35% of all new students were transfers into all classes. 621 transfer applications were received, 493 were accepted. Application deadline is August 1 for fall; January 1 for spring. Minimum 2.0 GPA required. Lowest course grade accepted is "D." Maximum number of transferable credits is 90 quarter hours. At least 45 quarter hours must be completed at the university to receive degree.
**Admissions contact:** James Hutto, Dean of Enrollment Services. 205 670-3179.

**FINANCIAL AID. Available aid:** Pell grants, SEOG, state scholarships and grants, school scholarships, private scholarships, ROTC scholarships, academic merit scholarships, and athletic scholarships. Perkins Loans (NDSL), PLUS, Stafford Loans (GSL), and SLS.
**Supporting data/closing dates:** FAFSA/FAF: Priority filing date is May 1. School's own aid application: Priority filing date is May 1. State aid form: Priority filing date is May 1. Notification of awards begins June 1.
**Financial aid contact:** Jeff Golden, Director of Financial Aid. 205 670-3176.

**STUDENT EMPLOYMENT.** College Work/Study Program. 8% of full-time undergraduates work on campus during school year. Students may expect to earn an average of $2,040 during school year. Off-campus part-time employment opportunities rated "fair."

**COMPUTER FACILITIES.** 17 IBM/IBM-compatible microcomputers. Computer languages and software packages include COBOL, FORTRAN. Computer facilities are available to all students.
**Fees:** None.
**Hours:** 9 AM-9 PM.

**GRADUATE CAREER DATA.** 40% of graduates choose careers in business and industry.

# Tuskegee University

**Tuskegee, AL 36088** **205 727-8011**

**1994-95 Costs.** Tuition: $6,834. Room & board: $3,894. Fees, books, misc. academic expenses (school's estimate): $600.
**Enrollment.** Undergraduates: 1,523 men, 1,732 women (full-time). Freshman class: 2,867 applicants, 1,995 accepted, 913 enrolled. Graduate enrollment: 103 men, 92 women.
**Test score averages/ranges.** Average SAT scores: 355 verbal, 450 math.
**Faculty.** 249 full-time; 10 part-time. 62% of faculty holds doctoral degree. Student/faculty ratio: 13 to 1.
**Selectivity rating.** Less competitive.

**PROFILE.** Tuskegee, founded in 1881, is a private, comprehensive university. Programs are offered through the College of Arts and Sciences and the Schools of Agriculture and Home Economics, Business, Education, Engineering and Architecture, Nursing and Allied Health, and Veterinary Medicine. Its 5,000-acre campus, located in Tuskegee, has been designated a National Historic Landmark.

**Accreditation:** SACS. Professionally accredited by the Accreditation Board for Engineering and Technology, the American Dietetic Association, the Council on Education American Veterinary Medical Association, the Council on Social Work Education, the National Architecture Accrediting Board, the National League for Nursing.
**Religious orientation:** Tuskegee University is nonsectarian; no religious requirements.
**Library:** Collections totaling over 293,656 volumes, 1,092 periodical subscriptions, and 131,412 microform items.
**Special facilities/museums:** Agricultural and natural history museum, electron microscopes, two nursery schools.

**STUDENT BODY. Undergraduate profile:** 21% are state residents. 1% Asian-American, 88% Black, 3% Hispanic, 1% Native American, 4% White, 3% Other. Average age of undergraduates is 20.
**Freshman profile:** 83% of freshmen come from public schools.
**Undergraduate achievement:** 60% of fall 1991 freshmen returned for fall 1992 term. 23% of entering class graduated.
**Foreign students:** 138 students are from out of the country. 34 countries represented in all.

**PROGRAMS OF STUDY. Degrees:** B.A., B.Arch., B.S.
**Majors:** Accounting, Agribusiness Education, Animal/Poultry Sciences, Architecture, Biology, Business Administration, Chemical Engineering, Chemistry, Computer Sciences, Construction Science/Management, Early Childhood Education, Economics, Electrical Engineering, Elementary Education, English, Fashion Merchandising, Finance, Food/Nutritional Science, General Dietetics, General Science, Health Education, History, Home Economics Education, Hospitality Management, Industrial Arts Education, Language Arts, Management Science, Marketing, Mathematics, Mechanical Engineering, Medical Technology, Mental Retardation, Nursing, Occupational Therapy, Physical Education, Physics, Plant/Soil Science, Political Science, Psychology, Social Work, Sociology.
**Distribution of degrees:** The majors with the highest enrollment are electrical engineering, biology, and business administration; medical technology and home econmonics education have the lowest.
**Requirements:** General education requirement.
**Special:** Minors offered in banking/finance, foreign languages, general science, math, pre-law, and pre-medicine. Courses offered in art, geography, music, and social science. Honors program includes seminars, summer readings, sophomore and senior comprehensive exams, and senior thesis. Dual degrees. Pass/fail grading option. Internships. Cooperative education programs. Graduate school at which undergraduates may take graduate-level courses. Preprofessional programs in law, medicine, veterinary science, and dentistry. 3-2 programs in engineering. Member of Alabama Center of Higher Education. Teacher certification in elementary, secondary, and vo-tech education. Certification in specific subject areas. ROTC and AFROTC.
**Honors:** Honors program. Honor societies.
**Academic Assistance:** Remedial reading, writing, math, and study skills. Nonremedial tutoring.

**STUDENT LIFE. Housing:** All freshmen, sophomores, and first-year transfer students must live on campus unless living with family. Women's and men's dorms. Off-campus privately-owned housing. On-campus married-student housing. 55% of students live in college housing.
**Social atmosphere:** "The student body at Tuskegee is considered a 'family'," reports the student newspaper. "There is a certain unity among the students that can only be found at Tuskegee." Popular events include Homecoming, the Special Olympics, the Tuskegee Relays, and choir concerts. The most influential groups on campus are AKA's, Delta's, Kappa's, Alpha's, the football team, and the freshman class. Favorite student meeting spots include the Avenue, the fountain, and the cafeteria. Off campus, students frequent Twenty Grand, the lake, and The Modulator.
**Services and counseling/handicapped student services:** Placement services. Health service. Day care. Counseling services for military and veteran students. Birth control and personal counseling. Career and academic guidance services.
**Campus organizations:** Undergraduate student government. Student newspaper (Campus Digest, published once/month). Yearbook. Chapel orchestra, choir, men's and women's glee clubs, marching and concert bands, Little Theatre, professional and special-interest groups. Four fraternities, no chapter houses; four sororities, no chapter houses. 6% of men join a fraternity. 5% of women join a sorority.

**ATHLETICS. Physical education requirements:** Two semesters of physical education required.
**Intercollegiate competition:** 2% of students participate. Baseball (M), basketball (M,W), cross-country (M,W), football (M), tennis (M,W), track and field (outdoor) (M,W), volleyball (W). Member of NCAA Division II, Southern Intercollegiate Athletic Conference.
**Intramural and club sports:** Intramural basketball, flag football, slow-pitch softball, volleyball.

**ADMISSIONS. Academic basis for candidate selection** (in order of priority): Standardized test scores, secondary school record, class rank, school's recommendation, essay.
**Nonacademic basis for candidate selection:** Character and personality are emphasized. Extracurricular participation and particular talent or ability are considered.
**Requirements:** Graduation from secondary school is required; GED is not accepted. 16 units and the following program of study are required: 4 units of English, 3 units of math, 2 units of science, 3 units of social studies, 4 units of electives. Minimum combined SAT score of 800 and minimum 2.0 GPA required; combined score of 900 and 2.5 GPA recommended. National League of Nursing exam required for nursing program applicants. Conditional admission possible for applicants not meeting standard requirements. SAT is required; ACT may be substituted. ACH recommended. No off-campus interviews.
**Procedure:** Suggest filing application by March 31. Application deadline is April 15. Notification of admission on rolling basis. $300 nonrefundable room deposit. Freshmen accepted for terms other than fall.
**Special programs:** Admission may be deferred one year. Placement may be granted through CEEB Advanced Placement exams. Credit and/or placement may be granted through CLEP general and subject exams. Credit and placement may be granted through challenge exams and military and life experience. Early entrance/early admission program.
**Transfer students:** Transfer students accepted for terms other than fall. Application deadline is July 15 for fall; November 31 for spring. Minimum 2.0 GPA required. Lowest course grade accepted is "C." Maximum number of transferable credits is 30 semester hours. At least 30 semester hours must be completed at the university to receive degree.
**Admissions contact:** Lee Young, Director of Admissions. 205 727-8500.

**FINANCIAL AID. Available aid:** Pell grants, SEOG, Federal Nursing Student Scholarships, state scholarships and grants, school scholarships and grants, and private scholarships and grants. Perkins Loans (NDSL), PLUS, Stafford Loans (GSL), NSL, and state loans.
**Financial aid statistics:** In 1993-94, 93% of all undergraduate applicants received aid; 88% of freshman applicants.
**Supporting data/closing dates:** FAFSA/FAF: Deadline is March 31. Notification of awards on rolling basis.
**Financial aid contact:** Barbara Blair, Director of Financial Aid. 205 727-8210, 205 727-8201.

**STUDENT EMPLOYMENT.** College Work/Study Program. 65% of full-time undergraduates work on campus during school year. Students may expect to earn an average of $1,602 during school year. Off-campus part-time employment opportunities rated "good."

**COMPUTER FACILITIES.** 75 IBM/IBM-compatible microcomputers; 25 are networked. Students may access Digital minicomputer/mainframe systems. Computer languages and software packages include Ada, Assembly, BASIC, C, COBOL, FORTRAN, Pascal; 12 in all. Computer facilities are available to all students.
**Fees:** Computer fee is included in tuition/fees.
**Hours:** 24 hours.

**GRADUATE CAREER DATA.** Graduate school percentages: 1% enter law school. 2% enter medical school. 3% enter graduate business programs. 7% enter graduate arts and sciences programs. Highest graduate school enrollments: Tuskegee U, Indiana U, UCLA. 29% of graduates choose careers in business and industry.

**PROMINENT ALUMNI/AE.** Daniel James, General, U.S. Air Force; R.D. Morrison, President Emeritus, Alabama A&M U; Lionel Richie, singer-songwriter.

# University of Alabama at Birmingham

**Birmingham, AL 35294** **205 934-8000**

**1993-94 Costs.** Tuition: $2,100 (state residents), $4,200 (out-of-state). Room & board: $4,590. Fees, books, misc. academic expenses (school's estimate): $978.
**Enrollment.** Undergraduates: 3,144 men, 3,816 women (full-time). Freshman class: 2,153 applicants, 1,524 accepted, 1,140 enrolled. Graduate enrollment: 1,859 men, 2,396 women.
**Test score averages/ranges.** Average ACT scores: 22 English, 20 math, 21 composite. Range of ACT scores of middle 50%: 18-24 English, 18-23 math.
**Faculty.** 1,695 full-time; 138 part-time. 86% of faculty holds doctoral degree. Student/faculty ratio: 17 to 1.
**Selectivity rating.** Less competitive.

**PROFILE.** U Alabama at Birmingham, founded in 1969, is a public university and medical center complex. Programs are offered through the Schools of Arts and Humanities, Business, Dentistry, Education, Engineering, Health-Related Professions, Medicine, Natural Sciences and Mathematics, Optometry, Social and Behavioral Sciences, and Public Health. The 265-acre campus is located six blocks from downtown Birmingham.

**Accreditation:** SACS. Professionally accredited by the Accreditation Board for Engineering and Technology, the American Assembly of Collegiate Schools of Business, the American Dental Association, the American Medical Association (CAHEA), the Council on Social Work Education, the National Association of Schools of Art and Design, the National Association of Schools of Music, the National Council for Accreditation of Teacher Education, the National League for Nursing.
**Religious orientation:** University of Alabama at Birmingham is nonsectarian; no religious requirements.
**Library:** Collections totaling over 1,471,689 volumes, 5,577 periodical subscriptions, and 1,073,622 microform items.
**Special facilities/museums:** Museum of health sciences.
**Athletic facilities:** Gymnasium, basketball, handball/racquetball, tennis, and squash courts, track, dance, gymnastics, and weight rooms, indoor swimming pool, intramural football, softball, and soccer fields.

**STUDENT BODY. Undergraduate profile:** 96% are state residents; 54% are transfers. 2% Asian-American, 21% Black, 1% Hispanic, 73% White, 3% Other. Average age of undergraduates is 25.
**Freshman profile:** 91% of accepted applicants took ACT. 92% of freshmen come from public schools.
**Undergraduate achievement:** 67% of fall 1992 freshmen returned for fall 1993 term. 16% of entering class graduated. 10% of students who completed a degree program immediately went on to graduate study.
**Foreign students:** 198 students are from out of the country. Countries represented include Canada, China, Japan, Jordan, Malaysia, and Sweden; 48 in all.

**PROGRAMS OF STUDY. Degrees:** B.A., B.F.A., B.S.
**Majors:** Accounting, Allied Health, Anthropology, Art History, Arts Education, Biology, Chemistry, Civil Engineering, Communication Studies, Computer/Information Sciences, Criminal Justice, Cytotechnology, Dance, Dental Hygiene, Early Childhood Education, Economics, Electrical Engineering, Elementary Education, English, Finance, French, Geology, German, Health Education, High School Education, History, Industrial Distribution, International Studies, Linguistics, Management, Marketing, Materials Engineering, Mathematics, Mechanical Engineering, Medical Records Administration, Medical Technology, Music, Music Education, Natural Science, Nuclear Medicine Technology, Nursing, Occupational Therapy, Philosophy, Physical Education, Physics, Political Science, Psychology, Radiologic Sciences, Social Work, Sociology, Spanish, Special Education, Studio Art, Surgeon's Assistant, Theatre.
**Distribution of degrees:** The majors with the highest enrollment are biology, nursing, and psychology.
**Requirements:** General education requirement.
**Academic regulations:** Freshmen must maintain minimum 1.75 GPA; sophomores, 1.85 GPA; juniors, 1.95 GPA; seniors, 2.00 GPA.
**Special:** Minors offered in most majors. Courses offered in astronomy, business law, classics, earth science, environmental science, Greek, and Latin. Division of Special Studies offers nontraditional course scheduling. University College's preprofessional programs enable students to pursue bachelor's degrees from Schools of Health-Related Professions and Nursing. Self-designed majors. Double majors. Dual degrees. Independent study. Internships. Cooperative education programs. Graduate school at which undergraduates may take graduate-level courses. Preprofessional programs in law, medicine, dentistry, and optometry. Five-year B.S./M.Acct. program. Member of Alabama Marine Environmental Sciences Consortium; off-campus study possible at Dauphin Island Sea Lab. Cross-registration with Birmingham-Southern Coll, Jefferson State Junior Coll, Miles Coll, and Samford U. Teacher certification in early childhood, elementary, secondary, and special education. Member of International Student Exchange Program (ISEP). Study abroad in the Bahamas, Brazil, England, and Mexico. ROTC. AFROTC at Samford U.
**Honors:** Honors program. Honor societies.
**Academic Assistance:** Remedial reading, writing, math, and study skills. Nonremedial tutoring.

**STUDENT LIFE. Housing:** Students may live on or off campus. Coed dorms. School-owned/operated apartments. On-campus married-student housing. 9% of students live in college housing.
**Social atmosphere:** Favorite gathering places include the library, the university center, the Mill, and Five Points South Area. There are no influential groups, according to the editor of the student newspaper: "It's like we're 16,000 total strangers." Basketball games and student art movies are popular events. "UAB is primarily an urban commuter university. We are a very diverse group of students in a million metro population. It's a good school, strong in research."
**Services and counseling/handicapped student services:** Placement services. Health service. Women's center. Day care. Counseling services for minority and veteran students. Personal counseling. Career and academic guidance services. Physically disabled student services. Learning disabled program/services. Notetaking services. Tape recorders. Tutors. Reader services for the blind.
**Campus organizations:** Undergraduate student government. Student newspaper (Kaleidoscope, published once/week). Literary magazine. Arts program, chorus, ballet, theatre, Ambassadors, Cercle Francais, Spanish Club, nuclear war prevention group, College Democrats, College Republicans, Gaming Society, Chess Club, Students for a Better Earth, Campus Civitan, 200 organizations in all. 10 fraternities, no chapter houses; seven sororities, no chapter houses. 6% of men join a fraternity. 5% of women join a sorority.
**Religious organizations:** Baptist Student Union, Catholic Student Association, Fellowship of Christian Athletes, Intervarsity Christian Fellowship, Latter-Day Saints Student Association, Muslim Student Association, United Methodist Campus Ministry, Presbyterian Ministry.
**Minority/foreign student organizations:** Black Student Awareness. International Student Association, African Student Association, Chinese Student Association, Association of Indian Students, Iranian Student Association, Korean Students Association, Union of Palestine Students.

**ATHLETICS. Physical education requirements:** None.
**Intercollegiate competition:** 4% of students participate. Baseball (M), basketball (M,W), cross-country (M,W), football (M), golf (M,W), riflery (M,W), soccer (M), tennis (M,W), track (W), track (indoor) (M,W), track (outdoor) (M,W), volleyball (W). Member of Great Midwest Conference, NCAA Division I.
**Intramural and club sports:** Intramural badminton, basketball, billiards, bowling, flag football, horseshoes, putt-putt golf, racquetball, soccer, softball, squash, swimming, table tennis, tennis, ultimate frisbee, volleyball.

**ADMISSIONS. Academic basis for candidate selection** (in order of priority): Standardized test scores, secondary school record.
**Requirements:** Graduation from secondary school is required; GED is accepted. 12 units and the following program of study are required: 4 units of English, 2 units of math, 2 units of science, 2 units of social studies. Minimum composite ACT score of 20 and minimum 2.0 GPA required. 4 units of college-preparatory math (2 algebra, 1 geometry, 1 trigonometry), 1 unit of chemistry, and composite ACT score of 20 or total of 40 on math and science required of engineering program applicants. Conditional admission possible for applicants not meeting standard requirements. ACT is required; SAT may be substituted. Campus visit recommended. No off-campus interviews.
**Procedure:** Suggest filing application by August 1; no deadline. Notification of admission on rolling basis. No set date by which applicants must accept offer. Freshmen accepted for terms other than fall.
**Special programs:** Admission may be deferred one year. Credit may be granted through CEEB Advanced Placement for scores of 3 or higher. Credit may be granted through CLEP general and subject exams, and military and life experience. Early entrance/early admission program. Concurrent enrollment program.
**Transfer students:** Transfer students accepted for terms other than fall. In fall 1993, 54% of all new students were transfers into all classes. 2,585 transfer applications were received, 2,125 were accepted. Minimum 2.0 GPA required. Lowest course grade accepted is "D." Maximum number of transferable credits is 64 semester hours. At least 32 semester hours must be completed at the university to receive degree.
**Admissions contact:** Michael Bridges, Director of Admissions. 205 934-8221.

**FINANCIAL AID. Available aid:** Pell grants, SEOG, state scholarships and grants, school scholarships, private scholarships, ROTC scholarships, academic merit scholarships, and athletic scholarships. Perkins Loans (NDSL), PLUS, Stafford Loans (GSL), Health Professions Loans, state loans, school loans, private loans, and SLS.
**Financial aid statistics:** 20% of aid is not need-based. In 1993-94, 31% of all undergraduate applicants received aid; 47% of freshman applicants. Average amounts of aid awarded freshmen: Scholarships and grants, $1,500; loans, $2,500.
**Supporting data/closing dates:** FAFSA/FAF/FFS: Priority filing date is June 1; accepted on rolling basis. School's own aid application: Priority filing date is June 1; accepted on rolling basis. Notification of awards on rolling basis.
**Financial aid contact:** Claude E. McCann, Director of Financial Aid. 205 934-8223.

**STUDENT EMPLOYMENT.** College Work/Study Program. Institutional employment. 15% of full-time undergraduates work on campus during school year. Students may expect to earn an average of $2,400 during school year. Off-campus part-time employment opportunities rated "excellent."

**COMPUTER FACILITIES.** IBM/IBM-compatible and Macintosh/Apple microcomputers. Students may access Cray, Digital, Hewlett-Packard, IBM, Prime, Sequent, SUN, UNISYS minicomputer/mainframe systems, BITNET, Internet. Computer languages and software packages include AppleWriter, AutoCAD, DataStar, dBASE, Lotus 1-2-3, Multiplan, PFS, ReportStar, Symphony, VisiCalc, WordStar. Computer facilities are available to all students.
**Fees:** $21 computer fee per computer course.
**Hours:** 24 hours.

**GRADUATE CAREER DATA.** Graduate school percentages: 3% enter law school. 5% enter medical school. 2% enter dental school. 9% enter graduate business programs. 5% enter graduate arts and sciences programs. 1% enter theological school/seminary. Highest graduate school enrollments: U Alabama, U Alabama at Birmingham, Samford U. 60% of graduates choose careers in business and industry. Companies and businesses that hire graduates: Alabama Power, AmSouth Bank, area hospitals, Bell South, Central Bank.

# University of Alabama in Huntsville

**Huntsville, AL 35899** **205 895-6295**

**1994-95 Costs.** Tuition: $2,480 (state residents), $4,960 (out-of-state). Room: $2,500. Board: $1,000. Fees, books, misc. academic expenses (school's estimate): $600.
**Enrollment.** Undergraduates: 1,449 men, 1,278 women (full-time). Freshman class: 1,376 applicants, 957 accepted, 478 enrolled. Graduate enrollment: 1,282 men, 776 women.
**Test score averages/ranges.** Average SAT scores: 456 verbal, 536 math. Range of SAT scores of middle 50%: 390-520 verbal, 460-620 math. Average ACT scores: 22 English, 22 math, 23 composite. Range of ACT scores of middle 50%: 19-22 English, 18-21 math.
**Faculty.** 288 full-time; 168 part-time. 85% of faculty holds doctoral degree. Student/faculty ratio: 17 to 1.
**Selectivity rating.** Less competitive.

**PROFILE.** U Alabama in Huntsville is a public university. Founded in 1950, it joined the state university system in 1960. Degrees are offered through the Schools of Administrative Science, Humanities and Behavioral Science, Science and Engineering, Nursing, and Graduate Studies. Its 337-acre main campus is located in northwest Huntsville; its medical campus is in the downtown medical district.
**Accreditation:** SACS. Professionally accredited by the Accreditation Board for Engineering and Technology, the Computing Sciences Accreditation Board, the Liaison Committee on Medical Education, the National League for Nursing.
**Religious orientation:** University of Alabama in Huntsville is nonsectarian; no religious requirements.
**Library:** Collections totaling over 300,000 volumes, 3,000 periodical subscriptions, and 300,000 microform items.
**Special facilities/museums:** Art museum and galleries, optics building, centers for applied optics, micro-gravity research, robotics, solar research, space plasma, and aeronomic research.
**Athletic facilities:** Gymnasium, swimming pool, racquetball and tennis courts, soccer and softball fields, weight room.

**STUDENT BODY. Undergraduate profile:** 89% are state residents; 30% are transfers. 4% Asian-American, 8% Black, 1% Hispanic, 1% Native American, 83% White, 3% Other. Average age of undergraduates is 23.
**Freshman profile:** 1% of freshmen who took SAT scored 700 or over on verbal, 12% scored 700 or over on math; 13% scored 600 or over on verbal, 33% scored 600 or over on math; 35% scored 500 or over on verbal, 64% scored 500 or over on math; 70% scored 400 or over on verbal, 85% scored 400 or over on math; 94% scored 300 or over on verbal, 97% scored 300 or over on math. 6% of freshmen who took ACT scored 30 or over on English, 9% scored 30 or over on math, 8% scored 30 or over on composite; 41% scored 24 or over on English, 40% scored 24 or over on math, 45% scored 24 or over on composite; 82% scored 18 or over on English, 80% scored 18 or over on math, 89% scored 18 or over on composite; 97% scored 12 or over on English, 97% scored 12 or over on math, 99% scored 12 or over on composite; 98% scored 6 or over on English, 99% scored 6 or over on math, 100% scored 6 or over on composite. 24% of accepted applicants took SAT; 76% took ACT.
**Undergraduate achievement:** 65% of fall 1992 freshmen returned for fall 1993 term.
**Foreign students:** 63 students are from out of the country. Countries represented include Australia, Canada, China, Egypt, India, and Indonesia; 25 in all.

**PROGRAMS OF STUDY. Degrees:** B.A., B.S.
**Majors:** Accounting, Art, Biology, Chemical Engineering, Chemistry, Civil/Environmental Engineering, Communication Arts, Computer Engineering, Computer Science, Economics, Electrical Engineering, Elementary Education, English, Finance, Foreign Language/International Trade, French, German, History, Industrial/Systems Engineering, Management, Management Information Systems, Marketing, Mathematics, Mathematics Education, Mechanical Engineering, Music, Music Education, Nursing, Optical Engineering, Optical Science, Philosophy, Physics, Political Science, Procurement Management, Psychology, Slavic Studies, Sociology, Spanish.
**Distribution of degrees:** The majors with the highest enrollment are electrical engineering, nursing, and management information systems; Slavic studies, philosophy, and computer engineering have the lowest.
**Requirements:** General education requirement.
**Academic regulations:** Minimum 2.0 GPA must be maintained.
**Special:** Minors offered. Certificate programs in accounting, environmental science, and production planning/control. Double majors. Independent study. Internships. Cooperative education programs. Graduate school at which undergraduates may take graduate-level courses. Preprofessional programs in law, medicine, and dentistry. Cross-registration with Alabama A&M U, Athens State Coll, John C. Calhoun State Comm Coll, Oakwood Coll, U of Alabama at Birmingham, and U of Alabama at Tuscaloosa. Teacher certification in elementary and secondary education. Certification in specific subject areas. ROTC at Alabama A&M U. AFROTC at Samford U.
**Honors:** Honors program. Honor societies.
**Academic Assistance:** Remedial study skills. Nonremedial tutoring.

**STUDENT LIFE. Housing:** Freshmen must live on campus or with relatives. Coed dorms. School-owned/operated apartments. On-campus married-student housing. 10% of students live in college housing.
**Social atmosphere:** On campus, students gather at University Center, the Engineering building, and the Baptist Student Union. Off campus, students frequent Mr. Gatti's Pizza, the University Inn, and the Koffee Klatch. Groups with widespread influence on campus include athletes, Greeks, the student government, and Students for the Exploration and Development of Space. Students enjoy the annual Fall-Der-All, Springfest, Homecoming, campus films, hockey games, guest lectures, and plays by the Broadway Theatre League. The student newspaper reports that student social groups tend to form according to majors. The student government helps students get out and about by providing tickets to off-campus events at reduced rates.
**Services and counseling/handicapped student services:** Placement services. Health service. Counseling services for minority, veteran, and older students. Personal and psychological counseling. Career and academic guidance services. Religious counseling. Physically disabled student services. Learning disabled services. Notetaking services. Reader services for the blind.
**Campus organizations:** Undergraduate student government. Student newspaper (Exponent, published once/week). Literary magazine. Choir, chorus, Village Singers, Premier Singers, Collegium Musicum, University Playhouse, film and lecture series, Circle K, Model UN, Medical Student Association, Society of Women Engineers, Lancers, engineering council, business, history, chemistry, forensic, and math clubs, athletic, departmental, service, and special-interest groups, 90 organizations in all. Five fraternities, three chapter houses; five sororities, no chapter houses. 11% of men join a fraternity. 7% of women join a sorority.
**Religious organizations:** Baptist Student Union, Campus Ministry Association, Christian Students Organization, Episcopal Student Fellowship, Presbyterian Student Fellowship.
**Minority/foreign student organizations:** Black Student Association. International Student Organization, Indian Student Organization, Chinese and Muslim student groups.

**ATHLETICS. Physical education requirements:** None.
**Intercollegiate competition:** 2% of students participate. Basketball (M,W), cross-country (M,W), ice hockey (M), soccer (M), tennis (M,W), volleyball (W). Member of Gulf South Athletic Conference, NCAA Division II, Southeastern Athletic Association.
**Intramural and club sports:** 3% of students participate. Intramural basketball, football, floor hockey, racquetball, softball, tennis, weight lifting. Men's club crew. Women's club crew.

**ADMISSIONS. Academic basis for candidate selection** (in order of priority): Standardized test scores, secondary school record.
**Requirements:** Graduation from secondary school is recommended; GED is accepted. 20 units and the following program of study are required: 4 units of English, 3 units of math, 2 units of science, 3 units of social studies, 8 units of electives. Minimum composite ACT score of 17 and minimum 3.25 GPA, or minimum composite ACT score of 24 and minimum 1.15 GPA, required. 1 unit of chemistry/physics and minimum composite ACT score of 21 (combined SAT score of 900) required of applicants to Colleges of Engineering and Science. 1 unit each of algebra II and trigonometry required of applicants to College of Engineering. Conditional admission possible for applicants not meeting standard requirements. SAT or ACT is required. Campus visit recommended. No off-campus interviews.
**Procedure:** Take SAT or ACT by May of 12th year. Application deadline is August 13. Notification of admission on rolling basis. No set date by which applicants must accept offer. $100 room deposit, refundable until published deadline. Freshmen accepted for terms other than fall.
**Special programs:** Admission may be deferred one year. Credit and/or placement may be granted through CEEB Advanced Placement exams for scores of 3 or higher. Credit may be granted through CLEP general and subject exams, and military experience. Credit and placement may be granted through challenge exams. Early entrance/early admission program. Concurrent enrollment program.
**Transfer students:** Transfer students accepted for terms other than fall. In fall 1993, 30% of all new students were transfers into all classes. 635 transfer applications were received, 576 were accepted. Application deadline is August 15 for fall; December 15 for spring. Minimum 2.0 GPA required. Lowest course grade accepted is "C." Maximum number of transferable credits is 64 semester hours. At least 32 semester hours must be completed at the university to receive degree.
**Admissions contact:** Ron R. Koger, Ed.D., Asst. VP for Enrollment Management. 205 895-6070, 800 UAH-CALL.

**FINANCIAL AID. Available aid:** Pell grants, SEOG, state grants, school scholarships, private scholarships, ROTC scholarships, academic merit scholarships, and athletic scholarships. Perkins Loans (NDSL), PLUS, Stafford Loans (GSL), and SLS. Institutional monthly payment plan.
**Financial aid statistics:** 50% of aid is not need-based. In 1993-94, 33% of all undergraduate applicants received aid; 28% of freshman applicants. Average amounts of aid awarded freshmen: Scholarships and grants, $1,600; loans, $1,600.
**Supporting data/closing dates:** FAFSA: Priority filing date is April 1. Notification of awards on rolling basis.
**Financial aid contact:** James B. Gibson, M.S., Director of Financial Aid. 205 895-6241.

**STUDENT EMPLOYMENT.** College Work/Study Program. Institutional employment. 8% of full-time undergraduates work on campus during school year. Students may expect to earn an average of $3,000 during school year. Off-campus part-time employment opportunities rated "excellent."

**COMPUTER FACILITIES.** 238 IBM/IBM-compatible and Macintosh/Apple microcomputers. Students may access Cray, Digital, Hewlett-Packard, SUN, UNISYS minicomputer/mainframe systems, BITNET. Client/LAN operating systems include Apple/Macintosh, DOS, Windows NT, Novell. Computer languages and software packages include Assembler, AutoCAD, BASIC, BMD, C, COBOL, DMS, FORTRAN, Microsoft Works, MINITAB, Pascal, PL/1, SPSS-X, WINGZ; 50 in all. Computer facilities are available to all students.
**Fees:** Computer fee is included in tuition/fees.
**Hours:** 8 AM-1 AM.

**GRADUATE CAREER DATA.** Companies and businesses that hire graduates: Huntsville Hospital, Intergraph, MICOM, NASA, SCI, Teledyne Brown, U.S. Army.

**PROMINENT ALUMNI/AE.** Dr. N. Jan Davis, NASA astronaut; John Hendricks, founder and CEO, Discovery Channel; Martha Simms, Board of Trustees, U of Alabama System; Steve Hettinger, mayor, Huntsville.

# University of Alabama, Tuscaloosa

Tuscaloosa, AL 35487-0132 205 348-6300

**1993-94 Costs.** Tuition: $2,172 (state residents), $5,424 (out-of-state). Room & board: $3,520. Fees, books, misc. academic expenses (school's estimate): $580.

**Enrollment.** Undergraduates: 6,928 men, 6,821 women (full-time). Freshman class: 7,677 applicants, 6,007 accepted, 2,628 enrolled. Graduate enrollment: 2,005 men, 2,146 women.

**Test score averages/ranges.** Average ACT scores: 23 English, 22 math, 23 composite. Range of ACT scores of middle 50%: 23-24 English, 21-22 math.

**Faculty.** 895 full-time; 270 part-time. 96% of faculty holds highest degree in specific field. Student/faculty ratio: 15 to 1.

**Selectivity rating.** Less competitive.

**PROFILE.** UAlabama at Tuscaloosa is a public institution. Programs are offered through the Colleges of Arts and Sciences, Commerce and Business Administration, Education, and Engineering; the Schools of Human Environmental Sciences and Social Work; New College; and Capstone College of Nursing. Its 1,000-acre campus is located in west central Alabama.

**Accreditation:** SACS. Professionally accredited by the Accreditation Board for Engineering and Technology, the Accrediting Council on Education in Journalism and Mass Communication, the American Assembly of Collegiate Schools of Business, the American Bar Association, the American Dietetic Association, the American Home Economics Association, the American Library Association, the American Psychological Association, the American Speech-Language-Hearing Association, the Council on Rehabilitation Education, the Council on Social Work Education, the Foundation for Interior Design Education Research, the Liaison Committee on Medical Education, the National Association of Schools of Art and Design, the National Association of Schools of Music, the National Council for Accreditation of Teacher Education, the National League for Nursing.

**Religious orientation:** University of Alabama, Tuscaloosa is nonsectarian; no religious requirements.

**Library:** Collections totaling over 1,902,000 volumes, 16,164 periodical subscriptions, and 2,800,000 microform items.

**Special facilities/museums:** Art gallery, natural history museum, concert hall, archaeologic site and museum, arboretum, observatory, simulated coal mine, robotics lab, wind tunnel, artificial intelligence lab, jet propulsion engine mini-lab.

**Athletic facilities:** Recreation center, intramural fields.

**STUDENT BODY. Undergraduate profile:** 72% are state residents; 35% are transfers. 1% Asian-American, 11% Black, 1% Hispanic, 84% White, 3% Other. Average age of undergraduates is 21.

**Freshman profile:** 7% of freshmen who took ACT scored 30 or over on English, 5% scored 30 or over on math, 7% scored 30 or over on composite; 47% scored 24 or over on English, 30% scored 24 or over on math, 38% scored 24 or over on composite; 93% scored 18 or over on English, 83% scored 18 or over on math, 95% scored 18 or over on composite; 103% scored 12 or over on English, 98% scored 12 or over on math, 100% scored 12 or over on composite. 85% of accepted applicants took ACT. 85% of freshmen come from public schools.

**Undergraduate achievement:** 80% of fall 1992 freshmen returned for fall 1993 term. 19% of entering class graduated.

**Foreign students:** 462 students are from out of the country. Countries represented include China, Hong Kong, India, Japan, Saudi Arabia, and Taiwan; 78 in all.

**PROGRAMS OF STUDY. Degrees:** B.A., B.F.A., B.Mus., B.S., B.Soc.Work.

**Majors:** Accounting, Advertising, Aerospace Engineering, American Studies, Anthropology, Applied Mathematics, Applied Physics, Art, Art Education, Banking/Financial Services, Biology, Chemical Engineering, Chemistry, Civil/Environmental Engineering, Classics, Clothing/Textiles/Design, Commerce/Business Administration, Communicative Disorders, Computer-Based Management Systems, Computer Science, Consumer Sciences, Coordinated Program in General Dietetics, Corporate Finance/Investment Management, Criminal Justice, Dance, Early Childhood Education, Economics, Electrical Engineering, Elementary Education, English, Family Studies, Fashion Retailing, Food/Nutrition, Foreign Language, French, General Studies/Human Environmental Sciences, Geography, Geology, German, Health Care Management, Health Education, History, Home Economics Education, Human Development, Industrial Engineering, Industrial Management, Insurance, Interdisciplinary, Interior Design, International Relations, Journalism, Latin American Studies, Management, Management Science, Marine Science, Marketing, Mathematical Statistics, Mathematics, Mechanical Engineering, Medical Technology, Metallurgical Engineering, Microbiology, Mineral Engineering, Music, Music Administration, Music Education, Music Therapy, Nursing, Philosophy, Physical Education, Physics, Political Science, Psychology, Public Archaeology, Public Relations, Real Estate, Regional/Urban Planning, Religious Studies, Restaurant/Hospitality Management, Russian/East European Studies, Secondary Education, Social Work, Sociology, Spanish, Special Education, Special Studies, Speech Communication, Statistics, Telecommunications/Film, Theatre, Transportation, Urban/Regional Planning/Program Management.

**Distribution of degrees:** The majors with the highest enrollment are marketing, accounting, and corporate finance/investment management; Latin American studies and religious studies have the lowest.

**Requirements:** General education requirement.

**Academic regulations:** Freshmen must maintain minimum 1.4 GPA; sophomores, 1.6 GPA; juniors, 1.8 GPA; seniors, 1.9 GPA.

**Special:** Self-designed and double minors. Interdisciplinary certificate program in urban and regional planning. Several concentrations available in art, business, commerce, education, mineral engineering, and music. Self-designed majors. Double majors. Dual degrees. Independent study. Pass/fail grading option. Internships. Cooperative education programs. Graduate school at which undergraduates may take graduate-level courses. Preprofessional programs in law, medicine, veterinary science, pharmacy, dentistry, and optometry. 2-2 engineering, nursing, and social work programs with Stillman Coll. 3-2 M.B.A. program. Member of American Council on Education, Oak Ridge Associated Universities, Southern Association of Colleges and Schools, Inc., and several other associations. Washington Semester. State Capitol Semester. Member of National Student Exchange (NSE). Teacher certification in early childhood, elementary, secondary, and special education. Certification in specific subject areas. Exchange programs abroad in Australia (Queensland U of Tech), Belgium (Hautes Etudes Commerciales), China, England (U of Hull), France, Germany (U of Mannheim and Padagogische Hochschule-Weingarten), Japan (Chiba U and Kansai U of Foreign Studies), Korea (Pusan National U), Latin American countries, former Soviet Republics, and Spain (U de Extremadura). Study abroad also in Denmark, Latvia, and the Netherlands. ROTC and AFROTC.

**Honors:** Phi Beta Kappa. Honors program. Honor societies.

**Academic Assistance:** Remedial reading, writing, math, and study skills. Nonremedial tutoring.

**STUDENT LIFE. Housing:** Students may live on or off campus. Women's and men's dorms. Sorority and fraternity housing. School-owned/operated apartments. On-campus married-student housing. 27% of students live in college housing.

**Social atmosphere:** According to the editor of the student newspaper, a few of the Greek organizations "control campus politics" at the University of Alabama. Popular events on campus include gymnastics meets and basketball and football games, especially those against Auburn U and U of Tennessee. Students gather at the recreation center, the quad, and the library on campus. Off campus, they frequent Egan's, Solomon's, and the Boothe.

**Services and counseling/handicapped student services:** Placement services. Health service. Women's center. Day care. Counseling services for minority, military, veteran, and older students. Birth control, personal, and psychological counseling. Career and academic guidance services. Physically disabled student services. Learning disabled program/services. Notetaking services. Tape recorders. Tutors. Reader services for the blind.

**Campus organizations:** Undergraduate student government. Student newspaper (Crimson White, published four times/week). Literary magazine. Yearbook. Radio and TV stations. Studio theatre, dance and music groups, Fantasy Game Club, ROTC clubs, environmental groups, Amnesty International, Circle K, Students 'R Us, academic, athletic, departmental, and special-interest groups, 254 organizations in all. 25 fraternities, all with chapter houses; 19 sororities, 18 chapter houses. 16% of men join a fraternity. 20% of women join a sorority.

**Religious organizations:** Baptist Campus Ministries, Campus Crusade for Christ, Christian Action Fellowship, Christian Science College Group, Disciple Student Fellowship, Fellowship of Christian Athletes, Great Commission Students, Navigators, Bahai, Catholic, Church of Christ, Episcopal, Jewish, Lutheran, Methodist, Muslim, and other religious groups.

**Minority/foreign student organizations:** African-American Association, NAACP, Minorities for Careers in Communication, National Society of Black Engineers, Society of Women Engineers, University NOW. International Student Association, Chinese, Indian, Japanese, and Korean groups.

**ATHLETICS. Physical education requirements:** None.

**Intercollegiate competition:** 2% of students participate. Baseball (M), basketball (M,W), cross-country (M,W), diving (M,W), football (M), golf (M,W), gymnastics (W), swimming (M,W), tennis (M,W), track (indoor) (M,W), track (outdoor) (M,W), track and field (indoor) (M,W), track and field (outdoor) (M,W), volleyball (W). Member of NCAA Division I, Southeastern Conference.

**Intramural and club sports:** Intramural basketball, football, golf, softball, swimming, tennis.

**ADMISSIONS. Academic basis for candidate selection** (in order of priority): Secondary school record, standardized test scores, school's recommendation, class rank.

**Nonacademic basis for candidate selection:** Particular talent or ability is considered.

**Requirements:** Graduation from secondary school is required; GED is accepted. 21 units and the following program of study are recommended: 4 units of English, 3 units of math, 3 units of science, 2 units of foreign language, 4 units of social studies, 1 unit of history, 4 units of electives. Minimum composite ACT score of 22 (combined SAT score of 920) and minimum 2.0 GPA required. Portfolio required of art program applicants. Audition required of music program applicants. Summer Trial Admission Program for applicants not meeting standard requirements. SAT or ACT is required. Campus visit recommended. No off-campus interviews.

**Procedure:** Suggest filing application by April 15. Application deadline is August 1. Notification of admission on rolling basis. No set date by which applicants must accept offer. $100 room deposit, refundable until July. Freshmen accepted for fall term only.

**Special programs:** Credit and/or placement may be granted through CEEB Advanced Placement exams for scores of 3 or higher. Credit and/or placement may be granted through CLEP general and subject exams. Placement may be granted through challenge exams. Credit and placement may be granted through DANTES exams and military and life experience. Early entrance/early admission program. Concurrent enrollment program.

**Transfer students:** Transfer students accepted for terms other than fall. In fall 1993, 35% of all new students were transfers into all classes. 2,696 transfer applications were received, 2,141 were accepted. Application deadline is August 1 for fall; December 10 for spring. Minimum 2.0 GPA required. Lowest course grade accepted is "C." Maximum number of transferable credits is 64 semester hours from a two-year school and 96 semester hours from a four-year school. At least 32 semester hours must be completed at the university to receive degree.

**Admissions contact:** Roy C. Smith, Ph.D., Director of Admissions and Registrar. 205 348-5666.

**FINANCIAL AID. Available aid:** Pell grants, SEOG, Federal Nursing Student Scholarships, state scholarships and grants, school scholarships and grants, private scholarships and grants, ROTC scholarships, academic merit scholarships, athletic scholarships, and aid for undergraduate foreign students. Perkins Loans (NDSL), PLUS, Stafford Loans (GSL), school loans, private loans, and SLS. Deferred payment plan.

**Financial aid statistics:** 33% of aid is not need-based. In 1993-94, 88% of all undergraduate applicants received aid; 69% of freshman applicants. Average amounts of aid awarded freshmen: Scholarships and grants, $2,529; loans, $2,256.
**Supporting data/closing dates:** FAFSA: Priority filing date is March 1. School's own aid application: Priority filing date is March 1. Notification of awards begins April 15.
**Financial aid contact:** Molly Lawrence, M.A., Director of Financial Aid. 205 348-6756.

**STUDENT EMPLOYMENT.** College Work/Study Program. Institutional employment. 21% of full-time undergraduates work on campus during school year. Students may expect to earn an average of $1,200 during school year. Off-campus part-time employment opportunities rated "fair."

**COMPUTER FACILITIES.** 914 IBM/IBM-compatible and Macintosh/Apple microcomputers; 800 are networked. Students may access Cray, IBM minicomputer/mainframe systems, BITNET, Internet. Residence halls may be equipped with stand-alone microcomputers. Client/LAN operating systems include Apple/Macintosh, DOS, UNIX/XENIX/AIX, LocalTalk/AppleTalk, Novell. Computer languages and software packages include APL, BASIC, C, COBOL, DISSPLA, FORTRAN, ImSL, LISP, MINITAB, Pascal, REDUCE, SAS, SPSS-X, TEX, VAST; 37 in all. Computer access depends on course, major, or residence hall.
**Fees:** $39 computer fee per semester; included in tuition/fees.

**GRADUATE CAREER DATA.** Companies and businesses that hire graduates: Alabama Power Co., AmSouth Bank, Arthur Andersen, Ernst & Young, Parisian's.

**PROMINENT ALUMNI/AE.** William Roper, Head of Centers for Disease Control; Winton M. Blount, president, Blount, Inc., former Postmaster General and former U.S. Chamber of Commerce president; O.H. Delchamps, Jr., presidents, Delchamps, Inc. and U.S. Chamber of Commerce president; Harper Lee, Pulitzer Prize-winning novelist, *To Kill a Mockingbird;* Gay Talese, novelist; E.O. Wilson, Pulitzer prize-winning biologist; John Cochrane (NBC) and Mary Tillotson (CNN), broadcast journalists.

## University of Mobile

**Mobile, AL 36663-0220** **205 675-5990**

**1993-94 Costs.** Tuition: $5,850. Room & board: $3,480. Fees, books, misc. academic expenses (school's estimate): $520.
**Enrollment.** Undergraduates: 508 men, 768 women (full-time). Freshman class: 452 applicants, 331 accepted, 269 enrolled. Graduate enrollment: 55 men, 104 women.
**Test score averages/ranges.** Average ACT scores: 21 composite. Range of ACT scores of middle 50%: 21-25 composite.
**Faculty.** 93 full-time; 67 part-time. 65% of faculty holds doctoral degree. Student/faculty ratio: 18 to 1.
**Selectivity rating.** Competitive.

**PROFILE.** Mobile is a private university. It was founded in 1961 as a church-affiliated liberal arts college. It gained university status in 1993. Its 700-acre campus is located in Mobile, 10 miles from downtown.

**Accreditation:** SACS. Professionally accredited by the National Association of Schools of Music, the National League for Nursing.
**Religious orientation:** University of Mobile is affiliated with the Baptist Church; two semesters of religion/theology required.
**Library:** Collections totaling over 131,186 volumes, 532 periodical subscriptions, and 79,563 microform items.
**Special facilities/museums:** Art gallery, mineral museum, on-campus day care/early childhood learning center.
**Athletic facilities:** Basketball and tennis courts, jogging trail, swimming pool, weight room, soccer and softball fields, gymnasium.

**STUDENT BODY. Undergraduate profile:** 89% are state residents; 45% are transfers. 1% Asian-American, 12% Black, 1% Hispanic, 1% Native American, 82% White, 3% Other. Average age of undergraduates is 27.
**Freshman profile:** 95% of accepted applicants took ACT. 88% of freshmen come from public schools.
**Undergraduate achievement:** 68% of fall 1992 freshmen returned for fall 1993 term. 38% of entering class graduated.
**Foreign students:** 17 students are from out of the country. Countries represented include Canada, England, Mexico, Nicaragua, Sweden, and Trinidad; 13 in all.

**PROGRAMS OF STUDY. Degrees:** B.A., B.S.
**Majors:** Accounting, Archaeology, Art, Behavioral Science, Biology, Business Administration, Chemistry, Church Recreation, Communications, Computer Science, Early Childhood Education, Economics/Finance, Elementary Education, English, Environmental Technology, Finance, Foreign Languages, French, General Science, General Studies, Health/Physical Education/Recreation, History, Latin American Studies, Management, Marketing, Mathematics, Music, Nursing, Political Science, Psychology, Religion, Social Sciences, Sociology, Theatre.
**Distribution of degrees:** The majors with the highest enrollment are nursing, education, and business administration; general studies, chemistry, and art have the lowest.
**Requirements:** General education requirement.
**Academic regulations:** Freshmen must maintain minimum 1.5 GPA; sophomores, 1.75 GPA; juniors, 2.0 GPA; seniors, 2.0 GPA.
**Special:** Minors offered in some majors. Associate's degrees offered. Double majors. Dual degrees. Independent study. Accelerated study. Internships. Cooperative education programs. Graduate school at which undergraduates may take graduate-level courses. Preprofessional programs in law and medicine. Law program with Tulane U. Engineering program with Auburn U. Five-year medical program with U of Alabama at Birmingham. Teacher certification in early childhood, elementary, and secondary education. Certification in specific subject areas. Exchange program abroad in Nicaragua (U of Mobile Latin American Branch Campus). ROTC and AFROTC.
**Honors:** Honor societies.
**Academic Assistance:** Remedial writing, math, and study skills.

**STUDENT LIFE. Housing:** All unmarried students under age 21 must live on campus unless living near campus with relatives. Women's and men's dorms. 25% of students live in college housing.
**Services and counseling/handicapped student services:** Placement services. Health service. Day care. Counseling services for veteran and older students. Personal and psychological counseling. Career and academic guidance services. Religious counseling. Physically disabled student services. Notetaking services. Tutors.
**Campus organizations:** Undergraduate student government. Student newspaper. Musical and drama groups, academic, service, and special-interest groups, 37 organizations in all.
**Religious organizations:** Baptist Christian Ministries, Fellowship of Christian Athletes.

**ATHLETICS. Physical education requirements:** Four semesters of physical education required.
**Intercollegiate competition:** 18% of students participate. Baseball (M), basketball (M,W), cheerleading (M,W), cross-country (M,W), golf (M), soccer (M,W), softball (W), tennis (M,W). Member of Gulf Coast Athletic Conference, NAIA.
**Intramural and club sports:** 10% of students participate. Intramural basketball, beach volleyball, flag football, golf, softball, swimming, table tennis, tennis, volleyball.

**ADMISSIONS. Academic basis for candidate selection** (in order of priority): Secondary school record, standardized test scores, class rank, school's recommendation, essay.
**Nonacademic basis for candidate selection:** Character and personality, extracurricular participation, and particular talent or ability are important. Alumni/ae relationship is considered.
**Requirements:** Graduation from secondary school is required; GED is accepted. 22 units and the following program of study are recommended: 4 units of English, 3 units of math, 2 units of science, 4 units of foreign language, 2 units of social studies, 2 units of history, 5 units of electives. Minimum composite ACT score of 18, rank in top half of secondary school class, and minimum 2.0 GPA required. 1 unit of chemistry required of nursing program applicants. Audition required of music program applicants. Conditional admission possible for applicants not meeting standard requirements. ACT is required; SAT may be substituted. Campus visit and interview recommended. Off-campus interviews available with an admissions representative.
**Procedure:** Take SAT or ACT by fall of 12th year. Visit college for interview by November 30 of 12th year. Suggest filing application by March. Application deadline is August. Notification of admission on rolling basis. No set date by which applicants must accept offer. $25 room deposit, refundable until end of year. Freshmen accepted for terms other than fall.
**Special programs:** Admission may be deferred one year. Credit may be granted through CEEB Advanced Placement for scores of 3 or higher. Credit may be granted through CLEP general and subject exams, DANTES and challenge exams, and military experience. Early entrance/early admission program.
**Transfer students:** Transfer students accepted for terms other than fall. In fall 1993, 45% of all new students were transfers into all classes. 491 transfer applications were received, 370 were accepted. Application deadline is rolling for fall; rolling for spring. Minimum 2.0 GPA required. Lowest course grade accepted is "C." Maximum number of transferable credits is 64 semester hours. At least 30 semester hours must be completed at the university to receive degree.
**Admissions contact:** Kim Leosis, M.B.A., Director of Admissions. 205 675-5990.

**FINANCIAL AID. Available aid:** Pell grants, SEOG, state scholarships and grants, school scholarships and grants, private scholarships and grants, ROTC scholarships, academic merit scholarships, athletic scholarships, and aid for undergraduate foreign students. Perkins Loans (NDSL), PLUS, Stafford Loans (GSL), NSL, and SLS.
**Financial aid statistics:** 27% of aid is not need-based. In 1993-94, 94% of all undergraduate applicants received aid; 96% of freshman applicants. Average amounts of aid awarded freshmen: Scholarships and grants, $4,200; loans, $2,625.
**Supporting data/closing dates:** FAFSA/FAF/FFS: Priority filing date is March 31; accepted on rolling basis. School's own aid application: Priority filing date is March 31; accepted on rolling basis. State aid form: Priority filing date is September 15; accepted on rolling basis. Notification of awards on rolling basis.
**Financial aid contact:** Lydia Herrington, Director of Financial Aid. 205 675-5990, extension 239.

**STUDENT EMPLOYMENT.** College Work/Study Program. Institutional employment. 12% of full-time undergraduates work on campus during school year. Students may expect to earn an average of $1,275 during school year. Off-campus part-time employment opportunities rated "good."

**COMPUTER FACILITIES.** 47 IBM/IBM-compatible and Macintosh/Apple microcomputers; 20 are networked. Students may access Digital minicomputer/mainframe systems. Client/LAN operating systems include Novell. Computer languages and software packages include BASIC, C, COBOL, dBASE, FORTRAN, Lotus 1-2-3, SPSS, Unix, WordPerfect; 12 in all. Computer facilities are available to all students.
**Fees:** $50 computer fee per course.
**Hours:** 8 AM-9 PM (M-Th).

**GRADUATE CAREER DATA.** Highest graduate school enrollments: Auburn U, U of Alabama, U of Southern Mississippi. 37% of graduates choose careers in business and industry. Companies and businesses that hire graduates: CIBA-GEIGY, Degussa, QMS.

**PROMINENT ALUMNI/AE.** Ricky Payne, pediatrician; Bibb Lamar, president, First Bank of Mobile; Dr. Michael Magnoli, president, U of Mobile.

# University of Montevallo

**Montevallo, AL 35115-6000 205 665-6000**

**1994-95 Costs.** Tuition: $2,340 (state residents), $4,680 (out-of-state). Room: $2,158. Board: $992. Fees, books, misc. academic expenses (school's estimate): $670.
**Enrollment.** Undergraduates: 777 men, 1,609 women (full-time). Freshman class: 1,351 applicants, 899 accepted, 570 enrolled. Graduate enrollment: 135 men, 463 women.
**Test score averages/ranges.** Average ACT scores: 22 English, 20 math, 21 composite. Range of ACT scores of middle 50%: 19-25 English, 17-22 math.
**Faculty.** 127 full-time; 55 part-time. 71% of faculty holds doctoral degree. Student/faculty ratio: 24 to 1.
**Selectivity rating.** Competitive.

**PROFILE.** The University of Montevallo, founded in 1896, is a public, liberal arts institution. Programs are offered through the Colleges of Arts and Sciences, Business, Education, and Fine Arts. Its 157-acre campus is located in Montevallo, 30 miles south of Birmingham.

**Accreditation:** SACS. Professionally accredited by the American Assembly of Collegiate Schools of Business, the American Dietetic Association, the American Home Economics Association, the American Speech-Language-Hearing Association, the Council on Social Work Education, the National Association of Schools of Art and Design, the National Association of Schools of Music, the National Council for Accreditation of Teacher Education.
**Religious orientation:** University of Montevallo is nonsectarian; no religious requirements.
**Library:** Collections totaling over 238,658 volumes, 1,232 periodical subscriptions, and 569,725 microform items.
**Special facilities/museums:** Art gallery, centers for child development, speech and hearing, traffic safety, undergraduate liberal studies, mass communications center with cable TV broadcasting capabilities.
**Athletic facilities:** Gymnasium, swimming pool, baseball, intramural, soccer, and softball fields, track, basketball, handball, racquetball, and tennis courts, golf driving range, lake, bowling lanes.

**STUDENT BODY. Undergraduate profile:** 97% are state residents; 34% are transfers. 10% Black, 87% White, 3% Other. Average age of undergraduates is 21.
**Freshman profile:** 5% of accepted applicants took SAT; 95% took ACT. 90% of freshmen come from public schools.
**Undergraduate achievement:** 70% of fall 1992 freshmen returned for fall 1993 term. 21% of students who completed a degree program immediately went on to graduate study.
**Foreign students:** 19 students are from out of the country. Countries represented include Canada, England, Guatemala, Japan, Malaysia, and Sweden; 11 in all.

**PROGRAMS OF STUDY. Degrees:** B.A., B.Bus.Admin., B.F.A., B.Mus., B.Mus.Ed., B.S.
**Majors:** Accounting, Art, Biology, Ceramics, Chemistry, Counseling/Guidance, Early Childhood Education, Education of the Hearing Impaired, Elementary Education, English, French, General Business, Health/Physical Education/Recreation, History, Home Economics, Home Economics Education, Home Economics Merchandising, International/Intercultural Studies, Management, Marketing, Mass Communications, Mathematics, Music Composition, Music Education, Music Performance, Piano Pedagogy, Political Science, Psychology, Social Science, Social Work, Sociology, Spanish, Speech, Speech/Language Pathology, Studio Art, Theatre, Traffic/Safety Education.
**Distribution of degrees:** The majors with the highest enrollment are elementary education/early childhood, health/physical education/recreation, and business management; general science, chemistry, and international/intercultural studies have the lowest.
**Requirements:** General education requirement.
**Academic regulations:** Minimum 2.0 GPA must be maintained.
**Special:** Minors offered in most majors and in approximately 15 other fields. Lecture series. Double majors. Independent study. Accelerated study. Internships. Cooperative education programs. Graduate school at which undergraduates may take graduate-level courses. Preprofessional programs in law, medicine, pharmacy, dentistry, and optometry. 3-2 engineering program with U of Alabama at Birmingham and Auburn U. Member of Alabama Consortium for Development of Higher Education, ACHE Consortium for the Advancement of Foreign Language Education, and Consortium of University Spanish Abroad Programs. Teacher certification in early childhood, elementary, secondary, and special education. Certification in specific subject areas. Exchange program abroad in Peru (Catholic U). Study abroad also in Europe. ROTC at U of Alabama at Birmingham. AFROTC at Samford U.
**Honors:** Honors program. Honor societies.
**Academic Assistance:** Remedial writing, math, and study skills. Nonremedial tutoring.

**STUDENT LIFE. Housing:** All unmarried students under age 19 must live on campus unless living with family. Women's and men's dorms. School-owned/operated apartments. 45% of students live in college housing.
**Social atmosphere:** Popular on-campus gathering spots include the Student Union Building and the cafeteria. Off campus, students head for JeRoe's Deli and the Underground Bar & Grill. The school newspaper reports, "although Greek life, athletes, and church groups do exist, the University of Montevallo is known and admired for outstanding theatre, music, and art programs. Students within these fields have widespread influence. Our campus TV news show and our school newspaper also hold influence and draw attention." Favorite events are College Night and Founder's Day. "The personal size of our school creates a friendly atmosphere for both resident and non-residents students. Located in the small town of Montevallo, the university provides the pleasure of small-town life, but the action of a big city; Birmingham, our state's largest city, is only 30 minutes away. Our diverse student body and our comprehensive liberal arts curriculum provide students with a thoroughly enjoyable college experience."
**Services and counseling/handicapped student services:** Placement services. Health service. Counseling services for minority, military, veteran, and older students. Birth control, personal, and psychological counseling. Career and academic guidance services. Physically disabled student services. Learning disabled services. Notetaking services. Tape recorders. Tutors. Reader services for the blind.
**Campus organizations:** Undergraduate student government. Student newspaper (Alabamian, published once/two weeks). Literary magazine. Yearbook. TV station. Choral and drama groups, orchestra, jazz bands, opera, musical theatre, debating, academic, professional, and special-interest groups, 72 organizations in all. Seven fraternities, two chapter houses; seven sororities, no chapter houses. 23% of men join a fraternity. 23% of women join a sorority.
**Religious organizations:** Baptist Student Union, Main Event, New Life Ministries, Presbyterian Fellowship, Wesley Fellowship.
**Minority/foreign student organizations:** African-American Society, Betterment of Black Males Coalition, Alpha Phi Alpha, Kappa Alpha Psi, Alpha Kappa Alpha, Delta Sigma Theta. International Student Association.

**ATHLETICS. Physical education requirements:** Four semesters of physical education required.
**Intercollegiate competition:** Baseball (M), basketball (M,W), cheerleading (M,W), golf (M), volleyball (W). Member of NAIA, Southern States Conference.
**Intramural and club sports:** Intramural badminton, basketball, bowling, flag football, golf, softball, volleyball, soccer. Men's club soccer.

**ADMISSIONS. Academic basis for candidate selection** (in order of priority): Secondary school record, standardized test scores, class rank, school's recommendation.
**Nonacademic basis for candidate selection:** Character and personality, extracurricular participation, particular talent or ability, and alumni/ae relationship are considered.
**Requirements:** Graduation from secondary school is required; GED is accepted. 16 units and the following program of study are required: 4 units of English, 2 units of math, 2 units of lab science, 2 units of social studies, 2 units of history, 4 units of academic electives. Minimum composite ACT score of 18 (combined SAT score of 900), rank in top half of secondary school class, and minimum 2.0 GPA required. Conditional admission summer program for applicants not normally admissible. ACT is required; SAT may be substituted. Campus visit and interview recommended. Off-campus interviews available with an admissions representative.
**Procedure:** Take SAT or ACT by October of 12th year. Visit college for interview by December of 12th year. Suggest filing application by December 1. Application deadline is August 1. Notification of admission on rolling basis. $100 room deposit, refundable until August 1. Freshmen accepted for terms other than fall.
**Special programs:** Admission may be deferred. Credit and/or placement may be granted through CEEB Advanced Placement exams for scores of 3 or higher. Credit may be granted through military experience. Early entrance/early admission program. Concurrent enrollment program.
**Transfer students:** Transfer students accepted for terms other than fall. In fall 1993, 34% of all new students were transfers into all classes. 458 transfer applications were received, 349 were accepted. Application deadline is August 1 for fall; December 1 for spring. Minimum 2.0 GPA required. Lowest course grade accepted is "D." Maximum number of transferable credits is 65 semester hours from a two-year school and 100 semester hours from a four-year school. At least 30 semester hours must be completed at the university to receive degree.
**Admissions contact:** Robert A. Doyle, Director of Admissions. 205 665-6030.

**FINANCIAL AID. Available aid:** Pell grants, SEOG, state scholarships and grants, school scholarships and grants, private scholarships and grants, ROTC scholarships, academic merit scholarships, and athletic scholarships. Perkins Loans (NDSL), PLUS, Stafford Loans (GSL), state loans, private loans, and SLS. University partial payment plan.
**Financial aid statistics:** 15% of aid is not need-based. In 1993-94, 63% of all undergraduate applicants received aid; 61% of freshman applicants. Average amounts of aid awarded freshmen: Scholarships and grants, $2,000; loans, $2,100.
**Supporting data/closing dates:** FAFSA: Priority filing date is April 1. School's own aid application: Priority filing date is April 1. Income tax forms: Accepted on rolling basis. Notification of awards on rolling basis.
**Financial aid contact:** William E. Gentry, M.A., Director of Financial Aid. 205 665-6050.

**STUDENT EMPLOYMENT.** College Work/Study Program. Institutional employment. 13% of full-time undergraduates work on campus during school year. Students may expect to earn an average of $2,000 during school year. Off-campus part-time employment opportunities rated "good."

**COMPUTER FACILITIES.** 110 IBM/IBM-compatible and Macintosh/Apple microcomputers; 50 are networked. Students may access Digital minicomputer/mainframe systems. Computer languages and software packages include AppleWorks, BASIC, COBOL, Excel, FORTRAN, Harvard Graphics, Lotus 1-2-3, Microsoft Word, PageMaker, Plan Perfect, SPSS, WordPerfect. Computer facilities are available to all students.
**Fees:** None.
**Hours:** 8 AM-11 PM.

**GRADUATE CAREER DATA.** Graduate school percentages: 18% enter law school. 1% enter medical school. 1% enter dental school. 1% enter graduate business programs. Highest graduate school enrollments: U of Alabama, U of Alabama at Birmingham, U of Montevallo. 24% of graduates choose careers in business and industry. Companies and businesses that hire graduates: AmSouth Bank, Bell South, federal government, state educational institutions.

**PROMINENT ALUMNI/AE.** Polly Holliday, actress; Jeanne Appleton Voltz, former food editor, *Woman's Day* magazine; Dr. Bonnie Strickland, president, American Psychological Association; Rebecca Luker, actress, *Phantom of the Opera*.

## University of North Alabama

**Florence, AL 35632-0001** **205 760-4100**

**1994-95 Costs.** Tuition: $1,566 (state residents), $2,166 (out-of-state). Room: $1,200. Board: $1,484. Fees, books, misc. academic expenses (school's estimate): $600.
**Enrollment.** Undergraduates: 1,566 men, 2,206 women (full-time). Freshman class: 1,087 applicants, 702 accepted, 625 enrolled. Graduate enrollment: 174 men, 429 women.
**Test score averages/ranges.** Average ACT scores: 21 English, 19 math, 20 composite.
**Faculty.** 217 full-time; 58 part-time. 62% of faculty holds doctoral degree. Student/faculty ratio: 24 to 1.
**Selectivity rating.** Competitive.

**PROFILE.** The University of North Alabama is a public institution. Founded in 1872, it adopted coeducation in 1874. Programs are offered through the Schools of Arts and Sciences, Business, Education, and Nursing. Its 92-acre campus is located in a residential section of Florence.
**Accreditation:** SACS. Professionally accredited by the Council on Social Work Education, the National Association of Schools of Art and Design, the National Association of Schools of Music, the National Council for Accreditation of Teacher Education, the National League for Nursing.
**Religious orientation:** University of North Alabama is nonsectarian; no religious requirements.
**Library:** Collections totaling over 274,426 volumes, 2,129 periodical subscriptions, and 706,086 microform items.
**Special facilities/museums:** On-campus lab school (N-6), planetarium, observatory.
**Athletic facilities:** Gymnasiums, field house, basketball, tennis, and volleyball courts, golf course, track, baseball, football, intramural, and softball fields, weight rooms, physical fitness center.
**STUDENT BODY. Undergraduate profile:** 81% are state residents; 55% are transfers. 1% Asian-American, 9% Black, 1% Hispanic, 1% Native American, 87% White, 1% Other. Average age of undergraduates is 22.
**Freshman profile:** 7% of accepted applicants took SAT; 93% took ACT. 89% of freshmen come from public schools.
**Undergraduate achievement:** 54% of fall 1992 freshmen returned for fall 1993 term.
**Foreign students:** 33 students are from out of the country. Countries represented include Canada, Germany, Guatemala, Japan, Sweden, and Turkey; 19 in all.
**PROGRAMS OF STUDY. Degrees:** B.A., B.F.A., B.Gen.Studies, B.Mus., B.Mus.Ed., B.S., B.Soc.Work.
**Majors:** Accounting, Administrative Office Services, Art, Biology, Chemistry, Commercial French, Commercial German, Commercial Music, Commercial Spanish, Communication Arts, Computer Information Systems, Computer Science, Criminal Justice, Early Childhood Education, Economics, Elementary Education, English, Environmental Biology, Fashion Merchandising, Finance, Fine Arts, French, General Studies, Geography, Geology, German, Health/Physical Education/Recreation, History, Home Economics, Industrial Hygiene, Interiors, Journalism, Management, Marine Biology, Marketing, Mathematics, Music Performance, Nursing, Physics, Political Science, Professional Biology, Professional Chemistry, Professional Geography, Professional Writing, Psychology, Public Relations, Radio/Television/Film, Secondary Education, Social Work, Sociology, Spanish, Special Education, Theatre.
**Distribution of degrees:** The majors with the highest enrollment are marketing, management, and accounting.
**Requirements:** General education requirement.
**Academic regulations:** Freshmen must maintain minimum 1.60 GPA; sophomores, 1.85 GPA; juniors, 1.95 GPA; seniors, 2.00 GPA.
**Special:** Minors offered in most majors and in art history, business administration, foods and nutrition, military science, photography, real estate/insurance, and retailing/clothing. Several concentrations available in biology, chemistry, French, geography, German, home economics, and Spanish. Secretarial training program. Commercial music program offers hands-on training at Muscle Shoals recording studios. Double majors. Independent study. Cooperative education programs. Graduate school at which undergraduates may take graduate-level courses. Preprofessional programs in law, medicine, veterinary science, pharmacy, dentistry, theology, optometry, agriculture/forestry, engineering, dental hygiene, medical technology, occupational therapy, physical therapy, and podiatry. Member of Alabama Marine Environmental Sciences consortium; off-campus study possible at Dauphin Island sea lab. Member of Consortium for Overseas Teaching. Teacher certification in early childhood, elementary, secondary, and special education. Certification in specific subject areas. ROTC.
**Honors:** Phi Beta Kappa. Honor societies.
**Academic Assistance:** Remedial reading, writing, and math. Nonremedial tutoring.
**STUDENT LIFE. Housing:** Students may live on or off campus. Women's and men's dorms. Sorority and fraternity housing. On-campus married-student housing. 15% of students live in college housing.
**Social atmosphere:** Popular gathering spots include the Guillet University Center, the amphitheater, the Rodeo, Club XIII, and McFarland Park. Groups with widespread influence include the Student Government Association, the University Program Council, the Football team, Greeks, and Cooperative Campus Ministries. Favorite events include Spring Fling, Homecoming, football and basketball games, alcohol awareness week, lectures, concerts, United Way Drive, and Yulefest. "Not much happens on the weekends around campus," reports the editor of the student newspaper. "Within the classroom, however, UNA is second to none. Classes are small, so students have a much better chance to get to know their professors. And between student organizations and Greek affiliations, students here really have a voice in their own education."
**Services and counseling/handicapped student services:** Placement services. Health service. Day care. Personal and psychological counseling. Career and academic guidance services. Physically disabled student services. Notetaking services. Tutors. Reader services for the blind.
**Campus organizations:** Undergraduate student government. Student newspaper (The Flor-Ala, published once/week). Literary magazine. Yearbook. Bands, chorales, ensembles, University Players, Re-entering Students Association, Commuters Association, College Republicans, Young Democrats, 91 organizations in all. Six fraternities, five chapter houses; six sororities, no chapter houses. 10% of men join a fraternity. 9% of women join a sorority.
**Religious organizations:** Alpha Omega Ministries, Baptist Student Union, Christian Student Fellowship, Main Event, Wesley Foundation, Cooperative Campus Ministry, Catholic Campus Ministry, Ascending Voices, Catholic Connection, Episcopal Alternative, Baptist Campus Ministry, Campus Outreach.
**Minority/foreign student organizations:** Black Student Alliance. International Club.
**ATHLETICS. Physical education requirements:** Two semesters of physical education required.
**Intercollegiate competition:** 6% of students participate. Baseball (M), basketball (M,W), cheerleading (M,W), cross-country (M,W), football (M), golf (M), softball (W), tennis (M,W), volleyball (W). Member of Gulf South Conference, NCAA Division II.
**Intramural and club sports:** 40% of students participate. Intramural basketball, billiards, flag football, golf, softball, table tennis, volleyball.
**ADMISSIONS. Academic basis for candidate selection** (in order of priority): Standardized test scores, class rank, secondary school record.
**Requirements:** Graduation from secondary school is required; GED is accepted. 12 units and the following program of study are required: 4 units of English, 2 units of math, 2 units of science, 2 units of social studies, 2 units of academic electives. Minimum combined SAT score of 700 (minimum composite ACT score of 18), rank in top half of secondary school class, and minimum 2.0 GPA required. Portfolio required of art program applicants. Audition required of music program applicants. Conditional admission possible for applicants not meeting standard requirements. SAT or ACT is required. No off-campus interviews.
**Procedure:** Take SAT or ACT by May of 12th year. Application deadline is July 1. Notification of admission on rolling basis. $50 refundable room deposit. Freshmen accepted for terms other than fall.
**Special programs:** Admission may be deferred two years. Credit may be granted through CEEB Advanced Placement for scores of 3 or higher. Credit may be granted through CLEP subject exams and military experience. Concurrent enrollment program.
**Transfer students:** Transfer students accepted for terms other than fall. In fall 1993, 55% of all new students were transfers into all classes. 931 transfer applications were received, 755 were accepted. Application deadline is July 1 for fall; December 1 for spring. Minimum 2.0 GPA required. Lowest course grade accepted is "C." At least 30 semester hours must be completed at the university to receive degree.
**Admissions contact:** G. Daniel Howard, Ph.D., Acting Dean of Enrollment Managment. 205 760-4608.
**FINANCIAL AID. Available aid:** SEOG, Federal Nursing Student Scholarships, state scholarships and grants, school scholarships and grants, private scholarships and grants, ROTC scholarships, academic merit scholarships, and athletic scholarships. Perkins Loans (NDSL), PLUS, Stafford Loans (GSL), NSL, private loans, and SLS. Tuition Plan Inc. and family tuition reduction.
**Financial aid statistics:** In 1993-94, 80% of all undergraduate applicants received aid; 70% of freshman applicants. Average amounts of aid awarded freshmen: Scholarships and grants, $1,374; loans, $1,800.
**Supporting data/closing dates:** FAFSA/FAF/FFS: Priority filing date is April 1; accepted on rolling basis. Notification of awards on rolling basis.
**Financial aid contact:** Jo Ann Weaver, Ph.D., Director of Financial Aid. 205 760-4278.
**STUDENT EMPLOYMENT.** College Work/Study Program. Institutional employment. 10% of full-time undergraduates work on campus during school year. Students may expect to earn an average of $1,740 during school year. Freshmen are discouraged from working during their first term. Off-campus part-time employment opportunities rated "good."
**COMPUTER FACILITIES.** 120 IBM/IBM-compatible and Macintosh/Apple microcomputers; 10 are networked. Students may access IBM minicomputer/mainframe systems. 9 major computer languages and software packages available. Students must be enrolled in a computer course to use facilities.
**Fees:** $30 computer fee per course.
**Hours:** 8 AM-10 PM (M-Th); 8 AM-7 PM (F).
**PROMINENT ALUMNI/AE.** T.S. Stribling, Pulitzer Prize-winning author; Ronnie Flippo, U.S. congressman; George "Goober" Lindsey and Will Stutts, actors; Harlon Hill, all-American football player; Frank Fleming, internationally recognized sculptor; Wendell Wilkie Gunn, former special assistant to President Reagan.

## University of South Alabama

**Mobile, AL 36688-0002** **205 460-6101**

**1994-95 Costs.** Tuition: $2,208 (state residents), $2,808 (out-of-state). Room & board: $3,060. Fees, books, misc. academic expenses (school's estimate): $733.
**Enrollment.** Undergraduates: 3,385 men, 4,131 women (full-time). Freshman class: 2,157 applicants, 1,965 accepted, 955 enrolled. Graduate enrollment: 524 men, 1,013 women.
**Test score averages/ranges.** Average ACT scores: 23 English, 21 math, 23 composite. Range of ACT scores of middle 50%: 19-24 English, 18-23 math.
**Faculty.** 439 full-time; 197 part-time. 82% of faculty holds doctoral degree. Student/faculty ratio: 26 to 1.
**Selectivity rating.** Less competitive.

**PROFILE.** The University of South Alabama, founded in 1963, is a public, comprehensive institution. Programs are offered through the Colleges of Arts and Sciences, Business and Management Studies, Education, and Engineering; the Divisions of Allied Health

Professions and Computer and Information Sciences; the School of Nursing; the Special Division; and the Graduate School. Its 1,200-acre campus is located in Mobile.

**Accreditation:** SACS. Professionally accredited by the Accreditation Board for Engineering and Technology, the American Assembly of Collegiate Schools of Business, the American Medical Association (CAHEA), the American Physical Therapy Association, the American Speech-Language-Hearing Association, the Computing Sciences Accreditation Board, the National Association of Schools of Music, the National Council for Accreditation of Teacher Education, the National League for Nursing.
**Religious orientation:** University of South Alabama is nonsectarian; no religious requirements.
**Library:** Collections totaling over 425,706 volumes, 4,084 periodical subscriptions, and 1,212,379 microform items.
**Special facilities/museums:** Museum/gallery complex, three hospitals, center for clinical education in health programs, engineering labs.
**Athletic facilities:** Gymnasium, swimming pool, tennis courts, weight room, track, sports medicine complex.

**STUDENT BODY. Undergraduate profile:** 68% are state residents; 52% are transfers. 3% Asian-American, 10% Black, 1% Hispanic, 1% Native American, 79% White, 6% Other. Average age of undergraduates is 23.
**Freshman profile:** 11% of accepted applicants took SAT; 89% took ACT. 91% of freshmen come from public schools.
**Undergraduate achievement:** 63% of fall 1992 freshmen returned for fall 1993 term. 10% of entering class graduated. 18% of students who completed a degree program immediately went on to graduate study.
**Foreign students:** 176 students are from out of the country. Countries represented include Bangladesh, Germany, Japan, Malaysia, Pakistan, and Vietnam; 50 in all.

**PROGRAMS OF STUDY. Degrees:** B.A., B.F.A., B.Mus., B.S.
**Majors:** Accounting, Anthropology, Art, Art History, Biological Sciences, Biomedical Sciences, Business Economics, Cardiorespiratory Sciences, Chemical Engineering, Chemistry, Civil Engineering, Communication, Computer/Information Sciences, Criminal Justice, Dramatic Arts, Early Childhood Education, Economics, Electrical Engineering, Elementary Education, English, Finance, French, General Business, Geography, Geology, German, Health Education, History, International Studies, Leisure Services, Management, Marketing, Mathematics, Mechanical Engineering, Medical Technology, Music, Music Education, Music Performance, Nursing, Occupational Therapy, Personalized Studies, Personalized Study Program for Adults, Philosophy, Physical Education, Physical Therapy, Physics, Political Science, Psychology, Russian, Secondary Education, Sociology, Spanish, Special Education, Speech/Hearing Sciences, Statistics, Studio Art.
**Distribution of degrees:** The majors with the highest enrollment are nursing, elementary education, and communication; French, physics, and dramatic arts have the lowest.
**Requirements:** General education requirement.
**Academic regulations:** Minimum 2.0 GPA must be maintained.
**Special:** Minors offered in most majors. Self-designed majors. Double majors. Dual degrees. Accelerated study. Pass/fail grading option. Internships. Cooperative education programs. Graduate school at which undergraduates may take graduate-level courses. Preprofessional programs in law, medicine, veterinary science, pharmacy, dentistry, and optometry. Member of Alabama Marine Environmental Science Consortium; off-campus study possible at Dauphin Island Sea Lab. Sea Semester. Teacher certification in early childhood, elementary, secondary, and special education. Certification in specific subject areas. Study abroad in England, France, and Mexico. ROTC and AFROTC.
**Honors:** Honor societies.
**Academic Assistance:** Remedial reading, writing, math, and study skills. Nonremedial tutoring.

**STUDENT LIFE. Housing:** Students may live on or off campus. Coed dorms. Fraternity housing. School-owned/operated apartments. On-campus married-student housing. 28% of students live in college housing.
**Social atmosphere:** Favorite student haunts include Poor Richard's, Haley's, Hurricane's, Wild Wild West, Rooster's, Solomon's, Sundowner, Hooter's, The Rec Center, The UC Game Room, Movies 10, G.T. Henry's, Culture Shock, and Vincent Van Go-Go. Among the groups with the most widespread influence on campus life are the Residence Life Council, Baptist Campus Ministries, S.G.A., Jaguar Productions, Panhellenic Interfraternity Council, Black Student Union, and the Gay/Lesbian/Bisexual Alliance. Frat parties, "Pink House" parties, baseball and basketball games, intermurals, Homecoming, and *The Rocky Horror Picture Show* are popular campus events. According to the editor of the student newspaper, "On-campus life isn't much: just you and your friends or your club/frat."
**Services and counseling/handicapped student services:** Placement services. Health service. Counseling services for minority, military, veteran, and older students. Personal and psychological counseling. Career and academic guidance services. Physically disabled student services. Notetaking services. Tape recorders. Tutors. Reader services for the blind.
**Campus organizations:** Undergraduate student government. Student newspaper (Vanguard, published once/week). Literary magazine. Yearbook. Bands, choir, chorale, opera theatre, Theatre for the Performing Arts, professional, social, and special-interest groups, 110 organizations in all. 10 fraternities, all with chapter houses; eight sororities, no chapter houses. 9% of men join a fraternity. 7% of women join a sorority.
**Religious organizations:** Baptist Campus Ministries, Campus Outreach, Chi Alpha Campus Ministry, Muslim Student Association, Newman Club, Wesley Fellowship.
**Minority/foreign student organizations:** Abenefoo Kuo, American Association of Black Engineers, Black Student Union, Students Together Against Racism. International Council, International Studies Group, Arab, Asian, Caribbean, Chinese, European, Hispanic, Indian, Latin American, Malaysian, Nigerian, Pakistani, and Vietnamese student groups.

**ATHLETICS. Physical education requirements:** Six quarter hours of physical education required.
**Intercollegiate competition:** 1% of students participate. Baseball (M), basketball (M,W), cross-country (M,W), golf (M,W), soccer (M), tennis (M,W), track and field (indoor) (M,W), track and field (outdoor) (M,W). Member of NCAA Division I, Sun Belt Conference.
**Intramural and club sports:** 40% of students participate. Intramural basketball, bowling, dodgeball, eightball, flag football, indoor soccer, kickball, putt-putt golf, racquetball, softball, table tennis, tennis, volleyball, walleyball, water polo, Wiffle ball. Men's club indoor track and field, outdoor track and field. Women's club soccer.

**ADMISSIONS. Academic basis for candidate selection** (in order of priority): Standardized test scores, secondary school record, school's recommendation.
**Nonacademic basis for candidate selection:** Character and personality are important. Extracurricular participation and particular talent or ability are considered.
**Requirements:** Graduation from secondary school is required; GED is accepted. 16 units and the following program of study are recommended: 4 units of English, 3 units of math, 2 units of science, 2 units of social studies, 2 units of history, 3 units of academic electives. Minimum composite ACT score of 19 and minimum 2.0 GPA recommended. 4 units of English, 4 units of math (2 algebra, 1 geometry, 1/2 trigonometry, and 1/2 advanced algebra or higher math), 2 units of lab science (physics, chemistry, or biology), and 2 units of history, social sciences, or foreign language required of engineering program applicants. Audition required of music program applicants. Conditional admission possible for applicants not meeting standard requirements. Developmental Studies Program for applicants not normally admissible. ACT is required; SAT may be substituted. Off-campus interviews available with an admissions representative.
**Procedure:** Take SAT or ACT by October of 12th year. Application deadline is September 10. Notification of admission on rolling basis. No set date by which applicants must accept offer. $50 refundable room deposit. Freshmen accepted for terms other than fall.
**Special programs:** Credit and/or placement may be granted through CEEB Advanced Placement exams for scores of 3 or higher. Credit and/or placement may be granted through CLEP general and subject exams. Credit may be granted through challenge exams and military experience. Placement may be granted through ACT PEP exams. Early entrance/early admission program. Concurrent enrollment program.
**Transfer students:** Transfer students accepted for terms other than fall. In fall 1993, 52% of all new students were transfers into all classes. 2,249 transfer applications were received, 1,894 were accepted. Application deadline is September 10 for fall; March 10 for spring. Minimum 2.0 GPA recommended. Lowest course grade accepted is "C." Maximum number of transferable credits is 96 quarter hours. 48 credit hours of upper-division course work must be completed at the university to receive degree.
**Admissions contact:** Catherine King, M.S., Director of Admissions. 205 460-6141, 800 872-5247.

**FINANCIAL AID. Available aid:** Pell grants, SEOG, state grants, school scholarships, ROTC scholarships, academic merit scholarships, and athletic scholarships. Perkins Loans (NDSL), PLUS, Stafford Loans (GSL), Health Professions Loans, and SLS.
**Financial aid statistics:** 18% of aid is not need-based. In 1993-94, 79% of all undergraduate applicants received aid; 73% of freshman applicants. Average amounts of aid awarded freshmen: Scholarships and grants, $2,083; loans, $1,985.
**Supporting data/closing dates:** FAFSA: Accepted on rolling basis. School's own aid application: Accepted on rolling basis. Income tax forms: Accepted on rolling basis. Notification of awards on rolling basis.
**Financial aid contact:** Grady Collins, M.A., Director of Financial Aid. 205 460-6231.

**STUDENT EMPLOYMENT.** College Work/Study Program. Institutional employment. 10% of full-time undergraduates work on campus during school year. Students may expect to earn an average of $2,000 during school year. Off-campus part-time employment opportunities rated "excellent."

**COMPUTER FACILITIES.** 249 IBM/IBM-compatible, Macintosh/Apple, and RISC-/UNIX-based microcomputers; 155 are networked. Students may access Cray, Digital, IBM, SUN minicomputer/mainframe systems, BITNET, Internet. Residence halls may be equipped with stand-alone microcomputers, networked terminals, modems. Client/LAN operating systems include Apple/Macintosh, DOS, UNIX/XENIX/AIX, X-windows, LocalTalk/AppleTalk, Novell. Computer languages and software packages include Assembler, ASSIST, BASIC, C, C++, COBOL, dBASE, FORTRAN, IMSL, Lotus 1-2-3, Microsoft Word, PageMaker, Pascal, PL/1, SAS, Script, SPSS, STATPAK, WATFIV, WordPerfect. Computer facilities are available to all students.
**Fees:** $10-15/course.
**Hours:** 7 AM-midn. for microcomputers; 6 AM-2 AM for mainframe.

**GRADUATE CAREER DATA.** Graduate school percentages: 1% enter law school. 1% enter medical school. 1% enter dental school. 3% enter graduate business programs. 12% enter graduate arts and sciences programs. 75% of graduates choose careers in business and industry. Companies and businesses that hire graduates: Alabama Power, AmSouth, Army Corps of Engineers, CIBA-GEIGY, Mobile County Schools, Scott Paper.

# Alaska

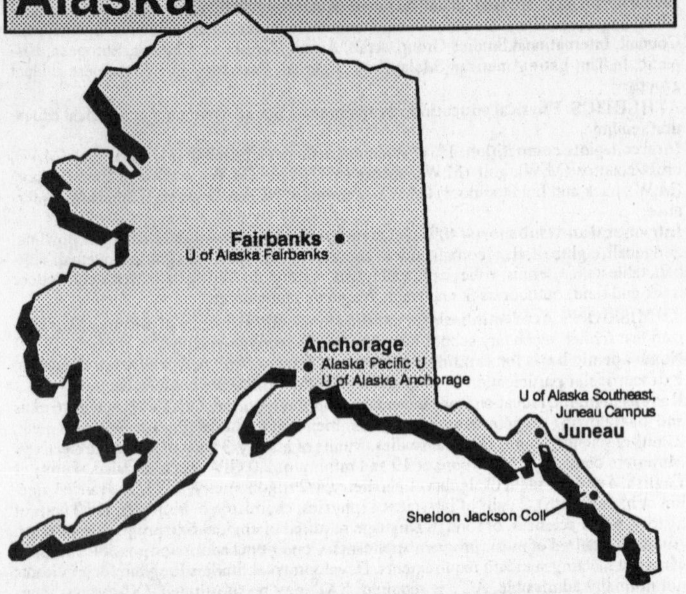


## Alaska Pacific University

**Anchorage, AK 99508** **907 561-1266**

**1993-94 Costs.** Tuition: $7,200. Room & board: $4,050. Fees, books, misc. academic expenses (school's estimate): $880.
**Enrollment.** Undergraduates: 82 men, 181 women (full-time). Freshman class: 193 applicants, 146 accepted, 55 enrolled. Graduate enrollment: 83 men, 151 women.
**Test score averages/ranges.** Average SAT scores: 482 verbal, 490 math. Range of SAT scores of middle 50%: 430-550 verbal, 440-530 math. Average ACT scores: 20 English, 19 math, 20 composite. Range of ACT scores of middle 50%: 16-24 English, 15-22 math.
**Faculty.** 22 full-time; 65 part-time. 40% of faculty holds doctoral degree. Student/faculty ratio: 7 to 1.
**Selectivity rating.** Competitive.

**PROFILE.** Alaska Pacific, founded in 1959, is a church-affiliated university. Undergraduate academic divisions include the Core Curriculum; General Studies; Human Resources and Education; Humanities, Arts, and Communication; Natural Sciences and Management; and Social Sciences, Philosophy, and Religion. Its 270-acre campus lies eight miles from the center of Anchorage.

**Accreditation:** NASC.
**Religious orientation:** Alaska Pacific University is affiliated with the United Methodist Church; no religious requirements.
**Library:** Collections totaling over 384,698 volumes, and 37,619 microform items.
**Athletic facilities:** Swimming pool, gymnasium, weight and wrestling rooms, Nordic skiing trails, soccer field, climbing wall.
**STUDENT BODY. Undergraduate profile:** 84% are state residents; 38% are transfers. 3% Asian-American, 5% Black, 4% Hispanic, 10% Native American, 70% White, 8% Other. Average age of undergraduates is 25.
**Freshman profile:** 3% of freshmen who took SAT scored 700 or over on verbal, 3% scored 700 or over on math; 9% scored 600 or over on verbal, 14% scored 600 or over on math; 43% scored 500 or over on verbal, 45% scored 500 or over on math; 83% scored 400 or over on verbal, 85% scored 400 or over on math; 97% scored 300 or over on verbal, 99% scored 300 or over on math. 3% of freshmen who took ACT scored 30 or over on English, 3% scored 30 or over on composite; 28% scored 24 or over on English, 14% scored 24 or over on math, 21% scored 24 or over on composite; 53% scored 18 or over on English, 53% scored 18 or over on math, 75% scored 18 or over on composite; 96% scored 12 or over on English, 96% scored 12 or over on math, 100% scored 12 or over on composite; 99% scored 6 or over on English, 99% scored 6 or over on math. 66% of accepted applicants took SAT; 53% took ACT. 98% of freshmen come from public schools.
**Undergraduate achievement:** 45% of fall 1992 freshmen returned for fall 1993 term. 5% of entering class graduated.
**Foreign students:** 26 students are from out of the country. Countries represented include Canada, China, Japan, Korea, Singapore, and Taiwan; eight in all.
**PROGRAMS OF STUDY. Degrees:** B.A.
**Majors:** Accounting/Finance, Art, Comparative Literature/Languages, Elementary Education, Environmental Science, History, Hospitality Management, Human Services, Intercultural Communications, International Business, Management/Marketing, Music, Natural Resources Management, Organizational Administration, Outdoor Studies, Pacific Rim Studies, Philosophy/Religion, Pre-Law, Psychology, Social Sciences, Speech Communication, Theatre, Travel Industry Management.
**Distribution of degrees:** The majors with the highest enrollment are organizational administration, elementary education, and social sciences; environmental science, speech communications, and intercultural communication have the lowest.
**Requirements:** General education requirement.
**Academic regulations:** Freshmen must maintain minimum 1.75 GPA; sophomores, 1.85 GPA; juniors, 1.95 GPA; seniors, 2.0 GPA.
**Special:** Associate's degrees offered. Double majors. Independent study. Pass/fail grading option. Internships. Graduate school at which undergraduates may take graduate-level courses. Preprofessional programs in law and theology. Teacher certification in elementary education. Exchange programs abroad in Japan (Nagoya Gakuin U) and Taiwan (Soochow U). Study abroad may also be arranged in other countries.
**Academic Assistance:** Remedial reading, writing, math, and study skills. Nonremedial tutoring.
**ADMISSIONS. Academic basis for candidate selection** (in order of priority): Secondary school record, standardized test scores, class rank, school's recommendation, essay.
**Nonacademic basis for candidate selection:** Character and personality, extracurricular participation, particular talent or ability, geographical distribution, and alumni/ae relationship are considered.
**Requirements:** Graduation from secondary school is required; GED is accepted. No specific distribution of secondary school units required. Minimum combined SAT score of 800 (composite ACT score of 17) and minimum 2.5 GPA required. Provisional admission for applicants not meeting standard requirements. SAT or ACT is required. Campus visit recommended. Off-campus interviews available with an admissions representative.
**Procedure:** Take SAT or ACT by December 31 of 12th year. Visit college for interview by February 1 of 12th year. Suggest filing application by December 31. Application deadline is August 15. Notification of admission on rolling basis. Reply is required by August 15. $100 nonrefundable tuition deposit. $100 room deposit, refundable until August 1. Freshmen accepted for terms other than fall.
**Special programs:** Admission may be deferred one year. Credit may be granted through CEEB Advanced Placement for scores of 3 or higher. Credit may be granted through CLEP general and subject exams, Regents College, ACT PEP, DANTES, and challenge exams, and military and life experience. Early entrance/early admission program. Concurrent enrollment program.
**Transfer students:** Transfer students accepted for terms other than fall. In fall 1993, 38% of all new students were transfers into all classes. Application deadline is August 15 for fall; December 15 for spring. Minimum 2.0 GPA required. Lowest course grade accepted is "C." Maximum number of transferable credits is 64 semester hours. At least 32 semester hours must be completed at the university to receive degree.
**Admissions contact:** Lois Bender, M.A.T., Director of Admissions. 907 564-8248.
**FINANCIAL AID. Available aid:** Pell grants, SEOG, state grants, school scholarships and grants, private scholarships and grants, academic merit scholarships, and aid for undergraduate foreign students. Stafford Loans (GSL), state loans, school loans, private loans, and SLS. Deferred payment plan.
**Supporting data/closing dates:** FAFSA/FAF: Priority filing date is March 15. Notification of awards on rolling basis.
**Financial aid contact:** Joye Freeman, Director of Financial Aid. 907 564-8248.

## Sheldon Jackson College

**Sitka, AK 99835-7699** **907 747-5220**

**1993-94 Costs.** Tuition: $9,000. Room & board: $4,800. Fees, books, misc. academic expenses (school's estimate): $950.
**Enrollment.** Undergraduates: 102 men, 101 women (full-time). Freshman class: 152 applicants, 149 accepted, 54 enrolled.
**Test score averages/ranges.** Average SAT scores: 915 combined. Average ACT scores: 21 composite.
**Faculty.** 20 full-time; 12 part-time. 42% of faculty holds highest degree in specific field. Student/faculty ratio: 10 to 1.
**Selectivity rating.** Noncompetitive.

**PROFILE.** Sheldon Jackson, founded in 1878, is a private, church-affiliated, liberal arts college. Its 450-acre campus is located in Sitka, 100 miles from Juneau.

**Accreditation:** NASC.
**Religious orientation:** Sheldon Jackson College is affiliated with the Presbyterian Church USA; three semester hours of religion required.
**Library:** Collections totaling over 70,000 volumes, 490 periodical subscriptions, and 21,000 microform items.
**Special facilities/museums:** Museum of Alaskan native artifacts and art, on-campus salmon hatchery, 60-foot motor vessel.
**Athletic facilities:** Athletic center.
**STUDENT BODY. Undergraduate profile:** 36% are state residents; 32% are transfers. 1% Asian-American, 1% Black, 26% Native American, 70% White, 2% Other. Average age of undergraduates is 22.
**Undergraduate achievement:** 60% of fall 1992 freshmen returned for fall 1993 term.
**Foreign students:** Five students are from out of the country. Five countries represented in all.
**PROGRAMS OF STUDY. Degrees:** B.A., B.S.
**Majors:** Aquatic Resources, Business Administration, Elementary Education, Interdisciplinary Studies, Liberal Arts, Natural Resource Management/Development, Secondary Education.
**Distribution of degrees:** The majors with the highest enrollment are elementary education and business.
**Requirements:** General education requirement.
**Academic regulations:** Freshmen must maintain minimum 1.75 GPA; sophomores, juniors, seniors, 2.0 GPA.
**Special:** Associate's degrees offered. Self-designed majors. Double majors. Independent study. Internships. Cooperative education programs. Teacher certification in elementary and secondary education. Certification in specific subject areas.
**Academic Assistance:** Remedial reading, writing, math, and study skills. Nonremedial tutoring.

**ADMISSIONS. Academic basis for candidate selection** (in order of priority): Secondary school record, essay, school's recommendation, standardized test scores, class rank.
**Nonacademic basis for candidate selection:** Character and personality are important. Extracurricular participation, particular talent or ability, and geographical distribution are considered.
**Requirements:** Graduation from secondary school is required; GED is accepted. No specific distribution of secondary school units required. Open admissions policy. Minimum 2.0 GPA recommended. SAT or ACT is recommended. Off-campus interviews available with an admissions representative.
**Procedure:** Notification of admission on rolling basis. $100 refundable room deposit. Freshmen accepted for terms other than fall.
**Special programs:** Admission may be deferred one semester. Credit and/or placement may be granted through CEEB Advanced Placement exams for scores of 3 or higher. Credit and/or placement may be granted through CLEP general and subject exams. Credit may be granted through challenge exams and military and life experience. Credit and placement may be granted through DANTES exams. Early entrance/early admission program. Concurrent enrollment program.
**Transfer students:** Transfer students accepted for terms other than fall. In fall 1993, 32% of all new students were transfers into all classes. 92 transfer applications were received, 90 were accepted. Lowest course grade accepted is "C-." Maximum number of transferable credits is 100 semester hours. At least 24 semester hours must be completed at the college to receive degree.
**Admissions contact:** Dennis Trotter, Director of Admissions. 907 747-5221.

**FINANCIAL AID. Available aid:** Pell grants, SEOG, state scholarships and grants, school scholarships and grants, private scholarships and grants, and academic merit scholarships. Perkins Loans (NDSL), PLUS, Stafford Loans (GSL), state loans, and SLS. Tuition Plan Inc. and guaranteed tuition.
**Financial aid statistics:** In 1993-94, 93% of all undergraduate applicants received aid; 87% of freshman applicants. Average amounts of aid awarded freshmen: Scholarships and grants, $4,250.
**Supporting data/closing dates:** FAFSA: Priority filing date is March 1. Income tax forms: Accepted on rolling basis. Notification of awards on rolling basis.
**Financial aid contact:** Dick Goff, M.A.Ed., Director of Financial Aid. 907 747-5241.

# University of Alaska Anchorage

**Anchorage, AK 99508 — 907 786-1800**

**1994-95 Costs.** Tuition: $1,794 (state residents), $5,000 (out-of-state). Room & board: $5,410. Fees, books, misc. academic expenses (school's estimate): $664.
**Enrollment.** Undergraduates: 2,446 men, 2,900 women (full-time). Freshman class: 4,324 applicants, 3,297 accepted, 2,390 enrolled. Graduate enrollment: 244 men, 347 women.
**Test score averages/ranges.** N/A.
**Faculty.** 362 full-time; 800 part-time. 41% of faculty holds doctoral degree. Student/faculty ratio: 22 to 1.
**Selectivity rating.** N/A.

**PROFILE.** The University of Alaska at Anchorage, founded in 1962, is a public, comprehensive institution. The present institution is the result of the urban university's 1987 merger with several community colleges and extension programs. Its modern campus is located near downtown Anchorage.

**Accreditation:** NASC. Professionally accredited by the Accreditation Board for Engineering and Technology, the Accrediting Council on Education in Journalism and Mass Communication, the Council on Social Work Education, the National Association of Schools of Art and Design, the National League for Nursing.
**Religious orientation:** University of Alaska at Anchorage is nonsectarian; no religious requirements.
**Library:** Collections totaling over 384,698 volumes, 3,479 periodical subscriptions, and 37,619 microform items.
**Special facilities/museums:** Justice center, center for international business, center for alcohol and addiction studies, circumpolar health institute, center for high-latitude research.
**Athletic facilities:** Gymnasium, swimming pool, track, ice rink, racquetball and squash courts, weight room.

**STUDENT BODY. Undergraduate profile:** 95% are state residents; 52% are transfers. 4% Asian-American, 6% Black, 3% Hispanic, 6% Native American, 79% White, 2% Other. Average age of undergraduates is 31.
**Foreign students:** 175 students are from out of the country. Countries represented include China, England, Finland, Mexico, Russia, and Spain; 41 in all.

**PROGRAMS OF STUDY. Degrees:** B.A., B.Bus.Admin., B.Ed., B.F.A., B.Mus., B.S., B.Soc.Work.
**Majors:** Accounting, Anthropology, Art, Biological Sciences, Chemistry, Civil Engineering, Computer Science, Economics, Elementary Education, English, Finance, Health Sciences, History, Interdisciplinary Studies, Journalism/Public Communications, Justice, Management, Management Information Systems, Marketing, Mathematics, Music, Natural Science, Nursing, Physical Education, Political Science, Psychology, Secondary Education, Social Work, Sociology, Surveying/Mapping, Technology, Theatre.
**Distribution of degrees:** The majors with the highest enrollment are elementary education, nursing, and accounting; sociology and theatre have the lowest.
**Requirements:** General education requirement.
**Academic regulations:** Minimum 2.0 GPA must be maintained.
**Special:** Minors offered in most majors and in Canadian and women's studies. Associate's degrees offered. Self-designed majors. Double majors. Dual degrees. Independent study. Pass/fail grading option. Internships. Cooperative education programs. Graduate school at which undergraduates may take graduate-level courses. Preprofessional programs in law. Member of National Student Exchange (NSE). Teacher certification in elementary and secondary education. Certification in specific subject areas. Exchange program abroad in England (American Coll in London). Study abroad also in France, Germany, and Italy.
**Honors:** Honor societies.
**Academic Assistance:** Remedial reading, writing, math, and study skills. Nonremedial tutoring.

**STUDENT LIFE. Housing:** Students may live on or off campus. School-owned/operated apartments. 3% of students live in college housing.
**Social atmosphere:** The student newspaper reports, "We are mostly a transient student body and have just built student housing recently, so some 'student life' is appearing. But the great majority of students come to class and leave right after it's over." The most popular sports event of the year is the Great Alaska Shootout in men's basketball. Favorite student gathering spots include Chilkoot Charlie's, Houlihan's Old Place, and Yesterday's.
**Services and counseling/handicapped student services:** Placement services. Health service. Women's center. Day care. Counseling services for minority, military, veteran, and older students. Birth control, personal, and psychological counseling. Career and academic guidance services. Religious counseling. Physically disabled student services. Learning disabled services. Notetaking services. Tape recorders.
**Campus organizations:** Undergraduate student government. Student newspaper (Northern Lights, published once/week). Literary magazine. Yearbook. Radio station. Jazz ensemble, accounting club, American Society of Civil Engineers, Student Nurse Association, University Free Press, Circumpolar Health Club, 64 organizations in all.
**Religious organizations:** Bahai group, Community Ministry, Intervarsity Christian Fellowship, Korean Campus Crusade for Christ.
**Minority/foreign student organizations:** African-American Association, Native Student Organization. Korean-American Association, Russian Club, La Experiencia, Nichiren Shoshu Sokagakkai Group.

**ATHLETICS. Physical education requirements:** None.
**Intercollegiate competition:** 1% of students participate. Alpine skiing (M,W), basketball (M,W), cheerleading (M,W), cross-country (M), diving (M), gymnastics (W), ice hockey (M), Nordic skiing (M,W), swimming (M), volleyball (W). Member of NCAA Division I for ice hockey, NCAA Division II, Pacific West Conference for basketball, Western Collegiage Hockey Association.
**Intramural and club sports:** 3% of students participate. Intramural basketball, broomball, ice hockey, racquetball, squash, volleyball, water polo. Men's club soccer. Women's club ice hockey.

**ADMISSIONS. Academic basis for candidate selection** (in order of priority): Secondary school record, school's recommendation, standardized test scores.
**Requirements:** Graduation from secondary school is recommended; GED is accepted. No specific distribution of secondary school units required. Minimum 2.5 GPA required. 45 college credits and score of 176 on Pre-Professional Skills Test (PPST) required of B.Ed. program applicants. Portfolio required of art program applicants. R.N. required of nursing program applicants. SAT or ACT is required. Campus visit recommended.
**Procedure:** Take SAT or ACT by May of 12th year. Suggest filing application by February 1; no deadline. No set date by which applicants must accept offer. $25 nonrefundable room deposit. Freshmen accepted for terms other than fall.
**Special programs:** Admission may be deferred seven years. Credit may be granted through CEEB Advanced Placement for scores of 3 or higher. Credit may be granted through CLEP general and subject exams, Regents College, ACT PEP, DANTES, and challenge exams, and military and life experience. Early decision program. In fall 1992, 2,233 applied for early decision and 1,334 were accepted. Deadline for applying for early decision is April 9. Early entrance/early admission program. Concurrent enrollment program.
**Transfer students:** Transfer students accepted for terms other than fall. In fall 1992, 52% of all new students were transfers into all classes. 2,882 transfer applications were received, 2,198 were accepted. Application deadline is rolling for fall; rolling for spring. Minimum 2.0 GPA required. Lowest course grade accepted is "C." At least 30 semester hours must be completed at the university to receive degree.
**Admissions contact:** Linda Berg Smith, Associate Vice Chancellor of Student Services. 907 786-1480.

**FINANCIAL AID. Available aid:** Pell grants, SEOG, state grants, school scholarships and grants, private scholarships, academic merit scholarships, and athletic scholarships. Perkins Loans (NDSL), PLUS, Stafford Loans (GSL), state loans, school loans, and SLS.
**Financial aid statistics:** In 1992-93, 67% of all undergraduate applicants received aid; 67% of freshman applicants.
**Supporting data/closing dates:** FAFSA/FAF/FFS: Priority filing date is April 1; accepted on rolling basis. School's own aid application: Priority filing date is April 1; accepted on rolling basis. State aid form: Priority filing date is May 15; accepted on rolling basis. Income tax forms: Priority filing date is April 1; accepted on rolling basis. Notification of awards begins June 1.
**Financial aid contact:** James Upchurch, M.Ed., Director of Financial Aid. 907 786-1585.

**STUDENT EMPLOYMENT.** College Work/Study Program. Institutional employment. 2% of full-time undergraduates work on campus during school year. Students may expect to earn an average of $2,500 during school year. Off-campus part-time employment opportunities rated "good."

**COMPUTER FACILITIES.** 140 IBM/IBM-compatible and Macintosh/Apple microcomputers; 25 are networked. Students may access Digital, IBM, Prime minicomputer/mainframe systems, BITNET, Internet. Client/LAN operating systems include Apple/Macintosh. Computer languages and software packages include Ada, LISP, BASIC, C, COBOL, FORTRAN, Pascal, RPG, SimScript; 30 in all. Some computers are available only to computer science majors.
**Fees:** None.
**Hours:** 24 hours.

**GRADUATE CAREER DATA.** Companies and businesses that hire graduates: Big Six accounting firms, CIA, FBI, other federal agencies, state agencies.

**PROMINENT ALUMNI/AE.** Colette LaRose, Alaska consulate in France; Roy Hundorf, president, Cook Inlet Regional Corp.; Daniel O'Tierney, commissioner, Alaska Public Utilities.

# University of Alaska Fairbanks

Fairbanks, AK 99775-7480 907 474-7521

**1994-95 Costs.** Tuition: $1,742 (state residents), $5,226 (out-of-state). Room: $1,800. Board: $1,890. Fees, books, misc. academic expenses (school's estimate): $960.
**Enrollment.** Undergraduates: 1,881 men, 1,768 women (full-time). Freshman class: 1,852 applicants, 1,427 accepted, 928 enrolled. Graduate enrollment: 439 men, 317 women.
**Test score averages/ranges.** Average SAT scores: 463 verbal, 490 math. Range of SAT scores of middle 50%: 380-550 verbal, 410-590 math. Average ACT scores: 21 English, 20 math. Range of ACT scores of middle 50%: 17-25 English, 16-24 math.
**Faculty.** 524 full-time; 193 part-time. 65% of faculty holds doctoral degree. Student/faculty ratio: 14 to 1.
**Selectivity rating.** Less competitive.

**PROFILE.** The University of Alaska at Fairbanks, founded in 1917, is a public institution. Its three colleges and six schools offer more than 70 fields of study and many technical and vocational programs. The 2,250-acre main campus is located four miles from downtown Fairbanks, in central Alaska.

**Accreditation:** NASC. Professionally accredited by the Accreditation Board for Engineering and Technology, the Accrediting Council on Education in Journalism and Mass Communication, the American Assembly of Collegiate Schools of Business, the Computing Sciences Accreditation Board, the Council on Social Work Education, the National Association of Schools of Music, the National Council for Accreditation of Teacher Education.
**Religious orientation:** University of Alaska at Fairbanks is nonsectarian; no religious requirements.
**Library:** Collections totaling over 750,000 volumes, 4,500 periodical subscriptions, and 850,000 microform items.
**Special facilities/museums:** Museum of natural/cultural history of Alaska and the North, Cray supercomputer, extensive telecommunication network, geophysical institute, NASA earth station, Poker Flat rocket range, electron microscope, microprobe.
**Athletic facilities:** Gymnasium, swimming pool, cross-country ski trails, bowling lanes, racquetball courts, ice arena, rifle/pistol ranges, free weight and Universal rooms, saunas, soccer and softball fields, sledding hill, fitness trail.
**STUDENT BODY. Undergraduate profile:** 89% are state residents; 20% are transfers. 2% Asian-American, 2% Black, 2% Hispanic, 17% Native American, 70% White, 7% Other. Average age of undergraduates is 24.
**Freshman profile:** 1% of freshmen who took SAT scored 700 or over on verbal, 4% scored 700 or over on math; 14% scored 600 or over on verbal, 23% scored 600 or over on math; 42% scored 500 or over on verbal, 51% scored 500 or over on math; 73% scored 400 or over on verbal, 78% scored 400 or over on math; 93% scored 300 or over on verbal, 96% scored 300 or over on math. 5% of freshmen who took ACT scored 30 or over on English, 4% scored 30 or over on math, 6% scored 30 or over on composite; 35% scored 24 or over on English, 31% scored 24 or over on math, 37% scored 24 or over on composite; 71% scored 18 or over on English, 66% scored 18 or over on math, 75% scored 18 or over on composite; 96% scored 12 or over on English, 99% scored 12 or over on math, 99% scored 12 or over on composite; 100% scored 6 or over on English, 100% scored 6 or over on math, 100% scored 6 or over on composite. 54% of accepted applicants took SAT; 59% took ACT. 90% of freshmen come from public schools.
**Undergraduate achievement:** 61% of fall 1992 freshmen returned for fall 1993 term.
**Foreign students:** 86 students are from out of the country. Countries represented include Canada, China, Germany, India, Japan, and Russia; 47 in all.
**PROGRAMS OF STUDY. Degrees:** B.A., B.Bus.Admin., B.Ed., B.F.A., B.Mus., B.S., B.Tech.
**Majors:** Accounting, Alaska Native Studies, Anthropology, Applied Physics, Art, Biological Sciences, Biology, Broadcasting, Business Administration, Chemistry, Civil Engineering, Computer Science, Earth Science, Economics, Electrical Engineering, Elementary Education, English, Eskimo, Exercise Science, Fisheries, Foreign Languages, General Science, Geography, Geological Engineering, Geology, History, Human Services, Interdisciplinary Studies, Journalism, Justice, Linguistics, Mathematics, Mechanical Engineering, Mining Engineering, Music, Natural Resources Management, Northern Studies, Petroleum Engineering, Philosophy, Physical Education, Physics, Political Science, Psychology, Rural Development, Russian Studies, Social Work, Sociology, Speech Communication, Statistics, Technology, Theatre.
**Distribution of degrees:** The majors with the highest enrollment are education, business administration, and biological sciences; Alaska native studies and human services have the lowest.
**Requirements:** General education requirement.
**Academic regulations:** Minimum 2.0 GPA must be maintained.
**Special:** Minors offered in Alaska native languages, Asian studies, athletic coaching, computer information systems, film studies, food science/nutrition, forestry, law/society, medical technology, ROTC, and women's studies. Associate's degrees offered. Self-designed majors. Double majors. Dual degrees. Independent study. Accelerated study. Pass/fail grading option. Graduate school at which undergraduates may take graduate-level courses. Preprofessional programs in law, medicine, veterinary science, dentistry, library science, nursing, and physical therapy. 2-2 medical technology program with U of Washington. Combined forestry program with Northern Arizona U, combined food science and technology program with Oregon State U, combined medical technician program with U of Washington. Member of National Student Exchange (NSE) and Western Undergraduate Exchange of Wiche. Teacher certification in early childhood, elementary, and secondary education. Certification in specific subject areas. Member of Northwest Interinstitutional Council on Study Abroad. Exchange programs abroad in Canada (McGill U), Denmark (U of Copenhagen), Japan (Hokkaido U, Nagoya Gakuin U), Mexico (U of Guadalajara), Norway (Agricultural U of Norway), Sweden (Lulea U), Venezuela (U of the Andes), and Russia (Yakutsk State U and Magadan U). Study abroad also in England, France, Germany, and Italy. ROTC.
**Honors:** Honors program. Honor societies.
**Academic Assistance:** Remedial reading, writing, math, and study skills. Nonremedial tutoring.
**STUDENT LIFE. Housing:** Students may live on or off campus. Coed, women's, and men's dorms. School-owned/operated apartments. On-campus married-student housing. 20% of students live in college housing.
**Social atmosphere:** According to the editor of the student newspaper, "The campus is very diverse. Included in social and cultural events are Eskimo-Indian native events, Chinese clubs and organizations, black student groups, Bahai Peace Club of Jewish faith, and increasing Russian cultural events." Popular on-campus gathering spots are the Wood Center Pub, Itza Pizza, and the Howling Dog Saloon. Influential groups on campus include Associated Students of University of Alaska Fairbanks and several Christian groups. The Christmas Ball, Starvation Gulch, Meltdown, World Eskimo-Indian Olympics, hockey and basketball games are among the year's favorite events.
**Services and counseling/handicapped student services:** Health service. Women's center. Day care. Counseling services for minority, military, veteran, and older students. Birth control, personal, and psychological counseling. Career and academic guidance services. Religious counseling. Physically disabled student services. Learning disabled services. Notetaking services. Tape recorders. Tutors. Reader services for the blind.
**Campus organizations:** Undergraduate student government. Student newspaper (Sun Star, published once/week). Literary magazine. Radio and TV stations. Band, choral groups, alpine club, contradancing, Melting Pot, Young Democrats, Young Republicans, 68 organizations in all. One fraternity, no chapter house; one sorority, no chapter house.
**Religious organizations:** Bahai Peace Club, Baptist Student Union, Campus Bible Ministries, Christian Fellowship, Jewish Study Group, Latter-Day Saints Student Association, St. Mark's Catholic University Parish, United Campus Ministry.
**Minority/foreign student organizations:** Black Awareness Student Union, Festival of Native Arts, Native Student Organization, Rural Student Services. Chinese Student and Scholar Association, Northern Star Chinese Association.
**ATHLETICS. Physical education requirements:** None.
**Intercollegiate competition:** 2% of students participate. Basketball (M,W), cross-country (M,W), ice hockey (M), Nordic skiing (M,W), riflery (M,W), volleyball (W). Member of CCHA for ice hockey, NCAA Division I for ice hockey, NCAA Division II, Pacific West Conference.
**Intramural and club sports:** 30% of students participate. Intramural arm wrestling, badminton, baseball, basketball, bowling, broomball, diving, flag football, free throw contest, homerun contest, ice hockey, indoor soccer, marathon, Nordic skiing, power lifting, racquetball, rifle, running, slow-pitch softball, snow shoe races, soccer, swimming, tug-of-war, volleyball, water polo, wrestling. Men's club cheerleading, fencing. Women's club cheerleading, fencing.
**ADMISSIONS. Academic basis for candidate selection** (in order of priority): Secondary school record, standardized test scores.
**Requirements:** Graduation from secondary school is required; GED is accepted. 16 units and the following program of study are required: 4 units of English, 3 units of math, 3 units of science including 1 unit of lab, 3 units of social studies, 3 units of academic electives. Minimum 2.0 cumulative GPA required; 2.5 GPA in 16 credit core. For engineering program applicants, 3.5 years of math is required; for math, statistics, and computer science program applicants, 4 years of math is required. SAT or ACT is required. Campus visit recommended. Off-campus interviews available with an admissions representative.
**Procedure:** Take SAT or ACT by August 1 of 12th year. Application deadline is August 1. Notification of admission on rolling basis. No set date by which applicants must accept offer. $250 refundable room deposit. Freshmen accepted for terms other than fall.
**Special programs:** Admission may be deferred one year. Credit and/or placement may be granted through CEEB Advanced Placement exams for scores of 3 or higher. Credit may be granted through CLEP general and subject exams, DANTES, challenge exams, and military and life experience. Concurrent enrollment program.
**Transfer students:** Transfer students accepted for terms other than fall. In fall 1993, 20% of all new students were transfers into all classes. 854 transfer applications were received, 673 were accepted. Application deadline is August 1 for fall; December 1 for spring. Minimum 2.0 GPA required. Lowest course grade accepted is "C." At least 30 semester hours must be completed at the university to receive degree.
**Admissions contact:** James T. Mansfield, M.A., Associate Director of Admissions and Records. 907 474-7521.
**FINANCIAL AID. Available aid:** Pell grants, SEOG, state grants, school scholarships and grants, private scholarships and grants, ROTC scholarships, academic merit scholarships, and athletic scholarships. PLUS, Stafford Loans (GSL), state loans, school loans, and SLS. Deferred payment plan and guaranteed tuition.
**Financial aid statistics:** 20% of aid is not need-based. In 1993-94, 90% of all undergraduate applicants received aid; 90% of freshman applicants.
**Supporting data/closing dates:** FAFSA: Priority filing date is May 15; accepted on rolling basis. FAF/FFS: Accepted on rolling basis. State aid form: Priority filing date is May 15; accepted on rolling basis. Notification of awards on rolling basis.
**Financial aid contact:** Donald Scheaffer, M.P.A., Director of Financial Aid. 907 474-7256.
**STUDENT EMPLOYMENT.** College Work/Study Program. Institutional employment. 20% of full-time undergraduates work on campus during school year. Freshmen are discouraged from working during their first term. Off-campus part-time employment opportunities rated "fair."
**COMPUTER FACILITIES.** 150 IBM/IBM-compatible and Macintosh/Apple microcomputers; 130 are networked. Students may access Cray, Digital, Hewlett-Packard, IBM, SUN, UNISYS minicomputer/mainframe systems, BITNET, Internet. Residence halls may be equipped with networked terminals. Client/LAN operating systems include Apple/Macintosh, DOS, UNIX/XENIX/AIX, X-windows, DEC, LocalTalk/AppleTalk. Computer languages and software packages include Ada, APL, Assembler, BASIC, BMDP, COBOL, FORTRAN, LINDO, MINITAB, PILOT, Pascal, SAS, SPSS; 50 in all. Computer facilities are available to all students.
**Fees:** None.

**Hours:** 24 hours in some locations.
**GRADUATE CAREER DATA.** Highest graduate school enrollments: U of Alaska at Fairbanks. Companies and businesses that hire graduates: State of Alaska Peace Corps, Big Six accounting firms, British Petroleum, K-Mart, school districts.

**PROMINENT ALUMNI/AE.** Grace Schaeble, attorney general of Alaska; Joseph Usibelli, Alaskan businessman; Sun-Ichi Akasofu, physicist, director of Geophysical Institute; J. Hammond, former governor of Alaska; Joseph Flakney, conservationist.

# University of Alaska Southeast, Juneau Campus

**Juneau, AK 99801** **907 465-6462**

**1993-94 Costs.** Tuition: $1,664 (state residents), $2496 (through Western Undergraduate Exchange program), $4,992 (out-of-state). Room: $1,870-$2,200. No meal plan. Fees, books, misc. academic expenses (school's estimate): $584.
**Enrollment.** Undergraduates: 232 men, 288 women (full-time). Freshman class: 142 applicants, 135 accepted, 114 enrolled. Graduate enrollment: 22 men, 36 women.
**Test score averages/ranges.** N/A.
**Faculty.** 105 full-time; 95 part-time. 35% of faculty holds doctoral degree. Student/faculty ratio: 10 to 1.
**Selectivity rating.** N/A.

**PROFILE.** University of Alaska Southeast, founded in 1972, is a public institution. Programs are offered through the Schools of Business and Public Administration; Education, Liberal Arts, and Science; and Regional Vocational/Technical Education and through its Offices of Continuing Education and Outreach Education. Its Ketchikan and Sitka Campuses offer technical training and associate's degrees. The campus is located on Auke Lake in Juneau.

**Accreditation:** NASC.
**Religious orientation:** University of Alaska Southeast, Juneau Campus is nonsectarian; no religious requirements.
**Library:** Collections totaling over 100,000 volumes, and 1,500 periodical subscriptions.
**STUDENT BODY. Undergraduate profile:** 7% Asian-American, 2% Black, 2% Hispanic, 17% Native American, 70% White, 2% Other. Average age of undergraduates is 24.
**Freshman profile:** 94% of freshmen come from public schools.
**Foreign students:** 10 students are from out of the country. Countries represented include Canada, Ethiopia, and Mexico; eight in all.
**PROGRAMS OF STUDY. Degrees:** B.A., B.Bus.Admin., B.Ed., B.Lib.Arts, B.S.
**Majors:** Accounting, Biology, Business Administration, Computer Information Systems, Early Childhood Education, Elementary Education, Government, Liberal Arts, Management, Marine Biology, Music, Public Administration/Law, Secondary Education.
**Distribution of degrees:** The majors with the highest enrollment are education, business administration, and liberal arts.
**Requirements:** General education requirement.
**Special:** Associate's degrees offered. Self-designed majors. Double majors. Independent study. Pass/fail grading option. Internships. Cooperative education programs. Graduate school at which undergraduates may take graduate-level courses. Preprofessional programs in law, medicine, and veterinary science. Teacher certification in early childhood, elementary, and secondary education. Certification in specific subject areas. Exchange programs abroad in Russia (U of Moscow, U of the Far East).
**Honors:** Honors program.
**Academic Assistance:** Remedial reading, writing, math, and study skills. Nonremedial tutoring.
**ADMISSIONS. Academic basis for candidate selection** (in order of priority): Secondary school record, essay, standardized test scores.
**Requirements:** Graduation from secondary school is required; GED is accepted. 11 units and the following program of study are recommended: 4 units of English, 2 units of math, 2 units of science, 3 units of social studies. Minimum 2.0 GPA required. Essay required of B.Ed. and B.Lib.Arts program applicants. SAT or ACT is recommended. No off-campus interviews.
**Procedure:** Take SAT or ACT by June of 12th year. Notification of admission on rolling basis. Reply is required by September 1. $100 refundable room deposit. Freshmen accepted for terms other than fall.
**Special programs:** Admission may be deferred one year. Credit and/or placement may be granted through CEEB Advanced Placement exams for scores of 3 or higher. Credit and/or placement may be granted through CLEP general and subject exams. Credit may be granted through challenge exams. Credit and placement may be granted through DANTES exams and military experience. Early decision program. In fall 1991, 100 applied for early decision and 97 were accepted. Deadline for applying for early decision is May 1. Early entrance/early admission program. Concurrent enrollment program.
**Transfer students:** Transfer students accepted for terms other than fall. Application deadline is rolling for fall; rolling for spring. Minimum 2.0 GPA required. Lowest course grade accepted is "C." At least 30 semester hours must be completed at the university to receive degree.
**Admissions contact:** Greg Wagner, M.S., Coordinator of Admissions and Placement. 907 465-6462.
**FINANCIAL AID. Available aid:** Pell grants, SEOG, state scholarships and grants, school scholarships and grants, private scholarships and grants, and academic merit scholarships. Perkins Loans (NDSL), Stafford Loans (GSL), state loans, school loans, and SLS. Tuition Management Systems and deferred payment plan. Advance tuition payment plan.
**Supporting data/closing dates:** FAFSA/FAF/FFS: Accepted on rolling basis. School's own aid application: Deadline is March 30. Notification of awards begins May 1.
**Financial aid contact:** Barbara Carlson-Burnett, M.Ed., Director of Financial Aid. 907 465-6255.

# Arizona

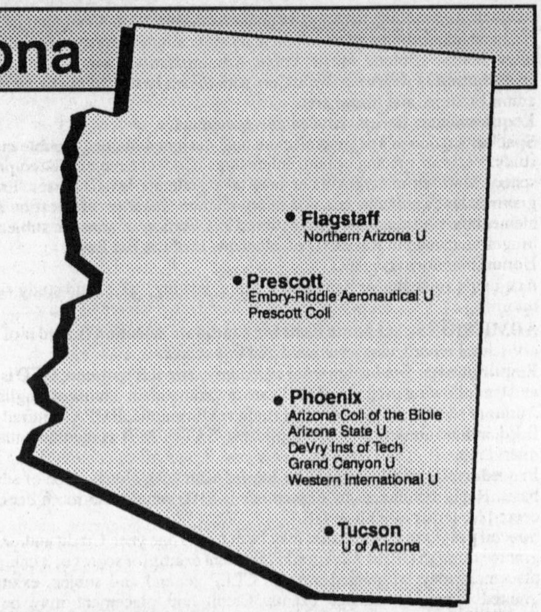


## Arizona College of the Bible

**Phoenix, AZ 85021** **602 995-2670**

**1993-94 Costs.** Tuition: $4,570. Room: $1,450. Fees, books, misc. academic expenses (school's estimate): $400.
**Enrollment.** Undergraduates: 50 men, 22 women (full-time). Freshman class: 69 applicants, 52 accepted, 42 enrolled.
**Test score averages/ranges.** N/A.
**Faculty.** 6 full-time; 9 part-time. 50% of faculty holds doctoral degree. Student/faculty ratio: 8 to 1.
**Selectivity rating.** Less competitive.

**PROFILE.** Arizona College of the Bible, founded in 1971, is a college with religious orientation. Its seven-acre campus is located near downtown Phoenix.

**Accreditation:** AABC.
**Religious orientation:** Arizona College of the Bible is a nondenominational Christian school; no religious requirements.
**Library:** Collections totaling over 30,597 volumes, 181 periodical subscriptions, and 2,000 microform items.
**Athletic facilities:** Gymnasium.
**STUDENT BODY. Undergraduate profile:** 81% are state residents; 12% are transfers. 2% Asian-American, 12% Black, 12% Hispanic, 1% Native American, 72% White, 1% Other. Average age of undergraduates is 24.
**Freshman profile:** 20% of freshmen who took SAT scored 600 or over on math; 20% scored 500 or over on verbal, 40% scored 500 or over on math; 40% scored 400 or over on verbal; 100% scored 300 or over on verbal, 100% scored 300 or over on math. 33% of freshmen who took ACT scored 18 or over on composite; 83% scored 12 or over on composite; 100% scored 6 or over on composite. Majority of accepted applicants took ACT.
**Undergraduate achievement:** 37% of fall 1991 freshmen returned for fall 1992 term. 40% of entering class graduated. 4% of students who completed a degree program went on to graduate study within one year.
**PROGRAMS OF STUDY. Degrees:** B.A., B.Church Mus.
**Majors:** Biblical Studies, Biblical Studies/Church Music, Biblical Studies/Elementary Education, Christian Education, Cross-Cultural Studies, Pastoral Ministry, Youth Ministry.
**Distribution of degrees:** The majors with the highest enrollment are biblical studies and biblical studies/elementary education.
**Requirements:** General education requirement.
**Academic regulations:** Minimum 2.0 GPA must be maintained.
**Special:** Associate's degrees offered. Self-designed majors. Double majors. Preprofessional programs in theology. Teacher certification in elementary education.
**ADMISSIONS. Academic basis for candidate selection** (in order of priority): Essay, secondary school record, school's recommendation, standardized test scores, class rank.
**Nonacademic basis for candidate selection:** Character and personality are emphasized. Extracurricular participation, particular talent or ability, geographical distribution, and alumni/ae relationship are considered.
**Requirements:** Graduation from secondary school is required; GED is accepted. No specific distribution of secondary school units required. Minimum 2.0 GPA recommended. Audition required of music program applicants. SAT or ACT is required. Campus visit and interview recommended. No off-campus interviews.
**Procedure:** Suggest filing application by July 15; no deadline. Notification of admission on rolling basis. Reply is required by registration day. $50 refundable room deposit. Freshmen accepted for terms other than fall.
**Special programs:** Admission may be deferred one year. Credit may be granted through CLEP general and subject exams. Placement may be granted through challenge exams. Credit and placement may be granted through military experience. Concurrent enrollment program.
**Transfer students:** Transfer students accepted for terms other than fall. In fall 1992, 12% of all new students were transfers into all classes. 26 transfer applications were received, 26 were accepted. Application deadline is day of registration for fall; day of registration for spring. Minimum 2.0 GPA required. Lowest course grade accepted is "C." Maximum number of transferable credits is 100 semester hours. At least 24 semester hours must be completed at the college to receive degree.
**Admissions contact:** Frances Scoggin, Director of Admissions. 602 995-2670, extension 46.
**FINANCIAL AID. Available aid:** Pell grants, SEOG, state grants, school scholarships, and academic merit scholarships. PLUS, Stafford Loans (GSL), school loans, and SLS. Deferred payment plan and family tuition reduction.
**Financial aid statistics:** 5% of aid is not need-based. In 1992-93, 90% of all undergraduate applicants received aid; 34% of freshman applicants.
**Supporting data/closing dates:** FAFSA/FFS: Accepted on rolling basis. Income tax forms: Accepted on rolling basis. Notification of awards on rolling basis.
**Financial aid contact:** Ruth Wilcoxson, Director of Financial Aid. 602 995-2670, extension 48.

## Arizona State University–Main Campus

**Tempe, AZ 85287-1203** **602 965-9011**

**1994-95 Costs.** Tuition: $1,828 (state residents), $7,434 (out-of-state). Room: $3,360. Board: $1,490. Fees, books, misc. academic expenses (school's estimate): $766.
**Enrollment.** Undergraduates: 11,664 men, 10,929 women (full-time). Freshman class: 12,809 applicants, 10,308 accepted, 3,761 enrolled. Graduate enrollment: 5,450 men, 5,622 women.
**Test score averages/ranges.** Average SAT scores: 442 verbal, 520 math. Range of SAT scores of middle 50%: 390-510 verbal, 450-590 math. Average ACT scores: 22 English, 22 math, 23 composite. Range of ACT scores of middle 50%: 19-25 English, 19-25 math.
**Faculty.** 1,774 full-time; 48 part-time. 93% of faculty holds highest degree in specific field. Student/faculty ratio: 20 to 1.
**Selectivity rating.** Less competitive.

**PROFILE.** Arizona State University is a public, comprehensive university. Founded as a Normal school in 1885, it gained university status in 1958. Its 700-acre campus is near downtown Tempe, close to the center of metropolitan Phoenix.

**Accreditation:** NCACS. Professionally accredited by the Accreditation Board for Engineering and Technology, the Accrediting Council on Education in Journalism and Mass Communication, the American Assembly of Collegiate Schools of Business, the American Council for Construction Education, the American Psychological Association, the American Speech-Language-Hearing Association, the Council on Social Work Education, the Foundation for Interior Design Education Research, the National Architecture Accrediting Board, the National Association of Schools of Music, the National Association of Schools of Public Affairs and Administration, the National Council for Accreditation of Teacher Education, the National League for Nursing.
**Religious orientation:** Arizona State University is nonsectarian; no religious requirements.
**Library:** Collections totaling over 2,698,607 volumes, 29,084 periodical subscriptions, and 4,684,743 microform items.
**Special facilities/museums:** Art, anthropology, geology, history, and sports museums, early childhood development lab, herbarium, wind tunnel, robotics lab, semiconductor clean room, high-resolution electron microscope facility, gamma cell irradiation chamber, solar research facilities, nuclear reactor.
**Athletic facilities:** Stadium, badminton, basketball, racquetball, squash, tennis, and volleyball courts, baseball, football, intramural, practice, soccer, and softball fields, aquatic center, golf course, exercise, martial arts, and weight rooms, gymnasiums, wellness center.
**STUDENT BODY. Undergraduate profile:** 72% are state residents; 51% are transfers. 4% Asian-American, 3% Black, 9% Hispanic, 2% Native American, 77% White, 5% Other. Average age of undergraduates is 23.
**Freshman profile:** 1% of freshmen who took SAT scored 700 or over on verbal, 5% scored 700 or over on math; 6% scored 600 or over on verbal, 23% scored 600 or over on math; 31% scored 500 or over on verbal, 62% scored 500 or over on math; 74% scored 400 or over on verbal, 89% scored 400 or over on math; 100% scored 300 or over on verbal, 100% scored 300 or over on math. 4% of freshmen who took ACT scored 30 or over on English, 7% scored 30 or over on math, 5% scored 30 or over on composite; 37% scored 24 or over on English, 39% scored 24 or over on math, 41% scored 24 or over on composite; 85% scored 18 or over on English, 86% scored 18 or over on math, 91% scored 18 or over on composite; 100% scored 12 or over on English, 100% scored 12 or over on math, 100% scored 12 or over on composite. 69% of accepted applicants took SAT; 51% took ACT.
**Undergraduate achievement:** 70% of fall 1992 freshmen returned for fall 1993 term. 15% of entering class graduated.
**Foreign students:** 289 students are from out of the country. Countries represented include Canada, China, India, Indonesia, Japan, and Pakistan; 32 in all.
**PROGRAMS OF STUDY. Degrees:** B.A., B.F.A., B.Mus., B.S., B.Soc.Work.
**Majors:** Accountancy, Aeronautical Engineering Technology, Aeronautical Management Technology, Aerospace Engineering, Agribusiness, Anthropology, Architectural Studies, Art, Asian Languages, Bioengineering, Biology, Botany, Broadcasting, Chemical Engineering, Chemistry, Choral/General Music, Civil Engineering, Clinical Laboratory Sciences, Communication, Computer Information Systems, Computer Science, Computer Systems Engineering, Construction, Dance, Design Science, Economics, Electrical Engineering, Electronics Engineering Technology, Elementary Education, Engineering Interdisciplinary Studies, Engineering Special Programs, English, Environmental Resources in Agriculture, Exercise Science/Physical Education, Family Resources/Human Development, Finance, French, Geography, Geology, German, History, Housing/Urban

Development, Humanities, Industrial Design, Industrial Engineering, Industrial Technology, Instrumental Music, Interdisciplinary Studies, Interior Design, Italian, Journalism, Justice Studies, Landscape Architecture, Management, Manufacturing Engineering Technology, Marketing, Materials Science/Engineering, Mathematics, Mechanical Engineering, Microbiology, Music, Music Performance, Music Theory/Composition, Music Therapy, Nursing, Philosophy, Physics, Political Science, Psychology, Purchasing/Logistics Management, Real Estate, Recreation, Religious Studies, Russian, Secondary Education, Selected Studies in Education, Social Work, Sociology, Spanish, Special Education, Speech/Hearing Sciences, Theatre, Urban Planning, Wildlife Conservation Biology, Women's Studies, Zoology.
**Distribution of degrees:** The majors with the highest enrollment are management, marketing, and finance.
**Requirements:** General education requirement.
**Academic regulations:** Freshmen must maintain minimum 1.6 GPA; sophomores, 1.75 GPA; juniors, 2.0 GPA; seniors, 2.0 GPA.
**Special:** Minors offered in most majors. Interdisciplinary programs include adult development/aging; city/regional and energy planning; and environmental, film, Islamic, linguistic, medieval/Renaissance, and women's studies. Optional one-semester Campus Match program for freshmen. Double majors. Dual degrees. Independent study. Pass/fail grading option. Internships. Graduate school at which undergraduates may take graduate-level courses. Preprofessional programs in law, medicine, and veterinary science. 2-2 communication, justice, and M.P.A. programs. 3-2 engineering and construction programs. Washington Semester. Exchange programs with Northern Arizona U and U of Arizona. Teacher certification in early childhood, elementary, secondary, special education, and bilingual/bicultural education. Exchange programs abroad in Bolivia, France, Germany, Japan, Mexico, the Netherlands, Norway, the United Kingdom, and the former Yugoslav Republic. Study abroad also in France, Israel, Italy, Portugal, Spain, and Wales. ROTC and AFROTC.
**Honors:** Phi Beta Kappa. Honors program. Honor societies.
**Academic Assistance:** Remedial reading, writing, math, and study skills. Nonremedial tutoring.

**STUDENT LIFE. Housing:** Students may live on or off campus. Coed, women's, and men's dorms. Sorority and fraternity housing. School-owned/operated apartments. 10% of students live in college housing.
**Social atmosphere:** The student newspaper reports, "ASU offers many diverse and interesting cultural programs and university-wide social events. Football is definitely the Number One social/athletic event at ASU. ASASU concerts also have a big draw." Favorite student gathering spots include the Dash Inn, the Memorial Union, Flakey Jake's, the Vine Tavern, After the Gold Rush, the Devilhouse, the Warehouse, and Bandersnatch Pub.
**Services and counseling/handicapped student services:** Placement services. Health service. Women's center. Day care. Counseling services for minority, military, veteran, and older students. Birth control, personal, and psychological counseling. Career and academic guidance services. Religious counseling. Physically disabled student services. Learning disabled program/services. Notetaking services. Tape recorders. Tutors. Reader services for the blind.
**Campus organizations:** Undergraduate student government. Student newspaper (State Press, published five days/week). Literary magazine. Yearbook. Radio and TV stations. Chorus, concert choir, orchestra, band, ensembles, academic, political, service, and special-interest groups, 330 organizations in all. 26 fraternities, no chapter houses; 15 sororities, 14 chapter houses. 12% of men join a fraternity. 10% of women join a sorority.
**Religious organizations:** Chi Alpha College Fellowship, Campus Ambassadors, Hillel, Jewish Student Center, Campus Crusade for Christ, Fellowship of Christian Athletes, numerous other religious groups.
**Minority/foreign student organizations:** MEChA, Native American Student Association, Black Business Student Association, Asian Students Association, other minority student groups. International Student Council, African, Asian, Chinese, Indian, and other foreign student groups.

**ATHLETICS. Physical education requirements:** None.
**Intercollegiate competition:** 3% of students participate. Baseball (M), basketball (M,W), cheerleading (M,W), cross-country (M,W), diving (M,W), football (M), golf (M,W), gymnastics (W), softball (W), swimming (M,W), tennis (M,W), track and field (indoor) (M,W), track and field (outdoor) (M,W), volleyball (W), wrestling (M). Member of NCAA Division I, Pacific 10 Conference.
**Intramural and club sports:** 50% of students participate. Intramural badminton, basketball, billiards, bowling, flag football, free throw, golf, racquetball, running, sand volleyball, soccer, softball, swimming, tennis, track and field, volleyball, weight lifting, wrestling. Men's club Alpine skiing, canoe, fencing, gymnastics, ice hockey, lacrosse, martial arts, racquetball, rifle, rodeo, roller blading, rugby, soccer, squash, table tennis, tennis, volleyball, water polo, weight lifting. Women's club Alpine skiing, canoe, fencing, lacrosse, martial arts, racquetball, rifle, rodeo, roller blading, rugby, soccer, squash, table tennis, tennis, volleyball, weight lifting.

**ADMISSIONS. Academic basis for candidate selection** (in order of priority): Secondary school record, class rank, standardized test scores, school's recommendation.
**Nonacademic basis for candidate selection:** Particular talent or ability is considered.
**Requirements:** Graduation from secondary school is required; GED is accepted. 11 units and the following program of study are required: 4 units of English, 3 units of math, 2 units of lab science, 1 unit of social studies, 1 unit of history. Minimum combined SAT score of 930 (composite ACT score of 22), rank in top quarter of secondary school class, or minimum 3.0 GPA recommended of in-state applicants; minimum combined SAT score of 1010 (composite ACT score of 24), rank in top quarter of secondary school class, or minimum 3.0 GPA recommended of out-of state applicants. Audition required of music program applicants. Conditional admission possible for applicants not meeting standard requirements. SAT or ACT is required. Campus visit recommended. No off-campus interviews.
**Procedure:** Take SAT or ACT by April of 12th year. Suggest filing application by April 15. Application deadline is August 10. Notification of admission on rolling basis. Reply is required by beginning of term. $150 room deposit; $100 of which is refundable. Freshmen accepted for terms other than fall.
**Special programs:** Credit and/or placement may be granted through CEEB Advanced Placement exams for scores of 3 or higher. Credit and/or placement may be granted through CLEP general and subject exams. Credit and placement may be granted through challenge exams. Early entrance/early admission program. Concurrent enrollment program.
**Transfer students:** Transfer students accepted for terms other than fall. In fall 1993, 51% of all new students were transfers into all classes. 10,085 transfer applications were received, 7,584 were accepted. Application deadline is August 10 for fall; January 14 for spring. Minimum 2.0 GPA required of in-state applicants; 2.5 for out-of-state applicants. Lowest course grade accepted is "C." Maximum number of transferable credits is 64 semester hours from a two-year school and 96 semester hours from a four-year school. At least 30 semester hours must be completed at the university to receive degree.
**Admissions contact:** Susan R. Dolbert, M.A., Director of Admissions. 602 965-2604.

**FINANCIAL AID. Available aid:** Pell grants, SEOG, state scholarships, school scholarships and grants, private scholarships and grants, ROTC scholarships, academic merit scholarships, and athletic scholarships. Perkins Loans (NDSL), PLUS, Stafford Loans (GSL), school loans, private loans, and SLS. Tuition Plan Inc. and AMS.
**Financial aid statistics:** 14% of aid is not need-based. In 1992-93, 52% of all undergraduate applicants received aid; 40% of freshman applicants. Average amounts of aid awarded freshmen: Scholarships and grants, $1,960; loans, $2,400.
**Supporting data/closing dates:** FAFSA/FAF/FFS: Priority filing date is March 1; accepted on rolling basis. Income tax forms: Priority filing date is April 1; accepted on rolling basis. Notification of awards begins April 1.
**Financial aid contact:** Kate Dosil, Director of Financial Aid. 602 965-4045.

**STUDENT EMPLOYMENT.** College Work/Study Program. Institutional employment. 17% of full-time undergraduates work on campus during school year. Students may expect to earn an average of $1,900 during school year. Off-campus part-time employment opportunities rated "excellent."

**COMPUTER FACILITIES.** 750 IBM/IBM-compatible, Macintosh/Apple, and RISC-/UNIX-based microcomputers; all are networked. Students may access minicomputer/mainframe systems, BITNET, Internet. Residence halls may be equipped with stand-alone microcomputers, networked microcomputers. Client/LAN operating systems include Apple/Macintosh, DOS, Banyan, LocalTalk/AppleTalk. 150 major computer languages and software packages available. Computer facilities are available to all students.
**Fees:** None.
**Hours:** 24 hours for some.

**PROMINENT ALUMNI/AE.** Steve Allen, entertainer; Reggie Jackson, professional baseball player; Wayne Doran, real estate developer.

## DeVry Institute of Technology

**Phoenix, AZ 85021** — **602 870-9222**

**1994-95 Costs.** Tuition: $5,962. Housing: None. Fees, books, misc. academic expenses (school's estimate): $580.
**Enrollment.** Undergraduates: 1,767 men, 407 women (full-time). Freshman class: 1,442 applicants, 1,339 accepted, 634 enrolled.
**Test score averages/ranges.** N/A.
**Faculty.** 60 full-time; 28 part-time. Student/faculty ratio: 33 to 1.
**Selectivity rating.** N/A.

**PROFILE.** DeVry/Phoenix, founded in 1967, is a private institution specializing in electronics technology and computer information systems. It is a member of a network of technical institutes with nine campuses in the U.S. and two in Canada. Its 18-acre campus is located in Phoenix.

**Accreditation:** NCACS. Professionally accredited by the Accreditation Board for Engineering and Technology.
**Religious orientation:** DeVry Institute of Technology is nonsectarian; no religious requirements.
**Library:** Collections totaling over 12,654 volumes, 230 periodical subscriptions and 141 microform items.
**Athletic facilities:** YMCA, game rooms, La Mancha Health and Racquet Club.

**STUDENT BODY. Undergraduate profile:** 41% are state residents; 60% are transfers. 6% Asian-American, 5% Black, 11% Hispanic, 3% Native American, 71% White, 4% Other. Average age of undergraduates is 24.
**Freshman profile:** 5% of accepted applicants took SAT; 11% took ACT.
**Undergraduate achievement:** 46% of fall 1992 freshmen returned for fall 1993 term. 32% of entering class graduated.
**Foreign students:** 66 students are from out of the country. Countries represented include Canada, Indonesia, Panama, Saudi Arabia, Taiwan, and Thailand.

**PROGRAMS OF STUDY. Degrees:** B.S.
**Majors:** Accounting, Business Operations, Computer Information Systems, Electronics Engineering Technology.
**Distribution of degrees:** The majors with the highest enrollment are electronics engineering technology, computer information systems, and business operations.
**Requirements:** General education requirement.
**Academic regulations:** Minimum 2.0 GPA must be maintained.
**Special:** Associate's degrees offered. Accelerated study. Cooperative education programs.
**Honors:** Honor societies.
**Academic Assistance:** Nonremedial tutoring.

**STUDENT LIFE. Housing:** Commuter campus; no student housing.
**Services and counseling/handicapped student services:** Placement services. Career and academic guidance services. Physically disabled student services. Notetaking services. Reader services for the blind.

**Campus organizations:** Undergraduate student government. Jazz band, photography and recording clubs, professional groups, Student Activity Association, billiards club, 15 organizations in all.
**Minority/foreign student organizations:** Society of Women Engineers, National Society of Black Engineers.

**ATHLETICS. Physical education requirements:** None.
**Intramural and club sports:** Intramural basketball, football, racquetball, soccer, softball, volleyball.

**ADMISSIONS. Academic basis for candidate selection** (in order of priority): Standardized test scores.
**Requirements:** Graduation from secondary school is required; GED is accepted. No specific distribution of secondary school units required. SAT or ACT is recommended. Applicants not submitting SAT or ACT must pass DeVry entrance exam. Admissions interview required. Off-campus interviews available with an admissions representative.
**Procedure:** Notification of admission on rolling basis. Reply is required by registration. $75 tuition deposit, refundable until beginning of classes. Freshmen accepted for terms other than fall.
**Special programs:** Admission may be deferred one year. Credit may be granted through CLEP subject exams, DANTES, and challenge exams.
**Transfer students:** Transfer students accepted for terms other than fall. In fall 1993, 60% of all new students were transfers into all classes. Application deadline is rolling for fall; rolling for spring. Minimum 2.0 GPA required. Lowest course grade accepted is "C." Maximum number of transferable semester hours is 65% of total required for degree. At least 35% of total semester hours must be completed at the institute to receive degree.
**Admissions contact:** Mr. Kim Galetti, Director of Admissions. 602 870-9201.

**FINANCIAL AID. Available aid:** Pell grants, SEOG, state scholarships and grants, school scholarships, and academic merit scholarships. Perkins Loans (NDSL), PLUS, Stafford Loans (GSL), state loans, and SLS. EDUCARD Plan.
**Financial aid statistics:** In 1993-94, 82% of all undergraduate applicants received aid; 80% of freshman applicants.
**Supporting data/closing dates:** FAFSA: Accepted on rolling basis. Notification of awards on rolling basis.
**Financial aid contact:** Scott Morrison, M.B.A., Director of Financial Aid.

**STUDENT EMPLOYMENT.** College Work/Study Program. Institutional employment. 4% of full-time undergraduates work on campus during school year. Students may expect to earn an average of $5,000 during school year. Freshmen are discouraged from working during their first term. Off-campus part-time employment opportunities rated "fair."

**COMPUTER FACILITIES.** 173 IBM/IBM-compatible microcomputers; all are networked. Students may access IBM minicomputer/mainframe systems. Client/LAN operating systems include DOS, UNIX/XENIX/AIX. Computer languages and software packages include BASIC, COBOL, FOCUS, Pascal, RPG; database, graphics, spreadsheet, word processing programs; 30 in all. Computer facilities are available to all students.
**Fees:** Computer fee is included in tuition/fees.

**GRADUATE CAREER DATA.** 93% of graduates choose careers in business and industry. Companies and businesses that hire graduates: ESA, Honeywell, Mayo Clinic, Micro-Rel, Motorola.

# Embry-Riddle Aeronautical University

**Prescott, AZ 86301** — **602 776-3728**

**1994-95 Costs.** Tuition: $7,370. Room & board: $3,755. Fees, books, misc. academic expenses (school's estimate): $400.
**Enrollment.** Undergraduates: 1,219 men, 231 women (full-time). Freshman class: 1,078 applicants, 922 accepted, 270 enrolled.
**Test score averages/ranges.** Average SAT scores: 471 verbal, 542 math. Average ACT scores: 23 English, 24 math, 24 composite.
**Faculty.** 63 full-time; 21 part-time. 48% of faculty holds highest degree in specific field. Student/faculty ratio: 17 to 1.
**Selectivity rating.** Competitive.

**PROFILE.** Embry-Riddle, founded in 1926, is a private university devoted exclusively to the field of aviation. Its 510-acre Arizona campus is located two miles from Prescott's airport and 90 miles from Phoenix.

**Accreditation:** SACS. Professionally accredited by the Accreditation Board for Engineering and Technology.
**Religious orientation:** Embry-Riddle Aeronautical University is nonsectarian; no religious requirements.
**Library:** Collections totaling over 26,170 volumes, 592 periodical subscriptions, and 135,523 microform items.
**Special facilities/museums:** Wind tunnels, aircraft structures and design labs, fully equipped aircraft, training simulators, aviation safety center.
**Athletic facilities:** Gymnasiums, racquetball, tennis, and volleyball courts, swimming pool, aerobics and weight rooms, athletic fields, fitness trails.

**STUDENT BODY. Undergraduate profile:** 7% are state residents; 30% are transfers. 6% Asian-American, 1% Black, 4% Hispanic, 1% Native American, 85% White, 3% Other. Average age of undergraduates is 22.
**Freshman profile:** 1% of freshmen who took SAT scored 700 or over on verbal, 6% scored 700 or over on math; 8% scored 600 or over on verbal, 31% scored 600 or over on math; 38% scored 500 or over on verbal, 72% scored 500 or over on math; 80% scored 400 or over on verbal, 97% scored 400 or over on math; 98% scored 300 or over on verbal, 98% scored 300 or over on math. 61% of accepted applicants took SAT; 39% took ACT.
**Undergraduate achievement:** 65% of fall 1992 freshmen returned for fall 1993 term. 2% of students who completed a degree program went on to graduate study within one year.
**Foreign students:** 64 students are from out of the country. Countries represented include Canada, France, India, Korea, the Netherlands, and the Philippines; 28 in all.

**PROGRAMS OF STUDY. Degrees:** B.S.
**Majors:** Aeronautical Science, Aerospace Engineering, Aerospace Studies, Aviation Business Administration, Aviation Computer Science, Aviation Maintenance Management, Electrical Engineering, Management of Technical Operations, Professional Aeronautics.
**Distribution of degrees:** The majors with the highest enrollment are aeronautical science, aviation business administration, and aerospace engineering; aviation maintenance management, electrical engineering, and aviation computer science have the lowest.
**Requirements:** General education requirement.
**Academic regulations:** Minimum 2.0 GPA must be maintained.
**Special:** Minors offered in air traffic control, aviation business administration, aviation safety, computer science, humanities, mathematics, psychology, and space studies. Double majors. Dual degrees. Independent study. Internships. Cooperative education programs. Study abroad in France, Germany, Greece, Italy, the Netherlands, Portugal, Spain, Sweden, and the United Kingdom. ROTC and AFROTC.
**Honors:** Phi Beta Kappa.
**Academic Assistance:** Remedial study skills. Nonremedial tutoring.

**STUDENT LIFE. Housing:** Students may live on or off campus. Coed dorms. School-owned/operated apartments. 50% of students live in college housing.
**Social atmosphere:** A popular on-campus gathering spot is the school courtyard; off campus, students head for the local bars. According to the editor of the student newspaper, "The university has a very diverse atmosphere and no one group dominates to any extent." Although there is a "leaning toward the conservative side, all groups are represented. The university also has a very developed social structure for such a small campus, and it has a very pleasant atmosphere. It has a beautiful mountain location." Homecoming is a popular student event.
**Services and counseling/handicapped student services:** Health service. Personal and psychological counseling. Career and academic guidance services. Learning disabled services.
**Campus organizations:** Undergraduate student government. Student newspaper (Horizons, published once/two weeks). Yearbook. Radio station. Angel Flight, Arnold Air Society, Aviation Pathfinders, skydiving club, Brothers of the Wind, Flight Team, management and photography groups, parachute club, Phi Beta Lambda, Golden Eagles, Screaming Eagles, Strike Eagles, veterans group, 55 organizations in all. Two fraternities, all with chapter houses; two sororities, no chapter houses.
**Religious organizations:** Campus Crusade for Christ, Campus Ministry.
**Minority/foreign student organizations:** International Student Association.

**ATHLETICS. Physical education requirements:** None.
**Intercollegiate competition:** 17% of students participate. Wrestling (M). Member of NAIA.
**Intramural and club sports:** 82% of students participate. Intramural badminton, basketball, cross-country, flashball, floor hockey, golf, racquetball, softball, swimming, table tennis, tennis, volleyball, water basketball. Men's club Alpine skiing, fencing, lacrosse, rugby, sky diving, soccer, volleyball. Women's club fencing, Alpine skiing, sky diving.

**ADMISSIONS. Academic basis for candidate selection** (in order of priority): Secondary school record, standardized test scores, class rank, essay, school's recommendation.
**Nonacademic basis for candidate selection:** Character and personality, extracurricular participation, and particular talent or ability are considered.
**Requirements:** Graduation from secondary school is required; GED is accepted. 13 units and the following program of study are recommended: 4 units of English, 3 units of math, 3 units of science, 3 units of social studies. Minimum SAT scores of 500 math and 450 verbal, rank in top half of secondary school class, and minimum 2.0 GPA required. FAA Medical Certificate (Class I or II) required of flight applicants. Conditional admission possible for applicants not meeting standard requirements. SAT or ACT is required. Campus visit and interview recommended. No off-campus interviews.
**Procedure:** Take SAT or ACT by December of 12th year. Final application filing date is 30 days prior to beginning of semester. Notification of admission on rolling basis. Reply is required within four weeks of notice of acceptance. $150 tuition deposit, refundable until 60 days prior to registration. $150 room deposit, refundable until 60 days prior to registration. Freshmen accepted for terms other than fall.
**Special programs:** Admission may be deferred one year. Credit and/or placement may be granted through CEEB Advanced Placement exams for scores of 3 or higher. Credit may be granted through CLEP general and subject exams, Regents College, ACT PEP, DANTES, and challenge exams. Credit and placement may be granted through military and life experience.
**Transfer students:** Transfer students accepted for terms other than fall. In fall 1993, 30% of all new students were transfers into all classes. 264 transfer applications were received, 217 were accepted. Application deadline is 30 days before beginning of semester for fall; 30 days before beginning of semester for spring. Minimum 2.0 GPA required. Lowest course grade accepted is "D." At least 30 semester hours must be completed at the university to receive degree.
**Admissions contact:** Darryl W. Niemeyer, Director of Admissions. 602 776-3857.

**FINANCIAL AID. Available aid:** Pell grants, SEOG, state scholarships and grants, ROTC scholarships, academic merit scholarships, and athletic scholarships. Perkins Loans (NDSL), PLUS, Stafford Loans (GSL), state loans, school loans, private loans, and SLS. Knight Tuition Plans and deferred payment plan.
**Financial aid statistics:** 20% of aid is not need-based. In 1993-94, 100% of all undergraduate applicants received aid; 100% of freshman applicants. Average amounts of aid awarded freshmen: Scholarships and grants, $1,700; loans, $2,600.
**Supporting data/closing dates:** FAFSA: Priority filing date is April 15. Notification of awards on rolling basis.
**Financial aid contact:** Daniel A. Lupin, Director of Financial Aid. 602 776-3765.

**STUDENT EMPLOYMENT.** College Work/Study Program. Institutional employment. 20% of full-time undergraduates work on campus during school year. Students may expect to earn an average of $2,300 during school year. Off-campus part-time employment opportunities rated "good."

**COMPUTER FACILITIES.** 120 IBM/IBM-compatible microcomputers; 30 are networked. Students may access SUN minicomputer/mainframe systems. Client/LAN operating systems include DOS, OS/2, Windows NT, X-windows, Novell. Computer languages and software packages include Ada, Assembly, BASIC, C, COBOL, dBASE, Derive, Enable, FORTRAN, Lotus 1-2-3, Pascal, WordPerfect. Computer facilities are available to all students.
**Fees:** Computer fee is included in tuition/fees.
**Hours:** 8 AM-midn. (M-Th); 8 AM-5 PM (F); noon-7 PM (Sa); 10 AM-midn. (Su).

**GRADUATE CAREER DATA.** Highest graduate school enrollments: Embry-Riddle Aeronautical U (Florida campus), U of Central Florida. 39% of graduates choose careers in business and industry. Companies and businesses that hire graduates: Air Desert Pacific, Diversified International Services Corp., Embry-Riddle Aeronautical U, Lockheed.

# Grand Canyon University

**Phoenix, AZ 85017** **602 589-2500**

**1994-95 Costs.** Tuition: $7,170. Room & board: $2,850-$2,950. Fees, books, misc. academic expenses (school's estimate): $770.
**Enrollment.** Undergraduates: 475 men, 767 women (full-time). Freshman class: 921 applicants, 694 accepted, 400 enrolled. Graduate enrollment: 36 men, 68 women.
**Test score averages/ranges.** N/A.
**Faculty.** 66 full-time; 66 part-time. 53% of faculty holds doctoral degree. Student/faculty ratio: 19 to 1.
**Selectivity rating.** N/A.

**PROFILE.** Grand Canyon, founded in 1949, is a church-affiliated, liberal arts university. Programs are offered through the Colleges of Business, Arts and Sciences, Education, and Performing Arts, and the Samaritan College of Nursing. Its 70-acre campus is located in the northwest area of Phoenix.

**Accreditation:** NCACS.
**Religious orientation:** Grand Canyon University is affiliated with the Southern Baptist Convention; two semesters of religion required.
**Library:** Collections totaling over 120,000 volumes, 635 periodical subscriptions, and 34,200 microform items.
**Special facilities/museums:** Art gallery, dynamical systems laboratory.
**Athletic facilities:** Gymnasium, swimming pool, tennis courts, martial arts, weight rooms, baseball and soccer fields.

**STUDENT BODY. Undergraduate profile:** 87% are state residents. 1% Asian-American, 4% Black, 5% Hispanic, 3% Native American, 80% White, 7% Other. Average age of undergraduates is 24.
**Freshman profile:** Majority of accepted applicants took ACT.
**Undergraduate achievement:** 48% of fall 1992 freshmen returned for fall 1993 term. 37% of entering class graduated.
**Foreign students:** 45 students are from out of the country. Countries represented include Canada, China, England, Japan, and Kenya; 21 in all.

**PROGRAMS OF STUDY. Degrees:** B.A., B.Gen.Studies, B.Mus., B.S.
**Majors:** Accounting, Art Education, Biology, Business Education, Chemistry, Christian Studies, Church Music, Communications, Communications/Commercial Music, Computer Science, Economics, Elementary Education, English, Finance, General Studies, Graphic Design, History, Human Resource Development, International Business, Justice Studies, Marketing, Mathematics, Music Education, Music Performance, Nursing, Physical Education, Piano Performance, Psychology, Science Education, Social Sciences, Sociology, Spanish, Special Education, Speech/Theatre, Studio Art, Theatre/Drama, Theatre/Speech, Vocal Performance.
**Distribution of degrees:** The majors with the highest enrollment are elementary education, nursing, and psychology; mathematics, chemistry, and church music have the lowest.
**Requirements:** General education requirement.
**Academic regulations:** Minimum 2.0 GPA must be maintained.
**Special:** Minors offered in many majors and in over 10 other fields. Minor required in most majors for graduation. Double majors. Dual degrees. Independent study. Internships. Graduate school at which undergraduates may take graduate-level courses. Preprofessional programs in law, medicine, veterinary science, pharmacy, dentistry, and optometry. 3-2 engineering program with Arizona State U. Member of Christian College Coalition. American Studies Program (Washington, D.C.). Teacher certification in elementary, secondary, and special education. Certification in specific subject areas. Study abroad in China, Costa Rica, Hungary, Mexico, the former Soviet Republics, and Spain. ROTC and AFROTC at Arizona State U.
**Honors:** Honors program.
**Academic Assistance:** Remedial reading and study skills. Nonremedial tutoring.

**STUDENT LIFE. Housing:** All freshmen under age 20 must live on campus unless living with family. Women's and men's dorms. School-owned/operated apartments. 33% of students live in college housing.
**Social atmosphere:** According to the editor of the student newspaper, "I appreciate the Christian atmosphere and the small size. It's a great place to go to school, with lots of room for involvement." Popular campus events include the Harvest Festival and baseball games. Influential student groups include the Baptist Student Union and the Associated Students of GCC. On campus, students frequent the cafeteria ("No student union yet!"). The Sun Devil House is a favorite dance club.
**Services and counseling/handicapped student services:** Placement services. Health service. Personal counseling. Career and academic guidance services. Physically disabled student services. Tape recorders. Reader services for the blind.
**Campus organizations:** Undergraduate student government. Student newspaper (Canyon Echoes, published once/two weeks). Literary magazine. Yearbook. Jazz band, ensembles, trios/quartets, Choralaires, opera workshop, chamber orchestra, Oratorio Society, debating, forensics, guitar, drama, and ski clubs, departmental, professional, and service groups.
**Religious organizations:** Baptist Student Union, Fellowship of Christian Athletes, Intervarsity Christian Fellowship, Ministerial Association, Mission Service Association, SOWERS (foreign mission group).
**Minority/foreign student organizations:** Native American Club. International Student Club.

**ATHLETICS. Physical education requirements:** Two semesters of physical education required.
**Intercollegiate competition:** 10% of students participate. Baseball (M), basketball (M,W), cheerleading (W), cross-country (M,W), golf (M), soccer (M), tennis (W), volleyball (W). Member of NCAA Division I (baseball), NCAA Division II, Pacific West Conference.
**Intramural and club sports:** 20% of students participate. Intramural basketball, football, karate, softball, tennis, volleyball, weight lifting. Men's club martial arts, volleyball.

**ADMISSIONS. Academic basis for candidate selection** (in order of priority): Secondary school record, class rank, standardized test scores, essay, school's recommendation.
**Requirements:** Graduation from secondary school is required; GED is accepted. No specific distribution of secondary school units required. SAT or ACT scores in top half of national percentiles, rank in top half of secondary school class, or minimum 2.5 GPA required. Conditional admission possible for applicants not meeting standard requirements. SAT or ACT is required. Campus visit recommended. Off-campus interviews available with an admissions representative.
**Procedure:** Take SAT or ACT by March 1 of 12th year. Suggest filing application by March 1. Application deadline is August 1. Notification of admission on rolling basis. $100 tuition deposit, refundable until August 1. $150 room deposit, $125 of which is refundable. Freshmen accepted for terms other than fall.
**Special programs:** Admission may be deferred one year. Credit may be granted through CEEB Advanced Placement for scores of 4 or higher. Credit may be granted through CLEP general and subject exams, ACT PEP, DANTES exams, and military experience. Credit and placement may be granted through challenge exams. Early entrance/early admission program.
**Transfer students:** Transfer students accepted for terms other than fall. Application deadline is August 1 for fall; January 1 for spring. Minimum 2.0 GPA required. Lowest course grade accepted is "C." Maximum number of transferable credits is 64 semester hours. At least 30 semester hours must be completed at the university to receive degree.
**Admissions contact:** Sherri Willborn, Director of Admissions and Enrollment Planning. 602 589-2855.

**FINANCIAL AID. Available aid:** Pell grants, SEOG, state grants, school scholarships, private scholarships, ROTC scholarships, academic merit scholarships, and athletic scholarships. Indian Health Services grants and other aid for Native Americans. Scholarships for children of Southern Baptist ministers. Perkins Loans (NDSL), PLUS, Stafford Loans (GSL), and SLS. Monthly payment plan.
**Financial aid statistics:** In 1993-94, 93% of all undergraduate applicants received aid; 91% of freshman applicants. Average amounts of aid awarded freshmen: Scholarships and grants, $1,788; loans, $2,859.
**Supporting data/closing dates:** FAFSA/FAF/FFS: Priority filing date is March 15; accepted on rolling basis. School's own aid application: Priority filing date is March 15; accepted on rolling basis. Income tax forms. Notification of awards begins March 29.
**Financial aid contact:** Ted Malone, Director of Financial Aid. 602 589-2885.

**STUDENT EMPLOYMENT.** College Work/Study Program. Institutional employment. 15% of full-time undergraduates work on campus during school year. Students may expect to earn an average of $1,500 during school year. Off-campus part-time employment opportunities rated "good."

**COMPUTER FACILITIES.** 62 IBM/IBM-compatible and Macintosh/Apple microcomputers; all are networked. Students may access Digital minicomputer/mainframe systems. Client/LAN operating systems include Apple/Macintosh, LocalTalk/AppleTalk. Computer languages and software packages include Ada, BASIC, C, COBOL, FORTRAN, LISP, Pascal, Prolog; 200 in all. Computer facilities are available to all students.
**Fees:** $85 computer fee per semester.
**Hours:** 7 AM-2 AM.

**GRADUATE CAREER DATA.** 40% of graduates choose careers in business and industry.

**PROMINENT ALUMNI/AE.** Bill Williams, president, Grand Canyon U; Mark Dickerson, general counsel, Talley Industries; Mitchell C. Laird, Mitchell C. Laird & Associates; Dianne Day, missionary.

# Northern Arizona University

**Flagstaff, AZ 86011** **602 523-9011**

**1993-94 Costs.** Tuition: $1,844 (state residents), $6,596 (out-of-state). Room: $1,456. Board: $1,558. Fees, books, misc. academic expenses (school's estimate): $700.
**Enrollment.** Undergraduates: 5,315 men, 5,934 women (full-time). Freshman class: 5,891 applicants, 4,931 accepted, 1,973 enrolled. Graduate enrollment: 1,484 men, 3,402 women.
**Test score averages/ranges.** Average SAT scores: 930 combined. Average ACT scores: 21 composite.
**Faculty.** 543 full-time; 179 part-time. 80% of faculty holds highest degree in specific field. Student/faculty ratio: 22 to 1.
**Selectivity rating.** Competitive.

**PROFILE.** Northern Arizona is a public, comprehensive university. Founded in 1899 as a teacher training school, it gained university status in 1966. Programs are offered through the Colleges of Arts and Science, Business Administration, Creative and Communication Arts, Engineering and Technology, and Social and Behavioral Sciences; the Center for Excellence in Education; and the Schools of Communication, Forestry, Health Professions, and Hotel and Restaurant Management. Its 730-acre campus is located in Flagstaff.

**Accreditation:** NCACS. Professionally accredited by the Accreditation Board for Engineering and Technology, the American Assembly of Collegiate Schools of Business, the American Dental Association, the American Dietetic Association, the American Physical Therapy Association, the National Association of Schools of Music, the National Council for Accreditation of Teacher Education, the National League for Nursing, the Society of American Foresters.
**Religious orientation:** Northern Arizona University is nonsectarian; no religious requirements.
**Library:** Collections totaling over 1,363,882 volumes, 5,831 periodical subscriptions, and 581,470 microform items.
**Special facilities/museums:** Art gallery, art and music studios, observatory, multidisciplinary research center, 4,000-acre experimental forest.
**Athletic facilities:** Dome, field house, natatorium, gymnasium, activity centers, track.

**STUDENT BODY. Undergraduate profile:** 84% are state residents; 49% are transfers. 2% Asian-American, 1% Black, 8% Hispanic, 6% Native American, 80% White, 3% Other. Average age of undergraduates is 22.
**Freshman profile:** Majority of accepted applicants took ACT.
**Undergraduate achievement:** 69% of fall 1992 freshmen returned for fall 1993 term. 26% of students who completed a degree program went on to graduate study within five years.
**Foreign students:** 265 students are from out of the country. Countries represented include Canada, China, Hong Kong, Japan, Malaysia, and Taiwan; 65 in all.

**PROGRAMS OF STUDY. Degrees:** B.A., B.F.A., B.Mus., B.Mus.Ed., B.S.
**Majors:** Accountancy, Advertising, Anthropology, Applied Sociology, Art, Art Education, Arts Management, Astronomy, Biology, Botany, Broadcasting, Business Economics, Chemistry, Civil Engineering, Computer Information Systems, Computer Science/ Engineering, Criminal Justice, Dental Hygiene, Early Childhood, Economics, Electrical Engineering, Elementary Education, English, Environmental Engineering, Environmental Science, Fashion Merchandising, Finance, Food/Nutrition, Forestry, French, General Studies, Geography, Geology, German, Health Education, History, Hotel/Restaurant Management, Humanities, Industrial Arts Education, Industrial Supervision, Interior Design, International Affairs, Management, Marketing, Mathematics, Mechanical Engineering, Microbiology, Music, Music Education, Nursing, Philosophy, Physical Education, Physical Science, Physics, Political Science, Psychology, Public Administration, Public Planning, Public Relations, Recreation/Leisure Services, Religious Studies, Secondary Education, Social Science, Social Work, Sociology, Spanish, Special Education, Speech Communication, Speech Pathology/Audiology, Technology Education, Theatre, Vocational Education, Zoology.
**Distribution of degrees:** The majors with the highest enrollment are hotel/restaurant management, elementary education, and psychology; forestry has the lowest.
**Requirements:** General education requirement.
**Academic regulations:** Freshmen must maintain minimum 1.7 GPA; sophomores, 1.9 GPA; juniors, 2.0 GPA; seniors, 2.0 GPA.
**Special:** Minors offered in some majors and in art history, German, library science, and statistics. Double majors. Dual degrees. Independent study. Accelerated study. Pass/fail grading option. Internships. Cooperative education programs. Graduate school at which undergraduates may take graduate-level courses. Preprofessional programs in law, medicine, veterinary science, pharmacy, dentistry, theology, optometry, forensic chemistry, and podiatry. Traveling Scholars Program with Arizona State U and U of Arizona. Member of National Student Exchange (NSE). Teacher certification in early childhood, elementary, secondary, and special education. Certification in specific subject areas. Study abroad in Australia, China, England, France, Germany, Israel, Italy, Japan, Mexico, the Netherlands, Russia, Spain, and Wales. ROTC and AFROTC.
**Honors:** Honors program.
**Academic Assistance:** Remedial study skills. Nonremedial tutoring.

**STUDENT LIFE. Housing:** Students may live on or off campus. Coed, women's, and men's dorms. Sorority and fraternity housing. On-campus married-student housing. 47% of students live in college housing.
**Social atmosphere:** The student newspaper reports, "Parties are the main social event." Popular gathering spots around NAU are Fiddlestix, the Mad Italian, Monsoons, Oak Creek Canyon, and Lake Powell. The Associated Students of NAU and the Peace and Justice Coalition are among the influential organizations on campus. A favorite social event during the year is Homecoming.
**Services and counseling/handicapped student services:** Placement services. Health service. Counseling services for minority, military, veteran, and older students. Personal and psychological counseling. Career and academic guidance services. Physically disabled student services. Learning disabled services. Notetaking services. Tutors. Reader services for the blind.
**Campus organizations:** Undergraduate student government. Student newspaper (Lumberjack, published once/week). Literary magazine. Radio station. A cappella choir, bands, orchestra, drama group, debating, 180 organizations in all. Eight fraternities, no chapter houses; five sororities, no chapter houses. 5% of men join a fraternity. 8% of women join a sorority.
**Religious organizations:** Bahai Campus Club, Baptist Student Union, Campus Ambassadors, Campus Crusade for Christ, Christian Science Organization, Fellowship of Christian Athletes, Hillel, Intervarsity Christian Fellowship, Knights of Columbus, Lutheran Student Movement, Muslim Student Association, Path Finders.
**Minority/foreign student organizations:** Black Student Union, MEChA, Native American student groups. International Club, Chinese and Malaysian groups.

**ATHLETICS. Physical education requirements:** None.
**Intercollegiate competition:** Basketball (M,W), cheerleading (M,W), cross-country (M,W), diving (M,W), football (M), swimming (M,W), tennis (M,W), track and field (indoor) (M,W), track and field (outdoor) (M,W), volleyball (W). Member of Big Sky Conference, NCAA Division I, NCAA Division I-AA for football.
**Intramural and club sports:** Intramural basketball, billiards, flag football, rugby, running, soccer, softball, tennis, volleyball, water polo.

**ADMISSIONS. Academic basis for candidate selection** (in order of priority): Secondary school record, class rank, standardized test scores, school's recommendation.
**Requirements:** Graduation from secondary school is required; GED is accepted. 16 units and the following program of study are required: 4 units of English, 3 units of math, 2 units of lab science, 2 units of social studies. Rank in top half of secondary school class, minimum 2.5 GPA, or minimum composite ACT score of 22 (combined SAT score of 930) required of in-state applicants; rank in top half of secondary school class, minimum 2.5 GPA, or minimum composite ACT score of 24 (combined SAT score of 1010) required of out-of-state applicants. Additional admissions requirements for business, dental hygiene, education, engineering, forestry, nursing, physical therapy, and speech pathology/audiology program applicants. ACT is required; SAT may be substituted. Campus visit recommended. No off-campus interviews.
**Procedure:** Take SAT or ACT by December of 12th year. Suggest filing application by April 15; no deadline. Notification of admission on rolling basis. $150 room deposit, refundable until May 15. Freshmen accepted for terms other than fall.
**Special programs:** Admission may be deferred one semester. Credit and/or placement may be granted through CEEB Advanced Placement exams for scores of 4 or higher. Credit may be granted through CLEP general and subject exams and military experience. Credit and placement may be granted through challenge exams. Early entrance/early admission program. Concurrent enrollment program.
**Transfer students:** Transfer students accepted for terms other than fall. In fall 1993, 49% of all new students were transfers into all classes. 3,974 transfer applications were received, 3,190 were accepted. Application deadline is July 1 for fall; December 1 for spring. Minimum 2.0 GPA required. Lowest course grade accepted is "C." Maximum number of transferable credits is 60 semester hours. At least 65 semester hours must be completed at the university to receive degree.
**Admissions contact:** Molly S. Carder, M.A., Director of Admissions. 602 523-5511.

**FINANCIAL AID. Available aid:** Pell grants, SEOG, state scholarships and grants, school scholarships and grants, private scholarships and grants, ROTC scholarships, academic merit scholarships, athletic scholarships, and aid for undergraduate foreign students. Perkins Loans (NDSL), PLUS, Stafford Loans (GSL), and NSL.
**Financial aid statistics:** In 1993-94, 60% of all undergraduate applicants received aid; 60% of freshman applicants. Average amounts of aid awarded freshmen: Scholarships and grants, $1,700; loans, $1,700.
**Supporting data/closing dates:** FAFSA/FAF/FFS: Priority filing date is April 15. School's own aid application: Priority filing date is April 15. State aid form: Priority filing date is April 15. Income tax forms: Priority filing date is April 15. Notification of awards on rolling basis.
**Financial aid contact:** James Pritchard, M.A., Director of Financial Aid. 602 523-4951.

**STUDENT EMPLOYMENT.** College Work/Study Program. Institutional employment. 26% of full-time undergraduates work on campus during school year. Students may expect to earn an average of $1,400 during school year. Off-campus part-time employment opportunities rated "good."

**COMPUTER FACILITIES.** 500 IBM/IBM-compatible, Macintosh/Apple, and RISC-/UNIX-based microcomputers. Students may access Digital, IBM minicomputer/ mainframe systems, BITNET, Internet. Residence halls may be equipped with stand-alone microcomputers. Client/LAN operating systems include Apple/Macintosh, DOS, UNIX/ XENIX/AIX, LocalTalk/AppleTalk. Computer languages and software packages include C, COBOL, Excel, FORTRAN, Microsoft, Paradox, Quattro Pro, Quick BASIC, WordPerfect; 20 in all. Computer facilities are available to all students.
**Fees:** None.

# Prescott College

**Prescott, AZ 86301** **602 778-2090**

**1994-95 Costs.** Tuition: $9,800. Housing: None. Fees, books, misc. academic expenses (school's estimate): $545.
**Enrollment.** Undergraduates: 198 men, 158 women (full-time). Freshman class: 321 applicants, 227 accepted, 129 enrolled.
**Test score averages/ranges.** N/A.
**Faculty.** 40 full-time; 50 part-time. 47% of faculty holds highest degree in specific field. Student/faculty ratio: 9 to 1.
**Selectivity rating.** N/A.

**PROFILE.** Prescott, founded in 1966, is a private college. Its two-acre campus is located in Prescott, 100 miles from Phoenix.

**Accreditation:** NCACS.
**Religious orientation:** Prescott College is nonsectarian; no religious requirements.
**Library:** Collections totaling over 12,000 volumes, 325 periodical subscriptions and 100 microform items.

**STUDENT BODY. Undergraduate profile:** 2% are state residents; 75% are transfers. .2% Asian-American, .5% Black, 1.3% Hispanic, 95% White, 3% Other. Average age of undergraduates is 22.
**Freshman profile:** Majority of accepted applicants took SAT. 66% of freshmen come from public schools.
**Undergraduate achievement:** 56% of fall 1992 freshmen returned for fall 1993 term. 26% of entering class graduated.
**Foreign students:** 10 students are from out of the country. Countries represented include Canada, Germany, Japan, Latvia, and Norway.

**PROGRAMS OF STUDY. Degrees:** B.A.
**Majors:** Cultural/Regional Studies, Environmental Studies, Human Development, Humanities, Outdoor Action.
**Distribution of degrees:** The majors with the highest enrollment are environmental studies, humanities, and human development.
**Special:** Minors offered in all fields of study. Students design their own programs within the broad areas of cultural/regional studies, environmental studies, human development, humanities, and outdoor action. Grades given upon request. Self-designed majors. Double majors. Independent study. Pass/fail grading option. Internships. Teacher certifi-

cation in early childhood, elementary, secondary, special education, and bilingual/bicultural education. Certification in specific subject areas. Exchange program abroad in Germany (Bremen Coll). Study abroad also in Costa Rica, Mexico, and the United Kingdom.
**Academic Assistance:** Remedial writing, math, and study skills. Nonremedial tutoring.

**ADMISSIONS.**
**Nonacademic basis for candidate selection:** Character and personality are emphasized. Particular talent or ability is important. Extracurricular participation is considered.
**Requirements:** Graduation from secondary school is required; GED is accepted. No specific distribution of secondary school units required. Conditional admission possible for applicants not meeting standard requirements. SAT is recommended; ACT may be substituted. Campus visit and interview recommended. No off-campus interviews.
**Procedure:** Suggest filing application by February 1; no deadline. Notification of admission on rolling basis. Applicants should accept offer of admission six months prior to anticipated enrollment. $100 nonrefundable tuition deposit. Freshmen accepted for terms other than fall.
**Special programs:** Credit and/or placement may be granted through CEEB Advanced Placement exams for scores of 4 or higher. Placement may be granted through CLEP general and subject exams, DANTES and challenge exams, and military and life experience.
**Transfer students:** Transfer students accepted for terms other than fall. In fall 1993, 75% of all new students were transfers into all classes. 240 transfer applications were received, 170 were accepted. Application deadline is rolling for fall; rolling for spring. Lowest course grade accepted is "C."
**Admissions contact:** Shari Sterling, Director of Resident Degree Program Admissions. 602 776-5180.

**FINANCIAL AID. Available aid:** Pell grants, SEOG, state scholarships and grants, school scholarships and grants, private scholarships and grants, academic merit scholarships, and aid for undergraduate foreign students. Perkins Loans (NDSL), PLUS, Stafford Loans (GSL), private loans, and SLS. Deferred payment plan.
**Financial aid statistics:** 42% of aid is not need-based. In 1993-94, 90% of all undergraduate applicants received aid. Average amounts of aid awarded freshmen: Scholarships and grants, $2,500; loans, $2,625.
**Supporting data/closing dates:** FAFSA: Priority filing date is April 15; accepted on rolling basis. Income tax forms: Accepted on rolling basis. Notification of awards on rolling basis.
**Financial aid contact:** Ray Ceo, Director of Financial Aid. 602 776-5168.

# University of Arizona

**Tucson, AZ 85721-0007** **602 621-2211**

**1993-94 Costs.** Tuition: $1,778 (state residents), $5,506 (out-of-state). Room & board: $3,986. Fees, books, misc. academic expenses (school's estimate): $686.
**Enrollment.** Undergraduates: 11,009 men, 10,662 women (full-time). Freshman class: 14,079 applicants, 12,298 accepted, 4,529 enrolled. Graduate enrollment: 4,578 men, 4,142 women.
**Test score averages/ranges.** Average SAT scores: 460 verbal, 529 math. Range of SAT scores of middle 50%: 400-520 verbal, 460-590 math. Average ACT scores: 23 composite. Range of ACT scores of middle 50%: 20-26 composite.
**Faculty.** 1,576 full-time; 76 part-time. 86% of faculty holds highest degree in specific field. Student/faculty ratio: 20 to 1.
**Selectivity rating.** Less competitive.

**PROFILE.** The University of Arizona, founded in 1885, is a public institution. Programs are offered through the Colleges of Agriculture, Architecture, Arts and Sciences, Business and Public Administration, Education, Engineering and Mines, Law, Medicine, Nursing, and Pharmacy; the Schools of Family and Consumer Resources and Health-Related Professions; and the Graduate College. Its 325-acre campus is located in a residential area of Tucson.

**Accreditation:** NCACS. Numerous professional accreditations.
**Religious orientation:** University of Arizona is nonsectarian; no religious requirements.
**Library:** Collections totaling over 3,800,000 volumes, 31,919 periodical subscriptions, and 4,100,000 microform items.
**Special facilities/museums:** Art, photography, and natural history museums, tree-ring lab, planetarium, optical sciences center, nuclear reactor.
**Athletic facilities:** Gymnasium, weight room, swimming pool, athletic fields, indoor and outdoor track, fitness center, racquetball courts.

**STUDENT BODY. Undergraduate profile:** 71% are state residents; 35% are transfers. 4% Asian-American, 2% Black, 11% Hispanic, 2% Native American, 77% White, 4% Other. Average age of undergraduates is 22.
**Freshman profile:** 1% of freshmen who took SAT scored 700 or over on verbal, 4% scored 700 or over on math; 7% scored 600 or over on verbal, 23% scored 600 or over on math; 34% scored 500 or over on verbal, 59% scored 500 or over on math; 77% scored 400 or over on verbal, 88% scored 400 or over on math; 98% scored 300 or over on verbal, 99% scored 300 or over on math. 7% of freshmen who took ACT scored 30 or over on composite; 38% scored 24 or over on composite; 88% scored 18 or over on composite; 100% scored 12 or over on composite. 79% of accepted applicants took SAT; 49% took ACT. 90% of freshmen come from public schools.
**Undergraduate achievement:** 76% of fall 1992 freshmen returned for fall 1993 term. 17% of entering class graduated.
**Foreign students:** 677 students are from out of the country. Countries represented include China, India, Japan, Mexico, South Korea, and Taiwan; 120 in all.

**PROGRAMS OF STUDY. Degrees:** B.A., B.Arch., B.F.A., B.Land.Arch., B.Mus., B.S.
**Majors:** Accounting, Aerospace Engineering, Agricultural Economics, Agricultural Education, Agricultural Engineering, Agriculture/Biosystems Engineering, Agriculture/Biosystems Technology, Agronomy, Animal Sciences, Anthropology, Architecture, Art Education, Art History, Astronomy, Atmospheric Science, Biochemistry, Biology, Business Economics, Cellular/Molecular Biology, Chemical Engineering, Chemistry, Civil Engineering, Classics, Communication, Computer Engineering, Computer Science, Creative Writing, Criminal Justice Administration, Dance, Drama Education, Drama/Production, Dramatic Theory, Early Childhood Education, East Asian Studies, Economics, Electrical Engineering, Elementary Education, Engineering Mathematics, Engineering Physics, English, Entomology, Exercise Sciences, Family/Consumer Resources, Family Studies, Finance, French, General Agriculture, General Business Administration, General Home Economics, General Studies, Geography, Geological Engineering, Geosciences, German, Greek, Health Education, Health/Human Services Administration, History, Home Economics Education, Horticulture, Hydrology, Industrial Engineering, Interdisciplinary Studies, Italian, Jazz Studies, Journalism, Latin, Latin American Studies, Linguistics, Management Information Systems, Marketing, Mathematics, Mechanical Engineering, Media Arts, Medical Technology, Merchandising/Consumer Studies, Mexican-American Studies, Microbiology, Mining Engineering, Music, Music Education, Music Education/Instrumental, Music Education/Vocal, Music Theatre, Music Theory/Composition, Nuclear Engineering, Nursing, Nutritional Sciences, Occupational Safety/Health Technology, Operations Management, Optical Engineering, Performance, Personnel Management, Pharmacy, Philosophy, Physical Education, Physics, Plant Pathology, Plant Sciences, Political Science, Portuguese, Psychology, Public Management, Radio/Television, Range Management, Real Estate, Regional Development, Rehabilitation, Religious Studies, Russian, Secondary Education, Sociology, Soil/Water Science, Spanish, Speech/Hearing Sciences, Studio Art, Systems Engineering, Theatre Arts Education, Theatre Production, Veterinary Science, Watershed Management, Wildlife/Fisheries Science.
**Distribution of degrees:** The majors with the highest enrollment are political science, psychology, and interdisciplinary studies; agricultural engineering, entomology, and Greek have the lowest.
**Requirements:** General education requirement.
**Academic regulations:** Minimum 2.0 GPA must be maintained.
**Special:** Minors offered in numerous fields; students in arts and sciences may elect minor in another college. Self-designed majors. Double majors. Dual degrees. Independent study. Pass/fail grading option. Internships. Cooperative education programs. Graduate school at which undergraduates may take graduate-level courses. Preprofessional programs in law, medicine, veterinary science, pharmacy, dentistry, and optometry. 3-2 M.B.A. program. Sea Semester. Teacher certification in early childhood, elementary, secondary, special education, and bilingual/bicultural education. Certification in specific subject areas. Exchange programs abroad in Brazil, Cyprus, England, France, Germany, Italy, Japan, Mexico, Spain, and Taiwan. ROTC, NROTC, and AFROTC.
**Honors:** Phi Beta Kappa. Honors program.
**Academic Assistance:** Remedial reading, writing, math, and study skills. Nonremedial tutoring.

**STUDENT LIFE. Housing:** Students may live on or off campus. Coed, women's, and men's dorms. Sorority and fraternity housing. School-owned/operated apartments. Off-campus married-student housing. 20% of students live in college housing.
**Social atmosphere:** The student newspaper reports, "As with any university this size, the cultural and social lives of the students are too diverse to list in categories. In general, though, sports are very popular, and the different international activities sponsored on campus are varyingly popular, depending on the culture and time of year. Wildcat basketball (we're number 1 in the nation) is by far the most popular sport, followed by football. Centennial Hall gives Broadway performances and has become the theatrical hub of Tucson. Greeks and their social patterns have a large influence on campus residents, though little on off-campus residents. In a college this size (31,000) and in a city this size (600,000), people pretty much do their own thing."
**Services and counseling/handicapped student services:** Placement services. Health service. Women's center. Counseling services for minority, military, veteran, and older students. Birth control, personal, and psychological counseling. Career and academic guidance services. Religious counseling. Physically disabled student services. Learning disabled program/services. Notetaking services. Tape recorders. Tutors. Reader services for the blind.
**Campus organizations:** Undergraduate student government. Student newspaper (Arizona Daily Wildcat). Literary magazine. Yearbook. Radio station. 250 registered organizations. 23 fraternities, 20 chapter houses; 13 sororities, 11 chapter houses. 13% of men join a fraternity. 12% of women join a sorority.
**Religious organizations:** Numerous religious groups.
**Minority/foreign student organizations:** Numerous minority student groups. Numerous foreign student groups.

**ATHLETICS. Physical education requirements:** None.
**Intercollegiate competition:** 6% of students participate. Baseball (M), basketball (M,W), cross-country (M,W), diving (M,W), football (M), golf (M,W), gymnastics (W), softball (W), swimming (M,W), tennis (M,W), track and field (M,W), track and field (outdoor) (M,W), volleyball (W). Member of NCAA Division I, Pacific 10 Conference.
**Intramural and club sports:** 25% of students participate. Intramural badminton, co-recreational football, co-recreational speed soccer, flag football, indoor softball, racquetball, sand volleyball, softball, swimming, table tennis, team tennis, trivia ball, turkey shoot. Men's club boxing, cheerleading, cycling, fencing, field hockey, ice hockey, lacrosse, martial arts, Nordic skiing, racquetball, rifle, rodeo, rugby, soccer, ultimate frisbee, volleyball, water polo, wrestling. Women's club cheerleading, cycling, fencing, field hockey, lacrosse, martial arts, Nordic skiing, racquetball, rodeo, rugby, soccer.

**ADMISSIONS. Academic basis for candidate selection** (in order of priority): Secondary school record, class rank, standardized test scores, school's recommendation, essay.
**Nonacademic basis for candidate selection:** Extracurricular participation and particular talent or ability are important. Character and personality, geographical distribution, and alumni/ae relationship are considered.
**Requirements:** Graduation from secondary school is required; GED is accepted. 11 units and the following program of study are required: 4 units of English, 3 units of math, 2 units of lab science, 1 unit of social studies, 1 unit of history. 18 units recommended. Minimum combined SAT score of 930 (composite ACT score of 22), rank in top half of secondary school class, or minimum 2.5 GPA required of in-state applicants; minimum combined SAT score of 1010 (composite ACT score of 24), rank in top quarter of secondary school class, or minimum 3.0 GPA required of out-of-state applicants. Additional requirements

for architecture, education, engineering, music and pharmacy program applicants. SAT or ACT is required. Campus visit recommended. No off-campus interviews.
**Procedure:** Take SAT or ACT by November of 12th year. Suggest filing application by March 1. Application deadline is April 1. Notification of acceptance by December 1 and January 15; on rolling basis after January 15. Reply is required by May 1. $150 partially refundable room deposit. Freshmen accepted for terms other than fall.
**Special programs:** Admission may be deferred one year. Credit may be granted through CEEB Advanced Placement for scores of 3 or higher. Credit may be granted through CLEP general and subject exams, ACT PEP, DANTES, challenge exams, and military experience. Early entrance/early admission program. Concurrent enrollment program.
**Transfer students:** Transfer students accepted for terms other than fall. In fall 1993, 35% of all new students were transfers into all classes. 5,781 transfer applications were received, 4,334 were accepted. Application deadline is June 1 for fall; December 1 for spring. Minimum 2.0 GPA required. Lowest course grade accepted is "C." Maximum number of transferable credits is 72 semester hours. At least 30 semester hours must be completed at the university to receive degree.
**Admissions contact:** Loyd V. Bell, M.A., Director of Admissions. 602 621-3237.

**FINANCIAL AID. Available aid:** Pell grants, SEOG, Federal Nursing Student Scholarships, state scholarships and grants, school scholarships and grants, private scholarships and grants, ROTC scholarships, academic merit scholarships, athletic scholarships, and aid for undergraduate foreign students. Perkins Loans (NDSL), PLUS, Stafford Loans (GSL), NSL, state loans, school loans, private loans, and SLS.
**Supporting data/closing dates:** FAFSA/FAF/FFS: Priority filing date is March 1; accepted on rolling basis. School's own aid application: Priority filing date is March 1; accepted on rolling basis. Notification of awards on rolling basis.
**Financial aid contact:** Phyllis B. Bannister, M.A., Director of Financial Aid. 602 621-1858.

**STUDENT EMPLOYMENT.** College Work/Study Program. Institutional employment. 19% of full-time undergraduates work on campus during school year. Students may expect to earn an average of $1,861 during school year. Off-campus part-time employment opportunities rated "good."

**COMPUTER FACILITIES.** 1,700 IBM/IBM-compatible and Macintosh/Apple microcomputers; 400 are networked. Students may access Digital, IBM minicomputer/mainframe systems, BITNET, Internet, CompuServe. Client/LAN operating systems include Apple/Macintosh. 150 major computer languages and software packages available. Computer facilities are available to all students.
**Fees:** Computer fee is included in tuition/fees.
**Hours:** 7 AM-11 PM for some; 24 hours for others.

**PROMINENT ALUMNI/AE.** Dennis DeConcini, U.S. senator, Arizona; Robert Dole, U.S. senator, Kansas; Barry Goldwater, former U.S. senator and presidential candidate; Morris Udall, U.S. congressman, Arizona; Karl Eller, president, Circle K Corp.

# Western International University

**Phoenix, AZ 85021** **602 943-2311**

**1994-95 Costs.** Tuition: $3,600 (state residents), $4,680 (international students). Housing: None. Fees, books, misc. academic expenses (school's estimate): $500.
**Enrollment.** Undergraduates: 351 men, 243 women (full-time). Graduate enrollment: 239 men, 134 women.
**Test score averages/ranges.** N/A.
**Faculty.** 62 part-time. 62% of faculty holds doctoral degree. Student/faculty ratio: 18 to 1.
**Selectivity rating.** N/A.

**PROFILE.** Western International University, founded in 1978, is a private university established to serve the needs of the adult learner. Its four-acre campus is located in Phoenix.

**Accreditation:** NCACS.
**Religious orientation:** Western International University is nonsectarian; no religious requirements.
**Library:** Collections totaling over 7,500 volumes, 106 periodical subscriptions and 100 microform items.

**STUDENT BODY. Undergraduate profile:** 75% are state residents. 4% Asian-American, 6% Black, 5% Hispanic, 1% Native American, 57% White, 27% Other. Average age of undergraduates is 31.
**Foreign students:** Countries represented include India, Japan, Mexico, Pakistan, Taiwan, and Thailand.

**PROGRAMS OF STUDY. Degrees:** B.A., B.S.
**Majors:** Accounting, Aviation Management, Behavioral Science, Finance, General Business, General Studies, Information Systems, International Business, International Studies, Management, Marketing.
**Distribution of degrees:** The majors with the highest enrollment are management, information systems, and general business; finance, behavioral studies, and marketing have the lowest.
**Requirements:** General education requirement.
**Special:** Associate's degrees offered. Independent study. Study abroad available through the university's London campus.
**Honors:** Honor societies.
**Academic Assistance:** Nonremedial tutoring.

**ADMISSIONS. Academic basis for candidate selection** (in order of priority): Secondary school record, class rank, school's recommendation, essay, standardized test scores.
**Requirements:** Graduation from secondary school is required; GED is accepted. No specific distribution of secondary school units required.
**Procedure:** Notification of admission on rolling basis. Freshmen accepted for terms other than fall.
**Special programs:** Admission may be deferred one year. Credit and/or placement may be granted through CEEB Advanced Placement for scores for scores of 3 or higher. Credit may be granted through CLEP general and subject exams, ACT PEP, DANTES exams, and military and life experience.
**Transfer students:** Transfer students accepted for terms other than fall. Application deadline is rolling for fall; rolling for spring. Minimum 2.0 GPA required. Lowest course grade accepted is "C." Maximum number of transferable credits is 90 semester hours. At least 36 semester hours must be completed at the university to receive degree.
**Admissions contact:** Kathie Westerfield, M.B.A., Director of Admissions. 602 943-2311, extension 138.

**FINANCIAL AID. Available aid:** Pell grants, SEOG, state scholarships and grants, school scholarships, and private scholarships. PLUS, Stafford Loans (GSL), private loans, and SLS. Tuition Plan Inc. and deferred payment plan.
**Financial aid statistics:** 70% of aid is not need-based. In 1993-94, 100% of all undergraduate applicants received aid. Average amounts of aid awarded freshmen: Scholarships and grants, $2,000; loans, $2,625.
**Supporting data/closing dates:** FAFSA: Accepted on rolling basis. Income tax forms: Accepted on rolling basis.
**Financial aid contact:** John Medley, Director of Financial Aid. 602 943-2311, extension 140.

# Arkansas

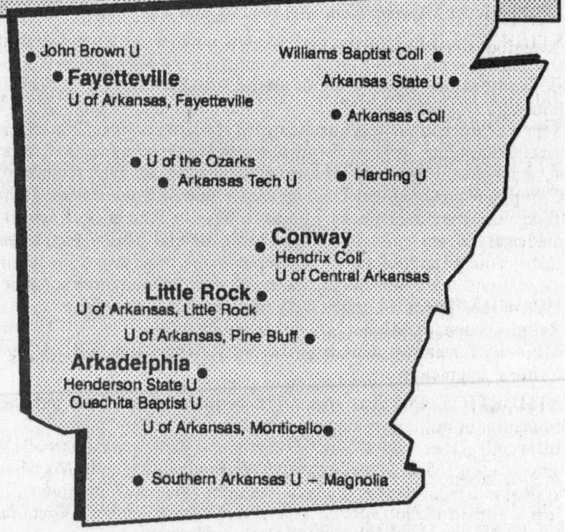


## Arkansas State University

**State University, AR 72467 800 382-3030 (in-state)**

**1994-95 Costs.** Tuition: $1,800 (state residents), $3,600 (out-of-state). Room & board: $2,410. Fees, books, misc. academic expenses (school's estimate): $720.
**Enrollment.** Undergraduates: 3,266 men, 3,946 women (full-time). Freshman class: 2,688 applicants, 2,633 accepted, 1,573 enrolled. Graduate enrollment: 338 men, 631 women.
**Test score averages/ranges.** Average ACT scores: 22 English, 20 math, 21 composite. Range of ACT scores of middle 50%: 18-25 English, 17-22 math.
**Faculty.** 404 full-time; 81 part-time. 85% of faculty holds highest degree in specific field. Student/faculty ratio: 24 to 1.
**Selectivity rating.** Noncompetitive.

**PROFILE.** Arkansas State, founded in 1909, is a public, comprehensive university. Programs are offered through the Department of Military Science and the Colleges of Arts and Sciences; Business; Communications; Education; Engineering, Agriculture, and Applied Sciences; Fine Arts; and Nursing and Health Professions. Its 800-acre campus is located in Jonesboro, 75 miles from Memphis.

**Accreditation:** NCACS. Professionally accredited by the Accreditation Board for Engineering and Technology, the Accrediting Council on Education in Journalism and Mass Communication, the American Assembly of Collegiate Schools of Business, the American Medical Association (CAHEA), the Council on Rehabilitation Education, the Council on Social Work Education, the National Association of Schools of Music, the National Association of Schools of Public Affairs and Administration, the National Council for Accreditation of Teacher Education, the National League for Nursing.
**Religious orientation:** Arkansas State University is nonsectarian; no religious requirements.
**Library:** Collections totaling over 471,500 volumes, 2,426 periodical subscriptions, and 357,000 microform items.
**Special facilities/museums:** Art gallery, museum of Native American cultures and Arkansas artifacts.
**Athletic facilities:** Gymnasiums, field house, baseball, football, and softball fields, track, basketball, tennis, and volleyball courts, stadium.

**STUDENT BODY. Undergraduate profile:** 83% are state residents; 32% are transfers. 2% Asian-American, 11% Black, 85% White, 2% Other. Average age of undergraduates is 23.
**Freshman profile:** 4% of freshmen who took ACT scored 30 or over on English, 1% scored 30 or over on math, 2% scored 30 or over on composite; 36% scored 24 or over on English, 17% scored 24 or over on math, 30% scored 24 or over on composite; 79% scored 18 or over on English, 71% scored 18 or over on math, 79% scored 18 or over on composite; 98% scored 12 or over on English, 99% scored 12 or over on math, 99% scored 12 or over on composite; 100% scored 6 or over on English, 100% scored 6 or over on math, 100% scored 6 or over on composite. 97% of accepted applicants took ACT. 98% of freshmen come from public schools.
**Undergraduate achievement:** 63% of fall 1992 freshmen returned for fall 1993 term. 32% of entering class graduated.
**Foreign students:** 244 students are from out of the country. Countries represented include China, Japan, Kuwait, Malaysia, Pakistan, and Saudi Arabia; 54 in all.

**PROGRAMS OF STUDY. Degrees:** B.A., B.F.A., B.Gen.Studies, B.Mus., B.Mus.Ed., B.S.
**Majors:** Accounting, Administrative Services, Agricultural Business/Economics, Agricultural Education, Agricultural Engineering, Animal Science, Art, Art Education, Biology, Biology/Chemistry/Physics Education, Botany, Business Administration, Business Economics, Business Education, Chemistry, Communicative Disorders, Computer Applications, Computer Information Systems, Computer Science, Criminology, Early Childhood Education, Economics, Elementary Education, Engineering, English, English/Education, Finance, French, General Agriculture, General Studies, Geography, Graphic Design, Health Services Administration, History, Instrumental Music, International Business Studies, Journalism, Management, Manufacturing Technology, Marketing, Mathematics, Mathematics Education, Medical Technology, Music, Nursing, Performance, Philosophy, Physical Education, Physical Therapy, Physics, Plant Science, Political Science, Printing, Printing/Education, Psychology, Radio/Television, Real Estate/Insurance, Sacred Music, Social Science Education, Social Work, Sociology, Spanish, Spanish Education, Special Education/Elementary Education, Speech Communication Education, Speech Communication/Theatre Arts, Theatre Arts, Transportation, Urban/Regional Affairs, Vocal Music, Wildlife Management, Zoology.
**Distribution of degrees:** The majors with the highest enrollment are elementary education, early childhood education, and accounting; agricultural engineering and French have the lowest.
**Requirements:** General education requirement.
**Academic regulations:** Freshmen must maintain minimum 1.25 GPA; sophomores, 1.65 GPA; juniors, 1.85 GPA; seniors, 2.0 GPA.
**Special:** Minors offered in many majors and in agronomy, art history, general business, German, health education, horticulture, military science, and recreation. Associate's degrees offered. Double majors. Cooperative education programs. Graduate school at which undergraduates may take graduate-level courses. Preprofessional programs in law, medicine, veterinary science, pharmacy, dentistry, optometry, chiropractic, forestry, occupational therapy, and respiratory therapy. Teacher certification in early childhood, elementary, secondary, special education, and vo-tech education. Certification in specific subject areas. Member of International Student Exchange Program (ISEP). ROTC.
**Honors:** Honors program. Honor societies.
**Academic Assistance:** Remedial reading, writing, math, and study skills. Nonremedial tutoring.

**STUDENT LIFE. Housing:** Unmarried students under age 21 who have completed fewer than 60 semester hours must live on campus unless living with family. Women's and men's dorms. Fraternity housing. On-campus married-student housing. Sorority suites.
**Social atmosphere:** The 501 and Jubilation (clubs), Indian Mall, and Wal-Mart Supercenter are popular off-campus hangouts. On campus, the Reng Center is a favored haunt because the cafeteria and restaurant are located there. Student groups with the most influence on campus social life include Greeks, religious organizations, Student Government Association, and the Student Activities Board. Homecoming and fall rush are big events on campus. Basketball and volleyball games are also popular. The Convocation Center is the site for many live performances. "The city of Jonesboro is a perfect size town for a college," reports the editor of the student newspaper. "It's not too big or too small, and it's located close to both Little Rock and Memphis, TN. It's a dry county, though, which makes many students travel out of town often. Overall, ASU is a commuter-type school, but the administration and other campus organizations are trying to find attractions to keep students from going home on the weekends."
**Services and counseling/handicapped student services:** Placement services. Health service. Personal counseling. Career and academic guidance services. Physically disabled student services. Learning disabled services. Notetaking services. Tutors. Reader services for the blind.
**Campus organizations:** Undergraduate student government. Student newspaper (Herald, published twice/week). Literary magazine. Yearbook. Radio and TV stations. Concert choir, madrigal singers, Art Student Union, drama group, Student Activities Board, debating, photography club, Young Democrats, Republican Club, Model UN, Circle K, bowling and racquetball clubs, drill team, Adult Student Union, 140 organizations in all. 13 fraternities, six chapter houses; eight sororities, no chapter houses. 10% of men join a fraternity. 10% of women join a sorority.
**Religious organizations:** Baptist Student Union, Canterbury House, Chi Alpha, Christ on Campus Fellowship, Church of God in Christ, Fellowship of Christian Students, Islamic Association, Koinonia, Latter-Day Saints Association, Missionary Baptist Fellowship, Newman Club, Wesley Foundation.
**Minority/foreign student organizations:** Black Student Association. Malaysian Student Association, International Student Association.

**ATHLETICS. Physical education requirements:** Two semesters of physical education required.
**Intercollegiate competition:** 2% of students participate. Baseball (M), basketball (M,W), cheerleading (M,W), cross-country (M,W), football (M), golf (M,W), tennis (W), track and field (indoor) (M,W), track and field (outdoor) (M,W), volleyball (W). Member of Big West Conference, NCAA Division I, Sun Belt Conference.
**Intramural and club sports:** 5% of students participate. Intramural archery, badminton, basketball, bowling, cross-country, fencing, flag football, horseshoes, racquetball, soccer, softball, swimming, table tennis, tennis, track and field, volleyball.

**ADMISSIONS. Academic basis for candidate selection** (in order of priority): Secondary school record, standardized test scores, class rank, school's recommendation.
**Nonacademic basis for candidate selection:** Particular talent or ability is considered.
**Requirements:** Graduation from secondary school is required; GED is accepted. No specific distribution of secondary school units required. Minimum 2.15 GPA and minimum composite ACT score of 19 or minimum 2.0 GPA in college prep courses and minimum composite ACT score of 24 required. Conditional admission possible for applicants not meeting standard requirements. PASS Program for applicants not normally admissible. ACT is required; SAT may be substituted. Campus visit recommended. No off-campus interviews.
**Procedure:** Take SAT or ACT by July 31 of 12th year. Suggest filing application by July 31; no deadline. Notification of admission on rolling basis. Reply is required 30 days prior to registration. $40 room deposit, refundable until 45 days before registration. Freshmen accepted for terms other than fall.
**Special programs:** Admission may be deferred one year. Credit may be granted through CEEB Advanced Placement for scores of 3 or higher. Credit may be granted through CLEP general and subject exams, challenge exams, and military experience. Placement may be granted through ACT PEP exams. Early decision program. Deadline for applying for early decision is July 31. Early entrance/early admission program. Concurrent enrollment program.
**Transfer students:** Transfer students accepted for terms other than fall. In fall 1993, 32% of all new students were transfers into all classes. 1,414 transfer applications were received, 1,379 were accepted. Application deadline is July 31 for fall; December 31 for spring. Minimum 2.0 GPA required. Lowest course grade accepted is "C." At least 57 semester hours must be completed at the university to receive degree.

**Admissions contact:** Leonard McDaniel, M.S., Director of Admissions and Records. 501 972-3024.

**FINANCIAL AID. Available aid:** Pell grants, SEOG, state scholarships and grants, school scholarships and grants, private scholarships, ROTC scholarships, academic merit scholarships, and athletic scholarships. Perkins Loans (NDSL), PLUS, Stafford Loans (GSL), NSL, state loans, private loans, and SLS. Deferred payment plan.
**Financial aid statistics:** Average amounts of aid awarded freshmen: Scholarships and grants, $1,600; loans, $950.
**Supporting data/closing dates:** FAFSA/FAF/FFS: Priority filing date is May 1; accepted on rolling basis. Notification of awards on rolling basis.
**Financial aid contact:** Gerald Craig, M.S., Director of Financial Aid. 501 972-2310.

**STUDENT EMPLOYMENT.** College Work/Study Program. Institutional employment. 10% of full-time undergraduates work on campus during school year. Students may expect to earn an average of $2,300 during school year. Off-campus part-time employment opportunities rated "fair."

**COMPUTER FACILITIES.** 986 IBM/IBM-compatible and Macintosh/Apple microcomputers; 189 are networked. Students may access Digital, IBM minicomputer/mainframe systems, Internet. Residence halls may be equipped with stand-alone microcomputers. Computer languages and software packages include Assembler, BASIC, C, COBOL, FORTRAN, Pascal, RPG, SAS, SPSS. Computer facilities are available to all students.
**Fees:** None.
**Hours:** 7 AM-midn.

**GRADUATE CAREER DATA.** Highest graduate school enrollments: Arkansas State U.

**PROMINENT ALUMNI/AE.** Earl Bell and Al Joyner, 1984 Olympic medalists, track.

# Arkansas Tech University

**Russellville, AR 72801** **501 968-0389**

**1994-95 Costs.** Tuition: $1,730 (state residents), $3,460 (out-of-state). Room & board: $2,650. Fees, books, misc. academic expenses (school's estimate): $560.
**Enrollment.** Undergraduates: 1,704 men, 1,898 women (full-time). Freshman class: 1,738 applicants, 1,733 accepted, 953 enrolled. Graduate enrollment: 53 men, 136 women.
**Test score averages/ranges.** Average ACT scores: 20 English, 18 math, 19 composite. Range of ACT scores of middle 50%: 16-22 English, 16-20 math.
**Faculty.** 180 full-time; 70 part-time. 57% of faculty holds doctoral degree. Student/faculty ratio: 18 to 1.
**Selectivity rating.** Noncompetitive.

**PROFILE.** Arkansas Tech, founded in 1909, is a public, multipurpose university. Programs are offered through the Schools of Education, Liberal and Fine Arts, Physical and Life Sciences, and Systems Science. Its 475-acre campus is adjacent to Lake Dardanelle, in Russellville, 78 miles west of Little Rock.

**Accreditation:** NCACS. Professionally accredited by the American Medical Association (CAHEA), the National Association of Schools of Music, the National Council for Accreditation of Teacher Education, the National League for Nursing.
**Religious orientation:** Arkansas Tech University is nonsectarian; no religious requirements.
**Library:** Collections totaling over 203,487 volumes, 1,198 periodical subscriptions, and 659,685 microform items.
**Athletic facilities:** Gymnasium, field house, swimming pool, basketball, tennis, and volleyball courts, track, baseball, football, intramural, and softball fields, coliseum.

**STUDENT BODY. Undergraduate profile:** 98% are state residents; 31% are transfers. 1% Asian-American, 2% Black, 1% Hispanic, 1% Native American, 95% White. Average age of undergraduates is 22.
**Freshman profile:** 1% of freshmen who took ACT scored 30 or over on English, 1% scored 30 or over on math, 1% scored 30 or over on composite; 24% scored 24 or over on English, 12% scored 24 or over on math, 21% scored 24 or over on composite; 68% scored 18 or over on English, 57% scored 18 or over on math, 71% scored 18 or over on composite; 98% scored 12 or over on English, 99% scored 12 or over on math, 99% scored 12 or over on composite; 100% scored 6 or over on English, 100% scored 6 or over on math. 56% of accepted applicants took ACT. 97% of freshmen come from public schools.
**Undergraduate achievement:** 77% of fall 1992 freshmen returned for fall 1993 term.
**Foreign students:** 23 students are from out of the country. Countries represented include Canada, India, Indonesia, and Japan; 15 in all.

**PROGRAMS OF STUDY. Degrees:** B.A., B.F.A., B.S.
**Majors:** Accounting, Agricultural Business, Art, Art Education, Biological Sciences, Biology, Business Administration, Business Education, Chemistry, Computer Science, Creative Writing, Economics/Finance, Elementary Education, Engineering, English, Fishery/Wildlife Management, French, Geology, German, Health Information Management, Health/Physical Education, History/Political Science, Hotel/Restaurant Management, Journalism, Mathematics, Medical Technology, Music, Music Education, Nursing, Office Management, Physical Sciences, Psychology, Recreation/Park Administration, Secondary Education, Sociology, Spanish, Special Major.
**Distribution of degrees:** The majors with the highest enrollment are elementary education, business administration, and history; physical sciences, geology, and music have the lowest.
**Requirements:** General education requirement.
**Academic regulations:** Freshmen must maintain minimum 1.5 GPA; sophomores, juniors, seniors, 2.0 GPA.
**Special:** Courses offered in allied health science, anthropology, driver/safety education, educational media, library media, philosophy, physics, political science, and theatre. Associate's degrees offered. Double majors. Graduate school at which undergraduates may take graduate-level courses. Preprofessional programs in law, medicine, veterinary science, pharmacy, and dentistry. Exchange program with Westfield State Coll. Teacher certification in elementary and secondary education. Exchange program abroad in Japan (Komazawa U).
**Honors:** Honor societies.
**Academic Assistance:** Remedial reading and study skills. Nonremedial tutoring.

**STUDENT LIFE. Housing:** All freshmen under age 21 and students with fewer than 60 semester hours must live on campus unless living with family. Women's and men's dorms. Both on-campus and off-campus married-student housing. 20% of students live in college housing.
**Services and counseling/handicapped student services:** Placement services. Health service. Counseling services for military and veteran students. Career and academic guidance services. Physically disabled student services. Tape recorders. Tutors.
**Campus organizations:** Undergraduate student government. Student newspaper (Arka Tech, published once/week). Literary magazine. Yearbook. Radio and TV stations. Choir, madrigal singers, orchestra, brass choir, several bands, departmental and professional clubs, Young Democrats, Young Republicans, service and special-interest groups, 88 organizations in all. Six fraternities, no chapter houses; three sororities, no chapter houses. 19% of men join a fraternity. 12% of women join a sorority.
**Religious organizations:** Several religious groups.
**Minority/foreign student organizations:** Association of Black Students. Association for Cultural Interaction.

**ATHLETICS. Physical education requirements:** Two semester hours of physical education or military science required.
**Intercollegiate competition:** 6% of students participate. Baseball (M), basketball (M,W), cheerleading (M,W), cross-country (W), football (M), golf (M), riflery (M), tennis (M,W), volleyball (W). Member of Arkansas Intercollegiate Conference, NAIA.
**Intramural and club sports:** 21% of students participate. Intramural basketball, football, handball, soccer, softball, tennis, track, volleyball.

**ADMISSIONS. Academic basis for candidate selection** (in order of priority): Secondary school record, standardized test scores, class rank, school's recommendation.
**Requirements:** Graduation from secondary school is recommended; GED is accepted. 15 secondary school units recommended, including 4 units of English, 3 units of math, and 8 units of science, social studies, or electives. Nongraduates may be admitted on basis of 15 solid secondary school units and recommendation of secondary school principal or superintendent. Campus visit recommended. No off-campus interviews.
**Procedure:** Notification of admission on rolling basis. $50 room deposit, refundable until July 15. Freshmen accepted for terms other than fall.
**Special programs:** Admission may be deferred. Credit may be granted through CLEP general and subject exams, challenge exams, and life experience. Early entrance/early admission program. Concurrent enrollment program.
**Transfer students:** Transfer students accepted for terms other than fall. In fall 1993, 31% of all new students were transfers into all classes. 542 transfer applications were received, 534 were accepted. Application deadline is 30 days before registration for fall; 30 days before registration for spring. Minimum 2.0 GPA required. Lowest course grade accepted is "C." Maximum number of transferable credits is 68 semester hours. At least 30 semester hours must be completed at the university to receive degree.
**Admissions contact:** Harold Cornett, M.A., Director of Admissions. 501 968-0343.

**FINANCIAL AID. Available aid:** Pell grants, SEOG, state scholarships and grants, school scholarships, private scholarships, academic merit scholarships, and athletic scholarships. Perkins Loans (NDSL), PLUS, Stafford Loans (GSL), and SLS.
**Financial aid statistics:** 30% of aid is not need-based. Average amounts of aid awarded freshmen: Scholarships and grants, $1,650.
**Supporting data/closing dates:** FAFSA/FAF/FFS: Priority filing date is May 1. School's own aid application: Priority filing date is May 1. Notification of awards begins June 1.
**Financial aid contact:** Shirley Goines, Director of Financial Aid. 501 968-0399.

**STUDENT EMPLOYMENT.** College Work/Study Program. Institutional employment. 10% of full-time undergraduates work on campus during school year. Students may expect to earn an average of $1,150 during school year. Off-campus part-time employment opportunities rated "good."

**COMPUTER FACILITIES.** 400 IBM/IBM-compatible and Macintosh/Apple microcomputers; 4 are networked. Students may access IBM minicomputer/mainframe systems. Computer languages and software packages include all major languages and software programs. Computer use in some labs limited to specific fields.
**Fees:** None.
**Hours:** 100 hours/week.

# Harding University

**Searcy, AR 72149** **501 279-4000**

**1994-95 Costs.** Tuition: $5,100. Room & board: $3,500. Fees, books, misc. academic expenses (school's estimate): $1,200.
**Enrollment.** Undergraduates: 1,471 men, 1,666 women (full-time). Freshman class: 1,621 applicants, 1,067 accepted, 841 enrolled. Graduate enrollment: 83 men, 106 women.
**Test score averages/ranges.** Average SAT scores: 520 verbal, 530 math. Range of SAT scores of middle 50%: 460-540 verbal, 470-550 math. Average ACT scores: 23 English, 24 math, 24 composite. Range of ACT scores of middle 50%: 21-26 English, 22-27 math.
**Faculty.** 183 full-time; 2 part-time. 70% of faculty holds doctoral degree. Student/faculty ratio: 18 to 1.
**Selectivity rating.** More competitive.

**PROFILE.** Harding, founded in 1924, is a private university with religious orientation. Programs are offered through the Colleges of Arts and Sciences and the Schools of Bible and Religion, Business, Education, and Nursing. Its 200-acre campus is located in Searcy, 45 miles northeast of Little Rock.

**Accreditation:** NCACS. Professionally accredited by the Council on Social Work Education, the National Association of Schools of Music, the National Council for Accreditation of Teacher Education, the National League for Nursing.
**Religious orientation:** Harding University is an interdenominational Christian school; eight semester hours of religion required.
**Library:** Collections totaling over 350,000 volumes, 1,320 periodical subscriptions, and 75,000 microform items.
**Special facilities/museums:** On-campus academy (prep school grades 1-12).
**Athletic facilities:** Gymnasiums, field houses, basketball, racquetball, tennis, and volleyball courts, baseball, football, intramural, soccer, and softball fields, swimming pools, gymnastics and weight rooms, bowling alley, golf practice area.

**STUDENT BODY. Undergraduate profile:** 28% are state residents; 8% are transfers. 3% Asian-American, 5% Black, 4% Hispanic, 1% Native American, 87% White. Average age of undergraduates is 21.
**Freshman profile:** 25% of accepted applicants took SAT; 75% took ACT. 75% of freshmen come from public schools.
**Undergraduate achievement:** 75% of fall 1992 freshmen returned for fall 1993 term. 60% of entering class graduated. 20% of students who completed a degree program immediately went on to graduate study.
**Foreign students:** Countries represented include Australia, Guatemala, Honduras, Japan, Mexico, and Nicaragua.

**PROGRAMS OF STUDY. Degrees:** B.A., B.Bus.Admin., B.F.A., B.Mus., B.Mus.Ed., B.S., B.Soc.Work.
**Majors:** Accounting, Advertising, American Studies, Applied Music, Applied Sociology, Art, Bible, Bible/Religion, Biblical Languages, Biochemistry, Biology, Business Education, Chemistry, Child Development, Computer Information Systems, Computer Science, Dietary Technology, Dietetics, Dietetics/Food Service Management, Education, Elementary Education, English, Fashion Merchandising, Food Merchandising, French, General Science, Gerontology, History, Home Economics, Interior Design, International Studies, Journalism, Kindergarten Education, Management, Marketing, Mass Communications, Mass Media, Mathematics, Mathematics Education, Medical Technology, Missions, Music, Music Education, Nursing, Office Systems, Physical Education, Physics, Piano, Political Science, Print Journalism, Psychology, Public Administration, Public Relations, Religious Education, Secondary Education, Secretarial Science, Social Science, Social Work, Sociology, Spanish, Special Education, Speech, Speech Therapy, Sport Management, Television/Radio, Viola/Violin, Vocational Home Economics, Voice.
**Distribution of degrees:** The majors with the highest enrollment are accounting, management, and elementary education.
**Requirements:** General education requirement.
**Academic regulations:** Freshmen must maintain minimum 1.5 GPA; sophomores, 1.75 GPA; juniors, 2.0 GPA; seniors, 2.0 GPA.
**Special:** Minors offered in all majors and in Greek. Associate's degrees offered. Double majors. Independent study. Accelerated study. Internships. Cooperative education programs. Graduate school at which undergraduates may take graduate-level courses. Preprofessional programs in law, medicine, veterinary science, pharmacy, dentistry, theology, optometry, agriculture, and architecture. 3-2 engineering programs with U of Arkansas at Fayetteville, Louisiana Tech U, and U of Missouri at Rolla. 3-2 dentistry, law, medical technology, medicine, and nursing programs. Teacher certification in early childhood, elementary, secondary, and special education. Study abroad in England, Greece, and Italy. ROTC at U of Arkansas at Little Rock.
**Honors:** Honors program. Honor societies.
**Academic Assistance:** Remedial reading, writing, math, and study skills. Nonremedial tutoring.

**STUDENT LIFE. Housing:** All unmarried students under age 23 must live on campus unless living with family. Women's and men's dorms. School-owned/operated apartments. Off-campus privately-owned housing. Both on-campus and off-campus married-student housing. 85% of students live in college housing.
**Social atmosphere:** The Student Center, front lawn, and the old gym are popular on-campus gathering spots. Student social life centers around the university's many social clubs and service organizations. Popular events include Homecoming, Club Pledge Week, Spring Sing, and the American Studies Lecture Series. Because the university is located in a small town, "the social and cultural life is very campus-centered," reports the editor of the student newspaper. The Student Association schedules regular movies, concerts, and other performances, and large numbers of students participate in social clubs and sports.
**Services and counseling/handicapped student services:** Placement services. Health service. Day care. Personal and psychological counseling. Career and academic guidance services. Physically disabled student services. Notetaking services. Tape recorders. Tutors. Reader services for the blind.
**Campus organizations:** Undergraduate student government. Student newspaper (Bison, published once/week). Yearbook. Radio and TV stations. A cappella chorus, chorale, band, orchestra, Belles and Beaux, drama club, forensics, debating, intercollegiate business games, JOY, Big Brothers, 75 organizations in all. 20 fraternities, no chapter houses; 23 sororities, no chapter houses.
**Religious organizations:** Campus Ministry.
**Minority/foreign student organizations:** Ujima (African-American club). Association for Foreign Students.

**ATHLETICS. Physical education requirements:** Three semester hours of physical education required.
**Intercollegiate competition:** 9% of students participate. Baseball (M), basketball (M,W), cheerleading (M,W), cross-country (M,W), football (M), golf (M), tennis (M,W), track and field (indoor) (M,W), track and field (outdoor) (M,W), volleyball (W). Member of Arkansas Intercollegiate Conference, NAIA.
**Intramural and club sports:** 80% of students participate. Intramural archery, badminton, basketball, flag football, racquetball, softball, swimming, tennis, volleyball. Men's club soccer.

**ADMISSIONS. Academic basis for candidate selection** (in order of priority): Secondary school record, standardized test scores, school's recommendation, class rank.
**Nonacademic basis for candidate selection:** Character and personality are important. Extracurricular participation, particular talent or ability, geographical distribution, and alumni/ae relationship are considered.
**Requirements:** Graduation from secondary school is required; GED is not accepted. No specific distribution of secondary school units required. Minimum composite ACT score of 19, rank in top half of secondary school class, and minimum 2.5 GPA required. Portfolio required of art program applicants. Audition required of music program applicants. ACT is required; SAT may be substituted. Campus visit and interview required. Off-campus interviews available with admissions and alumni representatives.
**Procedure:** Take SAT or ACT by April 1 of 12th year. Suggest filing application by March 1. Application deadline is June 1. Notification of admission on rolling basis. Reply is required by May 1. $125 room deposit, refundable until May 1. Freshmen accepted for terms other than fall.
**Special programs:** Admission may be deferred one year. Placement may be granted through CEEB Advanced Placement exams for scores of 3 or higher. Credit and/or placement may be granted through CLEP general and subject exams. Credit and placement may be granted through challenge exams. Early decision program. In fall 1993, 50 applied for early decision and 50 were accepted. Early entrance/early admission program.
**Transfer students:** Transfer students accepted for terms other than fall. In fall 1993, 8% of all new students were transfers into all classes. 292 transfer applications were received, 218 were accepted. Application deadline is May 1 for fall; October 1 for spring. Minimum 2.5 GPA recommended. Lowest course grade accepted is "D."
**Admissions contact:** Mike Williams, Director of Admissions. 501 279-4407.

**FINANCIAL AID. Available aid:** Pell grants, SEOG, Federal Nursing Student Scholarships, state scholarships and grants, school scholarships and grants, private scholarships and grants, academic merit scholarships, athletic scholarships, and aid for undergraduate foreign students. The Stephens Scholars Program (for African-American students). Perkins Loans (NDSL), PLUS, Stafford Loans (GSL), state loans, school loans, private loans, and SLS. Tuition Plan Inc. University's own plan.
**Financial aid statistics:** 20% of aid is not need-based. In 1993-94, 77% of all undergraduate applicants received aid; 77% of freshman applicants. Average amounts of aid awarded freshmen: Scholarships and grants, $1,000; loans, $1,200.
**Supporting data/closing dates:** FAFSA: Priority filing date is April 1. FAF/FFS: Deadline is April 1. State aid form: Priority filing date is April 1; deadline is August 1. Notification of awards on rolling basis.
**Financial aid contact:** Zearl Watson, Director of Financial Aid. 501 279-4257.

**STUDENT EMPLOYMENT.** College Work/Study Program. Institutional employment. 30% of full-time undergraduates work on campus during school year. Students may expect to earn an average of $1,100 during school year. Off-campus part-time employment opportunities rated "excellent."

**COMPUTER FACILITIES.** 250 IBM/IBM-compatible and Macintosh/Apple microcomputers. Students may access Digital minicomputer/mainframe systems, Internet. Client/LAN operating systems include Apple/Macintosh, DOS, Windows NT, X-windows, DEC. Computer languages and software packages include Assembler, BASIC, C, COBOL, FORTRAN, Pascal, PL/1; database, graphics, publishing, statistical, word processing programs. Computer facilities are available to all students.
**Fees:** $10 computer fee per class.
**Hours:** 24 hours.

**GRADUATE CAREER DATA.** Graduate school percentages: 2% enter law school. 3% enter medical school. 1% enter dental school. 2% enter graduate business programs. 15% enter graduate arts and sciences programs. 2% enter theological school/seminary. Highest graduate school enrollments: U of Arkansas, Florida State U, U of Tennessee, U of Texas. 60% of graduates choose careers in business and industry. Companies and businesses that hire graduates: Arthur Andersen, Pennzoil, Texas Instruments.

**PROMINENT ALUMNI/AE.** Jack McNutt, president, Murphy Oil; Kenneth Starr, U.S. solicitor general.

## Henderson State University

**Arkadelphia, AR 71923** 501 246-5511

**1994-95 Costs.** Tuition: $1,560 (state residents), $3,120 (out-of-state). Room & board: $2,400. Fees, books, misc. academic expenses (school's estimate): $600.
**Enrollment.** Undergraduates: 1,357 men, 1,608 women (full-time). Freshman class: 1,220 accepted, 733 enrolled. Graduate enrollment: 106 men, 281 women.
**Test score averages/ranges.** Average ACT scores: 21 composite.
**Faculty.** 150 full-time; 30 part-time. 60% of faculty holds doctoral degree. Student/faculty ratio: 20 to 1.
**Selectivity rating.** Less competitive.

**PROFILE.** Henderson State, founded in 1980, is a public, multipurpose university. Programs are offered through the Schools of Business, Education, Fine Arts, Liberal Arts, and Natural Sciences and Mathematics. Its 127-acre campus is located in Arkadelphia, 60 miles southwest of Little Rock.

**Accreditation:** NCACS. Professionally accredited by the National Council for Accreditation of Teacher Education, the National League for Nursing.
**Religious orientation:** Henderson State University is nonsectarian; no religious requirements.
**Library:** Collections totaling over 250,000 volumes.
**Special facilities/museums:** Natural history museum, closed-circuit TV studio.
**Athletic facilities:** Baseball, football, and softball fields, swimming pool, weight room, basketball, racquetball, tennis, and volleyball courts.

**STUDENT BODY. Undergraduate profile:** 95% are state residents. 14% Black, 86% White. Average age of undergraduates is 21.
**Freshman profile:** Majority of accepted applicants took ACT.
**Undergraduate achievement:** 80% of fall 1992 freshmen returned for fall 1993 term. 60% of entering class graduated.
**Foreign students:** 21 students are from out of the country. Countries represented include Canada, Germany, Hong Kong, Lebanon, Malaysia, and Pakistan; seven in all.

**PROGRAMS OF STUDY. Degrees:** B.A., B.F.A., B.Mus., B.Mus.Ed., B.S.

**Majors:** Accounting, Art, Aviation, Biological Science, Chemistry, Communication Disorders, Computer Science, Elementary Education, English, Graphic Design, History, Home Economics, Human Services, Journalism, Management, Marketing, Mathematics, Music, Nursing, Physical Education, Physics, Political Science, Psychology, Public Administration, Recreation, Secondary Education, Social Sciences, Sociology, Spanish, Speech/Theatre, Studio Art.
**Distribution of degrees:** The majors with the highest enrollment are elementary education, business management, and nursing; general science, physics, and studio art have the lowest.
**Requirements:** General education requirement.
**Academic regulations:** Freshmen must maintain minimum 1.25 GPA; sophomores, 1.75 GPA; juniors, 2.0 GPA; seniors, 2.0 GPA.
**Special:** Minors offered in all majors. National standardized test, such as GRE or National Teacher Exam, required in order to graduate. Courses offered in anthropology, geography, philosophy, and physical science. Associate's degrees offered. Double majors. Pass/fail grading option. Graduate school at which undergraduates may take graduate-level courses. Preprofessional programs in law, medicine, pharmacy, dentistry, and engineering. Member of Joint Education Consortium. Teacher certification in early childhood, elementary, secondary, and special education.
**Honors:** Honors program.
**Academic Assistance:** Remedial reading. Nonremedial tutoring.
**STUDENT LIFE. Housing:** All freshmen must live on campus. Women's and men's dorms. On-campus married-student housing. 50% of students live in college housing.
**Social atmosphere:** Spring Fling, Fite Nite, the HSU-Ouachita Baptist Univeristy football game, and the Swamp Stomp are the most popular campus events reports the student newspaper. Students gather at the student union pub and several fast-food chains.
**Services and counseling/handicapped student services:** Placement services. Health service. Counseling services for minority, veteran, and older students. Personal counseling. Career and academic guidance services. Physically disabled student services. Learning disabled services. Notetaking services. Tape recorders. Tutors. Reader services for the blind.
**Campus organizations:** Undergraduate student government. Student newspaper (Oracle, published once/week). Literary magazine. Yearbook. Radio station. Choir, orchestra, symphonic band, marching and pep bands, drama group, Big Brothers. Five fraternities, two chapter houses; six sororities, all with chapter houses. 15% of men join a fraternity. 10% of women join a sorority.
**Religious organizations:** Several religious groups.
**Minority/foreign student organizations:** Confederation of Black Students.
**ATHLETICS. Physical education requirements:** Two semesters of physical education required.
**Intercollegiate competition:** 1% of students participate. Baseball (M), basketball (M,W), cheerleading (M,W), cross-country (M,W), diving (M,W), football (M), golf (M), swimming (M,W), tennis (M,W), track (indoor) (M), track (outdoor) (M), track and field (indoor) (M), track and field (outdoor) (M,W), volleyball (W). Member of Gulf South Conference, NCAA Division II, New South Intercollegiate Swim League.
**Intramural and club sports:** Intramural basketball, flag football, softball, volleyball. Men's club soccer. Women's club soccer.
**ADMISSIONS. Academic basis for candidate selection** (in order of priority): Standardized test scores, secondary school record, class rank.
**Nonacademic basis for candidate selection:** Character and personality are emphasized. Extracurricular participation is important. Particular talent or ability is considered.
**Requirements:** Graduation from secondary school is required; GED is accepted. 15 units required and the following program of study recommended: 4 units of English, 2 units of math, 2 units of science, 2 units of foreign language, 2 units of social studies, 1 unit of history, 2 units of electives. Minimum composite ACT score of 16 and minimum 2.5 GPA required. Conditional admission possible for applicants not meeting standard requirements. ACT is required; SAT may be substituted. Campus visit and interview recommended. No off-campus interviews.
**Procedure:** Take SAT or ACT by March of 12th year. Application deadline is August 26. Notification of admission on rolling basis. No set date by which applicants must accept offer. $40 refundable room deposit. Freshmen accepted for terms other than fall.
**Special programs:** Admission may be deferred. Credit may be granted through CEEB Advanced Placement for scores of 3 or higher. Credit may be granted through CLEP general and subject exams, ACT PEP, challenge exams, and military experience. Early entrance/early admission program. Concurrent enrollment program.
**Transfer students:** Transfer students accepted for terms other than fall. Minimum 2.0 GPA required. Maximum number of transferable credits is 67 semester hours from a two-year school and 94 semester hours from a four-year school. At least 30 semester hours must be completed at the university to receive degree.
**Admissions contact:** Tom Gattin, M.S.E., Director of Admissions. 501 246-5511, extension 3270.
**FINANCIAL AID. Available aid:** Pell grants, SEOG, state scholarships and grants, school scholarships, private scholarships and grants, academic merit scholarships, and athletic scholarships. Perkins Loans (NDSL), PLUS, Stafford Loans (GSL), school loans, and SLS. Installment plan for room and board payments.
**Financial aid statistics:** In 1993-94, 65% of all undergraduate applicants received aid; 85% of freshman applicants. Average amounts of aid awarded freshmen: Scholarships and grants, $500; loans, $1,000.
**Supporting data/closing dates:** State aid form: Priority filing date is May 1.
**Financial aid contact:** Nelda Branstine, Director of Financial Aid. 501 246-5511, extension 3270.
**STUDENT EMPLOYMENT.** College Work/Study Program. Institutional employment. 20% of full-time undergraduates work on campus during school year. Students may expect to earn an average of $1,000 during school year. Off-campus part-time employment opportunities rated "fair."
**COMPUTER FACILITIES.** 50 IBM/IBM-compatible microcomputers; all are networked. Students may access IBM minicomputer/mainframe systems. Computer languages and software packages include Ada, Assembly, BASIC, C, COBOL, dBASE, DisplayWrite, FORTRAN, Lotus 1-2-3, Multiplan, Pascal, RPG, Select. Computer facilities are available to all students.
**Hours:** 7 AM-10 PM (M-F); 8 AM-5 PM (Sa); 1 PM-10 PM (Su).

# Hendrix College

**Conway, AR 72032-3080** **501 329-6811**

**1994-95 Costs.** Tuition: $8,800. Room: $1,260. Board: $1,935. Fees, books, misc. academic expenses (school's estimate): $628.
**Enrollment.** Undergraduates: 444 men, 542 women (full-time). Freshman class: 817 applicants, 743 accepted, 337 enrolled.
**Test score averages/ranges.** Average SAT scores: 532 verbal, 557 math. Range of SAT scores of middle 50%: 1050-1150 combined. Average ACT scores: 26 composite. Range of ACT scores of middle 50%: 24-28 composite.
**Faculty.** 74 full-time; 12 part-time. 80% of faculty holds doctoral degree. Student/faculty ratio: 14 to 1.
**Selectivity rating.** Highly competitive.

**PROFILE.** Hendrix, founded in 1876, is a church-affiliated, liberal arts college. Programs are offered in the areas of Humanities, Natural Science, and Social Science. Its 155-acre campus is located in Conway, 25 miles north of Little Rock.

**Accreditation:** NCACS. Professionally accredited by the National Association of Schools of Music, the National Council for Accreditation of Teacher Education.
**Religious orientation:** Hendrix College is affiliated with the United Methodist Church; no religious requirements.
**Library:** Collections totaling over 195,000 volumes, 586 periodical subscriptions, and 143,608 microform items.
**Special facilities/museums:** Language lab.
**Athletic facilities:** Gymnasiums, weight rooms, swimming pool, basketball, racquetball, tennis, and volleyball courts, track, intramural fields, fitness course.
**STUDENT BODY. Undergraduate profile:** 75% are state residents; 3% are transfers. 2% Asian-American, 6% Black, 1% Hispanic, 90% White, 1% Other. Average age of undergraduates is 19.
**Freshman profile:** 2% of freshmen who took SAT scored 700 or over on verbal, 7% scored 700 or over on math; 27% scored 600 or over on verbal, 37% scored 600 or over on math; 67% scored 500 or over on verbal, 78% scored 500 or over on math; 90% scored 400 or over on verbal, 93% scored 400 or over on math; 99% scored 300 or over on verbal, 99% scored 300 or over on math. 42% of accepted applicants took SAT; 92% took ACT.
**Undergraduate achievement:** 75% of fall 1991 freshmen returned for fall 1992 term. 54% of entering class graduated. 36% of students who completed a degree program immediately went on to graduate study.
**PROGRAMS OF STUDY. Degrees:** B.A.
**Majors:** Art, Biology, Chemistry, Economics/Business, Elementary Education, English, French, German, History, Humanities Area, Integrative Studies, Mathematics, Music, Philosophy, Philosophy/Religion, Physical Education, Physics, Political Science, Psychology, Religion, Sociology, Spanish, Theatre Arts.
**Distribution of degrees:** The majors with the highest enrollment are biology, economics/business, and political science; French, German, and philosophy/religion have the lowest.
**Requirements:** General education requirement.
**Academic regulations:** Minimum 2.0 GPA must be maintained.
**Special:** Self-designed majors. Dual degrees. Independent study. Pass/fail grading option. Internships. Preprofessional programs in law, medicine, veterinary science, pharmacy, dentistry, theology, engineering, and social work. 3-2 engineering programs with Columbia U, Vanderbilt U, and Washington U. Member of Associated Colleges of the South. Washington Semester. Gulf Coast Research Lab summer courses. Exchange program with Southern College University Union. Tuition exchange program. Teacher certification in elementary and secondary education. Certification in specific subject areas. Exchange programs abroad in Austria (Karl Franzens U) and Japan (Nanzan U). Member of International Student Exchange Program (ISEP), Association of Colleges and Universities for International and Intercultural Studies, and the Experiment in International Living. Study abroad also in England. ROTC at U of Central Arkansas
**Academic Assistance:** Nonremedial tutoring.
**ADMISSIONS. Academic basis for candidate selection** (in order of priority): Secondary school record, standardized test scores, school's recommendation, essay.
**Nonacademic basis for candidate selection:** Extracurricular participation is important. Character and personality, particular talent or ability, and geographical distribution are considered.
**Requirements:** Graduation from secondary school is recommended; GED is accepted. 13 units and the following program of study are recommended: 4 units of English, 3 units of math, 2 units of science, 1 unit of foreign language, 3 units of social studies. SAT or ACT is recommended. Campus visit and interview recommended. Off-campus interviews available with an admissions representative. No off-campus interviews.
**Procedure:** Take SAT or ACT by December of 12th year. Suggest filing application by April 1. Notification of admission on rolling basis. Reply is required by May 1. $175 tuition deposit, refundable until May 1. $75 room deposit, refundable until May 1. Freshmen accepted for terms other than fall.
**Special programs:** Admission may be deferred one year. Credit may be granted through CEEB Advanced Placement for scores of 4 or higher. Credit may be granted through CLEP general and subject exams. Early entrance/early admission program.
**Transfer students:** Transfer students accepted for terms other than fall. In fall 1992, 3% of all new students were transfers into all classes. 49 transfer applications were received, 37 were accepted. Application deadline is August 1 for fall; March 1 for spring. Lowest course grade accepted is "C." At least 18 quarter hours must be completed at the college to receive degree.
**Admissions contact:** Rudy Pollan, M.B.A., Director of Admissions. 501 450-1362, extension 1362.
**FINANCIAL AID. Available aid:** Pell grants, SEOG, state scholarships and grants, school scholarships and grants, private scholarships and grants, ROTC scholarships, academic merit scholarships, and aid for undergraduate foreign students. Perkins Loans (NDSL), PLUS, Stafford Loans (GSL), private loans, and SLS. Tuition Plan Inc.

**Financial aid statistics:** 35% of aid is not need-based. In 1992-93, 97% of all undergraduate applicants received aid; 95% of freshman applicants. Average amounts of aid awarded freshmen: Scholarships and grants, $3,612; loans, $2,314.
**Supporting data/closing dates:** FAFSA: Priority filing date is April 1; accepted on rolling basis. FAF/FFS: Priority filing date is April 1. Notification of awards on rolling basis.
**Financial aid contact:** Carlia Sproles, M.B.A., Director of Financial Aid. 501 450-1368, extension 1368.

# John Brown University

**Siloam Springs, AR 72761** **501 524-3131**

**1994-95 Costs.** Tuition: $6,938. Room & board: $3,672. Fees, books, misc. academic expenses (school's estimate): $548.
**Enrollment.** Undergraduates: 463 men, 444 women (full-time). Freshman class: 514 applicants, 406 accepted, 230 enrolled.
**Test score averages/ranges.** Average SAT scores: 460 verbal, 490 math. Average ACT scores: 23 composite.
**Faculty.** 63 full-time; 25 part-time. 65% of faculty holds doctoral degree. Student/faculty ratio: 16 to 1.
**Selectivity rating.** Less competitive.

**PROFILE.** John Brown, founded in 1919, is a liberal arts university with religious orientation. Its 200-acre campus is located in the town of Siloam Springs, 25 miles from Fayetteville.

**Accreditation:** NCACS. Professionally accredited by the National Council for Accreditation of Teacher Education.
**Religious orientation:** John Brown University is an interdenominational Christian school; four semesters of religion required.
**Library:** Collections totaling over 92,000 volumes, 620 periodical subscriptions and 125 microform items.
**Special facilities/museums:** Wellness assessment center, human anatomy lab, television studio.
**Athletic facilities:** Gymnasiums, field house, badminton, basketball, racquetball, tennis, and volleyball courts, track, baseball, intramural, and soccer fields, aerobics center, swimming pool.
**STUDENT BODY. Undergraduate profile:** 27% are state residents; 21% are transfers. 1% Asian-American, 2% Black, 1% Hispanic, 1% Native American, 84% White, 12% Foreign. Average age of undergraduates is 21.
**Freshman profile:** 2% of freshmen who took SAT scored 700 or over on verbal, 3% scored 700 or over on math; 5% scored 600 or over on verbal, 14% scored 600 or over on math; 31% scored 500 or over on verbal, 42% scored 500 or over on math; 74% scored 400 or over on verbal, 82% scored 400 or over on math; 97% scored 300 or over on verbal, 98% scored 300 or over on math. 56% of accepted applicants took SAT; 64% took ACT. 65% of freshmen come from public schools.
**Undergraduate achievement:** 73% of fall 1991 freshmen returned for fall 1992 term. 42% of entering class graduated. 20% of students who completed a degree program went on to graduate study within one year.
**Foreign students:** 40 students are from out of the country. Countries represented include China, Costa Rica, Ethiopia, Guatemala, Honduras, and Nicaragua; 25 in all.
**PROGRAMS OF STUDY. Degrees:** B.A., B.Mus., B.Mus.Ed., B.S.
**Majors:** Accounting, Art/Design, Bible, Biochemistry, Biology, Biology Teaching, Broadcasting, Business Administration, Business Teaching, Camping Ministries, Chemistry, Chemistry Teaching, Church Ministry, Community/Corporate Wellness, Computer Systems/Engineering, Construction Engineering, Construction Management, Electrical Engineering, Elementary Education, Engineering, Engineering Management, English, English Teaching, Family Ministries, History, Intercultural Studies, Interdisciplinary Studies, Journalism, Mathematics, Medical Technology, Missions, Music, Music Teaching, Office Administration, Pastoral Studies, Physical Education, Pretheological Studies, Psychology, Public Relations, Social Studies, Social Studies Teaching, Sports Medicine, Youth Ministries.
**Distribution of degrees:** The majors with the highest enrollment are business administration, elementary education, and broadcasting; Bible, history, and community/corporate wellness have the lowest.
**Requirements:** General education requirement.
**Academic regulations:** Freshmen must maintain minimum 1.75 GPA; sophomores, 1.75 GPA; juniors, 1.75 GPA; seniors, 2.0 GPA.
**Special:** Minors offered in many majors and in business computer information systems, computer science, economics, general science, physics, religion/philosophy, and sociology. Associate's degrees offered. Double majors. Independent study. Internships. Preprofessional programs in law, medicine, veterinary science, pharmacy, dentistry, theology, and optometry. 3-1 medical technology program with hospital in Joplin, Mo. Member of Christian College Consortium. Washington Semester. American Studies Program (Washington, D.C.), other off-campus programs through Christian College Consortium. Latin American Studies Program. Teacher certification in early childhood, elementary, secondary, and special education. Certification in specific subject areas. Study abroad in Israel. Summer ministry program with overseas missionary experience. ROTC at U of Arkansas.
**Honors:** Honors program. Honor societies.
**Academic Assistance:** Remedial reading, writing, math, and study skills. Nonremedial tutoring.
**ADMISSIONS. Academic basis for candidate selection** (in order of priority): Secondary school record, standardized test scores, class rank, school's recommendation, essay.
**Nonacademic basis for candidate selection:** Character and personality are emphasized. Particular talent or ability and alumni/ae relationship are important. Extracurricular participation and geographical distribution are considered.
**Requirements:** Graduation from secondary school is required; GED is accepted. 21 units and the following program of study are recommended: 4 units of English, 4 units of math, 3 units of science, 2 units of foreign language, 3 units of social studies, 2 units of history, 4 units of electives. Rank in top 40th percentile on SAT or ACT, rank in top half of secondary school class, and minimum 2.5 GPA required. Additional math and science units required of engineering program applicants. Conditional admission possible for applicants not meeting standard requirements. ACT is required; SAT may be substituted. Campus visit and interview recommended. Off-campus interviews available with an admissions representative.
**Procedure:** Take SAT or ACT by October of 12th year. Visit college for interview by May of 12th year. Suggest filing application by December 1. Application deadline is July 15. Notification of admission on rolling basis. Reply is required within 30 days of acceptance. $50 tuition deposit, refundable until June 1. $50 room deposit, refundable until August 1. Freshmen accepted for terms other than fall.
**Special programs:** Credit and/or placement may be granted through CEEB Advanced Placement exams for scores of 3 or higher. Credit and/or placement may be granted through CLEP general and subject exams, ACT PEP, DANTES exams, and military experience. Early entrance/early admission program. Concurrent enrollment program.
**Transfer students:** Transfer students accepted for terms other than fall. In fall 1992, 21% of all new students were transfers into all classes. 128 transfer applications were received, 112 were accepted. Application deadline is July 15 for fall; November 1 for spring. Minimum 2.0 GPA required. Lowest course grade accepted is "C." Maximum number of transferable credits is 84 semester hours. At least 40 semester hours must be completed at the university to receive degree.
**Admissions contact:** Don Crandall, M.S., Director of Enrollment Management. 800 634-6969.
**FINANCIAL AID. Available aid:** Pell grants, SEOG, state scholarships and grants, school scholarships and grants, private scholarships, academic merit scholarships, and athletic scholarships. Perkins Loans (NDSL), PLUS, Stafford Loans (GSL), and SLS. Monthly installment plan.
**Financial aid statistics:** 24% of aid is not need-based. In 1992-93, 89% of all undergraduate applicants received aid; 95% of freshman applicants. Average amounts of aid awarded freshmen: Scholarships and grants, $1,400; loans, $2,300.
**Supporting data/closing dates:** FAFSA/FAF/FFS: Priority filing date is March 1. State aid form: Priority filing date is April 1. Income tax forms: Priority filing date is April 1. Notification of awards on rolling basis.

# Lyon College

**Batesville, AR 72503** **501 793-9813**

**1993-94 Costs.** Tuition: $8,060. Room & board: $3,536.
**Enrollment.** Undergraduates: 233 men, 297 women (full-time). Freshman class: 708 applicants, 334 accepted, 166 enrolled.
**Test score averages/ranges.** Average SAT scores: 490 verbal, 542 math. Range of ACT scores of middle 50%: 23-28 English, 20-25 math.
**Faculty.** 42 full-time; 12 part-time. 76% of faculty holds doctoral degree. Student/faculty ratio: 11 to 1.
**Selectivity rating.** More competitive.

**PROFILE.** Lyon College, founded in 1872, is a church-affiliated, liberal arts institution. Formerly Arkansas College, it changed its name in 1994. Its 125-acre campus is predominantly modern and is located in Batesville, 90 miles north of Little Rock.

**Accreditation:** NCACS. Professionally accredited by the Council on Social Work Education, the National Council for Accreditation of Teacher Education.
**Religious orientation:** Arkansas College is affiliated with the Presbyterian Church USA; one semester of religion required.
**Library:** Collections totaling over 105,000 volumes, 900 periodical subscriptions, and 6,000 microform items.
**Special facilities/museums:** Art gallery, regional studies collection, computer controlled audio-visual equipped auditorium and classrooms, state-of-the-art science instrumentation.
**Athletic facilities:** Gymnasium, field house, swimming pool, track, basketball, tennis, and volleyball courts, athletic fields, weight room, cross-country trail, baseball complex.
**STUDENT BODY. Undergraduate profile:** 79% are state residents; 16% are transfers. .6% Asian-American, 4.3% Black, .7% Hispanic, .4% Native American, 93.9% White, .1% Other. Average age of undergraduates is 21.
**Freshman profile:** 14% of freshmen who took ACT scored 30 or over on English, 4% scored 30 or over on math, 8% scored 30 or over on composite; 63% scored 24 or over on English, 41% scored 24 or over on math, 61% scored 24 or over on composite; 97% scored 18 or over on English, 94% scored 18 or over on math, 100% scored 18 or over on composite; 101% scored 12 or over on English, 100% scored 12 or over on math. 14% of accepted applicants took SAT; 98% took ACT. 90% of freshmen come from public schools.
**Undergraduate achievement:** 75% of fall 1992 freshmen returned for fall 1993 term. 35% of entering class graduated. 14% of students who completed a degree program immediately went on to graduate study.
**Foreign students:** Two students are from out of the country. Countries represented include Scotland.
**PROGRAMS OF STUDY. Degrees:** B.A., B.S.
**Majors:** Art, Biology, Chemistry, Economics, Elementary Education, English, History, Mathematics, Music, Politics, Psychology, Religion/Philosophy, Theatre.
**Distribution of degrees:** The majors with the highest enrollment are elementary education, English, and biology; art and psychology have the lowest.
**Requirements:** General education requirement.
**Academic regulations:** Freshmen must maintain minimum 1.75 GPA; sophomores, 1.9 GPA; juniors, 2.0 GPA; seniors, 2.0 GPA.
**Special:** Minors offered in all majors and in computer science, French, physics/math, regional studies, and Spanish. Professional concentrations offered in accounting, journalism, management, and secondary education. Self-designed majors. Double majors. Dual degrees. Independent study. Pass/fail grading option. Internships. Cooperative education programs. Preprofessional programs in law, medicine, veterinary science, pharmacy, dentistry, theology, and engineering. 2-2 engineering program with U of Missouri at Rolla. 2-2 nursing program with U of Central Arkansas. Teacher certification in elementary and sec-

ondary education. Certification in specific subject areas. Study abroad in the Caribbean, England, France, Germany, and Turkey.
**Honors:** Honors program. Honor societies.
**Academic Assistance:** Nonremedial tutoring.

**ADMISSIONS. Academic basis for candidate selection** (in order of priority): Secondary school record, standardized test scores, school's recommendation, essay, class rank.
**Nonacademic basis for candidate selection:** Extracurricular participation and particular talent or ability are emphasized. Character and personality are important. Geographical distribution and alumni/ae relationship are considered.
**Requirements:** Graduation from secondary school is required; GED is accepted. 18 units and the following program of study are recommended: 4 units of English, 3 units of math, 3 units of science, 1 unit of foreign language, 1 unit of social studies, 2 units of history, 4 units of electives. Competitive applicants typically are "A/B" students with standardized test scores in the top 10% nationally. Conditional admission possible for applicants not meeting standard requirements. SAT or ACT is required. ACH recommended. Campus visit and interview recommended. Off-campus interviews available with admissions and alumni representatives.
**Procedure:** Take SAT or ACT by February of 12th year. Take ACH by February of 12th year. Visit college for interview by April 1 of 12th year. Suggest filing application by March 1. Application deadline is August 1. Notification of admission on rolling basis. Reply is required by May 1. $100 tuition deposit, refundable until May 1. $100 room deposit, refundable until May 1. Freshmen accepted for terms other than fall.
**Special programs:** Admission may be deferred one year. Credit and/or placement may be granted through CEEB Advanced Placement exams for scores of 3 or higher. Credit may be granted through CLEP general and subject exams, DANTES exams, and military experience. Credit and placement may be granted through challenge exams. Early entrance/early admission program. Concurrent enrollment program.
**Transfer students:** Transfer students accepted for terms other than fall. In fall 1993, 16% of all new students were transfers into all classes. 93 transfer applications were received, 50 were accepted. Application deadline is August 1 for fall; January 15 for spring. Lowest course grade accepted is "C." Maximum number of transferable credits is 67 semester hours from a two-year school and 96 semester hours from a four-year school. At least 24 semester hours must be completed at the college to receive degree.
**Admissions contact:** Jonathan Stroud, M.S., Dean of Admissions and Financial Aid. 800 423-2542.

**FINANCIAL AID. Available aid:** Pell grants, SEOG, state scholarships and grants, school scholarships and grants, private scholarships and grants, academic merit scholarships, athletic scholarships, and aid for undergraduate foreign students. Perkins Loans (NDSL), PLUS, Stafford Loans (GSL), school loans, private loans, and SLS. School's own monthly payment plan.
**Financial aid statistics:** 25% of aid is not need-based. In 1993-94, 99% of all undergraduate applicants received aid; 99% of freshman applicants. Average amounts of aid awarded freshmen: Scholarships and grants, $6,832; loans, $2,192.
**Supporting data/closing dates:** FAFSA: Priority filing date is March 1. School's own aid application: Priority filing date is March 1. Notification of awards on rolling basis.
**Financial aid contact:** Martha Stewart, C.P.A., Director of Financial Aid. 501 698-4250.

# Ouachita Baptist University

**Arkadelphia, AR 71998-0001 501 245-5000**

**1994-95 Costs.** Tuition: $6,530. Room: $1,200. Board: $1,600. Fees, books, misc. academic expenses (school's estimate): $500.

**Enrollment.** Undergraduates: 646 men, 659 women (full-time). Freshman class: 845 applicants, 710 accepted, 450 enrolled.

**Test score averages/ranges.** Average ACT scores: 24 English, 21 math, 23 composite. Range of ACT scores of middle 50%: 22-26 English, 19-23 math.

**Faculty.** 91 full-time; 20 part-time. 58% of faculty holds doctoral degree. Student/faculty ratio: 13 to 1.

**Selectivity rating.** Less competitive.

**PROFILE.** Ouachita Baptist, founded in 1886, is a church-affiliated, liberal arts university. Its 200-acre campus is located in Arkadelphia, 70 miles southwest of Little Rock.

**Accreditation:** NCACS. Professionally accredited by the American Dietetic Association, the National Association of Schools of Music, the National Council for Accreditation of Teacher Education.
**Religious orientation:** Ouachita Baptist University is affiliated with the Arkansas Baptist State Convention; two semesters of religion required.
**Library:** Collections totaling over 122,000 volumes, 1,100 periodical subscriptions, and 350,000 microform items.
**Special facilities/museums:** Historical archives, language lab, TV studio.
**Athletic facilities:** Basketball, racquetball, tennis, and volleyball courts, arena, intramural gymnasium, weight room, swimming pool, track, football, soccer, and softball fields.

**STUDENT BODY. Undergraduate profile:** 80% are state residents; 4% are transfers. 5% Black, 1% Hispanic, 88% White, 6% Other. Average age of undergraduates is 20.
**Freshman profile:** 10% of freshmen who took ACT scored 30 or over on English, 6% scored 30 or over on math, 8% scored 30 or over on composite; 59% scored 24 or over on English, 46% scored 24 or over on math, 54% scored 24 or over on composite; 92% scored 18 or over on English, 89% scored 18 or over on math, 91% scored 18 or over on composite; 100% scored 12 or over on English, 100% scored 12 or over on math, 100% scored 12 or over on composite. 20% of accepted applicants took SAT; 80% took ACT. 85% of freshmen come from public schools.
**Undergraduate achievement:** 74% of fall 1992 freshmen returned for fall 1993 term. 32% of entering class graduated. 40% of students who completed a degree program went on to graduate study within five years.
**Foreign students:** 79 students are from out of the country. Countries represented include Brazil, China, Japan, Sweden, the United Kingdom, and Uzbekistan; 32 in all.

**PROGRAMS OF STUDY. Degrees:** B.A., B.Mus., B.Mus.Ed., B.S.
**Majors:** Accounting, Applied Music, Art, Biology, Chemistry, Church Music, Communication, Computer Science, Drama, Economics, Elementary Education, English, Family Life Ministry, Finance, French, General Business, History, Management, Marketing, Mathematics/Computer Science, Music Education, Music Theory/Composition, Musical Theatre, Pastoral Ministry, Philosophy, Physical Education, Physics, Political Science/Government, Professional Accountancy, Professional Chemistry, Psychology, Religion, Religious Education, Secondary Education, Sociology, Spanish, Speech, Speech Pathology.
**Distribution of degrees:** The majors with the highest enrollment are education, business, and music; philosophy and physics have the lowest.
**Requirements:** General education requirement.
**Academic regulations:** Freshmen must maintain minimum 1.5 GPA; sophomores, 1.7 GPA; juniors, 1.9 GPA; seniors, 2.0 GPA.
**Special:** Double majors. Independent study. Accelerated study. Pass/fail grading option. Internships. Cooperative education programs. Preprofessional programs in law, medicine, pharmacy, dentistry, theology, dental hygiene, dietetics, engineering, landscape architecture, medical technology, nursing, and physical therapy. 3-2 programs in dentistry, engineering, several medical fields, and pharmacy. Cross-registration with Henderson State U. Teacher certification in early childhood, elementary, and secondary education. Certification in specific subject areas. Exchange programs abroad in Austria, China, England, Japan, Kazakhstan, Russia, and Uzbekistan.
**Honors:** Honors program. Honor societies.
**Academic Assistance:** Remedial reading, writing, math, and study skills. Nonremedial tutoring.

**STUDENT LIFE. Housing:** All unmarried students under age 21 must live on campus unless living near campus with relatives. Women's and men's dorms. On-campus married-student housing. 82% of students live in college housing.
**Services and counseling/handicapped student services:** Placement services. Health service. Counseling services for minority and veteran students. Personal and psychological counseling. Career and academic guidance services. Religious counseling. Physically disabled student services. Learning disabled services. Tape recorders. Tutors.
**Campus organizations:** Undergraduate student government. Student newspaper (Signal). Literary magazine. Yearbook. Music and drama groups, debating, literary club, Young Democrats, Association of Women Students, service and special-interest groups, 40 organizations in all. Four fraternities, no chapter houses; four sororities, no chapter houses. 20% of men join a fraternity. 15% of women join a sorority.
**Religious organizations:** Baptist Student Union, Ministerial Alliance.
**Minority/foreign student organizations:** Black American Student Society. International Student Club.

**ATHLETICS. Physical education requirements:** Four semesters of physical education required.
**Intercollegiate competition:** 24% of students participate. Baseball (M), basketball (M,W), cheerleading (M,W), diving (M,W), football (M), golf (M), swimming (M,W), track (indoor) (M), track (outdoor) (M), track and field (indoor) (M), track and field (outdoor) (M), volleyball (W). Member of Arkansas Intercollegiate Conference, NAIA.
**Intramural and club sports:** 38% of students participate. Intramural basketball, football, softball, volleyball. Men's club soccer, volleyball.

**ADMISSIONS. Academic basis for candidate selection** (in order of priority): Secondary school record, standardized test scores, class rank, school's recommendation.
**Nonacademic basis for candidate selection:** Character and personality, extracurricular participation, and particular talent or ability are important. Geographical distribution and alumni/ae relationship are considered.
**Requirements:** Graduation from secondary school is required; GED is accepted. 19 units and the following program of study are required: 4 units of English, 2 units of math, 2 units of science, 3 units of social studies, 8 units of electives including 6 units of academic electives. Electives should be in English, foreign languages, social science, and math. Secondary school graduates with minimum 2.5 GPA and nongraduates with minimum "B" average and recommendations are generally admitted. Audition required of music program applicants. ACT is required; SAT may be substituted. Campus visit and interview recommended. Off-campus interviews available with an admissions representative.
**Procedure:** Suggest filing application by May 1. Notification of admission on rolling basis. No set date by which applicants must accept offer. $50 room deposit, refundable until July 1. Freshmen accepted for terms other than fall.
**Special programs:** Admission may be deferred one year. Credit may be granted through CEEB Advanced Placement for scores of 3 or higher. Credit may be granted through CLEP general and subject exams, ACT PEP, and challenge exams. Early entrance/early admission program.
**Transfer students:** Transfer students accepted for terms other than fall. In fall 1993, 4% of all new students were transfers into all classes. 84 transfer applications were received. Minimum 1.75 GPA recommended. Lowest course grade accepted is "C-." Maximum number of transferable credits is 66 semester hours from a two-year school and 104 semester hours from a four-year school. At least 24 semester hours must be completed at the university to receive degree.
**Admissions contact:** Randy Garner, Director of Admissions Counseling. 501 245-5110, extension 5110.

**FINANCIAL AID. Available aid:** Pell grants, SEOG, state scholarships and grants, school scholarships, private scholarships, academic merit scholarships, athletic scholarships, and aid for undergraduate foreign students. Ministerial scholarships. Perkins Loans (NDSL), PLUS, Stafford Loans (GSL), school loans, and SLS. Tuition Plan Inc. and deferred payment plan.
**Financial aid statistics:** 50% of aid is not need-based. In 1993-94, 75% of all undergraduate applicants received aid; 80% of freshman applicants. Average amounts of aid awarded freshmen: Scholarships and grants, $1,500; loans, $2,000.
**Supporting data/closing dates:** FAFSA: Priority filing date is May 1. Notification of awards begins May 1.
**Financial aid contact:** Harold Johnson, M.B.A., Director of Student Financial Aid. 501 245-5570, extension 5570.

**STUDENT EMPLOYMENT.** College Work/Study Program. Institutional employment. 53% of full-time undergraduates work on campus during school year. Students may expect to earn an average of $1,400 during school year. Off-campus part-time employment opportunities rated "fair."

**COMPUTER FACILITIES.** 90 IBM/IBM-compatible and Macintosh/Apple microcomputers; 30 are networked. Students may access Digital minicomputer/mainframe systems. Computer languages and software packages include BASIC, C, COBOL, DataTrieve, dBASE, FORTRAN, Lotus 1-2-3, Pascal, RPG, SPSS, WordPerfect, WordStar. Computer facilities are available to all students.
**Fees:** None.
**Hours:** 8 AM-10 PM (M-Th); 8 AM-5 PM (F); 10 AM-4 PM (Sa); 1 PM-5 PM (Su).

**GRADUATE CAREER DATA.** Graduate school percentages: 4% enter law school. 4% enter medical school. 5% enter dental school. 4% enter graduate business programs. 8% enter graduate arts and sciences programs. 8% enter theological school/seminary. 20% of graduates choose careers in business and industry.

## Southern Arkansas University–Magnolia

**Magnolia, AR 71753** **501 235-4000**

**1994-95 Costs.** Tuition: $1,632 (state residents), $2,544 (out-of-state). Room & board: $2,410. Fees, books, misc. academic expenses (school's estimate): $600.

**Enrollment.** Undergraduates: 1,026 men, 1,238 women (full-time). Freshman class: 792 applicants, 792 accepted, 532 enrolled. Graduate enrollment: 33 men, 104 women.

**Test score averages/ranges.** Average ACT scores: 20 English, 19 math, 20 composite.

**Faculty.** 128 full-time; 30 part-time. 51% of faculty holds doctoral degree. Student/faculty ratio: 20 to 1.

**Selectivity rating.** Less competitive.

**PROFILE.** Southern Arkansas, founded in 1909, is a public, comprehensive university. Programs are offered through the Schools of Business Administration, Education, Liberal and Performing Arts, and Science and Technology and the Division of General Studies. Its 120-acre campus is located in Magnolia, in southwestern Arkansas.

**Accreditation:** NCACS. Professionally accredited by the National Council for Accreditation of Teacher Education, the National League for Nursing.
**Religious orientation:** Southern Arkansas University at Magnolia is nonsectarian; no religious requirements.
**Library:** Collections totaling over 152,198 volumes, 906 periodical subscriptions, and 93,059 microform items.
**Athletic facilities:** Gymnasium, track, baseball, football, and intramural fields, swimming pool, basketball, sand volleyball, and tennis courts, weight room.

**STUDENT BODY. Undergraduate profile:** 80% are state residents; 10% are transfers. 1% Asian-American, 19% Black, 1% Hispanic, 79% White. Average age of undergraduates is 24.
**Freshman profile:** 100% of accepted applicants took ACT. 95% of freshmen come from public schools.
**Undergraduate achievement:** 60% of fall 1992 freshmen returned for fall 1993 term.
**Foreign students:** 35 students are from out of the country. Countries represented include Bangladesh, Canada, China, Indonesia, Malaysia, and Nepal.

**PROGRAMS OF STUDY. Degrees:** B.A., B.Bus.Admin., B.Mus.Ed., B.S.
**Majors:** Accounting, Art, Art Education, Athletic Training, Biological Science/Agriculture, Biological Science Education, Biological Sciences, Business/Agriculture, Business/Computer Science, Business Education, Chemistry, Chemistry/Agriculture, Chemistry Education, Commercial Art, Commercial Design, Computer Science, Distributive/Industrial Education, Economics, Elementary Education, Engineering/Physics, English, English Education, Finance, General Business, General Science, General Science Education, General Studies, Health/Physical Education/Recreation, History, Industrial Cooperative Training, Industrial Management, Management, Marketing, Mass Communication, Mathematics, Mathematics Education, Medical Technology, Music, Music Education, Office Administration, Painting, Physics, Physics Education, Political Science, Printmaking, Psychology, Recreation/Community Services, Regional Studies, Sculpture, Social Studies Education, Social Work, Sociology, Spanish, Spanish Education, Speech Education, Theatre, Vocational Agricultural Education.
**Distribution of degrees:** The majors with the highest enrollment are elementary education and accounting; art has the lowest.
**Requirements:** General education requirement.
**Academic regulations:** Freshmen must maintain minimum 1.5 GPA; sophomores, 1.7 GPA; juniors, 1.9 GPA; seniors, 2.0 GPA.
**Special:** Minors offered in many majors and in agriculture, French, geography, geology, health education, horticulture, journalism, library science, physical sciences, and special education. Associate's degrees offered. Double majors. Internships. Graduate school at which undergraduates may take graduate-level courses. Preprofessional programs in law, medicine, veterinary science, pharmacy, and dentistry. Teacher certification in early childhood, elementary, secondary, special education, and vo-tech education.
**Honors:** Honor societies.
**Academic Assistance:** Remedial reading, writing, math, and study skills.

**STUDENT LIFE. Housing:** All unmarried students under age 21 must live on campus unless living near campus with relatives. Women's and men's dorms. On-campus married-student housing. 50% of students live in college housing.
**Social atmosphere:** The student newspaper reports that Greeks, the Black Students Association, religious organizations, Student Government, and the Resident Hall Association are prominent groups on campus. Some of the favorite campus events include Homecoming, Parents' Day, Spring Fling, Rush Week, Sadie Hawkins, and the End of the World Party. Students like to gather on campus at the Bruce Center, the fairgrounds, the Pavilion, and the Beef and Bisquit.
**Services and counseling/handicapped student services:** Placement services. Health service. Counseling services for minority and older students. Personal and psychological counseling. Academic guidance services. Physically disabled student services. Tape recorders. Tutors.
**Campus organizations:** Undergraduate student government. Student newspaper (Bray, published once/week). Literary magazine. Yearbook. Radio station. Campus Activities Board, agriculture, biology, and psychology clubs, Archaeological Society, Nursing Student Association, Society of Collegiate Journalists, Society of Physics Students, Music Educators National Conference, Newsmasters Art Club, College Republicans, 59 organizations in all. Seven fraternities, no chapter houses; seven sororities, no chapter houses. 10% of men join a fraternity. 10% of women join a sorority.
**Religious organizations:** Association of Baptist Students, Baptist Student Union, Church of Christ Student Center, Fellowship of Christian Athletes, missionary group, United Voices for Christ, Wesley Foundation.
**Minority/foreign student organizations:** Black Student Association. International Student Association.

**ATHLETICS. Physical education requirements:** Two semesters of physical education required.
**Intercollegiate competition:** 13% of students participate. Baseball (M), basketball (M,W), cheerleading (M,W), cross-country (M,W), football (M), golf (M), rodeo (M,W), tennis (M,W), track (indoor) (M), track (outdoor) (M,W), track and field (outdoor) (M,W), volleyball (W). Member of Arkansas Intercollegiate Conference, NAIA.
**Intramural and club sports:** 25% of students participate. Intramural badminton, basketball, sand volleyball, softball, table tennis, tennis, touch football, track and field, volleyball, water basketball.

**ADMISSIONS. Academic basis for candidate selection** (in order of priority): Standardized test scores, class rank, secondary school record, school's recommendation, essay.
**Nonacademic basis for candidate selection:** Extracurricular participation and geographical distribution are emphasized. Character and personality, particular talent or ability, and alumni/ae relationship are important.
**Requirements:** Graduation from secondary school is required; GED is accepted. 16 units and the following program of study are recommended: 4 units of English, 3 units of math, 3 units of science, 1 unit of foreign language, 3 units of social studies, 2 units of history. Minimum ACT score of 20, rank in top half of secondary school class, and minimum 2.0 GPA required of out-of-state applicants. Audition required of music program applicants. ACT is required; SAT may be substituted. Campus visit and interview recommended. Off-campus interviews available with admissions and alumni representatives.
**Procedure:** Take SAT or ACT by October of 12th year. Visit college for interview by fall of 12th year. Suggest filing application by fall; no deadline. Notification of admission on rolling basis. No set date by which applicants must accept offer. $40 room deposit, refundable until August 1. Freshmen accepted for terms other than fall.
**Special programs:** Admission may be deferred one year. Credit and/or placement may be granted through CEEB Advanced Placement exams for scores of 3 or higher. Credit may be granted through CLEP general and subject exams, military and life experience. Early decision program. In fall 1992, two applied for early decision and two were accepted. Early entrance/early admission program. Concurrent enrollment program.
**Transfer students:** Transfer students accepted for terms other than fall. In fall 1993, 10% of all new students were transfers into all classes. 382 transfer applications were received, 380 were accepted. Application deadline is rolling for fall; rolling for spring. Minimum 2.0 GPA recommended. Lowest course grade accepted is "C." Maximum number of transferable credits is 68 semester hours. At least 30 semester hours must be completed at the university to receive degree.
**Admissions contact:** Sonny Whittington, M.S.Ed., Director of Admissions. 501 235-4040.

**FINANCIAL AID. Available aid:** Pell grants, SEOG, state scholarships and grants, school scholarships, private scholarships and grants, academic merit scholarships, and athletic scholarships. Perkins Loans (NDSL), PLUS, Stafford Loans (GSL), and NSL. Deferred payment plan.
**Financial aid statistics:** 20% of aid is not need-based. In 1993-94, 62% of all undergraduate applicants received aid; 55% of freshman applicants. Average amounts of aid awarded freshmen: Scholarships and grants, $1,200; loans, $2,500.
**Supporting data/closing dates:** FAFSA/FFS: Accepted on rolling basis. Notification of awards on rolling basis.
**Financial aid contact:** Dorothy Duncan, Director of Financial Aid. 501 235-4023.

**STUDENT EMPLOYMENT.** College Work/Study Program. Institutional employment. 80% of full-time undergraduates work on campus during school year. Students may expect to earn an average of $1,200 during school year. Off-campus part-time employment opportunities rated "fair."

**COMPUTER FACILITIES.** IBM/IBM-compatible and Macintosh/Apple microcomputers. Students may access BITNET, Internet, CompuServe. Client/LAN operating systems include Apple/Macintosh, DOS. All major computer languages and software packages are available. Computer facilities are available to all students.
**Fees:** Computer fee is included in tuition/fees.

## University of Arkansas, Fayetteville

**Fayetteville, AR 72701** **501 575-2000**

**1994-95 Costs.** Tuition: $1,824 (state residents), $4,848 (out-of-state). Room & board: $3,462. Fees, books, misc. academic expenses (school's estimate): $972.

**Enrollment.** Undergraduates: 5,466 men, 4,512 women (full-time). Freshman class: 3,235 applicants, 3,108 accepted, 2,133 enrolled. Graduate enrollment: 1,570 men, 1,202 women.

**Test score averages/ranges.** Average ACT scores: 22 English, 21 math, 22 composite.

**Faculty.** 807 full-time; 64 part-time. 77% of faculty holds doctoral degree. Student/faculty ratio: 18 to 1.

**Selectivity rating.** Less competitive.

**PROFILE.** U Arkansas at Fayetteville, founded in 1871, is a public, land-grant institution. Undergraduate programs are offered through its Colleges of Agriculture and Home Economics, Business Administration, Education, and Engineering; the J. William Fulbright

College of Arts and Sciences; and the School of Architecture. Graduate programs are also offered. Its 420-acre campus is located in the Ozark Mountains in northwestern Arkansas.

**Accreditation:** NCACS. Professionally accredited by the Accreditation Board for Engineering and Technology, the Accrediting Council on Education in Journalism and Mass Communication, the American Assembly of Collegiate Schools of Business, the American Bar Association, the American Dental Association, the American Dietetic Association, the American Psychological Association, the American Society of Landscape Architects, the American Speech-Language-Hearing Association, the Association of American Law Schools, the Council on Social Work Education, the National Architecture Accrediting Board, the National Association of Schools of Music, the National Council for Accreditation of Teacher Education, the National League for Nursing.
**Religious orientation:** University of Arkansas, Fayetteville is nonsectarian; no religious requirements.
**Library:** Collections totaling over 1,392,403 volumes, 16,540 periodical subscriptions, and 1,656,466 microform items.
**Special facilities/museums:** Natural history museum, engineering research center, laser lab, electron diffractometer, G.C. mass spectrometer, scanning electron microscope.
**Athletic facilities:** Recreation facility, track, tennis courts, football, soccer, and softball fields.

**STUDENT BODY. Undergraduate profile:** 88% are state residents; 33% are transfers. 2% Asian-American, 6% Black, 1% Hispanic, 1% Native American, 87% White, 3% Other. Average age of undergraduates is 20.
**Freshman profile:** 6% of freshmen who took ACT scored 30 or over on English, 5% scored 30 or over on math, 5% scored 30 or over on composite; 41% scored 24 or over on English, 29% scored 24 or over on math, 40% scored 24 or over on composite; 81% scored 18 or over on English, 77% scored 18 or over on math, 87% scored 18 or over on composite; 99% scored 12 or over on English, 99% scored 12 or over on math, 99% scored 12 or over on composite; 100% scored 6 or over on English, 100% scored 6 or over on math. 3% of accepted applicants took SAT; 97% took ACT. 95% of freshmen come from public schools.
**Undergraduate achievement:** 73% of fall 1992 freshmen returned for fall 1993 term. 18% of entering class graduated. 17% of students who completed a degree program immediately went on to graduate study.
**Foreign students:** 321 students are from out of the country. Countries represented include Canada, India, Malaysia, Panama, Singapore, and the United Kingdom; 79 in all.

**PROGRAMS OF STUDY. Degrees:** B.A., B.F.A., B.Mus., B.S.
**Majors:** Accounting, Accounting/Computer Information Systems, Administrative Management, Agricultural Business, Agricultural Economics, Agricultural Education, Agricultural Mechanization, Agronomy, Animal Science, Anthropology, Architectural Studies, Art, Art Education, Biological/Agricultural Engineering, Biology, Botany, Business Economics, Chemical Engineering, Chemistry, Civil Engineering, Classical Studies, Clothing/Textiles, Communication, Computer Information Systems/Quantitative Analysis, Computer Science, Computer Science Engineering, Criminal Justice, Dairy Science, Domestic Animal Biology, Domestic/International Agricultural Marketing, Drama, Economics, Electrical Engineering, Elementary Education, English, Finance/Banking, Finance/Insurance, Finance/Real Estate, Financial Management, Food/Nutrition, Food Science, French, General Business, General Home Economics, Geography, Geology, German, Health Education, History, Home Economics Education, Horticulture, Human Development/Family Studies, Human Resource Management, Industrial Engineering, Industrial Management, Industrial Marketing, Interior Design/Housing, International Economics, Journalism, Landscape Design/Urban Horticulture, Marketing Management, Mathematics, Mechanical Engineering, Microbiology, Music, Music Education, Nursing, Office Systems Management, Philosophy, Physical Education, Physics, Plant Protection/Pest Management, Political Science, Poultry Science, Psychology, Public Administration, Recreation/Dance Education, Retail Marketing, Secondary Education, Small Business/Entrepreneurship, Social Work, Sociology, Spanish, Special Education, Speech Pathology/Audiology, Transportation, Vocational Education, Zoology.
**Distribution of degrees:** The majors with the highest enrollment are marketing, elementary education, and finance.
**Requirements:** General education requirement.
**Academic regulations:** Minimum 2.0 GPA must be maintained.
**Special:** Numerous minors offered. Associate's degrees offered. Double majors. Dual degrees. Independent study. Internships. Cooperative education programs. Graduate school at which undergraduates may take graduate-level courses. Preprofessional programs in law, medicine, veterinary science, pharmacy, dentistry, optometry, and chiropractic. 3-2 engineering programs and 3-3 law programs. Five-year M.A.T. program. Combined degree program in medical science/dentistry. Oak Ridge Science Semester (Tennessee). Teacher certification in elementary, secondary, special education, and vo-tech education. Certification in specific subject areas. Exchange programs abroad in Finland (U of Helsinki), Honduras (Elzamorano Sch of Agriculture), and Japan (Kansai U of Foreign Studies). Study abroad also in Austria, Costa Rica, England, France, Germany, Ireland, Italy, the former Soviet Republics, and Spain. ROTC and AFROTC.
**Honors:** Phi Beta Kappa. Honors program. Honor societies.
**Academic Assistance:** Remedial reading, writing, math, and study skills. Nonremedial tutoring.

**STUDENT LIFE. Housing:** All unmarried students under age 21 must live on campus unless living near campus with relatives. Coed, women's, and men's dorms. Sorority and fraternity housing. School-owned/operated apartments. On-campus married-student housing. 30% of students live in college housing.
**Social atmosphere:** Razorback sports, Greek rush, and the "Red Eye" are the big events at UA Fayetteville, reports the student newspaper. The Fulbright Symposium is well received, but the general comment on the cultural scene is, "What cultural life?" On campus, students frequent the Arkansas Union, Brough Common, the HPER Building, Razorback Stadium, and Barnhill Arena. Favorite off-campus nightspots include Norma Jean's, Old Post Office, City Lights, and Lily's.
**Services and counseling/handicapped student services:** Placement services. Health service. Day care. Women's health clinic. Counseling services for minority, veteran, and older students. Birth control, personal, and psychological counseling. Career and academic guidance services. Physically disabled student services. Learning disabled services. Notetaking services. Tutors. Reader services for the blind.

**Campus organizations:** Undergraduate student government. Student newspaper (Arkansas Traveler, published twice/week). Yearbook. Radio station. Chorus, band, orchestra, entertainment clubs, academic, professional, service, and special-interest groups, 225 organizations in all. 19 fraternities, 16 chapter houses; 12 sororities, 10 chapter houses. 17% of men join a fraternity. 18% of women join a sorority.
**Religious organizations:** Campus Connection, Campus Crusade for Christ, Chi Alpha, Christ on Campus, Christian Legal Society, Intervarsity Christian Fellowship, other religious groups.
**Minority/foreign student organizations:** Black Student Association, Native American Student Association. International Club, International Student Foundation, Chinese, German, Indian, Malaysian, Russian, Singapore, Vietnamese, and other foreign student groups.

**ATHLETICS. Physical education requirements:** None.
**Intercollegiate competition:** 3% of students participate. Baseball (M), basketball (M,W), cross-country (M,W), diving (M,W), football (M), golf (M), soccer (W), swimming (M,W), tennis (M,W), track (indoor) (M,W), track (outdoor) (M,W), track and field (indoor) (M,W), track and field (outdoor) (M,W). Member of NCAA Division I, Southeastern Conference.
**Intramural and club sports:** 45% of students participate. Intramural badminton, basketball, bowling, darts, football, golf, horseshoes, indoor soccer, pickleball, racquetball, soccer, softball, swimming, table tennis, team handball, tennis, track, volleyball, walleyball, water volleyball. Men's club rugby.

**ADMISSIONS. Academic basis for candidate selection** (in order of priority): Secondary school record.
**Requirements:** Graduation from secondary school is required; GED is accepted. 16 units and the following program of study are required: 4 units of English, 3 units of math, 3 units of science including 2 units of lab, 3 units of social studies, 3 units of academic electives. Minimum 2.75 GPA required. Portfolio required of art program applicants. Audition required of music program applicants. Conditional admission possible for applicants not meeting standard requirements. SAT or ACT is required. Campus visit and interview recommended. No off-campus interviews.
**Procedure:** Take SAT or ACT by February of 12th year. Suggest filing application by February 1. Application deadline is August 15. Notification of admission on rolling basis. $100 room deposit, refundable until July 1. Freshmen accepted for terms other than fall.
**Special programs:** Admission may be deferred. Credit and/or placement may be granted through CEEB Advanced Placement exams for scores of 3 or higher. Credit and/or placement may be granted through CLEP general and subject exams. Credit and placement may be granted through ACT PEP and challenge exams. Early entrance/early admission program. Concurrent enrollment program.
**Transfer students:** Transfer students accepted for terms other than fall. In fall 1993, 33% of all new students were transfers into all classes. 1,614 transfer applications were received, 1,496 were accepted. Application deadline is August 15 for fall; January 1 for spring. Minimum 2.0 GPA required. Lowest course grade accepted is "C." Maximum number of transferable credits is 68 semester hours. At least 30 semester hours must be completed at the university to receive degree.
**Admissions contact:** Maribeth Lynes and Linda Stafstrom, Ph.D., Co-Directors of Admissions. 501 575-5346.

**FINANCIAL AID. Available aid:** Pell grants, SEOG, state scholarships and grants, school scholarships, private scholarships, ROTC scholarships, academic merit scholarships, and athletic scholarships. Perkins Loans (NDSL), PLUS, Stafford Loans (GSL), state loans, and SLS.
**Financial aid statistics:** 48% of aid is not need-based. In 1993-94, 57% of all undergraduate applicants received aid; 70% of freshman applicants. Average amounts of aid awarded freshmen: Scholarships and grants, $1,824; loans, $1,968.
**Supporting data/closing dates:** FAFSA/FAF/FFS: Priority filing date is April 1. School's own aid application: Priority filing date is April 1; accepted on rolling basis. Notification of awards begins April 1.
**Financial aid contact:** Lenthon Clark, Ph.D., Director of Financial Aid. 501 575-3806.

**STUDENT EMPLOYMENT.** College Work/Study Program. Institutional employment. 13% of full-time undergraduates work on campus during school year. Students may expect to earn an average of $1,500 during school year. Off-campus part-time employment opportunities rated "fair."

**COMPUTER FACILITIES.** 800 IBM/IBM-compatible, Macintosh/Apple, and RISC-/UNIX-based microcomputers; 500 are networked. Students may access Cray, Hewlett-Packard, IBM, SUN minicomputer/mainframe systems, BITNET, Internet. Residence halls may be equipped with stand-alone microcomputers, networked microcomputers. Client/LAN operating systems include Apple/Macintosh, DOS, OS/2, UNIX/XENIX/AIX, X-windows, LocalTalk/AppleTalk, Novell. Computer languages and software packages include Assembler, BASIC, C, C++, COBOL, FORTRAN, ImSL, Modula 2, Pascal, PL/1, Prolog, SAS, Script, SPSS-X; 50 in all. Computer facilities are available to all students.
**Fees:** None.
**Hours:** 24 hours.

**GRADUATE CAREER DATA.** Graduate school percentages: 1% enter law school. 2% enter medical school. 3% enter graduate business programs. 8% enter graduate arts and sciences programs. Highest graduate school enrollments: U Arkansas at Fayetteville, U Arkansas at Little Rock. 41% of graduates choose careers in business and industry. Companies and businesses that hire graduates: Conoco, Datatronics, Dillards, Exxon, Halliburton, Tyson Foods, Wal-Mart.

**PROMINENT ALUMNI/AE.** David Pryor, U.S. senator; Sarah Caldwell, director, Boston Opera Co.; Don Tyson, chairman and CEO, Tyson Foods; Pat Summerall, CBS sports announcer; James Walton, CEO, Walton Bank Holding Co.; Charles Kittrell, executive vice-president, Phillips Petroleum; E. Fay Jones, architect; J. William Fulbright, former U.S. senator.

## University of Arkansas at Little Rock

**Little Rock, AR 72204** **501 569-3000**

**1994-95 Costs.** Tuition: $1,950 (state residents), $4,926 (out-of-state). Room: $2,340. No meal plan. Fees, books, misc. academic expenses (school's estimate): $698.
**Enrollment.** Undergraduates: 2,660 men, 3,219 women (full-time). Freshman class: 1,774 applicants, 1,330 accepted, 1,202 enrolled. Graduate enrollment: 734 men, 1,345 women.
**Test score averages/ranges.** Average ACT scores: 19 composite. Range of ACT scores of middle 50%: 18-23 composite.
**Faculty.** 481 full-time; 244 part-time. 47% of faculty holds highest degree in specific field.
**Selectivity rating.** Less competitive.

**PROFILE.** U Arkansas at Little Rock is a public institution. It was founded as a junior college in 1927, became a private, four-year college in 1957, and joined the state university system when it merged with the University of Arkansas in 1969. Programs are offered through the Colleges of Business Administration, Education, Professional and Public Affairs, and Science and Engineering Technology; the Graduate School; and the School of Law. Its 150-acre, predominantly modern campus is located in southwest Little Rock.

**Accreditation:** NCACS. Professionally accredited by the Accreditation Board for Engineering and Technology, the Accrediting Commission on Education for Health Services Administration, the Accrediting Council on Education in Journalism and Mass Communication, the American Assembly of Collegiate Schools of Business, the American Bar Association, the American Speech-Language-Hearing Association, the Association of American Law Schools, the Council on Social Work Education, the National Association of Schools of Art and Design, the National Association of Schools of Music, the National Council for Accreditation of Teacher Education, the National League for Nursing.
**Religious orientation:** University of Arkansas at Little Rock is nonsectarian; no religious requirements.
**Library:** Collections totaling over 367,648 volumes, 2,322 periodical subscriptions, and 691,612 microform items.
**Special facilities/museums:** Language lab, observatory, planetarium, electron microscope, particle accelerator, nuclear magnetic resonator.
**Athletic facilities:** Gymnasium, basketball, racquetball, and tennis courts, swimming pool baseball, football, and soccer fields, golf course, driving range, bowling lanes, field house, weight room.
**STUDENT BODY. Undergraduate profile:** 95% are state residents; 47% are transfers. 3.8% Asian-American, 14.7% Black, 1.3% Hispanic, .4% Native American, 79.7% White, .1% Other. Average age of undergraduates is 26.
**Freshman profile:** 1% of accepted applicants took SAT; 99% took ACT.
**Undergraduate achievement:** 24% of students who completed a degree program went on to graduate study within one year.
**Foreign students:** 435 students are from out of the country. Countries represented include China, India, Japan, Kuwait, Malaysia, and Saudi Arabia; 65 in all.
**PROGRAMS OF STUDY. Degrees:** B.A., B.Bus.Admin., B.Mus., B.S.
**Majors:** Accounting, Advertising, Art, Art History, Biology, Chemistry, Communicative Disorders, Computer Engineering Technology, Computer Information Systems, Computer Science, Construction Engineering Technology, Criminal Justice, Economics, Electronic Engineering Technology, Elementary Education, Engineering Technology, English, Environmental Health, Finance, French, General Business, Geology, Health Education, Health Professions, History, Industrial Management, International Studies, Journalism, Liberal Arts, Management, Manufacturing Engineering Technology, Marketing, Mathematics, Mechanical Engineering Technology, Music, Philosophy, Physics, Political Science, Professional/Technical Writing, Psychology, Radio/Television/Film, Sociology/Anthropology, Spanish, Special Education for the Deaf, Speech Communication, Speech Pathology, Surveying/Land Information Systems, Theatre Arts.
**Distribution of degrees:** The majors with the highest enrollment are elementary education, accounting, and psychology; physics, geology, and philosophy have the lowest.
**Requirements:** General education requirement.
**Academic regulations:** Minimum 2.0 GPA must be maintained.
**Special:** Minors offered in most majors and in approximately 70 other fields. Scholars program. Associate's degrees offered. Self-designed majors. Double majors. Dual degrees. Independent study. Accelerated study. Pass/fail grading option. Internships. Graduate school at which undergraduates may take graduate-level courses. Preprofessional programs in medicine and dentistry. Two-year pharmacy and engineering transfer programs. Bachelor's degree possible for students who enter approved dental or medical school after completing three-year preprofessional curriculum. Teacher certification in early childhood, elementary, secondary, and special education. Study abroad in Austria, France, Mexico (U Autonoma de Guadalajara), and Spain. ROTC.
**Honors:** Honors program.
**Academic Assistance:** Remedial reading, writing, math, and study skills. Nonremedial tutoring.
**STUDENT LIFE. Housing:** Coed dorms. 3% of students live in college housing.
**Social atmosphere:** Students meet at the Donaghey Student Center, Cajun's Wharf, and Shug's Bar & Grill. According to the editor of the student newspaper, "UALR is mostly a commuter school, and the campus population is very diverse."
**Services and counseling/handicapped student services:** Placement services. Health service. Women's center. Day care. Counseling services for minority and veteran students. Psychological counseling. Career and academic guidance services. Physically disabled student services. Learning disabled services. Notetaking services. Tape recorders. Tutors. Reader services for the blind.
**Campus organizations:** Undergraduate student government. Student newspaper (Forum, published once/week). Literary magazine. Radio station. Band, choir, organ and theatre guilds, tutoring programs, Young Democrats, Young Republicans, Chancellor's Leadership Class, Student Bar Association, Student Theatre Guild, departmental and service groups, special-interest groups, 50 organizations in all. Six fraternities, five chapter houses; five sororities, three chapter houses. 5% of men join a fraternity. 3% of women join a sorority.
**Religious organizations:** Baptist Student Union, Logos, United Methodist Student Center, Muslim Student Association, Catholic Campus Organization.
**Minority/foreign student organizations:** Minority student education group. International Student Club.
**ATHLETICS. Physical education requirements:** Two semesters of physical education required.
**Intercollegiate competition:** Baseball (M,W), basketball (M,W), cheerleading (W), cross-country (M,W), diving (M,W), golf (M,W), soccer (M,W), swimming (M,W), tennis (M,W), track (indoor) (M,W), track (outdoor) (M,W), track and field (indoor) (M,W), track and field (outdoor) (M,W), volleyball (W), water polo (M). Member of American Sun Belt Conference, Eastern Water Polo Association, NCAA Division I, New South Independent Swimming League.
**Intramural and club sports:** Intramural badminton, basketball, billiards, bowling, flag football, free throw, golf, horseshoes, softball, swimming, tennis, trap shooting, volleyball. Men's club rugby.
**ADMISSIONS. Academic basis for candidate selection** (in order of priority): Secondary school record, standardized test scores.
**Requirements:** Graduation from secondary school is recommended; GED is accepted. Distribution of required secondary school units varies with program. Minimum combined SAT score of 750 (composite ACT score of 19) and minimum 2.0 GPA required. Conditional admission possible for applicants not meeting standard requirements. SAT or ACT is required. Campus visit and interview recommended. No off-campus interviews.
**Procedure:** Take SAT or ACT by April of 12th year. Suggest filing application by August 1; no deadline. Notification of admission on rolling basis. No set date by which applicants must accept offer. $100 refundable room deposit. Freshmen accepted for terms other than fall.
**Special programs:** Admission may be deferred indefinitely. Credit may be granted through CEEB Advanced Placement for scores of 3 or higher. Credit may be granted through CLEP subject exams, ACT PEP, challenge exams, and military experience. Early entrance/early admission program. Concurrent enrollment program.
**Transfer students:** Transfer students accepted for terms other than fall. In fall 1993, 47% of all new students were transfers into all classes. 1,483 transfer applications were received, 1,266 were accepted. Application deadline is August 1 for fall; December 1 for spring. Minimum 2.0 GPA required. Lowest course grade accepted is "C." At least 30 must be completed at the university to receive degree.
**Admissions contact:** D. Sue Pine, M.P.A., Director of Admissions. 501 569-3127.
**FINANCIAL AID. Available aid:** Pell grants, SEOG, state scholarships and grants, school scholarships, private scholarships, ROTC scholarships, and athletic scholarships. Perkins Loans (NDSL), PLUS, Stafford Loans (GSL), and school loans. Deferred payment plan.
**Financial aid statistics:** 26% of aid is not need-based.
**Supporting data/closing dates:** FAFSA/FAF/FFS: Priority filing date is May 1. State aid form: Priority filing date is May 1. Notification of awards on rolling basis.
**STUDENT EMPLOYMENT.** College Work/Study Program. Institutional employment. 4% of full-time undergraduates work on campus during school year. Students may expect to earn an average of $1,400 during school year. Off-campus part-time employment opportunities rated "good."
**COMPUTER FACILITIES.** 305 IBM/IBM-compatible and Macintosh/Apple microcomputers; 15 are networked. Students may access Digital minicomputer/mainframe systems, BITNET. Computer languages and software packages include COBOL, FORTRAN; 48 in all. Restricted access to some computers.
**Fees:** $12 computer fee per course.
**GRADUATE CAREER DATA.** Highest graduate school enrollments: U of Arkansas at Little Rock Law Sch.

## University of Arkansas at Monticello

**Monticello, AR 71655** **501 460-1020**

**1993-94 Costs.** Tuition: $1,392 (state residents), $3,216 (out-of-state). Room: $780. Board: $1,300. Fees, books, misc. academic expenses (school's estimate): $808.
**Enrollment.** Undergraduates: 1,016 men, 1,159 women (full-time). Freshman class: 656 applicants, 573 accepted, 524 enrolled.
**Test score averages/ranges.** N/A.
**Faculty.** 116 full-time; 28 part-time. 56% of faculty holds doctoral degree. Student/faculty ratio: 20 to 1.
**Selectivity rating.** Less competitive.

**PROFILE.** U Arkansas at Monticello is a public institution. It was founded as an agricultural school in 1909, became a four-year college in 1940, and joined the state university system in 1971. Programs are offered through the Departments of Agriculture; Business Administration; Communication Arts; Education; Fine Arts; Forest Resources; Health, Physical Education, and Recreation; Mathematics and Physics; Natural Sciences; Nursing; and Social and Behavioral Sciences. Its 1,600-acre campus is located in southeastern Arkansas.

**Accreditation:** NCACS. Professionally accredited by the National Association of Schools of Music, the National Council for Accreditation of Teacher Education, the National League for Nursing, the Society of American Foresters.
**Religious orientation:** University of Arkansas at Monticello is nonsectarian; no religious requirements.

**Library:** Collections totaling over 126,229 volumes, 862 periodical subscriptions, and 9,794 microform items.
**Special facilities/museums:** Natural history museum, language lab, university farm and forest, instructional resource center, planetarium.
**Athletic facilities:** Gymnasium, field house, baseball, football, intramural, and softball fields, track, basketball, handball, and tennis courts, weight room, swimming pool.

**STUDENT BODY. Undergraduate profile:** 98% are state residents; 7% are transfers. 1% Asian-American, 13% Black, 1% Hispanic, 85% White.
**Freshman profile:** 5% of accepted applicants took SAT; 95% took ACT. 100% of freshmen come from public schools.
**Undergraduate achievement:** 54% of fall 1992 freshmen returned for fall 1993 term. 24% of entering class graduated.
**Foreign students:** Three students are from out of the country. Two countries represented in all.

**PROGRAMS OF STUDY. Degrees:** B.A., B.S.
**Majors:** Accounting, Agriculture, Art, Biology, Business Administration, Business Education, Chemistry, Computer Science, Elementary Education, English, Forestry, Geology, Health/Physical Education, History, Management, Marketing, Mathematics, Music, Nursing, Office Administration, Physical Sciences, Physics, Political Science, Psychology, Wildlife/Fish Management.
**Distribution of degrees:** The majors with the highest enrollment are business administration, elementary education, and nursing; chemistry, physical sciences, and history have the lowest.
**Requirements:** General education requirement.
**Academic regulations:** Minimum 2.0 GPA must be maintained.
**Special:** Minors offered in all majors and in French, human services, and sociology. Courses offered in anthropology, geography, journalism, philosophy, and Spanish. Unlimited Potential Program offers evening courses. Associate's degrees offered. Double majors. Dual degrees. Independent study. Accelerated study. Preprofessional programs in law, medicine, veterinary science, and pharmacy. Teacher certification in early childhood, elementary, secondary, and special education.
**Academic Assistance:** Remedial reading, writing, math, and study skills. Nonremedial tutoring.

**STUDENT LIFE. Housing:** Students may live on or off campus. Women's and men's dorms. On-campus married-student housing. 27% of students live in college housing.
**Social atmosphere:** One school official notes that UAM's location–in a small, rural community in southeastern Arkansas–dictates most social and cultural activities which revolve around on-campus events. Popular events include football and basketball games, the spring musical theatre production, and "big name" concerts. "UAM has a strong Greek system, and religious organizations are very active on campus."
**Services and counseling/handicapped student services:** Placement services. Health service. Counseling services for minority students. Career and academic guidance services. Physically disabled student services. Reader services for the blind.
**Campus organizations:** Undergraduate student government. Yearbook. A cappella choir, University Singers, band, stage band, grand chorus, Board Treaders (drama), debating, Judicial Council, Activities Board, Young Democrats and Republicans, Student Ambassadors, departmental and service groups, special-interest groups, 44 organizations in all. Seven fraternities, no chapter houses; three sororities, no chapter houses.
**Religious organizations:** Christians in Action, Wesley Foundation, Student Mobilization, Christian Outreach Club, Church of Christ, missionary groups.

**ATHLETICS. Physical education requirements:** None.
**Intercollegiate competition:** 9% of students participate. Baseball (M), basketball (M,W), cheerleading (M,W), cross-country (M,W), football (M), golf (M), track (indoor) (M,W), track (outdoor) (M,W), track and field (indoor) (M,W), track and field (outdoor) (M,W). Member of Arkansas Intercollegiate Conference, NAIA.
**Intramural and club sports:** 25% of students participate. Intramural basketball, flag football, racquetball, soccer, softball, table tennis, tennis, volleyball.

**ADMISSIONS. Academic basis for candidate selection** (in order of priority): Secondary school record, standardized test scores, class rank.
**Requirements:** Graduation from secondary school is required; GED is accepted. 20 units are recommended. Separate application required of nursing program applicants. Campus visit and interview recommended. Off-campus interviews available with an admissions representative.
**Procedure:** Take SAT or ACT by February of 12th year. Visit college for interview by March 12 of 12th year. Notification of admission on rolling basis. $40 room deposit, refundable until August 15. Freshmen accepted for terms other than fall.
**Special programs:** Credit and/or placement may be granted through CLEP general and subject exams. Placement may be granted through ACT PEP exams. Concurrent enrollment program.
**Transfer students:** Transfer students accepted for terms other than fall. In fall 1993, 7% of all new students were transfers into all classes. 214 transfer applications were received, 210 were accepted. Application deadline is August 15. Minimum 2.0 GPA. Lowest course grade accepted is "D." Maximum number of transferable credits is 68 semester hours. At least 30 semester hours must be completed at the university to receive degree.
**Admissions contact:** JoBeth Johnson, M.A., Director of Admissions. 501 460-1026.

**FINANCIAL AID. Available aid:** Pell grants, SEOG, state scholarships and grants, school scholarships and grants, private scholarships and grants, academic merit scholarships, and athletic scholarships. Perkins Loans (NDSL), PLUS, and Stafford Loans (GSL). VISA/Master Card. Room and board payment plan.
**Financial aid statistics:** 29% of aid is not need-based. In 1993-94, 70% of all undergraduate applicants received aid; 74% of freshman applicants. Average amounts of aid awarded freshmen: Scholarships and grants, $2,502; loans, $1,750.
**Supporting data/closing dates:** FAFSA/FAF/FFS: Deadline is April 15. Notification of awards on rolling basis.
**Financial aid contact:** Judy Lassiter, Financial Aid Director. 501 460-1050.

**STUDENT EMPLOYMENT.** College Work/Study Program. Institutional employment. 17% of full-time undergraduates work on campus during school year. Students may expect to earn an average of $1,000 during school year. Off-campus part-time employment opportunities rated "good."

**COMPUTER FACILITIES.** 450 IBM/IBM-compatible and Macintosh/Apple microcomputers; 100 are networked. Students may access Digital minicomputer/mainframe systems, BITNET, Internet. Residence halls may be equipped with stand-alone microcomputers. Client/LAN operating systems include Apple/Macintosh, DOS, LocalTalk/AppleTalk, Novell. Computer languages and software packages include BASIC, COBOL, dBASE, FORTRAN, Harvard Graphics, Lotus, Pascal, QuattroPro, TURBOC, SAS, WordPerfect; 12 in all. Computer facilities are available to all students.
**Fees:** None.
**Hours:** 8 AM-4:30 PM.

**GRADUATE CAREER DATA.** 55% of graduates choose careers in business and industry.

**PROMINENT ALUMNI/AE.** Otto Ledford, Gemini astronaut; Jim Ed Brown, entertainer; James Curlin, secretary, Department of the Interior; Dale Robertson, chief, U.S. Forest Service; Dwayne Powell, syndicated political cartoonist; Frank Hickingbotham, founder and board chairperson, TCBY.

# University of Arkansas at Pine Bluff

**Pine Bluff, AR 71601-2799 — 501 543-8000**

**1994-95 Costs.** Tuition: $1,464 (state residents), $3,384 (out-of-state). Room & board: $2,228-$2,408. Fees, books, misc. academic expenses (school's estimate): $550.
**Enrollment.** Undergraduates: 1,118 men, 1,730 women (full-time). Freshman class: 1,654 applicants, 1,073 accepted, 718 enrolled. Graduate enrollment: 11 men, 42 women.
**Test score averages/ranges.** N/A.
**Faculty.** 167 full-time; 26 part-time. 54% of faculty holds doctoral degree. Student/faculty ratio: 19 to 1.
**Selectivity rating.** N/A.

**PROFILE.** U Arkansas at Pine Bluff is a public, multipurpose, land-grant institution. It was founded as a Normal school in 1873, became a four-year college in 1933, and merged with the University of Arkansas in 1972. Its 295-acre campus is located in Pine Bluff, 38 miles north of Little Rock.

**Accreditation:** NCACS. Professionally accredited by the American Home Economics Association, the National Association of Schools of Music, the National Council for Accreditation of Teacher Education, the National League for Nursing.
**Religious orientation:** University of Arkansas at Pine Bluff is nonsectarian; no religious requirements.
**Library:** Collections totaling over 113,658 volumes, 810 periodical subscriptions, and 96,255 microform items.
**Special facilities/museums:** Fine arts gallery, child care center, 240-acre farm.
**Athletic facilities:** Swimming pool, racquetball and tennis courts, gymnastic and weight rooms.

**STUDENT BODY. Undergraduate profile:** 85% are state residents. 81% Black, 18% White, 1% Other. Average age of undergraduates is 19.
**Freshman profile:** Majority of accepted applicants took ACT.
**Undergraduate achievement:** 66% of fall 1991 freshmen returned for fall 1992 term.

**PROGRAMS OF STUDY. Degrees:** B.A., B.S.
**Majors:** Accounting, Agricultural Economics, Agricultural Education, Agronomy, Animal Science, Art Education, Art Functional, Automotive Technology Management, Biology, Business Administration, Business Education, Chemistry, Child Development, Community Recreation, Computer Science, Criminal Justice, Early Childhood Development, Economics, Educational Media, Elementary Education, English, English Education, Fashion Merchandising, Fisheries Biology, Food Sciences/Human Nutrition, Health/Physical Education, History, Home Economics Education, Industrial Arts Education, Industrial Technology, Law Enforcement, Mathematics, Mathematics Education, Music, Music Education, Nursing, Physics, Political Science, Pre-Engineering, Psychology, Regulatory Science/Agriculture, Regulatory Science/Environmental Biology, Regulatory Science/Industrial Health/Safety, Science Education, Social Science Education, Social Sciences, Social Welfare, Sociology, Special Education, Speech/Drama, Speech/Dramatic Arts Education, Trade/Industrial Education.
**Distribution of degrees:** The majors with the highest enrollment are business administration, criminal justice, and accounting; animal science, physics, and English have the lowest.
**Requirements:** General education requirement.
**Academic regulations:** Freshmen must maintain minimum 1.65 GPA; sophomores, 1.83 GPA; juniors, 1.96 GPA; seniors, 2.0 GPA.
**Special:** Associate's degrees offered. Double majors. Internships. Preprofessional programs in law, medicine, engineering, medical technology, and nursing. Teacher certification in early childhood, elementary, secondary, special education, and vo-tech education. ROTC.
**Honors:** Honors program.
**Academic Assistance:** Remedial reading, writing, math, and study skills. Nonremedial tutoring.

**STUDENT LIFE. Housing:** Students may live on or off campus. Women's and men's dorms. 27% of students live in college housing.
**Social atmosphere:** "School spirit is on the rise," according to the editor of the student newspaper. Students like to meet at the L.A. Davis Student Union, the front steps of the Watson library, and the recreational center. The Greeks are active in student social life. Some popular events include Homecoming week, Arkansas Classic, Spring Emphasis week, and Black History month.
**Services and counseling/handicapped student services:** Placement services. Health service. Day care. Counseling services for minority, military, veteran, and older students. Personal and psychological counseling. Career and academic guidance services.

**Campus organizations:** Undergraduate student government. Student newspaper. Yearbook. Choir, military and marching bands, home town clubs, speech and drama club, Lyceum Program. Four fraternities, no chapter houses; four sororities, no chapter houses. 5% of men join a fraternity. 2% of women join a sorority.
**Religious organizations:** Several religious groups.

**ATHLETICS. Physical education requirements:** Two semesters of physical education required.
**Intercollegiate competition:** 2% of students participate. Basketball (M,W), cheerleading (M,W), cross-country (M,W), football (M,W), golf (M), track (indoor) (M,W), track (outdoor) (M,W), track and field (indoor) (M,W), track and field (outdoor) (M,W), volleyball (W). Member of NAIA.
**Intramural and club sports:** 40% of students participate. Intramural basketball, football, racquetball, softball, swimming, tennis, track.

**ADMISSIONS. Academic basis for candidate selection** (in order of priority): Secondary school record, class rank, standardized test scores, school's recommendation.
**Nonacademic basis for candidate selection:** Character and personality are important. Extracurricular participation and alumni/ae relationship are considered.
**Requirements:** Graduation from secondary school is required; GED is accepted. No specific distribution of secondary school units required. Minimum composite ACT score of 19 and minimum "C" grade point average required. Conditional admission possible for applicants not meeting standard requirements. ACT is required. Campus visit recommended. Off-campus interviews available with an admissions representative.
**Procedure:** Take ACT by February of 12th year. Suggest filing application by fall. Application deadline is July 25. Notification of admission on rolling basis. $10 refundable room deposit. Freshmen accepted for terms other than fall.
**Special programs:** Admission may be deferred. Credit and/or placement may be granted through CLEP general and subject exams. Early entrance/early admission program. Concurrent enrollment program.
**Transfer students:** Transfer students accepted for terms other than fall. In fall 1992, 496 transfer applications were received, 408 were accepted. Minimum 2.0 GPA recommended. Maximum number of transferable credits is 68 semester hours.
**Admissions contact:** Kwurly M. Floyd, M.Ed., Registrar. 501 543-8492, 800 264-6585.

**FINANCIAL AID. Available aid:** Pell grants, SEOG, state scholarships, school scholarships, private scholarships and grants, ROTC scholarships, academic merit scholarships, and athletic scholarships. Perkins Loans (NDSL), PLUS, Stafford Loans (GSL), school loans, and SLS. Tuition Plan Inc.
**Financial aid statistics:** 24% of aid is not need-based. Average amounts of aid awarded freshmen: Loans, $2,000.
**Supporting data/closing dates:** FAFSA/FAF/FFS: Priority filing date is April 15; accepted on rolling basis. School's own aid application: Deadline is May 1. Income tax forms: Priority filing date is May 15; accepted on rolling basis. Notification of awards on rolling basis.
**Financial aid contact:** Ray Watley, Director of Financial Aid. 501 543-8301, 800 264-6523.

**STUDENT EMPLOYMENT.** College Work/Study Program. Institutional employment. 40% of full-time undergraduates work on campus during school year. Students may expect to earn an average of $600 during school year. Off-campus part-time employment opportunities rated "good."

**COMPUTER FACILITIES.** 27 IBM/IBM-compatible microcomputers. Students may access Digital minicomputer/mainframe systems. Residence halls may be equipped with stand-alone microcomputers. Computer languages and software packages include BASIC, COBOL, Database Management, FORTRAN, Harvard Graphics, Lotus 1-2-3, SPSS-X, WordStar, WordPerfect. Computer facilities are available to all students.
**Fees:** None.
**Hours:** 7:30 AM-10 PM (M-F); 9 AM-5 PM (Sa).

# University of Central Arkansas

**Conway, AR 72035-0001** **501 450-5000**

**1994-95 Costs.** Tuition: $1,586 (state residents), $3,172 (out-of-state). Room & board: $1,300. Fees, books, misc. academic expenses (school's estimate): $914.
**Enrollment.** Undergraduates: 2,982 men, 4,393 women (full-time). Freshman class: 2,797 applicants, 3,329 accepted, 1,856 enrolled. Graduate enrollment: 286 men, 725 women.
**Test score averages/ranges.** Average ACT scores: 22 English, 20 math, 22 composite. Range of ACT scores of middle 50%: 18-24 composite.
**Faculty.** 360 full-time; 163 part-time. 78% of faculty holds doctoral degree. Student/faculty ratio: 20 to 1.
**Selectivity rating.** Less competitive.

**PROFILE.** The University of Central Arkansas is a public institution. It was founded as a teachers college in 1907, became a state college in 1967, and gained university status in 1975. Programs are offered through the Colleges of Business Administration, Education, Fine and Applied Arts and Sciences, and Sciences and Humanities; the Division of Continuing Education; and the Honors College. Its 256-acre campus is located in Conway, 30 miles from Little Rock.

**Accreditation:** NCACS. Professionally accredited by the American Assembly of Collegiate Schools of Business, the American Medical Association (CAHEA), the American Physical Therapy Association, the American Speech-Language-Hearing Association, the National Association of Schools of Music, the National Council for Accreditation of Teacher Education, the National League for Nursing.
**Religious orientation:** University of Central Arkansas is nonsectarian; no religious requirements.
**Library:** Collections totaling over 353,730 volumes, 2,612 periodical subscriptions, and 602,066 microform items.
**Special facilities/museums:** Greenhouse, observatory.
**Athletic facilities:** Gymnasiums, field house, basketball, racquetball, tennis, and volleyball courts, swimming pool, track, fitness center, baseball, football, and intramural fields.

**STUDENT BODY. Undergraduate profile:** 98% are state residents. 1% Asian-American, 12% Black, 1% Hispanic, 1% Native American, 85% White. Average age of undergraduates is 21.
**Freshman profile:** 2% of freshmen who took ACT scored 30 or over on composite; 34% scored 24 or over on composite; 86% scored 18 or over on composite; 100% scored 12 or over on composite. 2% of accepted applicants took SAT; 97% took ACT. 99% of freshmen come from public schools.
**Undergraduate achievement:** 60% of fall 1992 freshmen returned for fall 1993 term. 25% of entering class graduated.
**Foreign students:** 168 students are from out of the country. Countries represented include Bangladesh, Bulgaria, Malaysia, Nigeria, Panama, and Singapore; 31 in all.

**PROGRAMS OF STUDY. Degrees:** B.A., B.Bus.Admin., B.Mus., B.Mus.Ed., B.S.
**Majors:** Accounting, Administration of Special Education, Art, Automated Office Management, Biology, Biology Education, Business/Commerce/Distributive, Business Economics, Business Education, Business/Management, Business Management/Administration, Chemistry, Communication, Computer Science, Counseling, Counseling Psychology, Dietetics, Dramatic Arts, Early Childhood Education, Economics, Education, Education of the Mentally Retarded, Educational Administration, Educational Psychology, Educational Supervision, Elementary Education, English, English Education, Finance, Fine/Applied Arts, French, General Business/Commerce, Geography, German, Gifted Education, Health, Health Education, Health Professions, History, Home Economics, Industrial Arts Education, Industrial Education, Interior Design, International Trade, Journalism, Junior High School Education, Kinesiology, Learning Disabilities, Library Science, Manual Arts Therapy, Marketing, Marketing Education, Mathematics, Mathematics Education, Medical Laboratory Technologies, Music, Music Education, Nuclear Medical Technology, Nursing, Occupational Therapy, Personnel Management, Physical Education, Physical Sciences, Physical Therapy, Physically Handicapped, Physics, Political Science/Government, Pre-Architecture, Pre-Dental Hygiene, Pre-Dentistry, Pre-Elementary Education, Pre-Engineering, Pre-Law, Pre-Medicine, Pre-Optometry, Pre-Pharmacy, Pre-Veterinary, Psychology, Public Administration, Radiography, Reading, Respiratory Therapy, School Psychology, Science, Social Sciences, Sociology, Spanish, Spanish Education, Special Education, Speech Correction, Speech/Debate/Forensics, Student Personnel, Vocational Technological Education.
**Distribution of degrees:** The majors with the highest enrollment are business, education, and health.
**Requirements:** General education requirement.
**Academic regulations:** Freshmen must maintain minimum 1.5 GPA; sophomores, 1.75 GPA; juniors, 2.0 GPA; seniors, 2.0 GPA.
**Special:** Minors offered in most majors. Independent study. Internships. Graduate school at which undergraduates may take graduate-level courses. Preprofessional programs in law, medicine, veterinary science, pharmacy, dentistry, and optometry. 3-2 engineering program with Arkansas State U. Teacher certification in early childhood, elementary, secondary, and special education. Certification in specific subject areas. ROTC.
**Honors:** Honors program.
**Academic Assistance:** Remedial reading, writing, math, and study skills. Nonremedial tutoring.

**STUDENT LIFE. Housing:** All freshmen must live on campus. Women's and men's dorms. 20% of students live in college housing.
**Social atmosphere:** The student newspaper reports that the university benefits from being only 30 minutes from Little Rock. UCA students frequent Beaver Park Lake and Toad Such State Park and meet at the nearby Wendy's. Groups that have widespread influence on campus include the Student Senate, Students for the Propagation of Black Culture, the Association of International Students, and the Royal Rooters. Popular events on campus include Bears football and baseball, the Board of Trustees lecture series, and the Honors College Challenge Week.
**Services and counseling/handicapped student services:** Placement services. Health service. Women's center. Counseling services for minority, military, and veteran students. Personal and psychological counseling. Career and academic guidance services. Physically disabled student services. Learning disabled services. Tape recorders. Tutors.
**Campus organizations:** Undergraduate student government. Student newspaper (Echo, published once/week). Yearbook. Radio and TV stations. Brass choir, marching and jazz bands, Dixieland band, saxophone and wind ensembles, madrigal singers, Stepperettes, majorettes, cheerleaders, UCA Players, debating, rifle corps, Student Activity Board, Blue/Gray Association, Young Democrats. 10 fraternities, one chapter house; eight sororities, no chapter houses. 30% of men join a fraternity. 20% of women join a sorority.
**Religious organizations:** Association of Baptists Students, Baptist Student Union, Chi Alpha Club, Church of Christ Student Union, Confraternity of Catholic Students, COGIC Club, Latter-Day Saints Student Association, Lutheran Student Association, Wesley Foundation.
**Minority/foreign student organizations:** Ebony Singers, Omega Pearls, Propagation of Black Culture. International Student Club.

**ATHLETICS. Physical education requirements:** Two semesters of physical education required.
**Intercollegiate competition:** 3% of students participate. Baseball (M), cross-country (W), football (M), golf (M), tennis (M,W), track (outdoor) (M), track and field (outdoor) (M), volleyball (W). Member of Gulf South Conference, NCAA Division II.
**Intramural and club sports:** 80% of students participate. Intramural badminton, basketball, bowling, cycling, golf, softball, table tennis, tennis, track, volleyball. Men's club cheerleading. Women's club cheerleading.

**ADMISSIONS. Academic basis for candidate selection** (in order of priority): Class rank, standardized test scores, secondary school record.
**Requirements:** Graduation from secondary school is required; GED is accepted. No specific distribution of secondary school units required. Minimum composite ACT score of 19, minimum 2.5 GPA, rank in top half of secondary school class, or completion of all required remedial courses required. ACT is required; SAT may be substituted. No off-campus interviews.
**Procedure:** Take SAT or ACT by April of 12th year. Application deadline is August 15. Notification of admission on rolling basis. No set date by which applicants must accept

offer. $100 room deposit, refundable until July 1. $100 room deposit, fully refundable until July 1, $50 refundable until August 20. Freshmen accepted for terms other than fall.
**Special programs:** Admission may be deferred one year. Credit and/or placement may be granted through CEEB Advanced Placement exams for scores of 3 or higher. Credit and/or placement may be granted through CLEP general and subject exams. Credit may be granted through military and life experience. Early entrance/early admission program. Concurrent enrollment program.
**Transfer students:** Transfer students accepted for terms other than fall. In fall 1993, 1,219 transfer applications were received, 1,014 were accepted. Application deadline is August 15 for fall; December 20 for spring. Minimum 2.0 GPA required. Lowest course grade accepted is "C." Maximum number of transferable credits is 60 semester hours from a two-year school and 90 semester hours from a four-year school. At least 24 credits must be completed at the university to receive degree.
**Admissions contact:** Joe F. Darling, M.S.E., Director of Admissions. 501 450-3128.

**FINANCIAL AID. Available aid:** Pell grants, SEOG, Federal Nursing Student Scholarships, state scholarships and grants, school scholarships, private scholarships, ROTC scholarships, academic merit scholarships, and athletic scholarships. Perkins Loans (NDSL), PLUS, Stafford Loans (GSL), NSL, and SLS.
**Financial aid statistics:** In 1993-94, 63% of all undergraduate applicants received aid; 60% of freshman applicants. Average amounts of aid awarded freshmen: Scholarships and grants, $1,850.
**Supporting data/closing dates:** FAFSA/FFS: Priority filing date is April 15; accepted on rolling basis. State aid form: Accepted on rolling basis. Notification of awards on rolling basis.
**Financial aid contact:** Sherry Byrd, Director of Financial Aid. 501 450-3140.

**STUDENT EMPLOYMENT.** College Work/Study Program. Institutional employment. 12% of full-time undergraduates work on campus during school year. Students may expect to earn an average of $1,500 during school year. Freshmen are discouraged from working during their first term. Off-campus part-time employment opportunities rated "good."

**COMPUTER FACILITIES.** 200 IBM/IBM-compatible and Macintosh/Apple microcomputers; 75 are networked. Students may access IBM minicomputer/mainframe systems. Residence halls may be equipped with modems. Client/LAN operating systems include Apple/Macintosh, DOS, UNIX/XENIX/AIX, LocalTalk/AppleTalk, Novell. Computer languages and software packages include Assembler, COBOL, FORTRAN, MUSIC, PL/1, SPSS. Computer facilities are available to all students.
**Fees:** None.
**Hours:** 7 AM-11 PM (M-F); 1 PM-5 PM (Sa); 1 PM-11 PM (Su).

**GRADUATE CAREER DATA.** Highest graduate school enrollments: U of Arkansas at Little Rock, U of Central Arkansas.

**PROMINENT ALUMNI/AE.** Sheffield Nelson, attorney, past president and chairperson of board, Arkla Gas; Jimmy Driftwood, songwriter, folklorist, Grammy award winner; Jim Bridges, screenwriter, motion picture director; Dee Brown, author, *Bury My Heart at Wounded Knee*.

# University of the Ozarks

**Clarksville, AR 72830 — 501 754-3839**

**1993-94 Costs.** Tuition: $4,800. Room & board: $2,850. Fees, books, misc. academic expenses (school's estimate): $720.
**Enrollment.** Undergraduates: 241 men, 270 women (full-time). Freshman class: 126 enrolled. Graduate enrollment: 2 men, 7 women.
**Test score averages/ranges.** Average ACT scores: 21 English, 18 math, 21 composite. Range of ACT scores of middle 50%: 16-25 English, 16-21 math.
**Faculty.** 39 full-time; 14 part-time. 46% of faculty holds doctoral degree. Student/faculty ratio: 15 to 1.
**Selectivity rating.** Noncompetitive.

**PROFILE.** The University of the Ozarks, founded in 1834, is a church-affiliated institution. Programs are offered through the Divisions of Business Enterprise, Education, Humanities and Fine Arts, Natural Science and Mathematics, and Social Sciences. Its 56-acre campus, including two central malls dominated by a Gothic memorial chapel, is located in Clarksville.

**Accreditation:** NCACS. Professionally accredited by the National Council for Accreditation of Teacher Education.
**Religious orientation:** University of the Ozarks is an interdenominational Christian school; one semester of religion required.
**Library:** Collections totaling over 81,624 volumes, 610 periodical subscriptions, and 9,623 microform items.
**Special facilities/museums:** Fine arts building and science center.
**Athletic facilities:** Gymnasium, dance studio, baseball, football, and softball fields, racquetball, tennis, and volleyball courts, swimming pool, track.

**STUDENT BODY. Undergraduate profile:** 81% are state residents; 27% are transfers. 3% Black, 1% Hispanic, 1% Native American, 81% White, 14% Other. Average age of undergraduates is 23.
**Freshman profile:** Majority of accepted applicants took ACT.
**Undergraduate achievement:** 57% of fall 1991 freshmen returned for fall 1992 term.
**Foreign students:** 92 students are from out of the country. Countries represented include Costa Rica, El Salvador, Guatemala, Malaysia, Nicaragua, and Panama; 11 in all.

**PROGRAMS OF STUDY. Degrees:** B.A., B.Gen.Studies, B.Mus.Ed., B.S.
**Majors:** Accounting, Art, Art Education, Biology, Business Administration, Business Education, Chemistry, Communications, Composite Science, Elementary Education, English, Environmental Studies, History, History/Political Science, History/Sociology, Management, Marketing, Mathematics, Medical Technology, Music, Music Business, Music Education, Philosophy/Religion/Christian Education, Physical Education, Physical Science, Political Science/Sociology, Pre-Professional, Psychology, Psychology/Sociology, Public Administration, Radiography, Respiratory Therapy, Social Studies, Social Studies Education.
**Distribution of degrees:** The majors with the highest enrollment are business administration, elementary education, and accounting.
**Requirements:** General education requirement.
**Academic regulations:** Freshmen must maintain minimum 1.37 GPA; sophomores, 1.62 GPA; juniors, 1.87 GPA; seniors, 2.0 GPA.
**Special:** Minors offered in many majors and in computer science, political science, and health. Associate's degrees offered. Double majors. Graduate school at which undergraduates may take graduate-level courses. Preprofessional programs in law, medicine, veterinary science, pharmacy, dentistry, and theology. 3-2 engineering program with U of Arkansas. Theology program with U of Dubuque. Native American Theological Education Consortium (NATEC). Teacher certification in early childhood, elementary, secondary, and special education. Certification in specific subject areas. Exchange program abroad in Japan (Shikoku Christian Coll). ROTC at U of Arkansas at Little Rock.
**Academic Assistance:** Remedial reading, writing, and study skills. Nonremedial tutoring.

**STUDENT LIFE. Housing:** All unmarried students under age 21 must live on campus unless living near campus with relatives. Women's and men's dorms. 75% of students live in college housing.
**Social atmosphere:** Popular events during the school year include basketball games and dances reports the student newspaper. Favorite student gathering spots include Curly's, Pizza Hut, and Weiderer's.
**Services and counseling/handicapped student services:** Placement services. Health service. Personal counseling. Career and academic guidance services. Religious counseling. Learning disabled program/services.
**Campus organizations:** Undergraduate student government. Student newspaper (Mountain Eagle, published once/week). Literary magazine. Yearbook. Radio and TV stations. Jazz ensemble, drama group, Freshmen Singers, Senior Chorale, Student Education Association, Ozark Area Mission, Young Democrats, Young Republicans, outdoors club.
**Religious organizations:** Baptist Student Union, Campus Christian Association, Fellowship of Christian Athletes, Catholic Youth.
**Minority/foreign student organizations:** Afro-American Club. International Club.

**ATHLETICS. Physical education requirements:** Four semester hours of physical education required.
**Intercollegiate competition:** 5% of students participate. Basketball (M,W), cheerleading (M), golf (M), tennis (M,W), track (outdoor) (M,W), track and field (outdoor) (M,W). Member of Arkansas Intercollegiate Conference, NAIA.
**Intramural and club sports:** 10% of students participate. Intramural basketball, football, racquetball, softball, tennis, volleyball. Men's club football, racquetball, soccer, softball, volleyball. Women's club football, racquetball, softball, volleyball.

**ADMISSIONS. Academic basis for candidate selection** (in order of priority): Secondary school record, class rank, standardized test scores, school's recommendation, essay.
**Nonacademic basis for candidate selection:** Character and personality, extracurricular participation, particular talent or ability, and geographical distribution are emphasized. Alumni/ae relationship is considered.
**Requirements:** Graduation from secondary school is recommended; GED is accepted. 15 units and the following program of study are required: 4 units of English, 2 units of math, 2 units of science including 1 unit of lab, 2 units of foreign language, 2 units of social studies, 2 units of history. Minimum composite ACT score of 18 (combined SAT score of 800) and minimum 2.0 GPA required. Conditional admission possible for applicants not meeting standard requirements. ACT is required; SAT may be substituted. Campus visit recommended. No off-campus interviews.
**Procedure:** Take SAT or ACT by January of 12th year. Suggest filing application by March 15. Application deadline is August 15. Notification of admission on rolling basis. Reply is required by June 1. Freshmen accepted for terms other than fall.
**Special programs:** Admission may be deferred one semester. Credit and/or placement may be granted through CEEB Advanced Placement exams for scores of 3 or higher. Credit may be granted through CLEP general and subject exams, DANTES exams, and military experience. Early entrance/early admission program. Concurrent enrollment program.
**Transfer students:** Transfer students accepted for terms other than fall. In fall 1992, 27% of all new students were transfers into all classes. 58 transfer applications were received, 58 were accepted. Application deadline is March 15 for fall; January 7 for spring. Minimum 2.0 GPA required. Lowest course grade accepted is "C." Maximum number of transferable credits is 66 semester hours from a two-year school and 90 semester hours from a four-year school. At least 30 semester hours must be completed at the university to receive degree.
**Admissions contact:** Tim McElroy, Ph.D., Director of Admissions. 501 754-3839, extension 231.

**FINANCIAL AID. Available aid:** Pell grants, SEOG, state scholarships and grants, school scholarships and grants, private scholarships and grants, academic merit scholarships, and athletic scholarships. Perkins Loans (NDSL), PLUS, Stafford Loans (GSL), school loans, and SLS. AMS.
**Financial aid statistics:** In 1992-93, 86% of all undergraduate applicants received aid; 78% of freshman applicants. Average amounts of aid awarded freshmen: Scholarships and grants, $1,800; loans, $2,000.
**Supporting data/closing dates:** FAFSA/FAF/FFS: Priority filing date is June 1; accepted on rolling basis. School's own aid application: Priority filing date is June 1; accepted on rolling basis. State aid form: Priority filing date is June 1; accepted on rolling basis. Income tax forms: Priority filing date is June 1; accepted on rolling basis. CSS: Priority filing date is June 1; accepted on rolling basis. Notification of awards on rolling basis.
**Financial aid contact:** Rex Anderson, Director of Financial Aid. 501 754-3839, extension 220.

**STUDENT EMPLOYMENT.** College Work/Study Program. Institutional employment. 35% of full-time undergraduates work on campus during school year. Students may expect to earn an average of $1,444 during school year. Off-campus part-time employment opportunities rated "fair."

**COMPUTER FACILITIES.** IBM/IBM-compatible microcomputers. Computer facilities are available to all students.
**Fees:** None.

# Williams Baptist College

Walnut Ridge, AR 72476 501 886-6741

**1994-95 Costs.** Tuition: $3,952. Room & board: $2,292. Fees, books, misc. academic expenses (school's estimate): $600.
**Enrollment.** Undergraduates: 186 men, 261 women (full-time). Freshman class: 307 applicants, 250 accepted, 198 enrolled.
**Test score averages/ranges.** Average ACT scores: 20 English, 18 math, 19 composite.
**Faculty.** 26 full-time; 12 part-time. 42% of faculty holds doctoral degree. Student/faculty ratio: 18 to 1.
**Selectivity rating.** Less competitive.

**PROFILE.** Williams Baptist is a church-affiliated college. It was founded as a two-year college in 1941, became a four-year college in 1983, and changed its name from Southern Baptist College in 1990. Its 175-acre campus is located three miles from Walnut Ridge, in northeastern Arkansas, 30 miles north of Jonesboro.

**Accreditation:** NCACS.
**Religious orientation:** Williams Baptist College is affiliated with the Southern Baptist Church; two semesters of religion required.
**Library:** Collections totaling over 76,816 volumes, 366 periodical subscriptions, and 40,002 microform items.
**Athletic facilities:** Sports center.
**STUDENT BODY. Undergraduate profile:** 79% are state residents; 6% are transfers. 3% Black, 91% White, 6% Other. Average age of undergraduates is 23.
**Freshman profile:** 3% of freshmen who took ACT scored 30 or over on English; 23% scored 24 or over on English, 8% scored 24 or over on math, 16% scored 24 or over on composite; 63% scored 18 or over on English, 41% scored 18 or over on math, 60% scored 18 or over on composite; 90% scored 12 or over on English, 87% scored 12 or over on math, 88% scored 12 or over on composite; 92% scored 6 or over on English, 89% scored 6 or over on math, 89% scored 6 or over on composite. 89% of accepted applicants took ACT. 95% of freshmen come from public schools.
**Undergraduate achievement:** 46% of fall 1992 freshmen returned for fall 1993 term. 2% of entering class graduated.
**Foreign students:** 33 students are from out of the country. Countries represented include Hong Kong, Japan, and Malayasia; 11 in all.
**PROGRAMS OF STUDY. Degrees:** B.A., B.S.
**Majors:** Art/Secondary, Business Administration, Church Music, Elementary Education, Music/Secondary, Pastoral Ministry, Physical Education, Psychology, Religious Education, Youth Ministry.
**Distribution of degrees:** The majors with the highest enrollment are elementary education and business administration.
**Requirements:** General education requirement.
**Academic regulations:** Freshmen must maintain minimum 1.5 GPA; sophomores, 1.5 GPA; juniors, 2.0 GPA; seniors, 2.0 GPA.
**Special:** Minors offered in some majors and in history and social science. Associate's degrees offered. Internships. Preprofessional programs in theology. Teacher certification in early childhood, elementary, and secondary education.
**Honors:** Honor societies.
**Academic Assistance:** Remedial reading, writing, and study skills. Nonremedial tutoring.
**ADMISSIONS. Academic basis for candidate selection** (in order of priority): Standardized test scores, secondary school record.
**Nonacademic basis for candidate selection:** Character and personality are emphasized. Particular talent or ability is important. Alumni/ae relationship is considered.
**Requirements:** Graduation from secondary school is recommended; GED is accepted. 16 units and the following program of study are required: 4 units of English, 2 units of math, 2 units of science, 3 units of history, 5 units of electives including 4 units of academic electives. Minimum composite ACT score of 19 and minimum 2.0 GPA recommended. Portfolio required of art program applicants. Audition required of music program applicants. Conditional admission possible for applicants not meeting standard requirements. ACT is required; SAT may be substituted. Campus visit and interview recommended. Off-campus interviews available with an admissions representative.
**Procedure:** Take SAT or ACT by June of 12th year. Notification of admission on rolling basis. No set date by which applicants must accept offer. $35 room deposit, refundable until two weeks prior to school opening. Freshmen accepted for terms other than fall.
**Special programs:** Credit may be granted through CLEP general and subject exams, challenge exams, and military experience. Early entrance/early admission program. Concurrent enrollment program.
**Transfer students:** Transfer students accepted for terms other than fall. In fall 1993, 6% of all new students were transfers into all classes. 65 transfer applications were received, 58 were accepted. Application deadline is September 6 for fall; January 24 for spring. Minimum 2.0 GPA recommended. Maximum number of transferable credits is 66 semester hours. At least 32 semester hours must be completed at the college to receive degree.
**Admissions contact:** Scott Wright, M.S., Director of Admissions. 501 886-6741, extension 127.

**FINANCIAL AID. Available aid:** Pell grants, SEOG, state scholarships and grants, school scholarships, private scholarships, academic merit scholarships, and athletic scholarships. Perkins Loans (NDSL), PLUS, Stafford Loans (GSL), school loans, and SLS.
**Financial aid statistics:** 3% of aid is not need-based. In 1993-94, 100% of all undergraduate applicants received aid. Average amounts of aid awarded freshmen: Scholarships and grants, $4,038; loans, $2,624.
**Supporting data/closing dates:** FAFSA: Priority filing date is May 1. School's own aid application: Priority filing date is May 1; accepted on rolling basis. Notification of awards on rolling basis.
**Financial aid contact:** Bob Womack, M.S., Director of Financial Aid. 501 886-6741, extension 122.

# California

## Academy of Art College

**San Francisco, CA 94105** **415 274-2200**

**1993-94 Costs.** Tuition: $9,000. Room: $4,900–$5,900. No meal plan. Fees: $70.
**Enrollment.** Undergraduates: 791 men, 876 women (full-time). Freshman class: 1,300 applicants, 1,300 accepted, 820 enrolled. Graduate enrollment: 161 men, 266 women.
**Test score averages/ranges.** N/A.
**Faculty.** 40 full-time; 210 part-time. 2% of faculty holds doctoral degree. Student/faculty ratio: 8 to 1.
**Selectivity rating.** N/A.

**PROFILE.** The Academy of Art College, founded in 1929, is a private institution. Its urban campus is located in San Francisco.

**Accreditation:** CCA-ACTTS. Professionally accredited by the Foundation for Interior Design Education Research, the National Association of Schools of Art and Design.
**Religious orientation:** Academy of Art College is nonsectarian; no religious requirements.
**Library:** Collections totaling over 16,000 volumes, 250 periodical subscriptions and 250 microform items.
**Special facilities/museums:** Art galleries, exhibit, foundry.

**STUDENT BODY. Undergraduate profile:** 90% are state residents; 60% are transfers. 36% Asian, 2% Black, 4% Hispanic, 2% Native American, 45% White, 11% Other. Average age of undergraduates is 23.
**Freshman profile:** 10% of accepted applicants took SAT; 15% took ACT. 75% of freshmen come from public schools.
**Undergraduate achievement:** 65% of fall 1992 freshmen returned for fall 1993 term. 55% of entering class graduated. 15% of students who completed a degree program went on to graduate study within five years.
**Foreign students:** 930 students are from out of the country. Countries represented include Hong Kong, Indonesia, Japan, Korea, Taiwan, and Thailand; 48 in all.

**PROGRAMS OF STUDY. Degrees:** B.F.A.
**Majors:** Advertising Design, Fashion, Fine Art, Graphic Design, Illustration, Interior Design, Motion Picture, Photography, Product Design.
**Distribution of degrees:** The majors with the highest enrollment are graphic design, interior design, and illustration; motion pictures, product design, and fashion have the lowest.
**Requirements:** General education requirement.
**Academic regulations:** Minimum 2.0 GPA must be maintained.
**Special:** Independent study. Internships. Cooperative education programs. Teacher certification in secondary education. Certification in specific subject areas.
**Academic Assistance:** Remedial reading, writing, and study skills.

**STUDENT LIFE. Housing:** Students may live on or off campus. Coed dorms. School-owned/operated apartments. 3% of students live in college housing.
**Social atmosphere:** Professional art and design organizations such as Western Art Directors' Club, American Society of Interior Designers, and International Sculpture Center have a strong influence on campus social life. Popular campus events include student exhibit openings and receptions, end of term project reviews, and the print sale. According to the student newspaper, "the academy is very diverse and multicultural, with a 30% international student population. The focus of students here is on professionalism."
**Services and counseling/handicapped student services:** Placement services. Health service. Counseling services for veteran students. Personal counseling. Academic guidance services. Physically disabled student services. Learning disabled services. Notetaking services.
**Campus organizations:** Undergraduate student government. Student newspaper (Academy Newsletter, published once/week).
**Minority/foreign student organizations:** International Student Club, Circle of Nations, Chinese Society, Korean Student Association, Gateway International, Taiwanese Student Association.

**ATHLETICS. Physical education requirements:** None.

**ADMISSIONS. Academic basis for candidate selection** (in order of priority): Secondary school record, school's recommendation.
**Nonacademic basis for candidate selection:** Particular talent or ability is emphasized. Character and personality and geographical distribution are considered.
**Requirements:** Graduation from secondary school is required; GED is accepted. No specific distribution of secondary school units required. Portfolio required for credit transfer. Advanced placement granted on the basis of artistic talent and relevant experience. Campus visit and interview recommended. Off-campus interviews available with an admissions representative.

**Procedure:** Priority filing dates: June 1 (Fall), November 1 (Spring), May 1 (Summer). Final filing dates: September 1 (Fall), January 15 (Spring), June 15 (Summer). Notification of admission on rolling basis. $100 nonrefundable tuition deposit. $500 nonrefundable room deposit. Freshmen accepted for terms other than fall.
**Special programs:** Admission may be deferred two semesters. Placement may be granted through CEEB Advanced Placement exams for scores of 4 or higher. Placement may be granted through military and life experience. Concurrent enrollment program.
**Transfer students:** Transfer students accepted for terms other than fall. In fall 1993, 60% of all new students were transfers into all classes. 700 transfer applications were received, 700 were accepted. Application deadline is rolling for fall; rolling for spring. Minimum 2.0 GPA recommended. Lowest course grade accepted is "C." Maximum number of transferable credits is 68 semester hours. At least 64 semester hours must be completed at the college to receive degree.
**Admissions contact:** Chris Garigliano, M.P.M., Director of Admissions. 415 274-2200.
**FINANCIAL AID. Available aid:** Pell grants, SEOG, state grants, school scholarships, and private scholarships. PLUS, Stafford Loans (GSL), private loans, and SLS. Deferred payment plan.
**Financial aid statistics:** 15% of aid is not need-based. In 1993-94, 60% of all undergraduate applicants received aid; 62% of freshman applicants. Average amounts of aid awarded freshmen: Scholarships and grants, $2,000; loans, $7,000.
**Supporting data/closing dates:** FAFSA: Accepted on rolling basis. School's own aid application: Accepted on rolling basis. State aid form: Accepted on rolling basis. Notification of awards on rolling basis.
**Financial aid contact:** Nancy Waltz, Director of Financial Aid. 415 274-2217.
**STUDENT EMPLOYMENT.** College Work/Study Program. Institutional employment. 3% of full-time undergraduates work on campus during school year. Students may expect to earn an average of $5,000 during school year. Freshmen are discouraged from working during their first term. Off-campus part-time employment opportunities rated "excellent."
**COMPUTER FACILITIES.** 65 Macintosh/Apple microcomputers; all are networked. Students may access minicomputer/mainframe systems. Client/LAN operating systems include Apple/Macintosh, LocalTalk/AppleTalk. Computer languages and software packages include Art-related programs and software, including Adobe Illustrator, Fractal, Macro Mind Director, Photoshop, and QuarkXPress. Computer facilities available only to students enrolled in computer courses.
**Fees:** $45 computer fee per semester.
**Hours:** 9 AM-12 AM.
**GRADUATE CAREER DATA.** Highest graduate school enrollments: Academy of Art Coll, Parsons Sch of Design, Rhode Island Sch of Design, San Francisco Art Inst. Companies and businesses that hire graduates: advertising agencies, banks, design firms, fashion companies, interior design firms, magazine publishers, real estate firms, television stations.
**PROMINENT ALUMNI/AE.** Millard Sheets, Howard Brodie, Doug Kingman, Barnaby Conrad.

## Art Center College of Design

**Pasadena, CA 91103** **818 584-5000**

**1993-94 Costs.** Tuition: $13,040. Housing: None. Fees, books, misc. academic expenses (school's estimate): $4,000.
**Enrollment.** Undergraduates: 816 men, 459 women (full-time). Freshman class: 582 applicants, 264 accepted, 223 enrolled.
**Test score averages/ranges.** Average SAT scores: 500 verbal, 500 math.
**Faculty.** 56 full-time; 254 part-time. Student/faculty ratio: 12 to 1.
**Selectivity rating.** Competitive.

**PROFILE.** Art Center, founded in 1930, is a private institution. Its 175-acre campus is located near Pasadena's Rose Bowl.

**Accreditation:** WASC. Professionally accredited by the National Association of Schools of Art and Design.
**Religious orientation:** Art Center College of Design is nonsectarian; no religious requirements.
**Library:** Collections totaling over 40,000 volumes and 400 periodical subscriptions.
**Special facilities/museums:** Galleries for student exhibits, photo/film stages, computer graphics facilities, industrial design labs, photography labs, shooting studios, sculpture garden.
**STUDENT BODY. Undergraduate profile:** 96% are transfers. 22% Asian-American, 2% Black, 9% Hispanic, 1% Native American, 65% White, 1% Other. Average age of undergraduates is 25.
**Undergraduate achievement:** 90% of fall 1991 freshmen returned for fall 1992 term. 68% of entering class graduated.
**Foreign students:** Countries represented include Germany, Hong Kong, Japan, Korea, Switzerland, and Taiwan; 37 in all.
**PROGRAMS OF STUDY. Degrees:** B.F.A., B.S.
**Majors:** Advertising, Environmental Design, Film, Fine Arts, Graphic/Packaging Design, Illustration, Industrial Design, Painting, Photography, Product Design, Transportation Design.
**Distribution of degrees:** The majors with the highest enrollment are graphic/packaging design, illustration, and photography; environmental design, film, and fine arts have the lowest.
**Requirements:** General education requirement.
**Academic regulations:** Minimum 2.5 GPA must be maintained.
**Special:** Minors offered in fine arts, illustration, and photography. Most classes are held once/week for full day. Courses offered in art history, humanities, natural sciences, philosophy, and social/behavioral sciences. Exchange programs with Caltech and Occidental Coll. Exchange program abroad in Switzerland (Art Center).
**Honors:** Honors program.
**STUDENT LIFE. Housing:** Commuter campus; no student housing.
**Social atmosphere:** The Industrial Designers Society of America Student Chapter is one of the most influential groups on campus. The mid-term all-school party is the most popular campus social event, but students also enjoy attending the various films and lectures. "Our students are all a little older than the average college student," notes the public relations coordinator. "They come to Art Center for a professional education and the opportunity to work with corporate sponsors; thus, they don't spend much time socializing on campus."
**Services and counseling/handicapped student services:** Placement services. Personal and psychological counseling. Career guidance services.
**Campus organizations:** Undergraduate student government. Student newspaper (Bulletin, published once/week).
**ATHLETICS. Physical education requirements:** None.
**ADMISSIONS. Academic basis for candidate selection** (in order of priority): Secondary school record, class rank, essay, standardized test scores, school's recommendation.
**Nonacademic basis for candidate selection:** Particular talent or ability is emphasized.
**Requirements:** Graduation from secondary school is required; GED is accepted. No specific distribution of secondary school units required. Portfolio required. SAT or ACT is required. Campus visit and interview recommended. No off-campus interviews.
**Procedure:** Suggest filing application by March 1; no deadline. Notification of admission on rolling basis. No set date by which applicants must accept offer. $200 nonrefundable tuition deposit. Freshmen accepted for terms other than fall.
**Special programs:** Admission may be deferred one semester.
**Transfer students:** Transfer students accepted for terms other than fall. In fall 1992, 96% of all new students were transfers into all classes. Application deadline is rolling for fall; rolling for spring. Minimum 2.5 GPA recommended. Lowest course grade accepted is "C." At least four semesters must be completed at the college to receive degree.
**Admissions contact:** Gregory Price, Director of Admissions. 818 584-5035.
**FINANCIAL AID. Available aid:** Pell grants, SEOG, state scholarships and grants, and school scholarships and grants. Perkins Loans (NDSL), PLUS, Stafford Loans (GSL), state loans, school loans, and SLS. Deferred payment plan.
**Financial aid statistics:** In 1992-93, 97% of all undergraduate applicants received aid; 95% of freshman applicants. Average amounts of aid awarded freshmen: Loans, $3,989.
**Supporting data/closing dates:** FAFSA/FAF/FFS: Priority filing date is February 1; accepted on rolling basis. School's own aid application: Priority filing date is February 1; accepted on rolling basis. State aid form: Priority filing date is March 1; accepted on rolling basis. Income tax forms: Accepted on rolling basis. Notification of awards on rolling basis.
**Financial aid contact:** Jerry Sims, Director of Financial Aid. 818 584-5137.
**STUDENT EMPLOYMENT.** College Work/Study Program. Institutional employment. 43% of full-time undergraduates work on campus during school year. Freshmen are discouraged from working during their first term. Off-campus part-time employment opportunities rated "fair."
**COMPUTER FACILITIES.** IBM/IBM-compatible and Macintosh/Apple microcomputers. Numerous computer languages and software packages available. Computer facilities are available to all students.
**Fees:** None.
**Hours:** 24 hours.
**GRADUATE CAREER DATA.** Companies and businesses that hire graduates: Chrysler, Ford, General Electric, General Motors, Hasbro Toys, J. Walter Thompson, Leo Burnett, Lockheed, Mattel, Mitsubishi, Ogilvy Mather, Omega Watch.

## Azusa Pacific University

**Azusa, CA 91702** **818 815-6000**

**1993-94 Costs.** Tuition: $10,788. Room & board: $3,950. Fees, books, misc. academic expenses (school's estimate): $696.
**Enrollment.** Undergraduates: 818 men, 1,214 women (full-time). Freshman class: 1,801 applicants, 1,481 accepted, 849 enrolled. Graduate enrollment: 784 men, 985 women.
**Test score averages/ranges.** Average SAT scores: 425 verbal, 471 math. Average ACT scores: 18 composite.
**Faculty.** 156 full-time; 181 part-time. 48% of faculty holds highest degree in specific field. Student/faculty ratio: 18 to 1.
**Selectivity rating.** Less competitive.

**PROFILE.** Azusa Pacific is a church-affiliated university. Founded in 1965, it gained university status in 1981. Programs are offered through the College of Liberal Arts and Sciences; the Schools of Business and Management, Music, Nursing, and Professional and Behavioral Studies; and the Graduate School of Theology. Its 50-acre campus is located 25 minutes east of Los Angeles.

**Accreditation:** WASC. Professionally accredited by the Council on Social Work Education, the National League for Nursing.
**Religious orientation:** Azusa Pacific University is a nondenominational Christian school; six semesters of religion/theology required.
**Library:** Collections totaling over 580,000 volumes, 950 periodical subscriptions, and 470,000 microform items.
**Special facilities/museums:** Electron microscope.
**Athletic facilities:** Gymnasium, baseball, football, and soccer fields, track, basketball and volleyball courts, weight room.
**STUDENT BODY. Undergraduate profile:** 79% are state residents. 5% Asian-American, 4% Black, 10% Hispanic, 2% Native American, 70% White, 9% Other. Average age of undergraduates is 22.
**Freshman profile:** 4% of freshmen who took SAT scored 600 or over on verbal, 11% scored 600 or over on math; 22% scored 500 or over on verbal, 39% scored 500 or over on math; 64% scored 400 or over on verbal, 74% scored 400 or over on math; 92% scored 300

or over on verbal, 95% scored 300 or over on math. Majority of accepted applicants took SAT.
**Undergraduate achievement:** 83% of fall 1992 freshmen returned for fall 1993 term.
**Foreign students:** 300 students are from out of the country. Countries represented include Canada, Indonesia, Japan, South Korea, Taiwan, and Thailand; 24 in all.
**PROGRAMS OF STUDY. Degrees:** B.A., B.S.
**Majors:** Accounting, Applied Health, Art, Biblical Literature, Biochemistry, Biology, Business Administration, Chemistry, Communication, Computer Science, English, History, International Studies, Liberal Studies, Life Science, Management Information Systems, Marketing, Mathematics/Physics, Music, Nursing, Philosophy, Physical Education, Physical Education/Athletic Training, Physical Science, Political Science, Psychology, Religion, Social Science, Social Work, Sociology.
**Distribution of degrees:** The majors with the highest enrollment are liberal studies, business administration, and nursing.
**Requirements:** General education requirement.
**Special:** Minors offered. Double majors. Independent study. Internships. Graduate school at which undergraduates may take graduate-level courses. Preprofessional programs in law, medicine, dentistry, and engineering. Washington Semester. Teacher certification in elementary and secondary education. Study abroad in Costa Rica, Ecuador, Japan, and Taiwan. ROTC at Claremont Coll.
**Honors:** Honors program.
**Academic Assistance:** Remedial reading, writing, math, and study skills. Nonremedial tutoring.
**STUDENT LIFE. Housing:** Students may live on or off campus. Women's and men's dorms. School-owned/operated apartments. 62% of students live in college housing.
**Services and counseling/handicapped student services:** Placement services. Health service. Personal and psychological counseling. Career and academic guidance services. Religious counseling.
**Campus organizations:** Undergraduate student government. Student newspaper (Clause, published once/week). Yearbook. Music groups, gospel choir, drama club, surf club, cheerleading, College Republicans, College Democrats, 14 organizations in all.
**Religious organizations:** Fellowship of Christian Athletes.
**Minority/foreign student organizations:** Hawaiian Club, MESA. Multi-ethnic organization.
**ATHLETICS. Physical education requirements:** Four semesters of physical education required.
**Intercollegiate competition:** 10% of students participate. Baseball (M), basketball (M,W), cross-country (M,W), football (M), soccer (M,W), softball (W), tennis (M), track and field (indoor) (M,W), track and field (outdoor) (M,W), volleyball (W). Member of Golden State Athletic Conference, NAIA.
**Intramural and club sports:** 4% of students participate. Intramural Alpine skiing, badminton, basketball, cycling, flag football, rock climbing, softball, tennis, volleyball. Men's club volleyball.
**ADMISSIONS. Academic basis for candidate selection** (in order of priority): Secondary school record, school's recommendation, essay, standardized test scores, class rank.
**Nonacademic basis for candidate selection:** Character and personality are emphasized. Extracurricular participation is important. Particular talent or ability and alumni/ae relationship are considered.
**Requirements:** Graduation from secondary school is recommended; GED is accepted. No specific distribution of secondary school units required. Minimum 2.5 GPA required. Conditional admission possible for applicants not meeting standard requirements. SAT is required; ACT may be substituted. Campus visit and interview recommended. Off-campus interviews available with an admissions representative.
**Procedure:** Take SAT or ACT by May 15 of 12th year. Visit college for interview by June 15 of 12th year. Notification of admission on rolling basis. No set date by which applicants must accept offer. $250 room deposit, refundable until July 15. Freshmen accepted for terms other than fall.
**Special programs:** Admission may be deferred two years. Credit may be granted through CEEB Advanced Placement for scores of 3 or higher. Credit may be granted through CLEP general and subject exams. Early entrance/early admission program. Concurrent enrollment program.
**Transfer students:** Transfer students accepted for terms other than fall. In fall 1993, 595 transfer applications were received, 339 were accepted. Application deadline is rolling for fall; rolling for spring. Minimum 2.0 GPA required. Lowest course grade accepted is "C." Maximum number of transferable credits is 64 semester hours. At least 30 semester hours must be completed at the university to receive degree.
**Admissions contact:** Deana Porterfield, Director of Admissions. 818 812-3016, 800 TALK-APU.
**FINANCIAL AID. Available aid:** Pell grants, SEOG, state scholarships and grants, school scholarships and grants, private scholarships and grants, ROTC scholarships, academic merit scholarships, and athletic scholarships. Perkins Loans (NDSL), PLUS, Stafford Loans (GSL), NSL, state loans, school loans, private loans, and SLS. Deferred payment plan and family tuition reduction.
**Financial aid statistics:** In 1993-94, 85% of all undergraduate applicants received aid.
**Supporting data/closing dates:** FAFSA: Priority filing date is January; accepted on rolling basis. FAF: Accepted on rolling basis. School's own aid application: Accepted on rolling basis. Income tax forms: Accepted on rolling basis. GPA verification form: Priority filing date is March 2; accepted on rolling basis. Notification of awards on rolling basis.
**Financial aid contact:** Beverly Jordan, Director of Financial Aid. 818 815-6000, extension 3009.
**STUDENT EMPLOYMENT.** College Work/Study Program. Institutional employment. 78% of full-time undergraduates work on campus during school year. Students may expect to earn an average of $1,440 during school year. Off-campus part-time employment opportunities rated "excellent."
**COMPUTER FACILITIES.** IBM/IBM-compatible and Macintosh/Apple microcomputers. Students may access Hewlett-Packard minicomputer/mainframe systems. Computer languages and software packages include BASIC, C, COBOL, FORTRAN, LISP, Pascal, SPSS-X. Computer facilities are available to all students.
**Hours:** 8 AM-11 PM (M-F); 8:30 AM-8 PM (Sa-Su).

# Biola University

**La Mirada, CA 90639** **310 903-6000**

**1994-95 Costs.** Tuition: $11,388. Room & board: $4,736. Fees, books, misc. academic expenses (school's estimate): $500.
**Enrollment.** Undergraduates: 729 men, 1,161 women (full-time). Freshman class: 1,118 applicants, 896 accepted, 461 enrolled. Graduate enrollment: 579 men, 285 women.
**Test score averages/ranges.** Average SAT scores: 440 verbal, 500 math. Average ACT scores: 23 English, 22 math, 22 composite.
**Faculty.** 126 full-time; 93 part-time. 65% of faculty holds doctoral degree. Student/faculty ratio: 17 to 1.
**Selectivity rating.** Less competitive.

**PROFILE.** Biola, founded in 1908, is a university with religious orientation. Programs are offered through the Schools of Arts and Sciences, Intercultural Studies, Psychology, and Theology. Its 100-acre campus is located in La Mirada, 22 miles from Los Angeles.

**Accreditation:** WASC. Professionally accredited by the American Psychological Association, the Association of Theological Schools in the United States and Canada, the National Association of Schools of Music, the National League for Nursing.
**Religious orientation:** Biola University is a nondenominational Christian school; 30 semester hours of religion/theology required.
**Library:** Collections totaling over 257,000 volumes, 1,000 periodical subscriptions, and 166,000 microform items.
**Special facilities/museums:** Art gallery, electron microscope, radio station, TV production facility, film editing facility.
**Athletic facilities:** Gymnasium, baseball and soccer fields, basketball and volleyball courts, track.
**STUDENT BODY. Undergraduate profile:** 70% are state residents; 27% are transfers. 14.3% Asian-American, 3.2% Black, 7.2% Hispanic, .5% Native American, 71.8% White, 3% Other. Average age of undergraduates is 21.
**Freshman profile:** 1% of freshmen who took SAT scored 700 or over on verbal, 3% scored 700 or over on math; 8% scored 600 or over on verbal, 20% scored 600 or over on math; 36% scored 500 or over on verbal, 54% scored 500 or over on math; 73% scored 400 or over on verbal, 83% scored 400 or over on math; 95% scored 300 or over on verbal, 98% scored 300 or over on math. Majority of accepted applicants took SAT.
**Undergraduate achievement:** 78% of fall 1992 freshmen returned for fall 1993 term. 49% of entering class graduated. 20% of students who completed a degree program immediately went on to graduate study.
**Foreign students:** 28 students are from out of the country. Countries represented include Canada, Hong Kong, Kenya, and the Philippines; 16 in all.
**PROGRAMS OF STUDY. Degrees:** B.A., B.Mus., B.S.
**Majors:** Applied Music, Art, Biblical Studies/Theology, Biochemistry, Biological Sciences, Business Administration, Chemistry, Christian Education, Communication, Computer Science, Economics, Education, English, Geography, Greek, Hebrew, History, Humanities, Intercultural Studies, Latin, Liberal/General Studies, Literature, Mathematical Science, Music, Music Education, Music Theory/Composition, Nursing, Philosophy, Physical Education, Physical Science, Print Media, Psychology, Radio/Television, Social Sciences, Sociology, Spanish, Speech Disorders.
**Distribution of degrees:** The majors with the highest enrollment are business administration, communication, and psychology; humanities, philosophy, and biochemistry have the lowest.
**Requirements:** General education requirement.
**Academic regulations:** Minimum 2.0 GPA must be maintained.
**Special:** Minors offered in most majors. Courses offered in anthropology, French, and German. Self-designed majors. Double majors. Internships. Cooperative education programs. Graduate school at which undergraduates may take graduate-level courses. Preprofessional programs in law, medicine, and theology. 3-2 engineering program with U of Southern California. Member of Christian College Consortium. Washington Semester. Exchange programs with Au Sable Inst of Environmental Studies and Los Angeles Film Inst. Teacher certification in elementary and secondary education. Study abroad in England (U of Sheffield and Oxford U), Latin America, Israel, Korea (Yonsei U), Japan, and Russia. ROTC, AFROTC at CalPoly at Pomona, CSU at Long Beach, and USC. NROTC at UCLA.
**Academic Assistance:** Remedial reading, writing, math, and study skills. Nonremedial tutoring.
**STUDENT LIFE. Housing:** All students under age 21 must live on campus unless living with family. Women's and men's dorms. School-owned/operated apartments. On-campus married-student housing. 65% of students live in college housing.
**Social atmosphere:** The student newspaper reports, "La Mirada is not really a college town but this is a fun campus with a close-knit group of students." Students gather on campus at the student union building and the Eagle's Nest, while off campus they frequent Rutabegorz and Gorky's. Popular social events at Biola include the lip sync contest, the Club's entertainment and concerts, BAB Week, and the Spring Banquet.
**Services and counseling/handicapped student services:** Placement services. Health service. Counseling services for minority, military, and veteran students. Personal and psychological counseling. Career and academic guidance services. Religious counseling. Physically disabled student services. Learning disabled services. Notetaking services. Tape recorders. Tutors. Reader services for the blind.
**Campus organizations:** Undergraduate student government. Student newspaper (Chimes, published once/week). Literary magazine. Yearbook. Radio and TV stations. Concert band, chorale, chamber singers, drama groups, debating, departmental, service, and special-interest groups, 25 organizations in all.
**Religious organizations:** Student Missionary Union, Brothers and Sisters in Christ.
**Minority/foreign student organizations:** Asian and Filipino clubs. Korean Student Association.

**ATHLETICS. Physical education requirements:** Four semesters of physical education required.
**Intercollegiate competition:** 1% of students participate. Baseball (M), basketball (M,W), cross-country (M,W), soccer (M), tennis (W), track and field (M,W), volleyball (W). Member of NAIA.
**Intramural and club sports:** 1% of students participate. Intramural basketball, football, soccer, volleyball.
**ADMISSIONS. Academic basis for candidate selection** (in order of priority): Secondary school record, standardized test scores, essay, school's recommendation.
**Nonacademic basis for candidate selection:** Character and personality are emphasized. Extracurricular participation, particular talent or ability, geographical distribution, and alumni/ae relationship are considered.
**Requirements:** Graduation from secondary school is required; GED is accepted. 16 units and the following program of study are required: 3 units of English, 2 units of math, 1 unit of science, 2 units of foreign language, 2 units of social studies, 6 units of electives. 1 unit each of chemistry and algebra required of nursing program applicants. 4 units of math and 1 unit each of chemistry and physics required of biology program applicants. Deficiencies may be made up. Audition required of music program applicants. Conditional admission possible for applicants not meeting standard requirements. SAT is required; ACT may be substituted. Campus visit recommended. Off-campus interviews available with admissions and alumni representatives.
**Procedure:** Take SAT or ACT by December of 12th year. Visit college for interview by March 1 of 12th year. Suggest filing application by February 1. Application deadline is June 1. Notification of admission on rolling basis. Reply is required by May 1. $100 nonrefundable tuition deposit. $100 room deposit, refundable until July 1. Freshmen accepted for terms other than fall.
**Special programs:** Admission may be deferred two years. Credit may be granted through CEEB Advanced Placement for scores of 3 or higher. Credit may be granted through CLEP general and subject exams. Credit and placement may be granted through challenge exams and military experience. Early entrance/early admission program. Concurrent enrollment program.
**Transfer students:** Transfer students accepted for terms other than fall. In fall 1993, 27% of all new students were transfers into all classes. 340 transfer applications were received, 261 were accepted. Application deadline is June 1 for fall; January 1 for spring. Minimum 2.25 GPA recommended. Lowest course grade accepted is "C." Maximum number of transferable credits is 70 semester hours. At least 30 semester hours must be completed at the university to receive degree.
**Admissions contact:** Greg Vaughan, M.A., Director of Enrollment Management. 310 903-4752.
**FINANCIAL AID. Available aid:** Pell grants, SEOG, state scholarships and grants, school scholarships and grants, private scholarships and grants, ROTC scholarships, academic merit scholarships, athletic scholarships, and aid for undergraduate foreign students. Perkins Loans (NDSL), PLUS, Stafford Loans (GSL), NSL, school loans, and SLS. Tuition Plan Inc. and deferred payment plan.
**Financial aid statistics:** 37% of aid is not need-based. In 1992-93, 87% of all undergraduate applicants received aid; 90% of freshman applicants. Average amounts of aid awarded freshmen: Scholarships and grants, $2,500; loans, $3,000.
**Supporting data/closing dates:** FAFSA/FAF: Priority filing date is March 2. School's own aid application: Accepted on rolling basis. Notification of awards on rolling basis.
**Financial aid contact:** George Jenkins, M.A., Director of Financial Aid. 310 903-4742.
**STUDENT EMPLOYMENT.** College Work/Study Program. Institutional employment. 32% of full-time undergraduates work on campus during school year. Students may expect to earn an average of $2,000 during school year. Off-campus part-time employment opportunities rated "excellent."
**COMPUTER FACILITIES.** 100 IBM/IBM-compatible, Macintosh/Apple, and RISC-/UNIX-based microcomputers; all are networked. Students may access Digital, Hewlett-Packard minicomputer/mainframe systems, BITNET, Internet. Residence halls may be equipped with stand-alone microcomputers, networked microcomputers. Client/LAN operating systems include Apple/Macintosh, DOS, UNIX/XENIX/AIX, X-windows, Artisoft, DEC, LocalTalk/AppleTalk. Computer languages and software packages include Ada, Adobe Illustrator, Adobe Photoshop, Aldus FreeHand, Aldus PageMaker, ASSEMBLY, C, C++, FORTRAN, LISP, MS Word, MS Excel, PASCAL, QuarkXPress. Computer facilities are available to all students.
**Fees:** $25 computer fee per semester.
**Hours:** 24 hours.
**GRADUATE CAREER DATA.** Highest graduate school enrollments: Rosemead Sch of Psychology, Sch of Intercultural Studies, Talbot Sch of Theology. 25% of graduates choose careers in business and industry.
**PROMINENT ALUMNI/AE.** Josh McDowell, theologian, author, and lecturer; John McArthur, theologian and college president; Rich Bueler, KRRT Radio; J. Richard Chase, president, Wheaton Coll (Ill.); John Campbell, vice-president, Ambassador Advertising; Todd Worrell, Christian educator and pitcher, St. Louis Cardinals; Robert Vernon, assistant police chief, Los Angeles.

## California Baptist College

**Riverside, CA 92504** — **909 689-5771**

**1994-95 Costs.** Tuition: $7,800. Room: $2,000. Board: $2,300. Fees, books, misc. academic expenses (school's estimate): $1,575.
**Enrollment.** Undergraduates: 228 men, 272 women (full-time). Freshman class: 504 applicants, 415 accepted, 252 enrolled. Graduate enrollment: 16 men, 26 women.
**Test score averages/ranges.** Average SAT scores: 395 verbal, 441 math. Average ACT scores: 20 English, 19 math, 19 composite.
**Faculty.** 46 full-time; 38 part-time. 70% of faculty holds doctoral degree. Student/faculty ratio: 12 to 1.
**Selectivity rating.** Competitive.

**PROFILE.** California Baptist, founded in 1950, is a church-affiliated, liberal arts college. Its 75-acre campus is located in Riverside, 50 miles east of Los Angeles. Thirteen campus buildings are Spanish in style.

**Accreditation:** WASC. Professionally accredited by the National Association of Schools of Music.
**Religious orientation:** California Baptist College is affiliated with the Southern Baptist Convention; six units of religion/theology required.
**Library:** Collections totaling over 110,000 volumes, 400 periodical subscriptions, and 7,986 microform items.
**Athletic facilities:** Gymnasium, badminton, basketball, sand volleyball, tennis, and volleyball courts, aerobics, weight rooms, baseball, soccer, and softball fields, field house.
**STUDENT BODY. Undergraduate profile:** 83% are state residents; 33% are transfers. 4% Asian-American, 8% Black, 6% Hispanic, 1% Native American, 51% White, 30% Other.
**Freshman profile:** 81% of accepted applicants took SAT; 19% took ACT.
**Foreign students:** 76 students are from out of the country. Countries represented include China, Hong Kong, Indonesia, Japan, Korea, and United Arab Emirates; 23 in all.
**PROGRAMS OF STUDY. Degrees:** B.A., B.Mus., B.S.
**Majors:** Art, Behavioral Science, Biology, Business Administration, Communication Arts, English, Government, History, Liberal Arts, Music, Physical Education, Physical Science, Psychology, Recreation, Religion, Social Science, Sociology, Spanish.
**Distribution of degrees:** The majors with the highest enrollment are business administration and religion.
**Requirements:** General education requirement.
**Special:** Minors offered in 25 fields. Courses offered in American studies, economics, French, German, and world studies. Double majors. Independent study. Pass/fail grading option. Internships. Preprofessional programs in law and medicine. Washington Semester. Teacher certification in elementary and secondary education. Study abroad in China. ROTC at California State U at San Bernardino.
**Honors:** Honors program.
**Academic Assistance:** Remedial reading, writing, and math.
**ADMISSIONS. Academic basis for candidate selection** (in order of priority): Secondary school record, standardized test scores, class rank, essay, school's recommendation.
**Nonacademic basis for candidate selection:** Character and personality are emphasized. Extracurricular participation is important. Particular talent or ability and alumni/ae relationship are considered.
**Requirements:** Graduation from secondary school is required; GED is accepted. No specific distribution of secondary school units required. Minimum combined SAT score of 800 (composite ACT score of 19) and minimum 2.0 GPA required. Minimum 2.5 GPA and testing required of teacher education program applicants. Audition required of music program applicants. SAT or ACT is required. Campus visit recommended. Off-campus interviews available with an admissions representative.
**Procedure:** Take SAT or ACT by May of 12th year. Notification of admission within two weeks of completion of file. $100 refundable room deposit. Freshmen accepted for terms other than fall.
**Special programs:** Admission may be deferred one year. Credit and/or placement may be granted through CEEB Advanced Placement exams for scores of 3 or higher. Credit and/or placement may be granted through CLEP general and subject exams. Early entrance/early admission program. Concurrent enrollment program.
**Transfer students:** Transfer students accepted for terms other than fall. In fall 1992, 33% of all new students were transfers into all classes. Application deadline is rolling for fall; rolling for spring. Minimum 2.0 GPA required. Lowest course grade accepted is "D" for up to six units not in major, "C" for more than six units. Maximum number of transferable credits is 70 semester hours from a two-year school and 100 semester hours from a four-year school. At least 24 semester hours must be completed at the college to receive degree.
**Admissions contact:** L. Kent Dacus, Director of Admissions. 909 689-5771, extension 212.
**FINANCIAL AID. Available aid:** Pell grants, SEOG, state scholarships and grants, school scholarships and grants, private scholarships and grants, academic merit scholarships, and athletic scholarships. Perkins Loans (NDSL), PLUS, and Stafford Loans (GSL). Tuition Management Systems and deferred payment plan.
**Financial aid statistics:** Average amounts of aid awarded freshmen: Scholarships and grants, $1,800; loans, $2,500.
**Supporting data/closing dates:** FAFSA: Priority filing date is March 2. School's own aid application: Priority filing date is April 1. Income tax forms: Priority filing date is April 15. Notification of awards on rolling basis.

## California College of Arts and Crafts

**Oakland, CA 94618** — **510 653-8118**

**1994-95 Costs.** Tuition: $12,760. Room: $2,300. Board: $2,124. Fees, books, misc. academic expenses (school's estimate): $730.
**Enrollment.** Undergraduates: 952 (full-time). Freshman class: 247 applicants, 148 accepted, 59 enrolled. Graduate enrollment: 79.
**Test score averages/ranges.** N/A.
**Faculty.** 32 full-time; 146 part-time. 71% of faculty holds highest degree in specific field. Student/faculty ratio: 7 to 1.
**Selectivity rating.** Less competitive.

**PROFILE.** California College of Arts and Crafts, founded in 1907, is a private institution. Its four-acre campus is located in Oakland, overlooking San Francisco Bay.

**Accreditation:** WASC. Professionally accredited by the Foundation for Interior Design Education Research, the National Architecture Accrediting Board, the National Association of Schools of Art and Design.

**Religious orientation:** California College of Arts and Crafts is nonsectarian; no religious requirements.
**Library:** Collections totaling over 33,400 volumes, 240 periodical subscriptions and 450 microform items.
**Special facilities/museums:** Art gallery.

**STUDENT BODY. Undergraduate profile:** 83% are state residents; 69% are transfers. 11% Asian-American, 4% Black, 6% Hispanic, 1% Native American, 61% White, 17% International/Unknown. Average age of undergraduates is 26.
**Undergraduate achievement:** 78% of fall 1992 freshmen returned for fall 1993 term. 50% of entering class graduated.
**Foreign students:** 122 students are from out of the country. Countries represented include Hong Kong, Indonesia, Japan, Korea, Singapore, and Taiwan; 27 in all.

**PROGRAMS OF STUDY. Degrees:** B.Arch., B.F.A.
**Majors:** Architecture, Ceramics, Drawing, Film/Video/Performance, Glass, Graphic Design, Illustration, Individualized Major, Industrial Design, Interior Architecture, Metals/Jewelry, Painting, Photography, Printmaking, Sculpture, Textiles, Wood/Furniture.
**Distribution of degrees:** The majors with the highest enrollment are graphic design and architecture; wood/furniture and textiles have the lowest.
**Requirements:** General education requirement.
**Academic regulations:** Minimum 2.0 GPA must be maintained.
**Special:** Self-designed majors. Double majors. Independent study. Internships. Cross-registration with Holy Names Coll and Mills Coll. Mobility program with Association of Independent Colleges of Art and Design (AICAD).
**Academic Assistance:** Remedial reading, writing, and study skills.

**ADMISSIONS. Academic basis for candidate selection** (in order of priority): Secondary school record, essay, school's recommendation, standardized test scores.
**Nonacademic basis for candidate selection:** Particular talent or ability is important. Character and personality and extracurricular participation are considered.
**Requirements:** Graduation from secondary school is required; GED is accepted. 16 units and the following program of study are recommended: 4 units of English, 2 units of math, 2 units of social studies. Minimum 2.0 GPA required. Portfolio required of art program applicants. SAT is recommended; ACT may be substituted. Campus visit recommended. Off-campus interviews available with an admissions representative.
**Procedure:** Suggest filing application by March 1; no deadline. Notification of admission on rolling basis. Reply is required by May 1. $150 nonrefundable tuition deposit. $200 nonrefundable room deposit. Freshmen accepted for terms other than fall.
**Special programs:** Admission may be deferred one term. Credit and/or placement may be granted through CEEB Advanced Placement exams for scores of 3 or higher. Placement may be granted through challenge exams.
**Transfer students:** Transfer students accepted for terms other than fall. In fall 1993, 69% of all new students were transfers into all classes. 448 transfer applications were received, 343 were accepted. Application deadline is March 1 (priority). Minimum 2.0 GPA required. Lowest course grade accepted is "C." Maximum number of transferable credits is 75 semester hours. At least 51 semester hours must be completed at the college to receive degree.
**Admissions contact:** Sheri Sivin McKenzie, M.A., Director of Admissions. 510 653-6522, extension 300.

**FINANCIAL AID. Available aid:** Pell grants, SEOG, state grants, school scholarships, and academic merit scholarships. Perkins Loans (NDSL), PLUS, Stafford Loans (GSL), and SLS. Deferred payment plan.
**Financial aid statistics:** 5% of aid is not need-based. In 1993-94, 100% of all undergraduate applicants received aid. Average amounts of aid awarded freshmen: Scholarships and grants, $3,400; loans, $3,000.
**Supporting data/closing dates:** FAFSA: Priority filing date is March 2; accepted on rolling basis. School's own aid application: Priority filing date is March 2; accepted on rolling basis. State aid form: Priority filing date is March 2; accepted on rolling basis. Income tax forms: Priority filing date is March 1; accepted on rolling basis. Verification Requirement Form: Priority filing date is March 2; accepted on rolling basis. Notification of awards begins in April.
**Financial aid contact:** Alice Knudson, M.S., Director of Financial Aid. 510 653-6522, extension 300.

## California Institute of the Arts

**Valencia, CA 91355** 805 255-1050

**1994-95 Costs.** Tuition: $14,600. Room: $3,250. Board: $2,910. Fees, books, misc. academic expenses (school's estimate): $1,700.
**Enrollment.** Undergraduates: 390 men, 260 women (full-time). Graduate enrollment: 194 men, 125 women.
**Test score averages/ranges.** N/A.
**Faculty.** 73 full-time; 105 part-time. Student/faculty ratio: 7 to 1.
**Selectivity rating.** N/A.

**PROFILE.** California Institute of the Arts, a private insitution, was founded through the 1961 merger of the L.A. Conservatory of Music and the Chouinard Art Institute. Its 60-acre campus is located in Valencia, overlooking the Santa Clarita Valley, 30 miles north of Los Angeles.

**Accreditation:** WASC. Professionally accredited by the National Association of Schools of Art and Design, the National Association of Schools of Music.
**Religious orientation:** California Institute of the Arts is nonsectarian; no religious requirements.
**Library:** Collections totaling over 64,164 volumes, 556 periodical subscriptions, and 6,958 microform items.
**Special facilities/museums:** Art museum/gallery, TV studio.

**STUDENT BODY. Undergraduate profile:** 40% are state residents. 7% Asian-American, 7% Black, 7% Hispanic, 1% Native American, 68% White, 10% Other. Average age of undergraduates is 23.
**Undergraduate achievement:** 90% of fall 1991 freshmen returned for fall 1992 term. 60% of entering class graduated.
**Foreign students:** 42 students are from out of the country. Countries represented include Brazil, China, Finland, France, Germany, and Iceland; 35 in all.

**PROGRAMS OF STUDY. Degrees:** B.F.A.
**Majors:** Acting, Character Animation, Dance, Directing for Theatre/Video/Cinema, Film Graphics Animation, Fine Arts, General Music, Graphic Design, Jazz, Live Action Film/Video, Music Composition, Music Performance, Photography, Technical Theatre.
**Requirements:** General education requirement.
**Special:** Self-designed majors. Independent study. Accelerated study. Internships. Cooperative education programs.
**Academic Assistance:** Nonremedial tutoring.

**ADMISSIONS.**
**Requirements:** Graduation from secondary school is required; GED is accepted. No specific distribution of secondary school units required. Portfolio required of visual arts and music composition program applicants. Audition required of performing arts program applicants. Conditional admission possible for applicants not meeting standard requirements. No off-campus interviews.
**Procedure:** Suggest filing application by February 1; deadlines vary by program. Notification of admission on rolling basis. Reply is required by May 1 if accepted by April 15. $300 nonrefundable tuition deposit. $200 refundable room deposit. Freshmen accepted for fall term only.
**Special programs:** Admission may be deferred in some majors for one year. Credit and/or placement may be granted through CEEB Advanced Placement exams for scores of 3 or higher. Credit and/or placement may be granted through CLEP general and subject exams.
**Transfer students:** Transfer students accepted for terms other than fall. In fall 1992, 250 transfer applications were received, 150 were accepted. Application deadline is February 1 (suggested) for fall; November 1 for spring. Lowest course grade accepted is "C." Maximum number of transferable credits is 22.
**Admissions contact:** Kenneth Young, Director of Admissions. 805 255-2185.

**FINANCIAL AID. Available aid:** Pell grants, SEOG, state scholarships and grants, school scholarships and grants, and private scholarships and grants. Perkins Loans (NDSL), PLUS, Stafford Loans (GSL), school loans, and SLS. Deferred payment plan.
**Financial aid statistics:** In 1992-93, 80% of all undergraduate applicants received aid.
**Supporting data/closing dates:** FAFSA/FAF/FFS: Priority filing date is March 2. Income tax forms: Accepted on rolling basis. Notification of awards begins April 1.
**Financial aid contact:** Bobbi Hever, Director of Financial Aid. 805 255-7869.

## California Institute of Technology

**Pasadena, CA 91125** 818 395-6811

**1994-95 Costs.** Tuition: $15,900. Room & board: $6,135. Fees, books, misc. academic expenses (school's estimate): $910.
**Enrollment.** Undergraduates: 662 men, 238 women (full-time). Freshman class: 1,916 applicants, 466 accepted, 210 enrolled. Graduate enrollment: 849 men, 228 women.
**Test score averages/ranges.** Average SAT scores: 660 verbal, 760 math. Range of SAT scores of middle 50%: 600-710 verbal, 720-780 math.
**Faculty.** 295 full-time. 100% of faculty holds doctoral degree. Student/faculty ratio: 3 to 1.
**Selectivity rating.** Most competitive.

**PROFILE.** Caltech, founded in 1891, is a private university and research center. Programs are offered through the Divisions of Biology, Chemistry and Chemical Engineering; Engineering and Applied Science; Geological and Planetary Sciences; the Humanities and Social Sciences; and Physics, Mathematics, and Astronomy. Its 124-acre campus is located in Pasadena, 10 miles from Los Angeles.

**Accreditation:** WASC. Professionally accredited by the Accreditation Board for Engineering and Technology.
**Religious orientation:** California Institute of Technology is nonsectarian; no religious requirements.
**Library:** Collections totaling over 487,000 volumes, and 6,500 periodical subscriptions.
**Special facilities/museums:** Industrial relations center, Palomar and Mt. Wilson observatories, aeronautical, environmental quality, jet propulsion, marine, and seismological labs.
**Athletic facilities:** Gymnasiums, swimming pools, weight room, track, baseball, football, soccer, and softball fields, basketball, racquetball, squash, tennis, and volleyball courts.

**STUDENT BODY. Undergraduate profile:** 30% are state residents; 6% are transfers. 30% Asian-American, 1% Black, 4% Hispanic, 1% Native American, 53% White, 11% Other. Average age of undergraduates is 18.
**Freshman profile:** 21% of freshmen who took SAT scored 700 or over on verbal, 93% scored 700 or over on math; 84% scored 600 or over on verbal, 100% scored 600 or over on math; 100% scored 500 or over on verbal. 100% of accepted applicants took SAT. 80% of freshmen come from public schools.
**Undergraduate achievement:** 95% of fall 1992 freshmen returned for fall 1993 term. 80% of entering class graduated. 61% of students who completed a degree program immediately went on to graduate study.
**Foreign students:** 85 students are from out of the country.

**PROGRAMS OF STUDY. Degrees:** B.S.
**Majors:** Applied Mathematics, Applied Physics, Astronomy, Biology, Chemical Engineering, Chemistry, Economics, Electrical Engineering, Engineering/Applied Science, Geochemistry, Geology, Geophysics, History, Independent Studies, Literature, Mathematics, Physics, Planetary Science, Social Sciences.

**Distribution of degrees:** The majors with the highest enrollment are engineering, physics, and biology.
**Requirements:** General education requirement.
**Academic regulations:** Minimum 1.9 GPA must be maintained.
**Special:** Self-designed majors. Double majors. Independent study. Pass/fail grading option. Internships. Graduate school at which undergraduates may take graduate-level courses. Host institution for 3-2 engineering program. ROTC at UCLA. AFROTC at U of Southern California.
**Academic Assistance:** Remedial writing.
**STUDENT LIFE. Housing:** All freshmen must live on campus. Coed dorms. School-owned/operated apartments. 80% of students live in college housing.
**Social atmosphere:** The Coffeehouse, the Espresso Bar, and Ralph's are hot spots. Caltech Christian Fellowship and Interhouse Committee are influential student groups. Popular social events include Drop Day, OPE, BDR, and Intrahouse. "Social life is close to nil," reports the student newspaper. "Not much time for fun, but the activities that exist are pursued with relish."
**Services and counseling/handicapped student services:** Placement services. Health service. Women's center. Counseling services for minority students. Birth control, personal, and psychological counseling. Career and academic guidance services. Religious counseling. Learning disabled services.
**Campus organizations:** Undergraduate student government. Student newspaper (California Tech, published once/week). Yearbook. Chamber music ensemble, jazz band, orchestra, choral groups, art classes, photo labs, drama club, Society of Women Engineers, service and political groups, special-interest groups.
**Religious organizations:** Christian Fellowship, Hillel, Newman Club.
**ATHLETICS. Physical education requirements:** Two terms of physical education required.
**Intercollegiate competition:** 35% of students participate. Baseball (M), basketball (M), cross-country (M,W), diving (M,W), fencing (M,W), golf (M,W), soccer (M), swimming (M,W), tennis (M,W), track (outdoor) (M,W), track and field (outdoor) (M,W), volleyball (W), water polo (M). Member of NCAA Division III, Southern California Intercollegiate Athletic Conference.
**Intramural and club sports:** 86% of students participate. Intramural basketball, flag football, soccer, softball, swimming, tennis, track and field, ultimate frisbee, volleyball. Men's club football, ice hockey, ultimate frisbee, volleyball. Women's club soccer.
**ADMISSIONS. Academic basis for candidate selection** (in order of priority): Secondary school record, standardized test scores, school's recommendation, class rank, essay.
**Nonacademic basis for candidate selection:** Character and personality and extracurricular participation are emphasized. Particular talent or ability is important.
**Requirements:** Graduation from secondary school is recommended; GED is not accepted. 15 units and the following program of study are required: 3 units of English, 4 units of math, 2 units of lab science, 1 unit of history. Remaining units may include additional English or history, foreign language, geology, biology, or other lab sciences, drawing, shop, or commercial subjects. SAT is required. ACH required. Campus visit recommended. No off-campus interviews.
**Procedure:** Take SAT by December of 12th year. Take ACH by December of 12th year. Application deadline is January 1. Notification of admission by March 15. Reply is required by May 1. $100 nonrefundable tuition deposit. Freshmen accepted for fall term only.
**Special programs:** Admission may be deferred one year. Placement may be granted through challenge exams. Early decision program. In fall 1993, 76 applied for early decision and 22 were accepted. Deadline for applying for early decision is October 15. Early entrance/early admission program.
**Transfer students:** Transfer students accepted for fall term only. In fall 1993, 6% of all new students were transfers into all classes. 300 transfer applications were received, 12 were accepted. Application deadline is March 1. Minimum 3.0 GPA required. Maximum number of transferable credits is 60 semester hours.
**Admissions contact:** Carole Snow, Ph.D., Director of Admissions. 818 564-8136.
**FINANCIAL AID. Available aid:** Pell grants, SEOG, state grants, school grants, and ROTC scholarships. Perkins Loans (NDSL), PLUS, Stafford Loans (GSL), school loans, and SLS. Tuition Plan Inc., Education Plan Inc., Knight Tuition Plans, AMS, EFI Fund Management, and Tuition Management Systems.
**Financial aid statistics:** 2% of aid is not need-based. In 1993-94, 80% of all undergraduate applicants received aid; 80% of freshman applicants. Average amounts of aid awarded freshmen: Scholarships and grants, $12,500; loans, $2,800.
**Supporting data/closing dates:** FAFSA/FAF: Priority filing date is February 1. State aid form: Deadline is March 2. Income tax forms: Priority filing date is May 1. Notification of awards begins March 20.
**Financial aid contact:** David Levy, M.A., Director of Financial Aid. 818 395-6341.
**STUDENT EMPLOYMENT.** College Work/Study Program. Institutional employment. 60% of full-time undergraduates work on campus during school year. Students may expect to earn an average of $1,800 during school year. Freshmen are discouraged from working during their first term. Off-campus part-time employment opportunities rated "good."
**COMPUTER FACILITIES.** IBM/IBM-compatible, Macintosh/Apple, and RISC-/UNIX-based microcomputers. Students may access Cray, Digital, IBM, SUN minicomputer/mainframe systems, BITNET, Internet, CompuServe. Residence halls may be equipped with stand-alone microcomputers, networked microcomputers, networked terminals, modems. Client/LAN operating systems include Apple/Macintosh, DOS, UNIX/XENIX/AIX. Numerous computer languages and software programs available. Computer facilities are available to all students.
**Fees:** None.
**Hours:** 24 hours.
**GRADUATE CAREER DATA.** Graduate school percentages: 2% enter medical school. 48% enter graduate arts and sciences programs. Highest graduate school enrollments: UC Berkeley, Harvard U, MIT, Princeton U, Stanford U. 16% of graduates choose careers in business and industry. Companies and businesses that hire graduates: Aerospace, petroleum, and research firms.
**PROMINENT ALUMNI/AE.** Linus Pauling, Nobel Prize-winning chemist; Richard Feynman, Nobel Prize-winning physicist; Rudy Marcus, Nobel Prize-winning chemist.

## California Lutheran University

**Thousand Oaks, CA 913602787** — **805 492-2411**

**1993-94 Costs.** Tuition: $11,860. Room & board: $5,200. Fees, books, misc. academic expenses (school's estimate): $780.
**Enrollment.** Undergraduates: 649 men, 778 women (full-time). Freshman class: 756 applicants, 572 accepted, 379 enrolled. Graduate enrollment: 368 men, 551 women.
**Test score averages/ranges.** Average SAT scores: 436 verbal, 495 math. Range of SAT scores of middle 50%: 400-600 verbal, 400-600 math.
**Faculty.** 112 full-time; 145 part-time. 72% of faculty holds doctoral degree. Student/faculty ratio: 14 to 1.
**Selectivity rating.** Less competitive.

**PROFILE.** California Lutheran, founded in 1961, is a church-affiliated, liberal arts university. Programs are offered through the Divisions of Humanities, Creative Arts and Education, Natural Sciences, and Social Sciences. Its 295-acre campus is located in the Conejo Valley, 50 miles northwest of Los Angeles.

**Accreditation:** WASC.
**Religious orientation:** California Lutheran University is affiliated with the Evangelical Lutheran Church in America; two semesters of religion required.
**Library:** Collections totaling over 115,000 volumes, 700 periodical subscriptions, and 5,000 microform items.
**Special facilities/museums:** On-campus elementary school, hypermedia lab, science center.
**Athletic facilities:** Gymnasium, athletic fields, tennis courts, swimming pool, track, weight room.
**STUDENT BODY. Undergraduate profile:** 90% are state residents; 44% are transfers. 4% Asian-American, 3% Black, 11% Hispanic, 1% Native American, 81% White. Average age of undergraduates is 20.
**Freshman profile:** 2% of freshmen who took SAT scored 700 or over on math; 4% scored 600 or over on verbal, 16% scored 600 or over on math; 23% scored 500 or over on verbal, 53% scored 500 or over on math; 67% scored 400 or over on verbal, 85% scored 400 or over on math; 95% scored 300 or over on verbal, 98% scored 300 or over on math. 90% of accepted applicants took SAT; 10% took ACT. 88% of freshmen come from public schools.
**Undergraduate achievement:** 80% of fall 1992 freshmen returned for fall 1993 term. 50% of entering class graduated. 40% of students who completed a degree program went on to graduate study within four years.
**Foreign students:** 126 students are from out of the country. Countries represented include Finland, Japan, Mexico, Norway, Singapore, and Sweden; 40 in all.
**PROGRAMS OF STUDY. Degrees:** B.A., B.S.
**Majors:** Accounting, Art, Athletic Training, Biological Sciences, Business Administration, Chemistry, Communication Arts, Computer Science, Criminal Justice, Drama, Economics, Education/Liberal Arts, English, French, Geology, German, History, Information Systems, Interdisciplinary, Mathematics, Music, Philosophy, Philosophy/Religion, Physical Education, Physics/Computer Science, Political Science, Psychology, Religion, Sociology, Spanish, Speech.
**Distribution of degrees:** The majors with the highest enrollment are business administration, communications, and psychology; mathematics, religion, and music have the lowest.
**Requirements:** General education requirement.
**Academic regulations:** Minimum 2.0 GPA must be maintained.
**Special:** Minors offered in most majors and in environmental studies, coaching, international business, and women's studies. Courses offered in Greek and international studies. Humanities and social science tutorial programs. Self-designed majors. Double majors. Dual degrees. Independent study. Accelerated study. Internships. Cooperative education programs. Graduate school at which undergraduates may take graduate-level courses. Preprofessional programs in law and medicine. 3-2 engineering program with Washington U. Sea Semester. Exchange program with Wagner Coll. Teacher certification in elementary, secondary, special education, and bilingual/bicultural education. Certification in specific subject areas. Study abroad in Austria, England, France, Germany, Mexico, the Netherlands, Norway, Spain, and Wales. ROTC and AFROTC at UC Santa Barbara.
**Honors:** Honors program. Honor societies.
**Academic Assistance:** Remedial writing and study skills. Nonremedial tutoring.
**STUDENT LIFE. Housing:** All freshmen must live on campus unless living with family. Coed dorms. 70% of students live in college housing.
**Social atmosphere:** The student newspaper reports that intramural sports, the Student Senate, and Campus Ministries are influential groups on campus. The Spring Formal, Homecoming, sporting events, Beach Day, and Showcase are among the year's favorite events. On-campus, students tend to meet at the Student Union Building, the library, the cafeteria, and Kingman Park. Hangouts off campus include the Thousand Oaks Mall, the Red Onion, and Rueben's.
**Services and counseling/handicapped student services:** Placement services. Health service. Women's center. Counseling services for minority, veteran, and older students. Birth control, personal, and psychological counseling. Career and academic guidance services. Religious counseling.
**Campus organizations:** Undergraduate student government. Student newspaper (Echo, published once/week). Literary magazine. Yearbook. Radio station. Choirs, string ensembles, concert orchestra, band, dance team, Rotaract, Circle K, 35 organizations in all.
**Religious organizations:** Fellowship of Christian Athletes, Campus Ministry, Lord of Life Congregation.
**Minority/foreign student organizations:** Asian American Association, Black Student Union, Latino American Organization. United Students of the World, Latin American student group.
**ATHLETICS. Physical education requirements:** Three semesters of physical education required.

**Intercollegiate competition:** 20% of students participate. Baseball (M), basketball (M,W), cross-country (M,W), football (M), golf (M), soccer (M,W), softball (W), tennis (M,W), track (outdoor) (M,W), volleyball (W). Member of NCAA Division III, Southern California Intercollegiate Athletic Conference.
**Intramural and club sports:** 60% of students participate. Intramural archery, badminton, basketball, flag football, soccer, tennis, volleyball. Men's club rugby.

**ADMISSIONS. Academic basis for candidate selection** (in order of priority): Secondary school record, essay, standardized test scores, school's recommendation, class rank.
**Nonacademic basis for candidate selection:** Character and personality and extracurricular participation are important. Particular talent or ability and alumni/ae relationship are considered.
**Requirements:** Graduation from secondary school is required; GED is accepted. 12 units and the following program of study are required: 4 units of English, 2 units of math, 2 units of science including 1 unit of lab, 2 units of foreign language, 2 units of social studies. Additional units in math, science, language, and social studies recommended. Minimum combined SAT score of 800 or rank in top 15% of secondary school class and minimum 2.5 GPA required. California High School Proficiency Exam also accepted. PLUS Program for applicants not normally admissible. SAT is required; ACT may be substituted. PSAT is recommended. Campus visit and interview recommended. No off-campus interviews.
**Procedure:** Take SAT or ACT by December 1 of 12th year. Visit college for interview by March 1 of 12th year. Suggest filing application by March 1. Application deadline is June 1. Notification of admission on rolling basis. Reply is required by May 1. $200 nonrefundable tuition deposit. Freshmen accepted for terms other than fall.
**Special programs:** Admission may be deferred one year. Credit and/or placement may be granted through CEEB Advanced Placement exams for scores of 4 or higher. Credit may be granted through CLEP subject exams, challenge exams, and military and life experience.
**Transfer students:** Transfer students accepted for terms other than fall. In fall 1993, 44% of all new students were transfers into all classes. 496 transfer applications were received, 368 were accepted. Application deadline is June 1 for fall; January 1 for spring. Minimum 2.3 GPA required. Lowest course grade accepted is "D." Maximum number of transferable credits is 70 semester hours. At least 30 semester hours must be completed at the university to receive degree.
**Admissions contact:** Ernie Sandlin, M.P.A., Director of Admissions. 805 493-3135.

**FINANCIAL AID. Available aid:** Pell grants, SEOG, state scholarships and grants, school scholarships and grants, private scholarships and grants, ROTC scholarships, academic merit scholarships, and aid for undergraduate foreign students. Perkins Loans (NDSL), PLUS, Stafford Loans (GSL), private loans, and SLS. Tuition Plan Inc. and family tuition reduction.
**Financial aid statistics:** 20% of aid is not need-based. In 1993-94, 92% of all undergraduate applicants received aid; 85% of freshman applicants. Average amounts of aid awarded freshmen: Scholarships and grants, $4,900; loans, $3,000.
**Supporting data/closing dates:** FAFSA: Priority filing date is March 1; accepted on rolling basis. Income tax forms: Accepted on rolling basis. Notification of awards begins April 1.
**Financial aid contact:** Betsy Kocher, Director of Financial Aid. 805 493-3115.

**STUDENT EMPLOYMENT.** College Work/Study Program. Institutional employment. 45% of full-time undergraduates work on campus during school year. Students may expect to earn an average of $1,200 during school year. Off-campus part-time employment opportunities rated "good."

**COMPUTER FACILITIES.** 110 IBM/IBM-compatible and Macintosh/Apple microcomputers; 65 are networked. Students may access Digital, Hewlett-Packard minicomputer/mainframe systems. Residence halls may be equipped with stand-alone microcomputers. Computer languages and software packages include BASIC, dBASE, Lotus 1-2-3, Pascal, WordPerfect. Computer facilities are available to all students.
**Fees:** None.
**Hours:** 8 AM-midn.

**GRADUATE CAREER DATA.** Graduate school percentages: 5% enter law school. 4% enter medical school. 1% enter dental school. 10% enter graduate business programs. 15% enter graduate arts and sciences programs. 1% enter theological school/seminary. Highest graduate school enrollments: UC Davis, UC San Diego, Ohio State U, Pepperdine U, U of Southern California. 50% of graduates choose careers in business and industry. Companies and businesses that hire graduates: Deluxe Check Printers, Ernst & Young, Prudential-Bache.

## California Maritime Academy

**Vallejo, CA 94590** **707 648-4200**

**1994-95 Costs.** Tuition: $1,807 (state residents), $7,897 (out-of-state). Room & board: $4,770. Fees, books, misc. academic expenses (school's estimate): $2,463.
**Enrollment.** Undergraduates: 430 men, 57 women (full-time). Freshman class: 321 applicants, 199 accepted, 117 enrolled.
**Test score averages/ranges.** N/A.
**Faculty.** 27 full-time; 13 part-time. 23% of faculty holds doctoral degree. Student/faculty ratio: 13 to 1.
**Selectivity rating.** Competitive.

**PROFILE.** The California Maritime Academy is a public institution. Founded in 1929, it adopted coeducation in 1973. Its 67-acre campus is located on the edge of San Francisco Bay, 30 miles from San Francisco.

**Accreditation:** WASC. Professionally accredited by the Accreditation Board for Engineering and Technology.
**Religious orientation:** California Maritime Academy is nonsectarian; no religious requirements.
**Library:** Collections totaling over 22,800 volumes, 220 periodical subscriptions, and 12,200 microform items.
**Special facilities/museums:** Computer, engineering, nuclear propulsion, oceanographic, radar simulation, and welding labs, tanker loading simulator, yachts, sloops, dinghies, motor cruiser.
**Athletic facilities:** Swimming pool, gymnasium, badminton, racquetball, tennis, and volleyball courts, weight and wrestling rooms, baseball, flag football, soccer, and softball fields.

**STUDENT BODY. Undergraduate profile:** 88% are state residents; 24% are transfers. 13% Asian-American, 4% Black, 6% Hispanic, 1% Native American, 73% White, 3% Other. Average age of undergraduates is 22.
**Freshman profile:** 1% of freshmen who took SAT scored 700 or over on verbal, 1% scored 700 or over on math; 8% scored 600 or over on verbal, 15% scored 600 or over on math; 24% scored 500 or over on verbal, 52% scored 500 or over on math; 60% scored 400 or over on verbal, 88% scored 400 or over on math; 100% scored 300 or over on verbal, 100% scored 300 or over on math. 75% of accepted applicants took SAT; 10% took ACT. 83% of freshmen come from public schools.
**Undergraduate achievement:** 80% of fall 1992 freshmen returned for fall 1993 term. 58% of entering class graduated. 15% of students who completed a degree program went on to graduate study within 10 years.
**Foreign students:** 12 students are from out of the country. Countries represented include the Bahamas, Mexico, Panama, and West Africa.

**PROGRAMS OF STUDY. Degrees:** B.S.
**Majors:** Business Administration, Marine Engineering Technology, Marine Transportation, Mechanical Engineering.
**Distribution of degrees:** The majors with the highest enrollment are mechanical engineering, marine transportation, and business administration.
**Requirements:** General education requirement.
**Academic regulations:** Minimum 2.0 GPA required for graduation.
**Special:** Minors offered in engineering, naval, and marine sciences. Merchant Marine Licensing Program qualifies students for Merchant Marine officer's license and Reserve Commission as an ensign in the U.S. Naval Reserve or Coast Guard Reserve. Cadet Shipping Training Program includes eight-week summer cruises on training ship following freshman, sophomore, and junior years. Double majors. Internships. Cooperative education programs. NROTC at UC Berkeley.
**Academic Assistance:** Remedial math and study skills. Nonremedial tutoring.

**STUDENT LIFE. Housing:** All freshmen and all unmarried students under 24 must live on campus. Coed dorms. 85% of students live in college housing.
**Services and counseling/handicapped student services:** Placement services. Health service. Counseling services for minority and veteran students.
**Campus organizations:** Undergraduate student government. Student newspaper (Binnacle, published three times/semester). Yearbook. Color guard, drill team, Corps of Midshipmen, camera, sailing, scuba, propeller, outing and ski clubs, service groups, 16 organizations in all.
**Religious organizations:** Bible Club.

**ATHLETICS. Physical education requirements:** One semester of physical education required.
**Intercollegiate competition:** 25% of students participate. Baseball (M), basketball (M), crew (M,W), golf (M,W), sailing (M,W), soccer (M), volleyball (M,W), water polo (M). Member of California Coastal Conference, Northern California Intercollegiate rowing Association, Northern California Yacht Racing Association.
**Intramural and club sports:** 65% of students participate. Intramural Alpine skiing, badminton, basketball, boxing, canoeing, flag football, horseback riding, indoor soccer, inner-tube water polo, running, rowing, sailing, softball, swimming, table tennis, tennis, volleyball. Men's club racquetball, sailing, scuba, tae kwon do. Women's club racquetball, sailing, scuba, tae kwon do.

**ADMISSIONS. Academic basis for candidate selection** (in order of priority): Secondary school record, standardized test scores, essay, class rank, school's recommendation.
**Nonacademic basis for candidate selection:** Character and personality, extracurricular participation, and particular talent or ability are important.
**Requirements:** Graduation from secondary school is required; GED is accepted. No specific distribution of secondary school units required. Preparation in science or math should be strong. SAT or ACT is required. Campus visit and interview recommended. Off-campus interviews available with an admissions representative.
**Procedure:** Take SAT or ACT by January of 12th year. Suggest filing application by March 15. Application deadline is July 1. Notification of admission on rolling basis. Reply is required by May 1. Freshmen accepted for fall term only.
**Special programs:** Credit may be granted through CEEB Advanced Placement for scores of 3 or higher. Credit may be granted through CLEP subject exams, challenge exams, and military experience.
**Transfer students:** Transfer students accepted for fall term only. In fall 1993, 24% of all new students were transfers into all classes. 55 transfer applications were received, 30 were accepted. Application deadline is March 15. Minimum 2.0 GPA required. Lowest course grade accepted is "C." At least three years of course work must be completed at the academy to receive degree.
**Admissions contact:** Albert T. Perkins, M.M., Director of Admissions. 707 648-4222.

**FINANCIAL AID. Available aid:** Pell grants, SEOG, state scholarships and grants, private scholarships, ROTC scholarships, and academic merit scholarships. Perkins Loans (NDSL), PLUS, Stafford Loans (GSL), private loans, and SLS.
**Financial aid statistics:** 10% of aid is not need-based. In 1993-94, 57% of all undergraduate applicants received aid; 48% of freshman applicants. Average amounts of aid awarded freshmen: Scholarships and grants, $1,555; loans, $2,300.
**Supporting data/closing dates:** FAFSA: Priority filing date is March 2. Notification of awards on rolling basis.
**Financial aid contact:** Paul Bidinger, M.A., Director of Financial Aid. 707 648-4227.

**STUDENT EMPLOYMENT.** College Work/Study Program. Institutional employment. 35% of full-time undergraduates work on campus during school year. Students may expect to earn an average of $720 during school year. Freshmen are discouraged from working during their first term. Off-campus part-time employment opportunities rated "fair."

**COMPUTER FACILITIES.** 24 IBM/IBM-compatible microcomputers. Students may access Hewlett-Packard minicomputer/mainframe systems. Client/LAN operating systems include DOS, Windows NT. Computer languages and software packages include BASIC, dBASE, Lotus 1-2-3, Pascal, WordPerfect, WordStar. Computer facilities are available to all students.
**Fees:** Computer fee is included in tuition/fees.
**Hours:** 24 hours.

**GRADUATE CAREER DATA.** Highest graduate school enrollments: UC Berkeley, California State U at Hayward, UC San Diego, San Francisco State, U of Southern California. 99% of graduates choose careers in business and industry. Companies and businesses that hire graduates: Arco Marine, Chevron, Crowley, Exxon, General Electric, Matson, Pacific Gas & Electric, Westinghouse.

**PROMINENT ALUMNI/AE.** Capt. Jerry Asplano, president, Arco Marine; Matt Franich, developer; Jean Arnold, marine chief engineer; Kim Estes, marine personnel director, Arco Marine.

# California Polytechnic State University, San Luis Obispo

**San Luis Obispo, CA 93407-0005 805 756-0111**

**1994-95 Costs.** Tuition: None (state residents), $7,380 (out-of-state). Room: $2,283. Board: $2,480. Fees, books, misc. academic expenses (school's estimate): $2,829.
**Enrollment.** Undergraduates: 7,604 men, 5,307 women (full-time). Freshman class: 7,744 applicants, 3,696 accepted, 1,650 enrolled. Graduate enrollment: 489 men, 643 women.
**Test score averages/ranges.** Average SAT scores: 1030 combined.
**Faculty.** 690 full-time; 263 part-time. 63% of faculty holds doctoral degree. Student/faculty ratio: 19 to 1.
**Selectivity rating.** Competitive.

**PROFILE.** Cal Poly, San Luis Obispo, founded in 1901, is a public university. Programs are offered through the Schools of Agriculture, Architecture and Environmental Design, Business, Engineering, Liberal Arts, Professional Studies and Education, and Science and Mathematics. Its 5,000-acre campus is located in San Luis Obispo, midway between Los Angeles and San Fransico.

**Accreditation:** WASC. Professionally accredited by the Accreditation Board for Engineering and Technology, the National Architecture Accrediting Board.
**Religious orientation:** California Polytechnic State University, San Luis Obispo is nonsectarian; no religious requirements.
**Library:** Collections totaling over 731,615 volumes, 2,983 periodical subscriptions, and 2,869,965 microform items.
**Athletic facilities:** Gymnasiums, swimming pools, weight rooms, bowling lanes, track, athletic fields.
**STUDENT BODY. Undergraduate profile:** 91% are state residents; 43% are transfers. 12.8% Asian-American, 2% Black, 14% Hispanic, 1.2% Native American, 61% White, 9% Other. Average age of undergraduates is 23.
**Freshman profile:** Majority of accepted applicants took SAT. 92% of freshmen come from public schools.
**Undergraduate achievement:** 83% of fall 1992 freshmen returned for fall 1993 term. 4% of entering class graduated. 16% of students who completed a degree program immediately went on to graduate study.
**Foreign students:** 1,257 students are from out of the country. Countries represented include China, Hong Kong, Mexico, South Korea, the Philippines, and Vietnam; 84 in all.
**PROGRAMS OF STUDY. Degrees:** B.A., B.Arch., B.Land.Arch., B.S.
**Majors:** Aeronautical Engineering, Agricultural Business, Agricultural Engineering, Agricultural Engineering Technology, Agricultural Management, Agricultural Sciences, Animal Science, Applied Art/Design, Architectural Engineering, Architecture, Biochemistry, Biological Sciences, Business Administration, Chemistry, City/Regional Planning, Civil Engineering, Computer Engineering, Computer Science, Construction Management, Crop Science, Dairy Science, Ecology/Systematic Biology, Economics, Electrical Engineering, Electronic Engineering, Engineering Science, English, Environmental Engineering, Food Science, Forestry, Fruit Science, Graphic Communications, History, Human Development, Industrial Engineering, Industrial Technology, Journalism, Landscape Architecture, Liberal Studies, Manufacturing Engineering, Materials Engineering, Mathematics, Mechanical Engineering, Microbiology, Nutritional Science, Ornamental Horticulture, Physical Education/Kinesiology, Physical Sciences, Physics, Plant Protection Science, Political Science, Poultry Industry, Recreation Administration, Social Sciences, Soil Science, Speech Communication, Statistics.
**Distribution of degrees:** The majors with the highest enrollment are business administration, agricultural business, and architectural engineering; poultry industry and physical science have the lowest.
**Requirements:** General education requirement.
**Academic regulations:** Minimum 2.0 GPA must be maintained.
**Special:** Courses offered in ethnic studies, foreign languages, music, philosophy, psychology, and public administration. Double majors. Dual degrees. Independent study. Pass/fail grading option. Internships. Cooperative education programs. Graduate school at which undergraduates may take graduate-level courses. Teacher certification in elementary, secondary, special education, and bilingual/bicultural education. Certification in specific subject areas. Study abroad in England and in over 25 other countries. ROTC.
**Academic Assistance:** Remedial reading, writing, math, and study skills. Nonremedial tutoring.
**STUDENT LIFE. Housing:** Students may live on or off campus. Coed dorms. Off-campus privately-owned housing. 15% of students live in college housing.
**Social atmosphere:** As reported by the student newspaper, the university is "casual, conservative (politically), close to the beach. Wonderful small-town atmosphere, campus of 15,000 students. San Luis Obispo is nicknamed SLO Town for good reason!" The Greeks, who hold open parties, and Christian groups are the most socially influential organizations on campus. The biggest event of the year is "Poly Royal, an annual open house throughout campus with a carnival-like atmosphere; last year's attendance was over 100,000, with people coming from all over California."
**Services and counseling/handicapped student services:** Placement services. Health service. Women's center. Day care. Counseling services for minority, veteran, and older students. Birth control, personal, and psychological counseling. Career and academic guidance services. Physically disabled student services. Learning disabled services. Notetaking services. Tape recorders. Tutors. Reader services for the blind.
**Campus organizations:** Undergraduate student government. Student newspaper (Mustang Daily). Radio station. Jazz, marching, and symphonic bands, orchestra, men's and women's glee clubs, theatre group, debating, community service groups, athletic and departmental clubs, special-interest groups. 27 fraternities, no chapter houses; eight sororities, no chapter houses. 8% of men join a fraternity. 5% of women join a sorority.
**Religious organizations:** Numerous religious groups.
**Minority/foreign student organizations:** ADELA, Afro-American Student Union, Black Students in Architecture, Hispanic engineering society, Latinos in Agriculture, MEChA, United Black Student Awareness. Arab, Iranian, and other foreign student groups.
**ATHLETICS. Physical education requirements:** Three to five units of physical activity or health education required, depending on school.
**Intercollegiate competition:** 35% of students participate. Baseball (M), basketball (M,W), cross-country (M,W), football (M), soccer (M,W), softball (W), swimming (M,W), tennis (M,W), track (M,W), track (outdoor) (M), track and field (outdoor) (M,W), volleyball (W), wrestling (M). Member of American West Conference, California Collegiate Athletic Association, NCAA Division I for volleyball and wrestling, NCAA Division II, Pacific 10 Conference.
**Intramural and club sports:** 60% of students participate. Intramural archery, badminton, basketball, crew, fencing, golf, hockey, lacrosse, martial arts, racquetball, rugby, sailing, soccer, skiing, swimming, ultimate frisbee, volleyball, walleyball, water polo. Men's club badminton, crew, fencing, lacrosse, roller hockey, rugby, sailing team, ultimate frisbee, volleyball, wheelmen, water polo. Women's club Alpine skiing, badminton, crew, fencing, sailing, ultimate frisbee, wheelmen, water polo.
**ADMISSIONS. Academic basis for candidate selection** (in order of priority): Secondary school record, standardized test scores.
**Nonacademic basis for candidate selection:** Extracurricular participation and geographical distribution are considered.
**Requirements:** Graduation from secondary school is required; GED is accepted. 15 units and the following program of study are required: 4 units of English, 3 units of math, 1 unit of lab science, 2 units of foreign language, 1 unit of history, 4 units of electives. Electives should include 1 unit of visual/performing arts. Minimum grade of "C" in listed secondary school courses and minimum eligibility index score based on GPA and SAT scores (different for in-state and out-of-state applicants) required. In-state applicants with minimum 3.0 GPA and out-of-state applicants with minimum 3.6 GPA are eligible regardless of test scores. Portfolio required of art program applicants. Audition required of music program applicants. EOP for applicants not normally admissible. Conditional admission possible for applicants not meeting standard requirements. SAT is required; ACT may be substituted. Campus visit recommended. Off-campus interviews available with an admissions representative.
**Procedure:** Take SAT or ACT by December of 12th year. Application deadline is November 30. Notification of acceptance on rolling basis beginning February 1. Reply is required by beginning of registration. Freshmen accepted for terms other than fall.
**Special programs:** Credit may be granted through CEEB Advanced Placement for scores of 3 or higher. Credit may be granted through CLEP general and subject exams, DANTES and challenge exams, and military experience. Concurrent enrollment program.
**Transfer students:** Transfer students accepted for terms other than fall. In fall 1993, 43% of all new students were transfers into all classes. 3,996 transfer applications were received, 1,824 were accepted. Application deadline is November 30 for fall; August 31 for spring. Minimum 2.0 GPA required. Lowest course grade accepted is "C." Maximum number of transferable credits is 105 quarter hours. At least 50 quarter hours must be completed at the university to receive degree.
**Admissions contact:** Jim Maraviglia, M.S., Director of Admissions. 805 756-2311.
**FINANCIAL AID. Available aid:** Pell grants, SEOG, state grants, school scholarships, private scholarships, ROTC scholarships, academic merit scholarships, and athletic scholarships. Perkins Loans (NDSL), PLUS, Stafford Loans (GSL), state loans, and school loans. Deferred payment plan.
**Financial aid statistics:** 36% of aid is not need-based. In 1993-94, 40% of all undergraduate applicants received aid; 38% of freshman applicants. Average amounts of aid awarded freshmen: Scholarships and grants, $4,242; loans, $2,000.
**Supporting data/closing dates:** FAFSA: Priority filing date is March 1; deadline is May 1. FAF/FFS: Deadline is March 1. School's own aid application: Deadline is March 1. State aid form: Deadline is March 1. Income tax forms: Deadline is March 1. Notification of awards begins in July.
**Financial aid contact:** Diane Ryan, Ph.D., Director of Financial Aid. 805 756-2927.
**STUDENT EMPLOYMENT.** College Work/Study Program. Institutional employment. 2% of full-time undergraduates work on campus during school year. Students may expect to earn an average of $1,500 during school year. Off-campus part-time employment opportunities rated "good."
**COMPUTER FACILITIES.** 1,006 IBM/IBM-compatible, Macintosh/Apple, and RISC-/UNIX-based microcomputers. Students may access Digital, IBM, SUN minicomputer/mainframe systems. Client/LAN operating systems include Apple/Macintosh, OS/2. Computer languages and software packages include BASIC, C, COBOL, FORTRAN, MINITAB, Pascal, SAS, SPSS, SPSS-X. Computer facilities are available to all students.
**Fees:** None.
**Hours:** 24 hours in most locations.
**PROMINENT ALUMNI/AE.** Commander Robert "Hoot" Gibson, astronaut, NASA Space Shuttle Project; John Madden, sportscaster and Oakland Raiders football coach; Ozzie Smith, shortstop, St. Louis Cardinals; Mike Krukow, pitcher, San Francisco Giants.

# California State Polytechnic University, Pomona

Pomona, CA 91768-4019 909 869-7659

**1994-95 Costs.** Tuition: None (state residents), $7,380 (out-of-state). Room & board: $4,862. Fees, books, misc. academic expenses (school's estimate): $2,548.
**Enrollment.** Undergraduates: 6,666 men, 4,556 women (full-time). Freshman class: 6,008 applicants, 3,931 accepted, 1,566 enrolled. Graduate enrollment: 733 men, 969 women.
**Test score averages/ranges.** Average SAT scores: 387 verbal, 508 math. Range of SAT scores of middle 50%: 320-460 verbal, 440-580 math. Average ACT scores: 20 English, 22 math, 21 composite. Range of ACT scores of middle 50%: 16-23 English, 19-26 math.
**Faculty.** 638 full-time; 231 part-time. 60% of faculty holds doctoral degree. Student/faculty ratio: 20 to 1.
**Selectivity rating.** Competitive.

**PROFILE.** Cal Poly, Pomona, is a public university. Founded in 1938 as a branch of Cal Poly, San Luis Obispo, it gained independent status in 1966. Programs are offered through the Colleges of Agriculture, Arts, Business Administration, Engineering, Environmental Design, and Science. Its 1,437-acre campus is located 30 miles from Los Angeles. Campus architecture includes Spanish style as well as modern design.

**Accreditation:** WASC. Professionally accredited by the Accreditation Board for Engineering and Technology, the American Society of Landscape Architects, the National Architecture Accrediting Board.
**Religious orientation:** California State Polytechnic University, Pomona is nonsectarian; no religious requirements.
**Library:** Collections totaling over 577,687 volumes, 2,919 periodical subscriptions, and 1,955,043 microform items.
**Special facilities/museums:** Citrus packing house, meat processing building, poultry plant, feed mill, beef, sheep, swine, Arabian horse units, horse show arena, and aerospace wind tunnel.
**Athletic facilities:** Gymnasiums, basketball, racquetball, and tennis courts, archery range, track, baseball, soccer, and softball fields, aerobics and weight rooms, swimming pool.

**STUDENT BODY. Undergraduate profile:** 99% are state residents. 37.4% Asian-American, 3.7% Black, 19% Hispanic, .6% Native American, 39.3% White. Average age of undergraduates is 23.
**Freshman profile:** 90% of accepted applicants took SAT; 10% took ACT. 90% of freshmen come from public schools.
**Undergraduate achievement:** 77% of fall 1992 freshmen returned for fall 1993 term. 21% of entering class graduated.
**Foreign students:** 621 students are from out of the country. Countries represented include China, Hong Kong, Indonesia, Mexico, Taiwan, and Vietnam.

**PROGRAMS OF STUDY. Degrees:** B.A., B.Arch., B.S.
**Majors:** Accounting, Aerospace Engineering, Agricultural Biology, Agricultural Business Management, Agricultural Engineering, Agricultural Science, Agronomy, American Studies, Animal Science, Anthropology, Architecture, Art, Behavioral Science, Biology, Biotechnology, Botany, Chemical Engineering, Chemistry, Civil Engineering, Communication Arts, Computer Information Systems, Computer Science, Earth Sciences, Economics, Electrical Engineering, Engineering Technology, English, Finance/Real Estate/Law, Foods/Nutrition, Fruit Industries, Geography, Geology, History, Home Economics, Horticulture, Hotel/Restaurant Management, Humanities, Industrial Engineering, International Agriculture, International Business, Land Irrigation Science, Landscape Architecture, Liberal Studies, Management/Human Resources, Manufacturing Engineering, Marketing Management, Mathematics, Mechanical Engineering, Microbiology, Music, Operations Management, Park Administration, Philosophy, Physical Education, Physics, Political Science, Psychology, Social Sciences, Sociology, Soil Science, Theatre, Urban/Regional Planning, Zoology.
**Distribution of degrees:** The majors with the highest enrollment are liberal studies, marketing, and finance; manufacturing engineering, American studies, and fruit industries have the lowest.
**Requirements:** General education requirement.
**Academic regulations:** Minimum 2.0 GPA must be maintained.
**Special:** Minors offered in some majors and other fields. Certificate programs offered through Office of Continuing Education. Double majors. Dual degrees. Pass/fail grading option. Internships. Cooperative education programs. Graduate school at which undergraduates may take graduate-level courses. Preprofessional programs in medicine, veterinary science, and dentistry. Member of Southern California Ocean Studies and Desert Studies Consortium. Member of National Student Exchange (NSE). Teacher certification in elementary, secondary, special education, and bilingual/bicultural education. Certification in specific subject areas. Exchange programs abroad in Australia, China, France, Germany, Japan, Mexico, and Norway. Study abroad also in 16 other countries. ROTC.
**Honors:** Honors program. Honor societies.
**Academic Assistance:** Remedial reading, writing, math, and study skills. Nonremedial tutoring.

**STUDENT LIFE. Housing:** Students may live on or off campus. Coed dorms. School-owned/operated apartments. 10% of students live in college housing.
**Services and counseling/handicapped student services:** Placement services. Health service. Women's center. Day care. Re-entry services. Counseling services for minority, military, and older students. Birth control, personal, and psychological counseling. Career and academic guidance services. Physically disabled student services. Learning disabled services. Notetaking services. Tape recorders. Tutors. Reader services for the blind.
**Campus organizations:** Undergraduate student government. Student newspaper (Poly Post, published biweekly). Yearbook. Academic groups, music and drama groups, service and special-interest groups, 123 organizations in all. 11 fraternities, no chapter houses; four sororities, no chapter houses. 2% of men join a fraternity. 1% of women join a sorority.
**Religious organizations:** Bahai Club, Campus Crusade for Christ, Christian Science Organization, Coptic-Orthodox Christian Club, Hillel, Newman Club, Studies in the Word, other religious groups.
**Minority/foreign student organizations:** Black Student Union, Hawaiian Club, MEChA, other minority student groups. Armenian, Asian-Pacific, Cambodian, Chinese, Filipino, Indonesian, Korean, Laotian, Pakistani, Thai, and other foreign student groups.

**ATHLETICS. Physical education requirements:** None.
**Intercollegiate competition:** 2% of students participate. Baseball (M), basketball (M,W), cheerleading (W), cross-country (M,W), soccer (M,W), tennis (M,W), track (outdoor) (M,W), track and field (outdoor) (M,W), volleyball (W). Member of CCAA, NCAA Division II.
**Intramural and club sports:** 4% of students participate. Intramural badminton, basketball, flag football, golf, inner-tube water polo, racquetball, soccer, softball, swimming, tennis, volleyball, wrestling. Men's club Alpine skiing, bowling, cycling, football, golf, horsemanship, rodeo, rugby, volleyball. Women's club Alpine skiing, bowling, cycling, field hockey, golf, horsemanship, rodeo.

**ADMISSIONS. Academic basis for candidate selection** (in order of priority): Secondary school record, standardized test scores, class rank.
**Requirements:** Graduation from secondary school is recommended; GED is accepted. 15 units and the following program of study are required: 4 units of English, 3 units of math, 1 unit of lab science, 2 units of foreign language, 1 unit of history, 4 units of electives. Electives should include 1 unit of visual/performing arts. Minimum grade of "C" in listed secondary school courses and minimum eligibility index of 2800 for SAT (694 for ACT) required of in-state applicants; minimum eligibility index of 3402 for SAT (842 for ACT) required of out-of-state applicants. In-state applicants with minimum 3.0 GPA and out-of-state applicants with minimum 3.6 GPA are eligible regardless of test scores. Higher GPA required of architecture program applicants; out-of-state applicants not admitted to this program. EOP for applicants not normally admissible. SAT or ACT is required. Campus visit recommended. No off-campus interviews.
**Procedure:** Take SAT or ACT by December of 12th year. Suggest filing application by November 30; no deadline. Notification of admission on rolling basis. Reply is required by beginning of term. $50 room deposit, refundable when students leave dorms (amount is payable each year). Freshmen accepted for terms other than fall.
**Special programs:** Credit and/or placement may be granted through CEEB Advanced Placement exams for scores of 3 or higher. Credit and/or placement may be granted through CLEP general and subject exams. Credit and placement may be granted through DANTES and challenge exams, and military experience. Early entrance/early admission program. Concurrent enrollment program.
**Transfer students:** Transfer students accepted for terms other than fall. In fall 1993, 3,905 transfer applications were received, 2,338 were accepted. Application deadline is November 30 for fall; August 31 for spring. Minimum 2.0 GPA required. Lowest course grade accepted is "D." Maximum number of transferable credits is 105 quarter hours. At least 50 quarter hours must be completed at the university to receive degree.
**Admissions contact:** Joseph Marshall, M.A., Acting Director of Admissions. 909 869-2000.

**FINANCIAL AID. Available aid:** Pell grants, SEOG, state scholarships and grants, school scholarships and grants, private scholarships and grants, ROTC scholarships, academic merit scholarships, and athletic scholarships. Perkins Loans (NDSL), PLUS, Stafford Loans (GSL), state loans, school loans, and SLS.
**Financial aid statistics:** 10% of aid is not need-based. In 1993-94, 30% of all undergraduate applicants received aid; 33% of freshman applicants. Average amounts of aid awarded freshmen: Scholarships and grants, $750; loans, $2,625.
**Supporting data/closing dates:** FAFSA/FAF: Priority filing date is March 2. State aid form: Priority filing date is March 2. Income tax forms: Priority filing date is May 1. Scholarship Form: Priority filing date is March 1; deadline is May 1. Notification of awards on rolling basis.
**Financial aid contact:** Al Andino, M.A., Director of Financial Aid. 909 869-3700.

**STUDENT EMPLOYMENT.** College Work/Study Program. Institutional employment. 5% of full-time undergraduates work on campus during school year. Students may expect to earn an average of $1,367 during school year. Freshmen are discouraged from working during their first term. Off-campus part-time employment opportunities rated "fair."

**COMPUTER FACILITIES.** 1,450 IBM/IBM-compatible, Macintosh/Apple, and RISC-/UNIX-based microcomputers; 700 are networked. Students may access AT&T, Digital, SUN minicomputer/mainframe systems, Internet. Client/LAN operating systems include Apple/Macintosh, DOS, OS/2, UNIX/XENIX/AIX, Windows NT, X-windows, DEC, LocalTalk/AppleTalk, Novell. Computer languages and software packages include BASIC, C, C++, COBOL, FORTRAN, MINITAB, Pascal, SAS, SQL, Spice, SPSS. Computer facilities are available to all students.
**Fees:** None.
**Hours:** 24 hours for some.

**GRADUATE CAREER DATA.** 71% of graduates choose careers in business and industry. Companies and businesses that hire graduates: General Dynamics, Hughes Aircraft, Jet Propulsion Lab, Metropolitan Water District, Northrop, Rockwell International, Southern California Edison, Southern California Gas, TRW, Xerox.

**PROMINENT ALUMNI/AE.** Carol Vaness, soprano, Metropolitan Opera; John Brewer, editor in chief, New York Times; Gene Lu, president/CEO, Advanced Logic Research.

## California State University, Bakersfield

**Bakersfield, CA 93311-1099** **805 664-2011**

**1993-94 Costs.** Tuition: None (state residents), $7,400 (out-of-state). Room & board: $4,100. Fees, books, misc. academic expenses (school's estimate): $2,700.
**Enrollment.** Undergraduates: 1,157 men, 1,767 women (full-time). Freshman class: 1,101 applicants, 617 accepted, 376 enrolled. Graduate enrollment: 438 men, 843 women.
**Test score averages/ranges.** Average SAT scores: 404 verbal, 433 math. Average ACT scores: 20 English, 21 math, 21 composite.
**Faculty.** 235 full-time; 114 part-time. 92% of faculty holds doctoral degree. Student/faculty ratio: 16 to 1.
**Selectivity rating.** Competitive.

**PROFILE.** California State at Bakersfield, founded in 1965, is a public university. Programs are offered through the Schools of Arts and Sciences, Business and Public Administration, and Education. Its 375-acre campus is located in Bakersfield.

**Accreditation:** WASC. Professionally accredited by the American Assembly of Collegiate Schools of Business, the American Medical Association (CAHEA), the National Council for Accreditation of Teacher Education, the National League for Nursing.
**Religious orientation:** California State University, Bakersfield is nonsectarian; no religious requirements.
**Library:** Collections totaling over 315,000 volumes, 2,700 periodical subscriptions, and 453,448 microform items.
**Athletic facilities:** Swimming pool, gymnasium, basketball, racquetball, tennis, and volleyball courts, track, combatives, weight, wrestling rooms, intramural, soccer, and softball fields.

**STUDENT BODY. Undergraduate profile:** 99% are state residents; 46% are transfers. 8% Asian-American, 6% Black, 22% Hispanic, 2% Native American, 53% White, 9% Other. Average age of undergraduates is 26.
**Freshman profile:** 50% of accepted applicants took SAT; 50% took ACT. 98% of freshmen come from public schools.
**Undergraduate achievement:** 73% of fall 1992 freshmen returned for fall 1993 term.
**Foreign students:** 101 students are from out of the country. Countries represented include Bhutan, El Salvador, India, Japan, Taiwan, and the Philippines; 58 in all.

**PROGRAMS OF STUDY. Degrees:** B.A., B.S.
**Majors:** Anthropology, Art, Biology, Business Administration, Chemistry, Child Development, Clinical Sciences, Communication, Computer Science, Counseling, Economics, Education, English, Fine Arts, Geology, History, Land Resource Management, Liberal Studies, Mathematics, Nursing, Philosophy, Physical Education, Physics, Political Science, Psychology, Public Administration, Religious Studies, Sociology, Spanish, Special Major.
**Distribution of degrees:** The majors with the highest enrollment are business administration, liberal studies, and nursing.
**Requirements:** General education requirement.
**Special:** Minors offered in many majors and in approximately 15 other fields. Self-designed majors. Double majors. Dual degrees. Independent study. Accelerated study. Pass/fail grading option. Internships. Cooperative education programs. Graduate school at which undergraduates may take graduate-level courses. Preprofessional programs in law, medicine, veterinary science, pharmacy, and engineering. Member of Consortium of the California State U. Semester/term-away study programs within CSU system; Visitors Program with 19 campuses. Member of National Student Exchange (NSE). Teacher certification in early childhood, elementary, secondary, and special education. Study abroad in approximately 15 countries.
**Honors:** Honors program.
**Academic Assistance:** Remedial reading, writing, math, and study skills.

**STUDENT LIFE. Housing:** Students may live on or off campus. Coed and women's dorms. 5% of students live in college housing.
**Social atmosphere:** The Pub, John Bryan's, Woody's, and Goose Loonie's are popular gathering spots for students. Greeks are influential in school social life. Some of the most popular social and cultural events are the radio rain dances, basketball games, and the Kern Shakespeare festival. According to the student newspaper, the average student age is 28, and the school is mostly a commuter campus.
**Services and counseling/handicapped student services:** Placement services. Health service. Day care. Counseling services for minority and older students. Birth control, personal, and psychological counseling. Career and academic guidance services. Religious counseling. Physically disabled student services. Learning disabled program/services. Notetaking services. Tutors. Reader services for the blind.
**Campus organizations:** Undergraduate student government. Student newspaper (Runner, published once/week). Literary magazine. Radio station. Choral groups, athletic, departmental, and service groups. Four fraternities, no chapter houses; three sororities, no chapter houses. 5% of men join a fraternity. 5% of women join a sorority.
**Religious organizations:** Intervarsity Christian Fellowship, Newman Club.
**Minority/foreign student organizations:** Afro-American Student Union, Estudiantes Unidas, MEChA, Asian Club. International Student Club.

**ATHLETICS. Physical education requirements:** None.
**Intercollegiate competition:** 6% of students participate. Basketball (M), diving (M,W), soccer (M), softball (W), swimming (M,W), tennis (W), track (outdoor) (M,W), track and field (outdoor) (M,W), volleyball (W), wrestling (M). Member of California Collegiate Athletic Association, NCAA Division II, NCAA Divison I for men's wrestling, Pacific Ten Conference.
**Intramural and club sports:** 5% of students participate. Intramural baseball, basketball, flag football, volleyball.

**ADMISSIONS. Academic basis for candidate selection** (in order of priority): Secondary school record, standardized test scores, school's recommendation, class rank.
**Nonacademic basis for candidate selection:** Character and personality, extracurricular participation, particular talent or ability, and geographical distribution are important.
**Requirements:** Graduation from secondary school is required; GED is accepted. 15 units and the following program of study are required: 4 units of English, 3 units of math, 1 unit of lab science, 2 units of foreign language, 1 unit of history, 4 units of electives. Electives should include 1 unit of visual/performing arts. Minimum grade of "C" in listed secondary school courses and minimum eligibility index of 2800 for SAT (694 for ACT) required of in-state applicants; minimum eligibility index of 3402 for SAT (842 for ACT) required of out-of-state applicants. In-state applicants with minimum 3.0 GPA and out-of-state applicants with minimum 3.6 GPA are eligible regardless of test scores. Prerequisite courses and interview required of nursing program applicants. EOP for applicants not normally admissible. SAT or ACT is required. Campus visit recommended. Off-campus interviews available with an admissions representative.
**Procedure:** Take SAT or ACT in November or December of 12th year. Suggest filing application by November. File only at first-choice campus of CSU system (alternative may be noted). Notification of admission on rolling basis. $500 room deposit, refundable within 30 days. Freshmen accepted for terms other than fall.
**Special programs:** Credit and/or placement may be granted through CEEB Advanced Placement exams for scores of 3 or higher. Credit and/or placement may be granted through CLEP general and subject exams. Credit and placement may be granted through Regents College and challenge exams, and military experience. Early decision program. Early entrance/early admission program. Concurrent enrollment program.
**Transfer students:** Transfer students accepted for terms other than fall. In fall 1993, 46% of all new students were transfers into all classes. 1,447 transfer applications were received, 1,015 were accepted. Application deadline is rolling for fall; rolling for spring. Minimum 2.0 GPA required. Lowest course grade accepted is "D." Maximum number of transferable credits is 105 quarter hours. At least 45 quarter hours must be completed at the university to receive degree.
**Admissions contact:** Homer S. Montalvo, Ed.D., Associate Dean of Admissions and Records. 805 664-3036.

**FINANCIAL AID. Available aid:** Pell grants, SEOG, Federal Nursing Student Scholarships, state scholarships and grants, school scholarships, and private scholarships. Perkins Loans (NDSL), PLUS, Stafford Loans (GSL), and NSL.
**Financial aid statistics:** In 1993-94, 25% of all undergraduate applicants received aid; 50% of freshman applicants. Average amounts of aid awarded freshmen: Scholarships and grants, $873; loans, $2,000.
**Supporting data/closing dates:** State aid form: Priority filing date is March 2. Notification of awards on rolling basis.
**Financial aid contact:** Steve Herndon, Ph.D., Director of Financial Aid. 805 664-3016.

**STUDENT EMPLOYMENT.** College Work/Study Program. Institutional employment. 9% of full-time undergraduates work on campus during school year. Students may expect to earn an average of $2,500 during school year. Off-campus part-time employment opportunities rated "good."

**COMPUTER FACILITIES.** 127 IBM/IBM-compatible, Macintosh/Apple, and RISC-/UNIX-based microcomputers. Students may access CDC Cyber, Digital, Prime minicomputer/mainframe systems. Computer languages and software packages include Ada, Assembly, BASIC, C, COBOL, dBASE, FORTRAN, Lotus 1-2-3, MacDraw, MacPaint, Pascal, PL/1, WordPerfect. Computer facilities are available to all students.
**Fees:** None.
**Hours:** 8 AM-11 PM (M-Th); 8 AM-5 PM (F); 1 PM-6 PM (Sa-Su).

**GRADUATE CAREER DATA.** Companies and businesses that hire graduates: American National Security, Bank of America, Conetel, Kraft Foods, Price Waterhouse, SAV-ON Drugs, Shell Oil, Tenneco.

**PROMINENT ALUMNI/AE.** Pauline Larwood and Roy Ashburn, county supervisors; Blas Hernandez, medical doctor; Esther Torrez and Bette Cutbirth, company CEOs.

## California State University, Chico

**Chico, CA 95929-0720** **916 898-6116**

**1993-94 Costs.** Tuition: None (state residents), $7,380 (out-of-state). Room & board: $2,510–$4,464. Fees (school's estimate): $891.
**Enrollment.** Undergraduates: 5,914 men, 5,914 women (full-time). Freshman class: 4,816 applicants, 3,922 accepted, 1,278 enrolled. Graduate enrollment: 645 men, 890 women.
**Test score averages/ranges.** Average SAT scores: 420 verbal, 479 math. Range of SAT scores of middle 50%: 370-480 verbal, 420-540 math. Average ACT scores: 20 English, 20 math, 21 composite. Range of ACT scores of middle 50%: 18-23 English, 17-21 math.
**Faculty.** 631 full-time; 213 part-time. 66% of faculty holds doctoral degree. Student/faculty ratio: 21 to 1.
**Selectivity rating.** Less competitive.

**PROFILE.** California State at Chico, founded in 1887, is a public, comprehensive university. Programs are offered through the Colleges of Agriculture; Behavioral and Social Sciences; Business; Communications; Education; Engineering, Computer Science, and Technology; Humanities and Fine Arts; and Natural Sciences and the Graduate School. Its 130-acre campus is located in the Sierra foothills, 90 miles from Sacramento. Campus architecture is influenced by Spanish and Victorian styles.

**Accreditation:** WASC. Professionally accredited by the Accreditation Board for Engineering and Technology, the American Assembly of Collegiate Schools of Business, the American Council for Construction Education, the American Dietetic Association, the American Home Economics Association, the American Speech-Language-Hearing

Association, the Council on Social Work Education, the National Association of Schools of Art and Design, the National Association of Schools of Music, the National Council for Accreditation of Teacher Education, the National League for Nursing, the National Recreation and Park Association.
**Religious orientation:** California State University, Chico is nonsectarian; no religious requirements.
**Library:** Collections totaling over 1,315,481 volumes, 3,413 periodical subscriptions, and 927,111 microform items.
**Special facilities/museums:** Anthropology museum, center for intercultural studies, instructional media center, satellite communication dishes, biological field station, university farm, electron microscope.
**Athletic facilities:** Gymnasiums, stadiums, swimming pool, weight rooms, track, athletic fields.

**STUDENT BODY. Undergraduate profile:** 99% are state residents; 54% are transfers. 5% Asian-American, 2% Black, 8% Hispanic, 2% Native American, 76% White, 7% Other. Average age of undergraduates is 23.
**Freshman profile:** 1% of freshmen who took SAT scored 700 or over on math; 2% scored 600 or over on verbal, 11% scored 600 or over on math; 17% scored 500 or over on verbal, 45% scored 500 or over on math; 62% scored 400 or over on verbal, 83% scored 400 or over on math; 92% scored 300 or over on verbal, 97% scored 300 or over on math. 2% of freshmen who took ACT scored 30 or over on composite; 22% scored 24 or over on English, 16% scored 24 or over on math, 19% scored 24 or over on composite; 77% scored 18 or over on English, 73% scored 18 or over on math, 83% scored 18 or over on composite; 98% scored 12 or over on English, 100% scored 12 or over on math, 100% scored 12 or over on composite; 100% scored 6 or over on English. 82% of accepted applicants took SAT. 87% of freshmen come from public schools.
**Undergraduate achievement:** 81% of fall 1992 freshmen returned for fall 1993 term. 13% of entering class graduated.
**Foreign students:** 216 students are from out of the country. Countries represented include Hong Kong, Indonesia, Japan, Lebanon, Malaysia, and Taiwan; 41 in all.

**PROGRAMS OF STUDY. Degrees:** B.A., B.F.A., B.S., B.Voc.Ed.
**Majors:** Agricultural Business, Agriculture, American Studies, Anthropology, Art, Biological Sciences, Business Administration, Chemistry, Child Development, Civil Engineering, Computer Engineering, Computer Information Systems, Computer Science, Construction Management, Dietetics/Food Administration, Economics, Electrical/Electronics Engineering, English, Ethnic Studies, French, Geography, Geology, German, Health Science, History, Humanities, Industrial Arts, Industrial Technology, Information/Communication Studies, Instructional Technology, International Relations, Journalism, Latin American Studies, Liberal Studies, Mathematics, Mechanical Engineering, Microbiology, Music, Nursing, Philosophy, Physical Education, Physical Science, Physics, Political Science, Psychology, Public Administration, Recreation Administration, Religious Studies, Social Science, Social Work, Sociology, Spanish, Special Major, Speech Pathology, Theatre Arts, Vocational Education.
**Distribution of degrees:** The majors with the highest enrollment are business administration, liberal studies, and information/communication studies; vocational education, physics, and American studies have the lowest.
**Requirements:** General education requirement.
**Academic regulations:** Minimum 2.0 GPA must be maintained.
**Special:** Minors offered in many majors. Area and interdisciplinary program. Self-designed majors. Double majors. Dual degrees. Independent study. Pass/fail grading option. Internships. Cooperative education programs. Graduate school at which undergraduates may take graduate-level courses. Preprofessional programs in law, medicine, veterinary science, pharmacy, dentistry, theology, optometry, forestry, library science, and physical therapy. Member of Consortium of the California State U. Member of National Student Exchange (NSE). Teacher certification in elementary, secondary, special education, vo-tech, and bilingual/bicultural education. Certification in specific subject areas. Exchange programs abroad in China, Costa Rica, Germany, Ireland, Japan, Mexico, Sweden, and Taiwan. Study abroad also in Canada, Denmark, France, Israel, Italy, New Zealand, Spain, the United Kingdom, and Zimbabwe.
**Honors:** Phi Beta Kappa. Honors program. Honor societies.
**Academic Assistance:** Remedial writing, math, and study skills. Nonremedial tutoring.

**STUDENT LIFE. Housing:** Students may live on or off campus. Coed dorms. Sorority and fraternity housing. School-owned/operated apartments. Off-campus privately-owned housing. 12% of students live in college housing.
**Social atmosphere:** The student newspaper reports, "Recently, *Playboy* magazine named Chico State the Number One party school in the nation. Although Chico State students do party quite heartily, the academic programs here require more seriousness toward the books than that article gave us credit for. Greeks seem to have the widest influence on student life, although many students are influenced by what they want to be influenced by. Pioneer Days is by far the biggest event of the year; not many things come close." Popular student gathering spots include the Madison Bear Garden, the Graduate, and Bidwell Park.
**Services and counseling/handicapped student services:** Placement services. Health service. Women's center. Day care. Counseling services for minority, veteran, and older students. Birth control, personal, and psychological counseling. Career and academic guidance services. Physically disabled student services. Learning disabled services. Notetaking services. Tape recorders. Tutors. Reader services for the blind.
**Campus organizations:** Undergraduate student government. Student newspaper (Orion, published once/week). Yearbook. Radio station. Bands, choirs, jazz ensemble, drama group, debating, flying and chess clubs, BACCHUS, Amnesty International, Republican and Democratic clubs, Libertarian Club, Educational and Support Program for Women, 190 organizations in all. 19 fraternities, 11 chapter houses; 16 sororities, eight chapter houses. 12% of men join a fraternity. 12% of women join a sorority.
**Religious organizations:** Asian Christian Fellowship, Baptist Student Union, Calvary on Campus, Campus Crusade for Christ, Chi Alpha, Christian Science Organization, Christians in Action, Faith Fellowship, International Neighbors, Intervarsity Christian Fellowship, Jewish Student Union, Latter-Day Saints Association, Alpha Omega, Bahai Association.
**Minority/foreign student organizations:** American Indian Club, MEChA, Concilio. International Student Club, Palestine Union, African, Arab, Asian, Italian, Malaysian, Pakistani, and Vietnamese groups.

**ATHLETICS. Physical education requirements:** None.
**Intercollegiate competition:** 4% of students participate. Baseball (M), basketball (M,W), cheerleading (M,W), cross-country (M,W), football (M), soccer (M,W), softball (W), track and field (outdoor) (M,W), volleyball (W). Member of NCAA Division II, Northern California Athletic Conference.
**Intramural and club sports:** 80% of students participate. Intramural aerobics, badminton, ballroom dancing, basketball, bowling, cycling, field hockey, flag football, floor hockey, golf, racquetball, soccer, softball, swimming, tennis, volleyball, walleyball, water hockey. Men's club Alpine skiing, badminton, cycling, fencing, field hockey, football, lacrosse, Nordic skiing, rugby, swimming, tennis, track, ultimate frisbee, volleyball. Women's club Alpine skiing, badminton, cycling, footbag, fencing, field hockey, lacrosse, Nordic skiing, swimming, tennis, track, ultimate frisbee.

**ADMISSIONS. Academic basis for candidate selection** (in order of priority): Secondary school record, standardized test scores.
**Requirements:** Graduation from secondary school is required; GED is accepted. 15 units and the following program of study are required: 4 units of English, 3 units of math, 1 unit of lab science, 2 units of foreign language, 1 unit of history, 4 units of electives. Electives should include 1 unit of visual/performing arts. Minimum grade of "C" in listed secondary school courses and minimum eligibility index of 2800 for SAT (694 for ACT) required of in-state applicants; minimum eligibility index of 3402 for SAT (842 for ACT) required of out-of-state applicants. In-state applicants with minimum 3.0 GPA and out-of-state applicants with minimum 3.61 GPA are eligible regardless of test scores. EOP for applicants not normally admissible. Conditional admission possible for applicants not meeting standard requirements. SAT or ACT is required. Campus visit recommended. No off-campus interviews.
**Procedure:** Take SAT or ACT by December of 12th year. Suggest filing application by November 31. Notification of admission on rolling basis. No set date by which applicants must accept offer. Freshmen accepted for terms other than fall.
**Special programs:** Admission may be deferred one semester. Credit and/or placement may be granted through CEEB Advanced Placement exams for scores of 3 or higher. Credit and/or placement may be granted through CLEP general and subject exams. Credit may be granted through DANTES exams and military and life experience. Credit and placement may be granted through Regents College and challenge exams. Early decision program. Early entrance/early admission program. Concurrent enrollment program.
**Transfer students:** Transfer students accepted for terms other than fall. In fall 1993, 54% of all new students were transfers into all classes. 4,161 transfer applications were received, 2,818 were accepted. Application deadline is November 30 for fall; August 31 for spring. Minimum 2.0 GPA required. Lowest course grade accepted is "D." Maximum number of transferable credits is 70 semester hours. At least 30 semester hours must be completed at the university to receive degree.
**Admissions contact:** Kenneth C. Edson, Ph.D., Director of Admissions. 916 898-6321.

**FINANCIAL AID. Available aid:** Pell grants, SEOG, state scholarships and grants, school scholarships, private scholarships, and academic merit scholarships. Perkins Loans (NDSL), PLUS, Stafford Loans (GSL), and SLS. Short-term emergency loans.
**Financial aid statistics:** In 1993-94, 63% of all undergraduate applicants received aid. Average amounts of aid awarded freshmen: Scholarships and grants, $1,600; loans, $1,986.
**Supporting data/closing dates:** FAFSA: Priority filing date is March 2. Notification of awards on rolling basis.
**Financial aid contact:** David G. Cook, M.A., Director of Financial Aid. 916 898-5065.

**STUDENT EMPLOYMENT.** College Work/Study Program. Institutional employment. 9% of full-time undergraduates work on campus during school year. Students may expect to earn an average of $2,400 during school year. Freshmen are discouraged from working during their first term. Off-campus part-time employment opportunities rated "fair."

**COMPUTER FACILITIES.** 1,000 IBM/IBM-compatible, Macintosh/Apple, and RISC-/UNIX-based microcomputers; 200 are networked. Students may access CDC Cyber, Digital, Hewlett-Packard, IBM, SUN minicomputer/mainframe systems, BITNET, Internet. Residence halls may be equipped with stand-alone microcomputers, networked terminals. Client/LAN operating systems include Apple/Macintosh, DOS, UNIX/XENIX/AIX, LocalTalk/AppleTalk, Novell. Computer languages and software packages include Assembly, BASIC, C, COBOL, CompuStat, FORTRAN, LISP, Pascal, Prolog, SAS, SPSS; numerous software packages. Computer facilities are available to all students.

**GRADUATE CAREER DATA.** Companies and businesses that hire graduates: Bank of America, Heublein, Hewlett-Packard, Macy's, Wilson's.

**PROMINENT ALUMNI/AE.** Rusty Areias and Mike Thompson, California state legislators; Ed Rollins, political consultant.

# California State University, Dominguez Hills

**Carson, CA 90747** **213 516-3300**

**1993-94 Costs.** Tuition: None (state residents), $7,380 (out-of-state). Room & board: $4,650. Fees, books, misc. academic expenses (school's estimate): $2,571.
**Enrollment.** Undergraduates: 1,614 men, 2,658 women (full-time). Freshman class: 1,493 applicants, 1,198 accepted. Graduate enrollment: 938 men, 1,805 women.
**Test score averages/ranges.** N/A.
**Faculty.** 286 full-time; 478 part-time. 90% of faculty holds doctoral degree. Student/faculty ratio: 18 to 1.
**Selectivity rating.** N/A.

**PROFILE.** California State at Dominguez Hills, founded in 1965, is a public, comprehensive university. Its 350-acre campus is located 20 miles from Los Angeles.

**Accreditation:** WASC. Professionally accredited by the National Association of Schools of Art and Design, the National Association of Schools of Music, the National Council for Accreditation of Teacher Education.
**Religious orientation:** California State University, Dominguez Hills is nonsectarian; no religious requirements.
**Library:** Collections totaling over 411,000 volumes, 2,222 periodical subscriptions, and 602,004 microform items.
**Athletic facilities:** Gymnasium, cross-country trail, baseball, soccer, and softball fields, tennis courts, track, combatives, dance, and weight rooms, swimming pool.

**STUDENT BODY. Undergraduate profile:** 96% are state residents; 52% are transfers. 9% Asian-American, 31% Black, 24% Hispanic, 1% Native American, 30% White, 5% Other. Average age of undergraduates is 22.
**Freshman profile:** 84% of freshmen come from public schools.
**Undergraduate achievement:** 69% of fall 1991 freshmen returned for fall 1992 term. 2% of entering class graduated.
**Foreign students:** 705 students are from out of the country. Countries represented include African countries, China, Japan, Mexico, and the Philippines; 86 in all.

**PROGRAMS OF STUDY. Degrees:** B.A., B.S.
**Majors:** African-American Studies, Anthropology, Art, Behavioral Sciences, Biology, Business Administration, Chemistry, Clinical Sciences, Communications, Computer Science, Economics, English, French, Geography, Health Science, History, Human Services, Interdisciplinary Studies, Labor Studies, Liberal Studies, Mathematics, Mexican-American Studies, Music, Nursing, Philosophy, Physical Education, Physics, Political Science, Psychology, Public Administration, Recreation, Sociology, Spanish, Special Major, Theatre Arts.
**Distribution of degrees:** The majors with the highest enrollment are business administration, liberal studies, and interdisciplinary studies; French, Mexican-American studies, and earth sciences have the lowest.
**Requirements:** General education requirement.
**Academic regulations:** Minimum 2.0 GPA must be maintained.
**Special:** Minors offered in many majors and in over 25 other fields. Small College offers creative, accelerated program with its own facilities, faculty, and individualized programs. Certificate programs in civilization, environmental studies, general studies, human studies, and science/technology/society. Double majors. Independent study. Internships. Graduate school at which undergraduates may take graduate-level courses. Preprofessional programs in law, medicine, veterinary science, pharmacy, dentistry, optometry, osteopathy, and podiatry. Member of Consortium of the California State U and California Desert Studies Consortium. Member of National Student Exchange (NSE). Teacher certification in special education. Certification in specific subject areas. Study abroad in 15 countries, including England, France, Germany, Italy, Peru, Spain, and Sweden. ROTC on campus and at CSU Long Beach. AFROTC at UCLA and Loyola Marymount U.
**Honors:** Honors program. Honor societies.
**Academic Assistance:** Remedial reading, writing, and math. Nonremedial tutoring.

**STUDENT LIFE. Housing:** Students may live on or off campus. School-owned/operated apartments. On-campus married-student housing. 6% of students live in college housing.
**Services and counseling/handicapped student services:** Placement services. Health service. Women's center. Day care. Counseling services for minority, veteran, and older students. Birth control, personal, and psychological counseling. Career and academic guidance services. Physically disabled student services. Learning disabled services. Notetaking services. Reader services for the blind.
**Campus organizations:** Undergraduate student government. Student newspaper (Dominguez News). Literary magazine. Yearbook. TV station. Numerous student groups. Four fraternities, no chapter houses; three sororities, no chapter houses.
**Religious organizations:** Campus Crusade for Christ, Ecumenical Campus Ministry Club, Intervarsity Christian Fellowship, Lutheran Student Association.
**Minority/foreign student organizations:** Black Student Union, Black Business Student Association, Latin American Culture Club, MEChA. International Student Club, Chinese, French, Korean, Malaysian, and Polynesian groups.

**ATHLETICS. Physical education requirements:** None.
**Intercollegiate competition:** 2% of students participate. Baseball (M), basketball (M,W), golf (M), soccer (M,W), softball (W), volleyball (W). Member of California Collegiate Athletic Association, NCAA Division II.
**Intramural and club sports:** 20% of students participate. Intramural basketball, dance, soccer, volleyball, weight training. Men's club cheerleading, cycling. Women's club cheerleading, cycling.

**ADMISSIONS. Academic basis for candidate selection** (in order of priority): Secondary school record, standardized test scores, school's recommendation, essay.
**Nonacademic basis for candidate selection:** Particular talent or ability is considered.
**Requirements:** Graduation from secondary school is required; GED is accepted. 15 units and the following program of study are required: 4 units of English, 3 units of math, 1 unit of lab science, 2 units of foreign language, 1 unit of history, 4 units of electives. Electives should include 1 unit of visual/performing arts. Minimum grade of "C" in listed secondary school courses and minimum eligibility index of 2994 for SAT (722 for ACT) required of in-state applicants; minimum eligibility index of 3402 for SAT (826 for ACT) required of out-of-state applicants. In-state applicants with minimum 3.0 GPA and out-of-state applicants with minimum 3.6 GPA are eligible regardless of test scores. R.N. required of nursing program applicants. EOP for applicants not normally admissible. SAT or ACT is required. Campus visit and interview recommended. Off-campus interviews available with an admissions representative.
**Procedure:** Suggest filing application by November 1; no deadline. Notification of admission on rolling basis. $10 room deposit, refundable upon moving out of room. Freshmen accepted for terms other than fall.
**Special programs:** Credit may be granted through CEEB Advanced Placement for scores of 3 or higher. Credit may be granted through CLEP general and subject exams, DANTES and challenge exams, and military and life experience. Early entrance/early admission program. Concurrent enrollment program.
**Transfer students:** Transfer students accepted for terms other than fall. In fall 1993, 52% of all new students were transfers into all classes. 1,823 transfer applications were received, 1,657 were accepted. Application deadline is June 1 for fall; November 23 for spring. Minimum 2.0 GPA required. Lowest course grade accepted is "D." Maximum number of transferable credits is 70 semester hours. At least 30 semester hours must be completed at the university to receive degree.
**Admissions contact:** Anita Gash, M.P.A., Director of Admissions. 213 516-3600.

**FINANCIAL AID. Available aid:** Pell grants, SEOG, state scholarships and grants, school scholarships, private scholarships and grants, academic merit scholarships, and athletic scholarships. Perkins Loans (NDSL), PLUS, Stafford Loans (GSL), state loans, school loans, private loans, and SLS.
**Financial aid statistics:** 15% of aid is not need-based. In 1993-94, 60% of all freshman applicants received aid. Average amounts of aid awarded freshmen: Scholarships and grants, $1,200; loans, $1,500.
**Supporting data/closing dates:** FAFSA/FAF/FFS: Priority filing date is April 16. School's own aid application: Priority filing date is April 16. State aid form: Priority filing date is April 16. Income tax forms: Priority filing date is April 16. Notification of awards begins April 19.
**Financial aid contact:** James Woods, Financial Aid Director. 213 516-3691.

**STUDENT EMPLOYMENT.** College Work/Study Program. Institutional employment. 7% of full-time undergraduates work on campus during school year. Students may expect to earn an average of $3,000 during school year. Off-campus part-time employment opportunities rated "excellent."

**COMPUTER FACILITIES.** 196 IBM/IBM-compatible, Macintosh/Apple, and RISC-/UNIX-based microcomputers; 115 are networked. Students may access CDC Cyber, Digital minicomputer/mainframe systems, BITNET, Internet. Residence halls may be equipped with stand-alone microcomputers. Client/LAN operating systems include Apple/Macintosh, DOS, OS/2, UNIX/XENIX/AIX, LocalTalk/AppleTalk, Novell. Computer languages and software packages include Ada, BASIC, C, COBOL, dBASE, Excel, FORTRAN, LISP, Lotus 1-2-3, HyperCard, PageMaker, Pascal, WordPerfect. Computer facilities are available to all students.
**Fees:** None.
**Hours:** 11 AM-10 PM (M-Th); 11 AM-4 PM (F); 8:30 AM-4 PM (Sa).

**GRADUATE CAREER DATA.** 62% of graduates choose careers in business and industry.

**PROMINENT ALUMNI/AE.** Clarence Gilyard, actor; Clarence Tucker, U.S. Assemblyman; Larry Lee, retired CEO, chairperson of the board, Western Airlines; Stephanie Lee-Miller, assistant secretary for public affairs, U.S. Department of Health and Human Services.

# California State University, Fresno

**Fresno, CA 93740-0047** **209 278-4240**

**1993-94 Costs.** Tuition: None (state residents), $7,380 (out-of-state). Room & board: $4,302. Fees, books, misc. academic expenses (school's estimate): $1,490.
**Enrollment.** Undergraduates: 6,474 men, 7,020 women (full-time). Freshman class: 4,823 applicants, 3,825 accepted, 1,483 enrolled. Graduate enrollment: 1,219 men, 2,050 women.
**Test score averages/ranges.** Average SAT scores: 393 verbal, 458 math. Average ACT scores: 18 English, 19 math, 19 composite.
**Faculty.** 708 full-time; 242 part-time. 62% of faculty holds doctoral degree. Student/faculty ratio: 18 to 1.
**Selectivity rating.** Competitive.

**PROFILE.** California State at Fresno is a public, comprehensive university. It was founded as a Normal school in 1911, joined the state university system in 1961, and was granted university status in 1972. Programs are offered through the Division of Graduate Studies and Research and the Schools of Agricultural Sciences and Technology, Arts and Humanities, Business and Administrative Sciences, Education and Human Development, Engineering, Health and Social Work, Natural Sciences, and Social Sciences. Its 220-acre campus and 1,190-acre university farm are located several miles from downtown Fresno.

**Accreditation:** WASC.
**Religious orientation:** California State University, Fresno is nonsectarian; no religious requirements.
**Library:** Collections totaling over 852,607 volumes, 2,975 periodical subscriptions, and 1,128,691 microform items.
**Special facilities/museums:** Marine lab.
**Athletic facilities:** Swimming pool, baseball/softball field, basketball, racquetball, and tennis courts.

**STUDENT BODY. Undergraduate profile:** 99% are state residents; 57% are transfers. 10% Asian-American, 5% Black, 25% Hispanic, 1% Native American, 59% White. Average age of undergraduates is 22.
**Freshman profile:** 1% of freshmen who took SAT scored 700 or over on math; 1% scored 600 or over on verbal, 11% scored 600 or over on math; 13% scored 500 or over on verbal, 36% scored 500 or over on math; 50% scored 400 or over on verbal, 71% scored 400 or over on math; 85% scored 300 or over on verbal, 95% scored 300 or over on math. 69% of accepted applicants took SAT; 16% took ACT. 98% of freshmen come from public schools.
**Undergraduate achievement:** 80% of fall 1992 freshmen returned for fall 1993 term.
**Foreign students:** 545 students are from out of the country. Countries represented include Hong Kong, Indonesia, Japan, Malaysia, Singapore, and Taiwan; 67 in all.

**PROGRAMS OF STUDY. Degrees:** B.A., B.S., B.Voc.Ed.
**Majors:** Agricultural Business, Agricultural Education, Agricultural Sciences, Animal Science, Anthropology, Art, Biology, Business Administration, Chemistry, Child Devel-

opment, Civil Engineering, Communicative Disorders, Computer Engineering, Computer Science, Criminology, Economics, Electrical Engineering, English, Food/Nutritional Sciences, French, Geography, Geology, German, Health Sciences, History, Home Economics, Industrial Arts, Industrial Engineering, Industrial Technology, Interior Design, Journalism, Liberal Studies, Linguistics, Mathematics, Mechanical Engineering, Microbiology, Music, Nursing, Philosophy, Physical Education, Physical Therapy, Physics, Plant Science, Political Science, Psychology, Public Administration, Recreation Administration, Russian, Social Science, Social Work, Sociology, Spanish, Special Major, Speech Communication, Surveying Engineering, Telecommunications, Theatre Arts, Vocational Arts.

**Distribution of degrees:** The majors with the highest enrollment are liberal studies, business administration, and agricultural sciences; economics, physics, and geology have the lowest.

**Requirements:** General education requirement.

**Special:** Minors offered in many majors and in aerospace, African-American, Armenian, Asian, Asian-American, Chicano/Latino, classical, ethnic, Latin American, peace/conflict, Russian area, urban, and women's studies and in gerontology, humanities, Japanese, Latin, military science, and physical sciences. Self-designed majors. Double majors. Dual degrees. Independent study. Pass/fail grading option. Internships. Cooperative education programs. Graduate school at which undergraduates may take graduate-level courses. Preprofessional programs in law, medicine, veterinary science, pharmacy, dentistry, optometry, and library science. Member of Consortium of the California State U. Member of National Student Exchange (NSE). Teacher certification in early childhood, elementary, secondary, and special education. Study abroad in Australia, Brazil, Canada, Denmark, France, Germany, Israel, Italy, Jamaica, Japan, Mexico, New Zealand, the former Soviet Republics, Sweden, Taiwan, and the United Kingdom. ROTC and AFROTC.

**Honors:** Phi Beta Kappa. Honors program.

**Academic Assistance:** Remedial reading, writing, math, and study skills. Nonremedial tutoring.

**STUDENT LIFE. Housing:** Students may live on or off campus. Coed, women's, and men's dorms. 5% of students live in college housing.

**Social atmosphere:** The Bucket is a popular on campus gathering-spot; off campus, students frequent Wiliker's Bar & Grill, Stuart Anderson's Black Angus, Butterfield's, and Bisla's. Athletes, Greeks, and Christian groups are some of the influential groups on the Fresno campus. Popular events include Vintage Days in mid-April and long weekends of parties. "On campus, Fresno State is pretty boring," reports the school newspaper. "It is a commuter campus mainly, so most of the socializing and parties are off-campus. The education is excellent, although the campus itself has no identity, drab architecture."

**Services and counseling/handicapped student services:** Placement services. Health service. Day care. Counseling services for minority, military, veteran, and older students. Personal and psychological counseling. Career and academic guidance services. Physically disabled student services. Notetaking services. Tape recorders. Tutors. Reader services for the blind.

**Campus organizations:** Student newspaper (Daily Collegian). Literary magazine. 200 registered organizations. 13 fraternities, seven chapter houses; eight sororities, six chapter houses. 7% of men join a fraternity. 5% of women join a sorority.

**Religious organizations:** Several religious groups.

**Minority/foreign student organizations:** Various minority student groups. Several foreign student groups.

**ATHLETICS. Physical education requirements:** None.

**Intercollegiate competition:** 1% of students participate. Baseball (M), basketball (M,W), cross-country (M,W), football (M), golf (M), soccer (M), softball (W), swimming (M,W), tennis (M,W), track (M,W), volleyball (W), water polo (M), wrestling (M). Member of NCAA Division I.

**ADMISSIONS. Academic basis for candidate selection** (in order of priority): Secondary school record, standardized test scores, class rank.

**Requirements:** Graduation from secondary school is required; GED is accepted. 15 units and the following program of study are required: 4 units of English, 3 units of math, 1 unit of lab science, 2 units of foreign language, 1 unit of history, 4 units of electives. Electives should include 1 unit of visual/performing arts. Minimum grade of "C" in listed secondary school courses and eligibility index of 2800 for SAT (694 for ACT) required of in-state applicants; minimum eligibility index of 3402 for SAT (842 for ACT) required of out-of-state applicants. In-state applicants with minimum 3.0 GPA and out-of-state applicants with minimum 3.6 GPA are eligible regardless of test scores. Specific college-level courses required of nursing and physical therapy program applicants; out-of-state applicants not admitted to physical therapy program. EOP for applicants not normally admissible. Conditional admission possible for applicants not meeting standard requirements. SAT or ACT is required. Off-campus interviews available with an admissions representative.

**Procedure:** Take SAT or ACT by March of 12th year. Visit college for interview by January of 12th year. Suggest filing application by November; no deadline. Notification of admission on rolling basis. Freshmen accepted for terms other than fall.

**Special programs:** Credit and/or placement may be granted through CEEB Advanced Placement exams for scores of 3 or higher. Credit and/or placement may be granted through CLEP general and subject exams. Placement may be granted through Regents College exams. Credit and placement may be granted through ACT PEP, DANTES, and challenge exams and military experience. Concurrent enrollment program.

**Transfer students:** Transfer students accepted for terms other than fall. In fall 1993, 57% of all new students were transfers into all classes. 3,554 transfer applications were received, 2,660 were accepted. Application deadline is June 1 for fall; October 16 for spring. Minimum 2.0 GPA required of in-state applicants; 2.4 GPA of out-of-state applicants. Lowest course grade accepted is "D-." Maximum number of transferable credits is 70 semester hours.

**Admissions contact:** Richard L. Backer, Ph.D., Director of Admissions. 209 278-6283.

**FINANCIAL AID. Available aid:** Pell grants, SEOG, state scholarships and grants, school scholarships and grants, private scholarships, ROTC scholarships, academic merit scholarships, and athletic scholarships. Perkins Loans (NDSL), PLUS, Stafford Loans (GSL), NSL, school loans, and SLS. Education Plan Inc. and deferred payment plan. Military service plan.

**Supporting data/closing dates:** FAFSA/FAF/FFS: Priority filing date is March 2. State aid form: Priority filing date is March 2. Notification of awards on rolling basis.

**Financial aid contact:** Joseph Heuston, Jr., M.A., Director of Financial Aid. 209 278-2183.

**STUDENT EMPLOYMENT.** College Work/Study Program. Institutional employment. Students may expect to earn an average of $2,275 during school year. Freshmen are discouraged from working during their first term. Off-campus part-time employment opportunities rated "good."

**COMPUTER FACILITIES.** 600 IBM/IBM-compatible, Macintosh/Apple, and RISC-/UNIX-based microcomputers. Students may access IBM minicomputer/mainframe systems. Computer languages and software packages include BMDP, C, COBOL, FORTRAN, LISP, Pascal, SAS, SPSS. Some computers are restricted.

**Fees:** None.

**Hours:** 8 AM-midn. (M-Th); 8 AM-5 PM (F); 9 AM-5 PM (Sa); noon-midn. (Su).

**PROMINENT ALUMNI/AE.** Ezunial Burts, executive director, port of Los Angeles; John Lewis, CEO, Amdahl; Col. Steven Nagel, astronaut; Paul O'Neill, CEO, Alcoa; Shirley Williams, poet, author.

# California State University, Fullerton

**Fullerton, CA 92634** **714 773-2011**

**1994-95 Costs.** Tuition: None (state residents), $5,904 (out-of-state). Room: $3,476. No meal plan. Fees, books, misc. academic expenses (school's estimate): $2,124.

**Enrollment.** Undergraduates: 5,332 men, 6,815 women (full-time). Freshman class: 6,469 applicants, 4,923 accepted, 1,895 enrolled. Graduate enrollment: 1,511 men, 2,226 women.

**Test score averages/ranges.** Average SAT scores: 396 verbal, 478 math. Range of SAT scores of middle 50%: 330-450 verbal, 400-530 math. Average ACT scores: 21 composite. Range of ACT scores of middle 50%: 17-23 composite.

**Faculty.** 88% of faculty holds doctoral degree. Student/faculty ratio: 22 to 1.

**Selectivity rating.** Less competitive.

**PROFILE.** California State at Fullerton, founded in 1957, is a public university. Programs are offered through the Schools of the Arts, Business Administration and Economics, Engineering and Computer Science, Human Development and Community Service, Humanities and Social Sciences, and Natural Science and Mathematics. Its 225-acre campus is located in Fullerton, 35 miles from Los Angeles.

**Accreditation:** WASC. Professionally accredited by the Accreditation Board for Engineering and Technology, the Accrediting Council on Education in Journalism and Mass Communication, the American Assembly of Collegiate Schools of Business, the American Speech-Language-Hearing Association, the National Association of Schools of Art and Design, the National Association of Schools of Music, the National Association of Schools of Public Affairs and Administration, the National Council for Accreditation of Teacher Education, the National League for Nursing.

**Religious orientation:** California State University, Fullerton is nonsectarian; no religious requirements.

**Library:** Collections totaling over 689,976 volumes, 5,416 periodical subscriptions, and 920,742 microform items.

**Special facilities/museums:** Centers for international business, economic education, and governmental studies, institutes of geophysics and molecular biology, wildlife sanctuary, 20-acre arboretum.

**Athletic facilities:** Gymnasium, weight room, swimming pool, intramural, soccer, and softball fields, basketball, racquetball, and tennis courts, putting green.

**STUDENT BODY. Undergraduate profile:** 99% are state residents; 11% are transfers. 16.8% Asian-American, 2.8% Black, 16.1% Hispanic, .7% Native American, 47.8% White, 15.8% Other. Average age of undergraduates is 24.

**Freshman profile:** 1% of freshmen who took SAT scored 700 or over on math; 2% scored 600 or over on verbal, 12% scored 600 or over on math; 15% scored 500 or over on verbal, 41% scored 500 or over on math; 49% scored 400 or over on verbal, 78% scored 400 or over on math; 87% scored 300 or over on verbal, 97% scored 300 or over on math. 2% of freshmen who took ACT scored 30 or over on composite; 24% scored 24 or over on composite; 80% scored 18 or over on composite; 99% scored 12 or over on composite; 100% scored 6 or over on composite. 90% of accepted applicants took SAT; 10% took ACT. 81% of freshmen come from public schools.

**Undergraduate achievement:** 73% of fall 1992 freshmen returned for fall 1993 term. 19% of entering class graduated.

**Foreign students:** 601 students are from out of the country. Countries represented include China, Indonesia, Japan, Mexico, South Korea, and Taiwan; 76 in all.

**PROGRAMS OF STUDY. Degrees:** B.A., B.F.A., B.Mus., B.S.

**Majors:** Accounting, Acting, Advertising, Afro-American Studies, American Studies, Anthropology, Applied Mathematics, Art/Design, Art History, Biochemistry, Biology, Botany, Business Economics, Cell/Molecular Biology, Ceramics, Chemistry, Chicano Studies, Child Development, Civil Engineering/Engineering Mechanics, Commercial Music, Communications, Communicative Disorders, Comparative Literature, Computer Science, Crafts, Creative Photography, Criminal Justice, Dance, Directing, Drawing/Painting, Ecology, Economics, Electrical Engineering, Elementary/Secondary Teacher Education, Engineering Science, English, Environmental Analysis, Environmental Design, Finance, French, Genetics, Geography, Geology, German, Graphic Design, History, Human Services, Illustration, Instrumental Music, International Business, Journalism Education, Keyboard Music, Latin American Studies, Liberal Studies, Linguistics, Management, Management Information Systems, Management Science, Marine Biology, Marketing, Mathematics, Mechanical Engineering, Medical Biology/Microbiology, Music/Accompanying Specialization, Music Composition, Music Education, Music History/Theory, Music/Liberal Arts, Musical Theatre, News/Editorial, Nursing, Philosophy,

Photocommunications, Physical Education, Physics, Playwriting, Political Science, Printmaking, Probability/Statistics, Psychology, Public Administration, Public Relations, Radio/Television/Film, Religious Studies, Russian/East European Area Studies, Sculpture, Sociology, Spanish, Special Major, Speech Communication, Television, Theatre Arts/Professional Emphasis, Theatre Arts/Teaching Emphasis, Theatre Arts/Technical Production/Design, Theatre History/Theory, Urban Geography, Voice, Zoology.

**Distribution of degrees:** The majors with the highest enrollment are communications, finance, and accounting; comparative literature and Russian studies have the lowest.

**Requirements:** General education requirement.

**Academic regulations:** Minimum 2.0 GPA must be maintained.

**Special:** Minors offered in many majors and in ethnic studies, gerontology, health promotion, international politics, Jewish studies, military science, Pacific Rim studies, peace studies, Portuguese, and women's studies. Self-designed majors. Double majors. Dual degrees. Independent study. Pass/fail grading option. Internships. Cooperative education programs. Graduate school at which undergraduates may take graduate-level courses. Preprofessional programs in law, medicine, dentistry, theology, optometry, podiatry, and social welfare. Member of Consortium of the California State U, California Desert Studies Consortium, and Southern California Ocean Studies Consortium. Teacher certification in elementary, secondary, and special education. Exchange programs abroad in China, France, Japan, and Mexico. Study abroad also in Brazil, Canada, Denmark, Germany, Israel, Italy, New Zealand, Peru, Spain, Sweden, Taiwan, and the United Kingdom. ROTC.

**Honors:** Honors program.

**Academic Assistance:** Remedial reading, writing, math, and study skills. Nonremedial tutoring.

**STUDENT LIFE. Housing:** Students may live on or off campus. School-owned/operated apartments. 2% of students live in college housing.

**Social atmosphere:** Popular gathering spots include the Quad, the University Center, the Tastery, and the library and humanities building. Influential groups on campus include the Associated Students and Greeks. Popular social events include Homecoming, Greek Week, Rush Week, Comm Week, and noon concerts. According to the student newspaper, CSU Fullerton is for the most part a commuter university, with only about 5% out-of-state students attending. About 75% of the student body works on or off campus.

**Services and counseling/handicapped student services:** Placement services. Health service. Women's center. Day care. Counseling services for minority, veteran, and older students. Birth control, personal, and psychological counseling. Career and academic guidance services. Physically disabled student services. Learning disabled services. Notetaking services.

**Campus organizations:** Undergraduate student government. Student newspaper (Daily Titan). Literary magazine. Numerous musical, debating, drama, departmental, professional, political, service, and special-interest groups. 13 fraternities, eight chapter houses; seven sororities, six chapter houses. 8% of men join a fraternity. 4% of women join a sorority.

**Religious organizations:** Campus Catholic Ministry, Campus Christian Fellowship, Campus Crusade for Christ, Latter-Day Saints Association, Newman Club.

**Minority/foreign student organizations:** Association of Afro-Ethnic Students, Black Business Student Association, Chinese-American groups, Latino Business Students, MEChA. Arab Student Association, Japanese International, Partners, Vietnamese Student Association.

**ATHLETICS. Physical education requirements:** None.

**Intercollegiate competition:** 4% of students participate. Baseball (M), basketball (M,W), cross-country (M,W), fencing (M,W), gymnastics (W), soccer (M,W), softball (W), tennis (W), track and field (outdoor) (M,W), volleyball (W), wrestling (M). Member of Big West Conference, NCAA Division I.

**Intramural and club sports:** 20% of students participate. Intramural badminton, basketball, billiards, bowling, flag football, golf, racquetball, soccer, softball, table tennis, tennis, ultimate frisbee, volleyball, warball. Men's club Alpine skiing, bowling, cycling, rugby, snowboarding, surfing, triathlon. Women's club Alpine skiing, bowling, cycling, snowboarding, surfing, triathlon.

**ADMISSIONS. Academic basis for candidate selection** (in order of priority): Secondary school record, standardized test scores, class rank, school's recommendation.

**Nonacademic basis for candidate selection:** Particular talent or ability and geographical distribution are important.

**Requirements:** Graduation from secondary school is required; GED is accepted. 15 units and the following program of study are required: 4 units of English, 3 units of math, 1 unit of lab science, 2 units of foreign language, 1 unit of history, 4 units of electives. Electives should include 1 unit of visual/performing arts. Minimum grade of "C" in listed secondary school courses. In-state applicants with minimum 3.0 GPA and out-of-state applicants with minimum 3.6 GPA are eligible regardless of test scores. Audition required of music program applicants. R.N. required of nursing program applicants. EOP for applicants not normally admissible. SAT or ACT is required. Campus visit recommended. No off-campus interviews.

**Procedure:** Take SAT or ACT by June of 12th year. Suggest filing application by November 30; no deadline. Notification of admission on rolling basis. Freshmen accepted for terms other than fall.

**Special programs:** Credit may be granted through CEEB Advanced Placement for scores of 3 or higher. Credit may be granted through CLEP general and subject exams. Credit and placement may be granted through military experience. Early decision program. Early entrance/early admission program. Concurrent enrollment program.

**Transfer students:** Transfer students accepted for terms other than fall. In fall 1993, 11% of all new students were transfers into all classes. 5,637 transfer applications were received, 3,388 were accepted. Application deadline is rolling for fall; rolling for spring. Minimum 2.0 GPA required. Lowest course grade accepted is "C." Maximum number of transferable credits is 70 semester hours from a two-year school and 94 semester hours from a four-year school. At least 30 semester hours must be completed at the university to receive degree.

**Admissions contact:** Nancy Dority, Admissions Officer. 714 773-2370.

**FINANCIAL AID. Available aid:** Pell grants, SEOG, state scholarships and grants, school scholarships and grants, private scholarships and grants, ROTC scholarships, academic merit scholarships, and athletic scholarships. Perkins Loans (NDSL), PLUS, Stafford Loans (GSL), school loans, and SLS.

**Financial aid statistics:** In 1993-94, 85% of all undergraduate applicants received aid; 22% of freshman applicants. Average amounts of aid awarded freshmen: Scholarships and grants, $2,175; loans, $1,500.

**Supporting data/closing dates:** FAFSA. Notification of awards begins in June.

**Financial aid contact:** Deborah Gordon, Director of Financial Aid. 714 773-3125.

**STUDENT EMPLOYMENT.** College Work/Study Program. Institutional employment. Off-campus part-time employment opportunities rated "good."

**COMPUTER FACILITIES.** 1,073 IBM/IBM-compatible and Macintosh/Apple microcomputers. Students may access Digital, IBM minicomputer/mainframe systems, Internet. Computer languages and software packages include BASIC, COBOL, FORTRAN, numerous others. Computer facilities are available to all students.

**Fees:** None.

**Hours:** 24 hours.

**PROMINENT ALUMNI/AE.** Gareth Chang, president, McDonnell Douglas (China); Edward Royce, state legislator, California; Diana Griego, Pulitzer Prize-winning journalist; Vicki Vargas, TV journalist, KNBC-TV, Los Angeles; Kevin Costner, actor.

# California State University, Hayward

**Hayward, CA 94542** **510 881-3000**

**1993-94 Costs.** Tuition: None (state residents), $7,380 (out-of-state). Room: $2,700. No meal plan. Fees, books, misc. academic expenses (school's estimate): $1,823.

**Enrollment.** Undergraduates: 2,629 men, 4,161 women (full-time). Freshman class: 2,121 applicants, 1,126 accepted, 698 enrolled. Graduate enrollment: 1,282 men, 2,050 women.

**Test score averages/ranges.** N/A.

**Faculty.** 440 full-time; 138 part-time. 80% of faculty holds doctoral degree. Student/faculty ratio: 19 to 1.

**Selectivity rating.** N/A.

**PROFILE.** California State at Hayward, founded in 1957, is a public university. Programs are offered through the Schools of Arts, Letters, and Social Sciences; Business and Economics; Education; and Science. Its 354-acre campus overlooks the San Francisco Bay area.

**Accreditation:** WASC. Professionally accredited by the American Assembly of Collegiate Schools of Business, the American Speech-Language-Hearing Association, the National Association of Schools of Art and Design, the National Association of Schools of Music, the National Council for Accreditation of Teacher Education, the National League for Nursing.

**Religious orientation:** California State University, Hayward is nonsectarian; no religious requirements.

**Library:** Collections totaling over 800,000 volumes, 2,509 periodical subscriptions, and 670,000 microform items.

**Special facilities/museums:** Anthropology museum, art gallery, Asian-American cultural center, marine lab, ecological field station, geology summer camp, electron microscope.

**Athletic facilities:** Track, swimming pool, racquetball and tennis courts, weight rooms, baseball, soccer, and softball fields.

**STUDENT BODY. Undergraduate profile:** 89% are state residents. 24% Asian-American, 13% Black, 10% Hispanic, 1% Native American, 49% White, 3% Other. Average age of undergraduates is 25.

**Freshman profile:** 95% of freshmen come from public schools.

**Foreign students:** 180 students are from out of the country. Countries represented include China, Hong Kong, Japan, Korea, Taiwan, and the Philippines; 50 in all.

**PROGRAMS OF STUDY. Degrees:** B.A., B.S.

**Majors:** Anthropology, Art, Biological Sciences, Business Administration, Chemistry, Computer Science, Criminal Justice Administration, Economics, English, Environmental Studies, Ethnic Studies, French, Geography, Geology, German, Health Sciences, History, Human Development, Latin American Studies, Liberal Studies, Mass Communication, Mathematics, Music, Nursing, Philosophy, Physical Education, Physical Science, Physics, Political Science, Psychology, Recreation, Sociology, Spanish, Special Major, Speech Communication, Speech Pathology/Audiology, Statistics, Theatre.

**Distribution of degrees:** The majors with the highest enrollment are business administration, computer science, and liberal studies; psychology and biology have the lowest.

**Requirements:** General education requirement.

**Special:** Minors offered in most majors and in approximately 25 other fields. Many options and areas of specialization available in majors. Self-designed majors. Double majors. Independent study. Pass/fail grading option. Internships. Cooperative education programs. Graduate school at which undergraduates may take graduate-level courses. Preprofessional programs in law, medicine, dentistry, and engineering. Member of National Student Exchange (NSE). Teacher certification in elementary, secondary, special education, and bilingual/bicultural education. Exchange programs abroad in England (Middlesex Polytechnic, others) and Italy. Study abroad also possible in other countries. ROTC, NROTC, and AFROTC at UC Berkeley.

**Honors:** Honors program. Honor societies.

**Academic Assistance:** Remedial writing and math.

**STUDENT LIFE. Housing:** Students may live on or off campus. School-owned/operated apartments. 3% of students live in college housing.

**Social atmosphere:** Students gather at the University Union, Sweet River Saloon, Bronco Billy's Pizza, and Buffalo Bill's Brewery. Influential groups include Greeks, athletes, some Christian groups, student ethnic groups, and various campus clubs. Theatre produc-

tions, the "Alfresco" campus festival, and sporting events are popular campus happenings. The student newspaper reports, "both the city and the campus are culturally and ethnically diverse. The proximity to San Francisco, Berkeley, and Oakland provide access to any number of events."
**Services and counseling/handicapped student services:** Placement services. Health service. Personal counseling. Career guidance services. Physically disabled student services. Learning disabled services. Notetaking services. Tape recorders. Tutors. Reader services for the blind.
**Campus organizations:** Undergraduate student government. Student newspaper (Pioneer, published once/week). Literary magazine. Radio and TV stations. Circle K, College Republicans, drama group, Toastmasters, academic groups, 85 organizations in all. Six fraternities, no chapter houses; seven sororities, no chapter houses.
**Religious organizations:** Asian-American Christian Fellowship, Baptist Campus Ministry Club, Campus Advance, Campus Crusade for Christ, Chinese Campus Evangelical Fellowship, Chinese for Christ Fellowship, Korean Campus for Christ, Newman Club.
**Minority/foreign student organizations:** MEChA. Afghan, African, Asian, Asian-Pacific American, Chinese, Filipino, French, German, Japanese, and Vietnamese groups.

**ATHLETICS. Physical education requirements:** None.
**Intercollegiate competition:** 2% of students participate. Baseball (M), basketball (M,W), cheerleading (W), football (M), soccer (M,W), softball (W), track and field (M,W), volleyball (W). Member of NCAA Division II, NCAC.

**ADMISSIONS. Academic basis for candidate selection** (in order of priority): Standardized test scores, secondary school record, class rank.
**Requirements:** Graduation from secondary school is required; GED is accepted. 15 units and the following program of study are required: 4 units of English, 3 units of math, 1 unit of lab science, 2 units of foreign language, 1 unit of history, 4 units of academic electives. Electives should include 1 unit of visual/performing arts. Minimum grade of "C" in listed secondary school courses and minimum eligibility index of 2800 for SAT (694 for ACT) required of in-state applicants; minimum eligibility index of 3402 for SAT (842 for ACT) required of out-of-state applicants. In-state applicants with minimum 3.0 GPA and out-of-state applicants with minimum 3.6 GPA are eligible regardless of test scores. EOP for applicants not normally admissible. Conditional admission possible for applicants not meeting standard requirements. SAT is required; ACT may be substituted. Campus visit recommended. Off-campus interviews available with an admissions representative.
**Procedure:** Take SAT or ACT by June 13 of 12th year. Suggest filing application by May 15. Application deadline is June 12. Notification of admission on rolling basis. No set date by which applicants must accept offer. Freshmen accepted for terms other than fall.
**Special programs:** Admission may be deferred two terms. Credit may be granted through CEEB Advanced Placement for scores of 3 or higher. Credit may be granted through CLEP subject exams (math and chemistry only), DANTES and challenge exams, and military experience. Early decision program. Concurrent enrollment program.
**Transfer students:** Transfer students accepted for terms other than fall. In fall 1992, 3,349 transfer applications were received, 2,495 were accepted. Application deadline is June 1. Minimum 2.0 GPA required. Lowest course grade accepted is "D." Maximum number of transferable credits is 84 quarter hours. At least 45 quarter hours must be completed at the university to receive degree.
**Admissions contact:** Maria DeAnda-Ramos, Ed.D., Director of Admissions and Outreach. 510 881-3817.

**FINANCIAL AID. Available aid:** Pell grants, SEOG, state grants, and school grants. Perkins Loans (NDSL), Stafford Loans (GSL), and SLS.
**Supporting data/closing dates:** School's own aid application: Priority filing date is May 2; accepted on rolling basis. State aid form: Accepted on rolling basis. Notification of awards begins May 2.
**Financial aid contact:** Janis Linfield, M.S., Director of Financial Aid. 510 881-3616.

**STUDENT EMPLOYMENT.** College Work/Study Program. 50% of full-time undergraduates work on campus during school year. Off-campus part-time employment opportunities rated "fair."

**COMPUTER FACILITIES.** 50 IBM/IBM-compatible and Macintosh/Apple microcomputers. Computer languages and software packages include BASIC, C, COBOL, dBASE, FORTRAN, Lotus 1-2-3, Pascal, WordStar. Computer facilities are available to all students.
**Fees:** None.
**Hours:** 8 AM-midn.

**PROMINENT ALUMNI/AE.** Bill Lockyer, state senator, California; Elihu Harris, mayor, Oakland; Johan Klehs, state assemblymen, California.

## California State University, Long Beach

**Long Beach, CA 90840** **310 985-4111**

**1994-95 Costs.** Tuition: None (state residents), $7,380 (out-of-state). Room & board: $4,900. Fees, books, misc. academic expenses (school's estimate): $1,847.
**Enrollment.** Undergraduates: 6,804 men, 8,065 women (full-time). Freshman class: 6,839 applicants, 6,237 accepted, 2,016 enrolled. Graduate enrollment: 2,462 men, 3,187 women.
**Test score averages/ranges.** Average SAT scores: 362 verbal, 438 math.
**Faculty.** 745 full-time; 433 part-time. 86% of faculty holds doctoral degree. Student/faculty ratio: 21 to 1.
**Selectivity rating.** Less competitive.

**PROFILE.** California State at Long Beach is a public, comprehensive university. Founded as a state college in 1949, it gained university status in 1972. Programs are offered through the Center for International Education; the Graduate Center for Public Policy and Administration; and the Schools of Applied Arts and Sciences, Business Administration, Education, Engineering, Fine Arts, Humanities, Natural Science, and Social and Behavioral Sciences. Its 322-acre campus is located 25 miles from Los Angeles.
**Accreditation:** WASC. Professionally accredited by the Accreditation Board for Engineering and Technology, the Accrediting Council on Education in Journalism and Mass Communication, the American Assembly of Collegiate Schools of Business, the American Dietetic Association, the American Home Economics Association, the American Physical Therapy Association, the American Speech-Language-Hearing Association, the Council on Social Work Education, the National Association of Schools of Art and Design, the National Association of Schools of Dance, the National Association of Schools of Music, the National Association of Schools of Theatre, the National League for Nursing, the National Recreation and Park Association.
**Religious orientation:** California State University, Long Beach is nonsectarian; no religious requirements.
**Library:** Collections totaling over 1,012,596 volumes, 3,618 periodical subscriptions, and 1,354,316 microform items.
**Special facilities/museums:** Art and science museums, Japanese garden.
**Athletic facilities:** Gymnasiums, swimming pools, track, athletic fields, basketball, racquetball, sand volleyball, tennis, and volleyball courts, weight room.

**STUDENT BODY. Undergraduate profile:** 99% are state residents; 61% are transfers. 23% Asian-American, 7% Black, 16% Hispanic, 1% Native American, 43% White, 10% Other. Average age of undergraduates is 22.
**Freshman profile:** 76% of accepted applicants took SAT; 1% took ACT. 81% of freshmen come from public schools.
**Undergraduate achievement:** 74% of fall 1992 freshmen returned for fall 1993 term. 2% of entering class graduated.
**Foreign students:** 125 students are from out of the country. Countries represented include China, Hong Kong, Indonesia, Japan, Korea, and Taiwan; 70 in all.

**PROGRAMS OF STUDY. Degrees:** B.A., B.F.A., B.Mus., B.S., B.Voc.Ed.
**Majors:** American Studies, Anthropology, Art, Asian Studies, Biochemistry, Biology, Black Studies, Business Administration, Chemical Engineering, Chemistry, Chicano/Latino Studies, Civil Engineering, Communicative Disorders, Comparative Literature, Computer Sciences, Criminal Justice, Dance, Dietetics, Earth Science, Economics, Electrical Engineering, Engineering, Engineering Technology, English, French, Geography, Geology, German, Graphic Design, Health Care Administration, Health Science, History, Home Economics, Human Development, Industrial Design, Interior Design, International Studies, Japanese, Journalism, Liberal Studies, Marine Biology, Mathematics, Mechanical Engineering, Microbiology, Music, Nursing, Philosophy, Physical Education, Physical Therapy, Physics, Political Science, Psychology, Radio/Television/Film, Recreation, Religious Studies, Social Work, Sociology, Spanish, Special Major, Speech Communication, Theatre Arts, Vocational Education, Zoology.
**Distribution of degrees:** The majors with the highest enrollment are liberal studies and psychology; earth science and German have the lowest.
**Requirements:** General education requirement.
**Academic regulations:** Minimum 2.0 GPA must be maintained.
**Special:** Minors offered. Certificates offered in Asian studies, black studies, cartography, environmental studies, gerontology, international business, legal studies, medieval/Renaissance studies, transportation policy/planning, women's studies, and other areas. Self-designed majors. Double majors. Independent study. Pass/fail grading option. Internships. Cooperative education programs. Graduate school at which undergraduates may take graduate-level courses. Preprofessional programs in law, medicine, and dentistry. Teacher certification in early childhood, elementary, secondary, special education, vo-tech, and bilingual/bicultural education. Certification in specific subject areas. Study abroad in Australia, Austria, Brazil, Canada, China, Denmark, Egypt, France, Germany, Israel, Italy, Japan, Jordan, Mexico, New Zealand, the Philippines, South Korea, Spain, Sweden, Taiwan, Thailand, the United Kingdom, and Zimbabwe. ROTC.
**Honors:** Phi Beta Kappa. Honors program.
**Academic Assistance:** Remedial reading, writing, math, and study skills. Nonremedial tutoring.

**STUDENT LIFE. Housing:** Students may live on or off campus. Coed dorms. 5% of students live in college housing.
**Social atmosphere:** According to the editor of the student newspaper, "With a campus of over 36,000 students, faculty, and staff, we are a very diversified community. CSULB is primarily a commuter college, and over 90% of the students are employed." Favorite gathering spots include the Nugget (on campus), Avenue No. 3 Pizza, Barwinkle's, El Paseo, Bobby McGee's, Corrigan's, Stanley's, and the Red Onion. Homecoming, Kaleidoscope, and the Blues Festival are all popular events on campus.
**Services and counseling/handicapped student services:** Placement services. Health service. Women's center. Day care. Counseling services for minority, military, veteran, and older students. Birth control, personal, and psychological counseling. Career and academic guidance services. Religious counseling. Physically disabled student services. Learning disabled services. Notetaking services. Reader services for the blind.
**Campus organizations:** Undergraduate student government. Student newspaper (Daily Forty-Niner). Literary magazine. Yearbook. Radio and TV stations. Orchestra, opera club, concert band, dance and drama groups, service and departmental groups, special-interest groups, 300 organizations in all. 20 fraternities, eight chapter houses; 12 sororities, six chapter houses. 9% of men join a fraternity. 5% of women join a sorority.
**Religious organizations:** Asian-American Christian Fellowship, Baptist Student Union, Hillel, Catholic Newman Club, Latter-Day Saints Student Association, Methodist Wesley Foundation, Navigators, Network Christian Fellowship, other religious groups.
**Minority/foreign student organizations:** Black Cultural Program Committee, Black Scholars, Black Student Union, American Indian Student Council, La Raza Student Association. International Student Association; African, Cambodian, Chinese, Filipino, Indian, Indonesian, Iranian, Japanese, Korean, Lebanese, Malaysian, Pakistani, Palestinian, Turkish, and Vietnamese groups.

**ATHLETICS. Physical education requirements:** None.
**Intercollegiate competition:** 4% of students participate. Baseball (M), basketball (M,W), cross-country (M,W), fencing (M,W), golf (M,W), softball (W), tennis (W), track and field (outdoor) (M,W), volleyball (M,W), water polo (M). Member of Big West Conference, Mountain Pacific Sports Federation, NCAA Division I.

**Intramural and club sports:** 11% of students participate. Intramural badminton, baseball, basketball, flag football, softball, tennis, track and field, volleyball. Men's club Alpine skiing, archery, badminton, bowling, cheerleading, crew, cycling, fencing, martial arts, rugby, sailing, soccer, water skiing. Women's club Alpine skiing, archery, badminton, bowling, cheerleading, crew, cycling, fencing, martial arts, sailing, soccer, water polo, water skiing.

**ADMISSIONS. Academic basis for candidate selection** (in order of priority): Secondary school record, standardized test scores, class rank.
**Nonacademic basis for candidate selection:** Particular talent or ability is important.
**Requirements:** Graduation from secondary school is required; GED is accepted. 15 units and the following program of study are required: 4 units of English, 3 units of math, 1 unit of lab science, 2 units of foreign language, 1 unit of history, 4 units of electives. Electives should include 1 unit of visual/performing arts. Minimum grade of "C" in listed secondary school courses and minimum eligibility index of 2994 for SAT (722 for ACT) required of in-state applicants; minimum eligibility index of 3402 for SAT (822 for ACT) required of out-of-state applicants. In-state applicants with GPA above 3.0 and out-of-state applicants with GPA above 3.6 are eligible regardless of test scores. Portfolios required of design applicants. EOP for applicants not normally admissible. SAT or ACT is required. Campus visit recommended. No off-campus interviews.
**Procedure:** Take SAT or ACT by November of 12th year. Suggest filing application by November 1; no deadline. Notification of admission on rolling basis. Freshmen accepted for terms other than fall.
**Special programs:** Credit may be granted through CEEB Advanced Placement for scores of 3 or higher. Credit and/or placement may be granted through CLEP general and subject exams. Credit and placement may be granted through challenge exams. Early entrance/early admission program. Concurrent enrollment program.
**Transfer students:** Transfer students accepted for terms other than fall. In fall 1993, 61% of all new students were transfers into all classes. 5,654 transfer applications were received, 5,321 were accepted. Application deadline is rolling for fall; rolling for spring. Minimum 2.0 GPA required. Lowest course grade accepted is "C." Maximum number of transferable credits is 70 semester hours from a two-year school and 94 semester hours from a four-year school. At least 30 semester hours must be completed at the university to receive degree.
**Admissions contact:** Gloria Kapp, Ph.D., Director of Enrollment Services and Financial Aid. 310 985-4141.

**FINANCIAL AID. Available aid:** Pell grants, SEOG, state scholarships and grants, school scholarships, private scholarships and grants, ROTC scholarships, academic merit scholarships, and athletic scholarships. Eduational Opportunity Program Grants. Perkins Loans (NDSL), PLUS, Stafford Loans (GSL), school loans, and SLS. Installment plan.
**Financial aid statistics:** 20% of aid is not need-based. In 1993-94, 60% of all undergraduate applicants received aid. Average amounts of aid awarded freshmen: Scholarships and grants, $1,000; loans, $2,000.
**Supporting data/closing dates:** FAFSA/FAF/FFS: Deadline is March 2. Income tax forms: Priority filing date is May 7. Notification of awards on rolling basis.
**Financial aid contact:** Gloria Kapp, Ph.D., Director of Enrollment Services and Financial Aid. 310 985-8403.

**STUDENT EMPLOYMENT.** College Work/Study Program. Institutional employment. 5% of full-time undergraduates work on campus during school year. Students may expect to earn an average of $3,000 during school year. Off-campus part-time employment opportunities rated "good."

**COMPUTER FACILITIES.** 1,901 IBM/IBM-compatible, Macintosh/Apple, and RISC-/UNIX-based microcomputers; 901 are networked. Students may access Digital minicomputer/mainframe systems, BITNET, Internet. Client/LAN operating systems include Apple/Macintosh, DOS, UNIX/XENIX/AIX, Windows NT, Banyan, Novell. Computer languages and software packages include ADA, BASIC, BIOMED, C, Cobol, FORTRAN, Macro, MINITAB, Pascal, SAS, SPSS; 52 in all. Computer facilities are available to all students.
**Fees:** Computer fee is included in tuition/fees.

# California State University, Northridge

**Northridge, CA 91330** **818 885-1200**

**1994-95 Costs.** Tuition: None (state residents), $7,424 (out-of-state). Room: $5,900. Board: $2,090. Fees, books, misc. academic expenses (school's estimate): $1,904.
**Enrollment.** Undergraduates: 6,762 men, 8,094 women (full-time). Freshman class: 6,837 applicants, 5,376 accepted, 1,826 enrolled. Graduate enrollment: 1,992 men, 3,609 women.
**Test score averages/ranges.** Average SAT scores: 365 verbal, 444 math.
**Faculty.** 846 full-time; 446 part-time. 83% of faculty holds doctoral degree. Student/faculty ratio: 21 to 1.
**Selectivity rating.** Less competitive.

**PROFILE.** California State at Northridge, founded in 1958, is a public, comprehensive university. Programs are offered through the Schools of Arts, Business Administration and Economics, Communication and Professional Studies, Education, Engineering and Computer Science, Humanities, Science and Mathematics, and Social and Behavioral Sciences. Its 350-acre campus is located in the San Fernando Valley, 15 miles from Los Angeles.

**Accreditation:** WASC. Professionally accredited by the Accreditation Board for Engineering and Technology, the Accrediting Council on Education in Journalism and Mass Communication, the American Assembly of Collegiate Schools of Business, the American Home Economics Association, the American Medical Association (CAHEA), the American Physical Therapy Association, the National Association of Schools of Music, the National Recreation and Park Association.
**Religious orientation:** California State University, Northridge is nonsectarian; no religious requirements.
**Library:** Collections totaling over 1,000,000 volumes, 3,700 periodical subscriptions, and 2,500,000 microform items.
**Special facilities/museums:** Anthropology museum, art galleries, deafness center, urban archives, map library, cancer research/developmental biology center, planetarium, observatory.
**Athletic facilities:** Gymnasiums, swimming pool, basketball, tennis, and volleyball courts, track stadium, athletic fields.

**STUDENT BODY. Undergraduate profile:** 98% are state residents; 60% are transfers. 14.3% Asian-American, 8.8% Black, 20.9% Hispanic, .8% Native American, 51.2% White, 4% Filipino. Average age of undergraduates is 24.
**Freshman profile:** 1% of freshmen who took SAT scored 700 or over on math; 1% scored 600 or over on verbal, 7% scored 600 or over on math; 8% scored 500 or over on verbal, 30% scored 500 or over on math; 35% scored 400 or over on verbal, 62% scored 400 or over on math; 70% scored 300 or over on verbal, 90% scored 300 or over on math. Majority of accepted applicants took SAT.
**Undergraduate achievement:** 70% of fall 1992 freshmen returned for fall 1993 term. 3% of entering class graduated.
**Foreign students:** 360 students are from out of the country. Countries represented include China, India, Iran, Japan, Korea, and Taiwan; 60 in all.

**PROGRAMS OF STUDY. Degrees:** B.A., B.Mus., B.S.
**Majors:** African-American Studies, Anthropology, Art, Biochemistry, Biology, Business Administration, Business Education, Chemistry, Child Development, Communicative Disorders, Computer Science, Deaf Studies, Earth Science, Economics, Engineering, English, Environmental/Occupational Health/Safety, French, Geography, Geology, German, Health Sciences, History, Home Economics, Humanities, Journalism, Liberal Studies, Linguistic Studies, Mathematics, Mexican-American Studies, Music, Nursing, Philosophy, Physical Education, Physics, Political Science, Psychology, Radio/Television Broadcasting, Recreation, Religious Studies, Sociology, Spanish, Special Major, Speech Communication, Theatre Arts, Urban Studies.
**Distribution of degrees:** The majors with the highest enrollment are business administration, psychology, and liberal studies; French and linguistic studies have the lowest.
**Requirements:** General education requirement.
**Academic regulations:** Minimum 2.0 GPA must be maintained.
**Special:** Minors offered in many majors and in African studies, American Indian studies, Asian studies, classics, classical Greek/Roman civilization, English as a Second Language, gerontology, human sexuality, Italian, Jewish studies, leadership/human relations, pan-African studies, Russian, and women's studies. Interdisciplinary semesters. Individual study possible in courses listed in catalog but not offered in particular semester. Self-designed majors. Double majors. Dual degrees. Independent study. Pass/fail grading option. Internships. Graduate school at which undergraduates may take graduate-level courses. Preprofessional programs in law, medicine, veterinary science, pharmacy, dentistry, optometry, and physical therapy. Member of Consortium of the California State U, California Desert Studies Consortium, and Southern California Ocean Studies Consortium. Member of National Student Exchange (NSE). Teacher certification in early childhood, elementary, secondary, and special education. Study abroad in Australia, Brazil, Canada, Denmark, England, France, Germany, Israel, Italy, Japan, Mexico, New Zealand, Spain, Sweden, Taiwan, and Zimbabwe. ROTC and AFROTC at UCLA.
**Honors:** Honors program.
**Academic Assistance:** Remedial reading, writing, math, and study skills.

**STUDENT LIFE. Housing:** Students may live on or off campus. School-owned/operated apartments. 10% of students live in college housing.
**Social atmosphere:** According to the editor of the student newspaper, CSU Northridge is a commuter campus with most students working at least part-time. "On-campus activities are sparsely attended because of off-campus entertainment." Gathering spots on campus include the Roof eatery and the Student Union; Greek Week and Homecoming are popular annual events. Off campus, students attend political rallies and take advantage of the numerous cultural opportunities of the greater Los Angeles area. There is a "heavy Greek influence" on campus, and the numerous minority social groups, CISPES, the Associated Student Senate, and religious organizations are also active.
**Services and counseling/handicapped student services:** Placement services. Health service. Women's center. Day care. Counseling services for minority, military, veteran, and older students. Birth control, personal, and psychological counseling. Career and academic guidance services. Physically disabled student services. Learning disabled program/services. Notetaking services. Tape recorders. Tutors. Reader services for the blind.
**Campus organizations:** Undergraduate student government. Student newspaper (Daily Sundial, published four times/week). Literary magazine. Yearbook. Radio and TV stations. Marching band, choral groups, debating, departmental and service groups, special-interest groups, 180 organizations in all. 23 fraternities, no chapter houses; 13 sororities, no chapter houses.
**Religious organizations:** Numerous religious groups.
**Minority/foreign student organizations:** Numerous minority student groups.

**ATHLETICS. Physical education requirements:** None.
**Intercollegiate competition:** 2% of students participate. Baseball (M), basketball (M,W), cross-country (M,W), diving (M,W), football (M), golf (M), soccer (M), softball (W), swimming (M,W), tennis (W), track (indoor) (M,W), track (outdoor) (M,W), track and field (indoor) (M,W), track and field (outdoor) (M,W), volleyball (M,W). Member of Mountain Pacific Conference, NCAA Division I, NCAA Division I-AA for football, Pacific Collegiate Conference, Western Athletic Conference, Western Football Conference.
**Intramural and club sports:** Intramural badminton, basketball, eightball, flag football, foosball, grass volleyball, racquetball, soccer, softball, swimming, table tennis, tennis, track and field, ultimate frisbee, volleyball. Men's club Alpine skiing, bowling, cheerleading, cycling, martial arts, ultimate frisbee, water skiing. Women's club Alpine skiing, bowling, cheerleading, cycling, martial arts, soccer, ultimate frisbee, water skiing.

**ADMISSIONS. Academic basis for candidate selection** (in order of priority): Secondary school record, standardized test scores.

**Requirements:** Graduation from secondary school is required; GED is accepted. 15 units and the following program of study are required: 4 units of English, 3 units of math, 1 unit of lab science, 2 units of foreign language, 1 unit of history, 4 units of electives. Electives should include 1 unit of visual/performing arts. Minimum grade of "C" in listed secondary school courses and minimum eligibility index of 2800 for SAT (694 for ACT) required of in-state applicants; minimum eligibility index of 3402 for SAT (842 for ACT) required of out-of-state applicants. In-state applicants with minimum 3.0 GPA and out-of-state applicants with minimum 3.6 GPA are eligible regardless of test scores. Additional requirements for business, computer science, engineering, and physical therapy program applicants. EOP for applicants not normally admissible. SAT or ACT is required. Campus visit recommended. Off-campus interviews available with an admissions representative.
**Procedure:** Take SAT or ACT by December of 12th year. Suggest filing application by November 30; no deadline. Notification of admission on rolling basis. No set date by which applicants must accept offer. $600 room deposit, $100 of which is refundable. Freshmen accepted for terms other than fall.
**Special programs:** Credit and/or placement may be granted through CEEB Advanced Placement exams for scores of 3 or higher. Credit and/or placement may be granted through CLEP general and subject exams. Credit may be granted through military experience. Credit and placement may be granted through DANTES and challenge exams. Early decision program. Early entrance/early admission program. Concurrent enrollment program.
**Transfer students:** Transfer students accepted for terms other than fall. In fall 1993, 60% of all new students were transfers into all classes. 7,822 transfer applications were received, 5,789 were accepted. Application deadline is November 30 for fall; August 31 for spring. Minimum 2.0 GPA required of in-state applicants; 2.4 GPA of out-of-state applicants. Lowest course grade accepted is "D." Maximum number of transferable credits is 70 semester hours. At least 30 semester hours must be completed at the university to receive degree.
**Admissions contact:** Lorraine Newlon, M.B.A., Director of Admissions. 818 885-3700.

**FINANCIAL AID. Available aid:** Pell grants, SEOG, state scholarships and grants, school scholarships and grants, private scholarships and grants, academic merit scholarships, and athletic scholarships. EOP. Perkins Loans (NDSL), PLUS, Stafford Loans (GSL), school loans, and SLS.
**Financial aid statistics:** 2% of aid is not need-based. In 1993-94, 50% of all undergraduate applicants received aid; 50% of freshman applicants.
**Supporting data/closing dates:** School's own aid application: Priority filing date is March 2. State aid form: Priority filing date is March 2; accepted on rolling basis. Notification of awards on rolling basis.
**Financial aid contact:** Leon King, Th.M., Director of Financial Aid. 818 885-2374.

**STUDENT EMPLOYMENT.** College Work/Study Program. Institutional employment. Students may expect to earn an average of $2,500 during school year. Off-campus part-time employment opportunities rated "good."

**COMPUTER FACILITIES.** 1,700 IBM/IBM-compatible, Macintosh/Apple, and RISC-/UNIX-based microcomputers; 400 are networked. Students may access AT&T, Digital, IBM minicomputer/mainframe systems, Internet. Client/LAN operating systems include Apple/Macintosh. Computer languages and software packages include COBOL, FORTRAN, Pascal; statistical, data management packages. Computer facilities are available to all students.
**Fees:** None.
**Hours:** 24 hours.

**GRADUATE CAREER DATA.** 70% of graduates choose careers in business and industry.

# California State University, Sacramento

**Sacramento, CA 95819** **916 278-6011**

**1994-95 Costs.** Tuition: None (state residents), $7,380 (out-of-state). Room & board: $4,600. Fees, books, misc. academic expenses (school's estimate): $2,550.
**Enrollment.** Undergraduates: 6,411 men, 7,250 women (full-time). Freshman class: 4,348 applicants, 3,026 accepted, 1,286 enrolled. Graduate enrollment: 1,688 men, 2,952 women.
**Test score averages/ranges.** Average SAT scores: 408 verbal, 476 math. Average ACT scores: 19 composite.
**Faculty.** 790 full-time; 332 part-time. 80% of faculty holds highest degree in specific field. Student/faculty ratio: 21 to 1.
**Selectivity rating.** Less competitive.

**PROFILE.** California State at Sacramento, founded in 1947, is a public, comprehensive university. Its 288-acre campus is located on the eastern edge of Sacramento, along the American River.

**Accreditation:** WASC. Professionally accredited by the Accreditation Board for Engineering and Technology, the American Assembly of Collegiate Schools of Business, the National Association of Schools of Art and Design, the National Association of Schools of Music, the National Council for Accreditation of Teacher Education, the National League for Nursing.
**Religious orientation:** California State University, Sacramento is nonsectarian; no religious requirements.
**Library:** Collections totaling over 916,408 volumes, 5,666 periodical subscriptions, and 1,400,000 microform items.
**Special facilities/museums:** Center for community study and service, engineering/computer science building.
**Athletic facilities:** Gymnasiums, stadium, basketball, racquetball, and tennis courts, weight and wrestling rooms, baseball, intramural, practice, soccer, and softball fields, archery range, swimming pool, diving well, track.

**STUDENT BODY. Undergraduate profile:** 99% are state residents; 70% are transfers. 13% Asian-American, 6% Black, 11% Hispanic, 1% Native American, 57% White, 12% Other. Average age of undergraduates is 24.
**Freshman profile:** 1% of freshmen who took SAT scored 700 or over on math; 3% scored 600 or over on verbal, 12% scored 600 or over on math; 18% scored 500 or over on verbal, 44% scored 500 or over on math; 56% scored 400 or over on verbal, 78% scored 400 or over on math; 91% scored 300 or over on verbal, 95% scored 300 or over on math. 95% of accepted applicants took SAT; 5% took ACT.
**Undergraduate achievement:** 75% of fall 1992 freshmen returned for fall 1993 term. 10% of entering class graduated.
**Foreign students:** 430 students are from out of the country. Countries represented include India, Indonesia, Japan, Malaysia, Pakistan, and Taiwan; 100 in all.

**PROGRAMS OF STUDY. Degrees:** B.A., B.Mus., B.S.
**Majors:** Anthropology, Art, Biological Sciences, Business Administration, Chemistry, Child Development, Civil Engineering, Communications Studies, Computer Engineering, Computer Science, Criminal Justice, Drama, Economics, Electrical/Electronic Engineering, Engineering Technology, English, Environmental Studies, Ethnic Studies, Forensic Science, French, Geography, Geology, German, Government, Government/Journalism, Health/Safety Studies, History, Home Economics, Humanities, Interior Design, Journalism, Liberal Studies, Mathematics, Mechanical Engineering, Music, Nursing, Philosophy, Physical Education, Physical Science, Physics, Psychology, Recreation Administration, Social Science, Social Work, Sociology, Spanish, Special Major, Speech Pathology/Audiology.
**Distribution of degrees:** The majors with the highest enrollment are business administration, liberal studies, and psychology; German and physical science have the lowest.
**Requirements:** General education requirement.
**Academic regulations:** Minimum 2.0 GPA must be maintained.
**Special:** Minors offered in most majors and in approximately 15 other fields. Self-designed majors. Double majors. Independent study. Pass/fail grading option. Internships. Cooperative education programs. Graduate school at which undergraduates may take graduate-level courses. Preprofessional programs in law and medicine. Member of the Capital Education Consortium. Overseas study. Teacher certification in early childhood, elementary, secondary, special education, and bilingual/bicultural education. Certification in specific subject areas. Exchange programs and other study-abroad opportunities in numerous countries. ROTC and AFROTC.
**Honors:** Phi Beta Kappa. Honor societies.
**Academic Assistance:** Remedial reading, writing, math, and study skills. Nonremedial tutoring.

**STUDENT LIFE. Housing:** Students may live on or off campus. Coed, women's, and men's dorms. 4% of students live in college housing.
**Social atmosphere:** According to the editor of the student newspaper, "Sacramento is not a very hip city," but students frequent its bar scene and hang out at coffeehouses, record stores, and movies. "The campus seems to be very segregated and each group holds its own functions and hangs out in different areas. We have Greeks, Asian clubs, black fraternities and sororities, etc. But, no one set group dominates social life." In addition, campus life is influenced by the fact that CSU-S is a commuter campus, with many students over age 25. Some of the popular campus events are the Causeway Classic football game versus arch-rival UC Davis, the Greek Sing, and the New American Music Festival; getting away to San Francisco or Lake Tahoe is also popular.
**Services and counseling/handicapped student services:** Placement services. Health service. Women's center. Day care. Counseling services for minority, military, veteran, and older students. Personal and psychological counseling. Career and academic guidance services. Physically disabled student services. Learning disabled program/services. Notetaking services. Tape recorders. Tutors. Reader services for the blind.
**Campus organizations:** Undergraduate student government. Student newspaper (Hornet, published twice/week). Literary magazine. Radio and TV stations. Chorus, orchestra, bands, forensic team, 250 organizations in all. 20 fraternities, no chapter houses; 13 sororities, no chapter houses.
**Religious organizations:** Campus Crusade for Christ, Fellowship of Christian Athletes, Intervarsity Christian Fellowship.
**Minority/foreign student organizations:** Black and Mexican-American groups, Minority Engineering Program, multicultural center, many ethnic/cultural student groups. Vietnamese and many foreign student other groups.

**ATHLETICS. Physical education requirements:** None.
**Intercollegiate competition:** 14% of students participate. Baseball (M), basketball (M,W), cross-country (M,W), football (M), golf (M), gymnastics (W), soccer (M), softball (W), tennis (M,W), track and field (indoor) (M,W), track and field (outdoor) (M,W), volleyball (W). Member of Big West, Mountain Pacific Sports Federation, NCAA Division I, NCAA Division I–AA for football, Western Athletic Conference.
**Intramural and club sports:** 38% of students participate. Intramural basketball, bowling, crew, cycling, flag football, racquetball, rugby, soccer, softball, ultimate frisbee, volleyball, water skiing. Men's club volleyball.

**ADMISSIONS. Academic basis for candidate selection** (in order of priority): Secondary school record, standardized test scores.
**Requirements:** Graduation from secondary school is required; GED is accepted. 15 units and the following program of study are required: 4 units of English, 3 units of math, 1 unit of lab science, 2 units of foreign language, 1 unit of history, 4 units of academic electives. Electives should include 1 unit of visual/performing arts. Minimum grade of "C" in listed secondary school courses and minimum eligibility index of 2800 for SAT (694 for ACT) and class rank in top third required of in-state applicants; minimum eligibility index of 3402 for SAT (842 for ACT) required of out-of-state applicants. In-state applicants with minimum 3.0 GPA and out-of-state applicants with minimum 3.6 GPA are eligible regardless of test scores. 3-1/2 units of math and 1 unit of chemistry and/or physics recommended of engineering, math, and science program applicants. EOP for applicants not normally admissible. SAT or ACT is required. Off-campus interviews available with an admissions representative.
**Procedure:** Take SAT or ACT by January of 12th year. Suggest filing application by November 30; no deadline. Notification of admission on rolling basis. No set date by which applicants must accept offer. Freshmen accepted for terms other than fall.

**Special programs:** Credit and/or placement may be granted through CEEB Advanced Placement exams for scores of 3 or higher. Credit may be granted through CLEP general and subject exams, DANTES exams, and military experience. Credit and placement may be granted through challenge exams. Early decision program. In fall 1993, 2,200 applied for early decision and 2,000 were accepted. Deadline for applying for early decision is November 30. Concurrent enrollment program.
**Transfer students:** Transfer students accepted for terms other than fall. In fall 1993, 70% of all new students were transfers into all classes. 6,797 transfer applications were received, 4,798 were accepted. Application deadline is November 30 for fall; August 31 for spring. Minimum 2.0 GPA required. Lowest course grade accepted is "D-." Maximum number of transferable credits is 70 semester hours. At least 30 semester hours must be completed at the university to receive degree.
**Admissions contact:** Larry Glasmire, Director of Admissions and Records. 916 278-3901, 800 722-4748.

**FINANCIAL AID. Available aid:** Pell grants, SEOG, state grants, school scholarships, ROTC scholarships, academic merit scholarships, and athletic scholarships. Perkins Loans (NDSL), PLUS, Stafford Loans (GSL), NSL, school loans, and SLS.
**Financial aid statistics:** In 1993-94, 24% of all undergraduate applicants received aid.
**Supporting data/closing dates:** FAFSA: Priority filing date is March 2; accepted on rolling basis. Notification of awards on rolling basis.
**Financial aid contact:** Starla Harris, M.A., Director of Financial Aid. 916 278-6554.

**STUDENT EMPLOYMENT.** College Work/Study Program. Institutional employment. Off-campus part-time employment opportunities rated "good."

**COMPUTER FACILITIES.** 400 IBM/IBM-compatible and Macintosh/Apple microcomputers. Students may access AT&T, CDC Cyber, Digital, IBM minicomputer/mainframe systems, Internet. Residence halls may be equipped with stand-alone microcomputers, networked terminals. Client/LAN operating systems include Apple/Macintosh, DOS, UNIX/XENIX/AIX, Windows NT, Banyan, LocalTalk/AppleTalk, Novell. Computer languages and software packages include BASIC, COBOL, Pascal, RPG. Computer facilities are available to all students.
**Fees:** None.

## California State University, San Bernardino

**San Bernardino, CA 92407-2397 — 714 880-5000**

**1993-94 Costs.** Tuition: None (state residents), $5,132 (out-of-state). Room & board: $3,962-$4,913.
**Enrollment.** Freshman class: 787 enrolled. Graduate enrollment: 3,291.
**Test score averages/ranges.** N/A.
**Faculty.** 350 full-time; 100 part-time. Student/faculty ratio: 20 to 1.
**Selectivity rating.** N/A.

**PROFILE.** California State at San Bernardino, founded in 1962, is a public university. Programs are offered through the Schools of Business and Public Administration, Humanities, Natural Sciences, and Social and Behavioral Sciences. Its 430-acre campus is located 55 miles east of Los Angeles.

**Accreditation:** WASC. Professionally accredited by the National Association of Schools of Art and Design, the National League for Nursing.
**Religious orientation:** California State University, San Bernardino is nonsectarian; no religious requirements.
**Library:** Collections totaling over 525,000 volumes, and 3,200 periodical subscriptions.
**Special facilities/museums:** Simulation labs, electronic music studios, language lab, desert studies center.
**Athletic facilities:** Gymnasium, swimming pool, soccer and softball fields, running trails.

**STUDENT BODY. Undergraduate profile:** 3% Asian-American, 7% Black, 12% Hispanic, 2% Native American, 75% White, 1% Other.
**Foreign students:** Countries represented include India, Indonesia, Japan, Saudi Arabia, and Taiwan.

**PROGRAMS OF STUDY. Degrees:** B.A., B.S., B.Voc.Ed.
**Majors:** Accounting, Administration, Administrative Data Processing, American Studies, Anthropology, Art, Biology, Business Economics, Chemistry, Communication, Computer Science, Criminal Justice, Economics, English, Environmental Studies, Finance, Foods/Nutrition, French, Geography, Health Science, History, Human Development, Human Services, Humanities, Industrial Technology, Information Management, Internal Auditing, International Business, Liberal Studies, Management, Management Accounting, Management Science, Marketing, Mathematics, Music, Nursing, Philosophy, Physical Education, Physics, Political Science, Psychology, Public Accounting, Public Administration, Small Business Management, Social Sciences, Sociology, Spanish, Special Major, Theatre Arts, Vocational Education.
**Distribution of degrees:** The majors with the highest enrollment are administration and liberal studies; philosophy, physics, and environmental studies have the lowest.
**Requirements:** General education requirement.
**Special:** National security studies program. Independent study. Internships. Cooperative education programs. Graduate school at which undergraduates may take graduate-level courses. Preprofessional programs in law, medicine, veterinary science, pharmacy, dentistry, and engineering. Teacher certification in elementary, secondary, special education, vo-tech, and bilingual/bicultural education. Study abroad in Brazil, Canada, Denmark, France, Germany, Israel, Italy, Japan, Mexico, New Zealand, Peru, Spain, Sweden, and Taiwan. ROTC. AFROTC at UCLA.
**Honors:** Honors program. Honor societies.
**Academic Assistance:** Remedial reading, writing, math, and study skills.

**STUDENT LIFE. Housing:** Students may live on or off campus. Coed, women's, and men's dorms. 3% of students live in college housing.
**Social atmosphere:** The student newspaper reports, "CSUSB is on the way to becoming a big school. Socially, things are better than they used to be, but we still have a long way to go. The Pub has a lot of good bands in the evening. Dorms have parties and so do the Greeks. Comedy nights are also popular." Influential student groups include the various Greek organizations and the Associated Students. Favorite off-campus gathering spots include Harry C's, the Red Onion, Celebrities, local movie theaters, and student parties.
**Services and counseling/handicapped student services:** Placement services. Health service. Women's center. Day care. Counseling services for minority and older students. Personal counseling. Career and academic guidance services. Physically disabled student services. Learning disabled program/services. Notetaking services.
**Campus organizations:** Undergraduate student government. Student newspaper (Chronicle, published once/week). Radio station. Choral group, drama group, outdoor leisure program, Student Union, student/faculty committees, academic, political, service, and special-interest groups, 45 organizations in all.
**Religious organizations:** Bahai Club, Baptist Student Ministry, Campus Crusade for Christ, Light Company, Newman Club, other religious groups.
**Minority/foreign student organizations:** Black Student Union, MEChA. International Student Association, Chinese, Indonesian, and Vietnamese groups.

**ATHLETICS. Physical education requirements:** Two semesters of physical education required.
**Intercollegiate competition:** 1% of students participate. Baseball (M), basketball (M,W), cheerleading (M,W), cross-country (M,W), golf (M), soccer (M,W), softball (W), swimming (M,W), tennis (M,W), water polo (M). Member of NCAA Division III.

**ADMISSIONS. Academic basis for candidate selection** (in order of priority): Secondary school record, standardized test scores, school's recommendation.
**Requirements:** Graduation from secondary school is required; GED is accepted. 13 units and the following program of study are required: 3 units of English, 2 units of math, 1 unit of lab science, 2 units of foreign language, 1 unit of social studies, 1 unit of history, 3 units of electives. Minimum grade of "C" in listed secondary school courses and minimum eligibility index of 3072 for SAT (741 for ACT) required of in-state applicants; minimum eligibility index of 3402 for SAT (822 for ACT) required of out-of-state applicants. In-state applicants with minimum 3.1 GPA and out-of-state applicants with minimum 3.6 GPA are eligible regardless of test scores. EOP for applicants not normally admissible. SAT or ACT is required. Campus visit recommended. No off-campus interviews.
**Procedure:** Take SAT or ACT by October of 12th year. Visit college for interview by December of 12th year. Suggest filing application by November 30. Application deadline is August 1. Notification of admission on rolling basis. No set date by which applicants must accept offer. Freshmen accepted for terms other than fall.
**Special programs:** Credit and/or placement may be granted through CEEB Advanced Placement exams for scores of 3 or higher. Credit may be granted through CLEP subject exams and challenge exams. Credit and placement may be granted through military experience. Early decision program. Deadline for applying for early decision is April 1. Early entrance/early admission program. Concurrent enrollment program.
**Transfer students:** Transfer students accepted for terms other than fall.
**Admissions contact:** Lydia Ortega, Director of Admissions. 714 880-5200.

**FINANCIAL AID. Available aid:** Pell grants, SEOG, state grants, private scholarships, and academic merit scholarships. Perkins Loans (NDSL), Stafford Loans (GSL), and SLS. Deferred payment plan.
**Supporting data/closing dates:** FAFSA/FAF/FFS: Priority filing date is March 2. State aid form: Priority filing date is March 2. Income tax forms: Priority filing date is April 15. Notification of awards begins May 1.
**Financial aid contact:** Ted Krug, M.A., Director of Financial Aid. 714 880-5220.

**STUDENT EMPLOYMENT.** College Work/Study Program. Institutional employment. 80% of full-time undergraduates work on campus during school year. Students may expect to earn an average of $4,100 during school year. Freshmen are discouraged from working during their first term. Off-campus part-time employment opportunities rated "good."

**COMPUTER FACILITIES.** 500 IBM/IBM-compatible and Macintosh/Apple microcomputers; 200 are networked. Students may access Digital, IBM minicomputer/mainframe systems, Internet. Computer languages and software packages include Assembly, BASIC, C, COBOL, dBASE, FORTRAN, Quattro Pro, WordPerfect. Computer facilities are available to all students.
**Fees:** None.

## California State University, Stanislaus

**Turlock, CA 95381 — 209 667-3122**

**1994-95 Costs.** Tuition: None (state residents), $2,952 (out-of-state). Room & board: $4,887. Fees, books, misc. academic expenses (school's estimate): $2,361.
**Enrollment.** Undergraduates: 1,433 men, 1,960 women (full-time). Freshman class: 1,042 applicants, 830 accepted, 461 enrolled. Graduate enrollment: 429 men, 854 women.
**Test score averages/ranges.** Average SAT scores: 400 verbal, 449 math.
**Faculty.** 187 full-time; 184 part-time. 87% of faculty holds highest degree in specific field. Student/faculty ratio: 18 to 1.
**Selectivity rating.** Competitive.

**PROFILE.** California State at Stanislaus is a public, comprehensive university. Founded as an upper-division college in 1957, it incorporated lower-division courses when it moved to the present campus in 1965. Its 230-acre campus is located midway between the San Francisco Bay area and the Sierra Nevada Mountains.

**Accreditation:** WASC. Professionally accredited by the Computing Sciences Accreditation Board, the National Association of Schools of Art and Design, the National Association of Schools of Music, the National Association of Schools of Public Affairs and Ad-

ministration, the National Association of Schools of Theatre, the National Council for Accreditation of Teacher Education, the National League for Nursing.
**Religious orientation:** California State University, Stanislaus is nonsectarian; no religious requirements.
**Library:** Collections totaling over 290,000 volumes, 4,000 periodical subscriptions, and 725,000 microform items.
**Special facilities/museums:** Marine sciences station, electron microscope.
**Athletic facilities:** Track, gymnasium, weight room, swimming pool, golf driving range, athletic fields.

**STUDENT BODY. Undergraduate profile:** 89% are state residents; 65% are transfers. 7.4% Asian-American, 3.5% Black, 16.4% Hispanic, 1.6% Native American, 65.5% White, 5.6% Other. Average age of undergraduates is 25.
**Freshman profile:** 60% of accepted applicants took SAT; 10% took ACT. 98% of freshmen come from public schools.
**Undergraduate achievement:** 80% of fall 1992 freshmen returned for fall 1993 term. 60% of entering class graduated. 60% of students who completed a degree program went on to graduate study within five years.
**Foreign students:** 67 students are from out of the country. Countries represented include Indonesia, Japan, Korea, and Taiwan; 30 in all.

**PROGRAMS OF STUDY. Degrees:** B.A., B.S., B.Voc.Ed.
**Majors:** Accounting, Anthropology, Applied Liberal Studies, Art, Art History, Biological Sciences, Business Administration, Chemistry, Child Development, Cognitive Studies, Computer Information Systems, Computer Science, Criminal Justice, Drama, Economics, English, Environmental Studies, Ethnic Studies, French, Geography, Geology, Gerontology, History, Interdepartmental Social Sciences, Liberal Studies, Marine Science, Mathematics, Modern Languages, Multidisciplinary Studies, Music, Nursing, Organizational Communications, Philosophy, Physical Education, Physical Sciences, Physics, Political Science, Psychology, Public Administration, Social Sciences, Sociology, Spanish, Teaching English to Speakers of Other Languages, Vocational Education, Zoology.
**Requirements:** General education requirement.
**Academic regulations:** Minimum 2.0 GPA must be maintained.
**Special:** Minors offered in some majors and in exceptional children/youth, German, interpersonal studies, journalism, microelectronics, Russian/Soviet studies, technology/change, and women's studies. Self-designed majors. Double majors. Independent study. Accelerated study. Pass/fail grading option. Internships. Cooperative education programs. Graduate school at which undergraduates may take graduate-level courses. Preprofessional programs in law, medicine, veterinary science, pharmacy, dentistry, optometry, medical technology, and physical therapy. Member of Consortium of the California State U and Higher Education of Central California Colleges (HECCC). CSU Visitors Status Exchange programs offered with all California St U campuses. Teacher certification in elementary, secondary, special education, and bilingual/bicultural education. Certification in specific subject areas. Study abroad in Australia, Brazil, Canada, Denmark, France, Germany, Israel, Italy, Japan, Mexico, New Zealand, Peru, Spain, Taiwan, the United Kingdom, and Zimbabwe.
**Honors:** Honors program.
**Academic Assistance:** Remedial reading, writing, math, and study skills. Nonremedial tutoring.

**STUDENT LIFE. Housing:** Coed dorms. School-owned/operated apartments. 5% of students live in college housing.
**Social atmosphere:** According to the editor of the student newspaper, the campus is "nice and quiet," but it could benefit from an infusion of energy. Sports, especially basketball, are popular, and athletes are influential. Students also enjoy campus events such as Warrior Day, the Spring Formal, and comedy shows and dances. On campus, students like to go to Mom's Pub and Grub. Off campus, they head for the Tree Frog and Pavillion nightclubs in Modesto.
**Services and counseling/handicapped student services:** Placement services. Health service. Day care. Counseling services for minority, military, veteran, and older students. Birth control, personal, and psychological counseling. Career and academic guidance services. Physically disabled student services. Learning disabled services. Notetaking services. Tape recorders. Tutors. Reader services for the blind.
**Campus organizations:** Undergraduate student government. Student newspaper (Signal). Literary magazine. Radio station. Orchestra, wind ensemble, string quartet, jazz ensemble, theatre group, debating, political, service, and special-interest groups, 58 organizations in all. Three fraternities, no chapter houses; two sororities, no chapter houses.
**Religious organizations:** Campus Ambassadors, Catholic Campus Community, Intervarsity Christian Fellowship.
**Minority/foreign student organizations:** Chicanos in Law, MEChA, Native American Club, UMOJA. World Student Association, Chinese, Hmong, and Vietnamese groups.

**ATHLETICS. Physical education requirements:** One semester of physical education required.
**Intercollegiate competition:** 5% of students participate. Baseball (M), basketball (M,W), cheerleading (M,W), cross-country (M,W), golf (M), soccer (M), softball (W), track and field (outdoor) (M,W), volleyball (W). Member of NCAA Division II, Northern California Athletic Conference.
**Intramural and club sports:** 10% of students participate. Intramural basketball, football, soccer, softball, volleyball. Men's club volleyball.

**ADMISSIONS. Academic basis for candidate selection** (in order of priority): Secondary school record, standardized test scores, school's recommendation.
**Nonacademic basis for candidate selection:** Character and personality, extracurricular participation, particular talent or ability, geographical distribution, and alumni/ae relationship are considered.
**Requirements:** Graduation from secondary school is required; GED is accepted. 15 units and the following program of study are required: 4 units of English, 3 units of math, 1 unit of lab science, 2 units of foreign language, 1 unit of history, 4 units of electives. Electives should include 1 unit of visual/performing arts. Minimum grade of "C" in listed secondary school courses and minimum eligibility index of 2800 for SAT (694 for ACT) required of in-state applicants; minimum eligibility index of 3402 for SAT (842 for ACT) required of out-of-state applicants. In-state applicants with minimum 3.0 GPA and out-of-state applicants with minimum 3.6 GPA may be exempt from submission of test scores. Audition required of music program applicants. R.N. required of nursing program applicants. EOP for applicants not normally admissible. Conditional admission possible for applicants not meeting standard requirements. California Veterans, Adult Re-entry Students SAT or ACT is required. Off-campus interviews available with admissions and alumni representatives.
**Procedure:** Take SAT or ACT by December of 12th year. Suggest filing application by November 1. Application deadline is August 1. Notification of admission on rolling basis. Reply is required before beginning of term. $50 refundable room deposit. Freshmen accepted for terms other than fall.
**Special programs:** Admission may be deferred one year. Credit and/or placement may be granted through CEEB Advanced Placement exams for scores of 3 or higher. Credit and/or placement may be granted through CLEP general and subject exams. Credit and placement may be granted through Regents College, ACT PEP, DANTES, and challenge exams and military experience. Early decision program. In fall 1993, 150 applied for early decision and 100 were accepted. Deadline for applying for early decision is November 30. Early entrance/early admission program. Concurrent enrollment program.
**Transfer students:** Transfer students accepted for terms other than fall. In fall 1993, 65% of all new students were transfers into all classes. 1,733 transfer applications were received, 1,504 were accepted. Application deadline is August 1 for fall; December 1 for spring. Minimum 2.0 GPA required of in-state applicants; 2.4 GPA of out-of-state applicants. Lowest course grade accepted is "D." Maximum number of transferable credits is 70 semester hours from a two-year school and 94 semester hours from a four-year school. At least 30 semester hours must be completed at the university to receive degree.
**Admissions contact:** Edward J. Aubert, M.B.A., Director of Enrollment Services. 209 667-3081.

**FINANCIAL AID. Available aid:** Pell grants, SEOG, state scholarships and grants, school scholarships, private scholarships, and academic merit scholarships. Perkins Loans (NDSL), PLUS, Stafford Loans (GSL), school loans, private loans, and SLS. Deferred payment plan.
**Financial aid statistics:** 10% of aid is not need-based. In 1993-94, 54% of all undergraduate applicants received aid.
**Supporting data/closing dates:** FAFSA: Priority filing date is March 2. FAF/FFS: Deadline is March 2. State aid form: Deadline is March 2. Income tax forms: Deadline is March 2. Notification of awards on rolling basis.
**Financial aid contact:** Joan Hillery, Director of Financial Aid. 209 667-3336.

**STUDENT EMPLOYMENT.** College Work/Study Program. Institutional employment. 6% of full-time undergraduates work on campus during school year. Students may expect to earn an average of $5,800 during school year. Off-campus part-time employment opportunities rated "good."

**COMPUTER FACILITIES.** 150 IBM/IBM-compatible and Macintosh/Apple microcomputers; all are networked. Students may access CDC Cyber, Digital, IBM, SUN minicomputer/mainframe systems, Internet. Residence halls may be equipped with standalone microcomputers, networked microcomputers, networked terminals, modems. Client/LAN operating systems include Apple/Macintosh, DOS, UNIX/XENIX/AIX, Windows NT, Banyan, LocalTalk/AppleTalk, Novell. Computer languages and software packages include BASIC, C, COBOL, CompuStat, dBASE, Excel, FORTRAN, Lotus 1-2-3, Microsoft Works, Pascal, PC Focus, Plato, SPSS, Word, and WordPerfect. Computer facilities are available to all students.
**Fees:** None.
**Hours:** During office hours, evenings, weekends, and by appointment.

# Chapman University

**Orange, CA 92666** **714 997-6815**

**1994-95 Costs.** Tuition: $17,153. Room & board: $5,896. Fees, books, misc. academic expenses (school's estimate): $1,025.
**Enrollment.** Undergraduates: 720 men, 942 women (full-time). Freshman class: 908 applicants, 739 accepted, 351 enrolled. Graduate enrollment: 331 men, 728 women.
**Test score averages/ranges.** Average SAT scores: 456 verbal, 501 math. Range of SAT scores of middle 50%: 400-500 verbal, 430-560 math. Average ACT scores: 22 English, 22 math, 22 composite. Range of ACT scores of middle 50%: 18-24 English, 17-24 math.
**Faculty.** 110 full-time; 147 part-time. 81% of faculty holds highest degree in specific field. Student/faculty ratio: 12 to 1.
**Selectivity rating.** Less competitive.

**PROFILE.** Chapman is a church-affiliated, liberal arts university. Founded in 1861, it gained university status in 1991. Its 32-acre campus is located in Orange, 30 miles southeast of Los Angeles.

**Accreditation:** WASC.
**Religious orientation:** Chapman University is affiliated with the Christian Church (Disciples of Christ); no religious requirements.
**Library:** Collections totaling over 155,000 volumes, 1,200 periodical subscriptions, and 300 microform items.
**Special facilities/museums:** Art gallery, TV studio.
**Athletic facilities:** Gymnasium, weight room, tennis courts, soccer/lacrosse field.

**STUDENT BODY. Undergraduate profile:** 50% are transfers. 9% Asian-American, 5% Black, 10% Hispanic, 1% Native American, 71% White, 4% Other. Average age of undergraduates is 22.
**Freshman profile:** 3% of freshmen who took SAT scored 700 or over on math; 5% scored 600 or over on verbal, 14% scored 600 or over on math; 27% scored 500 or over on verbal, 47% scored 500 or over on math; 75% scored 400 or over on verbal, 88% scored 400 or over on math; 98% scored 300 or over on verbal, 99% scored 300 or over on math. 83% of accepted applicants took SAT; 24% took ACT. 76% of freshmen come from public schools.
**Undergraduate achievement:** 68% of fall 1992 freshmen returned for fall 1993 term. 23% of entering class graduated.

**Foreign students:** 126 students are from out of the country. Countries represented include France, Indonesia, Japan, Korea, Taiwan and the United Kingdom; 33 in all.

**PROGRAMS OF STUDY. Degrees:** B.A., B.F.A., B.Mus., B.S.
**Majors:** Accounting, Applied Mathematics, Art, Biology, Business Administration, Chemistry, Communications, Composition, Computer Information Systems, Computer Science, Conducting, Criminal Justice, Economics, English, Environmental Science, Film/Television, Food Science/Nutrition, French, Health Science, History, Instrumental Performance, Legal Studies, Liberal Studies, Movement/Exercise Science, Music, Music Education/Instrumental, Music Education/Vocal, Natural Science, Peace Studies, Philosophy, Political Science, Psychology, Religion, Social Science, Sociology, Spanish, Theatre/Dance, Vocal Performance.
**Distribution of degrees:** The majors with the highest enrollment are communications, business administration, and liberal studies; chemistry, computer science, and French have the lowest.
**Requirements:** General education requirement.
**Academic regulations:** Minimum 2.0 GPA must be maintained.
**Special:** Minors offered. Associate's degrees offered. Self-designed majors. Double majors. Independent study. Pass/fail grading option. Internships. Cooperative education programs. Graduate school at which undergraduates may take graduate-level courses. Preprofessional programs in law, medicine, veterinary science, and dentistry. Washington Semester. Teacher certification in elementary, secondary, special education, and bilingual/bicultural education. Certification in specific subject areas. Exchange program abroad in England (King Alfred's Coll). Study abroad also in Australia, Austria, Denmark, France, Germany, Greece, Ireland, Israel, Italy, Japan, Kenya, Mexico, Russia, and Spain. ROTC and AFROTC at Loyola Marymount U.
**Honors:** Honors program. Honor societies.
**Academic Assistance:** Remedial reading, writing, math, and study skills. Nonremedial tutoring.

**STUDENT LIFE. Housing:** All freshmen and sophomores must live on campus unless living with family within a 20-mile radius. Coed dorms. School-owned/operated apartments. Off-campus school-owned housing. 41% of students live in college housing.
**Social atmosphere:** The student newspaper reports, "There's a place for everyone–many clubs and organizations. Since the school is so small, everyone pretty much knows everyone else. Greeks are very much an influence on student social life. ASB (the Associated Student Body) is also a big factor. Often, Greeks and ASB co-sponsor to create bigger and better events, including Greek dances and parties." Students like to gather at the ASB office, the Davis Apartment Complexes, the dorm lounges, Spoons, Islands, Norm's 24-hour Coffee Shop, and TGI Friday's.
**Services and counseling/handicapped student services:** Placement services. Health service. Day care. Counseling services for minority, military, veteran, and older students. Birth control, personal, and psychological counseling. Career and academic guidance services. Religious counseling. Physically disabled student services. Learning disabled services. Notetaking services. Tape recorders. Tutors. Reader services for the blind.
**Campus organizations:** Undergraduate student government. Student newspaper (Panther, published once/week). Literary magazine. Yearbook. Radio station. Concert choir, orchestra, ensembles, Habitat for Humanity, women's groups, environmental, political, and social groups, 50 organizations in all. Five fraternities, no chapter houses; four sororities, no chapter houses. 21% of men join a fraternity. 16% of women join a sorority.
**Religious organizations:** Disciples on Campus, Hillel, Newman Club.
**Minority/foreign student organizations:** Asian Student Union, Black Student Union, Chapman University Pride Association, Macondo. International Club, Korean Club.

**ATHLETICS. Physical education requirements:** Four semesters of physical education required.
**Intercollegiate competition:** 9% of students participate. Baseball (M), basketball (M,W), cross-country (M,W), football (M), golf (M,W), soccer (M,W), softball (W), swimming (W), tennis (M,W), track and field (outdoor) (W), volleyball (W), water polo (M). Member of NAIA, NCAA Division II.
**Intramural and club sports:** 14% of students participate. Intramural Alpine skiing, archery, badminton, baseball, basketball, billiards, bowling, golf, racquetball, relays, soccer, table tennis, tennis, ultimate frisbee, volleyball. Men's club lacrosse.

**ADMISSIONS. Academic basis for candidate selection** (in order of priority): Secondary school record, standardized test scores, essay, school's recommendation, class rank.
**Nonacademic basis for candidate selection:** Character and personality, extracurricular participation, and particular talent or ability are important.
**Requirements:** Graduation from secondary school is required; GED is accepted. 11 units and the following program of study are required: 2 units of English, 2 units of math, 2 units of science, 2 units of foreign language, 3 units of social studies. Minimum combined SAT score of 850 and minimum 2.5 GPA recommended. SAT or ACT is required. Campus visit and interview recommended. Off-campus interviews available with an admissions representative.
**Procedure:** Take SAT or ACT by fall of 12th year. Visit college for interview by March 1 of 12th year. Suggest filing application by March 1; no deadline. Notification of admission on rolling basis. Reply is required by June 1. $100 nonrefundable tuition deposit. $100 nonrefundable room deposit. Freshmen accepted for terms other than fall.
**Special programs:** Credit and/or placement may be granted through CEEB Advanced Placement exams for scores of 3 or higher. Credit and/or placement may be granted through CLEP general and subject exams. Placement may be granted through challenge exams. Credit and placement may be granted through military experience. Concurrent enrollment program.
**Transfer students:** Transfer students accepted for terms other than fall. In fall 1993, 50% of all new students were transfers into all classes. 584 transfer applications were received, 506 were accepted. Application deadline is March 1 for fall; December 15 for spring. Minimum 2.0 GPA required. Lowest course grade accepted is "D." Maximum number of transferable credits is 100 semester hours. At least 24 semester hours must be completed at the university to receive degree.
**Admissions contact:** Michael Drummy, Director of Admissions. 714 997-6711.

**FINANCIAL AID. Available aid:** Pell grants, SEOG, state scholarships, school scholarships and grants, private scholarships, and academic merit scholarships. Perkins Loans (NDSL), PLUS, Stafford Loans (GSL), school loans, and SLS. Knight Tuition Plans. Monthly payment plan.
**Financial aid statistics:** 33% of aid is not need-based. In 1993-94, 100% of all undergraduate applicants received aid; 100% of freshman applicants. Average amounts of aid awarded freshmen: Scholarships and grants, $11,600; loans, $3,400.
**Supporting data/closing dates:** FAFSA/FAF: Priority filing date is March 2; accepted on rolling basis. State aid form: Priority filing date is March 2. Income tax forms: Priority filing date is March 2; accepted on rolling basis. Notification of awards begins March 15.
**Financial aid contact:** Phyllis Bell-Coldiron, Director of Financial Aid. 714 997-6741.

**STUDENT EMPLOYMENT.** College Work/Study Program. Institutional employment. 39% of full-time undergraduates work on campus during school year. Students may expect to earn an average of $2,000 during school year. Off-campus part-time employment opportunities rated "excellent."

**COMPUTER FACILITIES.** 130 IBM/IBM-compatible and Macintosh/Apple microcomputers; 90 are networked. Students may access Digital, NCR minicomputer/mainframe systems, BITNET, Internet. Client/LAN operating systems include Apple/Macintosh, DOS, UNIX/XENIX/AIX, Novell. Computer languages and software packages include Ada, Adobe Illustrator, Adobe PhotoShop, APL, COBOL, FORTRAN, HyperCard, LISP, Lotus 1-2-3, Lotus for Windows, Microsoft Excel, Microsoft Windows, Microsoft Word, PageMaker, Prolog, SNOBOL, WordPerfect. Computer facilities are available to all students.
**Fees:** None.
**Hours:** 8 AM-11 PM (M-Th); 8 AM-5 PM (F); 10 AM-5 PM (Sa); 10 AM-10 PM (Su).

**GRADUATE CAREER DATA.** Highest graduate school enrollments: Chapman U. Companies and businesses that hire graduates: Big Six accounting firms, area companies, Orange County school districts.

**PROMINENT ALUMNI/AE.** George L. Argyros, businessman; Marjorie Laird Corter, judge; Bob Einstein, actor.

## Christian Heritage College

**El Cajon, CA 92019** **619 441-2200**

**1993-94 Costs.** Tuition: $8,000. Room & board: $4,000. Fees, books, misc. academic expenses (school's estimate): $350.
**Enrollment.** Undergraduates: 137 men, 139 women (full-time). Freshman class: 145 applicants, 110 accepted, 68 enrolled.
**Test score averages/ranges.** N/A.
**Faculty.** 22 full-time; 15 part-time. 48% of faculty holds doctoral degree. Student/faculty ratio: 14 to 1.
**Selectivity rating.** N/A.

**PROFILE.** Christian Heritage, founded in 1970, is a church-affiliated college offering programs in the liberal arts and in preprofessional areas. Its 30-acre campus is located two miles from downtown El Cajon and 20 miles from San Diego.

**Accreditation:** WASC.
**Religious orientation:** Christian Heritage College is a nondenominational Christian school; eight semesters of religion required.
**Library:** Collections totaling over 70,000 volumes, 350 periodical subscriptions, and 5,000 microform items.
**Special facilities/museums:** Institute for creation research.
**Athletic facilities:** Gymnasium, swimming pool, soccer field, tennis courts, athletic center.

**STUDENT BODY. Undergraduate profile:** 67% are state residents; 48% are transfers. 7% Asian-American, 8% Black, 5% Hispanic, 1% Native American, 79% White. Average age of undergraduates is 21.
**Freshman profile:** 95% of accepted applicants took SAT; 5% took ACT. 63% of freshmen come from public schools.
**Undergraduate achievement:** 60% of fall 1991 freshmen returned for fall 1992 term. 20% of entering class graduated. 30% of students who completed a degree program immediately went on to graduate study.
**Foreign students:** 10 students are from out of the country. Countries represented include Canada, Hong Kong, Mexico, and Taiwan; five in all.

**PROGRAMS OF STUDY. Degrees:** B.A., B.S.
**Majors:** Aviation Technology, Biblical Studies, Business, Church Music, Counseling, English, History, Intercultural Studies, International Business, Liberal Studies, Pastoral Studies, Physical Education, Social Sciences, Women's Studies.
**Distribution of degrees:** The majors with the highest enrollment are business, counseling, and liberal studies; English, history, and physical education have the lowest.
**Requirements:** General education requirement.
**Special:** Minors offered in English and social sciences. Teacher certification in elementary and secondary education. ROTC, NROTC, and AFROTC at San Diego State U.
**Academic Assistance:** Remedial writing, math, and study skills. Nonremedial tutoring.

**ADMISSIONS. Academic basis for candidate selection** (in order of priority): Essay, school's recommendation, secondary school record, standardized test scores, class rank.
**Nonacademic basis for candidate selection:** Character and personality are important.
**Requirements:** Graduation from secondary school is required; GED is accepted. 15 units and the following program of study are recommended: 4 units of English, 3 units of math, 3 units of science, 2 units of foreign language, 3 units of social studies. Minimum combined SAT score of 700 and minimum 2.5 GPA required. SAT is required; ACT may be substituted. Campus visit and interview recommended. Off-campus interviews available with an admissions representative.
**Procedure:** Take SAT or ACT by June 1 of 12th year. Suggest filing application by June 1. Application deadline is August 1. Notification of admission on rolling basis. No set date by which applicants must accept offer. $100 nonrefundable tuition deposit. Freshmen accepted for terms other than fall.

**Special programs:** Admission may be deferred one year. Credit may be granted through CEEB Advanced Placement for scores of 3 or higher. Credit may be granted through CLEP general and subject exams, Regents College and DANTES exams. Credit and placement may be granted through ACT PEP and challenge exams.
**Transfer students:** Transfer students accepted for terms other than fall. In fall 1992, 48% of all new students were transfers into all classes. 130 transfer applications were received, 100 were accepted. Application deadline is August 1 for fall; January 1 for spring. Minimum 2.0 GPA recommended. Lowest course grade accepted is "C." Maximum number of transferable credits is 90 semester hours. At least 32 semester hours must be completed at the college to receive degree.
**Admissions contact:** Pam Daly, Director of Admissions. 800 676-2242.
**FINANCIAL AID. Available aid:** Pell grants, SEOG, state scholarships, school scholarships, private scholarships, ROTC scholarships, athletic scholarships, and aid for undergraduate foreign students. Perkins Loans (NDSL), PLUS, Stafford Loans (GSL), private loans, and SLS. Tuition Plan Inc. and deferred payment plan. Education Credit Corp.
**Financial aid statistics:** 15% of aid is not need-based. In 1992-93, 90% of all undergraduate applicants received aid; 90% of freshman applicants. Average amounts of aid awarded freshmen: Loans, $2,625.
**Supporting data/closing dates:** FAFSA/FAF: Accepted on rolling basis. State aid form: Accepted on rolling basis. Notification of awards on rolling basis.
**Financial aid contact:** Bryce Cline, Director of Financial Aid. 619 440-3043.

# Claremont McKenna College

**Claremont, CA 91711** **909 621-8000**

**1994-95 Costs.** Tuition: $17,000. Room: $2,850. Board: $3,160. Fees, books, misc. academic expenses (school's estimate): $640.
**Enrollment.** Undergraduates: 522 men, 365 women (full-time). Freshman class: 1,860 applicants, 767 accepted, 227 enrolled.
**Test score averages/ranges.** Average SAT scores: 600 verbal, 670 math. Range of SAT scores of middle 50%: 550-640 verbal, 610-710 math. Average ACT scores: 27 English, 28 math, 28 composite. Range of ACT scores of middle 50%: 26-29 English, 25-30 math.
**Faculty.** 92 full-time; 15 part-time. 99% of faculty holds doctoral degree. Student/faculty ratio: 8 to 1.
**Selectivity rating.** Most competitive.

**PROFILE.** Claremont McKenna, founded in 1946, is a private, liberal arts college. It is one of the Claremont Colleges, a group of five undergraduate colleges and one graduate school with adjoining campuses and shared facilities and services. Its 56-acre campus is located at the base of the San Gabriel Mountains, 35 miles east of Los Angeles.

**Accreditation:** WASC.
**Religious orientation:** Claremont McKenna College is nonsectarian; no religious requirements.
**Library:** Collections totaling over 1,795,552 volumes, 5,941 periodical subscriptions, and 1,076,864 microform items.
**Special facilities/museums:** Art galleries, Athenaeum complex, centers for Black and Chicano studies, computer lab, leadership lab, science center.
**Athletic facilities:** Field house, swimming pool, basketball and tennis courts, track, baseball, football, intramural, and soccer fields, gymnasium.
**STUDENT BODY. Undergraduate profile:** 63% are state residents; 16% are transfers. 19% Asian-American, 6% Black, 12% Hispanic, 1% Native American, 63% White. Average age of undergraduates is 20.
**Freshman profile:** 4% of freshmen who took SAT scored 700 or over on verbal, 37% scored 700 or over on math; 56% scored 600 or over on verbal, 82% scored 600 or over on math; 94% scored 500 or over on verbal, 98% scored 500 or over on math; 100% scored 400 or over on verbal, 100% scored 400 or over on math. 20% of freshmen who took ACT scored 30 or over on English, 33% scored 30 or over on math, 30% scored 30 or over on composite; 87% scored 24 or over on English, 79% scored 24 or over on math, 91% scored 24 or over on composite; 100% scored 18 or over on English, 100% scored 18 or over on math, 100% scored 18 or over on composite. 99% of accepted applicants took SAT; 26% took ACT. 70% of freshmen come from public schools.
**Undergraduate achievement:** 92% of fall 1992 freshmen returned for fall 1993 term. 81% of entering class graduated. 80% of students who completed a degree program went on to graduate study within five years.
**Foreign students:** 38 students are from out of the country. Countries represented include Hong Kong, Indonesia, Japan, Singapore, Switzerland and the United Kingdom; 20 in all.
**PROGRAMS OF STUDY. Degrees:** B.A.
**Majors:** American Studies, Asian Studies, Biology, Chemistry, Drama, Economics, Economics/Accounting, European Studies, Film Studies, Fine Arts, French, German, Government, History, International Relations, Latin American Studies, Literature, Management/Engineering, Mathematics, Modern Languages, Philosophy, Physics, Psychology, Religion, Spanish, Women's Studies.
**Distribution of degrees:** The majors with the highest enrollment are economics, government, and international relations; film studies has the lowest.
**Requirements:** General education requirement.
**Special:** Dual minors offered. Interdisciplinary programs offered in many areas. Courses offered in black studies, Greek, Italian, Japanese, Korean, Latin, Mexican-American studies, Russian, and written/oral expression. Special programs in politics/philosophy/economics, environment/economics/politics, and management/engineering. Self-designed majors. Double majors. Dual degrees. Independent study. Accelerated study. Pass/fail grading option. Internships. Preprofessional programs in law, medicine, veterinary science, and business. B.A./B.S.Eng. management/engineering program with UC Berkeley, Harvey Mudd Coll, Stanford U, and others. 3-3 B.A./LL.B. program with Columbia U. B.A./M.B.A. and B.A./M.I.S. programs with Claremont Graduate Sch. Member of consortium with other Claremont Colleges, including Claremont Graduate Sch; qualified undergraduates may take graduate-level courses. Washington Semester. Exchange programs with Colby Coll, Haverford Coll, and Spelman Coll. Study abroad in Australia, Austria, China, England, Egypt, France, Germany, Hong Kong, Israel, Italy, Japan, Nepal, Spain, Sweden, Zimbabwe, and 25 other countries. ROTC and AFROTC. NROTC at U of Southern California.
**Honors:** Phi Beta Kappa. Honors program.
**Academic Assistance:** Nonremedial tutoring.
**STUDENT LIFE. Housing:** Coed dorms. School-owned/operated apartments. Off-campus privately-owned housing. 96% of students live in college housing.
**Social atmosphere:** "We're a close-knit community with a small and intimate campus, yet are close to L.A. and other areas for entertainment and diversion," reports the student newspaper. "The proximity of the six [Claremont] colleges creates competition and broader, if limited, comraderie." On campus, students gather at The Hub (Emett Student Center). Popular annual events include Monte Carlo Night, the Talent Show, and Stag Soccer Nationals. The Student Activities Committee and Associated Students of CMC are influential groups on campus.
**Services and counseling/handicapped student services:** Placement services. Health service. Women's center. Counseling services for minority and military students. Birth control, personal, and psychological counseling. Career and academic guidance services. Religious counseling. Physically disabled student services. Tape recorders. Tutors. Reader services for the blind.
**Campus organizations:** Undergraduate student government. Student newspaper (CMC Forum and Collage, published once/week). Literary magazine. Yearbook. Radio station. Concert choir, orchestra, drama group, intercollegiate forensics, international relations group, Amnesty International, Model UN, community service program, ski club, 250 organizations in all.
**Religious organizations:** Christian Fellowship, Hillel-Jewish College Community, services for most major religions.
**Minority/foreign student organizations:** Office of Black Student Affairs, Chicano Studies Center, Hui Laule'a (Hawaiian Club), Asian Student Association, Korean Student Association. International Club, International Place.
**ATHLETICS. Physical education requirements:** Three semesters of physical education required.
**Intercollegiate competition:** 30% of students participate. Baseball (M), basketball (M,W), cross-country (M,W), diving (M,W), football (M), golf (M), lacrosse (W), rugby (M), soccer (M,W), softball (W), swimming (M,W), tennis (M,W), track (outdoor) (M,W), track and field (outdoor) (M,W), volleyball (W), water polo (M). Member of NCAA Division III, Southern California Intercollegiate Athletic Conference.
**Intramural and club sports:** 80% of students participate. Intramural Alpine skiing, badminton, bowling, climbing, cycling, fencing, fly fishing, lacrosse, rugby, sailing, volleyball, water polo. Men's club cycling, fencing, lacrosse, volleyball. Women's club water polo.
**ADMISSIONS. Academic basis for candidate selection** (in order of priority): Secondary school record, standardized test scores, school's recommendation, essay, class rank.
**Nonacademic basis for candidate selection:** Character and personality and extracurricular participation are emphasized. Particular talent or ability is important. Alumni/ae relationship is considered.
**Requirements:** Graduation from secondary school is recommended; GED is accepted. 12 units and the following program of study are required: 4 units of English, 3 units of math, 2 units of science, 2 units of foreign language, 1 unit of history. Electives from listed areas recommended. Full program of intellectually challenging work is more important than specific number or distribution of units. SAT or ACT is required. ACH recommended. Campus visit and interview recommended. Off-campus interviews available with an alumni representative.
**Procedure:** Take SAT or ACT by January of 12th year. Take ACH by January of 12th year. Visit college for interview by January of 12th year. Application deadline is February 1. Notification of admission by April 1. Reply is required by May 1. $200 nonrefundable tuition deposit. Freshmen accepted for fall term only.
**Special programs:** Admission may be deferred one year. Credit and/or placement may be granted through CEEB Advanced Placement exams for scores of 4 or higher. Credit may be granted through challenge exams. Early decision program. In fall 1993, 82 applied for early decision and 28 were accepted. Deadline for applying for early decision is November 15. Early entrance/early admission program.
**Transfer students:** Transfer students accepted for terms other than fall. In fall 1993, 16% of all new students were transfers into all classes. 168 transfer applications were received, 64 were accepted. Application deadline is April 15 for fall; November 1 for spring. Minimum 3.5 GPA recommended. Lowest course grade accepted is "C." Maximum number of transferable credits is the equivalent of two years of course work. At least two years of course work must be completed at the college to receive degree.
**Admissions contact:** Richard C. Vos, Vice President/Dean of Admission and Financial Aid. 909 621-8088.
**FINANCIAL AID. Available aid:** Pell grants, SEOG, state scholarships and grants, school scholarships and grants, private scholarships, ROTC scholarships, and academic merit scholarships. Perkins Loans (NDSL), PLUS, Stafford Loans (GSL), school loans, and SLS. Knight Tuition Plans and deferred payment plan. 10-month payment plan.
**Financial aid statistics:** 17% of aid is not need-based. In 1993-94, 89% of all undergraduate applicants received aid; 85% of freshman applicants. Average amounts of aid awarded freshmen: Scholarships and grants, $9,771; loans, $3,000.
**Supporting data/closing dates:** State aid form: Deadline is February 1. Income tax forms: Deadline is May 1. Notification of awards begins April 1.
**Financial aid contact:** Georgette R. DeVeres, Director of Financial Aid. 909 621-8356.
**STUDENT EMPLOYMENT.** College Work/Study Program. Institutional employment. 37% of full-time undergraduates work on campus during school year. Students may expect to earn an average of $900 during school year. Off-campus part-time employment opportunities rated "fair."
**COMPUTER FACILITIES.** 60 IBM/IBM-compatible and Macintosh/Apple microcomputers. Students may access Digital, Hewlett-Packard minicomputer/mainframe systems, BITNET, Internet. Client/LAN operating systems include Apple/Macintosh, DOS, OS/2, UNIX/XENIX/AIX, Windows NT, X-windows. Computer languages and software packages include APL, BASIC, Cricket, dBASE, DCL, Excel, FORTRAN, Graph, Har-

vard Graphics, LISP, Lotus 1-2-3, MacDraw, MacLink Plus, MacPaint, Mathematica, Microsoft Word, Pascal, Prolog, WordPerfect, and others. Computer facilities are available to all students.
**Fees:** None.
**Hours:** 20 hours/day.

**GRADUATE CAREER DATA.** Graduate school percentages: 25% enter law school. 7% enter medical school. 1% enter dental school. 25% enter graduate business programs. 15% enter graduate arts and sciences programs. Highest graduate school enrollments: UC Berkeley, UCLA, Columbia U, Harvard U, Northwestern U, Princeton U, U of Southern California, Stanford U, Yale U. 65% of graduates choose careers in business and industry. Companies and businesses that hire graduates: Deloitte & Touche, First Interstate Bank, KPMG Peat Marwick, Xerox.

**PROMINENT ALUMNI/AE.** Henry Kravis and George Roberts, partners/founders of Kohlberg, Kravis & Roberts; David Dreier, U.S. congressman; Paul Brickman, film director, *Risky Business;* Douglas Day Stewart, screenwriter, *Officer and a Gentleman.*

## Cogswell Polytechnical College

Cupertino, CA 95014 — 408 252-5550

**1993-94 Costs.** Tuition: $6,600. Housing: None. Fees, books, misc. academic expenses (school's estimate): $700.
**Enrollment.** Undergraduates: 146 men, 19 women (full-time). Freshman class: 140 applicants, 125 accepted, 98 enrolled.
**Test score averages/ranges.** N/A.
**Faculty.** 12 full-time; 36 part-time. 33% of faculty holds doctoral degree. Student/faculty ratio: 9 to 1.
**Selectivity rating.** N/A.

**PROFILE.** Cogswell, founded in 1887, is a private college of technology. Its campus is located in the city of Cupertino, four miles from San Jose.

**Accreditation:** WASC. Professionally accredited by the Accreditation Board for Engineering and Technology.
**Religious orientation:** Cogswell Polytechnical College is nonsectarian; no religious requirements.
**Library:** Collections totaling over 1,200 volumes, 125 periodical subscriptions and 300 microform items.

**STUDENT BODY. Undergraduate profile:** 50% are state residents; 60% are transfers. 18% Asian-American, 12% Black, 10% Hispanic, 60% White. Average age of undergraduates is 28.
**Freshman profile:** 80% of freshmen come from public schools.
**Undergraduate achievement:** 80% of fall 1992 freshmen returned for fall 1993 term. 20% of students who completed a degree program went on to graduate study within five years.
**Foreign students:** 15 students are from out of the country. Countries represented include Japan, Korea, Malaysia, Saudi Arabia, and Taiwan; 10 in all.

**PROGRAMS OF STUDY. Degrees:** B.A., B.S.
**Majors:** Computer Engineering Technology, Computer/Video Imaging, Electrical Engineering, Electronics Engineering Technology, Fire Administration Management, Fire Protection Technology, Manufacturing Engineering Technology, Mechanical Engineering Technology, Music Engineering Technology, Software Engineering.
**Distribution of degrees:** The majors with the highest enrollment are electronics engineering technology, computer/video imaging, and music engineering technology; mechanical engineering technology has the lowest.
**Requirements:** General education requirement.
**Academic regulations:** Minimum 2.0 GPA must be maintained.
**Special:** Associate's degrees offered. Double majors.
**Academic Assistance:** Nonremedial tutoring.

**ADMISSIONS. Academic basis for candidate selection** (in order of priority): School's recommendation, secondary school record, essay, standardized test scores, class rank.
**Nonacademic basis for candidate selection:** Character and personality and particular talent or ability are important.
**Requirements:** Graduation from secondary school is required; GED is accepted. No specific distribution of secondary school units required. Minimum SAT scores of 500 in both verbal and math and minimum 2.5 GPA recommended. SAT or ACT is recommended. Campus visit and interview recommended. No off-campus interviews.
**Procedure:** Take SAT or ACT by fall of 12th year. Visit college for interview by spring of 12th year. Notification of admission on rolling basis. Freshmen accepted for terms other than fall.
**Special programs:** Admission may be deferred one year. Credit may be granted through CEEB Advanced Placement for scores of 3 or higher. Credit may be granted through CLEP general and subject exams, Regents College, ACT PEP, DANTES, and challenge exams, and military and life experience. Early entrance/early admission program. Concurrent enrollment program.
**Transfer students:** Transfer students accepted for terms other than fall. In fall 1993, 60% of all new students were transfers into all classes. 75 transfer applications were received, 70 were accepted. Application deadline is rolling for fall; rolling for spring. Minimum 2.5 GPA recommended. Lowest course grade accepted is "C." Maximum number of transferable credits is 70 semester hours from a two-year school and 94 semester hours from a four-year school. At least 36 semester hours must be completed at the college to receive degree.
**Admissions contact:** Paul A. Schreivogel, Dean of Student Services. 408 252-5550, extension 239.

**FINANCIAL AID. Available aid:** Pell grants, SEOG, state grants, school scholarships, private scholarships, and academic merit scholarships. Perkins Loans (NDSL), PLUS, Stafford Loans (GSL), and SLS. Deferred payment plan. Tuition Assurance.
**Financial aid statistics:** In 1993-94, 10% of all freshman applicants received aid. Average amounts of aid awarded freshmen: Scholarships and grants, $3,000; loans, $1,500.
**Supporting data/closing dates:** FAFSA/FAF/FFS: Priority filing date is July 1; accepted on rolling basis. School's own aid application: Accepted on rolling basis. State aid form: Priority filing date is July 1; accepted on rolling basis. Income tax forms: Priority filing date is July 1; accepted on rolling basis. Notification of awards on rolling basis.
**Financial aid contact:** Barbara Bell, Director of Financial Aid. 408 252-5550, extension 248.

## College of Notre Dame

Belmont, CA 94002 — 415 593-1601

**1993-94 Costs.** Tuition: $11,750. Room & board: $5,700. Fees, books, misc. academic expenses (school's estimate): $612.
**Enrollment.** Undergraduates: 172 men, 266 women (full-time). Freshman class: 377 applicants, 317 accepted, 114 enrolled. Graduate enrollment: 173 men, 572 women.
**Test score averages/ranges.** Range of SAT scores of middle 50%: 360-470 verbal, 390-510 math. Range of ACT scores of middle 50%: 18-23 composite.
**Faculty.** 52 full-time; 57 part-time. 78% of faculty holds highest degree in specific field. Student/faculty ratio: 10 to 1.
**Selectivity rating.** Competitive.

**PROFILE.** The College of Notre Dame is a private, church-affiliated, liberal arts college. Founded as a women's college in 1868, it adopted coeducation in 1968. Its 80-acre campus, located in Belmont, is the former summer estate of William C. Ralston and is listed as a National Historic Landmark.

**Accreditation:** WASC. Professionally accredited by the National Association of Schools of Music, the National Council for Accreditation of Teacher Education.
**Religious orientation:** College of Notre Dame is affiliated with the Roman Catholic Church (Sisters of Notre Dame de Namur); six units of religion/theology required.
**Library:** Collections totaling over 97,471 volumes, 595 periodical subscriptions, and 15,513 microform items.
**Special facilities/museums:** Student art museum, professional art gallery, archives of modern Christian art, theatre, early learning center for Montessori credential training, on-campus elementary school.
**Athletic facilities:** Tennis courts, gymnasium, cross-country trail, soccer and softball fields, fitness/weight room.

**STUDENT BODY. Undergraduate profile:** 81% are state residents; 69% are transfers. 25% Asian-American, 6% Black, 13% Hispanic, 1% Native American, 38% White, 17% International. Average age of undergraduates is 22.
**Freshman profile:** 80% of accepted applicants took SAT; 22% took ACT. 77% of freshmen come from public schools.
**Undergraduate achievement:** 75% of fall 1991 freshmen returned for fall 1992 term. 53% of entering class graduated. 11% of students who completed a degree program immediately went on to graduate study.
**Foreign students:** 77 students are from out of the country. Countries represented include Indonesia, Japan, Korea, Philippines, Taiwan, and Thailand; 20 in all.

**PROGRAMS OF STUDY. Degrees:** B.A., B.F.A., B.Mus., B.S.
**Majors:** Art, Art/Advertising Graphics, Art/Interior Design, Behavioral Science, Biochemistry, Biology, Business Administration, Communications, Computer Science, English, French, History, Humanities, Latin American Studies, Liberal Studies, Liberal Studies/Elementary Education, Music, Philosophy, Physical Science, Political Science, Psychology, Religious Studies, Social Science, Sociology, Theatre Arts.
**Distribution of degrees:** The majors with the highest enrollment are business administration, liberal studies, and psychology; religious studies, history, and sociology have the lowest.
**Requirements:** General education requirement.
**Academic regulations:** Minimum 2.0 GPA must be maintained.
**Special:** Minors offered in all majors. Business administration major includes several concentrations. Self-designed majors. Double majors. Dual degrees. Independent study. Pass/fail grading option. Internships. Preprofessional programs in law, medicine, veterinary science, pharmacy, and dentistry. Exchange programs with Emmanuel Coll (Boston, Mass.) and Trinity Coll (Washington, D.C.). Teacher certification in early childhood, elementary, and secondary education. Certification in specific subject areas. Study abroad in France, Greece, Japan, Spain, the United Kingdom, and other countries. ROTC, NROTC, and AFROTC at UC Berkeley.
**Honors:** Honor societies.
**Academic Assistance:** Remedial reading, writing, math, and study skills. Nonremedial tutoring.

**ADMISSIONS. Academic basis for candidate selection** (in order of priority): Secondary school record, standardized test scores, essay, school's recommendation, class rank.
**Nonacademic basis for candidate selection:** Particular talent or ability is important. Character and personality, extracurricular participation, and alumni/ae relationship are considered.
**Requirements:** Graduation from secondary school is required; GED is accepted. 13 units and the following program of study are required: 4 units of English, 2 units of math, 1 unit of lab science, 2 units of foreign language, 2 units of social studies, 2 units of academic electives. Audition required of music program applicants. Conditional admission possible for applicants not meeting standard requirements. SAT is required; ACT may be substituted. PSAT is recommended. Campus visit recommended. No off-campus interviews.
**Procedure:** Take SAT or ACT by December of 12th year. Suggest filing application by March 2. Application deadline is June 1. Notification of admission on rolling basis. Reply is required by May 1 or within three weeks of acceptance. $200 nonrefundable tuition de-

posit. $150 room deposit, refundable until July 1. Freshmen accepted for terms other than fall.
**Special programs:** Admission may be deferred one year. Credit and/or placement may be granted through CEEB Advanced Placement exams for scores of 3 or higher. Credit and/or placement may be granted through CLEP general and subject exams. Credit and placement may be granted through ACT PEP, DANTES, and challenge exams, and military experience. Concurrent enrollment program.
**Transfer students:** Transfer students accepted for terms other than fall. In fall 1992, 69% of all new students were transfers into all classes. 415 transfer applications were received, 376 were accepted. Application deadline is August 1 for fall; December 1 for spring. Minimum 2.0 GPA required. Lowest course grade accepted is "C." Maximum number of transferable credits is 78 semester hours from a two-year school and 90 semester hours from a four-year school. At least 30 semester hours must be completed at the college to receive degree.
**Admissions contact:** Gregory Smith, Ph.D., Director of Admission. 415 508-3607.
**FINANCIAL AID. Available aid:** Pell grants, SEOG, state scholarships and grants, school scholarships and grants, private scholarships and grants, ROTC scholarships, and academic merit scholarships. Perkins Loans (NDSL), PLUS, Stafford Loans (GSL), private loans, and SLS. AMS.
**Financial aid statistics:** 10% of aid is not need-based. In 1992-93, 80% of all undergraduate applicants received aid; 87% of freshman applicants. Average amounts of aid awarded freshmen: Scholarships and grants, $7,900; loans, $2,938.
**Supporting data/closing dates:** FAFSA/FAF/FFS: Priority filing date is March 2; accepted on rolling basis. State aid form: Priority filing date is March 2; accepted on rolling basis. Income tax forms: Accepted on rolling basis. Notification of awards begins April 15.
**Financial aid contact:** Sunhoong Ow, M.S.W., Director of Financial Aid. 415 508-3509.

# Concordia University

**Irvine, CA 92715 — 714 854-8002**

**1994-95 Costs.** Tuition: $10,800. Room: $2,520. Board: $1,920. Fees, books, misc. academic expenses (school's estimate): $1,260.
**Enrollment.** Undergraduates: 252 men, 389 women (full-time). Freshman class: 688 applicants, 497 accepted, 144 enrolled. Graduate enrollment: 17 men, 24 women.
**Test score averages/ranges.** Average SAT scores: 420 verbal, 485 math. Average ACT scores: 22 composite.
**Faculty.** 39 full-time; 45 part-time. 65% of faculty holds doctoral degree. Student/faculty ratio: 18 to 1.
**Selectivity rating.** Less competitive.

**PROFILE.** Concordia is a church-affiliated university. Founded in 1972, its name changed from Christ College Irvine in 1993. Its 70-acre campus is located 50 miles south of Los Angeles, on a plateau overlooking Orange County.

**Accreditation:** WASC.
**Religious orientation:** Concordia University is affiliated with the Lutheran Church-Missouri Synod; four semesters of religion required.
**Library:** Collections totaling over 85,000 volumes, 630 periodical subscriptions, and 20,540 microform items.
**Athletic facilities:** Gymnasium, baseball, soccer, and softball fields, track, arena, badminton, basketball, tennis, volleyball, and sand volleyball courts, weight room.
**STUDENT BODY. Undergraduate profile:** 80% are state residents; 42% are transfers. 12% Asian-American, 3% Black, 7% Hispanic, 76% White, 2% Other. Average age of undergraduates is 21.
**Freshman profile:** 2% of freshmen who took SAT scored 700 or over on math; 3% scored 600 or over on verbal, 16% scored 600 or over on math; 25% scored 500 or over on verbal, 49% scored 500 or over on math; 62% scored 400 or over on verbal, 82% scored 400 or over on math; 90% scored 300 or over on verbal, 96% scored 300 or over on math. 85% of accepted applicants took SAT; 15% took ACT.
**Undergraduate achievement:** 81% of fall 1992 freshmen returned for fall 1993 term. 40% of entering class graduated. 28% of students who completed a degree program immediately went on to graduate study.
**Foreign students:** 73 students are from out of the country. Countries represented include Canada, Hong Kong, Japan, Korea, and Taiwan; 10 in all.
**PROGRAMS OF STUDY. Degrees:** B.A.
**Majors:** Behavioral Science, Biology, Business Administration, Early Childhood Education, English, Humanities, Liberal Studies, Mathematics, Music, Physical Education, Psychology, Religion, Religious Studies, Social Science/History.
**Distribution of degrees:** The majors with the highest enrollment are business administration, liberal studies, and behavioral science.
**Requirements:** General education requirement.
**Academic regulations:** Minimum 2.0 GPA must be maintained.
**Special:** Minors offered in some majors and in American studies, art, biblical languages, chemistry, communications, history, multicultural studies, sociology, theatre, and writing. Associate's degrees offered. Independent study. Internships. Cooperative education programs. Graduate school at which undergraduates may take graduate-level courses. Preprofessional programs in law, medicine, dentistry, and theology. Exchange programs with Concordia U System. Teacher certification in early childhood, elementary, and secondary education. Exchange program abroad in Japan (Notre Dame Sheishin U). Study abroad also in Mexico.
**Academic Assistance:** Remedial reading, writing, math, and study skills. Nonremedial tutoring.
**ADMISSIONS. Academic basis for candidate selection** (in order of priority): Secondary school record, class rank, school's recommendation, standardized test scores, essay.
**Nonacademic basis for candidate selection:** Character and personality are emphasized. Extracurricular participation and particular talent or ability are considered.
**Requirements:** Graduation from secondary school is required; GED is accepted. No specific distribution of secondary school units required. Minimum 2.6 GPA and rank in top half of secondary class required. Conditional admission possible for applicants not meeting standard requirements. SAT is required; ACT may be substituted. ACH recommended. Campus visit and interview recommended. Off-campus interviews available with an admissions representative.
**Procedure:** Take SAT or ACT by fall of 12th year. Visit college for interview by fall of 12th year. Suggest filing application by December 31; no deadline. Notification of admission on rolling basis. Reply is required by May 1. $100 nonrefundable tuition deposit. $100 refundable room deposit. Freshmen accepted for terms other than fall.
**Special programs:** Admission may be deferred one year. Credit and/or placement may be granted through CEEB Advanced Placement exams for scores of 3 or higher. Credit and/or placement may be granted through CLEP subject exams.
**Transfer students:** Transfer students accepted for terms other than fall. In fall 1993, 42% of all new students were transfers into all classes. 252 transfer applications were received, 175 were accepted. Application deadline is July 1 for Fall:, November 1 for winter; February 1 for spring. Minimum 2.0 GPA required. Lowest course grade accepted is "C." Maximum number of transferable credits is 144 quarter hours. At least 48 quarter hours must be completed at the university to receive degree.
**Admissions contact:** Stan Meyer, M.B.A., Dean of of Enrollment Services. 714 854-8002.
**FINANCIAL AID. Available aid:** Pell grants, SEOG, state grants, school scholarships and grants, private scholarships, academic merit scholarships, and athletic scholarships. PLUS, Stafford Loans (GSL), and SLS. FACTS.
**Financial aid statistics:** 25% of aid is not need-based. In 1993-94, 90% of all undergraduate applicants received aid; 90% of freshman applicants. Average amounts of aid awarded freshmen: Scholarships and grants, $3,500; loans, $2,625.
**Supporting data/closing dates:** FAFSA: Priority filing date is March 2. State aid form: Priority filing date is March 2; deadline is May 15. Income tax forms: Priority filing date is April 15. Institutional Application: Priority filing date is April 15.
**Financial aid contact:** Lonnie Lee, Director of Financial Aid. 714 854-8002.

# DeVry Institute of Technology

**Pomona, CA 91768 — 909 622-8866**

**1994-95 Costs.** Tuition: $5,962. Housing: None. Fees, books, misc. academic expenses (school's estimate): $580.
**Enrollment.** Undergraduates: 1,721 men, 441 women (full-time). Freshman class: 1,377 applicants, 1,264 accepted, 800 enrolled.
**Test score averages/ranges.** N/A.
**Faculty.** 49 full-time; 51 part-time. Student/faculty ratio: 32 to 1.
**Selectivity rating.** N/A.

**PROFILE.** DeVry/Los Angeles, founded in 1983, is a private institution specializing in electronics technology and computer information systems. It is a member of a network of technical institutes with eight campuses in the U.S. and two in Canada. Its campus is located in the City of Industry, a commercial and residential complex, 19 miles from downtown Los Angeles.

**Accreditation:** NCACS. Professionally accredited by the Accreditation Board for Engineering and Technology.
**Religious orientation:** DeVry Institute of Technology is nonsectarian; no religious requirements.
**Library:** Collections totaling over 6,000 volumes, 200 periodical subscriptions and 81 microform items.
**Special facilities/museums:** Electronics labs, computer lab.
**STUDENT BODY. Undergraduate profile:** 94% are state residents; 54% are transfers. 19% Asian-American, 12% Black, 30% Hispanic, 1% Native American, 37% White, 1% Other. Average age of undergraduates is 24.
**Undergraduate achievement:** 48% of fall 1992 freshmen returned for fall 1993 term. 39% of entering class graduated.
**Foreign students:** 57 students are from out of the country. Countries represented include India, Indonesia, South Korea, Taiwan, Thailand, and the Philippines; 26 in all.
**PROGRAMS OF STUDY. Degrees:** B.S.
**Majors:** Accounting, Business Operations, Computer Information Systems, Electronics Engineering Technology, Telecommunications Management.
**Distribution of degrees:** The majors with the highest enrollment are electronics engineering technology, telecommunications management, and business operations.
**Requirements:** General education requirement.
**Academic regulations:** Minimum 2.0 GPA must be maintained.
**Special:** Associate's degrees offered. Accelerated study. Cooperative education programs.
**Honors:** Honor societies.
**Academic Assistance:** Nonremedial tutoring.
**STUDENT LIFE. Housing:** Commuter campus; no student housing.
**Services and counseling/handicapped student services:** Placement services. Career and academic guidance services. Physically disabled student services. Notetaking services. Reader services for the blind.
**Campus organizations:** Undergraduate student government. Student newspaper (DeVry Times). Toastmasters, Associated Student Body, professional groups, 18 organizations in all.
**Minority/foreign student organizations:** Society of Hispanic Professional Engineers, National Society of Black Engineers, Black Student Union.
**ATHLETICS. Physical education requirements:** None.
**Intramural and club sports:** 5% of students participate. Intramural basketball, football, softball, volleyball. Men's club basketball, football, soccer, softball, tennis, volleyball.
**ADMISSIONS. Academic basis for candidate selection** (in order of priority): Standardized test scores.

**Requirements:** Graduation from secondary school is required; GED is accepted. No specific distribution of secondary school units required. Applicants not submitting SAT or ACT must pass DeVry entrance exam. SAT or ACT is recommended. Campus visit and interview required. Off-campus interviews available with an admissions representative.
**Procedure:** Notification of admission on rolling basis. Reply is required by registration. $75 tuition deposit, refundable until beginning of classes. Freshmen accepted for terms other than fall.
**Special programs:** Admission may be deferred one year. Credit may be granted through CLEP subject exams, DANTES, and challenge exams.
**Transfer students:** Transfer students accepted for terms other than fall. In fall 1993, 54% of all new students were transfers into all classes. Application deadline is rolling for fall; rolling for spring. Minimum 2.0 GPA required. Lowest course grade accepted is "C." Maximum number of transferable semester hours is half of total required for degree. At least half of total semester hours must be completed at institute to receive degree.
**Admissions contact:** Keith Paridy, M.B.A., Director of Admissions. 909 622-8866.

**FINANCIAL AID. Available aid:** Pell grants, SEOG, state scholarships and grants, and school scholarships. Perkins Loans (NDSL), PLUS, Stafford Loans (GSL), state loans, and SLS. EDUCARD Plan.
**Financial aid statistics:** In 1993-94, 81% of all undergraduate applicants received aid; 79% of freshman applicants.
**Supporting data/closing dates:** FAFSA: Accepted on rolling basis. Notification of awards on rolling basis.
**Financial aid contact:** Lynn Taylor, Director of Financial Aid.

**STUDENT EMPLOYMENT.** College Work/Study Program. Institutional employment. 8% of full-time undergraduates work on campus during school year. Students may expect to earn an average of $5,000 during school year. Off-campus part-time employment opportunities rated "good."

**COMPUTER FACILITIES.** 122 IBM/IBM-compatible microcomputers; 120 are networked. Students may access IBM minicomputer/mainframe systems. Client/LAN operating systems include DOS, OS/2, UNIX/XENIX/AIX, Novell. 25 major computer languages and software packages available. Computer facilities are available to all students.
**Fees:** Computer fee is included in tuition/fees.

**GRADUATE CAREER DATA.** Companies and businesses that hire graduates: Advanced Micro Devices, Hughes Space and Communication, Northrop, Thermco Systems.

# Dominican College of San Rafael

**San Rafael, CA 94901-8008 — 415 457-4440**

**1994-95 Costs.** Tuition: $12,790. Room & board: $6,100. Fees, books, misc. academic expenses (school's estimate): $875.
**Enrollment.** Undergraduates: 150 men, 498 women (full-time). Freshman class: 213 applicants, 173 accepted, 75 enrolled. Graduate enrollment: 80 men, 220 women.
**Test score averages/ranges.** Average SAT scores: 432 verbal, 452 math. Range of SAT scores of middle 50%: 380-470 verbal, 390-520 math.
**Faculty.** 36 full-time; 74 part-time. 42% of faculty holds doctoral degree. Student/faculty ratio: 12 to 1.
**Selectivity rating.** Less competitive.

**PROFILE.** Dominican is a church-affiliated, liberal arts college. Founded as a women's college in 1890, it adopted coeducation in 1971. Its 80-acre campus is located in Marin County, half an hour from San Francisco.

**Accreditation:** WASC. Professionally accredited by the National League for Nursing.
**Religious orientation:** Dominican College of San Rafael is affiliated with the Roman Catholic Church; six units of religion/theology required.
**Library:** Collections totaling over 92,088 volumes, 295 periodical subscriptions, and 2,284 microform items.
**Special facilities/museums:** Art gallery, school for disabled children, natural history museum, movement lab.
**Athletic facilities:** Gymnasium, swimming pool, tennis courts, weight room, soccer field, fitness center.

**STUDENT BODY. Undergraduate profile:** 97% are state residents; 47% are transfers. 10% Asian-American, 6% Black, 10% Hispanic, 1% Native American, 73% White. Average age of undergraduates is 30.
**Freshman profile:** 5% of freshmen who took SAT scored 600 or over on verbal, 5% scored 600 or over on math; 22% scored 500 or over on verbal, 32% scored 500 or over on math; 72% scored 400 or over on verbal, 72% scored 400 or over on math; 94% scored 300 or over on verbal, 95% scored 300 or over on math. 83% of accepted applicants took SAT; 8% took ACT. 50% of freshmen come from public schools.
**Undergraduate achievement:** 71% of fall 1992 freshmen returned for fall 1993 term. 29% of entering class graduated. 18% of students who completed a degree program went on to graduate study within one year.
**Foreign students:** 26 students are from out of the country. Countries represented include China, Japan, Switzerland, Taiwan, Thailand, and the Philippines; 11 in all.

**PROGRAMS OF STUDY. Degrees:** B.A., B.F.A., B.Mus., B.S.
**Majors:** Art, Art History, Biology, Business Administration, English, English Literature/Writing Emphasis, History, Humanities, Interdisciplinary Studies, International Business, International Studies, Liberal Studies, Mathematics, Music, Nursing, Political Science, Psychology, Religious Studies.
**Distribution of degrees:** The majors with the highest enrollment are nursing, psychology, and international studies; music, biology, and humanities have the lowest.
**Requirements:** General education requirement.
**Academic regulations:** Minimum 2.0 GPA must be maintained.
**Special:** Minors offered in many majors and in foreign language and area studies. Self-designed majors. Double majors. Dual degrees. Independent study. Pass/fail grading option. Internships. Graduate school at which undergraduates may take graduate-level courses. Preprofessional programs in law, medicine, veterinary science, pharmacy, and dentistry. Exchange programs with Aquinas Coll, Barry U, and St. Thomas Aquinas Coll. Teacher certification in elementary and secondary education. Study abroad possible. AFROTC at UC Berkeley.
**Honors:** Honors program. Honor societies.
**Academic Assistance:** Remedial writing, math, and study skills. Nonremedial tutoring.

**ADMISSIONS. Academic basis for candidate selection** (in order of priority): Secondary school record, standardized test scores, school's recommendation, class rank, essay.
**Nonacademic basis for candidate selection:** Extracurricular participation and particular talent or ability are emphasized. Character and personality are important. Geographical distribution is considered.
**Requirements:** Graduation from secondary school is recommended; GED is accepted. 16 units and the following program of study are required: 4 units of English, 2 units of math, 1 unit of lab science, 2 units of foreign language, 1 unit of history, 5 units of electives. Minimum combined SAT score of 800 and minimum 2.5 GPA required. Audition required of music program applicants. SAT is required; ACT may be substituted. Campus visit and interview recommended. Off-campus interviews available with admissions and alumni representatives.
**Procedure:** Take SAT or ACT by January 1 of 12th year. Visit college for interview by August 15 of 12th year. Suggest filing application by February 1. Application deadline is August 15. Notification of admission on rolling basis. Reply is required by September 1. $150 nonrefundable tuition deposit. $150 nonrefundable room deposit. Freshmen accepted for terms other than fall.
**Special programs:** Admission may be deferred one year. Credit and/or placement may be granted through CEEB Advanced Placement exams for scores of 4 or higher. Credit and/or placement may be granted through CLEP general and subject exams. Credit and placement may be granted through challenge exams and military and life experience. Early entrance/early admission program. Concurrent enrollment program.
**Transfer students:** Transfer students accepted for terms other than fall. In fall 1993, 47% of all new students were transfers into all classes. 292 transfer applications were received, 249 were accepted. Application deadline is August 15 for fall; January 1 for spring. Minimum 2.0 GPA required. Lowest course grade accepted is "C." Maximum number of transferable credits is 70 semester hours from a two-year school and 94 semester hours from a four-year school. At least 30 semester hours must be completed at the college to receive degree.
**Admissions contact:** Lydia Hull, Director of Admissions. 415 485-3204.

**FINANCIAL AID. Available aid:** Pell grants, SEOG, Federal Nursing Student Scholarships, state scholarships and grants, school scholarships and grants, private scholarships and grants, academic merit scholarships, and athletic scholarships. Perkins Loans (NDSL), PLUS, Stafford Loans (GSL), private loans, and SLS. Deferred payment plan. 12-month installment plan.
**Financial aid statistics:** 9% of aid is not need-based. In 1993-94, 100% of all undergraduate applicants received aid. Average amounts of aid awarded freshmen: Scholarships and grants, $5,940; loans, $2,363.
**Supporting data/closing dates:** FAFSA: Priority filing date is March 2. School's own aid application: Priority filing date is March 2. Income tax forms: Priority filing date is June 1; accepted on rolling basis. Notification of awards on rolling basis.
**Financial aid contact:** Jean Lavane, Director of Financial Aid. 415 485-3204.

# Fresno Pacific College

**Fresno, CA 93702 — 209 453-2000**

**1994-95 Costs.** Tuition: $9,900. Room & board: $3,670. Fees, books, misc. academic expenses (school's estimate): $750.
**Enrollment.** Undergraduates: 291 men, 426 women (full-time). Freshman class: 346 applicants, 274 accepted, 146 enrolled. Graduate enrollment: 148 men, 530 women.
**Test score averages/ranges.** Average SAT scores: 477 verbal, 532 math. Average ACT scores: 20 composite.
**Faculty.** 40 full-time; 39 part-time. 55% of faculty holds doctoral degree. Student/faculty ratio: 15 to 1.
**Selectivity rating.** More competitive.

**PROFILE.** Fresno Pacific, founded in 1944, is a church-affiliated, liberal arts college. Programs are offered through the Divisions of Biblical and Religious Studies, Humanities, Natural Sciences and Mathematics, Social Sciences, and Education. Its 40-acre campus is located in Fresno.

**Accreditation:** WASC.
**Religious orientation:** Fresno Pacific College is affiliated with the Mennonite Brethren Church; four semesters of religion required.
**Library:** Collections totaling over 139,000 volumes, 900 periodical subscriptions, and 160,000 microform items.
**Special facilities/museums:** On-campus English language training institute, teacher center.
**Athletic facilities:** Gymnasium, swimming pool, weight room, racquetball, and tennis courts, soccer field.

**STUDENT BODY. Undergraduate profile:** 95% are state residents; 59% are transfers. 4% Asian-American, 3% Black, 14% Hispanic, 64% White, 15% Other.
**Freshman profile:** 88% of accepted applicants took SAT.
**Undergraduate achievement:** 73% of fall 1992 freshmen returned for fall 1993 term. 44% of entering class graduated.
**Foreign students:** 48 students are from out of the country. Countries represented include Armenia, Brazil, Canada, Japan, Mexico, and Russia; 20 in all.

**PROGRAMS OF STUDY. Degrees:** B.A.

**Majors:** Accounting, Biblical/Religious Studies, Biology, Business, Business/Accounting, Business Administration, Child Development, Communication, Computer Science, Contemporary Ministries, Drama, Education, Elementary Education, English, English Education, English Literature, Health Sciences, History, Humanities, Liberal Arts/General Studies, Liberal Arts/Mexican-American Studies, Life Science Education, Mathematics, Mathematics Education, Missions, Music, Music Education, Music Performance/Composition, Natural Science, Physical Education, Physical Therapy, Psychology, Recreation, Social Science, Social Science Education, Social Service, Spanish Language/Culture, Writing.
**Distribution of degrees:** The majors with the highest enrollment are education, business, and biblical/religious studies.
**Requirements:** General education requirement.
**Academic regulations:** Minimum 2.0 GPA must be maintained.
**Special:** Minors in all majors and conflict resolution, environmental studies, philosophy, political science, and theatre. Bible certificate program. Associate's degrees offered. Self-designed majors. Double majors. Independent study. Internships. Graduate school at which undergraduates may take graduate-level courses. Preprofessional programs in law and medicine. Member of San Joaquin Consortium and California Student Opportunity and Access Program. Washington Semester. Urban Studies Program (Chicago). Teacher certification in early childhood, elementary, secondary, special education, and bilingual/bicultural education. Study abroad in Asian countries, England, France, Germany, Israel, and Mexico.
**Academic Assistance:** Nonremedial tutoring.

**ADMISSIONS. Academic basis for candidate selection** (in order of priority): Secondary school record, standardized test scores, school's recommendation, class rank.
**Nonacademic basis for candidate selection:** Character and personality are important. Extracurricular participation, particular talent or ability, and alumni/ae relationship are considered.
**Requirements:** Graduation from secondary school is required; GED is accepted. 13 units and the following program of study are required: 4 units of English, 3 units of math, 1 unit of lab science, 2 units of foreign language, 2 units of social studies. 1 unit of visual/performing arts recommended. SAT or ACT is required. Campus visit and interview recommended. Off-campus interviews available with an admissions representative.
**Procedure:** Take SAT or ACT by March 2 of 12th year. Visit college for interview by March 2 of 12th year. Suggest filing application by January 31. Application deadline is July 31. Notification of admission by July 31. $100 nonrefundable tuition deposit. $50 refundable room deposit. Freshmen accepted for terms other than fall.
**Special programs:** Credit may be granted through CEEB Advanced Placement for scores of 3 or higher. Credit may be granted through CLEP general exams. Early decision program.
**Transfer students:** Transfer students accepted for terms other than fall. In fall 1993, 59% of all new students were transfers into all classes. 230 transfer applications were received, 182 were accepted. Application deadline is July 31 for fall; December 5 for spring. Minimum 2.4 GPA required. Lowest course grade accepted is "C." Maximum number of transferable credits is 70 semester hours. At least 24 semester hours must be completed at the college to receive degree.
**Admissions contact:** Cary Templeton, Director of Admissions. 209 453-2039.

**FINANCIAL AID. Available aid:** Pell grants, SEOG, state scholarships and grants, school scholarships and grants, private scholarships and grants, academic merit scholarships, and athletic scholarships. Perkins Loans (NDSL), PLUS, Stafford Loans (GSL), private loans, and SLS. Tuition Plan Inc., Education Plan Inc., deferred payment plan, and installment plan.
**Financial aid statistics:** Average amounts of aid awarded freshmen: Loans, $2,625.
**Supporting data/closing dates:** School's own aid application: Priority filing date is March 2. Income tax forms: Priority filing date is June 15. SAAC/FAFAS: Priority filing date is March 2. Notification of awards on rolling basis.
**Financial aid contact:** Bruce Steffensen, Director of Financial Aid. 209 453-2041.

# Golden Gate University

**San Francisco, CA 94105** **415 442-7000**

**1994-95 Costs.** Tuition: $5,880. Housing: None. Fees, books, misc. academic expenses (school's estimate): $810.
**Enrollment.** Undergraduates: 235 men, 318 women (full-time). Freshman class: 213 applicants, 169 accepted, 82 enrolled. Graduate enrollment: 2,446 men, 2,046 women.
**Test score averages/ranges.** N/A.
**Faculty.** 53 full-time; 401 part-time. 49% of faculty holds doctoral degree. Student/faculty ratio: 16 to 1.
**Selectivity rating.** N/A.

**PROFILE.** Golden Gate, founded in 1901, is a private university. Programs are offered through the Schools of Accounting, Finance, Humanities and Social Sciences, Law, Management, Public Administration, Taxation, Technology Management and the College of Special Programs. Its one-building campus is located in San Francisco's downtown financial district.

**Accreditation:** WASC. Professionally accredited by the American Bar Association, the Association of American Law Schools.
**Religious orientation:** Golden Gate University is nonsectarian; no religious requirements.
**Library:** Collections totaling over 118,919 volumes, 4,480 periodical subscriptions, and 493,659 microform items.

**STUDENT BODY. Undergraduate profile:** 80% are state residents; 74% are transfers. 16% Asian-American, 11% Black, 6% Hispanic, 1% Native American, 63% White, 3% Other. Average age of undergraduates is 21.
**Undergraduate achievement:** 87% of fall 1991 freshmen returned for fall 1992 term. 45% of entering class graduated.
**Foreign students:** 389 students are from out of the country. Countries represented include China, Hong Kong, Indonesia, Japan, Malaysia, and Taiwan; 66 in all.

**PROGRAMS OF STUDY. Degrees:** B.A., B.S.
**Majors:** Accounting, Administrative Management, Business Economics, Business/Humanities, Finance, Human Relations, Information Systems, Institutional/Hotel/Restaurant Management, International Management, Management, Marketing, Political Science, Pre-Legal Studies, Telecommunications Management, Transportation/Distribution Management.
**Distribution of degrees:** The majors with the highest enrollment are management, information systems, and institutional/hotel/restaurant management.
**Requirements:** General education requirement.
**Academic regulations:** Minimum 2.0 GPA must be maintained.
**Special:** Certificate programs offered in advertising/marketing/sales, applied politics, hotel/restaurant/institutional management, information systems, management, insurance, programming, real estate, and transportation. Associate's degrees offered. Independent study. Accelerated study. Internships. Cooperative education programs. Graduate school at which undergraduates may take graduate-level courses. Preprofessional programs in law. Member of San Francisco Consortium. AFROTC at San Francisco State U.
**Academic Assistance:** Remedial writing and math. Nonremedial tutoring.

**ADMISSIONS. Academic basis for candidate selection** (in order of priority): Secondary school record, standardized test scores, essay, school's recommendation.
**Nonacademic basis for candidate selection:** Character and personality, extracurricular participation, and particular talent or ability are considered.
**Requirements:** Graduation from secondary school is required; GED is accepted. 16 units required and the following program of study recommended: 3 units of English, 2 units of math, 1 unit of science, 1 unit of foreign language, 1 units of social studies. Minimum 3.0 GPA required. SAT or ACT required of applicants lacking in specified units or GPA. EOP for applicants not normally admissible. Conditional admission possible for applicants not meeting standard requirements. Campus visit recommended. Off-campus interviews available with an alumni representative.
**Procedure:** Suggest filing application by July 1; no deadline. Notification of admission on rolling basis. No set date by which applicants must accept offer. Freshmen accepted for terms other than fall.
**Special programs:** Admission may be deferred one year. Credit and/or placement may be granted through CEEB Advanced Placement exams for scores of 3 or higher. Credit and/or placement may be granted through CLEP general and subject exams. Credit may be granted through DANTES exams and military experience. Credit and placement may be granted through ACT PEP and challenge exams. Early entrance/early admission program. Concurrent enrollment program.
**Transfer students:** Transfer students accepted for terms other than fall. In fall 1992, 74% of all new students were transfers into all classes. 418 transfer applications were received, 385 were accepted. Application deadline is rolling for fall; rolling for spring. Minimum 2.0 GPA required. Lowest course grade accepted is "C." Maximum number of transferable credits is 70 semester hours from a two-year school and 93 semester hours from a four-year school. At least 30 semester hours must be completed at the university to receive degree.
**Admissions contact:** Archie Porter, M.Ed., Director of Admissions. 415 442-7200.

**FINANCIAL AID. Available aid:** Pell grants, SEOG, state grants, school scholarships and grants, private scholarships, and academic merit scholarships. Perkins Loans (NDSL), PLUS, Stafford Loans (GSL), school loans, private loans, and SLS. Deferred payment plan.
**Financial aid statistics:** 45% of aid is not need-based. In 1993-94, 89% of all undergraduate applicants received aid; 89% of freshman applicants. Average amounts of aid awarded freshmen: Scholarships and grants, $2,570; loans, $4,100.
**Supporting data/closing dates:** FAFSA: Priority filing date is March 2. School's own aid application: Priority filing date is February 15. State aid form: Deadline is March 2. Income tax forms: Priority filing date is April 22. Notification of awards on rolling basis.
**Financial aid contact:** Marilyn LeBlanc, M.P.A., Director of Financial Aid. 415 442-7270.

# Harvey Mudd College

**Claremont, CA 91711-5990** **909 621-8000**

**1993-94 Costs.** Tuition: $16,410. Room & board: $6,436. Fees, books, misc. academic expenses (school's estimate): $1,066.
**Enrollment.** Undergraduates: 505 men, 149 women (full-time). Freshman class: 1,377 applicants, 572 accepted, 178 enrolled. Graduate enrollment: 10 men, 2 women.
**Test score averages/ranges.** Range of SAT scores of middle 50%: 580-690 verbal, 710-770 math.
**Faculty.** 69 full-time; 9 part-time. 100% of faculty holds doctoral degree. Student/faculty ratio: 8 to 1.
**Selectivity rating.** Most competitive.

**PROFILE.** Harvey Mudd, founded in 1955, is a private college of engineering and science. It is one of the Claremont Colleges, a group of five undergraduate colleges and one graduate school with adjoining campuses and shared facilities and services. Its 18-acre campus is located at the base of the San Gabriel Mountains, 35 miles east of Los Angeles.

**Accreditation:** WASC. Professionally accredited by the Accreditation Board for Engineering and Technology.
**Religious orientation:** Harvey Mudd College is nonsectarian; no religious requirements.
**Library:** Collections totaling over 1,843,798 volumes, 5,922 periodical subscriptions, and 1,200,836 microform items.
**Special facilities/museums:** Observatory.

**Athletic facilities:** Swimming pools, sand volleyball courts, soccer field, tennis and basketball courts, track, weight room. Facilities at Claremont McKenna also available, including gymnasiums, track, pool, soccer fields, outdoor half basketball, sand volleyball, squash, and tennis courts.

**STUDENT BODY. Undergraduate profile:** 49% are state residents; 1% are transfers. 22% Asian-American, 2% Black, 4% Hispanic, 1% Native American, 71% White. Average age of undergraduates is 19.
**Freshman profile:** 20% of freshmen who took SAT scored 700 or over on verbal, 85% scored 700 or over on math; 75% scored 600 or over on verbal, 100% scored 600 or over on math; 98% scored 500 or over on verbal; 100% scored 400 or over on verbal. 100% of accepted applicants took SAT. 80% of freshmen come from public schools.
**Undergraduate achievement:** 91% of fall 1992 freshmen returned for fall 1993 term. 65% of entering class graduated. 53% of students who completed a degree program immediately went on to graduate study.
**Foreign students:** 12 students are from out of the country. Countries represented include Canada, India, South Korea, and Taiwan; nine in all.

**PROGRAMS OF STUDY. Degrees:** B.S.
**Majors:** Biology, Chemistry, Computer Science, Engineering, Mathematics, Physics.
**Distribution of degrees:** The majors with the highest enrollment are engineering and physics; biology and computer science have the lowest.
**Requirements:** General education requirement.
**Academic regulations:** Minimum 2.0 GPA required for graduation.
**Special:** Minors offered in humanities and social science fields. Self-designed majors. Double majors. Dual degrees. Independent study. Pass/fail grading option. Internships. Graduate school at which undergraduates may take graduate-level courses. 3-2 engineering/management program with Claremont McKenna Coll. Five-year M.Math. program with Claremont Graduate Sch. Five-year M.Eng. program. Member of consortium with other Claremont Colleges. Exchange programs with Rensselaer Polytechnic Inst and Swarthmore Coll. Exchange program abroad in France (ESIEE, Paris). Other study abroad programs with other Claremont Colleges. AFROTC. ROTC at Claremont McKenna Coll.
**Academic Assistance:** Nonremedial tutoring.

**STUDENT LIFE. Housing:** All freshmen must live on campus. Coed dorms. 97% of students live in college housing.
**Services and counseling/handicapped student services:** Placement services. Health service. Women's center. Writing center. Counseling services for minority students. Birth control, personal, and psychological counseling. Career and academic guidance services. Religious counseling. Learning disabled services.
**Campus organizations:** Undergraduate student government. Student newspaper (Collage, published once/week). Literary magazine. Yearbook. Radio station. Orchestras, stage and jazz bands, concert and chamber choirs, debating, drama groups, community service program, political and departmental groups, ski and sailing clubs, unicycle club, technological journal.
**Religious organizations:** Black Christian Fellowship, Christian Science Organization, Hillel-Jewish Collegiate Community, Muslim Student Association, other five-college groups.
**Minority/foreign student organizations:** Asian Student Association, Black Student Union, Chicano Studies Center, Hawaiian Club, MEChA, Office of Black Student Affairs. Etudiants des Science, Intercultural Association, Korean Student Association.

**ATHLETICS. Physical education requirements:** Three semesters of physical education required.
**Intercollegiate competition:** 5% of students participate. Baseball (M), basketball (M,W), cross-country (M,W), diving (M,W), football (M), golf (M,W), soccer (M,W), softball (W), swimming (M,W), tennis (M,W), track (M,W), track and field (outdoor) (M,W), volleyball (W), water polo (M,W). Member of NCAA Division III, Southern California Intercollegiate Athletic Conference (SCIAC).
**Intramural and club sports:** 1% of students participate. Intramural Alpine skiing, badminton, ballroom dancing, basketball, cricket, cycling, fencing, flag football, floor hockey, fly fishing, lacrosse, rock climbing, rugby, water polo. Men's club Alpine skiing, cricket, cycling, fencing, fly fishing, lacrosse, rock climbing, rugby. Women's club Alpine skiing, cycling, fly fishing, lacrosse, rock climbing.

**ADMISSIONS. Academic basis for candidate selection** (in order of priority): Secondary school record, standardized test scores, class rank, school's recommendation, essay.
**Nonacademic basis for candidate selection:** Character and personality, extracurricular participation, and particular talent or ability are emphasized. Alumni/ae relationship is considered.
**Requirements:** Graduation from secondary school is required; GED is not accepted. No specific distribution of secondary school units required. Minimum SAT scores of 500 verbal and 680 math and rank in top tenth of secondary school class recommended. SAT is required. ACH required. Campus visit and interview recommended. Off-campus interviews available with admissions and alumni representatives.
**Procedure:** Take SAT by January of 12th year. Take ACH by January of 12th year. Visit college for interview by February of 12th year. Application deadline is February 1. Notification of admission by April 1. Reply is required by May 1. $100 nonrefundable tuition deposit. $150 room deposit, refundable until July 15. Freshmen accepted for fall term only.
**Special programs:** Admission may be deferred one year. Credit and/or placement may be granted through CEEB Advanced Placement exams for scores of 5 or higher. Credit and placement may be granted through challenge exams. Early decision program. In fall 1993, 130 applied for early decision and 53 were accepted. Deadline for applying for early decision is December 1. Early entrance/early admission program.
**Transfer students:** Transfer students accepted for fall term only. In fall 1993, 1% of all new students were transfers into all classes. 63 transfer applications were received, 20 were accepted. Application deadline is May 1. Minimum 3.5 GPA recommended. Lowest course grade accepted is "C." Maximum number of transferable credits is the equivalent of four semesters of course work. At least 63 semester hours must be completed at the college to receive degree.
**Admissions contact:** Patricia Coleman, M.Ed., Dean of Admissions. 909 621-8011.

**FINANCIAL AID. Available aid:** Pell grants, SEOG, state scholarships and grants, school scholarships and grants, private scholarships and grants, and ROTC scholarships. Perkins Loans (NDSL), PLUS, Stafford Loans (GSL), school loans, and SLS. Tuition Plan Inc., Education Plan Inc., Knight Tuition Plans, AMS, EFI Fund Management, Tuition Management Systems, and deferred payment plan.
**Financial aid statistics:** In 1993-94, 99% of all undergraduate applicants received aid; 98% of freshman applicants. Average amounts of aid awarded freshmen: Scholarships and grants, $11,780; loans, $2,600.
**Supporting data/closing dates:** FAFSA: Priority filing date is February 1. School's own aid application: Priority filing date is February 1. Income tax forms: Priority filing date is March 1; accepted on rolling basis. Notification of awards begins April 1.
**Financial aid contact:** Noe Ortiz, Director of Financial Aid. 909 621-8055.

**STUDENT EMPLOYMENT.** College Work/Study Program. Institutional employment. 57% of full-time undergraduates work on campus during school year. Students may expect to earn an average of $1,374 during school year. Freshmen are discouraged from working during their first term. Off-campus part-time employment opportunities rated "good."

**COMPUTER FACILITIES.** 100 IBM/IBM-compatible, Macintosh/Apple, and RISC-/UNIX-based microcomputers; 80 are networked. Students may access Digital, Hewlett-Packard, IBM, Sequent, SUN minicomputer/mainframe systems, BITNET, Internet. Client/LAN operating systems include Apple/Macintosh, DOS, UNIX/XENIX/AIX, DEC, LocalTalk/AppleTalk, Novell. Computer languages and software packages include Ada, BASIC, C, FORTRAN, IDEAS, LISP, Maple, MATLAB, Pascal, SPSS-X; spreadsheet and word processing packages. Computer facilities are available to all students.
**Fees:** Computer fee is included in tuition/fees.
**Hours:** 24 hours.

**GRADUATE CAREER DATA.** Highest graduate school enrollments: UC Berkeley, Caltech, Carnegie Mellon U, Cornell U, U of Illinois/Urbana-Champaign, Johns Hopkins U, MIT, Stanford U, U of Wisconsin at Madison. 41% of graduates choose careers in business and industry. Companies and businesses that hire graduates: Andersen Consulting, Hewlett-Packard, Honeywell, Hughes, Jet Propulsion Lab, Lawrence Livermore Labs, Lockheed, Microsoft, Northrop, Stanford Research International, Teradyne.

**PROMINENT ALUMNI/AE.** George "Pinky" Nelson, physicist and space shuttle astronaut/crew member; Frederick Sontag, owner and president, Unison Industries; Michael G. Wilson, director of James Bond films; Dr. Kenneth Brown, heart surgeon.

# Holy Names College

**Oakland, CA 94619-1699** **510 436-1000**

**1994-95 Costs.** Tuition: $11,480. Room: $2,480. Board: $1,630. Fees, books, misc. academic expenses (school's estimate): $720.
**Enrollment.** Undergraduates: 95 men, 178 women (full-time). Freshman class: 258 applicants, 157 accepted, 43 enrolled. Graduate enrollment: 90 men, 286 women.
**Test score averages/ranges.** Average SAT scores: 448 verbal, 450 math. Range of SAT scores of middle 50%: 400-499 verbal, 400-499 math.
**Faculty.** 39 full-time; 13 part-time. 75% of faculty holds doctoral degree. Student/faculty ratio: 11 to 1.
**Selectivity rating.** Less competitive.

**PROFILE.** Holy Names College is a church-affiliated, liberal arts institution. It was founded as a girls' school in 1868, began granting bachelor's degrees in 1926, and adopted coeducation in 1971. Its 60-acre campus overlooks Oakland and San Francisco Bay.

**Accreditation:** WASC. Professionally accredited by the National Association of Schools of Music, the National League for Nursing.
**Religious orientation:** Holy Names College is affiliated with the Roman Catholic Church; no religious requirements.
**Library:** Collections totaling over 108,575 volumes, 634 periodical subscriptions, and 44,500 microform items.
**Special facilities/museums:** Art gallery, folk music collection, school for learning disabled children and adults.
**Athletic facilities:** Gymnasium, swimming pool, weight rooms, tennis courts, soccer and softball fields.

**STUDENT BODY. Undergraduate profile:** 79% are state residents; 42% are transfers. 7% Asian-American, 25% Black, 9% Hispanic, 1% Native American, 35% White, 23% Other. Average age of undergraduates is 23.
**Freshman profile:** Majority of accepted applicants took SAT. 74% of freshmen come from public schools.
**Undergraduate achievement:** 68% of fall 1992 freshmen returned for fall 1993 term.
**Foreign students:** 96 students are from out of the country. Countries represented include Hong Kong, Indonesia, Japan, Kenya, Korea, and Taiwan; 10 in all.

**PROGRAMS OF STUDY. Degrees:** B.A., B.Mus., B.S.
**Majors:** Biological Science, Business Administration, Business Administration/Communications, Business Administration/Economics, Business Administration/Philosophy, English, English Studies for Internationals, History, Human Services, Humanities, International Affairs, Liberal Studies, Mathematics, Mathematics or Science/Engineering, Music, Nursing, Philosophy, Psychology, Religious Studies, Sociology, Spanish.
**Distribution of degrees:** The majors with the highest enrollment are nursing, business administration/economics, and liberal studies; sociology, religious studies, and mathematics have the lowest.
**Requirements:** General education requirement.
**Academic regulations:** Minimum 2.0 GPA must be maintained.
**Special:** Minors offered in most majors and in art, chemistry, communication arts, and drama. Academic concentrations in economics, management, and political science. Religious studies concentration in youth ministry. Self-designed majors. Double majors. Dual degrees. Independent study. Pass/fail grading option. Internships. Graduate school at which undergraduates may take graduate-level courses. Preprofessional programs in law, medicine, veterinary science, pharmacy, dentistry, and theology. 3-2 engineering program with UC Berkeley. Member of Regional Association of East Bay Colleges and Universi-

ties; cross-registration possible. Exchange program with Anna Maria Coll. Exchange program abroad in Japan (Kansai U of Foreign Studies). Study abroad also in other countries. ROTC and AFROTC at UC Berkeley.
**Honors:** Honors program. Honor societies.
**Academic Assistance:** Remedial writing, math, and study skills. Nonremedial tutoring.

**ADMISSIONS. Academic basis for candidate selection** (in order of priority): Secondary school record, standardized test scores, essay, school's recommendation, class rank.
**Nonacademic basis for candidate selection:** Character and personality, extracurricular participation, and particular talent or ability are important.
**Requirements:** Graduation from secondary school is required; GED is accepted. 15 units and the following program of study are required: 4 units of English, 3 units of math, 1 unit of lab science, 2 units of foreign language, 1 unit of history, 4 units of electives including 1 unit of academic electives. Minimum combined SAT score of 880 and minimum 2.8 GPA required. R.N. required of nursing program applicants. Conditional admission possible for applicants not meeting standard requirements. SAT or ACT is required. Campus visit and interview recommended. Off-campus interviews available with admissions and alumni representatives.
**Procedure:** Take SAT or ACT by November of 12th year. Suggest filing application by November 30. Application deadline is August 1. Notification of admission on rolling basis. Reply is requested within four weeks of acceptance. $100 tuition deposit, refundable until May 1. $100 refundable room deposit. Freshmen accepted for terms other than fall.
**Special programs:** Admission may be deferred two years. Credit may be granted through CEEB Advanced Placement for scores of 3 or higher. Credit may be granted through CLEP general and subject exams, and challenge exams.
**Transfer students:** Transfer students accepted for terms other than fall. In fall 1993, 42% of all new students were transfers into all classes. 100 transfer applications were received, 70 were accepted. Application deadline is August 1 for fall; January 1 for spring. Minimum 2.2 GPA required. Lowest course grade accepted is "D." Maximum number of transferable credits is 66 semester hours. At least 24 semester hours must be completed at the college to receive degree.
**Admissions contact:** Carol Sellman, S.N.J.M., M.M., V.P. for Institutional Research/Planning. 510 436-1321.

**FINANCIAL AID. Available aid:** Pell grants, SEOG, state scholarships and grants, school scholarships and grants, private scholarships and grants, and academic merit scholarships. Perkins Loans (NDSL), PLUS, Stafford Loans (GSL), and SLS. Emergency loans. Deferred payment plan.
**Financial aid statistics:** 40% of aid is not need-based. In 1993-94, 95% of all undergraduate applicants received aid; 95% of freshman applicants. Average amounts of aid awarded freshmen: Scholarships and grants, $3,700; loans, $2,500.
**Supporting data/closing dates:** FAFSA: Priority filing date is March 2. School's own aid application: Priority filing date is March 2. State aid form: Priority filing date is March 2. Notification of awards begins April 1.
**Financial aid contact:** Paula Lehrberger, M.S., Director of Financial Aid. 510 436-1327.

## Humphreys College

**Stockton, CA 95207-3896** **209 478-0800**

**1994-95 Costs.** Tuition: $5,082. Room & board: $3,141. Fees, books, misc. academic expenses (school's estimate): $612.
**Enrollment.** Undergraduates: 62 men, 352 women (full-time). Freshman class: 92 applicants, 92 accepted, 84 enrolled. Graduate enrollment: 49 men, 45 women.
**Test score averages/ranges.** N/A.
**Faculty.** 29 full-time; 39 part-time. 38% of faculty holds doctoral degree. Student/faculty ratio: 11 to 1.
**Selectivity rating.** N/A.

**PROFILE.** Humphreys, founded in 1896, is a private college. Its 10-acre campus is in Stockton, 50 miles from Sacremento.

**Accreditation:** WASC.
**Religious orientation:** Humphreys College is nonsectarian; no religious requirements.
**Library:** Collections totaling over 20,000 volumes, 120 periodical subscriptions and 600 microform items.

**STUDENT BODY. Undergraduate profile:** 95% are state residents; 13% are transfers. 8% Asian-American, 8% Black, 16% Hispanic, 2% Native American, 66% White. Average age of undergraduates is 25.
**Freshman profile:** Majority of accepted applicants took SAT. 97% of freshmen come from public schools.
**Undergraduate achievement:** 80% of fall 1992 freshmen returned for fall 1993 term. 50% of entering class graduated.
**Foreign students:** Three students are from out of the country. Countries represented include Canada, China, and Japan; three in all.

**PROGRAMS OF STUDY. Degrees:** B.S.
**Majors:** Accounting, Business Management, Computer Management Information Systems, Paralegal Studies.
**Distribution of degrees:** The majors with the highest enrollment are paralegal studies, accounting, and business management; computer management information systems have the lowest.
**Requirements:** General education requirement.
**Academic regulations:** Minimum 2.0 GPA must be maintained.
**Special:** Associate's degrees offered. Double majors. Dual degrees. Independent study. Accelerated study. Internships. Cooperative education programs. Preprofessional programs in law.
**Honors:** Honor societies.
**Academic Assistance:** Remedial reading, writing, math, and study skills. Nonremedial tutoring.

**ADMISSIONS. Requirements:** Graduation from secondary school is recommended; GED is accepted. 13 units and the following program of study are recommended: 4 units of English, 3 units of math, 2 units of science including 1 unit of lab, 1 unit of foreign language, 2 units of social studies, 1 unit of history. Open admissions policy. SAT or ACT is recommended. PSAT is recommended. Campus visit and interview recommended. Off-campus interviews available with an admissions representative.
**Procedure:** Take SAT or ACT by May of 12th year. Take ACH by May of 12th year. Visit college for interview by June of 12th year. Suggest filing application by June 1. Application deadline is September 25. Notification of admission on rolling basis. No set date by which applicants must accept offer. $275 refundable room deposit. Freshmen accepted for terms other than fall.
**Special programs:** Admission may be deferred one year. Credit and/or placement may be granted through CEEB Advanced Placement exams for scores of 3 or higher. Credit and/or placement may be granted through CLEP general and subject exams. Placement may be granted through military and life experience. Credit and placement may be granted through challenge exams. Early entrance/early admission program. Concurrent enrollment program.
**Transfer students:** Transfer students accepted for terms other than fall. In fall 1993, 13% of all new students were transfers into all classes. 110 transfer applications were received, 110 were accepted. Application deadline is September 25 for fall; January 3 for spring. Minimum 2.0 GPA recommended. Lowest course grade accepted is "C." Maximum number of transferable credits is 120 quarter hours from a two-year school and 144 quarter hours from a four-year school. At least 36 quarter hours must be completed at the college to receive degree.
**Admissions contact:** Pamela Knapp, Admissions Counselor. 209 478-0800, extension 14.

**FINANCIAL AID. Available aid:** Pell grants, SEOG, state grants, school scholarships, and academic merit scholarships. PLUS, Stafford Loans (GSL), and SLS. Deferred payment plan.
**Financial aid statistics:** 5% of aid is not need-based. In 1993-94, 67% of all undergraduate applicants received aid; 83% of freshman applicants. Average amounts of aid awarded freshmen: Scholarships and grants, $3,500; loans, $2,625.
**Supporting data/closing dates:** FAFSA: Priority filing date is March 1; deadline is May 2. Cal Grant Application: Priority filing date is March 1; deadline is May 2. Notification of awards on rolling basis.
**Financial aid contact:** Michael Yahner, Financial Aid Director. 209 478-0800, ext. 12.

## John F. Kennedy University

**Orinda, CA 94563** **510 254-0200**

**1993-94 Costs.** Tuition: $7,848. Housing: None. Fees, books, misc. academic expenses (school's estimate): $844.
**Enrollment.** Undergraduates: 10 men, 45 women (full-time). Freshman class: 91 applicants, 82 accepted, 50 enrolled. Graduate enrollment: 401 men, 988 women.
**Test score averages/ranges.** N/A.
**Faculty.** 82 full-time. 42% of faculty holds doctoral degree. Student/faculty ratio: 12 to 1.
**Selectivity rating.** N/A.

**PROFILE.** John F. Kennedy University, founded in 1964, is a private, upper-division institution. Programs are offered through the Graduate Schools of Law, Liberal and Professional Arts, and Management and through the Graduate Schools of Consciousness Studies and Professional Psychology. Its campus is located in Orinda, five miles from Berkeley and 20 miles from San Francisco.

**Accreditation:** WASC.
**Religious orientation:** John F. Kennedy University is nonsectarian; no religious requirements.
**Library:** Collections totaling over 59,650 volumes, 645 periodical subscriptions and 29 microform items.
**Athletic facilities:** Playing fields.

**STUDENT BODY. Undergraduate profile:** 3% Asian-American, 8% Black, 5% Hispanic, 2% Native American, 77% White, 5% Other. Average age of undergraduates is 37.
**Foreign students:** 41 students are from out of the country. Countries represented include Canada, Germany, Japan, Switzerland, the Philippines, and the United Kingdom; 17 in all.

**PROGRAMS OF STUDY. Degrees:** B.A., B.S.
**Majors:** Accounting, Business Administration, Food Industry Management, General Management, Liberal Studies, Psychology, Public Administration.
**Requirements:** General education requirement.
**Special:** Minors offered in interdisciplinary studies, living systems, and psychology. Self-designed majors. Double majors. Independent study. Accelerated study. Pass/fail grading option. Internships. Cooperative education programs. B.A./M.A., B.A./J.D., and B.S./M.B.A. programs. Teacher certification in elementary and secondary education.
**Academic Assistance:** Remedial writing.

**ADMISSIONS. Academic basis for candidate selection** (in order of priority): Class rank.
**Nonacademic basis for candidate selection:** Character and personality are emphasized. Particular talent or ability is important. Extracurricular participation is considered.
**Requirements:** Graduation from secondary school is recommended; GED is accepted. No specific distribution of secondary school units required. Minimum 2.0 GPA required. Campus visit recommended. Off-campus interviews available with an admissions representative.
**Procedure:** Notification of admission on rolling basis. Freshmen accepted for terms other than fall.
**Special programs:** Admission may be deferred one year. Credit may be granted through CLEP general and subject exams, DANTES exams, and military and life experience. Placement may be granted through challenge exams.

**Transfer students:** Transfer students accepted for terms other than fall. Lowest course grade accepted is "D." Maximum number of transferable credits is 105 quarter hours.
**Admissions contact:** Ellena Bloedorn, M.A., Director of Admissions. 510 253-2213.

**FINANCIAL AID. Available aid:** Pell grants, SEOG, state scholarships and grants, school scholarships, and private scholarships. Perkins Loans (NDSL), PLUS, Stafford Loans (GSL), state loans, school loans, private loans, and SLS. Deferred payment plan.
**Financial aid statistics:** In 1992-93, 90% of all undergraduate applicants received aid. Average amounts of aid awarded freshmen: Loans, $2,625.
**Supporting data/closing dates:** FAFSA/FAF/FFS: Accepted on rolling basis. School's own aid application: Accepted on rolling basis. State aid form: Accepted on rolling basis. Income tax forms: Accepted on rolling basis. Notification of awards begins in May.
**Financial aid contact:** Janet Bullard, Director of Financial Aid. 510 254-0200.

## LaSierra University

**Riverside, CA 92515 — 800 874-5587**

**1994-95 Costs.** Tuition: $12,180. Room: $2,190. Board: $1,695. Fees, books, misc. academic expenses (school's estimate): $575.
**Enrollment.** Undergraduates: 575 men, 635 women (full-time). Freshman class: 684 applicants, 576 accepted, 325 enrolled. Graduate enrollment: 68 men, 83 women.
**Test score averages/ranges.** Average SAT scores: 420 verbal, 468 math. Range of SAT scores of middle 50%: 350-470 verbal, 380-520 math. Average ACT scores: 20 English, 20 math, 21 composite. Range of ACT scores of middle 50%: 17-23 English, 17-22 math.
**Faculty.** 95 full-time; 10 part-time. 70% of faculty holds doctoral degree. Student/faculty ratio: 13 to 1.
**Selectivity rating.** Less competitive.

**PROFILE.** LaSierra is a church-affiliated university. Founded in 1922, its name was changed in 1991 from Loma Linda University. Programs are offered through the Center for Lifelong Learning; the College of Arts and Sciences; the Graduate School; and the Schools of Education, Business and Management, and Religion. Its 40-acre campus is located in Riverside, 58 miles from Los Angeles.

**Accreditation:** WASC. Professionally accredited by the Council on Social Work Education.
**Religious orientation:** LaSierra University is affiliated with the Seventh-day Adventist Church; 16 quarter units of religion/theology required.
**Library:** Collections totaling over 220,000 volumes, 1,650 periodical subscriptions, and 270,000 microform items.
**Special facilities/museums:** Natural history, art museums.
**Athletic facilities:** Gymnasium, gymnastics and weight rooms, swimming pool, track, baseball and soccer fields, tennis courts, golf course.

**STUDENT BODY. Undergraduate profile:** 75% are state residents. 35% Asian-American, 7% Black, 18% Hispanic, 1% Native American, 39% White. Average age of undergraduates is 22.
**Freshman profile:** 1% of freshmen who took SAT scored 700 or over on verbal, 2% scored 700 or over on math; 7% scored 600 or over on verbal, 13% scored 600 or over on math; 21% scored 500 or over on verbal, 42% scored 500 or over on math; 57% scored 400 or over on verbal, 73% scored 400 or over on math; 89% scored 300 or over on verbal, 95% scored 300 or over on math. 3% of freshmen who took ACT scored 30 or over on English, 5% scored 30 or over on math, 5% scored 30 or over on composite; 19% scored 24 or over on English, 16% scored 24 or over on math, 22% scored 24 or over on composite; 72% scored 18 or over on English, 70% scored 18 or over on math, 75% scored 18 or over on composite; 99% scored 12 or over on English, 99% scored 12 or over on math, 100% scored 12 or over on composite; 100% scored 6 or over on English, 100% scored 6 or over on math. 67% of accepted applicants took SAT; 33% took ACT. 35% of freshmen come from public schools.
**Foreign students:** 303 students are from out of the country. Countries represented include China, Indonesia, Japan, Korea, Mexico, and Philippines; 61 in all.

**PROGRAMS OF STUDY. Degrees:** B.A., B.Bus.Admin., B.F.A., B.Mus., B.S., B.Soc.Work.
**Majors:** Art, Biology, Business/Economics, Chemistry, Communication, English, Health, History/Political Science, Liberal Arts, Mathematics/Computers, Modern Languages, Music, Office Management/Business Education, Physical Education, Physical Education/Recreation, Physics, Psychology, Religion, Social Work, Sociology.
**Distribution of degrees:** The majors with the highest enrollment are biology and business administration; physics has the lowest.
**Requirements:** General education requirement.
**Academic regulations:** Minimum 2.0 GPA must be maintained.
**Special:** Concentrations offered in all departments and programs. Transfer programs between schools include anesthesia, cytotechnology, dental hygiene, dietetics, medical records administration, medical technology, nursing, occupational therapy, physical therapy, public health science, radiological technology, and respiratory therapy. Associate's degrees offered. Independent study. Pass/fail grading option. Internships. Preprofessional programs in law, medicine, veterinary science, pharmacy, dentistry, theology, and optometry. Teacher certification in elementary, secondary, and special education. Study abroad in Austria, France, and Spain.
**Honors:** Honors program.
**Academic Assistance:** Remedial reading, writing, math, and study skills.

**STUDENT LIFE. Housing:** All unmarried students under age 23 must live on campus unless living with family. Women's and men's dorms. School-owned/operated apartments. Both on-campus and off-campus married-student housing. 50% of students live in college housing.
**Services and counseling/handicapped student services:** Placement services. Health service. Counseling services for minority students. Personal and psychological counseling. Career and academic guidance services. Religious counseling.
**Campus organizations:** Undergraduate student government. Student newspaper. Yearbook. Chamber singers, choir, orchestra, concert band, string ensemble, wind and percussion ensemble, athletic, service, and special-interest groups.
**Religious organizations:** Several religious groups.
**Minority/foreign student organizations:** Black Student Association, Spanish-American Organization. International Student Organization.

**ATHLETICS. Physical education requirements:** Five terms of physical education required.
**Intercollegiate competition:** 10% of students participate. Basketball (M,W), volleyball (M,W). Member of California Coastal Conference.
**Intramural and club sports:** 20% of students participate. Intramural badminton, baseball, basketball, flag football, floor hockey, golf, soccer, softball, table tennis, tennis, volleyball, weight lifting. Men's club gymnastics, soccer, tennis. Women's club gymnastics, softball, tennis.

**ADMISSIONS. Academic basis for candidate selection** (in order of priority): Secondary school record, school's recommendation, standardized test scores.
**Nonacademic basis for candidate selection:** Character and personality are emphasized.
**Requirements:** Graduation from secondary school is required; GED is accepted. No specific distribution of secondary school units required. Conditional admission possible for applicants not meeting standard requirements. SAT or ACT is required. Campus visit and interview recommended. Off-campus interviews available with an admissions representative.
**Procedure:** Take SAT or ACT by May 30 of 12th year. Visit college for interview by May 30 of 12th year. Suggest filing application by August 15; no deadline. Notification of admission on rolling basis. $100 room deposit, refundable until September 1. Freshmen accepted for terms other than fall.
**Special programs:** Admission may be deferred one year. Credit may be granted through CEEB Advanced Placement for scores of 3 or higher. Credit may be granted through CLEP general and subject exams, and challenge exams. Early entrance/early admission program.
**Transfer students:** Transfer students accepted for terms other than fall. In fall 1993, 437 transfer applications were received, 305 were accepted. Application deadline is August 15. Minimum 2.0 GPA required. Lowest course grade accepted is "D." Maximum number of transferable credits is 105 quarter units. At least 36 of last 44 quarter units must be completed at the university to receive degree.
**Admissions contact:** Myrna Costa, Director of Admissions. 909 785-2176.

**FINANCIAL AID. Available aid:** Pell grants, SEOG, state scholarships and grants, school scholarships and grants, private scholarships and grants, and academic merit scholarships. Perkins Loans (NDSL), Stafford Loans (GSL), state loans, school loans, private loans, and SLS. Tuition Plan Inc.
**Financial aid statistics:** 20% of aid is not need-based. In 1993-94, 70% of all undergraduate applicants received aid; 70% of freshman applicants. Average amounts of aid awarded freshmen: Scholarships and grants, $1,000; loans, $2,600.
**Supporting data/closing dates:** FAFSA: Priority filing date is March 2. FAF: Deadline is March 15. School's own aid application: Deadline is May 1. Notification of awards begins in June.
**Financial aid contact:** Delia Martinez, Director of Financial Aid. 909 785-2175.

**STUDENT EMPLOYMENT.** College Work/Study Program. Institutional employment. 60% of full-time undergraduates work on campus during school year. Students may expect to earn an average of $2,400 during school year. Off-campus part-time employment opportunities rated "good."

**COMPUTER FACILITIES.** 40 IBM/IBM-compatible and Macintosh/Apple microcomputers; all are networked. Students may access Digital, Sequent minicomputer/mainframe systems, BITNET, Internet. Residence halls may be equipped with networked terminals, modems. Client/LAN operating systems include Apple/Macintosh, DOS, Windows NT, Artisoft, DEC, LocalTalk/AppleTalk. Computer languages and software packages include ADA, Basic, C, COBOL, FORTRAN, Pascal, graphics, spreadsheet, CAD programs. Computer facilities are available to all students.
**Fees:** None.

**GRADUATE CAREER DATA.** Highest graduate school enrollments: Loma Linda U.

## Loyola Marymount University

**Los Angeles, CA 90045-2699 — 310 338-2700**

**1994-95 Costs.** Tuition: $13,592. Room & board: $5,346. Fees, books, misc. academic expenses (school's estimate): $721.
**Enrollment.** Undergraduates: 1,571 men, 1,974 women (full-time). Freshman class: 3,767 applicants, 2,662 accepted, 753 enrolled. Graduate enrollment: 476 men, 515 women.
**Test score averages/ranges.** Average SAT scores: 473 verbal, 535 math. Range of SAT scores of middle 50%: 420-520 verbal, 470-580 math. Average ACT scores: 24 composite.
**Faculty.** 258 full-time; 207 part-time. 81% of faculty holds doctoral degree. Student/faculty ratio: 15 to 1.
**Selectivity rating.** Competitive.

**PROFILE.** Loyola Marymount is a church-affiliated university. It is the product of the 1973 merger of Marymount College and Loyala University. Programs are offered through the Colleges of Business Administration, Communication and Fine Arts, Liberal Arts, and Science and Engineering; the Graduate Division; and the School of Law. Its 100-acre campus is located in a residential area of Los Angeles. Campus architecture includes postmodern style buildings.

**Accreditation:** WASC. Professionally accredited by the Accreditation Board for Engineering and Technology, the American Assembly of Collegiate Schools of Business, the American Bar Association, the National Association of Schools of Art and Design.

**Religious orientation:** Loyola Marymount University is affiliated with the Roman Catholic Church (Society of Jesus/Marymount); two semesters of theology required.
**Library:** Collections totaling over 431,469 volumes, 8,362 periodical subscriptions, and 253,471 microform items.
**Special facilities/museums:** Art gallery, computer graphics lab.
**Athletic facilities:** Gymnasiums, racquetball and tennis courts, swimming pools, baseball stadium, weight rooms, intramural, rugby, soccer, and softball fields.

**STUDENT BODY. Undergraduate profile:** 87% are state residents; 33% are transfers. 15% Asian-American, 6% Black, 19% Hispanic, 1% Native American, 54% White, 5% Other. Average age of undergraduates is 20.
**Freshman profile:** 1% of freshmen who took SAT scored 700 or over on verbal, 4% scored 700 or over on math; 9% scored 600 or over on verbal, 22% scored 600 or over on math; 38% scored 500 or over on verbal, 69% scored 500 or over on math; 86% scored 400 or over on verbal, 96% scored 400 or over on math; 98% scored 300 or over on verbal, 99% scored 300 or over on math. 96% of accepted applicants took SAT; 4% took ACT. 49% of freshmen come from public schools.
**Undergraduate achievement:** 87% of fall 1992 freshmen returned for fall 1993 term. 59% of entering class graduated.
**Foreign students:** 178 students are from out of the country. Countries represented include Hong Kong, Indonesia, Japan, Mexico, Spain, and the Philippines; 53 in all.

**PROGRAMS OF STUDY. Degrees:** B.A., B.Bus.Admin., B.S.
**Majors:** Accounting, Afro-American Studies, Art History, Biochemistry, Biology, Business Administration, Chemistry, Chicano Studies, Civil Engineering, Classical Civilization, Classics, Communication Arts, Communication Studies, Computer Science, Dance, Economics, Electrical Engineering, Engineering Physics, English, European Studies, French, Greek, History, Humanities, Individualized Studies, Latin, Liberal/General Studies, Mathematics, Mechanical Engineering, Music, Natural Science, Philosophy, Physics, Political Science, Psychology, Sociology, Spanish, Studio Arts, Theatre Arts, Theology, Urban Studies.
**Distribution of degrees:** The majors with the highest enrollment are business administration, communication arts, and psychology; engineering physics, French, and biochemistry have the lowest.
**Requirements:** General education requirement.
**Academic regulations:** Minimum 2.0 GPA must be maintained.
**Special:** Minors offered in most majors and in alcohol/drug studies, Asian/Pacific studies, German, Hispanic business, Italian, pastoral studies, peace studies, and women's studies. Self-designed majors. Double majors. Dual degrees. Independent study. Accelerated study. Pass/fail grading option. Internships. Graduate school at which undergraduates may take graduate-level courses. Preprofessional programs in law, medicine, veterinary science, pharmacy, dentistry, and optometry. Washington Semester. Teacher certification in elementary, secondary, and special education. Certification in specific subject areas. Study abroad in Germany, Mexico, and Monaco and in other countries by arrangement. AFROTC. ROTC and NROTC at UCLA.
**Honors:** Honors program. Honor societies.
**Academic Assistance:** Remedial study skills. Nonremedial tutoring.

**STUDENT LIFE. Housing:** Students may live on or off campus. Coed, women's, and men's dorms. School-owned/operated apartments. 48% of students live in college housing.
**Social atmosphere:** The student newspaper reports, "Los Angeles is a great place to go to school, and a university is a great environment to be in–the world is at your fingertips in both instances. There seem to be a lot of parties and activities on campus and any imaginable off-campus activity in the city." Basketball games, the Awareness Music Festival, Oktoberfest, Spring Luau, Homecoming, Mardi Gras, and the Mass of the Holy Spirit Day Picnic are the most popular social events of the year. The Campus Ministry, the basketball team, and the student newspaper are influential on campus. Students frequent the Bird Nest, Hannon Loft, the Lair, Toes Tavern, Tower Pizza, and Islands.
**Services and counseling/handicapped student services:** Placement services. Health service. Counseling services for minority and older students. Personal and psychological counseling. Career and academic guidance services. Religious counseling. Physically disabled student services. Learning disabled services. Tutors.
**Campus organizations:** Undergraduate student government. Student newspaper (Loyolan, published once/week). Literary magazine. Yearbook. Radio station. Men's and women's choruses, debating, prelegal society, Arnold Air Society, sailing club, academic, service, social, and special-interest groups, 117 organizations in all. Six fraternities, no chapter houses; four sororities, no chapter houses. 13% of men join a fraternity. 11% of women join a sorority.
**Religious organizations:** Campus Ministry.
**Minority/foreign student organizations:** Asian-Pacific Student Association, Black Student Union, Filipino-American Society, MEChA. International Student Association.

**ATHLETICS. Physical education requirements:** None.
**Intercollegiate competition:** 10% of students participate. Baseball (M), basketball (M,W), crew (M,W), cross-country (M,W), golf (M), soccer (M), softball (W), swimming (W), tennis (M,W), volleyball (M,W), water polo (M). Member of NCAA Division I, Southern California Rugby Football League, West Coast Athletic Conference, Western Intercollegiate Volleyball Association, Western International Rowing Association.
**Intramural and club sports:** 30% of students participate. Intramural basketball, football, sailing, soccer, surfing, tennis, ultimate frisbee, volleyball. Men's club lacrosse, rugby. Women's club cheerleading, soccer.

**ADMISSIONS. Academic basis for candidate selection** (in order of priority): Secondary school record, standardized test scores, essay, school's recommendation, class rank.
**Nonacademic basis for candidate selection:** Particular talent or ability is important. Character and personality, extracurricular participation, and alumni/ae relationship are considered.
**Requirements:** Graduation from secondary school is required; GED is accepted. 16 units and the following program of study are recommended: 4 units of English, 3 units of math, 2 units of lab science, 3 units of foreign language, 3 units of social studies, 1 unit of electives. 4 units of math required of computer science, engineering, and mathematics program applicants. Audition required of music program applicants. SAT is required; ACT may be substituted. Campus visit and interview recommended. Off-campus interviews available with an alumni representative.
**Procedure:** Take SAT or ACT by fall of 12th year. Suggest filing application by February 1; no deadline. Notification of admission on rolling basis. Reply is required by May 1. $200 nonrefundable tuition deposit. $200 nonrefundable room deposit. Freshmen accepted for terms other than fall.
**Special programs:** Admission may be deferred one year. Credit and/or placement may be granted through CEEB Advanced Placement exams for scores of 3 or higher. Placement may be granted through CLEP general exams and DANTES exams. Credit and/or placement may be granted through CLEP subject exams. Credit and placement may be granted through challenge exams. Early entrance/early admission program.
**Transfer students:** Transfer students accepted for terms other than fall. In fall 1993, 33% of all new students were transfers into all classes. 995 transfer applications were received, 603 were accepted. Application deadline is July 1 for fall; December 1 for spring. Minimum 2.75 GPA required. Lowest course grade accepted is "C." Maximum number of transferable credits is 60 semester hours from a two-year school and 90 semester hours from a four-year school. At least 30 semester hours must be completed at the university to receive degree.
**Admissions contact:** Matthew X. Fissinger, M.A., Director of Admissions. 310 338-2750.

**FINANCIAL AID. Available aid:** Pell grants, SEOG, state grants, school scholarships and grants, private scholarships and grants, ROTC scholarships, academic merit scholarships, and athletic scholarships. Perkins Loans (NDSL), PLUS, Stafford Loans (GSL), state loans, school loans, private loans, and SLS. Knight Tuition Plans and deferred payment plan.
**Financial aid statistics:** 4% of aid is not need-based. In 1993-94, 67% of all undergraduate applicants received aid; 95% of freshman applicants. Average amounts of aid awarded freshmen: Scholarships and grants, $8,638; loans, $4,147.
**Supporting data/closing dates:** FAFSA/FAF/FFS: Priority filing date is February 15. State aid form: Priority filing date is February 15; deadline is March 2. Income tax forms: Priority filing date is April 16; accepted on rolling basis. Notification of awards on rolling basis.
**Financial aid contact:** Donna M. Palmer, M.A., Director of Financial Aid. 310 338-2753.

**STUDENT EMPLOYMENT.** College Work/Study Program. Institutional employment. 45% of full-time undergraduates work on campus during school year. Students may expect to earn an average of $2,400 during school year. Off-campus part-time employment opportunities rated "excellent."

**COMPUTER FACILITIES.** 200 IBM/IBM-compatible and Macintosh/Apple microcomputers; 180 are networked. Students may access IBM minicomputer/mainframe systems, BITNET, Internet. Client/LAN operating systems include DOS, Windows NT. Computer languages and software packages include Ada, BASIC, dBASE, Excel, FORTRAN, Framework, Lotus 1-2-3, PageMaker, Pascal, PL/1, Quattro, SAS, SPSS-X, Storm, WordPerfect. Computer facilities are available to all students.
**Fees:** None.
**Hours:** 8 AM-2 AM (M-F).

**GRADUATE CAREER DATA.** Highest graduate school enrollments: UCLA, U of Southern California. Companies and businesses that hire graduates: IBM, TRW, Xerox.

**PROMINENT ALUMNI/AE.** Tony Coelho, former U.S. congressman; Daniel Travanti, TV actor; Don Kosterman, sports manager; Richard Adelman, NBA coach; Dave Roberti, president, California State Senate; Sr. Elizabeth Mary Strub, superior general; Albert Rabeteau, dean, Princeton U; Winfred C. Hervey-Stallworth, producer, *Golden Girls*.

# The Master's College

**Newhall, CA 91321 — 805 259-3540**

**1994-95 Costs.** Tuition: $9,084. Room & board: $2,100. Fees, books, misc. academic expenses (school's estimate): $500.
**Enrollment.** Undergraduates: 367 men, 386 women (full-time). Freshman class: 364 applicants, 312 accepted, 162 enrolled. Graduate enrollment: 7 men, 32 women.
**Test score averages/ranges.** Average SAT scores: 456 verbal, 488 math. Range of SAT scores of middle 50%: 430-470 verbal, 440-490 math. Average ACT scores: 24 English, 22 math, 23 composite. Range of ACT scores of middle 50%: 18-25 English, 19-23 math.
**Faculty.** 44 full-time; 41 part-time. 43% of faculty holds doctoral degree. Student/faculty ratio: 19 to 1.
**Selectivity rating.** Less competitive.

**PROFILE.** The Master's College, founded in 1927, is a private, church-affiliated college. Programs are offered in the Division of Biblical Studies, Humanities, Natural Sciences, and Social Sciences. Its 100-acre campus is located in Newhall, 35 miles from Los Angeles.

**Accreditation:** WASC.
**Religious orientation:** The Master's College is a nondenominational Christian school; eight semesters of theology required.
**Library:** Collections totaling over 110,000 volumes, 456 periodical subscriptions, and 5,000 microform items.
**Athletic facilities:** Gymnasium, athletic fields, swimming pool, tennis and volleyball courts, fitness center.

**STUDENT BODY. Undergraduate profile:** 73% are state residents; 41% are transfers. 3% Asian-American, 2% Black, 3% Hispanic, 1% Native American, 87% White, 4% Other. Average age of undergraduates is 23.
**Freshman profile:** 1% of freshmen who took SAT scored 700 or over on verbal, 4% scored 700 or over on math; 8% scored 600 or over on verbal, 21% scored 600 or over on math; 33% scored 500 or over on verbal, 48% scored 500 or over on math; 69% scored 400 or over on verbal, 77% scored 400 or over on math; 94% scored 300 or over on verbal, 93%

scored 300 or over on math. 7% of freshmen who took ACT scored 30 or over on English, 2% scored 30 or over on math, 5% scored 30 or over on composite; 42% scored 24 or over on English, 32% scored 24 or over on math, 38% scored 24 or over on composite; 95% scored 18 or over on English, 70% scored 18 or over on math, 90% scored 18 or over on composite; 100% scored 12 or over on English, 100% scored 12 or over on math, 100% scored 12 or over on composite. 75% of accepted applicants took SAT; 25% took ACT. 64% of freshmen come from public schools.
**Undergraduate achievement:** 50% of fall 1991 freshmen returned for fall 1992 term. 10% of students who completed a degree program immediately went on to graduate study.
**Foreign students:** 31 students are from out of the country. Countries represented include Argentina, the Bahamas, Canada, Japan, New Zealand, and Switzerland; 17 in all.
**PROGRAMS OF STUDY. Degrees:** B.A., B.S.
**Majors:** Biblical Counseling, Biblical Studies, Biological Sciences, Business Administration, Communication, English, History, Home Economics, Liberal Studies, Liberal Studies/Teaching Credential, Mathematics, Music, Natural Science, Nursing, Physical Education, Political Studies.
**Distribution of degrees:** The majors with the highest enrollment are biblical studies and liberal studies; music, home economics, and mathematics have the lowest.
**Requirements:** General education requirement.
**Academic regulations:** Minimum 2.0 GPA must be maintained.
**Special:** Minor offered in biblical studies. Independent study. Preprofessional programs in theology. 3-2 nursing program with Coll of the Canyons. Member of Christian College Coalition. Washington Semester. Teacher certification in elementary, secondary, and special education. Certification in specific subject areas. Exchange program abroad in Israel/Jordan (Institute of Holy Land Studies).
**Academic Assistance:** Remedial math. Nonremedial tutoring.
**ADMISSIONS. Academic basis for candidate selection** (in order of priority): Essay, secondary school record, standardized test scores, class rank, school's recommendation.
**Nonacademic basis for candidate selection:** Character and personality are emphasized. Extracurricular participation, particular talent or ability, and alumni/ae relationship are considered.
**Requirements:** Graduation from secondary school is required; GED is accepted. 15 units and the following program of study are required: 3 units of English, 3 units of math, 2 units of lab science, 2 units of foreign language, 2 units of history, 3 units of academic electives. SAT verbal score in top 30th percentile and minimum 2.0 GPA required. The Master's Institute for applicants not normally admissible. SAT or ACT is required. ACH recommended. Campus visit and interview recommended. Off-campus interviews available with an admissions representative.
**Procedure:** Take SAT or ACT by June of 12th year. Take ACH by December of 12th year. Visit college for interview by June of 12th year. Suggest filing application by June 15. Application deadline is August 15. Notification of admission on rolling basis. Reply is required by August 20. $100 tuition deposit, refundable until August 1. $150 room deposit, refundable until August 1. Freshmen accepted for terms other than fall.
**Special programs:** Admission may be deferred one year. Credit and/or placement may be granted through CEEB Advanced Placement exams for scores of 3 or higher. Credit and/or placement may be granted through CLEP subject exams. Credit may be granted through military experience. Concurrent enrollment program.
**Transfer students:** Transfer students accepted for terms other than fall. In fall 1992, 41% of all new students were transfers into all classes. 255 transfer applications were received, 216 were accepted. Application deadline is August 15 for fall; January 1 for spring. Minimum 2.0 GPA required. Lowest course grade accepted is "C." Maximum number of transferable credits is 94 semester hours. At least 28 semester hours must be completed at the college to receive degree.
**Admissions contact:** Don Gilmore, Director of Admissions. 800 568-6248.
**FINANCIAL AID. Available aid:** Pell grants, SEOG, state grants, school scholarships, private scholarships, academic merit scholarships, and athletic scholarships. Perkins Loans (NDSL), PLUS, Stafford Loans (GSL), and SLS. Deferred payment plan.
**Financial aid statistics:** In 1992-93, 78% of all undergraduate applicants received aid; 44% of freshman applicants. Average amounts of aid awarded freshmen: Scholarships and grants, $3,044; loans, $1,552.
**Supporting data/closing dates:** FAFSA/FAF: Priority filing date is March 2; deadline is August 1. School's own aid application: Priority filing date is March 31; deadline is August 1. State aid form: Deadline is March 2. Income tax forms: Priority filing date is March 31; deadline is August 1. Notification of awards begins April 15.
**Financial aid contact:** Roxanne Robson, Director of Financial Aid. 805 259-3540.

# Menlo College

**Atherton, CA 94027-4301 — 415 323-6141**

**1993-94 Costs.** Tuition: $13,975. Room & board: $6,200. Fees, books, misc. academic expenses (school's estimate): $700.
**Enrollment.** Undergraduates: 313 men, 217 women (full-time). Freshman class: 430 applicants, 422 accepted, 138 enrolled.
**Test score averages/ranges.** Average SAT scores: 382 verbal, 447 math. Average ACT scores: 19 composite.
**Faculty.** 31 full-time; 19 part-time. 52% of faculty holds doctoral degree. Student/faculty ratio: 16 to 1.
**Selectivity rating.** Noncompetitive.

**PROFILE.** Menlo, founded in 1927, is a private, multipurpose college. Programs are offered in the Schools of Letters and Science and Business Administration. Its 62-acre campus is located in Atherton, 30 miles south of San Francisco.
**Accreditation:** WASC.
**Religious orientation:** Menlo College is nonsectarian; no religious requirements.
**Library:** Collections totaling over 80,000 volumes, 12,000 periodical subscriptions, and 640 microform items.
**Special facilities/museums:** Psychology lab, observation room.
**Athletic facilities:** Gymnasium, athletic fields, swimming pools, tennis courts, track, pavilion.
**STUDENT BODY. Undergraduate profile:** 60% are state residents. Average age of undergraduates is 20.
**Freshman profile:** 1% of freshmen who took SAT scored 700 or over on verbal, 2% scored 700 or over on math; 2% scored 600 or over on verbal, 8% scored 600 or over on math; 9% scored 500 or over on verbal, 31% scored 500 or over on math; 42% scored 400 or over on verbal, 66% scored 400 or over on math; 84% scored 300 or over on verbal, 98% scored 300 or over on math. 92% of accepted applicants took SAT; 15% took ACT. 49% of freshmen come from public schools.
**Undergraduate achievement:** 70% of fall 1991 freshmen returned for fall 1992 term. 32% of entering class graduated. 15% of students who completed a degree program went on to graduate study within five years.
**Foreign students:** 65 students are from out of the country. Countries represented include France, Germany, India, Japan, Philippines, and Spain; 25 in all.
**PROGRAMS OF STUDY. Degrees:** B.A., B.S.
**Majors:** Biotechnology Management/Biological Sciences, Business Administration, Communication, Computer Information Systems, Computer Science, General Studies, Humanities, Psychology.
**Distribution of degrees:** The majors with the highest enrollment are business administration, communication, and general studies; psychology, humanities, and biological sciences have the lowest.
**Requirements:** General education requirement.
**Academic regulations:** Minimum 2.0 GPA must be maintained.
**Special:** Minors offered in all majors and in art, French, history, literature, philosophy, and Spanish. Two-year transfer program in the School of Letters and Sciences. Liberal arts core curriculum requirements for bachelor's degree candidates. Associate's degrees offered. Double majors. Dual degrees. Independent study. Accelerated study. Internships. Preprofessional programs in allied health, nursing, biotechnology management, and biological sciences. ROTC at Santa Clara U.
**Academic Assistance:** Nonremedial tutoring.
**ADMISSIONS. Academic basis for candidate selection** (in order of priority): Secondary school record, standardized test scores, school's recommendation, essay, class rank.
**Nonacademic basis for candidate selection:** Extracurricular participation and particular talent or ability are important. Character and personality and alumni/ae relationship are considered.
**Requirements:** Graduation from secondary school is required; GED is accepted. 12 units and the following program of study are recommended: 4 units of English, 3 units of math, 3 units of science, 3 units of foreign language, 2 units of social studies, 2 units of history. Minimum 2.0 GPA recommended. SAT is required; ACT may be substituted. Campus visit and interview recommended. Off-campus interviews available with an admissions representative.
**Procedure:** Take SAT or ACT by December of 12th year. Take ACH by December of 12th year. Suggest filing application by December 1; no deadline. Notification of admission on rolling basis. No set date by which applicants must accept offer. $450 tuition deposit, refundable until May 1. Freshmen accepted for terms other than fall.
**Special programs:** Admission may be deferred one year. Credit and/or placement may be granted through CEEB Advanced Placement exams for scores of 3 or higher. Placement may be granted through challenge exams. Credit and placement may be granted through ACT PEP exams. Early decision program. Deadline for applying for early decision is December 1. Early entrance/early admission program.
**Transfer students:** Transfer students accepted for terms other than fall. In fall 1992, 80 transfer applications were received, 60 were accepted. Application deadline is rolling for fall; rolling for spring. Minimum 2.0 GPA required. Lowest course grade accepted is "C." Maximum number of transferable credits is 90 semester hours. At least 30 semester hours must be completed at the college to receive degree.
**Admissions contact:** Jim Whitaker, Dean of Enrollment Management. 415 688-3753, 800 55-MENLO.
**FINANCIAL AID. Available aid:** Pell grants, SEOG, state scholarships and grants, school scholarships, private scholarships, and academic merit scholarships. Perkins Loans (NDSL), PLUS, Stafford Loans (GSL), and SLS. Tuition Plan Inc. and Knight Tuition Plans.
**Financial aid statistics:** In 1992-93, 90% of all undergraduate applicants received aid; 90% of freshman applicants. Average amounts of aid awarded freshmen: Scholarships and grants, $13,310; loans, $2,200.
**Supporting data/closing dates:** FAFSA/FAF/FFS: Priority filing date is March 2. SAAC: Priority filing date is March 2. Notification of awards on rolling basis.
**Financial aid contact:** Adria Olender, Financial Aid Counselor. 415 688-3753, 800 55-MENLO.

# Mills College

**Oakland, CA 94613 — 510 430-2255**

**1993-94 Costs.** Tuition: $14,100. Room & board: $6,000. Fees, books, misc. academic expenses (school's estimate): $890.
**Enrollment.** 824 women (full-time). Freshman class: 490 applicants, 414 accepted, 132 enrolled. Graduate enrollment: 55 men, 258 women.
**Test score averages/ranges.** Average SAT scores: 535 verbal, 536 math. Range of SAT scores of middle 50%: 470-610 verbal, 480-600 math. Average ACT scores: 25 English, 23 math, 25 composite.
**Faculty.** 71 full-time; 72 part-time. 78% of faculty holds doctoral degree. Student/faculty ratio: 11 to 1.
**Selectivity rating.** More competitive.

**PROFILE.** Mills, founded in 1852, is a private, liberal arts college for women. Its 135-acre campus is located in Oakland, 18 miles east of San Francisco.

**Accreditation:** WASC.
**Religious orientation:** Mills College is nonsectarian; no religious requirements.
**Library:** Collections totaling over 207,632 volumes, 657 periodical subscriptions, and 7,900 microform items.
**Special facilities/museums:** Art galleries, center for contemporary music, on-campus elementary school, botanical gardens.
**Athletic facilities:** Swimming pool, gymnasium, basketball, tennis, and volleyball courts, boathouse, cross-country trail, aerobics and weight room, fitness center, soccer field.

**STUDENT BODY. Undergraduate profile:** 71% are state residents; 58% are transfers. 14% Asian-American, 7% Black, 6% Hispanic, 1% Native American, 69% White, 3% Other. Average age of undergraduates is 23.
**Freshman profile:** 3% of freshmen who took SAT scored 700 or over on verbal, 6% scored 700 or over on math; 28% scored 600 or over on verbal, 29% scored 600 or over on math; 66% scored 500 or over on verbal, 69% scored 500 or over on math; 93% scored 400 or over on verbal, 94% scored 400 or over on math; 98% scored 300 or over on verbal, 100% scored 300 or over on math. 15% of freshmen who took ACT scored 30 or over on composite; 47% scored 24 or over on composite; 91% scored 18 or over on composite; 100% scored 12 or over on composite. 98% of accepted applicants took SAT; 26% took ACT. 77% of freshmen come from public schools.
**Undergraduate achievement:** 67% of fall 1992 freshmen returned for fall 1993 term. 62% of entering class graduated. 20% of students who completed a degree program immediately went on to graduate study.
**Foreign students:** 40 students are from out of the country. Countries represented include Canada, Hong Kong, Japan, South Korea, and Taiwan; 20 in all.

**PROGRAMS OF STUDY. Degrees:** B.A.
**Majors:** American Civilization, Art History, Biochemistry, Biology, Business Economics, Chemistry, Child Development, College Major Interest, Communication, Comparative Literature, Computer Science, Dance, Dramatic Arts, Economics, English, Environmental Studies, Ethnic Studies, French Studies, German Studies, Government, Hispanic Studies, History, International Relations, Liberal Studies, Mathematics, Music, Philosophy, Political/Legal/Economic Analysis, Psychology, Sociology, Sociology/Anthropology, Studio Art, Women's Studies.
**Distribution of degrees:** The majors with the highest enrollment are political/legal/economic analysis, communication, and biology; American civilization, comparative literature, and sociology/anthropology have the lowest.
**Requirements:** General education requirement.
**Academic regulations:** Minimum 2.0 GPA must be maintained.
**Special:** Minors offered. Departmental, divisional, and interdivisional majors. College major is student-designed interdisciplinary major. Self-designed majors. Double majors. Dual degrees. Independent study. Accelerated study. Pass/fail grading option. Internships. Graduate school at which undergraduates may take graduate-level courses. Preprofessional programs in medicine. 3-2 engineering programs with Boston U, UC Berkeley, and Stanford U. Five-year bachelor's/master's computer science program with Stanford U. Combined-degree statistics program with Stanford U. Cross-registration with California Coll of Arts and Crafts, UC Berkeley, California State U at Hayward, Chabot Coll, Coll of Alameda, Contra Costa Coll, Graduate Theological Union, Holy Names Coll, Laney Coll, Merritt Coll, St. Mary's Coll, Sonoma State U, and Vista Coll. Washington Semester. Exchange programs with Agnes Scott Coll, Fisk U, Howard U, Manhattanville Coll, Mount Holyoke Coll, Russell Sage Coll, Simmons Coll, Spelman Coll, Swarthmore Coll, and Wheaton Coll. Special visiting programs with Barnard Coll, Hollins Coll, and Wellesley Coll. Teacher certification in early childhood, elementary, and secondary education. Certification in specific subject areas. Study abroad in Austria, Denmark, England, France, Israel, Japan, Korea, Spain, and other countries.
**Honors:** Phi Beta Kappa. Honor societies.
**Academic Assistance:** Nonremedial tutoring.

**ADMISSIONS. Academic basis for candidate selection** (in order of priority): Secondary school record, standardized test scores, essay, school's recommendation, class rank.
**Nonacademic basis for candidate selection:** Alumni/ae relationship is emphasized. Character and personality, extracurricular participation, and geographical distribution are important. Particular talent or ability is considered.
**Requirements:** Graduation from secondary school is required; GED is accepted. No specific distribution of secondary school units required. Minimum 3.0 GPA required. Audition required of music scholarship applicants. Conditional admission possible for applicants not meeting standard requirements. Summer Academic Workshop for applicants not meeting standard requirements. SAT is required; ACT may be substituted. ACH recommended. Campus visit and interview recommended. Off-campus interviews available with admissions and alumni representatives.
**Procedure:** Take SAT or ACT by fall of 12th year. Visit college for interview by fall of 12th year. Application deadline is July 15. Notification of admission on rolling basis. Reply is required by May 1. $300 tuition deposit, refundable until May 1. $150 room deposit, refundable until May 1. Freshmen accepted for terms other than fall.
**Special programs:** Admission may be deferred one year. Credit may be granted through CEEB Advanced Placement for scores of 3 or higher. Credit may be granted through CLEP subject exams. Placement may be granted through challenge exams. Early entrance/early admission program. Concurrent enrollment program.
**Transfer students:** Transfer students accepted for terms other than fall. In fall 1993, 58% of all new students were transfers into all classes. 390 transfer applications were received, 310 were accepted. Application deadline is July 15 for fall; December 1 for spring. Minimum 3.0 GPA recommended. Lowest course grade accepted is "C." Maximum number of transferable credits is 67 semester hours from a two-year school and 77 semester hours from a four-year school. Maximum number of transferable credits is 77 semester hours; 110 quarter hours. At least 42 semester hours must be completed at the college to receive degree.
**Admissions contact:** Genevieve A. Flaherty, M.A., Director of Admissions. 510 430-2135, 800 87-MILLS.

**FINANCIAL AID. Available aid:** Pell grants, SEOG, state scholarships and grants, school scholarships and grants, private scholarships and grants, academic merit scholarships, and aid for undergraduate foreign students. Perkins Loans (NDSL), PLUS, Stafford Loans (GSL), state loans, school loans, and SLS. Knight Tuition Plans. Institutional installment plan.
**Financial aid statistics:** 15% of aid is not need-based. In 1993-94, 70% of all undergraduate applicants received aid; 75% of freshman applicants. Average amounts of aid awarded freshmen: Scholarships and grants, $11,908; loans, $3,250.
**Supporting data/closing dates:** FAFSA/FAF: Priority filing date is February 15. State aid form: Deadline is March 2. Notification of awards begins April 1.
**Financial aid contact:** Roberta Johnson, Ed.D., Director of Financial Aid. 510 430-2134.

# Mount St. Mary's College

**Los Angeles, CA 90049 — 310 476-2237**

**1994-95 Costs.** Tuition: $12,474. Room & board: $5,600. Fees, books, misc. academic expenses (school's estimate): $840.
**Enrollment.** Undergraduates: 75 men, 1,430 women (full-time). Freshman class: 577 applicants, 534 accepted, 270 enrolled. Graduate enrollment: 104 men, 234 women.
**Test score averages/ranges.** Range of SAT scores of middle 50%: 860-1080 combined.
**Faculty.** 66 full-time; 133 part-time. 58% of faculty holds highest degree in specific field. Student/faculty ratio: 15 to 1.
**Selectivity rating.** Less competitive.

**PROFILE.** Mount Saint Mary's, founded in 1925, is a church-affiliated, liberal arts college for women; men are admitted to undergraduate music and nursing programs and graduate programs. Its 53-acre campus, in white Spanish colonial style, is located in Los Angeles.

**Accreditation:** WASC. Professionally accredited by the American Physical Therapy Association, the National Association of Schools of Music, the National League for Nursing.
**Religious orientation:** Mount St. Mary's College is affiliated with the Roman Catholic Church (Sisters of St. Joseph of Carondolet); five semesters of religion/theology required.
**Library:** Collections totaling over 140,000 volumes, 690 periodical subscriptions, and 4,760 microform items.
**Athletic facilities:** Tennis courts, swimming pools, fitness centers.

**STUDENT BODY. Undergraduate profile:** 87% are state residents; 25% are transfers. 16% Asian-American, 10% Black, 35% Hispanic, 1% Native American, 29% White, 9% Other. Average age of undergraduates is 22.
**Freshman profile:** 1% of freshmen who took SAT scored 700 or over on verbal, 4% scored 700 or over on math; 10% scored 600 or over on verbal, 14% scored 600 or over on math; 36% scored 500 or over on verbal, 53% scored 500 or over on math; 75% scored 400 or over on verbal, 94% scored 400 or over on math; 96% scored 300 or over on verbal, 99% scored 300 or over on math. 91% of accepted applicants took SAT; 22% took ACT. 76% of freshmen come from public schools.
**Undergraduate achievement:** 81% of fall 1992 freshmen returned for fall 1993 term. 45% of entering class graduated. 37% of students who completed a degree program went on to graduate study within one year.
**Foreign students:** Five students are from out of the country. Countries represented include Japan, Korea, and the Philippines.

**PROGRAMS OF STUDY. Degrees:** B.A., B.Mus., B.S.
**Majors:** American Studies, Art, Biochemistry, Biological Science, Biological Sciences, Business, Chemistry, Child Development, Diversified Major, Elementary Teaching, English, French, Gerontology, Health Services Administration, History, Mathematics/Computer Studies, Music, Nursing, Philosophy, Political Science, Pre-Dentistry, Pre-Law, Pre-Medicine, Psychology, Religious Studies, Secondary Teaching, Social Science, Sociology, Spanish.
**Distribution of degrees:** The majors with the highest enrollment are nursing, psychology, and biology; philosophy, chemistry, and American studies have the lowest.
**Requirements:** General education requirement.
**Academic regulations:** Minimum 2.0 GPA must be maintained.
**Special:** Associate's degrees offered. Self-designed majors. Double majors. Dual degrees. Independent study. Pass/fail grading option. Internships. Graduate school at which undergraduates may take graduate-level courses. Preprofessional programs in law, medicine, veterinary science, dentistry, physical therapy, and health sciences. Cross-registration with UCLA. Washington Semester. Member of Carondolet College Exchange. Teacher certification in early childhood, elementary, secondary, and special education. Exchange programs abroad in Japan. Study abroad also in England, France, Mexico, Spain, and several other countries. ROTC and NROTC at UCLA. AFROTC at Loyola Marymount U.
**Honors:** Honors program.
**Academic Assistance:** Remedial reading, writing, math, and study skills. Nonremedial tutoring.

**ADMISSIONS. Academic basis for candidate selection** (in order of priority): Secondary school record, standardized test scores, class rank, essay, school's recommendation.
**Nonacademic basis for candidate selection:** Character and personality and extracurricular participation are important. Particular talent or ability, geographical distribution, and alumni/ae relationship are considered.
**Requirements:** Graduation from secondary school is required; GED is accepted. 16 units and the following program of study are recommended: 4 units of English, 3 units of math, 3 units of science, 2 units of foreign language, 2 units of social studies, 2 units of history. Combined SAT score of 900, rank in top quarter of secondary school class, and minimum 3.0 GPA recommended. Applicants not admissible to bachelor's degree program may be admitted to associate's degree program. SAT is required; ACT may be substituted. Campus visit and interview recommended. Off-campus interviews available with an admissions representative.
**Procedure:** Take SAT or ACT by November of 12th year. Suggest filing application by March 1; no deadline. Notification of admission is sent on a rolling basis beginning Janu-

ary 1. Reply is required by May 1. $100 nonrefundable tuition deposit. $100 nonrefundable room deposit. Freshmen accepted for terms other than fall.
**Special programs:** Admission may be deferred one year. Credit and/or placement may be granted through CEEB Advanced Placement exams for scores of 3 or higher. Credit may be granted through CLEP subject exams and challenge exams. Credit and placement may be granted through military and life experience. Early entrance/early admission program. Concurrent enrollment program.
**Transfer students:** Transfer students accepted for terms other than fall. In fall 1993, 25% of all new students were transfers into all classes. 316 transfer applications were received, 280 were accepted. Application deadline is rolling for fall; rolling for spring. Minimum 2.25 GPA required. Lowest course grade accepted is "D." Maximum number of transferable credits is 60 semester hours from a two-year school and 94 semester hours from a four-year school. At least 30 semester hours must be completed at the college to receive degree.
**Admissions contact:** Katy Murphy, Director of Admissions. 310 471-9516, 800 999-9893.

**FINANCIAL AID. Available aid:** Pell grants, SEOG, Federal Nursing Student Scholarships, state scholarships and grants, school scholarships and grants, private scholarships and grants, ROTC scholarships, academic merit scholarships, and athletic scholarships. Perkins Loans (NDSL), PLUS, Stafford Loans (GSL), NSL, school loans, and SLS. AMS and deferred payment plan.
**Financial aid statistics:** In 1993-94, 85% of all undergraduate applicants received aid; 77% of freshman applicants. Average amounts of aid awarded freshmen: Scholarships and grants, $4,500.
**Supporting data/closing dates:** FAFSA/FAF: Accepted on rolling basis. Notification of awards on rolling basis.
**Financial aid contact:** Beverly Porter, M.A., Director of Financial Aid. 310 471-9505.

## New College of California

**San Francisco, CA 94110** **415 241-1300**

**1993-94 Costs.** Tuition: $70. Housing: None. Fees, books, misc. academic expenses (school's estimate): $350.
**Enrollment.** Undergraduates: 111 men, 152 women (full-time). Graduate enrollment: 104 men, 166 women.
**Test score averages/ranges.** N/A.
**Faculty.** 17 full-time; 33 part-time. 50% of faculty holds doctoral degree. Student/faculty ratio: 10 to 1.
**Selectivity rating.** N/A.

**PROFILE.** The New College of California, founded in 1971, is a private, liberal arts college. Its one-acre campus is in San Francisco.

**Accreditation:** WASC.
**Religious orientation:** New College of California is nonsectarian; no religious requirements.
**Special facilities/museums:** Arts studio, video editing lab.

**STUDENT BODY. Undergraduate profile:** 87% are state residents; 75% are transfers. 9% Asian-American, 10% Black, 8% Hispanic, 3% Native American, 66% White, 4% Other. Average age of undergraduates is 28.
**Undergraduate achievement:** 70% of fall 1991 freshmen returned for fall 1992 term.
**Foreign students:** Countries represented include Argentina, Brazil, England, France, Germany, and Japan.

**PROGRAMS OF STUDY. Degrees:** B.A.
**Majors:** Anthropology, Arts/Social Change, Ecological Studies, Integrated Health Studies, Jazz Studies, Latin American Studies, Poetics, Politics/Society, Psychology, Self-Designed Emphasis, Sports in Society, Writing/Literature.
**Requirements:** General education requirement.
**Academic regulations:** Minimum 2.0 GPA must be maintained.
**Special:** Minors offered in all majors ("emphasis areas"); areas may be combined. Tutorials, student-directed seminars. Associate's degrees offered. Self-designed majors. Double majors. Independent study. Accelerated study. Pass/fail grading option. Internships. Graduate school at which undergraduates may take graduate-level courses. Combined B.A./M.A. poetics program. Summer off-campus field study opportunities. Teacher certification in bilingual/bicultural education. Study abroad in Mexico.
**Academic Assistance:** Remedial study skills.

**ADMISSIONS. Academic basis for candidate selection** (in order of priority): Standardized test scores, essay.
**Requirements:** Graduation from secondary school is recommended; GED is accepted. No specific distribution of secondary school units required. Campus visit and interview recommended. No off-campus interviews.
**Procedure:** Visit college for interview by August of 12th year. Suggest filing application by August 1. Application deadline is August 31. Notification of admission on rolling basis. Reply is required by end of late registration period. Freshmen accepted for terms other than fall.
**Special programs:** Admission may be deferred two years. Credit may be granted through CLEP general and subject exams, and life experience.
**Transfer students:** Transfer students accepted for terms other than fall. In fall 1992, 75% of all new students were transfers into all classes. Application deadline is August 31 for fall; January 31 for spring. Lowest course grade accepted is "C." Maximum number of transferable credits is 90 semester hours; 136 quarter hours. At least 30 semester hours must be completed at the college to receive degree.
**Admissions contact:** Katrina Fullman, Admissions Coordinator. 415 626-0884.

**FINANCIAL AID. Available aid:** Pell grants, SEOG, state scholarships and grants, school scholarships, and private scholarships and grants. PLUS, Stafford Loans (GSL), and SLS. Deferred payment plan. Institutional payment plan.
**Financial aid statistics:** In 1992-93, 80% of all undergraduate applicants received aid.
**Supporting data/closing dates:** FAFSA/FAF: Priority filing date is March 1; accepted on rolling basis. School's own aid application: Priority filing date is May 15; accepted on rolling basis. State aid form: Priority filing date is March 1; accepted on rolling basis. Income tax forms: Priority filing date is May 15; accepted on rolling basis. Notification of awards begins June 15.
**Financial aid contact:** Jan Murray, Acting Director of Financial Aid. 415 241-1300, extension 342.

## Northrop-Rice Aviation Institute of Technology

**Inglewood, CA 90301** **310 337-4444**

**1994-95 Costs.** Tuition: $8,424. Room & board: $6,930. Fees, books, misc. academic expenses (school's estimate): $500.
**Enrollment.** Undergraduates: 200 men, 36 women (full-time).
**Test score averages/ranges.** N/A.
**Faculty.** 29 full-time; 12 part-time. 10% of faculty holds highest degree in specific field. Student/faculty ratio: 20 to 1.
**Selectivity rating.** N/A.

**PROFILE.** Northrop-Rice Aviation Institute of Technology is a private institution. Founded in 1942, it changed its name from Northrop University in 1991.
**Accreditation:** SACS. Professionally accredited by the Accreditation Board for Engineering and Technology.
**Religious orientation:** Northrop-Rice Aviation Institute of Technology is nonsectarian; no religious requirements.
**Library:** Collections totaling over 10,500 volumes and 50 periodical subscriptions.
**Athletic facilities:** Fitness center, karate studio.

**STUDENT BODY. Undergraduate profile:** 80% are state residents. Average age of undergraduates is 28.

**PROGRAMS OF STUDY. Degrees:** B.S.
**Majors:** Aircraft Maintenance Engineering Technology.
**Requirements:** General education requirement.
**Special:** FAA-approved certificate programs in airframe and powerplant technology, avionics, and aircraft electrical systems. Associate's degrees offered.

**ADMISSIONS. Academic basis for candidate selection** (in order of priority): Secondary school record, class rank, school's recommendation, standardized test scores.
**Nonacademic basis for candidate selection:** Alumni/ae relationship is emphasized.
**Requirements:** Graduation from secondary school is required; GED is accepted. No specific distribution of secondary school units required. Campus visit recommended. Off-campus interviews available with an admissions representative.
**Procedure:** Notification of admission on rolling basis. Reply is required within 30 days of acceptance. $100 refundable tuition deposit. Freshmen accepted for terms other than fall.
**Special programs:** Admission may be deferred one year. Credit may be granted through CEEB Advanced Placement, CLEP general and subject exams, Regents College, ACT PEP, DANTES, and challenge exams. Concurrent enrollment program.
**Transfer students:** Transfer students accepted for terms other than fall. Application deadline is in August for fall; in February for spring. Minimum 2.25 GPA required. Lowest course grade accepted is "C." At least 99 quarter hours must be completed at the institute to receive degree.

**FINANCIAL AID. Available aid:** Pell grants and private scholarships and grants. PLUS, Stafford Loans (GSL), and school loans. Deferred payment plan.
**Supporting data/closing dates:** FAFSA/FAF/FFS: Priority filing date is April 1. Notification of awards on rolling basis.

## Occidental College

**Los Angeles, CA 90041** **213 259-2500**

**1994-95 Costs.** Tuition: $16,560. Room & board: $5,440. Fees, books, misc. academic expenses (school's estimate): $892.
**Enrollment.** Undergraduates: 761 men, 838 women (full-time). Freshman class: 2,638 applicants, 1,400 accepted, 440 enrolled. Graduate enrollment: 14 men, 16 women.
**Test score averages/ranges.** Average SAT scores: 540 verbal, 600 math. Range of SAT scores of middle 50%: 470-590 verbal, 540-640 math.
**Faculty.** 135 full-time; 49 part-time. 93% of faculty holds highest degree in specific field. Student/faculty ratio: 10 to 1.
**Selectivity rating.** Highly competitive.

**PROFILE.** Occidental, founded in 1887, is a private, liberal arts college. Its 120-acre campus, including buildings of Italian Renaissance architectural style, is located in Los Angeles.

**Accreditation:** WASC.
**Religious orientation:** Occidental College is nonsectarian; no religious requirements.
**Library:** Collections totaling over 520,000 volumes, 1,936 periodical subscriptions, and 175,197 microform items.
**Special facilities/museums:** Ornithology museum.

**Athletic facilities:** Gymnasiums, swimming pool, baseball, intramural, soccer, and softball fields, tennis and volleyball courts, weight room, dance studio, sports medicine center.

**STUDENT BODY. Undergraduate profile:** 55% are state residents; 15% are transfers. 16% Asian-American, 6% Black, 14% Hispanic, 1% Native American, 60% White, 3% Other. Average age of undergraduates is 20.
**Freshman profile:** 5% of freshmen who took SAT scored 700 or over on verbal, 10% scored 700 or over on math; 26% scored 600 or over on verbal, 49% scored 600 or over on math; 68% scored 500 or over on verbal, 85% scored 500 or over on math; 93% scored 400 or over on verbal, 97% scored 400 or over on math; 100% scored 300 or over on verbal, 100% scored 300 or over on math. 98% of accepted applicants took SAT; 2% took ACT. 62% of freshmen come from public schools.
**Undergraduate achievement:** 87% of fall 1991 freshmen returned for fall 1992 term. 70% of entering class graduated. 22% of students who completed a degree program immediately went on to graduate study.
**Foreign students:** 50 students are from out of the country. Countries represented include China, Hong Kong, Japan, the Philippines, South Africa, and Spain; 28 in all.

**PROGRAMS OF STUDY. Degrees:** B.A.
**Majors:** American Studies, Art, Asian Studies, Biochemistry, Biology, Chemistry, Classical Studies, Cognitive Science, Computer Science, Diplomacy/World Affairs, Economics, Engineering, English/Comparative Literary Studies, Exercise Science, French, Geochemistry, Geology, Geophysics, German, History, Languages/Literatures, Mathematics, Music, Philosophy, Physics, Politics, Psychobiology, Psychology, Public Policy, Religious Studies, Sociology/Anthropology, Spanish, Studio Art, Theatre, Women's Studies.
**Distribution of degrees:** The majors with the highest enrollment are English, economics, and psychology; geology, physics, and theatre arts have the lowest.
**Requirements:** General education requirement.
**Academic regulations:** Minimum 2.0 GPA must be maintained.
**Special:** Minors offered in all majors and in marine biology and Chinese, Hispanic/Latin American, Japanese, Latin, and Russian studies. Interdepartmental programs in area studies, health professions, and urban studies. Environmental science emphasis possible within biology and geology majors. Self-designed majors. Double majors. Independent study. Pass/fail grading option. Internships. Graduate school at which undergraduates may take graduate-level courses. Preprofessional programs in law, medicine, veterinary science, pharmacy, dentistry, theology, optometry, business administration, diplomacy/foreign service, engineering, government service, library science, music, personnel work, physical education, public administration, social work, and writing. 3-2 engineering programs with Caltech and Columbia U. 3-3 law program with Columbia U. Member of Southern California Consortium on International Studies. Washington Semester and UN Semester. Exchange program with Art Center Coll of Design. Teacher certification in early childhood, elementary, secondary, and special education. Certification in specific subject areas. Study abroad in China, England, France, Germany, Japan, Peru, Mexico, the former Soviet Republics, and Spain. ROTC and AFROTC at UCLA and U of Southern California.
**Honors:** Phi Beta Kappa. Honors program. Honor societies.
**Academic Assistance:** Nonremedial tutoring.

**STUDENT LIFE. Housing:** All freshmen must live on campus. Coed and women's dorms. Sorority and fraternity housing. 80% of students live in college housing.
**Social atmosphere:** The student newspaper reports, "Whatever one is interested in, there are two or three people, minimum, who are also into it and willing to get together. In an urban environment such as Oxy's, there is always more going on around campus than on campus, and it's a tough choice to decide when to find time to study. The Occidental student body is so diverse and eclectic that there are no identifiable groups, certainly not with real influence." Popular campus events include the Oxy Fall Weekend and Da Getaway. Concerning popular gathering spots, "On campus it's the quad in front of Freeman Union, where people gather to see and be seen. Off campus, perhaps the Big O, Troy's Burgers, Tommy's World Famous, and Julio's Itza Pizza."
**Services and counseling/handicapped student services:** Placement services. Health service. Women's center. Day care. Counseling services for minority, military, and older students. Birth control, personal, and psychological counseling. Career and academic guidance services. Religious counseling. Physically disabled student services. Notetaking services. Tape recorders. Tutors. Reader services for the blind.
**Campus organizations:** Undergraduate student government. Student newspaper (Occidental, published once/week). Literary magazine. Yearbook. Glee club, choir, jazz ensemble, orchestra, pep band, dance theatre, forensics union, Amnesty International, Anti-Apartheid Coalition, Project Literacy, Feminist Consciousness Coalition, athletic, departmental, political, and special-interest groups, 80 organizations in all. Four fraternities, all with chapter houses; three sororities, all with chapter houses. 18% of men join a fraternity. 18% of women join a sorority.
**Religious organizations:** Buddhist Organization, Canterbury Community, Christian Science Organization, Fellowship of Christian Athletes, Hillel, Interfaith Student Council, Latter-Day Saints Student Organization, Newman Club, Protestant Christian Fellowship.
**Minority/foreign student organizations:** Black Student Alliance, MEChA/ALAS, Latina Support Group, Asian-Pacific Alliance, Korean Club, Armenian Student Association. International Student Organization, Asian, Chinese, Filipino, and Japanese groups.

**ATHLETICS. Physical education requirements:** None.
**Intercollegiate competition:** 30% of students participate. Baseball (M), basketball (M,W), cross-country (M,W), diving (M,W), football (M), golf (M,W), soccer (M,W), softball (W), swimming (M,W), tennis (M,W), track and field (outdoor) (M,W), volleyball (W), water polo (M,W). Member of NCAA Division III, Southern California Intercollegiate Athletic Conference.
**Intramural and club sports:** 65% of students participate. Intramural basketball, flag football, indoor soccer, inner-tube water polo, softball, volleyball. Men's club bowling, fencing, lacrosse, martial arts, rugby, ultimate frisbee, volleyball. Women's club bowling, cheerleading, fencing, field hockey, lacrosse, martial arts, ultimate frisbee, water polo.

**ADMISSIONS. Academic basis for candidate selection** (in order of priority): Secondary school record, class rank, essay, school's recommendation, standardized test scores.
**Nonacademic basis for candidate selection:** Extracurricular participation and particular talent or ability are emphasized. Character and personality are important. Alumni/ae relationship is considered.
**Requirements:** Graduation from secondary school is required; GED is accepted. 16 units and the following program of study are recommended: 4 units of English, 3 units of math, 2 units of science, 3 units of foreign language, 2 units of history. 4 units of math, physics, and chemistry required of science and engineering program applicants. SAT is required; ACT may be substituted. ACH recommended. Campus visit and interview recommended. Off-campus interviews available with admissions and alumni representatives.
**Procedure:** Take SAT or ACT by January of 12th year. Take ACH by January of 12th year. Visit college for interview by February 1 of 12th year. Application deadline is February 1. Notification of admission by April 1. Reply is required by May 1. Nonrefundable $200 deposit required. Freshmen accepted for fall term only.
**Special programs:** Admission may be deferred one year. Credit and/or placement may be granted through CEEB Advanced Placement exams for scores of 4 or higher. Credit may be granted through challenge exams. Early decision program. In fall 1992, 65 applied for early decision and 23 were accepted. Deadline for applying for early decision is November 15. Early entrance/early admission program.
**Transfer students:** Transfer students accepted for fall term only. In fall 1992, 15% of all new students were transfers into all classes. 206 transfer applications were received, 100 were accepted. Application deadline is April 15 for fall; November 15 for spring. Minimum 3.0 GPA recommended. Lowest course grade accepted is "D." Maximum number of transferable credits is 18 courses. At least 17 courses must be completed at the college to receive degree.
**Admissions contact:** Charlene Liebau, M.A., Dean of Admission. 213 259-2700.

**FINANCIAL AID. Available aid:** Pell grants, SEOG, state scholarships and grants, school scholarships and grants, private scholarships and grants, academic merit scholarships, and aid for undergraduate foreign students. Perkins Loans (NDSL), PLUS, Stafford Loans (GSL), state loans, school loans, private loans, and SLS. Knight Tuition Plans and deferred payment plan.
**Financial aid statistics:** 15% of aid is not need-based. In 1992-93, 93% of all undergraduate applicants received aid; 95% of freshman applicants. Average amounts of aid awarded freshmen: Scholarships and grants, $12,412; loans, $4,438.
**Supporting data/closing dates:** FAFSA/FAF/FFS: Priority filing date is February 1. State aid form: Deadline is March 2. Income tax forms: Priority filing date is April 19. Notification of awards begins April 1.
**Financial aid contact:** Youlonda Copeland-Morgan, M.B.A., Director of Financial Aid. 213 259-2548.

**STUDENT EMPLOYMENT.** College Work/Study Program. Institutional employment. 43% of full-time undergraduates work on campus during school year. Students may expect to earn an average of $1,626 during school year. Off-campus part-time employment opportunities rated "good."

**COMPUTER FACILITIES.** 35 IBM/IBM-compatible and Macintosh/Apple microcomputers; all are networked. Students may access Prime, SUN minicomputer/mainframe systems, Internet. Residence halls may be equipped with stand-alone microcomputers. Client/LAN operating systems include Apple/Macintosh. Computer languages and software packages include BASIC, Pascal, SPSS, WordPerfect, Word Quattro Pro; 35 in all. Computer facilities are available to all students.
**Fees:** None.
**Hours:** 7 AM-2 AM.

**GRADUATE CAREER DATA.** Graduate school percentages: 5% enter law school. 4% enter medical school. 1% enter dental school. 10% enter graduate business programs. 20% enter graduate arts and sciences programs. Highest graduate school enrollments: Columbia U, Harvard U, Stanford U, UC Berkeley, UCLA. 30% of graduates choose careers in business and industry. Companies and businesses that hire graduates: Banks, investment houses, political and social agencies.

**PROMINENT ALUMNI/AE.** Robinson Jeffers, poet; Jim Mora, head coach, New Orleans Saints; Jack Kemp, former secretary, U.S. Department of Housing and Urban Development.

# Otis College of Art and Design

**Los Angeles, CA 90057** 213 251-0500

**1993-94 Costs.** Tuition: $12,285. Room & board: $4,266. Fees, books, misc. academic expenses (school's estimate): $1,957.
**Enrollment.** Undergraduates: 259 men, 408 women (full-time). Freshman class: 532 applicants, 303 accepted, 159 enrolled. Graduate enrollment: 13 men, 11 women.
**Test score averages/ranges.** Average SAT scores: 412 verbal, 458 math.
**Faculty.** 22 full-time; 150 part-time. 85% of faculty holds highest degree in specific field. Student/faculty ratio: 4 to 1.
**Selectivity rating.** Competitive.

**PROFILE.** Otis/Parsons School of Art and Design is a private, fine arts institute. Founded in 1918 as a coeducational institution, it merged with Parsons School of Design in 1978. Its three-acre campus is located in Los Angeles.

**Accreditation:** WASC. Professionally accredited by the National Association of Schools of Art and Design.
**Religious orientation:** Otis College of Art and Design is nonsectarian; no religious requirements.
**Library:** Collections totaling over 25,844 volumes, 168 periodical subscriptions and 154 microform items.
**Special facilities/museums:** Art gallery, student gallery.

**STUDENT BODY. Undergraduate profile:** 78% are state residents; 34% are transfers. 24% Asian-American, 6% Black, 11% Hispanic, 1% Native American, 39% White, 19% Other. Average age of undergraduates is 23.
**Freshman profile:** Majority of accepted applicants took SAT.
**Undergraduate achievement:** 85% of fall 1992 freshmen returned for fall 1993 term. 30% of students who completed a degree program immediately went on to graduate study.
**Foreign students:** 113 students are from out of the country. Countries represented include England, Hong Kong, Japan, Korea, Singapore, and Sweden; 32 in all.
**PROGRAMS OF STUDY. Degrees:** B.F.A.
**Majors:** Academy of Freedom, Ceramics, Communication Arts, Environmental Arts, Fashion Design, Fine Arts, Illustration, Photographics, Photography, Surface Design.
**Distribution of degrees:** The majors with the highest enrollment are fine arts and illustration; ceramics and photography have the lowest.
**Requirements:** General education requirement.
**Academic regulations:** Minimum 2.0 GPA must be maintained.
**Special:** Associate's degrees offered. Graduate school at which undergraduates may take graduate-level courses. 3-2 B.A./B.F.A. programs in communication design, environmental design, illustration, and photography with Whittier Coll. Member of East Coast Consortium. Exchange programs with Cooper Union, Parsons Sch of Design, Rhode Island Sch of Design, and Sch of the Art Inst of Chicago. Exchange program abroad in England (Ravensbourne Coll of Design and Communication), France (Ecole Parsons a Paris), and Sweden (Konstfack National Coll of Art, Craft, and Design).
**Academic Assistance:** Remedial reading and writing.
**ADMISSIONS. Academic basis for candidate selection** (in order of priority): Secondary school record, standardized test scores, school's recommendation, class rank, essay.
**Nonacademic basis for candidate selection:** Particular talent or ability is emphasized. Character and personality and extracurricular participation are important. Alumni/ae relationship is considered.
**Requirements:** Graduation from secondary school is required; GED is accepted. No specific distribution of secondary school units required. College-preparatory program recommended. Portfolio and home exam required of all applicants. SAT is required; ACT may be substituted. Campus visit and interview recommended. No off-campus interviews.
**Procedure:** Suggest filing application by March 1. Application deadline is September 1. Notification of admission on rolling basis. Reply is required within two weeks of acceptance. $250 nonrefundable tuition deposit. $200 nonrefundable room deposit. Freshmen accepted for terms other than fall.
**Special programs:** Admission may be deferred one year. Credit may be granted through CEEB Advanced Placement for scores of 4 or higher. Early decision program. In fall 1993, 365 applied for early decision and 129 were accepted. Deadline for applying for early decision is March 1. Early entrance/early admission program. Concurrent enrollment program.
**Transfer students:** Transfer students accepted for terms other than fall. In fall 1993, 34% of all new students were transfers into all classes. 143 transfer applications were received, 111 were accepted. Application deadline is September 1 for fall; January 1 for spring. Minimum 2.5 GPA required. Lowest course grade accepted is "C." Maximum number of transferable credits is 60 semester hours. At least 70 semester hours must be completed at the college to receive degree.
**Admissions contact:** Joseph Suszynski, Director of Admissions. 213 251-0505, 800 527-6847.
**FINANCIAL AID. Available aid:** Pell grants, SEOG, state scholarships and grants, school scholarships and grants, and private scholarships and grants. PLUS, Stafford Loans (GSL), and SLS. AMS.
**Financial aid statistics:** 10% of aid is not need-based. In 1993-94, 75% of all undergraduate applicants received aid; 70% of freshman applicants. Average amounts of aid awarded freshmen: Scholarships and grants, $4,000; loans, $2,625.
**Supporting data/closing dates:** FAFSA/FAF: Priority filing date is March 1; accepted on rolling basis. School's own aid application: Priority filing date is March 1; accepted on rolling basis. State aid form: Priority filing date is March 1; accepted on rolling basis. Notification of awards begins March 1.
**Financial aid contact:** Wende McQueen, Assistant Director of Financial Aid. 213 251-0542.

# Pacific Christian College

**Fullerton, CA 92631** **714 879-3901**

**1993-94 Costs.** Tuition: $6,500. Room & board: $2,995. Fees, books, misc. academic expenses (school's estimate): $915.
**Enrollment.** Undergraduates: 176 men, 187 women (full-time). Freshman class: 276 applicants, 242 accepted, 144 enrolled. Graduate enrollment: 122 men, 18 women.
**Test score averages/ranges.** Average SAT scores: 482 verbal, 463 math.
**Faculty.** 24 full-time; 33 part-time. 40% of faculty holds doctoral degree. Student/faculty ratio: 18 to 1.
**Selectivity rating.** Less competitive.

**PROFILE.** Pacific Christian, founded in 1928, is a church-affiliated, multipurpose college. Programs are offered in the Divisions of Biblical Studies, General Studies, and Major Studies, and the Graduate Division. Its 12-acre campus is located in Fullerton, southeast of Los Angeles.

**Accreditation:** AABC, WASC.
**Religious orientation:** Pacific Christian College is affiliated with the Church of Christ; eight semesters of religion required.
**Library:** Collections totaling over 60,000 volumes, 460 periodical subscriptions, and 1,000 microform items.
**Special facilities/museums:** On-campus preschool, learning lab.
**Athletic facilities:** Swimming pool, weight room, basketball and volleyball courts.

**STUDENT BODY. Undergraduate profile:** 65% are state residents; 45% are transfers. 6% Asian-American, 4% Black, 6% Hispanic, 83% White, 1% Other. Average age of undergraduates is 20.
**Freshman profile:** 87% of accepted applicants took SAT; 13% took ACT. 85% of freshmen come from public schools.
**Undergraduate achievement:** 65% of fall 1991 freshmen returned for fall 1992 term. 42% of entering class graduated. 25% of students who completed a degree program immediately went on to graduate study.
**Foreign students:** 24 students are from out of the country. Countries represented include Cambodia, China, Kenya, Korea, and Mexico; 14 in all.
**PROGRAMS OF STUDY. Degrees:** B.A.
**Majors:** Associate Ministry, Child Development, Children's Ministry, Communications, Early Childhood Education, Elementary Education, English, General Education, General Social Science, Management, Missions, Music, Physical Education, Preaching, Psychology, Secondary Education/Social Science, Social Work, Youth Ministry.
**Distribution of degrees:** The majors with the highest enrollment are education, ministry, and psychology.
**Requirements:** General education requirement.
**Academic regulations:** Minimum 2.0 GPA must be maintained.
**Special:** Associate's degrees offered. Double majors. Dual degrees. Independent study. Pass/fail grading option. Internships. Cooperative education programs. Graduate school at which undergraduates may take graduate-level courses. Preprofessional programs in theology. Study abroad in England.
**Honors:** Honor societies.
**Academic Assistance:** Remedial reading, writing, and math.
**ADMISSIONS. Academic basis for candidate selection** (in order of priority): Secondary school record, standardized test scores, essay, school's recommendation, class rank.
**Nonacademic basis for candidate selection:** Character and personality are considered.
**Requirements:** Graduation from secondary school is required; GED is accepted. 17 units and the following program of study are recommended: 4 units of English, 2 units of math, 2 units of science, 2 units of foreign language, 2 units of social studies, 2 units of history, 3 units of electives. Minimum 2.5 GPA required. Conditional admission possible for applicants not meeting standard requirements. SAT is required; ACT may be substituted. Campus visit and interview recommended. Off-campus interviews available with admissions and alumni representatives.
**Procedure:** Take SAT or ACT by February of 12th year. Visit college for interview by May of 12th year. Suggest filing application by December 1. Application deadline is July 1. Notification of admission on rolling basis. Reply is required by July 1. $200 tuition deposit, refundable until July 1. $100 room deposit, refundable until July 1. Freshmen accepted for terms other than fall.
**Special programs:** Admission may be deferred one year. Credit may be granted through CEEB Advanced Placement for scores of 3 or higher. Credit may be granted through CLEP general and subject exams, challenge exams, and military and life experience. Early decision program. In fall 1992, 40 applied for early decision and 28 were accepted. Deadline for applying for early decision is December 1. Concurrent enrollment program.
**Transfer students:** Transfer students accepted for terms other than fall. In fall 1992, 45% of all new students were transfers into all classes. 100 transfer applications were received, 94 were accepted. Application deadline is July 1 for fall; December 1 for spring. Minimum 2.0 GPA required. Lowest course grade accepted is "C." Maximum number of transferable credits is 90 semester hours. At least 30 semester hours must be completed at the college to receive degree.
**Admissions contact:** Diane LeJeune, Director of Admissions. 714 879-3901, extension 290.
**FINANCIAL AID. Available aid:** Pell grants, SEOG, state scholarships and grants, school scholarships and grants, private scholarships and grants, and academic merit scholarships. Perkins Loans (NDSL), PLUS, Stafford Loans (GSL), and SLS. AMS.
**Financial aid statistics:** In 1992-93, 90% of all undergraduate applicants received aid; 90% of freshman applicants. Average amounts of aid awarded freshmen: Scholarships and grants, $2,000; loans, $2,500.
**Supporting data/closing dates:** FAFSA/FAF: Priority filing date is March 2; accepted on rolling basis. School's own aid application: Priority filing date is March 2; accepted on rolling basis. State aid form: Priority filing date is March 1; accepted on rolling basis. Income tax forms: Priority filing date is March 1; accepted on rolling basis. Notification of awards begins April 1.
**Financial aid contact:** Cheryl Foster, Director of Financial Aid. 714 879-3901, extension 207.

# Pacific Union College

**Angwin, CA 94508** **707 965-6336**

**1994-95 Costs.** Tuition: $12,150. Room & board: $3,525. Books (school's estimate): $300.
**Enrollment.** Undergraduates: 598 men, 725 women (full-time). Freshman class: 512 applicants, 452 accepted, 368 enrolled. Graduate enrollment: 1 man, 3 women.
**Test score averages/ranges.** Average ACT scores: 20 English, 20 math, 21 composite. Range of ACT scores of middle 50%: 17-24 English, 17-22 math.
**Faculty.** 109 full-time; 18 part-time. 44% of faculty holds doctoral degree. Student/faculty ratio: 14 to 1.
**Selectivity rating.** Less competitive.

**PROFILE.** Pacific Union, founded in 1882, is a church-affiliated, liberal arts college. Its 2,000-acre campus is located in Angwin, 70 miles northeast of San Francisco.

**Accreditation:** WASC. Professionally accredited by the Council on Social Work Education, the National Association of Schools of Music, the National League for Nursing.
**Religious orientation:** Pacific Union College is affiliated with the Seventh-day Adventist Church; six terms of religion required.

**Library:** Collections totaling over 141,228 volumes, 999 periodical subscriptions, and 9,768 microform items.
**Special facilities/museums:** Art gallery, natural history collection, on-campus elementary and high schools.

**STUDENT BODY. Undergraduate profile:** 78% are state residents; 3% are transfers. 14% Asian-American, 3% Black, 8% Hispanic, 1% Native American, 61% White, 13% Other. Average age of undergraduates is 19.
**Freshman profile:** Majority of accepted applicants took ACT.
**Undergraduate achievement:** 16% of fall 1991 freshmen returned for fall 1992 term.
**Foreign students:** 112 students are from out of the country. Countries represented include Japan; 15 in all.

**PROGRAMS OF STUDY. Degrees:** B.A., B.Bus.Admin., B.Mus., B.S., B.Soc.Work
**Majors:** Advertising Design, Applied Mathematics, Art History, Art/Studio, Behavioral Science, Biology, Biophysics, Business Administration, Business Education, Chemistry, Communication, Computer Science, Consumer/Family Science, Early Childhood Education, Engineering Technology, English, Fashion Merchandising, Fine Art, Foods/Nutrition, French, History, History/Government, Industrial Technology Education, Industrial Technology/Management, Interdisciplinary Studies, International Communication, Journalism, Liberal Studies, Mathematics, Medical Technology, Music, Nursing, Office Administration, Physical Education, Physical Science, Physics, Psychology, Public Relations, Recreation, Religion, Residential Interior Design, Social Studies, Social Work, Spanish, Theology.
**Distribution of degrees:** The majors with the highest enrollment are business administration, nursing, and liberal studies.
**Requirements:** General education requirement.
**Academic regulations:** Minimum 2.0 GPA must be maintained.
**Special:** Minors offered in most majors and in outdoor leadership and political science. Business administration, computer science, engineering technology, music, physical education, and physics majors include several options. Associate's degrees offered. Self-designed majors. Double majors. Independent study. Internships. Cooperative education programs. Graduate school at which undergraduates may take graduate-level courses. Preprofessional programs in law, medicine, veterinary science, pharmacy, dentistry, theology, optometry, and architecture. 3-1 medical technology programs with Hinsdale Hospital (Hinsdale, Ill.) and LaSierra U. Teacher certification in early childhood, elementary, and secondary education. Certification in specific subject areas. Exchange programs abroad in Austria (Bogenhofen Seminary), France (French Adventist Seminary), and Spain (Spanish Adventist Seminary).
**Honors:** Honors program.
**Academic Assistance:** Remedial reading, writing, math, and study skills.

**STUDENT LIFE. Housing:** All unmarried students under age 21 must live on campus unless living near campus with relatives. Women's and men's dorms. On-campus married-student housing. 66% of students live in college housing.
**Social atmosphere:** Favorite gathering spots include the cafeteria, dorm lobby, campus center, Taco Bell, and Lake Berryessa. Influential student groups include Seventh-day Adventists, the Student Assocation, the Asian Student Association, and the Hawaiian club. Popular events include movies, Vespers, Afterglow, Week of Prayer, varsity sporting events, fall picnic, and fall and spring festivals. "The social and cultural life is completely what you make it to be," reports the editor of the student newspaper. "Urban opportunities are endless because of proximity to San Francisco, Berkeley, and Napa."
**Services and counseling/handicapped student services:** Health service. Religious counseling. Learning disabled services.
**Campus organizations:** Undergraduate student government. Student newspaper (Campus Chronicle, published once/two weeks). Yearbook. Radio station. Concert and lecture series, recreational activities.
**Religious organizations:** Campus Ministry, Student Missions.
**Minority/foreign student organizations:** Hawaiian Club. International Club, Chinese Club, Korean Club.

**ATHLETICS. Physical education requirements:** Five terms of physical education required.
**Intramural and club sports:** Intramural basketball, floor hockey, football, handball, indoor and outdoor soccer, softball, tennis, volleyball.

**ADMISSIONS. Academic basis for candidate selection** (in order of priority): Secondary school record, school's recommendation, standardized test scores, class rank, essay.
**Nonacademic basis for candidate selection:** Character and personality are important.
**Requirements:** Graduation from secondary school is required; GED is accepted. No specific distribution of secondary school units required. Minimum 2.3 GPA recommended. Audition required of music program applicants. Conditional admission possible for applicants not meeting standard requirements. ACT is required. Off-campus interviews available with an admissions representative.
**Procedure:** Notification of admission on rolling basis. $1000 refundable tuition deposit. $100 room deposit, refundable until September 15. Freshmen accepted for terms other than fall.
**Special programs:** Admission may be deferred one year. Credit may be granted through CEEB Advanced Placement for scores of 3 or higher. Credit may be granted through CLEP subject exams and military experience. Placement may be granted through challenge exams. Concurrent enrollment program.
**Transfer students:** Transfer students accepted for terms other than fall. In fall 1992, 3% of all new students were transfers into all classes. 246 transfer applications were received, 177 were accepted. Minimum 2.0 GPA recommended. Lowest course grade accepted is "D-." Maximum number of transferable credits is 108 quarter hours. At least 36 quarter hours must be completed at the college to receive degree.
**Admissions contact:** Gary D. Gifford, Ed.D., Director of Admissions. 800 862-6336.

**FINANCIAL AID. Available aid:** Pell grants, SEOG, state grants, and school scholarships and grants. BIA grants. Perkins Loans (NDSL), PLUS, Stafford Loans (GSL), state loans, school loans, and SLS. Tuition Plan Inc. and guaranteed tuition.
**Financial aid statistics:** In 1992-93, 70% of all undergraduate applicants received aid; 70% of freshman applicants. Average amounts of aid awarded freshmen: Scholarships and grants, $4,800; loans, $1,200.
**Supporting data/closing dates:** FAFSA/FAF: Priority filing date is April 1. State aid form: Priority filing date is March 2. Notification of awards on rolling basis.
**Financial aid contact:** Tom Hopmann, M.B.A., Director of Financial Aid. 707 965-7200.

**STUDENT EMPLOYMENT.** College Work/Study Program. Institutional employment. 50% of full-time undergraduates work on campus during school year. Students may expect to earn an average of $2,300 during school year. Off-campus part-time employment opportunities rated "good."

**COMPUTER FACILITIES.** 50 IBM/IBM-compatible, Macintosh/Apple, and RISC-/UNIX-based microcomputers; 25 are networked. Students may access Sequent minicomputer/mainframe systems, Internet. Client/LAN operating systems include Apple/Macintosh, LocalTalk/AppleTalk, Novell. Computer languages and software packages include C, FORTRAN 77, LISP, Lotus 1-2-3, PageMaker, Pascal, Professional Write, WordPerfect. Computer facilities are available to all students.
**Fees:** None.

**GRADUATE CAREER DATA.** Highest graduate school enrollments: LaSierra U.

# Patten College

**Oakland, CA 94601** 510 533-8306

**1994-95 Costs.** Tuition: $4,780. Room & board: $5,076. Fees, books, misc. academic expenses (school's estimate): $860.
**Enrollment.** Undergraduates: 86 men, 60 women (full-time). Freshman class: 90 applicants, 88 accepted, 75 enrolled.
**Test score averages/ranges.** N/A.
**Faculty.** 10 full-time; 16 part-time. 50% of faculty holds doctoral degree. Student/faculty ratio: 10 to 1.
**Selectivity rating.** N/A.

**PROFILE.** Patten, founded in 1944, is a private, church-affiliated, liberal arts college. Its five-acre campus is located in a residential section of Oakland.

**Accreditation:** WASC.
**Religious orientation:** Patten College is affiliated with the Christian Cathedral Evangelical Church; eight semesters of biblical studies required.
**Library:** Collections totaling over 35,000 volumes and 200 periodical subscriptions.

**STUDENT BODY. Undergraduate profile:** 98% are state residents; 45% are transfers. 22% Asian-American, 29% Black, 8% Hispanic, 1% Native American, 38% White, 2% Other. Average age of undergraduates is 25.
**Freshman profile:** 40% of freshmen come from public schools.
**Undergraduate achievement:** 60% of fall 1992 freshmen returned for fall 1993 term. 40% of entering class graduated. 75% of students who completed a degree program immediately went on to graduate study.
**Foreign students:** 13 students are from out of the country. Countries represented include China, India, Jamaica, Japan, and Korea.

**PROGRAMS OF STUDY. Degrees:** B.A.
**Majors:** Business/Organizational Management, Christian Education, Elective, Liberal Studies, Pastoral Studies, Pre-Seminary, Sacred Music.
**Distribution of degrees:** The majors with the highest enrollment are liberal studies, pastoral studies, and Christian education; sacred music and pre-seminary have the lowest.
**Requirements:** General education requirement.
**Academic regulations:** Minimum 2.0 GPA must be maintained.
**Special:** Associate's degrees offered. Preprofessional programs in theology. Teacher certification in elementary education. Certification in specific subject areas.
**Academic Assistance:** Remedial reading, writing, math, and study skills. Nonremedial tutoring.

**ADMISSIONS. Academic basis for candidate selection** (in order of priority): Secondary school record, essay, school's recommendation, standardized test scores, class rank.
**Nonacademic basis for candidate selection:** Character and personality, extracurricular participation, and alumni/ae relationship are important. Particular talent or ability is considered.
**Requirements:** Graduation from secondary school is required; GED is accepted. 22 units and the following program of study are required: 4 units of English, 2 units of math, 2 units of science, 1 unit of foreign language, 4 units of social studies, 1 unit of history, 8 units of electives. Minimum 2.0 GPA required. Conditional admission possible for applicants not meeting standard requirements. SAT or ACT is recommended. Campus visit required. No off-campus interviews.
**Procedure:** Application deadline is July 15. Notification of admission on rolling basis. $50 nonrefundable room deposit. Freshmen accepted for terms other than fall.
**Special programs:** Admission may be deferred six months. Credit and/or placement may be granted through CLEP general and subject exams. Placement may be granted through military and life experience. Credit and placement may be granted through Regents College, ACT PEP, DANTES, and challenge exams.
**Transfer students:** Transfer students accepted for terms other than fall. In fall 1993, 45% of all new students were transfers into all classes. 85 transfer applications were received, 80 were accepted. Application deadline is July 15 for fall; December 10 for spring. Minimum 2.0 GPA required. Lowest course grade accepted is "C." Maximum number of transferable credits is 90 semester hours. At least 30 semester hours must be completed at the college to receive degree.
**Admissions contact:** Sharon Barta, Associate Director of Admissions. 510 533-8306, extension 250.

**FINANCIAL AID. Available aid:** Pell grants, SEOG, state scholarships and grants, school scholarships, academic merit scholarships, and athletic scholarships. Music scholarship. Minority scholarship. Perkins Loans (NDSL), PLUS, Stafford Loans (GSL), and SLS. AMS. Individual payment plans may be arranged.
**Financial aid statistics:** 20% of aid is not need-based. In 1993-94, 75% of all undergraduate applicants received aid; 80% of freshman applicants. Average amounts of aid awarded freshmen: Scholarships and grants, $2,500; loans, $2,500.

**Supporting data/closing dates:** FAFSA: Priority filing date is March 2; accepted on rolling basis. FAF/FFS: Accepted on rolling basis. School's own aid application: Priority filing date is March 2. State aid form: Accepted on rolling basis. Income tax forms: Accepted on rolling basis. Notification of awards on rolling basis.
**Financial aid contact:** Juanita Marshall-Bell, Director of Financial Aid. 510 533-8306, extension 247.

# Pepperdine University

**Malibu, CA 90263-4392 — 310 456-4000**

**1994-95 Costs.** Tuition: $18,200. Room: $3,750. Board: $3,020. Fees, books, misc. academic expenses (school's estimate): $870.
**Enrollment.** Undergraduates: 1,134 men, 1,511 women (full-time). Freshman class: 2,883 applicants, 1,738 accepted, 601 enrolled. Graduate enrollment: 75 men, 58 women.
**Test score averages/ranges.** Average SAT scores: 503 verbal, 567 math. Range of SAT scores of middle 50%: 440-540 verbal, 500-620 math. Average ACT scores: 25 composite. Range of ACT scores of middle 50%: 22-28 composite.
**Faculty.** 153 full-time; 144 part-time. 89% of faculty holds doctoral degree. Student/faculty ratio: 14 to 1.
**Selectivity rating.** More competitive.

**PROFILE.** Pepperdine, founded in 1937, is a private, church-affiliated, arts and sciences university. Programs are offered through the Schools of Business and Management and Law and the Graduate School of Education and Psychology. Its 830-acre campus is located in Malibu, 12 miles from Santa Monica.

**Accreditation:** WASC. Professionally accredited by the National Association of Schools of Music.
**Religious orientation:** Pepperdine University is affiliated with the Church of Christ; three semesters of religion required.
**Library:** Collections totaling over 465,695 volumes, 3,148 periodical subscriptions, and 438,896 microform items.
**Special facilities/museums:** Art museum.
**Athletic facilities:** Indoor and outdoor swimming pools, ski cabin on Mt. Hood, fencing, handball, and squash courts, all major sports facilities.
**STUDENT BODY. Undergraduate profile:** 40% are state residents; 14% are transfers. 6% Asian-American, 3% Black, 7% Hispanic, 1% Native American, 72% White, 11% Other. Average age of undergraduates is 21.
**Freshman profile:** 1% of freshmen who took SAT scored 700 or over on verbal, 5% scored 700 or over on math; 10% scored 600 or over on verbal, 33% scored 600 or over on math; 49% scored 500 or over on verbal, 78% scored 500 or over on math; 90% scored 400 or over on verbal, 97% scored 400 or over on math; 100% scored 300 or over on verbal, 100% scored 300 or over on math. 88% of accepted applicants took SAT; 23% took ACT. 60% of freshmen come from public schools.
**Undergraduate achievement:** 85% of fall 1991 freshmen returned for fall 1992 term. 49% of entering class graduated.
**Foreign students:** 42 students are from out of the country. Countries represented include England, Hong Kong, Indonesia, Japan, Mexico, and United Arab Emirates; 23 in all.
**PROGRAMS OF STUDY. Degrees:** B.A., B.S.
**Majors:** Accounting, Advertising, American Studies, Art, Biology, Business Administration, Chemistry, Communication, Communication Theory, Creative Writing, Economics, Elementary Education, English, Foreign Languages, French, German, History, Humanities, International Studies, Journalism, Liberal Arts, Literature, Mathematics, Mathematics/Computer Science, Music, Natural Science, Nutrition/Food Science, Philosophy, Physical Education/Kinesiology, Political Science, Psychology, Public Relations, Religion, Secondary Education, Social Science, Sociology, Spanish, Speech, Sports Medicine, Telecommunications, Theatre.
**Distribution of degrees:** The majors with the highest enrollment are business administration, interdisciplinary major, and telecommunications; chemistry, mathematics/computer science, and philosophy have the lowest.
**Requirements:** General education requirement.
**Special:** Minors offered in some majors and in computer science, nutritional science, and youth/human service administration. Double majors. Independent study. Accelerated study. Internships. Graduate school at which undergraduates may take graduate-level courses. Preprofessional programs in medicine, veterinary science, and dentistry. Teacher certification in elementary and secondary education. Study abroad in Asian countries, Australia, England, France, Germany, Greece, Israel, Italy, Japan, Russia, and Spain. ROTC at UCLA. AFROTC at U of Southern California.
**STUDENT LIFE. Housing:** All freshmen and sophomores under age 21 must live on campus unless living with family. Women's and men's dorms. 62% of students live in college housing.
**Social atmosphere:** The student newspaper reports, "Cultural life on campus is readily available with an art gallery, theater and entertainment productions. Off campus, cultural life could not be better; we are a half-hour drive from Hollywood, Beverly Hills, and Westwood." Popular gathering spots on campus are The Oasis, The Fountain, and the track. Off campus, students congregate at Carlo's, Pepe's, and the beach. Prominent organizations on campus include Greeks, Student Government Association, and Campus Crusade for Christ. Homecoming, Songfest Annual Production, and Oktoberfest are among the year's favorite events.
**Services and counseling/handicapped student services:** Health service. Personal and psychological counseling. Career and academic guidance services. Physically disabled student services. Learning disabled services. Notetaking services. Tape recorders. Reader services for the blind.
**Campus organizations:** Undergraduate student government. Student newspaper (Graphic, published once/week). Literary magazine. Yearbook. Radio and TV stations. A cappella chorus, choral ensemble, orchestra, drama club, debating and public speaking groups, news magazine, volunteer program, departmental, service, and special-interest groups. Seven fraternities, no chapter houses; four sororities, no chapter houses. 15% of men join a fraternity. 10% of women join a sorority.
**ATHLETICS. Physical education requirements:** Four semesters of physical education required.
**Intercollegiate competition:** 7% of students participate. Baseball (M), basketball (M,W), cross-country (M,W), diving (W), golf (M,W), swimming (W), tennis (M,W), volleyball (M,W), water polo (M). Member of NCAA Division I.
**ADMISSIONS. Academic basis for candidate selection** (in order of priority): Secondary school record, standardized test scores, school's recommendation, essay, class rank.
**Nonacademic basis for candidate selection:** Character and personality are important. Extracurricular participation, particular talent or ability, and alumni/ae relationship are considered.
**Requirements:** Graduation from secondary school is required; GED is accepted. 21 units and the following program of study are required: 4 units of English, 3 units of math, 2 units of science, 12 units of academic electives. Minimum combined SAT score of 1100 (composite ACT score of 26) and minimum 3.4 GPA recommended. Summer Bridge Program for applicants not normally admissible. SAT or ACT is required. Campus visit and interview recommended. Off-campus interviews available with an admissions representative.
**Procedure:** Take SAT or ACT by February 1 of 12th year. Visit college for interview by March 1 of 12th year. Application deadline is February 1. Admission notification on April 1 for applications received by February 1; thereafter if space is available. Reply is required by May 1. $150 nonrefundable tuition deposit. $250 room deposit, refundable until May 30. Freshmen accepted for terms other than fall.
**Special programs:** Admission may be deferred one semester. Credit and/or placement may be granted through CEEB Advanced Placement exams for scores of 3 or higher. Credit and/or placement may be granted through CLEP general and subject exams. Early decision program. In fall 1992, 433 applied for early decision and 227 were accepted. Deadline for applying for early decision is November 15. Concurrent enrollment program.
**Transfer students:** Transfer students accepted for terms other than fall. In fall 1992, 14% of all new students were transfers into all classes. 297 transfer applications were received, 167 were accepted. Application deadline is March 1 for fall; October 15 for spring. Minimum 2.7 GPA required. Lowest course grade accepted is "C." Maximum number of transferable credits is 70 semester hours. At least 28 semester hours must be completed at the university to receive degree.
**Admissions contact:** Paul Long, M.A., Dean of Admission. 310 456-4392.
**FINANCIAL AID. Available aid:** Pell grants, SEOG, state scholarships and grants, school scholarships and grants, private scholarships and grants, ROTC scholarships, academic merit scholarships, athletic scholarships, and aid for undergraduate foreign students. Perkins Loans (NDSL), PLUS, Stafford Loans (GSL), state loans, school loans, private loans, and SLS. AMS, deferred payment plan, and guaranteed tuition.
**Financial aid statistics:** 65% of aid is not need-based. In 1992-93, 70% of all undergraduate applicants received aid; 55% of freshman applicants. Average amounts of aid awarded freshmen: Scholarships and grants, $8,653; loans, $2,625.
**Supporting data/closing dates:** FAFSA/FAF/FFS: Deadline is March 1. School's own aid application: Priority filing date is December 1; deadline is March 1. Income tax forms: Priority filing date is February 15. Notification of awards begins April 1.
**Financial aid contact:** Israel Rodriquez, M.A., Director of Financial Aid. 310 456-4301.
**STUDENT EMPLOYMENT.** College Work/Study Program. Institutional employment. 47% of full-time undergraduates work on campus during school year. Students may expect to earn an average of $1,400 during school year. Off-campus part-time employment opportunities rated "excellent."
**COMPUTER FACILITIES.** 180 IBM/IBM-compatible and Macintosh/Apple microcomputers; 140 are networked. Students may access Hewlett-Packard, IBM, SUN minicomputer/mainframe systems. Residence halls may be equipped with networked microcomputers. Client/LAN operating systems include Apple/Macintosh, Novell. Computer languages and software packages include communication/graphics, database, word processing, spreadsheet, statistical, mathematical programs; 25 in all. Computer facilities are available to all students.
**Fees:** None.
**Hours:** 8 AM-11 PM (M-Th); 8 AM-9 PM (F); 10 AM-6 PM (Sa); noon-11 PM (Su).
**GRADUATE CAREER DATA.** Companies and businesses that hire graduates: Big Six accounting firms, finance, banking, and insurance companies.
**PROMINENT ALUMNI/AE.** Christopher Chetsanga, Nobel Prize nominee for cancer research and professor and dean of science, U of Zimbabwe; Kenneth Hahn, supervisor, county of Los Angeles; Norman Coulson, chairperson and CEO, Glendale Federal Bank; Terry Giles, president, Giles Enterprises.

# Pitzer College

**Claremont, CA 91711 — 909 621-8000**

**1994-95 Costs.** Tuition: $18,198. Room & board: $5,582. Fees, books, misc. academic expenses (school's estimate): $1,800.
**Enrollment.** Undergraduates: 360 men, 390 women (full-time). Freshman class: 1,150 applicants, 600 accepted, 225 enrolled.
**Test score averages/ranges.** Average SAT scores: 560 verbal, 580 math. Range of SAT scores of middle 50%: 500-640 verbal, 520-690 math. Average ACT scores: 25 English, 27 math, 26 composite.
**Faculty.** 60 full-time; 20 part-time. 99% of faculty holds doctoral degree. Student/faculty ratio: 10 to 1.
**Selectivity rating.** Highly competitive.

**PROFILE.** Pitzer is a private, liberal arts college. It is one of the Claremont Colleges, a group of five undergraduate colleges and one graduate school with adjoining campuses and shared facilities and services. Its 30-acre campus is located in Claremont, 35 miles east of Los Angeles.

**Accreditation:** WASC.

**Religious orientation:** Pitzer College is nonsectarian; no religious requirements.

**Library:** Collections totaling over 2,000,000 volumes, and 50,000 periodical subscriptions.

**Special facilities/museums:** Theatre arts center, black and Chicano study centers, film, TV, and videotape studios, botanical garden, biological field station, medical center.

**Athletic facilities:** Handball, racquetball, squash, tennis, and walleyball courts, swimming pools, track, baseball, football, and soccer fields, gymnasium.

**STUDENT BODY. Undergraduate profile:** 45% are state residents; 5% are transfers. 8% Asian-American, 8% Black, 12% Hispanic, 2% Native American, 70% White. Average age of undergraduates is 20.

**Freshman profile:** 10% of freshmen who took SAT scored 700 or over on verbal, 12% scored 700 or over on math; 35% scored 600 or over on verbal, 39% scored 600 or over on math; 68% scored 500 or over on verbal, 71% scored 500 or over on math; 98% scored 400 or over on verbal, 99% scored 400 or over on math; 100% scored 300 or over on verbal, 100% scored 300 or over on math. 92% of accepted applicants took SAT; 8% took ACT. 45% of freshmen come from public schools.

**Undergraduate achievement:** 95% of fall 1992 freshmen returned for fall 1993 term. 75% of entering class graduated. 70% of students who completed a degree program went on to graduate study within five years.

**Foreign students:** 70 students are from out of the country. Countries represented include England, France, Italy, Japan, Spain, and Switzerland; 27 in all.

**PROGRAMS OF STUDY. Degrees:** B.A.

**Majors:** American Studies, Anthropology, Art, Asian Studies, Biology, Chemistry, Chicano Studies, Classics, Economics, English, Environmental Studies, European Studies, Film Studies, Folklore, French, German, History, Human Biology, Latin American Studies, Linguistics, Mathematics, Music/Theatre, Organizational Studies, Philosophy, Physics, Political Studies, Psychobiology, Psychology, Sociology, Spanish, Women's Studies.

**Distribution of degrees:** The majors with the highest enrollment are psychology, English, and sociology; mathematics has the lowest.

**Requirements:** General education requirement.

**Academic regulations:** Minimum 2.0 GPA must be maintained.

**Special:** Self-designed majors. Double majors. Dual degrees. Independent study. Accelerated study. Pass/fail grading option. Internships. Graduate school at which undergraduates may take graduate-level courses. Preprofessional programs in law, medicine, and dentistry. 3-2 business administration, management, and engineering programs with Claremont Graduate Sch. Member of consortium with other Claremont Colleges, including Claremont Graduate Sch; qualified undergraduates may take graduate-level courses. Washington Semester. Over 100 exchange programs. Study abroad in Asian, Central and South American, and European countries; over 100 locations in all.

**Honors:** Phi Beta Kappa. Honors program.

**ADMISSIONS. Academic basis for candidate selection** (in order of priority): Secondary school record, standardized test scores, school's recommendation, essay, class rank.

**Nonacademic basis for candidate selection:** Character and personality, extracurricular participation, and geographical distribution are important. Particular talent or ability and alumni/ae relationship are considered.

**Requirements:** Graduation from secondary school is required; GED is accepted. 16 units and the following program of study are required: 4 units of English, 2 units of math, 2 units of lab science, 2 units of foreign language, 3 units of social studies. Electives chosen from listed subject areas preferred; full program of intellectually challenging work is more important than specific number of units. Minimum SAT scores of 500 in both verbal and math, rank in top quarter of secondary school class, and minimum 3.0 GPA recommended. SAT or ACT is required. ACH recommended. Campus visit and interview recommended. Off-campus interviews available with admissions and alumni representatives.

**Procedure:** Take SAT or ACT by November 1 of 12th year. Visit college for interview by February 1 of 12th year. Application deadline is February 1. Notification of admission by April 1. Reply is required by May 1. $300 tuition deposit, refundable until July 1. $200 nonrefundable room deposit. Freshmen accepted for terms other than fall.

**Special programs:** Admission may be deferred one year. Credit and/or placement may be granted through CEEB Advanced Placement exams for scores of 4 or higher. Early entrance/early admission program. Concurrent enrollment program.

**Transfer students:** Transfer students accepted for terms other than fall. In fall 1993, 5% of all new students were transfers into all classes. 256 transfer applications were received, 80 were accepted. Application deadline is April 1 for fall; December 1 for spring. Minimum 3.0 GPA recommended. Lowest course grade accepted is "C." Maximum number of transferable credits is the equivalent of two years of course work. At least two years of course work must be completed at the college to receive degree.

**Admissions contact:** Lisa Meyer, M.A., Director of Admissions. 909 621-8129.

**FINANCIAL AID. Available aid:** Pell grants, state scholarships and grants, school scholarships and grants, and private scholarships and grants. Perkins Loans (NDSL), PLUS, Stafford Loans (GSL), school loans, private loans, and SLS. Tuition Plan Inc., Knight Tuition Plans, and deferred payment plan. Institutional payment plans.

**Financial aid statistics:** In 1993-94, 100% of all undergraduate applicants received aid. Average amounts of aid awarded freshmen: Scholarships and grants, $9,000; loans, $2,200.

**Supporting data/closing dates:** FAFSA: Priority filing date is February 1. FAF: Deadline is February 1. State aid form: Deadline is February 1. Income tax forms: Deadline is May 1. Notification of awards begins April 1.

**Financial aid contact:** Abigail Parsons, Director of Financial Aid. 909 621-8208.

# Point Loma Nazarene College

**San Diego, CA 92106-2899** **619 221-2200**

**1993-94 Costs.** Tuition: $9,408. Room & board: $3,990. Fees, books, misc. academic expenses (school's estimate): $484.

**Enrollment.** Undergraduates: 746 men, 1,143 women (full-time). Freshman class: 809 applicants, 687 accepted, 426 enrolled. Graduate enrollment: 114 men, 264 women.

**Test score averages/ranges.** Average SAT scores: 425 verbal, 472 math. Range of SAT scores of middle 50%: 360-490 verbal, 390-540 math. Average ACT scores: 21 composite. Range of ACT scores of middle 50%: 19-23 composite.

**Faculty.** 118 full-time; 21 part-time. 60% of faculty holds doctoral degree. Student/faculty ratio: 16 to 1.

**Selectivity rating.** Less competitive.

**PROFILE.** Point Loma Nazarene, founded in 1902, is a private, church-affiliated, liberal arts college. Its 90-acre campus is five miles from downtown San Diego.

**Accreditation:** WASC. Professionally accredited by the National League for Nursing.

**Religious orientation:** Point Loma Nazarene College is affiliated with the Church of the Nazarene; three courses of religion required.

**Library:** Collections totaling over 155,904 volumes, 656 periodical subscriptions, and 36,934 microform items.

**Special facilities/museums:** Language lab, on-campus preschool, electron microscope.

**Athletic facilities:** Gymnasium, weight room, track, tennis courts, golf green, baseball, soccer, and softball fields.

**STUDENT BODY. Undergraduate profile:** 87% are state residents; 39% are transfers. 4% Asian-American, 3% Black, 7% Hispanic, 1% Native American, 80% White, 5% Other. Average age of undergraduates is 21.

**Freshman profile:** 1% of freshmen who took SAT scored 700 or over on verbal, 2% scored 700 or over on math; 4% scored 600 or over on verbal, 13% scored 600 or over on math; 23% scored 500 or over on verbal, 41% scored 500 or over on math; 62% scored 400 or over on verbal, 74% scored 400 or over on math; 93% scored 300 or over on verbal, 95% scored 300 or over on math. 2% of freshmen who took ACT scored 30 or over on composite; 21% scored 24 or over on composite; 86% scored 18 or over on composite; 100% scored 12 or over on composite; 1% scored 6 or over on English. 86% of accepted applicants took SAT; 15% took ACT. 77% of freshmen come from public schools.

**Undergraduate achievement:** 69% of fall 1992 freshmen returned for fall 1993 term. 28% of students who completed a degree program went on to graduate study.

**Foreign students:** 65 students are from out of the country. Countries represented include Japan, Mexico, South Korea, Spain, Sweden, and the Philippines; 25 in all.

**PROGRAMS OF STUDY. Degrees:** B.A., B.S.Nurs.

**Majors:** Accounting, Applied Communication, Art, Athletic Training, Biology, Biology/Chemistry, Business Administration, Business Education, Chemistry, Child Development, Church Music/Youth Ministries, Communication/Business, Computer Science, Dietetics, Drama, Economics, Engineering/Physics, Family Life Services, Graphic Communications, History, History/Political Science, Home Economics, Human Environmental Sciences/Business, Industrial/Organizational Psychology, Journalism, Liberal Studies, Literature, Management Information Systems, Mass Communications, Mathematics, Ministerial Studies, Music, Music Business, Nursing, Office Administration, Philosophy, Physical Education, Physics, Political Science, Psychology, Religion, Sociology, Spanish, Speech.

**Distribution of degrees:** The majors with the highest enrollment are business administration, liberal studies, and nursing; art, mathematics, and philosophy have the lowest.

**Requirements:** General education requirement.

**Academic regulations:** Freshmen must maintain minimum 1.7 GPA; sophomores, juniors, seniors, 2.0 GPA.

**Special:** Pass/fail grading option. Internships. Graduate school at which undergraduates may take graduate-level courses. Preprofessional programs in law, medicine, dentistry, and engineering. Member of Christian College Coalition. Washington Semester. American Studies Program (Washington, D.C.) and other off-campus study opportunities. Teacher certification in early childhood, elementary, secondary, special education, and bilingual/bicultural education. Certification in specific subject areas. Study abroad in Israel. ROTC and AFROTC at San Diego State U. NROTC at San Diego State U and U of San Diego.

**Honors:** Honors program. Honor societies.

**Academic Assistance:** Remedial writing, math, and study skills. Nonremedial tutoring.

**STUDENT LIFE. Housing:** All unmarried, full-time undergraduate students under age 25 must live on campus. Women's and men's dorms. School-owned/operated apartments. Off-campus married-student housing. 53% of students live in college housing.

**Social atmosphere:** According to the editor of the student newspaper, the most popular social events are Homecoming, the Kappa Phi Kappa Car Rally, Spiritual Emphasis Week, and contemporary Christian concerts. Most influential groups are the Campus Ministry, Beta Gamma Chi, the Surf Club, Covenant groups, Surfers for Christ, and Kappa Phi Kappa. On campus, students are avid fans of the basketball games and meet at the Tank, a meeting and recreation room. Off campus, they head for Horton Plaza, The Strand (an old movie theatre), Ocean Beach, Seaport Village, and The Caf.

**Services and counseling/handicapped student services:** Placement services. Health service. Counseling services for military and veteran students. Personal and psychological counseling. Career and academic guidance services. Religious counseling. Physically disabled student services. Learning disabled services. Notetaking services. Tape recorders. Tutors. Reader services for the blind.

**Campus organizations:** Undergraduate student government. Student newspaper (Point, published once/week). Literary magazine. Yearbook. Radio station. Vocal and instrumental groups, drama groups, debating, student teacher group, business, literature, and nursing clubs, professional groups, 22 organizations in all. Three fraternities, no chapter houses; three sororities, no chapter houses. 15% of men join a fraternity. 3% of women join a sorority.

**Religious organizations:** Ocean Beach Ministries, Habitat for Humanity, Urban Ministries, Mexico Outreach, Elderly Outreach, Project AIM.

**Minority/foreign student organizations:** African American Students Union, Hispanic Club.

**ATHLETICS. Physical education requirements:** Two courses of physical education required.

**Intercollegiate competition:** 11% of students participate. Baseball (M), basketball (M,W), cross-country (M,W), golf (M), soccer (M), softball (W), tennis (M,W), track and field (outdoor) (M,W), volleyball (W). Member of Golden State Athletic Conference, NAIA.

**Intramural and club sports:** 21% of students participate. Intramural badminton, basketball, bowling, flag football, sailing, softball, tennis, track, volleyball. Men's club volleyball.

**ADMISSIONS. Academic basis for candidate selection** (in order of priority): Secondary school record, standardized test scores, school's recommendation, class rank, essay.

**Nonacademic basis for candidate selection:** Character and personality are emphasized. Extracurricular participation is considered.

**Requirements:** Graduation from secondary school is required; GED is accepted. 9 units and the following program of study are recommended: 3 units of English, 2 units of math, 1 unit of science, 2 units of foreign language, 1 unit of history. Minimum 2.5 GPA required. Conditional admission possible for applicants not meeting standard requirements. SAT is recommended; ACT may be substituted. Campus visit recommended. Off-campus interviews available with an admissions representative.

**Procedure:** Take SAT or ACT by summer of 12th year. Notification of admission on rolling basis. No set date by which applicants must accept offer. $200 room deposit, refundable until 30 days prior to entering term. Freshmen accepted for terms other than fall.

**Special programs:** Admission may be deferred by agreement. Credit may be granted through CEEB Advanced Placement for scores of 3 or higher. Credit may be granted through CLEP subject exams. Credit and placement may be granted through ACT PEP and challenge exams, and military experience. Early decision program. In fall 1992, 237 applied for early decision and 151 were accepted. Deadline for applying for early decision is February 1. Early entrance/early admission program. Concurrent enrollment program.

**Transfer students:** Transfer students accepted for terms other than fall. In fall 1993, 39% of all new students were transfers into all classes. 614 transfer applications were received, 522 were accepted. Application deadline is rolling for fall; rolling for spring. Minimum 2.0 GPA required. Lowest course grade accepted is "D." Maximum number of transferable credits is 105 semester hours. At least 24 semester hours must be completed at the college to receive degree.

**Admissions contact:** William J. Young, Jr., Executive Director for Enrollment Services. 619 221-2273.

**FINANCIAL AID. Available aid:** Pell grants, SEOG, Federal Nursing Student Scholarships, state scholarships and grants, school scholarships and grants, private scholarships and grants, ROTC scholarships, academic merit scholarships, and athletic scholarships. Perkins Loans (NDSL), PLUS, Stafford Loans (GSL), NSL, state loans, private loans, and SLS. Tuition Plan Inc., Knight Tuition Plans, and AMS. Educational Credit Corp.

**Financial aid statistics:** 50% of aid is not need-based.

**Supporting data/closing dates:** FAFSA/FAF: Priority filing date is April 10. School's own aid application: Priority filing date is April 10. State aid form: Priority filing date is January 1; deadline is March 2. Notification of awards on rolling basis.

**Financial aid contact:** Jack Scharn, Associate Director for Enrollment Services/Financial Aid. 619 221-2296.

**STUDENT EMPLOYMENT.** College Work/Study Program. Institutional employment. 20% of full-time undergraduates work on campus during school year. Off-campus part-time employment opportunities rated "fair."

**COMPUTER FACILITIES.** 82 IBM/IBM-compatible and Macintosh/Apple microcomputers; 75 are networked. Students may access IBM minicomputer/mainframe systems, Internet. Client/LAN operating systems include Apple/Macintosh, DOS, UNIX/XENIX/AIX, LocalTalk/AppleTalk, Novell. Computer languages and software packages include Ada, AppleWorks, BASIC, C, COBOL, dBase, FORTRAN, Lotus, Microsoft Word, Microsoft Works, Pascal, SAS, SPSS-X, WordPerfect. Computer facilities are available to all students.

**Fees:** None.

**Hours:** 7:15 AM-11 PM (M-Th); 7:15 AM-5 PM (F); 9 AM-5 PM (Sa).

**GRADUATE CAREER DATA.** Graduate school percentages: 2% enter law school. 2% enter medical school. 2% enter graduate business programs. 20% enter graduate arts and sciences programs. 2% enter theological school/seminary. Highest graduate school enrollments: Nazarene Theological Seminary, Point Loma Nazarene Coll.

**PROMINENT ALUMNI/AE.** James Dobson, psychologist and writer; Ramon Cortines, superintendent of schools, New York City school district.

# Pomona College

**Claremont, CA 91711-6312** **909 621-8000**

**1993-94 Costs.** Tuition: $16,720. Room & board: $6,920. Fees, books, misc. academic expenses (school's estimate): $880.

**Enrollment.** Undergraduates: 726 men, 671 women (full-time). Freshman class: 3,036 applicants, 1,150 accepted, 390 enrolled.

**Test score averages/ranges.** Average SAT scores: 640 verbal, 700 math. Range of SAT scores of middle 50%: 600-680 verbal, 650-730 math.

**Faculty.** 153 full-time; 30 part-time. 100% of faculty holds highest degree in specific field. Student/faculty ratio: 9 to 1.

**Selectivity rating.** Most competitive.

**PROFILE.** Pomona, founded in 1887, is a private, liberal arts college. It is one of the Claremont Colleges, a group of five undergraduate colleges and one graduate school with adjoining campuses and shared facilities and services. Its 160-acre campus, with a Spanish-influenced architectural style, is located 35 miles east of Los Angeles.

**Accreditation:** WASC.

**Religious orientation:** Pomona College is nonsectarian; no religious requirements.

**Library:** Collections totaling over 1,800,000 volumes, 7,000 periodical subscriptions, and 1,100,000 microform items.

**Special facilities/museums:** Art gallery, botanical garden, biological field station, observatory.

**Athletic facilities:** Track, baseball, football, soccer, and softball fields, swimming pools, gymnasiums, basketball, racquetball, squash, and tennis courts, fitness center, rehabilitation center, dance studio.

**STUDENT BODY. Undergraduate profile:** 43% are state residents; 5% are transfers. 21% Asian-American, 4% Black, 11% Hispanic, 1% Native American, 56% White, 7% Other. Average age of undergraduates is 20.

**Freshman profile:** 13% of freshmen who took SAT scored 700 or over on verbal, 51% scored 700 or over on math; 72% scored 600 or over on verbal, 89% scored 600 or over on math; 94% scored 500 or over on verbal, 97% scored 500 or over on math; 100% scored 400 or over on verbal, 100% scored 400 or over on math. 94% of accepted applicants took SAT; 6% took ACT. 71% of freshmen come from public schools.

**Undergraduate achievement:** 98% of fall 1992 freshmen returned for fall 1993 term. 28% of students who completed a degree program immediately went on to graduate study.

**Foreign students:** 23 students are from out of the country. Countries represented include Canada, China, Mexico, the Philippines, and South Korea.

**PROGRAMS OF STUDY. Degrees:** B.A.

**Majors:** American Studies, Anthropology, Art, Asian Studies, Biology, Chemistry, Chinese, Classics, Computer Science, Economics, English, Foreign Language, Foreign Literature, French, Geology, German, Government, History, International Relations, Japanese, Linguistics, Literature, Mathematics, Media Studies, Molecular Biology, Music, Neuroscience, Philosophy, Philosophy/Politics/Economics, Physics, Psychology, Public Policy, Religion, Russian, Science/Technology/Society, Sociology, Spanish, Theatre, Women's Studies.

**Distribution of degrees:** The majors with the highest enrollment are molecular biology, politics, and economics.

**Requirements:** General education requirement.

**Academic regulations:** Minimum 6.0 GPA must be maintained (on a 12.0 scale).

**Special:** Interdepartmental concentrations. Black and Chicano study programs. Student participation in astronomy, biochemistry, biophysics, botany, chemistry, economics, geology, government, physics, psychology, sociology, and zoology research projects. Qualified students may earn credit for summer reading or research courses. Self-designed majors. Double majors. Dual degrees. Independent study. Pass/fail grading option. Internships. Preprofessional programs in law and medicine. 3-2 engineering programs with Caltech and Washington U. Member of consortium with other Claremont Colleges, including Claremont Graduate Sch; qualified undergraduates may take graduate-level courses. Washington Semester. Exchange programs with Colby Coll, Fisk U, Smith Coll, Spelman Coll, and Swarthmore Coll. Study abroad in Australia, the Dominican Republic, France, Great Britain, Israel, Japan, Kenya, Nepal, Spain, Zimbabwe, and other countries.

**Honors:** Phi Beta Kappa.

**Academic Assistance:** Nonremedial tutoring.

**STUDENT LIFE. Housing:** All freshmen must live on campus. Coed dorms. 93% of students live in college housing.

**Services and counseling/handicapped student services:** Placement services. Health service. Women's center. Counseling services for minority students. Birth control, personal, and psychological counseling. Career and academic guidance services. Religious counseling. Physically disabled student services. Notetaking services.

**Campus organizations:** Undergraduate student government. Student newspaper (Student Life, published once/week). Literary magazine. Yearbook. Radio station. Band, jazz ensemble, orchestra, chamber music group, choir, glee club, dance group, drama productions, computer science study group, Crossroads Africa, Volunteers in Asia, forensic society, Model UN, Women's Coalition, 280 organizations in all.

**Religious organizations:** Christian Fellowship, Hillel.

**Minority/foreign student organizations:** Chicano Studies Center, Office of Black Student Affairs, Black Student Union, MEChA. Asian Student Association, International Place.

**ATHLETICS. Physical education requirements:** One semester of physical education required.

**Intercollegiate competition:** 40% of students participate. Baseball (M), basketball (M,W), cross-country (M,W), diving (M,W), football (M), golf (M,W), soccer (M,W), softball (W), swimming (M,W), tennis (M,W), track (outdoor) (M,W), track and field (outdoor) (M,W), volleyball (W), water polo (M,W). Member of NCAA Division III, Southern California Intercollegiate Athletic Conference.
**Intramural and club sports:** 80% of students participate. Intramural badminton, basketball, billiards, cycling, fencing, field hockey, golf, inner-tube water polo, lacrosse, racquetball, rock climbing, softball, squash, swimming, table tennis, tennis, track, ultimate frisbee, volleyball, walleyball. Men's club Alpine skiing, archery, cycling, fencing, lacrosse, martial arts, racquetball, rugby, squash, ultimate frisbee. Women's club Alpine skiing, archery, fencing, field hockey, lacrosse, martial arts, racquetball.
**ADMISSIONS. Academic basis for candidate selection** (in order of priority): Secondary school record, standardized test scores, essay, school's recommendation, class rank.
**Nonacademic basis for candidate selection:** Character and personality and extracurricular participation are important. Particular talent or ability, geographical distribution, and alumni/ae relationship are considered.
**Requirements:** Graduation from secondary school is recommended; GED is accepted. No specific distribution of secondary school units required. College-preparatory program expected of all applicants. SAT or ACT is required. ACH recommended. Campus visit and interview recommended. Off-campus interviews available with an alumni representative.
**Procedure:** Take SAT or ACT by December of 12th year. Visit college for interview by January 31 of 12th year. Suggest filing application by fall. Application deadline is January 15. Notification of acceptance by early April. Reply is required by May 1. $300 nonrefundable tuition deposit. Freshmen accepted for fall term only.
**Special programs:** Admission may be deferred one year. Credit and/or placement may be granted through CEEB Advanced Placement exams for scores of 4 or higher. Early decision program. In fall 1993, 149 applied for early decision and 81 were accepted. Deadline for applying for early decision is November 15. Early entrance/early admission program.
**Transfer students:** Transfer students accepted for terms other than fall. In fall 1993, 5% of all new students were transfers into all classes. 224 transfer applications were received, 53 were accepted. Application deadline is April 1 for fall; November 15 for spring. Lowest course grade accepted is "C-." At least 64 semester hours must be completed at the college to receive degree.
**Admissions contact:** Bruce J. Poch, Ed.M., Dean of Admissions. 909 621-8134.
**FINANCIAL AID. Available aid:** Pell grants, SEOG, state scholarships and grants, school scholarships and grants, private scholarships and grants, and aid for undergraduate foreign students. Perkins Loans (NDSL), PLUS, Stafford Loans (GSL), school loans, private loans, and SLS. Institutional payment plan.
**Financial aid statistics:** In 1993-94, 92% of all undergraduate applicants received aid; 86% of freshman applicants. Average amounts of aid awarded freshmen: Scholarships and grants, $13,700; loans, $2,950.
**Supporting data/closing dates:** FAFSA/FAF: Deadline is February 11. Income tax forms: Accepted on rolling basis. Business/Farm supplement. Divorced/Separated Parent form. Notification of awards begins in mid-April.
**Financial aid contact:** Patricia Coye, Director of Financial Aid. 909 621-8205.
**STUDENT EMPLOYMENT.** College Work/Study Program. Institutional employment. 65% of full-time undergraduates work on campus during school year. Students may expect to earn an average of $1,800 during school year. Off-campus part-time employment opportunities rated "good."
**COMPUTER FACILITIES.** 80 IBM/IBM-compatible and Macintosh/Apple microcomputers; 70 are networked. Students may access Digital, SUN minicomputer/mainframe systems, BITNET, Internet. Computer languages and software packages include APL, BASIC, C, FORTRAN, LISP, Microsoft Word, Pascal, PL/1, SAS, SPSS, SPSS-X. Computer facilities are available to all students.
**Hours:** 8 AM-midn.; 24 hours during exams.
**GRADUATE CAREER DATA.** Graduate school percentages: 10% enter law school. 9% enter medical school. 9% enter graduate business programs. 47% enter graduate arts and sciences programs. Highest graduate school enrollments: UC Berkeley, UCLA, Columbia U, Harvard U, Stanford U, U of Chicago. 32% of graduates choose careers in business and industry.
**PROMINENT ALUMNI/AE.** R. Stanton Avery, founder and chairperson of the board, Avery International; Frank Wells, president, Disney Co.; Bill Keller, Moscow bureau chief, *New York Times;* John Cage, musician; Paul Fussell, author; Kris Kristofferson, actor and singer; Richard Chamberlain, actor.

# Saint Mary's College

**Moraga, CA 94575** — **510 631-4224**

**1994-95 Costs.** Tuition: $13,332. Room & board: $6,354. Fees, books, misc. academic expenses (school's estimate): $500.
**Enrollment.** Undergraduates: 1,026 men, 1,063 women (full-time). Freshman class: 2,619 applicants, 1,663 accepted, 465 enrolled.
**Test score averages/ranges.** Average SAT scores: 494 verbal, 529 math. Range of SAT scores of middle 50%: 460-600 verbal, 510-600 math. Average ACT scores: 23 composite.
**Faculty.** 139 full-time. 91% of faculty holds doctoral degree. Student/faculty ratio: 16 to 1.
**Selectivity rating.** More competitive.

**PROFILE.** Saint Mary's is a church-affiliated, multipurpose college. Founded in 1863, it adopted coeducation in 1970. Its 400-acre campus, with a Spanish architectural style, is located in Moraga, 35 miles from Oakland.

**Accreditation:** WASC.
**Religious orientation:** Saint Mary's College is affiliated with the Roman Catholic Church (Christian Brothers); two semesters of religion/theology required.
**Library:** Collections totaling over 171,906 volumes, 1,116 periodical subscriptions, and 129,188 microform items.
**Special facilities/museums:** Art gallery.
**Athletic facilities:** Gymnasiums, athletic fields, swimming pool, weight room, basketball and tennis courts.
**STUDENT BODY. Undergraduate profile:** 81% are state residents; 28% are transfers. 9% Asian-American, 4% Black, 11% Hispanic, 1% Native American, 75% White. Average age of undergraduates is 21.
**Freshman profile:** 3% of freshmen who took SAT scored 700 or over on verbal, 5% scored 700 or over on math; 15% scored 600 or over on verbal, 21% scored 600 or over on math; 67% scored 500 or over on verbal, 72% scored 500 or over on math; 96% scored 400 or over on verbal, 100% scored 400 or over on math; 100% scored 300 or over on verbal. 81% of accepted applicants took SAT; 19% took ACT. 60% of freshmen come from public schools.
**Undergraduate achievement:** 91% of fall 1992 freshmen returned for fall 1993 term. 64% of entering class graduated.
**Foreign students:** 93 students are from out of the country. Countries represented include Hong Kong, Japan, Korea, the Philippines, and Taiwan; 27 in all.
**PROGRAMS OF STUDY. Degrees:** B.A., B.S.
**Majors:** Accounting, American Studies, Anthropology/Sociology, Art, Biology, Business Administration, Chemistry, Classical Languages, Communication Disorders, Cross-Cultural Studies, Diversified Liberal Arts, Economics, English/Drama, European Studies, French, Government, Health/Physical Education/Recreation, History, Integral Curriculum, Latin American Studies, Mathematics, Nursing, Performing Arts, Philosophy, Physics, Psychology, Religious Studies, Spanish.
**Requirements:** General education requirement.
**Special:** Self-designed majors. Double majors. Dual degrees. Independent study. Internships. Cooperative education programs. Graduate school at which undergraduates may take graduate-level courses. Preprofessional programs in law, medicine, veterinary science, pharmacy, dentistry, optometry, business, management sciences, medical technology, nursing, physical therapy, and psychology. 3-2 engineering programs with USC and Washington U. Cross-registration with Holy Names Coll and Mills Coll. Washington Semester. Teacher certification in elementary, secondary, and special education. Study abroad in Belgium, England, France, Germany, Greece, Ireland, Italy, Mexico, and Peru. ROTC, NROTC, and AFROTC at UC Berkeley.
**Honors:** Honor societies.
**Academic Assistance:** Nonremedial tutoring.
**STUDENT LIFE. Housing:** Students may live on or off campus. Coed dorms. School-owned/operated apartments. 70% of students live in college housing.
**Social atmosphere:** The student newspaper reports that social and cultural life is "not bad, not enough money to put on 'big' events." The most influential students are "members of the student council and social committee, who organize all the social activities." Popular events include Santa Clara athletic events, Casino Night, comedy acts, and formal dances. On campus, students frequent the Mission Road Inn Pizza Pub. Moraga Barn Bar is a favorite off-campus nightspot.
**Services and counseling/handicapped student services:** Placement services. Health service. Testing service. Counseling services for minority students. Personal and psychological counseling. Career and academic guidance services. Religious counseling. Physically disabled student services. Learning disabled services. Notetaking services. Tape recorders. Tutors. Reader services for the blind.
**Campus organizations:** Undergraduate student government. Student newspaper. Literary magazine. Yearbook. Radio and TV stations. Coed cheerleaders-songleaders, glee club, Outward Bound, departmental and special-interest groups.
**Religious organizations:** Campus Ministry.
**Minority/foreign student organizations:** Black Student Union, Chicano Student Organization, Pacific-Islanders Club. International Student Club.
**ATHLETICS. Physical education requirements:** None.
**Intercollegiate competition:** 20% of students participate. Baseball (M), basketball (M,W), crew (M,W), cross-country (M,W), football (M), golf (M), rugby (M), soccer (M,W), softball (W), tennis (M,W), volleyball (W). Member of NCAA Division I, NCAA Division I-AA for football, West Coast Conference.
**Intramural and club sports:** 50% of students participate. Intramural basketball, flag football, soccer, softball. Men's club cheerleading, ice hockey, lacrosse, volleyball. Women's club cheerleading, lacrosse.
**ADMISSIONS. Academic basis for candidate selection** (in order of priority): Secondary school record, standardized test scores, school's recommendation, class rank, essay.
**Nonacademic basis for candidate selection:** Character and personality and particular talent or ability are important. Extracurricular participation, geographical distribution, and alumni/ae relationship are considered.
**Requirements:** Graduation from secondary school is required; GED is accepted. 17 units and the following program of study are recommended: 4 units of English, 3 units of math, 2 units of science, 2 units of foreign language, 2 units of social studies, 1 unit of history, 2 units of electives. Algebra I and II, plane geometry, trigonometry, physics, and chemistry recommended of applicants to the School of Science. EOP for applicants not normally admissible. SAT or ACT is required. Campus visit and interview recommended. Off-campus interviews available with admissions and alumni representatives.
**Procedure:** Take SAT or ACT by January of 12th year. Suggest filing application by November 30. Application deadline is March 1. Notification of admission on rolling basis. Reply is required by May 1. $200 nonrefundable tuition deposit. $200 nonrefundable room deposit. Freshmen accepted for terms other than fall.
**Special programs:** Admission may be deferred. Credit and/or placement may be granted through CEEB Advanced Placement exams for scores of 3 or higher. Credit may be granted through CLEP subject exams and challenge exams. Early entrance/early admission program. Concurrent enrollment program.
**Transfer students:** Transfer students accepted for terms other than fall. In fall 1993, 28% of all new students were transfers into all classes. 611 transfer applications were received, 406 were accepted. Application deadline is July 1 for fall; December 1 for spring. Minimum 2.3 GPA required. Lowest course grade accepted is "C." Maximum number of transferable credits is 60 semester hours. At least 32 semester hours must be completed at the college to receive degree.
**Admissions contact:** Michael Beseda, M.A., Director of Admissions. 510 631-4224.

**FINANCIAL AID. Available aid:** Pell grants, SEOG, state grants, school scholarships and grants, athletic scholarships, and aid for undergraduate foreign students. Perkins Loans (NDSL), PLUS, Stafford Loans (GSL), private loans, and SLS. Tuition Plan Inc. and deferred payment plan. Education Funds, Inc.
**Financial aid statistics:** 2% of aid is not need-based. In 1993-94, 52% of all undergraduate applicants received aid; 52% of freshman applicants. Average amounts of aid awarded freshmen: Scholarships and grants, $8,797; loans, $3,116.
**Supporting data/closing dates:** FAFSA: Priority filing date is March 2. FAF/FFS: Priority filing date is March 1. School's own aid application: Priority filing date is March 1. State aid form: Deadline is March 2. Notification of awards begins April 15.
**Financial aid contact:** Billie Jones, M.A., Director of Financial Aid. 510 631-4370.

**STUDENT EMPLOYMENT.** Institutional employment. 60% of full-time undergraduates work on campus during school year. Students may expect to earn an average of $2,106 during school year. Off-campus part-time employment opportunities rated "excellent."

**COMPUTER FACILITIES.** 100 IBM/IBM-compatible and Macintosh/Apple microcomputers; 63 are networked. Students may access SUN minicomputer/mainframe systems, Internet. Computer languages and software packages include Excel, Lotus, Windows, Word, WordPerfect, Wordstar, Works; 15 in all. Computer facilities are available to all students.
**Fees:** None.
**Hours:** 8 AM-10:30 PM (M-Th); 9 AM-7 PM (Sa); 9 AM-10:30 PM (Su).

# Samuel Merritt College

**Oakland, CA 94609** **510 420-6011**

**1993-94 Costs.** Tuition: $11,865. Room & board: $5,520. Fees, books, misc. academic expenses (school's estimate): $1,509.
**Enrollment.** Undergraduates: 19 men, 263 women (full-time). Freshman class: 91 applicants, 40 accepted, 13 enrolled. Graduate enrollment: 28 men, 116 women.
**Test score averages/ranges.** Average SAT scores: 453 verbal, 459 math.
**Faculty.** 23 full-time; 16 part-time. 30% of faculty holds doctoral degree. Student/faculty ratio: 9 to 1.
**Selectivity rating.** Competitive.

**PROFILE.** Samuel Merritt, founded in 1909, is a private college. Its one-acre campus is located in Oakland.

**Accreditation:** WASC. Professionally accredited by the National League for Nursing.
**Religious orientation:** Samuel Merritt College is nonsectarian; two semesters of religion required.
**Library:** Collections totaling over 7,000 volumes, 360 periodical subscriptions and 600 microform items.
**Special facilities/museums:** Therapeutic exercise lab, anatomy lab, nursing resource lab, video production studio, medical center.

**STUDENT BODY. Undergraduate profile:** 90% are state residents; 50% are transfers. 9% Asian-American, 6% Black, 5% Hispanic, 2% Native American, 77% White, 1% Other.
**Freshman profile:** 17% of freshmen who took SAT scored 500 or over on verbal, 17% scored 500 or over on math; 100% scored 400 or over on verbal, 100% scored 400 or over on math. 100% of accepted applicants took SAT. 70% of freshmen come from public schools.
**Undergraduate achievement:** 82% of fall 1992 freshmen returned for fall 1993 term. 30% of students who completed a degree program went on to graduate study within five years.
**Foreign students:** Three students are from out of the country. Countries represented include the Philippines and Taiwan.

**PROGRAMS OF STUDY. Degrees:** B.S.Nurs.
**Majors:** Nursing.
**Requirements:** General education requirement.
**Academic regulations:** Minimum 2.0 GPA must be maintained.
**Special:** Program offered in conjunction with St. Mary's Coll (Moraga); nursing courses taught at Merritt Peralta Medical Center campus, general education courses at St. Mary's Coll. Double majors. Independent study. Accelerated study. Pass/fail grading option. Internships. Rural Health Semester. ROTC, NROTC, and AFROTC at St. Mary's Coll.
**Honors:** Honor societies.
**Academic Assistance:** Nonremedial tutoring.

**ADMISSIONS. Academic basis for candidate selection** (in order of priority): Secondary school record, standardized test scores, class rank, school's recommendation, essay.
**Nonacademic basis for candidate selection:** Character and personality, extracurricular participation, and particular talent or ability are considered.
**Requirements:** Graduation from secondary school is required; GED is accepted. No specific distribution of secondary school units required. Minimum combined SAT score of 800 and minimum 2.5 GPA required. SAT is required; ACT may be substituted. ACH recommended. Campus visit recommended. No off-campus interviews.
**Procedure:** Notification of admission on rolling basis. No set date by which applicants must accept offer. $200 nonrefundable tuition deposit. $100 room deposit, refundable until September 1. Freshmen accepted for terms other than fall.
**Special programs:** Admission may be deferred one year. Credit may be granted through CEEB Advanced Placement. Credit and/or placement may be granted through CLEP general and subject exams. Credit and placement may be granted through ACT PEP and challenge exams. Early decision program. Early entrance/early admission program.
**Transfer students:** Transfer students accepted for terms other than fall. In fall 1993, 50% of all new students were transfers into all classes. 306 transfer applications were received, 118 were accepted. Application deadline is May 1 for fall; October 1 for spring. Minimum 2.5 GPA required. Lowest course grade accepted is "C."
**Admissions contact:** Charisse Hughen, Director of Admissions. 510 420-6076.

**FINANCIAL AID. Available aid:** Pell grants, SEOG, Federal Nursing Student Scholarships, state scholarships and grants, school scholarships and grants, private scholarships and grants, academic merit scholarships, and United Negro College Fund. PLUS, Stafford Loans (GSL), NSL, state loans, school loans, private loans, and SLS. Tuition Management Systems and deferred payment plan.
**Financial aid statistics:** 8% of aid is not need-based. In 1993-94, 100% of all undergraduate applicants received aid; 100% of freshman applicants.
**Supporting data/closing dates:** State aid form: Priority filing date is March 1; deadline is June 1. Notification of awards on rolling basis.
**Financial aid contact:** Mary E. Robinson, Director of Financial Aid. 510 420-6131.

# San Diego State University

**San Diego, CA 92182-0771** **619 594-5200**

**1993-94 Costs.** Tuition: None (state residents), $5,904 (out-of-state). Room & board: $4,070. Fees, books, misc. academic expenses (school's estimate): $2,342.
**Enrollment.** Undergraduates: 7,961 men, 8,446 women (full-time). Freshman class: 8,187 applicants, 7,319 accepted, 2,151 enrolled. Graduate enrollment: 1,807 men, 2,388 women.
**Test score averages/ranges.** Average SAT scores: 394 verbal, 457 math. Range of SAT scores of middle 50%: 330-460 verbal, 390-520 math. Average ACT scores: 19 English, 20 math, 20 composite. Range of ACT scores of middle 50%: 16-21 English, 17-21 math.
**Faculty.** 1,199 full-time; 1,480 part-time. 88% of faculty holds doctoral degree. Student/faculty ratio: 19 to 1.
**Selectivity rating.** Less competitive.

**PROFILE.** San Diego State, founded in 1897, is a public, multipurpose university. Programs are offered through the Colleges of Arts and Letters, Business Administration, Education, Professional Studies and Fine Arts, Engineering, Human Services, and Sciences. The main quadrangle of the 300-acre campus, located in San Diego, is still surrounded by the original seven mission-styled buildings.
**Accreditation:** WASC.
**Religious orientation:** San Diego State University is nonsectarian; no religious requirements.
**Library:** Collections totaling over 1,062,800 volumes, 10,100 periodical subscriptions, and 3,400,000 microform items.
**Special facilities/museums:** Research bureaus for labor economics, marine studies and social science, audio-visual center.
**Athletic facilities:** Athletic center, gymnasium, stadium, swimming pool, tennis and racquetball courts, athletic fields.

**STUDENT BODY. Undergraduate profile:** 97% are state residents. 14% Asian-American, 5% Black, 15% Hispanic, 1% Native American, 55% White, 10% Other. Average age of undergraduates is 22.
**Freshman profile:** 1% of freshmen who took SAT scored 700 or over on math; 2% scored 600 or over on verbal, 9% scored 600 or over on math; 14% scored 500 or over on verbal, 35% scored 500 or over on math; 49% scored 400 or over on verbal, 74% scored 400 or over on math; 87% scored 300 or over on verbal, 96% scored 300 or over on math. 1% of freshmen who took ACT scored 30 or over on English, 2% scored 30 or over on math; 18% scored 24 or over on English, 16% scored 24 or over on math, 13% scored 24 or over on composite; 63% scored 18 or over on English, 69% scored 18 or over on math, 69% scored 18 or over on composite; 94% scored 12 or over on English, 100% scored 12 or over on math, 100% scored 12 or over on composite; 100% scored 6 or over on English. Majority of accepted applicants took SAT.
**Undergraduate achievement:** 71% of fall 1992 freshmen returned for fall 1993 term. 4% of entering class graduated.

**PROGRAMS OF STUDY. Degrees:** B.A., B.Mus., B.S., B.Voc.Ed.
**Majors:** Accounting, Aerospace Engineering, Afro-American Studies, American Studies, Anthropology, Art, Asian Studies, Astronomy, Biology, Botany, Chemical Physics, Chemistry, Child Development, Civil Engineering, Classics, Comparative Literature, Computer Science, Criminal Justice Administration, Drama, Economics, Electrical Engineering, Engineering, English, Environmental Health, European Studies, Finance, Financial Services, Foods/Nutrition, French, Geography, Geological Sciences, German, Health Sciences, History, Home Economics, Industrial Arts, Information Systems, Journalism, Latin American Studies, Liberal Studies, Linguistics, Management, Marketing, Mathematics, Mechanical Engineering, Mexican-American Studies, Microbiology, Music, Nursing, Philosophy, Physical Education, Physical Sciences, Physics, Political Science, Psychology, Public Administration, Real Estate, Recreation Administration, Religious Studies, Russian, Russian/East European Studies, Social Science, Social Work, Sociology, Spanish, Speech Communication, Speech Pathology/Audiology, Television/Radio, Vocational Arts, Women's Studies, Zoology.
**Requirements:** General education requirement.
**Academic regulations:** Minimum 2.0 GPA must be maintained.
**Special:** Internships. Graduate school at which undergraduates may take graduate-level courses. Preprofessional programs in law, medicine, veterinary science, and dentistry. Exchange program with U of New Hampshire. Teacher certification in early childhood, elementary, secondary, and special education. Exchange program abroad in England. Study abroad also in Brazil, Canada, Denmark, France, Germany, Israel, Italy, Japan, Mexico, New Zealand, Peru, Spain, Sweden, and Taiwan. ROTC, NROTC, and AFROTC.
**Honors:** Phi Beta Kappa.
**Academic Assistance:** Remedial reading, writing, math, and study skills.

**STUDENT LIFE. Housing:** Students may live on or off campus. Coed dorms. Sorority and fraternity housing. School-owned/operated apartments. 8% of students live in college housing.
**Social atmosphere:** According to the editor of the student newspaper, the social scene has "a lot of frat parties on weekends and lots of drinking–a very casual approach to school." Students meet on campus at Love Library, Aztec Center, and Food Court Commons; Aztec

Amusement, Rubio's, Woodstock's, and Winter's are popular off-campus spots. Greeks dominate social life; Greek Week and the Greek Show are two of the biggest events at SDSU. A.S. elections and Homecoming are also popular.
**Services and counseling/handicapped student services:** Placement services. Health service. Women's center. Day care. Personal counseling. Career and academic guidance services. Physically disabled student services. Notetaking services. Tape recorders. Tutors.
**Campus organizations:** Undergraduate student government. Student newspaper (Daily Aztec). Radio and TV stations. Music and drama groups, athletic, departmental, service, gay and lesbian, and special-interest groups, 292 organizations in all. 17 fraternities, all with chapter houses; 12 sororities, all with chapter houses. 7% of men join a fraternity. 6% of women join a sorority.
**Religious organizations:** Several religious groups.
**Minority/foreign student organizations:** African-American, Asian-American, Hispanic/Latino, and Native American groups. International Student Club.

**ATHLETICS. Physical education requirements:** Two semesters of physical education required.
**Intercollegiate competition:** 15% of students participate. Baseball (M), basketball (M,W), cross-country (M,W), football (M), soccer (M,W), softball (W), tennis (M,W), track and field (outdoor) (W), volleyball (M,W). Member of Big West, Mountain Pacific Sports Federation, NCAA Division I, Western Athletic Conference.
**Intramural and club sports:** 50% of students participate. Intramural basketball, football, soccer, softball, volleyball, walleyball. Men's club Alpine skiing, bowling, crew, cycling, fencing, ice hockey, lacrosse, rugby, sailing, ultimate frisbee, volleyball, water polo, water skiing. Women's club Alpine skiing, bowling, crew, cycling, fencing, sailing, soccer, ultimate frisbee, volleyball, water polo, water skiing.

**ADMISSIONS. Academic basis for candidate selection** (in order of priority): Standardized test scores.
**Requirements:** Graduation from secondary school is required; GED is accepted. 15 units and the following program of study are required: 4 units of English, 3 units of math, 1 unit of lab science, 2 units of foreign language, 1 unit of history, 4 units of electives. Electives should include 1 unit of visual/performing arts. Minimum grade of "C" in listed secondary school courses required. Minimum eligibility index of 2800 for SAT (674 for ACT) required of in-state applicants; minimum eligibility index of 3402 for SAT (822 for ACT) required of out-of-state applicants. In-state applicants with minimum 3.0 GPA and out-of-state applicants with minimum 3.6 GPA are eligible regardless of test scores. Approval and specific GPA required of nursing and radio/TV program applicants. Specific GPA required of engineering and business program applicants. EOP for applicants not normally admissible. SAT or ACT is required. Campus visit recommended. No off-campus interviews.
**Procedure:** Take SAT or ACT by July of 12th year. Suggest filing application by November 30; no deadline. Notification of admission on rolling basis. No set date by which applicants must accept offer. Freshmen accepted for terms other than fall.
**Special programs:** Credit may be granted through CEEB Advanced Placement for scores of 3 or higher. Credit may be granted through CLEP general and subject exams. Concurrent enrollment program.
**Transfer students:** Transfer students accepted for terms other than fall. Application deadline is November 30 for fall; August 30 for spring. Minimum 2.0 GPA required. Lowest course grade accepted is "C." At least 30 semester hours must be completed at the university to receive degree.
**Admissions contact:** Nancy C. Sprotte, Ph.D., Director of Admissions. 619 594-6871.

**FINANCIAL AID. Available aid:** Pell grants, SEOG, state grants, school scholarships and grants, private scholarships and grants, ROTC scholarships, academic merit scholarships, and athletic scholarships. Perkins Loans (NDSL), PLUS, Stafford Loans (GSL), school loans, and SLS. Deferred payment plan.
**Financial aid statistics:** 1% of aid is not need-based. In 1993-94, 88% of all undergraduate applicants received aid; 85% of freshman applicants. Average amounts of aid awarded freshmen: Scholarships and grants, $1,500; loans, $2,000.
**Supporting data/closing dates:** FAFSA: Priority filing date is March 2. State aid form: Priority filing date is March 2. Notification of awards begins in January.
**Financial aid contact:** William Boyd, Director of Financial Aid. 619 594-4161.

**STUDENT EMPLOYMENT.** College Work/Study Program. Off-campus part-time employment opportunities rated "good."

**COMPUTER FACILITIES.** 1,448 IBM/IBM-compatible and Macintosh/Apple microcomputers; 60 are networked. Students may access Cray, Digital, IBM, SUN minicomputer/mainframe systems, BITNET, Internet, CompuServe. Residence halls may be equipped with stand-alone microcomputers. Client/LAN operating systems include Apple/Macintosh, DOS, UNIX/XENIX/AIX, Windows NT, X-windows, DEC, LocalTalk/AppleTalk, Microsoft, Novell. Computer languages and software packages include Ada, COBOL, C+, FORTRAN, PL/I. Computer facilities are available to all students.
**Fees:** None.

# San Francisco Art Institute

**San Francisco, CA 94133** **415 771-7020**

**1994-95 Costs.** Tuition: $14,500. Housing: None. Fees, books, misc. academic expenses (school's estimate): $1,400.
**Enrollment.** Undergraduates: 229 men, 206 women (full-time). Freshman class: 177 applicants, 136 accepted, 41 enrolled. Graduate enrollment: 58 men, 75 women.
**Test score averages/ranges.** N/A.
**Faculty.** 29 full-time; 34 part-time. 62% of faculty holds highest degree in specific field. Student/faculty ratio: 9 to 1.
**Selectivity rating.** N/A.

**PROFILE.** The San Francisco Art Institute, founded in 1871, is a private institution for the arts. Its four-acre campus is located in downtown San Francisco.

**Accreditation:** WASC. Professionally accredited by the National Association of Schools of Art and Design.
**Religious orientation:** San Francisco Art Institute is nonsectarian; no religious requirements.
**Library:** Collections totaling over 26,000 volumes and 175 periodical subscriptions.
**Special facilities/museums:** Art gallery.

**STUDENT BODY. Undergraduate profile:** 60% are state residents; 77% are transfers. 5% Asian-American, 3% Black, 4% Hispanic, 1% Native American, 77% White, 10% Other. Average age of undergraduates is 27.
**Freshman profile:** 50% of accepted applicants took SAT; 10% took ACT.
**Undergraduate achievement:** 74% of fall 1992 freshmen returned for fall 1993 term.
**Foreign students:** 59 students are from out of the country. Countries represented include Canada, China, England, Germany, Japan, and Korea; 20 in all.

**PROGRAMS OF STUDY. Degrees:** B.F.A.
**Majors:** Film, New Genres, Painting/Drawing, Performance/Video/Computer Arts, Photography, Sculpture/Ceramics/Printmaking.
**Distribution of degrees:** The majors with the highest enrollment are painting, photography, and film; printmaking and performance have the lowest.
**Requirements:** General education requirement.
**Special:** Post-baccalaureate studio program. Self-designed majors. Double majors. Independent study. Internships. Member of Alliance of Independent Colleges of Art and Design (AICAD); exchange possible. Study abroad in China, France, Italy, and Japan.
**Academic Assistance:** Remedial reading and writing. Nonremedial tutoring.

**ADMISSIONS. Academic basis for candidate selection** (in order of priority): Secondary school record, standardized test scores, essay, school's recommendation, class rank.
**Nonacademic basis for candidate selection:** Character and personality and particular talent or ability are emphasized.
**Requirements:** Graduation from secondary school is required; GED is accepted. No specific distribution of secondary school units required. Portfolio required of all applicants. Minimum verbal SAT score of 420 (English ACT score of 20) recommended. SAT or ACT is required. Campus visit and interview recommended. Off-campus interviews available with an admissions representative.
**Procedure:** Take SAT or ACT by January of 12th year. Visit college for interview by March of 12th year. Suggest filing application by March 1. Application deadline is August 1. Notification of admission on rolling basis. Reply is required by May 1. $300 tuition deposit, refundable until May 1. Freshmen accepted for terms other than fall.
**Special programs:** Admission may be deferred one year. Credit may be granted through CEEB Advanced Placement for scores of 3 or higher. Credit may be granted through CLEP general and subject exams.
**Transfer students:** Transfer students accepted for terms other than fall. In fall 1993, 77% of all new students were transfers into all classes. 370 transfer applications were received, 309 were accepted. Application deadline is rolling for fall; rolling for spring. Minimum 2.0 GPA recommended. Lowest course grade accepted is "C." Maximum number of transferable credits is 90 semester hours. At least 30 semester hours must be completed at the institute to receive degree.
**Admissions contact:** Tim Robison, M.F.A., Director of Admissions and Financial Aid. 415 749-4500.

**FINANCIAL AID. Available aid:** Pell grants, SEOG, state scholarships and grants, school scholarships and grants, and academic merit scholarships. PLUS, Stafford Loans (GSL), and SLS. Deferred payment plan.
**Financial aid statistics:** 15% of aid is not need-based. In 1993-94, 90% of all undergraduate applicants received aid; 83% of freshman applicants. Average amounts of aid awarded freshmen: Scholarships and grants, $5,200.
**Supporting data/closing dates:** FAFSA/FAF: Priority filing date is April 1; accepted on rolling basis. School's own aid application: Priority filing date is April 1; accepted on rolling basis. State aid form: Priority filing date is April 1; accepted on rolling basis. Income tax forms: Priority filing date is April 1; accepted on rolling basis. Notification of awards begins April 1.

# San Francisco Conservatory of Music

**San Francisco, CA 94122** **415 564-8086**

**1993-94 Costs.** Tuition: $12,000. Housing: None. Fees, books, misc. academic expenses (school's estimate): $850.
**Enrollment.** Undergraduates: 59 men, 83 women (full-time). Freshman class: 69 applicants, 38 accepted, 23 enrolled. Graduate enrollment: 40 men, 68 women.
**Test score averages/ranges.** Average SAT scores: 468 verbal, 547 math. Range of SAT scores of middle 50%: 400-590 verbal, 480-660 math.
**Faculty.** 23 full-time; 45 part-time. 29% of faculty holds doctoral degree. Student/faculty ratio: 7 to 1.
**Selectivity rating.** N/A.

**PROFILE.** The San Francisco Conservatory of Music, founded in 1917, is a private conservatory of music. Its five-acre campus, in the Spanish Mission Revival style, is located in downtown San Francisco.

**Accreditation:** WASC. Professionally accredited by the National Association of Schools of Music.
**Religious orientation:** San Francisco Conservatory of Music is nonsectarian; no religious requirements.
**Library:** Collections totaling over 33,500 volumes and 73 periodical subscriptions.
**Special facilities/museums:** Performance hall, electronic composition studio.

**STUDENT BODY. Undergraduate profile:** 80% are state residents; 63% are transfers. 34% Asian-Am rican, 3% Black, 3% Hispanic, 60% White. Average age of undergraduates is 22.

**Freshman profile:** 70% of accepted applicants took SAT. 64% of freshmen come from public schools.
**Undergraduate achievement:** 80% of fall 1992 freshmen returned for fall 1993 term. 53% of entering class graduated. 25% of students who completed a degree program immediately went on to graduate study.
**Foreign students:** 41 students are from out of the country. Countries represented include Canada, Hong Kong, Japan, Singapore, South Korea, and Taiwan; 15 in all.

**PROGRAMS OF STUDY. Degrees:** B.Mus.
**Majors:** Bassoon, Clarinet, Classical Guitar, Composition, Double Bass, Flute, French Horn, Harp, Harpsichord, Oboe, Organ, Percussion, Piano, Trombone, Trumpet, Tuba, Viola, Violin, Violoncello, Voice.
**Distribution of degrees:** The majors with the highest enrollment are piano, guitar, and voice; flute, oboe, and trombone have the lowest.
**Requirements:** General education requirement.
**Academic regulations:** Minimum 2.0 GPA must be maintained.
**Special:** Independent study. Accelerated study.
**Academic Assistance:** Remedial writing.

**ADMISSIONS. Academic basis for candidate selection** (in order of priority): Secondary school record, school's recommendation, standardized test scores, class rank.
**Nonacademic basis for candidate selection:** Particular talent or ability is emphasized. Character and personality and extracurricular participation are considered.
**Requirements:** Graduation from secondary school is recommended; GED is accepted. No specific distribution of secondary school units required; 3 units of English and 3 units of a foreign language recommended. Minimum 2.0 GPA required; minimum 3.0 GPA recommended. Auditions required of all applicants. SAT is required; ACT may be substituted. No off-campus interviews.
**Procedure:** Take SAT or ACT by April of 12th year. Suggest filing application by April 1. Application deadline is July 1. Notification of admission on rolling basis. Reply is required by June 1. $200 nonrefundable tuition deposit. Freshmen accepted for terms other than fall.
**Special programs:** Credit may be granted through CEEB Advanced Placement for scores of 4 or higher. Credit may be granted through CLEP general and subject exams. Credit and placement may be granted through challenge exams. Early entrance/early admission program.
**Transfer students:** Transfer students accepted for terms other than fall. In fall 1993, 63% of all new students were transfers into all classes. 128 transfer applications were received, 64 were accepted. Application deadline is April 1 for fall; November 15 for spring. Minimum 2.0 GPA recommended. Lowest course grade accepted is "C." Maximum number of transferable credits is 68 semester hours. At least 28 semester hours must be completed at the conservatory to receive degree.
**Admissions contact:** Kate Murdock, Admission Officer. 415 759-3431.

**FINANCIAL AID. Available aid:** Pell grants, SEOG, state grants, school scholarships, private scholarships, and aid for undergraduate foreign students. Perkins Loans (NDSL), PLUS, Stafford Loans (GSL), and SLS. Institutional monthly payment plan.
**Financial aid statistics:** 5% of aid is not need-based. In 1993-94, 90% of all undergraduate applicants received aid; 90% of freshman applicants. Average amounts of aid awarded freshmen: Scholarships and grants, $4,700; loans, $3,000.
**Supporting data/closing dates:** FAFSA/FAF: Priority filing date is April 1. School's own aid application: Priority filing date is April 1. Notification of awards on rolling basis.
**Financial aid contact:** Colleen Katzowitz, Director of Student Services. 415 759-3422.

# San Francisco State University

**San Francisco, CA 94132** **415 338-1111**

**1993-94 Costs.** Tuition: None (state residents), $7,380 (out-of-state). Room & board: $4,192. Fees, books, misc. academic expenses (school's estimate): $1,656.
**Enrollment.** Undergraduates: 5,406 men, 7,454 women (full-time). Freshman class: 5,040 applicants, 3,531 accepted, 1,263 enrolled. Graduate enrollment: 2,775 men, 4,420 women.
**Test score averages/ranges.** Average SAT scores: 371 verbal, 438 math. Average ACT scores: 18 English, 18 math, 18 composite.
**Faculty.** 833 full-time; 596 part-time. Student/faculty ratio: 21 to 1.
**Selectivity rating.** Less competitive.

**PROFILE.** San Francisco State, founded in 1899, is a public, comprehensive university. Programs are offered through the Schools of Behavioral and Social Sciences; Business; Creative Arts; Education; Ethnic Studies; Health, Physical Education, and Leisure Studies; Humanities; and Science. Its 130-acre campus is located in San Francisco.

**Accreditation:** WASC. Professionally accredited by the Accreditation Board for Engineering and Technology, the Accrediting Council on Education in Journalism and Mass Communication, the American Assembly of Collegiate Schools of Business, the American Home Economics Association, the Council on Social Work Education, the National Association of Schools of Art and Design, the National Association of Schools of Music, the National Council for Accreditation of Teacher Education, the National League for Nursing.
**Religious orientation:** San Francisco State University is nonsectarian; no religious requirements.
**Library:** Collections totaling over 675,000 volumes, 4,300 periodical subscriptions, and 800,000 microform items.
**Special facilities/museums:** Museum of anthropology and ancient Egyptian artifacts, on-campus elementary school, telescopes.
**Athletic facilities:** Gymnasiums, swimming pool, tennis, basketball, handball and racquetball courts, playing fields, track.

**STUDENT BODY. Undergraduate profile:** 9% are transfers. 27% Asian-American, 7% Black, 10% Hispanic, 1% Native American, 43% White, 12% Other. Average age of undergraduates is 23.
**Freshman profile:** 2% of freshmen who took SAT scored 600 or over on verbal, 5% scored 600 or over on math; 10% scored 500 or over on verbal, 21% scored 500 or over on math; 28% scored 400 or over on verbal, 44% scored 400 or over on math; 49% scored 300 or over on verbal, 63% scored 300 or over on math. 75% of accepted applicants took SAT; 25% took ACT. 80% of freshmen come from public schools.
**Foreign students:** 733 students are from out of the country. Countries represented include China, Hong Kong, Indonesia, Japan, the Philippines, and Taiwan; 62 in all.

**PROGRAMS OF STUDY. Degrees:** B.A., B.Mus., B.S., B.Voc.Ed.
**Majors:** American Studies, Anthropology, Applied Mathematics, Art, Biochemistry, Biology, Black Studies, Botany, Business Administration, Business Education, Chemistry, Chinese, Civil Engineering, Classics, Clinical Psychology, Clinical Science, Communicative Disorders, Comparative Literature, Computer Science, Creative Arts, Creative Writing, Dance, Developmental Psychology, Drama, Ecology, Economics, Electrical Engineering, Engineering, English, English Language Studies, English Literature, Experimental Psychology, Film, French, Geography, Geology, German, Health Sciences, History, Home Economics, Human Factors Psychology, Human Movement, Humanities, Individualized Science, Industrial Arts, Industrial Organizational Psychology, Italian, Japanese, Journalism, La Raza Studies, Labor Studies, Liberal Studies, Marine Biology, Mathematics, Mechanical Engineering, Meteorology, Microbiology, Molecular Biology, Music, Nursing, Philosophy, Philosophy/Religion, Physical Education, Physical Sciences, Physics, Physics/Astronomy, Physiology, Political Science, Pre-Physical Therapy, Psychological Services, Radio/Television, Recreation, Russian, Science, Social Sciences, Social Welfare, Sociology, Spanish, Special Major, Speech, Statistics, Urban Studies, Vocational Education, Women's Studies, Zoology.
**Distribution of degrees:** The majors with the highest enrollment are business administration and liberal studies; science and meteorology have the lowest.
**Requirements:** General education requirement.
**Special:** Minors offered. Interdisciplinary creative arts and social science programs. Aerospace and area studies programs. Many professional certificate programs offered. Field work in archaeology, geology, political science, and social welfare. Programs in cooperation with California Youth Authority. Self-designed majors. Double majors. Independent study. Accelerated study. Pass/fail grading option. Internships. Preprofessional programs in law, medicine, and dentistry. Member of San Francisco Consortium; cross-registration possible. Teacher certification in early childhood, elementary, secondary, and special education. Study abroad in Brazil, Canada, Denmark, France, Germany, Israel, Italy, Japan, Mexico, New Zealand, Peru, Taiwan, Spain, Sweden, and the United Kingdom. AFROTC at UC Berkeley.
**Honors:** Phi Beta Kappa.
**Academic Assistance:** Remedial reading. Nonremedial tutoring.

**STUDENT LIFE. Housing:** Students may live on or off campus. Coed dorms. School-owned/operated apartments. 5% of students live in college housing.
**Social atmosphere:** As reported by the student newspaper, "Because USF is approximately one-half commuter students, social life is not as vibrant as in other schools. However, the return of basketball, bar life and the weekend games have had a profound influence in improving social life." The Cable Car Parade is one of the most popular events of the year. Influential organizations on campus include the ZBT social fraternity, St. Ignatius Institute (Great Books honor program), and Associated Students. Popular gathering spots are the Upper Division Pub, Rack N' Cue, and the Ecumenical House.
**Services and counseling/handicapped student services:** Health service. Women's center. Day care. Counseling services for minority, military, veteran, and older students. Career and academic guidance services. Physically disabled student services. Notetaking services. Tape recorders. Tutors. Reader services for the blind.
**Campus organizations:** Undergraduate student government. Student newspaper (Golden Gater, published twice/week). Literary magazine. Radio and TV stations. Debating, public speaking, music and drama groups, special-interest groups, 100 organizations in all. 12 fraternities, no chapter houses; nine sororities, no chapter houses. 1% of men join a fraternity. 1% of women join a sorority.
**Religious organizations:** Islamic student group.
**Minority/foreign student organizations:** Black Engineers Society, Hispanic Engineers Society, La Raza Organization, La Raza in Broadcasting. Central American, Chinese, German, Filipino, Indian, Indonesian, Japanese, Korean, Palestinian, and Vietnamese student groups.

**ATHLETICS. Physical education requirements:** None.
**Intercollegiate competition:** 2% of students participate. Baseball (M), basketball (M,W), cross-country (M,W), football (M), soccer (M,W), softball (W), swimming (M,W), track and field (M,W), track and field (outdoor) (M,W), volleyball (W), wrestling (M). Member of NCAA Division II, NCAC.
**Intramural and club sports:** 2% of students participate. Intramural badminton, basketball, racquetball, softball, ultimate frisbee, volleyball, weight lifting.

**ADMISSIONS. Academic basis for candidate selection** (in order of priority): Standardized test scores, secondary school record, class rank, school's recommendation, essay.
**Nonacademic basis for candidate selection:** Geographical distribution is emphasized. Extracurricular participation and particular talent or ability are considered.
**Requirements:** Graduation from secondary school is required; GED is not accepted. No specific distribution of secondary school units required. Minimum grade of "C" required in listed secondary school courses. Minimum eligibility index of 2800 for SAT (694 for ACT) required of in-state applicants; minimum eligibility index of 3402 for SAT (842 for ACT) required of out-of-state applicants. In-state applicants with minimum 3.0 GPA and out-of-state applicants with minimum 3.6 GPA are eligible regardless of test scores. Portfolio required of art program applicants. Audition required of music program applicants. EOP for applicants not normally admissible. SAT or ACT is recommended. No off-campus interviews.
**Procedure:** Take SAT or ACT by January of 12th year. Suggest filing application by June 1; no deadline. Notification of admission on rolling basis. No set date by which applicants must accept offer. Freshmen accepted for terms other than fall.

**Special programs:** Credit may be granted through CEEB Advanced Placement for scores of 3 or higher. Placement may be granted through military and life experience. Early entrance/early admission program.
**Transfer students:** Transfer students accepted for terms other than fall. In fall 1992, 9% of all new students were transfers into all classes. 6,109 transfer applications were received, 4,050 were accepted. Application deadline is November 30 for fall; September for spring. Minimum 2.0 GPA required. Maximum number of transferable credits is 56 semester hours.
**Admissions contact:** Pat Wade, Acting Director of Admissions. 415 338-2017.

**FINANCIAL AID. Available aid:** Pell grants, SEOG, state grants, school scholarships, private scholarships, and academic merit scholarships. Perkins Loans (NDSL) and Stafford Loans (GSL).
**Financial aid statistics:** 5% of aid is not need-based.
**Supporting data/closing dates:** FAFSA/FAF/FFS: Deadline is May 1. Notification of awards on rolling basis.
**Financial aid contact:** Jeffrey Baker, M.S., Director of Financial Aid. 415 338-1581.

**STUDENT EMPLOYMENT.** College Work/Study Program. Institutional employment. 7% of full-time undergraduates work on campus during school year. Students may expect to earn an average of $6,000 during school year. Off-campus part-time employment opportunities rated "good."

**COMPUTER FACILITIES.** 935 IBM/IBM-compatible and Macintosh/Apple microcomputers. Students may access Digital, IBM, SUN minicomputer/mainframe systems, BITNET. Computer facilities are available to all students.
**Fees:** None.
**Hours:** 24 hours.

**PROMINENT ALUMNI/AE.** Johnnie Mathis, singer and entertainer; Rene Enriques, movie and TV actor *Hill Street Blues;* Danny Glover, Annette Bening, Dana Carvey, actors; Mike Holmgren, head coach, Green Bay Packers.

# San Jose State University

**San Jose, CA 95192-0186** **408 924-1000**

**1993-94 Costs.** Tuition: None (state residents), $7,380 (out-of-state). Room & board: $5,772. Fees, books, misc. academic expenses (school's estimate): $2,672.
**Enrollment.** Undergraduates: 8,078 men, 8,079 women (full-time). Freshman class: 5,997 applicants, 4,668 accepted, 1,787 enrolled. Graduate enrollment: 2,660 men, 3,759 women.
**Test score averages/ranges.** Average SAT scores: 382 verbal, 475 math. Range of SAT scores of middle 50%: 305-445 verbal, 400-540 math. Average ACT scores: 19 English, 20 math, 19 composite. Range of ACT scores of middle 50%: 15-21 English, 17-22 math.
**Faculty.** 958 full-time; 1,237 part-time. 50% of faculty holds doctoral degree. Student/faculty ratio: 18 to 1.
**Selectivity rating.** Noncompetitive.

**PROFILE.** San Jose State, founded in 1857, is a public, comprehensive university. Programs are offered through the Schools of Applied Arts and Sciences, Business, Education, Engineering, Humanities and Arts, Science, Social Science, and Social Work. Its 104-acre campus reflects many architectural styles from Spanish to Romanesque to modernist. The campus is located in San Jose, 50 miles south of San Francisco.

**Accreditation:** WASC.
**Religious orientation:** San Jose State University is nonsectarian; no religious requirements.
**Library:** Collections totaling over 1,000,000 volumes, 5,700 periodical subscriptions, and 650,000 microform items.
**Special facilities/museums:** Child development lab, Chicano resource center, Beethoven studies center, John Steinbeck research center, art metal foundry, natural history living museum (science education) and science resource center, deep-sea research ship, electro-acoustical and recording studios, nuclear science and engineering labs.
**Athletic facilities:** Baseball, football, soccer, and softball fields, events center, gymnasiums, swimming pools, stadiums, basketball, tennis, and volleyball courts.

**STUDENT BODY. Undergraduate profile:** 99% are state residents; 44% are transfers. 24% Asian-American, 4% Black, 10% Hispanic, 1% Native American, 47% White, 14% Other. Average age of undergraduates is 23.
**Freshman profile:** 2% of freshmen who took SAT scored 700 or over on math; 2% scored 600 or over on verbal, 13% scored 600 or over on math; 14% scored 500 or over on verbal, 42% scored 500 or over on math; 44% scored 400 or over on verbal, 78% scored 400 or over on math; 80% scored 300 or over on verbal, 97% scored 300 or over on math. 14% of accepted applicants took SAT; 2% took ACT.
**Foreign students:** 979 students are from out of the country. Countries represented include China, Hong Kong, India, Iran, Taiwan, and Vietnam; 124 in all.

**PROGRAMS OF STUDY. Degrees:** B.A., B.F.A., B.Mus., B.S.
**Majors:** Advertising, Aerospace Engineering, Anthropology, Applied/Computational Mathematics, Art, Asian Studies, Aviation, Behavioral Science, Biological Science, Business Administration, Chemical Engineering, Chemistry, Child Development, Chinese, Civil Engineering, Computer Engineering, Computer Science, Creative Arts, Criminal Justice Administration, Dance, Economics, Electrical Engineering, Engineering, English, Environmental Studies, French, Geography, Geology, German, Graphic Design, Health Science, History, Hospitality Management, Humanities, Industrial Arts, Industrial Design, Industrial/Systems Engineering, Industrial Technology, Interior Design, Japanese, Journalism, Liberal Studies, Linguistics, Materials Engineering, Mathematics, Mechanical Engineering, Meteorology, Music, Natural Science, Nursing, Nutritional Science, Occupational Therapy, Philosophy, Physical Education, Physics, Political Science, Psychology, Public Relations, Radio/Television, Recreation, Religious Studies, Social Science, Social Work, Sociology, Spanish, Special Major, Speech Communication, Speech Pathology/Audiology, Theatre Arts.
**Requirements:** General education requirement.
**Special:** Minors offered in many majors and in over 40 other fields. Minors required of some for graduation. Self-designed majors. Double majors. Independent study. Accelerated study. Pass/fail grading option. Internships. Cooperative education programs. Graduate school at which undergraduates may take graduate-level courses. Preprofessional programs in law, medicine, and dentistry. Teacher certification in early childhood, elementary, secondary, and special education. Study abroad in 16 countries. ROTC and AFROTC. NROTC at UC Berkeley.
**Honors:** Honors program.
**Academic Assistance:** Nonremedial tutoring.

**STUDENT LIFE. Housing:** Students may live on or off campus. Coed dorms. Sorority and fraternity housing. School-owned/operated apartments. 7% of students live in college housing.
**Social atmosphere:** According to the student newspaper, "The campus is very segmented, except for those living on campus." Popular events include Homecoming, rush weeks, and "others which are scheduled at various times during the year–we even draw some national acts." Favorite off-campus nightspots include Club Oasis, D.B. Cooper's, One Step Beyond (new wave/alternative music), and Paradise Beach.
**Services and counseling/handicapped student services:** Placement services. Health service. Women's center. Day care. Counseling services for minority, military, veteran, and older students. Birth control, personal, and psychological counseling. Career and academic guidance services. Physically disabled student services. Learning disabled program/services. Notetaking services. Tape recorders. Tutors. Reader services for the blind.
**Campus organizations:** Undergraduate student government. Student newspaper (Spartan Daily). Literary magazine. Radio and TV stations. Bands, orchestras, ensembles, singing groups, drama groups, special-interest organizations, academic clubs, 220 organizations in all. 17 fraternities, 14 chapter houses; 10 sororities, six chapter houses.
**Religious organizations:** Asian-American Christian Fellowship, Campus Crusade for Christ, Bahai, Baptist, Catholic, Christian Science, Taoist, and other religious groups.
**Minority/foreign student organizations:** Black Alliance groups, Black Masque, MEChA. Chinese, Filipino, German, Indian, Italian, Palestinian, and Spanish student groups.

**ATHLETICS. Physical education requirements:** Two semester of physical education required.
**Intercollegiate competition:** 3% of students participate. Baseball (M), basketball (M,W), bowling (M,W), cheerleading (M,W), diving (W), fencing (M,W), football (M), golf (M,W), gymnastics (M,W), martial arts (M,W), rugby (M), sailing (M), soccer (M), softball (W), swimming (W), tennis (M,W), volleyball (W). Member of Big West Conference, Mountain Pacific Sports Conference for men's soccer, NCAA Division I, NCAA Division I-A for football.
**Intramural and club sports:** 15% of students participate. Intramural basketball, flag football, indoor soccer, inner-tube water polo, soccer, softball, tennis, volleyball. Men's club Alpine skiing, archery, bowling, ice hockey, lacrosse, outdoor track, rifle, rugby, sailing, volleyball, water polo. Women's club Alpine skiing, archery, bowling, outdoor track, sailing.

**ADMISSIONS. Academic basis for candidate selection** (in order of priority): Secondary school record, standardized test scores.
**Requirements:** Graduation from secondary school is required; GED is accepted. 15 units and the following program of study are required: 4 units of English, 3 units of math, 1 unit of lab science, 2 units of foreign language, 1 unit of history, 4 units of electives. Electives should include 1 unit of visual/performing arts. Minimum grade of "C" required in listed secondary school courses. Minimum eligibility index of 2800 for SAT (694 for ACT) required of in-state applicants; minimum eligibility index of 3402 for SAT (842 for ACT) required of out-of-state applicants. In-state applicants with minimum 3.0 GPA and out-of-state applicants with minimum 3.6 GPA are eligible regardless of test scores. Portfolio required of graphic and interior design program applicants. Additional requirements for "impacted" programs for which the number of applicants exceeds available space; list of impacted programs is issued each fall. EOP for applicants not normally admissible. Exception Admissions for applicants not meeting standard requirements. SAT or ACT is required. No off-campus interviews.
**Procedure:** Take SAT or ACT by fall of 12th year. Suggest filing application by November 30; no deadline. Notification of admission on rolling basis. No set date by which applicants must accept offer. Freshmen accepted for terms other than fall.
**Special programs:** Credit and/or placement may be granted through CEEB Advanced Placement exams for scores of 5 or higher. Credit and/or placement may be granted through CLEP general and subject exams. Credit and placement may be granted through challenge exams. Early decision program. Concurrent enrollment program.
**Transfer students:** Transfer students accepted for terms other than fall. In fall 1991, 44% of all new students were transfers into all classes. 8,139 transfer applications were received, 6,074 were accepted. Application deadline is November for fall; August for spring. Minimum 2.0 GPA required. Maximum number of transferable units is 105 quarter hours; 70 semester hours. At least 30 semester hours must be completed at the university to receive degree.
**Admissions contact:** Marilyn Radisch, Director of Admissions. 408 924-2000.

**FINANCIAL AID. Available aid:** Pell grants, SEOG, state grants, school scholarships, private scholarships, ROTC scholarships, and athletic scholarships. Perkins Loans (NDSL), PLUS, Stafford Loans (GSL), school loans, and SLS.
**Financial aid statistics:** 1% of aid is not need-based.
**Supporting data/closing dates:** FAFSA/FAF/FFS: Priority filing date is March 2; accepted on rolling basis. Notification of awards on rolling basis.
**Financial aid contact:** Donald P. Ryan, M.A., Director of Student Financial Aid. 408 924-6100.

**STUDENT EMPLOYMENT.** College Work/Study Program. Institutional employment. 50% of full-time undergraduates work on campus during school year. Students may expect to earn an average of $6,000 during school year. Off-campus part-time employment opportunities rated "good."

**COMPUTER FACILITIES.** 150 IBM/IBM-compatible and Macintosh/Apple microcomputers. Students may access IBM minicomputer/mainframe systems, BITNET, Inter-

net. Computer languages and software packages include Assembly, BASIC, C, dBASE, Excel, FORTRAN, ImSL, Lotus 1-2-3, MacDraw, MacWrite, Microsoft Word, Pascal, SAS, SPSS, WordPerfect. Computer facilities are available to all students.
**Fees:** None.
**Hours:** 9 AM-10 PM.

**PROMINENT ALUMNI/AE.** Peter Ueberroth, former baseball commissioner; Lyn Nofziger, former Reagan aide; the Smothers Brothers, entertainers; Stevie Nicks, singer; Carmen Dragon, musical arranger/conductor; Donald Beall, president, Rockwell International; Luiz Valdez, playwright.

# Santa Clara University

**Santa Clara, CA 95053 — 408 554-4764**

**1993-94 Costs.** Tuition: $12,879. Room: $3,378. Board: $2,525. Fees, books, misc. academic expenses (school's estimate): $576.
**Enrollment.** Undergraduates: 1,875 men, 2,016 women (full-time). Freshman class: 4,019 applicants, 2,779 accepted, 888 enrolled. Graduate enrollment: 2,117 men, 1,542 women.
**Test score averages/ranges.** Range of SAT scores of middle 50%: 450-560 verbal, 520-640 math.
**Faculty.** 296 full-time; 105 part-time. 90% of faculty holds highest degree in specific field. Student/faculty ratio: 14 to 1.
**Selectivity rating.** Competitive.

**PROFILE.** Santa Clara, founded in 1851, is a private, church-affiliated, comprehensive university. Programs are offered through the College of Arts and Sciences, the Schools of Business Administration and Engineering, and the Division of Counseling Psychology and Education. Its 104-acre campus is located in Santa Clara, 45 miles south of San Francisco.

**Accreditation:** WASC. Professionally accredited by the Accreditation Board for Engineering and Technology, the American Assembly of Collegiate Schools of Business.
**Religious orientation:** Santa Clara University is affiliated with the Roman Catholic Church (Society of Jesus); three terms of religion required.
**Library:** Collections totaling over 579,860 volumes, 5,081 periodical subscriptions, and 540,751 microform items.
**Special facilities/museums:** Art and history museum, mission church, theatre, media lab, retail management institute, computer design center, engineering labs.
**Athletic facilities:** Stadium, athletic center, pavillion, playing fields.

**STUDENT BODY. Undergraduate profile:** 66% are state residents; 23% are transfers. 19% Asian-American, 3% Black, 13% Hispanic, 1% Native American, 60% White, 4% Other. Average age of undergraduates is 21.
**Freshman profile:** 1% of freshmen who took SAT scored 700 or over on verbal, 8% scored 700 or over on math; 11% scored 600 or over on verbal, 41% scored 600 or over on math; 47% scored 500 or over on verbal, 83% scored 500 or over on math; 90% scored 400 or over on verbal, 97% scored 400 or over on math; 99% scored 300 or over on verbal, 99% scored 300 or over on math. 99% of accepted applicants took SAT. 56% of freshmen come from public schools.
**Undergraduate achievement:** 17% of students who completed a degree program immediately went on to graduate study.
**Foreign students:** 65 students are from out of the country. Countries represented include China, Hong Kong, Mexico, the Philippines, Singapore, and Vietnam; 23 in all.

**PROGRAMS OF STUDY. Degrees:** B.A., B.S.
**Majors:** Accounting, Anthropology, Art, Biology, Business Administration, Chemistry, Civil Engineering, Classics, Combined Sciences, Communication, Computer Engineering, Computer Science, Decision/Information Sciences, Economics, Electrical Engineering, Engineering, Engineering Physics, English, Finance, French, German, History, Individual Studies, Italian, Liberal Studies, Marketing, Mathematics, Mechanical Engineering, Music, Organizational Analysis/Management, Philosophy, Physics, Political Science, Psychology, Religious Studies, Sociology, Spanish, Theatre/Dance.
**Distribution of degrees:** The majors with the highest enrollment are political science, finance, and psychology; dance, music, and classics have the lowest.
**Requirements:** General education requirement.
**Academic regulations:** Freshmen must maintain minimum 1.6 GPA; sophomores, juniors, seniors, 2.0 GPA.
**Special:** Minors offered in most majors in College of Arts and Sciences and also in general business, general engineering, and computer engineering. Self-designed majors. Double majors. Independent study. Accelerated study. Pass/fail grading option. Internships. Cooperative education programs. Graduate school at which undergraduates may take graduate-level courses. Preprofessional programs in law, medicine, dentistry, business, and education. Washington Semester. Capital Program (Sacramento). Teacher certification in elementary, secondary, and special education. Certification in specific subject areas. Exchange program abroad in France (Ecole Superieure de Commerce de Rouen). Study abroad also in Austria, England, Germany, Italy, Japan, Mexico, and Spain. ROTC. NROTC at UC Berkeley. AFROTC at San Jose State U.
**Honors:** Phi Beta Kappa. Honors program. Honor societies.
**Academic Assistance:** Nonremedial tutoring.

**STUDENT LIFE. Housing:** Students may live on or off campus. Coed dorms. Sorority and fraternity housing. School-owned/operated apartments. 45% of students live in college housing.
**Services and counseling/handicapped student services:** Placement services. Health service. Women's center. Day care. Counseling services for minority, military, veteran, and older students. Personal counseling. Career and academic guidance services. Religious counseling. Physically disabled student services. Notetaking services. Tape recorders. Tutors. Reader services for the blind.
**Campus organizations:** Undergraduate student government. Student newspaper (Santa Clara, published once/week). Literary magazine. Yearbook. Radio station. Chorus, jazz band, orchestra, ballet ensemble, drama groups, debating, Community Action Program, Multicultural Program Board, 100 organizations in all. Four fraternities, all with chapter houses; three sororities, all with chapter houses. 15% of men join a fraternity. 17% of women join a sorority.
**Religious organizations:** Intervarsity Christian Fellowship.
**Minority/foreign student organizations:** MEChA, Ka Mana O'Hawaii. Asian Pacific Student Union, The Barkada, Chinese Student Association, Igwebuike, Intandesh, Overseas Chinese Student Club.

**ATHLETICS. Physical education requirements:** None.
**Intercollegiate competition:** 10% of students participate. Baseball (M), basketball (M,W), crew (M,W), cross-country (M,W), golf (M,W), soccer (M,W), softball (W), tennis (M,W), volleyball (W), water polo (M). Member of NCAA Division I, West Coast Conference.
**Intramural and club sports:** 80% of students participate. Intramural aerobics, badminton, basketball, fitness, football, golf, bowling, boxing, lacrosse, scuba diving, soccer, softball, tennis, volleyball, weight training. Men's club bowling, boxing, lacrosse, rugby, swimming, volleyball. Women's club lacrosse, swimming.

**ADMISSIONS. Academic basis for candidate selection** (in order of priority): Secondary school record, standardized test scores, school's recommendation, class rank, essay.
**Nonacademic basis for candidate selection:** Extracurricular participation is important. Character and personality, particular talent or ability, geographical distribution, and alumni/ae relationship are considered.
**Requirements:** Graduation from secondary school is required; GED is not accepted. 16 units and the following program of study are recommended: 4 units of English, 3 units of math, 1 unit of science, 3 units of foreign language, 1 unit of history, 4 units of electives. Electives should be chosen from advanced courses in language, math, lab science, or history. SAT is required; ACT may be substituted. Campus visit and interview recommended. Off-campus interviews available with an alumni representative.
**Procedure:** Take SAT or ACT by January of 12th year. Application deadline is February 1. Notification of admission on rolling basis. Reply is required by May 1. $200 nonrefundable tuition deposit. $200 nonrefundable room deposit. Freshmen accepted for terms other than fall.
**Special programs:** Credit and/or placement may be granted through CEEB Advanced Placement exams for scores of 4 or higher. Concurrent enrollment program.
**Transfer students:** Transfer students accepted for terms other than fall. In fall 1993, 23% of all new students were transfers into all classes. 670 transfer applications were received, 415 were accepted. Application deadline is May 1 for fall; February 1 for spring. Minimum 3.0 GPA recommended. Lowest course grade accepted is "C." Maximum number of transferable credits is 90 quarter units. At least 85 quarter units must be completed at the university to receive degree.
**Admissions contact:** Daniel J. Saracino, M.A., Dean of Admissions. 408 554-4700.

**FINANCIAL AID. Available aid:** Pell grants, SEOG, state scholarships and grants, school scholarships and grants, private scholarships and grants, ROTC scholarships, academic merit scholarships, and athletic scholarships. Perkins Loans (NDSL), PLUS, Stafford Loans (GSL), school loans, private loans, and SLS. Tuition Plan Inc., Knight Tuition Plans, AMS, family tuition reduction, and guaranteed tuition.
**Financial aid statistics:** 2% of aid is not need-based. In 1993-94, 62% of all undergraduate applicants received aid; 66% of freshman applicants. Average amounts of aid awarded freshmen: Scholarships and grants, $8,843; loans, $2,517.
**Supporting data/closing dates:** FAFSA/FAF: Priority filing date is February 1. State aid form: Deadline is March 1. Notification of awards on rolling basis.
**Financial aid contact:** Richard J. Toomey, J.D., Director of Student Records and Financial Services. 408 554-4505.

**STUDENT EMPLOYMENT.** College Work/Study Program. Institutional employment. 30% of full-time undergraduates work on campus during school year. Students may expect to earn an average of $1,800 during school year. Freshmen are discouraged from working during their first term. Off-campus part-time employment opportunities rated "good."

**COMPUTER FACILITIES.** 332 IBM/IBM-compatible microcomputers; 290 are networked. Students may access Digital minicomputer/mainframe systems, BITNET, Internet. Client/LAN operating systems include DOS. Computer languages and software packages include Ada, APL, BASIC, C, COBOL, dBASE, DECGraph, FinalWord, FORTRAN, GKS, Kermit, LISP, LOGO, Lotus 1-2-3, Oracle, Pascal, Progress, Prolog, RDB, Regis, SAS, SimScript, Simula, SLAM:II, SNOBOL, SPSS-X, VAX Assembler, WordPerfect, WordStar. Some computers restricted to use by School of Engineering students.
**Fees:** None.
**Hours:** 8 AM-midn. (Su-Sa); 24-hour dial-up access.

**GRADUATE CAREER DATA.** Graduate school percentages: 5% enter law school. 3% enter medical school. 2% enter dental school. 23% enter graduate business programs. 19% enter graduate arts and sciences programs. 1% enter theological school/seminary. Highest graduate school enrollments: UCLA, UC San Francisco, UC Santa Cruz, St. Louis Medical Sch, Santa Clara U. 72% of graduates choose careers in business and industry. Companies and businesses that hire graduates: Andersen Consulting, Ernst & Young, Hewlett-Packard, Lockheed.

**PROMINENT ALUMNI/AE.** Dr. Lisa Sowle Cahill, theologian, author; A. Michael Espy, U.S. congressman, Mississippi; Jack D. Kuehler, president, IBM.

# Scripps College

**Claremont, CA 91711** **909 621-8000**

**1993-94 Costs.** Tuition: $16,442. Room: $3,350. Board: $3,700. Fees, books, misc. academic expenses (school's estimate): $108.
**Enrollment.** 600 women (full-time). Freshman class: 780 applicants, 600 accepted, 164 enrolled.
**Test score averages/ranges.** Range of SAT scores of middle 50%: 520-620 verbal, 540-640 math. Average ACT scores: 26 composite. Range of ACT scores of middle 50%: 24-30 composite.
**Faculty.** 58 full-time; 27 part-time. 100% of faculty holds highest degree in specific field. Student/faculty ratio: 9 to 1.
**Selectivity rating.** Highly competitive.

**PROFILE.** Scripps, founded in 1926, is a private, liberal arts college for women. It is one of the Claremont Colleges, a group of five undergraduate colleges and one graduate school with adjoining campuses and shared facilities and services. Its 28-acre campus is located in Claremont, 35 miles east of Los Angeles.

**Accreditation:** WASC.
**Religious orientation:** Scripps College is nonsectarian; no religious requirements.
**Library:** Collections totaling over 1,900,000 volumes, 6,800 periodical subscriptions, and 1,100,000 microform items.
**Special facilities/museums:** Art gallery, humanities museum and institute, on-campus school, new joint science center with other Claremont Colleges.
**Athletic facilities:** Football stadium, heated swimming pool, gymnasiums, weight room, baseball, soccer, and intramural fields.

**STUDENT BODY. Undergraduate profile:** 56% are state residents; 9% are transfers. 11% Asian-American, 3% Black, 10% Hispanic, 1% Native American, 72% White, 3% Other. Average age of undergraduates is 21.
**Freshman profile:** 3% of freshmen who took SAT scored 700 or over on verbal, 9% scored 700 or over on math; 38% scored 600 or over on verbal, 49% scored 600 or over on math; 78% scored 500 or over on verbal, 87% scored 500 or over on math; 98% scored 400 or over on verbal, 99% scored 400 or over on math; 100% scored 300 or over on verbal, 100% scored 300 or over on math. 96% of accepted applicants took SAT; 4% took ACT. 65% of freshmen come from public schools.
**Undergraduate achievement:** 89% of fall 1991 freshmen returned for fall 1992 term. 75% of entering class graduated. 33% of students who completed a degree program immediately went on to graduate study.
**Foreign students:** 13 students are from out of the country. Countries represented include Hong Kong, India, Japan, Korea, Taiwan, and the United Kingdom; 12 in all.

**PROGRAMS OF STUDY. Degrees:** B.A.
**Majors:** American Studies, Anthropology, Art, Art History, Asian Studies, Biochemistry, Biology, Black Studies, Chemistry, Chicano Studies, Chinese, Classics, Computer Science, Dance, Economics, Engineering, English, Environmental Studies, European Studies, Film Studies, Foreign Languages/Literatures, French Literature/Civilization, Geology, German Literature/Modern German Studies, Government, Hispanic Studies, History, Human Biology, International Relations, Italian, Japanese, Latin American Studies, Legal Studies, Linguistics, Literature, Mathematics, Music, Organizational Studies, Philosophy, Physics, Political Science, Psychobiology, Psychology, Religion, Russian, Science/Technology/Society, Sociology, Spanish Literature/Civilization, Theatre, Women's Studies, World Literature.
**Distribution of degrees:** The majors with the highest enrollment are psychology, international relations, and history; literature and film studies have the lowest.
**Requirements:** General education requirement.
**Academic regulations:** Minimum 2.0 GPA required for graduation.
**Special:** Minors offered in all majors. Corporate training program. Self-designed majors. Double majors. Dual degrees. Independent study. Accelerated study. Pass/fail grading option. Internships. Affiliated with Claremont Graduate School; qualified undergraduates may take graduate-level courses. Preprofessional programs in law, medicine, veterinary science, pharmacy, and dentistry. Some majors offered in cooperation with other Claremont Colleges. Bachelor's/master's programs in business administration, government, international studies, public policy, and religion with Claremont Graduate Sch. 3-2 engineering programs with Harvey Mudd Coll and Stanford U. Member of consortium with other Claremont Colleges. Washington Semester and UN Semester. Sacramento Semester. Exchange programs with Caltech, Colby Coll, and Spelman Coll. Exchange programs abroad in Ecuador, France, Germany, Hungary, and Zimbabwe. Study abroad also in Australia, Cameroon, Denmark, Israel, Japan, Spain, and numerous other countries. ROTC and AFROTC.
**Honors:** Phi Beta Kappa. Honors program.
**Academic Assistance:** Nonremedial tutoring.

**ADMISSIONS. Academic basis for candidate selection** (in order of priority): Secondary school record, standardized test scores, class rank, school's recommendation, essay.
**Nonacademic basis for candidate selection:** Character and personality are important. Extracurricular participation, particular talent or ability, geographical distribution, and alumni/ae relationship are considered.
**Requirements:** Graduation from secondary school is required; GED is accepted. No specific distribution of secondary school units required. Rank in top tenth of secondary school class and minimum 3.4 GPA recommended. Portfolio, audition, or tape recommended of art, dance, and music program applicants. SAT or ACT is required. ACH recommended. Campus visit and interview recommended. Off-campus interviews available with admissions and alumni representatives.
**Procedure:** Take SAT or ACT by December of 12th year. Take ACH by January of 12th year. Visit college for interview by February 1 of 12th year. Application deadline is February 1. Notification of admission by April 1. Reply is required by May 1. $350 nonrefundable tuition deposit. Freshmen accepted for terms other than fall.
**Special programs:** Admission may be deferred one year. Credit may be granted through CEEB Advanced Placement for scores of 4 or higher. Early decision program. In fall 1992, 30 applied for early decision and 15 were accepted. Deadline for applying for early decision is November 15. Early entrance/early admission program.
**Transfer students:** Transfer students accepted for terms other than fall. In fall 1992, 9% of all new students were transfers into all classes. 87 transfer applications were received, 48 were accepted. Application deadline is April 1 for fall; November 15 for spring. Minimum 3.0 GPA required. Lowest course grade accepted is "C." Maximum number of transferable credits is 64 semester hours. At least 64 semester hours must be completed at the college to receive degree.
**Admissions contact:** Leslie A. Miles, M.Ed., Dean of Admissions and Financial Aid. 909 621-8149.

**FINANCIAL AID. Available aid:** Pell grants, SEOG, state grants, school scholarships and grants, private scholarships and grants, ROTC scholarships, and academic merit scholarships. Perkins Loans (NDSL), PLUS, Stafford Loans (GSL), school loans, and SLS. Tuition Plan Inc., Knight Tuition Plans, and deferred payment plan.
**Financial aid statistics:** 4% of aid is not need-based. In 1992-93, 98% of all undergraduate applicants received aid; 51% of freshman applicants. Average amounts of aid awarded freshmen: Scholarships and grants, $13,500; loans, $2,400.
**Supporting data/closing dates:** FAFSA/FAF: Priority filing date is February 1. State aid form: Priority filing date is February 1. Free Federal Form: Priority filing date is February 1. Notification of awards begins April 1.
**Financial aid contact:** Leslie A. Miles, M.Ed., Dean of Admissions and Financial Aid. 909 621-8275.

# Simpson College

**Redding, CA 96003-8606** **916 224-5600**

**1993-94 Costs.** Tuition: $6,600. Room & board: $3,690. Fees, books, misc. academic expenses (school's estimate): $839.
**Enrollment.** Undergraduates: 187 men, 320 women (full-time). Graduate enrollment: 40 men, 94 women.
**Test score averages/ranges.** N/A.
**Faculty.** 50% of faculty holds highest degree in specific field. Student/faculty ratio: 18 to 1.
**Selectivity rating.** N/A.

**PROFILE.** Simpson, founded in 1921, is a private, church-affiliated, liberal arts college. Its 60-acre campus is located in Redding, north of San Francisco.

**Accreditation:** WASC.
**Religious orientation:** Simpson College is affiliated with the Christian and Missionary Alliance; 30 credits of theology and Bible required.
**Library:** Collections totaling over 53,390 volumes, 246 periodical subscriptions, and 57,960 microform items.
**Athletic facilities:** Athletic field, gymnasium.

**STUDENT BODY. Undergraduate profile:** 76% are state residents. 8% Asian-American, 1% Black, 2% Hispanic, 2% Native American, 86% White, 1% Other.
**Freshman profile:** Majority of accepted applicants took SAT.
**Foreign students:** Five students are from out of the country. Countries represented include Canada, Ecuador, and Japan.

**PROGRAMS OF STUDY. Degrees:** B.A.
**Majors:** Accounting, Biblical Studies, Business Administration, Business/Human Resources Management, Christian Education, Cross-Cultural Mission, Diversified Liberal Arts, Elementary Education, English, History, Music, Music Education, Pastoral Studies, Psychology, Secondary Education, Social Science, Youth Ministries.
**Requirements:** General education requirement.
**Special:** Associate's degrees offered. Self-designed majors. Double majors. Independent study. Internships. Graduate school at which undergraduates may take graduate-level courses. Preprofessional programs in theology. Member of Christian College Coalition. Teacher certification in elementary and secondary education. Certification in specific subject areas.
**Academic Assistance:** Remedial reading, writing, math, and study skills. Nonremedial tutoring.

**ADMISSIONS. Academic basis for candidate selection** (in order of priority): Secondary school record, standardized test scores, school's recommendation, class rank.
**Nonacademic basis for candidate selection:** Character and personality are emphasized. Extracurricular participation is important. Particular talent or ability and alumni/ae relationship are considered.
**Requirements:** Graduation from secondary school is required; GED is accepted. No specific distribution of secondary school units required. SAT or ACT scores in top half for applicant's ethnic group and minimum 2.0 GPA required. Conditional admission possible for applicants not meeting standard requirements. SAT or ACT is required. Campus visit recommended. No off-campus interviews.
**Procedure:** Take SAT or ACT by fall of 12th year. Suggest filing application by February 1; no deadline. Notification of admission on rolling basis. Reply is required by May 1 or within two weeks of acceptance. $100 tuition deposit, refundable until May 1. Freshmen accepted for terms other than fall.
**Special programs:** Admission may be deferred one semester. Credit and/or placement may be granted through CEEB Advanced Placement exams for scores of 3 or higher. Credit and/or placement may be granted through CLEP general exams. Credit may be granted through CLEP subject exams. Credit and placement may be granted through challenge exams and military experience.
**Transfer students:** Transfer students accepted for terms other than fall. Minimum 2.0 GPA required. Lowest course grade accepted is "C." At least 30 semester hours must be completed at the college to receive degree.
**Admissions contact:** Marion S. Brown, M.S.Ed., Director of Admissions. 800 598-2493, 916 224-5606.

**FINANCIAL AID. Available aid:** Pell grants, SEOG, state scholarships and grants, school scholarships and grants, academic merit scholarships, and aid for undergraduate foreign students. Perkins Loans (NDSL), PLUS, Stafford Loans (GSL), school loans, and SLS. AMS.

**Financial aid statistics:** In 1993-94, 100% of all undergraduate applicants received aid; 100% of freshman applicants. Average amounts of aid awarded freshmen: Scholarships and grants, $4,200; loans, $2,625.

**Supporting data/closing dates:** FAFSA: Priority filing date is March 2. FAF/FFS: Priority filing date is March 31. School's own aid application: Priority filing date is March 31. State aid form: Priority filing date is March 31. Income tax forms: Accepted on rolling basis. Notification of awards begins May 1.

**Financial aid contact:** Christopher Kinnier, Director of Financial Aid.

## Sonoma State University

**Rohnert Park, CA 94928 — 707 664-2880**

**1992-93 Costs.** Tuition: None (state residents), $7,438 (out-of-state). Room & board: $5,161. Fees, books, misc. academic expenses (school's estimate): $2,110.

**Enrollment.** Undergraduates: 1,788 men, 2,706 women (full-time). Freshman class: 2,865 applicants, 1,789 accepted, 601 enrolled. Graduate enrollment: 369 men, 947 women.

**Test score averages/ranges.** Average SAT scores: 486 verbal, 482 math.

**Faculty.** 261 full-time; 161 part-time. 76% of faculty holds doctoral degree. Student/faculty ratio: 20 to 1.

**Selectivity rating.** Less competitive.

**PROFILE.** Sonoma State, founded in 1960, is a public, comprehensive university. Its 220-acre campus is located in Rohnert Park, 45 miles north of San Francisco.

**Accreditation:** WASC. Professionally accredited by the National Association of Schools of Art and Design, the National Association of Schools of Music, the National League for Nursing.

**Religious orientation:** Sonoma State University is nonsectarian; no religious requirements.

**Library:** Collections totaling over 458,073 volumes, 3,397 periodical subscriptions, and 1,250,000 microform items.

**Special facilities/museums:** Performing arts center, observatory, electron microscope, seismograph.

**Athletic facilities:** Gymnasiums, swimming pool, track, tennis and handball courts, weight room, athletic fields.

**STUDENT BODY. Undergraduate profile:** 98% are state residents; 59% are transfers. 4% Asian-American, 4% Black, 7% Hispanic, 1% Native American, 60% White, 24% Other. Average age of undergraduates is 23.

**Freshman profile:** 2% of freshmen who took SAT scored 600 or over on verbal, 8% scored 600 or over on math; 21% scored 500 or over on verbal, 40% scored 500 or over on math; 67% scored 400 or over on verbal, 85% scored 400 or over on math; 94% scored 300 or over on verbal, 99% scored 300 or over on math. Majority of accepted applicants took SAT.

**Undergraduate achievement:** 12% of students who completed a degree program immediately went on to graduate study.

**Foreign students:** 126 students are from out of the country. Countries represented include Germany, Hong Kong, Indonesia, Japan, Sweden, and Taiwan; 30 in all.

**PROGRAMS OF STUDY. Degrees:** B.A., B.S.

**Majors:** Afro-American Studies, Anthropology, Art, Biology, Chemistry, Communication Studies, Computer/Information Science, Criminal Justice Administration, Economics, English, Environmental Studies, French, Geography, Geology, German, History, India Studies, Interdisciplinary Special Major, Liberal Studies, Management, Mathematics, Mexican-American Studies, Music, Nursing, Philosophy, Physical Education/Health Sciences, Physics, Political Science, Psychology, Sociology, Spanish, Special Major, Theatre Arts.

**Distribution of degrees:** The majors with the highest enrollment are psychology and liberal studies; Afro-American studies, French, and German have the lowest.

**Requirements:** General education requirement.

**Special:** Minors offered in most majors and in over 15 other fields. Self-designed majors. Double majors. Dual degrees. Independent study. Internships. Cooperative education programs. Graduate school at which undergraduates may take graduate-level courses. Preprofessional programs in law, medicine, veterinary science, pharmacy, and dentistry. Combined bachelor's/M.B.A. and bachelor's/M.P.A. programs. Member of consortium with UC Berkeley and Mills Coll. London Semester. Member of National Student Exchange (NSE). Teacher certification in early childhood, elementary, secondary, special education, and bilingual/bicultural education. Certification in specific subject areas. Study abroad in Australia, Canada, Denmark, France, Germany, Israel, Japan, Mexico, New Zealand, Peru, Spain, Sweden, the United Kingdom, and Zimbabwe.

**Honors:** Phi Beta Kappa. Honor societies.

**Academic Assistance:** Remedial reading, writing, math, and study skills. Nonremedial tutoring.

**STUDENT LIFE. Housing:** Students may live on or off campus. Coed, women's, and men's dorms. School-owned/operated apartments. 12% of students live in college housing.

**Social atmosphere:** Favorite student hangouts include the Pub, Markey's, and Tubbey's. According to the editor of the student newspaper, social life at Sonoma State U is "slow."

**Services and counseling/handicapped student services:** Placement services. Health service. Women's center. Day care. Counseling services for minority, military, veteran, and older students. Birth control, personal, and psychological counseling. Career and academic guidance services. Physically disabled student services. Learning disabled services. Notetaking services. Tape recorders. Tutors. Reader services for the blind.

**Campus organizations:** Undergraduate student government. Student newspaper (STAR, published once/week). Literary magazine. Radio station. Gospel choir, jazz productions, Stage One, ceramics guild, athletic clubs, aquatics club, cycling group, American Market Association, International Business Association, accounting forum, gay/lesbian alliance, women's clubs, Young Republicans, Young Democrats, Community Involvement Program, 86 organizations in all. Five fraternities, no chapter houses; five sororities, no chapter houses. 3% of men join a fraternity. 3% of women join a sorority.

**Religious organizations:** Bahai Club, Christian Student Ministries, Hillel, Intervarsity Christian Fellowship, Newman Club.

**Minority/foreign student organizations:** Black Student Union, Native American Association, MEChA, Pre-Law for Women and Minorities. International Student Association, African-Pacific Islander group, African Culture Club, Chinese Student Association.

**ATHLETICS. Physical education requirements:** None.

**Intercollegiate competition:** 15% of students participate. Baseball (M), basketball (M,W), cheerleading (M,W), football (M), soccer (M,W), softball (W), volleyball (W). Member of NCAA Division II, Northern California Athletic Conference.

**Intramural and club sports:** 11% of students participate. Intramural athletic program. Men's club lacrosse, sailing, volleyball. Women's club sailing.

**ADMISSIONS. Academic basis for candidate selection** (in order of priority): Secondary school record, standardized test scores.

**Requirements:** Graduation from secondary school is required; GED is accepted. 15 units and the following program of study are required: 4 units of English, 3 units of math, 1 unit of lab science, 2 units of foreign language, 1 unit of history, 4 units of electives. Electives should include 1 unit of visual/performing arts. Minimum grade of "C" required in listed secondary school courses. Minimum eligibility index of 2800 for SAT (694 for ACT) required of in-state applicants; minimum eligibility index of 3402 for SAT (842 for ACT) required of out-of-state applicants. Portfolio required of art program applicants. Audition required of music program applicants. R.N. required of nursing program applicants. EOP for applicants not normally admissible. Special admission by petition for state residents not normally admissible. SAT or ACT is required. Campus visit recommended. No off-campus interviews.

**Procedure:** Take SAT or ACT by December of 12th year. Suggest filing application by November 30; no deadline. Notification of admission on rolling basis. No set date by which applicants must accept offer. $100 refundable room deposit. Freshmen accepted for terms other than fall.

**Special programs:** Credit and/or placement may be granted through CEEB Advanced Placement exams for scores of 3 or higher. Credit may be granted through CLEP general exams, ACT PEP, and DANTES exams, and military and life experience. Credit and/or placement may be granted through CLEP subject exams. Credit and placement may be granted through challenge exams. Concurrent enrollment program.

**Transfer students:** Transfer students accepted for terms other than fall. In fall 1992, 59% of all new students were transfers into all classes. 6,108 transfer applications were received, 3,609 were accepted. Application deadline is November 30 for fall; August 31 for spring. Minimum 2.0 GPA required. Lowest course grade accepted is "D-." Maximum number of transferable credits is 70 semester hours. At least 30 semester hours must be completed at the university to receive degree.

**Admissions contact:** Frank Tansey, Ph.D., Dean of Admissions and Records. 707 664-2778.

**FINANCIAL AID. Available aid:** Pell grants, SEOG, Federal Nursing Student Scholarships, state scholarships and grants, school scholarships and grants, private scholarships and grants, and academic merit scholarships. Perkins Loans (NDSL), PLUS, Stafford Loans (GSL), NSL, and SLS.

**Financial aid statistics:** In 1992-93, 85% of all undergraduate applicants received aid; 60% of freshman applicants. Average amounts of aid awarded freshmen: Scholarships and grants, $1,100.

**Supporting data/closing dates:** FAFSA/FAF/FFS: Priority filing date is March 2. State aid form: Priority filing date is March 2; accepted on rolling basis. Notification of awards begins May 1.

**Financial aid contact:** Drew Calandrella, Director of Financial Aid. 707 664-2389.

**STUDENT EMPLOYMENT.** College Work/Study Program. Institutional employment. 8% of full-time undergraduates work on campus during school year. Students may expect to earn an average of $1,500 during school year. Off-campus part-time employment opportunities rated "good."

**COMPUTER FACILITIES.** 850 IBM/IBM-compatible, Macintosh/Apple, and RISC-/UNIX-based microcomputers; 800 are networked. Students may access Digital, IBM minicomputer/mainframe systems, Internet. Client/LAN operating systems include Apple/Macintosh. Computer languages and software packages include APL, BASIC, C, COBOL, dBASE, Dynamo, Excel, FORTRAN, Lotus 1-2-3, Oracle, Pascal, SAS, SPSS, STELLA, WordPerfect; 100 in all. Computer facilities are available to all students.

**Fees:** None.

**Hours:** 24 hours.

**GRADUATE CAREER DATA.** Highest graduate school enrollments: UC Berkeley, UC Davis, San Francisco State U, Sonoma State U. 48% of graduates choose careers in business and industry. Companies and businesses that hire graduates: Bank of America, Deloitte & Touche, Hewlett-Packard, Kaiser Foundation, Sonoma County, State Farm Insurance.

**PROMINENT ALUMNI/AE.** Jack Hemingway, author; Tamara Loring, musician; Davis Campbell, Ph.D., former director, California School Board.

## Southern California College

**Costa Mesa, CA 92626** **714 556-3610**

**1994-95 Costs.** Tuition: $9,220. Room: $2,144. Board: $1,980. Fees, books, misc. academic expenses (school's estimate): $930.
**Enrollment.** Undergraduates: 384 men, 400 women (full-time). Freshman class: 502 applicants, 444 accepted, 222 enrolled. Graduate enrollment: 33 men, 32 women.
**Test score averages/ranges.** Average SAT scores: 410 verbal, 460 math. Average ACT scores: 20 English, 20 math, 21 composite.
**Faculty.** 45 full-time; 6 part-time. 67% of faculty holds doctoral degree. Student/faculty ratio: 16 to 1.
**Selectivity rating.** Competitive.

**PROFILE.** Southern California, founded in 1920, is a church-affiliated, liberal arts college. Its 40-acre campus is located in Costa Mesa, 45 miles southeast of Los Angeles.

**Accreditation:** WASC.
**Religious orientation:** Southern California College is affiliated with the Assemblies of God; 16 semester hours of religion required.
**Library:** Collections totaling over 115,000 volumes, 810 periodical subscriptions, and 8,300 microform items.
**Athletic facilities:** Gymnasium, baseball, intramural, soccer, and softball fields, training and weight rooms, track, tennis courts.

**STUDENT BODY. Undergraduate profile:** 75% are state residents; 31% are transfers. 6% Asian-American, 3% Black, 12% Hispanic, 1% Native American, 74% White, 4% Other. Average age of undergraduates is 22.
**Freshman profile:** 1% of freshmen who took SAT scored 700 or over on math; 4% scored 600 or over on verbal, 11% scored 600 or over on math; 19% scored 500 or over on verbal, 34% scored 500 or over on math; 53% scored 400 or over on verbal, 65% scored 400 or over on math; 89% scored 300 or over on verbal, 93% scored 300 or over on math. 2% of freshmen who took ACT scored 30 or over on math; 38% scored 24 or over on English, 12% scored 24 or over on math; 71% scored 18 or over on English, 69% scored 18 or over on math; 95% scored 12 or over on English, 100% scored 12 or over on math; 100% scored 6 or over on English. 84% of accepted applicants took SAT; 16% took ACT. 70% of freshmen come from public schools.
**Undergraduate achievement:** 71% of fall 1992 freshmen returned for fall 1993 term. 30% of entering class graduated.
**Foreign students:** 26 students are from out of the country. Countries represented include Canada, Japan, Kenya, Sweden, and Zaire; 14 in all.

**PROGRAMS OF STUDY. Degrees:** B.A.
**Majors:** Accounting, Biblical Studies, Biology, Broadcasting, Chemistry, Communications, Cross-Cultural Ministries, Cultural Anthropology, Education, Educational Ministries, English, Finance, History/Political Science, Humanities, Journalism, Liberal Studies, Management, Marketing, Mathematics, Ministries, Music, Music Education, Pastoral Ministry, Physical Education/Sports Science, Physical Education/Teaching/Coaching, Pre-Law, Pre-Medicine, Pre-Veterinary, Psychology, Public Address, Social Science/History/Political Science, Social Science/Psychology, Sociology, Sociology Applied, Speech, Theatre, TV/Film.
**Requirements:** General education requirement.
**Academic regulations:** Minimum 2.0 GPA must be maintained.
**Special:** Double majors. Dual degrees. Independent study. Pass/fail grading option. Internships. Graduate school at which undergraduates may take graduate-level courses. Preprofessional programs in law, medicine, veterinary science, and dentistry. Washington Semester. Teacher certification in early childhood, elementary, and secondary education. Study abroad in Costa Rica, Mexico, and Middle Eastern countries.
**Academic Assistance:** Remedial reading, writing, and math.

**ADMISSIONS. Academic basis for candidate selection** (in order of priority): Essay, secondary school record, standardized test scores, class rank, school's recommendation.
**Nonacademic basis for candidate selection:** Character and personality are important. Extracurricular participation and alumni/ae relationship are considered.
**Requirements:** Graduation from secondary school is required; GED is accepted. 12 units and the following program of study are required: 4 units of English, 2 units of math, 2 units of science, 3 units of social studies. Minimum 2.5 GPA required. Audition required of music program applicants. SAT or ACT is required. ACH recommended. Campus visit recommended. No off-campus interviews.
**Procedure:** Take SAT or ACT by April of 12th year. Suggest filing application by March 2. Application deadline is July 31. Notification of admission on rolling basis. Reply is required by September 1. Deposit of 70% of tuition and board, refundable until first week of classes. $50 nonrefundable room deposit. Freshmen accepted for terms other than fall.
**Special programs:** Admission may be deferred one year. Credit and/or placement may be granted through CEEB Advanced Placement exams for scores of 3 or higher. Credit and/or placement may be granted through CLEP general and subject exams. Credit may be granted through military experience. Credit and placement may be granted through DANTES exams. Concurrent enrollment program.
**Transfer students:** Transfer students accepted for terms other than fall. In fall 1993, 31% of all new students were transfers into all classes. 225 transfer applications were received, 192 were accepted. Application deadline is July 31 for fall; November 30 for spring. Minimum 2.0 GPA recommended. Lowest course grade accepted is "C-." Maximum number of transferable credits is 60 semester hours. At least 24 semester hours must be completed at the college to receive degree.
**Admissions contact:** Richard Hardy, M.A., Assistant Dean for Enrollment Management. 714 556-3610, extension 217.

**FINANCIAL AID. Available aid:** Pell grants, SEOG, state grants, school scholarships, private scholarships and grants, academic merit scholarships, athletic scholarships, and aid for undergraduate foreign students. Perkins Loans (NDSL), PLUS, Stafford Loans (GSL), and SLS. Tuition Plan Inc. and AMS.
**Financial aid statistics:** In 1993-94, 80% of all undergraduate applicants received aid; 80% of freshman applicants. Average amounts of aid awarded freshmen: Scholarships and grants, $1,350; loans, $2,000.
**Supporting data/closing dates:** School's own aid application: Deadline is April 1. State aid form: Deadline is March 2. Notification of awards on rolling basis.
**Financial aid contact:** Randy Hawkins, Director of Financial Aid. 714 556-3610, extension 355.

## Southern California Institute of Architecture

**Los Angeles, CA 90066** **310 574-1123**

**1992-93 Costs.** Tuition: $10,050. Housing: None. Fees, books, misc. academic expenses (school's estimate): $1,400.
**Enrollment.** Undergraduates: 150 men, 66 women (full-time). Freshman class: 200 applicants, 100 accepted, 70 enrolled. Graduate enrollment: 180 men, 60 women.
**Test score averages/ranges.** N/A.
**Faculty.** 40 full-time; 49 part-time. Student/faculty ratio: 13 to 1.
**Selectivity rating.** N/A.

**PROFILE.** Southern California Institute, founded in 1972, is a private institution of architecture. Its two-acre campus is located in Santa Monica, 10 miles from downtown Los Angeles.

**Accreditation:** Professionally accredited by the National Architecture Accrediting Board.
**Religious orientation:** Southern California Institute of Architecture is nonsectarian; no religious requirements.
**Library:** Collections totaling over 9,000 volumes and 60 periodical subscriptions.
**Special facilities/museums:** Art gallery, darkroom, video and photography labs, wood and metal shops, graphics center.

**STUDENT BODY. Undergraduate profile:** 55% are state residents; 80% are transfers. 18% Asian-American, 1% Black, 6% Hispanic, 74% White, 1% Other. Average age of undergraduates is 23.
**Foreign students:** Countries represented include England, Germany, Iceland, Iran, Iraq, and Israel; 22 in all.

**PROGRAMS OF STUDY. Degrees:** B.Arch.
**Majors:** Architecture.
**Requirements:** General education requirement.
**Special:** Independent study. Pass/fail grading option. Internships. Cooperative education programs. Graduate school at which undergraduates may take graduate-level courses. Exchange programs abroad in England (Bartlett) and Germany (Staedeschule). Study abroad also in Australia, Japan, and Switzerland.
**Academic Assistance:** Remedial reading and writing.

**STUDENT LIFE. Housing:** Commuter campus; no student housing.
**Services and counseling/handicapped student services:** Personal counseling. Career and academic guidance services.
**Campus organizations:** Undergraduate student government. Student newspaper (Termite, published four times/year). Literary magazine. Women in Architecture.
**Minority/foreign student organizations:** Diversity Committee.

**ATHLETICS. Physical education requirements:** None.

**ADMISSIONS. Academic basis for candidate selection** (in order of priority): Essay, class rank, school's recommendation, secondary school record, standardized test scores.
**Nonacademic basis for candidate selection:** Character and personality and particular talent or ability are emphasized. Extracurricular participation is considered.
**Requirements:** Graduation from secondary school is required; GED is accepted. No specific distribution of secondary school units required. One semester of college-level general physics, trigonometry, and English required. Minimum 2.0 GPA recommended. Design placement exam required of all applicants. Portfolio required to qualify for advanced standing. Conditional admission possible for applicants not meeting standard requirements. SAT or ACT is required. Campus visit and interview recommended; required of Los Angeles residents. No off-campus interviews.
**Procedure:** Suggest filing application by February 15. Application deadline is August. Notification of admission by April 1. Reply is required by May 1. $500 nonrefundable tuition deposit. Freshmen accepted for terms other than fall.
**Special programs:** Admission may be deferred one year. Credit and/or placement may be granted through CEEB Advanced Placement exams for scores of 3 or higher. Credit and/or placement may be granted through CLEP subject exams. Credit and placement may be granted through military and life experience.
**Transfer students:** Transfer students accepted for terms other than fall. In fall 1993, 80% of all new students were transfers into all classes. 90 transfer applications were received, 70 were accepted. Application deadline is February 15 for fall; November 4 for spring. Minimum 2.0 GPA recommended. Lowest course grade accepted is "C-." Maximum number of transferable credits is 90 semester hours. At least 60 semester hours must be completed at the institute to receive degree.
**Admissions contact:** Stephen Pite, Director of Admissions. 310 574-3625.

**FINANCIAL AID. Available aid:** Pell grants, SEOG, state grants, school scholarships and grants, private scholarships and grants, and academic merit scholarships. Perkins Loans (NDSL), PLUS, Stafford Loans (GSL), private loans, and SLS.
**Financial aid statistics:** In 1993-94, 80% of all undergraduate applicants received aid; 80% of freshman applicants.

**Supporting data/closing dates:** FAFSA/FAF: Priority filing date is March 1; accepted on rolling basis. State aid form: Priority filing date is March 1. Income tax forms: Priority filing date is March 1; accepted on rolling basis. Notification of awards begins May 1.
**Financial aid contact:** Sherri Colburn, Director of Financial Aid. 310 574-1123.

**STUDENT EMPLOYMENT.** College Work/Study Program. Institutional employment. 6% of full-time undergraduates work on campus during school year. Students may expect to earn an average of $1,500 during school year. Freshmen are discouraged from working during their first term. Off-campus part-time employment opportunities rated "excellent."

**COMPUTER FACILITIES.** 12 Macintosh/Apple microcomputers. Computer languages and software packages include BASIC, FORTRAN, LISP, Pascal. Computer facilities are available to all students.
**Fees:** None.
**Hours:** 24 hours.

**PROMINENT ALUMNI/AE.** Michael Rotondi and Annie Chu, architects; David Hertz, architect and furniture designer.

# Stanford University

**Stanford, CA 94305 — 415 723-2300**

**1994-95 Costs.** Tuition: $18,669. Room & board: $6,795. Fees, books, misc. academic expenses (school's estimate): $850.
**Enrollment.** Undergraduates: 3,500 men, 3,073 women (full-time). Freshman class: 13,608 applicants, 2,926 accepted, 1,616 enrolled. Graduate enrollment: 5,115 men, 2,314 women.
**Test score averages/ranges.** Range of SAT scores of middle 50%: 590-690 verbal, 660-750 math. Range of ACT scores of middle 50%: 28-33 composite.
**Faculty.** 1,398 full-time. 100% of faculty holds doctoral degree. Student/faculty ratio: 10 to 1.
**Selectivity rating.** Most competitive.

**PROFILE.** Stanford, founded in 1891, is a private, comprehensive university. Programs are offered through the Schools of Earth Sciences, Education, Engineering, Humanities and Sciences, Law, and Medicine and the Graduate Business School. The layout and character of Stanford's Quadrangle were developed by Frederick Olmsted, designer of New York's Central Park. The 8,200-acre campus includes Moorish Spanish and French Romanesque architecture. It is located in Stanford, 30 miles south of San Francisco.

**Accreditation:** WASC. Professionally accredited by the Accreditation Board for Engineering and Technology, the Accrediting Council on Education in Journalism and Mass Communication, the American Assembly of Collegiate Schools of Business.
**Religious orientation:** Stanford University is nonsectarian; no religious requirements.
**Library:** Collections totaling over 6,300,000 volumes, 60,000 periodical subscriptions, and 3,593,497 microform items.
**Special facilities/museums:** Art museum, food research institute, marine station, observatory, biological preserve, linear accelerator.
**Athletic facilities:** Gymnasiums, swimming pools, athletic pavilion, stadium, weight rooms, track, golf course, basketball, squash, tennis, and volleyball courts, baseball, lacrosse, rugby, and soccer fields.

**STUDENT BODY. Undergraduate profile:** 40% are state residents; 7% are transfers. 24% Asian-American, 8% Black, 11% Hispanic, 1% Native American, 52% White, 4% Other.
**Freshman profile:** 22% of freshmen who took SAT scored 700 or over on verbal, 59% scored 700 or over on math; 72% scored 600 or over on verbal, 89% scored 600 or over on math; 94% scored 500 or over on verbal, 99% scored 500 or over on math; 100% scored 400 or over on verbal, 100% scored 400 or over on math. 91% of accepted applicants took SAT; 18% took ACT. 70% of freshmen come from public schools.
**Undergraduate achievement:** 98% of fall 1992 freshmen returned for fall 1993 term. 75% of entering class graduated.
**Foreign students:** 283 students are from out of the country. Countries represented include Canada, China, India, Japan, Korea, and Taiwan; 28 in all.

**PROGRAMS OF STUDY. Degrees:** A.B., B.Arts/Sci., B.S.
**Majors:** African/Afro-American Studies, American Studies, Anthropology, Art, Biological Sciences, Chemical Engineering, Chemistry, Civil Engineering, Classics, Communication, Computer Science Engineering, Drama, Earth Sciences, East Asian Studies, Economics, Electrical Engineering, English, English/French Literatures, English/German Literatures, English/Italian Literatures, English/Spanish Literatures, Foreign Languages, French/English Literatures, French/Italian Literatures, History, Human Biology, Humanities, Industrial Engineering, International Relations, Italian/English Literatures, Italian/French Literatures, Latin American Studies, Linguistics, Materials Science/Engineering, Mathematical/Computational Science, Mathematics, Mechanical Engineering, Microbiology/Immunology, Music, Philosophy, Philosophy/Religious Studies, Physics, Political Science, Psychology, Public Policy, Religious Studies, Slavic Languages/Literatures, Sociology, Symbolic Systems, Urban Studies, Values/Technology/Science/Society.
**Distribution of degrees:** The majors with the highest enrollment are economics, English, and engineering; urban studies and Latin American studies have the lowest.
**Requirements:** General education requirement.
**Special:** Courses offered in feminist studies, history of science, and Jewish studies. Workshop on social and political issues. Voluntary small-group seminars for freshmen. Tutorials, seminars for sophomores and juniors. Self-designed majors. Double majors. Dual degrees. Independent study. Pass/fail grading option. Internships. Graduate school at which undergraduates may take graduate-level courses. 3-2 engineering programs with Claremont Coll and others. 3-2 bachelor's/master's degree programs. Member of Consortium on Financing Higher Education. Washington Semester. Exchange program with Howard U. Exchange program abroad in England (Oxford U). Study abroad also in Chile, France, Germany, Italy, Japan, and Russia, and in other countries by special arrangement. ROTC at Santa Clara U. NROTC at UC Berkeley. AFROTC at San Jose State U.
**Honors:** Phi Beta Kappa. Honors program.
**Academic Assistance:** Nonremedial tutoring.

**STUDENT LIFE. Housing:** All freshmen must live on campus. Coed and women's dorms. Fraternity housing. School-owned/operated apartments. On-campus married-student housing. 92% of students live in college housing.
**Services and counseling/handicapped student services:** Placement services. Health service. Women's center. Day care. Counseling services for minority, veteran, and older students. Birth control, personal, and psychological counseling. Career and academic guidance services. Religious counseling. Physically disabled student services. Notetaking services. Tape recorders. Tutors. Reader services for the blind.
**Campus organizations:** Undergraduate student government. Student newspaper (Stanford Daily). Many honor societies. Literary magazine. Yearbook. Radio and TV stations. Glee club, male choir, male and mixed choruses, orchestra, symphonic and marching bands, drama groups, debating, special-interest groups, 300 organizations in all. 18 fraternities, nine chapter houses; eight sororities, no chapter houses. 10% of men join a fraternity. 10% of women join a sorority.
**Religious organizations:** Several religious groups.
**Minority/foreign student organizations:** Several minority student groups. Several foreign student groups.

**ATHLETICS. Physical education requirements:** None.
**Intercollegiate competition:** 10% of students participate. Baseball (M), basketball (M,W), crew (M,W), cross-country (M,W), diving (M,W), fencing (M,W), field hockey (W), football (M), golf (M,W), gymnastics (M,W), sailing (M,W), soccer (M,W), squash (W), swimming (M,W), tennis (M,W), track (indoor) (M,W), track (outdoor) (M,W), track and field (indoor) (M,W), track and field (outdoor) (M,W), volleyball (M,W), water polo (M), wrestling (M). Member of NCAA Division I, Pacific Ten Conference.
**Intramural and club sports:** 40% of students participate. Men's club Alpine skiing, badminton, bowling, cricket, cycling, handball, horsemanship, ice hockey, lacrosse, martial arts, Nordic skiing, polo, racquetball, rugby, sailing, squash, ultimate frisbee. Women's club Alpine skiing, badminton, bowling, cricket, cycling, lacrosse, martial arts, Nordic skiing, polo, racquetball, rugby, sailing, squash, synchronized swimming, ultimate frisbee, water polo.

**ADMISSIONS. Requirements:** Graduation from secondary school is recommended; GED is accepted. No specific distribution of secondary school units required. Solid secondary school program recommended of applicants, including strongest possible background in English, math, science, one foreign language, and social studies. SAT or ACT is required. ACH recommended. Campus visit recommended. No off-campus interviews.
**Procedure:** Take SAT or ACT by December of 12th year. Take ACH by January of 12th year. Application deadline is December 15. Notification of admission by first week in April. Reply is required by May 1. Freshmen accepted for fall term only.
**Special programs:** Admission may be deferred one year. Credit and/or placement may be granted through CEEB Advanced Placement exams for scores of 4 or higher.
**Transfer students:** Transfer students accepted for fall term only. In fall 1993, 7% of all new students were transfers into all classes. 1,340 transfer applications were received, 155 were accepted. Application deadline is March 15 (subject to change). Lowest course grade accepted is "C." Maximum number of transferable credits is 90 quarter hours. At least 45 quarter hours must be completed at the university to receive degree.
**Admissions contact:** James M. Montoya, M.A., Dean of Undergraduate Admissions. 415 723-2091.

**FINANCIAL AID. Available aid:** Pell grants, SEOG, state scholarships and grants, school scholarships and grants, private scholarships and grants, ROTC scholarships, athletic scholarships, and aid for undergraduate foreign students. Perkins Loans (NDSL), PLUS, Stafford Loans (GSL), school loans, and SLS. Knight Tuition Plans and deferred payment plan. SHARE. CONSERN. ABLE.
**Financial aid statistics:** In 1993-94, 63% of all undergraduate applicants received aid; 54% of freshman applicants. Average amounts of aid awarded freshmen: Scholarships and grants, $12,163.
**Supporting data/closing dates:** FAFSA/FAF/FFS: Deadline is February 1. School's own aid application: Deadline is February 1. State aid form: Deadline is March 1. Income tax forms: Deadline is August 1. SAAC: Deadline is February 1. Notification of awards begins April 1.
**Financial aid contact:** Robert P. Huff, Ph.D., Director of Financial Aid. 415 723-3058.

**STUDENT EMPLOYMENT.** College Work/Study Program. Institutional employment. 50% of full-time undergraduates work on campus during school year. Students may expect to earn an average of $1,500 during school year. Off-campus part-time employment opportunities rated "good."

**COMPUTER FACILITIES.** IBM/IBM-compatible, Macintosh/Apple, and RISC-/UNIX-based microcomputers. Students may access Cray, Digital, Hewlett-Packard, IBM, SUN minicomputer/mainframe systems, BITNET, Internet. Residence halls may be equipped with stand-alone microcomputers, networked microcomputers, networked terminals, modems. Client/LAN operating systems include Apple/Macintosh, DOS, OS/2, UNIX/XENIX/AIX, Windows NT, X-windows, DEC, LocalTalk/AppleTalk, Microsoft, Novell. Numerous computer languages and software programs. Computer facilities are available to all students.
**Fees:** None.

**GRADUATE CAREER DATA.** Companies and businesses that hire graduates: 3 COM, Bain & Co., Booz, Allen & Hamilton, Boston Consulting Group, Deloitte & Touche, Hewlett-Packard, Microsoft, Shearson Lehman Hutton.

**PROMINENT ALUMNI/AE.** Herbert Hoover, U.S. president; William Rehnquist, chief justice, U.S. Supreme Court; Sandra Day O'Connor and Anthony Kennedy, justices, U.S. Supreme Court; John Steinbeck, author; Warren Christopher, U.S. secretary of state; Sally K. Ride, astronaut.

# Thomas Aquinas College

Santa Paula, CA 93060 805 525-4417

**1994-95 Costs.** Tuition: $12,790. Room & board: $5,110. Fees, books, misc. academic expenses (school's estimate): $250.
**Enrollment.** Undergraduates: 109 men, 99 women (full-time). Freshman class: 163 applicants, 87 accepted, 67 enrolled.
**Test score averages/ranges.** Average SAT scores: 583 verbal, 589 math. Range of SAT scores of middle 50%: 510-660 verbal, 550-650 math. Average ACT scores: 27 English, 24 math, 27 composite. Range of ACT scores of middle 50%: 23-30 English, 21-25 math.
**Faculty.** 19 full-time; 1 part-time. 65% of faculty holds doctoral degree. Student/faculty ratio: 10 to 1.
**Selectivity rating.** More competitive.

**PROFILE.** Thomas Aquinas, founded in 1969, is a church-affiliated, liberal arts college. Its 170-acre campus is located in Santa Paula, 65 miles northwest of Los Angeles.

**Accreditation:** WASC.
**Religious orientation:** Thomas Aquinas College is affiliated with the Roman Catholic Church; eight semesters of theology required.
**Library:** Collections totaling over 33,500 volumes and 40 periodical subscriptions.
**Athletic facilities:** Tennis, volleyball and basketball courts, athletic field.

**STUDENT BODY. Undergraduate profile:** 31% are state residents. 4% Asian-American, 1% Black, 3% Hispanic, 87% White, 5% Other. Average age of undergraduates is 20.
**Freshman profile:** 14% of freshmen who took SAT scored 700 or over on verbal, 10% scored 700 or over on math; 44% scored 600 or over on verbal, 46% scored 600 or over on math; 80% scored 500 or over on verbal, 88% scored 500 or over on math; 100% scored 400 or over on verbal, 100% scored 400 or over on math. 33% of freshmen who took ACT scored 30 or over on English, 6% scored 30 or over on math, 11% scored 30 or over on composite; 72% scored 24 or over on English, 56% scored 24 or over on math, 88% scored 24 or over on composite; 100% scored 18 or over on English, 100% scored 18 or over on math, 100% scored 18 or over on composite. 74% of accepted applicants took SAT; 26% took ACT. 55% of freshmen come from public schools.
**Undergraduate achievement:** 81% of fall 1992 freshmen returned for fall 1993 term. 69% of entering class graduated.
**Foreign students:** 31 students are from out of the country. Countries represented include Bulgaria, Canada, England, Ghana, Ireland, and Lithuania; eight in all.

**PROGRAMS OF STUDY. Degrees:** B.A.Lib.Arts.
**Requirements:** General education requirement.
**Academic regulations:** Minimum 2.0 GPA must be maintained.
**Special:** One curriculum required of all students; no majors or electives offered. All students are full-time and complete four-year program using only Great Books (no textbooks) and classroom discussions. Required classes are four years of history, lab sciences, literature, mathematics, philosophy, political science, psychology, and theology, two years of language, and one year of music.
**Academic Assistance:** Nonremedial tutoring.

**ADMISSIONS. Academic basis for candidate selection** (in order of priority): Essay, secondary school record, standardized test scores, school's recommendation, class rank.
**Nonacademic basis for candidate selection:** Character and personality are emphasized. Extracurricular participation and particular talent or ability are considered.
**Requirements:** Graduation from secondary school is recommended; GED is accepted. 17 units and the following program of study are recommended: 4 units of English, 3 units of math, 2 units of science, 2 units of foreign language, 1 unit of social studies, 5 units of academic electives. SAT or ACT is required. Campus visit and interview recommended. Off-campus interviews available with an admissions representative.
**Procedure:** Take SAT or ACT by May of 12th year. Visit college for interview by May of 12th year. Notification of admission on rolling basis. Reply is required by September 1. $100 nonrefundable tuition deposit. Freshmen accepted for fall term only.
**Special programs:** Admission may be deferred one year. Early entrance/early admission program.
**Admissions contact:** Thomas J. Susanka, Jr., Director of Admissions. 800 634-9797.

**FINANCIAL AID. Available aid:** School scholarships and grants and private scholarships and grants. PLUS, Stafford Loans (GSL), state loans, school loans, private loans, and SLS. Institutional payment plans.
**Financial aid statistics:** In 1993-94, 99% of all undergraduate applicants received aid; 98% of freshman applicants. Average amounts of aid awarded freshmen: Scholarships and grants, $6,478; loans, $2,625.
**Supporting data/closing dates:** FAFSA/FAF/FFS: Deadline is September 1. School's own aid application: Deadline is September 1. Notification of awards on rolling basis.
**Financial aid contact:** E. William Sockey III, Director of Financial Aid.

# United States International University

San Diego, CA 92131 619 271-4300

**1994-95 Costs.** Tuition: $11,760. Room & board: $4,225-$5,150. Fees, books, misc. academic expenses (school's estimate): $900.
**Enrollment.** Undergraduates: 151 men, 86 women (full-time). Freshman class: 812 applicants, 533 accepted. Graduate enrollment: 534 men, 647 women.
**Test score averages/ranges.** Average SAT scores: 440 verbal, 440 math. Range of SAT scores of middle 50%: 340-480 verbal, 370-700 math. Average ACT scores: 18 composite.
**Faculty.** 90 full-time; 127 part-time. 78% of faculty holds doctoral degree. Student/faculty ratio: 15 to 1.
**Selectivity rating.** Less competitive.

**PROFILE.** United States International, founded in 1952, is a private university. Programs are offered through the Schools of Business and Management, Education, Engineering and Applied Science, Hospitality Management, Human Behavior, International and Intercultural Studies, and Performing and Visual Arts. Its 200-acre U.S. campus is located in San Diego, about 20 minutes from the center of the city.

**Accreditation:** WASC. Professionally accredited by the Accreditation Board for Engineering and Technology.
**Religious orientation:** United States International University is nonsectarian; no religious requirements.
**Library:** Collections totaling over 200,000 volumes, 1,200 periodical subscriptions, and 225,000 microform items.
**Athletic facilities:** Indoor soccer field, gymnasium, outdoor fields for soccer, softball and baseball, tennis courts, bowling lanes.

**STUDENT BODY. Undergraduate profile:** 50% are state residents; 6% are transfers. 6.5% Asian-American, 5% Black, 9.5% Hispanic, 1% Native American, 26% White, 52% International. Average age of undergraduates is 23.
**Freshman profile:** 7% of freshmen who took SAT scored 700 or over on math; 7% scored 600 or over on verbal; 21% scored 500 or over on verbal, 28% scored 500 or over on math; 57% scored 400 or over on verbal, 71% scored 400 or over on math; 93% scored 300 or over on verbal, 100% scored 300 or over on math. 84% of accepted applicants took SAT; 16% took ACT. 65% of freshmen come from public schools.
**Undergraduate achievement:** 80% of fall 1991 freshmen returned for fall 1992 term. 70% of entering class graduated.
**Foreign students:** 161 students are from out of the country. Countries represented include China, Japan, Korea, Taiwan, Thailand, and Turkey; 88 in all.

**PROGRAMS OF STUDY. Degrees:** B.A., B.S.
**Majors:** Business Administration, Diversified Liberal Studies, Hotel/Restaurant/Tourism Management, Interdisciplinary Studies, International Business Administration, International Relations, Physical Education, Pre-Law/Human Behavior, Psychology, Social Psychology, Social Sciences, Teaching English to Speakers of Other Languages, World Literature.
**Distribution of degrees:** The majors with the highest enrollment are business administration, diversified liberal studies, and psychology.
**Requirements:** General education requirement.
**Academic regulations:** Minimum 2.0 GPA must be maintained.
**Special:** Minors in most majors and communications, comparative philosophy, creative writing, environmental studies, finance, gender studies, information systems, Japanese, Latin American studies, management, marketing, Spanish, U.S. history, U.S. politics, and U.S. studies. Psychology program with specialization in chemical dependency. Middle University admits secondary school juniors and seniors to programs featuring individualized academic counseling. Associate's degrees offered. Double majors. Dual degrees. Accelerated study. Pass/fail grading option. Internships. Graduate school at which undergraduates may take graduate-level courses. Teacher certification in early childhood, elementary, secondary, special education, and bilingual/bicultural education. Certification in specific subject areas. Study abroad at USIU's international campuses in Kenya and Mexico. ROTC at San Diego State U.
**Academic Assistance:** Remedial writing.

**ADMISSIONS. Academic basis for candidate selection** (in order of priority): Secondary school record, standardized test scores, school's recommendation, essay, class rank.
**Nonacademic basis for candidate selection:** Character and personality, extracurricular participation, and particular talent or ability are emphasized. Geographical distribution is considered.
**Requirements:** Graduation from secondary school is required; GED is accepted. 17 units and the following program of study are required: 4 units of English, 2 units of math, 2 units of science, 3 units of social studies, 1 unit of history, 5 units of electives including 4 units of academic electives. Minimum combined SAT score of 800 (composite ACT score of 15) and minimum 2.5 GPA required. SAT or ACT is required. Off-campus interviews available with an admissions representative.
**Procedure:** Take SAT or ACT by spring of 12th year. Notification of admission on rolling basis. Reply is required prior to start of quarter. $100 nonrefundable tuition deposit. $150 nonrefundable room deposit. Freshmen accepted for terms other than fall.
**Special programs:** Credit may be granted through CEEB Advanced Placement for scores of 3 or higher. Credit may be granted through CLEP general and subject exams.
**Transfer students:** Transfer students accepted for terms other than fall. In fall 1993, 6% of all new students were transfers into all classes. 78 transfer applications were received. Ap-

plication deadline is August for fall; March for spring. Minimum 2.5 GPA required. Lowest course grade accepted is "C." Maximum number of transferable credits is 105 quarter hours from a two-year school and 135 quarter hours from a four-year school. At least 45 quarter hours must be completed at the university to receive degree.
**Admissions contact:** Darla J. Wilson, M.S., Director of Admissions. 619 693-4772.

**FINANCIAL AID. Available aid:** Pell grants, SEOG, state scholarships and grants, school scholarships and grants, private scholarships and grants, and academic merit scholarships. Perkins Loans (NDSL), PLUS, Stafford Loans (GSL), private loans, and SLS. Deferred payment plan.
**Financial aid statistics:** In 1993-94, 47% of all undergraduate applicants received aid. Average amounts of aid awarded freshmen: Scholarships and grants, $5,900; loans, $4,200.
**Supporting data/closing dates:** FAFSA/FAF/FFS: Priority filing date is April 15. School's own aid application: Priority filing date is April 15; accepted on rolling basis. State aid form: Accepted on rolling basis. Income tax forms: Accepted on rolling basis. Notification of awards on rolling basis.
**Financial aid contact:** Mary Hausauer, M.S., Director of Financial Aid. 619 693-4558.

# University of California, Berkeley

**Berkeley, CA 94720** **510 642-2000**

**1994-95 Costs.** Tuition: None (state residents), $11,931 (out-of-state). Room & board: $6,246. Books (school's estimate): $635.
**Enrollment.** Undergraduates: 11,660 men, 10,181 women (full-time). Freshman class: 20,281 applicants, 8,700 accepted, 3,420 enrolled. Graduate enrollment: 5,164 men, 3,617 women.
**Test score averages/ranges.** Range of SAT scores of middle 50%: 500-640 verbal, 600-730 math.
**Faculty.** 1,466 full-time. 98% of faculty holds doctoral degree. Student/faculty ratio: 17 to 1.
**Selectivity rating.** Highly competitive.

**PROFILE.** UC Berkeley, founded in 1868, is a public university. Programs are offered through the Colleges of Letters and Science, Natural Resources, Chemistry, Engineering, and Environmental Design and the Schools of Business Administration, Journalism, and Optometry. Its 1,200-acre campus is located in Berkeley, on San Francisco Bay.

**Accreditation:** WASC. Professionally accredited by the Accreditation Board for Engineering and Technology, the Accrediting Council on Education in Journalism and Mass Communication, the American Assembly of Collegiate Schools of Business, the American Bar Association, the American Dietetic Association, the American Optometric Association, the American Society of Landscape Architects, the Council on Social Work Education, the National Architecture Accrediting Board, the Society of American Foresters.
**Religious orientation:** University of California, Berkeley is nonsectarian; no religious requirements.
**Library:** Collections totaling over 7,700,000 volumes, 87,500 periodical subscriptions, and 4,397,000 microform items.
**Special facilities/museums:** Anthropology, history, and art museums, space sciences lab, research institutes, electron microscope, seismograph, nuclear reactor.
**Athletic facilities:** Swimming pools, racquetball, squash, and tennis courts, gymnasiums, stadiums, aquatics complex, tracks, weight rooms, fitness center, athletic fields, boat houses, coliseum.

**STUDENT BODY. Undergraduate profile:** 90% are state residents; 31% are transfers. 30% Asian-American, 6% Black, 15% Hispanic, 1% Native American, 37% White, 11% Other. Average age of undergraduates is 20.
**Freshman profile:** 8% of freshmen who took SAT scored 700 or over on verbal, 44% scored 700 or over on math; 41% scored 600 or over on verbal, 77% scored 600 or over on math; 75% scored 500 or over on verbal, 93% scored 500 or over on math; 94% scored 400 or over on verbal, 99% scored 400 or over on math; 99% scored 300 or over on verbal, 100% scored 300 or over on math. Majority of accepted applicants took SAT. 83% of freshmen come from public schools.
**Foreign students:** 799 students are from out of the country. Countries represented include Canada, China, India, Japan, Korea, and Taiwan; 100 in all.

**PROGRAMS OF STUDY. Degrees:** B.A., B.S.
**Majors:** Afro-American Studies, Ancient Near Eastern Archaeology/Art History, Anthropology, Applied Mathematics, Architecture, Art, Art History, Asian-American Studies, Asian Studies, Astrophysics, Bioengineering, Bioresource Sciences, Business Administration, Chemical Engineering, Chemistry, Chicano Studies, Civil Engineering, Classical Civilization, Classical Languages, Cognitive Science, Comparative Literature, Computer Science, Conservation/Resource Studies, Development Studies, Dramatic Art, Dramatic Art/Dance, Dutch Studies, Earth Science, Economics, Electrical Engineering/Computer Sciences, Engineering, Engineering Geoscience, Engineering Mathematics/Statistics, Engineering Physics, English, Entomology, Environmental Sciences, Ethnic Studies, Film, Forest Products, Forestry, French, Geography, Geology, Geophysics, German, Greek, History, Humanities, Industrial Engineering/Operations Research, Integrative Biology, Interdisciplinary Studies, Italian, Landscape Architecture, Latin, Latin American Studies, Legal Studies, Linguistics, Manufacturing Engineering, Mass Communications, Materials Science/Engineering, Mathematics, Mechanical Engineering, Middle Eastern Studies, Mineral Engineering, Molecular/Cell Biology, Music, Native American Studies, Naval Architecture, Near Eastern Studies, Nuclear Engineering, Nutrition/Clinical Dietetics, Nutrition/Food Science, Optometry, Oriental Languages, Peace/Conflict Studies, Petroleum Engineering, Philosophy, Physical Education, Physical Sciences, Physics, Plant Biology, Political Economy of Industrialized Societies, Political Economy of Natural Resources, Political Science, Psychology, Religious Studies, Rhetoric, Scandinavian, Slavic Languages/Literatures, Social Sciences, Social Welfare, Sociology, Soil Environment, South/Southeast Asian Studies, Spanish, Statistics, Vision Science, Women's Studies.
**Distribution of degrees:** The majors with the highest enrollment are English, molecular/cell biology, and political science.
**Requirements:** General education requirement.
**Special:** Self-designed majors. Double majors. Dual degrees. Independent study. Accelerated study. Pass/fail grading option. Internships. Cooperative education programs. Graduate school at which undergraduates may take graduate-level courses. Preprofessional programs in veterinary science. Washington Semester. Exchange programs with California State U at Hayward, Howard U, Mills Coll, and Sonoma State U. Study abroad in Australia, Austria, Brazil, Canada, China, Costa Rica, Denmark, Ecuador, Egypt, France, Germany, Hungary, India, Indonesia, Ireland, Israel, Italy, Japan, Kenya, Korea, Mexico, New Zealand, Norway, Portugal, Russia, Scotland, Spain, Sweden, Thailand, Togo, and the United Kingdom. ROTC, NROTC, and AFROTC.
**Honors:** Phi Beta Kappa. Honors program.
**Academic Assistance:** Remedial reading, writing, math, and study skills. Nonremedial tutoring.

**STUDENT LIFE. Housing:** Students may live on or off campus. Coed, women's, and men's dorms. Sorority and fraternity housing. School-owned/operated apartments. Off-campus married-student housing. 28% of students live in college housing.
**Social atmosphere:** Popular on-campus gathering spots include Bear's Lair and Pappy's Pub. Influential campus organizations include Greeks and cultural organizations such as Movimiento Estudianti Chicano de Aztlan, Chinese Student Union, and Muslim Student Union. Football games at Memorial Stadium are popular events, especially the big game between Berkeley and Stanford. Weekend concerts at the Hearst Greek Theatre are also popular. According to the editor of the student newspaper, "students at Cal make what they want out of their social life. Many students, however, have a general feeling that Berkeley doesn't have much to offer; consequently, they flock to San Francisco for late night dancing and entertainment."
**Services and counseling/handicapped student services:** Placement services. Health service. Women's center. Day care. Optometry clinic. Athletic study center. Counseling services for minority, military, veteran, and older students. Birth control, personal, and psychological counseling. Career and academic guidance services. Physically disabled student services. Learning disabled services. Notetaking services. Tutors. Reader services for the blind.
**Campus organizations:** Undergraduate student government. Student newspaper (Daily Californian). Literary magazine. Yearbook. Radio station. Jazz, marching, and concert bands, chorus, men's glee club, women's Treble Clef Society, drama and modern dance groups, debating, radio/TV theatre, humor magazine, Community Project Committee, academic, professional, service, and special-interest groups, 350 organizations in all. 42 fraternities, no chapter houses; 17 sororities, no chapter houses. 14% of men join a fraternity. 13% of women join a sorority.
**Religious organizations:** Asian American Christian Fellowship, Bahai College Club, Campus Advance, Campus Crusade for Christ, Campus Evangelical Fellowship, Christian Science Organization, Grace, Intervarsity Christian Fellowship, Korean Baptist Student Union, Korean Presbyterian Campus Fellowship, Latter-Day Saints Student Association, Newman Club, ReJOYce in Jesus Campus Ministry, Students for the Truth, Studies in the Old and New Testament, University Christian Fellowship, other religious groups.
**Minority/foreign student organizations:** Asian American Student Association, Association for Raza Talent, Black Board, Black Women for Black Women Support Group, Cal Hawaii Club, Hermanos Unidos, MEChA, Mujeres en Marcha, Multiethnic/Interracial Student Coalition, My Brother's Keeper, Raices Latinas. African, Armenian, Asian-Pacific, Chinese, Filipino, Hong Kong, Indonesian, Iranian, Japanese, Khmer, Korean, Laotian, Lithuanian, Pakistani, Sikh, Singapore/Malaysian, Taiwanese, Thai, Vietnamese, and other foreign student groups.

**ATHLETICS. Physical education requirements:** None.
**Intercollegiate competition:** 9% of students participate. Baseball (M), basketball (M,W), crew (M,W), cross-country (M,W), diving (M,W), field hockey (W), football (M), golf (M), gymnastics (M,W), rugby (M), soccer (M,W), softball (W), swimming (M,W), tennis (M,W), track and field (indoor) (M,W), track and field (outdoor) (M,W), volleyball (W), water polo (M). Member of NCAA Division I, NORPAC Conference, Northern California Rugby Football Union, Pacific Coast Collegiate Conference, Pacific-10.
**Intramural and club sports:** 60% of students participate. Intramural aerobics, badminton, basketball, bowling, flag football, handball, indoor soccer, inner-tube water polo, racquetball, rock climbing, sailing, sand volleyball, soccer, softball, squash, street hockey, swimming, tennis, ultimate frisbee, volleyball, walleyball, water skiing, weight lifting. Men's club Alpine skiing, badminton, basketball, bowling, boxing, cheerleading, crew, cycling, dance, fencing, field hockey, gymnastics, handball, ice hockey, lacrosse, martial arts, mini-soccer, Nordic skiing, racquetball, rangers, sailing, squash, triathlon, ultimate frisbee, volleyball. Women's club Alpine skiing, badminton, basketball, bowling, boxing, cheerleading, crew, cycling, dance, fencing, field hockey, gymnastics, handball, ice hockey, lacrosse, martial arts, mini-soccer, Nordic skiing, racquetball, sailing, soccer, squash, synchronized swimming, triathlon, ultimate frisbee, water polo.

**ADMISSIONS. Academic basis for candidate selection** (in order of priority): Secondary school record, standardized test scores, essay, school's recommendation.
**Nonacademic basis for candidate selection:** Character and personality, extracurricular participation, particular talent or ability, and geographical distribution are considered.
**Requirements:** Graduation from secondary school is required; GED is accepted. 15 units and the following program of study are required: 4 units of English, 3 units of math, 2 units of lab science, 2 units of foreign language, 2 units of history, 2 units of academic electives. Electives should include 1 unit of visual/performing arts. Minimum grade of "C" in listed secondary school courses required of in-state applicants; minimum 3.4 GPA required of out-of-state applicants. In-state applicants with minimum 3.3 GPA are eligible regardless of test scores. Applicants with minimum combined SAT score of 1300 (composite ACT score of 31) and minimum combined ACH scores of 1650 (in-state) or 1730 (out-of-state), with no score below 500 on any one test, are eligible on the basis of test scores alone. Audition required of music program applicants. Special Action review for applicants not nor-

mally admissible; eligibility requirements may be waived for up to 5% of admitted applicants. SAT or ACT is required. ACH required. Campus visit recommended. No off-campus interviews.
**Procedure:** Take SAT or ACT by December of 12th year. Take ACH by December of 12th year. Suggest filing application by November 30; no deadline. Notification of admission by March 15. Reply is required by May 1. $100 nonrefundable tuition deposit. $25 room application fee. Freshmen accepted for terms other than fall.
**Special programs:** Credit and/or placement may be granted through CEEB Advanced Placement exams for scores of 3 or higher. Concurrent enrollment program.
**Transfer students:** Transfer students accepted for terms other than fall. In fall 1992, 31% of all new students were transfers into all classes. 6,277 transfer applications were received, 2,392 were accepted. Application deadline is November 30 for fall; July 31 for spring. Minimum 2.4 GPA required of in-state applicants; 2.8 GPA of out-of-state applicants. Lowest course grade accepted is "D." Maximum number of transferable credits is 70 semester hours.
**Admissions contact:** Bob Laird, M.A., Director of Office of Undergraduate Admission. 510 642-3175.

**FINANCIAL AID. Available aid:** Pell grants, SEOG, state scholarships and grants, school scholarships and grants, private scholarships and grants, ROTC scholarships, academic merit scholarships, and athletic scholarships. Perkins Loans (NDSL), PLUS, Stafford Loans (GSL), Health Professions Loans, school loans, private loans, and SLS.
**Financial aid statistics:** 5% of aid is not need-based. In 1992-93, 50% of all undergraduate applicants received aid; 51% of freshman applicants. Average amounts of aid awarded freshmen: Scholarships and grants, $3,700; loans, $2,100.
**Supporting data/closing dates:** FAFSA/FAF/FFS: Priority filing date is March 2. Notification of awards on rolling basis.
**Financial aid contact:** Richard W. Black, M.A., Director of Financial Aid. 510 642-6442.

**STUDENT EMPLOYMENT.** College Work/Study Program. Institutional employment. 34% of full-time undergraduates work on campus during school year. Students may expect to earn an average of $2,218 during school year. Off-campus part-time employment opportunities rated "excellent."

**COMPUTER FACILITIES.** IBM/IBM-compatible and Macintosh/Apple microcomputers. Students may access Digital, IBM minicomputer/mainframe systems. Residence halls may be equipped with stand-alone microcomputers, networked terminals, modems. Client/LAN operating systems include Apple/Macintosh. Computer languages and software packages include major communications, legal, medical, scientific, and other specialized software. Computer facilities are available to all students.
**Fees:** None.

**GRADUATE CAREER DATA.** Highest graduate school enrollments: UC Berkeley, UCLA, Harvard U, Stanford U. Companies and businesses that hire graduates: Bank of America, Bechtel, Chevron, Hewlett-Packard, IBM.

**PROMINENT ALUMNI/AE.** Gregory Peck, actor; Irving Stone, Maxine Hong Kingston, and Joan Didion, authors; Steve Wozniak and Steven Jobs, co-founders, Apple Computer; John Kenneth Galbraith, economist; Earl Warren, former chief justice, U.S. Supreme Court; Melvin Belli, attorney; Edwin Meese, former U.S. attorney general.

# University of California, Davis

**Davis, CA 95616-8678** **916 752-1011**

**1994-95 Costs.** Tuition: None (state residents), $7,699 (out-of-state). Room & board: $5,285. Fees, books, misc. academic expenses (school's estimate): $5,173.
**Enrollment.** Undergraduates: 8,169 men, 8,559 women (full-time). Freshman class: 16,343 applicants, 11,399 accepted, 3,124 enrolled. Graduate enrollment: 2,941 men, 2,339 women.
**Test score averages/ranges.** Average SAT scores: 485 verbal, 585 math. Range of SAT scores of middle 50%: 420-560 verbal, 520-650 math. Average ACT scores: 24 composite. Range of ACT scores of middle 50%: 21-27 composite.
**Faculty.** 1,370 full-time; 204 part-time. 98% of faculty holds highest degree in specific field. Student/faculty ratio: 19 to 1.
**Selectivity rating.** More competitive.

**PROFILE.** UC Davis, founded in 1908, is a public, comprehensive university. Programs are offered through the Colleges of Agricultural and Environmental Sciences, Engineering, and Letters and Science; the Graduate Division; the Graduate School of Management; and the Schools of Law, Medicine, and Veterinary Medicine. Its 3,555-acre campus is located in Davis, 15 miles from Sacramento.

**Accreditation:** WASC. Professionally accredited by the Accreditation Board for Engineering and Technology, the American Society of Landscape Architects.
**Religious orientation:** University of California, Davis is nonsectarian; no religious requirements.
**Library:** Collections totaling over 2,659,270 volumes, 50,298 periodical subscriptions, and 3,177,893 microform items.
**Special facilities/museums:** Art galleries, 150-acre university arboretum, equestrian center, craft center, student experimental farm, nuclear lab, human performance lab, prairie reserve, early childhood lab, raptor center, primate research center.
**Athletic facilities:** Stadium, tennis courts, equestrian trails, swimming pools, bowling alley, track, gymnasiums, athletic fields, recreation hall.

**STUDENT BODY. Undergraduate profile:** 97% are state residents; 32% are transfers. 25% Asian-American, 4% Black, 11% Hispanic, 1% Native American, 52% White, 7% Other. Average age of undergraduates is 21.
**Freshman profile:** 8% of freshmen who took ACT scored 30 or over on composite; 52% scored 24 or over on composite; 94% scored 18 or over on composite; 100% scored 12 or over on composite. 98% of accepted applicants took SAT; 24% took ACT. 86% of freshmen come from public schools.
**Undergraduate achievement:** 91% of fall 1992 freshmen returned for fall 1993 term. 24% of entering class graduated. 43% of students who completed a degree program went on to graduate study within one year.
**Foreign students:** 217 students are from out of the country. Countries represented include Hong Kong, Indonesia, Japan, Korea, and Taiwan; 32 in all.

**PROGRAMS OF STUDY. Degrees:** A.B., B.Appl.Sci., B.S.
**Majors:** Aeronautical Science/Engineering, African-American/African Studies, Agricultural Engineering, Agricultural/Managerial Economics, Agricultural Systems/Environment, American Studies, Animal Science, Animal Science/Management, Anthropology, Applied Behavioral Science, Applied Physics, Art History, Art Studio, Atmospheric Science, Avian Sciences, Biochemistry, Biological Sciences, Biological Systems Engineering, Botany, Chemical Engineering, Chemical Engineering/Materials Science/Engineering, Chemistry, Chicano/Mexican-American Studies, Chinese, Civil Engineering, Civil Engineering/Materials Science/Engineering, Classical Civilization, Community Nutrition, Comparative Literature, Computer Engineering, Computer Science, Computer Science/Engineering, Design, Dietetics, Dramatic Arts, East Asian Studies, Economics, Electrical Engineering, Electrical Engineering/Materials Science/Engineering, English, Entomology, Environmental Biology/Management, Environmental Policy/Analysis/Planning, Environmental/Resource Sciences, Environmental Toxicology, Fermentation Science, Fiber/Polymer Science, Food Biochemistry, Food Engineering, Food Science, French, Genetics, Geography, Geology, German, Greek, History, Human Development, Individual Majors, International Agricultural Development, International Relations, Italian, Japanese, Landscape Architecture, Latin, Linguistics, Materials Science/Engineering, Mathematics, Mechanical Engineering, Mechanical Engineering/Materials Science/Engineering, Medieval Studies, Microbiology, Music, Native American Studies, Nutrition Science, Philosophy, Physical Education, Physics, Physiology, Plant Science, Political Science, Political Science/Public Service, Psychology, Range/Wildlands Science, Religious Studies, Rhetoric/Communication, Russian, Sociology, Sociology/Organizational Studies, Soil/Water Science, Spanish, Statistics, Textiles/Clothing, Wildlife/Fisheries Biology, Women's Studies, Zoology.
**Distribution of degrees:** The majors with the highest enrollment are biological sciences, psychology, and international relations; medieval studies, range/wildlands science, and women's studies have the lowest.
**Requirements:** General education requirement.
**Academic regulations:** Minimum 2.0 GPA must be maintained.
**Special:** Minors offered in most majors and in aging/adult development, agricultural computing/information systems, agricultural entomology, apiculture, applied biological systems/technology, education, energy policy, environmental geology, food service management, geophysics, history/philosophy of science, insect ecology, medical-veterinary entomology, nature/culture, nematology, nutrition/food, recreation, war-peace studies. Self-designed majors. Double majors. Dual degrees. Independent study. Pass/fail grading option. Internships. Cooperative education programs. Graduate school at which undergraduates may take graduate-level courses. Washington Semester. Teacher certification in elementary, secondary, and bilingual/bicultural education. Certification in specific subject areas. Study abroad in 32 countries. ROTC.
**Honors:** Phi Beta Kappa. Honors program. Honor societies.
**Academic Assistance:** Remedial reading, writing, math, and study skills.

**STUDENT LIFE. Housing:** Students may live on or off campus. Coed and women's dorms. Sorority and fraternity housing. School-owned/operated apartments. On-campus married-student housing. Three cooperative-living houses. 22% of students live in college housing.
**Social atmosphere:** As reported by the student newspaper, "Davis students are serious about academic life, but casual about social and cultural life, which is for the most part informal, spontaneous, and centered on campus activities. When they want to get away, students are 20 minutes from good food and entertainment in Sacramento, one hour from great food and entertainment in San Francisco, and two hours from either the Pacific coast beaches or Lake Tahoe and the Sierra Nevada." Popular campus events include the "Whole Earth Festival," a spring regeneration and hippie revival, and Picnic Day, an annual celebration of Davis' roots as an agricultural school. Favorite off-campus spots include the Graduate and Mansion Cellars.
**Services and counseling/handicapped student services:** Placement services. Health service. Women's center. Day care. Counseling services for minority, veteran, and older students. Birth control, personal, and psychological counseling. Career and academic guidance services. Physically disabled student services. Learning disabled services. Notetaking services. Tape recorders. Tutors. Reader services for the blind.
**Campus organizations:** Undergraduate student government. Student newspaper (California Aggie, published five days/week). Literary magazine. Yearbook. Radio station. Marching band, modern dance group, square dancers, comedy troupe, outing club, Spirit Squad, Amnesty International, Model UN, Circle K, 350 organizations in all. 31 fraternities, 14 chapter houses; 20 sororities, nine chapter houses. 12% of men join a fraternity. 9% of women join a sorority.
**Religious organizations:** Numerous religious groups.
**Minority/foreign student organizations:** Numerous minority student groups. American Field Service, Japanese Culture Club, Model United Nations.

**ATHLETICS. Physical education requirements:** None.
**Intercollegiate competition:** 13% of students participate. Baseball (M), basketball (M,W), cross-country (M,W), diving (M,W), football (M), golf (M), gymnastics (W), soccer (M,W), softball (W), swimming (M,W), tennis (M,W), track and field (outdoor) (M,W), volleyball (W), water polo (M), wrestling (M). Member of NCAA Division I for wrestling and gymnastics, NCAA Division II, Northern California Athletic Conference.
**Intramural and club sports:** 70% of students participate. Intramural badminton, basketball, bowling, flag football, floor hockey, golf, inner-tube water polo, racquetball, soccer, softball, table tennis, tennis, ultimate frisbee, volleyball. Men's club Alpine skiing, archery, bowling, crew, cycling, horsemanship, ice hockey, lacrosse, martial arts, Nordic skiing, polo, racquetball, rifle, rodeo, rugby, sailing, squash, ultimate frisbee, volleyball, water skiing, weight lifting. Women's club Alpine skiing, archery, bowling, crew, cycling, horsemanship, lacrosse, martial arts, Nordic skiing, polo, racquetball, rifle, rodeo, sailing, squash, ultimate frisbee, water skiing, weight lifting.

**ADMISSIONS. Academic basis for candidate selection** (in order of priority): Secondary school record, standardized test scores, essay, school's recommendation.
**Nonacademic basis for candidate selection:** Particular talent or ability is important. Character and personality, extracurricular participation, and geographical distribution are considered.
**Requirements:** Graduation from secondary school is required; GED is accepted. 15 units and the following program of study are required: 4 units of English, 3 units of math, 2 units of lab science, 2 units of foreign language, 2 units of social studies/history, 2 units of academic electives. Minimum 3.30 GPA required of in-state applicants and no minimum SAT or ACT score required; 2.82-3.29 GPA requires specific SAT or ACT scores. Minimum 3.4 GPA required of out-of-state applicants. Applicants with minimum combined SAT score of 1300 (composite ACT score of 27) and minimum combined ACH scores of 1650 (in-state) or 1730 (out-of-state) with no score below 500 on any one test, are eligible on the basis of test scores alone. Eligibility requirements may be waived for up to 6% of enrolled applicants. SAT or ACT is required. ACH required. Campus visit recommended. No off-campus interviews.
**Procedure:** Take SAT or ACT by December of 12th year. Take ACH by December of 12th year. Suggest filing application by November 30; no deadline. Notification of admission by March 15. Reply is required by May 1. $100 nonrefundable tuition deposit. $450 nonrefundable room deposit. Freshmen accepted for terms other than fall.
**Special programs:** Admission may be deferred one year. Credit and/or placement may be granted through CEEB Advanced Placement exams for scores of 3 or higher. Credit may be granted through DANTES and challenge exams. Concurrent enrollment program.
**Transfer students:** Transfer students accepted for terms other than fall. In fall 1993, 32% of all new students were transfers into all classes. 5,142 transfer applications were received, 2,796 were accepted. Application deadline is November 30 for fall; October 31 for spring. Minimum 2.4 GPA required of in-state applicants, 2.8 GPA for out-of-state applicants. Lowest course grade accepted is "D." Maximum number of transferable credits is 105 quarter hours. Unlimited number of credits may be transferred from four-year program. At least 35 quarter hours must be completed at the university to receive degree.
**Admissions contact:** Gary Tudor, Ed.D., Director of Undergraduate Admissions. 916 752-2971.

**FINANCIAL AID. Available aid:** Pell grants, SEOG, state grants, school scholarships and grants, private scholarships and grants, ROTC scholarships, and academic merit scholarships. Perkins Loans (NDSL), PLUS, Stafford Loans (GSL), Health Professions Loans, school loans, and SLS. Knight Tuition Plans and AMS.
**Financial aid statistics:** 34% of aid is not need-based. In 1993-94, 75% of all undergraduate applicants received aid.
**Supporting data/closing dates:** FAFSA: Priority filing date is January 1; accepted on rolling basis. State aid form: Deadline is March 2. Notification of awards on rolling basis.
**Financial aid contact:** Ronald Johnson, Director of Financial Aid. 916 752-2390.

**STUDENT EMPLOYMENT.** College Work/Study Program. Institutional employment. Freshmen are discouraged from working during their first term. Off-campus part-time employment opportunities rated "good."

**COMPUTER FACILITIES.** IBM/IBM-compatible, Macintosh/Apple, and RISC-/UNIX-based microcomputers. Students may access Cray, Digital, Hewlett-Packard, IBM, SUN minicomputer/mainframe systems, Internet. Residence halls may be equipped with stand-alone microcomputers, networked microcomputers. Client/LAN operating systems include Apple/Macintosh, DOS, OS/2, UNIX/XENIX/AIX, Windows NT, X-windows, DEC, LocalTalk/AppleTalk, Microsoft, Novell. Computer languages and software packages include ALGOL, BASIC, C, COBOL, FORTH, FORTRAN, Pascal; numerous software packages available. Computer facilities are available to all students.
**Fees:** None.
**Hours:** 8 AM-midn.

**GRADUATE CAREER DATA.** Graduate school percentages: 4% enter law school. 5% enter medical school. 1% enter graduate business programs. 18% enter graduate arts and sciences programs. Highest graduate school enrollments: UC Berkeley, UC Davis, UCLA, UC San Francisco. 59% of graduates choose careers in business and industry.

**PROMINENT ALUMNI/AE.** Deborah K. Butterfield, sculptor of horses; Martin Yan, chef and host, *Yan Can Cook;* Mark and Delia Owens, zoologists, ecologists, and authors, *Cry of the Kalahari* and *The Eye of the Elephant.*

## University of California, Irvine

Irvine, CA 92717 714 856-6345

**1993-94 Costs.** Tuition: None (state residents), $7,699 (out-of-state). Room & board: $12,680. Fees, books, misc. academic expenses (school's estimate): $4,619.
**Enrollment.** Undergraduates: 6,390 men, 7,151 women (full-time). Freshman class: 15,698 applicants, 10,775 accepted, 2,479 enrolled. Graduate enrollment: 1,322 men, 778 women.
**Test score averages/ranges.** Average SAT scores: 455 verbal, 574 math.
**Faculty.** 96% of faculty holds highest degree in specific field. Student/faculty ratio: 17 to 1.
**Selectivity rating.** Competitive.

**PROFILE.** UC Irvine, founded in 1965, is a public university. Programs are offered through the Schools of Biological Sciences, Fine Arts, Humanities, Physical Sciences, Social Sciences, and Engineering; the Department of Information and Computer Science; the Graduate School of Management; and the Program in Social Ecology. Its 1,150-acre campus is located near Newport Beach, 40 miles south of Los Angeles.

**Accreditation:** WASC. Professionally accredited by the Accreditation Board for Engineering and Technology, the American Assembly of Collegiate Schools of Business, the American Medical Association (CAHEA), the National Association of Schools of Theatre, the National Council for Accreditation of Teacher Education.
**Religious orientation:** University of California, Irvine is nonsectarian; no religious requirements.
**Library:** Collections totaling over 1,500,000 volumes, 17,500 periodical subscriptions, and 1,465,012 microform items.
**Special facilities/museums:** Museum of systemic biology, freshwater marsh reserve, electron microscope, nuclear reactor, laser institute, research facilities.
**Athletic facilities:** Gymnasium, swimming pool, basketball, racquetball, and tennis courts, fitness room, track, athletic fields.

**STUDENT BODY. Undergraduate profile:** 96% are state residents; 30% are transfers. 46.6% Asian-American, 2.7% Black, 12% Hispanic, .5% Native American, 32.3% White, 5.9% Other. Average age of undergraduates is 21.
**Freshman profile:** Majority of accepted applicants took SAT. 87% of freshmen come from public schools.
**Undergraduate achievement:** 88% of fall 1992 freshmen returned for fall 1993 term.

**PROGRAMS OF STUDY. Degrees:** B.A., B.Mus., B.S.
**Majors:** Anatomy/Neurobiology, Anthropology, Biological Chemistry, Biological Sciences, Chemistry, Civil Engineering/Environmental Engineering, Classics, Cognitive Sciences, Comparative Culture, Comparative Literature, Dance, Developmental/Cell Biology, Drama, East Asian Languages/Literatures, Ecology/Evolutionary Biology, Economics, Electrical Engineering/Computer Engineering, English, Film Studies, Fine Arts, French, Geography, Geosciences, German, History, History of Art, Humanities, Information/Computer Science, Italian, Linguistics, Mathematics, Mechanical Engineering/Aerospace Engineering, Microbiology/Molecular Genetics, Molecular Biology/Biochemistry, Music, Philosophy, Physics, Physiology/Biophysics, Politics/Society, Portuguese, Psychobiology, Russian, Social Sciences, Sociology, Spanish, Studio Art.
**Distribution of degrees:** The majors with the highest enrollment are biological sciences and economics.
**Requirements:** General education requirement.
**Special:** Minors offered in most majors. Interdisciplinary studies programs in African American studies, Asian American studies, Chicano/Latino studies, global peace/conflict studies, Latin American studies, history/philosophy of science, transportation science, and women's studies. Public Policy Research Organization offers experience for students in information/computer science, social ecology, and social sciences. Double majors. Dual degrees. Independent study. Accelerated study. Pass/fail grading option. Internships. Graduate school at which undergraduates may take graduate-level courses. Preprofessional programs in law, medicine, business/management, and health-related sciences. 3-2 program with Graduate School of Management. Member of consortium with other UC campuses. Washington Semester. Education at Home Program offered through UC Riverside and in Williamsburg, Va., Philadelphia, Pa., and Washington, D.C. Exchange program with all UC system schools. Teacher certification in early childhood, elementary, and secondary education. Study abroad in Australia, Austria, Brazil, Canada, Chile, China, Costa Rica, Denmark, Egypt, France, Germany, Ghana, Hong Kong, Hungary, India, Indonesia, Israel, Italy, Japan, Mexico, New Zealand, Norway, Russia, Spain, Sweden, Thailand, and the United Kingdom. ROTC at CSU at Long Beach. NROTC at UCLA. AFROTC at USC, CSU, UCLA, and Loyola Marymount U.
**Honors:** Phi Beta Kappa. Honors program. Honor societies.
**Academic Assistance:** Remedial reading, writing, math, and study skills. Nonremedial tutoring.

**STUDENT LIFE. Housing:** Students may live on or off campus. Coed and women's dorms. School-owned/operated apartments. Both on-campus and off-campus married-student housing. RV park. 29% of students live in college housing.
**Services and counseling/handicapped student services:** Placement services. Health service. Women's center. Day care. Counseling services for minority and older students. Birth control, personal, and psychological counseling. Career and academic guidance services. Religious counseling. Physically disabled student services. Learning disabled services. Notetaking services. Tape recorders. Tutors. Reader services for the blind.
**Campus organizations:** Undergraduate student government. Student newspaper (New University, published once/week). Yearbook. Radio station. Gospel choir, band, musical groups, folk dance and drama groups, Kabuki Theatre, speech and debating, USEE-EYES (optometry club), Commuter Club, Amnesty International, Comedy Club, Pep Squad, University Ambassadors, surf club, academic and special interest groups. 17 fraternities, no chapter houses; 12 sororities, no chapter houses.
**Religious organizations:** Numerous religious organizations.
**Minority/foreign student organizations:** Numerous minority student organizations and international student organizations.

**ATHLETICS. Physical education requirements:** None.
**Intercollegiate competition:** 7% of students participate. Basketball (M,W), crew (M,W), cross-country (M,W), diving (M,W), golf (M), sailing (M,W), soccer (M,W), swimming (M,W), tennis (M,W), track (outdoor) (M,W), track and field (M,W), volleyball (M,W), water polo (M). Member of Big West Conference, NCAA Division I.
**Intramural and club sports:** 62% of students participate. Intramural badminton, basketball, billiards, flag football, pyramid ball, racquetball, soccer, softball, swimming, tennis, track, ultimate frisbee, volleyball, wrestling. Men's club Alpine skiing, badminton, cheerleading, cycling, fencing, floor hockey, lacrosse, martial arts, rugby, scuba diving, surfing, ultimate frisbee, wrestling. Women's club Alpine skiing, badminton, cheerleading, cycling, fencing, floor hockey, lacrosse, martial arts, scuba diving, softball, surfing, ultimate frisbee, water polo.

**ADMISSIONS. Academic basis for candidate selection** (in order of priority): Secondary school record, standardized test scores, essay, class rank, school's recommendation.
**Nonacademic basis for candidate selection:** Extracurricular participation is important. Particular talent or ability is considered.
**Requirements:** Graduation from secondary school is required; GED is accepted. 15 units and the following program of study are required: 4 units of English, 3 units of math, 1 unit of lab science, 2 units of foreign language, 2 units of history, 4 units of electives. Applicants who attain a minimum secondary school GPA of 3.3 will be considered eligible for admission regardless of their standardized test scores. Applicants whose GPA is below 3.3 but above 2.81 may be considered for admission if they achieve the composite or combined test score specified on the Eligibility Index. Civil engineering, economics, electrical engineering, mechanical engineering, and psychology program applicants must meet

higher standards. EOP for applicants not normally admissible. SAT or ACT is required. ACH required. No off-campus interviews.
**Procedure:** Take SAT or ACT by December of 12th year. Suggest filing application by November 1. Application deadline is November 30. Notification of admission on rolling basis. Reply is required by May 1. $50 tuition deposit, refundable until May 1. $100 nonrefundable room deposit. Freshmen accepted for terms other than fall.
**Special programs:** Credit may be granted through CEEB Advanced Placement for scores of 3 or higher. Early entrance/early admission program. Concurrent enrollment program.
**Transfer students:** Transfer students accepted for fall term only. In fall 1993, 30% of all new students were transfers into all classes. 4,545 transfer applications were received, 2,426 were accepted. Application deadline is November 30. Minimum 2.0 GPA required. Lowest course grade accepted is "C." Maximum number of transferable credits is 105 quarter units.
**Admissions contact:** Sue Wilbur, Ph.D., Director of Admissions. 714 856-6703.

**FINANCIAL AID. Available aid:** Pell grants, SEOG, state scholarships and grants, school scholarships and grants, private scholarships, ROTC scholarships, academic merit scholarships, athletic scholarships, and aid for undergraduate foreign students. Perkins Loans (NDSL), PLUS, Stafford Loans (GSL), Health Professions Loans, school loans, and SLS.
**Financial aid statistics:** 16% of aid is not need-based. In 1993-94, 46% of all freshman applicants received aid. Average financial aid amounts (1993-94): $6,288; total financial aid: $42,545,990.
**Supporting data/closing dates:** FAFSA: Priority filing date is March 1. Income tax forms: Priority filing date is March 2. Notification of awards on rolling basis.
**Financial aid contact:** Otto W. Reyer, Director of Financial Aid. 714 856-6261.

**STUDENT EMPLOYMENT.** College Work/Study Program. Institutional employment. 10% of full-time undergraduates work on campus during school year. Students may expect to earn an average of $5,500 during school year. Off-campus part-time employment opportunities rated "excellent."

**COMPUTER FACILITIES.** 500 microcomputers. Students may access Digital, Sequent minicomputer/mainframe systems. Computer languages and software packages include APL, BASIC, COBOL, FORTRAN, IGL, ImSL, LISP, MINITAB, Pascal, SPSS-X; numerous statistical, graphics, text formatting, test scoring, financial modeling, computer-assisted design, and database management packages. Computer facilities are available to all students.
**Fees:** None.
**Hours:** 24 hours.

**PROMINENT ALUMNI/AE.** J. Hillis Miller and Murray Krieger, professors of English and comparative literature; F. Sherwood Rowland, professor of chemistry.

# University of California, Los Angeles

**Los Angeles, CA 90024** **310 825-4321**

**1993-94 Costs.** Tuition: None (state residents), $7,699 (out-of-state). Room & board: $5,410. Fees, books, misc. academic expenses (school's estimate): $4,594.
**Enrollment.** Undergraduates: 11,854 men, 11,795 women (full-time). Freshman class: 23,340 applicants, 9,837 accepted, 3,460 enrolled. Graduate enrollment: 6,528 men, 5,162 women.
**Test score averages/ranges.** Average SAT scores: 528 verbal, 624 math.
**Faculty.** 100% of faculty holds highest degree in specific field. Student/faculty ratio: 17 to 1.
**Selectivity rating.** More competitive.

**PROFILE.** UCLA is a public, comprehensive university. Founded as a Normal school in 1919, it later became the first branch of the University of California system. Programs are offered through the Colleges of Letters and Science and Fine Arts; the Schools of Engineering and Applied Science, Dentistry, Law, Medicine, Nursing, and Public Health; and the Graduate Schools of Architecture and Urban Planning, Education, Library and Information Science, and Management. Its 419-acre campus is located in Westwood Village, within the corporate limits of Los Angeles. Campus architecture contains Tudor-Gothic, Italian Romanesque, and modernist styles.
**Accreditation:** WASC. Professionally accredited by the Accreditation Board for Engineering and Technology, the American Psychological Association, the National League for Nursing.
**Religious orientation:** University of California, Los Angeles is nonsectarian; no religious requirements.
**Library:** Collections totaling over 6,247,320 volumes, 94,156 periodical subscriptions, and 6,577,644 microform items.
**Special facilities/museums:** Art gallery, cultural history museum, sculpture garden, graphic arts center, numerous study centers, research institutes.
**Athletic facilities:** Gymnasiums, basketball, handball, racquetball, tennis, and volleyball courts, tracks, athletics center, baseball, football, intramural, soccer, and softball fields, boathouse, stadiums, weight rooms, swimming pools.

**STUDENT BODY. Undergraduate profile:** 96% are state residents; 37% are transfers. 30% Asian-American, 6% Black, 17% Hispanic, 1% Native American, 41% White, 5% Other. Average age of undergraduates is 21.
**Freshman profile:** 3% of freshmen who took SAT scored 700 or over on verbal, 27% scored 700 or over on math; 25% scored 600 or over on verbal, 63% scored 600 or over on math; 63% scored 500 or over on verbal, 87% scored 500 or over on math; 90% scored 400 or over on verbal, 96% scored 400 or over on math; 97% scored 300 or over on verbal, 98% scored 300 or over on math. 98% of accepted applicants took SAT. 85% of freshmen come from public schools.
**Undergraduate achievement:** 94% of fall 1991 freshmen returned for fall 1992 term. 60% of students who completed a degree program went on to graduate study.
**Foreign students:** Countries represented include China, Hong Kong, India, Japan, Korea, and Taiwan.

**PROGRAMS OF STUDY. Degrees:** B.A., B.S.
**Majors:** Aerospace Engineering, African Languages, Afro-American Studies, Ancient Near Eastern Civilizations, Anthropology, Applied Mathematics, Arabic, Art, Art History, Astrophysics, Atmospheric Sciences, Biochemistry, Biology, Business Economics, Chemical Engineering, Chemistry, Chemistry/Materials Science, Chicano Studies, Chinese, Civil Engineering, Classical Civilization, Classics, Cognitive Science, Communications Studies, Computer Science, Computer Science/Engineering, Cybernetics, Dance, Design, Development Studies, Earth Sciences, East Asian Studies, Economics, Economics/International Area Studies, Electrical Engineering, Engineering, English, English/Greek, English/Latin, Ethnomusicology, French, French/Linguistics, General Chemistry, General Mathematics, Geography, Geography/Environmental Studies, Geology, Geology/Engineering Geology, Geology/Paleobiology, Geophysics/Applied Geophysics, Geophysics/Space Physics, German, Greek, Hebrew, History, History/Art History, Individual Fields of Concentration, Iranian Studies, Italian, Italian/Special Fields, Japanese, Jewish Studies, Kinesiology, Latin, Latin American Studies, Linguistics, Linguistics/Anthropology, Linguistics/Computer Science, Linguistics/East Asian Languages/Cultures, Linguistics/English, Linguistics/French, Linguistics/Italian, Linguistics/Philosophy, Linguistics/Psychology, Linguistics/Scandinavian Languages, Linguistics/Spanish, Materials Engineering, Mathematics, Mathematics/Applied Science, Mathematics of Computation, Mechanical Engineering, Microbiology/Molecular Genetics, Motion Picture/Television, Music, Musicology, Near Eastern Studies, Nursing, Philosophy, Physics, Political Science, Portuguese, Psychobiology, Psychology, Russian Language/Literature, Russian Studies, Scandinavian Languages, Slavic Languages/Literatures, Sociology, Spanish, Spanish/Linguistics, Spanish/Portuguese, Study of Religion, Theater, Women's Studies, World Arts/Cultures.
**Distribution of degrees:** The majors with the highest enrollment are economics, psychology, and biology; African languages, Greek, and Arabic have the lowest.
**Requirements:** General education requirement.
**Academic regulations:** Minimum 2.0 GPA required for graduation.
**Special:** Self-designed majors. Double majors. Dual degrees. Independent study. Accelerated study. Pass/fail grading option. Internships. Graduate school at which undergraduates may take graduate-level courses. Preprofessional programs in law, pharmacy, optometry, dental hygiene, physical therapy, and public health. Teacher certification in elementary and bilingual/bicultural education. Study abroad in Australia, China, Egypt, Germany, Hungary, Israel, Kenya, Mexico, New Zealand, Peru, Sweden, Thailand, and numerous other countries. ROTC, NROTC, and AFROTC.
**Honors:** Phi Beta Kappa. Honors program.
**Academic Assistance:** Remedial reading, writing, math, and study skills.

**STUDENT LIFE. Housing:** Students may live on or off campus. Coed dorms. Sorority and fraternity housing. School-owned/operated apartments. Off-campus married-student housing. 24% of students live in college housing.
**Social atmosphere:** The student newspaper reports, "Cultural life (art, music, dance, theatre) is wonderful and very accessible to students. Socially one can be very active if one finds the time." On-campus hangouts include the Kerckhoff Coffee House, North Campus Restaurant, and LuValle Common; the Elysee Coffee Shop, Santo Pietro Restaurant, and Yesterday's are favorite off-campus spots. The Greek system and cultural and ethnic groups are influential groups on campus. Some popular events are the USC-UCLA football game, Mardi Gras in May, and Homecoming Week.
**Services and counseling/handicapped student services:** Placement services. Health service. Women's center. Day care. Counseling services for minority, military, veteran, and older students. Birth control, personal, and psychological counseling. Career and academic guidance services. Physically disabled student services. Learning disabled services. Notetaking services. Tape recorders. Tutors. Reader services for the blind.
**Campus organizations:** Undergraduate student government. Student newspaper (Daily Bruin). Yearbook. Radio station. Music groups, dance and drama groups, academic, community service, professional, and special-interest groups, 700 organizations in all. 32 fraternities, 24 chapter houses; 20 sororities, 13 chapter houses. 14% of men join a fraternity. 14% of women join a sorority.
**Religious organizations:** Campus Crusade for Christ, Maranatha Campus Ministries, Newman Club, Chabad House, Sri Chinmoy Meditation Society, Bible study groups, Bahai, Baptist, Christian Science, Lutheran, Methodist, Presbyterian, and other religious groups.
**Minority/foreign student organizations:** American Indian Student Association, Association of Chinese-Americans, Black Student Alliance, Black Entrepreneurs, MEChA, other minority student groups. International Student Association, African, Asian, Brazilian, Chinese, Colombian, Dutch, Egyptian, Filipino, Hawaiian, Iranian, Korean, Lithuanian, Mexican, Turkish, Vietnamese, and other foreign student groups.

**ATHLETICS. Physical education requirements:** None.
**Intercollegiate competition:** 10% of students participate. Baseball (M), basketball (M,W), cross-country (M,W), diving (M,W), football (M), golf (M,W), gymnastics (M,W), soccer (M,W), softball (W), swimming (M,W), tennis (M,W), track (indoor) (M,W), track (outdoor) (M,W), track and field (indoor) (M,W), track and field (outdoor) (M,W), volleyball (M,W), water polo (M). Member of NCAA Division I, NCAA Division I-A for football, Pacific 10 Conference.
**Intramural and club sports:** 75% of students participate. Intramural badminton, basketball, bowling, cricket, cycling, flag football, golf, handball, racquetball, sailing, skiing, softball, swimming, table tennis, tennis, track, volleyball, water polo. Men's club Alpine skiing, bowling, crew, cycling, fencing, ice hockey, lacrosse, Nordic skiing, rugby, sailing, surfing. Women's club Alpine skiing, bowling, crew, cycling, fencing, lacrosse, Nordic skiing, sailing, soccer, surfing, water polo.

**ADMISSIONS. Academic basis for candidate selection** (in order of priority): Secondary school record, standardized test scores, essay, school's recommendation.
**Nonacademic basis for candidate selection:** Particular talent or ability and geographical distribution are important. Extracurricular participation is considered.
**Requirements:** Graduation from secondary school is required; GED is accepted. 15 units and the following program of study is required: 4 units of English, 3 units of math, 2 units

of lab science, 2 units of foreign language, 2 units of history, 2 units of academic electives including 1 unit of visual/performing arts. Minimum 2.78 GPA required of in-state applicants; minimum 3.4 GPA required of out-of-state applicants. In-state applicants with minimum 3.3 GPA are eligible regardless of test scores; in-state applicants with minimum combined SAT score of 1100 (composite ACT score of 27) and minimum combined ACH score of 1650 (with minimum score of 500 on any one ACH) are eligible by examination alone. Additional requirements for applicants to School of the Arts and School of Theater, Film, and Television. Portfolio required of art program applicants. Audition required of music program applicants. Educational and economic disadvantages are considered in admissions process. SAT or ACT is required. ACH required. Campus visit recommended. No off-campus interviews.
**Procedure:** Take SAT or ACT by December of 12th year. Take ACH by December of 12th year. Suggest filing application by November 1; no deadline. Notification of admission by March 15. Reply is required by May 1. $100 nonrefundable registration fee. $20 nonrefundable housing application fee. Freshmen accepted for fall term only.
**Special programs:** Credit and/or placement may be granted through CEEB Advanced Placement exams for scores of 3 or higher. Placement may be granted through challenge exams. Concurrent enrollment program.
**Transfer students:** Transfer students accepted for terms other than fall. In fall 1992, 37% of all new students were transfers into all classes. 8,078 transfer applications were received, 3,413 were accepted. Application deadline is November 1 for fall; October 31 for spring. Minimum 2.4 GPA required. Lowest course grade accepted is "D." Maximum number of transferable credits is 70 semester hours.
**Admissions contact:** Rae Lee Siporin, Ph.D., Director of Undergraduate Admissions. 310 825-3101.

**FINANCIAL AID. Available aid:** Pell grants, SEOG, Federal Nursing Student Scholarships, state scholarships and grants, school scholarships and grants, private scholarships and grants, ROTC scholarships, academic merit scholarships, and athletic scholarships. Perkins Loans (NDSL), PLUS, Stafford Loans (GSL), NSL, Health Professions Loans, state loans, school loans, private loans, and SLS.
**Financial aid statistics:** 20% of aid is not need-based. In 1992-93, 89% of all undergraduate applicants received aid; 72% of freshman applicants. Average amounts of aid awarded freshmen: Scholarships and grants, $5,339; loans, $4,000.
**Supporting data/closing dates:** FAFSA/FAF/FFS: Deadline is March 2. Notification of awards begins July 1.
**Financial aid contact:** Larry Burt, Ph.D., Director of Financial Aid. 310 206-0400.

**STUDENT EMPLOYMENT.** College Work/Study Program. Institutional employment. 79% of full-time undergraduates work on campus during school year. Students may expect to earn an average of $6,378 during school year. Off-campus part-time employment opportunities rated "good."

**COMPUTER FACILITIES.** IBM/IBM-compatible and Macintosh/Apple microcomputers. Students may access IBM minicomputer/mainframe systems. Residence halls may be equipped with stand-alone microcomputers, networked terminals, modems. 160 major computer languages and software packages available.
**Fees:** None.
**Hours:** 24 hours.

**GRADUATE CAREER DATA.** Graduate school percentages: 11% enter law school. 5% enter medical school. 1% enter dental school. 4% enter graduate business programs. 16% enter graduate arts and sciences programs. 63% of graduates choose careers in business and industry.

## University of California, Riverside

Riverside, CA 92521 — 909 787-1012

**1994-95 Costs.** Tuition: None (state residents), $8,299 (out-of-state). Room & board: $5,430. Fees, books, misc. academic expenses (school's estimate): $5,248.
**Enrollment.** Undergraduates: 3,293 men, 3,629 women (full-time). Freshman class: 9,798 applicants, 7,567 accepted, 1,470 enrolled. Graduate enrollment: 769 men, 721 women.
**Test score averages/ranges.** Average SAT scores: 440 verbal, 542 math. Range of SAT scores of middle 50%: 360-510 verbal, 470-620 math.
**Faculty.** 554 full-time; 155 part-time. 98% of faculty holds highest degree in specific field. Student/faculty ratio: 14 to 1.
**Selectivity rating.** Less competitive.

**PROFILE.** UC Riverside, founded as an agricultural research center in 1907, is a public, comprehensive university. Programs are offered through the Colleges of Natural and Agricultural Sciences, Humanities and Social Sciences, and Engineering; the School of Education; the Graduate Division; and the Graduate School of Management. Its 1,200-acre campus is located 60 miles east of Los Angeles.

**Accreditation:** WASC. Professionally accredited by the American Medical Association (CAHEA).
**Religious orientation:** University of California, Riverside is nonsectarian; no religious requirements.
**Library:** Collections totaling over 1,561,000 volumes, 12,900 periodical subscriptions, and 1,365,000 microform items.
**Special facilities/museums:** Art gallery, photography museum, botanical gardens, audio-visual resource center/studios, media resource center, statistical consulting center, citrus research center and agricultural experiment station, air pollution research center, center for environmental research and technology, center for social and behavioral science research, dry lands research institute, water resources center, geophysics and planetary physics institutes, center for bibliographical studies.
**Athletic facilities:** Gymnasium, swimming pool.

**STUDENT BODY. Undergraduate profile:** 98% are state residents; 29% are transfers. 37% Asian-American, 4% Black, 14% Hispanic, 1% Native American, 44% White. Average age of undergraduates is 21.
**Freshman profile:** 1% of freshmen who took SAT scored 700 or over on verbal, 9% scored 700 or over on math; 8% scored 600 or over on verbal, 31% scored 600 or over on math; 31% scored 500 or over on verbal, 67% scored 500 or over on math; 67% scored 400 or over on verbal, 92% scored 400 or over on math; 93% scored 300 or over on verbal, 100% scored 300 or over on math. 99% of accepted applicants took SAT; 1% took ACT. 88% of freshmen come from public schools.
**Undergraduate achievement:** 89% of fall 1992 freshmen returned for fall 1993 term. 47% of entering class graduated. 47% of students who completed a degree program went on to graduate study within one year.
**Foreign students:** 23 students are from out of the country. Countries represented include China and Japan; 12 in all.

**PROGRAMS OF STUDY. Degrees:** B.A., B.S.
**Majors:** Administrative Studies, Anthropology, Art History, Asian Studies, Biochemistry, Biology, Biomedical Science, Botany/Plant Science, Business Administration, Business Economics, Chemical/Biochemical Engineering, Chemistry, Classical Studies, Comparative Literature, Computer Science, Creative Writing, Dance, Economics, Electrical Engineering, English, Entomology, Environmental Engineering, Environmental Science, Ethnic Studies, French, Geography, Geology, Geophysics, German, History, Human Development, Humanities/Social Sciences, Individual Major, Language, Latin American Studies, Liberal Studies, Linguistics, Mathematics, Music, Philosophy, Physical Sciences, Physics, Political Science, Psychobiology, Psychology, Public Service, Religious Studies, Russian Studies, Social Relations, Sociology, Soil Science, Spanish, Statistics, Studio Art, Theatre, Women's Studies.
**Distribution of degrees:** The majors with the highest enrollment are business administration, biology, and psychology.
**Requirements:** General education requirement.
**Academic regulations:** Minimum 2.0 GPA must be maintained.
**Special:** Minors offered in most majors and in Chicano studies, Chinese, international relations, journalism, Marxist studies, urban studies, and Western American studies. Self-designed majors. Double majors. Dual degrees. Independent study. Accelerated study. Pass/fail grading option. Internships. Cooperative education programs. Graduate school at which undergraduates may take graduate-level courses. Preprofessional programs in law, medicine, veterinary science, pharmacy, dentistry, and optometry. Seven-year B.S./M.D. biomedical sciences program with UCLA. Member of U of California Consortium on Mexico and the U.S. Washington Semester. Teacher certification in elementary, secondary, special education, and bilingual/bicultural education. Certification in specific subject areas. Study abroad in 29 countries. Reciprocity program in conjunction with Education Abroad Program. ROTC at California State U at San Bernardino. AFROTC at UCLA, USC, and Loyola Marymount U.
**Honors:** Phi Beta Kappa. Honors program. Honor societies.
**Academic Assistance:** Remedial reading, writing, math, and study skills. Nonremedial tutoring.

**STUDENT LIFE. Housing:** Students may live on or off campus. Coed dorms. Sorority and fraternity housing. School-owned/operated apartments. Off-campus privately-owned housing. On-campus married-student housing. 31% of students live in college housing.
**Social atmosphere:** According to the editor of the student newspaper, UC Riverside "tries to be culturally aware." Influential groups include Greeks as well as ethnically oriented student service groups and various political groups. Popular events include basketball and women's volleyball games, Spectrum '89 (a cultural awareness happening), and Open House, which attracts thousands. Noon concerts by various bands also draw a crowd. Some popular places to socialize are the Barn, the Bull-n-Mouth, the Pub, and See's Coffeehouse.
**Services and counseling/handicapped student services:** Placement services. Health service. Women's center. Day care. Campus ombudsman. Counseling services for minority and older students. Birth control, personal, and psychological counseling. Career and academic guidance services. Physically disabled student services. Learning disabled services. Notetaking services. Tape recorders. Tutors. Reader services for the blind.
**Campus organizations:** Undergraduate student government. Student newspaper (Highlander, published once/week). Literary magazine. Radio station. Bands, jazz ensemble, film society, folk dance club, service groups, Human Corps Program, Student BEAR FACTS orientation, performing arts program, academic clubs, recreation and environmental clubs, 136 organizations in all. 14 fraternities, no chapter houses; 12 sororities, no chapter houses. 10% of men join a fraternity. 14% of women join a sorority.
**Religious organizations:** Several religious groups.
**Minority/foreign student organizations:** Numerous minority student groups. Numerous foreign student groups.

**ATHLETICS. Physical education requirements:** None.
**Intercollegiate competition:** 4% of students participate. Baseball (M), basketball (M,W), cheerleading (M,W), cross-country (M,W), martial arts (M,W), softball (W), tennis (M,W), track (outdoor) (M,W), volleyball (W), water polo (M). Member of CCAA, NCAA Division II.
**Intramural and club sports:** 15% of students participate. Men's club golf, lacrosse, rugby, soccer. Women's club soccer.

**ADMISSIONS. Academic basis for candidate selection** (in order of priority): Secondary school record, standardized test scores, class rank, essay, school's recommendation.
**Nonacademic basis for candidate selection:** Extracurricular participation and particular talent or ability are important. Geographical distribution is considered.
**Requirements:** Graduation from secondary school is required; GED is accepted. 15 units and the following program of study are required: 4 units of English, 3 units of math, 2 units of lab science, 2 units of foreign language, 2 units of history, 2 units of academic electives. Minimum grade of "C" in listed secondary school courses required of in-state applicants; minimum 3.4 GPA required of out-of-state applicants. In-state applicants with minimum 3.3 GPA are eligible regardless of test scores. Applicants with minimum combined SAT score of 1300 (composite ACT score of 31) and minimum combined ACH scores of 1650 (in-state) or 1730 (out-of-state), with no score below 500 on any one test, are eligible on the basis of test scores alone. EOP for applicants not normally admissible. Student Affirmative Action for in-state applicants not normally admissible. SAT or ACT is required.

ACH required. Campus visit recommended. Off-campus interviews available with an admissions representative.
**Procedure:** Take SAT or ACT by December of 12th year. Take ACH by December of 12th year. Suggest filing application by November 30; no deadline. Notification of admission by March 15. Reply is required by May 1. $100 nonrefundable tuition deposit. $630 room deposit, partially refundable until September 1. Freshmen accepted for terms other than fall.
**Special programs:** Credit and/or placement may be granted through CEEB Advanced Placement exams for scores of 3 or higher. Placement may be granted through challenge exams. Early entrance/early admission program. Concurrent enrollment program.
**Transfer students:** Transfer students accepted for terms other than fall. In fall 1993, 29% of all new students were transfers into all classes. 2,628 transfer applications were received, 1,760 were accepted. Application deadline is rolling for fall; rolling for spring. Minimum 2.0 GPA required of in-state applicants; 2.4 GPA of out-of-state applicants. Lowest course grade accepted is "C." Maximum number of transferable credits is 105 quarter hours from a two-year school and 120 quarter hours from a four-year school. At least 35 quarter hours must be completed at the university to receive degree.
**Admissions contact:** R. Fred Zuker, Ph.D., Vice Chancellor, Enrollment Management. 909 787-4531, 909 787-3411.

**FINANCIAL AID. Available aid:** Pell grants, SEOG, state scholarships and grants, school scholarships and grants, private scholarships and grants, ROTC scholarships, academic merit scholarships, and athletic scholarships. Perkins Loans (NDSL), PLUS, Stafford Loans (GSL), school loans, private loans, and SLS. Deferred payment plan. 60-day short-term loans for fees.
**Supporting data/closing dates:** FAFSA: Priority filing date is March 2. Notification of awards begins May 1.
**Financial aid contact:** James W. Sandoval, M.A., Director of Financial Aid. 909 787-3878.

**STUDENT EMPLOYMENT.** College Work/Study Program. Institutional employment. 20% of full-time undergraduates work on campus during school year. Freshmen are discouraged from working during their first term. Off-campus part-time employment opportunities rated "good."

**COMPUTER FACILITIES.** 170 IBM/IBM-compatible, Macintosh/Apple, and RISC-/UNIX-based microcomputers. Students may access Digital, IBM minicomputer/mainframe systems, BITNET, Internet. Residence halls may be equipped with stand-alone microcomputers, networked microcomputers. Client/LAN operating systems include Apple/Macintosh, DOS, UNIX/XENIX/AIX. Computer languages and software packages include Apple Scan, Apple Share, BASIC, BMDP, C, COBOL, Cricket, dBASE, Excel, FORTRAN, GCG, Harvard Graphics, ImSL, LINDO, Lisp, Lotus 1-2-3, MacDraw, MacWrite, MINITAB, Microsoft Word, Pascal, RS/1, SAS, SCA, SPSS-X, WordPerfect. Computer facilities are available to all students.
**Fees:** Computer fee is included in tuition/fees.
**Hours:** 8 AM-midn. (M-Th); 8 AM-6 PM (F); 10 AM-6 PM (Sa); 1 PM-midn. (Su).

**PROMINENT ALUMNI/AE.** Charles E. Young, chancellor, UCLA; Butch Johnson, professional football player; Michael Huerta, commissioner, Port Authority of New York.

# University of California, San Diego

**La Jolla, CA 92093 — 619 534-2230**

**1993-94 Costs.** Tuition: None (state residents), $7,699 (out-of-state). Room & board: $6,562. Fees, books, misc. academic expenses (school's estimate): $4,620.
**Enrollment.** Undergraduates: 7,611 men, 7,246 women (full-time). Freshman class: 19,117 applicants, 11,338 accepted, 2,650 enrolled. Graduate enrollment: 2,179 men, 1,205 women.
**Test score averages/ranges.** Average SAT scores: 520 verbal, 622 math.
**Faculty.** 1,175 full-time; 209 part-time. 94% of faculty holds doctoral degree. Student/faculty ratio: 19 to 1.
**Selectivity rating.** More competitive.

**PROFILE.** UC San Diego, founded in 1959, is a public, comprehensive university. Its 1,200-acre campus is located in La Jolla, 12 miles north of San Diego.

**Accreditation:** WASC. Professionally accredited by the Accreditation Board for Engineering and Technology.
**Religious orientation:** University of California, San Diego is nonsectarian; no religious requirements.
**Library:** Collections totaling over 2,188,722 volumes, 24,388 periodical subscriptions, and 2,137,223 microform items.
**Special facilities/museums:** Art galleries, center for U.S.-Mexican studies, music recording studio, audio-visual center, center for music experimentation, aquarium, oceanographic institute, structural lab, supercomputer, electron microscopes.
**Athletic facilities:** Gymnasiums, athletic, baseball, soccer, and softball fields, track, basketball, racquetball, tennis, and volleyball courts, swimming pool, golf driving range.

**STUDENT BODY. Undergraduate profile:** 93% are state residents; 22% are transfers. 22% Asian-American, 2% Black, 11% Hispanic, 1% Native American, 55% White, 9% Other. Average age of undergraduates is 21.
**Freshman profile:** 95% of accepted applicants took SAT; 5% took ACT. 87% of freshmen come from public schools.
**Undergraduate achievement:** 92% of fall 1991 freshmen returned for fall 1992 term. 31% of students who completed a degree program went on to graduate study within one year.
**Foreign students:** 199 students are from out of the country. Countries represented include China, Germany, India, Japan, Taiwan, and the United Kingdom; 70 in all.

**PROGRAMS OF STUDY. Degrees:** B.A., B.S.
**Majors:** Animal Physiology, Anthropology, Applied Mathematics, Applied Mathematics/Scientific Programming, Applied Mechanics, Applied Physics, Architecture, Art History/Criticism, Biochemistry/Cell Biology, Bioengineering, Bioengineering/Pre-Medical, Biophysics, Biophysics/Pre-Medical, Chemical Education, Chemical Engineering, Chemistry, Chemistry/Biochemistry, Chemistry/Chemical Physics, Chemistry Education, Chemistry with Specialization in Earth Sciences, Chinese Studies, Classical Studies, Cognitive Science, Communication, Computer Engineering, Computer Science, Dual Major in Literature, Earth Sciences, Ecology/Behavior/Evolution, Economics, Electrical Engineering, Engineering Physics, Engineering Science, English/American Literature, Ethnic Studies, French Literature, General Biology, General Literature, General Physics, German Literature, History, Individual Majors, Information Science, Italian Literature, Italian Studies, Judaic Studies, Linguistics, Mathematics, Mathematics/Computer Science, Mechanical Engineering, Media, Microbiology, Molecular Biology, Muir Special Project Major, Music, Music/Humanities, Philosophy, Physics/Specialization in Earth Sciences, Political Science, Psychology, Quantitative Economics/Decision Sciences, Religious Studies, Russian Literature, Sociology, Spanish Literature, Structural Engineering, Studio Visual Arts, Systems/Control Engineering, Theatre, Third World Studies, Urban Studies/Planning, Visual Arts, Women's Studies, Writing/Literature.
**Distribution of degrees:** The majors with the highest enrollment are biology, economics, and political science; classical studies, Italian studies, and Third World studies have the lowest.
**Requirements:** General education requirement.
**Academic regulations:** Minimum 2.0 GPA must be maintained.
**Special:** Minors offered. Minor required in some majors for graduation. Science/technology/public affairs program. Five-college system: Revelle Coll offers curriculum with Renaissance perspective; Muir Coll stresses flexibility of curriculum; Third Coll focuses on social change and development in the modern world; Warren Coll links studies to personal and professional goals; Fifth Coll provides international focus. Self-designed majors. Double majors. Dual degrees. Independent study. Pass/fail grading option. Internships. Graduate school at which undergraduates may take graduate-level courses. Exchange programs with Dartmouth Coll, Morehouse Coll, and Spelman Coll. Teacher certification in elementary and secondary education. Study abroad in 35 countries.
**Honors:** Phi Beta Kappa. Honors program. Honor societies.
**Academic Assistance:** Nonremedial tutoring.

**STUDENT LIFE. Housing:** Students may live on or off campus. Coed dorms. School-owned/operated apartments. Both on-campus and off-campus married-student housing. 33% of students live in college housing.
**Services and counseling/handicapped student services:** Placement services. Health service. Women's center. Day care. Counseling services for minority, military, veteran, and older students. Birth control, personal, and psychological counseling. Career and academic guidance services. Religious counseling. Physically disabled student services. Learning disabled services. Notetaking services. Tape recorders. Tutors. Reader services for the blind.
**Campus organizations:** Undergraduate student government. Student newspaper (Guardian, published twice/week). Literary magazine. Yearbook. Radio and TV stations. Theatre and music activities, Model UN, Society for Creative Anachronism, over 250 organizations in all. 14 fraternities, no chapter houses; eight sororities, no chapter houses. 12% of men join a fraternity. 12% of women join a sorority.
**Religious organizations:** Bahai Club, Campus Crusade for Christ, Chi Alpha Fellowship, In The World, Intervarsity Christian Fellowship, Latter-Day Saints Student Association, Lutheran Community, Navigators, Young Life, other religious groups.
**Minority/foreign student organizations:** African-American Student Union, Hawaii Club, MEChA, Native American Student Alliance, other minority student groups. International Club, Chinese Student Association, Korean-American Association, Asian-Pacific Islander group, Vietnamese Student Association, Sangam Indian Club, other foreign student groups.

**ATHLETICS. Physical education requirements:** None.
**Intercollegiate competition:** 10% of students participate. Baseball (M), basketball (M,W), crew (M,W), cross-country (M,W), diving (M,W), fencing (M,W), golf (M), soccer (M,W), softball (W), swimming (M,W), tennis (M,W), track (outdoor) (M,W), track and field (outdoor) (M,W), volleyball (M,W), water polo (M,W). Member of NCAA Division III.
**Intramural and club sports:** 60% of students participate. Intramural badminton, basketball, bowling, flag football, floor hockey, golf, inner-tube water polo, racquetball, soccer, softball, tennis, track/field, ultimate frisbee, volleyball. Men's club Alpine skiing, cycling, flying, ice hockey, lacrosse, martial arts, rugby, sailing, surfing, ultimate disc, water skiing. Women's club Alpine skiing, cycling, flying, lacrosse, martial arts, sailing, surfing, ultimate disc, water skiing.

**ADMISSIONS. Academic basis for candidate selection** (in order of priority): Secondary school record, standardized test scores, essay, class rank, school's recommendation.
**Nonacademic basis for candidate selection:** Extracurricular participation is important. Particular talent or ability is considered.
**Requirements:** Graduation from secondary school is required; GED is accepted. 15 units and the following program of study are required: 4 units of English, 3 units of math, 2 units of lab science, 2 units of foreign language, 2 units of history, 2 units of electives. Minimum grade of "C" in listed secondary school courses required of in-state applicants; minimum 3.4 GPA required of out-of-state applicants. In-state applicants with minimum 3.3 GPA are eligible regardless of test scores. Applicants with minimum combined SAT score of 1100 (composite ACT score of 27) and minimum combined ACH scores of 1650 (in-state) or 1730 (out-of-state), with no score below 500 on any one test, are eligible on the basis of test scores alone. EOP and Student Affirmative Action program for applicants not normally admissible. SAT or ACT is required. ACH required. Campus visit recommended. No off-campus interviews.
**Procedure:** Take SAT or ACT by December of 12th year. Take ACH by December of 12th year. Application deadline is November 30. Notification of admission by March 15. Reply is required by May 1. $100 nonrefundable tuition deposit. $350 room deposit, sometimes refundable. Freshmen accepted for fall term only.
**Special programs:** Credit and/or placement may be granted through CEEB Advanced Placement exams for scores of 3 or higher. Credit may be granted through military experi-

ence. Placement may be granted through challenge exams. Early entrance/early admission program. Concurrent enrollment program.
**Transfer students:** Transfer students accepted for terms other than fall. In fall 1992, 22% of all new students were transfers into all classes. 4,144 transfer applications were received, 2,461 were accepted. Application deadline is November 30 for fall; October 31 for spring. Minimum 2.4 GPA required of in-state applicants; 2.8 GPA of out-of-state applicants. Lowest course grade accepted is "D." Maximum number of transferable credits is 105 quarter hours. At least 36 quarter hours must be completed at the university to receive degree.
**Admissions contact:** Registrar and Admissions Officer. 619 534-4831.

**FINANCIAL AID. Available aid:** Pell grants, SEOG, state scholarships and grants, school scholarships and grants, private scholarships and grants, academic merit scholarships, and United Negro College Fund. Perkins Loans (NDSL), PLUS, Stafford Loans (GSL), school loans, and SLS.
**Financial aid statistics:** In 1992-93, 43% of all undergraduate applicants received aid; 41% of freshman applicants. Average amounts of aid awarded freshmen: Scholarships and grants, $3,500; loans, $3,500.
**Supporting data/closing dates:** FAFSA/FAF/FFS: Priority filing date is March 2; deadline is May 1. School's own aid application: Deadline is November 30. State aid form: Priority filing date is March 2; deadline is May 1. Income tax forms: Priority filing date is March 2; deadline is May 1. Notification of awards begins in April.
**Financial aid contact:** Thomas M. Rutter, M.B.A., Financial Aid Officer. 619 534-4480.

**STUDENT EMPLOYMENT.** College Work/Study Program. Institutional employment. 50% of full-time undergraduates work on campus during school year. Off-campus part-time employment opportunities rated "good."

**COMPUTER FACILITIES.** IBM/IBM-compatible and Macintosh/Apple microcomputers; 300 are networked. Students may access AT&T, SUN, UNISYS minicomputer/mainframe systems, BITNET, Internet. Client/LAN operating systems include Apple/Macintosh. Computer languages and software packages include BASIC, C, C++, FORTRAN, LISP, Maple, Mathematica, Pascal, SAS, SPSS. Computer facilities are available to all students.
**Fees:** Computer fee is included in tuition/fees.
**Hours:** 24 hours.

**GRADUATE CAREER DATA.** Graduate school percentages: 5% enter law school. 6% enter medical school. 2% enter graduate business programs. 9% enter graduate arts and sciences programs. Highest graduate school enrollments: Other UC schools. 69% of graduates choose careers in business and industry.

**PROMINENT ALUMNI/AE.** Lucy Killea, California state senator; Susuma Toneqawa, 1987 Nobel laureate in medicine; Angela Davis, writer and social activist; Bill Atkinson, co-founder, Apple Computer; John Slaughter, president, Occidental Coll.

# University of California, Santa Barbara

**Santa Barbara, CA 93106** **805 893-2311**

**1993-94 Costs.** Tuition: None (state residents), $7,698 (out-of-state). Room & board: $5,816–$6,463. Fees, books, misc. academic expenses (school's estimate): $3,617.
**Enrollment.** Undergraduates: 8,057 men, 8,220 women (full-time). Freshman class: 17,402 applicants, 13,917 accepted, 3,218 enrolled. Graduate enrollment: 1,463 men, 915 women.
**Test score averages/ranges.** Average SAT scores: 480 verbal, 565 math. Range of SAT scores of middle 50%: 440-500 verbal, 520-640 math.
**Faculty.** 718 full-time. 100% of faculty holds highest degree in specific field. Student/faculty ratio: 18 to 1.
**Selectivity rating.** Competitive.

**PROFILE.** UC Santa Barbara is a public, comprehensive university. Founded as a Normal school in 1909, it joined the University of California system in 1944. Programs are offered through the Colleges of Creative Studies, Engineering, and Letters and Science; the Graduate Division; and the Graduate School of Education. Its 813-acre campus is located in Santa Barbara, 90 miles from Los Angeles.

**Accreditation:** WASC. Professionally accredited by the Accreditation Board for Engineering and Technology, the American Psychological Association, the American Speech-Language-Hearing Association.
**Religious orientation:** University of California, Santa Barbara is nonsectarian; no religious requirements.
**Library:** Collections totaling over 2,000,000 volumes, and 15,000 periodical subscriptions.
**Special facilities/museums:** Art museum, centers for black studies, Chicano studies, and study of developing nations, institutes for applied behavioral sciences, community/organizational research, marine science, and theoretical physics, Channel Islands field station.
**Athletic facilities:** Gymnasiums, swimming pool, basketball and tennis courts, outdoor track, stadium, baseball, intramural, and softball fields, Nautilus weight facility, aerobics studio, events center.

**STUDENT BODY. Undergraduate profile:** 94% are state residents; 27% are transfers. 13% Asian-American, 3% Black, 11% Hispanic, 1% Native American, 69% White, 3% Other. Average age of undergraduates is 21.
**Freshman profile:** 1% of freshmen who took SAT scored 700 or over on verbal, 6% scored 700 or over on math; 8% scored 600 or over on verbal, 38% scored 600 or over on math; 42% scored 500 or over on verbal, 80% scored 500 or over on math; 85% scored 400 or over on verbal, 96% scored 400 or over on math; 97% scored 300 or over on verbal, 99% scored 300 or over on math. 97% of accepted applicants took SAT; 19% took ACT. 84% of freshmen come from public schools.
**Undergraduate achievement:** 88% of fall 1991 freshmen returned for fall 1992 term. 36% of entering class graduated. 26% of students who completed a degree program went on to graduate study within one year.
**Foreign students:** 177 students are from out of the country. Countries represented include China, England, India, and Norway; 45 in all.

**PROGRAMS OF STUDY. Degrees:** B.A., B.F.A., B.Mus., B.S.
**Majors:** Anthropology, Art, Art History, Art Studio, Asian Studies, Biochemistry/Molecular Biology, Biological Sciences, Biology, Biopsychology, Black Studies, Botany, Business Economics, Chemical Engineering, Chemistry, Chicano Studies, Chinese, Classical Archaeology, Classical Civilization, Classics, Communication, Comparative Literature, Computer Science, Dance, Dramatic Arts, Ecology/Evolution, Economics, Economics/Mathematics, Electrical Engineering, English, Environmental Studies, Film Studies, French, Geography, Geological Sciences, Geophysics, German, Greek, History, Italian, Japanese, Latin, Latin American/Iberian Studies, Law/Society, Liberal Studies, Linguistics, Literature, Materials, Mathematical Sciences, Mathematics, Mechanical Engineering, Medieval Studies, Microbiology, Music, Music Composition, Music History, Music Performance, Music Theory, Nuclear Engineering, Painting, Pharmacology, Philosophy, Physics, Physiology/Cell Biology, Political Science, Portuguese, Psychology, Religious Studies, Renaissance Studies, Sculpture, Slavic Languages/Literatures, Sociology, Spanish, Speech/Hearing Sciences, Statistical Science, Theatre, Women's Studies, Zoology.
**Distribution of degrees:** The majors with the highest enrollment are economics, political science, and biology.
**Requirements:** General education requirement.
**Academic regulations:** Minimum 2.0 GPA must be maintained.
**Special:** Double majors. Accelerated study. Pass/fail grading option. Internships. Graduate school at which undergraduates may take graduate-level courses. Preprofessional programs in medicine, dentistry, and speech therapy. Exchange program with other UC campuses. Teacher certification in early childhood, elementary, secondary, and bilingual/bicultural education. Study abroad in over 26 countries. ROTC.
**Honors:** Phi Beta Kappa. Honors program. Honor societies.

**STUDENT LIFE. Housing:** Students may live on or off campus. Coed dorms. Married-student housing. 16% of students live in college housing.
**Social atmosphere:** The student newspaper reports, "People tend to be involved in their own groups or small organizations. The only organized social events are either Greek oriented or sponsored by the Associated Students. Dorms have their own social events, and off-campus events are mostly small groups getting together." Popular gathering spots at UCSB are The Pub, Cafe Roma, McBurley's, and Sam's Sandwiches. Greeks and Associated Students have some student influence, "but there is no one organization that the school centers on." Football and basketball are well-attended events during the school year.
**Services and counseling/handicapped student services:** Placement services. Health service. Women's center. Day care. Counseling services for minority, military, and veteran students. Birth control, personal, and psychological counseling. Career and academic guidance services. Physically disabled student services. Notetaking services. Tutors. Reader services for the blind.
**Campus organizations:** Undergraduate student government. Student newspaper (Daily Nexus). Literary magazine. Yearbook. Radio station. Modern Chorale, Musica Antiqua, chamber singers, opera workshop, glee clubs, orchestra, Schubertians, drama and dance group, Community Affairs Board, career, departmental, political, recreational, service, social action, and special-interest groups. 18 fraternities, all with chapter houses; 15 sororities, all with chapter houses. 14% of men join a fraternity. 16% of women join a sorority.
**Religious organizations:** Asian American Christian Fellowship, Bahai Club, Baptist Student Union, Campus Crusade for Christ, Christian Science Organization, Episcopal Students, Gaucho Christian Fellowship, Hillel, Korean Christian Fellowship, Latter-Day Saints Student Association, Lott Carey Christian Fellowship, Muslim Student Association, Orthodox Christian Fellowship, St. Mark's Catholic Student Organization, Sri Chimnoy Association, Studies in the Old and New Testament, United Christian Student Movement, University Christian Fellowship, University Unitarians.
**Minority/foreign student organizations:** Akanke, American Indian Association, Asian Culture Committee, Asian Student Coalition, Black Business Association, Chi Delta Theta, Chicano Graduation Committee, Chinese Student Association, El Congreso/La Mesa, Undergraduate Chinese Society, Upward Bound Associates. International Student Association, Filipino, Indian, Italian, Japanese, Korean, Russian, and Vietnamese groups.

**ATHLETICS. Physical education requirements:** None.
**Intercollegiate competition:** 3% of students participate. Alpine skiing (M,W), baseball (M), basketball (M,W), bowling (M,W), cheerleading (W), crew (M,W), cross-country (M,W), cycling (M,W), diving (M,W), fencing (M,W), golf (M), gymnastics (M,W), lacrosse (M,W), rugby (M), sailing (M,W), soccer (M,W), softball (W), swimming (M,W), tennis (M,W), track and field (outdoor) (M,W), ultimate frisbee (M,W), volleyball (M,W), water polo (M). Member of Big West Conference, Mountain Pacific Sports Federation, NCAA Division I.
**Intramural and club sports:** 39% of students participate. Intramural badminton, basketball, bowling, cross-country, flag football, floor hockey, golf, indoor soccer, inner-tube water polo, pool, soccer, softball, tennis, ultimate frisbee, volleyball, wrestling. Men's club bowling, crew, cycling, fencing, lacrosse, rugby, sailing, skiing, triathlon, ultimate frisbee, water skiing. Women's club bowling, crew, cycling, fencing, golf, lacrosse, sailing, skiing, surfing, triathlon, ultimate frisbee, water polo, water skiing.

**ADMISSIONS. Academic basis for candidate selection** (in order of priority): Secondary school record, standardized test scores, essay.
**Nonacademic basis for candidate selection:** Character and personality, extracurricular participation, and particular talent or ability are emphasized. Geographical distribution is considered.
**Requirements:** Graduation from secondary school is required; GED is accepted. 15 units and the following program of study are required: 4 units of English, 3 units of math, 1 unit of lab science, 2 units of foreign language, 1 unit of history, 4 units of electives. Electives should include 1 unit of visual/performing arts. Minimum 2.82 GPA required of in-state applicants; those with minimum combined SAT score of 1300 (composite ACT score of 31) and combined ACH score of 1650 (with minimum score of 500 on any one ACH) are eligible by exam alone. Minimum 3.4 GPA required of out-of-state applicants; those with combined SAT score of 1300 (composite ACT score of 31) and combined ACH score of

1730 (with minimum score of 500 on any one ACH) are eligible by exam alone. Audition or portfolio required of art, music, and performing arts applicants. SAT is required; ACT may be substituted. ACH required. Campus visit recommended. No off-campus interviews.
**Procedure:** Take SAT or ACT by December of 12th year. Take ACH by December of 12th year. Application deadline is November 30. Notification of admission by March 15. Reply is required by May 1. $100 nonrefundable tuition deposit. $200 nonrefundable room deposit. Freshmen accepted for terms other than fall.
**Special programs:** Admission may be deferred. Credit and/or placement may be granted through CEEB Advanced Placement exams for scores of 3 or higher. Credit may be granted through DANTES exams. Placement may be granted through challenge exams. Concurrent enrollment program.
**Transfer students:** Transfer students accepted for terms other than fall. In fall 1992, 27% of all new students were transfers into all classes. 4,750 transfer applications were received, 2,854 were accepted. Application deadline is November 30 for fall; October 31 for spring. Minimum 2.4 GPA required of in-state applicants; 2.8 GPA of out-of-state applicants. Lowest course grade accepted is "D." Maximum number of transferable credits is 105 course units. At least 45 course units must be completed at the university to receive degree.
**Admissions contact:** William J. Villa, Director of Admissions. 805 893-2485.

**FINANCIAL AID. Available aid:** Pell grants, SEOG, state scholarships and grants, school scholarships and grants, private scholarships and grants, ROTC scholarships, academic merit scholarships, athletic scholarships, and aid for undergraduate foreign students. Perkins Loans (NDSL), PLUS, Stafford Loans (GSL), and school loans.
**Financial aid statistics:** 80% of aid is not need-based. In 1991-92, 33% of all undergraduate applicants received aid; 17% of freshman applicants. Average amounts of aid awarded freshmen: Scholarships and grants, $4,651; loans, $1,957.
**Supporting data/closing dates:** FAFSA/FAF/FFS: Deadline is March 2. Notification of awards on rolling basis.
**Financial aid contact:** Ron Andrade, Director of Student Financial Services. 805 893-2432.

**STUDENT EMPLOYMENT.** College Work/Study Program. Institutional employment. 17% of full-time undergraduates work on campus during school year. Off-campus part-time employment opportunities rated "fair."

**COMPUTER FACILITIES.** 4,000 IBM/IBM-compatible, Macintosh/Apple, and RISC-/UNIX-based microcomputers; 2,000 are networked. Students may access Digital, Hewlett-Packard, IBM, SUN minicomputer/mainframe systems, BITNET, Internet. Residence halls may be equipped with stand-alone microcomputers. Client/LAN operating systems include Apple/Macintosh. Computer languages and software packages include APL, BASIC, C, COBOL, Excel, FORTRAN, Microsoft Word, Multiplan, PageMaker, Pascal, SAS, WordPerfect. Some computers are available only to students in specific programs.
**Fees:** None.
**Hours:** 7 AM-1 AM in Open Access lab; 24 hours during last two weeks of each quarter.

**GRADUATE CAREER DATA.** Graduate school percentages: 16% enter law school. 8% enter medical school. 5% enter graduate business programs. 13% enter graduate arts and sciences programs. Highest graduate school enrollments: UC Berkeley, UCLA, UC San Diego, UC Santa Barbara, California State Universities, Caltech, Stanford U, U of Southern California. 67% of graduates choose careers in business and industry. Companies and businesses that hire graduates: Applied Magnetics, Arthur Andersen, Hewlett-Packard, Hughes Aircraft, IBM, KPMG Peat Marwick.

**PROMINENT ALUMNI/AE.** Robert J. Lagomarsino, U.S. congressman, California; Mary P. Ryan, historian, winner of 1982 Bancroft Prize; Robert Ballard, senior scientist, Woods Hole Oceanographic Lab; Michael Douglas, actor and producer; Barbara Rush, actress; Max Jamiesson, CEO, Hyundai Motor America.

# University of California, Santa Cruz

**Santa Cruz, CA 95064** — **408 459-0111**

**1994-95 Costs.** Tuition: None (state residents), $7,699 (out-of-state). Room & board: $6,081. Fees, books, misc. academic expenses (school's estimate): $6,682.
**Enrollment.** Undergraduates: 3,953 men, 5,311 women (full-time). Freshman class: 10,717 applicants, 8,372 accepted, 1,810 enrolled. Graduate enrollment: 534 men, 457 women.
**Test score averages/ranges.** Average SAT scores: 515 verbal, 560 math.
**Faculty.** 405 full-time; 140 part-time. 99% of faculty holds doctoral degree. Student/faculty ratio: 19 to 1.
**Selectivity rating.** Highly competitive.

**PROFILE.** UC Santa Cruz, founded in 1965, is a public, comprehensive university. Its 2,000-acre campus is located on a former ranch, overlooking Monterey Bay, the Pacific Ocean, and downtown Santa Cruz.

**Accreditation:** WASC.
**Religious orientation:** University of California, Santa Cruz is nonsectarian; no religious requirements.
**Library:** Collections totaling over 1,004,772 volumes, 10,004 periodical subscriptions, and 548,215 microform items.
**Special facilities/museums:** Art museums, arboretum, agroecology farm, Lick Observatory, electron microscopes, institute for particle physics, institute of marine sciences, center for nonlinear science, institute of tectonics.
**Athletic facilities:** Swimming pool, basketball, handball, racquetball, tennis, and volleyball courts, weight room, track, softball fields, dance studio, martial arts room.

**STUDENT BODY. Undergraduate profile:** 85% are state residents; 32% are transfers. 12% Asian-American, 3% Black, 12% Hispanic, 2% Native American, 68% White, 3% Other. Average age of undergraduates is 21.
**Freshman profile:** Majority of accepted applicants took SAT. 70% of freshmen come from public schools.
**Undergraduate achievement:** 88% of fall 1991 freshmen returned for fall 1992 term. 31% of entering class graduated. 33% of students who completed a degree program immediately went on to graduate study.
**Foreign students:** 200 students are from out of the country. Countries represented include Australia, China, Germany, India, Japan, and United Kingdom; 52 in all.

**PROGRAMS OF STUDY. Degrees:** B.A., B.S.
**Majors:** American Studies, Anthropology, Art, Art History, Biochemistry/Molecular Biology, Biology, Chemistry, Community Studies, Computer Engineering, Computer/Information Sciences, Earth Sciences, Economics, Environmental Studies, History, Language Studies, Latin American Studies, Legal Studies, Linguistics, Literature, Marine Biology, Mathematics, Music, Philosophy, Physics, Politics, Psychobiology, Psychology, Sociology, Theatre Arts, Western Studies, Women's Studies.
**Distribution of degrees:** The majors with the highest enrollment are psychology, literature, and economics; legal studies, marine biology, and physics have the lowest.
**Requirements:** General education requirement.
**Special:** Minors offered in many majors and in East Asian and South/Southeast Asian studies. Students affiliate with one of eight small residential colleges but have access to all courses and facilities. Comprehensive exam or senior thesis required in major. Self-designed majors. Double majors. Dual degrees. Independent study. Pass/fail grading option. Internships. Graduate school at which undergraduates may take graduate-level courses. Preprofessional programs in law, medicine, pharmacy, dentistry, and optometry. 3-2 engineering program with UC Berkeley. Exchange program with U of New Hampshire and U of New Mexico. Teacher certification in elementary, secondary, and bilingual/bicultural education. Study abroad in Australia, Austria, Brazil, China, Costa Rica, Denmark, Ecuador, France, Germany, Hungary, India, Italy, Japan, Korea, Portugal, Spain, Thailand, and other countries.
**Honors:** Phi Beta Kappa.
**Academic Assistance:** Remedial reading, writing, math, and study skills.

**STUDENT LIFE. Housing:** Students may live on or off campus. Coed, women's, and men's dorms. School-owned/operated apartments. On-campus married-student housing. RV park, special-interest housing. 48% of students live in college housing.
**Services and counseling/handicapped student services:** Health service. Women's center. Day care. Counseling services for minority, veteran, and older students. Birth control, personal, and psychological counseling. Career and academic guidance services. Religious counseling. Physically disabled student services. Learning disabled services. Notetaking services. Tape recorders. Tutors. Reader services for the blind.
**Campus organizations:** Undergraduate student government. Student newspaper (City on a Hill, published once/week). Radio station. Gospel group, Artists Union, Filmmakers Union, Circle K, College Democrats, College Republicans, Amnesty International, other political groups, special-interest groups, 100 organizations in all.
**Religious organizations:** Bahai, Buddhist, and Muslim groups, Canterbury Foundation, Intervarsity Christian Fellowship, Lutheran Campus Ministry, Meditation Fellowship, Orthodox Christian Fellowship, United Campus Christian Ministry.
**Minority/foreign student organizations:** African/Black Student Alliance, African/Black Women United, MEChA, North American Indian group. Asian-Pacific Islander, Chinese, Filipino, Indian, Iranian, Korean, Mexican, Palestinian, South African, Vietnamese, and other foreign student groups.

**ATHLETICS. Physical education requirements:** None.
**Intercollegiate competition:** Basketball (M,W), diving (M,W), fencing (M,W), soccer (M,W), swimming (M,W), tennis (M,W), volleyball (M,W). Member of Independent, NCAA Division III.
**Intramural and club sports:** Intramural basketball, fencing, flag football, floor hockey, racquetball, soccer. Men's club cycling, lacrosse, martial arts, rugby, sailing, ultimate frisbee, water polo. Women's club cheerleading, cycling, lacrosse, martial arts, sailing, ultimate frisbee, water polo.

**ADMISSIONS. Academic basis for candidate selection** (in order of priority): Secondary school record, standardized test scores, essay, school's recommendation, class rank.
**Nonacademic basis for candidate selection:** Extracurricular participation and particular talent or ability are important. Character and personality are considered.
**Requirements:** Graduation from secondary school is required; GED is accepted. 15 units and the following program of study are required: 4 units of English, 2 units of science including 1 unit of lab, 2 units of foreign language, 1 unit of social studies, 1 unit of history, 2 units of academic electives. Electives should include 1 unit of visual/performing arts. Minimum grade of "C" in listed secondary school courses required of in-state applicants; minimum 3.5 GPA required of out-of-state applicants. In-state applicants with minimum 3.3 GPA are eligible regardless of test scores. Applicants with minimum combined SAT score of 1100 (composite ACT score of 27) and minimum combined ACH scores of 1650 (in-state) or 1730 (out-of-state), with no score below 500 on any one test, are eligible on the basis of test scores alone. EOP for applicants not normally admissible. SAT or ACT is required. ACH required. Campus visit recommended. No off-campus interviews.
**Procedure:** Take SAT or ACT by December of 12th year. Take ACH by December of 12th year. Application deadline is November 30. Notification of admission begins in mid-February. Reply is required by May 1. $100 nonrefundable tuition deposit. $150 nonrefundable room deposit. Freshmen accepted for terms other than fall.
**Special programs:** Credit may be granted through CEEB Advanced Placement for scores of 3 or higher. Credit may be granted through DANTES exams. Concurrent enrollment program.
**Transfer students:** Transfer students accepted for terms other than fall. In fall 1992, 32% of all new students were transfers into all classes. 3,330 transfer applications were received, 2,036 were accepted. Application deadline is November 30 for fall; October 31 for spring. Minimum 2.4 GPA required. Lowest course grade accepted is "D." Maximum number of transferable credits is 130 quarter hours. At least 45 quarter hours must be completed at the university to receive degree.
**Admissions contact:** Joseph P. Allen, M.A., Dean of Admissions. 408 459-4008.

**FINANCIAL AID. Available aid:** Pell grants, SEOG, state grants, school grants, private scholarships and grants, and academic merit scholarships. Perkins Loans (NDSL), PLUS, Stafford Loans (GSL), school loans, private loans, and SLS. Knight Tuition Plans. Institutional payment plans for fees and housing.
**Financial aid statistics:** 5% of aid is not need-based. Average amounts of aid awarded freshmen: Scholarships and grants, $4,134; loans, $2,625.
**Supporting data/closing dates:** FAFSA: Priority filing date is March 2; deadline is May 2. FAF/FFS: Deadline is March 2. State aid form: Deadline is March 2. Income tax forms: Priority filing date is May 1. Notification of awards on rolling basis.
**Financial aid contact:** Esperanza Nee, M.Ed., Director of Financial Aid. 408 459-2963.

**STUDENT EMPLOYMENT.** College Work/Study Program. Institutional employment. 3% of full-time undergraduates work on campus during school year. Students may expect to earn an average of $1,500 during school year. Off-campus part-time employment opportunities rated "good."

**COMPUTER FACILITIES.** 150 IBM/IBM-compatible and Macintosh/Apple microcomputers; all are networked. Students may access minicomputer/mainframe systems, BITNET, Internet. Client/LAN operating systems include Apple/Macintosh. Computer languages and software packages include Assembly, BASIC, BMDP, C+, COBOL, FOCUS, FORTRAN, PL/1, Pascal, SAS, SPSS. Computer facilities are available to all students.
**Fees:** None.
**Hours:** 24 hours for some; 9 AM-9 PM for others.

**GRADUATE CAREER DATA.** Graduate school percentages: 4% enter law school. 1% enter medical school. 3% enter graduate business programs. 12% enter graduate arts and sciences programs. Highest graduate school enrollments: UC and CSU system schools. 45% of graduates choose careers in business and industry.

**PROMINENT ALUMNI/AE.** Kent Nagano, music director/conductor, Berkeley Symphony Orchestra; Art Torres, state senator; Kathryn Sullivan, astronaut, first American woman to walk in space.

## University of Judaism–Lee College

**Los Angeles, CA 90077** **310 476-9777**

**1994-95 Costs.** Tuition: $10,560. Room & board: $6,200. Fees, books, misc. academic expenses (school's estimate): $1,228.
**Enrollment.** Undergraduates: 37 men, 54 women (full-time). Freshman class: 51 applicants, 38 accepted, 18 enrolled. Graduate enrollment: 49 men, 53 women.
**Test score averages/ranges.** Average SAT scores: 565 verbal, 565 math. Range of SAT scores of middle 50%: 450-590 verbal, 500-600 math.
**Faculty.** 17 full-time; 13 part-time. 88% of faculty holds highest degree in specific field. Student/faculty ratio: 6 to 1.
**Selectivity rating.** More competitive.

**PROFILE.** The University of Judaism, founded in 1947, is an university of research in Judaica and the related humanities; Lee College is its undergraduate division. Programs are offered through the David Lieber Graduate School, the Graduate School of Judaica, Lee College, and the University College of Jewish Studies. Its 28-acre campus is located in the Santa Monica Mountains of Los Angeles.

**Accreditation:** WASC.
**Religious orientation:** University of Judaism-Lee College is affiliated with the Jewish faith; no religious requirements.
**Library:** Collections totaling over 100,000 volumes, 600 periodical subscriptions, and 4,500 microform items.
**Special facilities/museums:** Art gallery, educational resource center for curriculum development, documentation center covering issues of interest to Jewish community.
**Athletic facilities:** All UCLA athletic facilities are fully available to students.

**STUDENT BODY. Undergraduate profile:** 35% are state residents; 18% are transfers. 1% Asian-American, 1% Black, 3% Hispanic, 95% White. Average age of undergraduates is 23.
**Freshman profile:** 7% of freshmen who took SAT scored 700 or over on math; 36% scored 600 or over on verbal, 36% scored 600 or over on math; 72% scored 500 or over on verbal, 79% scored 500 or over on math; 100% scored 400 or over on verbal, 100% scored 400 or over on math. Majority of accepted applicants took SAT. 80% of freshmen come from public schools.
**Undergraduate achievement:** 90% of fall 1992 freshmen returned for fall 1993 term. 44% of entering class graduated. 5% of students who completed a degree program immediately went on to graduate study.
**Foreign students:** 15 students are from out of the country. Countries represented include Australia, Canada, Israel, Mexico, South Africa, and Spain; seven in all.

**PROGRAMS OF STUDY. Degrees:** B.A., B.Lit.
**Majors:** Bioethics, Business, Interdisciplinary Major, Judaic Studies, Literature, Political Science, Psychology.
**Distribution of degrees:** The majors with the highest enrollment are psychology, Judaic studies, and literature; business and political science have the lowest.
**Requirements:** General education requirement.
**Academic regulations:** Minimum 2.0 GPA must be maintained.
**Special:** Minors offered in all majors. Bioethics program offered in conjunction with Mount St. Mary's Coll. Self-designed majors. Double majors. Independent study. Accelerated study. Pass/fail grading option. Internships. Graduate school at which undergraduates may take graduate-level courses. Preprofessional programs in law, medicine, and theology. Bachelor's/M.B.A. and Judaic studies/M.A.Ed. programs. Member of consortium with Mount St. Mary's Coll. Exchange programs abroad in Israel (Hebrew U, Tel Aviv U). Study abroad also in other countries.
**Academic Assistance:** Remedial writing and study skills. Nonremedial tutoring.

**ADMISSIONS. Academic basis for candidate selection** (in order of priority): Secondary school record, essay, standardized test scores, school's recommendation, class rank.
**Nonacademic basis for candidate selection:** Character and personality and extracurricular participation are important. Particular talent or ability is considered.
**Requirements:** Graduation from secondary school is required; GED is accepted. No specific distribution of secondary school units required. Minimum 3.2 GPA required; minimum combined SAT score of 1100 recommended. SAT or ACT is required. Campus visit and interview recommended. Off-campus interviews available with an admissions representative.
**Procedure:** Take SAT or ACT by December 15 of 12th year. Suggest filing application by January 31. Application deadline is June 30. Notification of admission on rolling basis after January 31, within one month of completion of file. Reply is required by May 1. $200 nonrefundable tuition deposit. $300 room deposit, refundable until August 1. Freshmen accepted for terms other than fall.
**Special programs:** Admission may be deferred one year. Credit may be granted through CEEB Advanced Placement for scores of 4 or higher. Credit may be granted through challenge exams. Early decision program. In fall 1992, three applied for early decision and two were accepted. Deadline for applying for early decision is November 15. Concurrent enrollment program.
**Transfer students:** Transfer students accepted for terms other than fall. In fall 1993, 18% of all new students were transfers into all classes. 37 transfer applications were received. Application deadline is April 15 for fall; November 1 for spring. Minimum 3.0 GPA required. Lowest course grade accepted is "C." Maximum number of transferable semester hours is 70 from two-year schools; no limit from four-year schools. At least 34 semester hours must be completed at the university to receive degree.
**Admissions contact:** Tamara Greenebaum, Dean of Admissions. 310 476-0236.

**FINANCIAL AID. Available aid:** Pell grants, SEOG, state scholarships and grants, school scholarships and grants, private scholarships and grants, academic merit scholarships, and aid for undergraduate foreign students. PLUS, Stafford Loans (GSL), and SLS. AMS.
**Financial aid statistics:** 18% of aid is not need-based. In 1993-94, 97% of all undergraduate applicants received aid; 92% of freshman applicants. Average amounts of aid awarded freshmen: Scholarships and grants, $10,715; loans, $2,625.
**Supporting data/closing dates:** FAFSA: Priority filing date is March 2. School's own aid application: Priority filing date is March 2. State aid form: Priority filing date is March 2. Income tax forms: Priority filing date is March 2. Notification of awards begins April 15.
**Financial aid contact:** Therese Eyermann, M.S.Ed., Financial Aid Administrator. 310 476-9777, extension 252.

## University of LaVerne

**LaVerne, CA 91750** **714 593-3511**

**1993-94 Costs.** Tuition: $12,775. Room & board: $4,550. Fees, books, misc. academic expenses (school's estimate): $600.
**Enrollment.** Undergraduates: 684 men, 805 women (full-time). Freshman class: 1,078 applicants, 861 accepted, 225 enrolled. Graduate enrollment: 573 men, 642 women.
**Test score averages/ranges.** Average SAT scores: 430 verbal, 460 math.
**Faculty.** 87 full-time; 200 part-time. 94% of faculty holds doctoral degree. Student/faculty ratio: 17 to 1.
**Selectivity rating.** Competitive.

**PROFILE.** LaVerne, founded in 1891, is a church-affiliated university. Programs are offered through the Colleges of Arts and Sciences, Graduate and Professional Studies, and Law; the American Armenian International College; and the Schools of Business and Economics and Continuing Education. Its 26-acre campus is located in LaVerne, 35 miles east of Los Angeles.

**Accreditation:** WASC.
**Religious orientation:** University of LaVerne is an interdenominational Christian school; no religious requirements.
**Library:** Collections totaling over 1,600,000 volumes, 436 periodical subscriptions, and 2,000 microform items.
**Special facilities/museums:** Natural history museum.
**Athletic facilities:** Gymnasium, weight room, track, football, soccer, and softball fields.

**STUDENT BODY. Undergraduate profile:** 86% are state residents; 34% are transfers. 7% Asian-American, 10% Black, 30% Hispanic, 2% Native American, 46% White, 5% Other. Average age of undergraduates is 20.
**Freshman profile:** 1% of freshmen who took SAT scored 700 or over on verbal, 1% scored 700 or over on math; 13% scored 600 or over on verbal, 15% scored 600 or over on math; 39% scored 500 or over on verbal, 49% scored 500 or over on math; 82% scored 400 or over on verbal, 86% scored 400 or over on math; 99% scored 300 or over on verbal, 99% scored 300 or over on math. 96% of accepted applicants took SAT; 4% took ACT. 63% of freshmen come from public schools.
**Undergraduate achievement:** 87% of fall 1991 freshmen returned for fall 1992 term. 43% of entering class graduated. 46% of students who completed a degree program immediately went on to graduate study.
**Foreign students:** 53 students are from out of the country. Countries represented include England, Greece, Japan, Korea, and Spain; 21 in all.

**PROGRAMS OF STUDY. Degrees:** B.A., B.S.
**Majors:** Accounting, Armenian Studies, Art, Behavioral Science, Biology, Broadcasting, Business/Finance, Business Management, Chemistry, Child Development, Communications, Computer Engineering, Computer Science, Criminal Justice, Economics/Business Administration, Electronics Engineering, Elementary Education, English, Environmental Biology, Environmental Health Care, Environmental Management, Foreign Languages/Literatures, French, German, Health Care Management, History, Human Development, Human Services, International Business/Language, International Studies, Journalism, Marketing, Mathematics, Music, Natural History, Philosophy, Physical Education/Health/

Recreation, Physics, Political Science, Psychology, Public Administration, Radio, Religion, Social Sciences, Sociology, Spanish, Television, Theatre Arts, Vocational Education.
**Distribution of degrees:** The majors with the highest enrollment are business, communications, and English.
**Requirements:** General education requirement.
**Academic regulations:** Minimum 2.0 GPA must be maintained.
**Special:** Minors offered in most majors. Associate's degrees offered. Self-designed majors. Double majors. Dual degrees. Accelerated study. Internships. Graduate school at which undergraduates may take graduate-level courses. Preprofessional programs in law, medicine, veterinary science, pharmacy, dentistry, theology, and optometry. 3-3 bachelor's/J.D. program. 3-4 medical/osteopathic program with Coll of Osteopathic Medicine of the Pacific. Exchange programs with Bridgewater Coll, Elizabethtown Coll, Juniata Coll, Manchester Coll, and McPherson Coll. Teacher certification in early childhood, elementary, and secondary education. Study abroad in China, Ecuador, England, France, Germany, Greece, Italy, Japan, and Mexico.
**Honors:** Honors program. Honor societies.
**Academic Assistance:** Remedial reading, writing, math, and study skills.

**STUDENT LIFE. Housing:** Students may live on or off campus. Coed, women's, and men's dorms. Fraternity housing. 54% of students live in college housing.
**Social atmosphere:** Students gather on campus at Warehouse Pizza and The Spot; off campus, students frequent Nick's Cafe Trevi, The Haven, and Newport Beach. The Latino Student Forum and Greeks are influential groups on campus. Popular events include Homecoming, Cinco de Mayo, football and basketball games, movies, the Spring Formal, and Rush Week. "Since the University of LaVerne is a small private school, social activities are usually within walking distance of the campus. The unspoken tradition at ULV is to never, never go to a dance before 11 PM," comments the Campus Times.
**Services and counseling/handicapped student services:** Placement services. Health service. Women's center. Day care. Counseling services for minority, military, veteran, and older students. Birth control, personal, and psychological counseling. Career and academic guidance services. Religious counseling. Learning disabled services.
**Campus organizations:** Undergraduate student government. Student newspaper (Campus Times, published once/week). Yearbook. Radio and TV stations. Choir, chorus, chamber singers, band, orchestra, drama club, debating, Model UN, athletic, departmental, and special-interest groups, 56 organizations in all. Six fraternities, one chapter house; six sororities, no chapter houses. 21% of men join a fraternity. 27% of women join a sorority.
**Religious organizations:** Newman Club, Nondenominational Club.
**Minority/foreign student organizations:** Black Student Union, Hawaiian Club, Latino Club. International Student Club, Asian Club.

**ATHLETICS. Physical education requirements:** Two semesters of physical education required.
**Intercollegiate competition:** 33% of students participate. Baseball (M), basketball (M,W), cheerleading (M,W), cross-country (M,W), football (M), golf (M), soccer (M,W), softball (W), tennis (M,W), track and field (outdoor) (M,W), volleyball (M,W). Member of NCAA Division III, Pacific Coast Volleyball Conference, SCIAC.
**Intramural and club sports:** 20% of students participate. Intramural basketball, billiards, flag football, table tennis, volleyball. Men's club skiing. Women's club skiing.

**ADMISSIONS. Academic basis for candidate selection** (in order of priority): Secondary school record, standardized test scores, class rank, school's recommendation, essay.
**Nonacademic basis for candidate selection:** Character and personality are important. Extracurricular participation, particular talent or ability, and alumni/ae relationship are considered.
**Requirements:** Graduation from secondary school is required; GED is accepted. 16 units and the following program of study are required: 4 units of English, 3 units of math, 2 units of science including 1 unit of lab, 2 units of foreign language, 2 units of social studies, 1 unit of history, 2 units of academic electives. Minimum combined SAT score of 800 and minimum 2.5 GPA required. Conditional admission possible for applicants not meeting standard requirements. SAT is required; ACT may be substituted. Campus visit and interview recommended. Off-campus interviews available with an admissions representative.
**Procedure:** Take SAT or ACT by December 15 of 12th year. Visit college for interview by April 1 of 12th year. Suggest filing application by March 1. Application deadline is August 1. Notification of admission on rolling basis. Reply is required by May 1. $100 nonrefundable tuition deposit. $100 room deposit, refundable until September 10. Freshmen accepted for terms other than fall.
**Special programs:** Admission may be deferred one year. Credit and/or placement may be granted through CEEB Advanced Placement exams for scores of 3 or higher. Credit may be granted through CLEP general and subject exams, challenge exams, and military experience.
**Transfer students:** Transfer students accepted for terms other than fall. In fall 1992, 34% of all new students were transfers into all classes. 226 transfer applications were received, 187 were accepted. Application deadline is August 1 for fall; January 15 for spring. Minimum 2.0 GPA required. Lowest course grade accepted is "C." Maximum number of transferable credits is 70 semester hours. At least 24 semester hours must be completed at the university to receive degree.
**Admissions contact:** K. Douglas Wible, Director of Admissions. 714 593-3511, extension 4026.

**FINANCIAL AID. Available aid:** Pell grants, SEOG, state scholarships and grants, school scholarships and grants, private scholarships and grants, and academic merit scholarships. Perkins Loans (NDSL), PLUS, Stafford Loans (GSL), school loans, private loans, and SLS. AMS, deferred payment plan, and family tuition reduction.
**Financial aid statistics:** In 1992-93, 73% of all undergraduate applicants received aid; 71% of freshman applicants. Average amounts of aid awarded freshmen: Scholarships and grants, $4,700; loans, $3,800.
**Supporting data/closing dates:** FAFSA/FAF: Priority filing date is March 1; deadline is August 1. School's own aid application: Priority filing date is March 1; deadline is August 1. State aid form: Priority filing date is March 1; deadline is August 1. Notification of awards begins March 15.
**Financial aid contact:** Bob Peters, M.A., Director of Financial Aid. 714 593-3511, extension 4135.

**STUDENT EMPLOYMENT.** College Work/Study Program. Institutional employment. 43% of full-time undergraduates work on campus during school year. Students may expect to earn an average of $1,500 during school year. Off-campus part-time employment opportunities rated "good."
**COMPUTER FACILITIES.** 92 IBM/IBM-compatible and Macintosh/Apple microcomputers. Computer facilities are available to all students.
**Fees:** None.

# University of the Pacific

**Stockton, CA 95211** **209 946-2211**

**1994-95 Costs.** Tuition: $16,670. Room & board: $5,300. Fees, books, misc. academic expenses (school's estimate): $700.
**Enrollment.** Undergraduates: 1,482 men, 1,845 women (full-time). Freshman class: 2,459 applicants, 1,997 accepted, 582 enrolled. Graduate enrollment: 199 men, 383 women.
**Test score averages/ranges.** Average SAT scores: 444 verbal, 531 math. Range of SAT scores of middle 50%: 400-540 verbal, 460-620 math.
**Faculty.** 247 full-time; 75 part-time. 84% of faculty holds highest degree in specific field. Student/faculty ratio: 15 to 1.
**Selectivity rating.** Less competitive.

**PROFILE.** The University of the Pacific, founded in 1851, is a private, comprehensive university. Programs are offered through the College of the Pacific; the Schools of Education, Engineering, International Studies, Pharmacy, and Business and Public Administration; and the Conservatory of Music. Its 150-acre campus is located in Stockton, 85 miles east of San Francisco.

**Accreditation:** WASC. Professionally accredited by the Accreditation Board for Engineering and Technology, the American Assembly of Collegiate Schools of Business, the American Council on Pharmaceutical Education, the American Speech-Language-Hearing Association, the National Association of Schools of Music, the National Council for Accreditation of Teacher Education.
**Religious orientation:** University of the Pacific is affiliated with the Methodist Church; no religious requirements.
**Library:** Collections totaling over 432,661 volumes, 2,304 periodical subscriptions, and 502,888 microform items.
**Special facilities/museums:** Language labs, John Muir library collection.
**Athletic facilities:** Gymnasiums, fitness center, basketball, sand volleyball, and tennis courts, swimming pool, fitness course.

**STUDENT BODY. Undergraduate profile:** 87% are state residents; 46% are transfers. 23% Asian-American, 4% Black, 8% Hispanic, 1% Native American, 59% White, 5% Other. Average age of undergraduates is 20.
**Freshman profile:** Majority of accepted applicants took SAT. 81% of freshmen come from public schools.
**Undergraduate achievement:** 84% of fall 1992 freshmen returned for fall 1993 term. 63% of entering class graduated. 30% of students who completed a degree program immediately went on to graduate study.
**Foreign students:** 250 students are from out of the country. Countries represented include Hong Kong, Japan, Kuwait, Saudi Arabia, Singapore, and Taiwan; 50 in all.

**PROGRAMS OF STUDY. Degrees:** B.A., B.F.A., B.Mus., B.S.
**Majors:** Applied Mathematics/Physics, Art, Art History, Biochemistry, Biological Sciences, Black Studies, Brass, Business Administration, Chemistry, Chemistry/Biology, Civil Engineering, Classics, Communication, Communicative Disorders, Computer Engineering, Computer Science, Cultural Anthropology, Development/Cultural Change, Drama, Economics, Electrical Engineering, Elementary Education, Engineering Physics, English, French, Geology, Geophysics, German, Graphic Design, Greek, Guitar, Harp, History, Information Systems, International/Regional Studies, International Relations, International Relations/Economic Emphasis, Japanese, Latin, Liberal Studies, Life Sciences, Linguistics, Management Engineering, Mathematics, Mathematics/Economics, Mechanical Engineering, Medicinal Chemistry, Music, Music Education, Music History, Music Management, Music Theory/Composition, Music Therapy, Organ, Percussion, Philosophy, Physical Sciences, Physics, Piano, Political Economy, Political Science, Pre-Law, Pre-Ministry, Pre-Pharmacy, Psychology, Religious Studies, Secondary Education, Social Policy/Urban Affairs, Social Science, Sociology, Spanish, Special Education, Sports Sciences, Strings, Studio Art, Voice, Woodwinds.
**Distribution of degrees:** The majors with the highest enrollment are pharmacy, business, and engineering; classics, drama, and mathematics have the lowest.
**Requirements:** General education requirement.
**Academic regulations:** Minimum 2.0 GPA must be maintained.
**Special:** Concentrations in accounting, arts and entertainment management, entrepreneurship, finance, general business, international management, marketing, organizational management, public management, and real estate in the Sch of Business and Public Administration. Self-designed majors. Double majors. Independent study. Accelerated study. Pass/fail grading option. Internships. Cooperative education programs. Preprofessional programs in law, medicine, pharmacy, dentistry, theology, engineering, and physical therapy. Sch of Pharmacy offers Doctor of Pharmacy degrees (three-year professional program after two years of prepharmacy); trimester system. Sch of Dentistry is located in San Francisco; McGeorge Sch of Law in Sacramento. Concurrent registration possible in two or more colleges or schools on Stockton campus. Washington Semester and UN Semester. Teacher certification in elementary, secondary, special education, and bilingual/bicultural education. Certification in specific subject areas. Over 200 study-abroad programs in more than 60 countries. AFROTC at California State U at Sacramento.
**Honors:** Honors program. Honor societies.
**Academic Assistance:** Remedial reading, writing, and math. Nonremedial tutoring.

**STUDENT LIFE. Housing:** All unmarried freshmen and sophomores must live on campus unless living with parents. Coed dorms. Sorority and fraternity housing. School-owned/operated apartments. Off-campus privately-owned housing. Theme houses including international, health and wellness, honors, quiet, professional pharmacy. 50% of students live in college housing.
**Social atmosphere:** As reported by the student newspaper, "Greeks are by far the most visible group." Homecoming, Band Frolic, and the Anchor Splash are the most popular events of the year. Students like to spend free time at the University Center, El Torito, Chili's, and Carlos Murphy's.
**Services and counseling/handicapped student services:** Placement services. Health service. Educational Resource Center. Counseling services for minority and older students. Birth control, personal, and psychological counseling. Career and academic guidance services. Religious counseling. Physically disabled student services. Learning disabled services. Notetaking services. Tape recorders. Tutors. Reader services for the blind.
**Campus organizations:** Undergraduate student government. Student newspaper (Pacifican, published once/week). Literary magazine. Yearbook. Radio station. Drama and debate groups, bands, choirs, and musical groups, symphony, special-interest groups, 120 organizations in all. Seven fraternities, four chapter houses; six sororities, four chapter houses. 17% of men join a fraternity. 18% of women join a sorority.
**Religious organizations:** College Life Christian Fellowship, Catholic Campus Ministry, Chi Alpha Radical Reality Christian Fellowship, Hillel Foundation/Jewish Students Association, Intervarsity Christian Fellowship.
**Minority/foreign student organizations:** African American Student Union, MeChA, Society of Hispanic Professional Engineers. Asian Alliance, Gulf Students Club, Association for International Chinese Students, International Student Association, International Association of Students in Economics and Business Administration, Vietnamese Students Association.

**ATHLETICS. Physical education requirements:** None.
**Intercollegiate competition:** 15% of students participate. Baseball (M), basketball (M,W), cheerleading (W), cross-country (W), field hockey (W), football (M), golf (M), ice hockey (M), lacrosse (M,W), soccer (W), softball (W), swimming (M,W), tennis (M,W), volleyball (M,W), water polo (M). Member of Big West Conference, NCAA Division I-A, NorPac Conference for field hockey.
**Intramural and club sports:** 50% of students participate. Intramural badminton, basketball, flag football, free-throw shooting, golf, racquetball, soccer, softball, tennis, turkey trot, ultimate frisbee, volleyball. Men's club crew, soccer. Women's club crew, lacrosse.

**ADMISSIONS. Academic basis for candidate selection** (in order of priority): Secondary school record, standardized test scores, school's recommendation, essay, class rank.
**Nonacademic basis for candidate selection:** Character and personality, extracurricular participation, particular talent or ability, geographical distribution, and alumni/ae relationship are considered.
**Requirements:** Graduation from secondary school is required; GED is accepted. 16 units and the following program of study are recommended: 4 units of English, 3 units of math, 2 units of lab science, 2 units of foreign language, 1 unit of history, 4 units of academic electives. Substantial record of grades ("A" or "B") in college-preparatory subjects required. Four years of math and three years of lab science recommended for science and technical program applicants. Audition required of music program applicants. Freshman Advantage Program for applicants not normally admissible. Community Involvement Program admits limited number of students from city of Stockton. SAT or ACT is required. Campus visit and interview recommended. No off-campus interviews.
**Procedure:** Take SAT or ACT by December of 12th year. Visit college for interview by April 1 of 12th year. Suggest filing application by March 1; no deadline. Notification of admission on rolling basis. Reply is required by May 1. $200 tuition deposit, refundable until May 1. Freshmen accepted for terms other than fall.
**Special programs:** Admission may be deferred one semester. Credit and/or placement may be granted through CEEB Advanced Placement exams for scores of 3 or higher. Credit and/or placement may be granted through CLEP general and subject exams. Early entrance/early admission program.
**Transfer students:** Transfer students accepted for terms other than fall. In fall 1993, 46% of all new students were transfers into all classes. 1,786 transfer applications were received, 793 were accepted. Application deadline is May 1 for fall; December 15 for spring. Minimum 2.3 GPA required. Lowest course grade accepted is "D." Maximum number of transferable credits is 64 semester hours. 32 out of the last 40 semester hours must be completed at the university to receive degree.
**Admissions contact:** Ed Schoenberg, M.A., Dean of Admissions. 209 946-2211, 800 959-2UOP.

**FINANCIAL AID. Available aid:** Pell grants, SEOG, state scholarships and grants, school scholarships and grants, private scholarships and grants, ROTC scholarships, academic merit scholarships, athletic scholarships, and aid for undergraduate foreign students. Perkins Loans (NDSL), PLUS, Stafford Loans (GSL), Health Professions Loans, school loans, private loans, and SLS. Deferred payment plan. Family Loan Program.
**Financial aid statistics:** 5% of aid is not need-based. In 1993-94, 100% of all undergraduate applicants received aid; 100% of freshman applicants. Average amounts of aid awarded freshmen: Scholarships and grants, $8,700; loans, $2,950.
**Supporting data/closing dates:** FAFSA: Priority filing date is March 2. School's own aid application: Priority filing date is March 2. Notification of awards on rolling basis.
**Financial aid contact:** Lynn Fox, Director of Financial Aid. 209 946-2421.

**STUDENT EMPLOYMENT.** College Work/Study Program. Institutional employment. 23% of full-time undergraduates work on campus during school year. Students may expect to earn an average of $1,200 during school year. Off-campus part-time employment opportunities rated "good."

**COMPUTER FACILITIES.** 157 IBM/IBM-compatible, Macintosh/Apple, and RISC-/UNIX-based microcomputers. Students may access Digital, SUN minicomputer/mainframe systems, Internet. Residence halls may be equipped with stand-alone microcomputers. Client/LAN operating systems include Apple/Macintosh, DOS, UNIX/XENIX/AIX, Windows NT, X-windows, LocalTalk/AppleTalk, Novell. Computer languages and software packages include Ada, BASIC, C, COBOL, Concurrent Euclid, FORTRAN, ImSO, MATHLAB, Pascal, PLOT 10, SCADA, SLAM, SMP, SPICE, SPSS, TEX, Turbo C++, Turbo Pascal. Computer facilities are available to all students.
**Fees:** None.
**Hours:** 8 AM-midn. (M-Th); 8 AM-5 PM (F); 10 AM-5 PM (Sa); noon-midn. (Su).

**GRADUATE CAREER DATA.** Highest graduate school enrollments: UC Davis, UC San Francisco, Hastings Coll of Law, U of the Pacific, USC, Stanford U.

**PROMINENT ALUMNI/AE.** Eddie LeBaron, football player; Alex G. Spanos, builder/developer and owner, San Diego Chargers; Dave Brubeck, jazz artist/composer.

# University of Redlands

**Redlands, CA 92373-0999** **909 793-2121**

**1994-95 Costs.** Tuition: $16,530. Room: $3,410. Board: $2,795. Fees, books, misc. academic expenses (school's estimate): $965.
**Enrollment.** Undergraduates: 672 men, 718 women (full-time). Freshman class: 1,429 applicants, 1,163 accepted, 366 enrolled. Graduate enrollment: 17 men, 83 women.
**Test score averages/ranges.** Average SAT scores: 511 verbal, 544 math. Average ACT scores: 24 composite.
**Faculty.** 106 full-time; 50 part-time. 76% of faculty holds doctoral degree. Student/faculty ratio: 13 to 1.
**Selectivity rating.** More competitive.

**PROFILE.** Redlands, founded in 1907, is a private, liberal arts university. Its 130-acre campus is located in Redlands, 65 miles east of Los Angeles.
**Accreditation:** WASC. Professionally accredited by the National Association of Schools of Music.
**Religious orientation:** University of Redlands is affiliated with the American Baptist Church; no religious requirements.
**Library:** Collections totaling over 227,000 volumes, 1,027 periodical subscriptions, and 45,000 microform items.
**Special facilities/museums:** Art gallery, Far East art collection, Southwest collection, center for communicative disorders, language lab.
**Athletic facilities:** Gymnasium, indoor swimming pool, weight room, dance studio, racquetball, basketball, and tennis courts, baseball, soccer, and football fields.

**STUDENT BODY. Undergraduate profile:** 65% are state residents; 24% are transfers. 8% Asian-American, 4% Black, 7% Hispanic, 1% Native American, 67% White, 13% Other. Average age of undergraduates is 19.
**Freshman profile:** 84% of accepted applicants took SAT; 16% took ACT. 85% of freshmen come from public schools.
**Undergraduate achievement:** 77% of fall 1991 freshmen returned for fall 1992 term. 55% of entering class graduated. 20% of students who completed a degree program immediately went on to graduate study.
**Foreign students:** 38 students are from out of the country. Countries represented include Hong Kong, Japan, Pakistan, and Taiwan; 25 in all.

**PROGRAMS OF STUDY. Degrees:** B.A., B.Mus., B.S.
**Majors:** Accounting, Art, Asian Studies, Biology, Business Administration, Chemistry, Communicative Disorders, Computer Science, Economics, Education, English Literature/Writing, Environmental Studies, Ethnic Studies, French, German, Government, History, International Relations, Mathematics, Music, Philosophy, Physics, Pre-Law, Pre-Medicine, Psychology, Religion, Sociology/Anthropology, Spanish, Women's Studies.
**Distribution of degrees:** The majors with the highest enrollment are liberal studies, government, and education; philosophy, religion, and modern languages have the lowest.
**Requirements:** General education requirement.
**Academic regulations:** Minimum 2.0 GPA must be maintained.
**Special:** Johnston Center for Individualized Learning emphasizes interpersonal, intercultural, international, and environmental dimensions of learning; curriculum based on contractual system, with written evaluations rather than grades; majors are self-designed and involve independent study, seminars, and tutorials. Interdisciplinary Honors Program. Self-designed majors. Double majors. Independent study. Pass/fail grading option. Internships. Cooperative education programs. Graduate school at which undergraduates may take graduate-level courses. Preprofessional programs in law, medicine, and health sciences. Washington Semester. Exchange program with 4-1-4 schools nationwide during January interim. Teacher certification in elementary and secondary education. Study abroad in African countries, Australia, Austria, China, England, France, Germany, Japan, Russia, South American countries, and Spain. ROTC and AFROTC at California State U at San Bernardino.
**Honors:** Phi Beta Kappa. Honors program. Honor societies.
**Academic Assistance:** Remedial writing, math, and study skills. Nonremedial tutoring.

**STUDENT LIFE. Housing:** All unmarried students under age 21 must live on campus unless living near campus with relatives. Coed and women's dorms. Sorority and fraternity housing. School-owned/operated apartments. On-campus married-student housing. 93% of students live in college housing.
**Services and counseling/handicapped student services:** Placement services. Health service. Women's center. Personal counseling. Career and academic guidance services. Religious counseling. Learning disabled services.
**Campus organizations:** Undergraduate student government. Student newspaper (Bulldog Weekly). Literary magazine. Yearbook. Radio station. Phi Mu Alpha Sinfonia, theatre, dance company, Model UN, Amnesty International, mock trials, academic, athletic, departmental, social-awareness, and special-interest groups, 60 organizations in all. Six fraternities, five chapter houses; four sororities, all with chapter houses. 15% of men join a fraternity. 20% of women join a sorority.
**Religious organizations:** Campus Crusade for Christ, Hillel, Intervarsity Christian Fellowship, Newman Club.
**Minority/foreign student organizations:** Black Student Union, MEChA, Hawaii Club. International Student Club, Asian Club.

**ATHLETICS. Physical education requirements:** None.
**Intercollegiate competition:** 2% of students participate. Baseball (M), basketball (M,W), cheerleading (M,W), cross-country (M,W), football (M), golf (M,W), soccer (M,W), soft-

ball (W), swimming (M,W), tennis (M,W), track (M,W), volleyball (W), water polo (M). Member of NCAA Division III, Southern California Intercollegiate Athletic Conference.
**Intramural and club sports:** 3% of students participate.

**ADMISSIONS. Academic basis for candidate selection** (in order of priority): Secondary school record, standardized test scores, school's recommendation, essay, class rank.
**Nonacademic basis for candidate selection:** Extracurricular participation is important. Character and personality, particular talent or ability, and alumni/ae relationship are considered.
**Requirements:** Graduation from secondary school is recommended; GED is accepted. No specific distribution of secondary school units required. Minimum combined SAT score of 950 and minimum 2.85 GPA recommended. Interview required of applicants to Johnston Center for Individualized Learning. Audition required of music program applicants. SAT or ACT is required. Campus visit and interview recommended. Off-campus interviews available with an admissions representative.
**Procedure:** Take SAT or ACT by January of 12th year. Take ACH by February of 12th year. Suggest filing application by January 1. Application deadline is April 1. Notification of admission on rolling basis. Reply is required by May 1. $200 tuition deposit, $100 of which is refundable until June 15. Freshmen accepted for terms other than fall.
**Special programs:** Admission may be deferred one year. Credit and/or placement may be granted through CEEB Advanced Placement exams for scores of 3 or higher. Credit and placement may be granted through challenge exams. Early entrance/early admission program.
**Transfer students:** Transfer students accepted for terms other than fall. In fall 1992, 24% of all new students were transfers into all classes. 351 transfer applications were received, 200 were accepted. Application deadline is April 1 for fall; January 24 for spring. Minimum 2.5 GPA recommended. Lowest course grade accepted is "C." Maximum number of transferable credits is 60 semester hours.
**Admissions contact:** Paul M. Driscoll, M.A., Director of Admissions. 909 335-4074.

**FINANCIAL AID. Available aid:** Pell grants, state grants, school scholarships and grants, private scholarships and grants, and academic merit scholarships. Perkins Loans (NDSL), Stafford Loans (GSL), school loans, and SLS.
**Supporting data/closing dates:** School's own aid application: Priority filing date is March 1. State aid form: Priority filing date is March 1. Notification of awards on rolling basis.
**Financial aid contact:** Sue Jarvis, Director of Financial Aid. 909 335-4047.

**STUDENT EMPLOYMENT.** College Work/Study Program. Institutional employment. 40% of full-time undergraduates work on campus during school year. Students may expect to earn an average of $1,200 during school year. Off-campus part-time employment opportunities rated "good."

**COMPUTER FACILITIES.** 90 IBM/IBM-compatible and Macintosh/Apple microcomputers; all are networked. Computer languages and software packages include BASIC, CAD, CAS, COBOL, Dynamo, FORTRAN, GE EDT, GPSS, ImSL, Pascal, SCSS, SORT; 100 in all. Computer facilities are available to all students.

**GRADUATE CAREER DATA.** Graduate school percentages: 13% enter law school. 1% enter medical school. 1% enter dental school. 5% enter graduate business programs. 51% enter graduate arts and sciences programs. 1% enter theological school/seminary. Highest graduate school enrollments: California State U at San Bernardino, UC Riverside, U of Colorado at Boulder, Drexel U, Hastings, U of Redlands, U of Southern California, U of Virginia, U of Washington. 23% of graduates choose careers in business and industry.

**PROMINENT ALUMNI/AE.** Glen Charles and Les Charles, creators of *Cheers* and *Taxi;* Robert Pierpoint and Gary Reeves, CBS news correspondents; Warren Christopher, U.S. Secretary of State; David Boies, CBS defense attorney in Westmoreland trial; Dan Petrie, screenwriter.

# University of San Diego

**San Diego, CA 92110** **619 260-4600**

**1993-94 Costs.** Tuition: $12,890. Room & board: $6,270. Fees, books, misc. academic expenses (school's estimate): $700.
**Enrollment.** Undergraduates: 1,611 men, 2,094 women (full-time). Freshman class: 3,586 applicants, 2,546 accepted, 930 enrolled. Graduate enrollment: 404 men, 710 women.
**Test score averages/ranges.** Range of SAT scores of middle 50%: 410-520 verbal, 460-580 math.
**Faculty.** 263 full-time; 203 part-time. 97% of faculty holds highest degree in specific field. Student/faculty ratio: 18 to 1.
**Selectivity rating.** Less competitive.

**PROFILE.** The University of San Diego, founded in 1949, is a private, church-affiliated university. Programs are offered through the College of Arts and Sciences and Schools of Business Administration, Education, Law, and Nursing. The 180-acre suburban campus, with Spanish architectural style, is located in San Diego.
**Accreditation:** WASC. Professionally accredited by the Accreditation Board for Engineering and Technology, the American Assembly of Collegiate Schools of Business, the American Bar Association, the National League for Nursing.
**Religious orientation:** University of San Diego is affiliated with the Roman Catholic Church; three semesters of religion required.
**Library:** Collections totaling over 660,000 volumes, and 5,800 periodical subscriptions.
**Special facilities/museums:** Art gallery, child development center, language labs.
**Athletic facilities:** Gymnasium, swimming pool, dance and weight rooms, baseball, football, intramural, soccer, and softball fields, tennis and volleyball courts.

**STUDENT BODY. Undergraduate profile:** 62% are state residents; 21% are transfers. 8% Asian-American, 2% Black, 11% Hispanic, 1% Native American, 76% White, 2% Other. Average age of undergraduates is 21.
**Freshman profile:** Majority of accepted applicants took SAT. 64% of freshmen come from public schools.
**Undergraduate achievement:** 90% of fall 1991 freshmen returned for fall 1992 term. 58% of entering class graduated. 46% of students who completed a degree program went on to graduate study within one year.
**Foreign students:** 152 students are from out of the country. Countries represented include Canada, France, Japan, Mexico, Norway, and Spain; 54 in all.

**PROGRAMS OF STUDY. Degrees:** B.A., B.Acct., B.S.
**Majors:** Accounting, Anthropology, Art, Biology, Business Administration, Business Economics, Chemistry, Communications Studies, Computer Science, Diversified Liberal Arts, Economics, Electrical Engineering, English, French, Hispanic/Latin American Studies, History, Interdisciplinary Humanities, International Relations, Marine Science, Mathematics, Music, Nursing, Ocean Studies, Philosophy, Physics, Political Science, Psychology, Religious Studies, Sociology, Spanish.
**Distribution of degrees:** The majors with the highest enrollment are business administration, communications studies, and accounting; anthropology and physics have the lowest.
**Requirements:** General education requirement.
**Academic regulations:** Minimum 2.0 GPA must be maintained.
**Special:** Minors offered in all majors and in art history, environmental studies, gender studies, German, information science, Italian, leadership, special education, studio arts, and theatre arts. American Humanics and Emerging Leader programs. Certificate program in art management. Double majors. Dual degrees. Pass/fail grading option. Internships. Cooperative education programs. Graduate school at which undergraduates may take graduate-level courses. Preprofessional programs in law, medicine, veterinary science, pharmacy, dentistry, and optometry. Teacher certification in elementary, secondary, special education, and bilingual/bicultural education. Certification in specific subject areas. Exchange programs abroad in England (Center for Medieval Studies, St. Clare's Hall), France (Ecole Superieur de Commerce, U of Avignon, U of Toulon and du Var), Germany (U of Freiburg), Italy (Scuola Lorenzo di Medici), Mexico, and Spain. NROTC. ROTC and AFROTC at San Diego State U.
**Honors:** Honors program. Honor societies.
**Academic Assistance:** Remedial reading, writing, math, and study skills. Nonremedial tutoring.

**STUDENT LIFE. Housing:** All unmarried freshmen under age 21 must live on campus unless living with family. Coed, women's, and men's dorms. School-owned/operated apartments. 50% of students live in college housing.
**Social atmosphere:** Students frequent The Deli, The Grill, The Pennant, The Mission, and the beach. Influential groups include Associated Students, Sigma Chi, and The United Front. Popular events are concerts, San Diego Padres and Chargers games, surf competitions, Halloween, and Derby Days. "Since USD is five minutes from the beach, much of student life revolves around the ocean culture," reports the editor of the school newspaper. "Since there are only about 3,500 students, it's a fairly close-knit campus. Also, it attracts well-off students and families with large disposable incomes!"
**Services and counseling/handicapped student services:** Health service. Counseling services for minority, military, and veteran students. Personal and psychological counseling. Career and academic guidance services. Religious counseling. Physically disabled student services. Learning disabled services. Tutors. Reader services for the blind.
**Campus organizations:** Undergraduate student government. Student newspaper (Vista, published once/week). Literary magazine. Yearbook. Chorale, orchestra, pep band, drama group, Model UN, Young Democrats, Young Republicans, conservation club, sailing club, cheerleaders, academic, athletic, and special-interest groups, 65 organizations in all. Four fraternities, no chapter houses; four sororities, no chapter houses. 20% of men join a fraternity. 20% of women join a sorority.
**Religious organizations:** Campus Ministry.
**Minority/foreign student organizations:** Black Student Union, Hispanos Unidos, MEChA. International Student Organization, Asian Student Association.

**ATHLETICS. Physical education requirements:** None.
**Intercollegiate competition:** 10% of students participate. Baseball (M), basketball (M,W), cheerleading (M,W), crew (M,W), cross-country (M,W), diving (W), football (M), golf (M), soccer (M,W), softball (W), swimming (W), tennis (M,W), volleyball (W). Member of NCAA Division I, NCAA Division I-AA for football, Pacific Collegiate Swimming Conference, Pioneer Football League, West Coast Conference, Western Intercollegiate Rowing Association, Western Intercollegiate Softball League.
**Intramural and club sports:** 85% of students participate. Intramural aerobics, ballet, basketball, bowling, cycling, dance, floor hockey, football, golf, horsemanship, martial arts, rowing, sailing, scuba diving, soccer, softball, surfing, tennis, volleyball, water polo. Men's club cheerleading, cycling, lacrosse, Nordic skiing, rugby, surfing, volleyball, water skiing, wrestling. Women's club cheerleading, cycling, Nordic skiing, surfing, water skiing.

**ADMISSIONS. Academic basis for candidate selection** (in order of priority): Secondary school record, standardized test scores, school's recommendation, essay.
**Nonacademic basis for candidate selection:** Extracurricular participation is important. Character and personality, particular talent or ability, and alumni/ae relationship are considered.
**Requirements:** Graduation from secondary school is required; GED is accepted. 20 units and the following program of study are recommended: 4 units of English, 4 units of math, 3 units of science, 4 units of foreign language, 2 units of social studies, 2 units of history, 1 unit of electives. Minimum combined SAT score of 1050 and minimum 3.2 GPA recommended. Audition required of Choral Scholar Program applicants. R.N. required of nursing program applicants. EOP for applicants not normally admissible. SAT is required; ACT may be substituted. PSAT is recommended. Campus visit recommended. No off-campus interviews.
**Procedure:** Take SAT or ACT by December of 12th year. Application deadline is February 5. Notification of admission on rolling basis. Reply is required by May 1. $100 tuition deposit, refundable until May 1. $150 room deposit, refundable until May 1. Freshmen accepted for terms other than fall.
**Special programs:** Admission may be deferred one year. Credit and/or placement may be granted through CEEB Advanced Placement exams for scores of 3 or higher. Credit may be granted through CLEP general and subject exams, ACT PEP exams, and military experience. Placement may be granted through challenge exams. Early entrance/early admission program.

**Transfer students:** Transfer students accepted for terms other than fall. In fall 1992, 21% of all new students were transfers into all classes. 865 transfer applications were received, 435 were accepted. Application deadline is February 5 for fall; November 1 for spring. Minimum 2.7 GPA required. Lowest course grade accepted is "C." At least 30 semester hours must be completed at the university to receive degree.
**Admissions contact:** Warren W. Muller, M.A.L.S., Director of Admissions. 619 260-4506.
**FINANCIAL AID. Available aid:** Pell grants, SEOG, state grants, school scholarships and grants, private scholarships and grants, ROTC scholarships, academic merit scholarships, and athletic scholarships. Perkins Loans (NDSL), PLUS, Stafford Loans (GSL), school loans, private loans, and SLS.
**Financial aid statistics:** 13% of aid is not need-based. In 1992-93, 100% of all undergraduate applicants received aid; 100% of freshman applicants. Average amounts of aid awarded freshmen: Scholarships and grants, $9,157; loans, $3,977.
**Supporting data/closing dates:** FAFSA/FAF/FFS: Priority filing date is February 20. State aid form: Priority filing date is February 20. Notification of awards on rolling basis.
**Financial aid contact:** Judith Lewis Logue, M.S., Director of Financial Aid. 619 260-4514.
**STUDENT EMPLOYMENT.** College Work/Study Program. Institutional employment. 29% of full-time undergraduates work on campus during school year. Students may expect to earn an average of $2,300 during school year. Off-campus part-time employment opportunities rated "good."
**COMPUTER FACILITIES.** 120 IBM/IBM-compatible, Macintosh/Apple, and RISC-/UNIX-based microcomputers; all are networked. Students may access Digital minicomputer/mainframe systems, BITNET, Internet. Computer languages and software packages include BASIC, C, C++, FORTRAN, Modula-2, Pasca; 12 in all. Computer facilities are available to all students.
**Hours:** 8 AM-11 PM
**GRADUATE CAREER DATA.** 40% of graduates choose careers in business and industry.

## University of San Francisco

### San Francisco, CA 94117-1080

**1994-95 Costs.** Tuition: $12,478. Room & board: $5,830. Fees, books, misc. academic expenses (school's estimate): $2,600.
**Enrollment.** Undergraduates: 1,201 men, 1,918 women (full-time). Freshman class: 2,307 applicants, 1,733 accepted, 537 enrolled. Graduate enrollment: 1,171 men, 1,507 women.
**Test score averages/ranges.** Average SAT scores: 463 verbal, 514 math. Range of SAT scores of middle 50%: 350-550 verbal, 450-600 math. Average ACT scores: 21 composite. Range of ACT scores of middle 50%: 20-24 composite.
**Faculty.** 218 full-time. 86% of faculty holds highest degree in specific field. Student/faculty ratio: 17 to 1.
**Selectivity rating.** Less competitive.

**PROFILE.** The University of San Francisco, founded in 1855, is a private, church-affiliated university. Programs are offered through the Colleges of Business, Liberal Arts and Sciences, and Professional Studies and the Schools of Education, Nursing, and Law. The 52-acre campus is located in San Francisco.
**Accreditation:** WASC. Professionally accredited by the American Assembly of Collegiate Schools of Business, the National League for Nursing.
**Religious orientation:** University of San Francisco is affiliated with the Roman Catholic Church (Society of Jesus); two semesters of religion required.
**Library:** Collections totaling over 695,312 volumes, 2,689 periodical subscriptions, and 725,716 microform items.
**Special facilities/museums:** Language lab, institute for Chinese-Western cultural history, electron microscope.
**Athletic facilities:** Baseball, football, intramural, soccer, and softball fields, tennis courts, gymnasium, stadium, recreation center.
**STUDENT BODY. Undergraduate profile:** 65% are state residents; 50% are transfers. 21% Asian-American, 4% Black, 8% Hispanic, 1% Native American, 45% White, 21% Other. Average age of undergraduates is 21.
**Freshman profile:** 1% of freshmen who took SAT scored 700 or over on verbal, 5% scored 700 or over on math; 11% scored 600 or over on verbal, 23% scored 600 or over on math; 35% scored 500 or over on verbal, 54% scored 500 or over on math; 74% scored 400 or over on verbal, 90% scored 400 or over on math; 97% scored 300 or over on verbal, 100% scored 300 or over on math. 5% of freshmen who took ACT scored 30 or over on composite; 30% scored 24 or over on composite; 97% scored 18 or over on composite; 100% scored 12 or over on composite. 91% of accepted applicants took SAT; 21% took ACT. 45% of freshmen come from public schools.
**Undergraduate achievement:** 86% of fall 1992 freshmen returned for fall 1993 term. 30% of entering class graduated. 40% of students who completed a degree program went on to graduate study within one year.
**Foreign students:** 487 students are from out of the country. Countries represented include Hong Kong, Indonesia, Japan, Norway, Singapore, and Taiwan; 70 in all.
**PROGRAMS OF STUDY. Degrees:** B.A., B.F.A., B.Pub.Admin., B.S.
**Majors:** Accounting, Advertising, Applied Economics, Applied Science/Business, Biology, Biophysics, Chemistry, Communication, Computer Engineering, Computer Science, Economics, Electronics Physics, Engineering Physics, English, Environmental Science, Exercise/Sports Science, Fine Arts, French, Global Management, Graphic Design, History, Hospitality Management, Illustration, Individual Major, Information Systems Management, Interior Design, Liberal Studies, Mathematics, Nursing, Organizational Behavior, Philosophy, Photography, Physics, Politics, Psychological Services, Psychology, Psychology/Religion, Public Administration, Religious Studies, Sociology, Spanish, Theology, Theology/Religious Studies.
**Distribution of degrees:** The majors with the highest enrollment are nursing, management, and communication; mathematics, theology, and physics have the lowest.
**Requirements:** General education requirement.
**Academic regulations:** Minimum 2.0 GPA must be maintained.
**Special:** Minors offered in business and in most arts and sciences disciplines. Adult Education division offers majors in applied economics, information systems management, organizational behavior, and public administration. St. Ignatius Institute offers degree programs with Catholic liberal arts curriculum. Interdisciplinary program in natural sciences. Certificate program. Ethnic studies department. Center for Pacific Rim Studies offers credit and noncredit programs and minor in Asian-Pacific studies. Self-designed majors. Double majors. Independent study. Internships. Graduate school at which undergraduates may take graduate-level courses. Preprofessional programs in law, medicine, dentistry, and optometry. 4-1 B.A./M.B.A. program in economics. 3-3 law program. Member of San Francisco Consortium; cross-registration possible. Exchange programs with Fordham U. Teacher certification in elementary, secondary, and bilingual/bicultural education. Exchange program abroad in Japan (Sophia U). Study abroad also in numerous other countries. ROTC. AFROTC at San Francisco State U.
**Honors:** Honors program.
**Academic Assistance:** Remedial study skills. Nonremedial tutoring.
**STUDENT LIFE. Housing:** All unmarried students under age 21 must live on campus unless living near campus with relatives. Coed and women's dorms. 28% of students live in college housing.
**Social atmosphere:** The student newspaper reports, "San Francisco offers a variety of cultural experiences. USF's student population is 20 percent international students who add to the cultural experience." Favorite off-campus gathering spots include Pat O'Shea's Bar, Pasquale's Pizzeria, and the DVS Club. Popular campus activities include Zeta Beta Tau's Boat Dance, the Senior Ball, basketball games, bands playing at the campus pub, the Hawaiian Luau, the Nurses' Fashion Show, and the Foghorn Evening with the Stars.
**Services and counseling/handicapped student services:** Placement services. Health service. Counseling services for older students. Personal and psychological counseling. Career and academic guidance services. Religious counseling. Physically disabled student services. Learning disabled services. Tape recorders. Tutors.
**Campus organizations:** Undergraduate student government. Student newspaper (Foghorn, published once/week). Literary magazine. Yearbook. Radio station. College Players, debating, Knights of Columbus, Student Teachers Association, Young Democrats, Young Republicans, departmental, professional, and special-interest groups, 55 organizations in all. Four fraternities, one chapter house; three sororities, no chapter houses. 2% of men join a fraternity. 2% of women join a sorority.
**Religious organizations:** Intervarsity Christian Fellowship, Muslim Student Association.
**Minority/foreign student organizations:** Society of Black Students, Club Latino, Phil-Am Society. Several international groups.
**ATHLETICS. Physical education requirements:** None.
**Intercollegiate competition:** 7% of students participate. Baseball (M), basketball (M,W), cross-country (M,W), golf (M,W), riflery (M,W), soccer (M,W), tennis (M,W), volleyball (W). Member of NCAA Division I, West Coast Athletic Conference.
**Intramural and club sports:** 50% of students participate. Intramural badminton, basketball, crew, diving, fencing, lacrosse, martial arts, racquetball, soccer, swimming, tennis, volleyball, weight lifting.
**ADMISSIONS. Academic basis for candidate selection** (in order of priority): Secondary school record, school's recommendation, class rank, standardized test scores, essay.
**Nonacademic basis for candidate selection:** Extracurricular participation is important. Character and personality, particular talent or ability, and alumni/ae relationship are considered.
**Requirements:** Graduation from secondary school is required; GED is accepted. 22 units and the following program of study are recommended: 4 units of English, 3 units of math, 2 units of science, 2 units of foreign language, 3 units of social studies, 2 units of history, 6 units of electives. Rank in top quarter of secondary school class and minimum 3.0 GPA recommended. Conditional admission possible for applicants not meeting standard requirements. SAT is required; ACT may be substituted. Campus visit and interview recommended. Off-campus interviews available with admissions and alumni representatives.
**Procedure:** Take SAT or ACT by January of 12th year. Visit college for interview by February of 12th year. Suggest filing application by March 2; no deadline. Notification of admission on rolling basis. Reply is required by May 1. $100 tuition deposit, refundable until May 1. $250 room deposit, refundable until May 1. Freshmen accepted for terms other than fall.
**Special programs:** Admission may be deferred one year. Credit and/or placement may be granted through CEEB Advanced Placement exams for scores of 3 or higher. Credit may be granted through CLEP general exams, ACT PEP, and DANTES exams, and military and life experience. Credit and/or placement may be granted through CLEP subject exams. Credit and placement may be granted through challenge exams. Early entrance/early admission program.
**Transfer students:** Transfer students accepted for terms other than fall. In fall 1993, 50% of all new students were transfers into all classes. 1,768 transfer applications were received, 1,130 were accepted. Application deadline is March 2 for fall; December 15 for spring. Minimum 2.5 GPA required. Lowest course grade accepted is "D." Maximum number of transferable credits is 70 semester hours. At least 30 semester hours must be completed at the university to receive degree.
**Admissions contact:** William A. Henley, M.A., Director of Admissions. 415 666-6563.
**FINANCIAL AID. Available aid:** Pell grants, SEOG, Federal Nursing Student Scholarships, state scholarships and grants, school scholarships and grants, private scholarships and grants, ROTC scholarships, academic merit scholarships, athletic scholarships, and aid for undergraduate foreign students. Perkins Loans (NDSL), PLUS, Stafford Loans (GSL), private loans, and SLS. Tuition Plan Inc., Knight Tuition Plans, and family tuition reduction. Institutional payment plan.
**Financial aid statistics:** 13% of aid is not need-based. In 1993-94, 48% of all undergraduate applicants received aid; 59% of freshman applicants. Average amounts of aid awarded freshmen: Scholarships and grants, $7,756; loans, $533.
**Supporting data/closing dates:** FAFSA: Priority filing date is March 2. FAF/FFS: Priority filing date is March 2; accepted on rolling basis. State aid form: Priority filing date is March 2; accepted on rolling basis. Notification of awards begins April 1.
**Financial aid contact:** Susan Murphy, M.A., Director of Financial Aid. 415 666-6303.

**STUDENT EMPLOYMENT.** College Work/Study Program. Institutional employment. 35% of full-time undergraduates work on campus during school year. Students may expect to earn an average of $1,800 during school year. Off-campus part-time employment opportunities rated "good."

**COMPUTER FACILITIES.** 162 IBM/IBM-compatible, Macintosh/Apple, and RISC-/UNIX-based microcomputers; 50 are networked. Students may access Digital minicomputer/mainframe systems, Internet. Residence halls may be equipped with stand-alone microcomputers. Client/LAN operating systems include Apple/Macintosh, DOS, UNIX/XENIX/AIX. Computer languages and software packages include Assembler, BASIC, C, Pascal; 25 in all. Some facilities restricted to science students only.

**Hours:** 24 hours.

**GRADUATE CAREER DATA.** Graduate school percentages: 5% enter law school. 6% enter medical school. 15% enter graduate business programs.

**PROMINENT ALUMNI/AE.** Pierre Salinger, politician and journalist; Richard Egan, actor; Mary Callanan, treasurer, San Francisco; Pete Rozelle, former football commissioner; K.C. Jones, former coach, Boston Celtics; Bill Russell and Bill Cartwright, professional basketball players.

# University of Southern California

**Los Angeles, CA 90089 — 213 740-2311**

**1994-95 Costs.** Tuition: $17,230. Room: $3,566. Board: $2,916. Fees, books, misc. academic expenses (school's estimate): $930.

**Enrollment.** Undergraduates: 13,331 (full-time). Freshman class: 12,229 applicants, 8,498 accepted, 2,474 enrolled. Graduate enrollment: 12,600.

**Test score averages/ranges.** Range of SAT scores of middle 50%: 470-570 verbal, 540-650 math. Range of ACT scores of middle 50%: 23-28 composite.

**Faculty.** 1,643 full-time; 693 part-time. 94% of faculty holds highest degree in specific field. Student/faculty ratio: 14 to 1.

**Selectivity rating.** Highly competitive.

**PROFILE.** USC, founded in 1880, is a private, comprehensive university. The main campus is located in downtown Los Angeles.

**Accreditation:** WASC. Professionally accredited by the Accreditation Board for Engineering and Technology, the Accrediting Commission on Education for Health Services Administration, the Accrediting Council on Education in Journalism and Mass Communication, the American Assembly of Collegiate Schools of Business, the American Bar Association, the American Council on Pharmaceutical Education, the American Medical Association (CAHEA), the American Physical Therapy Association, the American Psychological Association, the Council on Social Work Education, the Liaison Committee on Medical Education, the National Architecture Accrediting Board, the National Association of Schools of Music, the National Association of Schools of Public Affairs and Administration, the National League for Nursing.

**Religious orientation:** University of Southern California is nonsectarian; no religious requirements.

**Library:** Collections totaling over 3,168,668 volumes, 16,500 periodical subscriptions, and 1,500,000 microform items.

**Special facilities/museums:** Art museums, wind tunnels, cinema scoring sound stage.

**Athletic facilities:** Gymnasiums, athletic stadiums, athletic fields, swimming pools, basketball, racquetball, tennis, and volleyball courts, weight rooms, tracks, sports arena.

**STUDENT BODY. Undergraduate profile:** 61% are state residents; 39% are transfers. 21% Asian-American, 7% Black, 12% Hispanic, 1% Native American, 49% White, 10% Other. Average age of undergraduates is 22.

**Freshman profile:** 2% of freshmen who took SAT scored 700 or over on verbal, 13% scored 700 or over on math; 18% scored 600 or over on verbal, 48% scored 600 or over on math; 50% scored 500 or over on verbal, 85% scored 500 or over on math; 100% scored 400 or over on verbal, 100% scored 400 or over on math. 97% of accepted applicants took SAT; 20% took ACT. 65% of freshmen come from public schools.

**Undergraduate achievement:** 90% of fall 1992 freshmen returned for fall 1993 term. 68% of entering class graduated.

**Foreign students:** 1,272 students are from out of the country. Countries represented include Hong Kong and Indonesia; 100 in all.

**PROGRAMS OF STUDY. Degrees:** B.A., B.Arch., B.F.A., B.Mus., B.S.

**Majors:** Accounting, Aerospace Engineering, American Studies, Anthropology, Applied Mechanics, Architecture, Astronomy, Biological Sciences, Biological Sciences/Marine Biology and Ecology, Biological Sciences/Molecular Biology and Biochemistry, Biological Sciences/Neurobiology and Physiology, Biomedical Engineering, Broadcast Journalism, Business Administration, Chemical Engineering, Chemical Engineering/Environmental Engineering, Chemical Engineering/Petroleum Engineering, Chemical Engineering/Polymer Science, Chemistry, Cinema/Television, Civil Engineering, Civil Engineering/Building Science, Civil Engineering/Construction Engineering, Civil Engineering/Environmental Engineering, Civil Engineering/Structural Engineering, Civil Engineering/Water Resources, Classical Civilization, Classics, Communication Arts/Sciences, Comparative Literature, Composition, Composition/Film Scoring, Computer Engineering, Computer Engineering/Computer Science, Computer Science, Dental Hygiene, Dental Science, East Asian Area Studies, East Asian Languages/Cultures, Economics, Electrical Engineering, Electrical Engineering/Computer Science, Electroacoustic Media, English, English/American Literature, English/Creative Writing, English/Literature/Language, Environmental Engineering, Environmental Studies, Ethnic Studies, Exercise Science, Film Writing, Fine Arts, Fine Arts/Art History, Fine Arts/Studio Arts, French, General Studies, Geography, Geological Sciences, German, Gerontology, Greek, History, Humanities/Classics, Humanities/Comparative Literature, Humanities/East Asian Languages/Cultures, Humanities/English, Humanities/French, Humanities/German, Humanities/Greek, Humanities/Italian, Humanities/Latin, Humanities/Music, Humanities/Philosophy, Humanities/Religion, Humanities/Slavic Languages/Literatures, Humanities/Spanish, Humanities/Theatre, Industrial/Systems Engineering, Interdisciplinary Studies, International Relations, Jazz Studies, Latin, Linguistics, Mathematics, Mechanical Engineering, Mechanical Engineering/Petroleum Engineering, Music, Music Education, Music Recording, Natural Sciences/Mathematics, Natural Sciences/Mathematics/Astronomy, Nursing, Occupational Therapy, Performance, Philosophy, Philosophy/Ethics, Philosophy/History, Philosophy/Science, Physical Sciences, Physician Assistant Practice, Physics, Planning/Development, Political Science, Print Journalism, Psychobiology, Psychology, Public Policy/Management/Planning, Public Policy/Public Management, Public Relations, Religion, Religion/Judaic Studies, Russian, Safety/Health, Social Sciences/Communication, Sociology, Spanish, Still Photography, Study of Women/Men in Society, Theatre, Theatre/Acting, Theatre/Design, Theatre/Stage Management, Theatre/Technical Direction, Theory, Urban Applied Anthropology.

**Distribution of degrees:** The majors with the highest enrollment are business, engineering, and social science.

**Requirements:** General education requirement.

**Academic regulations:** Minimum 2.0 GPA must be maintained.

**Special:** Minors offered in many majors and related fields. Self-designed majors. Double majors. Dual degrees. Accelerated study. Pass/fail grading option. Internships. Cooperative education programs. Graduate school at which undergraduates may take graduate-level courses. Preprofessional programs in law, medicine, pharmacy, and dentistry. Students may enroll in professional schools of dentistry and pharmacy after two years of undergraduate work. 3-2 program in engineering. Five-year programs in accounting, economics, history, and mathematics. Washington Semester and Sea Semester. Exchange programs with Howard U and Hebrew Union Coll. Teacher certification in elementary, secondary, and bilingual/bicultural education. Certification in specific subject areas. Study abroad in Australia, Austria, China, England, France, Germany, Israel, Italy, Japan, Kenya, Mexico, Russia, and Zimbabwe. ROTC, NROTC, and AFROTC.

**Honors:** Phi Beta Kappa. Honors program. Honor societies.

**Academic Assistance:** Remedial reading, writing, math, and study skills. Nonremedial tutoring.

**STUDENT LIFE. Housing:** Students may live on or off campus. Coed, women's, and men's dorms. Sorority and fraternity housing. School-owned/operated apartments. Off-campus privately-owned housing. Both on-campus and off-campus married-student housing. 31% of students live in college housing.

**Social atmosphere:** Students gather on campus at Center Plaza. Off campus, students choose destinations from Los Angeles' array of beaches, clubs, and sporting events. "Twenty percent of students belong to a Greek house, so they're very influential. Athletes, volunteer service groups, and some religious groups have an effect on university life, too," reports the Daily Trojan. Popular events include Songfest (a school-wide musical), the Springfest Concert, and football games.

**Services and counseling/handicapped student services:** Placement services. Health service. Women's center. Day care. Counseling services for minority, veteran, and older students. Birth control, personal, and psychological counseling. Career and academic guidance services. Physically disabled student services. Learning disabled services. Notetaking services. Tutors. Reader services for the blind.

**Campus organizations:** Undergraduate student government. Student newspaper (Daily Trojan). Literary magazine. Yearbook. Radio and TV stations. Bands, orchestra, string quartet, Chamber Singers, choirs, men's and women's glee clubs, film series, drama group, speakers committee, debating, academic, political, professional, recreational, service, and social groups, 300 organizations in all. 18% of men join a fraternity. 18% of women join a sorority.

**Religious organizations:** Baha'i Club, Baptist Student Union, Campus Crusade for Christ, Muslim Student Association, Newman Center, Rejoice in Jesus.

**Minority/foreign student organizations:** Asian-Pacific Student Services, Black Student Services, El Centro Chicano. International Student Assembly, numerous other foreign student groups.

**ATHLETICS. Physical education requirements:** None.

**Intercollegiate competition:** 4% of students participate. Baseball (M), basketball (M,W), crew (M,W), cross-country (M,W), diving (M,W), football (M), golf (M,W), sailing (M,W), soccer (W), swimming (M,W), tennis (M,W), volleyball (M,W), water polo (M). Member of NCAA Division I, Pacific 10 Conference.

**Intramural and club sports:** 50% of students participate. Intramural badminton, backgammon, basketball, billiards, bowling, football, inner tube water polo, racquetball, soccer, softball, squash, superstars, swimming, tennis, track and field, volleyball. Coed club Alpine skiing, amateur radio, badminton, bowling, cycling, dance, equestrian sports, fencing, frisbee, polo, racquetball, sailing, soccer, squash, table tennis, tennis, triathlon, volleyball, windsurfing, wrestling, ice hockey, lacrosse, rugby, waterskiing, surfing.

**ADMISSIONS. Academic basis for candidate selection** (in order of priority): Secondary school record, class rank, standardized test scores, school's recommendation, essay.

**Nonacademic basis for candidate selection:** Character and personality, extracurricular participation, particular talent or ability, and alumni/ae relationship are considered.

**Requirements:** Graduation from secondary school is required; GED is not accepted. 16 units and the following program of study are required: 4 units of English, 3 units of math, 2 units of science, 2 units of foreign language, 2 units of social studies, 3 units of electives. Supplemental application required of cinema/TV program applicants. Portfolio required of art program applicants. Audition required of music program applicants. University Access Program for applicants not normally admissible. SAT is required; ACT may be substituted. ACH recommended. Campus visit and interview recommended. Off-campus interviews available with admissions and alumni representatives.

**Procedure:** Take SAT or ACT by fall of 12th year. Visit college for interview by February of 12th year. Suggest filing application by December 15. Application deadline is February 1. Notification of admission on rolling basis. Reply is required by May 1. $250 nonrefundable tuition deposit. $200 room deposit, refundable until February 1. Freshmen accepted for terms other than fall.

**Special programs:** Admission may be deferred one year. Credit and/or placement may be granted through CEEB Advanced Placement exams for scores of 3 or higher. Early entrance/early admission program.

**Transfer students:** Transfer students accepted for terms other than fall. In fall 1993, 39% of all new students were transfers into all classes. 4,291 transfer applications were received, 2,663 were accepted. Application deadline is May 1 for fall; November 1 for

spring. Minimum 2.75 GPA required. Lowest course grade accepted is "C-." Maximum number of transferable credits is 70 semester hours from a two-year school and 80 semester hours from a four-year school. At least 128 semester hours must be completed at the university to receive degree.
**Admissions contact:** Duncan Murdoch, M.S.Ec., Associate Dean/Director of Admission. 213 740-1111.
**FINANCIAL AID. Available aid:** Pell grants, SEOG, state scholarships and grants, school scholarships and grants, private scholarships and grants, ROTC scholarships, academic merit scholarships, and athletic scholarships. Perkins Loans (NDSL), PLUS, Stafford Loans (GSL), Health Professions Loans, school loans, private loans, and SLS. Tuition Plan Inc.
**Financial aid statistics:** 30% of aid is not need-based. In 1993-94, 65% of all undergraduate applicants received aid; 57% of freshman applicants.
**Supporting data/closing dates:** FAFSA/FAF: Priority filing date is February 15; deadline is March 1. School's own aid application: Priority filing date is February 15; deadline is March 1. State aid form: Priority filing date is February 15; deadline is March 1. Income tax forms: Priority filing date is April 15; deadline is May 1. Notification of awards on rolling basis.
**Financial aid contact:** Catherine Thomas, M.S.Ed., Associate Dean/Director of Financial Aid. 213 740-1111.
**STUDENT EMPLOYMENT.** College Work/Study Program. Institutional employment. 11% of full-time undergraduates work on campus during school year. Students may expect to earn an average of $2,700 during school year. Off-campus part-time employment opportunities rated "good."
**COMPUTER FACILITIES.** 960 IBM/IBM-compatible and Macintosh/Apple microcomputers. Students may access IBM minicomputer/mainframe systems. Computer languages and software packages include Ada, BASIC, C, COBOL, dBASE, FORTH, FORTRAN, ISPF, Lotus 1-2-3, Pascal, Prolog, WordStar. Computer facilities are available to all students.
**Hours:** 24 hours.
**PROMINENT ALUMNI/AE.** Robert Foman, president, E.F. Hutton; George Lucas, movie director, *Star Wars;* Leo Buscaglia, educator, writer; Neil Armstrong, astronaut; Lionel Hampton, musician; Marilyn Horne, mezzo-soprano; O.J. Simpson, athlete, sportscaster; Frank O. Gehry, architect; Michael Tilson-Thomas; conductor; David Wolper, producer.

# West Coast University

**Los Angeles, CA 90020-1765 — 213 487-4433**

**1994-95 Costs.** Tuition: $9,000. Housing: None. Fees, books, misc. academic expenses (school's estimate): $720.
**Enrollment.** Undergraduates: 300 men, 200 women (full-time). Graduate enrollment: 800 men, 400 women.
**Test score averages/ranges.** N/A.
**Faculty.** 25 full-time; 130 part-time. Student/faculty ratio: 12 to 1.
**Selectivity rating.** N/A.

**PROFILE.** West Coast, founded in 1909, is a private university offering programs in business administration, computer science, engineering, and technology. Its campus is in Los Angeles.
**Accreditation:** WASC.
**Religious orientation:** West Coast University is nonsectarian; no religious requirements.
**Library:** Collections totaling over 25,000 volumes, 500 periodical subscriptions, and 5,000 microform items.
**STUDENT BODY.**
**Foreign students:** 200 students are from out of the country. Countries represented include Japan, Korea, Philippines, Taiwan, and Thailand; 30 in all.
**PROGRAMS OF STUDY. Degrees:** B.S.
**Majors:** Accounting, Acquisition/Contract Management, Business Administration, Business Information Systems, Computer Science, Engineering, Industrial Technology, Logistics Management.
**Distribution of degrees:** The majors with the highest enrollment are business administration, engineering, and computer science.
**Requirements:** General education requirement.
**Special:** Associate's degrees offered. Dual degrees. Preprofessional programs in medicine, pharmacy, dentistry, chiropractic, and health.
**Academic Assistance:** Remedial reading, writing, and math.
**ADMISSIONS. Academic basis for candidate selection** (in order of priority): Secondary school record.
**Requirements:** Graduation from secondary school is required; GED is accepted. 15 units and the following program of study are recommended: 3 units of English, 4.5 units of math, 4.5 units of science, 3 units of social studies. No off-campus interviews.
**Procedure:** Freshmen accepted for fall term only.
**Special programs:** Admission may be deferred one year. Credit and/or placement may be granted through CEEB Advanced Placement exams for scores of 3 or higher. Credit and/or placement may be granted through CLEP general and subject exams. Credit and placement may be granted through Regents College, ACT PEP, DANTES, and challenge exams, and military and life experience.
**Transfer students:** Transfer students accepted for terms other than fall. Application deadline is rolling for fall; rolling for spring.
**Admissions contact:** Roger A. Miller, Dean of Admissions and Registrar. 213 487-4433.
**FINANCIAL AID. Available aid:** Pell grants and SEOG. Perkins Loans (NDSL), Stafford Loans (GSL), and SLS.
**Financial aid statistics:** In 1993-94, 15% of all undergraduate applicants received aid.
**Supporting data/closing dates:** FAFSA/FAF: Accepted on rolling basis.
**Financial aid contact:** Fe Santos. 213 487-4433.

# Westmont College

**Santa Barbara, CA 93108-1099 — 805 565-6000**

**1994-95 Costs.** Tuition: $14,320. Room: $3,080. Board: $2,224. Fees, books, misc. academic expenses (school's estimate): $1,356.
**Enrollment.** Undergraduates: 505 men, 771 women (full-time). Freshman class: 950 applicants, 713 accepted, 351 enrolled.
**Test score averages/ranges.** Average SAT scores: 501 verbal, 550 math. Range of SAT scores of middle 50%: 450-550 verbal, 480-620 math. Average ACT scores: 24 English, 24 math, 24 composite. Range of ACT scores of middle 50%: 21-27 English, 21-26 math.
**Faculty.** 79 full-time; 36 part-time. 81% of faculty holds doctoral degree. Student/faculty ratio: 15 to 1.
**Selectivity rating.** Competitive.

**PROFILE.** Westmont, founded in 1940, is a liberal arts college with religious orientation. Its 133-acre campus is located four miles from the center of Santa Barbara.
**Accreditation:** WASC.
**Religious orientation:** Westmont College is an interdenominational Christian school; four semesters of religion required.
**Library:** Collections totaling over 150,000 volumes, 710 periodical subscriptions, and 20,687 microform items.
**Special facilities/museums:** Art gallery, observatory, nuclear magnetic resonance spectrometer, electron microscope, pre-med center.
**Athletic facilities:** Gymnasium, training/weight room, racquetball and tennis courts, baseball and soccer fields, track, swimming pool.
**STUDENT BODY. Undergraduate profile:** 76% are state residents; 23% are transfers. 3.6% Asian-American, 1% Black, 3.5% Hispanic, 1.2% Native American, 88.1% White, 2.6% Foreign National. Average age of undergraduates is 20.
**Freshman profile:** 1% of freshmen who took SAT scored 700 or over on verbal, 7% scored 700 or over on math; 13% scored 600 or over on verbal, 32% scored 600 or over on math; 56% scored 500 or over on verbal, 72% scored 500 or over on math; 91% scored 400 or over on verbal, 96% scored 400 or over on math; 99% scored 300 or over on verbal, 100% scored 300 or over on math. 8% of freshmen who took ACT scored 30 or over on English, 7% scored 30 or over on math, 6% scored 30 or over on composite; 54% scored 24 or over on English, 53% scored 24 or over on math, 55% scored 24 or over on composite; 97% scored 18 or over on English, 94% scored 18 or over on math, 99% scored 18 or over on composite; 100% scored 12 or over on English, 100% scored 12 or over on math, 100% scored 12 or over on composite. 95% of accepted applicants took SAT; 31% took ACT. 78% of freshmen come from public schools.
**Undergraduate achievement:** 81% of fall 1992 freshmen returned for fall 1993 term. 30% of students who completed a degree program immediately went on to graduate study.
**Foreign students:** 13 students are from out of the country. Countries represented include Canada, Ecuador, Ethiopia, Kenya, Papua New Guinea, and Portugal; 11 in all.
**PROGRAMS OF STUDY. Degrees:** B.A., B.S.
**Majors:** Alternative Major, Art, Biology, Chemistry, Communication Studies, Computer Science, Economics/Business, Elementary Education, Engineering/Physics, English, English/Modern Language, French, History, Interdisciplinary Studies, International Studies, Mathematics, Music, Natural Science, Philosophy, Physical Education/Kinesiology, Physics, Political Science, Psychology, Religious Studies, Secondary Education, Social Science, Sociology/Anthropology, Spanish, Theatre Arts.
**Distribution of degrees:** The majors with the highest enrollment are economics/business, English, and education; French, Spanish, and English/modern language have the lowest.
**Requirements:** General education requirement.
**Academic regulations:** Minimum 2.0 GPA must be maintained.
**Special:** Minors offered in most majors. Teaching credential program. Self-designed majors. Double majors. Dual degrees. Accelerated study. Pass/fail grading option. Internships. Cooperative education programs. Preprofessional programs in law, medicine, veterinary science, pharmacy, dentistry, theology, optometry, engineering, and physical therapy. 3-2 engineering programs with California Polytech State U, UC Berkeley, UCLA, USC, Stanford U, Washington U. Member of Christian College Consortium. Washington Semester. Au Sable Institute of Environmental Studies in Michigan, Los Angeles Film Studies Semester, San Francisco Urban Semester. Exchange program with other Christian colleges through Consortium Visitor Program. Teacher certification in elementary and secondary education. Certification in specific subject areas. Study abroad in Asian countries, Latin American countries, European countries, Israel, and South Africa. ROTC at UC Santa Barbara.
**Honors:** Honors program. Honor societies.
**Academic Assistance:** Remedial writing, math, and study skills. Nonremedial tutoring.
**STUDENT LIFE. Housing:** Students may live on or off campus. Coed dorms. School-owned/operated apartments. Off-campus married-student housing. 85% of students live in college housing.
**Social atmosphere:** The student newspaper reports, "Since it is such a close campus, our social lives consist of hanging out with our friends at one of the many beautiful places in Santa Barbara. The city has many cultural opportunities for theater, visual arts, etc." Popular gathering spots at the school are The Study, Peabodys, Carrows, and the beach. Christian organizations, The Young Republicans, and the Surf Club are influential groups on campus. The Spring Sing, Fall Follies, Potters Clay, and basketball and volleyball games are among the favorite events on campus.
**Services and counseling/handicapped student services:** Placement services. Health service. Women's center. Counseling services for minority, military, veteran, and older students. Birth control, personal, and psychological counseling. Career and academic guidance services. Religious counseling. Physically disabled student services. Learning disabled services. Notetaking services. Tape recorders. Tutors. Reader services for the blind.
**Campus organizations:** Undergraduate student government. Student newspaper (Horizon, published once/week). Literary magazine. Yearbook. Radio station. Zephaniah (music group), band and instrumental ensembles, chamber orchestra, choir, vespers, drama

group, career clubs, majors clubs, community service organizations, leadership development group, political organizations, special-interest groups, 40 organizations in all.
**Religious organizations:** Christian Services Association.
**Minority/foreign student organizations:** African-American, Asian, and Hispanic groups. Foreign student group.
**ATHLETICS. Physical education requirements:** Four semesters of physical education required.
**Intercollegiate competition:** 15% of students participate. Baseball (M), basketball (M), cross-country (M,W), soccer (M,W), tennis (M,W), track (outdoor) (M,W), track and field (outdoor) (M,W), volleyball (W). Member of Golden State Athletic Conference, NAIA.
**Intramural and club sports:** 40% of students participate. Intramural badminton, basketball, fencing, flag football, frisbee golf, inner-tube water polo, pickleball, racquetball, softball, table tennis, tennis, ultimate frisbee, volleyball. Men's club cheerleading, rugby, volleyball. Women's club cheerleading, lacrosse.
**ADMISSIONS. Academic basis for candidate selection** (in order of priority): Secondary school record, standardized test scores, class rank, essay, school's recommendation.
**Nonacademic basis for candidate selection:** Character and personality, extracurricular participation, particular talent or ability, and alumni/ae relationship are considered.
**Requirements:** Graduation from secondary school is required; GED is accepted. 16 units and the following program of study are required: 4 units of English, 2 units of math, 2 units of science including 1 unit of lab, 2 units of foreign language, 2 units of social studies, 2 units of history, 1 unit of academic electives. Minimum combined SAT score of 900 and minimum 2.7 GPA recommended. SAT or ACT is required. Campus visit and interview recommended. Off-campus interviews available with admissions and alumni representatives.
**Procedure:** Take SAT or ACT by January of 12th year. Visit college for interview by January of 12th year. Suggest filing application by December 1. Application deadline is February 15. Notification of admission by March 15. Reply is required by May 1. $200 nonrefundable tuition deposit. Freshmen accepted for terms other than fall.
**Special programs:** Admission may be deferred one year. Credit and/or placement may be granted through CEEB Advanced Placement exams for scores of 4 or higher. Credit and/or placement may be granted through CLEP general and subject exams. Credit and placement may be granted through challenge exams.
**Transfer students:** Transfer students accepted for terms other than fall. In fall 1993, 23% of all new students were transfers into all classes. 292 transfer applications were received, 184 were accepted. Application deadline is March 15 for fall; November 1 for spring. Minimum 2.0 GPA recommended. Lowest course grade accepted is "C." Maximum number of transferable credits is 64 semester hours. At least one-half of upper-division units required for major and the final two full-time semesters (32 of the last 40 semester hours) must be completed at the college to receive degree.
**Admissions contact:** David A. Morley, M.A., Director of Admissions. 805 565-6200.
**FINANCIAL AID. Available aid:** Pell grants, SEOG, state grants, school scholarships and grants, private scholarships and grants, academic merit scholarships, athletic scholarships, and aid for undergraduate foreign students. Perkins Loans (NDSL), PLUS, Stafford Loans (GSL), state loans, school loans, private loans, and SLS. Deferred payment plan. 10-month payment plan. Discount payment plan.
**Financial aid statistics:** 41% of aid is not need-based. In 1993-94, 95% of all undergraduate applicants received aid; 95% of freshman applicants. Average amounts of aid awarded freshmen: Scholarships and grants, $5,000; loans, $4,000.
**Supporting data/closing dates:** FAFSA/FAF/FFS: Priority filing date is March 1. Income tax forms: Priority filing date is August 1; accepted on rolling basis. Notification of awards begins April 15.
**Financial aid contact:** Alice V. Meyers, Director of Financial Aid. 805 565-6063.
**STUDENT EMPLOYMENT.** College Work/Study Program. Institutional employment. 60% of full-time undergraduates work on campus during school year. Students may expect to earn an average of $1,200 during school year. Freshmen are discouraged from working during their first term. Off-campus part-time employment opportunities rated "good."
**COMPUTER FACILITIES.** 24 IBM/IBM-compatible and Macintosh/Apple microcomputers; 21 are networked. Students may access IBM minicomputer/mainframe systems, Internet. Client/LAN operating systems include Apple/Macintosh, DOS, UNIX/XENIX/AIX, Artisoft, LocalTalk/AppleTalk. Computer languages and software packages include Ada, BASIC, C, FORTRAN, LISP, Pascal, PERL, SPSS-X, Scheme, Turing. Computer facilities are available to all students.
**Hours:** 7:45 AM-midn.
**GRADUATE CAREER DATA.** Graduate school percentages: 90% enter medical school. 40% enter graduate business programs. Highest graduate school enrollments: Arizona State U, UC system schools, U of Chicago, Colorado State U, Dallas Seminary, Fuller Seminary, Princeton U, Stanford U, Washington U. Companies and businesses that hire graduates: Apple Computer, Arthur Andersen, AT&T, Clorox, IBM, ITT, Martin Marietta, Merrill Lynch, Procter & Gamble.
**PROMINENT ALUMNI/AE.** Dennis Cope, M.D., director of internal medicine, UCLA Medical Center; David Hubbard, president, Fuller Theological Seminary; William Kliewar, executive director, World Vision; John Crew, M.D., vascular surgeon, UC San Francisco; Dr. Alvin Austin, president, LeTourneau Coll.

# Whittier College

**Whittier, CA 90608 — 310 907-4200**

**1994-95 Costs.** Tuition: $16,249. Room & board: $5,699. Fees, books, misc. academic expenses (school's estimate): $1,094.
**Enrollment.** Undergraduates: 562 men, 668 women (full-time). Freshman class: 1,681 applicants, 1,069 accepted, 345 enrolled. Graduate enrollment: 398 men, 263 women.
**Test score averages/ranges.** Average SAT scores: 454 verbal, 507 math. Range of SAT scores of middle 50%: 390-510 verbal, 430-580 math. Average ACT scores: 23 composite.
**Faculty.** 82 full-time; 36 part-time. 89% of faculty holds highest degree in specific field. Student/faculty ratio: 15 to 1.
**Selectivity rating.** Competitive.

**PROFILE.** Whittier, founded in 1887, is a private, liberal arts college. Its 105-acre campus is located in Whittier, 18 miles east of Los Angeles.
**Accreditation:** WASC. Professionally accredited by the American Bar Association, the Council on Social Work Education.
**Religious orientation:** Whittier College is nonsectarian; no religious requirements.
**Library:** Collections totaling over 416,005 volumes, 1,357 periodical subscriptions, and 13,025 microform items.
**Special facilities/museums:** Performing arts center, on-campus preschool/elementary school, image processing lab.
**Athletic facilities:** Football stadium, activities center, aquatic center, track, tennis courts, baseball and soccer fields.
**STUDENT BODY. Undergraduate profile:** 70% are state residents; 8% are transfers. 9% Asian-American, 4% Black, 23% Hispanic, 1% Native American, 59% White, 4% Other. Average age of undergraduates is 20.
**Freshman profile:** 1% of freshmen who took SAT scored 700 or over on verbal, 3% scored 700 or over on math; 7% scored 600 or over on verbal, 20% scored 600 or over on math; 30% scored 500 or over on verbal, 57% scored 500 or over on math; 74% scored 400 or over on verbal, 88% scored 400 or over on math; 97% scored 300 or over on verbal, 99% scored 300 or over on math. 90% of accepted applicants took SAT; 10% took ACT. 73% of freshmen come from public schools.
**Undergraduate achievement:** 77% of fall 1992 freshmen returned for fall 1993 term. 48% of entering class graduated. 32% of students who completed a degree program immediately went on to graduate study.
**Foreign students:** 38 students are from out of the country. Countries represented include Canada, Denmark, India, Japan, and the United Kingdom; 15 in all.
**PROGRAMS OF STUDY. Degrees:** B.A.
**Majors:** Art, Art History, Biology, Business Administration, Chemistry, Child Development, Comparative Cultures, Earth Science, Economics, English, French, Geology, History, International Studies, Latin American Studies, Mathematics, Mathematics/Business Administration, Music, Music Education, Music History/Literature, Music Performance, Philosophy, Physical Education/Recreation, Physics, Political Science, Psychology, Religious Studies, Social Work, Sociology, Sociology/Anthropology, Spanish, Speech Pathology/Audiology, Theatre Arts.
**Distribution of degrees:** The majors with the highest enrollment are business administration, political science, and English; geology and music have the lowest.
**Requirements:** General education requirement.
**Academic regulations:** Minimum 2.0 GPA must be maintained.
**Special:** Minors offered. Environmental studies and freshman writing programs. Self-designed majors. Double majors. Independent study. Pass/fail grading option. Internships. Cooperative education programs. Graduate school at which undergraduates may take graduate-level courses. Preprofessional programs in law, medicine, veterinary science, pharmacy, dentistry, and optometry. 4-1 social work program. 3-2 engineering programs with Case Western Reserve U, Colorado State U, Columbia U, Dartmouth Coll, U of Southern California, and Washington U. Washington Semester. Teacher certification in elementary and secondary education. Certification in specific subject areas. Exchange programs abroad in Denmark (U of Copenhagen) and India (Madurai Kamaraj U). Study abroad also in many other countries. ROTC and AFROTC at U Southern California.
**Honors:** Honor societies.
**Academic Assistance:** Nonremedial tutoring.
**STUDENT LIFE. Housing:** All freshmen, sophomores, and juniors must live on campus unless living with family. Coed dorms. 60% of students live in college housing.
**Social atmosphere:** "The campus social life focuses on smaller parties, with lots of party hopping," according to the student newspaper. "Scholars Film Series provides art films on Friday nights." Popular campus events include the spring formal, Luminarias, the spring talent show, Spring Sing, and the Mona Kai dance. "Sachsen, a coed society, is one of the more popular organized groups. Lacrosse games are popular and influential. Whittier has societies similar to national sororities and fraternities." Whittier students frequent restaurants in the Uptown area.
**Services and counseling/handicapped student services:** Placement services. Health service. Counseling services for minority students. Personal and psychological counseling. Career and academic guidance services. Religious counseling.
**Campus organizations:** Undergraduate student government. Student newspaper (Quaker Campus, published once/week). Literary magazine. Yearbook. Radio station. A cappella choir, orchestra, major plays and shows, forensic groups, ski club, Associated Students of Whittier College, Residence Hall Association, departmental and special-interest groups, 45 organizations in all. Four fraternities, no chapter houses; five sororities, no chapter houses. 17% of men join a fraternity. 24% of women join a sorority.
**Religious organizations:** Several religious groups.
**Minority/foreign student organizations:** Black Student Union, Whittier Islander Club, Hispanic Student Association, Iota Chi, Jewish Student Union. International Students, Asian Student Association.
**ATHLETICS. Physical education requirements:** None.
**Intercollegiate competition:** 35% of students participate. Baseball (M), basketball (M,W), cross-country (M,W), diving (M,W), football (M), golf (M), lacrosse (M), soccer (M,W), softball (W), swimming (M,W), tennis (M,W), track (outdoor) (M,W), track and field (outdoor) (M,W), volleyball (W), water polo (M,W). Member of NCAA Division III, Southern California Intercollegiate Athletic Conference.
**Intramural and club sports:** Intramural basketball, billiards, bowling, flag football, inner-tube water polo, racquetball, softball, table tennis, tennis, track, volleyball, walleyball. Men's club ice hockey, volleyball. Women's club cheerleading, lacrosse.
**ADMISSIONS. Academic basis for candidate selection** (in order of priority): Secondary school record, school's recommendation, standardized test scores, class rank, essay.
**Nonacademic basis for candidate selection:** Character and personality are important. Extracurricular participation, particular talent or ability, and alumni/ae relationship are considered.
**Requirements:** Graduation from secondary school is required; GED is not accepted. 17 units and the following program of study are recommended: 4 units of English, 3 units of math, 3 units of science, 2 units of foreign language, 2 units of social studies, 3 units of history. SAT or ACT is required. Campus visit and interview recommended. Off-campus interviews available with an admissions representative.

**Procedure:** Take SAT or ACT by March of 12th year. Suggest filing application by February 15; no deadline. Notification of admission on rolling basis. Reply is required by May 1. $300 nonrefundable tuition deposit. $100 nonrefundable room deposit. Freshmen accepted for terms other than fall.
**Special programs:** Admission may be deferred one year. Credit and/or placement may be granted through CEEB Advanced Placement exams for scores of 4 or higher. Placement may be granted through challenge exams. Early decision program. In fall 1993, 65 applied for early decision and 57 were accepted. Deadline for applying for early decision is December 10.
**Transfer students:** Transfer students accepted for terms other than fall. In fall 1993, 8% of all new students were transfers into all classes. 319 transfer applications were received, 155 were accepted. Application deadline is April 20 for fall; December 15 for spring. Minimum 2.5 GPA recommended. Lowest course grade accepted is "C-." Maximum number of transferable credits is 90 semester hour. At least 30 semester hours must be completed at the college to receive degree.
**Admissions contact:** Tom Enders, M.M., Dean of Enrollment. 310 907-4238.

**FINANCIAL AID. Available aid:** Pell grants, SEOG, state scholarships and grants, school scholarships and grants, private scholarships and grants, ROTC scholarships, academic merit scholarships, and aid for undergraduate foreign students. Perkins Loans (NDSL), PLUS, Stafford Loans (GSL), school loans, private loans, and SLS. AMS.
**Financial aid statistics:** 25% of aid is not need-based. In 1993-94, 98% of all undergraduate applicants received aid; 98% of freshman applicants. Average amounts of aid awarded freshmen: Scholarships and grants, $10,568; loans, $2,338.
**Supporting data/closing dates:** FAFSA: Priority filing date is February 15. FAF: Priority filing date is February 15; accepted on rolling basis. State aid form: Deadline is March 2. Notification of awards begins April 1.
**Financial aid contact:** Kathy Street, M.S., Associate Dean of Enrollment. 310 907-4285.

**STUDENT EMPLOYMENT.** College Work/Study Program. Institutional employment. 41% of full-time undergraduates work on campus during school year. Students may expect to earn an average of $1,250 during school year. Off-campus part-time employment opportunities rated "good."

**COMPUTER FACILITIES.** 50 Macintosh/Apple microcomputers; all are networked. Students may access Digital, IBM minicomputer/mainframe systems, Internet. Residence halls may be equipped with networked microcomputers. Client/LAN operating systems include Apple/Macintosh, UNIX/XENIX/AIX, LocalTalk/AppleTalk. Computer languages and software packages include C and Pascal; some Apple Macintosh and IBM software. Computer facilities are available to all students.
**Fees:** None.
**Hours:** 8 AM-1 AM.

**GRADUATE CAREER DATA.** Graduate school percentages: 5% enter law school. 4% enter medical school. 2% enter dental school. 2% enter graduate business programs. 4% enter graduate arts and sciences programs. 1% enter theological school/seminary. Highest graduate school enrollments: UC Los Angeles, the California State U campuses, U of Hawaii, U of Washington. 23% of graduates choose careers in business and industry. Companies and businesses that hire graduates: Bullocks/Macy's, Crawford & Co., Expediturs International, Parker-Hannifin Corp., State Farm Insurance.

# Woodbury University

**Burbank, CA 91510-7846** **818 767-0888**

**1994-95 Costs.** Tuition: $12,180, $12,660 for B.Arch. program. Room & board: $5,490. Fees, books, misc. academic expenses (school's estimate): $1,740.
**Enrollment.** Undergraduates: 345 men, 393 women (full-time). Freshman class: 389 applicants, 345 accepted, 136 enrolled. Graduate enrollment: 89 men, 76 women.
**Test score averages/ranges.** Average SAT scores: 365 verbal, 437 math. Range of SAT scores of middle 50%: 290-420 verbal, 380-500 math. Average ACT scores: 21 composite. Range of ACT scores of middle 50%: 19-22 composite.
**Faculty.** 23 full-time; 100 part-time. 46% of faculty holds highest degree in specific field. Student/faculty ratio: 18 to 1.
**Selectivity rating.** Less competitive.

**PROFILE.** Woodbury, founded in 1884, is a private university of business administration and professional design. Its 22-acre campus is located in Burbank, in the Los Angeles metropolitan area.

**Accreditation:** WASC. Professionally accredited by the Foundation for Interior Design Education Research.
**Religious orientation:** Woodbury University is nonsectarian; no religious requirements.
**Library:** Collections totaling over 61,000 volumes, 600 periodical subscriptions, and 77,000 microform items.
**Athletic facilities:** Gymnasium, basketball and volleyball courts, track, swimming pool, football and soccer fields, aerobics, recreation, and weight rooms, dance studio.

**STUDENT BODY. Undergraduate profile:** 44% are transfers. 15% Asian-American, 6% Black, 22% Hispanic, 1% Native American, 45% White, 11% Other. Average age of undergraduates is 23.
**Freshman profile:** 1% of freshmen who took SAT scored 600 or over on verbal, 4% scored 600 or over on math; 9% scored 500 or over on verbal, 27% scored 500 or over on math; 32% scored 400 or over on verbal, 69% scored 400 or over on math; 74% scored 300 or over on verbal, 97% scored 300 or over on math. 9% of freshmen who took ACT scored 24 or over on composite; 78% scored 18 or over on composite; 100% scored 12 or over on composite. 93% of accepted applicants took SAT; 7% took ACT.
**Undergraduate achievement:** 74% of fall 1991 freshmen returned for fall 1992 term.
**Foreign students:** 160 students are from out of the country. Countries represented include Indonesia, Japan, Korea, Taiwan, and Thailand; 34 in all.

**PROGRAMS OF STUDY. Degrees:** B.Arch., B.S.
**Majors:** Accounting, Architecture, Computer Information Systems, Fashion Design, Fashion Marketing, Finance, Graphic Design, Interior Design, International Business, Management, Marketing.
**Distribution of degrees:** The majors with the highest enrollment are business, interior design, and architecture; computer information systems, management, and marketing have the lowest.
**Requirements:** General education requirement.
**Academic regulations:** Minimum 2.0 GPA must be maintained.
**Special:** Double majors. Independent study. Internships.
**Honors:** Honor societies.
**Academic Assistance:** Remedial reading, writing, math, and study skills. Nonremedial tutoring.

**STUDENT LIFE. Housing:** Students may live on or off campus. Coed dorms. 20% of students live in college housing.
**Social atmosphere:** According to the student newspaper, the university's recent move to a new campus in Burbank offers students many facilities and amenities not previously available: "a residence hall, recreation facilities, a full-service cafeteria, and trees and grass" instead of concrete. "Most of us feel that the move will have a big impact on campus life, making students more interested and willing to stick around and get involved." Concerning the most influential student organizations, "Greeks and the business fraternity are stronger than most."
**Services and counseling/handicapped student services:** Placement services. Health service. Counseling services for minority, veteran, and older students. Personal and psychological counseling. Career and academic guidance services. Physically disabled student services. Learning disabled services. Tutors.
**Campus organizations:** Undergraduate student government. American Institute of Architecture, Fashion Guild, Data Processing Management group, Institute of Business Designers, Residence Hall Council, Students in Free Enterprise, student curriculum committee, 33 organizations in all. Three fraternities, one chapter house; three sororities, no chapter houses. 15% of men join a fraternity. 8% of women join a sorority.
**Religious organizations:** Chinese Christian Fellowship, Newman Club.
**Minority/foreign student organizations:** African-American Student Union, Latin Culture Club. International Connection, accounting conversation groups for international students, Chinese, Japanese, and Korean groups.

**ATHLETICS. Physical education requirements:** None.
**Intramural and club sports:** 25% of students participate. Intramural aerobics, basketball, bowling, cycling, dance, football, ice skating, roller skating, soccer, volleyball, weight lifting, yoga.

**ADMISSIONS. Academic basis for candidate selection** (in order of priority): Secondary school record, essay, standardized test scores, school's recommendation, class rank.
**Nonacademic basis for candidate selection:** Character and personality and particular talent or ability are important. Extracurricular participation, geographical distribution, and alumni/ae relationship are considered.
**Requirements:** Graduation from secondary school is required; GED is accepted. 15 units and the following program of study are recommended: 4 units of English, 3 units of math, 2 units of science, 2 units of foreign language, 2 units of social studies, 2 units of history. Minimum 2.5 GPA recommended. Conditional admission possible for applicants not meeting standard requirements. SAT is required; ACT may be substituted. Campus visit and interview recommended. Off-campus interviews available with an admissions representative.
**Procedure:** Suggest filing application by March 1; no deadline. Notification of admission on rolling basis. No set date by which applicants must accept offer. $100 nonrefundable tuition deposit. $150 nonrefundable room deposit. Freshmen accepted for terms other than fall.
**Special programs:** Admission may be deferred one year. Credit may be granted through CEEB Advanced Placement for scores of 3 or higher. Credit may be granted through CLEP general and subject exams, ACT PEP, and DANTES exams, and military experience.
**Transfer students:** Transfer students accepted for terms other than fall. In fall 1992, 44% of all new students were transfers into all classes. 199 transfer applications were received, 174 were accepted. Application deadline is April 15 for fall; one month prior to beginning of quarter for spring. Minimum 2.0 GPA required. Lowest course grade accepted is "C." At least 68 quarter hours must be completed at the university to receive degree.
**Admissions contact:** Patrick N. Contrades, Director of Admission. 818 767-0888, extension 221.

**FINANCIAL AID. Available aid:** Pell grants, SEOG, state grants, school scholarships and grants, and private scholarships. Perkins Loans (NDSL), PLUS, Stafford Loans (GSL), state loans, and SLS. Deferred payment plan. Institutional payment plan.
**Financial aid statistics:** 11% of aid is not need-based. In 1992-93, 83% of all undergraduate applicants received aid; 77% of freshman applicants. Average amounts of aid awarded freshmen: Scholarships and grants, $3,406; loans, $2,450.
**Supporting data/closing dates:** FAFSA/FAF: Accepted on rolling basis. School's own aid application: Accepted on rolling basis. State aid form: Priority filing date is March 2. Income tax forms: Accepted on rolling basis. Notification of awards on rolling basis.
**Financial aid contact:** William T. Wagoner, Director of Financial Aid. 818 767-0888, extension 273.

**STUDENT EMPLOYMENT.** College Work/Study Program. Institutional employment. 9% of full-time undergraduates work on campus during school year. Students may expect to earn an average of $1,200 during school year. Off-campus part-time employment opportunities rated "good."

**COMPUTER FACILITIES.** 63 IBM/IBM-compatible and Macintosh/Apple microcomputers; 32 are networked. Students may access Digital minicomputer/mainframe systems, BITNET. Client/LAN operating systems include Apple/Macintosh. Computer languages and software packages include C, COBOL, dBASE, Excelerator, Lotus 1-2-3, Pascal, WordPerfect. Computer facilities are available to all students.
**Fees:** Computer fee is included in tuition/fees.
**Hours:** 7:30 AM-midn. (seven days).

**PROMINENT ALUMNI/AE.** Don Maxwell, vice-president and controller, Times Mirror Co.; Helen Gurley Brown, editor, *Cosmopolitan* magazine; Stephen Gamble, president and CEO, Hospital Council of Southern California; Jane Singer, president, Jane Singer.

# Colorado

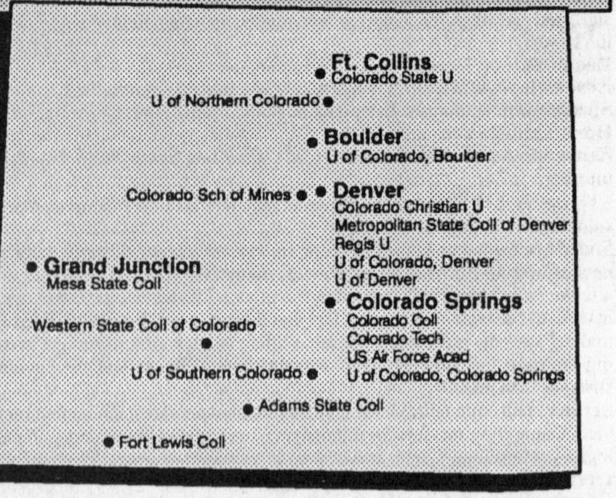


## Adams State College

**Alamosa, CO 81102** **719 589-7712**

**1994-95 Costs.** Tuition: $1,380 (state residents), $4,700 (out-of-state). Room: $1,750. Board: $1,980. Fees, books, misc. academic expenses (school's estimate): $880.
**Enrollment.** Undergraduates: 874 men, 941 women (full-time). Freshman class: 1,346 applicants, 1,212 accepted, 501 enrolled. Graduate enrollment: 90 men, 246 women.
**Test score averages/ranges.** Average SAT scores: 440 verbal, 470 math. Average ACT scores: 21 composite.
**Faculty.** 104 full-time; 16 part-time. 68% of faculty holds highest degree in specific field. Student/faculty ratio: 20 to 1.
**Selectivity rating.** Competitive.

**PROFILE.** Adams State, founded in 1921 as a Normal school, is a public college. Programs are offered through the Division of Library Science and the Schools of Art and Letters; Business; Education and Behavioral Science; and Science, Mathematics, and Technology. Its 90-acre campus is located in the San Luis Valley of south central Colorado.

**Accreditation:** NCACS. Professionally accredited by the National Council for Accreditation of Teacher Education.
**Religious orientation:** Adams State College is nonsectarian; no religious requirements.
**Library:** Collections totaling over 57,137 volumes, 1,000 periodical subscriptions, and 650,099 microform items.
**Special facilities/museums:** Art and area history museum, planetarium, observatory.
**Athletic facilities:** Swimming pool, basketball, tennis, and racquetball courts, indoor track, weight room.

**STUDENT BODY. Undergraduate profile:** 80% are state residents; 20% are transfers. 1% Asian-American, 2% Black, 26% Hispanic, 3% Native American, 68% White.
**Freshman profile:** 15% of accepted applicants took SAT; 84% took ACT. 95% of freshmen come from public schools.
**Undergraduate achievement:** 65% of fall 1992 freshmen returned for fall 1993 term. 19% of students who completed a degree program went on to graduate study within one year.
**Foreign students:** Nine students are from out of the country.

**PROGRAMS OF STUDY. Degrees:** B.A., B.S.
**Majors:** Art, Biology, Business Administration, Chemistry, Elementary Education, English, Exercise Physiology/Leisure Science, Geology, Hispanic/Southwest Studies, History/Government, Industrial Technology, Mathematics, Medical Technology, Music, Physics, Psychology, Selected Studies, Sociology, Spanish, Speech/Theatre.
**Distribution of degrees:** The majors with the highest enrollment are business administration, elementary education, and biology.
**Requirements:** General education requirement.
**Special:** Minors offered in most majors and in accounting, advertising, athletic coaching, business computer systems, business education, earth science, economics, environmental science, finance, journalism, management, marketing, office management, philosophy, and reading. Selected Studies Curriculum has no major requirement. Associate's degrees offered. Self-designed majors. Double majors. Dual degrees. Accelerated study. Internships. Graduate school at which undergraduates may take graduate-level courses. Preprofessional programs in law, medicine, veterinary science, pharmacy, dentistry, optometry, and physical therapy. Member of State Colleges in Colorado consortium. Teacher certification in early childhood, elementary, secondary, and special education.
**Academic Assistance:** Remedial reading, writing, and math. Nonremedial tutoring.

**STUDENT LIFE. Housing:** All unmarried freshmen and sophomores must live on campus unless living with family. Coed and women's dorms. School-owned/operated apartments. On-campus married-student housing. 43% of students live in college housing.
**Social atmosphere:** Influential groups at Adams State College include Greeks, cross-country athletes, and wrestlers. Students enjoy sporting events such as cross-country meets and wrestling matches as well as plays and parties.
**Services and counseling/handicapped student services:** Placement services. Day care. Counseling services for minority, veteran, and older students. Personal counseling. Career and academic guidance services. Learning disabled services.
**Campus organizations:** Undergraduate student government. Student newspaper (South Coloradan, published once/week). Literary magazine. Yearbook. Radio station. Choir, band, jazz band, Adams State Players, residence hall councils, Student Ambassadors, Student Mobilization Committee, Young Democrats, Young Republicans, 57 organizations in all.
**Religious organizations:** Baptist Student Union, Newman Center, Fellowship of Christian Athletes.
**Minority/foreign student organizations:** Black Student Organization, Native American Club, Hispanic Student Organization. Foreign Student Club.

**ATHLETICS. Physical education requirements:** One semester of physical education required.
**Intercollegiate competition:** 15% of students participate. Basketball (M,W), cheerleading (M,W), cross-country (M,W), football (M), golf (M), softball (W), volleyball (W), wrestling (M). Member of NCAA Division II, Rocky Mountain Athletic Conference.
**Intramural and club sports:** 20% of students participate. Intramural basketball, bowling, football, softball, tennis, track and field, volleyball, water polo. Women's club soccer.

**ADMISSIONS. Academic basis for candidate selection** (in order of priority): Secondary school record, standardized test scores, class rank, school's recommendation, essay.
**Nonacademic basis for candidate selection:** Character and personality, extracurricular participation, particular talent or ability, geographical distribution, and alumni/ae relationship are considered.
**Requirements:** Graduation from secondary school is required; GED is accepted. 15 units and the following program of study are required: 3 units of English, 2 units of math, 2 units of science, 3 units of social studies, 5 units of electives. Minimum composite ACT score of 21 (combined SAT score of 850), rank in top half of secondary school class, and minimum 2.5 GPA required. ACT is required; SAT may be substituted. Campus visit recommended. Off-campus interviews available with an admissions representative.
**Procedure:** Take SAT or ACT by October of 12th year. Suggest filing application by January 30. Application deadline is August 1. Notification of admission on rolling basis. No set date by which applicants must accept offer. $100 room deposit, refundable under certain circumstances. $100 room deposit, $75 of which is refundable until June 1. Freshmen accepted in terms other than fall.
**Special programs:** Admission may be deferred one year. Credit and/or placement may be granted through CEEB Advanced Placement exams for scores of 3 or higher. Credit and/or placement may be granted through CLEP general and subject exams. Credit and placement may be granted through challenge exams and military experience. Early entrance/early admission program. Concurrent enrollment program.
**Transfer students:** Transfer students accepted for terms other than fall. In fall 1993, 20% of all new students were transfers into all classes. 343 transfer applications were received, 317 were accepted. Application deadline is August 1 for fall; December 1 for spring. Minimum 2.0 GPA required. Lowest course grade accepted is "C." Maximum number of transferable credits is 62 semester hours. At least 62 semester hours must be completed at the college to receive degree.
**Admissions contact:** Cheryl Billingsley, M.A., Director of Admissions. 800 824-6494.

**FINANCIAL AID. Available aid:** Pell grants, SEOG, state scholarships and grants, private scholarships and grants, academic merit scholarships, athletic scholarships, and aid for undergraduate foreign students. Perkins Loans (NDSL), PLUS, and Stafford Loans (GSL). Tuition Plan Inc., EFI Fund Management, and deferred payment plan.
**Financial aid statistics:** 25% of aid is not need-based. In 1993-94, 95% of all undergraduate applicants received aid; 98% of freshman applicants. Average amounts of aid awarded freshmen: Scholarships and grants, $1,824; loans, $1,100.
**Supporting data/closing dates:** FAFSA: Priority filing date is April 15. Notification of awards on rolling basis.
**Financial aid contact:** Ted Laws, M.A., Director of Financial Aid. 719 589-7306.

**STUDENT EMPLOYMENT.** College Work/Study Program. Institutional employment. 32% of full-time undergraduates work on campus during school year. Students may expect to earn an average of $1,350 during school year. Off-campus part-time employment opportunities rated "fair."

**COMPUTER FACILITIES.** 125 microcomputers; 80 are networked. Students may access minicomputer/mainframe systems. Residence halls may be equipped with stand-alone microcomputers. Computer languages and software packages include BASIC, C, COBOL, FORTRAN, Pascal; 20 in all. Computer facilities are available to all students.
**Fees:** $25 computer fee per year.

**GRADUATE CAREER DATA.** Graduate school percentages: 6% enter law school. 2% enter medical school. 6% enter graduate business programs. 5% enter graduate arts and sciences programs.

## Colorado Christian University

**Lakewood, CO 80226** **303 238-5386**

**1993-94 Costs.** Tuition: $6,000. Room & board: $3,400. Fees, books, misc. academic expenses (school's estimate): $750.
**Enrollment.** Undergraduates: 461 men, 540 women (full-time). Freshman class: 175 enrolled. Graduate enrollment: 47 men, 50 women.
**Test score averages/ranges.** Average SAT scores: 422 verbal, 445 math. Average ACT scores: 21 composite.
**Faculty.** 22 full-time; 50 part-time. 46% of faculty holds doctoral degree. Student/faculty ratio: 21 to 1.
**Selectivity rating.** Noncompetitive.

**PROFILE.** Colorado Christian is a university with religious orientation. Founded in 1914, the current institution is the result of the 1985 merger of Rockmont College and Western Bible College. Its 25-acre campus is located in Lakewood, 10 miles from Denver.

**Accreditation:** AABC, NCACS.
**Religious orientation:** Colorado Christian University is a nondenominational Christian school; 18 hours of religion required.

**Library:** Collections totaling over 42,500 volumes, 320 periodical subscriptions and 25 microform items.
**Special facilities/museums:** Music recording studio, electron microscope.
**Athletic facilities:** Field house, gymnasium, basketball, and volleyball courts, soccer field, weight room.

**STUDENT BODY. Undergraduate profile:** 65% are state residents. Average age of undergraduates is 21.
**Freshman profile:** 2% of freshmen who took ACT scored 30 or over on composite; 13% scored 24 or over on composite; 44% scored 18 or over on composite; 86% scored 12 or over on composite; 100% scored 6 or over on composite. Majority of accepted applicants took SAT. 62% of freshmen come from public schools.
**Undergraduate achievement:** 45% of fall 1992 freshmen returned for fall 1993 term.
**Foreign students:** 14 students are from out of the country. Countries represented include Belgium, Canada, China, Japan, Russia, and Zimbabwe; 10 in all.

**PROGRAMS OF STUDY. Degrees:** B.A., B.Mus.Ed., B.S.
**Majors:** Accounting, Art, Biblical Studies, Biology, Business Education, Communications, Computer Management, English, General Science, History/Political Science, Humanities, Liberal Arts, Management, Marketing, Mathematics, Music, Music Ministry, Organizational Management, Psychology, Science, Social Studies, Theatre, Youth Ministry.
**Distribution of degrees:** The majors with the highest enrollment are psychology and liberal arts: art, social studies, and communication have the lowest.
**Requirements:** General education requirement.
**Academic regulations:** Minimum 2.0 GPA must be maintained.
**Special:** Minors offered in many majors and in broadcasting, business, and missions. Associate's degrees offered. Double majors. Independent study. Pass/fail grading option. Internships. Cooperative education programs. Graduate school at which undergraduates may take graduate-level courses. Preprofessional programs in medicine and theology. Member of Christian College Coalition. Teacher certification in elementary and secondary education. ROTC and AFROTC at U Colorado at Boulder.
**Academic Assistance:** Remedial study skills.

**STUDENT LIFE. Housing:** All first-time freshmen must live on campus. School-owned/operated apartments. 50% of students live in college housing.
**Services and counseling/handicapped student services:** Placement services. Health service. Personal and psychological counseling. Career and academic guidance services. Religious counseling.
**Campus organizations:** Undergraduate student government. Student newspaper (Sword, published once/week). Literary magazine. Yearbook. Radio and TV stations. Choir, ensembles, cross-cultural concerts, Fellowship of the Performing Arts, Artist Lecture Series, outdoor club.
**Religious organizations:** Baptist Student Union, Bible study groups, Dare to Care, Fellowship of Christian Athletes.

**ATHLETICS. Physical education requirements:** None.
**Intercollegiate competition:** 20% of students participate. Basketball (M,W), cheerleading (W), golf (M), soccer (M,W), tennis (M,W), volleyball (W). Member of Colorado Athletic Conference, NCAA Division II.
**Intramural and club sports:** 80% of students participate. Intramural Alpine skiing, basketball, hiking, mountain biking, soccer, table tennis, volleyball.

**ADMISSIONS. Academic basis for candidate selection** (in order of priority): Secondary school record, standardized test scores, school's recommendation, essay, class rank.
**Nonacademic basis for candidate selection:** Character and personality are emphasized. Extracurricular participation and particular talent or ability are considered.
**Requirements:** Graduation from secondary school is recommended; GED is accepted. No specific distribution of secondary school units required. Minimum combined SAT score of 800 (composite ACT score of 18) and minimum 2.0 GPA required. Audition required of music program applicants. Conditional admission possible for applicants not meeting standard requirements. SAT or ACT is required. Campus visit and interview recommended. Off-campus interviews available with an admissions representative.
**Procedure:** Take SAT or ACT by December 1 of 12th year. Visit college for interview by April 1 of 12th year. Application deadline is August 15. Notification of admission on rolling basis. No set date by which applicants must accept offer. $100 nonrefundable tuition deposit. $100 nonrefundable room deposit. Freshmen accepted in terms other than fall.
**Special programs:** Admission may be deferred one year. Credit and/or placement may be granted through CEEB Advanced Placement exams for scores of 4 or higher. Credit may be granted through CLEP general and subject exams, and military experience. Early entrance/early admission program.
**Transfer students:** Transfer students accepted for terms other than fall. In fall 1993, 284 transfer applications were received, 116 were accepted. Application deadline is August 15 for fall; January 15 for spring. Minimum 2.0 GPA required. Lowest course grade accepted is "C." Maximum number of transferable credits is 104 semester hours. At least 32 semester hours must be completed at the university to receive degree.
**Admissions contact:** Anna DiTorrice, Director of Admissions. 303 238-5386, extension 125.

**FINANCIAL AID. Available aid:** Pell grants, SEOG, school scholarships and grants, academic merit scholarships, and athletic scholarships. Perkins Loans (NDSL), PLUS, Stafford Loans (GSL), and private loans. Tuition Plan Inc. and family tuition reduction.
**Financial aid statistics:** 10% of aid is not need-based. In 1993-94, 75% of all undergraduate applicants received aid; 75% of freshman applicants. Average amounts of aid awarded freshmen: Scholarships and grants, $1,500; loans, $2,625.
**Supporting data/closing dates:** FAFSA: Priority filing date is March 15. School's own aid application: Priority filing date is March 15. FAT and verification form: Priority filing date is March 15. Notification of awards begins April 1.
**Financial aid contact:** Candice Failing, Director of Financial Aid. 303 238-5386, extension 117.

**STUDENT EMPLOYMENT.** College Work/Study Program. Institutional employment. Students may expect to earn an average of $2,160 during school year. Off-campus part-time employment opportunities rated "excellent."

**COMPUTER FACILITIES.** 50 IBM/IBM-compatible and Macintosh/Apple microcomputers. Client/LAN operating systems include Apple/Macintosh, DOS, UNIX/XENIX/AIX, Windows NT. Computer facilities are available to all students.
**Fees:** $50 computer fee per semester.

**GRADUATE CAREER DATA.** Highest graduate school enrollments: Denver U, U of Colorado.

**PROMINENT ALUMNI/AE.** Ivan Olson, founder, Bercan Fundamentalist Fellowship; Alex Strauch, author of best-selling book on church leadership; Dr. Thomas Graham, director, California State University System; Danny Ee, evangelist and leader, Youth for Christ; Duncan Wilkie, founder, FCFFI (Christian Firefighters); Bert Banzhaf, Campus for Christ in South Africa.

# Colorado College

**Colorado Springs, CO 80903** **719 389-6000**

**1993-94 Costs.** Tuition: $15,942. Room: $2,006. Board: $1,970. Fees, books, misc. academic expenses (school's estimate): $570.
**Enrollment.** Undergraduates: 922 men, 965 women (full-time). Freshman class: 3,207 applicants, 1,577 accepted, 490 enrolled. Graduate enrollment: 7 men, 23 women.
**Test score averages/ranges.** Range of SAT scores of middle 50%: 510-610 verbal, 560-670 math. Range of ACT scores of middle 50%: 25-29 composite.
**Faculty.** 152 full-time; 48 part-time. 95% of faculty holds highest degree in specific field. Student/faculty ratio: 13 to 1.
**Selectivity rating.** Highly competitive.

**PROFILE.** Colorado College, founded in 1874, is a private, liberal arts college. Its 90-acre campus is located at the foot of the Rocky Mountains in Colorado Springs.

**Accreditation:** NCACS. Professionally accredited by the National Association of Schools of Music.
**Religious orientation:** Colorado College is nonsectarian; no religious requirements.
**Library:** Collections totaling over 480,000 volumes, 1,600 periodical subscriptions, and 20,000 microform items.
**Special facilities/museums:** Herbarium, sound studio, graphics workstations, telescope, electron microscope, Fourier transform nuclear magnetic resonance spectrometer.
**Athletic facilities:** Gymnasiums, weight room, basketball, racquetball, squash, and tennis courts, tracks, swimming pool, ice rink, intramural and soccer fields.

**STUDENT BODY. Undergraduate profile:** 30% are state residents; 12% are transfers. 2.9% Asian-American, 2.3% Black, 5.2% Hispanic, 1.5% Native American, 74.9% White, 13.2% Other. Average age of undergraduates is 20.
**Freshman profile:** 4% of freshmen who took SAT scored 700 or over on verbal, 14% scored 700 or over on math; 35% scored 600 or over on verbal, 59% scored 600 or over on math; 81% scored 500 or over on verbal, 92% scored 500 or over on math; 98% scored 400 or over on verbal, 99% scored 400 or over on math; 100% scored 300 or over on verbal, 100% scored 300 or over on math. 88% of accepted applicants took SAT; 57% took ACT. 72% of freshmen come from public schools.
**Undergraduate achievement:** 92% of fall 1992 freshmen returned for fall 1993 term. 71% of entering class graduated. 30% of students who completed a degree program immediately went on to graduate study.
**Foreign students:** 50 students are from out of the country. Countries represented include Canada, China, Japan, Mexico, Spain, and Sweden; 18 in all.

**PROGRAMS OF STUDY. Degrees:** B.A.
**Majors:** Anthropology, Art, Biochemistry, Biology, Chemistry, Classics, Classics/International Affairs, Comparative Literature, Dance, Drama, Economics, English, Environmental Geology, French, French/Romance Languages, Geology, Geology/International Affairs, German, History, History/Philosophy, History/Political Science, Liberal Arts/Sciences, Mathematics, Mathematics/Computer Science, Medical Technology, Music, Philosophy, Philosophy/Political Science, Physics, Political Economy, Political Science, Political Science/International Affairs, Psychology, Religion, Sociology, Spanish.
**Distribution of degrees:** The majors with the highest enrollment are English, biology, and economics; dance, French/Romance languages, and philosophy/political science have the lowest.
**Requirements:** General education requirement.
**Special:** Thematic minors offered. Programs offered in American ethnic, Asian-Pacific, Latin American, North American Russian, Southwest, environmental, urban, and women's studies, and war and peace in the nuclear age. Courses offered in dance, education, humanities, Italian, physical therapy, and Russian. Off-campus courses and special course sequences may be developed to meet individual needs. Freshman tutorials emphasize writing. Self-designed majors. Independent study. Pass/fail grading option. Internships. Cooperative education programs. Graduate school at which undergraduates may take graduate-level courses. Preprofessional programs in law, medicine, veterinary science, and dentistry. 2-2 medical technology and nursing programs with Rush U. 3-2 engineering programs with Columbia U, Rensselaer Polytech Inst, U of Southern California, and Washington U. 3-2 forestry and environmental studies program with Duke U. Six-year B.A./J.D. program with Columbia U. Member of Associated Colleges of the Midwest. Washington Semester. Oak Ridge Lab Science Semester (Tennessee), Newberry Library Program in the Humanities (Illinois), Urban Studies Program (Chicago), Wilderness Field Station Program (Wisconsin). Teacher certification in elementary and secondary education. Certification in specific subject areas. Exchange programs abroad in England (U of Manchester), Germany (U of Goettingen, U of Regensburg), and Japan (Kansai Gaidai U). Study abroad also in China, Costa Rica, the Czech Republic, England, Hong Kong, India, Italy, Mexico, Russia, Zimbabwe, and other countries. ROTC at U of Colorado at Colorado Springs.

**Honors:** Phi Beta Kappa.
**Academic Assistance:** Nonremedial tutoring.

**STUDENT LIFE. Housing:** All students except seniors must live on campus. Coed, women's, and men's dorms. Fraternity housing. On-campus married-student housing. 68% of students live in college housing.
**Services and counseling/handicapped student services:** Placement services. Health service. Counseling services for minority students. Birth control, personal, and psychological counseling. Career and academic guidance services. Religious counseling.
**Campus organizations:** Undergraduate student government. Student newspaper (Catalyst, published once/week). Literary magazine. Yearbook. Radio station. Collegium Musicum, chamber choir, ensemble, theatre and dance workshops, film series committee, outdoor recreation groups, Feminist Collective, Bisexual/Gay/Lesbian Alliance, environmental action group, community service center, 60 organizations in all. Four fraternities, all with chapter houses; four sororities, all with chapter houses. 20% of men join a fraternity. 20% of women join a sorority.
**Religious organizations:** Chavarim, Intervarsity Christian Fellowship, Chapel Council.
**Minority/foreign student organizations:** Black Student Union, Native American Association, MEChA, Hawaii-ti Club, Asian American Student Union. International Student Organization.

**ATHLETICS. Physical education requirements:** None.
**Intercollegiate competition:** 30% of students participate. Baseball (M), basketball (M), cross-country (M,W), diving (M,W), football (M), golf (M), ice hockey (M), lacrosse (M), soccer (M,W), swimming (M,W), tennis (M,W), track (indoor) (M,W), track (outdoor) (M,W), track and field (indoor) (M,W), track and field (outdoor) (M,W), volleyball (W). Member of ISL, NCAA Division I for men's ice hockey and women's soccer, NCAA Division III, RMIGA, Rocky Mountain Intercollegiate Lacrosse Association, Rocky Mountain Intercollegiate Ski Conference, Rocky Mountain Intercollegiate Soccer League, Western Collegiate Hockey Association.
**Intramural and club sports:** 60% of students participate. Intramural badminton, basketball, flag football, ice hockey, pickleball, racquetball, soccer, softball, tennis, track, ultimate frisbee, volleyball. Men's club Alpine skiing, cycling, field hockey, ice hockey, rugby, squash, volleyball. Women's club Alpine skiing, cycling, field hockey, ice hockey, lacrosse, soccer, squash.

**ADMISSIONS. Academic basis for candidate selection** (in order of priority): Secondary school record, class rank, standardized test scores, essay, school's recommendation.
**Nonacademic basis for candidate selection:** Particular talent or ability is emphasized. Character and personality and extracurricular participation are important. Geographical distribution and alumni/ae relationship are considered.
**Requirements:** Graduation from secondary school is recommended; GED is accepted. 16 secondary school units required. SAT or ACT is required. Campus visit recommended. No off-campus interviews.
**Procedure:** Take SAT or ACT by December of 12th year. Application deadline is January 15. Notification of admission by April 15. Reply is required by May 1. $100 nonrefundable tuition deposit. $125 room deposit, refundable until July 1. Freshmen accepted in terms other than fall.
**Special programs:** Admission may be deferred one year. Credit and/or placement may be granted through CEEB Advanced Placement exams for scores of 3 or higher. Early entrance/early admission program.
**Transfer students:** Transfer students accepted for terms other than fall. In fall 1993, 12% of all new students were transfers into all classes. 330 transfer applications were received, 112 were accepted. Application deadline is April 1 for fall; November 1 for spring. Lowest course grade accepted is "C." At least eight units (one year) must be completed at the college to receive degree.
**Admissions contact:** Terrance K. Swenson, M.A., Dean of Admissions and Financial Aid. 719 389-6344.

**FINANCIAL AID. Available aid:** Pell grants, SEOG, state scholarships and grants, school scholarships and grants, academic merit scholarships, and athletic scholarships. Perkins Loans (NDSL), PLUS, Stafford Loans (GSL), and SLS. Knight Tuition Plans, AMS, and deferred payment plan.
**Financial aid statistics:** 10% of aid is not need-based. In 1993-94, 78% of all undergraduate applicants received aid; 79% of freshman applicants. Average amounts of aid awarded freshmen: Scholarships and grants, $10,300; loans, $2,780.
**Supporting data/closing dates:** FAFSA/FAF: Priority filing date is February 15. Income tax forms: Priority filing date is March 1. Notification of awards begins April 1.
**Financial aid contact:** James Swanson, Director of Financial Aid. 719 389-6651.

**STUDENT EMPLOYMENT.** College Work/Study Program. Institutional employment. 42% of full-time undergraduates work on campus during school year. Students may expect to earn an average of $1,200 during school year. Off-campus part-time employment opportunities rated "fair."

**COMPUTER FACILITIES.** 190 IBM/IBM-compatible, Macintosh/Apple, and RISC-/UNIX-based microcomputers. Students may access Digital, IBM, Prime minicomputer/mainframe systems, BITNET, Internet. Residence halls may be equipped with networked microcomputers. Computer languages and software packages include BASIC, C, FORTRAN, LISP, Multiplan, Paradox, QuattroPro, Turbo Pascal, WordPerfect; statistical packages. Computer facilities are available to all students.
**Fees:** None.
**Hours:** 8 AM-midn. for some; 8 AM-2 AM for some; 24 hours for others.

**GRADUATE CAREER DATA.** Graduate school percentages: 5% enter law school. 5% enter medical school. 3% enter graduate business programs. 16% enter graduate arts and sciences programs.

**PROMINENT ALUMNI/AE.** William I. Spencer, retired president and CAO, Citicorp and Citibank; Harold E. Berg, retired chairperson of the board and CEO, Getty Oil; Glenna Goodacre, artist, creator of Women's Vietnam Memorial; Donna Wolf Steigerwaldt, chairperson of the board and CEO, Jockey International.

# Colorado School of Mines

**Golden, CO 80401-9952** **303 273-3000**

**1993-94 Costs.** Tuition: $4,100 (state residents), $11,360 (out-of-state). Room & board: $4,050. Fees, books, misc. academic expenses (school's estimate): $1,104.
**Enrollment.** Undergraduates: 1,585 men, 483 women (full-time). Freshman class: 1,494 applicants, 1,210 accepted, 495 enrolled. Graduate enrollment: 774 men, 197 women.
**Test score averages/ranges.** Average SAT scores: 550 verbal, 650 math. Range of SAT scores of middle 50%: 485-615 verbal, 590-710 math. Average ACT scores: 28 composite. Range of ACT scores of middle 50%: 26-31 composite.
**Faculty.** 175 full-time; 25 part-time. 90% of faculty holds doctoral degree. Student/faculty ratio: 14 to 1.
**Selectivity rating.** Highly competitive.

**PROFILE.** The Colorado School of Mines, founded in 1874, is a public college of engineering and science studies. Its 207-acre campus is located in Golden, 20 miles west of Denver.

**Accreditation:** NCACS. Professionally accredited by the Accreditation Board for Engineering and Technology.
**Religious orientation:** Colorado School of Mines is nonsectarian; no religious requirements.
**Library:** Collections totaling over 395,000 volumes, 2,500 periodical subscriptions, and 2,600 microform items.
**Special facilities/museums:** Geology museum, experimental mine, field camps, geophysical lab, energy research institute, other research institutes.
**Athletic facilities:** Gymnasium, swimming pool, sauna, field house, weight and wrestling rooms, racquetball and tennis courts, athletic fields, tracks.

**STUDENT BODY. Undergraduate profile:** 69% are state residents; 18% are transfers. 3% Asian-American, 2% Black, 5% Hispanic, 1% Native American, 82% White, 7% Other. Average age of undergraduates is 20.
**Freshman profile:** 1% of freshmen who took SAT scored 700 or over on verbal, 10% scored 700 or over on math; 12% scored 600 or over on verbal, 80% scored 600 or over on math; 77% scored 500 or over on verbal, 100% scored 500 or over on math; 99% scored 400 or over on verbal; 100% scored 300 or over on verbal. 25% of freshmen who took ACT scored 30 or over on composite; 95% scored 24 or over on composite; 100% scored 18 or over on composite. Majority of accepted applicants took SAT. 85% of freshmen come from public schools.
**Undergraduate achievement:** 85% of fall 1992 freshmen returned for fall 1993 term. 35% of entering class graduated. 15% of students who completed a degree program went on to graduate study within one year.
**Foreign students:** 202 students are from out of the country. Countries represented include China, Indonesia, Malaysia, Saudi Arabia, United Arab Emirates, and Venezuela; 67 in all.

**PROGRAMS OF STUDY. Degrees:** B.S.
**Majors:** Chemical Engineering, Chemistry, Engineering, Geological Engineering, Geophysical Engineering, Mathematics, Metallurgical/Materials Engineering, Mining Engineering, Petroleum Engineering, Physics.
**Distribution of degrees:** The majors with the highest enrollment are engineering, chemical engineering, and petroleum engineering; mining engineering, geophysical engineering, and chemistry have the lowest.
**Requirements:** General education requirement.
**Academic regulations:** Minimum 2.0 GPA must be maintained.
**Special:** Minors offered in computer science, environmental science, mineral economics, and various areas of engineering. Engineering major includes civil, electrical, and mechanical concentrations. Courses offered in area studies, economics, English, German, history, philosophy, psychology, Russian, sociology, and Spanish. Double majors. Dual degrees. Accelerated study. Cooperative education programs. Graduate school at which undergraduates may take graduate-level courses. Host school for 2-2 and 3-2 engineering programs with Adams State Coll, Comm Coll of Denver, Fort Lewis Coll, Front Range Comm Coll, and Mesa State Coll. Professional degrees offered in science and engineering; require one year beyond B.S. degree. Exchange program abroad in Austria (Mining U of Leoben) and Sweden (Lulea U). ROTC. AFROTC at U of Colorado at Boulder.
**Honors:** Honors program. Honor societies.
**Academic Assistance:** Remedial reading, writing, math, and study skills.

**STUDENT LIFE. Housing:** Students may live on or off campus. Coed and men's dorms. Sorority and fraternity housing. Off-campus privately-owned housing. On-campus married-student housing. 24% of students live in college housing.
**Social atmosphere:** According to the editor of the student newspaper, "On-campus events are limited. Off campus, there are a wide variety of social and cultural events happening year-round." Popular campus events include Engineers' Day, Homecoming, The Big Event, Oktoberfest, and Greek Golf. Favorite off-campus gathering spots include Jose O'Shea's, the Ace, the Golden Eagle, the Mercantile, and Kenrow's.
**Services and counseling/handicapped student services:** Placement services. Health service. Day care. Counseling services for minority, military, and veteran students. Birth control, personal, and psychological counseling. Career and academic guidance services. Religious counseling. Physically disabled student services. Notetaking services. Tutors. Reader services for the blind.

**Campus organizations:** Undergraduate student government. Student newspaper (Oredigger, published once/week). Literary magazine. Yearbook. Bands, mixed chorus, "M" Club, Mines Flyfishers, Little Theatre, science fiction club, professional societies, 40 organizations in all. Seven fraternities, all with chapter houses; two sororities, all with chapter houses. 19% of men join a fraternity. 20% of women join a sorority.

**Religious organizations:** Agape House, Baptist Student Union, Chi Alpha, Christian Science Organization, Intervarsity Christian Fellowship, MINT, Newman Club, Sonlight Fellowship.

**Minority/foreign student organizations:** American Indian Society for Science and Engineering, National Society of Black Engineers, Society of Hispanic Professional Engineers. Asian Student Association, International Council, Muslim Student Association.

**ATHLETICS. Physical education requirements:** Four semesters of physical education required.

**Intercollegiate competition:** 27% of students participate. Baseball (M), basketball (M,W), cross-country (M,W), diving (M,W), football (M), golf (M), lacrosse (M), soccer (M), softball (W), swimming (M,W), tennis (M), track (indoor) (M,W), track (outdoor) (M,W), track and field (indoor) (M,W), track and field (outdoor) (M,W), volleyball (W), wrestling (M). Member of NCAA Division II, Rocky Mountain Athletic Conference.

**Intramural and club sports:** 62% of students participate. Intramural badminton, basketball, cross-country, flag football, frisbee, racquetball, soccer, softball, swimming, tennis, track, volleyball, wrestling. Men's club rugby. Women's club soccer.

**ADMISSIONS. Academic basis for candidate selection** (in order of priority): Secondary school record, class rank, standardized test scores, school's recommendation, essay.

**Nonacademic basis for candidate selection:** Extracurricular participation, geographical distribution, and alumni/ae relationship are considered.

**Requirements:** Graduation from secondary school is required; GED is accepted. 16 units and the following program of study are required: 4 units of English, 4 units of math, 3 units of lab science, 2 units of social studies, 3 units of academic electives. Rank in top third of secondary school class recommended. Conditional admission possible for applicants not meeting standard requirements. SAT or ACT is required. Campus visit and interview recommended. Off-campus interviews available with an alumni representative.

**Procedure:** Take SAT or ACT by December 1 of 12th year. Visit college for interview by April 1 of 12th year. Suggest filing application by April 1. Application deadline is June 1. Notification of admission on rolling basis. Reply is required by May 1. $50 refundable room deposit. $50 room deposit, half of which is refundable until July 1. Freshmen accepted in terms other than fall.

**Special programs:** Admission may be deferred one year. Credit and/or placement may be granted through CEEB Advanced Placement exams for scores of 4 or higher. Credit and placement may be granted through challenge exams. Early entrance/early admission program. Concurrent enrollment program.

**Transfer students:** Transfer students accepted for terms other than fall. In fall 1993, 18% of all new students were transfers into all classes. 240 transfer applications were received, 161 were accepted. Application deadline is August 1 for fall; December 15 for spring. Minimum 2.5 GPA required. Lowest course grade accepted is "C." At least 30 semester hours must be completed at the institute to receive degree.

**Admissions contact:** Bill Young, M.S., Director of Enrollment Management. 303 273-3220.

**FINANCIAL AID. Available aid:** Pell grants, SEOG, state scholarships and grants, school scholarships and grants, private scholarships, ROTC scholarships, academic merit scholarships, and athletic scholarships. Perkins Loans (NDSL), PLUS, Stafford Loans (GSL), state loans, school loans, private loans, and SLS. Knight Tuition Plans and AMS.

**Financial aid statistics:** 25% of aid is not need-based. In 1993-94, 95% of all undergraduate applicants received aid; 95% of freshman applicants. Average amounts of aid awarded freshmen: Scholarships and grants, $3,685; loans, $3,470.

**Supporting data/closing dates:** FAFSA/FAF: Priority filing date is March 1; accepted on rolling basis. School's own aid application: Priority filing date is March 1; accepted on rolling basis. Notification of awards begins April 1.

**Financial aid contact:** Roger A. Koester, M.B.A., Director of Financial Aid. 303 273-3301.

**STUDENT EMPLOYMENT.** College Work/Study Program. Institutional employment. 30% of full-time undergraduates work on campus during school year. Students may expect to earn an average of $800 during school year. Off-campus part-time employment opportunities rated "fair."

**COMPUTER FACILITIES.** 250 IBM/IBM-compatible, Macintosh/Apple, and RISC-/UNIX-based microcomputers; 175 are networked. Students may access Digital, IBM minicomputer/mainframe systems, BITNET, Internet. Residence halls may be equipped with networked terminals. Client/LAN operating systems include Apple/Macintosh, DOS, UNIX/XENIX/AIX. Computer languages and software packages include AutoCAD, BASIC, C, Excel, FORTRAN, Harvard Graphics, Lotus 1-2-3, MINITAB, Modula 2, SPSS, Turbo Pascal, Word, WordPerfect, Z. Computer facilities are available to all students.

**Fees:** Computer fee is included in tuition/fees.

**Hours:** 7 AM-midn. (M-F); 9 AM-5 PM (Sa); 9 AM-midn. (Su).

**GRADUATE CAREER DATA.** Graduate school percentages: 1% enter law school. 1% enter medical school. 2% enter graduate business programs. 85% of graduates choose careers in business and industry. Companies and businesses that hire graduates: Dow Chemical, Exxon, US West, Environmental Scientists and Engineering, Inc.

**PROMINENT ALUMNI/AE.** William Erickson, Colorado supreme court justice; Robert Waterman, author and consultant; Donald Miller, president, Gates Corp; Harry Conger, president, Homestake Mining.

# Colorado State University

**Fort Collins, CO 80523** **303 491-1101**

**1994-95 Costs.** Tuition: $2,123 (state residents), $8,413 (out-of-state). Room & board: $3,886-$4,224. Fees, books, misc. academic expenses (school's estimate): $1,014.

**Enrollment.** Undergraduates: 8,098 men, 7,550 women (full-time). Freshman class: 8,294 applicants, 5,799 accepted, 2,225 enrolled. Graduate enrollment: 2,005 men, 1,633 women.

**Test score averages/ranges.** Average SAT scores: 472 verbal, 539 math. Range of SAT scores of middle 50%: 410-530 verbal, 470-670 math. Average ACT scores: 24 composite. Range of ACT scores of middle 50%: 22-26 composite.

**Faculty.** 1,019 full-time. 84% of faculty holds doctoral degree. Student/faculty ratio: 13 to 1.

**Selectivity rating.** Competitive.

**PROFILE.** Colorado State is a public university. Founded in 1870, it became a land-grant college in 1879, and was granted university status in 1957. Programs are offered through the Colleges of Agricultural Sciences; Applied Human Sciences; Arts, Humanities, and Social Sciences; Business; Engineering; Forestry and Natural Resources; Natural Sciences; and Veterinary Medicine and Biomedical Sciences. Its 833-acre main campus is located at the foot of the Rocky Mountains, in Fort Collins, 65 miles north of Denver.

**Accreditation:** NCACS. Professionally accredited by the Accreditation Board for Engineering and Technology, the Accrediting Council on Education in Journalism and Mass Communication, the American Assembly of Collegiate Schools of Business, the American Council for Construction Education, the American Medical Association (CAHEA), the American Psychological Association, the American Society of Landscape Architects, the American Speech-Language-Hearing Association, the American Veterinary Medical Association, the Council on Social Work Education, the National Association of Schools of Music, the National Council for Accreditation of Teacher Education, the Society of American Foresters.

**Religious orientation:** Colorado State University is nonsectarian; no religious requirements.

**Library:** Collections totaling over 1,804,316 volumes, 20,853 periodical subscriptions, and 2,500,124 microform items.

**Athletic facilities:** Gymnasiums, badminton, basketball, racquetball, tennis, and volleyball courts, track, swimming pools, aerobics and weight rooms, athletic fields.

**STUDENT BODY. Undergraduate profile:** 78% are state residents; 49% are transfers. 2% Asian-American, 2% Black, 5% Hispanic, 1% Native American, 87% White, 3% Other. Average age of undergraduates is 22.

**Freshman profile:** 69% of accepted applicants took SAT; 77% took ACT.

**Foreign students:** 175 students are from out of the country. Countries represented include China, India, Japan, Korea, Saudi Arabia, and Taiwan; 93 in all.

**PROGRAMS OF STUDY. Degrees:** B.A., B.F.A., B.S.

**Majors:** Accounting, Actuarial Science, Adapted-Corrective, Adult Technical Education, Agricultural Biotechnology, Agricultural Business, Agricultural Economics, Agricultural Education, Agricultural Engineering, Agricultural/Natural Resources Journalism, Agronomic Production Management, Agronomy, Animal Science, Anthropology, Apparel Design/Production, Apparel/Merchandising, Applied Mathematics, Applied Physics, Art, Art Education, Art History, Arts/Humanities, Bioagricultural Science, Biochemistry, Biological Sciences, Botany, Business Administration, Chemical Engineering, Chemistry, Civil Engineering, Coaching, Commercial Recreation/Tourism, Computer Engineering, Computer Science, Construction Management, Consumer Sciences, Creative Writing, Crop Science, Dance, Dietetics, Drawing, Economics, Electrical Engineering, Electronic Reporting, Engineering Science, English, Entomology, Environmental Health, Environmental Soil Science, Equine Science, Exercise/Sport Science, Farm/Ranch Management, Fibers, Finance/Real Estate, Fishery Biology, Floriculture, Food Industry Management, Food Science/Technology, Forest Biology, Forest Fire Science, Forest Management, Forestry, Forestry/Business, French, General Business, Geology, German, Graphic Design, History, Home Economics, Horticultural Business Management, Horticultural Food Crops, Horticulture, Human Development/Family Studies, Human Nutrition/Dietetics, Industrial Sciences/Technology, Industrial Technology, Industrial Training, Industry, Information Systems, Interior Design, International Agronomy, Land Rehabilitation, Landscape Architecture, Landscape Design/Construction, Landscape Horticulture, Language, Liberal Arts, Management, Marketing, Mathematics, Mathematics Education, Mechanical Engineering, Merchandising, Metalsmithing, Microbiology, Music, Music Education, Music Performance, Music Therapy, Natural Resource Economics, Natural Resources Management, News/Editorial, Nursery/Landscape Management, Nutrition/Fitness, Nutritional Sciences, Occupational Therapy, Painting, Performing Arts, Philosophy, Philosophy/Bioethics, Philosophy/Religion, Photo Image Making, Physical Science, Physics, Plant Pathology, Plant Protection, Political Science, Pottery, Printmaking, Psychology, Public Relations, Range Ecology, Range/Forest Management, Recreation Resource Administration, Recreation Resources Administration, Recreation Resources Management, Resource Interpretation, Restaurant Management, Science, Sculpture, Social Sciences, Social Studies Teaching, Social Work, Sociology, Soil Resources/Conservation, Spanish, Speech/Broadcasting, Speech Communication, Sports Medicine, Statistics, Studio Art, Teacher Education, Technical Journalism, Technical/Specialized Journalism, Technology Education, Theatre, Trade/Industrial Education, Turf Management, Watershed Sciences, Wellness Program Management, Wildlife Biology, Wood Science/Technology, Zoology.

**Distribution of degrees:** The majors with the highest enrollment are general business, social sciences/biological sciences, and human development/family studies; agricultural journalism and statistics have the lowest.

**Requirements:** General education requirement.
**Academic regulations:** Minimum 2.0 GPA must be maintained.
**Special:** Minors offered in over 50 fields. Interdisciplinary programs in biotechnology, conservation biology, criminal justice, gerontology, youth agency administration and in Asian, Hispano-American, Central European, Latin American, religious, Russian, and women's studies. Self-designed majors. Double majors. Dual degrees. Independent study. Pass/fail grading option. Internships. Cooperative education programs. Graduate school at which undergraduates may take graduate-level courses. Preprofessional programs in law, medicine, veterinary science, pharmacy, dentistry, and nursing. National External Degree Consortium. Teacher certification in elementary and secondary education. Certification in specific subject areas. Study abroad possible. ROTC and AFROTC.
**Honors:** Phi Beta Kappa. Honors program.
**Academic Assistance:** Nonremedial tutoring.

**STUDENT LIFE. Housing:** All unmarried students under age 21 must live on campus unless living near campus with relatives. Coed dorms. Sorority and fraternity housing. On-campus married-student housing. 25% of students live in college housing.
**Social atmosphere:** The hot spots for students are Lory Student Center, Paris on the Poudre, Washington's Bar & Grill, C.B., and POH's. Greeks have widespread influence on campus. Homecoming is the most popular social event for students. The student newspaper reports that most social life revolves around drinking, mountain climbing, and snow activities.
**Services and counseling/handicapped student services:** Placement services. Health service. Women's center. Day care. Counseling services for minority, military, veteran, and older students. Birth control, personal, and psychological counseling. Career and academic guidance services. Physically disabled student services. Learning disabled services. Notetaking services. Tape recorders. Tutors. Reader services for the blind.
**Campus organizations:** Undergraduate student government. Student newspaper (The Rocky Mountain Collegian, published once/day). Yearbook. Radio station. Political and recreational groups, tutorial groups, theatre, Special Events Board, 300 organizations in all. 11 fraternities, all with chapter houses; nine sororities, all with chapter houses. 6% of men join a fraternity. 6% of women join a sorority.
**Religious organizations:** Numerous religious groups.
**Minority/foreign student organizations:** Black Student Services, Asian-American Student Services, Native American Student Services, Hispanic Student Services. Foreign Student Office.

**ATHLETICS. Physical education requirements:** Two semester hours of physical education required.
**Intercollegiate competition:** 2% of students participate. Basketball (M,W), cross-country (M,W), diving (W), football (M), golf (M,W), swimming (W), tennis (M,W), track and field (indoor) (M,W), track and field (outdoor) (M,W). Member of NCAA Division I, NCAA Division I-A for football, Western Athletic Conference.
**Intramural and club sports:** 50% of students participate. Intramural basketball, flag football, golf, inner-tube water polo, racquetball, soccer, softball, tennis, triathlon, volleyball. Men's club Alpine skiing, bowling, cricket, cycling, fencing, ice hockey, lacrosse, martial arts, Nordic skiing, polo, racquetball, rodeo, rugby, soccer, ultimate frisbee, volleyball, water polo, wrestling. Women's club Alpine skiing, bowling, cycling, fencing, lacrosse, martial arts, Nordic skiing, polo, racquetball, rodeo, rugby, soccer, ultimate frisbee.

**ADMISSIONS. Academic basis for candidate selection** (in order of priority): Secondary school record, class rank, standardized test scores, essay, school's recommendation.
**Nonacademic basis for candidate selection:** Extracurricular participation, particular talent or ability, geographical distribution, and alumni/ae relationship are considered.
**Requirements:** Graduation from secondary school is required; GED is accepted. No specific distribution of secondary school units required. Minimum combined SAT score of 950 (composite ACT score of 23), rank in top third of secondary school class, and minimum 3.0 GPA recommended. 4 units of math (including 2 algebra, 1 geometry, 1/2 trigonometry), 1 unit of chemistry, and 1 unit of another science (preferably physics) recommended of engineering program applicants. SAT or ACT is required. Off-campus interviews available with an admissions representative.
**Procedure:** Take SAT or ACT by January of 12th year. Suggest filing application by July 1; no deadline. Notification of admission on rolling basis. Reply is required by May 1. $150 refundable room deposit. Freshmen accepted in terms other than fall.
**Special programs:** Admission may be deferred one term. Credit and/or placement may be granted through CEEB Advanced Placement exams for scores of 3 or higher. Credit and/or placement may be granted through CLEP general and subject exams. Credit and placement may be granted through DANTES and challenge exams, and military experience. Concurrent enrollment program.
**Transfer students:** Transfer students accepted for terms other than fall. In fall 1992, 49% of all new students were transfers into all classes. 3,359 transfer applications were received, 3,039 were accepted. Application deadline is rolling for fall; rolling for spring. Minimum 2.0 GPA recommended. Lowest course grade accepted is "C." Maximum number of transferable credits is 64 semester hours. At least 32 semester hours must be completed at the university to receive degree.
**Admissions contact:** Mary Ontiveros, M.Ed., Director of Admissions. 303 491-6909.

**FINANCIAL AID. Available aid:** Pell grants, SEOG, state scholarships and grants, school scholarships and grants, private scholarships, ROTC scholarships, academic merit scholarships, and athletic scholarships. Perkins Loans (NDSL), PLUS, Stafford Loans (GSL), Health Professions Loans, and SLS.
**Financial aid statistics:** 20% of aid is not need-based. In 1992-93, 65% of all undergraduate applicants received aid; 80% of freshman applicants.
**Supporting data/closing dates:** FAFSA/SINGLEFILE: Accepted on rolling basis. Notification of awards on rolling basis.
**Financial aid contact:** Kay Jacks, M.Ed., Director of Financial Aid. 303 491-6321.

**STUDENT EMPLOYMENT.** College Work/Study Program. Institutional employment. Off-campus part-time employment opportunities rated "good."

**COMPUTER FACILITIES.** 2,000 IBM/IBM-compatible and Macintosh/Apple microcomputers; all are networked. Students may access AT&T, Data General, Digital, Hewlett-Packard, IBM, NCR, SUN minicomputer/mainframe systems, BITNET, Internet. Residence halls may be equipped with stand-alone microcomputers, networked microcomputers, modems. Client/LAN operating systems include UNIX/XENIX/AIX. Numerous computer languages and software programs available. Computer facilities are available to all students.
**Fees:** None.
**Hours:** 8 AM-midn.

**PROMINENT ALUMNI/AE.** Roy Romer, governor of Colorado; Trudi Morrison, member of President Reagan's staff; Robert Anderson, chairperson and CEO, Rockwell International; Bill Parzybock, vice-president, Hewlett-Packard; Mary Cleave, NASA astronaut.

# Colorado Tech

**Colorado Springs, CO 80907** **719 598-0200**

**1994-95 Costs.** Tuition: $5,850. Housing: None. Fees, books, misc. academic expenses (school's estimate): $1,930.
**Enrollment.** Undergraduates: 398 men, 76 women (full-time). Freshman class: 421 applicants, 364 accepted, 326 enrolled. Graduate enrollment: 249 men, 54 women.
**Test score averages/ranges.** Average SAT scores: 500 verbal, 600 math.
**Faculty.** 31 full-time; 39 part-time. 38% of faculty holds doctoral degree. Student/faculty ratio: 19 to 1.
**Selectivity rating.** More competitive.

**PROFILE.** Colorado Tech, founded in 1965, is a private institution offering career-oriented engineering, computer, and technology studies. Its five-acre campus is located in the business and industrial section of Colorado Springs.

**Accreditation:** NCACS. Professionally accredited by the Accreditation Board for Engineering and Technology.
**Religious orientation:** Colorado Tech is nonsectarian; no religious requirements.
**Library:** Collections totaling over 11,050 volumes, 350 periodical subscriptions, and 15,000 microform items.

**STUDENT BODY. Undergraduate profile:** 95% are state residents; 78% are transfers. 3% Asian-American, 6% Black, 5% Hispanic, 1% Native American, 72% White, 13% Other. Average age of undergraduates is 29.
**Freshman profile:** 3% of freshmen who took SAT scored 700 or over on verbal, 2% scored 700 or over on math; 20% scored 600 or over on verbal, 17% scored 600 or over on math; 100% scored 500 or over on verbal, 100% scored 500 or over on math. 3% of freshmen who took ACT scored 30 or over on composite; 100% scored 24 or over on composite. Majority of accepted applicants took SAT.
**Undergraduate achievement:** 86% of fall 1992 freshmen returned for fall 1993 term. 5% of students who completed a degree program immediately went on to graduate study.
**Foreign students:** 36 students are from out of the country. Countries represented include Honduras, Korea, and United Arab Emirates; 14 in all.

**PROGRAMS OF STUDY. Degrees:** B.S.
**Majors:** Computer Engineering, Computer Science, Electrical Engineering, Electronic Engineering Technology, Logistics Systems Management, Systems Management, Telecommunications Electronic Technology.
**Distribution of degrees:** The majors with the highest enrollment are electrical engineering, computer science, and logistics systems management; computer engineering and telecommunication electronic technology have the lowest.
**Requirements:** General education requirement.
**Academic regulations:** Minimum 2.0 GPA must be maintained.
**Special:** Professional certificates available. Associate's degrees offered. Double majors. Dual degrees. Accelerated study. Internships. Cooperative education programs. 2-2 programs in logistics systems management and systems management. ROTC at U of Colorado at Colorado Springs.
**Honors:** Honor societies.

**ADMISSIONS. Academic basis for candidate selection** (in order of priority): Standardized test scores.
**Requirements:** Graduation from secondary school is required; GED is accepted. No specific distribution of secondary school units required. Minimum composite ACT score of 24 (combined SAT score of 1050 with minimum math score of 550) recommended. SAT or ACT is recommended. ACH recommended. Campus visit and interview recommended. No off-campus interviews.
**Procedure:** Application deadline is September. Notification of admission on rolling basis. Reply is required by September. Freshmen accepted in terms other than fall.
**Special programs:** Admission may be deferred one year. Credit and/or placement may be granted through CEEB Advanced Placement exams for scores of 3 or higher. Credit and/or placement may be granted through CLEP general and subject exams. Credit and placement may be granted through DANTES and challenge exams, and military and life experience. Early entrance/early admission program.
**Transfer students:** Transfer students accepted for terms other than fall. In fall 1993, 78% of all new students were transfers into all classes. Application deadline is in September for fall; in December for winter; in March for spring; in June for summer. College transcripts required of all transfer applicants. Lowest course grade accepted is "C." Maximum number of transferable credits is 70 quarter hours from a two-year school and 140 quarter hours from a four-year school. At least 30 quarter hours must be completed at the college to receive degree.
**Admissions contact:** Tom McDonald, Director of Admissions. 719 598-0200.

**FINANCIAL AID. Available aid:** Pell grants, SEOG, state scholarships and grants, school scholarships, ROTC scholarships, and academic merit scholarships. Perkins Loans (NDSL), PLUS, Stafford Loans (GSL), and SLS. Monthly payment plan.
**Financial aid statistics:** In 1993-94, 85% of all undergraduate applicants received aid; 75% of freshman applicants. Average amounts of aid awarded freshmen: Scholarships and grants, $2,500; loans, $2,625.

**Supporting data/closing dates:** FAFSA: Accepted on rolling basis. School's own aid application: Accepted on rolling basis. State aid form: Accepted on rolling basis. Income tax forms: Accepted on rolling basis. Notification of awards on rolling basis.
**Financial aid contact:** Linda Vosler, Director of Financial Aid. 719 598-0200.

# Fort Lewis College

**Durango, CO 81301** **303 247-7010**

**1993-94 Costs.** Tuition: $1,450 (state residents), $6,198 (out-of-state). Room: $1,500. Board: $1,820. Fees, books, misc. academic expenses (school's estimate): $827.
**Enrollment.** Undergraduates: 1,938 men, 1,700 women (full-time). Freshman class: 3,440 applicants, 2,823 accepted, 1,119 enrolled.
**Test score averages/ranges.** Average ACT scores: 21 composite. Range of ACT scores of middle 50%: 20-25 composite.
**Faculty.** 180 full-time; 70 part-time. 87% of faculty holds doctoral degree. Student/faculty ratio: 20 to 1.
**Selectivity rating.** Competitive.

**PROFILE.** Fort Lewis, founded in 1911, is a public, liberal arts college. Programs are offered through the Schools of Arts and Sciences, Business Administration, and Education and the Center of Southwest Studies. Its 250-acre campus is located southwest of Durango's business district, in southern Colorado.

**Accreditation:** NCACS. Professionally accredited by the American Assembly of Collegiate Schools of Business, the National Association of Schools of Music.
**Religious orientation:** Fort Lewis College is nonsectarian; no religious requirements.
**Library:** Collections totaling over 180,000 volumes, 1,525 periodical subscriptions, and 37,466 microform items.
**Special facilities/museums:** Southwest studies center, archaeological dig site.
**Athletic facilities:** Gymnasium, swimming pool, exercise, fitness, training, and weight rooms, sand volleyball courts, football, intramural, soccer, and softball fields, performance lab.
**STUDENT BODY. Undergraduate profile:** 70% are state residents; 24% are transfers. 1% Asian-American, 1% Black, 4% Hispanic, 11% Native American, 78% White, 5% Other. Average age of undergraduates is 20.
**Freshman profile:** 30% of accepted applicants took SAT; 70% took ACT. 85% of freshmen come from public schools.
**Undergraduate achievement:** 65% of fall 1992 freshmen returned for fall 1993 term. 20% of entering class graduated. 25% of students who completed a degree program immediately went on to graduate study.
**Foreign students:** 73 students are from out of the country. Countries represented include Canada, Ecuador, Germany, Japan, Mexico, and the Netherlands; 14 in all.
**PROGRAMS OF STUDY. Degrees:** B.A., B.S.
**Majors:** Accounting, Agribusiness, Agriculture, Anthropology, Art, Athletic Training, Biology, Business Administration, Chemistry, Communication, Computer Science, Computer Science Information Systems, Economics, Elementary Education, Engineering Management, English, Finance, Geology, History, Humanities, International Business, Management, Marketing, Mathematics, Music, Philosophy, Physical Education, Physical Sciences, Physics, Political Science, Psychology, Sociology/Human Services, Southwest Studies, Spanish, Tourism/Resort Management.
**Distribution of degrees:** The majors with the highest enrollment are business administration, English, and psychology; Southwest studies, agriculture, and music have the lowest.
**Requirements:** General education requirement.
**Academic regulations:** Minimum 2.0 GPA must be maintained.
**Special:** Minors offered in some majors. Intercultural program. Four-week special projects in major possible during spring/summer term. Associate's degrees offered. Self-designed majors. Double majors. Independent study. Accelerated study. Internships. Preprofessional programs in law, medicine, veterinary science, pharmacy, and dentistry. Combined engineering/math program with Colorado State U. Member of National Student Exchange (NSE). Teacher certification in early childhood, elementary, secondary, and bilingual/bicultural education. Study abroad in Japan and Mexico.
**Honors:** Honors program.
**Academic Assistance:** Remedial reading, writing, math, and study skills. Nonremedial tutoring.
**STUDENT LIFE. Housing:** Unmarried first-time freshmen under age 21 not living near campus with relatives must live in school housing. Coed, women's, and men's dorms. School-owned/operated apartments. On-campus married-student housing. 37% of students live in college housing.
**Social atmosphere:** Students gather at the snack bar on campus and at the Steamin' Bean Coffee Company, Carver's Bakery, and various bars in Durango. Popular events include Weekend Wipeout (spring celebration), Snowdown (winter celebration), and concerts on campus and in town. "Fort Lewis brags of its cultural diversity but recognizes that it needs to improve racial relationships. Because of the nearby Native American population and our Native American students, we know the importance of acceptance and appreciation of different cultures," reports the student newspaper.
**Services and counseling/handicapped student services:** Placement services. Health service. Day care. Counseling services for minority, veteran, and older students. Birth control, personal, and psychological counseling. Career and academic guidance services. Religious counseling. Physically disabled student services. Learning disabled services. Notetaking services. Tape recorders. Tutors. Reader services for the blind.
**Campus organizations:** Undergraduate student government. Student newspaper (Independent, published once/week). Literary magazine. Radio and TV stations. Chamber singers, concert choir, concert band, marching band, orchestra, theatre program, Outdoor Pursuits Program, United Coalition Against Prejudice; academic, athletic, service, and special-interest groups, 50 organizations in all.
**Religious organizations:** Campus Ambassadors, College Baptists, Latter-Day Saints group, Newman Club, other religious groups.
**Minority/foreign student organizations:** Black Student Union, Hispanic Student Center, Intercultural Center, Keepers of the Sacred Trust (Native American). International Student Club.
**ATHLETICS. Physical education requirements:** Two semesters of physical education required.
**Intercollegiate competition:** 7% of students participate. Basketball (M,W), cheerleading (M,W), cross-country (M,W), football (M), golf (M), soccer (M), softball (W), volleyball (W), wrestling (M). Member of Colorado Athletic Conference, NCAA Division II, Rocky Mountain Athletic Conference Associate Member.
**Intramural and club sports:** 75% of students participate. Intramural aerobic dance, Alpine skiing, basketball, cross-country, cycling, indoor soccer, mountain biking, Nordic skiing, polo, soccer, softball, swimming, tennis, triathlon, volleyball, water polo, wrestling. Men's club Alpine skiing, lacrosse. Women's club Alpine skiing, soccer.
**ADMISSIONS. Academic basis for candidate selection** (in order of priority): Secondary school record, class rank, standardized test scores.
**Nonacademic basis for candidate selection:** Character and personality, extracurricular participation, and particular talent or ability are important.
**Requirements:** Graduation from secondary school is required; GED is accepted. 15 units and the following program of study are required: 4 units of English, 2 units of math, 2 units of science, 2 units of social studies, 2 units of history, 3 units of electives. Minimum composite ACT score of 20 (combined SAT score of 800) and minimum 2.5 GPA generally required, but sliding scale is used and each application is reviewed individually. ACT is required; SAT may be substituted. Campus visit and interview recommended. Off-campus interviews available with admissions and alumni representatives.
**Procedure:** Take SAT or ACT by December of 12th year. Application deadline is June 30. Notification of admission on rolling basis. No set date by which applicants must accept offer. $100 room deposit, refundable until one month prior to beginning of term. Freshmen accepted in terms other than fall.
**Special programs:** Admission may be deferred one year. Credit and/or placement may be granted through CEEB Advanced Placement exams for scores of 3 or higher. Credit and/or placement may be granted through CLEP general and subject exams. Credit may be granted through challenge exams and military experience. Concurrent enrollment program.
**Transfer students:** Transfer students accepted for terms other than fall. In fall 1993, 24% of all new students were transfers into all classes. 1,001 transfer applications were received, 750 were accepted. Application deadline is one month prior to beginning of term for fall; one month prior to beginning of term for spring. Minimum 2.0 GPA required. Lowest course grade accepted is "C." Maximum number of transferable credits is 72 semester hours from a two-year school and 100 semester hours from a four-year school. At least 28 semester hours must be completed at the college to receive degree.
**Admissions contact:** Dean Garland, Director of Admissions. 303 247-7184.
**FINANCIAL AID. Available aid:** Pell grants, SEOG, state scholarships and grants, school scholarships and grants, private scholarships and grants, academic merit scholarships, and athletic scholarships. Perkins Loans (NDSL), PLUS, Stafford Loans (GSL), school loans, private loans, and SLS. Deferred payment plan. Alternative financing plan.
**Financial aid statistics:** In 1993-94, 66% of all undergraduate applicants received aid; 80% of freshman applicants. Average amounts of aid awarded freshmen: Scholarships and grants, $750; loans, $1,700.
**Supporting data/closing dates:** FAFSA: Priority filing date is February 15. Notification of awards on rolling basis.
**Financial aid contact:** Rick Willis, M.A., Director of Financial Aid. 303 247-7142.
**STUDENT EMPLOYMENT.** College Work/Study Program. Institutional employment. 30% of full-time undergraduates work on campus during school year. Students may expect to earn an average of $1,500 during school year. Off-campus part-time employment opportunities rated "excellent."
**COMPUTER FACILITIES.** 120 IBM/IBM-compatible and Macintosh/Apple microcomputers; 40 are networked. Students may access Digital minicomputer/mainframe systems, Internet. Residence halls may be equipped with stand-alone microcomputers, networked terminals. Client/LAN operating systems include Apple/Macintosh. Computer languages and software packages include BASIC, C, COBOL, dBASE, FORTRAN, LISP, Lotus 1-2-3, Microsoft Works, Modula 2, Multinet, Oracle, Pascal, WordPerfect. Computer facilities are available to all students.
**Fees:** None.
**Hours:** 96 hours/week.
**GRADUATE CAREER DATA.** Graduate school percentages: 3% enter law school. 2% enter medical school. 10% enter graduate business programs. 20% enter graduate arts and sciences programs. Highest graduate school enrollments: Colorado State U, U of Colorado. 60% of graduates choose careers in business and industry. Companies and businesses that hire graduates: Arthur Andersen, CIA, FBI, Federal Reserve Bank, K mart, NCR.
**PROMINENT ALUMNI/AE.** Susan Witkin, broadcaster, San Francisco; Scott McInnis, U.S. congressman; Christopher Schauble, news anchor, Michigan.

# Mesa State College

**Grand Junction, CO 81502** **303 248-1020**

**1993-94 Costs.** Tuition: $1,728 (state residents), $4,606 (out-of-state). Room: $1,518. Board: $1,826. Fees, books, misc. academic expenses (school's estimate): $400.
**Enrollment.** Undergraduates: 1,585 men, 1,869 women (full-time). Freshman class: 1,903 applicants, 1,903 accepted, 1,125 enrolled.
**Test score averages/ranges.** Average SAT scores: 407 verbal, 439 math. Average ACT scores: 19 composite.
**Faculty.** 152 full-time; 45 part-time. 50% of faculty holds highest degree in specific field. Student/faculty ratio: 19 to 1.
**Selectivity rating.** Noncompetitive.

**PROFILE.** Mesa State is a multipurpose, public college. Established as a two-year college in 1925, it became a four-year state college in 1988. Programs are offered through the

Schools of Business, Humanities and Fine Arts, Industry and Technology, Natural Sciences and Mathematics, Nursing and Allied Health, and Social and Behavioral Sciences. Its 42-acre campus is located in Grand Junction, in western Colorado.

**Accreditation:** NCACS. Professionally accredited by the American Medical Association (CAHEA), the National League for Nursing.
**Religious orientation:** Mesa State College is nonsectarian; no religious requirements.
**Library:** Collections totaling over 191,000 volumes, 893 periodical subscriptions, and 380,869 microform items.
**Special facilities/museums:** Art gallery, experimental farm, early childhood education center, electron microscopes, television studio.

**STUDENT BODY. Undergraduate profile:** 93% are state residents; 33% are transfers. 1% Asian-American, 1% Black, 5% Hispanic, 1% Native American, 88% White, 4% Other. Average age of undergraduates is 26.
**Freshman profile:** 98% of freshmen come from public schools.
**Undergraduate achievement:** 38% of fall 1992 freshmen returned for fall 1993 term.
**Foreign students:** 87 students are from out of the country. Countries represented include Japan, Malaysia, the Netherlands, Norway, and Saudi Arabia; 30 in all.

**PROGRAMS OF STUDY. Degrees:** B.A., B.Bus.Admin., B.S.
**Majors:** Accounting, Administrative Office Management, Art, Biological/Agricultural Sciences, Biology, Business Administration, Business Computer Information Systems, Business Economics, Computer Science, Economics, Engineering, English, Environmental Restoration/Waste Management, Finance, Geology, History, Human Performance/Wellness, Management, Marketing, Mass Communication, Mathematics, Music, Music Theatre, Nursing, Parks/Recreation Resource Management, Physical/Mathematics Sciences, Physics, Political Science, Psychology, Social Science, Sociology, Theatre.
**Distribution of degrees:** The majors with the highest enrollment are management and accounting; business economics has the lowest.
**Requirements:** General education requirement.
**Academic regulations:** Freshmen must maintain minimum 1.7 GPA; sophomores, 1.9 GPA; juniors, 2.0 GPA; seniors, 2.0 GPA.
**Special:** Certificate programs offered in data processing, dental assisting, electric lineman, emergency medical technician, heavy equipment/diesel mechanics, job entry training, legal secretary, medical office assistant, nursing, office clerical/secretary, and welding. Associate's degrees offered. Self-designed majors. Double majors. Dual degrees. Independent study. Accelerated study. Internships. Member of State Colleges in Colorado consortium. Washington Semester. Teacher certification in early childhood, elementary, and secondary education.
**Honors:** Honors program. Honor societies.
**Academic Assistance:** Remedial reading, writing, math, and study skills. Nonremedial tutoring.

**STUDENT LIFE. Housing:** All freshmen and sophomores under 21 must live on campus. Coed dorms. School-owned/operated apartments. 16% of students live in college housing.
**Social atmosphere:** Students get together at Gladstone's, Blue Moon, The Rose, and Powderhorn Ski Resort. The Student Body Association and the Cultural Awareness Board influence campus life. Homecoming is the most popular event of the year. "Western Colorado is great for sports and outdoors enthusiasts. We enjoy biking, skiing, and fishing," states the editor of the student newspaper.
**Services and counseling/handicapped student services:** Placement services. Health service. Day care. Counseling services for minority and veteran students. Personal and psychological counseling. Career guidance services. Physically disabled student services. Notetaking services. Tape recorders. Reader services for the blind.
**Campus organizations:** Undergraduate student government. Student newspaper (Criterion, published once/week). Literary magazine. Radio station. Concert choir, chamber choir, jazz and string ensembles, drama group, debating, Interresidence Hall Council, Young Democrats, Young Republicans, academic, professional, and special-interest groups, 60 organizations in all.
**Religious organizations:** Baptist Student Union, Bahai Club, Newman Center, Intervarsity Christian Fellowship, Latter-Day Saints Association.
**Minority/foreign student organizations:** Black Student Alliance, Hispanic Student Association, Polynesian Club. International Student Association.

**ATHLETICS. Physical education requirements:** Four credit hours of physical education required (waived for veterans or students over age 25).
**Intercollegiate competition:** 8% of students participate. Baseball (M), basketball (M,W), football (M), softball (W), tennis (M,W), volleyball (W). Member of NCAA Division II, Rocky Mountain Athletic Conference.
**Intramural and club sports:** 20% of students participate. Intramural flag football, hiking, hunting, kayaking, mountain biking, rafting, skiing, soccer, softball, swimming, volleyball. Men's club soccer.

**ADMISSIONS. Academic basis for candidate selection** (in order of priority): Secondary school record, class rank, school's recommendation, standardized test scores, essay.
**Nonacademic basis for candidate selection:** Particular talent or ability is emphasized.
**Requirements:** Graduation from secondary school is required; GED is accepted. No specific distribution of secondary school units required. Minimum composite ACT score of 21 (combined SAT score of 850) and rank in top two-thirds of secondary school class or minimum 2.3 GPA recommended. Nursing and allied health program applicants must apply to specific program. ACT is required; SAT may be substituted. Campus visit recommended. Off-campus interviews available with an admissions representative.
**Procedure:** Take SAT or ACT by January of 12th year. Application deadline is August 15. Notification of admission on rolling basis. No set date by which applicants must accept offer. $100 room deposit, refundable up to 30 days before registration. Freshmen accepted in terms other than fall.
**Special programs:** Admission may be deferred one year. Credit and/or placement may be granted through CEEB Advanced Placement exams for scores of 3 or higher. Credit and/or placement may be granted through CLEP subject exams. Concurrent enrollment program.
**Transfer students:** Transfer students accepted for terms other than fall. In fall 1993, 33% of all new students were transfers into all classes. 733 transfer applications were received, 733 were accepted. Application deadline is August 15 for fall; January 1 for spring; May 1 for summer. Minimum 2.0 GPA required. Lowest course grade accepted is "C." At least 28 semester hours must be completed at the college to receive degree.
**Admissions contact:** Sherri Pe'a, M.A., Director of Admissions. 303 248-1376, 800 921-MESA.

**FINANCIAL AID. Available aid:** Pell grants, SEOG, state scholarships and grants, private scholarships, and athletic scholarships. Perkins Loans (NDSL), PLUS, Stafford Loans (GSL), state loans, school loans, and SLS.
**Financial aid statistics:** In 1993-94, 80% of all undergraduate applicants received aid; 65% of freshman applicants. Average amounts of aid awarded freshmen: Loans, $3,000.
**Supporting data/closing dates:** FAFSA/FAF/FFS: Priority filing date is March 1; accepted on rolling basis. Notification of awards on rolling basis.
**Financial aid contact:** Phillip Swille, M.A., Director of Financial Aid. 303 248-1396.

**STUDENT EMPLOYMENT.** College Work/Study Program. Institutional employment. 15% of full-time undergraduates work on campus during school year. Students may expect to earn an average of $1,400 during school year. Off-campus part-time employment opportunities rated "excellent."

**COMPUTER FACILITIES.** 300 IBM/IBM-compatible and Macintosh/Apple microcomputers; 150 are networked. Students may access AT&T minicomputer/mainframe systems, Internet, CompuServe. Residence halls may be equipped with stand-alone microcomputers. Client/LAN operating systems include Apple/Macintosh, DOS, UNIX/XENIX/AIX. Computer languages and software packages include Ada, BASIC, C, COBOL, FORTRAN, Pascal, Twin 132, WordPerfect; 70 in all. Computer facilities are available to all students.
**Fees:** $13 computer fee per semester.
**Hours:** 8 AM-10:30 PM (M-Th); 8 AM-5 PM (F); 10 AM-3 PM (Sa); 3 PM-10:30 PM (Su).

**PROMINENT ALUMNI/AE.** William Spencer, former chairperson of the board, Citicorp; Dr. Louis Englehart, retired journalism professor; Tony Martin, professional football player; William Ela, district judge; Ted Brumbaugh, public school administrator; Dalton Tannanaka, TV news reporter; Dr. Rey Ingraham, retired professor of dentistry.

# Metropolitan State College of Denver

**Denver, CO 80217-3362 — 303 556-3058**

**1993-94 Costs.** Tuition: $1,344 (state residents), $4,992 (out-of-state). Housing: None. Fees, books, misc. academic expenses (school's estimate): $757.
**Enrollment.** Undergraduates: 4,608 men, 4,877 women (full-time). Freshman class: 4,919 applicants, 4,242 accepted, 2,359 enrolled.
**Test score averages/ranges.** Average SAT scores: 407 verbal, 448 math. Range of SAT scores of middle 50%: 340-460 verbal, 380-500 math. Average ACT scores: 20 composite. Range of ACT scores of middle 50%: 17-22 composite.
**Faculty.** 394 full-time; 437 part-time. 74% of faculty holds doctoral degree. Student/faculty ratio: 24 to 1.
**Selectivity rating.** Less competitive.

**PROFILE.** Metropolitan State, founded in 1965, is a multipurpose, public college. Programs are offered through the Schools of Business; Letters, Arts, and Sciences; and Professional Studies; Institutes for Intercultural Studies and Services and Women's Studies and Services. Its 169-acre campus is located in Denver.

**Accreditation:** NCACS. Professionally accredited by the Accreditation Board for Engineering and Technology, the National Association of Schools of Music, the National Council for Accreditation of Teacher Education, the National League for Nursing, the National Recreation and Park Association.
**Religious orientation:** Metropolitan State College of Denver is nonsectarian; no religious requirements.
**Library:** Collections totaling over 699,976 volumes, 3,347 periodical subscriptions, and 644,956 microform items.
**Special facilities/museums:** Art gallery, child care center, flight simulators, historic brewery building, on-campus lab school, world indoor airport.
**Athletic facilities:** Swimming pool, basketball, squash, racquetball, tennis, and volleyball courts, baseball, football, soccer, and softball fields, track, weight room, fitness center.

**STUDENT BODY. Undergraduate profile:** 97% are state residents; 53% are transfers. 4% Asian-American, 5% Black, 10% Hispanic, 1% Native American, 77% White, 3% Other. Average age of undergraduates is 27.
**Freshman profile:** 1% of freshmen who took SAT scored 700 or over on math; 2% scored 600 or over on verbal, 9% scored 600 or over on math; 15% scored 500 or over on verbal, 30% scored 500 or over on math; 55% scored 400 or over on verbal, 70% scored 400 or over on math; 91% scored 300 or over on verbal, 95% scored 300 or over on math. 1% of freshmen who took ACT scored 30 or over on composite; 12% scored 24 or over on composite; 69% scored 18 or over on composite; 100% scored 12 or over on composite. 11% of accepted applicants took SAT; 39% took ACT. 96% of freshmen come from public schools.
**Undergraduate achievement:** 56% of fall 1992 freshmen returned for fall 1993 term. 2% of entering class graduated.
**Foreign students:** 156 students are from out of the country. Countries represented include Canada, Ethiopia, Iran, Japan, Mexico, and Vietnam; 80 in all.

**PROGRAMS OF STUDY. Degrees:** B.A., B.F.A., B.S.
**Majors:** Accounting, African American Studies, Anthropology, Art, Aviation Management, Aviation Technology, Behavioral Science, Biology, Chemistry, Chicano Studies, Civil Engineering Technology, Computer Information Systems/Management Science, Computer Science, Criminal Justice/Criminology, Economics, Electronics Engineering Technology, English, Finance, Health Care Management, History, Hospitality/Meeting/Travel Administration, Human Performance/Sport, Human Services, Industrial Design, Industrial/Technical Studies, Journalism, Land Use, Leisure Studies, Management, Mar-

keting, Mathematics, Mechanical Engineering Technology, Meteorology, Modern Foreign Languages, Music Education, Music Performance, Nursing, Philosophy, Physics, Political Science, Psychology, Social Welfare, Sociology, Spanish, Speech Communications, Surveying/Mapping, Technical Communications Multi-Major, Technical/Industrial Administration, Urban Studies.
**Distribution of degrees:** The majors with the highest enrollment are accounting, management, and psychology; industrial/technical studies, modern languages, and industrial design have the lowest.
**Requirements:** General education requirement.
**Academic regulations:** Minimum 2.0 GPA must be maintained.
**Special:** Minors offered in many majors and in approximately 20 other fields. Self-designed majors. Double majors. Dual degrees. Independent study. Accelerated study. Pass/fail grading option. Internships. Cooperative education programs. Member of Consortium of State Colleges in Colorado. Teacher certification in early childhood, elementary, and secondary education. Certification in specific subject areas. Study abroad in Australia, England, Mexico, and Scotland. ROTC and AFROTC.
**Honors:** Honors program. Honor societies.
**Academic Assistance:** Nonremedial tutoring.

**STUDENT LIFE. Housing:** Commuter campus; no student housing.
**Social atmosphere:** The student newspaper reports that having three schools (Metropolitan State College, University of Colorado at Denver, and the Community College of Denver) on one shared campus and as many night students as day students creates "a very diverse group of over 30,000." Although the student body is still primarily nontraditional, the number of 18- to 22-year-olds has been growing over the past few years, resulting in a greater interest in on-campus activities. Favorite off-campus nightspots include Tivoli Mall, Rocky Rococo, Wazee Lounge, and My Brother's Bar.
**Services and counseling/handicapped student services:** Placement services. Health service. Women's center. Day care. Counseling services for minority, veteran, and older students. Birth control, personal, and psychological counseling. Career and academic guidance services. Physically disabled student services. Learning disabled services. Notetaking services. Tape recorders. Tutors. Reader services for the blind.
**Campus organizations:** Undergraduate student government. Student newspaper (Metropolitan, published once/week). Literary magazine. Art club, clay club, Metro Marketing Club, Auraria Gamers, BACCHUS, Young Democrats, College Republicans, Democratic Socialists of America, Coalition of Gay, Lesbian, and Bisexual People, professional and special-interest groups, academic organizations, 80 organizations in all.
**Religious organizations:** Asian Christian Fellowship, Auraria Catholics, Bahai Club, Baptist Student Union, Hillel, Intervarsity Christian Fellowship, Menorah Ministries, Muslim Student Association.
**Minority/foreign student organizations:** Black Men of Campus, Black Student Alliance, Hispanic Leadership Association, LaRaza Coalition, MEChA, Metro American Indian Students for Equality (MAISE), National Society for Black Engineers. International Student Organization, Asian and Vietnamese groups.

**ATHLETICS. Physical education requirements:** None.
**Intercollegiate competition:** 1% of students participate. Baseball (M), basketball (M,W), diving (M,W), soccer (M,W), swimming (M,W), tennis (M,W), volleyball (W). Member of Colorado Athletic Conference, NCAA Division II.
**Intramural and club sports:** 25% of students participate. Intramural badminton, basketball, flag football, floor hockey, golf, indoor soccer, mountain cycling, polo, paintball, racquetball, running, sand volleyball, slam dunk, softball, squash, tennis, volleyball, ultimate frisbee. Men's club Alpine skiing, cheerleading, indoor soccer, lacrosse, martial arts, Nordic skiing, rugby, volleyball, weight lifting. Women's club Alpine skiing, cheerleading, indoor soccer, martial arts, Nordic skiing, rugby, weight lifting.

**ADMISSIONS. Academic basis for candidate selection** (in order of priority): Secondary school record, standardized test scores, class rank, school's recommendation.
**Requirements:** Graduation from secondary school is required; GED is accepted. No specific distribution of secondary school units required. Audition required of music program applicants. Redirect program with Community Coll of Denver. ACT is required; SAT may be substituted. No off-campus interviews.
**Procedure:** Take SAT or ACT by March 1 of 12th year. Suggest filing application by May 1. Application deadline is August 1. Notification of admission on rolling basis. No set date by which applicants must accept offer. Freshmen accepted in terms other than fall.
**Special programs:** Admission may be deferred one year. Credit and/or placement may be granted through CEEB Advanced Placement exams for scores of 2 or higher. Credit may be granted through CLEP general and subject exams, challenge exams, and military experience. Placement may be granted through ACT PEP exams. Credit and placement may be granted through life experience. Early decision program. In fall 1993, 171 applied for early decision and 160 were accepted. Deadline for applying for early decision is January 1. Early entrance/early admission program. Concurrent enrollment program.
**Transfer students:** Transfer students accepted for terms other than fall. In fall 1993, 53% of all new students were transfers into all classes. 3,375 transfer applications were received, 3,193 were accepted. Application deadline is August 1 for fall; December 20 for spring. Minimum 2.0 GPA required. ACT or SAT required of transfer applicants under 20 years of age; recommended of applicants 20 years of age or older. All transcripts required of transfer applicants under 20 years of age and degree-seeking transfer applicants 20 years of age or older. Lowest course grade accepted is "C." Maximum number of transferable credits is 64 semester hours from a two-year school and 90 semester hours from a four-year school. At least 30 semester hours must be completed at the college to receive degree.
**Admissions contact:** Kenneth C. Curtis, Ph.D., Dean of Admissions and Records. 303 556-3058.

**FINANCIAL AID. Available aid:** Pell grants, SEOG, Federal Nursing Student Scholarships, state scholarships and grants, school scholarships, private scholarships and grants, academic merit scholarships, and athletic scholarships. Veterans Administration grants, National Merit Scholarships. Perkins Loans (NDSL), PLUS, Stafford Loans (GSL), private loans, and SLS.
**Supporting data/closing dates:** FAFSA/FAF/FFS: Priority filing date is March 1; accepted on rolling basis. Income tax forms: Priority filing date is April 4; accepted on rolling basis. SINGLEFILE: Priority filing date is March 1; accepted on rolling basis. Notification of awards on rolling basis.
**Financial aid contact:** Cheryl Judson, Ph.D., Assistant Vice President, Financial Aid. 303 534-6501.

**STUDENT EMPLOYMENT.** College Work/Study Program. Institutional employment. 6% of full-time undergraduates work on campus during school year. Students may expect to earn an average of $2,100 during school year. Off-campus part-time employment opportunities rated "excellent."

**COMPUTER FACILITIES.** 240 IBM/IBM-compatible, Macintosh/Apple, and RISC-/UNIX-based microcomputers; 230 are networked. Students may access Digital, Hewlett-Packard minicomputer/mainframe systems, BITNET, Internet. Client/LAN operating systems include Apple/Macintosh, DOS, UNIX/XENIX/AIX, Banyan. Computer languages and software packages include BASIC, COBOL, dBASE, Excel, Lotus 1-2-3, Microsoft Word, Microsoft Works, Pascal, SPSS, WordPerfect; database, spreadsheet, word processing programs; 20 in all. Computer facilities are available to all students.
**Fees:** $16 computer fee per semester.
**Hours:** 8 AM-10 PM (M-Th); 8 AM-5 PM (F); 8 AM-8 PM (Sa). Some labs have extended hours.

**PROMINENT ALUMNI/AE.** Peter Boyles, radio talk show host, Denver; Richard T. Castro, director of Agency for Human Rights and Community Relations and former state legislator; Edna Wilson Mosley, director of Women's Bank, Denver; Ruth Pelton-Roby, lawyer, urban planner, and artist; Peter Alan Simon, concert pianist.

# Regis University

**Denver, CO 80221-1099 — 303 458-4100**

**1994-95 Costs.** Tuition: $12,700. Room: $2,780. Board: $2,700. Fees, books, misc. academic expenses (school's estimate): $570.
**Enrollment.** Undergraduates: 473 men, 669 women (full-time). Freshman class: 950 applicants, 904 accepted, 307 enrolled.
**Test score averages/ranges.** Average SAT scores: 487 verbal, 442 math. Average ACT scores: 22 composite.
**Faculty.** 70 full-time; 20 part-time. 90% of faculty holds doctoral degree. Student/faculty ratio: 16 to 1.
**Selectivity rating.** Less competitive.

**PROFILE.** Regis is a church-affiliated, liberal arts university. It was founded as a school for men in 1877, adopted coeducation in 1968, and gained university status in 1991. Undergraduates apply to and attend Regis College, a division of the university. Its 90-acre campus is located in Denver.

**Accreditation:** NCACS. Professionally accredited by the National Council for Accreditation of Teacher Education.
**Religious orientation:** Regis University is affiliated with the Roman Catholic Church (Society of Jesus); three semesters of theology required.
**Library:** Collections totaling over 246,839 volumes, 2,232 periodical subscriptions, and 86,273 microform items.
**Special facilities/museums:** Language lab, wellness center, seismic observatory.
**Athletic facilities:** Field house, swimming pool, handball, racquetball, and tennis courts, gymnasiums, baseball, intramural, soccer, and softball fields, stadium.

**STUDENT BODY. Undergraduate profile:** 60% are state residents. 3% Asian-American, 2% Black, 9% Hispanic, .5% Native American, 80% White, 5.5% Other. Average age of undergraduates is 22.
**Freshman profile:** 59% of accepted applicants took SAT; 74% took ACT. 57% of freshmen come from public schools.
**Undergraduate achievement:** 65% of fall 1992 freshmen returned for fall 1993 term. 67% of entering class graduated. 14% of students who completed a degree program immediately went on to graduate study.
**Foreign students:** 22 students are from out of the country. Countries represented include Belize, Guatemala, Mexico, and Spain; seven in all.

**PROGRAMS OF STUDY. Degrees:** B.A., B.S.
**Majors:** Biology, Business Administration, Chemistry, Communications, Computer Science, Economics, Education, Engineering, English, Environmental Science, French, History, Mathematics, Nursing, Philosophy, Political Science, Pre-Dentistry, Pre-Law, Pre-Medicine, Professional Accounting, Psychology, Religious Studies, Sociology, Spanish.
**Distribution of degrees:** The majors with the highest enrollment are business administration, communications, and nursing; French, religious studies, and environmental science have the lowest.
**Requirements:** General education requirement.
**Academic regulations:** Minimum 2.0 GPA must be maintained.
**Special:** Minors offered in all majors. Interdivisional concentrations. Courses offered in anthropology, art, astronomy, criminal justice, geology, German, Greek, Hispanic studies, humanities, Latin, marketing, music, physical education, physics, and speech. Self-designed majors. Double majors. Independent study. Pass/fail grading option. Internships. Graduate school at which undergraduates may take graduate-level courses. Preprofessional programs in law, medicine, and dentistry. 3-2 engineering program with Washington U. Exchange programs with other Jesuit colleges and universities. Teacher certification in elementary and secondary education. Study abroad possible. ROTC at Metropolitan State Coll. AFROTC at U of Colorado at Boulder.
**Honors:** Honors program.
**Academic Assistance:** Nonremedial tutoring.

**STUDENT LIFE. Housing:** All unmarried freshmen and sophomores under age 21 must live on campus unless living with family. Coed dorms. 48% of students live in college housing.

**Social atmosphere:** Favorite off-campus gathering spots include the Hilltop Bar, Common Grounds Coffee House, and Hamlin's Restaurant. On-campus, student frequent the Pub, the Snack Bar, and the Quad. The Program Activities Council (PAC) and the Student Executive Board have considerable influence over campus social life. Popular events include Ranger Day, Thursday Thrills, Faith and Justice Institute, Parent's Weekend, Casino Night, Censorship Day, Martin Luther King, Jr. Day, Media Day, and the Mass of the Holy Spirit. According to the editor of the student newspaper, "There is rarely a day that goes by that there isn't some kind of social event at Regis." The university's location in north Denver allows many opportunities for social and cultural experiences.

**Services and counseling/handicapped student services:** Placement services. Health service. Personal and psychological counseling. Career and academic guidance services. Religious counseling. Learning disabled program/services.

**Campus organizations:** Undergraduate student government. Student newspaper (Highlander, published twice/month). Literary magazine. Yearbook. Radio station. Leadership program, activities council, 19 organizations in all.

**Religious organizations:** Campus Ministry, Pax Christi.

**Minority/foreign student organizations:** Minority student club.

**ATHLETICS. Physical education requirements:** None.

**Intercollegiate competition:** 24% of students participate. Baseball (M), basketball (M,W), golf (M,W), soccer (M,W), softball (W), tennis (M,W), volleyball (W). Member of Colorado Athletic Conference, NCAA Division II.

**Intramural and club sports:** 50% of students participate. Intramural basketball, flag football, soccer, softball, tennis, volleyball, walleyball. Men's club lacrosse, volleyball.

**ADMISSIONS. Academic basis for candidate selection** (in order of priority): Secondary school record, standardized test scores, school's recommendation, essay, class rank.

**Nonacademic basis for candidate selection:** Character and personality and extracurricular participation are important. Particular talent or ability and alumni/ae relationship are considered.

**Requirements:** Graduation from secondary school is required; GED is accepted. 16 units and the following program of study are recommended: 4 units of English, 2 units of math, 2 units of science, 2 units of foreign language, 2 units of social studies, 1 unit of history. Minimum 2.5 GPA recommended. Freshman Success Program and Freshmen Commitment Program for applicants not normally admissible. SAT or ACT is required. Off-campus interviews available with an admissions representative.

**Procedure:** Take SAT or ACT by January of 12th year. Visit college for interview by April of 12th year. Suggest filing application by May 1; no deadline. Notification of admission on rolling basis. Reply is required by May 1. $100 nonrefundable tuition deposit. $100 nonrefundable room deposit. Freshmen accepted in terms other than fall.

**Special programs:** Admission may be deferred one year. Credit may be granted through CEEB Advanced Placement for scores of 3 or higher. Credit and/or placement may be granted through CLEP general and subject exams. Credit may be granted through challenge exams. Concurrent enrollment program.

**Transfer students:** Transfer students accepted for terms other than fall. In fall 1993, 340 transfer applications were received, 323 were accepted. Application deadline is August 15 for fall; December 15 for spring. Minimum 2.0 GPA required. Lowest course grade accepted is "C." Maximum number of transferable credits is 98 semester hours. At least 30 semester hours must be completed at the university to receive degree.

**Admissions contact:** Robert Blust, M.A., Director of Admissions. 303 458-4900, 800 388-2366.

**FINANCIAL AID. Available aid:** Pell grants, SEOG, state scholarships and grants, school scholarships and grants, private scholarships and grants, academic merit scholarships, and athletic scholarships. Perkins Loans (NDSL), PLUS, Stafford Loans (GSL), NSL, private loans, and SLS. Tuition Plan Inc., Knight Tuition Plans, and AMS.

**Financial aid statistics:** 51% of aid is not need-based. In 1993-94, 100% of all undergraduate applicants received aid. Average amounts of aid awarded freshmen: Scholarships and grants, $8,600; loans, $2,900.

**Supporting data/closing dates:** School's own aid application: Priority filing date is March 15. Notification of awards begins January.

**Financial aid contact:** Audrey Matson, M.S., Director of Financial Aid. 303 458-4066.

**STUDENT EMPLOYMENT.** College Work/Study Program. Institutional employment. 60% of full-time undergraduates work on campus during school year. Students may expect to earn an average of $1,500 during school year. Off-campus part-time employment opportunities rated "good."

**COMPUTER FACILITIES.** 200 IBM/IBM-compatible microcomputers; 64 are networked. Students may access Digital, Hewlett-Packard minicomputer/mainframe systems. Residence halls may be equipped with stand-alone microcomputers, networked terminals. Client/LAN operating systems include DOS, Windows NT, DEC, Novell. Computer languages and software packages include BASIC, C, C++, dBASE, Paradox, Pascal, Quattro, WordPerfect; 40 in all. Computer facilities are available to all students.

**Fees:** None.

**Hours:** 24 hours.

**GRADUATE CAREER DATA.** Highest graduate school enrollments: Columbia Coll, U of Colorado Health Center, U of Denver. Companies and businesses that hire graduates: Arthur Andersen, Ernst & Young, Federal Reserve Bank, State Farm Insurance, U.S. Department of Energy.

**PROMINENT ALUMNI/AE.** Bill Murray, actor; Edward Feulner, president, Heritage Foundation; Edward R. Beauvais, president, America West Airlines.

# United States Air Force Academy

**USAF Academy, CO 80840-5025 719 472-1818**

**1994-95 Costs.** Tuition: None.

**Enrollment.** Undergraduates: 3,687 men, 549 women (full-time). Freshman class: 9,557 applicants, 1,605 accepted, 1,160 enrolled.

**Test score averages/ranges.** Average SAT scores: 569 verbal, 663 math. Range of SAT scores of middle 50%: 520-600 verbal, 610-700 math. Average ACT scores: 27 English, 29 math. Range of ACT scores of middle 50%: 25-29 English, 26-30 math.

**Faculty.** 517 full-time. 40% of faculty holds doctoral degree. Student/faculty ratio: 8 to 1.

**Selectivity rating.** Most competitive.

**PROFILE.** The U.S. Air Force Academy is a public service academy. Founded in 1955, it adopted coeducation in 1976. Its 18,325-acre campus is located in Colorado Springs.

**Accreditation:** NCACS. Professionally accredited by the Accreditation Board for Engineering and Technology.

**Religious orientation:** United States Air Force Academy is nonsectarian; no religious requirements.

**Library:** Collections totaling over 116,000 volumes, 3,555 periodical subscriptions, and 543,000 microform items.

**Special facilities/museums:** Art gallery, aeronautics, instrumentation, research, and radio frequency systems labs, two 3,500-foot runways, planetarium.

**Athletic facilities:** Gymnasiums, swimming pools, ice rink, tracks, baseball, football, flickerball, lacrosse, rugby, soccer, and softball fields, stadium, golf course, racquetball, squash, tennis, and volleyball courts, boxing rings.

**STUDENT BODY. Undergraduate profile:** 8% are state residents. 4% Asian-American, 6% Black, 6% Hispanic, 1% Native American, 82% White, 1% Other. Average age of undergraduates is 21.

**Freshman profile:** 1% of freshmen who took SAT scored 700 or over on verbal, 24% scored 700 or over on math; 32% scored 600 or over on verbal, 85% scored 600 or over on math; 93% scored 500 or over on verbal, 100% scored 500 or over on math; 100% scored 400 or over on verbal. 49% of accepted applicants took SAT; 51% took ACT.

**Undergraduate achievement:** 85% of fall 1992 freshmen returned for fall 1993 term. 68% of entering class graduated. 4% of students who completed a degree program immediately went on to graduate study.

**Foreign students:** 40 students are from out of the country. Countries represented include Chile, Guatemala, Korea, the Philippines, Thailand, and Turkey; 21 in all.

**PROGRAMS OF STUDY. Degrees:** B.S.

**Majors:** Aeronautical Engineering, Astronautical Engineering, Basic Sciences, Behavioral Science, Biology, Chemistry, Civil Engineering, Computer Science, Economics, Electrical Engineering, Engineering Sciences, English, General Engineering, Geography, History, Humanities, International Affairs, Legal Studies, Management, Mathematical Sciences, Operations Research, Physics, Political Sciences, Social Sciences, Space Science.

**Distribution of degrees:** The majors with the highest enrollment are engineering sciences and social sciences; computer science, biology, and management have the lowest.

**Requirements:** General education requirement.

**Academic regulations:** Minimum 2.0 GPA must be maintained.

**Special:** Minor offered in foreign languages. Double majors. Independent study. Accelerated study. Exchange programs with U.S. Coast Guard, Merchant Marine, Military, and Naval Academies. Exchange program abroad in France (French Air Force Academy).

**Honors:** Honors program.

**Academic Assistance:** Nonremedial tutoring.

**STUDENT LIFE. Housing:** All cadets must live on campus. Coed dorms. 100% of students live in college housing.

**Services and counseling/handicapped student services:** Health service. Counseling services for minority and military students. Personal and psychological counseling. Career and academic guidance services. Religious counseling.

**Campus organizations:** Undergraduate student government. Student newspaper. Yearbook. Radio and TV stations. Blue Bards, chorale, drum and bugle corps, forensic association, 70 organizations in all.

**Minority/foreign student organizations:** Way of Life Committee, Los Padrinos.

**ATHLETICS. Physical education requirements:** 14 semester hours of physical education required.

**Intercollegiate competition:** 35% of students participate. Baseball (M), basketball (M,W), boxing (M), cheerleading (M,W), cross-country (M,W), diving (M,W), fencing (M,W), football (M), golf (M), gymnastics (M,W), ice hockey (M), lacrosse (M), riflery (M,W), soccer (M,W), swimming (M,W), tennis (M,W), track (indoor) (M,W), track (outdoor) (M,W), track and field (indoor) (M,W), track and field (outdoor) (M,W), volleyball (W), water polo (M), wrestling (M). Member of Colorado Athletic Conference, NCAA Division I for men's athletics, NCAA Division II for women's athletics, NCBA, Western Athletic Conference.

**Intramural and club sports:** 100% of students participate. Intramural aerobics, basketball, boxing, cross-country, flickerball, flag football, handball, mountain cycling, racquetball, rugby, soccer, softball, swimming, tennis, ultimate frisbee, volleyball, walleyball, water polo, wrestling. Men's club Alpine skiing, archery, bowling, cycling, handball, martial arts, Nordic skiing, pistol, racquetball, rodeo, rugby, scuba, skeet, squash, team handball, weight lifting. Women's club Alpine skiing, archery, bowling, cycling, handball, martial arts, Nordic skiing, pistol, racquetball, rodeo, rugby, scuba, skeet, softball, squash, team handball, weight lifting.

**ADMISSIONS. Academic basis for candidate selection** (in order of priority): Secondary school record, class rank, standardized test scores, school's recommendation, essay.
**Nonacademic basis for candidate selection:** Character and personality and extracurricular participation are emphasized. Particular talent or ability is important.
**Requirements:** Graduation from secondary school is recommended; GED is accepted. No specific distribution of secondary school units required. Minimum SAT scores of 500 verbal and 550 math (ACT scores of 21 English and 24 math) required. Nomination by members of Congress, the Vice President, or the President of the United States required. High leadership, academic, extracurricular, and physical fitness standards (as determined by interview with Air Force Admissions Liaison Officer). Submission of writing sample and satisfactory completion of medical exam and fitness test also required. SAT or ACT is required. PSAT is recommended. Campus visit recommended. Off-campus interviews available with an admissions representative.
**Procedure:** Take SAT or ACT by January of 12th year. Application deadline is January 31. Notification of admission by May 10. Reply is required by May 1. Freshmen accepted for fall term only.
**Special programs:** Credit and/or placement may be granted through CEEB Advanced Placement exams for scores of 4 or higher. Credit and placement may be granted through DANTES exams.
**Transfer students:** Transfer students accepted for fall term. Application deadline is January 31. Minimum 3.0 GPA. At least 43.5 must be completed at the service academy to receive degree. Four years must be completed at the academy to receive degree.
**Admissions contact:** Col. Robert Y. Foerster, M.S., Director of Admissions. 719 472-2520.

**FINANCIAL AID. Available aid:** Private scholarships and academic merit scholarships.

**COMPUTER FACILITIES.** 200 IBM/IBM-compatible microcomputers; all are networked. Students may access Digital minicomputer/mainframe systems. Residence halls may be equipped with stand-alone microcomputers, networked terminals. Client/LAN operating systems include DOS, OS/2, X-windows, Microsoft, Novell. Computer languages and software packages include Ada, ALGOL, C, FORTRAN, GPSS, LISP, Pascal, SLAM, SPSS; many educational packages. Computer facilities are available to all students.
**Fees:** None.
**Hours:** 7:30 AM-11 PM.

**GRADUATE CAREER DATA.** Graduate school percentages: 2% enter medical school. Highest graduate school enrollments: Columbia U, Harvard U, MIT, Oxford U, Purdue U, U of Washington. Companies and businesses that hire graduates: U.S. Air Force.

**PROMINENT ALUMNI/AE.** John E. Blaha, Karol J. Bobko, and Richard O. Covey, astronauts; Alonzo C. Babers, Olympic gold-medal winner.

# University of Colorado at Boulder

**Boulder, CO 80309** **303 492-1411**

**1993-94 Costs.** Tuition: $2,120 (state residents), $11,630 (out-of-state). Room & board: $3,850. Fees, books, misc. academic expenses (school's estimate): $880.
**Enrollment.** Undergraduates: 9,904 men, 8,700 women (full-time). Freshman class: 13,761 applicants, 10,473 accepted, 3,604 enrolled. Graduate enrollment: 2,980 men, 2,066 women.
**Test score averages/ranges.** Range of SAT scores of middle 50%: 450-550 verbal, 520-630 math. Range of ACT scores of middle 50%: 22-27 English, 22-28 math.
**Faculty.** 961 full-time; 232 part-time. 91% of faculty holds highest degree in specific field. Student/faculty ratio: 19 to 1.
**Selectivity rating.** Competitive.

**PROFILE.** U Colorado at Boulder, founded in 1876, is a comprehensive, public university. Programs are offered through the Colleges of Arts and Sciences, Business and Administration, Engineering and Applied Science, Environmental Design, and Music; the Graduate School; the Graduate School of Business Administration; and the Schools of Education, Journalism and Mass Communication, Law, and Pharmacy. Its 600-acre campus is located in Boulder, 27 miles northwest of Denver.

**Accreditation:** NCACS. Professionally accredited by the Accreditation Board for Engineering and Technology, the Accrediting Council on Education in Journalism and Mass Communication, the American Assembly of Collegiate Schools of Business, the American Bar Association, the Association of American Law Schools, the National Association of Schools of Music, the National Council for Accreditation of Teacher Education.
**Religious orientation:** University of Colorado at Boulder is nonsectarian; no religious requirements.
**Library:** Collections totaling over 2,400,000 volumes, 27,313 periodical subscriptions, and 4,500,000 microform items.
**Special facilities/museums:** Natural history museum, planetarium, electron microscope.
**Athletic facilities:** Recreation center, swimming pool, basketball, handball, racquetball, squash, tennis, and volleyball courts, field house, gymnasium, baseball, intramural, lacrosse, and soccer fields, weight rooms, tracks.

**STUDENT BODY. Undergraduate profile:** 65% are state residents; 7% are transfers. 6% Asian-American, 2% Black, 6% Hispanic, 1% Native American, 82% White, 3% Other.
**Freshman profile:** 83% of accepted applicants took SAT; 61% took ACT.
**Undergraduate achievement:** 82% of fall 1991 freshmen returned for fall 1992 term. 33% of entering class graduated.
**Foreign students:** 191 students are from out of the country. 80 countries represented in all.

**PROGRAMS OF STUDY. Degrees:** B.A., B.Env.Design, B.Mus., B.Mus.Ed., B.S.
**Majors:** Accounting, Advertising, Aerospace Engineering Sciences, American Folk Music, American Studies, Anthropology, Applied Mathematics, Architectural Engineering, Art History, Arts Management, Asian Studies, Biological Sciences, Black Studies, Broadcast News, Broadcast Production Management, Central/East European Studies, Chemical Engineering, Chemistry, Chinese, Choral Music, Church Music, Civil Engineering, Classics, Communication, Communication Disorders/Speech Science, Composition, Computer Science, Computer Science Applications, Dance, Distributed Studies, Drama, Economics, Electrical Engineering, Electrical Engineering/Computer Science, Elementary Education, Elementary/Secondary Education, Engineering Physics, English, Entrepreneurship/Small Business Management, Environmental Conservation, Environmental Design, Film Studies, Finance, French, General Music, Geography, Geology, German, Guitar, History, History/Literature, Humanities, Individually Structured Major, Information Systems, Instrumental Music, International Affairs, International Business, Italian, Japanese, Jazz Studies, Kinesiology, Latin, Latin American Studies, Linguistics, Marketing, Mathematics, Mechanical Engineering, Music/Broadcasting, Music Business, Music History/Literature, Music Journalism/Broadcasting, Music Pedagogy, Music Performance, Music/Theatre, Music Theory/Composition, News/Editorial, Organ, Organization Management, Personnel/Human Resource Management, Pharmacy, Philosophy, Physics, Piano, Political Science, Psychology, Public Relations, Real Estate, Religious Studies, Russian, Science, Social Studies, Sociology, Spanish, String, Studio Arts, Theatre, Tourism/Recreation Management, Transportation/Distribution Management, Voice/Performance or Theatre, Wind/Percussion Music Education, Women's Studies.
**Distribution of degrees:** The majors with the highest enrollment are psychology, marketing, and English; black studies, dance, and Chinese have the lowest.
**Requirements:** General education requirement.
**Special:** Residential hall academic program. Vacation Coll program in January. Self-designed majors. Double majors. Dual degrees. Independent study. Pass/fail grading option. Internships. Cooperative education programs. Graduate school at which undergraduates may take graduate-level courses. Preprofessional programs in law, medicine, veterinary science, dentistry, architecture, medical technology, nursing, and physical therapy. Five-year B.S. program in engineering and business. Sea Semester. Teacher certification in elementary, secondary, and bilingual/bicultural education. Study abroad in Costa Rica, England, France, Germany, Israel, Italy, Japan, Mexico, and Spain. ROTC, NROTC, and AFROTC.
**Honors:** Phi Beta Kappa. Honors program.
**Academic Assistance:** Remedial reading, writing, math, and study skills. Nonremedial tutoring.

**STUDENT LIFE. Housing:** All freshmen under age 20 must live on campus unless living with family. Coed, women's, and men's dorms. Sorority and fraternity housing. School-owned/operated apartments. On-campus married-student housing. 25% of students live in college housing.
**Social atmosphere:** The student newspaper reports, "The town of Boulder and CU are known for their liberalism and, because of that, they attract many diverse groups. Much focus is put on a clean environment, and many students come to CU because of the beautifully landscaped campus and for the skiing and hiking, which can be done in the nearby mountains." Among the most popular activities: "an annual Alfred Packer Day, in honor of Colorado's only cannibal. The day includes an eating contest, with such foods as raw meat, red onions, and Rocky Mountain oysters. We also have an annual Trivia Bowl competition, which attracts contestants from all over the country. Our annual World Affairs Conference attracts foreign speakers in different occupations."
**Services and counseling/handicapped student services:** Placement services. Health service. Women's center. Day care. Counseling services for minority, veteran, and older students. Birth control, personal, and psychological counseling. Career and academic guidance services. Physically disabled student services. Learning disabled program/services.
**Campus organizations:** Undergraduate student government. Student newspaper (Colorado Daily; Campus Press, published once/week). Yearbook. Radio station. Orchestra, bands, festival chorus, choirs, men's and women's glee clubs, intercollegiate debating, theatre, modern dance group, musical comedy group, community service program, special-interest groups, 250 organizations in all. 25 fraternities, 22 chapter houses; 15 sororities, 12 chapter houses. 13% of men join a fraternity. 18% of women join a sorority.
**Religious organizations:** Several religious groups.
**Minority/foreign student organizations:** Black Student Association, Oyate Indian Club, United Mexican Student Association, Minority Student Access Center, Third World Center, other minority student groups. Eight foreign student groups.

**ATHLETICS. Physical education requirements:** None.
**Intercollegiate competition:** 3% of students participate. Alpine skiing (M,W), basketball (M,W), cheerleading (M,W), cross-country (M,W), football (M), golf (M,W), Nordic skiing (M,W), tennis (M,W), track and field (indoor) (M,W), track and field (outdoor) (M,W), volleyball (W). Member of Big Eight Conference, NCAA Division I.
**Intramural and club sports:** 75% of students participate. Intramural basketball, broomball, flag football, handball, ice hockey, lacrosse, racquetball, rugby, soccer, softball, squash, tennis, ultimate frisbee, volleyball. Men's club baseball, cycling, ice hockey, lacrosse, rugby, soccer, swimming, ultimate frisbee. Women's club cycling, field hockey, rugby, swimming.

**ADMISSIONS. Academic basis for candidate selection** (in order of priority): Secondary school record, class rank, standardized test scores, school's recommendation, essay.
**Nonacademic basis for candidate selection:** Geographical distribution and alumni/ae relationship are emphasized. Character and personality, extracurricular participation, and particular talent or ability are important.
**Requirements:** Graduation from secondary school is required; GED is accepted. 16 units and the following program of study are required: 4 units of English, 3 units of math, 3 units of science including 2 units of lab, 2 units of foreign language, 2 units of social studies. 4 units of math required of architecture/planning, business/administration and engineering/applied science program applicants. Chemistry and physics required of engineering/applied science program applicants. 3 units of foreign language and 3 units of social studies required of arts/sciences and business/administration program applicants. Audition required of music program applicants. CU Opportunity Program for applicants not normally admissible. SAT or ACT is required. Campus visit recommended. No off-campus interviews.

**Procedure:** Take SAT or ACT by January of 12th year. Application deadline is February 15. Notification of admission on rolling basis. Reply is required by May 1. $200 nonrefundable tuition deposit. $100 room deposit, partially refundable. Freshmen accepted in terms other than fall.
**Special programs:** Credit and/or placement may be granted through CEEB Advanced Placement exams for scores of 3 or higher. Credit and/or placement may be granted through CLEP subject exams. Placement may be granted through challenge exams. Concurrent enrollment program.
**Transfer students:** Transfer students accepted for terms other than fall. In fall 1992, 7% of all new students were transfers into all classes. 3,841 transfer applications were received, 2,502 were accepted. Application deadline is April 1 for fall; November 1 for spring. Minimum 2.5 GPA required. Lowest course grade accepted is "C-." Maximum number of transferable credits is 60 semester hours from a two-year school and 90 semester hours from a four-year school. At least 30 semester hours must be completed at the university to receive degree.
**Admissions contact:** Gary M. Kelsey, M.A., Director of Admissions. 303 492-6301.
**FINANCIAL AID. Available aid:** Pell grants, SEOG, state scholarships and grants, school scholarships and grants, private scholarships and grants, ROTC scholarships, academic merit scholarships, and athletic scholarships. Perkins Loans (NDSL), PLUS, Stafford Loans (GSL), state loans, school loans, and SLS. Deferred payment plan.
**Financial aid statistics:** 10% of aid is not need-based. Average amounts of aid awarded freshmen: Scholarships and grants, $1,750; loans, $1,300.
**Supporting data/closing dates:** FAFSA/FAF/FFS: Priority filing date is April 1; accepted on rolling basis. Income tax forms: Priority filing date is April 1; accepted on rolling basis. Notification of awards on rolling basis.
**Financial aid contact:** Gerald Sullivan, M.A., Director of Financial Aid. 303 492-5091.
**STUDENT EMPLOYMENT.** College Work/Study Program. Institutional employment. 70% of full-time undergraduates work on campus during school year. Students may expect to earn an average of $1,500 during school year. Off-campus part-time employment opportunities rated "excellent."
**COMPUTER FACILITIES.** IBM/IBM-compatible and Macintosh/Apple microcomputers. Students may access Digital minicomputer/mainframe systems, BITNET. Residence halls may be equipped with stand-alone microcomputers, networked microcomputers, networked terminals. Computer languages and software packages include BASIC, C, COBOL, FORTRAN, LISP, Pascal, SNOBOL. Computer facilities are available to all students.
**Fees:** Computer fee is included in tuition/fees.
**PROMINENT ALUMNI/AE.** Roy Romer, governor of Colorado; Byron White, U.S. Supreme Court justice; David Bokn, retired U.S. ambassador; Judy Collins, folk singer; Joan Van Ark, actress; Robert Redford and Larry Linville, actors; Hale Irwin, professional golfer; Scott Carpenter, astronaut.

## University of Colorado at Colorado Springs

**Colorado Springs, CO 80933-7150 719 593-3000**

**1993-94 Costs.** Tuition: $2,131 (state residents), $7,187 (out-of-state). Housing: None. Fees, books, misc. academic expenses (school's estimate): $793.
**Enrollment.** Undergraduates: 1,112 men, 1,458 women (full-time). Freshman class: 826 applicants, 620 accepted, 373 enrolled. Graduate enrollment: 805 men, 780 women.
**Test score averages/ranges.** Range of SAT scores of middle 50%: 380-510 verbal, 450-560 math. Range of ACT scores of middle 50%: 22-26 English, 20-26 math.
**Faculty.** 189 full-time; 180 part-time. 90% of faculty holds highest degree in specific field. Student/faculty ratio: 15 to 1.
**Selectivity rating.** Less competitive.

**PROFILE.** U Colorado at Colorado Springs, founded in 1965, is a public university. Programs are offered through the Colleges of Letters, Arts, and Sciences; Business and Administration; and Engineering and Applied Science; the Schools of Dentistry, Education, Journalism, Law, Medicine, Nursing, and Pharmacy; the Graduate School; and the Graduate School of Public Affairs. Its 400-acre campus is located in Colorado Springs, 60 miles from Denver.
**Accreditation:** NCACS. Professionally accredited by the Accreditation Board for Engineering and Technology, the American Assembly of Collegiate Schools of Business, the National Association of Schools of Public Affairs and Administration, the National Council for Accreditation of Teacher Education.
**Religious orientation:** University of Colorado at Colorado Springs is nonsectarian; no religious requirements.
**Library:** Collections totaling over 280,654 volumes, 2,440 periodical subscriptions, and 431,382 microform items.
**Special facilities/museums:** Gallery of contemporary art.
**Athletic facilities:** Gymnasium, fitness center, football, soccer, and softball fields, tennis and volleyball courts.
**STUDENT BODY. Undergraduate profile:** 87% are state residents; 56% are transfers. 3% Asian-American, 3% Black, 6% Hispanic, 1% Native American, 85% White, 2% Other. Average age of undergraduates is 27.
**Freshman profile:** Majority of accepted applicants took ACT.
**Undergraduate achievement:** 62% of fall 1992 freshmen returned for fall 1993 term.
**Foreign students:** 38 students are from out of the country. Countries represented include China, Germany, India, Spain, Taiwan, and the United Kingdom; 17 in all.
**PROGRAMS OF STUDY. Degrees:** B.A., B.S.
**Majors:** Accounting, Anthropology, Applied Mathematics, Biology, Chemistry, Communication, Computer Science, Distributed Studies, Economics, Electrical Engineering, Elementary Education, English, Finance, Fine Arts, Geography/Environmental Studies, History, Information Science, Marketing, Mathematics, Organizational Management, Personnel/Human Resource Management, Philosophy, Physics, Political Science/Government, Production/Operations Management, Psychology, Public Agency Administration, Secondary Education, Small Business Management/Ownership, Sociology, Spanish.
**Distribution of degrees:** The majors with the highest enrollment are business, communication, and psychology; chemistry, mathematics, and anthropology have the lowest.
**Requirements:** General education requirement.
**Academic regulations:** Minimum 2.0 GPA must be maintained.
**Special:** Double majors. Dual degrees. Independent study. Pass/fail grading option. Graduate school at which undergraduates may take graduate-level courses. Preprofessional programs in law, medicine, pharmacy, dentistry, education, environmental design, journalism, nursing, and physical therapy. Exchange program with U of Colorado at Boulder. Teacher certification in elementary and secondary education. ROTC.
**Honors:** Honors program. Honor societies.
**Academic Assistance:** Nonremedial tutoring.
**STUDENT LIFE. Housing:** Commuter campus; no student housing.
**Social atmosphere:** Students gather on campus at the University Center, the Pub, the Patio, and the cafeteria. Minority student groups, student clubs, and the programming board are influential on campus. Students enjoy events such as Comedy Night, Casino Night, and women's basketball games. "We are a commuter campus so it is hard to get students involved. Activities that are successful every year usually get the most participation. New events have less commitment from students," comments the editor of the Scribe.
**Services and counseling/handicapped student services:** Placement services. Women's center. Day care. Counseling services for minority, veteran, and older students. Birth control, personal, and psychological counseling. Career and academic guidance services. Physically disabled student services. Learning disabled program/services. Notetaking services. Tape recorders. Tutors. Reader services for the blind.
**Campus organizations:** Undergraduate student government. Student newspaper (Scribe, published once/week). Literary magazine. Choir, drama group, Performing Arts Guild; academic, service, and recreation groups, 55 organizations in all.
**Religious organizations:** Bahai Club, Baptist Student Union, Campus Advance, High Country College Ministry, Intervarsity Christian Fellowship, Latter-Day Saints Student Association, Tag.
**Minority/foreign student organizations:** Black Student Union, MEChA, Asian and Islander Club. International Student Club.
**ATHLETICS. Physical education requirements:** None.
**Intercollegiate competition:** 3% of students participate. Basketball (M,W), golf (M), soccer (M), softball (W), tennis (M,W), volleyball (W). Member of Colorado Athletic Conference, NCAA Division II.
**Intramural and club sports:** 3% of students participate. Intramural badminton, basketball, bowling, softball, volleyball. Men's club Alpine skiing, cycling, football, martial arts. Women's club Alpine skiing, cycling, martial arts.
**ADMISSIONS. Academic basis for candidate selection** (in order of priority): Secondary school record, class rank, standardized test scores, school's recommendation.
**Nonacademic basis for candidate selection:** Character and personality, extracurricular participation, particular talent or ability, and alumni/ae relationship are considered.
**Requirements:** Graduation from secondary school is required; GED is accepted. 16 units and the following program of study are required: 4 units of English, 3 units of math, 3 units of science including 2 units of lab, 2 units of foreign language, 2 units of social studies, 1 unit of academic electives. Minimum composite ACT score of 24 recommended. Minimum requirements are higher for business and engineering program applicants. CU Opportunity Program for applicants not meeting standard requirements. SAT or ACT is required. Campus visit recommended. No off-campus interviews.
**Procedure:** Take SAT or ACT by fall of 12th year. Suggest filing application by December 1. Application deadline is July 1. Notification of admission on rolling basis. Reply is required by registration day. Freshmen accepted in terms other than fall.
**Special programs:** Admission may be deferred one year. Credit and/or placement may be granted through CEEB Advanced Placement exams for scores of 3 or higher. Credit and/or placement may be granted through CLEP subject exams. Credit may be granted through military experience. Early decision program. Concurrent enrollment program.
**Transfer students:** Transfer students accepted for terms other than fall. In fall 1993, 56% of all new students were transfers into all classes. 1,064 transfer applications were received, 890 were accepted. Application deadline is July 1 for fall; December 1 for spring. Minimum 2.0 GPA required. Lowest course grade accepted is "C." Maximum number of transferable credits is 72 semester hours from a two-year school and 102 semester hours from a four-year school. At least 30 semester hours must be completed at the university to receive degree.
**Admissions contact:** Randall E. Kouba, M.P.A., Director of Admissions. 719 593-3383.
**FINANCIAL AID. Available aid:** Pell grants, SEOG, Federal Nursing Student Scholarships, state scholarships and grants, school scholarships, private scholarships, ROTC scholarships, academic merit scholarships, and athletic scholarships. Perkins Loans (NDSL), PLUS, Stafford Loans (GSL), school loans, private loans, and SLS. AMS.
**Financial aid statistics:** 20% of aid is not need-based. In 1993-94, 85% of all undergraduate applicants received aid; 79% of freshman applicants. Average amounts of aid awarded freshmen: Scholarships and grants, $1,840; loans, $2,650.
**Supporting data/closing dates:** FAFSA/FFS: Priority filing date is April 1. School's own aid application: Priority filing date is April 1. Income tax forms: Priority filing date is April 1. IVF: Priority filing date is April 1. Notification of awards on rolling basis.
**Financial aid contact:** Lee Ingalls Noble, M.A., Director of Financial Aid. 719 593-3460.
**STUDENT EMPLOYMENT.** College Work/Study Program. Institutional employment. 15% of full-time undergraduates work on campus during school year. Students may expect to earn an average of $700 during school year. Off-campus part-time employment opportunities rated "good."
**COMPUTER FACILITIES.** 250 IBM/IBM-compatible and Macintosh/Apple microcomputers; 200 are networked. Students may access Digital minicomputer/mainframe systems, BITNET, Internet. Computer languages and software packages include Ada, BASIC, C, COBOL, dBASE, FORTRAN, IFPS, INGRES, LISP, Lotus 1-2-3, Pascal, SAS, SPSS, WordPerfect; 30 in all. Computer facilities are available to all students.

**Fees:** $10 computer fee per semester.
**Hours:** 24 hours (mainframe lab); 10 AM-10 PM (microcomputer lab).

**GRADUATE CAREER DATA.** Highest graduate school enrollments: U of Colorado at Boulder, U of Colorado at Colorado Springs, U of Colorado Health Sciences Center, U of Denver.

## University of Colorado at Denver

**Denver, CO 80217-3364** **303 556-2400**

**1994-95 Costs.** Tuition: $1,740 (state residents), $8,404 (out-of-state). Housing: None. Fees, books, misc. academic expenses (school's estimate): $735.
**Enrollment.** Undergraduates: 1,746 men, 1,955 women (full-time). Freshman class: 1,199 applicants, 562 accepted, 261 enrolled. Graduate enrollment: 2,091 men, 2,532 women.
**Test score averages/ranges.** Average SAT scores: 478 verbal, 526 math. Average ACT scores: 23 English, 24 math, 23 composite.
**Faculty.** 360 full-time; 200 part-time. 83% of faculty holds doctoral degree. Student/faculty ratio: 16 to 1.
**Selectivity rating.** Competitive.

**PROFILE.** U Colorado at Denver, founded in 1912, is a public university. Programs are offered through the Colleges of Business and Administration, Engineering and Applied Science, and Liberal Arts and Sciences; the Graduate School; the Graduate Schools of Business Administration and Public Affairs; the Military Science program; and the Schools of Architecture and Planning and Education. Its 169-acre campus is located in downtown Denver.

**Accreditation:** NCACS. Professionally accredited by the Accreditation Board for Engineering and Technology, the American Assembly of Collegiate Schools of Business, the National Association of Schools of Music, the National Council for Accreditation of Teacher Education.
**Religious orientation:** University of Colorado at Denver is nonsectarian; no religious requirements.
**Library:** Collections totaling over 507,914 volumes, 3,332 periodical subscriptions, and 644,956 microform items.
**Athletic facilities:** Gymnasium, swimming pool, track and field, handball and racquetball courts.

**STUDENT BODY. Undergraduate profile:** 95% are state residents; 41% are transfers. 7% Asian-American, 4% Black, 9% Hispanic, 1% Native American, 71% White, 8% Other. Average age of undergraduates is 26.
**Freshman profile:** 3% of freshmen who took SAT scored 700 or over on verbal, 3% scored 700 or over on math; 15% scored 600 or over on verbal, 25% scored 600 or over on math; 41% scored 500 or over on verbal, 60% scored 500 or over on math; 79% scored 400 or over on verbal, 94% scored 400 or over on math; 95% scored 300 or over on verbal, 98% scored 300 or over on math. 51% of accepted applicants took SAT; 87% took ACT. 92% of freshmen come from public schools.
**Undergraduate achievement:** 68% of fall 1992 freshmen returned for fall 1993 term. 40% of students who completed a degree program immediately went on to graduate study.
**Foreign students:** 324 students are from out of the country. Countries represented include China, India, Indonesia, Japan, Taiwan, and Thailand; 54 in all.

**PROGRAMS OF STUDY. Degrees:** B.A., B.F.A., B.S.
**Majors:** Anthropology, Applied Mathematics, Biology, Business Administration, Chemistry, Civil Engineering, Communication/Theatre, Computer Science/Engineering, Economics, Electrical Engineering, English, Fine Arts, French, Geography, Geology, German, History, Individually-Structured Major, Mathematics, Mechanical Engineering, Music, Philosophy, Physics, Political Science, Psychology, Sociology, Spanish, Writing Program.
**Distribution of degrees:** The major with the highest enrollment is business administration; German has the lowest.
**Requirements:** General education requirement.
**Academic regulations:** Minimum 2.0 GPA must be maintained.
**Special:** Minors offered. Self-designed majors. Double majors. Dual degrees. Independent study. Pass/fail grading option. Internships. Cooperative education programs. Graduate school at which undergraduates may take graduate-level courses. Preprofessional programs in medicine and dentistry. Five-year engineering/business program. Cross-registration with Community Coll of Denver-Auraria and Metropolitan State Coll of Denver. Teacher certification in early childhood, elementary, secondary, special education, and bilingual/bicultural education. Certification in specific subject areas. Study abroad in France, Germany, and Russia. ROTC. AFROTC at U of Colorado at Boulder.
**Honors:** Phi Beta Kappa. Honors program. Honor societies.
**Academic Assistance:** Remedial study skills. Nonremedial tutoring.

**STUDENT LIFE. Housing:** Commuter campus; no student housing.
**Social atmosphere:** Rockies Deli and 9th Street Park are popular on-campus locations for students. Favorite places off-campus are St. Mark's Coffeehouse, the Market, and Skyline Park. Student Government/Student Events, CoPIRG (Colorado Public Interest Research Group), honor societies, academic clubs, and the Student Advisory Committee to the Auraria Board are influential in student life. Fall Fest, Halloween Scream, AIDS awareness month, and Spring Fling are popular social/educational events. Since this is a non-residential campus, the student median age is higher than average and the student body is more diverse and disconnected than at residential universities. "However, the student newspaper and other small groups provide students with many entertainment and lifestyle opportunities and information," according to the editor of the student newspaper.
**Services and counseling/handicapped student services:** Placement services. Health service. Women's center. Day care. Counseling services for minority, veteran, and older students. Personal counseling. Career and academic guidance services. Physically disabled student services. Learning disabled program/services. Notetaking services. Tutors. Reader services for the blind.
**Campus organizations:** Undergraduate student government. Student newspaper (Advocate, published once/week). Literary magazine. Chorale, jazz band, electronic music group, debating, drama group, departmental and political groups, professional groups, special-interest groups, 43 organizations in all.
**Religious organizations:** Several religious groups.
**Minority/foreign student organizations:** Asian-American Student Alliance, Black Student Alliance, Native American Organization, United Mexican-American Students. International Club.

**ATHLETICS. Physical education requirements:** None.
**Intercollegiate competition:** 1% of students participate.
**Intramural and club sports:** Intramural football, racquetball, soccer, tennis, track and field.

**ADMISSIONS. Academic basis for candidate selection** (in order of priority): Secondary school record, standardized test scores, class rank, school's recommendation.
**Nonacademic basis for candidate selection:** Particular talent or ability and alumni/ae relationship are considered.
**Requirements:** Graduation from secondary school is required; GED is accepted. 15 units and the following program of study are required: 4 units of English, 3 units of math, 3 units of science including 2 units of lab, 2 units of foreign language, 2 units of social studies, 1 unit of academic electives. Minimum composite ACT score of 26 (combined SAT score of 1070) and rank in top fifth of secondary school class recommended. Audition required of music program applicants. EOP and conditional admission possible for applicants not meeting standard requirements. SAT or ACT is required. Campus visit recommended. No off-campus interviews.
**Procedure:** Take SAT or ACT by October of 12th year. Suggest filing application by May 1. Application deadline is July 22. Notification of admission on rolling basis. No set date by which applicants must accept offer. Freshmen accepted in terms other than fall.
**Special programs:** Admission may be deferred one term. Credit and/or placement may be granted through CEEB Advanced Placement exams for scores of 4 or higher. Credit may be granted through CLEP subject exams, DANTES and challenge exams, and military experience. Early entrance/early admission program. Concurrent enrollment program.
**Transfer students:** Transfer students accepted for terms other than fall. In fall 1993, 41% of all new students were transfers into all classes. 1,965 transfer applications were received, 1,643 were accepted. Application deadline is July 22 for fall; December 1 for spring. Minimum 2.0 GPA required. Lowest course grade accepted is "C." Maximum number of transferable credits is 60 semester hours from a two-year school and 90 semester hours from a four-year school. At least 30 semester hours must be completed at the university to receive degree.
**Admissions contact:** Barbara Schneider, Ph.D., Asst. Vice Chancellor for Enrollment and Student Services. 303 556-3287.

**FINANCIAL AID. Available aid:** Pell grants, SEOG, state scholarships and grants, school scholarships and grants, private scholarships, and academic merit scholarships. Perkins Loans (NDSL), PLUS, Stafford Loans (GSL), school loans, private loans, and SLS. Deferred payment plan.
**Financial aid statistics:** 48% of aid is not need-based. In 1993-94, 65% of all undergraduate applicants received aid; 65% of freshman applicants. Average amounts of aid awarded freshmen: Scholarships and grants, $800; loans, $2,000.
**Supporting data/closing dates:** FAFSA: Priority filing date is March 1. School's own aid application: Priority filing date is March 31. Notification of awards begins April 15.
**Financial aid contact:** Ellie Miller, M.A., Director of Financial Aid. 303 556-2886.

**STUDENT EMPLOYMENT.** College Work/Study Program. Institutional employment. 10% of full-time undergraduates work on campus during school year. Students may expect to earn an average of $2,000 during school year. Off-campus part-time employment opportunities rated "good."

**COMPUTER FACILITIES.** 450 IBM/IBM-compatible and Macintosh/Apple microcomputers; all are networked. Students may access Digital, Sequent, SUN minicomputer/mainframe systems, BITNET, Internet. Client/LAN operating systems include Apple/Macintosh, DOS, UNIX/XENIX/AIX, Banyan, LocalTalk/AppleTalk. 50 major computer languages and software packages available. Computer facilities are available to all students.
**Fees:** $10 computer fee per semester.
**Hours:** 8 AM-11 PM.

**GRADUATE CAREER DATA.** 70% of graduates choose careers in business and industry.

**PROMINENT ALUMNI/AE.** Ralph Sargent III, Vice President, Public Service Co. of Colorado; Al Stecklein, President, North American Operation Gates Rubber Tire.

## University of Denver

**Denver, CO 80208** **303 871-2000**

**1994-95 Costs.** Tuition: $15,192. Room & board: $4,578. Fees, books, misc. academic expenses (school's estimate): $730.
**Enrollment.** Undergraduates: 1,296 men, 1,379 women (full-time). Freshman class: 2,484 applicants, 2,001 accepted, 582 enrolled. Graduate enrollment: 2,467 men, 2,528 women.
**Test score averages/ranges.** Average SAT scores: 470 verbal, 540 math. Average ACT scores: 24 composite. Range of ACT scores of middle 50%: 21-27 composite.
**Faculty.** 378 full-time; 21 part-time. 91% of faculty holds highest degree in specific field. Student/faculty ratio: 13 to 1.
**Selectivity rating.** Competitive.

**PROFILE.** The University of Denver, founded in 1864, is a church-affiliated institution. Programs are offered through the Colleges of Business Administration, Human Services, and Law; the Faculties of Arts and Humanities, Mathematical and Computer Sciences, Natural Sciences, and Social Sciences; and the Graduate Schools of Business and Public Management, International Studies, and Social Work. Its 125-acre main campus is located seven miles from downtown Denver.

**Accreditation:** NCACS. Professionally accredited by the Accreditation Board for Engineering and Technology, the American Assembly of Collegiate Schools of Business, the National Association of Schools of Music.
**Religious orientation:** University of Denver is an interdenominational Christian school; no religious requirements.
**Library:** Collections totaling over 1,057,979 volumes, 4,796 periodical subscriptions, and 845,127 microform items.
**Special facilities/museums:** Center for Latin American studies, museum of anthropology, center for gifted and talented children, regional conservation center, observatory, electron microscope.
**Athletic facilities:** Field house, gymnasiums, swimming pool, ice rink, basketball, racquetball, tennis, and volleyball courts, weight room, baseball and intramural fields.

**STUDENT BODY. Undergraduate profile:** 32% are state residents; 10% are transfers. 4.9% Asian-American, 2.8% Black, 4.6% Hispanic, .4% Native American, 75.9% White, 11.4% Other. Average age of undergraduates is 21.
**Freshman profile:** 1% of freshmen who took SAT scored 700 or over on verbal, 2% scored 700 or over on math; 9% scored 600 or over on verbal, 21% scored 600 or over on math; 38% scored 500 or over on verbal, 64% scored 500 or over on math; 83% scored 400 or over on verbal, 91% scored 400 or over on math; 99% scored 300 or over on verbal, 100% scored 300 or over on math. 73% of accepted applicants took SAT; 65% took ACT.
**Undergraduate achievement:** 81% of fall 1992 freshmen returned for fall 1993 term. 58% of entering class graduated. 27% of students who completed a degree program went on to graduate study within one year.
**Foreign students:** 279 students are from out of the country. Countries represented include Canada, Indonesia, Japan, Korea, Malaysia, and United Arab Emirates; 71 in all.

**PROGRAMS OF STUDY. Degrees:** B.A., B.Bus.Admin., B.F.A., B.Mus., B.Mus.Ed., B.S.
**Majors:** Accounting, Animal Technology, Anthropology, Art, Biological Sciences, Chemistry, Classical Studies, Commercial Art, Communications, Computer Science, Decision Sciences, Economics, Electrical Engineering, Engineering, English, Environmental Sciences, Finance, Finance/Marketing, Finance/Real Estate, French, General Business, Geography, German, Graphic Communication Design, History, Hospitality Management/Tourism, Human Communication, International Business, International Studies, Journalism, Latin American Studies, Marketing, Mass Communications, Mathematics, Mechanical Engineering, Music, Philosophy, Physics, Political Science, Psychology, Public Affairs, Real Estate/Construction Management, Religious Studies, Russian, Russian Area Studies, Science, Social Science, Sociology, Spanish, Speech Communication, Statistics, Studio Art, Theatre, Women's Studies.
**Distribution of degrees:** The majors with the highest enrollment are general business, mass communications, and journalism; theatre and religious studies have the lowest.
**Requirements:** General education requirement.
**Academic regulations:** Minimum 2.0 GPA must be maintained.
**Special:** Minors offered in most majors. Double majors. Dual degrees. Independent study. Accelerated study. Internships. Cooperative education programs. Graduate school at which undergraduates may take graduate-level courses. Preprofessional programs in law, medicine, veterinary science, and dentistry. 3-2 liberal arts/business and engineering programs. Teacher certification in elementary, secondary, and special education. Certification in specific subject areas. Exchange programs abroad in Denmark (Southern Denmark Business Sch), England (Brighton U), France (U of Paris), and Germany (U of Tubingen). Study abroad also in Canada and in African, Asian, Australian, European, and Latin American countries. ROTC and AFROTC at U of Colorado at Boulder.
**Honors:** Phi Beta Kappa. Honors program. Honor societies.

**STUDENT LIFE. Housing:** All unmarried freshmen and sophomores under age 21 must live on campus unless living with family within a 90-mile radius. Coed dorms. Sorority and fraternity housing. School-owned/operated apartments. 56% of students live in college housing.
**Social atmosphere:** As reported by the student newspaper, the most popular events are Geneva Glenn, Winter Carnival, Spring Week, Homecoming, and hockey games, especially those against rival Colorado College. The most influential groups on campus include the hockey and basketball teams, the Greek organizations, and the Campus Crusade for Christ. Favorite student gathering spots are the D.U. Pub, the Border, Sweet Marie Cafe, and the Pearl St. Bar & Grill.
**Services and counseling/handicapped student services:** Placement services. Health service. Counseling services for minority, military, veteran, and older students. Birth control, personal, and psychological counseling. Career and academic guidance services. Religious counseling. Physically disabled student services. Learning disabled program/services. Notetaking services. Tape recorders. Tutors. Reader services for the blind.
**Campus organizations:** Undergraduate student government. Student newspaper (Clarion, published once/week). Literary magazine. Yearbook. Radio station. Bands, choir, chorale, ensembles, Program Board, Access, Alpine Club, BACCHUS, Care, Circle K, forensics group, 82 organizations in all. Nine fraternities, all with chapter houses; five sororities, all with chapter houses. 41% of men join a fraternity. 24% of women join a sorority.
**Religious organizations:** Intervarsity Christian Fellowship, Baptist Student Union, B'nai B'rith, Hillel, Campus Ambassadors, Catholic Campus Ministries, Christian Science Ministry, Day Springs Ministry, Episcopal Canterbury Club, Latter-Day Saints Student Association, Presbyterian Fellowship, United Methodist group.
**Minority/foreign student organizations:** Asian Law Student Association, Black Student Alliance, Black Law Students Association, Hispanic Student Alliance, Hispanic Law Students Association, Ka-ohana club, Native American Law Students Association, Vietnamese Student Alliance. International Student Organization, Indonesian Students, Japanese Association, Korean, Malaysian, and Thai student groups.

**ATHLETICS. Physical education requirements:** None.
**Intercollegiate competition:** 15% of students participate. Alpine skiing (M,W), baseball (M), basketball (M,W), cheerleading (M,W), diving (M,W), golf (M), gymnastics (W), ice hockey (M), lacrosse (M), Nordic skiing (M,W), soccer (M,W), swimming (M,W), tennis (M,W), volleyball (W). Member of Colorado Athletic Conference, Intermountain Swimming League, NCAA Division I for men's ice hockey and women's gymnastics, NCAA Division II, Rocky Mountain Intercollegiate Lacrosse Conference, Western Collegiate Hockey Association.
**Intramural and club sports:** 60% of students participate. Intramural Alpine skiing, badminton, basketball, bowling, broomball, canoeing, cross-country, flag football, golf, ice hockey, kayaking, racquetball, soccer, softball, tennis, volleyball, water basketball, water polo. Men's club Alpine skiing, ice hockey, lacrosse, martial arts, Nordic skiing, rugby, volleyball, water polo. Women's club Alpine skiing, lacrosse, martial arts, Nordic skiing.

**ADMISSIONS. Academic basis for candidate selection** (in order of priority): Secondary school record, standardized test scores, class rank, school's recommendation, essay.
**Nonacademic basis for candidate selection:** Character and personality, extracurricular participation, and particular talent or ability are important. Alumni/ae relationship is considered.
**Requirements:** Graduation from secondary school is required; GED is accepted. No specific distribution of secondary school units required. Minimum combined SAT score of 850 (composite ACT score of 18), rank in top three-fifths of secondary school class, and minimum 2.8 GPA recommended. Portfolio recommended of art program applicants. Audition required of music program applicants. SAT or ACT is required. Campus visit and interview recommended. Off-campus interviews available with an admissions representative.
**Procedure:** Take SAT or ACT by December of 12th year. Visit college for interview by April of 12th year. Suggest filing application by December 20. Application deadline is March 1. Notification of admission on rolling basis. Reply is required by May 1. $200 nonrefundable tuition deposit. $100 room deposit, refundable until beginning of term. Freshmen accepted in terms other than fall.
**Special programs:** Admission may be deferred two years. Credit and/or placement may be granted through CEEB Advanced Placement exams for scores of 3 or higher. Credit and/or placement may be granted through CLEP general and subject exams. Placement may be granted through challenge exams. Early entrance/early admission program. Concurrent enrollment program.
**Transfer students:** Transfer students accepted for terms other than fall. In fall 1993, 10% of all new students were transfers into all classes. 596 transfer applications were received, 517 were accepted. Application deadline is August 1 for fall; December 1 for winter; February 15 for spring. Minimum 2.0 GPA required. Lowest course grade accepted is "C." Maximum number of transferable credits is 90 quarter hours from a two-year school and 138 quarter hours from a four-year school. At least 43 quarter hours must be completed at the university to receive degree.
**Admissions contact:** Roger Campbell, Dean of Admission and Financial Aid. 303 871-2036.

**FINANCIAL AID. Available aid:** Pell grants, SEOG, state scholarships and grants, school scholarships and grants, private scholarships and grants, ROTC scholarships, academic merit scholarships, athletic scholarships, and aid for undergraduate foreign students. Perkins Loans (NDSL), PLUS, Stafford Loans (GSL), school loans, private loans, and SLS. Tuition Plan Inc., Knight Tuition Plans, AMS, and deferred payment plan.
**Financial aid statistics:** 35% of aid is not need-based. In 1993-94, 97% of all undergraduate applicants received aid; 96% of freshman applicants. Average amounts of aid awarded freshmen: Scholarships and grants, $7,182; loans, $2,800.
**Supporting data/closing dates:** FAFSA: Priority filing date is February 20. Income tax forms: Accepted on rolling basis. Notification of awards begins April 1.
**Financial aid contact:** Colleen Hillmeyer, M.Ed., Director of Financial Aid. 303 871-2681.

**STUDENT EMPLOYMENT.** College Work/Study Program. Institutional employment. 25% of full-time undergraduates work on campus during school year. Students may expect to earn an average of $1,618 during school year. Off-campus part-time employment opportunities rated "excellent."

**COMPUTER FACILITIES.** 410 IBM/IBM-compatible and Macintosh/Apple microcomputers; all are networked. Students may access Digital, IBM minicomputer/mainframe systems, BITNET, Internet. Residence halls may be equipped with networked microcomputers, modems. Client/LAN operating systems include Apple/Macintosh, DOS, UNIX/XENIX/AIX, LocalTalk/AppleTalk, Novell. Computer languages and software packages include Ada, BASIC, BMDP, C, COBOL, dBASE, Excel, FORTRAN, Gopher, INGRES, LISP, Maple, Microsoft Word, MINITAB, PowerPoint, Prolog, SAS, Shazam!, SPSS, Windows, WordPerfect. Computer facilities are available to all students.
**Fees:** None.
**Hours:** 24 hours.

**GRADUATE CAREER DATA.** Graduate school percentages: 5% enter law school. 2% enter medical school. 4% enter graduate business programs. 11% enter graduate arts and sciences programs. 1% enter theological school/seminary. Highest graduate school enrollments: Columbia U, Pepperdine U, U of California at Berkeley, U of Chicago, U of Colorado, U of Denver, U of Notre Dame, U of Pennsylania, U of Texas, Yale U. 60% of graduates choose careers in business and industry. Companies and businesses that hire graduates: Arthur Andersen, CitiCorp, Great West Life, Hughes Aircraft, Hyatt, MCI, Southern Pacific Transportation, United Airlines, Walt Disney World.

**PROMINENT ALUMNI/AE.** Marc Nathanson, chairman and CEO, Falcon Cable TV; Peter Morton, founder, Hard Rock America; Pete Domenici, U.S. senator.

# University of Northern Colorado

**Greeley, CO 80639 303 351-1890**

**1993-94 Costs.** Tuition: $1,742 (state residents), $7,028 (out-of-state). Room & board: $3,894. Fees, books, misc. academic expenses (school's estimate): $892.
**Enrollment.** Undergraduates: 3,374 men, 4,651 women (full-time). Freshman class: 5,530 applicants, 4,007 accepted, 1,721 enrolled. Graduate enrollment: 586 men, 1,011 women.
**Test score averages/ranges.** Average SAT scores: 436 verbal, 480 math. Range of SAT scores of middle 50%: 380-480 verbal, 420-540 math. Average ACT scores: 21 English, 21 math, 22 composite. Range of ACT scores of middle 50%: 18-24 English, 18-23 math.
**Faculty.** 426 full-time; 130 part-time. 75% of faculty holds doctoral degree. Student/faculty ratio: 21 to 1.
**Selectivity rating.** Less competitive.

**PROFILE.** The University of Northern Colorado is a public university. Founded as a Normal school in 1890, it gained university status in 1970. Programs are offered through the Colleges of Arts and Sciences, Business Administration, Education, Health and Human Services, Human Performance and Leisure Studies, Performing and Visual Arts, and the Graduate School. Its 236-acre campus is located in Greeley, 50 miles north of Denver.
**Accreditation:** NCACS. Professionally accredited by the American Assembly of Collegiate Schools of Business, the American Dietetic Association, the American Psychological Association, the American Speech-Language-Hearing Association, the Council on Education for Public Health, the Council on Rehabilitation Education, the National Association of Schools of Music, the National Council for Accreditation of Teacher Education, the National League for Nursing.
**Religious orientation:** University of Northern Colorado is nonsectarian; no religious requirements.
**Library:** Collections totaling over 901,042 volumes, 4,289 periodical subscriptions, and 859,964 microform items.
**Special facilities/museums:** Art museum, music library, on-campus lab school (K-12).
**Athletic facilities:** Gymnasium, field house, natatorium, baseball and football fields, track, tennis courts.

**STUDENT BODY. Undergraduate profile:** 89% are state residents; 37% are transfers. 2% Asian-American, 2% Black, 7% Hispanic, 1% Native American, 85% White, 3% Other. Average age of undergraduates is 22.
**Freshman profile:** 2% of freshmen who took SAT scored 700 or over on math; 4% scored 600 or over on verbal, 10% scored 600 or over on math; 22% scored 500 or over on verbal, 45% scored 500 or over on math; 68% scored 400 or over on verbal, 81% scored 400 or over on math; 97% scored 300 or over on verbal, 97% scored 300 or over on math. 2% of freshmen who took ACT scored 30 or over on English, 1% scored 30 or over on math, 1% scored 30 or over on composite; 31% scored 24 or over on English, 21% scored 24 or over on math, 31% scored 24 or over on composite; 81% scored 18 or over on English, 79% scored 18 or over on math, 89% scored 18 or over on composite; 99% scored 12 or over on English, 100% scored 12 or over on math, 99% scored 12 or over on composite; 100% scored 6 or over on English. 48% of accepted applicants took SAT; 85% took ACT. 95% of freshmen come from public schools.
**Undergraduate achievement:** 66% of fall 1992 freshmen returned for fall 1993 term. 15% of entering class graduated. 9% of students who completed a degree program went on to graduate study within one year.
**Foreign students:** 88 students are from out of the country. Countries represented include Japan, Korea, and Mexico; 43 in all.

**PROGRAMS OF STUDY. Degrees:** B.A., B.Mus., B.Mus.Ed., B.S.
**Majors:** Biological Science, Black Studies, Business Administration, Chemistry, Communication, Communication Disorders/Audiology, Communication Disorders/Speech/Language Pathology, Dietetics, Earth Sciences, Economics, English, French, Geography, German, Gerontology, Health, Hispanic Studies, History, Human Rehabilitative Services, Interdisciplinary Studies, Journalism, Kinesiology, Mathematics, Medical Technology, Music, Musical Theatre, Nursing, Philosophy, Physical Sciences, Physics, Political Science, Psychology, Recreation, Social Science, Sociology, Spanish, Theatre Arts, Visual Arts.
**Distribution of degrees:** The majors with the highest enrollment are business administration, psychology, and sociology; medical technology, foreign languages, and gerontology have the lowest.
**Requirements:** General education requirement.
**Academic regulations:** Minimum 2.0 GPA must be maintained.
**Special:** Minors offered in most majors and in anthropology, applied statistics, community health education, computer information systems, computer science, dance, early childhood, environmental studies, food/nutrition, humanities, legal studies, Mexican-American studies, military science, physical education, reading, school health education, special education, teaching English as a second language, women's studies, and writing. Self-designed majors. Double majors. Dual degrees. Independent study. Accelerated study. Pass/fail grading option. Internships. Graduate school at which undergraduates may take graduate-level courses. Preprofessional programs in law, medicine, veterinary science, pharmacy, dentistry, optometry, and engineering. Member of National Student Exchange (NSE). Teacher certification in early childhood, elementary, secondary, and special education. Certification in specific subject areas. Member of International Student Exchange Program (ISEP). Exchange program abroad in England (Oxford U). Study abroad also in France, Germany, and Spain. ROTC and AFROTC.
**Honors:** Honors program. Honor societies.
**Academic Assistance:** Remedial reading, writing, math, and study skills. Nonremedial tutoring.

**STUDENT LIFE. Housing:** All unmarried freshman under age 21 not living with relatives must live on campus. Coed and women's dorms. Sorority and fraternity housing. School-owned/operated apartments. Both on-campus and off-campus married-student housing. 30% of students live in college housing.
**Services and counseling/handicapped student services:** Placement services. Health service. Day care. Counseling services for minority, military, and older students. Birth control, personal, and psychological counseling. Career and academic guidance services. Physically disabled student services. Learning disabled services. Notetaking services. Reader services for the blind.
**Campus organizations:** Undergraduate student government. Student newspaper (Mirror, published three times/week). Literary magazine. Yearbook. Radio station. Chorus, band, orchestra, debating, Little Theatre, service fraternities, departmental, political, and special-interest groups, 72 organizations in all. Nine fraternities, all with chapter houses; five sororities, all with chapter houses. 9% of men join a fraternity. 6% of women join a sorority.
**Religious organizations:** Numerous religious groups.
**Minority/foreign student organizations:** Black Student Union, Organization of Hispanic Students. International Student Association.

**ATHLETICS. Physical education requirements:** One semester of physical education required.
**Intercollegiate competition:** 11% of students participate. Baseball (M), basketball (M,W), cross-country (W), diving (W), football (M), golf (M), soccer (W), swimming (W), tennis (M,W), track and field (indoor) (M,W), track and field (outdoor) (M,W), volleyball (W), wrestling (M). Member of NCAA Division II, North Central Intercollegiate Athletic Conference.
**Intramural and club sports:** 60% of students participate. Intramural basketball, flag football, floor hockey, inner-tube water polo, soccer, softball, volleyball. Men's club cycling, golf, karate, lacrosse, racquetball, rugby, soccer, volleyball. Women's club cycling, karate, racquetball, rugby.

**ADMISSIONS. Academic basis for candidate selection** (in order of priority): Secondary school record, class rank, standardized test scores, school's recommendation.
**Nonacademic basis for candidate selection:** Character and personality, extracurricular participation, particular talent or ability, and geographical distribution are considered.
**Requirements:** Graduation from secondary school is required; GED is accepted. 15 units required and the following program of study recommended: 4 unit of English, 3 units of math, 2 units of science, 2 units of social studies. Composite ACT score of 22 (combined SAT score of 890), rank in top two-fifths of secondary school class, and 2.8 GPA recommended. Audition required of music program applicants. Conditional admission possible for applicants not meeting standard requirements. SAT or ACT is required. Campus visit recommended. Off-campus interviews available with an admissions representative.
**Procedure:** Take SAT or ACT by November of 12th year. Suggest filing application by November. Application deadline is August 1. Notification of admission on rolling basis. No set date by which applicants must accept offer. $100 room deposit, refundable until May 31. Freshmen accepted in terms other than fall.
**Special programs:** Credit and/or placement may be granted through CEEB Advanced Placement exams for scores of 3 or higher. Credit and/or placement may be granted through CLEP subject exams. Credit may be granted through challenge exams and military experience. Early entrance/early admission program. Concurrent enrollment program.
**Transfer students:** Transfer students accepted for terms other than fall. In fall 1993, 37% of all new students were transfers into all classes. 2,022 transfer applications were received, 1,773 were accepted. Application deadline is August 1 for fall; January 1 for spring. Minimum 2.0 GPA required. Lowest course grade accepted is "C." Maximum number of transferable credits is 64 semester hours from a two-year school and 90 semester hours from a four-year school. At least 30 semester hours must be completed at the university to receive degree.
**Admissions contact:** Gary Gullickson, Director of Admissions. 303 351-2881.

**FINANCIAL AID. Available aid:** Pell grants, SEOG, state scholarships and grants, school scholarships and grants, private scholarships and grants, ROTC scholarships, academic merit scholarships, and athletic scholarships. Perkins Loans (NDSL), PLUS, Stafford Loans (GSL), school loans, and SLS. Deferred payment plan.
**Financial aid statistics:** 16% of aid is not need-based. In 1993-94, 91% of all undergraduate applicants received aid; 89% of freshman applicants. Average amounts of aid awarded freshmen: Scholarships and grants, $937; loans, $1,846.
**Supporting data/closing dates:** FAFSA: Priority filing date is March 1. Notification of awards begins April 15.
**Financial aid contact:** Michael E. Maestas, Director of Financial Aid. 303 351-2502.

**STUDENT EMPLOYMENT.** College Work/Study Program. Institutional employment. 30% of full-time undergraduates work on campus during school year. Students may expect to earn an average of $1,290 during school year. Off-campus part-time employment opportunities rated "good."

**COMPUTER FACILITIES.** 600 IBM/IBM-compatible and Macintosh/Apple microcomputers; 120 are networked. Students may access Digital, IBM minicomputer/mainframe systems, Internet. Residence halls may be equipped with stand-alone microcomputers. Client/LAN operating systems include Apple/Macintosh, DOS, UNIX/XENIX/AIX, LocalTalk/AppleTalk, Novell. Computer languages and software packages include COBOL, FORTRAN, GPSS/H, SAS, SPSS. Computer facilities are available to all students.
**Fees:** $3 computer fee per credit hour; included in tuition/fees.

**PROMINENT ALUMNI/AE.** Nick Nolte and Lee Horsley, actors; James Michener, author; Steve Antonopulos, athletic trainer, Denver Broncos; Dr. Gerald Schmidt, research fellow, NATO.

# University of Southern Colorado

**Pueblo, CO 81001** **719 549-2100**

**1993-94 Costs.** Tuition: $1,536 (state residents), $6,088 (out-of-state). Room: $1,600. Board: $2,000. Fees, books, misc. academic expenses (school's estimate): $797.
**Enrollment.** Undergraduates: 1,786 men, 1,912 women (full-time). Freshman class: 1,402 applicants, 1,262 accepted, 698 enrolled. Graduate enrollment: 98 men, 87 women.
**Test score averages/ranges.** Average SAT scores: 860 combined. Range of SAT scores of middle 50%: 330-480 verbal, 380-550 math. Average ACT scores: 20 composite. Range of ACT scores of middle 50%: 13-26 English, 14-26 math.
**Faculty.** 168 full-time; 110 part-time. 84% of faculty holds highest degree in specific field. Student/faculty ratio: 18 to 1.
**Selectivity rating.** Noncompetitive.

**PROFILE.** University of Southern Colorado is a public, polytechnic university. It was founded as a two-year institution in 1933, became a four-year college in 1963, and gained university status in 1975. Its 800-acre campus is located in Pueblo, 40 miles south of Colorado Springs.

**Accreditation:** NCACS. Professionally accredited by the Accreditation Board for Engineering and Technology, the Council on Social Work Education, the National Association of Schools of Music, the National League for Nursing.
**Religious orientation:** University of Southern Colorado is nonsectarian; no religious requirements.
**Library:** Collections totaling over 185,600 volumes, 1,300 periodical subscriptions, and 6,440 microform items.
**Special facilities/museums:** Recital hall, communication center, electron microscope.
**Athletic facilities:** Racquetball and tennis courts, baseball, football, softball, and soccer fields, gymnasium, swimming pool, weight room, climbing wall.

**STUDENT BODY. Undergraduate profile:** 95% are state residents; 37% are transfers. 1% Asian-American, 3% Black, 23% Hispanic, 1% Native American, 68% White, 4% Other. Average age of undergraduates is 23.
**Freshman profile:** 1% of freshmen who took ACT scored 30 or over on composite; 25% scored 24 or over on composite; 70% scored 18 or over on composite; 100% scored 12 or over on composite. 11% of accepted applicants took SAT; 96% took ACT.
**Foreign students:** 138 students are from out of the country. Countries represented include Germany, Indonesia, Japan, Pakistan, Saudi Arabia, and Thailand; 33 in all.

**PROGRAMS OF STUDY. Degrees:** B.A., B.S., B.Soc.Work.
**Majors:** Accounting, Art, Automotive Parts/Service Management, Biology, Business Administration, Chemistry, Civil Engineering Technology, Computer Science Technology, Economics, Electronics Engineering Technology, English, History, Industrial Engineering, Industrial Science/Technology, Management/Marketing, Mass Communications, Mathematics, Mechanical Engineering Technology, Music, Nursing, Physical Education, Physics, Political Science, Psychology, Recreation, Social Science, Social Work, Sociology/Anthropology, Spanish, Speech Communication/Theatre, Sports Medicine.
**Distribution of degrees:** The majors with the highest enrollment are management/marketing, mass communications, and biology; history, English, and chemistry have the lowest.
**Requirements:** General education requirement.
**Academic regulations:** Minimum 2.0 GPA must be maintained.
**Special:** Minors offered in many majors and in Chicano studies, education, and foreign languages. Double majors. Dual degrees. Independent study. Internships. Cooperative education programs. Graduate school at which undergraduates may take graduate-level courses. Preprofessional programs in law, medicine, veterinary science, pharmacy, dentistry, optometry, and physical therapy. 2-2 engineering program with Colorado State U. Member of Colorado State University System. Member of National Student Exchange (NSE). Teacher certification in elementary, secondary, and bilingual/bicultural education. Certification in specific subject areas. Study abroad in Germany, Italy, and Mexico.
**Honors:** Honors program.
**Academic Assistance:** Nonremedial tutoring.

**STUDENT LIFE. Housing:** All unmarried, nonveteran freshmen must live on campus unless living with family within a 50-mile radius. Coed dorms. 9% of students live in college housing.
**Social atmosphere:** According to the student newspaper, "USC is the perfect size for a school with approximately 5,000 students, large enough for quality faculty but small enough not to get lost in the shuffle. In the last couple of years, there has been a synergy created between USC and Pueblo, a community of 100,000 middle-income families." The most influential campus group is the Student Activities Board. Students enjoy attending the basketball tournament, the Colorado State Fair, and Party Gras. On campus, they frequent La Cantina, The Wall, and Fountain Plaza; off campus, they head for Easy Street, the Savoy, the Cavalcade, Riverside, and the Irish Pub.
**Services and counseling/handicapped student services:** Placement services. Health service. Women's center. Counseling services for minority, military, veteran, and older students. Birth control, personal, and psychological counseling. Career and academic guidance services. Religious counseling. Physically disabled student services. Learning disabled services. Notetaking services. Tape recorders. Tutors. Reader services for the blind.
**Campus organizations:** Undergraduate student government. Student newspaper (USC Today, published once/week). Radio and TV stations. 33 registered organizations. One fraternity, no chapter house.
**Religious organizations:** Baptist Student Union, Campus Ministry, Intervarsity Christian Fellowship.
**Minority/foreign student organizations:** Black Student Organization. International Student Association, Nigerian Student Association.

**ATHLETICS. Physical education requirements:** None.
**Intercollegiate competition:** 6% of students participate. Baseball (M), basketball (M,W), cheerleading (W), golf (M), soccer (M,W), softball (W), tennis (M,W), volleyball (W), wrestling (M). Member of Colorado Athletic Conference, NCAA Division II.
**Intramural and club sports:** 10% of students participate. Intramural basketball, flag football, racquetball, softball, volleyball, weight lifting. Men's club rodeo. Women's club rodeo.

**ADMISSIONS. Academic basis for candidate selection** (in order of priority): Secondary school record, standardized test scores, class rank, school's recommendation, essay.
**Nonacademic basis for candidate selection:** Character and personality, extracurricular participation, and particular talent or ability are considered.
**Requirements:** Graduation from secondary school is required; GED is accepted. No specific distribution of secondary school units required. Minimum composite ACT score of 18 (combined SAT score of 720), rank in top half of secondary school class, and minimum 2.5 GPA recommended. Separate applications required of nursing and industrial engineering program applicants. EOP for applicants not normally admissible. SAT or ACT is required. Campus visit and interview recommended. Off-campus interviews available with an admissions representative.
**Procedure:** Take SAT or ACT by July 21 of 12th year. Visit college for interview by April 15 of 12th year. Application deadline is July 21. Notification of admission on rolling basis. $100 room deposit, refundable until six weeks before beginning of term. Freshmen accepted in terms other than fall.
**Special programs:** Admission may be deferred one year. Credit may be granted through CEEB Advanced Placement for scores of 3 or higher. Credit may be granted through CLEP general and subject exams, ACT PEP and challenge exams, and military and life experience. Early entrance/early admission program. Concurrent enrollment program.
**Transfer students:** Transfer students accepted for terms other than fall. In fall 1992, 37% of all new students were transfers into all classes. 832 transfer applications were received, 696 were accepted. Application deadline is July 21 for fall; November 1 for spring. Minimum 2.0 GPA required. Lowest course grade accepted is "C." Maximum number of transferable credits is 96 semester hours. At least 32 semester hours must be completed at the university to receive degree.
**Admissions contact:** Martha G. Wade, Ph.D., Director of Admissions and Records. 719 549-2461.

**FINANCIAL AID. Available aid:** Pell grants, SEOG, state scholarships and grants, school scholarships and grants, private scholarships, academic merit scholarships, and athletic scholarships. Perkins Loans (NDSL), PLUS, Stafford Loans (GSL), state loans, school loans, private loans, and SLS. AMS.
**Financial aid statistics:** 31% of aid is not need-based. In 1992-93, 84% of all undergraduate applicants received aid; 49% of freshman applicants. Average amounts of aid awarded freshmen: Scholarships and grants, $1,200; loans, $1,000.
**Supporting data/closing dates:** FAFSA/FAF/FFS: Priority filing date is March 1. School's own aid application: Priority filing date is March 1. Income tax forms: Priority filing date is April 15.
**Financial aid contact:** Gina Mestas, Director of Financial Aid. 719 549-2753.

**STUDENT EMPLOYMENT.** College Work/Study Program. Institutional employment. 25% of full-time undergraduates work on campus during school year. Students may expect to earn an average of $1,740 during school year. Off-campus part-time employment opportunities rated "fair."

**COMPUTER FACILITIES.** 160 IBM/IBM-compatible and Macintosh/Apple microcomputers. Students may access Prime minicomputer/mainframe systems, Internet. Residence halls may be equipped with stand-alone microcomputers. Computer languages and software packages include BASIC, COBOL, dBASE, FORTRAN, IFPS, LINDO, LISP, Lotus 1-2-3, Paradox, Pascal, PL/1, Quattro Pro, SPSS-X, 20/20, WordPerfect. Computer facilities are available to all students.
**Fees:** None.
**Hours:** 8 AM-10 PM (M-F); 11 AM-5 PM (Sa); 1 PM-10 PM (Su).

**GRADUATE CAREER DATA.** Graduate school percentages: 1% enter medical school. 1% enter dental school. 5% enter graduate business programs. 9% enter graduate arts and sciences programs. Highest graduate school enrollments: Colorado State U, U of Colorado, U of Denver, U of Southern Colorado. Companies and businesses that hire graduates: local medical centers and school district.

**PROMINENT ALUMNI/AE.** Raymond P. Kogosvek, former U.S. congressman; James Robert Issac, mayor, Colorado Springs; Carl Tony Capozzoloa, actor, writer, and attorney.

# Western State College of Colorado

**Gunnison, CO 81231** **303 943-3035**

**1994-95 Costs.** Tuition: $1,312 (state residents), $5,411 (out-of-state). Room: $1,805. Board: $1,936. Fees, books, misc. academic expenses (school's estimate): $907.
**Enrollment.** Undergraduates: 1,374 men, 941 women (full-time). Freshman class: 2,676 applicants, 2,039 accepted, 604 enrolled.
**Test score averages/ranges.** Average SAT scores: 435 verbal, 475 math. Average ACT scores: 21 composite.
**Faculty.** 112 full-time; 26 part-time. 70% of faculty holds doctoral degree. Student/faculty ratio: 20 to 1.
**Selectivity rating.** Less competitive.

**PROFILE.** Western State, founded in 1911, is a public, multipurpose college. Its 228-acre campus is located in Gunnison, in the Rocky Mountains, southwest of Denver.

**Accreditation:** NCACS. Professionally accredited by the National Association of Schools of Music.

**Religious orientation:** Western State College of Colorado is nonsectarian; no religious requirements.
**Library:** Collections totaling over 110,000 volumes, 630 periodical subscriptions, and 661,000 microform items.
**Special facilities/museums:** Botanical garden.
**Athletic facilities:** Field house, gymnasium, stadium, track, swimming pool, basketball and racquetball courts, aerobics and weight rooms.

**STUDENT BODY. Undergraduate profile:** 65% are state residents; 29% are transfers. 1% Asian-American, 2% Black, 3% Hispanic, 1% Native American, 92% White, 1% Other. Average age of undergraduates is 21.
**Freshman profile:** 2% of freshmen who took SAT scored 600 or over on verbal, 7% scored 600 or over on math; 16% scored 500 or over on verbal, 33% scored 500 or over on math; 56% scored 400 or over on verbal, 74% scored 400 or over on math; 93% scored 300 or over on verbal, 97% scored 300 or over on math. 31% of accepted applicants took SAT; 70% took ACT.
**Undergraduate achievement:** 48% of fall 1992 freshmen returned for fall 1993 term.
**Foreign students:** 29 students are from out of the country. Countries represented include Canada, Germany, Japan, New Zealand, Spain, and Sweden; 12 in all.

**PROGRAMS OF STUDY. Degrees:** B.A.
**Majors:** Accounting, Art, Biology, Business, Chemistry, Communication/Theatre, Economics, Education, English, French, Geography, Geology, History, Kinesiology, Mathematics, Music, Physics, Political Science, Psychology, Recreation, Sociology, Spanish.
**Distribution of degrees:** The majors with the highest enrollment are business and communication/theatre; physics, economics, and Spanish have the lowest.
**Requirements:** General education requirement.
**Academic regulations:** Freshmen must maintain minimum 1.5 GPA; sophomores, 1.88 GPA; juniors, 2.0 GPA; seniors, 2.0 GPA.
**Special:** Minors offered in most majors and in anthropology, coaching, computer science, health education, journalism, literature, and small business. Mentor Program. Freshman Advisory Core. Self-designed majors. Double majors. Independent study. Pass/fail grading option. Internships. Cooperative education programs. Preprofessional programs in law, medicine, veterinary science, dentistry, physical therapy, and forestry. Combined engineering and forestry programs with Colorado State U. Member of Consortium of State Colleges in Colorado. Member of National Student Exchange (NSE); semester/year exchange in one of 39 states, including Hawaii, the Virgin Islands, and Puerto Rico. Teacher certification in elementary and secondary education. Certification in specific subject areas. Study abroad possible.
**Honors:** Honors program. Honor societies.
**Academic Assistance:** Remedial reading, writing, and math. Nonremedial tutoring.

**STUDENT LIFE. Housing:** All unmarried freshmen under age 21 must live on campus unless living with family. Coed, women's, and men's dorms. Fraternity housing. School-owned/operated apartments. Off-campus privately-owned housing. Both on-campus and off-campus married-student housing. 45% of students live in college housing.
**Social atmosphere:** Packers (the Union snack bar), Crested Butte Mountain Resort (ski area), the Dos Rios Lounge, the Alamo Bar, and the Steaming Bean Coffee Shop are favorite student haunts. Influential groups on campus include the Student Government Association, Greeks, BACCHUS, the Newman Club, and Campus Crusade for Christ. Outdoor sports -- skiing, mountain biking, road biking, and hiking -- as well as basketball games and the "'Coldest Spot in the Nation' Celebration" are the most popular activities during the school year. According to the school newspaper, "Many students are very involved in campus organizations. The town of Gunnison is very small, located in a high mountain valley. Many of the activities students are involved in are of an outdoor nature."
**Services and counseling/handicapped student services:** Placement services. Mental Health Services. Personal and psychological counseling. Career and academic guidance services. Physically disabled student services. Learning disabled services. Notetaking services. Tape recorders. Tutors. Reader services for the blind.
**Campus organizations:** Undergraduate student government. Student newspaper (Top O' The World, published once/week). Literary magazine. Yearbook. Radio and TV stations. Jazz and marching bands, jazz singers, opera workshop, orchestra, debating, Mountain Players, veterans club, Young Democrats, Young Republicans, 60 organizations in all. Six fraternities, one chapter house; three sororities, no chapter houses. 5% of men join a fraternity. 2% of women join a sorority.
**Religious organizations:** Baptist Student Union, Campus Crusade for Christ, Fellowship of Christian Athletes, Newman Club.
**Minority/foreign student organizations:** NAACP and other minority groups. International student groups.

**ATHLETICS. Physical education requirements:** None.
**Intercollegiate competition:** 18% of students participate. Alpine skiing (M,W), basketball (M,W), cross-country (M,W), football (M), Nordic skiing (M,W), track and field (indoor) (M,W), track and field (outdoor) (M,W), volleyball (W), wrestling (M). Member of NCAA Division I for Alpine and Nordic skiing, NCAA Division II, Rocky Mountain Athletic Conference.
**Intramural and club sports:** 29% of students participate. Intramural Alpine skiing, basketball, bowling, cycling, flag football, golf, lacrosse, mountain climbing, Nordic skiing, rugby, snow boarding, soccer. Men's club baseball, cycling, lacrosse, rodeo, rugby, soccer. Women's club cycling, rodeo, soccer, softball.

**ADMISSIONS. Academic basis for candidate selection** (in order of priority): Secondary school record, standardized test scores, class rank, essay, school's recommendation.
**Nonacademic basis for candidate selection:** Character and personality are important. Extracurricular participation, particular talent or ability, and alumni/ae relationship are considered.
**Requirements:** Graduation from secondary school is recommended; GED is accepted. No specific distribution of secondary school units required. Minimum combined SAT score of 820 (composite ACT score of 20), rank in top two-thirds of secondary school class, and minimum 2.5 GPA recommended. SAT or ACT is required. Campus visit and interview recommended. Off-campus interviews available with an admissions representative.
**Procedure:** Take SAT or ACT by December of 12th year. Suggest filing application by April 15. Notification of admission on rolling basis. No set date by which applicants must accept offer. $100 room deposit, refundable until July 1. Freshmen accepted in terms other than fall.
**Special programs:** Admission may be deferred two years. Credit and/or placement may be granted through CEEB Advanced Placement exams for scores of 3 or higher. Credit and/or placement may be granted through CLEP general and subject exams. Placement may be granted through challenge exams. Concurrent enrollment program.
**Transfer students:** Transfer students accepted for terms other than fall. In fall 1993, 29% of all new students were transfers into all classes. 570 transfer applications were received, 425 were accepted. Application deadline is April 15 for fall; February 1 for spring. Minimum 2.0 GPA required. Lowest course grade accepted is "C." Maximum number of transferable credits is 64 semester hours from a two-year school and 90 semester hours from a four-year school. At least 30 semester hours must be completed at the college to receive degree.
**Admissions contact:** Monica Bruning, M.P.A., Director of Admissions. 303 943-2119.

**FINANCIAL AID. Available aid:** Pell grants, SEOG, state scholarships and grants, school scholarships and grants, private scholarships and grants, academic merit scholarships, and athletic scholarships. Perkins Loans (NDSL), PLUS, Stafford Loans (GSL), school loans, and SLS. AMS. Installment plan. Manufacturers Hanover plan.
**Financial aid statistics:** 50% of aid is not need-based. In 1993-94, 70% of all undergraduate applicants received aid; 70% of freshman applicants. Average amounts of aid awarded freshmen: Scholarships and grants, $1,700; loans, $2,600.
**Supporting data/closing dates:** FAFSA: Priority filing date is April 1. Notification of awards begins April 15.
**Financial aid contact:** Marty Somero, M.S., Director of Financial Aid. 303 943-3085.

**STUDENT EMPLOYMENT.** College Work/Study Program. Institutional employment. 35% of full-time undergraduates work on campus during school year. Students may expect to earn an average of $1,000 during school year. Off-campus part-time employment opportunities rated "good."

**COMPUTER FACILITIES.** 110 IBM/IBM-compatible and Macintosh/Apple microcomputers; 33 are networked. Client/LAN operating systems include Apple/Macintosh, DOS. Computer languages and software packages include Banner, BASIC, COBOL, FORTRAN, Lotus 1-2-3, Pascal, SQL, WordPerfect. Computer facilities are available to all students.
**Fees:** $25 computer fee per year.
**Hours:** 7:30 AM-11 PM.

**PROMINENT ALUMNI/AE.** James R. Richard, U.S. inspector general; Michael Callahan, lieutenant governor of Colorado; Monica Shea, supervisor, U.S. headquarters of Mitsubishi Motors; Lisa Lyden, news anchor person, KOAA-TV, Colorado Springs; Roxanne Bradshaw, secretary-treasurer, National Education Association.

# Connecticut

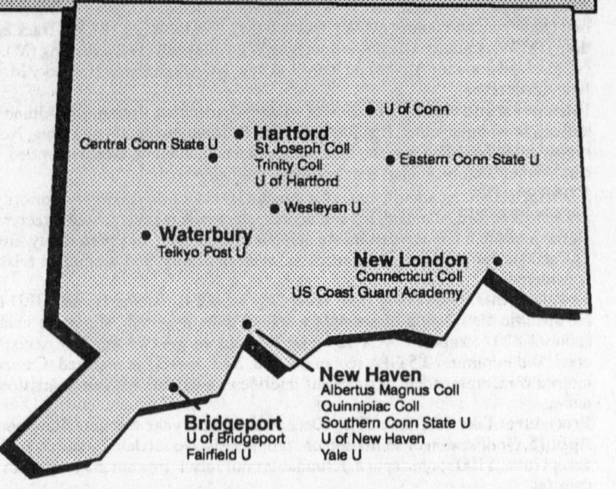


## Albertus Magnus College

**New Haven, CT 06511-1189** **203 773-8550**

**1993-94 Costs.** Tuition: $11,420. Room & board: $5,240. Fees, books, misc. academic expenses (school's estimate): $900.
**Enrollment.** Undergraduates: 155 men, 261 women (full-time). Freshman class: 317 applicants, 313 accepted, 72 enrolled. Graduate enrollment: 3 men, 6 women.
**Test score averages/ranges.** Average SAT scores: 391 verbal, 414 math. Range of SAT scores of middle 50%: 400-420 verbal, 450-470 math.
**Faculty.** 36 full-time; 32 part-time. 65% of faculty holds doctoral degree. Student/faculty ratio: 11 to 1.
**Selectivity rating.** Less competitive.

**PROFILE.** Albertus Magnus is a church-affiliated, liberal arts college. Founded in 1925, the college admitted only women until becoming coed in 1985. The 50-acre campus is located between New Haven and Hamden.

**Accreditation:** NEASC.
**Religious orientation:** Albertus Magnus College is affiliated with the Roman Catholic Church (Dominican Sisters of St. Mary of the Springs); one semester of religion required.
**Library:** Collections totaling over 100,000 volumes, 425 periodical subscriptions, and 5,500 microform items.
**Athletic facilities:** Racquetball and tennis courts, track, softball and soccer fields, swimming pool, gymnasium, dance, aerobics, and weight rooms.
**STUDENT BODY. Undergraduate profile:** 65% are state residents; 30% are transfers. 2% Asian-American, 9% Black, 3% Hispanic, 1% Native American, 75% White, 10% Other. Average age of undergraduates is 21.
**Freshman profile:** 4% of freshmen who took SAT scored 700 or over on math; 8% scored 600 or over on verbal, 19% scored 600 or over on math; 21% scored 500 or over on verbal, 38% scored 500 or over on math; 60% scored 400 or over on verbal, 75% scored 400 or over on math; 95% scored 300 or over on verbal, 100% scored 300 or over on math. 100% of accepted applicants took SAT. 41% of freshmen come from public schools.
**Undergraduate achievement:** 75% of fall 1992 freshmen returned for fall 1993 term. 83% of entering class graduated.
**Foreign students:** 65 students are from out of the country. Countries represented include Brazil, China, Japan, Kenya, Korea, and Nigeria; 10 in all.
**PROGRAMS OF STUDY. Degrees:** B.A., B.F.A., B.S.
**Majors:** Art, Art History, Art Therapy, Biology, Biology/Chemistry, Business/Economics, Chemistry, Classics, Communications, Community Psychology, Computer Science, Criminal Justice, Dramatic Arts, Economics, English, Finance, Foreign Languages/Multiple Emphasis, French, General Studies, Health Care Management, History, Human Services, Humanities, Industrial/Organizational Psychology, Italian, Management, Management Information Systems, Marketing, Mathematics, Performance Art Theatre, Philosophy, Physical Sciences, Political Science, Psychology, Religious Studies, Romance Languages, Social Sciences, Social Welfare, Sociology, Spanish, Studio Art, Urban Studies.
**Distribution of degrees:** The majors with the highest enrollment are business/economics, English, and psychology; romance languages, mathematics, and classics have the lowest.
**Requirements:** General education requirement.
**Academic regulations:** Freshmen must maintain minimum 1.7 GPA; sophomores, 1.8 GPA; juniors, 1.9 GPA; seniors, 2.0 GPA.
**Special:** Minors offered in all majors. Associate's degrees offered. Self-designed majors. Double majors. Dual degrees. Independent study. Accelerated study. Pass/fail grading option. Internships. Graduate school at which undergraduates may take graduate-level courses. Preprofessional programs in law, medicine, veterinary science, dentistry, and optometry. Cross-registration with U of New Haven, Paier Coll of Art, and Quinnipiac Coll. Washington Semester. Study abroad possible.
**Honors:** Honor societies.
**Academic Assistance:** Remedial reading, writing, math, and study skills. Nonremedial tutoring.
**ADMISSIONS. Academic basis for candidate selection** (in order of priority): Secondary school record, class rank, school's recommendation, standardized test scores.
**Nonacademic basis for candidate selection:** Extracurricular participation is emphasized. Character and personality and particular talent or ability are important. Geographical distribution and alumni/ae relationship are considered.
**Requirements:** Graduation from secondary school is required; GED is accepted. 16 units and the following program of study are required: 4 units of English, 3 units of math, 2 units of lab science, 2 units of foreign language, 2 units of social studies, 2 units of history, 1 unit of academic electives. Minimum combined SAT score of 800, rank in top half of secondary school class, and minimum 2.3 GPA recommended. Portfolio recommended of art program applicants. Conditional admission possible for applicants not meeting standard requirements. SAT is required; ACT may be substituted. ACH recommended. Campus visit and interview recommended. Off-campus interviews available with an admissions representative.
**Procedure:** Take SAT or ACT by December of 12th year. Take ACH by February of 12th year. Visit college for interview by April of 12th year. Suggest filing application by March 1. Application deadline is June 1. Notification of admission on rolling basis. Reply is required by May 1. $200 tuition deposit, refundable until May 1. $250 room deposit, refundable until May 1. Freshmen accepted for terms other than fall.
**Special programs:** Admission may be deferred one year. Credit and/or placement may be granted through CEEB Advanced Placement exams for scores of 4 or higher. Credit may be granted through CLEP general and subject exams, and challenge exams. Credit and placement may be granted through ACT PEP exams and military experience. Early entrance/early admission program. Concurrent enrollment program.
**Transfer students:** Transfer students accepted for terms other than fall. In fall 1993, 30% of all new students were transfers into all classes. 65 transfer applications were received, 53 were accepted. Application deadline is rolling for fall; rolling for spring. Minimum 2.0 GPA required. Lowest course grade accepted is "C." Maximum number of transferable credits is 60 semester hours from a two-year school and 90 semester hours from a four-year school. At least 30 semester hours must be completed at the college to receive degree.
**Admissions contact:** Richard Lolatte, M.A., Director of Admissions. 203 773-8501, 800 578-9160.
**FINANCIAL AID. Available aid:** Pell grants, SEOG, state scholarships and grants, school scholarships and grants, and private scholarships. Perkins Loans (NDSL), PLUS, Stafford Loans (GSL), and SLS. Tuition Plan Inc. and deferred payment plan.
**Financial aid statistics:** 15% of aid is not need-based. In 1993-94, 95% of all undergraduate applicants received aid; 74% of freshman applicants. Average amounts of aid awarded freshmen: Scholarships and grants, $3,064; loans, $2,504.
**Supporting data/closing dates:** FAFSA/FAF/FFS: Priority filing date is February 15. School's own aid application: Priority filing date is February 15. State aid form: Priority filing date is February 15. Income tax forms: Priority filing date is February 15. Notification of awards begins April 1.
**Financial aid contact:** Mary Young, Director of Financial Aid. 203 773-8508.

## Central Connecticut State University

**New Britain, CT 06050** **203 827-7000**

**1994-95 Costs.** Tuition: $1,842 (state residents), $5,962 (out-of-state). Room: $2,584. Board: $2,110. Fees, books, misc. academic expenses (school's estimate): $1,848-$2,656.
**Enrollment.** Undergraduates: 3,079 men, 3,315 women (full-time). Freshman class: 4,158 applicants, 2,532 accepted, 902 enrolled. Graduate enrollment: 772 men, 1,618 women.
**Test score averages/ranges.** Average SAT scores: 419 verbal, 462 math. Range of SAT scores of middle 50%: 370-460 verbal, 400-510 math.
**Faculty.** 390 full-time; 339 part-time. 70% of faculty holds doctoral degree. Student/faculty ratio: 17 to 1.
**Selectivity rating.** Less competitive.

**PROFILE.** Central Connecticut is a public university. Founded in 1849, it gained university status in 1985. Programs are offered through the Schools of Arts and Sciences, Business, Education and Professional Studies, and Technology. Its 152-acre campus is located in a residential area of New Britain, nine miles from Hartford.

**Accreditation:** NEASC. Professionally accredited by the Accreditation Board for Engineering and Technology, the National Council for Accreditation of Teacher Education, the National League for Nursing.
**Religious orientation:** Central Connecticut State University is nonsectarian; three credits of religion/theology required.
**Library:** Collections totaling over 452,468 volumes, 2,961 periodical subscriptions, and 54,579 microform items.
**Special facilities/museums:** Art gallery, language lab, childhood center, planetarium and space science center, center for economic education, TV studio.
**Athletic facilities:** Gymnasium, swimming pool, badminton, basketball, tennis, and volleyball courts, indoor tennis courts, weight rooms, baseball, football, soccer, and softball fields, training track.
**STUDENT BODY. Undergraduate profile:** 95% are state residents; 37% are transfers. 2% Asian-American, 7% Black, 4% Hispanic, 85% White, 2% Other. Average age of undergraduates is 22.
**Freshman profile:** 1% of freshmen who took SAT scored 700 or over on math; 1% scored 600 or over on verbal, 7% scored 600 or over on math; 14% scored 500 or over on verbal, 34% scored 500 or over on math; 63% scored 400 or over on verbal, 76% scored 400 or

over on math; 97% scored 300 or over on verbal, 99% scored 300 or over on math. 97% of accepted applicants took SAT.
**Undergraduate achievement:** 73% of fall 1992 freshmen returned for fall 1993 term. 33% of entering class graduated. 19% of students who completed a degree program immediately went on to graduate study.
**Foreign students:** 131 students are from out of the country. Countries represented include China, Germany, Jamaica, Japan, Taiwan, and the United Kingdom; 45 in all.

**PROGRAMS OF STUDY. Degrees:** B.A., B.F.A., B.S.
**Majors:** Accounting, Actuarial Sciences, Anthropology, Art, Art Education, Biology, Business Administrative Science, Business Education, Chemistry, Communication, Computer Science, Construction Engineering Technology, Early Childhood Education, Earth Science, East Asian Studies, Economics, Elementary Education, English, Finance, French, General Science, Geography, German, History, Industrial Production Technology, Industrial Systems Engineering Technology, International Business, International Studies, Italian, Management Information Systems, Manufacturing Engineering Technology, Marketing, Marketing Education, Mathematics, Mechanical Engineering Technology, Music, Music Education, Nursing, Office Administration, Philosophy, Physical Education, Physical Sciences, Physics, Political Science, Psychology, Social Sciences, Social Work, Sociology, Spanish, Special Education, Special Studies, Technology Education, Theatre, Vocational/Technical Education.
**Distribution of degrees:** The majors with the highest enrollment are business administrative science, accounting, and marketing.
**Requirements:** General education requirement.
**Academic regulations:** Minimum 2.0 GPA required for graduation.
**Special:** Minors or concentrations offered in many majors and in Afro-American studies, archaeology, Chinese, criminal justice, geology, journalism, linguistics, meteorology, reading, religion, Russian, science, Soviet/East European studies, speech pathology, TESOL, and writing. Self-designed majors. Double majors. Independent study. Pass/fail grading option. Internships. Cooperative education programs. Graduate school at which undergraduates may take graduate-level courses. Exchange programs with U of Connecticut and all public colleges in Connecticut. Engineering transfer program with U of Connecticut. Teacher certification in early childhood, elementary, secondary, and special education. Certification in specific subject areas. Member of International Student Exchange Program (ISEP). ROTC and AFROTC at U of Connecticut.
**Honors:** Honors program. Honor societies.
**Academic Assistance:** Remedial reading, writing, math, and study skills. Nonremedial tutoring.

**STUDENT LIFE. Housing:** Students may live on or off campus. Coed, women's, and men's dorms. 25% of students live in college housing.
**Social atmosphere:** The student newspaper reports, "There's always something going on." Popular social events include Winter Weekend, Spring Weekend, Homecoming/United Way Week, and the Halloween Dance. Favorite off-campus gathering spots include Elmer's Place, Sean Patrick's, the Russian Lady, and the Brass Lion.
**Services and counseling/handicapped student services:** Placement services. Health service. Women's center. Day care. Counseling services for minority, military, veteran, and older students. Personal and psychological counseling. Career and academic guidance services. Physically disabled student services. Learning disabled program/services. Notetaking services. Tape recorders. Tutors. Reader services for the blind.
**Campus organizations:** Undergraduate student government. Student newspaper (Central Recorder). Literary magazine. Yearbook. Radio station. Dance, drama, academic, and special-interest groups, 100 organizations in all. One fraternity, no chapter house; two sororities, no chapter houses. 1% of men join a fraternity. 1% of women join a sorority.
**Religious organizations:** Newman Club, Hillel, Christian and Muslim groups.
**Minority/foreign student organizations:** African-American, Latin American, Native American groups. International Relations Club, African, Chinese, East Asian, French, Italian, Japanese, and Korean groups.

**ATHLETICS. Physical education requirements:** Two credits of physical education required.
**Intercollegiate competition:** 4% of students participate. Baseball (M), basketball (M,W), cheerleading (M,W), cross-country (M,W), diving (M,W), football (M), golf (M), soccer (M), softball (W), swimming (M,W), tennis (M,W), track (indoor) (M,W), track and field (indoor) (M,W), track and field (outdoor) (M,W), volleyball (W), wrestling (M). Member of East Coast Conference, ECAC, NCAA Division I, NCAA Division I-AA for football.
**Intramural and club sports:** 10% of students participate. Intramural badminton, basketball, flag football, floor hockey, softball, tennis, volleyball. Men's club Alpine skiing, boxing, crew, cycling, fencing, horsemanship, ice hockey, lacrosse, martial arts, rugby, volleyball, weight lifting, wrestling. Women's club Alpine skiing, crew, cycling, fencing, horsemanship, martial arts, soccer.

**ADMISSIONS. Academic basis for candidate selection** (in order of priority): Secondary school record, class rank, standardized test scores, school's recommendation, essay.
**Nonacademic basis for candidate selection:** Extracurricular participation, particular talent or ability, and alumni/ae relationship are considered.
**Requirements:** Graduation from secondary school is recommended; GED is accepted. 13 units and the following program of study are required: 4 units of English, 3 units of math, 2 units of science including 1 unit of lab, 2 units of social studies. Minimum combined SAT score of 800, rank in top half of secondary school class, and minimum 2.0 GPA recommended. R.N. required of B.S.N. program applicants. EOP for applicants not normally admissible. CONNCAP (Connecticut Collegiate Awareness and Preparation Program) for applicants not normally admissible. SAT is required. Campus visit recommended. No off-campus interviews.
**Procedure:** Take SAT by November of 12th year. Visit college for interview by December of 12th year. Suggest filing application by December 1. Application deadline is May 1. Notification of admission on rolling basis. Reply is required by May 1. $90 nonrefundable tuition deposit. $100 nonrefundable room deposit. Freshmen accepted for terms other than fall.
**Special programs:** Admission may be deferred. Credit may be granted through CEEB Advanced Placement for scores of 4 or higher. Credit may be granted through CLEP subject exams, DANTES exams, and military experience.
**Transfer students:** Transfer students accepted for terms other than fall. In fall 1993, 37% of all new students were transfers into all classes. 1,428 transfer applications were received, 1,036 were accepted. Application deadline is May 1 for fall; November 1 for spring. Minimum 2.0 GPA required. Lowest course grade accepted is "C." At least 45 semester hours must be completed at the university to receive degree.
**Admissions contact:** Charlotte Bisson, M.S., Director of Admissions. 203 827-7543.

**FINANCIAL AID. Available aid:** Pell grants, SEOG, state scholarships and grants, school scholarships and grants, private scholarships and grants, academic merit scholarships, and athletic scholarships. Perkins Loans (NDSL), PLUS, Stafford Loans (GSL), state loans, and SLS. AMS and deferred payment plan.
**Financial aid statistics:** 33% of aid is not need-based. In 1993, 79% of all undergraduate applicants received aid. Average amounts of aid awarded freshmen: Scholarships and grants, $4,700.
**Supporting data/closing dates:** FAFSA: Priority filing date is February 15; deadline is march 15. Income tax forms: Priority filing date is May 1. Notification of awards begins June 15.
**Financial aid contact:** John Taylor, M.S., Director of Financial Aid. 203 827-7330.

**STUDENT EMPLOYMENT.** College Work/Study Program. Institutional employment. 10% of full-time undergraduates work on campus during school year. Students may expect to earn an average of $1,200 during school year. Off-campus part-time employment opportunities rated "good."

**COMPUTER FACILITIES.** 145 IBM/IBM-compatible and Macintosh/Apple microcomputers; 125 are networked. Students may access Digital minicomputer/mainframe systems, Internet. Residence halls may be equipped with stand-alone microcomputers. Client/LAN operating systems include Apple/Macintosh, DOS, DEC, LocalTalk/AppleTalk, Novell. Computer languages and software packages include Assembler, BASIC, COBOL, DataTrieve, FOCUS, FORTRAN, MINITAB, Modula 2, Pascal, SAS, Smartstar. Computer facilities are available to all students.
**Fees:** Computer fee is included in tuition/fees.
**Hours:** 8:30 AM-midn. (M-Th); 8:30-6 PM (F); 9 AM-6 PM (Sa); 1 PM-10 PM (Su).

**GRADUATE CAREER DATA.** Graduate school percentages: 5% enter graduate business programs. 14% enter graduate arts and sciences programs. Highest graduate school enrollments: Central Connecticut State U, Hartford Graduate Center, U of Connecticut, U of Hartford. 65% of graduates choose careers in business and industry. Companies and businesses that hire graduates: Aetna Insurance, Arthur Anderson & Co., Blum Shapiro, Bob's Stores, CIGNA, Coopers & Lybrand, Ernst & Young, ITT Hartford, Travelers Insurance, United Technologies, State of Connecticut.

**PROMINENT ALUMNI/AE.** David C. Campa, secondary coach, Dallas Cowboys; Carmen E. Espinosa, superior court judge; John B. Larson, president pro tempore, Connecticut State Senate.

# Connecticut College

**New London, CT 06320-4196 — 203 447-1911**

**1994-95 Costs.** Tuition: $18,740. Room & board: $6,300. Fees, books, misc. academic expenses (school's estimate): $710.
**Enrollment.** Undergraduates: 699 men, 931 women (full-time). Freshman class: 3,035 applicants, 1,546 accepted, 438 enrolled. Graduate enrollment: 14 men, 71 women.
**Test score averages/ranges.** Range of SAT scores of middle 50%: 540-636 verbal, 570-670 math.
**Faculty.** 167 full-time; 64 part-time. 91% of faculty holds doctoral degree. Student/faculty ratio: 12 to 1.
**Selectivity rating.** Highly competitive.

**PROFILE.** Connecticut College is a private, liberal arts institution. Founded as a women's college in 1911, it adopted coeducation in 1969. Its 702-acre campus (including the 426-acre Connecticut Arboretum) is located two miles from downtown New London.

**Accreditation:** NEASC.
**Religious orientation:** Connecticut College is nonsectarian; no religious requirements.
**Library:** Collections totaling over 464,894 volumes, 1,723 periodical subscriptions, and 252,764 microform items.
**Special facilities/museums:** Art museum, children's school, language lab, 426-acre arboretum, botanic garden, greenhouse, environment control labs, transmission and scanning electron microscope, ion accelerator, refracting telescope, observatory.
**Athletic facilities:** Basketball, paddle tennis, racquetball, squash, tennis, and volleyball courts, swimming pool, Universal, Hydro gymnasiums, hockey rink, athletic fields, jogging and cross-country trails, fitness/wellness center, boat house, rowing tanks.

**STUDENT BODY. Undergraduate profile:** 19% are state residents; 7% are transfers. 3% Asian-American, 4% Black, 3% Hispanic, 1% Native American, 89% White. Average age of undergraduates is 20.
**Freshman profile:** 95% of accepted applicants took SAT. 51% of freshmen come from public schools.
**Undergraduate achievement:** 92% of fall 1992 freshmen returned for fall 1993 term. 84% of entering class graduated. 20% of students who completed a degree program immediately went on to graduate study.
**Foreign students:** 12 students are from out of the country. Countries represented include Brazil and Japan; 12 in all.

**PROGRAMS OF STUDY. Degrees:** B.A.
**Majors:** Africana Studies, Anthropology, Art History/Appreciation, Asian Studies, Biochemistry, Biology, Botany, Chemistry, Child Development, Chinese, Classics, Dance, Economics, English, French, German, German Studies, Government, Hispanic Studies, History, Human Ecology/Environmental Studies, Human Relations, International Relations, Italian, Italian Studies, Japanese, Mathematical Science, Mathematics, Medieval Studies, Modern European Studies, Music, Music/Technology, Philosophy, Physics, Psychology, Religious Studies, Russian Studies, Sociology, Studio Art, Theatre, Urban Studies, Zoology.

**Distribution of degrees:** The majors with the highest enrollment are government, history, and English.
**Requirements:** General education requirement.
**Academic regulations:** Minimum 2.0 GPA required for graduation.
**Special:** Minors offered in approximately 43 fields. Self-designed majors. Double majors. Dual degrees. Independent study. Accelerated study. Pass/fail grading option. Internships. Graduate school at which undergraduates may take graduate-level courses. Preprofessional programs in law, medicine, and health. 3-2 engineering program with Washington U. Member of American Collegiate Consortium for East-West Cultural Academic Exchange. Administrative and accrediting agent for the Associated Kyoto Program. Cross-registration with Trinity Coll, U.S. Coast Guard Academy, and Wesleyan U. Washington Semester and Sea Semester. National Theatre Institute Semester (Connecticut). Williams-Mystic Seaport Semester (Connecticut). Member of Twelve College Exchange Program. Teacher certification in early childhood, elementary, and secondary education. Exchange program abroad in England (Westminster Coll). Study abroad also in Austria, China, France, Germany, Ireland, Israel, Italy, Japan, Mexico, Scotland, Singapore, Spain, and Taiwan.
**Honors:** Phi Beta Kappa. Honors program. Honor societies.
**Academic Assistance:** Nonremedial tutoring.

**STUDENT LIFE. Housing:** All unmarried students under age 21 must live on campus unless living near campus with relatives. Coed dorms. 98% of students live in college housing.
**Social atmosphere:** Popular gathering spots on and off campus include the campus bar, the snack shop, the Brown Derby, Margarita's, and Casino. The most anticipated event on campus is Floralia, an annual bacchanalian celebration. Other highlights include lacrosse and soccer playoff games and various cultural events. According to the editor of the student newspaper, "Social life at Connecticut College is neither very diverse nor exciting. Crush parties, 80s parties, and formals add some variety, but too often it is the same people doing the same things. Some events can be fun, but most social life occurs on campus, not much off campus."
**Services and counseling/handicapped student services:** Placement services. Health service. Women's center. Counseling services for minority and older students. Birth control, personal, and psychological counseling. Career and academic guidance services. Religious counseling. Physically disabled student services. Learning disabled services. Notetaking services. Tape recorders. Tutors. Reader services for the blind.
**Campus organizations:** Undergraduate student government. Student newspaper (College Voice, published once/week). Literary magazine. Yearbook. Radio station. Choral groups, orchestra, ensembles, debating, theatre group, film society, folk dancing, Journal of Arts and Sciences, Big Brothers/Big Sisters, Young Democrats, Young Republicans, college governance participation, departmental groups, special-interest groups.
**Religious organizations:** Campus Ministry, Chavarah, Christian Science advisers, Southern Baptist Mission Board, Intervarsity Christian Fellowship.
**Minority/foreign student organizations:** Asian Student Association, La Unidad, minority cultural center, UMOJA, SOAR, I-PRIDE.

**ATHLETICS. Physical education requirements:** None.
**Intercollegiate competition:** 25% of students participate. Basketball (M,W), crew (M,W), cross-country (M,W), diving (M,W), field hockey (W), ice hockey (M), lacrosse (M,W), sailing (M,W), soccer (M,W), squash (M,W), swimming (M,W), tennis (M,W), track (outdoor) (M,W), track and field (outdoor) (M,W), volleyball (W). Member of ECAC, NCAA Division III, New England Small College Athletic Conference.
**Intramural and club sports:** 85% of students participate. Intramural basketball, cross-country, flag football, floor hockey, indoor soccer, outdoor soccer, racquetball, softball, team tennis, volleyball, water polo (coed). Men's club Alpine skiing, baseball, cycling, golf, ice hockey, indoor soccer, lacrosse, martial arts, Nordic skiing, rugby, ultimate frisbee. Women's club Alpine skiing, cycling, golf, horsemanship, ice hockey, indoor soccer, lacrosse, martial arts, Nordic skiing, rugby, softball.

**ADMISSIONS. Academic basis for candidate selection** (in order of priority): Secondary school record, class rank, standardized test scores, school's recommendation, essay.
**Nonacademic basis for candidate selection:** Character and personality, extracurricular participation, and particular talent or ability are emphasized. Geographical distribution is important. Alumni/ae relationship is considered.
**Requirements:** Graduation from secondary school is required; GED is not accepted. 18 units and the following program of study are required: 4 units of English, 3 units of math, 2 units of science including 1 unit of lab, 3 units of foreign language, 2 units of social studies, 4 units of academic electives. Audition required of dance program applicants. SAT is required; ACT may be substituted. ACH required. Campus visit and interview recommended. Off-campus interviews available with admissions and alumni representatives.
**Procedure:** Take SAT or ACT by December of 12th year. Take ACH by December of 12th year. Visit college for interview by January 15 of 12th year. Application deadline is January 15. Notification of admission by April 1. Reply is required by May 1. $250 refundable tuition deposit. Freshmen accepted for fall term only.
**Special programs:** Admission may be deferred one year. Credit and/or placement may be granted through CEEB Advanced Placement exams for scores of 4 or higher. Early decision program. In fall 1993, 195 applied for early decision and 112 were accepted. Deadline for applying for early decision is November 15.
**Transfer students:** Transfer students accepted for terms other than fall. In fall 1993, 7% of all new students were transfers into all classes. 151 transfer applications were received, 77 were accepted. Application deadline is April 1 for fall; December 1 for spring. Minimum 3.0 GPA required. Lowest course grade accepted is "C." Maximum number of transferable credits is 64 semester hours. At least 64 semester hours must be completed at the college to receive degree.
**Admissions contact:** Claire K. Matthews, Dean of Admissions. 203 439-2200.

**FINANCIAL AID. Available aid:** Pell grants, SEOG, state scholarships and grants, and school scholarships and grants. Perkins Loans (NDSL), PLUS, Stafford Loans (GSL), and school loans. Knight Tuition Plans and AMS.
**Financial aid statistics:** In 1993-94, 96% of all undergraduate applicants received aid; 90% of freshman applicants. Average amounts of aid awarded freshmen: Scholarships and grants, $13,564; loans, $2,000.
**Supporting data/closing dates:** FAFSA: Deadline is February 15. School's own aid application: Deadline is February 15. Income tax forms: Deadline is February 15. Notification of awards begins April 1.
**Financial aid contact:** Elaine F. Solinga, Director of Financial Aid. 203 439-2059.

**STUDENT EMPLOYMENT.** College Work/Study Program. Institutional employment. 70% of full-time undergraduates work on campus during school year. Students may expect to earn an average of $1,050 during school year. Off-campus part-time employment opportunities rated "good."

**COMPUTER FACILITIES.** 130 IBM/IBM-compatible and Macintosh/Apple microcomputers; all are networked. Students may access Digital minicomputer/mainframe systems, Internet. Computer languages and software packages include Ada, Assembler, BASIC, C, COBOL, Excel, FORTRAN, LISP, LOGO, Microsoft Windows, MINITAB, Pascal, Prolog, SAS, SETL, SNOBOL, SPSS-X, WordPerfect. Computer facilities are available to all students.
**Fees:** None.
**Hours:** 24 hours.

**GRADUATE CAREER DATA.** Graduate school percentages: 4% enter law school. 3% enter medical school. 2% enter graduate business programs. 11% enter graduate arts and sciences programs. Highest graduate school enrollments: Boston U, U of Connecticut, New York U, Tufts U, Yale U. 27% of graduates choose careers in business and industry.

**PROMINENT ALUMNI/AE.** Anita DeFrantz, first black woman on International Olympic Committee; David Grantz, actor; Robert Hernandez, senior assistant editor, *National Geographic*; Claire L. Guadiani, president, Connecticut Coll; Amy Gross, editor, *Mirabella* magazine; Jim Gabarra, member, U.S. National Soccer Team.

# Eastern Connecticut State University

**Willimantic, CT 06226** **203 456-5400**

**1994-95 Costs.** Tuition: $1,754 (state residents), $5,678 (out-of-state). Room & board: $4,020. Fees, books, misc. academic expenses (school's estimate): $500.
**Enrollment.** Undergraduates: 1,269 men, 1,497 women (full-time). Freshman class: 2,172 applicants, 1,493 accepted, 564 enrolled. Graduate enrollment: 44 men, 231 women.
**Test score averages/ranges.** Average SAT scores: 430 verbal, 460 math.
**Faculty.** 127 full-time; 65 part-time. 78% of faculty holds doctoral degree. Student/faculty ratio: 17 to 1.
**Selectivity rating.** Less competitive.

**PROFILE.** Eastern Connecticut State is a public university. It was founded as a state Normal school in 1889, became a state college in 1959, and gained university status in 1983. Programs are offered through the Schools of Arts and Sciences, Professional Studies, and Continuing Education. Its 100-acre campus is located in Willimantic, 28 miles from Hartford.

**Accreditation:** NEASC.
**Religious orientation:** Eastern Connecticut State University is nonsectarian; no religious requirements.
**Library:** Collections totaling over 212,000 volumes, 1,850 periodical subscriptions, and 350,000 microform items.
**Special facilities/museums:** Art gallery, electron microscope, planetarium with teaching facilities, center for Connecticut studies, media center with TV studio.
**Athletic facilities:** Gymnasiums, racquetball and tennis courts, field house, swimming pool, dance studio, weight room, outdoor playing fields.

**STUDENT BODY. Undergraduate profile:** 90% are state residents; 35% are transfers. 1% Asian-American, 9% Black, 5% Hispanic, 1% Native American, 82% White, 2% International. Average age of undergraduates is 20.
**Freshman profile:** 1% of freshmen who took SAT scored 700 or over on verbal, 1% scored 700 or over on math; 3% scored 600 or over on verbal, 6% scored 600 or over on math; 17% scored 500 or over on verbal, 31% scored 500 or over on math; 61% scored 400 or over on verbal, 74% scored 400 or over on math; 98% scored 300 or over on verbal, 98% scored 300 or over on math. 100% of accepted applicants took SAT. 88% of freshmen come from public schools.
**Undergraduate achievement:** 86% of fall 1992 freshmen returned for fall 1993 term. 50% of entering class graduated. 32% of students who completed a degree program went on to graduate study within one year.
**Foreign students:** 103 students are from out of the country. Countries represented include Bangladesh, England, Hong Kong, Jamaica, Pakistan, and Sri Lanka; 31 in all.

**PROGRAMS OF STUDY. Degrees:** B.A., B.Gen.Studies, B.S.
**Majors:** Accounting, Biology, Business Administration/Management, Communications, Computer Sciences, Dance, Early Childhood Education, Economics, Elementary Education, English, Environmental Earth Science, Fine Arts, History, History/Social Science, Junior High Education, Mathematics, Music, Physical Education, Psychology, Public Policy/Government, Secondary Education, Sociology/Applied Social Relations, Spanish, Theatre, Visual Arts.
**Distribution of degrees:** The majors with the highest enrollment are business administration, education, and psychology.
**Requirements:** General education requirement.
**Academic regulations:** Freshmen must maintain minimum 1.8 GPA; sophomores, 1.9 GPA; juniors, 2.0 GPA; seniors, 2.0 GPA.
**Special:** Minors offered in 36 areas. Associate's degrees offered. Self-designed majors. Double majors. Independent study. Accelerated study. Pass/fail grading option. Internships. Cooperative education programs. Graduate school at which undergraduates may take graduate-level courses. Preprofessional programs in law, medicine, veterinary science, pharmacy, dentistry, and optometry. Library science program through Southern

Connecticut State U. One course/semester may be taken at U of Connecticut and at other Connecticut state universities. Washington Semester. Member of National Student Exchange (NSE). Teacher certification in early childhood, elementary, and secondary education. Certification in specific subject areas. Study abroad in Australia, Canada, France, Hong Kong, Kenya, Mexico, Spain, and the United Kingdom. ROTC and AFROTC at U of Connecticut.
**Honors:** Honors program. Honor societies.
**Academic Assistance:** Remedial reading, writing, math, and study skills. Nonremedial tutoring.

**STUDENT LIFE. Housing:** Students may live on or off campus. Coed and women's dorms. School-owned/operated apartments. 60% of students live in college housing.
**Social atmosphere:** Off campus, students head for Blarney's, Snack East, Hot Shots, Jonathan's, Eastbrook Mall, and Danny's Adult World. Groups such as the Nubian Society, the Campus Lantern (newspaper), the Olas Club, the SCUBA club, and the National Student Exchange have a considerable influence on campus social life. Popular events of the school year include Fall Fest, Spring Fest, Hump Day, and the Wacky Olympics. Students also enjoy activities such as free weekend movies, dance, formals, and "Stop the Hate" forums. "This is pretty much a commuter school," notes the editor of the student newspaper. "Things are very dead on the weekends."
**Services and counseling/handicapped student services:** Placement services. Health service. Women's center. Day care. Counseling services for minority, military, veteran, and older students. Birth control, personal, and psychological counseling. Career and academic guidance services. Religious counseling. Physically disabled student services. Learning disabled services. Notetaking services. Tape recorders. Tutors. Reader services for the blind.
**Campus organizations:** Undergraduate student government. Student newspaper (Campus Lantern, published once/week). Literary magazine. Yearbook. Radio and TV stations. Drama and outing clubs, 45 organizations in all.
**Religious organizations:** Campus Ministry.
**Minority/foreign student organizations:** NUBIAN Society, Organization of Latin American Students. International Student Club.

**ATHLETICS. Physical education requirements:** Three semesters of physical education required.
**Intercollegiate competition:** 11% of students participate. Baseball (M), basketball (M,W), cheerleading (M,W), cross-country (M,W), soccer (M,W), softball (W), track (outdoor) (M,W), volleyball (W). Member of ECAC, Little East Conference, NCAA Division III, New England State Athletic Conference.
**Intramural and club sports:** 70% of students participate. Intramural badminton, basketball, bowling, floor hockey, flag football, golf, racquetball, soccer, softball, swimming, tennis, volleyball, water polo, weight lifting. Men's club ice hockey, weight lifting.

**ADMISSIONS. Academic basis for candidate selection** (in order of priority): Secondary school record, class rank, school's recommendation, standardized test scores, essay.
**Nonacademic basis for candidate selection:** Character and personality, extracurricular participation, and particular talent or ability are considered.
**Requirements:** Graduation from secondary school is required; GED is accepted. 16 units and the following program of study are required: 4 units of English, 3 units of math, 2 units of science including 1 unit of lab, 2 units of social studies, 3 units of electives including 2 units of academic electives. Minimum combined SAT score of 850, rank in top half of secondary school class, and minimum 2.5 GPA recommended. Contract Admissions Program for applicants not normally admissible. SAT is required. Campus visit and interview recommended. Off-campus interviews available with an admissions representative.
**Procedure:** Take SAT by December of 12th year. Visit college for interview by February 1 of 12th year. Suggest filing application by February 1. Application deadline is May 1. Notification of admission on rolling basis. Reply is required by May 1. $90 nonrefundable tuition deposit. $100 nonrefundable room deposit. Freshmen accepted for terms other than fall.
**Special programs:** Admission may be deferred one year. Credit and/or placement may be granted through CEEB Advanced Placement exams for scores of 3 or higher. Credit and/or placement may be granted through CLEP general and subject exams. Credit and placement may be granted through Regents College, ACT PEP, and DANTES exams, and military and life experience. Early entrance/early admission program. Concurrent enrollment program.
**Transfer students:** Transfer students accepted for terms other than fall. In fall 1993, 35% of all new students were transfers into all classes. 742 transfer applications were received, 601 were accepted. Application deadline is July 1 for fall; January 1 for spring. Minimum 2.5 GPA recommended. Lowest course grade accepted is "C-." Maximum number of transferable credits is 90 semester hours. At least 30 semester hours must be completed at the university to receive degree.
**Admissions contact:** Arthur C. Forst, Jr., Ph.D., Director of Admissions and Enrollment Planning. 203 456-5286.

**FINANCIAL AID. Available aid:** Pell grants, SEOG, state scholarships and grants, school scholarships and grants, private scholarships, and ROTC scholarships. Perkins Loans (NDSL), PLUS, Stafford Loans (GSL), state loans, school loans, and SLS. AMS.
**Financial aid statistics:** In 1993-94, 60% of all undergraduate applicants received aid; 60% of freshman applicants. Average amounts of aid awarded freshmen: Scholarships and grants, $3,500; loans, $3,500.
**Supporting data/closing dates:** FAFSA: Priority filing date is March 15. FAF: Deadline is March 15. Income tax forms: Deadline is March 15. Notification of awards begins May 1.
**Financial aid contact:** Richard Savage, Director of Financial Aid. 203 456-5205.

**STUDENT EMPLOYMENT.** College Work/Study Program. Institutional employment. 22% of full-time undergraduates work on campus during school year. Students may expect to earn an average of $1,300 during school year. Off-campus part-time employment opportunities rated "good."

**COMPUTER FACILITIES.** 150 IBM/IBM-compatible and Macintosh/Apple microcomputers; 100 are networked. Students may access Digital minicomputer/mainframe systems, BITNET, Internet. Residence halls may be equipped with networked microcomputers. Client/LAN operating systems include Apple/Macintosh, DOS, DEC. Computer languages and software packages include BASIC, C, COBOL, FORTRAN, GPSS, LISP, Pascal, SAS. Computer facilities are available to all students.
**Fees:** None.
**Hours:** 8 AM-11 PM (M-F).

**PROMINENT ALUMNI/AE.** Faith Middleton, radio host, Connecticut Public Radio.

## Fairfield University

**Fairfield, CT 06430-7524** **203 254-4000**

**1994-95 Costs.** Tuition: $15,000. Room & board: $6,200. Fees, books, misc. academic expenses (school's estimate): $750.
**Enrollment.** Undergraduates: 1,344 men, 1,640 women (full-time). Freshman class: 4,784 applicants, 3,346 accepted, 773 enrolled. Graduate enrollment: 161 men, 595 women.
**Test score averages/ranges.** Average SAT scores: 504 verbal, 562 math. Range of SAT scores of middle 50%: 460-540 verbal, 510-610 math.
**Faculty.** 177 full-time; 105 part-time. 90% of faculty holds highest degree in specific field. Student/faculty ratio: 16 to 1.
**Selectivity rating.** Competitive.

**PROFILE.** Fairfield, founded in 1942, is a church-affiliated, liberal arts university. Programs are offered through the College of Arts and Sciences and the Schools of Business and Nursing. Its 225-acre campus is located two miles from Long Island Sound and 60 miles from New York City.

**Accreditation:** NEASC. Professionally accredited by the National League for Nursing.
**Religious orientation:** Fairfield University is affiliated with the Roman Catholic Church (Society of Jesus); no religious requirements.
**Library:** Collections totaling over 298,220 volumes, 1,798 periodical subscriptions, and 416,354 microform items.
**Special facilities/museums:** Center for the arts, media center, TV studio, language labs, computer center for teacher education.
**Athletic facilities:** Gymnasium, swimming pool, basketball, racquetball, tennis, and volleyball courts, weight room, baseball, football, lacrosse, rugby, soccer, and softball fields.

**STUDENT BODY. Undergraduate profile:** 32% are state residents; 1% are transfers. 4% Asian-American, 2% Black, 4% Hispanic, 1% Native American, 89% White. Average age of undergraduates is 20.
**Freshman profile:** 4% of freshmen who took SAT scored 700 or over on math; 11% scored 600 or over on verbal, 31% scored 600 or over on math; 53% scored 500 or over on verbal, 83% scored 500 or over on math; 95% scored 400 or over on verbal, 98% scored 400 or over on math; 99% scored 300 or over on verbal, 99% scored 300 or over on math. 100% of accepted applicants took SAT. 50% of freshmen come from public schools.
**Undergraduate achievement:** 89% of fall 1992 freshmen returned for fall 1993 term. 84% of entering class graduated. 18% of students who completed a degree program went on to graduate study within one year.
**Foreign students:** 23 students are from out of the country. Countries represented include Canada, France, Ireland, Japan, Spain, and Sweden; 17 in all.

**PROGRAMS OF STUDY. Degrees:** B.A., B.S.
**Majors:** Accounting, American Studies, Art, Biology, Chemistry, Communications Art, Computer Science, Economics, English, Finance, Fine Arts, French, German, History, Information Systems, International Business, Management, Marketing, Mathematics, Modern Languages, Music, Nursing, Philosophy, Physics, Politics, Psychology, Religious Studies, Sociology, Spanish, Theatre.
**Distribution of degrees:** The majors with the highest enrollment are English, accounting, and biology; religious studies, philosophy, and modern languages have the lowest.
**Requirements:** General education requirement.
**Academic regulations:** Freshmen must maintain minimum 1.8 GPA; sophomores, 1.8 GPA; juniors, 1.9 GPA; seniors, 2.0 GPA.
**Special:** Minors offered in all majors and in Asian, Latin American, and women's studies and the Faith, Peace, and Justice Program. Double majors. Internships. Graduate school at which undergraduates may take graduate-level courses. Preprofessional programs in law, medicine, and dentistry. 3-2 engineering program with Columbia U, Rensselaer Polytech Inst, and U of Connecticut. 3-2 dental program with New York U. Washington Semester and Sea Semester. Exchange programs with Sacred Heart U and U of Bridgeport. Teacher certification in secondary and special education. Certification in specific subject areas. Member of International Student Exchange Program (ISEP).
**Honors:** Honors program. Honor societies.
**Academic Assistance:** Nonremedial tutoring.

**STUDENT LIFE. Housing:** All freshmen and sophomores must live on campus unless living with family. Coed dorms. School-owned/operated apartments. Off-campus privately-owned housing. 80% of students live in college housing.
**Social atmosphere:** According to the editor of the student newspaper, "The Campus Center is a popular on-campus spot." On campus, students participate in a variety of volunteer programs and Student Government organizations. Annual events include Harvest Weekend in the fall. The men's basketball games always draw a large crowd. "Many students also travel to different clubs, movies, concerts, and plays in the cities near Fairfield, such as New Haven, Bridgeport, and New York City."
**Services and counseling/handicapped student services:** Placement services. Health service. Women's center. Counseling services for minority, veteran, and older students. Personal and psychological counseling. Career and academic guidance services. Religious counseling. Physically disabled student services. Tutors. Reader services for the blind.
**Campus organizations:** Undergraduate student government. Student newspaper (Mirror, published once/week). Literary magazine. Yearbook. Radio and TV stations. Chorale, glee club, vocal ensemble, chamber orchestra, pep band, coffeehouse, drama group, debating, public affairs and radio clubs, film society, 60 organizations in all.
**Religious organizations:** Campus Ministry.
**Minority/foreign student organizations:** SALSA (Spanish and Latin Student Association), Asian Student Association, UMOJA. International Club.

**ATHLETICS. Physical education requirements:** None.

**Intercollegiate competition:** 20% of students participate. Baseball (M), basketball (M,W), cheerleading (M,W), cross-country (M,W), diving (M,W), field hockey (W), golf (M), ice hockey (M), lacrosse (M), rugby (M), soccer (M,W), softball (W), swimming (M,W), tennis (M,W), volleyball (W). Member of ECAC, MAAC, NCAA Division I.
**Intramural and club sports:** 76% of students participate. Intramural aerobics, basketball, flag football, racquetball, soccer, softball, volleyball, walleyball, water polo. Men's club Alpine skiing, crew, fencing, lacrosse, martial arts, rugby, sailing. Women's club Alpine skiing, crew, fencing, lacrosse, martial arts, sailing, soccer.

**ADMISSIONS. Academic basis for candidate selection** (in order of priority): Secondary school record, class rank, standardized test scores, school's recommendation.
**Nonacademic basis for candidate selection:** Character and personality are emphasized. Extracurricular participation, particular talent or ability, and alumni/ae relationship are considered.
**Requirements:** Graduation from secondary school is required; GED is not accepted. 17 units and the following program of study are required: 3 units of English, 3 units of math, 2 units of science including 1 unit of lab, 2 units of foreign language, 3 units of social studies, 1 unit of history, 3 units of electives. Rank in top two-fifths of secondary school class recommended. SAT is required; ACT may be substituted. ACH recommended. Campus visit and interview recommended. No off-campus interviews.
**Procedure:** Take SAT or ACT by December 1 of 12th year. Take ACH by May 1 of 12th year. Visit college for interview by March 1 of 12th year. Application deadline is March 1. Notification of admission by April 1. Reply is required by May 1. $200 nonrefundable tuition deposit. $200 nonrefundable room deposit. Freshmen accepted for fall term only.
**Special programs:** Admission may be deferred one year. Placement may be granted through CEEB Advanced Placement exams for scores of 4 or higher. Placement may be granted through CLEP subject exams and challenge exams. Early decision program. In fall 1993, 140 applied for early decision and 105 were accepted. Deadline for applying for early decision is December 1.
**Transfer students:** Transfer students accepted for terms other than fall. In fall 1993, 1% of all new students were transfers into all classes. 217 transfer applications were received, 53 were accepted. Application deadline is June 1 for fall; December 1 for spring. Minimum 2.5 GPA recommended. Lowest course grade accepted is "B." Maximum number of transferable credits is 60 semester hours. At least 60 semester hours must be completed at the university to receive degree.
**Admissions contact:** David M. Flynn, M.S., Dean of Admission and Financial Aid. 203 254-4100.

**FINANCIAL AID. Available aid:** Pell grants, SEOG, state scholarships and grants, school scholarships and grants, private scholarships and grants, academic merit scholarships, and athletic scholarships. Perkins Loans (NDSL), PLUS, Stafford Loans (GSL), NSL, state loans, private loans, and SLS. Excel and Alliance (Teri) loans. EFI Fund Management and family tuition reduction.
**Financial aid statistics:** 11% of aid is not need-based. In 1993-94, 100% of all undergraduate applicants received aid. Average amounts of aid awarded freshmen: Scholarships and grants, $7,225; loans, $2,855.
**Supporting data/closing dates:** FAFSA/FAF: Deadline is February 1. Income tax forms: Deadline is May 1. Notification of awards begins April 1.
**Financial aid contact:** James T. Anderson, M.S., Director of Financial Aid. 203 254-4000, extension 2485.

**STUDENT EMPLOYMENT.** College Work/Study Program. Institutional employment. 10% of full-time undergraduates work on campus during school year. Students may expect to earn an average of $1,200 during school year. Off-campus part-time employment opportunities rated "good."

**COMPUTER FACILITIES.** 136 IBM/IBM-compatible and Macintosh/Apple microcomputers; 60 are networked. Students may access Digital minicomputer/mainframe systems, Internet. Client/LAN operating systems include Apple/Macintosh, DOS, UNIX/XENIX/AIX, DEC. Computer languages and software packages include APL, BASIC, FORTRAN, Pascal. Computer facilities are available to all students.
**Fees:** Computer fee is included in tuition/fees.
**Hours:** 8 AM-midn.

**GRADUATE CAREER DATA.** Graduate school percentages: 5% enter law school. 4% enter medical school. 3% enter dental school. 3% enter graduate business programs. 2% enter graduate arts and sciences programs. Highest graduate school enrollments: Columbia, Fordham, Georgetown U, New York U, U of Connecticut. 70% of graduates choose careers in business and industry. Companies and businesses that hire graduates: Aetna, Big Six accounting firms, Caldors, IBM, Chase Manhattan Bank.

**PROMINENT ALUMNI/AE.** E. Gerald Corrigan, president, New York Federal Reserve Bank; Michael Farren, U.S. undersecretary of commerce; Lisa Schwabe, vice-president, Chase Manhattan Bank; Joyce Tabory Phillips, vice-president, Citibank; Eddie Rodriguez, Connecticut supreme court justice; John Swanhaus, president, Pepsico Wines and Spirits International.

# Quinnipiac College

**Hamden, CT 06518** **203 288-5251**

**1993-94 Costs.** Tuition: $11,250. Room & board: $5,790. Fees, books, misc. academic expenses (school's estimate): $1,560.
**Enrollment.** Undergraduates: 1,219 men, 1,489 women (full-time). Freshman class: 3,712 applicants, 2,153 accepted, 672 enrolled. Graduate enrollment: 607 men, 615 women.
**Test score averages/ranges.** Average SAT scores: 510 verbal, 535 math. Range of SAT scores of middle 50%: 450-550 verbal, 480-580 math. Average ACT scores: 23 composite.
**Faculty.** 208 full-time; 125 part-time. 85% of faculty holds highest degree in specific field. Student/faculty ratio: 15 to 1.
**Selectivity rating.** More competitive.

**PROFILE.** Quinnipiac, founded in 1929, is a private, multipurpose college. Programs are offered through the Schools of Allied Health and Natural Sciences, Business, and Liberal Arts and the Division of Continuing Education. Its 170-acre campus is located in Hamden, nine miles from metropolitan New Haven.

**Accreditation:** NEASC. Professionally accredited by the American Bar Association, the American Medical Association (CAHEA), the American Physical Therapy Association, the American Veterinary Medical Association, the National League for Nursing.
**Religious orientation:** Quinnipiac College is nonsectarian; no religious requirements.
**Library:** Collections totaling over 440,000 volumes, 4,100 periodical subscriptions, and 155,750 microform items.
**Special facilities/museums:** Electron microscope, computer, radiology, and television and radio broadcast and editing labs.
**Athletic facilities:** Gymnasium, weight rooms, tennis courts, baseball, softball, soccer, and intramural fields.

**STUDENT BODY. Undergraduate profile:** 45% are state residents; 24% are transfers. 1% Asian-American, 5% Black, 3% Hispanic, 89% White, 2% Other. Average age of undergraduates is 21.
**Freshman profile:** 4% of freshmen who took SAT scored 700 or over on verbal, 6% scored 700 or over on math; 18% scored 600 or over on verbal, 20% scored 600 or over on math; 22% scored 500 or over on verbal, 65% scored 500 or over on math; 70% scored 400 or over on verbal, 100% scored 400 or over on math. 99% of accepted applicants took SAT; 1% took ACT. 58% of freshmen come from public schools.
**Undergraduate achievement:** 84% of fall 1992 freshmen returned for fall 1993 term. 65% of entering class graduated. 70% of students who completed a degree program went on to graduate study within one year.
**Foreign students:** 25 students are from out of the country. Countries represented include the Bahamas, China, Greece, Ireland, Japan, and Oman; eight in all.

**PROGRAMS OF STUDY. Degrees:** B.A., B.S., B.S.Hlth.Sci.
**Majors:** Accounting, Animal Technology, Biochemistry, Biology, Business Administration, Chemistry, Clinical Microbiology, Computer Science, Economics, English, Financial Management, General Management, Gerontology, Health Management, History, International Business, Legal Studies, Marketing, Mass Communications, Mathematics, Medical Laboratory Sciences, Medical Technology, Microbiology, Microbiology/Biotechnology, Nursing, Occupational Therapy, Physical Therapy, Political Science, Psychobiology, Psychology, Radiography, Respiratory Therapy, Social Service, Sociology.
**Distribution of degrees:** The majors with the highest enrollment are physical therapy, occupational therapy, and marketing.
**Requirements:** General education requirement.
**Academic regulations:** Freshmen must maintain minimum 1.5 GPA; sophomores, 1.7 GPA; juniors, 2.0 GPA; seniors, 2.0 GPA.
**Special:** Minors offered in actuarial science, anthropology, art, drama and theatre, French, geography, German, Japanese, music, political science, and Spanish. Self-designed majors. Double majors. Dual degrees. Independent study. Accelerated study. Internships. Cooperative education programs. Graduate school at which undergraduates may take graduate-level courses. Preprofessional programs in law, medicine, veterinary science, pharmacy, dentistry, physical therapy, and pathologist's assistant. 3-4 podiatric medicine programs with Coll of Podiatric Medicine and Surgery (Iowa) and New York Coll of Podiatric Medicine. 3-4 chiropractic program with National Coll of Chiropractic (Illinois). Five-year M.B.A. and M.A.T. programs. 4 1/2-year chemistry cooperation. Exchange possible with Albertus Magnus Coll, American U, U of New Haven. Teacher certification in secondary education. Certification in specific subject areas. Exchange programs abroad in Barbados (U of the West Indies), Canada, China (Beijing Information Tech Inst, Nankai U, Zhejiang U), England (Lansdowne Independent University Coll), Greece (Southeastern Coll), Israel (Hebrew U), Italy (John Cabot U), Japan (Kansai U), and Switzerland (American Coll of Switzerland). Study abroad also in Austria, France, Germany, and Spain. AFROTC at U of Connecticut.
**Honors:** Honors program. Honor societies.
**Academic Assistance:** Remedial reading, writing, math, and study skills. Nonremedial tutoring.

**STUDENT LIFE. Housing:** Students may live on or off campus. Coed and women's dorms. 75% of students live in college housing.
**Social atmosphere:** According to the student newspaper, social life is "low key, especially due to a more stringent alcohol policy." Greeks, though accounting for only a small proportion of students, are influential on campus. Greek and non-Greek semiformals, the Spring Break Mixer, and May Weekend are popular events on campus. Students congregate at the campus Rathskeller, on-campus apartments, and area nightclubs.
**Services and counseling/handicapped student services:** Placement services. Health service. Women's center. Day care. Counseling services for minority and older students. Birth control, personal, and psychological counseling. Career and academic guidance services. Religious counseling. Physically disabled student services. Learning disabled services. Notetaking services. Tape recorders. Tutors. Reader services for the blind.
**Campus organizations:** Undergraduate student government. Student newspaper (Chronicle, published once/two weeks). Literary magazine. Yearbook. Radio station. Choir, Jazz Connection, theatre workshop, dance company, debating, martial arts, and ski clubs, Amnesty International, Greenpeace, women's group, academic, athletic, departmental, and special-interest groups, 65 organizations in all. Four fraternities, no chapter houses; three sororities, no chapter houses. 3% of men join a fraternity. 3% of women join a sorority.
**Religious organizations:** Catholic Community, Christian Fellowship, Hillel.
**Minority/foreign student organizations:** Black Student Union. International Club.

**ATHLETICS. Physical education requirements:** One semester of physical education required.
**Intercollegiate competition:** 6% of students participate. Baseball (M), basketball (M,W), cheerleading (W), cross-country (M,W), golf (M), ice hockey (M), lacrosse (M), soccer (M,W), softball (W), tennis (M,W), volleyball (W). Member of ECAC, NCAA Division II, NCAA Division III for ice hockey, NECAC, Northeast-10 Conference.
**Intramural and club sports:** 2% of students participate. Intramural basketball, bowling, field hockey, soccer, softball, touch football, volleyball.

**ADMISSIONS. Academic basis for candidate selection** (in order of priority): Secondary school record, class rank, school's recommendation, standardized test scores, essay.

**Nonacademic basis for candidate selection:** Character and personality are important. Extracurricular participation, particular talent or ability, geographical distribution, and alumni/ae relationship are considered.

**Requirements:** Graduation from secondary school is required; GED is accepted. 16 units and the following program of study are required: 4 units of English, 3 units of math, 2 units of science including 1 unit of lab, 1 unit of social studies, 2 units of history, 4 units of electives including 2 units of academic electives. Minimum combined SAT score of 950, rank in top half of secondary school class, and minimum 2.5 GPA recommended. Physics and pre-calculus required of physical therapy program applicants. Chemistry required of nursing program applicants. Chemistry, algebra, and fourth year science and math required of occupational therapy program applicants. Academic Assistance Program for applicants not normally admissible. SAT is required; ACT may be substituted. Campus visit and interview recommended. No off-campus interviews.

**Procedure:** Take SAT or ACT by November of 12th year. Visit college for interview by February of 12th year. Suggest filing application by March 1; no deadline. Notification of admission on rolling basis. Reply is required by May 1. $200 tuition deposit, refundable until May 1. $350 room deposit, refundable until May 1. Freshmen accepted for terms other than fall.

**Special programs:** Admission may be deferred one year. Credit may be granted through CEEB Advanced Placement for scores of 3 or higher. Credit and/or placement may be granted through CLEP general and subject exams. Credit and placement may be granted through challenge exams and military and life experience.

**Transfer students:** Transfer students accepted for terms other than fall. In fall 1993, 24% of all new students were transfers into all classes. 479 transfer applications were received, 380 were accepted. Application deadline is rolling for fall; rolling for spring. Minimum 2.0 GPA required. Lowest course grade accepted is "C." At least 45 semester hours must be completed at the college to receive degree.

**Admissions contact:** Joan Isaac Mohr, M.A., Vice President and Dean of Admissions. 203 281-8600, 800 462-1944.

**FINANCIAL AID. Available aid:** Pell grants, SEOG, Federal Nursing Student Scholarships, state scholarships and grants, school scholarships and grants, private scholarships and grants, ROTC scholarships, academic merit scholarships, and athletic scholarships. Students of Color scholarship. Perkins Loans (NDSL), PLUS, Stafford Loans (GSL), NSL, state loans, private loans, and SLS. EXEL, TERI, FELP, and ABLE loans. Knight Tuition Plans and deferred payment plan.

**Financial aid statistics:** 27% of aid is not need-based. In 1993-94, 70% of all undergraduate applicants received aid; 83% of freshman applicants. Average amounts of aid awarded freshmen: Scholarships and grants, $6,599; loans, $2,625.

**Supporting data/closing dates:** FAFSA: Priority filing date is March 1. School's own aid application: Priority filing date is March 1; accepted on rolling basis. State aid form: Accepted on rolling basis. Income tax forms: Accepted on rolling basis. Notification of awards on rolling basis.

**Financial aid contact:** Margaret Bridle, M.B.A., Director of Financial Aid. 203 281-8750.

**STUDENT EMPLOYMENT.** College Work/Study Program. Institutional employment. 5% of full-time undergraduates work on campus during school year. Students may expect to earn an average of $1,500 during school year. Off-campus part-time employment opportunities rated "good."

**COMPUTER FACILITIES.** 130 IBM/IBM-compatible and Macintosh/Apple microcomputers; 120 are networked. Students may access Digital, IBM minicomputer/mainframe systems. Client/LAN operating systems include Apple/Macintosh, DOS, DEC. Computer languages and software packages include Assembler, BASIC, C, C++, COBOL, dBASE, FORTRAN, Lotus 1-2-3, Paradox, Pascal, RPG, Windows, WordPerfect. Computer facilities are available to all students.

**Fees:** Computer fee is included in tuition/fees.

**Hours:** 8 AM-midn. (M-Th); 8 AM-10 PM (F); 10 AM-6 PM (Sa); 1 PM-midn. (Su).

**GRADUATE CAREER DATA.** Graduate school percentages: 6% enter law school. 7% enter graduate business programs. 8% enter medical/dental school. 5% enter graduate arts and sciences programs. Highest graduate school enrollments: Quinnipiac Coll, U of Connecticut, U of Hartford, U of New Haven. 60% of graduates choose careers in business and industry. Companies and businesses that hire graduates: Aetna, Bristol-Myers, Gaylord Rehab Hospital, Internal Revenue Service, IBM, Miles Pharmaceutical, Pratt & Whitney, Sikorsky, Travelers Insurance, U.S. Surgical, Yale New Haven Hospital.

**PROMINENT ALUMNI/AE.** Murray Lender, founder, Lender's Bagels; Albert Magnoli, producer/director, *Purple Rain;* Robert Haversat, CEO, ESSTAR.

# Saint Joseph College

**West Hartford, CT 06117** **203 232-4571**

**1994-95 Costs.** Tuition: $12,200. Room: $2,200. Board: $2,400.

**Enrollment.** 543 women (full-time). Freshman class: 332 applicants, 241 accepted, 96 enrolled. Graduate enrollment: 93 men, 674 women.

**Test score averages/ranges.** Average SAT scores: 430 verbal, 450 math. Range of SAT scores of middle 50%: 370-510 verbal, 380-540 math.

**Faculty.** 68 full-time; 76 part-time. 70% of faculty holds doctoral degree. Student/faculty ratio: 12 to 1.

**Selectivity rating.** Competitive.

**PROFILE.** Saint Joseph, founded in 1932, is a private, church-affiliated college for women; qualified men offered admission to graduate division and continuing education programs. Its 84-acre campus is located in West Hartford, three miles from Hartford.

**Accreditation:** NEASC. Professionally accredited by the American Dietetic Association, the Council on Social Work Education, the National League for Nursing.

**Religious orientation:** Saint Joseph College is affiliated with the Roman Catholic Church (Sisters of Mercy); two semesters of religion required.

**Library:** Collections totaling over 120,000 volumes, 736 periodical subscriptions, and 10,200 microform items.

**Special facilities/museums:** Art gallery, computer lab, language lab, nursing lab, nursery school/kindergarten, school for exceptional children.

**Athletic facilities:** Gymnasium, swimming pool, weight room, soccer and softball fields, dance studio, track, basketball, paddle tennis, tennis, and volleyball courts.

**STUDENT BODY. Undergraduate profile:** 94% are state residents; 51% are transfers. 1% Asian-American, 5% Black, 2% Hispanic, 1% Native American, 91% White. Average age of undergraduates is 21.

**Freshman profile:** 1% of freshmen who took SAT scored 700 or over on math; 6% scored 600 or over on verbal, 8% scored 600 or over on math; 20% scored 500 or over on verbal, 34% scored 500 or over on math; 70% scored 400 or over on verbal, 70% scored 400 or over on math; 98% scored 300 or over on verbal, 98% scored 300 or over on math. 98% of accepted applicants took SAT. 81% of freshmen come from public schools.

**Undergraduate achievement:** 88% of fall 1992 freshmen returned for fall 1993 term. 60% of entering class graduated. 5% of students who completed a degree program immediately went on to graduate study.

**PROGRAMS OF STUDY. Degrees:** B.A., B.S.

**Majors:** Accounting, American Studies, Art History, Biology, Biology/Chemistry, Business Administration, Chemistry, Child Study, Dietetics/Food/Nutrition, Economics/Finance, English, French, History, History/Political Science, Home Economics Education, Humanities, Life Resource Management, Management, Mathematics, Mathematics/Computer Science, Mathematics/Economics, Medical Technology, Music Education, Natural Sciences, Nursing, Philosophy, Political Science, Psychology, Religious Studies, Social Science/History, Social Work, Sociology, Spanish, Special Education.

**Distribution of degrees:** The majors with the highest enrollment are child study, nursing, and special education.

**Requirements:** General education requirement.

**Academic regulations:** Minimum 2.0 GPA must be maintained.

**Special:** Minors offered in many majors and in approximately 15 other fields. Self-designed majors. Double majors. Independent study. Pass/fail grading option. Internships. Graduate school at which undergraduates may take graduate-level courses. Preprofessional programs in law and medicine. Business/M.B.A. program with U of Hartford. Math/physics/engineering program with George Washington U. Member of Hartford Consortium for Higher Education; cross-registration possible. Teacher certification in early childhood, elementary, secondary, and special education. Certification in specific subject areas. Exchange program abroad in Japan (Seissen Junior Coll). ROTC at U of Hartford.

**Honors:** Honors program.

**Academic Assistance:** Nonremedial tutoring.

**ADMISSIONS. Academic basis for candidate selection** (in order of priority): Secondary school record, class rank, standardized test scores, school's recommendation.

**Nonacademic basis for candidate selection:** Character and personality, extracurricular participation, and particular talent or ability are considered.

**Requirements:** Graduation from secondary school is required; GED is accepted. 16 units are required and the following program of study is recommended: 4 units of English, 3 units of math, 3 units of science, 2 units of foreign language, 2 units of social studies, 2 units of history. SAT is required. ACH recommended. Campus visit and interview recommended. Off-campus interviews available with an admissions representative.

**Procedure:** Take SAT by fall of 12th year. Application deadline is May 1. Notification of admission on rolling basis. Reply is required by May 1 or by date specified in letter of acceptance. $100 nonrefundable tuition deposit. Freshmen accepted for terms other than fall.

**Special programs:** Admission may be deferred. Credit and/or placement may be granted through CEEB Advanced Placement exams for scores of 4 or higher. Credit may be granted through CLEP general and subject exams, challenge exams, and military and life experience. Early decision program. In fall 1993, three applied for early decision and three were accepted. Deadline for applying for early decision is November 15. Early entrance/early admission program. Concurrent enrollment program.

**Transfer students:** Transfer students accepted for terms other than fall. In fall 1993, 51% of all new students were transfers into all classes. 202 transfer applications were received, 141 were accepted. Application deadline is July 1 for fall; December 1 for spring. Minimum 2.7 GPA recommended. Lowest course grade accepted is "C-." At least 60 semester hours must be completed at the college to receive degree.

**Admissions contact:** Mary C. Demo, M.A., Director of Admissions. 203 232-4571.

**FINANCIAL AID. Available aid:** Pell grants, SEOG, state scholarships and grants, school scholarships and grants, private scholarships and grants, and academic merit scholarships. Perkins Loans (NDSL), PLUS, Stafford Loans (GSL), NSL, state loans, private loans, and SLS. AMS and deferred payment plan.

**Financial aid statistics:** 10% of aid is not need-based. In 1993-94, 91% of all undergraduate applicants received aid; 98% of freshman applicants. Average amounts of aid awarded freshmen: Scholarships and grants, $5,574; loans, $3,735.

**Supporting data/closing dates:** FAFSA/FAF: Priority filing date is February 1; accepted on rolling basis. School's own aid application: Priority filing date is February 1; accepted on rolling basis. Income tax forms: Priority filing date is February 1; accepted on rolling basis. Notification of awards on rolling basis.

**Financial aid contact:** Philip Malinsoki, Director of Financial Aid. 203 232-4571.

## Southern Connecticut State University

**New Haven, CT 06515** **203 397-4000**

**1994-95 Costs.** Tuition: $1,842 (state residents), $5,962 (out-of-state). Room: $2,616. Board: $2,180. Fees, books, misc. academic expenses (school's estimate): $1,461-$2,269.

**Enrollment.** Undergraduates: 2,740 men, 3,402 women (full-time). Freshman class: 3,852 applicants, 2,378 accepted, 928 enrolled. Graduate enrollment: 880 men, 2,665 women.

**Test score averages/ranges.** Average SAT scores: 460 verbal, 440 math.

**Faculty.** 369 full-time; 379 part-time. 67% of faculty holds doctoral degree. Student/faculty ratio: 19 to 1.

**Selectivity rating.** Less competitive.

**PROFILE.** Southern Connecticut State, founded in 1893, is a public, liberal arts university. Its 158-acre campus is located in New Haven, 35 miles from Hartford.

**Accreditation:** NEASC. Professionally accredited by the American Library Association, the Council on Social Work Education, the National Council for Accreditation of Teacher Education, the National League for Nursing.

**Religious orientation:** Southern Connecticut State University is nonsectarian; no religious requirements.

**Library:** Collections totaling over 369,838 volumes, 3,146 periodical subscriptions, and 671,485 microform items.

**Special facilities/museums:** Art gallery, language lab, child development center, communication disorders center, planetarium and observatory, closed-circuit TV center.

**Athletic facilities:** Field house, indoor track, swimming pool, weight training room, gymnasium, human performance lab.

**STUDENT BODY. Undergraduate profile:** 91% are state residents; 40% are transfers. 1% Asian-American, 7% Black, 2% Hispanic, 1% Native American, 88% White, 1% Other. Average age of undergraduates is 21.

**Freshman profile:** 2% of freshmen who took SAT scored 600 or over on verbal, 3% scored 600 or over on math; 13% scored 500 or over on verbal, 27% scored 500 or over on math; 58% scored 400 or over on verbal, 74% scored 400 or over on math; 100% scored 300 or over on verbal, 100% scored 300 or over on math. Majority of accepted applicants took SAT.

**Undergraduate achievement:** 65% of fall 1991 freshmen returned for fall 1992 term. 33% of students who completed a degree program went on to graduate study.

**Foreign students:** 156 students are from out of the country. Countries represented include China, England, and Germany; 14 in all.

**PROGRAMS OF STUDY. Degrees:** B.A., B.S.

**Majors:** Accounting, Art, Athletic Training, Biology, Business Economics, Chemistry, Communication, Communication Disorders, Computer Science, Earth Sciences, Education, English, Finance, Foreign Languages, French, Geography, German, History, Human Performance, Interdisciplinary Major, Italian, Journalism, Library Science, Library Science/Instructional Technology, Literature, Management, Marketing, Mathematics, Nursing, Philosophy, Physical Education, Physics, Political Science, Psychology, Public Health, Recreation, School Health Education, Social Work, Sociology, Spanish, Special Education, Theatre.

**Distribution of degrees:** The majors with the highest enrollment are business, education, and communications; theatre, philosophy, and geography have the lowest.

**Requirements:** General education requirement.

**Academic regulations:** Minimum 2.0 GPA required for graduation.

**Special:** Minors offered in some majors and in African, Asian, and Soviet/East European studies, anthropology, criminal justice, dance, environmental studies, marine biology/aquatic studies, public health administration, religious studies, women's studies, and several other fields. Associate's degrees offered. Double majors. Dual degrees. Independent study. Pass/fail grading option. Internships. Cooperative education programs. Graduate school at which undergraduates may take graduate-level courses. Preprofessional programs in law, medicine, veterinary science, and dentistry. Member of New England Regional Student Program. Exchange programs with other members of state university system. Teacher certification in early childhood, elementary, secondary, and special education. Study abroad in England, France, and Spain. ROTC and AFROTC at U of Connecticut.

**Honors:** Honors program.

**Academic Assistance:** Nonremedial tutoring.

**STUDENT LIFE. Housing:** Students may live on or off campus. Coed dorms. School-owned/operated apartments. 60% of students live in college housing.

**Social atmosphere:** The student newspaper reports, "New Haven is a hotbed of activity. Most students take advantage of this. A majority of the students live off campus and go to the lectures, exhibits, festivals, etc., off campus rather than staying on campus." Popular campus activities include Homecoming Weekend, Springfest, soccer games and gymnastics meets, and various speakers throughout the year. Favorite off-campus gathering spots include the New West Cafe, 127 West, Toad's Place, and Skidder's.

**Services and counseling/handicapped student services:** Placement services. Health service. Women's center. Day care. Counseling services for minority, veteran, and older students. Birth control, personal, and psychological counseling. Career and academic guidance services. Physically disabled student services. Learning disabled services. Notetaking services. Tape recorders. Tutors. Reader services for the blind.

**Campus organizations:** Undergraduate student government. Student newspaper (Southern News, published once/week). Literary magazine. Yearbook. Radio station. Band, orchestra, choir, chorus, Crescent Players Dance Theatre, debating, Environmental Awareness Council, Student Tenant Organization, Young Democrats, Young Republicans, departmental, social, and special-interest groups, 100 organizations in all. Five fraternities, no chapter houses; four sororities, no chapter houses.

**Religious organizations:** Christian Baptist Campus Ministries, Newman Club, Organization of Jewish Students, United Ministry of Higher Education.

**Minority/foreign student organizations:** Black Student Union, Latin American organization. People to People.

**ATHLETICS. Physical education requirements:** One semester of physical education required.

**Intercollegiate competition:** 4% of students participate. Baseball (M), basketball (M,W), cheerleading (W), cross-country (M,W), field hockey (W), football (M), gymnastics (M,W), soccer (M), softball (W), swimming (M,W), track and field (indoor) (M,W), track and field (outdoor) (M,W), volleyball (W), wrestling (M). Member of ECAC, NCAA Division I for men's gymnastics, NCAA Division II, NECC.

**Intramural and club sports:** 1% of students participate. Intramural aerobics, badminton, basketball, floor hockey, football, golf, gymnastics, jogging, karate, soccer, softball, tennis, turkey trot, swimming, volleyball, water polo, weight training, Wiffle ball. Men's club fencing, ice hockey, karate, rugby, skiing. Women's club cheerleading, fencing, karate, rugby, skiing.

**ADMISSIONS. Academic basis for candidate selection** (in order of priority): Secondary school record, class rank, standardized test scores, essay, school's recommendation.

**Requirements:** Graduation from secondary school is required; GED is accepted. 16 units and the following program of study are required: 4 units of English, 3 units of math, 2 units of science including 1 unit of lab, 2 units of foreign language, 2 units of social studies, 1 unit of history, 3 units of academic electives. Minimum combined SAT score of 800 required; 900 recommended. EOP for applicants not normally admissible. SAT or ACT is required. Campus visit recommended. No off-campus interviews.

**Procedure:** Take SAT or ACT by March of 12th year. Suggest filing application by May 1. Application deadline is August 1. Notification of admission on rolling basis beginning December 1. Reply is required by May 1 or within two weeks of acceptance. $90 nonrefundable tuition deposit. $100 nonrefundable room deposit. Freshmen accepted for terms other than fall.

**Special programs:** Admission may be deferred one year. Credit may be granted through CEEB Advanced Placement for scores of 3 or higher. Credit may be granted through CLEP general and subject exams, DANTES exams, and military experience. Credit and placement may be granted through challenge exams. Concurrent enrollment program.

**Transfer students:** Transfer students accepted for terms other than fall. In fall 1992, 40% of all new students were transfers into all classes. Application deadline is July 1 for fall; January 1 for spring. Minimum 2.0 GPA required. Lowest course grade accepted is "C." Maximum number of transferable credits is 63 semester hours from a two-year school and 90 semester hours from a four-year school. At least 30 semester hours must be completed at the university to receive degree.

**Admissions contact:** Sharon A. Brennan, M.A., Director of Admissions. 203 397-4450.

**FINANCIAL AID. Available aid:** Pell grants, SEOG, state scholarships and grants, school grants, and academic merit scholarships. Perkins Loans (NDSL), PLUS, Stafford Loans (GSL), and SLS. AMS.

**Financial aid statistics:** In 1992-93, 38% of all undergraduate applicants received aid; 30% of freshman applicants. Average amounts of aid awarded freshmen: Scholarships and grants, $2,500; loans, $1,000.

**Supporting data/closing dates:** FAFSA/FAF: Deadline is March 15. School's own aid application: Deadline is March 15. Notification of awards on rolling basis.

**Financial aid contact:** Kenneth D. Maginniss, M.Ed., Director of Financial Aid. 203 397-4232.

**STUDENT EMPLOYMENT.** College Work/Study Program. Institutional employment. 15% of full-time undergraduates work on campus during school year. Students may expect to earn an average of $1,200 during school year. Freshmen are discouraged from working during their first term. Off-campus part-time employment opportunities rated "good."

**COMPUTER FACILITIES.** 200 IBM/IBM-compatible and Macintosh/Apple microcomputers. Students may access Digital minicomputer/mainframe systems. Computer languages and software packages include Ada, BASIC, COBOL, FORTRAN, LISP, MINITAB, Pascal, SAS, SPSS-X. Computer facilities are available to all students.

**Fees:** Computer fee is included in tuition/fees.

**Hours:** 8 AM-10 PM (M-F); 16 hours on weekends. Modem lines provide 24-hour access.

**PROMINENT ALUMNI/AE.** Michael J. Adanti, president, Southern Connecticut State U; Gerald Tirozzi, president, Wheelock Coll; Leo Connors, president, Founders Bank; John Williamson, vice-president, Houghton Mifflin; Mary Galvin, prosecutor, Connecticut Attorney General's office; Charles Gill, Superior Court judge; Dan Lauria, actor.

## Teikyo Post University

**Waterbury, CT 06723-2540** **203 596-4500**

**1994-95 Costs.** Tuition: $11,300. Room & board: $5,400. Fees, books, misc. academic expenses (school's estimate): $750.

**Enrollment.** Undergraduates: 220 men, 391 women (full-time). Freshman class: 645 applicants, 577 accepted, 201 enrolled.

**Test score averages/ranges.** N/A.

**Faculty.** 25 full-time; 168 part-time. 27% of faculty holds doctoral degree. Student/faculty ratio: 17 to 1.

**Selectivity rating.** N/A.

**PROFILE.** Teikyo Post is a private university. It was founded as a business school in 1890, and in 1990 its name was changed from Post College. Programs are offered through the Schools of Arts and Sciences and Business Administration. Its 70-acre campus is located in Waterbury, 30 miles west of Hartford.

**Accreditation:** NEASC.

**Religious orientation:** Teikyo Post University is nonsectarian; no religious requirements.

**Library:** Collections totaling over 45,000 volumes, 625 periodical subscriptions, and 4,200 microform items.

**Special facilities/museums:** Government documents collection.
**Athletic facilities:** Swimming pool, gymnasium, basketball, racquetball, and tennis courts, weight room, soccer, and softball fields, sauna, steam room, whirlpool.

**STUDENT BODY. Undergraduate profile:** 65% are state residents; 43% are transfers. 6% Asian-American, 5% Black, 5% Hispanic, 82% White, 2% Other. Average age of undergraduates is 24.
**Foreign students:** Countries represented include Canada, Japan, Nepal, and Puerto Rico; 32 in all.

**PROGRAMS OF STUDY. Degrees:** B.A., B.S.
**Majors:** Accounting, English, Equine Management, Fashion Merchandising, Finance, General Studies, History, Hospitality Management, Interior Design, International Business, Legal Assistant, Management, Marketing, Psychology, Sociology.
**Distribution of degrees:** The majors with the highest enrollment are business management, psychology, and social sciences.
**Requirements:** General education requirement.
**Academic regulations:** Minimum 2.0 GPA must be maintained.
**Special:** Minors offered in all majors and in management information systems. Self-designed majors. Double majors. Accelerated study. Cooperative education programs. Preprofessional programs in law and optometry. Member of Teikyo U International Consortium. Teacher certification in early childhood education. Study abroad in England, Germany, Japan, the Netherlands, and Poland. ROTC at Southern Connecticut State U.
**Honors:** Phi Beta Kappa. Honor societies.
**Academic Assistance:** Remedial reading, writing, math, and study skills. Nonremedial tutoring.

**ADMISSIONS. Academic basis for candidate selection** (in order of priority): Secondary school record, class rank, standardized test scores, school's recommendation, essay.
**Nonacademic basis for candidate selection:** Character and personality are important. Extracurricular participation, particular talent or ability, and alumni/ae relationship are considered.
**Requirements:** Graduation from secondary school is required; GED is accepted. 16 units and the following program of study are required: 4 units of English. SAT or ACT is recommended. Campus visit and interview recommended. Off-campus interviews available with admissions and alumni representatives.
**Procedure:** Visit college for interview by January of 12th year. Notification of admission on rolling basis. Reply is required by May 1 or within one month of acceptance. $100 tuition deposit, refundable until May 1. $100 room deposit, refundable until May 1. Freshmen accepted for terms other than fall.
**Special programs:** Admission may be deferred one year. Credit and/or placement may be granted through CEEB Advanced Placement exams for scores of 2 or higher. Credit may be granted through CLEP general and subject exams, DANTES exams, and life experience. Placement may be granted through Regents College, ACT PEP, and challenge exams. Credit and placement may be granted through military experience. Early entrance/early admission program. Concurrent enrollment program.
**Transfer students:** Transfer students accepted for terms other than fall. In fall 1992, 43% of all new students were transfers into all classes. Application deadline is rolling for fall; rolling for spring. Minimum 2.0 GPA recommended. Lowest course grade accepted is "C-." Maximum number of transferable credits is 90 semester hours. At least 30 semester hours must be completed at the university to receive degree.
**Admissions contact:** Aline Rossiter, Director of Admissions. 203 596-4520.

**FINANCIAL AID. Available aid:** Pell grants, SEOG, state scholarships and grants, school scholarships and grants, private scholarships and grants, and athletic scholarships. Perkins Loans (NDSL), PLUS, Stafford Loans (GSL), private loans, and SLS. AMS, Tuition Management Systems, and deferred payment plan. University payment plans.
**Financial aid statistics:** 25% of aid is not need-based. In 1992-93, 80% of all undergraduate applicants received aid; 75% of freshman applicants. Average amounts of aid awarded freshmen: Scholarships and grants, $4,000; loans, $2,625.
**Supporting data/closing dates:** FAFSA/FAF: Priority filing date is March 13. School's own aid application: Priority filing date is March 15. State aid form: Priority filing date is February 15. Income tax forms: Priority filing date is March 15. Notification of awards begins February.
**Financial aid contact:** Claire Dwyer, Director of Financial Aid. 203 596-4527.

# Trinity College

**Hartford, CT 06016 — 203 297-2000**

**1994-95 Costs.** Tuition: $18,810. Room: $3,540. Board: $2,150. Fees, books, misc. academic expenses (school's estimate): 1,280.
**Enrollment.** Undergraduates: 911 men, 852 women (full-time). Freshman class: 2,851 applicants, 1,731 accepted, 475 enrolled. Graduate enrollment: 100 men, 100 women.
**Test score averages/ranges.** Average SAT scores: 560 verbal, 610 math. Range of SAT scores of middle 50%: 520-610 verbal, 560-660 math. Average ACT scores: 26 composite. Range of ACT scores of middle 50%: 23-29 composite.
**Faculty.** 152 full-time; 62 part-time. 97% of faculty holds doctoral degree. Student/faculty ratio: 10 to 1.
**Selectivity rating.** Highly competitive.

**PROFILE.** Trinity, founded in 1823, is a private, liberal arts college. The architectural design of the present campus, developed in the 1870's, was influenced by the English institutions Oxford and Cambridge. Its 96-acre, urban campus is located in Hartford.

**Accreditation:** NEASC.
**Religious orientation:** Trinity College is nonsectarian; no religious requirements.
**Library:** Collections totaling over 847,696 volumes, 2,181 periodical subscriptions, and 249,869 microform items.
**Special facilities/museums:** Collections of early American texts, maritime history, Native American history.
**Athletic facilities:** Gymnasiums, field house, swimming pool, basketball, squash, tennis, and volleyball courts, training, weight, and wrestling rooms, rowing tanks, tracks, athletic fields.

**STUDENT BODY. Undergraduate profile:** 22% are state residents; 4% are transfers. 6% Asian-American, 6% Black, 4% Hispanic, 82% White, 2% Other. Average age of undergraduates is 20.
**Freshman profile:** 3% of freshmen who took SAT scored 700 or over on verbal, 8% scored 700 or over on math; 25% scored 600 or over on verbal, 52% scored 600 or over on math; 82% scored 500 or over on verbal, 92% scored 500 or over on math; 100% scored 400 or over on verbal, 100% scored 400 or over on math. 14% of freshmen who took ACT scored 30 or over on composite; 74% scored 24 or over on composite; 100% scored 18 or over on composite. 91% of accepted applicants took SAT; 9% took ACT. 49% of freshmen come from public schools.
**Undergraduate achievement:** 95% of fall 1991 freshmen returned for fall 1992 term. 85% of entering class graduated.
**Foreign students:** 30 students are from out of the country. 25 countries represented in all.

**PROGRAMS OF STUDY. Degrees:** B.A., B.S.
**Majors:** American Studies, Area Studies, Art History, Biochemistry, Biology, Biomedical Engineering, Chemistry, Classics, Comparative Literature, Computer Science, Computer Coordinate, Economics, Educational Studies, Engineering, English, French, German, History, Italian, Mathematics, Modern Languages, Music, Neuroscience, Philosophy, Physical Sciences, Physics/Astronomy, Political Science, Psychology, Public Policy Studies, Religion, Russian, Sociology, Spanish, Studio Art, Theatre Arts/Dance, Urban/Environmental Studies, Women's Studies.
**Distribution of degrees:** The majors with the highest enrollment are economics, history, and English.
**Requirements:** General education requirement.
**Special:** Approximately 30 interdisciplinary minors offered. Self-designed majors. Double majors. Independent study. Pass/fail grading option. Internships. Graduate school at which undergraduates may take graduate-level courses. Preprofessional programs in law, medicine, veterinary science, and dentistry. Five-year engineering/M.S. program with Rensselaer Polytechnic Inst. Member of Hartford Consortium for Higher Education. Washington Semester. National Theatre Institute Semester (Connecticut) and Williams-Mystic Seaport Semester (Connecticut). Member of Twelve College Exchange Program. Teacher certification in elementary, secondary, and special education. Study abroad in numerous countries. ROTC at U of Connecticut.
**Honors:** Phi Beta Kappa.
**Academic Assistance:** Remedial writing, math, and study skills. Nonremedial tutoring.

**STUDENT LIFE. Housing:** Students may live on or off campus. Coed dorms. Sorority and fraternity housing. Off-campus privately-owned housing. 92% of students live in college housing.
**Social atmosphere:** According to the student newspaper, Trinity is "not a suitcase school. Not too many people go off campus, and sports are popular. The Cinestudio Theatre runs quality films, and the Arts Center provides something every weekend." A favorite on-campus hangout is the Cave, a snackbar. Off campus, students head for the College View Cafe. The Trinity College Activities Committee sponsors popular events, and the fraternities hold regular parties. Yearly events to attend are the Halloween Party at Delta Kappa Epsilon, the Bantam Ball in January, the Crew Semiformal in February, and Spring Weekend.
**Services and counseling/handicapped student services:** Placement services. Health service. Women's center. Day care. Counseling services for minority and older students. Birth control, personal, and psychological counseling. Career and academic guidance services. Religious counseling. Physically disabled student services. Learning disabled services. Tape recorders. Tutors. Reader services for the blind.
**Campus organizations:** Undergraduate student government. Student newspaper (Trinity Tripod, published once/week). Literary magazine. Yearbook. Radio station. Band, chamber group, chapel choir, concert choir, informal singing groups, Society of Carilloneurs, student organists association, drama group, film society, political forum, PIRG, departmental, service, and special-interest groups, 70 organizations in all. Nine fraternities, all with chapter houses; two sororities, no chapter houses. 33% of men join a fraternity. 11% of women join a sorority.
**Religious organizations:** Christian Fellowship, Hillel, Newman Club.
**Minority/foreign student organizations:** Pan-African Alliance, La Voz Latina, ASIA, Coalition of Black Women, Vietnamese Club, Indian Club. International Club.

**ATHLETICS. Physical education requirements:** None.
**Intercollegiate competition:** 55% of students participate. Baseball (M), basketball (M,W), crew (M,W), cross-country (M,W), diving (M,W), field hockey (W), football (M), golf (M), ice hockey (M), lacrosse (M,W), soccer (M,W), softball (W), squash (M,W), swimming (M,W), tennis (M,W), track and field (indoor) (M,W), track and field (outdoor) (M,W), volleyball (W), wrestling (M). Member of ECAC, NCAA Division III, NESCAC.
**Intramural and club sports:** 70% of students participate. Intramural basketball, flag football, physical fitness, soccer, softball, squash, tennis, volleyball. Men's club Alpine skiing, fencing, rugby, ultimate frisbee, volleyball, water polo. Women's club Alpine skiing, cheerleading, fencing, horsemanship, rugby, water polo.

**ADMISSIONS. Academic basis for candidate selection** (in order of priority): Secondary school record, school's recommendation, class rank, standardized test scores, essay.
**Nonacademic basis for candidate selection:** Character and personality, extracurricular participation, and particular talent or ability are important. Geographical distribution and alumni/ae relationship are considered.
**Requirements:** Graduation from secondary school is required; GED is accepted. 12 units and the following program of study are required: 4 units of English, 3 units of math, 1 unit of lab science, 2 units of foreign language, 1 unit of history. SAT or ACT is required. ACH required. Campus visit and interview recommended. Off-campus interviews available with an alumni representative.
**Procedure:** Take SAT or ACT by November of 12th year. Take ACH by December of 12th year. Visit college for interview by January 15 of 12th year. Application deadline is January 15. Acceptance notification by early April. Reply is required by May 1. Freshmen accepted for fall term only.
**Special programs:** Admission may be deferred one year. Credit and/or placement may be granted through CEEB Advanced Placement exams for scores of 4 or higher. Early decision

program. In fall 1992, 160 applied for early decision and 95 were accepted. Deadline for applying for early decision is December 1 (Option I); February 1 (Option II). Early entrance/early admission program.
**Transfer students:** Transfer students accepted for terms other than fall. In fall 1992, 4% of all new students were transfers into all classes. 113 transfer applications were received, 55 were accepted. Application deadline is March 15 for fall; November 15 for spring. Minimum 3.2 GPA recommended. Lowest course grade accepted is "C-." Maximum number of transferable credits is 18 course credits from a two-year school and 20 course credits from a four-year school. At least 16 course credits must be completed at the college to receive degree.
**Admissions contact:** David M. Borus, Ph.D., Dean of Admission and Financial Aid. 203 297-2180.
**FINANCIAL AID. Available aid:** Pell grants, SEOG, state scholarships and grants, school scholarships and grants, private scholarships and grants, ROTC scholarships, and aid for undergraduate foreign students. Perkins Loans (NDSL), PLUS, Stafford Loans (GSL), state loans, school loans, and SLS. Tuition Plan Inc., Knight Tuition Plans, and AMS.
**Financial aid statistics:** Average amounts of aid awarded freshmen: Scholarships and grants, $13,725; loans, $2,625.
**Supporting data/closing dates:** FAFSA/FAF/FFS: Deadline is February 1. School's own aid application: Deadline is February 15. Income tax forms. Notification of awards begins April 1.
**Financial aid contact:** Anne M. Zartarian, Ph.D., Director of Financial Aid. 203 297-2046.
**STUDENT EMPLOYMENT.** College Work/Study Program. Institutional employment. 50% of full-time undergraduates work on campus during school year. Students may expect to earn an average of $1,400 during school year. Off-campus part-time employment opportunities rated "good."
**COMPUTER FACILITIES.** 120 IBM/IBM-compatible and Macintosh/Apple microcomputers; all are networked. Students may access AT&T, SUN minicomputer/mainframe systems, BITNET, Internet. Residence halls may be equipped with modems. Client/LAN operating systems include Apple/Macintosh. Computer languages and software packages include BASIC, Excel, FORTRAN, Graph, Hyper Card, LISP, Lotus 1-2-3, Pascal, SAS, Scribe, WordPerfect. Computer facilities are available to all students.
**Fees:** None.
**Hours:** 24 hours.

# United States Coast Guard Academy

**New London, CT 06320-4195 — 203 444-8444**

**1994-95 Costs.** Tuition: None.
**Enrollment.** Undergraduates: 761 men, 169 women (full-time). Freshman class: 2,591 applicants, 466 accepted, 277 enrolled.
**Test score averages/ranges.** Average SAT scores: 542 verbal, 644 math. Range of SAT scores of middle 50%: 539-605 verbal, 598-700 math. Average ACT scores: 26 English, 28 math. Range of ACT scores of middle 50%: 24-29 English, 25-30 math.
**Faculty.** 112 full-time. 30% of faculty holds highest degree in specific field.
**Selectivity rating.** Highly competitive.

**PROFILE.** The U.S. Coast Guard Academy is a public service academy. Founded in 1876, it adopted coeducation in 1976. Its 110-acre campus is located in New London, on the Long Island Sound, 45 miles southeast of Hartford.

**Accreditation:** NEASC. Professionally accredited by the Accreditation Board for Engineering and Technology.
**Religious orientation:** United States Coast Guard Academy is nonsectarian; no religious requirements.
**Library:** Collections totaling over 180,000 volumes, 850 periodical subscriptions, and 60,000 microform items.
**Special facilities/museums:** Coast Guard historical museum.
**Athletic facilities:** Swimming pools, gymnasiums, indoor and outdoor tracks, handball and tennis courts, boat house, sailing center, soccer field, weight rooms, football stadium.
**STUDENT BODY. Undergraduate profile:** 7% are state residents. 8% Asian-American, 4% Black, 5% Hispanic, 1% Native American, 80% White, 2% Other. Average age of undergraduates is 21.
**Freshman profile:** Majority of accepted applicants took SAT. 83% of freshmen come from public schools.
**Undergraduate achievement:** 86% of fall 1992 freshmen returned for fall 1993 term. 65% of entering class graduated.
**Foreign students:** 23 students are from out of the country. 11 countries represented in all.
**PROGRAMS OF STUDY. Degrees:** B.S.
**Majors:** Civil Engineering, Electrical Engineering, Government, Management, Marine Science, Mathematical/Computer Sciences, Mechanical Engineering, Naval Architecture/Marine Engineering.
**Distribution of degrees:** The majors with the highest enrollment are government, civil engineering, and marine science; mathematical/computer sciences, electrical engineering, and naval architecture/marine engineering have the lowest.
**Requirements:** General education requirement.
**Special:** Independent study. Internships. Graduate school at which undergraduates may take graduate-level courses. One-semester exchange programs with U.S. Air Force Academy, U.S. Military Academy, and U.S. Naval Academy.
**Honors:** Honors program.
**Academic Assistance:** Remedial writing, math, and study skills. Nonremedial tutoring.
**STUDENT LIFE. Housing:** All cadets must live on campus. Coed dorms. 100% of students live in college housing.
**Social atmosphere:** According to the editor of the student newspaper, "Social life on and off campus is good with Connecticut College across the street and numerous colleges in the area. New York City and Boston are only about two hours away, if students need some city life." Students enjoy the many sports clubs and special-interest groups such as the Scuba Club, Bowling Club, Pep Band, Idlers, Icebreakers, Glee Club, Genesis Club, Drill Team, Speech and Debate teams, and many others. On the whole, the academy is run as a military organization, and there are no really influential groups. Popular events include Parents Weekend, Christmas and Valentine formals, Graduation Ball, and the various mixers held throughout the year.
**Services and counseling/handicapped student services:** Counseling services for minority, military, and older students. Birth control, personal, and psychological counseling. Career and academic guidance services. Religious counseling.
**Campus organizations:** Undergraduate student government. Student newspaper (Howling Gale, published once/month). Literary magazine. Yearbook. Choir, glee club, small vocal and instrumental groups, marching and dance bands, rock group, drama group, debating, Big Brothers/Big Sisters, Boy Scouts, bicycle and radio clubs, athletic groups, special-interest groups.
**Religious organizations:** Fellowship of Christian Athletes, Officers Christian Fellowship.
**Minority/foreign student organizations:** Genesis Club.
**ATHLETICS. Physical education requirements:** Eight semesters of physical education required.
**Intercollegiate competition:** 80% of students participate. Baseball (M), basketball (M,W), crew (M,W), cross-country (M,W), diving (M), football (M), pistol (M,W), riflery (M,W), sailing (M,W), soccer (M), softball (W), swimming (M), tennis (M), track and field (indoor) (M,W), track and field (outdoor) (M,W), volleyball (M), wrestling (M). Member of Constitution Conference, ECAC, Freedom Football Conference, NCAA Division III, New England Women's Athletic Conference.
**Intramural and club sports:** 100% of students participate. Men's club ice hockey, lacrosse, rugby. Women's club golf, soccer.
**ADMISSIONS. Academic basis for candidate selection** (in order of priority): Standardized test scores, class rank, secondary school record, school's recommendation, essay.
**Nonacademic basis for candidate selection:** Character and personality and extracurricular participation are emphasized. Alumni/ae relationship is considered.
**Requirements:** Graduation from secondary school is required; GED is accepted. 15 units and the following program of study are required: 3 units of English, 3 units of math, 9 units of academic electives. Trigonometry, physics, and chemistry strongly recommended. Minimum combined SAT score of 950 (minimum 500 math) or minimum math ACT score of 21 required. The academy tenders appointments solely on the basis of an annual nationwide competition; no congressional nominations or geographical quotas. All entrants must have reached the age of 17 but must not have reached the age of 22 by July 1 of the year of admission. All applicants must be unmarried U.S. citizens (foreign nationals with approval) with no parental obligations or responsibilities. SAT or ACT is required. Campus visit recommended. No off-campus interviews.
**Procedure:** Take SAT or ACT by December of 12th year. Application deadline is December 15. Notification of admission on rolling basis. Reply is required by May 1. $1,500 acceptance fee required. Freshmen accepted for fall term only.
**Special programs:** Placement may be granted through challenge exams.
**Admissions contact:** R.W. Thorne, USCG, M.S., Director of Admissions. 203 444-8501.
**COMPUTER FACILITIES.** Macintosh/Apple microcomputers. Students may access Digital, Sequent, SUN, UNISYS minicomputer/mainframe systems, Internet. Residence halls may be equipped with stand-alone microcomputers, networked microcomputers, networked terminals, modems. Client/LAN operating systems include Apple/Macintosh. Computer languages and software packages include C, Excel, FORTRAN, MacSurf, Microsoft Word, Pascal, True BASIC. Computer facilities are available to all students.
**Fees:** None.
**Hours:** 6 AM-midn.

# University of Bridgeport

**Bridgeport, CT 06601 — 203 576-4000**

**1993-94 Costs.** Tuition: $12,020. Room & board: $6,540. Fees, books, misc. academic expenses (school's estimate): $1,374.
**Enrollment.** Undergraduates: 258 men, 269 women (full-time). Freshman class: 598 applicants, 441 accepted, 153 enrolled. Graduate enrollment: 381 men, 385 women.
**Test score averages/ranges.** Average SAT scores: 422 verbal, 489 math. Range of SAT scores of middle 50%: 350-490 verbal, 420-550 math.
**Faculty.** 92 full-time; 131 part-time. 58% of faculty holds doctoral degree. Student/faculty ratio: 8 to 1.
**Selectivity rating.** Less competitive.

**PROFILE.** The University of Bridgeport is a private institution. Founded as a junior college in 1927, it became a four-year institution in 1947. Programs are offered through the Colleges of Arts and Humanities, Business and Public Management, Health and Human Services, and Science and Engineering; the School of Law; and Metropolitan College. Its 86-acre campus is located on the former estate of P.T. Barnum in Bridgeport, 60 miles from New York City.

**Accreditation:** NEASC. Professionally accredited by the Accreditation Board for Engineering and Technology, the American Assembly of Collegiate Schools of Business, the American Dental Association, the National Association of Schools of Art and Design.
**Religious orientation:** University of Bridgeport is nonsectarian; no religious requirements.
**Library:** Collections totaling over 208,000 volumes, 1,000 periodical subscriptions, and 943,000 microform items.
**Special facilities/museums:** Art gallery, language lab.

**Athletic facilities:** Field house, swimming pool, gymnasium, racquetball and tennis courts, athletic fields, recreation center, sauna/steam room, track.

**STUDENT BODY. Undergraduate profile:** 79% are state residents; 43% are transfers. 4% Asian-American, 17% Black, 9% Hispanic, 43% White, 27% International. Average age of undergraduates is 23.

**Freshman profile:** 2% of freshmen who took SAT scored 700 or over on math; 6% scored 600 or over on verbal, 19% scored 600 or over on math; 23% scored 500 or over on verbal, 51% scored 500 or over on math; 56% scored 400 or over on verbal, 74% scored 400 or over on math; 81% scored 300 or over on verbal, 85% scored 300 or over on math. 97% of accepted applicants took SAT; 3% took ACT. 93% of freshmen come from public schools.

**Undergraduate achievement:** 70% of fall 1992 freshmen returned for fall 1993 term. 48% of entering class graduated. 10% of students who completed a degree program immediately went on to graduate study.

**Foreign students:** 141 students are from out of the country. Countries represented include China, Greece, Japan, Korea, Malaysia, and the former Soviet Republics; 39 in all.

**PROGRAMS OF STUDY. Degrees:** B.A., B.Elective Studies, B.F.A., B.Mus., B.S.

**Majors:** Accounting, Advertising, Art, Biology, Business Economics, Chemistry, Cinema, Communications, Computer Applications/Information Systems, Computer Engineering, Computer Science, Dental Hygiene, Elective Studies, Electrical Engineering, English, Fashion Merchandising, Finance, Fine Arts, General Administration, Graphic Design, History, Human Services, Illustration, Industrial Design, Interior Design, International Business, Journalism, Management/Industrial Relations, Marketing, Mathematics, Mechanical Engineering, Medical Technology, Music, Physics, Political Science, Psychology, Respiratory Therapy.

**Distribution of degrees:** The majors with the highest enrollment are elective studies, electrical engineering, and mechanical engineering; history, communications, and economics have the lowest.

**Requirements:** General education requirement.

**Academic regulations:** Minimum 2.0 GPA must be maintained.

**Special:** Minors offered in many majors and in computer information systems, economics, education, and legal studies. Associate's degrees offered. Self-designed majors. Double majors. Dual degrees. Independent study. Accelerated study. Pass/fail grading option. Internships. Cooperative education programs. Graduate school at which undergraduates may take graduate-level courses. Preprofessional programs in law, medicine, dentistry, and chiropractic. Coll of Chiropractic offers Doctor of Chiropractic. Fones Sch of Dental Hygiene. Human Nutrition Program. Five-year bachelor's/master's program in business administration. Teacher certification in early childhood, elementary, and secondary education. Certification in specific subject areas. Study abroad in the Bahamas, England, France, Italy, Spain, and Switzerland. ROTC.

**Honors:** Honors program. Honor societies.

**Academic Assistance:** Remedial reading, writing, math, and study skills. Nonremedial tutoring.

**ADMISSIONS. Academic basis for candidate selection** (in order of priority): Secondary school record, standardized test scores, essay, school's recommendation, class rank.

**Nonacademic basis for candidate selection:** Character and personality, particular talent or ability, and alumni/ae relationship are important. Extracurricular participation is considered.

**Requirements:** Graduation from secondary school is required; GED is accepted. 16 units and the following program of study are required: 4 units of English, 3 units of math, 1 unit of lab science, 1 unit of social studies, 7 units of academic electives. Portfolio required of art program applicants. Audition required of music program applicants. Conditional admission possible for applicants not meeting standard requirements. Basic Studies Division for applicants not normally admissible. SAT or ACT is required. Campus visit and interview recommended. Off-campus interviews available with an admissions representative.

**Procedure:** Take SAT or ACT by December of 12th year. Visit college for interview by February of 12th year. Suggest filing application by April 1; no deadline. Notification of admission begins by March 1. Reply is required by May 1. $200 tuition deposit, refundable until June 1. $200 room deposit, refundable until June 1. Freshmen accepted for terms other than fall.

**Special programs:** Admission may be deferred one year. Credit and/or placement may be granted through CEEB Advanced Placement exams for scores of 3 or higher. Credit may be granted through CLEP subject exams, challenge exams, and military and life experience. Early entrance/early admission program.

**Transfer students:** Transfer students accepted for terms other than fall. In fall 1993, 43% of all new students were transfers into all classes. 298 transfer applications were received, 272 were accepted. Application deadline is July 1 for fall; December 1 for spring. Minimum 2.0 GPA required. Lowest course grade accepted is "C-." Maximum number of transferable credits is 66 semester hours from a two-year school and 90 semester hours from a four-year school. At least 30 semester hours must be completed at the university to receive degree.

**Admissions contact:** Andrew G. Nelson, M.A., Dean of Admissions & Financial Aid. 203 576-4552.

**FINANCIAL AID. Available aid:** Pell grants, SEOG, state scholarships and grants, school scholarships and grants, private scholarships and grants, ROTC scholarships, academic merit scholarships, athletic scholarships, and aid for undergraduate foreign students. Perkins Loans (NDSL), PLUS, Stafford Loans (GSL), state loans, private loans, and SLS. Tuition Plan Inc., Education Plan Inc., Knight Tuition Plans, AMS, deferred payment plan, and family tuition reduction.

**Financial aid statistics:** 10% of aid is not need-based. In 1993-94, 100% of all undergraduate applicants received aid. Average amounts of aid awarded freshmen: Scholarships and grants, $13,875; loans, $3,800.

**Supporting data/closing dates:** FAFSA: Priority filing date is January 1. School's own aid application: Priority filing date is April 1; accepted on rolling basis. State aid form: Priority filing date is April 1; accepted on rolling basis. Income tax forms: Priority filing date is April 1; accepted on rolling basis. Notification of awards begins March 1.

**Financial aid contact:** Harry White, M.S., Director of Admissions & Financial Aid. 203 576-4568.

**PROMINENT ALUMNI/AE.** Robert Kowalski, leader in artificial intelligence; Andrew Robostelli, member of NFL Hall of Fame; William Smitrovich, actor, *Life Goes On*.

# University of Connecticut

**Storrs, CT 06269** — **203 486-2000**

**1994-95 Costs.** Tuition: $3,824 (state residents), $11,656 (out-of-state). Room & board: $5,072. Fees, books, misc. academic expenses (school's estimate): $1,458.

**Enrollment.** Undergraduates: 5,569 men, 5,697 women (full-time). Freshman class: 9,735 applicants, 7,187 accepted, 2,064 enrolled. Graduate enrollment: 3,124 men, 3,216 women.

**Test score averages/ranges.** Average SAT scores: 481 verbal, 551 math. Range of SAT scores of middle 50%: 430-530 verbal, 490-610 math.

**Faculty.** 1,211 full-time; 42 part-time. 90% of faculty holds highest degree in specific field.

**Selectivity rating.** Competitive.

**PROFILE.** The University of Connecticut, founded in 1881, is a public, comprehensive university. Programs are offered through the Colleges of Agriculture and Natural Resources and Liberal Arts and Sciences; the Schools of Allied Health Professions, Business Administration, Education, Engineering, Family Studies, Fine Arts, Nursing, and Pharmacy; and Ratcliffe Hicks School of Agriculture. Its 3,100-acre campus is located in Storrs, 30 miles from Hartford.

**Accreditation:** NEASC. Professionally accredited by the Accreditation Board for Engineering and Technology, the American Assembly of Collegiate Schools of Business, the American Council on Pharmaceutical Education, the American Dietetic Association, the American Medical Association (CAHEA), the American Physical Therapy Association, the American Speech-Language-Hearing Association, the National Association of Schools of Art and Design, the National Association of Schools of Music, the National Council for Accreditation of Teacher Education, the National League for Nursing.

**Religious orientation:** University of Connecticut is nonsectarian; no religious requirements.

**Library:** Collections totaling over 1,854,452 volumes, 9,594 periodical subscriptions, and 2,600,000 microform items.

**Special facilities/museums:** Art and natural history museums, child development labs, national undersea research center, arboretum, institute for social inquiry, institute of materials science, electron microscope labs.

**Athletic facilities:** Gymnasiums, field house, swimming pools, ice rink, badminton, basketball, racquetball, squash, tennis, and volleyball courts, weight rooms, track, baseball, field hockey, football, intramural, soccer, and softball fields, arena, fitness center.

**STUDENT BODY. Undergraduate profile:** 85% are state residents; 19% are transfers. 4% Asian-American, 4% Black, 3% Hispanic, 88% White, 1% Other. Average age of undergraduates is 21.

**Freshman profile:** 1% of freshmen who took SAT scored 700 or over on verbal, 5% scored 700 or over on math; 7% scored 600 or over on verbal, 26% scored 600 or over on math; 36% scored 500 or over on verbal, 65% scored 500 or over on math; 81% scored 400 or over on verbal, 92% scored 400 or over on math; 99% scored 300 or over on verbal, 99% scored 300 or over on math. 99% of accepted applicants took SAT.

**Undergraduate achievement:** 87% of fall 1992 freshmen returned for fall 1993 term. 34% of entering class graduated. 15% of students who completed a degree program went on to graduate study within one year.

**Foreign students:** 79 students are from out of the country. Countries represented include Hong Kong and Japan.

**PROGRAMS OF STUDY. Degrees:** B.A., B.F.A., B.Gen.Studies, B.Mus., B.S.

**Majors:** Accounting, Acting, Agricultural Education, Agricultural/Resource Economics, Agronomy, Animal Science, Anthropology, Applied Mathematical Sciences, Applied Music, Art History, Biological Sciences, Biophysics, Ceramics, Chemical Engineering, Chemical Engineering/Materials Engineering, Chemistry, Civil Engineering, Civil Engineering/Materials Engineering, Classics, Communication Sciences, Computer Science/Engineering, Cytotechnology, Design/Resource Management, Design/Technical Theatre, Dietetics, Economics, Electrical Engineering, Electrical Engineering/Materials Engineering, Elementary Education, English, Finance, French, General Program in Dramatic Arts, General Program in Music, General Studies/Agriculture/Natural Resources, Geography, Geology/Geophysics, German, Graphic Design, Health Systems Management, History, Horticulture, Human Development/Family Relations, Individualized Major, Italian, Journalism, Landscape Architecture, Latin American Studies, Leisure Science, Linguistics/Philosophy, Management, Management Information Systems, Marketing, Mathematics, Mathematics/Actuarial Science, Mathematics/Statistics, Mechanical Engineering, Mechanical Engineering/Materials Engineering, Medical Cytogenetic Technology, Medical Technology, Middle East Studies, Molecular/Cell Biology, Music Education, Nursing, Nutritional Sciences, Painting, Pathobiology, Pharmacy, Philosophy, Photography, Physical Therapy, Physics, Physiology/Neurobiology, Political Science, Portuguese, Printmaking, Psychology, Puppetry, Real Estate/Urban Economics, Renewable Natural Resources, Risk Management/Insurance, Russian, Sculpture, Secondary Education, Slavic/East European Studies, Sociology, Spanish, Special Education, Sport Pedagogy, Sport Science, Statistics, Urban Studies, Women's Studies.

**Distribution of degrees:** The majors with the highest enrollment are English, economics, and psychology; agricultural/resource economics, linguistics/philosophy, and biophysics have the lowest.

**Requirements:** General education requirement.

**Academic regulations:** Freshmen must maintain minimum 1.6 GPA; sophomores, 1.9 GPA; juniors, seniors, 2.0 GPA.

**Special:** Self-designed majors. Double majors. Dual degrees. Independent study. Accelerated study. Pass/fail grading option. Internships. Cooperative education programs. Graduate school at which undergraduates may take graduate-level courses. Preprofessional programs in law, medicine, and dentistry. B.S./M.B.A. programs in engineering and pharmacy. Urban Semester Program (Connecticut). Teacher certification in elementary, secondary, and special education. Certification in specific subject areas. Study abroad in

Austria, Canada, the Dominican Republic, England, France, Italy, Japan, the Netherlands, Peru, and Spain. ROTC and AFROTC.
**Honors:** Phi Beta Kappa. Honors program. Honor societies.
**Academic Assistance:** Remedial reading, writing, math, and study skills. Nonremedial tutoring.

**STUDENT LIFE. Housing:** Students may live on or off campus. Coed, women's, and men's dorms. Special-interest housing. 68% of students live in college housing.
**Social atmosphere:** The Student Union, the Upper Deck, Bidwell Tavern, Woody's, Chuck's & Margarita's, and Ted's are popular gathering-spots. Greeks, student government, and UConn PIRG are influential groups on campus life. Highlights of the school year include Homecoming, Spring Weekend, men's and women's basketball games, and the Yale Bowl. According to the editor of the student newspaper, there's "never a dull moment."
**Services and counseling/handicapped student services:** Placement services. Health service. Women's center. Day care. Counseling services for minority, military, veteran, and older students. Birth control, personal, and psychological counseling. Career and academic guidance services. Religious counseling. Physically disabled student services. Learning disabled program/services. Notetaking services. Tape recorders. Tutors. Reader services for the blind.
**Campus organizations:** Undergraduate student government. Student newspaper (Daily Campus). Literary magazine. Yearbook. Radio station. Band, drama group, theatre, Women's Government Association, debating, athletic, departmental, professional, service, and special-interest groups, 200 organizations in all. 16 fraternities, five chapter houses; nine sororities, four chapter houses. 10% of men join a fraternity. 10% of women join a sorority.
**Religious organizations:** Baptist Student Union, Campus Crusade for Christ, Christian Scientist Organization, Faith Christian Fellowship, St.Thomas Aquinas Club, Navigators, University Jewish Students, Hillel.
**Minority/foreign student organizations:** Asian, black, Puerto Rican, and Native American groups. Various foreign student groups.

**ATHLETICS. Physical education requirements:** None.
**Intercollegiate competition:** 5% of students participate. Baseball (M), basketball (M,W), cross-country (M,W), diving (M,W), field hockey (W), football (M), golf (M), ice hockey (M), soccer (M,W), softball (W), swimming (M,W), tennis (M,W), track and field (indoor) (M,W), track and field (outdoor) (M,W), volleyball (W). Member of Big East Conference, ECAC, NCAA Division I, NCAA Division I-AA for football, Yankee Conference.
**Intramural and club sports:** 60% of students participate. Intramural badminton, basketball, cross-country, free throw, indoor soccer, inner-tube water polo, racquetball, soccer, softball, squash, swimming, table tennis, track and field, volleyball. Men's club bowling, crew, cycling, fencing, martial arts, Nordic skiing, rugby, sailing, swimming, volleyball. Women's club bowling, crew, cycling, fencing, ice hockey, lacrosse, martial arts, Nordic skiing, rugby, sailing, swimming.

**ADMISSIONS. Academic basis for candidate selection** (in order of priority): Secondary school record, class rank, standardized test scores, school's recommendation, essay.
**Nonacademic basis for candidate selection:** Particular talent or ability is important. Character and personality, extracurricular participation, geographical distribution, and alumni/ae relationship are considered.
**Requirements:** Graduation from secondary school is required; GED is accepted. 16 units and the following program of study are required: 4 units of English, 3 units of math, 2 units of lab science, 2 units of foreign language, 2 units of social studies, 3 units of electives including 2 units of academic electives. Minimum combined SAT score of 900 and rank in top half of secondary school class recommended of in-state applicants; minimum combined SAT score of 1000 and rank in top quarter of secondary school class recommended of out-of-state applicants. Audition required of music and drama program applicants. Center for Academic Programs (CAP) and Minority Engineering Program (MEP) for applicants not normally admissible. SAT is required. Campus visit recommended. No off-campus interviews.
**Procedure:** Take SAT by January of 12th year. Application deadline is April 1. Notification of admission on rolling basis. Reply is required by May 1. $150 nonrefundable tuition deposit. $140 room deposit, refundable partially until August 1. Freshmen accepted for terms other than fall.
**Special programs:** Admission may be deferred one year. Credit and/or placement may be granted through CEEB Advanced Placement exams for scores of 3 or higher. Credit and/or placement may be granted through CLEP subject exams. Credit and placement may be granted through DANTES and challenge exams and military experience. Early entrance/early admission program.
**Transfer students:** Transfer students accepted for terms other than fall. In fall 1993, 19% of all new students were transfers into all classes. 2,059 transfer applications were received, 938 were accepted. Application deadline is May 1 for fall; October 15 for spring. Minimum 2.5 GPA recommended. Lowest course grade accepted is "C." At least 30 semester hours must be completed at the university to receive degree.
**Admissions contact:** Ann L. Huckenbeck, Ph.D., Director of Admissions. 203 486-3137.

**FINANCIAL AID. Available aid:** Pell grants, SEOG, state scholarships and grants, school scholarships and grants, private scholarships, academic merit scholarships, and athletic scholarships. Perkins Loans (NDSL), PLUS, Stafford Loans (GSL), and SLS. AMS.
**Financial aid statistics:** 15% of aid is not need-based. In 1993-94, 65% of all undergraduate applicants received aid; 65% of freshman applicants. Average amounts of aid awarded freshmen: Scholarships and grants, $1,858; loans, $1,500.
**Supporting data/closing dates:** FAFSA: Priority filing date is February 15. Notification of awards begins April 1.
**Financial aid contact:** Richard Bishop, Interim Director of Financial Aid. 203 486-2819.

**STUDENT EMPLOYMENT.** College Work/Study Program. Institutional employment. 20% of full-time undergraduates work on campus during school year. Students may expect to earn an average of $1,500 during school year. Off-campus part-time employment opportunities rated "good."

**COMPUTER FACILITIES.** 1,800 IBM/IBM-compatible and Macintosh/Apple microcomputers. Students may access IBM minicomputer/mainframe systems, BITNET, Internet. Residence halls may be equipped with stand-alone microcomputers. Client/LAN operating systems include Apple/Macintosh, LocalTalk/AppleTalk. Computer languages and software packages include COBOL, FORTRAN, Pascal, PL/1; 250 in all. Computer facilities are available to all students.
**Fees:** None.
**Hours:** 8 AM-midn. daily.

**PROMINENT ALUMNI/AE.** Franklin Chang-Diaz, astronaut; Edward A. Horrigan, CEO, R.J. Reynolds; Sidney Marland, former Secretary of Education; Richard Gamble, United Technologies; Gustav Mehlquist, botanist.

# University of Hartford

**West Hartford, CT 06117 — 203 768-4100**

**1993-94 Costs.** Tuition: $13,600. Room & board: $5,598. Fees, books, misc. academic expenses (school's estimate): $660.
**Enrollment.** Undergraduates: 1,917 men, 1,851 women (full-time). Freshman class: 5,117 applicants, 4,141 accepted, 1,200 enrolled. Graduate enrollment: 956 men, 1,123 women.
**Test score averages/ranges.** Average SAT scores: 447 verbal, 503 math.
**Faculty.** 333 full-time; 450 part-time. 77% of faculty holds highest degree in specific field. Student/faculty ratio: 11 to 1.
**Selectivity rating.** Less competitive.

**PROFILE.** The University of Hartford, founded in 1877, is a private, comprehensive institution. Programs are offered through the Colleges of Arts and Sciences; Basic Studies; Education, Nursing, and Health Professions; and Engineering. Additional programs are offered through the Barney School of Business and Public Administration, Hartford Art School, Hartt School of Music, and S.I. Ward College of Technology. Its 300-acre campus is located in West Hartford, two miles from downtown Hartford.
**Accreditation:** NEASC. Professionally accredited by the Accreditation Board for Engineering and Technology, the American Medical Association (CAHEA), the National Association of Schools of Art and Design, the National Association of Schools of Music, the National Council for Accreditation of Teacher Education, the National League for Nursing.
**Religious orientation:** University of Hartford is nonsectarian; no religious requirements.
**Library:** Collections totaling over 389,487 volumes, 2,450 periodical subscriptions, and 220,000 microform items.
**Special facilities/museums:** Museum of presidential memorabilia, off-campus child care center for student teaching, learning skills and language lab, audio-visual aids center, 8,000-acre environmental center.
**Athletic facilities:** Gymnasium, intramural, soccer, and softball fields, weight room, basketball, racquetball, squash, tennis, and volleyball courts, swimming pools, saunas.

**STUDENT BODY. Undergraduate profile:** 35% are state residents; 18% are transfers. 2% Asian-American, 7% Black, 4% Hispanic, 81% White, 6% International.
**Freshman profile:** 3% of freshmen who took SAT scored 700 or over on math; 4% scored 600 or over on verbal, 19% scored 600 or over on math; 26% scored 500 or over on verbal, 57% scored 500 or over on math; 78% scored 400 or over on verbal, 94% scored 400 or over on math; 99% scored 300 or over on verbal, 100% scored 300 or over on math. 79% of freshmen come from public schools.
**Undergraduate achievement:** 74% of fall 1992 freshmen returned for fall 1993 term. 47% of entering class graduated. 21% of students who completed a degree program immediately went on to graduate study.
**Foreign students:** 250 students are from out of the country. Countries represented include India, Japan, Malaysia, South Korea, and Thailand; 59 in all.

**PROGRAMS OF STUDY. Degrees:** B.A., B.F.A., B.Mus., B.S.
**Majors:** Accounting, Actuarial Sciences, Architectural Engineering Technology, Art History, Audio Engineering Technology, Biology, Chemistry, Chemistry/Biology, Civil Engineering, Communication, Computer Engineering, Computer Science, Criminal Justice, Dance, Design, Drawing, Early Childhood Education, Economics, Economics/Finance, Electrical Engineering, Electronic Engineering Technology, Elementary Education, Engineering, English, Experimental Studies, Film/Video, Fine/Applied Arts, Foreign Languages/Literatures, Foreign Languages/Multiple Emphasis, French, German, Health Sciences, History, Human Services, Illustration, Insurance, Insurance/Finance, Italian, Legal Studies, Linguistics, Management, Management Information Systems, Marketing, Mathematics, Mathematics/Management Science, Mechanical Engineering, Mechanical Engineering Technology, Medical Technology, Music, Music Composition, Music Education, Music History, Music Management, Musical Theatre, Nursing, Occupational Therapy, Painting, Philosophy, Photography, Physics, Political Economy, Politics/Government, Pre-Optometry, Psychology, Public Administration, Radiologic Technology, Respiratory Therapy, Sculpture, Secondary Education, Sociology, Spanish, Special Education, Theatre Arts.
**Distribution of degrees:** The majors with the highest enrollment are communication, marketing, and mechanical engineering; chemistry, public administration, and theatre arts have the lowest.
**Requirements:** General education requirement.
**Academic regulations:** Freshmen must maintain minimum 1.8 GPA; sophomores, 1.9 GPA; juniors, 1.9 GPA; seniors, 2.0 GPA.
**Special:** Minors offered in many areas including health, Judaic, religious, and women's studies. Associate's degrees offered. Self-designed majors. Double majors. Dual degrees. Independent study. Pass/fail grading option. Internships. Cooperative education programs. Graduate school at which undergraduates may take graduate-level courses. Preprofessional programs in law, optometry, and health. 3-2 engineering program. 3-4 optometry program with New England Coll of Optometry. Five-year combined programs with School of Business and Public Administration. Member of Hartford Consortium for Higher Education; cross-registration and use of library facilities possible. Washington Semester. Teacher certification in early childhood, elementary, secondary, and special education. Certification in specific subject areas. Exchange programs abroad in England (Bristol Polytech), France (French American Inst for Management), and Italy. Study

abroad also in Israel and Poland. ROTC at U of Connecticut (Hartford branch campus). AFROTC at U of Connecticut (Storrs).
**Honors:** Honors program.
**Academic Assistance:** Nonremedial tutoring.

**STUDENT LIFE. Housing:** Students may live on or off campus. Coed, women's, and men's dorms. School-owned/operated apartments. 75% of students live in college housing.
**Social atmosphere:** The student newspaper reports, "Hartford becomes the nightspot on weekends with many clubs and cultural events. On campus there are parties or events one night of the weekend. Most of the action takes place in the Village Apartments." Popular events include a concert series held after basketball games, the beach party, and fall and spring weekends. Greeks are active at UH.The Student Association has influence on campus. Favorite off-campus clubs are the Russian Lady, Bopper's, J.P.'s, and the Civic Pub.
**Services and counseling/handicapped student services:** Placement services. Health service. Women's center. Learning Skills Center. Counseling services for veteran and older students. Birth control, personal, and psychological counseling. Career and academic guidance services. Religious counseling. Learning disabled services.
**Campus organizations:** Undergraduate student government. Student newspaper (Informer, published once/week). Literary magazine. Yearbook. Radio and TV stations. Chorus, jazz ensemble, orchestra, University Players, film series, art magazine, amateur radio club, Residence Hall Association, Student Union Board of Governors, Program Council, Commuter/Transfer Association, 75 organizations in all. Nine fraternities, no chapter houses; five sororities, no chapter houses. 12% of men join a fraternity. 12% of women join a sorority.
**Religious organizations:** Hillel, Newman Club, Intervarsity Christian Fellowship, Muslim Student Association, Protestant Student Organization.
**Minority/foreign student organizations:** African-American and Spanish-speaking student groups. International Student Association, Arab, French, Korean, Malaysian, and Spanish clubs.

**ATHLETICS. Physical education requirements:** None.
**Intercollegiate competition:** 15% of students participate. Baseball (M), basketball (M,W), cheerleading (M,W), cross-country (M,W), golf (M,W), lacrosse (M), soccer (M,W), softball (W), tennis (M,W), track and field (indoor) (M,W), track and field (outdoor) (M,W), volleyball (W). Member of ECAC, NCAA Division I, North Atlantic Conference.
**Intramural and club sports:** 75% of students participate. Intramural basketball, indoor soccer, racquetball, soccer, softball, squash, street hockey, tennis, touch football, ultimate frisbee, volleyball, walleyball. Men's club badminton, cycling, racquetball, rugby, swimming, volleyball. Women's club badminton, rugby, swimming.

**ADMISSIONS. Academic basis for candidate selection** (in order of priority): Secondary school record, class rank, standardized test scores, school's recommendation, essay.
**Nonacademic basis for candidate selection:** Character and personality and extracurricular participation are important. Alumni/ae relationship is considered.
**Requirements:** Graduation from secondary school is recommended; GED is accepted. 16 units and the following program of study are recommended: 4 units of English, 2 units of math, 2 units of science, 2 units of foreign language, 2 units of social studies, 3 units of electives. Portfolio required of art program applicants. Audition required of music program applicants. R.N. required of nursing program applicants. SAT is required; ACT may be substituted. ACH recommended. Campus visit and interview recommended. No off-campus interviews.
**Procedure:** Take SAT or ACT by November of 12th year. Take ACH by November of 12th year. Suggest filing application by February 1; no deadline. Notification of admission on rolling basis. Reply is required by May 1. $150 nonrefundable tuition deposit. $200 room deposit, refundable until May 1. Freshmen accepted for terms other than fall.
**Special programs:** Admission may be deferred one year. Credit and/or placement may be granted through CEEB Advanced Placement exams for scores of 3 or higher. Credit may be granted through CLEP general and subject exams, Regents College, ACT PEP, and DANTES exams. Credit and placement may be granted through challenge exams and military and life experience. Early entrance/early admission program. Concurrent enrollment program.
**Transfer students:** Transfer students accepted for terms other than fall. In fall 1993, 18% of all new students were transfers into all classes. 691 transfer applications were received, 575 were accepted. Application deadline is rolling (February 1 recommended) for fall; rolling (December 1 recommended) for spring. Minimum 2.25 GPA recommended. Lowest course grade accepted is "C-." At least 30 semester hours must be completed at the university to receive degree.
**Admissions contact:** Richard A. Zeiser, M.S.Ed., Director of Admissions. 203 768-4296.

**FINANCIAL AID. Available aid:** Pell grants, SEOG, state scholarships and grants, school scholarships and grants, private scholarships and grants, academic merit scholarships, athletic scholarships, and aid for undergraduate foreign students. Perkins Loans (NDSL), PLUS, Stafford Loans (GSL), state loans, school loans, and SLS. AMS and family tuition reduction.
**Financial aid statistics:** In 1993-94, 72% of all undergraduate applicants received aid; 76% of freshman applicants. Average amounts of aid awarded freshmen: Scholarships and grants, $7,200; loans, $2,800.
**Supporting data/closing dates:** FAFSA: Priority filing date is February 1. School's own aid application: Priority filing date is February 1. Income tax forms: Priority filing date is March 1. Notification of awards begins March 15.
**Financial aid contact:** Joseph Martinkovic, M.S., Director of Financial Aid. 203 768-4296.

**STUDENT EMPLOYMENT.** College Work/Study Program. Institutional employment. 20% of full-time undergraduates work on campus during school year. Students may expect to earn an average of $1,000 during school year. Off-campus part-time employment opportunities rated "good."

**COMPUTER FACILITIES.** 300 IBM/IBM-compatible, Macintosh/Apple, and RISC-/UNIX-based microcomputers. Students may access Digital minicomputer/mainframe systems, BITNET, Internet. Computer languages and software packages include BASIC, FORTRAN, Lotus 1-2-3, MacWrite, Multimate, Pascal; 100 in all. Computer facilities are available to all students.
**Fees:** None.
**Hours:** 24 hours.

**GRADUATE CAREER DATA.** Graduate school percentages: 3% enter law school. 2% enter medical school. 22% enter graduate business programs. 33% enter graduate arts and sciences programs. Highest graduate school enrollments: Boston U, U of Connecticut, George Washington U, Hartford Graduate Center, U of Hartford, Yale Music School. 85% of graduates choose careers in business and industry. Companies and businesses that hire graduates: Aetna, United Technologies.

**PROMINENT ALUMNI/AE.** Dionne Warwick, singer.

# University of New Haven

**West Haven, CT 06516** **203 932-7000**

**1994-95 Costs.** Tuition: $10,600. Room: $3,120. Board: $1,810–$1,980. Fees, books, misc. academic expenses (school's estimate): $690.
**Enrollment.** Undergraduates: 1,012 men, 412 women (full-time). Freshman class: 1,773 applicants, 1,426 accepted, 350 enrolled. Graduate enrollment: 1,591 men, 921 women.
**Test score averages/ranges.** Range of SAT scores of middle 50%: 350-550 verbal, 400-600 math.
**Faculty.** 151 full-time; 250 part-time. 90% of faculty holds highest degree in specific field. Student/faculty ratio: 19 to 1.
**Selectivity rating.** Less competitive.

**PROFILE.** The University of New Haven, founded in 1920, is a private university. Programs are offered through the Schools of Arts and Sciences; Business; Engineering; Hotel, Restaurant, and Tourism Administration; and Professional Studies and Continuing Education. Its 73-acre campus is located in West Haven, two miles from New Haven.
**Accreditation:** NEASC. Professionally accredited by the Accreditation Board for Engineering and Technology.
**Religious orientation:** University of New Haven is nonsectarian; no religious requirements.
**Library:** Collections totaling over 339,404 volumes, 1,299 periodical subscriptions, and 53,770 microform items.
**Special facilities/museums:** Art gallery, forensic science labs.
**Athletic facilities:** Gymnasium, baseball, football, lacrosse, soccer, and softball fields, basketball, racquetball, tennis, and volleyball courts, fitness and weight rooms.

**STUDENT BODY. Undergraduate profile:** 63% are state residents; 40% are transfers. 1% Asian-American, 8% Black, 2% Hispanic, 81% White, 8% Other. Average age of undergraduates is 20.
**Freshman profile:** Majority of accepted applicants took SAT. 80% of freshmen come from public schools.
**Foreign students:** 197 students are from out of the country. Countries represented include China, India, Israel, Korea, Taiwan, and Thailand; 52 in all.

**PROGRAMS OF STUDY. Degrees:** B.A., B.S.
**Majors:** Accounting, Air Transportation Management, Arson Investigation, Art, Aviation Science, Biology, Biomedical Computing, Business Administration, Business Economics, Chemical Engineering, Chemistry, Civil Engineering, Communication, Computer Science, Criminal Justice, Economics, Electrical Engineering, English, Environmental Science, Finance, Fire/Occupational Safety, Fire Protection Engineering, Fire Science, Forensic Science, General Dietetics, Graphic Design, History, Hotel/Restaurant Management, Industrial Engineering, Interior Design, International Business, Management of Sports Industries, Marketing, Materials Technology, Mathematics, Mechanical Engineering, Music, Music/Sound Recording, Occupational Safety/Health Administration, Occupational Safety/Health Technology, Political Science, Psychology, Public Administration, Sociology, Tourism/Travel Administration.
**Distribution of degrees:** The majors with the highest enrollment are business administration and engineering.
**Requirements:** General education requirement.
**Academic regulations:** Minimum 2.0 GPA must be maintained.
**Special:** Minors offered. Associate's degrees offered. Double majors. Dual degrees. Accelerated study. Internships. Cooperative education programs. Graduate school at which undergraduates may take graduate-level courses. Preprofessional programs in law, medicine, veterinary science, dentistry, and architecture. Exchange program with Albertus Magnus Coll. AFROTC.
**Honors:** Honors program. Honor societies.
**Academic Assistance:** Remedial writing, math, and study skills. Nonremedial tutoring.

**STUDENT LIFE. Housing:** Students may live on or off campus. Coed dorms. School-owned/operated apartments.
**Social atmosphere:** According to the editor of the student newspaper, "There is a strong social calendar sponsored by the Day Student Government. Further, New Haven provides many entertainment opportunities. Students are generally friendly and parties are common. Greeks in general are very influential, especially the fraternities. The Black Student Union is also very influential." Popular social events include Delta Sigma Alpha's Hawaiian Beach Party, the annual John Valby concert, and Homecoming tailgate parties. Popular on-campus gathering places are the Tavern and the Day Student Government office. Off-campus hotspots include Toad's Place and Nemery's (bars), and friends' apartments.
**Services and counseling/handicapped student services:** Placement services. Health service. Counseling services for minority, veteran, and older students. Birth control, personal, and psychological counseling. Career and academic guidance services. Physically disabled student services. Learning disabled services. Notetaking services. Reader services for the blind.
**Campus organizations:** Undergraduate student government. Student newspaper (Charger Bulletin, published once/week). Literary magazine. Yearbook. Radio station. Evening Council, professional, social, and special-interest groups, 40 organizations in all.

Five fraternities, no chapter houses; three sororities, no chapter houses. 8% of men join a fraternity. 8% of women join a sorority.
**Minority/foreign student organizations:** Black Student Union, Latino Association. International Student Club, Arab and Malaysian groups.

**ATHLETICS. Physical education requirements:** None.
**Intercollegiate competition:** 22% of students participate. Baseball (M), basketball (M,W), cheerleading (W), cross-country (M), football (M), lacrosse (M), soccer (M,W), softball (W), tennis (W), track (indoor) (M), track (outdoor) (M), volleyball (W). Member of ECAC, NCAA Division II, New England Collegiate Conference.
**Intramural and club sports:** 30% of students participate. Intramural basketball, bowling, racquetball, softball, tennis, touch football, volleyball. Women's club indoor track, outdoor track.

**ADMISSIONS. Academic basis for candidate selection** (in order of priority): Secondary school record, school's recommendation, standardized test scores.
**Nonacademic basis for candidate selection:** Extracurricular participation is important. Character and personality, particular talent or ability, and alumni/ae relationship are considered.
**Requirements:** Graduation from secondary school is recommended; GED is accepted. 16 units and the following program of study are recommended: 4 units of English, 3 units of math, 2 units of science, 2 units of foreign language, 2 units of social studies, 3 units of electives. Minimum combined SAT score of 750 recommended. Portfolio recommended of art program applicants. Conditional admission possible for applicants not meeting standard requirements. SAT is required; ACT may be substituted. Campus visit and interview recommended. No off-campus interviews.
**Procedure:** Suggest filing application by March 1; no deadline. Notification of admission on rolling basis. No set date by which applicants must accept offer. $200 tuition deposit, refundable until May 1. $150 nonrefundable room deposit. Freshmen accepted for terms other than fall.
**Special programs:** Admission may be deferred one year. Credit and/or placement may be granted through CEEB Advanced Placement exams for scores of 3 or higher. Credit and/or placement may be granted through CLEP general and subject exams. Credit may be granted through DANTES exams and military experience. Credit and placement may be granted through challenge exams. Concurrent enrollment program.
**Transfer students:** Transfer students accepted for terms other than fall. In fall 1992, 40% of all new students were transfers into all classes. 576 transfer applications were received, 550 were accepted. Application deadline is rolling for fall; rolling for spring. Minimum 2.0 GPA required. Lowest course grade accepted is "C." Maximum number of transferable credits is 60 semester hours from a two-year school and 90 semester hours from a four-year school. At least 30 semester hours must be completed at the university to receive degree.
**Admissions contact:** Steven Briggs, M.Ed., Dean of Admissions. 203 932-7319.

**FINANCIAL AID. Available aid:** Pell grants, SEOG, state grants, school scholarships and grants, academic merit scholarships, and athletic scholarships. Perkins Loans (NDSL), PLUS, Stafford Loans (GSL), and SLS. Tuition Plan Inc., AMS, and family tuition reduction.
**Financial aid statistics:** In 1992-93, 71% of all undergraduate applicants received aid; 50% of freshman applicants. Average amounts of aid awarded freshmen: Scholarships and grants, $6,320; loans, $2,336.
**Supporting data/closing dates:** FAFSA/FAF/FFS: Priority filing date is March 15. School's own aid application: Priority filing date is March 15. Income tax forms: Priority filing date is March 15. Notification of awards on rolling basis.
**Financial aid contact:** Jane Sangeloty, Director of Financial Aid. 203 932-7314.

**STUDENT EMPLOYMENT.** College Work/Study Program. Institutional employment. 12% of full-time undergraduates work on campus during school year. Students may expect to earn an average of $1,000 during school year. Off-campus part-time employment opportunities rated "good."

**COMPUTER FACILITIES.** 140 IBM/IBM-compatible, Macintosh/Apple, and RISC-/UNIX-based microcomputers; 20 are networked. Students may access Data General, Prime minicomputer/mainframe systems. Computer languages and software packages include Assembler, BASIC, C, COBOL, dBASE, FORTRAN, LISP, Lotus 1-2-3, Pascal, PL/1, Quattro Pro, RPG, WordPerfect; 34 in all. Computer facilities are available to all students.
**Fees:** Computer fee is included in tuition/fees.
**Hours:** 24 hours.

**GRADUATE CAREER DATA.** Highest graduate school enrollments: Central Connecticut State U, Fairfield U, U of Connecticut, U of New Haven. Companies and businesses that hire graduates: AT&T, General Dynamics, Northeast Utilities, SNET Co., Textron, United Illuminating, United Technologies.

# Wesleyan University

**Middletown, CT 06457** **203 347-9411**

**1994-95 Costs.** Tuition: $18,780. Room: $3,160. Board: $2,230. Fees, books, misc. academic expenses (school's estimate): $1,130.
**Enrollment.** Undergraduates: 1,372 men, 1,299 women (full-time). Freshman class: 4,772 applicants, 2,029 accepted, 713 enrolled. Graduate enrollment: 94 men, 81 women.
**Test score averages/ranges.** Average SAT scores: 630 verbal, 660 math. Range of SAT scores of middle 50%: 570-670 verbal, 610-710 math. Average ACT scores: 30 composite.
**Faculty.** 293 full-time; 61 part-time. 95% of faculty holds highest degree in specific field. Student/faculty ratio: 11 to 1.
**Selectivity rating.** Highly competitive.

**PROFILE.** Wesleyan is a private, liberal arts university. Founded in 1831 as a university for men, it was coeducational from 1872 to 1912, then readopted coeducation in 1968. Its 120-acre campus is located in Middletown, 15 miles south of Hartford.

**Accreditation:** NEASC.
**Religious orientation:** Wesleyan University is nonsectarian; no religious requirements.
**Library:** Collections totaling over 1,212,000 volumes, 3,343 periodical subscriptions, and 198,000 microform items.
**Special facilities/museums:** Art center, art galleries, center for Afro-American studies, music hall, public affairs center, language lab, electron microscope, observatory, nuclear magnetic resonance spectrometers.
**Athletic facilities:** Gymnasium, field house, swimming pool, basketball, racquetball, squash, tennis, and volleyball courts, ice rink, indoor and outdoor tracks, wrestling room, athletic fields, weight room, fitness center.
**STUDENT BODY. Undergraduate profile:** 9% are state residents; 6% are transfers. 11% Asian-American, 9% Black, 7% Hispanic, 67% White, 6% Other. Average age of undergraduates is 20.
**Freshman profile:** 99% of accepted applicants took SAT; 1% took ACT. 57% of freshmen come from public schools.
**Undergraduate achievement:** 93% of fall 1992 freshmen returned for fall 1993 term. 88% of entering class graduated. 90% of students who completed a degree program went on to graduate study within five years.
**Foreign students:** 19 students are from out of the country. Countries represented include Canada, China, England, Germany, and Korea; 15 in all.
**PROGRAMS OF STUDY. Degrees:** B.A.
**Majors:** African Studies, Afro-American Studies, American Studies, Anthropology, Anthropology/Sociology, Art History, Asian Languages/Literatures, Astronomy, Biology, Chemistry, Chinese, Classical Civilization, Classics, Dance, Earth/Environmental Science, East Asian Studies, Economics, Educational Studies, English, Film, French, German Language/Literature, Government, Greek, History, Italian, Japanese, Latin, Latin American Studies, Letters, Mathematics, Mathematics/Economics, Medieval Studies, Molecular Biology/Biochemistry, Music, Philosophy, Physics, Psychology, Psychology/Sociology, Religion, Romance Languages/Literature, Russian Language/Literature, Science in Society, Social Studies, Sociology, Spanish, Studio Art, Theatre, University Major/Individualized, Women's Studies.
**Distribution of degrees:** The majors with the highest enrollment are English, government, and American studies.
**Academic regulations:** Minimum 2.0 GPA must be maintained.
**Special:** Self-designed majors. Double majors. Independent study. Accelerated study. Pass/fail grading option. Internships. Graduate school at which undergraduates may take graduate-level courses. Preprofessional programs in law and medicine. 3-2 engineering programs with Caltech and Columbia U. Washington Semester and Sea Semester. Member of Twelve College Exchange. Study abroad in China, France, Germany, Great Britain, Israel, Italy, Japan, Latin American countries, the former Soviet Republics, and Spain. ROTC, NROTC, and AFROTC at U of Connecticut.
**Honors:** Phi Beta Kappa. Honors program. Honor societies.
**Academic Assistance:** Nonremedial tutoring.
**STUDENT LIFE. Housing:** All first-year students must live on campus. Coed, women's, and men's dorms. Fraternity housing. School-owned/operated apartments. Special-interest housing. 95% of students live in college housing.
**Social atmosphere:** On campus, students frequently gather at the campus center, the science center, and in fraternity houses and dorm lounges. Off-campus, popular haunts include Wes Wings (restaurant), Atticus Bookstore/Cafe, Foss Hill, and the cinema. Influential groups on campus include the Student of Color Council, Queer Alliance (lesbian, gay, and bisexual students), Greeks, and a variety of ethnic and cultural groups. However, the editor of the student newspaper observes, "Groups have less of an effect on the culture of Wesleyan than do more personal issues." Among the most popular events of the school year are the Spring Fling and Fall Ball, two all-day outdoor pop-music concerts, and fall football games. Other noteworthy events include political rallies, speak-outs (against rape, racism, homophobia, etc.), special speakers, poetry recitals, and the jazz series. "Wesleyan is not a school where students spend a lot of time thinking about their social lives. It lacks the patriotic cohesion to the alma mater that dominates other colleges. People tend not to go to big events, but rather go off and do their own thing. This is mostly because Wesleyan is so ethnically, culturally, and politically diverse."
**Services and counseling/handicapped student services:** Placement services. Health service. Counseling services for minority and older students. Birth control, personal, and psychological counseling. Career and academic guidance services. Religious counseling.
**Campus organizations:** Undergraduate student government. Student newspaper (Argus, published twice/week). Literary magazine. Yearbook. Radio station. Bands, orchestra, glee club, choirs, a cappella singing groups, community service groups, debating, theatre, dance groups, film series, outing club, departmental, political, and social action groups, 150 organizations in all. Nine fraternities, four chapter houses; four sororities, no chapter houses. 10% of men join a fraternity. 2% of women join a sorority.
**Religious organizations:** Christian Fellowship, Havurah.
**Minority/foreign student organizations:** Ajua-Campos (Latino student group), Student of Color Council, UJAMAA (black student group), WAASU (Asian-American student group).
**ATHLETICS. Physical education requirements:** None.
**Intercollegiate competition:** 75% of students participate. Baseball (M), basketball (M,W), crew (M,W), cross-country (M,W), diving (M,W), field hockey (W), football (M), golf (M), ice hockey (M,W), lacrosse (M,W), soccer (M,W), softball (W), squash (M,W), swimming (M,W), tennis (M,W), track (indoor) (M,W), track (outdoor) (M,W), volleyball (W), wrestling (M). Member of ECAC, NCAA Division III, NESCAC, NIAC.
**Intramural and club sports:** 65% of students participate. Intramural badminton, basketball, bowling, cross-country, floor hockey, ice hockey, inner-tube water polo, racquetball, soccer, softball, squash, table tennis, tennis, volleyball. Men's club Alpine skiing, cycling, horsemanship, rugby, sailing, ultimate frisbee, volleyball, water polo. Women's club Alpine skiing, cycling, horsemanship, rugby, sailing, ultimate frisbee, water polo.
**ADMISSIONS. Academic basis for candidate selection** (in order of priority): Secondary school record, class rank, standardized test scores, school's recommendation, essay.

**Nonacademic basis for candidate selection:** Character and personality are important. Extracurricular participation, particular talent or ability, geographical distribution, and alumni/ae relationship are considered.
**Requirements:** Graduation from secondary school is required; GED is not accepted. 16 units and the following program of study are recommended: 4 units of English, 3 units of math, 3 units of science, 3 units of foreign language, 3 units of social studies. SAT or ACT is required. ACH required. Campus visit and interview recommended. Off-campus interviews available with admissions and alumni representatives.
**Procedure:** Take SAT or ACT by December of 12th year. Visit college for interview by January of 12th year. Suggest filing application by January 15; no deadline. Notification of admission by April 15. Reply is required by May 1. $300 nonrefundable tuition deposit. Freshmen accepted for fall term only.
**Special programs:** Admission may be deferred one year. Credit and/or placement may be granted through CEEB Advanced Placement exams for scores of 4 or higher. Early decision program. In fall 1993, 454 applied for early decision and 226 were accepted. Deadline for applying for early decision is November 15. Early entrance/early admission program.
**Transfer students:** Transfer students accepted for terms other than fall. In fall 1993, 6% of all new students were transfers into all classes. 422 transfer applications were received, 166 were accepted. Application deadline is November 1 for fall; March 1 for spring. Minimum 3.0 GPA recommended. Lowest course grade accepted is "C-." Maximum number of transferable credits is 18 semester credits. At least 16 semester credits must be completed at the university to receive degree.
**Admissions contact:** Barbara-Jan Wilson, M.A., Director of Admissions. 203 347-9411, extension 2900.

**FINANCIAL AID. Available aid:** Pell grants, SEOG, state scholarships and grants, school scholarships and grants, and private scholarships and grants. Perkins Loans (NDSL), PLUS, Stafford Loans (GSL), state loans, school loans, and private loans. Tuition Plan Inc. and deferred payment plan. Insured payment plan. SHARE Loan Program.
**Financial aid statistics:** In 1993-94, 48% of all freshman applicants received aid. Average amounts of aid awarded freshmen: Scholarships and grants, $11,739; loans, $2,000.
**Supporting data/closing dates:** FAFSA/FAF/FFS: Deadline is January 15. School's own aid application: Deadline is January 15. Notification of awards begins April 10.
**Financial aid contact:** Edwin Below, Director of Financial Aid. 203 347-9411, extension 2304.

**STUDENT EMPLOYMENT.** College Work/Study Program. Institutional employment. 64% of full-time undergraduates work on campus during school year. Students may expect to earn an average of $1,200 during school year. Off-campus part-time employment opportunities rated "good."

**COMPUTER FACILITIES.** 300 IBM/IBM-compatible and Macintosh/Apple microcomputers; 200 are networked. Students may access Digital minicomputer/mainframe systems, BITNET, Internet. Residence halls may be equipped with modems. Computer languages and software packages include C, COBOL, FORTRAN, KERMIT, LISP, MINITAB, Pascal, Prolog, SAS, SPSS, SuperCalc, WordPerfect, WordStar; various instructional programs. Computer facilities are available to all students.
**Fees:** None.
**Hours:** 24 hours in some locations.

**GRADUATE CAREER DATA.** Graduate school percentages: 20% enter law school. 15% enter medical school. 10% enter graduate business programs. 25% enter graduate arts and sciences programs. Highest graduate school enrollments: Columbia U, Harvard U, Yale U. Companies and businesses that hire graduates: Bain & Co., Goldman Sachs, Peace Corps, Procter & Gamble.

## Yale University

**New Haven, CT 06520-8234 203 432-4771**

**1994-95 Costs.** Tuition: $19,840. Room & board: $6,510.
**Enrollment.** Undergraduates: 2,789 men, 2,430 women (full-time). Freshman class: 10,705 applicants, 2,453 accepted, 1,317 enrolled. Graduate enrollment: 3,096 men, 2,558 women.
**Test score averages/ranges.** Range of SAT scores of middle 50%: 600-710 verbal, 650-750 math.
**Faculty.** 95% of faculty holds highest degree in specific field.
**Selectivity rating.** Most competitive.

**PROFILE.** Yale is a private, Ivy League, liberal arts university. Founded in 1701, it adopted coeducation in 1969. Its 175-acre main campus is located near the center of New Haven. Campus buildings are primarily in the collegiate Gothic style.

**Accreditation:** NEASC. Professionally accredited by the Accreditation Board for Engineering and Technology, the Accrediting Commission on Education for Health Services Administration, the American Bar Association, the American Medical Association (CAHEA), the American Psychological Association, the Association of Theological Schools, the Council on Education for Public Health, the Liaison Committee on Medical Education, the National Architecture Accrediting Board, the National Association of Schools of Music, the National Council for Accreditation of Teacher Education, the National League for Nursing, the Society of American Foresters.
**Religious orientation:** Yale University is nonsectarian; no religious requirements.
**Library:** Collections totaling over 10,200,000 volumes, 54,601 periodical subscriptions, and 4,000,000 microform items.
**Special facilities/museums:** Art and history museums, observatory, electron microscopes, nuclear accelerators.
**Athletic facilities:** Gymnasium, athletic fields, tracks, tennis courts, ice rink, rowing tanks, lagoon, golf course, polo/equestrian center, sailing center, outdoor education center (woodlands with lake).

**STUDENT BODY. Undergraduate profile:** 10% are state residents; 1% are transfers. 16% Asian-American, 9% Black, 6% Hispanic, 69% White. Average age of undergraduates is 20.
**Freshman profile:** Majority of accepted applicants took SAT. 60% of freshmen come from public schools.
**Undergraduate achievement:** 98% of fall 1992 freshmen returned for fall 1993 term. 33% of students who completed a degree program went on to graduate study within one year.
**Foreign students:** 233 students are from out of the country. Countries represented include Canada, China, England, France, India, and South Korea; 51 in all.

**PROGRAMS OF STUDY. Degrees:** B.A., B.Lib.Studies, B.S.
**Majors:** African/African-American Studies, American Studies, Anthropology, Applied Mathematics, Applied Physics, Archaeological Studies, Architecture, Art, Astronomy, Astronomy/Physics, Biology, Chemical Engineering, Chemistry, Chinese, Classical Civilization, Classics, Comparative Literature, Computer Science, Computer Science/Mathematics, Computer Science/Psychology, East Asian Studies, Economics, Economics/Mathematics, Electrical Engineering, Engineering Science, English, Ethics/Politics/Economics, Film Studies, French, Geology/Geophysics, German, German Studies, History, History of Art, History of Science/History of Medicine, Humanities, International Studies, Italian, Japanese, Judaic Studies, Latin American Studies, Linguistics, Literature, Mathematics, Mathematics/Philosophy, Mathematics/Physics, Mechanical Engineering, Molecular Biophysics/Biochemistry, Music, Near Eastern Languages/Civilizations, Organismal Biology, Philosophy, Physics, Physics/Philosophy, Political Science, Psychology, Religious Studies, Renaissance Studies, Russian, Russian/East European Studies, Sociology, Spanish, Special Divisional Major, Studies in the Environment, Theatre Studies, Women's Studies.
**Distribution of degrees:** The majors with the highest enrollment are history, English, and biology.
**Requirements:** General education requirement.
**Special:** Self-designed majors. Double majors. Dual degrees. Independent study. Accelerated study. Pass/fail grading option. Internships. Graduate school at which undergraduates may take graduate-level courses. Member of Consortium on Financing Higher Education. Teacher certification in secondary and special education. Study abroad in France, Germany, Italy, Spain, and other countries. ROTC at Southern Conn. State U and U of Bridgeport. AFROTC at U of Connecticut.
**Honors:** Phi Beta Kappa.
**Academic Assistance:** Nonremedial tutoring.

**STUDENT LIFE. Housing:** All freshmen must live on campus. Coed dorms. School-owned/operated apartments. On-campus married-student housing. 86% of students live in college housing.
**Services and counseling/handicapped student services:** Placement services. Health service. Women's center. Day care. Counseling services for minority students. Birth control, personal, and psychological counseling. Career and academic guidance services. Physically disabled student services. Notetaking services. Tape recorders. Tutors. Reader services for the blind.
**Campus organizations:** Undergraduate student government. Student newspaper (Daily News). Literary magazine. Yearbook. Radio station. Orchestra, jazz groups, concert and marching bands, choir, glee club, Slavic, Russian, and other singing groups, drama groups, film societies, debating, dance groups, numerous student publications, cultural, departmental, political, social, and special-interest groups, 209 organizations in all.
**Religious organizations:** Black Church, Campus Crusade for Christ, Bahai, Baptist, Buddhist, Catholic, Christian Science, Church of Christ, Episcopal, Friends, Jewish, Latter-Day Saints, Lutheran, Orthodox Christian, and Unitarian groups.
**Minority/foreign student organizations:** Afro-American Cultural Center, Asian-American Students Association, Black Pre-Professional Council, Black Student Alliance, Despierta Boricua, MEChA. Caribbean Club, Irish Education Committee, International Forum, Canadian, Chinese, Filipino, Japanese, Latin American, South Asian, and Vietnamese groups.

**ATHLETICS. Physical education requirements:** None.
**Intercollegiate competition:** 20% of students participate. Baseball (M), basketball (M,W), crew (M,W), cross-country (M,W), diving (M,W), fencing (M,W), field hockey (W), football (M), golf (M,W), gymnastics (W), ice hockey (M,W), lacrosse (M,W), soccer (M,W), softball (W), squash (M,W), swimming (M,W), tennis (M,W), track (indoor) (M,W), track (outdoor) (M,W), track and field (indoor) (M,W), track and field (outdoor) (M,W), volleyball (W). Member of ECAC, Ivy League, NCAA Division I.
**Intramural and club sports:** 52% of students participate. Intramural baseball, basketball, billiards, bowling, crew, field hockey, football, golf, racquetball, soccer, softball, swimming, table tennis, tennis, ultimate frisbee, volleyball, water polo, wrestling. Men's club Alpine skiing, badminton, ballroom dancing, cricket, croquet, cycling, equestrian sports, fishing, ultimate frisbee, handball, judo, kayak, kendo, kung-fu, Nordic skiing, outing, pistol, pony polo, powerlifting, rifle, rugby, sailing, shotokan karate, skeet/trap shooting, table tennis, tae kwon do, triathlon, volleyball, water polo, windsurfing, weight training, wrestling. Women's club Alpine skiing, badminton, ballroom dancing, cricket, croquet, cycling, equestrian sports, fishing, handball, judo, kayak, kendo, kung-fu, Nordic skiing, outing, pistol, pony polo, powerlifting, rifle, rugby, sailing, shotokan karate, skeet & trap, table tennis, tae kwon do, triathlon, ultimate frisbee, volleyball, water polo, windsurfing, weight training, wrestling.

**ADMISSIONS. Academic basis for candidate selection** (in order of priority): Secondary school record, standardized test scores, class rank, school's recommendation, essay.
**Nonacademic basis for candidate selection:** Character and personality and extracurricular participation are emphasized. Particular talent or ability and alumni/ae relationship are important. Geographical distribution is considered.
**Requirements:** Graduation from secondary school is recommended; GED is accepted. No specific distribution of secondary school units required. Applicants urged to take honors and advanced placement courses. SAT or ACT is required. ACH required. Admissions interview recommended. Off-campus interviews available with an alumni representative.
**Procedure:** Take SAT or ACT by January of 12th year. Take ACH by January of 12th year. Suggest filing application by December 31; no deadline. Notification of admission by April 15. Reply is required by May 1. Freshmen accepted for fall term only.

**Special programs:** Admission may be deferred one year. Credit and/or placement may be granted through CEEB Advanced Placement exams. Placement may be granted through challenge exams. Early action program. In fall 1993, 1,687 applied for early action and 556 were accepted. Deadline for applying for early action is November 1. Early entrance/early admission program.

**Transfer students:** Transfer students accepted for terms other than fall. In fall 1993, 1% of all new students were transfers into all classes. 582 transfer applications were received, 28 were accepted. Application deadline is March 11. Lowest course grade accepted is "C." Maximum number of transferable credits is the equivalent of two full terms of study. At least 18 course credits must be completed at Yale to receive degree.

**Admissions contact:** Richard H. Shaw, Jr., Dean of Admissions. 203 432-1900.

**FINANCIAL AID. Available aid:** Pell grants, SEOG, state scholarships and grants, school grants, private scholarships and grants, ROTC scholarships, and aid for undergraduate foreign students. Perkins Loans (NDSL), PLUS, Stafford Loans (GSL), state loans, school loans, private loans, and SLS. Tuition Plan Inc., Knight Tuition Plans, AMS, and guaranteed tuition. University prepayment plan.

**Financial aid statistics:** In 1992-93, 91% of all undergraduate applicants received aid; 82% of freshman applicants. Average amounts of aid awarded freshmen: Scholarships and grants, $13,837; loans, $2,625.

**Supporting data/closing dates:** FAFSA/FAF: Deadline is February 1. Notification of awards begins around April 1. School's own aid application: Deadline is February 1. State aid form: Accepted on rolling basis. Income tax forms: Accepted on rolling basis.

**Financial aid contact:** James Tilton, Director of Undergraduate Financial Aid. 203 432-0360.

**STUDENT EMPLOYMENT.** College Work/Study Program. Institutional employment. Students may expect to earn an average of $2,205 during school year. Off-campus part-time employment opportunities rated "good."

**COMPUTER FACILITIES.** 250 IBM/IBM-compatible and Macintosh/Apple microcomputers. Students may access Digital, IBM, SUN minicomputer/mainframe systems. Residence halls may be equipped with networked microcomputers. Client/LAN operating systems include Apple/Macintosh, DOS, LocalTalk/AppleTalk. Computer facilities are available to all students.

**Fees:** None.

**Hours:** 24 hours.

**GRADUATE CAREER DATA.** Graduate school percentages: 8% enter law school. 9% enter medical school. 1% enter graduate business programs. 11% enter graduate arts and sciences programs. Highest graduate school enrollments: Columbia U, Harvard U, New York U, UC Berkeley, Yale U. 17% of graduates choose careers in business and industry.

**PROMINENT ALUMNI/AE.** George Bush, former President of the United States; Richard Cheyney, former U.S. secretary of defense; Jodie Foster and Vincent Price, actors; Gary Trudeau, cartoonist; William F. Buckley, Jr., journalist; Dick Cavett, TV host; Maya Lin, architect; Sinclair Lewis, author; Eli Whitney, inventor.

# Delaware

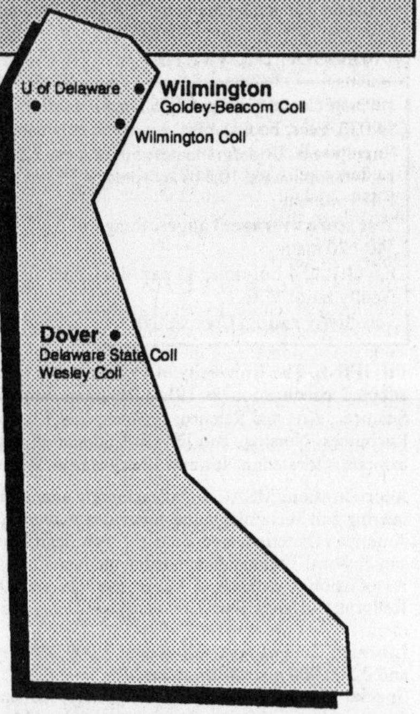


## Delaware State College

**Dover, DE 19901-2275** **302 739-4917**

**1993-94 Costs.** Tuition: $1,788 (state residents), $4,346 (out-of-state). Room: $2,046. Board: $1,418. Fees, books, misc. academic expenses (school's estimate): $1,650.
**Enrollment.** Undergraduates: 1,024 men, 1,220 women (full-time). Freshman class: 1,998 applicants, 1,475 accepted, 580 enrolled. Graduate enrollment: 76 men, 164 women.
**Test score averages/ranges.** N/A.
**Faculty.** 166 full-time; 16 part-time. 57% of faculty holds highest degree in specific field. Student/faculty ratio: 15 to 1.
**Selectivity rating.** N/A.

**PROFILE.** Delaware State, founded in 1891, is a public college. Its 400-acre campus is located one mile north of Dover's city limits.

**Accreditation:** MSACS. Professionally accredited by the Council on Social Work Education, the National League for Nursing.
**Religious orientation:** Delaware State College is nonsectarian; no religious requirements.
**Library:** Collections totaling over 161,565 volumes, 2,739 periodical subscriptions, and 73,266 microform items.
**Special facilities/museums:** Art gallery, language lab, observatory, herbarium.
**Athletic facilities:** Gymnasium, swimming pool, racquetball courts, track, playing fields.
**STUDENT BODY. Undergraduate profile:** 60% are state residents. 1% Asian-American, 62% Black, 1% Hispanic, 34% White, 2% Other. Average age of undergraduates is 21.
**Freshman profile:** 80% of freshmen come from public schools.
**Undergraduate achievement:** 9% of entering class graduated.
**Foreign students:** Countries represented include Bermuda, Cameroon, China, Honduras, Kenya, and Nigeria; 46 in all.
**PROGRAMS OF STUDY. Degrees:** B.A., B.S., B.Tech.
**Majors:** Accounting, Agribusiness, Agribusiness Technology, Agricultural Education, Agriculture, Airway Science, Art/Business, Art Education, Biology, Botany, Business Administration, Business Education, Business/Secretarial Technologies, Chemical Engineering, Chemical Laboratory Technology/Environmental Technology, Chemistry, Chemistry/Chemical Engineering, Child Development/Family Relations, Civil Engineering, Clothing/Textiles/Related Arts, Community Health, Criminal Justice Technology, Data Processing, Dental Assisting Technology, Distributive Education, Drama/Speech Communication Education, Early Childhood Education, Early Childhood/Exceptional Children, Economics, Electrical Engineering, Elementary Education, Engineering Technology, English, Environmental Health, Fire Protection, Fisheries Management, Food Service Management Technology, Foods/Nutrition, French, General Arts, General Resource Management, Health Education, Health/Physical Education, History, Home Economics, Home Economics Education, Human Services Technology, Journalism, Library Studies, Library Technology, Marketing, Marketing Education, Mathematics, Mathematics/Computer Science, Mathematics Education, Mathematics/Mechanical Engineering, Mechanical/Aerospace Engineering, Medical Laboratory Technologies, Music, Natural Resources Technology, Nursing, Occupational Teacher Education, Occupational/Vocational Guidance of Children, Park Administration/Natural Resources, Park Management/Recreation, Physics, Physics/Civil Engineering, Physics Education, Physics/Electrical Engineering, Physics/Mechanical/Aerospace Engineering, Plant Sciences, Political Science, Pre-Study in Medically Allied Fields, Psychology, Recreation, Science Education, Science Education Technology, Secretarial/Related Business Subjects, Secretarial Science, Social Studies, Social Work, Sociology, Soil/Water Management, Spanish, Special Education, Theatre, Urban Affairs, Vegetation Management.
**Distribution of degrees:** The majors with the highest enrollment are business administration, marketing, and accounting; physics education has the lowest.
**Requirements:** General education requirement.
**Academic regulations:** Minimum 1.7 GPA must be maintained.
**Special:** Minors offered in black studies and women's studies. Courses offered in astronomy and philosophy. Technology program. Self-designed majors. Double majors. Dual degrees. Independent study. Accelerated study. Pass/fail grading option. Internships. Cooperative education programs. Graduate school at which undergraduates may take graduate-level courses. Preprofessional programs in law, veterinary science, and dentistry. Exchange program with U of Delaware. Teacher certification in early childhood, elementary, secondary, and special education. Study abroad in China. ROTC and AFROTC.
**Honors:** Honors program.
**Academic Assistance:** Remedial reading, writing, math, and study skills. Nonremedial tutoring.

**STUDENT LIFE. Housing:** Students may live on or off campus. Women's and men's dorms. Off-campus married-student housing. 66% of students live in college housing.
**Social atmosphere:** The student newspaper reports that students with common geographic backgrounds tend to hang out together. Favorite activities include the back to school concert, athletic events, and Homecoming. Fraternities and sororities have the most social influence on campus. While on campus, students congregate at the Martin Luther King Student Center, particularly in the canteen and game room, and in front of the dorms during the cooler months.
**Services and counseling/handicapped student services:** Placement services. Health service. Day care. Counseling services for veteran students. Career and academic guidance services. Physically disabled student services. Notetaking services. Tape recorders.
**Campus organizations:** Undergraduate student government. Student newspaper (Hornet, published once/month). Yearbook. Radio station. Art, writers, and jazz clubs, band and choir, debating, drama guild, athletic and departmental groups, commuter club, 53 organizations in all. Five fraternities, no chapter houses. 4% of men join a fraternity.
**Minority/foreign student organizations:** International Student Association.
**ATHLETICS. Physical education requirements:** None.
**Intercollegiate competition:** 10% of students participate. Baseball (M), basketball (M,W), cheerleading (M,W), cross-country (M,W), football (M), softball (W), tennis (M,W), track (indoor) (M,W), track (outdoor) (M,W), track and field (indoor) (M,W), track and field (outdoor) (M,W), volleyball (W), wrestling (M). Member of ECAC, Mid-Eastern Athletic Conference, NCAA Division I, NCAA Division I-AA for football.
**Intramural and club sports:** 12% of students participate. Intramural basketball, bowling, football, jogging, racquetball, softball, swimming, tennis, track/field, volleyball, weight lifting. Men's club soccer.
**ADMISSIONS. Academic basis for candidate selection** (in order of priority): Secondary school record, standardized test scores, school's recommendation, class rank, essay.
**Nonacademic basis for candidate selection:** Character, personality, and extracurricular participation are important. Particular talent or ability and alumni/ae relationship are considered.
**Requirements:** Graduation from secondary school is required; GED is accepted. 15 units and the following program of study are required: 4 units of English, 2 units of math, 2 units of science including 1 unit of lab, 2 units of social studies, 5 units of academic electives. Minimum 2.0 GPA required. SAT or ACT is required. Campus visit and interview recommended. Off-campus interviews available with an admissions representative.
**Procedure:** Take SAT or ACT by July of 12th year. Suggest filing application by June 1. Application deadline is November 1. Notification of admission on rolling basis. Reply is required by June 30. $100 nonrefundable room deposit. Freshmen accepted for terms other than fall.
**Special programs:** Placement may be granted through CEEB Advanced Placement exams. Credit and/or placement may be granted through CLEP general and subject exams. Credit and placement may be granted through DANTES exams and military experience. Concurrent enrollment program.
**Transfer students:** Transfer students accepted for terms other than fall. In fall 1992, 613 transfer applications were received, 370 were accepted. Application deadline is June 1 for fall; November 1 for spring. Minimum 2.0 GPA required. Lowest course grade accepted is "C." At least 30 semester hours must be completed at the college to receive degree.
**Admissions contact:** Jethro C. Williams, Director of Admissions. 302 739-4917.

**FINANCIAL AID. Available aid:** Pell grants, SEOG, state scholarships and grants, school scholarships and grants, private scholarships and grants, ROTC scholarships, academic merit scholarships, and athletic scholarships. Perkins Loans (NDSL), Stafford Loans (GSL), state loans, school loans, and private loans. Deferred payment plan.
**Financial aid statistics:** In 1992-93, 67% of all undergraduate applicants received aid; 60% of freshman applicants. Average amounts of aid awarded freshmen: Scholarships and grants, $600; loans, $2,625.
**Supporting data/closing dates:** FAFSA/FAF/FFS: Priority filing date is May 1. Notification of awards on rolling basis.
**Financial aid contact:** Leo R. LeCompte, M.A., Director of Financial Aid. 302 739-4908.
**STUDENT EMPLOYMENT.** College Work/Study Program. Institutional employment. 5% of full-time undergraduates work on campus during school year. Students may expect to earn an average of $2,000 during school year. Off-campus part-time employment opportunities rated "excellent."

**COMPUTER FACILITIES.** 192 IBM/IBM-compatible microcomputers; 88 are networked. Students may access IBM minicomputer/mainframe systems. Computer languages and software packages include Banner, BASIC, COBOL, FORTRAN, Harvard Graphics, Lotus, MINITAB, SPSS, Windows, WordPerfect. Computer facilities are available to all students.
**Fees:** None.
**GRADUATE CAREER DATA.** Companies and businesses that hire graduates: Du Pont, Kodak, Hercules, banks, retail firms.
**PROMINENT ALUMNI/AE.** Kent Amos, former vice president, Xerox; John Sims, vice-president, Digital Equipment Corp.; William Granville, vice-president, Mobil Oil; Wayne Gilcrest, Maryland congressman; Wanda Wilson, veterinarian.

# Goldey-Beacom College

**Wilmington, DE 19808** **302 998-8814**

**1994-95 Costs.** Tuition: $6,120. Room: $2,985. Fees, books, misc. academic expenses (school's estimate): $500.
**Enrollment.** Undergraduates: 313 men, 539 women (full-time). Freshman class: 633 applicants, 468 accepted, 284 enrolled.
**Test score averages/ranges.** Average SAT scores: 378 verbal, 424 math.
**Faculty.** 24 full-time; 49 part-time. 25% of faculty holds doctoral degree. Student/faculty ratio: 33 to 1.
**Selectivity rating.** Less competitive.

**PROFILE.** Goldey-Beacom, founded in 1886, is a private college of business. Its 23-acre campus is located 15 miles from downtown Wilmington.
**Accreditation:** MSACS.
**Religious orientation:** Goldey-Beacom College is nonsectarian; no religious requirements.
**Library:** Collections totaling over 25,000 volumes and 400 periodical subscriptions.
**Athletic facilities:** Basketball, handball, tennis, and volleyball courts, soccer and softball fields fitness trail, weight room, rented gymnasium.
**STUDENT BODY. Undergraduate profile:** 60% are state residents; 26% are transfers. 6% Asian-American, 10% Black, 2.4% Hispanic, .3% Native American, 81% White, .3% Other. Average age of undergraduates is 21.
**Freshman profile:** 1% of freshmen who took SAT scored 600 or over on verbal, 8% scored 600 or over on math; 8% scored 500 or over on verbal, 40% scored 500 or over on math; 69% scored 400 or over on verbal, 94% scored 400 or over on math; 100% scored 300 or over on verbal, 100% scored 300 or over on math. 63% of accepted applicants took SAT.
**Undergraduate achievement:** 65% of fall 1992 freshmen returned for fall 1993 term. 43% of entering class graduated.
**Foreign students:** 100 students are from out of the country. Countries represented include China, northern European countries, India, Indonesia, and Korea; 34 in all.
**PROGRAMS OF STUDY. Degrees:** B.S.
**Majors:** Accounting, Administrative Office Management, Business Communication, Computer Information Systems, International Business, Management, Management Information Systems, Marketing.
**Distribution of degrees:** The majors with the highest enrollment are accounting and management; computer information systems has the lowest.
**Requirements:** General education requirement.
**Academic regulations:** Minimum 2.0 GPA must be maintained.
**Special:** Postgraduate certificate program in computer information systems. Courses offered in computer programming, economics, English, history, law, mathematics, philosophy, political science, psychology, sociology, and statistics. Associate's degrees offered. Double majors. Internships. Cooperative education programs. Study abroad in England and Scotland.
**Honors:** Honors program. Honor societies.
**Academic Assistance:** Remedial reading, writing, math, and study skills. Nonremedial tutoring.
**ADMISSIONS. Academic basis for candidate selection** (in order of priority): Secondary school record, standardized test scores, school's recommendation, class rank.
**Nonacademic basis for candidate selection:** Character and personality, extracurricular participation, particular talent or ability, and alumni/ae relationship are considered.
**Requirements:** Graduation from secondary school is required; GED is accepted. No specific distribution of secondary school units required. Minimum combined SAT score of 700 and minimum 2.5 GPA recommended. College Board Descriptive Test required; test administered every month by the college. Algebra I or II and geometry required of B.S. applicants. SAT is recommended; ACT may be substituted. Campus visit recommended. Off-campus interviews available with an admissions representative.
**Procedure:** Notification of admission on rolling basis within three weeks of receipt of all credentials. Reply is requested within one month of acceptance. $150 tuition deposit, refundable until May 1. $375 room deposit, refundable until May 1. Freshmen accepted for terms other than fall.
**Special programs:** Admission may be deferred two semesters. Credit and/or placement may be granted through CEEB Advanced Placement exams for scores of 3 or higher. Credit and/or placement may be granted through CLEP general and subject exams. Credit may be granted through military experience. Credit and placement may be granted through challenge exams. Early entrance/early admission program.
**Transfer students:** Transfer students accepted for terms other than fall. In fall 1993, 26% of all new students were transfers into all classes. 133 transfer applications were received, 113 were accepted. Application deadline is rolling for fall; rolling for spring. Minimum 2.5 GPA recommended. Lowest course grade accepted is "C." Maximum number of transferable credits is 65 semester hours from a two-year school and 75 semester hours from a four-year school. At least 50 semester hours must be completed at the college to receive degree.
**Admissions contact:** Patricia M. Buhler, M.B.A., Acting Director of Admissions. 302 998-8814.
**FINANCIAL AID. Available aid:** Pell grants, SEOG, state scholarships and grants, school scholarships, academic merit scholarships, and athletic scholarships. Perkins Loans (NDSL), PLUS, Stafford Loans (GSL), and SLS. AMS, deferred payment plan, and family tuition reduction.
**Financial aid statistics:** 15% of aid is not need-based. In 1993-94, 77% of all undergraduate applicants received aid; 79% of freshman applicants. Average amounts of aid awarded freshmen: Loans, $2,400.
**Supporting data/closing dates:** FAFSA: Priority filing date is February 15. Notification of awards on rolling basis.
**Financial aid contact:** Jane Lysle, Director of Financial Aid. 302 998-8814.

# University of Delaware

**Newark, DE 19716** **302 831-2000**

**1993-94 Costs.** Tuition: $3,550 (state residents), $9,650 (out-of-state). Room & board: $4,030. Fees, books, misc. academic expenses (school's estimate): $963.
**Enrollment.** Undergraduates: 5,821 men, 7,663 women (full-time). Freshman class: 14,446 applicants, 10,516 accepted, 3,252 enrolled. Graduate enrollment: 1,624 men, 1,459 women.
**Test score averages/ranges.** Range of SAT scores of middle 50%: 460-530 verbal, 540-620 math.
**Faculty.** 954 full-time; 43 part-time. 78% of faculty holds doctoral degree. Student/faculty ratio: 17 to 1.
**Selectivity rating.** Competitive.

**PROFILE.** The University of Delaware is a land grant institution. Founded in 1833, it adopted coeducation in 1914. Programs are offered in the Colleges of Agricultural Sciences; Arts and Science; Business and Economics; Education; Engineering; Human Resources; Nursing; and Physical Education, Athletics, and Recreation. Its 1,100-acre campus is located in Newark, 12 miles from Wilmington and 30 miles from Philadelphia.
**Accreditation:** MSACS. Professionally accredited by the Accreditation Board for Engineering and Technology, the American Assembly of Collegiate Schools of Business, the American Dietetic Association, the American Medical Association (CAHEA), the American Physical Therapy Association, the American Psychological Association, the National Association of Schools of Music, the National League for Nursing.
**Religious orientation:** University of Delaware is nonsectarian; no religious requirements.
**Library:** Collections totaling over 2,000,000 volumes, 21,000 periodical subscriptions, and 2,300,000 microform items.
**Special facilities/museums:** Art gallery, ice skating science development center, language lab, center for composite materials, 434-acre experimental farm, human performance lab, on-campus preschool.
**Athletic facilities:** Gymnasiums, weight rooms, field house, ice arenas, swimming pool, basketball, racquetball, squash, tennis, and volleyball courts, fitness trails, ropes course, track, baseball, field hockey, football, intramural, lacrosse, soccer, and softball fields.
**STUDENT BODY. Undergraduate profile:** 42% are state residents; 18% are transfers. 2% Asian-American, 5% Black, 1% Hispanic, 91% White, 1% Other. Average age of undergraduates is 21.
**Freshman profile:** 99% of accepted applicants took SAT; 1% took ACT. 77% of freshmen come from public schools.
**Undergraduate achievement:** 86% of fall 1992 freshmen returned for fall 1993 term. 50% of entering class graduated. 20% of students who completed a degree program went on to graduate study within one year.
**Foreign students:** 148 students are from out of the country. Countries represented include China, France, Germany, India, Korea, and Taiwan; 85 in all.
**PROGRAMS OF STUDY. Degrees:** B.A., B.Chem.Eng., B.Elec.Eng., B.F.A., B.Mech. Eng., B.Mus., B.Mus.Ed., B.S.
**Majors:** Accounting, Agricultural Business Management, Agricultural Economics, Agricultural Education, Agricultural Engineering Technology, Animal Science, Anthropology, Anthropology Education, Apparel Design, Applied Music, Applied Nutrition, Art, Art Conservation, Art History, Athletic Training, Biochemistry, Biological Sciences, Biological Sciences/Biotechnology Interest, Biological Sciences Education, Business Administration, Chemical Engineering, Chemistry, Chemistry Education, Civil Engineering, Communication Interest, Comparative Literature, Computer/Information Sciences, Consumer Economics, Criminal Justice, Dietetics, Early Childhood Development/Education, Earth Science Education, Economics, Economics Education, Educational Studies, Electrical Engineering, Elementary Teacher Education, English, English Education, Entomology, Entomology/Plant Pathology, Environmental Science, Environmental Soil Science, Family/Community Services, Finance, Food Science, French, French Education, General Agriculture, Geography, Geography Education, Geology, Geophysics, German, German Education, History, History Education, Hotel/Restaurant/Institutional Management, Human Development/Family Processes, Interdisciplinary Studies, International Relations, Languages, Latin, Latin American Studies, Latin Education, Mathematics, Mathematics Education, Mechanical Engineering, Medical Technology Interest, Music, Music Education, Music Theory/Composition, Nursing, Nutritional Sciences, Philosophy, Physical Education/Health Education, Physical Education Studies, Physics, Physics Education, Plant Sciences, Political Science, Political Science Education, Psychology, Psychology Education, Recreation/Park Administration, Russian, Russian Education, Sociology, Sociology Education, Spanish, Spanish Education, Special Education, Statistics, Textile Science, Textiles/Clothing Merchandising, Theatre Production, Women's Studies.
**Distribution of degrees:** The majors with the highest enrollment are English, psychology, and elementary teacher education.
**Requirements:** General education requirement.
**Academic regulations:** Minimum 2.0 GPA required for graduation.
**Special:** Minors offered in many majors and in black American, East Asian, educational, Irish, jazz, Jewish, legal, medical, medieval, music, religious, and women's studies, classics, cognitive science, international business, Italian, linguistics, medical humanities, management information systems/decision support systems, nutrition, public administration, science/technology/society, and theatre. Many majors include options. Dean's Scholar Program. Humanities Semester. Liberal Studies Program. Undergraduate Research Program. Self-designed majors. Double majors. Dual degrees. Independent study. Accelerated study. Pass/fail grading option. Internships. Cooperative education programs. Graduate school at which undergraduates may take graduate-level courses. Preprofessional programs in law, medicine, veterinary science, and dentistry. 2-2 engineering technology program with Delaware Tech. 5-1/2-year B.S. engineering/M.B.A. program for highly qualified students. Washington Semester. Member of National Student Exchange (NSE). Teacher certification in early childhood, elementary, secondary, special

education, and bilingual/bicultural education. Certification in specific subject areas. Study abroad in Austria, China, Costa Rica, England, France, Germany, Greece, Israel, Italy, Mexico, Russia, Scotland, Spain, and Switzerland. ROTC and AFROTC.
**Honors:** Phi Beta Kappa. Honors program. Honor societies.
**Academic Assistance:** Remedial reading, writing, math, and study skills. Nonremedial tutoring.

**STUDENT LIFE. Housing:** All freshmen must live on campus unless living with parent or guardian. Coed and women's dorms. Sorority and fraternity housing. School-owned/operated apartments. On-campus married-student housing. 53% of students live in college housing.
**Social atmosphere:** The student newspaper reports, "There is a heavy emphasis on local nightlife at bars, clubs, and off-campus parties," as well as many lectures and cultural events on campus. Popular events include Spring Fling, which is a day of outdoor music and games, and Delaware football games "with accompanying tailgate parties before and after the games." Favorite off-campus nightspots include the Stone Balloon, Deer Park, and the Down Under.
**Services and counseling/handicapped student services:** Placement services. Health service. Women's center. Counseling services for minority, military, veteran, and older students. Birth control, personal, and psychological counseling. Career and academic guidance services. Religious counseling. Physically disabled student services. Learning disabled services. Notetaking services. Tape recorders. Tutors. Reader services for the blind.
**Campus organizations:** Undergraduate student government. Student newspaper (Review, published twice/week). Yearbook. Radio station. Theatre groups, gospel ensemble, College Democrats and Republicans, Young Libertarians, Toastmasters Club, juggling group, Wildlife Conservation Club, Amnesty International, Student Programming Association, Campus Coalition for Human Rights, Student Environmental Action Coalition, numerous other athletic, departmental, service, and special-interest groups, 150 organizations in all. 24 fraternities, 10 chapter houses; 14 sororities, five chapter houses. 10% of men join a fraternity. 14% of women join a sorority.
**Religious organizations:** Baptist Campus Ministry, Campus Crusade for Christ, Chabad House, Christians in Action, Episcopal Campus Ministry, Hillel, Intervarsity Christian Fellowship, Jewish Student Union, Latter-Day Saints Student Association, Lutheran Student Association, Muslim Student Association, Phoenix Community, Thomas More Oratory, Wesley Foundation Ministry, Word of Life Campus Ministry.
**Minority/foreign student organizations:** Black Student Union, Black Greek Alliance, HOLA, Minorities in Agriculture, Natural Resources, and Related Sciences, NAACP, Society of Black Engineers. Arab-American Student Association, Chinese Student Association, Cosmopolitan Club, Delaware Israel Public Affairs Committee, Indian Student Association, People United Against Apartheid, Russian Circle, Turkish-American Student Association.

**ATHLETICS. Physical education requirements:** None.
**Intercollegiate competition:** 12% of students participate. Baseball (M), basketball (M,W), cross-country (M,W), diving (M,W), field hockey (W), football (M), golf (M), lacrosse (M,W), soccer (M,W), softball (W), swimming (M,W), tennis (M,W), track and field (indoor) (M,W), track and field (outdoor) (M,W), volleyball (W). Member of Colonial Athletic Association for women's lacrosse, ECAC, NCAA Division I, NCAA Division I-AA for football, North Atlantic Conference, Yankee Conference for football.
**Intramural and club sports:** 60% of students participate. Intramural basketball, bowling, field hockey, flag football, golf, indoor lacrosse, indoor soccer, inner-tube water polo, racquetball, road racing, soccer, softball, street hockey, tennis, ultimate frisbee, volleyball, walleyball. Men's club cheerleading, ice hockey, martial arts, Nordic skiing, rugby, sailing. Women's club crew, martial arts, Nordic skiing, rugby, sailing.

**ADMISSIONS. Academic basis for candidate selection** (in order of priority): Secondary school record, standardized test scores, class rank, school's recommendation, essay.
**Nonacademic basis for candidate selection:** Particular talent or ability, geographical distribution, and alumni/ae relationship are considered.
**Requirements:** Graduation from secondary school is required; GED is accepted. 16 units and the following program of study are required: 4 units of English, 2 units of math, 2 units of science including 1 unit of lab, 2 units of foreign language, 1 unit of social studies, 2 units of history, 3 units of academic electives. SAT is required; ACT may be substituted. ACH recommended. Campus visit recommended. No off-campus interviews.
**Procedure:** Take SAT or ACT by November of 12th year. Suggest filing application by January 1. Application deadline is March 1. Notification of admission on rolling basis. Reply is required by May 1. $200 nonrefundable tuition deposit. Half of room deposit is refundable until June 15. Freshmen accepted for terms other than fall.
**Special programs:** Admission may be deferred one semester. Credit may be granted through CEEB Advanced Placement for scores of 3 or higher. Credit may be granted through challenge exams. Early decision program. Deadline for applying for early decision is November 15. Early entrance/early admission program. Concurrent enrollment program.
**Transfer students:** Transfer students accepted for terms other than fall. In fall 1993, 18% of all new students were transfers into all classes. 1,760 transfer applications were received, 1,147 were accepted. Application deadline is March 1 for fall; November 15 for spring. Minimum 2.5 GPA required. Lowest course grade accepted is "C." At least 30 semester hours must be completed at the university to receive degree.
**Admissions contact:** N. Bruce Walker, Ed.D., Associate Provost, Admissions and Financial Aid. 302 831-8123, FAX 302 831-6905.

**FINANCIAL AID. Available aid:** Pell grants, SEOG, state scholarships and grants, school scholarships and grants, private scholarships and grants, ROTC scholarships, academic merit scholarships, and athletic scholarships. Perkins Loans (NDSL), PLUS, Stafford Loans (GSL), NSL, and SLS. Deferred payment plan and family tuition reduction.
**Financial aid statistics:** In 1993-94, 90% of all undergraduate applicants received aid; 98% of freshman applicants. Average amounts of aid awarded freshmen: Scholarships and grants, $4,000; loans, $2,625.
**Supporting data/closing dates:** FAFSA: Priority filing date is February 15; deadline is May 1. Notification of awards begins April 1.
**Financial aid contact:** Johnie Burton, M.A., Director, Financial Aid. 302 831-8761.

**STUDENT EMPLOYMENT.** College Work/Study Program. Institutional employment. 15% of full-time undergraduates work on campus during school year. Students may expect to earn an average of $1,000 during school year. Off-campus part-time employment opportunities rated "fair."

**COMPUTER FACILITIES.** 605 IBM/IBM-compatible, Macintosh/Apple, and RISC-/UNIX-based microcomputers; 460 are networked. Students may access IBM, SUN minicomputer/mainframe systems, BITNET, Internet. Residence halls may be equipped with networked microcomputers, modems. Client/LAN operating systems include Apple/Macintosh, DOS, UNIX/XENIX/AIX, X-windows, LocalTalk/AppleTalk, Novell. Computer languages and software packages include Ada, APL, Assembler, BASIC, BMDP, C, C++, COBOL, FORTRAN, IMSL, LINDO, LISP, Maple, MINITAB, Modula 2, NAG, NCAR Graphics, PV-Wave, Pascal, SAS, Scheme, SDRC Ideas, SPlus, SPSS-X, SYSTAT, TEX, WORDGAMS, WordPerfect. Computer facilities are available to all students.
**Fees:** None.
**Hours:** 24 hours for mainframes; limited hours for microcomputers.

**GRADUATE CAREER DATA.** Graduate school percentages: 4% enter law school. 1% enter medical school. 3% enter graduate business programs. Highest graduate school enrollments: U of Delaware, U of Maryland, Ohio St U, Rutgers U, Temple U, Villanova U, Widener U School of Law. Companies and businesses that hire graduates: AT&T, Big Six accounting firms, Chase Manhattan, DuPont, MBNA-America, Price-Waterhouse, Wilmington Savings Fund Society.

**PROMINENT ALUMNI/AE.** Joseph R. Biden, Jr., U.S. senator; Thomas R. Carper, U.S. congressman; Bryan Gordan, Academy Award-winning director/writer; G. Dallas Green, manager, New York Mets; Dr. Mary Patterson McPherson, president, Bryn Mawr Coll; Dr. Daniel Nathans, Nobel laureate in medicine; Thomas Turcol, Pulitzer Prize-winning journalist; Rich Gannon, quarterback, Washington Redskins.

## Wesley College

**Dover, DE 19901 — 302 736-2300**

**1994-95 Costs.** Tuition: $9,890. Room: $2,450. Board: $2,224. Fees, books, misc. academic expenses (school's estimate): $785.
**Enrollment.** Undergraduates: 412 men, 460 women (full-time). Freshman class: 839 applicants, 807 accepted, 350 enrolled. Graduate enrollment: 632 men, 688 women.
**Test score averages/ranges.** Average SAT scores: 439 verbal, 448 math.
**Faculty.** 50 full-time; 48 part-time. 50% of faculty holds doctoral degree. Student/faculty ratio: 16 to 1.
**Selectivity rating.** Less competitive.

**PROFILE.** Wesley is a church-affiliated college. Founded as an academy in 1873, it became a two-year college in 1922 and a four-year college in 1978. Its 12-acre campus is located in Dover, 76 miles southeast of Philadelphia.

**Accreditation:** MSACS. Professionally accredited by the American Bar Association, the National League for Nursing.
**Religious orientation:** Wesley College is affiliated with the United Methodist Church; one semester of religion required.
**Library:** Collections totaling over 65,000 volumes.
**Athletic facilities:** Gymnasium, swimming pool, baseball, field hockey, fitness center, football, intramural, lacrosse, soccer, and softball fields, weight room, basketball, tennis, and volleyball courts, golf course.

**STUDENT BODY. Undergraduate profile:** 22% are state residents; 24% are transfers. 2% Asian-American, 12% Black, 7% Hispanic, 1% Native American, 75% White, 3% Other. Average age of undergraduates is 20.
**Freshman profile:** 95% of accepted applicants took SAT; 5% took ACT. 85% of freshmen come from public schools.
**Undergraduate achievement:** 68% of fall 1992 freshmen returned for fall 1993 term. 48% of entering class graduated.
**Foreign students:** 20 students are from out of the country. Countries represented include the Bahamas, the Cayman Islands, Germany, Japan, and Saudi Arabia; 15 in all.

**PROGRAMS OF STUDY. Degrees:** B.A., B.S.
**Majors:** Accounting, Applied Communications, Biology, Computer Information Systems, Computer Science, Economics, English, Environmental Sciences, Fashion Marketing, Management, Marketing, Medical Technology, Physical Education, Political Science/Government, Psychology.
**Distribution of degrees:** The majors with the highest enrollment are management and marketing.
**Requirements:** General education requirement.
**Academic regulations:** Minimum 2.00 GPA required for graduation.
**Special:** Courses offered in drama, geography, health and sociology, modern languages, nursing, paralegal studies, philosophy, physical science, religion, and speech. Associate's degrees offered. Independent study. Internships. Preprofessional programs in law, medicine, and veterinary science. 2-2 fashion marketing programs. Exchange program with Centre Coll. Teacher certification in elementary and secondary education. Certification in specific subject areas. Study abroad in England, France, Spain, and Wales.
**Academic Assistance:** Remedial reading, writing, math, and study skills.

**ADMISSIONS. Academic basis for candidate selection** (in order of priority): Secondary school record, class rank, standardized test scores, school's recommendation.
**Nonacademic basis for candidate selection:** Character and personality, extracurricular participation, and particular talent or ability are important.
**Requirements:** Graduation from secondary school is required; GED is accepted. 18 units and the following program of study are recommended: 4 units of English, 3 units of math, 2 units of science, 2 units of foreign language, 3 units of social studies, 4 units of history, 5 units of electives. SAT is required; ACT may be substituted. Campus visit and interview recommended. No off-campus interviews.

**Procedure:** Take SAT or ACT by March of 12th year. Visit college for interview by April of 12th year. Suggest filing application by March; no deadline. Notification of admission on rolling basis. Reply is required within three weeks of acceptance. $150 nonrefundable tuition deposit. Freshmen accepted for terms other than fall.
**Special programs:** Admission may be deferred one year. Credit and/or placement may be granted through CEEB Advanced Placement exams for scores of 3 or higher. Credit and/or placement may be granted through CLEP general and subject exams. Early decision program. In fall 1993, 100 applied for early decision and 95 were accepted. Deadline for applying for early decision is November 1. Early entrance/early admission program. Concurrent enrollment program.
**Transfer students:** Transfer students accepted for terms other than fall. In fall 1993, 24% of all new students were transfers into all classes. 209 transfer applications were received, 150 were accepted. Minimum 2.0 GPA required. Lowest course grade accepted is "C."
**Admissions contact:** Joseph R. Slights, Jr., M.Ed., Director of Admissions. 302 736-2400.

**FINANCIAL AID. Available aid:** Pell grants, SEOG, state scholarships and grants, school scholarships and grants, private scholarships and grants, academic merit scholarships, and aid for undergraduate foreign students. Perkins Loans (NDSL), Stafford Loans (GSL), state loans, and SLS. AMS.
**Financial aid statistics:** 15% of aid is not need-based. In 1993-94, 68% of all undergraduate applicants received aid; 64% of freshman applicants. Average amounts of aid awarded freshmen: Scholarships and grants, $2,000.
**Supporting data/closing dates:** FAFSA/FAF/FFS: Priority filing date is April 1. State aid form: Priority filing date is March 1. Income tax forms: Priority filing date is April 1. Notification of awards begins March 1.
**Financial aid contact:** Marilyn Ambrose, M.A., Director of Financial Aid. 302 736-2338.

## Wilmington College

**New Castle, DE 19720** 302 328-9401

**1993-94 Costs.** Tuition: $4,160. Housing: None. Fees, books, misc. academic expenses (school's estimate): $625.
**Enrollment.** Undergraduates: 221 men, 362 women (full-time). Graduate enrollment: 215 men, 269 women.
**Test score averages/ranges.** N/A.
**Faculty.** 28 full-time; 300 part-time. 40% of faculty holds doctoral degree. Student/faculty ratio: 22 to 1.
**Selectivity rating.** N/A.

**PROFILE.** Wilmington, founded in 1967, is a private college. Its 15-acre main campus is located in New Castle, six miles south of Wilmington.

**Accreditation:** MSACS. Professionally accredited by the National League for Nursing.
**Religious orientation:** Wilmington College is nonsectarian; no religious requirements.
**Library:** Collections totaling over 76,827 volumes, 332 periodical subscriptions, and 6,300 microform items.
**Athletic facilities:** Gymnasium, weight room.
**STUDENT BODY. Undergraduate profile:** 97% are state residents; 62% are transfers. 1% Asian-American, 16% Black, 1% Hispanic, 82% White. Average age of undergraduates is 30.
**Undergraduate achievement:** 80% of fall 1992 freshmen returned for fall 1993 term. 68% of entering class graduated. 35% of students who completed a degree program went on to graduate study within 10 years.
**Foreign students:** 16 students are from out of the country. Countries represented include African countries, India, and Taiwan; five in all.

**PROGRAMS OF STUDY. Degrees:** B.A., B.S., B.S.Nurs.
**Majors:** Accounting, Aviation Management, Banking/Finance, Behavioral Science, Business Management, Communication Arts, Criminal Justice, Elementary Education, Human Resource Management, Nursing.
**Distribution of degrees:** The majors with the highest enrollment are business management, nursing, and human resources management; communications arts has the lowest.
**Requirements:** General education requirement.
**Academic regulations:** Freshmen must maintain minimum 1.60 GPA; sophomores, 1.80 GPA; juniors, 1.80 GPA; seniors, 2.00 GPA.
**Special:** Minors offered in business and management information systems. Associate's degrees offered. Independent study. Internships. Graduate school at which undergraduates may take graduate-level courses. Teacher certification in early childhood and elementary education. ROTC and AFROTC at U of Delaware.
**Academic Assistance:** Remedial reading, writing, math, and study skills. Nonremedial tutoring.

**ADMISSIONS. Academic basis for candidate selection** (in order of priority): Secondary school record, school's recommendation, class rank, standardized test scores.
**Nonacademic basis for candidate selection:** Character and personality are emphasized.
**Requirements:** Graduation from secondary school is required; GED is accepted. No specific distribution of secondary school units required. R.N. required of nursing program applicants. SAT is recommended; ACT may be substituted. Admissions interview recommended. Off-campus interviews available with an admissions representative.
**Procedure:** Take SAT or ACT by spring of 12th year. Suggest filing application by June. Application deadline is August 1. Notification of admission on rolling basis. Reply is required by September 6. Freshmen accepted for terms other than fall.
**Special programs:** Admission may be deferred. Credit may be granted through CEEB Advanced Placement. Credit and/or placement may be granted through CLEP general and subject exams. Credit and placement may be granted through ACT PEP exams.
**Transfer students:** Transfer students accepted for terms other than fall. In fall 1993, 62% of all new students were transfers into all classes. 691 transfer applications were received, 682 were accepted. Application deadline is August 1 for fall; December 1 for spring. Minimum 2.0 GPA recommended. Lowest course grade accepted is "C." Maximum number of transferable credits is 75 semester hours. At least 45 semester hours must be completed at the college to receive degree.
**Admissions contact:** Michael Lee, Dean of Admissions and Financial Aid. 302 328-9407.

**FINANCIAL AID. Available aid:** Pell grants, SEOG, state grants, school scholarships, private scholarships, academic merit scholarships, and athletic scholarships. PLUS, Stafford Loans (GSL), state loans, and SLS. Deferred payment plan.
**Financial aid statistics:** 20% of aid is not need-based. In 1993-94, 85% of all undergraduate applicants received aid; 80% of freshman applicants. Average amounts of aid awarded freshmen: Scholarships and grants, $2,400; loans, $2,625.
**Supporting data/closing dates:** FAFSA/FAF/FFS: Priority filing date is April 30. Income tax forms: Accepted on rolling basis. Notification of awards on rolling basis.
**Financial aid contact:** J.L. Iocono, Director of Financial Aid. 302 329-9437.

# District of Columbia

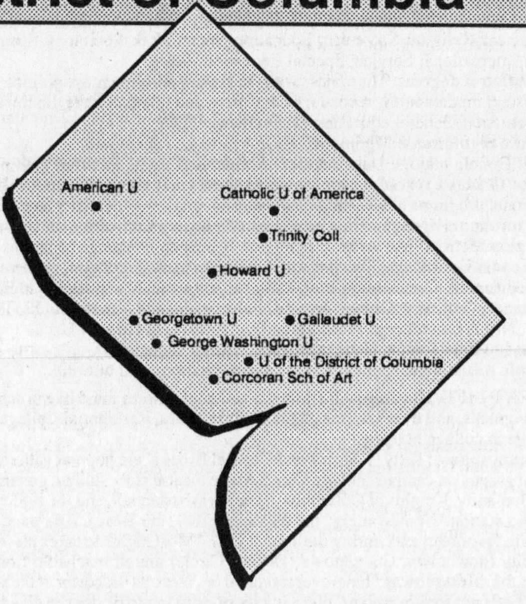


## The American University

**Washington, DC 20016-8001** **202 885-1000**

**1994-95 Costs.** Tuition: $15,934. Room: $3,960. Board: $2,440. Fees, books, misc. academic expenses (school's estimate): $660.
**Enrollment.** Undergraduates: 1,835 men, 2,642 women (full-time). Freshman class: 4,597 applicants, 3,581 accepted, 1,094 enrolled. Graduate enrollment: 1,673 men, 2,022 women.
**Test score averages/ranges.** Average SAT scores: 550 verbal, 582 math. Range of SAT scores of middle 50%: 1030-1210 combined. Average ACT scores: 26 composite. Range of ACT scores of middle 50%: 23-28 composite.
**Faculty.** 570 full-time; 765 part-time. 92% of faculty holds doctoral degree. Student/faculty ratio: 14 to 1.
**Selectivity rating.** More competitive.

**PROFILE.** The American University, founded in 1891, is a church-affiliated, comprehensive institution. Programs are offered through the College of Arts and Sciences; the Schools of Communication, Education, International Affairs, and Public Affairs; the Kogod College of Business Administration; and the Washington College of Law. The 78-acre main campus is located in northwest Washington.

**Accreditation:** MSACS. Professionally accredited by the Accrediting Council on Education in Journalism and Mass Communication, the American Assembly of Collegiate Schools of Business, the American Psychological Association, the National Association of Schools of Music, the National Council for Accreditation of Teacher Education.
**Religious orientation:** The American University is affiliated with the Methodist Church; no religious requirements.
**Library:** Collections totaling over 584,000 volumes, 3,500 periodical subscriptions, and 690,000 microform items.
**Special facilities/museums:** Radio and TV facilities.
**Athletic facilities:** Basketball, racquetball, squash, and tennis courts, indoor track, weight room, swimming pools, field hockey, and soccer fields, arena.

**STUDENT BODY. Undergraduate profile:** 10% are state residents; 26% are transfers. 5% Asian-American, 7% Black, 4% Hispanic, 1% Native American, 74% White, 9% Other.
**Freshman profile:** 3% of freshmen who took SAT scored 700 or over on verbal, 8% scored 700 or over on math; 28% scored 600 or over on verbal, 46% scored 600 or over on math; 77% scored 500 or over on verbal, 89% scored 500 or over on math; 100% scored 400 or over on verbal, 100% scored 400 or over on math. 87% of accepted applicants took SAT. 60% of freshmen come from public schools.
**Undergraduate achievement:** 86% of fall 1992 freshmen returned for fall 1993 term. 62% of entering class graduated. 39% of students who completed a degree program immediately went on to graduate study.
**Foreign students:** 420 students are from out of the country. Countries represented include Germany, Japan, Korea, Saudi Arabia, Turkey and the United Kingdom; 125 in all.

**PROGRAMS OF STUDY. Degrees:** B.A., B.F.A., B.S.
**Majors:** Accounting, American Studies, Anthropology, Applied Mathematics, Art History, Audio Technology, Biology, Broadcast Journalism, Business Management, Chemistry, Communication/Legal Institutions/Economics/Government, Computer Information Systems, Computer Science, Design, Economic Theory, Economics, Elementary Education, Environmental Studies, Finance, Fine Arts, Foreign Language/Communication Media, French, French/West European Studies, German, German/West European Studies, History, Interdisciplinary Studies, International Business, International Communication, International Comparative/Regional Studies, International Development, International Economic Policy, International Politics, International Studies, Jewish Studies, Justice, Language/Area Studies, Law/Society, Liberal Studies, Literature, Literature/Cinema Studies, Marketing, Mathematics, Music, Music/Technology, Music Theater, Peace Studies/Conflict Resolution, Philosophy, Physics, Political Science, Print Journalism, Psychology, Public Communication, Real Estate/Urban Development, Religion, Russian, Russian/East European Studies, Secondary Education Certification, Sociology, Spanish, Spanish/Latin American Area Studies, Statistics, Studio Art, Theatre, U.S. Foreign Policy, Visual Media.
**Distribution of degrees:** The majors with the highest enrollment are communication, international studies, and finance; Jewish studies, music, German, and religion have the lowest.
**Requirements:** General education requirement.
**Academic regulations:** Minimum 2.0 GPA required for graduation.
**Special:** Minors offered in most majors. Students in arts and sciences may elect courses in other undergraduate divisions. Associate's degrees offered. Double majors. Independent study. Pass/fail grading option. Internships. Cooperative education programs. Graduate school at which undergraduates may take graduate-level courses. Preprofessional programs in law, medicine, veterinary science, and dentistry. 3-2 engineering programs with U of Maryland and Washington U. Member of Consortium of Universities of the Washington Metropolitan Area. Member of Marine Science Consortium; off-campus study possible at Wallops Island, Va. Washington Semester. Summer Public Affairs Lab. Teacher certification in early childhood, elementary, secondary, and bilingual/bicultural education. Certification in specific subject areas. Study abroad in Argentina, Austria, Belgium, Chile, China, the Czech Republic, Denmark, England, Hungary, Italy, Poland, Russia, and Slovakia. ROTC at Georgetown U. NROTC at George Washington U. AFROTC at Howard U.
**Honors:** Honors program. Honor societies.
**Academic Assistance:** Remedial reading, writing, and math. Nonremedial tutoring.

**STUDENT LIFE. Housing:** Coed dorms. School-owned/operated apartments. Honors housing. Living and learning centers. 60% of students live in college housing.
**Social atmosphere:** On campus, students gather at the Tavern in the Mary Gradon Center and on the Quad when the sun is shining. Off campus, students gather at Quigley's and at Maggie's, both local restaurant/bars. Greeks, basketball players, the campus newspaper, and the campus radio station are influential groups. The most popular events of the year are the Student Union Board's spring and fall concerts, featuring popular rock groups; Artemas Ward Weekend, with carnival rides and food on the Quad; and International Week, with international music, food, and dances on the Quad. The student newspaper reports, "The campus has a very mixed atmosphere because there are people from all over the country and the world on campus. AU is a great place to be because the school is in a safe suburban neighborhood, and D.C. is there for everything from museums to restaurants to clubs to internships."
**Services and counseling/handicapped student services:** Placement services. Health service. Day care. Counseling services for minority and older students. Birth control, personal, and psychological counseling. Career and academic guidance services. Religious counseling. Physically disabled student services. Learning disabled program/services. Notetaking services. Tape recorders. Tutors. Reader services for the blind.
**Campus organizations:** Undergraduate student government. Student newspaper (Eagle, published once/week). Literary magazine. Yearbook. Radio and TV stations. Chorus, orchestra, music club, theatre group, political groups, business organizations, academic clubs, professional fraternities, service fraternities, departmental groups, 119 organizations in all. Seven fraternities, no chapter houses; six sororities, no chapter houses. 25% of men join a fraternity. 19% of women join a sorority.
**Religious organizations:** Protestant Student Organization, Muslim Student Association, Catholic Student Association, Christian Network, Hillel, Christian Fellowship, Korean Christian Fellowship, Buddhist groups.
**Minority/foreign student organizations:** Black Student Alliance, Japan-American Society, Fieri. Global Friendship, African, Arab, Caribbean, Chinese, Egyptian, Greek, Indian, Korean, and Mexican groups.

**ATHLETICS. Physical education requirements:** None.
**Intercollegiate competition:** 5% of students participate. Basketball (M,W), cheerleading (M,W), cross-country (M,W), diving (M,W), field hockey (W), golf (M), lacrosse (W), soccer (M,W), swimming (M,W), tennis (M,W), volleyball (W), wrestling (M). Member of Colonial Athletic Association, ECAC, NCAA Division I.
**Intramural and club sports:** 40% of students participate. Intramural basketball, floor hockey, football, racquetball, soccer, softball, squash, swimming, tennis, volleyball, wrestling. Men's club crew, rugby, track. Women's club crew, track.

**ADMISSIONS. Academic basis for candidate selection** (in order of priority): Secondary school record, class rank, standardized test scores, school's recommendation, essay.
**Nonacademic basis for candidate selection:** Extracurricular participation is emphasized. Character and personality, particular talent or ability, and alumni/ae relationship are important. Geographical distribution is considered.
**Requirements:** Graduation from secondary school is required; GED is accepted. 15 units and the following program of study are required: 4 units of English, 3 units of math, 2 units of foreign language. Portfolio required of art program applicants. Special admissions program for local and adult applicants not normally admissible. SAT is required; ACT may be substituted. ACH recommended. Campus visit recommended. Off-campus interviews available with admissions and alumni representatives.
**Procedure:** Take SAT or ACT by November of 12th year. Take ACH by November of 12th year. Application deadline is February 1. Notification of admission by April 1. Reply is required by May 1. $200 nonrefundable tuition deposit. Freshmen accepted for terms other than fall.
**Special programs:** Admission may be deferred one year. Credit and/or placement may be granted through CEEB Advanced Placement exams for scores of 3 or higher. Credit may be granted through CLEP general exams, military and life experience. Credit and/or placement may be granted through CLEP subject exams. Early decision program. In fall 1993, 280 applied for early decision and 235 were accepted. Deadline for applying for early decision is November 15. Early entrance/early admission program.
**Transfer students:** Transfer students accepted for terms other than fall. In fall 1993, 26% of all new students were transfers into all classes. 820 transfer applications were received, 640 were accepted. Application deadline is July 1 for fall; November 1 for spring. Minimum 2.5 GPA required. Lowest course grade accepted is "C." Maximum number of

transferable credits is 60 semester hours from a two-year school and 75 semester hours from a four-year school.
**Admissions contact:** Marcelle Heerschap, M.A., Director of Admissions. 202 885-6000.
**FINANCIAL AID. Available aid:** Pell grants, SEOG, state scholarships and grants, school scholarships and grants, private scholarships and grants, academic merit scholarships, and athletic scholarships. Perkins Loans (NDSL), PLUS, Stafford Loans (GSL), and SLS. Deferred payment plan.
**Financial aid statistics:** 65% of aid is not need-based. In 1993-94, 90% of all undergraduate applicants received aid; 90% of freshman applicants. Average amounts of aid awarded freshmen: Scholarships and grants, $4,800; loans, $2,800.
**Supporting data/closing dates:** FAFSA/FAF: Priority filing date is March 1. Notification of awards begins March 15.
**Financial aid contact:** Robin Robinson, M.A., Director of Financial Aid. 202 885-6100.
**STUDENT EMPLOYMENT.** College Work/Study Program. Institutional employment. Students may expect to earn an average of $1,500 during school year. Off-campus part-time employment opportunities rated "excellent."
**COMPUTER FACILITIES.** 200 IBM/IBM-compatible and Macintosh/Apple microcomputers; 80 are networked. Students may access AT&T, Hewlett-Packard, IBM, SUN minicomputer/mainframe systems, BITNET, Internet. Client/LAN operating systems include Apple/Macintosh, DOS, OS/2, X-windows, Novell. Computer languages and software packages include Assembly, BASIC, C, COBOL, dBASE, FORTRAN, Lotus 1-2-3, Pascal, PL/1, Quattro Pro, WordPerfect; 36 in all. Computer facilities are available to all students.
**Fees:** None.
**Hours:** 24 hours.
**GRADUATE CAREER DATA.** Graduate school percentages: 28% enter law school.

## The Catholic University of America

**Washington, DC 20064** **202 319-5200**

**1994-95 Costs.** Tuition: $13,712. Room: $3,622. Board: $2,786. Fees, books, misc. academic expenses (school's estimate): $986.
**Enrollment.** Undergraduates: 979 men, 1,180 women (full-time). Freshman class: 1,754 applicants, 1,465 accepted, 515 enrolled. Graduate enrollment: 1,851 men, 1,926 women.
**Test score averages/ranges.** Range of SAT scores of middle 50%: 460-570 verbal, 490-610 math. Average ACT scores: 24 English, 24 math, 25 composite. Range of ACT scores of middle 50%: 21-27 English, 20-27 math.
**Faculty.** 302 full-time; 239 part-time. 95% of faculty holds highest degree in specific field. Student/faculty ratio: 9 to 1.
**Selectivity rating.** Competitive.

**PROFILE.** The Catholic University of America, founded in 1887, is a church-affiliated institution. Programs are offered through the Schools of Arts and Sciences, Engineering and Architecture, Law, Library Information and Science, Music, Nursing, Philosophy, Religious Studies, and Social Service, and the University College. Its 155-acre campus is located in northeast Washington.

**Accreditation:** MSACS. Professionally accredited by the Accreditation Board for Engineering and Technology, the American Psychological Association, the Council on Social Work Education, the National Architecture Accrediting Board, the National Association of Schools of Music, the National Council for Accreditation of Teacher Education, the National League for Nursing.
**Religious orientation:** The Catholic University of America is affiliated with the Roman Catholic Church; four courses of religion/theology required.
**Library:** Collections totaling over 1,300,000 volumes, 8,600 periodical subscriptions, and 1,000,000 microform items.
**Special facilities/museums:** Anthropology and art museums, rare book collection, youth and development building, nuclear reactor, electron microscope, vitreous-state labs.
**Athletic facilities:** Swimming pool, weight room, basketball, racquetball, tennis, and volleyball courts, tracks, baseball, football, soccer, and softball fields.
**STUDENT BODY. Undergraduate profile:** 4% are state residents; 22% are transfers. 3% Asian-American, 7% Black, 5% Hispanic, 85% White. Average age of undergraduates is 20.
**Freshman profile:** 9% of freshmen who took ACT scored 30 or over on English, 12% scored 30 or over on math, 13% scored 30 or over on composite; 53% scored 24 or over on English, 50% scored 24 or over on math, 61% scored 24 or over on composite; 92% scored 18 or over on English, 90% scored 18 or over on math, 98% scored 18 or over on composite; 100% scored 12 or over on English, 100% scored 12 or over on math, 100% scored 12 or over on composite. 96% of accepted applicants took SAT; 18% took ACT. 39% of freshmen come from public schools.
**Undergraduate achievement:** 85% of fall 1992 freshmen returned for fall 1993 term. 65% of entering class graduated. 45% of students who completed a degree program immediately went on to graduate study.
**Foreign students:** 228 students are from out of the country. Countries represented include China, India, Japan, Panama, South Korea, and the Philippines; 73 in all.
**PROGRAMS OF STUDY. Degrees:** B.A., B.Arch., B.Civil Eng., B.Elec.Eng., B.F.A., B.Mech.Eng., B.Mus., B.Phil., B.S.
**Majors:** Accounting, American Studies, Anthropology, Architecture, Art, Art History, Biochemistry, Biology, Biomedical Engineering, Business Administration, Chemical Physics, Chemistry, Civil Engineering, Classics, Communications, Computer Science, Construction, Data Processing, Drama, Early Childhood Education, Economics, Education, Electrical Engineering, Elementary Education, Elementary Music Education, Elementary Special Education, English, Financial Management, Foreign Languages, French, General Studies, German, Greek, History, Human Resource Management, Interdisciplinary Studies, Latin, Mathematics, Mechanical Engineering, Medical Technology, Medieval Studies, Music, Music Education, Music History/Literature, Music Theatre, Nursing, Orchestral Instruments, Organ, Peace Studies, Philosophy, Philosophy/Honors, Philosophy/Pre-Law, Physics, Piano, Politics, Psychology, Public Administration, Quantitative Management, Religion, Secondary Education, Social Work, Sociology, Spanish, Spanish/Foreign/International Service, Special Education, Voice.
**Distribution of degrees:** The majors with the highest enrollment are politics, architecture, and nursing; mathematics, secondary education, and German have the lowest.
**Requirements:** General education requirement.
**Academic regulations:** Minimum 2.0 GPA must be maintained.
**Special:** Double majors. Dual degrees. Accelerated study. Pass/fail grading option. Internships. Graduate school at which undergraduates may take graduate-level courses. Preprofessional programs in law, medicine, veterinary science, dentistry, and optometry. 3-2 architecture and civil engineering programs. Member of Consortium of Universities of the Washington Metropolitan Area. Washington Semester. Exchange programs with Depaul U and Loyola U, Chicago. Teacher certification in early childhood, elementary, and secondary education. Certification in specific subject areas. Study abroad in Belgium, England, France, Germany, Greece, Ireland, Italy, Spain, and Venezuela. ROTC at Georgetown U. NROTC at George Washington U. AFROTC at Howard U.
**Honors:** Phi Beta Kappa. Honors program. Honor societies.
**Academic Assistance:** Remedial study skills. Nonremedial tutoring.

**STUDENT LIFE. Housing:** All freshmen and sophomores must live in school housing. Coed, women's, and men's dorms. "Quiet" dormitories, Residential College. 51% of students live in college housing.
**Social atmosphere:** Kitty O'Shea's and Colonel Brooks' are popular gathering-spots. Influential groups on campus include Center Stage theatre club, student government, Habitat for Humanity, Knights of Columbus, intramural basketball, and the student newspaper and radio station. Homecoming, the Mistletoe Ball, the Beaux Arts dance, and rugby games are favorite events during the school year. "Most nightlife takes place off campus, as the city (downtown, Georgetown, Dupont Circle) are all reachable from the Metro, which is the safest subway I have ever travelled on," reports the editor of the student newspaper. "Let's not fool ourselves, there is a lot of drinking to be done at CU, but you don't have to participate."
**Services and counseling/handicapped student services:** Placement services. Health service. Day care. Counseling services for minority, military, veteran, and older students. Personal and psychological counseling. Career and academic guidance services. Religious counseling. Physically disabled student services. Learning disabled services. Notetaking services. Tape recorders. Tutors. Reader services for the blind.
**Campus organizations:** Undergraduate student government. Student newspaper (Tower, published once/week). Literary magazine. Yearbook. Radio station. Center Stage Dance Theatre Company, Dance Theatre, Eccentric Theatre Company, Habitat for Humanity, Appalachia Club, 120 organizations in all. One fraternity, no chapter house; one sorority, no chapter house. 1% of men join a fraternity. 1% of women join a sorority.
**Religious organizations:** Back Door Club, Shenandoah Club, The House, CUA Praise, Caldwell Chapel Community Organization, Communion and Liberation, Fools for Jesus, Women in Theology.
**Minority/foreign student organizations:** Asian/Pacific American Law Student Association, Black Law Student Association, Black Organization of Students at CUA, CUA Hispanic Association, Native American Law Student Association. International Student Association, Idente Youth, International Law Society, European Club, Filipino Organization of CUA Students, Gaelic Society, Indian Student Association, Lebanese Cultural Club, Muslim Student Association, Republic of China Student Association, Vietnamese Student Association.

**ATHLETICS. Physical education requirements:** None.
**Intercollegiate competition:** 25% of students participate. Baseball (M), basketball (M,W), cheerleading (M,W), cross-country (M,W), field hockey (W), football (M), soccer (M,W), softball (W), swimming (M,W), tennis (M,W), track (indoor) (M,W), track (outdoor) (M,W), track and field (indoor) (M,W), track and field (outdoor) (M,W), volleyball (W). Member of Capitol Athletic Conference, ECAC, NCAA Division III, South Region Conference.
**Intramural and club sports:** 60% of students participate. Intramural basketball, football, free throw, homerun contest, indoor soccer, indoor track, inner-tube water polo, racquetball, running, soccer, softball, superstars, tennis, volleyball, weight lifting, Wiffle ball. Men's club crew, lacrosse, rugby. Women's club crew.

**ADMISSIONS. Academic basis for candidate selection** (in order of priority): Secondary school record, class rank, school's recommendation, essay, standardized test scores.
**Nonacademic basis for candidate selection:** Character and personality, extracurricular participation, and particular talent or ability are emphasized. Alumni/ae relationship is considered.
**Requirements:** Graduation from secondary school is required; GED is accepted. 17 units and the following program of study are required: 4 units of English, 3 units of math, 3 units of science including 1 unit of lab, 2 units of foreign language, 4 units of social studies, 1 unit of academic electives. Biology, chemistry, language, math, and social science required of nursing program applicants. Audition required of music program applicants. SAT or ACT is required. ACH recommended. Campus visit recommended. Off-campus interviews available with an alumni representative. No off-campus interviews.
**Procedure:** Take SAT or ACT by February of 12th year. Application deadline is February 15. Acceptance notification from March 15 to April 15. Reply is required by May 1. $200 nonrefundable tuition deposit. $400 room deposit, refundable if notified in writing by June 1. Freshmen accepted for terms other than fall.
**Special programs:** Admission may be deferred one year. Credit and/or placement may be granted through CEEB Advanced Placement exams for scores of 3 or higher. Credit and placement may be granted through challenge exams. Early decision program. In fall 1993, 170 applied for early decision and 95 were accepted. Deadline for applying for early decision is November 15.
**Transfer students:** Transfer students accepted for terms other than fall. In fall 1993, 22% of all new students were transfers into all classes. 440 transfer applications were received, 320 were accepted. Application deadline is March 1 for fall; November 1 for spring. Minimum 3.0 GPA recommended. Lowest course grade accepted is "C." Maximum number of transferable credits is 60 semester hours from a two-year school and 90 semester hours

from a four-year school. At least 30 semester hours must be completed at the university to receive degree.
**Admissions contact:** David R. Gibson, M.A., Dean of Admissions. 800-673-2772.
**FINANCIAL AID. Available aid:** Pell grants, SEOG, state scholarships and grants, school scholarships and grants, private scholarships and grants, ROTC scholarships, and academic merit scholarships. Minority scholarships. Perkins Loans (NDSL), PLUS, Stafford Loans (GSL), school loans, and private loans. AMS and deferred payment plan.
**Financial aid statistics:** 39% of aid is not need-based. In 1993-94, 92% of all undergraduate applicants received aid; 90% of freshman applicants. Average amounts of aid awarded freshmen: Scholarships and grants, $7,849; loans, $4,961.
**Supporting data/closing dates:** FAFSA/FAF/FFS: Deadline is February 28. School's own aid application: Deadline is February 28. State aid form: Deadline is February 28. Income tax forms: Deadline is February 28. Notification of awards begins April 1.
**Financial aid contact:** Paul Patelunas, M.A., Director of Financial Aid. 202 319-5307.
**STUDENT EMPLOYMENT.** College Work/Study Program. Institutional employment. 35% of full-time undergraduates work on campus during school year. Students may expect to earn an average of $1,000 during school year. Off-campus part-time employment opportunities rated "excellent."
**COMPUTER FACILITIES.** 950 IBM/IBM-compatible and Macintosh/Apple microcomputers; 250 are networked. Students may access Digital, SUN minicomputer/mainframe systems, BITNET, Internet. Residence halls may be equipped with stand-alone microcomputers, networked microcomputers, networked terminals, modems. Client/LAN operating systems include Apple/Macintosh, DOS, UNIX/XENIX/AIX, X-windows, DEC, LocalTalk/AppleTalk, Microsoft. Computer languages and software packages include AutoCAD, BASIC, BMDP, C, COBOL, dBASE IV, ETHNO, ExpertChoice, FORTRAN, Harvard Graphics, MATLAB, MINITAB, Paradox, Pascal, QuattroPro, SAS, SPSS, WordPerfect. Computer facilities are available to all students.
**Fees:** None.
**Hours:** 24 hours.
**GRADUATE CAREER DATA.** Graduate school percentages: 26% enter law school. 9% enter medical school. 3% enter dental school. 10% enter graduate business programs. 37% enter graduate arts and sciences programs. 5% enter theological school/seminary. Highest graduate school enrollments: Catholic U of America, George Washington U, Georgetown U, Johns Hopkins U, U of Maryland. Companies and businesses that hire graduates: Catholic U, NASA, National Institute of Health, U.S. government, World Bank.
**PROMINENT ALUMNI/AE.** Thomas Harkin, U.S. senator, Iowa; Ed McMahon, TV personality; John, Cardinal O'Connor, archbishop, New York; Rear Admiral Julia Plotnick, deputy surgeon general.

## The Corcoran School of Art

**Washington, DC 20006** — **202 628-9484**

**1993-94 Costs.** Tuition: $10,480. Room: $3,500. Fees, books, misc. academic expenses (school's estimate): $1,800.
**Enrollment.** Undergraduates: 107 men, 161 women (full-time). Freshman class: 220 applicants, 132 accepted, 59 enrolled.
**Test score averages/ranges.** Average SAT scores: 450 verbal, 480 math. Range of SAT scores of middle 50%: 350-550 verbal, 360-600 math. Average ACT scores: 19 composite. Range of ACT scores of middle 50%: 16-22 composite.
**Faculty.** 45 full-time; 36 part-time. 8% of faculty holds doctoral degree. Student/faculty ratio: 8 to 1.
**Selectivity rating.** Competitive.

**PROFILE.** The Corcoran School of Art, founded in 1890, is a private college. Its four-acre campus is located in Washington, D.C.

**Accreditation:** MSACS. Professionally accredited by the National Association of Schools of Art and Design.
**Religious orientation:** The Corcoran School of Art is nonsectarian; no religious requirements.
**Library:** Collections totaling over 13,300 volumes and 120 periodical subscriptions.
**Special facilities/museums:** Art gallery.
**STUDENT BODY. Undergraduate profile:** 61% are state residents; 39% are transfers. 7% Asian-American, 6% Black, 4% Hispanic, 79% White, 4% Other. Average age of undergraduates is 20.
**Freshman profile:** 10% of freshmen who took SAT scored 600 or over on verbal, 20% scored 600 or over on math; 50% scored 500 or over on verbal, 80% scored 500 or over on math; 95% scored 400 or over on verbal, 98% scored 400 or over on math; 98% scored 300 or over on verbal, 99% scored 300 or over on math. 5% of freshmen who took ACT scored 24 or over on composite; 95% scored 18 or over on composite; 100% scored 12 or over on composite. 90% of accepted applicants took SAT; 5% took ACT. 75% of freshmen come from public schools.
**Undergraduate achievement:** 75% of fall 1991 freshmen returned for fall 1992 term. 63% of entering class graduated. 20% of students who completed a degree program went on to graduate study within one year.
**Foreign students:** 18 students are from out of the country. Countries represented include Canada, China, Korea, Norway, Spain, and Sweden; 18 in all.
**PROGRAMS OF STUDY. Degrees:** B.F.A.
**Majors:** Fine Arts, Graphic Design, Photography.
**Requirements:** General education requirement.
**Academic regulations:** Minimum 2.0 GPA must be maintain.
**Special:** Internships. Member of Alliance of Independent Colleges of Art. Semester-away programs with other art schools and studios. Member of Art College Exchange.
**Academic Assistance:** Remedial reading, writing, and study skills.
**ADMISSIONS. Academic basis for candidate selection** (in order of priority): Secondary school record, standardized test scores, class rank, school's recommendation.
**Nonacademic basis for candidate selection:** Particular talent or ability is emphasized. Character and personality are considered.
**Requirements:** Graduation from secondary school is recommended; GED is accepted. No specific distribution of secondary school units required. Art as an elective recommended of all applicants. Portfolio required of all applicants. SAT is recommended; ACT may be substituted. Campus visit and interview recommended. No off-campus interviews.
**Procedure:** Take SAT or ACT by December of 12th year. Visit college for interview by March 15 of 12th year. Suggest filing application by March 15; no deadline. Notification of admission on rolling basis. Reply is required within two weeks of acceptance. $200 tuition deposit, refundable until May 1. $100 nonrefundable room deposit. Freshmen accepted for terms other than fall.
**Special programs:** Admission may be deferred one year. Credit may be granted through CEEB Advanced Placement for scores of 5 or higher. Early entrance/early admission program. Concurrent enrollment program.
**Transfer students:** Transfer students accepted for terms other than fall. In fall 1992, 39% of all new students were transfers into all classes. 88 transfer applications were received, 60 were accepted. Application deadline is rolling. Minimum 2.0 GPA recommended. Lowest course grade accepted is "C." Maximum number of transferable credits is 63 semester hours. At least 63 semester hours must be completed at the college to receive degree.
**Admissions contact:** Mark Sistek, Director of Admissions. 202 628-9484.
**FINANCIAL AID. Available aid:** Pell grants, SEOG, state scholarships and grants, school scholarships and grants, private scholarships and grants, and aid for undergraduate foreign students. Perkins Loans (NDSL), PLUS, Stafford Loans (GSL), and SLS. AMS.
**Financial aid statistics:** In 1992-93, 65% of all undergraduate applicants received aid; 65% of freshman applicants. Average amounts of aid awarded freshmen: Scholarships and grants, $1,325; loans, $2,625.
**Supporting data/closing dates:** FAFSA/FAF/FFS: Priority filing date is March 15; accepted on rolling basis. School's own aid application: Priority filing date is March 15; accepted on rolling basis. Income tax forms: Priority filing date is March 15; accepted on rolling basis. Notification of awards on rolling basis.
**Financial aid contact:** Wandra Miller, Director of Financial Aid. 202 628-9484, extension 730.

## Gallaudet University

**Washington, DC 20002** — **202 651-5000**

**1994-95 Costs.** Tuition: $4,700. Room & board: $6,950. Fees, books, misc. academic expenses (school's estimate): $880.
**Enrollment.** Undergraduates: 729 men, 812 women (full-time). Freshman class: 820 applicants, 640 accepted, 424 enrolled. Graduate enrollment: 68 men, 303 women.
**Test score averages/ranges.** N/A.
**Faculty.** 300 full-time; 30 part-time. 57% of faculty holds doctoral degree.
**Selectivity rating.** N/A.

**PROFILE.** Gallaudet, founded in 1864, is a private, liberal arts university for deaf and hard-of-hearing students. Programs are offered through the College of Arts and Sciences and the Schools of Communication, Education and Human Services, Management, and Preparatory Studies. Its 93-acre campus is located in northeast Washington, D.C.; a separate nine-acre campus for the School of Preparatory Studies is in the northwest section of the city.

**Accreditation:** MSACS. Professionally accredited by the American Speech-Language-Hearing Association, the Council on Rehabilitation Education, the Council on Social Work Education, the National Council for Accreditation of Teacher Education.
**Religious orientation:** Gallaudet University is nonsectarian; no religious requirements.
**Library:** Collections totaling over 189,500 volumes, 1,415 periodical subscriptions, and 290,000 microform items.
**Special facilities/museums:** Demonstration elementary school and model secondary school for the deaf, TV/film studio, national information center, national center for laws, and international center for the deaf.
**Athletic facilities:** Gymnasiums, swimming pool, racquetball and tennis courts, track, baseball, football, and softball fields, field house, Cybex, training, and weight rooms.

**STUDENT BODY. Undergraduate profile:** 2% are state residents. 2% Asian-American, 10% Black, 1% Native American, 79% White, 8% Other. Average age of undergraduates is 23.
**Freshman profile:** 48% of freshmen come from public schools.
**Undergraduate achievement:** 66% of fall 1992 freshmen returned for fall 1993 term. 75% of entering class graduated.
**Foreign students:** 285 students are from out of the country. Countries represented include Canada, Japan, Nigeria, and Sweden; 53 in all.

**PROGRAMS OF STUDY. Degrees:** B.A., B.S.
**Majors:** Accounting, Advertising Art, American Studies, Art, Art Education, Art History/Museum Studies, Biology, Business Administration, Chemistry, Child Development, Communication Arts, Computer Engineering Technology, Computer Information Systems, Computer Mathematics, Drama Production/Performance, Early Childhood Education, Economics, Education, Elementary Education, Engineering, English, French, General Science, German, Government, History, Home Economics, Home Economics Education, International Studies, Leadership/Programming, Mathematics, Nutrition/Foods, Philosophy, Philosophy/Religion, Physical Education, Physics, Psychology, Recreation/Leisure Studies, Recreation Therapy, Romance Languages, Secondary Education, Sign Communication, Social Philosophy, Social Work, Sociology, Spanish, Theatre Arts, TV/Film/Photography.
**Distribution of degrees:** The majors with the highest enrollment are psychology and accounting; art history/museum studies, French, and theatre arts have the lowest.
**Requirements:** General education requirement.

**Special:** Double majors. Independent study. Pass/fail grading option. Internships. Cooperative education programs. 3-2 engineering program with George Washington U. Member of Consortium of Universities of the Washington Metropolitan Area. Exchange programs with Oberlin Coll and Western Maryland Coll. Teacher certification in early childhood, elementary, and secondary education. Study abroad in Germany.
**Honors:** Honors program.
**Academic Assistance:** Remedial reading, writing, and math. Nonremedial tutoring.

**STUDENT LIFE. Housing:** Students may live on or off campus. Coed dorms. 90% of students live in college housing.
**Social atmosphere:** According to the student newspaper, "Students are politically active and are aware of many little things that leaders have done. 'Deaf' students love loud music, and on weekends go to Georgetown bars." Popular events include Homecoming, an annual rock festival in the spring, and the Student Body Elections in February. Influential groups include Greeks, the Student Body Government, the Student Congress, and the Student Affairs Office. On campus, students meet at the Ely Center and the cafeteria. Off-campus spots include G & G Villa, among others.
**Services and counseling/handicapped student services:** Placement services. Health service. Day care. Career and academic guidance services.
**Campus organizations:** Undergraduate student government. Student newspaper (Buff and Blue, published once/month). Yearbook. Theatre, dance company, special-interest groups. Three fraternities, no chapter houses; three sororities, no chapter houses. 20% of men join a fraternity. 15% of women join a sorority.
**Religious organizations:** Ephphatha Club, Gamma Delta, Hillel, Newman Community, Wesley Foundation.
**Minority/foreign student organizations:** Ebony Harambee Club. International Club, German Club.

**ATHLETICS. Physical education requirements:** Four semester hours of physical education required.
**Intercollegiate competition:** 25% of students participate. Baseball (M), basketball (M,W), cheerleading (W), cross-country (M,W), football (M), soccer (M), softball (W), swimming (W), tennis (M,W), track and field (indoor) (M,W), track and field (outdoor) (M,W), volleyball (W), wrestling (M). Member of Capital Athletic Conference, NCAA Division III.
**Intramural and club sports:** 45% of students participate. Intramural basketball, cycling, football, horseshoes, shuffleboard, softball, table tennis, volleyball. Men's club cheerleading, gymnastics. Women's club cheerleading, gymnastics.

**ADMISSIONS. Academic basis for candidate selection** (in order of priority): Secondary school record, school's recommendation, class rank.
**Nonacademic basis for candidate selection:** Character and personality and particular talent or ability are emphasized. Extracurricular participation is important. Alumni/ae relationship is considered.
**Requirements:** Graduation from secondary school is required; GED is accepted. No specific distribution of secondary school units required. College-preparatory program including algebra recommended. Audiogram required of all applicants; results must indicate that hearing impairment would affect attendance at other colleges or universities where programs are designed for those with normal hearing. Entrance exam, including achievement and aptitude tests, also required. New students enter either the School of Preparatory Studies or the freshman class. Campus visit and interview recommended.
**Procedure:** Suggest filing application by April 15; no deadline. Acceptance notification on rolling basis beginning in October. Closing date is June 15. Reply is required by May 1. $50 nonrefundable tuition deposit. $150 refundable room deposit. Freshmen accepted for terms other than fall.
**Special programs:** Admission may be deferred one year. Placement may be granted through CEEB Advanced Placement exams. Credit may be granted through CLEP general and subject exams. Early decision program. Early entrance/early admission program.
**Transfer students:** Transfer students accepted for terms other than fall. Application deadline is May 1. Minimum 2.0 GPA required. Lowest course grade accepted is "C."
**Admissions contact:** Debra DeStefano, M.A., Director of Admissions. 202 651-5750.

**FINANCIAL AID. Available aid:** Pell grants, SEOG, state scholarships and grants, school scholarships and grants, private scholarships and grants, academic merit scholarships, and aid for undergraduate foreign students. Perkins Loans (NDSL), PLUS, Stafford Loans (GSL), and SLS. Deferred payment plan.
**Supporting data/closing dates:** FAFSA/FAF: Priority filing date is May 1. School's own aid application: Accepted on rolling basis. Income tax forms: Priority filing date is May 1. Notification of awards on rolling basis.
**Financial aid contact:** Nancy L. Cowan, Director of Financial Aid. 202 651-5290.

**STUDENT EMPLOYMENT.** Institutional employment. Off-campus part-time employment opportunities rated "good."

**COMPUTER FACILITIES.** 200 IBM/IBM-compatible and Macintosh/Apple microcomputers. Students may access Digital minicomputer/mainframe systems. Residence halls may be equipped with stand-alone microcomputers, networked microcomputers. Computer languages and software packages include BASIC, BLISS, C, COBOL, DataTrieve, FORTRAN, LISP, Pascal, Prolog, Scribe, SNOBOL, SPSS-X, System 1032, WordPerfect; word processing packages. Computer facilities are available to all students.
**Fees:** None.

**GRADUATE CAREER DATA.** Companies and businesses that hire graduates: educational/nonprofit institutions, federal government agencies, private business and industry.

# Georgetown University

**Washington, DC 20057** **202 687-5055**

**1993-94 Costs.** Tuition: $17,430. Room & board: $6,824. Fees, books, misc. academic expenses (school's estimate): $156.
**Enrollment.** Undergraduates: 2,841 men, 3,040 women (full-time). Freshman class: 11,113 applicants, 2,881 accepted, 1,391 enrolled. Graduate enrollment: 3,275 men, 2,759 women.
**Test score averages/ranges.** Range of SAT scores of middle 50%: 540-650 verbal, 590-690 math. Range of ACT scores of middle 50%: 26-31 composite.
**Faculty.** 504 full-time; 250 part-time. 90% of faculty holds highest degree in specific field. Student/faculty ratio: 11 to 1.
**Selectivity rating.** Most competitive.

**PROFILE.** Georgetown, founded in 1789, is a church-affiliated, liberal arts university. Programs are offered through the College of Arts and Sciences; the Graduate School; and the Schools of Business Administration, Dentistry, Foreign Service, Languages and Linguistics, Law, Medicine, and Nursing. Its 110-acre campus is located in Washington, D.C. The oldest campus building dates from 1795 and is in the Flemish Renaissance style.

**Accreditation:** MSACS. Professionally accredited by the American Assembly of Collegiate Schools of Business, the National League for Nursing.
**Religious orientation:** Georgetown University is affiliated with the Roman Catholic Church (Society of Jesus); two semesters of theology required.
**Library:** Collections totaling over 1,910,000 volumes, 24,763 periodical subscriptions, and 383,744 microform items.
**Special facilities/museums:** Language lab, seismological observatory.
**Athletic facilities:** Gymnasium, field house, basketball, racquetball, squash, and volleyball courts, dance, exercise, and weight rooms, swimming pool, track, athletic fields.

**STUDENT BODY. Undergraduate profile:** 3% are state residents; 19% are transfers. 7% Asian-American, 7% Black, 6% Hispanic, 1% Native American, 68% White, 11% Other. Average age of undergraduates is 20.
**Freshman profile:** 8% of freshmen who took SAT scored 700 or over on verbal, 24% scored 700 or over on math; 53% scored 600 or over on verbal, 75% scored 600 or over on math; 87% scored 500 or over on verbal, 95% scored 500 or over on math; 99% scored 400 or over on verbal, 99% scored 400 or over on math; 100% scored 300 or over on verbal, 100% scored 300 or over on math. 98% of accepted applicants took SAT; 21% took ACT. 45% of freshmen come from public schools.
**Undergraduate achievement:** 96% of fall 1992 freshmen returned for fall 1993 term. 88% of entering class graduated. 25% of students who completed a degree program immediately went on to graduate study.
**Foreign students:** 152 students are from out of the country. Countries represented include Germany, India, Japan, Korea, Spain, and the United Kingdom; 105 in all.

**PROGRAMS OF STUDY. Degrees:** B.A., B.S.
**Majors:** Accounting, American Studies, Arabic, Biology, Chemistry, Chinese, Classics, Comparative/Regional Studies, Computer Science, Economics, English, Finance, Fine Arts, French, German, Government, History, History/Diplomacy, Humanities/International Affairs, Individualized Program, Interdisciplinary Studies, International Business, International Economics, International Politics, Italian, Japanese, Linguistics, Marketing, Mathematics, Nursing, Philosophy, Physics, Portuguese, Psychology, Russian, Sociology, Spanish, Theology.
**Distribution of degrees:** The majors with the highest enrollment are international affairs, government, and English; interdisciplinary studies, computer science, and classics have the lowest.
**Requirements:** General education requirement.
**Academic regulations:** Minimum 2.0 GPA must be maintained.
**Special:** Minors offered in most majors. Self-designed majors. Double majors. Independent study. Accelerated study. Pass/fail grading option. Internships. Graduate school at which undergraduates may take graduate-level courses. Preprofessional programs in medicine and dentistry. 3-2 engineering program with Catholic U. Member of Consortium of Universities of the Washington Metropolitan Area. Teacher certification in secondary education. Study abroad in 34 countries; university owns villas in Italy and Turkey. ROTC. NROTC at George Washington U. AFROTC at Howard U.
**Honors:** Phi Beta Kappa. Honors program.
**Academic Assistance:** Nonremedial tutoring.

**STUDENT LIFE. Housing:** All freshmen and sophomores must live on campus unless living with family. Coed dorms. School-owned/operated apartments. Special-interest housing. 80% of students live in college housing.
**Social atmosphere:** Georgetown students frequent the Tombs, Hoya's, Booeymonger's, the Pub, and Cafe Northwest. The GU Student Association, men's and women's basketball teams, class committees, and the two student newspapers are influential on student social life. Favorite events during the school year include the Cherry Tree Massacre (an a capella festival), SpringFest, the Diplomatic Ball, and basketball games. "Since Georgetown is in Washington, students tend to spread out on the weekends," reports the Georgetown Voice. "Many students visit the taverns five blocks from campus on Wisconsin and M Streets; there are always open parties hosted in on- and off-campus apartments and houses."
**Services and counseling/handicapped student services:** Placement services. Health service. Women's center. Counseling services for minority and military students. Personal and psychological counseling. Career and academic guidance services. Physically disabled student services. Learning disabled services. Notetaking services. Tape recorders. Tutors. Reader services for the blind.
**Campus organizations:** Undergraduate student government. Student newspapers (Hoya; Voice; both published twice/week). Literary magazine. Yearbook. Radio station. Band, orchestra, string quartet, Collegium Musicum, glee club, choir, debating and public speaking groups, theatre, poetry magazine, Mask and Bauble Society, Young Democrats,

Young Republicans, community service group, special-interest groups, over 100 organizations in all.
**Religious organizations:** Campus Ministry, Fellowship of Christian Athletes, Jewish Student Association.
**Minority/foreign student organizations:** Black Alliance and theatre group, NAACP, Center for Minority Student Affairs, Student Coalition Against Racism, Mexican-American group. Arab, Brazilian, Chinese, Japanese, Korean, Latin American, and South Asian groups.
**ATHLETICS. Physical education requirements:** None.
**Intercollegiate competition:** 10% of students participate. Baseball (M), basketball (M,W), cheerleading (M,W), crew (M,W), cross-country (M,W), diving (M,W), field hockey (W), football (M), golf (M), lacrosse (M,W), sailing (M,W), soccer (M,W), swimming (M,W), tennis (M,W), track and field (indoor) (M,W), track and field (outdoor) (M,W), volleyball (W). Member of Big East Conference, NCAA Division I, NCAA Division I-AA for football.
**Intramural and club sports:** 55% of students participate. Intramural basketball, flag football, golf, racquetball, soccer, softball, squash, tennis, track, volleyball.
**ADMISSIONS. Academic basis for candidate selection** (in order of priority): Secondary school record, standardized test scores, class rank, school's recommendation, essay.
**Nonacademic basis for candidate selection:** Extracurricular participation is emphasized. Character and personality, particular talent or ability, geographical distribution, and alumni/ae relationship are important.
**Requirements:** Graduation from secondary school is required; GED is accepted. No specific distribution of secondary school units required but only academic subjects may be counted. 4 units of math and 3 units of science required of math and science program applicants. Chemistry, biology, and physics required of nursing program applicants. Language background required of foreign service and language program applicants. SAT or ACT is required. ACH recommended. Campus visit recommended. Off-campus interviews available with an alumni representative.
**Procedure:** Take SAT or ACT by December of 12th year. Application deadline is January 10. Notification of admission by April 1. Reply is required by May 1. $800 nonrefundable tuition deposit. Freshmen accepted for fall term only.
**Special programs:** Admission may be deferred one year. Credit and/or placement may be granted through CEEB Advanced Placement exams for scores of 4 or higher. Early action program. In fall 1993, 2,635 applied for early action and 632 were accepted. Deadline for applying for early action is November 1.
**Transfer students:** Transfer students accepted for fall term only. In fall 1993, 19% of all new students were transfers into all classes. 1,457 transfer applications were received, 485 were accepted. Application deadline is March 1. Minimum 3.0 GPA required. Lowest course grade accepted is "C." Maximum number of transferable credits is 60 semester hours. At least 60 semester hours must be completed at the university to receive degree.
**Admissions contact:** Charles A. Deacon, M.A., Dean of Undergraduate Admissions. 202 687-3600.
**FINANCIAL AID. Available aid:** Pell grants, SEOG, Federal Nursing Student Scholarships, state scholarships and grants, school scholarships and grants, private scholarships and grants, ROTC scholarships, and athletic scholarships. Perkins Loans (NDSL), PLUS, Stafford Loans (GSL), NSL, private loans, and SLS. Deferred payment plan. Institutional payment plan.
**Financial aid statistics:** 22% of aid is not need-based. In 1993-94, 94% of all undergraduate applicants received aid; 92% of freshman applicants. Average amounts of aid awarded freshmen: Scholarships and grants, $10,524; loans, $3,713.
**Supporting data/closing dates:** FAFSA/FAF: Priority filing date is February 1; accepted on rolling basis. Income tax forms: Priority filing date is May 15; accepted on rolling basis. Notification of awards begins April 1.
**Financial aid contact:** Patricia A. McWade, M.Ed., Dean of Financial Aid. 202 687-4547.
**STUDENT EMPLOYMENT.** College Work/Study Program. Institutional employment. 48% of full-time undergraduates work on campus during school year. Students may expect to earn an average of $2,500 during school year. Off-campus part-time employment opportunities rated "excellent."
**COMPUTER FACILITIES.** 200 IBM/IBM-compatible microcomputers. Students may access Digital, IBM minicomputer/mainframe systems, BITNET, Internet. Client/LAN operating systems include DOS, Windows NT. Computer languages and software packages include C, COBOL, FORTRAN, Lotus 1-2-3, MacroAssembler, Pascal, R:BASE, SAS, WordPerfect. Computer facilities are available to all students.
**Fees:** $40 computer fee per semester.
**Hours:** 8 AM-11 PM; extended hours during exams.
**GRADUATE CAREER DATA.** Graduate school percentages: 8% enter law school. 4% enter medical school. 1% enter graduate business programs. 11% enter graduate arts and sciences programs. 30% of graduates choose careers in business and industry.
**PROMINENT ALUMNI/AE.** Patrick Ewing, center, New York Knicks; William Clinton, president of the U.S.; Patrick Buchanan, journalist; Maria Shriver, journalist.

## The George Washington University

**Washington, DC 20052** **202 994-1000**

**1992-93 Costs.** Tuition: $15,980. Room: $3,980. Board: $2,330. Fees, books, misc. academic expenses (school's estimate): $890.

**Enrollment.** Undergraduates: 2,549 men, 2,721 women (full-time). Freshman class: 7,875 applicants, 5,062 accepted, 1,531 enrolled. Graduate enrollment: 5,781 men, 4,310 women.

**Test score averages/ranges.** Range of SAT scores of middle 50%: 490-600 verbal, 530-650 math. Range of ACT scores of middle 50%: 24-29 composite.

**Faculty.** 653 full-time; 639 part-time. 93% of faculty holds highest degree in specific field. Student/faculty ratio: 14 to 1.

**Selectivity rating.** More competitive.

**PROFILE.** The George Washington University, founded in 1821, is a private institution. Programs are offered through the Columbian College of Arts and Sciences and the Schools of Education and Human Development, Engineering and Applied Science, Government and Business Administration, Medicine and Health Sciences, and Public and International Affairs. Its 45-acre campus is located in the federal section of Washington, D.C., several blocks from the White House.

**Accreditation:** MSACS. Professionally accredited by the Accreditation Board for Engineering and Technology, the American Assembly of Collegiate Schools of Business, the American Medical Association (CAHEA), the American Psychological Association, the American Speech-Language-Hearing Association, the National Association of Schools of Music, the National Council for Accreditation of Teacher Education.
**Religious orientation:** The George Washington University is nonsectarian; no religious requirements.
**Library:** Collections totaling over 1,692,638 volumes, 13,596 periodical subscriptions, and 1,923,935 microform items.
**Special facilities/museums:** Art gallery, language lab, word processing center.
**Athletic facilities:** Athletic center, gymnasium, swimming pool.

**STUDENT BODY. Undergraduate profile:** 13% are state residents; 20% are transfers. 11% Asian-American, 8% Black, 5% Hispanic, 1% Native American, 65% White, 10% Other. Average age of undergraduates is 21.
**Freshman profile:** 3% of freshmen who took SAT scored 700 or over on verbal, 11% scored 700 or over on math; 29% scored 600 or over on verbal, 51% scored 600 or over on math; 74% scored 500 or over on verbal, 90% scored 500 or over on math; 98% scored 400 or over on verbal, 100% scored 400 or over on math; 100% scored 300 or over on verbal. 21% of freshmen who took ACT scored 30 or over on composite; 80% scored 24 or over on composite; 100% scored 18 or over on composite. 87% of accepted applicants took SAT; 7% took ACT. 80% of freshmen come from public schools.
**Undergraduate achievement:** 87% of fall 1992 freshmen returned for fall 1993 term. 61% of entering class graduated. 48% of students who completed a degree program immediately went on to graduate study.
**Foreign students:** 157 students are from out of the country. Countries represented include Canada, India, Japan, Korea, Saudi Arabia, and Turkey; 116 in all.

**PROGRAMS OF STUDY. Degrees:** B.A., B.Acct., B.Bus.Admin., B.Human Services, B.Mus., B.S.
**Majors:** Accountancy, Anthropology, Applied Mathematics, Archaeology, Art History, Art History/Fine Arts, Biology, Business Economics/Public Policy, Chemistry, Chinese Language/Literature, Civil Engineering, Classical Archaeology/Classics, Classical Humanities, Clinical Laboratory Sciences, Communications, Computer Science, Criminal Justice, Dance, Diagnostic Medical Sonography, Early Modern European Studies, East Asian Studies, Economics, Electrical Engineering, Emergency Medical Services, English, Environmental Studies, Exercise/Sport Science, Finance, Fine Arts, French Language/Literature, General Liberal Arts, Geography, Geology, Germanic Languages/Literatures, History, Human Resource Management, Human Services, Information Systems, International Affairs, International Business, Journalism, Judaic Studies, Latin American Studies, Marketing, Mathematics, Mechanical Engineering, Medical Technology, Music, Philosophy, Physician Assistant, Physics, Political Communication, Political Science, Psychology, Radio/Television, Religion, Russian Language/Literature, Russian Literature/Culture, Sociology, Spanish American Literature, Spanish Language/Literature, Speech/Hearing Science, Statistics, Systems Analysis, Theatre.
**Distribution of degrees:** The majors with the highest enrollment are international affairs, business administration, and pre-medicine; Chinese, dance, and physics have the lowest.
**Requirements:** General education requirement.
**Academic regulations:** Minimum 2.0 GPA must be maintained.
**Special:** Minors offered in most majors and in applied ethics, biological anthropology, creative writing, cross-cultural communication, dance education, dance history and criticism, Japanese, peace studies, sociocultural anthropology, and women's studies. Interschool study in five undergraduate divisions. Residential living and learning programs in politics and values, exploration of Western cultures, and technology and society. Associate's degrees offered. Self-designed majors. Double majors. Dual degrees. Independent study. Accelerated study. Pass/fail grading option. Internships. Cooperative education programs. Graduate school at which undergraduates may take graduate-level courses. Preprofessional programs in law, medicine, and dentistry. Seven-year integrated B.A./M.D. program. 3-2 chemical toxicology and art therapy programs with George Washington U Graduate School of Arts and Sciences. 3-2 engineering programs with Bowie State U, Gallaudet U, Georgian Court Coll, Hood Coll, Southeastern Coll (Athens, Greece), St. Joseph's Coll, St. Thomas Aquinas Coll, and Wheaton Coll. Five-year B.A./M.A. program in economics, five-year B.S./M.S. in systems analysis and engineering/operations research, five-year B.S./M.A. in systems analysis and engineering/economics, and five-year B.A./M.S. in economics/operations research or engineering/economics. Member of Consortium of Universities of the Washington Metropolitan Area and Washington Research Library Consortium. Exchange programs abroad in Brazil (U Federal do Rio de Janiero), Chile (U de Chile and U de Santiago), China (Beijing U, Fudan U), the Czech Republic (Charles U), England (East Anglia U, Essex U, Lancaster U, Manchester U), France (American U of Paris), Germany (U of Bamberg), and Peru (U Catolica). Study abroad also in Japan, Israel, and Spain. NROTC. ROTC at Georgetown U and Howard U. AFROTC at Howard U and U of Maryland.
**Honors:** Phi Beta Kappa. Honors program. Honor societies.
**Academic Assistance:** Nonremedial tutoring.

**STUDENT LIFE. Housing:** Students may live on or off campus. Coed and women's dorms. School-owned/operated apartments. 54% of students live in college housing.
**Social atmosphere:** Students gather at the Marrin Center on campus and at Odd's, Quigley's, and landmarks on the mall off campus. Greeks and international student groups influence campus life. Basketball games are the favorite events on campus. According to the student newspaper, George Washington's large international student population and the atmosphere of the city make politics a constant topic of conversation and debate.
**Services and counseling/handicapped student services:** Placement services. Health service. Counseling services for minority, military, veteran, and older students. Birth control, personal, and psychological counseling. Career and academic guidance services. Religious counseling. Physically disabled student services. Learning disabled services. Notetaking services. Tape recorders. Reader services for the blind.

**Campus organizations:** Undergraduate student government. Student newspaper (Hatchet, published twice/week). Literary magazine. Yearbook. Radio and TV stations. Numerous service and professional societies, and performing arts groups, 215 organizations in all. 12 fraternities, eight chapter houses; eight sororities, no chapter houses. 15% of men join a fraternity. 14% of women join a sorority.
**Religious organizations:** Bahai Club, Baptist Fellowship, Christian Science Organization, College and Young Adult Fellowship, Convenant Ministries, G-Force, International Christian Fellowship, Intervarsity Christian Fellowship, Latter-Day Saints student group, Navigators-KACF, University Bible Fellowship, CARP, Hillel, Ecumenical Christian Ministry, Religious Society of Friends, Lutheran Students Association, Muslim Student Association, Newman Catholic Center.
**Minority/foreign student organizations:** Numerous minority student organizations. Numerous foreign student organizations.

**ATHLETICS. Physical education requirements:** None.
**Intercollegiate competition:** 5% of students participate. Baseball (M), basketball (M,W), cheerleading (M,W), crew (M,W), cross-country (M,W), diving (M,W), golf (M), gymnastics (W), soccer (M,W), swimming (M,W), tennis (M,W), volleyball (W), water polo (M). Member of Atlantic 10, ECAC, NCAA Division I.
**Intramural and club sports:** 45% of students participate. Intramural aikido, badminton, basketball, beach volleyball, boating, bowling, cycling, dance, flag football, floor hockey, free throw, fun runs, golf, horseback riding, horseshoes, indoor soccer, kickboxing, lacrosse, miniature golf, oofball, racquetball, rugby, sailing, shotokan karate, shuto karate, softball, squash, swimming, table tennis, tae kwon do, tennis, tong leong, turkey trot, volleyball, Wiffle ball.

**ADMISSIONS. Academic basis for candidate selection** (in order of priority): Secondary school record, class rank, standardized test scores, school's recommendation, essay.
**Nonacademic basis for candidate selection:** Character and personality, extracurricular participation, particular talent or ability, geographical distribution, and alumni/ae relationship are considered.
**Requirements:** Graduation from secondary school is required; GED is not accepted. 16 units and the following program of study are required: 4 units of English, 3 units of math, 2 units of science including 1 unit of lab, 2 units of foreign language, 1 unit of social studies, 1 unit of history, 3 units of academic electives. Minimum combined SAT score of 1000 (composite ACT score of 23), rank in top one-third of secondary school class, and minimum 3.0 GPA recommended. 4 units of math (2 algebra, 1 plane geometry, 1/2 plane trigonometry, 1/2 precalculus), 1 unit of physics, and 1 unit of chemistry required of engineering program applicants. Audition required of music program applicants. EOP for applicants not normally admissible. SAT or ACT is required. ACH recommended. Campus visit and interview recommended. Off-campus interviews available with admissions and alumni representatives.
**Procedure:** Take SAT or ACT by December of 12th year. Take ACH by December of 12th year. Application deadlines are December 1 (Part I) and February 1 (Part II). Notification of regular admission begins in early March and continues through mid-April. Reply is required by May 1. $325 nonrefundable tuition deposit. $300 nonrefundable room deposit. Freshmen accepted for terms other than fall.
**Special programs:** Admission may be deferred one year. Credit and/or placement may be granted through CEEB Advanced Placement exams for scores of 5 or higher. Credit and/or placement may be granted through CLEP general and subject exams. Credit and placement may be granted through DANTES exams. Early decision program. In fall 1992, 224 applied for early decision and 150 were accepted. Deadline for applying for early decision is November 1 (Part I); December 1 (Part II). Early entrance/early admission program. Concurrent enrollment program.
**Transfer students:** Transfer students accepted for terms other than fall. In fall 1993, 20% of all new students were transfers into all classes. 1,467 transfer applications were received, 717 were accepted. Application deadline is May 1 for Part I; June 1 for Part II. Minimum 2.75 GPA recommended. Lowest course grade accepted is "C." At least 30 semester hours must be completed at the university to receive degree.
**Admissions contact:** Frederic A. Siegel, M.A., Director of Admissions. 202 994-6040.

**FINANCIAL AID. Available aid:** Pell grants, SEOG, state scholarships and grants, school scholarships and grants, private scholarships and grants, ROTC scholarships, academic merit scholarships, athletic scholarships, and aid for undergraduate foreign students. Perkins Loans (NDSL), PLUS, Stafford Loans (GSL), and SLS. Tuition Plan Inc., Knight Tuition Plans, deferred payment plan, and family tuition reduction.
**Financial aid statistics:** 26% of aid is not need-based. In 1993-94, 92% of all undergraduate applicants received aid; 94% of freshman applicants. Average amounts of aid awarded freshmen: Scholarships and grants, $13,487; loans, $4,849.
**Supporting data/closing dates:** FAFSA/FAF: Priority filing date is February 1. Income tax forms: Priority filing date is March 15. W-2 forms: Priority filing date is March 15. Notification of awards begins April 1.
**Financial aid contact:** Vicki J. Baker, M.A., Director of Student Financial Assistance. 202 994-6620.

**STUDENT EMPLOYMENT.** College Work/Study Program. Institutional employment. Students may expect to earn an average of $1,510 during school year. Off-campus part-time employment opportunities rated "excellent."

**COMPUTER FACILITIES.** 550 IBM/IBM-compatible, Macintosh/Apple, and RISC-/UNIX-based microcomputers; all are networked. Students may access Hewlett-Packard, IBM, Sequent, SUN minicomputer/mainframe systems, BITNET. Residence halls may be equipped with stand-alone microcomputers, networked microcomputers, networked terminals, modems. Client/LAN operating systems include UNIX/XENIX/AIX, Novell. Computer languages and software packages include Ada, BMDP, COBOL, Excel, FORTRAN, LISP, WordPerfect, Pascal, PL/1, Quattro Pro, SAS, SPSS-X; 200 in all. Computer facilities are available to all students.
**Fees:** None.
**Hours:** 24 hours.

**GRADUATE CAREER DATA.** Graduate school percentages: 12% enter law school. 9% enter medical school. 8% enter graduate arts and sciences programs. Companies and businesses that hire graduates: federal government agencies, financial services, engineering and retail firms.

**PROMINENT ALUMNI/AE.** William Fulbright and Daniel Inouye, U.S. senators; Leon Jaworski; George Romney; John Foster Dulles; J. Edgar Hoover; Jacqueline Kennedy Onassis; Margaret Truman; Frederick Gregory, astronaut; Mary Hartwood-Futrell, president, National Education Association; Henry Cisneros, secretary of housing and urban development, U.S. government; Colin Powell, former chairperson, Joint Chiefs of Staff.

# Howard University

**Washington, DC 20059** — **202 806-6100**

**1993-94 Costs.** Tuition: $7,130. Room & board: $4,150. Fees, books, misc. academic expenses (school's estimate): $1,005.
**Enrollment.** Undergraduates: 2,659 men, 4,242 women (full-time). Freshman class: 5,732 applicants, 2,801 accepted, 1,340 enrolled. Graduate enrollment: 1,330 men, 1,637 women.
**Test score averages/ranges.** Average SAT scores: 426 verbal, 452 math. Average ACT scores: 20 English, 19 math, 20 composite.
**Faculty.** 1,319 full-time; 702 part-time. Student/faculty ratio: 7 to 1.
**Selectivity rating.** Less competitive.

**PROFILE.** Howard, founded in 1867, is a private, comprehensive, historically black university. Programs are offered through the Divisions of Academic Affairs and Health Affairs. Its 89-acre main campus is located in central Washington; its 22-acre West Campus is located near Rock Creek Park in northwest Washington.

**Accreditation:** MSACS.
**Religious orientation:** Howard University is nonsectarian; no religious requirements.
**Library:** Collections totaling over 1,816,927 volumes, 24,966 periodical subscriptions, and 2,266,115 microform items.
**Special facilities/museums:** Three art galleries, language labs, hospital, research center with comprehensive collection on Africa and persons of African descent.
**Athletic facilities:** Gymnasiums, weight room, basketball, tennis, and volleyball courts, swimming pool, track, baseball, football, intramural, and soccer fields.

**STUDENT BODY. Undergraduate profile:** 20% are state residents; 36% are transfers. 1% Asian-American, 90% Black, 9% Other. Average age of undergraduates is 20.
**Freshman profile:** 3% of freshmen who took SAT scored 600 or over on verbal, 5% scored 600 or over on math; 17% scored 500 or over on verbal, 28% scored 500 or over on math; 60% scored 400 or over on verbal, 69% scored 400 or over on math; 96% scored 300 or over on verbal, 97% scored 300 or over on math. 1% of freshmen who took ACT scored 30 or over on English, 1% scored 30 or over on composite; 16% scored 24 or over on English, 9% scored 24 or over on math, 10% scored 24 or over on composite; 58% scored 18 or over on English, 51% scored 18 or over on math, 62% scored 18 or over on composite; 81% scored 12 or over on English, 81% scored 12 or over on math, 76% scored 12 or over on composite; 87% scored 6 or over on English, 83% scored 6 or over on math, 77% scored 6 or over on composite. 95% of accepted applicants took SAT; 5% took ACT. 80% of freshmen come from public schools.
**Undergraduate achievement:** 75% of fall 1991 freshmen returned for fall 1992 term. 16% of entering class graduated. 40% of students who completed a degree program immediately went on to graduate study.
**Foreign students:** Countries represented include the Bahamas, Bermuda, Canada, China, Jamaica, and Trinidad/Tobago; 110 in all.

**PROGRAMS OF STUDY. Degrees:** B.A., B.Arch., B.Bus.Admin., B.F.A., B.Mus., B.Mus.Ed., B.S.
**Majors:** Accounting, Administration of Justice, Afro-American Study, Anthropology, Applied Music, Architecture, Art, Art Education, Art History, Astronomy, Biology, Broadcast Management, Broadcast Production, Ceramics, Chemical Engineering, Chemistry, Civil Engineering, Classics, Communication Sciences/Disorders, Composition, Computer Information Systems, Computer System Engineering, Consumer Affairs Management, Design, Drama, Economics, Electrical Engineering, Elementary Education, English, Environmental Sciences, Experimental Studio, Fashion Fundamentals, Film Directing, Finance, French, Geography, Geology, German, Graphic Art, History, Hotel/Motel Management, Human Communication Studies, Human Development, Insurance, Interior Design, International Business, Jazz Studies, Journalism, Management, Marketing, Mathematics, Mechanical Engineering, Medical Technology, Military Science, Music History/Literature, Music Therapy, Musical Theatre, Nursing, Nutritional Sciences, Occupational Therapy, Painting, Pharmacy, Philosophy, Photography, Physical Education/Recreation, Physical Therapy, Physician's Assistant, Physics, Political Science, Printmaking, Psychology, Russian, Sculpture, Sociology, Spanish, Theatre/Speech Education.
**Distribution of degrees:** The majors with the highest enrollment are business administration, electrical engineering, and zoology; German, classics, and Afro-American studies have the lowest.
**Requirements:** General education requirement.
**Academic regulations:** Minimum 2.0 GPA must be maintained.
**Special:** Dual degrees. Independent study. Accelerated study. Pass/fail grading option. Internships. Graduate school at which undergraduates may take graduate-level courses. Preprofessional programs in medicine, veterinary science, pharmacy, dentistry, optometry, allied health, medicine, osteopathy, and podiatry. J.D./M.B.A., B.S./M.D., and B.S./D.D.S. programs. Member of Consortium of Universities of the Washington, D.C., Metropolitan Area. Exchange programs with Duke U, Harvard U, Mills Coll, Smith Coll, Reed Coll, Stanford U, Tufts U, U of California at Berkeley, U of Southern California, and Vassar Coll. Teacher certification in early childhood, elementary, and secondary education. Certification in specific subject areas. Member of International Student Exchange Program (ISEP). ROTC and AFROTC.
**Honors:** Phi Beta Kappa. Honors program.
**Academic Assistance:** Remedial reading, math, and study skills.

**STUDENT LIFE. Housing:** All freshmen and transfer students must live on campus. Coed, women's, and men's dorms. School-owned/operated apartments. Both on-campus and off-campus married-student housing. 38% of students live in college housing.
**Social atmosphere:** According to the student newspaper, influential organizations include Greeks, geographical clubs, international clubs, sports clubs, and professional soci-

eties. Students gather at the bronze sculpture and reflecting pool in front of the Blackburn Center when on campus. Off-campus, favorite hangouts are Punch Out, Ritz, Takoma Station, and Georgetown. Social activities include Homecoming, Spring Festival, Charter Day, and Graduation.

**Services and counseling/handicapped student services:** Placement services. Health service. Day care. Counseling services for veteran students. Personal and psychological counseling. Career and academic guidance services. Physically disabled student services. Notetaking services. Reader services for the blind.

**Campus organizations:** Undergraduate student government. Student newspaper (Hilltop, published once/week). Yearbook. Radio and TV stations. Gospel choir, string ensemble, band, jazz society, dance group, drama groups, debating, state and city geographical clubs, professional clubs. Four fraternities, no chapter houses; four sororities, no chapter houses. 1% of men join a fraternity. 1% of women join a sorority.

**Religious organizations:** Absalom Jones Student Association, Adventist Community, Baptist Student Union, Methodist Fellowship.

**Minority/foreign student organizations:** African Cultural Ensemble, Caribbean Student Association, Pan-African Association.

**ATHLETICS. Physical education requirements:** Four semesters of physical education required.

**Intercollegiate competition:** 1% of students participate. Baseball (M), basketball (M,W), cross-country (M,W), football (M), soccer (M), swimming (M,W), tennis (M,W), track and field (W), track and field (indoor) (M), track and field (outdoor) (M), volleyball (W), wrestling (M). Member of Mid Eastern Athletic Conference, NCAA Division I, NCAA Division I-AA for football.

**Intramural and club sports:** 10% of students participate. Intramural badminton, basketball, bowling, handball, lacrosse, soccer, softball, swimming, table tennis, tennis, touch football, weight lifting. Men's club basketball, cheerleading, football, lacrosse, soccer, swimming, tennis, wrestling. Women's club basketball, cheerleading, soccer, swimming, tennis.

**ADMISSIONS. Academic basis for candidate selection** (in order of priority): Class rank, secondary school record, standardized test scores, school's recommendation.

**Nonacademic basis for candidate selection:** Extracurricular participation, particular talent or ability, and alumni/ae relationship are considered.

**Requirements:** Graduation from secondary school is required; GED is accepted. 16 units and the following program of study are required: 4 units of English, 2 units of math, 2 units of science, 2 units of foreign language, 4 units of academic electives. Audition, tape, or portfolio required of applicants to the College of Fine Arts. Center for Academic Reinforcement for applicants not normally admissible. SAT or ACT is required. Campus visit recommended. No off-campus interviews.

**Procedure:** Take SAT or ACT by December of 12th year. Suggest filing application by November 1. Application deadline is April 15. Notification of admission on rolling basis, within five days of receipt of completed application. Reply is required within 30 days of notification. $150 nonrefundable tuition deposit. $100 nonrefundable room deposit. Freshmen accepted for terms other than fall.

**Special programs:** Admission may be deferred one semester. Credit and/or placement may be granted through CEEB Advanced Placement exams for scores of 3 or higher. Early entrance/early admission program. Concurrent enrollment program.

**Transfer students:** Transfer students accepted for terms other than fall. In fall 1992, 36% of all new students were transfers into all classes. 2,476 transfer applications were received, 1,301 were accepted. Application deadline is April 1 for fall; November 1 for spring. Minimum 2.5 GPA. Lowest course grade accepted is "C." At least 30 semester hours must be completed at the university to receive degree.

**Admissions contact:** Emmett R. Griffin, Jr., M.S., Director of Admissions. 202 806-2752.

**FINANCIAL AID. Available aid:** Pell grants, SEOG, Federal Nursing Student Scholarships, state scholarships and grants, school scholarships and grants, private scholarships and grants, ROTC scholarships, academic merit scholarships, athletic scholarships, and aid for undergraduate foreign students. Perkins Loans (NDSL), PLUS, Stafford Loans (GSL), and Health Professions Loans. Deferred payment plan.

**Supporting data/closing dates:** FAFSA/FAF/FFS: Priority filing date is April 1. Notification of awards on rolling basis.

**Financial aid contact:** Adrienne M. Price, Director of Financial Aid. 202 806-2800.

**STUDENT EMPLOYMENT.** College Work/Study Program. Institutional employment. 6% of full-time undergraduates work on campus during school year. Students may expect to earn an average of $200 during school year. Freshmen are discouraged from working during their first term. Off-campus part-time employment opportunities rated "good."

**COMPUTER FACILITIES.** 150 IBM/IBM-compatible and Macintosh/Apple microcomputers. Students may access IBM minicomputer/mainframe systems. Computer languages and software packages include APL, BASIC, COBOL, dBASE, Display Write, FORTRAN, Lotus 1-2-3, PL/1, SPSS, WordStar. Computer facilities are available to all students.

**Fees:** None.

**GRADUATE CAREER DATA.** Graduate school percentages: 10% enter law school. 12% enter medical school. 9% enter dental school. 4% enter graduate business programs. 15% enter graduate arts and sciences programs. 3% enter theological school/seminary. Highest graduate school enrollments: American U, Howard U, U of Maryland. 14% of graduates choose careers in business and industry. Companies and businesses that hire graduates: AT&T, IBM, ITT.

**PROMINENT ALUMNI/AE.** Thurgood Marshall, former U.S. Supreme Court justice; Edward W. Brooke, former U.S. senator; Phyllicia Rashad, actress; Kenneth Clark, psychologist; Sirjang Lai Tandon, computer entrepreneur; Andrew Young, former mayor of Atlanta.

# Trinity College

**Washington, DC 200171094 — 202 939-5000**

**1992-93 Costs.** Tuition: $11,080. Room & board: $6,430. Fees, books, misc. academic expenses (school's estimate): $650.

**Enrollment.** 309 women (full-time). Freshman class: 253 applicants, 217 accepted, 100 enrolled. Graduate enrollment: 212 women.

**Test score averages/ranges.** Average SAT scores: 500 verbal, 510 math. Range of SAT scores of middle 50%: 570-440 verbal, 580-460 math. Average ACT scores: 22 English, 21 math, 24 composite. Range of ACT scores of middle 50%: 18-26 English, 18-21 math.

**Faculty.** 48 full-time; 62 part-time. 88% of faculty holds highest degree in specific field. Student/faculty ratio: 8 to 1.

**Selectivity rating.** More competitive.

**PROFILE.** Trinity, founded in 1897, is a church-affiliated, liberal arts college for women. The 28-acre campus is located three miles north of downtown Washington. The oldest of the college facilities dates from 1909. The Byzantine-style Chapel of Notre Dame was completed in 1924.

**Accreditation:** MSACS.

**Religious orientation:** Trinity College is affiliated with the Roman Catholic Church (Sisters of Notre Dame de Namur); two semesters of theology required.

**Library:** Collections totaling over 178,232 volumes, 620 periodical subscriptions, and 5,392 microform items.

**Special facilities/museums:** Art gallery, writing center, computer center.

**Athletic facilities:** Aerobic rooms, athletic fields, basketball court, fitness center, indoor running track, swimming pool, tennis courts, weight room.

**STUDENT BODY. Undergraduate profile:** 11% are state residents; 19% are transfers. 4% Asian-American, 28% Black, 9% Hispanic, 55% White, 4% Other. Average age of undergraduates is 19.

**Freshman profile:** 14% of freshmen who took ACT scored 30 or over on math; 42% scored 24 or over on English, 28% scored 24 or over on math, 63% scored 24 or over on composite; 71% scored 18 or over on English, 71% scored 18 or over on math, 76% scored 18 or over on composite; 100% scored 12 or over on English, 100% scored 12 or over on math, 100% scored 12 or over on composite. 94% of accepted applicants took SAT; 6% took ACT. 50% of freshmen come from public schools.

**Undergraduate achievement:** 89% of fall 1992 freshmen returned for fall 1993 term. 50% of students who completed a degree program went on to graduate study within one year.

**Foreign students:** Countries represented include China, Colombia, Japan, Saudi Arabia, the former Soviet republics, and Taiwan.

**PROGRAMS OF STUDY. Degrees:** B.A., B.S.

**Majors:** Art History, Biochemistry, Biology, Business Administration, Communications, Economics, Education, Elementary Education, English, Environmental Science, French, History, Human Relations, International Studies, Language/Culture Studies, Mathematics, Political Science, Psychology.

**Distribution of degrees:** The majors with the highest enrollment are business administration, political science, and psychology.

**Requirements:** General education requirement.

**Academic regulations:** Minimum 2.0 GPA required for graduation.

**Special:** Minors offered in bioethics, music, philosophy, physics, secondary education, sociology, Spanish, theology, and women's studies. Self-designed majors. Double majors. Dual degrees. Independent study. Pass/fail grading option. Internships. Graduate school at which undergraduates may take graduate-level courses. Preprofessional programs in law and medicine. Five-year B.A./M.A.T. in education. Member of Consortium of Universities of the Washington Metropolitan Area and Council for International Educational Exchange (CIEE). Member of Marine Science Consortium; off-campus study possible at Wallops Island, Va. SND Exchange. Teacher certification in early childhood, elementary, secondary, and special education. Study abroad possible in Argentina, Australia, Belgium, Brazil, Chile, China, Costa Rica, the Czech Republic/Slovenkia, Costa Rica, the Dominican Republic, France, Germany, Hungary, Indonesia, Japan, Mexico, the Netherlands, Poland, Russia, Spain, Thailand, the United Kingdom, and Vietnam. ROTC, NROTC, and AFROTC through consortium.

**Honors:** Phi Beta Kappa. Honor societies.

**Academic Assistance:** Remedial reading, writing, math, and study skills. Nonremedial tutoring.

**ADMISSIONS. Academic basis for candidate selection** (in order of priority): Secondary school record, standardized test scores, school's recommendation, essay, class rank.

**Nonacademic basis for candidate selection:** Character and personality, extracurricular participation, particular talent or ability, and geographical distribution are important. Alumni/ae relationship is considered.

**Requirements:** Graduation from secondary school is required; GED is accepted. 17 units and the following program of study are required: 4 units of English, 3 units of math, 2 units of lab science, 3 units of foreign language, 3 units of social studies, 2 units of academic electives. Combined SAT score of 900, rank in top half of secondary school class, and "B" average recommended. Conditional admission possible for applicants not meeting standard requirements. SAT or ACT is required. Campus visit and interview recommended. Off-campus interviews available with admissions and alumni representatives.

**Procedure:** Take SAT or ACT by November of 12th year. Visit college for interview by April of 12th year. Suggest filing application by February 1. Notification of admission on rolling basis. Reply is required by May 1. $200 tuition deposit, refundable until May 1. Freshmen accepted for terms other than fall.

**Special programs:** Admission may be deferred one year. Credit and/or placement may be granted through CEEB Advanced Placement exams for scores of 4 or higher. Credit and/or placement may be granted through CLEP general exams. Credit may be granted through CLEP subject exams. Placement may be granted through challenge exams. Credit and placement may be granted through life experience. Early entrance/early admission program.
**Transfer students:** Transfer students accepted for terms other than fall. In fall 1993, 19% of all new students were transfers into all classes. 51 transfer applications were received, 44 were accepted. Application deadline is rolling for fall; rolling for spring. Minimum 2.0 GPA required. Lowest course grade accepted is "C." Maximum number of transferable credits is 96 semester hours. At least 32 semester hours must be completed at the college to receive degree.
**Admissions contact:** Mary-Agnes D. Evans, Director of Admissions. 202 939-5040, 800 492-6882.

**FINANCIAL AID. Available aid:** Pell grants, SEOG, state grants, school scholarships and grants, private scholarships and grants, and academic merit scholarships. Perkins Loans (NDSL), PLUS, Stafford Loans (GSL), private loans, and SLS. Tuition Plan Inc., AMS, Tuition Management Systems, and deferred payment plan.
**Financial aid statistics:** Average amounts of aid awarded freshmen: Scholarships and grants, $6,000; loans, $2,500.
**Supporting data/closing dates:** FAFSA/FAF: Priority filing date is February 1; deadline is May 1. Income tax forms: Priority filing date is March 15; deadline is June 15. Notification of awards on rolling basis.
**Financial aid contact:** Penelope Grubik, Director of Financial Aid. 202 939-5047.

## University of the District of Columbia

**Washington, DC 20008** 202 282-7300

**1994-95 Costs.** Tuition: $864 (state residents), $3,456 (out-of-state). Housing: None. Fees, books, misc. academic expenses (school's estimate): $910.
**Enrollment.** Undergraduates: 1,664 men, 1,994 women (full-time). Freshman class: 3,895 applicants, 3,866 accepted, 1,917 enrolled. Graduate enrollment: 268 men, 355 women.
**Test score averages/ranges.** N/A.
**Faculty.** 265 full-time; 225 part-time. 52% of faculty holds doctoral degree. Student/faculty ratio: 13 to 1.
**Selectivity rating.** N/A.

**PROFILE.** The University of the District of Columbia, founded in 1976, is a public university. Programs are offered through the Colleges of Business and Public Management; Education and Human Ecology; Liberal and Fine Arts; Life Sciences; and Physical Science, Engineering, and Technology. Its 21-acre campus is located in Washington, D.C.

**Accreditation:** MSACS. Professionally accredited by the Accreditation Board for Engineering and Technology.
**Religious orientation:** University of the District of Columbia is nonsectarian; no religious requirements.
**Library:** Collections totaling over 575,457 volumes, 2,137 periodical subscriptions, and 602,144 microform items.
**Special facilities/museums:** Theatre, greenhouse.
**Athletic facilities:** Gymnasium, swimming pool, racquetball and tennis courts, weight room, exercise rooms, athletic field.

**STUDENT BODY. Undergraduate profile:** 85% are state residents; 15% are transfers. 3% Asian-American, 72% Black, 3% Hispanic, 3% White, 19% Other. Average age of undergraduates is 29.
**Freshman profile:** 90% of freshmen come from public schools.
**Undergraduate achievement:** 25% of fall 1992 freshmen returned for fall 1993 term. 25% of entering class graduated. 10% of students who completed a degree program immediately went on to graduate study.
**Foreign students:** 1,273 students are from out of the country. Countries represented include Cameroon, Ethiopia, Gambia, Kenya, Nigeria, and Trinidad/Tobago; 133 in all.

**PROGRAMS OF STUDY. Degrees:** B.A., B.S.
**Majors:** Accounting, Acting, Art Education, Biology, Business Education, Chemistry, Civil Engineering, Clothing/Textiles, Community Planning/Development, Computer Science, Computer Systems/Science, Construction Management, Directing, Early Childhood Education, Economics, Electrical Engineering, Elementary Education, English Studies, Environmental Science, Family Living/Child Development, Film Production/Cinematography, Finance, Food/Nutrition, Food Science, Forestry Management, French, General Theatre, Geography, Geoscience, German, Health Education, History, Home Economics Education, Humanities, Industrial Arts Education, Journalism, Library/Media Technology, Management, Mass Media, Mathematics, Mechanical Engineering, Media Science, Music, Music Education, Nursing, Office Administration, Ornamental Horticulture, Philosophy, Physical Education, Physics, Political Science, Printing Management, Procurement/Public Contracting, Psychology, Public Administration, Recreation Education, Social Welfare/Rehabilitation, Sociology, Spanish, Special Education, Speech/Language Pathology, Studio Art, Technical Theatre, Technical Vocational Education, Television Production, Theatre, Urban Studies, Wildlife Management, Writing.
**Distribution of degrees:** The majors with the highest enrollment are business and education; social sciences have the lowest.
**Requirements:** General education requirement.
**Academic regulations:** Minimum 2.3 GPA required for graduation.
**Special:** Associate's degrees offered. Double majors. Independent study. Internships. Cooperative education programs. Graduate school at which undergraduates may take graduate-level courses. Member of Consortium of Universities of the Washington Metropolitan Area. Teacher certification in early childhood, elementary, and special education. ROTC and AFROTC at Howard U. NROTC at Naval Science Inst.
**Honors:** Honors program.
**Academic Assistance:** Remedial reading and math.

**STUDENT LIFE. Housing:** Commuter campus; no student housing.
**Social atmosphere:** As reported by the student newspaper, "The nation's capital is a city that is rich in cultural and social diversity." The biggest events on campus in recent years have been the NCAA Division II basketball tournament, Homecoming events, rallies against apartheid, fundraiser dances, symposia, and career-oriented conferences. Influential groups include Greeks, student political science organizations, and student government members. Students frequent nightclubs with dancing, jazz, and reggae in Adams Morgan, Georgetown, and Capitol Hill.
**Services and counseling/handicapped student services:** Placement services. Health service. Counseling services for veteran and older students. Career and academic guidance services.
**Campus organizations:** Undergraduate student government. Student newspaper (Trilogy, published once/month). Yearbook. Radio station. Arts ensemble, departmental groups, jazz ensemble, marching band, The Voices chorale, music interest group, music senate, political science organization, modern dance group, special-interest organizations. Three fraternities, no chapter houses; three sororities, no chapter houses. 5% of men join a fraternity. 5% of women join a sorority.

**ATHLETICS. Physical education requirements:** 1-1/2 semesters of physical education required.
**Intercollegiate competition:** 5% of students participate. Basketball (M,W), cheerleading (W), cross-country (M,W), soccer (M), tennis (M,W), track and field (M,W), volleyball (W). Member of Independent, NCAA Division II.
**Intramural and club sports:** 10% of students participate. Intramural basketball, flag football, racquetball, softball, swimming, table tennis, tennis, weight training. Men's club swimming, volleyball. Women's club swimming.

**ADMISSIONS. Academic basis for candidate selection** (in order of priority): Secondary school record.
**Requirements:** Graduation from secondary school is required; GED is accepted. No specific distribution of secondary school units required. Open admissions policy to graduates of accredited secondary schools or the equivalent. Portfolio required of art program applicants. Audition required of music program applicants. Conditional admission possible for applicants not meeting standard requirements. Campus visit and interview recommended. No off-campus interviews.
**Procedure:** Suggest filing application by June 1. Application deadline is August 1. Notification of admission on rolling basis. Freshmen accepted for terms other than fall.
**Special programs:** Admission may be deferred one year. Placement may be granted through CEEB Advanced Placement exams for scores of 4 or higher. Credit may be granted through CLEP general and subject exams. Early decision program. Early entrance/early admission program. Concurrent enrollment program.
**Transfer students:** Transfer students accepted for terms other than fall. In fall 1992, 15% of all new students were transfers into all classes. Application deadline is June 14 for fall; November 15 for spring. Minimum 2.0 GPA required. Lowest course grade accepted is "C." At least 60 semester hours must be completed at the university to receive degree.
**Admissions contact:** Sandra Dolphin, M.A., Director of Admissions and Recruitment. 202 282-3200.

**FINANCIAL AID. Available aid:** Pell grants, SEOG, state scholarships and grants, school scholarships and grants, private scholarships, academic merit scholarships, and athletic scholarships. Perkins Loans (NDSL), PLUS, Stafford Loans (GSL), school loans, private loans, and SLS. Deferred payment plan.
**Financial aid statistics:** 7% of aid is not need-based. In 1993-94, 40% of all undergraduate applicants received aid; 50% of freshman applicants. Average amounts of aid awarded freshmen: Scholarships and grants, $450; loans, $600.
**Supporting data/closing dates:** FAFSA: Priority filing date is March 15; accepted on rolling basis. FAF/FFS: Accepted on rolling basis. Notification of awards on rolling basis.
**Financial aid contact:** Kenneth Howard, M.A., Director of Financial Aid. 202 282-3239.

**STUDENT EMPLOYMENT.** College Work/Study Program. Institutional employment. 2% of full-time undergraduates work on campus during school year. Students may expect to earn an average of $1,000 during school year. Off-campus part-time employment opportunities rated "good."

**COMPUTER FACILITIES.** 100 IBM/IBM-compatible microcomputers. Students may access Digital, IBM minicomputer/mainframe systems. Computer languages and software packages include APL, Assembler, COBOL, FORTRAN, PL/1, SAS, SPSS. Computer facilities are available to all students.
**Fees:** None.
**Hours:** 24 hours.

**GRADUATE CAREER DATA.** Graduate school percentages: 1% enter law school. 1% enter medical school. 1% enter dental school. 3% enter graduate business programs. 15% of graduates choose careers in business and industry. Companies and businesses that hire graduates: IBM, Kodak, Naval Air Systems Command, Xerox, Washington D.C. and federal governments.

**PROMINENT ALUMNI/AE.** Maggie Taylor, director of community services, HUD Office of Contracts; Marilyn Thornton, executive director, Arts D.C.; Warren E. Connley, aerospace engineer, Naval Air Systems Command.

# Florida

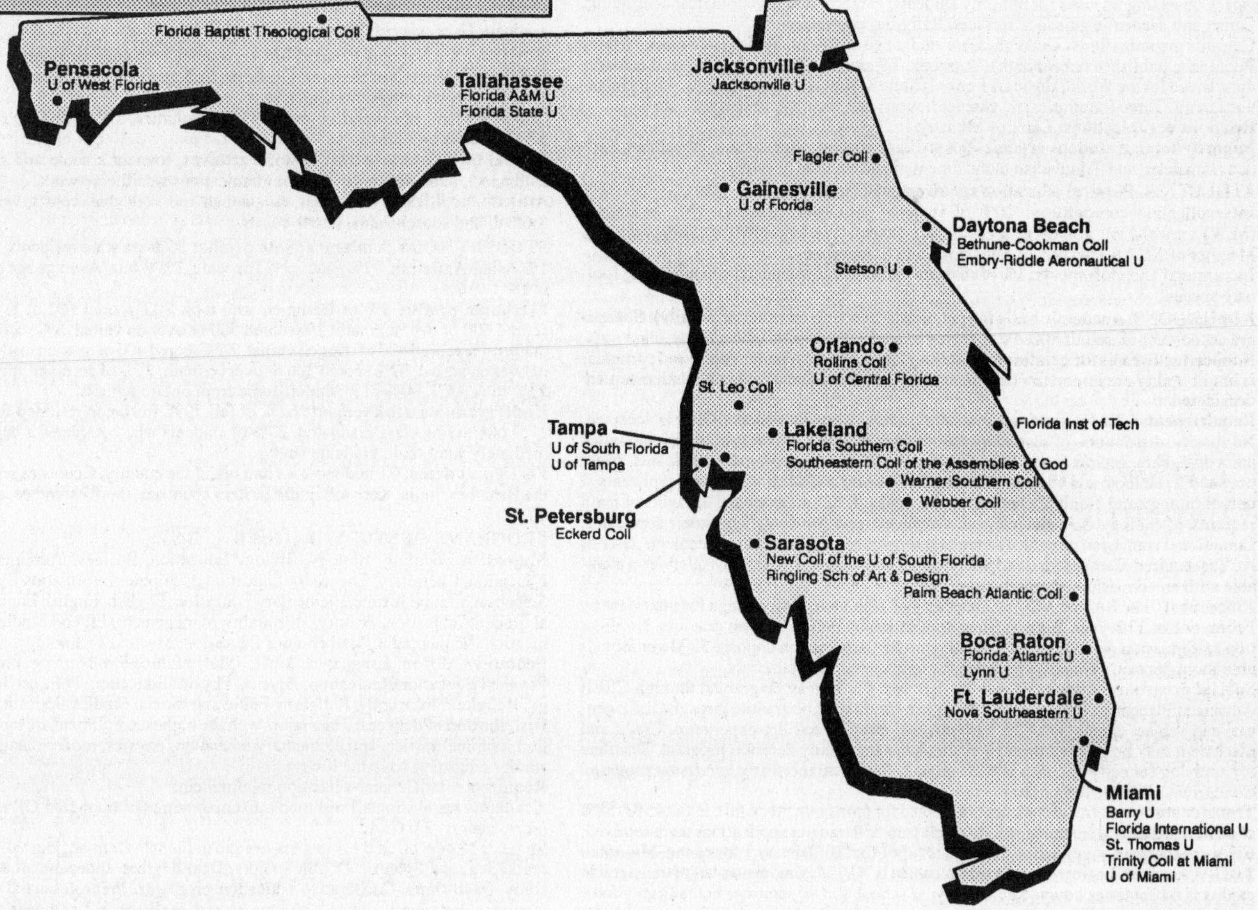


## Barry University

**Miami Shores, FL 33161** **305 899-3000**

**1994-95 Costs.** Tuition: $10,490. Room & board: $5,620. Fees, books, misc. academic expenses (school's estimate): $300.
**Enrollment.** Undergraduates: 668 men, 1,152 women (full-time). Freshman class: 878 applicants, 643 accepted, 266 enrolled. Graduate enrollment: 547 men, 1,253 women.
**Test score averages/ranges.** Average SAT scores: 454 verbal, 493 math. Range of SAT scores of middle 50%: 840-1040 combined. Average ACT scores: 20 composite. Range of ACT scores of middle 50%: 18-23 composite.
**Faculty.** 168 full-time; 228 part-time. 75% of faculty holds doctoral degree. Student/faculty ratio: 14 to 1.
**Selectivity rating.** Less competitive.

**PROFILE.** Barry, founded in 1940, is a church-affiliated, liberal arts university. Programs are offered through the Schools of Arts and Sciences, Business, Computer Science, Education, Nursing, and Social Work, and the Frank J. Rooney School of Adult and Continuing Education. Its 90-acre campus is located in Miami Shores.

**Accreditation:** SACS. Professionally accredited by the Council on Social Work Education, the National Council for Accreditation of Teacher Education, the National League for Nursing.
**Religious orientation:** Barry University is affiliated with the Roman Catholic Church (Adrian Dominican Sisters); two semesters of religion/theology required.
**Library:** Collections totaling over 500,000 volumes, 2,000 periodical subscriptions, and 300,000 microform items.
**Special facilities/museums:** Language lab, human performance lab.
**Athletic facilities:** Gymnasium, basketball, racquetball, tennis, and volleyball courts, training and weight rooms, swimming pool, baseball, intramural, soccer, and softball fields, track.
**STUDENT BODY. Undergraduate profile:** 68% are state residents; 58% are transfers. 1% Asian-American, 12% Black, 26% Hispanic, 50% White, 11% Other. Average age of undergraduates is 18.
**Freshman profile:** 1% of freshmen who took SAT scored 700 or over on verbal; 4% scored 600 or over on verbal, 10% scored 600 or over on math; 19% scored 500 or over on verbal, 38% scored 500 or over on math; 64% scored 400 or over on verbal, 78% scored 400 or over on math; 100% scored 300 or over on verbal, 100% scored 300 or over on math. 84% of accepted applicants took SAT; 30% took ACT.

**Undergraduate achievement:** 68% of fall 1992 freshmen returned for fall 1993 term. 41% of entering class graduated.
**Foreign students:** 442 students are from out of the country. Countries represented include the Bahamas, Canada, Equador, Jamaica, Trinidad, and Venezuela; 68 in all.
**PROGRAMS OF STUDY. Degrees:** B.A., B.F.A., B.Lib.Studies, B.Prof.Studies, B.S.
**Majors:** Accounting, Art, Art Management, Biology, Broadcast Communication, Cardiovascular Perfusion, Chemistry, Communication Arts, Computer Science, Criminal Justice, Cytotechnology, Diagnostic Medical Ultrasound Technology, Economics/Finance, Elementary/Early Childhood Education, English, Exercise Science, French, History, International Studies, Journalism, Liberal Studies, Literature, Management, Management Information Systems, Marketing, Mathematical Sciences, Medical Technology, Nuclear Medical Technology, Nursing, Occupational Therapy, Philosophy, Photography, Physical Education, Political Science, Pre-Law, Professional Writing, Psychology, Public Relations, Secondary Education, Sociology, Spanish, Sport Management, Sports Information, Sports Management/Diving Industry, Sports Medicine/Athletic Training, Theatre, Theatre Management, Theology.
**Distribution of degrees:** The majors with the highest enrollment are accounting, management, and nursing.
**Requirements:** General education requirement.
**Academic regulations:** Minimum 2.0 GPA must be maintained.
**Special:** Minors offered in all majors and in music and secondary education. Double majors. Dual degrees. Accelerated study. Pass/fail grading option. Internships. Graduate school at which undergraduates may take graduate-level courses. Preprofessional programs in law, medicine, veterinary science, pharmacy, and dentistry. 3-2 engineering program with U of Miami. Exchange programs with Aquinas Coll, Dominican Coll, St. Mary's Dominican Coll, and St. Thomas Aquinas Coll. Teacher certification in early childhood, elementary, and secondary education. Certification in specific subject areas. Exchange program abroad in England (Manchester Coll of Oxford). Study abroad also in Belgium, France, Luxembourg, and the Netherlands. ROTC and AFROTC at U of Miami.
**Honors:** Honors program. Honor societies.
**Academic Assistance:** Remedial reading, writing, math, and study skills. Nonremedial tutoring.

**STUDENT LIFE. Housing:** Coed and women's dorms. 44% of students live in college housing.
**Social atmosphere:** Influential student groups include Fellowship of Christian Athletes, Trinidadian Club, Student Activities Department, White Boys of Rap, and Ahern and Leval's Comedy Club. Basketball is popular. Special events include the Halloween Dance, Rat Dances, Carnival Day, Spring Formal, intramural sports, Lady Buc Women's Soccer Invitational, Disney World and Epcot trip, David Brinkley Communications Award ceremony, and Barry Weekender. Favorite off-campus gathering spots include the Mayfair, UKE, Orange Bowl, Tugboat Annie's, and East Side Mario's, which features crab races.

On campus, students frequent the Houndstooth, Buccaneer office, Earl and James Halls, and the swimming pool.
**Services and counseling/handicapped student services:** Placement services. Health service. Counseling services for minority students. Personal and psychological counseling. Career and academic guidance services. Religious counseling.
**Campus organizations:** Undergraduate student government. Student newspaper (Barry Buccaneer, published once/month). Yearbook. TV station. Chorale, Key Notes, Ambassadors, Bread for the World, Business Forum, Circle K, special-interest groups, 43 organizations in all. Three fraternities, no chapter houses; one sorority, no chapter house.
**Religious organizations:** Campus Ministry.
**Minority/foreign student organizations:** Black student organization, Bahamian, Haitian, Jamaican, and Trinidadian clubs. International Student Services.
**ATHLETICS. Physical education requirements:** None.
**Intercollegiate competition:** 10% of students participate. Baseball (M), basketball (M,W), crew (M,W), golf (M), soccer (M,W), softball (W), tennis (M,W), volleyball (W). Member of NCAA Division II, Sunshine State Conference.
**Intramural and club sports:** 1% of students participate. Intramural basketball, flag football, soccer.
**ADMISSIONS. Academic basis for candidate selection** (in order of priority): Secondary school record, standardized test scores, school's recommendation, essay, class rank.
**Nonacademic basis for candidate selection:** Extracurricular participation and particular talent or ability are important. Character and personality and alumni/ae relationship are considered.
**Requirements:** Graduation from secondary school is recommended; GED is accepted. No specific distribution of secondary school units required. 3.5 units of math including 2 units of algebra, geometry, and trigonometry required of math program applicants. Algebra I and II, biology, and chemistry required of nursing and science program applicants. 1 unit of biology and 1 unit of chemistry with grade of "C" or better and 2.5 units of math required of biology (pre-medical, pre-veterinary, and pre-dental) program applicants. Conditional admission possible for applicants not meeting standard requirements. SAT or ACT is required. Campus visit and interview recommended. Off-campus interviews available with an admissions representative.
**Procedure:** Take SAT or ACT by October 1 of 12th year. Visit college for interview by February 1 of 12th year. Suggest filing application by February 1; no deadline. Notification of admission on rolling basis. $100 nonrefundable tuition deposit. $200 nonrefundable room deposit. Freshmen accepted for terms other than fall.
**Special programs:** Admission may be deferred. Credit may be granted through CEEB Advanced Placement for scores of 3 or higher. Credit may be granted through CLEP general and subject exams, DANTES exams, and military and life experience. Credit and placement may be granted through challenge exams. Early decision program. Deadline for applying for early decision is November 1. Early entrance/early admission program. Concurrent enrollment program.
**Transfer students:** Transfer students accepted for terms other than fall. In fall 1993, 58% of all new students were transfers into all classes. 878 transfer applications were received, 637 were accepted. Application deadline is July 1 for fall; January 1 for spring. Minimum 2.0 GPA required. Lowest course grade accepted is "C." Maximum number of transferable credits is 64 semester hours from a two-year school and 90 semester hours from a four-year school. At least 30 semester hours must be completed at the university to receive degree.
**Admissions contact:** Robin R. Roberts, Dean of Admissions. 305 899-3100.
**FINANCIAL AID. Available aid:** Pell grants, SEOG, state scholarships and grants, school scholarships and grants, private scholarships and grants, academic merit scholarships, and athletic scholarships. PLUS, Stafford Loans (GSL), Health Professions Loans, state loans, school loans, private loans, and SLS. Knight Tuition Plans, AMS, Tuition Management Systems, deferred payment plan, and family tuition reduction.
**Financial aid statistics:** 40% of aid is not need-based. In 1993-94, 68% of all undergraduate applicants received aid; 82% of freshman applicants. Average amounts of aid awarded freshmen: Scholarships and grants, $1,000; loans, $2,000.
**Supporting data/closing dates:** FAFSA/FAF/FFS: Priority filing date is March 1. School's own aid application: Priority filing date is March 1. State aid form: Priority filing date is March 1. Income tax forms: Accepted on rolling basis. Notification of awards on rolling basis.
**Financial aid contact:** Valerie Turner, Director of Financial Aid. 305 899-3673.
**STUDENT EMPLOYMENT.** College Work/Study Program. Institutional employment. 20% of full-time undergraduates work on campus during school year. Students may expect to earn an average of $1,000 during school year. Off-campus part-time employment opportunities rated "fair."
**COMPUTER FACILITIES.** 400 IBM/IBM-compatible and Macintosh/Apple microcomputers; 250 are networked. Students may access Digital minicomputer/mainframe systems, BITNET, Internet. Computer languages and software packages include Ada, BASIC, C, COBOL, RPG II; 40 in all. Computer facilities are available to all students.
**Fees:** None.
**Hours:** 8 AM-midn.

## Bethune-Cookman College

**Daytona Beach, FL 32114-3099 — 904 255-1401**

**1994-95 Costs.** Tuition: $5,138. Room & board: $3,396. Fees, books, misc. academic expenses (school's estimate): $1,027.
**Enrollment.** Undergraduates: 868 men, 1,260 women (full-time). Freshman class: 1,646 applicants, 1,150 accepted, 549 enrolled.
**Test score averages/ranges.** Average SAT scores: 367 verbal, 408 math. Average ACT scores: 16 English, 16 math, 16 composite.
**Faculty.** 125 full-time; 87 part-time. 48% of faculty holds doctoral degree. Student/faculty ratio: 15 to 1.
**Selectivity rating.** Less competitive.

**PROFILE.** Bethune-Cookman is a church-affiliated, historically black college. It is the product of the 1923 merger of Cookman Institute for Boys (founded in 1872) and the Daytona Normal and Industrial Institute for Girls (founded in 1904). Its 52-acre campus is located near the downtown section of Daytona Beach.

**Accreditation:** SACS. Professionally accredited by the American Medical Association (CAHEA), the National Council for Accreditation of Teacher Education.
**Religious orientation:** Bethune-Cookman College is affiliated with the United Methodist Church; two semesters of religion required.
**Library:** Collections totaling over 145,864 volumes, 770 periodical subscriptions, and 37,118 microform items.
**Special facilities/museums:** Historic archives, founder's home and gravesite (historic landmark), outreach center, telecommunications satellite network.
**Athletic facilities:** Gymnasium, racquetball and volleyball courts, weight room, track, football and soccer fields, tennis courts.
**STUDENT BODY. Undergraduate profile:** 86% are state residents; 1% are transfers. 1% Asian-American, 97% Black, 1% Hispanic, 1% White. Average age of undergraduates is 18.
**Freshman profile:** 1% of freshmen who took SAT scored 600 or over on verbal, 1% scored 600 or over on math; 2% scored 500 or over on verbal, 3% scored 500 or over on math; 14% scored 400 or over on verbal, 24% scored 400 or over on math; 50% scored 300 or over on verbal, 69% scored 300 or over on math. 27% of accepted applicants took SAT; 23% took ACT. 90% of freshmen come from public schools.
**Undergraduate achievement:** 67% of fall 1992 freshmen returned for fall 1993 term. 17% of entering class graduated. 23% of students who completed a degree program immediately went on to graduate study.
**Foreign students:** 67 students are from out of the country. Countries represented include the Bahamas, India, Kenya, Middle Eastern countries, the West Indies, and Uganda; 10 in all.
**PROGRAMS OF STUDY. Degrees:** B.A., B.S.
**Majors:** Accounting, Biology, Biology Education, Business Administration, Business Education, Chemistry, Chemistry Education, Computer Information Systems, Computer Science, Criminal Justice, Elementary Education, English, English Education, Exceptional Student Education, History, Hospitality Management, Liberal Studies, Mass Communication, Mathematics, Mathematics Education, Medical Technology, Modern Language Education, Modern Languages, Music, Music Education, Nursing, Physical Education, Physical Education/Recreation, Physics, Physics Education, Political Science, Psychology, Religion/Philosophy, Religious Education, Social Studies Education, Sociology.
**Distribution of degrees:** The majors with the highest enrollment are business administration, criminal justice, and elementary education; physics, modern languages, and social studies education have the lowest.
**Requirements:** General education requirement.
**Academic regulations:** Freshmen must maintain minimum 1.85 GPA; sophomores, juniors, seniors, 2.0 GPA.
**Special:** Minors offered in most majors and in French, German, journalism, management, marketing, and Spanish. Double majors. Dual degrees. Independent study. Accelerated study. Internships. Cooperative education programs. Preprofessional programs in law, medicine, veterinary science, pharmacy, and dentistry. 3-2 engineering programs with Florida A&M U, Florida Atlantic U, U of Florida, and Tuskegee U. Teacher certification in elementary, secondary, and special education. Study abroad in France, Germany, and Spain. ROTC and AFROTC at Embry-Riddle Aeronautical U.
**Honors:** Honors program. Honor societies.
**Academic Assistance:** Remedial reading, writing, math, and study skills. Nonremedial tutoring.
**STUDENT LIFE. Housing:** All freshmen must live on campus unless living with family. Women's and men's dorms. 57% of students live in college housing.
**Social atmosphere:** As reported by the student newspaper, "There needs to be more of a balance between educational, cultural, and social events on campus. We have no student union." Students like to gather on campus at The Quad and the Snackbar. Some favorite off-campus hang outs include C.G. Happs, the Dollar Movies, the Volusia Mall, and the beach. Influential groups on campus are Religious Life Fellowship, the Marching Wildcats, and the Wildcat football team. Popular campus events are Homecoming, Founder's Day, concerts, and football games.
**Services and counseling/handicapped student services:** Placement services. Health service. Counseling services for minority, military, veteran, and older students. Birth control, personal, and psychological counseling. Career and academic guidance services. Religious counseling. Physically disabled student services. Tape recorders. Tutors.
**Campus organizations:** Undergraduate student government. Student newspaper (Voice, published once/month). Yearbook. Radio station. Concert chorale, gospel choir, marching band, drama group, Men's Senate, Women's Senate, 40 organizations in all. Four fraternities, no chapter houses; four sororities, no chapter houses. 2% of men join a fraternity. 5% of women join a sorority.
**Religious organizations:** Religion and Philosophy Club, Religious Fellowship Club.
**Minority/foreign student organizations:** NAACP. International Relations Club, Federation of Bahamian Students.
**ATHLETICS. Physical education requirements:** Two semesters of physical education required.
**Intercollegiate competition:** 12% of students participate. Baseball (M), basketball (M,W), cheerleading (M,W), cross-country (M,W), football (M), golf (M,W), softball (W), tennis (M,W), track (indoor) (W), track (outdoor) (M,W), track and field (indoor) (W), track and field (outdoor) (M,W), volleyball (W). Member of MEAC, NCAA Division I, NCAA Division I-AA for football.
**Intramural and club sports:** 1% of students participate. Intramural baseball, basketball, football, softball, table tennis, volleyball. Men's club soccer.
**ADMISSIONS. Academic basis for candidate selection** (in order of priority): Secondary school record, school's recommendation, class rank, essay, standardized test scores.
**Nonacademic basis for candidate selection:** Character and personality are emphasized. Extracurricular participation and particular talent or ability are important.
**Requirements:** Graduation from secondary school is required; GED is accepted. 26 units and the following program of study are required: 4 units of English, 3 units of math, 3 units

of science, 2 units of foreign language, 5 units of social studies, 9 units of academic electives. Minimum 2.0 GPA required. Special Services program for applicants not meeting standard requirements. SAT or ACT is recommended. No off-campus interviews.
**Procedure:** Take SAT or ACT by July of 12th year. Visit college for interview by January of 12th year. Application deadline is July 30. Notification of admission on rolling basis. $100 room deposit, refundable until registration. Freshmen accepted for terms other than fall.
**Special programs:** Admission may be deferred one year. Credit may be granted through CEEB Advanced Placement for scores of 3 or higher. Credit may be granted through CLEP general and subject exams. Early decision program.
**Transfer students:** Transfer students accepted for terms other than fall. In fall 1993, 1% of all new students were transfers into all classes. 140 transfer applications were received, 100 were accepted. Application deadline is July 30 for fall; November 30 for spring. Minimum 2.0 GPA required. Lowest course grade accepted is "C." Maximum number of transferable credits is 60 semester hours. At least 30 semester hours must be completed at the college to receive degree.
**Admissions contact:** Roberto Barragan, Jr., Ed.D., Director of Admissions. 904 238-3803, 800 448-0228.

**FINANCIAL AID. Available aid:** Pell grants, SEOG, Federal Nursing Student Scholarships, state scholarships and grants, school scholarships and grants, private scholarships and grants, ROTC scholarships, academic merit scholarships, athletic scholarships, aid for undergraduate foreign students, and United Negro College Fund. Perkins Loans (NDSL), PLUS, Stafford Loans (GSL), state loans, private loans, and SLS. Tuition Plan Inc., AMS, and deferred payment plan.
**Financial aid statistics:** 22% of aid is not need-based. In 1993-94, 85% of all undergraduate applicants received aid; 95% of freshman applicants. Average amounts of aid awarded freshmen: Scholarships and grants, $2,450; loans, $2,695.
**Supporting data/closing dates:** FAFSA/FAF/FFS: Priority filing date is March 1. Notification of awards begins May 1.
**Financial aid contact:** Joseph L. Coleman, Director of Financial Aid. 904 255-1401.

**STUDENT EMPLOYMENT.** College Work/Study Program. Institutional employment. 18% of full-time undergraduates work on campus during school year. Students may expect to earn an average of $1,400 during school year. Off-campus part-time employment opportunities rated "fair."

**COMPUTER FACILITIES.** 150 IBM/IBM-compatible and Macintosh/Apple microcomputers; 100 are networked. Students may access Digital minicomputer/mainframe systems. Residence halls may be equipped with stand-alone microcomputers. Computer languages and software packages include BASIC, C, COBOL, FORTRAN, LISP, Pascal. Computer facilities are available to all students.
**Fees:** $20 computer fee per academic year.
**Hours:** 8 AM-10 PM.

**GRADUATE CAREER DATA.** Graduate school percentages: 2% enter law school. 1% enter medical school. 9% enter graduate business programs. 5% enter graduate arts and sciences programs. 1% enter theological school/seminary. Highest graduate school enrollments: Florida A&M U, Florida International U, Nova U, U of Central Florida. 30% of graduates choose careers in business and industry. Companies and businesses that hire graduates: IBM, Bell South, State Farm Insurance, Wal-Mart, Sears, local school districts.

**PROMINENT ALUMNI/AE.** Anthony Godbolt, Theodore Nicholson, and David Moore, physicians; Zelle Blunt, neurosurgeon; Andre Samuels, Tampa Bay Buccaneers; Ricky Claitt, Washington Redskins; Carl Cannon and Edward Dawkins, lawyers; Dr. Oswald P. Bronson, Sr., college president.

# Eckerd College

**St. Petersburg, FL 33711 — 813 867-1166**

**1994-95 Costs.** Tuition: $15,360. Room & board: $4,080. Fees, books, misc. academic expenses (school's estimate): $920.
**Enrollment.** Undergraduates: 677 men, 715 women (full-time). Freshman class: 1,422 applicants, 1,109 accepted, 366 enrolled.
**Test score averages/ranges.** Average SAT scores: 517 verbal, 559 math. Range of SAT scores of middle 50%: 460-580 verbal, 510-620 math. Average ACT scores: 25 composite. Range of ACT scores of middle 50%: 22-28 composite.
**Faculty.** 87 full-time; 52 part-time. 90% of faculty holds doctoral degree. Student/faculty ratio: 14 to 1.
**Selectivity rating.** Competitive.

**PROFILE.** Eckerd, founded in 1958, is a church-affiliated college of liberal arts and sciences. Its 267-acre campus is located on Boca Ciega Bay in St. Petersburg, 25 miles from Tampa.

**Accreditation:** SACS.
**Religious orientation:** Eckerd College is affiliated with the Presbyterian Church USA; no religious requirements.
**Library:** Collections totaling over 120,000 volumes, 1,100 periodical subscriptions, and 13,000 microform items.
**Special facilities/museums:** Language lab.
**Athletic facilities:** Gymnasium, swimming pool, weight room, baseball, soccer, and softfields, tennis courts, waterfront facility for sailing and water skiing (fleet of over 50 boats), fitness course.

**STUDENT BODY. Undergraduate profile:** 28% are state residents; 17% are transfers. 2% Asian-American, 3% Black, 3% Hispanic, 1% Native American, 81% White, 10% Other. Average age of undergraduates is 20.
**Freshman profile:** 1% of freshmen who took SAT scored 700 or over on verbal, 5% scored 700 or over on math; 16% scored 600 or over on verbal, 31% scored 600 or over on math; 57% scored 500 or over on verbal, 78% scored 500 or over on math; 96% scored 400 or over on verbal, 97% scored 400 or over on math; 100% scored 300 or over on verbal, 100% scored 300 or over on math. 11% of freshmen who took ACT scored 30 or over on composite; 64% scored 24 or over on composite; 99% scored 18 or over on composite; 100% scored 12 or over on composite. 85% of accepted applicants took SAT; 46% took ACT. 80% of freshmen come from public schools.
**Undergraduate achievement:** 80% of fall 1992 freshmen returned for fall 1993 term. 60% of entering class graduated. 45% of students who completed a degree program immediately went on to graduate study.
**Foreign students:** 143 students are from out of the country. Countries represented include Brazil, France, Germany, India, Japan, and Sweden; 55 in all.

**PROGRAMS OF STUDY. Degrees:** B.A., B.S.
**Majors:** American Studies, Anthropology, Biology, Business Administration, Chemistry, Comparative Education Studies, Comparative Literature, Computer Science, Creative Writing, Economics, Elementary Education, Environmental Studies, French, German, History, Human Development, Humanities, International Business, International Studies, Literature, Management, Marine Science, Mathematics, Modern Languages, Music, Philosophy, Philosophy/Religion, Physics, Political Science, Psychology, Religious Studies, Russian Studies, Sociology, Spanish, Theatre, Visual Arts, Women's/Gender Studies.
**Distribution of degrees:** The majors with the highest enrollment are management, international business, and psychology; humanities, music, and Russian studies have the lowest.
**Requirements:** General education requirement.
**Academic regulations:** Freshmen must maintain minimum 1.80 GPA; sophomores, 1.90 GPA; juniors, 2.00 GPA; seniors, 2.00 GPA.
**Special:** Minors offered in all majors. Student-created majors and concentrations. Self-designed majors. Double majors. Dual degrees. Independent study. Accelerated study. Pass/fail grading option. Internships. Preprofessional programs in law, medicine, veterinary science, dentistry, and theology. 3-2 engineering programs with Auburn U, Columbia U, Georgia Tech, and Washington U. Sea Semester. Exchange programs with other 4-1-4 colleges and universities. Teacher certification in elementary and secondary education. Certification in specific subject areas. Member of International Student Exchange Program (ISEP). Exchange programs abroad in England (London Study Center) and Japan (Kansai U of Foreign Studies). ROTC and AFROTC at U of South Florida.
**Honors:** Honors program. Honor societies.
**Academic Assistance:** Nonremedial tutoring.

**STUDENT LIFE. Housing:** All first-time freshmen must live on campus unless living with family. Coed, women's, and men's dorms. Off-campus privately-owned housing. 78% of students live in college housing.
**Social atmosphere:** The student newspaper reports that students are most likely to be found in the Pub or "wherever a party is happening. The social life is controlled by the parties happening on campus. No group has any significance on the student social life; the dorms create the social environment." Popular social events include Zeta Halloween, Homelycoming, Jello Jam, Spring Ball, and Spring Beta.
**Services and counseling/handicapped student services:** Placement services. Health service. Women's center. Counseling services for minority, veteran, and older students. Birth control, personal, and psychological counseling. Career and academic guidance services. Religious counseling. Physically disabled student services. Tutors. Reader services for the blind.
**Campus organizations:** Undergraduate student government. Student newspaper (Triton Tribune, published once/week). Literary magazine. Yearbook. Radio and TV stations. Concert choir, theatre workshop, Young Republicans, Young Democrats, World Concerns, College Bowl Society, Earth Society, water safety and rescue team, special-interest groups, 62 organizations in all.
**Religious organizations:** Campus Ministry, Fellowship of Christian Athletes.
**Minority/foreign student organizations:** Afro-American Society. International Student Organization.

**ATHLETICS. Physical education requirements:** None.
**Intercollegiate competition:** 12% of students participate. Baseball (M), basketball (M,W), cross-country (M,W), golf (M), sailing (M,W), soccer (M), softball (W), tennis (M,W), volleyball (W). Member of NCAA Division II, Sunshine State Conference.
**Intramural and club sports:** 22% of students participate. Intramural basketball, sailing, softball, swimming, tennis, touch football, track, volleyball. Men's club volleyball.

**ADMISSIONS. Academic basis for candidate selection** (in order of priority): Secondary school record, standardized test scores, essay, class rank, school's recommendation.
**Nonacademic basis for candidate selection:** Particular talent or ability is emphasized. Character and personality and extracurricular participation are important.
**Requirements:** Graduation from secondary school is required; GED is accepted. 18 units and the following program of study are required: 4 units of English, 3 units of math, 3 units of lab science, 2 units of foreign language, 2 units of social studies, 2 units of history, 2 units of electives. Minimum combined SAT score of 850 (composite ACT score of 20) and minimum 2.5 GPA recommended. SAT or ACT is required. PSAT is recommended. ACH recommended. Campus visit and interview recommended. Off-campus interviews available with an admissions representative.
**Procedure:** Take SAT or ACT by December 15 of 12th year. Take ACH by December 15 of 12th year. Visit college for interview by March 1 of 12th year. Suggest filing application by January 15; no deadline. Notification of admission on rolling basis. Reply is required by May 1. $100 tuition deposit, refundable until May 1. Freshmen accepted for terms other than fall.
**Special programs:** Admission may be deferred one year. Credit and/or placement may be granted through CEEB Advanced Placement exams for scores of 4 or higher. Credit and/or placement may be granted through CLEP subject exams. Credit and placement may be granted through Regents College, DANTES, and challenge exams. Early entrance/early admission program.
**Transfer students:** Transfer students accepted for terms other than fall. In fall 1993, 17% of all new students were transfers into all classes. 231 transfer applications were received, 146 were accepted. Application deadline is April 1 for fall; November 1 for spring. Minimum 2.5 GPA recommended. Lowest course grade accepted is "C." Maximum number of transferable credits is 63 semester hours. At least 63 semester hours must be completed at the college to receive degree.
**Admissions contact:** Richard R. Hallin, Ph.D., Dean of Admissions. 813 864-8331.

**FINANCIAL AID. Available aid:** Pell grants, SEOG, state scholarships and grants, school scholarships and grants, private scholarships and grants, ROTC scholarships, academic merit scholarships, athletic scholarships, and aid for undergraduate foreign students. Perkins Loans (NDSL), PLUS, Stafford Loans (GSL), school loans, and SLS. AMS.
**Financial aid statistics:** 20% of aid is not need-based. In 1993-94, 100% of all undergraduate applicants received aid; 100% of freshman applicants. Average amounts of aid awarded freshmen: Scholarships and grants, $9,000; loans, $3,000.
**Supporting data/closing dates:** FAFSA: Priority filing date is April 1. Notification of awards begins March 1.
**Financial aid contact:** Margaret W. Morris, M.A., Director of Financial Aid. 813 864-8334.

**STUDENT EMPLOYMENT.** College Work/Study Program. Institutional employment. 43% of full-time undergraduates work on campus during school year. Students may expect to earn an average of $1,000 during school year. Off-campus part-time employment opportunities rated "excellent."

**COMPUTER FACILITIES.** 50 IBM/IBM-compatible, Macintosh/Apple, and RISC-/UNIX-based microcomputers; 35 are networked. Students may access SUN minicomputer/mainframe systems, BITNET, Internet. Client/LAN operating systems include Apple/Macintosh, DOS, UNIX/XENIX/AIX, Windows NT, X-windows, LocalTalk/AppleTalk, Novell. 25 major computer languages and software packages available. Computer facilities are available to all students.
**Fees:** Computer fee is included in tuition/fees.
**Hours:** 8:30 AM-12 midn.

**GRADUATE CAREER DATA.** Graduate school percentages: 8% enter law school. 5% enter medical school. 1% enter dental school. 13% enter graduate business programs. 25% enter graduate arts and sciences programs. 2% enter theological school/seminary. Highest graduate school enrollments: Emory U, Florida State U, Vanderbilt U, U of Florida, U of South Florida. 50% of graduates choose careers in business and industry. Companies and businesses that hire graduates: Allstate Insurance, Chase Banks, Raymond James Associates, Templeton Mutual Funds.

**PROMINENT ALUMNI/AE.** Sterling Watson, teacher and novelist; Chris Trakas, opera singer; Jane Petro, medical doctor; Susan Russ, Rhodes Scholar.

## Embry-Riddle Aeronautical University

**Daytona Beach, FL 32114-3900 904 226-6000**

**1994-95 Costs.** Tuition: $7,370. Room: $1,800. Board: $1,430. Fees, books, misc. academic expenses (school's estimate): $400.

**Enrollment.** Undergraduates: 3,102 men, 401 women (full-time). Freshman class: 3,092 applicants, 2,496 accepted, 688 enrolled. Graduate enrollment: 152 men, 27 women.

**Test score averages/ranges.** Average SAT scores: 446 verbal, 530 math. Average ACT scores: 22 English, 23 math, 23 composite.

**Faculty.** 226 full-time; 41 part-time. 58% of faculty holds highest degree in specific field. Student/faculty ratio: 17 to 1.

**Selectivity rating.** Less competitive.

**PROFILE.** Embry-Riddle, founded in 1926, is a private university devoted exclusively to the field of aviation. Its Daytona Beach campus, established in 1965, is located at Daytona Beach Regional Airport.

**Accreditation:** SACS. Professionally accredited by the Accreditation Board for Engineering and Technology.
**Religious orientation:** Embry-Riddle Aeronautical University is nonsectarian; no religious requirements.
**Library:** Collections totaling over 53,350 volumes, 1,242 periodical subscriptions, and 159,484 microform items.
**Special facilities/museums:** Fully equipped aircraft, training simulators, airway science simulation lab, wind tunnel.
**Athletic facilities:** Swimming pool, basketball, racquetball, tennis, and volleyball courts, weight room, athletic and softball fields.

**STUDENT BODY. Undergraduate profile:** 28% are state residents; 28% are transfers. 5% Asian-American, 5% Black, 6% Hispanic, .3% Native American, 78.2% White, 5.5% Other. Average age of undergraduates is 22.
**Freshman profile:** 1% of freshmen who took SAT scored 700 or over on verbal, 3% scored 700 or over on math; 4% scored 600 or over on verbal, 25% scored 600 or over on math; 28% scored 500 or over on verbal, 67% scored 500 or over on math; 75% scored 400 or over on verbal, 92% scored 400 or over on math; 96% scored 300 or over on verbal, 99% scored 300 or over on math. Majority of accepted applicants took SAT.
**Foreign students:** 457 students are from out of the country. Countries represented include Canada, India, Kuwait, Malaysia, South Korea, and United Arab Emirates; 85 in all.

**PROGRAMS OF STUDY. Degrees:** B.S.
**Majors:** Aeronautical Science, Aerospace Engineering, Aerospace Studies, Aircraft Engineering Technology, Aviation Business Administration, Aviation Computer Science, Aviation Maintenance Management, Aviation Technology, Avionics Engineering Technology, Engineering Physics, Management of Technical Operations, Professional Aeronautics.
**Distribution of degrees:** The majors with the highest enrollment are aeronautical science, aviation business administration, and aerospace engineering; management of technical operations, aerospace studies, and aviation computer science have the lowest.
**Requirements:** General education requirement.
**Academic regulations:** Minimum 2.0 GPA must be maintained.
**Special:** Minors offered in air traffic control, aviation business administration, aviation safety, computer science, humanities, mathematics, psychology, and space studies. Associate's degrees offered. Double majors. Dual degrees. Independent study. Internships. Cooperative education programs. Graduate school at which undergraduates may take graduate-level courses. Member of American Higher Educational Center Consortium and Florida Space Grant Consortium. Study abroad in France and Germany. ROTC and AFROTC.
**Honors:** Phi Beta Kappa. Honor societies.
**Academic Assistance:** Remedial reading, writing, and math. Nonremedial tutoring.

**STUDENT LIFE. Housing:** Students may live on or off campus. Coed dorms. Fraternity housing. School-owned/operated apartments. Off-campus privately-owned housing. 24% of students live in college housing.
**Social atmosphere:** The student newspaper reports, "Aviation topics or activities are always occurring. Surfing and other beach activities are a big topic." The big events of the year are the Daytona 24-hour auto race, the Daytona 500, spring break festivities, the Halloween dance, the Sky Fest Airshow, and aviation and space guest speakers. Influential groups on campus include ROTC, Aviators, the entertainment committee, and the student newspaper staff. Favorite off-campus destinations include the 701 South Club, Mr. Gatti's Restaurant, the beach, and the Kennedy Space Center.
**Services and counseling/handicapped student services:** Health service. Counseling services for minority, military, veteran, and older students. Birth control, personal, and psychological counseling. Career and academic guidance services. Religious counseling. Physically disabled student services. Learning disabled services. Tutors.
**Campus organizations:** Undergraduate student government. Student newspaper (Avion, published once/week). Yearbook. Radio station. Angel Flight, Brothers of the Wind, Flight Team, Screaming Eagles, WERU broadcast club, parachute and photography clubs, veteran clubs, preprofessional groups, special-interest groups, 83 organizations in all. Seven fraternities, three chapter houses; two sororities, no chapter houses. 5% of men join a fraternity. 2% of women join a sorority.
**Religious organizations:** Christian Fellowship Club, Muslim Students Association.
**Minority/foreign student organizations:** African Student Aviation Association, Hispanic club. Caribbean Association, EuroConnections in America, Icelandic Student Association, Emirates National Student Union, Korean Student Association.

**ATHLETICS. Physical education requirements:** None.
**Intercollegiate competition:** 20% of students participate. Baseball (M), basketball (M), cheerleading (M,W), golf (M), soccer (M), tennis (M). Member of Florida Sun Conference, NAIA.
**Intramural and club sports:** 60% of students participate. Intramural basketball, bowling, flag football, golf, racquetball, sailing, scuba diving, sky diving, soccer, softball, swimming, wind surfing, wrestling. Men's club bowling, cycling, fencing, golf, lacrosse, martial arts, racquetball, sailing, soccer, volleyball, water skiing, wrestling. Women's club bowling, cycling, fencing, golf, martial arts, racquetball, sailing, soccer, volleyball, water skiing.

**ADMISSIONS. Academic basis for candidate selection** (in order of priority): Secondary school record, standardized test scores, class rank, essay, school's recommendation.
**Nonacademic basis for candidate selection:** Character and personality, extracurricular participation, and particular talent or ability are considered.
**Requirements:** Graduation from secondary school is required; GED is accepted. 13 units and the following program of study are recommended: 4 units of English, 3 units of math, 3 units of science, 3 units of social studies. Minimum SAT scores of 450 verbal and 500 math, rank in top half of secondary school class, and minimum 2.0 GPA required. FAA Medical Certificate (Class I or II) required of flight school program applicants. SAT or ACT is required. Campus visit and interview recommended. No off-campus interviews.
**Procedure:** Take SAT or ACT by December of 12th year. Take ACH by December of 12th year. Application deadline is 30 days prior to beginning of semester. Notification of admission on rolling basis. Reply is required within four weeks of acceptance. $150 tuition deposit, refundable until 60 days prior to registration. $150 room deposit, refundable until 60 days prior to registration. Freshmen accepted for terms other than fall.
**Special programs:** Admission may be deferred one year. Credit and/or placement may be granted through CEEB Advanced Placement exams for scores of 3 or higher. Credit may be granted through CLEP general and subject exams, Regents College, ACT PEP, DANTES, and challenge exams. Credit and placement may be granted through military and life experience.
**Transfer students:** Transfer students accepted for terms other than fall. In fall 1993, 28% of all new students were transfers into all classes. 690 transfer applications were received, 515 were accepted. Application deadline is 30 days prior to beginning of semester for fall; 30 days prior to beginning of semester for spring. Minimum 2.0 GPA required. Lowest course grade accepted is "D." At least 30 semester hours must be completed at the university to receive degree.
**Admissions contact:** Darryl W. Niemeyer, Director of Admissions. 800 222-ERAU, 904 226-6100.

**FINANCIAL AID. Available aid:** Pell grants, SEOG, state scholarships and grants, school scholarships, private scholarships, ROTC scholarships, academic merit scholarships, and athletic scholarships. U.S. Dept. of Veterans' Affairs Education Benefits. Perkins Loans (NDSL), PLUS, Stafford Loans (GSL), state loans, school loans, private loans, and SLS. Knight Tuition Plans and deferred payment plan.
**Financial aid statistics:** In 1993-94, 100% of all undergraduate applicants received aid. Average amounts of aid awarded freshmen: Scholarships and grants, $1,700; loans, $2,600.
**Supporting data/closing dates:** FAFSA: Priority filing date is April 15. Notification of awards on rolling basis.
**Financial aid contact:** Claudia Geary, Director of Financial Aid. 904 226-6300.

**STUDENT EMPLOYMENT.** College Work/Study Program. Institutional employment. 21% of full-time undergraduates work on campus during school year. Students may expect to earn an average of $2,500 during school year. Off-campus part-time employment opportunities rated "excellent."

**COMPUTER FACILITIES.** 140 IBM/IBM-compatible and RISC-/UNIX-based microcomputers; 120 are networked. Students may access IBM, SUN minicomputer/mainframe systems, Internet. Client/LAN operating systems include DOS, UNIX/XENIX/AIX, Novell. Computer languages and software packages include Ada, Assembly, AutoCAD, Autosketch, BASIC, C, COBOL, Enable, FORTRAN, Grammatik, Harvard Graphics, LISP,

Lotus 1-2-3, Lotus Smart-Suite for Windows, Oracle, Pascal, Tracon, WordPerfect, WordStar. Computer facilities are available to all students.
**Fees:** Computer fee is included in tuition/fees.
**Hours:** 11 AM-6 PM (Su-F); 9 AM-6 PM (Sa).

**GRADUATE CAREER DATA.** Highest graduate school enrollments: Embry-Riddle Aeronautical U. 47% of graduates choose careers in business and industry. Companies and businesses that hire graduates: Delta, Federal Aviation Administration, General Electric.

# Flagler College

**Saint Augustine, FL 32085-1027 904 829-6481**

**1994-95 Costs.** Tuition: $5,120. Room: $1,260. Board: $1,940. Fees, books, misc. academic expenses (school's estimate): $500.
**Enrollment.** Undergraduates: 545 men, 800 women (full-time). Freshman class: 1,415 applicants, 714 accepted, 338 enrolled.
**Test score averages/ranges.** Average SAT scores: 476 verbal, 513 math. Range of SAT scores of middle 50%: 430-520 verbal, 460-560 math. Average ACT scores: 23 English, 21 math, 22 composite. Range of ACT scores of middle 50%: 20-25 English, 18-23 math.
**Faculty.** 48 full-time; 70 part-time. 52% of faculty holds doctoral degree. Student/faculty ratio: 19 to 1.
**Selectivity rating.** Competitive.

**PROFILE.** Flagler, founded in 1968, is a private, liberal arts college. Its 36-acre campus is located in the center of St. Augustine at the former Ponce de Leon Hotel, a Spanish-style resort.

**Accreditation:** SACS. Numerous professional accreditations.
**Religious orientation:** Flagler College is nonsectarian; no religious requirements.
**Library:** Collections totaling over 120,000 volumes, 450 periodical subscriptions, and 32,000 microform items.
**Special facilities/museums:** Museum/theatre, learning disabilities clinic for student teachers.
**Athletic facilities:** Gymnasium, aerobics, martial arts, and weight training rooms, racquetball and tennis courts, swimming pool, baseball, intramural, soccer, and softball fields.

**STUDENT BODY. Undergraduate profile:** 60% are state residents; 26% are transfers. 1% Asian-American, 1% Black, 3% Hispanic, 95% White. Average age of undergraduates is 20.
**Freshman profile:** 2% of freshmen who took SAT scored 700 or over on math; 5% scored 600 or over on verbal, 15% scored 600 or over on math; 36% scored 500 or over on verbal, 57% scored 500 or over on math; 91% scored 400 or over on verbal, 99% scored 400 or over on math; 100% scored 300 or over on verbal, 100% scored 300 or over on math. 3% of freshmen who took ACT scored 30 or over on English, 3% scored 30 or over on math, 2% scored 30 or over on composite; 38% scored 24 or over on English, 25% scored 24 or over on math, 36% scored 24 or over on composite; 96% scored 18 or over on English, 87% scored 18 or over on math, 98% scored 18 or over on composite; 100% scored 12 or over on English, 100% scored 12 or over on math, 100% scored 12 or over on composite. 82% of accepted applicants took SAT; 46% took ACT. 78% of freshmen come from public schools.
**Undergraduate achievement:** 71% of fall 1992 freshmen returned for fall 1993 term. 40% of entering class graduated. 10% of students who completed a degree program immediately went on to graduate study.
**Foreign students:** 32 students are from out of the country. Countries represented include Canada, Denmark, England, Germany, the Netherlands, and Sweden; 20 in all.

**PROGRAMS OF STUDY. Degrees:** B.A.
**Majors:** Accounting, Art Education, Business Administration, Communications, Deaf Education, Drama, Elementary Education, English, Fine Art, Graphic Design, History, Latin American Studies/Spanish, Mathematics, Philosophy/Religion, Physical Education, Psychology, Recreation, Secondary Education, Social Sciences, Spanish.
**Distribution of degrees:** The majors with the highest enrollment are business administration, communications, and elementary education; drama, mathematics, and history have the lowest.
**Requirements:** General education requirement.
**Academic regulations:** Freshmen must maintain minimum 1.5 GPA; sophomores, 1.67 GPA; juniors, 1.75 GPA; seniors, 2.0 GPA.
**Special:** Minors offered in advertising, anthropology, coaching, economics, French, gerontology, international studies, journalism, mental retardation, political science, sociology, specific learning disabilities, and written communications. Self-designed majors. Double majors. Independent study. Internships. Preprofessional programs in law and youth ministry. Member of Northeast Florida Educational Consortium for the Hearing Impaired. Teacher certification in elementary, secondary, special education, and bilingual/bicultural education. Certification in specific subject areas. Member of Council on International Educational Exchange. Study abroad in Central and South American countries, Italy, Mexico, and other countries.
**Honors:** Honor societies.
**Academic Assistance:** Remedial reading, writing, math, and study skills.

**STUDENT LIFE. Housing:** All freshmen under age 21 must live on campus unless living with family. Women's and men's dorms. 50% of students live in college housing.
**Social atmosphere:** According to the editor of the student newspaper, "Flagler is a small college with 55% of the students residing on campus. Whether you're visiting an on- or off-campus spot, you're bound to see someone you know." Popular gathering spots on campus include the Snack Bar, the Rotunda, the student lounge, and the Breezeway and Lewis House lounges. Off campus, students often go to El Toro's, Churchill's Attic, St. George's Tavern, the Milltop, Jeff's Place, the Bayfront, and St. George Street. Influential groups include the Student Government Association, Surf Club, Society for Advancement of Management (SAM), and Women's Club. Other popular pastimes include Ponce Players drama productions, men's basketball games, intramural sports, and formal dances.
**Services and counseling/handicapped student services:** Placement services. Health service. Counseling services for veteran students. Personal counseling. Career and academic guidance services.
**Campus organizations:** Undergraduate student government. Student newspaper (Gargoyle, published once/three weeks). Literary magazine. Yearbook. Radio station. Chorus, Art Exhibition Club, drama group, Chrysalis (environmental group), Deaf Awareness Club, Circle K, women's service group, Rotaract, Best Buddies, departmental groups, 22 organizations in all.
**Religious organizations:** Intervarsity Christian Fellowship.

**ATHLETICS. Physical education requirements:** None.
**Intercollegiate competition:** 12% of students participate. Baseball (M), basketball (M,W), cheerleading (M,W), cross-country (M,W), golf (M), soccer (M), tennis (M,W), volleyball (W). Member of Florida Sun Conference, NAIA.
**Intramural and club sports:** 35% of students participate. Intramural basketball, flag football, soccer, softball, surfing, volleyball. Men's club volleyball. Women's club soccer.

**ADMISSIONS. Academic basis for candidate selection** (in order of priority): Secondary school record, standardized test scores, class rank, school's recommendation, essay.
**Nonacademic basis for candidate selection:** Character and personality, extracurricular participation, particular talent or ability, and alumni/ae relationship are considered.
**Requirements:** Graduation from secondary school is required; GED is accepted. 16 units and the following program of study are required: 4 units of English, 3 units of math, 2 units of science including 1 unit of lab, 3 units of social studies, 1 unit of history, 3 units of academic electives. SAT or ACT scores in top 40th percentile, rank in top half of secondary school class, and minimum 2.5 GPA recommended. SAT or ACT scores in top 45th percentile and minimum 2.5 GPA required of education program applicants. SAT or ACT is required. Campus visit and interview recommended. No off-campus interviews.
**Procedure:** Take SAT or ACT by December of 12th year. Visit college for interview by March 1 of 12th year. Suggest filing application by December 1. Application deadline is March 1. Acceptance notification on January 1, February 15, and March 30. Reply is required within three weeks of acceptance. $100 nonrefundable tuition deposit. $200 nonrefundable room deposit. Freshmen accepted for terms other than fall.
**Special programs:** Admission may be deferred one year. Credit and/or placement may be granted through CEEB Advanced Placement exams for scores of 3 or higher. Credit and/or placement may be granted through CLEP general exams. Early entrance/early admission program. Concurrent enrollment program.
**Transfer students:** Transfer students accepted for terms other than fall. In fall 1993, 26% of all new students were transfers into all classes. 398 transfer applications were received, 178 were accepted. Application deadline is March 1 for fall; November 15 for spring. Minimum 2.0 GPA required. Lowest course grade accepted is "C." Maximum number of transferable credits is 64 semester hours from a two-year school and 90 semester hours from a four-year school. At least 30 semester hours must be completed at the college to receive degree.
**Admissions contact:** Marc G. Williar, M.B.A., Director of Admissions. 904 829-6481, extension 220.

**FINANCIAL AID. Available aid:** Pell grants, SEOG, state scholarships and grants, school scholarships and grants, private scholarships and grants, academic merit scholarships, and athletic scholarships. Perkins Loans (NDSL), PLUS, Stafford Loans (GSL), school loans, private loans, and SLS. Tuition Plan Inc. and Knight Tuition Plans.
**Financial aid statistics:** 30% of aid is not need-based. In 1993-94, 75% of all undergraduate applicants received aid; 70% of freshman applicants. Average amounts of aid awarded freshmen: Scholarships and grants, $2,250; loans, $2,150.
**Supporting data/closing dates:** FAFSA/FAF/FFS: Priority filing date is March 15; accepted on rolling basis. School's own aid application: Priority filing date is March 15. State aid form: Deadline is May 15. Income tax forms: Priority filing date is March 15; accepted on rolling basis. Notification of awards begins March 1.
**Financial aid contact:** Reuben Sitton, Director of Financial Aid. 904 829-6481, extension 225.

**STUDENT EMPLOYMENT.** College Work/Study Program. Institutional employment. 22% of full-time undergraduates work on campus during school year. Students may expect to earn an average of $800 during school year. Off-campus part-time employment opportunities rated "good."

**COMPUTER FACILITIES.** 96 IBM/IBM-compatible and Macintosh/Apple microcomputers. Client/LAN operating systems include Apple/Macintosh, DOS, LocalTalk/AppleTalk. Computer languages and software packages include AppleWorks, Assembly, BASIC, C, COBOL, dBASE, Enable, Lotus 1-2-3, MacWrite, PageMaker, Pascal, QuarkXPress, SuperPaint, WordPerfect. Computer facilities are available to all students.
**Fees:** Computer fee is included in tuition/fees.
**Hours:** 8 AM-11 PM (M-F); 9 AM-1 PM (Sa); 1 PM-11 PM (Su).

**GRADUATE CAREER DATA.** Graduate school percentages: 5% enter law school. 25% enter graduate business programs. 20% enter graduate arts and sciences programs. 5% enter theological school/seminary. Highest graduate school enrollments: Columbia Theological Seminary, Florida State U, U of North Florida. 50% of graduates choose careers in business and industry. Companies and businesses that hire graduates: State Boards of Education, accounting firms, banking industry, small businesses.

# Florida Agricultural and Mechanical University

Tallahassee, FL 32307 904 599-3000

**1994-95 Costs.** Tuition: $1,749 (state residents), $6,651 (out-of-state). Room & board: $2,822. Fees, books, misc. academic expenses (school's estimate): $480.

**Enrollment.** Undergraduates: 3,281 men, 4,524 women (full-time). Freshman class: 4,880 applicants, 2,899 accepted, 1,463 enrolled. Graduate enrollment: 220 men, 415 women.

**Test score averages/ranges.** Average SAT scores: 489 verbal, 440 math. Average ACT scores: 14 English, 16 math, 20 composite.

**Faculty.** 610 full-time; 6 part-time. 51% of faculty holds doctoral degree. Student/faculty ratio: 13 to 1.

**Selectivity rating.** Less competitive.

**PROFILE.** Florida Agricultural and Mechanical University, founded in 1887, is a public, historically black university. Programs are offered through the Colleges of Arts and Sciences; Education; Engineering Sciences, Technology, and Agriculture; Pharmacy and Pharmaceutical Sciences and the Schools of Allied Health Sciences; Architecture; Business and Industry; General Studies; Journalism, Media, and Graphic Arts; Nursing; and Graduate Studies, Research, and Continuing Education. Its 419-acre campus is located in Tallahassee.

**Accreditation:** SACS. Professionally accredited by the Accreditation Board for Engineering and Technology, the Accrediting Council on Education in Journalism and Mass Communication, the National Architecture Accrediting Board, the National Council for Accreditation of Teacher Education.

**Religious orientation:** Florida Agricultural and Mechanical University is nonsectarian; no religious requirements.

**Library:** Collections totaling over 485,985 volumes, 3,300 periodical subscriptions, and 82,000 microform items.

**Athletic facilities:** Gymnasium, baseball and softball fields, track, swimming pool, tennis courts.

**STUDENT BODY. Undergraduate profile:** 72% are state residents; 24% are transfers. 1% Asian-American, 89% Black, 1% Hispanic, 7% White, 2% Other. Average age of undergraduates is 23.

**Freshman profile:** 1% of freshmen who took SAT scored 700 or over on verbal, 2% scored 700 or over on math; 6% scored 600 or over on verbal, 12% scored 600 or over on math; 22% scored 500 or over on verbal, 41% scored 500 or over on math; 64% scored 400 or over on verbal, 78% scored 400 or over on math; 95% scored 300 or over on verbal, 98% scored 300 or over on math. 1% of freshmen who took ACT scored 30 or over on English, 1% scored 30 or over on math; 13% scored 24 or over on English, 10% scored 24 or over on math, 9% scored 24 or over on composite; 59% scored 18 or over on English, 56% scored 18 or over on math, 66% scored 18 or over on composite; 97% scored 12 or over on English, 99% scored 12 or over on math, 100% scored 12 or over on composite. Majority of accepted applicants took ACT. 80% of freshmen come from public schools.

**Undergraduate achievement:** 80% of fall 1992 freshmen returned for fall 1993 term.

**Foreign students:** 133 students are from out of the country. Countries represented include the Bahamas, Bermuda, China, Jamaica, Montserrat, Nigeria; 43 in all.

**PROGRAMS OF STUDY. Degrees:** B.A., B.S., B.Tech.

**Majors:** Accounting, Agricultural Business, Animal Science, Architecture, Art Education, Biology, Broadcast Journalism, Business Administration, Business/Commerce/Distributive Education, Chemical Engineering, Chemistry, Civil Engineering, Civil Engineering Technology, Computer Information Science, Construction Engineering Technology, Criminal Justice/Corrections, Dramatic Arts/Theatre, Economics, Electrical Engineering, Electronic Engineering Technology, Elementary Education, English, English Education, Fine Arts, Graphic Arts Technology, Graphic Design, Health Care Administration, History, Industrial Arts Vocational/Technical Education, Industrial Engineering, Journalism, Magazine Production, Mathematics, Mathematics Education, Mechanical Engineering, Medical Records Administration, Music, Music Composition, Music Education, Music Performance, Music Theory, Newspaper Journalism, Nursing, Occupational Therapy, Ornamental Horticulture/Landscape Design, Pharmacy, Philosophy/Religion, Photography, Physical Education, Physical Therapy, Physics, Political Science/Public Management, Printing Management, Psychology, Public Relations, Religious Studies, Respiratory Therapy, Science Education, Secondary Education, Social Studies Education, Social Welfare, Sociology.

**Distribution of degrees:** The majors with the highest enrollment are business administration, health professions, and liberal arts; animal science, chemistry, and physics have the lowest.

**Requirements:** General education requirement.

**Academic regulations:** Minimum 2.0 GPA must be maintained.

**Special:** Double majors. Independent study. Pass/fail grading option. Internships. Graduate school at which undergraduates may take graduate-level courses. Preprofessional programs in law, medicine, and dentistry. Washington Semester. Architecture semester (Virginia). Teacher certification in early childhood, elementary, secondary, and special education. Study abroad in England and Italy. ROTC and NROTC. AFROTC at Florida State U.

**Honors:** Honors program. Honor societies.

**Academic Assistance:** Remedial reading and math. Nonremedial tutoring.

**STUDENT LIFE. Housing:** All freshmen must live on campus unless living with family. Women's and men's dorms. On-campus married-student housing. 28% of students live in college housing.

**Social atmosphere:** According to the editor of the student newspaper, social and cultural life on campus is "relatively slow" and involves mostly weekend activities. Homecoming, Greek Weeks, and Harambee are some of the popular events. Students gather at the Student Union and an outdoor cafeteria commonly called "The Set." Most of the Greek organizations are influential on campus.

**Services and counseling/handicapped student services:** Placement services. Health service. Day care. Counseling services for minority, military, veteran, and older students. Birth control, personal, and psychological counseling. Career and academic guidance services. Religious counseling. Physically disabled student services. Learning disabled services. Notetaking services. Tape recorders. Tutors. Reader services for the blind.

**Campus organizations:** Undergraduate student government. Student newspaper (Famuan, published once/week). Yearbook. Radio and TV stations. Music and drama groups, literary guild, cheerleaders, departmental, political, service, and special-interest groups. Four fraternities, three chapter houses; four sororities, two chapter houses.

**Religious organizations:** Bahai Fellowship, Baptist Campus Ministry, Canterbury Club, Council of Religious Activities, Methodist Student Organization.

**Minority/foreign student organizations:** NAACP, Pan-African Cultural Club. International Student Association, Bilalian Student Alliance, Nigerian Student Alliance.

**ATHLETICS. Physical education requirements:** None.

**Intercollegiate competition:** 3% of students participate. Baseball (M), basketball (M,W), cross-country (M,W), diving (M,W), football (M), golf (M), softball (W), swimming (M,W), tennis (M,W), track and field (indoor) (M,W), track and field (outdoor) (M,W), volleyball (W). Member of Mid Eastern Athletic Conference, NCAA Division I, NCAA Division I-AA for football, New South Women's Athletic Conference.

**Intramural and club sports:** 34% of students participate. Intramural basketball, flag football, soccer, softball, tennis, track, volleyball.

**ADMISSIONS. Academic basis for candidate selection** (in order of priority): Secondary school record, standardized test scores, school's recommendation, class rank, essay.

**Requirements:** Graduation from secondary school is required; GED is accepted. 19 units and the following program of study are required: 4 units of English, 3 units of math, 3 units of science including 2 units of lab, 2 units of foreign language, 3 units of social studies, 4 units of electives. Minimum combined SAT score of 900 (composite ACT score of 19) and minimum 2.5 GPA required. SAT or ACT is required. Campus visit recommended. No off-campus interviews.

**Procedure:** Take SAT or ACT by December 1 of 12th year. Suggest filing application by February 1. Application deadline is May 1. Notification of admission on rolling basis. No set date by which applicants must accept offer. $250 room deposit, refundable until August 1. Freshmen accepted for terms other than fall.

**Special programs:** Admission may be deferred one year. Credit may be granted through CEEB Advanced Placement for scores of 3 or higher. Credit may be granted through CLEP general and subject exams, military and life experience. Early entrance/early admission program. Concurrent enrollment program.

**Transfer students:** Transfer students accepted for terms other than fall. In fall 1993, 24% of all new students were transfers into all classes. 2,164 transfer applications were received, 823 were accepted. Application deadline is May 1 for fall; November 1 for spring. Minimum 2.0 GPA required. Lowest course grade accepted is "C." Maximum number of transferable credits is 90 semester hours. At least 30 semester hours must be completed at the university to receive degree.

**Admissions contact:** Roland H. Gaines, M.A., Director of Admissions. 904 599-3796.

**FINANCIAL AID. Available aid:** Pell grants, SEOG, state scholarships and grants, school scholarships and grants, private scholarships and grants, ROTC scholarships, academic merit scholarships, and athletic scholarships. Perkins Loans (NDSL), PLUS, Stafford Loans (GSL), state loans, school loans, private loans, and SLS.

**Financial aid statistics:** 40% of aid is not need-based. In 1993-94, 72% of all undergraduate applicants received aid; 88% of freshman applicants. Average amounts of aid awarded freshmen: Scholarships and grants, $969; loans, $310.

**Supporting data/closing dates:** FAFSA: Priority filing date is April 1. Notification of awards on rolling basis.

**Financial aid contact:** Alton W. Royal, M.A., Director of Financial Aid. 904 599-3730.

**STUDENT EMPLOYMENT.** College Work/Study Program. Institutional employment. 10% of full-time undergraduates work on campus during school year. Students may expect to earn an average of $1,360 during school year. Freshmen are discouraged from working during their first term. Off-campus part-time employment opportunities rated "good."

**COMPUTER FACILITIES.** 100 IBM/IBM-compatible and Macintosh/Apple microcomputers. Students may access IBM minicomputer/mainframe systems. Computer languages and software packages include Assembler, BASIC, COBOL, DW 370, FORTRAN, LISP, Pascal, PL/1, SPSS, SQL. Computer facilities are available to all students. Fees: None.

**GRADUATE CAREER DATA.** 35% of graduates choose careers in business and industry. Companies and businesses that hire graduates: federal government agencies, banking and accounting firms, retail companies.

**PROMINENT ALUMNI/AE.** Dr. Lasalle Lefall, cancer researcher; Andre Dawson and Vince Coleman, athletes; Maj. Gen. Eugene Cromartie, U.S. Army; Davidson Hepburn, UN ambassador to the Bahamas.

# Florida Atlantic University

Boca Raton, FL 33431-0991 407 367-3000

**1993-94 Costs.** Tuition: $1,735 (state residents), $6,493 (out-of-state). Room & board: $3,975. Fees, books, misc. academic expenses (school's estimate): $600.

**Enrollment.** Undergraduates: 2,707 men, 3,207 women (full-time). Freshman class: 2,977 applicants, 1,980 accepted, 819 enrolled. Graduate enrollment: 1,779 men, 2,231 women.

**Test score averages/ranges.** Average SAT scores: 462 verbal, 528 math. Range of SAT scores of middle 50%: 910-1080 combined. Average ACT scores: 22 composite. Range of ACT scores of middle 50%: 20-24 composite.

**Faculty.** 528 full-time; 20 part-time. 78% of faculty holds highest degree in specific field. Student/faculty ratio: 20 to 1.

**Selectivity rating.** Less competitive.

**PROFILE.** Florida Atlantic, founded in 1961, is a public, multipurpose university. Its 900-acre main campus is located in Boca Raton, 20 miles from Fort Lauderdale.

**Accreditation:** SACS. Professionally accredited by the Accreditation Board for Engineering and Technology, the American Assembly of Collegiate Schools of Business, the National Association of Schools of Music, the National Council for Accreditation of Teacher Education, the National League for Nursing.
**Religious orientation:** Florida Atlantic University is nonsectarian; no religious requirements.
**Library:** Collections totaling over 592,131 volumes, 4,571 periodical subscriptions, and 2,515,820 microform items.
**Special facilities/museums:** Art gallery, on-campus elementary school, robotics lab, marine research facilities.
**Athletic facilities:** Gymnasium, basketball, tennis, and volleyball courts, weight room, baseball, intramural, soccer, and softball fields, aerobics studio.

**STUDENT BODY. Undergraduate profile:** 93% are state residents; 60% are transfers. 5% Asian-American, 9% Black, 9% Hispanic, 1% Native American, 75% White, 1% Other. Average age of undergraduates is 26.
**Freshman profile:** 1% of freshmen who took SAT scored 700 or over on verbal, 3% scored 700 or over on math; 6% scored 600 or over on verbal, 21% scored 600 or over on math; 33% scored 500 or over on verbal, 66% scored 500 or over on math; 84% scored 400 or over on verbal, 99% scored 400 or over on math; 99% scored 300 or over on verbal, 100% scored 300 or over on math. 84% of accepted applicants took SAT; 45% took ACT.
**Undergraduate achievement:** 83% of fall 1992 freshmen returned for fall 1993 term. 25% of entering class graduated.
**Foreign students:** 1,579 students are from out of the country. Countries represented include Canada, China, India, and the United Kingdom; 80 in all.

**PROGRAMS OF STUDY. Degrees:** B.A., B.Bus.Admin., B.F.A., B.Hlth.Sci., B.Pub.Aff., B.S., B.Soc.Work.
**Majors:** Accounting, Anthropology, Art, Biological Sciences, Botany, Chemistry, Communication, Computer/Information Systems, Computer Science, Criminal Justice, Economics, Electrical Engineering, Elementary Education, English, Exceptional Student Education, Exercise/Wellness, Finance, French, General Management, Geography, Geology, German, Health Services Administration, History, Human Resources Management, Humanities, Interdisciplinary Science, International Business Management, Language/Linguistics, Marine Biology, Marketing, Mathematics, Mechanical Engineering, Medical Technology, Microbiology, Music, Nursing, Ocean Engineering, Philosophy, Physics, Political Science, Psychology, Public Affairs, Real Estate, Social Psychology, Social Work, Sociology, Spanish, Theatre, Urban/Regional Planning, Zoology.
**Distribution of degrees:** The majors with the highest enrollment are elementary education, accounting, and management; philosophy, physics, and public affairs have the lowest.
**Requirements:** General education requirement.
**Academic regulations:** Minimum 2.0 GPA must be maintained.
**Special:** Minors offered in the College of Liberal Arts and College of Urban and Public Affairs and in ethnic studies, governmental/political reporting, Latin American studies, and women's studies. Several concentrations available in communication. Self-designed majors. Independent study. Accelerated study. Pass/fail grading option. Internships. Cooperative education programs. Graduate school at which undergraduates may take graduate-level courses. Preprofessional programs in law, medicine, veterinary science, and dentistry. 3-2 engineering programs with Bethune-Cookman Coll and Florida Memorial Coll. Exchange programs with various state schools in Florida. Teacher certification in early childhood, elementary, secondary, special education, and bilingual/bicultural education. Certification in specific subject areas. Exchange program abroad in England and Spain (Polytech U of Madrid). Study abroad also in Israel.
**Honors:** Honors program. Honor societies.
**Academic Assistance:** Nonremedial tutoring.

**STUDENT LIFE. Housing:** Students may live on or off campus. Coed and women's dorms. 8% of students live in college housing.
**Social atmosphere:** According to the editor of the student newspaper, "The people who want to get involved, do!" Popular events include Freaker's Ball, Sam's Ballroom Launch, the student government Special Olympics, and FAU basketball games. Students meet at the Rat on campus and frequent Club Key Largo, Nipper's, Weekends, Lakeside, Bounty, and Club Boca off campus. Greeks, the student government, and the Program Board are all influential on campus.
**Services and counseling/handicapped student services:** Placement services. Health service. Day care. Counseling services for minority, military, veteran, and older students. Birth control, personal, and psychological counseling. Career and academic guidance services. Religious counseling. Physically disabled student services. Learning disabled services. Notetaking services. Tape recorders. Tutors. Reader services for the blind.
**Campus organizations:** Undergraduate student government. Student newspaper. Literary magazine. Yearbook. Radio station. Jazz band, NOW, science club, art groups, academic and special-interest groups, 113 organizations in all. Four fraternities, no chapter houses; four sororities, no chapter houses. 1% of men join a fraternity. 1% of women join a sorority.
**Religious organizations:** Hillel, United Campus Ministries, Muslim Student Organization, Catholic Student Union, Campus Crusade for Christ.
**Minority/foreign student organizations:** Pan-African Student Association, Hispanic Student Association. International Student Association, Chinese Student Association, Carribean Connection, Asian, Bahamian, Japanese, and Latin American student groups.

**ATHLETICS. Physical education requirements:** None.
**Intercollegiate competition:** 1% of students participate. Baseball (M), basketball (M,W), cross-country (M,W), diving (M,W), golf (M,W), soccer (M,W), swimming (M,W), tennis (M,W), volleyball (W). Member of NCAA Division II.
**Intramural and club sports:** 1% of students participate. Intramural aerobics, basketball, flag football, floor hockey, ice hockey, martial arts, soccer, softball, track, volleyball.

**ADMISSIONS. Academic basis for candidate selection** (in order of priority): Secondary school record, standardized test scores, school's recommendation, essay, class rank.
**Nonacademic basis for candidate selection:** Particular talent or ability is emphasized. Extracurricular participation is important. Character and personality and alumni/ae relationship are considered.
**Requirements:** Graduation from secondary school is required; GED is accepted. 19 units and the following program of study are required: 4 units of English, 3 units of math, 3 units of science including 2 units of lab, 2 units of foreign language, 3 units of social studies, 4 units of academic electives. Minimum combined SAT score of 900 and minimum 2.5 GPA recommended. Audition required of music program applicants. Summer remedial course work required of applicants not meeting standard requirements. SAT or ACT is required. Campus visit recommended. No off-campus interviews.
**Procedure:** Take SAT or ACT by December of 12th year. Suggest filing application by January 1. Application deadline is May 1. Notification of admission on rolling basis. Reply is required by May 1. $200 room deposit, refundable partially until May 15. Freshmen accepted for terms other than fall.
**Special programs:** Admission may be deferred one year. Credit may be granted through CEEB Advanced Placement for scores of 3 or higher. Credit may be granted through CLEP general and subject exams, Regents College, ACT PEP, and DANTES exams and military experience. Early entrance/early admission program. Concurrent enrollment program.
**Transfer students:** Transfer students accepted for terms other than fall. In fall 1993, 60% of all new students were transfers into all classes. 3,832 transfer applications were received, 3,304 were accepted. Application deadline is June 1 for fall; October 15 for spring. Minimum 2.0 GPA required. Lowest course grade accepted is "D." Maximum number of transferable credits is 60 semester hours from a two-year school and 90 semester hours from a four-year school. At least 30 semester hours must be completed at the university to receive degree.
**Admissions contact:** Brian Levin-Stankevich, Ph.D., Director of Admissions. 407 367-3040.

**FINANCIAL AID. Available aid:** Pell grants, SEOG, state scholarships and grants, school scholarships, private scholarships and grants, academic merit scholarships, and athletic scholarships. Perkins Loans (NDSL), PLUS, Stafford Loans (GSL), school loans, private loans, and SLS. Deferred payment plan. Prepaid Tuition-State of Florida.
**Financial aid statistics:** In 1993-94, 74% of all undergraduate applicants received aid; 64% of freshman applicants. Average amounts of aid awarded freshmen: Scholarships and grants, $2,128; loans, $2,584.
**Supporting data/closing dates:** FAFSA: Priority filing date is April 1; accepted on rolling basis. School's own aid application: Priority filing date is April 1; accepted on rolling basis. Income tax forms: Priority filing date is April 1; accepted on rolling basis. Notification of awards on rolling basis.
**Financial aid contact:** Olga Moas, M.A., Director of Financial Aid. 407 367-3530.

**STUDENT EMPLOYMENT.** College Work/Study Program. Institutional employment. 5% of full-time undergraduates work on campus during school year. Students may expect to earn an average of $2,500 during school year. Off-campus part-time employment opportunities rated "excellent."

**COMPUTER FACILITIES.** 262 IBM/IBM-compatible and Macintosh/Apple microcomputers; 125 are networked. Students may access Digital, IBM minicomputer/mainframe systems, BITNET, Internet. Client/LAN operating systems include Apple/Macintosh, DOS, UNIX/XENIX/AIX, DEC. Computer languages and software packages include C, COBOL, FORTRAN, Pascal. Computer facilities are available to all students. Fees: None.

**PROMINENT ALUMNI/AE.** Daniel Mica, former U.S. congressman; Dr. Carolyn Macleod, AIDS researcher; Richard C. Asher, deputy superintendent of salvage, U.S. Navy; Robert C. Maxson, president, U of Nevada (Las Vegas); Robert J. Criswell, president, Amoco; Clarence E. Anthony, president, C.E. Anthony Associates.

# Florida Baptist Theological College

Graceville, FL 32440 904 263-3261

**1994-95 Costs.** Tuition: $2,250. Room: $1,350. Fees, books, misc. academic expenses (school's estimate): $354.

**Enrollment.** Undergraduates: 355 men, 84 women (full-time). Freshman class: 168 applicants, 156 accepted, 126 enrolled.

**Test score averages/ranges.** N/A.

**Faculty.** 13 full-time; 9 part-time. 85% of faculty holds doctoral degree. Student/faculty ratio: 23 to 1.

**Selectivity rating.** N/A.

**PROFILE.** Florida Baptist Theological College, founded in 1943, is a church-affiliated institution. Its 150-acre campus is located in Graceville.

**Accreditation:** SACS.
**Religious orientation:** Florida Baptist Theological College is affiliated with the Southern Baptist Convention; five semesters of religion required.
**Library:** Collections totaling over 49,036 volumes, 325 periodical subscriptions and 645 microform items.
**Athletic facilities:** Basketball, tennis, and volleyball courts, table tennis, softball and touch football fields, driving range.

**STUDENT BODY. Undergraduate profile:** 57% are state residents; 58% are transfers. 1% Asian-American, 3% Black, 4% Hispanic, 1% Native American, 90% White, 1% Other. Average age of undergraduates is 31.
**Freshman profile:** 90% of freshmen come from public schools.
**Undergraduate achievement:** 77% of fall 1992 freshmen returned for fall 1993 term. 14% of entering class graduated. 2% of students who completed a degree program immediately went on to graduate study.
**Foreign students:** Five students are from out of the country. Countries represented include Bermuda, Canada, Germany, Mexico, and Romania.

**PROGRAMS OF STUDY. Degrees:** B.A., B.Minis., B.Mus.Minis., B.Relig.Ed., Theol.B.
**Majors:** Music/Conducting, Music Ministry, Music/Piano, Music/Voice, Religious Education, Theology.
**Requirements:** General education requirement.
**Academic regulations:** Freshmen must maintain minimum 1.0 GPA; sophomores, 1.33 GPA; juniors, 1.66 GPA; seniors, 2.0 GPA.
**Special:** Minors offered in conducting, evangelism/preaching, organ, piano, psychology, and voice. Associate's degrees offered. Dual degrees.
**Academic Assistance:** Remedial reading, writing, and math.

**ADMISSIONS. Academic basis for candidate selection** (in order of priority): School's recommendation, essay.
**Nonacademic basis for candidate selection:** Character and personality, extracurricular participation, and particular talent or ability are important.
**Requirements:** Graduation from secondary school is required; GED is accepted. No specific distribution of secondary school units required. Church recommendation (from church of membership) and one year of approved Christian experience after conversion required. SAT or ACT is required. Campus visit and interview recommended. Off-campus interviews available with admissions and alumni representatives.
**Procedure:** Suggest filing application by May 1. Application deadline is August 1. Notification of admission on rolling basis. No set date by which applicants must accept offer. $20 nonrefundable tuition deposit. $25 room deposit, refundable until August 1. Freshmen accepted for terms other than fall.
**Special programs:** Admission may be deferred one year. Credit may be granted through CLEP subject exams, DANTES exams, and military experience.
**Transfer students:** Transfer students accepted for terms other than fall. In fall 1993, 58% of all new students were transfers into all classes. Application deadline is August 1 for fall; December 15 for spring. Minimum 2.0 GPA required. Lowest course grade accepted is "C." Maximum number of transferable credits is 92 semester hours. At least 38 semester hours must be completed at the college to receive degree.
**Admissions contact:** Rev. O. Lavan Wilson, M.A., Director of Admissions. 904 263-3261, extension 63.

**FINANCIAL AID. Available aid:** Pell grants, SEOG, school scholarships and grants, private scholarships, and academic merit scholarships. PLUS, Stafford Loans (GSL), school loans, and SLS. Tuition Plan Inc.
**Financial aid statistics:** 35% of aid is not need-based. In 1993-94, 90% of all undergraduate applicants received aid; 75% of freshman applicants. Average amounts of aid awarded freshmen: Scholarships and grants, $1,500.
**Supporting data/closing dates:** FAFSA/FFS: Priority filing date is April; accepted on rolling basis. Income tax forms: Priority filing date is April; accepted on rolling basis. Notification of awards begins May.
**Financial aid contact:** Donna Neel, Director of Financial Aid. 904 263-3261, extension 61.

## Florida Institute of Technology

**Melbourne, FL 32901-6988** **407 768-8000**

**1994-95 Costs.** Tuition: $13,700. Room & board: $4,140. Fees, books, misc. academic expenses (school's estimate): $985.

**Enrollment.** Undergraduates: 1,342 men, 521 women (full-time). Freshman class: 1,947 applicants, 1,580 accepted, 523 enrolled. Graduate enrollment: 1,863 men, 1,023 women.

**Test score averages/ranges.** Average SAT scores: 500 verbal, 596 math. Range of SAT scores of middle 50%: 450-499 verbal, 550-599 math.

**Faculty.** 226 full-time; 251 part-time. 86% of faculty holds doctoral degree. Student/faculty ratio: 12 to 1.

**Selectivity rating.** More competitive.

**PROFILE.** Florida Institute of Technology, founded in 1958, is a private institution. Programs are offered through the Colleges of Science and Engineering and Applied Technology and the Schools of Aeronautics, Management and Humanities, and Psychology. Its 146-acre campus is located in Melbourne, 60 miles from Orlando.

**Accreditation:** SACS. Professionally accredited by the Accreditation Board for Engineering and Technology, the American Psychological Association.
**Religious orientation:** Florida Institute of Technology is nonsectarian; no religious requirements.
**Library:** Collections totaling over 233,930 volumes, 1,463 periodical subscriptions, and 187,605 microform items.
**Special facilities/museums:** Medical genetics lab, research vessel, observatory, electron microscopes.
**Athletic facilities:** Gymnasium, swimming pools, weight room, soccer, baseball and softball fields, handball and tennis courts.

**STUDENT BODY. Undergraduate profile:** 38% are state residents; 30% are transfers. 2% Asian-American, 2% Black, 6% Hispanic, .5% Native American, 65% White, 24.5% Other. Average age of undergraduates is 22.
**Freshman profile:** 1% of freshmen who took SAT scored 700 or over on verbal, 11% scored 700 or over on math; 10% scored 600 or over on verbal, 47% scored 600 or over on math; 46% scored 500 or over on verbal, 83% scored 500 or over on math; 85% scored 400 or over on verbal, 98% scored 400 or over on math; 97% scored 300 or over on verbal, 100% scored 300 or over on math. 73% of accepted applicants took SAT; 15% took ACT. 80% of freshmen come from public schools.
**Undergraduate achievement:** 75% of fall 1992 freshmen returned for fall 1993 term. 55% of entering class graduated. 23% of students who completed a degree program immediately went on to graduate study.
**Foreign students:** 434 students are from out of the country. Countries represented include France, India, Kenya, Korea, the Netherlands Antilles, and Taiwan; 90 in all.

**PROGRAMS OF STUDY. Degrees:** B.A., B.S.
**Majors:** Accounting, Aeronautics, Aerospace Engineering, Aircraft Systems Management, Airway Science Management, Applied Mathematics, Applied Science, Aquaculture, Aviation Management, Aviation Management/Flight Technology, Biochemistry, Biological Sciences, Biological Sciences/Aquaculture, Biological Sciences/Biochemistry, Biological Sciences/Cell and Molecular Biology, Biological Sciences/Ecology, Biological Sciences/General Biology, Biological Sciences/Marine Biology, Biological Sciences/Preprofessional Biology, Business Administration, Business Communications, Chemical Engineering, Chemical Management, Chemistry, Chemistry Research, Civil Engineering, Communications, Communications/Business, Communications/Technical, Computer Engineering, Computer Science, Data Processing/Computer Science, Ecology, Economics, Electrical Engineering, Environmental Engineering, Environmental Science, Finance, General Biology, General Business, Humanities, Management, Management Science, Marine Biology, Marketing, Mechanical Engineering, Ocean Engineering, Oceanography, Oceanography/Biological, Oceanography/Chemical, Oceanography/Geological, Oceanography/Physical, Physics, Pre-Law, Procurement/Materials Management, Productions/Operations Management, Psychology, Psychology/Aviation, Science Education, Science Education/Aviation-Aerospace, Science Education/Biology, Science Education/Chemistry, Science Education/Computer Science, Science Education/Earth/Space Science, Science Education/General Science, Science Education/Mathematics, Science Education/Physics, Space Science.
**Distribution of degrees:** The majors with the highest enrollment are aeronautics, electrical engineering, and marine biology; humanities, business communications, and chemistry have the lowest.
**Requirements:** General education requirement.
**Academic regulations:** Minimum 2.0 GPA must be maintained.
**Special:** Internships. Cooperative education programs. Graduate school at which undergraduates may take graduate-level courses. Preprofessional programs in law, medicine, veterinary science, and dentistry. Member of Independent Colleges and Universities of Florida. Teacher certification in secondary education. Certification in specific subject areas. ROTC.
**Honors:** Honor societies.
**Academic Assistance:** Remedial reading, writing, math, and study skills. Nonremedial tutoring.

**STUDENT LIFE. Housing:** All unmarried freshmen with fewer than 30 semester hours must live on campus. Coed, women's, and men's dorms. Fraternity housing. School-owned/operated apartments. On-campus married-student housing. 50% of students live in college housing.
**Social atmosphere:** The College Campus Cafe and the Lazy Bean are popular on-campus hangouts; off campus, students can be found at the Rathskellar Bar, The 'Shroom, The Panther Pit, and the beach. Student government, Greeks, the Campus Activities Board, and the student radio station are influential groups on campus social life. Popular events of the school year include basketball and soccer games, Campus Activities Board events, Annual Greek Week, and "Tie Night" at the Beachside Hilton. FIT is a "very culturally diverse campus, small and friendly," reports the student newspaper. "There is some Greek life, but it's not necessary to be Greek to belong!"
**Services and counseling/handicapped student services:** Placement services. Health service. Counseling services for military and veteran students. Personal and psychological counseling. Career and academic guidance services. Religious counseling. Physically disabled student services. Learning disabled services. Tutors.
**Campus organizations:** Undergraduate student government. Student newspaper (Crimson, published once/week). Yearbook. Radio and TV stations. Stage band, College Players, video club, environmental group, 70 organizations in all. Seven fraternities, three chapter houses; three sororities, no chapter houses. 5% of men join a fraternity. 3% of women join a sorority.
**Religious organizations:** Intervarsity Christian Fellowship, Newman Club, Hillel.
**Minority/foreign student organizations:** Spanish-Speaking Student Society. Caribbean, Chinese, Greek, Indian, Korean, and Pakistani student groups.

**ATHLETICS. Physical education requirements:** None.
**Intercollegiate competition:** 10% of students participate. Baseball (M), basketball (M,W), cheerleading (M,W), crew (M,W), cross-country (M,W), soccer (M), softball (W), tennis (M), volleyball (W). Member of NCAA Division II, Sunshine State Conference.
**Intramural and club sports:** 60% of students participate. Intramural basketball, cricket, flag football, frisbee, golf, racquetball, soccer, softball, swimming, tennis, volleyball, water polo, weight lifting, Wiffle ball. Men's club diving, fencing, karate, lacrosse, sailing, surfing. Women's club diving, fencing, karate, lacrosse, surfing.

**ADMISSIONS. Academic basis for candidate selection** (in order of priority): Secondary school record, class rank, standardized test scores, school's recommendation.
**Requirements:** Graduation from secondary school is recommended; GED is accepted. 16 units and the following program of study are required: 4 units of English, 4 units of math, 3 units of science. Minimum combined SAT score of 1000, rank in top third of secondary school class, or minimum 2.8 GPA recommended. SAT is required; ACT may be substituted. Campus visit and interview recommended. Off-campus interviews available with admissions and alumni representatives.
**Procedure:** Take SAT or ACT by December of 12th year. Visit college for interview by December of 12th year. Suggest filing application by February 1; no deadline. Notification of admission on rolling basis. Reply is required by May 1. $250 nonrefundable tuition deposit. $200 room deposit, refundable until August 10. Freshmen accepted for terms other than fall.
**Special programs:** Admission may be deferred one year. Credit and/or placement may be granted through CEEB Advanced Placement exams for scores of 5 or higher. Credit and/or placement may be granted through CLEP general exams. Credit may be granted through CLEP subject exams and challenge exams. Early entrance/early admission program. Concurrent enrollment program.
**Transfer students:** Transfer students accepted for terms other than fall. In fall 1993, 30% of all new students were transfers into all classes. 456 transfer applications were received, 337 were accepted. Application deadline is July 1 for fall; November 1 for spring. Minimum 2.5 GPA recommended. Lowest course grade accepted is "C." Maximum number of transferable credits is 94 semester hours. At least 30 semester hours must be completed at the institute to receive degree.
**Admissions contact:** Louis T. Levy, Ed.S., Dean of Admissions. 800 888-4348.

**FINANCIAL AID. Available aid:** Pell grants, SEOG, state scholarships and grants, school scholarships and grants, private scholarships and grants, ROTC scholarships, academic merit scholarships, and athletic scholarships. Perkins Loans (NDSL), PLUS, Stafford Loans (GSL), state loans, private loans, and SLS. Tuition Plan Inc. Florida Tech Time Payment Plan.
**Financial aid statistics:** 51% of aid is not need-based. In 1993-94, 70% of all undergraduate applicants received aid; 77% of freshman applicants. Average amounts of aid awarded freshmen: Scholarships and grants, $2,263; loans, $2,824.
**Supporting data/closing dates:** FAFSA/FAF: Deadline is February 1. State aid form: Deadline is April 15. Notification of awards on rolling basis.
**Financial aid contact:** Leonard Gude, M.S., Director of Student Financial Aid. 800 666-4348.

**STUDENT EMPLOYMENT.** College Work/Study Program. Institutional employment. 25% of full-time undergraduates work on campus during school year. Students may expect to earn an average of $1,500 during school year. Freshmen are discouraged from working during their first term. Off-campus part-time employment opportunities rated "good."

**COMPUTER FACILITIES.** 80 IBM/IBM-compatible, Macintosh/Apple, and RISC-/UNIX-based microcomputers; 50 are networked. Students may access Digital minicomputer/mainframe systems, Internet. Client/LAN operating systems include Apple/Macintosh, DOS, OS/2, UNIX/XENIX/AIX, Windows NT, X-windows, Novell. Computer languages and software packages include Ada, ASPEN, C, CHEMSHARE, COBOL, EXCEL, FORTRAN, IMSL, NASTRAM, Pascal, SPSS, WordPerfect. Computer facilities are available to all students.
**Fees:** None.
**Hours:** 100 hours/week.

**GRADUATE CAREER DATA.** Graduate school percentages: 2% enter law school. 2% enter medical school. 2% enter dental school. 11% enter graduate business programs. Highest graduate school enrollments: Florida Inst of Tech, Rutgers U, U of Central Florida, U of Miami. 70% of graduates choose careers in business and industry. Companies and businesses that hire graduates: DIGICON, Grumman, Harris, Lockheed, NASA, Norfolk Naval Shipyard.

# Florida International University

Miami, FL 33199 — 305 348-2000

**1994-95 Costs.** Tuition: $1,760 (state residents), $6,600 (out-of-state). Room: $2,400. Board: $1,700. Fees, books, misc. academic expenses (school's estimate): $830.
**Enrollment.** Undergraduates: 4,123 men, 5,579 women (full-time). Freshman class: 3,468 applicants, 1,861 accepted, 1,036 enrolled. Graduate enrollment: 1,831 men, 2,626 women.
**Test score averages/ranges.** Average SAT scores: 476 verbal, 543 math. Range of SAT scores of middle 50%: 470-530 verbal, 540-590 math. Average ACT scores: 23 composite. Range of ACT scores of middle 50%: 22-25 composite.
**Faculty.** 758 full-time; 385 part-time. 79% of faculty holds doctoral degree. Student/faculty ratio: 16 to 1.
**Selectivity rating.** More competitive.

**PROFILE.** Florida International is a public university. Founded as an upper-level institution in 1965, it adopted a four-year undergraduate program in 1981. Programs are offered through the Colleges of Arts and Sciences, Business Administration, Education, and Engineering and Applied Sciences and the Schools of Health Sciences, Hospitality Management, Nursing, and Public Affairs and Services. Its 344-acre campus is located 10 miles from downtown Miami.
**Accreditation:** SACS. Professionally accredited by the Accreditation Board for Engineering and Technology, the Accrediting Council on Education in Journalism and Mass Communication, the American Assembly of Collegiate Schools of Business, the American Council for Construction Education, the American Dietetic Association, the American Medical Association (CAHEA), the American Physical Therapy Association, the Council on Social Work Education, the National League for Nursing.
**Religious orientation:** Florida International University is nonsectarian; no religious requirements.
**Library:** Collections totaling over 942,882 volumes, 9,151 periodical subscriptions, and 2,710,463 microform items.
**Special facilities/museums:** Art gallery, consumer affairs institute, center for economic studies, women's studies center, robotics lab.
**Athletic facilities:** Fitness center, basketball, racquetball, and tennis courts, swimming pool, intramural and softball fields, arena, baseball and soccer stadiums.

**STUDENT BODY. Undergraduate profile:** 92% are state residents; 67% are transfers. 3% Asian-American, 10% Black, 49% Hispanic, 32% White, 6% Other. Average age of undergraduates is 23.
**Freshman profile:** 1% of freshmen who took SAT scored 700 or over on verbal, 4% scored 700 or over on math; 7% scored 600 or over on verbal, 25% scored 600 or over on math; 37% scored 500 or over on verbal, 73% scored 500 or over on math; 87% scored 400 or over on verbal, 98% scored 400 or over on math; 99% scored 300 or over on verbal, 100% scored 300 or over on math. 4% of freshmen who took ACT scored 30 or over on composite; 35% scored 24 or over on composite; 98% scored 18 or over on composite; 100% scored 12 or over on composite. 78% of accepted applicants took SAT; 50% took ACT. 61% of freshmen come from public schools.
**Foreign students:** 936 students are from out of the country. Countries represented include the Bahamas, China, Jamaica, Peru, Taiwan, and Venezuela; 106 in all.

**PROGRAMS OF STUDY. Degrees:** B.A., B.Acct., B.Bus.Admin., B.F.A., B.Hlth.Serv.Admin., B.Mus., B.Pub.Admin., B.S., B.S.Nurs.
**Majors:** Accounting, Apparel Management, Architectural Technology, Art, Art Education, Biology, Biology Education, Chemistry, Chemistry Education, Civil Engineering, Communication, Computer Engineering, Computer Science, Construction Management, Criminal Justice, Dance, Dietetics/Nutrition, Economics, Electrical Engineering, Elementary Education, Emotional Disturbances, English, English Education, Environmental Studies, Finance, French, Geology, German, Health Information Management, Health Occupations Education, Health Services Administration, History, History Education, Home Economics Education, Hospitality Management, Humanities, Industrial Arts Education, Industrial Engineering, Interior Design, International Business, International Relations, Italian, Liberal Studies, Management, Management Information Systems, Marketing, Mathematical Sciences, Mathematics, Mathematics Education, Mechanical Engineering, Medical Technology, Mental Retardation, Modern Language Education, Music, Music Education, Nursing, Occupational Therapy, Parks/Recreation Administration, Personnel Management, Philosophy, Physical Education, Physical Therapy, Physics, Political Science, Portuguese, Prosthetics/Orthotics, Psychology, Public Administration, Religious Studies, Science Education, Social Studies Education, Social Work, Sociology/Anthropology, Spanish, Specific Learning Disability, Statistics, Technical Education, Theatre, Vocational Industrial Education.
**Distribution of degrees:** The majors with the highest enrollment are elementary education, hospitality management, and finance; geology and health occupations education have the lowest.
**Requirements:** General education requirement.
**Academic regulations:** Minimum 2.0 GPA must be maintained.
**Special:** Minors offered in many arts and sciences majors and in advertising, art history, broadcasting, geography, journalism, mass communications, public relations, and visual arts. Academic and professional certificate programs in all college and school divisions. Associate's degrees offered. Double majors. Dual degrees. Independent study. Accelerated study. Pass/fail grading option. Cooperative education programs. Graduate school at which undergraduates may take graduate-level courses. Preprofessional programs in law, medicine, veterinary science, and dentistry. 2-2 art, music, and theatre programs with New World School of the Arts. Member of Southeast Florida Educational Consortium. Member of National Student Exchange (NSE). Teacher certification in early childhood, elementary, secondary, special education, vo-tech, and bilingual/bicultural education. Certification in specific subject areas. Study abroad in China, Costa Rica, England, France, Grenada, St. Lucia, and Spain. ROTC and AFROTC at U of Miami.
**Honors:** Honors program. Honor societies.
**Academic Assistance:** Remedial reading, writing, math, and study skills. Nonremedial tutoring.

**STUDENT LIFE. Housing:** Students may live on or off campus. Coed dorms. School-owned/operated apartments. On-campus married-student housing. 5% of students live in college housing.
**Services and counseling/handicapped student services:** Placement services. Health service. Women's center. Counseling services for minority, military, veteran, and older students. Birth control, personal, and psychological counseling. Career and academic guidance services. Physically disabled student services. Learning disabled services. Notetaking services. Tape recorders. Tutors. Reader services for the blind.
**Campus organizations:** Undergraduate student government. Student newspaper (Beacon, published once/week). 129 registered organizations. Eight fraternities, no chapter houses; five sororities, no chapter houses. 8% of men join a fraternity. 7% of women join a sorority.
**Religious organizations:** Eight religious groups.
**Minority/foreign student organizations:** Seven minority student groups. 16 foreign student groups.

**ATHLETICS. Physical education requirements:** None.
**Intercollegiate competition:** 2% of students participate. Baseball (M), basketball (M,W), cross-country (M,W), golf (M,W), soccer (M,W), tennis (M,W), track and field (indoor) (M,W), track and field (outdoor) (M,W), volleyball (W). Member of NCAA Division I-AAA, Trans America Conference.
**Intramural and club sports:** 10% of students participate. Intramural basketball, bowling, fishing, flag football, golf, racquetball, running, soccer, softball, tennis, volleyball, walleyball. Men's club boxing, crew, fencing, rugby, SCUBA. Women's club crew, fencing, SCUBA, softball.

**ADMISSIONS. Academic basis for candidate selection** (in order of priority): Secondary school record, standardized test scores, class rank, school's recommendation.

**Nonacademic basis for candidate selection:** Character and personality, extracurricular participation, and particular talent or ability are considered.
**Requirements:** Graduation from secondary school is recommended; GED is accepted. 19 units and the following program of study are required: 4 units of English, 3 units of math, 3 units of science including 2 units of lab, 2 units of foreign language, 2 units of social studies, 1 unit of history, 4 units of electives. Minimum combined SAT score of 1000, rank in top fifth of secondary school class, and minimum 3.0 GPA recommended. Audition required of music and theatre program applicants. Portfolio required of art program applicants. SAT is required; ACT may be substituted. Campus visit recommended. No off-campus interviews.
**Procedure:** Take SAT or ACT by December of 12th year. Suggest filing application by February 1. Application deadline is June 1. Notification of admission on rolling basis. Reply is required by August 1. $100 nonrefundable room deposit. Freshmen accepted for terms other than fall.
**Special programs:** Admission may be deferred one year. Credit and/or placement may be granted through CEEB Advanced Placement exams for scores of 3 or higher. Credit and/or placement may be granted through CLEP general and subject exams. Credit and placement may be granted through DANTES and challenge exams. Early entrance/early admission program. Concurrent enrollment program.
**Transfer students:** Transfer students accepted for terms other than fall. In fall 1992, 67% of all new students were transfers into all classes. 4,905 transfer applications were received, 3,177 were accepted. Application deadline is June 1 for fall; October 1 for spring. Minimum 2.5 GPA required. Lowest course grade accepted is "D." Maximum number of transferable credits is 60 semester hours from a two-year school and 90 semester hours from a four-year school. At least 30 semester hours must be completed at the university to receive degree.
**Admissions contact:** Carmen Brown, M.A., Director of Admissions. 305 348-2363.

**FINANCIAL AID. Available aid:** Pell grants, SEOG, state scholarships and grants, school scholarships and grants, private scholarships and grants, academic merit scholarships, athletic scholarships, and aid for undergraduate foreign students. Perkins Loans (NDSL), PLUS, Stafford Loans (GSL), state loans, school loans, private loans, and SLS. Florida Pre-Paid Tuition Plan.
**Financial aid statistics:** 31% of aid is not need-based. In 1992-93, 50% of all undergraduate applicants received aid; 46% of freshman applicants. Average amounts of aid awarded freshmen: Scholarships and grants, $1,338; loans, $2,244.
**Supporting data/closing dates:** FAFSA/FAF/FFS: Priority filing date is February 1; deadline is March 15. School's own aid application: Priority filing date is February 1; deadline is March 15. State aid form: Priority filing date is February 1. Income tax forms: Priority filing date is February 1. Notification of awards begins April 15.
**Financial aid contact:** Ana Sarasti, M.A., Director of Financial Aid. 305 348-2431.

**STUDENT EMPLOYMENT.** College Work/Study Program. Institutional employment. 4% of full-time undergraduates work on campus during school year. Students may expect to earn an average of $1,663 during school year. Off-campus part-time employment opportunities rated "good."

**COMPUTER FACILITIES.** 1,500 IBM/IBM-compatible and Macintosh/Apple microcomputers; 1,400 are networked. Students may access Digital, SUN minicomputer/mainframe systems, BITNET, Internet. Computer languages and software packages include dBASE III, Lotus 1-2-3, SuperCalc, Symphony; 100 in all. Computer facilities are available to all students.
**Fees:** None.
**Hours:** 8 AM-4 AM.

**GRADUATE CAREER DATA.** Graduate school percentages: 4% enter law school. 3% enter medical school. 11% enter graduate business programs. 8% enter graduate arts and sciences programs. Highest graduate school enrollments: Florida International U, Florida State U, U of Florida, U of Miami. 40% of graduates choose careers in business and industry. Companies and businesses that hire graduates: Accounting firms, Barnett Bank, Caterpillar, U.S. government, IBM, Nabisco, Xerox.

**PROMINENT ALUMNI/AE.** Pat Bradley, professional golfer; Ileana Ros-Lehtinen, congresswoman; Andy Garcia, actor.

# Florida Southern College

**Lakeland, FL 33801-5698 — 813 680-4111**

**1993-94 Costs.** Tuition: $7,100. Room & board: $4,600. Fees, books, misc. academic expenses (school's estimate): $1,110.
**Enrollment.** Undergraduates: 771 men, 803 women (full-time). Freshman class: 1,404 applicants, 1,058 accepted, 338 enrolled. Graduate enrollment: 52 men, 20 women.
**Test score averages/ranges.** Average SAT scores: 468 verbal, 532 math. Range of SAT scores of middle 50%: 910-1100 combined. Average ACT scores: 23 composite.
**Faculty.** 96 full-time; 4 part-time. 63% of faculty holds doctoral degree. Student/faculty ratio: 15 to 1.
**Selectivity rating.** Competitive.

**PROFILE.** Florida Southern, founded in 1885, is a church-affiliated college of liberal arts and sciences. Its 100-acre campus is located in Lakeland, 45 miles from Tampa and Orlando. The campus, containing buildings designed by Frank Lloyd Wright, is listed with the National Register of Historic Places.

**Accreditation:** SACS.
**Religious orientation:** Florida Southern College is affiliated with the Methodist Church; two semesters of religion required.
**Library:** Collections totaling over 200,000 volumes, 792 periodical subscriptions, and 205,556 microform items.
**Special facilities/museums:** Preschool lab, radio and TV studios.
**Athletic facilities:** Gymnasium, basketball and tennis courts, weight room, baseball, football, soccer, and softball fields.

**STUDENT BODY. Undergraduate profile:** 64% are state residents; 24% are transfers. 1% Asian-American, 2% Black, 2% Hispanic, 95% White. Average age of undergraduates is 20.
**Freshman profile:** 1% of freshmen who took SAT scored 700 or over on verbal, 3% scored 700 or over on math; 6% scored 600 or over on verbal, 23% scored 600 or over on math; 31% scored 500 or over on verbal, 63% scored 500 or over on math; 86% scored 400 or over on verbal, 97% scored 400 or over on math; 100% scored 300 or over on verbal, 100% scored 300 or over on math. 2% of freshmen who took ACT scored 30 or over on English, 2% scored 30 or over on math, 2% scored 30 or over on composite; 27% scored 24 or over on English, 18% scored 24 or over on math, 29% scored 24 or over on composite; 91% scored 18 or over on English, 86% scored 18 or over on math, 100% scored 18 or over on composite; 100% scored 12 or over on English, 100% scored 12 or over on math. 62% of accepted applicants took SAT; 38% took ACT. 75% of freshmen come from public schools.
**Foreign students:** 102 students are from out of the country. Countries represented include the Bahamas, Germany, Hong Kong, Japan, Korea, and South American countries; 29 in all.

**PROGRAMS OF STUDY. Degrees:** B.A., B.Mus., B.Mus.Ed., B.S.
**Majors:** Accounting, Art, Art Communications, Biology, Business Administration, Chemistry, Citrus/Horticulture, Criminology, Economics, Elementary Education, English, Health/Physical Education, History, Humanities, Journalism, Mass Communications, Mathematics, Medical Technology, Music, Music Education, Music Management, Physical Education, Physics, Political Science, Primary Education, Psychology, Recreation, Religion, Sacred Music, Social Sciences, Sociology, Spanish, Sports Management, Theatre.
**Distribution of degrees:** The major with the highest enrollment is business administration; art has the lowest.
**Requirements:** General education requirement.
**Special:** Minors offered in most majors. Double majors. Independent study. Pass/fail grading option. Internships. Preprofessional programs in law, medicine, veterinary science, pharmacy, dentistry, theology, optometry, forestry, and nursing. 3-1 medical technology program. 3-2 forestry and environmental studies programs with Duke U and U of Florida. 3-2 engineering programs with U of Miami and Washington U. Member of Independent Colleges and Universities of Florida. Washington Semester and UN Semester. Other off-campus study opportunities. Teacher certification in early childhood, elementary, secondary, and special education. Certification in specific subject areas. Study abroad in Belgium, England, France, Germany, Ireland, the Netherlands, Scotland, and Spain. ROTC. AFROTC at U of South Florida.
**Academic Assistance:** Nonremedial tutoring.

**STUDENT LIFE. Housing:** Unmarried students under age 24 must live on campus. Women's and men's dorms. Sorority and fraternity housing. 87% of students live in college housing.
**Services and counseling/handicapped student services:** Placement services. Health service. Chaplain. Hotline. Counseling services for veteran students. Personal and psychological counseling. Career and academic guidance services. Religious counseling. Physically disabled student services. Tape recorders.
**Campus organizations:** Undergraduate student government. Student newspaper (Southern News). Yearbook. Choir, band, civic and political groups, resident hall councils, cheerleaders, Vagabonds (drama group), Association of Women Students, special-interest groups. Eight fraternities, all with chapter houses; six sororities, all with chapter houses. 40% of men join a fraternity. 40% of women join a sorority.
**Religious organizations:** All-Campus Fellowship, BCM, Canterbury Club, Hillel, John Wesley Club, Newman Club, Preministry Society.
**Minority/foreign student organizations:** International Club.

**ATHLETICS. Physical education requirements:** Two semesters of physical education required.
**Intercollegiate competition:** 20% of students participate. Baseball (M), basketball (M,W), cross-country (M,W), golf (M), soccer (M), softball (W), tennis (W), volleyball (W). Member of NCAA Division II, Sunshine State Conference.
**Intramural and club sports:** 65% of students participate. Intramural basketball, bowling, cross-country, soccer, softball, tennis, touch football, volleyball. Men's club water skiing. Women's club soccer, water skiing.

**ADMISSIONS. Academic basis for candidate selection** (in order of priority): Secondary school record, standardized test scores, class rank, school's recommendation, essay.
**Nonacademic basis for candidate selection:** Character and personality are emphasized. Extracurricular participation and particular talent or ability are important.
**Requirements:** Graduation from secondary school is required; GED is accepted. 18 units and the following program of study are recommended: 4 units of English, 3 units of math, 2 units of science, 2 units of foreign language, 1 unit of social studies, 2 units of history, 4 units of electives. Minimum combined SAT score of 900 (composite ACT score of 20) required of education applicants. SAT or ACT is required. Campus visit and interview recommended. Off-campus interviews available with an admissions representative.
**Procedure:** Take SAT or ACT by March of 12th year. Suggest filing application by April. Application deadline is August 1. Notification of admission on rolling basis. Reply required within four weeks of acceptance. $250 tuition deposit, refundable until May 1. Freshmen accepted for terms other than fall.
**Special programs:** Admission may be deferred. Credit and/or placement may be granted through CEEB Advanced Placement exams for scores of 3 or higher. Credit and/or placement may be granted through CLEP general and subject exams. Credit may be granted through military experience. Early entrance/early admission program. Concurrent enrollment program.
**Transfer students:** Transfer students accepted for terms other than fall. In fall 1992, 24% of all new students were transfers into all classes. 360 transfer applications were received, 243 were accepted. Application deadline is August 1 for fall; December 1 for spring. Minimum 2.0 GPA required. Lowest course grade accepted is "C." Maximum number of transferable credits is 62 semester hours from a two-year school and 94 semester hours from a four-year school. At least 30 semester hours must be completed at the college to receive degree.
**Admissions contact:** William B. Stephens, Jr., Director of Admissions. 813 680-4131.

**FINANCIAL AID. Available aid:** Pell grants, SEOG, state scholarships and grants, school scholarships and grants, private scholarships and grants, ROTC scholarships, academic merit scholarships, and athletic scholarships. $300 tuition grant for simultaneously enrolled family members. $1400 grant for unmarried children of Florida Methodist ministers, $300 for children of other ministers. Perkins Loans (NDSL), PLUS, Stafford Loans (GSL), school loans, private loans, and SLS. Tuition Plan Inc., Knight Tuition Plans, AMS, Tuition Management Systems, and family tuition reduction.
**Financial aid statistics:** 50% of aid is not need-based. In 1992-93, 90% of all undergraduate applicants received aid; 90% of freshman applicants. Average amounts of aid awarded freshmen: Scholarships and grants, $3,000; loans, $2,000.
**Supporting data/closing dates:** FAFSA/FAF: Priority filing date is April 15. School's own aid application: Priority filing date is April 15. Notification of awards begins March 1.
**Financial aid contact:** Robert L. Sterling, M.S., Director of Financial Aid. 813 680-4140.

**STUDENT EMPLOYMENT.** College Work/Study Program. Institutional employment. 25% of full-time undergraduates work on campus during school year. Students may expect to earn an average of $1,000 during school year. Off-campus part-time employment opportunities rated "good."

**COMPUTER FACILITIES.** 75 IBM/IBM-compatible and Macintosh/Apple microcomputers; 45 are networked. Students may access IBM minicomputer/mainframe systems. Computer languages and software packages include BASIC, COBOL, FORTRAN, Pascal. Computer facilities are available to all students.
**Fees:** $50 computer fee.
**Hours:** 8 AM-11 PM.

# Florida State University

**Tallahassee, FL 32306-1009 — 904 644-2525**

**1993-94 Costs.** Tuition: $1,780 (state residents), $6,680 (out-of-state). Room: $2,150. Board: $1,910. Fees, books, misc. academic expenses (school's estimate): $600.
**Enrollment.** Undergraduates: 8,588 men, 10,281 women (full-time). Freshman class: 11,651 applicants, 8,683 accepted, 3,023 enrolled. Graduate enrollment: 2,452 men, 2,663 women.
**Test score averages/ranges.** Range of SAT scores of middle 50%: 460-560 verbal, 510-630 math. Range of ACT scores of middle 50%: 22-27 English, 22-27 math.
**Faculty.** 1,397 full-time; 146 part-time. 90% of faculty holds highest degree in specific field.
**Selectivity rating.** Competitive.

**PROFILE.** Florida State, founded in 1857, is a public, comprehensive university. Its 418-acre campus is located within a mile of downtown Tallahassee.

**Accreditation:** SACS. Professionally accredited by the Accreditation Board for Engineering and Technology, the American Assembly of Collegiate Schools of Business, the American Bar Association, the American Dietetic Association, the American Home Economics Association, the American Library Association, the American Psychological Association, the American Speech-Language-Hearing Association, the Association of American Law Schools, the Council on Rehabilitation Education, the Council on Social Work Education, the Foundation for Interior Design Education Research, the National Association of Schools of Music, the National Council for Accreditation of Teacher Education, the National League for Nursing, the National Recreation and Park Association.
**Religious orientation:** Florida State University is nonsectarian; no religious requirements.
**Library:** Collections totaling over 2,028,509 volumes, 18,420 periodical subscriptions, and 4,103,578 microform items.
**Special facilities/museums:** Art gallery, museum, developmental research school, marine lab, oceanographic institute, tandem Van de Graaff accelerator, national high magnetic field lab.
**Athletic facilities:** Gymnasiums, basketball, racquetball, and tennis courts, athletic fields, swimming pool, track, golf course, bowling lanes, recreation center.

**STUDENT BODY. Undergraduate profile:** 85% are state residents; 45% are transfers. 2% Asian-American, 9% Black, 5% Hispanic, 1% Native American, 83% White. Average age of undergraduates is 22.
**Freshman profile:** 1% of freshmen who took SAT scored 700 or over on verbal, 7% scored 700 or over on math; 14% scored 600 or over on verbal, 39% scored 600 or over on math; 56% scored 500 or over on verbal, 81% scored 500 or over on math; 93% scored 400 or over on verbal, 98% scored 400 or over on math; 100% scored 300 or over on verbal, 100% scored 300 or over on math. Majority of accepted applicants took SAT. 85% of freshmen come from public schools.
**Foreign students:** 160 students are from out of the country. Countries represented include Canada, China, India, Korea, Taiwan, and the United Kingdom; 100 in all.

**PROGRAMS OF STUDY. Degrees:** B.A., B.F.A., B.Mus., B.Mus.Ed., B.S.
**Majors:** Accounting, American Studies, Anthropology, Art Education, Art History, Asian Studies, Audiology/Speech Pathology, Biochemistry, Biological Sciences, Business Administration, Chemical Engineering, Chemical Science, Chemistry, Civil Engineering, Classics, Clothing/Textile/Fashion Merchandising, Communication, Computer Science, Criminology, Dance, Early Childhood Education, Economics, Electrical Engineering, Elementary Education, Emotional Disturbances/Learning Disabilities, English, English Education, Entrepreneurship/Small Business Management, Family/Child/Consumer Sciences, Finance, Food/Nutrition, French, Geography, Geology, German, Greek, Health Education, History, Home Economics Education, Hospitality Administration, Human Resources Management, Human Sciences, Humanities, Industrial Engineering, Interior Design, International Affairs, Italian, Latin, Latin American/Caribbean Studies, Leisure Services/Studies, Management, Management Information Systems, Marketing, Mathematics, Mathematics Education, Mechanical Engineering, Mental Retardation, Meteorology, Motion Picture/Television/Recording Arts, Multilingual/Multicultural Education, Multinational Business, Music, Music Composition, Music Education, Music History, Music Performance, Music Theory, Music Therapy, Nursing, Operations Management, Philosophy, Physical Education, Physics, Political Science, Psychology, Real Estate, Rehabilitation Services, Religion, Risk Management/Insurance, Russian, Russian/East European Studies, Science Education, Secondary Science/Math Teaching, Social Science, Social Science Education, Social Work, Sociology, Spanish, Statistics, Studio Art, Theatre, Visual Disabilities.
**Distribution of degrees:** The majors with the highest enrollment are criminology, psychology, and biological sciences.
**Requirements:** General education requirement.
**Academic regulations:** Minimum 2.0 GPA must be maintained.
**Special:** Minors offered in most majors and in aerospace studies, black studies, child development, Chinese, classical languages/literature/civilization, film studies, housing, linguistics, military science, peace studies, Portuguese, public administration, Serbo-Croatian, urban and regional planning, and women's studies. All first-year students except dance and music majors enter undergraduate studies and transfer as upperclass students to specific academic division. Associate's degrees offered. Double majors. Dual degrees. Independent study. Accelerated study. Pass/fail grading option. Internships. Graduate school at which undergraduates may take graduate-level courses. Preprofessional programs in law, medicine, veterinary science, pharmacy, dentistry, theology, and optometry. Cooperative programs with Florida A&M U, Tallahassee Comm Coll, and other institutions. Medical science program with U of Florida Coll of Medicine. Teacher certification in early childhood, elementary, secondary, special education, and bilingual/bicultural education. Certification in specific subject areas. Study abroad in Costa Rica, England, France, Italy, Panama, Russia, Spain, Switzerland, and the former Yugoslav Republics. ROTC and AFROTC. NROTC at Florida A&M U.
**Honors:** Phi Beta Kappa. Honors program. Honor societies.
**Academic Assistance:** Nonremedial tutoring.

**STUDENT LIFE. Housing:** Students may live on or off campus. Coed, women's, and men's dorms. Sorority and fraternity housing. School-owned/operated apartments. On-campus married-student housing. 18% of students live in college housing.
**Social atmosphere:** The student newspaper reports, "Bars for drinking and dancing, and the outdoors for gonzo and intramural sports, seem to be most popular with the majority of students." Sororities, fraternities, and the football team have the biggest social influence on campus. Popular events include football games, Homecoming, Valentine's Day, and concerts at the civic center. Favorite off-campus nightspots include The Phyrst and Finale's.
**Services and counseling/handicapped student services:** Placement services. Health service. Women's center. Day care. Counseling services for minority, military, veteran, and older students. Birth control, personal, and psychological counseling. Career and academic guidance services. Religious counseling. Physically disabled student services. Learning disabled services. Notetaking services. Tape recorders. Tutors. Reader services for the blind.
**Campus organizations:** Undergraduate student government. Student newspaper (Florida Flambeau, published once/day). Literary magazine. Yearbook. Radio and TV stations. Debating, ensembles, bands, theatre and dance groups, academic, cultural, departmental, professional, social service, and special-interest groups, 290 organizations in all. 25 fraternities, 21 chapter houses; 19 sororities, 16 chapter houses. 20% of men join a fraternity. 20% of women join a sorority.
**Religious organizations:** Baptist Campus Ministry, Catholic Campus Ministry, Christian Science Organization, Christians in Action, Fellowship of Christian Athletes, Hillel, Latter-Day Saints Association, Muslim Student Organization, Navigators, Wesley Foundation.
**Minority/foreign student organizations:** Black Student Union, Caribbean Club, Chinese Students and Scholars Association, Hispanic Student Union, United Latin Society. African, Arab, Chinese, Egyptian, Latin, Nigerian, and Thai student groups.

**ATHLETICS. Physical education requirements:** None.
**Intercollegiate competition:** Baseball (M), basketball (M,W), cross-country (M,W), diving (M,W), football (M), golf (M,W), softball (W), swimming (M,W), tennis (M,W), track and field (indoor) (M,W), track and field (outdoor) (M,W), volleyball (W). Member of Atlantic Coast Conference, NCAA Division I-A.
**Intramural and club sports:** Intramural badminton, basketball, beach volleyball, bench press, bowling, eightball, flag football, foul shooting, golf, inner-tube water polo, putt-putt golf, racquetball, running, soccer, softball, swimming, table tennis, tennis, track and field, volleyball, wrestling. Men's club bowling, crew, fencing, lacrosse, martial arts, racquetball, rugby, sailing, soccer, ultimate frisbee, volleyball, water polo, water skiing, wrestling. Women's club bowling, martial arts, racquetball, rugby, sailing, soccer, ultimate frisbee, water polo, water skiing.

**ADMISSIONS. Academic basis for candidate selection** (in order of priority): Secondary school record, standardized test scores, class rank, school's recommendation, essay.
**Nonacademic basis for candidate selection:** Particular talent or ability is important. Character and personality, extracurricular participation, geographical distribution, and alumni/ae relationship are considered.
**Requirements:** Graduation from secondary school is required; GED is accepted. 19 units and the following program of study are required: 4 units of English, 3 units of math, 3 units of science including 2 units of lab, 2 units of foreign language, 3 units of social studies, 4 units of electives. Minimum "B" average in secondary school subjects and a minimum composite ACT score of 24 (combined SAT score of 1000) required of in-state applicants. Higher standards required of out-of-state applicants. Audition required of dance, music, and B.F.A. program applicants. Departmental application required of motion picture, television, and recording arts program applicants. Portfolio required of art program applicants. Horizons Unlimited Program and Summer Enrichment Program for applicants not normally admissible. SAT or ACT is required. Campus visit recommended. No off-campus interviews.
**Procedure:** Take SAT or ACT by January of 12th year. Suggest filing application by December. Application deadline is March 1. Notification of admission on rolling basis. No set date by which applicants must accept offer. $225 refundable room deposit. Freshmen accepted for terms other than fall.
**Special programs:** Credit and/or placement may be granted through CEEB Advanced Placement exams for scores of 3 or higher. Credit and/or placement may be granted through CLEP general and subject exams. Credit and placement may be granted through

challenge exams and military experience. Early entrance/early admission program. Concurrent enrollment program.
**Transfer students:** Transfer students accepted for terms other than fall. In fall 1993, 45% of all new students were transfers into all classes. 6,239 transfer applications were received, 4,194 were accepted. Application deadline is June 20 for fall; November 1 for spring. Lowest course grade accepted is "D." Final 30 semester hours must be completed at the university to receive degree.
**Admissions contact:** John Barnhill, M.S., Director of Admissions. 904 644-6200.

**FINANCIAL AID. Available aid:** Pell grants, SEOG, state scholarships and grants, school scholarships and grants, private scholarships and grants, academic merit scholarships, and athletic scholarships. Perkins Loans (NDSL), PLUS, Stafford Loans (GSL), state loans, school loans, and SLS. Deferred payment plan. Prepaid Tuition Plan.
**Financial aid statistics:** 40% of aid is not need-based. In 1993-94, 45% of all undergraduate applicants received aid; 42% of freshman applicants. Average amounts of aid awarded freshmen: Scholarships and grants, $2,000; loans, $2,620.
**Supporting data/closing dates:** FAFSA/FAF/FFS: Priority filing date is March 1. School's own aid application: Priority filing date is March 1. State aid form: Priority filing date is March 1. Income tax forms: Priority filing date is March 1. Florida Student Assistant Grant Application: Deadline is April 15. Notification of awards begins in May.
**Financial aid contact:** Robert L. McCloud, Director of Financial Aid. 904 644-5871.

**STUDENT EMPLOYMENT.** College Work/Study Program. Institutional employment. 10% of full-time undergraduates work on campus during school year. Students may expect to earn an average of $1,600 during school year. Off-campus part-time employment opportunities rated "good."

**COMPUTER FACILITIES.** 75 IBM/IBM-compatible and Macintosh/Apple microcomputers; all are networked. Students may access CDC Cyber, Cray, Digital, IBM, SUN minicomputer/mainframe systems, BITNET, Internet. Residence halls may be equipped with stand-alone microcomputers, networked microcomputers, networked terminals, modems. Client/LAN operating systems include Apple/Macintosh, DOS, UNIX/XENIX/AIX, X-windows, LocalTalk/AppleTalk, Novell. Computer languages and software packages include Ada, Assembly, BASIC, C, COBOL, FORTRAN, LISP, Pascal. Some computers are available to departmental majors only.
**Fees:** Computer fee is included in tuition/fees.

**GRADUATE CAREER DATA.** Companies and businesses that hire graduates: Arthur Andersen; Barnett Bank, First Florida Bank; Burdines; Information Systems of Florida; Maas Brothers; Price Waterhouse; Xerox.

**PROMINENT ALUMNI/AE.** Reubin Askew, former governor of Florida; Norman Thagard, astronaut; Burt Reynolds and Robert Urich, actors.

# Jacksonville University

**Jacksonville, FL 32211** **904 744-3950**

**1994-95 Costs.** Tuition: $9,600. Room: $2,020. Board: $2,360. Fees, books, misc. academic expenses (school's estimate): $1,180.
**Enrollment.** Undergraduates: 841 men, 723 women (full-time). Freshman class: 1,347 applicants, 1,119 accepted, 305 enrolled. Graduate enrollment: 155 men, 179 women.
**Test score averages/ranges.** N/A.
**Faculty.** 110 full-time; 125 part-time. 64% of faculty holds highest degree in specific field. Student/faculty ratio: 18 to 1.
**Selectivity rating.** Less competitive.

**PROFILE.** Jacksonville, founded in 1934, is a private university. Programs are offered through the Colleges of Arts and Science, Business Administration, and Fine Arts. Its 214-acre campus is located near downtown Jacksonville.

**Accreditation:** SACS. Professionally accredited by the National Association of Schools of Art and Design, the National Association of Schools of Music, the National League for Nursing.
**Religious orientation:** Jacksonville University is nonsectarian; no religious requirements.
**Library:** Collections totaling over 284,706 volumes, 733 periodical subscriptions, and 97,395 microform items.
**Special facilities/museums:** Art museum, dance pavilion, concert hall, on-campus elementary school, air field.
**Athletic facilities:** Swimming pool, gymnasium, baseball, football, lacrosse, and soccer fields, basketball, racquetball, and tennis courts, golf course, weight room, archery range.

**STUDENT BODY. Undergraduate profile:** 61% are state residents; 34% are transfers. 3% Asian-American, 8% Black, 5% Hispanic, 1% Native American, 79% White, 4% Other. Average age of undergraduates is 23.
**Freshman profile:** 1% of freshmen who took SAT scored 700 or over on verbal, 3% scored 700 or over on math; 9% scored 600 or over on verbal, 18% scored 600 or over on math; 30% scored 500 or over on verbal, 50% scored 500 or over on math; 70% scored 400 or over on verbal, 85% scored 400 or over on math; 98% scored 300 or over on verbal, 98% scored 300 or over on math. Majority of accepted applicants took SAT.
**Foreign students:** 143 students are from out of the country. Countries represented include the Bahamas, Bermuda, Canada, England, Japan, and the Netherlands; 57 in all.

**PROGRAMS OF STUDY. Degrees:** B.A., B.Art Ed., B.F.A., B.Gen.Studies, B.Mus., B.Mus.Ed., B.S., B.S.Nurs.
**Majors:** Accounting, Applied Music, Art, Art Education, Art History, Aviation Management/Flight Operations, Biology, Business, Chemistry, Church Music, Communications, Computer Art/Design, Computer Science, Dance, Dance Education, Economics, Electrical Engineering, Elementary Education, English, Entrepreneurial Studies, Environmental Science, Exceptional Child Education, Finance, French, Geography, German, History, Humanities, International Affairs, Liberal Studies, Management, Marine Science, Marketing, Mathematics, Mechanical Engineering, Medical Technology, Music, Music/Business, Music Composition/Theory, Music Education, Music History, Music/Theatre, Nursing, Philosophy, Physical Education, Physics, Political Science, Psychology, Public Management, Sociology, Spanish, Speech/Theatre, Studio Art, Theatre Arts, Visual Communications, Voice/Opera.
**Distribution of degrees:** The majors with the highest enrollment are business administration, communications, and nursing.
**Requirements:** General education requirement.
**Academic regulations:** Minimum 2.0 GPA must be maintained.
**Special:** Minors offered in most majors. Courses offered in contemporary world studies, naval science, physical science, religion, speech, women's studies. Self-designed majors. Double majors. Dual degrees. Independent study. Pass/fail grading option. Internships. Cooperative education programs. Graduate school at which undergraduates may take graduate-level courses. Preprofessional programs in law, medicine, and veterinary science. Dual-degree engineering programs with Columbia U, U of Florida, Georgia Tech, Mercer U, U of Miami, Stevens Inst of Tech, and Washington U. Teacher certification in early childhood, elementary, secondary, and special education. NROTC. ROTC at U of North Florida.
**Honors:** Honors program. Honor societies.
**Academic Assistance:** Remedial reading, writing, math, and study skills.

**STUDENT LIFE. Housing:** Women's and men's dorms. 50% of students live in college housing.
**Social atmosphere:** "JU is basically a quiet and conservative campus of upper middle-class to wealthy students," according to the student newspaper, "but always welcomes new and stimulating activities." Influential student groups on campus include "Christian groups, athletes, over a dozen national fraternities and sororities, various professional and extracurricular groups." On campus, students gather at the Wolfson Student Center. Favorite off-campus spots are Cindy's Good Times Pub and Crabshaw's.
**Services and counseling/handicapped student services:** Placement services. Health service. Counseling services for minority students. Personal and psychological counseling. Career and academic guidance services. Religious counseling. Physically disabled student services. Learning disabled services. Notetaking services. Reader services for the blind.
**Campus organizations:** Undergraduate student government. Student newspaper (Navigator, published once/week). Literary magazine. Yearbook. Radio station. Chorus, orchestra, wind ensembles, opera workshop, JU Players, dance theatre, Childhood Education International, 73 organizations in all. Seven fraternities, no chapter houses; five sororities, no chapter houses. 30% of men join a fraternity. 23% of women join a sorority.
**Religious organizations:** Canterbury Club, Catholic Student Ministry, Hillel, Baptist Student Union, Interfaith Council.
**Minority/foreign student organizations:** United Minority Alliance. International Student Association.

**ATHLETICS. Physical education requirements:** Two semesters of physical education required.
**Intercollegiate competition:** 16% of students participate. Baseball (M), basketball (M), cheerleading (M,W), crew (M,W), cross-country (M,W), golf (M,W), soccer (M), tennis (M,W), track (outdoor) (W), volleyball (W). Member of NCAA Division I, Sun Belt Conference.
**Intramural and club sports:** 28% of students participate. Intramural badminton, basketball, bowling, football, lacrosse, soccer, softball, volleyball. Men's club cycling, racquetball, rugby, softball, volleyball.

**ADMISSIONS. Academic basis for candidate selection** (in order of priority): Secondary school record, standardized test scores, class rank, essay, school's recommendation.
**Nonacademic basis for candidate selection:** Extracurricular participation and particular talent or ability are emphasized. Character and personality and alumni/ae relationship are considered.
**Requirements:** Graduation from secondary school is required; GED is accepted. 22 units and the following program of study are required: 4 units of English, 3 units of math, 2 units of science, 2 units of social studies, 2 units of history, 5 units of electives. Rank in top half of secondary school class recommended. Portfolio required of art program applicants. SAT or ACT is required. Campus visit and interview recommended. Off-campus interviews available with an admissions representative.
**Procedure:** Take SAT or ACT by March of 12th year. Visit college for interview by June 30 of 12th year. Application deadline is August 1. Notification of admission on rolling basis. Reply is required by May 1. $100 tuition deposit for commuters; $200 deposit for residents, partially refundable until June 30. Freshmen accepted for terms other than fall.
**Special programs:** Admission may be deferred one year. Credit and/or placement may be granted through CEEB Advanced Placement exams for scores of 3 or higher. Credit may be granted through CLEP general and subject exams, DANTES and challenge exams and military experience. Credit and placement may be granted through life experience. Early entrance/early admission program. Concurrent enrollment program.
**Transfer students:** Transfer students accepted for terms other than fall. In fall 1993, 34% of all new students were transfers into all classes. 511 transfer applications were received, 396 were accepted. Application deadline is August 1 for fall; December 1 for spring. Minimum 2.0 GPA required. Lowest course grade accepted is "C." Maximum number of transferable credits is 64 semester hours from a two-year school and 96 semester hours from a four-year school. At least 32 semester hours must be completed at the university to receive degree.
**Admissions contact:** Frank J. Vastola, M.S., Director of Admissions. 904 745-7000.

**FINANCIAL AID. Available aid:** Pell grants, SEOG, Federal Nursing Student Scholarships, state scholarships and grants, school scholarships and grants, private scholarships and grants, ROTC scholarships, academic merit scholarships, and athletic scholarships. Perkins Loans (NDSL), PLUS, Stafford Loans (GSL), school loans, private loans, and SLS. Unsubsidized Stafford Loans. Tuition Plan Inc., Knight Tuition Plans, AMS, and family tuition reduction.
**Financial aid statistics:** 48% of aid is not need-based. In 1993-94, 96% of all undergraduate applicants received aid; 100% of freshman applicants. Average amounts of aid awarded freshmen: Scholarships and grants, $6,406; loans, $3,200.
**Supporting data/closing dates:** FAFSA: Priority filing date is March 15. School's own aid application: Priority filing date is March 15. Notification of awards on rolling basis.
**Financial aid contact:** William K. Spiers, Director of Financial Aid. 904 745-7060.

**STUDENT EMPLOYMENT.** College Work/Study Program. Institutional employment. 16% of full-time undergraduates work on campus during school year. Students may expect to earn an average of $1,000 during school year. Freshmen are discouraged from working during their first term. Off-campus part-time employment opportunities rated "good."

**COMPUTER FACILITIES.** 87 IBM/IBM-compatible and Macintosh/Apple microcomputers; 20 are networked. Students may access Hewlett-Packard minicomputer/mainframe systems, Internet. Residence halls may be equipped with stand-alone microcomputers. Client/LAN operating systems include Apple/Macintosh, DOS, UNIX/XENIX/AIX, LocalTalk/AppleTalk. Computer languages and software packages include BASIC, C, COBOL, dBASE, FORTRAN, Lotus 1-2-3, Microsoft Word, Pascal, WordPerfect. Computer facilities are available to all students.
**Fees:** Computer fee is included in tuition/fees.
**Hours:** 9 AM-10 PM (M-Th); 9 AM-5 PM (F); noon-5 PM (Sa); noon-10 PM (Su).

# Lynn University

**Boca Raton, FL 33431-5598 407 994-0770**

**1993-94 Costs.** Tuition: $12,900. Room & board: $5,100. Fees, books, misc. academic expenses (school's estimate): $1,700.
**Enrollment.** Undergraduates: 624 men, 576 women (full-time). Freshman class: 1,630 applicants, 1,200 accepted, 429 enrolled. Graduate enrollment: 47 men, 49 women.
**Test score averages/ranges.** Average SAT scores: 440 verbal, 470 math. Average ACT scores: 21 composite.
**Faculty.** 40 full-time; 35 part-time. 53% of faculty holds doctoral degree. Student/faculty ratio: 20 to 1.
**Selectivity rating.** Less competitive.

**PROFILE.** Lynn University is a private institution. Founded as a junior college for women in 1963, it adopted coeducation when it became a four-year institution in 1971. Programs are offered through the Divisions of Arts and Sciences; Business; and Hotel, Restaurant, and Tourism Management. Its 123-acre campus is located in Boca Raton, 20 miles from Fort Lauderdale and Palm Beach.
**Accreditation:** SACS.
**Religious orientation:** Lynn University is nonsectarian; no religious requirements.
**Library:** Collections totaling over 66,161 volumes, 400 periodical subscriptions, and 2,000 microform items.
**Athletic facilities:** Gymnasium, swimming pool, basketball and tennis courts, weight room, baseball, soccer, and softball fields.

**STUDENT BODY. Undergraduate profile:** 30% are state residents; 27% are transfers. 3% Asian-American, 5% Black, 9% Hispanic, 1% Native American, 82% White. Average age of undergraduates is 19.
**Freshman profile:** 82% of accepted applicants took SAT; 18% took ACT. 38% of freshmen come from public schools.
**Foreign students:** 80 students are from out of the country. Countries represented include Caribbean Islands, England, France, Japan, Peru, and Venezuela; 35 in all.

**PROGRAMS OF STUDY. Degrees:** B.A., B.F.A., B.S.
**Majors:** Accounting, Applied Studies, Art/Design, Aviation Management, Behavioral Science, Business Administration, Club/Recreation Management, Communications, Design, Elementary Education, Fashion Marketing, Health/Human Services, History/Political Science, Hotel/Restaurant Management, Humanities, Liberal Arts, Marketing, Pre-Elementary Education, Psychology, Sociology, Sports Management, Travel/Tourism.
**Distribution of degrees:** The majors with the highest enrollment are business administration, hotel/restaurant management, and liberal arts.
**Requirements:** General education requirement.
**Academic regulations:** Minimum 2.0 GPA must be maintained.
**Special:** Associate's degrees offered. Independent study. Accelerated study. Internships. Graduate school at which undergraduates may take graduate-level courses. Preprofessional programs in law. Member of Florida Association of Private College and University Admissions and Independent Colleges and Universities of Florida. Teacher certification in early childhood and elementary education. Study abroad in England, France, Ireland, Sweden, and other countries.
**Honors:** Honors program.
**Academic Assistance:** Remedial reading, writing, math, and study skills. Nonremedial tutoring.

**STUDENT LIFE. Housing:** Freshmen and sophomores must live on campus. Women's and men's dorms. 70% of students live in college housing.
**Social atmosphere:** According to the student newspaper, "A full round of social and cultural activities is available on and off campus." Golf, tennis, soccer, and baseball are popular, as are campus dances and weekend trips to Florida sights. Among the socially influential groups on campus is the KOR, Knights of the Roundtable.
**Services and counseling/handicapped student services:** Placement services. Health service. Counseling services for minority and older students. Birth control, personal, and psychological counseling. Career and academic guidance services. Religious counseling. Physically disabled student services. Learning disabled program/services. Notetaking services. Tape recorders.
**Campus organizations:** Undergraduate student government. Student newspaper (Collegiate). Hospitality groups, Knights of the Roundtable, weekend trips, cocurricular clubs, service groups.
**Religious organizations:** Hillel, Newman Club.
**Minority/foreign student organizations:** International Student Organization.

**ATHLETICS. Physical education requirements:** None.
**Intercollegiate competition:** 10% of students participate. Baseball (M), basketball (M,W), cheerleading (M,W), golf (M,W), soccer (M,W), tennis (M,W). Member of NAIA.
**Intramural and club sports:** 20% of students participate. Intramural basketball, flag football, soccer, softball, tennis, volleyball. Men's club ice hockey, lacrosse, swimming. Women's club swimming.

**ADMISSIONS. Academic basis for candidate selection** (in order of priority): Secondary school record, class rank, school's recommendation, standardized test scores, essay.
**Nonacademic basis for candidate selection:** Character and personality are important. Extracurricular participation, particular talent or ability, and alumni/ae relationship are considered.
**Requirements:** Graduation from secondary school is required; GED is accepted. 20 units and the following program of study are recommended: 4 units of English, 3 units of math, 3 units of science, 1 unit of foreign language, 2 units of social studies, 2 units of history, 5 units of electives. Portfolio required of art program applicants. SAT or ACT is required. Campus visit and interview recommended. Off-campus interviews available with admissions and alumni representatives.
**Procedure:** Take SAT or ACT by May of 12th year. Visit college for interview by June of 12th year. Notification of admission on rolling basis. Reply is required by August 1. $200 nonrefundable tuition deposit. $300 nonrefundable room deposit. Freshmen accepted for terms other than fall.
**Special programs:** Admission may be deferred. Credit and/or placement may be granted through CEEB Advanced Placement exams for scores of 3 or higher. Credit and/or placement may be granted through CLEP general and subject exams. Early entrance/early admission program. Concurrent enrollment program.
**Transfer students:** Transfer students accepted for terms other than fall. In fall 1993, 27% of all new students were transfers into all classes. Application deadline is rolling for fall; rolling for spring. Minimum 2.0 GPA required. Lowest course grade accepted is "C." Maximum number of transferable credits is 90 semester hours. At least 30 semester hours must be completed at the university to receive degree.
**Admissions contact:** Charles Somma, M.A., Director of Admissions. 407 994-0770, extension 157.

**FINANCIAL AID. Available aid:** Pell grants, SEOG, state scholarships and grants, school scholarships and grants, private scholarships and grants, academic merit scholarships, athletic scholarships, and aid for undergraduate foreign students. Perkins Loans (NDSL), Stafford Loans (GSL), state loans, and private loans. Knight Tuition Plans.
**Supporting data/closing dates:** FAFSA/FAF/FFS: Priority filing date is February 15. Notification of awards on rolling basis.
**Financial aid contact:** Evelyn Nelson, Director of Financial Aid. 407 994-0770, extension 127.

**STUDENT EMPLOYMENT.** College Work/Study Program. Institutional employment. 5% of full-time undergraduates work on campus during school year. Students may expect to earn an average of $600 during school year. Off-campus part-time employment opportunities rated "excellent."

**COMPUTER FACILITIES.** 60 IBM/IBM-compatible microcomputers. Computer facilities are available to all students.
**Fees:** None.

# New College of the University of South Florida

**Sarasota, FL 34243-2197 813 359-4269**

**1993-94 Costs.** Tuition: $2,030 (state residents), $7,913 (out-of-state). Room: $1,930. Board: $1,737. Fees, books, misc. academic expenses (school's estimate): $700.
**Enrollment.** Undergraduates: 260 men, 276 women (full-time). Freshman class: 803 applicants, 283 accepted, 146 enrolled.
**Test score averages/ranges.** Range of SAT scores of middle 50%: 570-660 verbal, 580-690 math. Range of ACT scores of middle 50%: 27-31 composite.
**Faculty.** 53 full-time. 97% of faculty holds doctoral degree. Student/faculty ratio: 10 to 1.
**Selectivity rating.** Highly competitive.

**PROFILE.** New College, founded in 1960, is a public university. Its 120-acre campus, including the former estate of Charles Ringling, is located in Sarasota, 50 miles south of Tampa.
**Accreditation:** SACS.
**Religious orientation:** New College of the University of South Florida is nonsectarian; no religious requirements.
**Library:** Collections totaling over 228,000 volumes, 1,100 periodical subscriptions, and 400,000 microform items.
**Special facilities/museums:** Ringling Museum of Art, anthropology, psychology, and environmental studies labs, music and fine arts facility.
**Athletic facilities:** Fitness center, basketball, racquetball, tennis, and volleyball courts, outdoor swimming pool, aerobics studio, exercise room, whirlpool.

**STUDENT BODY. Undergraduate profile:** 60% are state residents; 30% are transfers. 6% Asian-American, 1% Black, 5% Hispanic, 1% Native American, 87% White. Average age of undergraduates is 21.
**Freshman profile:** 15% of freshmen who took SAT scored 700 or over on verbal, 27% scored 700 or over on math; 61% scored 600 or over on verbal, 74% scored 600 or over on math; 97% scored 500 or over on verbal, 97% scored 500 or over on math; 100% scored 400 or over on verbal, 100% scored 400 or over on math. 47% of freshmen who took ACT scored 30 or over on composite; 99% scored 24 or over on composite; 100% scored 18 or over on composite. 97% of accepted applicants took SAT; 53% took ACT. 80% of freshmen come from public schools.
**Undergraduate achievement:** 80% of fall 1992 freshmen returned for fall 1993 term. 62% of entering class graduated. 70% of students who completed a degree program went on to graduate study within five years.
**Foreign students:** 21 students are from out of the country. Countries represented include Canada, England, and Hong Kong.

**PROGRAMS OF STUDY. Degrees:** B.A.

**Majors:** Anthropology, Art History, Biology, Chemistry, Classics, Computer Science, Economics, Environmental Studies, Fine Arts, French, German, Greek, History, Literature, Mathematics, Music, Philosophy, Physics, Political Science, Psychology, Religion, Russian, Sociology, Spanish.
**Distribution of degrees:** The majors with the highest enrollment are literature, psychology, and biology; physics, history, and French have the lowest.
**Special:** Self-designed majors. Double majors. Independent study. Accelerated study. Pass/fail grading option. Internships. Exchange programs abroad in England (U of Newcastle upon Tyne) and Scotland (U of Glasgow). Study abroad also in Florence, London, and other cities. ROTC and AFROTC at U of South Florida at Tampa.
**Honors:** Honors program.
**Academic Assistance:** Nonremedial tutoring.

**STUDENT LIFE. Housing:** All freshmen must live on campus. Coed dorms. 60% of students live in college housing.
**Social atmosphere:** Popular on-campus gathering spots include the lawn behind College Hall (the old Ringling Mansion) that overlooks the bay and has a great view of the sunset, and Palm Court where there is outdoor dancing and parties. Influential groups include Queer Culture (gay, lesbian, bisexual alliance), New College Student Alliance, Woman's Action Group, Multi-cultural Society, and the Food Service Committee. Among the most popular events of the school year are the Palm Court parties held on Halloween, Valentine's Day, and Graduation, the Semi-Normal (semi-formal), and the Crucial Barbeque. "We're academically intense and socially crazy," reports the editor of the student newspaper. "We're the most interesting social misfits around because everyone fits in here. If you graduate New College, you'll feel it for the rest of your life!"
**Services and counseling/handicapped student services:** Placement services. Health service. Counseling services for veteran students. Birth control, personal, and psychological counseling. Career and academic guidance services. Religious counseling. Physically disabled student services. Notetaking services. Tape recorders. Tutors. Reader services for the blind.
**Campus organizations:** Undergraduate student government. Student newspaper. Literary magazine. Chorus, drama and film groups, science fiction club, international arts association, public interest and research groups, other student groups.

**ATHLETICS. Physical education requirements:** None.
**Intramural and club sports:** 10% of students participate. Intramural aerobics, basketball, cycling, floor hockey, martial arts, racquetball, running, soccer, softball, swimming, tennis, touch football, volleyball, yoga. Men's club camping, canoeing, cycling, sailing, scuba. Women's club camping, canoeing, cycling, sailing, scuba.

**ADMISSIONS. Academic basis for candidate selection** (in order of priority): Secondary school record, essay, standardized test scores, school's recommendation.
**Nonacademic basis for candidate selection:** Character and personality are emphasized. Extracurricular participation is important. Alumni/ae relationship is considered.
**Requirements:** Graduation from secondary school is recommended; GED is accepted. 19 units and the following program of study are required: 4 units of English, 3 units of math, 3 units of science including 2 units of lab, 2 units of foreign language, 3 units of social studies, 4 units of academic electives. SAT or ACT is required. Campus visit recommended. Off-campus interviews available with an alumni representative.
**Procedure:** Take SAT or ACT by December of 12th year. Suggest filing application by February 1. Application deadline is May 1. Notification of admission on rolling basis. Reply is required by May 1 or within two weeks if accepted after April 15. $200 refundable room deposit. Freshmen accepted for terms other than fall.
**Special programs:** Admission may be deferred one year. Early entrance/early admission program.
**Transfer students:** Transfer students accepted for terms other than fall. In fall 1993, 30% of all new students were transfers into all classes. 265 transfer applications were received, 65 were accepted. Application deadline is May 1 for fall; December 1 for spring. Lowest course grade accepted is "C." At least two years of academic work must be completed at the college to receive degree.
**Admissions contact:** David L. Anderson, M.S., Director of Admissions. 813 359-4269.

**FINANCIAL AID. Available aid:** Pell grants, SEOG, state scholarships and grants, school scholarships and grants, private scholarships and grants, and academic merit scholarships. Perkins Loans (NDSL), PLUS, Stafford Loans (GSL), state loans, school loans, private loans, and SLS. Florida Prepaid Tuition Plan.
**Financial aid statistics:** 35% of aid is not need-based. In 1993-94, 85% of all undergraduate applicants received aid; 90% of freshman applicants. Average amounts of aid awarded freshmen: Scholarships and grants, $2,802; loans, $3,800.
**Supporting data/closing dates:** FAFSA/FAF/FFS: Priority filing date is March 1; accepted on rolling basis. Notification of awards begins April 15.
**Financial aid contact:** Peter Fazio, Financial Aid Coordinator. 813 359-4257.

**STUDENT EMPLOYMENT.** College Work/Study Program. Institutional employment. 15% of full-time undergraduates work on campus during school year. Students may expect to earn an average of $1,800 during school year. Off-campus part-time employment opportunities rated "excellent."

**COMPUTER FACILITIES.** 30 IBM/IBM-compatible and Macintosh/Apple microcomputers; 10 are networked. Students may access IBM, SUN minicomputer/mainframe systems, Internet. Client/LAN operating systems include Apple/Macintosh. Computer languages and software packages include C, Pascal, Mathematica. Mainframe access is limited to coursework.
**Fees:** Computer fee is included in tuition/fees.
**Hours:** 24 hours in Macintosh lab.

**GRADUATE CAREER DATA.** Highest graduate school enrollments: Harvard U, New York U, U of Florida, U of Miami, Yale U.

**PROMINENT ALUMNI/AE.** William Thurston, math professor, Princeton U, and 1983 winner of Fields Medal in Mathematics; John Cranor, CEO, Kentucky Fried Chicken Worldwide.

## Nova Southeastern University

**Fort Lauderdale, FL 33314** **305 475-7300**

**1994-95 Costs.** Tuition: $8,500. Room: $2,880. Board: $1,800. Fees, books, misc. academic expenses (school's estimate): $600.
**Enrollment.** Undergraduates: 800 men, 1,254 women (full-time). Freshman class: 1,200 applicants, 900 accepted, 360 enrolled. Graduate enrollment: 3,361 men, 5,089 women.
**Test score averages/ranges.** Average SAT scores: 441 verbal, 468 math. Range of SAT scores of middle 50%: 390-490 verbal, 410-500 math.
**Faculty.** 51 full-time. 85% of faculty holds doctoral degree. Student/faculty ratio: 16 to 1.
**Selectivity rating.** Less competitive.

**PROFILE.** Nova Southeastern, founded in 1964, is a private university. Programs are offered through the Divisions of Behavioral and Social Sciences, Business and Administrative Studies, Cluster Studies, Computer Science and Engineering, and Education. Its 200-acre campus is located 10 miles from Fort Lauderdale.

**Accreditation:** SACS. Several professional accreditations.
**Religious orientation:** Nova Southeastern University is nonsectarian; no religious requirements.
**Library:** Collections totaling over 220,000 volumes, 6,538 periodical subscriptions, and 73,659 microform items.
**Special facilities/museums:** Early childhood family center, university school for prekindergarten to grade 12, oceanographic center and lab, biofeedback and learning technology labs, and psychology clinics.
**Athletic facilities:** Basketball, tennis, and volleyball courts, training and weight rooms, baseball and soccer fields, swimming pool.

**STUDENT BODY. Undergraduate profile:** 86% are state residents; 42% are transfers. 2% Asian-American, 18% Black, 18% Hispanic, 60% White, 2% Other. Average age of undergraduates is 29.
**Freshman profile:** 2% of freshmen who took SAT scored 600 or over on verbal, 4% scored 600 or over on math; 21% scored 500 or over on verbal, 36% scored 500 or over on math; 74% scored 400 or over on verbal, 87% scored 400 or over on math; 99% scored 300 or over on verbal, 98% scored 300 or over on math. Majority of accepted applicants took SAT. 62% of freshmen come from public schools.
**Undergraduate achievement:** 79% of fall 1992 freshmen returned for fall 1993 term. 30% of students who completed a degree program went on to graduate study within five years.
**Foreign students:** 258 students are from out of the country. Countries represented include the Bahamas, Canada, Cyprus, Jamaica, and Panama; 20 in all.

**PROGRAMS OF STUDY. Degrees:** B.A., B.S.
**Majors:** Accounting, Administrative Studies, Business Administration, Computer Information Systems, Computer Science, Computer Systems, Elementary Education, Exceptional Education, Legal Studies, Liberal Arts, Ocean Studies, Pre-Medicine, Pre-Optometry, Pre-Pharmacy, Psychology, Secondary Education.
**Distribution of degrees:** The majors with the highest enrollment are business administration, education, and psychology.
**Requirements:** General education requirement.
**Academic regulations:** Freshmen must maintain minimum 1.50 GPA; sophomores, 1.90 GPA; juniors, 2.00 GPA; seniors, 2.00 GPA.
**Special:** Double majors. Independent study. Accelerated study. Internships. Cooperative education programs. Graduate school at which undergraduates may take graduate-level courses. Preprofessional programs in law, medicine, pharmacy, and optometry. 3-4 premedicine program with Southeastern U of the Health Sciences. Study abroad in Brazil, Mexico, and Peru.
**Honors:** Honor societies.
**Academic Assistance:** Remedial reading, writing, math, and study skills. Nonremedial tutoring.

**STUDENT LIFE. Housing:** Freshmen from outside the tri-county area must live on campus. Coed dorms. School-owned/operated apartments. On-campus married-student housing. 5% of students live in college housing.
**Services and counseling/handicapped student services:** Counseling services for minority, veteran, and older students. Personal and psychological counseling. Career and academic guidance services.
**Campus organizations:** Undergraduate student government. Student newspaper (Nova Knight). Yearbook. Radio station. 32 registered organizations. Three fraternities, no chapter houses; two sororities, no chapter houses. 11% of men join a fraternity. 11% of women join a sorority.
**Religious organizations:** Hillel, Catholic Campus Ministries, Fellowship of Christian Athletes.
**Minority/foreign student organizations:** Black Student Association. International Student Association.

**ATHLETICS. Physical education requirements:** None.
**Intercollegiate competition:** 14% of students participate. Baseball (M), basketball (M), cheerleading (W), cross-country (M,W), golf (M), soccer (M), tennis (W), volleyball (W). Member of Florida Sun Conference, NAIA District 7.
**Intramural and club sports:** 28% of students participate. Intramural basketball, bowling, football, golf, softball, volleyball. Men's club rugby.

**ADMISSIONS. Nonacademic basis for candidate selection:** Extracurricular participation is considered.
**Requirements:** Graduation from secondary school is required; GED is accepted. No specific distribution of secondary school units required. Minimum 2.0 GPA recommended. 4 units of science required of life sciences (premedicine) dual enrollment program applicants.

SAT is required; ACT may be substituted. Campus visit and interview recommended. Off-campus interviews available with an admissions representative.
**Procedure:** Notification of admission on rolling basis. No set date by which applicants must accept offer; June recommended. $200 nonrefundable tuition deposit. $150 nonrefundable room deposit. Freshmen accepted for terms other than fall.
**Special programs:** Admission may be deferred one year. Credit and/or placement may be granted through CEEB Advanced Placement exams for scores of 3 or higher. Credit and/or placement may be granted through CLEP general and subject exams. Credit and placement may be granted through DANTES and challenge exams and military and life experience. Early entrance/early admission program.
**Transfer students:** Transfer students accepted for terms other than fall. In fall 1992, 42% of all new students were transfers into all classes. Application deadline is rolling for fall; rolling for spring. Minimum 2.2 GPA recommended. Lowest course grade accepted is "C." Maximum number of transferable credits is 90 semester hours. At least 30 semester hours must be completed at the university to receive degree.
**Admissions contact:** Jean Lewis, M.A., Acting Director of Admissions. 305 475-7360.

**FINANCIAL AID. Available aid:** Pell grants, SEOG, state scholarships and grants, school scholarships and grants, private scholarships and grants, academic merit scholarships, and athletic scholarships. Perkins Loans (NDSL), PLUS, Stafford Loans (GSL), Health Professions Loans, state loans, private loans, and SLS. Deferred payment plan.
**Financial aid statistics:** In 1993-94, 85% of all undergraduate applicants received aid; 87% of freshman applicants. Average amounts of aid awarded freshmen: Scholarships and grants, $3,000; loans, $2,500.
**Supporting data/closing dates:** FAFSA/FAF/FFS: Priority filing date is April 1; deadline is May 1. School's own aid application: Priority filing date is April 1. State aid form. Notification of awards on rolling basis.
**Financial aid contact:** Stephania Naim, Assistant Director of Financial Aid. 305 475-7411.

**STUDENT EMPLOYMENT.** College Work/Study Program. Institutional employment. 12% of full-time undergraduates work on campus during school year. Students may expect to earn an average of $2,800 during school year. Off-campus part-time employment opportunities rated "good."

**COMPUTER FACILITIES.** 300 IBM/IBM-compatible and Macintosh/Apple microcomputers; 200 are networked. Students may access Digital, SUN minicomputer/mainframe systems, Internet. Residence halls may be equipped with stand-alone microcomputers, networked microcomputers. Client/LAN operating systems include Apple/Macintosh, DOS, UNIX/XENIX/AIX. Numerous computer languages and software programs available. Some computers dedicated to specific programs and centers.
**Fees:** None.
**Hours:** 8 AM-11 PM (M-F); 8 AM-6 PM (Sa); noon-8 PM (Su).

# Palm Beach Atlantic College

**West Palm Beach, FL 33416-4708 407 650-7700**

**1993-94 Costs.** Tuition: $7,200. Room & board: $3,220. Fees, books, misc. academic expenses (school's estimate): $700.
**Enrollment.** Undergraduates: 618 men, 814 women (full-time). Freshman class: 729 applicants, 352 accepted, 349 enrolled. Graduate enrollment: 57 men, 44 women.
**Test score averages/ranges.** Average SAT scores: 950 combined. Average ACT scores: 22 composite.
**Faculty.** 68 full-time; 42 part-time. 73% of faculty holds doctoral degree. Student/faculty ratio: 21 to 1.
**Selectivity rating.** Competitive.

**PROFILE.** Palm Beach Atlantic, founded in 1968, is a church-affiliated, liberal arts college. Its 23-acre campus is located in West Palm Beach, 60 miles north of Fort Lauderdale.
**Accreditation:** SACS.
**.01Religious orientation:** Palm Beach Atlantic College is affiliated with the Baptist Church; two semesters of religion required.
**Library:** Collections totaling over 65,000 volumes, 350 periodical subscriptions, and 10,000 microform items.
**Special facilities/museums:** Learning research center.
**Athletic facilities:** Gymnasium, basketball, tennis, and volleyball courts, swimming pools, baseball and soccer fields.

**STUDENT BODY. Undergraduate profile:** 63% are state residents; 39% are transfers. 1% Asian-American, 5% Black, 4% Hispanic, 1% Native American, 84% White, 5% Other. Average age of undergraduates is 20.
**Freshman profile:** 57% of accepted applicants took SAT; 43% took ACT. 60% of freshmen come from public schools.
**Undergraduate achievement:** 57% of fall 1992 freshmen returned for fall 1993 term. 22% of entering class graduated.
**Foreign students:** 38 students are from out of the country. Countries represented include the Bahamas, Bolivia, Brazil, Canada, and Sweden; 20 in all.

**PROGRAMS OF STUDY. Degrees:** B.A., B.S.
**Majors:** Accounting, Art, Biology, Business Administration, Communication/Speech, Computer Science, Drama Education, Economics, Elementary Education, English, Finance, History/Political Science, International Business, Management, Marketing, Mathematics, Music, Natural Science, Physical Education, Psychology, Religion, Theatre Arts.
**Distribution of degrees:** The majors with the highest enrollment are business administration, education, and psychology; communication/speech and English have the lowest.
**Requirements:** General education requirement.
**Special:** Minors offered in some majors and in biblical languages, chemistry, computer science, oceanography, philosophy, secondary education, sociology, and Spanish. 50 hours of service/semester required for first two years through Workship Program; opportunities offered for volunteer participation in local church or in community service through local agencies such as schools, convalescent homes, and mental health facilities. Double majors. Independent study. Pass/fail grading option. Internships. Graduate school at which undergraduates may take graduate-level courses. Preprofessional programs in law, medicine, veterinary science, and health professional. Washington Semester. Teacher certification in early childhood, elementary, secondary, and special education. Certification in specific subject areas. Study abroad in England.
**Honors:** Honors program.
**Academic Assistance:** Remedial reading, writing, math, and study skills. Nonremedial tutoring.

**STUDENT LIFE. Housing:** All unmarried students under age 20 must live on campus unless living with family. Women's and men's dorms. 40% of students live in college housing.
**Social atmosphere:** According to the student newspaper, "The climate on our campus is best described as being extremely caring and friendly. The social and cultural life tends to be enthusiastically fun and joyful, while at all times maintaining high Christian principles. Some of the most popular events include the Winter Games, Almost Anything Goes, Studio 77, the Lip Sync contest, the Homecoming Banquet at the Flagler Mansion, contemporary Christian concerts, Christian Awareness Week, and basketball games. Students favor the beach, the malls, walks along the intracoastal waterway."
**Services and counseling/handicapped student services:** Placement services. Psychological counseling. Academic guidance services. Religious counseling. Learning disabled services.
**Campus organizations:** Undergraduate student government. Student newspaper (Compass, published once/week). Yearbook. Singing and jazz ensembles, Student Music Educators Conference, drama club, science club, 30 organizations in all.
**Religious organizations:** Baptist Campus Ministries, Campus Baptist Young Women, Fellowship of Christian Athletes, Ministerial Fellowship, Newman Club, share teams.

**ATHLETICS. Physical education requirements:** Two semesters of physical education required.
**Intercollegiate competition:** 15% of students participate. Baseball (M), basketball (M), cheerleading (W), soccer (M), volleyball (W). Member of Florida Sun Conference, NAIA.
**Intramural and club sports:** 25% of students participate. Intramural basketball, billiards, flag football, foosball, soccer, softball, table tennis, tennis, volleyball.

**ADMISSIONS. Academic basis for candidate selection** (in order of priority): Secondary school record, standardized test scores, class rank, essay, school's recommendation.
**Nonacademic basis for candidate selection:** Character and personality are emphasized. Extracurricular participation is important. Particular talent or ability is considered.
**Requirements:** Graduation from secondary school is required; GED is accepted. 22 units and the following program of study are recommended: 4 units of English, 4 units of math, 3 units of science, 2 units of foreign language, 3 units of social studies, 1 unit of history, 2 units of electives. Minimum combined SAT score of 800 (composite ACT score of 19), and minimum 2.0 GPA recommended. Audition required of music program applicants. Conditional admission possible for applicants not meeting standard requirements. SAT or ACT is required. Campus visit and interview recommended. Off-campus interviews available with admissions and alumni representatives.
**Procedure:** Take SAT or ACT by March of 12th year. Visit college for interview by May 15 of 12th year. Notification of admission on rolling basis. $100 nonrefundable tuition deposit. $125 nonrefundable room deposit. Freshmen accepted for terms other than fall.
**Special programs:** Admission may be deferred one year. Credit may be granted through CEEB Advanced Placement for scores of 3 or higher. Credit and/or placement may be granted through CLEP general and subject exams. Early entrance/early admission program. Concurrent enrollment program.
**Transfer students:** Transfer students accepted for terms other than fall. In fall 1993, 39% of all new students were transfers into all classes. 424 transfer applications were received, 263 were accepted. Application deadline is rolling. Minimum 2.0 GPA required. Lowest course grade accepted is "C." Maximum number of transferable credits is 67 semester hours. At least 32 semester hours must be completed at the college to receive degree.
**Admissions contact:** Rich Grimm, M.Div., Dean of Admissions. 407 835-4309, 800-238-3998.

**FINANCIAL AID. Available aid:** Pell grants, SEOG, state scholarships and grants, school scholarships and grants, private scholarships and grants, academic merit scholarships, athletic scholarships, and aid for undergraduate foreign students. Perkins Loans (NDSL), PLUS, Stafford Loans (GSL), and SLS. AMS.
**Financial aid statistics:** 27% of aid is not need-based. In 1993-94, 98% of all undergraduate applicants received aid.
**Supporting data/closing dates:** FAFSA/FAF/FFS: Priority filing date is May 1; accepted on rolling basis. Notification of awards on rolling basis.
**Financial aid contact:** Donna Coons, Director of Financial Aid. 407 835-4321.

**STUDENT EMPLOYMENT.** College Work/Study Program. 50% of full-time undergraduates work on campus during school year. Off-campus part-time employment opportunities rated "excellent."

**COMPUTER FACILITIES.** 75 RISC-/UNIX-based microcomputers; all are networked. Students may access SUN minicomputer/mainframe systems, Internet. Residence halls may be equipped with stand-alone microcomputers. Client/LAN operating systems include DOS, UNIX/XENIX/AIX, X-windows, Novell. Computer languages and software packages include BASIC, COBOL, Pascal. Computer facilities are available to all students.
**Fees:** None.
**Hours:** 9 AM-11 PM.

# Ringling School of Art and Design

**Sarasota, FL 34234** **813 351-4614**

**1993-94 Costs.** Tuition: $10,350. Room & board: $5,400. Fees, books, misc. academic expenses (school's estimate): $1,585.
**Enrollment.** Undergraduates: 360 men, 340 women (full-time). Freshman class: 800 applicants, 342 accepted, 240 enrolled.
**Test score averages/ranges.** N/A.
**Faculty.** 73 full-time; 8 part-time. 1% of faculty holds doctoral degree. Student/faculty ratio: 13 to 1.
**Selectivity rating.** N/A.

**PROFILE.** Ringling, founded in 1931, is a private school of art and design. Its 30-acre campus is located in Sarasota, 50 miles from Tampa.

**Accreditation:** SACS. Professionally accredited by the Foundation for Interior Design Education Research, the National Association of Schools of Art and Design.
**Religious orientation:** Ringling School of Art and Design is nonsectarian; no religious requirements.
**Library:** Collections totaling over 13,000 volumes and 268 periodical subscriptions.
**Athletic facilities:** Volleyball and basketball courts.
**STUDENT BODY. Undergraduate profile:** 50% are state residents; 25% are transfers. 2% Asian-American, 5% Black, 12% Hispanic, 81% White. Average age of undergraduates is 22.
**Freshman profile:** 85% of freshmen come from public schools.
**Foreign students:** Countries represented include Brazil, Canada, Colombia, and England; 12 in all.
**PROGRAMS OF STUDY. Degrees:** B.F.A.
**Majors:** Computer Graphics, Fine Arts, Graphic Design, Illustration, Interior Design.
**Distribution of degrees:** The majors with the highest enrollment are graphic design, illustration, and interior design; computer graphics and fine arts have the lowest.
**Requirements:** General education requirement.
**Academic regulations:** Minimum 2.0 GPA must be maintained.
**Special:** Minor offered in photography. Internships. Graduate school at which undergraduates may take graduate-level courses. Member of Art College Exchange Consortium. Study abroad program in France (American Coll); liberal arts and art history requirements may be earned.
**ADMISSIONS. Academic basis for candidate selection** (in order of priority): Secondary school record, school's recommendation, essay.
**Nonacademic basis for candidate selection:** Particular talent or ability is emphasized. Character and personality, extracurricular participation, and alumni/ae relationship are considered.
**Requirements:** Graduation from secondary school is required; GED is accepted. No specific distribution of secondary school units required. Each applicant must submit a slide portfolio of original work or complete the required visual presentation exercises. Portfolio should contain at least ten color slides or photographs (not originals) of drawings, paintings, sculpture, etc. Conditional admission possible for applicants not meeting standard requirements. SAT is recommended; ACT may be substituted. Campus visit and interview recommended. No off-campus interviews.
**Procedure:** Suggest filing application by March 15; no deadline. Notification of admission on rolling basis. Reply is required by May 1. $250 tuition deposit, refundable until May 1. $100 room deposit, refundable until May 1. Freshmen accepted for fall term only.
**Special programs:** Admission may be deferred one year. Credit and/or placement may be granted through CEEB Advanced Placement exams for scores of 3 or higher. Credit and/or placement may be granted through CLEP general and subject exams.
**Transfer students:** Transfer students accepted for terms other than fall. In fall 1992, 25% of all new students were transfers into all classes. 60 transfer applications were received, 41 were accepted. Application deadline is rolling for fall; rolling for spring. Minimum 2.0 GPA recommended. Lowest course grade accepted is "C." Maximum number of transferable credits is 45 semester hours. At least 60 semester hours must be completed at Ringling to receive degree.
**Admissions contact:** James H. Dean, M.A., Director of Admissions. 813 359-7523.
**FINANCIAL AID. Available aid:** Pell grants, SEOG, state grants, school scholarships, and private scholarships. PLUS, Stafford Loans (GSL), and SLS. AMS.
**Supporting data/closing dates:** FAFSA/FAF: Priority filing date is March 15. School's own aid application: Priority filing date is March 15. Income tax forms: Priority filing date is March 15. Notification of awards on rolling basis.
**Financial aid contact:** Kurt Wolf, M.A., Director of Financial Aid. 813 359-7534.

# Rollins College

**Winter Park, FL 32789** **407 646-2000**

**1993-94 Costs.** Tuition: $15,495. Room & board: $4,925. Fees, books, misc. academic expenses (school's estimate): $1,055.
**Enrollment.** Undergraduates: 621 men, 791 women (full-time). Freshman class: 1,730 applicants, 1,125 accepted, 382 enrolled. Graduate enrollment: 297 men, 350 women.
**Test score averages/ranges.** Range of SAT scores of middle 50%: 500-550 verbal, 500-610 math. Range of ACT scores of middle 50%: 23-27 composite.
**Faculty.** 124 full-time. 88% of faculty holds doctoral degree. Student/faculty ratio: 12 to 1.
**Selectivity rating.** Competitive.

**PROFILE.** Rollins, founded in 1885, is a private, liberal arts college. Its 65-acre campus of traditional Spanish-Mediterranean architecture is located in Winter Park, a suburb of Orlando.

**Accreditation:** SACS. Professionally accredited by the National Association of Schools of Music.
**Religious orientation:** Rollins College is nonsectarian; no religious requirements.
**Library:** Collections totaling over 259,971 volumes, 1,536 periodical subscriptions, and 32,935 microform items.
**Special facilities/museums:** Art museum, theatres, fine arts center, language lab, skills development building, child development center, psychology center.
**Athletic facilities:** Field house, tennis courts, swimming pool, fitness course, baseball and soccer fields, baseball stadium, lake, boathouse.
**STUDENT BODY. Undergraduate profile:** 40% are state residents; 18% are transfers. 4% Asian-American, 3% Black, 6% Hispanic, 85% White, 2% Other. Average age of undergraduates is 20.
**Freshman profile:** 96% of accepted applicants took SAT; 36% took ACT. 54% of freshmen come from public schools.
**Undergraduate achievement:** 88% of fall 1992 freshmen returned for fall 1993 term. 73% of entering class graduated. 21% of students who completed a degree program immediately went on to graduate study.
**Foreign students:** 63 students are from out of the country. Countries represented include the Bahamas, Brazil, Canada, England, Norway, and Spain; 24 in all.
**PROGRAMS OF STUDY. Degrees:** B.A.
**Majors:** Anthropology, Art, Biology, Chemistry, Classical Studies, Computer Science, Economics, Elementary Education, English, Environmental Studies, Foreign Languages, French, German, History, History of Art, International Relations, Latin American/Caribbean Affairs, Mathematics, Music, Philosophy, Physics, Political Science, Psychology, Religious Studies, Sociology, Spanish, Studio Art, Theatre Arts.
**Distribution of degrees:** The majors with the highest enrollment are political science, psychology, and English; classical studies, music, and religious studies have the lowest.
**Requirements:** General education requirement.
**Academic regulations:** Freshmen must maintain minimum 1.8 GPA; sophomores, juniors, seniors, 2.0 GPA.
**Special:** Minors offered in all majors and in African/Afro-American studies, Australian studies, business, communication, dance, Irish studies, Russian, secondary school teaching, and women's studies. Community of Learners features a small group of students, with faculty member, studying three related courses for one semester and conducting a student-run seminar focusing on a central theme. Science Community Year. Self-designed majors. Double majors. Dual degrees. Independent study. Accelerated study. Pass/fail grading option. Internships. Graduate school at which undergraduates may take graduate-level courses. Preprofessional programs in law, medicine, veterinary science, pharmacy, dentistry, optometry, engineering, and management. 3-2 M.B.A. program with Rollins Crummer Graduate Sch. 3-2 engineering programs with Auburn U, Case Western Reserve U, Columbia U, Georgia Tech, and Washington U. 3-2 forestry/environmental studies and medical technology programs with Duke U. Nursing program with Emory U. Member of Southern Consortium and Associated Colleges of the South. Washington Semester. Philadelphia Urban Semester, Arts Program in New York, Oak Ridge Science Semester (Tennessee), and Newberry Library Program in the Humanities (Illinois). Exchange program with American U. Teacher certification in elementary and secondary education. Exchange programs abroad in England (Cambridge U) and France (American U). Study abroad also in Australia, Germany, Ireland, Mexico, and Spain.
**Honors:** Honors program. Honor societies.
**Academic Assistance:** Remedial reading, writing, math, and study skills. Nonremedial tutoring.
**STUDENT LIFE. Housing:** Students may live on or off campus. Coed dorms. Sorority and fraternity housing. Special-interest housing. 80% of students live in college housing.
**Services and counseling/handicapped student services:** Placement services. Health service. Counseling services for minority, veteran, and older students. Birth control, personal, and psychological counseling. Career and academic guidance services. Religious counseling. Physically disabled student services. Learning disabled services. Notetaking services. Tape recorders. Tutors. Reader services for the blind.
**Campus organizations:** Undergraduate student government. Student newspaper (New Sandspur, published once/week). Literary magazine. Yearbook. Radio and TV stations. Choral society, off-campus student group, women's group, Rollins Players, greenhouse, World Hunger Committee, ADEPT, departmental clubs, 75 organizations in all. Six fraternities, five chapter houses; six sororities, five chapter houses. 35% of men join a fraternity. 35% of women join a sorority.
**Religious organizations:** Jewish Student League, Newman Club, Fellowship of Christian Athletes.
**Minority/foreign student organizations:** Black Student Union, Latin American Student Association, Asian American Student Association, Cultural Action Committee. International Student Organization.
**ATHLETICS. Physical education requirements:** Four courses of physical education required.
**Intercollegiate competition:** 22% of students participate. Baseball (M), basketball (M,W), cheerleading (M,W), crew (M,W), cross-country (M,W), golf (M,W), sailing (M,W), soccer (M), softball (W), tennis (M,W), volleyball (M), water skiing (M). Member of NCAA Division II, Sunshine State Conference.
**Intramural and club sports:** 45% of students participate. Intramural basketball, bowling, flag football, golf, soccer, softball, swimming, table tennis, tennis, track, volleyball. Men's club swimming. Women's club soccer, swimming.
**ADMISSIONS. Academic basis for candidate selection** (in order of priority): Secondary school record, class rank, standardized test scores, essay, school's recommendation.
**Nonacademic basis for candidate selection:** Character and personality, extracurricular participation, and particular talent or ability are important. Geographical distribution and alumni/ae relationship are considered.
**Requirements:** Graduation from secondary school is required; GED is accepted. No specific distribution of secondary school units required. SAT or ACT is required. ACH recommended. Campus visit and interview recommended. No off-campus interviews.

**Procedure:** Take SAT or ACT by January 1 of 12th year. Take ACH by January 1 of 12th year. Suggest filing application by February 15; no deadline. Notification of admission by April 1. Reply is required by May 1. $500 nonrefundable tuition deposit. Freshmen accepted for terms other than fall.
**Special programs:** Admission may be deferred one year. Credit and/or placement may be granted through CEEB Advanced Placement exams for scores of 4 or higher. Credit and/or placement may be granted through CLEP general exams. Placement may be granted through challenge exams. Credit and placement may be granted through ACT PEP exams and military experience. Early decision program. In fall 1993, 140 applied for early decision and 75 were accepted. Deadline for applying for early decision is November 15 for Round I, January 15 for Round II. Early entrance/early admission program. Concurrent enrollment program.
**Transfer students:** Transfer students accepted for terms other than fall. In fall 1993, 18% of all new students were transfers into all classes. 288 transfer applications were received, 184 were accepted. Application deadline is April 15 for fall; November 15 for spring. Minimum 2.5 GPA recommended. Lowest course grade accepted is "C." Maximum number of transferable credits is 60 semester hours. At least 60 semester hours must be completed at the college to receive degree.
**Admissions contact:** David G. Erdmann, M.A., Dean of Admissions. 407 646-2161.

**FINANCIAL AID. Available aid:** Pell grants, SEOG, state scholarships and grants, school scholarships and grants, private scholarships and grants, academic merit scholarships, and athletic scholarships. Perkins Loans (NDSL), PLUS, Stafford Loans (GSL), state loans, school loans, and SLS. Tuition Plan Inc., Knight Tuition Plans, and guaranteed tuition. Institutional monthly payment plan.
**Financial aid statistics:** 31% of aid is not need-based. In 1993-94, 58% of all undergraduate applicants received aid; 50% of freshman applicants. Average amounts of aid awarded freshmen: Scholarships and grants, $11,000; loans, $2,600.
**Supporting data/closing dates:** FAFSA/FAF/FFS: Priority filing date is March 1. School's own aid application: Priority filing date is March 1. Income tax forms: Accepted on rolling basis. Notification of awards begins March 1.
**Financial aid contact:** Linda Downing, M.S.M., Director of Financial Aid. 407 646-2395.

**STUDENT EMPLOYMENT.** College Work/Study Program. Institutional employment. 15% of full-time undergraduates work on campus during school year. Students may expect to earn an average of $891 during school year. Off-campus part-time employment opportunities rated "good."

**COMPUTER FACILITIES.** 100 IBM/IBM-compatible and Macintosh/Apple microcomputers; 20 are networked. Students may access Digital minicomputer/mainframe systems, BITNET. Residence halls may be equipped with stand-alone microcomputers, networked microcomputers, networked terminals, modems. Client/LAN operating systems include Apple/Macintosh. Computer languages and software packages include BASIC, DataCalc, FORTRAN, Hyper Card, Lotus 1-2-3, MacDraw, MacPaint, MacWrite, Microsoft Word, MINITAB, PageMaker, Pascal, Quattro, SAS, Star Graphics, WordPerfect. Computer facilities are available to all students.
**Fees:** Computer fee is included in tuition/fees.
**Hours:** 8 AM-midn.

**GRADUATE CAREER DATA.** Graduate school percentages: 3% enter law school. 2% enter medical school. 2% enter graduate business programs. 12% enter graduate arts and sciences programs. Highest graduate school enrollments: Duke U, Emory U, Florida State U, U of Florida, Georgetown U, U of Miami, U of South Florida, Tulane U, Wake Forest U, Washington U. 44% of graduates choose careers in business and industry. Companies and businesses that hire graduates: Aerotek, Barnett Bank, Nations Bank, Sears, Universal Studios, Upjohn Pharmaceuticals

**PROMINENT ALUMNI/AE.** Anthony Perkins, actor; John Reardon, baritone with Metropolitan Opera; Dana Ivey, Broadway actress; Donald J. Cram, winner of 1987 Nobel Prize in chemistry and professor at UCLA; Fred Rogers, creator of "Mister Rogers' Neighborhood" TV show; Charles Rice, CEO, Barnett Banks; Paul Dye, golf course architect; Ted Alfond, president, Dexter Shoes.

## Saint Leo College

**Saint Leo, FL 33574** **904 588-8200**

**1994-95 Costs.** Tuition: $9,150. Room: $2,310. Board: $2,340. Fees, books, misc. academic expenses (school's estimate): $1,200.
**Enrollment.** Undergraduates: 410 men, 369 women (full-time). Freshman class: 1,100 applicants, 759 accepted, 315 enrolled.
**Test score averages/ranges.** Average SAT scores: 407 verbal, 446 math. Range of SAT scores of middle 50%: 370-450 verbal, 400-500 math. Average ACT scores: 19 composite.
**Faculty.** 57 full-time; 19 part-time. 56% of faculty holds highest degree in specific field. Student/faculty ratio: 17 to 1.
**Selectivity rating.** Less competitive.

**PROFILE.** Saint Leo is a private, church-affiliated, liberal arts college. Founded in 1889, it continues to offer a military education program. Its 170-acre campus, including buildings with a Spanish Florida baroque architectural style, is located in Saint Leo.

**Accreditation:** SACS. Professionally accredited by the Council on Social Work Education.
**Religious orientation:** Saint Leo College is affiliated with the Roman Catholic Church (Benedictine Order); two three-credit courses of religion/theology required.
**Library:** Collections totaling over 95,460 volumes, 750 periodical subscriptions, and 25,712 microform items.
**Athletic facilities:** Gymnasium, basketball, racquetball, tennis, and volleyball courts, weight room, dance studios, swimming pool, baseball, soccer, and softball fields, track, golf course, lake.

**STUDENT BODY. Undergraduate profile:** 60% are state residents; 25% are transfers.5% Asian-American, 3% Black, 6% Hispanic, .5% Native American, 80% White, 10% Other. Average age of undergraduates is 22.
**Freshman profile:** Majority of accepted applicants took SAT. 64% of freshmen come from public schools.
**Undergraduate achievement:** 71% of fall 1992 freshmen returned for fall 1993 term.
**Foreign students:** 43 students are from out of the country. Countries represented include the Bahamas, the Cayman Islands, Honduras, Jamaica, and Tanzania; 21 in all.

**PROGRAMS OF STUDY. Degrees:** B.A., B.S., B.Soc.Work
**Majors:** Art, Art Education, Biology, Business Administration, Criminology, Elementary Education, English, English/Secondary Education, Health Care Administration, Health Services Management, History, History/Secondary Education, Human Resources Administration, International Studies, Management, Marketing, Mathematics/Secondary Education, Medical Technology, Music, Music/Elementary to Secondary Education, Physical Education Teacher Training, Political Science, Political Science/Secondary Education, Pre-Law, Psychology, Public Administration, Religious Studies, Restaurant/Hotel Management, Social Work, Sociology, Specific Learning Disabilities, Sports Management, Technology Management.
**Distribution of degrees:** The majors with the highest enrollment are business administration, psychology, and sports management; math/secondary education and religious studies have the lowest.
**Requirements:** General education requirement.
**Academic regulations:** Freshmen must maintain minimum 1.60 GPA; sophomores, juniors, seniors, 2.0 GPA.
**Special:** Minors offered in some majors and in chemistry, computer information systems, economics, philosophy, and Spanish. Courses offered in fine arts, French, geography, humanities, math, physics, and speech. Freshman Studies Program. Associate's degrees offered. Double majors. Independent study. Accelerated study. Internships. Preprofessional programs in law, medicine, veterinary science, and dentistry. Teacher certification in elementary, secondary, and special education. Certification in specific subject areas. ROTC. AFROTC at U of South Florida.
**Honors:** Honors program. Honor societies.
**Academic Assistance:** Remedial reading, writing, math, and study skills.

**ADMISSIONS. Academic basis for candidate selection** (in order of priority): Secondary school record, standardized test scores, school's recommendation, essay, class rank.
**Nonacademic basis for candidate selection:** Character and personality are emphasized. Extracurricular participation is important. Particular talent or ability and alumni/ae relationship are considered.
**Requirements:** Graduation from secondary school is required; GED is accepted. 16 units and the following program of study are required: 4 units of English, 3 units of math, 2 units of science, 3 units of social studies, 4 units of electives. Conditional admission possible for applicants not meeting standard requirements. SAT or ACT is required. ACH recommended. Campus visit and interview recommended. Off-campus interviews available with admissions and alumni representatives.
**Procedure:** Take SAT or ACT by February of 12th year. Visit college for interview by fall of 12th year. Application deadline is August 1. Notification of admission on rolling basis. Reply is required by May 1. $100 nonrefundable tuition deposit. $150 nonrefundable room deposit. Freshmen accepted for terms other than fall.
**Special programs:** Admission may be deferred one semester. Credit may be granted through CEEB Advanced Placement for scores of 3 or higher. Credit may be granted through CLEP general and subject exams, DANTES and challenge exams, and military experience. Early entrance/early admission program. Concurrent enrollment program.
**Transfer students:** Transfer students accepted for terms other than fall. In fall 1993, 25% of all new students were transfers into all classes. 422 transfer applications were received, 295 were accepted. Application deadline is August 1 for fall; December 1 for spring. Minimum 2.0 GPA required. Lowest course grade accepted is "D." Maximum number of transferable credits is 64 semester hours. At least 30 semester hours must be completed at the college to receive degree.
**Admissions contact:** Bonnie L. Black, M.Ed., Director of Admissions. 904 588-8283.

**FINANCIAL AID. Available aid:** Pell grants, SEOG, state scholarships and grants, school scholarships and grants, private scholarships, academic merit scholarships, and athletic scholarships. Perkins Loans (NDSL), PLUS, Stafford Loans (GSL), and SLS. Knight Tuition Plans and AMS.
**Financial aid statistics:** 35% of aid is not need-based. In 1993-94, 60% of all undergraduate applicants received aid; 50% of freshman applicants. Average amounts of aid awarded freshmen: Scholarships and grants, $3,700; loans, $2,625.
**Supporting data/closing dates:** FAFSA/FFS: Priority filing date is April 1; accepted on rolling basis. School's own aid application: Priority filing date is April 1; accepted on rolling basis. State aid form: Priority filing date is April 1. Income tax forms: Priority filing date is April 1; accepted on rolling basis. Notification of awards on rolling basis.
**Financial aid contact:** Richard Ritzman, Director of Financial Aid. 904 588-8270.

## St. Thomas University

**Miami, FL 33054** **305 625-6000**

**1993-94 Costs.** Tuition: $9,300. Room & board: $4,600. Fees, books, misc. academic expenses (school's estimate): $780.
**Enrollment.** Undergraduates: 482 men, 643 women (full-time). Freshman class: 1,099 applicants, 832 accepted, 518 enrolled. Graduate enrollment: 503 men, 481 women.
**Test score averages/ranges.** Average SAT scores: 390 verbal, 440 math. Range of SAT scores of middle 50%: 375-425 verbal, 390-440 math.
**Faculty.** 68 full-time; 80 part-time. 59% of faculty holds doctoral degree. Student/faculty ratio: 15 to 1.
**Selectivity rating.** Less competitive.

**PROFILE.** St. Thomas, is a private, church-affiliated, liberal arts university. Founded in 1961, it adopted coeducation in 1975. Its 140-acre campus is located in Miami.

**Accreditation:** SACS.
**Religious orientation:** St. Thomas University is affiliated with the Roman Catholic Church (Archdiocese of Miami); nine semester hours of religion/theology required.
**Library:** Collections totaling over 151,000 volumes, 900 periodical subscriptions, and 16,500 microform items.
**Special facilities/museums:** Multimedia computer equipment, TV studio.
**Athletic facilities:** Swimming pool, basketball and tennis courts, weight room, baseball, flag football, lacrosse, soccer, and softball fields.

**STUDENT BODY. Undergraduate profile:** 85% are state residents; 48% are transfers. 1% Asian-American, 17.2% Black, 51% Hispanic, .4% Native American, 17.4% White, 13% Other. Average age of undergraduates is 25.
**Freshman profile:** 66% of freshmen come from public schools.
**Foreign students:** 197 students are from out of the country. Countries represented include the Bahamas, Colombia, Jamaica, Japan, Spain, and Trinidad/Tobago; 44 in all.

**PROGRAMS OF STUDY. Degrees:** B.A., B.Bus.Admin.
**Majors:** Accounting, Biology, Business/Management, Chemistry, Communication Arts, Computer/Information Systems, Computer Science, Criminal Justice, Elementary Education, English, Finance, History, Human Resources, International Management, Liberal Studies, Marketing Management, Political Science, Psychology, Public Administration, Religious Studies, Secondary Education, Social Studies, Sociology, Spanish, Sports Administration, Tourism/Hospitality Management.
**Distribution of degrees:** The majors with the highest enrollment are human resources, communication arts, and business/management; public administration has the lowest.
**Requirements:** General education requirement.
**Academic regulations:** Minimum 2.00 GPA must be maintained.
**Special:** Minors offered in most majors and in American studies, economics, environmental studies, marketing, mathematics, pastoral ministries, and peacemaker of the community. Double majors. Internships. Preprofessional programs in law, medicine, veterinary science, and dentistry. Member of EDUCOM (Interuniversity Communications Council) and Southeast Florida Higher Education Consortium. Teacher certification in elementary and secondary education. Certification in specific subject areas. Study abroad in Ecuador, Italy, and Spain.
**Honors:** Honors program. Honor societies.
**Academic Assistance:** Remedial reading, writing, math, and study skills. Nonremedial tutoring.

**STUDENT LIFE. Housing:** Students may live on or off campus. Coed, women's, and men's dorms. 34% of students live in college housing.
**Social atmosphere:** "Only a small number of students are housed on campus but everyone is friendly and there is plenty to keep a person occupied," reports the student newspaper. Influential groups on campus include Greeks, Minority Student Union, International Student Organization, and Student Government. The Halloween Party, Land and Water Olympics, SGA Carnival, and sporting events are among the year's favorite events. Popular hangouts are The Rathskellar, the pool, the beach, and Hooligans.
**Services and counseling/handicapped student services:** Placement services. Health service. Personal and psychological counseling. Career and academic guidance services. Religious counseling. Physically disabled student services. Learning disabled services. Notetaking services. Tape recorders. Tutors. Reader services for the blind.
**Campus organizations:** Undergraduate student government. Student newspaper (Informer, published twice/month). Literary magazine. Yearbook. Radio and TV stations. Accounting Association, Computer Science Association, Students for Global Preservation, Political Action Club, Student Government Association, Circle K, Society for Premedical Studies, Business Student Association, Inter-dorm Council, 26 organizations in all. Two fraternities, no chapter houses; one sorority, no chapter house.
**Religious organizations:** Campus Ministry, St. Thomas Cares, St. Thomas Proud, Catholic Student Lawyers Guild.
**Minority/foreign student organizations:** Minority Student Union. International Student Organization.

**ATHLETICS. Physical education requirements:** None.
**Intercollegiate competition:** 8% of students participate. Baseball (M), basketball (M), cheerleading (W), soccer (M,W), softball (W), tennis (W). Member of Florida Sun Conference, NAIA.
**Intramural and club sports:** 10% of students participate. Intramural aerobics, basketball, bowling, cross-country, flag football, golf, soccer, softball, tennis, volleyball. Men's club golf, lacrosse.

**ADMISSIONS. Academic basis for candidate selection** (in order of priority): Secondary school record, class rank, standardized test scores, school's recommendation, essay.
**Nonacademic basis for candidate selection:** Character and personality, extracurricular participation, particular talent or ability, geographical distribution, and alumni/ae relationship are considered.
**Requirements:** Graduation from secondary school is required; GED is accepted. 18 units and the following program of study are required: 4 units of English, 3 units of math, 2 units of science, 3 units of social studies. Rank in top three-fifths of secondary school class and minimum 2.0 GPA required. Conditional admission possible for applicants not meeting standard requirements. SAT or ACT is required. Campus visit and interview recommended. Off-campus interviews available with an admissions representative.
**Procedure:** Take SAT or ACT by December of 12th year. Notification of admission on rolling basis. Applicant must accept offer admission by date specified in letter of acceptance. $150 tuition deposit, refundable until May 1. $200 room deposit, refundable until May 1. Freshmen accepted for terms other than fall.
**Special programs:** Admission may be deferred one year. Credit and/or placement may be granted through CEEB Advanced Placement exams for scores of 3 or higher. Credit may be granted through CLEP general and subject exams and life experience. Placement may be granted through challenge exams. Concurrent enrollment program.
**Transfer students:** Transfer students accepted for terms other than fall. In fall 1993, 48% of all new students were transfers into all classes. 521 transfer applications were received, 399 were accepted. Application deadline is rolling for fall; rolling for spring. Minimum 2.0 GPA required. Lowest course grade accepted is "C." Maximum number of transferable credits is 60 semester hours from a two-year school and 90 semester hours from a four-year school. At least 30 semester hours must be completed at the university to receive degree.
**Admissions contact:** John Letvinchuk, Ed.M., Director of Admissions. 305 628-6546.

**FINANCIAL AID. Available aid:** Pell grants, SEOG, state scholarships and grants, school scholarships and grants, private scholarships, ROTC scholarships, academic merit scholarships, athletic scholarships, and aid for undergraduate foreign students. Perkins Loans (NDSL), PLUS, Stafford Loans (GSL), and private loans. Tuition Management Systems and deferred payment plan.
**Financial aid statistics:** 23% of aid is not need-based. In 1993-94, 89% of all undergraduate applicants received aid; 89% of freshman applicants. Average amounts of aid awarded freshmen: Scholarships and grants, $1,500; loans, $3,250.
**Supporting data/closing dates:** FAFSA: Priority filing date is April 1; accepted on rolling basis. School's own aid application: Priority filing date is April 1; accepted on rolling basis. State aid form: Priority filing date is April 15; accepted on rolling basis. Notification of awards begins April 1.
**Financial aid contact:** Laura Galvis, Director of Financial Aid. 305 628-6547.

**STUDENT EMPLOYMENT.** College Work/Study Program. Institutional employment. 21% of full-time undergraduates work on campus during school year. Students may expect to earn an average of $2,400 during school year. Off-campus part-time employment opportunities rated "good."

**COMPUTER FACILITIES.** 50 IBM/IBM-compatible microcomputers; 21 are networked. Students may access Prime minicomputer/mainframe systems. Computer languages and software packages include BASIC, C, COBOL, Lotus 1-2-3, WordPerfect; 100 in all. Computer facilities are available to all students.
**Fees:** Computer fee is included in tuition/fees.

# Southeastern College of the Assemblies of God

**Lakeland, FL 33801** **813 665-4404**

**1994-95 Costs.** Tuition: $3,744. Room & board: $2,772. Fees, books, misc. academic expenses (school's estimate): $948.
**Enrollment.** Undergraduates: 550 men, 528 women (full-time). Freshman class: 542 applicants, 410 enrolled.
**Test score averages/ranges.** N/A.
**Faculty.** 52 full-time; 33 part-time. 50% of faculty holds doctoral degree. Student/faculty ratio: 21 to 1.
**Selectivity rating.** N/A.

**PROFILE.** Southeastern College, founded in 1935, is a private, church-affiliated college. Its 57-acre campus is located in Lakeland, 15 miles from Tampa.

**Accreditation:** AABC, SACS.
**Religious orientation:** Southeastern College of the Assemblies of God is affiliated with the Assemblies of God; eight semesters of religion/theology required.
**Library:** Collections totaling over 77,194 volumes, 537 periodical subscriptions, and 23,286 microform items.
**Athletic facilities:** Gymnasium, beach volleyball, racquetball, and tennis courts, baseball, intramural, and soccer fields, weight room.

**STUDENT BODY. Undergraduate profile:** 43% are state residents; 13% are transfers. 2% Asian-American, 2% Black, 8% Hispanic, 1% Native American, 86% White, 1% Other.
**Undergraduate achievement:** 35% of fall 1992 freshmen returned for fall 1993 term. 35% of entering class graduated.
**Foreign students:** 22 students are from out of the country. Countries represented include the Bahamas, Belize, Canada, India, and Puerto Rico; nine in all.

**PROGRAMS OF STUDY. Degrees:** B.A.
**Majors:** Church Ministries, Elementary Education, Middle Grades Education, Music Education, Primary Education, Psychology, Sacred Music, Secondary Education, Teacher Education.
**Distribution of degrees:** The majors with the highest enrollment are teacher education and church ministries; sacred music and psychology have the lowest.
**Requirements:** General education requirement.
**Academic regulations:** Minimum 2.0 GPA must be maintained.
**Special:** Minors offered in administration and leadership, biblical languages, business/office administration, Christian education, English, Greek, history, missions, pastoral counseling, preaching, psychology, sociology, Spanish, speech-communications, and theology. Courses offered in French, natural science, philosophy, and secretarial science. All students required to complete four semesters of an approved student ministry. Double majors. Independent study. Internships. Preprofessional programs in theology. Teacher certification in early childhood, elementary, and secondary education. Certification in specific subject areas. Study abroad in England. ROTC at Florida Southern Coll.
**Honors:** Honor societies.
**Academic Assistance:** Remedial reading, writing, math, and study skills. Nonremedial tutoring.

**STUDENT LIFE. Housing:** All unmarried students under age 25 must live on campus unless living with family. Women's and men's dorms. School-owned/operated apartments. Off-campus privately-owned housing. Both on-campus and off-campus married-student housing. 65% of students live in college housing.
**Social atmosphere:** Popular gathering spots include the snack shop, library, gym, TV room, Lake Hollingsworth, skating rink, and park. Student ministry groups and the English Honor Society influence student social life. Favorite social events include Homecoming, basketball games, Junior/Senior Banquet, and the Valentine's Day Banquet.

**Services and counseling/handicapped student services:** Placement services. Health service. Personal and psychological counseling. Career and academic guidance services. Religious counseling. Learning disabled services.
**Campus organizations:** Undergraduate student government. Student newspaper (Flame, published once/month). Yearbook. TV station. College band, choir, women's and men's choruses, chorale, drama group, Caring Couples Fellowship, Cultural Awareness Movement, departmental groups, 50 organizations in all.
**Religious organizations:** Mission associations, student ministry groups.
**Minority/foreign student organizations:** Spanish and international clubs.

**ATHLETICS. Physical education requirements:** Two semesters of physical education required.
**Intercollegiate competition:** 8% of students participate. Baseball (M), basketball (M,W), soccer (M), tennis (M), volleyball (W). Member of Florida Christian College Conference, NCCAA.
**Intramural and club sports:** 20% of students participate. Intramural basketball, beach volleyball, flag football, floor hockey, martial arts, racquetball, softball, tennis, volleyball. Women's club cheerleading.

**ADMISSIONS. Academic basis for candidate selection** (in order of priority): Secondary school record, school's recommendation, standardized test scores.
**Nonacademic basis for candidate selection:** Character and personality are important. Extracurricular participation and particular talent or ability are considered.
**Requirements:** Graduation from secondary school is required; GED is accepted. No specific distribution of secondary school units required. Applicants who have not graduated from secondary school or who do not have GED may be considered for admission as special students. Evidence of gaining secondary school diploma or equivalent within one year from enrollment at college required; no more than 24 credit hours may be earned until secondary school diploma or GED is awarded. Minimum 2.0 GPA recommended. Minimum composite ACT score of 21 (combined SAT score of 84) required of education program applicants. Audition required of music program applicants. SAT or ACT is required. No off-campus interviews.
**Procedure:** Take SAT or ACT by spring of 12th year. Suggest filing application by fall. Application deadline is August 1. Notification of admission on rolling basis. No specific date by which applicants must accept offer. $100 room deposit, refundable until August 1 for fall. Freshmen accepted for terms other than fall.
**Special programs:** Admission may be deferred one year. Credit may be granted through CEEB Advanced Placement for scores of 3 or higher. Credit may be granted through CLEP general and subject exams ACT PEP, DANTES, and challenge exams and military experience. Early entrance/early admission program.
**Transfer students:** Transfer students accepted for terms other than fall. In fall 1993, 13% of all new students were transfers into all classes. 184 transfer applications were received, 183 were accepted. Application deadline is August 1 for fall; December 1 for spring. Minimum 2.0 GPA recommended. Lowest course grade accepted is "C." Maximum number of transferable credits is 100 semester hours. At least 30 semester hours must be completed at the college to receive degree.
**Admissions contact:** Royce M. Shelton, M.A., M.Div., Director of Admissions and Records. 813 665-4404, extension 210.

**FINANCIAL AID. Available aid:** Pell grants, SEOG, state scholarships and grants, school scholarships, private scholarships, ROTC scholarships, and academic merit scholarships. Perkins Loans (NDSL), PLUS, Stafford Loans (GSL), state loans, school loans, private loans, and SLS. AMS and deferred payment plan.
**Financial aid statistics:** 32% of aid is not need-based. In 1993-94, 70% of all undergraduate applicants received aid; 55% of freshman applicants. Average amounts of aid awarded freshmen: Loans, $2,100.
**Supporting data/closing dates:** FAFSA: Priority filing date is April 15. School's own aid application: Priority filing date is April 15; accepted on rolling basis. State aid form: Priority filing date is April 15. Income tax forms: Accepted on rolling basis. Notification of awards on rolling basis.
**Financial aid contact:** Carol Bradley, Director of Financial Aid. 813 665-4404, extension 222.

**STUDENT EMPLOYMENT.** College Work/Study Program. Institutional employment. 2% of full-time undergraduates work on campus during school year. Students may expect to earn an average of $1,500 during school year. Off-campus part-time employment opportunities rated "good."

**COMPUTER FACILITIES.** 29 IBM/IBM-compatible and Macintosh/Apple microcomputers; 14 are networked. Client/LAN operating systems include Apple/Macintosh, DOS. Computer languages and software packages include AppleWorks, BASIC, DOS, WordPerfect. Students must pay computer access fee.
**Fees:** $50 computer fee per semester.
**Hours:** 20-25 hours/week (outside of instruction).

# Stetson University

**DeLand, FL 32720** **904 822-7000**

**1993-94 Costs.** Tuition: $11,510. Room: $2,335. Board: $2,105. Fees, books, misc. academic expenses (school's estimate): $1,085.
**Enrollment.** Undergraduates: 888 men, 1,142 women (full-time). Freshman class: 1,630 applicants, 1,337 accepted, 503 enrolled. Graduate enrollment: 441 men, 524 women.
**Test score averages/ranges.** Range of SAT scores of middle 50%: 420-540 verbal, 470-610 math. Range of ACT scores of middle 50%: 21-27 composite.
**Faculty.** 152 full-time; 36 part-time. 80% of faculty holds doctoral degree. Student/faculty ratio: 12 to 1.
**Selectivity rating.** Competitive.

**PROFILE.** Stetson, founded in 1883, is a private, church-affiliated university. Programs are offered through the College of Liberal Arts and the Schools of Business Administration and Music. Its 117-acre campus is located in DeLand, 35 miles north of Orlando.

**Accreditation:** SACS. Professionally accredited by the American Assembly of Collegiate Schools of Business, the American Bar Association, the Association of American Law Schools, the National Association of Schools of Music.
**Religious orientation:** Stetson University is affiliated with the Baptist Church; one semester of religion required.
**Library:** Collections totaling over 300,000 volumes, and 1,400 periodical subscriptions.
**Special facilities/museums:** Language lab, art gallery, greenhouse with growth chambers, mineral museum, electron microscopes.
**Athletic facilities:** Gymnasium, tennis courts, weight room, swimming pool, driving range, athletic fields.

**STUDENT BODY. Undergraduate profile:** 78% are state residents; 25% are transfers. 2% Asian-American, 2% Black, 4% Hispanic, 1% Native American, 89% White, 2% Other. Average age of undergraduates is 20.
**Freshman profile:** 1% of freshmen who took SAT scored 700 or over on verbal, 4% scored 700 or over on math; 10% scored 600 or over on verbal, 25% scored 600 or over on math; 40% scored 500 or over on verbal, 65% scored 500 or over on math; 86% scored 400 or over on verbal, 95% scored 400 or over on math; 100% scored 300 or over on verbal, 100% scored 300 or over on math. 65% of accepted applicants took SAT; 35% took ACT. 72% of freshmen come from public schools.
**Undergraduate achievement:** 80% of fall 1991 freshmen returned for fall 1992 term. 55% of entering class graduated. 45% of students who completed a degree program went on to graduate study within one year.
**Foreign students:** 59 students are from out of the country. Countries represented include Canada, Germany, Latin American countries, Spain, and the West Indies; 28 in all.

**PROGRAMS OF STUDY. Degrees:** B.A., B.Bus.Admin., B.M., B.Mech.Eng., B.S.
**Majors:** Accounting, American Studies, Art, Biology, Business Administration, Chemistry, Church Music, Computer Science, Economics, English, Finance, French, Geography, German, History, Management/Marketing, Mathematics, Music, Music Education, Music Theory, Orchestra/Instruments, Philosophy, Physical Education, Physics, Political Science, Pre-Engineering, Pre-Law, Pre-Medicine, Psychology, Religion, Russian Studies, Sociology, Spanish, Voice.
**Distribution of degrees:** The majors with the highest enrollment are business administration, psychology, and education; American studies, German, and geography have the lowest.
**Requirements:** General education requirement.
**Academic regulations:** Minimum 2.0 GPA must be maintained.
**Special:** Minors offered in most majors. Interdepartmental major in urban studies. Roland George Investment Program. Hollis Leadership Development Program. Self-designed majors. Double majors. Dual degrees. Independent study. Accelerated study. Pass/fail grading option. Internships. Graduate school at which undergraduates may take graduate-level courses. Preprofessional programs in law, medicine, and engineering. 3-2 forestry and environmental studies program with Duke U. 3-2 medical technology programs with Baptist Medical Center, Duke U, Florida Hospital, Tallahassee Memorial Regional Medical Center, and Tampa General Hospital. Member of Associated Mid-Florida Colleges; cross-registration possible. Washington Semester. Exchange programs with Austin Coll, Berea Coll, Eckerd Coll, Gustav Adolphus Coll, Hamline U, Macalester Coll, Rollins Coll, St. Olaf Coll, and U of Redlands. Teacher certification in elementary, secondary, and special education. Exchange programs abroad in England (Nottingham Polytech), France (U of Dijon), Germany (U of Freiburg), Russia (Moscow State U), and Spain (U of Madrid). Study abroad also in Latin American countries. ROTC at Embry-Riddle Aeronautical U.
**Honors:** Phi Beta Kappa. Honors program.
**Academic Assistance:** Remedial study skills.

**STUDENT LIFE. Housing:** All unmarried students under age 21 must live on campus unless living near campus with relatives. Coed, women's, and men's dorms. Sorority and fraternity housing. 75% of students live in college housing.
**Social atmosphere:** Students gather at the Commons on campus, and at Half Times, Rossi's, and Gator's off campus. Greeks and the Student Union Board influence campus life. Popular events include Homecoming, Parents Weekend, Bahama Blue, the Viking Party, Orlando Magic basketball games, Greek Week, and Greenfeather.
**Services and counseling/handicapped student services:** Placement services. Health service. Career guidance services. Physically disabled student services. Learning disabled services. Reader services for the blind.
**Campus organizations:** Undergraduate student government. Student newspaper (Stetson Reporter, published twice/week). Literary magazine. Yearbook. Band, chorus, jazz ensemble, orchestra, opera workshop, drama group, debating, public speaking, departmental clubs, special-interest groups, 86 organizations in all. Seven fraternities, no chapter houses; seven sororities, no chapter houses. 43% of men join a fraternity. 43% of women join a sorority.
**Religious organizations:** Baptist Campus Ministry, Canterbury House, Christian Science group, Wesley Foundation, Westminster Fellowship, Catholic Campus Ministry, Religious Life Council, Ministerial Association.
**Minority/foreign student organizations:** Afro-American Society. International House.

**ATHLETICS. Physical education requirements:** Two semesters of physical education required.
**Intercollegiate competition:** 17% of students participate. Baseball (M), basketball (M,W), cheerleading (M,W), crew (M,W), cross-country (M,W), golf (M,W), soccer (M,W), softball (W), tennis (M,W), volleyball (W). Member of NCAA Division I, Trans America Athletic Conference.
**Intramural and club sports:** 70% of students participate. Intramural badminton, basketball, flag football, racquetball, soccer, softball, table tennis, volleyball. Men's club volleyball.

**ADMISSIONS. Academic basis for candidate selection** (in order of priority): Class rank, secondary school record, standardized test scores, school's recommendation, essay.

**Nonacademic basis for candidate selection:** Character and personality, extracurricular participation, particular talent or ability, and alumni/ae relationship are emphasized. Geographical distribution is considered.
**Requirements:** Graduation from secondary school is required; GED is accepted. 16 units and the following program of study are required: 4 units of English, 3 units of math, 3 units of science, 2 units of foreign language, 2 units of social studies, 2 units of academic electives. Audition required of music program applicants. Summer Opportunity Program for applicants not normally admissible. SAT or ACT is required. Campus visit and interview recommended. Off-campus interviews available with an admissions representative.
**Procedure:** Take SAT or ACT by fall of 12th year. Suggest filing application by fall. Application deadline is March 1. Notification of admission by April 1. Reply is required by May 1. $400 tuition deposit, refundable until May 1. $200 room deposit, refundable until May 15. Freshmen accepted for terms other than fall.
**Special programs:** Credit and/or placement may be granted through CEEB Advanced Placement exams for scores of 4 or higher. Credit and/or placement may be granted through CLEP subject exams. Credit and placement may be granted through challenge exams. Early decision program. Deadline for applying for early decision is November 15. Early entrance/early admission program.
**Transfer students:** Transfer students accepted for terms other than fall. In fall 1992, 25% of all new students were transfers into all classes. 380 transfer applications were received, 274 were accepted. Application deadline is March 1. Minimum 2.0 GPA required. Lowest course grade accepted is "C-." Maximum number of transferable credits is 64 semester hours. At least 48 semester hours must be completed at the university to receive degree.
**Admissions contact:** Linda Glover, Dean of Admissions. 904 822-7100.

**FINANCIAL AID. Available aid:** Pell grants, SEOG, state scholarships and grants, school scholarships and grants, private scholarships and grants, ROTC scholarships, academic merit scholarships, athletic scholarships, and aid for undergraduate foreign students. Perkins Loans (NDSL), PLUS, Stafford Loans (GSL), state loans, school loans, and private loans. Knight Tuition Plans.
**Financial aid statistics:** In 1992-93, 90% of all undergraduate applicants received aid; 80% of freshman applicants. Average amounts of aid awarded freshmen: Scholarships and grants, $3,000; loans, $2,610.
**Supporting data/closing dates:** FAFSA/FAF/FFS: Deadline is March 15. School's own aid application: Deadline is March 15. State aid form: Deadline is March 15. Income tax forms: Deadline is March 15. Notification of awards on rolling basis.
**Financial aid contact:** Jack Agett, M.S., Director of Financial Aid. 904 822-7120.

**STUDENT EMPLOYMENT.** College Work/Study Program. Institutional employment. 37% of full-time undergraduates work on campus during school year. Students may expect to earn an average of $1,300 during school year. Off-campus part-time employment opportunities rated "good."

**COMPUTER FACILITIES.** IBM/IBM-compatible and Macintosh/Apple microcomputers. Students may access Digital minicomputer/mainframe systems. Computer languages and software packages include BASIC, C, COBOL, dBASE III+, FORTRAN, IFPS+, Lotus 1-2-3, Microsoft Works, MINITAB, Pascal, SPSS-X, WordPerfect. Computer facilities are available to all students.
**Fees:** None.

**GRADUATE CAREER DATA.** Highest graduate school enrollments: Florida State U, Stetson Law Sch, Stetson U, U of Central Florida, U of Florida. Companies and businesses that hire graduates: Barnett, Martin Marietta, Prudential.

**PROMINENT ALUMNI/AE.** Mark Hollis, president and CEO, Publix Supermarkets; Dan Davis, president and CEO, Winn Dixie Supermarkets; Hon. Carolyn Parr, judge, U.S. Tax Court; Don Iverson, president, Iverson Technology.

## Trinity College at Miami

**Miami, FL 33101-9674** | **305 577-4600**

**1993-94 Costs.** Tuition: $6,300. Room & board: $3,080. Fees, books, misc. academic expenses (school's estimate): $550.
**Enrollment.** Undergraduates: 121 men, 82 women (full-time). Freshman class: 70 applicants, 64 accepted, 52 enrolled.
**Test score averages/ranges.** Average ACT scores: 16 composite.
**Faculty.** 9 full-time; 12 part-time. 45% of faculty holds doctoral degree. Student/faculty ratio: 15 to 1.
**Selectivity rating.** Noncompetitive.

**PROFILE.** Trinity College at Miami is a private college with religious orientation. Founded in 1949, its name changed from Miami Christian College in 1993. Its campus is located in Miami.

**Accreditation:** NCACS.
**Religious orientation:** Trinity College at Miami is an interdenominational Christian school; 42 semester hours of Bible and theology required.
**Library:** Collections totaling over 36,569 volumes, 185 periodical subscriptions and 167 microform items.
**Athletic facilities:** Soccer and softball fields, tennis courts.

**STUDENT BODY. Undergraduate profile:** 88% are state residents; 18% are transfers. 1% Asian-American, 27% Black, 26% Hispanic, 1% Native American, 43% White, 2% Other. Average age of undergraduates is 25.
**Undergraduate achievement:** 50% of fall 1991 freshmen returned for fall 1992 term. 30% of entering class graduated. 27% of students who completed a degree program went on to graduate study within five years.
**Foreign students:** Four students are from out of the country. Countries represented include the Dominican Republic, Jamaica, Kenya, and Nigeria.

**PROGRAMS OF STUDY. Degrees:** B.A.
**Majors:** Biblical Studies, Business Management, Communication, Elementary Education, General Studies, Psychology.
**Distribution of degrees:** The majors with the highest enrollment are elementary education, biblical studies, and psychology.
**Requirements:** General education requirement.
**Academic regulations:** Minimum 2.0 GPA required for graduation.
**Special:** Minors offered in some majors. Double majors. Independent study. Pass/fail grading option. Internships. Preprofessional programs in theology. Teacher certification in elementary education. Study abroad in Israel.

**ADMISSIONS. Academic basis for candidate selection** (in order of priority): Secondary school record, essay, standardized test scores, class rank, school's recommendation.
**Nonacademic basis for candidate selection:** Character and personality are important. Extracurricular participation is considered.
**Requirements:** Graduation from secondary school is required; GED is accepted. 16 units and the following program of study are recommended: 3 units of English, 2 units of math, 2 units of science, 2 units of foreign language, 2 units of social studies, 3 units of electives. Minimum combined SAT score of 770 (composite ACT score of 17), rank in top half of secondary school class, and minimum 2.0 GPA required. Requirements vary according to program. ACT is required; SAT may be substituted. Campus visit and interview recommended. Off-campus interviews available with an admissions representative.
**Procedure:** Take SAT or ACT by December of 12th year. Notification of admission on rolling basis. Reply is required within 30 days of notification. $100 nonrefundable tuition deposit. $50 refundable room deposit. Freshmen accepted for terms other than fall.
**Special programs:** Admission may be deferred one semester. Credit may be granted through CEEB Advanced Placement for scores of 3 or higher. Credit may be granted through CLEP subject exams, ACT PEP and challenge exams, and military experience. Early entrance/early admission program. Concurrent enrollment program.
**Transfer students:** Transfer students accepted for terms other than fall. Application deadline is rolling for fall; rolling for spring. Minimum 2.0 GPA required. Lowest course grade accepted is "C." Maximum number of transferable credits is 64 semester hours from a two-year school and 96 semester hours from a four-year school. At least 30 semester hours must be completed at the college to receive degree.
**Admissions contact:** Gary Larson, Director of Admissions. 305 577-4600, extension 135.

**FINANCIAL AID. Available aid:** Pell grants, SEOG, state scholarships and grants, school scholarships and grants, private scholarships and grants, and academic merit scholarships. PLUS, Stafford Loans (GSL), and SLS. AMS and deferred payment plan.
**Supporting data/closing dates:** FAFSA/FAF/FFS: Priority filing date is April 15. Notification of awards on rolling basis.
**Financial aid contact:** Marilyn S. Meyers, Director of Financial Aid. 305 577-4600, extension 145.

## University of Central Florida

**Orlando, FL 32816** | **407 823-2000**

**1993-94 Costs.** Tuition: $1,662 (state residents), $6,564 (out-of-state). Room: $2,260. Board: $2,046. Fees, books, misc. academic expenses (school's estimate): $755.
**Enrollment.** Undergraduates: 5,856 men, 6,432 women (full-time). Freshman class: 6,999 applicants, 2,962 accepted, 1,903 enrolled. Graduate enrollment: 1,544 men, 1,476 women.
**Test score averages/ranges.** Average SAT scores: 464 verbal, 533 math. Average ACT scores: 23 composite.
**Faculty.** 590 full-time; 411 part-time. 80% of faculty holds doctoral degree. Student/faculty ratio: 17 to 1.
**Selectivity rating.** Competitive.

**PROFILE.** The University of Central Florida, founded in 1963, is a public, comprehensive university. Programs are offered through the Colleges of Arts and Sciences, Business Administration, Education, Engineering, and Health. Its 1,227-acre campus is located in Orlando.

**Accreditation:** SACS. Professionally accredited by the Accreditation Board for Engineering and Technology, the American Assembly of Collegiate Schools of Business, the American Medical Association (CAHEA), the American Speech-Language-Hearing Association, the Council on Social Work Education, the National Association of Schools of Music, the National Council for Accreditation of Teacher Education, the National League for Nursing.
**Religious orientation:** University of Central Florida is nonsectarian; no religious requirements.
**Library:** Collections totaling over 955,903 volumes, 4,838 periodical subscriptions, and 1,261,086 microform items.
**Special facilities/museums:** Media center, language lab.
**Athletic facilities:** Gymnasium, baseball, football, soccer, and softball fields, swimming pool, tennis and volleyball courts.

**STUDENT BODY. Undergraduate profile:** 94% are state residents; 51% are transfers. 5% Asian-American, 5% Black, 9% Hispanic, 79% White, 2% Other. Average age of undergraduates is 24.
**Freshman profile:** 4% of freshmen who took SAT scored 700 or over on verbal, 7% scored 700 or over on math; 9% scored 600 or over on verbal, 24% scored 600 or over on math; 31% scored 500 or over on verbal, 62% scored 500 or over on math; 78% scored 400 or over on verbal, 92% scored 400 or over on math; 98% scored 300 or over on verbal, 100% scored 300 or over on math. 3% of freshmen who took ACT scored 30 or over on composite; 35% scored 24 or over on composite; 91% scored 18 or over on composite; 100% scored 12 or over on composite. 71% of accepted applicants took SAT; 29% took ACT.
**Undergraduate achievement:** 73% of fall 1992 freshmen returned for fall 1993 term. 68% of entering class graduated.
**Foreign students:** 400 students are from out of the country. Countries represented include China, India, Korea, and Taiwan; 90 in all.

**PROGRAMS OF STUDY. Degrees:** B.A., B.F.A., B.Mus., B.Mus.Ed., B.S., B.Soc.Work.

**Majors:** Accounting, Aerospace Engineering, Anthropology, Art, Art Education, Biology, Botany, Business Education, Cardiopulmonary Sciences, Chemistry, Civil Engineering, Communicative Disorders, Computer Engineering, Computer Science, Criminal Justice, Design Engineering Technology, Early Childhood Education, Economics, Electrical Engineering, Electronics Engineering Technology, Elementary Education, English, English Language Arts Education, Environmental Engineering, Exceptional Child Education, Finance, Foreign Language Combination, Foreign Language Education, Forensic Science, French, General Business Administration, General Studies, Health Information Management, Health Services Administration, History, Hospitality Management, Humanities, Industrial Engineering, Interpersonal Communication, Journalism, Legal Studies, Liberal Arts, Limnology, Management, Marketing, Mathematics, Mathematics Education, Mechanical Engineering, Medical Laboratory Sciences, Medical Records Administration, Molecular Biology/Microbiology, Motion Picture Technology, Music, Music Education, Nursing, Organization Communication, Philosophy, Physical Education, Physical Therapy, Physics, Political Science, Psychology, Public Administration, Radio/Television, Radiologic Sciences, Science Education, Social Science Education, Social Science Interdisciplinary, Social Work, Sociology, Spanish, Statistics, Technical/Vocational Education, Theatre, Zoology.
**Distribution of degrees:** The majors with the highest enrollment are psychology, elementary education, and electrical engineering; visual/performing arts, allied health sciences, and life sciences have the lowest.
**Requirements:** General education requirement.
**Academic regulations:** Minimum 2.0 GPA must be maintained.
**Special:** Minors offered in most majors and in over 25 other fields. Self-designed majors. Double majors. Dual degrees. Independent study. Internships. Cooperative education programs. Graduate school at which undergraduates may take graduate-level courses. Preprofessional programs in medicine, veterinary science, pharmacy, dentistry, optometry, and podiatry. 3-1 programs arranged but not encouraged. Teacher certification in early childhood, elementary, secondary, special education, and vo-tech education. Exchange programs abroad in France (Inst des Sciences Appliquees de Lyon) and Spain (U of Oviedo). Study abroad also in Italy and Venezuela. ROTC and AFROTC.
**Honors:** Honors program.

**STUDENT LIFE. Housing:** Students may live on or off campus. Coed, women's, and men's dorms. Sorority and fraternity housing. 6% of students live in college housing.
**Social atmosphere:** As reported by the student newspaper, popular gathering spots in and around campus are the library, Wild Pizza, Hooters, All-Pro Subs, Visage, and Pleasure Island. Amnesty International, the Environmental Society, Student Government, Greeks, and ROTC are influential organizations on campus. Some of the favorite events during the school year are Greek Rush, Homecoming, Shakespeare Festival, Studio E Productions, and Greek Week.
**Services and counseling/handicapped student services:** Placement services. Health service. Day care. Counseling services for minority and veteran students. Personal counseling. Career and academic guidance services. Physically disabled student services. Learning disabled services. Notetaking services. Tape recorders. Tutors. Reader services for the blind.
**Campus organizations:** Undergraduate student government. Student newspaper (Central Florida Future, published twice/week). Literary magazine. Yearbook. Radio station. Concerts, cinema, cultural arts, and speakers committees, Knight's Roundtable, Arts Alliance, cinematography association, debate club, Society of Women Engineers, Student Council for Exceptional Children, Human Factors Society, academic, service, and special-interest groups, 150 organizations in all. 13 fraternities, four chapter houses; six sororities, all with chapter houses. 9% of men join a fraternity. 6% of women join a sorority.
**Religious organizations:** Bahai Association, Baptist Campus Ministry, Campus Community Church, Campus Crusade for Christ, Collegiate Adventist Fellowship, Intervarsity Christian Fellowship, Jewish Student Union/Hillel, Moslem Student Association, Newman Club, Wesley Foundation, Fellowship of Christian Athletes.
**Minority/foreign student organizations:** Black Student Union, Chinese American Student Association, Hispanic American Student Association, Indian, Korean, Palestinian, and Vietnamese clubs. International Student Association, Caribbean, French, and Italian clubs.

**ATHLETICS. Physical education requirements:** None.
**Intercollegiate competition:** 1% of students participate. Baseball (M), basketball (M,W), cross-country (M,W), football (M), golf (M,W), soccer (M,W), tennis (M,W), track (indoor) (M,W), track (outdoor) (M,W), track and field (indoor) (M,W), track and field (outdoor) (M,W), volleyball (W). Member of American South Conference, NCAA Division I, NCAA Division I-AA for football.
**Intramural and club sports:** Intramural badminton, basketball, bench press, cross-country, disk golf, floor hockey, flag football, racquetball, soccer, softball, swimming, tennis, track and field, volleyball, Wiffle ball, wrestling.

**ADMISSIONS. Academic basis for candidate selection** (in order of priority): Secondary school record, standardized test scores, school's recommendation, class rank.
**Nonacademic basis for candidate selection:** Particular talent or ability and alumni/ae relationship are considered.
**Requirements:** Graduation from secondary school is required; GED is accepted. 19 units and the following program of study are required: 4 units of English, 3 units of math, 3 units of science, 2 units of foreign language, 3 units of social studies, 4 units of electives. Specific requirements vary greatly for specific programs. EOP for applicants not normally admissible. Conditional admission possible for applicants not meeting standard requirements. SAT or ACT is required. No off-campus interviews.
**Procedure:** Take SAT or ACT by December of 12th year. Suggest filing application by January. Application deadline is March 15. Notification of admission on rolling basis. $150 refundable room deposit. Freshmen accepted for terms other than fall.
**Special programs:** Admission may be deferred one year. Credit may be granted through CEEB Advanced Placement for scores of 3 or higher. Credit may be granted through CLEP general and subject exams. Early entrance/early admission program. Concurrent enrollment program.
**Transfer students:** Transfer students accepted for terms other than fall. In fall 1993, 51% of all new students were transfers into all classes. 6,583 transfer applications were received, 4,946 were accepted. Application deadline is March 15 for fall; October 15 for spring. Minimum 2.0 GPA required. Lowest course grade accepted is "D." At least 30 semester hours must be completed at the university to receive degree.
**Admissions contact:** Susan McKinnon, M.Ed., Acting Director of Admissions. 407 823-3000.

**FINANCIAL AID. Available aid:** Pell grants, SEOG, state scholarships and grants, school scholarships and grants, private scholarships, ROTC scholarships, academic merit scholarships, and athletic scholarships. Perkins Loans (NDSL), PLUS, Stafford Loans (GSL), school loans, and SLS. Florida Pre-Paid Tuition Program.
**Financial aid statistics:** 15% of aid is not need-based. In 1992-93, 83% of all undergraduate applicants received aid; 99% of freshman applicants. Average amounts of aid awarded freshmen: Scholarships and grants, $2,879; loans, $3,060.
**Supporting data/closing dates:** FAFSA: Priority filing date is March 1. FAF/FFS: Priority filing date is March 15; accepted on rolling basis. School's own aid application: Accepted on rolling basis. Institutional application: Accepted on rolling basis. Notification of awards begins June 1.
**Financial aid contact:** Mary H. McKinney, M.P.A., Director of Financial Aid. 407 823-2827.

**STUDENT EMPLOYMENT.** College Work/Study Program. Institutional employment. 15% of full-time undergraduates work on campus during school year. Students may expect to earn an average of $2,200 during school year. Off-campus part-time employment opportunities rated "excellent."

**COMPUTER FACILITIES.** 250 IBM/IBM-compatible and Macintosh/Apple microcomputers; 245 are networked. Computer languages and software packages include BASIC, C, COBOL, dBASE, FORTRAN, LISP, Pascal, SAS, SPSS; database, spreadsheet, tutorial, word processing packages. Computer facilities are available to all students.
**Fees:** Computer fee is included in tuition/fees.
**Hours:** 24 hours.

# University of Florida

**Gainesville, FL 32611** 904 392-3261

**1994-95 Costs.** Tuition: $1,820 (state residents), $7,090 (out-of-state). Room & board: $4,180. Fees, books, misc. academic expenses (school's estimate): $600.
**Enrollment.** Undergraduates: 12,851 men, 11,235 women (full-time). Freshman class: 12,445 applicants, 8,836 accepted, 3,623 enrolled. Graduate enrollment: 4,905 men, 3,600 women.
**Test score averages/ranges.** Range of SAT scores of middle 50%: 480-590 verbal, 560-680 math. Range of ACT scores of middle 50%: 24-28 composite.
**Faculty.** 1,622 full-time; 58 part-time. 86% of faculty holds doctoral degree. Student/faculty ratio: 17 to 1.
**Selectivity rating.** Highly competitive.

**PROFILE.** The University of Florida, founded in 1853, is a public, comprehensive university. Programs are offered through the Colleges of Agriculture, Architecture, Business Administration, Education, Engineering, Fine Arts, Health and Human Performance, Health Related Professions, Journalism and Communications, Liberal Arts and Sciences, Nursing, and Pharmacy; the Schools of Building Construction and Forest Resources and Conservation; and the Fisher School of Accounting. Its 2,000-acre campus is located in Gainesville.

**Accreditation:** SACS. Professionally accredited by the Accreditation Board for Engineering and Technology, the Accrediting Council on Education in Journalism and Mass Communication, the American Assembly of Collegiate Schools of Business, the American Council for Construction Education, the American Council on Pharmaceutical Education, the American Dietetic Association, the American Physical Therapy Association, the American Society of Landscape Architects, the Foundation for Interior Design Education Research, the National Association of Schools of Dance, the National Association of Schools of Theatre, the National Council for Accreditation of Teacher Education, the National League for Nursing, the Society of American Foresters.
**Religious orientation:** University of Florida is nonsectarian; no religious requirements.
**Library:** Collections totaling over 3,022,768 volumes, 24,191 periodical subscriptions, and 5,282,887 microform items.
**Special facilities/museums:** Natural history museum, art museum, art gallery, center for the performing arts, Aeolian Skinner organ, cast-bell carillon, citrus research center, coastal engineering wave tank, 100-kilowatt training and research reactor, academic computing center, self-contained intensive care hyperbaric chamber.
**Athletic facilities:** Gymnasium, racquetball and tennis courts, track, baseball, football, and intramural fields, swimming pool.

**STUDENT BODY. Undergraduate profile:** 93% are state residents. 4.8% Asian-American, 5.5% Black, 7.1% Hispanic, .2% Native American, 77.2% White, 5.2% Foreign national. Average age of undergraduates is 22.
**Freshman profile:** 74% of accepted applicants took SAT; 26% took ACT.
**Undergraduate achievement:** 88% of fall 1992 freshmen returned for fall 1993 term. 28% of entering class graduated.
**Foreign students:** 436 students are from out of the country. Countries represented include Brazil, Canada, China, India, Korea, and Taiwan; 114 in all.

**PROGRAMS OF STUDY. Degrees:** B.A., B.Design, B.F.A., B.Hlth.Sci., B.Land.Arch., B.Mus., B.S., B.S.Pharm.
**Majors:** Accounting, Advertising, Aerospace Engineering, Agricultural Education/Communication, Agricultural Engineering, Agricultural Operations Management, Agronomy, Allied Health, American Studies, Animal Science, Anthropology, Architecture, Art, Art Education, Asian Studies, Astronomy, Botany, Building Construction, Chemical Engineering, Chemistry, Civil Engineering, Classical Studies, Communication Processes/Disorders, Computer Engineering, Computer/Information Sciences, Creative Photography, Criminal Justice, Dairy Science, East Asian Languages/Literatures, Economics, Electrical Engineering, Elementary Education, Engineering Science, English, Entomology/Nematology, Environmental Engineering Sciences, Exercise/Sport Sciences,

Finance, Food/Resource Economics, Food Science/Human Nutrition, Forestry, French, Geography, Geology, German, Graphic Arts, Health Science Education, History, History of Art, Horticultural Science, Industrial/Systems Engineering, Insurance, Interdisciplinary Engineering Studies, Interdisciplinary Studies, Interior Design, Jewish Studies, Journalism, Landscape Architecture, Linguistics, Management, Marketing, Materials Science/Engineering, Mathematics, Mechanical Engineering, Microbiology/Cell Science, Music, Music Education, Music History/Literature, Natural Resource Conservation, Nuclear Engineering, Nuclear Engineering Sciences, Nursing, Occupational Therapy, Pharmacological Sciences, Pharmacy, Philosophy, Physical Therapy, Physician Assistant, Physics, Plant Pathology, Plant Sciences, Political Science, Portuguese, Poultry Science, Psychology, Public Relations, Real Estate/Urban Analysis, Recreation, Religion, Russian, Sociology, Soil/Water Sciences, Spanish, Special Education, Statistics, Surveying/Mapping, Telecommunication, Theatre Performance, Theatre Production, Wildlife Ecology, Zoology.

**Distribution of degrees:** The majors with the highest enrollment are finance, psychology, and marketing; botany, agronomy, and linguistics have the lowest.

**Requirements:** General education requirement.

**Academic regulations:** Minimum 2.0 GPA must be maintained.

**Special:** Minors offered in many majors and in actuarial science, African studies, business administration, education, environmental horticulture, gerontology, Latin American studies, mass communication, secondary education, and women's studies. Certificate programs in some minors and in African studies, Afro-American studies, business and economic history, environmental studies, Greek studies, humanities/agriculture, Latin American studies, and Soviet/East European area studies. Associate's degrees offered. Self-designed majors. Double majors. Dual degrees. Independent study. Accelerated study. Pass/fail grading option. Internships. Cooperative education programs. Graduate school at which undergraduates may take graduate-level courses. Preprofessional programs in law, medicine, veterinary science, pharmacy, and dentistry. 3-2 accounting/M.B.S. program. 3-2 mathematics/M.B.A. or M.B.S. program. 4-2 industrial systems engineering/M.B.A. program. Member of Association of American Universities (AAU) and the Alliance for Undergraduate Education (AUE). Exchange programs with Florida State U, Stetson U, U of Georgia, U of New Orleans, and all other state university system institutions. Teacher certification in elementary, secondary, and special education. Certification in specific subject areas. Study abroad in Argentina, Australia, Austria, Brazil, Chile, China, Costa Rica, Denmark, England, Finland, France, Germany, Greece, Hong Kong, Hungary, Indonesia, Israel, Italy, Japan, Mexico, the Netherlands, Nigeria, Norway, Poland, Russia, Scotland, Spain, Taiwan, Tanzania, Uganda, Venezuela, Vietnam, and Zimbabwe. Study abroad also in other countries through other Florida state university system institutions. ROTC, NROTC, and AFROTC.

**Honors:** Phi Beta Kappa. Honors program. Honor societies.

**Academic Assistance:** Remedial reading, writing, math, and study skills. Nonremedial tutoring.

**STUDENT LIFE. Housing:** Students may live on or off campus. Coed, women's, and men's dorms. Sorority and fraternity housing. School-owned/operated apartments. On-campus married-student housing. 18% of students live in college housing.

**Social atmosphere:** According to the editor of the student newspaper, "Fitness is big on campus," and the campus has an "active Greek life." Students meet at Orange & Brew on campus while the Purple Porpoise and C.J.'s are popular off-campus spots. Football games and Gator Growl, the largest student-produced pep rally in the country, highlight the school year.

**Services and counseling/handicapped student services:** Placement services. Health service. Women's center. Day care. Counseling services for minority, military, veteran, and older students. Birth control, personal, and psychological counseling. Career and academic guidance services. Religious counseling. Physically disabled student services. Learning disabled services. Notetaking services. Tape recorders. Tutors. Reader services for the blind.

**Campus organizations:** Undergraduate student government. Student newspaper (Independent Florida Alligator). Yearbook. Radio and TV stations. Instrumental and choral groups, Florida Players, debating, professional groups, 420 organizations in all. 28 fraternities, 24 chapter houses; 18 sororities, 16 chapter houses. 15% of men join a fraternity. 15% of women join a sorority.

**Religious organizations:** Several religious groups.

**Minority/foreign student organizations:** Black Student Union, NAACP, minority fraternities/sororities, Hispania Student Association. Several foreign student groups.

**ATHLETICS. Physical education requirements:** None.

**Intercollegiate competition:** 11% of students participate. Baseball (M), basketball (M,W), cheerleading (M,W), cross-country (M,W), diving (M,W), football (M), golf (M,W), gymnastics (W), swimming (M,W), tennis (M,W), track (indoor) (M,W), track (outdoor) (M,W), track and field (indoor) (M,W), track and field (outdoor) (M,W), volleyball (W). Member of NCAA Division I, Southeastern Conference.

**Intramural and club sports:** 70% of students participate. Intramural basketball, flag football, golf, raquetball, soccer, softball, swimming, tennis, track/field, volleyball. Men's club archery, badminton, bowling, canoe/kayak, crew, cycling, fencing, field hockey, floor hockey, folk dancing, horsemanship, lacrosse, martial arts, mountain biking, rifle, rugby, sailing, scuba, soccer, surfing, table tennis, shooting triathalon, ultimate frisbee, volleyball, water polo, water skiing, wrestling. Women's club archery, badminton, bowling, canoe/kayak, crew, cycling, fencing, field hockey, floor hockey, folk dancing, horsemanship, martial arts, mountain biking, rifle, rugby, sailing, scuba, soccer, surfing, table tennis, shooting triathalon, ultimate frisbee, volleyball, water polo, water skiing.

**ADMISSIONS. Academic basis for candidate selection** (in order of priority): Secondary school record, standardized test scores, school's recommendation, essay.

**Nonacademic basis for candidate selection:** Character and personality, extracurricular participation, particular talent or ability, geographical distribution, and alumni/ae relationship are considered.

**Requirements:** Graduation from secondary school is required; GED is accepted. 19 units and the following program of study are required: 4 units of English, 3 units of math, 3 units of science including 2 units of lab, 2 units of foreign language, 3 units of social studies, 4 units of electives. Minimum combined SAT score of 840 (minimum verbal score of 340 and math score of 400) or minimum composite ACT score of 19 (minimum verbal and math scores of 16), and minimum "C" average as computed by university required. Audition required of music and theatre program applicants. Portfolio required of art program applicants. Admissions Committee review for applicants not normally admissible. SAT is required; ACT may be substituted. Campus visit recommended. No off-campus interviews.

**Procedure:** Take SAT or ACT by December of 12th year. Suggest filing application by November 1. Application deadline is February 1. Notification of admission by March 26. Reply is required within three weeks of acceptance. $175 room deposit, refundable until May 1. $20 administrative charge if refund is requested after student has left the university. Freshmen accepted for terms other than fall.

**Special programs:** Credit and/or placement may be granted through CEEB Advanced Placement exams for scores of 3 or higher. Credit and/or placement may be granted through CLEP general and subject exams. Credit may be granted through military experience. Credit and placement may be granted through challenge exams. Early decision program. In fall 1993, 20 applied for early decision and 11 were accepted. Deadline for applying for early decision is October 1. Early entrance/early admission program. Concurrent enrollment program.

**Transfer students:** Transfer students accepted for terms other than fall. In fall 1993, 6,304 transfer applications were received, 2,591 were accepted. Application deadline is June 10 for fall; November 1 for spring. Minimum 2.0 GPA required. Lowest course grade accepted is "D." Maximum number of transferable credits is 64 semester hours. At least 30 semester hours must be completed at the university to receive degree.

**Admissions contact:** William Kolb, M.A., Director of Admissions. 904 392-1365.

**FINANCIAL AID. Available aid:** Pell grants, SEOG, state scholarships and grants, school scholarships and grants, private scholarships and grants, ROTC scholarships, academic merit scholarships, and athletic scholarships. Perkins Loans (NDSL), PLUS, Stafford Loans (GSL), Health Professions Loans, state loans, school loans, private loans, and SLS. Tuition Plan Inc., Education Plan Inc., and Knight Tuition Plans.

**Financial aid statistics:** 45% of aid is not need-based. In 1993-94, 65% of all freshman applicants received aid. Average amounts of aid awarded freshmen: Scholarships and grants, $3,000; loans, $2,500.

**Supporting data/closing dates:** FAFSA: Priority filing date is April 15. School's own aid application: Priority filing date is April 15. Notification of awards on rolling basis.

**Financial aid contact:** Karen Fooks, Director of Financial Aid. 904 392-1275.

**STUDENT EMPLOYMENT.** College Work/Study Program. Institutional employment. 21% of full-time undergraduates work on campus during school year. Students may expect to earn an average of $1,800 during school year. Freshmen are discouraged from working during their first term. Off-campus part-time employment opportunities rated "fair."

**COMPUTER FACILITIES.** 612 IBM/IBM-compatible and Macintosh/Apple microcomputers; all are networked. Students may access Digital, IBM, SUN minicomputer/mainframe systems, BITNET, Internet. Residence halls may be equipped with modems. Client/LAN operating systems include Apple/Macintosh, DOS, UNIX/XENIX/AIX, X-windows, LocalTalk/AppleTalk, Novell. Computer languages and software packages include Apple OS, BASIC, C, COBOL, FORTRAN, Pascal, SAS, SCRIPT. Computer facilities are available to all students.

**Fees:** None.

**Hours:** 9 AM-5 PM some computers; 24 hours for others. 8 AM-midn. (M-Th); 8 AM-5 PM (F); noon-6 PM (S); noon-8 PM (Su) for CIRCA/CSE labs.

# University of Miami

**Coral Gables, FL 33124** **305 284-2211**

**1994-95 Costs.** Tuition: $16,665. Room & board: $6,535. Fees, books, misc. academic expenses (school's estimate): $630.

**Enrollment.** Undergraduates: 4,017 men, 3,625 women (full-time). Freshman class: 7,112 applicants, 5,386 accepted, 1,643 enrolled. Graduate enrollment: 2,821 men, 2,385 women.

**Test score averages/ranges.** Range of SAT scores of middle 50%: 920-1170 combined. Range of ACT scores of middle 50%: 21-28 composite.

**Faculty.** 623 full-time; 435 part-time. 87% of faculty holds doctoral degree. Student/faculty ratio: 8 to 1.

**Selectivity rating.** Competitive.

**PROFILE.** The University of Miami, founded in 1925, is a private, comprehensive university. Its 260-acre main campus is located in Coral Gables, south of downtown Miami.

**Accreditation:** SACS. Professionally accredited by the Accreditation Board for Engineering and Technology, the Accrediting Council on Education in Journalism and Mass Communication, the American Assembly of Collegiate Schools of Business, the American Psychological Association, the National Architecture Accrediting Board, the National Association of Schools of Music, the National Association of Schools of Theatre, the National Council for Accreditation of Teacher Education, the National League for Nursing.

**Religious orientation:** University of Miami is nonsectarian; no religious requirements.

**Library:** Collections totaling over 1,875,556 volumes, 18,890 periodical subscriptions, and 3,192,822 microform items.

**Special facilities/museums:** Art museum, concert hall.

**Athletic facilities:** Sports complex, athletic center, track and field complex, tennis courts, arena, baseball and football stadiums, intramural fields, wellness center.

**STUDENT BODY. Undergraduate profile:** 51% are state residents; 27% are transfers. 4% Asian-American, 9% Black, 24% Hispanic, 52% White, 11% Other. Average age of undergraduates is 19.

**Freshman profile:** 2% of freshmen who took SAT scored 700 or over on verbal, 9% scored 700 or over on math; 14% scored 600 or over on verbal, 38% scored 600 or over on math; 46% scored 500 or over on verbal, 72% scored 500 or over on math; 83% scored 400 or over on verbal, 94% scored 400 or over on math; 98% scored 300 or over on verbal, 100% scored 300 or over on math. 95% of accepted applicants took SAT; 5% took ACT.

**Foreign students:** 901 students are from out of the country. Countries represented include Brazil, Columbia, Peru, Spain, and Venezuela; 110 in all.

**PROGRAMS OF STUDY. Degrees:** A.B., B.A., B.Arch., B.Bus.Admin., B.Comp.Sci., B.F.A., B.Gen.Studies, B.Hlth.Sci., B.Mus., B.S.
**Majors:** Accounting, Advertising Communication, Aerospace Engineering, African/Afro-American Studies, American Studies, Anthropology, Architectural Engineering, Architecture, Art, Art History, Audio Engineering, Biochemistry, Biology, Biomedical Engineering, Broadcast Journalism, Broadcasting, Business Management/Organization, Caribbean Studies, Chemistry, Civil Engineering, Computer Information Systems, Computer Science, Criminology, Economics, Electrical Engineering, Electrical Engineering/Computer Science, Elementary Education, Engineering Science, English, Entrepreneurship, Environmental Engineering, Environmental Science, Finance, Foreign Language, French, General Business, Geography, Geology, German, Health Sciences, History, Human Resources, Human Resources Management, Industrial Engineering, International/Comparative Studies, International Business, International Marketing, Journalism, Judaic Studies, Latin American Studies, Law/Economics, Legal Studies, Manufacturing Engineering, Marine Affairs, Marine Biology, Marine Science, Marketing, Mathematics, Mechanical Engineering, Meteorology, Microbiology, Motion Picture, Music, Music Education, Music Engineering Technology, Music Industry, Music Literature, Music Performance, Music Therapy, Musical Theatre, Nursing, Organizational Communication, Philosophy, Photography, Physics, Politics, Politics/Public Affairs, Psychobiology, Psychology, Public Affairs, Public Relations, Real Estate, Religious Studies, Secondary Education, Sociology, Spanish, Special Education, Speech Communication, Sports Management, Studio Music/Jazz/Instrumental, Studio Music/Jazz/Vocal, Studio Music/Music Performance, Systems Analysis, Theatre Arts, Theory/Composition, Video/Film, Women's Studies.
**Distribution of degrees:** The majors with the highest enrollment are psychology, biology, and accounting.
**Requirements:** General education requirement.
**Academic regulations:** Minimum 2.0 GPA required for graduation.
**Special:** Minors required in most departments of College of Arts and Sciences. Minors offered in more than 100 fields. Self-designed majors. Double majors. Dual degrees. Independent study. Accelerated study. Pass/fail grading option. Internships. Graduate school at which undergraduates may take graduate-level courses. Preprofessional programs in law, medicine, and dentistry. Dual-admission honors programs offered; six-year B.S./M.D. program, seven-year B.A. or B.S./J.D. program, B.S./Ph.D. program in marine/atmospheric science, B.A. or B.S./M.B.A. program in business administration, and eight-year B.S./M.D. programs in engineering and medicine. Member of Southern Consortium of Colleges and Universities. Teacher certification in elementary, secondary, and special education. Certification in specific subject areas. Study abroad in Argentina, Australia, Austria, Belgium, Chile, Colombia, Costa Rica, the Czech Republic, Ecuador, England, France, Germany, Guatemala, Israel, Italy, Japan, Scotland, Slovakia, Spain, Sweden, Switzerland, Thailand, and Wales. ROTC and AFROTC.
**Honors:** Phi Beta Kappa. Honors program. Honor societies.
**Academic Assistance:** Remedial reading, writing, math, and study skills. Nonremedial tutoring.

**STUDENT LIFE. Housing:** All freshmen must live in a residential college unless living with family. Residential colleges. 43% of students live in college housing.
**Social atmosphere:** According to the editor of the student newspaper, "The student body is extremely diverse, therefore each of the groups are very splintered. The huge number of things that can attract students attentions makes participation in everything very hard." Popular locations at UM are The Rat, Sundays on the Bay, Hooligans Pub, and Tony Roma's. Greeks, the football team, Resident Assistants, the Student Activities department, and the Residential Colleges are influential groups on campus. Favorite events during the year are football games, Sportsfest, Homecoming, Greek Week, and Fall Ball.
**Services and counseling/handicapped student services:** Placement services. Health service. Counseling services for minority students. Personal and psychological counseling. Career and academic guidance services. Physically disabled student services. Learning disabled services. Notetaking services. Tape recorders. Tutors. Reader services for the blind.
**Campus organizations:** Undergraduate student government. Student newspaper (Miami Hurricane, published twice/week). Literary magazine. Yearbook. Radio and TV stations. Drama productions, seven professional magazines, community service opportunities, Rathskeller, professional groups, special-interest groups, 200 organizations in all. 15 fraternities, seven chapter houses; 11 sororities, no chapter houses. 16% of men join a fraternity. 18% of women join a sorority.
**Religious organizations:** American Friends Service group, Baptist Campus Ministry, Catholic Student Center, Christian Science Organization, Episcopal Church Center, Hillel, Intervarsity Christian Fellowship, Methodist Center.
**Minority/foreign student organizations:** United Black Student, African Student Union. Jamaican Unity, Haitian Student Association, Caribbean Association, Muslim Student Organization.

**ATHLETICS. Physical education requirements:** None.
**Intercollegiate competition:** 20% of students participate. Baseball (M), basketball (M,W), cheerleading (M,W), crew (M,W), cross-country (M,W), diving (M,W), football (M), golf (W), swimming (M,W), tennis (M,W), track (indoor) (M,W), track (outdoor) (M,W), track and field (M,W), track and field (indoor) (M,W), track and field (outdoor) (M,W). Member of Big East Conference, NCAA Division I.
**Intramural and club sports:** 50% of students participate. Intramural badminton, basketball, bowling, floor hockey, golf, inner-tube water polo, racquetball, soccer, softball, swimming, tennis, touch football, track, volleyball, water polo. Men's club aikido, badminton, cricket, fencing, frisbee, lacrosse, outdoor recreation, rugby, sailing, scuba, soccer, table tennis, volleyball. Women's club aikido, badminton, cricket, fencing, frisbee, lacrosse, outdoor recreation, rugby, sailing, scuba, soccer, table tennis, volleyball.

**ADMISSIONS. Academic basis for candidate selection** (in order of priority): Secondary school record, class rank, school's recommendation, standardized test scores, essay.
**Nonacademic basis for candidate selection:** Character and personality, extracurricular participation, particular talent or ability, geographical distribution, and alumni/ae relationship are important.
**Requirements:** Graduation from secondary school is required; GED is accepted. No specific distribution of secondary school units required. Applicants who have been awarded secondary school equivalency certificates or diplomas in accordance with home-state education policies are considered. Three ACH (English, chemistry, and math level II) required of applicants to dual-admission medical school program. (Program is for Florida residents only.) Audition required of music program applicants. SAT or ACT is required. PSAT is recommended. Off-campus interviews available with an admissions representative.
**Procedure:** Take SAT or ACT by fall of 12th year. Suggest filing application by November 15. Application deadline is March 1. Notification of admission no later than April 15 for applications completed by March 1. Reply is required by May 1. $200 nonrefundable tuition deposit. $200 nonrefundable enrollment deposit required. $150 room deposit, refundable until June 1. Freshmen accepted for terms other than fall.
**Special programs:** Admission may be deferred one year. Credit and/or placement may be granted through CEEB Advanced Placement exams for scores of 3 or higher. Credit and/or placement may be granted through CLEP general and subject exams. Early decision program. In fall 1993, 793 applied for early decision and 643 were accepted. Deadline for applying for early decision is November 1. Early entrance/early admission program. Concurrent enrollment program.
**Transfer students:** Transfer students accepted for terms other than fall. In fall 1993, 27% of all new students were transfers into all classes. 1,947 transfer applications were received, 1,240 were accepted. Application deadline is July 1 for fall; November 1 for spring. Minimum 2.5 GPA recommended. Lowest course grade accepted is "C." At least 45 semester hours must be completed at the university to receive degree.
**Admissions contact:** Edward M. Gillis, Assoc. Dean of Enrollment and Dir. of Admissions. 305 284-4323.

**FINANCIAL AID. Available aid:** Pell grants, SEOG, Federal Nursing Student Scholarships, state scholarships and grants, school scholarships and grants, private scholarships and grants, ROTC scholarships, academic merit scholarships, and athletic scholarships. Perkins Loans (NDSL), PLUS, Stafford Loans (GSL), school loans, private loans, and SLS. Guaranteed tuition. Monthly payment plan.
**Supporting data/closing dates:** FAFSA/FAF: Priority filing date is March 1; accepted on rolling basis. School's own aid application: Priority filing date is March 1; accepted on rolling basis. State aid form: Priority filing date is March 1. Notification of awards begins March 1.
**Financial aid contact:** Martin J. Carney, Director of Financial Aid. 305 284-5212.

**STUDENT EMPLOYMENT.** College Work/Study Program. Institutional employment. 33% of full-time undergraduates work on campus during school year. Students may expect to earn an average of $2,000 during school year. Off-campus part-time employment opportunities rated "good."

**COMPUTER FACILITIES.** 2,000 IBM/IBM-compatible and Macintosh/Apple microcomputers. Students may access Digital, IBM minicomputer/mainframe systems, BITNET, Internet. Residence halls may be equipped with stand-alone microcomputers, networked microcomputers, networked terminals, modems. Computer languages and software packages include BMDP, SAS, SOL. Computer facilities are available to all students.
**Fees:** None.
**Hours:** 24 hours (Tu-Sa); 2 PM-7 AM (Su-M).

**PROMINENT ALUMNI/AE.** Dante Fascell, U.S. congressman; Marvis Marvin, New York Metropolitan Opera; Bruce Hornsby, Grammy award winner; Jon Secada, Grammy award winner.

# University of South Florida

**Tampa, FL 33620** **813 974-2011**

**1994-95 Costs.** Tuition: $2,000 (state residents), $7,200 (out-of-state). Room: $1,806. Board: $1,900.
**Enrollment.** Undergraduates: 9,522 men, 12,148 women (full-time). Freshman class: 7,589 applicants, 4,676 accepted, 1,878 enrolled. Graduate enrollment: 2,538 men, 3,426 women.
**Test score averages/ranges.** Average SAT scores: 492 verbal, 553 math. Range of SAT scores of middle 50%: 430-550 verbal, 500-610 math. Average ACT scores: 23 composite. Range of ACT scores of middle 50%: 20-25 composite.
**Faculty.** 1,320 full-time; 184 part-time. 63% of faculty holds doctoral degree. Student/faculty ratio: 15 to 1.
**Selectivity rating.** Competitive.

**PROFILE.** The University of South Florida, founded in 1956, is a public, comprehensive university. Programs are offered through the Colleges of Arts and Sciences, Business, Education, Engineering, and Fine Arts. Its 1,700-acre campus is located 10 miles from the center of Tampa.

**Accreditation:** SACS. Professionally accredited by the Accreditation Board for Engineering and Technology, the Accrediting Council on Education in Journalism and Mass Communication, the American Assembly of Collegiate Schools of Business, the American Medical Association (CAHEA), the Council on Social Work Education, the National Association of Schools of Music, the National Council for Accreditation of Teacher Education, the National League for Nursing.
**Religious orientation:** University of South Florida is nonsectarian; no religious requirements.
**Library:** Collections totaling over 826,552 volumes, and 2,126,233 microform items.
**Special facilities/museums:** Art museum and galleries, planetarium.
**Athletic facilities:** Gymnasium, basketball and tennis courts, golf course, baseball, intramural, soccer, and softball fields, stadiums.

**STUDENT BODY. Undergraduate profile:** 89% are state residents; 54% are transfers. 4% Asian-American, 6% Black, 7% Hispanic, 81% White, 2% Other. Average age of undergraduates is 25.

**Freshman profile:** 2% of freshmen who took SAT scored 700 or over on verbal, 8% scored 700 or over on math; 14% scored 600 or over on verbal, 32% scored 600 or over on math; 48% scored 500 or over on verbal, 75% scored 500 or over on math; 87% scored 400 or over on verbal, 96% scored 400 or over on math; 99% scored 300 or over on verbal, 100% scored 300 or over on math. 8% of freshmen who took ACT scored 30 or over on composite; 44% scored 24 or over on composite; 92% scored 18 or over on composite; 100% scored 12 or over on composite. Majority of accepted applicants took SAT.

**Undergraduate achievement:** 36% of entering class graduated.

**Foreign students:** 382 students are from out of the country. Countries represented include China, France, France, India, Taiwan, and the United Kingdom; 88 in all.

**PROGRAMS OF STUDY. Degrees:** B.A., B.Eng.Tech., B.F.A., B.S., B.Secr.Sci., B.Soc.Work.

**Majors:** Accounting, African/Afro-American Studies, American Studies, Anthropology, Art Education, Art History, Biology, Biology Education, Botany, Botany Education, Business/Office Education, Chemical Engineering, Chemistry, Chemistry Education, Civil Engineering, Classics, Clinical Chemistry, Communication, Computer Engineering, Computer Science, Criminology, Dance/Ballet, Dance/Modern, Distributive/Marketing Education, Economics, Electrical Engineering, Elementary/Early Childhood Education, Elementary Education, Engineering, Engineering Science, English, English Education, Finance, Foreign Language Education, French, General Business Administration, Geography, Geology, German, Gerontology, History, Humanities, Humanities Education, Industrial Engineering, Industrial/Technical Education, Information Systems, Interdisciplinary Social Science, International Studies, Italian, Latin, Liberal Studies, Management, Management Information Systems, Marketing, Mass Communications, Mass Communications English Education, Mathematics, Mathematics Education, Mechanical Engineering, Medical Technology, Microbiology, Music Composition, Music Education, Music/Jazz Composition, Music/Jazz Performance, Music Performance, Music/Piano Pedagogy, Natural Sciences Interdisciplinary, Philosophy, Physical Education, Physics, Physics Education, Political Science, Psychology, Religious Studies, Russian, Social Science Education, Social Work, Sociology, Spanish, Special Education, Speech Communication English Education, Studio Art, Theatre Arts, Theatre Design, Theatre Performance, Women's Studies, Zoology, Zoology Education.

**Distribution of degrees:** The majors with the highest enrollment are elementary education, accounting, and finance; Afro-American studies, American studies, and botany have the lowest.

**Requirements:** General education requirement.

**Academic regulations:** Minimum 2.00 GPA must be maintained.

**Special:** Minors offered in many majors and in African and Asian studies, creative writing, English/American literature, Greek, human services, interdisciplinary studies, linguistics, and manual communications. Double majors. Independent study. Accelerated study. Pass/fail grading option. Internships. Cooperative education programs. Graduate school at which undergraduates may take graduate-level courses. Preprofessional programs in law, medicine, veterinary science, pharmacy, dentistry, optometry, osteopathy, physical therapy, and podiatry. Off-campus term offers opportunities for social action projects and independent research. Member of National Student Exchange (NSE) and International Student Exchange Program (ISEP). Education exchange program with U of Maine at Farmington. Teacher certification in early childhood, elementary, secondary, and special education. Certification in specific subject areas. Exchange program in Europe. Study abroad in England, Italy, and other countries. ROTC and AFROTC.

**Honors:** Honors program.

**Academic Assistance:** Nonremedial tutoring.

**STUDENT LIFE. Housing:** Students may live on or off campus. Coed, women's, and men's dorms. School-owned/operated apartments. Honor housing. 15% of students live in college housing.

**Social atmosphere:** USF is "very much a commuter school," reports the student newspaper. "There is not a whole lot of social/cultural life." Popular events include Homecoming, Bull Run, Black Emphasis Month, Women's Awareness Week, and Intercultural Week. Favorite off-campus spots include Kasey's Cove, Chili's, and Skipper's Smokehouse. On campus, students meet at The Empty Keg, Crescent Hill, and Martin Luther King Jr. Plaza.

**Services and counseling/handicapped student services:** Placement services. Health service. Day care. Counseling services for minority, military, veteran, and older students. Birth control, personal, and psychological counseling. Career and academic guidance services. Physically disabled student services. Learning disabled services. Notetaking services. Tape recorders. Tutors. Reader services for the blind.

**Campus organizations:** Undergraduate student government. Student newspaper (Oracle, published once/day). Literary magazine. Radio and TV stations. Economics Society, Math Education Club, Society of Women Engineers, Argos Events Council, Homecoming Steering Committee, service and political groups, athletic and departmental groups, special-interest groups, 300 organizations in all. 21 fraternities, two chapter houses; 11 sororities, no chapter houses. 5% of men join a fraternity. 5% of women join a sorority.

**Religious organizations:** Campus Ministry, Catholic Student Union, Christian Science group, Episcopal Center, Hillel, Navigators, Chapel Fellowship.

**Minority/foreign student organizations:** Black Student Union, Black Panhellenic Council, minority social sciences group, Minority Engineers, Hispanic Organization to Promote Education (HOPE). International Student Association, Intercultural Organization. Caribbean, Indian, Latin American, Pakistani, Thai, and Vietnamese student groups.

**ATHLETICS. Physical education requirements:** None.

**Intercollegiate competition:** 1% of students participate. Baseball (M), basketball (M,W), cheerleading (M,W), cross-country (M,W), golf (M,W), soccer (M), softball (W), tennis (M,W), track (indoor) (M,W), track (outdoor) (M,W), track and field (indoor) (M,W), track and field (outdoor) (M,W), volleyball (W). Member of Metro Conference, NCAA Division I, Sun Belt Conference.

**Intramural and club sports:** 3% of students participate. Intramural basketball, basketball jamboree, bowling, 5K run, flag football, floor hockey, golf, homerun hitting, punt/pass/kick, racquetball, soccer, softball, sports trivia bowl, swimming, tennis, track and field, ultimate frisbee, volleyball, wrestling. Men's club aikido, bicycle racing, bowling, chito ryu karate, cycling, frisbee, ice hockey, lacrosse, roller hockey, rugby, sailing/windsurfing, SCUBA, skydiving, surfing, tae kwon do, uechi ryu karate, shotokan karate, volleyball, wado kai karate, water skiing, weight training. Women's club aikido, bicycle racing, bowling, chito ryu karate, cycling, frisbee, ice hockey, lacrosse, roller hockey, rugby, sailing/windsurfing, SCUBA, skydiving, surfing, tae kwon do, uechi ryu karate, shotokan karate, volleyball, wado kai karate, water skiing, weight training.

**ADMISSIONS. Academic basis for candidate selection** (in order of priority): Secondary school record, standardized test scores, school's recommendation.

**Nonacademic basis for candidate selection:** Character and personality are important. Extracurricular participation and particular talent or ability are considered.

**Requirements:** Graduation from secondary school is required; GED is accepted. 19 units and the following program of study are required: 4 units of English, 3 units of math, 3 units of science including 2 units of lab, 2 units of foreign language, 3 units of social studies, 4 units of academic electives. Minimum combined SAT score of 900 and minimum 2.5 GPA required. Portfolio required of art program applicants. Audition required of music program applicants. Special services program for applicants not normally admissible. SAT or ACT is required. Campus visit recommended. No off-campus interviews.

**Procedure:** Take SAT or ACT by March of 12th year. Application deadline is June 1. Notification of admission on rolling basis. Freshmen accepted for terms other than fall.

**Special programs:** Credit may be granted through CEEB Advanced Placement for scores of 3 or higher. Credit may be granted through CLEP general and subject exams and military experience. Placement may be granted through challenge exams. Credit and placement may be granted through ACT PEP exams. Early entrance/early admission program. Concurrent enrollment program.

**Transfer students:** Transfer students accepted for terms other than fall. In fall 1993, 54% of all new students were transfers into all classes. 7,143 transfer applications were received, 5,639 were accepted. Application deadline is June 1 for fall; October 25 for spring. Minimum 2.0 GPA required. Lowest course grade accepted is "D." At least 30 semester hours must be completed at the university to receive degree.

**Admissions contact:** Vicki W. Ahrens, M.A., Director of Admissions. 813 974-3350.

**FINANCIAL AID. Available aid:** Pell grants, SEOG, state scholarships and grants, school scholarships and grants, private scholarships, ROTC scholarships, academic merit scholarships, and athletic scholarships. Perkins Loans (NDSL), PLUS, Stafford Loans (GSL), NSL, state loans, school loans, and SLS.

**Financial aid statistics:** 25% of aid is not need-based. In 1993-94, 65% of all undergraduate applicants received aid; 57% of freshman applicants. Average amounts of aid awarded freshmen: Scholarships and grants, $1,000; loans, $2,100.

**Supporting data/closing dates:** FAFSA: accepted on rolling basis. Notification of awards begins April 15.

**Financial aid contact:** Gwyn Francis, Director of Financial Aid. 813 974-4700.

**STUDENT EMPLOYMENT.** College Work/Study Program. Institutional employment. 25% of full-time undergraduates work on campus during school year. Students may expect to earn an average of $2,500 during school year. Off-campus part-time employment opportunities rated "excellent."

**COMPUTER FACILITIES.** IBM/IBM-compatible and Macintosh/Apple microcomputers. Students may access IBM minicomputer/mainframe systems. Computer facilities are available to all students.

**Fees:** None.

**Hours:** 24 hours for some computers.

**PROMINENT ALUMNI/AE.** Charles Olcott, former CEO, Burger King; John Cornell; president, Harris Corp.; Richard Rohn, chief economist, National Chamber of Commerce; Richard Oppel, editor in chief, *Charlotte Observer*; Tony LaRussa, manager, Oakland Athletics.

# University of Tampa

**Tampa, FL 33606** **813 253-3333**

**1993-94 Costs.** Tuition: $11,895. Room & board: $4,400. Fees, books, misc. academic expenses (school's estimate): $1,070.

**Enrollment.** Undergraduates: 740 men, 712 women (full-time). Freshman class: 1,600 applicants, 1,200 accepted, 305 enrolled.

**Test score averages/ranges.** Average SAT scores: 420 verbal, 471 math. Average ACT scores: 24 composite.

**Faculty.** 120 full-time; 62 part-time. 85% of faculty holds highest degree in specific field. Student/faculty ratio: 16 to 1.

**Selectivity rating.** Less competitive.

**PROFILE.** The University of Tampa, founded in 1931, is a private, comprehensive university. Programs are offered through the College of Business; the Departments of Aerospace Studies and Military Science; the Divisions of Economics and Business, Education, Fine Arts, Humanities, Nursing, Science and Mathematics, and Social Sciences; and the Graduate Program. Its 69-acre campus is located in central Tampa. Plant Hall, dating from 1891, is the campus landmark; it is a combination of Moorish, Turkish, Spanish, and American Victorian styles.

**Accreditation:** SACS. Professionally accredited by the National Association of Schools of Music, the National League for Nursing.

**Religious orientation:** University of Tampa is nonsectarian; no religious requirements.

**Library:** Collections totaling over 250,000 volumes, 1,883 periodical subscriptions, and 50,000 microform items.

**Special facilities/museums:** Victorian art and furniture museum, theatres, studios, music center, language lab, fully equipped research vessel for marine science.

**Athletic facilities:** Gymnasium, swimming pool, track, stadium, baseball, intramural, soccer, and softball fields, racquetball and tennis courts, aerobics and weight rooms.

**STUDENT BODY. Undergraduate profile:** 46% are state residents; 12% are transfers. 1% Asian-American, 3% Black, 6% Hispanic, 1% Native American, 78% White, 11% Other. Average age of undergraduates is 19.
**Freshman profile:** 95% of accepted applicants took SAT; 3% took ACT. 70% of freshmen come from public schools.
**Undergraduate achievement:** 70% of fall 1992 freshmen returned for fall 1993 term. 40% of entering class graduated.
**Foreign students:** 117 students are from out of the country. Countries represented include the Bahamas, Canada, the Cayman Islands, the Netherlands Antilles, the United Kingdom, and the Virgin Islands; 44 in all.

**PROGRAMS OF STUDY. Degrees:** B.A., B.F.A., B.Mus., B.S., B.S.Nurs.
**Majors:** Accounting, Art, Banking/Finance, Biochemistry, Biology, Business Administration/Management, Chemistry, Communications, Computer/Information Sciences, Criminology, Economics, Education, English, French, History, International Business, International Studies, Marine Science, Marketing, Mathematics, Medical Technology, Music, Nursing, Philosophy, Physical Education, Political Science/Government, Psychology, Social Sciences, Social Work, Spanish, Writing.
**Distribution of degrees:** The majors with the highest enrollment are business management, communications, and psychology.
**Requirements:** General education requirement.
**Academic regulations:** Freshmen must maintain minimum 1.6 GPA; sophomores, juniors, seniors, 2.0 GPA.
**Special:** Minors offered in aerospace studies, art history, dance, recreation, religious studies, speech/drama, sports management, and women's studies. English majors take comprehensive exam. Social work majors take practicum in senior year. Medical technology students work 15 months at any approved lab or hospital and must earn six semester hours during summer following completion of program. Nursing major is for upper division only. Associate's degrees offered. Independent study. Pass/fail grading option. Internships. Preprofessional programs in law, medicine, veterinary science, dentistry, and engineering. Washington Semester. Teacher certification in secondary education. Study abroad possible. ROTC. AFROTC at U of South Florida.
**Honors:** Honors program.
**Academic Assistance:** Remedial reading, writing, math, and study skills.

**STUDENT LIFE. Housing:** Students may live on or off campus. Coed, women's, and men's dorms. School-owned/operated apartments. 60% of students live in college housing.
**Social atmosphere:** Social life on campus is dominated by a variety of distinct crowds, including Greeks, Long Islanders, and "an influential crowd of progressives and socialites," according to the student newspaper. On campus, students meet in the lobby of Plant Hall and the Rat; Hyde Park shops, Gio's Club, the Masquerade, and Club 911 are favorite off-campus hangouts. Tampa boasts some "excellent post-mod clubs." Popular social events include Harold's Club's Semiformal Casino Night, Homecoming in February, the Gasparilla Parade, and the President's Cup Regatta.
**Services and counseling/handicapped student services:** Placement services. Health service. Counseling services for minority, military, veteran, and older students. Birth control, personal, and psychological counseling. Career and academic guidance services. Religious counseling. Physically disabled student services. Learning disabled services. Notetaking services.
**Campus organizations:** Undergraduate student government. Student newspaper (Minaret, published once/week). Literary magazine. Yearbook. Radio station. Community choir, general chorus, concert chorus, orchestra, band, lab theatre, film society, poetry review, participation in state opera, university Diplomats and Hosts, accounting club, special-interest groups, 52 organizations in all. Five fraternities, one chapter house; three sororities, no chapter houses. 7% of men join a fraternity. 7% of women join a sorority.
**Religious organizations:** Baptist Ministry, Hillel, Newman Club.
**Minority/foreign student organizations:** Association of Minority Collegiates. International Student Organization.

**ATHLETICS. Physical education requirements:** None.
**Intercollegiate competition:** 20% of students participate. Baseball (M), basketball (M,W), cheerleading (M,W), crew (M,W), cross-country (M,W), golf (M), soccer (M), softball (W), swimming (M,W), tennis (M,W), volleyball (W). Member of NCAA Division II, Sunshine State Conference.
**Intramural and club sports:** 20% of students participate. Intramural basketball, football, golf, karate, softball, tennis, volleyball.

**ADMISSIONS. Academic basis for candidate selection** (in order of priority): Secondary school record, class rank, school's recommendation, standardized test scores, essay.
**Nonacademic basis for candidate selection:** Extracurricular participation is emphasized. Particular talent or ability is important. Character and personality and alumni/ae relationship are considered.
**Requirements:** Graduation from secondary school is required; GED is accepted. 15 units and the following program of study are required: 4 units of English, 2 units of math, 2 units of lab science, 2 units of social studies, 5 units of academic electives. Portfolio required of art program applicants. Audition required of music program applicants. R.N. required of nursing program applicants. Conditional admission possible for applicants not meeting standard requirements. Academic Skills Program for applicants not meeting standard requirements. SAT or ACT is required. Campus visit and interview recommended. Off-campus interviews available with admissions and alumni representatives.
**Procedure:** Suggest filing application by December 31. Notification of admission on rolling basis. $200 tuition deposit, refundable until May 1. $200 nonrefundable room deposit. Freshmen accepted for terms other than fall.
**Special programs:** Admission may be deferred one year. Credit and/or placement may be granted through CEEB Advanced Placement exams for scores of 3 or higher. Credit and/or placement may be granted through CLEP general and subject exams. Credit and placement may be granted through DANTES exams and military and life experience. Early decision program. Early entrance/early admission program.
**Transfer students:** Transfer students accepted for terms other than fall. In fall 1993, 12% of all new students were transfers into all classes. 478 transfer applications were received, 406 were accepted. Application deadline is rolling for fall; rolling for spring. Minimum 2.0 GPA required. Lowest course grade accepted is "C." At least 31 semester hours must be completed at the university to receive degree.
**Admissions contact:** Ronald J. Ingersoll, Ph.D., Vice President for Enrollment. 813 253-6228.

**FINANCIAL AID. Available aid:** Pell grants, SEOG, state scholarships and grants, school scholarships and grants, private scholarships and grants, ROTC scholarships, academic merit scholarships, and athletic scholarships. Perkins Loans (NDSL), PLUS, Stafford Loans (GSL), school loans, and SLS. University payment plan.
**Financial aid statistics:** 60% of aid is not need-based. In 1993-94, 80% of all undergraduate applicants received aid; 82% of freshman applicants. Average amounts of aid awarded freshmen: Scholarships and grants, $4,000; loans, $2,000.
**Supporting data/closing dates:** FAFSA/FAF/FFS: Priority filing date is March 15; accepted on rolling basis. State aid form: Priority filing date is April 15. Notification of awards on rolling basis.
**Financial aid contact:** Thomas J. Judge, M.A., Director of Financial Aid. 813 253-6219.

**STUDENT EMPLOYMENT.** College Work/Study Program. Institutional employment. 50% of full-time undergraduates work on campus during school year. Students may expect to earn an average of $1,200 during school year. Off-campus part-time employment opportunities rated "good."

**COMPUTER FACILITIES.** 110 IBM/IBM-compatible and Macintosh/Apple microcomputers; 91 are networked. Students may access Digital, NCR minicomputer/mainframe systems. Computer languages and software packages include BASIC, C, COBOL, FORTRAN. Computer facilities are available to all students.
**Fees:** None.
**Hours:** 8 AM-10 PM.

**PROMINENT ALUMNI/AE.** Robert Martinez, governor of Florida; Freddie Solomon, wide receiver of San Francisco '49ers.

# University of West Florida

**Pensacola, FL 32514-5750** **904 474-2000**

**1993-94 Costs.** Tuition: $1,702 (state residents), $6,604 (out-of-state). Room & board: $2,960. Fees, books, misc. academic expenses (school's estimate): $523.
**Enrollment.** Undergraduates: 1,654 men, 2,147 women (full-time). Freshman class: 1,558 applicants, 1,254 accepted, 472 enrolled. Graduate enrollment: 533 men, 628 women.
**Test score averages/ranges.** Average SAT scores: 465 verbal, 526 math. Average ACT scores: 23 English, 22 math, 23 composite.
**Faculty.** 221 full-time. 81% of faculty holds doctoral degree. Student/faculty ratio: 26 to 1.
**Selectivity rating.** Less competitive.

**PROFILE.** The University of West Florida, founded in 1963, is a public institution. Its 1,000-acre campus is located in Pensacola, 60 miles from Mobile, Ala.

**Accreditation:** SACS. Professionally accredited by the Accrediting Council on Education in Journalism and Mass Communication, the Council on Social Work Education, the National Association of Schools of Music, the National League for Nursing.
**Religious orientation:** University of West Florida is nonsectarian; no religious requirements.
**Library:** Collections totaling over 539,995 volumes, 3,409 periodical subscriptions, and 998,091 microform items.
**Special facilities/museums:** Instructional media center, biology, chemistry, physics, and psychology labs, property on the Gulf of Mexico for marine and ecology research.
**Athletic facilities:** Swimming pool, baseball, football, soccer, and softball fields, track, racquetball and tennis courts, aerobics, dance, martial arts, and weight rooms, cross-country and fitness trails, gymnasium, canoes, sailboats, water skiing facilities.

**STUDENT BODY. Undergraduate profile:** 98% are state residents; 39% are transfers. 3.1% Asian-American, 6.4% Black, 2.2% Hispanic, .7% Native American, 86.3% White, 1.3% Other. Average age of undergraduates is 23.
**Freshman profile:** 42% of accepted applicants took SAT; 78% took ACT. 90% of freshmen come from public schools.
**Undergraduate achievement:** 80% of fall 1992 freshmen returned for fall 1993 term. 19% of entering class graduated.
**Foreign students:** 88 students are from out of the country. Countries represented include Canada, Taiwan, and the United Kingdom; 35 in all.

**PROGRAMS OF STUDY. Degrees:** B.A., B.F.A., B.S., B.S.Bus.Admin., B.S.Nurs.
**Majors:** Accounting, Anthropology, Art Education, Art History/Appreciation, Art Studio, Biology, Biology Education, Building Construction, Business Teacher Education, Chemistry, Chemistry Education, Communication, Communication Arts Education, Computer Science, Criminal Justice, Early Childhood Education, Economics, Electrical Engineering Technology, Elementary Education, English, English Education, Environmental Resource Management/Planning, Finance, Fine Arts, French, French Education, Health Education, History, History Education, Humanities, Industrial Technology, International Studies, Legal Administration, Management, Management Information Systems, Marine Biology, Marketing, Mathematics, Mathematics Education, Medical Technology, Middle/Junior High School Education, Music, Music Education, Nursing, Philosophy, Physical Education, Physics, Physics Education, Political Science Education, Political Science/Government, Psychology, Religious Studies, Sciences, Social Sciences, Social Work, Sociology, Spanish, Spanish Education, Special Education, Special Education/Mentally Handicapped, Systems Science, Theatre, Trade/Industrial Education.
**Distribution of degrees:** The majors with the highest enrollment are elementary education, psychology, and accounting; physics, French, and religious studies have the lowest.
**Requirements:** General education requirement.
**Academic regulations:** Minimum 2.00 GPA must be maintained.

**Special:** Minors offered in many majors and in several other fields. Associate's degrees offered. Independent study. Pass/fail grading option. Internships. Cooperative education programs. Graduate school at which undergraduates may take graduate-level courses. Preprofessional programs in law, medicine, veterinary science, pharmacy, and dentistry. 3-2 engineering programs with Florida State U and Florida A&M U. Teacher certification in early childhood, elementary, secondary, special education, and vo-tech education. Certification in specific subject areas. Exchange program abroad in Ireland (University Coll). Study abroad also in Japan and Norway. ROTC.
**Honors:** Honors program. Honor societies.
**Academic Assistance:** Remedial reading, writing, and math.

**STUDENT LIFE. Housing:** Students may live on or off campus. Coed and women's dorms. Sorority housing. School-owned/operated apartments. On-campus married-student housing. 9% of students live in college housing.
**Social atmosphere:** According to the student newspaper, "We are an older-student college, but with recent addition of lower-division undergraduates, the average age of students is dropping rapidly. We provide a high quality of cultural events which is enhanced by the community cultural events." Popular gathering spots include the Great Hall, the Rathskellar, Macguire's Irish Pub, and Trader John's. Greek and athletic organizations are influential on campus. Favorite events during the year are Homecoming, Greek Rush, and the comedian series.
**Services and counseling/handicapped student services:** Placement services. Day care. Counseling services for minority, veteran, and older students. Personal and psychological counseling. Career and academic guidance services. Religious counseling. Physically disabled student services. Learning disabled services. Notetaking services. Tutors.
**Campus organizations:** Undergraduate student government. Student newspaper (Voyager, published once/week). Literary magazine. Radio station. Band, chorale, dance, outing, and sports clubs, Young Democrats, College Republicans, departmental clubs, Education Student Association, Medieval Society, professional organizations, 108 organizations in all. Six fraternities, one chapter house; five sororities, no chapter houses. 5% of men join a fraternity. 5% of women join a sorority.
**Religious organizations:** Baptist Student Union, Catholic Campus Ministries, Christians in Action, Jewish Campus Community, Muslim Student Association, Wesley Foundation.
**Minority/foreign student organizations:** Alpha Kappa Alpha, Alpha Phi Alpha, Delta Sigma Theta, Black Student Union. International Club, Chinese Student Association, Spanish-American Student Association.

**ATHLETICS. Physical education requirements:** 60 credit hours of physical education required.
**Intercollegiate competition:** 3% of students participate. Baseball (M), basketball (M,W), cheerleading (W), cross-country (M,W), golf (M), soccer (M,W), softball (W), tennis (M,W). Member of Gulf South Conference, NAIA, NCAA II, Southern States.
**Intramural and club sports:** 6% of students participate. Intramural badminton, bowling, flag football, handball, melonball, pickleball, racquetball, softball, tennis, volleyball. Men's club canoe/kayak, cross-country, fencing, football, martial arts, racquetball, sailing, soccer, swimming, volleyball, water skiing. Women's club canoe/kayak, cheerleading, cross-country, fencing, football, martial arts, racquetball, sailing, swimming, volleyball, water skiing.

**ADMISSIONS. Academic basis for candidate selection** (in order of priority): Secondary school record, standardized test scores, class rank, school's recommendation.
**Nonacademic basis for candidate selection:** Extracurricular participation and particular talent or ability are important. Character and personality and alumni/ae relationship are considered.
**Requirements:** Graduation from secondary school is required; GED is accepted. 19 units and the following program of study are required: 4 units of English, 3 units of math, 3 units of science including 2 units of lab, 2 units of foreign language, 3 units of social studies, 4 units of electives. Social studies requirement may include units in history, civics, political science, economics, sociology, psychology, or geography. Minimum combined SAT score of 900 (composite ACT score of 19) and minimum 3.0 GPA required. Portfolio required of art program applicants. Audition required of music program applicants. R.N. required of nursing program applicants. Conditional admission possible for applicants not meeting standard requirements. SAT or ACT is required. Campus visit recommended.
**Procedure:** Take SAT or ACT by December of 12th year. Application deadline is June 1. Notification of admission on rolling basis. Freshmen accepted for terms other than fall.
**Special programs:** Credit may be granted through CEEB Advanced Placement for scores of 3 or higher. Credit may be granted through CLEP general and subject exams, ACT PEP, DANTES, and challenge exams, and military experience. Early entrance/early admission program. Concurrent enrollment program.
**Transfer students:** Transfer students accepted for terms other than fall. In fall 1993, 39% of all new students were transfers into all classes. 1,061 transfer applications were received, 972 were accepted. Application deadline is June 1 for fall; November 15 for spring. Minimum 2.0 GPA required. Lowest course grade accepted is "D." Maximum number of transferable credits is 60 semester hours. At least 60 semester hours must be completed at the university to receive degree.
**Admissions contact:** Peter F. Metarko, Ph.D., Director of Enrollment Services. 904 474-2230.

**FINANCIAL AID. Available aid:** Pell grants, SEOG, state scholarships and grants, school scholarships and grants, private scholarships and grants, ROTC scholarships, academic merit scholarships, and athletic scholarships. Perkins Loans (NDSL), PLUS, Stafford Loans (GSL), and school loans.
**Financial aid statistics:** In 1993-94, 40% of all undergraduate applicants received aid; 30% of freshman applicants. Average amounts of aid awarded freshmen: Scholarships and grants, $750; loans, $3,800.
**Supporting data/closing dates:** FAFSA/FAF/FFS: Priority filing date is April 1; accepted on rolling basis. School's own aid application: Priority filing date is April 1. State aid form: Priority filing date is April 15. Income tax forms: Priority filing date is April 1. Notification of awards on rolling basis.
**Financial aid contact:** C.R. Bennett, Ph.D., Director of Financial Aid. 904 474-2398.

**STUDENT EMPLOYMENT.** College Work/Study Program. Institutional employment. Off-campus part-time employment opportunities rated "good."

**COMPUTER FACILITIES.** 750 IBM/IBM-compatible and Macintosh/Apple microcomputers; 300 are networked. Students may access IBM, SUN minicomputer/mainframe systems, BITNET. Client/LAN operating systems include Apple/Macintosh, DOS, OS/2, UNIX/XENIX/AIX, LocalTalk/AppleTalk, Novell. Computer languages and software packages include Ada, BASIC, COBOL, FORTRAN, SAS, SPSS; 20 in all. Computer facilities are available to all students.
**Fees:** None.
**Hours:** 24 hours.

**PROMINENT ALUMNI/AE.** Col. James F. Buchli, astronaut, part of 1989 Shuttle Discovery crew; Steve Bultman, 1992 U.S. Olympic Swim Team coach; Lacey Collier, U.S. District judge.

# Warner Southern College

**Lake Wales, FL 33853** **813 638-1426**

**1993-94 Costs.** Tuition: $6,100. Room: $1,500. Board: $1,770. Fees, books, misc. academic expenses (school's estimate): $1,250.
**Enrollment.** Undergraduates: 227 men, 242 women (full-time). Freshman class: 249 applicants, 191 accepted, 72 enrolled.
**Test score averages/ranges.** Average SAT scores: 795 combined. Range of SAT scores of middle 50%: 690-950 combined. Average ACT scores: 20 composite. Range of ACT scores of middle 50%: 17-23 composite.
**Faculty.** 19 full-time; 38 part-time. 53% of faculty holds doctoral degree. Student/faculty ratio: 11 to 1.
**Selectivity rating.** Less competitive.

**PROFILE.** Warner Southern, founded in 1967, is church-affiliated college. Its 380-acre campus is located in Lake Wales, 50 miles south of Orlando.

**Accreditation:** SACS.
**Religious orientation:** Warner Southern College is affiliated with the Church of God (Anderson, Ind.); four semesters of religion required.
**Library:** Collections totaling over 74,000 volumes, 314 periodical subscriptions, and 6,758 microform items.
**Special facilities/museums:** Archives, computer lab, curriculum lab.
**Athletic facilities:** Gymnasium, fitness center, tennis courts, soccer field.

**STUDENT BODY. Undergraduate profile:** 89% are state residents; 66% are transfers. 11% Black, 5% Hispanic, 82% White, 2% Non-Resident.
**Freshman profile:** 71% of accepted applicants took SAT; 41% took ACT. 77% of freshmen come from public schools.
**Undergraduate achievement:** 48% of fall 1992 freshmen returned for fall 1993 term. 21% of entering class graduated. 30% of students who completed a degree program went on to graduate study within five years.
**Foreign students:** Five students are from out of the country. Countries represented include Bermuda, Grand Cayman Island, Jamaica, Japan, and Trinidad.

**PROGRAMS OF STUDY. Degrees:** B.A.
**Majors:** Accounting, Business Administration, Church Ministries/Biblical Studies, Church Ministries/Missions, Church Ministries/Music, Church Ministries/Pastoral Ministry, Church Ministries/Youth Ministry, Communication/English, Elementary Education, Exercise Science, Music Education, Organizational Management, Physical Education, Psychology, Secondary Education/Biology, Secondary Education/English, Social Work, Sport/Leisure Management.
**Distribution of degrees:** The majors with the highest enrollment are organizational management, elementary education, and business administration; music education, communications, and science education have the lowest.
**Requirements:** General education requirement.
**Academic regulations:** Minimum 2.0 GPA must be maintained.
**Special:** Optional minors offered in biblical studies, biology, business, Christian education, communication, English, missions, music, pastoral ministries, and physical education and recreation. Associate's degrees offered. Double majors. Internships. Los Angeles Film Study (California). Teacher certification in elementary and secondary education. Certification in specific subject areas.
**Honors:** Honor societies.
**Academic Assistance:** Remedial reading, writing, math, and study skills. Nonremedial tutoring.

**ADMISSIONS. Academic basis for candidate selection** (in order of priority): Secondary school record, class rank, standardized test scores, school's recommendation, essay.
**Nonacademic basis for candidate selection:** Character and personality are important. Extracurricular participation and particular talent or ability are considered.
**Requirements:** Graduation from secondary school is required; GED is accepted. 18 units and the following program of study are recommended: 4 units of English, 3 units of math, 3 units of science, 2 units of foreign language, 3 units of social studies, 3 units of history. Minimum composite ACT score of 18 (combined SAT score of 720), rank in upper two-fifths of secondary school class, and 2.25 GPA required. Provisional Admission. ACT is required; SAT may be substituted. Campus visit and interview recommended. Off-campus interviews available with admissions and alumni representatives.
**Procedure:** Take SAT or ACT by March 2 of 12th year. Visit college for interview by March 2 of 12th year. Application deadline is August 15. Notification of admission on rolling basis. $50 nonrefundable tuition deposit. $50 nonrefundable room deposit. Freshmen accepted for terms other than fall.
**Special programs:** Admission may be deferred one year. Credit may be granted through CEEB Advanced Placement for scores of 3 or higher. Credit may be granted through CLEP general and subject exams, military and life experience. Early entrance/early admission program. Concurrent enrollment program.
**Transfer students:** Transfer students accepted for terms other than fall. In fall 1993, 66% of all new students were transfers into all classes. 149 transfer applications were received, 89 were accepted. Application deadline is rolling for fall; rolling for spring. Minimum 2.0

GPA required. Lowest course grade accepted is "C." At least 32 semester hours must be completed at the college to receive degree.
**Admissions contact:** Valerie S. Rutland, Director of Enrollment Management. 813 638-2109.

**FINANCIAL AID. Available aid:** Pell grants, SEOG, state scholarships and grants, school scholarships and grants, private scholarships and grants, and athletic scholarships. Perkins Loans (NDSL), PLUS, Stafford Loans (GSL), state loans, and school loans.
**Financial aid statistics:** Average amounts of aid awarded freshmen: Scholarships and grants, $825; loans, $1,452.
**Supporting data/closing dates:** FAFSA/FAF/FFS: Accepted on rolling basis. School's own aid application: Accepted on rolling basis. State aid form: Priority filing date is April 1. Income tax forms: Accepted on rolling basis. Notification of awards on rolling basis.
**Financial aid contact:** Jean Fitterling, Associate Director of Financial Aid. 813 638-1426, ext. 205.

# Webber College

**Babson Park, FL 33827 — 813 638-1431**

**1994-95 Costs.** Tuition: $5,790. Room: $990. Board: $1,930. Fees, books, misc. academic expenses (school's estimate): $500.
**Enrollment.** Undergraduates: 149 men, 172 women (full-time). Freshman class: 383 applicants, 256 accepted, 157 enrolled.
**Test score averages/ranges.** Average SAT scores: 374 verbal, 454 math. Range of SAT scores of middle 50%: 350-450 verbal, 375-475 math. Average ACT scores: 18 composite. Range of ACT scores of middle 50%: 17-19 composite.
**Faculty.** 19 full-time; 13 part-time. 47% of faculty holds doctoral degree. Student/faculty ratio: 13 to 1.
**Selectivity rating.** Less competitive.

**PROFILE.** Webber is a private college of business. Founded as a college for women in 1927, it adopted coeducation in 1971. Its 110-acre campus is located in Babson Park, 60 miles southwest of Orlando.

**Accreditation:** SACS.
**Religious orientation:** Webber College is nonsectarian; no religious requirements.
**Library:** Collections totaling over 35,000 volumes, 148 periodical subscriptions, and 16,424 microform items.
**Special facilities/museums:** Antique clothing collection.
**Athletic facilities:** Gymnasiums, tennis courts, swimming pool, weight room, soccer and softball fields, lake, horseshoe pits, outdoor volleyball courts.
**STUDENT BODY. Undergraduate profile:** 67% are state residents; 38% are transfers. 1% Asian-American, 11% Black, 4% Hispanic, 69% White, 15% Other. Average age of undergraduates is 22.
**Freshman profile:** 2% of freshmen who took SAT scored 600 or over on verbal, 2% scored 600 or over on math; 15% scored 500 or over on verbal, 17% scored 500 or over on math; 54% scored 400 or over on verbal, 60% scored 400 or over on math; 98% scored 300 or over on verbal, 98% scored 300 or over on math. 67% of accepted applicants took SAT; 11% took ACT. 87% of freshmen come from public schools.
**Undergraduate achievement:** 72% of fall 1992 freshmen returned for fall 1993 term. 42% of entering class graduated. 12% of students who completed a degree program went on to graduate study within one year.
**Foreign students:** 27 students are from out of the country. Countries represented include Bulgaria, Curacao, Germany, India, Japan, and Sweden; 22 in all.
**PROGRAMS OF STUDY. Degrees:** B.Bus.Admin., B.S.
**Majors:** Accounting, Business Management, Club/Recreation Management, Finance, Hotel/Restaurant Management, International Travel/Tourism, Marketing, Retail Management.
**Distribution of degrees:** The major with the highest enrollment is business management.
**Requirements:** General education requirement.
**Academic regulations:** Freshmen must maintain minimum 1.85 GPA; sophomores, 1.97 GPA; juniors, 2.00 GPA; seniors, 2.00 GPA.
**Special:** Associate's degrees offered. Double majors. Internships. 2-2 programs. Study abroad in Spain and the United Kingdom.
**Honors:** Honor societies.
**Academic Assistance:** Remedial reading, writing, math, and study skills. Nonremedial tutoring.

**ADMISSIONS. Academic basis for candidate selection** (in order of priority): Secondary school record, standardized test scores, school's recommendation, essay, class rank.
**Nonacademic basis for candidate selection:** Character and personality are emphasized. Extracurricular participation and alumni/ae relationship are considered.
**Requirements:** Graduation from secondary school is required; GED is accepted. 16 units and the following program of study are recommended: 4 units of English, 4 units of math, 3 units of science. Minimum combined SAT score of 800 (composite ACT score of 17), rank in top half of secondary class, and minimum 2.0 GPA required. Conditional admission possible for applicants not meeting standard requirements. SAT or ACT is required. Campus visit and interview recommended. Off-campus interviews available with an admissions representative.
**Procedure:** Take SAT or ACT by June of 12th year. Visit college for interview by July of 12th year. Suggest filing application by July 15. Application deadline is August 15. Notification of admission on rolling basis. Reply is required by August 1. $150 tuition deposit, refundable until August 1. $200 room deposit, refundable until August 1. Freshmen accepted for terms other than fall.
**Special programs:** Admission may be deferred one year. Credit may be granted through CEEB Advanced Placement for scores of 3 or higher. Credit and/or placement may be granted through CLEP general and subject exams. Credit may be granted through Regents College and DANTES exams. Credit and placement may be granted through challenge exams and military experience. Early decision program. In fall 1993, 15 applied for early decision and eight were accepted. Deadline for applying for early decision is December 1. Early entrance/early admission program. Concurrent enrollment program.
**Transfer students:** Transfer students accepted for terms other than fall. In fall 1993, 38% of all new students were transfers into all classes. 90 transfer applications were received, 86 were accepted. Application deadline is August 15 for fall; December 20 for spring. Minimum 2.0 GPA required. Lowest course grade accepted is "C." Maximum number of transferable credits is 62 credits from a two-year school and 90 credits from a four-year school. At least 30 credits must be completed at the college to receive degree.
**Admissions contact:** Deborah Milliken, D.M.D., Dean of Student Development. 813 638-2910.

**FINANCIAL AID. Available aid:** Pell grants, SEOG, state scholarships and grants, school scholarships, private scholarships and grants, academic merit scholarships, and athletic scholarships. Perkins Loans (NDSL), PLUS, Stafford Loans (GSL), and SLS. AMS, deferred payment plan, and family tuition reduction.
**Financial aid statistics:** 36% of aid is not need-based. In 1993-94, 85% of all undergraduate applicants received aid; 80% of freshman applicants. Average amounts of aid awarded freshmen: Scholarships and grants, $1,100; loans, $1,200.
**Supporting data/closing dates:** FAFSA: Priority filing date is April 1; accepted on rolling basis. School's own aid application: Priority filing date is April 1; accepted on rolling basis. State aid form: Priority filing date is April 1; deadline is April 15. Income tax forms: Priority filing date is April 1; accepted on rolling basis. Notification of awards begins May 15.
**Financial aid contact:** Kathleen Wilson, Registrar and Director of Financial Aid. 813 638-1431, extension 30.

# Georgia

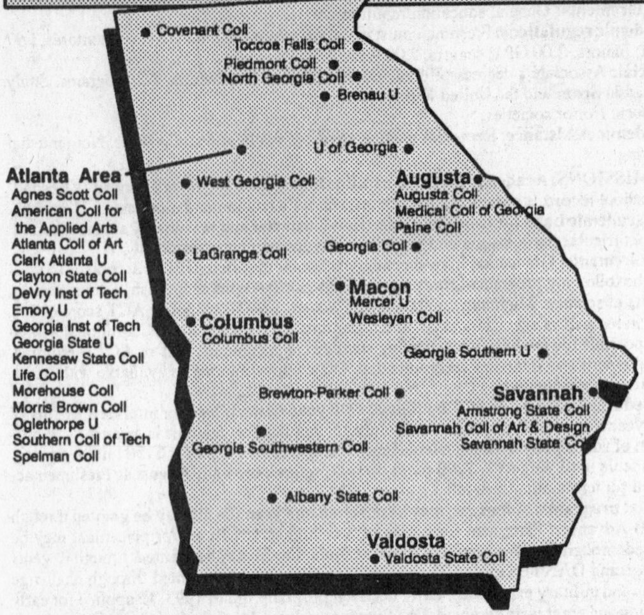


## Agnes Scott College

**Decatur, GA 30030** **404 638-6000**

**1994-95 Costs.** Tuition: $12,960. Room & board: $5,450. Fees, books, misc. academic expenses (school's estimate): $485.
**Enrollment.** 510 women (full-time). Freshman class: 417 applicants, 349 accepted, 137 enrolled. Graduate enrollment: 3 men, 24 women.
**Test score averages/ranges.** Range of SAT scores of middle 50%: 470-600 verbal, 490-610 math.
**Faculty.** 66 full-time; 16 part-time. 97% of faculty holds highest degree in specific field. Student/faculty ratio: 8 to 1.
**Selectivity rating.** More competitive.

**PROFILE.** Agnes Scott, founded in 1889, is a church-affiliated, liberal arts college for women. Its 100-acre campus is located in Decatur, six miles from Atlanta. Campus buildings are Gothic and Victorian in style.

**Accreditation:** SACS.
**Religious orientation:** Agnes Scott College is affiliated with the Presbyterian Church USA; one semester of religion/theology or philosophy required.
**Library:** Collections totaling over 191,325 volumes, 816 periodical subscriptions, and 24,000 microform items.
**Special facilities/museums:** Art galleries, collaborative learning center, language lab, electron microscope, observatory, 30-inch Beck telescope in dark-sky viewing site, interactive learning center.
**Athletic facilities:** Gymnasium, swimming pool, Nautilus, basketball, racquetball, tennis, and volleyball courts, track, soccer field.
**STUDENT BODY. Undergraduate profile:** 51% are state residents; 7% are transfers. 2% Asian-American, 12% Black, 3% Hispanic, 76% White, 7% Other. Average age of undergraduates is 21.
**Freshman profile:** 94% of accepted applicants took SAT; 6% took ACT. 87% of freshmen come from public schools.
**Undergraduate achievement:** 71% of fall 1992 freshmen returned for fall 1993 term. 51% of entering class graduated. 35% of students who completed a degree program immediately went on to graduate study.
**Foreign students:** 17 students are from out of the country. Countries represented include the Dominican Republic, Germany, and Japan; 12 in all.
**PROGRAMS OF STUDY. Degrees:** B.A.
**Majors:** Art, Art History/English Literature, Art History/History, Art/Psychology, Astrophysics, Bible/Religion, Biology, Biology/Psychology, Chemistry, Classical Languages/Literature, Classical Studies, Economics, Economics/Business, English, English Literature/Creative Writing, French, German, Greek, History, History/English Literature, International Relations, Latin, Latin American Studies, Mathematics, Mathematics/Economics, Mathematics/Physics, Music, Philosophy, Physics, Political Science, Psychology, Sociology, Sociology/Anthropology, Spanish, Theatre.
**Distribution of degrees:** The majors with the highest enrollment are English, psychology, and economics; Latin American studies, Greek, and Latin have the lowest.
**Requirements:** General education requirement.
**Academic regulations:** Freshmen must maintain minimum 1.5 GPA; sophomores, 1.75 GPA; juniors, 1.91 GPA; seniors, 2.0 GPA.
**Special:** Minors offered in most majors and in dance, studio art, and women's studies. Self-designed majors. Double majors. Dual degrees. Independent study. Accelerated study. Pass/fail grading option. Internships. Graduate school at which undergraduates may take graduate-level courses. Preprofessional programs in law, medicine, veterinary science, and dentistry. 3-2 biotechnology, engineering, information/computer sciences, industrial management, and management science programs with Georgia Tech. 3-4 architecture and art programs with Washington U. Member of University Center (Georgia) and Public Leadership Education Network (PLEN). Washington Semester and UN Semester. PLEN Public Policy Semester. Exchange program with Mills Coll. Teacher certification in early childhood, elementary, and secondary education. Certification in specific subject areas. Exchange programs abroad in France (U Catholique de L'Ouest), Germany (Johannes Gutenberg U Mainz), and Japan (Kinjo Gakuin). Study abroad also in the Republic of Georgia, Japan, Russia, and South Africa. NROTC and AFROTC at Georgia Tech.
**Honors:** Phi Beta Kappa. Honor societies.
**Academic Assistance:** Nonremedial tutoring.
**ADMISSIONS. Academic basis for candidate selection** (in order of priority): Secondary school record, class rank, standardized test scores, school's recommendation, essay.
**Nonacademic basis for candidate selection:** Character and personality, extracurricular participation, and particular talent or ability are important.
**Requirements:** Graduation from secondary school is required; GED is accepted. 16 units and the following program of study are recommended: 4 units of English, 3 units of math, 1 unit of lab science, 2 units of foreign language, 1 unit of social studies. Rank in top third of secondary school class recommended. SAT or ACT is required. ACH recommended. Campus visit and interview recommended. Off-campus interviews available with admissions and alumni representatives.
**Procedure:** Take SAT or ACT by January of 12th year. Take ACH by January of 12th year. Suggest filing application by March 1; no deadline. Acceptance notification on a rolling basis beginning March 1. Reply is required by May 1. $250 tuition deposit, refundable until May 1. Freshmen accepted for terms other than fall.
**Special programs:** Admission may be deferred one year. Credit and/or placement may be granted through CEEB Advanced Placement exams for scores of 4 or higher. Early decision program. In fall 1993, 34 applied for early decision and 29 were accepted. Deadline for applying for early decision is November 15. Early entrance/early admission program. Concurrent enrollment program.
**Transfer students:** Transfer students accepted for terms other than fall. In fall 1993, 7% of all new students were transfers into all classes. 44 transfer applications were received, 28 were accepted. Application deadline is rolling for fall; rolling for spring. Minimum 2.5 GPA recommended. Lowest course grade accepted is "C." At least 60 semester hours must be completed at the college to receive degree.
**Admissions contact:** Jenifer Cooper, Director of Admission. 404 371-6285.
**FINANCIAL AID. Available aid:** Pell grants, SEOG, state scholarships and grants, school scholarships and grants, private scholarships, academic merit scholarships, and aid for undergraduate foreign students. PLUS, Stafford Loans (GSL), school loans, and SLS. Knight Tuition Plans.
**Financial aid statistics:** 46% of aid is not need-based. In 1993-94, 100% of all undergraduate applicants received aid. Average amounts of aid awarded freshmen: Scholarships and grants, $8,581; loans, $2,625.
**Supporting data/closing dates:** FAFSA/FAF: Priority filing date is March 15. Income tax forms: Priority filing date is May 1. Notification of awards on rolling basis.
**Financial aid contact:** Tansill H. Hille, M.B.A., Director of Financial Aid. 404 371-6395.

## Albany State College

**Albany, GA 31705** **912 430-4600**

**1993-94 Costs.** Tuition: $1,773 (state residents), $2,763 (out-of-state). Room: $1,170-$1,800. Board: $1,425. Fees, books, misc. academic expenses (school's estimate): $1,099.
**Enrollment.** Undergraduates: 844 men, 1,456 women (full-time). Freshman class: 1,649 applicants, 1,250 accepted, 673 enrolled. Graduate enrollment: 134 men, 210 women.
**Test score averages/ranges.** N/A.
**Faculty.** 133 full-time; 15 part-time. 56% of faculty holds doctoral degree. Student/faculty ratio: 20 to 1.
**Selectivity rating.** Less competitive.

**PROFILE.** Albany State, a public, liberal arts college, was founded in 1903 as the Albany Bible and Manual Training Institute. In 1932 it became a member of the state university system, and in 1954 assumed its present name. Its 202-acre campus is located in southwest Georgia, 180 miles from Atlanta.

**Accreditation:** SACS. Professionally accredited by the National Council for Accreditation of Teacher Education, the National League for Nursing.
**Religious orientation:** Albany State College is nonsectarian; no religious requirements.
**Library:** Collections totaling over 158,585 volumes, 1,628 periodical subscriptions, and 516,732 microform items.
**Special facilities/museums:** Electron microscope lab.
**Athletic facilities:** Gymnasium, tennis courts, weight room, swimming pool, athletic fields.
**STUDENT BODY. Undergraduate profile:** 90% are state residents; 50% are transfers. 84% Black, 16% White. Average age of undergraduates is 20.
**Freshman profile:** 90% of accepted applicants took SAT; 10% took ACT. 99% of freshmen come from public schools.
**Undergraduate achievement:** 71% of fall 1991 freshmen returned for fall 1992 term. 65% of entering class graduated. 10% of students who completed a degree program immediately went on to graduate study.
**Foreign students:** 10 students are from out of the country.
**PROGRAMS OF STUDY. Degrees:** B.A., B.Bus.Admin., B.S., B.Soc.Work.
**Majors:** Accounting, Allied Health, Allied Sciences, Art, Biology, Business, Business Administration, Chemistry, Clinical Chemistry, Computer Science, Criminal Justice, Early Childhood Education, English, French, Health/Physical Education, History, Management, Marketing, Mass Communications, Mathematics, Middle School Education,

Music, Nursing, Office Administration, Political Science, Psychology, Secondary Education, Social Work, Sociology, Spanish, Special Education, Special Major, Speech/Theatre.
**Distribution of degrees:** The majors with the highest enrollment are criminal justice, nursing, and accounting; art, computer science, and chemistry have the lowest.
**Requirements:** General education requirement.
**Academic regulations:** Freshmen must maintain minimum 1.5 GPA; sophomores, 1.75 GPA; juniors, 2.0 GPA; seniors, 2.0 GPA.
**Special:** Courses offered in black studies, geography, German, humanities, and physics. Double majors. Dual degrees. Internships. Cooperative education programs. Preprofessional programs in law, medicine, pharmacy, and dentistry. 2-2 and 3-2 engineering programs with Georgia Tech. Teacher certification in early childhood, elementary, and secondary education. Certification in specific subject areas. ROTC.
**Honors:** Honors program. Honor societies.
**Academic Assistance:** Remedial reading, writing, math, and study skills.

**STUDENT LIFE. Housing:** Students may live on or off campus. Women's and men's dorms. 31% of students live in college housing.
**Services and counseling/handicapped student services:** Health service. Counseling services for minority, military, and veteran students. Personal counseling. Career and academic guidance services.
**Campus organizations:** Undergraduate student government. Student newspaper (Student Voice, published once/quarter). Radio station. Concert and gospel choirs, concert and marching band, theatre group, 18 organizations in all. Four fraternities, no chapter houses; four sororities, no chapter houses. 15% of men join a fraternity. 15% of women join a sorority.
**Religious organizations:** Baptist Student Union, Religious Life Organization.

**ATHLETICS. Physical education requirements:** Three semesters of physical education required.
**Intercollegiate competition:** 5% of students participate. Baseball (M), basketball (M,W), cheerleading (M,W), cross-country (M,W), football (M), track and field (M,W), volleyball (W). Member of NCAA Division II, SIAC.
**Intramural and club sports:** 5% of students participate. Intramural basketball, flag football, swimming, tennis.

**ADMISSIONS. Academic basis for candidate selection** (in order of priority): Secondary school record, standardized test scores.
**Requirements:** Graduation from secondary school is required; GED is accepted. 15 units and the following program of study are required: 4 units of English, 3 units of math, 3 units of lab science, 2 units of foreign language, 3 units of social studies. Minimum combined SAT score of 700 (composite ACT score of 17) required. College placement exams and/or development studies courses required of applicants not meeting standard requirements. SAT or ACT is required. Campus visit recommended. No off-campus interviews.
**Procedure:** Suggest filing application by April 15. Application deadline is June 1. Notification of admission on rolling basis. No set date by which applicants must accept offer. $50 nonrefundable room deposit. Freshmen accepted for terms other than fall.
**Special programs:** Admission may be deferred. Credit and/or placement may be granted through CEEB Advanced Placement exams. Credit may be granted through CLEP general exams and life experience. Early decision program. Deadline for applying for early decision is September 1. Early entrance/early admission program. Concurrent enrollment program.
**Transfer students:** Transfer students accepted for fall term only. In fall 1992, 50% of all new students were transfers into all classes. 408 transfer applications were received, 260 were accepted. Application deadline is September 1 for fall; March 1 for spring. Minimum 2.0 GPA required. Lowest course grade accepted is "C." Maximum number of transferable credits is 135 quarter hours. At least 45 quarter hours must be completed at the college to receive degree.
**Admissions contact:** Kathleen Caldwell, M.S., Director of Admissions and Financial Aid. 912 430-4646.

**FINANCIAL AID. Available aid:** Pell grants, SEOG, Federal Nursing Student Scholarships, state scholarships and grants, school scholarships, private scholarships, and ROTC scholarships. Perkins Loans (NDSL), PLUS, Stafford Loans (GSL), NSL, state loans, private loans, and SLS.
**Financial aid statistics:** 13% of aid is not need-based. In 1992-93, 87% of all undergraduate applicants received aid; 85% of freshman applicants.
**Supporting data/closing dates:** FAFSA/FAF/FFS: Priority filing date is April 15. School's own aid application: Priority filing date is April 15; accepted on rolling basis. Income tax forms: Accepted on rolling basis. Notification of awards on rolling basis.
**Financial aid contact:** Kathleen Caldwell, M.S., Director of Admissions and Financial Aid. 912 430-4650.

**STUDENT EMPLOYMENT.** College Work/Study Program. Institutional employment. 60% of full-time undergraduates work on campus during school year. Students may expect to earn an average of $800 during school year. Freshmen are discouraged from working during their first term. Off-campus part-time employment opportunities rated "good."

**COMPUTER FACILITIES.** 90 IBM/IBM-compatible and Macintosh/Apple microcomputers. Computer languages and software packages include Assembler, BASIC, COBOL, DisplayWrite, FORTRAN, Pascal, WordPerfect, WordStar. Computer facilities are available to all students.
**Fees:** None.
**Hours:** 8 AM-5 PM (M-F).

**GRADUATE CAREER DATA.** Graduate school percentages: 1% enter law school. 2% enter medical school. 2% enter dental school. 1% enter graduate business programs. 1% enter graduate arts and sciences programs. Highest graduate school enrollments: Albany State Coll, Georgia Tech, Iowa State U, Medical Coll of Georgia, Ohio State U. Companies and businesses that hire graduates: Miller Brewing Co., AT&T, Procter & Gamble.

**PROMINENT ALUMNI/AE.** Joseph Jordan and Benjamin Jaudon, medical doctors; Daryl Chapman, dentist; Robert White, plant manager, Procter & Gamble; Sam Russell, Miller Brewing Co.

# American College for the Applied Arts

**Atlanta, GA 30326** **404 231-9000**

**1994-95 Costs.** Tuition: $8,220. Room: $3,850. Fees, books, misc. academic expenses (school's estimate): $480.
**Enrollment.** Undergraduates: 100 men, 400 women (full-time). Freshman class: 306 applicants, 189 accepted, 185 enrolled.
**Test score averages/ranges.** N/A.
**Faculty.** 12 full-time; 48 part-time. 95% of faculty holds highest degree in specific field.
**Selectivity rating.** N/A.

**PROFILE.** The American College for the Applied Arts, founded in 1977, is a private institution. Its one-acre campus is located in Atlanta.
**Accreditation:** SACS. Professionally accredited by the Foundation for Interior Design Education Research.
**Religious orientation:** American College for the Applied Arts is nonsectarian; no religious requirements.
**Library:** Collections totaling over 24,680 volumes, 205 periodical subscriptions and 180 microform items.
**STUDENT BODY. Undergraduate profile:** 60% are state residents; 30% are transfers. 1% Asian-American, 28% Black, 4% Hispanic, 67% White. Average age of undergraduates is 24.
**Undergraduate achievement:** 81% of fall 1992 freshmen returned for fall 1993 term. 67% of entering class graduated. 2% of students who completed a degree program immediately went on to graduate study.
**Foreign students:** 105 students are from out of the country. Countries represented include the Bahamas, Jamaica, Japan, Korea, Nigeria, and Saudi Arabia; 80 in all.
**PROGRAMS OF STUDY. Degrees:** B.A.
**Majors:** Business Administration, Commercial Art, Fashion Design, Fashion Marketing, Interior Design.
**Distribution of degrees:** The majors with the highest enrollment are interior design, fashion marketing, and commercial art; business administration and fashion design have the lowest.
**Requirements:** General education requirement.
**Academic regulations:** Minimum 2.0 GPA must be maintained.
**Special:** Minors available in aviation administration and photography. Associate's degrees offered. Double majors. Independent study. Accelerated study. Internships. Study abroad in England.
**Academic Assistance:** Remedial writing and math.
**ADMISSIONS. Academic basis for candidate selection** (in order of priority): School's recommendation, secondary school record, essay, standardized test scores, class rank.
**Nonacademic basis for candidate selection:** Character and personality are important.
**Requirements:** Graduation from secondary school is required; GED is accepted. No specific distribution of secondary school units required. Campus visit and interview recommended. Off-campus interviews available with an admissions representative.
**Procedure:** Notification of admission on rolling basis. No set date by which applicants must accept offer. $260 tuition deposit, refundable until 30 days prior to beginning of term. $100 nonrefundable room deposit. Freshmen accepted for terms other than fall.
**Special programs:** Admission may be deferred three years. Early decision program. In fall 1993, 109 applied for early decision and 87 were accepted. Early entrance/early admission program. Concurrent enrollment program.
**Transfer students:** Transfer students accepted for terms other than fall. In fall 1993, 30% of all new students were transfers into all classes. 260 transfer applications were received, 230 were accepted. Application deadline is rolling for fall; rolling for spring. Minimum 2.0 GPA recommended. Lowest course grade accepted is "C." Maximum number of transferable credits is 30 quarter hours from a two-year school and 60 quarter hours from a four-year school. At least 130 quarter hours must be completed at the college to receive degree.
**Admissions contact:** Suzanne McBride, Director of Admissions. 404 231-9000.
**FINANCIAL AID. Available aid:** Pell grants, SEOG, and school scholarships and grants. PLUS, Stafford Loans (GSL), and SLS. Payment plans arranged on individual basis.
**Financial aid statistics:** 5% of aid is not need-based. In 1993-94, 60% of all undergraduate applicants received aid; 80% of freshman applicants. Average amounts of aid awarded freshmen: Scholarships and grants, $1,050; loans, $2,625.
**Supporting data/closing dates:** FAFSA: Priority filing date is January; accepted on rolling basis. FAF/FFS: Accepted on rolling basis. School's own aid application: Priority filing date is January; accepted on rolling basis. Federal Form: Accepted on rolling basis. Notification of awards on rolling basis.
**Financial aid contact:** Constance King, M.P.A., Director of Financial Aid. 404 231-9000.

# Armstrong State College

**Savannah, GA 31419** **912 927-5275**

**1993-94 Costs.** Tuition: $1,521 (state residents), $4,203 (out-of-state). Room & board: $3,144-$3,624. Fees, books, misc. academic expenses (school's estimate): $450.
**Enrollment.** Undergraduates: 1,327 men, 2,843 women (full-time). Freshman class: 1,773 applicants, 1,662 accepted, 1,207 enrolled. Graduate enrollment: 346.
**Test score averages/ranges.** N/A.
**Faculty.** 138 full-time; 10 part-time. 53% of faculty holds doctoral degree. Student/faculty ratio: 18 to 1.
**Selectivity rating.** N/A.

**PROFILE.** Armstrong State is a public institution. Founded as a junior college in 1935, it became a four-year institution in 1964. Programs offered include criminal justice, social work, teaching, and the health professions; the college is a designated Health Professions Education Center. Its 250-acre campus is located 10 miles from downtown Savannah.

**Accreditation:** SACS. Professionally accredited by the American Dental Association, the American Medical Association (CAHEA), the National Association of Schools of Music, the National Council for Accreditation of Teacher Education, the National League for Nursing.
**Religious orientation:** Armstrong State College is nonsectarian; no religious requirements.
**Library:** Collections totaling over 148,647 volumes, 806 periodical subscriptions, and 466,000 microform items. Library also has collection of 35,000 records, slides, motion picture kits, and videotapes.
**Special facilities/museums:** Language lab.
**Athletic facilities:** Gymnasium, swimming pool, baseball and soccer fields, tennis courts, weight room, athletic training room.

**STUDENT BODY. Undergraduate profile:** 93% are state residents; 30% are transfers. 1% Asian-American, 14% Black, 1% Hispanic, 1% Native American, 83% White. Average age of undergraduates is 25.
**Undergraduate achievement:** 75% of fall 1991 freshmen returned for fall 1992 term. 40% of entering class graduated.
**Foreign students:** 39 students are from out of the country. Countries represented include African countries, Canada, China, Sweden, and the United Kingdom.

**PROGRAMS OF STUDY. Degrees:** B.A., B.Dent.Hyg.Ed., B.Gen.Studies, B.Hlth.Sci., B.Media Tech., B.Mus.Ed., B.S., B.S.Ed., B.S.Nurs.
**Majors:** Art Education, Biology, Chemistry, Criminal Justice, Dental Hygiene, Early Elementary Education, English, Health Education/Recreation, History, Mass Communications, Media Technology, Middle School Education, Music, Music Education, Nursing, Political Science, Psychology, Secondary Education, Social Work.
**Distribution of degrees:** The majors with the highest enrollment are education, history, and political science.
**Requirements:** General education requirement.
**Special:** Minors offered in many majors and in approximately 25 other fields. Courses offered at Marine Science Center. Exit exam in major and reading and writing competency tests are required. Associate's degrees offered. Self-designed majors. Double majors. Dual degrees. Independent study. Cooperative education programs. Graduate school at which undergraduates may take graduate-level courses. Preprofessional programs in law, medicine, veterinary science, pharmacy, dentistry, optometry, engineering, forestry, and industrial management. 2-2 and 3-2 engineering programs with Georgia Tech. Member of Brunswick Center Consortium. Exchange program with Savannah State Coll. Teacher certification in early childhood, elementary, secondary, and special education. ROTC. NROTC at Savannah State Coll.
**Honors:** Honors program.
**Academic Assistance:** Nonremedial tutoring.

**STUDENT LIFE. Housing:** Students may live on or off campus. Coed dorms. 10% of students live in college housing.
**Services and counseling/handicapped student services:** Placement services. Day care. Counseling services for minority and veteran students. Personal counseling. Career and academic guidance services.
**Campus organizations:** Undergraduate student government. Student newspaper (Inkwell, published bimonthly). Literary magazine. Yearbook. Band, glee club, chorus, vocal ensemble, Masquers, summer theatre, Women of Worth, Marauders, Young Republicans, numerous professional groups. One fraternity, no chapter house; two sororities, no chapter houses. 1% of men join a fraternity. 1% of women join a sorority.
**Religious organizations:** Baptist Student Union.
**Minority/foreign student organizations:** Ebony Coalition. International Student Association.

**ATHLETICS. Physical education requirements:** Six hours of physical education required.
**Intercollegiate competition:** 6% of students participate. Baseball (M), basketball (M,W), cheerleading (M,W), cross-country (M,W), tennis (M,W), volleyball (W). Member of NCAA Division II, Peach Belt Athletic Conference.
**Intramural and club sports:** 14% of students participate. Intramural aerobics, badminton, basketball, bowling, flag football, inner-tube water polo, running, soccer, table tennis, tennis, volleyball.

**ADMISSIONS. Academic basis for candidate selection** (in order of priority): Standardized test scores, secondary school record.
**Requirements:** Graduation from secondary school is required; GED is accepted. No specific distribution of secondary school units required. Minimum SAT scores of 380 in both verbal and math (composite ACT score of 16) and minimum 2.0 GPA required. Minimum college 2.5 GPA required of B.S.N. program applicants. Conditional admission possible for applicants not meeting standard requirements. SAT is required; ACT may be substituted. Campus visit recommended. Off-campus interviews available with an admissions representative.
**Procedure:** Take SAT or ACT by June of 12th year. Suggest filing application by June. Application deadline is August 30. Notification of admission on rolling basis. $100 nonrefundable room deposit. Freshmen accepted for terms other than fall.
**Special programs:** Admission may be deferred one year. Credit may be granted through CEEB Advanced Placement for scores of 3 or higher. Credit may be granted through CLEP general and subject exams, ACT PEP and DANTES exams, and military experience. Early decision program. Early entrance/early admission program. Concurrent enrollment program.
**Transfer students:** Transfer students accepted for terms other than fall. In fall 1992, 30% of all new students were transfers into all classes. Application deadline is August 1 for fall; March 1 for spring. Minimum 2.0 GPA recommended. Lowest course grade accepted is "D." Maximum number of transferable credits is 100 quarter hours. At least half of courses required for major must be completed at the college to receive degree.
**Admissions contact:** Kim West, M.H.S., Director of Admissions. 912 927-5277.

**FINANCIAL AID. Available aid:** Pell grants, SEOG, state grants, school scholarships, ROTC scholarships, academic merit scholarships, and athletic scholarships. Perkins Loans (NDSL), PLUS, Stafford Loans (GSL), Health Professions Loans, school loans, and SLS.
**Supporting data/closing dates:** FAFSA/FAF: Priority filing date is January 1; deadline is May 31. School's own aid application: Priority filing date is January 1; deadline is May 31. Income tax forms: Priority filing date is January 1; deadline is May 31. Notification of awards on rolling basis.
**Financial aid contact:** Ellen Shaw, Director of Financial Aid. 912 927-5272.

**STUDENT EMPLOYMENT.** College Work/Study Program. Institutional employment. 4% of full-time undergraduates work on campus during school year. Students may expect to earn an average of $1,800 during school year. Off-campus part-time employment opportunities rated "good."

**COMPUTER FACILITIES.** Macintosh/Apple microcomputers. Students may access AT&T minicomputer/mainframe systems. Computer facilities are available to all students.
**Fees:** None.

# Atlanta College of Art

**Atlanta, GA 30309** **404 898-1164**

**1994-95 Costs.** Tuition: $9,850. Room: $3,150.
**Enrollment.** Undergraduates: 221 men, 200 women (full-time). Freshman class: 440 applicants, 286 accepted, 132 enrolled.
**Test score averages/ranges.** Average SAT scores: 942 combined. Average ACT scores: 21 composite.
**Faculty.** 24 full-time; 24 part-time. 100% of faculty holds highest degree in specific field. Student/faculty ratio: 12 to 1.
**Selectivity rating.** Less competitive.

**PROFILE.** The Atlanta College of Art, founded in 1928, is a private institution. The college is part of the Woodruff Arts Center, which includes the High Museum of Art, the Atlanta Symphony, and the Alliance Theatre Company/Atlanta Children's Theatre. Its six-acre campus is located in Atlanta's midtown area.

**Accreditation:** SACS. Professionally accredited by the National Association of Schools of Art and Design.
**Religious orientation:** Atlanta College of Art is nonsectarian; no religious requirements.
**Library:** Collections totaling over 27,000 volumes and 250 periodical subscriptions. Library also offers 60,000 slides.
**Special facilities/museums:** Art galleries, sculpture building with foundry and wood shop, individual painting, design, and sculpture studios, darkrooms.

**STUDENT BODY. Undergraduate profile:** 36% are state residents; 48% are transfers. 4% Asian-American, 13% Black, 3% Hispanic, 1% Native American, 68% White, 11% Other. Average age of undergraduates is 19.
**Freshman profile:** 55% of accepted applicants took SAT; 15% took ACT. 80% of freshmen come from public schools.
**Undergraduate achievement:** 71% of fall 1991 freshmen returned for fall 1992 term.
**Foreign students:** Countries represented include Bermuda, the Caribbean Islands, China, Japan, the U.S. Virgin Islands, and United Arab Emirates.

**PROGRAMS OF STUDY. Degrees:** B.F.A.
**Majors:** Communication Design, Drawing, Electronic Arts, Interior Design, Painting, Photography, Printmaking, Sculpture.
**Distribution of degrees:** The majors with the highest enrollment are communication design, painting, and photography; drawing, printmaking, and sculpture have the lowest.
**Requirements:** General education requirement.
**Special:** College shares facilities and works in cooperation with High Museum of Art, Atlanta Symphony, and Alliance Theatre. Concentrations in advertising and graphic design, illustration, computer art and graphics, and video. Self-designed majors. Double majors. Independent study. Internships. Cooperative education programs. Dual degree program with Oglethorpe U. Member of Independent Colleges of Art and Design.

**ADMISSIONS. Academic basis for candidate selection** (in order of priority): Secondary school record, class rank, school's recommendation, essay, standardized test scores.
**Nonacademic basis for candidate selection:** Particular talent or ability is important. Character and personality, extracurricular participation, geographical distribution, and alumni/ae relationship are considered.
**Requirements:** Graduation from secondary school is required; GED is accepted. No specific distribution of secondary school units required. Minimum 2.0 GPA and portfolio required. Conditional admission possible for applicants not meeting standard requirements. SAT or ACT is required. Campus visit and interview recommended. Off-campus interviews available with an admissions representative.
**Procedure:** Take SAT or ACT by June of 12th year. Notification of admission on rolling basis. No set date by which applicants must accept offer. $150 tuition deposit, refundable until May 1. $350 nonrefundable room deposit. Freshmen accepted for terms other than fall.
**Special programs:** Admission may be deferred two years. Credit may be granted through CEEB Advanced Placement for scores of 4 or higher. Early entrance/early admission program.
**Transfer students:** Transfer students accepted for terms other than fall. In fall 1992, 48% of all new students were transfers into all classes. 159 transfer applications were received, 110 were accepted. Application deadline is rolling for fall; rolling for spring. Lowest course grade accepted is "C." Maximum number of transferable credits is 81 semester hours. At least 31 semester hours must be completed at the college to receive degree.
**Admissions contact:** John A. Farkas, M.S., Director of Enrollment Management. 800 832-2104.

**FINANCIAL AID. Available aid:** Pell grants, SEOG, state scholarships and grants, school scholarships and grants, private scholarships and grants, academic merit scholarships, and aid for undergraduate foreign students. Perkins Loans (NDSL), PLUS, Stafford Loans (GSL), school loans, private loans, and SLS. Knight Tuition Plans.

**Financial aid statistics:** 35% of aid is not need-based. In 1992-93, 86% of all undergraduate applicants received aid; 73% of freshman applicants. Average amounts of aid awarded freshmen: Scholarships and grants, $1,242; loans, $2,606.
**Supporting data/closing dates:** FAFSA/FAF: Priority filing date is March 15. School's own aid application: Priority filing date is March 15. Income tax forms: Priority filing date is March 15. Notification of awards on rolling basis.
**Financial aid contact:** Teresa Tantillo, M.A., Director of Financial Aid. 800 832-2104.

**STUDENT EMPLOYMENT.** College Work/Study Program. Institutional employment. 19% of full-time undergraduates work on campus during school year. Students may expect to earn an average of $1,400 during school year. Off-campus part-time employment opportunities rated "fair."

**COMPUTER FACILITIES.** 24 IBM/IBM-compatible and Macintosh/Apple microcomputers. Computer facilities are available to all students.
**Fees:** None.
**Hours:** 9 AM-5 PM.

**GRADUATE CAREER DATA.** Highest graduate school enrollments: Georgia State U, Massachusetts Coll of Art, Rochester Inst of Tech. 30% of graduates choose careers in business and industry. Companies and businesses that hire graduates: IBM.

**PROMINENT ALUMNI/AE.** Joseph Spencer, illustrator; Tomas Gonzales, art director, Coca-Cola USA; Kim Youngblood, president, Youngblood Sweat & Tears; Preston Rose, president, Preston Rose Printing Co.; Gudmund Vigtel, director, High Museum of Art; Victor Beitzell, filmmaker.

# Augusta College

**Augusta, GA 30910 — 706 737-1405**

**1993-94 Costs.** Tuition: $1,542 (state residents), $4,224 (out-of-state). Housing: None. Fees, books, misc. academic expenses (school's estimate): $370.
**Enrollment.** Undergraduates: 1,168 men, 1,758 women (full-time). Freshman class: 1,423 applicants, 1,089 accepted, 813 enrolled. Graduate enrollment: 333 men, 500 women.
**Test score averages/ranges.** Average SAT scores: 450 verbal, 490 math.
**Faculty.** 174 full-time; 51 part-time. 66% of faculty holds doctoral degree. Student/faculty ratio: 28 to 1.
**Selectivity rating.** Less competitive.

**PROFILE.** Augusta is a public, comprehensive college. Founded as a postgraduate academy in 1783, it became a junior college in 1925, was incorporated into the state university system, and began granting four-year degrees in 1967. Its 80-acre campus is located on a former plantation in Augusta.

**Accreditation:** SACS. Professionally accredited by the National Association of Schools of Music, the National Council for Accreditation of Teacher Education, the National League for Nursing.
**Religious orientation:** Augusta College is nonsectarian; no religious requirements.
**Library:** Collections totaling over 465,000 volumes, 270,000 periodical subscriptions, and 1,200,000 microform items.
**Athletic facilities:** 18-hole golf course, indoor swimming pool, tennis courts, gymnasium, volleyball court, athletic fields, lake.

**STUDENT BODY. Undergraduate profile:** 97% are state residents; 24% are transfers. 2% Asian-American, 16% Black, 1% Hispanic, 80% White, 1% Other. Average age of undergraduates is 24.
**Freshman profile:** 1% of freshmen who took SAT scored 700 or over on verbal, 3% scored 700 or over on math; 7% scored 600 or over on verbal, 14% scored 600 or over on math; 26% scored 500 or over on verbal, 45% scored 500 or over on math; 72% scored 400 or over on verbal, 85% scored 400 or over on math; 99% scored 300 or over on verbal, 100% scored 300 or over on math. 95% of accepted applicants took SAT; 5% took ACT.
**Undergraduate achievement:** 77% of fall 1991 freshmen returned for fall 1992 term.
**Foreign students:** 38 students are from out of the country. Countries represented include Bermuda, France, India, Israel, Sweden, and the United Kingdom; 22 in all.

**PROGRAMS OF STUDY. Degrees:** B.A., B.Bus.Admin., B.F.A., B.S.
**Majors:** Accounting, Art, Art Education, Biology, Business Education, Chemistry, Communication, Computer Science, Criminal Justice, Economics, Elementary Education, English, Executive Secretarial, Finance/Insurance/Real Estate, General Business, Health/Physical Education, History, Management, Marketing, Mathematics, Medical Technology, Music Education, Music Performance, Physical Science, Physics, Political Science, Psychology, Sociology, Special Education, Studio Art.
**Distribution of degrees:** The majors with the highest enrollment are accounting, psychology, and management; music performance and studio art have the lowest.
**Requirements:** General education requirement.
**Academic regulations:** Freshmen must maintain minimum 1.3 GPA; sophomores, 1.6 GPA; juniors, 1.9 GPA; seniors, 2.0 GPA.
**Special:** Minors offered in some majors and in anthropology, British studies, business administration, drama education, French, general studies, German, gerontology, humanities, international studies, military science, philosophy, social science, social work, and Spanish. Associate's degrees offered. Double majors. Accelerated study. Internships. Cooperative education programs. Graduate school at which undergraduates may take graduate-level courses. Preprofessional programs in law, medicine, veterinary science, pharmacy, and dentistry. Combined-degree programs in engineering with Georgia Tech and in allied health with Medical Coll of Georgia. Ph.D. offered in cooperation with Georgia Southern U. Washington Semester. Teacher certification in early childhood, elementary, and special education. Study abroad in Italy, Japan, and Sweden. ROTC.
**Honors:** Phi Beta Kappa.
**Academic Assistance:** Remedial reading, writing, math, and study skills. Nonremedial tutoring.

**STUDENT LIFE. Housing:** Commuter campus; no student housing.
**Social atmosphere:** "Since we are a commuter college, most students' social life is not centered here," reports the student newspaper. On campus, students gather at the College Activity Center; off-campus hangouts include the Post Office and the Red Lion. Octoberfest, Homecoming, and basketball games are the most popular social events on campus.
**Services and counseling/handicapped student services:** Placement services. Day care. Counseling services for minority, military, veteran, and older students. Personal and psychological counseling. Career and academic guidance services. Physically disabled student services. Learning disabled services. Notetaking services. Tape recorders. Tutors. Reader services for the blind.
**Campus organizations:** Undergraduate student government. Student newspaper (Bell Ringer, published once/week). Literary magazine. Yearbook. Radio station. Choir, 38 organizations in all. Two fraternities, no chapter houses; one sorority, no chapter house. 3% of men join a fraternity. 2% of women join a sorority.
**Religious organizations:** Baptist Student Union, Newman Club.
**Minority/foreign student organizations:** Black Student Union.

**ATHLETICS. Physical education requirements:** Six quarters of physical education required.
**Intercollegiate competition:** 4% of students participate. Baseball (M), basketball (M,W), cheerleading (M,W), cross-country (M,W), golf (M), soccer (M), softball (W), tennis (M,W), volleyball (W). Member of Big South Conference, NCAA Division II, Peach Belt Athletic Conference.
**Intramural and club sports:** 2% of students participate. Intramural basketball, flag football, softball, volleyball. Men's club crew, table tennis. Women's club crew.

**ADMISSIONS. Academic basis for candidate selection** (in order of priority): Secondary school record, standardized test scores.
**Requirements:** Graduation from secondary school is required; GED is accepted. No specific distribution of secondary school units required. Minimum SAT scores of 350 in both verbal and math and minimum 2.0 GPA required. Additional admission requirements for nursing program applicants. Conditional admission possible for applicants not meeting standard requirements. SAT is required; ACT may be substituted. Campus visit recommended. No off-campus interviews.
**Procedure:** Take SAT or ACT by end of 12th year. Notification of admission on rolling basis. Reply is required by date of registration. Freshmen accepted for terms other than fall.
**Special programs:** Admission may be deferred. Credit and/or placement may be granted through CEEB Advanced Placement exams for scores of 5. Credit may be granted through CLEP general and subject exams, ACT PEP and challenge exams. Concurrent enrollment program.
**Transfer students:** Transfer students accepted for terms other than fall. In fall 1992, 24% of all new students were transfers into all classes. 678 transfer applications were received, 537 were accepted. Application deadline is August 21 for fall; February 23 for spring. Minimum 2.0 GPA required. Lowest course grade accepted is "D." At least 45 quarter hours must be completed at the college to receive degree.
**Admissions contact:** Luanne H. Baroni, M.B.A., Director of Admissions. 706 737-1405.

**FINANCIAL AID. Available aid:** Pell grants, SEOG, state scholarships and grants, school scholarships and grants, private scholarships, ROTC scholarships, academic merit scholarships, and athletic scholarships. Perkins Loans (NDSL), PLUS, Stafford Loans (GSL), state loans, school loans, and SLS. Credit card payment plan.
**Financial aid statistics:** 5% of aid is not need-based. In 1992-93, 77% of all undergraduate applicants received aid; 59% of freshman applicants. Average amounts of aid awarded freshmen: Scholarships and grants, $1,830; loans, $2,625.
**Supporting data/closing dates:** FAFSA/FAF: Accepted on rolling basis. School's own aid application: Accepted on rolling basis. Notification of awards on rolling basis.
**Financial aid contact:** Kevin Wellwood, Director of Financial Aid. 706 737-1431.

**STUDENT EMPLOYMENT.** College Work/Study Program. Institutional employment. Students may expect to earn an average of $2,400 during school year. Off-campus part-time employment opportunities rated "good."

**COMPUTER FACILITIES.** 600 IBM/IBM-compatible and Macintosh/Apple microcomputers; 320 are networked. Students may access Digital, IBM, SUN minicomputer/mainframe systems, BITNET, Internet. Computer languages and software packages include COBOL, dBASE, FORTRAN, Lotus 1-2-3, Paradox, Pascal, Quattro Pro, SPSS, WordPerfect, WordStar. Computer facilities are available to all students.
**Fees:** Computer fee is included in tuition/fees.
**Hours:** 24 hours in several locations.

**PROMINENT ALUMNI/AE.** Charles A. DeVaney, mayor of Augusta; Paul S. Simon, president, Morris Communications; D. Douglas Barnard, U.S. congressman.

# Brenau University

**Gainesville, GA 30501 — 404 534-6299**

**1994-95 Costs.** Tuition: $9,592. Room & board: $5,879. Fees, books, misc. academic expenses (school's estimate): $500.
**Enrollment.** Undergraduates: 111 men, 806 women (full-time). Freshman class: 380 applicants, 284 accepted, 155 enrolled. Graduate enrollment: 129 men, 196 women.
**Test score averages/ranges.** Average SAT scores: 453 verbal, 479 math.
**Faculty.** 104 full-time; 154 part-time. 80% of faculty holds doctoral degree. Student/faculty ratio: 13 to 1.
**Selectivity rating.** Less competitive.

**PROFILE.** Brenau, founded in 1878, is a private, liberal arts college for women. Its 37-acre campus is located in a residential area of Gainesville.

**Accreditation:** SACS. Professionally accredited by the Foundation for Interior Design Education Research, the National League for Nursing.
**Religious orientation:** Brenau University is nonsectarian; no religious requirements.
**Library:** Collections totaling over 75,730 volumes, 476 periodical subscriptions, and 159,668 microform items.
**Special facilities/museums:** Art museum, media lab.

**Athletic facilities:** Gymnasium, natatorium, tennis courts.

**STUDENT BODY. Undergraduate profile:** 74% are state residents; 69% are transfers. 1% Asian-American, 14% Black, 1% Hispanic, 82% White, 2% Other. Average age of undergraduates is 21.

**Freshman profile:** 90% of accepted applicants took SAT; 10% took ACT. 85% of freshmen come from public schools.

**Undergraduate achievement:** 61% of fall 1992 freshmen returned for fall 1993 term. 52% of entering class graduated. 66% of students who completed a degree program went on to graduate study within five years.

**Foreign students:** 41 students are from out of the country. Countries represented include Columbia, France, Germany, India, Japan, and Korea; 19 in all.

**PROGRAMS OF STUDY. Degrees:** B.A., B.F.A., B.Mus., B.Mus.Ed., B.S., B.S.Nurs.

**Majors:** Accounting, Allied Health Sciences, Applied Mathematics, Arts Administration, Ballet Pedagogy, Ballet Performance, Biology, Broadcasting, Business Administration, Church Music, Commercial Art, Conservation Law Enforcement, Criminal Justice, Dance/Theatre, Early Childhood Education, English, Fashion Merchandising, History, Human Resources Management, Interior Design, Journalism, Medical Technology, Middle Grade Education, Music Education, Nursing, Performing Arts, Political Science, Pre-Law, Pre-Medicine, Pre-Occupational Therapy, Pre-Pharmacy, Pre-Physical Therapy, Pre-Veterinary, Psychology, Public Administration, Public Relations, Special Education/Mentally Retarded, Studio Art, Theatre, Theatre Education, Visual Arts.

**Distribution of degrees:** The majors with the highest enrollment are education, business, and nursing; English, music performance, and studio art have the lowest.

**Requirements:** General education requirement.

**Academic regulations:** Minimum 2.0 GPA must be maintained.

**Special:** Minors offered in most majors. Courses offered in anthropology, business education, geography, math, philosophy, physical science, and religion. Self-designed majors. Double majors. Independent study. Pass/fail grading option. Internships. Graduate school at which undergraduates may take graduate-level courses. Preprofessional programs in law, medicine, veterinary science, pharmacy, dentistry, pre-occupational therapy, and prephysical therapy. Junior year at Fashion Inst of Tech for fashion merchandising majors. Teacher certification in early childhood, elementary, and special education. Study abroad in Austria, China, England, France, Italy, Mexico, the Netherlands, Spain, Switzerland, and Wales. ROTC.

**Honors:** Honors program. Honor societies.

**Academic Assistance:** Remedial reading, writing, math, and study skills. Nonremedial tutoring.

**ADMISSIONS. Academic basis for candidate selection** (in order of priority): Secondary school record, standardized test scores, school's recommendation, class rank.

**Nonacademic basis for candidate selection:** Character and personality, extracurricular participation, and particular talent or ability are important. Alumni/ae relationship is considered.

**Requirements:** Graduation from secondary school is required; GED is accepted. No specific distribution of secondary school units required. Minimum combined SAT score of 800 and minimum 2.2 GPA recommended. Audition required of performing arts program applicants. Portfolio required of visual arts program applicants. "Plan B" program for applicants not meeting standard requirements. SAT or ACT is required. Campus visit and interview recommended. Off-campus interviews available with an admissions representative.

**Procedure:** Take SAT or ACT by November of 12th year. Visit college for interview by March of 12th year. Application deadline is September 1. Notification of admission on rolling basis. No set date by which applicants must accept offer. $250 tuition deposit, refundable until May 1. $100 refundable room deposit. Freshmen accepted for terms other than fall.

**Special programs:** Admission may be deferred one year. Credit and/or placement may be granted through CEEB Advanced Placement exams for scores of 3 or higher. Credit and/or placement may be granted through CLEP general and subject exams. Credit and placement may be granted through challenge exams. Early decision program. Deadline for applying for early decision is November 15. Early entrance/early admission program. Concurrent enrollment program.

**Transfer students:** Transfer students accepted for terms other than fall. In fall 1993, 69% of all new students were transfers into all classes. 517 transfer applications were received, 481 were accepted. Application deadline is September 1 for fall; January 1 for spring. Minimum 2.0 GPA required. Lowest course grade accepted is "D." Maximum number of transferable credits is 155 quarter hours. At least 45 quarter hours must be completed at the university to receive degree.

**Admissions contact:** John D. Upchurch, M.M., D.M., Dean of Admissions. 404 534-6100.

**FINANCIAL AID. Available aid:** Pell grants, SEOG, state scholarships and grants, school scholarships and grants, private scholarships and grants, ROTC scholarships, academic merit scholarships, athletic scholarships, and aid for undergraduate foreign students. Minority and leadership scholarships. Perkins Loans (NDSL), PLUS, Stafford Loans (GSL), state loans, private loans, and SLS. AMS and deferred payment plan. CIC Tuition Exchange.

**Financial aid statistics:** 40% of aid is not need-based. In 1993-94, 81% of all undergraduate applicants received aid; 82% of freshman applicants. Average amounts of aid awarded freshmen: Scholarships and grants, $6,131; loans, $4,039.

**Supporting data/closing dates:** FAFSA: Priority filing date is April 15. FAF: Priority filing date is April 15; accepted on rolling basis. School's own aid application: Priority filing date is May 15; accepted on rolling basis. State aid form: Accepted on rolling basis. Income tax forms: Priority filing date is May 15; accepted on rolling basis. Notification of awards on rolling basis. 9933

**Financial aid contact:** Pam Barrett, Director of Financial Aid. 404 534-6152.

# Brewton-Parker College

**Mt. Vernon, GA 30445-0197** **912 583-2241**

**1994-95 Costs.** Tuition: $4,500. Room & board: $2,400. Fees, books, misc. academic expenses (school's estimate): $600.

**Enrollment.** Undergraduates: 603 men, 521 women (full-time). Freshman class: 1,436 applicants, 1,202 accepted.

**Test score averages/ranges.** Average SAT scores: 373 verbal, 393 math.

**Faculty.** 60 full-time; 171 part-time. 60% of faculty holds doctoral degree. Student/faculty ratio: 14 to 1.

**Selectivity rating.** Less competitive.

**PROFILE.** Brewton-Parker, founded in 1904, is a private, church-affiliated, liberal arts college. Its 136-acre campus is located in Mt. Vernon, 85 miles from Macon.

**Accreditation:** SACS. Professionally accredited by the National Association of Schools of Music.

**Religious orientation:** Brewton-Parker College is an interdenominational Christian school; 10 credit hours of religion/theology required.

**Library:** Collections totaling over 41,756 volumes, 399 periodical subscriptions and 153 microform items.

**Athletic facilities:** Baseball and soccer fields, fitness center, gym, pool, tennis courts, volleyball pit.

**STUDENT BODY. Undergraduate profile:** 95% are state residents. 1% Asian-American, 23% Black, 1% Hispanic, 75% White. Average age of undergraduates is 24.

**Freshman profile:** Majority of accepted applicants took SAT. 90% of freshmen come from public schools.

**Undergraduate achievement:** 55% of fall 1992 freshmen returned for fall 1993 term. 10% of entering class graduated. 14% of students who completed a degree program immediately went on to graduate study.

**Foreign students:** One student is from out of the country.

**PROGRAMS OF STUDY. Degrees:** B.A., B.Minis., B.Mus., B.S.

**Majors:** Business Administration, Business Education, Christianity, Early Childhood Education, English, English Education, General Studies, Health/Physical Education/Recreation, History, History Education, Learning Disabilities Education, Middle Grades Education, Ministry, Music, Music Education, Office Administration, Psychology, Science Education, Sociology.

**Distribution of degrees:** The majors with the highest enrollment are teacher education and business administration; music and Christianity have the lowest.

**Requirements:** General education requirement.

**Academic regulations:** Freshmen must maintain minimum 1.6 GPA; sophomores, 1.9 GPA; juniors, 2.0 GPA; seniors, 2.0 GPA.

**Special:** Minors offered in some majors and in philosophy and political science. Associate's degrees offered. Double majors. Independent study. Pass/fail grading option. Preprofessional programs in law, medicine, veterinary science, pharmacy, dentistry, optometry, and pre-dental hygiene. Teacher certification in early childhood, elementary, and secondary education. Certification in specific subject areas.

**Honors:** Honors program. Honor societies.

**Academic Assistance:** Remedial reading, writing, math, and study skills. Nonremedial tutoring.

**STUDENT LIFE. Housing:** Women's and men's dorms. School-owned/operated apartments. 42% of students live in college housing.

**Services and counseling/handicapped student services:** Placement services. Counseling services for minority students. Career guidance services. Physically disabled student services. Tape recorders. Tutors. Reader services for the blind.

**Campus organizations:** Undergraduate student government. Student newspaper (Proud and Mighty, published once/month). Yearbook. 24 registered organizations. Four fraternities, no chapter houses; four sororities, no chapter houses. 16% of men join a fraternity. 11% of women join a sorority.

**Religious organizations:** Baptist Student Union, Ministerial Association.

**Minority/foreign student organizations:** International Student Organization.

**ATHLETICS. Physical education requirements:** Up to 15 credit hours of physical education required.

**Intercollegiate competition:** Baseball (M,W), basketball (M,W), golf (M), soccer (M,W), softball (W), tennis (M,W). Member of NAIA.

**Intramural and club sports:** Intramural baseball, basketball, flag football, soccer, swimming, tennis, volleyball.

**ADMISSIONS. Academic basis for candidate selection** (in order of priority): Standardized test scores, secondary school record, class rank, essay, school's recommendation.

**Requirements:** Graduation from secondary school is recommended; GED is accepted. 13 units and the following program of study are recommended: 4 units of English, 2 units of math, 2 units of science, 2 units of foreign language, 3 units of social studies. Open admissions. Audition required of music program applicants. SAT is recommended; ACT may be substituted. Campus visit and interview recommended. Off-campus interviews available with admissions and alumni representatives.

**Procedure:** Notification of admission on rolling basis. $100 room deposit, refundable until 30 days before beginning of quarter. Freshmen accepted for terms other than fall.

**Special programs:** Admission may be deferred. Early entrance/early admission program. Concurrent enrollment program.

**Transfer students:** Transfer students accepted for terms other than fall. Application deadline is by first day of registration for fall; by first day of registration for spring. Lowest course grade accepted is "D." Final 45 quarter hours must be completed at the college to receive degree. At least 30 quarter hours must be completed at the school to receive degree.

**Admissions contact:** Jill O'Neal, Director of Admissions. 912 583-2241, extension 268.

**FINANCIAL AID. Available aid:** Pell grants, SEOG, state scholarships and grants, school scholarships and grants, private scholarships and grants, academic merit scholarships, athletic scholarships, and aid for undergraduate foreign students. Perkins Loans (NDSL), PLUS, Stafford Loans (GSL), state loans, and SLS. Deferred payment plan.
**Financial aid statistics:** 22% of aid is not need-based. In 1993-94, 83% of all undergraduate applicants received aid; 85% of freshman applicants. Average amounts of aid awarded freshmen: Scholarships and grants, $1,450; loans, $2,400.
**Supporting data/closing dates:** FAFSA: Accepted on rolling basis. School's own aid application: Priority filing date is June 1; accepted on rolling basis. State aid form: Accepted on rolling basis. Income tax forms: Priority filing date is September 15; accepted on rolling basis. Notification of awards on rolling basis.
**Financial aid contact:** Cecilia Hightower. 912 583-2241, extension 213.
**STUDENT EMPLOYMENT.** College Work/Study Program. Institutional employment. 9% of full-time undergraduates work on campus during school year. Students may expect to earn an average of $900 during school year. Off-campus part-time employment opportunities rated "good."
**COMPUTER FACILITIES.** 18 IBM/IBM-compatible microcomputers; 8 are networked. Computer languages and software packages include C, COBOL, dBase, Lotus 1-2-3, Paradox, Pascal, Stat Plus, Word Star, WordPerfect. Computer facilities are available to all students.
**Fees:** None.
**Hours:** 30 hours/week.
**GRADUATE CAREER DATA.** Graduate school percentages: 2% enter graduate business programs. 5% enter graduate arts and sciences programs. 7% enter theological school/seminary. Highest graduate school enrollments: Georgia Southern U, Southern Baptist Theological Seminary. 22% of graduates choose careers in business and industry. Companies and businesses that hire graduates: Georgia public schools, Department of Family and Children's Services.

# Clark Atlanta University

**Atlanta, GA 30314** — **404 880-8000**

**1993-94 Costs.** Tuition: $11,400. Room & board: $3,940. Fees, books, misc. academic expenses (school's estimate): $630.
**Enrollment.** Undergraduates: 954 men, 2,198 women (full-time). Freshman class: 5,749 applicants, 2,840 accepted, 797 enrolled. Graduate enrollment: 456 men, 773 women.
**Test score averages/ranges.** N/A.
**Faculty.** 251 full-time; 21 part-time. Student/faculty ratio: 19 to 1.
**Selectivity rating.** N/A.

**PROFILE.** Clark Atlanta, founded in 1869, is a private university. Academic divisions include General Education, Humanities, Natural Sciences and Mathematics, and Sociocultural Studies. Its campus is located one mile west of downtown Atlanta.

**Accreditation:** SACS. Professionally accredited by the American Dietetic Association, the American Physical Therapy Association, the Council on Social Work Education, the National Council for Accreditation of Teacher Education.
**Religious orientation:** Clark Atlanta University is affiliated with the United Methodist Church; no religious requirements.
**Library:** Collections totaling over 750,000 volumes.
**Special facilities/museums:** Language lab.
**Athletic facilities:** Swimming pool, gymnasium, weight room, football fields, basketball, tennis courts.
**STUDENT BODY. Undergraduate profile:** 50% are state residents; 35% are transfers. 1% Asian-American, 96% Black, 1% Hispanic, 2% White. Average age of undergraduates is 20.
**Undergraduate achievement:** 75% of fall 1991 freshmen returned for fall 1992 term.
**PROGRAMS OF STUDY. Degrees:** B.A., B.S., B.Soc.Work
**Majors:** Accounting, Art, Art Education, Biology, Bookkeeping, Business Administration, Business Education, Chemistry, Child Development, Computer Science, Dietetics, Drama, Early Childhood, Educational Studies, Elementary Education, English, Fine Arts, French, German, History, Home Economics Education, Human Resources, Mass Communications, Mathematics, Medical Illustration, Medical Records Administration, Medical Technology, Music, Music Education, Nutrition, Office Administration, Philosophy, Physical Education, Physical Therapy, Physics, Political Science, Psychology, Religion, Restaurant/Institutional Management, Social Welfare, Sociology, Spanish, Speech Communication.
**Requirements:** General education requirement.
**Academic regulations:** Freshmen must maintain minimum 1.76 GPA.
**Special:** Established and self-designed interdepartmental majors. Cooperative general science program for non-science majors. Required freshman orientation seminars. Double majors. Dual degrees. Independent study. Accelerated study. Pass/fail grading option. 3-2 engineering program with Georgia Tech. All undergraduate majors offered through Atlanta University Center are open to CAU students. Member of Atlanta University Center Consortium. Affiliated with Southern Center for Studies in Public Policy. Teacher certification in early childhood, elementary, secondary, and special education. Study abroad possible. ROTC, NROTC, and AFROTC.
**Honors:** Honors program.
**Academic Assistance:** Remedial reading, writing, math, and study skills. Nonremedial tutoring.
**STUDENT LIFE. Housing:** Students may live on or off campus. Coed, women's, and men's dorms. 40% of students live in college housing.
**Social atmosphere:** "Because we are located within walking distance of four other colege campuses, the daily interaction is a main event," reports the student newspaper. "The social life is excellent and every weekend, at least four major functions are held." Popular campus hangouts are the Soul Source Bookstore, Stegal's Shop, Jomandi Theater, the Color Box Club, Screamin Wheels, and Crickets. Greek organizations are influential on campus. Homecoming, The Mug, and the Labor Day Classic are among the year's favorite events.
**Services and counseling/handicapped student services:** Placement services. Health service. Counseling services for veteran students. Personal and psychological counseling. Career and academic guidance services. Religious counseling. Physically disabled student services. Tutors.
**Campus organizations:** Undergraduate student government. Student newspaper (Panther, published once/week). Yearbook. Radio and TV stations. Band, choir, orchestra, jazz ensemble, musical theatre, community service projects, special-interest groups, 60 organizations in all. Four fraternities, no chapter houses; four sororities, no chapter houses.
**Religious organizations:** Campus Ministry.
**ATHLETICS. Physical education requirements:** Two semesters of physical education required.
**Intercollegiate competition:** 1% of students participate. Basketball (M,W), cheerleading (W), football (M), track and field (outdoor) (M,W), volleyball (W). Member of NCAA Division II, Southern Intercollegiate Athletic Conference.
**Intramural and club sports:** 1% of students participate. Intramural basketball, softball, swimming, volleyball, weight lifting. Men's club baseball.
**ADMISSIONS. Academic basis for candidate selection** (in order of priority): Secondary school record, standardized test scores.
**Nonacademic basis for candidate selection:** Particular talent or ability is important. Extracurricular participation and alumni/ae relationship are considered.
**Requirements:** Graduation from secondary school is required; GED is accepted. 16 units and the following program of study are recommended: 4 units of English, 3 units of math, 2 units of science, 2 units of foreign language, 2 units of social studies, 5 units of electives. Applicants whose preparation varies from recommended distribution will be considered. SAT is required; ACT may be substituted. No off-campus interviews.
**Procedure:** Suggest filing application by March 1; no deadline. Notification of admission on rolling basis. $100 tuition deposit, refundable until July 1. $750 room deposit, refundable until July 1. Freshmen accepted for terms other than fall.
**Special programs:** Early entrance/early admission program. Concurrent enrollment program.
**Transfer students:** Transfer students accepted for terms other than fall. In fall 1992, 35% of all new students were transfers into all classes. 1,138 transfer applications were received, 604 were accepted. Application deadline is March 1 for fall; November 1 for spring. Minimum 2.0 GPA required. Lowest course grade accepted is "C." At least 30 semester hours must be completed at the university to receive degree.
**Admissions contact:** Clifton B. Rawles, M.A., Director of Admissions. 404 880-8017.
**FINANCIAL AID. Available aid:** Pell grants, SEOG, state scholarships and grants, school scholarships and grants, ROTC scholarships, academic merit scholarships, athletic scholarships, and United Negro College Fund. Perkins Loans (NDSL), PLUS, Stafford Loans (GSL), and SLS. Deferred payment plan.
**Financial aid statistics:** In 1992-93, 89% of all undergraduate applicants received aid; 94% of freshman applicants. Average amounts of aid awarded freshmen: Scholarships and grants, $5,800; loans, $2,625.
**Supporting data/closing dates:** FAFSA/FAF: Priority filing date is April 30. Notification of awards begins May 1.
**Financial aid contact:** Marjorie Belton, M.P.A., Director of Financial Aid. 404 880-8066.
**STUDENT EMPLOYMENT.** College Work/Study Program. Institutional employment. 3% of full-time undergraduates work on campus during school year. Students may expect to earn an average of $2,000 during school year. Off-campus part-time employment opportunities rated "fair."
**COMPUTER FACILITIES.** IBM/IBM-compatible microcomputers. Computer facilities are available to all students.
**Fees:** Computer fee is included in tuition/fees.

# Clayton State College

**Morrow, GA 30260** — **404 961-3400**

**1993-94 Costs.** Tuition: $1,440 (state residents), $4,122 (out-of-state). Housing: None. Fees, books, misc. academic expenses (school's estimate): $400.
**Enrollment.** Undergraduates: 779 men, 999 women (full-time). Freshman class: 1,702 applicants, 1,126 accepted, 821 enrolled.
**Test score averages/ranges.** Average SAT scores: 380 verbal, 410 math. Average ACT scores: 17 English, 17 math, 18 composite.
**Faculty.** 108 full-time; 85 part-time. 56% of faculty holds doctoral degree.
**Selectivity rating.** Less competitive.

**PROFILE.** Clayton State, founded in 1969, is a public, multipurpose institution. Programs are offered through the Schools of Arts and Sciences, Business, and Health Sciences. Its 150-acre campus is located in Morrow, 10 miles from Atlanta.

**Accreditation:** SACS. Professionally accredited by the National League for Nursing.
**Religious orientation:** Clayton State College is nonsectarian; no religious requirements.
**STUDENT BODY. Undergraduate profile:** 97% are state residents. 3% Asian-American, 20% Black, 3% Hispanic, 74% White.
**Freshman profile:** 75% of accepted applicants took SAT; 100% took ACT.
**Undergraduate achievement:** 48% of fall 1992 freshmen returned for fall 1993 term.
**Foreign students:** 56 students are from out of the country. Countries represented include India, Jamaica, Kenya, Nigeria, and Vietnam; 10 in all.
**PROGRAMS OF STUDY. Degrees:** B.A., B.Bus.Admin., B.Mus., B.S.Nurs.
**Majors:** Accounting, Composition, Computer Information Systems, General Business, Instrument Building, Management, Middle Level Education, Nursing, Performance.
**Distribution of degrees:** The majors with the highest enrollment are accounting and nursing.
**Requirements:** General education requirement.
**Academic regulations:** Minimum 2.0 GPA must be maintained.
**Special:** Associate's degrees offered. Accelerated study. Internships. Cooperative education programs.

**Honors:** Phi Beta Kappa. Honors program.
**Academic Assistance:** Remedial reading, writing, math, and study skills. Nonremedial tutoring.

**STUDENT LIFE. Housing:** Commuter campus; no student housing.
**Services and counseling/handicapped student services:** Placement services. Counseling services for minority, veteran, and older students. Personal counseling. Career guidance services. Physically disabled student services. Learning disabled services. Tutors.
**Campus organizations:** Undergraduate student government. Student newspaper (Bent Tree, published once/month). Multicultural Awareness Task Force, Students Supporting Other Students.
**Religious organizations:** Baptist Student Union, United Methodist Fellowship.
**Minority/foreign student organizations:** Black Cultural Awareness Association. International Awareness Club.

**ATHLETICS. Physical education requirements:** Three quarters of physical education required.

**ADMISSIONS. Academic basis for candidate selection** (in order of priority): Secondary school record, standardized test scores.
**Requirements:** Graduation from secondary school is required; GED is accepted. 18 units and the following program of study are required: 4 units of English, 3 units of math, 3 units of science including 2 units of lab, 2 units of foreign language, 3 units of social studies, 2 units of history, 1 unit of electives. SAT or ACT is required. Campus visit recommended. No off-campus interviews.
**Procedure:** Take SAT or ACT by April of 12th year. Notification of admission on rolling basis. Freshmen accepted for terms other than fall.
**Special programs:** Admission may be deferred one year. Credit and/or placement may be granted through CEEB Advanced Placement exams for scores of 3 or higher. Credit may be granted through CLEP general and subject exams, Regents College and challenge exams. Early decision program. Concurrent enrollment program.
**Transfer students:** Transfer students accepted for terms other than fall. Application deadline is September 1 for fall; March 1 for spring. Minimum 2.0 GPA recommended. Lowest course grade accepted is "D." Maximum number of transferable credits is 30 quarter hours.
**Admissions contact:** Tonya R. Hobson, M.A., Director of Admissions. 404 961-3500.

**FINANCIAL AID. Available aid:** Pell grants, SEOG, Federal Nursing Student Scholarships, state scholarships and grants, school scholarships and grants, private scholarships and grants, academic merit scholarships, and athletic scholarships. State of Georgia Hope Grants. Perkins Loans (NDSL), Stafford Loans (GSL), NSL, state loans, and SLS.
**Financial aid statistics:** In 1993-94, 90% of all undergraduate applicants received aid.
**Supporting data/closing dates:** FAFSA/FAF/FFS: Accepted on rolling basis. School's own aid application: Accepted on rolling basis. Notification of awards on rolling basis.
**Financial aid contact:** Vera Brooks, M.A., Director of Financial Aid. 404 961-3511.

**STUDENT EMPLOYMENT.** College Work/Study Program. Institutional employment. Off-campus part-time employment opportunities rated "excellent."

**COMPUTER FACILITIES.** 500 IBM/IBM-compatible and Macintosh/Apple microcomputers; 300 are networked. Students may access CDC Cyber, IBM minicomputer/mainframe systems, BITNET, Internet. Client/LAN operating systems include Apple/Macintosh, DOS, OS/2, UNIX/XENIX/AIX, Novell. Computer facilities are available to all students.
**Fees:** None.

**GRADUATE CAREER DATA.** Highest graduate school enrollments: Georgia State U, U of Georgia. 60% of graduates choose careers in business and industry. Companies and businesses that hire graduates: Delta Airlines.

# Columbus College

**Columbus, GA 31993-2399 706 568-2001**

**1994-95 Costs.** Tuition: $1,601 (state residents), $4,364 (out-of-state). Room & board: $2,916. Fees, books, misc. academic expenses (school's estimate): $500.
**Enrollment.** Undergraduates: 1,134 men, 1,739 women (full-time). Freshman class: 1,196 enrolled. Graduate enrollment: 242 men, 390 women.
**Test score averages/ranges.** Average SAT scores: 418 verbal, 464 math.
**Faculty.** 180 full-time; 48 part-time. 64% of faculty holds doctoral degree. Student/faculty ratio: 14 to 1.
**Selectivity rating.** Noncompetitive.

**PROFILE.** Columbus is a public college. Founded in 1958, it became a senior member of the University System of Georgia in 1965. Programs are offered through the Schools of Arts and Letters, Business, Education, and Science. Its 132-acre modern campus is located in Columbus, 100 miles from Atlanta.

**Accreditation:** SACS. Professionally accredited by the American Dental Association, the American Medical Association (CAHEA), the National Association of Schools of Music, the National Council for Accreditation of Teacher Education, the National League for Nursing.
**Religious orientation:** Columbus College is nonsectarian; no religious requirements.
**Library:** Collections totaling over 235,000 volumes, 8,308 periodical subscriptions, and 742,043 microform items.
**Athletic facilities:** Two gymnasiums, swimming pool, baseball and softball fields, soccer field, intramural fields, tennis courts.

**STUDENT BODY. Undergraduate profile:** 97% are state residents. 3% Asian-American, 22% Black, 3% Hispanic, 72% White. Average age of undergraduates is 26.
**Freshman profile:** 1% of freshmen who took SAT scored 700 or over on math; 3% scored 600 or over on verbal, 7% scored 600 or over on math; 18% scored 500 or over on verbal, 35% scored 500 or over on math; 57% scored 400 or over on verbal, 79% scored 400 or over on math; 97% scored 300 or over on verbal, 99% scored 300 or over on math. Majority of accepted applicants took SAT. 98% of freshmen come from public schools.
**Foreign students:** 53 students are from out of the country. Countries represented include Argentina, China, Germany, Honduras, Japan, and Mexico; 32 in all.

**PROGRAMS OF STUDY. Degrees:** B.A., B.Bus.Admin., B.Mus., B.S.
**Majors:** Accounting, Art, Art Education, Biology, Business Administration, Chemistry, Communicative Disorders/Speech/Language Pathology, Computer Information Management, Criminal Justice, Drama, Early Childhood Education, Economics, English Language/Literature, Finance, General Studies, Geology, Health, History, Management, Marketing, Mathematical Science/Computers, Medical Technology, Middle Grades Education, Music, Music Education/Vocal/Instrumental, Nursing, Piano Pedagogy/Performance, Political Science, Psychology, Public Administration, Recreation/Park Administration, Secondary Education, Sociology, Special Education/Mental Retardation, Speech Communication.
**Distribution of degrees:** The majors with the highest enrollment are criminal justice, general studies, and management; drama, geology, and sociology have the lowest.
**Requirements:** General education requirement.
**Academic regulations:** Freshmen must maintain minimum 1.35 GPA; sophomores, 1.45 GPA; juniors, 1.55 GPA; seniors, 1.65 GPA.
**Special:** Minors offered in many majors and in approximately five other fields. Major in middle grades education requires two or more areas of concentration; at least one must be from science, social science, language arts, or math; other areas of concentration are art, music, and health/physical education. Secondary education majors must select at least one area of concentration from biology, chemistry, English, history, math, political science, or social science. GRE required for graduation in some programs. Associate's degrees offered. Internships. Graduate school at which undergraduates may take graduate-level courses. Preprofessional programs in law, medicine, veterinary science, pharmacy, dentistry, engineering, and forestry. 2-2 engineering program with Georgia Tech. Member of consortium with University System of Georgia. Teacher certification in early childhood, secondary, and special education. Study abroad in Asian, African, European, and Central and South American countries. ROTC.
**Honors:** Honors program. Honor societies.
**Academic Assistance:** Remedial reading, writing, math, and study skills. Nonremedial tutoring.

**STUDENT LIFE. Housing:** Sorority and fraternity housing. School-owned/operated apartments. Referral service for privately owned off-campus housing. 6% of students live in college housing.
**Social atmosphere:** According to the student newspaper, "We are basically a commuter school, but many activities occur on and off campus." Popular student hangouts include the Davidson Center and area malls. The Greeks, the Baptist Student Union, and the Saber staff have widespread influence on student social life. The college's Halloween carnival and Homecoming are the most popular social events of the year.
**Services and counseling/handicapped student services:** Placement services. Health service. Counseling services for minority, military, veteran, and older students. Personal counseling. Career and academic guidance services. Physically disabled student services. Learning disabled services. Notetaking services. Tape recorders. Tutors. Reader services for the blind.
**Campus organizations:** Undergraduate student government. Student newspaper (Saber, published once/week). Literary magazine. Yearbook. Academic and professional groups, bands, orchestra, ensembles, choirs, Choral Interpreters, theatre, special-interest organizations, 50 organizations in all. Four fraternities, one chapter house; four sororities, one chapter house.
**Religious organizations:** Baptist Student Union.
**Minority/foreign student organizations:** Afro-American Student Union. International Student Association.

**ATHLETICS. Physical education requirements:** Three quarter hours of physical education required.
**Intercollegiate competition:** 1% of students participate. Baseball (M), basketball (M), cross-country (M), golf (M), soccer (M), softball (W), tennis (M,W), volleyball (W). Member of NAIA, NCAA Division II.
**Intramural and club sports:** Intramural basketball, flag football, golf, softball, tennis, volleyball.

**ADMISSIONS. Academic basis for candidate selection** (in order of priority): Standardized test scores, secondary school record.
**Requirements:** Graduation from secondary school is recommended; GED is accepted. 16 units and the following program of study are required: 4 units of English, 3 units of math, 3 units of lab science, 2 units of foreign language, 3 units of social studies. Minimum SAT score of 350 in both verbal and math and minimum 1.8 GPA required. Interview required of applicants to health science, nursing, and other programs. Developmental Studies Program for applicants not normally admissible. SAT or ACT is required. Campus visit recommended. No off-campus interviews.
**Procedure:** Take SAT or ACT by winter of 12th year. Suggest filing application by July. Application deadline is August. Notification of admission on rolling basis. No set date by which applicants must accept offer. $100 refundable room deposit. Freshmen accepted for terms other than fall.
**Special programs:** Admission may be deferred one year. Credit may be granted through CEEB Advanced Placement for scores of 3 or higher. Credit may be granted through CLEP general and subject exams, challenge exams, and military and life experience. Placement may be granted through Regents College exams. Early entrance/early admission program. Concurrent enrollment program.
**Transfer students:** Transfer students accepted for terms other than fall. Application deadline is September 7 for fall; March 15 for spring. Minimum 2.0 GPA. Lowest course grade accepted is "D." Maximum number of transferable credits is 101 quarter hours. At least 45 quarter hours must be completed at the college to receive degree.
**Admissions contact:** Patty L. Ross, M.S., Director of Admissions. 404 568-2035.

**FINANCIAL AID. Available aid:** Pell grants, SEOG, Federal Nursing Student Scholarships, state scholarships and grants, school scholarships, ROTC scholarships, academic merit scholarships, and athletic scholarships. Perkins Loans (NDSL), PLUS, Stafford Loans (GSL), state loans, school loans, and SLS.
**Financial aid statistics:** Average amounts of aid awarded freshmen: Scholarships and grants, $1,227; loans, $900.
**Supporting data/closing dates:** FAFSA/FAF: Accepted on rolling basis. Notification of awards on rolling basis.

**Financial aid contact:** Al Pinckney, M.Ed., Director of Financial Aid. 404 568-2036.
**STUDENT EMPLOYMENT.** College Work/Study Program. Institutional employment. 2% of full-time undergraduates work on campus during school year. Off-campus part-time employment opportunities rated "excellent."
**COMPUTER FACILITIES.** 265 IBM/IBM-compatible, Macintosh/Apple, and RISC-/UNIX-based microcomputers; 225 are networked. Students may access CDC Cyber, IBM, SUN minicomputer/mainframe systems, BITNET. Client/LAN operating systems include Apple/Macintosh, DOS, Windows NT, Novell. Computer languages and software packages include Assembler, CH, COBOL, dBASE, Lotus 1-2-3, SPSS/PC, Turbo Pascal. Computer facilities are available to all students.
**Fees:** None.
**Hours:** 16 hours (M-F); 8 hours (Sa-Su).
**PROMINENT ALUMNI/AE.** Jean M. Hartin, vice-president of nursing services, Medical Center Hospital; James D. Yancey, president, SYNOVUS; Kenneth E. Evans, executive vice-president, Total Systems.

# Covenant College

**Lookout Mountain, GA 30750 706 820-1560**

**1993-94 Costs.** Tuition: $8,400. Room & board: $3,510. Fees, books, misc. academic expenses (school's estimate): $730.
**Enrollment.** Undergraduates: 273 men, 332 women (full-time). Freshman class: 407 applicants, 317 accepted, 181 enrolled. Graduate enrollment: 20 men, 21 women.
**Test score averages/ranges.** Average SAT scores: 515 verbal, 550 math. Range of SAT scores of middle 50%: 450-580 verbal, 490-620 math. Average ACT scores: 25 composite. Range of ACT scores of middle 50%: 22-27 composite.
**Faculty.** 40 full-time; 19 part-time. 70% of faculty holds doctoral degree. Student/faculty ratio: 14 to 1.
**Selectivity rating.** Competitive.

**PROFILE.** Covenant, founded in 1955, is a church-affiliated, liberal arts college. Its 70-acre campus is located in Lookout Mountain, across the state line from Chattanooga, Tenn.

**Accreditation:** SACS.
**Religious orientation:** Covenant College is affiliated with the Presbyterian Church in America; four semesters of religion/theology required.
**Library:** Collections totaling over 80,860 volumes, 500 periodical subscriptions, and 27,196 microform items.
**Athletic facilities:** Gymnasium, football and soccer fields, tennis courts, weight room.
**STUDENT BODY. Undergraduate profile:** 19% are state residents; 22% are transfers. .5% Asian-American, 3% Black, 1% Hispanic, .5% Native American, 93% White, 2% Other. Average age of undergraduates is 20.
**Freshman profile:** 3% of freshmen who took SAT scored 700 or over on verbal, 8% scored 700 or over on math; 24% scored 600 or over on verbal, 31% scored 600 or over on math; 52% scored 500 or over on verbal, 72% scored 500 or over on math; 90% scored 400 or over on verbal, 98% scored 400 or over on math; 100% scored 300 or over on verbal, 100% scored 300 or over on math. Majority of accepted applicants took SAT.
**Undergraduate achievement:** 74% of fall 1992 freshmen returned for fall 1993 term. 35% of entering class graduated.
**Foreign students:** 24 students are from out of the country. Countries represented include China, France, Germany, India, Japan, and South Africa; 15 in all.
**PROGRAMS OF STUDY. Degrees:** B.A., B.Mus., B.S.
**Majors:** Applied Music, Biblical Studies/Missions, Biology, Business Administration, Chemistry, Computer Science, Elementary Education, English, History, Interdisciplinary Studies, Music, Music Education, Natural Science, Organizational Behavior, Psychology, Sociology.
**Distribution of degrees:** The majors with the highest enrollment are business administration, elementary education, and interdisciplinary studies; chemistry, applied music, and music have the lowest.
**Requirements:** General education requirement.
**Academic regulations:** Freshmen must maintain minimum 1.9 GPA; sophomores, juniors, seniors 2.0 GPA.
**Special:** Minors offered in most majors and in accounting, art, information systems management, interpersonal counseling, marketing, mathematics, philosophy, physical education, physics, Spanish, and youth ministry. Associate's degrees offered. Double majors. Dual degrees. Independent study. Pass/fail grading option. Preprofessional programs in law, medicine, theology, and nursing. 3-2 engineering program with Georgia Tech. Member of Christian College Coalition. Teacher certification in elementary and secondary education. Certification in specific subject areas. Study abroad in Costa Rica, France, Germany, Israel, and Spain. ROTC U of Tennessee at Chattanooga.
**Honors:** Honors program.
**Academic Assistance:** Remedial writing. Nonremedial tutoring.
**ADMISSIONS. Academic basis for candidate selection** (in order of priority): Standardized test scores, secondary school record, essay.
**Requirements:** Graduation from secondary school is recommended; GED is accepted. 16 units and the following program of study are recommended: 4 units of English, 3 units of math, 2 units of science, 2 units of foreign language, 2 units of social studies, 3 units of electives. Minimum combined SAT score of 900 (composite ACT score of 21) and minimum 2.5 GPA required. Minimum of five years of work experience and two years of college required of organizational behavior program applicants. Special admissions criteria required of pre-medicine and pre-engineering program applicants. Audition required of music program applicants. Limited Load for applicants not meeting standard requirements. SAT is required; ACT may be substituted. Campus visit recommended. Off-campus interviews available with an admissions representative.
**Procedure:** Take SAT or ACT by spring of 12th year. Visit college for interview by spring of 12th year. Suggest filing application by March 31. Application deadline is June 1. Notification of admission on rolling basis. Reply is required by May 1, or within 30 days of notification of acceptance. $100 nonrefundable tuition deposit. $100 refundable room deposit. Room deposit is refundable if written request received by June 1; if received by July 1, half of deposit refunded. Freshmen accepted for terms other than fall.
**Special programs:** Admission may be deferred indefinitely. Credit and/or placement may be granted through CEEB Advanced Placement exams for scores of 3 or higher. Credit and/or placement may be granted through CLEP general and subject exams. Credit may be granted through life experience.
**Transfer students:** Transfer students accepted for terms other than fall. In fall 1993, 22% of all new students were transfers into all classes. 100 transfer applications were received, 78 were accepted. Application deadline is rolling for fall; November 1 for spring. Minimum 2.0 GPA recommended. Lowest course grade accepted is "C-." Maximum number of transferable credits is 70 semester hours. At least 30 semester hours must be completed at the college to receive degree.
**Admissions contact:** Charlie Phillips, Vice President for Development and Admissions. 706 820-1560, extension 1140.
**FINANCIAL AID. Available aid:** Pell grants, SEOG, state scholarships and grants, school scholarships and grants, private scholarships, ROTC scholarships, academic merit scholarships, athletic scholarships, and aid for undergraduate foreign students. Education and music scholarships. Perkins Loans (NDSL), PLUS, Stafford Loans (GSL), and state loans. AMS and deferred payment plan. Bank card center of American National Bank and Trust.
**Financial aid statistics:** 18% of aid is not need-based. In 1993-94, 100% of all undergraduate applicants received aid. Average amounts of aid awarded freshmen: Scholarships and grants, $4,163; loans, $1,773.
**Supporting data/closing dates:** FAFSA: Priority filing date is March 31; accepted on rolling basis. School's own aid application: Priority filing date is March 31; accepted on rolling basis. Income tax forms: Priority filing date is March 31. Merit Scholarship Forms: Priority filing date is March 31. Notification of awards on rolling basis.
**Financial aid contact:** Becky Bigger, Director of Financial Aid. 796 820-1560, extension 1150.

# DeVry Institute of Technology

**Decatur, GA 30030 404 292-7900**

**1994-95 Costs.** Tuition: $5,962. Housing: None. Fees, books, misc. academic expenses (school's estimate): $580.
**Enrollment.** Undergraduates: 1,692 men, 608 women (full-time). Freshman class: 1,956 applicants, 1,741 accepted, 826 enrolled.
**Test score averages/ranges.** N/A.
**Faculty.** 72 full-time; 13 part-time. Student/faculty ratio: 32 to 1.
**Selectivity rating.** N/A.

**PROFILE.** DeVry/Atlanta, founded in 1969, is a private institution specializing in electronics technology and computer information systems. It is a member of a network of technical institutes with eight campuses in the U.S. and two in Canada. Its 21-acre campus is located in Decatur, on the eastern edge of Atlanta.

**Accreditation:** NCACS. Professionally accredited by the Accreditation Board for Engineering and Technology.
**Religious orientation:** DeVry Institute of Technology is nonsectarian; no religious requirements.
**Library:** Collections totaling over 13,500 volumes, 200 periodical subscriptions, and 111 microform items.
**Special facilities/museums:** Electronics lab.
**Athletic facilities:** Gymnasium, recreation center.
**STUDENT BODY. Undergraduate profile:** 44% are state residents; 49% are transfers. 3% Asian-American, 61% Black, 2% Hispanic, 1% Native American, 32% White, 1% Other. Average age of undergraduates is 24.
**Undergraduate achievement:** 34% of fall 1992 freshmen returned for fall 1993 term. 25% of entering class graduated.
**Foreign students:** 41 students are from out of the country. Countries represented include the Bahamas, India, Japan, Pakistan, United Arab Emirates, and the United Kingdom; 16 in all.
**PROGRAMS OF STUDY. Degrees:** B.S.
**Majors:** Accounting, Business Operations, Computer Information Systems, Electronics Engineering Technology.
**Distribution of degrees:** The majors with the highest enrollment are computer information systems, electronics engineering technology, and business operations.
**Requirements:** General education requirement.
**Academic regulations:** Minimum 2.0 GPA must be maintained.
**Special:** Electronics technician diploma program. Lock-Step Curriculum with three 15-week trimesters; B.S. degree possible in three years through continuous enrollment. Associate's degrees offered. Accelerated study. Cooperative education programs.
**Honors:** Honor societies.
**Academic Assistance:** Nonremedial tutoring.
**STUDENT LIFE. Housing:** Commuter campus; no student housing.
**Social atmosphere:** DeVry students frequent the Commons. Peer advisors, the DeVry Christian Fellowhsip, and the Student Association are influential groups on campus. Popular events are the "Taste of DeVry," the Alpha Experience, the Martin Luther King, Jr. March, and the Schick 3-on-3 Basketball Tournament. A school administrator reports, "This is a close-knit campus with many of its social and cultural events sponsored by the Student Association."
**Services and counseling/handicapped student services:** Placement services. Career and academic guidance services. Physically disabled student services. Notetaking services. Reader services for the blind.
**Campus organizations:** Undergraduate student government. New Generation mass choir, accounting, business, computer and electronics clubs, service fraternities, peer advisors, Toastmasters, 14 organizations in all.

**Religious organizations:** Christian Fellowship.
**Minority/foreign student organizations:** National Society of Black Engineers, Association of Women in Science, Black DP Association. International Student Club.

**ATHLETICS. Physical education requirements:** None.
**Intercollegiate competition:** 1% of students participate.
**Intramural and club sports:** 12% of students participate. Intramural basketball, flag football, golf, soccer, softball, volleyball. Men's club flag football, volleyball.

**ADMISSIONS. Academic basis for candidate selection** (in order of priority): Standardized test scores.
**Requirements:** Graduation from secondary school is required; GED is accepted. No specific distribution of secondary school units required. SAT or ACT recommended. Applicants not submitting SAT or ACT must pass DeVry entrance exam. Applicants must have graduated from secondary school at their application time and be at least age 17 on or before first day of classes. Minimum SAT or ACT scores vary by program; generally SAT math score of 400-480 (ACT math score of 16-18) required. Campus visit recommended. Off-campus interviews available with an admissions representative.
**Procedure:** Notification of admission on rolling basis. Reply is required by registration. $75 tuition deposit, refundable until beginning of classes. Freshmen accepted for terms other than fall.
**Special programs:** Admission may be deferred one year. Credit may be granted through CLEP subject exams, DANTES and challenge exams.
**Transfer students:** Transfer students accepted for terms other than fall. In fall 1993, 49% of all new students were transfers into all classes. Application deadline is rolling for fall; rolling for spring. Minimum 2.0 GPA required. Lowest course grade accepted is "C." Maximum number of transferable semester hours is 65% of total required for degree. At least 35% of total semester hours must be completed at the institute to receive degree.
**Admissions contact:** Susann Anderson-Hirst, Director of Admissions. 404 292-2645.

**FINANCIAL AID. Available aid:** Pell grants, SEOG, state scholarships and grants, school scholarships, and academic merit scholarships. Perkins Loans (NDSL), PLUS, Stafford Loans (GSL), state loans, and SLS. EduCard Plan.
**Financial aid statistics:** In 1993-94, 75% of all undergraduate applicants received aid; 73% of freshman applicants.
**Supporting data/closing dates:** FAFSA: Accepted on rolling basis. Notification of awards on rolling basis.
**Financial aid contact:** Loretta Franklin, M.Ed., Dean of Student Finance.

**STUDENT EMPLOYMENT.** College Work/Study Program. Institutional employment. 9% of full-time undergraduates work on campus during school year. Students may expect to earn an average of $930 during school year. Freshmen are discouraged from working during their first term. Off-campus part-time employment opportunities rated "poor."

**COMPUTER FACILITIES.** 450 IBM/IBM-compatible microcomputers; 232 are networked. Students may access IBM minicomputer/mainframe systems. Client/LAN operating systems include DOS, UNIX/XENIX/AIX, Novell. Computer languages and software packages include Assembly, C++, MASM, Turbo C, Visual BASIC, WordPerfect; 20 in all. Computer facilities are available to all students.
**Fees:** Computer fee is included in tuition/fees.
**Hours:** 7:30 AM-11 PM

**GRADUATE CAREER DATA.** 84% of graduates choose careers in business and industry. Companies and businesses that hire graduates: Applied Materials, Hewlett-Packard, Microsoft, Geico.

# Emory University

**Atlanta, GA 30322** **404 727-6123**

**1994-95 Costs.** Tuition: $17,600. Room: $3,600. Board: $2,400. Fees, books, misc. academic expenses (school's estimate): $830.
**Enrollment.** Undergraduates: 2,464 men, 3,056 women (full-time). Freshman class: 8,506 applicants, 4,245 accepted, 1,166 enrolled. Graduate enrollment: 2,305 men, 2,326 women.
**Test score averages/ranges.** Average SAT scores: 570 verbal, 650 math. Range of SAT scores of middle 50%: 530-610 verbal, 600-700 math. Average ACT scores: 27 composite. Range of ACT scores of middle 50%: 26-30 composite.
**Faculty.** 519 full-time; 167 part-time. 96% of faculty holds doctoral degree. Student/faculty ratio: 10 to 1.
**Selectivity rating.** Highly competitive.

**PROFILE.** Emory is a church-affiliated, comprehensive university. Founded as a college in Oxford, Ga. in 1836, Emory was granted university status when it moved to Atlanta in 1919. Its 631-acre campus is located in a residential area north of Atlanta's downtown. Campus architecture includes Italian Renaissance style.
**Accreditation:** SACS. Professionally accredited by the American Assembly of Collegiate Schools of Business, the Liaison Committee on Medical Education, the National Council for Accreditation of Teacher Education, the National League for Nursing.
**Religious orientation:** Emory University is affiliated with the United Methodist Church; no religious requirements.
**Library:** Collections totaling over 2,200,000 volumes, 22,842 periodical subscriptions, and 2,400,000 microform items.
**Special facilities/museums:** Museum of art and archaeology, U.S. centers for disease control, Carter presidential center, primate research center.
**Athletic facilities:** Gymnasium, badminton, basketball, racquetball, squash, tennis, and volleyball courts, swimming pool, combatives, and weight rooms, dance studio, track, baseball, intramural, and soccer fields, court hockey rink, stadium.

**STUDENT BODY. Undergraduate profile:** 20% are state residents; 8% are transfers. 10% Asian-American, 9% Black, 3% Hispanic, 76% White, 2% Other. Average age of undergraduates is 19.
**Freshman profile:** 4% of freshmen who took SAT scored 700 or over on verbal, 21% scored 700 or over on math; 37% scored 600 or over on verbal, 77% scored 600 or over on math; 92% scored 500 or over on verbal, 100% scored 500 or over on math; 100% scored 400 or over on verbal. 82% of accepted applicants took SAT; 21% took ACT. 65% of freshmen come from public schools.
**Undergraduate achievement:** 90% of fall 1992 freshmen returned for fall 1993 term. 80% of entering class graduated. 66% of students who completed a degree program immediately went on to graduate study.
**Foreign students:** 88 students are from out of the country. Countries represented include Canada, China, Korea, and the United Kingdom; 40 in all.

**PROGRAMS OF STUDY. Degrees:** B.A., B.Bus.Admin., B.S., B.S.Nurs.
**Majors:** African/Afro-American Studies, Anthropology, Anthropology/Human Ecology/Environmental Science, Applied Physics, Art History, Biology, Business Administration, Chemistry, Classical Civilization, Classical Studies, Classics, Creative Writing, Economics, Educational Studies, Elementary Education, English, Film Studies, French, French Cultural Studies, German, German Studies, Greek, Hispanic/Latin American Studies, History, International Studies, Italian Studies, Judaic Language/Literature, Judaic Studies, Latin, Latin American Studies, Liberal Studies, Literature, Mathematics, Mathematics/Computer Science, Medieval/Renaissance Studies, Music, Near Eastern Studies, Nursing, Philosophy, Physics, Political Science, Psychology, Religion, Russian, Sociology, Spanish, Theatre Studies, Women's Studies.
**Distribution of degrees:** The majors with the highest enrollment are psychology, biology, and political science; German studies, classical studies, and Near Eastern studies have the lowest.
**Requirements:** General education requirement.
**Academic regulations:** Freshmen must maintain minimum 1.50 GPA; sophomores, 1.60 GPA; juniors, 1.70 GPA; seniors, 2.00 GPA.
**Special:** Minors offered in some majors and in Arabic, art history, Hebrew, Italian, and Soviet and East European studies. 15 joint concentrations and nine interdepartmental programs offered, which may include joint majors in economics and history, economics and math, history and political science, and English and history. School of Business and School of Nursing are entered after sophomore year. Carter Center offers Latin American and Caribbean studies and has committee on comparative cultural changes. Associate's degrees offered. Double majors. Dual degrees. Accelerated study. Pass/fail grading option. Internships. Graduate school at which undergraduates may take graduate-level courses. Preprofessional programs in law, medicine, veterinary science, dentistry, and theology. 3-2 engineering program with Georgia Tech. Member of Southern College Consortium and Atlanta University Center Consortium. Washington Semester. Teacher certification in early childhood, elementary, and secondary education. Certification in specific subject areas. Exchange programs abroad in Austria (Johannes Kepler U), Scotland (St. Andrews U), and the former Soviet Republics (Tbilisi State U). Study abroad also in China, England, France, Germany, Israel, Italy, Japan, and Spain.
**Honors:** Phi Beta Kappa. Honors program. Honor societies.
**Academic Assistance:** Nonremedial tutoring.

**STUDENT LIFE. Housing:** All freshmen must live on campus unless living with family in metro Atlanta. Coed and women's dorms. Sorority and fraternity housing. School-owned-operated apartments. On-campus married-student housing. 70% of students live in college housing.
**Social atmosphere:** According to the editor of the student newspaper, Emory students enjoy Atlanta's diverse cultural opportunities. Socially, the campus is very active, with the Greeks greatly influencing student social life. Fraternity parties, the Halloween Ball, Homecoming, and Dooley's Week highlight the school year. The Candler Library, Fraternity Row, and Lullwater Park are popular on-campus meeting spots, while students frequent Moe's & Joe's, Limerick Junction, and Atkins Park off campus.
**Services and counseling/handicapped student services:** Placement services. Health service. Women's center. Day care. Counseling services for minority students. Birth control, personal, and psychological counseling. Career and academic guidance services. Religious counseling. Physically disabled student services. Learning disabled services. Notetaking services. Tape recorders. Tutors. Reader services for the blind.
**Campus organizations:** Undergraduate student government. Student newspapers (Emory Voice; Wheel). Literary magazine. Yearbook. Radio station. Glee club, women's chorale, orchestra, drama groups, intercollegiate debate, Barkley Forum, Environmental Committee, PIRG, Volunteer Emory, Women's Liberation Organization, Young Democrats, Young Republicans, 200 organizations in all. 15 fraternities, all with chapter houses; 10 sororities, all with chapter houses. 35% of men join a fraternity. 35% of women join a sorority.
**Religious organizations:** Baptist Student Union, Christian Fellowship, Fellowship for Friends, Hillel, Bahai Club, Muslim Student Association, Westminster Fellowship, Wesley Fellowship, other religious groups.
**Minority/foreign student organizations:** Academic Support Program, All-Star Leaguer program, Black Student Alliance, Faculty Mentor Program. International Association, Central American Network, Chinese, French, German, Italian, Korean, and Spanish groups.

**ATHLETICS. Physical education requirements:** Four semesters of physical education required.
**Intercollegiate competition:** 16% of students participate. Baseball (M), basketball (M,W), cross-country (M,W), diving (M,W), golf (M), soccer (M,W), swimming (M,W), tennis (M,W), track and field (indoor) (M,W), track and field (outdoor) (M,W), volleyball (W). Member of NCAA Division III, University Athletic Assocation.
**Intramural and club sports:** 80% of students participate. Intramural archery, badminton, baseball, basketball, bowling, cross-country, darts, fencing, flag football, floor hockey, golf, hacky sack, handball, indoor soccer, inner-tube water polo, racquetball, run-pass-kick, skiing, soccer, softball, squash, stickball, swimming, table tennis, tennis, track and field, triathlon, turkey trot, ultimate frisbee, volleyball, walleyball, weight lifting, wrestling. Men's club badminton, bowling, cheerleading, crew, cycling, fencing, ice hockey, lacrosse, martial arts, racquetball, rugby, sailing, ultimate frisbee, water polo, water skiing, wrestling. Women's club badminton, bowling, cheerleading, crew, cycling, fencing, field hockey, golf, lacrosse, martial arts, racquetball, rugby, sailing, ultimate frisbee, water skiing.

**ADMISSIONS. Academic basis for candidate selection** (in order of priority): Secondary school record, standardized test scores, school's recommendation, essay, class rank.
**Nonacademic basis for candidate selection:** Extracurricular participation, particular talent or ability, geographical distribution, and alumni/ae relationship are important. Character and personality are considered.

**Requirements:** Graduation from secondary school is required; GED is not accepted. 16 units and the following program of study are required: 4 units of English, 3 units of math, 2 units of lab science, 2 units of foreign language, 2 units of social studies, 3 units of academic electives. Solid "B" to "B+" average in advanced secondary school coursework required. Audition required of music program applicants. SAT or ACT is required. ACH recommended. Campus visit recommended. No off-campus interviews.
**Procedure:** Take SAT or ACT by December of 12th year. Take ACH by January of 12th year. Suggest filing application by January 15. Application deadline is January 15. Notification of admission by April 1. Reply is required by May 1. $350 nonrefundable tuition deposit. Freshmen accepted for fall term only.
**Special programs:** Admission may be deferred one year. Credit and/or placement may be granted through CEEB Advanced Placement exams for scores of 4 or higher. Placement may be granted through challenge exams. Early decision program. In fall 1993, 439 applied for early decision and 318 were accepted. Deadline for applying for early decision is November 1. Early entrance/early admission program. Concurrent enrollment program.
**Transfer students:** Transfer students accepted for terms other than fall. In fall 1993, 8% of all new students were transfers into all classes. 500 transfer applications were received, 250 were accepted. Application deadline is July 1 for fall; November 1 for spring. Minimum 3.0 GPA recommended. Lowest course grade accepted is "C." Maximum number of transferable credits is 64 semester hours. At least 64 semester hours must be completed at the university to receive degree.
**Admissions contact:** Daniel C. Walls, M.S., Dean of Admissions. 404 727-6036, 800 727-6036.

**FINANCIAL AID. Available aid:** Pell grants, SEOG, Federal Nursing Student Scholarships, state scholarships and grants, school scholarships and grants, private scholarships, and academic merit scholarships. Perkins Loans (NDSL), PLUS, Stafford Loans (GSL), NSL, Health Professions Loans, state loans, school loans, private loans, and SLS. Guaranteed tuition. Emory Payment Plan (installments).
**Financial aid statistics:** 25% of aid is not need-based. In 1993-94, 98% of all undergraduate applicants received aid; 98% of freshman applicants. Average amounts of aid awarded freshmen: Scholarships and grants, $10,000; loans, $3,099.
**Supporting data/closing dates:** FAFSA/FAF: Deadline is April 1. State aid form: Accepted on rolling basis. Income tax forms: Deadline is May 1. Notification of awards begins April 15.
**Financial aid contact:** Anne Sturtevant, M.S., Director of Financial Aid. 404 727-6039.

**STUDENT EMPLOYMENT.** College Work/Study Program. Institutional employment. 40% of full-time undergraduates work on campus during school year. Students may expect to earn an average of $1,400 during school year. Off-campus part-time employment opportunities rated "good."

**COMPUTER FACILITIES.** 483 IBM/IBM-compatible and Macintosh/Apple microcomputers; 468 are networked. Students may access Digital, IBM, SUN minicomputer/mainframe systems, BITNET, Internet. Residence halls may be equipped with stand-alone microcomputers, networked microcomputers, networked terminals. Client/LAN operating systems include Apple/Macintosh, DOS, OS/2, Windows NT, DEC, LocalTalk/AppleTalk, Novell. Computer languages and software packages include ACK, BASIC, C, COBOL, FORTRAN, MacPascal, MSC; desktop publishing, graphics, math, simulation, statistical, text processing programs; 87 in all. Computer facilities are available to all students.
**Fees:** Computer fee is included in tuition/fees.
**Hours:** 8 AM-5 PM (mainframes); 24 hrs. (microcomputers).

**GRADUATE CAREER DATA.** Graduate school percentages: 22% enter law school. 18% enter medical school. 2% enter graduate business programs. 24% enter graduate arts and sciences programs. 1% enter theological school/seminary. Highest graduate school enrollments: Duke U, Johns Hopkins U, Stanford U, U of Chicago, U of Virginia, Yale U.

**PROMINENT ALUMNI/AE.** C. Vann Woodward, David Potter, and Dumas Malone, Pulitzer Prize-winning historians; Claude Sitton, Pulitzer Prize-winning journalist; Sam Nunn and Wyche Fowler, U.S. senators; George Page, PBS executive and host.

# Georgia College

**Milledgeville, GA 31061** **912 453-5004**

**1993-94 Costs.** Tuition: $1,694 (state residents), $4,457 (out-of-state). Room: $1,305. Board: $1,434. Fees, books, misc. academic expenses (school's estimate): $450.
**Enrollment.** Undergraduates: 1,273 men, 2,194 women (full-time). Freshman class: 1,858 applicants, 1,788 accepted, 792 enrolled. Graduate enrollment: 393 men, 641 women.
**Test score averages/ranges.** Average SAT scores: 433 verbal, 483 math. Range of SAT scores of middle 50%: 420-499 verbal, 440-519 math.
**Faculty.** 184 full-time; 78 part-time. 68% of faculty holds doctoral degree. Student/faculty ratio: 25 to 1.
**Selectivity rating.** Less competitive.

**PROFILE.** Georgia College, founded in 1889, is a public college. Programs are offered through the Schools of Arts and Sciences, Business, and Education. Its 42-acre campus is located in Milledgeville, 30 miles from Macon.

**Accreditation:** SACS. Professionally accredited by the Association of Collegiate Business Schools and Programs, the National Association of Schools of Music, the National Council for Accreditation of Teacher Education, the National League for Nursing.
**Religious orientation:** Georgia College is nonsectarian; no religious requirements.
**Library:** Collections totaling over 161,877 volumes, 1,138 periodical subscriptions, and 441,638 microform items.
**Special facilities/museums:** Education archives museum, on-campus nursery and kindergarten.
**Athletic facilities:** Swimming pool, gymnasium, badminton, basketball, handball, racquetball, tennis, and volleyball courts, lake, track, soccer, and softball fields.

**STUDENT BODY. Undergraduate profile:** 96% are state residents; 12% are transfers. 1% Asian-American, 17% Black, 1% Hispanic, 80% White, 1% Other. Average age of undergraduates is 23.
**Freshman profile:** 1% of freshmen who took SAT scored 700 or over on math; 2% scored 600 or over on verbal, 9% scored 600 or over on math; 16% scored 500 or over on verbal, 44% scored 500 or over on math; 80% scored 400 or over on verbal, 92% scored 400 or over on math; 98% scored 300 or over on verbal, 99% scored 300 or over on math. 98% of accepted applicants took SAT; 20% took ACT. 81% of freshmen come from public schools.
**Undergraduate achievement:** 83% of fall 1992 freshmen returned for fall 1993 term. 19% of entering class graduated.
**Foreign students:** 80 students are from out of the country. Countries represented include China, India, Japan, Pakistan, Sri Lanka, and the United Kingdom; 31 in all.

**PROGRAMS OF STUDY. Degrees:** B.A., B.Bus.Admin., B.Gen.Studies, B.Mus., B.Mus.Ed., B.Mus.Ther., B.S., B.S.Nurs.
**Majors:** Accounting, Art, Art Education, Art Marketing, Biology, Business Administration, Business Information Systems, Chemistry, Community Health Education, Computer Information Systems, Criminal Justice, Early Childhood Education, Economics, English, French, General Business, General Studies, Health Education, History, Journalism, Legal Assistance Studies, Management, Marketing, Mathematics, Middle Grade Education, Music, Music Theory, Nursing, Office Administration, Physical Education, Political Science, Psychology, Public Administration, Secondary Education, Sociology, Spanish, Special Education, Vocal/Instrumental Concentration.
**Distribution of degrees:** The majors with the highest enrollment are management, nursing, and early childhood education; voice and social science have the lowest.
**Requirements:** General education requirement.
**Academic regulations:** Freshmen must maintain minimum 1.4 GPA; sophomores, 1.6 GPA; juniors, 1.8 GPA; seniors, 2.0 GPA.
**Special:** Minors offered in most majors. Self-designed majors. Double majors. Dual degrees. Independent study. Accelerated study. Internships. Cooperative education programs. Graduate school at which undergraduates may take graduate-level courses. Preprofessional programs in law, medicine, veterinary science, pharmacy, dentistry, theology, optometry, dental hygiene, engineering, forestry, health service administration, horticulture, medical records administration, medical technician, occupational therapy, osteopathy, physical therapy, podiatry, and respiratory therapy. 2-2 and 3-2 engineering programs with Georgia Tech. Teacher certification in early childhood, secondary, and special education. Certification in specific subject areas. Exchange program abroad in England (Demontfort U) and Spain (U of Valladolid). Study abroad also in numerous countries. ROTC.
**Honors:** Honors program. Honor societies.
**Academic Assistance:** Remedial reading, writing, math, and study skills. Nonremedial tutoring.

**STUDENT LIFE. Housing:** Students may live on or off campus. Women's and men's dorms. Off-campus privately-owned housing. 21% of students live in college housing.
**Social atmosphere:** According to the student newspaper, "Some students enjoy going to parties and socializing, but we do have many who are concerned about their grades." Favorite gathering spots are the Maxwell College Union, the Colonial Cafe, Lanier Arts and Sciences Courtyard, and Beesen Field. Off campus, students frequent Shooter's, Justin's, and the Opera House. Social life revolves around the Greeks, the Baptist Student Union, and the American Marketing Association. Popular events are the Spring Concert, Greek Rush, basketball and baseball games, and the various school plays.
**Services and counseling/handicapped student services:** Placement services. Health service. Day care. Counseling services for minority, military, veteran, and older students. Birth control, personal, and psychological counseling. Career and academic guidance services. Religious counseling. Physically disabled student services. Learning disabled services. Notetaking services. Tape recorders. Tutors. Reader services for the blind.
**Campus organizations:** Undergraduate student government. Student newspaper (Colonnade, published once/week). Literary magazine. Yearbook. Radio and TV stations. Brass choir, choir, concert band, theatre, dance groups, departmental clubs, entertainment committee, service groups, 80 organizations in all. Eight fraternities, five chapter houses; six sororities, one chapter house. 20% of men join a fraternity. 20% of women join a sorority.
**Religious organizations:** Baptist Student Union, Wesley Foundation.
**Minority/foreign student organizations:** Black Student Alliance. International Student Association.

**ATHLETICS. Physical education requirements:** Six quarter hours of physical education required.
**Intercollegiate competition:** 5% of students participate. Baseball (M), basketball (M,W), cheerleading (M,W), cross-country (M,W), golf (M), softball (W), tennis (M,W). Member of NAIA, NCAA Division II, Peach Belt Athletic Conference.
**Intramural and club sports:** 18% of students participate. Intramural badminton, basketball, football, golf, soccer, softball, table tennis, tennis, track, volleyball. Men's club fencing, soccer, water skiing. Women's club fencing, water skiing.

**ADMISSIONS. Academic basis for candidate selection** (in order of priority): Secondary school record, standardized test scores.
**Requirements:** Graduation from secondary school is required; GED is not accepted. 15 units and the following program of study are required: 4 units of English, 3 units of math, 3 units of lab science, 2 units of foreign language, 1 unit of social studies, 2 units of history. Minimum combined SAT score of 740, minimum 1.8 GPA, and completion of state's College Preparatory Curriculum required. Additional requirements for applicants to Schools of Business and Nursing. Portfolio required of art program applicants. Audition required of music program applicants. Conditional admission possible for applicants not meeting standard requirements. SAT or ACT is required. Campus visit and interview recommended. Off-campus interviews available with an admissions representative.
**Procedure:** Take SAT or ACT by January of 12th year. Visit college for interview by January of 12th year. Application deadline is September. Notification of admission on rolling basis. $75 room deposit, refundable until 30 days prior to entering term. Freshmen accepted for terms other than fall.
**Special programs:** Admission may be deferred one year. Credit may be granted through CEEB Advanced Placement for scores of 3 or higher. Credit may be granted through CLEP general and subject exams, DANTES and challenge exams and military experience. Early entrance/early admission program. Concurrent enrollment program.

**Transfer students:** Transfer students accepted for terms other than fall. In fall 1993, 12% of all new students were transfers into all classes. 828 transfer applications were received, 818 were accepted. Application deadline is September 1 for fall; December 1 for winter; March 1 for spring. Minimum 2.0 GPA required. Lowest course grade accepted is "D." Maximum number of transferable credits is 101 quarter hours from a two-year school and 126 quarter hours from a four-year school. At least 60 quarter hours must be completed at the college to receive degree.
**Admissions contact:** Larry A. Peevy, M.Ed., Associate Vice President for Admissions and Records. 912 453-5004.

**FINANCIAL AID. Available aid:** Pell grants, SEOG, Federal Nursing Student Scholarships, state scholarships and grants, school scholarships and grants, private scholarships and grants, ROTC scholarships, academic merit scholarships, athletic scholarships, and aid for undergraduate foreign students. Perkins Loans (NDSL), PLUS, Stafford Loans (GSL), NSL, Health Professions Loans, state loans, private loans, and SLS.
**Financial aid statistics:** 6% of aid is not need-based. In 1993-94, 64% of all undergraduate applicants received aid; 58% of freshman applicants. Average amounts of aid awarded freshmen: Scholarships and grants, $1,600; loans, $1,800.
**Supporting data/closing dates:** FAFSA: Deadline is May 1. FAF: Priority filing date is April 15; deadline is May 1. School's own aid application: Priority filing date is April 15; deadline is May 1. Income tax forms. Notification of awards on rolling basis.
**Financial aid contact:** Aurelia Dykes, Director of Financial Aid. 912 453-5149.

**STUDENT EMPLOYMENT.** College Work/Study Program. Institutional employment. 15% of full-time undergraduates work on campus during school year. Students may expect to earn an average of $1,800 during school year. Off-campus part-time employment opportunities rated "good."

**COMPUTER FACILITIES.** 180 IBM/IBM-compatible and Macintosh/Apple microcomputers; 100 are networked. Students may access Digital minicomputer/mainframe systems. Client/LAN operating systems include Apple/Macintosh, DOS, Novell. Computer languages and software packages include BASIC, COBOL, dBASE, FORTRAN, Lotus 1-2-3, Pascal; word processing, graphics packages. Computer facilities are available to all students.
**Fees:** None.
**Hours:** 80 hours/week.

**PROMINENT ALUMNI/AE.** Flannery O'Connor, author.

# Georgia Institute of Technology

**Atlanta, GA 30332** **404 894-2000**

**1994-95 Costs.** Tuition: $1,937 (state residents), $7,637 (out-of-state). Room & board: $4,559. Fees, books, misc. academic expenses (school's estimate): $1,248.
**Enrollment.** Undergraduates: 6,334 men, 2,194 women (full-time). Freshman class: 7,947 applicants, 4,536 accepted, 1,771 enrolled. Graduate enrollment: 2,870 men, 794 women.
**Test score averages/ranges.** Average SAT scores: 559 verbal, 673 math. Range of SAT scores of middle 50%: 550-570 verbal, 670-690 math.
**Faculty.** 615 full-time. 91% of faculty holds doctoral degree. Student/faculty ratio: 21 to 1.
**Selectivity rating.** Highly competitive.

**PROFILE.** Georgia Tech, founded in 1888, is a public institute of technology. Programs are offered through the Colleges of Architecture, Engineering, Management, and Sciences and Liberal Studies. Its 330-acre campus is located near downtown Atlanta.

**Accreditation:** SACS. Professionally accredited by the Accreditation Board for Engineering and Technology, the American Assembly of Collegiate Schools of Business, the National Architecture Accrediting Board.
**Religious orientation:** Georgia Institute of Technology is nonsectarian; no religious requirements.
**Library:** Collections totaling over 1,770,000 volumes, 11,381 periodical subscriptions, and 3,400,000 microform items.
**Special facilities/museums:** Advanced technology development center, research institute, oceanography institute, nuclear research center, nuclear reactor, electron microscope.
**Athletic facilities:** Gymnasiums, field house, basketball, racquetball, squash, tennis, and volleyball courts, swimming pool, weight room, workout studios, athletic fields.

**STUDENT BODY. Undergraduate profile:** 66% are state residents; 16% are transfers. 9% Asian-American, 9% Black, 3% Hispanic, 79% White.
**Freshman profile:** Majority of accepted applicants took SAT. 86% of freshmen come from public schools.
**Undergraduate achievement:** 83% of fall 1992 freshmen returned for fall 1993 term. 30% of entering class graduated.
**Foreign students:** 238 students are from out of the country. Countries represented include China, France, India, Korea, Pakistan, and Taiwan; 54 in all.

**PROGRAMS OF STUDY. Degrees:** B.A.Eng., B.Aero.Eng., B.Bus.Admin., B.Cer.Eng., B.Chem.Eng., B.Civil Eng., B.Comp.Eng., B.Elec.Eng., B.Indust.Eng., B.Mat.Eng., B.Mech.Eng., B.Nuc.Eng., B.S., B.S.Textile Eng.
**Majors:** Aerospace Engineering, Applied Biology, Applied Mathematics, Applied Physics, Applied Psychology, Architecture, Building Construction, Business Administration, Ceramic Engineering, Chemical Engineering, Chemistry, Civil Engineering, Computer Engineering, Discrete Mathematics, Economics, Electrical Engineering, Engineering Science/Mechanics, Health Physics, History/Technology/Society, Industrial Design, Industrial Engineering, Information/Computer Science, International Affairs, Management, Management Science, Materials Engineering, Mathematics, Mechanical Engineering, Nuclear Engineering, Physics, Psychology, Science/Technology/Culture, Textile Chemistry, Textile Engineering, Textiles.
**Distribution of degrees:** The majors with the highest enrollment are electrical engineering, mechanical engineering, and management; ceramic engineering, history/technology/society, and science/technology/culture have the lowest.
**Requirements:** General education requirement.
**Academic regulations:** Freshmen must maintain minimum 1.7 GPA; sophomores, 1.9 GPA; juniors, 2.0 GPA; seniors, 2.0 GPA.
**Special:** Certificate programs in accounting, American literature, computer integration, drama, economics, history, international affairs, management technology, and technical communications. Double majors. Dual degrees. Accelerated study. Pass/fail grading option. Cooperative education programs. Graduate school at which undergraduates may take graduate-level courses. Five-year cooperative plan alternates college and industrial quarters and offers courses in all chemistry, engineering, information computer science, management, and physics majors. Six-year master's program in architecture. Host institute for 3-2 degree program in Regents Engineering Transfer Program (RETP). Member of Oak Ridge Associated Universities and Southeast Consortium for Minorities in Engineering. Teacher certification in secondary education. Certification in specific subject areas. Exchange electrical engineering program in France. Study abroad also in Germany. ROTC, NROTC, and AFROTC.
**Honors:** Honors program. Honor societies.
**Academic Assistance:** Remedial reading, writing, math, and study skills.

**STUDENT LIFE. Housing:** Coed, women's, and men's dorms. Sorority and fraternity housing. On-campus married-student housing. 44% of students live in college housing.
**Social atmosphere:** The student newspaper reports that students gather at the Student Center on campus. Off-campus destinations include Bashriprock's, Lenox, PT's, Grumpy's, and the Wreck Room. Influential groups at the institute are the Technique staff and the Greeks. Homecoming and basketball games the biggest annual events on campus.
**Services and counseling/handicapped student services:** Placement services. Health service. Women's center. Counseling services for minority, military, veteran, and older students. Birth control, personal, and psychological counseling. Career and academic guidance services. Physically disabled student services. Learning disabled services. Notetaking services. Tape recorders. Tutors. Reader services for the blind.
**Campus organizations:** Undergraduate student government. Student newspapers (Technique; North Avenue Review). Literary magazine. Yearbook. Radio station. Yellow Jacket Band, chamber orchestra, jazz ensemble, chorale, DramaTech, 250 organizations in all. 31 fraternities, 28 chapter houses; eight sororities, six chapter houses. 30% of men join a fraternity. 24% of women join a sorority.
**Religious organizations:** Bahai Club, Campus Crusade for Christ, Canterbury Association, Christian Campus Fellowship, Fellowship of Christian Athletes, Great Commission, Navigators, Wesley Foundation, Baptist, Catholic, Christian Science, Jewish, Lutheran, Muslim, and Presbyterian groups.
**Minority/foreign student organizations:** African-American Association, National Organization of Minority Architects, Society of Black Engineers, Society of Hispanic Professional Engineers, Society of Women Engineers. Hellenic Society, League of Latin American Citizens, Lebanon Club, Spanish-Speaking Organization, Chinese, French, Indian, Korean, Pakistani, Turkish, and Vietnamese student groups.

**ATHLETICS. Physical education requirements:** Two terms of physical education required.
**Intercollegiate competition:** 6% of students participate. Baseball (M), basketball (M,W), cheerleading (M,W), cross-country (M,W), diving (M), football (M), golf (M), softball (W), swimming (M), tennis (M,W), track (indoor) (M,W), track (outdoor) (M,W), track and field (indoor) (M,W), track and field (outdoor) (M,W), volleyball (W). Member of Atlantic Coast Conference, NCAA Division I.
**Intramural and club sports:** 43% of students participate. Intramural basketball, bowling, boxing, field hockey, flag football, hockey, racquetball, rugby, soccer, softball, swimming, volleyball. Men's club ballet, barbell, bowling, cycling, discus, hapkido, hockey, judo, karate, lacrosse, rowing, rugby, sailing, soccer, parachuting, swimming, table tennis, volleyball, water polo, water skiing. Women's club ballet, barbell, bowling, cycling, discus, hapkido, hockey, judo, karate, lacrosse, rowing, rugby, sailing, soccer, parachuting, swimming, table tennis, volleyball, water polo, water skiing.

**ADMISSIONS. Academic basis for candidate selection** (in order of priority): Secondary school record, standardized test scores.
**Nonacademic basis for candidate selection:** Alumni/ae relationship is important. Particular talent or ability is considered.
**Requirements:** Graduation from secondary school is recommended; GED is accepted. 16 units and the following program of study are required: 4 units of English, 4 units of math, 3 units of science including 2 units of lab, 2 units of foreign language, 1 unit of social studies, 2 units of history. Chemistry required of engineering and science program applicants. 3 units of math recommended of management program applicants. SAT is required; ACT may be substituted. Campus visit recommended. No off-campus interviews.
**Procedure:** Take SAT or ACT by December 1 of 12th year. Suggest filing application by February 1; no deadline. Notification of admission by March 15. Reply is required by May 1. $250 tuition deposit, refundable after enrollment $120 room deposit, refundable partially until July. Freshmen accepted for terms other than fall.
**Special programs:** Credit may be granted through CEEB Advanced Placement for scores of 3 or higher. Credit and placement may be granted through challenge exams. Early decision program. In fall 1993, 4,000 applied for early decision and 1,500 were accepted. Deadline for applying for early decision is February 1. Early entrance/early admission program. Concurrent enrollment program.
**Transfer students:** Transfer students accepted for terms other than fall. In fall 1993, 16% of all new students were transfers into all classes. 1,114 transfer applications were received, 419 were accepted. Application deadline is June 1 for fall; January 1 for spring. Minimum 2.7 GPA required. Lowest course grade accepted is "C." At least 50 quarter hours must be completed at the institute to receive degree.
**Admissions contact:** Deborah Smith, M.Ed., Director of Admissions. 404 894-4154.

**FINANCIAL AID. Available aid:** Pell grants, SEOG, state scholarships and grants, school scholarships and grants, private scholarships and grants, ROTC scholarships, academic merit scholarships, and athletic scholarships. Hope Grant. Perkins Loans (NDSL), PLUS, Stafford Loans (GSL), state loans, school loans, and private loans. Tuition Plan Inc. and Knight Tuition Plans.

**Financial aid statistics:** In 1993-94, 78% of all undergraduate applicants received aid. Average amounts of aid awarded freshmen: Scholarships and grants, $1,000; loans, $2,625.
**Supporting data/closing dates:** FAFSA: Deadline is March 1. School's own aid application: Accepted on rolling basis; deadline is March 1. Notification of awards begins April 15.
**Financial aid contact:** Curley Williams, Acting Director of Financial Planning and Services. 404 894-4160.

**STUDENT EMPLOYMENT.** College Work/Study Program. Institutional employment. Off-campus part-time employment opportunities rated "excellent."

**COMPUTER FACILITIES.** 5,000 IBM/IBM-compatible, Macintosh/Apple, and RISC-/UNIX-based microcomputers. Students may access CDC Cyber, Cray, Digital, IBM, Sequent, SUN minicomputer/mainframe systems, BITNET, Internet. Residence halls may be equipped with networked microcomputers, modems. Client/LAN operating systems include Apple/Macintosh, DOS, OS/2, UNIX/XENIX/AIX, DEC, Novell. Computer languages and software packages include APL, BASIC, C, COBOL, FORTRAN, Pascal. Computer facilities are available to all students.
**Fees:** None.
**Hours:** 24 hours.

**GRADUATE CAREER DATA.** Highest graduate school enrollments: Georgia Tech, Stanford, UC Berkeley, Purdue U. Companies and businesses that hire graduates: Northern Telecom/BNR, General Electric, Milliken, Anderson Consulting, Shaw Industries.

**PROMINENT ALUMNI/AE.** Jimmy Carter, former U.S. president; Sam Nunn, U.S. senator; Ivan Allen, former mayor of Atlanta; Frank Freeman, president, Paramount Pictures; Henry Grady, editor, *Atlanta Constitution*; Dick Truly, head, Space Shuttle Program; John Young, head, Astronaut Training, NASA; John Portman, architect; David Garrett, CEO, Delta Airlines; Bobby Jones, golfer.

## Georgia Southern University

**Statesboro, GA 30460-8024 912 681-5611**

**1993-94 Costs.** Tuition: $1,382 (state residents), $4,145 (out-of-state). Room: $1,380. Board: $1,410. Fees, books, misc. academic expenses (school's estimate): $906.
**Enrollment.** Undergraduates: 5,434 men, 5,971 women (full-time). Freshman class: 8,388 applicants, 5,423 accepted, 3,759 enrolled. Graduate enrollment: 527 men, 1,253 women.
**Test score averages/ranges.** Average SAT scores: 438 verbal, 480 math.
**Faculty.** 570 full-time; 79 part-time. 58% of faculty holds doctoral degree. Student/faculty ratio: 24 to 1.
**Selectivity rating.** Less competitive.

**PROFILE.** Georgia Southern is a public university. It was founded in 1906, joined the state university system in 1931, and gained university status in 1989. Programs are offered through the Graduate School and the Schools of Arts and Sciences; Business; Education; Health, Physical Education, Recreation, and Nursing; and Technology. Its 457-acre campus is located in Statesboro, 50 miles from Savannah.

**Accreditation:** SACS. Professionally accredited by the Accreditation Board for Engineering and Technology, the American Assembly of Collegiate Schools of Business, the American Dietetic Association, the American Home Economics Association, the National Association of Schools of Music, the National Council for Accreditation of Teacher Education, the National League for Nursing.
**Religious orientation:** Georgia Southern University is nonsectarian; no religious requirements.
**Library:** Collections totaling over 451,292 volumes, 3,511 periodical subscriptions, and 744,451 microform items.
**Special facilities/museums:** Art galleries, teaching museum, lab school, broadcasting studios, institute of arthropodology and parasitology, planetarium, public school.
**Athletic facilities:** Gymnasiums, swimming pool, weight training area, football, soccer, and softball fields, basketball, handball, racquetball, tennis, and volleyball courts, archery and golf ranges, exercise trail, stadium, field house.

**STUDENT BODY. Undergraduate profile:** 90% are state residents; 16% are transfers. 1% Asian-American, 19% Black, 1% Hispanic, 1% Native American, 78% White and Other. Average age of undergraduates is 21.
**Freshman profile:** Majority of accepted applicants took SAT.
**Undergraduate achievement:** 72% of fall 1992 freshmen returned for fall 1993 term.
**Foreign students:** 127 students are from out of the country. Countries represented include Canada, China, Germany, Honduras, Japan, and Turkey; 62 in all.

**PROGRAMS OF STUDY. Degrees:** B.A., B.Bus.Admin., B.F.A., B.Mus., B.S.
**Majors:** Accounting, Anthropology, Apparel Design, Apparel Manufacturing, Art, Art Education, Band or Orchestral Instrument, Biology, Building Construction/Contracting, Business Education, Business/Home/Consumer Services, Chemistry, Civil Engineering Technology, Communication Arts, Community Education, Community Health Education, Computer Science, Early Childhood, Economics, Economics/Agribusiness, Electrical Engineering Technology, English, Exceptional Child Education, Family/Child Studies, Finance, Fine Arts Education, Food Service Management, French, General Business Management, Geology, German, Health/Fitness Promotion, Health/Physical Education, History, Industrial Engineering Technology, Industrial Management, Information Systems, Interior Design/Housing, Journalism, Justice Studies, Keyboard Instruments, Manufacturing Technology, Marketing/Fashion Merchandising, Mathematics, Mechanical Engineering, Medical Technology, Music, Music Theory/Composition, Nursing, Organ/Church Music, Physical Education, Physics, Political Science, Printing Management, Psychology, Recreation/Outdoor/Public/Therapeutic, Restaurant/Hotel/Institutional Administration, School Music, Secondary Education, Sociology, Spanish, Sport Management, Textiles/Clothing, Trade/Industrial Education, Upper Elementary Education, Voice.
**Distribution of degrees:** The majors with the highest enrollment are business and education.
**Requirements:** General education requirement.
**Academic regulations:** Minimum 2.0 GPA must be maintained.
**Special:** Minors offered in some majors and in African American studies, American studies, geography, interdisciplinary areas, Latin American studies, library science, linguistics, philosophy, and religious studies. Associate's degrees offered. Double majors. Dual degrees. Internships. Cooperative education programs. Graduate school at which undergraduates may take graduate-level courses. Preprofessional programs in law, medicine, veterinary science, pharmacy, and dentistry. Two-year transfer program in agriculture with U of Georgia. 3-2 engineering program with Georgia Tech. Member of Brunswick Consortium. Teacher certification in early childhood, elementary, secondary, and special education. Study abroad in Austria, Belgium, Canada, England, France, Germany, Mexico, Spain, and the former Soviet Republics. ROTC.
**Honors:** Phi Beta Kappa. Honors program.
**Academic Assistance:** Remedial reading, writing, math, and study skills. Nonremedial tutoring.

**STUDENT LIFE. Housing:** Women's and men's dorms. School-owned/operated apartments. 22% of students live in college housing.
**Services and counseling/handicapped student services:** Placement services. Health service. Counseling services for minority and older students. Career and academic guidance services. Religious counseling. Learning disabled program/services.
**Campus organizations:** Undergraduate student government. Student newspapers (George-Anne; Eagle, each published once/week). Literary magazine. Yearbook. Radio station. Band, musical societies, Sinfonia, debating group, Masquers, puppetry guild, TV/radio production studio, student governing council, departmental and service groups, special-interest organizations, 150 organizations in all. 15 fraternities, four chapter houses; nine sororities, one chapter house. 21% of men join a fraternity. 21% of women join a sorority.
**Religious organizations:** Baptist Student Union, Campus Crusade for Christ, Canterbury Club, Fellowship of Christian Athletes, Good News Bible Study, Hillel Counselorship, Life Ministries, Lutheran group, Newman Club, Wesley Foundation, Muslim Student Association.
**Minority/foreign student organizations:** Afro-American choir, Black Student Alliance, NAACP. International Club.

**ATHLETICS. Physical education requirements:** Four terms of physical education required.
**Intercollegiate competition:** Baseball (M), basketball (M,W), cheerleading (M,W), cross-country (M,W), diving (M,W), football (M), golf (M), soccer (M,W), softball (W), swimming (M,W), tennis (M,W), volleyball (W). Member of NCAA Division I, NCAA Division I-AA for football, Southern Conference.
**Intramural and club sports:** Intramural badminton, basketball, flag football, soccer, softball, volleyball. Men's club rugby, volleyball. Women's club soccer.

**ADMISSIONS. Academic basis for candidate selection** (in order of priority): Standardized test scores, secondary school record, school's recommendation.
**Requirements:** Graduation from secondary school is recommended; GED is accepted. 17 units and the following program of study are required: 4 units of English, 3 units of math, 3 units of science including 2 units of lab, 2 units of foreign language, 3 units of social studies. Minimum SAT scores of 370 verbal and 380 math and minimum 2.0 GPA required. SAT or ACT is required. Campus visit and interview recommended. No off-campus interviews.
**Procedure:** Take SAT or ACT by September 1 of 12th year. Application deadline is August 1. Notification of admission on rolling basis. Reply is required by May 1. $50 room deposit, refundable until July 1. Freshmen accepted for terms other than fall.
**Special programs:** Credit and/or placement may be granted through CEEB Advanced Placement exams for scores of 3 or higher. Credit and/or placement may be granted through CLEP general exams. Credit may be granted through CLEP subject exams. Placement may be granted through challenge exams. Early entrance/early admission program. Concurrent enrollment program.
**Transfer students:** Transfer students accepted for terms other than fall. In fall 1993, 16% of all new students were transfers into all classes. 1,652 transfer applications were received, 924 were accepted. Application deadline is August 1 for fall; March 1 for spring. Minimum 2.0 GPA required. Lowest course grade accepted is "C." Maximum number of transferable credits is 101 quarter hours. At least 45 quarter hours must be completed at the university to receive degree.
**Admissions contact:** W. Dale Wasson, Ed.D., Director of Admissions. 912 681-5531.

**FINANCIAL AID. Available aid:** Pell grants, SEOG, Federal Nursing Student Scholarships, state scholarships and grants, school scholarships and grants, private scholarships and grants, ROTC scholarships, academic merit scholarships, and athletic scholarships. Perkins Loans (NDSL), PLUS, Stafford Loans (GSL), state loans, school loans, private loans, and SLS.
**Financial aid statistics:** 25% of aid is not need-based. Average amounts of aid awarded freshmen: Loans, $1,500.
**Supporting data/closing dates:** FAFSA: Priority filing date is April 15. School's own aid application: Priority filing date is April 15. Income tax forms: Priority filing date is April 15. Notification of awards begins June 1.
**Financial aid contact:** Tolly Nagy, M.Ed., Director of Financial Aid. 912 681-5413.

**STUDENT EMPLOYMENT.** College Work/Study Program. Institutional employment. 20% of full-time undergraduates work on campus during school year. Students may expect to earn an average of $2,500 during school year. Off-campus part-time employment opportunities rated "fair."

**COMPUTER FACILITIES.** 92 IBM/IBM-compatible and Macintosh/Apple microcomputers. Students may access CDC Cyber minicomputer/mainframe systems. Computer languages and software packages include BASIC, COBOL, dBASE, FORTRAN, Lotus 1-2-3, Pascal, SPSS, SuperCalc, WordPerfect; 100 in all. Computer facilities are available to all students.
**Fees:** Computer fee is included in tuition/fees.
**Hours:** 24 hrs.

## Georgia Southwestern College

**Americus, GA 31709-4693 912 928-1279**

**1992-93 Costs.** Tuition: $1,650 (state residents), $4,332 (out-of-state). Room: $1,110-$1,560. Board: $1,155-$1,410. Fees, books, misc. academic expenses (school's estimate): $838.

**Enrollment.** Undergraduates: 667 men, 873 women (full-time). Freshman class: 935 applicants, 786 accepted, 417 enrolled. Graduate enrollment: 88 men, 250 women.

**Test score averages/ranges.** Average ACT scores: 19 English, 19 math, 20 composite.

**Faculty.** 127 full-time; 21 part-time. 63% of faculty holds doctoral degree. Student/faculty ratio: 18 to 1.

**Selectivity rating.** Noncompetitive.

**PROFILE.** Georgia Southwestern, founded in 1906, is a public college. Programs are offered through the Divisions of Arts and Sciences, Business Administration, Computer and Applied Sciences, Education, Nursing, and Graduate Studies. Its 187-acre campus is located in Americus, 135 miles south of Atlanta.

**Accreditation:** SACS. Professionally accredited by the National Council for Accreditation of Teacher Education, the National League for Nursing.
**Religious orientation:** Georgia Southwestern College is nonsectarian; no religious requirements.
**Library:** Collections totaling over 1,566,457 volumes, 845 periodical subscriptions, and 469,857 microform items.
**Special facilities/museums:** Electron microscope.
**Athletic facilities:** Gymnasiums, athletic fields, swimming pool, tennis courts, weight rooms.
**STUDENT BODY. Undergraduate profile:** 97% are state residents; 27% are transfers. 1% Asian-American, 18% Black, 1% Hispanic, 80% White. Average age of undergraduates is 24.
**Freshman profile:** 3% of freshmen who took SAT scored 600 or over on verbal, 5% scored 600 or over on math; 13% scored 500 or over on verbal, 22% scored 500 or over on math; 48% scored 400 or over on verbal, 59% scored 400 or over on math; 95% scored 300 or over on verbal, 98% scored 300 or over on math. 88% of accepted applicants took SAT; 5% took ACT.
**Undergraduate achievement:** 61% of fall 1991 freshmen returned for fall 1992 term.
**Foreign students:** 60 students are from out of the country. Countries represented include the Bahamas, India, Japan, Panama, South Korea, and Taiwan; 17 in all.
**PROGRAMS OF STUDY. Degrees:** B.A., B.Bus.Admin., B.F.A., B.S., B.S.Ed.
**Majors:** Accounting, Agribusiness, Art, Art/Commercial Studio, Art Education, Biological Science, Biology, Business Administration, Business Education, Business Systems, Chemistry, Clerical, Computer Science, Early Childhood, Earth/Space Sciences, Education, English, Finance, Fine Arts, French, General Business, Geology, Health/Physical Education, History, Human Services, Management, Marketing, Mathematics, Middle Grades Education, Music Education, Nursing, Office Administration, Physics Education, Political Science, Psychology, Recreation, Secretarial, Social Science, Sociology, Spanish, Special Education, Speech/Drama.
**Distribution of degrees:** The majors with the highest enrollment are education, business administration, and computer science.
**Requirements:** General education requirement.
**Academic regulations:** Freshmen must maintain minimum 1.0 GPA; sophomores, 1.6 GPA; juniors, 1.8 GPA; seniors, 1.9 GPA.
**Special:** Minors offered. Courses offered in anthropology, electronic data processing, geography, journalism, library science, linguistics, and philosophy. International business program. Exit exam requirements. Associate's degrees offered. Dual degrees. Cooperative education programs. Graduate school at which undergraduates may take graduate-level courses. Preprofessional programs in law, medicine, pharmacy, and dentistry. 3-2 engineering program with Georgia Tech. Teacher certification in elementary, secondary, and special education. ROTC.
**Academic Assistance:** Remedial reading, writing, and math. Nonremedial tutoring.
**STUDENT LIFE. Housing:** Freshmen and sophomores under age 21 must live on campus unless living with family. Women's and men's dorms. 25% of students live in college housing.
**Social atmosphere:** On-campus gathering-spots include the Canes Den, the Marshall Student Center, the cafeteria, and the art department. A variety of student groups contribute to on-campus social life, including Greeks, the Non-Traditional League (NTL), the Baptist Student Union, and Gamma Beta Phi honor society. Homecoming, basketball and baseball season, and the Ms. SABU and Mr. GSW Pageants are highlights of the school year.
**Services and counseling/handicapped student services:** Placement services. Health service. Counseling services for minority, military, and older students. Personal and psychological counseling. Physically disabled student services. Notetaking services.
**Campus organizations:** Undergraduate student government. Student newspaper (Sou'-Wester, published once/week). Literary magazine. Yearbook. Band, choir, gospel choir, theatre, Young Democrats, outdoor club, Student Activities Office, Association for Women Students, departmental and special-interest groups. Seven fraternities, three chapter houses; six sororities, no chapter houses.
**Religious organizations:** Baptist Student Union, Catholic Campus Ministry, Presbyterian Student Center, Wesley Foundation.
**Minority/foreign student organizations:** Black Greek Council, SABU. International Friendship Club.
**ATHLETICS. Physical education requirements:** Six terms of physical education required.
**Intercollegiate competition:** 10% of students participate. Baseball (M), basketball (M,W), cheerleading (W), cross-country (M,W), golf (M), tennis (M,W), volleyball (W). Member of Georgia Intercollegiate Athletic Conference, NAIA.
**Intramural and club sports:** 50% of students participate. Intramural badminton, basketball, flag football, soccer, softball, tennis, volleyball.
**ADMISSIONS. Academic basis for candidate selection** (in order of priority): Secondary school record, standardized test scores, class rank, school's recommendation.
**Requirements:** Graduation from secondary school is required; GED is accepted. 18 units and the following program of study are required: 4 units of English, 3 units of math, 3 units of science including 2 units of lab, 2 units of foreign language, 3 units of social studies. Minimum SAT score of 350 in both verbal and math and minimum 1.8 GPA required. Physical exam required of nursing program applicants. Conditional admission possible for applicants not meeting standard requirements. SAT is required; ACT may be substituted. Campus visit recommended. No off-campus interviews.
**Procedure:** Take SAT or ACT by August of 12th year. Notification of admission on rolling basis. $25 tuition deposit, refundable until 20 days prior to start of fall quarter. $50 room deposit, refundable until 20 days prior to start of fall quarter. Freshmen accepted for terms other than fall.
**Special programs:** Admission may be deferred two quarters. Credit may be granted through CEEB Advanced Placement for scores of 3 or higher. Credit may be granted through CLEP general and subject exams and military experience. Credit and placement may be granted through challenge exams. Early entrance/early admission program. Concurrent enrollment program.
**Transfer students:** Transfer students accepted for terms other than fall. In fall 1992, 27% of all new students were transfers into all classes. 292 transfer applications were received, 261 were accepted. Application deadline is prior to registration for fall; prior to registration for spring. Minimum 2.0 GPA required. Lowest course grade accepted is "D." Maximum number of transferable credits is 100 quarter hours. At least 45 of final 60 quarter hours must be completed at the college to receive degree.
**Admissions contact:** Diane P. Burns, M.Ed., Director of Admissions. 912 928-1273.
**FINANCIAL AID. Available aid:** Pell grants, SEOG, state scholarships and grants, school scholarships and grants, private scholarships and grants, ROTC scholarships, academic merit scholarships, athletic scholarships, and aid for undergraduate foreign students. Perkins Loans (NDSL), PLUS, Stafford Loans (GSL), NSL, state loans, school loans, private loans, and SLS.
**Financial aid statistics:** Average amounts of aid awarded freshmen: Scholarships and grants, $2,000; loans, $1,700.
**Supporting data/closing dates:** FAFSA/FAF: Accepted on rolling basis. School's own aid application: Deadline is May 1. State aid form: Accepted on rolling basis. Income tax forms: Accepted on rolling basis. Notification of awards on rolling basis.
**Financial aid contact:** Freida Jones, M.Ed., Director of Financial Aid. 912 928-1378.
**STUDENT EMPLOYMENT.** College Work/Study Program. Institutional employment. 21% of full-time undergraduates work on campus during school year. Students may expect to earn an average of $740 during school year. Off-campus part-time employment opportunities rated "good."
**COMPUTER FACILITIES.** 183 IBM/IBM-compatible and Macintosh/Apple microcomputers; 50 are networked. Students may access IBM minicomputer/mainframe systems, Internet. Computer languages and software packages include BASIC, C, COBOL, FORTRAN; database, desktop publishing, graphics, spreadsheet, text editor packages. Computer facilities are available to all students.
**Fees:** None.
**Hours:** 8 AM-10 PM (M-F); weekend hours vary.
**GRADUATE CAREER DATA.** Highest graduate school enrollments: Georgia Southwestern Coll, U of Georgia. 20% of graduates choose careers in business and industry. Companies and businesses that hire graduates: Regional service and retail companies.
**PROMINENT ALUMNI/AE.** Griffin Bell, lawyer; Jimmy Carter, former U.S. President.

## Georgia State University

**Atlanta, GA 30303 404 651-2000**

**1994-95 Costs.** Tuition: $1,845 (state residents), $6,277 (out-of-state). Housing: None. Fees, books, misc. academic expenses (school's estimate): $894.

**Enrollment.** Undergraduates: 3,298 men, 4,434 women (full-time). Freshman class: 2,620 applicants, 1,271 accepted, 699 enrolled. Graduate enrollment: 2,819 men, 4,046 women.

**Test score averages/ranges.** Average SAT scores: 455 verbal, 506 math. Range of SAT scores of middle 50%: 420-540 verbal, 450-610 math. Average ACT scores: 23 composite. Range of ACT scores of middle 50%: 19-27 composite.

**Faculty.** 738 full-time; 143 part-time. 85% of faculty holds doctoral degree.

**Selectivity rating.** Competitive.

**PROFILE.** Georgia State, founded in 1913, is a public university. Programs are offered through the Colleges of Arts and Sciences, Business Administration, Education, Health Sciences, Law, and Public and Urban Affairs and the Division of Developmental Studies. Its 57-acre campus is located in Atlanta.

**Accreditation:** SACS. Professionally accredited by the Accrediting Commission on Education for Health Services Administration, the American Assembly of Collegiate Schools of Business, the American Association for Counseling and Development, the American Bar Association, the American Dietetic Association, the American Physical Therapy Association, the American Psychological Association, the Council on Rehabilitation Education, the Council on Social Work Education, the National Association of Schools of Art and Design, the National Association of Schools of Music, the National Council for Accreditation of Teacher Education, the National League for Nursing.
**Religious orientation:** Georgia State University is nonsectarian; no religious requirements.
**Library:** Collections totaling over 1,500,000 volumes, 12,270 periodical subscriptions, and 1,785,000 microform items.
**Special facilities/museums:** Art gallery, language lab, on-campus day care center for education majors, economic forecasting center, small business development center.
**Athletic facilities:** Sports arena, weight room, tennis courts, swimming pool, baseball, soccer, and softball fields.

**STUDENT BODY. Undergraduate profile:** 92% are state residents; 64% are transfers. 5% Asian-American, 19% Black, 2% Hispanic, 1% Native American, 73% White. Average age of undergraduates is 26.
**Freshman profile:** 1% of freshmen who took SAT scored 700 or over on math; 4% scored 600 or over on verbal, 12% scored 600 or over on math; 28% scored 500 or over on verbal, 51% scored 500 or over on math; 86% scored 400 or over on verbal, 97% scored 400 or over on math; 97% scored 300 or over on verbal, 100% scored 300 or over on math. 1% of freshmen who took ACT scored 30 or over on composite; 29% scored 24 or over on composite; 97% scored 18 or over on composite; 100% scored 12 or over on composite. 89% of accepted applicants took SAT; 12% took ACT.
**Foreign students:** 742 students are from out of the country. Countries represented include China, Colombia, India, Japan, Korea, and Nigeria; 95 in all.

**PROGRAMS OF STUDY. Degrees:** B.A., B.Bus.Admin., B.F.A., B.Interdis.Studies, B.Mus., B.S., B.S.Ed., B.S.Nurs., B.Soc.Work.
**Majors:** Accounting, Actuarial Sciences, Anthropology, Art, Art Education, Biological Sciences, Business Management, Chemistry, Classics, Commercial Music/Recording, Community Health Nutrition, Comprehensive Business Education, Computer Science, Criminal Justice, Dance, Decision Sciences, Early Childhood Education, Economics, Education of the Mentally Retarded, Elementary Education, English, English Education, Exercise Science, Film/Video, Finance, French, Geography, Geology, German, Health Education, History, Hotel/Restaurant/Travel Administration, Human Resources Development, Information Systems, Insurance, Journalism, Management, Marketing, Marketing/Distributive Education, Mathematics, Mathematics Education, Medical Technology, Mental Health, Middle Childhood Education, Music, Nursing, Philosophy, Physical Education, Physical Therapy, Physics, Political Science, Psychology, Real Estate/Urban Affairs, Respiratory Therapy, Secondary Education, Social Work, Sociology, Spanish, Speech, Studio Art, Theatre, Urban Studies, Vocational Education.
**Distribution of degrees:** The majors with the highest enrollment are management, marketing, and psychology; classics, philosophy, and foreign language have the lowest.
**Requirements:** General education requirement.
**Academic regulations:** Minimum 2.0 GPA must be maintained.
**Special:** Minors offered in all majors. Courses offered in astronomy, Dutch, folklore, Hebrew, industrial relations, Italian, library media, legal studies, linguistics, quantitative methods, Russian, and Scandinavian. Self-designed majors. Internships. Cooperative education programs. Graduate school at which undergraduates may take graduate-level courses. Preprofessional programs in law, medicine, and veterinary science. Member of Atlanta University Center Consortium. Teacher certification in early childhood, elementary, secondary, special education, vo-tech, and bilingual/bicultural education. Member of Consortium for Overseas Student Teaching. Study abroad in Canada, Israel, Mexico, and many Western European countries. ROTC. NROTC and AFROTC at Georgia Tech.
**Honors:** Honors program.
**Academic Assistance:** Remedial reading, writing, math, and study skills. Nonremedial tutoring.

**STUDENT LIFE. Housing:** Commuter campus; no student housing.
**Social atmosphere:** "GSU is a one hundred percent commuter school," reports the student newspaper. "Most people are employed full-time or part-time. The average age is 27, but the bulk of the social activities take place among the traditional age students. Most activities take place all around town since we are located in downtown Atlanta." Popular events include Greek-sponsored activities, GSU sports, and Atlanta Hawks, Braves, and Falcons games. Favorite nightspots include Good Ol' Days, American Pie, Livingston's Library, Club Rio, Sneakers, the Beer Mug, Fat Tuesday's, and Peachtree Cafe.
**Services and counseling/handicapped student services:** Placement services. Health service. Day care. Counseling services for minority, veteran, and older students. Personal and psychological counseling. Career and academic guidance services. Religious counseling. Physically disabled student services. Learning disabled services. Notetaking services. Tape recorders. Tutors. Reader services for the blind.
**Campus organizations:** Undergraduate student government. Student newspaper (Signal, published once/week). Literary magazine. Yearbook. Radio and TV stations. Georgia State Players, jazz band, Amnesty International, Young Republicans and Democrats, special-interest groups, 107 organizations in all. 11 fraternities, no chapter houses; nine sororities, no chapter houses. 6% of men join a fraternity. 3% of women join a sorority.
**Religious organizations:** Ecumenical Council, Baptist Student Union, Catholic Student Union, Episcopal Campus Ministry, Wesley Foundation, Chi Alpha Christian Fellowship, Muslim Student Association.
**Minority/foreign student organizations:** Black Freshman Network, NAACP, Black Student Alliance. ESL Student Club, International Student Association, Caribbean, Indian, Korean, Latin American, and Pakistani student groups.

**ATHLETICS. Physical education requirements:** None.
**Intercollegiate competition:** 1% of students participate. Baseball (M), basketball (M,W), cheerleading (M,W), cross-country (M,W), golf (M,W), soccer (M,W), softball (W), tennis (M,W), volleyball (W), wrestling (M). Member of NCAA Division I-AAA, Trans America Athletic Conference.
**Intramural and club sports:** 5% of students participate. Intramural basketball, climbing, flag football, golf, pool, soccer, softball, street hockey, tennis, volleyball, wrestling.

**ADMISSIONS. Academic basis for candidate selection** (in order of priority): Secondary school record, standardized test scores, essay, school's recommendation.
**Nonacademic basis for candidate selection:** Character and personality, extracurricular participation, particular talent or ability, and alumni/ae relationship are considered.
**Requirements:** Graduation from secondary school is required; GED is accepted. 15 units and the following program of study are required: 4 units of English, 3 units of math, 3 units of science including 2 units of lab, 2 units of foreign language, 1 unit of social studies, 2 units of history. Minimum SAT scores of 400 in both verbal and math (ACT scores of 21 English and 19 math) and minimum 2.0 GPA required. Separate application required of physical and respiratory therapy program applicants. Audition and theory placement tests required of music program applicants. Developmental studies recommended for applicants not meeting standard requirements. SAT or ACT is required. Campus visit and interview recommended. Off-campus interviews available with an admissions representative.
**Procedure:** Application deadline is July 15. Notification of admission on rolling basis. Freshmen accepted for terms other than fall.
**Special programs:** Credit and/or placement may be granted through CEEB Advanced Placement exams for scores of 3 or higher. Credit may be granted through CLEP subject exams. Placement may be granted through challenge exams. Early entrance/early admission program. Concurrent enrollment program.
**Transfer students:** Transfer students accepted for terms other than fall. In fall 1993, 64% of all new students were transfers into all classes. 4,913 transfer applications were received, 3,979 were accepted. Application deadline is July 15 for fall; November 15 for winter; February 15 for spring. Minimum 2.0 GPA required. Lowest course grade accepted is "C." Maximum number of transferable credits is 90 quarter hours from a two-year school and 140 quarter hours from a four-year school. At least 45 quarter hours must be completed at the university to receive degree.
**Admissions contact:** Ernest Beals, D.Ed., Dean of Admissions. 404 651-2365.

**FINANCIAL AID. Available aid:** Pell grants, SEOG, Federal Nursing Student Scholarships, state scholarships and grants, school scholarships and grants, private scholarships and grants, ROTC scholarships, academic merit scholarships, and athletic scholarships. Perkins Loans (NDSL), PLUS, Stafford Loans (GSL), NSL, state loans, and SLS.
**Financial aid statistics:** 20% of aid is not need-based. In 1993-94, 30% of all undergraduate applicants received aid; 30% of freshman applicants. Average amounts of aid awarded freshmen: Scholarships and grants, $2,000; loans, $2,625.
**Supporting data/closing dates:** FAFSA/FAF: Accepted on rolling basis. School's own aid application: Priority filing date is May 1; accepted on rolling basis. Income tax forms: Accepted on rolling basis. SINGLEFILE: Priority filing date is May 1. Notification of awards on rolling basis.
**Financial aid contact:** Thomas J. McTier, Director of Financial Aid. 404 651-2227.

**STUDENT EMPLOYMENT.** College Work/Study Program. Institutional employment. 5% of full-time undergraduates work on campus during school year. Off-campus part-time employment opportunities rated "excellent."

**COMPUTER FACILITIES.** 1,200 IBM/IBM-compatible and Macintosh/Apple microcomputers. Students may access UNISYS minicomputer/mainframe systems. Computer languages and software packages include BASIC, C, COBOL, FORTRAN, Pascal, GPSS, SAS; 35 in all. Computer facilities are available to all students.
**Fees:** None.
**Hours:** 24 hours.

# Kennesaw State College

**Marietta, GA 30061** **404 423-6000**

**1994-95 Costs.** Tuition: $1,500 (state residents), $4,500 (out-of-state). Housing: None. Fees, books, misc. academic expenses (school's estimate): $632.
**Enrollment.** Undergraduates: 2,255 men, 3,188 women (full-time). Freshman class: 2,209 applicants, 1,824 accepted, 1,190 enrolled. Graduate enrollment: 494 men, 771 women.
**Test score averages/ranges.** Average SAT scores: 446 verbal, 482 math.
**Faculty.** 350 full-time; 179 part-time. 71% of faculty holds doctoral degree. Student/faculty ratio: 30 to 1.
**Selectivity rating.** Less competitive.

**PROFILE.** Kennesaw State, founded in 1963, is a public, liberal arts college. Programs are offered through the Schools of Arts and Behavioral Sciences, Business, Education, and Science and Allied Health. Its 185-acre campus is located in Marietta, 25 miles from Atlanta.

**Accreditation:** SACS. Professionally accredited by the National Association of Schools of Music, the National League for Nursing, the Society of American Foresters.
**Religious orientation:** Kennesaw State College is nonsectarian; no religious requirements.
**Library:** Collections totaling over 450,000 volumes, 3,300 periodical subscriptions, and 750,000 microform items.
**Special facilities/museums:** Rare book collection, center for excellence in teaching and learning.
**Athletic facilities:** Gymnasiums, swimming pool, softball and other athletic fields, weight room.

**STUDENT BODY. Undergraduate profile:** 97% are state residents; 42% are transfers. 2% Asian-American, 6% Black, 1% Hispanic, 91% White. Average age of undergraduates is 26.
**Freshman profile:** 1% of freshmen who took SAT scored 700 or over on math; 3% scored 600 or over on verbal, 11% scored 600 or over on math; 23% scored 500 or over on verbal, 42% scored 500 or over on math; 76% scored 400 or over on verbal, 89% scored 400 or over on math; 99% scored 300 or over on verbal, 100% scored 300 or over on math. 95% of accepted applicants took SAT; 5% took ACT.
**Undergraduate achievement:** 68% of fall 1992 freshmen returned for fall 1993 term. 46% of entering class graduated. 6% of students who completed a degree program immediately went on to graduate study.
**Foreign students:** 362 students are from out of the country. Countries represented include Canada, Iran, Japan, Kenya, Nigeria, and the United Kingdom; 67 in all.

**PROGRAMS OF STUDY. Degrees:** B.A., B.Bus.Admin., B.Mus., B.S., B.S.Nurs.
**Majors:** Accounting, Art, Biology, Biology Education, Business Education, Chemistry, Communications, Computer Science, Economics/Finance, Elementary Education, English, Exercise Science, French, French Education, Health/Physical Education, Health Promotion/Wellness, History, International Affairs, Management, Marketing, Mathematics, Music, Music Education, Nursing, Political Science, Pre-Dentistry, Pre-Engineering, Pre-Forestry, Pre-Law, Pre-Medicine, Pre-Pharmacy, Pre-Veterinary, Professional Selling, Psychology, Secondary Education, Social Services, Spanish, Spanish Education, Sports Management.
**Distribution of degrees:** The majors with the highest enrollment are management, marketing, and accounting; chemistry, secondary education, and French have the lowest.
**Requirements:** General education requirement.
**Academic regulations:** Minimum 2.0 GPA must be maintained.
**Special:** Minors offered in some majors and in art history, American literature, coaching education, defense studies, economics, English literature, health/physical education,

international studies, legal studies, Native American studies, women's studies, and writing. Associate's degrees offered. Double majors. Internships. Cooperative education programs. Preprofessional programs in law, medicine, veterinary science, pharmacy, dentistry, engineering, and forestry. Member of Atlanta University Center Consortium; cross-registration possible. Teacher certification in early childhood, elementary, and secondary education. Certification in specific subject areas. Study abroad in France, Mexico, and Spain. ROTC.
**Honors:** Honor societies.
**Academic Assistance:** Remedial reading, writing, math, and study skills. Nonremedial tutoring.

**STUDENT LIFE. Housing:** Commuter campus; no student housing.
**Social atmosphere:** Favorite hangouts include the student center, Taco Mac, Rio Bravo, town center, and mall. Influential student groups include Theta Chi, Delta Phi Epsilon, Phi Mu, Baptist Student Union, African American Student Alliance, Student Government Association, and Pi Kappa Phi. Popular social events include KSC Day and Homecoming. "Due to the fact that KSC is a commuter school, there is less emphasis on on-campus socialization," reports the editor of the student newspaper.
**Services and counseling/handicapped student services:** Placement services. Lifelong Learning Center Counseling services for minority and older students. Personal counseling. Career and academic guidance services. Physically disabled student services. Learning disabled services. Notetaking services. Tape recorders. Tutors. Reader services for the blind.
**Campus organizations:** Undergraduate student government. Student newspaper (Sentinel, published once/week). Literary magazine. Yearbook. Orchestra, chorale, singers, music ensembles, jazz band, Art Guild, media and photography clubs, STRIVE, SOAR, Rotaract, departmental groups, 62 organizations in all. Two fraternities, no chapter houses; three sororities, no chapter houses. 2% of men join a fraternity. 2% of women join a sorority.
**Religious organizations:** Bahai Club, Baptist Student Union, Campus Crusade for Christ.
**Minority/foreign student organizations:** African-American Student Alliance. International Affairs Council.

**ATHLETICS. Physical education requirements:** Six quarter hours of physical education required.
**Intercollegiate competition:** 2% of students participate. Baseball (M), basketball (M,W), cheerleading (W), cross-country (M,W), golf (M), softball (W), tennis (W). Member of NCAA Division II, Peach Belt Athletic Conference.
**Intramural and club sports:** 20% of students participate. Intramural basketball, badminton, flag football, racquetball, softball, swimming, tennis, volleyball.

**ADMISSIONS. Academic basis for candidate selection** (in order of priority): Secondary school record, standardized test scores, school's recommendation.
**Requirements:** Graduation from secondary school is required; GED is accepted. 19 units and the following program of study are required: 4 units of English, 3 units of math, 3 units of science including 2 units of lab, 2 units of foreign language, 3 units of social studies. Minimum combined SAT score of 650 (composite ACT score of 17) and minimum 2.0 GPA required. Additional application required of nursing program applicants. SAT is required; ACT may be substituted. Campus visit recommended. No off-campus interviews.
**Procedure:** Take SAT or ACT by June of 12th year. Suggest filing application by June 1. Application deadline is September 3. Notification of admission on rolling basis. Freshmen accepted for terms other than fall.
**Special programs:** Admission may be deferred two years. Credit may be granted through CEEB Advanced Placement for scores of 3 or higher. Credit may be granted through CLEP subject exams. Credit and placement may be granted through challenge exams. Early entrance/early admission program. Concurrent enrollment program.
**Transfer students:** Transfer students accepted for terms other than fall. In fall 1993, 42% of all new students were transfers into all classes. 2,034 transfer applications were received, 1,902 were accepted. Application deadline is September 3 for fall; December 1 for spring. Minimum 2.0 GPA required. Lowest course grade accepted is "D." At least 45 quarter hours must be completed at the college to receive degree.
**Admissions contact:** Joe F. Head, M.Ed., Director of Admissions. 404 423-6300.

**FINANCIAL AID. Available aid:** Pell grants, SEOG, state scholarships and grants, school scholarships, private scholarships, and athletic scholarships. Perkins Loans (NDSL), PLUS, Stafford Loans (GSL), state loans, school loans, and SLS.
**Financial aid statistics:** 25% of aid is not need-based. In 1993-94, 90% of all undergraduate applicants received aid; 90% of freshman applicants. Average amounts of aid awarded freshmen: Scholarships and grants, $1,200; loans, $2,000.
**Supporting data/closing dates:** FAFSA/FAF/FFS: Priority filing date is April 15; accepted on rolling basis. School's own aid application. Notification of awards on rolling basis.
**Financial aid contact:** Terry Faust, M.Ed., Director of Financial Aid. 404 423-6074.

**STUDENT EMPLOYMENT.** College Work/Study Program. Institutional employment. 5% of full-time undergraduates work on campus during school year. Students may expect to earn an average of $2,000 during school year. Off-campus part-time employment opportunities rated "good."

**COMPUTER FACILITIES.** 78 IBM/IBM-compatible and Macintosh/Apple microcomputers. Students may access CDC Cyber, SUN minicomputer/mainframe systems, BITNET, Internet. Client/LAN operating systems include Apple/Macintosh, DOS, UNIX/XENIX/AIX, LocalTalk/AppleTalk, Novell. Computer languages and software packages include BASIC, COBOL, dBASE, LOGO, Lotus 1-2-3, Modula 2, Pascal, PC-Write. Computer facilities are available to all students.
**Fees:** None.
**Hours:** 8 AM-11 PM (M-Th); 8 AM-5 PM (F); 10 AM-6 PM (Sa); noon-8 PM (Su).

**GRADUATE CAREER DATA.** Graduate school percentages: 5% enter law school. 5% enter medical school. 5% enter dental school. 18% enter graduate business programs. 53% enter graduate arts and sciences programs. Highest graduate school enrollments: Emory U, Georgia State U, Kennesaw State Coll. 65% of graduates choose careers in business and industry. Companies and businesses that hire graduates: Coopers & Lybrand, Georgia Pacific, IBM, Institute of Nuclear Power, Southern Bell, Veterans Administration, Wachovia Bank.

# LaGrange College

**LaGrange, GA 30240** **706 882-2911**

**1994-95 Costs.** Tuition: $7,650. Room & board: $1,220. Fees, books, misc. academic expenses (school's estimate): $1,025.
**Enrollment.** Undergraduates: 275 men, 325 women (full-time). Freshman class: 554 applicants, 439 accepted, 196 enrolled. Graduate enrollment: 28 men, 26 women.
**Test score averages/ranges.** Average SAT scores: 410 verbal, 370 math.
**Faculty.** 78 full-time; 15 part-time. 83% of faculty holds highest degree in specific field. Student/faculty ratio: 15 to 1.
**Selectivity rating.** Less competitive.

**PROFILE.** LaGrange, founded in 1831, is a church-affiliated, liberal arts college. Its 35-acre campus is located in LaGrange, 65 miles southwest of Atlanta.

**Accreditation:** SACS. Professionally accredited by the National League for Nursing.
**Religious orientation:** LaGrange College is affiliated with the United Methodist Church; one term of religion required.
**Library:** Collections totaling over 102,614 volumes, 409 periodical subscriptions, and 1,955 microform items.
**Special facilities/museums:** Art center, center for the performing arts, language lab.
**Athletic facilities:** Athletic fields, fitness center, tennis courts, gymnasium.

**STUDENT BODY. Undergraduate profile:** 85% are state residents; 27% are transfers. 11% Black, 2% Hispanic, 81% White, 6% Other. Average age of undergraduates is 24.
**Freshman profile:** 1% of freshmen who took SAT scored 600 or over on verbal, 5% scored 600 or over on math; 11% scored 500 or over on verbal, 25% scored 500 or over on math; 100% scored 400 or over on verbal, 100% scored 400 or over on math. Majority of accepted applicants took SAT. 60% of freshmen come from public schools.
**Undergraduate achievement:** 89% of fall 1992 freshmen returned for fall 1993 term. 35% of students who completed a degree program went on to graduate study within one year.
**Foreign students:** 65 students are from out of the country. Countries represented include the Republic of Georgia, Germany, Japan, Mauritius, the Netherlands, and Spain; 13 in all.

**PROGRAMS OF STUDY. Degrees:** B.A., B.Bus.Admin., B.S.
**Majors:** Art/Design, Art Education, Biology, Business Administration, Chemistry, Christian Education, Computer Science, Early Childhood Education, Economics, English, History, International Business, Mathematics, Middle Childhood Education, Music, Physics, Political Science, Psychology, Religion, Secondary Education, Social Work, Spanish, Speech Communication/Theatre.
**Distribution of degrees:** The majors with the highest enrollment are business administration, education, and art; Spanish and computer science have the lowest.
**Requirements:** General education requirement.
**Academic regulations:** Freshmen must maintain minimum 1.65 GPA; sophomores, 1.75 GPA; juniors, 1.85 GPA; seniors, 2.00 GPA.
**Special:** Minors offered in most majors and in French and German. Associate's degrees offered. Double majors. Dual degrees. Independent study. Internships. Preprofessional programs in law, medicine, veterinary science, pharmacy, dentistry, optometry, engineering, and physical therapy. 3-2 engineering programs with Auburn U and Georgia Tech. Medical programs with Auburn U and Medical Coll of Georgia. Teacher certification in early childhood and secondary education. Certification in specific subject areas. Study abroad in France, Mexico, the former Soviet Republics, and Spain.
**Honors:** Phi Beta Kappa. Honor societies.

**ADMISSIONS. Academic basis for candidate selection** (in order of priority): Secondary school record, standardized test scores, essay.
**Nonacademic basis for candidate selection:** Character and personality, extracurricular participation, particular talent or ability, geographical distribution, and alumni/ae relationship are considered.
**Requirements:** Graduation from secondary school is recommended; GED is accepted. 11 units and the following program of study are required: 4 units of English, 2 units of math, 2 units of science, 3 units of social studies. Minimum SAT scores of 400 verbal and 400 math and minimum 2.5 GPA required. Conditional admission possible for applicants not meeting standard requirements. SAT is required; ACT may be substituted. Campus visit and interview recommended. Off-campus interviews available with an admissions representative.
**Procedure:** Take SAT or ACT by December of 12th year. Visit college for interview by April of 12th year. Application deadline is August 1. Notification of admission on rolling basis. $150 room deposit, refundable until July 15. Freshmen accepted for terms other than fall.
**Special programs:** Admission may be deferred one year. Credit and/or placement may be granted through CEEB Advanced Placement exams for scores of 4 or higher. Credit may be granted through CLEP general and subject exams. Early entrance/early admission program. Concurrent enrollment program.
**Transfer students:** Transfer students accepted for terms other than fall. In fall 1993, 27% of all new students were transfers into all classes. Application deadline is August 1 for fall; February 1 for spring. Minimum 2.0 GPA recommended. Lowest course grade accepted is "C." Maximum number of transferable credits is 135 quarter units. At least 60 quarter units must be completed at the college to receive degree.
**Admissions contact:** Phil Dodson, Director of Admission. 706 882-2911.

**FINANCIAL AID. Available aid:** Pell grants, SEOG, state scholarships and grants, school grants, and private scholarships. Perkins Loans (NDSL), PLUS, Stafford Loans (GSL), state loans, private loans, and SLS. Tuition Plan Inc. and AMS.
**Financial aid statistics:** In 1993-94, 73% of all undergraduate applicants received aid; 78% of freshman applicants. Average amounts of aid awarded freshmen: Scholarships and grants, $2,203; loans, $2,625.
**Supporting data/closing dates:** FAFSA/FAF: Accepted on rolling basis. School's own aid application: Priority filing date is May 1; accepted on rolling basis. Notification of awards begins May 1.
**Financial aid contact:** Sylvia Smith, Director of Financial Aid. 706 882-2911.

## Life College

**Marietta, GA 30060** **404 424-0554**

**1993-94 Costs.** Tuition: $10,900. Housing: None. Fees, books, misc. academic expenses (school's estimate): $850.
**Enrollment.** Undergraduates: 500 men, 300 women (full-time). Freshman class: 150 applicants, 125 accepted, 100 enrolled. Graduate enrollment: 1,800 men, 700 women.
**Test score averages/ranges.** N/A.
**Faculty.** 15 full-time; 10 part-time. 85% of faculty holds doctoral degree. Student/faculty ratio: 18 to 1.
**Selectivity rating.** N/A.

**PROFILE.** Life College, founded in 1974, is a specialized private college with a four-year program leading to a Doctor of Chiropractic degree. Programs are also offered in business, nutrition and sports health science. Its 100-acre campus is located in Marietta, 20 miles northwest of Atlanta.

**Accreditation:** SACS. Professionally accredited by the Council on Chiropractic Education.
**Religious orientation:** Life College is nonsectarian; no religious requirements.
**Athletic facilities:** Gymnasium, weight room, cross-country trail, rugby and soccer fields.

**STUDENT BODY. Undergraduate profile:** 30% are state residents; 2% are transfers. Average age of undergraduates is 25.
**Freshman profile:** 80% of accepted applicants took SAT; 20% took ACT. 90% of freshmen come from public schools.
**Undergraduate achievement:** 90% of fall 1992 freshmen returned for fall 1993 term. 50% of entering class graduated.
**Foreign students:** 100 students are from out of the country. Countries represented include Australia, Canada, China, France, South Africa, and South Korea; 45 in all.

**PROGRAMS OF STUDY. Degrees:** B.A., B.S.
**Majors:** Business, Nutrition.
**Requirements:** General education requirement.
**Special:** Athletic coaching. Graduate school at which undergraduates may take graduate-level courses. Preprofessional programs in chiropractic. Four-year Doctor of Chiropractic program.
**Academic Assistance:** Remedial reading, writing, and math.

**ADMISSIONS. Academic basis for candidate selection** (in order of priority): Secondary school record, standardized test scores, class rank, school's recommendation, essay.
**Nonacademic basis for candidate selection:** Character and personality are important. Extracurricular participation and alumni/ae relationship are considered.
**Requirements:** Graduation from secondary school is required; GED is accepted. No specific distribution of secondary school units required. Minimum combined SAT score of 750 and minimum 2.0 GPA required. SAT or ACT is required. Campus visit and interview recommended. No off-campus interviews.
**Procedure:** Take SAT or ACT by January of 12th year. Take ACH by January of 12th year. Suggest filing application by November 1. Application deadline is April 1. Notification of admission on rolling basis. Reply is required by June 1. Freshmen accepted for terms other than fall.
**Special programs:** Admission may be deferred one year. Credit may be granted through CLEP subject exams, DANTES and challenge exams, and military experience.
**Transfer students:** Transfer students accepted for terms other than fall. In fall 1993, 2% of all new students were transfers into all classes. 15 transfer applications were received, 15 were accepted. Application deadline is July 1 for fall; January 1 for spring. Minimum 2.0 GPA required. Lowest course grade accepted is "C." Maximum number of transferable credits is 45 quarter hours. At least 45 quarter hours must be completed at the college to receive degree.
**Admissions contact:** Melvin L. Reynolds, M.A., Director of Admissions. 404 424-0554, ext. 231, 232.

**FINANCIAL AID. Available aid:** Pell grants, SEOG, state grants, school scholarships and grants, athletic scholarships, and aid for undergraduate foreign students. Perkins Loans (NDSL), PLUS, Stafford Loans (GSL), Health Professions Loans, school loans, and SLS. Deferred payment plan.
**Supporting data/closing dates:** FAFSA/FAF/FFS: Accepted on rolling basis. School's own aid application: Accepted on rolling basis. State aid form: Accepted on rolling basis. Income tax forms: Accepted on rolling basis. Notification of awards on rolling basis.
**Financial aid contact:** David Haygood, M.A., Director of Financial Aid. 404 424-0554, ext. 601.

## Medical College of Georgia

**Augusta, GA 30912** **706 721-0211**

**1993-94 Costs.** Tuition: $1,845 (state residents), $5,535 (out-of-state). Room: $1,095. Board: $2,466. Fees, books, misc. academic expenses (school's estimate): $740.
**Enrollment.** Undergraduates: 173 men, 651 women (full-time). Freshman class: 307 applicants, 40 accepted, 37 enrolled. Graduate enrollment: 716 men, 472 women.
**Test score averages/ranges.** N/A.
**Faculty.** 83% of faculty holds doctoral degree.
**Selectivity rating.** N/A.

**PROFILE.** The Medical College of Georgia in Augusta, founded in 1828, is a public college. Programs are offered in the School of Allied Health Sciences, Dentistry, Nursing, Medicine, and Graduate Studies. Its 95-acre campus is located in downtown Augusta, 85 miles southwest of Columbia, S.C.

**Accreditation:** SACS. Professionally accredited by the American Dental Association, the American Medical Association (CAHEA), the American Physical Therapy Association, the National League for Nursing.
**Religious orientation:** Medical College of Georgia is nonsectarian; no religious requirements.
**Library:** Collections totaling over 151,810 volumes, 1,527 periodical subscriptions, and 4,934 microform items.
**Special facilities/museums:** 600-bed teaching hospital on campus.
**Athletic facilities:** Tennis courts, putting green, off-campus gymnasium.

**STUDENT BODY. Undergraduate profile:** 91% are state residents. 2% Asian-American, 10% Black, 1% Hispanic, 87% White.
**Freshman profile:** Majority of accepted applicants took SAT.
**Undergraduate achievement:** 98% of fall 1992 freshmen returned for fall 1993 term.
**Foreign students:** Three students are from out of the country; three countries represented in all.

**PROGRAMS OF STUDY. Degrees:** B.S., B.S.Nurs.
**Majors:** Dental Hygiene, Diagnostic Medical Sonography, Health Information Management, Medical Technology, Nuclear Medical Technology, Nursing, Occupational Therapy, Physical Therapy, Physician's Assistant, Radiation Therapy, Radiologic Technology, Respiratory Therapy.
**Distribution of degrees:** The majors with the highest enrollment are nursing, occupational therapy, and physical therapy; medical technology, health information management, and dental hygiene have the lowest.
**Requirements:** General education requirement.
**Academic regulations:** Minimum 2.0 GPA must be maintained.
**Special:** Associate's degrees offered.

**ADMISSIONS. Academic basis for candidate selection** (in order of priority): Standardized test scores, secondary school record, class rank, school's recommendation, essay.
**Nonacademic basis for candidate selection:** Character and personality are emphasized.
**Requirements:** Graduation from secondary school is required; GED is accepted. No specific distribution of secondary school units required. Unit requirements vary with each program. Preference given to applicants with strong science background. SAT or ACT is required. Campus visit recommended. No off-campus interviews.
**Procedure:** Take SAT or ACT by fall of 12th year. Suggest filing application by fall; no deadline. Notification of admission on rolling basis. Reply is required within 15 days of receipt of acceptance. $50 tuition deposit, refundable until registration day. $50 room deposit, refundable until checkout. Freshmen accepted for fall term only.
**Special programs:** Credit may be granted through CLEP general and subject exams and ACT PEP exams.
**Transfer students:** Transfer students accepted for fall term only. In fall 1993, 2,138 transfer applications were received, 534 were accepted. Application deadline is rolling. Minimum 2.0 GPA required. Lowest course grade accepted is "D." Maximum number of transferable credits is 100 quarter hours from a two-year school and 145 quarter hours from a four-year school. At least 45 quarter hours must be completed at the university to receive degree.
**Admissions contact:** Elizabeth Griffin, M.A., Director of Undergraduate Admissions. 706 721-2725.

**FINANCIAL AID. Available aid:** Pell grants, SEOG, Federal Nursing Student Scholarships, state scholarships and grants, school scholarships, private scholarships, and academic merit scholarships. Perkins Loans (NDSL), PLUS, Stafford Loans (GSL), NSL, Health Professions Loans, state loans, school loans, private loans, and SLS.
**Financial aid statistics:** 5% of aid is not need-based. In 1993-94, 91% of all undergraduate applicants received aid.
**Supporting data/closing dates:** FAFSA/FAF: Priority filing date is February 15. School's own aid application: Priority filing date is February 15. Income tax forms: Priority filing date is March 15. Financial Aid transcript: Priority filing date is March 15. Notification of awards begins April.
**Financial aid contact:** Sandra Fowler, M.Ed., Director of Financial Aid. 706 721-4901.

## Mercer University

**Macon, GA 31207** **912 752-2700**

**1994-95 Costs.** Tuition: $11,985. Room & board: $4,081. Fees, books, misc. academic expenses (school's estimate): $400.
**Enrollment.** Undergraduates: 1,309 men, 1,634 women (full-time). Freshman class: 2,029 applicants, 1,699 accepted, 571 enrolled. Graduate enrollment: 623 men, 810 women.
**Test score averages/ranges.** Average SAT scores: 473 verbal, 529 math. Range of SAT scores of middle 50%: 400-600 verbal, 500-600 math. Average ACT scores: 25 composite.
**Faculty.** 170 full-time; 29 part-time. 93% of faculty holds highest degree in specific field. Student/faculty ratio: 12 to 1.
**Selectivity rating.** Competitive.

**PROFILE.** Mercer, founded in 1833, is a private, church-affiliated university. Programs are offered through the College of Liberal Arts and the Schools of Business and Economics, Engineering, Law, and Medicine. Its 150-acre campus is located in Macon, 75 miles south of Atlanta.

**Accreditation:** SACS. Professionally accredited by the Accreditation Board for Engineering and Technology, the National Association of Schools of Music.
**Religious orientation:** Mercer University is affiliated with the Baptist Convention of Georgia; one term of religion required.
**Library:** Collections totaling over 494,755 volumes, 5,341 periodical subscriptions, and 8,687 microform items.
**Athletic facilities:** Gymnasiums, baseball, intramural, soccer, and softball fields, racquetball courts.

**STUDENT BODY. Undergraduate profile:** 66% are state residents; 28% are transfers. 2% Asian-American, 13% Black, 1% Hispanic, 1% Native American, 81% White, 2% Other. Average age of undergraduates is 20.
**Freshman profile:** 1% of freshmen who took SAT scored 700 or over on verbal, 3% scored 700 or over on math; 6% scored 600 or over on verbal, 21% scored 600 or over on math; 32% scored 500 or over on verbal, 55% scored 500 or over on math; 75% scored 400 or over on verbal, 88% scored 400 or over on math; 97% scored 300 or over on verbal, 99% scored 300 or over on math. 80% of accepted applicants took SAT; 20% took ACT. 78% of freshmen come from public schools.
**Undergraduate achievement:** 82% of fall 1992 freshmen returned for fall 1993 term. 30% of entering class graduated. 33% of students who completed a degree program went on to graduate study within five years.
**Foreign students:** 45 students are from out of the country. Countries represented include France, India, Japan, Panama, the United Kingdom, and Zaire; 24 in all.

**PROGRAMS OF STUDY. Degrees:** B.A., B.Bus.Admin., B.Mus., B.Mus.Ed., B.S.
**Majors:** Accounting, African American Studies, Art, Biology, Biomedical Engineering, Chemistry, Christianity, Communication/Theatre Arts, Computer Science, Earth Science, Economics, Education, Electrical Engineering, English, Environmental Engineering, Finance, French, General Business, German, Greek, History, Individualized Majors, Industrial Administration, Industrial Engineering, Latin, Management, Marketing, Mathematics, Mechanical Engineering, Music, Music Education, Music Performance, Natural Sciences, Philosophy, Physics, Political Science, Psychology, Sacred Music, Sociology, Spanish, Special Education.
**Distribution of degrees:** The majors with the highest enrollment are early childhood education, business management, and psychology; earth science, French, and German have the lowest.
**Requirements:** General education requirement.
**Academic regulations:** Minimum 2.0 GPA required for graduation.
**Special:** Minors offered in most majors and in anthropology, business, criminal justice, gender studies, health physics, photography, technical communication/manufacturing, and women's studies. Distributional general education program; instead of regular major-minor program, students may choose concentrations in African-American studies, classical studies, communication, early childhood education, learning disabilities, middle grades education, natural sciences, service learning, or social studies, or choose self-designed or double majors. Roberts School of Christianity offers courses in biblical studies, Christian ethics, Christian history, and Christian thought. Freshman Seminar Program. Great Books Program. Senior Capstone. Program in Learning Services. Self-designed majors. Double majors. Dual degrees. Independent study. Accelerated study. Pass/fail grading option. Internships. Cooperative education programs. Graduate school at which undergraduates may take graduate-level courses. Preprofessional programs in law, medicine, veterinary science, pharmacy, dentistry, and forestry. 3-1 medical technology program in cooperation with any NAACLS-approved school of medical technology. 3-3 pharmacy program with Mercer Sch of Pharmacy. Six-year law program with Walter F. George Sch of Law. Cooperative programs in dentistry and medicine. 3-2 forestry program with Duke U. Member of Atlanta University Center Consortium. Teacher certification in early childhood, elementary, secondary, and special education. Certification in specific subject areas. Study abroad in England, France, Italy, and Spain. ROTC.
**Honors:** Honor societies.
**Academic Assistance:** Nonremedial tutoring.

**ADMISSIONS. Academic basis for candidate selection** (in order of priority): Secondary school record, standardized test scores, school's recommendation, class rank.
**Nonacademic basis for candidate selection:** Character and personality are important. Extracurricular participation, particular talent or ability, and alumni/ae relationship are considered.
**Requirements:** Graduation from secondary school is required; GED is accepted. 17 units and the following program of study are required: 4 units of English, 3 units of math, 3 units of science, 2 units of foreign language, 3 units of social studies, 2 units of electives. SAT or ACT is required. Campus visit and interview recommended. No off-campus interviews.
**Procedure:** Take SAT or ACT by fall of 12th year. Suggest filing application by winter. Acceptance notification on rolling basis beginning in September. No set date by which applicants must accept offer. $150 tuition deposit, refundable until May 1. $100 room deposit, refundable until May 1. Freshmen accepted for terms other than fall.
**Special programs:** Credit and/or placement may be granted through CEEB Advanced Placement exams for scores of 3 or higher. Credit and/or placement may be granted through CLEP general and subject exams. Early decision program. In fall 1993, 42 applied for early decision and 39 were accepted. Deadline for applying for early decision is December 1. Early entrance/early admission program.
**Transfer students:** Transfer students accepted for terms other than fall. In fall 1993, 28% of all new students were transfers into all classes. 376 transfer applications were received, 320 were accepted. Application deadline is before start of classes for fall; before start of classes for spring. Minimum 2.0 GPA required. SAT/ACT scores required of transfer applicants with fewer than 30 semester credits. Both secondary school and college transcripts required for transfer applicants with fewer than 30 semester credits. Lowest course grade accepted is "C." Maximum number of transferable credits is 90 quarter hours from a two-year school and 135 quarter hours from a four-year school. At least 45 credit hours must be completed at the university to receive degree.
**Admissions contact:** Lynell A. Cadray, Director of Admissions. 912 752-2650.

**FINANCIAL AID. Available aid:** Pell grants, SEOG, state scholarships and grants, school scholarships and grants, private scholarships and grants, ROTC scholarships, academic merit scholarships, athletic scholarships, and aid for undergraduate foreign students. Special fund providing aid to students preparing for church-related vocations. Perkins Loans (NDSL), PLUS, Stafford Loans (GSL), state loans, school loans, and SLS. Tuition Plan Inc., Knight Tuition Plans, AMS, EFI Fund Management, and Tuition Management Systems.
**Financial aid statistics:** 32% of aid is not need-based. In 1993-94, 99% of all undergraduate applicants received aid; 99% of freshman applicants. Average amounts of aid awarded freshmen: Scholarships and grants, $7,740; loans, $4,214.
**Supporting data/closing dates:** FAFSA: Accepted on rolling basis; deadline is May 1. School's own aid application: Deadline is May 1. State aid form: Accepted on rolling basis. Notification of awards on rolling basis.
**Financial aid contact:** Carol Williams, Director of Financial Aid. 912 752-2670.

# Morehouse College

**Atlanta, GA 30314** **404 681-2800**

**1993-94 Costs.** Tuition: $6,650. Room & board: $5,224. Fees, books, misc. academic expenses (school's estimate): $1,800.
**Enrollment.** 2,787 men (full-time). Freshman class: 3,526 applicants, 1,491 accepted, 660 enrolled.
**Test score averages/ranges.** Average SAT scores: 483 verbal, 529 math. Average ACT scores: 22 English, 25 math, 24 composite.
**Faculty.** 150 full-time; 28 part-time. 74% of faculty holds highest degree in specific field. Student/faculty ratio: 17 to 1.
**Selectivity rating.** More competitive.

**PROFILE.** Morehouse, founded in 1867, is a private, liberal arts college. Its 47-acre campus is located in downtown Atlanta.

**Accreditation:** SACS.
**Religious orientation:** Morehouse College is nonsectarian; one semester of religion required.
**Library:** Collections totaling over 500,000 volumes, 3,000 periodical subscriptions, and 100,000 microform items.
**Athletic facilities:** Athletic field, track, swimming pool, gymnasium, bowling alley.

**STUDENT BODY. Undergraduate profile:** 18% are state residents; 13% are transfers. 98% Black, 2% Other. Average age of undergraduates is 20.
**Freshman profile:** 2% of freshmen who took SAT scored 700 or over on verbal, 4% scored 700 or over on math; 19% scored 600 or over on verbal, 25% scored 600 or over on math; 58% scored 500 or over on verbal, 69% scored 500 or over on math; 100% scored 400 or over on verbal, 100% scored 400 or over on math. 79% of accepted applicants took SAT; 21% took ACT. 79% of freshmen come from public schools.
**Undergraduate achievement:** 77% of fall 1991 freshmen returned for fall 1992 term. 52% of entering class graduated.
**Foreign students:** 56 students are from out of the country. Countries represented include the Bahamas, Bermuda, India, Jamaica, Nigeria, and Pakistan; 18 in all.

**PROGRAMS OF STUDY. Degrees:** B.A., B.S.
**Majors:** Accounting, Architecture, Art, Banking/Finance, Biology, Business Administration, Chemistry, Computer Science, Drama, Economics, Education, Engineering, English, French, German, Health/Physical Education, History, International Studies, Management, Marketing, Mathematics, Music, Philosophy, Physics, Political Science, Psychology, Real Estate, Religion, Social Welfare, Sociology, Spanish, Urban Studies.
**Distribution of degrees:** The majors with the highest enrollment are engineering, business administration, and biology/premedical; education, art, and German have the lowest.
**Requirements:** General education requirement.
**Academic regulations:** Minimum 2.0 GPA must be maintained.
**Special:** Minors offered in African studies, Afro-American studies, Caribbean studies, and library science. Courses offered in non-Western studies, Russian, and Swahili. Interdepartmental B.S. degree. Double majors. Dual degrees. Independent study. Internships. Cooperative education programs. Preprofessional programs in law, medicine, veterinary science, and dentistry. 3-2 engineering programs with Auburn U, Boston U, Georgia Tech, and Rochester Inst of Tech. Combined architecture program with U of Michigan. Member of Atlanta University Center Consortium and of Associated Colleges of the South. Exchange programs with Dartmouth Coll, U of California at San Diego, and Vassar Coll. Teacher certification in early childhood, elementary, and secondary education. Study abroad in England, Germany, Italy, Spain, and Zimbabwe. ROTC and NROTC. AFROTC at Georgia Tech.
**Honors:** Phi Beta Kappa. Honors program. Honor societies.
**Academic Assistance:** Remedial reading, math, and study skills. Nonremedial tutoring.

**STUDENT LIFE. Housing:** Freshmen encouraged to live on campus, but all students may live on or off campus. Men's dorms. School-owned/operated apartments. 55% of students live in college housing.
**Services and counseling/handicapped student services:** Placement services. Health service. Counseling services for military, veteran, and older students. Birth control, personal, and psychological counseling. Career and academic guidance services. Religious counseling. Learning disabled services.
**Campus organizations:** Undergraduate student government. Student newspaper (Maroon Tiger, published twice/month). Literary magazine. Yearbook. Glee club, marching band, jazz ensemble, King Players, forensics, Mathletes, 55 organizations in all. Six fraternities, no chapter houses. 3% of men join a fraternity.
**Minority/foreign student organizations:** International Student Association.

**ATHLETICS. Physical education requirements:** Two semesters of physical education required.
**Intercollegiate competition:** 5% of students participate. Basketball (M), football (M), tennis (M), track (M). Member of NCAA Division II, Southern Intercollegiate Athletic Conference.
**Intramural and club sports:** 1% of students participate. Intramural basketball, bowling, flag football, softball, swimming, track, volleyball.

**ADMISSIONS. Academic basis for candidate selection** (in order of priority): Secondary school record, standardized test scores, class rank, school's recommendation, essay.
**Nonacademic basis for candidate selection:** Character and personality and extracurricular participation are emphasized. Particular talent or ability and alumni/ae relationship are considered.
**Requirements:** Graduation from secondary school is required; GED is accepted. 16 units and the following program of study are required: 4 units of English, 3 units of math, 2 units of lab science, 2 units of social studies, 5 units of academic electives. 2 units of foreign language and 2 units of history recommended. Minimum combined SAT score of 980 (composite ACT score of 21), rank in top half of secondary school class, and minimum 2.5 GPA required. SAT is required; ACT may be substituted. Campus visit recommended. Off-campus interviews available with admissions and alumni representatives.

**Procedure:** Take SAT or ACT by January of 12th year. Visit college for interview by November of 12th year. Suggest filing application by November 1. Application deadline is February 15. Notification of admission by April 1. Reply is required by May 1. $200 nonrefundable tuition deposit. $3,165 room deposit, refundable until October 1. Freshmen accepted for terms other than fall.
**Special programs:** Admission may be deferred one year. Credit and/or placement may be granted through CEEB Advanced Placement exams for scores of 3 or higher. Credit and/or placement may be granted through CLEP general and subject exams. Placement may be granted through challenge exams and military experience. Credit and placement may be granted through DANTES exams. Early entrance/early admission program. Concurrent enrollment program.
**Transfer students:** Transfer students accepted for terms other than fall. In fall 1992, 13% of all new students were transfers into all classes. 497 transfer applications were received, 193 were accepted. Application deadline is February 15 for fall; October 1 for spring. Minimum 2.5 GPA required. Lowest course grade accepted is "C." At least 64 semester hours must be completed at the college to receive degree.
**Admissions contact:** Sterling H. Hudson III, M.A., Director of Admissions. 800 992-0642.
**FINANCIAL AID. Available aid:** Pell grants, SEOG, state scholarships and grants, school scholarships and grants, private scholarships and grants, ROTC scholarships, academic merit scholarships, athletic scholarships, and United Negro College Fund. Perkins Loans (NDSL), PLUS, Stafford Loans (GSL), private loans, and SLS. Tuition Plan Inc. and AMS.
**Financial aid statistics:** 35% of aid is not need-based. In 1992-93, 77% of all undergraduate applicants received aid; 62% of freshman applicants. Average amounts of aid awarded freshmen: Scholarships and grants, $3,000; loans, $2,500.
**Supporting data/closing dates:** FAFSA/FAF: Priority filing date is February 15; deadline is April 1. State aid form: Priority filing date is February 15. Income tax forms: Deadline is April 1. Notification of awards begins April 15.
**Financial aid contact:** Johnny Nimes, M.A., Director of Financial Aid. 404 215-2638.
**STUDENT EMPLOYMENT.** College Work/Study Program. Institutional employment. 18% of full-time undergraduates work on campus during school year. Students may expect to earn an average of $1,300 during school year. Off-campus part-time employment opportunities rated "fair."
**COMPUTER FACILITIES.** 250 IBM/IBM-compatible and Macintosh/Apple microcomputers. Students may access Digital, Prime, SUN minicomputer/mainframe systems. Residence halls may be equipped with stand-alone microcomputers, modems. Computer facilities are available to all students.
**Fees:** Computer fee is included in tuition/fees.
**Hours:** 9 AM-11 PM.
**GRADUATE CAREER DATA.** 31% of graduates choose careers in business and industry. Companies and businesses that hire graduates: Coca-Cola, Monsanto.
**PROMINENT ALUMNI/AE.** Martin Luther King, Jr., civil rights leader and Nobel Prize winner; Lerone Bennett, editor and historian; Maynard Jackson, mayor of Atlanta; Louis Sullivan, M.D., former secretary, U.S. Department of Health and Human Services; Edwin Moses, Olympic athlete; Spike Lee, filmmaker.

# Morris Brown College

**Atlanta, GA 30314 — 404 220-0270**

**1993-94 Costs.** Tuition: $6,770. Room & board: $4,438. Fees, books, misc. academic expenses (school's estimate): $1,426.
**Enrollment.** Undergraduates: 819 men, 1,088 women (full-time). Freshman class: 1,762 applicants, 1,753 accepted, 415 enrolled.
**Test score averages/ranges.** Average SAT scores: 340 verbal, 372 math. Range of SAT scores of middle 50%: 300-340 verbal, 320-380 math.
**Faculty.** 102 full-time; 43 part-time. 70% of faculty holds doctoral degree. Student/faculty ratio: 14 to 1.
**Selectivity rating.** Noncompetitive.

**PROFILE.** Morris Brown, founded in 1881, is a private, church-affiliated, historically black college. Programs are offered through the Divisions of Education and Psychology, Humanities, Natural Science and Mathematics, and Social Science. Its 18-acre campus is located in Atlanta.

**Accreditation:** SACS.
**Religious orientation:** Morris Brown College is affiliated with the African Methodist Episcopal Church; no religious requirements.
**Library:** Collections totaling over 366,407 volumes, 45,659 periodical subscriptions, and 233,796 microform items.
**Special facilities/museums:** Art gallery, language lab, electron microscope.
**STUDENT BODY. Undergraduate profile:** 56% are state residents; 18% are transfers. 1% Asian-American, 97% Black, 1% Native American, 1% White. Average age of undergraduates is 19.
**Freshman profile:** 1% of freshmen who took SAT scored 600 or over on math; 2% scored 500 or over on verbal, 6% scored 500 or over on math; 13% scored 400 or over on verbal, 20% scored 400 or over on math; 39% scored 300 or over on verbal, 45% scored 300 or over on math. Majority of accepted applicants took SAT.
**Foreign students:** 94 students are from out of the country. Countries represented include the Bahamas, Bermuda, Jamaica, Kenya, and Nigeria; 21 in all.
**PROGRAMS OF STUDY. Degrees:** B.A., B.S.
**Majors:** Accounting, Airway Computer Science, Allied Health, Art, Biology, Business Administration, Business Education, Business Management, Chemistry, Computer Science, Criminal Justice, Early Childhood Education, Economics, Engineering, History, Hospitality Administration, Information Processing, Marketing, Mass Communications, Mathematics, Music, Nursing, Paralegal Studies, Political Science, Psychology, Religion, Sociology, Spanish, Therapeutic Recreation.
**Distribution of degrees:** The majors with the highest enrollment are business administration, engineering, and computer science; chemistry and economics have the lowest.
**Requirements:** General education requirement.
**Academic regulations:** Minimum 2.00 GPA must be maintained.
**Special:** Minors offered in some majors and in analysis, computer/information science, English language and literature, information processing management, and recreation. All students in first two years follow prescribed distribution of courses in lower division; upper division is designed for specialization. Dual degrees. Cooperative education programs. Graduate school at which undergraduates may take graduate-level courses. Preprofessional programs in medicine, pharmacy, and dentistry. Combined degree programs in architecture, building construction, industrial design, and engineering with Georgia Tech. 3-3 program in law with St. John U; 3-3 program in medicine with Boston U. Member of Atlanta University Center Consortium. Teacher certification in early childhood, elementary, and special education. ROTC, NROTC, and AFROTC.
**Academic Assistance:** Remedial reading, writing, math, and study skills.
**STUDENT LIFE. Housing:** Freshmen must live on campus. Women's and men's dorms. 37% of students live in college housing.
**Services and counseling/handicapped student services:** Placement services. Health service. Counseling services for veteran students. Birth control, personal, and psychological counseling. Career and academic guidance services. Religious counseling. Physically disabled student services. Notetaking services.
**Campus organizations:** Undergraduate student government. Student newspaper (Wolverine Observer, published once/month). Yearbook. Choir, glee clubs, orchestra, band, drama league, Sinfonette Society, debating club, academic groups, Association for Computer Machinery, Florida Club, Hospitality Management Association, Pre-Alumni Council. Four fraternities, no chapter houses; four sororities, no chapter houses. 50% of men join a fraternity. 50% of women join a sorority.
**Religious organizations:** Several religious associations.
**Minority/foreign student organizations:** International Student Organization, Pan Hellenic Council.
**ATHLETICS. Physical education requirements:** Two semesters of physical education required.
**Intercollegiate competition:** Basketball (M,W), cross-country (M,W), football (M), tennis (M,W), track (M,W), volleyball (W). Member of NCAA Division II.
**Intramural and club sports:** Intramural basketball, bowling, chess, pool, table tennis, tag football, volleyball.
**ADMISSIONS. Academic basis for candidate selection** (in order of priority): Secondary school record, standardized test scores, class rank, school's recommendation, essay.
**Nonacademic basis for candidate selection:** Character and personality are important. Extracurricular participation and alumni/ae relationship are considered.
**Requirements:** Graduation from secondary school is required; GED is accepted. 15 units and the following program of study are required: 4 units of English, 3 units of math, 3 units of science, 2 units of foreign language, 3 units of social studies. Minimum 2.0 GPA required. Conditional admission possible for applicants not meeting standard requirements. SAT is required; ACT may be substituted. No off-campus interviews.
**Procedure:** Take SAT or ACT by November 15 of 12th year. Notification of admission on rolling basis. Applicant must accept offer of admission within four weeks. $50 refundable tuition deposit. $50 refundable room deposit. Freshmen accepted for terms other than fall.
**Special programs:** Admission may be deferred one year. Credit and/or placement may be granted through CLEP general and subject exams. Early entrance/early admission program. Concurrent enrollment program.
**Transfer students:** Transfer students accepted for terms other than fall. In fall 1991, 18% of all new students were transfers into all classes. Minimum 2.0 GPA required. Lowest course grade accepted is "C." Maximum number of transferable credits is 92 semester hours. At least 32 semester hours must be completed at the college to receive degree.
**Admissions contact:** Tyrone P. Fletcher, M.P.A., Director of Admissions. 404 220-0152.
**FINANCIAL AID. Available aid:** Pell grants, SEOG, Federal Nursing Student Scholarships, state scholarships and grants, school scholarships, private grants, ROTC scholarships, academic merit scholarships, athletic scholarships, and United Negro College Fund. Perkins Loans (NDSL), PLUS, Stafford Loans (GSL), NSL, state loans, and SLS. AMS and Tuition Management Systems.
**Financial aid statistics:** 10% of aid is not need-based. In 1991-92, 88% of all undergraduate applicants received aid; 83% of freshman applicants. Average amounts of aid awarded freshmen: Scholarships and grants, $3,200; loans, $3,000.
**Supporting data/closing dates:** FAFSA/FAF: Priority filing date is March 15; accepted on rolling basis. School's own aid application: Priority filing date is March 15; accepted on rolling basis. State aid form: Priority filing date is March 15; accepted on rolling basis. Income tax forms: Priority filing date is March 15; accepted on rolling basis. Notification of awards on rolling basis.
**Financial aid contact:** Willie Williams, M.S., Director of Financial Aid. 404 220-0133.
**STUDENT EMPLOYMENT.** College Work/Study Program. Institutional employment. 11% of full-time undergraduates work on campus during school year. Students may expect to earn an average of $1,200 during school year. Off-campus part-time employment opportunities rated "excellent."
**COMPUTER FACILITIES.** 500 IBM/IBM-compatible and Macintosh/Apple microcomputers; 45 are networked. Students may access IBM minicomputer/mainframe systems. Residence halls may be equipped with stand-alone microcomputers, networked microcomputers, networked terminals, modems. Client/LAN operating systems include Novell. Computer languages and software packages include Assembly, C, COBOL, dBASE, FORTRAN, Excel, Lotus 1-2-3, Pascal, Quattro, RPG, SQL/DS, WordPerfect, WS; 55 in all. Computer facilities are available to all students.
**Fees:** $75 computer fee per year.
**Hours:** 24 hours.
**GRADUATE CAREER DATA.** Graduate school percentages: 4% enter medical school. 4% enter dental school. 10% enter graduate business programs. 5% enter graduate arts and sciences programs. Highest graduate school enrollments: Clark Atlanta U, U of Georgia. Companies and businesses that hire graduates: AT&T, Atlanta Gas Light Company, Atlanta Board of Education, BellSouth, Delta Airlines, Georgia Power, IBM, Mobil Oil, Northfolk Southern Railway, United Parcel Service, Xerox.

**PROMINENT ALUMNI/AE.** James McPherson, Pulitzer Prize-winner author; Rachelle and James G. Reddick, prominent in nuclear energy field; Beverly J. Harvard, deputy chief of police, Atlanta; Calvin Mapp, judge, Dade County, Florida; Robert James, bank president; Mary Taylor Williams, MD, neurosurgeon.

# North Georgia College

**Dahlonega, GA 30597** **706 864-1800**

**1994-95 Costs.** Tuition: $1,450 (state residents), $4,351 (out-of-state). Room & board: $2,583. Fees, books, misc. academic expenses (school's estimate): $744.
**Enrollment.** Undergraduates: 835 men, 1,275 women (full-time). Freshman class: 1,923 applicants, 1,369 accepted, 715 enrolled. Graduate enrollment: 74 men, 285 women.
**Test score averages/ranges.** Average SAT scores: 440 verbal, 484 math.
**Faculty.** 145 full-time. 61% of faculty holds doctoral degree. Student/faculty ratio: 20 to 1.
**Selectivity rating.** Less competitive.

**PROFILE.** North Georgia, founded in 1873, is a public, military college. Its 150-acre campus, on the site of the original U.S. Government Gold Mint, is located in Dahlonega, 70 miles northeast of Atlanta.

**Accreditation:** SACS. Professionally accredited by the National Council for Accreditation of Teacher Education, the National League for Nursing.
**Religious orientation:** North Georgia College is nonsectarian; no religious requirements.
**Library:** Collections totaling over 112,000 volumes, 817 periodical subscriptions, and 386,850 microform items.
**Athletic facilities:** Gymnasium, football, soccer, and softball fields, track, swimming pool, weight room.
**STUDENT BODY. Undergraduate profile:** 97% are state residents; 41% are transfers. 2% Black, 97% White, 1% Other. Average age of undergraduates is 20.
**Freshman profile:** 95% of accepted applicants took SAT; 5% took ACT. 80% of freshmen come from public schools.
**Undergraduate achievement:** 80% of fall 1992 freshmen returned for fall 1993 term. 40% of entering class graduated. 20% of students who completed a degree program went on to graduate study within five years.
**Foreign students:** Eight students are from out of the country. Countries represented include Cameroon, Canada, England, Nigeria, and Sweden.
**PROGRAMS OF STUDY. Degrees:** B.A., B.Bus.Admin., B.S., B.S.Nurs.
**Majors:** Accounting, Art, Art Education, Biology, Business Education, Chemistry, Computer/Information Sciences, Craft Design, Criminal Justice, Early Childhood Education, Economics, English, French, History, Management, Marketing, Mathematics, Middle Grade Education, Music Education, Physical Education, Physics, Political Science, Psychology, Recreation, Secretarial, Social Sciences, Sociology, Special Education.
**Distribution of degrees:** The majors with the highest enrollment are business and education.
**Requirements:** General education requirement.
**Academic regulations:** Sophomores must maintain minimum 1.7 GPA; juniors, 1.8 GPA; seniors, 1.9 GPA.
**Special:** Minors offered in most majors. Comprehensive exams required of seniors. All male resident students must join Corps of Cadets and complete 18 hours of military science instruction. Associate's degrees offered. Double majors. Dual degrees. Accelerated study. Internships. 3-2 engineering programs with Clemson U and Georgia Tech. 3-3 program leading to M.S. in physical therapy. Teacher certification in early childhood, elementary, secondary, and special education. Certification in specific subject areas. ROTC.
**Honors:** Phi Beta Kappa. Honor societies.
**Academic Assistance:** Remedial reading, writing, math, and study skills. Nonremedial tutoring.
**STUDENT LIFE. Housing:** Unmarried, nonveteran students under age 23 must live on campus unless living with family within 40 miles. Women's and men's dorms. 38% of students live in college housing.
**Social atmosphere:** According to the editor of the student newspaper, North Georgia is the only coed, liberal arts, military school in the country to have non-military females in its student population. The Greek organizations and the College Union Board influence student social life. Students meet at the Student Center, Pine Valley, and the canteen on campus and at Beauregard's off campus. Basketball games, the Sweetheart Ball, and the Military Ball highlight the school year.
**Services and counseling/handicapped student services:** Placement services. Health service. Counseling services for minority, military, and veteran students. Personal and psychological counseling. Career and academic guidance services.
**Campus organizations:** Undergraduate student government. Student newspaper (Collegiate Voice, published biweekly). Yearbook. Concert band, chorus, chorale, drama club, military groups, parachutist club, Resident Women's, special-interest groups. Six fraternities, no chapter houses; four sororities, no chapter houses. 21% of men join a fraternity. 14% of women join a sorority.
**Religious organizations:** Baptist Student Union, Wesley Foundation, Newman Club, Latter-Day Saints Club, Westminster Club.
**Minority/foreign student organizations:** Students for Social Awareness.
**ATHLETICS. Physical education requirements:** Five terms of physical education required.
**Intercollegiate competition:** 1% of students participate. Basketball (M,W), cross-country (M,W), riflery (M), soccer (M), softball (W), tennis (M,W), track and field (outdoor) (M,W). Member of Georgia Intercollegiate Athletic Conference, NAIA.
**Intramural and club sports:** 40% of students participate. Intramural football, softball, swimming, track and field, volleyball. Women's club soccer.
**ADMISSIONS. Academic basis for candidate selection** (in order of priority): Secondary school record, standardized test scores, school's recommendation.
**Nonacademic basis for candidate selection:** Character and personality are important.
**Requirements:** Graduation from secondary school is required; GED is not accepted. No specific distribution of secondary school units required. Minimum combined SAT score of 800 and minimum 2.0 GPA required. Higher GPA and SAT scores required of nursing program applicants. Specific GPA required of teacher education and computer science program applicants. Conditional admission possible for applicants not meeting standard requirements. SAT or ACT is required. Campus visit and interview recommended. No off-campus interviews.
**Procedure:** Take SAT or ACT by October of 12th year. Take ACH by October of 12th year. Visit college for interview by November of 12th year. Application deadline is September 1. Notification of admission on rolling basis. Reply is required by May 1. $100 room deposit, refundable until July 1. Freshmen accepted for terms other than fall.
**Special programs:** Admission may be deferred. Credit may be granted through CEEB Advanced Placement exams, CLEP subject exams, and military experience. Credit and placement may be granted through ACT PEP and challenge exams. Early entrance/early admission program. Concurrent enrollment program.
**Transfer students:** Transfer students accepted for terms other than fall. In fall 1993, 41% of all new students were transfers into all classes. Application deadline is September 1. Minimum 2.0 GPA required. Maximum number of transferable credits is 95 quarter hours. At least 45 quarter hours must be completed at the college to receive degree.
**Admissions contact:** Gary R. Steffey, M.B.A., M.Ed., Director of Admissions and Enrollment Management. 706 864-1800.
**FINANCIAL AID. Available aid:** Pell grants, SEOG, state scholarships and grants, school scholarships, private scholarships, ROTC scholarships, academic merit scholarships, and athletic scholarships. Perkins Loans (NDSL), PLUS, Stafford Loans (GSL), state loans, school loans, private loans, and SLS.
**Financial aid statistics:** 50% of aid is not need-based. In 1993-94, 90% of all undergraduate applicants received aid; 90% of freshman applicants. Average amounts of aid awarded freshmen: Scholarships and grants, $750; loans, $1,800.
**Supporting data/closing dates:** FAFSA: Priority filing date is June 1. Income tax forms: Priority filing date is June 1; accepted on rolling basis. Notification of awards on rolling basis.
**Financial aid contact:** Deborah Barbone, M.Ed., Director of Financial Aid. 706 864-1410.
**STUDENT EMPLOYMENT.** College Work/Study Program. Institutional employment. 10% of full-time undergraduates work on campus during school year. Students may expect to earn an average of $1,500 during school year. Freshmen are discouraged from working during their first term. Off-campus part-time employment opportunities rated "poor."
**COMPUTER FACILITIES.** 100 IBM/IBM-compatible and RISC-/UNIX-based microcomputers; all are networked. Client/LAN operating systems include DOS, UNIX/XENIX/AIX. Computer languages and software packages include BASIC, C++, COBOL, FORTRAN, LOGO, Lotus 1-2-3, Quattro Pro, Paradox, WordPerfect. Computer facilities are available to all students.
**Fees:** None.
**Hours:** 8 AM-10 PM (M-Th); 8 AM-5 PM (F); 5-10 PM (Su).
**GRADUATE CAREER DATA.** Graduate school percentages: 5% enter law school. 2% enter medical school. 1% enter dental school. 3% enter graduate business programs. Highest graduate school enrollments: Georgia State, U of Georgia, Medical Coll of Georgia. 80% of graduates choose careers in business and industry. Companies and businesses that hire graduates: numerous companies; U.S. Army.
**PROMINENT ALUMNI/AE.** Tom Murphy, Speaker, Georgia House of Representatives; Brooks Pennington, CEO, Pennington Agribusiness.

# Oglethorpe University

**Atlanta, GA 30319-2797** **404 261-1441**

**1994-95 Costs.** Tuition: $12,990. Room & board: $4,340. Fees, books, misc. academic expenses (school's estimate): $660.
**Enrollment.** Undergraduates: 318 men, 451 women (full-time). Freshman class: 792 applicants, 648 accepted, 186 enrolled. Graduate enrollment: 5 men, 61 women.
**Test score averages/ranges.** Average SAT scores: 549 verbal, 570 math. Range of SAT scores of middle 50%: 490-610 verbal, 510-630 math. Average ACT scores: 27 composite. Range of ACT scores of middle 50%: 24-30 composite.
**Faculty.** 44 full-time; 67 part-time. 93% of faculty holds doctoral degree. Student/faculty ratio: 17 to 1.
**Selectivity rating.** Highly competitive.

**PROFILE.** Oglethorpe, founded in 1835, is a private, comprehensive university. Programs are offered through the Divisions of Humanities, History and Political Studies, Science, Education and Behavioral Sciences, Economics and Business Administration, and Graduate Studies. Its 90-acre campus, including buildings of neo-Gothic design, is located in Atlanta.

**Accreditation:** SACS. Professionally accredited by the National Council for Accreditation of Teacher Education.
**Religious orientation:** Oglethorpe University is nonsectarian; no religious requirements.
**Library:** Collections totaling over 101,000 volumes and 760 periodical subscriptions.
**Special facilities/museums:** Art museum, Japanese elementary school, scanning electron microscope.
**Athletic facilities:** Field house, track, baseball and soccer fields, tennis courts, swimming pool, weight room.
**STUDENT BODY. Undergraduate profile:** 62% are state residents; 22% are transfers. 4% Asian-American, 7% Black, 2% Hispanic, 1% Native American, 81% White, 5% Other. Average age of undergraduates is 21.
**Freshman profile:** 1% of freshmen who took SAT scored 700 or over on verbal, 7% scored 700 or over on math; 26% scored 600 or over on verbal, 38% scored 600 or over on math; 72% scored 500 or over on verbal, 82% scored 500 or over on math; 99% scored 400 or over on verbal, 99% scored 400 or over on math; 100% scored 300 or over on verbal,

100% scored 300 or over on math. 26% of freshmen who took ACT scored 30 or over on composite; 81% scored 24 or over on composite; 100% scored 18 or over on composite. 80% of accepted applicants took SAT; 47% took ACT. 72% of freshmen come from public schools.

**Undergraduate achievement:** 83% of fall 1992 freshmen returned for fall 1993 term. 56% of entering class graduated. 15% of students who completed a degree program immediately went on to graduate study.

**Foreign students:** 53 students are from out of the country. Countries represented include Japan, the Netherlands, Pakistan, Spain, Turkey, and Venezuela; 28 in all.

**PROGRAMS OF STUDY. Degrees:** B.A., B.Bus.Admin., B.S.

**Majors:** Accounting, American Studies, Biology, Business Administration, Business Administration/Behavioral Science, Business Administration/Computer Science, Chemistry, Communications, Early Childhood Education, Economics, Engineering, English, History, Individually Planned Major, International Studies, Mathematics, Mathematics/Computer Science, Medical Technology, Middle Grades Education, Philosophy, Physics, Political Studies, Psychology, Secondary Education, Social Work/Sociology, Sociology.

**Distribution of degrees:** The majors with the highest enrollment are history, accounting, and business administration; art, American studies, and early childhood education have the lowest.

**Requirements:** General education requirement.

**Academic regulations:** Freshmen must maintain minimum 1.50 GPA; sophomores, 1.75 GPA; juniors, 2.00 GPA; seniors, 2.00 GPA.

**Special:** Minors offered in many majors and in art, computer science, French, music, theatre, and writing. Curriculum is organized according to functions represented by divisions: Behavioral Sciences, Education, Business and Economics, Humanities, Science, and Social Studies. Self-designed majors. Double majors. Dual degrees. Independent study. Accelerated study. Pass/fail grading option. Internships. Cooperative education programs. Graduate school at which undergraduates may take graduate-level courses. Preprofessional programs in law, medicine, veterinary science, pharmacy, dentistry, theology, and optometry. 2-2-1/2 art program with Atlanta Coll of Art. 3-2 engineering programs with Auburn U, U of Florida, Georgia Tech, and U of Southern California. Professional option bachelor's degree possible for students who enter an accredited professional school after completing junior year. Member of Atlanta University Center Consortium. Washington Semester. Cross-registration with all Atlanta University Center Consortium members. Teacher certification in early childhood, elementary, and secondary education. Certification in specific subject areas. Exchange program abroad in Japan (Seigauin U). Study abroad also in Argentina (U de Belgrano), France (Lycee J.A. Marguerite), and the Netherlands (Inst of Higher European Studies). ROTC at Georgia State U. AFROTC at Georgia Tech.

**Honors:** Honors program. Honor societies.

**Academic Assistance:** Nonremedial tutoring.

**ADMISSIONS. Academic basis for candidate selection** (in order of priority): Secondary school record, standardized test scores, school's recommendation, class rank, essay.

**Nonacademic basis for candidate selection:** Character and personality and extracurricular participation are important. Alumni/ae relationship is considered.

**Requirements:** Graduation from secondary school is required; GED is accepted. 18 units and the following program of study are required: 4 units of English, 3 units of math, 2 units of lab science, 2 units of social studies. Minimum combined SAT score of 950 and minimum 2.8 GPA required. SAT or ACT is required. Campus visit and interview recommended. Off-campus interviews available with an admissions representative.

**Procedure:** Take SAT or ACT by fall of 12th year. Visit college for interview by fall of 12th year. Suggest filing application by February 1. Application deadline is August 15. Acceptance notification will be mailed on February 1 if application is received by January 21; rolling basis for applications received after January 21. Reply is required by May 1. $100 nonrefundable tuition deposit. $100 nonrefundable room deposit. Freshmen accepted for terms other than fall.

**Special programs:** Admission may be deferred one year. Credit and/or placement may be granted through CEEB Advanced Placement exams for scores of 3 or higher. Credit and/or placement may be granted through CLEP general and subject exams. Early decision program. In fall 1993, 54 applied for early decision and 52 were accepted. Deadline for applying for early decision is December 1. Early entrance/early admission program. Concurrent enrollment program.

**Transfer students:** Transfer students accepted for terms other than fall. In fall 1993, 22% of all new students were transfers into all classes. 144 transfer applications were received, 111 were accepted. Application deadline is August 1 for fall; January 1 for spring. Minimum 2.5 GPA required. Lowest course grade accepted is "C." Maximum number of transferable credits is 60 semester hours from a two-year school and 75 semester hours from a four-year school. At least 45 semester hours must be completed at the university to receive degree.

**Admissions contact:** Dennis T. Matthews, M.A., Director of Admissions. 404 364-8307, 800 428-4484 (outside Atlanta).

**FINANCIAL AID. Available aid:** Pell grants, SEOG, state scholarships and grants, school scholarships and grants, private scholarships and grants, academic merit scholarships, and aid for undergraduate foreign students. Perkins Loans (NDSL), PLUS, Stafford Loans (GSL), state loans, school loans, private loans, and SLS. AMS, deferred payment plan, family tuition reduction, and guaranteed tuition.

**Financial aid statistics:** 57% of aid is not need-based. In 1993-94, 100% of all undergraduate applicants received aid. Average amounts of aid awarded freshmen: Scholarships and grants, $8,720; loans, $5,625.

**Supporting data/closing dates:** FAFSA: Priority filing date is May 1. School's own aid application: Accepted on rolling basis. State aid form: Accepted on rolling basis. Income tax forms: Accepted on rolling basis. Verification documents: Accepted on rolling basis. Notification of awards on rolling basis.

**Financial aid contact:** Pamela Beaird, Director of Financial Aid. 404 364-8356.

# Paine College

**Augusta, GA 30910** 706 821-8200

**1993-94 Costs.** Tuition: $5,460. Room: $1,110. Board: $1,704. Fees, books, misc. academic expenses (school's estimate): $800.

**Enrollment.** Undergraduates: 188 men, 401 women (full-time). Freshman class: 1,143 applicants, 636 accepted, 225 enrolled.

**Test score averages/ranges.** Average SAT scores: 328 verbal, 371 math. Range of SAT scores of middle 50%: 260-390 verbal, 300-430 math. Average ACT scores: 15 composite. Range of ACT scores of middle 50%: 14-18 composite.

**Faculty.** 55 full-time; 8 part-time. 44% of faculty holds doctoral degree. Student/faculty ratio: 11 to 1.

**Selectivity rating.** Less competitive.

**PROFILE.** Paine, founded in 1882, is a private, church-affiliated, historically black college. Its 41-acre campus is situated in the center of Augusta, east of Atlanta.

**Accreditation:** SACS.

**Religious orientation:** Paine College is affiliated with the Christian Methodist Episcopal and United Methodist Churches; one semester of religion/theology required.

**Library:** Collections totaling over 85,025 volumes, 437 periodical subscriptions, and 10,024 microform items.

**Special facilities/museums:** Early childhood development center.

**STUDENT BODY. Undergraduate profile:** 77% are state residents; 44% are transfers. 98% Black, 1% White, 1% Other.

**Freshman profile:** 72% of accepted applicants took SAT; 20% took ACT.

**Undergraduate achievement:** 60% of fall 1991 freshmen returned for fall 1992 term. 11% of entering class graduated.

**Foreign students:** 13 students are from out of the country. Countries represented include African countries and the Bahamas.

**PROGRAMS OF STUDY. Degrees:** B.A., B.S.

**Majors:** Biology, Business Administration, Chemistry, Early Childhood Education, English, History, Mass Communications, Mathematics, Middle Grade Education, Music Education, Philosophy/Religion, Psychology, Sociology.

**Distribution of degrees:** The majors with the highest enrollment are business administration, sociology, education, and biology; philosophy/religion, English, and mathematics have the lowest.

**Requirements:** General education requirement.

**Academic regulations:** Freshmen must maintain minimum 1.7 GPA; sophomores, 1.8 GPA; juniors, 1.9 GPA; seniors, 2.0 GPA.

**Special:** Minors offered in all majors and in art, French, German, health/physical education, music, physics, and secondary education. Courses offered in economics, geography, and political science. Developmental courses. Dual degrees. Independent study. Internships. Cooperative education programs. 3-2 engineering programs with Florida A&M U and Georgia Tech. Combined biomedical science and chemistry programs with Meharry Medical Coll. Combined mass communications program with Clark Atlanta U. Cross-registration with Augusta Coll. Teacher certification in early childhood, elementary, and secondary education. ROTC.

**Honors:** Honors program. Honor societies.

**Academic Assistance:** Remedial reading, writing, math, and study skills. Nonremedial tutoring.

**ADMISSIONS. Academic basis for candidate selection** (in order of priority): Secondary school record, standardized test scores, school's recommendation, essay, class rank.

**Nonacademic basis for candidate selection:** Particular talent or ability is important. Character and personality, extracurricular participation, and alumni/ae relationship are considered.

**Requirements:** Graduation from secondary school is required; GED is accepted. 15 units and the following program of study are recommended: 4 units of English, 2 units of math, 1 unit of science, 2 units of foreign language, 1 unit of social studies, 1 unit of history, 4 units of electives. Electives may include commercial/vocational courses, fine arts, foreign language, health, and physical education. Minimum 2.0 GPA recommended. Conditional admission possible for applicants not meeting standard requirements. SAT or ACT is required. Campus visit and interview recommended. Off-campus interviews available with admissions and alumni representatives.

**Procedure:** Take SAT or ACT by December of 12th year. Suggest filing application by March. Application deadline is August 1. Notification of admission on rolling basis. $25 refundable room deposit. Freshmen accepted for terms other than fall.

**Special programs:** Admission may be deferred. Credit may be granted through CEEB Advanced Placement for scores of 3 or higher. Credit may be granted through CLEP general and subject exams, military and life experience. Early entrance/early admission program. Concurrent enrollment program.

**Transfer students:** Transfer students accepted for terms other than fall. In fall 1992, 44% of all new students were transfers into all classes. 111 transfer applications were received, 59 were accepted. Minimum 2.0 GPA required. Lowest course grade accepted is "C." At least 42 semester hours must be completed at the college to receive degree.

**Admissions contact:** Phillis Wyatt-Woodruff, M.S., Director of Enrollment Management. 706 821-8320.

**FINANCIAL AID. Available aid:** Pell grants, SEOG, state scholarships, school scholarships and grants, private scholarships and grants, ROTC scholarships, academic merit scholarships, athletic scholarships, and aid for undergraduate foreign students. Perkins Loans (NDSL), PLUS, and Stafford Loans (GSL). Deferred payment plan and family tuition reduction.

**Financial aid statistics:** In 1992-93, 98% of all undergraduate applicants received aid; 98% of freshman applicants.

**Supporting data/closing dates:** FAFSA/FAF: Priority filing date is March 1. School's own aid application: Priority filing date is March 1. State aid form: Priority filing date is March 1. Income tax forms: Priority filing date is March 1. Notification of awards on rolling basis.
**Financial aid contact:** Ardrina Scott-Elliott, Director of Financial Aid. 706 821-8320.

# Piedmont College

**Demorest, GA 30535** **706 778-3000**

**1993-94 Costs.** Tuition: $4,920. Room & board: $3,620. Fees, books, misc. academic expenses (school's estimate): $600.
**Enrollment.** Undergraduates: 268 men, 373 women (full-time). Freshman class: 663 applicants, 562 accepted, 266 enrolled.
**Test score averages/ranges.** Average SAT scores: 452 verbal, 499 math.
**Faculty.** 43 full-time; 12 part-time. 75% of faculty holds doctoral degree. Student/faculty ratio: 14 to 1.
**Selectivity rating.** Less competitive.

**PROFILE.** Piedmont, founded in 1897, is a private, church-affiliated, multipurpose college. Programs are offered in the Divisions of Humanities, Social Sciences, Natural Sciences, Commerce, and Education. Its 200-acre campus is located in Demorest, northeast of Atlanta.

**Accreditation:** SACS.
**Religious orientation:** Piedmont College is affiliated with the National Association of Congregational Christian Churches; one semester of religion required.
**Library:** Collections totaling over 105,000 volumes, 442 periodical subscriptions, and 9,000 microform items.
**Special facilities/museums:** Art gallery, child development center.
**Athletic facilities:** Gymnasium, golf course, baseball, soccer, and softball fields, tennis and volleyball courts.

**STUDENT BODY. Undergraduate profile:** 93% are state residents. 1% Asian-American, 5% Black, 1% Hispanic, 1% Native American, 92% White. Average age of undergraduates is 26.
**Freshman profile:** 95% of accepted applicants took SAT; 5% took ACT.
**Foreign students:** 16 students are from out of the country. Countries represented include the Bahamas, Cameroon, China, Germany, Japan, and Nepal.

**PROGRAMS OF STUDY. Degrees:** B.A., B.S.
**Majors:** Accounting, Art, Art Education, Art History, Biology, Business Administration, Business Economics, Chemistry, Computer Information Systems, Computer Science/Mathematics, Early Childhood Education, Economics, English, Health Science, History, Mathematics, Middle Grades Education, Music, Music Education, Psychology, Sociology, Spanish, Special Education, Theatre Arts.
**Distribution of degrees:** The majors with the highest enrollment are business administration, early childhood education, and history; music education, music, and art education have the lowest.
**Requirements:** General education requirement.
**Academic regulations:** Freshmen must maintain minimum 1.3 GPA; sophomores, 1.5 GPA; juniors, 1.8 GPA; seniors, 2.0 GPA.
**Special:** Minors offered in most majors and in anthropology, French, physical education, physical science, political science, religion, and secondary education. Double majors. Internships. Preprofessional programs in law, medicine, veterinary science, pharmacy, dentistry, theology, optometry, and nursing. 3-2 B.A./B.S. nursing program with Emory U. Teacher certification in early childhood, elementary, secondary, and special education. Certification in specific subject areas.
**Honors:** Honors program. Honor societies.
**Academic Assistance:** Remedial reading, writing, math, and study skills. Nonremedial tutoring.

**ADMISSIONS. Academic basis for candidate selection** (in order of priority): Secondary school record, standardized test scores, class rank, school's recommendation, essay.
**Nonacademic basis for candidate selection:** Character and personality, extracurricular participation, particular talent or ability, and alumni/ae relationship are considered.
**Requirements:** Graduation from secondary school is recommended; GED is accepted. 21 units and the following program of study are recommended: 4 units of English, 3 units of math, 2 units of science, 2 units of foreign language, 1 unit of social studies, 2 units of history. Minimum combined SAT score of 800 and minimum 2.0 GPA required. Portfolio required of art program applicants. Audition required of music program applicants. Conditional admission possible for applicants not meeting standard requirements. SAT is required; ACT may be substituted. Campus visit and interview recommended. Off-campus interviews available with an admissions representative.
**Procedure:** Take SAT or ACT by March of 12th year. Visit college for interview by summer of 12th year. Suggest filing application by January. Application deadline is July. Notification of admission on rolling basis. $100 tuition deposit, refundable until one month prior to beginning of term. $75 room deposit, refundable until student moves out of room. Freshmen accepted for terms other than fall.
**Special programs:** Admission may be deferred one year. Credit and/or placement may be granted through CEEB Advanced Placement exams for scores of 3 or higher. Credit and/or placement may be granted through CLEP general and subject exams. Credit and placement may be granted through DANTES exams. Early entrance/early admission program. Concurrent enrollment program.
**Transfer students:** Transfer students accepted for terms other than fall. Application deadline is July 15 for fall; January 1 for spring. Minimum 2.0 GPA required. Lowest course grade accepted is "D." Maximum number of transferable credits is 90 semester hours. At least 30 semester hours must be completed at the college to receive degree.
**Admissions contact:** Penny L. Graber, Director of Admissions. 800 277-7020.

**FINANCIAL AID. Available aid:** Pell grants, SEOG, state scholarships and grants, school scholarships and grants, private scholarships and grants, academic merit scholarships, and athletic scholarships. Perkins Loans (NDSL), PLUS, Stafford Loans (GSL), state loans, school loans, private loans, and SLS. AMS.
**Financial aid statistics:** 43% of aid is not need-based. In 1993-94, 95% of all undergraduate applicants received aid; 94% of freshman applicants. Average amounts of aid awarded freshmen: Scholarships and grants, $1,800; loans, $2,300.
**Supporting data/closing dates:** FAFSA: Accepted on rolling basis. State aid form: Accepted on rolling basis. Notification of awards on rolling basis.
**Financial aid contact:** Kenneth Owen, Director of Financial Aid. 706 778-3000.

# The Savannah College of Art and Design

**Savannah, GA 31401** **912 238-2400**

**1994-95 Costs.** Tuition: $9,900. Room: $3,000-$3,500. Board: $2,250. Fees, books, misc. academic expenses (school's estimate): $1,200.
**Enrollment.** Undergraduates: 1,088 men, 914 women (full-time). Freshman class: 2,355 applicants, 1,225 accepted, 777 enrolled. Graduate enrollment: 66 men, 78 women.
**Test score averages/ranges.** Average SAT scores: 460 verbal, 520 math. Range of SAT scores of middle 50%: 470-550 verbal, 490-560 math. Average ACT scores: 24 composite. Range of ACT scores of middle 50%: 22-24 composite.
**Faculty.** 106 full-time; 21 part-time. 99% of faculty holds highest degree in specific field. Student/faculty ratio: 19 to 1.
**Selectivity rating.** Competitive.

**PROFILE.** The Savannah College of Art and Design, founded in 1978, is a private college of the arts. Its three-acre campus is located in Savannah.

**Accreditation:** SACS. Professionally accredited by the National Architecture Accrediting Board.
**Religious orientation:** The Savannah College of Art and Design is nonsectarian; no religious requirements.
**Library:** Collections totaling over 32,000 volumes and 350 periodical subscriptions.
**Special facilities/museums:** Art galleries, computer, video, photography, and design labs.
**Athletic facilities:** Equipment available for crew, soccer, and volleyball teams.

**STUDENT BODY. Undergraduate profile:** 22% are state residents. 1% Asian-American, 7% Black, 2% Hispanic, 1% Native American, 89% White. Average age of undergraduates is 20.
**Freshman profile:** 1% of freshmen who took SAT scored 700 or over on verbal, 1% scored 700 or over on math; 13% scored 600 or over on verbal, 13% scored 600 or over on math; 41% scored 500 or over on verbal, 52% scored 500 or over on math; 90% scored 400 or over on verbal, 93% scored 400 or over on math; 100% scored 300 or over on verbal, 100% scored 300 or over on math. 95% of accepted applicants took SAT; 5% took ACT.
**Undergraduate achievement:** 65% of fall 1991 freshmen returned for fall 1992 term. 60% of entering class graduated. 10% of students who completed a degree program went on to graduate study within one year.
**Foreign students:** 140 students are from out of the country. Countries represented include the Bahamas, Canada, India, Japan, Taiwan, and Thailand; 50 in all.

**PROGRAMS OF STUDY. Degrees:** B.Arch., B.F.A.
**Majors:** Architecture, Art History, Computer Art, Fashion, Fibers, Graphic Design, Historic Preservation, Illustration, Interior Design, Painting, Photography, Video.
**Distribution of degrees:** The majors with the highest enrollment are graphic design, illustration, and interior design.
**Requirements:** General education requirement.
**Academic regulations:** Minimum 2.0 GPA must be maintained.
**Special:** Double majors. Dual degrees. Independent study. Internships. Summer quarter programs in New York City and Europe; apprenticeships with artists or designers and internships with museums, agencies, media production companies, architectural firms, and other companies in the U.S. or abroad. Study abroad in Egypt, England, France, Germany, Italy, and Spain.
**Academic Assistance:** Nonremedial tutoring.

**STUDENT LIFE. Housing:** Students may live on or off campus. Coed, women's, and men's dorms. School-owned/operated apartments. 35% of students live in college housing.
**Social atmosphere:** Popular student gathering spots include Design Works Cafe, Streamliner Diner, Bobbie's Diner, Folsyth Park, Madison Square, and Savannah restaurants, clubs, and coffee shops. The United Student Forum, the Student Activities Council, athletes, the Inter-cultural Student Association, the Residence Hall Council, the Expressionist Cafe, Cinema Obscura, the Pan African Association, and BACCHUS are influential campus groups. Popular campus events include the Masquerade Ball, the Beach Party, the Sidewalk Arts Festival, Late Night breakfasts, the International Festival, and campus concerts, films, and performances. The student newsletter reports, "Historic Savannah provides a lively backdrop for artistic, academic, and social activities. The beach at Tybee Island is 15 minutes away. River Street and City Market offer restaurants, bars, clubs, shops, and coffeehouses in restored buildings."
**Services and counseling/handicapped student services:** Placement services. Personal counseling. Career and academic guidance services.
**Campus organizations:** Undergraduate student government. Student newspaper (SCAD Scoops, published biweekly). Literary magazine. National Interior Design Society, Student Illustrators' Society, Student Preservation Association, academic organizations, 10 organizations in all.
**Minority/foreign student organizations:** Foreign Student Association.

**ATHLETICS. Physical education requirements:** None.
**Intercollegiate competition:** 30% of students participate. Baseball (M), basketball (M,W), cheerleading (M,W), crew (M,W), golf (M,W), rugby (M), soccer (M,W), softball (W), tennis (M,W), volleyball (W). Member of NCAA Division III.

**Intramural and club sports:** 25% of students participate. Intramural basketball, cycling, football, sailing, soccer, softball, ultimate frisbee, volleyball. Men's club crew, rugby, soccer. Women's club crew, soccer.

**ADMISSIONS. Academic basis for candidate selection** (in order of priority): Standardized test scores, secondary school record, school's recommendation, class rank.
**Nonacademic basis for candidate selection:** Particular talent or ability is emphasized. Character and personality and extracurricular participation are considered.
**Requirements:** Graduation from secondary school is recommended; GED is accepted. No specific distribution of secondary school units required. Minimum combined SAT score of 1000 (composite ACT score of 25), rank in top half of secondary school class, and minimum 3.0 GPA recommended. Minimum SAT math score of 520 (ACT math score of 24) required of architecture program applicants. Conditional admission possible for applicants not meeting standard requirements. SAT or ACT is required. Campus visit and interview recommended. Off-campus interviews available with an admissions representative.
**Procedure:** Take SAT or ACT by March 1 of 12th year. Visit college for interview by April 1 of 12th year. Suggest filing application by April 1; no deadline. Notification of admission on rolling basis. Reply is required within 30 days of acceptance. $400 nonrefundable tuition deposit. $500 nonrefundable room deposit. Freshmen accepted for terms other than fall.
**Special programs:** Credit/placement may be offered through CEEB Advanced Placement for scores of 5; minimum combined SAT score of 1000 required for AP credit. Early entrance/early admission program. Concurrent enrollment program.
**Transfer students:** Transfer students accepted for terms other than fall. Application deadline is rolling. Minimum 2.0 GPA required. Lowest course grade accepted is "C." Maximum number of transferable credits is 90 quarter hours. At least 90 quarter hours must be completed at the college to receive degree.
**Admissions contact:** Cissy Rudder, Dean of Admissions. 912 238-2483.

**FINANCIAL AID. Available aid:** Pell grants, SEOG, state grants, school scholarships, private scholarships, and academic merit scholarships. Perkins Loans (NDSL), PLUS, Stafford Loans (GSL), state loans, private loans, and SLS. Deferred payment plan.
**Financial aid statistics:** In 1992-93, 90% of all undergraduate applicants received aid; 90% of freshman applicants. Average amounts of aid awarded freshmen: Scholarships and grants, $1,100; loans, $2,500.
**Supporting data/closing dates:** FAFSA/FAF/FFS: Accepted on rolling basis. Notification of awards on rolling basis.
**Financial aid contact:** Cindy Bradley, Director of Financial Aid. 912 238-2400.

**STUDENT EMPLOYMENT.** College Work/Study Program. Institutional employment. 10% of full-time undergraduates work on campus during school year. Students may expect to earn an average of $900 during school year. Freshmen are discouraged from working during their first term. Off-campus part-time employment opportunities rated "excellent."

**COMPUTER FACILITIES.** 250 IBM/IBM-compatible and Macintosh/Apple microcomputers. Computer facilities are available to all students.
**Fees:** None.

**GRADUATE CAREER DATA.** Graduate school percentages: 10% enter graduate arts and sciences programs. Companies and businesses that hire graduates: art and architectural firms.

# Savannah State College

**Savannah, GA 31404** — **912 356-2186**

**1993-94 Costs.** Tuition: $1,686 (state residents), $4,368 (out-of-state). Room & board: $2,205. Fees, books, misc. academic expenses (school's estimate): $600.
**Enrollment.** Undergraduates: 648 men, 754 women (full-time). Freshman class: 1,133 applicants, 423 enrolled.
**Test score averages/ranges.** Average SAT scores: 390 verbal, 421 math. Average ACT scores: 18 composite.
**Faculty.** 129 full-time. 52% of faculty holds doctoral degree. Student/faculty ratio: 19 to 1.
**Selectivity rating.** Noncompetitive.

**PROFILE.** Savannah State is a public, multipurpose, historically black college. Founded in 1890, it adopted coeducation in 1921. Programs are offered through the Schools of Business, Humanities and Social Sciences, and Science and Technology. Its 165-acre campus is located in Savannah.

**Accreditation:** SACS. Professionally accredited by the Accreditation Board for Engineering and Technology.
**Religious orientation:** Savannah State College is nonsectarian; no religious requirements.
**Library:** Collections totaling over 140,000 volumes.
**Athletic facilities:** Gymnasium, baseball and practice fields, track, stadium.

**STUDENT BODY. Undergraduate profile:** 88% are state residents. 1% Asian-American, 79% Black, 2% Hispanic, 1% Native American, 17% White. Average age of undergraduates is 21.
**Freshman profile:** 94% of freshmen come from public schools.
**Foreign students:** 65 students are from out of the country. Countries represented include the Bahamas, Ethiopia, Kuwait, Nigeria, Pakistan, and the Virgin Islands; 18 in all.

**PROGRAMS OF STUDY. Degrees:** B.A., B.Bus.Admin., B.S., B.Soc.Work.
**Majors:** Accounting, Administrative Services, Biology, Chemistry, Civil Engineering Technology, Computer Science Technology, Criminal Justice, Economics, Electronics Engineering Technology, English Language/Literature, Environmental Studies, Finance, General Business Administration, History, Information Systems, Management, Marine Biology, Marketing, Mathematics, Mechanical Engineering Technology, Music, Political Science, Social Sciences, Sociology.
**Distribution of degrees:** The majors with the highest enrollment are accounting, computer science, and electronics engineering technology; English language/literature, music, and environmental studies have the lowest.
**Requirements:** General education requirement.
**Special:** Minors offered in several majors and in accounting, art, child development, computer science, disadvantaged/handicapped families, electronics/physics, engineering technology, English, French, German, gerontology, hotel management, mass communications, naval science, psychology, religious/philosophical studies, and Spanish. Associate's degrees offered. Double majors. Dual degrees. Independent study. Accelerated study. Internships. Cooperative education programs. Preprofessional programs in law, medicine, veterinary science, pharmacy, dentistry, engineering, medical illustration, medical secretary, medical social work, medical technology, nursing, and physical therapy. 3-2 dual degree engineering programs with Georgia Tech. Member of BJCC Consortium. ROTC and NROTC.
**Honors:** Honors program.
**Academic Assistance:** Nonremedial tutoring.

**STUDENT LIFE. Housing:** Freshmen, sophomores, and juniors must live on campus. Women's and men's dorms. School-owned/operated apartments. 50% of students live in college housing.
**Social atmosphere:** The student newspaper reports that popular gathering spots include the Student Center, Payne Hall, the Zoo, Raymond's, and Hollywood's. Influential groups on campus are Players by the Sea, Greeks, and ATOM (Association of the Original Man). Homecoming Week, the Queen Coronation, Midnight Breakfast, various talent shows, and a beach party are popular events.
**Services and counseling/handicapped student services:** Placement services. Health service. Counseling services for minority, military, veteran, and older students. Personal counseling. Career and academic guidance services. Learning disabled services.
**Campus organizations:** Undergraduate student government. Student newspaper (Tiger's Roar, published once/month). Yearbook. Radio station. Band, choral society, concert choir, gospel choir, special-interest groups. Five fraternities, no chapter houses; four sororities, no chapter houses. 38% of men join a fraternity. 39% of women join a sorority.

**ATHLETICS. Physical education requirements:** Six hours of physical education and/or health required.
**Intercollegiate competition:** 4% of students participate. Baseball (M), basketball (M,W), cheerleading (W), cross-country (W), football (M), tennis (W), track (outdoor) (M), volleyball (W). Member of NCAA Division II, Southeastern Intercollegiate Athletic Conference.
**Intramural and club sports:** 1% of students participate. Intramural basketball, flag football, softball.

**ADMISSIONS. Academic basis for candidate selection** (in order of priority): Standardized test scores.
**Requirements:** Graduation from secondary school is required; GED is accepted. No specific distribution of secondary school units required. Minimum combined SAT score of 750 (composite ACT score of 19) and minimum 2.0 GPA required. Conditional admission possible for applicants not meeting standard requirements. Developmental Studies Program for applicants not normally admissible. SAT or ACT is required. Campus visit and interview recommended. Off-campus interviews available with an admissions representative.
**Procedure:** Take SAT or ACT by December 10 of 12th year. Visit college for interview by May 1 of 12th year. Suggest filing application by March 1; application must be filed no later than 20 days before registration. Notification of admission on rolling basis. Reply is required by May 1. $50 refundable room deposit. Freshmen accepted for terms other than fall.
**Special programs:** Credit and/or placement may be granted through CEEB Advanced Placement exams for scores of 3 or higher. Credit may be granted through CLEP general and subject exams. Credit and placement may be granted through military experience. Early entrance/early admission program. Concurrent enrollment program.
**Transfer students:** Transfer students accepted for terms other than fall. Minimum 2.0 GPA required. Lowest course grade accepted is "D."
**Admissions contact:** Roy Jackson, Ph.D., Director of Admissions. 912 356-2181.

**FINANCIAL AID. Available aid:** Pell grants, SEOG, state scholarships and grants, school scholarships, private scholarships and grants, ROTC scholarships, academic merit scholarships, and athletic scholarships. Perkins Loans (NDSL), state loans, school loans, and private loans.
**Financial aid statistics:** In 1992-93, 95% of all undergraduate applicants received aid; 65% of freshman applicants.
**Supporting data/closing dates:** FAFSA/FAF/FFS: Priority filing date is July 18. School's own aid application: Deadline is July 18. Notification of awards on rolling basis.
**Financial aid contact:** Thelma Harris, C.P.A., Director of Financial Aid. 912 356-2253.

**STUDENT EMPLOYMENT.** College Work/Study Program. 45% of full-time undergraduates work on campus during school year. Students may expect to earn an average of $900 during school year. Freshmen are discouraged from working during their first term. Off-campus part-time employment opportunities rated "good."

**COMPUTER FACILITIES.** IBM/IBM-compatible and Macintosh/Apple microcomputers. Students may access Prime minicomputer/mainframe systems. Computer languages and software packages include BASIC, C, COBOL, dBASE II, FORTRAN 77, IBM Graphics, Lotus 1-2-3, Pascal, SuperCalc IV, WordPerfect. Computer facilities are available to all students.
**Fees:** None.
**Hours:** 8 AM-10 PM.

**GRADUATE CAREER DATA.** Highest graduate school enrollments: Georgia State U, Ohio State U, U of Georgia. 23% of graduates choose careers in business and industry.

# Southern College of Technology

**Marietta, GA 30060-2896** **404 528-7281**

**1994-95 Costs.** Tuition: $1,422 (state residents), $4,266 (out-of-state). Room: $1,500. Board: $2,100. Fees, books, misc. academic expenses (school's estimate): $767.
**Enrollment.** Undergraduates: 1,878 men, 352 women (full-time). Freshman class: 652 applicants, 503 accepted, 297 enrolled. Graduate enrollment: 234 men, 147 women.
**Test score averages/ranges.** Average SAT scores: 428 verbal, 512 math. Range of SAT scores of middle 50%: 380-470 verbal, 460-560 math. Average ACT scores: 22 English, 24 math, 22 composite. Range of ACT scores of middle 50%: 22-23 English, 22-23 math.
**Faculty.** 147 full-time; 60 part-time. 48% of faculty holds doctoral degree. Student/faculty ratio: 13 to 1.
**Selectivity rating.** Less competitive.

**PROFILE.** Southern College of Technology, founded in 1948, is a public college of technology. Its 200-acre campus is located in Marietta, 15 miles from Atlanta.

**Accreditation:** SACS. Professionally accredited by the Accreditation Board for Engineering and Technology, the American Council for Construction Education.
**Religious orientation:** Southern College of Technology is nonsectarian; no religious requirements.
**Library:** Collections totaling over 110,000 volumes, 1,500 periodical subscriptions, and 40,000 microform items.
**Athletic facilities:** Gymnasium, baseball field, tennis courts.
**STUDENT BODY. Undergraduate profile:** 97% are state residents; 58% are transfers. 3% Asian-American, 17% Black, 2% Hispanic, 75% White, 3% Other. Average age of undergraduates is 25.
**Freshman profile:** 2% of freshmen who took SAT scored 700 or over on math; 2% scored 600 or over on verbal, 15% scored 600 or over on math; 14% scored 500 or over on verbal, 61% scored 500 or over on math; 66% scored 400 or over on verbal, 94% scored 400 or over on math; 100% scored 300 or over on verbal, 100% scored 300 or over on math. 33% of freshmen who took ACT scored 24 or over on math, 17% scored 24 or over on composite; 83% scored 18 or over on English, 100% scored 18 or over on math, 100% scored 18 or over on composite; 100% scored 12 or over on English. 93% of accepted applicants took SAT; 2% took ACT. 93% of freshmen come from public schools.
**Undergraduate achievement:** 65% of fall 1992 freshmen returned for fall 1993 term. 5% of entering class graduated. 15% of students who completed a degree program went on to graduate study within one year.
**Foreign students:** 95 students are from out of the country. Countries represented include China, Ethiopia, India, Iran, Nigeria, and Pakistan; 48 in all.
**PROGRAMS OF STUDY. Degrees:** B.Arch., B.S.
**Majors:** Apparel Engineering Technology, Apparel/Textile Engineering Technology, Architecture, Civil Engineering Technology, Computer Engineering Technology, Computer Science, Construction, Electrical Engineering Technology, Environmental Development, Industrial Distribution, Industrial Engineering Technology, Manufacturing, Mathematics, Mechanical Engineering Technology, Physics, Technical/Professional Communication, Technology Management.
**Distribution of degrees:** The majors with the highest enrollment are electrical engineering technology, industrial engineering technology, and mechanical engineering technology; mathematics, physics, and apparel/textile engineering technology have the lowest.
**Requirements:** General education requirement.
**Academic regulations:** Freshmen must maintain minimum 1.80 GPA; sophomores, 1.90 GPA; juniors, 2.00 GPA; seniors, 2.00 GPA.
**Special:** Minors offered in some majors. Courses offered in chemistry, economics, English, geology, history, psychology, and social studies. Associate's degrees offered. Double majors. Dual degrees. Cooperative education programs. Graduate school at which undergraduates may take graduate-level courses. Study abroad in England. ROTC at Kennesaw State Coll. NROTC and AFROTC at Georgia Tech.
**Academic Assistance:** Remedial reading, writing, math, and study skills. Nonremedial tutoring.
**STUDENT LIFE. Housing:** Coed and men's dorms. Off-campus privately-owned housing. 10% of students live in college housing.
**Social atmosphere:** The student newspaper reports, "Southern Tech is a commuter college, so campus activities are somewhat restricted. Off campus, there are many activities in the Marietta and Atlanta area." Popular activities include Homecoming, Goat Week, and the Bathtub Race. "Greeks are the main social force at SCT." On campus, students gather at the student center. Off campus, they frequent Charades, Studebaker's, and Carlos McGee's.
**Services and counseling/handicapped student services:** Placement services. Health service. Group learning activities. Counseling services for minority and veteran students. Personal and psychological counseling. Career and academic guidance services. Physically disabled student services. Learning disabled services. Notetaking services. Tape recorders. Tutors. Reader services for the blind.
**Campus organizations:** Undergraduate student government. Student newspaper (Sting, published twice/month). Yearbook. Radio station. Engineering and professional groups, radio, chess and drama clubs, special-interest groups, 39 organizations in all. Seven fraternities, no chapter houses; two sororities, no chapter houses. 6% of men join a fraternity. 6% of women join a sorority.
**Religious organizations:** Baptist Student Union.
**Minority/foreign student organizations:** Black Men in Unity, National Society of Black Engineers. International Student Association.
**ATHLETICS. Physical education requirements:** None.
**Intercollegiate competition:** 2% of students participate. Baseball (M), basketball (M), tennis (M). Member of Georgia Intercollegiate Athletic Conference, NAIA.
**Intramural and club sports:** 2% of students participate. Intramural basketball, floor hockey, football, soccer, softball, volleyball.
**ADMISSIONS. Academic basis for candidate selection** (in order of priority): Standardized test scores, secondary school record.
**Requirements:** Graduation from secondary school is required; GED is accepted. No specific distribution of secondary school units required. Additional courses in math, science, and drawing recommended. Minimum test score requirement options: SAT scores of 350 verbal and 350 math (ACT scores of 18 English and 16 math). SAT or ACT is required. No off-campus interviews.
**Procedure:** Take SAT or ACT by April 1 of 12th year. Suggest filing application by March 1; no deadline. Notification of admission on rolling basis. No set date by which applicant must accept offer. $75 room deposit, refundable until one month prior to beginning of the quarter. Freshmen accepted for terms other than fall.
**Special programs:** Admission may be deferred one year. Credit and/or placement may be granted through CEEB Advanced Placement exams for scores of 3 or higher. Credit and/or placement may be granted through CLEP general and subject exams. Credit and placement may be granted through challenge exams and life experience. Early entrance/early admission program. Concurrent enrollment program.
**Transfer students:** Transfer students accepted for terms other than fall. In fall 1993, 58% of all new students were transfers into all classes. 595 transfer applications were received, 536 were accepted. Application deadline is August 31 for fall; March 10 for spring. Minimum 2.0 GPA recommended. Lowest course grade accepted is "C." Maximum number of transferable credits is 100 quarter hours from a two-year school and 160 quarter hours from a four-year school. At least 45 quarter hours must be completed at the college to receive degree.
**Admissions contact:** Virginia S. Head, M.Ed., Director of Admissions. 404 528-7281.
**FINANCIAL AID. Available aid:** Pell grants, SEOG, state scholarships and grants, school scholarships, private scholarships and grants, ROTC scholarships, academic merit scholarships, and athletic scholarships. Perkins Loans (NDSL), PLUS, Stafford Loans (GSL), private loans, and SLS.
**Financial aid statistics:** 8% of aid is not need-based. In 1993-94, 73% of all undergraduate applicants received aid; 75% of freshman applicants. Average amounts of aid awarded freshmen: Scholarships and grants, $1,500; loans, $1,850.
**Supporting data/closing dates:** FAFSA: Priority filing date is February 15. School's own aid application: Priority filing date is March 15. Income tax forms: Priority filing date is March 15. Notification of awards on rolling basis.
**Financial aid contact:** Emerelle McNair, Ed.D, Director of Financial Aid. 404 528-7290.
**STUDENT EMPLOYMENT.** College Work/Study Program. Institutional employment. 10% of full-time undergraduates work on campus during school year. Students may expect to earn an average of $1,000 during school year. Off-campus part-time employment opportunities rated "good."
**COMPUTER FACILITIES.** 700 IBM/IBM-compatible and Macintosh/Apple microcomputers; 200 are networked. Students may access IBM minicomputer/mainframe systems, Internet. Client/LAN operating systems include Apple/Macintosh, DOS, UNIX/XENIX/AIX, X-windows, LocalTalk/AppleTalk, Novell. Computer languages and software packages include Assembler, BASIC, COBOL, C++, FORTRAN, IFPS, ImSL, Maple, Microsoft Word, SPSS-X, Turbo Pascal, WordPerfect; 37 in all. Computer facilities are available to all students.
**Fees:** None.
**Hours:** 6 AM-2 AM.
**GRADUATE CAREER DATA.** Graduate school percentages: 5% enter graduate business programs. 10% enter graduate arts and sciences programs. Highest graduate school enrollments: Georgia State U, Southern Coll of Tech. 80% of graduates choose careers in business and industry. Companies and businesses that hire graduates: Georgia Department of Transportation, Georgia Power, Lockheed-Georgia Co., Scientific-Atlantic, Inc., Southern Bell, Southwire Co.
**PROMINENT ALUMNI/AE.** Earl Smith, president/owner of E. Smith Heating and Air Conditioning; Wesley E. Cantrell, president, Lanier Business Products; H. Raymond Eckman, president and CEO, LanTel.

# Spelman College

**Atlanta, GA 30314** **404 681-3643**

**1993-94 Costs.** Tuition: $6,480. Room & board: $5,250. Fees, books, misc. academic expenses (school's estimate): $1,322.
**Enrollment.** 1,971 women (full-time). Freshman class: 3,713 applicants, 1,049 accepted, 443 enrolled.
**Test score averages/ranges.** Average SAT scores: 1010 combined. Average ACT scores: 22 composite.
**Faculty.** 135 full-time; 67 part-time. 87% of faculty holds doctoral degree. Student/faculty ratio: 15 to 1.
**Selectivity rating.** More competitive.

**PROFILE.** Spelman, founded in 1881, is a private, historically black, liberal arts college for women. Its 32-acre campus is located one mile from downtown Atlanta.

**Accreditation:** SACS. Professionally accredited by the National Association of Schools of Music, the National Council for Accreditation of Teacher Education.
**Religious orientation:** Spelman College is nonsectarian; no religious requirements.
**Library:** Collections totaling over 404,991 volumes, 2,693 periodical subscriptions, and 385,538 microform items.
**Special facilities/museums:** Nursery-elementary school for child development majors, language lab, electron microscope.
**Athletic facilities:** Gymnasium, bowling lanes, swimming pool, badminton, basketball, tennis, and volleyball courts.
**STUDENT BODY. Undergraduate profile:** 21% are state residents; 7% are transfers. 99% Black, 1% Other. Average age of undergraduates is 20.

**Freshman profile:** 80% of accepted applicants took SAT; 20% took ACT. 83% of freshmen come from public schools.
**Undergraduate achievement:** 90% of fall 1992 freshmen returned for fall 1993 term. 61% of entering class graduated. 41% of students who completed a degree program immediately went on to graduate study.
**Foreign students:** 24 students are from out of the country. Countries represented include African countries, the Bahamas, Bermuda, and the Dominican Republic.

**PROGRAMS OF STUDY. Degrees:** B.A., B.S.
**Majors:** Art, Biochemistry, Biology, Chemistry, Child Development, Computer Sciences, Drama, Economics, Engineering, English, French, History, Independent Major, Mathematics, Music, Natural Sciences, Philosophy, Physics, Political Science, Psychology, Religion, Sociology, Spanish.
**Distribution of degrees:** The majors with the highest enrollment are psychology, English, and economics; religion, French, and philosophy have the lowest.
**Requirements:** General education requirement.
**Special:** Minors offered in several majors and in communication studies, dance, international studies, management and organization, and women's studies. Social welfare program. Freshman studies program offers pilot interdisciplinary core curriculum. Self-designed majors. Double majors. Dual degrees. Internships. Graduate school at which undergraduates may take graduate-level courses. Preprofessional programs in law, medicine, pharmacy, and dentistry. 3-2 engineering programs with Auburn U, Boston U, Georgia Tech, and Rochester U. Member of Atlanta University Center Consortium. Washington Semester. New York Semester. Exchange programs with Mills Coll, Mount Holyoke Coll, Pomona Coll, Simmons Coll, Smith Coll, Vassar Coll, and Wellesley Coll. Pre-medicine program with Boston U. Teacher certification in early childhood, elementary, and secondary education. Study abroad in numerous countries. ROTC and NROTC at Morehouse Coll. AFROTC at Georgia Tech.
**Honors:** Honors program.
**Academic Assistance:** Remedial reading, math, and study skills. Nonremedial tutoring.

**STUDENT LIFE. Housing:** All honors students must live on campus their freshmen year. Women's dorms. 67% of students live in college housing.
**Social atmosphere:** Popular gathering spots include the Lower Manley Student Center Plaza and Friday Market. Student Government Association, sororities, and AST (African Sisterhood) have widespread influence on student life. Eagerly anticipated social events include Homecoming Week, Founder's Week, Celebration in Black, Howard vs. Morehouse football game, and Upperclass Women Week. "There is a lot to do," reports the editor of the student newspaper. "Although we are a small private college, we are part of a larger university system. We are within walking distance of three other colleges/universities. We are also five minutes from the downtown Atlanta area."
**Services and counseling/handicapped student services:** Placement services. Health service. Women's center. Day care. Office of Freshman Studies. Counseling services for older students. Birth control, personal, and psychological counseling. Career and academic guidance services. Religious counseling. Learning disabled services.
**Campus organizations:** Undergraduate student government. Student newspaper (Spotlight, published bimonthly). Literary magazine. Yearbook. Players and Chorus (three-college), glee club and jazz band, dance theatres, tour guides, tutoring groups, debate group, departmental and political groups, service and special-interest groups. Three sororities, no chapter houses. 8% of women join a sorority.
**Religious organizations:** Several religious groups.
**Minority/foreign student organizations:** International Student Club.

**ATHLETICS. Physical education requirements:** Two semester of physical education required.
**Intercollegiate competition:** 5% of students participate. Basketball (W), tennis (W), track and field (outdoor) (W), volleyball (W).
**Intramural and club sports:** 5% of students participate. Intramural badminton, basketball, soccer, softball, swimming, tennis, volleyball.

**ADMISSIONS. Academic basis for candidate selection** (in order of priority): Secondary school record, standardized test scores, essay, school's recommendation, class rank.
**Nonacademic basis for candidate selection:** Extracurricular participation is important. Particular talent or ability, geographical distribution, and alumni/ae relationship are considered.
**Requirements:** Graduation from secondary school is required; GED is accepted. 15 units and the following program of study are required: 4 units of English, 2 units of math, 2 units of science including 1 unit of lab, 2 units of foreign language, 2 units of social studies, 2 units of electives. SAT or ACT is required. Campus visit recommended. No off-campus interviews.
**Procedure:** Take SAT or ACT by December of 12th year. Visit college for interview by January of 12th year. Application deadline is February 1. Notification of admission by March 15. Reply is required by May 1. $50 tuition deposit, refundable until July 1. Freshmen accepted for terms other than fall.
**Special programs:** Admission may be deferred one year. Credit may be granted through CEEB Advanced Placement for scores of 3 or higher. Credit may be granted through CLEP subject exams. Credit and placement may be granted through challenge exams. Early decision program. In fall 1993, 427 applied for early decision and 165 were accepted. Deadline for applying for early decision is November 15. Early entrance/early admission program. Concurrent enrollment program.
**Transfer students:** Transfer students accepted for terms other than fall. In fall 1993, 7% of all new students were transfers into all classes. 248 transfer applications were received, 59 were accepted. Application deadline is February 1 for fall; November 1 for spring. Minimum 2.0 GPA required. Lowest course grade accepted is "C." Maximum number of transferable credits is 90 semester hours. At least 32 semester hours must be completed at the college to receive degree.
**Admissions contact:** Aline Rivers-Jones, Ed.D., Director of Admissions. 404 681-3643, extension 2188.

**FINANCIAL AID. Available aid:** Pell grants, SEOG, state grants, school grants, private scholarships and grants, ROTC scholarships, academic merit scholarships, and aid for undergraduate foreign students. Perkins Loans (NDSL), PLUS, Stafford Loans (GSL), and SLS. Deferred payment plan.
**Supporting data/closing dates:** FAFSA/FAF/FFS: Deadline is April 1. School's own aid application: Deadline is April 1. Notification of awards begins April 2.
**Financial aid contact:** Shirley Scott, M.S., Director of Financial Aid. 404 681-3643, extension 1471.

**STUDENT EMPLOYMENT.** College Work/Study Program. Institutional employment. 25% of full-time undergraduates work on campus during school year. Students may expect to earn an average of $1,500 during school year. Off-campus part-time employment opportunities rated "fair."

**COMPUTER FACILITIES.** IBM/IBM-compatible microcomputers. Computer languages and software packages include all major computer languages. Computer facilities are available to all students.
**Fees:** None.
**Hours:** 8 AM-10 PM.

**PROMINENT ALUMNI/AE.** Marion Wright Edelman, founder and president, Children's Defense Fund; Alice Walker, author; Esther Rolle, actress; Varnette Honeywood, artist; Rolanda Watts, newscaster; Deborah Prolo-Stith, public health commissioner, Massachusetts; Col. Marchelite Jordan, first woman commander of an Air Force base.

# Toccoa Falls College

**Toccoa Falls, GA 30598** — **706 886-6831**

**1994-95 Costs.** Tuition: $6,072. Room & board: $3,636. Fees, books, misc. academic expenses (school's estimate): $800.
**Enrollment.** Undergraduates: 397 men, 384 women (full-time). Freshman class: 1,198 applicants, 935 accepted, 364 enrolled.
**Test score averages/ranges.** Average SAT scores: 433 verbal, 450 math. Average ACT scores: 21 composite.
**Faculty.** 40 full-time; 14 part-time. 42% of faculty holds doctoral degree. Student/faculty ratio: 18 to 1.
**Selectivity rating.** Less competitive.

**PROFILE.** Toccoa Falls, founded in 1907, is a liberal arts college with religious orientation. Its 1,100-acre campus is located two miles from Toccoa, in north Georgia, 100 miles northeast of Atlanta.

**Accreditation:** AABC, SACS. Professionally accredited by the National Association of Schools of Music.
**Religious orientation:** Toccoa Falls College is an interdenominational Christian school; 30 semester hours of theology required.
**Library:** Collections totaling over 88,648 volumes, 590 periodical subscriptions, and 6,647 microform items.
**Special facilities/museums:** Recital hall, music practice rooms, curriculum lab for elementary education majors, photography studio and lab, college archives, historic power plant.
**Athletic facilities:** Gymnasium, basketball, racquetball, and tennis courts, weight room, baseball, soccer, and softball fields.

**STUDENT BODY. Undergraduate profile:** 26% are state residents; 9% are transfers. 3% Asian-American, 2% Black, 4% Hispanic, 1% Native American, 90% White. Average age of undergraduates is 20.
**Freshman profile:** 65% of accepted applicants took SAT; 35% took ACT.
**Undergraduate achievement:** 58% of fall 1992 freshmen returned for fall 1993 term. 45% of entering class graduated. 25% of students who completed a degree program immediately went on to graduate study.
**Foreign students:** 48 students are from out of the country. Countries represented include the Bahamas, Canada, Hungary, Myanmar, Nigeria, and Zimbabwe; 21 in all.

**PROGRAMS OF STUDY. Degrees:** B.A., B.S., Theol.B.
**Majors:** Biblical Languages, Biblical Studies, Broadcasting, Christian Counseling, Christian Education, Church Music, Cross-Cultural Studies, Early Childhood Education, English, Family/Children's Ministries, Interpersonal/Organizational Communication, Journalism, Middle Grades Education, Missiology, Music Composition, Music Education, Music Performance, Pastoral Ministries, Philosophy/Religion, Pre-Seminary Studies, Psychology, Secondary Education, Youth Ministries.
**Distribution of degrees:** The majors with the highest enrollment are early childhood education, pastoral ministries, and interpersonal/organizational communication; philosophy/religion, pre-seminary studies, and music performance have the lowest.
**Requirements:** General education requirement.
**Academic regulations:** Freshmen must maintain minimum 1.5 GPA; sophomores, 1.7 GPA; juniors, 1.9 GPA; seniors, 2.0 GPA.
**Special:** Minors offered in most majors and in anthropology, behavioral science, church planting/enlargement, evangelism/renewal, Greek, history, interpersonal communication, missionary radio broadcasting, missions, New Testament, Old Testament, public relations, teacher education, TESOL, and theology. Foreign teaching internships available. Associate's degrees offered. Self-designed majors. Double majors. Independent study. Internships. Preprofessional programs in law. Five-year theology program. Teacher certification in early childhood, elementary, and secondary education. Certification in specific subject areas.
**Honors:** Phi Beta Kappa. Honors program. Honor societies.
**Academic Assistance:** Remedial reading, writing, and study skills. Nonremedial tutoring.

**ADMISSIONS. Academic basis for candidate selection** (in order of priority): Secondary school record, standardized test scores, class rank, school's recommendation.
**Nonacademic basis for candidate selection:** Character and personality are emphasized. Extracurricular participation is important. Particular talent or ability is considered.
**Requirements:** Graduation from secondary school is required; GED is accepted. No specific distribution of secondary school units required. Minimum combined SAT score of 1000 (composite ACT score of 20), rank in top 15% of secondary school class, and minimum 2.0 GPA recommended. Statement of Christian faith required of all applicants. Audition required of music program applicants. SAT or ACT is required. Campus visit and interview recommended. No off-campus interviews.

**Procedure:** Take SAT or ACT by February 1 of 12th year. Suggest filing application by August 1. Application deadline is August 15. Notification of admission on rolling basis. Reply is required within 60 days of acceptance. $50 tuition deposit, refundable until May 1. $50 room deposit, refundable until May 1. Freshmen accepted for terms other than fall.
**Special programs:** Admission may be deferred two years. Credit may be granted through CEEB Advanced Placement for scores of 3 or higher. Credit may be granted through CLEP general and subject exams, DANTES exams, and military experience. Early entrance/early admission program. Concurrent enrollment program.
**Transfer students:** Transfer students accepted for terms other than fall. In fall 1993, 9% of all new students were transfers into all classes. Application deadline is August 15 for fall; January 15 for spring. Minimum 2.0 GPA required. Lowest course grade accepted is "C-." Maximum number of transferable credits is 100 semester hours. At least 30 semester hours must be completed at the college to receive degree.
**Admissions contact:** Matthew L. King, Director of Admissions. 706 886-6831, 800 868-3257.

**FINANCIAL AID. Available aid:** Pell grants, SEOG, state scholarships and grants, school scholarships and grants, private scholarships and grants, and academic merit scholarships. Perkins Loans (NDSL), PLUS, Stafford Loans (GSL), state loans, school loans, and SLS. Deferred payment plan.
**Supporting data/closing dates:** FAFSA/FAF/FFS: Priority filing date is April 1. School's own aid application: Priority filing date is April 1. State aid form: Accepted on rolling basis. Notification of awards begins May 1.
**Financial aid contact:** Sylvia Eby, Director of Financial Aid. 706 886-6831.

# University of Georgia

**Athens, GA 30602** **706 542-3000**

**1993-94 Costs.** Tuition: $1,845 (state residents), $5,534 (out-of-state). Room & board: $3,285. Fees, books, misc. academic expenses (school's estimate): $909.
**Enrollment.** Undergraduates: 9,057 men, 10,414 women (full-time). Freshman class: 11,363 applicants, 7,304 accepted, 2,993 enrolled. Graduate enrollment: 2,903 men, 3,383 women.
**Test score averages/ranges.** Average SAT scores: 511 verbal, 567 math. Range of SAT scores of middle 50%: 460-560 verbal, 520-620 math.
**Faculty.** 1,792 full-time; 97 part-time. 83% of faculty holds doctoral degree. Student/faculty ratio: 14 to 1.
**Selectivity rating.** More competitive.

**PROFILE.** The University of Georgia, founded in 1785, is a public university. Programs are offered through the Colleges of Arts and Sciences, Agriculture, Pharmacy, Education, Business Administration, Home Economics, and Veterinary Medicine; the Schools of Forest Resources, Journalism and Mass Communication, Social Work, and Environmental Design; the Graduate School; and the Center for Continuing Education. Its 2,090-acre campus is located in Athens, 80 miles east of Atlanta.

**Accreditation:** SACS. Professionally accredited by the Accreditation Board for Engineering and Technology, the American Assembly of Collegiate Schools of Business, the American Bar Association, the American Council on Pharmaceutical Education, the American Dietetic Association, the American Home Economics Association, the American Psychological Association, the American Society of Landscape Architects, the American Speech-Language-Hearing Association, the American Veterinary Medical Association, the Council on Social Work Education, the Foundation for Interior Design Education Research, the National Association of Schools of Art and Design, the National Association of Schools of Music, the National Council for Accreditation of Teacher Education, the Society of American Foresters.
**Religious orientation:** University of Georgia is nonsectarian; no religious requirements.
**Library:** Collections totaling over 3,048,491 volumes, 53,516 periodical subscriptions, and 4,865,800 microform items.
**Special facilities/museums:** Art and natural history museums, state botanical garden, language lab.
**Athletic facilities:** Recreation hall, swimming pool, baseball and intramural fields, stadium, coliseum, tennis courts, track stadium, golf course.

**STUDENT BODY. Undergraduate profile:** 86% are state residents; 38% are transfers. 2% Asian-American, 6% Black, 1% Hispanic, 1% Native American, 90% White. Average age of undergraduates is 21.
**Freshman profile:** 2% of freshmen who took SAT scored 700 or over on verbal, 6% scored 700 or over on math; 15% scored 600 or over on verbal, 32% scored 600 or over on math; 52% scored 500 or over on verbal, 81% scored 500 or over on math; 94% scored 400 or over on verbal, 98% scored 400 or over on math; 99% scored 300 or over on verbal, 99% scored 300 or over on math. 99% of accepted applicants took SAT. 87% of freshmen come from public schools.
**Undergraduate achievement:** 84% of fall 1991 freshmen returned for fall 1992 term. 32% of entering class graduated.
**Foreign students:** Countries represented include Canada, India, Japan, Korea, Taiwan, and the United Kingdom; 90 in all.

**PROGRAMS OF STUDY. Degrees:** A.B.Journ., B.A., B.Bus.Admin., B.F.A., B.Land.Arch., B.Mus., B.S., B.Soc.Work.
**Majors:** Accounting, Advertising, Agribusiness, Agricultural Communications, Agricultural Economics, Agricultural Education, Agricultural Engineering, Agricultural Extension, Agricultural Technology Management, Agronomy, Animal Health, Animal Science, Anthropology, Area Studies Major, Art, Biochemistry, Biological Sciences, Biology, Botany, Broadcast News, Business, Business Administration/Industrial Geography, Chamber Music, Chemistry, Child Development, Child/Family Development, Church Music, Classical Culture, Clothing/Textiles, Communication Sciences/Disorders, Community Health, Community Nutrition, Comparative Literature, Computer Science, Consumer Economics/Home Management, Consumer Foods, Criminal Justice, Crop Science, Dairy Science, Dance, Dietetics/Institutional Management, Drama, Early Childhood, Early Childhood Education, Economics, Educational Psychology, Elementary Education, English, English/Speech, Entomology, Environmental Economics/Management, Environmental Health, Environmental Soil Science, Exercise/Sports Science, Family Development, Fashion Merchandising, Finance, Food Science, Food Service Management, Foreign Language, Forest Resources, French, Furnishings/Interiors, General Agriculture, General Business, Genetics, Geography, Geology, German, Germanic/Slavic Languages, Greek, Health, Health Occupations Education, Health/Physical Education, History, Home Economics Education, Home Economics/Journalism, Horticulture, Hotel/Restaurant Management, Housing, Industrial Arts, Industrial Relations, Interdisciplinary Studies, International Business, Italian, Japanese Language/Literature, Landscape Architecture, Landscape/Grounds Management, Language/Literature, Latin, Linguistics, Magazines, Management, Management Information Systems, Management Science, Marketing, Marketing Education, Mathematics, Mental Retardation, Microbiology, Middle School Education, Music, Music Composition, Music Education, Music Literature, Music Performance, Music Therapy, Newspapers, Nutritional Science, Organizational Management, Pharmacy, Philosophy, Physics, Physics/Astronomy, Plant Genetics, Plant Pathology, Plant Pathology/Plant Genetics, Plant Protection/Pest Management, Political Science, Political Science/Philosophy, Poultry Science, Psychology, Public Relations, Publication Management, Real Estate, Recreation/Leisure Studies, Recreation Resource Management, Religion, Risk Management/Insurance, Romance Languages, School Health, Science, Social Sciences, Social Work, Sociology, Spanish, Speech Communication, Speech Pathology/Audiology, Statistics, Telecommunication Arts, Therapeutic Recreation, Trade/Industrial Education, Zoology.
**Distribution of degrees:** The majors with the highest enrollment are general business, political science, and English.
**Requirements:** General education requirement.
**Academic regulations:** Minimum 2.0 GPA must be maintained.
**Special:** Minors offered in many majors and in Chinese, Portuguese, Russian language and literature, mass communication, and women's studies. Area studies major includes several concentrations. Five-year landscape architecture program. Associate's degrees offered. Self-designed majors. Double majors. Dual degrees. Independent study. Accelerated study. Internships. Cooperative education programs. Graduate school at which undergraduates may take graduate-level courses. Preprofessional programs in law, medicine, veterinary science, pharmacy, dentistry, theology, engineering, forest resources, journalism, landscape architecture, medical technology, and nursing. Combined dentistry program with Medical Coll of Georgia. 3-2 engineering program with Georgia Tech. Member of Southern Regional Education Board Consortium. Washington Semester. Governor's intern programs. Member of National Student Exchange (NSE). Teacher certification in early childhood, elementary, secondary, and special education. Study abroad in Belgium, Brazil, Canada, England, France, Germany, Greece, Italy, Japan, Mexico, and Spain. ROTC and AFROTC.
**Honors:** Phi Beta Kappa. Honors program. Honor societies.
**Academic Assistance:** Remedial reading, writing, math, and study skills. Nonremedial tutoring.

**STUDENT LIFE. Housing:** Coed, women's, and men's dorms. Sorority and fraternity housing. On-campus married-student housing. International housing. 29% of students live in college housing.
**Social atmosphere:** The student newspaper editor reports that the students really enjoy partying and do it well. Greeks, athletes, and religious groups have widespread social influence on campus. Football is the big sport at Georgia, especially the U Georgia/U Florida football game played in Jacksonville. On campus, students meet at the Tate Student Center. Off-campus favorite gathering spots are O'Malley's and Stonewalls.
**Services and counseling/handicapped student services:** Placement services. Health service. Counseling services for minority, military, veteran, and older students. Birth control, personal, and psychological counseling. Career and academic guidance services. Religious counseling. Physically disabled student services. Notetaking services. Tape recorders. Tutors. Reader services for the blind.
**Campus organizations:** Undergraduate student government. Student newspaper (Red and Black; Campus Times). Literary magazine. Yearbook. Radio station. Orchestra, ensembles, trombone choir, choral groups, Concert Dance Company, debating, Toastmasters, Young Democrats, Amnesty International, BACCHUS, Campus NOW, 4-H, Foodshare, Habitat for Humanity, academic and professional groups, 200 organizations in all. 27 fraternities, 21 chapter houses; 22 sororities, 18 chapter houses. 19% of men join a fraternity. 22% of women join a sorority.
**Religious organizations:** Alpha Omega, Bahai Association, Baptist Student Union, Campus Crusade for Christ, Catholic Student Fellowship, Hillel, Worldwide Discipleship Association, other religious groups.
**Minority/foreign student organizations:** Black Affairs Council, Black Theatrical Ensemble, Black Educational Support Team, Committee for Black Cultural Programs. Global Encounter Organization, Global Studies Student Association; African, Asian-American, Caribbean, Chinese, Egyptian, Filipino, Hispanic, Hong Kong/Macau, Indian, Indonesian, Japanese, Korean, Muslim, Nordic, Pakistani, Russian, and Thai groups.

**ATHLETICS. Physical education requirements:** Two terms of physical education required.
**Intercollegiate competition:** 5% of students participate. Baseball (M), basketball (M,W), cross-country (M,W), diving (M,W), football (M), golf (M,W), gymnastics (W), swimming (M,W), tennis (M,W), track and field (indoor) (M,W), track and field (outdoor) (M,W), volleyball (W). Member of NCAA Division I, Southeastern Conference.
**Intramural and club sports:** 36% of students participate. Intramural basketball, bench press, bowling, diving, flag football, golf, inner-tube water polo, putt-putt golf, racquetball, soccer, softball, swimming, tennis, track/field, volleyball, walleyball. Men's club bowling, crew, cycling, fencing, horsemanship, ice hockey, lacrosse, martial arts, racquetball, rugby, soccer, track, ultimate frisbee, volleyball, water skiing, wrestling. Women's club bowling, cycling, horsemanship, ice hockey, lacrosse, martial arts, racquetball, soccer, track, ultimate frisbee, volleyball, water skiing, wrestling.

**ADMISSIONS. Academic basis for candidate selection** (in order of priority): Secondary school record, standardized test scores, school's recommendation, essay.
**Nonacademic basis for candidate selection:** Particular talent or ability is considered.
**Requirements:** Graduation from secondary school is required; GED is accepted. 15 units and the following program of study are required: 4 units of English, 3 units of math, 3 units of science, 2 units of foreign language, 3 units of social studies. Minimum combined SAT score of 900 (or equivalent ACT score) and minimum 3.0 GPA recommended. Foreign

language ACH required of applicants planning to continue study of a language. Plane geometry, trigonometry, chemistry, and physics recommended of B.S. program applicants. Minimum "B+" average and combined SAT score of 1000 recommended of business administration program applicants. Audition required of music program applicants. Developmental Studies Program in reading, English, and math for in-state applicants not normally admissible. SAT is required; ACT may be substituted. Campus visit recommended. No off-campus interviews.
**Procedure:** Take SAT or ACT by January of 12th year. Application deadline is February 1. Early notification on rolling basis for top applicants; March 30 for all others. Reply is required by May 1. $50 room deposit, refundable until mid-summer. Freshmen accepted for terms other than fall.
**Special programs:** Admission may be deferred nine months. Credit and/or placement may be granted through CEEB Advanced Placement exams for scores of 3 or higher. Credit and/or placement may be granted through CLEP subject exams. Early entrance/early admission program. Concurrent enrollment program.
**Transfer students:** Transfer students accepted for terms other than fall. In fall 1992, 38% of all new students were transfers into all classes. 3,926 transfer applications were received, 2,476 were accepted. Application deadline is August 1 for fall; March 1 for spring. Minimum 2.2 GPA required. Lowest course grade accepted is "D." Maximum number of transferable credits is 105 quarter hours. At least 90 quarter hours must be completed at the university to receive degree.
**Admissions contact:** Claire C. Swann, Ed.D., Director of Admissions. 706 542-8776.

**FINANCIAL AID. Available aid:** Pell grants, SEOG, state scholarships and grants, school scholarships and grants, private scholarships and grants, ROTC scholarships, academic merit scholarships, and athletic scholarships. Perkins Loans (NDSL), PLUS, Stafford Loans (GSL), Health Professions Loans, state loans, school loans, private loans, and SLS.
**Financial aid statistics:** In 1992-93, 95% of all undergraduate applicants received aid. Average amounts of aid awarded freshmen: Scholarships and grants, $1,000; loans, $1,500.
**Supporting data/closing dates:** School's own aid application. Income tax forms.
**Financial aid contact:** Ray Tripp, Director of Student Financial Aid. 706 542-6147.

**STUDENT EMPLOYMENT.** College Work/Study Program. Institutional employment. 50% of full-time undergraduates work on campus during school year. Students may expect to earn an average of $2,500 during school year. Off-campus part-time employment opportunities rated "good."

**COMPUTER FACILITIES.** 950 IBM/IBM-compatible and Macintosh/Apple microcomputers. Residence halls may be equipped with stand-alone microcomputers. Numerous computer languages and programs available. Computer facilities in residence halls are not available to all students.
**Fees:** None.
**Hours:** 24 hours for some computers.

**GRADUATE CAREER DATA.** Highest graduate school enrollments: U of Florida, U of Georgia, U of North Carolina, U of Virginia. 65% of graduates choose careers in business and industry. Companies and businesses that hire graduates: Baxter Health Care, Black & Decker, Milliken, NCR.

**PROMINENT ALUMNI/AE.** Eugene Black, former president, World Bank; W. Tapley Bennett, assistant U.S. secretary of state; Francis Tarkenton, former NFL quarterback, TV personality, businessman; James G. Miller, chairperson, Federal Trade Commission; Charlayne Hunter-Gault, reporter/anchor, "MacNeil-Lehrer Report"; Richard B. Russell, former U.S. senator; W. Thomas Johnson, publisher.

# Valdosta State College

**Valdosta, GA 31698 — 912 333-5800**

**1993-94 Costs.** Tuition: $1,729 (state residents), $4,492 (out-of-state). Room: $1,290. Board: $1,650. Fees, books, misc. academic expenses (school's estimate): $600.
**Enrollment.** Undergraduates: 2,428 men, 3,554 women (full-time). Freshman class: 3,674 applicants, 2,663 accepted, 1,883 enrolled. Graduate enrollment: 344 men, 931 women.
**Test score averages/ranges.** Average SAT scores: 395 verbal, 431 math.
**Faculty.** 315 full-time; 75 part-time. 50% of faculty holds highest degree in specific field. Student/faculty ratio: 22 to 1.
**Selectivity rating.** Less competitive.

**PROFILE.** Valdosta State, founded in 1906, is a public, multipurpose college. Programs are offered through the Division of Aerospace Studies and the Schools of the Arts, Arts and Sciences, Business Administration, Education, and Nursing. Its two campuses, totaling over 168 acres, are located in Valdosta, in southern Georgia, 115 miles west of Jacksonville, Fla.

**Accreditation:** SACS. Professionally accredited by the National Association of Schools of Music, the National Council for Accreditation of Teacher Education, the National League for Nursing.
**Religious orientation:** Valdosta State College is nonsectarian; no religious requirements.
**Library:** Collections totaling over 367,718 volumes, 2,848 periodical subscriptions, and 821,877 microform items.
**Athletic facilities:** Swimming pool, basketball and tennis courts, baseball, football, and softball fields, weight room, indoor track, golf course.

**STUDENT BODY. Undergraduate profile:** 90% are state residents; 21% are transfers. 1% Asian-American, 18% Black, 1% Hispanic, 80% White. Average age of undergraduates is 21.
**Freshman profile:** 85% of accepted applicants took SAT; 15% took ACT. 95% of freshmen come from public schools.
**Foreign students:** 51 students are from out of the country. Countries represented include Japan and Korea.

**PROGRAMS OF STUDY. Degrees:** B.A., B.Bus.Admin., B.F.A., B.Gen.Studies, B.Mus., B.S., B.S.Crim.Just., B.S.Ed., B.S.Nurs.
**Majors:** Accounting, Anthropology, Applied Mathematics, Applied Music, Art, Art Education, Astronomy, Biology, Business Education, Business/Vocational Education, Chemistry, Computer Science, Criminal Justice, Early Childhood Education, Economics, English, Finance, French, Geology, History, Management, Management Information Systems, Marketing, Mathematics, Middle Childhood Education, Modern Foreign Languages, Music, Music Education, Nursing, Philosophy, Physical Education, Physics, Political Science, Secondary Education, Secretarial Administration, Sociology, Spanish, Special Education, Speech Communication, Speech/Drama, Speech Education, Sports Medicine, Sports Medicine Education, Theatre Arts, Trade/Industrial Education.
**Requirements:** General education requirement.
**Academic regulations:** Freshmen must maintain minimum 1.6 GPA; sophomores, 1.8 GPA; juniors, 2.00 GPA; seniors, 2.00 GPA.
**Special:** Minors, associate's degrees, and certificate programs offered. Double majors. Dual degrees. Independent study. Internships. Cooperative education programs. Preprofessional programs in law, medicine, veterinary science, pharmacy, dentistry, theology, and optometry. 2-2 engineering programs with Georgia Tech and Mercer U. Teacher certification in early childhood, elementary, secondary, and special education. Study abroad in Japan and the United Kingdom. AFROTC.
**Honors:** Honors program.
**Academic Assistance:** Remedial reading, writing, math, and study skills. Nonremedial tutoring.

**STUDENT LIFE. Housing:** All students under age 19 must live on campus unless living with family. Coed, women's, and men's dorms. Sorority and fraternity housing. School-owned/operated apartments. 30% of students live in college housing.
**Social atmosphere:** Gathering spots most often frequented by students include the campus game room, the quadrangle, the tennis courts, Blazer Cafe, YMCA, Valdosta Mall, and the Waffle House. Athletes, Greeks, the student newspaper, and the student government all contribute to campus social life. Popular events include Homecoming, Greek Week, The Happening, Mayhem, and football games.
**Services and counseling/handicapped student services:** Placement services. Health service. Women's center. Counseling services for minority, veteran, and older students. Career and academic guidance services. Physically disabled student services. Tutors. Reader services for the blind.
**Campus organizations:** Undergraduate student government. Student newspaper (Spectator, published once/week). Literary magazine. Radio station. Concert band, concert choir, ensembles, drama productions, departmental organizations and service groups. Nine fraternities, no chapter houses; nine sororities, no chapter houses.
**Religious organizations:** Baptist, Catholic, Christian, Church of Christ, Episcopal, Jewish, Lutheran, Methodist, and Presbyterian groups.
**Minority/foreign student organizations:** Black Student League. International Student Association.

**ATHLETICS. Physical education requirements:** One semester of physical education required.
**Intercollegiate competition:** 3% of students participate. Baseball (M), basketball (M,W), cross-country (M,W), football (M), golf (M), softball (W), tennis (M,W). Member of Gulf South Conference, NCAA Division II.
**Intramural and club sports:** Intramural basketball, flag football, oozeball, soccer, softball, tennis, volleyball, water polo. Men's club soccer.

**ADMISSIONS. Academic basis for candidate selection** (in order of priority): Secondary school record, standardized test scores.
**Requirements:** Graduation from secondary school is recommended; GED is accepted. 15 units and the following program of study are recommended: 4 units of English, 3 units of math, 3 units of science, 2 units of foreign language, 3 units of social studies. Minimum SAT scores of 300 verbal and 330 math and minimum 2.0 GPA required. Audition required of music program applicants. SAT or ACT is required. Campus visit recommended. No off-campus interviews.
**Procedure:** Take SAT or ACT by October of 12th year. Suggest filing application by January. Application deadline is September. Notification of admission on rolling basis. $75 room deposit, refundable until July. Freshmen accepted for terms other than fall.
**Special programs:** Admission may be deferred three years. Credit and/or placement may be granted through CEEB Advanced Placement exams for scores of 3 or higher. Credit and/or placement may be granted through CLEP general and subject exams. Credit and placement may be granted through DANTES exams. Early entrance/early admission program. Concurrent enrollment program.
**Transfer students:** Transfer students accepted for terms other than fall. In fall 1993, 21% of all new students were transfers into all classes. 1,209 transfer applications were received, 1,136 were accepted. Application deadline is September 1 for fall; March 1 for spring. Minimum 2.0 GPA required. Lowest course grade accepted is "D." Maximum number of transferable credits is 90 quarter hours from a two-year school and 135 quarter hours from a four-year school. At least 45 quarter hours must be completed at the college to receive degree.
**Admissions contact:** Walter H. Peacock, M.B.A., Director of Admissions. 912 333-5791.

**FINANCIAL AID. Available aid:** Pell grants, Federal Nursing Student Scholarships, school scholarships, ROTC scholarships, academic merit scholarships, and athletic scholarships. Perkins Loans (NDSL), PLUS, and Stafford Loans (GSL).
**Financial aid statistics:** In 1993-94, 87% of all undergraduate applicants received aid. Average amounts of aid awarded freshmen: Scholarships and grants, $2,000; loans, $1,500.
**Supporting data/closing dates:** FAFSA/FAF/FFS: Deadline is April 1. School's own aid application: Deadline is April 1. Notification of awards on rolling basis.
**Financial aid contact:** Tommy Moore, Director of Financial Aid. 912 333-5935.

**STUDENT EMPLOYMENT.** College Work/Study Program. Institutional employment. Students may expect to earn an average of $1,500 during school year. Off-campus part-time employment opportunities rated "good."

**COMPUTER FACILITIES.** 150 IBM/IBM-compatible and Macintosh/Apple microcomputers. Computer languages and software packages include BASIC, COBOL, dBASE, Pascal. Computer facilities are available to all students.
**Fees:** None.
**Hours:** 8 AM-midn.

## Wesleyan College

**Macon, GA 31297** **912 477-1110**

**1994-95 Costs.** Tuition: $11,500. Room & board: $4,500. Fees, books, misc. academic expenses (school's estimate): $980.
**Enrollment.** 386 women (full-time). Freshman class: 291 applicants, 287 accepted, 109 enrolled.
**Test score averages/ranges.** Average SAT scores: 510 verbal, 481 math. Range of SAT scores of middle 50%: 500-599 verbal, 460-570 math.
**Faculty.** 41 full-time; 11 part-time. 73% of faculty holds doctoral degree. Student/faculty ratio: 9 to 1.
**Selectivity rating.** Less competitive.

**PROFILE.** Wesleyan, founded in 1836, is a church-affiliated college for women. Its 240-acre campus is located in Macon, in central Georgia, 90 miles south of Atlanta.

**Accreditation:** SACS. Professionally accredited by the National Association of Schools of Music.
**Religious orientation:** Wesleyan College is affiliated with the United Methodist Church; no religious requirements.
**Library:** Collections totaling over 134,484 volumes, 556 periodical subscriptions, and 19,504 microform items.
**Special facilities/museums:** Art and history museums, special collection of Georgiana and Americana, early childhood center.
**Athletic facilities:** Gymnasium, aerobics and dance studios, weight room, soccer field, swimming pool, equestrian center, fitness trail, basketball, tennis, and volleyball courts, golf driving range.

**STUDENT BODY. Undergraduate profile:** 62% are state residents; 3% are transfers. 4% Asian-American, 11% Black, 3% Hispanic, 78% White, 4% Non-resident alien. Average age of undergraduates is 21.
**Freshman profile:** 6% of freshmen who took SAT scored 700 or over on verbal, 1% scored 700 or over on math; 32% scored 600 or over on verbal, 19% scored 600 or over on math; 60% scored 500 or over on verbal, 44% scored 500 or over on math; 100% scored 400 or over on verbal, 100% scored 400 or over on math. 82% of accepted applicants took SAT; 46% took ACT. 80% of freshmen come from public schools.
**Undergraduate achievement:** 65% of fall 1992 freshmen returned for fall 1993 term. 42% of entering class graduated. 36% of students who completed a degree program immediately went on to graduate study.
**Foreign students:** 16 students are from out of the country. Countries represented include Bangladesh, Bulgaria, China, Japan, Korea, and Taiwan; 15 in all.

**PROGRAMS OF STUDY. Degrees:** A.B., B.Mus.
**Majors:** Art History, Biology, Business Administration, Chemistry, Communications, Early Childhood Education, Education, English, English/Journalism, History, History/Political Science, Interdisciplinary Majors, International Relations, Mathematics, Middle Grades Education, Music, Organ Performance, Philosophy, Piano Performance, Psychology, Religion, Secondary Education, Sociology, Spanish, Studio Art, Voice Performance.
**Distribution of degrees:** The majors with the highest enrollment are business administraiton, psychology, and communication; music, religion, and self-designed interdisciplinary have the lowest.
**Requirements:** General education requirement.
**Academic regulations:** Freshmen must maintain minimum 1.7 GPA; sophomores, 1.9 GPA; juniors, 2.0 GPA; seniors, 2.0 GPA.
**Special:** Equestrian program with boarding on campus. Minors offered in several majors and computer information systems, economics, French, political science, theatre. Self-designed majors. Double majors. Dual degrees. Independent study. Internships. Graduate school at which undergraduates may take graduate-level courses. Preprofessional programs in law, medicine, veterinary science, pharmacy, dentistry, theology, optometry, and engineering. 3-2 engineering programs with Auburn U, Georgia Tech, and Mercer U. Washington Semester. Teacher certification in early childhood, elementary, and secondary education. Certification in specific subject areas. Exchange programs abroad in Bulgaria (U of Sophia) and Japan (International Christian U). Study abroad also in Australia, China, France, Germany, Italy, Spain, and the United Kingdom.
**Honors:** Honors program.
**Academic Assistance:** Nonremedial tutoring.

**ADMISSIONS. Academic basis for candidate selection** (in order of priority): Secondary school record, standardized test scores, school's recommendation, class rank, essay.
**Nonacademic basis for candidate selection:** Character and personality, extracurricular participation, and particular talent or ability are emphasized. Alumnae relationship is considered.
**Requirements:** Graduation from secondary school is required; GED is accepted. 16 units and the following program of study are required: 4 units of English, 3 units of math, 2 units of science, 3 units of social studies, 4 units of academic electives. Audition required of theatre program applicants. Portfolio required of art program applicants. Audition required of music program applicants. Conditional admission possible for applicants not meeting standard requirements. SAT or ACT is required. Campus visit and interview recommended. Off-campus interviews available with an admissions representative.
**Procedure:** Take SAT or ACT by December of 12th year. Visit college for interview by February of 12th year. Suggest filing application by November 1. Application deadline is March 1. Notification of admission on rolling basis. Reply is required by May 1. $150 tuition deposit, refundable until May 1. $100 room deposit, refundable until May 1. Freshmen accepted for terms other than fall.
**Special programs:** Admission may be deferred one year. Credit may be granted through CEEB Advanced Placement for scores of 4 or higher. Credit may be granted through CLEP general and subject exams, challenge exams, and military and life experience. Early decision program. Deadline for applying for early decision is November 1. Early entrance/early admission program. Concurrent enrollment program.
**Transfer students:** Transfer students accepted for terms other than fall. In fall 1993, 3% of all new students were transfers into all classes. 32 transfer applications were received, 29 were accepted. Application deadline is August 1 for fall; December 1 for spring. Minimum 2.0 GPA recommended. Lowest course grade accepted is "C." Maximum number of transferable credits is 60 semester hours from a two-year school and 90 semester hours from a four-year school. At least 30 semester hours must be completed at the college to receive degree.
**Admissions contact:** John A. Thompson, M.Ed., Dean of Admissions. 800 447-6610.

**FINANCIAL AID. Available aid:** Pell grants, SEOG, state scholarships and grants, school scholarships and grants, private scholarships and grants, academic merit scholarships, and aid for undergraduate foreign students. Perkins Loans (NDSL), PLUS, Stafford Loans (GSL), state loans, school loans, private loans, and SLS. AMS and family tuition reduction.
**Financial aid statistics:** 12% of aid is not need-based. In 1993-94, 90% of all undergraduate applicants received aid; 95% of freshman applicants. Average amounts of aid awarded freshmen: Scholarships and grants, $7,186; loans, $2,638.
**Supporting data/closing dates:** FAFSA/FAF/FFS: Priority filing date is April 1. School's own aid application: Priority filing date is April 1. Income tax forms: Priority filing date is April 1. Notification of awards begins April 1.
**Financial aid contact:** Melva B. Lord, Director of Financial Planning. 800 447-6610.

## West Georgia College

**Carrollton, GA 30118-0001** **404 836-6500**

**1994-95 Costs.** Tuition: $1,819 (state residents), $4,664 (out-of-state). Room: $1,329. Board: $1,236. Fees, books, misc. academic expenses (school's estimate): $450.
**Enrollment.** Undergraduates: 1,890 men, 2,688 women (full-time). Freshman class: 3,668 applicants, 2,690 accepted, 1,331 enrolled. Graduate enrollment: 457 men, 1,766 women.
**Test score averages/ranges.** Average SAT scores: 412 verbal, 456 math. Range of SAT scores of middle 50%: 360-450 verbal, 400-500 math. Average ACT scores: 20 English, 20 math, 20 composite. Range of ACT scores of middle 50%: 17-22 English, 18-22 math.
**Faculty.** 271 full-time; 74 part-time. 76% of faculty holds doctoral degree. Student/faculty ratio: 17 to 1.
**Selectivity rating.** Less competitive.

**PROFILE.** West Georgia, founded in 1906, is a public college. Its 393-acre campus is located in Carrollton, 45 miles west of Atlanta.

**Accreditation:** SACS. Professionally accredited by the American Assembly of Collegiate Schools of Business, the National Association of Schools of Music, the National Council for Accreditation of Teacher Education, the National League for Nursing.
**Religious orientation:** West Georgia College is nonsectarian; no religious requirements.
**Library:** Collections totaling over 295,260 volumes, 1,495 periodical subscriptions, and 824,949 microform items.
**Special facilities/museums:** Archaeological laboratory, art gallery, electron microscope, observatory, preschool.
**Athletic facilities:** Gymnasiums, basketball, handball, racquetball, tennis, and volleyball courts, track, athletic fields, swimming pool, weight room.

**STUDENT BODY. Undergraduate profile:** 97% are state residents; 24% are transfers. 1% Asian-American, 16% Black, 1% Hispanic, 82% White. Average age of undergraduates is 24.
**Freshman profile:** 1% of freshmen who took SAT scored 700 or over on math; 1% scored 600 or over on verbal, 6% scored 600 or over on math; 13% scored 500 or over on verbal, 30% scored 500 or over on math; 54% scored 400 or over on verbal, 81% scored 400 or over on math; 95% scored 300 or over on verbal, 100% scored 300 or over on math. 87% of accepted applicants took SAT; 7% took ACT. 95% of freshmen come from public schools.
**Undergraduate achievement:** 60% of fall 1992 freshmen returned for fall 1993 term. 13% of entering class graduated.
**Foreign students:** 62 students are from out of the country. Countries represented include China, France, Japan, and Turkey; 35 in all.

**PROGRAMS OF STUDY. Degrees:** A.B., B.A., B.Bus.Admin., B.F.A., B.Mus., B.S.
**Majors:** Accounting, Administrative Systems, Anthropology, Art, Biology, Bookkeeping/Business Management, Business Education, Business Information Systems, Chemistry, Computer/Information Sciences, Criminal Justice, Data Processing/Accounting, Early Childhood Education, Earth Science, Economics, Education, English, Finance, French, General Studies, Geography, Geology, History, International Economic Affairs, Management, Marketing, Mass Communications, Mathematics, Mathematics/Computer Science, Middle Grades Education, Music Education, Music Performance, Music Theory/Composition, Nursing, Philosophy, Physical Education, Physics, Political Science, Psychology, Real Estate, Recreation, Secondary Education/Science, Secondary Education/Social Science, Sociology, Spanish, Special Education, Special Education/Mental Retardation, Speech/Theatre Arts, Systems Economics.
**Distribution of degrees:** The majors with the highest enrollment are early childhood education, psychology, and marketing; theatre, secondary education/Spanish, and music theory/composition have the lowest.
**Requirements:** General education requirement.
**Academic regulations:** Minimum 2.00 GPA must be maintained.
**Special:** Minors offered in many majors and in art history, astronomy, business administration, classical studies, German, Latin, media, music, and religion. Associate's degrees offered. Dual degrees. Independent study. Internships. Cooperative education programs. Graduate school at which undergraduates may take graduate-level courses. Preprofessional programs in law, medicine, veterinary science, pharmacy, dentistry, and optometry. 3-2 engineering programs with Auburn U and Georgia Tech. Ed.D. program with U of Georgia. Teacher certification in early childhood, elementary, secondary, and special education education. Certification in specific subject areas. Study abroad possible. ROTC.
**Honors:** Phi Beta Kappa. Honors program. Honor societies.

**Academic Assistance:** Remedial reading, writing, math, and study skills. Nonremedial tutoring.

**STUDENT LIFE. Housing:** All unmarried freshmen under age 21 must live on campus unless living with family. Coed, women's, and men's dorms. Sorority housing. 33% of students live in college housing.

**Social atmosphere:** According to the editor of the student newspaper, "You have to be Greek to have a social life." Along with Greeks, Student Government, Baptist Student Union, and College Republicans are influential organizations on campus. Students tend to hang out at Bradley's Bar, Spyro Gyro, the "Wall" at the library, and the Lazy Donkey. Homecoming, Greek Week, Tyus T-Party, and Spring Fling are among the year's favorite events.

**Services and counseling/handicapped student services:** Placement services. Health service. Day care. Counseling services for minority, military, veteran, and older students. Birth control, personal, and psychological counseling. Career and academic guidance services. Religious counseling. Physically disabled student services. Learning disabled services. Tutors. Reader services for the blind.

**Campus organizations:** Undergraduate student government. Student newspaper (West Georgian, published once/week). Literary magazine. Radio and TV stations. Marching band, concert choir, wind ensemble, chamber singers, jazz ensemble, Fine Arts Festival, dance company, theatre, nontraditional student group, drill team, judo and aikido clubs, Chess Federation, National Organization for Women, Circle K, departmental groups, special-interest groups, 88 organizations in all. 10 fraternities, six chapter houses; nine sororities, three chapter houses. 24% of men join a fraternity. 14% of women join a sorority.

**Religious organizations:** Interfaith Council, Campus Outreach, Baptist Student Union, Fellowship of Christian Athletes, In Covenant with Christ, Jewish Student Union, Presbyterians in Action, Wesley Foundation.

**Minority/foreign student organizations:** Black Achievement Program, Black Greek Council, Black Student Alliance. International Club.

**ATHLETICS. Physical education requirements:** Six terms of physical education required.

**Intercollegiate competition:** 4% of students participate. Baseball (M), basketball (M,W), cheerleading (M,W), cross-country (M,W), football (M), golf (M), softball (W), tennis (M,W), volleyball (W). Member of Gulf South Conference, NCAA Division II.

**Intramural and club sports:** 4% of students participate. Intramural badminton, basketball, flag football, golf, hiking, soccer, softball, swimming, track and field, volleyball, weight lifting. Men's club soccer.

**ADMISSIONS. Academic basis for candidate selection** (in order of priority): Secondary school record, standardized test scores.

**Requirements:** Graduation from secondary school is required; GED is accepted. 18 units and the following program of study are required: 4 units of English, 3 units of math, 3 units of science including 2 units of lab, 2 units of foreign language, 1 unit of social studies, 2 units of history, 3 units of academic electives. Minimum SAT scores of 360 verbal and 400 math and minimum 2.0 GPA required. R.N. required of nursing program applicants. SAT or ACT is required. Campus visit and interview recommended. Off-campus interviews available with an admissions representative.

**Procedure:** Take SAT or ACT by March 1 of 12th year. Visit college for interview by February 1 of 12th year. Suggest filing application by January 1; no deadline. Notification of admission on rolling basis. $75 room deposit, refundable up to 30 days prior to term ending. Freshmen accepted for terms other than fall.

**Special programs:** Credit and/or placement may be granted through CEEB Advanced Placement exams for scores of 3 or higher. Credit and/or placement may be granted through CLEP subject exams. Credit and placement may be granted through DANTES exams and military experience. Early entrance/early admission program. Concurrent enrollment program.

**Transfer students:** Transfer students accepted for terms other than fall. In fall 1993, 24% of all new students were transfers into all classes. 863 transfer applications were received, 793 were accepted. Application deadline is rolling for fall; rolling for spring. Lowest course grade accepted is "C." Maximum number of transferable credits is 100 quarter hours from a two-year school and 140 quarter hours from a four-year school. At least 50 quarter hours must be completed at the college to receive degree.

**Admissions contact:** Jennifer W. Payne, M.Ed., Director of Admissions. 404 836-6416.

**FINANCIAL AID. Available aid:** Pell grants, SEOG, state scholarships and grants, school scholarships and grants, private scholarships and grants, ROTC scholarships, academic merit scholarships, and athletic scholarships. Perkins Loans (NDSL), PLUS, Stafford Loans (GSL), state loans, school loans, private loans, and SLS.

**Financial aid statistics:** 10% of aid is not need-based. In 1993-94, 79% of all undergraduate applicants received aid; 95% of freshman applicants. Average amounts of aid awarded freshmen: Scholarships and grants, $1,487; loans, $1,614.

**Supporting data/closing dates:** FAFSA: Priority filing date is March 15; accepted on rolling basis. Notification of awards on rolling basis.

**Financial aid contact:** Sue Meyers, Director of Financial Aid. 404 836-6421.

**STUDENT EMPLOYMENT.** College Work/Study Program. Institutional employment. 19% of full-time undergraduates work on campus during school year. Students may expect to earn an average of $955 during school year. Off-campus part-time employment opportunities rated "fair."

**COMPUTER FACILITIES.** 503 IBM/IBM-compatible, Macintosh/Apple, and RISC-/UNIX-based microcomputers. Students may access IBM, SUN minicomputer/mainframe systems, BITNET, Internet. Client/LAN operating systems include Apple/Macintosh, DOS, OS/2, UNIX/XENIX/AIX, X-windows, LocalTalk/AppleTalk, Microsoft, Novell. Computer languages and software packages include Assembler, BASIC, C, COBOL, FORTRAN, Pascal, RPG, SAS, SPSSX; 67 in all. Computer facilities are available to all students.

**Fees:** None.

**Hours:** 8 AM-11 PM.

# Hawaii

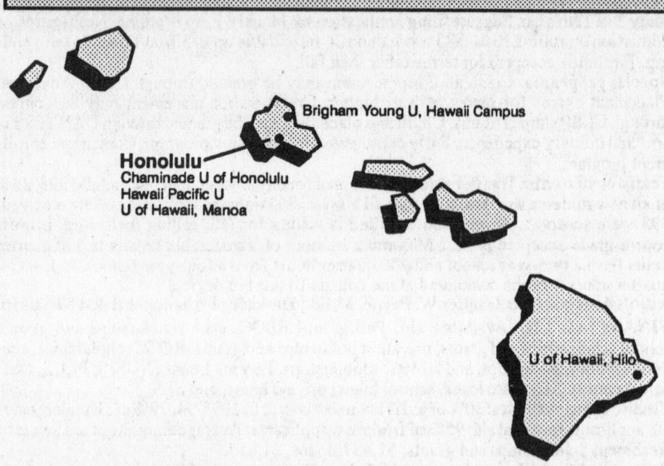


## Brigham Young University-Hawaii Campus

Laie, HI 96762-1294 808 293-3211

**1993-94 Costs.** Tuition: $2,375. Room & board: $4,375. Fees, books, misc. academic expenses (school's estimate): $630.
**Enrollment.** Undergraduates: 809 men, 1,046 women (full-time). Freshman class: 835 applicants, 589 accepted, 495 enrolled. Graduate enrollment: 9 women.
**Test score averages/ranges.** Average ACT scores: 20 English, 19 math, 20 composite.
**Faculty.** 153 full-time; 6 part-time. 64% of faculty holds doctoral degree. Student/faculty ratio: 20 to 1.
**Selectivity rating.** Competitive.

**PROFILE.** Brigham Young University-Hawaii Campus is a church-affiliated, liberal arts institution. Founded in 1955, it became affiliated with Brigham Young University in 1974. Its 60-acre campus is located in Laie, 38 miles from Honolulu.

**Accreditation:** WASC. Professionally accredited by the Council on Social Work Education.
**Religious orientation:** Brigham Young University-Hawaii Campus is affiliated with the Church of Jesus Christ of Latter-Day Saints; 14 credits of religion required.
**Library:** Collections totaling over 160,000 volumes, 1,050 periodical subscriptions, and 800,000 microform items.
**Special facilities/museums:** Natural history museum, Pacific institute and museum, Polynesian Cultural Center, English language institute.
**Athletic facilities:** Gymnasiums, activities center, athletic, rugby, and softball fields, swimming pool, racquetball and tennis courts, weight room.

**STUDENT BODY. Undergraduate profile:** 72% are state residents; 26% are transfers. 33% Asian-American, 1% Black, 2% Hispanic, 1% Native American, 32% White, 31% Foreign.
**Freshman profile:** 4% of freshmen who took ACT scored 30 or over on English, 2% scored 30 or over on math, 2% scored 30 or over on composite; 31% scored 24 or over on English, 17% scored 24 or over on math, 24% scored 24 or over on composite; 73% scored 18 or over on English, 62% scored 18 or over on math, 75% scored 18 or over on composite; 96% scored 12 or over on English, 98% scored 12 or over on math, 99% scored 12 or over on composite; 100% scored 6 or over on English, 100% scored 6 or over on math, 100% scored 6 or over on composite. 44% of accepted applicants took ACT.
**Undergraduate achievement:** 54% of fall 1992 freshmen returned for fall 1993 term.
**Foreign students:** 877 students are from out of the country. Countries represented include Hong Kong, Japan, Singapore, and Tonga; 52 in all.

**PROGRAMS OF STUDY. Degrees:** B.A., B.F.A., B.S., B.Soc.Work.
**Majors:** Accounting, Art, Art Education, Biological Sciences, Biological Sciences Education, Business Management, Chemistry, Elementary Education, English, Hotel/Restaurant Management, Information Systems, International Business Management, Mathematics, Pacific Island Studies, Physical Education/Recreation, Physical Science Education, Political Science, Psychology, Social Work, Sociology, Teaching English to Speakers of Other Languages, Travel Management.
**Distribution of degrees:** The majors with the highest enrollment are business management, accounting, and elementary education; art has the lowest.
**Requirements:** General education requirement.
**Academic regulations:** Minimum 2.0 GPA must be maintained.
**Special:** Minors or related concentrations offered in chemistry, Hawaiian studies, modern languages, Polynesian studies, psychology, religion, and speech communication. Courses offered in Chinese, clothing and textiles, economics, geography, geology, oceanography, and theatre. Home study possible. Credit by Examination. Associate's degrees offered. Accelerated study. Pass/fail grading option. Internships. Cooperative education programs. Preprofessional programs in law, medicine, and dentistry. Teacher certification in early childhood, elementary, and secondary education. ROTC and AFROTC.
**Honors:** Honors program. Honor societies.
**Academic Assistance:** Remedial reading, writing, math, and study skills. Nonremedial tutoring.

**STUDENT LIFE. Housing:** All freshman must live on campus. Women's and men's dorms. On-campus married-student housing. 72% of students live in college housing.
**Social atmosphere:** As reported by the student newspaper, "The student body is very international. A strong Student Association arranges on-campus and off-campus activities. The school has about 15 major fine arts events each year, featuring noted classic music groups and individuals." Students like to congregate at the Seasider, the Aloha Center, the Games Center, and Masa's. The Na Hoa Pageant and Ball, Foodfest International, and Homecoming are among the year's favorite events.
**Services and counseling/handicapped student services:** Placement services. Health service. Day care. Counseling services for minority and veteran students. Personal and psychological counseling. Career and academic guidance services. Religious counseling. Learning disabled services.
**Campus organizations:** Undergraduate student government. Student newspaper (Ke Alaka'i, published once/week). Music and drama groups, academic groups, special-interest groups, 35 organizations in all.
**Minority/foreign student organizations:** Hawaiian group. Chinese, Indian, Japanese, Korean, Latino, Pacific Islander, and Singapore/Malaysian groups.

**ATHLETICS. Physical education requirements:** Three credits of physical education required.
**Intercollegiate competition:** 5% of students participate. Basketball (M), cross-country (M,W), rugby (M), tennis (M,W), volleyball (W). Member of NAIA.
**Intramural and club sports:** 20% of students participate. Intramural badminton, basketball, flag football, golf, racquetball, power lifting, softball, table tennis, tennis, triathlon, volleyball, water basketball, water polo.

**ADMISSIONS. Academic basis for candidate selection** (in order of priority): Secondary school record, standardized test scores, class rank, school's recommendation, essay.
**Nonacademic basis for candidate selection:** Character and personality and geographical distribution are emphasized. Particular talent or ability is important. Extracurricular participation and alumni/ae relationship are considered.
**Requirements:** Graduation from secondary school is required; GED is not accepted. No specific distribution of secondary school units required. 12 secondary school units required. Minimum composite ACT score of 17 and minimum 2.5 GPA required. Portfolio required of art program applicants. ACT is required. Admissions interview required. Off-campus interviews available with an admissions representative.
**Procedure:** Take ACT by March 31 of 12th year. Application deadline is March 31. Notification of admission by April 15. Reply is required within 90 days or by August 15. $50 refundable room deposit. Freshmen accepted for terms other than fall.
**Special programs:** Credit may be granted through CLEP general and subject exams. Placement may be granted through ACT PEP exams. Credit and placement may be granted through challenge exams. Early entrance/early admission program. Concurrent enrollment program.
**Transfer students:** Transfer students accepted for terms other than fall. In fall 1993, 26% of all new students were transfers into all classes. 215 transfer applications were received, 152 were accepted. Application deadline is March 31 for fall; October 31 for spring. Minimum 2.5 GPA recommended. Lowest course grade accepted is "C-." Maximum number of transferable credits is 100 semester hours. At least 30 semester hours must be completed at the university to receive degree.
**Admissions contact:** Clark E. Hirschi, Coordinator of Admissions. 808 293-3738.

**FINANCIAL AID. Available aid:** Pell grants, school scholarships and grants, private scholarships and grants, academic merit scholarships, athletic scholarships, and aid for undergraduate foreign students. PLUS, Stafford Loans (GSL), and SLS.
**Financial aid statistics:** Average amounts of aid awarded freshmen: Loans, $2,000.
**Supporting data/closing dates:** FAFSA/FAF: Priority filing date is April 30. Notification of awards begins May 1.
**Financial aid contact:** Steven Bang, Director of Financial Aid. 808 293-3730.

**STUDENT EMPLOYMENT.** College Work/Study Program. Institutional employment. 45% of full-time undergraduates work on campus during school year. Students may expect to earn an average of $4,000 during school year. Off-campus part-time employment opportunities rated "excellent."

**COMPUTER FACILITIES.** 60 IBM/IBM-compatible and Macintosh/Apple microcomputers. Students may access Digital minicomputer/mainframe systems. Computer languages and software packages include COBOL, Lotus 1-2-3, Pascal, WordPerfect, WordStar. Use restricted to students enrolled in courses requiring computers.
**Fees:** $25 computer fee per semester.
**Hours:** 3 PM-11 PM.

## Chaminade University of Honolulu

Honolulu, HI 96816-1587 808 735-4711

**1994-95 Costs.** Tuition: $10,600. Room & board: $4,600. Fees, books, misc. academic expenses (school's estimate): $500.
**Enrollment.** Undergraduates: 289 men, 376 women (full-time). Freshman class: 650 applicants, 450 accepted, 250 enrolled. Graduate enrollment: 164 men, 100 women.
**Test score averages/ranges.** Average SAT scores: 400 verbal, 440 math. Average ACT scores: 19 composite.
**Faculty.** 57 full-time; 139 part-time. 48% of faculty holds highest degree in specific field. Student/faculty ratio: 16 to 1.
**Selectivity rating.** Less competitive.

**PROFILE.** Chaminade, founded in 1955, is a church-affiliated university. Programs are offered through the College of Arts and Sciences and the School of Business. Its 67-acre campus is located four miles east of downtown Honolulu and two miles north of Waikiki Beach.

**Accreditation:** WASC.
**Religious orientation:** Chaminade University of Honolulu is affiliated with the Roman Catholic Church (Society of Marianists); two semesters of religion/theology required.
**Library:** Collections totaling over 60,000 volumes and 500 periodical subscriptions.
**Special facilities/museums:** Montessori school, language lab, writing lab.
**Athletic facilities:** Gymnasium, field house, fitness center, basketball courts, tennis courts.

**STUDENT BODY. Undergraduate profile:** 75% are state residents; 37% are transfers. Average age of undergraduates is 19.
**Freshman profile:** Majority of accepted applicants took SAT. 45% of freshmen come from public schools.
**Foreign students:** 156 students are from out of the country. Countries represented include China, Hong Kong, Indonesia, Japan, the Philippines and Taiwan; 33 in all.

**PROGRAMS OF STUDY. Degrees:** B.A., B.Bus.Admin., B.F.A., B.S.
**Majors:** Accounting, Behavioral Science, Biology, Business Administration, Chemistry, Communication, Computer Science, Criminal Justice, Early Childhood Education, Economics, Elementary Education, English, History, Humanities, Interior Design, International Studies, Management, Marketing, Mathematics, Philosophy, Political Science, Psychology, Religious Studies, Secondary Education, Social Studies, Studio Art.
**Distribution of degrees:** The majors with the highest enrollment are management, criminal justice, and business administration; political science, religious studies, and early childhood education/elementary education have the lowest.
**Requirements:** General education requirement.
**Academic regulations:** Minimum 2.0 GPA must be maintained.
**Special:** Minors offered in all majors and in anthropology, drama, Japanese, physics, sociology, and Spanish. Courses offered in art, aerospace studies, developmental skills, earth science, English for non-native speakers, French, Hawaiian, military science, music, physical science, Spanish, and speech. Credit by examination offered in some courses. Associate's degrees offered. Double majors. Independent study. Accelerated study. Pass/fail grading option. Internships. Graduate school at which undergraduates may take graduate-level courses. Preprofessional programs in law, medicine, dentistry, optometry, biology, business management, chemistry, physical therapy, political science, and speech therapy. 3-2 math/engineering program with St. Mary's U. Cross-registration with Brigham Young U-Hawaii campus, U of Hawaii at Manoa, and Hawaii Pacific Coll. Exchange programs with St. Mary's U and U of Dayton. Teacher certification in early childhood, elementary, and secondary education. Study abroad in Japan (Ritsu Meikan and Doshisha U). ROTC and AFROTC at U of Hawaii at Manoa.
**Honors:** Honors program.
**Academic Assistance:** Remedial reading, writing, math, and study skills. Nonremedial tutoring.

**ADMISSIONS. Academic basis for candidate selection** (in order of priority): Secondary school record, standardized test scores, school's recommendation, essay, class rank.
**Nonacademic basis for candidate selection:** Character and personality and extracurricular participation are important.
**Requirements:** Graduation from secondary school is required; GED is accepted. 16 units and the following program of study are required: 4 units of English, 4 units of math, 1 unit of lab science, 2 units of foreign language, 3 units of social studies. Minimum combined SAT score of 800 (composite ACT score of 19) and minimum 2.0 GPA recommended. SAT or ACT is required. No off-campus interviews.
**Procedure:** Take SAT or ACT by December of 12th year. Notification of admission on rolling basis. No set date by which applicants must accept offer. $150 nonrefundable tuition deposit. $150 nonrefundable room deposit. Freshmen accepted for terms other than fall.
**Special programs:** Admission may be deferred one semester. Credit may be granted through CEEB Advanced Placement for scores of 3 or higher. Credit and/or placement may be granted through CLEP general exams. Credit and placement may be granted through DANTES and challenge exams, and military and life experience. Early decision program. Deadline for applying for early decision is April 1. Early entrance/early admission program. Concurrent enrollment program.
**Transfer students:** Transfer students accepted for terms other than fall. In fall 1992, 37% of all new students were transfers into all classes. 260 transfer applications were received, 220 were accepted. Application deadline is rolling for fall; rolling for spring. Minimum 2.0 GPA required. Lowest course grade accepted is "C." Maximum number of transferable credits is 94 semester hours. At least 30 semester hours must be completed at the university to receive degree.
**Admissions contact:** Faye Tiger Conquest, Ed.M., Director of Admissions. 808 735-4735.

**FINANCIAL AID. Available aid:** Pell grants, SEOG, state scholarships and grants, school scholarships and grants, private scholarships, ROTC scholarships, academic merit scholarships, athletic scholarships, and aid for undergraduate foreign students. Perkins Loans (NDSL), PLUS, Stafford Loans (GSL), school loans, private loans, and SLS. FACTS Tuition Plan.
**Financial aid statistics:** 25% of aid is not need-based. In 1992-93, 80% of all undergraduate applicants received aid; 50% of freshman applicants. Average amounts of aid awarded freshmen: Scholarships and grants, $4,300; loans, $2,625.
**Supporting data/closing dates:** FAFSA/FAF/FFS: Priority filing date is March 15. School's own aid application: Priority filing date is March 15. State aid form: Accepted on rolling basis. Income tax forms: Accepted on rolling basis. Notification of awards on rolling basis.
**Financial aid contact:** Gail Koki, Director of Financial Aid. 808 735-4780.

# Hawaii Pacific University

**Honolulu, HI 96813** **808 544-0200**

**1994-95 Costs.** Tuition: $6,300. Room & board: $6,500. Fees, books, misc. academic expenses (school's estimate): $650.
**Enrollment.** Undergraduates: 2,163 men, 2,181 women (full-time). Freshman class: 1,827 applicants, 1,409 accepted, 984 enrolled. Graduate enrollment: 527 men, 385 women.
**Test score averages/ranges.** Average SAT scores: 475 verbal, 529 math.
**Faculty.** 137 full-time; 314 part-time. 57% of faculty holds doctoral degree. Student/faculty ratio: 20 to 1.
**Selectivity rating.** Competitive.

**PROFILE.** Hawaii Pacific, founded in 1965, is a private, liberal arts university. Its urban campus is located in Honolulu.

**Accreditation:** WASC. Professionally accredited by the National League for Nursing.
**Religious orientation:** Hawaii Pacific University is nonsectarian; no religious requirements.
**Library:** Collections totaling over 115,000 volumes, 1,750 periodical subscriptions, and 157,000 microform items.
**Special facilities/museums:** Art gallery.
**Athletic facilities:** Full use of nearby YMCA facilities available.

**STUDENT BODY. Undergraduate profile:** 55% are state residents; 47% are transfers. 38% Asian-American, 12% Black, 6% Hispanic, 2% Native American, 38% White, 4% Other. Average age of undergraduates is 25.
**Freshman profile:** 3% of freshmen who took SAT scored 700 or over on verbal, 4% scored 700 or over on math; 11% scored 600 or over on verbal, 15% scored 600 or over on math; 35% scored 500 or over on verbal, 49% scored 500 or over on math; 80% scored 400 or over on verbal, 88% scored 400 or over on math; 95% scored 300 or over on verbal, 97% scored 300 or over on math. 70% of accepted applicants took SAT; 5% took ACT. 70% of freshmen come from public schools.
**Undergraduate achievement:** 75% of fall 1992 freshmen returned for fall 1993 term. 29% of students who completed a degree program immediately went on to graduate study.
**Foreign students:** 2,045 students are from out of the country. Countries represented include Hong Kong, Japan, Korea, Malaysia, Singapore, and Taiwan; 70 in all.

**PROGRAMS OF STUDY. Degrees:** B.A., B.S.
**Majors:** Accounting, American Studies, Asian Studies, Business Economics, Computer Information Systems, Computer Science, Corporate Communications, Credit Management, Economics, Engineering, Entrepreneurial Studies, Finance, Health Care Administration, History, Human Resource Development, Human Resources Management, Human Services, Humanities, Individualized Major, International Business, International Relations, International Studies, Justice Administration, Literature, Management, Marine Science, Marketing, Mathematics, Nursing, Pacific Studies, Political Science, Pre-Law, Pre-Medical Studies, Psychology, Public Administration, Science, Social Sciences, Sociology/Anthropology, Teaching English as a Second Language, Travel Industry Management.
**Distribution of degrees:** The majors with the highest enrollment are business management, computer information systems, and travel industry management; American studies, public administration, and pre-medical studies have the lowest.
**Requirements:** General education requirement.
**Academic regulations:** Freshmen must maintain minimum 1.6 GPA; sophomores, 1.8 GPA; juniors, 2.0 GPA; seniors, 2.0 GPA.
**Special:** Minors offered in most majors and in communications and organizational psychology. Studio art courses offered at Honolulu Acad of Arts. Associate's degrees offered. Self-designed majors. Double majors. Dual degrees. Independent study. Accelerated study. Pass/fail grading option. Internships. Cooperative education programs. Graduate school at which undergraduates may take graduate-level courses. Preprofessional programs in law, medicine, and theology. 3-2 engineering programs with U of Southern California and Washington U-St. Louis. Member of Hawaii Association of Independent Colleges and Universities. Certification in specific subject areas. Study abroad in Japan. ROTC and AFROTC at U of Hawaii at Manoa.
**Honors:** Honors program. Honor societies.
**Academic Assistance:** Remedial reading, writing, math, and study skills. Nonremedial tutoring.

**STUDENT LIFE. Housing:** Students may live on or off campus. Coed, women's, and men's dorms. Off-campus privately-owned housing. University-leased apartments. 10% of students live in college housing.
**Social atmosphere:** According to a school representative, "Student life at Hawaii Pacific university is lively and informal. Students come from Hawaii, the U.S. mainland states, and from 50 countries throughout the world. The student population is diverse, varying in age, religion, ethnic and cultural origin, philosophy and interests–the social activities reflect this rich diversity. From jungle trails and team sports to armchair adventure and quiet contemplation, from banquets and dances to luaus and moonlit cruises, and from lectures and cultural performances to community service projects–Hawaii Pacific has it all." Popular gathering spots on and off campus are Campus Crossroads, the HPU Club Room, Rumours, and the Hot Rod Cafe.
**Services and counseling/handicapped student services:** Placement services. Health service. Counseling services for military, veteran, and older students. Personal counseling. Career and academic guidance services. Religious counseling. Learning disabled services.
**Campus organizations:** Undergraduate student government. Student newspaper (Kalamalama). Literary magazine. Accounting, ad, psychology, and ecology clubs, pep band, American marketing and data processing management associations, graduate student,

student business, and travel industry management organizations, Rotaract, 32 organizations in all.
**Religious organizations:** Christian Fellowship.
**Minority/foreign student organizations:** Black Student Organization. International Student Organization, Chinese, European, Korean, Malaysian, Samoan, Singaporean, Taiwanese, and Tongan groups.
**ATHLETICS. Physical education requirements:** None.
**Intercollegiate competition:** 3% of students participate. Baseball (M), basketball (M), cheerleading (M,W), cross-country (M,W), soccer (M), softball (W), tennis (M,W), volleyball (W). Member of Hawaii Intercollegiate Athletic Conference, NAIA.
**Intramural and club sports:** 3% of students participate. Intramural archery, basketball, canoeing, flag football, softball, swimming, table tennis, tennis, volleyball. Men's club golf, softball, swimming, volleyball. Women's club golf, softball, swimming, volleyball.
**ADMISSIONS. Academic basis for candidate selection** (in order of priority): Secondary school record, school's recommendation, standardized test scores, class rank, essay.
**Nonacademic basis for candidate selection:** Character and personality are emphasized. Extracurricular participation and particular talent or ability are important.
**Requirements:** Graduation from secondary school is required; GED is accepted. 20 units and the following program of study are recommended: 3 units of English, 2 units of math, 1 unit of science, 2 units of foreign language, 3 units of social studies, 3 units of history, 4 units of electives. Minimum 2.5 GPA required. Minimum 3.0 GPA required of marine science program applicants. Conditional admission possible for applicants not meeting standard requirements. SAT or ACT is recommended. Campus visit and interview recommended. Off-campus interviews available with admissions and alumni representatives.
**Procedure:** Suggest filing application by August 1. Application deadline is August 31. Notification of admission on rolling basis. No set date by which applicants must accept offer. $400 nonrefundable room deposit. Freshmen accepted for terms other than fall.
**Special programs:** Admission may be deferred two years. Credit and/or placement may be granted through CEEB Advanced Placement exams for scores of 3 or higher. Credit and/or placement may be granted through CLEP general and subject exams, Regents College, ACT PEP, DANTES, and challenge exams, and military experience. Early entrance/early admission program.
**Transfer students:** Transfer students accepted for terms other than fall. In fall 1993, 47% of all new students were transfers into all classes. 1,441 transfer applications were received, 1,117 were accepted. Application deadline is August 15 for fall; December 15 for spring. Minimum 2.0 GPA required. Lowest course grade accepted is "C." Maximum number of transferable credits is 60 semester hours. At least 30 semester hours must be completed at the university to receive degree.
**Admissions contact:** Scott Stensrud, M.A., Director of Admissions. 808 544-0238.
**FINANCIAL AID. Available aid:** Pell grants, SEOG, Federal Nursing Student Scholarships, state scholarships and grants, school scholarships, private scholarships and grants, ROTC scholarships, academic merit scholarships, and athletic scholarships. Perkins Loans (NDSL), PLUS, Stafford Loans (GSL), NSL, private loans, and SLS. Credit card payment plan. Installment payment plan.
**Financial aid statistics:** 20% of aid is not need-based. In 1993-94, 100% of all undergraduate applicants received aid. Average amounts of aid awarded freshmen: Scholarships and grants, $3,200; loans, $4,800.
**Supporting data/closing dates:** FAFSA: Priority filing date is March 15; accepted on rolling basis. School's own aid application: Priority filing date is March 15; accepted on rolling basis. Notification of awards begins April 15.
**Financial aid contact:** Walter Fleming, Director of Financial Aid. 808 544-0251.
**STUDENT EMPLOYMENT.** College Work/Study Program. Institutional employment. 8% of full-time undergraduates work on campus during school year. Students may expect to earn an average of $2,500 during school year. Off-campus part-time employment opportunities rated "excellent."
**COMPUTER FACILITIES.** 200 IBM/IBM-compatible, Macintosh/Apple, and RISC-/UNIX-based microcomputers; 25 are networked. Students may access AT&T, SUN minicomputer/mainframe systems. Client/LAN operating systems include Apple/Macintosh, DOS, OS/2, UNIX/XENIX/AIX, Windows NT, LocalTalk/AppleTalk, Novell. Computer languages and software packages include Ada, Assembler, C, COBOL, dBASE, FORTRAN, Harvard Graphics, Lotus 1-2-3, Pascal, Prolog, RPG, WordStar; 50 in all. Computer facilities are available to all students.
**Fees:** $45 computer fee per course.
**Hours:** 8 AM-9 PM (M-F); 8 AM-5 PM (Sa-Su).
**GRADUATE CAREER DATA.** Graduate school percentages: 5% enter law school. 40% enter graduate business programs. 5% enter graduate arts and sciences programs. Highest graduate school enrollments: U of Hawaii, Hawaii Pacific U, U of Oregon, U of Southern California. 70% of graduates choose careers in business and industry. Companies and businesses that hire graduates: Big Six accounting firms, Hawaii and Pacific financial institutions, Hilton and Sheraton Hotels.
**PROMINENT ALUMNI/AE.** John Derby, senior vice-president, Bank of Hawaii; Djufrie N. Sentana, managing director, PT Surya Raya Idjman, Jakarta (hotel/resort development company); Kennio Frank, senator, Pohnpei Legislature.

# University of Hawaii at Hilo

**Hilo, HI 96720-4091 — 808 933-3311**

**1994-95 Costs.** Tuition: $480 (state residents), $2,900 (out-of-state). Room & board: $2,400. Fees, books, misc. academic expenses (school's estimate): $1,230.
**Enrollment.** Undergraduates: 833 men, 1,249 women (full-time). Freshman class: 976 applicants, 568 accepted, 309 enrolled.
**Test score averages/ranges.** Average SAT scores: 401 verbal, 473 math. Range of SAT scores of middle 50%: 380-470 verbal, 420-540 math.
**Faculty.** 206 full-time; 75 part-time. 87% of faculty holds highest degree in specific field. Student/faculty ratio: 13 to 1.
**Selectivity rating.** Competitive.

**PROFILE.** The University of Hawaii at Hilo, founded in 1970, is a public institution. Programs are offered through the Colleges of Agriculture and Arts and Sciences, the Hawaii Community College, and the Center for Continuing Education and Community Service. Its campuses of 137 acres are located in Hilo, on the island of Hawaii, 200 miles from Honolulu.

**Accreditation:** WASC.
**Religious orientation:** University of Hawaii at Hilo is nonsectarian; no religious requirements.
**Library:** Collections totaling over 200,000 volumes, and 1,600 periodical subscriptions.
**Special facilities/museums:** Theatre, small business development center, marine science center, 110-acre agricultural farm lab.
**Athletic facilities:** Gymnasiums, tennis courts, weight room, baseball field.
**STUDENT BODY. Undergraduate profile:** 94% are state residents; 40% are transfers. 34.1% Asian-American, .9% Black, 1.6% Hispanic, 18% Native American, 35% White, 10.4% Other. Average age of undergraduates is 27.
**Freshman profile:** 1% of freshmen who took SAT scored 700 or over on verbal, 2% scored 700 or over on math; 4% scored 600 or over on verbal, 13% scored 600 or over on math; 16% scored 500 or over on verbal, 42% scored 500 or over on math; 57% scored 400 or over on verbal, 80% scored 400 or over on math; 82% scored 300 or over on verbal, 97% scored 300 or over on math. 98% of accepted applicants took SAT; 2% took ACT. 81% of freshmen come from public schools.
**Undergraduate achievement:** 63% of fall 1992 freshmen returned for fall 1993 term.
**Foreign students:** 161 students are from out of the country. Countries represented include Canada, Hong Kong, Japan, Micronesia, Taiwan, and Vanuatu; 26 in all.
**PROGRAMS OF STUDY. Degrees:** B.A., B.Bus.Admin., B.S., B.S.Nurs.
**Majors:** Agriculture, Anthropology, Art, Biology, Business Administration, Chemistry, Computer Science, Economics, English, Geography, Geology, Hawaiian Studies, History, Japanese Studies, Liberal Studies, Linguistics, Marine Science, Mathematics, Music, Natural Science, Philosophy, Physics, Political Science, Psychology, Sociology, Speech.
**Distribution of degrees:** The majors with the highest enrollment are business, liberal studies, and psychology; economics, geology, and linguistics have the lowest.
**Requirements:** General education requirement.
**Academic regulations:** Minimum 2.0 GPA must be maintained.
**Special:** Minors offered in most majors. Self-designed majors. Double majors. Dual degrees. Independent study. Pass/fail grading option. Internships. Cooperative education programs. Preprofessional programs in law, medicine, and veterinary science. 2-2 program in engineering with U of Hawaii at Manoa. Member of National Student Exchange (NSE). Western Undergraduate Exchange. Teacher certification in elementary and secondary education. Certification in specific subject areas. Study abroad in England, Japan, Mexico, and Russia.
**Honors:** Honors program. Honor societies.
**Academic Assistance:** Nonremedial tutoring.
**STUDENT LIFE. Housing:** Students may live on or off campus. Coed dorms. School-owned/operated apartments. On-campus married-student housing. Privately managed on-campus apartment complex. 24% of students live in college housing.
**Social atmosphere:** According to the editor of the student newspaper, UH Hilo is a small university so there is a feeling of "team" among the the various clubs and sports teams. An atmosphere of "Ohana" (family) is evident to all who visit. UHH is very diversified culturally with a large group of overseas students. There is a very good atmosphere for academic concentration. Popular on campus are basketball and volleyball games, Homecoming, International Night, Mardi Gras, Halloween, Rocky Horror, and movies. Influential groups are athletes, International Student Association, and the professors. Students enjoy going to the Campus Center, game room, and Library Lanai. Off campus, there's the Fun Factory, Nihon, Fiascos, and Kailua-Kona.
**Services and counseling/handicapped student services:** Placement services. Health service. Women's center. Counseling services for minority and older students. Birth control, personal, and psychological counseling. Career and academic guidance services. Physically disabled student services. Learning disabled services. Notetaking services. Reader services for the blind.
**Campus organizations:** Undergraduate student government. Student newspaper (Ke Kalahea, published once/week). Literary magazine. Choir, stage band, wind ensemble, theatre group, art exhibitions, departmental, political, service, and special-interest groups, 43 organizations in all.
**Religious organizations:** Bahai University Club, Baptist Student Union, Campus Ministry, Impact Ministries, Latter-Day Saints Association, Newman Club.
**Minority/foreign student organizations:** Hui Malama Aina, Bayanihan, Chinese, Korean, Samoan, and Yapese groups. International Student Association, Chinese and Micronesian groups.
**ATHLETICS. Physical education requirements:** None.
**Intercollegiate competition:** 8% of students participate. Baseball (M), basketball (M), cheerleading (M,W), cross-country (M), golf (M), softball (W), tennis (M,W), volleyball (W). Member of Hawaii Intercollegiate Athletic Conference, NAIA, NCAA Division I for baseball, NCAA Division II, Pacific West Conference.
**Intramural and club sports:** 15% of students participate. Intramural badminton, basketball, bowling, golf, pool, soccer, softball, tennis, volleyball. Men's club bowling, soccer, weight lifting.
**ADMISSIONS. Academic basis for candidate selection** (in order of priority): Secondary school record, standardized test scores, class rank, school's recommendation.
**Nonacademic basis for candidate selection:** Extracurricular participation, particular talent or ability, and geographical distribution are considered.
**Requirements:** Graduation from secondary school is required; GED is accepted. 20 units and the following program of study are required: 4 units of English, 2 units of math, 2 units of lab science, 3 units of social studies, 2 units of history, 7 units of electives. Minimum 3.0 GPA or minimum 2.5 GPA and combined SAT score of 800 (composite ACT score of 19) required. Plane geometry, 2 units of algebra, and trigonometry recommended of business, engineering, mathematics, and science program applicants. Physics and mechanical drawing also recommended of engineering program applicants. Chemistry, biology, and 2 units of algebra recommended of agriculture program applicants. Conditional admission possible for applicants not meeting standard requirements. Agriculture Develop-

ment Program for applicants not normally admissible. SAT is required; ACT may be substituted. Admissions interview recommended. No off-campus interviews.
**Procedure:** Take SAT or ACT by November of 12th year. Application deadline is June 15. Notification of admission on rolling basis. Reply is required by June 15. Freshmen accepted for terms other than fall.
**Special programs:** Admission may be deferred one term. Credit may be granted through CEEB Advanced Placement for scores of 3 or higher. Credit may be granted through CLEP general and subject exams. Concurrent enrollment program.
**Transfer students:** Transfer students accepted for terms other than fall. In fall 1933, 40% of all new students were transfers into all classes. 950 transfer applications were received, 679 were accepted. Application deadline is June 15 for fall; November 15 for spring. Minimum 2.0 GPA required. Lowest course grade accepted is "C." Maximum number of transferable credits is 90 semester hours. At least 30 semester hours must be completed at the university to receive degree.
**Admissions contact:** James B. West, Director of Admissions. 808 933-3414.

**FINANCIAL AID. Available aid:** Pell grants, SEOG, state scholarships and grants, school scholarships and grants, private scholarships, academic merit scholarships, and athletic scholarships. Merit scholarships for foreign students from targeted Pacific-Asian regions. Perkins Loans (NDSL), PLUS, Stafford Loans (GSL), and state loans.
**Financial aid statistics:** 10% of aid is not need-based. In 1993-94, 92% of all undergraduate applicants received aid; 92% of freshman applicants. Average amounts of aid awarded freshmen: Scholarships and grants, $2,802; loans, $1,442.
**Supporting data/closing dates:** FAFSA: Priority filing date is March 1; accepted on rolling basis. Notification of awards begins April 9.
**Financial aid contact:** Jean Coffman, M.Ed., Director of Financial Aid. 808 933-3324.

**STUDENT EMPLOYMENT.** College Work/Study Program. Institutional employment. 23% of full-time undergraduates work on campus during school year. Students may expect to earn an average of $3,082 during school year. Off-campus part-time employment opportunities rated "fair."

**COMPUTER FACILITIES.** 108 IBM/IBM-compatible and Macintosh/Apple microcomputers. Students may access Digital minicomputer/mainframe systems, Internet. Residence halls may be equipped with stand-alone microcomputers. Client/LAN operating systems include DOS, UNIX/XENIX/AIX. Computer languages and software packages include BASIC, C, COBOL, FORTRAN, LISP, Pascal, RPG II, SAS, SPSS; database programs, electronic mail, word processing software. Computer facilities are available to all students.
**Fees:** None.
**Hours:** 7:45 AM-10:30 PM (M-F); 1 PM-10:30 PM (Sa-Su).

# University of Hawaii at Manoa

**Honolulu, HI 96822** **808 956-8975**

**1994-95 Costs.** Tuition: $1,460 (state residents), $4,460 (out-of-state). Room & board: $5,103. Fees, books, misc. academic expenses (school's estimate): $811.
**Enrollment.** Undergraduates: 4,980 men, 5,996 women (full-time). Freshman class: 4,053 applicants, 2,661 accepted, 1,684 enrolled. Graduate enrollment: 1,428 men, 1,667 women.
**Test score averages/ranges.** Average SAT scores: 441 verbal, 538 math. Range of SAT scores of middle 50%: 380-490 verbal, 470-600 math.
**Faculty.** 85% of faculty holds highest degree in specific field.
**Selectivity rating.** Less competitive.

**PROFILE.** The University of Hawaii at Manoa, founded in 1907, is a public institution. Programs are offered through the Colleges of Arts and Sciences, Business Administration, Continuing Education and Community Service, Education, Engineering, Health Sciences and Social Welfare, and Tropical Agriculture and Human Resources and the Schools of Architecture, Law, Library Studies, Medicine, Nursing, Public Health, and Social Work. Its 300-acre campus is located in Manoa Valley, a residential area near the center of metropolitan Honolulu.

**Accreditation:** WASC.
**Religious orientation:** University of Hawaii at Manoa is nonsectarian; no religious requirements.
**Library:** Collections totaling over 2,700,000 volumes, 36,592 periodical subscriptions, and 34 microform items.
**Special facilities/museums:** Language lab, urban and regional planning program, environmental center, water resources research center, institute of marine biology, biomedical research center, population genetics lab, institute of astronomy/geophysics.
**Athletic facilities:** Gymnasiums, athletic fields, weight room, swimming pools, tracks, basketball and tennis courts, dance studios.

**STUDENT BODY. Undergraduate profile:** 30% are state residents; 41% are transfers. 47% Asian-American, 1% Black, 1% Hispanic, 16% White, 35% Other. Average age of undergraduates is 23.
**Freshman profile:** 1% of freshmen who took SAT scored 700 or over on verbal, 6% scored 700 or over on math; 5% scored 600 or over on verbal, 25% scored 600 or over on math; 26% scored 500 or over on verbal, 67% scored 500 or over on math; 71% scored 400 or over on verbal, 96% scored 400 or over on math; 97% scored 300 or over on verbal, 100% scored 300 or over on math. 98% of accepted applicants took SAT; 2% took ACT. 62% of freshmen come from public schools.
**Undergraduate achievement:** 81% of fall 1992 freshmen returned for fall 1993 term.
**Foreign students:** 783 students are from out of the country. Countries represented include China, Hong Kong, India, Japan, Korea, and Taiwan; 75 in all.

**PROGRAMS OF STUDY. Degrees:** B.A., B.Arch., B.Bus.Admin., B.Ed., B.F.A., B.Mus., B.S., B.Soc.Work
**Majors:** Accounting, Agricultural/Resource Economics, Agronomy/Soil Science, American Studies, Animal Science, Animal Technology, Anthropology, Architecture, Art, Asian Studies, Biology, Botany, Business Economics/Quantitative Methods, Chemistry, Chinese, Civil Engineering, Classics, Communications, Computer Science, Dance Ethnology, Dance Theatre, Dental Hygiene, Drama/Theatre, Economics, Education, Elementary Education, Engineering/Electrical, English, Entomology, Ethnic Studies, Family Resources, Fashion Design/Merchandising, Finance, Food Science/Human Nutrition, French, General Agriculture, General Business, Geography, Geology, Geology/Geophysics, German, Hawaiian, Hawaiian Studies, Health/Physical Education/Recreation, History, Human Resource Management, International Business, Japanese, Journalism, Liberal Studies, Management, Management Information Systems, Marketing, Mathematics, Mechanical Engineering, Mechanized Agricultural Production, Medical Technology, Meteorology, Microbiology, Music, Nursing, Philosophy, Physics, Political Science, Psychology, Real Estate, Religion, Russian, Secondary Education, Social Work, Sociology, Spanish, Speech, Speech Pathology/Audiology, Travel Industry Management, Tropical Horticulture, Women's Studies, Zoology.
**Requirements:** General education requirement.
**Academic regulations:** Minimum 2.0 GPA must be maintained.
**Special:** Self-designed majors. Double majors. Dual degrees. Independent study. Pass/fail grading option. Internships. Cooperative education programs. Graduate school at which undergraduates may take graduate-level courses. Preprofessional programs in law, medicine, veterinary science, pharmacy, dentistry, optometry, business, education, medical technology, nursing, social work, speech pathology, and travel industry management. Member of National Student Exchange (NSE). Teacher certification in early childhood, elementary, and secondary education. Study abroad in Argentina, Denmark, England, France, Germany, Indonesia, Japan, Kenya, Mexico, Russia, Spain, Thailand, and Vietnam. ROTC and AFROTC.
**Honors:** Phi Beta Kappa. Honors program. Honor societies.
**Academic Assistance:** Nonremedial tutoring.

**STUDENT LIFE. Housing:** Students may live on or off campus. Coed, women's, and men's dorms. School-owned/operated apartments. On-campus married-student housing. 17% of students live in college housing.
**Social atmosphere:** The student newspaper reports, "The University of Hawaii at Manoa has a relaxed atmosphere and is situated five minutes from famed Waikiki. There are diverse ethnic groups that make up the campus. Parties are frequent in on-campus housing." Popular gathering spots include the Campus Center, Manoa Garden, Mama Mia's, Anna Bannana's, and beaches. Influential organizations on campus are the Associated Students Senate and the Society of Professional Journalists. Basketball games, football games, and dances are among the favorite events at the University.
**Services and counseling/handicapped student services:** Placement services. Health service. Women's center. Day care. Counseling services for minority, veteran, and older students. Birth control, personal, and psychological counseling. Career and academic guidance services. Physically disabled student services. Notetaking services. Tape recorders. Tutors. Reader services for the blind.
**Campus organizations:** Undergraduate student government. Student newspaper (Ka Leo O Hawaii, published five times/week). Literary magazine. Drama group, debating, departmental groups, special-interest groups, 250 organizations in all. Eight fraternities, no chapter houses; seven sororities, no chapter houses. 2% of men join a fraternity. 2% of women join a sorority.

**ATHLETICS. Physical education requirements:** None.
**Intercollegiate competition:** 2% of students participate. Baseball (M), basketball (M,W), cheerleading (M,W), cross-country (W), diving (M,W), football (M), golf (M,W), sailing (M,W), softball (W), swimming (M,W), tennis (M,W), volleyball (M,W). Member of Big West Conference, NCAA Division I, Pacific Coast Yacht Racing Association, Western Athletic Conference, Western Intercollegiate Volleyball Association.
**Intramural and club sports:** 32% of students participate. Intramural badminton, basketball, biathlon, golf, soccer, softball, tennis, volleyball, wrestling. Women's club cross-country.

**ADMISSIONS. Academic basis for candidate selection** (in order of priority): Secondary school record, standardized test scores, class rank, school's recommendation.
**Requirements:** Graduation from secondary school is required; GED is accepted. 20 units and the following program of study are required: 4 units of English, 2 units of math, 2 units of science, 12 units of electives. Minimum combined SAT score of 860 (composite ACT score of 20), rank in top two-fifths of secondary school class, and minimum 2.8 GPA required of in-state applicants; minimum combined SAT score of 960 (composite ACT score of 22), rank in top two-fifths of secondary school class, and minimum 3.2 GPA required of out-of-state applicants. Higher math standards required of engineering, math, biology, and physical sciences program applicants. College Opportunities Program for applicants not normally admissible. SAT or ACT is required. No off-campus interviews.
**Procedure:** Take SAT or ACT by December of 12th year. Application deadline is May 1. Notification of admission on rolling basis. Reply is required by date specified in letter of acceptance. $90 nonrefundable tuition deposit (non–resident); $27 nonrefundable tuition deposit (resident). $75 refundable room deposit. Freshmen accepted for terms other than fall.
**Special programs:** Credit and/or placement may be granted through CEEB Advanced Placement exams for scores of 3 or higher. Credit and/or placement may be granted through CLEP general and subject exams. Credit and placement may be granted through DANTES and challenge exams, and military experience. Early entrance/early admission program. Concurrent enrollment program.
**Transfer students:** Transfer students accepted for terms other than fall. In fall 1993, 41% of all new students were transfers into all classes. Application deadline is May 1 for fall; November 1 for spring. Minimum 2.5 GPA required. Lowest course grade accepted is "C." Maximum number of transferable credits is 60 semester hours from two–year schools; unlimited from four–year schools. At least 30 semester hours must be completed at the university to receive degree.
**Admissions contact:** David Robb, Ph.D., Director of Admissions and Records. 808 956-8975.

**FINANCIAL AID. Available aid:** Pell grants, SEOG, state scholarships, school scholarships, private scholarships, ROTC scholarships, academic merit scholarships, and athletic scholarships. Perkins Loans (NDSL), PLUS, Stafford Loans (GSL), NSL, state loans, and SLS.

**Financial aid statistics:** 10% of aid is not need-based. In 1993-94, 42% of all undergraduate applicants received aid; 19% of freshman applicants. Average amounts of aid awarded freshmen: Scholarships and grants, $2,450; loans, $1,955.

**Supporting data/closing dates:** FAFSA: Priority filing date is March 1. School's own aid application: Priority filing date is March 1. Income tax forms: Accepted on rolling basis. Notification of awards begins June 15.

**Financial aid contact:** Annabelle Fong, M.A., Director of Financial Aid. 808 956-7251.

**STUDENT EMPLOYMENT.** College Work/Study Program. Institutional employment. 18% of full-time undergraduates work on campus during school year. Students may expect to earn an average of $3,500 during school year. Off-campus part-time employment opportunities rated "good."

**COMPUTER FACILITIES.** 1,000 IBM/IBM-compatible, Macintosh/Apple, and RISC-/UNIX-based microcomputers; all are networked. Students may access CDC Cyber, Digital, IBM, SUN minicomputer/mainframe systems, BITNET, Internet. Client/LAN operating systems include Apple/Macintosh, DOS, OS/2, UNIX/XENIX/AIX, X-windows, LocalTalk/AppleTalk, Novell. Numerous computer language and programs available. Computer facilities are available to all students.

**Fees:** None.

**PROMINENT ALUMNI/AE.** Daniel K. Inouye, first U.S. Senator of Japanese descent; Richard Mamiya, early pioneer of open heart surgery; Bette Midler, film/recording artist.

# Idaho

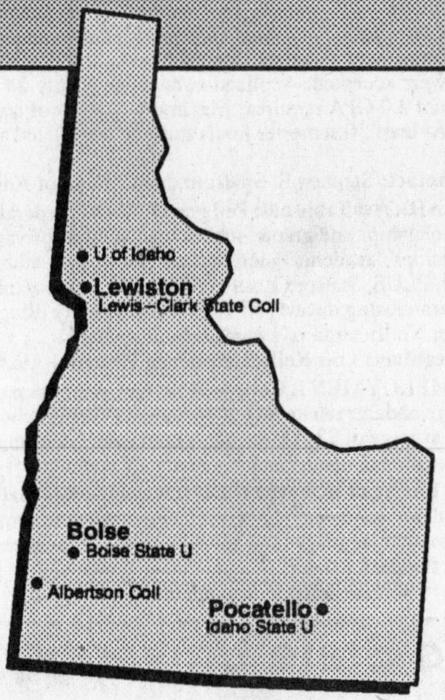


## Albertson College

**Caldwell, ID 83605** **208 459-5500**

**1994-95 Costs.** Tuition: $13,500. Room & board: $3,200. Fees, books, misc. academic expenses (school's estimate): $732.
**Enrollment.** Undergraduates: 330 men, 348 women (full-time). Freshman class: 587 applicants, 479 accepted, 158 enrolled. Graduate enrollment: 191.
**Test score averages/ranges.** Average SAT scores: 487 verbal, 524 math. Average ACT scores: 24 composite.
**Faculty.** 58 full-time; 44 part-time. 71% of faculty holds highest degree in specific field. Student/faculty ratio: 11 to 1.
**Selectivity rating.** Competitive.

**PROFILE.** Albertson College is a church-affiliated, liberal arts institution. Founded in 1891, its name was changed from the College of Idaho in 1991. Its 20-acre campus is located in Caldwell, 25 miles west of Boise.

**Accreditation:** NASC.
**Religious orientation:** Albertson College is nonsectarian; three units of religion required.
**Library:** Collections totaling over 158,769 volumes, 776 periodical subscriptions, and 45,925 microform items.
**Special facilities/museums:** Art and natural history museums, gem and mineral collections, observatory, planetarium, nuclear magnetic resonance spectrometer (NMR), gas chromatograph, gamma camera, graphic computer.
**Athletic facilities:** Gymnasium with weight room and dance studio, soccer and softball fields, tennis courts; ski resort nearby.

**STUDENT BODY. Undergraduate profile:** 78% are state residents; 25% are transfers. 4.4% Asian-American, .2% Black, 3.6% Hispanic, .5% Native American, 84% White, 7.3% Other. Average age of undergraduates is 20.
**Freshman profile:** 9% of freshmen who took ACT scored 30 or over on composite; 47% scored 24 or over on composite; 94% scored 18 or over on composite; 99% scored 12 or over on composite. 49% of accepted applicants took SAT; 78% took ACT. 95% of freshmen come from public schools.
**Undergraduate achievement:** 85% of fall 1992 freshmen returned for fall 1993 term. 50% of entering class graduated. 50% of students who completed a degree program went on to graduate study within three years.
**Foreign students:** 37 students are from out of the country. Countries represented include Brazil, Canada, France, and Japan; 11 in all.

**PROGRAMS OF STUDY. Degrees:** B.A., B.S.
**Majors:** Accounting, Anthropology, Art, Biology, Business Administration, Chemistry, Computer Science, Economics, Elementary Education, English, English Teaching, Exercise Science, French, History, Mathematics, Mathematics Teaching, Music, Philosophy, Physical Education Teaching, Physics, Politics/International Relations, Psychology, Religion, Social Studies Teaching, Sociology, Spanish, Sport/Fitness Center Management, Theatre.
**Distribution of degrees:** The majors with the highest enrollment are business administration, biology, and elementary education; French, anthropology, and physics have the lowest.
**Requirements:** General education requirement.
**Academic regulations:** Minimum 2.0 GPA must be maintained.
**Special:** Minors offered in all majors and in computer graphics and German. Self-designed majors. Double majors. Dual degrees. Independent study. Pass/fail grading option. Internships. Cooperative education programs. Graduate school at which undergraduates may take graduate-level courses. Preprofessional programs in law, medicine, veterinary science, dentistry, optometry, and physical therapy. 3-2 engineering programs with Columbia U, U of Idaho, and Washington U. Washington Semester. Teacher certification in elementary and secondary education. Certification in specific subject areas. Exchange programs abroad vary from year to year. Study abroad in various countries.
**Honors:** Honors program. Honor societies.

**ADMISSIONS. Academic basis for candidate selection** (in order of priority): Secondary school record, standardized test scores, school's recommendation, essay, class rank.
**Nonacademic basis for candidate selection:** Character and personality are important. Extracurricular participation, particular talent or ability, and alumni/ae relationship are considered.
**Requirements:** Graduation from secondary school is required; GED is accepted. 12 units and the following program of study are recommended: 4 units of English, 3 units of math, 2 units of science, 3 units of social studies. Audition required of applicants to some music programs. Conditional admission possible for applicants not meeting standard requirements. SAT or ACT is required. Campus visit and interview recommended. Off-campus interviews available with admissions and alumni representatives.
**Procedure:** Suggest filing application by February 15; no deadline. Notification of admission on rolling basis. No set date by which applicants must accept offer. $100 nonrefundable tuition deposit. $150 nonrefundable room deposit. Freshmen accepted for terms other than fall.
**Special programs:** Admission may be deferred one year. School has a no-increase tuition program, guaranteeing that students pay the same rate of tuition for each of their four years. Credit and/or placement may be granted through CEEB Advanced Placement exams for scores of 3 or higher. Credit and/or placement may be granted through CLEP general and subject exams. Placement may be granted through challenge exams. Concurrent enrollment program.
**Transfer students:** Transfer students accepted for terms other than fall. In fall 1993, 25% of all new students were transfers into all classes. 129 transfer applications were received, 98 were accepted. Application deadline is rolling for fall; rolling for spring. Minimum 2.0 GPA recommended. Lowest course grade accepted is "D." Maximum number of transferable credits is 62 semester hours. At least 30 semester hours must be completed at the college to receive degree.

**FINANCIAL AID. Available aid:** Pell grants, SEOG, state scholarships and grants, school scholarships and grants, private scholarships and grants, academic merit scholarships, and athletic scholarships. Perkins Loans (NDSL), PLUS, Stafford Loans (GSL), and school loans. Guaranteed tuition.
**Financial aid statistics:** 40% of aid is not need-based. In 1993-94, 93% of all undergraduate applicants received aid.
**Supporting data/closing dates:** FAFSA: Priority filing date is March 1. FAF/FFS: Priority filing date is March 1; accepted on rolling basis. Notification of awards on rolling basis.
**Financial aid contact:** Ann Grober, M.A., Director of Financial Aid. 800 635-0434 (out-of-state), 800 841-8648 (in-state).

**STUDENT EMPLOYMENT.** College Work/Study Program. Institutional employment. 36% of full-time undergraduates work on campus during school year. Students may expect to earn an average of $1,500 during school year. Off-campus part-time employment opportunities rated "good."

**COMPUTER FACILITIES.** 120 IBM/IBM-compatible microcomputers; 25 are networked. Students may access Hewlett-Packard minicomputer/mainframe systems. Computer languages and software packages include C, COBOL, dBASE, Excel, FORTRAN, LISP, Lotus 1-2-3, MathCad, Pascal, Prolog, Stat Pack Gold, WordPerfect; multigraphic packages; 50 in all. Computer facilities are available to all students.
**Fees:** None.

**GRADUATE CAREER DATA.** Highest graduate school enrollments: U of Idaho, U of Washington, Willamette U. 20% of graduates choose careers in business and industry.

**PROMINENT ALUMNI/AE.** Joe A. Albertson, founder, Albertson grocery stores; Dr. Lawrence Henry Gipson, Pulitzer Prize-winning author; Kris McDivitt, president, Patagonia Outerwear; Dr. Mary Shaw Shorb, medical researcher, co-discoverer of Vitamin B-12; Paul J. Smith, Academy Award-winning film music composer, Disney Studios.

## Boise State University

**Boise, ID 83725** **208 385-1011**

**1993-94 Costs.** Tuition: None (state residents), $2,650 (out-of-state). Room & board: $3,069. Fees, books, misc. academic expenses (school's estimate): $1,918.
**Enrollment.** Undergraduates: 3,602 men, 4,295 women (full-time). Freshman class: 3,873 applicants, 3,346 accepted, 2,023 enrolled. Graduate enrollment: 986 men, 2,249 women.
**Test score averages/ranges.** Average SAT scores: 419 verbal, 460 math. Average ACT scores: 20 English, 19 math, 20 composite.
**Faculty.** 455 full-time; 367 part-time. Student/faculty ratio: 19 to 1.
**Selectivity rating.** Less competitive.

**PROFILE.** Boise State is a public institution. It was founded as a junior college in 1932, became a four-year insitution in 1965, joined the state system in 1969, and gained university status in 1974. Programs are offered through the Colleges of Arts and Sciences, Business, Education, Health Science, and Technology; the Graduate College; and the Schools of Applied Technology, Social Sciences and Public Affairs, and Vocational Technical Education. Its 120-acre campus is located in downtown Boise.

**Accreditation:** NASC. Professionally accredited by the American Assembly of Collegiate Schools of Business, the American Dental Association, the American Medical Association (CAHEA), the Council on Social Work Education, the Liaison Committee on Medical Education, the National Association of Schools of Music, the National Council for Accreditation of Teacher Education, the National League for Nursing.
**Religious orientation:** Boise State University is nonsectarian; no religious requirements.
**Library:** Collections totaling over 403,393 volumes, 4,709 periodical subscriptions, and 988,137 microform items.
**Athletic facilities:** Football stadium, basketball and racquetball courts, weight room, wrestling facility, tracks, grass practice fields, gymnasiums, swimming pool.

**STUDENT BODY. Undergraduate profile:** 88% are state residents; 28% are transfers. 2% Asian-American, 1% Black, 3% Hispanic, 1% Native American, 85% White, 8% Other. Average age of undergraduates is 26.
**Freshman profile:** 1% of freshmen who took SAT scored 700 or over on verbal, 2% scored 700 or over on math; 5% scored 600 or over on verbal, 11% scored 600 or over on math; 25% scored 500 or over on verbal, 38% scored 500 or over on math; 62% scored 400 or over on verbal, 72% scored 400 or over on math; 94% scored 300 or over on verbal, 96% scored 300 or over on math. 1% of freshmen who took ACT scored 30 or over on composite; 20% scored 24 or over on composite; 77% scored 18 or over on composite; 99% scored 12 or over on composite; 100% scored 6 or over on composite. 28% of accepted applicants took SAT; 72% took ACT.
**Undergraduate achievement:** 78% of fall 1991 freshmen returned for fall 1992 term.
**Foreign students:** 117 students are from out of the country. Countries represented include the Bahamas, Canada, China, Hong Kong, Japan, and Malaysia; 55 in all.

**PROGRAMS OF STUDY. Degrees:** B.A., B.Appl.Sci., B.Bus.Admin., B.F.A., B.Interdis.Studies, B.Mus., B.S.
**Majors:** Accounting, Advertising Design, Anthropology, Art, Athletic Training, Bilingual/Multicultural Elementary Education, Biology, Chemistry, Communication, Communication/English, Computer Information Systems, Computer Science, Construction Management, Criminal Justice Administration, Economics, Elementary Education, English, Environmental Health, Finance, French, General Business, General Business Management, General Education, General Health Sciences, General Social Studies, Geology, Geophysics, German, History, Interdisciplinary Studies, International Business, Management, Manufacturing Engineering Technology, Marketing, Mathematics, Medical Technology, Military Science, Multiethnic Study, Music, Nursing, Philosophy, Physical Education, Physics, Political Science, Pre-Dental, Pre-Medical, Pre-Veterinary Medicine, Production/Operations Management, Psychology, Radiologic Technology, Social Science, Social Work, Sociology, Spanish, Theatre Arts.
**Distribution of degrees:** The majors with the highest enrollment are accounting, general business, and elementary education.
**Requirements:** General education requirement.
**Academic regulations:** Minimum 2.0 GPA required for graduation.
**Special:** Minors offered. Numerous certificate and diploma programs. Associate's degrees offered. Self-designed majors. Double majors. Independent study. Internships. Graduate school at which undergraduates may take graduate-level courses. Preprofessional programs in medicine, veterinary science, and dentistry. 2-2, 3-1, and 3-2 engineering programs. Member of National Student Exchange (NSE). Teacher certification in early childhood, elementary, secondary, special education, and bilingual/bicultural education. Certification in specific subject areas. Study abroad in England, France, Germany, Mexico, and Spain. ROTC.
**Honors:** Honors program. Honor societies.
**Academic Assistance:** Remedial writing, math, and study skills. Nonremedial tutoring.

**STUDENT LIFE. Housing:** Students may live on or off campus. Coed and women's dorms. School-owned/operated apartments. Off-campus privately-owned housing. Off-campus married-student housing. 10% of students live in college housing.
**Social atmosphere:** Students gather at the Student Union, Gainey's, the Emerald Club, and Dino's. According to the Arbiter, athletes are influential on campus. The most popular campus events include Homecoming and the Boise State vs. the University of Idaho football game. The Arbiter reports that campus cultural life is extremely varied due to the wide range of age and experience among the student population.
**Services and counseling/handicapped student services:** Placement services. Health service. Women's center. Day care. Multicultural center. Counseling services for minority, veteran, and older students. Birth control, personal, and psychological counseling. Career and academic guidance services. Physically disabled student services. Learning disabled services. Notetaking services. Tape recorders. Tutors. Reader services for the blind.
**Campus organizations:** Undergraduate student government. Student newspaper (Arbiter, published once/week). Radio and TV stations. A cappella choir, opera workshop, community orchestra, debating, athletic, departmental, service, and special-interest groups, 133 organizations in all. Four fraternities, all with chapter houses; four sororities, all with chapter houses. 3% of men join a fraternity. 2% of women join a sorority.
**Religious organizations:** Several religious groups.
**Minority/foreign student organizations:** Black Student Union, Native American Student Association, Organizacion de Estudiantes Latino-Americanos. International Student Association, Asian-American Association.

**ATHLETICS. Physical education requirements:** None.
**Intercollegiate competition:** 4% of students participate. Basketball (M,W), cheerleading (M,W), cross-country (M,W), football (M), golf (M,W), gymnastics (W), tennis (M,W), track (indoor) (M,W), track (outdoor) (M,W), track and field (indoor) (M,W), track and field (outdoor) (M,W), volleyball (W), wrestling (M). Member of Big Sky Athletic Conference, NCAA Division I, NCAA Division I-AA for football, Pacific 10 Conference.
**Intramural and club sports:** 29% of students participate. Intramural basketball, racquetball, soccer, softball, touch football, volleyball. Men's club baseball, bowling, cheerleading, fencing, martial arts, racquetball, rock climbing, rodeo, rugby, soccer, swimming. Women's club bowling, cheerleading, fencing, martial arts, racquetball, rock climbing, rodeo, rugby, soccer, swimming.

**ADMISSIONS. Academic basis for candidate selection** (in order of priority): Secondary school record, standardized test scores.
**Requirements:** Graduation from secondary school is required; GED is accepted. No specific distribution of secondary school units required. Minimum 2.0 GPA required. School of Vocational-Technical Education has special admissions requirements. R.N. required of nursing program applicants. Applicants not normally admissible may be admitted as special students. SAT or ACT is required. Campus visit recommended. No off-campus interviews.
**Procedure:** Take SAT or ACT by May 1 of 12th year. Application deadline is July 28. Notification of admission on rolling basis. $60 room deposit, refundable until July 15. Freshmen accepted for terms other than fall.
**Special programs:** Admission may be deferred one year. Credit may be granted through CEEB Advanced Placement for scores of 3 or higher. Credit may be granted through CLEP general and subject exams, ACT PEP and DANTES exams, and military and life experience. Credit and placement may be granted through challenge exams. Early entrance/early admission program. Concurrent enrollment program.
**Transfer students:** Transfer students accepted for terms other than fall. In fall 1992, 28% of all new students were transfers into all classes. 2,253 transfer applications were received, 1,997 were accepted. Application deadline is July 28 for fall; November 24 for spring. Minimum 2.0 GPA required. Maximum number of transferable credits is 70 semester hours. At least 30 semester hours must be completed at the university to receive degree.
**Admissions contact:** Stephen E. Spafford, M.A., Dean of Admissions. 208 385-1156.

**FINANCIAL AID. Available aid:** Pell grants, SEOG, Federal Nursing Student Scholarships, state scholarships and grants, school scholarships, private scholarships and grants, ROTC scholarships, academic merit scholarships, and athletic scholarships. Perkins Loans (NDSL), PLUS, Stafford Loans (GSL), NSL, school loans, and SLS.
**Supporting data/closing dates:** FAF or FAFSA: Priority filing date is March 1; accepted on rolling basis. Notification of awards on rolling basis.
**Financial aid contact:** Lois Kelly, Director of Financial Aid. 208 385-1664.

**STUDENT EMPLOYMENT.** College Work/Study Program. Institutional employment. 67% of full-time undergraduates work on campus during school year. Students may expect to earn an average of $3,000 during school year. Off-campus part-time employment opportunities rated "excellent."

**COMPUTER FACILITIES.** 450 IBM/IBM-compatible and Macintosh/Apple microcomputers. Students may access IBM minicomputer/mainframe systems, BITNET, Internet. 7 major computer languages and software packages available. Computer facilities are available to all students.
**Fees:** Computer fee is included in tuition/fees.

# Idaho State University

**Pocatello, ID 83209-0009** **208 236-3277**

**1993-94 Costs.** Tuition: None (state residents), $3,614 (out-of-state). Room & board: $2,840. Fees, books, misc. academic expenses (school's estimate): $2,102.
**Enrollment.** Undergraduates: 3,116 men, 3,431 women (full-time). Freshman class: 2,747 applicants, 1,996 accepted, 1,424 enrolled. Graduate enrollment: 830 men, 938 women.
**Test score averages/ranges.** Average ACT scores: 20 English, 19 math, 21 composite. Range of ACT scores of middle 50%: 16-22 English, 15-21 math.
**Faculty.** 434 full-time; 201 part-time. 88% of faculty holds doctoral degree. Student/faculty ratio: 18 to 1.
**Selectivity rating.** Less competitive.

**PROFILE.** Idaho State, founded in 1901, is a public university. Programs are offered through the Colleges of Business, Education, Health-Related Professions, Liberal Arts, and Pharmacy; the School of Engineering and Nuclear Science; and the Graduate School. Its campus is located in a residential area of Pocatello, in the southeastern corner of Idaho.
**Accreditation:** NASC. Professionally accredited by the Accreditation Board for Engineering and Technology, the American Assembly of Collegiate Schools of Business, the American Council on Pharmaceutical Education, the American Dental Association, the American Dietetic Association, the American Medical Association (CAHEA), the American Speech-Language-Hearing Association, the Council on Social Work Education, the National Association of Schools of Music, the National Council for Accreditation of Teacher Education, the National League for Nursing.
**Religious orientation:** Idaho State University is nonsectarian; no religious requirements.
**Library:** Collections totaling over 482,793 volumes, 3,326 periodical subscriptions, and 1,293,361 microform items.
**Special facilities/museums:** Museum of natural history.
**Athletic facilities:** Gymnasium, basketball and tennis courts, swimming pool, track, sports arena.

**STUDENT BODY. Undergraduate profile:** 93% are state residents; 52% are transfers. 1% Asian-American, 1% Black, 2% Hispanic, 1% Native American, 93% White, 2% Foreign national. Average age of undergraduates is 25.
**Freshman profile:** Majority of accepted applicants took ACT. 100% of freshmen come from public schools.
**Undergraduate achievement:** 60% of fall 1992 freshmen returned for fall 1993 term.
**Foreign students:** 236 students are from out of the country. Countries represented include Canada, China, Hong Kong, India, Malaysia, and Pakistan; 44 in all.

**PROGRAMS OF STUDY. Degrees:** B.A., B.Appl.Tech., B.Bus.Admin., B.F.A., B.Mech.Eng., B.Mus., B.Mus.Ed., B.S., B.Univ.Studies.
**Majors:** Accounting, American Studies, Anthropology, Applied Technology, Art, Biochemistry, Biology, Botany, Chemistry, Computer Information Systems, Computer Science, Corporate Training, Dental Hygiene, Dietetics, Early Childhood Education, Ecology, Economics, Elementary Education, Engineering, Engineering Management, English, Finance, French, General Studies, Geology, German, Health Care Administration, Health Education, History, Home Economics, International Studies, Management, Marketing, Mass Communications, Mathematics, Medical Technology, Microbiology, Middle School/Junior High Education, Music, Music Education, Nursing, Philosophy, Physical Education, Physics, Political Science, Psychology, Radiological Science, Secondary Education, Social Work, Sociology, Spanish, Speech Communication, Speech Pathology/Audiology, Technical/Vocational Education, Theatre, University Studies, Zoology.
**Distribution of degrees:** The majors with the highest enrollment are education, business administration, and health related professions.
**Requirements:** General education requirement.
**Academic regulations:** Freshmen must maintain minimum 1.0 GPA; sophomores, 1.6 GPA; juniors, 1.8 GPA; seniors, 2.0 GPA.
**Special:** Students in College of Arts and Sciences may take courses in other divisions. Radiation protection "training-study" program. Associate's degrees offered. Pass/fail grading option. Internships. Graduate school at which undergraduates may take graduate-

level courses. Preprofessional programs in medicine, veterinary science, and pharmacy. Dentistry program with Creighton U. B.S./M.S. chemistry program. Teacher certification in early childhood, elementary, secondary, special education, and vo-tech education. Certification in specific subject areas.
**Honors:** Honor societies.
**Academic Assistance:** Remedial reading, writing, math, and study skills. Nonremedial tutoring.

**STUDENT LIFE. Housing:** Students may live on or off campus. Coed, women's, and men's dorms. Fraternity housing. School-owned/operated apartments. On-campus married-student housing. 14% of students live in college housing.
**Social atmosphere:** As reported by the student newspaper, "Idaho State University draws a diverse student population, including traditonal students who frequent local lounges and adult students who maintain a more conservative lifestyle." On campus, students meet at the union building. Favorite off-campus spots: Freddy's, Sam's Town, and Locomotion. "Athletes and their 'groupies' seem to dictate, to some degree, where students converge."
**Services and counseling/handicapped student services:** Placement services. Health service. Women's center. Day care. Counseling services for minority, veteran, and older students. Birth control, personal, and psychological counseling. Career and academic guidance services. Physically disabled student services. Learning disabled program/services. Notetaking services. Tape recorders. Tutors. Reader services for the blind.
**Campus organizations:** Undergraduate student government. Student newspaper (Bengal, published once/week). Concert choir, ensembles, ROTC band, orchestra, crafts workshop, Young Republicans, Young Democrats, professional and special-interest groups, 105 organizations in all. Three fraternities, one chapter house; three sororities, no chapter houses. 1% of men join a fraternity. 1% of women join a sorority.
**Religious organizations:** Baptist Campus Ministries, Campus Crusade for Christ, Catholic Campus Ministry, Chi Alpha, Ecumenical Ministry, Lutheran Student Association, Muslim Student Association, Wesley Foundation.
**Minority/foreign student organizations:** Native Americans United, Black Student Association, Hispanic Awareness Leadership Organization. International Student Association, African, Pakistani, and Saudi Arabian groups.

**ATHLETICS. Physical education requirements:** None.
**Intercollegiate competition:** 3% of students participate. Basketball (M,W), cheerleading (M,W), cross-country (M,W), football (M), golf (M,W), tennis (M,W), track and field (indoor) (M,W), track and field (outdoor) (M,W), volleyball (W). Member of Big Sky Conference, NCAA Division I.
**Intramural and club sports:** Intramural badminton, basketball, billiards, bowling, football, golf, handball, horseshoes, pickleball, racquetball, soccer, softball, table tennis, tennis, volleyball.

**ADMISSIONS. Academic basis for candidate selection** (in order of priority): Secondary school record, standardized test scores.
**Nonacademic basis for candidate selection:** Extracurricular participation and particular talent or ability are considered.
**Requirements:** Graduation from secondary school is recommended; GED is accepted. No specific distribution of secondary school units required. Minimum 2.0 GPA required. 1 unit of advanced algebra or 1/2 unit of advanced algebra and 1/2 unit of solid geometry or trigonometry required of biology, forestry, and geology program applicants. 2 units of algebra, 1 unit of geometry, 1 unit of advanced math (including trigonometry), and physics recommended of chemistry, engineering, mathematics, and physics program applicants. Audition required of music program applicants. Conditional admission possible for applicants not meeting standard requirements. ACT is required; SAT may be substituted. Campus visit recommended.
**Procedure:** Take SAT or ACT by October of 12th year. Suggest filing application by February 15. Application deadline is July 1. Notification of admission on rolling basis. $20 nonrefundable tuition deposit. $75 refundable room deposit. Freshmen accepted for terms other than fall.
**Special programs:** Credit and/or placement may be granted through CEEB Advanced Placement exams for scores of 3 or higher. Credit may be granted through CLEP general and subject exams, and military experience. Credit and placement may be granted through challenge exams and life experience. Concurrent enrollment program.
**Transfer students:** Transfer students accepted for terms other than fall. In fall 1993, 52% of all new students were transfers into all classes. 1,588 transfer applications were received, 1,406 were accepted. Application deadline is March for fall; November for spring. Minimum 2.0 GPA required. Lowest course grade accepted is "C." At least 32 semester hours must be completed at the university to receive degree.
**Admissions contact:** Mike Echanis, M.Ed., Director of Admissions. 208 236-2475.

**FINANCIAL AID. Available aid:** Pell grants, SEOG, state scholarships and grants, school scholarships and grants, private scholarships and grants, academic merit scholarships, athletic scholarships, and aid for undergraduate foreign students. Perkins Loans (NDSL), PLUS, and Stafford Loans (GSL).
**Supporting data/closing dates:** FAFSA/FAF: Priority filing date is March 15. Notification of awards begins in spring.
**Financial aid contact:** Doug Severs, M.A., Director of Financial Aid. 208 236-2756.

**STUDENT EMPLOYMENT.** College Work/Study Program. Institutional employment. 24% of full-time undergraduates work on campus during school year. Students may expect to earn an average of $4,000 during school year. Off-campus part-time employment opportunities rated "fair."

**COMPUTER FACILITIES.** 310 IBM/IBM-compatible and Macintosh/Apple microcomputers; 225 are networked. Students may access Hewlett-Packard, IBM minicomputer/mainframe systems, Internet. Residence halls may be equipped with networked microcomputers. Computer languages and software packages include COBOL, dBASE, FORTRAN, FoxPro, Lotus 1-2-3, Quattro Pro, RPG II, SAS-PC, SPSS-PC, Turbo Pascal, WordPerfect; 50 in all. Computer facilities are available to all students.
**Fees:** $10 computer fee per semester.

**GRADUATE CAREER DATA.** 26% of graduates choose careers in business and industry. Companies and businesses that hire graduates: Arthur Andersen, Deloitte & Touche, Farmers Insurance, First Security Bank, K mart, Northwestern Mutual Life, West One Bank.

**PROMINENT ALUMNI/AE.** Dr. Claude ZoBell, marine microbiologist; Ray Dills, inventor; Roger Williams, pianist/entertainer; Amos Jordon, president and CEO, Center for Strategic and International Studies, Georgetown U; John Foreman, movie producer; Terrel H. Bell, former secretary, U.S. Department of Education; Hans Ashbaker, opera singer; Florence Bean James, theatre director; James McClure, former senator; Lewis G. Neal, president, NOXSO Corp.

## Lewis-Clark State College

**Lewiston, ID 83501-2698 — 208 799-LCSC**

**1992-93 Costs.** Tuition: None (state residents), $2,340 (out-of-state). Room & board: $2,300-$2,900. Fees, books, misc. academic expenses (school's estimate): $1,748.
**Enrollment.** Undergraduates: 832 men, 1,138 women (full-time). Freshman class: 700 applicants, 692 accepted, 399 enrolled.
**Test score averages/ranges.** N/A.
**Faculty.** 117 full-time; 185 part-time. 80% of faculty holds highest degree in specific field. Student/faculty ratio: 17 to 1.
**Selectivity rating.** N/A.

**PROFILE.** Lewis-Clark, founded in 1893, is a public, multipurpose institution. Programs are offered in Business, Education, Heavy Industrial Technologies, Humanities, Light Industrial Technologies, Natural Sciences, Nursing, and Social Sciences. Its 45-acre campus is located in a residential area of Lewiston.

**Accreditation:** NASC. Professionally accredited by the National Council for Accreditation of Teacher Education, the National League for Nursing.
**Religious orientation:** Lewis-Clark State College is nonsectarian; no religious requirements.
**Library:** Collections totaling over 167,000 volumes, 994 periodical subscriptions, and 98,691 microform items.
**Special facilities/museums:** Museum/art gallery, educational technology center.
**Athletic facilities:** Gymnasium, weight room, aerobic exercise room, indoor and outdoor tennis courts, outdoor physical activity/exercise paths, basketball courts, baseball diamond, outdoor volleyball courts.

**STUDENT BODY. Undergraduate profile:** 80% are state residents; 33% are transfers. 1% Asian-American, 1% Black, 1% Hispanic, 2% Native American, 95% White. Average age of undergraduates is 26.
**Freshman profile:** 92% of freshmen come from public schools.
**Undergraduate achievement:** 3% of students who completed a degree program immediately went on to graduate study.
**Foreign students:** 59 students are from out of the country. Countries represented include Australia, Canada, Honduras, Japan, Korea, and Malaysia; 29 in all.

**PROGRAMS OF STUDY. Degrees:** B.A., B.S., B.S.Nurs.
**Majors:** Applied Science, Applied Technology, Biology, Business Administration, Chemistry, Communication Arts, Corrections, Criminal Justice, Drama/Speech, Earth Sciences/Geology, Elementary Education, English, English/Business, General Studies, History, History/Political Science, Kinesiology, Law Enforcement, Management/Technology, Mathematics, Natural Science, Nursing, Pacific Rim Studies, Physical Education, Secondary Education, Social Sciences, Social Work, Special Education.
**Requirements:** General education requirement.
**Academic regulations:** Minimum 2.0 GPA must be maintained.
**Special:** Minors available in 35 subjects. 19 certificate programs. Associate's degrees offered. Self-designed majors. Double majors. Independent study. Internships. Cooperative education programs. Preprofessional programs in law, medicine, veterinary science, agriculture, engineering, forestry, and physical therapy. Teacher certification in elementary, secondary, and special education. Certification in specific subject areas. ROTC at U of Idaho.
**Academic Assistance:** Remedial reading, writing, math, and study skills. Nonremedial tutoring.

**STUDENT LIFE. Housing:** Students may live on or off campus. Coed, women's, and men's dorms. Off-campus privately-owned housing. 7% of students live in college housing.
**Social atmosphere:** With an average student age of 26, LCSC's social life differs somewhat from that of most colleges. The biggest events of the year are the NAIA World Series Baseball, other athletic events, the Dogwood Festival, dances, and the Lewiston Round-Up rodeo. Residence halls sponsor 20 to 25 events per semester. Favorite student spots around Lewiston include The Corner Pocket, Cafe Ole Restaurant, and Hellsgate State Park.
**Services and counseling/handicapped student services:** Placement services. Health service. Day care. Counseling services for minority, military, veteran, and older students. Birth control, personal, and psychological counseling. Career and academic guidance services. Physically disabled student services. Learning disabled services. Notetaking services. Tape recorders. Tutors. Reader services for the blind.
**Campus organizations:** Undergraduate student government. Student newspaper (Pathfinder, published twice/month). Cheerleaders, choir, jazz band, College Republicans, College Democrats, drama groups, men's and women's associations, professional organizations, special-interest groups.
**Religious organizations:** Baptist Student Ministries, Latter-Day Saints Association, Newman Club, nondenominational Christian group.
**Minority/foreign student organizations:** Indian People's Union. International Club.

**ATHLETICS. Physical education requirements:** None.
**Intercollegiate competition:** 1% of students participate. Baseball (M), basketball (M,W), tennis (M,W), volleyball (W). Member of NAIA.
**Intramural and club sports:** Intramural backpacking, baseball, basketball, horseback riding, rafting, snow skiing, tennis, volleyball. Men's club rodeo. Women's club rodeo.

**ADMISSIONS. Academic basis for candidate selection** (in order of priority): Secondary school record, standardized test scores.

**Requirements:** Graduation from secondary school is recommended; GED is accepted. No specific distribution of secondary school units required. Composite ACT score of 17 (composite SAT score of 690) and 2.0 GPA required. Special applications required of education and nursing program applicants. Employment Readiness Training and Project Self-Sufficiency for applicants not normally admissible. ACT is required; SAT may be substituted. Campus visit recommended. No off-campus interviews.
**Procedure:** Suggest filing application by May; no deadline. Notification of admission on rolling basis. Freshmen accepted for terms other than fall.
**Special programs:** Admission may be deferred. Credit and/or placement may be granted through CEEB Advanced Placement exams for scores of 3 or higher. Credit and/or placement may be granted through CLEP general and subject exams. Credit may be granted through life experience. Credit and placement may be granted through challenge exams. Concurrent enrollment program.
**Transfer students:** Transfer students accepted for terms other than fall. In fall 1993, 33% of all new students were transfers into all classes. 567 transfer applications were received, 291 were accepted. Minimum 2.0 GPA required. Lowest course grade accepted is "D." Maximum number of transferable credits is 70 semester hours from a two-year school and 96 semester hours from a four-year school. At least 32 semester hours must be completed at the college to receive degree.
**Admissions contact:** Steven J. Bussolini, M.A., Director of Enrollment Management. 208 799-2210.

**FINANCIAL AID. Available aid:** Pell grants, SEOG, state scholarships, school scholarships, private scholarships, academic merit scholarships, and athletic scholarships. Perkins Loans (NDSL), PLUS, Stafford Loans (GSL), NSL, and school loans. Deferred payment plan.
**Supporting data/closing dates:** FAFSA: Priority filing date is March 1. School's own aid application: Priority filing date is March 1. Notification of awards on rolling basis.
**Financial aid contact:** Harriet L. Rojas, M.A., Associate Director of Financial Aid. 208 799-2224.

**STUDENT EMPLOYMENT.** College Work/Study Program. Institutional employment. 5% of full-time undergraduates work on campus during school year. Students may expect to earn an average of $1,920 during school year. Off-campus part-time employment opportunities rated "good."

**COMPUTER FACILITIES.** 88 IBM/IBM-compatible and Macintosh/Apple microcomputers; 45 are networked. Students may access SUN minicomputer/mainframe systems. Residence halls may be equipped with stand-alone microcomputers. Client/LAN operating systems include Apple/Macintosh. Computer languages and software packages include BASIC, Pascal; file management, spreadsheet, word processing programs; 7 in all. Computer facilities are available to all students.
**Fees:** None.
**Hours:** 9 AM-9 PM.

**GRADUATE CAREER DATA.** Graduate school percentages: 1% enter law school. 3% enter graduate business programs. 2% enter graduate arts and sciences programs. 1% enter theological school/seminary. Highest graduate school enrollments: Gonzaga U, U of Idaho, Washington State U. 70% of graduates choose careers in business and industry. Companies and businesses that hire graduates: Idaho Department of Health and Welfare, Lewiston School District, Potlatch Corp., St. Joseph's Regional Medical Center.

**PROMINENT ALUMNI/AE.** Lovetta Eisle, mayor, city of Lewiston; Mel Spelde, president, Empire Airlines.

# University of Idaho

**Moscow, ID 83843** **208 885-6111**

**1993-94 Costs.** Tuition: None (state residents), $3,900 (out-of-state). Room & board: $3,400. Fees, books, misc. academic expenses (school's estimate): $2,196.
**Enrollment.** Undergraduates: 4,298 men, 2,944 women (full-time). Freshman class: 3,133 applicants, 2,799 accepted, 1,337 enrolled. Graduate enrollment: 1,725 men, 1,145 women.
**Test score averages/ranges.** Average SAT scores: 464 verbal, 520 math. Range of SAT scores of middle 50%: 400-520 verbal, 450-600 math. Average ACT scores: 22 English, 22 math, 23 composite. Range of ACT scores of middle 50%: 19-25 English, 19-25 math.
**Faculty.** 546 full-time; 55 part-time. 84% of faculty holds doctoral degree. Student/faculty ratio: 17 to 1.
**Selectivity rating.** Less competitive.

**PROFILE.** The University of Idaho, founded in 1889, is a public, comprehensive, land-grant institution. Programs are offered through the Colleges of Agriculture; Art and Architecture; Business and Economics; Education; Engineering; Forestry, Wildlife, and Range Sciences; Graduate Studies; Law; Letters and Science; and Mines and Earth Resources. Its 1,450-acre campus and university farm are located in Moscow, 90 miles southeast of Spokane, Wash.

**Accreditation:** NASC. Numerous professional accreditations.
**Religious orientation:** University of Idaho is nonsectarian; no religious requirements.
**Library:** Collections totaling over 932,760 volumes, 13,248 periodical subscriptions, and 1,289,222 microform items.
**Special facilities/museums:** On-campus preschool, experimental forest, electron microscope.
**Athletic facilities:** Gymnasiums, athletic center, golf course, outdoor track, multi-purpose indoor dome.

**STUDENT BODY. Undergraduate profile:** 71% are state residents; 38% are transfers. 2% Asian-American, 1% Black, 2% Hispanic, 1% Native American, 86% White, 8% Other. Average age of undergraduates is 22.
**Freshman profile:** 1% of freshmen who took SAT scored 700 or over on verbal, 5% scored 700 or over on math; 9% scored 600 or over on verbal, 26% scored 600 or over on math; 36% scored 500 or over on verbal, 59% scored 500 or over on math; 78% scored 400 or over on verbal, 87% scored 400 or over on math; 98% scored 300 or over on verbal, 99% scored 300 or over on math. 5% of freshmen who took ACT scored 30 or over on English, 7% scored 30 or over on math, 8% scored 30 or over on composite; 41% scored 24 or over on English, 37% scored 24 or over on math, 44% scored 24 or over on composite; 86% scored 18 or over on English, 87% scored 18 or over on math, 92% scored 18 or over on composite; 100% scored 12 or over on English, 100% scored 12 or over on math, 100% scored 12 or over on composite. 59% of accepted applicants took SAT; 71% took ACT. 96% of freshmen come from public schools.
**Undergraduate achievement:** 76% of fall 1992 freshmen returned for fall 1993 term. 11% of entering class graduated.
**Foreign students:** 192 students are from out of the country. Countries represented include Canada, Hong Kong, Japan, Malaysia, Pakistan, and the United Kingdom; 63 in all.

**PROGRAMS OF STUDY. Degrees:** B.A., B.Appl.Phys., B.Arch., B.Dance, B.F.A., B.Gen.Studies, B.Land.Arch., B.Mus., B.Naval Sci., B.S., B.Tech.
**Majors:** Accounting, Agribusiness, Agricultural Economics, Agricultural Education, Agricultural Engineering, Agricultural Mechanization, Agriculture, American Studies, Animal Science, Anthropology, Applied Mathematics, Applied Music, Architecture, Art, Art Education, Bacteriology, Biology, Botany, Business Education, Cartography, Chemical Engineering, Chemistry, Child Development/Family Relations, Civil Engineering, Classical Studies, Clothing/Textiles/Design, Communication, Computer Engineering, Computer Science, Criminal Justice, Crop Management, Crop Science, Dance, Economics, Electrical Engineering, Elementary Education, English, Entomology, Finance, Fishery Resources, Food/Nutrition, Foreign Languages, Forest Products, Forest Resources, French, General Studies, Geography, Geological Engineering, Geology, German, History, Home Economics, Home Economics Education, Horticultural Science, Human Resources Management, Industrial Technology, Industrial Technology Education, Information Systems, Interdisciplinary Studies, Interior Planning/Design, International Studies, Journalism, Landscape Architecture, Landscape Horticulture, Latin, Latin American Studies, Manufacturing Engineering, Marketing, Marketing Education, Mathematics, Mechanical Engineering, Medical Technology, Metallurgical Engineering, Mining Engineering, Music Composition, Music Education, Music Education/Instrumental, Music Education/Vocal, Music Education/Vocal/Instrumental, Music History/Literature, Music/Instrumental Performance, Music Theory, Music/Vocal Performance, Natural Resources/Rural Development, Naval Science, Office Administration, Office Occupations Education, Organizational Communication, Philosophy, Photography, Physical Education, Physics, Plant Protection, Political Science, Poultry Science, Production/Operations Management, Psychology, Range/Livestock Management, Range Resources, Recreation, Secondary Education, Sociology, Soil Science, Spanish, Special Education, Sport Science, Theatre Arts, Trade/Industrial/Technical Education, Veterinary Science, Visual Communication, Wildlife Resources, Zoology.
**Distribution of degrees:** The majors with the highest enrollment are accounting, elementary education, and electrical engineering.
**Requirements:** General education requirement.
**Academic regulations:** Minimum 2.0 GPA must be maintained.
**Special:** Minors offered in some majors and in over 20 other fields. Chemistry major has several specializations. Double majors. Pass/fail grading option. Internships. Cooperative education programs. Graduate school at which undergraduates may take graduate-level courses. Preprofessional programs in nursing. Member of National Student Exchange (NSE) and Washington, Oregon, Idaho Exchange (WOI). Teacher certification in early childhood, elementary, secondary, and vo-tech education. Study abroad possible. ROTC, NROTC, and AFROTC.
**Honors:** Honors program. Honor societies.
**Academic Assistance:** Remedial reading, writing, math, and study skills. Nonremedial tutoring.

**STUDENT LIFE. Housing:** Students may live on or off campus. Women's and men's dorms. Sorority and fraternity housing. School-owned/operated apartments. On-campus married-student housing. Co-op housing. 65% of students live in college housing.
**Social atmosphere:** The garden, Sub, and Wallace Cafeteria are favorite gathering places. Greeks are influential on campus life. Popular events include homecoming, UI/BSU football games, Mardi Gras, Renaissance Fair, and Jazz Festival.
**Services and counseling/handicapped student services:** Placement services. Health service. Women's center. Day care. Counseling services for minority and older students. Personal and psychological counseling. Career guidance services. Physically disabled student services. Learning disabled services. Notetaking services. Tutors. Reader services for the blind.
**Campus organizations:** Undergraduate student government. Student newspaper (Argonaut, published twice/week). Yearbook. Radio and TV stations. Associated Women Students, ballet, choral group, concert and pep bands, orchestra, University Singers, opera workshop, intercollegiate debating, drama productions, Young Democrats, Young Republicans, 139 organizations in all. 20 fraternities, 18 chapter houses; eight sororities, all with chapter houses. 26% of men join a fraternity. 19% of women join a sorority.
**Religious organizations:** Baptist Student Ministries, Campus Christian Fellowship, Adventist Christian Fellowship, Student Evangelical Fellowship.
**Minority/foreign student organizations:** Native American Student Association, MEChA, Minority Student Round Table. Basque, Indian, Korean, Muslim, Pakistani, and Vietnamese student groups.

**ATHLETICS. Physical education requirements:** None.
**Intercollegiate competition:** 5% of students participate. Basketball (M,W), cheerleading (M,W), cross-country (M,W), football (M), golf (M,W), track (indoor) (M,W), track (outdoor) (M,W), track and field (indoor) (M,W), track and field (outdoor) (M,W), volleyball (W). Member of Big Sky Athletic Conference, NCAA Division I, NCAA Division I-AA for football.
**Intramural and club sports:** Intramural Alpine skiing, badminton, basketball, bowling, flag football, golf, Nordic skiing, racquetball, soccer, softball, swimming, table tennis, tennis, ultimate frisbee, volleyball, walleyball, wrestling. Men's club baseball, ice hockey, rugby, skiing, soccer. Women's club rugby, skiing.

**ADMISSIONS. Academic basis for candidate selection** (in order of priority): Secondary school record, class rank, standardized test scores.
**Nonacademic basis for candidate selection:** Character and personality, geographical distribution, and alumni/ae relationship are considered.

**Requirements:** Graduation from secondary school is required; GED is accepted. No specific distribution of secondary school units required. Minimum composite ACT score of 19 (combined SAT score of 830) or minimum 2.5 GPA required. SAT or ACT is required. Campus visit recommended. Off-campus interviews available with an admissions representative.

**Procedure:** Suggest filing application by February 15. Application deadline is August 1. Notification of admission on rolling basis. No set date by which applicants must accept offer. $100 room deposit, refundable until August 1. Freshmen accepted for terms other than fall.

**Special programs:** Admission may be deferred. Credit and/or placement may be granted through CEEB Advanced Placement exams for scores of 3 or higher. Credit and/or placement may be granted through CLEP general and subject exams. Credit and placement may be granted through challenge exams. Early entrance/early admission program. Concurrent enrollment program.

**Transfer students:** Transfer students accepted for terms other than fall. In fall 1993, 38% of all new students were transfers into all classes. 1,363 transfer applications were received, 1,200 were accepted. Application deadline is August 1 for fall; December 15 for spring. Minimum 2.0 GPA required. Lowest course grade accepted is "D." Maximum number of transferable credits is 70 semester hours. At least 32 semester hours must be completed at the university to receive degree.

**Admissions contact:** Peter Brown, M.A.T., Director of Admissions. 208 885-6326.

**FINANCIAL AID. Available aid:** Pell grants, SEOG, state scholarships and grants, school scholarships and grants, private scholarships, ROTC scholarships, academic merit scholarships, and athletic scholarships. Perkins Loans (NDSL), PLUS, Stafford Loans (GSL), school loans, private loans, and SLS. Direct federal loans. Deferred payment plan.

**Financial aid statistics:** 38% of aid is not need-based. In 1993-94, 70% of all freshman applicants received aid. Average amounts of aid awarded freshmen: Scholarships and grants, $800; loans, $2,200.

**Supporting data/closing dates:** FAFSA/FAF/FFS: Priority filing date is January 30. School's own aid application: Priority filing date is February 15. Notification of awards on rolling basis.

**Financial aid contact:** Dan Davenport, Ph.D., Director of Financial Aid. 208 885-6312.

**STUDENT EMPLOYMENT.** College Work/Study Program. Institutional employment. 35% of full-time undergraduates work on campus during school year. Students may expect to earn an average of $1,200 during school year. Off-campus part-time employment opportunities rated "good."

**COMPUTER FACILITIES.** 800 IBM/IBM-compatible, Macintosh/Apple, and RISC-/UNIX-based microcomputers; 350 are networked. Students may access Hewlett-Packard, IBM, SUN minicomputer/mainframe systems. Residence halls may be equipped with networked microcomputers. Computer languages and software packages include COBOL, dBASE, Excel, Lotus 1-2-3, Microsoft Word, Pascal, WordPerfect. Computer facilities are available to all students.

**Fees:** Computer fee is included in tuition/fees.

**Hours:** 24 hours.

**PROMINENT ALUMNI/AE.** Philip Habib, statesman; James McClure and Steven Symms, U.S. senators; Terrell Bell, educator, former U.S. secretary of education.

# Illinois

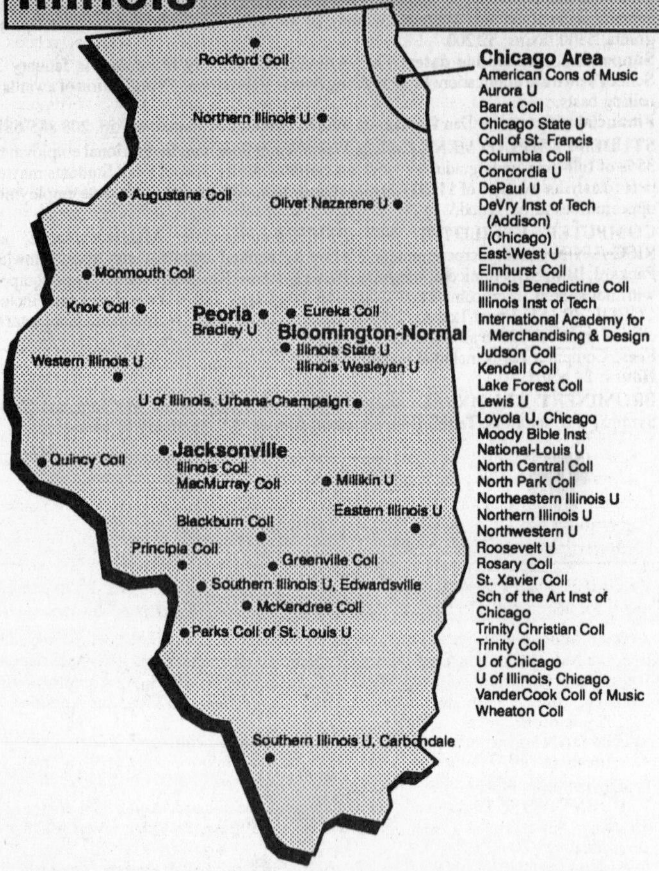


## American Conservatory of Music

**Chicago, IL 60602** **312 263-4161**

**1993-94 Costs.** Tuition: $4,680. Fees, books, misc. academic expenses (school's estimate): $550.
**Enrollment.** Undergraduates: 80 men, 35 women (full-time). Graduate enrollment: 107.
**Test score averages/ranges.** N/A.
**Faculty.** 12 full-time; 90 part-time. 20% of faculty holds doctoral degree. Student/faculty ratio: 2 to 1.
**Selectivity rating.** N/A.

**PROFILE.** The American Conservatory of Music, founded in 1886, is a private institution. Its campus is located in downtown Chicago, near the Chicago Symphony Orchestra and the Chicago Lyric Opera.

**Accreditation:** Professionally accredited by the National Association of Schools of Music.
**Religious orientation:** American Conservatory of Music is nonsectarian; no religious requirements.
**Library:** Collections totaling over 8,929 volumes, 309 periodical subscriptions and 929 microform items.
**STUDENT BODY. Undergraduate profile:** Average age of undergraduates is 26.
**Undergraduate achievement:** 70% of students who completed a degree program immediately went on to graduate study.
**Foreign students:** Countries represented include China, Indonesia, Japan, and Korea.
**PROGRAMS OF STUDY. Degrees:** B.Mus., B.Mus.Ed.
**Majors:** Composition, Jazz Composition/Arranging, Music Performance, Piano Pedagogy, Theory.
**Requirements:** General education requirement.
**Special:** Minors offered in guitar, piano, and voice. Piano Technician Department offers two-semester professional course. Certificate program offered in jazz and commercial music. Associate's degrees offered. Dual degrees. Independent study. Accelerated study. Graduate school at which undergraduates may take graduate-level courses. Preprofessional programs in music. Member of consortium with Roosevelt U and Sch of the Art Inst of Chicago. Teacher certification in elementary and secondary education.
**Academic Assistance:** Nonremedial tutoring.
**ADMISSIONS. Academic basis for candidate selection** (in order of priority): Secondary school record, school's recommendation.
**Nonacademic basis for candidate selection:** Character and personality and extracurricular participation are considered.
**Requirements:** Graduation from secondary school is required; GED is accepted. 15 units and the following program of study are required: 3 units of English, 3 units of math, 3 units of social studies, 6 units of academic electives. Electives should include foreign language. Students not normally admissible must eliminate deficiencies within one year of initial enrollment. SAT is recommended; ACT may be substituted. Campus visit and interview recommended. Off-campus interviews available with an admissions representative.
**Procedure:** Suggest filing application by August 1. Notification of admission on rolling basis. Freshmen accepted for terms other than fall.
**Special programs:** Admission may be deferred. Credit and/or placement may be granted through CLEP subject exams. Early decision program.
**Transfer students:** Transfer students accepted for terms other than fall. Lowest course grade accepted is "C."
**Admissions contact:** Joseph L. Miller, Ph.D., Dean of Admissions. 312 263-4161.
**FINANCIAL AID. Available aid:** Pell grants, SEOG, and state grants. Perkins Loans (NDSL), PLUS, and Stafford Loans (GSL). Deferred payment plan.
**Supporting data/closing dates:** FAFSA: Accepted on rolling basis. Notification of awards on rolling basis.
**Financial aid contact:** Linda Thomas, Business Manager. 312 263-4161.

## Augustana College

**Rock Island, IL 61201** **309 794-7000**

**1994-95 Costs.** Tuition: $13,353. Room & board: $4,173. Fees, books, misc. academic expenses (school's estimate): $1,093.
**Enrollment.** Undergraduates: 839 men, 1,111 women (full-time). Freshman class: 1,879 applicants, 1,658 accepted, 497 enrolled.
**Test score averages/ranges.** Average ACT scores: 25 composite. Range of ACT scores of middle 50%: 21-28 composite.
**Faculty.** 142 full-time; 33 part-time. 83% of faculty holds highest degree in specific field. Student/faculty ratio: 12 to 1.
**Selectivity rating.** Competitive.

**PROFILE.** Augustana, founded in 1860, is a church-affiliated, liberal arts college. Its 100-acre campus is located in Rock Island, in the Quad-City region between Chicago and Des Moines.

**Accreditation:** NCACS. Professionally accredited by the Council on Social Work Education, the National Association of Schools of Music, the National Council for Accreditation of Teacher Education.
**Religious orientation:** Augustana College is affiliated with the Evangelical Lutheran Church in America; six terms of religion/theology required.
**Library:** Collections totaling over 374,232 volumes, 1,489 periodical subscriptions, and 95,783 microform items.
**Special facilities/museums:** Art gallery, black culture house, Hispanic culture house, geology museum, on-campus preschool, immigration research center, scanning electron microscope, transmission electron microscope, nuclear magnetic resonance, atomic absorption, and diode array mass spectrophotometers, planetarium, observatory with celestron telescope, environmental field stations.
**Athletic facilities:** Physical education center, swimming pool, athletic fields, tennis courts.
**STUDENT BODY. Undergraduate profile:** 80% are state residents; 15% are transfers. 2% Asian-American, 3% Black, 2% Hispanic, 1% Native American, 92% White. Average age of undergraduates is 20.
**Freshman profile:** 34% of accepted applicants took SAT; 86% took ACT. 89% of freshmen come from public schools.
**Undergraduate achievement:** 85% of fall 1991 freshmen returned for fall 1992 term. 68% of entering class graduated. 33% of students who completed a degree program went on to graduate study within one year.
**Foreign students:** 54 students are from out of the country. Countries represented include India, Korea, Laos, and Sweden; 24 in all.
**PROGRAMS OF STUDY. Degrees:** A.B., B.A.
**Majors:** Accounting, Art, Art Education, Art History, Asian Studies, Biology, Business Administration, Chemistry, Classics, Clinical Lab Sciences, Computer Science, Computer Science/Mathematics, Earth Science Teaching, Economics, Elementary Education, Engineering Physics, English, French, Geography, Geology, German, History, Mathematics, Music, Music Education, Music/Instrumental, Music/Voice, Philosophy, Physical Education, Physics, Political Science, Pre-Dentistry, Pre-Medicine, Psychology, Public Administration/International Management, Religion, Scandinavian, Social Work, Sociology, Spanish, Speech Communication, Speech/Language Pathology, Theatre.
**Distribution of degrees:** The majors with the highest enrollment are business administration, biology, and English.
**Requirements:** General education requirement.
**Academic regulations:** Minimum 2.0 GPA must be maintained.
**Special:** Minors offered in most majors and in African American studies, anthropology, athletic training, biochemistry, coaching, environmental studies, ethics, journalism, Latin American studies, studio art, and women's studies. Foundations honors program offers interdisciplinary, team-taught courses. Double majors. Dual degrees. Independent study. Internships. Graduate school at which undergraduates may take graduate-level courses. Preprofessional programs in law, medicine, veterinary science, pharmacy, dentistry, theology, optometry, engineering, occupational therapy, and physical therapy. 3-2 engineering programs with Iowa State U, U of Illinois at Urbana-Champaign, and Washington U. 3-2 forestry and environmental studies program with Duke U. 3-2 landscape architecture program with U of Illinois at Urbana-Champaign. 3-2 occupational therapy program with Washington U. Combined medical technology program with U of Iowa, U of Wisconsin, and Hines V.A., Peoria Methodist Center, and Rockford Memorial Hospitals. Teacher certification in elementary and secondary education. Certification in specific subject

areas. Exchange programs abroad in China (Huazhong Normal U), Germany (U of Passau), Peru (U Catolica de Santa Maria), and Sweden (U of Karstad, U of Uppsala, U of Vaxjo). Study abroad also in Ecuador, France, Greece, Israel, and Italy. International internship program.
**Honors:** Phi Beta Kappa. Honors program. Honor societies.
**Academic Assistance:** Nonremedial tutoring.

**STUDENT LIFE. Housing:** All freshmen, sophomores, and juniors must live on campus. Coed, women's, and men's dorms. School-owned/operated apartments. Off-campus privately-owned housing. 63% of students live in college housing.
**Social atmosphere:** As reported by the student newspaper, social life is "dominated by Greek groups." Also influential is CUBOM, an organization that plans social events, trips, lectures, concerts, and movies. "CUBOM gets the entire campus involved." The big events of the year are Homecoming, the IS-IF Formal, Greek Week, the Humanities Festival, the Stagg Bowl football game, and the Campus Ministry's lecture series. Off campus, students frequent Whitey's ice cream shop, and Lee's and Grandinetti's, a couple of nightspots.
**Services and counseling/handicapped student services:** Placement services. Health service. Women's center. Counseling services for minority students. Personal and psychological counseling. Career and academic guidance services. Religious counseling. Physically disabled student services. Reader services for the blind.
**Campus organizations:** Undergraduate student government. Student newspaper (Observer, published once/week). Literary magazine. Yearbook. Radio station. Band, choir, chorus, jazz ensembles, orchestra, Handel Oratorio Society, Koto Ensemble, opera workshop, theatre group, dance company, cheerleading, Feminist Forum, Global Affect, Amnesty International, departmental, political, professional, and special-interest groups, 150 organizations in all. Seven fraternities, no chapter houses; seven sororities, no chapter houses. 40% of men join a fraternity. 40% of women join a sorority.
**Religious organizations:** Diakonos, Fellowship of Christian Athletes, Intervarsity Christian Fellowship, Windows of the World.
**Minority/foreign student organizations:** Black Student Union, LOVE, Majestic Gents, Latin American Council, Latinos Unidos. International Club.

**ATHLETICS. Physical education requirements:** Three terms of physical education required.
**Intercollegiate competition:** 28% of students participate. Baseball (M), basketball (M,W), cross-country (M,W), diving (M,W), football (M), golf (M), soccer (M,W), softball (W), swimming (M,W), tennis (M,W), track and field (indoor) (M,W), track and field (outdoor) (M,W), volleyball (W), wrestling (M). Member of College Conference of Illinois and Wisconsin, NCAA Division III.
**Intramural and club sports:** 20% of students participate. Intramural badminton, basketball, cross-country, football, golf, frisbee golf, racquetball, soccer, softball, swimming, table tennis, tennis, track/field, volleyball, water basketball, wrestling.

**ADMISSIONS. Academic basis for candidate selection** (in order of priority): Secondary school record, standardized test scores, class rank, school's recommendation, essay.
**Nonacademic basis for candidate selection:** Extracurricular participation and particular talent or ability are important. Character and personality, geographical distribution, and alumni/ae relationship are considered.
**Requirements:** Graduation from secondary school is required; GED is accepted. No specific distribution of secondary school units required. 1-1/2 units of algebra, 1 unit of plane geometry, and 1/2 unit of trigonometry recommended of science, engineering, and math program applicants. Campus visit and interview with faculty required of Foundations honor program applicants. Academic skills program for applicants not normally admissible. SAT or ACT is required. Campus visit and interview recommended. Off-campus interviews available with an admissions representative.
**Procedure:** Take SAT or ACT by January of 12th year. Visit college for interview by May of 12th year. Notification of admission on rolling basis. Reply is required by May 1. $200 nonrefundable tuition deposit. Freshmen accepted for terms other than fall.
**Special programs:** Admission may be deferred one year. Credit and/or placement may be granted through CEEB Advanced Placement exams for scores of 3 or higher. Placement may be granted through challenge exams.
**Transfer students:** Transfer students accepted for terms other than fall. In fall 1993, 15% of all new students were transfers into all classes. 208 transfer applications were received, 157 were accepted. Minimum 2.5 GPA recommended. Lowest course grade accepted is "D." Maximum number of transferable credits is 60 semester hours from two-year schools. At least 30 semester hours must be completed at the college to receive degree.
**Admissions contact:** Martin R. Saver, M.B.A., Director of Admissions/Associate Dean for Enrollment. 309 794-7341.

**FINANCIAL AID. Available aid:** Pell grants, SEOG, state scholarships and grants, school scholarships and grants, private scholarships and grants, academic merit scholarships, and aid for undergraduate foreign students. Perkins Loans (NDSL), PLUS, Stafford Loans (GSL), state loans, and SLS. Tuition Plan Inc., Knight Tuition Plans, AMS, and family tuition reduction.
**Financial aid statistics:** 33% of aid is not need-based. In 1993-94, 93% of all undergraduate applicants received aid; 96% of freshman applicants. Average amounts of aid awarded freshmen: Scholarships and grants, $7,714; loans, $2,855.
**Supporting data/closing dates:** FAFSA/FAF: Accepted on rolling basis. School's own aid application: Accepted on rolling basis. Income tax forms: Accepted on rolling basis. Notification of awards on rolling basis.
**Financial aid contact:** Sue Standley, Director of Financial Aid. 309 794-7207.

**STUDENT EMPLOYMENT.** College Work/Study Program. Institutional employment. 63% of full-time undergraduates work on campus during school year. Students may expect to earn an average of $850 during school year. Off-campus part-time employment opportunities rated "good."

**COMPUTER FACILITIES.** 550 IBM/IBM-compatible, Macintosh/Apple, and RISC-/UNIX-based microcomputers; 500 are networked. Students may access Digital, SUN minicomputer/mainframe systems, BITNET, Internet. Residence halls may be equipped with stand-alone microcomputers, networked microcomputers. Client/LAN operating systems include Apple/Macintosh, DOS, UNIX/XENIX/AIX, LocalTalk/AppleTalk, Novell. Computer languages and software packages include Ada, AutoCAD, BASIC, C, COBOL, Corel Draw, FORTRAN, LISP, MathCAD, Paradox, Pascal, Prolog, Quattro, WordPerfect; 75 in all. Some computers located in labs are available only to students in specific majors.
**Fees:** None.
**Hours:** 24 hours in residence halls.

**GRADUATE CAREER DATA.** Graduate school percentages: 4% enter law school. 5% enter medical school. 1% enter dental school. 3% enter graduate business programs. 17% enter graduate arts and sciences programs. 1% enter theological school/seminary. Highest graduate school enrollments: Duke U, Northwestern U, U of Chicago, U of Illinois, U of Iowa, U of Kansas, Washington U. 50% of graduates choose careers in business and industry. Companies and businesses that hire graduates: Arthur Andersen, AT&T, Deere & Co., Hewlett-Packard, IBM.

**PROMINENT ALUMNI/AE.** Robert Sweiringa, Financial Accounting Standard Board; Dr. Charlotte Erickson, historian; Ken Anderson, professional football player; Robert A. Hanson, retired CEO and board chair, Deere & Co.

# Aurora University

**Aurora, IL 60506** **708 892-6431**

**1994-95 Costs.** Tuition: $10,250. Room & Board: $3,850. Fees, books, misc. academic expenses (school's estimate): $500.
**Enrollment.** Undergraduates: 355 men, 432 women (full-time). Freshman class: 532 applicants, 481 accepted, 127 enrolled. Graduate enrollment: 151 men, 288 women.
**Test score averages/ranges.** Average ACT scores: 21 composite. Range of ACT scores of middle 50%: 18-25 composite.
**Faculty.** 83 full-time; 70 part-time. 43% of faculty holds doctoral degree. Student/faculty ratio: 14 to 1.
**Selectivity rating.** Less competitive.

**PROFILE.** Aurora, founded in 1893, is a private, liberal arts university. Its 26-acre campus is located in a residential area, less than an hour from downtown Chicago.

**Accreditation:** NCACS. Professionally accredited by the Council on Social Work Education, the National League for Nursing, the National Recreation and Park Association.
**Religious orientation:** Aurora University is nonsectarian; no religious requirements.
**Library:** Collections totaling over 132,996 volumes, 762 periodical subscriptions, and 79,523 microform items.
**Special facilities/museums:** Center for Native American culture.
**Athletic facilities:** Gymnasium, racquetball courts, weight room, baseball, football, soccer, and softball fields.

**STUDENT BODY. Undergraduate profile:** 89% are state residents; 55% are transfers. 3% Asian-American, 14% Black, 7% Hispanic, 75% White, 1% Other. Average age of undergraduates is 20.
**Freshman profile:** 3% of freshmen who took ACT scored 30 or over on composite; 25% scored 24 or over on composite; 81% scored 18 or over on composite; 99% scored 12 or over on composite. 2% of accepted applicants took SAT; 98% took ACT.
**Undergraduate achievement:** 12% of students who completed a degree program immediately went on to graduate study.

**PROGRAMS OF STUDY. Degrees:** B.A., B.S., B.S.Nurs., B.Soc.Work.
**Majors:** Accounting, Biology, Business Administration, Chemistry, Christian Studies, Communication, Computer Information Systems, Computer Science, Computer Science/Business, Criminal Justice, Criminal Justice Management, Economics, Elementary Education, Engineering Science, English, Environmental Science, Finance, Health Sciences, History, Industrial Management, Management, Marketing, Mathematics, Nursing, Philosophy, Physical Education, Political Science, Psychology, Recreation, Social Work, Sociology.
**Distribution of degrees:** The majors with the highest enrollment are nursing, business administration, and communication.
**Requirements:** General education requirement.
**Academic regulations:** Minimum 2.0 GPA must be maintained.
**Special:** Minors offered in many majors and in art, education, health education, music, physics, physiology, religion, and theatre. Concentrations in pre-law and secondary education. Certificate programs in accounting and management. Self-designed majors. Double majors. Independent study. Pass/fail grading option. Internships. Graduate school at which undergraduates may take graduate-level courses. Preprofessional programs in law, medicine, veterinary science, and dentistry. Member of four-college Council of West Suburban Colleges; cross-registration possible. Semester in the American West program. Nursing program offered both at main campus and at Illinois Masonic Medical Center in Chicago. Teacher certification in elementary and secondary education. Certification in specific subject areas. Exchange programs abroad in England (Edge Hill Coll, Lansdown Coll). Study abroad also in Spain. ROTC at Wheaton Coll.
**Honors:** Honors program. Honor societies.
**Academic Assistance:** Remedial study skills. Nonremedial tutoring.

**ADMISSIONS. Academic basis for candidate selection** (in order of priority): Standardized test scores, class rank, secondary school record, essay, school's recommendation.
**Nonacademic basis for candidate selection:** Extracurricular participation, geographical distribution, and alumni/ae relationship are important. Character and personality and particular talent or ability are considered.
**Requirements:** Graduation from secondary school is recommended; GED is accepted. No specific distribution of secondary school units required. College-preparatory program recommended. Minimum composite ACT score of 19, rank in top half of secondary school class, and minimum 2.0 GPA required. Separate admissions program for social work, nursing, and education program applicants. Conditional admission possible for applicants not meeting standard requirements. ACT is required; SAT may be substituted. Campus visit and interview recommended. Off-campus interviews available with an admissions representative.
**Procedure:** Take SAT or ACT by spring of 12th year. Notification of admission on rolling basis. $50 tuition deposit, refundable until May 1. $100 room deposit, refundable until May 1. Freshmen accepted for terms other than fall.

**Special programs:** Credit and/or placement may be granted through CEEB Advanced Placement exams for scores of 3 or higher. Credit and/or placement may be granted through CLEP general and subject exams. Placement may be granted through challenge exams. Credit and placement may be granted through ACT PEP and DANTES exams, and military and life experience.
**Transfer students:** Transfer students accepted for terms other than fall. In fall 1993, 55% of all new students were transfers into all classes. 357 transfer applications were received, 345 were accepted. Application deadline is rolling for fall; rolling for spring. Minimum 2.0 GPA required. SAT/ACT scores required of transfer applicants with fewer than 15 semester hours. Both secondary school and college transcripts required of transfer applicants with fewer than 15 semester hours. Lowest course grade accepted is "C." Maximum number of transferable credits is 60 semester hours from a two-year school and 90 semester hours from a four-year school. At least 30 semester hours must be completed at the university to receive degree.
**Admissions contact:** Frank Johnson, M.S., Director of Admissions. 708 896-1975.

**FINANCIAL AID. Available aid:** Pell grants, SEOG, state scholarships and grants, school scholarships and grants, private scholarships and grants, and academic merit scholarships. Perkins Loans (NDSL), PLUS, Stafford Loans (GSL), state loans, school loans, and SLS. Tuition Plan Inc. and Tuition Management Systems.
**Financial aid statistics:** 20% of aid is not need-based. In 1993-94, 90% of all undergraduate applicants received aid; 95% of freshman applicants.
**Supporting data/closing dates:** FAFSA: Accepted on rolling basis. Income tax forms: Accepted on rolling basis. Notification of awards begins March 1.
**Financial aid contact:** Heather Gutierrez, Director of Financial Aid. 708 844-5149.

# Barat College

**Lake Forest, IL 60045** **708 234-3000**

**1994-95 Costs.** Tuition: $10,560. Room & board: $4,500. Fees, books, misc. academic expenses (school's estimate): $440.
**Enrollment.** Undergraduates: 142 men, 311 women (full-time). Freshman class: 261 applicants, 192 accepted, 111 enrolled.
**Test score averages/ranges.** Average SAT scores: 468 verbal, 474 math. Range of SAT scores of middle 50%: 410-500 verbal, 440-510 math. Average ACT scores: 22 English, 20 math, 21 composite. Range of ACT scores of middle 50%: 18-24 English, 14-22 math.
**Faculty.** 40 full-time; 55 part-time. 60% of faculty holds doctoral degree. Student/faculty ratio: 12 to 1.
**Selectivity rating.** Noncompetitive.

**PROFILE.** Barat is a church-affiliated, liberal arts college. It was founded in 1858 as an academy for women, became a four-year college in 1919, and adopted coeducation in 1982. Its 30-acre campus is located in Lake Forest, 30 miles north of Chicago.

**Accreditation:** NCACS.
**Religious orientation:** Barat College is affiliated with the Roman Catholic Church; no religious requirements.
**Library:** Collections totaling over 98,952 volumes, 11,174 periodical subscriptions, and 4,508 microform items.
**Athletic facilities:** Gymnasium, fitness and weight rooms, basketball, tennis, and volleyball courts, athletic fields.

**STUDENT BODY. Undergraduate profile:** 81% are state residents; 57% are transfers. 4% Asian-American, 7% Black, 3% Hispanic, 85% White, 1% Other. Average age of undergraduates is 22.
**Freshman profile:** 5% of freshmen who took SAT scored 600 or over on verbal, 5% scored 600 or over on math; 37% scored 500 or over on verbal, 41% scored 500 or over on math; 82% scored 400 or over on verbal, 86% scored 400 or over on math; 100% scored 300 or over on verbal, 100% scored 300 or over on math. 2% of freshmen who took ACT scored 30 or over on English, 2% scored 30 or over on math; 27% scored 24 or over on English, 15% scored 24 or over on math, 22% scored 24 or over on composite; 86% scored 18 or over on English, 65% scored 18 or over on math, 89% scored 18 or over on composite; 100% scored 12 or over on English, 100% scored 12 or over on math, 100% scored 12 or over on composite. 25% of accepted applicants took SAT; 76% took ACT. 76% of freshmen come from public schools.
**Undergraduate achievement:** 80% of fall 1991 freshmen returned for fall 1992 term. 50% of entering class graduated. 25% of students who completed a degree program went on to graduate study within two years.
**Foreign students:** 42 students are from out of the country. Countries represented include Canada, China, England, Germany, Greece, and Japan; 15 in all.

**PROGRAMS OF STUDY. Degrees:** B.A., B.F.A., B.S., B.S.Nurs.
**Majors:** Accounting, Art Therapy, Banking/Finance, Ceramics, Chemistry, Communication Arts, Computing Information Systems, Dance, Dance Therapy, Economics, Education/Psychology, English, Fiber, Health Studies, Human Resources, Humanities, International Trade/Finance, Management/Business, Marketing Management/Research, Mathematics/Computer Studies, Nursing, Painting, Performing Arts, Photography, Political Science, Psychology, Science/Mathematics/Computer Studies, Sociology, Studio Art.
**Distribution of degrees:** The majors with the highest enrollment are management/business, education, and psychology; chemistry, economics, and sociology have the lowest.
**Requirements:** General education requirement.
**Academic regulations:** Minimum 2.0 GPA must be maintained.
**Special:** Minors offered in some majors and in approximately 14 other fields. Self-designed majors. Double majors. Independent study. Accelerated study. Pass/fail grading option. Internships. Graduate school at which undergraduates may take graduate-level courses. Preprofessional programs in law, medicine, and physical therapy. B.S.N. completion, 2-2 medical technology, 2-2 physician assistant, and 2-2 medical radiation physics programs with U of Health Sciences/Chicago Medical Sch. Cross-registration and cooperation with Lake Forest Coll. Teacher certification in elementary, secondary, and special education. Certification in specific subject areas. Study abroad in Australia and in African, European, Latin American, and South Asian countries.
**Honors:** Honor societies.
**Academic Assistance:** Remedial reading, writing, math, and study skills. Nonremedial tutoring.

**ADMISSIONS. Academic basis for candidate selection** (in order of priority): Secondary school record, class rank, standardized test scores, essay, school's recommendation.
**Nonacademic basis for candidate selection:** Character and personality, extracurricular participation, and particular talent or ability are important.
**Requirements:** Graduation from secondary school is required; GED is accepted. 16 units and the following program of study are recommended: 4 units of English, 2 units of math, 2 units of science, 2 units of foreign language, 2 units of social studies, 1 unit of history, 3 units of electives. Minimum composite ACT score of 18 (combined SAT score of 900), rank in top half of secondary school class, and minimum 2.5 GPA recommended. Auditions required of dance program applicants. R.N. required of nursing program applicants. Conditional admission possible for applicants not meeting standard requirements. SAT or ACT is required. Campus visit and interview recommended. Off-campus interviews available with an admissions representative.
**Procedure:** Notification of admission on rolling basis. $100 nonrefundable tuition deposit. $225 room deposit, refundable until May 1. Freshmen accepted for terms other than fall.

**Special programs:** Admission may be deferred one year. Credit and/or placement may be granted through CEEB Advanced Placement exams for scores of 3 or higher. Credit and/or placement may be granted through CLEP general and subject exams. Credit and placement may be granted through ACT PEP and DANTES exams and life experience.
**Transfer students:** Transfer students accepted for terms other than fall. In fall 1992, 57% of all new students were transfers into all classes. 232 transfer applications were received, 204 were accepted. Application deadline is rolling for fall; rolling for spring. Minimum 2.0 GPA required. Lowest course grade accepted is "C." Maximum number of transferable credits is 60 semester hours from a two-year school and 75 semester hours from a four-year school. At least 45 semester hours must be completed at the college to receive degree.
**Admissions contact:** Loretta Brickman, B.M.E., Director of Admissions. 708 234-3000.

**FINANCIAL AID. Available aid:** Pell grants, SEOG, state scholarships and grants, school scholarships, academic merit scholarships, and athletic scholarships. Perkins Loans (NDSL), PLUS, Stafford Loans (GSL), state loans, and SLS. Deferred payment plan.
**Financial aid statistics:** 18% of aid is not need-based. In 1992-93, 70% of all undergraduate applicants received aid; 92% of freshman applicants. Average amounts of aid awarded freshmen: Scholarships and grants, $1,500; loans, $2,625.
**Supporting data/closing dates:** FAFSA/FAF/FFS: Accepted on rolling basis. School's own aid application: Accepted on rolling basis. Income tax forms. Notification of awards on rolling basis.
**Financial aid contact:** Sharon Stang, M.A., Director of Financial Aid. 708 234-3000.

# Blackburn College

**Carlinville, IL 62626** **217 854-3231**

**1993-94 Costs.** Tuition: $7,820. Room & board: $1,000. Fees, books, misc. academic expenses (school's estimate): $800.
**Enrollment.** Undergraduates: 222 men, 225 women (full-time). Freshman class: 423 applicants, 329 accepted, 177 enrolled.
**Test score averages/ranges.** Average ACT scores: 21 composite.
**Faculty.** 37 full-time; 9 part-time. 82% of faculty holds highest degree in specific field. Student/faculty ratio: 14 to 1.
**Selectivity rating.** Competitive.

**PROFILE.** Blackburn, founded in 1837, is a church-affiliated, liberal arts college. Its 80-acre campus is located in Carlinville, 60 miles from St. Louis, Mo.

**Accreditation:** NCACS.
**Religious orientation:** Blackburn College is affiliated with the Presbyterian Church; no religious requirements.
**Library:** Collections totaling over 84,000 volumes, 283 periodical subscriptions, and 84,668 microform items.
**Special facilities/museums:** Electron microscope.
**Athletic facilities:** Swimming pool, basketball, racquetball, and tennis courts, weight rooms, playing fields, gymnasium.

**STUDENT BODY. Undergraduate profile:** 80% are state residents; 17% are transfers. 12% Black, 1% Hispanic, 1% Native American, 83% White, 3% Other. Average age of undergraduates is 19.
**Freshman profile:** 1% of freshmen who took ACT scored 30 or over on composite; 15% scored 24 or over on composite; 70% scored 18 or over on composite; 99% scored 12 or over on composite; 100% scored 6 or over on composite. 4% of accepted applicants took SAT; 96% took ACT. 85% of freshmen come from public schools.
**Undergraduate achievement:** 48% of fall 1991 freshmen returned for fall 1992 term. 29% of entering class graduated.
**Foreign students:** 14 students are from out of the country. Countries represented include African and Asian countries; seven in all.

**PROGRAMS OF STUDY. Degrees:** B.A.
**Majors:** Art, Biology, Business Administration/Accounting, Business Administration/Management, Chemistry, Computer/Information Sciences, Elementary Education, English/American Literature, History, Interdisciplinary Major, Mathematics, Medical Technology, Music, Physical Education, Political Science, Psychology, Public Administration, Secondary Teaching of English, Secondary Teaching of Social Sciences, Spanish.

**Distribution of degrees:** The majors with the highest enrollment are business administration, psychology, and elementary education; art, English/American literature, and music have the lowest.
**Requirements:** General education requirement.
**Academic regulations:** Freshmen must maintain minimum 1.6 GPA; sophomores, 1.8 GPA; juniors, 2.0 GPA; seniors, 2.0 GPA.
**Special:** Minors offered in several majors and in art history, economics, French, international relations, philosophy, public policy analysis, religion, secondary teaching of Spanish, and studio art. Associate's degrees offered. Self-designed majors. Double majors. Dual degrees. Independent study. Pass/fail grading option. Internships. Preprofessional programs in law, medicine, veterinary science, and dentistry. 3-1 medical technology program. 3-2 engineering program. Washington Semester. Teacher certification in elementary and secondary education. Study abroad in Europe and Mexico.
**Academic Assistance:** Nonremedial tutoring.

**ADMISSIONS. Academic basis for candidate selection** (in order of priority): Secondary school record, class rank, standardized test scores.
**Nonacademic basis for candidate selection:** Extracurricular participation and particular talent or ability are considered.
**Requirements:** Graduation from secondary school is required; GED is accepted. 12 units and the following program of study are recommended: 4 units of English, 2 units of math, 2 units of science, 2 units of foreign language, 2 units of social studies. Minimum composite ACT score of 18, rank in top half of secondary school class, and minimum 2.3 GPA required. SAT or ACT is required. Campus visit and interview recommended. Off-campus interviews available with admissions and alumni representatives.
**Procedure:** Take SAT or ACT by June of 12th year. Notification of admission on rolling basis. No set date by which applicants must accept offer. $50 room deposit, refundable until May 15. Freshmen accepted for terms other than fall.
**Special programs:** Admission may be deferred one year. Credit and/or placement may be granted through CEEB Advanced Placement exams for scores of 3 or higher. Credit and/or placement may be granted through CLEP general and subject exams. Credit may be granted through military experience. Early entrance/early admission program.
**Transfer students:** Transfer students accepted for terms other than fall. In fall 1992, 17% of all new students were transfers into all classes. Application deadline is rolling for fall; rolling for spring. Minimum 2.5 GPA recommended. Lowest course grade accepted is "C." At least 30 credits must be completed at the college to receive degree.
**Admissions contact:** John Malin, Director of Admissions. 217 854-3231, extension 215.

**FINANCIAL AID. Available aid:** Pell grants, SEOG, state scholarships and grants, school scholarships and grants, private scholarships, academic merit scholarships, and aid for undergraduate foreign students. Perkins Loans (NDSL), PLUS, Stafford Loans (GSL), school loans, and SLS. AMS and Tuition Management Systems.
**Financial aid statistics:** In 1992-93, 90% of all undergraduate applicants received aid; 91% of freshman applicants. Average amounts of aid awarded freshmen: Scholarships and grants, $6,800; loans, $1,880.
**Supporting data/closing dates:** FAFSA/FAF/FSS: Priority filing date is April 1; accepted on rolling basis. Income tax forms: Accepted on rolling basis. Notification of awards on rolling basis.
**Financial aid contact:** Cheryl A. Gardner, Director of Financial Aid. 217 854-3231, extension 292.

# Bradley University

**Peoria, IL 61625** **309 676-7611**

**1994-95 Costs.** Tuition: $10,880. Room & board: $4,400. Fees, books, misc. academic expenses (school's estimate): $500.
**Enrollment.** Undergraduates: 2,285 men, 2,246 women (full-time). Freshman class: 3,767 applicants, 3,414 accepted, 1,061 enrolled. Graduate enrollment: 447 men, 403 women.
**Test score averages/ranges.** Average SAT scores: 530 verbal, 590 math. Range of SAT scores of middle 50%: 450-600 verbal, 550-700 math. Average ACT scores: 25 composite. Range of ACT scores of middle 50%: 21-30 composite.
**Faculty.** 304 full-time. 80% of faculty holds highest degree in specific field. Student/faculty ratio: 16 to 1.
**Selectivity rating.** Competitive.

**PROFILE.** Bradley, founded in 1897, is a private university. Programs are offered through the Colleges of Business Administration, Communications and Fine Arts, Education and Health Sciences, Engineering and Technology, and Liberal Arts and Sciences and the Graduate School. Its 35-acre campus is located in a residential area of Peoria.

**Accreditation:** NCACS. Professionally accredited by the Accreditation Board for Engineering and Technology, the American Assembly of Collegiate Schools of Business, the American Council for Construction Education, the National Association of Schools of Art and Design, the National Association of Schools of Music, the National Council for Accreditation of Teacher Education, the National League for Nursing.
**Religious orientation:** Bradley University is nonsectarian; no religious requirements.
**Library:** Collections totaling over 521,265 volumes, 2,612 periodical subscriptions, and 21,521 microform items.
**Special facilities/museums:** Art museum, language lab, urban studies institute.
**Athletic facilities:** Recreation hall, field house, athletic fields, basketball and volleyball courts.

**STUDENT BODY. Undergraduate profile:** 76% are state residents; 27% are transfers. 3% Asian-American, 6% Black, 2% Hispanic, 87% White, 2% Other. Average age of undergraduates is 20.
**Freshman profile:** 4% of freshmen who took SAT scored 700 or over on verbal, 15% scored 700 or over on math; 26% scored 600 or over on verbal, 49% scored 600 or over on math; 64% scored 500 or over on verbal, 87% scored 500 or over on math; 95% scored 400 or over on verbal, 98% scored 400 or over on math; 99% scored 300 or over on verbal, 100% scored 300 or over on math. 30% of accepted applicants took SAT; 86% took ACT. 75% of freshmen come from public schools.
**Undergraduate achievement:** 87% of fall 1992 freshmen returned for fall 1993 term.
**Foreign students:** 239 students are from out of the country. Countries represented include India, Kuwait, Lebanon, Malaysia, Panama, and Saudi Arabia; 39 in all.

**PROGRAMS OF STUDY. Degrees:** B.A., B.F.A., B.Mus., B.Mus.Ed., B.S.
**Majors:** Accounting, Administration of Criminal Justice, Advertising, Art, Art Education, Art History, Biochemistry, Biology, Biotechnology, Business Computer Systems, Business Management/Administration, Ceramics, Chemistry, Civil Engineering, Communication, Computer Information Systems, Computer Science, Construction, Dietetics, Early Childhood Education, Economics, Electrical Engineering, Electrical Engineering Technology, Elementary Education, Engineering/Computers, Engineering Physics, English, Environmental Science, Fashion Merchandising, Finance, French, Geological Science, German, Graphic Design, History, Home Economics, Home Economics Education, Individualized Major, Industrial Engineering, International Business, International Studies, Kindergarten/Primary Education, Manufacturing Engineering, Manufacturing Engineering Technology, Marketing, Mathematics, Mechanical Engineering, Medical Technology, Music, Music Education, News, Nursing, Painting, Philosophy, Photography, Physical Therapy, Physics, Political Science, Printmaking, Psychology, Public Relations, Radio/Video/Photo, Religious Studies, Sculpture, Secondary Education, Social Services, Sociology, Spanish, Special Education, Speech, Theatre Arts.
**Distribution of degrees:** The majors with the highest enrollment are business management/administration, psychology, and advertising; religious studies, engineering physics, and individualized major have the lowest.
**Requirements:** General education requirement.
**Academic regulations:** Minimum 2.0 GPA required for graduation.
**Special:** Minors offered. Academic Exploration Program. Self-designed majors. Double majors. Dual degrees. Independent study. Pass/fail grading option. Internships. Cooperative education programs. Graduate school at which undergraduates may take graduate-level courses. Preprofessional programs in law, medicine, veterinary science, and dentistry. Washington Semester. Teacher certification in early childhood, elementary, secondary, and special education. Study abroad in Austria, Denmark, England, Hungary, Ireland, Israel, Japan, the Netherlands, the former Soviet Republics, and Sweden.
**Honors:** Honors program. Honor societies.
**Academic Assistance:** Remedial study skills. Nonremedial tutoring.

**STUDENT LIFE. Housing:** All freshmen and sophomores must live on campus. Coed and men's dorms. Sorority and fraternity housing. School-owned/operated apartments. 85% of students live in college housing.
**Social atmosphere:** Sully's Bar, Coffee Classics, Lucky Lady Saloon, Yankee Inn, and Lums are favorite gathering spots. Greeks, the Scout, and the activities council have widespread influence in student life. Fall Fest, Homecoming, Basketball games, and midnight movies are popular social/sporting events. "While a typical Bradley Student doesn't usually get involved in a lot of activities, some events, such as basketball or theatre shows, are very popular," reports the editor of the student newspaper.
**Services and counseling/handicapped student services:** Placement services. Health service. Counseling services for minority, veteran, and older students. Personal and psychological counseling. Career and academic guidance services. Learning disabled services.
**Campus organizations:** Undergraduate student government. Student newspaper (Scout, published once/week). Literary magazine. Yearbook. Radio station. Numerous musical groups, theatre, debating, athletic, professional, and special-interest groups, 210 organizations in all. 20 fraternities, 15 chapter houses; 11 sororities, seven chapter houses. 43% of men join a fraternity. 32% of women join a sorority.
**Religious organizations:** Numerous religious groups.
**Minority/foreign student organizations:** Numerous minority student groups. Numerous foreign student groups.

**ATHLETICS. Physical education requirements:** None.
**Intercollegiate competition:** 7% of students participate. Baseball (M), basketball (M,W), cheerleading (M,W), cross-country (M,W), diving (M,W), golf (M,W), soccer (M), softball (W), swimming (M,W), tennis (M,W), volleyball (W). Member of Missouri Valley Conference, NCAA Division I.
**Intramural and club sports:** Intramural badminton, basketball, bowling, football, golf, racquetball, soccer, softball, swimming, table tennis, track, volleyball, wrestling. Men's club fencing, ice hockey, table tennis, wrestling. Women's club fencing, ice hockey, table tennis.

**ADMISSIONS. Academic basis for candidate selection** (in order of priority): Secondary school record, standardized test scores, class rank, school's recommendation, essay.
**Nonacademic basis for candidate selection:** Extracurricular participation is emphasized. Character and personality are important. Particular talent or ability and alumni/ae relationship are considered.
**Requirements:** Graduation from secondary school is required; GED is accepted. 16 units and the following program of study are required: 3 units of English, 2 units of math, 1 unit of lab science, 2 units of social studies. Minimum composite ACT score of 20 (combined SAT score of 850) and rank in top half of secondary school class, or minimum 2.0 GPA, recommended. Departments may specify special admissions requirements. Portfolio required of art program applicants. Audition required of music program applicants. SAT or ACT is required. PSAT is recommended. Campus visit and interview recommended. Off-campus interviews available with an admissions representative.
**Procedure:** Suggest filing application by May 1. Application deadline is August. Notification of admission on rolling basis. Reply is required by May 1. $100 nonrefundable tuition deposit. $100 room deposit, refundable until June 1. Freshmen accepted for terms other than fall.
**Special programs:** Admission may be deferred one semester. Credit may be granted through CEEB Advanced Placement for scores of 3 or higher. Credit may be granted through CLEP general and subject exams. Early entrance/early admission program. Concurrent enrollment program.
**Transfer students:** Transfer students accepted for terms other than fall. In fall 1993, 27% of all new students were transfers into all classes. 699 transfer applications were received, 592 were accepted. Application deadline is July 30 for fall; December 15 for spring.

Minimum 2.0 GPA required. Lowest course grade accepted is "D." Maximum number of transferable credits is 66 semester hours. At least 30 semester hours must be completed at the university to receive degree.
**Admissions contact:** Gary Bergman, M.S., Director of Enrollment Management. 309 677-1000.

**FINANCIAL AID. Available aid:** Pell grants, SEOG, state grants, school scholarships and grants, private scholarships and grants, academic merit scholarships, and athletic scholarships. Perkins Loans (NDSL), PLUS, Stafford Loans (GSL), NSL, and SLS. Deferred payment plan.
**Financial aid statistics:** Average amounts of aid awarded freshmen: Scholarships and grants, $4,500; loans, $2,000.
**Supporting data/closing dates:** FAFSA/FAF: Priority filing date is March 1; accepted on rolling basis. Notification of awards on rolling basis.
**Financial aid contact:** David Pardieck, M.S., Director of Financial Assistance. 309 677-3089.

**STUDENT EMPLOYMENT.** College Work/Study Program. Institutional employment. 30% of full-time undergraduates work on campus during school year. Students may expect to earn an average of $1,000 during school year. Off-campus part-time employment opportunities rated "good."

**COMPUTER FACILITIES.** 1,600 IBM/IBM-compatible and Macintosh/Apple microcomputers; 1,500 are networked. Students may access CDC Cyber minicomputer/mainframe systems, BITNET. Residence halls may be equipped with networked microcomputers. Client/LAN operating systems include Apple/Macintosh. 50 major computer languages and software packages available. Computer facilities are available to all students.
**Fees:** None.
**Hours:** 24 hours.

**GRADUATE CAREER DATA.** Graduate school percentages: 2% enter law school. 2% enter medical school. Highest graduate school enrollments: Bradley U, Illinois State U, Northwestern U, Southern Illinois U, U of Illinois, U of Wisconsin. 80% of graduates choose careers in business and industry. Companies and businesses that hire graduates: Andersen Consulting, Boeing, Caterpillar, Methodist Medical Center, St. Francis Medical Center, State Farm Insurance.

**PROMINENT ALUMNI/AE.** Robert Michel, U.S. congressman and minority leader, U.S. House of Representatives; David Horowitz, broadcaster and writer; Judge Robert Morgan; Major Robert Lawrence, astronaut; Jerry Hadley, tenor, New York Opera; Richard E. Carver, assistant secretary of the Air Force; Albert Siepert, NASA's first deputy director of administration.

# Chicago State University

**Chicago, IL 60628** **312 995-2000**

**1994-95 Costs.** Tuition: $1,902 (state residents), $2,853 (out-of-state). Housing: None. Fees, books, misc. academic expenses (school's estimate): $1,193.
**Enrollment.** Total undergraduate men: 2259. Total undergraduate women: 4976. Freshman class: 3,553 applicants, 1,719 accepted, 802 enrolled. Graduate enrollment: 781 men, 1,491 women.
**Test score averages/ranges.** Average ACT scores: 17 composite.
**Faculty.** 370 full-time; 112 part-time. 62% of faculty holds doctoral degree. Student/faculty ratio: 30 to 1.
**Selectivity rating.** Less competitive.

**PROFILE.** Chicago State, a public university, was founded in 1867 as an experimental teacher training school. Programs are now offered through the Colleges of Allied Health, Arts and Sciences, Business and Administration, Education, and Nursing. Its 152-acre campus is located in a residential neighborhood on Chicago's South Side.

**Accreditation:** NCACS. Professionally accredited by the National Council for Accreditation of Teacher Education, the National League for Nursing.
**Religious orientation:** Chicago State University is nonsectarian; no religious requirements.
**Library:** Collections totaling over 270,000 volumes, 1,377 periodical subscriptions, and 388,028 microform items.
**Athletic facilities:** Gymnasium, dance, aerobic, and weight rooms, swimming pool, tennis courts, indoor and outdoor tracks, softball field.

**STUDENT BODY. Undergraduate profile:** 98% are state residents; 50% are transfers. 1% Asian-American, 84% Black, 3% Hispanic, 1% Native American, 10% White, 1% Other. Average age of undergraduates is 30.
**Freshman profile:** 38% of freshmen who took ACT scored 18 or over on composite; 100% scored 12 or over on composite. 84% of accepted applicants took ACT. 80% of freshmen come from public schools.
**Undergraduate achievement:** 55% of fall 1992 freshmen returned for fall 1993 term.
**Foreign students:** 82 students are from out of the country. Countries represented include Germany, Liberia, Nigeria, and South Korea; eight in all.

**PROGRAMS OF STUDY. Degrees:** B.A., B.S., B.S.Ed.
**Majors:** Accounting, Art, Bilingual/Bicultural Education, Biology, Business Education, Chemistry, Computer Science/Data Processing, Corrections, Early Childhood/Elementary Education, Economics, English, Finance, Geography, Health/Safety/Physical Education/Recreation, History, Hotel/Restaurant Management, Industrial Technology, Information Sciences/Systems, Management, Marketing Management/Research, Mathematics, Medical Records Administration, Music, Nursing, Occupational Education, Occupational Therapy, Physics, Political Science/Government, Professional/Technical Writing, Psychology, Radio/Television Broadcasting, Sociology/Anthropology, Spanish, Special Education.
**Distribution of degrees:** The majors with the highest enrollment are accounting, early childhood/elementary education, and nursing; industrial technology, Spanish, and geography have the lowest.
**Requirements:** General education requirement.
**Academic regulations:** Sophomores must maintain minimum 1.8 GPA; juniors, 1.9 GPA; seniors, 2.0 GPA.
**Special:** Minors offered in many majors and in anthropology, French, philosophy, physical science, real estate, religious studies, social work, theatre arts, and writing. Individualized curriculum, University Without Walls, and Board of Governors programs. Business Lab Program and Presidential Scholars Program. Self-designed majors. Double majors. Independent study. Internships. Cooperative education programs. Preprofessional programs in law, medicine, veterinary science, pharmacy, dentistry, optometry, and podiatry. 3-2 engineering programs with Illinois Inst of Tech and U of Illinois at Chicago. Teacher certification in early childhood, elementary, secondary, and special education. Certification in specific subject areas. Study abroad in Germany and Nigeria. ROTC. AFROTC at Illinois Inst of Tech.
**Honors:** Phi Beta Kappa. Honors program.
**Academic Assistance:** Remedial reading, writing, math, and study skills. Nonremedial tutoring.

**STUDENT LIFE. Housing:** Commuter campus; no student housing.
**Services and counseling/handicapped student services:** Placement services. Health service. Day care. Counseling services for minority, military, and veteran students. Personal counseling. Career and academic guidance services. Physically disabled student services. Notetaking services. Tape recorders.
**Campus organizations:** Undergraduate student government. Student newspaper (Tempo). Yearbook. Radio station. Musical, departmental, social, and special-interest groups, 50 organizations in all. Four fraternities, no chapter houses; four sororities, no chapter houses. 12% of men join a fraternity. 15% of women join a sorority.
**Religious organizations:** Campus Ministry.
**Minority/foreign student organizations:** Latin American Student Organization, Black Student Psychological Association.

**ATHLETICS. Physical education requirements:** Three semester hours of physical education required of education majors.
**Intercollegiate competition:** 2% of students participate. Baseball (M), basketball (M,W), cross-country (M,W), golf (W), tennis (M,W), track (indoor) (M,W), track (outdoor) (M,W), track and field (indoor) (M,W), track and field (outdoor) (M,W), volleyball (W), wrestling (M). Member of East Coast Conference, NCAA Division I.
**Intramural and club sports:** 2% of students participate. Intramural aerobics, basketball, softball, swimming, track, weight lifting. Women's club cheerleading.

**ADMISSIONS. Academic basis for candidate selection** (in order of priority): Class rank, standardized test scores, secondary school record.
**Requirements:** Graduation from secondary school is required; GED is accepted. 15 units and the following program of study are required: 4 units of English, 3 units of math, 3 units of lab science, 3 units of social studies, 2 units of electives. 2 units required of foreign language, music, or art. ACT scores meeting university's minimum standards and rank in top quarter of secondary school class required. After admission, completion of university exams and prerequisite courses required of applicants to certain programs. Provisional admission possible for applicants not meeting standard requirements. SAT or ACT is required. Campus visit and interview recommended. No off-campus interviews.
**Procedure:** Take SAT or ACT by April of 12th year. Application deadline is August 1. Notification of admission on rolling basis. No set date by which applicants must accept offer. Freshmen accepted for terms other than fall.
**Special programs:** Credit and/or placement may be granted through CEEB Advanced Placement exams for scores of 4 or higher. Credit and/or placement may be granted through CLEP general and subject exams. Credit and placement may be granted through life experience. Concurrent enrollment program.
**Transfer students:** Transfer students accepted for terms other than fall. In fall 1993, 50% of all new students were transfers into all classes. 2,877 transfer applications were received, 1,361 were accepted. Application deadline is August 1 for fall; December 1 for spring. Minimum 2.0 GPA required. Lowest course grade accepted is "C." Maximum number of transferable credits is 66 credit hours. At least 30 credit hours must be completed at the university to receive degree.
**Admissions contact:** Romi Lowe, Director of Admissions. 312 995-2513.

**FINANCIAL AID. Available aid:** Pell grants, SEOG, state scholarships and grants, school scholarships and grants, private scholarships, ROTC scholarships, academic merit scholarships, athletic scholarships, and aid for undergraduate foreign students. Perkins Loans (NDSL), PLUS, and Stafford Loans (GSL). Deferred payment plan.
**Financial aid statistics:** In 1993-94, 85% of all undergraduate applicants received aid; 80% of freshman applicants. Average amounts of aid awarded freshmen: Scholarships and grants, $1,868.
**Supporting data/closing dates:** FAFSA/FAF/FFS: Priority filing date is April 15. School's own aid application: Priority filing date is April 15.
**Financial aid contact:** George West, Director of Financial Aid. 312 995-2304.

**STUDENT EMPLOYMENT.** College Work/Study Program. Institutional employment. 38% of full-time undergraduates work on campus during school year. Students may expect to earn an average of $2,700 during school year. Off-campus part-time employment opportunities rated "fair."

**COMPUTER FACILITIES.** 40 IBM/IBM-compatible microcomputers. Students may access IBM minicomputer/mainframe systems. Client/LAN operating systems include DOS. Computer languages and software packages include BND, CICS, MINITAB, SAS, SPSS, UNIX. Computer facilities are available to all students.
**Fees:** None.
**Hours:** 8:30 AM-10 PM (M-F); 8:30 AM-5 PM (Sa); 1 PM-8 PM (Su).

**GRADUATE CAREER DATA.** Highest graduate school enrollments: DePaul U, Illinois State U, Loyola U, Roosevelt U, U of Chicago, U of Illinois at Chicago. Companies and businesses that hire graduates: Arthur Andersen, Chicago public schools, federal government, Xerox.

**PROMINENT ALUMNI/AE.** Edward Gardner, president, Soft Sheen Products; Dr. Margaret Burroughs, founder and president, DuSable Museum of Black History; Dr. James Birren, gerontologist; Jacqueline Vaughn, president, Chicago Teacher's Union; Jolyn Robichaux, president, Baldwin Ice Cream.

## College of St. Francis

**Joliet, IL 60435** **815 740-3360**

**1994-95 Costs.** Tuition: $9,810. Room & board: $4,160. Fees, books, misc. academic expenses (school's estimate): $580.
**Enrollment.** Undergraduates: 390 men, 427 women (full-time). Freshman class: 420 applicants, 310 accepted, 160 enrolled. Graduate enrollment: 370 men, 648 women.
**Test score averages/ranges.** Average ACT scores: 23 composite.
**Faculty.** 47 full-time; 52 part-time. 52% of faculty holds doctoral degree. Student/faculty ratio: 15 to 1.
**Selectivity rating.** Less competitive.

**PROFILE.** The College of St. Francis, founded in 1920, is a church-affiliated college of liberal arts and sciences. Its 16-acre campus is located in Joliet, 35 miles southwest of Chicago.

**Accreditation:** NCACS. Professionally accredited by the Council on Social Work Education.
**Religious orientation:** College of St. Francis is affiliated with the Roman Catholic Church (Franciscan Order); two semesters of religion required.
**Library:** Collections totaling over 186,000 volumes, 525 periodical subscriptions, and 185,384 microform items.
**Special facilities/museums:** Nuclear magnetic resonance spectrometer.
**Athletic facilities:** Gymnasium, field house, basketball, racquetball, tennis, and volleyball courts, weight room, baseball and softball fields, recreation center, football stadium.

**STUDENT BODY. Undergraduate profile:** 90% are state residents; 39% are transfers. 1% Asian-American, 5% Black, 4% Hispanic, 90% White. Average age of undergraduates is 23.
**Freshman profile:** 5% of freshmen who took ACT scored 30 or over on composite; 35% scored 24 or over on composite; 98% scored 18 or over on composite; 100% scored 12 or over on composite. 5% of accepted applicants took SAT; 95% took ACT. 55% of freshmen come from public schools.
**Undergraduate achievement:** 83% of fall 1992 freshmen returned for fall 1993 term. 64% of entering class graduated. 10% of students who completed a degree program immediately went on to graduate study.
**Foreign students:** Two students are from out of the country.

**PROGRAMS OF STUDY. Degrees:** B.A., B.Bus.Admin., B.S.
**Majors:** Accounting, Actuarial Science, Biology, Business Administration/Management, Computer/Information Sciences, Creative Arts, Elementary Education, English, Environmental Science, Finance, Health Arts, History, Journalism/Mass Communications, Management, Marketing, Mathematics, Medical Technology, Nuclear Medical Technology, Political Science/Government, Professional Arts, Psychology, Public Policy, Religious Studies, Social Work, Therapeutic Recreation.
**Distribution of degrees:** The majors with the highest enrollment are business, education, and computer science; fine arts, history, and English have the lowest.
**Requirements:** General education requirement.
**Academic regulations:** Minimum 2.0 GPA must be maintained.
**Special:** Minors offered in all majors and in chemistry, economics, and library science. Double majors. Independent study. Internships. Preprofessional programs in law, medicine, veterinary science, dentistry, and physical therapy. 3-1 nuclear medicine and medical technology programs with area hospitals. Member of Associated Colleges of the Chicagoland Area. Washington Semester. Teacher certification in elementary and secondary education. Certification in specific subject areas. Study abroad in Canada, England, Italy, Mexico, Russia, and Spain. ROTC at Wheaton Coll.
**Honors:** Honor societies.

**ADMISSIONS. Academic basis for candidate selection** (in order of priority): Secondary school record, class rank, standardized test scores, essay, school's recommendation.
**Nonacademic basis for candidate selection:** Particular talent or ability and geographical distribution are important. Character and personality, extracurricular participation, and alumni/ae relationship are considered.
**Requirements:** Graduation from secondary school is required; GED is accepted. 20 units and the following program of study are recommended: 4 units of English, 3 units of math, 2 units of science, 2 units of foreign language, 2 units of social studies, 2 units of history, 5 units of electives. Minimum composite ACT score of 20, rank in top half of secondary school class, and minimum 2.5 GPA required. ACT is required; SAT may be substituted. Campus visit and interview recommended. Off-campus interviews available with an admissions representative.
**Procedure:** Take SAT or ACT by April of 12th year. Visit college for interview by March 1 of 12th year. Suggest filing application by March 1. Application deadline is June 1. Notification of admission on rolling basis. Reply is required by May 31. $50 tuition deposit, refundable until May 1. $50 nonrefundable room deposit. Freshmen accepted for terms other than fall.
**Special programs:** Admission may be deferred one year. Credit and/or placement may be granted through CEEB Advanced Placement exams for scores of 3 or higher. Credit may be granted through CLEP general exams and military experience. Credit and/or placement may be granted through CLEP subject exams. Placement may be granted through challenge exams. Credit and placement may be granted through ACT PEP exams and life experience.
**Transfer students:** Transfer students accepted for terms other than fall. In fall 1993, 39% of all new students were transfers into all classes. 231 transfer applications were received, 159 were accepted. Application deadline is August 1 for fall; January 1 for spring. Minimum 2.0 GPA required. Lowest course grade accepted is "C." Maximum number of transferable credits is 70 semester hours. At least 32 semester hours must be completed at the college to receive degree.
**Admissions contact:** Charles M. Beutel, M.B.A., Director of Admissions. 815 740-3400.

**FINANCIAL AID. Available aid:** Pell grants, SEOG, state scholarships and grants, school scholarships and grants, private scholarships, academic merit scholarships, and athletic scholarships. Perkins Loans (NDSL), PLUS, Stafford Loans (GSL), state loans, and SLS. Family tuition reduction. Institutional payment plan.
**Financial aid statistics:** 30% of aid is not need-based. In 1993-94, 85% of all undergraduate applicants received aid; 85% of freshman applicants. Average amounts of aid awarded freshmen: Scholarships and grants, $4,000; loans, $2,500.
**Supporting data/closing dates:** FAFSA/FAF/FFS: Priority filing date is April 1; deadline is July 1. Notification of awards on rolling basis.
**Financial aid contact:** Bruce Foote, Director of Financial Aid. 815 740-3403.

## Columbia College

**Chicago, IL 60605-1996** **312 663-1600**

**1993-94 Costs.** Tuition: $6,928. Room: $4,100. No meal plan. Fees, books, misc. academic expenses (school's estimate): $590.
**Enrollment.** Undergraduates: 2,411 men, 2,298 women (full-time). Freshman class: 2,565 applicants, 2,308 accepted, 1,062 enrolled. Graduate enrollment: 170 men, 234 women.
**Test score averages/ranges.** N/A.
**Faculty.** 163 full-time; 628 part-time. 43% of faculty holds highest degree in specific field. Student/faculty ratio: 10 to 1.
**Selectivity rating.** N/A.

**PROFILE.** Columbia, founded in 1890, is a private college of liberal arts, public arts, and information media studies. Its facilities are located in high-rise buildings in Chicago.

**Accreditation:** NCACS.
**Religious orientation:** Columbia College is nonsectarian; no religious requirements.
**Library:** Collections totaling over 123,679 volumes, 906 periodical subscriptions, and 84,588 microform items.
**Special facilities/museums:** Art galleries, contemporary photography museum, dance center.

**STUDENT BODY. Undergraduate profile:** 98% are state residents; 54% are transfers. 5% Asian-American, 22% Black, 9% Hispanic, 63% White, 1% Other. Average age of undergraduates is 23.
**Freshman profile:** Majority of accepted applicants took SAT.
**Undergraduate achievement:** 60% of fall 1991 freshmen returned for fall 1992 term. 12% of students who completed a degree program went on to graduate study within one year.
**Foreign students:** 145 students are from out of the country. Countries represented include Greece, Hong Kong, Japan, Korea, Sweden, and Thailand; 40 in all.

**PROGRAMS OF STUDY. Degrees:** B.A.
**Majors:** Advertising, Art, Dance, Fashion Design, Fiction Writing, Film/Video, Graphic Design/Illustration/Advertising Art, Interior Design, Journalism, Management, Marketing Communication, Photography, Public Relations, Radio/Sound, Television, Theater/Music.
**Distribution of degrees:** The majors with the highest enrollment are marketing communication, television, and film/video; dance and music have the lowest.
**Requirements:** General education requirement.
**Academic regulations:** Minimum 2.0 GPA must be maintained.
**Special:** Courses in generative systems and science for nonscience majors combine practical and scientific principles with creative and aesthetic ones. Film and music/theatre programs stress performance and/or production. Writing department publishes efforts of story workshop class. Self-designed majors. Independent study. Internships. Graduate school at which undergraduates may take graduate-level courses. Cooperative arrangements with cultural and educational institutions in Chicago include study at the Adler Planetarium. Cooperative library privileges at Roosevelt U. Study abroad possible in England.
**Academic Assistance:** Remedial writing and math. Nonremedial tutoring.

**STUDENT LIFE. Housing:** Students may live on or off campus. Coed dorms.
**Social atmosphere:** According to the editor of the student newspaper, "Columbia is an urban commuter school, so most of the students have a social and cultural life off campus." However, some places to gather on campus include the Hokin Student Center and the Getz Theatre. Off campus, students head for the Heros Sports Bar, Cabaret Metro, and Doug's Place. The Greeks have a large influence on campus, and the Student Activities Board is a popular group. Favorite social and cultural events are the Class Bash, plays at the Getz, and presentations by guest lecturers.
**Services and counseling/handicapped student services:** Placement services. Counseling services for veteran students. Personal counseling. Career and academic guidance services. Physically disabled student services. Learning disabled services. Notetaking services. Tutors. Reader services for the blind.
**Campus organizations:** Student newspaper (Columbia College Chronicle, published once/week). Literary magazine. Radio station. Filmmakers festival, faculty/student theatre company, concert ensemble, dance troupe, art, literary, and photography magazines, photography exhibitions, Women's Coalition, Gay/Lesbian Alliance, 20 organizations in all. Five fraternities, no chapter houses; four sororities, no chapter houses. 4% of men join a fraternity. 3% of women join a sorority.
**Religious organizations:** Bible study group.
**Minority/foreign student organizations:** African-American Alliance, Latino Alliance, League of Black Women.

**ATHLETICS. Physical education requirements:** None.

**ADMISSIONS. Academic basis for candidate selection** (in order of priority): School's recommendation, secondary school record, class rank, standardized test scores.
**Nonacademic basis for candidate selection:** Character and personality, extracurricular participation, and particular talent or ability are considered.

**Requirements:** Graduation from secondary school is required; GED is accepted. No specific distribution of secondary school units required. College-preparatory program recommended. SAT or ACT is recommended. Campus visit recommended. No off-campus interviews.
**Procedure:** Take SAT or ACT by January of 12th year. Notification of admission on rolling basis. Reply is required within two weeks of notification of admission. $20 nonrefundable acceptance fee. $500 room deposit, partially refundable. Freshmen accepted for terms other than fall.
**Special programs:** Admission may be deferred one year. Credit and/or placement may be granted through CEEB Advanced Placement exams for scores of 4 or higher. Credit and/or placement may be granted through CLEP general and subject exams. Placement may be granted through life experience. Early entrance/early admission program.
**Transfer students:** Transfer students accepted for terms other than fall. In fall 1992, 54% of all new students were transfers into all classes. 2,384 transfer applications were received, 2,106 were accepted. Application deadline is rolling for fall; rolling for spring. Lowest course grade accepted is "C." Maximum number of transferable credits is 62 semester hours from a two-year school and 88 semester hours from a four-year school. At least 36 semester hours must be completed at the college to receive degree.
**Admissions contact:** Debra McGrath, M.F.A., Director of Admissions. 312 663-1600, extension 130.
**FINANCIAL AID. Available aid:** Pell grants, SEOG, state grants, school grants, private scholarships and grants, and academic merit scholarships. PLUS, Stafford Loans (GSL), and SLS. Deferred payment plan.
**Financial aid statistics:** 20% of aid is not need-based. In 1992-93, 55% of all undergraduate applicants received aid. Average amounts of aid awarded freshmen: Loans, $2,560.
**Supporting data/closing dates:** FAFSA/FAF/FFS: Accepted on rolling basis. Income tax forms: Accepted on rolling basis. FED: Accepted on rolling basis. Notification of awards on rolling basis.
**Financial aid contact:** John Olino, Director of Financial Aid. 312 663-1600, extension 140.
**STUDENT EMPLOYMENT.** College Work/Study Program. Institutional employment. 7% of full-time undergraduates work on campus during school year. Students may expect to earn an average of $2,000 during school year. Off-campus part-time employment opportunities rated "excellent."
**COMPUTER FACILITIES.** IBM/IBM-compatible and Macintosh/Apple microcomputers. Residence halls may be equipped with stand-alone microcomputers. Computer facilities are available to all students.
**Fees:** None.
**GRADUATE CAREER DATA.** Graduate school percentages: 1% enter law school. 1% enter medical school. 10% enter graduate arts and sciences programs.

## Concordia University

**River Forest, IL 60305-1499** **708 771-8300**

**1994-95 Costs.** Tuition: $9,216. Room & board: $4,191. Fees, books, misc. academic expenses (school's estimate): $530.
**Enrollment.** Undergraduates: 387 men, 781 women (full-time). Freshman class: 613 applicants, 488 accepted, 253 enrolled. Graduate enrollment: 211 men, 934 women.
**Test score averages/ranges.** Average ACT scores: 23 English, 22 math, 23 composite.
**Faculty.** 96 full-time; 120 part-time. 61% of faculty holds highest degree in specific field. Student/faculty ratio: 12 to 1.
**Selectivity rating.** Less competitive.

**PROFILE.** Concordia, founded in 1864, is a church-affiliated university. Its 40-acre campus is located in River Forest, 10 miles from Chicago.

**Accreditation:** NCACS. Professionally accredited by the National Council for Accreditation of Teacher Education, the National League for Nursing.
**Religious orientation:** Concordia University is affiliated with the Lutheran Church-Missouri Synod; no religious requirements.
**Library:** Collections totaling over 150,490 volumes, 600 periodical subscriptions, and 464,818 microform items.
**Special facilities/museums:** Natural history and art museums, early childhood education lab school, TV and radio studios.
**Athletic facilities:** Swimming pool, gymnastics and weight rooms, human performance lab, batting cages, gymnasiums, baseball, football, and softball fields, track, tennis courts, cross-country course, exercise hill.
**STUDENT BODY. Undergraduate profile:** 67% are state residents; 45% are transfers. 3% Asian-American, 16% Black, 2% Hispanic, 79% White.
**Freshman profile:** 5% of freshmen who took ACT scored 30 or over on composite; 44% scored 24 or over on composite; 93% scored 18 or over on composite; 100% scored 12 or over on composite. 94% of accepted applicants took ACT. 70% of freshmen come from public schools.
**Undergraduate achievement:** 73% of fall 1992 freshmen returned for fall 1993 term. 15% of students who completed a degree program immediately went on to graduate study.
**Foreign students:** Eight students are from out of the country. Countries represented include China, Greece, and Japan; five in all.
**PROGRAMS OF STUDY. Degrees:** B.A., B.Mus., B.Mus.Ed., B.S., B.S.Nurs.
**Majors:** Accounting, Art, Biology, Business Management, Chemistry, Communication/Theatre, Communications, Computer Information Systems, Computer Science, Coputer Science/Mathematics, Early Childhood Education, Earth Science, Elementary Education, English, Exercise Science/Fitness Management, Geography/Environmental Science, German, History, Mathematics, Music, Natural Science, Nursing, Philosophy, Political Science, Psychology, Secondary Education, Social Service, Sociology, Theological Languages, Theology.
**Distribution of degrees:** The majors with the highest enrollment are education, nursing, and business management; philosophy, political science, and geography have the lowest.
**Requirements:** General education requirement.
**Academic regulations:** Freshmen must maintain minimum 1.60 GPA; sophomores, 1.85 GPA; juniors, 1.90 GPA; seniors, 1.95 GPA.
**Special:** Minors offered in most majors and in biblical languages, foreign languages, and physics. Courses offered in economics, French, Greek, Hebrew, Latin, and Spanish. Careers for Christ retreat. Deaconess Program. Director of Christian Education and Director of Parish Music programs. Double majors. Independent study. Pass/fail grading option. Internships. Preprofessional programs in law, medicine, dentistry, and seminary. Nursing program in cooperation with West Suburban Hospital Coll of Nursing. Member of Chicago Consortium of Colleges and Universities and Associated Colleges of the Chicago Area. Teacher certification in early childhood, elementary, secondary, and special education. Certification in specific subject areas.
**Honors:** Phi Beta Kappa.
**Academic Assistance:** Nonremedial tutoring.
**ADMISSIONS. Academic basis for candidate selection** (in order of priority): Secondary school record, standardized test scores, class rank, school's recommendation.
**Nonacademic basis for candidate selection:** Character and personality, extracurricular participation, and particular talent or ability are considered.
**Requirements:** Graduation from secondary school is required; GED is accepted. 15 units and the following program of study are required: 3 units of English, 1 unit of math, 2 units of science, 1 unit of social studies. Minimum composite ACT score of 18, rank in top half of secondary school class, and minimum 2.0 GPA required. ACT is required; SAT may be substituted. Campus visit and interview recommended. Off-campus interviews available with an admissions representative.
**Procedure:** Take SAT or ACT by September 1 of 12th year. Notification of admission on rolling basis. Reply is required by May 1. $100 tuition deposit, refundable until May 1. $50 refundable room deposit. Freshmen accepted for terms other than fall.
**Special programs:** Admission may be deferred one year. Credit may be granted through CEEB Advanced Placement for scores of 3 or higher. Credit may be granted through CLEP general and subject exams, ACT PEP and challenge exams, and military experience.
**Transfer students:** Transfer students accepted for terms other than fall. In fall 1993, 45% of all new students were transfers into all classes. 355 transfer applications were received, 237 were accepted. Application deadline is rolling for fall; rolling for spring. Minimum 2.0 GPA recommended. Lowest course grade accepted is "D." Maximum number of transferable credits is 100 quarter hours. At least 48 quarter hours must be completed at the university to receive degree.
**Admissions contact:** Sara E. Dahms, M.A., Director of Admissions. 800 285-2668.
**FINANCIAL AID. Available aid:** Pell grants, SEOG, state grants, school scholarships and grants, private scholarships and grants, and academic merit scholarships. Perkins Loans (NDSL), PLUS, Stafford Loans (GSL), school loans, and SLS. AMS.
**Financial aid statistics:** Average amounts of aid awarded freshmen: Scholarships and grants, $996; loans, $1,659.
**Supporting data/closing dates:** FAFSA/FAF: Accepted on rolling basis. Income tax forms: Accepted on rolling basis. Notification of awards on rolling basis.
**Financial aid contact:** Deb Ness, M.Ed., Director of Financial Aid. 708 209-3113.

## DePaul University

**Chicago, IL 60604** **312 362-8000**

**1993-94 Costs.** Tuition: $10,500. Room & board: $5,500. Fees, books, misc. academic expenses (school's estimate): $340.
**Enrollment.** Undergraduates: 2,669 men, 3,400 women (full-time). Freshman class: 4,970 applicants, 4,093 accepted, 1,227 enrolled. Graduate enrollment: 3,539 men, 3,152 women.
**Test score averages/ranges.** Range of SAT scores of middle 50%: 440-560 verbal, 480-610 math. Range of ACT scores of middle 50%: 22-27 composite.
**Faculty.** 500 full-time; 565 part-time. 88% of faculty holds highest degree in specific field. Student/faculty ratio: 17 to 1.
**Selectivity rating.** Competitive.

**PROFILE.** DePaul, founded in 1898, is a private, church-affiliated university. Undergraduate programs are offered through the College of Commerce, the College of Liberal Arts and Sciences, the School of Education, the School of Music, the Theatre School, and the School for New Learning. Its 32-acre Lincoln Park campus is located three miles north of the Loop in Chicago; the Lewis Center is located in downtown Chicago.

**Accreditation:** NCACS. Professionally accredited by the American Assembly of Collegiate Schools of Business, the American Psychological Association, the Association of American Law Schools, the National Association of Schools of Music, the National Council for Accreditation of Teacher Education, the National League for Nursing.
**Religious orientation:** DePaul University is affiliated with the Roman Catholic Church (Vincentian Fathers); two term of religion required.
**Library:** Collections totaling over 637,100 volumes, 16,711 periodical subscriptions, and 295,644 microform items.
**Special facilities/museums:** Theatre.
**Athletic facilities:** Gymnasiums, field house, basketball, handball, racquetball, tennis, and volleyball courts, aerobics, weight rooms, swimming pool, athletic fields.
**STUDENT BODY. Undergraduate profile:** 75% are state residents; 47% are transfers. 6% Asian-American, 12% Black, 11% Hispanic, 1% Native American, 69% White, 1% Other. Average age of undergraduates is 22.
**Freshman profile:** 32% of accepted applicants took SAT; 68% took ACT. 67% of freshmen come from public schools.
**Undergraduate achievement:** 82% of fall 1992 freshmen returned for fall 1993 term. 63% of entering class graduated.
**Foreign students:** 99 students are from out of the country. Countries represented include China, Greece, India, Korea, Taiwan, and Thailand; 56 in all.
**PROGRAMS OF STUDY. Degrees:** B.A., B.F.A., B.M., B.S., B.S.Commerce.

**Majors:** Accountancy, Acting, American Studies, Art, Biological Sciences, Business Administration, Chemistry, Clinical Laboratory Sciences, Communications, Comparative Literature, Computer Education, Computer/Information Sciences, Costume Construction, Costume Design, Directing, Early Childhood Education, Economics, Elementary Education, English, Environmental Sciences, Finance, French, Geography, German, History, International Studies, Italian, Jazz Studies, Jewish Studies, Latin American Studies, Lighting Design, Management, Marketing, Mathematics, Music Business, Music Composition, Music Education, Music Performance, Nursing, Philosophy, Physical Education, Physics, Playwriting, Political Science/Government, Pre-Law Commerce, Pre-Law Liberal Arts, Production Management, Psychology, Recording/Sound Technology, Religious Studies, Scene Design, Secondary Education, Social Sciences, Sociology, Spanish, Theatre History/Criticism, Theatre Management, Theatre Production, Theatre Studies, Theatre Technology, Urban Studies, Women's Studies.
**Distribution of degrees:** The majors with the highest enrollment are accounting, finance, and marketing; theatre history and music business have the lowest.
**Requirements:** General education requirement.
**Academic regulations:** Minimum 2.0 GPA must be maintained.
**Special:** Minors offered in most majors. Double majors. Dual degrees. Accelerated study. Pass/fail grading option. Internships. Graduate school at which undergraduates may take graduate-level courses. Preprofessional programs in law, medicine, veterinary science, pharmacy, dentistry, and optometry. 3-2 engineering program with U of Detroit, U of Illinois at Urbana-Champaign, Iowa State U, Northwestern U, Notre Dame U, Ohio State U, and U of Southern California. Five-year M.Accountancy program. B.A./M.S program in industrial/organizational psychology and liberal studies. B.S./M.S. programs in applied mathematics, biology, chemistry, and physics. Teacher certification in early childhood, elementary, secondary, and bilingual/bicultural education. Certification in specific subject areas. Study abroad in China, England, France, Germany, Greece, Hungary, Israel, Italy, Japan, Malta, Mexico, Poland, Spain, Thailand, and Zimbabwe. ROTC.
**Honors:** Honors program. Honor societies.
**Academic Assistance:** Remedial reading, writing, math, and study skills. Nonremedial tutoring.

**STUDENT LIFE. Housing:** Students may live on or off campus. Coed dorms. 25% of students live in college housing.
**Services and counseling/handicapped student services:** Placement services. Health service. Counseling services for minority, military, veteran, and older students. Personal and psychological counseling. Career and academic guidance services. Religious counseling. Physically disabled student services. Learning disabled program/services. Notetaking services. Tape recorders. Tutors. Reader services for the blind.
**Campus organizations:** Undergraduate student government. Student newspaper (DePaulia, published once/week). Literary magazine. Yearbook. Radio station. Activities board, residence hall council, Amnesty International, Best Buddies, Habitat for Humanity, ARK (Animal Rights Koalition), AIDS/HIV Awareness Project, literacy and tutoring volunteer groups, women's and alumni associations, Bisexual/Gay/Lesbian Student Union, Elvis Golden Fan Club, Self-Defense Club, other academic, special-interest, and service groups, 85 organizations in all. Three fraternities, all with chapter houses; two sororities, all with chapter houses. 3% of men join a fraternity. 2% of women join a sorority.
**Religious organizations:** College Life Christian Fellowship, Hillel/Jewish Student Union.
**Minority/foreign student organizations:** African American Alliance, Korean American Student Organization. Students of the World, Asian Cultural Exchange, Croatian Club, Latin American and Japanese groups.

**ATHLETICS. Physical education requirements:** None.
**Intercollegiate competition:** 3% of students participate. Basketball (M,W), cross-country (M,W), golf (M), riflery (M,W), soccer (M), tennis (M,W), track (indoor) (M,W), track (outdoor) (M,W), track and field (indoor) (M,W), track and field (outdoor) (M,W), volleyball (W). Member of Chicagoland Collegiate Golf Conference, Mid Atlantic Rifle Conference, Mid-Continent (softball), NCAA Division I, The Great Midwest Conference.
**Intramural and club sports:** 80% of students participate. Intramural aerobics, basketball, flag football, floor hockey, handball, soccer, softball, tennis, volleyball, walleyball, weight lifting. Men's club baseball, cheerleading, ice hockey, volleyball. Women's club cheerleading, soccer.

**ADMISSIONS. Academic basis for candidate selection** (in order of priority): Secondary school record, class rank, standardized test scores, school's recommendation, essay.
**Nonacademic basis for candidate selection:** Character and personality and extracurricular participation are emphasized. Particular talent or ability and alumni/ae relationship are considered.
**Requirements:** Graduation from secondary school is required; GED is accepted. 16 units and the following program of study are required: 4 units of English, 2 units of math, 2 units of science, 2 units of social studies, 2 units of history, 4 units of academic electives. Additional units of math and science recommended. Audition required of theatre and music program applicants. R.N. required of nursing program applicants. Bridge Program for applicants not meeting standard requirements. SAT or ACT is required. Campus visit and interview recommended. Off-campus interviews available with admissions and alumni representatives.
**Procedure:** Take SAT or ACT by April of 12th year. Visit college for interview by April of 12th year. Suggest filing application by November 15. Application deadline is August 15. Notification is sent on rolling basis; Early Action Program applicants receive notification by December 1. Reply is required by May 1. $200 room deposit, refundable until May 1. Freshmen accepted for terms other than fall.
**Special programs:** Admission may be deferred one year. Credit and/or placement may be granted through CEEB Advanced Placement exams for scores of 3 or higher. Credit and/or placement may be granted through CLEP general and subject exams. Credit and placement may be granted through ACT PEP, DANTES, and challenge exams, and military and life experience. Early entrance/early admission program. Concurrent enrollment program.
**Transfer students:** Transfer students accepted for terms other than fall. In fall 1993, 47% of all new students were transfers into all classes. 2,413 transfer applications were received, 1,776 were accepted. Application deadline is August 15 for fall; December 1 (winter); February 30 for spring. Minimum 2.0 GPA required. Lowest course grade accepted is "D." Maximum number of transferable credits is 99 quarter hours from a two-year school and 132 quarter hours from a four-year school. At least 56 quarter hours must be completed at the university to receive degree.
**Admissions contact:** Lucy Leusch, Director of Admissions. 312 362-8300.

**FINANCIAL AID. Available aid:** Pell grants, SEOG, state scholarships and grants, school scholarships and grants, private scholarships and grants, ROTC scholarships, academic merit scholarships, and athletic scholarships. Perkins Loans (NDSL), PLUS, Stafford Loans (GSL), state loans, private loans, and SLS. Tuition Plan Inc., Knight Tuition Plans, AMS, EFI Fund Management, and deferred payment plan. Monthly installment plan.
**Financial aid statistics:** In 1993-94, 73% of all undergraduate applicants received aid; 78% of freshman applicants. Average amounts of aid awarded freshmen: Scholarships and grants, $2,800; loans, $2,460.
**Supporting data/closing dates:** FAFSA/FAF: Priority filing date is May 1. Notification of awards on rolling basis.
**Financial aid contact:** John Schoultz, Director of Financial Aid. 312 362-8526.

**STUDENT EMPLOYMENT.** College Work/Study Program. Institutional employment. 28% of full-time undergraduates work on campus during school year. Students may expect to earn an average of $2,000 during school year. Off-campus part-time employment opportunities rated "excellent."

**COMPUTER FACILITIES.** 750 IBM/IBM-compatible and Macintosh/Apple microcomputers; all are networked. Students may access Digital, IBM, SUN minicomputer/mainframe systems, BITNET, Internet. Residence halls may be equipped with stand-alone microcomputers. Client/LAN operating systems include Apple/Macintosh, DOS, UNIX/XENIX/AIX, Windows NT, X-windows, LocalTalk/AppleTalk, Microsoft. Computer languages and software packages include Ada, BASIC, C, COBOL, FORTRAN, LISP, LOGO, Pascal, PL/1; numerous software packages. Computer facilities are available to all students.
**Fees:** Computer fee is included in tuition/fees.
**Hours:** 24 hours by modem.

**GRADUATE CAREER DATA.** 70% of graduates choose careers in business and industry. Companies and businesses that hire graduates: Amoco, Baxter Health Care, Big Six accounting firms, Motorola, Quaker Oats.

**PROMINENT ALUMNI/AE.** William Smithburg, chairperson and CEO, Quaker Oats; Eugene Tracy, chairperson and CEO, Peoples Energy Corp.; Richard Daley, mayor, Chicago.

# DeVry Institute of Technology (Addison)

**Addison, IL 60101** **708 953-1300**

**1994-95 Costs.** Tuition: $5,962. Housing: None. Fees, books, misc. academic expenses (school's estimate): $580.
**Enrollment.** Undergraduates: 1,504 men, 339 women (full-time). Freshman class: 1,430 applicants, 1,317 accepted, 746 enrolled.
**Test score averages/ranges.** N/A.
**Faculty.** 54 full-time; 50 part-time. 2% of faculty holds doctoral degree. Student/faculty ratio: 29 to 1.
**Selectivity rating.** N/A.

**PROFILE.** DeVry/Addison is a private institution specializing in electronics technology and computer information systems. It is a member of a network of technical institutes with eight campuses in the U.S. and two in Canada. Its campus, founded in 1982, is located 20 miles west of downtown Chicago.

**Accreditation:** NCACS. Professionally accredited by the Accreditation Board for Engineering and Technology.
**Religious orientation:** DeVry Institute of Technology (Addison) is nonsectarian; no religious requirements.
**Library:** Collections totaling over 7,849 volumes, 165 periodical subscriptions and 84 microform items.

**STUDENT BODY. Undergraduate profile:** 78% are state residents; 65% are transfers. 6% Asian-American, 11% Black, 5% Hispanic, 78% White. Average age of undergraduates is 23.
**Undergraduate achievement:** 47% of fall 1992 freshmen returned for fall 1993 term. 40% of entering class graduated.
**Foreign students:** 16 students are from out of the country. Countries represented include Burma and India; 11 in all.

**PROGRAMS OF STUDY. Degrees:** B.S.
**Majors:** Accounting, Business Operations, Computer Information Systems, Electronic Engineering Technology, Telecommunications Management.
**Distribution of degrees:** The majors with the highest enrollment are electrical engineering technology, computer information systems, and business operations.
**Requirements:** General education requirement.
**Academic regulations:** Minimum 2.0 GPA must be maintained.
**Special:** Electronics technician diploma offered. Associate's degrees offered. Accelerated study. Cooperative education programs. ROTC at Wheaton Coll.
**Honors:** Honor societies.
**Academic Assistance:** Nonremedial tutoring.

**STUDENT LIFE. Housing:** Commuter campus; no student housing.
**Services and counseling/handicapped student services:** Placement services. Career and academic guidance services. Physically disabled student services. Notetaking services. Reader services for the blind.
**Campus organizations:** Undergraduate student government. Student newspaper (Compiler). Laser club, math and accounting clubs, computer users group, electronics

club, Student Activities Association, ski club, martial arts club, 11 organizations in all. Two fraternities, no chapter houses.
**Religious organizations:** Muslim Student Association.
**Minority/foreign student organizations:** Association for the Advancement of Hispanic Students, Black Leadership Association.

**ATHLETICS. Physical education requirements:** None.
**Intramural and club sports:** Intramural baseball, basketball, volleyball, weight lifting.

**ADMISSIONS. Academic basis for candidate selection** (in order of priority): Standardized test scores.
**Requirements:** Graduation from secondary school is required; GED is accepted. No specific distribution of secondary school units required. All applicants must be at least 17 years of age on first day of classes. SAT or ACT is recommended. Applicants not submitting SAT or ACT must pass DeVry entrance exam. Minimum score of 52% on DeVry math exams or minimum math SAT score of 400-480 (math ACT score of 16-18) required of electronics program applicants. Minimum score of 72% on DeVry arithmetic exam and 65% on DeVry logical reasoning exam or minimum combined SAT score of 840 (composite ACT score of 20) required of computer science and business program applicants. Campus visit recommended. Off-campus interviews available with an admissions representative.
**Procedure:** Take SAT, ACT, or DeVry entrance exam. Notification of admission on rolling basis. Reply is required by registration. $75 tuition deposit, refundable until beginning of classes. Freshmen accepted for terms other than fall.
**Special programs:** Admission may be deferred one year. Credit may be granted through CLEP subject exams, DANTES and challenge exams.
**Transfer students:** Transfer students accepted for terms other than fall. In fall 1993, 65% of all new students were transfers into all classes. Application deadline is rolling for fall; rolling for spring. Minimum 2.0 GPA required. Lowest course grade accepted is "C." Maximum number of transferable semester hours is 65% of total required for degree. At least 35% of total semester hours must be completed at DeVry to receive degree.
**Admissions contact:** Milt Kobus, Director of Admissions. 708 953-2000.

**FINANCIAL AID. Available aid:** Pell grants, SEOG, state scholarships and grants, school scholarships, and academic merit scholarships. Perkins Loans (NDSL), PLUS, Stafford Loans (GSL), state loans, and SLS. EDUCARD plan.
**Financial aid statistics:** In 1993-94, 71% of all undergraduate applicants received aid; 69% of freshman applicants.
**Supporting data/closing dates:** FAFSA: Accepted on rolling basis. Notification of awards on rolling basis.
**Financial aid contact:** Diane Battistella, Director of Financial Aid.

**STUDENT EMPLOYMENT.** College Work/Study Program. Institutional employment. 4% of full-time undergraduates work on campus during school year. Students may expect to earn an average of $4,500 during school year. Off-campus part-time employment opportunities rated "excellent."

**COMPUTER FACILITIES.** 210 IBM/IBM-compatible microcomputers; 130 are networked. Students may access IBM minicomputer/mainframe systems. Client/LAN operating systems include DOS, UNIX/XENIX/AIX, Novell. Computer languages and software packages include BASIC, COBOL, FoxPro, Pascal, RPG, Turbo C; database, graphics, spreadsheet, and word processing programs; 25 in all. Computer facilities are available to all students.
**Fees:** Computer fee is included in tuition/fees.

**GRADUATE CAREER DATA.** 89% of graduates choose careers in business and industry. Companies and businesses that hire graduates: AT&T Bell Laboratories, CBIS, CNA Insurance, State Farm Insurance,.

# DeVry Institute of Technology (Chicago)

**Chicago, IL 60618** **312 929-8500**

**1994-95 Costs.** Tuition: $5,962. Housing: None. Fees, books, misc. academic expenses (school's estimate): $580.
**Enrollment.** Undergraduates: 1,510 men, 513 women (full-time). Freshman class: 1,197 applicants, 1,049 accepted, 769 enrolled.
**Test score averages/ranges.** N/A.
**Faculty.** 55 full-time; 58 part-time. Student/faculty ratio: 20 to 1.
**Selectivity rating.** N/A.

**PROFILE.** DeVry/Chicago, founded in 1931, is a private institution specializing in electronics technology and computer information systems. It is a member of a network of technical institutes with eight campuses in the U.S. and two in Canada. Its campus is located in a residential area on the city's northwest side.

**Accreditation:** NCACS. Professionally accredited by the Accreditation Board for Engineering and Technology.
**Religious orientation:** DeVry Institute of Technology (Chicago) is nonsectarian; no religious requirements.
**Library:** Collections totaling over 14,566 volumes, 220 periodical subscriptions and 141 microform items.
**Athletic facilities:** Outdoor basketball court, baseball diamond, volleyball court.

**STUDENT BODY. Undergraduate profile:** 95% are state residents; 36% are transfers. 11% Asian-American, 33% Black, 22% Hispanic, 32% White, 2% Other. Average age of undergraduates is 24.
**Freshman profile:** Majority of accepted applicants took ACT.
**Undergraduate achievement:** 45% of fall 1992 freshmen returned for fall 1993 term. 35% of entering class graduated.
**Foreign students:** 82 students are from out of the country. Countries represented include India, Japan, Pakistan, the Philippines, Poland, and Thailand; 30 in all.

**PROGRAMS OF STUDY. Degrees:** B.S.
**Majors:** Accounting, Business Operations, Computer Information Systems, Electronics Engineering Technology.
**Distribution of degrees:** The majors with the highest enrollment are electronics engineering technology, computer information systems, and business operations.
**Requirements:** General education requirement.
**Academic regulations:** Minimum 2.0 GPA must be maintained.
**Special:** Associate's degrees offered. Accelerated study. Cooperative education programs.
**Honors:** Honor societies.
**Academic Assistance:** Nonremedial tutoring.

**STUDENT LIFE. Housing:** Commuter campus; no student housing.
**Social atmosphere:** Pablo's Cafe, the basketball court, and downtown Chicago are popular gathering spots for students. Student organizations with widespread influence are Kappa Alpha Rho, IEEE, Bible club, Society of Hispanic Engineers, Asian multicultural organization, African American student organization, accounting society, professional business organization, and Alpha Beta Gamma. Some of the most popular social/cultural events include the multi-racial unity party, Latinola awareness month, Taste of DeVry Fest, and Video Fun Flick Fest. Many of the school's events celebrate cultural heritage since it is a very diverse institution. Students are able to take advantage of Chicago's offering of art, music and dance.
**Services and counseling/handicapped student services:** Career and academic guidance services. Physically disabled student services. Notetaking services. Reader services for the blind.
**Campus organizations:** Undergraduate student government. Student newspaper (DeVry Hard Copy, published once/month). Accounting and business groups, electronics club, amateur radio club, laser club, developmental video association, 15 organizations in all.
**Religious organizations:** Bible club.
**Minority/foreign student organizations:** African-American Student Organization, Society of Hispanic Professional Engineers. Filipino Academic Support Club, Indo-Pak Society.

**ATHLETICS. Physical education requirements:** None.
**Intramural and club sports:** Intramural basketball, bowling, soccer, softball, table tennis, volleyball.

**ADMISSIONS. Academic basis for candidate selection** (in order of priority): Standardized test scores.
**Requirements:** Graduation from secondary school is required; GED is accepted. No specific distribution of secondary school units required. All applicants must be at least 17 years old on first day of classes. SAT or ACT is recommended. Applicants not submitting SAT or ACT must pass DeVry entrance exam. Satisfactory completion of DeVry entrance/placement exam and minimum math SAT score of 400-480 (math ACT score of 16-18) required of electronics program applicants. Satisfactory completion of math and logic entrance exam and minimum combined SAT score of 840 (composite ACT score of 20) required of computer science program applicants. Campus visit recommended. Off-campus interviews available with an admissions representative.
**Procedure:** Take SAT, ACT, or DeVry entrance exam. Notification of admission on rolling basis. Reply is required by registration. $75 tuition deposit, refundable until beginning of classes. Freshmen accepted for terms other than fall.
**Special programs:** Admission may be deferred one year. Credit may be granted through CLEP subject exams, DANTES and challenge exams.
**Transfer students:** Transfer students accepted for terms other than fall. In fall 1993, 36% of all new students were transfers into all classes. Application deadline is rolling for fall; rolling for spring. Minimum 2.0 GPA required. Lowest course grade accepted is "C." Maximum number of transferable semester hours is 65% of total required for degree. At least 35% of total semester hours must be completed at DeVry to receive degree.
**Admissions contact:** Richard Yaconis, Director of Admissions. 312 929-6550.

**FINANCIAL AID. Available aid:** Pell grants, SEOG, state scholarships and grants, and academic merit scholarships. Perkins Loans (NDSL), PLUS, Stafford Loans (GSL), state loans, and SLS. EDUCARD plan.
**Financial aid statistics:** In 1993-94, 79% of all undergraduate applicants received aid; 77% of freshman applicants.
**Supporting data/closing dates:** FAFSA: Accepted on rolling basis. Notification of awards on rolling basis.
**Financial aid contact:** Betty Glenn, M.P.M., Director of Financial Aid.

**STUDENT EMPLOYMENT.** College Work/Study Program. Institutional employment. 5% of full-time undergraduates work on campus during school year. Students may expect to earn an average of $5,350 during school year. Freshmen are discouraged from working during their first term. Off-campus part-time employment opportunities rated "excellent."

**COMPUTER FACILITIES.** 246 IBM/IBM-compatible microcomputers; 72 are networked. Students may access IBM minicomputer/mainframe systems. Client/LAN operating systems include DOS, UNIX/XENIX/AIX. Computer languages and software packages include BASIC, COBOL, Pascal, RPG; database, graphics, spreadsheet, and word processing packages; 29 in all. Computer facilities are available to all students.
**Fees:** Computer fee is included in tuition/fees.

**GRADUATE CAREER DATA.** 85% of graduates choose careers in business and industry. Companies and businesses that hire graduates: Cargill, Cotter Companies, Deluxe Checking, State Farm Insurance.

# East-West University

**Chicago, IL 60605 312 939-0111**

**1993-94 Costs.** Tuition: $6,150. Fees, books, misc. academic expenses (school's estimate): $395.
**Enrollment.** Undergraduates: 127 men, 145 women (full-time). Freshman class: 134 applicants, 121 accepted, 92 enrolled.
**Test score averages/ranges.** N/A.
**Faculty.** 6 full-time; 8 part-time. 55% of faculty holds doctoral degree. Student/faculty ratio: 16 to 1.
**Selectivity rating.** N/A.

**PROFILE.** East-West, founded in 1978, is a liberal arts university. Its campus is located in downtown Chicago.

**Accreditation:** NCACS.
**Religious orientation:** East-West University is nonsectarian; no religious requirements.
**STUDENT BODY. Undergraduate profile:** 80% are state residents; 30% are transfers. 8% Asian-American, 75% Black, 13% Hispanic, 2% White, 2% Other. Average age of undergraduates is 19.
**Freshman profile:** 90% of freshmen come from public schools.
**Undergraduate achievement:** 45% of fall 1992 freshmen returned for fall 1993 term. 8% of entering class graduated.
**Foreign students:** 36 students are from out of the country. Countries represented include Belgium, Korea, Nigeria, Pakistan, Sweden, and Vietnam.
**PROGRAMS OF STUDY. Degrees:** B.A., B.S.
**Majors:** Behavioral Science, Business Administration, Computer/Information Sciences, Electronics Engineering Technology, English/Communications, Mathematics.
**Distribution of degrees:** The major with the highest enrollment is business administration.
**Requirements:** General education requirement.
**Special:** Minors offered in all majors. Associate's degrees offered. Double majors. Independent study. Cooperative education programs. Graduate school at which undergraduates may take graduate-level courses.
**Academic Assistance:** Remedial reading, writing, math, and study skills. Nonremedial tutoring.
**ADMISSIONS. Requirements:** Graduation from secondary school is required; GED is accepted. No specific distribution of secondary school units required. ACT is recommended. Campus visit and interview recommended. Off-campus interviews available with an admissions representative.
**Procedure:** Take SAT or ACT by January of 12th year. Final filing date is ten days prior to registration. Application cut-off can be announced as part of effort to limit enrollment. Notification of admission on rolling basis. Freshmen accepted for terms other than fall.
**Special programs:** Admission may be deferred. Credit and/or placement may be granted through CEEB Advanced Placement exams. Credit and/or placement may be granted through CLEP general and subject exams. Credit and placement may be granted through DANTES exams.
**Transfer students:** In fall 1993, 30% of all new students were transfers into all classes. 56 transfer applications were received, 56 were accepted. Lowest course grade accepted is "C." At least 48 credits must be completed at the university to receive degree.
**Admissions contact:** Mettha M. Green, Director of Admissions.
**FINANCIAL AID. Available aid:** Pell grants, SEOG, state scholarships, and private scholarships. Tuition Plan Inc. and deferred payment plan.
**Supporting data/closing dates:** FAFSA/FAF/FFS. Notification of awards on rolling basis.
**Financial aid contact:** Elizabeth Guzman, Director of Financial Aid.

# Eastern Illinois University

**Charleston, IL 61920 217 581-5000**

**1994-95 Costs.** Tuition: $1,902 (state residents), $5,706 (out-of-state). Room & board: $3,066. Fees, books, misc. academic expenses (school's estimate): $902.
**Enrollment.** Undergraduates: 4,187 men, 4,974 women (full-time). Freshman class: 5,597 applicants, 4,253 accepted, 1,575 enrolled. Graduate enrollment: 509 men, 880 women.
**Test score averages/ranges.** Average ACT scores: 22 English, 21 math, 22 composite. Range of ACT scores of middle 50%: 19-24 English, 18-24 math.
**Faculty.** 603 full-time; 59 part-time. 62% of faculty holds doctoral degree. Student/faculty ratio: 15 to 1.
**Selectivity rating.** Less competitive.

**PROFILE.** Eastern Illinois, founded in 1895, is a public university. Programs are offered through the Colleges of Arts and Sciences; Business; Education; Fine Arts; and Health, Physical Education, and Recreation and the Graduate School. Its 325-acre campus is located in Charleston, 55 miles from Champaign-Urbana.

**Accreditation:** NCACS. Professionally accredited by the Accrediting Council on Education in Journalism and Mass Communication, the American Assembly of Collegiate Schools of Business, the American Home Economics Association, the American Speech-Language-Hearing Association, the National Association of Schools of Art and Design, the National Association of Schools of Music, the National Council for Accreditation of Teacher Education, the National Recreation and Park Association.
**Religious orientation:** Eastern Illinois University is nonsectarian; no religious requirements.

**Library:** Collections totaling over 905,650 volumes, 3,220 periodical subscriptions, and 1,300,000 microform items.
**Special facilities/museums:** Arts center, electron microscope.
**Athletic facilities:** Gymnasiums, field house, weight rooms, athletic fields, swimming pool, basketball, racquetball, and tennis courts, track, fitness trail, archery range, ski hill.
**STUDENT BODY. Undergraduate profile:** 97% are state residents; 42% are transfers. 1% Asian-American, 5% Black, 1% Hispanic, 92% White. Average age of undergraduates is 20.
**Freshman profile:** 3% of freshmen who took ACT scored 30 or over on English, 2% scored 30 or over on math, 2% scored 30 or over on composite; 32% scored 24 or over on English, 27% scored 24 or over on math, 28% scored 24 or over on composite; 86% scored 18 or over on English, 82% scored 18 or over on math, 92% scored 18 or over on composite; 99% scored 12 or over on English, 99% scored 12 or over on math, 99% scored 12 or over on composite. 98% of accepted applicants took ACT.
**Undergraduate achievement:** 81% of fall 1992 freshmen returned for fall 1993 term. 28% of entering class graduated. 31% of students who completed a degree program went on to graduate study within one year.
**Foreign students:** 46 students are from out of the country. Countries represented include Bangladesh, Canada, Ghana, Japan, and the United Kingdom; 17 in all.
**PROGRAMS OF STUDY. Degrees:** B.A., B.Mus., B.S., B.S.Bus., B.S.Ed.
**Majors:** Accounting, Administrative Information Systems, Afro-American Studies, Art, Board of Governors, Botany, Business Education, Career Occupations, Chemistry, Communication Disorders/Sciences, Computer Management, Economics, Elementary Education, Engineering, English, Environmental Biology, Finance, French, Geology, German, Health Studies, History, Home Economics, Industrial Technology, Journalism, Junior High Education, Management, Marketing, Mathematics, Mathematics/Computer Science, Medical Technology, Music, Philosophy, Physical Education, Physics, Political Science, Psychology, Recreation Administration, Social Science, Sociology, Spanish, Special Education, Speech Communication, Technology Education, Theatre Arts, Zoology.
**Distribution of degrees:** The majors with the highest enrollment are home economics, speech communication, and elementary education; technology education, French, and German have the lowest.
**Requirements:** General education requirement.
**Academic regulations:** Minimum 2.0 GPA must be maintained.
**Special:** Minors offered in many majors and in approximately 15 other fields. Double majors. Dual degrees. Independent study. Accelerated study. Internships. Graduate school at which undergraduates may take graduate-level courses. Preprofessional programs in law, medicine, veterinary science, pharmacy, dentistry, optometry, engineering, nursing, and physical therapy. 2-2 and 3-2 engineering programs with U of Illinois at Urbana-Champaign. Cooperative preprofessional programs leading to B.S. degree after one year of medical or dental school. Teacher certification in early childhood, elementary, secondary, and special education. Certification in specific subject areas. Study abroad in the Caribbean, Ireland, and Mexico. ROTC.
**Honors:** Honors program.
**Academic Assistance:** Remedial reading, math, and study skills. Nonremedial tutoring.
**STUDENT LIFE. Housing:** Unmarried freshmen must live on campus as space permits, unless living with family. Coed, women's, and men's dorms. Sorority and fraternity housing. School-owned/operated apartments. On-campus married-student housing. 52% of students live in college housing.
**Social atmosphere:** The Martin Luther King, Jr. University Union's video lounge and bowling alley, Marty's, the Dungeon, Stu's, Stix, and the Lighthouse are popular gathering spots. Greeks, Black Student Union, LASSO, LGBAU and the Wesley Foundation influence student life. Popular social events include Homecoming, Parents' weekend, Comedians, Spring Concert, Celebration, and Greek Week.
**Services and counseling/handicapped student services:** Placement services. Health service. Women's center. Counseling services for minority, military, and veteran students. Birth control, personal, and psychological counseling. Career and academic guidance services. Religious counseling. Physically disabled student services. Learning disabled services. Notetaking services. Tape recorders. Reader services for the blind.
**Campus organizations:** Undergraduate student government. Student newspaper (Daily Eastern News). Literary magazine. Yearbook. Radio and TV stations. Bands, choir, chorus, ensembles, orchestras, debating, drama group, College Democrats, Young Republicans, 135 organizations in all. 15 fraternities, 10 chapter houses; 13 sororities, eight chapter houses. 19% of men join a fraternity. 16% of women join a sorority.
**Religious organizations:** Wesley Foundation, Pax Christi, Newman Center, Intervarsity Christian Fellowship, Baptist Student Ministries, Unity Gospel Fellowship, Navigators.
**Minority/foreign student organizations:** Black Student Union, four black fraternities, four black sororities, Hispanic Student Union. International Student Association.
**ATHLETICS. Physical education requirements:** None.
**Intercollegiate competition:** 4% of students participate. Baseball (M), basketball (M,W), cheerleading (M,W), cross-country (M,W), diving (M,W), football (M), golf (M), soccer (M), softball (W), swimming (M,W), tennis (M,W), track and field (indoor) (M,W), track and field (outdoor) (M,W), volleyball (W), wrestling (M). Member of Gateway Football Conference, Mid-Continent Conference, NCAA Division I.
**Intramural and club sports:** 80% of students participate. Intramural archery, badminton, basketball, bowling, cross-country, flag football, free-throw shooting, frisbee golf, golf pitching, home run derby, indoor soccer, pickleball, powerlifting, punt-pass-kick, racquetball, riflery, soccer, softball, swimming, table tennis, tennis, track, trapshooting, volleyball, walleyball, water basketball, Wiffle ball, wrestling. Men's club bowling, ice hockey, lacrosse, rugby, weight lifting. Women's club bowling, soccer.
**ADMISSIONS. Academic basis for candidate selection** (in order of priority): Class rank, standardized test scores, secondary school record, school's recommendation.
**Requirements:** Graduation from secondary school is required; GED is accepted. 13 units and the following program of study are required: 4 units of English, 3 units of math, 3 units of lab science, 3 units of social studies. Minimum composite ACT score of 22 and rank in top three-quarters of secondary school class or minimum composite ACT score of 18 and rank in top half of secondary school class required. Audition required of theatre and music program applicants. Minority Admission Program for applicants not normally admissible.

ACT is required; SAT may be substituted. Campus visit and interview recommended. Off-campus interviews available with an admissions representative.
**Procedure:** Notification of admission on rolling basis. No set date by which applicants must accept offer. $50 room deposit, half of which is refundable until summer prior to entrance. Freshmen accepted for terms other than fall.
**Special programs:** Admission may be deferred one semester. Credit may be granted through CEEB Advanced Placement for scores of 3 or higher. Credit may be granted through CLEP general and subject exams, ACT PEP, DANTES, and challenge exams, and military and life experience. Early entrance/early admission program. Concurrent enrollment program.
**Transfer students:** Transfer students accepted for terms other than fall. In fall 1993, 42% of all new students were transfers into all classes. 2,042 transfer applications were received, 1,627 were accepted. Application deadline is rolling for fall; rolling for spring. Minimum 2.0 GPA required. Lowest course grade accepted is "C." At least 42 semester hours must be completed at the university to receive degree.
**Admissions contact:** Dale Wolf, M.S.E., Director of Admissions. 217 581-2223, 800 252-5711.

**FINANCIAL AID. Available aid:** Pell grants, SEOG, state scholarships and grants, school scholarships and grants, private scholarships, ROTC scholarships, academic merit scholarships, athletic scholarships, and aid for undergraduate foreign students. Perkins Loans (NDSL), PLUS, Stafford Loans (GSL), school loans, private loans, and SLS. Institutional installment plan.
**Financial aid statistics:** 32% of aid is not need-based.
**Supporting data/closing dates:** FAFSA: Priority filing date is April 15. School's own aid application: Priority filing date is April 15. Income tax forms: Priority filing date is April 15. Notification of awards on rolling basis.
**Financial aid contact:** John Flynn, M.S.Ed., Director of Financial Aid. 217 581-3713.

**STUDENT EMPLOYMENT.** College Work/Study Program. Institutional employment. 30% of full-time undergraduates work on campus during school year. Students may expect to earn an average of $850 during school year. Off-campus part-time employment opportunities rated "fair."

**COMPUTER FACILITIES.** 700 IBM/IBM-compatible and Macintosh/Apple microcomputers; 350 are networked. Students may access IBM, SUN minicomputer/mainframe systems, BITNET, Internet, CompuServe. Residence halls may be equipped with stand-alone microcomputers, networked microcomputers. Client/LAN operating systems include Apple/Macintosh, DOS, OS/2, UNIX/XENIX/AIX, LocalTalk/AppleTalk, Microsoft. Computer languages and software packages include BASIC, C++, CICS, Claris Works, COBOL, FORTRAN, Harvard Graphics, Lotus 1-2-3, MacWrite, Microsoft Works, ROSCOE, WordPerfect. Computer facilities are available to all students.
**Fees:** $10 computer fee per semester.
**Hours:** 8 AM-midn.

**GRADUATE CAREER DATA.** Graduate school percentages: 1% enter law school. 22% of graduates choose careers in business and industry.

**PROMINENT ALUMNI/AE.** Jim Edgar, Illinois governor; Jeff Gossett, professional football player; Joan Embery, San Diego Zoo; John Malkovich, actor; Burl Ives, entertainer.

# Elmhurst College

**Elmhurst, IL 60126-3296** **708 617-3400**

**1994-95 Costs.** Tuition: $9,124. Room: $2,100. Board: $2,000. Fees, books, misc. academic expenses (school's estimate): $500.
**Enrollment.** Undergraduates: 575 men, 1,030 women (full-time). Freshman class: 950 applicants, 663 accepted, 267 enrolled.
**Test score averages/ranges.** Average SAT scores: 421 verbal, 461 math. Average ACT scores: 21 composite. Range of ACT scores of middle 50%: 18-23 composite.
**Faculty.** 98 full-time; 38 part-time. 66% of faculty holds doctoral degree. Student/faculty ratio: 15 to 1.
**Selectivity rating.** Competitive.

**PROFILE.** Elmhurst, founded in 1871, is a church-affiliated, liberal arts college. Its 35-acre campus, a designated arboretum, is located in a suburb of Chicago, 16 miles west of the Loop.

**Accreditation:** NCACS. Professionally accredited by the National Council for Accreditation of Teacher Education, the National League for Nursing.
**Religious orientation:** Elmhurst College is affiliated with the United Church of Christ; one semester of theology required.
**Library:** Collections totaling over 216,500 volumes, 1,300 periodical subscriptions, and 42,000 microform items.
**Special facilities/museums:** Language lab, computer science/technology center, four electron microscopes.
**Athletic facilities:** Gymnasium, track, baseball, football, and soccer fields, tennis courts, weight room.

**STUDENT BODY. Undergraduate profile:** 93% are state residents; 58% are transfers. 4% Asian-American, 5% Black, 3% Hispanic, .5% Native American, 81% White, 6.5% Other. Average age of undergraduates is 22.
**Freshman profile:** 3% of freshmen who took ACT scored 30 or over on English, 2% scored 30 or over on math, 1% scored 30 or over on composite; 25% scored 24 or over on English, 22% scored 24 or over on math, 22% scored 24 or over on composite; 72% scored 18 or over on English, 67% scored 18 or over on math, 80% scored 18 or over on composite; 97% scored 12 or over on English, 99% scored 12 or over on math, 100% scored 12 or over on composite. 9% of accepted applicants took SAT; 96% took ACT. 80% of freshmen come from public schools.
**Undergraduate achievement:** 73% of fall 1992 freshmen returned for fall 1993 term. 41% of entering class graduated. 6% of students who completed a degree program immediately went on to graduate study.
**Foreign students:** 18 students are from out of the country. Countries represented include Greece and Japan; seven in all.

**PROGRAMS OF STUDY. Degrees:** B.A., B.Mus., B.S.
**Majors:** Accounting, American Studies, Art, Art Education, Arts Management, Athletic Training, Biochemistry, Biology, Business Administration, Chemistry, Computer Science, Economics, Elementary Education, English, Environmental Planning, Finance, French, Geography/Environmental Planning, German, Health Management, History, Human Resources Management, Information Systems, Interdepartmental Communication, International Business, Management, Marketing, Mathematics, Music, Music Business, Music Education, Nursing, Philosophy, Physical Education, Physics, Political Science, Psychology, Recreation Management, Secondary Education, Sociology, Spanish, Special Education, Speech Communication, Speech Education, Speech/Language Pathology, Theatre, Theology/Religion, Time Arts, Transportation Management.
**Distribution of degrees:** The majors with the highest enrollment are business administration, accounting, and marketing; theology, Spanish, and German have the lowest.
**Requirements:** General education requirement.
**Academic regulations:** Minimum 2.0 GPA must be maintained.
**Special:** Double majors. Independent study. Pass/fail grading option. Internships. Cooperative education programs. Preprofessional programs in law, medicine, veterinary science, pharmacy, dentistry, theology, and optometry. Combined-degree engineering programs with Illinois Inst of Tech, U of Illinois at Chicago, and Northwestern U. West Suburban Regional Academic Consortium, Higher Education Regional Consortium. Washington Semester. Teacher certification in early childhood, elementary, secondary, and special education. Certification in specific subject areas. Study abroad possible in Austria, England, France, Germany, Greece, Mexico, and Spain. ROTC at Wheaton Coll. AFROTC at Illinois Inst of Tech.
**Honors:** Honors program. Honor societies.
**Academic Assistance:** Remedial study skills. Nonremedial tutoring.

**STUDENT LIFE. Housing:** Coed, women's, and men's dorms. 35% of students live in college housing.
**Social atmosphere:** According to the editor of the student newspaper, the most popular social events of the year are Homecoming, Spring Dance, and Festival of Fools. Members of the Union Board, the Greek organizations, and the Campus Life Council exert the most social influence on campus. Favorite student gathering spots are the College Union Building and the game room on campus. Students frequent Oscar's, McGregor's, and comedy clubs, and enjoy downtown Chicago's night life.
**Services and counseling/handicapped student services:** Placement services. Health service. Counseling services for minority, veteran, and older students. Personal and psychological counseling. Career and academic guidance services. Religious counseling. Physically disabled student services. Learning disabled services. Tape recorders.
**Campus organizations:** Undergraduate student government. Student newspaper (Leader, published once/week). Literary magazine. Yearbook. Radio station. Union Board, choir, jazz band, vocal jazz ensemble, Orchesis, band, Theatre Guild, debating, pom pom/cheerleader squads, 53 organizations in all. Four fraternities, no chapter houses; three sororities, no chapter houses. 10% of men join a fraternity. 15% of women join a sorority.
**Religious organizations:** Campus Ministry Committee, Fellowship of Christian Athletes, Religious Life Committee, Campus Crusade for Christ, Christian Science Organization, gospel choir.
**Minority/foreign student organizations:** Black Student Union, Hablamos. International Club.

**ATHLETICS. Physical education requirements:** Two semesters of physical education required.
**Intercollegiate competition:** Baseball (M), basketball (M,W), cross-country (M,W), football (M), golf (M,W), softball (W), tennis (M,W), track (indoor) (M,W), track (outdoor) (M,W), track and field (indoor) (M,W), track and field (outdoor) (M,W), volleyball (W), wrestling (M). Member of College Conference of Illinois and Wisconsin, NCAA Division III.
**Intramural and club sports:** Intramural basketball, softball, volleyball. Men's club cheerleading. Women's club cheerleading.

**ADMISSIONS. Academic basis for candidate selection** (in order of priority): Secondary school record, class rank, standardized test scores, school's recommendation, essay.
**Nonacademic basis for candidate selection:** Character and personality are important. Extracurricular participation, particular talent or ability, geographical distribution, and alumni/ae relationship are considered.
**Requirements:** Graduation from secondary school is required; GED is accepted. 12 units and the following program of study are required: 3 units of English, 2 units of math, 2 units of lab science, 2 units of social studies, 1 unit of history. Minimum composite ACT score of 20 (combined SAT score of 800), rank in top half of secondary school class, and minimum 2.0 GPA recommended. Audition required of music program applicants. Limited load provision and special Freshmen Advising Program during first term for applicants not meeting standard requirements. ACT is required; SAT may be substituted. Campus visit and interview recommended. Off-campus interviews available with an admissions representative.
**Procedure:** Take SAT or ACT by June of 12th year. Visit college for interview by May of 12th year. Application deadline is August 1. Notification of admission on rolling basis. Reply is required by June 1 or within two weeks of acceptance. $100 tuition deposit, refundable until May 1. $100 room deposit, refundable until August 1. Freshmen accepted for terms other than fall.
**Special programs:** Admission may be deferred two years. Credit and/or placement may be granted through CEEB Advanced Placement exams for scores of 3 or higher. Credit and/or placement may be granted through CLEP general and subject exams. Credit and placement may be granted through ACT PEP, DANTES, and challenge exams, and military and life experience. Early entrance/early admission program. Concurrent enrollment program.
**Transfer students:** Transfer students accepted for terms other than fall. In fall 1993, 58% of all new students were transfers into all classes. 890 transfer applications were received, 716 were accepted. Application deadline is August 1 for fall; January 1 for spring. Minimum 2.0 GPA required. Lowest course grade accepted is "D." Maximum number of transferable credits is 64 semester hours from a two-year school and 96 semester hours from a

four-year school. At least 32 semester hours must be completed at the college to receive degree.
**Admissions contact:** John R. Hopkins, M.A., Director of Enrollment Development. 708 617-3400, 800 697-1871.

**FINANCIAL AID. Available aid:** Pell grants, SEOG, state scholarships and grants, school scholarships and grants, private scholarships and grants, and academic merit scholarships. Perkins Loans (NDSL), PLUS, Stafford Loans (GSL), state loans, private loans, and SLS. Deferred payment plan.
**Financial aid statistics:** 10% of aid is not need-based. In 1993-94, 60% of all undergraduate applicants received aid; 62% of freshman applicants. Average amounts of aid awarded freshmen: Scholarships and grants, $5,600; loans, $1,800.
**Supporting data/closing dates:** FAFSA: Priority filing date is April 15; accepted on rolling basis. School's own aid application: Priority filing date is April 15; accepted on rolling basis. Income tax forms: Priority filing date is April 15. Notification of awards begins March 15.
**Financial aid contact:** Gary F. Rold, M.Ed., Director of Financial Aid. 708 617-3075.

**STUDENT EMPLOYMENT.** College Work/Study Program. Institutional employment. 16% of full-time undergraduates work on campus during school year. Students may expect to earn an average of $1,200 during school year. Off-campus part-time employment opportunities rated "excellent."

**COMPUTER FACILITIES.** 110 IBM/IBM-compatible and Macintosh/Apple microcomputers; all are networked. Students may access AT&T, IBM minicomputer/mainframe systems, Internet. Residence halls may be equipped with modems. Client/LAN operating systems include Apple/Macintosh, DOS, OS/2, UNIX/XENIX/AIX, X-windows. Computer languages and software packages include Ada, BASIC, C++, CICS, COBOL, dBASE, FORTRAN, LISP, Lotus 1-2-3, Oracle, Pascal, QuattroPro, RPG, SPSS-X, UNIX, WordPerfect; 20 in all. Computer facilities are available to all students.
**Fees:** Computer fee is included in tuition/fees.
**Hours:** 24 hours/day.

**GRADUATE CAREER DATA.** Graduate school percentages: 2% enter law school. 1% enter medical school. 8% enter graduate business programs. 2% enter graduate arts and sciences programs. Highest graduate school enrollments: DePaul U, Loyola U, Northern Illinois U, Roosevelt U, U of Illinois at Chicago. 80% of graduates choose careers in business and industry. Companies and businesses that hire graduates: Allstate, Dominick's Food Store, Jewel, Lutheran General Hospital, Motorola, Performance Analytics, U.P.S., Walgreen's, Wolf & Co.

**PROMINENT ALUMNI/AE.** William Bauer, former chief justice, U.S. Court of Appeals, 7th Circuit, Illinois; Terri Hemmert, Chicago radio personality; George Sangmeister, congressman; Cathy Notari Davidson, educator; David Kuebler, operatic tenor; David Rasche, actor; Richard and Reinhold Niebuhr, theologians.

## Eureka College

Eureka, IL 61530 — 309 467-6350

**1994-95 Costs.** Tuition: $11,630. Room & board: $3,650. Fees, books, misc. academic expenses (school's estimate): $650.
**Enrollment.** Undergraduates: 246 men, 238 women (full-time). Freshman class: 560 applicants, 454 accepted, 113 enrolled.
**Test score averages/ranges.** Average ACT scores: 22 composite.
**Faculty.** 41 full-time; 16 part-time. 70% of faculty holds doctoral degree. Student/faculty ratio: 12 to 1.
**Selectivity rating.** Less competitive.

**PROFILE.** Eureka College, founded in 1855, is a church-affiliated, liberal arts institution. Its 112-acre campus is located in the town of Eureka, between the metropolitan centers of Peoria and Bloomington-Normal.

**Accreditation:** NCACS.
**Religious orientation:** Eureka College is affiliated with the Christian Church (Disciples of Christ); no religious requirements.
**Library:** Collections totaling over 80,000 volumes and 400 periodical subscriptions.
**Athletic facilities:** Field house, basketball, tennis, and volleyball courts, track, swimming pool, baseball, football, intramural, and softball fields.

**STUDENT BODY. Undergraduate profile:** 88% are state residents; 23% are transfers. 1% Asian-American, 4% Black, 2% Hispanic, 88% White, 5% Other. Average age of undergraduates is 21.
**Freshman profile:** 4% of freshmen who took ACT scored 30 or over on composite; 34% scored 24 or over on composite; 87% scored 18 or over on composite; 100% scored 12 or over on composite. 98% of accepted applicants took ACT. 95% of freshmen come from public schools.
**Undergraduate achievement:** 72% of fall 1992 freshmen returned for fall 1993 term. 58% of entering class graduated. 22% of students who completed a degree program immediately went on to graduate study.
**Foreign students:** 22 students are from out of the country. Countries represented include Japan.

**PROGRAMS OF STUDY. Degrees:** B.A., B.S.
**Majors:** Accounting, Art, Athletic Training, Biology, Business Administration, Chemistry, Communications, Computer Science, Economics, Economics/Business, Elementary Education, Engineering, English, Finance, History, Mathematics, Medical Technology, Music, Nursing, Philosophy/Religious Studies, Physical Education, Physical Fitness Leadership, Physical Science, Political Science/History, Psychology, Social Science/Business, Sociology, Sociology/Psychology, Speech Communication, Theatre Arts.
**Distribution of degrees:** The majors with the highest enrollment are education, business, and physical education; philosophy/religion and communications have the lowest.
**Requirements:** General education requirement.
**Academic regulations:** Freshmen must maintain minimum 1.70 GPA; sophomores, 1.80 GPA; juniors, 1.90 GPA; seniors, 2.00 GPA.
**Special:** Minors offered in all majors and in writing. Intensive Study Plan divides each semester into two eight-week terms; students take two or three courses during each term. Double majors. Independent study. Internships. Preprofessional programs in law, medicine, veterinary science, dentistry, and theology. 2-2 nursing program with Mennonite Coll of Nursing and St. Francis Sch of Nursing. 3-1 medical technology program with St. Francis Sch of Nursing and St. John's Hospital. 3-2 engineering program with Illinois Inst of Tech. Teacher certification in elementary and secondary education. Study abroad in Austria, France, Germany, Italy, Japan, Spain, and the United Kingdom.
**Honors:** Honors program. Honor societies.
**Academic Assistance:** Remedial reading, writing, and math. Nonremedial tutoring.

**ADMISSIONS. Academic basis for candidate selection** (in order of priority): Class rank, standardized test scores, secondary school record, school's recommendation.
**Nonacademic basis for candidate selection:** Character and personality, extracurricular participation, particular talent or ability, geographical distribution, and alumni/ae relationship are important.
**Requirements:** Graduation from secondary school is required; GED is accepted. No specific distribution of secondary school units required. Minimum composite ACT score of 21 and rank in top half of secondary school class recommended. ACT is required; SAT may be substituted. Campus visit recommended. Off-campus interviews available with an admissions representative.
**Procedure:** Take SAT or ACT by April of 12th year. Suggest filing application by March 1; no deadline. Notification of admission on rolling basis. Reply is required by date specified in letter of acceptance. $200 nonrefundable tuition deposit. $50 nonrefundable room deposit. Freshmen accepted for terms other than fall.
**Special programs:** Admission may be deferred one year. Credit may be granted through CEEB Advanced Placement for scores of 3 or higher. Concurrent enrollment program.
**Transfer students:** Transfer students accepted for terms other than fall. In fall 1993, 23% of all new students were transfers into all classes. 119 transfer applications were received, 76 were accepted. Application deadline is rolling for fall; rolling for spring. Minimum 2.0 GPA required. Lowest course grade accepted is "C." Maximum number of transferable credits is 68 semester hours from a two-year school and 94 semester hours from a four-year school. At least 84 semester hours must be completed at the college to receive degree.
**Admissions contact:** Susan R. Jordan, Dean of Admissions and Financial Aid. 800 322-3756.

**FINANCIAL AID. Available aid:** Pell grants, SEOG, state scholarships and grants, school scholarships and grants, private scholarships and grants, and academic merit scholarships. Perkins Loans (NDSL), PLUS, Stafford Loans (GSL), and SLS. Tuition Plan Inc.
**Financial aid statistics:** In 1993-94, 97% of all undergraduate applicants received aid; 96% of freshman applicants. Average amounts of aid awarded freshmen: Scholarships and grants, $4,900; loans, $2,412.
**Supporting data/closing dates:** FAFSA. Income tax forms: Accepted on rolling basis. Notification of awards on rolling basis.
**Financial aid contact:** Martin Stromberger, M.S., Director of Financial Aid. 309 467-6310.

## Greenville College

Greenville, IL 62246 — 618 664-1840

**1993-94 Costs.** Tuition: $9,910. Room & board: $4,160. Fees, books, misc. academic expenses (school's estimate): $620.
**Enrollment.** Undergraduates: 374 men, 397 women (full-time). Freshman class: 594 applicants, 379 accepted, 195 enrolled.
**Test score averages/ranges.** Average ACT scores: 21 English, 20 math, 22 composite. Range of ACT scores of middle 50%: 18-24 English, 17-23 math.
**Faculty.** 56 full-time; 7 part-time. 46% of faculty holds doctoral degree. Student/faculty ratio: 14 to 1.
**Selectivity rating.** Competitive.

**PROFILE.** Greenville, founded in 1892, is a church-affiliated, liberal arts college. Its eight-acre central campus is located two blocks from Greenville's town square and 50 miles east of St. Louis.

**Accreditation:** NCACS.
**Religious orientation:** Greenville College is affiliated with the Free Methodist Church; two semesters of religion required.
**Library:** Collections totaling over 119,621 volumes, 578 periodical subscriptions, and 10,287 microform items.
**Special facilities/museums:** Sculpture museum, sports training annex.
**Athletic facilities:** Gymnasiums, recreation center, aerobics and weight rooms, tennis courts, track, baseball, football, soccer, and softball fields, swimming pool, sauna.

**STUDENT BODY. Undergraduate profile:** 60% are state residents; 26% are transfers. 2% Asian-American, 8% Black, 3% Hispanic, 1% Native American, 84% White, 2% Other. Average age of undergraduates is 20.
**Freshman profile:** 2% of freshmen who took ACT scored 30 or over on English, 3% scored 30 or over on math, 2% scored 30 or over on composite; 26% scored 24 or over on English, 19% scored 24 or over on math, 28% scored 24 or over on composite; 62% scored 18 or over on English, 56% scored 18 or over on math, 65% scored 18 or over on composite; 78% scored 12 or over on English, 78% scored 12 or over on math, 79% scored 12 or over on composite; 79% scored 6 or over on English, 79% scored 6 or over on math. Majority of accepted applicants took ACT.
**Undergraduate achievement:** 68% of fall 1992 freshmen returned for fall 1993 term. 50% of entering class graduated. 15% of students who completed a degree program immediately went on to graduate study.
**Foreign students:** 13 students are from out of the country. Countries represented include Canada, China, Haiti, Japan, and the Dominican Republican; 11 in all.

**PROGRAMS OF STUDY. Degrees:** B.A., B.Mus.Ed., B.S.
**Majors:** Accounting, Art, Biology, Business, Business Management, Chemistry, Communications, Computer Science, Contemporary Christian Music, Drama, Education, English, French, Gerontology, History/Political Science, Marketing, Mathematics, Modern Languages, Music, Pastoral Ministries, Philosophy, Physics, Psychology, Psychology/Religion, Recreation, Religion, Religion/Philosophy, Social Work, Sociology, Spanish, Speech, Youth Ministries.
**Distribution of degrees:** The majors with the highest enrollment are education, business, and biology; Spanish, speech, and art have the lowest.
**Requirements:** General education requirement.
**Academic regulations:** Freshmen must maintain minimum 1.5 GPA; sophomores, 1.75 GPA; juniors, 2.0 GPA; seniors, 2.0 GPA.
**Special:** Minors offered in most majors and in coaching. Unlimited area majors offered through individually tailored Education Plan. Four-year theological curriculum allows students to qualify for conference membership and ordination without additional studies. Self-designed majors. Double majors. Independent study. Pass/fail grading option. Internships. Cooperative education programs. Preprofessional programs in law, medicine, veterinary science, pharmacy, dentistry, theology, optometry, and nursing. 3-2 engineering program with U of Illinois. 3-2 nursing program with Mennonite Coll of Nursing. 3-2 engineering and physical therapy programs with Washington U. Member of Christian College Consortium. Washington Semester. AuSable Inst of Environmental Studies Program (Michigan). Colorado Semester. Hollywood Film Semester. Teacher certification in early childhood, elementary, secondary, and special education. Certification in specific subject areas. Study abroad in the Dominican Republic, European countries, Kenya, and Mexico.
**Academic Assistance:** Remedial reading, writing, and study skills. Nonremedial tutoring.

**ADMISSIONS. Academic basis for candidate selection** (in order of priority): Secondary school record, school's recommendation, class rank, essay, standardized test scores.
**Nonacademic basis for candidate selection:** Character and personality, extracurricular participation, and particular talent or ability are important.
**Requirements:** Graduation from secondary school is required; GED is accepted. 16 units and the following program of study are required: 4 units of English, 2 units of math, 1 unit of lab science, 2 units of foreign language, 1 unit of history. Minimum composite ACT score of 18, rank in top half of secondary school class, and minimum 2.0 GPA required. Conditional admission possible for applicants not meeting standard requirements. SAT or ACT is required. Campus visit and interview recommended. Off-campus interviews available with admissions and alumni representatives.
**Procedure:** Take SAT or ACT by September 1 of 12th year. Notification of admission on rolling basis. No set date by which applicants must accept offer. $100 tuition deposit, refundable until July 1. Freshmen accepted for terms other than fall.
**Special programs:** Admission may be deferred two years. Credit may be granted through CEEB Advanced Placement for scores of 3 or higher. Credit may be granted through CLEP general and subject exams. Placement may be granted through life experience. Credit and placement may be granted through challenge exams and military experience. Concurrent enrollment program.
**Transfer students:** Transfer students accepted for terms other than fall. In fall 1993, 26% of all new students were transfers into all classes. 187 transfer applications were received, 96 were accepted. Application deadline is rolling for fall; rolling for spring. Minimum 2.0 GPA recommended. Lowest course grade accepted is "C." At least 40 semester hours must be completed at the college to receive degree.
**Admissions contact:** H. Kent Krober, M.S.Ed., Director of Admissions. 800 248-2288 (in-state), 800 345-4440 (out-of-state).

**FINANCIAL AID. Available aid:** Pell grants, SEOG, state scholarships and grants, school scholarships and grants, private scholarships and grants, and academic merit scholarships. Perkins Loans (NDSL), PLUS, Stafford Loans (GSL), state loans, school loans, and SLS. AMS. Institutional payment plans.
**Financial aid statistics:** 14% of aid is not need-based. In 1993-94, 98% of all undergraduate applicants received aid; 98% of freshman applicants. Average amounts of aid awarded freshmen: Scholarships and grants, $3,300; loans, $3,500.
**Supporting data/closing dates:** FAFSA: Priority filing date is June 1. Notification of awards begins March 1.
**Financial aid contact:** Marilyn Reinhard, M.S.Ed., Associate Director of Admissions for Financial Aid. 618 664-2800, extension 4421.

# Illinois Benedictine College

**Lisle, IL 60532-0900** **708 960-1500**

**1994-95 Costs.** Tuition: $10,500. Room & board: $4,348. Fees, books, misc. academic expenses (school's estimate): $800.
**Enrollment.** Undergraduates: 614 men, 614 women (full-time). Freshman class: 558 applicants, 497 accepted, 231 enrolled. Graduate enrollment: 472 men, 456 women.
**Test score averages/ranges.** Average ACT scores: 23 composite. Range of ACT scores of middle 50%: 19-25 composite.
**Faculty.** 79 full-time; 61 part-time. 78% of faculty holds doctoral degree. Student/faculty ratio: 15 to 1.
**Selectivity rating.** Less competitive.

**PROFILE.** Illinois Benedictine, founded in 1887, is a church-affiliated, liberal arts college. Its 108-acre campus is located in Lisle, 25 miles southwest of downtown Chicago.

**Accreditation:** NCACS. Professionally accredited by the American Dietetic Association, the National League for Nursing.
**Religious orientation:** Illinois Benedictine College is affiliated with the Roman Catholic (Benedictine Monks); two semesters of religion/theology required.
**Library:** Collections totaling over 162,874 volumes, 700 periodical subscriptions, and 109,591 microform items.
**Special facilities/museums:** Natural science and history museums, Ph.D.-level exercise physiology and robotics lab.
**Athletic facilities:** Gymnasium, field house, basketball, racquetball, and tennis courts, track, weight room, baseball, football, and softball fields, swimming pool.

**STUDENT BODY. Undergraduate profile:** 98% are state residents; 50% are transfers. 5% Asian-American, 5% Black, 3% Hispanic, 86% White, 1% Other. Average age of undergraduates is 25.
**Freshman profile:** 2% of accepted applicants took SAT; 96% took ACT. 71% of freshmen come from public schools.
**Undergraduate achievement:** 72% of fall 1992 freshmen returned for fall 1993 term. 54% of entering class graduated. 13% of students who completed a degree program immediately went on to graduate study.
**Foreign students:** 45 students are from out of the country. Countries represented include African and Asian countries, European countries, and Japan.

**PROGRAMS OF STUDY. Degrees:** B.A., B.S.
**Majors:** Accounting, Biochemistry, Biology, Business Economics, Chemistry, Clinical Laboratory Science, Computer Science, Economics, Elementary Education, Engineering Science, Health Sciences, Health Services Management, History, International Business/Economics, Literature/Communications, Mathematics, Music, Nuclear Medical Technology, Nursing, Nutrition, Philosophy, Physical Education, Physics, Political Science, Psychology, Religious Studies, Social Science/History, Social Sciences, Sociology, Spanish, Special Education.
**Distribution of degrees:** The majors with the highest enrollment are business economics, biology, and literature/communications; Spanish, history, and philosophy have the lowest.
**Academic regulations:** Minimum 2.0 GPA must be maintained.
**Special:** Minors offered in most majors and in art, gerontology, languages, and social work; students are encouraged to select a minor. Music majors choose one of the following concentrations: applied music, jazz studies, music education, sacred music, or music theory. Interdisciplinary program in business and humanities. Courses offered in criminal justice, French, German, and Latin. Double majors. Independent study. Internships. Graduate school at which undergraduates may take graduate-level courses. Preprofessional programs in law, medicine, veterinary science, pharmacy, dentistry, optometry, engineering, medical records administration, nursing, occupational therapy, physical therapy, and podiatry. 2-2 nursing program with Rush U. 3-2 engineering program; 2-2 pre-engineering transfer programs with U of Illinois, Marquette U, and U of Notre Dame; 2-3 pre-engineering transfer program with U of Detroit. Engineering program with Illinois Inst of Tech. 4-1 B.S. in health studies or nutrition with M.S. in exercise physiology. 4-1 B.A./M.B.A. or M.S. program. Member of Council of West Suburban Colleges and West Suburban Regional Academic Consortium. Cross-registration with Aurora U and North Central Coll. Teacher certification in early childhood, elementary, secondary, and special education. Certification in specific subject areas. Exchange program abroad in Japan (Chuo U). Study abroad also in Austria, China, Costa Rica, England, France, Germany, Greece, Mexico, Spain, Taiwan, and other countries. ROTC at Wheaton Coll. NROTC and AFROTC at Illinois Inst of Tech.
**Honors:** Honors program. Honor societies.
**Academic Assistance:** Remedial reading, writing, and study skills. Nonremedial tutoring.

**STUDENT LIFE. Housing:** Students may live on or off campus. Coed, women's, and men's dorms. 36% of students live in college housing.
**Social atmosphere:** Eagles Nest, Fireside Lounge, Jukebox, El Burrito Mexicano, and Cafe Trieste are hot spots on and off campus. Athletes, Union of Minority Students, Student Government Association, Music Department (Jazz), IBC Theatre, and Cultural Events Committee influence campus life. Eagerly anticipated social events include pub parties, Homecoming (football games, dance, week of activities/contests), theatre performances, Spring Semi-Formal, Senior Ball, volleyball and softball games, and Jazz at Noon. "Located in the suburbs of Chicago, there are abundant opportunities for social and cultural experiences in the city and surrounding areas: museums, theatres, concerts, restaurants, bars, etc.," reports the editor of the student newspaper.
**Services and counseling/handicapped student services:** Placement services. Health service. Day care. Counseling services for minority and older students. Personal and psychological counseling. Career and academic guidance services. Religious counseling. Physically disabled student services. Learning disabled services. Notetaking services. Tape recorders. Tutors.
**Campus organizations:** Undergraduate student government. Student newspaper (Candor, published once/week). Literary magazine. Yearbook. Radio and TV stations. Gospel choir, chorus, jazz bands, Commuter Association, psychology club, departmental and special-interest groups, Circle K, Knights of Columbus, Blue Key, 36 organizations in all.
**Religious organizations:** Campus Ministry.
**Minority/foreign student organizations:** Union of Minority Students. International Student Association.

**ATHLETICS. Physical education requirements:** None.
**Intercollegiate competition:** 23% of students participate. Baseball (M), basketball (M,W), cheerleading (M,W), cross-country (M,W), diving (M,W), football (M), golf (M,W), soccer (M), softball (W), swimming (M,W), tennis (M,W), track (indoor) (M,W), track (outdoor) (M,W), track and field (indoor) (M,W), track and field (outdoor) (M,W), volleyball (W). Member of NCAA Division III, Northern Illinois Intercollegiate Conference.
**Intramural and club sports:** 43% of students participate. Intramural aerobics, basketball, bowling, field hockey, olympics, softball, volleyball, water polo. Men's club volleyball, water polo. Women's club water polo.

**ADMISSIONS. Academic basis for candidate selection** (in order of priority): Secondary school record, class rank, standardized test scores, school's recommendation, essay.
**Nonacademic basis for candidate selection:** Particular talent or ability is important. Character and personality and extracurricular participation are considered.
**Requirements:** Graduation from secondary school is required; GED is accepted. 16 units and the following program of study are required: 4 units of English, 2 units of math, 1 unit of lab science, 2 units of foreign language, 1 unit of history, 6 units of electives including 2 units of academic electives. Minimum composite ACT score of 21, rank in top half of secondary school class, and minimum 2.0 GPA required. 3 units of math (including advanced algebra/trigonometry) strongly recommended of accounting, business economics, computer science, economics, math, and science program applicants. Additional science units recommended of science program applicants. Interview and essay required of Scholars Program applicants. Audition required of music program applicants. R.N. required of

nursing program applicants. Conditional admission possible for applicants not meeting standard requirements. ACT is required; SAT may be substituted. Campus visit and interview recommended. Off-campus interviews available with admissions and alumni representatives.

**Procedure:** Take SAT or ACT by June of 12th year. Notification of admission on rolling basis. $75 tuition deposit, refundable until May 1. $75 room deposit, refundable until May 1. Freshmen accepted for terms other than fall.

**Special programs:** Admission may be deferred two years. Credit and/or placement may be granted through CEEB Advanced Placement exams for scores of 3 or higher. Credit and/or placement may be granted through CLEP general and subject exams. Credit may be granted through ACT PEP exams and life experience. Placement may be granted through challenge exams. Early entrance/early admission program. Concurrent enrollment program.

**Transfer students:** Transfer students accepted for terms other than fall. In fall 1993, 50% of all new students were transfers into all classes. 490 transfer applications were received, 351 were accepted. Application deadline is rolling for fall; rolling for spring. Minimum 2.0 GPA required. Lowest course grade accepted is "C." Maximum number of transferable semester hours is 60 from two-year schools; 30 from four-year schools. At least 30 semester hours must be completed at the college to receive degree.

**Admissions contact:** Jane L. Smith, M.B.A., Director of Admissions. 708 960-1500, extension 4000.

**FINANCIAL AID. Available aid:** Pell grants, SEOG, state scholarships and grants, school scholarships and grants, private scholarships and grants, ROTC scholarships, academic merit scholarships, and aid for undergraduate foreign students. Perkins Loans (NDSL), PLUS, Stafford Loans (GSL), state loans, and SLS. Tuition Plan Inc., AMS, Tuition Management Systems, and family tuition reduction. College payment plan.

**Financial aid statistics:** 30% of aid is not need-based. In 1993-94, 95% of all undergraduate applicants received aid; 94% of freshman applicants. Average amounts of aid awarded freshmen: Scholarships and grants, $6,113; loans, $2,247.

**Supporting data/closing dates:** FAFSA/FAF/FFS: Accepted on rolling basis. School's own aid application: Accepted on rolling basis. Income tax forms: Accepted on rolling basis. Notification of awards on rolling basis.

**Financial aid contact:** Laura Day, Director of Financial Aid. 708 960-1500, extension 4105.

**STUDENT EMPLOYMENT.** College Work/Study Program. Institutional employment. 28% of full-time undergraduates work on campus during school year. Students may expect to earn an average of $1,200 during school year. Off-campus part-time employment opportunities rated "good."

**COMPUTER FACILITIES.** 58 IBM/IBM-compatible and Macintosh/Apple microcomputers; 47 are networked. Students may access Sequent minicomputer/mainframe systems, Internet. Residence halls may be equipped with modems. Computer languages and software packages include BASIC, C, COBOL, FORTRAN, Informix, LISP, Pstat, Pascal, Prolog, WordPerfect, WordStar; graphics programs; 15 in all. Computer facilities are available to all students.

**Fees:** Computer fee is included in tuition/fees.

**Hours:** 8 AM-11 PM (M-F); 10 AM-3 PM (Sa); 1 PM-11 PM (Su).

**GRADUATE CAREER DATA.** Graduate school percentages: 1% enter law school. 12% enter medical school. 1% enter dental school. 2% enter graduate business programs. Highest graduate school enrollments: Loyola U, U of Illinois, U of Michigan, Notre Dame U. 80% of graduates choose careers in business and industry. Companies and businesses that hire graduates: Amoco, Arthur Andersen, AT&T, Bell Labs, Nalco.

**PROMINENT ALUMNI/AE.** Most Rev. Daniel W. Kucera, O.S.B., archbishop, Dubuque, Iowa; Earl Burrell, retired CEO, Pittsburgh Plate Glass; Ronald Winters, M.D., general practice physician, Elgin, Ill.

## Illinois College

**Jacksonville, IL 62650 — 217 245-3000**

**1994-95 Costs.** Tuition: $8,050. Room & board: $3,850. Fees, books, misc. academic expenses (school's estimate): $500.

**Enrollment.** Undergraduates: 432 men, 477 women (full-time). Freshman class: 894 applicants, 787 accepted, 262 enrolled. Graduate enrollment: 448 men, 489 women.

**Test score averages/ranges.** Average SAT scores: 470 verbal, 545 math. Range of SAT scores of middle 50%: 370-580 verbal, 420-690 math. Average ACT scores: 23 composite. Range of ACT scores of middle 50%: 21-26 composite.

**Faculty.** 60 full-time; 25 part-time. 70% of faculty holds doctoral degree. Student/faculty ratio: 15 to 1.

**Selectivity rating.** Less competitive.

**PROFILE.** Illinois College, founded in 1829, is a church-affiliated institution. Its 62-acre campus is located in Jacksonville, 35 miles west of Springfield.

**Accreditation:** NCACS.

**Religious orientation:** Illinois College is affiliated with the United Presbyterian Church and United Church of Christ; two semesters of religion required.

**Library:** Collections totaling over 130,000 volumes and 600 periodical subscriptions.

**Special facilities/museums:** Art gallery, language lab.

**Athletic facilities:** Gymnasiums, field house, swimming pool, basketball, handball, and racquetball courts, weight room, baseball, football, intramural, soccer, and softball fields, batting cage, track, fitness center, stadium.

**STUDENT BODY. Undergraduate profile:** 94% are state residents; 18% are transfers. 2.2% Asian-American, 1.7% Black, .4% Hispanic, 95.6% White, .1% Other. Average age of undergraduates is 20.

**Freshman profile:** 4% of freshmen who took SAT scored 700 or over on verbal, 16% scored 700 or over on math; 12% scored 600 or over on verbal, 43% scored 600 or over on math; 47% scored 500 or over on verbal, 58% scored 500 or over on math; 67% scored 400 or over on verbal, 97% scored 400 or over on math; 100% scored 300 or over on verbal, 100% scored 300 or over on math. 4% of freshmen who took ACT scored 30 or over on composite; 41% scored 24 or over on composite; 99% scored 18 or over on composite; 100% scored 12 or over on composite. 10% of accepted applicants took SAT; 97% took ACT.

**Undergraduate achievement:** 85% of fall 1992 freshmen returned for fall 1993 term. 50% of entering class graduated. 20% of students who completed a degree program immediately went on to graduate study.

**Foreign students:** Six students are from out of the country. Countries represented include Bangladesh, Bulgaria, and Japan; three in all.

**PROGRAMS OF STUDY. Degrees:** B.A., B.S.

**Majors:** Accounting, Art, Biology, Chemistry, Communications/Theatre, Computer Science, Economics/Business Administration, Elementary Education, English, Finance, Fine Arts, French, German, History, Interdisciplinary Studies, International Studies, Management Information Systems, Mathematics, Music, Philosophy, Philosophy/Religion, Physical Education, Physics, Political Science, Psychology, Religious Studies, Sociology, Spanish, Speech.

**Distribution of degrees:** The majors with the highest enrollment are business administration, political science, and education.

**Requirements:** General education requirement.

**Academic regulations:** Freshmen must maintain minimum 1.6 GPA; sophomores, 1.8 GPA; juniors, 2.0 GPA; seniors, 2.0 GPA.

**Special:** Double majors. Dual degrees. Independent study. Pass/fail grading option. Internships. Preprofessional programs in law, medicine, veterinary science, dentistry, and engineering. 3-1 medical technology program with St. John's Hospital (Springfield). 3-1 cytotechnology program with Mayo Sch of Health-Related Sciences. 3-2 engineering programs with U of Illinois and Washington U. 3-2 occupational therapy program with Washington U. 3-2 nursing program with Mennonite Coll of Nursing. Urban Studies Program (Chicago). Teacher certification in elementary and secondary education. Certification in specific subject areas. Study abroad in England, France, Germany, Japan, and Spain.

**Honors:** Phi Beta Kappa. Honor societies.

**Academic Assistance:** Nonremedial tutoring.

**ADMISSIONS. Academic basis for candidate selection** (in order of priority): Secondary school record, class rank, standardized test scores, school's recommendation, essay.

**Nonacademic basis for candidate selection:** Character and personality, extracurricular participation, particular talent or ability, geographical distribution, and alumni/ae relationship are considered.

**Requirements:** Graduation from secondary school is required; GED is accepted. 15 units and the following program of study are required: 3 units of English, 3 units of math, 7 units of academic electives. Minimum composite ACT score of 20 (SAT scores of 400 in both verbal and math), rank in top half of secondary school class, and minimum 2.0 GPA required. SAT or ACT is required. Campus visit and interview recommended. Off-campus interviews available with admissions and alumni representatives.

**Procedure:** Take SAT or ACT by October of 12th year. Visit college for interview by February of 12th year. Suggest filing application by April 1. Application deadline is August 15. Notification of admission on rolling basis. Reply is required by May 1. $100 nonrefundable tuition deposit. $50 room deposit, refundable until May 1. Freshmen accepted for terms other than fall.

**Special programs:** Admission may be deferred one year. Credit and/or placement may be granted through CEEB Advanced Placement exams for scores of 4 or higher. Credit and/or placement may be granted through CLEP general and subject exams. Early decision program. Deadline for applying for early decision is May 1. Early entrance/early admission program. Concurrent enrollment program.

**Transfer students:** Transfer students accepted for terms other than fall. In fall 1993, 18% of all new students were transfers into all classes. 127 transfer applications were received, 101 were accepted. Application deadline is August 15 for fall; January 1 for spring. Minimum 2.0 GPA required. Lowest course grade accepted is "C." Maximum number of transferable credits is 66 semester hours. At least 60 semester hours must be completed at the college to receive degree.

**Admissions contact:** Gale F. Vaughn, Director of Enrollment. 217 245-3030.

**FINANCIAL AID. Available aid:** Pell grants, SEOG, state scholarships and grants, school scholarships and grants, and academic merit scholarships. Perkins Loans (NDSL), PLUS, Stafford Loans (GSL), and SLS. Tuition Plan Inc.

**Financial aid statistics:** 40% of aid is not need-based. In 1993-94, 99% of all undergraduate applicants received aid; 100% of freshman applicants. Average amounts of aid awarded freshmen: Scholarships and grants, $4,165; loans, $2,520.

**Supporting data/closing dates:** FAFSA: Priority filing date is April 15; deadline is May 1. Notification of awards on rolling basis.

**Financial aid contact:** Katherine Taylor, Director of Financial Aid. 217 245-3035.

# Illinois Institute of Technology

**Chicago, IL 60616** **312 567-3000**

**1993-94 Costs.** Tuition: $13,750. Room & board: $4,500. Fees, books, misc. academic expenses (school's estimate): $1,000.
**Enrollment.** Undergraduates: 1,334 men, 412 women (full-time). Freshman class: 1,312 applicants, 1,155 accepted, 399 enrolled. Graduate enrollment: 2,203 men, 768 women.
**Test score averages/ranges.** Average SAT scores: 510 verbal, 630 math. Range of SAT scores of middle 50%: 500-600 verbal, 590-680 math. Average ACT scores: 25 composite. Range of ACT scores of middle 50%: 22-27 composite.
**Faculty.** 336 full-time; 233 part-time. 87% of faculty holds highest degree in specific field. Student/faculty ratio: 12 to 1.
**Selectivity rating.** More competitive.

**PROFILE.** IIT, founded in 1940, is a private institute. Programs are offered through the Colleges of Architecture, Planning, and Design; Engineering; Law; and Sciences and Letters and the Schools of Business Administration and Advanced Studies. Its 120-acre campus is located three miles south of Chicago's Loop. The campus plan and many of its buildings were designed by Ludwig Mies van der Rohe.

**Accreditation:** NCACS. Professionally accredited by the Accreditation Board for Engineering and Technology, the American Bar Association, the American Psychological Association, the Association of American Law Schools, the Council on Rehabilitation Education, the National Architecture Accrediting Board.
**Religious orientation:** Illinois Institute of Technology is nonsectarian; no religious requirements.
**Library:** Collections totaling over 400,000 volumes, 2,500 periodical subscriptions, and 160,000 microform items.
**Special facilities/museums:** Environment chamber, wind tunnel, extrusion press, railroad simulator, electron microscope.
**Athletic facilities:** Gymnasium, swimming pool, basketball, handball, racquetball, tennis, and volleyball courts, weight-training and exercise facilities, baseball, intramural, and soccer fields, bowling lane.
**STUDENT BODY. Undergraduate profile:** 75% are state residents; 32% are transfers. 17% Asian-American, 14% Black, 7% Hispanic, 56% White, 6% Other. Average age of undergraduates is 20.
**Freshman profile:** 9% of freshmen who took SAT scored 700 or over on verbal, 14% scored 700 or over on math; 25% scored 600 or over on verbal, 57% scored 600 or over on math; 62% scored 500 or over on verbal, 89% scored 500 or over on math; 86% scored 400 or over on verbal, 99% scored 400 or over on math; 93% scored 300 or over on verbal, 100% scored 300 or over on math. 28% of accepted applicants took SAT; 75% took ACT. 60% of freshmen come from public schools.
**Undergraduate achievement:** 80% of fall 1991 freshmen returned for fall 1992 term. 18% of entering class graduated. 10% of students who completed a degree program immediately went on to graduate study.
**Foreign students:** 128 students are from out of the country. Countries represented include Hong Kong, India, Japan, Korea, Malaysia, and Taiwan; 70 in all.
**PROGRAMS OF STUDY. Degrees:** B.A., B.Arch., B.Bus.Admin., B.S.
**Majors:** Accounting, Aerospace Engineering, Architecture, Business Administration, Chemical Engineering, Chemistry, Civil Engineering, Computer Science, Design, Electrical Engineering, English, History, Mathematics, Mechanical Engineering, Metallurgical Engineering, Philosophy, Physics, Political Science, Psychology, Science/Technology in Context, Sociology.
**Distribution of degrees:** The majors with the highest enrollment are engineering, architecture, and computer science; psychology, political science, and sociology have the lowest.
**Requirements:** General education requirement.
**Academic regulations:** Minimum 1.85 GPA must be maintained.
**Special:** Numerous specialized minors offered; many are cross-disciplinary. Interdisciplinary and multidisciplinary programs in most majors. Double majors. Dual degrees. Accelerated study. Cooperative education programs. Graduate school at which undergraduates may take graduate-level courses. Preprofessional programs in law and medicine. B.S/M.S. medical physics and B.S./M.D. programs with Chicago Medical School. Bachelor's/J.D., bachelor's/M.B.A., and bachelor's/M.P.A. programs. Member of Illinois Consortium for Educational Opportunity. Exchange programs abroad in France (Inst of Applied Sciences) and Scotland (Robert Gordon Inst of Tech). Study abroad also in Germany. ROTC, NROTC, and AFROTC.
**Honors:** Honor societies.
**Academic Assistance:** Remedial reading, writing, and study skills. Nonremedial tutoring.
**STUDENT LIFE. Housing:** All full-time freshmen must live on campus unless living with family. Coed, women's, and men's dorms. Fraternity housing. School-owned/operated apartments. 53% of students live in college housing.
**Services and counseling/handicapped student services:** Placement services. Health service. Personal and psychological counseling. Career and academic guidance services. Physically disabled student services. Notetaking services. Tape recorders. Tutors. Reader services for the blind.
**Campus organizations:** Undergraduate student government. Student newspaper (Tech News, published once/week). Radio station. Jazz bands, drama club, Literary Society, sailing club, Midshipman Club, Society of Women Engineers, 75 organizations in all. 10 fraternities, nine chapter houses; two sororities, no chapter houses. 35% of men join a fraternity. 12% of women join a sorority.
**Religious organizations:** Christway Bible Fellowship, Roman Catholic Seminar, Chinese Evangelical Fellowship, Korean Bible Fellowship, Intervarsity Christian Fellowship, Moslem student group, ReJOYce in Jesus, Ambassadors for Christ.
**Minority/foreign student organizations:** Latinos Involved in Further Education, National Society of Black Engineers, Union of Concerned Black Students. International Student Organization, Arab, Chinese, Filipino, Indian, Malaysian, and Turkish groups.
**ATHLETICS. Physical education requirements:** Two semesters of physical education required.
**Intercollegiate competition:** 5% of students participate. Baseball (M), basketball (M,W), cross-country (M,W), diving (M,W), softball (W), swimming (M,W), volleyball (M,W). Member of Chicagoland Athletic Conference, NAIA.
**Intramural and club sports:** 20% of students participate. Intramural basketball, cross-country, handball, racquetball, soccer, softball, squash, swimming, tennis, touch football, turkey trot, volleyball, walleyball. Men's club hockey, sailing, wrestling. Women's club sailing.
**ADMISSIONS. Academic basis for candidate selection** (in order of priority): Secondary school record, class rank, standardized test scores, school's recommendation, essay.
**Nonacademic basis for candidate selection:** Extracurricular participation is considered.
**Requirements:** Graduation from secondary school is required; GED is accepted. 11.5 units and the following program of study are required: 4 units of English, 3.5 units of math, 2 units of lab science, 1 unit of social studies, 1 unit of history. SAT or ACT is required. Campus visit and interview recommended. Off-campus interviews available with admissions and alumni representatives.
**Procedure:** Take SAT or ACT by June of 12th year. Visit college for interview by April of 12th year. Suggest filing application by December 1; no deadline. Notification of admission on rolling basis. Reply is required by May 1 or within two weeks of acceptance if after May 1. $100 nonrefundable tuition deposit. $250 nonrefundable room deposit. Freshmen accepted for terms other than fall.
**Special programs:** Admission may be deferred one year. Credit and/or placement may be granted through CEEB Advanced Placement exams for scores of 4 or higher. Placement may be granted through challenge exams. Early decision program. In fall 1992, 514 applied for early decision and 435 were accepted. Deadline for applying for early decision is December 1. Early entrance/early admission program.
**Transfer students:** Transfer students accepted for terms other than fall. In fall 1992, 32% of all new students were transfers into all classes. 405 transfer applications were received, 301 were accepted. Application deadline is rolling for fall; rolling for spring. Minimum 3.0 GPA. Lowest course grade accepted is "C." Maximum number of transferable credits is 68 semester hours. At least 46 semester hours must be completed at the institute to receive degree.
**Admissions contact:** Director of Admissions. 312 567-3025.
**FINANCIAL AID. Available aid:** Pell grants, SEOG, state scholarships and grants, school scholarships and grants, private scholarships and grants, ROTC scholarships, academic merit scholarships, athletic scholarships, and aid for undergraduate foreign students. Perkins Loans (NDSL), PLUS, Stafford Loans (GSL), state loans, school loans, private loans, and SLS. Deferred payment plan.
**Financial aid statistics:** In 1992-93, 80% of all undergraduate applicants received aid; 90% of freshman applicants. Average amounts of aid awarded freshmen: Scholarships and grants, $6,300; loans, $2,600.
**Supporting data/closing dates:** FAFSA/FAF/FFS: Priority filing date is May 1. School's own aid application: Priority filing date is May 1. Notification of awards on rolling basis.
**Financial aid contact:** Walter O'Neill, Director of Financial Aid. 312 567-3303.
**STUDENT EMPLOYMENT.** College Work/Study Program. Institutional employment. 23% of full-time undergraduates work on campus during school year. Students may expect to earn an average of $1,500 during school year. Off-campus part-time employment opportunities rated "fair."
**COMPUTER FACILITIES.** 450 IBM/IBM-compatible and Macintosh/Apple microcomputers; 300 are networked. Students may access Digital, Prime minicomputer/mainframe systems, BITNET, Internet. Residence halls may be equipped with networked microcomputers, networked terminals. Computer languages and software packages include BASIC, C, FORTRAN, Icon, ImSL, Maple, Modula 2, Pascal, SAS, SPSS. Computer facilities are available to all students.
**Fees:** None.
**Hours:** 8 AM-midn.
**GRADUATE CAREER DATA.** Highest graduate school enrollments: Illinois Institute of Technology, Northwestern U. 10% of graduates choose careers in business and industry. Companies and businesses that hire graduates: Amoco, Arthur Andersen, AT&T, Commonwealth Edison, federal government, General Motors, Inland Steel, Kraft, Motorola.
**PROMINENT ALUMNI/AE.** Richard Ogilvie, attorney; Benny Goodman, jazz musician; Marvin Camras, electrical engineer; Bob Pritzker, industrial engineer; Susan Soloman, environmental engineer.

# Illinois State University

**Normal, IL 61761-6901** **309 438-2111**

**1994-95 Costs.** Tuition: $2,600 (state residents), $7,799 (out-of-state). Room & board: $3,403. Fees, books, misc. academic expenses (school's estimate): $1,355.
**Enrollment.** Undergraduates: 7,040 men, 8,623 women (full-time). Freshman class: 8,681 applicants, 6,695 accepted, 2,408 enrolled. Graduate enrollment: 1,083 men, 1,580 women.
**Test score averages/ranges.** Average ACT scores: 22 English, 21 math, 22 composite. Range of ACT scores of middle 50%: 18-24 English, 18-24 math.
**Faculty.** 809 full-time; 144 part-time. 70% of faculty holds doctoral degree. Student/faculty ratio: 21 to 1.
**Selectivity rating.** Less competitive.

**PROFILE.** Illinois State, founded in 1857, is a public, multipurpose university. Programs are offered through the Colleges of Applied Science and Technology, Arts and Sciences, Business, Education, and Fine Arts; the Graduate School; and the College of Continuing Education and Public Service. Its 50-acre campus is located in the urban area of Normal-Bloomington. Campus architecture ranges from a castle-like hall to modern 28-story residential towers.

**Accreditation:** NCACS. Professionally accredited by the American Assembly of Collegiate Schools of Business, the American Dietetic Association, the American Home Economics Association, the American Medical Association (CAHEA), the American Speech-Language-Hearing Association, the Council on Social Work Education, the National Association of Schools of Art and Design, the National Association of Schools of Music, the National Council for Accreditation of Teacher Education, the National Recreation and Park Association.

**Religious orientation:** Illinois State University is nonsectarian; no religious requirements.

**Library:** Collections totaling over 1,239,044 volumes, 9,963 periodical subscriptions, and 1,787,850 microform items.

**Special facilities/museums:** Art gallery, historical and cultural museums, on-campus elementary and secondary schools, greenhouse, farm, planetarium, radio station.

**Athletic facilities:** Gymnasiums, field house, stadium, swimming pools, basketball, mud volleyball, and tennis courts, weight rooms, tracks, baseball, football, intramural, soccer, and softball fields, golf course, climbing tower.

**STUDENT BODY. Undergraduate profile:** 98% are state residents; 45% are transfers. 2% Asian-American, 8% Black, 2% Hispanic, 88% White. Average age of undergraduates is 20.

**Freshman profile:** 3% of freshmen who took ACT scored 30 or over on English, 3% scored 30 or over on math, 2% scored 30 or over on composite; 32% scored 24 or over on English, 28% scored 24 or over on math, 32% scored 24 or over on composite; 83% scored 18 or over on English, 82% scored 18 or over on math, 90% scored 18 or over on composite; 99% scored 12 or over on English, 100% scored 12 or over on math, 100% scored 12 or over on composite. 97% of accepted applicants took ACT. 90% of freshmen come from public schools.

**Undergraduate achievement:** 73% of fall 1992 freshmen returned for fall 1993 term. 27% of entering class graduated. 34% of students who completed a degree program went on to graduate study within five years.

**Foreign students:** 95 students are from out of the country. Countries represented include China, Germany, India, Japan, Taiwan, and Thailand; 54 in all.

**PROGRAMS OF STUDY. Degrees:** B.A., B.F.A., B.Mus., B.Mus.Ed., B.S., B.S.Ed.

**Majors:** Accounting, Administrative Systems/Office Technology, Agribusiness, Agriculture, Anthropology, Applied Computer Science, Art, Biological Sciences, Business Administration, Business Education, Chemistry, Criminal Justice Sciences, Dance, Early Childhood Education, Economics, Elementary Education, English, Environmental Health, Finance, French, General Studies, Geography, Geology, German, Health Education, History, Home Economics, Industrial Technology, International Business, Junior High Education, Management, Marketing, Mass Communications, Mathematics, Medical Records Administration, Medical Technology, Music, Music Education, Music Performance, Philosophy, Physical Education, Physics, Political Science, Psychology, Public Relations, Recreation/Park Administration, Russian Studies, Safety, Social Sciences, Social Work, Sociology, Spanish, Special Education, Speech Communication, Speech Pathology/Audiology, Theatre.

**Distribution of degrees:** The majors with the highest enrollment are elementary education, special education, and accounting; Russian studies, dance, and German have the lowest.

**Requirements:** General education requirement.

**Academic regulations:** Minimum 2.0 GPA must be maintained.

**Special:** Minors offered in all majors and in cinema studies, community health, consumer education, ethnic and cultural studies, geohydrology, gerontology, instructional media, Japanese studies, journalism, Latin-American studies, military science, reading, religious studies, TESOL, women's studies, and writing. Selected studies (experimental and interdisciplinary courses), institutes, and workshops available. Self-designed majors. Double majors. Independent study. Pass/fail grading option. Internships. Cooperative education programs. Graduate school at which undergraduates may take graduate-level courses. Preprofessional programs in medicine and dentistry. Member of National Student Exchange (NSE). Teacher certification in early childhood, elementary, secondary, and special education. Certification in specific subject areas. Study abroad in Australia, Austria, England, France, Germany, Italy, Japan, Russia, Scotland, Spain, and Sweden. ROTC.

**Honors:** Honors program.

**Academic Assistance:** Remedial reading, writing, math, and study skills. Nonremedial tutoring.

**STUDENT LIFE. Housing:** All students entering as freshmen must live on campus for first four semesters; sophomore transfers for first two semesters. Coed, women's, and men's dorms. Sorority and fraternity housing. School-owned/operated apartments. Off-campus married-student housing. International House. 37% of students live in college housing.

**Social atmosphere:** The student newspaper reports, "There are numerous museums, art galleries, playhouses, and athletic activities on campus and throughout the Bloomington-Normal community. The Greek system, with approximately 2,000 members, has a large agenda for social and other activities, clearly the focus of organized social life." Students gather at the Bone Student Center, the library, and the campus recreation center on campus. Off-campus spots most frequented include Rocky's II, Big Rudy's Too, Pub II, The Cellar, and fraternity and sorority houses. Popular events include basketball and football games and rock concerts.

**Services and counseling/handicapped student services:** Placement services. Health service. Women's center. Day care. Counseling services for minority, military, veteran, and older students. Birth control, personal, and psychological counseling. Career and academic guidance services. Physically disabled student services. Learning disabled program/services. Notetaking services. Tape recorders. Tutors. Reader services for the blind.

**Campus organizations:** Undergraduate student government. Student newspaper (Vidette, published once/day). Radio and TV stations. Choral groups, orchestra, marching and concert bands, jazz and pep bands, musical theatre, drama group, debating, film society, ACLU, Gay Alliance, departmental and political groups, special-interest and service groups, 250 organizations in all. 25 fraternities, 22 chapter houses; 16 sororities, 12 chapter houses. 20% of men join a fraternity. 20% of women join a sorority.

**Religious organizations:** Baptist Student Union, Campus Crusade for Christ, Celebration Christian Fellowship, Chi Alpha Christian Fellowship, Chinese Bible Study Group, Church of Christ, other religious groups.

**Minority/foreign student organizations:** BAAC, Black Student Union, Black Writers Forum, Minority Professional Opportunities, NAACP. Third World Student Association, African, Chinese, European, Indian, Latin American, and Thai groups.

**ATHLETICS. Physical education requirements:** None.

**Intercollegiate competition:** 3% of students participate. Baseball (M), basketball (M,W), cross-country (M,W), diving (W), football (M), golf (M,W), gymnastics (W), soccer (M), softball (W), swimming (W), tennis (M,W), track and field (indoor) (M,W), track and field (outdoor) (M,W), volleyball (W), wrestling (M). Member of Gateway Conference for football, Missouri Valley Athletic Conference, NCAA Division I, NCAA Division I-AA for football.

**Intramural and club sports:** 37% of students participate. Intramural badminton, baseball, basketball, handball, hockey, lacrosse, racquetball, rock climbing, rugby, soccer, softball, swimming, ultimate frisbee, volleyball. Men's club field hockey, lacrosse, racquetball, rock climbing, rugby, swimming, ultimate frisbee, volleyball. Women's club rock climbing, soccer.

**ADMISSIONS. Academic basis for candidate selection** (in order of priority): Class rank, standardized test scores, secondary school record.

**Nonacademic basis for candidate selection:** Particular talent or ability is considered.

**Requirements:** Graduation from secondary school is required; GED is accepted. 15 units and the following program of study are required: 4 units of English, 3 units of math, 2 units of lab science, 2 units of foreign language or fine arts, 2 units of social studies, 2 units of electives. All applicants with rank in top half of secondary school class and minimum composite ACT score of 17 are admitted. Audition required of music program applicants. College Opportunities Admission Program (COAP), High Potential Student Program, Talent Program, Veterans Program, Adult Learner Program, and Summer Opportunity for Freshmen for applicants not normally admissible. ACT is required; SAT may be substituted. Campus visit recommended. Off-campus interviews available with an admissions representative.

**Procedure:** Take SAT or ACT by October of 12th year. Notification of admission on rolling basis. No set date by which applicants must accept offer. $150 room deposit, partially refundable. Freshmen accepted for terms other than fall.

**Special programs:** Credit and/or placement may be granted through CEEB Advanced Placement exams for scores of 3 or higher. Credit may be granted through CLEP general and subject exams, DANTES exams, and military experience. Credit and placement may be granted through challenge exams. Early entrance/early admission program. Concurrent enrollment program.

**Transfer students:** Transfer students accepted for terms other than fall. In fall 1993, 45% of all new students were transfers into all classes. 3,533 transfer applications were received, 3,239 were accepted. Application deadline is May 1. Minimum 2.0 GPA required. Lowest course grade accepted is "D." Maximum number of transferable credits is 66 semester hours. At least 30 semester hours must be completed at the university to receive degree.

**Admissions contact:** David Snyder, M.A., Director of Enrollment Management. 309 438-2181.

**FINANCIAL AID. Available aid:** Pell grants, SEOG, state scholarships and grants, school scholarships and grants, private scholarships, ROTC scholarships, academic merit scholarships, and athletic scholarships. Perkins Loans (NDSL), PLUS, Stafford Loans (GSL), state loans, and SLS. Deferred payment plan.

**Financial aid statistics:** In 1993-94, 70% of all freshman applicants received aid.

**Supporting data/closing dates:** FAFSA/FAF/FFS: Accepted on rolling basis. School's own aid application: Priority filing date is March 1. Notification of awards begins May 1.

**Financial aid contact:** Linda L. Maxwell, M.A., Director of Financial Aid. 309 438-2231.

**STUDENT EMPLOYMENT.** College Work/Study Program. Institutional employment. 21% of full-time undergraduates work on campus during school year. Students may expect to earn an average of $1,200 during school year. Off-campus part-time employment opportunities rated "excellent."

**COMPUTER FACILITIES.** 1,250 IBM/IBM-compatible and Macintosh/Apple microcomputers; 425 are networked. Students may access IBM, SUN minicomputer/mainframe systems, BITNET, Internet. Residence halls may be equipped with stand-alone microcomputers, networked microcomputers. Client/LAN operating systems include Apple/Macintosh, DOS, OS/2, UNIX/XENIX/AIX, LocalTalk/AppleTalk, Microsoft, Novell. Computer languages and software packages include BMDP, COBOL, dBASE, Excel, FORTRAN, GPSS, Lotus 1-2-3, Microsoft Word, PL/1, SAS, SPSS, SPSS-X, WATBOL, WATFIV, WordPerfect, WordStar. Students must purchase "compucard" in order to use computer facilities.

**Fees:** $10 or $45 computer fee per semester.

**Hours:** 24 hours.

**GRADUATE CAREER DATA.** Graduate school percentages: 1% enter law school. 1% enter medical school.

# Illinois Wesleyan University

**Bloomington, IL 61702-2900** **309 556-1000**

**1993-94 Costs.** Tuition: $13,295. Room & board: $3,985. Fees, books, misc. academic expenses (school's estimate): $500.

**Enrollment.** Undergraduates: 838 men, 971 women (full-time). Freshman class: 3,344 applicants, 1,519 accepted, 553 enrolled.

**Test score averages/ranges.** Average SAT scores: 580 verbal, 613 math. Range of SAT scores of middle 50%: 530-630 verbal, 590-680 math. Average ACT scores: 27 English, 26 math, 27 composite. Range of ACT scores of middle 50%: 25-29 English, 24-29 math.

**Faculty.** 143 full-time; 35 part-time. 75% of faculty holds doctoral degree. Student/faculty ratio: 13 to 1.

**Selectivity rating.** Highly competitive.

**PROFILE.** Illinois Wesleyan, founded in 1850, is a private university. Programs are offered through the Colleges of Liberal Arts, Fine Arts, and Nursing. Its 58-acre campus is located in a residential area of Bloomington-Normal. Many campus buildings were constructed just after World War II.

**Accreditation:** NCACS. Professionally accredited by the National Association of Schools of Music, the National League for Nursing.

**Religious orientation:** Illinois Wesleyan University is an interdenominational Christian school; one course unit of religion required.

**Library:** Collections totaling over 201,000 volumes, 1,260 periodical subscriptions, and 115,800 microform items.

**Special facilities/museums:** On-campus preschool, observatory, computerized music lab.

**Athletic facilities:** Gymnasium, field house, swimming pool, tennis courts, track.

**STUDENT BODY. Undergraduate profile:** 82% are state residents; 5% are transfers. 3% Asian-American, 2% Black, 2% Hispanic, 1% Native American, 87% White, 5% Other. Average age of undergraduates is 19.

**Freshman profile:** 14% of freshmen who took SAT scored 700 or over on verbal, 23% scored 700 or over on math; 37% scored 600 or over on verbal, 54% scored 600 or over on math; 83% scored 500 or over on verbal, 97% scored 500 or over on math; 100% scored 400 or over on verbal, 100% scored 400 or over on math. 42% of accepted applicants took SAT; 89% took ACT. 83% of freshmen come from public schools.

**Undergraduate achievement:** 95% of fall 1991 freshmen returned for fall 1992 term. 86% of entering class graduated. 30% of students who completed a degree program immediately went on to graduate study.

**Foreign students:** 95 students are from out of the country. Countries represented include China, Germany, India, Japan, and the former Soviet Republics; 34 in all.

**PROGRAMS OF STUDY. Degrees:** B.A., B.F.A., B.Mus., B.Mus.Ed., B.S., B.Sacred Mus.

**Majors:** Accounting, Art, Biology, Business Administration, Chemistry, Computer Science, Drama, Economics, Elementary Education, English, Finance/Insurance, Fine Arts, French, German, History, Instruments, International Business, Mathematics/Computer Science, Music Composition, Music Education, Music Theatre, Natural Sciences, Nursing, Orchestral Music, Organ, Philosophy, Physics, Piano, Piano Pedagogy, Political Science, Psychology, Religion, Sacred Music, Sociology/Anthropology, Spanish, Voice.

**Distribution of degrees:** The majors with the highest enrollment are business, nursing, and biology; natural sciences, music theatre, and German have the lowest.

**Requirements:** General education requirement.

**Academic regulations:** Freshmen must maintain minimum 1.5 GPA; sophomores, 1.8 GPA; juniors, 2.0 GPA; seniors, 2.0 GPA.

**Special:** Minors offered in all majors and in art management and international studies. During January short term, students select one course or pursue approved off-campus study. Courses offered in Russian and Japanese. Self-designed majors. Double majors. Dual degrees. Independent study. Pass/fail grading option. Internships. Preprofessional programs in law, medicine, veterinary science, pharmacy, dentistry, theology, engineering, forestry, human resources, journalism, medical technology, nursing, osteopathy, and physical therapy. 2-2 engineering programs with Dartmouth Coll and U of Illinois. 3-1 medical technology program. 3-2 engineering and pharmacy programs with Case Western Reserve U, Northwestern U, U of Illinois at Chicago, and Washington U. 3-2 forestry and environmental studies program with Duke U. Washington Semester and UN Semester. Teacher certification in elementary and secondary education. Certification in specific subject areas. Study abroad in Costa Rica, France, Germany, Italy, Japan, Mexico, Singapore, the former Soviet Republics, and Spain. ROTC at Illinois State U.

**Academic Assistance:** Nonremedial tutoring.

**STUDENT LIFE. Housing:** All students under age 21 must live on campus unless living with family. Coed, women's, and men's dorms. Sorority and fraternity housing. School-owned/operated apartments. 90% of students live in college housing.

**Services and counseling/handicapped student services:** Placement services. Health service. Counseling services for minority students. Personal and psychological counseling. Career and academic guidance services. Religious counseling. Physically disabled student services. Reader services for the blind.

**Campus organizations:** Undergraduate student government. Student newspaper (Argus, published once/week). Literary magazine. Yearbook. Radio station. Chamber and community orchestras, vocal and instrumental ensembles, concert and pep bands, women's chorus, opera theatre, contemporary dance theatre, Masquers, intercollegiate debating, community service projects. Six fraternities, all with chapter houses; six sororities, all with chapter houses. 17% of men join a fraternity. 18% of women join a sorority.

**Religious organizations:** Brothers and Sisters in Christ, Fellowship of Christian Athletes, Intervarsity Christian Fellowship, Religious Activities Commission, Catholic Collegiate Organization.

**Minority/foreign student organizations:** Black Student Union, CLASE. International Student Organization.

**ATHLETICS. Physical education requirements:** None.

**Intercollegiate competition:** 18% of students participate. Baseball (M), basketball (M,W), cross-country (M,W), diving (M,W), football (M), golf (M), soccer (M), softball (W), swimming (M,W), tennis (M,W), track (indoor) (M,W), track (outdoor) (M,W), volleyball (W). Member of College Conference of Illinois and Wisconsin, NCAA Division III.

**Intramural and club sports:** 3% of students participate. Intramural badminton, basketball, bowling, golf, softball, swimming, tennis, water polo. Men's club lacrosse, sailing, water polo. Women's club sailing, soccer, water polo.

**ADMISSIONS. Academic basis for candidate selection** (in order of priority): Secondary school record, class rank, standardized test scores, essay, school's recommendation.

**Nonacademic basis for candidate selection:** Particular talent or ability is emphasized. Extracurricular participation is important. Character and personality, geographical distribution, and alumni/ae relationship are considered.

**Requirements:** Graduation from secondary school is required; GED is accepted. 14 units and the following program of study are required: 4 units of English, 3 units of math, 3 units of lab science, 2 units of foreign language, 2 units of social studies. Minimum combined SAT score of 1000 (composite ACT score of 24), rank in top third of secondary school class, and minimum 3.0 GPA recommended. Audition required of music and drama program applicants. Biology, chemistry, algebra, and geometry required of nursing program applicants. Additional math and science required of pre-engineering and science program applicants. Portfolio required of art program applicants. Conditional admission possible for applicants not meeting standard requirements. SAT or ACT is required. PSAT is recommended. Campus visit and interview recommended. Off-campus interviews available with an admissions representative.

**Procedure:** Take SAT or ACT by October of 12th year. Visit college for interview by March 1 of 12th year. Notification of admission on rolling basis. Reply is required by May 1. $100 nonrefundable tuition deposit. $25 nonrefundable room deposit. Freshmen accepted for terms other than fall.

**Special programs:** Admission may be deferred one year. Credit and/or placement may be granted through CEEB Advanced Placement exams for scores of 3 or higher. Credit and/or placement may be granted through CLEP general and subject exams. Placement may be granted through challenge exams. Credit and placement may be granted through ACT PEP exams. Early entrance/early admission program.

**Transfer students:** Transfer students accepted for terms other than fall. Application deadline is March 1 for fall; December 1 for spring. Minimum 2.0 GPA recommended. Lowest course grade accepted is "C." Maximum number of transferable credits is 70 semester hours. At least 52 semester hours must be completed at the university to receive degree.

**Admissions contact:** James R. Ruoti, M.A., Director of Admissions. 800 332-2498.

**FINANCIAL AID. Available aid:** Pell grants, SEOG, Federal Nursing Student Scholarships, state scholarships and grants, school scholarships and grants, private scholarships and grants, ROTC scholarships, academic merit scholarships, and aid for undergraduate foreign students. Perkins Loans (NDSL), PLUS, Stafford Loans (GSL), NSL, state loans, school loans, and private loans. Monthly payment plan.

**Financial aid statistics:** 34% of aid is not need-based. In 1992-93, 100% of all undergraduate applicants received aid; 100% of freshman applicants. Average amounts of aid awarded freshmen: Loans, $2,900.

**Supporting data/closing dates:** FAFSA/FAF/FFS: Priority filing date is March 1; deadline is May 1. Income tax forms: Accepted on rolling basis. Notification of awards on rolling basis.

**Financial aid contact:** Lynn Nichelson, Director of Financial Aid. 309 556-3096.

**STUDENT EMPLOYMENT.** College Work/Study Program. Institutional employment. 5% of full-time undergraduates work on campus during school year. Students may expect to earn an average of $1,200 during school year. Off-campus part-time employment opportunities rated "excellent."

**COMPUTER FACILITIES.** IBM/IBM-compatible and Macintosh/Apple microcomputers; 200 are networked. Residence halls may be equipped with stand-alone microcomputers. Client/LAN operating systems include Apple/Macintosh. Computer languages and software packages include Easy CAD, FORTRAN, LOGO, Lotus 1-2-3, MacIntax, PageMaker, Pascal, PC Solve, Quattro, WordPerfect; 63 in all. Restrictions apply to faculty office equipment.

**Fees:** None.

**Hours:** 18 hours/day.

**GRADUATE CAREER DATA.** Graduate school percentages: 2% enter law school. 5% enter medical school. 2% enter dental school. 7% enter graduate business programs. 10% enter graduate arts and sciences programs. 1% enter theological school/seminary. Highest graduate school enrollments: Illinois State U, Northwestern U, Southern Illinois U, U of Chicago, U of Illinois, Washington U. 40% of graduates choose careers in business and industry. Companies and businesses that hire graduates: Archer Daniel Midland, Arthur Andersen, State Farm Insurance.

**PROMINENT ALUMNI/AE.** Edward B. Rust, Jr., CEO, State Farm Insurance; Dawn Upshaw, Metropolitan Opera; Jack Sikma, retired basketball player, Milwaukee Bucks; C. Virgil Martin, retired executive, Carson, Pirie, Scott; Edward Telling, retired CEO, Sears, Roebuck.

## International Academy for Merchandising and Design

**Chicago, IL 60602-3300** **312 541-3900**

**1994-95 Costs.** Tuition: $8,000. Housing: None. Fees, books, misc. academic expenses (school's estimate): $700.
**Enrollment.** Undergraduates: 39 men, 285 women (full-time). Freshman class: 283 applicants, 281 accepted, 236 enrolled. Graduate enrollment: 92 men, 565 women.
**Test score averages/ranges.** N/A.
**Faculty.** 53 part-time. 1% of faculty holds doctoral degree. Student/faculty ratio: 12 to 1.
**Selectivity rating.** N/A.

**PROFILE.** The International Academy for Merchandising and Design, founded in 1979, is a private academy. Its urban campus is located in downtown Chicago.
**Accreditation:** CCA-ACICS. Professionally accredited by the Foundation for Interior Design Education Research.
**Religious orientation:** International Academy for Merchandising and Design is nonsectarian; no religious requirements.
**STUDENT BODY. Undergraduate profile:** 93% are state residents; 65% are transfers. 4% Asian-American, 26% Black, 13% Hispanic, 1% Native American, 56% White. Average age of undergraduates is 28.
**Freshman profile:** 60% of freshmen come from public schools.
**Undergraduate achievement:** 79% of fall 1992 freshmen returned for fall 1993 term. 5% of entering class graduated. 5% of students who completed a degree program immediately went on to graduate study.
**Foreign students:** 15 students are from out of the country. Countries represented include Canada, Japan, Korea, and Poland; seven in all.
**PROGRAMS OF STUDY. Degrees:** B.A., B.F.A.
**Majors:** Advertising Design/Communication, Fashion Design, Interior Design, Merchandising Management.
**Distribution of degrees:** The majors with the highest enrollment are merchandising management, interior design, and fashion design.
**Requirements:** General education requirement.
**Academic regulations:** Freshmen must maintain minimum 1.5 GPA; sophomores, juniors, seniors, 2.0 GPA.
**Special:** Associate's degrees offered.
**Honors:** Honor societies.
**ADMISSIONS. Academic basis for candidate selection** (in order of priority): Secondary school record.
**Nonacademic basis for candidate selection:** Particular talent or ability is emphasized.
**Requirements:** Graduation from secondary school is required; GED is accepted. No specific distribution of secondary school units required. 2.0 minimum GPA recommended; 1.5 minimum GPA required. Campus visit and interview required. No off-campus interviews.
**Procedure:** Notification of admission on rolling basis. Freshmen accepted for terms other than fall.
**Special programs:** Admission may be deferred one year. Credit and/or placement may be granted through CLEP general and subject exams.
**Transfer students:** Transfer students accepted for terms other than fall. In fall 1993, 65% of all new students were transfers into all classes. 120 transfer applications were received, 120 were accepted. Minimum 1.5 GPA recommended. Maximum number of transferable credits is 69 quarter hours. At least 111 quarter hours must be completed at the school to receive degree.
**Admissions contact:** Cynthia Reynolds, Director of Admissions. 312 541-3900.
**FINANCIAL AID. Available aid:** Pell grants and SEOG. PLUS, Stafford Loans (GSL), and SLS. Deferred payment plan.
**Financial aid statistics:** 89% of aid is not need-based. In 1993-94, 90% of all undergraduate applicants received aid; 87% of freshman applicants. Average amounts of aid awarded freshmen: Scholarships and grants, $2,000; loans, $2,625.
**Supporting data/closing dates:** FAFSA: Accepted on rolling basis. Notification of awards on rolling basis.
**Financial aid contact:** Patrick James, Director of Financial Aid. 312 541-3910.

## Judson College

**Elgin, IL 60123** **708 695-2500**

**1993-94 Costs.** Tuition: $8,800. Room & board: $4,700. Fees, books, misc. academic expenses (school's estimate): $600.
**Enrollment.** Undergraduates: 273 men, 332 women (full-time). Freshman class: 356 applicants, 237 accepted, 133 enrolled.
**Test score averages/ranges.** Average SAT scores: 460 verbal, 460 math. Average ACT scores: 21 English, 21 math, 21 composite.
**Faculty.** 30 full-time; 76 part-time. 41% of faculty holds doctoral degree. Student/faculty ratio: 15 to 1.
**Selectivity rating.** Competitive.

**PROFILE.** Judson, founded in 1963, is a church-affiliated, liberal arts college. Its 80-acre campus is located 40 miles west of Chicago. Campus architecture includes brick colonial buildings.
**Accreditation:** NCACS.
**Religious orientation:** Judson College is affiliated with the American Baptist Church; three semesters of religion required.
**Library:** Collections totaling over 77,000 volumes, 420 periodical subscriptions, and 27,000 microform items.
**Special facilities/museums:** Radio lab.
**Athletic facilities:** Gymnasium, basketball, racquetball, and tennis courts, weight room, baseball, softball, and soccer fields, track.
**STUDENT BODY. Undergraduate profile:** 72% are state residents; 35% are transfers. 1% Asian-American, 5% Black, 5% Hispanic, 86% White, 3% Other. Average age of undergraduates is 20.
**Freshman profile:** 15% of accepted applicants took SAT; 85% took ACT. 82% of freshmen come from public schools.
**Undergraduate achievement:** 67% of fall 1991 freshmen returned for fall 1992 term. 43% of entering class graduated.
**Foreign students:** 12 students are from out of the country. Countries represented include Brazil, China, Jamaica, Japan, Korea, and Romania; seven in all.
**PROGRAMS OF STUDY. Degrees:** B.A.
**Majors:** Anthropology, Art, Bible Studies, Biology, Business Administration, Chemistry, Christian Ministries/Youth Ministries, Christian Religion, Computer/Information Science, Elementary Education, English, History, Human Services, Language/Literature, Mass Media, Mathematics, Music, Philosophy, Physical Education, Psychology, Sociology, Speech/Theatre.
**Distribution of degrees:** The majors with the highest enrollment are elementary education, psychology, and business administration; chemistry, biology, and sociology have the lowest.
**Requirements:** General education requirement.
**Academic regulations:** Freshmen must maintain minimum 1.8 GPA; sophomores, juniors, seniors, 2.0 GPA.
**Special:** Qualified computer/information science majors may work at Fermi Labs and at local firms while attending college. Double majors. Independent study. Accelerated study. Internships. Cooperative education programs. Graduate school at which undergraduates may take graduate-level courses. Preprofessional programs in law, medicine, veterinary science, dentistry, theology, engineering, and nursing. 2-2 nursing program with Rush U. 3-2 engineering programs with approved universities. Member of Christian College Coalition; exchange and cross-registration possible. Washington Semester. Teacher certification in elementary and secondary education. Study abroad possible. ROTC at Wheaton Coll.
**Honors:** Honors program. Honor societies.
**Academic Assistance:** Remedial reading, math, and study skills. Nonremedial tutoring.
**ADMISSIONS. Academic basis for candidate selection** (in order of priority): Secondary school record, standardized test scores, class rank, school's recommendation.
**Nonacademic basis for candidate selection:** Character and personality are important. Extracurricular participation and particular talent or ability are considered.
**Requirements:** Graduation from secondary school is required; GED is accepted. No specific distribution of secondary school units required. Minimum composite ACT score of 18 and rank in top half of secondary school class recommended. ACT is required; SAT may be substituted. Campus visit and interview recommended. Off-campus interviews available with an admissions representative.
**Procedure:** Take SAT or ACT by April of 12th year. Visit college for interview by May of 12th year. Suggest filing application by April; no deadline. Notification of admission on rolling basis. $100 nonrefundable tuition deposit. $100 refundable room deposit. Freshmen accepted for terms other than fall.
**Special programs:** Admission may be deferred two semesters. Credit and/or placement may be granted through CEEB Advanced Placement exams. Credit and/or placement may be granted through CLEP general and subject exams. Concurrent enrollment program.
**Transfer students:** Transfer students accepted for terms other than fall. In fall 1992, 35% of all new students were transfers into all classes. 158 transfer applications were received, 123 were accepted. Minimum 2.0 GPA required. Lowest course grade accepted is "C." Maximum number of transferable credits is 77 semester hours from a two-year school and 92 semester hours from a four-year school. At least 30 semester hours must be completed at the college to receive degree.
**Admissions contact:** Matthew Osborne, Director of Admissions. 708 695-2500, extension 2310.
**FINANCIAL AID. Available aid:** Pell grants, SEOG, state scholarships and grants, school grants, academic merit scholarships, athletic scholarships, and aid for undergraduate foreign students. Fine arts scholarship. Perkins Loans (NDSL), PLUS, and Stafford Loans (GSL). AMS and deferred payment plan.
**Financial aid statistics:** 58% of aid is not need-based. In 1992-93, 99% of all undergraduate applicants received aid; 97% of freshman applicants. Average amounts of aid awarded freshmen: Scholarships and grants, $5,358.
**Supporting data/closing dates:** FAFSA/FAF/FFS: Priority filing date is May 1. Notification of awards on rolling basis.
**Financial aid contact:** Alice Foreman, Director of Financial Aid. 708 695-2500, extension 2330.

## Kendall College

**Evanston, IL 60201** **708 866-1304**

**1994-95 Costs.** Tuition: $8,346. Room & board: $4,956. Fees, books, misc. academic expenses (school's estimate): $650.
**Enrollment.** Undergraduates: 285 men, 218 women (full-time). Freshman class: 332 applicants, 297 accepted, 231 enrolled.
**Test score averages/ranges.** Average ACT scores: 18 English, 16 math, 17 composite.
**Faculty.** 22 full-time; 15 part-time. 50% of faculty holds doctoral degree. Student/faculty ratio: 10 to 1.
**Selectivity rating.** Less competitive.

**PROFILE.** Kendall is a church-affiliated college. Founded as a junior college in 1934, it became a four-year college in 1979. Its one-acre campus is located in Evanston, 15 miles from Chicago.

**Accreditation:** NCACS.
**Religious orientation:** Kendall College is an interdenominational Christian school; no religious requirements.
**Library:** Collections totaling over 30,000 volumes, 2,500 periodical subscriptions, and 1,500 microform items.
**Special facilities/museums:** Native American Indian museum, nursery school, restaurant.

**STUDENT BODY. Undergraduate profile:** 84% are state residents; 50% are transfers. Average age of undergraduates is 22.
**Freshman profile:** 95% of accepted applicants took ACT. 85% of freshmen come from public schools.
**Undergraduate achievement:** 60% of fall 1992 freshmen returned for fall 1993 term. 30% of entering class graduated.
**Foreign students:** 16 students are from out of the country. Countries represented include African countries, China, Denmark, Japan, the Phillipines, and Sweden; eight in all.

**PROGRAMS OF STUDY. Degrees:** B.A.
**Majors:** American Studies, Applied Social Sciences, Business Administration, Early Childhood Education, Hospitality Management, Human Services, Independent Scholar.
**Distribution of degrees:** The majors with the highest enrollment are hospitality management, business administration, and human services; applied social science and American studies have the lowest.
**Requirements:** General education requirement.
**Academic regulations:** Minimum 2.0 GPA must be maintained.
**Special:** Associate's degrees offered. Self-designed majors. Internships. Teacher certification in early childhood education. Certification in specific subject areas. Study abroad in Hong Kong and Switzerland.
**Honors:** Phi Beta Kappa. Honor societies.
**Academic Assistance:** Remedial reading, writing, math, and study skills. Nonremedial tutoring.

**ADMISSIONS. Academic basis for candidate selection** (in order of priority): Secondary school record, class rank, standardized test scores, school's recommendation, essay.
**Nonacademic basis for candidate selection:** Particular talent or ability is important.
**Requirements:** Graduation from secondary school is required; GED is accepted. 14 units and the following program of study are recommended: 4 units of English, 2 units of math, 2 units of science, 2 units of social studies, 2 units of history, 2 units of electives. Minimum composite ACT score of 15 (combined SAT score of 800), rank in top half of secondary school class, and minimum 2.0 GPA required. Freshman Year Program for applicants not normally admissible. ACT is required; SAT may be substituted. Campus visit and interview recommended. Off-campus interviews available with an admissions representative.
**Procedure:** Take SAT or ACT by April of 12th year. Visit college for interview by April of 12th year. Notification of admission on rolling basis. Reply is required at least one month prior to beginning of term. $150 tuition deposit, refundable under certain conditions. $100 room deposit, refundable under certain conditions. Freshmen accepted for terms other than fall.
**Special programs:** Admission may be deferred one year. Credit may be granted through CLEP general and subject exams and life experience. Placement may be granted through challenge exams. Credit and placement may be granted through military experience.
**Transfer students:** Transfer students accepted for terms other than fall. In fall 1993, 50% of all new students were transfers into all classes. 75 transfer applications were received, 56 were accepted. Application deadline is rolling for fall; rolling for spring. Minimum 2.0 GPA required. Lowest course grade accepted is "C." Maximum number of transferable credits is 92 quarter hours from a two-year school and 139 quarter hours from a four-year school. At least 84 quarter hours must be completed at the college to receive degree.
**Admissions contact:** Ralph E. Stareuko, M.S., Director of Enrollment Management. 708 866-1304.

**FINANCIAL AID. Available aid:** Pell grants, SEOG, state scholarships and grants, school scholarships and grants, and academic merit scholarships. Perkins Loans (NDSL), PLUS, Stafford Loans (GSL), and SLS. Deferred payment plan, family tuition reduction, and guaranteed tuition.
**Financial aid statistics:** 20% of aid is not need-based. In 1993-94, 85% of all undergraduate applicants received aid; 85% of freshman applicants. Average amounts of aid awarded freshmen: Scholarships and grants, $4,000; loans, $2,500.
**Supporting data/closing dates:** FAFSA/FAF/FFS: Deadline is August 15. School's own aid application: Accepted on rolling basis. State aid form: Deadline is August 10. Income tax forms: Accepted on rolling basis. Notification of awards on rolling basis.
**Financial aid contact:** Helen Whyte, B.A., Director of Financial Aid. 708 866-1349.

# Knox College

**Galesburg, IL 61401** **309 343-0112**

**1994-95 Costs.** Tuition: $15,747. Room & board: $4,062. Fees, books, misc. academic expenses (school's estimate): $586.
**Enrollment.** Undergraduates: 461 men, 506 women (full-time). Freshman class: 1,040 applicants, 845 accepted, 286 enrolled.
**Test score averages/ranges.** Range of SAT scores of middle 50%: 470-590 verbal, 490-640 math. Range of ACT scores of middle 50%: 23-28 composite.
**Faculty.** 79 full-time; 9 part-time. 94% of faculty holds highest degree in specific field. Student/faculty ratio: 12 to 1.
**Selectivity rating.** More competitive.

**PROFILE.** Knox College, founded in 1837, is a private, liberal arts institution. Its 65-acre campus is located in Galesburg, 40 miles from Peoria. The campus's oldest building is a registered National Historical Landmark.

**Accreditation:** NCACS. Professionally accredited by the National Council for Accreditation of Teacher Education.
**Religious orientation:** Knox College is nonsectarian; no religious requirements.
**Library:** Collections totaling over 261,633 volumes, 750 periodical subscriptions, and 44,282 microform items.
**Special facilities/museums:** Anthropology, art, and field museums, theatre with revolving stage and computerized lighting, ceramics, sculpture, painting, and printmaking studios, 760-acre biological field station, environmental climate chambers, electron microscope.
**Athletic facilities:** Gymnasiums, field house, swimming pool, athletic fields, track, basketball, and tennis courts, weight room, golf course.

**STUDENT BODY. Undergraduate profile:** 64% are state residents; 10% are transfers. 5% Asian-American, 6% Black, 2% Hispanic, 1% Native American, 78% White, 8% International. Average age of undergraduates is 19.
**Freshman profile:** 4% of freshmen who took SAT scored 700 or over on verbal, 12% scored 700 or over on math; 25% scored 600 or over on verbal, 49% scored 600 or over on math; 69% scored 500 or over on verbal, 76% scored 500 or over on math; 95% scored 400 or over on verbal, 96% scored 400 or over on math; 100% scored 300 or over on verbal, 100% scored 300 or over on math. 44% of accepted applicants took SAT; 90% took ACT.
**Undergraduate achievement:** 83% of fall 1992 freshmen returned for fall 1993 term. 67% of entering class graduated. 24% of students who completed a degree program immediately went on to graduate study.
**Foreign students:** 75 students are from out of the country. Countries represented include China, India, Japan, Pakistan, Saudi Arabia, and Spain; 29 in all.

**PROGRAMS OF STUDY. Degrees:** B.A.
**Majors:** American Studies, Art History/Studio, Biochemistry, Biology, Chemistry, Classics, Computer Science, Economics, Educational Studies, Elementary Education, English, English Literature, English Writing, French, German, German Area Studies, History, Interdisciplinary Studies, International Relations, Mathematics, Modern Languages/Literature, Music, Philosophy, Physics, Political Science, Psychology, Russian, Russian Area Studies, Secondary Education, Sociology/Anthropology, Spanish, Theatre.
**Distribution of degrees:** The majors with the highest enrollment are political science, chemistry, and biology; American studies, classics, and German area studies have the lowest.
**Requirements:** General education requirement.
**Academic regulations:** Minimum 2.0 GPA must be maintained.
**Special:** Concentrations in black studies, environmental studies, religious studies, women's studies. Self-designed majors. Double majors. Dual degrees. Independent study. Accelerated study. Pass/fail grading option. Internships. Preprofessional programs in law, medicine, veterinary science, dentistry, theology, and social work. Combined degree programs in medicine and nursing/medical technology with Rush Medical U; in architecture with Washington U; in law with Columbia U and U of Chicago. 3-2 engineering programs with Columbia U, Rensselaer Polytech Inst, U of Illinois, and Washington U. 3-2 forestry and environmental studies program with Duke U. Member of Associated Colleges of the Midwest. Washington Semester. Argonne Science Semester (Illinois). Chicago Semester in the Arts. Newberry Library Program in the Humanities (Illinois). Oak Ridge Science Semester (Tennessee). Urban Education Program (Chicago). Urban Studies Program (Chicago). Exchange program with U of Chicago Business School. Teacher certification in elementary, secondary, and bilingual/bicultural education. Certification in specific subject areas. Study abroad in Austria, China, Costa Rica, the Czech Republic, England, France, Germany, Greece, India, Indonesia, Italy, Japan, the former Soviet Republics, Spain, and Zimbabwe.
**Honors:** Phi Beta Kappa. Honors program. Honor societies.
**Academic Assistance:** Remedial reading, writing, math, and study skills.

**ADMISSIONS. Academic basis for candidate selection** (in order of priority): Secondary school record, class rank, school's recommendation, essay, standardized test scores.
**Nonacademic basis for candidate selection:** Character and personality and extracurricular participation are important. Particular talent or ability, geographical distribution, and alumni/ae relationship are considered.
**Requirements:** Graduation from secondary school is required; GED is accepted. 15 units required and the following program of study recommended: 4 units of English, 3 units of math, 3 units of science, 2 units of foreign language, 3 units of social studies. Rank in top half of secondary school class required. Educational Development Program (EDP) for applicants not normally admissible. SAT or ACT is required. Campus visit and interview recommended. Off-campus interviews available with an admissions representative.
**Procedure:** Take SAT or ACT by December 15 of 12th year. Visit college for interview by February 15 of 12th year. Suggest filing application by February 15. Notification of admission by March 31. Reply is required by May 1. $100 nonrefundable tuition deposit. Freshmen accepted for terms other than fall.
**Special programs:** Admission may be deferred one year. Credit and/or placement may be granted through CEEB Advanced Placement exams for scores of 3 or higher. Credit and/or placement may be granted through CLEP general and subject exams. Placement may be granted through challenge exams. Early decision program. Early entrance/early admission program. Early action program. Concurrent enrollment program.
**Transfer students:** Transfer students accepted for terms other than fall. In fall 1993, 10% of all new students were transfers into all classes. 65 transfer applications were received, 43 were accepted. Application deadline is April 1 for fall; November 1 for winter; February 1 for spring. SAT/ACT scores required of transfer applicants with less than two years of college. Minimum 2.75 GPA recommended. Lowest course grade accepted is "C." 45 semester hours must be completed at the college to receive degree.
**Admissions contact:** Paul Steenis, Director of Admission. 309 343-0112, extension 123.

**FINANCIAL AID. Available aid:** Pell grants, SEOG, state scholarships and grants, school scholarships and grants, private scholarships and grants, academic merit scholarships, and aid for undergraduate foreign students. Perkins Loans (NDSL), PLUS, Stafford

Loans (GSL), state loans, school loans, and SLS. Tuition Plan Inc., AMS, and deferred payment plan.
**Financial aid statistics:** 6% of aid is not need-based. In 1993-94, 99% of all undergraduate applicants received aid; 98% of freshman applicants. Average amounts of aid awarded freshmen: Scholarships and grants, $10,468; loans, $3,100.
**Supporting data/closing dates:** FAFSA/FAF: Priority filing date is March 1. Income tax forms: Priority filing date is March 1; accepted on rolling basis. Notification of awards begins March 15.
**Financial aid contact:** Teresa Jackson, Director of Financial Aid. 309 343-0112, extension 149.

# Lake Forest College

**Lake Forest, IL 60045** **708 234-3100**

**1994-95 Costs.** Tuition: $16,880. Room: $2,230. Board: $1,740. Fees, books, misc. academic expenses (school's estimate): $650.
**Enrollment.** Undergraduates: 458 men, 511 women (full-time). Freshman class: 979 applicants, 683 accepted, 271 enrolled. Graduate enrollment: 3 men, 19 women.
**Test score averages/ranges.** Range of SAT scores of middle 50%: 440-560 verbal, 480-600 math. Range of ACT scores of middle 50%: 22-27 composite.
**Faculty.** 80 full-time; 32 part-time. 95% of faculty holds doctoral degree. Student/faculty ratio: 10 to 1.
**Selectivity rating.** More competitive.

**PROFILE.** Lake Forest, founded in 1857, is a church-affiliated, liberal arts college. Its 110-acre campus is located in Lake Forest, 25 miles from Chicago.
**Accreditation:** NCACS. Professionally accredited by the National Council for Accreditation of Teacher Education.
**Religious orientation:** Lake Forest College is affiliated with the Presbyterian Church; no religious requirements.
**Library:** Collections totaling over 374,543 volumes, 1,300 periodical subscriptions, and 27,473 microform items.
**Special facilities/museums:** Art gallery, language labs, electron microscope, computer molecular modeling equipment, fiber optic wired network, high-resolution FT-IR, NMR spectrometer, neutron howitzer, music/recording studio with synthesizers, 11 public access computer labs.
**Athletic facilities:** Gymnasium, ice rink, swimming pool, handball, racquetball, squash, tennis, and volleyball courts, weight room, saunas, athletic fields.
**STUDENT BODY. Undergraduate profile:** 36% are state residents; 20% are transfers. 3% Asian-American, 5% Black, 3% Hispanic, 88% White, 1% Other. Average age of undergraduates is 20.
**Freshman profile:** 60% of accepted applicants took SAT; 72% took ACT. 73% of freshmen come from public schools.
**Undergraduate achievement:** 77% of fall 1992 freshmen returned for fall 1993 term. 71% of entering class graduated. 21% of students who completed a degree program immediately went on to graduate study.
**Foreign students:** 55 students are from out of the country. Countries represented include Canada, Japan, and Spain; 29 in all.
**PROGRAMS OF STUDY. Degrees:** B.A.
**Majors:** American Studies, Area Studies, Art History, Asian Studies, Biology, Business, Chemistry, Comparative World Literature, Computer Science, Economics, Education, English, Environmental Studies, French, German, History, International Relations, Mathematics, Music, Philosophy, Physics, Politics, Psychology, Sociology/Anthropology, Spanish, Studio Art.
**Distribution of degrees:** The majors with the highest enrollment are psychology, economics, and English; music, comparative world literature, and area studies have the lowest.
**Academic regulations:** Freshmen must maintain minimum 1.5 GPA; sophomores, 1.8 GPA; juniors, 2.0 GPA; seniors, 2.0 GPA.
**Special:** Courses offered in African-American studies, ancient Mediterranean and French civilizations, dramatic arts, religion, urban studies, and women's studies. Adult programs. Freshman Interdisciplinary Seminar Program. Honors program for qualified juniors and seniors. Honors courses for freshmen in English, history, and math. Richter Apprentice Scholars Program provides opportunity for outstanding freshmen to conduct independent research. Self-designed majors. Double majors. Independent study. Pass/fail grading option. Internships. Preprofessional programs in law, medicine, veterinary science, and dentistry. 2-2 medical technology and nursing programs with Rush U. 3-2 engineering program with Washington U. 3-2 B.A./M.A. social service program with U of Chicago. Member of Associated Colleges of the Midwest. Washington Semester. Teacher certification in elementary and secondary education. Certification in specific subject areas. Study abroad programs in China, Costa Rica, the Czech Republic/Slovakia, England, France, Greece, India, Italy, Japan, Russia, Spain, and Zimbabwe. International Internship program in Paris and Madrid.
**Honors:** Phi Beta Kappa. Honors program. Honor societies.
**Academic Assistance:** Nonremedial tutoring.
**ADMISSIONS. Academic basis for candidate selection** (in order of priority): Secondary school record, school's recommendation, essay, class rank, standardized test scores.
**Nonacademic basis for candidate selection:** Character and personality and extracurricular participation are important. Particular talent or ability and alumni/ae relationship are considered.
**Requirements:** Graduation from secondary school is required; GED is accepted. No specific distribution of secondary school units required. Accelerated courses recommended. SAT or ACT is required. Campus visit and interview recommended. Off-campus interviews available with an admissions representative.
**Procedure:** Take SAT or ACT by February of 12th year. Visit college for interview by March 1 of 12th year. Suggest filing application by March 1; no deadline. Notification of admission by April 1. Reply is required by May 1. $100 nonrefundable tuition deposit. Freshmen accepted for terms other than fall.
**Special programs:** Admission may be deferred one year. Credit and/or placement may be granted through CEEB Advanced Placement exams for scores of 3 or higher. Early decision program. In fall 1993, 82 applied for early decision and 58 were accepted. Deadline for applying for early decision is January 1. Early entrance/early admission program.
**Transfer students:** Transfer students accepted for terms other than fall. In fall 1993, 20% of all new students were transfers into all classes. 219 transfer applications were received, 114 were accepted. Application deadline is July 15 for fall; December 15 for spring. Minimum 2.0 GPA. Lowest course grade accepted is "C-." Maximum number of transferable credits is 60 semester hours. At least 60 semester hours must be completed at the college to receive degree.
**Admissions contact:** William G. Metzer, Jr., Director of Admissions. 708 735-5000.
**FINANCIAL AID. Available aid:** Pell grants, SEOG, state scholarships and grants, school scholarships and grants, private scholarships and grants, academic merit scholarships, and aid for undergraduate foreign students. Perkins Loans (NDSL), Stafford Loans (GSL), school loans, and SLS. Tuition Management Systems.
**Financial aid statistics:** 1% of aid is not need-based. In 1993-94, 98% of all undergraduate applicants received aid; 97% of freshman applicants. Average amounts of aid awarded freshmen: Scholarships and grants, $12,711; loans, $2,000.
**Supporting data/closing dates:** School's own aid application: Priority filing date is March 1; accepted on rolling basis. Income tax forms: Accepted on rolling basis. Notification of awards on rolling basis.
**Financial aid contact:** Jerry E. Cebrzynski, M.A., Director of Financial Aid. 708 234-3100.

# Lewis University

**Romeoville, IL 60441** **815 838-0500**

**1993-94 Costs.** Tuition: $9,216. Room & board: $4,270. Fees, books, misc. academic expenses (school's estimate): $2,920.
**Enrollment.** Undergraduates: 1,101 men, 1,091 women (full-time). Freshman class: 1,297 applicants, 1,200 accepted, 633 enrolled. Graduate enrollment: 381 men, 347 women.
**Test score averages/ranges.** Average ACT scores: 20 English, 20 math, 20 composite. Range of ACT scores of middle 50%: 18-23 composite.
**Faculty.** 138 full-time. 59% of faculty holds doctoral degree. Student/faculty ratio: 16 to 1.
**Selectivity rating.** Less competitive.

**PROFILE.** Lewis, founded in 1932, is a church-affiliated university. Programs are offered through the Colleges of Arts and Sciences, Business, and Nursing. Its 450-acre campus is located in Romeoville, 30 miles southwest of Chicago.
**Accreditation:** NCACS. Professionally accredited by the National League for Nursing.
**Religious orientation:** Lewis University is affiliated with the Roman Catholic Church (Brothers of Christian Schools); two semesters of theology required.
**Library:** Collections totaling over 160,000 volumes, 506 periodical subscriptions, and 32,000 microform items.
**Special facilities/museums:** Aviation complex, theatre.
**Athletic facilities:** Sports center, gymnasium, baseball, playing, and softball fields track, mini-gymnasium, weight training room, basketball, handball, racquetball, tennis, and volleyball courts.
**STUDENT BODY. Undergraduate profile:** 99% are state residents; 12% are transfers. 2% Asian-American, 9% Black, 4% Hispanic, 1% Native American, 84% White. Average age of undergraduates is 24.
**Freshman profile:** 1% of freshmen who took ACT scored 30 or over on English, 1% scored 30 or over on math, 1% scored 30 or over on composite; 20% scored 24 or over on English, 16% scored 24 or over on math, 21% scored 24 or over on composite; 66% scored 18 or over on English, 64% scored 18 or over on math, 76% scored 18 or over on composite; 97% scored 12 or over on English, 97% scored 12 or over on math, 99% scored 12 or over on composite; 100% scored 6 or over on English, 100% scored 6 or over on math, 100% scored 6 or over on composite. 1% of accepted applicants took SAT; 99% took ACT.
**Foreign students:** 18 students are from out of the country. Countries represented include Greece, Hong Kong, India, Israel, and Japan; 12 in all.
**PROGRAMS OF STUDY. Degrees:** B.A., B.Elect.Studies, B.S., B.S.Nurs.
**Majors:** Accountancy, Airway Science, Applied Science, Art, Athletic Training, Athletics, Aviation Flight, Aviation Maintenance, Aviation Management, Aviation/Non-Destructive Evaluation, Avionics, Biology, Business Administration/Management, Chemistry, Coach Certification, Computer Science, Criminal/Social Justice, Economics, Economics/Social Science, Education, Elected Studies, English, Finance, History, Human Resources Management, Journalism, Liberal Arts, Management Information Systems, Marketing, Mathematics, Medical Technology, Military Science, Music, Music Merchandising, Nursing, Philosophy, Physics, Political Science, Psychology, Public Administration, Religious Studies, Social Work, Sociology, Speech/Drama/Communications, Television/Radio Broadcasting, Theatre.
**Distribution of degrees:** The majors with the highest enrollment are business administration, nursing, and criminal/social justice; applied science, music, and speech have the lowest.
**Requirements:** General education requirement.
**Academic regulations:** Minimum 2.00 GPA must be maintained.
**Special:** Minors offered in most majors. Associate's degrees offered. Double majors. Dual degrees. Independent study. Accelerated study. Pass/fail grading option. Internships. Preprofessional programs in law, medicine, veterinary science, pharmacy, dentistry, optometry, engineering, medical technology, and meteorology. Teacher certification in elementary and secondary education. Certification in specific subject areas. ROTC. NROTC and AFROTC at Illinois Inst of Tech.
**Honors:** Honors program.

**Academic Assistance:** Nonremedial tutoring.

**STUDENT LIFE. Housing:** Students may live on or off campus. Coed, women's, and men's dorms. 26% of students live in college housing.
**Social atmosphere:** The Den and Cody Hall are the most popular gathering spots on campus. Delta Sigma Theta sorority and the student government have widespread influence on student social life. The most popular events at Lewis include parties and The Auction of the DT's.
**Services and counseling/handicapped student services:** Placement services. Health service. Weekly freshman seminars. Counseling services for minority, veteran, and older students. Personal counseling. Career and academic guidance services. Religious counseling. Physically disabled student services. Notetaking services. Tape recorders. Reader services for the blind.
**Campus organizations:** Undergraduate student government. Student newspaper (Flyer, published once/week). Literary magazine. Radio and TV stations. Jazz and pep bands, Young Democrats, Student Nurses Association, Society for Physics, departmental and special-interest groups. Six fraternities, no chapter houses; four sororities, no chapter houses. 3% of men join a fraternity. 2% of women join a sorority.
**Religious organizations:** Campus Ministry.
**Minority/foreign student organizations:** Black Student Union, El Movimiento. International Student Association.

**ATHLETICS. Physical education requirements:** None.
**Intercollegiate competition:** 10% of students participate. Baseball (M), basketball (M,W), cross-country (M,W), golf (M,W), soccer (M,W), softball (W), tennis (M,W), track (indoor) (M,W), track (outdoor) (M,W), track and field (indoor) (M,W), track and field (outdoor) (M,W), volleyball (M,W). Member of Great Lakes Valley Conference, NCAA Division II.
**Intramural and club sports:** 60% of students participate. Intramural basketball, bowling, floor hockey, football, handball, horseshoes, golf, racquetball, softball, tennis, track, volleyball, walleyball. Men's club volleyball.

**ADMISSIONS. Academic basis for candidate selection** (in order of priority): Secondary school record, standardized test scores, class rank, school's recommendation, essay.
**Nonacademic basis for candidate selection:** Character and personality, extracurricular participation, particular talent or ability, and alumni/ae relationship are considered.
**Requirements:** Graduation from secondary school is required; GED is accepted. 15 secondary school units required, including 3 units of English. Rank in top half of secondary school class and minimum 2.0 GPA required. Open admissions policy for undergraduate applicants over age 23. Developmental Program for applicants not normally admissible. ACT is required; SAT may be substituted. PSAT is recommended. Campus visit and interview recommended. Off-campus interviews available with an admissions representative.
**Procedure:** Take SAT or ACT by October of 12th year. Suggest filing application by April 15. Application deadline is September 1. Notification of admission on rolling basis. $50 tuition deposit, refundable until June 15. $100 refundable room deposit. Freshmen accepted for terms other than fall.
**Special programs:** Admission may be deferred one year. Credit and/or placement may be granted through CEEB Advanced Placement exams for scores of 3 or higher. Credit may be granted through CLEP general and subject exams, military and life experience. Credit and placement may be granted through challenge exams. Early decision program. Early entrance/early admission program. Concurrent enrollment program.
**Transfer students:** Transfer students accepted for terms other than fall. In fall 1993, 12% of all new students were transfers into all classes. 780 transfer applications were received, 664 were accepted. Application deadline is September 1 for fall; January 15 for spring. Minimum 2.0 GPA required. Lowest course grade accepted is "C." Maximum number of transferable credits is 72 semester hours from a two-year school and 96 semester hours from a four-year school.
**Admissions contact:** Irish O'Reilly, M.S., Director of Admissions. 815 838-0500, extension 250.

**FINANCIAL AID. Available aid:** Pell grants, SEOG, state scholarships and grants, school scholarships and grants, private scholarships and grants, ROTC scholarships, academic merit scholarships, and athletic scholarships. Perkins Loans (NDSL), PLUS, Stafford Loans (GSL), NSL, private loans, and SLS. Deferred payment plan.
**Financial aid statistics:** 26% of aid is not need-based. In 1993-94, 98% of all undergraduate applicants received aid; 99% of freshman applicants.
**Supporting data/closing dates:** FAFSA/FAF/FFS: Accepted on rolling basis. School's own aid application: Priority filing date is April 1; accepted on rolling basis. Income tax forms: Priority filing date is April 1; accepted on rolling basis. Notification of awards on rolling basis.
**Financial aid contact:** Sally Floyd, Director of Financial Aid. 815 838-0500, extension 263.

**STUDENT EMPLOYMENT.** College Work/Study Program. Institutional employment. 16% of full-time undergraduates work on campus during school year. Students may expect to earn an average of $2,000 during school year. Off-campus part-time employment opportunities rated "good."

**COMPUTER FACILITIES.** IBM/IBM-compatible, Macintosh/Apple, and RISC-/UNIX-based microcomputers. Students may access IBM, Prime minicomputer/mainframe systems. Residence halls may be equipped with stand-alone microcomputers. Client/LAN operating systems include Apple/Macintosh, DOS, OS/2, UNIX/XENIX/AIX. Numerous computer languages and software programs available. Computer facilities are available to all students.
**Fees:** None.
**Hours:** 8 AM-midn.

## Loyola University, Chicago

**Chicago, IL 60611** **312 274-3000**

**1993-94 Costs.** Tuition: $10,470. Room & board: $5,310. Fees, books, misc. academic expenses (school's estimate): $800.
**Enrollment.** Undergraduates: 2,079 men, 3,165 women (full-time). Freshman class: 3,579 applicants, 2,959 accepted, 855 enrolled. Graduate enrollment: 2,248 men, 3,452 women.
**Test score averages/ranges.** Average SAT scores: 482 verbal, 529 math. Range of SAT scores of middle 50%: 420-540 verbal, 460-590 math. Average ACT scores: 23 English, 23 math, 24 composite. Range of ACT scores of middle 50%: 20-26 English, 20-26 math.
**Faculty.** 606 full-time; 501 part-time. 93% of faculty holds doctoral degree.
**Selectivity rating.** Competitive.

**PROFILE.** Loyola University, Chicago, founded in 1870, is a church-affiliated institution. The University is comprised of four campuses: Lake Shore Campus offers undergraduate courses in the arts and sciences and nursing; Water Tower Campus offers programs through the Schools of Education and Business and the College of Arts and Sciences; Mallinckrodt Campus offers select courses at the undergraduate and graduate level; and Loyola University Medical Center offers programs through the Schools of Medicine and Dentistry and graduate programs in the life sciences.

**Accreditation:** NCACS. Professionally accredited by the American Assembly of Collegiate Schools of Business, the Council on Social Work Education, the National Council for Accreditation of Teacher Education, the National League for Nursing.
**Religious orientation:** Loyola University, Chicago is affiliated with the Roman Catholic Church (Society of Jesus); three semesters of theology required.
**Library:** Collections totaling over 1,033,115 volumes, 10,229 periodical subscriptions, and 1,044,312 microform items.
**Special facilities/museums:** Renaissance art gallery, seismograph station.
**Athletic facilities:** Gymnasium, field house, swimming pool, basketball, handball, and racquetball courts, athletic fields, recreation center.

**STUDENT BODY. Undergraduate profile:** 83% are state residents; 34% are transfers. 10% Asian-American, 8% Black, 6% Hispanic, 1% Native American, 73% White, 2% Other. Average age of undergraduates is 21.
**Freshman profile:** 7% of freshmen who took ACT scored 30 or over on English, 7% scored 30 or over on math, 5% scored 30 or over on composite; 50% scored 24 or over on English, 45% scored 24 or over on math, 51% scored 24 or over on composite; 94% scored 18 or over on English, 91% scored 18 or over on math, 97% scored 18 or over on composite; 100% scored 12 or over on English, 100% scored 12 or over on math, 100% scored 12 or over on composite. 48% of accepted applicants took SAT; 92% took ACT. 60% of freshmen come from public schools.
**Undergraduate achievement:** 81% of fall 1992 freshmen returned for fall 1993 term. 35% of entering class graduated.
**Foreign students:** 75 students are from out of the country. Countries represented include Australia, Canada, China, India, Ireland, and Korea; 70 in all.

**PROGRAMS OF STUDY. Degrees:** B.A., B.A.Classics, B.Bus.Admin., B.S.
**Majors:** Anthropology, Applied Psychology, Biology, Chemistry, Classical Civilization, Communication, Computer Science, Criminal Justice, Economics, Elementary Education, English, Finance, Fine Arts, French, German, Greek, History, Information Systems Management, Italian, Latin, Managerial Accounting, Marketing, Mathematics, Mathematics/Computer Science, Music, Nursing, Personnel Management, Philosophy, Physics, Political Science, Production Management, Psychology, Public Accounting, Social Work, Sociology, Spanish, Special Education, Theatre, Theology.
**Distribution of degrees:** The majors with the highest enrollment are psychology, communications, and biology; German, Latin, and physics have the lowest.
**Requirements:** General education requirement.
**Academic regulations:** Freshmen must maintain minimum 1.76 GPA; sophomores, juniors, seniors, 2.0 GPA.
**Special:** African-American studies, Latin-American studies, and women's studies offered. Double majors. Dual degrees. Pass/fail grading option. Internships. Graduate school at which undergraduates may take graduate-level courses. Preprofessional programs in law, medicine, veterinary science, pharmacy, dentistry, and optometry. 3-2 engineering program with U of Illinois at Urbana-Champaign. 3-3 law program with Loyola U Sch of Law. Washington Semester. Teacher certification in elementary, secondary, and special education. Certification in specific subject areas. Study abroad in Italy and Mexico. ROTC at U of Illinois and Chicago. NROTC at Northwestern U. AFROTC at Illinois Inst of Tech.
**Honors:** Honors program.
**Academic Assistance:** Remedial study skills. Nonremedial tutoring.

**STUDENT LIFE. Housing:** Students may live on or off campus. Coed and women's dorms. Graduate student housing. 32% of students live in college housing.
**Social atmosphere:** Student government, Campus Life Union Board, and Greeks are the most influential groups on campus. Popular events during the school year include soccer and basketball games, theatre productions, the President's Ball, and the Valentine's Dance. "Being in Chicago provides the university with the unique opportunity of including the city in our campus," reports the editor of the student newspaper. "Most students take advantage of this and benefit from what the city offers."
**Services and counseling/handicapped student services:** Placement services. Health service. Women's center. Counseling services for minority, military, veteran, and older students. Personal and psychological counseling. Career and academic guidance services.

Religious counseling. Physically disabled student services. Learning disabled services. Notetaking services. Tape recorders. Tutors. Reader services for the blind.
**Campus organizations:** Undergraduate student government. Student newspaper (Phoenix, published once/week). Literary magazine. Radio station. Orchestra, chorus, jazz band, theatre, debating, ski club, Circle K, Amnesty International, athletic, departmental, social, and special-interest groups, 136 organizations in all. Six fraternities, three chapter houses; nine sororities, no chapter houses. 8% of men join a fraternity. 7% of women join a sorority.
**Religious organizations:** Hillel, Intervarsity Christian Fellowship, Muslim Student Association, Bahai, Christian Legal Society.
**Minority/foreign student organizations:** Black Cultural Center, Black Accountants Association, Afro-American group, Black Student Council, Latin American group, Asian Student Organization. International Student Organization.

**ATHLETICS. Physical education requirements:** None.
**Intercollegiate competition:** 25% of students participate. Basketball (M,W), cheerleading (M,W), cross-country (M,W), golf (M), soccer (M,W), softball (W), swimming (M), track (indoor) (M,W), track (outdoor) (M,W), track and field (indoor) (M,W), track and field (outdoor) (M,W), volleyball (W). Member of Midwestern Collegiate Conference, NCAA Division I.
**Intramural and club sports:** 65% of students participate. Intramural basketball, flag football, floor hockey, handball, racquetball, softball, tennis, touch football, volleyball.

**ADMISSIONS. Academic basis for candidate selection** (in order of priority): Class rank, standardized test scores, secondary school record, school's recommendation, essay.
**Nonacademic basis for candidate selection:** Character and personality, extracurricular participation, and particular talent or ability are considered.
**Requirements:** Graduation from secondary school is required; GED is accepted. 15 units and the following program of study are required: 4 units of English, 2 units of math, 1 unit of science, 1 unit of social studies. Minimum 2.0 GPA required. Biology and chemistry with labs required of nursing program applicants. LEAP (Learning Enrichment for Academic Progress) program for applicants not normally admissible. SAT or ACT is required. Campus visit and interview recommended. Off-campus interviews available with admissions and alumni representatives.
**Procedure:** Take SAT or ACT by May of 12th year. Application deadline is July 9. Notification of admission on rolling basis. Reply is required by May 1 or date specified in letter of acceptance. $100 nonrefundable tuition deposit. $100 room deposit, refundable until July 15. Freshmen accepted for terms other than fall.
**Special programs:** Credit and/or placement may be granted through CEEB Advanced Placement exams for scores of 3 or higher. Credit may be granted through CLEP general and subject exams, DANTES exams, and military experience.
**Transfer students:** Transfer students accepted for terms other than fall. In fall 1993, 34% of all new students were transfers into all classes. 963 transfer applications were received, 861 were accepted. Application deadline is July 9 for fall; December 3 for spring. Minimum 2.0 GPA required. Lowest course grade accepted is "C." Maximum number of transferable credits is 64 semester hours from a two-year school and 96 semester hours from a four-year school. At least 32 semester hours must be completed at the university to receive degree.
**Admissions contact:** Edward Moore, Director of Admissions. 312 915-6500.

**FINANCIAL AID. Available aid:** SEOG, Federal Nursing Student Scholarships, state scholarships and grants, school scholarships and grants, private scholarships and grants, ROTC scholarships, academic merit scholarships, and athletic scholarships. Perkins Loans (NDSL), PLUS, Stafford Loans (GSL), NSL, Health Professions Loans, state loans, school loans, private loans, and SLS. University Budget Plan.
**Financial aid statistics:** 35% of aid is not need-based. In 1993-94, 80% of all undergraduate applicants received aid; 70% of freshman applicants. Average amounts of aid awarded freshmen: Scholarships and grants, $3,370; loans, $2,125.
**Supporting data/closing dates:** FAFSA/FAF: Priority filing date is February 15; accepted on rolling basis. Notification of awards begins February 15.
**Financial aid contact:** Joseph Burkhart, Director of Student Financial Aids. 312 915-6639.

**STUDENT EMPLOYMENT.** College Work/Study Program. Institutional employment. 17% of full-time undergraduates work on campus during school year. Students may expect to earn an average of $2,200 during school year. Off-campus part-time employment opportunities rated "excellent."

**COMPUTER FACILITIES.** 207 IBM/IBM-compatible and Macintosh/Apple microcomputers. Residence halls may be equipped with networked microcomputers. Computer languages and software packages include COBOL, dBASE I and II, FORTRAN, Lotus 1-2-3, Pascal, SAS, SPSS, WordPerfect. Computer facilities are available to all students.
**Hours:** 9 AM-9 PM.

**PROMINENT ALUMNI/AE.** Bob Newhart, actor; Bill Plant, CBS White House correspondent; Michael Quinlan, president and CEO, McDonald's.

# MacMurray College

**Jacksonville, IL 62650** **217 479-7000**

**1994-95 Costs.** Tuition: $9,620. Room: $1,700. Board: $2,050. Fees, books, misc. academic expenses (school's estimate): $550.
**Enrollment.** Undergraduates: 272 men, 356 women (full-time). Freshman class: 885 applicants, 664 accepted, 211 enrolled.
**Test score averages/ranges.** Average ACT scores: 21 composite. Range of ACT scores of middle 50%: 18-23 composite.
**Faculty.** 53 full-time; 15 part-time. 47% of faculty holds doctoral degree. Student/faculty ratio: 12 to 1.
**Selectivity rating.** Less competitive.

**PROFILE.** MacMurray is a church-affiliated, liberal arts college. Founded as a women's college in 1848, it adopted coeducation in 1969. Its 60-acre campus is located in Jacksonville, 35 miles west of Springfield.

**Accreditation:** NCACS. Professionally accredited by the National Council for Accreditation of Teacher Education, the National League for Nursing.
**Religious orientation:** MacMurray College is affiliated with the United Methodist Church; no religious requirements.
**Library:** Collections totaling over 145,000 volumes, 450 periodical subscriptions, and 100 microform items.
**Special facilities/museums:** Art gallery, language lab.
**Athletic facilities:** Basketball courts, gymnasium, indoor swimming pool, wrestling room, weight room, tennis courts, athletic fields.

**STUDENT BODY. Undergraduate profile:** 90% are state residents; 23% are transfers. 1% Asian-American, 5% Black, 2% Hispanic, 1% Native American, 91% White. Average age of undergraduates is 21.
**Freshman profile:** 4% of freshmen who took SAT scored 700 or over on math; 14% scored 600 or over on math; 15% scored 500 or over on verbal, 40% scored 500 or over on math; 51% scored 400 or over on verbal, 63% scored 400 or over on math; 90% scored 300 or over on verbal, 100% scored 300 or over on math. 2% of freshmen who took ACT scored 30 or over on composite; 21% scored 24 or over on composite; 79% scored 18 or over on composite; 100% scored 12 or over on composite. 3% of accepted applicants took SAT; 97% took ACT. 90% of freshmen come from public schools.
**Undergraduate achievement:** 84% of fall 1992 freshmen returned for fall 1993 term. 40% of entering class graduated. 12% of students who completed a degree program immediately went on to graduate study.
**Foreign students:** Six students are from out of the country. Countries represented include Bangladesh, Japan, Liberia, Malaysia, and Zambia; five in all.

**PROGRAMS OF STUDY. Degrees:** B.A., B.S., B.S.Nurs.
**Majors:** Accountancy, Art, Biology, Business Administration, Chemistry, Computer Electronics, Computer Science, Criminal Justice, Elementary Education, English, French, Hearing Impaired Education, History, Journalism, Learning Disabilites and Social/Emotional Disorders, Management Information Systems, Marketing, Mathematics, Music, Nursing, Philosophy, Physical Education, Physics, Political Science, Pre-Dentistry, Pre-Engineering, Pre-Law, Pre-Medical Technology, Pre-Medicine, Pre-Occupational Therapy, Pre-Physical Therapy, Pre-Veterinary Medicine, Psychology, Religion, Social Work, Spanish, Sports Management.
**Distribution of degrees:** The majors with the highest enrollment are nursing, social work, and hearing impaired education; chemistry and physics have the lowest.
**Requirements:** General education requirement.
**Academic regulations:** Freshmen must maintain minimum 1.50 GPA; sophomores, juniors, seniors, 2.0 GPA. Nursing and education students must maintain minimum 2.5 GPA.
**Special:** Minors offered in several fields. Associate's degrees offered. Double majors. Dual degrees. Independent study. Accelerated study. Pass/fail grading option. Internships. Graduate school at which undergraduates may take graduate-level courses. Preprofessional programs in law, medicine, veterinary science, dentistry, occupational therapy, and physical therapy. 3-2 engineering program with Columbia U and Washington U. 3-2 occupational therapy program with Washington U. Member of Central Illinois Foreign Language and International Studies Consortium. Washington Semester. Teacher certification in elementary, secondary, and special education. Certification in specific subject areas.
**Honors:** Honors program. Honor societies.
**Academic Assistance:** Remedial study skills. Nonremedial tutoring.

**ADMISSIONS. Academic basis for candidate selection** (in order of priority): Secondary school record, class rank, essay, standardized test scores, school's recommendation.
**Nonacademic basis for candidate selection:** Particular talent or ability is emphasized. Character and personality and extracurricular participation are important. Alumni/ae relationship is considered.
**Requirements:** Graduation from secondary school is required; GED is accepted. 16 units and the following program of study are recommended: 4 units of English, 2 units of math, 2 units of science, 2 units of foreign language, 2 units of social studies, 4 units of electives. Minimum composite ACT score of 20, rank in top half of secondary school class, and minimum 2.5 GPA recommended. ACT is required; SAT may be substituted. Campus visit and interview recommended. Off-campus interviews available with admissions and alumni representatives.
**Procedure:** Take SAT or ACT by December of 12th year. Visit college for interview by April of 12th year. Application deadline is July 15. Notification of admission on rolling basis. Reply is required by August 1. $150 tuition deposit, refundable until May 1. Freshmen accepted for terms other than fall.
**Special programs:** Admission may be deferred. Credit and/or placement may be granted through CEEB Advanced Placement exams for scores of 3 or higher. Credit and/or placement may be granted through CLEP subject exams. Credit and placement may be granted through ACT PEP and DANTES exams. Early entrance/early admission program. Concurrent enrollment program.
**Transfer students:** Transfer students accepted for terms other than fall. In fall 1993, 23% of all new students were transfers into all classes. 136 transfer applications were received, 100 were accepted. Application deadline is July 15 for fall; January 15 for spring. Minimum 2.0 GPA required. Lowest course grade accepted is "C." Maximum number of transferable semester hours is 60 from two-year schools; unlimited from four-year schools. At least 30 semester hours must be completed at the college to receive degree.
**Admissions contact:** Ed Hockett, Ph.D., Dean of Admissions. 217 479-7056.

**FINANCIAL AID. Available aid:** Pell grants, SEOG, state scholarships and grants, school scholarships and grants, private scholarships and grants, academic merit scholarships, and aid for undergraduate foreign students. Perkins Loans (NDSL), PLUS, Stafford Loans (GSL), NSL, state loans, school loans, private loans, and SLS. Tuition Plan Inc. Monthly interest-free payment plan.
**Financial aid statistics:** 15% of aid is not need-based. In 1993-94, 95% of all undergraduate applicants received aid; 91% of freshman applicants. Average amounts of aid awarded freshmen: Scholarships and grants, $4,925; loans, $3,042.
**Supporting data/closing dates:** FAFSA: Accepted on rolling basis. Notification of awards on rolling basis.
**Financial aid contact:** Rebecca Waltrip, Director of Financial Aid. 217 479-7041.

# McKendree College

**Lebanon, IL 62254 — 618 537-4481**

**1994-95 Costs.** Tuition: $7,680. Room & board: $3,570. Fees, books, misc. academic expenses (school's estimate): $635.
**Enrollment.** Undergraduates: 360 men, 466 women (full-time). Freshman class: 1,002 applicants, 555 accepted.
**Test score averages/ranges.** Average ACT scores: 21 composite.
**Faculty.** 47 full-time; 30 part-time. 70% of faculty holds doctoral degree. Student/faculty ratio: 15 to 1.
**Selectivity rating.** Competitive.

**PROFILE.** McKendree, founded in 1828, is a liberal arts college. Programs offered in the Divisions of Business, Humanities, Nursing, Science and Mathematics, and Social Sciences and Education. Its 40-acre campus is located in Lebanon, 15 miles east of St. Louis.

**Accreditation:** NCACS.
**Religious orientation:** McKendree College is affiliated with the United Methodist Church; three semester hours of religion/theology required.
**Library:** Collections totaling over 65,310 volumes, 460 periodical subscriptions, and 16,932 microform items.
**Athletic facilities:** Gymnasiums, weight room, tennis courts, baseball, soccer, and softball fields.

**STUDENT BODY. Undergraduate profile:** 94% are state residents; 15% are transfers. 1% Asian-American, 10% Black, 1% Hispanic, 1% Native American, 86% White, 1% Other. Average age of undergraduates is 24.
**Freshman profile:** Majority of accepted applicants took ACT. 87% of freshmen come from public schools.
**Undergraduate achievement:** 73% of fall 1992 freshmen returned for fall 1993 term. 20% of entering class graduated. 10% of students who completed a degree program immediately went on to graduate study.
**Foreign students:** 21 students are from out of the country. Countries represented include Argentina, Canada, Japan, and Korea; four in all.

**PROGRAMS OF STUDY. Degrees:** B.A., B.Bus.Admin., B.F.A., B.S.
**Majors:** Accounting, Art, Art Education, Biology, Business Administration, Business Education, Chemistry, Christian Education, Computing/Information Science, Criminal Justice Studies, Elementary Education, English, History, International Relations, Management, Marketing, Mathematics, Medical Technology, Nursing, Occupational Therapy, Organizational Communication, Philosophy, Physical Education, Political Science, Psychology, Public Relations, Religious Studies, Social Science, Social Studies, Sociology, Speech Communication.
**Distribution of degrees:** The majors with the highest enrollment are business administration, computer science, and accounting; public relations, chemistry, and physical education have the lowest.
**Requirements:** General education requirement.
**Academic regulations:** Freshmen must maintain minimum 1.75 GPA; sophomores, 1.9 GPA; juniors, 2.0 GPA; seniors, 2.0 GPA.
**Special:** Minors offered in coaching, gerontology, journalism, and music. Self-designed majors. Double majors. Independent study. Accelerated study. Pass/fail grading option. Internships. Preprofessional programs in law, medicine, veterinary science, pharmacy, dentistry, and optometry. 3-2 occupational therapy program with Washington U, St. Louis, Mo. Teacher certification in elementary, physical, and secondary education. Certification in specific subject areas. Exchange program abroad in England (Harlaton Coll). AFROTC.
**Honors:** Honors program. Honor societies.
**Academic Assistance:** Remedial reading, writing, math, and study skills. Nonremedial tutoring.

**ADMISSIONS. Academic basis for candidate selection** (in order of priority): Standardized test scores, class rank, secondary school record, school's recommendation, essay.
**Nonacademic basis for candidate selection:** Character and personality, extracurricular participation, particular talent or ability, and alumni/ae relationship are considered.
**Requirements:** Graduation from secondary school is required; GED is accepted. No specific distribution of secondary school units required. Minimum composite ACT score of 18, rank in top half of secondary school class, and minimum 2.2 GPA required. R.N. required of nursing program applicants. Conditional admission possible for applicants not meeting standard requirements. ACT is required; SAT may be substituted. Campus visit and interview recommended. No off-campus interviews.
**Procedure:** Take SAT or ACT by May 31 of 12th year. Suggest filing application by July 1. Application deadline is August 1. Notification of admission on rolling basis. Reply is required by August 1. $50 nonrefundable tuition deposit. $50 room deposit, refundable until July 1. Freshmen accepted for terms other than fall.
**Special programs:** Admission may be deferred six months. Credit may be granted through CEEB Advanced Placement exams. Credit may be granted through CLEP general and subject exams.
**Transfer students:** Transfer students accepted for terms other than fall. In fall 1993, 15% of all new students were transfers into all classes. 283 transfer applications were received, 151 were accepted. Application deadline is August 1 for fall; January 1 for spring. Minimum 2.0 GPA required. Lowest course grade accepted is "C." Maximum number of transferable credits is 70 semester hours from a two-year school and 96 semester hours from a four-year school. At least 32 semester hours must be completed at the college to receive degree.
**Admissions contact:** Sue Cordon, Dean of Admissions. 800 232-7228 (800 BEAR CAT), extension 121.

**FINANCIAL AID. Available aid:** Pell grants, SEOG, state scholarships and grants, school scholarships, private scholarships, ROTC scholarships, academic merit scholarships, and athletic scholarships. Perkins Loans (NDSL), PLUS, Stafford Loans (GSL), and SLS. Tuition Plan Inc., Knight Tuition Plans, AMS, and Tuition Management Systems.
**Financial aid statistics:** 30% of aid is not need-based. In 1993-94, 75% of all undergraduate applicants received aid; 90% of freshman applicants. Average amounts of aid awarded freshmen: Scholarships and grants, $2,000; loans, $2,625.
**Supporting data/closing dates:** FAFSA: Priority filing date is June 1. FAF: Priority filing date is May 1. Notification of awards on rolling basis.
**Financial aid contact:** Tamie Comley, Director of Financial Aid. 618 537-4481, extension 117.

# Millikin University

**Decatur, IL 62522 — 217 424-6211**

**1994-95 Costs.** Tuition: $11,910. Room: $2,278. Board: $2,100. Fees, books, misc. academic expenses (school's estimate): $541.
**Enrollment.** Undergraduates: 767 men, 1,021 women (full-time). Freshman class: 1,439 applicants, 1,270 accepted, 456 enrolled.
**Test score averages/ranges.** Average SAT scores: 511 verbal, 541 math. Average ACT scores: 24 English, 22 math, 24 composite. Range of ACT scores of middle 50%: 21-27 English, 20-26 math.
**Faculty.** 125 full-time; 90 part-time. 64% of faculty holds doctoral degree. Student/faculty ratio: 14 to 1.
**Selectivity rating.** Competitive.

**PROFILE.** Millikin, founded in 1901, is a private, church-affiliated university. Programs are offered through the Colleges of Arts and Sciences, Fine Arts, and Nursing and the Tabor School of Business. Its 40-acre campus is located in Decatur, 40 miles east of Springfield.

**Accreditation:** NCACS. Professionally accredited by the National Association of Schools of Music, the National League for Nursing.
**Religious orientation:** Millikin University is affiliated with the Presbyterian Church USA; no religious requirements.
**Library:** Collections totaling over 147,921 volumes, 1,002 periodical subscriptions, and 18,679 microform items.
**Special facilities/museums:** Art museum, fitness/wellness center.
**Athletic facilities:** Gymnasium, field house, swimming pool, basketball, tennis, and volleyball courts, athletic fields, track, stadium.

**STUDENT BODY. Undergraduate profile:** 87% are state residents; 16% are transfers. 1% Asian-American, 3% Black, 1% Hispanic, 1% Native American, 93% White, 1% Other. Average age of undergraduates is 21.
**Freshman profile:** 5% of freshmen who took SAT scored 700 or over on math; 16% scored 600 or over on verbal, 24% scored 600 or over on math; 56% scored 500 or over on verbal, 73% scored 500 or over on math; 94% scored 400 or over on verbal, 96% scored 400 or over on math; 100% scored 300 or over on verbal, 99% scored 300 or over on math. 8% of freshmen who took ACT scored 30 or over on English, 7% scored 30 or over on math, 4% scored 30 or over on composite; 52% scored 24 or over on English, 41% scored 24 or over on math, 48% scored 24 or over on composite; 94% scored 18 or over on English, 93% scored 18 or over on math, 99% scored 18 or over on composite; 100% scored 12 or over on English, 100% scored 12 or over on math, 100% scored 12 or over on composite. 16% of accepted applicants took SAT; 93% took ACT. 85% of freshmen come from public schools.
**Undergraduate achievement:** 81% of fall 1992 freshmen returned for fall 1993 term. 53% of entering class graduated. 22% of students who completed a degree program immediately went on to graduate study.
**Foreign students:** 17 students are from out of the country. Countries represented include Bulgaria, China, France, Germany, Malaysia, and Poland; nine in all.

**PROGRAMS OF STUDY. Degrees:** B.A., B.F.A., B.Mus., B.S.
**Majors:** Accounting, American Studies, Applied Music, Art, Art Management, Art Therapy, Biology, Business Administration/Management, Chemistry, Church Music, Commercial Art/Computer Design, Commercial Music, Communications, Computer Science/Mathematics, Economics, Elementary Education, English, Experimental Psychology, Finance, Foreign Languages/Multiple Emphasis, French, German, History, Human Resources Management, Human Services, Instrumental Music, International Business, International Studies, Management Information Systems, Marketing, Mathematics, Music/Business, Music Education, Music Performance, Musical Theatre, Nursing, Philosophy, Physical Education, Physics, Political Science/Government, Production/Operations Management, Psychology, Religion, School Nursing, Social Sciences, Sociology, Spanish, Theatre, Writing.
**Distribution of degrees:** The majors with the highest enrollment are nursing, communications, and accounting; Spanish, philosophy/religion, and American studies/physics have the lowest.
**Requirements:** General education requirement.

**Academic regulations:** Minimum 2.0 GPA must be maintained.
**Special:** Minors offered in most majors and in astronomy and dance. Self-designed majors. Double majors. Dual degrees. Independent study. Pass/fail grading option. Internships. Preprofessional programs in law, medicine, dentistry, engineering, medical technology, occupational therapy, and physical therapy. 3-2 physical and occupational therapy programs. 3-2 engineering programs with Washington U. Member of Associated Colleges of Illinois and Federation of Independent Illinois Colleges and Universities. Washington Semester and UN Semester. Teacher certification in elementary and secondary education. Certification in specific subject areas. Study abroad in Australia, Austria, China, England, France, Germany, Italy, Japan, Mexico, Russia, Spain, Singapore, and Taiwan.
**Honors:** Honors program. Honor societies.
**Academic Assistance:** Remedial math and study skills. Nonremedial tutoring.

**STUDENT LIFE. Housing:** Unmarried freshmen, sophomores, and juniors must live on campus unless living with family. Coed, women's, and men's dorms. Sorority and fraternity housing. 67% of students live in college housing.
**Services and counseling/handicapped student services:** Placement services. Health service. Orientation course for freshmen during first semester. Counseling services for minority, military, veteran, and older students. Birth control, personal, and psychological counseling. Career and academic guidance services. Religious counseling. Physically disabled student services. Learning disabled services. Tape recorders. Tutors. Reader services for the blind.
**Campus organizations:** Undergraduate student government. Student newspaper (Decaturian, twice/month). Literary magazine. Yearbook. Radio station. Choir, chorus, vocal and instrumental ensembles, orchestra, band, jazz band, athletic and departmental groups, Alpha Phi Omega, Circle K, 68 organizations in all. Five fraternities, four chapter houses; four sororities, all with chapter houses. 27% of men join a fraternity. 25% of women join a sorority.
**Religious organizations:** Intervarsity Christian Fellowship, Newman Club, Brothers and Sisters of Christ, Presbyterian Student Fellowship, Fellowship of Christian Athletes, Theo-Socratic Society, Religious Life Committee.
**Minority/foreign student organizations:** Black Emphasis Association, Alpha Phi Alpha, Multicultural Association, Minority Student Newsletter. International Association, International Hospitality Program.

**ATHLETICS. Physical education requirements:** None.
**Intercollegiate competition:** 40% of students participate. Baseball (M), basketball (M,W), cheerleading (M,W), cross-country (M,W), football (M), golf (M), soccer (M), softball (W), swimming (M,W), tennis (M,W), track (indoor) (M), track (outdoor) (M,W), track and field (indoor) (M), track and field (outdoor) (M,W), volleyball (W), wrestling (M). Member of College Conference of Illinois and Wisconsin, NCAA Division III.
**Intramural and club sports:** 60% of students participate. Intramural basketball, bowling, football, handball, miniature golf, softball, table tennis, tennis, volleyball.

**ADMISSIONS. Academic basis for candidate selection** (in order of priority): Secondary school record, class rank, standardized test scores, school's recommendation.
**Nonacademic basis for candidate selection:** Character and personality, extracurricular participation, particular talent or ability, and geographical distribution are considered.
**Requirements:** Graduation from secondary school is required; GED is accepted. 15 units required and the following program of study recommended: 4 units of English, 3 units of math, 3 units of science, 2 units of foreign language, 2 units of social studies. Nonacademic subjects considered individually. Minimum combined SAT score of 900 (composite ACT score of 20), rank in top half of secondary school class, and minimum 2.2 GPA required. 4 units of math recommended of engineering, mathematics, and science program applicants. 3 units of lab science required of nursing program applicants. Portfolio required of art program applicants. Audition required of music program applicants. SAT or ACT is required. Campus visit and interview recommended. Off-campus interviews available with an admissions representative.
**Procedure:** Take SAT or ACT by February of 12th year. Notification of admission on rolling basis. No set date by which applicants must accept offer. $50 nonrefundable tuition deposit. $100 nonrefundable room deposit. Freshmen accepted for terms other than fall.
**Special programs:** Admission may be deferred one year. Credit and/or placement may be granted through CEEB Advanced Placement exams for scores of 3 or higher. Credit may be granted through CLEP general and subject exams. Credit and placement may be granted through challenge exams and military experience.
**Transfer students:** Transfer students accepted for terms other than fall. In fall 1993, 16% of all new students were transfers into all classes. 203 transfer applications were received, 163 were accepted. Application deadline is rolling for fall; rolling for spring. Minimum 2.0 GPA required. Lowest course grade accepted is "D." Maximum number of transferable credits is 66 semester hours. At least 33 semester hours must be completed at the university to receive degree.
**Admissions contact:** Lin Stoner, Dean of Admissions. 217 424-6210, 800 373-7733.

**FINANCIAL AID. Available aid:** Pell grants, SEOG, state scholarships and grants, school scholarships and grants, private scholarships and grants, academic merit scholarships, and aid for undergraduate foreign students. Perkins Loans (NDSL), PLUS, Stafford Loans (GSL), state loans, school loans, private loans, and SLS. TERI Loans. AMS.
**Financial aid statistics:** 13% of aid is not need-based. In 1993-94, 92% of all undergraduate applicants received aid; 92% of freshman applicants. Average amounts of aid awarded freshmen: Scholarships and grants, $5,100; loans, $2,475.
**Supporting data/closing dates:** FAFSA/FAF: Accepted on rolling basis. Income tax forms: Accepted on rolling basis. Notification of awards on rolling basis.
**Financial aid contact:** Michael W. Pope, M.S., Director of Financial Aid. 217 424-6343.

**STUDENT EMPLOYMENT.** College Work/Study Program. Institutional employment. 39% of full-time undergraduates work on campus during school year. Students may expect to earn an average of $700 during school year. Off-campus part-time employment opportunities rated "good."

**COMPUTER FACILITIES.** 115 IBM/IBM-compatible and Macintosh/Apple microcomputers; 90 are networked. Students may access Digital minicomputer/mainframe systems, BITNET, Internet. Client/LAN operating systems include Apple/Macintosh, DOS, X-windows, Novell. Computer languages and software packages include Aldus PageMaker, BASIC, cc:Mail, COBOL, dBASE, Derive, DrawPerfect, FORTRAN, Freelance Plus, INGRES, Lotus 1-2-3, Paradox, Pascal, Quattro Pro, SPSS-X, Turbo C++, Turbo Pascal, WordPerfect; 80 in all. Computer facilities are available to all students.
**Fees:** None.
**Hours:** 8 AM-11 PM daily.

**GRADUATE CAREER DATA.** Graduate school percentages: 2% enter law school. 2% enter medical school. 2% enter graduate business programs. 12% enter graduate arts and sciences programs. Highest graduate school enrollments: U of Illinois, Southern Illinois U, Washington U. 25% of graduates choose careers in business and industry. Companies and businesses that hire graduates: Archer Daniels Midland, Armstrong International, Rockwell International.

**PROMINENT ALUMNI/AE.** Dr. John Leighty, chemist who helped develop use for penicillin; Jodi Benson, Broadway singer/actor; Clarence Johnson, former president, Borg-Warner.

## Monmouth College

**Monmouth, IL 61462** — **309 457-2131**

**1994-95 Costs.** Tuition: $13,000. Room: $2,180. Board: $1,920. Fees, books, misc. academic expenses (school's estimate): $600.
**Enrollment.** Undergraduates: 326 men, 345 women (full-time). Freshman class: 700 applicants, 591 accepted, 261 enrolled.
**Test score averages/ranges.** Average ACT scores: 23 composite. Range of ACT scores of middle 50%: 23-27 composite.
**Faculty.** 53 full-time; 22 part-time. 90% of faculty holds doctoral degree. Student/faculty ratio: 12 to 1.
**Selectivity rating.** Less competitive.

**PROFILE.** Monmouth, founded in 1853, is a church-affiliated, liberal arts college. Its 36-acre campus is located in Monmouth, 60 miles west of Peoria.
**Accreditation:** NCACS.
**Religious orientation:** Monmouth College is affiliated with the Presbyterian Church USA; no religious requirements.
**Library:** Collections totaling over 225,000 volumes, 679 periodical subscriptions, and 68,000 microform items.
**Athletic facilities:** Gymnasium.

**STUDENT BODY. Undergraduate profile:** 75% are state residents; 14% are transfers. 2% Asian-American, 7% Black, 2% Hispanic, 89% White. Average age of undergraduates is 20.
**Freshman profile:** 9% of accepted applicants took SAT; 91% took ACT. 91% of freshmen come from public schools.
**Undergraduate achievement:** 78% of fall 1992 freshmen returned for fall 1993 term. 44% of entering class graduated. 35% of students who completed a degree program immediately went on to graduate study.
**Foreign students:** 11 students are from out of the country. Countries represented include France, India, and Japan; six in all.

**PROGRAMS OF STUDY. Degrees:** B.A.
**Majors:** Accounting, Art, Biology, Business Administration, Chemistry, Classics, Computer Science, Economics, Education, English, Environmental Science, Government, Greek, History, Latin, Mathematics, Music, Physical Education, Physics, Psychology, Religious/Philosophical Studies, Sociology, Spanish, Speech/Communication Arts, Topical Major.
**Distribution of degrees:** The majors with the highest enrollment are economics/business administration, education, and speech/communication; classics and religious studies/philosophy have the lowest.
**Requirements:** General education requirement.
**Academic regulations:** Freshmen must maintain minimum 1.8 GPA; sophomores, juniors, seniors, 2.0 GPA. Convocation attendance mandatory for freshmen.
**Special:** Minors offered in most majors. Courses offered in German, Pan-American studies, women's studies, and linguistics. Freshman seminar. Self-designed majors. Double majors. Independent study. Accelerated study. Internships. Graduate school at which undergraduates may take graduate-level courses. Preprofessional programs in law, medicine, veterinary science, dentistry, theology, architecture, Christian education, communications, computer science, engineering, library science, medical technology, occupational therapy, physical therapy, and social service. 3-2 engineering programs with Case Western Reserve U and Washington U. 3-2 nursing program with Rush U. Member of Associated Colleges of the Midwest; exchange possible. Washington Semester. Newberry Library Program in the Humanities (Illinois). Oak Ridge Science Semester (Tennessee). Urban Education Program (Chicago). Wilderness Field Station Program (Minnesota). Other off-campus study opportunities. Teacher certification in early childhood, elementary, secondary, and special education. Certification in specific subject areas. Study abroad in Costa Rica, Czech Republic/Slovakia, England, Hong Kong, India, Italy, Japan, Russia and Zimbabwe. ROTC at Western Illinois U.
**Honors:** Honors program.
**Academic Assistance:** Remedial study skills. Nonremedial tutoring.

**ADMISSIONS. Academic basis for candidate selection** (in order of priority): Secondary school record, standardized test scores, class rank, school's recommendation.
**Nonacademic basis for candidate selection:** Character and personality are emphasized. Extracurricular participation is important. Particular talent or ability, geographical distribution, and alumni/ae relationship are considered.
**Requirements:** Graduation from secondary school is required; GED is accepted. 15 units and the following program of study are required: 4 units of English, 3 units of math, 2 units of lab science, 2 units of foreign language, 2 units of social studies, 2 units of history. Minimum composite ACT score of 18, rank in top half of secondary school class, and minimum 2.0 GPA recommended. ACT is required; SAT may be substituted. Campus visit and interview recommended. Off-campus interviews available with an admissions representative.
**Procedure:** Take SAT or ACT by February of 12th year. Visit college for interview by February 1 of 12th year. Notification of admission on rolling basis. Reply is required by

May 1. $150 tuition deposit, refundable until May 1. Freshmen accepted for terms other than fall.
**Special programs:** Admission may be deferred one year. Credit and/or placement may be granted through CEEB Advanced Placement exams for scores of 3 or higher. Credit and/or placement may be granted through CLEP general and subject exams. Early decision program. In fall 1992, 28 applied for early decision and 20 were accepted. Deadline for applying for early decision is December 1. Early entrance/early admission program. Concurrent enrollment program.
**Transfer students:** Transfer students accepted for terms other than fall. In fall 1993, 14% of all new students were transfers into all classes. 80 transfer applications were received, 65 were accepted. Application deadline is August 1 for fall; December 1 for spring. Minimum 2.0 GPA required. Lowest course grade accepted is "C." Maximum number of transferable credits is 62 semester hours. At least 62 semester hours must be completed at the college to receive degree.
**Admissions contact:** Richard Valentine, Dean of Admission. 800 74-SCOTS.

**FINANCIAL AID. Available aid:** Pell grants, SEOG, state scholarships and grants, school scholarships and grants, private scholarships and grants, ROTC scholarships, academic merit scholarships, and aid for undergraduate foreign students. Perkins Loans (NDSL), PLUS, Stafford Loans (GSL), state loans, and SLS. Tuition Management Systems.
**Financial aid statistics:** 40% of aid is not need-based. In 1993-94, 98% of all undergraduate applicants received aid; 98% of freshman applicants. Average amounts of aid awarded freshmen: Scholarships and grants, $10,295; loans, $2,829.
**Supporting data/closing dates:** FAFSA: Priority filing date is April 30. School's own aid application. Income tax forms: Accepted on rolling basis. Notification of awards begins March 1.
**Financial aid contact:** Brian Pomeroy, Director of Financial Aid. 309 457-2129.

## Moody Bible Institute

**Chicago, IL 60610** — **312 329-4000**

**1993-94 Costs.** Tuition: None. Room & board: $4,400. Fees, books, misc. academic expenses (school's estimate): $1,150.
**Enrollment.** Undergraduates: 834 men, 532 women (full-time). Freshman class: 899 applicants, 753 accepted, 466 enrolled. Graduate enrollment: 38 men, 35 women.
**Test score averages/ranges.** Average ACT scores: 22 composite. Range of ACT scores of middle 50%: 19-24 composite.
**Faculty.** 60 full-time; 12 part-time. 42% of faculty holds doctoral degree. Student/faculty ratio: 20 to 1.
**Selectivity rating.** Less competitive.

**PROFILE.** Moody Bible, founded in 1886, is a private institution with religious orientation. Its 23-acre campus is located in Chicago.

**Accreditation:** AABC, NCACS. Professionally accredited by the National Association of Schools of Music.
**Religious orientation:** Moody Bible Institute is an interdenominational Christian school; eight semesters of religion/theology required.
**Library:** Collections totaling over 127,588 volumes, 900 periodical subscriptions, and 1,720 microform items.
**Special facilities/museums:** Audio-visual center.
**Athletic facilities:** Gymnasium, field house, basketball, racquetball, and volleyball courts, aerobics and weight rooms.

**STUDENT BODY. Undergraduate profile:** 27% are state residents; 36% are transfers. 4% Asian-American, 3% Black, 2% Hispanic, 91% White. Average age of undergraduates is 22.
**Freshman profile:** 2% of freshmen who took ACT scored 30 or over on composite; 33% scored 24 or over on composite; 84% scored 18 or over on composite; 99% scored 12 or over on composite; 100% scored 6 or over on composite. Majority of accepted applicants took ACT.
**Undergraduate achievement:** 50% of entering class graduated.
**Foreign students:** 140 students are from out of the country. Countries represented include Canada, England, Germany, India, Singapore, and South Korea; 50 in all.

**PROGRAMS OF STUDY. Degrees:** B.A., B.S., B.Sacred Mus.
**Majors:** Bible/Theology, Church Music, Communication, Educational Ministries, Evangelism/Discipleship, International Ministries, Jewish/Modern Israel Studies, Missionary Aviation, Pastoral Studies, Sacred Music, Urban Ministries, Youth Ministries.
**Distribution of degrees:** The majors with the highest enrollment are Bible/theology, international ministries, and pastoral studies; evangelism, church music, and sacred music have the lowest.
**Requirements:** General education requirement.
**Academic regulations:** Freshmen must maintain minimum 1.75 GPA; sophomores, 1.85 GPA; juniors, 1.95 GPA; seniors, 2.00 GPA.
**Special:** Independent study. Graduate school at which undergraduates may take graduate-level courses. Study abroad in Israel.

**STUDENT LIFE. Housing:** All unmarried students must live on campus. Women's and men's dorms. On-campus married-student housing. No housing available for students in missionary aviation program in Tennessee. 81% of students live in college housing.
**Social atmosphere:** Favorite student hangouts include Culby 2, Coffeecove, Solheim center, Plaza, Mr.G's, Checkers, Third Coast, Ed Debevic's, North Pier, and West Egg. STUCO, RACO, and Afro-Awareness influence student life. Popular events include Homecoming, volleyball and soccer games, Founder's Week, Timey Fitness Week, Bro/Sis Olympics, and Labor Day Blitz. "Spiritually strong on-campus environment," reports the editor of the student newspaper. "Lots of neat people. Chicago offers many diverse activities."
**Services and counseling/handicapped student services:** Placement services. Health service. Personal counseling. Academic guidance services. Religious counseling. Learning disabled services.
**Campus organizations:** Undergraduate student government. Student newspaper (Moody Student, published once/month). Yearbook. Radio station. Concert band, chorale, oratorio chorus, men's collegiate choir, women's concert choir, bell ensemble, Married Students Fellowship, pre-aviation club, volleyball club, Big Brother/Big Sister, Students Wives Fellowship.
**Religious organizations:** Selah, Student Missionary Fellowship.
**Minority/foreign student organizations:** Afro Awareness Fellowship. International Student Fellowship.

**ATHLETICS. Physical education requirements:** Three semesters of physical education required.
**Intercollegiate competition:** 10% of students participate. Basketball (M,W), soccer (M), volleyball (W). Member of NCCAA.
**Intramural and club sports:** 70% of students participate. Intramural badminton, basketball, floor hockey, indoor football, racquetball, volleyball, walleyball. Men's club volleyball.

**ADMISSIONS. Academic basis for candidate selection** (in order of priority): Essay, secondary school record, standardized test scores, class rank, school's recommendation.
**Nonacademic basis for candidate selection:** Character and personality are emphasized. Christian commitment and physical health are important. Particular talent or ability are considered.
**Requirements:** Graduation from secondary school is required; GED is accepted. No specific distribution of secondary school units required. 12 units recommended, including English grammar and college-preparatory courses. Minimum 2.3 GPA required. Flight camp evaluation required of missionary aviation program applicants; entrance tests required of premissionary aviation program applicants. Auditions and placement tests required of church music program applicants. ACT is required. Campus visit and interview recommended. No off-campus interviews.
**Procedure:** Take ACT by March 15 of 12th year. Suggest filing application by April 1. Application deadline is May 1. Notification of admission on rolling basis. Reply is required by July 1. $100 room deposit; half is refundable until July 15. Freshmen accepted for terms other than fall.
**Special programs:** Admission may be deferred one year. Credit may be granted through CLEP general and subject exams.
**Transfer students:** Transfer students accepted for terms other than fall. In fall 1992, 36% of all new students were transfers into all classes. 457 transfer applications were received. Application deadline is May 1 for fall; November 1 for spring. Minimum 2.0 GPA required. Lowest course grade accepted is "C." Maximum number of transferable credits is 98 semester hours. At least 32 semester hours must be completed at the institute to receive degree.
**Admissions contact:** Philip Van Wynen, M.Div., M.S., Dean of Enrollment Management. 312 329-4266.

**FINANCIAL AID. Available aid:** School grants and private scholarships and grants. Aid for "needy and deserving" students. Deferred payment plan.
**Financial aid statistics:** 2% of aid is not need-based. In 1992-93, 2% of all undergraduate applicants received aid. Average amounts of aid awarded freshmen: Loans, $700.
**Supporting data/closing dates:** School's own aid application: Accepted on rolling basis. Notification of awards on rolling basis.
**Financial aid contact:** Joe Gonzales, Director of Financial Aid. 312 329-4202.

**STUDENT EMPLOYMENT.** Institutional employment. 60% of full-time undergraduates work on campus during school year. Students may expect to earn an average of $3,000 during school year. Off-campus part-time employment opportunities rated "good."

**COMPUTER FACILITIES.** 12 IBM/IBM-compatible microcomputers; all are networked. Computer languages and software packages include First Publisher, Microsoft Works, NASB Computer Bible, WordStar, WordPerfect. Computer access restricted to students who have had computer instruction.
**Fees:** None.
**Hours:** 7:30 AM-9 PM (M-Th); 7:30 AM-5 PM (F); 9 AM-3 PM (Sa).

## National-Louis University

**Evanston, IL 60201** — **708 475-1100**

**1993-94 Costs.** Tuition: $9,090. Room & board: $4,128.
**Enrollment.** Undergraduates: 938 men, 1,812 women (full-time). Freshman class: 470 applicants, 353 accepted, 273 enrolled. Graduate enrollment: 612 men, 3,674 women.
**Test score averages/ranges.** Average ACT scores: 18 composite.
**Faculty.** 231 full-time; 12 part-time. 65% of faculty holds doctoral degree. Student/faculty ratio: 13 to 1.
**Selectivity rating.** Less competitive.

**PROFILE.** National-Louis, founded in 1886, is a private, comprehensive university. Its 14-acre campus is located in Evanston, 10 miles north of Chicago.

**Accreditation:** NCACS. Professionally accredited by the American Medical Association (CAHEA), the National Council for Accreditation of Teacher Education.
**Religious orientation:** National-Louis University is nonsectarian; no religious requirements.
**Library:** Collections totaling over 150,000 volumes, 1,255 periodical subscriptions, and 1,500,000 microform items.
**Special facilities/museums:** On-campus school (N-8).
**Athletic facilities:** Gymnasium, swimming pool, weight room, athletic fields.

**STUDENT BODY. Undergraduate profile:** 69% are state residents; 65% are transfers. 5% Asian-American, 20% Black, 9% Hispanic, 1% Native American, 65% White. Average age of undergraduates is 32.
**Freshman profile:** 3% of freshmen who took ACT scored 30 or over on composite; 15% scored 24 or over on composite; 45% scored 18 or over on composite; 98% scored 12 or

over on composite; 100% scored 6 or over on composite. 4% of accepted applicants took SAT; 28% took ACT.
**Undergraduate achievement:** 70% of fall 1991 freshmen returned for fall 1992 term. 45% of entering class graduated. 30% of students who completed a degree program went on to graduate study within one year.
**Foreign students:** Two students are from out of the country.

**PROGRAMS OF STUDY. Degrees:** B.A., B.S.
**Majors:** Accounting, Alcoholism Counseling, Allied Health Education, Allied Health Management, Anthropology, Applied Behavioral Sciences, Art, Asian Bilingual Multicultural Studies, Business Administration, Communication Arts, Computer Information Systems Management, Early Childhood Education, Elementary Education, English, Human Development, Human Services, Legal Studies, Management, Mathematics, Medical Technology, Multicultural Studies, Psychology, Quantitative Methods, Radiation Therapy Technology, Respiratory Therapy, Science, Social Science, Special Education, Sport Management, Theatre Arts.
**Distribution of degrees:** The majors with the highest enrollment are management, applied behavioral sciences, and elementary education; human development, social science, and respiratory therapy have the lowest.
**Requirements:** General education requirement.
**Academic regulations:** Minimum 2.0 GPA must be maintained.
**Special:** Minors offered in some majors and in fine arts/theatre, philosophy, and sports science. Double majors. Accelerated study. Internships. Graduate school at which undergraduates may take graduate-level courses. 3-1 medical technology program with Michael Reese Medical Center. Teacher certification in early childhood, elementary, special education, and bilingual/bicultural education. Certification in specific subject areas. Study abroad in England.
**Honors:** Honor societies.
**Academic Assistance:** Remedial reading, writing, math, and study skills. Nonremedial tutoring.

**STUDENT LIFE. Housing:** All freshmen must live on campus unless living with family. Coed dorms. 5% of students live in college housing.
**Services and counseling/handicapped student services:** Placement services. Health service. Counseling services for minority and older students. Personal counseling. Career and academic guidance services. Physically disabled student services. Learning disabled services. Tutors.
**Campus organizations:** Undergraduate student government. Student newspaper (Campus). Yearbook. Choir, Circle K, early childhood club, human services club, Student Education Association, Council on Exceptional Children, commuter student association, 12 organizations in all. One sorority, no chapter house. 5% of women join a sorority.
**Religious organizations:** Intervarsity Christian Fellowship.
**Minority/foreign student organizations:** Korean club.

**ATHLETICS. Physical education requirements:** Four terms of physical education required.
**Intercollegiate competition:** 13% of students participate. Basketball (W), soccer (M). Member of Chicagoland Collegiate Athletic Conference, NAIA.
**Intramural and club sports:** 6% of students participate. Intramural badminton, basketball, bowling, volleyball.

**ADMISSIONS. Academic basis for candidate selection** (in order of priority): Secondary school record, standardized test scores, class rank, school's recommendation.
**Nonacademic basis for candidate selection:** Character and personality are emphasized. Extracurricular participation and particular talent or ability are important. Alumni/ae relationship is considered.
**Requirements:** Graduation from secondary school is required; GED is accepted. 12 units and the following program of study are recommended: 4 units of English, 3 units of math, 2 units of science (1 science unit should be a lab science), 2 units of foreign language, 3 units of social studies. Rank in top half of secondary school class recommended. Conditional admission possible for applicants not meeting standard requirements. Communications Skills Lab for applicants not normally admissible. SAT or ACT is required. ACH recommended. Campus visit and interview recommended. Off-campus interviews available with an admissions representative.
**Procedure:** Take SAT or ACT by June 1 of 12th year. Visit college for interview by June 1 of 12th year. Application deadline is September 1. Notification of admission on rolling basis. $150 tuition deposit, refundable until May 1. $50 room deposit, refundable until July 1. Freshmen accepted for terms other than fall.
**Special programs:** Admission may be deferred two years. Credit and/or placement may be granted through CEEB Advanced Placement exams for scores of 3 or higher. Credit and/or placement may be granted through CLEP general and subject exams, military and life experience. Credit and placement may be granted through challenge exams. Early entrance/early admission program.
**Transfer students:** Transfer students accepted for terms other than fall. In fall 1992, 65% of all new students were transfers into all classes. 788 transfer applications were received, 569 were accepted. Application deadline is rolling for fall; rolling for spring. Minimum 2.0 GPA recommended. Lowest course grade accepted is "C." Maximum number of transferable quarter hours varies by program.
**Admissions contact:** Randall Berd, M.Ed., Director of Student Enrollment. 708 475-1100, extension 2225.

**FINANCIAL AID. Available aid:** Pell grants, SEOG, state grants, school scholarships and grants, private scholarships and grants, academic merit scholarships, and athletic scholarships. Perkins Loans (NDSL), PLUS, Stafford Loans (GSL), and SLS. Deferred payment plan and guaranteed tuition.
**Financial aid statistics:** 10% of aid is not need-based. In 1992-93, 90% of all undergraduate applicants received aid.
**Supporting data/closing dates:** School's own aid application: Priority filing date is July 15; accepted on rolling basis. Income tax forms: Accepted on rolling basis. SINGLEFILE: Accepted on rolling basis. Notification of awards on rolling basis.
**Financial aid contact:** Kendra Dane, Director of Financial Aid. 708 475-1100, extension 5770.

**STUDENT EMPLOYMENT.** College Work/Study Program. Institutional employment. Students may expect to earn an average of $1,800 during school year. Off-campus part-time employment opportunities rated "good."

**COMPUTER FACILITIES.** 200 IBM/IBM-compatible and Macintosh/Apple microcomputers; 30 are networked. Students may access IBM minicomputer/mainframe systems. Residence halls may be equipped with stand-alone microcomputers. Client/LAN operating systems include Novell. Computer languages and software packages include Apple educational programs, BASIC, dBASE, LOGO, Lotus 1-2-3, Pascal, PFS, PILOT, WordPerfect. Computer facilities are available to all students.
**Fees:** None.
**Hours:** 9 AM-9 PM (M-F) or class hours as scheduled (six labs).

**GRADUATE CAREER DATA.** Graduate school percentages: 5% enter graduate business programs. 25% enter graduate arts and sciences programs. 53% of graduates choose careers in business and industry.

# North Central College

**Naperville, IL 60566-7065** **708 420-3400**

**1994-95 Costs.** Tuition: $11,718. Room & board: $4,398. Fees, books, misc. academic expenses (school's estimate): $570.
**Enrollment.** Undergraduates: 701 men, 598 women (full-time). Freshman class: 1,127 applicants, 846 accepted, 308 enrolled. Graduate enrollment: 263 men, 150 women.
**Test score averages/ranges.** Average SAT scores: 483 verbal, 556 math. Range of SAT scores of middle 50%: 440-550 verbal, 480-630 math. Average ACT scores: 23 English, 24 math, 25 composite. Range of ACT scores of middle 50%: 20-26 English, 21-26 math.
**Faculty.** 97 full-time; 81 part-time. 71% of faculty holds doctoral degree. Student/faculty ratio: 13 to 1.
**Selectivity rating.** Competitive.

**PROFILE.** North Central, founded in 1861, is a private, church-affiliated college. Programs are offered through the Divisions of Creative Arts, Economics and Business Administration, Humanities, Language and Literature, Natural Science and Mathematics, and Social and Behavioral Sciences. Its 54-acre campus is located in a residential area of Naperville, west of metropolitan Chicago.
**Accreditation:** NCACS.
**Religious orientation:** North Central College is affiliated with the United Methodist Church; no religious requirements.
**Library:** Collections totaling over 110,000 volumes and 764 periodical subscriptions.
**Athletic facilities:** Indoor and outdoor tracks, field house, stadium, swimming pool, weight room, two gymnasiums, soccer field, baseball diamond, softball diamond, four tennis courts.

**STUDENT BODY. Undergraduate profile:** 80% are state residents; 18% are transfers. 2% Asian-American, 5% Black, 3% Hispanic, 1% Native American, 88% White, 1% Other. Average age of undergraduates is 20.
**Freshman profile:** 7% of freshmen who took SAT scored 700 or over on math; 11% scored 600 or over on verbal, 35% scored 600 or over on math; 45% scored 500 or over on verbal, 72% scored 500 or over on math; 70% scored 400 or over on verbal, 90% scored 400 or over on math; 90% scored 300 or over on verbal, 98% scored 300 or over on math. 32% of accepted applicants took SAT; 87% took ACT.
**Undergraduate achievement:** 75% of fall 1992 freshmen returned for fall 1993 term. 47% of entering class graduated. 17% of students who completed a degree program immediately went on to graduate study.
**Foreign students:** 23 students are from out of the country. Countries represented include China, Hong Kong, India, and Japan; 16 in all.

**PROGRAMS OF STUDY. Degrees:** B.A., B.S.
**Majors:** Accounting, Art, Athletic Training, Biochemistry, Biology, Business, Chemistry, Classics, Computer/Information Sciences, Economics, Education, English, Finance, Fitness Management, French, General Studies, German, History, Information Systems, International Business, International Studies, Japanese, Management, Management Information Systems, Marketing, Mathematics, Music, Organizational Communication, Philosophy, Physical Education, Physics, Political Science/Government, Psychology, Public Relations, Religious Studies, Social Studies, Sociology/Anthropology, Spanish, Speech Communications, Theatre.
**Distribution of degrees:** The majors with the highest enrollment are management, computer science, and accounting; classics, Japanese, and social studies have the lowest.
**Requirements:** General education requirement.
**Academic regulations:** Freshmen must maintain minimum 1.8 GPA; sophomores, juniors, seniors, 2.0 GPA.
**Special:** Minors offered in all majors and in journalism, organizational leadership, and women's studies. Interdisciplinary courses in aesthetics, ecology, environmental science, and music/drama workshops. Curriculum is divided into three areas: Foundation (students complete objectives within the six academic divisions); Exploration (designed to extend the student's interest); and Concentration (in single academic area, single division area, or interdisciplinary area). Program based on close student-faculty work. Mid-Winter Study and Research Team includes off-campus projects, intensified workshops, seminars, and independent study. Gulf Coast Research Lab. Self-designed majors. Double majors. Dual degrees. Independent study. Accelerated study. Internships. Graduate school at which undergraduates may take graduate-level courses. Preprofessional programs in law, medicine, veterinary science, pharmacy, and dentistry. 2-2 nursing program with Rush U. Cooperative programs with approved schools of dentistry, law, medicine, and medical technology. 3-2 engineering programs with Marquette U, U of Illinois at Urbana-Champaign, U of Minnesota, and Washington U. The Council of West Suburban Colleges. Washington Semester and UN Semester. Teacher certification in elementary and secondary education. Certification in specific subject areas. Exchange program abroad in Japan

(Osaka Jogakuin Junior Coll). Study abroad in over 60 countries. ROTC at Wheaton Coll. NROTC at Northern Illinois U. AFROTC at Illinois Inst of Tech.
**Honors:** Honors program.
**Academic Assistance:** Remedial reading, writing, math, and study skills. Nonremedial tutoring.

**STUDENT LIFE. Housing:** Students may live on or off campus. Coed, women's, and men's dorms. 65% of students live in college housing.
**Social atmosphere:** As reported by the student newspaper, many students go home on the weekends, though frequent trips to Chicago are also taken. Athletes influence student social life at North Central. Students gather in The Lantern, Features, and Maxwell & Millie's. Popular school-year events include Homecoming, Winter Dance, Spring Formal, College Union Activities Board entertainment, and theatre productions.
**Services and counseling/handicapped student services:** Placement services. Health service. Counseling services for minority students. Personal and psychological counseling. Career and academic guidance services. Religious counseling. Physically disabled student services. Learning disabled services. Notetaking services. Reader services for the blind.
**Campus organizations:** Undergraduate student government. Student newspaper (Chronicle, published twice/month). Literary magazine. Yearbook. Radio station. College-Community Orchestra, oratorio chorus, Theatre Guild, departmental groups, intercollegiate debate, Activities Board, political groups, special-interest groups, American Marketing Association, 30 organizations in all.
**Religious organizations:** Fellowship of Christian Athletes, New Visions choral group, Tuesday Night Life, Campus Ministry, United Methodist Students, Newman club.
**Minority/foreign student organizations:** Multicultural Student Association. International Student Association.

**ATHLETICS. Physical education requirements:** One course credit of physical education required.
**Intercollegiate competition:** 7% of students participate. Baseball (M), basketball (M,W), cross-country (M,W), football (M), golf (M), soccer (M,W), softball (W), swimming (M,W), tennis (M,W), track (M,W), track (indoor) (M,W), track (outdoor) (M,W), track and field (W), volleyball (W), wrestling (M). Member of College Conference of Illinois and Wisconsin, NCAA Division III.
**Intramural and club sports:** 4% of students participate. Intramural aerobics, basketball, bowling, flag football, softball, volleyball.

**ADMISSIONS. Academic basis for candidate selection** (in order of priority): Secondary school record, standardized test scores, class rank, school's recommendation, essay.
**Nonacademic basis for candidate selection:** Character and personality and extracurricular participation are important. Particular talent or ability, geographical distribution, and alumni/ae relationship are considered.
**Requirements:** Graduation from secondary school is required; GED is accepted. No specific distribution of secondary school units required. Minimum combined SAT score of 800 (composite ACT score of 20), rank in top half of secondary school class, and minimum 2.0 GPA required. SAT or ACT is required. Campus visit and interview recommended. Off-campus interviews available with an admissions representative.
**Procedure:** Take SAT or ACT by January of 12th year. Visit college for interview by March of 12th year. Notification of admission on rolling basis. Reply is required by May 1. $100 tuition deposit, refundable until May 1. $50 room deposit, refundable until May 1. Freshmen accepted for terms other than fall.
**Special programs:** Admission may be deferred one year. Credit and/or placement may be granted through CEEB Advanced Placement exams for scores of 4 or higher. Credit and/or placement may be granted through CLEP general and subject exams. Credit and placement may be granted through life experience. Early entrance/early admission program.
**Transfer students:** Transfer students accepted for terms other than fall. In fall 1993, 18% of all new students were transfers into all classes. 375 transfer applications were received, 308 were accepted. Application deadline is rolling for fall; rolling for spring. Minimum 2.0 GPA required. Lowest course grade accepted is "D." Maximum number of transferable credits is 67 semester hours from a two-year school and 90 semester hours from a four-year school. At least 30 semester hours must be completed at the college to receive degree.
**Admissions contact:** Marguerite Waters, Director of Admission. 708 420-3414.

**FINANCIAL AID. Available aid:** Pell grants, SEOG, state scholarships and grants, school scholarships and grants, private scholarships and grants, academic merit scholarships, and aid for undergraduate foreign students. Perkins Loans (NDSL), PLUS, Stafford Loans (GSL), state loans, school loans, private loans, and SLS. Tuition Management Systems.
**Financial aid statistics:** 27% of aid is not need-based.
**Supporting data/closing dates:** FAFSA: Priority filing date is April 1. School's own aid application: Priority filing date is April 1. Income tax forms: Priority filing date is April 1. Notification of awards on rolling basis.
**Financial aid contact:** Katherine Edmunds, Director of Financial Aid. 708 420-3420.

**STUDENT EMPLOYMENT.** College Work/Study Program. Institutional employment. 55% of full-time undergraduates work on campus during school year. Students may expect to earn an average of $748 during school year. Off-campus part-time employment opportunities rated "excellent."

**COMPUTER FACILITIES.** 110 IBM/IBM-compatible microcomputers; all are networked. Students may access Sequent minicomputer/mainframe systems. Residence halls may be equipped with stand-alone microcomputers. Computer languages and software packages include Assembler, BASIC, C, COBOL, dBASE, FORTRAN, Lotus 1-2-3, Pascal, WordPerfect; 42 in all. Computer facilities are available to all students.
**Fees:** Computer fee is included in tuition/fees.
**Hours:** 96 hours/week; seven days/week.

**GRADUATE CAREER DATA.** Highest graduate school enrollments: U of Illinois at Urbana/Champaign, Loyola U, North Central Coll, Northwestern U, Purdue U, U of Wisconsin at Madison. 59% of graduates choose careers in business and industry. Companies and businesses that hire graduates: Amoco Research, AT&T, Chemical Waste Management, Inc.

**PROMINENT ALUMNI/AE.** Dr. Daniel Ruge, personal physician to former President Reagan; Bertram Lee, co-owner of the Denver Nuggets and first minority owner of an NBA team.

# North Park College

**Chicago, IL 60625** **312 583-2700**

**1994-95 Costs.** Tuition: $12,580. Room: $2,390. Board: $2,020.
**Enrollment.** Undergraduates: 396 men, 483 women (full-time). Freshman class: 365 applicants, 284 accepted, 180 enrolled. Graduate enrollment: 201 men, 38 women.
**Test score averages/ranges.** Average ACT scores: 22 composite. Range of ACT scores of middle 50%: 17-24 composite.
**Faculty.** 62 full-time; 12 part-time. 72% of faculty holds highest degree in specific field. Student/faculty ratio: 12 to 1.
**Selectivity rating.** Less competitive.

**PROFILE.** North Park, founded in 1891, is a private, church-affiliated college. Programs are offered in the Divisions of Fine Arts, Humanities, Nursing, Science and Mathematics, and Social Science. Its 30-acre campus is located on the northwest side of Chicago.
**Accreditation:** NCACS. Professionally accredited by the National Association of Schools of Music, the National League for Nursing.
**Religious orientation:** North Park College is affiliated with the Evangelical Covenant Church; two terms of religion required.
**Library:** Collections totaling over 207,000 volumes, 1,000 periodical subscriptions, and 3,304 microform items.
**Special facilities/museums:** Art gallery, language lab, Swedish Historical Society Archives.
**Athletic facilities:** Gymnasium, weight rooms, swimming pool, baseball, football, soccer, and softball fields, track, basketball, tennis, and volleyball courts.

**STUDENT BODY. Undergraduate profile:** 55% are state residents; 11% are transfers. 9% Asian-American, 5% Black, 6% Hispanic, 78% White, 2% Other. Average age of undergraduates is 22.
**Freshman profile:** 5% of freshmen who took ACT scored 30 or over on composite; 32% scored 24 or over on composite; 71% scored 18 or over on composite; 100% scored 12 or over on composite. 37% of accepted applicants took SAT; 66% took ACT.
**Undergraduate achievement:** 75% of fall 1992 freshmen returned for fall 1993 term. 60% of entering class graduated.
**Foreign students:** 102 students are from out of the country. Countries represented include Canada, Korea, Norway, and Sweden; 22 in all.

**PROGRAMS OF STUDY. Degrees:** B.A., B.Mus., B.S.
**Majors:** Accounting, Art, Biblical/Theological Studies, Biology, Business Administration, Chemistry, Computer Science, Economics, Elementary Education, English, Exercise Science, Finance, History, Instrumental Music, International Affairs, International Business, Mathematics, Medical Technology, Music, Music Education, Music/Voice, Nursing Science, Occupational Therapy, Philosophy, Physical Education, Physics, Political Science, Psychology, Secondary Education, Social Studies, Sociology/Anthropology, Spanish, Speech/Communications, Swedish, Voice, Youth Ministry.
**Distribution of degrees:** The majors with the highest enrollment are business, life sciences, and education.
**Requirements:** General education requirement.
**Special:** Minors offered in all majors and in 22 interdisciplinary areas. Self-designed majors. Double majors. Dual degrees. Independent study. Accelerated study. Pass/fail grading option. Internships. Graduate school at which undergraduates may take graduate-level courses. Preprofessional programs in law, medicine, veterinary science, pharmacy, dentistry, and theology. 3-1 medical technology programs with Evanston Hospital, Lutheran General Hospital, and Michael Reese Hospital. 3-2 engineering programs with Case Western Reserve U, U of Illinois, U of Minnesota, Stanford U, and Washington U. 3-2 occupational therapy program with Washington U. Five-year M.B.A. program. Member of Christian College Consortium. Washington Semester. Other semester-away programs available. Exchange program in Hollywood. Teacher certification in early childhood, elementary, and secondary education. Winter term program in Mexico. Exchange programs abroad in Germany (Goethe Inst in Murnau) and Sweden (Sondra Vatterbygdens Folkhogskola in Jonkoping). AFROTC at Illinois Inst of Tech and U of Illinois.
**Honors:** Phi Beta Kappa. Honors program.
**Academic Assistance:** Remedial reading, writing, math, and study skills. Nonremedial tutoring.

**ADMISSIONS. Academic basis for candidate selection** (in order of priority): Standardized test scores, class rank, secondary school record, essay, school's recommendation.
**Nonacademic basis for candidate selection:** Character and personality are emphasized. Extracurricular participation and particular talent or ability are important.
**Requirements:** Graduation from secondary school is required; GED is accepted. No specific distribution of secondary school units required. Nonacademic subjects may be considered depending upon the tested aptitude of applicant. Minimum combined SAT score of 850 (composite ACT score of 18), rank in top half of secondary school class, and minimum 2.0 GPA recommended. Audition required of music program applicants. Provisional admission possible for applicants not meeting standard requirements. SAT or ACT is required. Campus visit and interview recommended. Off-campus interviews available with admissions and alumni representatives.
**Procedure:** Notification of admission on rolling basis. Reply is required within three weeks of notification. $100 tuition deposit, refundable until May 15. $75 room deposit, refundable until May 15. Freshmen accepted for terms other than fall.
**Special programs:** Admission may be deferred one term. Credit may be granted through CEEB Advanced Placement for scores of 3 or higher. Credit and/or placement may be granted through CLEP general and subject exams. Credit and placement may be granted through ACT PEP and challenge exams. Early decision program. Early entrance/early admission program.

**Transfer students:** Transfer students accepted for terms other than fall. In fall 1993, 11% of all new students were transfers into all classes. 161 transfer applications were received. Application deadline is rolling for fall; rolling for spring. Minimum 2.0 GPA required. Lowest course grade accepted is "D." Maximum number of transferable credits is 60 semester hours from a two-year school and 90 semester hours from a four-year school. Final 30 semester hours must be completed at the college to receive degree.
**Admissions contact:** John Schafer, M.A., Dean of Admissions and Financial Aid. 312 583-2700, extension 4500, 800 888-6728.

**FINANCIAL AID. Available aid:** Pell grants, SEOG, Federal Nursing Student Scholarships, state scholarships and grants, school scholarships and grants, private scholarships and grants, academic merit scholarships, and aid for undergraduate foreign students. Perkins Loans (NDSL), PLUS, Stafford Loans (GSL), NSL, state loans, and SLS. AMS and deferred payment plan.
**Financial aid statistics:** Average amounts of aid awarded freshmen: Scholarships and grants, $5,000.
**Supporting data/closing dates:** FAFSA/FAF/FFS: Priority filing date is July 1. School's own aid application: Accepted on rolling basis. Income tax forms: Accepted on rolling basis. Notification of awards on rolling basis.
**Financial aid contact:** Melvin Soderstrom, M.Ed., Director of Financial Aid. 312 583-2700, extension 4052.

# Northeastern Illinois University

**Chicago, IL 60625** **312 583-4050**

**1993-94 Costs.** Tuition: $1,848 (state residents), $5,544 (out-of-state). Housing: None. Fees, books, misc. academic expenses (school's estimate): $586.
**Enrollment.** Undergraduates: 1,754 men, 2,512 women (full-time). Freshman class: 2,320 applicants, 1,508 accepted, 810 enrolled. Graduate enrollment: 1,133 men, 2,188 women.
**Test score averages/ranges.** Average ACT scores: 17 English, 17 math, 17 composite. Range of ACT scores of middle 50%: 12-19 English, 12-18 math.
**Faculty.** 334 full-time; 199 part-time. 72% of faculty holds highest degree in specific field. Student/faculty ratio: 20 to 1.
**Selectivity rating.** Less competitive.

**PROFILE.** Northeastern Illinois, founded in 1867, is a public university. Programs are offered through the Colleges of Business, Liberal Arts and Sciences, Professional Studies, and Visual and Performing Arts. Its 460-acre campus is located eight miles from downtown Chicago.

**Accreditation:** NCACS. Professionally accredited by the National Council for Accreditation of Teacher Education.
**Religious orientation:** Northeastern Illinois University is nonsectarian; no religious requirements.
**Library:** Collections totaling over 580,000 volumes, 5,650 periodical subscriptions, and 692,000 microform items.
**Special facilities/museums:** Learning Center with audio-visual, TV, multimedia, film, photography, graphic arts, and electronic instructional equipment, listening room.
**Athletic facilities:** Gymnasiums, basketball, racquetball, tennis, and volleyball courts, swimming pool, weight room, baseball and softball fields, tracks.

**STUDENT BODY. Undergraduate profile:** 98% are state residents; 51% are transfers. 10% Asian-American, 12% Black, 19% Hispanic, 1% Native American, 57% White, 1% Other. Average age of undergraduates is 27.
**Freshman profile:** 1% of freshmen who took ACT scored 30 or over on English, 1% scored 30 or over on composite; 8% scored 24 or over on English, 4% scored 24 or over on math, 6% scored 24 or over on composite; 42% scored 18 or over on English, 37% scored 18 or over on math, 46% scored 18 or over on composite; 83% scored 12 or over on English, 98% scored 12 or over on math, 97% scored 12 or over on composite; 100% scored 6 or over on English, 100% scored 6 or over on math, 100% scored 6 or over on composite. 99% of accepted applicants took ACT. 52% of freshmen come from public schools.
**Undergraduate achievement:** 71% of fall 1992 freshmen returned for fall 1993 term.
**Foreign students:** 145 students are from out of the country. 20 countries represented in all.

**PROGRAMS OF STUDY. Degrees:** B.A., B.S.
**Majors:** Accounting, Anthropology, Art, Bilingual/Bicultural Education, Biology, Chemistry, Computer Science, Criminal Justice, Early Childhood Education, Earth Science, Economics, Elementary Education, English, Environmental Studies, Finance, French, General Business Administration, Geography/Environmental Studies, History, Human Resource Development, Inner City Studies, Leisure Studies, Linguistics, Management, Marketing, Mathematics, Music, Philosophy, Physical Education, Physics, Political Science, Psychology, Secondary Education, Social Sciences, Social Work, Sociology, Spanish, Special Education, Speech.
**Distribution of degrees:** The majors with the highest enrollment are elementary education and accounting; French and philosophy have the lowest.
**Requirements:** General education requirement.
**Academic regulations:** Minimum 2.0 GPA must be maintained.
**Special:** Minors offered in many majors and in Asian studies, dance, German, gerontology, Greek studies, Italian, public administration, Russian, and women's studies. Program for interdisciplinary education based on development of new curricular approaches, often off campus; up to 18 credits possible. Kaskaskia Plan offers nontraditional, individualized, multidisciplinary bachelor's degree program. Creative writing program maintains off-campus center for students and writers living in Chicago. Field centers in various parts of Chicago for the study of, and service to, communities. Self-designed majors. Double majors. Independent study. Pass/fail grading option. Internships. Graduate school at which undergraduates may take graduate-level courses. Preprofessional programs in law, medicine, pharmacy, and dentistry. Member of Union for Experimenting Colleges and Universities. University Without Walls center. Washington Center Program. Member of National Student Exchange (NSE). Teacher certification in early childhood, elementary, secondary, special education, and bilingual/bicultural education. Certification in specific subject areas. Study abroad in Canada, Costa Rica, and Mexico. ROTC at U of Illinois at Chicago. AFROTC at Illinois Institute of Technology.
**Honors:** Phi Beta Kappa. Honors program. Honor societies.
**Academic Assistance:** Remedial reading, writing, math, and study skills. Nonremedial tutoring.

**STUDENT LIFE. Housing:** Commuter campus; no student housing.
**Social atmosphere:** Students gather at the cafeteria, the Commuter Center, the Library, and near the vending machines. The student newspaper and the student senate are the most influential groups on campus. Favorite events include Homecoming, theatre productions, and musical performances.
**Services and counseling/handicapped student services:** Placement services. Health service. Women's center. Day care. Counseling services for minority, veteran, and older students. Personal and psychological counseling. Career and academic guidance services. Religious counseling. Physically disabled student services. Learning disabled services. Notetaking services. Tape recorders. Tutors. Reader services for the blind.
**Campus organizations:** Undergraduate student government. Student newspaper (Independent, published twice/month). Radio station. Women's and mixed choruses, band, orchestra, Collegium Musicum, instrumental ensembles, theatre, athletic, departmental, service, and special-interest groups, 51 organizations in all. One fraternity, no chapter house; one sorority, no chapter house.
**Religious organizations:** Bible Fellowship, Israel-Hillel Club, Muslim Student Association, Newman Community, Northeastern Christian Community.
**Minority/foreign student organizations:** Advocates for Accessibility, Black Caucus, Black Heritage, Comite Colombia, Nichiren Shoshu of America, Polish Student Alliance, Que Ondee Sola, Union for Puerto Rican Students. Arab Students Organization, Asian Affairs, Assyrian Student Association, Chimexla Student Union, Nigerian Student Association, Vietnamese Club.

**ATHLETICS. Physical education requirements:** None.
**Intercollegiate competition:** 15% of students participate. Baseball (M), basketball (M,W), cross-country (M,W), diving (M,W), golf (M,W), soccer (M), softball (W), swimming (M,W), tennis (M,W), volleyball (W). Member of NCAA Division I.
**Intramural and club sports:** 35% of students participate. Intramural badminton, basketball, flag football, racquetball, running, soccer, softball, swimming, table tennis, volleyball, walleyball, weight training. Men's club soccer.

**ADMISSIONS. Academic basis for candidate selection** (in order of priority): Class rank, standardized test scores, secondary school record.
**Requirements:** Graduation from secondary school is required; GED is accepted. 15 units and the following program of study are required: 4 units of English, 3 units of math, 3 units of science, 3 units of social studies, 2 units of electives. Minimum composite ACT score of 19 or rank in top half of secondary school class required. Minimum 2.5 GPA and specific exams required of applicants to the Colleges of Education and Business and Management. ACT is required; SAT may be substituted. Campus visit recommended. No off-campus interviews.
**Procedure:** Take SAT or ACT by November of 12th year. Application deadline is July 1. Notification of admission on rolling basis. Freshmen accepted for terms other than fall.
**Special programs:** Credit may be granted through CEEB Advanced Placement for scores of 4 or higher. Credit may be granted through CLEP general exams, DANTES and challenge exams, and military and life experience.
**Transfer students:** Transfer students accepted for terms other than fall. In fall 1993, 51% of all new students were transfers into all classes. 2,132 transfer applications were received, 1,288 were accepted. Application deadline is June 1 for fall; November 1 for spring. Minimum 2.0 GPA required. Lowest course grade accepted is "D." Maximum number of transferable credits is 60 semester hours from a two-year school and 90 semester hours from a four-year school. At least 30 semester hours must be completed at the university to receive degree.
**Admissions contact:** Miriam Rivera, M.A., Director of Admissions and Records. 312 794-2600.

**FINANCIAL AID. Available aid:** Pell grants, SEOG, state scholarships and grants, school scholarships and grants, private scholarships and grants, academic merit scholarships, and athletic scholarships. Perkins Loans (NDSL), PLUS, Stafford Loans (GSL), state loans, school loans, and SLS. Deferred payment plan and family tuition reduction.
**Supporting data/closing dates:** FAFSA: Priority filing date is April 1. FAF/FFS: Priority filing date is April 1; accepted on rolling basis. Notification of awards on rolling basis.
**Financial aid contact:** J. Marshall Jennings, M.A., Director of Financial Aid. 312 794-2900.

**STUDENT EMPLOYMENT.** College Work/Study Program. Institutional employment. 10% of full-time undergraduates work on campus during school year. Students may expect to earn an average of $1,800 during school year. Off-campus part-time employment opportunities rated "good."

**COMPUTER FACILITIES.** 50 IBM/IBM-compatible and Macintosh/Apple microcomputers. Students may access AT&T, Digital minicomputer/mainframe systems. Computer languages and software packages include Assembler, BASIC, C, COBOL, dBASE, FORTRAN, Lotus 1-2-3, Pascal, PL/1, SuperCalc, WordStar. Computer facilities are available to all students.
**Fees:** None.
**Hours:** 8 AM-10 PM (M-Th); 8 AM-6 PM (F); 8 AM-1 PM (Sa).

**PROMINENT ALUMNI/AE.** Dennis Meritt, assistant director, Lincoln Park Zoo.

# Northern Illinois University

**DeKalb, IL 60115** **815 753-1000**

**1994-95 Costs.** Tuition: $2,595 (state residents), $7,798 (out-of-state). Room & board: $3,316. Fees, books, misc. academic expenses (school's estimate): $1,343.
**Enrollment.** Undergraduates: 6,910 men, 7,916 women (full-time). Freshman class: 10,706 applicants, 7,219 accepted, 2,397 enrolled. Graduate enrollment: 2,753 men, 3,619 women.
**Test score averages/ranges.** Average ACT scores: 22 English, 22 math, 22 composite. Range of ACT scores of middle 50%: 18-25 English, 18-25 math.
**Faculty.** 1,049 full-time; 184 part-time. 71% of faculty holds doctoral degree. Student/faculty ratio: 18 to 1.
**Selectivity rating.** Less competitive.

**PROFILE.** Northern Illinois, founded in 1895, is a public university. Programs are offered through the Colleges of Business, Education, Engineering and Engineering Technology, Liberal Arts and Sciences, Professional Studies, and Visual and Performing Arts and the Graduate School. Its 460-acre campus is located in DeKalb, 65 miles west of Chicago.

**Accreditation:** NCACS. Professionally accredited by the Accreditation Board for Engineering and Technology, the American Assembly of Collegiate Schools of Business, the American Physical Therapy Association, the Council on Rehabilitation Education, the National Council for Accreditation of Teacher Education, the National League for Nursing.
**Religious orientation:** Northern Illinois University is nonsectarian; no religious requirements.
**Library:** Collections totaling over 1,299,353 volumes, 14,762 periodical subscriptions, and 1,873,516 microform items.
**Special facilities/museums:** Art museum, anthropology museum, plant molecular biology center.
**Athletic facilities:** Recreation center with basketball, volleyball, badminton, tennis, racquetball, and handball courts, track, swimming pools, field house.

**STUDENT BODY. Undergraduate profile:** 97% are state residents; 48% are transfers. 5% Asian-American, 8% Black, 5% Hispanic, 81% White, 1% Other. Average age of undergraduates is 22.
**Freshman profile:** 4% of freshmen who took ACT scored 30 or over on English, 5% scored 30 or over on math, 3% scored 30 or over on composite; 36% scored 24 or over on English, 36% scored 24 or over on math, 40% scored 24 or over on composite; 83% scored 18 or over on English, 85% scored 18 or over on math, 91% scored 18 or over on composite; 97% scored 12 or over on English, 100% scored 12 or over on math, 100% scored 12 or over on composite. 100% of accepted applicants took ACT.
**Undergraduate achievement:** 78% of fall 1992 freshmen returned for fall 1993 term. 25% of entering class graduated. 10% of students who completed a degree program immediately went on to graduate study.
**Foreign students:** 214 students are from out of the country. Countries represented include China, India, Malaysia, Norway, and Taiwan; 90 in all.

**PROGRAMS OF STUDY. Degrees:** B.A., B.F.A., B.Gen.Studies, B.S., B.S.Ed.
**Majors:** Accountancy, Anthropology, Art Education, Art History, Biological Sciences, Chemistry, Communications Studies, Communicative Disorders, Community Health, Computer Science, Dietetics/Nutrition/Food Service, Early Childhood, Economics, Electrical Engineering, Elementary Education, English, Family/Child Studies, Finance, French, General Studies, Geography, Geology, German, History, Home Economics Education, Industrial Engineering, Industry/Technology, Journalism, Management, Marketing, Mathematics, Mechanical Engineering, Medical Technology, Meteorology, Music, Nursing, Operations Management/Information Systems, Philosophy, Physical Education, Physical Therapy, Physics, Political Science, Psychology, Russian, Social Sciences, Sociology, Spanish, Special Education, Studio Art, Textiles/Clothing, Theatre Arts.
**Distribution of degrees:** The majors with the highest enrollment are communications studies and marketing; geology, physics, and philosophy have the lowest.
**Requirements:** General education requirement.
**Academic regulations:** Freshmen must maintain minimum 1.6 GPA; sophomores, juniors, seniors, 2.0 GPA.
**Special:** Minors offered in applied communication, classical studies, comparative literature, environmental studies, international relations, linguistics, public administration, Southeast Asian studies, urban studies, and women's studies. Self-designed majors. Double majors. Independent study. Pass/fail grading option. Internships. Cooperative education programs. Graduate school at which undergraduates may take graduate-level courses. Preprofessional programs in law, medicine, veterinary science, pharmacy, dentistry, optometry, osteopathy, and podiatry. 3-2 physics and engineering programs with U of Illinois. Teacher certification in early childhood, elementary, secondary, and special education. Study abroad in Austria, China, Denmark, England, Israel, Italy, Japan, Mexico, Norway, the former Soviet Republics, and Spain. ROTC. AFROTC at Illinois Inst of Tech.
**Honors:** Honors program.

**STUDENT LIFE. Housing:** All unmarried freshmen under age 21 must live on campus unless living with family. Coed dorms. School-owned/operated apartments. 30% of students live in college housing.
**Social atmosphere:** According to the editor of the student newspaper, "We're known as a suitcase college because there are not a whole lot of entertaining events during the weekend." Influential groups on campus include Greeks, the John Lennon Society, and The Northern Star. Popular events include NIU Jazz Ensemble concerts, Springfest, Homecoming, and NIU's Theatre Workshop performances. "NIU's football team is one of the worst in the nation so they're not very popular." Local bars that attract students include Otto's and McCabe's.
**Services and counseling/handicapped student services:** Health service. Women's center. Day care. Counseling services for minority, veteran, and older students. Birth control, personal, and psychological counseling. Career and academic guidance services. Learning disabled program/services.
**Campus organizations:** Undergraduate student government. Student newspaper (Northern Star, published five times/week). Literary magazine. Yearbook. Radio and TV stations. Band, orchestra, ensembles, chorus, choir, madrigals, theatre groups, extemporaneous speaking, intercollegiate debating, recreational clubs, University Artist Series, departmental, political, service, and special-interest groups, 200 organizations in all. 16 fraternities, 15 chapter houses; 11 sororities, nine chapter houses. 16% of men join a fraternity. 13% of women join a sorority.
**Religious organizations:** Several religious groups.
**Minority/foreign student organizations:** Several minority student groups.

**ATHLETICS. Physical education requirements:** None.
**Intercollegiate competition:** Baseball (M), basketball (M,W), diving (M,W), field hockey (W), football (M), golf (M,W), gymnastics (M,W), soccer (M), softball (W), swimming (M,W), tennis (M,W), volleyball (W), wrestling (M). Member of NCAA Division I, NCAA Division I-A for football, North Star Conference.
**Intramural and club sports:** Intramural Aikido, Alpine skiing, baseball, bowling, cycling, fencing, ice hockey, Judo, lacrosse, rugby, track, volleyall, water polo. Men's club Alpine skiing, bowling, cycling, fencing, ice hockey, lacrosse, rugby, volleyball, water polo. Women's club Alpine skiing, bowling, cycling, fencing, lacrosse, rugby, water polo.

**ADMISSIONS. Academic basis for candidate selection** (in order of priority): Standardized test scores, class rank, secondary school record.
**Nonacademic basis for candidate selection:** Particular talent or ability is considered.
**Requirements:** Graduation from secondary school is recommended; GED is accepted. 13 units and the following program of study are required: 4 units of English, 3 units of math, 3 units of science including 1 unit of lab, 2 units of social studies, 1 unit of academic electives. Minimum composite ACT score of 19 and rank in top half of secondary school class or minimum composite ACT score of 23 and rank in top two-thirds of secondary school class required. Audition required of music program applicants. Educational services and programs for applicants not normally admissible. ACT is required; SAT may be substituted. Campus visit recommended. No off-campus interviews.
**Procedure:** Application deadline is August 1. Notification of admission on rolling basis. Freshmen accepted for terms other than fall.
**Special programs:** Credit may be granted through CEEB Advanced Placement. Credit may be granted through CLEP general exams.
**Transfer students:** Transfer students accepted for terms other than fall. In fall 1993, 48% of all new students were transfers into all classes. 4,687 transfer applications were received, 3,867 were accepted. Application deadline is July 15 for fall; December 1 for spring. Minimum 2.0 GPA required. Lowest course grade accepted is "D." Maximum number of transferable credits is 94 semester hours. At least 30 semester hours must be completed at the university to receive degree.
**Admissions contact:** Daniel S. Oborn, Ed.D., Director of Admissions. 815 753-0446.

**FINANCIAL AID. Available aid:** Pell grants, SEOG, Federal Nursing Student Scholarships, state scholarships and grants, school scholarships and grants, private scholarships, ROTC scholarships, academic merit scholarships, and athletic scholarships. Perkins Loans (NDSL), PLUS, Stafford Loans (GSL), state loans, and SLS. Installment Payment Plan.
**Financial aid statistics:** 37% of aid is not need-based. In 1993-94, 61% of all undergraduate applicants received aid; 61% of freshman applicants. Average amounts of aid awarded freshmen: Scholarships and grants, $1,500; loans, $2,838.
**Supporting data/closing dates:** FAFSA/FAF: Priority filing date is March 1; deadline is May 1. School's own aid application: Priority filing date is March 1. Income tax forms: Priority filing date is March 1. Notification of awards begins June 1.
**Financial aid contact:** Jerry D. Augsburger, M.A., Director of Student Financial Aid. 815 753-1395.

**STUDENT EMPLOYMENT.** College Work/Study Program. Institutional employment. 20% of full-time undergraduates work on campus during school year. Students may expect to earn an average of $1,000 during school year. Off-campus part-time employment opportunities rated "excellent."

**COMPUTER FACILITIES.** 1,055 IBM/IBM-compatible microcomputers; 949 are networked. Students may access minicomputer/mainframe systems. Residence halls may be equipped with stand-alone microcomputers, networked microcomputers, networked terminals, modems. Computer languages and software packages include BMDP, COBOL, C, dBASE, FORTRAN, Lotus 123, PageMaker, Pascal, Quattro, R:BASE, SAS, SPSS, WordPerfect, Word Star. Some computer systems are restricted to colleges or departments.
**Fees:** $40 computer fee per semester.
**Hours:** 8 AM-4 AM in some locations.

**GRADUATE CAREER DATA.** Companies and businesses that hire graduates: Amoco, Arthur Andersen, Illinois Bell, Motorola.

**PROMINENT ALUMNI/AE.** Gary L. Watson, president, Gannett Community Newspaper Group; Richard Henderson, president, US Sprint Midwest; Dennis Hastert, congressman, Illinois; Dr. Pierre Guibor, oculoplastic surgeon, New York; Dr. Winifred Sawtell Cameron, NASA astrophysicist (retired); Joan Allen, Tony Award–winning actress.

# Northwestern University

Evanston, IL 60204-3060 708 491-3741

**1994-95 Costs.** Tuition: $16,404. Room & board: $5,520. Fees, books, misc. academic expenses (school's estimate): $759.

**Enrollment.** Undergraduates: 3,716 men, 3,734 women (full-time). Freshman class: 12,289 applicants, 5,200 accepted, 1,902 enrolled. Graduate enrollment: 2,642 men, 1,916 women.

**Test score averages/ranges.** Range of SAT scores of middle 50%: 530-630 verbal, 600-710 math. Range of ACT scores of middle 50%: 27-31 composite.

**Faculty.** 784 full-time; 147 part-time. 95% of faculty holds doctoral degree. Student/faculty ratio: 11 to 1.

**Selectivity rating.** Most competitive.

**PROFILE.** Northwestern, founded in 1851, is a private, comprehensive university. Programs are offered through the College of Arts and Sciences; the Schools of Education and Social Policy, Journalism, Law, Music, and Speech; and the Technological Institute. Its 250-acre campus is located in Evanston, 12 miles north of Chicago.

**Accreditation:** NCACS. Professionally accredited by the Accreditation Board for Engineering and Technology, the Accrediting Council on Education in Journalism and Mass Communication, the American Psychological Association, the American Speech-Language-Hearing Association, the National Association of Schools of Music.
**Religious orientation:** Northwestern University is nonsectarian; no religious requirements.
**Library:** Collections totaling over 3,600,000 volumes, 36,000 periodical subscriptions, and 40,500 microform items.
**Special facilities/museums:** Art gallery, learning sciences institute, communicative disorders building, materials and life sciences building, catalysis center, astronomical research center.
**Athletic facilities:** Gymnasiums, basketball, handball, racquetball, squash, and tennis courts, tracks, stadium, weight rooms, swimming pools, diving wells, athletic fields.

**STUDENT BODY. Undergraduate profile:** 26% are state residents; 5% are transfers. 15% Asian-American, 7% Black, 2% Hispanic, 1% Native American, 73% White, 2% Other. Average age of undergraduates is 20.
**Freshman profile:** 5% of freshmen who took SAT scored 700 or over on verbal, 33% scored 700 or over on math; 43% scored 600 or over on verbal, 78% scored 600 or over on math; 87% scored 500 or over on verbal, 96% scored 500 or over on math; 98% scored 400 or over on verbal, 99% scored 400 or over on math; 100% scored 300 or over on verbal, 100% scored 300 or over on math. 73% of accepted applicants took SAT; 35% took ACT. 75% of freshmen come from public schools.
**Undergraduate achievement:** 96% of fall 1992 freshmen returned for fall 1993 term. 78% of entering class graduated. 15% of students who completed a degree program immediately went on to graduate study.
**Foreign students:** 48 students are from out of the country. Countries represented include Canada, India, Japan, Korea, Malaysia, and Pakistan; 27 in all.

**PROGRAMS OF STUDY. Degrees:** B.A., B.A.Mus., B.Mus., B.Mus.Ed., B.Phil., B.S.Ed., B.S.Gen.Ed., B.S.Med., B.S.Speech
**Majors:** African-American Studies, American Culture, Anthropology, Applied Mathematics, Art History, Art Theory/Practice, Asian Studies, Astronomy, Biological Sciences, Biomedical Engineering, Chemical Engineering, Chemistry, Church Music/Organ, Civil Engineering, Classics, Cognitive Science, Communication Sciences/Disorders, Communication Studies, Computer Science, Computer Studies, Conducting, Dance, Economics, Electrical Engineering, English, Environmental Engineering, Environmental Sciences, French, Geography, Geological Sciences, German Language/Literature, Hispanic Studies, History, Industrial Engineering/Management Sciences, Integrated Science Program, International Studies, Italian, Journalism, Keyboard, Linguistics, Manufacturing Engineering, Materials Science/Engineering, Mathematical Methods in the Social Sciences, Mathematics, Mechanical Engineering, Music Education, Neuroscience, Organizational Studies/Psychological Services/Social Policy, Performance Studies, Philosophy, Physics, Political Science, Psychology, Radio/Television/Film, Religion, Secondary Teaching, Slavic Languages/Literatures, Sociology, Statistics, String Instruments, Theatre, Theory/Composition, Urban Studies, Voice, Winds/Percussion.
**Distribution of degrees:** The majors with the highest enrollment are economics, political science, and history; neuroscience and urban studies have the lowest.
**Requirements:** General education requirement.
**Academic regulations:** Minimum 2.0 GPA must be maintained.
**Special:** Special programs in American culture, comparative literature, neuroscience, urban affairs, and women's studies. Certificate programs in business institutions, humanities, integrated arts, leadership, and musical theatre. Writer's workshop. Freshman colloquia in history. 30 superior science students admitted to three-year B.A. integrated science program. 30 superior students admitted to mathematical methods in the social sciences program. Thematic residential colleges in commerce and industry, community studies, and philosophy and religion. Self-designed majors. Double majors. Dual degrees. Independent study. Pass/fail grading option. Internships. Cooperative education programs. Graduate school at which undergraduates may take graduate-level courses. Four-year master's programs in biology, chemistry, communication arts, economics, and foreign language. Combined degree honors programs in engineering management and undergraduate research. Seven-year honors program with Northwestern Medical Sch open by special application to 60 entering freshmen. Combined program leads to B.A. and professional degree from Northwestern Dental or Medical Sch. Medical technology and physical therapy programs in cooperation with Medical Sch. Five-year degree programs in journalism/engineering, music/liberal arts, and music/engineering. Member of COFHE and CIC. Washington Semester. Teacher certification in secondary education. Certification in specific subject areas. Exchange programs abroad in Canada (U of Laval), China (Beijing Normal U, Beijing U of Foreign Studies), England (U of Sussex), Germany (U of Munich), Italy (Intercollegiate Center for Classic Studies), and Spain (U of Seville). Study abroad also in France, Israel, Japan, Mexico, and Russia. NROTC. ROTC at Loyola U. AFROTC at Illinois Inst of Tech.
**Honors:** Phi Beta Kappa. Honors program. Honor societies.
**Academic Assistance:** Nonremedial tutoring.

**STUDENT LIFE. Housing:** Coed, women's, and men's dorms. Sorority and fraternity housing. 75% of students live in college housing.
**Social atmosphere:** As reported by the student newspaper, "NU is not known for its social life. The focus is definitely academic. But because we are so close to Chicago, there is always something to do. On-campus partying still revolves around the fraternities for the most part, but dorms are becoming more and more social." While the Gathering Place is the most popular on-campus spot, the PM Club, Clarke's, and J.K. Sweet's are the most popular off-campus hangouts. Greeks, For Members Only, Indian Student Organization, Chinese Student Association, and Associated Student Government are influential student groups. Waa Mu, Homecoming tailgating parties, the A & O Ball, Pumpkin Prom, May-fest, and Armadillo Day are popular social events.
**Services and counseling/handicapped student services:** Placement services. Health service. Women's center. Counseling services for minority and military students. Birth control, personal, and psychological counseling. Career and academic guidance services. Religious counseling. Physically disabled student services. Learning disabled services. Notetaking services. Tape recorders. Tutors. Reader services for the blind.
**Campus organizations:** Undergraduate student government. Student newspaper (Daily Northwestern, five times/week). Literary magazine. Yearbook. Radio and TV stations. Music and drama groups, NOVA (volunteers in mental health), Students for a Better Environment, annual music review, intercollegiate debating, volunteer network, 100 organizations in all. 21 fraternities, 20 chapter houses; 12 sororities, all with chapter houses. 40% of men join a fraternity. 39% of women join a sorority.
**Religious organizations:** Baptist Student Union, B'nai B'rith Hillel Foundation, Society of Friends, other religious groups.
**Minority/foreign student organizations:** Culture Connection, Hellenic-American Student Union, International Student Club, Korean-American Student Association, Casa Hispana, For Members Only.

**ATHLETICS. Physical education requirements:** None.
**Intercollegiate competition:** 8% of students participate. Baseball (M), basketball (M,W), cheerleading (M,W), diving (M,W), fencing (W), field hockey (W), football (M), golf (M,W), soccer (M,W), softball (W), swimming (M,W), tennis (M,W), volleyball (W), wrestling (M). Member of Big 10 Conference, NCAA Division I.
**Intramural and club sports:** 6% of students participate. Intramural badminton, basketball, bowling, broomball, football, floor hockey, frisbee, golf, handball, indoor soccer, racquetball, softball, swimming, tennis, volleyball, walleyball, water polo, Wiffle ball, wrestling. Men's club crew, rugby, ultimate frisbee. Women's club crew, soccer.

**ADMISSIONS. Academic basis for candidate selection** (in order of priority): Secondary school record, class rank, essay, standardized test scores, school's recommendation.
**Nonacademic basis for candidate selection:** Character and personality, extracurricular participation, and particular talent or ability are important. Alumni/ae relationship is considered.
**Requirements:** Graduation from secondary school is recommended; GED is accepted. 16 units and the following program of study are recommended: 4 units of English, 3 units of math, 2 units of science, 2 units of foreign language, 3 units of social studies, 2 units of electives. Electives may be chosen from all listed subjects. 3.5 to 4 units of math recommended of engineering program applicants. Audition required of music program applicants. SAT or ACT is required. ACH recommended. Campus visit and interview recommended. Off-campus interviews available with an alumni representative.
**Procedure:** Take SAT or ACT by December of 12th year. Take ACH by December of 12th year. Visit college for interview by January 1 of 12th year. Suggest filing application by November 1. Application deadline is January 1. Notification of admission by April 15. Reply is required by May 1. $200 nonrefundable tuition deposit. $200 nonrefundable room deposit. Freshmen accepted for terms other than fall.
**Special programs:** Admission may be deferred one year. Credit and/or placement may be granted through CEEB Advanced Placement exams for scores of 4 or higher. Placement may be granted through challenge exams. Early decision program. In fall 1993, 572 applied for early decision and 354 were accepted. Deadline for applying for early decision is November 1. Early entrance/early admission program.
**Transfer students:** Transfer students accepted for terms other than fall. In fall 1993, 5% of all new students were transfers into all classes. 636 transfer applications were received, 188 were accepted. Application deadline is June 1 for fall; November 1 for spring. Minimum 3.0 GPA recommended. Lowest course grade accepted is "D." Maximum number of transferable credits is 2 years. At least two years of full-time work must be completed at the university to receive degree.
**Admissions contact:** Carol Lunkenheimer, M.A., Director of Admissions. 708 491-7271.

**FINANCIAL AID. Available aid:** Pell grants, SEOG, state scholarships and grants, school grants, private scholarships and grants, ROTC scholarships, and athletic scholarships. Perkins Loans (NDSL), PLUS, Stafford Loans (GSL), Health Professions Loans, state loans, school loans, private loans, and SLS. Knight Tuition Plans and AMS. University nine-month payment plan.
**Financial aid statistics:** 3% of aid is not need-based. In 1993-94, 95% of all undergraduate applicants received aid; 95% of freshman applicants. Average amounts of aid awarded freshmen: Scholarships and grants, $8,200; loans, $2,900.
**Supporting data/closing dates:** FAFSA/FAF: Priority filing date is February 15. Income tax forms: Priority filing date is February 15. Notification of awards begins April 15.
**Financial aid contact:** Carolyn Lindley, M.A., Director of Financial Aid. 708 419-7400.

**STUDENT EMPLOYMENT.** College Work/Study Program. Institutional employment. 53% of full-time undergraduates work on campus during school year. Students may expect to earn an average of $1,500 during school year. Off-campus part-time employment opportunities rated "good."

**COMPUTER FACILITIES.** IBM/IBM-compatible, Macintosh/Apple, and RISC-/UNIX-based microcomputers. Students may access Digital, Hewlett-Packard, IBM, SUN minicomputer/mainframe systems, BITNET, Internet. Residence halls may be equipped with networked microcomputers, modems. Client/LAN operating systems include Apple/Macintosh, DOS, OS/2, UNIX/XENIX/AIX, Windows NT, X-windows, Artisoft, Banyan, LocalTalk/AppleTalk, Microsoft, Novell. Computer languages and

software packages include BASIC, C, COBOL, FORTRAN, Pascal. Computer facilities are available to all students.
**Fees:** None.
**Hours:** 24 hours for networked facilities; 16 hours/day for microcomputer labs.

**GRADUATE CAREER DATA.** Graduate school percentages: 10% enter law school. 10% enter medical school. 23% enter graduate business programs. 15% enter graduate arts and sciences programs. 70% of graduates choose careers in business and industry.

**PROMINENT ALUMNI/AE.** Saul Bellow, writer and Nobel laureate; Richard Gephardt, congressman; John Paul Stevens, U.S. Supreme Court justice; Charlton Heston and Cloris Leachman, actors.

# Olivet Nazarene University

**Kankakee, IL 60901** **815 939-5011**

**1993-94 Costs.** Tuition: $7,700. Room & board: $4,140. Fees, books, misc. academic expenses (school's estimate): $386.
**Enrollment.** Undergraduates: 674 men, 857 women (full-time). Graduate enrollment: 291 men, 372 women.
**Test score averages/ranges.** Average ACT scores: 22 composite.
**Faculty.** 80 full-time; 40 part-time. 52% of faculty holds doctoral degree. Student/faculty ratio: 18 to 1.
**Selectivity rating.** Less competitive.

**PROFILE.** Olivet Nazarene, founded in 1907, is a church-affiliated, liberal arts university. Programs are offered through the Divisions of Business, Communication, Education, Fine Arts, Health Sciences, Natural Sciences, Religion, and Social Sciences and the Graduate School. Its 160-acre campus is located in Kankakee, 60 miles from Chicago.

**Accreditation:** NCACS. Professionally accredited by the National Association of Schools of Music, the National Council for Accreditation of Teacher Education, the National League for Nursing.
**Religious orientation:** Olivet Nazarene University is affiliated with the Church of the Nazarene; four semesters of religion required.
**Library:** Collections totaling over 153,000 volumes, 900 periodical subscriptions, and 42,000 microform items.
**Special facilities/museums:** Natural history museum, planetarium.
**Athletic facilities:** Gymnasiums, field house, basketball, racquetball, sand volleyball, tennis, and volleyball courts, track, baseball, football, soccer, and softball fields, swimming pool, weight room, ice rink.

**STUDENT BODY. Undergraduate profile:** 24% are state residents; 23% are transfers. 1% Asian-American, 4% Black, 1% Hispanic, 92% White, 2% Other. Average age of undergraduates is 19.
**Freshman profile:** 95% of accepted applicants took ACT.
**Undergraduate achievement:** 74% of fall 1992 freshmen returned for fall 1993 term. 23% of students who completed a degree program went on to graduate study within five years.
**Foreign students:** 60 students are from out of the country. Countries represented include Canada, Japan, Kenya, Korea, Laos, and Vietnam; 19 in all.

**PROGRAMS OF STUDY. Degrees:** B.A., B.S., Theol.B.
**Majors:** Accounting, Art, Biblical Literature, Biology, Botany, Business Administration, Business Education, Chemistry, Child Development, Christian Education, Christian Education/Church Music, Church Music, Computer Science, Dietetics, Economics, Education, Engineering, Engineering Physics, English, Environmental Science, General Studies, Geology, History, Home Economics, Mathematics, Medical Technology, Music, Music Education, Music Performance, Nursing, Physical Education, Physical Sciences, Psychology, Religion, Religion/Philosophy, Romance Languages, Social Justice, Social Sciences, Social Work, Sociology, Speech Communication, Theology, Zoology.
**Distribution of degrees:** The majors with the highest enrollment are elementary education, business administration, and nursing.
**Requirements:** General education requirement.
**Special:** Minors offered in most majors and in several other fields. Self-designed majors. Double majors. Independent study. Accelerated study. Graduate school at which undergraduates may take graduate-level courses. Preprofessional programs in law, medicine, physical therapy, and seminary. Member of Christian College Consortium. American Studies Program (Washington, D.C.). Elected use of Argonne National Labs. Teacher certification in elementary and secondary education. ROTC.
**Honors:** Honors program.
**Academic Assistance:** Remedial reading, writing, math, and study skills. Nonremedial tutoring.

**STUDENT LIFE. Housing:** All unmarried students under age 23 must live on campus unless living with family. Women's and men's dorms. 80% of students live in college housing.
**Social atmosphere:** As reported by the student newspaper, "The social life on campus is better than that off campus. Many students feel Kankakee does not have much to offer. However, Chicago is only an hour away, and many students take advantage of Chicago's social life. We are a Christian school and have many ministry-related organizations. Also, our athletic events shape our social life." Popular events include Ollies Follies (class athletic and relay competition), the Mr. ONU Contest ("a talent and beauty competition for guys"), and Coronation and Homecoming.
**Services and counseling/handicapped student services:** Placement services. Health service. Personal and psychological counseling. Career and academic guidance services. Religious counseling.
**Campus organizations:** Undergraduate student government. Student newspaper (Glimmerglass). Yearbook. Radio station. Brass choir, string quartet, concert band, concert singers, orchestra, mixed chorus, public affairs club, community service, departmental, and special-interest groups, 24 organizations in all.
**Religious organizations:** Nurses Christian Fellowship, Fellowship of Christian Athletes, Ministerial Fellowship, Concerned Christians in Action, Spiritual Life Organization.

**ATHLETICS. Physical education requirements:** Four semesters of physical education required.
**Intercollegiate competition:** 31% of students participate. Baseball (M), basketball (M,W), cheerleading (M,W), cross-country (M,W), football (M), golf (M), soccer (M), softball (W), tennis (M,W), track (indoor) (M,W), track (outdoor) (M,W), track and field (indoor) (M,W), track and field (outdoor) (M,W), volleyball (W), wrestling (M). Member of Chicagoland Collegiate Athletic Conference, NAIA.
**Intramural and club sports:** 60% of students participate. Intramural badminton, basketball, flag football, sand volleyball, soccer, softball, table tennis, tennis, volleyball. Men's club volleyball. Women's club soccer.

**ADMISSIONS. Academic basis for candidate selection** (in order of priority): Secondary school record, school's recommendation, standardized test scores, class rank.
**Nonacademic basis for candidate selection:** Character and personality are emphasized. Extracurricular participation is important. Particular talent or ability is considered.
**Requirements:** Graduation from secondary school is required; GED is accepted. 15 units required and the following program of study recommended: 3 units of English, 2 units of math, 2 units of science, 2 units of foreign language, 2 units of social studies, 2 units of history. Minimum composite ACT score of 18, rank in top three-quarters of secondary school class, and minimum 2.0 GPA recommended. Conditional admission possible for applicants not meeting standard requirements. ACT is required. Campus visit and interview recommended. Off-campus interviews available with admissions and alumni representatives.
**Procedure:** Take ACT by April of 12th year. Visit college for interview by May of 12th year. Suggest filing application by May. Application deadline is August 1. Notification of admission on rolling basis. $30 room deposit, refundable until August 1. Freshmen accepted for terms other than fall.
**Special programs:** Admission may be deferred. Credit and/or placement may be granted through CLEP general and subject exams. Credit and placement may be granted through challenge exams.
**Transfer students:** Transfer students accepted for terms other than fall. In fall 1992, 23% of all new students were transfers into all classes. 260 transfer applications were received, 221 were accepted. Application deadline is August 1 for fall; January 2 for spring. Minimum 2.0 GPA required. Lowest course grade accepted is "D." Maximum number of transferable credits is 68 semester hours from a two-year school and 90 semester hours from a four-year school. At least 30 semester hours must be completed at the university to receive degree.
**Admissions contact:** John Mongerson, Director of Admissions. 815 939-5203.

**FINANCIAL AID. Available aid:** Pell grants, SEOG, state scholarships and grants, school scholarships and grants, private scholarships and grants, ROTC scholarships, academic merit scholarships, and athletic scholarships. Perkins Loans (NDSL), PLUS, Stafford Loans (GSL), private loans, and SLS. AMS and Tuition Management Systems.
**Financial aid statistics:** 60% of aid is not need-based. In 1993-94, 96% of all undergraduate applicants received aid; 98% of freshman applicants. Average amounts of aid awarded freshmen: Scholarships and grants, $4,200.
**Supporting data/closing dates:** FAFSA: Priority filing date is March 1; accepted on rolling basis. School's own aid application: Deadline is March 1. Income tax forms: Priority filing date is March 1; accepted on rolling basis. Verification Worksheet: Priority filing date is March 1; accepted on rolling basis. Notification of awards on rolling basis.
**Financial aid contact:** Laurel Hubbard, Director of Financial Aid. 815 939-5249.

**STUDENT EMPLOYMENT.** College Work/Study Program. Institutional employment. 26% of full-time undergraduates work on campus during school year. Students may expect to earn an average of $1,000 during school year. Off-campus part-time employment opportunities rated "good."

**COMPUTER FACILITIES.** 80 IBM/IBM-compatible and Macintosh/Apple microcomputers. Students may access AT&T, IBM minicomputer/mainframe systems, Internet. Computer languages and software packages include BASIC, C, COBOL, FORTRAN, Pascal. Computer facilities are available to all students.
**Fees:** Computer fee is included in tuition/fees.
**Hours:** 8 AM-10 PM.

**PROMINENT ALUMNI/AE.** Dr. Richard Jones, former president of Sears, Roebuck and chairman of Federal Savings Bank, Dallas, Tex.; Sharrell Miksell, vice-president, Owens-Corning.

# Parks College of St. Louis University

**Cahokia, IL 62206** **800 851-3048**

**1994-95 Costs.** Tuition: $9,140. Room: $1,680. Board: $2,320. Fees, books, misc. academic expenses (school's estimate): $850.
**Enrollment.** Undergraduates: 759 men, 88 women (full-time). Freshman class: 493 applicants, 374 accepted, 119 enrolled.
**Test score averages/ranges.** Average SAT scores: 1024 combined. Average ACT scores: 24 composite.
**Faculty.** 85 full-time; 15 part-time. 50% of faculty holds doctoral degree. Student/faculty ratio: 26 to 1.
**Selectivity rating.** Less competitive.

**PROFILE.** Parks College, founded in 1927, is a private, church-affiliated college of aeronautics and aviation. Its 113-acre campus is located in Cahokia, three miles from St. Louis, Mo.

**Accreditation:** NCACS. Professionally accredited by the Accreditation Board for Engineering and Technology.

**Religious orientation:** Parks College of St. Louis University is affiliated with the Roman Catholic Church (Society of Jesus); no religious requirements.
**Library:** Collections totaling over 35,076 volumes.
**Special facilities/museums:** Aerodynamics, aircraft maintenance engineering, meteorology, and other labs. Fleet of single- and twin-engine planes.
**Athletic facilities:** Gymnasium, basketball, racquetball, and tennis courts, weight room, baseball, soccer, and softball fields.

**STUDENT BODY. Undergraduate profile:** 41% are state residents; 45% are transfers. 5% Asian-American, 5% Black, 2% Hispanic, 88% White. Average age of undergraduates is 23.
**Freshman profile:** 50% of freshmen come from public schools.
**Undergraduate achievement:** 85% of fall 1991 freshmen returned for fall 1992 term. 65% of entering class graduated. 20% of students who completed a degree program went on to graduate study within five years.
**Foreign students:** 135 students are from out of the country. Countries represented include Malaysia, Saudi Arabia, Spain, and United Arab Emirates.

**PROGRAMS OF STUDY. Degrees:** B.S.
**Majors:** Aeronautical Administration, Aerospace Engineering, Aircraft Maintenance Engineering, Aircraft Maintenance Management, Airway Science, Aviation Science/Professional Pilot, Avionics, Computer Science, Electrical Engineering, Logistics, Meteorology, Transportation, Travel/Tourism.
**Distribution of degrees:** The majors with the highest enrollment are aerospace engineering, aviation science/ professional pilot, and aircraft maintenance engineering and management; travel/tourism, meteorology, and transportation have the lowest.
**Requirements:** General education requirement.
**Special:** Associate's degrees offered. Independent study. Accelerated study. Internships. Cooperative education programs. Graduate school at which undergraduates may take graduate-level courses. 3-2 program with St. Louis U (main campus). Study abroad in France, Germany, and Spain. AFROTC. ROTC and NROTC at Washington U.
**Academic Assistance:** Nonremedial tutoring.

**ADMISSIONS. Academic basis for candidate selection** (in order of priority): Secondary school record, class rank, school's recommendation, standardized test scores.
**Nonacademic basis for candidate selection:** Character and personality are emphasized. Extracurricular participation and geographical distribution are considered.
**Requirements:** Graduation from secondary school is required; GED is accepted. 16 units and the following program of study are recommended: 4 units of English, 2 units of math, 2 units of science, 2 units of social studies, 1 unit of history, 2 units of electives. Requirements for GPA, class rank, and math/science preparation vary by program. SAT or ACT is required. Campus visit and interview recommended. No off-campus interviews.
**Procedure:** Take SAT or ACT by December of 12th year. Visit college for interview by March of 12th year. Suggest filing application by December 1. Notification of admission on rolling basis. Reply is required by August 14. $250 nonrefundable tuition deposit. $200 nonrefundable room deposit. Freshmen accepted for terms other than fall.
**Special programs:** Admission may be deferred two years. Credit and/or placement may be granted through CEEB Advanced Placement exams for scores of 3 or higher. Credit and/or placement may be granted through CLEP subject exams. Credit and placement may be granted through challenge exams. Early decision program. Early entrance/early admission program. Concurrent enrollment program.
**Transfer students:** Transfer students accepted for terms other than fall. In fall 1992, 45% of all new students were transfers into all classes. 500 transfer applications were received, 400 were accepted. Lowest course grade accepted is "C."
**Admissions contact:** Sarah Nandor, Director of Admissions. 800 851-3048, extension 223.

**FINANCIAL AID. Available aid:** Pell grants, SEOG, state scholarships and grants, school scholarships, ROTC scholarships, and academic merit scholarships. Perkins Loans (NDSL), PLUS, and Stafford Loans (GSL). Tuition Plan Inc. and deferred payment plan.
**Financial aid statistics:** Average amounts of aid awarded freshmen: Scholarships and grants, $500.
**Supporting data/closing dates:** FAFSA/FAF/FFS: Accepted on rolling basis. School's own aid application: Accepted on rolling basis. Notification of awards on rolling basis.
**Financial aid contact:** Robert Doom, Manager of Financial Aid. 800 851-3048, extension 222.

## Principia College

**Elsah, IL 62028** **618 374-2131**

**1994-95 Costs.** Tuition: $12,816. Room: $2,634. Board: $2,790. Fees, books, misc. academic expenses (school's estimate): $531.
**Enrollment.** Undergraduates: 232 men, 295 women (full-time). Freshman class: 207 applicants, 184 accepted, 129 enrolled.
**Test score averages/ranges.** Average SAT scores: 496 verbal, 548 math. Range of SAT scores of middle 50%: 420-590 verbal, 470-660 math.
**Faculty.** 48 full-time; 28 part-time. 58% of faculty holds doctoral degree. Student/faculty ratio: 14 to 1.
**Selectivity rating.** Competitive.

**PROFILE.** Principia, founded in 1912, is a private, church-affiliated, liberal arts college. Its 3,000-acre campus is located in Elsah, 40 miles north of St. Louis.

**Accreditation:** NCACS.
**Religious orientation:** Principia College is affiliated with the Church of Christ, Scientist; two terms of religion/theology required.
**Library:** Collections totaling over 196,000 volumes, 900 periodical subscriptions, and 193,000 microform items.
**Special facilities/museums:** Arts and crafts museum, school of nations, language lab.
**Athletic facilities:** Badminton, basketball, racquetball, squash, tennis, and volleyball courts, swimming pool, baseball, football, soccer, and softball fields, field houses, weight room.

**STUDENT BODY. Undergraduate profile:** 13% are state residents; 21% are transfers. 1% Asian-American, 1% Black, 1% Hispanic, 88% White, 9% Other. Average age of undergraduates is 19.
**Freshman profile:** 1% of freshmen who took SAT scored 700 or over on verbal, 8% scored 700 or over on math; 18% scored 600 or over on verbal, 35% scored 600 or over on math; 43% scored 500 or over on verbal, 71% scored 500 or over on math; 93% scored 400 or over on verbal, 94% scored 400 or over on math; 100% scored 300 or over on verbal, 97% scored 300 or over on math. 95% of accepted applicants took SAT; 5% took ACT. 65% of freshmen come from public schools.
**Undergraduate achievement:** 89% of fall 1992 freshmen returned for fall 1993 term. 67% of entering class graduated. 26% of students who completed a degree program went on to graduate study within five years.
**Foreign students:** 47 students are from out of the country. Countries represented include Brazil, Canada, England, Germany, Ghana, and Nigeria; 18 in all.

**PROGRAMS OF STUDY. Degrees:** B.A., B.S.
**Majors:** Art History, Biology, Business Administration, Chemistry, Communications, Computer Science, Dramatic Art/Literature, Economics, Education, Engineering, English, Environmental Science, Fine Arts, Foreign Languages, French, German Studies, History, International Relations, Mathematics, Music, Musical Studies, Physics, Political Science, Religion/Philosophy, Russian Studies, Sociology/Anthropology, Spanish, Special Majors, Special Studies, Sports Management, Studio Art, World Perspectives.
**Distribution of degrees:** The majors with the highest enrollment are English, business administration, and history; foreign languages, sports management, and Russian studies have the lowest.
**Requirements:** General education requirement.
**Academic regulations:** Minimum 2.0 GPA must be maintained.
**Special:** Minors offered in most majors and in coaching fundamentals, earth sciences, philosophy, and women's studies. Courses offered in astronomy, dance, environmental studies, physical education, and world literature. Self-designed majors. Double majors. Independent study. Internships. 3-2 engineering science program with Southern Illinois U at Edwardsville, U of Southern California, and Washington U. Washington Semester. Off-campus study in San Francisco. Teacher certification in elementary and secondary education. Certification in specific subject areas. Study abroad in African countries, Argentina, Australia, China, England, France, Germany, Italy, Japan, Mexico, New Zealand, Russia, and Vietnam.
**Honors:** Honors program. Honor societies.
**Academic Assistance:** Remedial writing and study skills.

**ADMISSIONS. Academic basis for candidate selection** (in order of priority): Essay, secondary school record, standardized test scores, school's recommendation, class rank.
**Nonacademic basis for candidate selection:** Character and personality are important. Extracurricular participation and particular talent or ability are considered.
**Requirements:** Graduation from secondary school is required; GED is not accepted. 15 units and the following program of study are required: 4 units of English, 3 units of math, 2 units of lab science, 2 units of foreign language, 1 unit of social studies, 1 unit of history, 2 units of academic electives. Minimum combined SAT score of 800 and minimum 2.0 GPA required. Applicants must be Christian Scientists. SAT is required; ACT may be substituted. Campus visit and interview recommended. Off-campus interviews available with an admissions representative.
**Procedure:** Take SAT or ACT by June of 12th year. Take ACH by June of 12th year. Visit college for interview by June of 12th year. Suggest filing application by April 30. Application deadline is August 1. Notification of admission on rolling basis. Reply is required within one month of acceptance. $100 room deposit, refundable until July 1. Freshmen accepted for terms other than fall.
**Special programs:** Admission may be deferred one year. Credit may be granted through CEEB Advanced Placement for scores of 3 or higher. Credit may be granted through CLEP general and subject exams and life experience. Placement may be granted through challenge exams.
**Transfer students:** Transfer students accepted for terms other than fall. In fall 1993, 21% of all new students were transfers into all classes. 60 transfer applications were received, 46 were accepted. Application deadline is August 1 for fall; March 15 for spring. Minimum 2.0 GPA required. Lowest course grade accepted is "C-." At least 60 quarter hours must be completed at the college to receive degree.
**Admissions contact:** Martha Green Quirk, M.A., Director of Admissions and Enrollment. 800 851-1084.

**FINANCIAL AID. Available aid:** School scholarships and grants, private scholarships, academic merit scholarships, and aid for undergraduate foreign students. School loans and private loans. Knight Tuition Plans. Institutional Payment Plan.
**Financial aid statistics:** 10% of aid is not need-based. Average amounts of aid awarded freshmen: Scholarships and grants, $7,921; loans, $2,128.
**Supporting data/closing dates:** FAFSA/FAF: Accepted on rolling basis. School's own aid application: Accepted on rolling basis. Income tax forms: Accepted on rolling basis. Notification of awards on rolling basis.
**Financial aid contact:** Brooks Benjamin, M.L.S., Director of Financial Aid. 800 851-1084.

# Quincy University

**Quincy, IL 62301 217 222-8020**

**1994-95 Costs.** Tuition: $10,100. Room: $1,750. Board: $2,390. Fees, books, misc. academic expenses (school's estimate): $610.
**Enrollment.** Undergraduates: 540 men, 530 women (full-time). Freshman class: 1,025 applicants, 707 accepted, 297 enrolled. Graduate enrollment: 26 men, 22 women.
**Test score averages/ranges.** Average SAT scores: 496 verbal, 528 math. Range of SAT scores of middle 50%: 450-560 verbal, 490-590 math. Average ACT scores: 22 English, 23 math, 23 composite. Range of ACT scores of middle 50%: 21-25 English, 21-27 math.
**Faculty.** 70 full-time; 31 part-time. 68% of faculty holds doctoral degree. Student/faculty ratio: 12 to 1.
**Selectivity rating.** Less competitive.

**PROFILE.** Quincy is a private, church-affiliated university. Founded in 1860, it adopted coeducation in 1923. Its 73-acre campus is located in downtown Quincy, northwest of St. Louis.

**Accreditation:** NCACS. Professionally accredited by the Association of Collegiate Business Schools and Programs, the National Association of Schools of Music.
**Religious orientation:** Quincy University is affiliated with the Roman Catholic Church (Franciscan Friars); six semesters of religion/theology required.
**Library:** Collections totaling over 225,965 volumes, 645 periodical subscriptions, and 130,261 microform items.
**Special facilities/museums:** On-campus reading center for student teachers, computer art lab, computer writing lab.
**Athletic facilities:** Gymnasiums, weight room, tennis courts, baseball and football stadiums, soccer field.

**STUDENT BODY. Undergraduate profile:** 61% are state residents; 20% are transfers. 1% Asian-American, 5% Black, 1% Hispanic, 1% Native American, 91% White, 1% Other. Average age of undergraduates is 22.
**Freshman profile:** 8% of freshmen who took ACT scored 30 or over on composite; 40% scored 24 or over on composite; 98% scored 18 or over on composite; 100% scored 12 or over on composite. 5% of accepted applicants took SAT; 95% took ACT. 44% of freshmen come from public schools.
**Undergraduate achievement:** 88% of fall 1992 freshmen returned for fall 1993 term. 64% of entering class graduated. 21% of students who completed a degree program immediately went on to graduate study.
**Foreign students:** 10 students are from out of the country. Countries represented include Hong Kong, Ireland, Japan, and Mexico; eight in all.

**PROGRAMS OF STUDY. Degrees:** B.A., B.F.A., B.S.
**Majors:** Accounting, Art, Art Education, Arts Management, Athletic Training, Biological Sciences, Biology, Business Administration, Chemistry, Communication, Computer Science, Education, Elementary Education, English, Finance, General Biology, History, Human Resource Management, Humanities Interdisciplinary, International Studies, Management, Management Information Systems, Marketing, Mathematics, Medical Technology, Music, Music Business Studies, Music Education, Philosophy, Physical Education, Political Science, Psychology, Reading Education, Religious Education, Social Work, Sociology, Special Education/Learning Disabilities, Sports Management, Theology.
**Distribution of degrees:** The majors with the highest enrollment are elementary education, marketing, and business administration; humanities, religious education, and theology have the lowest.
**Requirements:** General education requirement.
**Academic regulations:** Minimum 2.0 GPA must be maintained.
**Special:** Minors offered in many majors and in art studio, art history, and writing. Self-designed majors. Double majors. Dual degrees. Independent study. Pass/fail grading option. Internships. Graduate school at which undergraduates may take graduate-level courses. Preprofessional programs in law, medicine, veterinary science, pharmacy, and dentistry. 3-2 engineering program with Washington U. Teacher certification in elementary, secondary, and special education. Certification in specific subject areas. Study abroad in Italy and Spain.
**Honors:** Honors program. Honor societies.
**Academic Assistance:** Remedial writing. Nonremedial tutoring.

**STUDENT LIFE. Housing:** All unmarried students under age 21 must live on campus unless living near campus with relatives. Coed, women's, and men's dorms. School-owned/operated apartments. Off-campus privately-owned housing. On-campus married-student housing. 70% of students live in college housing.
**Services and counseling/handicapped student services:** Placement services. Counseling services for minority, veteran, and older students. Personal and psychological counseling. Career and academic guidance services. Religious counseling. Physically disabled student services. Learning disabled services. Notetaking services. Tape recorders. Tutors. Reader services for the blind.
**Campus organizations:** Undergraduate student government. Student newspaper (Falcon, published once/week). Literary magazine. Yearbook. Radio and TV stations. Jazz and wind ensembles, other musical groups, theatre, cheerleading squads, athletic, departmental, service, and special-interest groups, 41 organizations in all.
**Religious organizations:** Bread for the World, Spiritual Life Organization, Needs of Our World.
**Minority/foreign student organizations:** Black Student Perspective, Intercultural Exchange. International Student Organization.

**ATHLETICS. Physical education requirements:** One semester of physical education required.
**Intercollegiate competition:** 19% of students participate. Baseball (M), basketball (M,W), football (M), soccer (M,W), softball (W), tennis (M,W), volleyball (M,W). Member of Midwest Intercollegiate Volleyball Association, NCAA Division II.
**Intramural and club sports:** 80% of students participate. Intramural aerobics, basketball, bowling, football, pickleball, soccer, softball, tennis, volleyball.

**ADMISSIONS. Academic basis for candidate selection** (in order of priority): Standardized test scores, secondary school record, class rank, school's recommendation.
**Nonacademic basis for candidate selection:** Extracurricular participation, particular talent or ability, and alumni/ae relationship are important. Character and personality and geographical distribution are considered.
**Requirements:** Graduation from secondary school is recommended; GED is accepted. 16 units and the following program of study are recommended: 4 units of English, 3 units of math, 3 units of science, 2 units of foreign language, 2 units of social studies, 2 units of history. Minimum composite ACT score of 20, rank in top half of secondary school class, and minimum 2.0 GPA required. Portfolio required of art program applicants. Audition required of music program applicants. SAT or ACT is required. Campus visit and interview recommended. Off-campus interviews available with an admissions representative.
**Procedure:** Take SAT or ACT by March of 12th year. Notification of admission on rolling basis. No specific date by which applicants must accept offer. $150 nonrefundable tuition deposit. $100 nonrefundable room deposit. Freshmen accepted for terms other than fall.
**Special programs:** Admission may be deferred. Credit and/or placement may be granted through CEEB Advanced Placement exams for scores of 4 or higher. Credit and/or placement may be granted through CLEP general and subject exams. Credit may be granted through ACT PEP and DANTES exams, and military and life experience. Credit and placement may be granted through challenge exams. Early entrance/early admission program. Concurrent enrollment program.
**Transfer students:** Transfer students accepted for terms other than fall. In fall 1993, 20% of all new students were transfers into all classes. 160 transfer applications were received, 115 were accepted. Minimum 2.0 GPA required. Lowest course grade accepted is "D." At least 30 semester hours must be completed at the university to receive degree.
**Admissions contact:** Frank Bevec, Director of Admissions. 212 228-5215.

**FINANCIAL AID. Available aid:** Pell grants, SEOG, state scholarships and grants, school scholarships and grants, private scholarships and grants, academic merit scholarships, and athletic scholarships. Perkins Loans (NDSL), PLUS, Stafford Loans (GSL), state loans, school loans, private loans, and SLS. Tuition Plan Inc., AMS, Tuition Management Systems, deferred payment plan, and family tuition reduction.
**Financial aid statistics:** 30% of aid is not need-based. In 1993-94, 100% of all undergraduate applicants received aid; 100% of freshman applicants. Average amounts of aid awarded freshmen: Scholarships and grants, $7,471; loans, $2,625.
**Supporting data/closing dates:** FAFSA. Income tax forms: Accepted on rolling basis. Notification of awards on rolling basis.
**Financial aid contact:** Linda Schuttler, Director of Financial Aid. 217 228-5260.

**STUDENT EMPLOYMENT.** College Work/Study Program. Institutional employment. 33% of full-time undergraduates work on campus during school year. Students may expect to earn an average of $700 during school year. Off-campus part-time employment opportunities rated "good."

**COMPUTER FACILITIES.** 132 IBM/IBM-compatible and Macintosh/Apple microcomputers; 96 are networked. Students may access AT&T, Digital minicomputer/mainframe systems, Internet. Residence halls may be equipped with stand-alone microcomputers. Client/LAN operating systems include DOS, OS/2, Novell. Computer languages and software packages include BASIC, C, C++, COBOL, dBASE V, FORTRAN, Grammatic, Lotus 1-2-3, Pascal, Paradox, Quattro Pro, WordPerfect, Writer's Workbench. Computer facilities are available to all students.
Fees: None.

**GRADUATE CAREER DATA.** Graduate school percentages: 3% enter law school. 2% enter medical school. 1% enter dental school. 3% enter graduate business programs. 12% enter graduate arts and sciences programs. Highest graduate school enrollments: U of Illinois, U of Notre Dame, St. Louis U, Washington U. 36% of graduates choose careers in business and industry. Companies and businesses that hire graduates: Arthur Andersen, McDonnell Douglas, Monsanto.

**PROMINENT ALUMNI/AE.** John Mahoney, actor; Robert Crutsinger, CEO, Wetteran Corp.

# Rockford College

**Rockford, IL 61101-2393 815 226-4000**

**1994-95 Costs.** Tuition: $12,400. Room & board: $4,080. Fees, books, misc. academic expenses (school's estimate): $950.
**Enrollment.** Undergraduates: 327 men, 571 women (full-time). Freshman class: 623 applicants, 537 accepted, 223 enrolled. Graduate enrollment: 173 men, 175 women.
**Test score averages/ranges.** Average SAT scores: 427 verbal, 474 math. Average ACT scores: 21 English, 20 math, 21 composite.
**Faculty.** 80 full-time; 55 part-time. 63% of faculty holds doctoral degree. Student/faculty ratio: 12 to 1.
**Selectivity rating.** Competitive.

**PROFILE.** Rockford is a private, liberal arts college. Founded in 1847, it adopted coeducation in 1958. Its 247-acre campus is located in Rockford, 90 miles from Chicago.

**Accreditation:** NCACS. Professionally accredited by the National League for Nursing.
**Religious orientation:** Rockford College is nonsectarian; no religious requirements.
**Library:** Collections totaling over 165,000 volumes, 700 periodical subscriptions, and 2,500 microform items.
**Special facilities/museums:** Language lab.
**Athletic facilities:** Gymnasium, swimming pool, fitness center, tennis courts, baseball, intramural, soccer, and softball fields.

**STUDENT BODY. Undergraduate profile:** 86% are state residents; 43% are transfers. 4% Asian-American, 5% Black, 3% Hispanic, .3% Native American, 85% White, 2.7% Other. Average age of undergraduates is 22.

**Freshman profile:** 21% of accepted applicants took SAT; 79% took ACT. 75% of freshmen come from public schools.
**Undergraduate achievement:** 62% of fall 1992 freshmen returned for fall 1993 term. 60% of entering class graduated. 16% of students who completed a degree program immediately went on to graduate study.
**Foreign students:** 29 students are from out of the country. Countries represented include France, Germany, Iceland, India, Japan, and Pakistan; 18 in all.

**PROGRAMS OF STUDY. Degrees:** B.A., B.F.A., B.S., B.S.Nurs.
**Majors:** Accounting, Anthropology/Sociology, Art, Art History, Biology, Business Administration/Management, Chemistry, Child Development, Classics, Computer Science, Criminal Justice, Economics, Education, English, French, German, History, Human Relations, Humanities, Latin, Management Information Systems, Mathematics, Music, Nursing, Philosophy, Physical Education, Political Science, Psychology, Social Studies, Sociology, Spanish, Theatre Arts, Urban Studies.
**Distribution of degrees:** The majors with the highest enrollment are business, education, and nursing; philosophy, classics, and music have the lowest.
**Requirements:** General education requirement.
**Academic regulations:** Minimum 2.0 GPA must be maintained.
**Special:** Minors offered in all majors. Interdivisional major in humanities. Divisional fields in child development, medical technology, science/mathematics, and social studies. Special studies courses. Faculty seminars. Double majors. Dual degrees. Internships. Graduate school at which undergraduates may take graduate-level courses. Preprofessional programs in law, medicine, veterinary science, dentistry, optometry, engineering, and physical therapy. 3-2 engineering program with Washington U. Five-year B.A. or B.S./M.B.A. program. Washington Semester and UN Semester. Exchange program with Regents Coll. Teacher certification in early childhood, elementary, secondary, and special education. Exchange program abroad in Japan (Kobe Coll). Study abroad also in Austria, Denmark, England, France, Germany, Ireland, Spain, and other countries. ROTC.
**Honors:** Phi Beta Kappa. Honors program. Honor societies.
**Academic Assistance:** Remedial reading, writing, math, and study skills. Nonremedial tutoring.

**ADMISSIONS. Academic basis for candidate selection** (in order of priority): Secondary school record, standardized test scores, class rank, school's recommendation, essay.
**Nonacademic basis for candidate selection:** Character and personality, extracurricular participation, and particular talent or ability are important. Geographical distribution is considered.
**Requirements:** Graduation from secondary school is recommended; GED is accepted. 16 units and the following program of study are required: 4 units of English, 2 units of math, 2 units of lab science, 2 units of foreign language, 1 unit of social studies, 3 units of history. Minimum composite ACT score of 18 (combined SAT score of 780), rank in top half of secondary school class, and minimum 2.5 GPA required. Audition required of theatre arts program applicants. Conditional admission possible for applicants not meeting standard requirements. ACT is required; SAT may be substituted. Campus visit and interview recommended. Off-campus interviews available with an admissions representative.
**Procedure:** Take SAT or ACT by fall of 12th year. Visit college for interview by fall of 12th year. Notification of admission on rolling basis. Reply is required by August 15. $200 refundable tuition deposit. $100 room deposit, refundable prior to May 1. Freshmen accepted for terms other than fall.
**Special programs:** Admission may be deferred two years. Credit and/or placement may be granted through CEEB Advanced Placement exams for scores of 4 or higher. Credit may be granted through CLEP general and subject exams. Early entrance/early admission program. Concurrent enrollment program.
**Transfer students:** Transfer students accepted for terms other than fall. In fall 1993, 43% of all new students were transfers into all classes. 331 transfer applications were received, 277 were accepted. Application deadline is rolling for fall; rolling for spring. Minimum 2.0 GPA required. Lowest course grade accepted is "C." Maximum number of transferable credits is 64 semester hours from a two-year school and 90 semester hours from a four-year school. At least 30 semester hours must be completed at the college to receive degree.
**Admissions contact:** Miriam King, M.A., Vice President for Enrollment Management. 815 226-4050.

**FINANCIAL AID. Available aid:** Pell grants, SEOG, Federal Nursing Student Scholarships, state scholarships and grants, school scholarships and grants, private scholarships and grants, ROTC scholarships, academic merit scholarships, and aid for undergraduate foreign students. Local scholarships. Perkins Loans (NDSL), PLUS, Stafford Loans (GSL), state loans, school loans, private loans, and SLS. Tuition Plan Inc., AMS, EFI Fund Management, and Tuition Management Systems.
**Financial aid statistics:** 36% of aid is not need-based. In 1993-94, 96% of all undergraduate applicants received aid; 98% of freshman applicants. Average amounts of aid awarded freshmen: Loans, $1,800.
**Supporting data/closing dates:** FAFSA: Priority filing date is April 15. State aid form: Deadline is April 15. Income tax forms: Priority filing date is April 15. Notification of awards on rolling basis.
**Financial aid contact:** D. Denny, M.A., Director of Financial Aid. 815 226-4050.

## Roosevelt University

**Chicago, IL 60605 — 312 341-3500**

**1993-94 Costs.** Tuition: $6,646. Room & board: $4,804. Fees, books, misc. academic expenses (school's estimate): $660.
**Enrollment.** Undergraduates: 714 men, 873 women (full-time). Freshman class: 422 applicants, 367 accepted, 218 enrolled. Graduate enrollment: 770 men, 1,175 women.
**Test score averages/ranges.** Average ACT scores: 20 composite.
**Faculty.** 159 full-time; 310 part-time. Student/faculty ratio: 14 to 1.
**Selectivity rating.** Less competitive.

**PROFILE.** Roosevelt, founded in 1945, is a private university. Programs are offered through the Colleges of Arts and Sciences, Business Administration, Continuing Education, and Education and the Chicago Musical College. Its urban campus is located in downtown Chicago.

**Accreditation:** NCACS. Professionally accredited by the American Bar Association, the National Association of Schools of Music, the National Council for Accreditation of Teacher Education.
**Religious orientation:** Roosevelt University is nonsectarian; no religious requirements.
**Library:** Collections totaling over 405,022 volumes, 1,601 periodical subscriptions, and 130,233 microform items.
**Athletic facilities:** Soccer field, tennis courts; Chicago area has many athletic facilities, some available at discount to students.

**STUDENT BODY. Undergraduate profile:** 85% are transfers. 3% Asian-American, 31% Black, 7% Hispanic, 53% White, 6% Other.
**Freshman profile:** 14% of accepted applicants took SAT; 18% took ACT.
**Foreign students:** 351 students are from out of the country. Countries represented include India, Japan, Korea, Pakistan, and Taiwan; 60 in all.

**PROGRAMS OF STUDY. Degrees:** B.A., B.F.A., B.Gen.Studies, B.Mus., B.S.
**Majors:** Accounting, Actuarial Sciences, Administrative Studies, African/Afro-American/Black Studies, Allied Health, American Studies, Anthropology, Applied Laboratory Science, Art, Art History, Biology, Business Education, Business Institutions, Chemistry, Choral Music Education, Classical Guitar, Communications, Comparative Literature, Composition, Comprehensive Music Education, Computer Science, Computing/Information, Cytotechnology, Data Processing, Early Childhood, Economics, Education, Electronic Composition, Electronic Engineering Technology, Elementary Teacher Education, English/Communication Arts, Finance, Fine Arts, French, Geography, Gerontology, Health Care Administration, History, Histotechnology, Hospitality Management, Individualized Programs, Industrial Engineering, Instrumental Music Education, Interior Design, International Studies, Jazz Composition, Jazz Education, Jazz Performance, Jazz Studies, Jewish Studies, Journalism, Jungian Perspectives in the Humanities, Keyboard Instruments, Labor Relations, Labor Studies, Languages, Legal Studies, Liberal Arts, Literature, Management, Marketing/Advertising, Mathematics, Medical Technology, Music, Music Business Education, Music Education, Music History, Music in Special Education, Music/Theatre, Music Theory, Nuclear Medical Technology, Orchestral/Band Instruments, Personnel Administration, Philosophy, Physics, Physics Technology, Piano, Piano Pedagogy, Podiatric Science, Political/Economic Institutions, Political Science, Psychology, Public Administration, Public Relations, Radiologic Technology, Radiological Technology, Secondary Teacher Education, Social Work, Sociology, Spanish, Speech Communication, Substance Abuse Counseling, Theatre, Therapeutic Radiation Technology, Traditional Composition, Urban Environmental Studies, Urban Studies, Voice, Women's Studies.
**Distribution of degrees:** The majors with the highest enrollment are computer science and accounting; interior design, French, and composition have the lowest.
**Requirements:** General education requirement.
**Academic regulations:** Freshmen must maintain minimum 2.0 GPA.
**Special:** Minors offered in most majors. Courses offered in cultural/area studies, Hebrew, Italian, physical education, and statistics. Accelerated B.Gen.Studies degree. Post-baccalaureate programs in pre-medicine and hospitality management. Self-designed majors. Double majors. Independent study. Accelerated study. Pass/fail grading option. Internships. Cooperative education programs. Graduate school at which undergraduates may take graduate-level courses. Preprofessional programs in law, medicine, veterinary science, pharmacy, and dentistry. Member of Chicago Consortium of Colleges and Universities. Cross-registration with Art Institute of Chicago and Spertus Coll of Judaica. Teacher certification in early childhood, elementary, secondary, and special education. Certification in specific subject areas.
**Honors:** Honors program. Honor societies.
**Academic Assistance:** Remedial reading, writing, math, and study skills. Nonremedial tutoring.

**STUDENT LIFE. Housing:** Students may live on or off campus. Coed, women's, and men's dorms. 40% of students live in college housing.
**Services and counseling/handicapped student services:** Placement services. Counseling services for older students. Personal and psychological counseling. Career and academic guidance services. Learning disabled program/services.
**Campus organizations:** Undergraduate student government. Student newspaper (Torch, published once/week). Literary magazine. Radio station. Jazz ensembles, opera studio and theatre, bands, orchestra, health and fitness group, natural science and business clubs, psychology club, student activities board. One fraternity, no chapter house; one sorority, no chapter house. 1% of men join a fraternity. 1% of women join a sorority.
**Religious organizations:** Christian Bible Study, Crown Center Fellowship, Intervarsity Christian Fellowship, Newman Club.
**Minority/foreign student organizations:** Black Student Union, African-American Women Student Union, African Student Association, Confederation of Latin American Students. International Student Union, Chinese, Korean, Latin American, and Malaysian groups.

**ATHLETICS. Physical education requirements:** None.
**Intercollegiate competition:** Member of Chicagoland Collegiate Athletic Conference.
**Intramural and club sports:** Intramural archery, badminton, basketball, billiards, bowling, chess, softball, table tennis, touch football, triathlon.

**ADMISSIONS. Academic basis for candidate selection** (in order of priority): Standardized test scores, class rank, secondary school record, school's recommendation.
**Nonacademic basis for candidate selection:** Character and personality and particular talent or ability are important. Extracurricular participation and alumni/ae relationship are considered.
**Requirements:** Graduation from secondary school is recommended; GED is accepted. 15 units and the following program of study are recommended: 4 units of English, 3 units of math, 2 units of science, 2 units of foreign language, 2 units of social studies, 1 unit of history, 1 unit of electives. Minimum composite ACT score of 20, rank in top half of secondary school class, and minimum 2.0 GPA required. Audition required of music program applicants. Conditional admission possible for applicants not meeting standard

requirements. Project Prime and Career and Academic Planning program for applicants not normally admissible. SAT or ACT is required. No off-campus interviews.
**Procedure:** Take SAT or ACT by April 30 of 12th year. Suggest filing application by August 1. Notification of admission on rolling basis. $250 room deposit, refundable up to one month prior to beginning of term. Freshmen accepted for terms other than fall.
**Special programs:** Admission may be deferred one year. Credit may be granted through CEEB Advanced Placement for scores of 3 or higher. Credit may be granted through CLEP general exams, DANTES exams, and life experience. Credit and/or placement may be granted through CLEP subject exams. Placement may be granted through challenge exams. Credit and placement may be granted through military experience. Early decision program. Deadline for applying for early decision is rolling. Early entrance/early admission program. Concurrent enrollment program.
**Transfer students:** Transfer students accepted for terms other than fall. In fall 1992, 85% of all new students were transfers into all classes. 1,164 transfer applications were received, 1,033 were accepted. Application deadline is rolling for fall; rolling for spring. Minimum 2.0 GPA required. Lowest course grade accepted is "D." Maximum number of transferable credits is 66 semester hours. At least 30 semester hours must be completed at the university to receive degree.
**Admissions contact:** Barbara Gianneschi, M.A., Dean of Enrollment Management. 312 341-3515.

**FINANCIAL AID. Available aid:** Pell grants, SEOG, state scholarships and grants, school scholarships, private scholarships and grants, academic merit scholarships, and United Negro College Fund. Perkins Loans (NDSL), PLUS, Stafford Loans (GSL), state loans, school loans, private loans, and SLS. Tuition Plan Inc. and deferred payment plan.
**Financial aid statistics:** In 1992-93, 95% of all undergraduate applicants received aid. Average amounts of aid awarded freshmen: Scholarships and grants, $2,000.
**Supporting data/closing dates:** FAFSA/FAF: Priority filing date is October 1; deadline is in May. State aid form: Priority filing date is October; deadline is in May. Notification of awards on rolling basis.
**Financial aid contact:** Stephen Bellin, M.A., Director of Financial Aid. 312 341-3565.

**STUDENT EMPLOYMENT.** College Work/Study Program. Institutional employment. Off-campus part-time employment opportunities rated "good."

**COMPUTER FACILITIES.** 52 IBM/IBM-compatible and Macintosh/Apple microcomputers; 20 are networked. Students may access minicomputer/mainframe systems. Computer languages and software packages include Assembler, C++, COBOL, Hyper Card, Microsoft Works, MINITAB, Pascal, SPSS, WordPerfect. Computer facilities are available to all students.
**Fees:** Computer fee is included in tuition/fees.
**Hours:** 9:30 AM-10:30 PM.

**GRADUATE CAREER DATA.** Highest graduate school enrollments: Loyola U, U of Chicago, U of Illinois. Companies and businesses that hire graduates: Allstate, Internal Revenue Service, Motorola, Sears.

**PROMINENT ALUMNI/AE.** Judy Rogala, president and CEO, Flagship Express; Thomas Burrell, CEO, Burrell Communications Group; Mark S. Handler, president, R.H. Macy.

## Rosary College

**River Forest, IL 60305 — 708 366-2490**

**1994-95 Costs.** Tuition: $10,950. Room & board: $4,600. Fees, books, misc. academic expenses (school's estimate): $595.
**Enrollment.** Undergraduates: 154 men, 470 women (full-time). Freshman class: 434 applicants, 321 accepted, 141 enrolled. Graduate enrollment: 314 men, 715 women.
**Test score averages/ranges.** Average ACT scores: 22 English, 21 math, 22 composite. Range of ACT scores of middle 50%: 18-23 composite.
**Faculty.** 60 full-time; 35 part-time. 65% of faculty holds doctoral degree. Student/faculty ratio: 11 to 1.
**Selectivity rating.** Less competitive.

**PROFILE.** Rosary, founded in 1901, is a private, liberal arts college. Its 30-acre campus of Gothic-style buildings is located in River Forest.

**Accreditation:** NCACS. Professionally accredited by the American Dietetic Association.
**Religious orientation:** Rosary College is affiliated with the Roman Catholic Church (Dominican Sisters of Sinsinawa); one semester of religion/theology required.
**Library:** Collections totaling over 292,000 volumes, 1,062 periodical subscriptions, and 10,200 microform items.
**Special facilities/museums:** Art gallery, radio workshop, language lab.
**Athletic facilities:** Gymnasiums, racquetball courts, weight room, swimming pool, track.

**STUDENT BODY. Undergraduate profile:** 91% are state residents; 50% are transfers. 2% Asian-American, 6% Black, 9% Hispanic, 78% White, 5% Other. Average age of undergraduates is 24.
**Freshman profile:** 3% of freshmen who took ACT scored 30 or over on composite; 30% scored 24 or over on composite; 80% scored 18 or over on composite; 100% scored 12 or over on composite. 5% of accepted applicants took SAT; 95% took ACT. 57% of freshmen come from public schools.
**Undergraduate achievement:** 81% of fall 1992 freshmen returned for fall 1993 term. 50% of entering class graduated. 40% of students who completed a degree program went on to graduate study within five years.
**Foreign students:** 31 students are from out of the country. Countries represented include China, India, Japan, Thailand, and Turkey; 27 in all.

**PROGRAMS OF STUDY. Degrees:** B.A.
**Majors:** Accounting, American Studies, Art, Arts Management, Biology, Biology/Chemistry, British Studies, Business Administration, Business Writing, Chemistry, Communication Arts/Sciences, Computer Information Systems, Computer Science, Corporate Communication, Economics, English, Environmental Science, European Studies, Fashion Design, Fashion Merchandising, Fine Arts, Food Science/Nutrition, Food Service Management, French, German, History, Home Economics Education, International Business, Italian, Latin American Studies, Mathematics, Mathematics/Computer Science, Nutrition/Dietetics, Philosophy, Political Science, Psychology, Religious Studies, Social Sciences, Sociology, Spanish.
**Distribution of degrees:** The majors with the highest enrollment are business administration, accounting, and psychology.
**Requirements:** General education requirement.
**Academic regulations:** Minimum 2.0 GPA must be maintained.
**Special:** Minors offered. Nonmajor programs in elementary or secondary education. Courses offered in geography, geology, health and physical education, linguistics, music, natural science, nursing, and physics. Double majors. Independent study. Accelerated study. Pass/fail grading option. Internships. Graduate school at which undergraduates may take graduate-level courses. Preprofessional programs in law, medicine, veterinary science, pharmacy, dentistry, and library science. 2-2 programs in nursing and medical technology with Rush U. Five-year B.A./M.B.A. program. 2-3 pharmacy program with Chicago Coll of Pharmacy. Washington Semester. Exchange program with Concordia U. Teacher certification in elementary and secondary education. Certification in specific subject areas. Study abroad in England, France, Germany, Italy, and Spain.
**Honors:** Honors program. Honor societies.
**Academic Assistance:** Remedial writing, math, and study skills. Nonremedial tutoring.

**ADMISSIONS. Academic basis for candidate selection** (in order of priority): Secondary school record, class rank, standardized test scores, school's recommendation, essay.
**Nonacademic basis for candidate selection:** Character and personality are important. Extracurricular participation, particular talent or ability, geographical distribution, and alumni/ae relationship are considered.
**Requirements:** Graduation from secondary school is required; GED is accepted. 16 secondary school units required, 14 of which should be distributed among English, math, lab science, foreign language, and social studies. Two units of electives also required. Rank in top half of secondary school class and minimum 2.5 GPA required. Portfolio required of art program applicants. Academic Potential Program for disadvantaged applicants not normally admissible. SAT or ACT is required. Campus visit and interview recommended. No off-campus interviews.
**Procedure:** Take SAT or ACT by February of 12th year. Notification of admission on rolling basis. Reply is required by May 1. $100 tuition deposit, refundable until May 1. Freshmen accepted for terms other than fall.
**Special programs:** Admission may be deferred one term. Credit may be granted through CEEB Advanced Placement for scores of 3 or higher. Credit and/or placement may be granted through CLEP general exams. Credit may be granted through CLEP subject exams. Credit and placement may be granted through life experience. Concurrent enrollment program.
**Transfer students:** Transfer students accepted for terms other than fall. In fall 1993, 50% of all new students were transfers into all classes. 288 transfer applications were received, 195 were accepted. Application deadline is rolling for fall; rolling for spring. Minimum 2.3 GPA required. Lowest course grade accepted within major is "C"; "D" for all other courses. Maximum number of transferable credits is 68 semester hours from a two-year school and 90 semester hours from a four-year school. At least 34 semester hours must be completed at the college to receive degree.
**Admissions contact:** Hildegarde Schmidt, M.B.A., Dean of Admissions and Financial Aid. 708 366-6800.

**FINANCIAL AID. Available aid:** Pell grants, SEOG, state scholarships and grants, school scholarships and grants, private scholarships, academic merit scholarships, athletic scholarships, and aid for undergraduate foreign students. Parish Leadership Awards, Community Service Awards. Perkins Loans (NDSL), PLUS, Stafford Loans (GSL), and SLS. Deferred payment plan and family tuition reduction.
**Financial aid statistics:** 20% of aid is not need-based. In 1993-94, 97% of all undergraduate applicants received aid; 99% of freshman applicants. Average amounts of aid awarded freshmen: Scholarships and grants, $6,594; loans, $2,430.
**Supporting data/closing dates:** FAFSA/FAF: Accepted on rolling basis. Income tax forms: Accepted on rolling basis. Notification of awards on rolling basis.
**Financial aid contact:** Howard Florine, M.B.A., Director of Financial Aid. 708 366-6809.

## Saint Xavier University

**Chicago, IL 60655 — 312 298-3000**

**1993-94 Costs.** Tuition: $10,230. Room & board: $4,360. Fees, books, misc. academic expenses (school's estimate): $555.
**Enrollment.** Undergraduates: 384 men, 979 women (full-time). Freshman class: 785 applicants, 635 accepted. Graduate enrollment: 783 men, 1,399 women.
**Test score averages/ranges.** N/A.
**Faculty.** Student/faculty ratio: 16 to 1.
**Selectivity rating.** Less competitive.

**PROFILE.** Saint Xavier is a private, church-affiliated, liberal arts college. Founded in 1847, it adopted coeducation in 1969. Its 47-acre suburban campus is located in Chicago.

**Accreditation:** NCACS. Professionally accredited by the National Association of Schools of Music, the National League for Nursing.
**Religious orientation:** Saint Xavier University is affiliated with the Roman Catholic Church (Sisters of Mercy); two semesters of religion/theology required.
**Athletic facilities:** Gymnasium, football complex, basketball and volleyball courts, baseball, soccer, and softball fields, weight room.

**STUDENT BODY. Undergraduate profile:** 77% are transfers. 2% Asian-American, 12% Black, 6% Hispanic, 1% Native American, 78% White, 1% Other. Average age of undergraduates is 24.

**Undergraduate achievement:** 95% of fall 1992 freshmen returned for fall 1993 term. 66% of entering class graduated. 40% of students who completed a degree program went on to graduate study within five years.
**Foreign students:** 31 students are from out of the country. Countries represented include France, India, Ireland, Japan, Lithuania, and Mexico; 18 in all.

**PROGRAMS OF STUDY. Degrees:** B.A., B.F.A., B.S.
**Majors:** Art, Biology, Business Administration/Management, Chemistry, Computer/Information Sciences, Criminal Justice, Early Childhood Education, Early Childhood Studies, Education, English, Family Studies, French, History, International Studies, Mass Communications, Mathematics, Music, Music Education, Music Performance, Nursing, Philosophy, Political Science/Government, Psychology, Religious Studies, Social Sciences, Sociology, Spanish, Speech/Language Pathology, Voice/Theatre.
**Distribution of degrees:** The majors with the highest enrollment are business administration/management, nursing, and education; international studies, philosophy, and social sciences have the lowest.
**Requirements:** General education requirement.
**Special:** Minors offered in many majors and in anthropology, journalism, physical education (coaching), speech communication/theatre, and theology. Advanced and Specialized Studies program in which student and adviser plan unified pattern of courses centering on particular discipline in one of the academic departments. Certificate programs in business, criminal justice, and family studies. Courses offered in German, humanities, physical science, and physics. January interim offers special courses and service projects on and off campus; individual programs arranged. Independent study. Internships. Graduate school at which undergraduates may take graduate-level courses. Preprofessional programs in law, medicine, veterinary science, pharmacy, dentistry, and optometry. 2-2 engineering program with Illinois Inst of Tech. Science students may take courses through Associated Colleges of the Chicago Area. Argonne Science Semester. Teacher certification in early childhood, elementary, and secondary education. Study abroad in Ireland and in European and South American countries. AFROTC at Illinois Inst of Tech.
**Academic Assistance:** Remedial reading, writing, and math. Nonremedial tutoring.

**STUDENT LIFE. Housing:** Students may live on or off campus. Coed dorms. 10% of students live in college housing.
**Social atmosphere:** Popular gathering places include McGuire Hall, the reception room, the student lounge, the cafeteria, Gilhooley's, Reilly's Daughter, Waltzing Matilda's, Brewbakers, and the Stingray. Student Government Association, Black Student Union, Fellowship of Christian Athletes, WXAV, Education Club, Theatre II, music department, football team, International Student Organization, and UNIDOS have widespread influence over campus life. Eagerly anticipated events include the Irish Fest, Homecoming, the Boat Bash, Theater II productions, the Barn Bash, Hunger Week, Saint Francis Xavier Day, and the International Food Fest. "Saint Xavier University is a multi-cultural school," reports the editor of the student newspaper. "Most of the students are commuters, and even those who live in the dorms tend to commute home on weekends."
**Services and counseling/handicapped student services:** Placement services. Day care. Speech and hearing clinic. Personal and psychological counseling. Career and academic guidance services. Learning disabled services.
**Campus organizations:** Undergraduate student government. Student newspaper (Xavierite, published once/two weeks). Literary magazine. Yearbook. Radio station. Choral group, drama group, Resident Council.
**Religious organizations:** Campus Ministry Council.
**Minority/foreign student organizations:** Black Student Organization, Hispanic Student Organization. International Student Association.

**ATHLETICS. Physical education requirements:** Two semesters of physical education required.
**Intercollegiate competition:** 4% of students participate. Baseball (M), basketball (M), cross-country (W), football (M), soccer (M), softball (W), volleyball (W). Member of Chicagoland Collegiate Athletic Conference, College Conference of Illinois and Wisconsin, Mid-States Football Association, NAIA.
**Intramural and club sports:** 5% of students participate. Intramural basketball, volleyball.

**ADMISSIONS. Academic basis for candidate selection** (in order of priority): Secondary school record, class rank, school's recommendation, standardized test scores.
**Nonacademic basis for candidate selection:** Character and personality, extracurricular participation, and particular talent or ability are important. Alumni/ae relationship is considered.
**Requirements:** Graduation from secondary school is required; GED is accepted. 16 units and the following program of study are recommended: 4 units of English, 3 units of math, 2 units of foreign language, 4 units of social studies. Remaining units may be selected from any subjects accepted by secondary school for graduation. 1 unit of chemistry required of nursing program applicants. ACT is required; SAT may be substituted. Campus visit and interview recommended. Off-campus interviews available with an alumni representative.
**Procedure:** Take SAT or ACT by January 1 of 12th year. Visit college for interview by May 1 of 12th year. Suggest filing application by May 1. Application deadline is August 15. Notification of admission on rolling basis. Reply is required by May 1. $50 nonrefundable tuition deposit. $50 room deposit, refundable until one month before entrance. Freshmen accepted for terms other than fall.
**Special programs:** Admission may be deferred one semester. Credit may be granted through CEEB Advanced Placement for scores of 3 or higher. Credit may be granted through CLEP general and subject exams, ACT PEP, DANTES, and challenge exams. Concurrent enrollment program.
**Transfer students:** Transfer students accepted for terms other than fall. In fall 1993, 77% of all new students were transfers into all classes. 830 transfer applications were received. Application deadline is August 15 for fall; January 15 for spring. Minimum 2.5 GPA required. Lowest course grade accepted is "C." Maximum number of transferable credits is 70 semester hours from a two-year school and 90 semester hours from a four-year school. At least 30 semester hours must be completed at the university to receive degree.
**Admissions contact:** Evelyn A. McKenna, Director of Admissions. 312 298-3050.

**FINANCIAL AID. Available aid:** Pell grants, SEOG, state scholarships and grants, school scholarships and grants, private scholarships and grants, academic merit scholarships, and athletic scholarships. Perkins Loans (NDSL), PLUS, Stafford Loans (GSL), school loans, and SLS. AMS and deferred payment plan.
**Financial aid statistics:** 30% of aid is not need-based. In 1993-94, 80% of all undergraduate applicants received aid; 67% of freshman applicants. Average amounts of aid awarded freshmen: Scholarships and grants, $4,383; loans, $3,364.
**Supporting data/closing dates:** FAFSA: Priority filing date is May 1. Notification of awards begins in February.
**Financial aid contact:** Sharon Sweeney, Director of Financial Aid. 312 298-3070.

**STUDENT EMPLOYMENT.** College Work/Study Program. Institutional employment. 10% of full-time undergraduates work on campus during school year. Students may expect to earn an average of $1,000 during school year. Off-campus part-time employment opportunities rated "good."

**COMPUTER FACILITIES.** 75 IBM/IBM-compatible and Macintosh/Apple microcomputers; 50 are networked. Students may access Digital minicomputer/mainframe systems. Client/LAN operating systems include Novell. Computer languages and software packages include AppleWorks, Assembler, BASIC, COBOL, Pascal, 20/20. Computer facilities are available to all students.
**Fees:** None.
**Hours:** 8 AM-10 PM.

# School of the Art Institute of Chicago

**Chicago, IL 60603** — **312 899-5100**

**1993-94 Costs.** Tuition: $13,350. Room: $1,800-$2,200. Fees, books, misc. academic expenses (school's estimate): $2,225.
**Enrollment.** Undergraduates: 558 men, 641 women (full-time). Freshman class: 706 applicants, 566 accepted, 227 enrolled. Graduate enrollment: 129 men, 223 women.
**Test score averages/ranges.** N/A.
**Faculty.** 93 full-time; 211 part-time. 87% of faculty holds highest degree in specific field. Student/faculty ratio: 12 to 1.
**Selectivity rating.** N/A.

**PROFILE.** The School of the Art Institute of Chicago, founded in 1866, is a private institution. The school occupies its own facilities adjoining the museum in downtown Chicago, overlooking Grant Park and Lake Michigan.

**Accreditation:** NCACS. Professionally accredited by the National Association of Schools of Art and Design.
**Religious orientation:** School of the Art Institute of Chicago is nonsectarian; no religious requirements.
**Library:** Collections totaling over 300,000 volumes, 450 periodical subscriptions, and 2,300 microform items.
**Special facilities/museums:** Art Institute of Chicago, slide library, film center, two school-affiliated galleries.

**STUDENT BODY. Undergraduate profile:** 38% are state residents; 62% are transfers. 7% Asian-American, 5% Black, 6% Hispanic, 1% Native American, 75% White, 6% Other. Average age of undergraduates is 23.
**Undergraduate achievement:** 16% of entering class graduated.
**Foreign students:** 57 students are from out of the country. Countries represented include Canada, Japan, South Korea, Taiwan, and the United Kingdom; 31 in all.

**PROGRAMS OF STUDY. Degrees:** B.F.A., B.Inter.Arch.
**Majors:** Art Education/Therapy, Art History, Art/Technology Studies, Ceramics, Fashion Design, Fiber/Fabric, Filmmaking, Interior Architecture, Painting/Drawing, Performance, Photography, Pottery, Printmaking, Sculpture, Sound/Music, Time Arts, Video, Visual Communication/Graphic Design.
**Requirements:** General education requirement.
**Special:** Students develop their own curriculum; major not required. Courses offered in English, humanities, history, natural sciences, and social sciences. First-year foundations program. Visiting artists program. Self-designed majors. Double majors. Independent study. Pass/fail grading option. Internships. Cooperative education programs. Graduate school at which undergraduates may take graduate-level courses. Member of Alliance of Independent Colleges of Art. Oxbow summer program. Studio program with Whitney Museum of American Art; other programs with Atlanta Coll of Art, Center for Creative Studies-Coll of Art and Design, Cleveland Inst of Art, Kansas City Art Inst, Maryland Inst Coll of Art, Otis/Parsons Sch of Art and Design, Rhode Island Sch of Design, and San Francisco Art Inst. Teacher certification in elementary and secondary education. Exchange programs abroad in Canada, France, Germany, Italy, Japan, and the United Kingdom.
**Academic Assistance:** Remedial reading, writing, math, and study skills. Nonremedial tutoring.

**STUDENT LIFE. Housing:** Coed dorms. No meal plan.
**Services and counseling/handicapped student services:** Health service. Career planning. Counseling services for minority and veteran students. Birth control, personal, and psychological counseling. Career and academic guidance services. Physically disabled student services. Learning disabled services. Notetaking services. Tape recorders. Tutors.
**Campus organizations:** Undergraduate student government. Student newspaper (F, published once/month). Literary magazine. Gay/Lesbian Union, 5 organizations in all.
**Religious organizations:** Bible study group, Jewish student group.
**Minority/foreign student organizations:** Ethnic American Students United, Artists of Color United, Hispanic and Asian student groups. Peer/mentor program.

**ATHLETICS. Physical education requirements:** None.
**Intramural and club sports:** Intramural soccer.

**ADMISSIONS. Academic basis for candidate selection** (in order of priority): Secondary school record, standardized test scores, school's recommendation, essay, class rank.

**Nonacademic basis for candidate selection:** Particular talent or ability is emphasized. Alumni/ae relationship is important. Character and personality, extracurricular participation, and geographical distribution are considered.
**Requirements:** Graduation from secondary school is required; GED is accepted. No specific distribution of secondary school units required. Minimum SAT score of 420 verbal (ACT English score of 18) required. Applicants should have as much art experience as possible. Portfolio required of art program applicants. SAT or ACT is required. Campus visit and interview recommended. Off-campus interviews available with an admissions representative.
**Procedure:** Take SAT or ACT by August 1 of 12th year. Visit college for interview by August 15 of 12th year. Suggest filing application by March 15. Application deadline is August 15. Notification of admission on rolling basis. Reply is required by August 15. $200 nonrefundable tuition deposit. Freshmen accepted for terms other than fall.
**Special programs:** Admission may be deferred one year. Credit and/or placement may be granted through CEEB Advanced Placement exams for scores of 3 or higher. Credit may be granted through CLEP general and subject exams, and military experience. Concurrent enrollment program.
**Transfer students:** Transfer students accepted for terms other than fall. In fall 1992, 62% of all new students were transfers into all classes. 497 transfer applications were received, 427 were accepted. Application deadline is August 15 for fall; January 1 for spring. Lowest course grade accepted is "C." Maximum number of transferable credits is 90 semester hours. At least 36 semester hours must be completed at the college to receive degree.
**Admissions contact:** Ellen Cropp, Director of Admissions. 312 899-5219.

**FINANCIAL AID. Available aid:** Pell grants, SEOG, state scholarships and grants, school scholarships and grants, private scholarships and grants, academic merit scholarships, and aid for undergraduate foreign students. Perkins Loans (NDSL), PLUS, Stafford Loans (GSL), state loans, and SLS. Tuition Management Systems. Institutional payment plan.
**Financial aid statistics:** 10% of aid is not need-based. In 1992-93, 95% of all undergraduate applicants received aid; 93% of freshman applicants. Average amounts of aid awarded freshmen: Scholarships and grants, $5,112; loans, $4,020.
**Supporting data/closing dates:** FAFSA/FAF: Accepted on rolling basis. School's own aid application: Priority filing date is April 1; accepted on rolling basis. Notification of awards on rolling basis.
**Financial aid contact:** Kathy Amato, Director of Financial Aid. 312 899-5106.

**STUDENT EMPLOYMENT.** College Work/Study Program. Institutional employment. 41% of full-time undergraduates work on campus during school year. Students may expect to earn an average of $1,515 during school year. Off-campus part-time employment opportunities rated "excellent."

**COMPUTER FACILITIES.** 7 IBM/IBM-compatible and Macintosh/Apple microcomputers. Computer languages and software packages include PageMaker, QuarkXPress, Adobe PhotoShop, FreeHand. Computer facilities are available to all students.
**Fees:** None.
**Hours:** 1 PM-10 PM (M,W,Th), 10 AM-10 PM (Tu), 10 AM-8 PM (F), 9 AM-6 PM (Sa), 11 AM-6 PM (Su).

**GRADUATE CAREER DATA.** Highest graduate school enrollments: SAIC, U of Illinois. 22% of graduates choose careers in business and industry.

**PROMINENT ALUMNI/AE.** Georgia O'Keefe, artist; Halston, fashion designer; Walt Disney, illustrator.

# Southern Illinois University at Carbondale

**Carbondale, IL 62901** **618 453-5351**

**1993-94 Costs.** Tuition: $2,250 (state residents), $6,750 (out-of-state). Room & board: $3,168. Fees, books, misc. academic expenses (school's estimate): $1,377.
**Enrollment.** Undergraduates: 10,172 men, 6,789 women (full-time). Freshman class: 9,907 applicants, 6,089 accepted, 2,243 enrolled. Graduate enrollment: 2,243 men, 2,178 women.
**Test score averages/ranges.** Average ACT scores: 22 composite.
**Faculty.** 1,076 full-time; 90 part-time. 65% of faculty holds doctoral degree. Student/faculty ratio: 17 to 1.
**Selectivity rating.** Competitive.

**PROFILE.** SIU-Carbondale, founded in 1869, is a public, comprehensive university. Programs are offered through the Colleges of Agriculture, Business and Administration, Communications and Fine Arts, Education, Engineering and Technology, Liberal Arts, Science, and Technical Careers; the Schools of Law and Medicine; and the Graduate School. Its 7,253-acre campus is located in Carbondale, 100 miles from St. Louis, Mo.

**Accreditation:** WASC, NCACS. Professionally accredited by the Accreditation Board for Engineering and Technology, the Accrediting Council on Education in Journalism and Mass Communication, the American Assembly of Collegiate Schools of Business, the American Bar Association, the American Dietetic Association, the American Library Association, the American Medical Association (CAHEA), the American Physical Therapy Association, the American Psychological Association, the Association of American Law Schools, the Council on Rehabilitation Education, the Council on Social Work Education, the Foundation for Interior Design Education Research, the Liaison Committee on Medical Education, the National Association of Schools of Art and Design, the National Association of Schools of Music, the National Association of Schools of Public Affairs and Administration, the National Council for Accreditation of Teacher Education, the National League for Nursing, the National Recreation and Park Association, the Society of American Foresters.
**Religious orientation:** Southern Illinois University at Carbondale is nonsectarian; no religious requirements.
**Library:** Collections totaling over 2,248,064 volumes, 17,047 periodical subscriptions, and 3,537,477 microform items.
**Special facilities/museums:** Art, natural history, and science museums, outdoor education center, center for crime studies, advertising and public relations agencies, child development lab, community human services center, airport training facility, archaeological research center, fisheries and wildlife research labs, coal research center, electron microscopy center.
**Athletic facilities:** Gymnasium, arena, baseball, field hockey, football, intramural, soccer, and softball fields, track, swimming pool, weight room, basketball, racquetball, squash, tennis, and volleyball courts, recreation center.

**STUDENT BODY. Undergraduate profile:** 90% are state residents; 56% are transfers. 1.6% Asian-American, 12% Black, 2% Hispanic, .4% Native American, 74% White, 10% Other. Average age of undergraduates is 23.
**Freshman profile:** 2% of accepted applicants took SAT; 90% took ACT. 88% of freshmen come from public schools.
**Undergraduate achievement:** 68% of fall 1992 freshmen returned for fall 1993 term. 17% of entering class graduated. 33% of students who completed a degree program immediately went on to graduate study.
**Foreign students:** 1,443 students are from out of the country. Countries represented include China, India, Japan, Korea, Malaysia, and Taiwan; 118 in all.

**PROGRAMS OF STUDY. Degrees:** B.A., B.F.A., B.Mus., B.S.
**Majors:** Accounting, Administration of Justice, Advanced Technical Studies, Agribusiness Economics, Animal Science, Anthropology, Art, Art Education, Aviation Management, Biological Sciences, Biological Sciences Education, Business/Administration, Business Economics, Business Education, Chemistry, Chemistry Education, Cinema/Photography, Civil Engineering, Classics, Communication Disorders/Sciences, Computer Science, Consumer Economics/Family Management, Design, Early Childhood Education, Economics, Electrical Engineering, Electronics Management, Elementary Education, Engineering Technology, English, English Education, Finance, Fire Science Management, Food/Nutrition, Foreign Language/International Trade, Foreign Languages Education, Forestry, French, French Education, General Agriculture, Geography, Geography Education, Geology, German, Health Care Management, Health Education, History, History Education, Home Economics, Industrial Technology, Interior Design, Journalism, Linguistics, Management, Marketing, Mathematics, Mathematics Education, Mechanical Engineering, Microbiology, Mining Engineering, Music, Music Education, Paralegal Studies, Philosophy, Physical Education, Physics, Physiology, Plant Biology, Plant/Soil Science, Political Science, Political Science Education, Psychology, Radio/Television, Russian, Social Studies Education, Social Work, Sociology, Spanish, Special Education, Speech Communication, Theater, University Studies, Vocational Education Studies, Zoology, Zoology Education.
**Distribution of degrees:** The majors with the highest enrollment are education, industrial technology, and aviation; classics, Russian, and French have the lowest.
**Requirements:** General education requirement.
**Academic regulations:** Minimum 2.0 GPA must be maintained.
**Special:** Minors offered in most majors and in approximately 20 other fields. Two-year Capstone program for transfer students with associate's degree in applied science or occupational equivalent provides alternative route to baccalaureate degree. Associate's degrees offered. Self-designed majors. Double majors. Dual degrees. Independent study. Accelerated study. Pass/fail grading option. Internships. Cooperative education programs. Graduate school at which undergraduates may take graduate-level courses. Preprofessional programs in law, medicine, veterinary science, pharmacy, dentistry, optometry, osteopathy, and podiatry. M.B.A./J.D., J.D./M.D., and M.Acct./J.D. programs. Member of Southern Illinois Common Market Consortium. Washington Semester. Teacher certification in early childhood, elementary, secondary, and special education. Certification in specific subject areas. Exchange program abroad in 37 countries. Study abroad also in Austria, Estonia, Japan, Latvia, and Lithuania. ROTC and AFROTC.
**Honors:** Honors program. Honor societies.
**Academic Assistance:** Remedial reading, writing, math, and study skills. Nonremedial tutoring.

**STUDENT LIFE. Housing:** All unmarried, nonveteran freshmen and sophomores under age 21 must live in school-approved housing unless living with family. Coed, women's, and men's dorms. Sorority and fraternity housing. School-owned/operated apartments. Off-campus privately-owned housing. On-campus married-student housing. 18% of students live in college housing.
**Social atmosphere:** According to the editor of the student newspaper, the most popular social events on campus are Homecoming, Spring Fest, and the Great Cardboard Boat Regatta. Influential groups are athletes, Greeks, some Christian groups, and several registered student organizations. Students like to gather at the Student Center and various bars on South Illinois Avenue.
**Services and counseling/handicapped student services:** Placement services. Health service. Women's center. Day care. Limited dental clinic. Counseling services for minority, military, veteran, and older students. Birth control, personal, and psychological counseling. Career and academic guidance services. Religious counseling. Physically disabled student services. Learning disabled program/services. Notetaking services. Tape recorders. Tutors. Reader services for the blind.
**Campus organizations:** Undergraduate student government. Student newspaper (Daily Egyptian). Yearbook. Radio and TV stations. Musical groups, drama productions, debating, public speaking groups, radio club, College Democrats, College Republicans, United We Stand, Students for Amnesty International, Circle K, departmental, recreational, service groups, and special-interest groups, 420 organizations in all. 16 fraternities, 11 chapter houses; eight sororities, four chapter houses. 4% of men join a fraternity. 2% of women join a sorority.
**Religious organizations:** American Baptist Students, B'nai B'rith Hillel Foundation, Campus Crusade for Christ, Chi Alpha, Christians Unlimited, Church of Christ Student Fellowship, International Christian Fellowship, Intervarsity Christian Fellowship, Latter-Day Saint Student Association, Lutheran Student Fellowship, Muslim Student Associa-

tion, Newman Student Organization, Student Bible Fellowship, Wesley Foundation, other religious groups.

**Minority/foreign student organizations:** Asian-American Student Coalition, Black Affairs Council, Friends for Native Americans, Hispanic Student Council, NAACP College Chapter. International Student Association, 35 foreign student groups.

**ATHLETICS. Physical education requirements:** Two semesters of physical education required.

**Intercollegiate competition:** 8% of students participate. Baseball (M), basketball (M,W), cheerleading (M,W), cross-country (M,W), diving (M,W), football (M), golf (M,W), softball (W), swimming (M,W), tennis (M,W), track (indoor) (M,W), track (outdoor) (M,W), track and field (indoor) (M,W), track and field (outdoor) (M,W), volleyball (W). Member of Gateway Collegiate Athletic Conference for football, Missouri Valley Conference, NCAA Division I, NCAA Division I-AA for football.

**Intramural and club sports:** 80% of students participate. Intramural aerobics, badminton, basketball, canoe, cycling, flag football, floor hockey, golf, handball, inner-tube water polo, racquetball, soccer, softball, squash, swimming, table tennis, tennis, track and field, ultimate frisbee, volleyball, walleyball. Men's club badminton, bowling, boxing, canoe/kayak, caving, cheerleading, cycling, fencing, horsemanship, ice hockey, martial arts, mountaineering, orienteering, racquetball, rugby, sailing, soccer, squash, ultimate frisbee, volleyball, water polo, water skiing, weight lifting, wrestling. Women's club badminton, bowling, canoe/kayak, caving, cheerleading, cycling, fencing, horsemanship, martial arts, mountaineering, orienteering, racquetball, sailing, squash, ultimate frisbee, volleyball, water skiing, weight lifting.

**ADMISSIONS. Academic basis for candidate selection** (in order of priority): Standardized test scores, class rank, secondary school record, school's recommendation.

**Nonacademic basis for candidate selection:** Character and personality, extracurricular participation, and particular talent or ability are considered.

**Requirements:** Graduation from secondary school is required; GED is accepted. 15 units and the following program of study are required: 4 units of English, 3 units of math, 3 units of lab science, 3 units of social studies, 2 units of electives. Minimum composite ACT score of 20 or rank in top half of secondary school class and composite ACT score of 18 required. Some programs require additional materials and screening, with entry requirements higher than standard minimums. Center for Basic Skills for applicants not normally admissible. ACT is required. Campus visit recommended. Off-campus interviews available with an admissions representative.

**Procedure:** Take ACT by October of 12th year. Notification of admission on rolling basis. No set date by which applicants must accept offer. Nonrefundable prepayment of $358 required. Freshmen accepted for terms other than fall.

**Special programs:** Credit and/or placement may be granted through CEEB Advanced Placement exams for scores of 3 or higher. Credit and/or placement may be granted through CLEP general and subject exams. Credit may be granted through challenge exams, and military and life experience. Credit and placement may be granted through DANTES exams. Concurrent enrollment program.

**Transfer students:** Transfer students accepted for terms other than fall. In fall 1993, 56% of all new students were transfers into all classes. 6,218 transfer applications were received, 4,415 were accepted. Application deadline is rolling for fall; rolling for spring. Minimum 2.0 GPA required. Lowest course grade accepted is "D." At least 30 semester hours must be completed at the university to receive degree.

**Admissions contact:** Roland E. Keim, M.S.Ed., Director of Admissions & Records. 618 453-4381.

**FINANCIAL AID. Available aid:** Pell grants, SEOG, state scholarships and grants, school scholarships and grants, private scholarships and grants, ROTC scholarships, academic merit scholarships, athletic scholarships, and aid for undergraduate foreign students. Perkins Loans (NDSL), PLUS, Stafford Loans (GSL), Health Professions Loans, state loans, and SLS. Deferred payment plan.

**Financial aid statistics:** 15% of aid is not need-based. In 1993-94, 95% of all undergraduate applicants received aid; 90% of freshman applicants.

**Supporting data/closing dates:** FAFSA: Priority filing date is April 1; accepted on rolling basis. Notification of awards begins May 1994.

**Financial aid contact:** Pam Britton, M.S., Director of Financial Aid. 618 453-4334.

**STUDENT EMPLOYMENT.** College Work/Study Program. Institutional employment. 33% of full-time undergraduates work on campus during school year. Students may expect to earn an average of $1,400 during school year. Off-campus part-time employment opportunities rated "good."

**COMPUTER FACILITIES.** 3,000 IBM/IBM-compatible and Macintosh/Apple microcomputers; 1,000 are networked. Students may access Data General, IBM, Prime, SUN minicomputer/mainframe systems, BITNET. Residence halls may be equipped with stand-alone microcomputers, networked terminals, modems. Client/LAN operating systems include OS/2. Computer languages and software packages include Assembler, COBOL, FORTRAN, RPG II, SAS; 200 in all. Computer facilities are available to all students.

**Fees:** None.

**Hours:** 7 AM-3 AM daily.

**GRADUATE CAREER DATA.** 42% of graduates choose careers in business and industry. Companies and businesses that hire graduates: Arthur Andersen, McDonnell Douglas, Texas Instruments.

**PROMINENT ALUMNI/AE.** Donald McHenry, former U.S. Ambassador to the United Nations; Kenneth Pontikes, chairman and president, Comdisco, Inc.; Walter Rodgers, *ABC Nightly News* correspondent; Dave Stieb, Toronto Blue Jays pitcher; Robert Lewis Taylor, Pulitzer Prize-winning author; James Belushi, actor; Dick Gregory, author, comedian.

# Southern Illinois University at Edwardsville

**Edwardsville, IL 62026-1083 — 618 692-2000**

**1993-94 Costs.** Tuition: $2,200 (state residents), $5,652 (out-of-state). Room: $1,500-$2,230. Board: $519-$1,299.

**Enrollment.** Undergraduates: 2,957 men, 3,825 women (full-time). Freshman class: 2,492 applicants, 2,169 accepted, 987 enrolled. Graduate enrollment: 1,230 men, 1,530 women.

**Test score averages/ranges.** Average ACT scores: 21 composite. Range of ACT scores of middle 50%: 18-23 composite.

**Faculty.** 76% of faculty holds doctoral degree. Student/faculty ratio: 16 to 1.

**Selectivity rating.** Competitive.

**PROFILE.** SIU-Edwardsville, founded in 1957, is a public, comprehensive university. Its 2,600-acre campus is located in Edwardsville, 15 miles southwest of St. Louis.

**Accreditation:** NCACS. Professionally accredited by the Accreditation Board for Engineering and Technology, the American Assembly of Collegiate Schools of Business, the American Association for Counseling and Development, the American Dental Association, the American Speech-Language-Hearing Association, the Council on Social Work Education, the National Association of Schools of Music, the National Council for Accreditation of Teacher Education, the National League for Nursing.

**Religious orientation:** Southern Illinois University at Edwardsville is nonsectarian; no religious requirements.

**Library:** Collections totaling over 797,000 volumes, 6,130 periodical subscriptions, and 1,157,961 microform items.

**Special facilities/museums:** Art gallery, anthropology museum, language lab, center for advanced manufacturing and production, technology commercialization center, electron microscope.

**Athletic facilities:** Gymnasiums, field house, baseball, intramural, soccer, and softball fields, swimming pools, aerobics and dance studios, sauna, basketball, racquetball, tennis, and volleyball courts, weight room, track, cross-country and cycling trails, lake, bowling alley.

**STUDENT BODY. Undergraduate profile:** 88% are state residents; 53% are transfers. 1% Asian-American, 16% Black, 1% Hispanic, 1% Native American, 80% White, 1% Other. Average age of undergraduates is 23.

**Freshman profile:** 1% of freshmen who took ACT scored 30 or over on composite; 21% scored 24 or over on composite; 79% scored 18 or over on composite; 99% scored 12 or over on composite; 100% scored 6 or over on composite. 92% of accepted applicants took ACT.

**Undergraduate achievement:** 65% of fall 1991 freshmen returned for fall 1992 term.

**Foreign students:** 82 students are from out of the country. Countries represented include China, Germany, India, Malaysia, Pakistan, and Taiwan; 47 in all.

**PROGRAMS OF STUDY. Degrees:** B.A., B.F.A., B.Lib.Studies, B.Mus., B.S.

**Majors:** Accounting, Anthropology, Art, Art/Design, Art Education, Art History, Arts/Drama, Biological Sciences, Business Administration, Business Economics, Chemistry, Civil Engineering, Computer Science, Construction, Dance, Early Childhood Education, Economics, Electrical Engineering, Elementary Education, English, Foreign Languages/Literatures, General Science/Mathematics, Geography, Health Education, History, Industrial Engineering, Liberal Studies, Management Information Systems, Mass Communications, Mathematical Studies/Statistics, Mechanical Engineering, Music, Nursing, Philosophy, Physical Education, Physical Science Education, Physics, Political Science, Psychology, Recreation, Social Work, Sociology, Special Education, Speech Communication, Speech Pathology/Audiology, Theatre.

**Distribution of degrees:** The majors with the highest enrollment are business administration, elementary education, and nursing; general science/mathematics and physical science education have the lowest.

**Requirements:** General education requirement.

**Academic regulations:** Minimum 3.0 GPA must be maintained.

**Special:** Minors offered in many majors and in aerospace studies, American studies, Black American studies, coaching, comparative literature, classical studies, instructional technology, Italian, Latin American studies, linguistics, peace studies, Russian area studies, and women's studies. Specializations offered in jazz, journalism, medical technology, music education, music merchandising, and radio/television. Double majors. Dual degrees. Internships. Cooperative education programs. Graduate school at which undergraduates may take graduate-level courses. Preprofessional programs in law, medicine, and dentistry. Teacher certification in early childhood, elementary, secondary, and special education. Certification in specific subject areas. Exchange programs abroad in England (Sheffield City Polytech), France (Ecole Superieure du Commerce Exterieur, Ecole Superieure des Sciences Commerciales d'Angers), Germany (International Business Sch), and the Netherlands (Haarlem Polytech). ROTC and AFROTC.

**Honors:** Honors program. Honor societies.

**Academic Assistance:** Remedial reading, writing, math, and study skills. Nonremedial tutoring.

**STUDENT LIFE. Housing:** Students may live on or off campus. School-owned/operated apartments. 10% of students live in college housing.

**Social atmosphere:** Students gather at the University Center and the recreational area, and at The Stagger Inn Again, The Kind Ground Coffee Shop, Rusty's, and Tommy's. College Democrats and campus "radicals" have widespread influence on SIUE student life. "SIUE provides something for everyone both on-campus and off," reports the student newspaper. "Edwardsville provides excellent restaurants and/or bars for people of all ages."

**Services and counseling/handicapped student services:** Placement services. Health service. Women's center. Day care. Counseling services for minority, military, veteran, and older students. Birth control and personal counseling. Career and academic guidance services. Religious counseling. Physically disabled student services. Learning disabled services. Notetaking services. Tape recorders. Tutors. Reader services for the blind.

**Campus organizations:** Undergraduate student government. Student newspaper (Alestle, published twice/week). Literary magazine. Radio station. Band and orchestra, choral groups, student opera, musical theatre, crafts workshop, athletic clubs, Student Leadership Series, Community Involvement Program, Disabled Student Association, political, service, and special-interest groups, 104 organizations in all. Nine fraternities, one chapter house; seven sororities, no chapter houses. 3% of men join a fraternity. 3% of women join a sorority.

**Religious organizations:** B'ahai College Club, Baptist Student Union, Chinese Christian Fellowship, Christian Student Fellowship, Deseret Club, Intervarsity Christian Fellowship, Knights of Columbus, Moslem Student Association, Newman Student Union, Upside Down Christian Fellowship.

**Minority/foreign student organizations:** Minority Business Students, Black Student Association, Association of Black Accountants, Black Literary Guild, Association of Black Journalists, National Society of Black Engineers, TRIBE, Indian Student Association, Native American Student Union, Indian Science and Engineering Society. International Student Council, Chinese, French, Indian, Korean, Latin American, and Pakistani groups.

**ATHLETICS. Physical education requirements:** None.

**Intercollegiate competition:** 6% of students participate. Baseball (M), basketball (M,W), cheerleading (M,W), cross-country (M,W), golf (M), soccer (M,W), softball (W), tennis (M,W), track and field (indoor) (M,W), track and field (outdoor) (M,W), wrestling (M). Member of NCAA Division I for men's soccer, NCAA Division II.

**Intramural and club sports:** Intramural badminton, basketball, bowling, golf, racquetball, soccer, softball, swimming, table tennis, tennis, volleyball. Women's club volleyball.

**ADMISSIONS. Academic basis for candidate selection** (in order of priority): Standardized test scores, class rank.

**Requirements:** Graduation from secondary school is recommended; GED is accepted. No specific distribution of secondary school units required. Additional admissions requirements vary by department. Portfolio required of art program applicants. Audition required of music program applicants. Conditional admission possible for applicants not meeting standard requirements. ACT is required; SAT may be substituted. Campus visit recommended. No off-campus interviews.

**Procedure:** Application deadline is August 2. Notification of admission on rolling basis. $75 refundable room deposit. Freshmen accepted for terms other than fall.

**Special programs:** Admission may be deferred. Credit may be granted through CEEB Advanced Placement for scores of 3 or higher. Credit and/or placement may be granted through CLEP general and subject exams. Credit may be granted through DANTES exams. Credit and placement may be granted through challenge exams. Early entrance/early admission program. Concurrent enrollment program.

**Transfer students:** Transfer students accepted for terms other than fall. In fall 1992, 53% of all new students were transfers into all classes. 1,774 transfer applications were received, 1,643 were accepted. Application deadline is August 2 for fall; December 20 for spring. Minimum 2.0 GPA required. Lowest course grade accepted is "C." At least 30 semester hours must be completed at the university to receive degree.

**Admissions contact:** Eugene J. Magac, M.S., Director of Admissions. 618 692-3705, 800 447-SIUE (in-state), 314 231-SIUE (St. Louis).

**FINANCIAL AID. Available aid:** Pell grants, SEOG, state scholarships and grants, school scholarships, private scholarships and grants, ROTC scholarships, academic merit scholarships, and athletic scholarships. Perkins Loans (NDSL), PLUS, Stafford Loans (GSL), Health Professions Loans, state loans, school loans, private loans, and SLS. AMS.

**Financial aid statistics:** 40% of aid is not need-based. In 1992-93, 80% of all undergraduate applicants received aid; 80% of freshman applicants. Average amounts of aid awarded freshmen: Scholarships and grants, $1,150; loans, $2,500.

**Supporting data/closing dates:** FAFSA: Priority filing date is April 1; accepted on rolling basis. School's own aid application: Priority filing date is April 1; accepted on rolling basis. Notification of awards begins June 15.

**Financial aid contact:** William Burns, Ph.D., Acting Director of Financial Aid. 618 692-3880.

**STUDENT EMPLOYMENT.** College Work/Study Program. Institutional employment. 20% of full-time undergraduates work on campus during school year. Students may expect to earn an average of $3,000 during school year. Off-campus part-time employment opportunities rated "good."

**COMPUTER FACILITIES.** IBM/IBM-compatible and Macintosh/Apple microcomputers. Students may access IBM minicomputer/mainframe systems. Residence halls may be equipped with stand-alone microcomputers. Numerous computer languages and software programs available. Computer facilities are available to all students.

# Trinity Christian College

**Palos Heights, IL 60463** **708 597-3000**

**1994-95 Costs.** Tuition: $10,400. Room: $2,050. Board: $1,940. Fees, books, misc. academic expenses (school's estimate): $515.

**Enrollment.** Undergraduates: 245 men, 363 women (full-time). Freshman class: 418 applicants, 315 accepted, 216 enrolled.

**Test score averages/ranges.** Average ACT scores: 22 composite. Range of ACT scores of middle 50%: 21-25 composite.

**Faculty.** 36 full-time; 9 part-time. 58% of faculty holds highest degree in specific field. Student/faculty ratio: 12 to 1.

**Selectivity rating.** Less competitive.

**PROFILE.** Trinity Christian, founded in 1959, is a church-affiliated college. The 52-acre campus in suburban Palos Heights is 25 miles south of Chicago.

**Accreditation:** NCACS. Professionally accredited by the National League for Nursing.

**Religious orientation:** Trinity Christian College is an interdenominational Christian school; two semesters of theology required.

**Library:** Collections totaling over 65,000 volumes, 300 periodical subscriptions, and 1,200 microform items.

**Special facilities/museums:** Dutch heritage museum.

**Athletic facilities:** Gymnasium, weight room, basketball, racquetball, and tennis courts, stadium, baseball, soccer, and softball fields, country club.

**STUDENT BODY. Undergraduate profile:** 61% are state residents; 24% are transfers. 1% Asian-American, 9% Black, 1% Hispanic, 89% White. Average age of undergraduates is 20.

**Freshman profile:** Majority of accepted applicants took ACT. 19% of freshmen come from public schools.

**Undergraduate achievement:** 83% of fall 1992 freshmen returned for fall 1993 term. 39% of entering class graduated.

**Foreign students:** Three students are from out of the country.

**PROGRAMS OF STUDY. Degrees:** B.A., B.S., B.S.Nurs.

**Majors:** Accounting, Art, Biology, Business Administration, Business Education, Chemistry, Communications, Computer Science, Computer Science/Mathematics, Elementary Education, English, History, Industrial Arts Education, Mathematics, Medical Technology, Music, Nursing, Philosophy, Physical Education, Psychology, Secondary Education, Sociology, Theology.

**Distribution of degrees:** The majors with the highest enrollment are business, nursing, and education.

**Requirements:** General education requirement.

**Special:** Minors offered in all majors. Double majors. Dual degrees. Independent study. Internships. Cooperative education programs. Graduate school at which undergraduates may take graduate-level courses. Preprofessional programs in law, medicine, veterinary science, dentistry, theology, optometry, allied health, chiropractic, and physical therapy. 3-1 medical technology programs with three area hospitals. Member of consortium with Chicago State U. Chicago Metropolitan Studies Program. Teacher certification in elementary and secondary education. Study abroad in the Netherlands (business exchange program) and Spain.

**Academic Assistance:** Nonremedial tutoring.

**ADMISSIONS. Academic basis for candidate selection** (in order of priority): Secondary school record, standardized test scores, class rank, school's recommendation, essay.

**Nonacademic basis for candidate selection:** Character and personality, extracurricular participation, and particular talent or ability are important. Geographical distribution and alumni/ae relationship are considered.

**Requirements:** Graduation from secondary school is required; GED is accepted. 16 units and the following program of study are required: 4 units of English, 2 units of math, 3 units of science, 2 units of social studies, 2 units of history. 2 units of foreign language recommended. Minimum composite ACT score of 18 and minimum 2.1 GPA required. SAT or ACT is required. Campus visit and interview recommended. Off-campus interviews available with an admissions representative.

**Procedure:** Take SAT or ACT by March of 12th year. Visit college for interview by March of 12th year. Suggest filing application by February 15. Application deadline is August 1. Notification of admission on rolling basis. Reply is required by May 1. $100 nonrefundable tuition deposit. $75 room deposit, refundable until September 1. Freshmen accepted for terms other than fall.

**Special programs:** Admission may be deferred one year. Credit and/or placement may be granted through CEEB Advanced Placement exams for scores of 3 or higher. Credit and/or placement may be granted through CLEP general and subject exams. Credit and placement may be granted through Regents College, ACT PEP, and DANTES exams. Concurrent enrollment program.

**Transfer students:** Transfer students accepted for terms other than fall. In fall 1993, 24% of all new students were transfers into all classes. 159 transfer applications were received, 106 were accepted. Application deadline is August 15 for fall; December 15 for spring. Minimum 2.1 GPA required. Lowest course grade accepted is "C." Maximum number of transferable credits is 65 semester hours. At least 30 semester hours must be completed at the college to receive degree.

**Admissions contact:** David Lageveen, Director of Admissions. 708 597-3000.

**FINANCIAL AID. Available aid:** Pell grants, SEOG, state scholarships and grants, school scholarships and grants, academic merit scholarships, and athletic scholarships. Perkins Loans (NDSL), PLUS, Stafford Loans (GSL), and NSL. Deferred payment plan.

**Supporting data/closing dates:** FAFSA/FAF/FFS: Priority filing date is February 15. Notification of awards begins in March.

**Financial aid contact:** Nancy Rietveld, Director of Financial Aid. 708 597-3000.

# Trinity College

**Deerfield, IL 60015** **708 948-8980**

**1994-95 Costs.** Tuition: $10,420. Room & board: $4,260. Fees, books, misc. academic expenses (school's estimate): $750.

**Enrollment.** Undergraduates: 408 men, 466 women (full-time). Freshman class: 311 applicants, 301 accepted, 149 enrolled.

**Test score averages/ranges.** Average ACT scores: 22 composite.

**Faculty.** 43 full-time; 20 part-time. 60% of faculty holds doctoral degree. Student/faculty ratio: 17 to 1.

**Selectivity rating.** Less competitive.

**PROFILE.** Trinity is a private, church-affiliated, liberal arts college. Its 120-acre campus is located in Deerfield, 20 miles north of Chicago.

**Accreditation:** NCACS. Professionally accredited by the American Council for Construction Education.

**Religious orientation:** Trinity College is affiliated with the Evangelical Free Church of America; four semesters of theology required.
**Library:** Collections totaling over 205,000 volumes, 1,700 periodical subscriptions, and 63,875 microform items.
**Athletic facilities:** Sports center, weight room, accessibility to indoor tennis and racquetball club.

**STUDENT BODY. Undergraduate profile:** 48% are state residents; 26% are transfers. 3% Asian-American, 8% Black, 3% Hispanic, 85% White, 1% Other. Average age of undergraduates is 20.
**Freshman profile:** Majority of accepted applicants took ACT.
**Undergraduate achievement:** 74% of fall 1992 freshmen returned for fall 1993 term. 56% of entering class graduated.
**Foreign students:** 28 students are from out of the country. Countries represented include Canada, China, Japan, Kenya, Nigeria, and Norway; six in all.

**PROGRAMS OF STUDY. Degrees:** B.A.
**Majors:** Biblical Studies, Biological Science, Business Administration, Chemistry, Computer Information Science, Computer Science, Elementary Education, English, English/Communications, General Studies, History, Mathematics, Medical Technology, Music, Philosophy, Physical Education, Sociology, Youth Ministries.
**Distribution of degrees:** The majors with the highest enrollment are elementary education and biblical studies; chemistry has the lowest.
**Requirements:** General education requirement.
**Academic regulations:** Freshmen must maintain minimum 1.50 GPA; sophomores, 1.75 GPA; juniors, 1.87 GPA; seniors, 2.00 GPA.
**Special:** Minors offered in most majors and in Christian ministries, computer information systems, oral communications, political science, and psychology. Courses offered in art, Christian education, computer programming, French, Greek, Hebrew, physical science, physics, Spanish, and special education. Double majors. Independent study. Internships. Graduate school at which undergraduates may take graduate-level courses. Preprofessional programs in law, medicine, dentistry, nursing, and physical therapy. Member of Christian College Consortium; exchange possible. American Studies Program (Washington D.C.). Other off-campus study opportunities. Teacher certification in elementary and secondary education. Certification in specific subject areas.
**Honors:** Honors program.
**Academic Assistance:** Remedial writing. Nonremedial tutoring.

**ADMISSIONS. Academic basis for candidate selection** (in order of priority): Secondary school record, standardized test scores, essay, class rank.
**Nonacademic basis for candidate selection:** Extracurricular participation and particular talent or ability are important. Character and personality are considered.
**Requirements:** Graduation from secondary school is recommended; GED is accepted. 15 units required and the following program of study recommended: 3 units of English, 2 units of math, 2 units of science, 2 units of foreign language, 2 units of social studies. Graduates of three-year schools must present 12 units (10 college preparatory). Minimum composite ACT score of 16 (combined SAT score of 740), rank in top half of secondary school class, and minimum 2.5 GPA required. Conditional admission possible for applicants not meeting standard requirements. Growth Assistance Program (GAP) for applicants not normally admissible. ACT is required; SAT may be substituted. Campus visit recommended. Off-campus interviews available with an admissions representative.
**Procedure:** Take SAT or ACT by July of 12th year. Visit college for interview by January of 12th year. Suggest filing application by January 1. Notification of admission on rolling basis. Reply is required within 15 days of receiving financial aid package. $150 tuition deposit, refundable until May 1. Freshmen accepted for terms other than fall.
**Special programs:** Admission may be deferred two years. Credit and/or placement may be granted through CEEB Advanced Placement exams for scores of 3 or higher.
**Transfer students:** Transfer students accepted for terms other than fall. In fall 1993, 26% of all new students were transfers into all classes. 251 transfer applications were received, 190 were accepted. Application deadline is rolling for fall; rolling for spring. Minimum 2.0 GPA recommended. Lowest course grade accepted is "C." Maximum number of transferable credits is 64 semester hours. At least 30 semester hours must be completed at the college to receive degree.
**Admissions contact:** Gary Larson, Director of Admissions. 708 317-7000.

**FINANCIAL AID. Available aid:** Pell grants, SEOG, state grants, school scholarships and grants, private scholarships and grants, academic merit scholarships, and athletic scholarships. Perkins Loans (NDSL), PLUS, Stafford Loans (GSL), school loans, and SLS. Trinity Alternative Payment Plan (TAPP).
**Financial aid statistics:** In 1993-94, 85% of all undergraduate applicants received aid. Average amounts of aid awarded freshmen: Scholarships and grants, $7,000; loans, $2,179.
**Supporting data/closing dates:** FAFSA: Priority filing date is April 1. School's own aid application: Accepted on rolling basis. Notification of awards on rolling basis.
**Financial aid contact:** Gary Larson, Director of Financial Aid. 708 317-8060.

## University of Chicago

**Chicago, IL 60637** **312 702-1234**

**1994-95 Costs.** Tuition: $18,930. Room: $3,310. Board: $3,070. Fees, books, misc. academic expenses (school's estimate): $1,314.
**Enrollment.** Undergraduates: 1,924 men, 1,442 women (full-time). Freshman class: 6,335 applicants, 2,994 accepted, 922 enrolled. Graduate enrollment: 4,686 men, 2,782 women.
**Test score averages/ranges.** Range of SAT scores of middle 50%: 570-680 verbal, 630-720 math. Range of ACT scores of middle 50%: 27-31 composite.
**Faculty.** 1,855 full-time. 100% of faculty holds doctoral degree. Student/faculty ratio: 6 to 1.
**Selectivity rating.** Most competitive.

**PROFILE.** The University of Chicago, founded in 1890, is a private, comprehensive university. Its 171-acre campus is located seven miles south of downtown Chicago.

**Accreditation:** NCACS.
**Religious orientation:** University of Chicago is nonsectarian; no religious requirements.
**Library:** Collections totaling over 5,500,000 volumes, 47,000 periodical subscriptions, and 2,000,000 microform items.
**Special facilities/museums:** Two art galleries, archaeology museum, court theatre, on-campus lab school (pre-K–12), Argonne National Lab, Enrico Fermi Institute, observatory, two telescopes, accelerator lab.
**Athletic facilities:** Baseball, football, lacrosse, rugby, soccer, and softball fields, badminton, basketball, handball, squash, tennis, and volleyball courts, field house, track, gymnastics, martial arts, weight lifting, and wrestling rooms, gymnasium, swimming pool, lake, lagoon, cross-country course.

**STUDENT BODY. Undergraduate profile:** 27% are state residents; 7% are transfers. 26% Asian-American, 5% Black, 4% Hispanic, 64% White, 1% Other. Average age of undergraduates is 20.
**Freshman profile:** 94% of accepted applicants took SAT; 46% took ACT. 69% of freshmen come from public schools.
**Undergraduate achievement:** 91% of fall 1992 freshmen returned for fall 1993 term. 75% of entering class graduated. 33% of students who completed a degree program immediately went on to graduate study.
**Foreign students:** 108 students are from out of the country. Countries represented include Canada, China, India, Japan, and Korea; 70 in all.

**PROGRAMS OF STUDY. Degrees:** B.A., B.S.
**Majors:** African/African-American Studies, Analysis of Ideas/the Study of Methods, Anatomy, Anthropology, Applied Mathematics, Art/Design, Art History, Biochemistry, Biological Chemistry, Biology, Biophysics/Theoretical Biology, Biopsychology, Chemistry, Classical Languages/Literature, Developmental Biology, Early Christian Literature, East Asian Languages/Civilizations, Economics, English, Environmental Studies, Evolutionary Biology, Fundamentals: Issues/Texts, General Studies/Humanities, Genetics, Geography, Geophysical Sciences, Germanic Languages/Literatures, History, History/Philosophy/Social Studies of Science/Medicine, Immunology, Jewish Studies, Latin American Studies, Law/Letters/Society, Linguistics, Mathematics, Mathematics/Computer Science, Medieval Studies, Microbiology, Music, Near Eastern Languages/Civilizations, Pathology, Pharmacological/Physiological Sciences, Philosophy, Physics, Political Science, Psychology, Public Policy Studies, Religion/Humanities, Romance Languages/Literature, Russian Civilization, Russian/Other Slavic Languages/Literatures, Sociology, South Asian Languages/Civilizations, South Asian Studies, Statistics, Tutorial Studies, Virology.
**Distribution of degrees:** The majors with the highest enrollment are economics, biological sciences, and English; tutorial studies and religion/humanities have the lowest.
**Requirements:** General education requirement.
**Academic regulations:** Minimum 1.75 GPA must be maintained.
**Special:** Self-designed majors. Double majors. Independent study. Accelerated study. Pass/fail grading option. Internships. Graduate school at which undergraduates may take graduate-level courses. Joint B.A./M.A. or B.S./M.S. programs in biology/biochemistry, chemistry/biochemistry, economics, geography, linguistics, math, Romance languages and literatures, and social sciences. 3-2 programs in business, law, public policy, and social work. Member of Associated Colleges of the Midwest, COFHE, and Committee on Institutional Cooperation. Chicago Semester in the Arts. Newberry Library Program in the Humanities (Illinois). Urban Education Program (Chicago). Urban Studies Program (Chicago). Oak Ridge Science Semester (Tennessee). Wilderness Field Station Program (Minnesota). Study abroad in over 30 countries, including China, Costa Rica, the Czech Republic, England, France, Germany, India, Italy, Japan, Mexico, the former Soviet Republics, Spain, and Zimbabwe. ROTC at U of Illinois-Chicago. AFROTC at Illinois Institute of Technology.
**Honors:** Phi Beta Kappa. Honors program. Honor societies.
**Academic Assistance:** Remedial math and study skills. Nonremedial tutoring.

**STUDENT LIFE. Housing:** First year, non-commuting students must live on campus. Coed dorms. Fraternity housing. Off-campus privately-owned housing. 66% of students live in college housing.
**Social atmosphere:** Popular student gathering places include C-Snoe, the library, Reynolds Club, Medici, Caffe Floriah, and record stores. COUP, the Maroon, university theater, DOC, MAB, and fraternities influence campus life. Eagerly anticipated social events include Kuviasuerk, Blues 'n Ribs, IM Basketball, and Scavenger Hunt. "Social life does not mean giant, inebriated, scam-fests at fraternity houses," reports the editor of the student newspaper. "Social life at the U of C means sitting with friends in a coffee shop, going to the North Side of Chicago to go dancing, and occasionally going to a fraternity or apartment party."
**Services and counseling/handicapped student services:** Placement services. Health service. Women's center. Counseling services for veteran students. Birth control, personal, and psychological counseling. Career and academic guidance services. Religious counseling. Physically disabled student services. Notetaking services. Reader services for the blind.
**Campus organizations:** Undergraduate student government. Student newspaper (Maroon, published twice/week). Literary magazine. Yearbook. Radio station. Choir, Collegium Musicum, orchestra, Gilbert and Sullivan group, theatre, debating, student-run snack shops, film societies, 150 organizations in all. Nine fraternities, seven chapter houses; two sororities, no chapter houses. 10% of men join a fraternity. 3% of women join a sorority.
**Religious organizations:** Korean-American Campus Ministry, Bahai, Buddhist, Catholic, Eastern Orthodox, Jewish, Muslim, and Protestant groups.
**Minority/foreign student organizations:** Numerous minority groups. Over 40 cultural groups.

**ATHLETICS. Physical education requirements:** Three terms of physical education required.
**Intercollegiate competition:** 40% of students participate. Baseball (M), basketball (M,W), cross-country (M,W), diving (M,W), fencing (M), football (M), soccer (M,W), softball (W), swimming (M,W), tennis (M,W), track (indoor) (M,W), track (outdoor)

(M,W), track and field (indoor) (M,W), track and field (outdoor) (M,W), volleyball (W), wrestling (M). Member of NCAA Division III, University Athletic Association.
**Intramural and club sports:** 70% of students participate. Intramural badminton, crew, cycling, fencing, gymnastics, handball, ice hockey, lacrosse, martial arts, rugby, sailing, squash, swimming, ultimate frisbee, volleyball. Men's club Alpine skiing, cheerleading, crew, cycling, gymnastics, ice hockey, lacrosse, martial arts, racquetball, rugby, sailing, squash, ultimate frisbee, volleyball, weight lifting. Women's club Alpine skiing, cheerleading, crew, cycling, fencing, gymnastics, lacrosse, martial arts, racquetball, sailing, squash, ultimate frisbee, weight lifting.

**ADMISSIONS. Academic basis for candidate selection** (in order of priority): Secondary school record, class rank, essay, school's recommendation, standardized test scores.
**Nonacademic basis for candidate selection:** Character and personality, extracurricular participation, and particular talent or ability are important.
**Requirements:** Graduation from secondary school is required; GED is accepted. 16 units and the following program of study are recommended: 4 units of English, 3 units of math, 3 units of science, 2 units of foreign language, 2 units of social studies, 2 units of history. Rank in top fifth of secondary school class recommended. SAT or ACT is required. Campus visit and interview recommended. Off-campus interviews available with an alumni representative.
**Procedure:** Take SAT or ACT by December of 12th year. Visit college for interview by March 2 of 12th year. Application deadline is January 15. Acceptance notification by early April. Reply is required by May 1. $200 nonrefundable tuition deposit. Freshmen accepted for fall term only.
**Special programs:** Admission may be deferred one year. Credit and/or placement may be granted through CEEB Advanced Placement exams for scores of 4 or higher. Credit and placement may be granted through challenge exams. Early decision program. In fall 1993, 511 applied for early decision and 386 were accepted. Deadline for applying for early decision is November 15. Early entrance/early admission program.
**Transfer students:** Transfer students accepted for fall term only. In fall 1993, 7% of all new students were transfers into all classes. 532 transfer applications were received, 132 were accepted. Application deadline is April 1 and May 1. Minimum 3.0 GPA required. Lowest course grade accepted is "C." At least 18 quarter units must be completed at the university to receive degree.
**Admissions contact:** Theodore A. O'Neill, M.A., Dean of Admissions. 312 702-8650.

**FINANCIAL AID. Available aid:** Pell grants, SEOG, state scholarships and grants, school scholarships and grants, private scholarships and grants, ROTC scholarships, academic merit scholarships, and aid for undergraduate foreign students. Perkins Loans (NDSL), PLUS, Stafford Loans (GSL), private loans, and SLS. Guaranteed tuition. Institutional payment plan.
**Financial aid statistics:** In 1993-94, 62% of all undergraduate applicants received aid; 68% of freshman applicants. Average amounts of aid awarded freshmen: Scholarships and grants, $10,700; loans, $2,450.
**Supporting data/closing dates:** FAFSA: Priority filing date is February 1. FAF: Deadline is February 1. School's own aid application: Priority filing date is February 1. Income tax forms: Accepted on rolling basis. Notification of awards begins April 1.
**Financial aid contact:** Alicia Reyes, Director of Financial Aid. 312 702-8666.

**STUDENT EMPLOYMENT.** College Work/Study Program. Institutional employment. 80% of full-time undergraduates work on campus during school year. Students may expect to earn an average of $2,200 during school year. Off-campus part-time employment opportunities rated "excellent."

**COMPUTER FACILITIES.** IBM/IBM-compatible, Macintosh/Apple, and RISC-/UNIX-based microcomputers. Students may access SUN minicomputer/mainframe systems, BITNET, Internet. Residence halls may be equipped with stand-alone microcomputers, networked microcomputers, networked terminals, modems. Client/LAN operating systems include Apple/Macintosh, DOS, UNIX/XENIX/AIX, X-windows. Computer languages and software packages include C, FORTRAN, LISP, Pascal. Computer facilities are available to all students.
**Fees:** None.
**Hours:** 24 hours; lab hours vary.

**GRADUATE CAREER DATA.** Graduate school percentages: 18% enter law school. 12% enter medical school. 7% enter graduate business programs. 54% enter graduate arts and sciences programs. Highest graduate school enrollments: New York U. Companies and businesses that hire graduates: Arthur Andersen, First Chicago.

**PROMINENT ALUMNI/AE.** Kurt Vonnegut, Jr. and Susan Sontag, authors; Katherine Graham, publisher, *Washington Post;* Carl Sagan, professor of astrophysics.

# University of Illinois at Chicago

**Chicago, IL 60680** **312 996-7000**

**1993-94 Costs.** Tuition: $2,262 (state residents), $6,456 (out-of-state). Room & board: $4,988. Fees, books, misc. academic expenses (school's estimate): $1,678.
**Enrollment.** Undergraduates: 6,564 men, 6,954 women (full-time). Freshman class: 8,384 applicants, 5,727 accepted, 2,710 enrolled. Graduate enrollment: 4,065 men, 4,671 women.
**Test score averages/ranges.** Average ACT scores: 20 English, 21 math, 21 composite. Range of ACT scores of middle 50%: 17-22 English, 18-23 math.
**Faculty.** 1,004 full-time; 213 part-time. 82% of faculty holds highest degree in specific field. Student/faculty ratio: 13 to 1.
**Selectivity rating.** Competitive.

**PROFILE.** The University of Illinois at Chicago was formed by the 1982 consolidation of two campuses: the University of Illinois at the Medical Center and the University of Illinois at Chicago Circle. Programs are offered through the Colleges of Architecture, Art, and Urban Planning; Associated Health Professionals; Business Administration; Education; Engineering; Health, Physical Education, and Recreation; Liberal Arts and Sciences; Nursing; and Social Work. Its 183-acre campus is located close to Chicago's business district.

**Accreditation:** NCACS. Professionally accredited by the Accreditation Board for Engineering and Technology, the American Assembly of Collegiate Schools of Business, the American Council on Pharmaceutical Education, the American Dental Association, the American Dietetic Association, the American Medical Association (CAHEA), the American Physical Therapy Association, the American Psychological Association, the Council on Education for Public Health, the Council on Social Work Education, the National Architecture Accrediting Board, the National Association of Schools of Art and Design, the National League for Nursing.
**Religious orientation:** University of Illinois at Chicago is nonsectarian; no religious requirements.
**Library:** Collections totaling over 1,782,637 volumes, 21,119 periodical subscriptions, and 2,112,590 microform items.
**Special facilities/museums:** Museum, integrated systems lab, center for research in criminal justice, energy resources center, urban systems lab, Jane Addams' Hull House, James Woodworth prairie preserve, convention/sports/entertainment center.
**Athletic facilities:** Handball, squash, racquetball, and tennis courts, stadium, swimming pool, training and weight rooms, baseball, soccer, and softball fields, all-weather track, gymnasiums, ice rink.

**STUDENT BODY. Undergraduate profile:** 95% are state residents; 44% are transfers. 18% Asian-American, 11% Black, 16% Hispanic, .3% Native American, 50% White, 4.7% Other. Average age of undergraduates is 22.
**Freshman profile:** 1% of freshmen who took ACT scored 30 or over on English, 3% scored 30 or over on math, 2% scored 30 or over on composite; 18% scored 24 or over on English, 23% scored 24 or over on math, 23% scored 24 or over on composite; 62% scored 18 or over on English, 68% scored 18 or over on math, 83% scored 18 or over on composite; 88% scored 12 or over on English, 89% scored 12 or over on math, 100% scored 12 or over on composite. Majority of accepted applicants took ACT. 60% of freshmen come from public schools.
**Undergraduate achievement:** 70% of fall 1992 freshmen returned for fall 1993 term. 11% of entering class graduated. 24% of students who completed a degree program went on to graduate study within one year.
**Foreign students:** 334 students are from out of the country. Countries represented include Canada, Greece, Hong Kong, Japan, Korea, and Pakistan; 49 in all.

**PROGRAMS OF STUDY. Degrees:** B.A., B.Arch., B.F.A., B.S., B.Soc.Work.
**Majors:** Accounting, Afro-American Studies, Anthropology, Architectural Studies, Architecture, Art Education, Biochemistry, Bioengineering, Biological Sciences, Business Administration, Chemical Engineering, Chemistry, Civil Engineering, Classical Civilization, Classical Languages/Literature, Communication/Theatre, Computer Engineering, Computer Science, Computer Science/Engineering, Criminal Justice, Dentistry, Design, Economics, Electrical Engineering, Elementary Education, Engineering, Engineering Management, Engineering Physics, English/American Literature, English Education, Finance, Foreign Languages Education, French, French Business Studies, Geography, Geological Sciences, German, Graphic Design, Health Information Management, History, History of Architecture/Art, Individual Plans of Study, Industrial Design, Industrial Engineering, Information/Decision Sciences, Italian, Judaic Studies, Kinesiology, Latin American Studies, Management, Marketing, Materials Science/Engineering, Mathematics, Mathematics/Computer Science, Mathematics Education, Mechanical Engineering, Medical Laboratory Sciences, Metallurgical Engineering, Music, Nursing, Nutrition/Medical Dietetics, Occupational Therapy, Pharmacy, Philosophy, Photography/Film/Electronic Media, Physical Therapy, Physics, Polish, Political Science, Psychology, Russian, Science Education, Secondary Education, Social Studies Education, Social Work, Sociology, Spanish, Statistics/Operation Research, Studio Arts.
**Distribution of degrees:** The majors with the highest enrollment are accounting, psychology, and biological sciences; Judaic studies, Italian, and geography have the lowest.
**Requirements:** General education requirement.
**Academic regulations:** Minimum 3.0 GPA must be maintained (on a 5.0 scale).
**Special:** Minors offered in most majors. Self-designed majors. Double majors. Independent study. Accelerated study. Pass/fail grading option. Internships. Cooperative education programs. Graduate school at which undergraduates may take graduate-level courses. Preprofessional programs in law, medicine, veterinary science, pharmacy, dentistry, health information management, medical lab sciences, nursing, nutrition, occupational therapy, physical therapy, and social work. 3-2 engineering programs. Cross-registration at other U of Illinois campuses and at City Colleges of Chicago. Exchange program with Tuskegee Inst. Teacher certification in elementary and secondary education. Certification in specific subject areas. Study abroad in Austria, Canada, France, Italy, Latin American countries, Mexico, Spain, and other countries. ROTC. NROTC and AFROTC at Illinois Inst of Tech.
**Honors:** Phi Beta Kappa. Honors program. Honor societies.
**Academic Assistance:** Remedial reading, writing, math, and study skills. Nonremedial tutoring.

**STUDENT LIFE. Housing:** Students may live on or off campus. Coed dorms. School-owned/operated apartments. 10% of students live in college housing.
**Social atmosphere:** Hot spots are Hawkeye's, Dugan's, Inner Circle, and Cousin's. Greeks influence student life. Hockey games and Tailgate parties are popular social/sports events. Students take advantage of all that Chicago has to offer.
**Services and counseling/handicapped student services:** Placement services. Health service. Women's center. Day care. Educational Assistance Program, Student Legal Service. Counseling services for minority, military, and veteran students. Birth control, personal, and psychological counseling. Career and academic guidance services. Physically disabled student services. Learning disabled services. Notetaking services. Tape recorders. Tutors. Reader services for the blind.
**Campus organizations:** Undergraduate student government. Student newspaper (Chicago Flames; UIC News, both published once/week). Literary magazine. UIC Jazz Festival, UIC Blues Concert, Cultural Festival, Monthly Fine Arts Series, 148 organizations in all. Eight fraternities, no chapter houses; five sororities, no chapter houses. 2% of men join a fraternity. 2% of women join a sorority.
**Religious organizations:** Religious groups.

**Minority/foreign student organizations:** Minority student groups. Foreign student groups.

**ATHLETICS. Physical education requirements:** None.

**Intercollegiate competition:** 1% of students participate. Baseball (M), basketball (M,W), cheerleading (M,W), cross-country (M,W), diving (M,W), gymnastics (M,W), ice hockey (M), soccer (M), softball (W), swimming (M,W), tennis (M,W), volleyball (W). Member of Central Collegiate Hockey Association, Mid-Continent Conference, NCAA Division I.

**Intramural and club sports:** 3% of students participate. Intramural badminton, basketball, football, racquetball, softball, tennis, volleyball, wrestling. Men's club rugby, volleyball.

**ADMISSIONS. Academic basis for candidate selection** (in order of priority): Class rank, standardized test scores, secondary school record, school's recommendation, essay.

**Nonacademic basis for candidate selection:** Particular talent or ability is important. Geographical distribution is considered.

**Requirements:** Graduation from secondary school is required; GED is accepted. 16 units and the following program of study are required: 4 units of English, 3 units of math, 3 units of lab science, 2 units of social studies, 1 unit of history, 3 units of electives including 1 unit of academic electives. Rank in top 70% of secondary school class required; 2 units of foreign language recommended. Specific subject recommendations may vary for individual colleges. Educational Assistance Program (EAP), African American Academic Network, Latin American Recruitment/Educational Services, Native American Support Program, and Center for Academic Potential for applicants not normally admissible. ACT is required; SAT may be substituted. Campus visit recommended. No off-campus interviews.

**Procedure:** Take SAT or ACT by fall of 12th year. Suggest filing application by February 28. Application deadline is June 17. Notification of admission on rolling basis. $125 room deposit, refundable until late May (fall) and mid-November (spring). Freshmen accepted for terms other than fall.

**Special programs:** Credit and/or placement may be granted through CEEB Advanced Placement exams for scores of 3 or higher. Credit may be granted through CLEP general and subject exams, and military experience. Credit and placement may be granted through challenge exams. Early entrance/early admission program. Concurrent enrollment program.

**Transfer students:** Transfer students accepted for terms other than fall. In fall 1993, 44% of all new students were transfers into all classes. 6,943 transfer applications were received, 3,729 were accepted. Application deadline is February 28 for fall; November 1 for spring. Minimum 2.0 GPA required. Lowest course grade accepted is "C." At least 60 semester hours must be completed at the university to receive degree.

**Admissions contact:** Marilyn Fiduccia, Ph.D., Director of Admissions. 312 996-4350.

**FINANCIAL AID. Available aid:** Pell grants, SEOG, Federal Nursing Student Scholarships, state scholarships and grants, school scholarships and grants, private scholarships and grants, ROTC scholarships, academic merit scholarships, and athletic scholarships. Perkins Loans (NDSL), PLUS, Stafford Loans (GSL), NSL, Health Professions Loans, state loans, school loans, and SLS.

**Financial aid statistics:** 30% of aid is not need-based.

**Supporting data/closing dates:** FAFSA: Priority filing date is March 1. School's own aid application: Priority filing date is March 1. Notification of awards on rolling basis.

**Financial aid contact:** Marsha Weiss, Director of Financial Aid. 312 996-3126.

**STUDENT EMPLOYMENT.** College Work/Study Program. Institutional employment. 21% of full-time undergraduates work on campus during school year. Students may expect to earn an average of $1,994 during school year. Off-campus part-time employment opportunities rated "good."

**COMPUTER FACILITIES.** 500 IBM/IBM-compatible, Macintosh/Apple, and RISC-/UNIX-based microcomputers. Students may access IBM minicomputer/mainframe systems, Internet. Residence halls may be equipped with networked microcomputers, networked terminals, modems. Client/LAN operating systems include Apple/Macintosh, DOS, OS/2, UNIX/XENIX/AIX, DEC, Microsoft, Novell. Computer languages and software packages include seven computer languages and 31 software programs. Computer facilities are available to all students.

**Hours:** 24 hours.

**GRADUATE CAREER DATA.** Graduate school percentages: 5% enter law school. 11% enter medical school. 2% enter dental school. 24% enter graduate business programs. 37% enter graduate arts and sciences programs. 59% of graduates choose careers in business and industry. Companies and businesses that hire graduates: Amoco, Baxter, Motorola.

**PROMINENT ALUMNI/AE.** Alfred B. Swanson, M.D., developed silicon implants to replace arthritic joints; Emo Philips, comedian; Ramsey Lewis, jazz pianist; Bob Thall, landscape photographer; Carol Mosely Braun, U.S. Senator; James Thompson, former governor of Illinois; Leo Malamed, former director and special counsel to Chicago Mercantile Exchange.

# University of Illinois at Urbana-Champaign

**Urbana, IL 61801** **217 333-1000**

**1993-94 Costs.** Tuition: $2,486 (state residents), $6,738 (out-of-state). Room & board: $4,358. Fees, books, misc. academic expenses (school's estimate): $1,420.

**Enrollment.** Undergraduates: 14,204 men, 11,218 women (full-time). Freshman class: 14,939 applicants, 11,652 accepted, 5,692 enrolled. Graduate enrollment: 5,973 men, 4,130 women.

**Test score averages/ranges.** Average SAT scores: 521 verbal, 616 math. Range of SAT scores of middle 50%: 470-590 verbal, 550-690 math. Average ACT scores: 26 English, 27 math, 27 composite.

**Faculty.** 2,095 full-time; 63 part-time. 92% of faculty holds doctoral degree. Student/faculty ratio: 12 to 1.

**Selectivity rating.** Highly competitive.

**PROFILE.** The University of Illinois at Urbana-Champaign, founded in 1867, is a public, comprehensive institution. Programs are offered through the Colleges of Agriculture, Applied Life Sciences, Commerce and Business Administration, Communications, Education, Engineering, Fine and Applied Arts, and Liberal Arts and Sciences; the Institute of Aviation; the Graduate School of Library and Information Science; and the School of Social Work. Its 705-acre campus is located in the Urbana-Champaign metropolitan area, 130 miles south of Chicago.

**Accreditation:** NCACS. Professionally accredited by the Accreditation Board for Engineering and Technology, the Accrediting Council on Education in Journalism and Mass Communication, the American Assembly of Collegiate Schools of Business, the American Dietetic Association, the American Home Economics Association, the American Psychological Association, the American Society of Landscape Architects, the American Speech-Language-Hearing Association, the American Veterinary Medical Association, the Council on Education for Public Health, the Council on Social Work Education, the National Architecture Accrediting Board, the National Association of Schools of Art and Design, the National Association of Schools of Dance, the National Association of Schools of Music, the National Council for Accreditation of Teacher Education, the National Recreation and Park Association, the Society of American Foresters.

**Religious orientation:** University of Illinois at Urbana-Champaign is nonsectarian; no religious requirements.

**Library:** Collections totaling over 8,096,000 volumes, and 93,850 periodical subscriptions.

**Special facilities/museums:** Art and natural history museums, performing arts center, national center for supercomputing applications.

**Athletic facilities:** Gymnasiums, field house, stadium, swimming pool, athletic fields, basketball, racquetball, squash, tennis, and volleyball courts, weight rooms.

**STUDENT BODY. Undergraduate profile:** 92% are state residents; 18% are transfers. 12% Asian-American, 7% Black, 5.3% Hispanic, .2% Native American, 73.9% White, 1.6% Other. Average age of undergraduates is 20.

**Freshman profile:** 34% of accepted applicants took SAT; 66% took ACT. 78% of freshmen come from public schools.

**Undergraduate achievement:** 52% of entering class graduated. 40% of students who completed a degree program went on to graduate study within one year.

**Foreign students:** 431 students are from out of the country. Countries represented include Austria, Germany, Hong Kong, Japan, Korea, and the United Kingdom; 57 in all.

**PROGRAMS OF STUDY. Degrees:** A.B., B.A.Urb.Plan., B.Arch., B.F.A., B.Land.Arch., B.Mus., B.S., B.Soc.Work, B.Vet.Med.

**Majors:** Accountancy, Actuarial Science, Advertising, Aeronautical/Astronautical Engineering, Agricultural Communications, Agricultural Core Curriculum, Agricultural Economics, Agricultural Education, Agricultural Engineering, Agricultural Mechanization, Agricultural Sciences, Agriculture, Agronomy, Aircraft Maintenance Technology, American Civilization, Animal Sciences, Anthropology, Architectural Studies, Art Education, Asian Studies, Astronomy, Audiology, Biochemistry, Bioengineering, Biology, Biology Education, Biophysics, Business Administration, Business Education, Business/Finance/Investments, Cell and Structural Biology, Ceramic Engineering, Chemical Engineering, Chemistry, Chemistry Education, Child and Family Welfare, Cinema Studies, Civil Engineering, Classics, Comparative Literature, Computer Engineering, Computer Science, Computer Science Education, Consumer Economics, Crafts, Curriculum/Instruction, Dance, Dietetics, Early Childhood Education, Earth Science Education, Ecology/Ethology/Evolution, Economics, Education, Education (General), Education of Persons with Moderate to Severe Disabilities, Electrical Engineering, Elementary Education, Engineering, Engineering Mechanics, Engineering Physics, English, English Education, Entomology, Entrepreneurship, Finance, Food/Agribusiness Management, Food in Business, Food Industry, Food Science, Foods/Nutrition, Forestry, French, French Education, Geography, Geology, German Education, German Language/Literature, Gerontology/Social Work, Graphic Design, Health Education/Health Promotion, Health Planning/Administration, Health/Rehabilitation, Hearing Science, History, History of Art, History/Philosophy of Science, Home Economics, Horticulture, Human Development/Family Studies, Industrial Design, Industrial Distribution Management, Industrial Engineering, Instrumental Music, Insurance/Risk Management, Italian, Journalism, Juvenile Delinquency/Criminal Justice/Social Work, Kinesiology, Landscape Architecture, Language Science Pathology, Latin American Studies, Leisure Studies, Linguistics, Management Information Systems, Management Science, Manufacturing Engineering, Marketing, Marketing Textiles/Apparels, Materials Science/Engineering, Mathematics, Mathematics/Computer Science, Mathematics Education, Mechanical Engineering, Medieval Civilization, Mental Health/Social Work, Metallurgical Engineering, Microbiology, Music, Music Composition, Music Education, Music History, News Editorial/Broadcast, News Editorial-Media Studies, Nuclear Engineering, Organization Administration, Ornamental Horticulture, Painting, Performance Studies, Philosophy, Photography, Physics, Physics Education, Physiology, Plant Biology, Political Science, Polymer Science/Engineering, Portuguese, Production/Commerce/Business Administration, Professional Pilot, Professional Studio in Acting, Professional Studio in Design/Technology, Psychology, Real Estate/Urban Economics, Religious Studies, Renaissance Studies, Restaurant Management, Rhetoric, Russian, Russian/East European Studies, Russian Education, Sculpture, Secondary Education/English, Secondary Education/Life Science, Secondary Education/Mathematics, Secondary Education/Physical Science, Secondary Education/Social Science, Secondary General Science Education, Social Studies Education, Social Work, Sociology, Soil Science, Spanish, Spanish Education, Speech Communication, Speech Education, Speech/Hearing Science, Speech Science, Statistics, Statistics/Computer Science, Substance Abuse/Social Work, Technical Education, Textiles/Apparel, Urban Regional Analysis/Planning, Vocational Consumer Home Economics Education, Voice.

**Distribution of degrees:** The majors with the highest enrollment are biology, psychology, and accountancy; secondary general science education has the lowest.

**Requirements:** General education requirement.

**Academic regulations:** Minimum 3.0 GPA must be maintained (on a 5.0 scale).

**Special:** International minor in engineering. Certificate programs in aviation. Special studies offered. Programs offered in arms control, disarmament, international security, and women's studies. Self-designed majors. Double majors. Dual degrees. Independent study. Accelerated study. Pass/fail grading option. Internships. Cooperative education programs. Graduate school at which undergraduates may take graduate-level courses. Preprofessional programs in medicine, veterinary science, pharmacy, dentistry, health information management, medical lab sciences, nursing, nutrition and medical dietetics, occupational therapy, and physical therapy. Five-year B.S. in engineering/B.S. or B.A. in liberal arts and sciences. Host university of 3-2 engineering program. Five-year B.S. in liberal arts and masters in business administration. Member of Committee on Institutional Cooperation and Midwest University Consortium for International Activities. Semester-away programs possible. Exchange programs with 30 colleges and universities. Teacher certification in early childhood, elementary, secondary, special education, and vo-tech education. Certification in specific subject areas. Study abroad programs in many countries. ROTC, NROTC, and AFROTC.

**Honors:** Phi Beta Kappa. Honors program. Honor societies.

**Academic Assistance:** Remedial reading, writing, math, and study skills. Nonremedial tutoring.

**STUDENT LIFE. Housing:** All freshmen must live in university-approved housing. Coed, women's, and men's dorms. Sorority and fraternity housing. School-owned/operated apartments. Off-campus privately-owned housing. Both on-campus and off-campus married-student housing. 32% of students live in college housing.

**Social atmosphere:** As reported by the student newspaper, "Greeks seem to dominate much of the scene but our school is big enough that there's something for everyone. The local music scene is pretty happening, though it doesn't receive enough support to be overflowing with new bands." On campus, students gather in campus bars, fraternity houses, the Illini Union, and the library. Popular school-year events include football and basketball games, Homecoming, Moms' and Dads' Days, and concerts.

**Services and counseling/handicapped student services:** Placement services. Health service. Women's center. Counseling services for minority, military, and veteran students. Birth control, personal, and psychological counseling. Career and academic guidance services. Physically disabled student services. Learning disabled services. Notetaking services. Tape recorders. Reader services for the blind.

**Campus organizations:** Undergraduate student government. Student newspaper (Daily Illini). Yearbook. Radio and TV stations. 700 registered organizations. 56 fraternities, 50 chapter houses; 28 sororities, 23 chapter houses. 22% of men join a fraternity. 26% of women join a sorority.

**Minority/foreign student organizations:** Black Greek Council, Caribbean Students United, Indian Student Association, Latino Peer Retention Program, United Colors, numerous other minority student groups.

**ATHLETICS. Physical education requirements:** None.

**Intercollegiate competition:** 2% of students participate. Baseball (M), basketball (M,W), cheerleading (M,W), cross-country (M,W), diving (M,W), fencing (M), football (M), golf (M,W), gymnastics (M,W), swimming (M,W), tennis (M,W), track (indoor) (M,W), track (outdoor) (M,W), track and field (indoor) (M,W), track and field (outdoor) (M,W), volleyball (W), wrestling (M). Member of Big 10 Conference, NCAA Division I.

**Intramural and club sports:** 28% of students participate. Intramural badminton, basketball, broomball, flag football, golf, ice hockey, racquetball, soccer, softball, swimming, table tennis, tennis, volleyball, water polo, wrestling. Men's club Alpine skiing, archery, cycling, fencing, gymnastics, ice hockey, lacrosse, martial arts, racquetball, rugby, sailing, scuba, soccer, table tennis, volleyball, water polo, wrestling. Women's club Alpine skiing, cycling, ice hockey, martial arts, racquetball, rugby, sailing, soccer, softball, ultimate frisbee, volleyball.

**ADMISSIONS. Academic basis for candidate selection** (in order of priority): Secondary school record, class rank, standardized test scores, essay, school's recommendation.

**Nonacademic basis for candidate selection:** Particular talent or ability and geographical distribution are considered.

**Requirements:** Graduation from secondary school is required; GED is accepted. 15 units and the following program of study are required: 4 units of English, 3 units of math, 2 units of lab science, 2 units of foreign language, 2 units of social studies, 2 units of academic electives. Professional interest statement recommended for some programs. Portfolio required of art program applicants. Audition required of music program applicants. EOP for applicants not normally admissible. SAT or ACT is required. Campus visit recommended. No off-campus interviews.

**Procedure:** Take SAT or ACT by June of 12th year. Suggest filing application by November 15. Application deadline is January 1. Notification of admission is sent on modified rolling basis. Reply is required by May 1. $100 room deposit, refundable partially. Freshmen accepted for terms other than fall.

**Special programs:** Admission may be deferred one year. Credit and/or placement may be granted through CEEB Advanced Placement exams for scores of 3 or higher. Credit and/or placement may be granted through CLEP general exams. Credit may be granted through CLEP subject exams and military experience. Credit and placement may be granted through challenge exams. Early entrance/early admission program. Concurrent enrollment program.

**Transfer students:** Transfer students accepted for terms other than fall. In fall 1993, 18% of all new students were transfers into all classes. 2,751 transfer applications were received, 1,645 were accepted. Application deadline is March 15 for fall; November 1 for spring. Minimum 3.25 GPA required. Lowest course grade accepted is "D." Maximum number of transferable credits is 60 semester hours from a two-year school and 90 semester hours from a four-year school. At least 30 semester hours must be completed at the university to receive degree.

**Admissions contact:** Patricia E. Askew, M.B.A., Director of Admissions and Records. 217 333-0302.

**FINANCIAL AID. Available aid:** Pell grants, SEOG, Federal Nursing Student Scholarships, state scholarships and grants, school scholarships and grants, private scholarships and grants, ROTC scholarships, academic merit scholarships, and athletic scholarships. Perkins Loans (NDSL), PLUS, Stafford Loans (GSL), NSL, state loans, school loans, private loans, and SLS. Three equal payments over semester.

**Financial aid statistics:** 60% of aid is not need-based. In 1993-94, 84% of all undergraduate applicants received aid; 78% of freshman applicants. Average amounts of aid awarded freshmen: Scholarships and grants, $1,750; loans, $2,500.

**Supporting data/closing dates:** FAFSA: Priority filing date is March 15. School's own aid application. Notification of awards begins May 15.

**Financial aid contact:** Orlo Austin, Ph.D., Director of Financial Aid. 217 333-0100.

**STUDENT EMPLOYMENT.** College Work/Study Program. Institutional employment. 45% of full-time undergraduates work on campus during school year. Students may expect to earn an average of $1,194 during school year. Off-campus part-time employment opportunities rated "good."

**COMPUTER FACILITIES.** 13,500 IBM/IBM-compatible, Macintosh/Apple, and RISC-/UNIX-based microcomputers; 11,000 are networked. Students may access Sequent, SUN minicomputer/mainframe systems, BITNET, Internet. Residence halls may be equipped with stand-alone microcomputers, networked microcomputers, modems. Client/LAN operating systems include Apple/Macintosh, DOS, OS/2, UNIX/XENIX/AIX, X-windows, LocalTalk/AppleTalk, Novell. Computer languages and software packages include all major languages and database, graphics, spreadsheet, word processing packages. Computer facilities are available to all students.

**Fees:** Computer fee is included in tuition/fees.

**Hours:** 24 hours.

**GRADUATE CAREER DATA.** 42% of graduates choose careers in business and industry. Companies and businesses that hire graduates: Amoco, Dow Chemical, Eli Lilly, General Mills, Kraft Foods.

**PROMINENT ALUMNI/AE.** Arnold O. Beckman, inventor and founder, Beckman Instruments; Rosalyn S. Yalow, Nobel Prize-winner for medicine; Roger Ebert, film critic.

# VanderCook College of Music

**Chicago, IL 60616** — **312 225-6288**

**1993-94 Costs.** Tuition: $8,930. Room & board: $4,600. Fees, books, misc. academic expenses (school's estimate): $750.

**Enrollment.** Undergraduates: 45 men, 40 women (full-time). Freshman class: 43 applicants, 31 accepted, 19 enrolled. Graduate enrollment: 47 men, 39 women.

**Test score averages/ranges.** Average SAT scores: 900 combined. Average ACT scores: 21 composite.

**Faculty.** 11 full-time; 29 part-time. 30% of faculty holds doctoral degree. Student/faculty ratio: 6 to 1.

**Selectivity rating.** Less competitive.

**PROFILE.** VanderCook, founded in 1909, is a private college of music education. Its two-acre campus is located in Chicago, three miles south of the Loop area.

**Accreditation:** NCACS. Professionally accredited by the National Association of Schools of Music.

**Religious orientation:** VanderCook College of Music is nonsectarian; no religious requirements.

**Library:** Collections totaling over 17,000 volumes and 80 periodical subscriptions.

**Athletic facilities:** Gymnasium, swimming pool, bowling lane, baseball field, tennis courts.

**STUDENT BODY. Undergraduate profile:** 80% are state residents; 15% are transfers. 26% Black, 2% Hispanic, 72% White. Average age of undergraduates is 21.

**Freshman profile:** Majority of accepted applicants took ACT. 80% of freshmen come from public schools.

**Undergraduate achievement:** 90% of fall 1992 freshmen returned for fall 1993 term. 54% of entering class graduated. 5% of students who completed a degree program immediately went on to graduate study.

**PROGRAMS OF STUDY. Degrees:** B.M.Ed.

**Majors:** Music Education/Instrumental, Music Education/Vocal.

**Requirements:** General education requirement.

**Academic regulations:** Minimum 2.0 GPA must be maintained.

**Special:** Independent study. Pass/fail grading option. Teacher certification in elementary and secondary education. Certification in specific subject areas.

**ADMISSIONS. Academic basis for candidate selection** (in order of priority): School's recommendation, secondary school record, class rank, essay, standardized test scores.

**Nonacademic basis for candidate selection:** Extracurricular participation and particular talent or ability are emphasized. Character and personality and alumni/ae relationship are considered.

**Requirements:** Graduation from secondary school is required; GED is accepted. No specific distribution of secondary school units required. Rank in top half of secondary school class and minimum 2.0 GPA required. Audition required of music program applicants. Conditional admission possible for applicants not meeting standard requirements. SAT or ACT is required. Campus visit recommended. Off-campus interviews available with admissions and alumni representatives.

**Procedure:** Take SAT or ACT by February 1 of 12th year. Visit college for interview by March 1 of 12th year. Application deadline is June 1. Notification of admission on rolling basis. Reply is required by May 1 or July 1. $400 nonrefundable tuition deposit. $150 nonrefundable room deposit. Freshmen accepted for terms other than fall.

**Special programs:** Admission may be deferred one year. Credit may be granted through CEEB Advanced Placement. Credit may be granted through CLEP general and subject exams, Regents College, ACT PEP, and DANTES exams, and military experience. Credit and placement may be granted through challenge exams. Early decision program. In fall 1993, five applied for early decision and three were accepted. Deadline for applying for early decision is December 1.

**Transfer students:** Transfer students accepted for terms other than fall. In fall 1993, 15% of all new students were transfers into all classes. 4 transfer applications were received, 4 were accepted. Application deadline is June 1 for fall; October 1 for spring. Minimum 2.0 GPA required. Lowest course grade accepted is "C." At least 30 semester hours must be completed at the college to receive degree.

**FINANCIAL AID. Available aid:** Pell grants, state scholarships and grants, school scholarships and grants, private scholarships and grants, and academic merit scholarships. PLUS, Stafford Loans (GSL), private loans, and SLS. Tuition Management Systems.

**Financial aid statistics:** In 1993-94, 100% of all undergraduate applicants received aid; 100% of freshman applicants. Average amounts of aid awarded freshmen: Scholarships and grants, $2,000.
**Supporting data/closing dates:** FAFSA: Accepted on rolling basis. Income tax forms. Notification of awards on rolling basis.
**Financial aid contact:** Ralph Mastro, M.B.A., Director of Financial Aid. 312 225-6288.

## Western Illinois University

**Macomb, IL 61455 309 295-1414**

**1994-95 Costs.** Tuition: $1,902 (state residents), $5,706 (out-of-state). Room & board: $3,193. Fees, books, misc. academic expenses (school's estimate): $1,305.
**Enrollment.** Undergraduates: 4,806 men, 4,209 women (full-time). Freshman class: 6,491 applicants, 5,027 accepted, 1,563 enrolled. Graduate enrollment: 954 men, 1,459 women.
**Test score averages/ranges.** Average ACT scores: 20 English, 20 math, 20 composite. Range of ACT scores of middle 50%: 20-21 English, 19-20 math.
**Faculty.** 658 full-time; 45 part-time. 65% of faculty holds doctoral degree. Student/faculty ratio: 18 to 1.
**Selectivity rating.** Competitive.

**PROFILE.** Western Illinois, founded in 1899, is a public, multipurpose university. Programs are offered through the Colleges of Applied Sciences; Arts and Sciences; Business; Education; Fine Arts; and Health, Physical Education, and Recreation and the Schools of Continuing Education and Graduate Studies. Its 1,050-acre campus is located in Macomb, 70 miles west of Peoria.

**Accreditation:** NCACS. Professionally accredited by the American Assembly of Collegiate Schools of Business, the National Council for Accreditation of Teacher Education.
**Religious orientation:** Western Illinois University is nonsectarian; no religious requirements.
**Library:** Collections totaling over 672,000 volumes, 200,000 periodical subscriptions, and 3,600 microform items.
**Special facilities/museums:** History museum, art gallery, on-campus elementary school, electron microscope.
**Athletic facilities:** Gymnasiums, field house, swimming pools, basketball, tennis, and volleyball courts, weight rooms, track, baseball, football, soccer, and softball fields.

**STUDENT BODY. Undergraduate profile:** 98% are state residents; 47% are transfers. 1% Asian-American, 8.1% Black, 2.1% Hispanic, .3% Native American, 81.4% White, 7.1% Other. Average age of undergraduates is 21.
**Freshman profile:** Majority of accepted applicants took ACT. 85% of freshmen come from public schools.
**Undergraduate achievement:** 68% of fall 1992 freshmen returned for fall 1993 term. 24% of entering class graduated. 23% of students who completed a degree program went on to graduate study within one year.
**Foreign students:** 268 students are from out of the country. Countries represented include Indonesia, Japan, Korea, Malaysia, and Thailand; 44 in all.

**PROGRAMS OF STUDY. Degrees:** B.A., B.Bus., B.F.A., B.S., B.Soc.Work.
**Majors:** Accounting, Agriculture, Applied Mathematics/Computer Science, Art, Bilingual/Bicultural Education, Biology, Board of Governors, Chemistry, Communication Arts/Sciences, Communication Sciences/Disorders, Computer Science, Economics, Education, Elementary Education, Engineering Technology, English, Finance, French, Geography, Geology, Health Science, History, Home Economics, Human Resource Management, Industrial Education, Industrial Technology, Information Management, Journalism, Kaskaskia, Law Enforcement, Management, Manufacturing, Marketing, Mathematics, Medical Technology, Music, Philosophy, Photography/Advertising Design, Photography/Media, Physical Education, Physics, Political Science, Psychology, Recreation/Park Administration, Social Work, Sociology, Spanish, Special Education, Theatre.
**Distribution of degrees:** The majors with the highest enrollment are law enforcement, recreation/park administration, and communications arts/sciences; industrial education has the lowest.
**Requirements:** General education requirement.
**Academic regulations:** Freshmen must maintain minimum 1.75 GPA; sophomores, 1.85 GPA; juniors, 2.0 GPA; seniors, 2.0 GPA.
**Special:** Minors offered in all majors. Self-designed majors. Double majors. Dual degrees. Independent study. Accelerated study. Pass/fail grading option. Internships. Cooperative education programs. Graduate school at which undergraduates may take graduate-level courses. Preprofessional programs in law, medicine, veterinary science, pharmacy, dentistry, optometry, agricultural engineering, architecture, chemical engineering, engineering, forestry, and nursing. 3-2 engineering program with U of Illinois. Teacher certification in early childhood, elementary, secondary, and special education. Study abroad in Germany, Spain, and the United Kingdom. ROTC.
**Honors:** Honors program.
**Academic Assistance:** Remedial reading, writing, and math.

**STUDENT LIFE. Housing:** All freshmen and sophomores must live on campus unless living with family. Coed, women's, and men's dorms. Sorority and fraternity housing. On-campus married-student housing. 47% of students live in college housing.
**Social atmosphere:** As reported by the student newspaper, "Sometimes WIU is wrongly termed a party school because of the high number of bars and parties. Actually, students socialize more because we are in a rural area and the only social spots are bars and parties. During the weekdays the University Union is the most traveled and popular spot on campus. On the weekends students frequent a number of bars or go to the movies. Since Macomb is a rural town with no city nearby, the cultural life is sometimes limited. For this reason students tend to socialize more often and the Greek system is highly popular."
**Services and counseling/handicapped student services:** Placement services. Health service. Women's center. Counseling services for minority, military, veteran, and older students. Psychological counseling. Career and academic guidance services. Physically disabled student services. Learning disabled services. Notetaking services. Reader services for the blind.
**Campus organizations:** Undergraduate student government. Student newspaper. Yearbook. Radio and TV stations. Swing choir, chorus, men's and women's glee clubs, orchestra, wind and percussion ensembles, woodwind quintet, university and marching bands, music theatre, jazz band, debating, service and special-interest groups. 20 fraternities, 15 chapter houses; 11 sororities, seven chapter houses. 10% of men join a fraternity. 5% of women join a sorority.
**Religious organizations:** Ambassadors for Christ, B'nai B'rith Hillel, Navigators, Baptist Student Union, Campus Crusade for Christ, Intervarsity Christian Fellowship, Latter-Day Saints Fellowship, Lutheran Student Center, Moslem Student Association, Mount Calvary Christian Youth, New Life Fellowship, Newman Center, Wesley Foundation.

**ATHLETICS. Physical education requirements:** None.
**Intercollegiate competition:** 25% of students participate. Baseball (M), basketball (M,W), cross-country (M,W), diving (M,W), football (M), golf (M), soccer (M), softball (W), swimming (M,W), tennis (M,W), track (indoor) (M,W), track (outdoor) (M,W), track and field (indoor) (M,W), track and field (outdoor) (M,W), volleyball (W). Member of Gateway Collegiate Conference, Mid-Continent Conference, NCAA Division I, NCAA Division I-AA for football.
**Intramural and club sports:** 75% of students participate. Intramural archery, badminton, basketball, billiards, bowling, cross-country, cycling, decathlon, eightball, fishing derby, fitness day, football, free throw, frisbee golf, golf, hole-in-one, indoor track, pentathlon, pickleball, putt-putt golf, racquetball, relays, rifle, skeet shooting, soccer, softball, swimming, table tennis, target shooting, team handball, tennis, track, tug-of-war, volleyball, weight lifting, wrestling. Men's club lacrosse, martial arts, rugby, scuba, volleyball, weight lifting. Women's club lacrosse, martial arts, rugby, scuba, soccer, volleyball, weight lifting.

**ADMISSIONS. Academic basis for candidate selection** (in order of priority): Class rank, standardized test scores, secondary school record.
**Requirements:** Graduation from secondary school is required; GED is accepted. 15 units and the following program of study are required: 4 units of English, 3 units of math, 3 units of lab science, 3 units of social studies, 2 units of electives. An additional 2 units of foreign language recommended. Minimum combined SAT score of 910 (composite ACT score of 22) or minimum combined SAT score of 720 (composite ACT score of 18) and rank in top half of secondary school class required. Academic Services Program gives special admission consideration for applicants not normally admissible. ACT is required; SAT may be substituted. ACH recommended. Campus visit and interview recommended. Off-campus interviews available with an admissions representative.
**Procedure:** Take SAT or ACT by June of 12th year. Take ACH by June of 12th year. Visit college for interview by June of 12th year. Suggest filing application by June. Notification of admission on rolling basis. $50 room deposit, refundable until July 1. Freshmen accepted for terms other than fall.
**Special programs:** Admission may be deferred one year. Credit may be granted through CLEP general and subject exams, ACT PEP, DANTES, and challenge exams, and military experience. Early entrance/early admission program. Concurrent enrollment program.
**Transfer students:** Transfer students accepted for terms other than fall. In fall 1993, 47% of all new students were transfers into all classes. 3,010 transfer applications were received, 2,202 were accepted. Application deadline is two weeks prior to term; same for spring. Minimum 2.0 GPA required. Lowest course grade accepted is "D." At least 30 semester hours must be completed at the university to receive degree.
**Admissions contact:** Tom Streveler, Ed.D., Director of Admissions. 309 298-3157.

**FINANCIAL AID. Available aid:** Pell grants, SEOG, state grants, school scholarships and grants, private scholarships, academic merit scholarships, and athletic scholarships. Perkins Loans (NDSL), PLUS, Stafford Loans (GSL), and SLS. Deferred payment plan.
**Financial aid statistics:** Average amounts of aid awarded freshmen: Scholarships and grants, $500.
**Supporting data/closing dates:** FAFSA/FAF/FFS: Priority filing date is March 15. School's own aid application: Priority filing date is March 15. Income tax forms: Priority filing date is March 15. Notification of awards begins May 1.
**Financial aid contact:** William Bushaw, M.S., Director of Financial Aid. 309 298-2446.

**STUDENT EMPLOYMENT.** College Work/Study Program. Institutional employment. 10% of full-time undergraduates work on campus during school year. Students may expect to earn an average of $800 during school year. Off-campus part-time employment opportunities rated "fair."

**COMPUTER FACILITIES.** 1,500 IBM/IBM-compatible and Macintosh/Apple microcomputers; 1,000 are networked. Students may access CDC Cyber, Digital, IBM minicomputer/mainframe systems, BITNET, Internet. Residence halls may be equipped with networked microcomputers. Client/LAN operating systems include Novell. 150 major computer languages and software packages available. Computer facilities are available to all students.
**Fees:** $35 computer fee per semester.
**Hours:** 8 AM-midn.

**PROMINENT ALUMNI/AE.** David R. Collins, author and poet; Lowell Fisher, professor, U of Illinois Department of English; Dan Isaacson, president, Sports Management International; Robert "Red" Miller, football coach, Denver Broncos; John C. Mowbray, justice, Supreme Court of Nevada, winner of NAACP Equal Justice Award; John Rosemond, psychologist, author; Paul Reuschel, baseball player.

# Wheaton College

**Wheaton, IL 60187** **708 752-5000**

**1993-94 Costs.** Tuition: $10,640. Room & board: $4,070. Fees, books, misc. academic expenses (school's estimate): $500.
**Enrollment.** Freshman class: 1,432 applicants, 920 accepted, 548 enrolled.
**Test score averages/ranges.** Range of SAT scores of middle 50%: 500-620 verbal, 560-670 math. Range of ACT scores of middle 50%: 25-30 composite.
**Faculty.** 155 full-time; 106 part-time. 84% of faculty holds doctoral degree. Student/faculty ratio: 15 to 1.
**Selectivity rating.** Highly competitive.

**PROFILE.** Wheaton, founded in 1860, is a liberal arts college with religious orientation. Its 80-acre campus is located in Wheaton, a residential suburb 25 miles west of Chicago.

**Accreditation:** NCACS. Professionally accredited by the National Association of Schools of Music, the National Association of Schools of Music, the National Council for Accreditation of Teacher Education.
**Religious orientation:** Wheaton College is a nondenominational Christian school; 14 semester hours of religion required.
**Library:** Collections totaling over 375,828 volumes, 2,209 periodical subscriptions, and 310,672 microform items.
**Special facilities/museums:** World evangelism museum, language lab, observatory.
**Athletic facilities:** Gymnasiums, swimming pool, fitness center, basketball and tennis courts, track, swimming pool, weight center, baseball, football, intramural, soccer, and softball fields.

**STUDENT BODY. Undergraduate profile:** 23% are state residents; 13% are transfers. 5% Asian-American, 1% Black, 1% Hispanic, 92% White, 1% Other. Average age of undergraduates is 20.
**Freshman profile:** 5% of freshmen who took SAT scored 700 or over on verbal, 17% scored 700 or over on math; 37% scored 600 or over on verbal, 58% scored 600 or over on math; 80% scored 500 or over on verbal, 95% scored 500 or over on math; 98% scored 400 or over on verbal, 99% scored 400 or over on math; 100% scored 300 or over on verbal, 100% scored 300 or over on math. 28% of freshmen who took ACT scored 30 or over on composite; 87% scored 24 or over on composite; 100% scored 18 or over on composite. 81% of accepted applicants took SAT; 58% took ACT. 70% of freshmen come from public schools.
**Undergraduate achievement:** 92% of fall 1992 freshmen returned for fall 1993 term. 70% of entering class graduated. 28% of students who completed a degree program went on to graduate study within one year.
**Foreign students:** 26 students are from out of the country. Countries represented include Canada, Hong Kong, Japan, Kenya, Mexico, and Spain.

**PROGRAMS OF STUDY. Degrees:** B.A., B.Mus., B.Mus.Ed., B.S.
**Majors:** Academy of Freedom, Ancient Languages, Archaeology, Art, Biblical Studies, Biology, Business Economics, Chemistry, Christian Education, Communication, Computer Science/Mathematics, Economics, Education, Environmental Science, Ethnomusicology, French, Geology, German, History, History/Social Science, Interdisciplinary Studies, Liberal Arts/Engineering, Liberal Arts/Nursing, Literature, Mathematics, Music Composition, Music History/Literature, Music Performance, Philosophy, Physical Education, Physics, Political Science, Psychology, Religious Studies, Sociology, Spanish.
**Distribution of degrees:** The majors with the highest enrollment are business economics, literature, and biblical studies; physics, archaeology, and ancient languages have the lowest.
**Requirements:** General education requirement.
**Academic regulations:** Freshmen must maintain minimum 1.8 GPA; sophomores, 1.9 GPA; juniors, 2.0 GPA; seniors, 2.0 GPA.
**Special:** Minors offered in most majors. Conservatory of Music. Special programs in human needs/global resources and Third World studies. Self-designed majors. Double majors. Independent study. Pass/fail grading option. Internships. Graduate school at which undergraduates may take graduate-level courses. Preprofessional programs in law, medicine, dentistry, theology, business, education, engineering, government service, and nursing. 3-2 nursing programs with Emory U, Goshen Nursing Sch, U of Rochester, and Rush U. 3-2 engineering program with Case Western Reserve U, Illinois Inst of Tech, U of Illinois, and Washington U. Member of Christian College Consortium. Washington Semester. Latin American Studies Program (Costa Rica); Film Studies Program (Los Angeles). Teacher certification in elementary and secondary education. Certification in specific subject areas. Summer study abroad in East Asian countries, England, France, Germany, Israel, Russia, and Spain. ROTC.
**Honors:** Honors program. Honor societies.

**ADMISSIONS. Academic basis for candidate selection** (in order of priority): Secondary school record, standardized test scores, class rank, school's recommendation, essay.
**Nonacademic basis for candidate selection:** Character and personality are emphasized. Extracurricular participation is important. Particular talent or ability and alumni/ae relationship are considered.
**Requirements:** Graduation from secondary school is required; GED is accepted. 16 units required and the following program of study recommended: 4 units of English, 3 units of math, 3 units of science, 2 units of foreign language, 2 units of social studies. Rank in top half of secondary school class required. Portfolio required of art program applicants. Audition required of music program applicants. SAT or ACT is required. ACH recommended. Campus visit recommended. Off-campus interviews available with an admissions representative.
**Procedure:** Take SAT or ACT by fall of 12th year. Visit college for interview by February 15 of 12th year. Suggest filing application by December 1. Application deadline is February 15. Notification of accceptance is sent by February 10 for applications received by December 1; by April 10 for others. Reply is required by May 1. $200 tuition deposit, refundable until May 1. Freshmen accepted for terms other than fall.
**Special programs:** Admission may be deferred one semester. Credit and/or placement may be granted through CEEB Advanced Placement exams for scores of 3 or higher. Credit and/or placement may be granted through CLEP subject exams. Credit and placement may be granted through challenge exams.
**Transfer students:** Transfer students accepted for terms other than fall. In fall 1993, 13% of all new students were transfers into all classes. 229 transfer applications were received, 136 were accepted. Application deadline is March 1 for fall; October 1 for spring. Minimum 3.0 GPA required. Lowest course grade accepted is "C-." Maximum number of transferable credits is 92 semester hours. At least 32 semester hours must be completed at the college to receive degree.
**Admissions contact:** A. Duane Litfin, M.A., Director of Admissions. 708 752-5011.

**FINANCIAL AID. Available aid:** Pell grants, SEOG, state scholarships and grants, school scholarships and grants, private scholarships and grants, ROTC scholarships, and academic merit scholarships. Perkins Loans (NDSL), PLUS, Stafford Loans (GSL), school loans, and SLS. Wheaton College Installment Plan.
**Financial aid statistics:** 4% of aid is not need-based. In 1993-94, 55% of all undergraduate applicants received aid; 61% of freshman applicants. Average amounts of aid awarded freshmen: Scholarships and grants, $5,412; loans, $3,242.
**Supporting data/closing dates:** FAFSA: Priority filing date is March 15. School's own aid application: Priority filing date is March 15. Notification of awards on rolling basis.
**Financial aid contact:** Donna Peltz, Director of Financial Aid. 708 752-5021.

**STUDENT EMPLOYMENT.** College Work/Study Program. Institutional employment. 43% of full-time undergraduates work on campus during school year. Students may expect to earn an average of $1,000 during school year. Off-campus part-time employment opportunities rated "excellent."

**COMPUTER FACILITIES.** 70 IBM/IBM-compatible, Macintosh/Apple, and RISC-/UNIX-based microcomputers; all are networked. Students may access Digital minicomputer/mainframe systems, Internet. Client/LAN operating systems include Apple/Macintosh, DOS, UNIX/XENIX/AIX, Windows NT, X-windows, DEC, LocalTalk/AppleTalk, Novell. Computer languages and software packages include BASIC, C, C++, FORTRAN, ICON, MINITAB, Modula 2, Paradox, Pascal, Quattro Pro, SAS, SPSS, WORD, WordPerfect; 30 in all. Computer facilities are available to all students.
**Fees:** Computer fee is included in tuition/fees.
**Hours:** 8 AM-midn. (M-Th); 9 AM-6 PM (F-Sa).

**GRADUATE CAREER DATA.** Graduate school percentages: 1% enter law school. 3% enter medical school. 1% enter dental school. 2% enter graduate business programs. 10% enter graduate arts and sciences programs. 6% enter theological school/seminary. Highest graduate school enrollments: U of Illinois, Northern Illinois U, Rush U, and Wheaton Coll.

**PROMINENT ALUMNI/AE.** Dr. William F. Graham, evangelist, Billy Graham Association; John Brobeck, M.D., scientist, National Academy of Sciences; Daniel Coats, U.S. Senator, Indiana; Dr. Richard Halvorsen, chaplain, U.S. Senate; Dr. Larry Ward, director, Food for the Hungry; John Nelson, orchestra conductor.

# Indiana

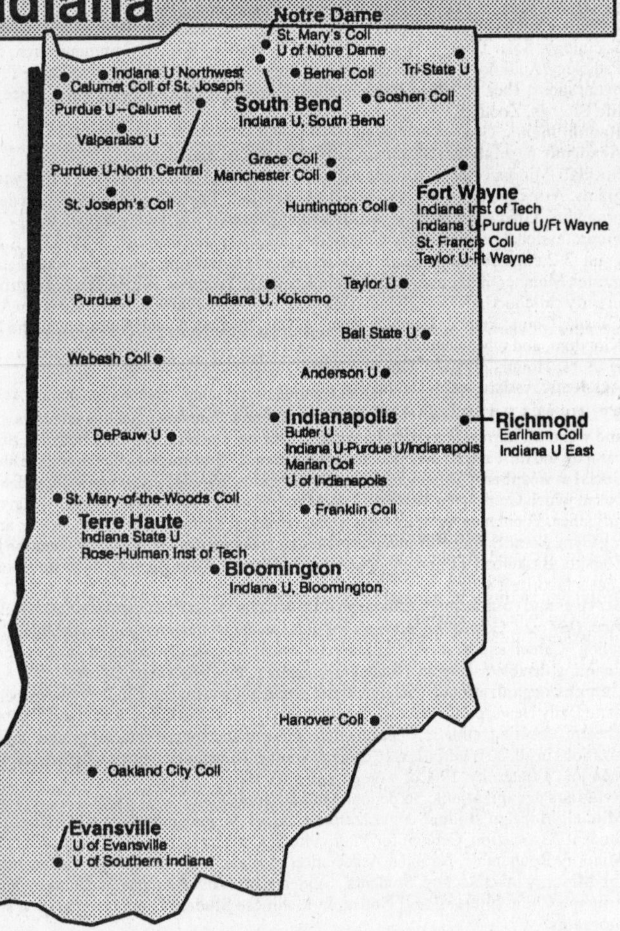


## Anderson University

**Anderson, IN 46012** **317 649-9071**

**1994-95 Costs.** Tuition: $10,100. Room & board: $3,520. Fees, books, misc. academic expenses (school's estimate): $750.
**Enrollment.** Undergraduates: 786 men, 1,032 women (full-time). Freshman class: 748 applicants, 701 accepted, 577 enrolled. Graduate enrollment: 105 men, 32 women.
**Test score averages/ranges.** Average SAT scores: 422 verbal, 461 math. Range of SAT scores of middle 50%: 360-490 verbal, 380-540 math. Average ACT scores: 21 English, 20 math. Range of ACT scores of middle 50%: 18-23 English, 17-23 math.
**Faculty.** 106 full-time; 63 part-time. 62% of faculty holds highest degree in specific field. Student/faculty ratio: 15 to 1.
**Selectivity rating.** Competitive.

**PROFILE.** Anderson, founded in 1917, is a church-affiliated, liberal arts university. Programs are offered through the Schools of Theoretical and Applied Science; Social and Professional Studies; and Arts, Culture, and Religion. Its 100-acre campus is located in Anderson, 40 miles from Indianapolis.

**Accreditation:** NCACS. Professionally accredited by the Council on Social Work Education, the National Association of Schools of Music, the National Council for Accreditation of Teacher Education, the National League for Nursing.
**Religious orientation:** Anderson University is affiliated with the Church of God; one semester of religion/theology required.
**Library:** Collections totaling over 215,800 volumes, 928 periodical subscriptions, and 184,890 microform items.
**Special facilities/museums:** Bible museum, art gallery, ancient Near Eastern museum.
**Athletic facilities:** Gymnasiums, field house, weight room, basketball, tennis, and volleyball courts, swimming pool, track, baseball, football, intramural, soccer, and softball fields, stadium.

**STUDENT BODY. Undergraduate profile:** 52% are state residents; 16% are transfers. 5% Black, 91% White, 4% Other. Average age of undergraduates is 23.
**Freshman profile:** 2% of freshmen who took SAT scored 700 or over on math; 3% scored 600 or over on verbal, 16% scored 600 or over on math; 21% scored 500 or over on verbal, 38% scored 500 or over on math; 60% scored 400 or over on verbal, 69% scored 400 or over on math; 92% scored 300 or over on verbal, 95% scored 300 or over on math. 4% of freshmen who took ACT scored 30 or over on English, 2% scored 30 or over on math; 30% scored 24 or over on English, 23% scored 24 or over on math; 80% scored 18 or over on English, 67% scored 18 or over on math; 98% scored 12 or over on English, 100% scored 12 or over on math; 100% scored 6 or over on English. 67% of accepted applicants took SAT; 51% took ACT.
**Undergraduate achievement:** 78% of fall 1991 freshmen returned for fall 1992 term. 15% of students who completed a degree program went on to graduate study within one year.
**Foreign students:** Countries represented include African countries, Canada, Caribbean countries, Greece, Japan, and Lebanon; 10 in all.

**PROGRAMS OF STUDY. Degrees:** B.A., B.S.Nurs.
**Majors:** Accounting, American Studies, Athletic Training, Bible, Biology, Business/Computer Science, Chemistry, Christian Ministries, Church Music, Computer Science, Computer Science/Business, Computer Science/Mathematics, Criminal Justice, Economics, Education, Elementary Education, English, Finance, French, German, Graphic Design, History, Management, Marketing, Marriage/Family Relations, Mass Communications, Mathematics, Mathematics/Computer Science, Medical Technology, Music, Music Business, Music Education, Music Performance, Nursing, Philosophy, Physical Education, Physics, Political Science, Psychology, Religion, Secondary Education, Social Work, Sociology, Spanish, Speech.
**Requirements:** General education requirement.
**Academic regulations:** Freshmen must maintain minimum 1.4 GPA; sophomores, 1.7 GPA; juniors, 1.8 GPA; seniors, 1.9 GPA.
**Special:** Minors offered in some majors and in classics, electrical engineering technology, management information systems, music theory/literature, statistics, and writing. Associate's degrees offered. Self-designed majors. Double majors. Independent study. Pass/fail grading option. Internships. Graduate school at which undergraduates may take graduate-level courses. Preprofessional programs in law, medicine, veterinary science, pharmacy, dentistry, theology, occupational therapy, physical therapy, and podiatry. 3-2 engineering program with Purdue U. Washington Semester. Teacher certification in early childhood, elementary, and secondary education. Certification in specific subject areas. Study abroad in France, Latin American countries, and Spain.
**Honors:** Honor societies.
**Academic Assistance:** Remedial study skills. Nonremedial tutoring.

**STUDENT LIFE. Housing:** All unmarried students under age 21 must live on campus unless living near campus with relatives. Women's and men's dorms. School-owned/operated apartments. Off-campus married-student housing. 48% of students live in college housing.
**Social atmosphere:** According to the student newspaper, "The Campus Activities Board (CAB) is a student organization which actively provides entertainment and social opportunities for students. AU's social clubs are a major source of fellowship and activity for the more than 400 participating students. Also, Campus Ministries provides opportunities for involvement in varied spiritual programs and events. The CAB-sponsored Air Band Contest is one of the most popular entertainment events of the semester. The Dativus social club's Zany Cheap Thrills show, usually staged twice a semester, is another popular entertainment production. The twice-weekly chapel/convocation service brings many renowned musical artists, religious leaders, sports figures, and other speakers to campus."
**Services and counseling/handicapped student services:** Placement services. Health service. Counseling services for minority and older students. Personal counseling. Career and academic guidance services. Religious counseling. Physically disabled student services. Learning disabled program/services. Tape recorders. Tutors. Reader services for the blind.
**Campus organizations:** Undergraduate student government. Student newspaper (Andersonian, published once/week). Yearbook. Radio station. A cappella choir, orchestra, Oratorio Society, band, mixed choral union, choral and instrumental ensembles, drama club, spring touring play, Forensic Society, political, social, and special-interest groups, 26 organizations in all.
**Religious organizations:** Christian Ministry, Search Groups, Work Camps, Christianity in Action, Agape Squad, Fellowship of Christian Athletes.
**Minority/foreign student organizations:** Multicultural Student Union. International Student Association.

**ATHLETICS. Physical education requirements:** None.
**Intercollegiate competition:** 25% of students participate. Baseball (M), basketball (M), cross-country (M,W), football (M), golf (M), soccer (M,W), softball (W), tennis (M,W), track (indoor) (M,W), track (outdoor) (M,W), track and field (indoor) (M,W), track and field (outdoor) (M,W), volleyball (W). Member of Indiana Collegiate Athletic Conference, NCAA Division III.
**Intramural and club sports:** 65% of students participate. Intramural basketball, football, soccer, softball, volleyball.

**ADMISSIONS. Academic basis for candidate selection** (in order of priority): Secondary school record, class rank, standardized test scores, school's recommendation, essay.
**Nonacademic basis for candidate selection:** Character and personality, extracurricular participation, and alumni/ae relationship are important. Particular talent or ability and geographical distribution are considered.
**Requirements:** Graduation from secondary school is required; GED is accepted. 18 units and the following program of study are recommended: 4 units of English, 4 units of math, 4 units of science, 2 units of foreign language, 2 units of social studies, 2 units of history. Minimum combined SAT score of 800, rank in top half of secondary school class, and minimum 2.0 GPA required. SAT or ACT is required. Campus visit and interview recommended. No off-campus interviews.
**Procedure:** Take SAT or ACT by September of 12th year. Suggest filing application by fall; no deadline. Notification of admission on rolling basis. Reply is required by May 1. $100 tuition deposit, refundable until May 1. Freshmen accepted for terms other than fall.
**Special programs:** Admission may be deferred three years. Credit and/or placement may be granted through CEEB Advanced Placement exams for scores of 3 or higher. Credit may be granted through CLEP general and subject exams, challenge exams, and military experience. Early decision program. Deadline for applying for early decision is December 1. Concurrent enrollment program.
**Transfer students:** Transfer students accepted for terms other than fall. for fall 1992, 16% of all new students were transfers into all classes. 147 transfer applications were received, 118 were accepted. Application deadline is August 1 for fall; December for spring. Minimum 2.0 GPA recommended. Lowest course grade accepted is "C." At least 24 semester hours must be completed at the university to receive degree.

**Admissions contact:** Ann E. Brandon, Director of Admissions. 317 641-4080.

**FINANCIAL AID. Available aid:** Pell grants, SEOG, state scholarships and grants, school scholarships and grants, private scholarships and grants, academic merit scholarships, and aid for undergraduate foreign students. Perkins Loans (NDSL), PLUS, Stafford Loans (GSL), and SLS. Deferred payment plan.
**Financial aid statistics:** 55% of aid is not need-based.
**Supporting data/closing dates:** FAFSA/FAF/FFS: Accepted on rolling basis. School's own aid application: Accepted on rolling basis. Notification of awards on rolling basis.
**Financial aid contact:** Kenneth Nieman, Director of Financial Aid. 317 641-4187.

**STUDENT EMPLOYMENT.** College Work/Study Program. Institutional employment. 40% of full-time undergraduates work on campus during school year. Students may expect to earn an average of $1,800 during school year. Off-campus part-time employment opportunities rated "fair."

**COMPUTER FACILITIES.** 125 IBM/IBM-compatible and Macintosh/Apple microcomputers. Students may access Hewlett-Packard minicomputer/mainframe systems. Client/LAN operating systems include Apple/Macintosh. Computer languages and software packages include C, COBOL, FORTRAN, Pascal, WordPerfect; desktop publishing, graphics, spreadsheet programs. Computer facilities are available to all students.
**Fees:** None.

# Ball State University

**Muncie, IN 47306** **317 289-1241**

**1994-95 Costs.** Tuition: $2,864 (state residents), $7,244 (out-of-state). Room & board: $3,608. Fees, books, misc. academic expenses (school's estimate): $500.
**Enrollment.** Undergraduates: 7,496 men, 8,652 women (full-time). Freshman class: 9,361 applicants, 7,601 accepted, 3,849 enrolled. Graduate enrollment: 1,025 men, 1,337 women.
**Test score averages/ranges.** Average SAT scores: 422 verbal, 473 math. Average ACT scores: 21 composite.
**Faculty.** 965 full-time; 186 part-time. 66% of faculty holds highest degree in specific field. Student/faculty ratio: 21 to 1.
**Selectivity rating.** Less competitive.

**PROFILE.** Ball State is a public, comprehensive university. Founded in 1918, it gained university status in 1965. Its 955-acre campus is located in a residential area one mile northwest of downtown Muncie. Campus architecture includes Tudor-Gothic and modern styles.

**Accreditation:** NCACS. Professionally accredited by the Accrediting Council on Education in Journalism and Mass Communication, the American Bar Association, the American Dietetic Association, the American Home Economics Association, the American Medical Association (CAHEA), the American Psychological Association, the American Society of Landscape Architects, the American Speech-Language-Hearing Association, the Council on Social Work Education, the Liaison Committee on Medical Education, the National Architecture Accrediting Board, the National Association of Schools of Music, the National Association of Schools of Public Affairs and Administration, the National Council for Accreditation of Teacher Education, the National League for Nursing.
**Religious orientation:** Ball State University is nonsectarian; no religious requirements.
**Library:** Collections totaling over 1,051,018 volumes, 3,807 periodical subscriptions, and 280,947 microform items.
**Special facilities/museums:** Art gallery, museum, on-campus school (K-12), learning center, weather station, physical therapy lab, human performance lab, planetarium/observatory, wildlife and nature preserve.
**Athletic facilities:** Gymnasiums, aquatic center, sports building, tennis courts, athletic fields, bowling alleys, arena.

**STUDENT BODY. Undergraduate profile:** 90% are state residents; 20% are transfers. 1% Asian-American, 4.5% Black, 1% Hispanic, .5% Native American, 90% White, 3% Other. Average age of undergraduates is 20.
**Freshman profile:** 1% of freshmen who took SAT scored 700 or over on verbal, 1% scored 700 or over on math; 3% scored 600 or over on verbal, 11% scored 600 or over on math; 19% scored 500 or over on verbal, 39% scored 500 or over on math; 100% scored 400 or over on verbal, 100% scored 400 or over on math. 90% of accepted applicants took SAT.
**Undergraduate achievement:** 77% of fall 1992 freshmen returned for fall 1993 term.
**Foreign students:** 186 students are from out of the country. Countries represented include China, Germany, India, Japan, South Korea, and Taiwan; 91 in all.

**PROGRAMS OF STUDY. Degrees:** B.A., B.Arch., B.F.A., B.Gen.Studies, B.Land.Arch., B.Mus., B.S., B.Soc.Work, B.Urban Plan./Dev.
**Majors:** Accounting, Actuarial Science, Advertising, Anthropology, Apparel Design, Aquatic Biology/Fisheries, Architecture, Art, Art Education, Athletic Training, Biology, Botany, Business Administration, Business Economics, Business Education/Office Administration, Cellular/Molecular Biology, Ceramics, Ceramics/Ceramic Sculpture, Chemistry, Chinese, Computer Science, Criminal Justice/Criminology, Dance, Dietetics, Drawing, Earth Science, Economics, Electronics, Elementary Education, English, Environmental Design, Exercise Science/Fitness Specialist, Fashion Merchandising, Finance, Food Management, Food/Nutrition, Foreign Languages, French, General Studies, Genetics, Geography, Geology, German, Graphic Arts Management, Graphic Design, Health/Safety Education, Hearing Impaired, History, Home Economics, Home Economics/ Vocational, Housing/Home Furnishings, Industrial Technology Education, Industry/ Technology, Insurance, Interdepartmental Studies, Interior/Environmental Design, International Business, Journalism, Junior High/Middle School Education, Landscape Architecture, Latin, Latin American Studies, Legal Administration, Magazine, Management Science, Marine Biology, Marketing, Mathematical Economics, Mathematical Sciences, Medical Technology, Metals, Microbiology, Music, Music Education, Music Engineering Technology, Music Theory/Composition, Natural Resources, News/Editorial, Nursing, Organ, Painting, Philosophy, Photography, Photojournalism, Physical Education, Physics, Physiology/Health Science, Piano, Political Science, Printmaking, Psychology, Public Relations, Religious Studies, School Media Services, Sculpture, Secondary Education, Social Work, Sociology, Solar Energy, Spanish, Special Education, Speech Communication, Speech Pathology/Audiology, Symphonic Instruments, Symphonic Instruments/Guitar, Telecommunications, Theatre, Urban Planning/Development, Visual Arts Education, Voice, Wildlife Biology, Zoology.
**Requirements:** General education requirement.
**Academic regulations:** Minimum 2.0 GPA must be maintained.
**Special:** Minors offered in some majors. B.Arch. and B.Land.Arch. are five-year programs. Associate's degrees offered. Double majors. Internships. Cooperative education programs. Graduate school at which undergraduates may take graduate-level courses. Preprofessional programs in law, medicine, pharmacy, and theology. 3-2 B.S./M.B.A. program. 3-2 engineering program with accredited engineering programs. Washington Semester. Member of International Student Exchange Program (ISEP). Teacher certification in early childhood, elementary, secondary, and special education. Study abroad in Austria, Canada, China, France, Jamaica, Japan, Korea, Mexico, Spain, Switzerland, the United Kingdom, and other countries. ROTC.
**Honors:** Honors program. Honor societies.
**Academic Assistance:** Nonremedial tutoring.

**STUDENT LIFE. Housing:** All freshmen and new transfers must live on campus. Coed and women's dorms. Fraternity housing. Off-campus privately-owned housing. Both on-campus and off-campus married-student housing. 27% of students live in college housing.
**Social atmosphere:** The student newspaper reports that Ball State is an independent campus in which Greeks, the Student Center Programming Board, and athletes all have some influence. Popular on-campus spots are the Bracken Library, the Student Center, and Irving Gym. Some favorite off-campus gathering areas are the Chug, Mugly's, and the Flying Tomato. Basketball games, the Watermelon Bust, and the Bike-A-Thon are among the year's favorite events.
**Services and counseling/handicapped student services:** Placement services. Health service. Day care. Counseling services for older students. Personal and psychological counseling. Career and academic guidance services. Physically disabled student services. Learning disabled services. Notetaking services. Tape recorders. Tutors.
**Campus organizations:** Undergraduate student government. Student newspaper (Ball State Daily News, published daily). Literary magazine. Yearbook. Radio and TV stations. Theatre, debating, athletic, departmental, service, and special-interest groups, 290 organizations in all. 20 fraternities, 16 chapter houses; 16 sororities, no chapter houses. 13% of men join a fraternity. 19% of women join a sorority.
**Religious organizations:** 36 denominational groups.
**Minority/foreign student organizations:** Asian American Student Association, Black Student Association, Council for Multicultural Concerns, Hispanic Student Association, Minority Roundtable, National Association of Black Journalists, National Organization for Minority Architecture Students, Students of Native American Culture, Voice of Triumph Choir. International House, Indochinese Student Club, international student programs.

**ATHLETICS. Physical education requirements:** One semester of physical education required. Three hours of physical education required.
**Intercollegiate competition:** 4% of students participate. Baseball (M), basketball (M,W), cheerleading (M,W), cross-country (M,W), diving (M,W), field hockey (W), football (M), golf (M), gymnastics (W), swimming (M,W), tennis (M,W), track (indoor) (M,W), track (outdoor) (M,W), track and field (indoor) (M,W), track and field (outdoor) (M,W), volleyball (M,W). Member of Mid-America Conference, Midwest Intercollegiate Volleyball Association (men), NCAA Division I, NCAA Division I-A for football.
**Intramural and club sports:** 20% of students participate. Men's club bowling, handball, horsemanship, martial arts, racquetball, soccer, ultimate frisbee, weight lifting. Women's club bowling, handball, horsemanship, martial arts, racquetball, soccer, ultimate frisbee, weight lifting.

**ADMISSIONS. Academic basis for candidate selection** (in order of priority): Class rank, standardized test scores, secondary school record, essay, school's recommendation.
**Nonacademic basis for candidate selection:** Character and personality, extracurricular participation, particular talent or ability, and alumni/ae relationship are considered.
**Requirements:** Graduation from secondary school is required; GED is accepted. 36 units and the following program of study are recommended: 8 units of English, 6 units of math, 4 units of science including 2 units of lab, 4 units of foreign language, 6 units of social studies, 2 units of history, 6 units of electives. Minimum combined SAT score of 800 (or composite ACT score of 19) and rank in top half of secondary school class required. Portfolio required of art program applicants. Audition required of music program applicants. Project Start for applicants not normally admissible. SAT or ACT is required. Campus visit and interview recommended. No off-campus interviews.
**Procedure:** Take SAT or ACT by January of 12th year. Visit college for interview by March of 12th year. Suggest filing application by March 1. Notification of admission on rolling basis. Reply is required by May 1. $50 tuition deposit, refundable until May 1. $25 room deposit, refundable until May 1. Freshmen accepted for terms other than fall.
**Special programs:** Admission may be deferred one and a half years. Credit and/or placement may be granted through CEEB Advanced Placement exams for scores of 3 or higher. Credit and/or placement may be granted through CLEP general and subject exams. Credit may be granted through DANTES exams. Concurrent enrollment program.
**Transfer students:** Transfer students accepted for terms other than fall. for fall 1993, 20% of all new students were transfers into all classes. 1,368 transfer applications were received, 1,007 were accepted. Application deadline is March 1 for fall; December 1 for spring. Minimum 2.0 GPA required. Lowest course grade accepted is "C." At least 30 semester hours must be completed at the university to receive degree.
**Admissions contact:** Ruth Vedvik, M.S., Director of Admissions. 317 285-8300, FAX 317 285-1632.

**FINANCIAL AID. Available aid:** Pell grants, SEOG, state scholarships and grants, school scholarships, private scholarships, ROTC scholarships, academic merit scholarships,

and athletic scholarships. Perkins Loans (NDSL), PLUS, Stafford Loans (GSL), and SLS. Deferred payment plan.
**Financial aid statistics:** 52% of aid is not need-based. In 1993-94, 83% of all undergraduate applicants received aid; 92% of freshman applicants. Average amounts of aid awarded freshmen: Scholarships and grants, $3,500; loans, $1,500.
**Supporting data/closing dates:** FAFSA: Priority filing date is March 1. School's own aid application: Priority filing date is March 1. Notification of awards begins in May.
**Financial aid contact:** Clarence L. Casazza, M.B.A., Ed.D., Director of Student Financial Assistance. 317 285-5600.

**STUDENT EMPLOYMENT.** College Work/Study Program. Institutional employment. 17% of full-time undergraduates work on campus during school year. Students may expect to earn an average of $1,500 during school year. Off-campus part-time employment opportunities rated "good."

**COMPUTER FACILITIES.** IBM/IBM-compatible and Macintosh/Apple microcomputers. Students may access Digital, IBM minicomputer/mainframe systems, BITNET, Internet. Residence halls may be equipped with stand-alone microcomputers, networked microcomputers, modems. Client/LAN operating systems include Apple/Macintosh, DOS, UNIX/XENIX/AIX, LocalTalk/AppleTalk, Novell. Numerous computer languages and software programs available. Computer facilities are available to all students.
**Fees:** None.
**Hours:** 24 hours (M-Th).

**PROMINENT ALUMNI/AE.** David Letterman, entertainer; Jim Davis, creator of *Garfield;* Cyndi Williams, actress.

# Bethel College

**Mishawaka, IN 46545 219 259-8511**

**1994-95 Costs.** Tuition: $9,300. Room: $1,300. Board: $1,850. Fees, books, misc. academic expenses (school's estimate): $200.
**Enrollment.** Undergraduates: 312 men, 421 women (full-time). Freshman class: 381 applicants, 319 accepted, 212 enrolled. Graduate enrollment: 22 men, 1 woman.
**Test score averages/ranges.** Average SAT scores: 453 verbal, 490 math. Range of SAT scores of middle 50%: 380-500 verbal, 410-570 math. Average ACT scores: 23 English, 21 math, 22 composite. Range of ACT scores of middle 50%: 18-26 English, 18-24 math.
**Faculty.** 53 full-time; 51 part-time. 48% of faculty holds doctoral degree. Student/faculty ratio: 19 to 1.
**Selectivity rating.** Less competitive.

**PROFILE.** Bethel, founded in 1947, is a church-affiliated college. Its 62-acre campus is located in Mishawaka, 90 miles from Chicago.

**Accreditation:** NCACS. Professionally accredited by the National League for Nursing.
**Religious orientation:** Bethel College is affiliated with the Missionary Church; three semesters of religion required.
**Library:** Collections totaling over 73,686 volumes, 415 periodical subscriptions, and 3,849 microform items.
**Athletic facilities:** Baseball field, soccer field, basketball court, volleyball court.

**STUDENT BODY. Undergraduate profile:** 83% are state residents. .3% Asian-American, 13% Black, .4% Hispanic, .1% Native American, 85% White, 1.2% Other. Average age of undergraduates is 27.
**Freshman profile:** 3% of freshmen who took SAT scored 700 or over on math; 5% scored 600 or over on verbal, 19% scored 600 or over on math; 28% scored 500 or over on verbal, 43% scored 500 or over on math; 66% scored 400 or over on verbal, 81% scored 400 or over on math; 98% scored 300 or over on verbal, 98% scored 300 or over on math. 10% of freshmen who took ACT scored 30 or over on English, 3% scored 30 or over on math, 7% scored 30 or over on composite; 43% scored 24 or over on English, 29% scored 24 or over on math, 36% scored 24 or over on composite; 82% scored 18 or over on English, 80% scored 18 or over on math, 85% scored 18 or over on composite; 100% scored 12 or over on English, 100% scored 12 or over on math, 100% scored 12 or over on composite. 70% of accepted applicants took SAT; 30% took ACT. 84% of freshmen come from public schools.
**Undergraduate achievement:** 70% of fall 1992 freshmen returned for fall 1993 term.
**Foreign students:** Five students are from out of the country.

**PROGRAMS OF STUDY. Degrees:** B.A., B.S.
**Majors:** Accounting, Art, Biblical Studies, Biology, Business Administration, Business Education, Chemistry, Christian Ministries, Church Music, Communication, Elementary Education, Engineering, English, English Education, Liberal Studies, Mathematics, Music, Music Education, Music Performance, Nursing, Organizational Management, Physical Education, Piano Pedagogy, Pre-Dentistry, Pre-Medicine, Psychology, Recreation Administration, Science Education, Social Sciences, Social Studies Education, Sociology, Visual Communications.
**Distribution of degrees:** The majors with the highest enrollment are elementary education, business administration, and nursing; art, computer science, and recreation administration have the lowest.
**Requirements:** General education requirement.
**Academic regulations:** Minimum 2.0 GPA must be maintained.
**Special:** Optional minors available in most majors and in Bible, biblical languages, biology education, chemistry education, drama, economics, economics education, French, health and safety education, history, journalism, mass media, math education, missions, psychology education, sociology education, Spanish, U.S. history education, world civilization education, and youth ministry. Associate's degrees offered. Double majors. Internships. Graduate school at which undergraduates may take graduate-level courses. Preprofessional programs in medicine and dentistry. 3-2 engineering program with U of Notre Dame. Member of Northern Indiana Consortium for Education. Teacher certification in early childhood, elementary, and secondary education. Certification in specific subject areas. Study abroad in Ecuador and Jamaica.
**Academic Assistance:** Remedial reading, writing, math, and study skills. Nonremedial tutoring.

**ADMISSIONS. Academic basis for candidate selection** (in order of priority): Standardized test scores, secondary school record, class rank, school's recommendation.
**Nonacademic basis for candidate selection:** Character and personality, extracurricular participation, and particular talent or ability are considered.
**Requirements:** Graduation from secondary school is required; GED is accepted. 12 units and the following program of study are required: 4 units of English, 2 units of math, 2 units of lab science, 2 units of foreign language, 1 unit of social studies, 1 unit of history. Minimum SAT scores of 360 in both verbal and math (ACT scores of 18 English and 17 math) required. Chemistry required of nursing program applicants. Audition required of music program applicants. Conditional admission possible for applicants not meeting standard requirements. SAT or ACT is required. Campus visit and interview recommended. Off-campus interviews available with an admissions representative.
**Procedure:** Take SAT or ACT by January of 12th year. Visit college for interview by June of 12th year. Notification of admission on rolling basis. Reply is required by May 1. $50 nonrefundable tuition deposit. $75 room deposit, refundable until March 1. Freshmen accepted for terms other than fall.
**Special programs:** Admission may be deferred two years. Credit and/or placement may be granted through CEEB Advanced Placement exams for scores of 3 or higher. Credit and/or placement may be granted through CLEP general and subject exams. Credit and placement may be granted through ACT PEP, DANTES, and challenge exams, and military and life experience. Early entrance/early admission program. Concurrent enrollment program.
**Transfer students:** Transfer students accepted for terms other than fall. for fall 1993, 112 transfer applications were received, 96 were accepted. Application deadline is rolling for fall; rolling for spring. Minimum 2.0 GPA required. Lowest course grade accepted is "C-." Maximum number of transferable credits is 94 semester hours. At least 30 semester hours must be completed at the college to receive degree.
**Admissions contact:** Stephen J. Matteson, M.S., Dean of Admissions. 219 257-3339.

**FINANCIAL AID. Available aid:** Pell grants, SEOG, state scholarships and grants, school scholarships and grants, private scholarships, academic merit scholarships, athletic scholarships, and aid for undergraduate foreign students. Perkins Loans (NDSL), PLUS, Stafford Loans (GSL), state loans, school loans, and SLS. AMS and family tuition reduction.
**Financial aid statistics:** In 1993-94, 85% of all undergraduate applicants received aid. Average amounts of aid awarded freshmen: Scholarships and grants, $4,000; loans, $2,771.
**Supporting data/closing dates:** FAFSA/FAF: Priority filing date is March 1. School's own aid application: Accepted on rolling basis. State aid form: Deadline is March 1. Notification of awards on rolling basis.
**Financial aid contact:** Guy Fisher, Director of Financial Aid. 219 257-3316.

# Butler University

**Indianapolis, IN 46208 317 283-8000**

**1994-95 Costs.** Tuition: $13,130. Room: $1,940. Board: $2,480. Fees, books, misc. academic expenses (school's estimate): $690.
**Enrollment.** Undergraduates: 1,041 men, 1,547 women (full-time). Freshman class: 2,362 applicants, 2,037 accepted, 700 enrolled. Graduate enrollment: 438 men, 556 women.
**Test score averages/ranges.** Average SAT scores: 484 verbal, 544 math. Range of SAT scores of middle 50%: 420-540 verbal, 480-610 math. Average ACT scores: 25 composite. Range of ACT scores of middle 50%: 22-28 composite.
**Faculty.** 210 full-time; 130 part-time. 78% of faculty holds doctoral degree. Student/faculty ratio: 13 to 1.
**Selectivity rating.** Competitive.

**PROFILE.** Butler, founded in 1855, is a private university. Programs are offered through the Colleges of Liberal Arts and Sciences, Business Administration, Education, and Pharmacy; the Jordan College of Fine Arts; and the University College. Its 300-acre campus is located in a residential area five miles from downtown Indianapolis.

**Accreditation:** NCACS. Professionally accredited by the American Council on Pharmaceutical Education, the National Association of Schools of Music, the National Council for Accreditation of Teacher Education.
**Religious orientation:** Butler University is nonsectarian; no religious requirements.
**Library:** Collections totaling over 282,195 volumes, 2,835 periodical subscriptions, and 218,207 microform items.
**Special facilities/museums:** Observatory and planetarium with 38-inch reflecting telescope.
**Athletic facilities:** Gymnasiums, field house, swimming pool, basketball, tennis, and volleyball courts, track, baseball, football, lacrosse, soccer, and softball fields.

**STUDENT BODY. Undergraduate profile:** 66% are state residents; 16% are transfers. 2% Asian-American, 6% Black, 1% Hispanic, 90% White, 1% Other. Average age of undergraduates is 20.
**Freshman profile:** 2% of freshmen who took SAT scored 700 or over on verbal, 4% scored 700 or over on math; 11% scored 600 or over on verbal, 30% scored 600 or over on math; 46% scored 500 or over on verbal, 70% scored 500 or over on math; 85% scored 400 or over on verbal, 95% scored 400 or over on math; 100% scored 300 or over on verbal, 100% scored 300 or over on math. 69% of accepted applicants took SAT; 31% took ACT. 78% of freshmen come from public schools.
**Undergraduate achievement:** 80% of fall 1992 freshmen returned for fall 1993 term. 47% of entering class graduated. 10% of students who completed a degree program immediately went on to graduate study.
**Foreign students:** 40 students are from out of the country. Countries represented include Canada, France, Germany, Japan, Korea, and Thailand; 28 in all.

**PROGRAMS OF STUDY. Degrees:** B.A., B.F.A., B.Mus., B.S., B.S.Econ., B.S.Journ., B.S.Pharm.
**Majors:** Accounting, Actuarial Sciences, American Studies, Arts Administration, Biology, Business Administration/Management, Chemistry, Computer/Information Sciences, Computer Information Systems, Dance, Economics, Elementary Education, English, Environmental Studies, Fine Arts, Foreign Language, French, General Science, German, Greek, Health/Safety, History, Journalism/Mass Communications, Latin, Mathematics, Music, Music Business, Music Education, Music Theory/Composition, Pharmacy, Philosophy, Physical Education, Physics, Political Science/Government, Psychology, Public/Corporate Communication, Radio/Television, Reading Education, Religion, Social Studies, Sociology, Spanish, Special Education, Speech, Speech Pathology, Theatre.
**Distribution of degrees:** The majors with the highest enrollment are pharmacy and elementary education; physics, philosophy, and theatre have the lowest.
**Requirements:** General education requirement.
**Academic regulations:** Minimum 2.0 GPA must be maintained.
**Special:** Double majors. Independent study. Accelerated study. Pass/fail grading option. Internships. Graduate school at which undergraduates may take graduate-level courses. Preprofessional programs in law, medicine, pharmacy, and dentistry. 3-2 engineering programs with U of Illinois, Marquette U, U of Notre Dame, Purdue U, Vanderbilt U, and Washington U. 3-2 forestry and environmental studies program with Duke U. Member of Consortium for Urban Education. Teacher certification in early childhood, elementary, secondary, and special education. Certification in specific subject areas. Study abroad in Australia, England, Ireland, New Zealand, and Scotland. ROTC and AFROTC at Indiana U-Purdue U at Indianapolis.
**Honors:** Honors program.
**Academic Assistance:** Nonremedial tutoring.

**STUDENT LIFE. Housing:** All unmarried students under age 21 must live on campus unless living near campus with relatives. Coed, women's, and men's dorms. Sorority and fraternity housing. Off-campus privately-owned housing. 71% of students live in college housing.
**Social atmosphere:** The student newspaper reports, "There is great influence by Greeks despite the fact that they comprise only one-third of all undergrads; social events often center around Greeks. Good cultural opportunities abound because of Butler's Starlight Theater, Clowes Hall, its ballet, the Jordan School of Fine Arts, and Indianapolis theater and symphonic events." Favorite off-campus gathering spots include the Bulldog Lounge, Melody Inn, Ike and Jonesy's, and Union Station. Popular campus events include Spring Weekend, Geneva Stunts, and Spring Sing. "Geneva Stunts and Spring Sing are student-written and produced musicals. Spring Weekend events include entertainment, Greek competitions, and games."
**Services and counseling/handicapped student services:** Placement services. Health service. Placement tests during Orientation Week. Counseling services for minority and veteran students. Birth control, personal, and psychological counseling. Career and academic guidance services. Religious counseling. Physically disabled student services. Notetaking services. Reader services for the blind.
**Campus organizations:** Undergraduate student government. Student newspaper (Butler Collegian, published once/week). Literary magazine. Yearbook. TV station. Ballet, debating, drama productions, extensive music activities, interest-group publications, departmental and service groups, 65 organizations in all. Seven fraternities, all with chapter houses; nine sororities, seven chapter houses. 38% of men join a fraternity. 37% of women join a sorority.
**Religious organizations:** Baptist Student Union, Campus Crusade for Christ, Fellowship of Christian Athletes, Intervarsity Christian Fellowship, Lutheran Student Movement, Newman Club, YMCA.
**Minority/foreign student organizations:** Black Student Union. International Student Club.

**ATHLETICS. Physical education requirements:** Two semesters of physical education required.
**Intercollegiate competition:** 20% of students participate. Baseball (M), basketball (M,W), cheerleading (M,W), cross-country (M,W), football (M), golf (M), lacrosse (M), soccer (M,W), softball (W), swimming (M,W), tennis (M,W), track and field (indoor) (M,W), track and field (outdoor) (M,W), volleyball (W). Member of Midwestern Collegiate Conference, NCAA Division I, NCAA Division I-AA for football.
**Intramural and club sports:** 10% of students participate. Intramural basketball, broom hockey, golf, racquetball, soccer, softball, swimming, track, volleyball. Men's club crew, cycling, rugby. Women's club crew, cycling.

**ADMISSIONS. Academic basis for candidate selection** (in order of priority): Class rank, essay, secondary school record, standardized test scores, school's recommendation.
**Requirements:** Graduation from secondary school is required; GED is accepted. 17 units and the following program of study are required: 4 units of English, 3 units of math, 3 units of science, 2 units of foreign language, 1 unit of social studies, 1 unit of history, 3 units of academic electives. Additional science and math units recommended of science, mathematics, and pharmacy program applicants. Additional math units recommended of business program applicants. Audition required of dance, music, radio/television, and theatre program applicants. SAT is required; ACT may be substituted. Campus visit and interview recommended. Off-campus interviews available with an admissions representative.
**Procedure:** Take SAT or ACT by December of 12th year. Visit college for interview by December 15 of 12th year. Suggest filing application by October 1. Application deadline is August 1. Notification of admission on rolling basis. No set date by which applicants must accept offer. $150 tuition deposit, refundable until June 1. $100 room deposit, refundable until June 1. Freshmen accepted for terms other than fall.
**Special programs:** Credit and/or placement may be granted through CEEB Advanced Placement exams for scores of 3 or higher. Credit and/or placement may be granted through CLEP general and subject exams. Credit may be granted through military experience. Early decision program. for fall 1993, 601 applied for early decision and 559 were accepted. Deadline for applying for early decision is October 1.
**Transfer students:** Transfer students accepted for terms other than fall. for fall 1993, 16% of all new students were transfers into all classes. 420 transfer applications were received, 255 were accepted. Minimum 2.0 GPA required. Lowest course grade accepted is "C." Maximum number of transferable credits is 64 semester hours from a two-year school and 98 semester hours from a four-year school. At least 30 semester hours must be completed at the university to receive degree.
**Admissions contact:** O'Neil Turner, M.A., Director of Admissions. 317 283-9255.

**FINANCIAL AID. Available aid:** Pell grants, SEOG, state scholarships and grants, school scholarships and grants, private scholarships and grants, ROTC scholarships, academic merit scholarships, athletic scholarships, and aid for undergraduate foreign students. Grants-in-aid for students showing promise in some area of intercollegiate competition or representation. Perkins Loans (NDSL), PLUS, Stafford Loans (GSL), state loans, and school loans.
**Financial aid statistics:** 53% of aid is not need-based. In 1993-94, 83% of all undergraduate applicants received aid; 89% of freshman applicants. Average amounts of aid awarded freshmen: Scholarships and grants, $5,549; loans, $3,472.
**Supporting data/closing dates:** FAFSA/FAF/FFS: Priority filing date is March 1. School's own aid application: Priority filing date is March 1. Notification of awards on rolling basis.
**Financial aid contact:** Richard Bellows, Director of Financial Aid. 317 283-9278.

**STUDENT EMPLOYMENT.** College Work/Study Program. Institutional employment. 20% of full-time undergraduates work on campus during school year. Students may expect to earn an average of $1,500 during school year. Freshmen are discouraged from working during their first term. Off-campus part-time employment opportunities rated "fair."

**COMPUTER FACILITIES.** 230 IBM/IBM-compatible and Macintosh/Apple microcomputers; 180 are networked. Students may access Digital minicomputer/mainframe systems, BITNET, Internet. Residence halls may be equipped with stand-alone microcomputers, networked microcomputers. Client/LAN operating systems include Apple/Macintosh, DOS, LocalTalk/AppleTalk. Computer languages and software packages include BASIC, C, COBOL, Excel, FORTRAN, Microsoft Word, Pascal, Poise, PL/1, VMS. Computer facilities are available to all students.
**Fees:** None.
**Hours:** 8 AM-11 PM.

**GRADUATE CAREER DATA.** Graduate school percentages: 1% enter law school. 1% enter medical school. 2% enter graduate business programs. 4% enter graduate arts and sciences programs. Highest graduate school enrollments: U of Illinois, Indiana U, Ohio State U. 50% of graduates choose careers in business and industry. Companies and businesses that hire graduates: Procter & Gamble, Indiana National Bank, IBM.

**PROMINENT ALUMNI/AE.** Richard L. Roudebush, former U.S. congressman and director of U.S. Veterans Administration; A. Byron Reed, retired chair of the board, Munsingwear, Inc.; Peter Lupus, TV star, *Mission Impossible.*

# Calumet College of St. Joseph

**Whiting, IN 46394** 219 473-7770

**1994-95 Costs.** Tuition: $4,650. Housing: None. Fees, books, misc. academic expenses (school's estimate): $500.
**Enrollment.** Undergraduates: 138 men, 306 women (full-time). Freshman class: 368 applicants, 309 accepted, 274 enrolled.
**Test score averages/ranges.** Average SAT scores: 340 verbal, 340 math. Average ACT scores: 17 composite.
**Faculty.** 35 full-time; 75 part-time. 51% of faculty holds highest degree in specific field. Student/faculty ratio: 11 to 1.
**Selectivity rating.** Less competitive.

**PROFILE.** Calumet, founded in 1951, is a church-affiliated, liberal arts college. Its 256-acre campus is located in Whiting, an urban area 10 miles from Chicago.

**Accreditation:** NCACS.
**Religious orientation:** Calumet College of St. Joseph is affiliated with the Roman Catholic Church; two semesters of theology required.
**Library:** Collections totaling over 111,742 volumes, 270 periodical subscriptions, and 3,838 microform items.
**Special facilities/museums:** Art gallery.

**STUDENT BODY. Undergraduate profile:** 75% are state residents; 75% are transfers. 1% Asian-American, 18% Black, 16% Hispanic, 65% White. Average age of undergraduates is 21.
**Freshman profile:** 13% of freshmen who took SAT scored 500 or over on verbal, 7% scored 500 or over on math; 33% scored 400 or over on verbal, 30% scored 400 or over on math; 70% scored 300 or over on verbal, 80% scored 300 or over on math. Majority of accepted applicants took SAT.
**Undergraduate achievement:** 68% of fall 1991 freshmen returned for fall 1992 term.
**Foreign students:** Two students are from out of the country. Countries represented include Jamaica.

**PROGRAMS OF STUDY. Degrees:** B.A., B.S., B.S.Ed.
**Majors:** Accounting, Addictionology, Biology, Business Education, Chemistry, Communication Arts, Computer Information Systems, Criminal Justice, Elementary Education, English, Fine Arts, General Science, General Studies, History, Industrial Relations, Liberal Arts, Management, Organizational Management, Philosophy, Political Science, Psychology, Science Education, Social Science, Social Science Education, Sociology, Sociology/Social Work, Theology.
**Distribution of degrees:** The majors with the highest enrollment are accounting, management, and criminal justice; English, history, and fine arts have the lowest.
**Requirements:** General education requirement.
**Academic regulations:** Freshmen must maintain minimum 1.50 GPA; sophomores, 1.75 GPA; juniors, 2.00 GPA; seniors, 2.00 GPA.
**Special:** Minors offered in most majors and in peace and justice. Associate's degrees offered. Self-designed majors. Double majors. Dual degrees. Independent study. Accelerated

study. Internships. Cooperative education programs. Preprofessional programs in law, medicine, and pharmacy. Teacher certification in elementary and secondary education.
**Honors:** Honors program.
**Academic Assistance:** Remedial reading, writing, math, and study skills. Nonremedial tutoring.

**ADMISSIONS. Academic basis for candidate selection** (in order of priority): Secondary school record, class rank, essay, standardized test scores, school's recommendation.
**Nonacademic basis for candidate selection:** Character and personality are emphasized. Extracurricular participation and particular talent or ability are considered.
**Requirements:** Graduation from secondary school is required; GED is accepted. 15 units and the following program of study are recommended: 4 units of English, 3 units of math, 2 units of science, 1 unit of foreign language, 2 units of social studies, 1 unit of history, 2 units of electives. Minimum combined SAT score of 800 (composite ACT score of 18), rank in top half of secondary school class, and minimum 2.0 GPA required. Conditional admission possible for applicants not meeting standard requirements. SAT or ACT is required. Campus visit and interview recommended. Off-campus interviews available with an admissions representative.
**Procedure:** Take SAT or ACT by May of 12th year. Visit college for interview by March 30 of 12th year. Suggest filing application by June 30. Application deadline is September 1. Notification of admission on rolling basis. $30 nonrefundable tuition deposit. Freshmen accepted for terms other than fall.
**Special programs:** Admission may be deferred one semester. Credit may be granted through CLEP general and subject exams, challenge exams, and military and life experience. Early decision program. for fall 1992, three applied for early decision and one was accepted. Deadline for applying for early decision is September 1. Early entrance/early admission program. Concurrent enrollment program.
**Transfer students:** Transfer students accepted for terms other than fall. for fall 1992, 75% of all new students were transfers into all classes. 189 transfer applications were received, 156 were accepted. Application deadline is September 1 for fall; December 15 for spring. Minimum 2.0 GPA required. Lowest course grade accepted is "C." Maximum number of transferable credits is 66 semester hours from a two-year school and 94 semester hours from a four-year school. At least 30 semester hours must be completed at the college to receive degree.
**Admissions contact:** Cynthia Hillman, M.A., Dean of Enrollment Management. 219 473-4215.

**FINANCIAL AID. Available aid:** Pell grants, SEOG, state scholarships and grants, school scholarships and grants, private scholarships and grants, and academic merit scholarships. Perkins Loans (NDSL), PLUS, Stafford Loans (GSL), and SLS. AMS.
**Financial aid statistics:** 9% of aid is not need-based. In 1992-93, 100% of all undergraduate applicants received aid. Average amounts of aid awarded freshmen: Scholarships and grants, $2,300.
**Supporting data/closing dates:** FAFSA: Priority filing date is March 1; accepted on rolling basis. School's own aid application: Priority filing date is June 1. State aid form: Priority filing date is March 1. Income tax forms: Accepted on rolling basis. Notification of awards on rolling basis.
**Financial aid contact:** Andre Wade, Director of Financial Aid. 219 473-4215.

# DePauw University

**Greencastle, IN 46135** **317 658-4800**

**1994-95 Costs.** Tuition: $14,300. Room & board: $5,020. Fees, books, misc. academic expenses (school's estimate): $750.
**Enrollment.** Undergraduates: 888 men, 1,059 women (full-time). Freshman class: 2,073 applicants, 1,721 accepted, 495 enrolled.
**Test score averages/ranges.** Range of SAT scores of middle 50%: 460-580 verbal, 510-650 math. Range of ACT scores of middle 50%: 24-28 composite.
**Faculty.** 156 full-time; 52 part-time. 78% of faculty holds doctoral degree. Student/faculty ratio: 12 to 1.
**Selectivity rating.** More competitive.

**PROFILE.** DePauw, founded in 1837, is a church-affiliated, liberal arts university. Programs are offered through the Asbury College of Liberal Arts, the School of Music, and the School of Nursing. Its 116-acre campus is located in a residential area of Greencastle, 40 miles west of Indianapolis. Its oldest building is listed in the National Register of Historical Monuments.

**Accreditation:** NCACS. Professionally accredited by the National Association of Schools of Music, the National Council for Accreditation of Teacher Education.
**Religious orientation:** DePauw University is affiliated with the United Methodist Church; no religious requirements.
**Library:** Collections totaling over 271,129 volumes, 1,249 periodical subscriptions, and 314,759 microform items.
**Special facilities/museums:** Language lab, performing arts center, anthropology and art museums, contemporary media center, nature preserve, observatory.
**Athletic facilities:** Gymnasium, field house, badminton, basketball, racquetball, tennis, and volleyball courts, weight rooms, sauna, dance studio, track, baseball, football, soccer, and softball fields, swimming pool.

**STUDENT BODY. Undergraduate profile:** 40% are state residents; 6% are transfers. 2% Asian-American, 7% Black, 3% Hispanic, 85% White, 3% International students. Average age of undergraduates is 20.
**Freshman profile:** 1% of freshmen who took SAT scored 700 or over on verbal, 10% scored 700 or over on math; 21% scored 600 or over on verbal, 46% scored 600 or over on math; 60% scored 500 or over on verbal, 82% scored 500 or over on math; 93% scored 400 or over on verbal, 97% scored 400 or over on math; 100% scored 300 or over on verbal, 100% scored 300 or over on math. 87% of accepted applicants took SAT; 68% took ACT. 83% of freshmen come from public schools.
**Undergraduate achievement:** 89% of fall 1992 freshmen returned for fall 1993 term. 72% of entering class graduated. 25% of students who completed a degree program immediately went on to graduate study.
**Foreign students:** 60 students are from out of the country. Countries represented include Argentina, Colombia, Japan, and the former Yugoslav Republics; 25 in all.

**PROGRAMS OF STUDY. Degrees:** B.A., B.Mus.
**Majors:** Anthropology, Art History, Biological Sciences, Chemistry, Classical Civilizations, Classical Languages, Communication Arts/Sciences, Computer Science, Earth Sciences, East Asian Studies, Economics, Elementary Education, English Writing, French, Geography, Geology, German, Greek, History, Interdisciplinary, Latin, Literature, Mathematics, Medical Technology, Music, Music Business, Music Composition, Music Double Major, Music Education, Music Performance, Philosophy, Physical Education, Physics, Political Science, Pre-Engineering, Pre-Nursing, Psychology, Religion, Romance Languages, Russian/Slavic Studies, Sociology, Spanish, Studio Art, Women's Studies.
**Distribution of degrees:** The majors with the highest enrollment are political science, economics, and communication arts/sciences; Latin, anthropology, and pre-engineering have the lowest.
**Requirements:** General education requirement.
**Academic regulations:** Minimum 2.0 GPA must be maintained.
**Special:** Minors offered in many majors and in Asian studies, black studies, business administration, and international business. Self-designed majors. Double majors. Dual degrees. Independent study. Pass/fail grading option. Internships. Preprofessional programs in law, medicine, veterinary science, dentistry, theology, engineering, speech language/pathology, and audiology. Pre-nursing degree program with Rush U. 3-2 engineering programs with Case Western Reserve U, Columbia U, Georgia Tech, and Washington U. Member of Great Lakes College Association. Washington Semester and UN Semester. Arts Program in New York, Newberry Library Program in the Humanities (Illinois), Oak Ridge Science Semester (Tennessee), Philadelphia Urban Semester. Teacher certification in elementary and secondary education. Certification in specific subject areas. Exchange programs abroad in Argentina (John F. Kennedy U) and Japan (Nanzan U). Year, semester, or summer abroad programs in African countries, Austria, China, England, France, Germany, Greece, India, Japan, Latin American countries, Scotland, the former Soviet Republics, Spain, and the former Yugoslav republics. ROTC at Rose-Hulman Inst of Tech. AFROTC at Indiana U.
**Honors:** Phi Beta Kappa. Honors program. Honor societies.
**Academic Assistance:** Nonremedial tutoring.

**STUDENT LIFE. Housing:** All unmarried students under age 23 must live on campus unless living with family. Coed dorms. Sorority and fraternity housing. 93% of students live in college housing.
**Social atmosphere:** According to the student newspaper, "Social life at DePauw centers around fraternities and sororities. DePauw is 90 percent Greek." Student plays draw good crowds. The most popular sports events are football games and the "Little 500" bike race. On campus, students socialize at The Hub cafeteria and Bowman Pond; off campus, they frequent several local bars including Topper's, Noble Roman's, Delaney's, and Marvin's.
**Services and counseling/handicapped student services:** Placement services. Health service. Women's center. Counseling services for minority students. Personal and psychological counseling. Career and academic guidance services. Religious counseling.
**Campus organizations:** Undergraduate student government. Student newspaper (DePauw, published twice/week). Literary magazine. Yearbook. Radio and TV stations. Festival choir, gospel choir, Little Theatre, debating, Habitat for Humanity, Amnesty International, investment club, Little 500 Board, women's groups, union board, residence hall association, fencing and cycling clubs, ice hockey and sailing clubs, 65 organizations in all. 13 fraternities, all with chapter houses; 10 sororities, eight chapter houses. 82% of men join a fraternity. 78% of women join a sorority.
**Religious organizations:** Chaplain's Living Unit Council, Canterbury Club, Intervarsity Christian Fellowship.
**Minority/foreign student organizations:** AAAS (black student group). International student group, ASIA.

**ATHLETICS. Physical education requirements:** None.
**Intercollegiate competition:** 29% of students participate. Baseball (M), basketball (M,W), cross-country (M,W), diving (M,W), field hockey (W), football (M), golf (M,W), soccer (M,W), swimming (M,W), tennis (M,W), track (outdoor) (M,W), track and field (outdoor) (M,W), volleyball (W). Member of Indiana Collegiate Athletic Conference, NCAA Division III.
**Intramural and club sports:** 35% of students participate. Intramural cheerleading, crew, cycling, fencing, lacrosse, rugby, sailing, volleyball. Men's club cheerleading, crew, cycling, fencing, lacrosse, rugby, sailing, volleyball. Women's club cheerleading, crew, cycling, fencing, lacrosse, rugby, sailing, softball.

**ADMISSIONS. Academic basis for candidate selection** (in order of priority): Secondary school record, class rank, standardized test scores, essay, school's recommendation.
**Nonacademic basis for candidate selection:** Character and personality, extracurricular participation, and particular talent or ability are emphasized. Geographical distribution and alumni/ae relationship are considered.
**Requirements:** Graduation from secondary school is required; GED is accepted. 15 units and the following program of study are required: 4 units of English, 3 units of math, 3 units of science including 2 units of lab, 2 units of foreign language, 1 unit of social studies, 2 units of history. Separate applications required for admission to Honor Scholars, Management Fellows, Media Fellows, and Science Research Fellows Programs. Audition required of music program applicants. SAT or ACT is required. Campus visit and interview recommended. Off-campus interviews available with an admissions representative.
**Procedure:** Take SAT or ACT by February 1 of 12th year. Suggest filing application by December 1. Application deadline is February 15. Notification of admission by April 1. Reply is required by May 1. $200 nonrefundable tuition deposit. $50 room deposit, refundable until May 15. Freshmen accepted for terms other than fall.
**Special programs:** Admission may be deferred one year. Credit and/or placement may be granted through CEEB Advanced Placement exams for scores of 4 or higher. Credit and/or placement may be granted through CLEP subject exams. Credit and placement may be granted through challenge exams. Early decision program. for fall 1993, 446 applied for

early decision and 422 were accepted. Deadline for applying for early decision is December 1. Early entrance/early admission program.

**Transfer students:** Transfer students accepted for terms other than fall. for fall 1992, 6% of all new students were transfers into all classes. 73 transfer applications were received, 55 were accepted. Application deadline is April 1 for fall; December 31 for spring. Minimum 3.0 GPA recommended. Lowest course grade accepted is "C." Six of final eight courses (24 of last 32 semester hours) must be completed at the university to receive degree.

**Admissions contact:** David C. Murray, M.Ed., Director of Admissions. 800 447-2495.

**FINANCIAL AID. Available aid:** Pell grants, SEOG, state scholarships and grants, school scholarships and grants, private scholarships and grants, ROTC scholarships, and academic merit scholarships. Perkins Loans (NDSL), PLUS, Stafford Loans (GSL), NSL, school loans, and SLS. Knight Tuition Plans and deferred payment plan.

**Financial aid statistics:** 32% of aid is not need-based. In 1993-94, 91% of all undergraduate applicants received aid; 95% of freshman applicants. Average amounts of aid awarded freshmen: Scholarships and grants, $8,137; loans, $2,836.

**Supporting data/closing dates:** FAFSA/FAF: Priority filing date is February 15. State aid form: Deadline is March 1. Income tax forms: Priority filing date is February 15. Notification of awards on rolling basis.

**Financial aid contact:** Alan Hill, M.A.T., Coordinator of Financial Aid. 317 658-4030.

**STUDENT EMPLOYMENT.** College Work/Study Program. Institutional employment. 30% of full-time undergraduates work on campus during school year. Students may expect to earn an average of $655 during school year. Off-campus part-time employment opportunities rated "good."

**COMPUTER FACILITIES.** 135 IBM/IBM-compatible and Macintosh/Apple microcomputers; 45 are networked. Students may access Digital minicomputer/mainframe systems, BITNET. Residence halls may be equipped with stand-alone microcomputers, networked terminals. Client/LAN operating systems include Apple/Macintosh, DOS. Computer languages and software packages include BASIC, C, FORTRAN, Kermit, MINITAB, Paradox, Quattro Pro, SPSS, Turbo Pascal, Vax Pascal, WordPerfect. Computer facilities are available to all students.

**Fees:** None.

**Hours:** 8 AM-midn.

**GRADUATE CAREER DATA.** Graduate school percentages: 6% enter law school. 4% enter medical school. 1% enter dental school. 3% enter graduate business programs. 6% enter graduate arts and sciences programs. 1% enter theological school/seminary. Highest graduate school enrollments: U of Chicago, U of Illinois, Indiana U, Northwestern U. 55% of graduates choose careers in business and industry. Companies and businesses that hire graduates: American National Bank, Arthur Andersen, Andersen Consulting, Deloitte & Touche, Eli Lilly, Enterprise Rent-A-Car, IBM, Northern Trust, Procter & Gamble, Ralston Purina.

**PROMINENT ALUMNI/AE.** J. Danforth Quayle, former Vice President of the U.S.; John Jakes, author, American Bicentennial Series; Vernon Jordan, former president, National Urban League; Gretchen Cryer and Nancy Ford Charles, lyricist team.

# Earlham College

**Richmond, IN 47374 — 317 983-1200**

**1994-95 Costs.** Tuition: $15,849. Room: $1,971. Board: $2,220. Fees, books, misc. academic expenses (school's estimate): $853.

**Enrollment.** Undergraduates: 447 men, 581 women (full-time). Freshman class: 1,358 applicants, 1,006 accepted, 274 enrolled. Graduate enrollment: 25 men, 24 women.

**Test score averages/ranges.** Average SAT scores: 540 verbal, 560 math. Range of SAT scores of middle 50%: 480-600 verbal, 500-630 math. Average ACT scores: 25 composite. Range of ACT scores of middle 50%: 22-29 composite.

**Faculty.** 90 full-time; 18 part-time. 95% of faculty holds highest degree in specific field. Student/faculty ratio: 11 to 1.

**Selectivity rating.** Competitive.

**PROFILE.** Earlham, founded in 1847, is a church-affiliated, liberal arts college. Its 800-acre campus is located in Richmond, 40 miles west of Dayton, Ohio.

**Accreditation:** NCACS.

**Religious orientation:** Earlham College is affiliated with the Society of Friends; two terms of religion required.

**Library:** Collections totaling over 338,740 volumes, 1,276 periodical subscriptions, and 170,590 microform items.

**Special facilities/museums:** Living history and natural history museums, cultural center, language labs, greenhouse, observatory, planetarium.

**Athletic facilities:** Gymnasiums, field house, swimming pool, baseball, field hockey, football, lacrosse, soccer, and softball fields, weight room, badminton, basketball, racquetball, tennis, and volleyball courts, climbing wall, track, wellness room.

**STUDENT BODY. Undergraduate profile:** 15% are state residents; 12% are transfers. 4% Asian-American, 9% Black, 1% Hispanic, 85% White, 1% Other. Average age of undergraduates is 20.

**Freshman profile:** 4% of freshmen who took SAT scored 700 or over on verbal, 8% scored 700 or over on math; 28% scored 600 or over on verbal, 37% scored 600 or over on math; 68% scored 500 or over on verbal, 75% scored 500 or over on math; 94% scored 400 or over on verbal, 93% scored 400 or over on math; 100% scored 300 or over on verbal, 100% scored 300 or over on math. 19% of freshmen who took ACT scored 30 or over on composite; 69% scored 24 or over on composite; 93% scored 18 or over on composite; 100% scored 12 or over on composite. 87% of accepted applicants took SAT; 39% took ACT. 74% of freshmen come from public schools.

**Undergraduate achievement:** 82% of fall 1992 freshmen returned for fall 1993 term. 69% of entering class graduated. 35% of students who completed a degree program immediately went on to graduate study.

**Foreign students:** 47 students are from out of the country. Countries represented include China, Israel, Japan, Kenya, South Africa, and Turkey; 19 in all.

**PROGRAMS OF STUDY. Degrees:** B.A.

**Majors:** African-American Studies, Art, Biology, Chemistry, Computer Science, Drama, Economics, Education, English, Environmental Science, French, Geology, German, History, Human Development/Social Relations, International Studies, Japanese Area Studies, Management, Mathematics, Music, Peace/Global Studies, Philosophy, Physics/Astronomy, Political Science, Psychology, Religion, Sociology/Anthropology, Spanish, Theatre Arts, Women's Studies.

**Distribution of degrees:** The majors with the highest enrollment are biology, English, and psychology; geology, philosophy, and computer science have the lowest.

**Requirements:** General education requirement.

**Academic regulations:** Minimum 2.0 GPA must be maintained.

**Special:** Minors offered in many majors and in art history and classics. Living-Learning Program integrates classroom and dormitory experiences. Self-designed majors. Double majors. Dual degrees. Independent study. Accelerated study. Internships. Cooperative education programs. Graduate school at which undergraduates may take graduate-level courses. Preprofessional programs in law, medicine, theology, architecture, business, engineering, forestry, and nursing. 3-2 engineering programs with Case Western Reserve U, Columbia U, U of Michigan, Rensselaer Polytech Inst, U of Rochester, and Washington U. 3-2 nursing program with Case Western Reserve U. 3-2 architecture program with Washington U. 3-2 forestry and environmental studies program with Duke U. Member of Great Lakes Colleges Association. Arts Program in New York. Newberry Library Program in the Humanities (Illinois). Oak Ridge Science Semester (Tennessee). Philadelphia Urban Semester. Wilderness Field Station Program (Minnesota). Other off-campus study opportunities. Teacher certification in elementary and secondary education. Certification in specific subject areas. Study abroad in 19 countries including Austria, England, France, Germany, Japan, Kenya, Mexico, and the Middle East.

**Honors:** Phi Beta Kappa. Honor societies.

**Academic Assistance:** Remedial study skills. Nonremedial tutoring.

**STUDENT LIFE. Housing:** All unmarried students under age 21 must live on campus unless living near campus with relatives. Coed dorms. School-owned/operated apartments. Off-campus married-student housing. Off-campus college-owned houses. 85% of students live in college housing.

**Social atmosphere:** According to the editor of the student newspaper, "This is a small campus and a small town, but thanks to the people here and the nearby cities, (Dayton, Cincinnati), it is a pretty good place to be." Popular gathering spots include the Runyan Center, the Coffeeshop, and the Promenade. Student Government, politically correct groups, and the Rape Awareness Group are influential on campus. Mayday, Sunsplash, Breadbox, and the Earlham Film Series are among the year's favorite events.

**Services and counseling/handicapped student services:** Health service. Women's center. Day care. Personal counseling. Career and academic guidance services. Religious counseling. Physically disabled student services. Learning disabled services. Notetaking services. Tape recorders. Tutors. Reader services for the blind.

**Campus organizations:** Undergraduate student government. Student newspaper (Earlham Word, published once/week). Literary magazine. Yearbook. Radio station. Chamber and madrigal singers, gospel choir, concert choir, orchestra, jazz band, instrumental ensembles, folk dancing, drama groups, recycling group, student food cooperatives, hunger action group, Amnesty International, coffeehouse, volunteer program, special-interest groups, 60 organizations in all.

**Religious organizations:** Young Friends, Catholic Organization, Christian Fellowship, Jewish Student Union, Council on Religion, Unitarian Universalist Fellowship, Baptist Student Union, other religious groups.

**Minority/foreign student organizations:** Black Leadership Coalition. International student group.

**ATHLETICS. Physical education requirements:** Four terms of physical education required.

**Intercollegiate competition:** 30% of students participate. Baseball (M), basketball (M,W), cross-country (M,W), field hockey (W), football (M), lacrosse (W), soccer (M,W), tennis (M,W), track and field (indoor) (M,W), track and field (outdoor) (M,W), volleyball (W). Member of NCAA Division III, North Coast Athletic Conference.

**Intramural and club sports:** 50% of students participate. Intramural basketball, bowling, racquetball, soccer, softball, tennis, triathlon, volleyball. Men's club lacrosse, swimming, ultimate frisbee, volleyball. Women's club cheerleading, swimming, ultimate frisbee.

**ADMISSIONS. Academic basis for candidate selection** (in order of priority): Secondary school record, class rank, essay, standardized test scores, school's recommendation.

**Nonacademic basis for candidate selection:** Character and personality are emphasized. Extracurricular participation and particular talent or ability are important. Geographical distribution and alumni/ae relationship are considered.

**Requirements:** Graduation from secondary school is recommended; GED is accepted. 15 units and the following program of study are required: 4 units of English, 3 units of math, 2 units of lab science, 2 units of foreign language, 2 units of social studies. Additional units of mathematics and social studies/history recommended. Minimum SAT scores of 500 in both verbal and math and minimum 2.8 GPA recommended. SAT is required; ACT may be substituted. Campus visit and interview recommended. Off-campus interviews available with admissions and alumni representatives.

**Procedure:** Take SAT or ACT by November of 12th year. Visit college for interview by February 1 of 12th year. Application deadline is February 15. Notification of admission by April 2. Reply is required by May 1. $200 nonrefundable tuition deposit. Freshmen accepted for terms other than fall.

**Special programs:** Admission may be deferred one year. Credit may be granted through CEEB Advanced Placement for scores of 4 or higher. Credit and/or placement may be granted through CLEP general and subject exams. Early decision program. for fall 1993, 48 applied for early decision and 45 were accepted. Deadline for applying for early decision is December 1. Early entrance/early admission program. Concurrent enrollment program.

**Transfer students:** Transfer students accepted for terms other than fall. for fall 1993, 12% of all new students were transfers into all classes. 87 transfer applications were received, 62 were accepted. Application deadline is April 1 for fall; March 1 for spring. Minimum 2.5 GPA recommended. Lowest course grade accepted is "C." Maximum number of

transferable credits is 18 course credits from a two-year school and 36 course credits from a four-year school. At least 9 course credits must be completed at the college to receive degree.
**Admissions contact:** Robert de Veer, M.A., Director of Admissions. 800 327-5426.
**FINANCIAL AID. Available aid:** Pell grants, SEOG, state scholarships and grants, school scholarships and grants, private scholarships and grants, academic merit scholarships, and aid for undergraduate foreign students. Perkins Loans (NDSL), PLUS, Stafford Loans (GSL), and school loans. Knight Tuition Plans and deferred payment plan.
**Financial aid statistics:** 5% of aid is not need-based. In 1993-94, 65% of all undergraduate applicants received aid; 59% of freshman applicants. Average amounts of aid awarded freshmen: Scholarships and grants, $9,050; loans, $2,785.
**Supporting data/closing dates:** FAFSA/FAF: Priority filing date is March 1. State aid form: Accepted on rolling basis. Income tax forms: Priority filing date is April 1. Notification of awards on rolling basis.
**Financial aid contact:** Robert Arnold, M.A., Director of Financial Aid. 317 983-1217.
**STUDENT EMPLOYMENT.** College Work/Study Program. Institutional employment. 42% of full-time undergraduates work on campus during school year. Students may expect to earn an average of $1,275 during school year. Off-campus part-time employment opportunities rated "poor."
**COMPUTER FACILITIES.** 50 IBM/IBM-compatible and Macintosh/Apple microcomputers; all are networked. Students may access Digital minicomputer/mainframe systems, Internet. Client/LAN operating systems include Apple/Macintosh. Computer languages and software packages include Bliss, C, FORTH, FORTRAN, LISP, Pascal, SPSS; 750 in all. Computer facilities are available to all students.
**Fees:** None.
**Hours:** 24 hours.
**GRADUATE CAREER DATA.** Graduate school percentages: 4% enter law school. 5% enter medical school. 2% enter dental school. 1% enter graduate business programs. 12% enter graduate arts and sciences programs. 2% enter theological school/seminary. Highest graduate school enrollments: Columbia U, Indiana U, U of Michigan. 32% of graduates choose careers in business and industry. Companies and businesses that hire graduates: SONY, Subaru/Isuzu.
**PROMINENT ALUMNI/AE.** Frances Moore Lappe, author/activist on food policy issues; Laura Sessions Streep, Pulitzer Prize-winning assistant editor, *Washington Post;* Wendel Stanley, Nobel Prize-winning chemist; Lindley Clark, economic news editor, *Wall Street Journal;* Jim Fowler, zoologist and natural park designer; Barbara Howard, Peabody Award-winning radio producer.

## Franklin College

**Franklin, IN 46131** **317 738-8062**

**1994-95 Costs.** Tuition: $10,390. Room & Board: $4,040. Fees, books, misc. academic expenses (school's estimate): $510.
**Enrollment.** Undergraduates: 375 men, 461 women (full-time). Freshman class: 723 applicants, 567 accepted, 282 enrolled.
**Test score averages/ranges.** Average SAT scores: 466 verbal, 528 math. Average ACT scores: 22 composite.
**Faculty.** 61 full-time; 34 part-time. 70% of faculty holds highest degree in specific field. Student/faculty ratio: 12 to 1.
**Selectivity rating.** Less competitive.

**PROFILE.** Franklin, founded in 1834, is a church-affiliated, liberal arts college. Its 74-acre campus is located in Franklin, 20 miles south of Indianapolis.

**Accreditation:** NCACS. Professionally accredited by the National Council for Accreditation of Teacher Education.
**Religious orientation:** Franklin College is affiliated with the Baptist Church (American Baptist Churches USA); no religious requirements.
**Library:** Collections totaling over 105,621 volumes, 496 periodical subscriptions and 354 microform items.
**Athletic facilities:** Gymnasium, field house, weight room, basketball, tennis, and volleyball courts, track, baseball, field hockey, football, soccer, and softball fields.
**STUDENT BODY. Undergraduate profile:** 90% are state residents; 1% are transfers. 1% Asian-American, 2% Black, 1% Hispanic, 96% White. Average age of undergraduates is 20.
**Freshman profile:** 1% of freshmen who took SAT scored 700 or over on math; 6% scored 600 or over on verbal, 24% scored 600 or over on math; 36% scored 500 or over on verbal, 67% scored 500 or over on math; 83% scored 400 or over on verbal, 91% scored 400 or over on math; 100% scored 300 or over on verbal, 100% scored 300 or over on math. Majority of accepted applicants took SAT.
**Undergraduate achievement:** 82% of fall 1991 freshmen returned for fall 1992 term. 72% of entering class graduated. 20% of students who completed a degree program went on to graduate study within five years.
**Foreign students:** 17 students are from out of the country. Countries represented include Australia, China, Greece, Japan, Sri Lanka, and Uganda; 14 in all.
**PROGRAMS OF STUDY. Degrees:** B.A.
**Majors:** Accounting, American Studies, Art, Biology, Business, Canadian Studies, Chemistry, Economics, Elementary Education, English, French, History, Journalism, Mathematics, Mathematics/Computing, Music, Philosophy, Physical Education, Physics, Political Science, Psychology, Religious Studies, Sociology, Spanish, Theatre.
**Distribution of degrees:** The majors with the highest enrollment are journalism, business, and education; philosophy, computer information science, and French have the lowest.
**Requirements:** General education requirement.
**Special:** Minors offered in all majors and in conservation/environmental science, fitness, international studies, reading, and rhetoric. Winter term provides one month of intensive study in a project of student's choice. Career cluster program prepares students for professional career interest. Double majors. Dual degrees. Independent study. Pass/fail grading option. Internships. Cooperative education programs. Graduate school at which undergraduates may take graduate-level courses. Preprofessional programs in law, medicine, veterinary science, dentistry, optometry, engineering, and forestry. 2-2 nursing program with Rush U. 3-1 medical technology program. 3-2 engineering and occupational therapy programs with Washington U. 3-2 forestry and environmental studies program with Duke U. Washington Semester, UN Semester, and Sea Semester. Teacher certification in early childhood, elementary, and secondary education. Exchange program abroad in Canada (Acadia U). Study abroad also in England, France, Germany, Italy, Peru, and Spain. ROTC at Indiana U–Purdue U at Indianapolis.
**Honors:** Honors program. Honor societies.
**Academic Assistance:** Nonremedial tutoring.
**ADMISSIONS. Academic basis for candidate selection** (in order of priority): Standardized test scores, secondary school record, class rank, school's recommendation.
**Nonacademic basis for candidate selection:** Character and personality are emphasized. Particular talent or ability is important. Extracurricular participation and alumni/ae relationship are considered.
**Requirements:** Graduation from secondary school is required; GED is accepted. 15 units and the following program of study are recommended: 4 units of English, 3 units of math, 2 units of science, 2 units of foreign language, 2 units of social studies, 2 units of history. Minimum SAT scores of 400 in both verbal and math, rank in top half of secondary school class, and minimum 2.0 GPA required. SAT or ACT is required. Campus visit and interview recommended. No off-campus interviews.
**Procedure:** Take SAT or ACT in spring of the 11th year or fall of 12th year. Suggest filing application as early as possible during 12th year. No deadline. Notification of admission on rolling basis. Applicant must accept offer and pay nonrefundable tuition deposit by date given in acceptance letter. $100 room deposit, refundable until May 1. Freshmen accepted for terms other than fall.
**Special programs:** Admission may be deferred one year. Credit may be granted through CEEB Advanced Placement for scores of 3 or higher. Credit may be granted through CLEP subject exams, DANTES exams, and military experience. Early entrance/early admission program. Concurrent enrollment program.
**Transfer students:** Transfer students accepted for terms other than fall. for fall 1992, 1% of all new students were transfers into all classes. Application deadline is rolling for fall; rolling for spring. Minimum 2.0 GPA required. Lowest course grade accepted is "C." Maximum number of transferable credits is 106 quarter hours. At least 136 quarter hours must be completed at the college to receive degree.
**Admissions contact:** B. Stephen Richards, Director of Admissions. 317 738-8062, 800 852-0232.
**FINANCIAL AID. Available aid:** Pell grants, SEOG, state scholarships and grants, school scholarships and grants, private scholarships, and academic merit scholarships. Perkins Loans (NDSL), PLUS, Stafford Loans (GSL), school loans, and SLS. AMS and deferred payment plan.
**Financial aid statistics:** In 1992-93, 95% of all undergraduate applicants received aid; 96% of freshman applicants. Average amounts of aid awarded freshmen: Scholarships and grants, $6,900; loans, $1,783.
**Supporting data/closing dates:** FAFSA/FAF/FFS: Priority filing date is March 1. State aid form: Priority filing date is March 1. Income tax forms: Accepted on rolling basis. Notification of awards on rolling basis.
**Financial aid contact:** Mike Roberts, Director of Financial Aid. 317 738-8075.

## Goshen College

**Goshen, IN 46526** **219 535-7000**

**1994-95 Costs.** Tuition: $9,420. Room: $1,800. Board: $1,930. Fees, books, misc. academic expenses (school's estimate): $600.
**Enrollment.** Undergraduates: 416 men, 540 women (full-time). Freshman class: 550 applicants, 460 accepted, 236 enrolled. Graduate enrollment: 474 men, 648 women.
**Test score averages/ranges.** Average SAT scores: 487 verbal, 519 math. Range of SAT scores of middle 50%: 450-499 verbal, 500-549 math.
**Faculty.** 85 full-time; 40 part-time. 63% of faculty holds doctoral degree. Student/faculty ratio: 14 to 1.
**Selectivity rating.** Competitive.

**PROFILE.** Goshen, founded in 1894, is a church-affiliated, liberal arts college. Its 135-acre campus is located in Goshen.

**Accreditation:** NCACS. Professionally accredited by the American Dietetic Association, the Council on Social Work Education, the National Council for Accreditation of Teacher Education, the National League for Nursing.
**Religious orientation:** Goshen College is affiliated with the Mennonite Church; three semesters of religion/theology required.
**Library:** Collections totaling over 115,000 volumes, 860 periodical subscriptions, and 45,000 microform items.
**Special facilities/museums:** X-ray precision lab, lab kindergarten, historical library.
**Athletic facilities:** Gymnasium; track; basketball, tennis, volleyball courts; baseball, soccer, softball fields.
**STUDENT BODY. Undergraduate profile:** 40% are state residents; 22% are transfers. 2% Asian-American, 2% Black, 3% Hispanic, 1% Native American, 85% White, 7% Other. Average age of undergraduates is 21.
**Freshman profile:** 3% of freshmen who took SAT scored 700 or over on verbal, 7% scored 700 or over on math; 15% scored 600 or over on verbal, 22% scored 600 or over on math; 41% scored 500 or over on verbal, 52% scored 500 or over on math; 71% scored 400 or over on verbal, 73% scored 400 or over on math; 86% scored 300 or over on verbal, 87% scored 300 or over on math. 85% of accepted applicants took SAT; 31% took ACT. 78% of freshmen come from public schools.
**Undergraduate achievement:** 80% of fall 1992 freshmen returned for fall 1993 term. 50% of entering class graduated.

**Foreign students:** 85 students are from out of the country. Countries represented include China, Germany, India, Indonesia, and Sri Lanka; 33 in all.

**PROGRAMS OF STUDY. Degrees:** B.A., B.S., B.S.Nurs.
**Majors:** Accounting, Art, Biblical Studies, Biology, Business, Chemistry, Church Ministries, Communication, Computer Science, Early Childhood Education, Economics, Elementary Education, English, Family Life, Foods/Nutrition, German, Hispanic Ministries, History, History/Investigative Skills, Mathematics, Music, Natural Science, Nursing, Physical Education, Physics, Politics/Society, Psychology, Religion, Social Work, Sociology, Spanish, Urban/Black Ministries.
**Distribution of degrees:** The majors with the highest enrollment are business, nursing, and elementary education; German, Spanish, and chemistry have the lowest.
**Requirements:** General education requirement.
**Academic regulations:** Minimum 2.0 GPA must be maintained.
**Special:** Minors offered in most majors and in church music, environmental studies, peace studies, piano pedagogy, teaching English as a second language, tropical agriculture, women's studies, and world service. On-the-spot course in marine biology. Double majors. Independent study. Pass/fail grading option. Internships. Preprofessional programs in law, medicine, pharmacy, dentistry, theology, optometry, physical therapy, engineering, medical technology, nursing, and social work. 3-1 medical technology program. 3-2 engineering programs with Case Western Reserve U, U of Illinois, Pennsylvania State U, and Washington U. Semester-away programs. Teacher certification in early childhood education. Study abroad in Costa Rica, the Dominican Republic, Germany, Indonesia, and the Ivory Coast.
**Academic Assistance:** Remedial reading, writing, math, and study skills. Nonremedial tutoring.

**ADMISSIONS. Academic basis for candidate selection** (in order of priority): Secondary school record, standardized test scores, school's recommendation, class rank, essay.
**Nonacademic basis for candidate selection:** Character and personality, extracurricular participation, and particular talent or ability are important.
**Requirements:** Graduation from secondary school is required; GED is accepted. 16 units and the following program of study are recommended: 4 units of English, 2 units of math, 2 units of science, 2 units of foreign language, 2 units of social studies. Minimum combined SAT score of 800 (composite ACT score of 21), rank in top half of secondary school class, and minimum 2.0 GPA required. Nursing, social work, and teacher education programs have separate admissions procedures, including prerequisite courses, references, and GPA requirements. Conditional admission possible for applicants not meeting standard requirements. SAT is required; ACT may be substituted. PSAT is recommended. Campus visit and interview recommended. Off-campus interviews available with an admissions representative.
**Procedure:** Take SAT or ACT by summer of 12th year. Suggest filing application by April 1. Application deadline is August. Notification of admission on rolling basis. Reply is required before classes begin. $100 tuition deposit, refundable until May 1. $100 nonrefundable room deposit. Freshmen accepted for terms other than fall.
**Special programs:** Admission may be deferred two years. Credit may be granted through CEEB Advanced Placement for scores of 3 or higher. Credit may be granted through CLEP general and subject exams. Credit and placement may be granted through life experience. Concurrent enrollment program.
**Transfer students:** Transfer students accepted for terms other than fall. for fall 1993, 22% of all new students were transfers into all classes. 126 transfer applications were received, 115 were accepted. Application deadline is August 15 for fall; December 15 for spring. Minimum 2.0 GPA required. Lowest course grade accepted is "C." Maximum number of transferable credits is 90 semester hours. At least 30 semester hours must be completed at the college to receive degree.
**Admissions contact:** Martha Lehman, M.S., Director of Admissions. 219 535-7535.

**FINANCIAL AID. Available aid:** Pell grants, SEOG, Federal Nursing Student Scholarships, state scholarships and grants, school scholarships and grants, private scholarships and grants, academic merit scholarships, athletic scholarships, and aid for undergraduate foreign students. Perkins Loans (NDSL), PLUS, Stafford Loans (GSL), NSL, state loans, school loans, private loans, and SLS. AMS.
**Financial aid statistics:** 25% of aid is not need-based. In 1993-94, 79% of all undergraduate applicants received aid; 85% of freshman applicants. Average amounts of aid awarded freshmen: Scholarships and grants, $1,350; loans, $3,015.
**Supporting data/closing dates:** FAFSA/FAF/FFS: Accepted on rolling basis. School's own aid application: Accepted on rolling basis. State aid form: Accepted on rolling basis. Income tax forms: Accepted on rolling basis. Notification of awards on rolling basis.
**Financial aid contact:** Walter Schmucker, Director of Financial Aid. 219 535-7523.

## Grace College

**Winona Lake, IN 46590** **219 372-5100**

**1994-95 Costs.** Tuition: $8,958. Room & board: $3,818. Fees, books, misc. academic expenses (school's estimate): $300.
**Enrollment.** Undergraduates: 276 men, 342 women (full-time). Freshman class: 687 applicants, 540 accepted, 234 enrolled. Graduate enrollment: 97 men, 2 women.
**Test score averages/ranges.** Average ACT scores: 21 English, 19 math, 22 composite.
**Faculty.** 30 full-time; 26 part-time. 43% of faculty holds doctoral degree. Student/faculty ratio: 14 to 1.
**Selectivity rating.** Less competitive.

**PROFILE.** Grace College, founded in 1948, is a church-affiliated, liberal arts college. Its 150-acre, modern campus is in the town of Winona Lake, centrally located between Detroit, Indianapolis, and Chicago.

**Accreditation:** NCACS.
**Religious orientation:** Grace College is affiliated with the Fellowship of Grace Brethren Churches; five semesters of religion required.
**Library:** Collections totaling over 143,000 volumes, 560 periodical subscriptions, and 42,000 microform items.
**Special facilities/museums:** Art gallery, language lab.
**Athletic facilities:** Tennis courts; baseball, soccer, softball fields; cross-country course; gymnasium; weight room; swimming facilities.

**STUDENT BODY. Undergraduate profile:** 33% are state residents; 19% are transfers. 1% Asian-American, 2% Black, 1% Hispanic, 1% Native American, 95% White. Average age of undergraduates is 20.
**Freshman profile:** Majority of accepted applicants took ACT. 64% of freshmen come from public schools.
**Undergraduate achievement:** 78% of fall 1992 freshmen returned for fall 1993 term. 38% of entering class graduated. 18% of students who completed a degree program immediately went on to graduate study.
**Foreign students:** 12 students are from out of the country. Countries represented include Canada, Germany, Mexico, and Switzerland; 11 in all.

**PROGRAMS OF STUDY. Degrees:** B.A., B.S.
**Majors:** Accounting, Art, Art Education, Behavioral Science, Bible Studies, Biblical Languages, Biology, Business Administration/Management, Christian Ministries, Communication, Counseling, Criminal Justice, Elementary Education, English, French, General Science, General Studies, German, Graphic Arts, Greek, Mathematics, Music, Music Education, Physical Education, Psychology, Russian, Science, Sociology, Spanish, Speech Communication.
**Distribution of degrees:** The majors with the highest enrollment are psychology, elementary education, and business administration; German, Russian, and mathematics have the lowest.
**Requirements:** General education requirement.
**Academic regulations:** Freshmen must maintain minimum 1.50 GPA; sophomores, 1.75 GPA; juniors, 2.00 GPA; seniors, 2.00 GPA.
**Special:** Minors offered in most majors and in coaching endorsement, computer science, health/safety education, information processing, journalism, pedagogy, physics, and teaching English as a second language. Courses offered in broadcasting, drama, Hebrew, linguistics, and philosophy. Two-year certification programs in art and biblical studies. Christian ministries major is an interdisciplinary program in preparation for seminary or youth/music ministry. Associate's degrees offered. Double majors. Internships. Graduate school at which undergraduates may take graduate-level courses. Preprofessional programs in law, medicine, veterinary science, pharmacy, dentistry, theology, and physical therapy. 2-2 engineering program with Tri-State U. Member of Christian College Coalition; exchange possible. Teacher certification in elementary and secondary education. Certification in specific subject areas. Study abroad in France, Germany, Mexico, Spain, and Russia.
**Honors:** Honor societies.
**Academic Assistance:** Remedial study skills. Nonremedial tutoring.

**ADMISSIONS. Academic basis for candidate selection** (in order of priority): Secondary school record, class rank, standardized test scores, school's recommendation.
**Nonacademic basis for candidate selection:** Character and personality are emphasized. Extracurricular participation, particular talent or ability, and geographical distribution are considered.
**Requirements:** Graduation from secondary school is required; GED is accepted. 14 units and the following program of study are recommended: 4 units of English, 2 units of math, 2 units of science, 2 units of foreign language, 2 units of social studies, 1 unit of history, 1 unit of electives. Minimum composite ACT score of 19 (minimum combined SAT score of 800), rank in top half of secondary school class, and minimum 2.0 GPA required. Pastor's reference required of all applicants. Portfolio required of art program applicants. Audition required of music program applicants. Conditional admission possible for applicants not meeting standard requirements. SAT or ACT is required. Campus visit and interview recommended. Off-campus interviews available with an admissions representative.
**Procedure:** Take SAT or ACT by June of 12th year. Visit college for interview by March 15 of 12th year. Suggest filing application by April 1. Application deadline is August 1. Notification of admission on rolling basis. Reply is required by June 1. $100 tuition deposit, refundable until August 1. Freshmen accepted for terms other than fall.
**Special programs:** Admission may be deferred one year. Credit and/or placement may be granted through CEEB Advanced Placement exams for scores of 4 or higher. Credit and/or placement may be granted through CLEP subject exams. Credit and placement may be granted through Regents College, ACT PEP, DANTES, and challenge exams, and military experience. Concurrent enrollment program.
**Transfer students:** Transfer students accepted for terms other than fall. for fall 1993, 19% of all new students were transfers into all classes. 122 transfer applications were received, 94 were accepted. Application deadline is August 1 for fall; December 1 for spring. Minimum 2.0 GPA required. Lowest course grade accepted is "C." At least 30 semester hours must be completed at the college to receive degree.
**Admissions contact:** Ron Henry, M.A., M.Div., Dean of Enrollment. 219 372-5131.

**FINANCIAL AID. Available aid:** Pell grants, SEOG, state scholarships and grants, school scholarships and grants, private scholarships and grants, academic merit scholarships, athletic scholarships, and aid for undergraduate foreign students. Perkins Loans (NDSL), PLUS, Stafford Loans (GSL), state loans, school loans, private loans, and SLS. AMS. School's own payment plan.
**Financial aid statistics:** 22% of aid is not need-based. In 1993-94, 95% of all undergraduate applicants received aid; 95% of freshman applicants. Average amounts of aid awarded freshmen: Scholarships and grants, $2,900; loans, $3,800.
**Supporting data/closing dates:** FAFSA: Priority filing date is March 1. FAF: Priority filing date is April 1. State aid form: Deadline is March 1. Notification of awards on rolling basis.
**Financial aid contact:** Clifton Palmer, Associate Director of Financial Aid. 219 372-5244.

# Hanover College

**Hanover, IN 47243** **812 866-7000**

**1994-95 Costs.** Tuition: $8,200. Room: $1,540. Board: $1,945. Fees, books, misc. academic expenses (school's estimate): $810.
**Enrollment.** Undergraduates: 457 men, 587 women (full-time). Freshman class: 1,006 applicants, 781 accepted, 320 enrolled.
**Test score averages/ranges.** Average SAT scores: 498 verbal, 542 math. Average ACT scores: 24 English, 26 math, 25 composite.
**Faculty.** 92 full-time; 11 part-time. 85% of faculty holds doctoral degree. Student/faculty ratio: 13 to 1.
**Selectivity rating.** Competitive.

**PROFILE.** Hanover, founded in 1827, is a church-affiliated, liberal arts college. Its 630-acre campus is located between Cincinnati, Louisville, and Indianapolis. Campus architecture is predominantly Georgian in style.

**Accreditation:** NCACS.
**Religious orientation:** Hanover College is affiliated with the Presbyterian Church; one term of theology required.
**Library:** Collections totaling over 325,000 volumes, 927 periodical subscriptions, and 169,321 microform items.
**Special facilities/museums:** Geological museum, electronic language lab, observatory.
**Athletic facilities:** Intramural and softball fields, swimming pool, handball, racquetball, and tennis courts, gymnasiums, track, billiard tables, bowling lanes.

**STUDENT BODY. Undergraduate profile:** 60% are state residents; 8% are transfers. 2% Asian-American, 2% Black, 1% Hispanic, 95% White. Average age of undergraduates is 20.
**Freshman profile:** 94% of accepted applicants took SAT; 5% took ACT. 80% of freshmen come from public schools.
**Undergraduate achievement:** 87% of fall 1992 freshmen returned for fall 1993 term. 62% of entering class graduated. 40% of students who completed a degree program immediately went on to graduate study.
**Foreign students:** 27 students are from out of the country. Countries represented include China, Japan, Kuwait, Pakistan, and Sri Lanka; 19 in all.

**PROGRAMS OF STUDY. Degrees:** B.A.
**Majors:** Anthropology, Art, Biology, Business Administration, Chemistry, Communication, Economics, Elementary Education, English, French, Geology, German, History, International Studies, Latin American Studies, Mathematics, Medieval/Renaissance Studies, Music, Philosophy, Physical Education, Physics, Political Science, Psychology, Sociology, Spanish, Theatre, Theology.
**Distribution of degrees:** The majors with the highest enrollment are business administration, communication, and history; theology, philosophy, and physics have the lowest.
**Requirements:** General education requirement.
**Academic regulations:** Freshmen must maintain minimum 2.0 GPA; sophomores, juniors, seniors 2.5 GPA.
**Special:** Minors offered in most majors and in accounting, banking, classics, and finance. Teacher-Assisted, Mastery-Based, Self-Paced Instruction (TAMBSPI) program with Ohio State U in Arabic, Chinese, Japanese, and Russian. Double majors. Independent study. Pass/fail grading option. Internships. Preprofessional programs in law, medicine, veterinary science, dentistry, and theology. 3-2 engineering program with Washington U. Member of Spring Term Consortium. Washington Semester. Philadelphia Urban Semester. Exchange programs with Alma Coll, Elmira Coll, U of Indianapolis, Northland Coll, Transylvania U, Wartburg Coll, and William Woods Coll. Teacher certification in elementary and secondary education. Certification in specific subject areas. Study abroad in England, France, Germany, and Spain.
**Honors:** Honor societies.
**Academic Assistance:** Remedial writing. Nonremedial tutoring.

**STUDENT LIFE. Housing:** All unmarried students under age 21 must live on campus unless living near campus with relatives. Women's and men's dorms. Sorority and fraternity housing. 95% of students live in college housing.
**Social atmosphere:** Popular student gathering spots include Louie's, Barley and Hops, the coffeehouse, and fraternity houses. The Student Programming Board and the Greek houses have a widespread influence on campus social life. Homecoming and fraternity rush are two of the most popular campus activities. "There is no culture in the town of Hanover," reports the student newspaper, "so the college must bring in its own cultural programming. Most of the socializing occurs on weekend nights at the fraternity houses."
**Services and counseling/handicapped student services:** Placement services. Health service. Day care. Counseling services for minority students. Personal and psychological counseling. Career and academic guidance services. Religious counseling. Physically disabled student services. Tutors.
**Campus organizations:** Undergraduate student government. Student newspaper (The Hanover College Triangle, published once/week). Literary magazine. Yearbook. Radio and TV stations. Choir, chamber singers, chamber orchestra, theatre, Interfraternity Council, Student Programming Board, 24 organizations in all. Five fraternities, all with chapter houses; four sororities, all with chapter houses. 62% of men join a fraternity. 62% of women join a sorority.
**Religious organizations:** Fellowship of Christian Athletes.
**Minority/foreign student organizations:** Positive Image. International Student Club.

**ATHLETICS. Physical education requirements:** Four terms of physical education required.
**Intercollegiate competition:** 30% of students participate. Baseball (M), basketball (M,W), cross-country (M,W), field hockey (W), football (M), golf (M,W), soccer (M), softball (W), tennis (M,W), track (indoor) (M,W), track (outdoor) (M,W), track and field (indoor) (M,W), track and field (outdoor) (M,W), volleyball (W). Member of Indiana Collegiate Athletic Conference, NCAA III.
**Intramural and club sports:** 50% of students participate. Intramural basketball, bowling, football, swimming, table tennis, tennis, track, volleyball.

**ADMISSIONS. Academic basis for candidate selection** (in order of priority): Secondary school record, class rank, school's recommendation, essay, standardized test scores.
**Nonacademic basis for candidate selection:** Character and personality are emphasized. Extracurricular participation is important. Particular talent or ability, geographical distribution, and alumni/ae relationship are considered.
**Requirements:** Graduation from secondary school is required; GED is not accepted. 18 units and the following program of study are required: 4 units of English, 2 units of math, 2 units of lab science, 2 units of foreign language, 2 units of social studies, 2 units of history, 2 units of academic electives. Minimum combined SAT score of 900 and rank in top half of secondary school class recommended. SAT is required; ACT may be substituted. Campus visit and interview recommended. Off-campus interviews available with an admissions representative.
**Procedure:** Take SAT or ACT by December of 12th year. Visit college for interview by February 15 of 12th year. Suggest filing application by November 15. Application deadline is March 15. Notification of admission on rolling basis. $200 room deposit, refundable until May 1. Freshmen accepted for terms other than fall.
**Special programs:** Admission may be deferred one year. Credit and/or placement may be granted through CEEB Advanced Placement exams for scores of 4 or higher.
**Transfer students:** Transfer students accepted for terms other than fall. for fall 1993, 8% of all new students were transfers into all classes. 68 transfer applications were received, 56 were accepted. Application deadline is March 15 for fall; November 15 for spring. Minimum 2.5 GPA required. Lowest course grade accepted is "C." Maximum number of transferable credits is 60 semester hours. At least 50 semester hours must be completed at the college to receive degree.
**Admissions contact:** C. Eugene McLemore, M.S., Director of Admissions. 812 866-7021.

**FINANCIAL AID. Available aid:** Pell grants, state scholarships and grants, school scholarships and grants, private scholarships and grants, academic merit scholarships, and aid for undergraduate foreign students. Perkins Loans (NDSL), PLUS, and Stafford Loans (GSL). AMS.
**Financial aid statistics:** 20% of aid is not need-based. In 1993-94, 70% of all undergraduate applicants received aid; 67% of freshman applicants. Average amounts of aid awarded freshmen: Scholarships and grants, $4,000; loans, $1,600.
**Supporting data/closing dates:** FAFSA/FAF/FFS: Priority filing date is February 15; deadline is April 15. Income tax forms: Deadline is April 15. Notification of awards on rolling basis.
**Financial aid contact:** Sue A. Allmon, M.S., Director of Financial Aid. 812 866-7030.

**STUDENT EMPLOYMENT.** Institutional employment. 30% of full-time undergraduates work on campus during school year. Students may expect to earn an average of $600 during school year. Off-campus part-time employment opportunities rated "fair."

**COMPUTER FACILITIES.** 30 IBM/IBM-compatible and Macintosh/Apple microcomputers; all are networked. Computer languages and software packages include BASIC, Excel, Microsoft Word, Paradox, Pascal, Quattro, WordPerfect. Computer facilities are available to all students.
**Fees:** None.
**Hours:** 60 hours/week.

**GRADUATE CAREER DATA.** Graduate school percentages: 4% enter law school. 5% enter medical school. 3% enter dental school. 15% enter graduate business programs. 8% enter graduate arts and sciences programs. 1% enter theological school/seminary. Highest graduate school enrollments: Indiana U, U of Louisville, Purdue U. 30% of graduates choose careers in business and industry. Companies and businesses that hire graduates: Eli Lilly, Procter & Gamble.

**PROMINENT ALUMNI/AE.** "Woody" Harrelson, actor; John Burlew, president, Cincinnati Bar Association; Brian J. Martin, assistant solicitor general of the U.S.; Thomas A. Hendricks, former Vice President of the U.S.; William B. Rossow, NASA scientist; Jim Near, CEO, Wendy's.

# Huntington College

**Huntington, IN 46750** **219 356-6000**

**1994-95 Costs.** Tuition: $9,240. Room & board: $3,780. Fees, books, misc. academic expenses (school's estimate): $600.
**Enrollment.** Undergraduates: 248 men, 255 women (full-time). Freshman class: 600 applicants, 480 accepted, 150 enrolled. Graduate enrollment: 57 men, 2 women.
**Test score averages/ranges.** Range of SAT scores of middle 50%: 390-470 verbal, 470-570 math. Average ACT scores: 21 composite. Range of ACT scores of middle 50%: 18-24 composite.
**Faculty.** 39 full-time; 7 part-time. 76% of faculty holds doctoral degree. Student/faculty ratio: 13 to 1.
**Selectivity rating.** Less competitive.

**PROFILE.** Huntington, founded in 1850, is a church-affiliated, liberal arts college. Its 110-acre campus is located on the edge of the city of Huntington, 20 miles from Fort Wayne.

**Accreditation:** NCACS.
**Religious orientation:** Huntington College is affiliated with the United Brethren in Christ; two semesters of theology required.
**Library:** Collections totaling over 71,275 volumes, 487 periodical subscriptions, and 29,352 microform items.

**Special facilities/museums:** Natural resource area and regional resource center with herbarium, arboretum, mammal pelt collection, and nature preserve, phase-contrast microscope, X-ray generator, tektronix oscilloscope, gamma-ray spectrometer.
**Athletic facilities:** Gymnasiums, swimming pool, baseball, soccer, and softball fields, track, racquetball and tennis courts, weight room, field house.

**STUDENT BODY. Undergraduate profile:** 64% are state residents; 5% are transfers. 1% Asian-American, 97% White, 2% Other. Average age of undergraduates is 21.

**Freshman profile:** 4% of freshmen who took SAT scored 700 or over on verbal, 3% scored 700 or over on math; 12% scored 600 or over on verbal, 10% scored 600 or over on math; 47% scored 500 or over on verbal, 44% scored 500 or over on math; 67% scored 400 or over on verbal, 65% scored 400 or over on math; 97% scored 300 or over on verbal, 98% scored 300 or over on math. 76% of accepted applicants took SAT; 20% took ACT. 97% of freshmen come from public schools.

**Undergraduate achievement:** 66% of fall 1992 freshmen returned for fall 1993 term. 41% of entering class graduated. 12% of students who completed a degree program immediately went on to graduate study.

**Foreign students:** 33 students are from out of the country. Countries represented include Canada, China, Jamaica, Japan, and Sierra Leone; 15 in all.

**PROGRAMS OF STUDY. Degrees:** B.A., B.Mus., B.S.

**Majors:** Accounting, Art Education, Bible/Religion, Biology, Biology Education, Broadcasting, Business, Business Education, Business Management, Camping Ministries, Chemistry, Chemistry Education, Choral Education, Church Ministries, Community/Commercial Recreation, Computer Information Science, Cross-Cultural Ministries, Economics, Education, Elementary Education, English, English Education, Fine Arts, Graphic Arts, History, Instrumental Education, Management, Mathematics, Medical Technology, Music, Music Education, Music Performance, Outdoor Recreation, Philosophy, Physical Education, Print Media, Psychology, Recreation Management, Secondary Education, Social Studies Education, Sociology, Theatre, Therapeutic Recreation, Youth Ministries.

**Distribution of degrees:** The majors with the highest enrollment are business and elementary education; biology, sociology, and chemistry have the lowest.

**Requirements:** General education requirement.

**Academic regulations:** Freshmen must maintain minimum 1.70 GPA; sophomores, 1.80 GPA; juniors, 1.90 GPA; seniors, 2.00 GPA.

**Special:** Minors offered in many fields. One-year diploma programs in foundations of Christian leadership and in secretarial science. January term provides extensive opportunity for internships, off-campus experiences, overseas travel, and individualized study; exchange possible during January with other schools offering January term. Associate's degrees offered. Double majors. Independent study. Pass/fail grading option. Internships. Graduate school at which undergraduates may take graduate-level courses. Preprofessional programs in law, medicine, veterinary science, dentistry, physical therapy, and nursing. 2-2 nursing program with Goshen Coll. Member of Christian College Coalition. American Studies Program (Washington, D.C.). AuSable Inst of Environmental Studies Program (Michigan). Latin American Studies Program. Oregon Extension Program. Teacher certification in elementary, secondary, and special education. Exchange programs abroad in Israel/Jordan (Inst for Holy Land Studies in Jerusalem), Japan, and Korea (Kangnamu). Study abroad also in England, Italy, Jamaica, and Mexico.

**Academic Assistance:** Remedial reading, writing, math, and study skills. Nonremedial tutoring.

**ADMISSIONS. Academic basis for candidate selection** (in order of priority): Secondary school record, class rank, standardized test scores, school's recommendation.

**Requirements:** Graduation from secondary school is required; GED is accepted. No specific distribution of secondary school units required. Minimum combined SAT score of 750, rank in top half of secondary school class, and minumum 2.3 GPA recommended. Audition required of music program applicants. Education program for applicants not normally admissible. SAT or ACT is required. PSAT is recommended. Campus visit and interview recommended. Off-campus interviews available with an admissions representative.

**Procedure:** Take SAT or ACT by April of 12th year. Suggest filing application by December 31. Application deadline is August 15. Notification of admission on rolling basis. Reply is required by May 1. $100 tuition deposit, refundable until May 15. $100 room deposit, refundable until May 15. Freshmen accepted for terms other than fall.

**Special programs:** Admission may be deferred one year. Credit may be granted through CEEB Advanced Placement for scores of 3 or higher. Credit may be granted through CLEP subject exams. Early entrance/early admission program. Concurrent enrollment program.

**Transfer students:** Transfer students accepted for terms other than fall. for fall 1993, 5% of all new students were transfers into all classes. 41 transfer applications were received, 35 were accepted. Minimum 2.0 GPA. Lowest course grade accepted is "C-." At least 30 semester hours must be completed at the college to receive degree.

**Admissions contact:** Chantler Thompson, M.A., Dean of Admissions. 800 642-6493.

**FINANCIAL AID. Available aid:** Pell grants, SEOG, state scholarships and grants, school scholarships and grants, private scholarships and grants, academic merit scholarships, athletic scholarships, and aid for undergraduate foreign students. Perkins Loans (NDSL), PLUS, Stafford Loans (GSL), school loans, and SLS. Tuition Plan Inc., AMS, and family tuition reduction.

**Financial aid statistics:** 30% of aid is not need-based. In 1993-94, 94% of all undergraduate applicants received aid; 89% of freshman applicants. Average amounts of aid awarded freshmen: Scholarships and grants, $4,000; loans, $2,200.

**Supporting data/closing dates:** FAFSA/FAF/FFS: Priority filing date is April 1. State aid form: Priority filing date is March 1. Notification of awards on rolling basis.

**Financial aid contact:** Sharon Woods, M.A., Director of Financial Aid. 219 356-6000, extension 1015.

# Indiana Institute of Technology

**Fort Wayne, IN 46803** **219 422-5561**

**1994-95 Costs.** Tuition: $8,120. Room & board: $3,790. Fees, books, misc. academic expenses (school's estimate): $1,700.
**Enrollment.** Undergraduates: 379 men, 166 women (full-time). Freshman class: 957 applicants, 892 accepted, 167 enrolled.
**Test score averages/ranges.** Average SAT scores: 453 verbal, 484 math. Average ACT scores: 22 composite.
**Faculty.** 22 full-time; 30 part-time. 30% of faculty holds doctoral degree. Student/faculty ratio: 18 to 1.
**Selectivity rating.** Less competitive.

**PROFILE.** Indiana Tech, founded in 1930, is a private institution. Its 25-acre campus is located near the center of Fort Wayne.

**Accreditation:** NCACS.
**Religious orientation:** Indiana Institute of Technology is nonsectarian; no religious requirements.
**Library:** Collections totaling over 40,000 volumes, 150 periodical subscriptions, and 11,000 microform items.
**Athletic facilities:** Gymnasium; weight room, indoor track, soccer field.

**STUDENT BODY. Undergraduate profile:** 51% are state residents; 2% are transfers. 1.2% Asian-American, 19% Black, 2% Hispanic, .2% Native American, 63% White, 14.6% Other. Average age of undergraduates is 20.
**Freshman profile:** 75% of accepted applicants took SAT; 25% took ACT.
**Undergraduate achievement:** 53% of fall 1992 freshmen returned for fall 1993 term. 27% of entering class graduated. 5% of students who completed a degree program immediately went on to graduate study.
**Foreign students:** 60 students are from out of the country. Countries represented include India, Indonesia, Korea, Malaysia, and Pakistan; 17 in all.

**PROGRAMS OF STUDY. Degrees:** B.S.
**Majors:** Accounting, Business, Computer Engineering, Computer Information Systems, Computer Science, Electrical Engineering, Electrical Engineering Technologies, Engineering, Engineering Management Technology, Human Services Management, Mechanical Engineering, Recreation Management, Technical Communications, Therapeutic Recreation.
**Distribution of degrees:** The majors with the highest enrollment are accounting, business administration, and engineering; technical communications, therapeutic recreation, and recreation management have the lowest.
**Requirements:** General education requirement.
**Academic regulations:** Minimum 2.00 GPA must be maintained.
**Special:** Competency-Based Education requires periodic evaluations in each of four competency areas (communication skills, major field, liberal arts, and integrated course work); the sum of the competency evaluations provides future employers with additional information regarding student potential. Associate's degrees offered. Double majors. Dual degrees. Independent study. Accelerated study. Pass/fail grading option. Internships. Cooperative education programs. Graduate school at which undergraduates may take graduate-level courses.
**Honors:** Honor societies.
**Academic Assistance:** Remedial reading, writing, math, and study skills. Nonremedial tutoring.

**ADMISSIONS. Academic basis for candidate selection** (in order of priority): Secondary school record, standardized test scores, class rank, school's recommendation.
**Requirements:** Graduation from secondary school is required; GED is accepted. 3-1/2 units of mathematics and 4 units of foreign language, social studies, and/or history required. Minimum combined SAT score of 700 and minimum 2.0 GPA required; rank in top third of secondary school class recommended. SAT or ACT is required. Campus visit and interview recommended. Off-campus interviews available with an admissions representative.
**Procedure:** Take SAT or ACT by May 15 of 12th year. Visit college for interview by August 15 of 12th year. Suggest filing application by January. Application deadline is August 20. Notification of admission on rolling basis. Reply is required by August 20. $100 tuition deposit, refundable until 90 days prior to start of semester. $200 room deposit, refundable until 90 days prior to start of semester. Freshmen accepted for terms other than fall.
**Special programs:** Admission may be deferred one year. Credit and/or placement may be granted through CEEB Advanced Placement exams for scores of 3 or higher. Credit and/or placement may be granted through CLEP general and subject exams. Credit and placement may be granted through Regents College, ACT PEP, DANTES, and challenge exams, and military and life experience. Early decision program. Early entrance/early admission program. Concurrent enrollment program.
**Transfer students:** Transfer students accepted for terms other than fall. for fall 1993, 2% of all new students were transfers into all classes. 35 transfer applications were received, 30 were accepted. Application deadline is August 20 for fall; December 20 for spring. Minimum 2.0 GPA required. Lowest course grade accepted is "C." Maximum number of transferable credits is 90 semester hours. At least 30 semester hours must be completed at the college to receive degree.
**Admissions contact:** Donald E. St. Clair, M.S., Director of Admissions. 219 422-5561, extension 205.

**FINANCIAL AID. Available aid:** Pell grants, SEOG, state scholarships and grants, school scholarships and grants, private scholarships and grants, academic merit

scholarships, and athletic scholarships. Perkins Loans (NDSL), PLUS, Stafford Loans (GSL), and SLS. Tuition Plan Inc.
**Financial aid statistics:** In 1993-94, 100% of all undergraduate applicants received aid. Average amounts of aid awarded freshmen: Scholarships and grants, $3,450.
**Supporting data/closing dates:** FAFSA/FAF/FFS: Priority filing date is March 1. School's own aid application. Notification of awards on rolling basis.
**Financial aid contact:** Teresa M. Vasquez, Director of Financial Aid. 219 422-5561, extension 208.

# Indiana State University

**Terre Haute, IN 47809** **812 237-2121**

**1994-95 Costs.** Tuition: $2,750 (state residents), $6,725 (out-of-state). Room & board: $3,588. Fees, books, misc. academic expenses (school's estimate): $600.
**Enrollment.** Undergraduates: 4,339 men, 4,260 women (full-time). Freshman class: 5,659 applicants, 4,761 accepted, 2,377 enrolled. Graduate enrollment: 763 men, 870 women.
**Test score averages/ranges.** Average SAT scores: 387 verbal, 427 math. Average ACT scores: 19 composite.
**Faculty.** 591 full-time; 127 part-time. 62% of faculty holds doctoral degree. Student/faculty ratio: 15 to 1.
**Selectivity rating.** Less competitive.

**PROFILE.** Indiana State, founded in 1865, is a public university. Programs are offered through the College of Arts and Sciences and the Schools of Business; Education; Graduate Studies; Health, Physical Education, and Recreation; Nursing; and Technology. Its 92-acre campus is located on the north side of Terre Haute's downtown business district, 60 miles from Indianapolis.

**Accreditation:** NCACS. Professionally accredited by the American Assembly of Collegiate Schools of Business, the American Dental Association, the American Dietetic Association, the American Home Economics Association, the American Medical Association (CAHEA), the American Psychological Association, the American Speech-Language-Hearing Association, the Foundation for Interior Design Education Research, the National Association of Schools of Art and Design, the National Association of Schools of Music, the National Athletic Trainers Association, the National Council for Accreditation of Teacher Education, the National League for Nursing.
**Religious orientation:** Indiana State University is nonsectarian; no religious requirements.
**Library:** Collections totaling over 1,160,450 volumes, 5,663 periodical subscriptions, and 853,470 microform items.
**Special facilities/museums:** Music hall, art gallery, civic center, museum, on-campus school, audio-visual center, observatory.
**Athletic facilities:** Gymnasiums, field house, track, stadium, golf course, baseball, football, intramural, and softball fields, basketball, tennis, and volleyball courts.

**STUDENT BODY. Undergraduate profile:** 95% are state residents; 22% are transfers. .4% Asian-American, 7% Black, .3% Hispanic, .3% Native American, 87% White, 5% Other. Average age of undergraduates is 21.
**Freshman profile:** 1% of freshmen who took SAT scored 600 or over on verbal, 5% scored 600 or over on math; 10% scored 500 or over on verbal, 25% scored 500 or over on math; 44% scored 400 or over on verbal, 60% scored 400 or over on math; 87% scored 300 or over on verbal, 92% scored 300 or over on math. Majority of accepted applicants took SAT.
**Undergraduate achievement:** 68% of fall 1992 freshmen returned for fall 1993 term. 27% of entering class graduated. 18% of students who completed a degree program immediately went on to graduate study.
**Foreign students:** 671 students are from out of the country. Countries represented include China, India, Japan, Malaysia, Singapore, and Taiwan; 70 in all.

**PROGRAMS OF STUDY. Degrees:** B.A., B.F.A., B.S.
**Majors:** Accounting, Administrative Systems/Business Education, Aerospace Technology, Afro-American Studies, Anthropology, Architectural Technology, Art, Athletic Training, Business/Nondesignated, CAD/CAM, Chemistry, Communication, Communication Disorders, Community Health Education, Computer Science, Counseling, Criminology, Early Childhood Education, Economics, Education/Nondesignated, Educational Administration, Educational Foundations/Media Technology, Electronics/Computer Technology, Elementary Education, English, Environmental Health Sciences, Finance, Fitness, Foreign Languages, Geography/Geology, Graphic Arts Management, Health/Safety, History, Home Economics, Human Resource Development, Humanities, Industrial Automotive Technology, Industrial/Mechanical Technology, Industrial Supervision, Industrial Technology Education, Insurance, Latin American Studies, Library Science, Life Sciences, Management, Manufacturing/Construction Technology, Marketing, Mathematics, Music, Nursing, Packaging Technology, Philosophy, Physical Education, Physics, Political Science, Pre-Physical Therapy, Pre-Professional Programs, Professional Pilot, Psychology, Recreation/Leisure Studies, Recreation Management, Recreational Sports, Safety Management, School Psychology, Science Teaching, Secondary Education, Social Science Teaching, Social Work, Sociology, Special Education, Sports Management, Sports Studies, Systems/Decision Science, Technology/Nondesignated, Theatre, Therapeutic Recreation, Urban/Regional Studies, Women's Studies.
**Distribution of degrees:** The majors with the highest enrollment are administrative systems/business education, nursing, and elementary education.
**Requirements:** General education requirement.
**Academic regulations:** Minimum 2.0 GPA must be maintained.
**Special:** Liberal arts major in interdisciplinary studies. Minors offered in biomedical electronics, classical studies, coaching, conservation, creative writing, dance, industrial hygiene, mechanical drafting, and occupational health. Associate's degrees offered. Double majors. Dual degrees. Independent study. Internships. Cooperative education programs. Graduate school at which undergraduates may take graduate-level courses. Preprofessional programs in law, medicine, veterinary science, pharmacy, dentistry, theology, optometry, chiropractic, osteopathy, physical therapy, and podiatry. Member of consortium with Rose-Hulman Inst of Tech and St. Mary-of-the-Woods Coll. Teacher certification in early childhood, elementary, secondary, and special education. Study abroad in Austria, Costa Rica, France, Germany, Russia, and Spain. ROTC and AFROTC.
**Honors:** Honors program. Honor societies.
**Academic Assistance:** Remedial study skills. Nonremedial tutoring.

**STUDENT LIFE. Housing:** All freshmen under age 20 must live on campus. Coed, women's, and men's dorms. Sorority and fraternity housing. Off-campus married-student housing. 45% of students live in college housing.
**Social atmosphere:** For night life, students head to the 4th Quarter for live music, the Indiana Theatre (an historic movie house), Sonka's Irish Pub, and The Coffee Grounds. Greeks, international students, and the Afro-American Association influence life on campus. The most popular events on campus are Homecoming, Battle of the Bands, Theatrefest, the Convocation Series, and the International Film Series. "Because Terre Haute is a rural community, students often have to make their own fun. The ISU Activities Committee sponsors movies, bands, and lectures. There's a strong music scene in the midwest, so a lot of great acts pass through. Bloomington and Indianapolis are each an hour away and are further repositories of culture," comments the student newspaper.
**Services and counseling/handicapped student services:** Placement services. Health service. Women's center. Day care. Counseling services for minority, military, veteran, and older students. Personal and psychological counseling. Career and academic guidance services. Religious counseling. Physically disabled student services. Learning disabled services. Tape recorders. Tutors.
**Campus organizations:** Undergraduate student government. Student newspaper (Indiana Statesman, published three times/week). Yearbook. Radio and TV stations. Ebony Majestic Choir, Performing Arts Ensemble, Sycamore Players, speech union, debating, broadcasting groups, cheerleaders, College Democrats, College Republicans, departmental and special-interest groups, 183 organizations in all. 21 fraternities, 10 chapter houses; 13 sororities, no chapter houses. 16% of men join a fraternity. 11% of women join a sorority.
**Religious organizations:** African Christian Fellowship, American Baptist Campus Ministries, Bahai Club, Church of Christ Campus Ministries, Fellowship of Christian Athletes, Intervarsity Christian Fellowship, Jewish Student Group, Latter-Day Saints Association, Lutheran Student Fellowship, Malaysian Students Islamic Study, Muslim Student Association, Nichrien Shoshu of America, St. Joseph's Catholic Center.
**Minority/foreign student organizations:** Afro-American Cultural Center, Black Greek Council, Black Theatre Network, Future Black Technologists. Chinese, Korean, Japanese, Malaysian, Nigerian, Palestinian, Singaporan, and Saudi Arabian groups.

**ATHLETICS. Physical education requirements:** Two semesters of physical education required.
**Intercollegiate competition:** 30% of students participate. Baseball (M), basketball (M,W), cheerleading (M,W), cross-country (M,W), football (M), softball (W), tennis (M,W), track (indoor) (M,W), track (outdoor) (M,W), track and field (indoor) (M,W), track and field (outdoor) (M,W), volleyball (W). Member of Gateway Collegiate Football Conference, Missouri Valley Conference, NCAA Division I-AA.
**Intramural and club sports:** 50% of students participate. Intramural basketball, flag football, racquetball, soccer, softball, swimming, table tennis, tennis, track, volleyball, walleyball, weight lifting, wrestling. Men's club bowling. Women's club bowling.

**ADMISSIONS. Academic basis for candidate selection** (in order of priority): Secondary school record, class rank, standardized test scores, school's recommendation, essay.
**Nonacademic basis for candidate selection:** Character and personality, extracurricular participation, and particular talent or ability are considered.
**Requirements:** Graduation from secondary school is required; GED is accepted. No specific distribution of secondary school units required. Rank in top half of secondary school class and minimum 2.0 GPA required; minimum combined SAT score of 800 recommended. Rank in top quarter of secondary school class and minimum combined SAT score of 900 recommended of nursing program applicants. Audition required of music program applicants. Conditional admission possible for applicants not meeting standard requirements. SAT or ACT is required. Campus visit and interview recommended. No off-campus interviews.
**Procedure:** Take SAT or ACT by May of 12th year. Visit college for interview by May of 12th year. Suggest filing application by May 1. Application deadline is August 15. Notification of admission on rolling basis. $50 room deposit, refundable until July 1. Freshmen accepted for terms other than fall.
**Special programs:** Admission may be deferred one year. Credit may be granted through CEEB Advanced Placement for scores of 3 or higher. Credit may be granted through CLEP general and subject exams, DANTES exams, and life experience. Credit and placement may be granted through challenge exams and military experience. Early entrance/early admission program. Concurrent enrollment program.
**Transfer students:** Transfer students accepted for terms other than fall. for fall 1993, 22% of all new students were transfers into all classes. 1,392 transfer applications were received, 1,086 were accepted. Application deadline is August 15 for fall; December 15 for spring. Minimum 2.0 GPA required. Lowest course grade accepted is "C." Maximum number of transferable credits is 62 semester hours from a two-year school and 92 semester hours from a four-year school. At least 30 semester hours must be completed at the university to receive degree.
**Admissions contact:** Richard J. Riehl, M.A., Director of Admissions. 812 237-2121, 800 742-0891.

**FINANCIAL AID. Available aid:** Pell grants, SEOG, state scholarships and grants, school scholarships, ROTC scholarships, academic merit scholarships, athletic scholarships, aid for undergraduate foreign students, and United Negro College Fund. Perkins Loans (NDSL), PLUS, Stafford Loans (GSL), and SLS. AMS and deferred payment plan.
**Financial aid statistics:** 63% of aid is not need-based. In 1993-94, 93% of all undergraduate applicants received aid; 92% of freshman applicants. Average amounts of aid awarded freshmen: Scholarships and grants, $1,155; loans, $3,089.
**Supporting data/closing dates:** FAFSA: Priority filing date is March 1. School's own aid application: Priority filing date is March 1; accepted on rolling basis. Notification of awards on rolling basis.

**Financial aid contact:** Michael Phillips, Director of Financial Aid. 812 237-2215.

**STUDENT EMPLOYMENT.** College Work/Study Program. Institutional employment. 22% of full-time undergraduates work on campus during school year. Students may expect to earn an average of $894 during school year. Off-campus part-time employment opportunities rated "excellent."

**COMPUTER FACILITIES.** 369 IBM/IBM-compatible, Macintosh/Apple, and RISC-/UNIX-based microcomputers; 205 are networked. Students may access Digital, IBM, Sequent, SUN minicomputer/mainframe systems, BITNET, Internet. Residence halls may be equipped with networked microcomputers. Client/LAN operating systems include Apple/Macintosh, DOS, OS/2, UNIX/XENIX/AIX, Novell. Computer languages and software packages include BASIC, COBOL, FOCUS, FORTRAN, Pascal. Computer facilities are available to all students.
**Fees:** None.
**Hours:** 24 hours.

**GRADUATE CAREER DATA.** Graduate school percentages: 1% enter law school. 1% enter medical school. 1% enter dental school. 1% enter graduate business programs. 15% enter graduate arts and sciences programs. 1% enter theological school/seminary. Highest graduate school enrollments: Indiana State U, Indiana U. 70% of graduates choose careers in business and industry. Companies and businesses that hire graduates: Aristocraft, Bemis, Digital Audio Disc Corp., federal government, Gibault School for Boys, Methodist Hospital, Regional Hospital, SONY, State Farm Insurance, state of Indiana, Union Hospital.

**PROMINENT ALUMNI/AE.** Larry Bird, former Boston Celtics forward; Gil Verlcamp, CEO and president, Aristocraft, Inc.; Bruce Baumgartner, Olympic wrestling champion.

# Indiana University Bloomington

**Bloomington, IN 47405** **812 855-4848**

**1993-94 Costs.** Tuition: $2,638 (state residents), $8,630 (out-of-state). Room & board: $3,729. Fees, books, misc. academic expenses (school's estimate): $500.

**Enrollment.** Undergraduates: 12,115 men, 14,128 women (full-time). Freshman class: 16,587 applicants, 13,243 accepted, 5,873 enrolled. Graduate enrollment: 3,945 men, 3,533 women.

**Test score averages/ranges.** Average SAT scores: 466 verbal, 530 math. Average ACT scores: 24 composite.

**Faculty.** 1,405 full-time; 170 part-time. 84% of faculty holds highest degree in specific field. Student/faculty ratio: 19 to 1.

**Selectivity rating.** Less competitive.

**PROFILE.** Indiana University Bloomington, founded in 1820, is a public, comprehensive institution. Programs are offered through the College of Arts and Sciences; the Division of Allied Health Sciences; and the Schools of Business, Education, Dentistry, Health/Physical Education/Recreation, Music, Nursing, Optometry, Public and Environmental Affairs, and Social Work. Its 1,800-acre campus is located in the city of Bloomington, 45 miles from Indianapolis.

**Accreditation:** NCACS. Professionally accredited by the Accrediting Council on Education in Journalism and Mass Communication, the American Medical Association (CAHEA), the American Physical Therapy Association, the National Association of Schools of Music, the National Council for Accreditation of Teacher Education, the National League for Nursing.
**Religious orientation:** Indiana University Bloomington is nonsectarian; no religious requirements.
**Library:** Collections totaling over 5,438,860 volumes, 39,755 periodical subscriptions, and 3,260,559 microform items.
**Special facilities/museums:** Museums of anthropology, art, folklore, history, outdoor educational center, cyclotron, two observatories.
**Athletic facilities:** Basketball, handball, outdoor tennis, racquetball, squash, and volleyball courts, exercise, martial arts, and weight rooms, gymnasiums, swimming pools, field house, jogging track, athletic fields.

**STUDENT BODY. Undergraduate profile:** 73% are state residents. 2.4% Asian-American, 4.4% Black, 1.6% Hispanic, 88% White, 3.6% Other. Average age of undergraduates is 20.
**Freshman profile:** 1% of freshmen who took SAT scored 700 or over on verbal, 4% scored 700 or over on math; 8% scored 600 or over on verbal, 26% scored 600 or over on math; 38% scored 500 or over on verbal, 65% scored 500 or over on math; 82% scored 400 or over on verbal, 93% scored 400 or over on math; 99% scored 300 or over on verbal, 100% scored 300 or over on math. 88% of accepted applicants took SAT; 45% took ACT.
**Undergraduate achievement:** 87% of fall 1992 freshmen returned for fall 1993 term. 48% of entering class graduated.
**Foreign students:** 728 students are from out of the country. Countries represented include Canada, China, India, Japan, South Korea, and Taiwan; 122 in all.

**PROGRAMS OF STUDY. Degrees:** B.A., B.F.A., B.Mus., B.Mus.Ed., B.S.
**Majors:** Accounting, Afro-American Studies, Anthropology, Apparel Merchandising/Interior Design, Astronomy/Astrophysics, Athletic Training, Audio Recording, Ballet, Biochemistry, Biology, Business Economics/Public Policy, Chemistry, Choral/General Teaching, Classical Greek, Classical Studies, Comparative Literature, Composition, Computer Information Systems, Computer Science, Criminal Justice, Cytotechnology, Dietetics, Early Music/Instrument, Early Music/Voice, East Asian Languages/Cultures, Economics, Elementary Education, English, Environmental Science/Management, Exercise Science, Finance, Finance/Insurance, Finance/Real Estate, Fine Arts, Folklore, French, Geography, Geological Sciences, Germanic Studies, Health Administration, Health Information Administration, History, Human Development/Family Studies, Human Resource Management, Individualized Major Program, Instrument Teaching, International Studies, Italian, Jazz Studies, Jewish Studies, Journalism, Junior High/Middle School, Kindergarten/Primary, Linguistics, Management, Marketing, Marketing/Distribution Management, Mathematics, Medical Technology, Microbiology, Music, Near Eastern Languages/Cultures, Nursing, Nutrition Science, Occupational Safety, Occupational Therapy, Opera Scenic Technique, Operations Management, Optometry, Orchestral Instrument, Organ, Outdoor Recreation/Resource Management, Parks/Recreation Management, Personnel/Industrial Relations, Philosophy, Physical Therapy, Physics, Piano, Political Science, Portuguese, Psychology, Public Financial Management, Public Health, Public Health/Dental Hygiene, Public Policy, Radiation Therapy Technology, Radiologic Sciences, Religious Studies, Respiration Therapy, Secondary, Secondary Education/Health, Slavic Languages/Literatures, Social Work, Sociology, Spanish, Special Education, Specialized Study/Public/Environmental Affairs, Speech Communication, Speech/Hearing Sciences, Sport Management, Sports Communications, Sports Marketing/Management, Teacher Preparation, Teaching All Grades, Teaching Area, Telecommunications, Theatre/Drama, Therapeutic Recreation, Tourism Management, Transportation, Voice, Woodwind Instruments.
**Distribution of degrees:** The majors with the highest enrollment are business, education, and biology; French/Italian, theatre/drama, and speech communication have the lowest.
**Requirements:** General education requirement.
**Academic regulations:** Minimum 2.00 GPA must be maintained.
**Special:** Minors offered in many areas. Associate's degrees offered. Self-designed majors. Double majors. Dual degrees. Independent study. Accelerated study. Pass/fail grading option. Internships. Cooperative education programs. Graduate school at which undergraduates may take graduate-level courses. Preprofessional programs in law, medicine, pharmacy, dentistry, and optometry. Member of several consortiums, including Consortium on Institutional Cooperation. Washington Semester. Many domestic exchange programs offered. Teacher certification in early childhood, elementary, secondary, and special education. Certification in specific subject areas. Study abroad possible in numerous countries. ROTC and AFROTC.
**Honors:** Phi Beta Kappa. Honors program.
**Academic Assistance:** Remedial reading, writing, math, and study skills. Nonremedial tutoring.

**STUDENT LIFE. Housing:** Students may live on or off campus. Coed and women's dorms. Sorority and fraternity housing. Off-campus privately-owned housing. 50% of students live in college housing.
**Social atmosphere:** The student newspaper reports, "Any type of student can find a place to fit in at IU. One of the largest Greek systems in America is housed at IU. Culturally, IU has a wealth of offerings from art exhibits to Broadway shows. The IU Opera Theatre is part of the number one music school in the world." Besides the Greeks, influential campus groups include the Union Board, football and basketball players, and members of the Dean of Students Office. Popular social events include football and basketball games against Purdue; and Rush, Homecoming, touring Broadway shows, and rock concerts.
**Services and counseling/handicapped student services:** Placement services. Health service. Women's center. Day care. Counseling services for minority, military, veteran, and older students. Birth control, personal, and psychological counseling. Career and academic guidance services. Religious counseling. Physically disabled student services. Learning disabled services. Notetaking services. Tape recorders. Tutors. Reader services for the blind.
**Campus organizations:** Undergraduate student government. Student newspaper (Daily Student, published five times/week). Literary magazine. Yearbook. Radio and TV stations. 252 registered organizations. 34 fraternities, 33 chapter houses; 27 sororities, 23 chapter houses. 12% of men join a fraternity. 11% of women join a sorority.
**Religious organizations:** Numerous religious groups.
**Minority/foreign student organizations:** Black Student Union, Latinos Unidos, numerous other minority groups. International Center, numerous international student groups.

**ATHLETICS. Physical education requirements:** None.
**Intercollegiate competition:** 5% of students participate. Baseball (M), basketball (M,W), cross-country (M,W), diving (M,W), football (M), golf (M,W), soccer (M,W), softball (W), swimming (M,W), tennis (M,W), track and field (indoor) (M,W), track and field (outdoor) (M,W), volleyball (W), wrestling (M). Member of Big 10 Conference, NCAA Division I.

**ADMISSIONS. Academic basis for candidate selection** (in order of priority): Secondary school record, class rank, school's recommendation, standardized test scores.
**Nonacademic basis for candidate selection:** Character and personality, extracurricular participation, particular talent or ability, and alumni/ae relationship are considered.
**Requirements:** Graduation from secondary school is required; GED is accepted. 19 secondary school units recommended. Rank in top third of secondary school class and completion of nineteen year-long academic courses recommended. Each application is reviewed with primary attention given to the number of strong college-preparatory courses taken, their level of difficulty, student's willingness to accept challenge, and grade trends. Students with modest class rank but rising grades in challenging academic programs are encouraged to apply. Audition required of music program applicants. SAT or ACT is required. Campus visit and interview recommended. No off-campus interviews.
**Procedure:** Suggest filing application by February 15; no deadline. Notification of admission on rolling basis. Reply is required by May 1. $100 nonrefundable tuition deposit. $120 nonrefundable room deposit. Freshmen accepted for terms other than fall.
**Special programs:** Admission may be deferred one year. Credit and/or placement may be granted through CEEB Advanced Placement exams for scores of 3 or higher. Credit and/or placement may be granted through CLEP subject exams. Credit and placement may be granted through DANTES and challenge exams, and military experience. Concurrent enrollment program.
**Transfer students:** Transfer students accepted for terms other than fall. for fall 1993, 1,564 transfer applications were received, 1,015 were accepted. Application deadline is July 15 for fall; December 1 for spring. Minimum GPA for in-state transfer applicants is 2.30; for out-of-state applicants, 2.70. Lowest course grade accepted is "C." At least 30 semester hours must be completed at the university to receive degree.
**Admissions contact:** Robert S. Magee, M.S., M.Div., Director of Admissions. 812 855-0661.

**FINANCIAL AID. Available aid:** Pell grants, SEOG, Federal Nursing Student Scholarships, state scholarships and grants, school scholarships and grants, private scholarships

and grants, ROTC scholarships, academic merit scholarships, and athletic scholarships. Perkins Loans (NDSL), PLUS, Stafford Loans (GSL), NSL, Health Professions Loans, state loans, private loans, and SLS. Deferred payment plan.
**Financial aid statistics:** 10% of aid is not need-based. In 1993-94, 70% of all undergraduate applicants received aid; 60% of freshman applicants. Average amounts of aid awarded freshmen: Scholarships and grants, $1,000; loans, $2,253.
**Supporting data/closing dates:** FAFSA: Priority filing date is March 1. School's own aid application: Priority filing date is March 1. Income tax forms: Accepted on rolling basis. Notification of awards on rolling basis.
**Financial aid contact:** Susan Pugh, Ph.D., Director of Student Financial Assistance. 812 855-0321.

**STUDENT EMPLOYMENT.** College Work/Study Program. Institutional employment. Off-campus part-time employment opportunities rated "excellent."

**COMPUTER FACILITIES.** 1,200 IBM/IBM-compatible, Macintosh/Apple, and RISC-/UNIX-based microcomputers; all are networked. Students may access Digital, Hewlett-Packard minicomputer/mainframe systems, BITNET, Internet, CompuServe. Residence halls may be equipped with networked microcomputers, modems. Client/LAN operating systems include Apple/Macintosh, DOS, OS/2, UNIX/XENIX/AIX, Windows NT, X-windows, LocalTalk/AppleTalk, Novell. Computer languages and software packages include dBASE, Lotus 1-2-3, PageMaker, SPSS, WordPerfect; most commercial software packages Computer facilities are available to all students.
**Fees:** $100 per semester for freshmen; less for upperclassmen.
**Hours:** 24 hours in many locations.

**PROMINENT ALUMNI/AE.** Dr. Otis Bowen, politician; Kevin Kline, actor; Jane Pauley, TV journalist; Isiah Thomas, athlete; J. Danforth Quayle, former vice president of the U.S.; Hoagy Carmichael, musician; James Watson, geneticist; Steve Tesich, screenwriter; Wendell Wilkie, politician; Sherman Minton, former justice, U.S. Supreme Court; Theodore Dreiser, novelist; Harold Poling, CEO, Ford Motor Co.; Ernie Pyle, writer.

# Indiana University East

**Richmond, IN 47374-1289** **317 973-8200**

**1994-95 Costs.** Tuition: $2,214 (state residents), $5,685 (out-of-state). Housing: None. Fees, books, misc. academic expenses (school's estimate): $675.
**Enrollment.** Undergraduates: 315 men, 675 women (full-time). Freshman class: 835 applicants, 835 accepted, 616 enrolled. Graduate enrollment: 7 men, 25 women.
**Test score averages/ranges.** Average SAT scores: 370 verbal, 410 math. Average ACT scores: 19 composite.
**Faculty.** 75 full-time; 120 part-time. 66% of faculty holds highest degree in specific field.
**Selectivity rating.** Noncompetitive.

**PROFILE.** Indiana University East, founded in 1971, is a public university. Programs are offered in behavioral and social sciences, business, English, and nursing. Its 200-acre campus is located in Richmond, 45 miles from Dayton, Ohio.

**Accreditation:** NCACS.
**Religious orientation:** Indiana University East is nonsectarian; no religious requirements.
**Library:** Collections totaling over 56,165 volumes, 598 periodical subscriptions, and 36,167 microform items.
**Athletic facilities:** Soccer and softball fields, sand volleyball and tennis courts, par course.

**STUDENT BODY. Undergraduate profile:** 98% are state residents; 13% are transfers. 1% Asian-American, 3% Black, 1% Hispanic, 95% White.
**Freshman profile:** 1% of freshmen who took SAT scored 600 or over on verbal, 5% scored 600 or over on math; 6% scored 500 or over on verbal, 21% scored 500 or over on math; 39% scored 400 or over on verbal, 52% scored 400 or over on math; 85% scored 300 or over on verbal, 90% scored 300 or over on math. 9% of freshmen who took ACT scored 24 or over on composite; 67% scored 18 or over on composite; 100% scored 12 or over on composite. 63% of accepted applicants took SAT; 13% took ACT.
**Undergraduate achievement:** 55% of fall 1992 freshmen returned for fall 1993 term.

**PROGRAMS OF STUDY. Degrees:** B.A., B.S.
**Majors:** Behavioral/Social Sciences, Business, Education, English, General Studies, Nursing.
**Academic regulations:** Minimum 2.0 GPA must be maintained.
**Special:** Minors offered in economics, history, and interdisciplinary studies. Associate's degrees offered. Double majors. Dual degrees. Independent study. Pass/fail grading option. Internships. Teacher certification in elementary and secondary education. Certification in specific subject areas.
**Honors:** Honor societies.
**Academic Assistance:** Remedial reading, writing, math, and study skills. Nonremedial tutoring.

**ADMISSIONS. Academic basis for candidate selection** (in order of priority): Secondary school record, school's recommendation, class rank, standardized test scores.
**Requirements:** Graduation from secondary school is required; GED is accepted. 14 units and the following program of study are recommended: 4 units of English, 3 units of math, 1 unit of science, 2 units of social studies, 4 units of electives. Minimum combined SAT score of 760 or minimum composite ACT score of 17, rank in top half of secondary school class, and minimum 2.0 GPA recommended. Conditional admission possible for applicants not meeting standard requirements. SAT or ACT is required. Campus visit recommended. Off-campus interviews available with an admissions representative.
**Procedure:** Application deadline is August 11. Notification of admission on rolling basis. Freshmen accepted for terms other than fall.
**Special programs:** Admission may be deferred. Credit may be granted through CEEB Advanced Placement for scores of 4 or higher. Credit may be granted through CLEP general exams, DANTES exams, and military and life experience. Concurrent enrollment program.
**Transfer students:** Transfer students accepted for terms other than fall. for fall 1993, 13% of all new students were transfers into all classes. 124 transfer applications were received, 124 were accepted. Application deadline is August 11 for fall; December 15 for spring. Minimum 2.0 GPA. Lowest course grade accepted is "C." At least 30 semester hours must be completed at the university to receive degree.

**FINANCIAL AID. Available aid:** Pell grants, SEOG, state scholarships and grants, school scholarships and grants, private scholarships and grants, and academic merit scholarships. Perkins Loans (NDSL), PLUS, Stafford Loans (GSL), and SLS.
**Financial aid statistics:** 10% of aid is not need-based. In 1993-94, 85% of all undergraduate applicants received aid; 91% of freshman applicants. Average amounts of aid awarded freshmen: Scholarships and grants, $2,000; loans, $2,000.
**Supporting data/closing dates:** FAFSA: Priority filing date is March 1. School's own aid application: Priority filing date is March 1. Notification of awards on rolling basis.
**Financial aid contact:** Patricia E. Lemmons, M.A., Director of Admissions and Financial Aid. 317 973-8206.

# Indiana University Kokomo

**Kokomo, IN 46902** **317 453-2000**

**1994-95 Costs.** Tuition: $1,896 (state residents), $4,920 (out-of-state). Housing: None. Fees, books, misc. academic expenses (school's estimate): $465.
**Enrollment.** Undergraduates: 390 men, 764 women (full-time). Freshman class: 1,120 applicants, 1,112 accepted.
**Test score averages/ranges.** Average SAT scores: 390 verbal, 421 math.
**Faculty.** 73 full-time; 110 part-time. 55% of faculty holds doctoral degree. Student/faculty ratio: 17 to 1.
**Selectivity rating.** Less competitive.

**PROFILE.** Indiana University Kokomo, founded in 1945, is a public university of liberal arts and teacher education. Its 50-acre urban campus is located in central Kokomo.

**Accreditation:** NCACS. Professionally accredited by the Accreditation Board for Engineering and Technology, the National Council for Accreditation of Teacher Education, the National League for Nursing.
**Religious orientation:** Indiana University Kokomo is nonsectarian; no religious requirements.
**Library:** Collections totaling over 111,342 volumes, 872 periodical subscriptions, and 70,363 microform items.
**Special facilities/museums:** Observatory.
**Athletic facilities:** YMCA, local high school gym.

**STUDENT BODY. Undergraduate profile:** 99% are state residents; 17% are transfers. 1% Asian-American, 2% Black, 1% Hispanic, 1% Native American, 95% White. Average age of undergraduates is 29.
**Freshman profile:** 1% of freshmen who took SAT scored 700 or over on math; 3% scored 600 or over on verbal, 11% scored 600 or over on math; 20% scored 500 or over on verbal, 43% scored 500 or over on math; 71% scored 400 or over on verbal, 77% scored 400 or over on math; 97% scored 300 or over on verbal, 98% scored 300 or over on math. 58% of accepted applicants took SAT.

**PROGRAMS OF STUDY. Degrees:** B.A., B.Gen.Studies, B.S., B.S.Ed., B.S.Nurs.
**Majors:** Accounting, Biological/Physical Sciences, Biology, Business Administration/Management, Communication, Data Processing/Information Systems, Electrical Engineering Technology, Elementary Education, English, General Studies, Humanities, Labor Studies, Mathematics, Medical Technology, Nursing, Psychology, Social/Behavioral Sciences, Sociology, Supervision.
**Requirements:** General education requirement.
**Special:** Certificate programs in business studies, labor studies, and secretarial studies. Courses offered in computer techology, economics, engineering graphics, health care management, home economics, industrial engineering technology, physical sciences, and secondary education. External degree programs in general studies. Associate's degrees offered. Self-designed majors. Dual degrees. Independent study. Accelerated study. Pass/fail grading option. Cooperative education programs. Graduate school at which undergraduates may take graduate-level courses. Preprofessional programs in law, medicine, and dentistry. 3-1 medical technology program. Washington Semester and UN Semester. Exchange programs with the Indiana U system and Purdue U. Teacher certification in elementary education. Study abroad in European countries, Israel, Mexico, Peru, and the former Soviet Republics. ROTC at Indiana U-Purdue U at Indianapolis.
**Academic Assistance:** Remedial reading, writing, and math. Nonremedial tutoring.

**ADMISSIONS. Academic basis for candidate selection** (in order of priority): Secondary school record, class rank, standardized test scores.
**Requirements:** Graduation from secondary school is required; GED is accepted. 28 units and the following program of study are recommended: 8 units of English, 6 units of math, 2 units of lab science, 4 units of foreign language, 2 units of social studies, 2 units of history. Above-average SAT (ACT) scores and rank in top half of secondary school class recommended of in-state applicants. Rank in top third of secondary school class and minimum "B" average required of out-of-state applicants. Guided Study Program for applicants not normally admissible. SAT or ACT is required. ACH in chemistry and foreign languages required of applicants who plan further study in those fields or in liberal studies. Campus visit and interview recommended. Off-campus interviews available with an admissions representative.
**Procedure:** Suggest filing application by July 1. Application deadline is July 29. Acceptance notification on rolling basis within one month of receipt of all credentials. Freshmen accepted for terms other than fall.
**Special programs:** Admission may be deferred one semester. Credit and/or placement may be granted through CEEB Advanced Placement exams. Credit and/or placement may be granted through CLEP subject exams. Credit and placement may be granted through

military experience. Early decision program. Early entrance/early admission program. Concurrent enrollment program.
**Transfer students:** Transfer students accepted for terms other than fall. for fall 1993, 17% of all new students were transfers into all classes. 225 transfer applications were received, 225 were accepted. Application deadline is July 1 for fall; December 1 for spring. Minimum 2.0 GPA recommended. Lowest course grade accepted is "C."
**Admissions contact:** Jack Tharp, Ed.D., Director of Admissions. 317 455-9217.

**FINANCIAL AID. Available aid:** Pell grants, SEOG, Federal Nursing Student Scholarships, state scholarships and grants, school scholarships and grants, private scholarships, and academic merit scholarships. PLUS, Stafford Loans (GSL), NSL, and private loans. Deferred payment plan.
**Supporting data/closing dates:** FAFSA/FAF: Priority filing date is March 1. School's own aid application: Priority filing date is March 1. Notification of awards on rolling basis.
**Financial aid contact:** Janet Bates, Director of Financial Aid. 317 455-9216.

# Indiana University Northwest

Gary, IN 46408 219 980-6500

**1994-95 Costs.** Tuition: $2,310 (state residents), $5,781 (out-of-state). Housing: None. Fees, books, misc. academic expenses (school's estimate): $295.
**Enrollment.** Undergraduates: 945 men, 1,754 women (full-time). Freshman class: 2,236 applicants, 1,784 accepted, 1,246 enrolled. Graduate enrollment: 210 men, 388 women.
**Test score averages/ranges.** N/A.
**Faculty.** 187 full-time; 187 part-time. 73% of faculty holds highest degree in specific field. Student/faculty ratio: 14 to 1.
**Selectivity rating.** N/A.

**PROFILE.** Indiana University Northwest, founded in 1922, is a public university. Programs are offered through the Divisions of Allied Health Sciences, Arts and Sciences, Business and Economics, Continuing Studies, Education, Nursing, and Public and Environmental Affairs and Political Science; Dental Auxiliary Education; Labor Studies; Library and Information Science; Medical Sciences; and Guided Studies. Its 240-acre campus is located in Gary.

**Accreditation:** NCACS. Professionally accredited by the American Assembly of Collegiate Schools of Business, the National Council for Accreditation of Teacher Education, the National League for Nursing.
**Religious orientation:** Indiana University Northwest is nonsectarian; no religious requirements.
**Library:** Collections totaling over 203,948 volumes, 1,100 periodical subscriptions, and 133,943 microform items.
**Special facilities/museums:** Art gallery, electron microscope.
**Athletic facilities:** Volleyball court, strength and aerobic training area.

**STUDENT BODY. Undergraduate profile:** 99% are state residents. 1% Asian-American, 21% Black, 8% Hispanic, 69% White, 1% Other. Average age of undergraduates is 24.
**Freshman profile:** 64% of accepted applicants took SAT. 95% of freshmen come from public schools.
**Undergraduate achievement:** 61% of fall 1992 freshmen returned for fall 1993 term. 14% of students who completed a degree program immediately went on to graduate study.

**PROGRAMS OF STUDY. Degrees:** B.A., B.Gen.Studies, B.S., B.S.Nurs.
**Majors:** Accounting, Afro-American Studies, Biology, Chemistry, Communications, Criminal Justice, Data Processing/Information Systems, Economics, Elementary Education, English, Fine Arts, French, General Studies, Geology, History, Labor Studies, Management/Administration, Mathematics, Medical Technology, Nursing, Policy/Administration, Political Science, Psychology, Secondary Education, Sociology, Spanish, Theatre, Urban Studies.
**Distribution of degrees:** The majors with the highest enrollment are nursing, elementary education, and management; French, geology, and Afro-American studies have the lowest.
**Requirements:** General education requirement.
**Academic regulations:** Minimum 2.0 GPA must be maintained.
**Special:** Associate's degrees offered. Double majors. Independent study. Pass/fail grading option. Internships. Cooperative education programs. Graduate school at which undergraduates may take graduate-level courses. Preprofessional programs in law, medicine, pharmacy, dentistry, and optometry. 3-1 medical technology program with Methodist Hospital and St. Mary Mercy Hospital (both in Gary). Teacher certification in elementary, secondary, and bilingual/bicultural education. Exchange programs abroad in England, France, Germany, Israel, Italy, Mexico, Peru, and Spain. Member of Council of International Educational Exchange. ROTC.
**Honors:** Honors program.
**Academic Assistance:** Remedial math. Nonremedial tutoring.

**STUDENT LIFE. Housing:** Commuter campus; no student housing.
**Services and counseling/handicapped student services:** Placement services. Day care. Counseling services for minority, veteran, and older students. Personal and psychological counseling. Career and academic guidance services. Physically disabled student services. Notetaking services.
**Campus organizations:** Undergraduate student government. Student newspaper (Phoenix). Literary magazine. Chorale, ensembles, theatre, Young Democrats, College Republicans, Student Guide Services, Student-Worker Alliance, Women's Caucus, athletic and departmental groups, service and special-interest groups, 40 organizations in all. Two fraternities, no chapter houses; two sororities, no chapter houses.
**Religious organizations:** IUN Bible Club, Cardinal Newman Catholic Center, several religious groups.
**Minority/foreign student organizations:** Black Student Union, Alianza Latina del Medio oeste de America (ALMA), Bilingual Education Student Organization (BESO).

**ATHLETICS. Physical education requirements:** None.
**Intercollegiate competition:** 1% of students participate.
**Intramural and club sports:** 1% of students participate. Intramural badminton, basketball, bowling, floor hockey, football, golf, table tennis, tennis, volleyball. Men's club baseball, basketball, golf, tennis. Women's club volleyball.

**ADMISSIONS. Academic basis for candidate selection** (in order of priority): Secondary school record, class rank, standardized test scores, school's recommendation.
**Requirements:** Graduation from secondary school is required; GED is accepted. 14 units and the following program of study are required: 4 units of English, 3 units of math, 1 unit of science, 2 units of social studies, 4 units of academic electives. Minimum combined SAT score of 860, rank in top half of secondary school class, and minimum 2.0 GPA required. 2 units of foreign language and 2 units of science required of allied health sciences, arts and science, and nursing program applicants. 2 units of algebra and 1 unit of trigonometry recommended of business and math program applicants. SAT or ACT is required. Off-campus interviews available with an admissions representative.
**Procedure:** Take SAT or ACT by fall of 12th year. Notification of admission on rolling basis. Freshmen accepted for terms other than fall.
**Special programs:** Admission may be deferred one year. Credit and/or placement may be granted through CEEB Advanced Placement exams for scores of 3 or higher. Credit and/or placement may be granted through CLEP general and subject exams. Early decision program. Concurrent enrollment program.
**Transfer students:** Transfer students accepted for terms other than fall. Minimum 2.0 GPA required. Lowest course grade accepted is "C." Maximum number of transferable credits is 90 credit hours. 30 credit hours must be completed at the university in the senior year to receive degree.
**Admissions contact:** William D. Lee, Director of Admissions. 219 980-6991.

**FINANCIAL AID. Available aid:** Pell grants, SEOG, state scholarships and grants, school scholarships and grants, private scholarships, ROTC scholarships, and academic merit scholarships. Perkins Loans (NDSL), PLUS, Stafford Loans (GSL), state loans, and SLS. Deferred payment plan.
**Supporting data/closing dates:** FAFSA: Priority filing date is March 1. School's own aid application: Priority filing date is March 1. State aid form: Priority filing date is March 1. Notification of awards on rolling basis.
**Financial aid contact:** Gene Blakely, Director of Financial Aid. 219 980-6777.

**STUDENT EMPLOYMENT.** College Work/Study Program. 15% of full-time undergraduates work on campus during school year. Students may expect to earn an average of $1,000 during school year. Off-campus part-time employment opportunities rated "good."

**COMPUTER FACILITIES.** 150 IBM/IBM-compatible and Macintosh/Apple microcomputers; 125 are networked. Students may access IBM, Prime minicomputer/mainframe systems, Internet. Client/LAN operating systems include Apple/Macintosh, DOS, Novell. Computer languages and software packages include BASIC, COBOL, dBASE, FORTRAN, Lotus 1-2-3, MacWrite, MINITAB, PC-Calc, PC-Write, SAS, SPSS-X. Computer facilities are available to all students.
**Fees:** $1.70 per credit hour.
**Hours:** 8 AM-10 PM.

**GRADUATE CAREER DATA.** Highest graduate school enrollments: U of Illinois at Chicago, Indiana U at Bloomington, Loyola U, Purdue U Calumet. Companies and businesses that hire graduates: Crowe, Chizek & Co., Inland Steel, KPMG Peat Marwick.

**PROMINENT ALUMNI/AE.** Peter Visclosky, congressman.

# Indiana University–Purdue University Fort Wayne

Fort Wayne, IN 46805-1499 219 481-6812

**1994-95 Costs.** Tuition: $2,400 (state residents), $6,000 (out-of-state). Housing: None. Fees, books, misc. academic expenses (school's estimate): $600.
**Enrollment.** Undergraduates: 2,135 men, 2,486 women (full-time). Freshman class: 2,306 applicants, 2,114 accepted, 1,714 enrolled. Graduate enrollment: 918.
**Test score averages/ranges.** Average SAT scores: 405 verbal, 459 math.
**Faculty.** 329 full-time; 338 part-time. 90% of faculty holds doctoral degree. Student/faculty ratio: 20 to 1.
**Selectivity rating.** Less competitive.

**PROFILE.** IPFW, founded in 1964, is a public, multipurpose university. Its 412-acre campus is located in Fort Wayne, 110 miles from Indianapolis.

**Accreditation:** NCACS. Professionally accredited by the Accreditation Board for Engineering and Technology, the American Assembly of Collegiate Schools of Business, the American Dental Association, the National Association of Schools of Music, the National Council for Accreditation of Teacher Education, the National League for Nursing.
**Religious orientation:** Indiana University-Purdue University at Fort Wayne is nonsectarian; no religious requirements.
**Library:** Collections totaling over 405,039 volumes, 2,100 periodical subscriptions, and 222,145 microform items.
**Special facilities/museums:** Biological research center nearby.
**Athletic facilities:** Gymnasium, field house, basketball, racquetball, sand volleyball, tennis, volleyball, and walleyball courts, weight room, track, baseball, soccer, and softball fields.

**STUDENT BODY. Undergraduate profile:** 97% are state residents; 42% are transfers. 1% Asian-American, 3% Black, 1% Hispanic, 95% White. Average age of undergraduates is 27.
**Freshman profile:** 80% of accepted applicants took SAT; 20% took ACT. 66% of freshmen come from public schools.
**Foreign students:** Countries represented include Canada, Ethiopia, India, Pakistan, the United Kingdom, and Venezuela; 57 in all.

**PROGRAMS OF STUDY. Degrees:** B.A., B.S.

**Majors:** Anthropology, Biology, Biology Teaching, Business, Chemistry, Chemistry Teaching, Computer Technology, Construction Technology, Dental Health Education, Electrical Technology, Elementary Education, Engineering, English, Fine Arts, French, General Science, General Science Teaching, General Studies, Geology, German, History, Individualized Majors, Industrial Engineering Technology, Interpersonal/Public Communication, Mathematics, Mathematics Teaching, Mechanical Technology, Medical Technology, Music, Music Education, Music Therapy, Nursing, Philosophy, Physics, Physics Teaching, Political Science/Government, Psychology, Public Affairs, Radio/Television/Film, Secondary Education, Sociology, Spanish, Speech Communication, Teaching Supervision, Theatre.
**Distribution of degrees:** The majors with the highest enrollment are business, education, and engineering; general studies, public affairs, and fine arts have the lowest.
**Requirements:** General education requirement.
**Special:** Minors offered. Interdisciplinary certificates. Self-designed majors. Double majors. Independent study. Pass/fail grading option. Internships. Cooperative education programs. Graduate school at which undergraduates may take graduate-level courses. Preprofessional programs in law, medicine, and dentistry. 3-1 programs in dentistry, medicine, and optometry possible. Transfer programs with other Indiana and Purdue campuses in agriculture, allied health occupations/health services management, audiology and speech sciences, consumer and family sciences, cytotechnology, engineering, industrial education, management, medical record administration, nursing, occupational therapy, prepharmacy, public health, radiologic sciences, and respiratory therapy. Member of National Student Exchange (NSE). Teacher certification in early childhood, elementary, and secondary education. Study abroad in England, Germany, Israel, Italy, Mexico, and Spain.
**Honors:** Phi Beta Kappa. Honors program.
**Academic Assistance:** Nonremedial tutoring.

**STUDENT LIFE. Housing:** Commuter campus; no student housing.
**Social atmosphere:** As reported by the student newspaper, "We are a commuter campus with no student housing, therefore the social life of students is generally filled with off-campus activities. Many students also work part-time and have limited free time." When students do have free time they gather at Our Place, Brubaker's, or Columbia Street West. On campus, students meet in the basement lounge, the classroom medical television lounge, or The Fort. Greeks, International Student Union, Arts Group, and Christian Fellowship are the influential groups on campus. The most popular social events include plays, parties, and the Greek Rush.
**Services and counseling/handicapped student services:** Placement services. Women's center. Day care. Counseling services for minority students. Personal and psychological counseling. Career and academic guidance services.
**Campus organizations:** Undergraduate student government. Student newspaper (Communicator, published once/week). TV station. University Singers, Art Student League, ceramics club, music therapy club speech and hearing club, Forensics League, Student Union Board, 49 organizations in all. Two fraternities, no chapter houses; three sororities, no chapter houses. 1% of men join a fraternity. 1% of women join a sorority.
**Religious organizations:** Campus Ministry.
**Minority/foreign student organizations:** Black Collegian Caucus. International Student Organization.

**ATHLETICS. Physical education requirements:** None.
**Intercollegiate competition:** 1% of students participate. Baseball (M), basketball (M,W), cross-country (M,W), soccer (M), softball (W), tennis (M,W), volleyball (M,W). Member of Great Lakes Valley Conference, Midwest Intercollegiate Volleyball Association, NCAA Division II.
**Intramural and club sports:** 3% of students participate. Intramural basketball, billiards, flag football, golf, racquetball, sand volleyball, table tennis, tennis, volleyball, walleyball.

**ADMISSIONS. Academic basis for candidate selection** (in order of priority): Secondary school record, class rank, standardized test scores, school's recommendation.
**Requirements:** Graduation from secondary school is required; GED is accepted. 10 units and the following program of study are required: 4 units of English, 3 units of math, 1 unit of lab science, 1 unit of foreign language, 1 unit of social studies, 1 unit of history. Minimum combined SAT score of 800 required. SAT or ACT is required. No off-campus interviews.
**Procedure:** Application deadline is August 1. Notification of admission on rolling basis. Freshmen accepted for terms other than fall.
**Special programs:** Credit may be granted through CEEB Advanced Placement for scores of 3 or higher. Credit may be granted through CLEP general and subject exams.
**Transfer students:** Transfer students accepted for terms other than fall. for fall 1992, 42% of all new students were transfers into all classes. Application deadline is August 1 for fall; November 15 for spring. Minimum 2.0 GPA required. Lowest course grade accepted is "C." Maximum number of transferable credits is 90 semester hours. At least 30 semester hours must be completed at the university to receive degree.
**Admissions contact:** Karl F. Zimmerman, M.S., Director of Admissions. 219 481-6812.

**FINANCIAL AID. Available aid:** Pell grants, SEOG, state grants, school scholarships and grants, academic merit scholarships, and athletic scholarships. Perkins Loans (NDSL), Stafford Loans (GSL), NSL, and SLS.
**Supporting data/closing dates:** FAFSA/FAF: Deadline is March 1.
**Financial aid contact:** Gina Roberts, M.S., Director of Financial Aid. 219 481-6820.

**STUDENT EMPLOYMENT.** College Work/Study Program. Institutional employment. Off-campus part-time employment opportunities rated "excellent."

**COMPUTER FACILITIES.** 150 IBM/IBM-compatible microcomputers; all are networked. Students may access Digital, IBM minicomputer/mainframe systems. Computer languages and software packages include BASIC, COBOL, FORTRAN, Mass-II, Pascal, WordPerfect; 19 in all. Computer facilities are available to all students.
**Fees:** Computer fee is included in tuition/fees.

**GRADUATE CAREER DATA.** 50% of graduates choose careers in business and industry. Companies and businesses that hire graduates: Magnavox, Lincoln National Life Insurance Co., North American Van Lines, General Electric, ITT, General Telephone Co.

**PROMINENT ALUMNI/AE.** Charles Conville, bank president; Dean Stanley, engineering vice-president, Navistar; Joseph Wiley, finance vice-president, AT&T Information Systems; Sharon Gabet, TV actress, *Another World*.

# Indiana University–Purdue University Indianapolis

**Indianapolis, IN 46202-5167** **317 274-5555**

**1993-94 Costs.** Tuition: $2,662 (state residents), $7,938 (out-of-state). Room & board: $3,015. Fees, books, misc. academic expenses (school's estimate): $800.
**Enrollment.** Undergraduates: 3,800 men, 5,416 women (full-time). Freshman class: 4,652 applicants, 3,688 accepted, 2,316 enrolled. Graduate enrollment: 3,400 men, 3,760 women.
**Test score averages/ranges.** Average SAT scores: 380 verbal, 420 math. Range of SAT scores of middle 50%: 330-440 verbal, 360-490 math. Average ACT scores: 18 English, 18 math, 19 composite. Range of ACT scores of middle 50%: 16-21 English, 16-20 math.
**Faculty.** 561 full-time; 712 part-time. 89% of faculty holds highest degree in specific field. Student/faculty ratio: 16 to 1.
**Selectivity rating.** Less competitive.

**PROFILE.** IUPUI is a public, comprehensive university. It was founded with the 1969 merger of Indiana University and Purdue University. Its urban campus is located in Indianapolis.

**Accreditation:** NCACS.
**Religious orientation:** Indiana University Purdue University Indianapolis is nonsectarian; no religious requirements.
**Library:** Collections totaling over 1,018,987 volumes, 12,387 periodical subscriptions, and 1,597,906 microform items.
**Athletic facilities:** Swimming pools, diving well, track, weight room, basketball, tennis, and volleyball courts, baseball, soccer, and softball fields.

**STUDENT BODY. Undergraduate profile:** 99% are state residents; 34% are transfers. 2% Asian-American, 8% Black, 1% Hispanic, 87% White, 2% Other. Average age of undergraduates is 27.
**Freshman profile:** 1% of freshmen who took SAT scored 600 or over on verbal, 4% scored 600 or over on math; 8% scored 500 or over on verbal, 18% scored 500 or over on math; 34% scored 400 or over on verbal, 45% scored 400 or over on math; 66% scored 300 or over on verbal, 69% scored 300 or over on math. 3% of freshmen who took ACT scored 24 or over on English, 2% scored 24 or over on math, 2% scored 24 or over on composite; 13% scored 18 or over on English, 11% scored 18 or over on math, 13% scored 18 or over on composite; 20% scored 12 or over on English, 20% scored 12 or over on math, 20% scored 12 or over on composite. Majority of accepted applicants took SAT.
**Undergraduate achievement:** 51% of fall 1992 freshmen returned for fall 1993 term. 5% of entering class graduated.
**Foreign students:** 179 students are from out of the country. Countries represented include Canada, India, Japan, People's Republic of China, South Korea, and Taiwan; 67 in all.

**PROGRAMS OF STUDY. Degrees:** B.A., B.A.Ed., B.Art Ed., B.F.A., B.Gen.Studies, B.S., B.S.Bus., B.S.Elec.Eng., B.S.Indust.Eng., B.S.Mech.Eng., B.S.Nurs., B.S.Phys.Ed., B.S.Pub.Aff., B.Soc.Work
**Majors:** Anthropology, Art Education, Art History, Biology, Business, Chemistry, Communication/Theatre, Computer Integrated Manufacturing Technology, Computer Science, Computer Technology, Construction Technology, Criminal Justice, Cytotechnology, Economics, Electrical Engineering, Electrical Engineering Technology, Elementary Education, English, Fine Arts, French, General Studies, Geography, Geology, German, Health Information Administration, Health Occupations Education, Health Services Management, History, Interdisciplinary Engineering, Journalism, Labor Studies, Mathematical Sciences, Mechanical Engineering, Mechanical Engineering Technology, Medical Imaging Technology, Medical Technology, Nuclear Medicine, Nursing, Occupational Therapy, Philosophy, Physical Education, Physical Therapy, Physics, Political Science, Psychology, Public Affairs, Public Health, Public Health/Dental Hygiene, Radiation Therapy, Religious Studies, Respiratory Therapy, Secondary Education, Social Studies Education, Social Work, Sociology, Spanish, Supervision.
**Distribution of degrees:** The majors with the highest enrollment are business, nursing, and engineering/technology; geology, public health/dental hygiene, and art history have the lowest.
**Requirements:** General education requirement.
**Special:** Minors offered in non-invasive cardiovascular technology, gerontology, museum studies, and international studies. Business major includes concentrations in accounting, business economics/public policy, finance, finance/insurance, finance/real estate, human resources management, management, marketing, and marketing/distribution management. Fine arts majors includes concentrations in ceramics, general fine arts, painting, photography, printmaking, sculpture, visual communications, and woodworking design. Certificate programs in business studies, dental assisting, environmental studies, hazardous materials management, labor relations analyst, labor studies, public affairs, public health, public management, and technical drafting. Associate's degrees offered. Self-designed majors. Double majors. Independent study. Accelerated study. Pass/fail grading option. Internships. Cooperative education programs. Graduate school at which undergraduates may take graduate-level courses. Preprofessional programs in law, medicine, and dentistry. Member of Consortium of Urban Education in Indianapolis. Teacher certification in elementary, secondary, and special education. Certification in specific subject areas. Study abroad possible. ROTC. NROTC at Indiana U. AFROTC at Purdue U.
**Honors:** Honors program. Honor societies.

**Academic Assistance:** Remedial reading, writing, math, and study skills. Nonremedial tutoring.

**STUDENT LIFE. Housing:** Students may live on or off campus. Coed dorms. School-owned/operated apartments. On-campus married-student housing. 1% of students live in college housing.

**Social atmosphere:** The student newspaper reports that IUPUI is primarily a commuter campus, yet social and cultural life on campus does exist. Popular on-campus gathering spots include University Place and Union Station. Off campus, students tend to socialize at the Slippery Noodle Inn and Broadripples. The Progressive Student Union, the Student Senate, and The Advocate are influential groups on campus. Popular campus events include the Penrod Festival, the Indianapolis 500, the Fall Festival, and the Spring Fling.

**Services and counseling/handicapped student services:** Placement services. Health service. Women's center. Day care. Counseling services for minority, military, veteran, and older students. Personal and psychological counseling. Career and academic guidance services. Physically disabled student services. Learning disabled services. Notetaking services. Tape recorders. Tutors. Reader services for the blind.

**Campus organizations:** Undergraduate student government. Student newspaper (Sagamore, published once/week). Literary magazine. Yearbook. Chamber singers, pep band, debating, University Theatre, Activity Board, Society of Women Engineers, departmental and special-interest groups, 202 organizations in all. Two fraternities, no chapter houses; two sororities, no chapter houses. 1% of men join a fraternity. 1% of women join a sorority.

**Minority/foreign student organizations:** Black Student Union, Society of Black Engineers. Chinese Culture Club, International Affairs Club.

**ATHLETICS. Physical education requirements:** None.

**Intercollegiate competition:** 2% of students participate. Baseball (M), basketball (M,W), cheerleading (M,W), soccer (M), softball (W), tennis (M,W), volleyball (W). Member of NAIA, NCAA Division II.

**Intramural and club sports:** 1% of students participate. Intramural basketball, flag football, golf, racquetball, softball, tennis, volleyball.

**ADMISSIONS. Academic basis for candidate selection** (in order of priority): Secondary school record, class rank, standardized test scores, school's recommendation, essay.

**Requirements:** Graduation from secondary school is required; GED is accepted. 14 units and the following program of study are required: 4 units of English, 3 units of math, 1 unit of lab science, 2 units of social studies, 4 units of academic electives. Rank in top half of secondary school class required. Score in top third on SAT and rank in top third of secondary school class recommended of out-of-state applicants. 2-1/2 units of algebra, 1 unit of geometry, 1/2 unit of trigonometry, 1 unit of chemistry, and minimum SAT scores of 400 verbal and 500 math required of engineering program applicants. 2-1/2 units of algebra, 1 unit of geometry, 1/2 unit of trigonometry, and minimum SAT scores of 400 in both verbal and math required of science program applicants. Chemistry and algebra required of nursing program applicants. Portfolio required of art program applicants. Undergraduate Education Center Preparatory Program for applicants not normally admissible. SAT or ACT is required. Campus visit recommended. No off-campus interviews.

**Procedure:** Take SAT or ACT by October of 12th year. Suggest filing application by June 15; no deadline. Notification of admission on rolling basis. Reply deadlines for nursing and allied health programs only. Freshmen accepted for terms other than fall.

**Special programs:** Admission may be deferred one year. Credit may be granted through CEEB Advanced Placement for scores of 3 or higher. Credit may be granted through CLEP general and subject exams, DANTES exams, and military and life experience. Credit and placement may be granted through challenge exams. Concurrent enrollment program.

**Transfer students:** Transfer students accepted for terms other than fall. for fall 1993, 34% of all new students were transfers into all classes. 2,567 transfer applications were received, 1,958 were accepted. Application deadline is June 1 for fall; October 1 for spring. Minimum 2.0 GPA required. Lowest course grade accepted is "C." At least 30 semester hours must be completed at the university to receive degree.

**Admissions contact:** Alan N. Crist, Ph.D., Director of Admissions. 317 274-4591.

**FINANCIAL AID. Available aid:** Pell grants, SEOG, state scholarships and grants, school scholarships and grants, private scholarships and grants, ROTC scholarships, academic merit scholarships, athletic scholarships, and aid for undergraduate foreign students. Perkins Loans (NDSL), PLUS, Stafford Loans (GSL), NSL, Health Professions Loans, school loans, and SLS. Deferred payment plan.

**Financial aid statistics:** 4% of aid is not need-based. In 1993-94, 86% of all undergraduate applicants received aid; 79% of freshman applicants. Average amounts of aid awarded freshmen: Scholarships and grants, $1,881; loans, $2,845.

**Supporting data/closing dates:** FAFSA: Priority filing date is March 1. Notification of awards on rolling basis.

**Financial aid contact:** Natala Hart, Director of Financial Aid. 317 274-4162.

**STUDENT EMPLOYMENT.** College Work/Study Program. Institutional employment. 5% of full-time undergraduates work on campus during school year. Students may expect to earn an average of $1,800 during school year. Off-campus part-time employment opportunities rated "excellent."

**COMPUTER FACILITIES.** 400 IBM/IBM-compatible and Macintosh/Apple microcomputers; 350 are networked. Students may access Digital, IBM minicomputer/mainframe systems, BITNET, Internet. Client/LAN operating systems include Apple/Macintosh, DOS, LocalTalk/AppleTalk. Computer languages and software packages include E-Mail, Lotus 1-2-3, dBASE, HyperCard, MacWrite, MacWrite II, Microsoft Word, Microsoft Works, Paradox, Quattro, VAX Notes, WordPerfect. Computer facilities are available to all students.

**Fees:** $75 computer fee per semester.

# Indiana University South Bend

**South Bend, IN 46634** — **219 237-4111**

**1993-94 Costs.** Tuition: $2,141 (state residents), $5,624 (out-of-state). Housing: None. Fees, books, misc. academic expenses (school's estimate): $725.

**Enrollment.** Undergraduates: 924 men, 1,662 women (full-time). Freshman class: 1,250 applicants, 1,100 accepted, 980 enrolled. Graduate enrollment: 614 men, 921 women.

**Test score averages/ranges.** Average SAT scores: 450 verbal, 450 math.

**Faculty.** 143 full-time; 155 part-time. 95% of faculty holds highest degree in specific field. Student/faculty ratio: 25 to 1.

**Selectivity rating.** Less competitive.

**PROFILE.** IUSB, founded in 1922, is a public, comprehensive institution. Programs are offered through the Divisions of Arts and Sciences, Business and Economics, Continuing Education, Education, Labor Studies, Music, and Public and Environmental Affairs and the Schools of Dentistry, Library and Information Science, Nursing, and Technology. Its 40-acre campus is located east of downtown South Bend.

**Accreditation:** NCACS. Professionally accredited by the American Assembly of Collegiate Schools of Business, the National Council for Accreditation of Teacher Education.

**Religious orientation:** Indiana University South Bend is nonsectarian; no religious requirements.

**Library:** Collections totaling over 250,000 volumes, 1,770 periodical subscriptions, and 169,000 microform items.

**Athletic facilities:** Rented gymnasium.

**STUDENT BODY. Undergraduate profile:** 99% are state residents. 6% Black, 1% Hispanic, 90% White, 3% Other. Average age of undergraduates is 23.

**Freshman profile:** 95% of accepted applicants took SAT; 5% took ACT. 90% of freshmen come from public schools.

**Undergraduate achievement:** 90% of fall 1992 freshmen returned for fall 1993 term. 34% of entering class graduated.

**Foreign students:** Countries represented include Canada and Asian countries.

**PROGRAMS OF STUDY. Degrees:** A.B., B.Gen.Studies, B.Mus., B.Mus.Ed., B.S., B.S.Ed., B.S.Nurs.

**Majors:** Accounting, Banking/Finance, Biological Sciences, Chemistry, Communication Arts, Computer Science, Criminal Justice, Dental Assisting, Dental Hygiene, Early Childhood Education, Economics, Electrical Engineering Technology, Elementary Education, Emergency Services Administration, English, Environmental Policy, Film Studies, Finance, Fine Arts, French, General Studies, German, History, Instrumental Music, Jazz/Commercial Music, Junior High/Middle School Education, Labor Studies, Management/Administration, Marketing, Marketing/Advertising, Mathematics, Mechanical Engineering Technology, Music Composition, Music Education, Nursing, Personnel/Industrial Relations, Philosophy, Physics, Policy/Administration, Political Science, Psychology, Religious Studies, Secondary Education, Sociology, Spanish, Special Education, Voice, Women's Studies.

**Requirements:** General education requirement.

**Special:** Several minors offered. All freshmen and sophomores enroll in University Division; courses may be taken in other divisions. Culture sequences offered include African, Afro-American, Ancient Greek/Roman, East/Southeast Asian, Latin American/Spanish, Russian, Sub-Saharan, and Western European (medieval/Renaissance and modern). Certificate programs in dental assisting, environmental studies, humanities, international studies, labor studies, management and administration, office management, sciences, social sciences, and urban studies. Double majors. Independent study. Pass/fail grading option. Internships. Graduate school at which undergraduates may take graduate-level courses. Preprofessional programs in law, medicine, veterinary science, pharmacy, dentistry, optometry, mortuary, occupational therapy, physical therapy, radiology, and respiratory therapy. Member of Northern Indiana Consortium for Education. Semester-away programs. Teacher certification in early childhood, elementary, secondary, and special education. Exchange programs abroad in Ireland (U of Belfast) and other countries. ROTC, NROTC, and AFROTC at U of Notre Dame.

**Honors:** Honors program.

**Academic Assistance:** Remedial reading, writing, math, and study skills. Nonremedial tutoring.

**STUDENT LIFE. Housing:** Commuter campus; no student housing.

**Social atmosphere:** Popular students hangouts include the Northside Lounge, the Greenlawn Lounge, Basix, Cheers, and the Oaken Bucket. College Republicans and the Student Association influence student life. Students enjoy the Student Association's Halloween Bash and the annual Breakfast with Santa. Art shows, plays, and concerts are also favorite activities. According to the student newspaper, students tend to congregate off campus. "Our campus is basically a commuter campus since we have no dorms. But the administration plans to build dorms, a student union, and a new liberal arts building."

**Services and counseling/handicapped student services:** Placement services. Women's center. Day care. Counseling services for minority, veteran, and older students. Personal and psychological counseling. Career and academic guidance services. Physically disabled student services. Learning disabled services. Notetaking services. Tape recorders. Tutors. Reader services for the blind.

**Campus organizations:** Undergraduate student government. Student newspaper (Preface, published once/two weeks). Literary magazine. Music and drama groups, chess club, community-oriented programs, debating and public speaking, athletic, departmental, service, and special-interest groups. Four fraternities, all with chapter houses; four sororities, three chapter houses.

**Religious organizations:** Campus Ministry.

**Minority/foreign student organizations:** Black Student Union. International Student Association.

**ATHLETICS. Physical education requirements:** None.

**Intercollegiate competition:** 1% of students participate. Basketball (M,W). Member of Chicagoland Conference, NAIA.

**Intramural and club sports:** 10% of students participate. Intramural basketball, soccer, volleyball.

**ADMISSIONS. Academic basis for candidate selection** (in order of priority): Secondary school record, class rank, standardized test scores, school's recommendation.

**Nonacademic basis for candidate selection:** Extracurricular participation and particular talent or ability are considered.

**Requirements:** Graduation from secondary school is required; GED is accepted. 13 units and the following program of study are required: 4 units of English, 2 units of math, 1 unit of lab science, 2 units of social studies, 4 units of electives. English units may include 1/2 unit each of speech and journalism. 2 or more units each of math, foreign language, and science recommended of arts and sciences program applicants. 2 or more units of algebra and trigonometry recommended of business program applicants. Interviews required of nursing and dental auxiliary program applicants. Continuing studies program has separate application. Audition required of music program applicants. Veterans are given admission preference. Special Services may sponsor disadvantaged or minority students. SAT or ACT is required. Campus visit and interview recommended. Off-campus interviews available with an admissions representative.

**Procedure:** Take SAT or ACT by March of 12th year. Notification of admission on rolling basis. Freshmen accepted for terms other than fall.

**Special programs:** Admission may be deferred one year. Credit may be granted through CLEP subject exams, DANTES and challenge exams, and military and life experience. Early entrance/early admission program. Concurrent enrollment program.

**Transfer students:** Transfer students accepted for terms other than fall. for fall 1993, Application deadline is July 1 for fall; December 1 for spring. Minimum 2.0 GPA required. Lowest course grade accepted is "C." Maximum number of transferable credits is 30 semester hours from a two-year school and 90 semester hours from a four-year school. At least 30 semester hours must be completed at the university to receive degree.

**Admissions contact:** Esker Ligon, M.A., Director of Admissions. 219 237-IUSB.

**FINANCIAL AID. Available aid:** Pell grants, SEOG, state scholarships and grants, school scholarships and grants, private scholarships, and academic merit scholarships. Perkins Loans (NDSL), PLUS, Stafford Loans (GSL), and school loans. Tuition Management Systems and deferred payment plan.

**Financial aid statistics:** 15% of aid is not need-based.

**Supporting data/closing dates:** FAFSA/FAF: Priority filing date is March 1. School's own aid application: Priority filing date is March 1. Income tax forms: Priority filing date is March 1. Notification of awards on rolling basis.

**Financial aid contact:** Stephen Cullen, Director of Financial Aid. 219 237-4357.

**STUDENT EMPLOYMENT.** College Work/Study Program. Students may expect to earn an average of $1,100 during school year. Off-campus part-time employment opportunities rated "fair."

**COMPUTER FACILITIES.** IBM/IBM-compatible and Macintosh/Apple microcomputers. Students may access IBM, SUN minicomputer/mainframe systems, BITNET, Internet. Client/LAN operating systems include Apple/Macintosh, DOS, Banyan. Numerous computer languages and software programs available. Computer facilities are available to all students.

**Fees:** None.

**Hours:** 8 AM-10 PM.

# Manchester College

**North Manchester, IN 46962-0365 219 982-5000**

**1994-95 Costs.** Tuition: $10,090. Room: $1,890. Board: $1,960. Fees, books, misc. academic expenses (school's estimate): $875.

**Enrollment.** Undergraduates: 464 men, 456 women (full-time). Freshman class: 967 applicants, 836 accepted, 241 enrolled. Graduate enrollment: 8 men, 10 women.

**Test score averages/ranges.** Average SAT scores: 442 verbal, 508 math. Average ACT scores: 22 composite.

**Faculty.** 83 full-time; 17 part-time. 60% of faculty holds doctoral degree. Student/faculty ratio: 14 to 1.

**Selectivity rating.** Less competitive.

**PROFILE.** Manchester, founded in 1889, is a church-affiliated, liberal arts college. Its 100-acre campus is located one mile from downtown North Manchester, 35 miles west of Fort Wayne.

**Accreditation:** NCACS. Professionally accredited by the Council on Social Work Education, the National Council for Accreditation of Teacher Education.

**Religious orientation:** Manchester College is affiliated with the Church of the Brethren; one semester of religion required.

**Library:** Collections totaling over 166,000 volumes, 860 periodical subscriptions, and 19,000 microform items.

**Special facilities/museums:** Language lab, observatory, environmental center and labs.

**Athletic facilities:** Gymnasium, stadium, track, weight room, baseball, football, soccer, and softball fields, basketball, racquetball, tennis, and volleyball courts.

**STUDENT BODY. Undergraduate profile:** 86% are state residents; 13% are transfers. 2% Asian-American, 3% Black, 1% Hispanic, 94% White. Average age of undergraduates is 20.

**Freshman profile:** 1% of freshmen who took SAT scored 700 or over on verbal, 1% scored 700 or over on math; 7% scored 600 or over on verbal, 18% scored 600 or over on math; 27% scored 500 or over on verbal, 55% scored 500 or over on math; 67% scored 400 or over on verbal, 87% scored 400 or over on math; 99% scored 300 or over on verbal, 99% scored 300 or over on math. Majority of accepted applicants took SAT. 99% of freshmen come from public schools.

**Undergraduate achievement:** 80% of fall 1992 freshmen returned for fall 1993 term. 55% of entering class graduated. 14% of students who completed a degree program went on to graduate study within one year.

**Foreign students:** 24 students are from out of the country. Countries represented include Bulgaria, China, Haiti, Honduras, Japan, and Turkey; 14 in all.

**PROGRAMS OF STUDY. Degrees:** B.A., B.S.

**Majors:** Accounting, Art, Athletic Training, Biology, Biology/Chemistry, Business Administration, Chemistry, Communications Studies, Computer Science, Corporate Finance, Economics, Elementary Education, Engineering Science, English, Environmental Studies, French, German, History, Individualized Interdisciplinary, International Business, Mathematics, Medical Technology, Music, Peace Studies, Philosophy, Physical Education, Physics, Political Science, Psychology, Religion, Social Work, Sociology, Spanish.

**Distribution of degrees:** The majors with the highest enrollment are education, accounting, and business; French, German, and religion have the lowest.

**Requirements:** General education requirement.

**Academic regulations:** Freshmen must maintain minimum 1.75 GPA; sophomores, juniors, seniors, 2.0 GPA.

**Special:** Minors offered in gerontology and journalism. Interdivisional senior seminars and gender studies. Associate's degrees offered. Self-designed majors. Double majors. Dual degrees. Independent study. Pass/fail grading option. Internships. Preprofessional programs in law, medicine, veterinary science, pharmacy, dentistry, theology, and optometry. 2-2 nursing program with Goshen Coll. 3-2 engineering programs with several schools. Teacher certification in early childhood, elementary, secondary, and special education. Certification in specific subject areas. Exchange programs abroad in China (Dalian Foreign Language Inst), Ecuador (U of Ecuador), England (Cheltenham Coll, Gloucester Coll), France (U of Nancy, U of Strasbourg), Germany (U of Marburg), Greece (U of LaVerne in Athens), Japan (Hokusei Gakuen U), and Spain (U of Barcelona).

**Honors:** Honors program.

**Academic Assistance:** Remedial reading, writing, math, and study skills. Nonremedial tutoring.

**ADMISSIONS. Academic basis for candidate selection** (in order of priority): Secondary school record, school's recommendation, class rank, standardized test scores.

**Nonacademic basis for candidate selection:** Character and personality and particular talent or ability are important. Extracurricular participation and alumni/ae relationship are considered.

**Requirements:** Graduation from secondary school is required; GED is accepted. 28 units and the following program of study are recommended: 8 units of English, 6 units of math, 6 units of science, 4 units of foreign language, 2 units of social studies, 2 units of history. Minimum combined SAT score of 800, rank in top half of secondary school class, and minimum 2.3 GPA recommended. Audition required of music program applicants. Academic Assistance Program for applicants not normally admissible. SAT is required; ACT may be substituted. Campus visit and interview recommended. No off-campus interviews.

**Procedure:** Take SAT or ACT by January of 12th year. Visit college for interview by March of 12th year. Suggest filing application by March 1. Application deadline is August 1. Notification of admission on rolling basis. Reply is required by May 1. $100 tuition deposit, refundable until May 1. $25 nonrefundable room deposit. Freshmen accepted for terms other than fall.

**Special programs:** Admission may be deferred one year. Credit may be granted through CEEB Advanced Placement for scores of 3 or higher. Credit may be granted through CLEP general and subject exams. Credit and placement may be granted through challenge exams. Concurrent enrollment program.

**Transfer students:** Transfer students accepted for terms other than fall. for fall 1993, 13% of all new students were transfers into all classes. 85 transfer applications were received, 56 were accepted. Application deadline is August 1 for fall; January 15 for spring. Minimum 2.0 GPA required. Lowest course grade accepted is "C." Maximum number of transferable credits is 64 semester hours from a two-year school and 96 semester hours from a four-year school. At least 32 semester hours must be completed at the college to receive degree.

**Admissions contact:** David McFadden, M.I.S., Dean of Enrollment Management. 219 982-5055.

**FINANCIAL AID. Available aid:** Pell grants, SEOG, state scholarships and grants, school scholarships and grants, private scholarships and grants, academic merit scholarships, and aid for undergraduate foreign students. Perkins Loans (NDSL), PLUS, Stafford Loans (GSL), school loans, private loans, and SLS. Tuition Management Systems, deferred payment plan, and family tuition reduction.

**Financial aid statistics:** 13% of aid is not need-based. In 1993-94, 97% of all undergraduate applicants received aid; 97% of freshman applicants. Average amounts of aid awarded freshmen: Scholarships and grants, $6,480; loans, $2,950.

**Supporting data/closing dates:** FAFSA: Accepted on rolling basis. Notification of awards begins March 1.

**Financial aid contact:** Steve Payne, M.S., Director of Financial Aid. 219 982-5066.

# Marian College

**Indianapolis, IN 46222** **317 929-0123**

**1993-94 Costs.** Tuition: $9,200. Room & board: $3,616. Fees, books, misc. academic expenses (school's estimate): $610.
**Enrollment.** Undergraduates: 312 men, 611 women (full-time). Freshman class: 770 applicants, 542 accepted, 257 enrolled.
**Test score averages/ranges.** Average SAT scores: 420 verbal, 466 math. Range of SAT scores of middle 50%: 380-460 verbal, 400-530 math.
**Faculty.** 91 full-time. 36% of faculty holds highest degree in specific field. Student/faculty ratio: 12 to 1.
**Selectivity rating.** Competitive.

**PROFILE.** Marian is a church-affiliated, liberal arts college. Founded in 1851, it adopted coeducation in 1954. Its 144-acre campus is located six miles from the center of Indianapolis. Allison Hall, located in the center of campus, is listed in the National Register of Historic Places.
**Accreditation:** NCACS. Professionally accredited by the National Council for Accreditation of Teacher Education, the National League for Nursing.
**Religious orientation:** Marian College is affiliated with the Roman Catholic Church (Sisters of St. Francis); two semesters of religion/theology required.
**Library:** Collections totaling over 112,000 volumes and 550 periodical subscriptions.
**Athletic facilities:** Physical education center, gymnasium, weight room, racquetball court.
**STUDENT BODY. Undergraduate profile:** 94% are state residents; 27% are transfers. 1% Asian-American, 12% Black, 1% Hispanic, 1% Native American, 85% White. Average age of undergraduates is 23.
**Freshman profile:** 3% of freshmen who took SAT scored 600 or over on verbal, 9% scored 600 or over on math; 13% scored 500 or over on verbal, 34% scored 500 or over on math; 64% scored 400 or over on verbal, 76% scored 400 or over on math; 96% scored 300 or over on verbal, 96% scored 300 or over on math. 92% of accepted applicants took SAT; 8% took ACT. 75% of freshmen come from public schools.
**Undergraduate achievement:** 75% of fall 1992 freshmen returned for fall 1993 term. 51% of entering class graduated.
**PROGRAMS OF STUDY. Degrees:** B.A., B.S., B.S.Nurs.
**Majors:** Accounting, Art, Biology, Business Administration, Chemistry, Computer Science, Dietetics, Education, English, French, German, History, Mathematics, Medical Technology, Music, Nursing, Philosophy, Physical Education, Psychology, Sociology, Spanish, Speech/Theatre, Theology.
**Distribution of degrees:** The majors with the highest enrollment are nursing, business, and elementary education; music and Spanish have the lowest.
**Requirements:** General education requirement.
**Academic regulations:** Freshmen must maintain minimum 1.5 GPA; sophomores, 1.9 GPA; juniors, 2.0 GPA; seniors, 2.0 GPA.
**Special:** Minors offered in most majors. Associate's degrees offered. Independent study. Accelerated study. Pass/fail grading option. Internships. Indianapolis Consortium for Urban Education. Teacher certification in early childhood, elementary, secondary, and special education. Certification in specific subject areas. Study abroad. AFROTC Indiana U Bloomington.
**Honors:** Honors program. Honor societies.
**Academic Assistance:** Remedial reading, writing, math, and study skills. Nonremedial tutoring.
**ADMISSIONS. Academic basis for candidate selection** (in order of priority): Standardized test scores, secondary school record, class rank, school's recommendation, essay.
**Nonacademic basis for candidate selection:** Particular talent or ability is emphasized. Character and personality and extracurricular participation are considered.
**Requirements:** Graduation from secondary school is required; GED is accepted. No specific distribution of secondary school units required. 2 units of foreign language recommended. Minimum combined SAT score of 700, rank in top half of secondary school class, and minimum 2.3 GPA recommended. Nursing program applicants must meet additional requirements. Conditional admission possible for applicants not meeting standard requirements. Project Challenge for applicants not normally admissible. SAT is required; ACT may be substituted. Campus visit recommended.
**Procedure:** Take SAT or ACT by June of 12th year. Notification of admission on rolling basis. $100 nonrefundable tuition deposit. $100 room deposit, refundable until August 1. Freshmen accepted for terms other than fall.
**Special programs:** Credit and/or placement may be granted through CEEB Advanced Placement exams. Credit and/or placement may be granted through CLEP general and subject exams. Credit may be granted through military experience. Concurrent enrollment program.
**Transfer students:** Transfer students accepted for terms other than fall. for fall 1993, 27% of all new students were transfers into all classes. 194 transfer applications were received, 177 were accepted. Minimum 2.0 GPA required. Lowest course grade accepted is "C." Maximum number of transferable credits is 49 semester hours from a two-year school and 98 semester hours from a four-year school. At least 30 semester hours must be completed at the college to receive degree.
**Admissions contact:** Brent Smith, Ph.D., Dean for Enrollment Management. 317 929-0321.
**FINANCIAL AID. Available aid:** Pell grants, SEOG, state scholarships and grants, school scholarships and grants, private scholarships and grants, academic merit scholarships, and athletic scholarships. Perkins Loans (NDSL), PLUS, Stafford Loans (GSL), private loans, and SLS. Tuition Plan Inc., AMS, EFI Fund Management, and family tuition reduction.
**Financial aid statistics:** 13% of aid is not need-based. In 1993-94, 97% of all undergraduate applicants received aid; 97% of freshman applicants. Average amounts of aid awarded freshmen: Scholarships and grants, $5,855; loans, $2,656.
**Supporting data/closing dates:** FAFSA/FAF: Accepted on rolling basis. School's own aid application: Priority filing date is April 20. State aid form: Priority filing date is March 1. Income tax forms: Priority filing date is April 20. Notification of awards on rolling basis.
**Financial aid contact:** John Shelton, M.S., Director of Financial Aid. 317 929-0234.

# Oakland City College

**Oakland City, IN 47660** **812 749-1231**

**1994-95 Costs.** Tuition: $7,200. Room & board: $2,984. Fees, books, misc. academic expenses (school's estimate): $950.
**Enrollment.** Undergraduates: 359 men, 381 women (full-time). Freshman class: 450 applicants, 360 enrolled. Graduate enrollment: 10 men, 1 woman.
**Test score averages/ranges.** Average SAT scores: 360 verbal, 370 math. Average ACT scores: 20 English, 22 math, 20 composite.
**Faculty.** 39 full-time; 15 part-time. 60% of faculty holds highest degree in specific field. Student/faculty ratio: 15 to 1.
**Selectivity rating.** Noncompetitive.

**PROFILE.** Oakland City, founded in 1885, is a private, church-affiliated, multipurpose college. Programs are offered in the Divisions of Arts and Sciences, Business, Education, Religious Studies, and Technical Studies. The campus is located in Oakland City, 30 miles north of Evansville.
**Accreditation:** NCACS.
**Religious orientation:** Oakland City College is affiliated with the General Baptist Church; two semesters of religion required.
**Library:** Collections totaling over 75,000 volumes, 370 periodical subscriptions, and 30,000 microform items.
**Athletic facilities:** Gymnasium; baseball, softball field; golf course.
**STUDENT BODY. Undergraduate profile:** 70% are state residents; 15% are transfers. 1% Asian-American, 1% Black, 93% White, 5% Other. Average age of undergraduates is 20.
**Freshman profile:** Majority of accepted applicants took SAT. 75% of freshmen come from public schools.
**Undergraduate achievement:** 90% of fall 1992 freshmen returned for fall 1993 term. 35% of entering class graduated. 30% of students who completed a degree program went on to graduate study within five years.
**Foreign students:** Seven students are from out of the country. Countries represented include China and India.
**PROGRAMS OF STUDY. Degrees:** B.A., B.S.
**Majors:** Accounting, Biology, Business Administration/Management, Business Education, Elementary Education, English, Humanities, Mathematics, Music, Physical Education, Religious Studies, Science, Visual Arts.
**Distribution of degrees:** The majors with the highest enrollment are elementary education, business administration, and accounting.
**Requirements:** General education requirement.
**Special:** Minors offered in some majors and in chemistry, Christian education, Christian missions, data processing, general business, history, kindergarten education, and ministry. Certificate programs offered in auto-diesel technology, computer technology, heating/air conditioning/refrigeration, ministerial, secretarial science, and welding. Associate's degrees offered. Double majors. Accelerated study. Pass/fail grading option. Cooperative education programs. Graduate school at which undergraduates may take graduate-level courses. Preprofessional programs in law, medicine, dentistry, theology, music performance, nuclear medical technology, and physical therapy. Teacher certification in elementary, secondary, and vo-tech education. Certification in specific subject areas.
**Honors:** Honors program. Honor societies.
**Academic Assistance:** Remedial reading, writing, math, and study skills. Nonremedial tutoring.
**ADMISSIONS. Academic basis for candidate selection** (in order of priority): Secondary school record, standardized test scores, school's recommendation, class rank, essay.
**Nonacademic basis for candidate selection:** Character and personality are emphasized. Extracurricular participation is important. Particular talent or ability is considered.
**Requirements:** Graduation from secondary school is required; GED is accepted. 16 units and the following program of study are recommended: 4 units of English, 2 units of math, 3 units of science, 2 units of foreign language, 2 units of social studies. Minimum combined SAT score of 700 (composite ACT score of 18) and minimum 2.0 GPA required. Recommendation of secondary school counselor required of learning disabled applicants who must participate in remedial services on campus. Project Opportunity for applicants not normally admissible. SAT or ACT is required. Campus visit and interview recommended. Off-campus interviews available with an admissions representative.
**Procedure:** Notification of admission on rolling basis. Reply is required by date specified in letter of acceptance. $50 tuition deposit, refundable until third week. $20 room deposit, refundable until third week. Freshmen accepted for terms other than fall.
**Special programs:** Admission may be deferred one semester. Credit and/or placement may be granted through CEEB Advanced Placement exams. Credit and/or placement may be granted through CLEP general and subject exams. Credit may be granted through life experience. Early decision program. Early entrance/early admission program. Concurrent enrollment program.
**Transfer students:** Transfer students accepted for terms other than fall. for fall 1993, 15% of all new students were transfers into all classes. 75 transfer applications were received, 40 were accepted. Minimum 2.0 GPA required. Lowest course grade accepted is "D."
**Admissions contact:** Faye Camp, Director of Admissions. 812 749-1222.
**FINANCIAL AID. Available aid:** Pell grants, SEOG, state scholarships and grants, school scholarships and grants, private scholarships and grants, ROTC scholarships, academic merit scholarships, and athletic scholarships. Perkins Loans (NDSL), PLUS, Stafford Loans (GSL), private loans, and SLS. Deferred payment plan.
**Financial aid statistics:** In 1993-94, 95% of all undergraduate applicants received aid; 98% of freshman applicants.

**Supporting data/closing dates:** FAFSA/FAF: Priority filing date is March 1; accepted on rolling basis. School's own aid application: Accepted on rolling basis. State aid form: Priority filing date is March 1. Notification of awards on rolling basis.
**Financial aid contact:** Caren Richeson, Director of Financial Aid. 812 749-1224.

## Purdue University

**West Lafayette, IN 47907** **317 494-4600**

**1994-95 Costs.** Tuition: $2,884 (state residents), $9,556 (out-of-state). Room & board: $4,230. Fees, books, misc. academic expenses (school's estimate): $590.
**Enrollment.** Undergraduates: 14,838 men, 11,112 women (full-time). Freshman class: 21,804 applicants, 18,744 accepted, 5,761 enrolled. Graduate enrollment: 4,170 men, 2,527 women.
**Test score averages/ranges.** Average SAT scores: 452 verbal, 543 math. Range of SAT scores of middle 50%: 390-510 verbal, 470-620 math. Average ACT scores: 23 English, 24 math, 24 composite. Range of ACT scores of middle 50%: 20-26 English, 21-28 math.
**Faculty.** 1,806 full-time; 87 part-time. 83% of faculty holds doctoral degree. Student/faculty ratio: 17 to 1.
**Selectivity rating.** Less competitive.

**PROFILE.** Purdue University is a public, comprehensive institution. Founded in 1869, it adopted coeducation in 1874. Its 1,565-acre campus is located in West Lafayette, 65 miles northwest of Indianapolis.
**Accreditation:** NCACS. Numerous professional accreditations.
**Religious orientation:** Purdue University is nonsectarian; no religious requirements.
**Library:** Collections totaling over 2,076,302 volumes, 14,139 periodical subscriptions, and 2,061,467 microform items.
**Special facilities/museums:** Hall of music, child development lab, speech and hearing clinic, small animal veterinary clinic, horticulture park, linear accelerator, tornado simulator, nuclear accelerator.
**Athletic facilities:** Gymnasiums, swimming pools, archery and riflery ranges, fitness, weight, and wrestling rooms, badminton, basketball, handball, racquetball, squash, tennis, volleyball, and walleyball courts, golf course, baseball, football, intramural, soccer, and softball fields, tracks, arena.
**STUDENT BODY. Undergraduate profile:** 74% are state residents; 12% are transfers. 4% Asian-American, 4% Black, 2% Hispanic, .5% Native American, 88% White, 1.5% International. Average age of undergraduates is 20.
**Freshman profile:** 8% of freshmen who took SAT scored 700 or over on math; 5% scored 600 or over on verbal, 31% scored 600 or over on math; 29% scored 500 or over on verbal, 65% scored 500 or over on math; 70% scored 400 or over on verbal, 87% scored 400 or over on math; 92% scored 300 or over on verbal, 95% scored 300 or over on math. 5% of freshmen who took ACT scored 30 or over on English, 13% scored 30 or over on math, 9% scored 30 or over on composite; 46% scored 24 or over on English, 54% scored 24 or over on math, 53% scored 24 or over on composite; 84% scored 18 or over on English, 86% scored 18 or over on math, 88% scored 18 or over on composite; 92% scored 12 or over on English, 92% scored 12 or over on math, 92% scored 12 or over on composite. Majority of accepted applicants took SAT.
**Undergraduate achievement:** 84% of fall 1992 freshmen returned for fall 1993 term. 30% of entering class graduated. 20% of students who completed a degree program went on to graduate study within one year.
**Foreign students:** 633 students are from out of the country. Countries represented include China, Hong Kong, India, Indonesia, Malaysia, and Taiwan; 76 in all.
**PROGRAMS OF STUDY. Degrees:** B.A., B.Phys.Ed., B.S., B.S.Agri.Eng., B.S.Chem., B.S.Chem.Eng., B.S.Civil Eng., B.S.Elec.Eng., B.S.Eng., B.S.Forestry, B.S.Indust.Mgmt., B.S.Land Surv., B.S.Land.Arch., B.S.Mech.Eng., B.S.Metal.Eng., B.S.Pharm.
**Majors:** Accounting, Actuarial Science, Advertising, Aeronautical/Astronautical Engineering, Afro-American Studies, Agri-Sales/Marketing, Agribusiness Management, Agricultural Communications, Agricultural Economics, Agricultural Education, Agricultural Engineering, Agricultural Finance, Agricultural Mechanization, Agricultural Meteorology, American Studies, Animal Agribusiness, Animal Production, Animal Products, Animal Science, Anthropology, Apparel Technology, Applied Mathematics, Art History, Athletic Training, Atmospheric Science/Meteorology, Audiology/Speech Sciences, Aviation Maintenance Technology, Aviation Technology, Biochemistry, Biology, Biology Teaching, Building Construction/Contracting, Cell/Developmental Biology, Chemical Engineering, Chemistry, Chemistry Teaching, Child Development/Family Studies, Civil Engineering, Coaching, Communication, Community Development, Community Health, Comparative Literature, Computer/Electrical Engineering, Computer Integrated Manufacturing Technology, Computer Sciences, Computer Technology, Construction Engineering/Management, Consumer Affairs, Consumer/Homemaking Education, Crafts, Creative Writing, Dietetics, Early Childhood Education, Earth/Space Science Teaching, Ecology/Evolutionary/Population Biology, Economics, Electrical Engineering, Electrical Engineering Technology, Elementary Education, Engineering Geology, English, Entomology, Environmental Health Science, Farm Management, Film Studies, Financial Counseling/Planning, Fine Arts, Fisheries/Aquatic Science, Food Business Management, Food Science, Food Service/Lodging Supervision, Foods/Nutrition in Business, French, General Agriculture, General Aviation Flight, General Health Sciences, General Science, Genetic Biology, Geochemistry/Mineralogy/Petrology, Geology, Geophysics, German, Health Physics, History, Horticultural Science/Technology, Industrial Arts Teaching, Industrial Design, Industrial Engineering, Industrial Hygiene, Industrial Management, Industrial Technology, Integrated Pest Management, Interdisciplinary Engineering, Interior Design, International Agriculture, International Agronomy, Interpersonal Communication, Journalistic Communication, Land Surveying, Landscape Architecture, Law/Society, Linguistics, Management, Mass Communication, Materials Engineering, Mathematics Teaching, Mechanical Engineering, Mechanical Engineering Technology, Medical Technology, Medieval Studies, Microbiology, Molecular Biology, Movement/Sport Sciences, Natural Resources/Environmental Science, Neurobiology/Animal Physiology, Nuclear Engineering, Nursing, Nutritional Science, Occupational Home Economics Education, Operations Research, Organizational Communication, Paleontology/Paleoecology, Pharmacy, Philosophy, Photography, Physical Education, Physics, Physics Teaching, Plant Molecular Biology/Physiology, Plant Science, Political Science, Pre-Forestry, Professional Writing, Psychology, Public Communication, Public Relations, Quantitative Agricultural Economics, Recreation Studies, Religious Studies, Restaurant/Hotel/Institutional Management, Restaurant/Hotel/Institutional/Tourism Management, Retail Management, Russian, Science/Culture, Social Science Education, Sociology, Soil/Crop Management, Soil/Crop Science, Solid Earth Sciences, Spanish, Special Education, Statistics, Supervision, Teacher Preparation, Technical Graphics, Telecommunication, Theatre, Turf Science, Urban/Industrial Pest Control, Visual Communication Design, Wildlife Science.
**Distribution of degrees:** The majors with the highest enrollment are communications, electrical engineering, and elementary education; food business management, medieval studies, and Afro-American studies have the lowest.
**Academic regulations:** Freshmen must maintain minimum 1.4 GPA; sophomores, 1.6 GPA; juniors, 1.8 GPA; seniors, 2.0 GPA.
**Special:** Minors offered. Associate's degrees offered. Self-designed majors. Double majors. Independent study. Accelerated study. Pass/fail grading option. Internships. Cooperative education programs. Graduate school at which undergraduates may take graduate-level courses. Preprofessional programs in law, medicine, veterinary science, pharmacy, dentistry, optometry, and pre-podiatry. 3-1 bachelor's/M.S. in industrial administration program. Five-year pharmacy program. Teacher certification in early childhood, elementary, secondary, special education, and vo-tech education. Certification in specific subject areas. Study abroad in England, France, Germany, Mexico, the former Soviet Republics, and Spain. ROTC, NROTC, and AFROTC.
**Honors:** Phi Beta Kappa. Honors program. Honor societies.
**Academic Assistance:** Remedial writing and study skills. Nonremedial tutoring.
**STUDENT LIFE. Housing:** Students may live on or off campus. Coed, women's, and men's dorms. Sorority and fraternity housing. School-owned/operated apartments. Off-campus privately-owned housing. On-campus married-student housing. Cooperative housing. 37% of students live in college housing.
**Social atmosphere:** The student newspaper reports, "Purdue has a big Greek system, but off-campus is active. Band people tend to stick together. Purdue Student Government sponsors activities and the residence halls do also." Purdue students like to hangout in local bars or on Slayter Hill, an outdoor stage where concerts are sometimes held. Special campus events include Homecoming, the Christmas Show, basketball season, and the Grand Prix go-cart race.
**Services and counseling/handicapped student services:** Placement services. Health service. Women's center. Day care. Women's health clinic Counseling services for minority, military, and older students. Personal and psychological counseling. Career and academic guidance services. Physically disabled student services. Learning disabled services. Note-taking services. Tape recorders. Tutors. Reader services for the blind.
**Campus organizations:** Undergraduate student government. Student newspaper (Exponent, published five times/week). Literary magazine. Yearbook. Radio station. Choir, bands, glee club, debating, theatre, special-interest groups, 528 organizations in all. 47 fraternities, 41 chapter houses; 24 sororities, 18 chapter houses. 20% of men join a fraternity. 18% of women join a sorority.
**Religious organizations:** Numerous religious groups.
**Minority/foreign student organizations:** Numerous minority groups. Numerous international groups.
**ATHLETICS. Physical education requirements:** None.
**Intercollegiate competition:** 1% of students participate. Basketball (M,W), cross-country (M,W), diving (M,W), football (M), golf (M,W), softball (W), swimming (M,W), tennis (M,W), track and field (indoor) (M,W), track and field (outdoor) (M,W), volleyball (W), wrestling (M). Member of Big 10 Conference, NCAA Division I.
**Intramural and club sports:** 50% of students participate. Intramural baseball, basketball, fencing, golf, handball, horseshoes, judo, softball, squash, swimming, table tennis, tennis, weight lifting, wrestling.
**ADMISSIONS. Academic basis for candidate selection** (in order of priority): Secondary school record, class rank, standardized test scores, school's recommendation, essay.
**Nonacademic basis for candidate selection:** Alumni/ae relationship is important. Character and personality, extracurricular participation, and particular talent or ability are considered.
**Requirements:** Graduation from secondary school is required; GED is accepted. No specific distribution of secondary school units required. 1 to 2 units of history and social studies also recommended. Out-of-state applicants must meet higher standards than in-state applicants; combination of class rank, standardized test scores, probability of success, GPA in subjects related to degree objectives, trends in achievement, and strength of preparatory program are considered. Minimum SAT scores of 400 verbal and 500 math (composite ACT scores of 21 English and 23 math) required of engineering program applicants. Interview required of veterinary technology program applicants. SAT or ACT is required. PSAT is recommended. Campus visit and interview recommended. No off-campus interviews.
**Procedure:** Take SAT or ACT by December of 12th year. Priority filing date for engineering, nursing, and flight technology applicants is November 15; December 15 for veterinary technology; rolling admissions for all other programs. Notification of admission on rolling basis. Reply is required by May 1. $50 refundable tuition deposit. $15 refundable until July 1. $10 nonrefundable room deposit. $10 room deposit, partially refundable. Freshmen accepted for terms other than fall.
**Special programs:** Credit and/or placement may be granted through CEEB Advanced Placement exams. Credit and/or placement may be granted through CLEP general and subject exams. Credit and placement may be granted through challenge exams.
**Transfer students:** Transfer students accepted for terms other than fall. for fall 1993, 12% of all new students were transfers into all classes. 2,923 transfer applications were received, 1,998 were accepted. Application deadline is rolling for fall; rolling for spring. Minimum 2.0 GPA required. Lowest course grade accepted is "C." At least 32 semester hours must be completed at the university to receive degree.
**Admissions contact:** William J. Murray, M.A., Director of Admissions. 317 494-1776.

**FINANCIAL AID. Available aid:** Pell grants, SEOG, state scholarships and grants, school scholarships and grants, private scholarships and grants, ROTC scholarships, academic merit scholarships, and athletic scholarships. Perkins Loans (NDSL), PLUS, Stafford Loans (GSL), Health Professions Loans, state loans, school loans, and SLS. Budget plan with 10 monthly payments.
**Financial aid statistics:** 9% of aid is not need-based. In 1993-94, 100% of all undergraduate applicants received aid. Average amounts of aid awarded freshmen: Scholarships and grants, $1,924; loans, $5,369.
**Supporting data/closing dates:** FAFSA: Priority filing date is March 1. School's own aid application: Priority filing date is March 1. Notification of awards begins April 15.
**Financial aid contact:** Joyce Hall, M.S., Director of Financial Aid. 317 494-5050.

**STUDENT EMPLOYMENT.** College Work/Study Program. Institutional employment. 6% of full-time undergraduates work on campus during school year. Students may expect to earn an average of $2,000 during school year. Off-campus part-time employment opportunities rated "good."

**COMPUTER FACILITIES.** IBM/IBM-compatible and Macintosh/Apple microcomputers. Students may access IBM, Sequent minicomputer/mainframe systems, BITNET, Internet. Residence halls may be equipped with networked microcomputers, networked terminals, modems. Client/LAN operating systems include Apple/Macintosh, DOS, UNIX/XENIX/AIX, Windows NT, X-windows, LocalTalk/AppleTalk, Novell. Numerous software packages and programs available. Computer facilities are available to all students.
**Fees:** None.
**Hours:** 24 hours.

**GRADUATE CAREER DATA.** Highest graduate school enrollments: Purdue U. 90% of graduates choose careers in business and industry. Companies and businesses that hire graduates: Arthur Andersen, Eli Lilly, Ford, General Electric, General Motors, Hook's Drugs, IBM, Marriott.

**PROMINENT ALUMNI/AE.** Neil Armstrong, astronaut and first man on the moon; Stephen Bechtel, chairperson of the board, Bechtel Corp.; Paul Oreffice, chairperson of the board, Dow Chemical.

# Purdue University–Calumet

**Hammond, IN 46323 219 989-2400**

**1994-95 Costs.** Tuition: $2,374 (state residents), $5,521 (out-of-state). Housing: None. Fees, books, misc. academic expenses (school's estimate): $525.
**Enrollment.** Undergraduates: 1,715 men, 1,760 women (full-time). Freshman class: 1,768 applicants, 1,738 accepted, 1,676 enrolled. Graduate enrollment: 294 men, 506 women.
**Test score averages/ranges.** Average SAT scores: 430 verbal, 480 math.
**Faculty.** 250 full-time; 207 part-time. 59% of faculty holds doctoral degree. Student/faculty ratio: 18 to 1.
**Selectivity rating.** Less competitive.

**PROFILE.** Purdue University-Calumet, founded in 1943, is a public, comprehensive university. Programs are offered in the Schools of Liberal Arts and Sciences, General Studies, and Professional Studies. Its 167-acre campus is located in Hammond, 26 miles from Chicago.

**Accreditation:** NCACS. Professionally accredited by the Accreditation Board for Engineering and Technology, the National Council for Accreditation of Teacher Education, the National League for Nursing.
**Religious orientation:** Purdue University- Calumet is nonsectarian; no religious requirements.
**Library:** Collections totaling over 215,830 volumes, 1,736 periodical subscriptions, and 481,678 microform items.
**Special facilities/museums:** Audio-visual services, urban development institute.
**Athletic facilities:** Recreation center, fitness center, weight room, gymnasium, track, basketball and racquetball courts, playing fields.

**STUDENT BODY. Undergraduate profile:** 92% are state residents; 29% are transfers. 1% Asian-American, 9% Black, 9% Hispanic, 1% Native American, 80% White. Average age of undergraduates is 27.
**Freshman profile:** 1% of freshmen who took SAT scored 700 or over on verbal, 1% scored 700 or over on math; 6% scored 600 or over on verbal, 7% scored 600 or over on math; 28% scored 500 or over on verbal, 26% scored 500 or over on math; 67% scored 400 or over on verbal, 76% scored 400 or over on math; 97% scored 300 or over on verbal, 94% scored 300 or over on math. 85% of accepted applicants took SAT; 10% took ACT. 88% of freshmen come from public schools.
**Undergraduate achievement:** 65% of fall 1992 freshmen returned for fall 1993 term.

**PROGRAMS OF STUDY. Degrees:** B.A., B.Phys.Ed., B.S., B.S.Eng., B.S.Mgmt.
**Majors:** Biology, Chemistry, Communication, Computer Programming, Computer Science, Electrical Technology, Elementary Education, Engineering, English, French, German, History, Industrial Engineering Technology, Information Systems/Computer Programming, Management, Mathematics, Mechanical Technology, Medical Technology, Nursing, Philosophy, Physics, Political Science, Psychology, Radio/Television, Radio/TV Teaching, Restaurant/Hotel/Institutional Management, School Media Services, Science Teaching, Social Studies Teaching, Sociology, Spanish, Speech Communication/Theatre Teaching, Supervision.
**Distribution of degrees:** The majors with the highest enrollment are engineering, management, and nursing; industrial engineering technology, physics, and math have the lowest.
**Requirements:** General education requirement.
**Academic regulations:** Freshmen must maintain minimum 3.5 GPA; sophomores, 3.9 GPA; juniors, 4.0 GPA; seniors, 4.0 GPA (on a 6.0 scale).
**Special:** Associate's degrees offered. Double majors. Internships. Cooperative education programs. Graduate school at which undergraduates may take graduate-level courses. Preprofessional programs in law, medicine, veterinary science, pharmacy, and dentistry. 2-2 nursing program. Teacher certification in early childhood, elementary, secondary, and special education. ROTC.
**Honors:** Honors program.
**Academic Assistance:** Remedial reading, writing, math, and study skills. Nonremedial tutoring.

**STUDENT LIFE. Housing:** Commuter campus; no student housing.
**Social atmosphere:** The student newspaper reports that, as a commuter campus with an average student age of 26, social and cultural activities on campus are limited. Students gather in the lounge in the library building, at the recreation center, and on the campus lawn. Local restaurants and bars are popular off-campus student spots. Popular school-year events include Homecoming and dances.
**Services and counseling/handicapped student services:** Placement services. Health service. Women's center. Day care. Counseling services for minority, military, veteran, and older students. Personal and psychological counseling. Career and academic guidance services. Physically disabled student services. Notetaking services. Tape recorders. Tutors. Reader services for the blind.
**Campus organizations:** Undergraduate student government. Student newspaper (Chronicle). Literary magazine. Musical, athletic, departmental, service, and special-interest groups. Three fraternities, no chapter houses; three sororities, no chapter houses. 1% of men join a fraternity. 1% of women join a sorority.
**Religious organizations:** Several religious groups.
**Minority/foreign student organizations:** Black Student Union, Los Latinos, Minority Assistance Club.

**ATHLETICS. Physical education requirements:** None.
**Intercollegiate competition:** 1% of students participate. Basketball (M,W), cheerleading (W), soccer (M), volleyball (W). Member of Chicagoland Collegiate Conference, NAIA.
**Intramural and club sports:** 12% of students participate. Intramural aerobic dance, basketball, football, racquetball, road racing, softball, volleyball, weight lifting. Men's club golf, wrestling. Women's club softball.

**ADMISSIONS. Academic basis for candidate selection** (in order of priority): Standardized test scores, secondary school record, class rank.
**Requirements:** Graduation from secondary school is required; GED is accepted. 16 units and the following program of study are required: 3 units of English, 2 units of math, 1 unit of lab science, 2 units of foreign language, 1 unit of social studies, 1 unit of history. Minimum SAT scores of 500 in both verbal and math required. 4 units of English required of education, humanities, and social science program applicants. Chemistry required of nursing program applicants. 2.5 units of math required of forestry program applicants. 3 units of math required of mathematics program applicants. Developmental Program for applicants not normally admissible. SAT is required; ACT may be substituted. Campus visit recommended. No off-campus interviews.
**Procedure:** Notification of admission on rolling basis. Reply is required by first week of classes. Freshmen accepted for terms other than fall.
**Special programs:** Admission may be deferred one year. Credit may be granted through CEEB Advanced Placement for scores of 3 or higher. Credit may be granted through CLEP subject exams. Concurrent enrollment program.
**Transfer students:** Transfer students accepted for terms other than fall. for fall 1992, 29% of all new students were transfers into all classes. Application deadline is rolling for fall; rolling for spring. Minimum 4.0 GPA required. Lowest course grade accepted is "C." Maximum number of transferable credits is 90 semester hours. At least 32 semester hours must be completed at the university to receive degree.
**Admissions contact:** Patricia W. Grady, M.A., Acting Director of Admissions. 219 989-2213.

**FINANCIAL AID. Available aid:** Pell grants, SEOG, state scholarships and grants, school scholarships, private scholarships and grants, academic merit scholarships, and athletic scholarships. Perkins Loans (NDSL), PLUS, Stafford Loans (GSL), private loans, and SLS. Deferred payment plan.
**Financial aid statistics:** 1% of aid is not need-based. In 1993-94, 69% of all undergraduate applicants received aid; 55% of freshman applicants.
**Supporting data/closing dates:** FAFSA/FAF/FFS: Priority filing date is March 1; accepted on rolling basis. School's own aid application. Notification of awards begins June 1.
**Financial aid contact:** Carl D. Curry, M.A., Director of Financial Aid. 219 989-2301.

**STUDENT EMPLOYMENT.** College Work/Study Program. Institutional employment. Off-campus part-time employment opportunities rated "excellent."

**COMPUTER FACILITIES.** 453 microcomputers; all are networked. Computer languages and software packages include BASIC, C, COBOL, dBASE, FORTRAN, Lotus 1-2-3, Microsoft Word, Pascal. Computer facilities are available to all students.
**Fees:** None.
**Hours:** 8 AM-11 PM (M-F).

**PROMINENT ALUMNI/AE.** Rev. Henry Williamson, national president, Operation Push.

# Purdue University–North Central

**Westville, IN 46391 219 785-5200**

**1993-94 Costs.** Tuition: $2,044. Housing: None. Fees, books, misc. academic expenses (school's estimate): $535.
**Enrollment.** Undergraduates: 1,268 (full-time). Freshman class: 2,088 accepted, 1,370 enrolled. Graduate enrollment: 44.
**Test score averages/ranges.** Average SAT scores: 429 verbal, 476 math. Average ACT scores: 21 composite.
**Faculty.** 88 full-time; 130 part-time. Student/faculty ratio: 16 to 1.
**Selectivity rating.** Less competitive.

**PROFILE.** Purdue-North Central, founded in 1967, is a public university. Its 264-acre campus is in Westville, 75 miles from Chicago.

**Accreditation:** MSACS.

**Religious orientation:** Purdue University - North Central is nonsectarian; no religious requirements.

**Library:** Collections totaling over 75,122 volumes and 356 periodical subscriptions.

**STUDENT BODY. Undergraduate profile:** 17% are transfers. 1% Asian-American, 3% Black, 2% Hispanic, 1% Native American, 93% White. Average age of undergraduates is 29.

**Freshman profile:** 1% of freshmen who took SAT scored 700 or over on verbal, 3% scored 700 or over on math; 9% scored 600 or over on verbal, 19% scored 600 or over on math; 35% scored 500 or over on verbal, 57% scored 500 or over on math; 84% scored 400 or over on verbal, 90% scored 400 or over on math; 100% scored 300 or over on verbal, 99% scored 300 or over on math. 75% of accepted applicants took SAT; 25% took ACT.

**Undergraduate achievement:** 56% of fall 1991 freshmen returned for fall 1992 term.

**PROGRAMS OF STUDY. Degrees:** B.A., B.Lib.Studies, B.S.

**Majors:** Elementary Education, English, Liberal Studies, Manufacturing Technology, Mechanical Engineering Technology, Nursing.

**Distribution of degrees:** The majors with the highest enrollment are liberal studies and elementary education; English and mechanical engineering technology have the lowest.

**Requirements:** General education requirement.

**Academic regulations:** Freshmen must maintain minimum 3.5 GPA; sophomores, 3.7 GPA; juniors, 4.0 GPA; seniors, 4.0 GPA (on a 6.0 scale).

**Special:** Associate's degrees offered.

**Honors:** Honors program.

**Academic Assistance:** Remedial reading, writing, math, and study skills.

**STUDENT LIFE. Housing:** Commuter campus; no student housing.

**Services and counseling/handicapped student services:** Placement services. Day care. Personal counseling. Career and academic guidance services. Physically disabled student services. Learning disabled services. Notetaking services. Tutors. Reader services for the blind.

**Campus organizations:** Student newspaper (Spectator). Student Senate, Students in Free Enterprise.

**Minority/foreign student organizations:** Student Cultural Society.

**ATHLETICS. Physical education requirements:** None.

**ADMISSIONS. Academic basis for candidate selection** (in order of priority): Secondary school record, standardized test scores, school's recommendation.

**Requirements:** Graduation from secondary school is required; GED is accepted. 10 units and the following program of study are required: 4 units of English, 2 units of math, 2 units of science including 1 unit of lab, 2 units of social studies. Community college Bridge Program. SAT or ACT is required. Campus visit and interview recommended. No off-campus interviews.

**Procedure:** Suggest filing application by July 1. Application deadline is August 1. Notification of admission on rolling basis. Freshmen accepted for terms other than fall.

**Special programs:** Admission may be deferred one year. Credit may be granted through CLEP general and subject exams, and DANTES exams. Credit and placement may be granted through challenge exams. Concurrent enrollment program.

**Transfer students:** Transfer students accepted for terms other than fall. for fall 1992, 17% of all new students were transfers into all classes. 410 transfer applications were received, 352 were accepted. Application deadline is July 15 for fall; December 1 for spring. Minimum 2.0 GPA required. Admissions interview recommended. Lowest course grade accepted is "C." At least 32 semester hours must be completed at the university to receive degree.

**Admissions contact:** Bill Barnett, M.S., Director of Admissions and Placement. 219 785-5458.

**FINANCIAL AID. Available aid:** Pell grants, SEOG, state scholarships and grants, and school scholarships. Perkins Loans (NDSL), PLUS, Stafford Loans (GSL), and SLS.

**Financial aid statistics:** In 1992-93, 85% of all undergraduate applicants received aid; 85% of freshman applicants. Average amounts of aid awarded freshmen: Scholarships and grants, $2,500.

**Supporting data/closing dates:** FAFSA: Priority filing date is March 1; accepted on rolling basis. School's own aid application: Priority filing date is March 1; accepted on rolling basis. Notification of awards begins June 1.

**Financial aid contact:** Gerald Lewis, M.S., Director of Financial Aid. 219 785-5279.

**STUDENT EMPLOYMENT.** College Work/Study Program. Institutional employment. 2% of full-time undergraduates work on campus during school year. Students may expect to earn an average of $1,200 during school year. Off-campus part-time employment opportunities rated "fair."

**COMPUTER FACILITIES.** 135 IBM/IBM-compatible and Macintosh/Apple microcomputers; all are networked. Students may access IBM minicomputer/mainframe systems. Client/LAN operating systems include Novell. Computer languages and software packages include Autocad, C, COBOL, dBASE, Lotus 1-2-3, Microsoft Works, RPG. Computer facilities are available to all students.

**Fees:** Computer fee is included in tuition/fees.

**Hours:** 8 AM-10 PM.

# Rose-Hulman Institute of Technology

**Terre Haute, IN 47803** **812 877-1511**

**1994-95 Costs.** Tuition: $13,200. Room & board: $4,200. Fees, books, misc. academic expenses (school's estimate): $1,360.

**Enrollment.** 1,310 men (full-time). Freshman class: 3,320 applicants, 2,082 accepted, 381 enrolled. Graduate enrollment: 50 men, 3 women.

**Test score averages/ranges.** Average SAT scores: 540 verbal, 670 math. Range of SAT scores of middle 50%: 540-650 verbal, 650-800 math. Average ACT scores: 24 English, 33 math, 30 composite.

**Faculty.** 100 full-time; 10 part-time. 94% of faculty holds doctoral degree. Student/faculty ratio: 13 to 1.

**Selectivity rating.** Highly competitive.

**PROFILE.** Rose-Hulman, founded in 1874, is a private, technological institution. Its 130-acre campus is located in a residential section of Terre Haute.

**Accreditation:** NCACS. Professionally accredited by the Accreditation Board for Engineering and Technology.

**Religious orientation:** Rose-Hulman Institute of Technology is nonsectarian; no religious requirements.

**Library:** Collections totaling over 55,000 volumes and 450 periodical subscriptions.

**Athletic facilities:** Field house, track, basketball and racquetball courts, weight lifting facilities, intramural fields, recreation center.

**STUDENT BODY. Undergraduate profile:** 60% are state residents; 1% are transfers. 2% Asian-American, 2% Black, 1% Hispanic, 95% White. Average age of undergraduates is 20.

**Freshman profile:** 4% of freshmen who took SAT scored 700 or over on verbal, 34% scored 700 or over on math; 22% scored 600 or over on verbal, 81% scored 600 or over on math; 69% scored 500 or over on verbal, 100% scored 500 or over on math; 100% scored 400 or over on verbal. 30% of freshmen who took ACT scored 30 or over on English, 95% scored 30 or over on math; 95% scored 24 or over on English, 100% scored 24 or over on math; 100% scored 18 or over on English. 75% of accepted applicants took SAT; 25% took ACT. 73% of freshmen come from public schools.

**Undergraduate achievement:** 90% of fall 1992 freshmen returned for fall 1993 term. 75% of entering class graduated. 50% of students who completed a degree program went on to graduate study within five years.

**Foreign students:** Seven students are from out of the country. Countries represented include Germany, Thailand, and United Arab Emirates.

**PROGRAMS OF STUDY. Degrees:** B.S.

**Majors:** Applied Optics, Chemical Engineering, Chemistry, Civil Engineering, Computer Engineering, Computer Science, Economics, Electrical Engineering, Mathematics, Mechanical Engineering, Physics.

**Distribution of degrees:** The majors with the highest enrollment are electrical engineering, mechanical engineering, and chemical engineering; economics, chemistry, and physics have the lowest.

**Requirements:** General education requirement.

**Academic regulations:** Freshmen must maintain minimum 1.8 GPA; sophomores, 1.8 GPA; juniors, 2.0 GPA; seniors, 2.0 GPA.

**Special:** Minors offered in applied optics and in several areas of humanities and social sciences. Interdepartmental courses. Student chooses department of specialization after first year. Technical translation certificates offered in German and Russian. Double majors. Independent study. Graduate school at which undergraduates may take graduate-level courses. Preprofessional programs in medicine. Study abroad programs in China, Germany, Ireland, and the former Soviet Republics. ROTC and AFROTC.

**Academic Assistance:** Remedial writing, math, and study skills. Nonremedial tutoring.

**STUDENT LIFE. Housing:** All freshmen must live on campus. Men's dorms. Fraternity housing. 65% of students live in college housing.

**Social atmosphere:** According to the student newspaper, "The academic load at Rose can be overwhelming. However, there are opportunities to do things that are not accessible to engineering students at other schools, such as running a campus newspaper and working a radio station." The Commons is a popular place to gather on campus. Off campus, students like to go to the Fourth Quarter, the Ballyhoo, and the Overpass. Popular groups on campus include Greeks and the operators of the school radio station. Homecoming, the Springfest concert, and the Rose Show are among the year's favorite events.

**Services and counseling/handicapped student services:** Placement services. Health service. Personal and psychological counseling. Academic guidance services.

**Campus organizations:** Undergraduate student government. Student newspaper (Thorn, published once/week). Yearbook. Radio station. Band, glee club, drama club, 50 organizations in all. Eight fraternities, all with chapter houses. 44% of men join a fraternity.

**Religious organizations:** Campus Fellowship.

**Minority/foreign student organizations:** Society of Black Engineers.

**ATHLETICS. Physical education requirements:** None.

**Intercollegiate competition:** 25% of students participate. Baseball (M), basketball (M), cheerleading (M), cross-country (M), diving (M), football (M), golf (M), riflery (M), soccer (M), swimming (M), tennis (M), track (indoor) (M), track (outdoor) (M), track and field (indoor) (M), track and field (outdoor) (M), wrestling (M). Member of Indiana College Athletic Conference, NCAA Division III.

**Intramural and club sports:** 85% of students participate. Intramural basketball, bowling, cross-country, football, racquetball, soccer, softball, tennis, track, ultimate frisbee, volleyball. Men's club fencing, ultimate frisbee, weight lifting.

**ADMISSIONS. Academic basis for candidate selection** (in order of priority): Secondary school record, class rank, standardized test scores, school's recommendation, essay.
**Nonacademic basis for candidate selection:** Character and personality are important. Extracurricular participation and particular talent or ability are considered.
**Requirements:** Graduation from secondary school is required; GED is not accepted. 16 units and the following program of study are required: 4 units of English, 4 units of math, 2 units of lab science, 2 units of social studies, 4 units of academic electives. Minimum combined SAT score of 1000 and rank in top quarter of secondary school class required; minimum combined SAT score of 1200 and rank in top fifth of secondary school class recommended. SAT or ACT is required. Campus visit and interview recommended. Off-campus interviews available with an alumni representative.
**Procedure:** Take SAT or ACT by March of 12th year. Suggest filing application by December 1. Application deadline is April 1. Notification of admission on rolling basis. Reply is required by May 1. $100 nonrefundable tuition deposit. $100 room deposit, refundable until June 1. Freshmen accepted for fall term only.
**Special programs:** Admission may be deferred one year. Credit and/or placement may be granted through CEEB Advanced Placement exams for scores of 4 or higher. Credit and placement may be granted through challenge exams.
**Transfer students:** Transfer students accepted for fall term. for fall 1993, 1% of all new students were transfers into all classes. 58 transfer applications were received, 45 were accepted. Application deadline is August 1. Minimum 3.0 GPA recommended. Lowest course grade accepted is "C."
**Admissions contact:** Charles G. Howard, M.S., Dean of Admissions. 812 877-1511, extension 213.

**FINANCIAL AID. Available aid:** Pell grants, SEOG, state scholarships and grants, school scholarships and grants, private scholarships and grants, ROTC scholarships, and academic merit scholarships. Perkins Loans (NDSL), PLUS, Stafford Loans (GSL), private loans, and SLS. Tuition Plan Inc., AMS, and Tuition Management Systems.
**Financial aid statistics:** 20% of aid is not need-based. In 1993-94, 90% of all undergraduate applicants received aid; 88% of freshman applicants. Average amounts of aid awarded freshmen: Scholarships and grants, $2,000; loans, $4,100.
**Supporting data/closing dates:** FAFSA/FAF/FFS: Priority filing date is March 1. School's own aid application: Priority filing date is February 1. State aid form: Accepted on rolling basis. Income tax forms: Accepted on rolling basis. Notification of awards on rolling basis.
**Financial aid contact:** R. Paul Steward, M.S., Director of Financial Aid. 812 877-1511, extension 259.

**STUDENT EMPLOYMENT.** College Work/Study Program. Institutional employment. 40% of full-time undergraduates work on campus during school year. Students may expect to earn an average of $1,000 during school year. Off-campus part-time employment opportunities rated "excellent."

**COMPUTER FACILITIES.** 700 IBM/IBM-compatible, Macintosh/Apple, and RISC-/UNIX-based microcomputers; 350 are networked. Students may access Digital minicomputer/mainframe systems, BITNET, Internet. Computer languages and software packages include Ada, Assembly, BASIC, C, COBOL, FORTRAN, LISP, Modula 2, Pascal; 11 in all. Computer facilities are available to all students.
**Fees:** Computer fee is included in tuition/fees.
**Hours:** 24 hours/day.

**GRADUATE CAREER DATA.** Graduate school percentages: 1% enter law school. 2% enter medical school. 5% enter graduate business programs. Highest graduate school enrollments: U of Illinois, MIT, Purdue U. 95% of graduates choose careers in business and industry. Companies and businesses that hire graduates: Eli Lilly, Ford, General Motors, Texas Instruments.

## Saint Francis College

**Fort Wayne, IN 46808** — **219 434-3100**

**1993-94 Costs.** Tuition: $8,300. Room & board: $3,630. Fees, books, misc. academic expenses (school's estimate): $400.
**Enrollment.** Undergraduates: 144 men, 331 women (full-time). Freshman class: 467 applicants, 384 accepted, 218 enrolled. Graduate enrollment: 77 men, 165 women.
**Test score averages/ranges.** Average SAT scores: 360 verbal, 459 math. Average ACT scores: 20 composite.
**Faculty.** 38 full-time; 39 part-time. 60% of faculty holds highest degree in specific field. Student/faculty ratio: 15 to 1.
**Selectivity rating.** Competitive.

**PROFILE.** Saint Francis, founded in 1890, is a church-affiliated, liberal arts college. Its 70-acre campus occupies a former estate centered on a Romanesque manor house, dating from 1887, and listed with the National Register of Historic Places. The campus is located in Fort Wayne.

**Accreditation:** NCACS. Professionally accredited by the Council on Social Work Education, the National Council for Accreditation of Teacher Education.
**Religious orientation:** Saint Francis College is affiliated with the Roman Catholic Church; two semesters of religion required.
**Library:** Collections totaling over 81,000 volumes, 700 periodical subscriptions, and 444,000 microform items.
**Athletic facilities:** Outdoor facilities, gymnasium.

**STUDENT BODY. Undergraduate profile:** 77% are state residents; 30% are transfers. 4% Asian-American, 5% Black, 2% Hispanic, 1% Native American, 88% White. Average age of undergraduates is 23.
**Freshman profile:** Majority of accepted applicants took SAT. 85% of freshmen come from public schools.
**Undergraduate achievement:** 68% of fall 1992 freshmen returned for fall 1993 term. 30% of students who completed a degree program went on to graduate study within five years.
**Foreign students:** 30 students are from out of the country. Countries represented include Taiwan.

**PROGRAMS OF STUDY. Degrees:** B.A., B.Bus.Admin., B.S., B.S.Ed., B.S.Nurs., B.Soc.Work.
**Majors:** Accounting, American Studies, Art, Art Education, Biology, Business Administration, Business Education, Chemistry, Communication, Elementary Education, English, English Education, Environmental Science, Fine/Commercial Art, General Sciences, Health/Safety, Health/Safety Education, Liberal Studies, Medical Technology, Nursing, Pre-Dentistry, Pre-Law, Pre-Medicine, Pre-Veterinary, Psychology, Religious Studies, Science Education, Secondary Education, Social Studies, Social Work, Special Education.
**Distribution of degrees:** The majors with the highest enrollment are art, business administration, and education.
**Requirements:** General education requirement.
**Academic regulations:** Minimum 2.0 GPA must be maintained.
**Special:** Minors offered in some majors and in coaching endorsement, earth science, philosophy, physical education, reading, science, and sociology. Associate's degrees offered. Double majors. Dual degrees. Independent study. Pass/fail grading option. Internships. Graduate school at which undergraduates may take graduate-level courses. Preprofessional programs in law, medicine, veterinary science, and dentistry. Teacher certification in elementary, secondary, and special education. Certification in specific subject areas.
**Honors:** Honors program.
**Academic Assistance:** Remedial reading, writing, math, and study skills. Nonremedial tutoring.

**ADMISSIONS. Academic basis for candidate selection** (in order of priority): Secondary school record, standardized test scores, class rank, essay, school's recommendation.
**Requirements:** Graduation from secondary school is required; GED is accepted. 16 units and the following program of study are recommended: 4 units of English, 3 units of math, 2 units of science, 2 units of foreign language, 2 units of social studies, 2 units of history, 1 unit of electives. Minimum combined SAT score of 800 (composite ACT score of 19), rank in top half of secondary school class, and minimum 2.0 GPA required. 1 unit each of algebra, biology, and chemistry required of nursing program applicants. SAT or ACT is required. Campus visit recommended. Off-campus interviews available with an admissions representative.
**Procedure:** Take SAT or ACT by December of 12th year. Visit college for interview by May of 12th year. Notification of admission on rolling basis. Reply is required by May 1. $50 tuition deposit, refundable until May 1. $50 room deposit, refundable until May 1. Freshmen accepted for terms other than fall.
**Special programs:** Admission may be deferred one year. Credit and/or placement may be granted through CEEB Advanced Placement exams for scores of 3 or higher. Credit and/or placement may be granted through CLEP general and subject exams. Credit and placement may be granted through Regents College, ACT PEP, DANTES, and challenge exams, and military and life experience. Early entrance/early admission program. Concurrent enrollment program.
**Transfer students:** Transfer students accepted for terms other than fall. for fall 1993, 30% of all new students were transfers into all classes. Application deadline is rolling for fall; rolling for spring. Minimum 2.0 GPA required. Lowest course grade accepted is "C." At least 32 semester hours must be completed at the college to receive degree.
**Admissions contact:** Michael Wank, M.A., Dean of Enrollment Services. 219 434-3279.

**FINANCIAL AID. Available aid:** Pell grants, SEOG, state scholarships and grants, school scholarships and grants, private scholarships and grants, academic merit scholarships, and athletic scholarships. Perkins Loans (NDSL), PLUS, Stafford Loans (GSL), private loans, and SLS. AMS.
**Financial aid statistics:** 22% of aid is not need-based. In 1993-94, 73% of all undergraduate applicants received aid; 77% of freshman applicants. Average amounts of aid awarded freshmen: Scholarships and grants, $4,938; loans, $2,280.
**Supporting data/closing dates:** FAFSA/FAF: Priority filing date is March 1. School's own aid application: Accepted on rolling basis. State aid form: Priority filing date is March 1. Notification of awards on rolling basis.
**Financial aid contact:** Cynthia Tremain, Director of Financial Aid. 219 434-3283.

## Saint Joseph's College

**Rensselaer, IN 47978** — **219 866-6000**

**1993-94 Costs.** Tuition: $10,500. Room & board: $3,900. Fees, books, misc. academic expenses (school's estimate): $830.
**Enrollment.** Undergraduates: 411 men, 404 women (full-time). Freshman class: 920 applicants, 777 accepted, 225 enrolled.
**Test score averages/ranges.** Average SAT scores: 432 verbal, 500 math. Range of SAT scores of middle 50%: 370-480 verbal, 400-550 math. Average ACT scores: 22 English, 22 math, 23 composite. Range of ACT scores of middle 50%: 21-24 composite.
**Faculty.** 53 full-time; 22 part-time. 66% of faculty holds highest degree in specific field. Student/faculty ratio: 15 to 1.
**Selectivity rating.** Less competitive.

**PROFILE.** Saint Joseph's, founded in 1891, is a private, church-affiliated college. Programs are offered in the Divisions of Commerce, Education and Arts, Humanities, Mathematics and Natural Science, and Social Sciences. Its 340-acre campus, including a Romanesque brick and stone chapel built in 1910, is located in Rensselaer, 75 miles from Chicago.

**Accreditation:** NCACS. Professionally accredited by the National Council for Accreditation of Teacher Education.
**Religious orientation:** Saint Joseph's College is affiliated with the Roman Catholic Church (Society of the Precious Blood); no religious requirements.
**Library:** Collections totaling over 165,000 volumes, 744 periodical subscriptions, and 44,428 microform items.
**Athletic facilities:** Gymnasium; field house; baseball, football, intramural, soccer, softball fields; track; basketball, racquetball, tennis, volleyball courts; recreation center; weight room.

**STUDENT BODY. Undergraduate profile:** 74% are state residents; 11% are transfers. .2% Asian-American, 4.7% Black, 2.6% Hispanic, 91.6% White, .9% Other. Average age of undergraduates is 24.
**Freshman profile:** 64% of accepted applicants took SAT; 36% took ACT. 56% of freshmen come from public schools.
**Undergraduate achievement:** 75% of fall 1992 freshmen returned for fall 1993 term. 55% of entering class graduated.
**Foreign students:** Five students are from out of the country.

**PROGRAMS OF STUDY. Degrees:** B.A., B.Bus.Admin., B.S.
**Majors:** Accountancy/Finance, Accounting/Finance, Accounting Information Systems, Biology, Biology/Chemistry, Business Administration, Chemistry, Communications/Theatre Arts, Computer Science, Creative Writing, Economics, Economics/Finance, Elementary Education, English, Finance/Accounting, Finance/Information Systems, Geobiology, Geology/Chemistry, Geology/Physics, History, Human Services, International Studies, Journalism, Management, Management/Marketing Information Systems, Marketing, Mathematics, Mathematics/Computer Science, Mathematics/Physics, Medical Technology, Music, Nursing, Philosophy, Physical Education, Political Science, Pre-Engineering, Psychology, Religion/Philosophy, Science Education, Sociology, Television/Radio.
**Distribution of degrees:** The majors with the highest enrollment are business administration, psychology, and elementary education; math/physics, sociology, and chemistry have the lowest.
**Requirements:** General education requirement.
**Academic regulations:** Freshmen must maintain minimum 1.8 GPA; sophomores, 1.8 GPA; juniors, 1.9 GPA; seniors, 1.9 GPA.
**Special:** Minors offered in most majors and in art, Latin, earth science, French, German, physics, secondary education, and Spanish. Associate's degrees offered. Double majors. Dual degrees. Pass/fail grading option. Internships. Preprofessional programs in law, medicine, veterinary science, pharmacy, dentistry, theology, engineering, and physical therapy. 3-2 program in engineering. 3-2 program in medical technology. Member of the Indiana Consortium for International Program. Washington Semester and UN Semester. Teacher certification in elementary and secondary education. Certification in specific subject areas. Study abroad in Austria, England, France, Germany, Mexico, the Netherlands, Spain, and Wales.
**Honors:** Honor societies.
**Academic Assistance:** Remedial reading, writing, and study skills. Nonremedial tutoring.

**ADMISSIONS. Academic basis for candidate selection** (in order of priority): Secondary school record, standardized test scores, class rank, school's recommendation, essay.
**Nonacademic basis for candidate selection:** Character and personality, extracurricular participation, particular talent or ability, and alumni/ae relationship are considered.
**Requirements:** Graduation from secondary school is required; GED is accepted. 20 units and the following program of study are required: 4 units of English, 4 units of math, 3 units of science including 2 units of lab, 2 units of foreign language, 2 units of social studies, 5 units of academic electives. Units in social studies include history. Rank in top half of secondary school class and minimum 2.0 GPA recommended. Freshman Academic Support Program for 25 applicants not normally admissible. SAT or ACT is required. Campus visit and interview recommended. Off-campus interviews available with an admissions representative.
**Procedure:** Take SAT or ACT by July of 12th year. Visit college for interview by August of 12th year. Application deadline is August 15. Notification of admission on rolling basis. Reply is required by May 1. $100 room deposit, refundable until May 1. Freshmen accepted for terms other than fall.
**Special programs:** Admission may be deferred. Credit and/or placement may be granted through CEEB Advanced Placement exams for scores of 3 or higher. Credit and/or placement may be granted through CLEP general and subject exams. Credit and placement may be granted through Regents College and challenge exams, and military and life experience.
**Transfer students:** Transfer students accepted for terms other than fall. for fall 1993, 11% of all new students were transfers into all classes. 99 transfer applications were received, 92 were accepted. Application deadline is August 15 for fall; January 1 for spring. Minimum 2.0 GPA recommended. Lowest course grade accepted is "C." Maximum number of transferable credits is 64 semester hours from a two-year school and 90 semester hours from a four-year school. At least 30 semester hours must be completed at the college to receive degree.
**Admissions contact:** Brian Kesse, M.A., Director of Admissions. 800 447-8781.

**FINANCIAL AID. Available aid:** Pell grants, SEOG, state scholarships and grants, school scholarships and grants, private scholarships and grants, academic merit scholarships, and athletic scholarships. Perkins Loans (NDSL), PLUS, Stafford Loans (GSL), and SLS. Knight Tuition Plans and family tuition reduction.
**Financial aid statistics:** 20% of aid is not need-based. In 1993-94, 99% of all undergraduate applicants received aid; 99% of freshman applicants. Average amounts of aid awarded freshmen: Scholarships and grants, $6,900; loans, $2,344.
**Supporting data/closing dates:** FAFSA. School's own aid application: Priority filing date is May 1; accepted on rolling basis. State aid form: Deadline is March 1. Notification of awards on rolling basis.
**Financial aid contact:** David H. Hoover, M.A., Director of Financial Aid. 219 866-6163.

# Saint Mary's College

**Notre Dame, IN 46556** **219 284-4000**

**1993-94 Costs.** Tuition: $12,010. Room & board: $4,252. Fees, books, misc. academic expenses (school's estimate): $1,289.
**Enrollment.** 1,523 women (full-time). Freshman class: 888 applicants, 734 accepted, 393 enrolled.
**Test score averages/ranges.** Average SAT scores: 488 verbal, 538 math. Range of SAT scores of middle 50%: 430-530 verbal, 490-600 math. Average ACT scores: 25 English, 23 math, 25 composite. Range of ACT scores of middle 50%: 23-27 composite.
**Faculty.** 117 full-time; 73 part-time. 74% of faculty holds doctoral degree. Student/faculty ratio: 11 to 1.
**Selectivity rating.** Competitive.

**PROFILE.** Saint Mary's, founded in 1844, is a private, church-affiliated, liberal arts college for women. Its 275-acre campus is located in Notre Dame, five miles from South Bend.

**Accreditation:** NCACS. Professionally accredited by the National Association of Schools of Art and Design, the National Association of Schools of Music, the National Council for Accreditation of Teacher Education, the National League for Nursing.
**Religious orientation:** Saint Mary's College is affiliated with the Roman Catholic Church (Sisters of the Holy Cross); two semesters of religion required.
**Library:** Collections totaling over 192,000 volumes, 790 periodical subscriptions, and 5,502 microform items.
**Special facilities/museums:** Art gallery, early childhood development center, language lab, electron microscope.
**Athletic facilities:** Swimming pool, basketball, racquetball, tennis, and volleyball courts, gymnasium, Nautilus equipment, soccer, and softball fields, tracks, fitness center, arena, gymnastics area.
**STUDENT BODY. Undergraduate profile:** 19% are state residents; 14% are transfers. 1% Asian-American, 1% Black, 2% Hispanic, 95% White, 1% Other. Average age of undergraduates is 20.
**Freshman profile:** 2% of freshmen who took SAT scored 700 or over on verbal, 2% scored 700 or over on math; 8% scored 600 or over on verbal, 26% scored 600 or over on math; 46% scored 500 or over on verbal, 72% scored 500 or over on math; 90% scored 400 or over on verbal, 96% scored 400 or over on math; 100% scored 300 or over on verbal, 100% scored 300 or over on math. 7% of freshmen who took ACT scored 30 or over on English, 5% scored 30 or over on math, 6% scored 30 or over on composite; 68% scored 24 or over on English, 51% scored 24 or over on math, 69% scored 24 or over on composite; 99% scored 18 or over on English, 82% scored 18 or over on math, 99% scored 18 or over on composite; 100% scored 12 or over on English, 90% scored 12 or over on math, 100% scored 12 or over on composite. 47% of accepted applicants took SAT; 53% took ACT. 52% of freshmen come from public schools.
**Undergraduate achievement:** 93% of fall 1992 freshmen returned for fall 1993 term. 68% of entering class graduated. 20% of students who completed a degree program immediately went on to graduate study.
**Foreign students:** 19 students are from out of the country. Countries represented include Bangladesh, Bolivia, Mexico, Panama, Tanzania, and the United Kingdom; 15 in all.
**PROGRAMS OF STUDY. Degrees:** B.A., B.Bus.Admin., B.F.A., B.Mus., B.S.
**Majors:** Accounting, Applied Music, Art, Biology, Chemistry, Communication, Economics, Elementary Education, English Literature, English Writing, Finance, French, History, Honors Program/Studio Art, Humanistic Studies, International Business Management, Management, Marketing, Mathematics, Music, Music Education, Music Literature/Theory, Nursing, Philosophy, Political Science, Psychology, Religious Studies, Social Work, Sociology, Spanish, Theatre.
**Distribution of degrees:** The majors with the highest enrollment are business administration, communication, and political science; theatre, Spanish, and economics have the lowest.
**Requirements:** General education requirement.
**Academic regulations:** Freshmen must maintain minimum 1.8 GPA; sophomores, 1.9 GPA; juniors, 2.0 GPA; seniors, 2.0 GPA.
**Special:** Minors offered in many majors and in American studies, anthropology, applied mathematics, art history, art studio, computer science, computer science/economics, dance, international studies, Italian, justice studies, Latin American studies, physics, professional writing, urban studies, and women's studies. Double majors. Dual degrees. Independent study. Pass/fail grading option. Internships. Graduate school at which undergraduates may take graduate-level courses. Preprofessional programs in law, medicine, and dentistry. 3-2 engineering program with U of Notre Dame. Member of Northern Indiana Consortium for Education. Cross-registration with U of Notre Dame. Washington Semester. Teacher certification in early childhood, elementary, secondary, and special education. Certification in specific subject areas. Study abroad in Australia, Austria, France, India, Ireland, Israel, Italy, Japan, Mexico, Spain, and the United Kingdom. ROTC, NROTC, and AFROTC at U of Notre Dame.
**Honors:** Honor societies.
**Academic Assistance:** Nonremedial tutoring.
**STUDENT LIFE. Housing:** Students may live on or off campus. Women's dorms. 89% of students live in college housing.
**Services and counseling/handicapped student services:** Placement services. Health service. Day care. Counseling services for minority students. Personal and psychological counseling. Academic guidance services. Religious counseling. Learning disabled services.
**Campus organizations:** Undergraduate student government. Student newspaper (Observer, published once/day). Literary magazine. Yearbook. Marching and concert bands, South Bend Symphony, mixed choral group, glee club, drama club, Toastmasters,

community tutoring program, volunteer services, Circle K, Student Alliance for Women's Colleges, Alcohol Education Council, Model UN, departmental groups, 51 organizations in all.
**Religious organizations:** World Hunger Coalition, Campus Fellowship, Right-to-Life, Campus Bible Fellowship, Fellowship of Christian Athletes.
**Minority/foreign student organizations:** FUERZA, Sisters of Nefertiti, Student Organization Unified for the Needs of Diversity (SOUND).

**ATHLETICS. Physical education requirements:** None.
**Intercollegiate competition:** 20% of students participate. Basketball (W), diving (W), soccer (W), softball (W), swimming (W), tennis (W), track (indoor) (W), track (outdoor) (W), track and field (outdoor) (W), volleyball (W). Member of NCAA Division III.
**Intramural and club sports:** 50% of students participate. Intramural aerobics, basketball, flag football, floor hockey, racquetball, soccer, tennis, volleyball, walleyball. Women's club crew, cross-country, equestrian sports, fencing, golf, gymnastics, lacrosse, Nordic skiing, racquetball, sailing.

**ADMISSIONS. Academic basis for candidate selection** (in order of priority): Secondary school record, class rank, school's recommendation, standardized test scores, essay.
**Nonacademic basis for candidate selection:** Character and personality, extracurricular participation, particular talent or ability, geographical distribution, and alumni/ae relationship are considered.
**Requirements:** Graduation from secondary school is required; GED is accepted. 16 units and the following program of study are required: 4 units of English, 3 units of math, 1 unit of lab science, 2 units of foreign language, 2 units of social studies, 4 units of academic electives. Additional math and science units recommended of mathematics, science, and nursing program applicants. Audition recommended of music program applicants. Portfolio recommended of art program applicants. SAT or ACT is required. ACH required. Campus visit and interview recommended. Off-campus interviews available with admissions and alumni representatives.
**Procedure:** Take SAT or ACT by December of 12th year. Take ACH by May of 12th year. Suggest filing application by March 1. Application deadline is August 1. Notification of admission on rolling basis. Reply is required by May 1. $200 tuition deposit, refundable until May 1. Freshmen accepted for terms other than fall.
**Special programs:** Admission may be deferred one year. Credit and/or placement may be granted through CEEB Advanced Placement exams for scores of 4 or higher. Credit and/or placement may be granted through CLEP general and subject exams. Credit and placement may be granted through challenge exams. Early decision program. for fall 1993, 160 applied for early decision and 140 were accepted. Deadline for applying for early decision is November 15. Early entrance/early admission program.
**Transfer students:** Transfer students accepted for terms other than fall. for fall 1993, 14% of all new students were transfers into all classes. 122 transfer applications were received, 81 were accepted. Application deadline is April 15 for fall; December 15 for spring. Minimum 3.0 GPA recommended. Lowest course grade accepted is "C." Maximum number of transferable credits is 68 semester hours. At least 60 semester hours must be completed at the college to receive degree.
**Admissions contact:** Mary Pat Nolan, M.A., Director of Admissions. 219 284-4587.

**FINANCIAL AID. Available aid:** Pell grants, SEOG, state scholarships and grants, school scholarships and grants, private scholarships, ROTC scholarships, and aid for undergraduate foreign students. Perkins Loans (NDSL), PLUS, Stafford Loans (GSL), school loans, private loans, and SLS. Tuition Plan Inc., Knight Tuition Plans, AMS, and family tuition reduction.
**Financial aid statistics:** 5% of aid is not need-based. In 1993-94, 93% of all undergraduate applicants received aid; 86% of freshman applicants. Average amounts of aid awarded freshmen: Scholarships and grants, $5,637; loans, $2,526.
**Supporting data/closing dates:** FAFSA/FAF: Priority filing date is March 1. Income tax forms: Priority filing date is April 30. Notification of awards on rolling basis.
**Financial aid contact:** Mary Nucciarone, Director of Financial Aid. 219 284-4557.

**STUDENT EMPLOYMENT.** College Work/Study Program. Institutional employment. 40% of full-time undergraduates work on campus during school year. Students may expect to earn an average of $1,400 during school year. Off-campus part-time employment opportunities rated "fair."

**COMPUTER FACILITIES.** 130 IBM/IBM-compatible and Macintosh/Apple microcomputers; 100 are networked. Students may access Hewlett-Packard minicomputer/mainframe systems, Internet. Residence halls may be equipped with stand-alone microcomputers, networked microcomputers, networked terminals. Client/LAN operating systems include Apple/Macintosh, DOS, UNIX/XENIX/AIX, Novell. Computer languages and software packages include Adobe Illustrator, BASIC, C++, ClarisWorks, COBOL, dBASE, DTP, Excel, FORTRAN, Harvard Graphics, Hypercard, Informix, Lotus 1-2-3, MacDraw, MacPaint, Microsoft Word, MINITAB, Multiplan, Paradox, Pascal, Quattro Pro, SPSS-X, Super Paint, WordPerfect; 50 in all. Computer facilities are available to all students.
**Fees:** None.
**Hours:** 24 hours.

**GRADUATE CAREER DATA.** Graduate school percentages: 3% enter law school. 1% enter medical school. 8% enter graduate business programs. 5% enter graduate arts and sciences programs. Highest graduate school enrollments: Georgetown U, U of Illinois, Indiana U, Northwestern U, U of Notre Dame, Rush U Medical Sch. 60% of graduates choose careers in business and industry. Companies and businesses that hire graduates: Anderson Consulting, AT&T, Big Six accounting firms, Eastman Kodak, IBM, Sears Roebuck, Chicago-area banks and hospitals.

**PROMINENT ALUMNI/AE.** Florence Dovlo, food consultant to African Government; Kathleen Buck-Battocchi, General Counsel, U.S. Air Force; and Gloria Ybarra, judge, Arizona Superior Court.

# Saint Mary-of-the-Woods College

**St. Mary-of-the-Woods, IN 47876 812 535-5106**

**1994-95 Costs.** Tuition: $10,800. Room: $1,640. Board: $2,620. Fees, books, misc. academic expenses (school's estimate): $870.
**Enrollment.** 325 women (full-time). Freshman class: 120 applicants, 117 accepted, 58 enrolled. Graduate enrollment: 77 women.
**Test score averages/ranges.** Average SAT scores: 457 verbal, 466 math. Average ACT scores: 22 composite.
**Faculty.** 50 full-time; 22 part-time. 65% of faculty holds highest degree in specific field. Student/faculty ratio: 11 to 1.
**Selectivity rating.** Less competitive.

**PROFILE.** Saint Mary-of-the-Woods, founded in 1840, is a private, church-affiliated college for women. Programs are offered through the Divisions of Arts and Letters; Science, Mathematics, and Home Economics; and Social and Behavioral Sciences. Its 67-acre campus, including several 19th- and early 20th-century buildings, is located in St. Mary-of-the-Woods, 70 miles from Indianapolis.

**Accreditation:** NCACS. Professionally accredited by the American Dietetic Association, the National Association of Schools of Music.
**Religious orientation:** Saint Mary-of-the-Woods College is an interdenominational Christian school; two semesters of theology required.
**Library:** Collections totaling over 142,000 volumes, 460 periodical subscriptions, and 1,676 microform items.
**Special facilities/museums:** On-campus pre-school.
**Athletic facilities:** Gymnasium, swimming pool, fitness trail, softball field.

**STUDENT BODY. Undergraduate profile:** 85% are state residents; 5% are transfers. 2% Asian-American, 3% Black, 5% Hispanic, 90% White. Average age of undergraduates is 23.
**Freshman profile:** 90% of accepted applicants took SAT; 10% took ACT. 90% of freshmen come from public schools.
**Foreign students:** 10 students are from out of the country. Countries represented include China and Japan.

**PROGRAMS OF STUDY. Degrees:** B.A., B.S.
**Majors:** Accounting, Art, Biology, Business Administration, Computer Information Systems, Early Childhood Education, Education, Elementary Education, English, Equine Studies, Fine Arts, French, General Science, History, Humanities, Journalism, Management, Marketing, Mathematics, Medical Technology, Music, Music Performance, Music Therapy, Paralegal, Political Science, Pre-School Special Education, Psychology, Secondary Education, Spanish, Special Education, Speech, Studio Art, Theatre/Allied Arts, Theatre/Technical, Theology, Voice, Voice/Theatre.
**Distribution of degrees:** The majors with the highest enrollment are business administration and elementary education; fine arts and general science have the lowest.
**Requirements:** General education requirement.
**Special:** Minors offered; individualized according to students' needs. Associate's degrees offered. Self-designed majors. Double majors. Independent study. Internships. Graduate school at which undergraduates may take graduate-level courses. Preprofessional programs in law, medicine, veterinary science, pharmacy, and dentistry. Member of consortium with Indiana State U. Teacher certification in early childhood, elementary, secondary, and special education. Exchange program abroad in Taiwan (Providence U). Study abroad also in Spain. ROTC at Rose-Hulman Inst of Tech.
**Academic Assistance:** Nonremedial tutoring.

**ADMISSIONS. Academic basis for candidate selection** (in order of priority): Secondary school record, standardized test scores, school's recommendation, class rank, essay.
**Nonacademic basis for candidate selection:** Character and personality are emphasized. Extracurricular participation, particular talent or ability, and alumni/ae relationship are important.
**Requirements:** Graduation from secondary school is required; GED is accepted. 24 units and the following program of study are recommended: 3 units of English, 3 units of math, 3 units of science, 3 units of foreign language, 2 units of social studies, 2 units of history, 8 units of electives. Portfolio required of art program applicants. Audition required of music program applicants. Restricted-status admission for applicants not meeting standard requirements. SAT or ACT is required. Campus visit recommended. Off-campus interviews available with admissions and alumni representatives.
**Procedure:** Take SAT or ACT by November of 12th year. Visit college for interview by March of 12th year. Suggest filing application by May; no deadline. Notification of admission on rolling basis. $50 nonrefundable tuition deposit. Freshmen accepted for terms other than fall.
**Special programs:** Admission may be deferred two years. Credit and/or placement may be granted through CEEB Advanced Placement exams for scores of 4 or higher. Credit and/or placement may be granted through CLEP general and subject exams. Credit may be granted through life experience. Early decision program. for fall 1992, 10 applied for early decision and 10 were accepted. Early entrance/early admission program.
**Transfer students:** Transfer students accepted for terms other than fall. for fall 1992, 5% of all new students were transfers into all classes. 30 transfer applications were received, 30 were accepted. Application deadline is rolling for fall; rolling for spring. Lowest course grade accepted is "C." At least 30 semester hours must be completed at the college to receive degree.
**Admissions contact:** Katherine K. Satchwill, M.B.A., Director of Admissions. 812 535-5151, 800 926-SMWC.

**FINANCIAL AID. Available aid:** Pell grants, SEOG, state scholarships and grants, school scholarships and grants, private scholarships and grants, and academic merit scholarships. Perkins Loans (NDSL), PLUS, Stafford Loans (GSL), and SLS. Tuition Management Systems and deferred payment plan.

**Financial aid statistics:** In 1992-93, 84% of all undergraduate applicants received aid. Average amounts of aid awarded freshmen: Loans, $2,649.

**Supporting data/closing dates:** FAFSA/FAF/FFS: Accepted on rolling basis. Income tax forms. Notification of awards on rolling basis.

**Financial aid contact:** Marylee Hagan, Director of Financial Aid. 812 535-5106.

# Taylor University

**Upland, IN 46989** **317 998-2751**

**1994-95 Costs.** Tuition: $10,965. Room: $1,900. Board: $2,100. Fees, books, misc. academic expenses (school's estimate): $710.

**Enrollment.** Undergraduates: 845 men, 918 women (full-time). Freshman class: 1,769 applicants, 1,041 accepted, 437 enrolled.

**Test score averages/ranges.** Average SAT scores: 545 verbal, 557 math.

**Faculty.** 109 full-time; 40 part-time. 70% of faculty holds highest degree in specific field. Student/faculty ratio: 18 to 1.

**Selectivity rating.** Highly competitive.

**PROFILE.** Taylor is a liberal arts university with religious orientation. Its 250-acre campus is located in Upland, in northeast Indiana, 50 miles from Fort Wayne.

**Accreditation:** NCACS. Professionally accredited by the Council on Social Work Education, the National Association of Schools of Music, the National Council for Accreditation of Teacher Education.

**Religious orientation:** Taylor University is an interdenominational Christian school; four semesters of religion required.

**Library:** Collections totaling over 167,275 volumes, 720 periodical subscriptions, and 8,238 microform items.

**Athletic facilities:** Gymnasium, football stadium, baseball, intramural, soccer, and softball fields, racquetball and tennis courts, fitness and Nautilus rooms, track.

**STUDENT BODY. Undergraduate profile:** 33% are state residents. 3% Asian-American, 2% Black, 1% Hispanic, 93% White, 1% Other. Average age of undergraduates is 20.

**Freshman profile:** 4% of freshmen who took SAT scored 700 or over on verbal, 6% scored 700 or over on math; 35% scored 600 or over on verbal, 35% scored 600 or over on math; 73% scored 500 or over on verbal, 72% scored 500 or over on math; 94% scored 400 or over on verbal, 99% scored 400 or over on math; 100% scored 300 or over on verbal, 100% scored 300 or over on math. 60% of accepted applicants took SAT; 40% took ACT. 79% of freshmen come from public schools.

**Undergraduate achievement:** 97% of fall 1992 freshmen returned for fall 1993 term. 12% of students who completed a degree program went on to graduate study within one year.

**Foreign students:** 44 students are from out of the country. Countries represented include the Bahamas, Canada, Japan, and Singapore; 12 in all.

**PROGRAMS OF STUDY. Degrees:** B.A., B.Mus., B.S.

**Majors:** Accounting, Art, Art/Computer Graphics, Bible, Biology, Business Administration, Chemistry, Christian Education, Communication Arts Education, Communication Studies, Composition, Computer Science, Economics, Elementary Education, English, Environmental Science, French, History, Individual Goal Oriented, International Studies, Management Information Systems, Mass Communications, Mathematics, Mathematics/Computer Systems, Music, Music Education, Natural Science, Performance, Philosophy of Religion, Physical Education, Physics, Political Science, Psychology, Recreational Leadership, Sacred Music, Science, Social Studies, Social Work, Sociology, Spanish, Theatre Arts.

**Distribution of degrees:** The majors with the highest enrollment are business, elementary education, and psychology; economics, individual goal-oriented, and natural science have the lowest.

**Requirements:** General education requirement.

**Academic regulations:** Freshmen must maintain minimum 1.7 GPA; sophomores, 1.8 GPA; juniors, 1.9 GPA; seniors, 2.0 GPA.

**Special:** Minors offered in many majors and in applied music, athletic training, biblical languages, Christian education, church music, philosophy, piano pedagogy, pre-law, and public relations. Career training in systems analysis and environmental studies. Associate's degrees offered. Self-designed majors. Double majors. Dual degrees. Independent study. Pass/fail grading option. Internships. Cooperative education programs. Preprofessional programs in law, medicine, pharmacy, dentistry, theology, medical technology, and physical therapy. 3-2 pre-engineering programs with Saint Louis U and Washington U. Member of Christian College Coalition. Washington Semester. American Studies Program (Washington, D.C.). AuSable Inst of Environmental Studies Program (Michigan). Oregon Extension Program. Member of Christian College Consortium; exchange possible. Teacher certification in early childhood, elementary, and secondary education. Certification in specific subject areas. Study abroad in African countries, China, England, Germany, Hong Kong, Israel, Singapore, the former Soviet Republics, and Spain. ROTC, NROTC, and AFROTC at Ball State U.

**Honors:** Honors program.

**Academic Assistance:** Remedial reading, writing, math, and study skills. Nonremedial tutoring.

**STUDENT LIFE. Housing:** Women's and men's dorms. School-owned/operated apartments. Off-campus married-student housing. 85% of students live in college housing.

**Services and counseling/handicapped student services:** Placement services. Health service. Counseling services for minority students. Personal and psychological counseling. Career and academic guidance services. Religious counseling.

**Campus organizations:** Undergraduate student government. Student newspaper (Echo, published once/week). Literary magazine. Yearbook. Radio and TV stations. Taylor Sounds, Taylor Ringers, Performing Artist Series, Fine Arts Festival, Religious Drama Company, Student Activities Council, Taylor Student Organization, special-interest groups.

**Religious organizations:** Fellowship of Christian Athletes, Campus Life, World Outreach.

**Minority/foreign student organizations:** Minority Student Organization. International Student Society, Mu Kappa.

**ATHLETICS. Physical education requirements:** Three semesters of physical education required.

**Intercollegiate competition:** 18% of students participate. Baseball (M), basketball (M,W), cheerleading (M,W), cross-country (M,W), football (M), golf (M), soccer (M), softball (W), tennis (M,W), track (outdoor) (M,W), track and field (outdoor) (M,W), volleyball (W). Member of MCC, NAIA, NCCAA.

**Intramural and club sports:** 65% of students participate. Intramural badminton, basketball, flag football, pool, racquetball, soccer, softball, table tennis, volleyball. Men's club horsemanship, volleyball. Women's club horsemanship.

**ADMISSIONS. Academic basis for candidate selection** (in order of priority): Secondary school record, standardized test scores, class rank, essay, school's recommendation.

**Nonacademic basis for candidate selection:** Character and personality are emphasized. Extracurricular participation is important. Particular talent or ability, geographical distribution, and alumni/ae relationship are considered.

**Requirements:** Graduation from secondary school is required; GED is accepted. 15 units and the following program of study are required: 4 units of English, 3 units of math, 3 units of lab science, 2 units of social studies. Minimum combined SAT score of 1000, rank in top quarter of secondary school class, and minimum 3.3 GPA required. Audition required of music program applicants. Retention Assistance Program (RAP) for applicants not normally admissible. SAT or ACT is required. Campus visit and interview recommended. Off-campus interviews available with an admissions representative.

**Procedure:** Take SAT or ACT by September of 12th year. Visit college for interview by February 15 of 12th year. Notification of admission on rolling basis. Reply is required by May 1. $150 tuition deposit, refundable until May 1. $50 room deposit, refundable until May 1. Freshmen accepted for terms other than fall.

**Special programs:** Credit and/or placement may be granted through CEEB Advanced Placement exams for scores of 3 or higher. Credit and/or placement may be granted through CLEP general and subject exams.

**Transfer students:** Transfer students accepted for terms other than fall. for fall 1993, 207 transfer applications were received, 101 were accepted. Minimum 2.5 GPA required. Lowest course grade accepted is "C." Maximum number of transferable credits is 66 semester hours. At least 62 semester hours must be completed at the university to receive degree.

**Admissions contact:** Herb W. Frye, M.A., Dean of Enrollment Management. 800 882-3456.

**FINANCIAL AID. Available aid:** Pell grants, state scholarships and grants, school scholarships and grants, private scholarships and grants, and academic merit scholarships. Minority scholarships. Music scholarships. Perkins Loans (NDSL), PLUS, Stafford Loans (GSL), state loans, school loans, private loans, and SLS. AMS.

**Financial aid statistics:** Average amounts of aid awarded freshmen: Loans, $2,650.

**Supporting data/closing dates:** FAFSA: Deadline is March 1. School's own aid application: Deadline is March 1. Income tax forms: Deadline is March 1. Notification of awards on rolling basis.

**Financial aid contact:** Tim Nace, M.S., Director of Financial Aid. 317 998-5125.

**STUDENT EMPLOYMENT.** College Work/Study Program. Institutional employment. 42% of full-time undergraduates work on campus during school year. Students may expect to earn an average of $1,030 during school year. Off-campus part-time employment opportunities rated "poor."

**COMPUTER FACILITIES.** 200 IBM/IBM-compatible, Macintosh/Apple, and RISC-/UNIX-based microcomputers; 153 are networked. Students may access Digital, SUN minicomputer/mainframe systems, BITNET. Residence halls may be equipped with networked terminals. Client/LAN operating systems include UNIX/XENIX/AIX, DEC. Computer languages and software packages include Ada, BASIC, C, COBOL, Pascal, SPSS. Some facilities are restricted to computer science majors.

**Fees:** Computer fee is included in tuition/fees.

**GRADUATE CAREER DATA.** Graduate school percentages: 2% enter medical school. 6% enter graduate arts and sciences programs. Highest graduate school enrollments: Ball State U, Purdue U. 44% of graduates choose careers in business and industry. Companies and businesses that hire graduates: Arthur Andersen, Digital Equipment Corp., Eli Lilly.

**PROMINENT ALUMNI/AE.** Jay Kesler, president, Taylor U; Dr. Fred Stockinger, heart surgeon; Ted Engstrom, president, World Vision; Dr. John Hershey, retired chairperson and president, Milton Hershey Sch; Dr. Joseph Brain, professor, Harvard U Sch of Public Health; Dr. Beverly Brightly, education specialist, State of New Jersey; Billy Melvin, National Association of Evangelicals.

# Taylor University, Fort Wayne Campus

**Fort Wayne, IN 46807** **219 456-2111**

**1994-95 Costs.** Tuition: $8,914. Room: $1,600. Board: $2,000. Fees, books, misc. academic expenses (school's estimate): $486.
**Enrollment.** Undergraduates: 105 men, 184 women (full-time). Freshman class: 553 applicants, 427 accepted, 150 enrolled.
**Test score averages/ranges.** Average SAT scores: 443 verbal, 470 math. Range of SAT scores of middle 50%: 437-000 verbal, 443-000 math. Average ACT scores: 20 English, 22 math, 21 composite. Range of ACT scores of middle 50%: 20-00 English, 22-00 math.
**Faculty.** 30 full-time; 10 part-time. 48% of faculty holds doctoral degree. Student/faculty ratio: 10 to 1.
**Selectivity rating.** Less competitive.

**PROFILE.** Taylor University, Fort Wayne Campus, founded in 1895 as Fort Wayne Bible College, is a private, church-affiliated, multipurpose college. Its 32-acre campus is located in Fort Wayne, 80 miles southeast of South Bend.

**Accreditation:** NCACS. Professionally accredited by the National Council for Accreditation of Teacher Education.
**Religious orientation:** Taylor University, Fort Wayne Campus is an interdenominational Christian school; four semesters of religion required.
**Library:** Collections totaling over 620,000 volumes, 365 periodical subscriptions and 776 microform items.
**Athletic facilities:** Gymnasiums, fitness and weight rooms, badminton, basketball, tennis, and volleyball courts, soccer field.
**STUDENT BODY. Undergraduate profile:** 68% are state residents; 9% are transfers. 1% Asian-American, 5% Black, 1% Hispanic, 1% Native American, 92% White. Average age of undergraduates is 22.
**Freshman profile:** 1% of freshmen who took SAT scored 700 or over on math; 5% scored 600 or over on verbal, 7% scored 600 or over on math; 32% scored 500 or over on verbal, 28% scored 500 or over on math; 88% scored 400 or over on verbal, 81% scored 400 or over on math; 99% scored 300 or over on verbal, 92% scored 300 or over on math. Majority of accepted applicants took SAT. 77% of freshmen come from public schools.
**Undergraduate achievement:** 72% of fall 1992 freshmen returned for fall 1993 term. 50% of students who completed a degree program went on to graduate study within five years.
**Foreign students:** Six students are from out of the country. Countries represented include the Bahamas, Canada, Israel, Jamaica, Liberia, and Switzerland.
**PROGRAMS OF STUDY. Degrees:** B.A., B.S.
**Majors:** Business Administration, Christian Education, Criminal Justice, Cross-Cultural Ministry, Elementary Education, Individual Goal Oriented, Pastoral Ministries, Psychology, Public Relations, Urban Ministries, Youth Ministry.
**Distribution of degrees:** The majors with the highest enrollment are pastoral ministries, psychology, and elementary education.
**Requirements:** General education requirement.
**Academic regulations:** Freshmen must maintain minimum 1.7 GPA; sophomores, 1.8 GPA; juniors, 1.9 GPA; seniors, 2.0 GPA.
**Special:** Minors offered in biblical studies, Christian ministry, early childhood education, and in kindergarten and junior high/middle school endorsement in language arts or science. Associate's degrees offered. Self-designed majors. Double majors. Dual degrees. Independent study. Pass/fail grading option. Internships. Cooperative education programs. Member of Christian College Coalition. Oxford Study Program. Teacher certification in elementary education. Certification in specific subject areas. Study abroad in England, Israel, and Jordan.
**Academic Assistance:** Remedial reading, writing, math, and study skills. Nonremedial tutoring.
**ADMISSIONS. Academic basis for candidate selection** (in order of priority): Secondary school record, class rank, standardized test scores, school's recommendation, essay.
**Nonacademic basis for candidate selection:** Character and personality are emphasized. Extracurricular participation, particular talent or ability, and alumni/ae relationship are considered.
**Requirements:** Graduation from secondary school is required; GED is accepted. No specific distribution of secondary school units required. Minimum combined SAT score of 850 (composite ACT score of 21), rank in top two-fifths of secondary school class, and minimum 2.8 GPA required. Retention Assistance Program possible for applicants not normally admissible. SAT or ACT is required. Campus visit and interview recommended. Off-campus interviews available with an admissions representative.
**Procedure:** Take SAT or ACT by August 15 of 12th year. Visit college for interview by June 1 of 12th year. Suggest filing application by December 15. Application deadline is August 20. Notification of admission on rolling basis. $100 tuition deposit, refundable until May 1. $50 room deposit, refundable until May 1. Freshmen accepted for terms other than fall.
**Special programs:** Admission may be deferred two years. Credit and/or placement may be granted through CEEB Advanced Placement exams for scores of 4 or higher. Credit and/or placement may be granted through CLEP general and subject exams. Placement may be granted through challenge exams. Concurrent enrollment program.
**Transfer students:** Transfer students accepted for terms other than fall. for fall 1993, 9% of all new students were transfers into all classes. 68 transfer applications were received, 44 were accepted. Application deadline is August 20 for fall; January 20 for spring. Minimum 2.5 GPA required. SAT/ACT scores required of all transfers under age 25. Lowest course grade accepted is "C." Maximum number of transferable credits is 66 semester hours from a two-year school and 98 semester hours from a four-year school. At least 30 semester hours must be completed at the university to receive degree.
**Admissions contact:** D. Nathan Phinney, Director of Admissions. 219 456-2111, extension 2274.
**FINANCIAL AID. Available aid:** Pell grants, SEOG, state scholarships and grants, school scholarships and grants, private scholarships and grants, academic merit scholarships, and United Negro College Fund. Church Matching Grant Program. Perkins Loans (NDSL), PLUS, Stafford Loans (GSL), school loans, private loans, and SLS. AMS.
**Financial aid statistics:** 29% of aid is not need-based. In 1993-94, 83% of all undergraduate applicants received aid; 80% of freshman applicants. Average amounts of aid awarded freshmen: Scholarships and grants, $2,500; loans, $3,500.
**Supporting data/closing dates:** FAFSA: Deadline is March 1. School's own aid application: Priority filing date is March 1. Notification of awards begins March 15.
**Financial aid contact:** Victoria Book, Director of Financial Aid. 219 456-2111, extension 2276.

# Tri-State University

**Angola, IN 46703-0307** **219 665-4100**

**1993-94 Costs.** Tuition: $9,456. Room & board: $4,200. Fees, books, misc. academic expenses (school's estimate): $96.
**Enrollment.** Undergraduates: 696 men, 282 women (full-time). Freshman class: 1,374 applicants, 1,204 accepted, 347 enrolled.
**Test score averages/ranges.** Average SAT scores: 410 verbal, 510 math. Range of SAT scores of middle 50%: 360-490 verbal, 430-580 math. Average ACT scores: 20 English, 23 math, 22 composite.
**Faculty.** 75 full-time; 12 part-time. 51% of faculty holds doctoral degree. Student/faculty ratio: 13 to 1.
**Selectivity rating.** Less competitive.

**PROFILE.** Tri-State, founded in 1884, is a private, comprehensive university. Programs are offered through the Schools of Arts and Sciences, Business, and Engineering and the Technology Division. Its 300-acre campus is located in Angola, 65 miles east of South Bend.
**Accreditation:** NCACS. Professionally accredited by the Accreditation Board for Engineering and Technology.
**Religious orientation:** Tri-State University is nonsectarian; no religious requirements.
**Library:** Collections totaling over 151,364 volumes, 457 periodical subscriptions, and 11,337 microform items.
**Special facilities/museums:** Museum.
**Athletic facilities:** Gymnasiums, swimming pool, racquetball and tennis courts, baseball, intramural, soccer, and softball fields, weight rooms, 18-hole golf course, fitness center, track, golf driving range, putting green.
**STUDENT BODY. Undergraduate profile:** 17% are transfers. 1% Asian-American, 2% Black, 1% Hispanic, 78% White, 18% Other. Average age of undergraduates is 22.
**Freshman profile:** 3% of freshmen who took SAT scored 700 or over on math; 3% scored 600 or over on verbal, 22% scored 600 or over on math; 16% scored 500 or over on verbal, 58% scored 500 or over on math; 61% scored 400 or over on verbal, 84% scored 400 or over on math; 100% scored 300 or over on verbal, 100% scored 300 or over on math. Majority of accepted applicants took SAT.
**Undergraduate achievement:** 67% of fall 1992 freshmen returned for fall 1993 term. 24% of entering class graduated. 20% of students who completed a degree program went on to graduate study within one year.
**Foreign students:** 144 students are from out of the country. Countries represented include India, Japan, Malaysia, Pakistan, Saudi Arabia, and Singapore; 28 in all.
**PROGRAMS OF STUDY. Degrees:** B.A., B.S.
**Majors:** Accounting, Aerospace Engineering, Biology, Business/Arts, Chemical Engineering, Chemistry, Civil Engineering, Communications, Computer-Assisted Drafting/Design, Computer Information Systems, Computer Science, Corporate English, Criminal Justice, Economics, Electrical Engineering, Elementary Education, Engineering Administration, Environmental Science, History, Individual Studies, Management, Marketing, Mathematics, Mechanical Engineering, Office Administration, Physical Education, Physical Science, Pre-Medical, Psychology, Secondary Education, Social Science, Technical Management.
**Distribution of degrees:** The majors with the highest enrollment are electrical engineering, mechanical engineering, and business administration; business/arts, history, and economics have the lowest.
**Academic regulations:** Freshmen must maintain minimum 1.75 GPA; sophomores, 1.9 GPA; juniors, 2.0 GPA; seniors, 2.0 GPA.
**Special:** Minors offered in most majors and in health/safety. Two-year programs in accounting, arts, business administration, computer technology, criminal justice, drafting and design, manufacturing technology, science, and secretarial science. ESL programs. Associate's degrees offered. Self-designed majors. Double majors. Internships. Cooperative education programs. Preprofessional programs in law and medicine. Combined degree programs in office administration and technical management. Teacher certification in elementary and secondary education. Certification in specific subject areas. Study abroad in Japan.
**Honors:** Honors program. Honor societies.
**Academic Assistance:** Remedial writing, math, and study skills. Nonremedial tutoring.
**ADMISSIONS. Academic basis for candidate selection** (in order of priority): Secondary school record, class rank, standardized test scores, school's recommendation.
**Nonacademic basis for candidate selection:** Extracurricular participation is important. Character and personality, particular talent or ability, and alumni/ae relationship are considered.
**Requirements:** Graduation from secondary school is required; GED is accepted. 18 units and the following program of study are required: 4 units of English, 2 units of math, 2 units of lab science, 1 unit of social studies, 2 units of history, 5 units of academic electives.

Minimum combined SAT score of 800 and rank in top half of secondary school class recommended. SAT or ACT is required. Campus visit and interview recommended. Off-campus interviews available with an admissions representative.
**Procedure:** Take SAT or ACT by February of 12th year. Suggest filing application by March 1. Application deadline is August 15. Notification of admission on rolling basis. No set date by which applicants must accept offer. $50 refundable tuition deposit. $150 refundable room deposit. Freshmen accepted for terms other than fall.
**Special programs:** Admission may be deferred one year. Credit and/or placement may be granted through CEEB Advanced Placement exams for scores of 3 or higher. Credit and/or placement may be granted through CLEP subject exams. Credit and placement may be granted through DANTES and challenge exams. Concurrent enrollment program.
**Transfer students:** Transfer students accepted for terms other than fall. for fall 1993, 17% of all new students were transfers into all classes. Application deadline is August 15 for fall; February 1 for spring. SAT/ACT scores required of transfer applicants with fewer than 16 quarter hours. Minimum 2.0 GPA required. Lowest course grade accepted is "C." At least 45 quarter hours must be completed at the university to receive degree.
**Admissions contact:** Kim Bryan, Director of Admissions. 219 665-4131, 219 665-4132.

**FINANCIAL AID. Available aid:** Pell grants, SEOG, state scholarships and grants, school scholarships and grants, private scholarships and grants, academic merit scholarships, athletic scholarships, and aid for undergraduate foreign students. Perkins Loans (NDSL), PLUS, Stafford Loans (GSL), and SLS. Tuition Plan Inc. and AMS.
**Financial aid statistics:** 50% of aid is not need-based. In 1993-94, 78% of all undergraduate applicants received aid; 85% of freshman applicants. Average amounts of aid awarded freshmen: Scholarships and grants, $3,581; loans, $2,456.
**Supporting data/closing dates:** FAFSA/FAF/FFS: Priority filing date is March 1. Notification of awards on rolling basis.
**Financial aid contact:** Susan Stroh, M.P.A., Director of Financial Aid. 219 665-4131.

## University of Evansville

**Evansville, IN 47722** **812 479-2000**

**1994-95 Costs.** Tuition: $11,800. Room: $1,820. Board: $2,520. Fees, books, misc. academic expenses (school's estimate): $900.

**Enrollment.** Undergraduates: 1,130 men, 1,515 women (full-time). Freshman class: 2,096 applicants, 1,626 accepted, 694 enrolled. Graduate enrollment: 21 men, 90 women.

**Test score averages/ranges.** Average SAT scores: 498 verbal, 538 math. Average ACT scores: 25 composite.

**Faculty.** 172 full-time; 3 part-time. 61% of faculty holds doctoral degree. Student/faculty ratio: 13 to 1.

**Selectivity rating.** Competitive.

**PROFILE.** Evansville, founded in 1854, is a church-affiliated, liberal arts university. Programs are offered through the Colleges of Arts and Sciences, Engineering and Computing Sciences, Fine Arts, and Graduate and Continuing Studies; the Schools of Business Administration, Education, and Nursing; and Harlaxton College in Grantham, England. Its 75-acre campus is located in southwestern Indiana.

**Accreditation:** NCACS. Professionally accredited by the Accreditation Board for Engineering and Technology, the American Bar Association, the American Physical Therapy Association, the National Association of Schools of Music, the National Council for Accreditation of Teacher Education, the National League for Nursing.
**Religious orientation:** University of Evansville is affiliated with the United Methodist Church; no religious requirements.
**Library:** Collections totaling over 233,412 volumes, 1,162 periodical subscriptions, and 291,407 microform items.
**Athletic facilities:** Gymnasium, basketball, tennis, and volleyball courts, swimming pool, weight room, track, baseball, football, soccer, and softball fields.

**STUDENT BODY. Undergraduate profile:** 54% are state residents; 15% are transfers. 1.3% Asian-American, 3.2% Black, .8% Hispanic, 88% White, 6.7% Other. Average age of undergraduates is 20.
**Freshman profile:** 1% of freshmen who took SAT scored 700 or over on verbal, 2% scored 700 or over on math; 15% scored 600 or over on verbal, 26% scored 600 or over on math; 51% scored 500 or over on verbal, 70% scored 500 or over on math; 87% scored 400 or over on verbal, 97% scored 400 or over on math; 99% scored 300 or over on verbal, 100% scored 300 or over on math. 16% of freshmen who took ACT scored 30 or over on composite; 71% scored 24 or over on composite; 100% scored 18 or over on composite. 74% of accepted applicants took SAT; 62% took ACT.
**Undergraduate achievement:** 83% of fall 1992 freshmen returned for fall 1993 term. 60% of entering class graduated. 18% of students who completed a degree program immediately went on to graduate study.
**Foreign students:** 167 students are from out of the country. Countries represented include Bulgaria, Germany, Japan, Malaysia, United Arab Emirates, and the United Kingdom; 40 in all.

**PROGRAMS OF STUDY. Degrees:** B.A., B.F.A., B.Lib.Studies, B.Mus.Ed., B.Mus.Ther., B.S.
**Majors:** Accounting, Archaeology/Art History, Art, Art Education, Art History, Art Therapy, Biology, Business Administration, Chemistry, Civil Engineering, Commercial Art, Communication, Computer Science, Economics, Electrical Engineering, Elementary Education, Engineering Management, English, Environmental Studies, Exercise Science, Foreign Languages, History, Instrumental Music, International Studies, Legal Administration, Liberal Studies, Mathematics, Mechanical Engineering, Medical Technology, Mineral Lands Management, Music, Music Education, Music Management, Music Performance, Music Therapy, Nursing, Philosophy, Physical Therapy, Physics, Political Science, Psychobiology, Psychology, Religion, Secondary Education, Sociology, Theatre, Theatre Design/Technology, Theatre Management, Vocal Music.
**Distribution of degrees:** The majors with the highest enrollment are business, engineering, and communication; physics, religion/philosophy, and archaeology have the lowest.
**Requirements:** General education requirement.
**Academic regulations:** Freshmen must maintain minimum 1.6 GPA; sophomores, 1.9 GPA; juniors, 2.0 GPA; seniors, 2.0 GPA.
**Special:** Minors offered in some majors and in anthropology, athletic training, criminal justice, geography, interpersonal communications, literature, mass communications, sports studies, and writing. Arts and sciences students may elect courses from other university divisions. Associate's degrees offered. Double majors. Dual degrees. Independent study. Pass/fail grading option. Internships. Cooperative education programs. Graduate school at which undergraduates may take graduate-level courses. Preprofessional programs in law, medicine, veterinary science, pharmacy, dentistry, theology, and optometry. 2-3 physical therapy program. Teacher certification in early childhood, elementary, secondary, and special education. Exchange program abroad in Germany (Osnabruck U). Member of International Student Exchange Program (ISEP).
**Honors:** Phi Beta Kappa. Honors program. Honor societies.
**Academic Assistance:** Remedial writing. Nonremedial tutoring.

**STUDENT LIFE. Housing:** All unmarried freshmen must live on campus unless living with family. Coed, women's, and men's dorms. Fraternity housing. School-owned/operated apartments. 73% of students live in college housing.
**Social atmosphere:** Students gather at the Wooden Indian, the Coffee Pot, Turoni's, Kiplee's, and Denny's. Kappa Chi (a Christian organization), theatre majors, Greeks, and athletes are influential groups on campus. Popular campus events include the Watermelon Bust, Masquerade Ball, Taco Salad Wednesday, Thursday night movies, and the Evansville vs. Xavier basketball game. "Because UE is a suitcase campus, things are usually pretty dead. When people do get together, it's usually in someone's room or apartment," reports the student newspaper.
**Services and counseling/handicapped student services:** Placement services. Health service. Counseling services for minority and veteran students. Birth control, personal, and psychological counseling. Career and academic guidance services. Religious counseling. Physically disabled student services. Learning disabled services. Tutors. Reader services for the blind.
**Campus organizations:** Undergraduate student government. Student newspaper (Crescent, published once/week). Literary magazine. Yearbook. Radio station. Band, choir, orchestra, glee club, chorale, musical ensembles, drama group, College Republicans, Panhellenic Council, IEEE, IFC, Greek Council, 124 organizations in all. Five fraternities, all with chapter houses; four sororities, no chapter houses. 31% of men join a fraternity. 17% of women join a sorority.
**Religious organizations:** Baptist Student Union, Chapel Deacons, Intervarsity Christian Fellowship, Kappa Chi, Latter-Day Christian Saints, Hillel, Newman Center, Student Christian Fellowship, Outward Bound, Lutheran Student Group.
**Minority/foreign student organizations:** Minority Student Association. Emiretes, International Student Club, Malaysian Student Club, Muslim Student Association, Turkish Club.

**ATHLETICS. Physical education requirements:** One semester of physical education required.
**Intercollegiate competition:** 15% of students participate. Baseball (M), basketball (M,W), cross-country (M,W), diving (M,W), football (M), golf (M), soccer (M), softball (W), swimming (M,W), tennis (M,W), volleyball (W). Member of Midwestern Collegiate Conference, NCAA Division I, NCAA Division IAA for football, Pioneer Football League.
**Intramural and club sports:** 1% of students participate. Intramural badminton, baseball, basketball, bowling, cross country, flag football, golf, racquetball, soccer, softball, swimming, table tennis, tennis, track, volleyball. Women's club soccer.

**ADMISSIONS. Academic basis for candidate selection** (in order of priority): Secondary school record, class rank, standardized test scores, school's recommendation, essay.
**Nonacademic basis for candidate selection:** Particular talent or ability is important. Character and personality, extracurricular participation, and alumni/ae relationship are considered.
**Requirements:** Graduation from secondary school is required; GED is accepted. No specific distribution of secondary school units required. 2 units each of foreign language, social studies, and electives recommended. Minimum combined SAT score of 850 (composite ACT score of 20) and rank in top half of secondary school class required. Audition required of theatre program applicants. Chemistry required of nursing program applicants. Four years of math required of engineering program applicants. Portfolio required of art program applicants. Audition required of music program applicants. Summer courses available at local college for applicants not meeting standard requirements. SAT or ACT is required. Campus visit and interview recommended. Off-campus interviews available with an admissions representative.
**Procedure:** Take SAT or ACT by November of 12th year. Visit college for interview by April of 12th year. Suggest filing application by December 1. Application deadline is February 15. Acceptance notification by December 15 and March 1. Reply is required by May 1. $200 nonrefundable tuition deposit. Freshmen accepted for terms other than fall.
**Special programs:** Admission may be deferred one year. Credit may be granted through CEEB Advanced Placement for scores of 4 or higher. Credit and/or placement may be granted through CLEP general and subject exams. Credit and placement may be granted through challenge exams. Early entrance/early admission program. Concurrent enrollment program.
**Transfer students:** Transfer students accepted for terms other than fall. for fall 1993, 15% of all new students were transfers into all classes. 308 transfer applications were received, 206 were accepted. Application deadline is rolling for fall; rolling for spring. Minimum 2.0 GPA required. Lowest course grade accepted is "C." Maximum number of transferable credits is 61 semester hours. At least 63 semester hours must be completed at the university to receive degree.
**Admissions contact:** John Byrd, Ph.D., Vice President. 812 479-2468.

**FINANCIAL AID. Available aid:** Pell grants, SEOG, state scholarships and grants, school scholarships and grants, private scholarships and grants, academic merit scholarships, athletic scholarships, and aid for undergraduate foreign students. Perkins Loans

(NDSL), PLUS, Stafford Loans (GSL), NSL, school loans, private loans, and SLS. Tuition Plan Inc., AMS, and EFI Fund Management. School's own payment plan.

**Financial aid statistics:** 23% of aid is not need-based. In 1993-94, 63% of all undergraduate applicants received aid; 96% of freshman applicants. Average amounts of aid awarded freshmen: Scholarships and grants, $6,289; loans, $2,916.

**Supporting data/closing dates:** FAFSA/FAF: Priority filing date is March 1. School's own aid application: Priority filing date is February 15. State aid form: Priority filing date is March 1. Notification of awards on rolling basis.

**Financial aid contact:** JoAnn Laugel and Verla Richardson, Co-Directors of Financial Aid. 812 479-2364.

**STUDENT EMPLOYMENT.** College Work/Study Program. Institutional employment. 23% of full-time undergraduates work on campus during school year. Students may expect to earn an average of $1,140 during school year. Off-campus part-time employment opportunities rated "good."

**COMPUTER FACILITIES.** 120 IBM/IBM-compatible and Macintosh/Apple microcomputers; 60 are networked. Students may access IBM minicomputer/mainframe systems. Computer languages and software packages include COBOL, FORTRAN, LIMDEP, LISP, Lotus, Quattro, SPSS, WordPerfect; 12 in all. Computer facilities are available to all students.

**Fees:** Computer fee is included in tuition/fees.

**Hours:** 8 AM-11 PM.

**GRADUATE CAREER DATA.** Graduate school percentages: 3% enter law school. 3% enter medical school. 1% enter dental school. 2% enter graduate business programs. 5% enter graduate arts and sciences programs. 1% enter theological school/seminary. Highest graduate school enrollments: Indiana U, U of Notre Dame, Purdue U. 60% of graduates choose careers in business and industry. Companies and businesses that hire graduates: ALCOA, Bristol-Myers, Ernst & Young, Intel, local schools and hospitals.

**PROMINENT ALUMNI/AE.** Matt Williams, former writer and producer, "The Cosby Show" and "Roseanne"; Ron Glass, actor; Jerry Sloan, head coach, Utah Jazz; Wayne Davidson, CEO, Bristol-Myers; J. Allen McCutchan, M.D., research physician; Major General John Conaway, Vice Chief of US National Guard, the Pentagon.

# University of Indianapolis

**Indianapolis, IN 46227-3697** **317 STU-DENT**

**1994-95 Costs.** Tuition: $11,120. Room & board: $4,080. Fees, books, misc. academic expenses (school's estimate): $525.

**Enrollment.** Undergraduates: 548 men, 870 women (full-time). Freshman class: 1,487 applicants, 1,276 accepted, 388 enrolled. Graduate enrollment: 289 men, 418 women.

**Test score averages/ranges.** Average SAT scores: 432 verbal, 487 math. Range of SAT scores of middle 50%: 370-490 verbal, 400-570 math. Average ACT scores: 21 English, 21 math, 21 composite. Range of ACT scores of middle 50%: 17-25 English, 17-24 math.

**Faculty.** 121 full-time; 155 part-time. 52% of faculty holds doctoral degree. Student/faculty ratio: 13 to 1.

**Selectivity rating.** Less competitive.

**PROFILE.** The University of Indianapolis, founded in 1902, is a church-affiliated, liberal arts institution. Programs are offered through the College of Arts and Sciences and the Schools of Business, Education, and Nursing. Its 60-acre campus is located southeast of downtown Indianapolis.

**Accreditation:** NCACS. Professionally accredited by the American Physical Therapy Association, the National Association of Schools of Music, the National Council for Accreditation of Teacher Education, the National League for Nursing.

**Religious orientation:** University of Indianapolis is affiliated with the United Methodist Church; one semester of religion required.

**Library:** Collections totaling over 165,000 volumes, 1,300 periodical subscriptions, and 5,500 microform items.

**Special facilities/museums:** Developmental pre-school, art gallery, observatory.

**Athletic facilities:** Gymnasiums, weight and wrestling rooms, basketball, racquetball, sand volleyball, tennis, and volleyball courts, stadium, fitness center, baseball, football, soccer, and softball fields, track, swimming pool, dance studio.

**STUDENT BODY. Undergraduate profile:** 89% are state residents. 6% Black, 87% White, 7% Other. Average age of undergraduates is 20.

**Freshman profile:** 1% of freshmen who took SAT scored 700 or over on verbal, 1% scored 700 or over on math; 4% scored 600 or over on verbal, 13% scored 600 or over on math; 21% scored 500 or over on verbal, 40% scored 500 or over on math; 60% scored 400 or over on verbal, 71% scored 400 or over on math; 93% scored 300 or over on verbal, 96% scored 300 or over on math. 4% of freshmen who took ACT scored 30 or over on English, 2% scored 30 or over on math, 6% scored 30 or over on composite; 32% scored 24 or over on English, 26% scored 24 or over on math, 31% scored 24 or over on composite; 73% scored 18 or over on English, 72% scored 18 or over on math, 82% scored 18 or over on composite; 99% scored 12 or over on English, 99% scored 12 or over on math, 100% scored 12 or over on composite; 100% scored 6 or over on English, 100% scored 6 or over on math. 75% of accepted applicants took SAT; 33% took ACT.

**Undergraduate achievement:** 75% of fall 1992 freshmen returned for fall 1993 term. 52% of entering class graduated.

**Foreign students:** 116 students are from out of the country. Countries represented include African countries, Cyprus, Greece, India, and Pakistan; 40 in all.

**PROGRAMS OF STUDY. Degrees:** B.A., B.S.

**Majors:** Accounting, Art, Art Therapy, Biology, Business Administration, Chemistry, Communications in Business, Communications Studies, Corrections, Earth/Space Sciences, Economics/Finance, Electrical Engineering, Electronic Media, English, French, General Science, German, History, History of Art, Industrial Management, International Business, Journalism, Law Enforcement, Management Information Systems, Marketing, Mathematics, Mechanical Engineering, Medical Technology, Music, Music Performance, Nursing, Philosophy, Physical Education, Physics, Political Science, Pre-Business, Psychology, Religion, Social Work, Sociology, Spanish, Sports Information, Theatre, Undeclared/General Studies, Visual Communications.

**Requirements:** General education requirement.

**Academic regulations:** Freshmen must maintain minimum 1.7 GPA; sophomores, 1.8 GPA; juniors, 1.9 GPA; seniors, 2.0 GPA.

**Special:** Minors offered in most majors and in anthropology, art history, athletic training, crafts, graphic design, health/safety, humanities, and several other fields. Associate's degrees offered. Double majors. Dual degrees. Independent study. Pass/fail grading option. Internships. Cooperative education programs. Graduate school at which undergraduates may take graduate-level courses. Preprofessional programs in law, medicine, veterinary science, dentistry, theology, engineering, occupational therapy, and physical therapy. 3-1 medical technology program with Methodist Hospital. 3-2 engineering program with Indiana U-Purdue U at Indianapolis. Member of Consortium for Urban Education. Teacher certification in elementary, secondary, and special education. Certification in specific subject areas. Study abroad in Cyprus. ROTC at Indiana U–Purdue U at Indianapolis.

**Honors:** Honors program. Honor societies.

**Academic Assistance:** Remedial writing, math, and study skills. Nonremedial tutoring.

**STUDENT LIFE. Housing:** Students may live on or off campus. Coed and women's dorms. School-owned/operated apartments. On-campus married-student housing. 60% of students live in college housing.

**Social atmosphere:** Favorite student gathering spots include The Greyhound Sports Bar, Schwitzer Center, and Street's Corner. Influential student groups include Indianapolis Student Government, Christian Life, Fellowship of Christian Athletes, and The Student/Reflector. The Top Dog Game, Homecoming, Brown County Day, and Mardi Gras are popular campus social events. "Students always complain that there is nothing to do," reports the editor of the student newspaper.

**Services and counseling/handicapped student services:** Placement services. Health service. Day care. Counseling center. Personal and psychological counseling. Career and academic guidance services. Religious counseling. Physically disabled student services. Learning disabled program/services.

**Campus organizations:** Undergraduate student government. Student newspaper (Student Reflector, published once/week). Yearbook. Radio and TV stations. Crimson Express, Crimson Steppers, pep and jazz bands, concert choir, ensembles, Oracle, drama society, departmental groups, Greyhound Ambassadors, 37 organizations in all.

**Religious organizations:** Christian Life, Deputation Teams, Fellowship of Christian Athletes.

**Minority/foreign student organizations:** Black Student Association. Intercultural Association, International Relations Club.

**ATHLETICS. Physical education requirements:** Four semesters of physical education required.

**Intercollegiate competition:** 22% of students participate. Baseball (M), basketball (M,W), cheerleading (M,W), cross-country (M,W), diving (M,W), football (M), golf (M,W), soccer (M,W), softball (W), swimming (M,W), tennis (M,W), track and field (indoor) (M,W), track and field (outdoor) (M,W), volleyball (W), wrestling (M). Member of Great Lakes Valley Conference, Midwest Intercollegiate Football Conference, NCAA Division II.

**Intramural and club sports:** 45% of students participate. Intramural basketball, bowling, flag football, racquetball, soccer, table tennis, tennis, volleyball, walleyball.

**ADMISSIONS. Academic basis for candidate selection** (in order of priority): Secondary school record, class rank, school's recommendation, standardized test scores.

**Nonacademic basis for candidate selection:** Character and personality, extracurricular participation, particular talent or ability, and alumni/ae relationship are considered.

**Requirements:** Graduation from secondary school is required; GED is accepted. No specific distribution of secondary school units required. Audition and portfolio required of music and art program scholarship applicants. Conditional admission possible for applicants not meeting standard requirements. SAT or ACT is required. Campus visit and interview recommended. Off-campus interviews available with an admissions representative.

**Procedure:** Take SAT or ACT by May of 12th year. Visit college for interview by May of 12th year. Suggest filing application by March 1. Application deadline is August 15. Notification of admission on rolling basis. Reply is required by May 1. $100 tuition deposit, refundable until May 1. $50 room deposit, refundable until May 1. Freshmen accepted for terms other than fall.

**Special programs:** Admission may be deferred one year. Credit may be granted through CEEB Advanced Placement for scores of 3 or higher. Credit may be granted through CLEP general and subject exams, ACT PEP and DANTES exams, and military experience. Credit and placement may be granted through challenge exams. Concurrent enrollment program.

**Transfer students:** Transfer students accepted for terms other than fall. for fall 1993, 400 transfer applications were received, 322 were accepted. Application deadline is August 15 for fall; December 15 for spring. Minimum 2.0 GPA required. Lowest course grade accepted is "C-." At least 30 semester hours must be completed at the university to receive degree.

**Admissions contact:** Mark T. Weigand, M.S., Director of Admissions. 317 788-3216.

**FINANCIAL AID. Available aid:** Pell grants, SEOG, state scholarships and grants, school scholarships and grants, private scholarships and grants, ROTC scholarships, academic merit scholarships, and athletic scholarships. Perkins Loans (NDSL), PLUS, Stafford Loans (GSL), private loans, and SLS. AMS and deferred payment plan.

**Financial aid statistics:** 35% of aid is not need-based. In 1993-94, 82% of all undergraduate applicants received aid; 82% of freshman applicants.

**Supporting data/closing dates:** FAFSA: Priority filing date is March 1. School's own aid application: Priority filing date is March 1. Notification of awards on rolling basis.

**Financial aid contact:** Linda B. Handy, M.S., Director of Financial Aid. 317 788-3217.

**STUDENT EMPLOYMENT.** College Work/Study Program. Institutional employment. 50% of full-time undergraduates work on campus during school year. Students may expect to earn an average of $1,400 during school year. Off-campus part-time employment opportunities rated "excellent."

**COMPUTER FACILITIES.** 200 IBM/IBM-compatible and Macintosh/Apple microcomputers. Students may access Digital minicomputer/mainframe systems, Internet. Computer languages and software packages include all major programs. Computer facilities are available to all students.
**Fees:** Computer fee is included in tuition/fees.
**PROMINENT ALUMNI/AE.** William Raspberry, syndicated columnist; Jim Magel, president and CEO, Merchants Bank; Larry Barrett, president, Great Lakes Bankcorp.

# University of Notre Dame

**Notre Dame, IN 46556 219 631-5000**

**1994-95 Costs.** Tuition: $16,840. Room & board: $4,260. Fees, books, misc. academic expenses (school's estimate): $550.
**Enrollment.** Undergraduates: 4,500 men, 3,100 women (full-time). Freshman class: 7,700 applicants, 3,700 accepted, 1,900 enrolled. Graduate enrollment: 1,480 men, 820 women.
**Test score averages/ranges.** Range of SAT scores of middle 50%: 540-640 verbal, 620-720 math.
**Faculty.** 620 full-time; 200 part-time. 90% of faculty holds doctoral degree. Student/faculty ratio: 12 to 1.
**Selectivity rating.** Most competitive.

**PROFILE.** Notre Dame, founded in 1842, is a church-affiliated, comprehensive university. Programs are offered through the Colleges of Arts and Letters, Business Administration, Engineering, and Science. Its 1,250-acre campus, with a dominant Victorian Gothic architectural style, is located in Notre Dame, five miles outside South Bend.
**Accreditation:** NCACS. Professionally accredited by the Accreditation Board for Engineering and Technology, the American Assembly of Collegiate Schools of Business, the National Architecture Accrediting Board, the National Association of Schools of Art and Design, the National Council for Accreditation of Teacher Education.
**Religious orientation:** University of Notre Dame is affiliated with the Roman Catholic Church (Congregation of the Holy Cross); two semesters of theology required.
**Library:** Collections totaling over 2,000,000 volumes, 20,500 periodical subscriptions, and 2,500,000 microform items.
**Special facilities/museums:** Art museum, language lab, accelerator lab, electron microscope.
**Athletic facilities:** Gymnasiums, field house, basketball, racquetball, tennis, and volleyball courts, ice rink, weight rooms, tracks, golf course, baseball, football, intramural, lacrosse, soccer, and softball fields, natatorium, stadiums.
**STUDENT BODY. Undergraduate profile:** 9% are state residents; 5% are transfers. 3% Asian-American, 3% Black, 6% Hispanic, 1% Native American, 84% White, 3% Other. Average age of undergraduates is 20.
**Freshman profile:** 5% of freshmen who took SAT scored 700 or over on verbal, 30% scored 700 or over on math; 39% scored 600 or over on verbal, 78% scored 600 or over on math; 87% scored 500 or over on verbal, 97% scored 500 or over on math; 98% scored 400 or over on verbal, 100% scored 400 or over on math; 100% scored 300 or over on verbal. 96% of accepted applicants took SAT; 4% took ACT. 56% of freshmen come from public schools.
**Undergraduate achievement:** 97% of fall 1992 freshmen returned for fall 1993 term. 92% of entering class graduated. 32% of students who completed a degree program immediately went on to graduate study.
**Foreign students:** 102 students are from out of the country. Countries represented include Bolivia, Canada, China, Hong Kong, India, and Panama; 35 in all.
**PROGRAMS OF STUDY. Degrees:** B.A., B.Arch., B.Bus.Admin., B.F.A., B.Mus., B.S.
**Majors:** Accountancy, Aerospace/Mechanical Engineering, American Studies, Anthropology, Art/Art History/Design, Biochemistry, Biological Sciences, Chemical Engineering, Chemistry, Civil Engineering, Classics, Communication/Theatre, Computer Engineering, Computer Science, Economics, Electrical Engineering, Engineering/Environmental Studies, English, Finance/Business Economics, French, Geological Sciences, German, Government/International Studies, History, Italian, Japanese, Liberal Studies, Management, Marketing, Mathematics, Medieval Studies, Music, Philosophy, Physics, Pre-Professional Studies, Psychology, Russian, Sociology, Spanish, Theology.
**Distribution of degrees:** The majors with the highest enrollment are accountancy, government, and finance; Greek, Russian, and Japanese have the lowest.
**Requirements:** General education requirement.
**Academic regulations:** Freshmen must maintain minimum 1.85 GPA; sophomores, juniors, seniors, 2.0 GPA.
**Special:** Programs offered in African-American, area, film/cultural, gender, and peace studies and in computer applications, public service, science/technology/values, and secondary education. Double majors. Dual degrees. Independent study. Accelerated study. Internships. Graduate school at which undergraduates may take graduate-level courses. Preprofessional programs in medicine, dentistry, theology, business, architecture, computer science, and education. 3-2 liberal arts/engineering programs with Bethel Coll, St. Anselm Coll, St. Mary's Coll, Coll of St. Thomas, and Carroll Coll. Washington Semester. American Studies Program (Washington, D.C.). Exchange programs with Xavier U (New Orleans) and Clark-Atlanta U. Teacher certification in secondary education offered through St. Mary's Coll. Certification in specific subject areas. Study abroad in Australia, Austria, Chile, Egypt, England, France, Ireland, Israel, Italy, Japan, Mexico, and Spain. ROTC, NROTC, and AFROTC.
**Honors:** Phi Beta Kappa. Honors program. Honor societies.
**Academic Assistance:** Remedial study skills. Nonremedial tutoring.
**STUDENT LIFE. Housing:** All freshmen must live on campus. Women's and men's dorms. Off-campus privately-owned housing. On-campus married-student housing. 84% of students live in college housing.
**Social atmosphere:** The student newspaper reports that the influential organizations on campus are the football team, the Student Union Board, and dorm groups. Football games, the Collegiate Jazz Festival, Bengal Bouts, the Morrissey Film Festival, and the Fisher Regatta are among the year's favorite events. Students gather on campus at the Huddle, the Oak Room, and the Senior Bar. Popular off-campus hangouts include Coach's, the Linebacker, Club 23, Bridget McGuire's, and Barnaby's.
**Services and counseling/handicapped student services:** Placement services. Health service. Day care. Counseling services for minority and military students. Personal and psychological counseling. Career and academic guidance services. Religious counseling. Physically disabled student services. Learning disabled services. Notetaking services. Tape recorders. Tutors. Reader services for the blind.
**Campus organizations:** Undergraduate student government. Student newspaper (Observer, published once/day). Literary magazine. Yearbook. Radio station. Choir, glee club, band, orchestra, debating, literary and technical quarterlies, Notre Dame-St. Mary's Theatre, media clubs, Society of Women Engineers, Women United for Justice and Peace, academic, athletic, service, special-interest, and volunteer groups, 200 organizations in all.
**Religious organizations:** Fellowship of Christian Athletes, Pax Christi, Muslim Students.
**Minority/foreign student organizations:** Black Cultural Arts Festival, African-American Student Alliance, League of Black Business Students, NAACP, Society of Black Engineers, Native American Student Association, Hispanic-American Organization, Asian-American Association, Cuban-American Union, American-Lebanese Club. International Student Organization, Filipino, Indian, Japanese, and Korean student groups.
**ATHLETICS. Physical education requirements:** Two semesters of physical education required.
**Intercollegiate competition:** 10% of students participate. Baseball (M), basketball (M,W), cross-country (M,W), diving (M,W), fencing (M,W), football (M), golf (M,W), ice hockey (M), lacrosse (M), soccer (M,W), softball (W), swimming (M,W), tennis (M,W), track (indoor) (M,W), track (outdoor) (M,W), track and field (indoor) (M,W), track and field (outdoor) (M,W), volleyball (W). Member of CCHA for hockey, Midwestern Collegiate Conference, NCAA Division I, NCAA Division I-A for football.
**Intramural and club sports:** 82% of students participate. Intramural aerobics, badminton, baseball, basketball, cricket, cross-country, cycling, flag football, floor hockey, handball, ice hockey, ice skating, lacrosse, Nordic skiing, racquetball, soccer, softball, squash, tackle football, tennis, ultimate frisbee, volleyball, walleyball, water aerobics, water polo, weight lifting. Men's club Alpine skiing, boxing, crew, equestrian sports, gymnastics, rugby, sailing, volleyball, water polo. Women's club Alpine skiing, crew, equestrian sports, gymnastics, sailing, synchronized swimming.
**ADMISSIONS. Academic basis for candidate selection** (in order of priority): Secondary school record, class rank, standardized test scores, school's recommendation, essay.
**Nonacademic basis for candidate selection:** Character and personality, extracurricular participation, and particular talent or ability are emphasized. Alumni/ae relationship is considered.
**Requirements:** Graduation from secondary school is required; GED is not accepted. 16 units and the following program of study are required: 4 units of English, 3 units of math, 2 units of lab science, 2 units of foreign language, 2 units of history, 3 units of academic electives. Portfolio required of art program applicants. Audition required of music program applicants. SAT is required; ACT may be substituted. PSAT is recommended. ACH recommended. Campus visit recommended. No off-campus interviews.
**Procedure:** Take SAT or ACT by January of 12th year. Visit college for tour by January of 12th year. Take ACH by June of 12th year. Suggest filing application by December 15. Application deadline is January 6. Notification of admission by April 7. Reply is required by May 1. $200 nonrefundable tuition deposit. Freshmen accepted for fall term only.
**Special programs:** Admission may be deferred one year. Credit and/or placement may be granted through CEEB Advanced Placement exams for scores of 4 or higher. Early decision program. for fall 1993, 818 applied for early decision and 600 were accepted. Deadline for applying for early decision is November 1.
**Transfer students:** Transfer students accepted for fall term. for fall 1993, 5% of all new students were transfers into all classes. 600 transfer applications were received, 300 were accepted. Application deadline is April 15 for fall; November 1 for spring. Minimum 3.0 GPA required. Lowest course grade accepted is "C." Maximum number of transferable credits is 60 semester hours. At least 60 semester hours must be completed at the university to receive degree.
**Admissions contact:** Kevin M. Rooney, M.S., Director of Admissions. 219 631-7505.
**FINANCIAL AID. Available aid:** Pell grants, SEOG, state scholarships and grants, school scholarships and grants, private scholarships and grants, ROTC scholarships, and athletic scholarships. Perkins Loans (NDSL), PLUS, Stafford Loans (GSL), state loans, private loans, and SLS. AMS.
**Financial aid statistics:** 44% of aid is not need-based. In 1993-94, 98% of all undergraduate applicants received aid; 99% of freshman applicants. Average amounts of aid awarded freshmen: Scholarships and grants, $7,100; loans, $4,650.
**Supporting data/closing dates:** FAFSA/FAF: Priority filing date is February 28. State aid form: Priority filing date is March 1. Income tax forms. Notification of awards on rolling basis.
**Financial aid contact:** Joseph A. Russo, M.S., Director of Financial Aid. 219 631-6436.
**STUDENT EMPLOYMENT.** College Work/Study Program. Institutional employment. 41% of full-time undergraduates work on campus during school year. Students may expect to earn an average of $1,150 during school year. Off-campus part-time employment opportunities rated "good."
**COMPUTER FACILITIES.** 455 IBM/IBM-compatible, Macintosh/Apple, and RISC-/UNIX-based microcomputers; all are networked. Students may access Digital, IBM, Prime, SUN minicomputer/mainframe systems. Residence halls may be equipped with stand-alone microcomputers, modems. Client/LAN operating systems include Apple/Macintosh, DOS. Computer languages and software packages include BASIC, C, COBOL, FORTRAN, LISP, Pascal, PL/1, REDUCE, SAS, SPSS. Computer facilities are available to all students.
**GRADUATE CAREER DATA.** Graduate school percentages: 9% enter law school. 8% enter medical school. 1% enter dental school. 1% enter graduate business programs. 11% enter graduate arts and sciences programs. 1% enter theological school/seminary. Highest graduate school enrollments: Columbia U, Duke U, Georgetown U, Northwestern U. 50%

of graduates choose careers in business and industry. Companies and businesses that hire graduates: Major public accounting firms, Procter & Gamble, IBM.
**PROMINENT ALUMNI/AE.** Bruce Babbitt, U.S. Secretary of the Interior; Adrian Dantley and Bill Laimbeer, NBA players.

# University of Southern Indiana

**Evansville, IN 47712 812 464-1765**

**1994-95 Costs.** Tuition: $2,040 (state residents), $4,972 (out-of-state). Room: $1,660. Fees, books, misc. academic expenses (school's estimate): $520.
**Enrollment.** Undergraduates: 1,689 men, 2,417 women (full-time). Freshman class: 2,412 applicants, 2,317 accepted, 2,100 enrolled. Graduate enrollment: 154 men, 114 women.
**Test score averages/ranges.** Average SAT scores: 391 verbal, 434 math. Average ACT scores: 18 composite.
**Faculty.** 168 full-time; 197 part-time. 58% of faculty holds doctoral degree. Student/faculty ratio: 20 to 1.
**Selectivity rating.** Competitive.

**PROFILE.** Southern Indiana, founded in 1965, is a public, comprehensive university. Its 300-acre campus is located in Evansville, in southwestern Indiana.

**Accreditation:** NCACS.
**Religious orientation:** University of Southern Indiana is nonsectarian; no religious requirements.
**Library:** Collections totaling over 170,000 volumes, 745 periodical subscriptions, and 232,716 microform items.
**Athletic facilities:** Gymnasiums, field house, training and weight rooms, badminton, basketball, tennis, and volleyball courts, swimming pool, baseball, intramural, soccer, and softball fields.
**STUDENT BODY. Undergraduate profile:** 95% are state residents; 14% are transfers. 1% Asian-American, 3% Black, 95% White, 1% Other.
**Freshman profile:** 1% of freshmen who took SAT scored 700 or over on verbal, 1% scored 700 or over on math; 7% scored 600 or over on verbal, 8% scored 600 or over on math; 16% scored 500 or over on verbal, 29% scored 500 or over on math; 50% scored 400 or over on verbal, 61% scored 400 or over on math; 89% scored 300 or over on verbal, 93% scored 300 or over on math. Majority of accepted applicants took SAT.
**Undergraduate achievement:** 80% of fall 1992 freshmen returned for fall 1993 term. 12% of students who completed a degree program immediately went on to graduate study.
**Foreign students:** 64 students are from out of the country. Countries represented include Austria, Bermuda, Jordan, Malaysia, Peru, and Turkey; 36 in all.
**PROGRAMS OF STUDY. Degrees:** B.A., B.S., B.S.Nurs.
**Majors:** Accounting, Administrative Systems, Art, Biology, Biophysics, Business Administration, Business Education/Secondary, Chemistry, Civil Engineering Technology, Communications, Computer Information Systems, Dental Hygiene Education, Economics, Electrical Engineering Technology, English Secondary Education, German, Health Services, Management, Marketing, Mathematics, Mathematics Education, Mechanical Engineering Technology, Medical Technology, Nursing, Occupational Therapy, Philosophy, Physical Education, Political Science, Pre-Dentistry, Pre-Law, Pre-Medicine, Pre-Nuclear Medicine, Pre-Optometry, Pre-Osteopathy, Psychology, Public Relations, Radio/Television, Radio/Television Education, Science Education, Secondary Education, Social Sciences, Social Studies Education, Social Work, Sociology, Spanish, Speech, Speech Communication/Theatre Education, Sports Medicine, Theatre, Visual Arts Education.
**Distribution of degrees:** The majors with the highest enrollment are business and communications; health services, civil engineering, and philosophy have the lowest.
**Requirements:** General education requirement.
**Academic regulations:** Minimum 2.0 GPA must be maintained.
**Special:** Minors offered in some majors and in early childhood education, environmental biology, geochemistry, geography, geology, geophysics, Latin American studies, metro-core education, physics, reading, recreation, and school library/audio-visual services. Associate's degrees offered. Double majors. Internships. Cooperative education programs. Graduate school at which undergraduates may take graduate-level courses. Preprofessional programs in law, medicine, veterinary science, pharmacy, dentistry, optometry, and pre-physical therapy. Teacher certification in early childhood, elementary, and secondary education.
**Academic Assistance:** Remedial reading, writing, math, and study skills. Nonremedial tutoring.

**STUDENT LIFE. Housing:** Students may live on or off campus. Coed dorms. No meal plan. Off-campus privately-owned housing. On-campus married-student housing. 17% of students live in college housing.
**Social atmosphere:** Favorite hangouts include the university center, Denny's, Jerry's, Breakers, and Shobar. Greeks and non-traditional students influence student life. Eagerly anticipated events include Eagle Grand Prix Bicycle Race, Sig Tau Gamma Big Chill, Kenny Kent Toyota National Shootout, Basketball Tournament, and Westside Nut Fall Festival. Basketball provides a lot of Evanville's entertainment. Even though USI's Greek system is small, fraternity parties are popular. On-campus, the Activities Programming Board brings in movies, comedians, and musicians.
**Services and counseling/handicapped student services:** Placement services. Health service. Day care. Counseling services for minority, veteran, and older students. Birth control, personal, and psychological counseling. Career and academic guidance services. Religious counseling. Physically disabled student services. Learning disabled services. Notetaking services. Tape recorders. Tutors. Reader services for the blind.
**Campus organizations:** Undergraduate student government. Student newspaper (Transitions, published once/month). Literary magazine. Yearbook. Radio station. Mid-America Singers, student government, Activities Programming Board, Young Democrats, Young Republicans, academic, service, social, and special-interest groups, 80 organizations in all. Five fraternities, two chapter houses; three sororities, no chapter houses. 20% of men join a fraternity. 20% of women join a sorority.
**Religious organizations:** Baptist Student Union, Fellowship of Christian Athletes, Intervarsity Christian Fellowship, Newman Club.
**Minority/foreign student organizations:** Black Student Union. International Club.
**ATHLETICS. Physical education requirements:** Two semesters of physical education required.
**Intercollegiate competition:** 2% of students participate. Baseball (M), basketball (M,W), cross-country (M,W), golf (M), soccer (M), softball (W), tennis (M,W), volleyball (W). Member of Great Lakes Valley Conference, NCAA Division I for men's soccer, NCAA Division II.
**Intramural and club sports:** 35% of students participate. Intramural badminton, basketball, golf, miniature golf, punt-pass-kick, pickleball, rugby, soccer, softball, tennis, tug-of-war, wrestling. Men's club rugby. Women's club soccer.
**ADMISSIONS. Academic basis for candidate selection** (in order of priority): Secondary school record.
**Nonacademic basis for candidate selection:** Extracurricular participation and particular talent or ability are important. Character and personality are considered.
**Requirements:** Graduation from secondary school is required; GED is accepted. No specific distribution of secondary school units required. Minimum 2.0 GPA required. Conditional admission possible for applicants not meeting standard requirements. SAT or ACT is required. Off-campus interviews available with an admissions representative.
**Procedure:** Take SAT or ACT by June of 12th year. Visit college for interview by August 15 of 12th year. Application deadline is August 15. Notification of admission on rolling basis. $100 room deposit, refundable until June. Freshmen accepted for terms other than fall.
**Special programs:** Admission may be deferred one semester. Credit may be granted through CEEB Advanced Placement for scores of 3 or higher. Credit may be granted through CLEP general and subject exams. Concurrent enrollment program.
**Transfer students:** Transfer students accepted for terms other than fall. for fall 1993, 14% of all new students were transfers into all classes. Application deadline is August 15 for fall; December 15 for spring. Minimum 2.0 GPA required. Lowest course grade accepted is "D." At least 30 semester hours must be completed at the university to receive degree.
**Admissions contact:** Timothy K. Buecher, M.A., Director of Admissions. 800 467-1965.

**FINANCIAL AID. Available aid:** Pell grants, SEOG, state scholarships and grants, school scholarships and grants, private scholarships and grants, academic merit scholarships, and athletic scholarships. Perkins Loans (NDSL), PLUS, Stafford Loans (GSL), private loans, and SLS. Deferred payment plan.
**Financial aid statistics:** 30% of aid is not need-based. In 1993-94, 85% of all undergraduate applicants received aid; 68% of freshman applicants. Average amounts of aid awarded freshmen: Scholarships and grants, $750; loans, $1,500.
**Supporting data/closing dates:** FAFSA/FAF: Priority filing date is March 1; accepted on rolling basis. School's own aid application: Priority filing date is March 1; accepted on rolling basis. Notification of awards on rolling basis.
**Financial aid contact:** James M. Patton, M.S., Director of Financial Aid. 800 467-1965.
**STUDENT EMPLOYMENT.** College Work/Study Program. Institutional employment. 7% of full-time undergraduates work on campus during school year. Students may expect to earn an average of $1,000 during school year. Off-campus part-time employment opportunities rated "good."
**COMPUTER FACILITIES.** 400 IBM/IBM-compatible microcomputers. Students may access minicomputer/mainframe systems. Computer languages and software packages include BASIC, COBOL, dBASE, FORTRAN, Lotus 1-2-3, Pascal, RPG, SPSS, Symphony, WordStar.
Fees: None.
**Hours:** 8 AM-midn. (M-Th); 8 AM-4:30 PM (F); 10 AM-6 PM (Sa); 2 PM-10 PM (Su).
**GRADUATE CAREER DATA.** Graduate school percentages: 3% enter graduate business programs. 25% enter graduate arts and sciences programs. 91% of graduates choose careers in business and industry.

# Valparaiso University

**Valparaiso, IN 46383-6493 219 464-5000**

**1993-94 Costs.** Tuition: $11,300. Room: $1,790. Board: $1,300. Fees, books, misc. academic expenses (school's estimate): $920.
**Enrollment.** Undergraduates: 1,122 men, 1,418 women (full-time). Freshman class: 2,466 applicants, 2,071 accepted, 723 enrolled. Graduate enrollment: 349 men, 412 women.
**Test score averages/ranges.** Range of SAT scores of middle 50%: 470-590 verbal, 530-670 math. Range of ACT scores of middle 50%: 25-30 composite.
**Faculty.** 263 full-time; 78 part-time. 75% of faculty holds doctoral degree. Student/faculty ratio: 14 to 1.
**Selectivity rating.** Highly competitive.

**PROFILE.** Valparaiso, founded in 1859, is a church-affiliated university. Programs are offered through Christ College; the Colleges of Arts and Sciences, Business Administration, Engineering, and Nursing; the Law School; and the Graduate Division. Its 310-acre campus is located in Valparaiso, 45 miles southeast of Chicago.

**Accreditation:** NCACS. Professionally accredited by the Accreditation Board for Engineering and Technology, the American Assembly of Collegiate Schools of Business, the American Bar Association, the Association of American Law Schools, the Council on Social Work Education, the National Association of Schools of Music, the National Council for Accreditation of Teacher Education, the National League for Nursing.
**Religious orientation:** Valparaiso University is affiliated with the Lutheran Church; three semesters of theology required.

**Library:** Collections totaling over 259,830 volumes, 1,560 periodical subscriptions, and 180,000 microform items.
**Special facilities/museums:** Art museum, galleries, audio-visual lab, language lab, subcritical nuclear reactor, particle accelerator, electron microscope, planetarium, observatory.
**Athletic facilities:** Gymnasium, swimming pool, badminton, basketball, handball, racquetball, tennis, and volleyball courts, track, baseball, football, intramural, and soccer fields, recreation center, stadium.

**STUDENT BODY. Undergraduate profile:** 31% are state residents. 1% Asian-American, 2% Black, 1% Hispanic, 1% Native American, 92% White, 3% Other. Average age of undergraduates is 20.
**Freshman profile:** 3% of freshmen who took SAT scored 700 or over on verbal, 15% scored 700 or over on math; 22% scored 600 or over on verbal, 50% scored 600 or over on math; 57% scored 500 or over on verbal, 83% scored 500 or over on math; 96% scored 400 or over on verbal, 97% scored 400 or over on math; 100% scored 300 or over on verbal, 100% scored 300 or over on math. 21% of freshmen who took ACT scored 30 or over on composite; 79% scored 24 or over on composite; 100% scored 18 or over on composite. 52% of accepted applicants took SAT; 48% took ACT. 80% of freshmen come from public schools.
**Undergraduate achievement:** 92% of fall 1992 freshmen returned for fall 1993 term. 64% of entering class graduated. 40% of students who completed a degree program went on to graduate study within five years.
**Foreign students:** 122 students are from out of the country. Countries represented include Finland, Germany, India, Japan, Korea, and Malaysia; 37 in all.

**PROGRAMS OF STUDY. Degrees:** B.A., B.Mus., B.Mus.Ed., B.S., B.S.Acct., B.S.Admin.Just., B.S.Bus.Admin., B.S.Civil Eng., B.S.Comp.Eng., B.S.Ed., B.S.Elec.Eng., B.S.Fine Arts, B.S.Mech.Eng., B.S.Nurs., B.S.Phys.Ed., B.Soc.Work
**Majors:** Accounting, American Studies, Art, Art Education, Athletic Training, Biochemistry, Biology, British Studies, Cartology/Map Making, Church Music, Civil Engineering, Classics, Communications, Computer Engineering, Computer Science, Criminal Justice, East Asian Studies, Economics, Education, Electrical Engineering, Elementary Education, English, Environmental Management/Land Use Analysis, Film Studies, Finance, Foreign Languages, Geography, Geology, History, Human Resource Management, Humanities, International Economics/Cultural Affairs, Journalism, Management, Marketing, Mathematics, Mechanical Engineering, Medical Technology, Meterology/Weather Forecasting, Music, Music Education, Music History, Music Merchandising, Music Performance, Music Theory, Nursing, Philosophy, Physical Education, Physics, Political Science, Psychology, Regional/Urban Planning, Secondary Education, Social Studies, Social Work, Sociology, Special Education, Speech/Drama, Studio Art, Theatre, Theology, Urban Studies.
**Distribution of degrees:** The majors with the highest enrollment are business administration, nursing, and education; philosophy, Latin, and classics have the lowest.
**Requirements:** General education requirement.
**Academic regulations:** Minimum 2.00 GPA must be maintained.
**Special:** Minors offered in many majors and in acting, gerontology, Hebrew, information systems, liberal arts/business, theatre design, theatre production, and writing. Interdepartmental courses. Honors students may enter additional undergraduate college, Christ Coll, in freshman year. Deaconess training program. Associate's degrees offered. Self-designed majors. Double majors. Dual degrees. Independent study. Accelerated study. Pass/fail grading option. Internships. Cooperative education programs. Graduate school at which undergraduates may take graduate-level courses. Preprofessional programs in law, medicine, veterinary science, dentistry, theology, optometry, physical therapy, and podiatry. Member of Associated Colleges of the Midwest and American Schools of Oriental Studies. Washington Semester and UN Semester. Urban Studies Program (Chicago). Teacher certification in elementary, secondary, and special education. Certification in specific subject areas. Study abroad in China, England, France, Germany, Japan, Mexico, and other countries.
**Honors:** Honors program.
**Academic Assistance:** Nonremedial tutoring.

**STUDENT LIFE. Housing:** All unmarried students under age 21 must live on campus unless living near campus with relatives. Coed, women's, and men's dorms. Sorority and fraternity housing. 92% of students live in college housing.
**Social atmosphere:** According to the student newspaper, Valparaiso is "extremely conservative with little in the way of non-Greek involvement. The university is fortunate in that it's near Chicago. Nearly 50 percent of the student population is Greek. It is far and away the greatest influence on social life at VU. The Lutheran affiliation of this university makes for much Christian group activity." Favorite off-campus spots include Jackson's, Restaurant Gasagallardo, and the Gathering Restaurant. Chicago, an hour's drive, is a popular destination. Popular school-year events include Jazz Fest, Spring Weekend, Madrigal Dinner, and Homecoming.
**Services and counseling/handicapped student services:** Placement services. Health service. Counseling services for minority, military, and veteran students. Personal and psychological counseling. Career and academic guidance services. Religious counseling.
**Campus organizations:** Undergraduate student government. Student newspaper (Torch, published once/week). Literary magazine. Yearbook. Radio and TV stations. Bands, orchestra, choirs, dance troupe, drama productions, debating, Union Board, service fraternity, variety magazine, professional and special-interest groups, 150 organizations in all. 12 fraternities, all with chapter houses; eight sororities, no chapter houses. 48% of men join a fraternity. 40% of women join a sorority.
**Religious organizations:** Campus Life, Christian Law Society, Intersorority Christian Fellowship, Nurses Christian Fellowship, Altar Guild, Thunderhouse-Newman Center, mime/clown ministry, other religious groups.
**Minority/foreign student organizations:** Black Student Organization, Black Cultural Center, Black American Law Student Group, Office of Minority Programs. International Student Association, Global Nomads, VISA.

**ATHLETICS. Physical education requirements:** One semester of physical education required.
**Intercollegiate competition:** 11% of students participate. Baseball (M), basketball (M,W), cheerleading (M,W), cross-country (M,W), football (M), soccer (M,W), softball (W), swimming (M,W), tennis (M,W), volleyball (W), wrestling (M). Member of Mid-Continent Conference, NCAA Division I, NCAA Division I-AA for football, Pioneer Football League.
**Intramural and club sports:** 65% of students participate. Intramural badminton, basketball, bike racing, billiards, bowling, cross-country, field day, football, golf, racquetball, soccer, softball, volleyball, water basketball. Women's club soccer.

**ADMISSIONS. Academic basis for candidate selection** (in order of priority): Secondary school record, class rank, standardized test scores, school's recommendation, essay.
**Nonacademic basis for candidate selection:** Character and personality and extracurricular participation are important. Particular talent or ability, geographical distribution, and alumni/ae relationship are considered.
**Requirements:** Graduation from secondary school is required; GED is accepted. No specific distribution of secondary school units required. Audition required of music program applicants. SAT or ACT is required. PSAT is recommended. Campus visit and interview recommended. Off-campus interviews available with an admissions representative.
**Procedure:** Take SAT or ACT by December of 12th year. Notification of admission on rolling basis. Reply is required by May 1. $50 tuition deposit, refundable until May 1. $150 room deposit, refundable until May 1. Freshmen accepted for terms other than fall.
**Special programs:** Admission may be deferred one year. Credit and/or placement may be granted through CEEB Advanced Placement exams for scores of 4 or higher. Credit may be granted through CLEP general and subject exams. Credit and placement may be granted through challenge exams. Concurrent enrollment program.
**Transfer students:** Transfer students accepted for terms other than fall. Application deadline is rolling for fall; rolling for spring. Minimum 2.0 GPA required. Lowest course grade accepted is "C-." Maximum number of transferable credits is 94 semester hours. At least 30 semester hours must be completed at the university to receive degree.
**Admissions contact:** Karen Foust, Director of Admissions Recruitment. 219 464-5011.

**FINANCIAL AID. Available aid:** Pell grants, SEOG, Federal Nursing Student Scholarships, state scholarships and grants, school scholarships and grants, private scholarships and grants, academic merit scholarships, athletic scholarships, and aid for undergraduate foreign students. Perkins Loans (NDSL), PLUS, Stafford Loans (GSL), NSL, state loans, school loans, private loans, and SLS. AMS and guaranteed tuition.
**Financial aid statistics:** In 1993-94, 80% of all undergraduate applicants received aid; 79% of freshman applicants. Average amounts of aid awarded freshmen: Scholarships and grants, $4,170; loans, $3,625.
**Supporting data/closing dates:** FAFSA: Priority filing date is March 1. School's own aid application: Priority filing date is March 1. State aid form: Deadline is March 1. Income tax forms: Accepted on rolling basis. Notification of awards begins March 15.
**Financial aid contact:** David Fevig, M.S., Director of Financial Aid. 219 464-5015.

**STUDENT EMPLOYMENT.** College Work/Study Program. Institutional employment. 36% of full-time undergraduates work on campus during school year. Students may expect to earn an average of $710 during school year. Off-campus part-time employment opportunities rated "fair."

**COMPUTER FACILITIES.** 325 IBM/IBM-compatible and Macintosh/Apple microcomputers; 276 are networked. Students may access Digital minicomputer/mainframe systems, Internet. Computer languages and software packages include BASIC, COBOL, FORTRAN, Pascal. Computer facilities are available to all students.
**Fees:** Computer fee is included in tuition/fees.
**Hours:** 7:30 AM-11 PM.

**GRADUATE CAREER DATA.** Graduate school percentages: 1% enter law school. 1% enter medical school. 1% enter graduate business programs. 20% enter graduate arts and sciences programs. Highest graduate school enrollments: U of Chicago, Indiana U, Northwestern U, Purdue U. Companies and businesses that hire graduates: Amoco, Arthur Andersen, Bethlehem Steel, Coopers & Lybrand, General Dynamics, General Motors, McDonnell Douglas, Mobil Oil, National Security Agency, Price Waterhouse, Rush-Presbyterian-St. Luke's Hospital, TRW, UNISYS, U.S. Air Force.

**PROMINENT ALUMNI/AE.** Ray Scherer, former NBC News White House correspondent; Gerhard Freche, president and CEO, New England Telephone; Donald Fites, president, Caterpillar, Inc.; David Ruprecht, actor; Bill Buhler, head trainer, Los Angeles Dodgers; William Dannemeyer, U.S. congressman; Jill L. Long, congresswoman.

# Wabash College

**Crawfordsville, IN 47933-0352 — 317 362-1400**

**1994-95 Costs.** Tuition: $12,925. Room: $1,480. Board: $2,715. Fees, books, misc. academic expenses (school's estimate): $750.
**Enrollment.** 801 men (full-time). Freshman class: 741 applicants, 623 accepted, 256 enrolled.
**Test score averages/ranges.** Range of SAT scores of middle 50%: 440-580 verbal, 540-660 math.
**Faculty.** 79 full-time; 5 part-time. 89% of faculty holds doctoral degree. Student/faculty ratio: 11 to 1.
**Selectivity rating.** Highly competitive.

**PROFILE.** Wabash, founded in 1832, is a private, liberal arts college for men. Its 50-acre campus is located in Crawfordsville, 45 miles northwest of Indianapolis.

**Accreditation:** NCACS.
**Religious orientation:** Wabash College is nonsectarian; no religious requirements.
**Library:** Collections totaling over 227,800 volumes, 864 periodical subscriptions, and 8,182 microform items.
**Special facilities/museums:** Two art galleries, language lab, electron microscope, atomic absorption, nuclear, infrared, electron paramagnetic resonance spectrometers.
**Athletic facilities:** Swimming pool, gymnasium, tracks, recreation, training, weight, and wrestling rooms, basketball, handball, racquetball, and tennis courts, baseball, football, rugby, and soccer fields, stadium.

**STUDENT BODY. Undergraduate profile:** 81% are state residents; 6% are transfers. 3% Asian-American, 6% Black, 3% Hispanic, 1% Native American, 82% White, 5% Other. Average age of undergraduates is 20.

**Freshman profile:** 2% of freshmen who took SAT scored 700 or over on verbal, 14% scored 700 or over on math; 22% scored 600 or over on verbal, 50% scored 600 or over on math; 60% scored 500 or over on verbal, 85% scored 500 or over on math; 91% scored 400 or over on verbal, 99% scored 400 or over on math; 100% scored 300 or over on verbal, 100% scored 300 or over on math. 98% of accepted applicants took SAT. 80% of freshmen come from public schools.
**Undergraduate achievement:** 86% of fall 1992 freshmen returned for fall 1993 term. 77% of entering class graduated. 43% of students who completed a degree program immediately went on to graduate study.
**Foreign students:** 42 students are from out of the country. Countries represented include Bangladesh, China, Gambia, Greece, India, and Malaysia; 25 in all.
**PROGRAMS OF STUDY. Degrees:** A.B.
**Majors:** Art, Biology, Chemistry, Classical Civilizations, Economics, English, French, German, Greek, History, Latin, Mathematics, Music, Philosophy, Physics, Political Science, Psychology, Religion, Spanish, Speech, Theatre.
**Distribution of degrees:** The majors with the highest enrollment are history, economics, and English; Greek, music, and German have the lowest.
**Requirements:** General education requirement.
**Academic regulations:** Freshmen must maintain minimum 1.10 GPA; sophomores, 1.40 GPA; juniors, 1.70 GPA; seniors, 2.0 GPA.
**Special:** Minors offered in all majors and in computer science. Far Eastern area and Afro-American studies programs. Courses not counted toward graduation requirements may be taken on credit/no credit basis; includes accounting, important books, computer science, and physical education. Independent study project may be substituted for one regular course otherwise taken in a concentration. Three marine biology summer sessions. Freshman Tutorial and Sophomore Cultures and Traditions programs. Double majors. Independent study. Pass/fail grading option. Internships. Preprofessional programs in law, medicine, dentistry, and engineering. 3-2 engineering programs with Columbia U and Washington U. 3-3 law program with Columbia U. Member of Great Lakes Colleges Association. Washington Semester and Sea Semester. Oak Ridge Science Semester (Tennessee), Newberry Library Semester (Chicago), New York Arts Semester. Teacher certification in secondary education. Study abroad in Austria, England, France, Germany, Scotland, and Spain.
**Honors:** Phi Beta Kappa. Honor societies.
**Academic Assistance:** Nonremedial tutoring.
**ADMISSIONS. Academic basis for candidate selection** (in order of priority): Secondary school record, class rank, standardized test scores, school's recommendation, essay.
**Nonacademic basis for candidate selection:** Character and personality are emphasized. Extracurricular participation, particular talent or ability, geographical distribution, and alumni/ae relationship are considered.
**Requirements:** Graduation from secondary school is recommended; GED is accepted. 15 units and the following program of study are recommended: 4 units of English, 3 units of math, 2 units of foreign language, 2 units of social studies, 2 units of history. Additional math units recommended. Minimum SAT scores of 450 in both math and verbal, rank in top third of secondary school class, and minimum 2.7 GPA recommended. SAT is required; ACT may be substituted. Campus visit and interview recommended. Off-campus interviews available with admissions and alumni representatives.
**Procedure:** Take SAT or ACT by December of 12th year. Suggest filing application by December 1. Application deadline is April 1. Notification of admission on rolling basis. Reply is required by May 1. $150 nonrefundable tuition deposit. $50 nonrefundable room deposit. Freshmen accepted for terms other than fall.
**Special programs:** Admission may be deferred one year. Credit and/or placement may be granted through CEEB Advanced Placement exams for scores of 3 or higher. Credit and/or placement may be granted through CLEP general and subject exams. Credit and placement may be granted through challenge exams. Early entrance/early admission program.
**Transfer students:** Transfer students accepted for terms other than fall. for fall 1993, 6% of all new students were transfers into all classes. 56 transfer applications were received, 24 were accepted. Application deadline is July 1 for fall; December 1 for spring. Minimum 2.5 GPA recommended. Lowest course grade accepted is "C." At least half of required semester hours must be completed at the college to receive degree.
**Admissions contact:** Greg Birk, Director of Admissions. 317 364-4225, 800 345-5385.
**FINANCIAL AID. Available aid:** Pell grants, SEOG, state scholarships and grants, school scholarships and grants, private scholarships and grants, academic merit scholarships, and aid for undergraduate foreign students. PLUS, Stafford Loans (GSL), school loans, and SLS. Knight Tuition Plans and AMS.
**Financial aid statistics:** In 1993-94, 70% of all undergraduate applicants received aid; 75% of freshman applicants. Average amounts of aid awarded freshmen: Scholarships and grants, $9,755; loans, $2,425.
**Supporting data/closing dates:** FAFSA: Priority filing date is March 1. FAF: Priority filing date is March 1; accepted on rolling basis. Income tax forms: Priority filing date is April 1; accepted on rolling basis. Notification of awards on rolling basis.
**Financial aid contact:** Lester L. Hearson, Ph.D., Director of Financial Aid. 317 364-4370.

# Iowa

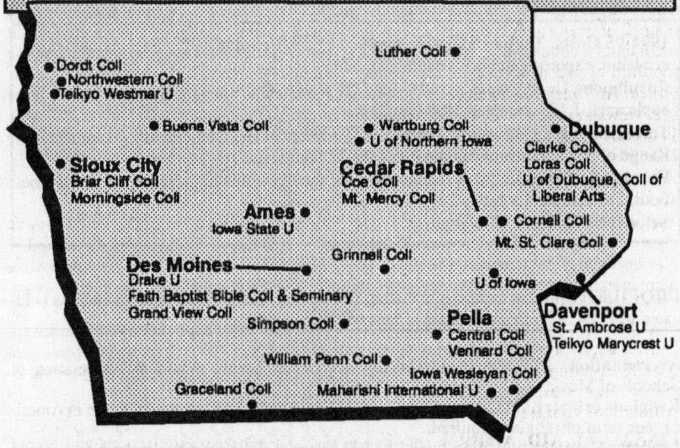


## Briar Cliff College

**Sioux City, IA 51104-2100** **712 279-5321**

**1994-95 Costs.** Tuition: $10,260. Room & board: $3,597. Fees, books, misc. academic expenses (school's estimate): $750.
**Enrollment.** Undergraduates: 255 men, 437 women (full-time). Freshman class: 426 applicants, 418 accepted, 155 enrolled.
**Test score averages/ranges.** Average SAT scores: 385 verbal, 410 math. Average ACT scores: 22 composite. Range of ACT scores of middle 50%: 17-24 English, 18-25 math.
**Faculty.** 64 full-time; 9 part-time. 65% of faculty holds highest degree in specific field. Student/faculty ratio: 12 to 1.
**Selectivity rating.** Less competitive.

**PROFILE.** Briar Cliff is a church-affiliated, liberal arts college. It was founded as a two-year college for women in 1930, became a four-year college in 1937, and adopted coeducation in 1966. Its 70-acre campus is located near downtown Sioux City.

**Accreditation:** NCACS. Professionally accredited by the Council on Social Work Education, the National League for Nursing.
**Religious orientation:** Briar Cliff College is affiliated with the Roman Catholic Church (Sisters of St. Francis of the Holy Family); three credit hours of theology or ethics required.
**Library:** Collections totaling over 100,773 volumes, 529 periodical subscriptions, and 31,397 microform items.
**Special facilities/museums:** Art gallery.
**Athletic facilities:** Gymnasium, field house, basketball, racquetball, tennis, and volleyball courts, weight rooms, baseball, intramural, soccer, and softball fields.
**STUDENT BODY. Undergraduate profile:** 70% are state residents; 25% are transfers. 1% Asian-American, 2% Black, 2% Hispanic, 1% Native American, 91% White, 3% Other. Average age of undergraduates is 20.
**Freshman profile:** 17% of freshmen who took SAT scored 700 or over on verbal; 17% scored 600 or over on math; 34% scored 400 or over on verbal, 34% scored 400 or over on math; 67% scored 300 or over on verbal, 101% scored 300 or over on math. 3% of freshmen who took ACT scored 30 or over on English, 3% scored 30 or over on math, 4% scored 30 or over on composite; 32% scored 24 or over on English, 29% scored 24 or over on math, 36% scored 24 or over on composite; 74% scored 18 or over on English, 70% scored 18 or over on math, 89% scored 18 or over on composite; 91% scored 12 or over on English, 91% scored 12 or over on math, 99% scored 12 or over on composite; 92% scored 6 or over on English, 100% scored 6 or over on composite. Majority of accepted applicants took ACT. 70% of freshmen come from public schools.
**Undergraduate achievement:** 71% of fall 1992 freshmen returned for fall 1993 term. 41% of entering class graduated. 13% of students who completed a degree program immediately went on to graduate study.
**Foreign students:** 27 students are from out of the country. Countries represented include Canada, China, India, Panama, Taiwan and the former Yugoslav Republics; 11 in all.
**PROGRAMS OF STUDY. Degrees:** B.A., B.S., B.S.Nurs.
**Majors:** Accounting, Art, Biology, Business Administration/Management, Chemistry, Computer Science, Criminal Justice, Education, English, Health/Physical Education/Recreation, History, Human Resource Management, Mass Communications, Mathematics, Medical Technology, Music, Nursing, Psychology, Radiologic Technology, Social Work, Sociology, Spanish, Theatre, Theology, Writing.
**Distribution of degrees:** The majors with the highest enrollment are business, psychology, and nursing; secondary education and computer science have the lowest.
**Requirements:** General education requirement.
**Academic regulations:** Minimum 2.0 GPA must be maintained.
**Special:** Minors offered in most majors and in management information systems, peace studies, philosophy, physics, political science, recreation/leisure, and speech/theatre. "Mini courses" for freshmen and sophomores. Freshmen Liberal Arts Program stresses identity in relation to the modern world. Vocations Discernment professional program for those considering religious vocations in the Catholic Church. Associate's degrees offered. Self-designed majors. Double majors. Dual degrees. Independent study. Pass/fail grading option. Internships. Preprofessional programs in law, medicine, veterinary science, pharmacy, dentistry, theology, optometry, chiropractic, engineering, occupational therapy, peace/conflict studies, physical therapy, and physician assistant. 2-2 and 3-2 engineering programs with Iowa State U. 3-1 medical technology program with St. Luke's Sch of Nursing. 1-3-1 radiologic technology program with Marian Health Center, Sch of Radiologic Tech. Member of Colleges of Mid-America Consortium. Washington Semester. Urban Studies Program (Chicago). Teacher certification in elementary and secondary education. Study abroad possible.
**Honors:** Honor societies.
**Academic Assistance:** Remedial reading, writing, math, and study skills. Nonremedial tutoring.

**ADMISSIONS. Academic basis for candidate selection** (in order of priority): Secondary school record, class rank, standardized test scores, school's recommendation.
**Nonacademic basis for candidate selection:** Extracurricular participation is emphasized. Particular talent or ability is important. Character and personality are considered.
**Requirements:** Graduation from secondary school is required; GED is accepted. 16 units and the following program of study are recommended: 4 units of English, 4 units of math, 3 units of science, 2 units of foreign language, 1 unit of social studies, 2 units of history. Two of the following are required: minimum composite ACT score of 19, rank in top half of secondary school class, minimum 2.25 GPA. Conditional admission possible for applicants not meeting standard requirements. ACT is required; SAT may be substituted. Campus visit and interview recommended. Off-campus interviews available with an admissions representative.
**Procedure:** Take SAT or ACT by October of 12th year. Suggest filing application by February 1; no deadline. Notification of admission on rolling basis. Reply is required within 30 days of acceptance. $50 tuition deposit, refundable until May 1. Freshmen accepted for terms other than fall.
**Special programs:** Admission may be deferred one year. Credit may be granted through CEEB Advanced Placement for scores of 3 or higher. Credit may be granted through CLEP general and subject exams. Credit and placement may be granted through ACT PEP exams and life experience. Early entrance/early admission program. Concurrent enrollment program.
**Transfer students:** Transfer students accepted for terms other than fall. In fall 1993, 25% of all new students were transfers into all classes. 98 transfer applications were received, 75 were accepted. Application deadline is rolling for fall; rolling for spring. Minimum 2.0 GPA required. Lowest course grade accepted is "D." Maximum number of transferable credits is 60 semester hours. At least 30 semester hours must be completed at the college to receive degree.
**Admissions contact:** Sharisue Wilcoxon, M.B.A., Executive Director of Marketing and Admissions. 712 279-5200, 800 662-3303.

**FINANCIAL AID. Available aid:** Pell grants, SEOG, state scholarships and grants, school scholarships and grants, private scholarships and grants, academic merit scholarships, athletic scholarships, and aid for undergraduate foreign students. Perkins Loans (NDSL), PLUS, Stafford Loans (GSL), school loans, private loans, and SLS. AMS.
**Financial aid statistics:** 30% of aid is not need-based. In 1993-94, 95% of all undergraduate applicants received aid; 98% of freshman applicants. Average amounts of aid awarded freshmen: Scholarships and grants, $4,900; loans, $3,700.
**Supporting data/closing dates:** FAFSA/FAF/FFS: Priority filing date is April; accepted on rolling basis. Notification of awards begins March 1.
**Financial aid contact:** Donald W. Duzik, Director of Financial Aid. 712 279-5440.

## Buena Vista College

**Storm Lake, IA 50588** **712 749-2351**

**1994-95 Costs.** Tuition: $13,306. Room & board: $3,797. Fees, books, misc. academic expenses (school's estimate): $450.
**Enrollment.** Undergraduates: 475 men, 493 women (full-time). Freshman class: 860 applicants, 688 accepted, 285 enrolled.
**Test score averages/ranges.** Average SAT scores: 521 verbal, 585 math. Range of SAT scores of middle 50%: 495-565 verbal, 565-595 math. Average ACT scores: 24 English, 25 math, 24 composite. Range of ACT scores of middle 50%: 23-26 English, 24-28 math.
**Faculty.** 68 full-time; 14 part-time. 65% of faculty holds doctoral degree. Student/faculty ratio: 14 to 1.
**Selectivity rating.** Competitive.

**PROFILE.** Buena Vista, founded in 1891, is a church-affiliated, liberal arts college. Its 50-acre campus is located in Storm Lake, 70 miles east of Sioux City.

**Accreditation:** NCACS. Professionally accredited by the National Council for Accreditation of Teacher Education.
**Religious orientation:** Buena Vista College is affiliated with the General Assembly of the Presbyterian Church USA; no religious requirements.
**Library:** Collections totaling over 131,000 volumes, 660 periodical subscriptions, and 15,000 microform items.
**Special facilities/museums:** Art gallery language lab, television station, radio station, satellite telecommunications system, computer labs/centers, electron microscope.
**Athletic facilities:** Gymnasium, field house, weight and wrestling rooms, swimming pool, basketball, racquetball, tennis, and volleyball courts, stadium, track, golf course, swimming pool, batting nets, aerobics/dance studio, athletic fields.
**STUDENT BODY. Undergraduate profile:** 76% are state residents; 18% are transfers. 1% Asian-American, 1% Black, 1% Hispanic, 93% White, 4% Other. Average age of undergraduates is 20.

**Freshman profile:** 10% of freshmen who took ACT scored 30 or over on composite; 76% scored 24 or over on composite; 97% scored 18 or over on composite; 100% scored 12 or over on composite. 15% of accepted applicants took SAT; 97% took ACT. 96% of freshmen come from public schools.

**Undergraduate achievement:** 72% of fall 1992 freshmen returned for fall 1993 term. 56% of entering class graduated. 12% of students who completed a degree program immediately went on to graduate study.

**Foreign students:** 40 students are from out of the country. Countries represented include China, Japan, Korea, Malaysia, and Taiwan; 10 in all.

**PROGRAMS OF STUDY. Degrees:** B.A., B.S.

**Majors:** Accounting, Art, Arts Management, Athletic Training, Banking/Finance, Biology, Business, Business Education, Chemistry, Computer/Information Sciences, Corporate Communications, Criminal Justice, Distributive Major, Economics, Elementary Education, English, General Science, Health/Physical Education, History, International Business, Management/Entrepreneurship, Management Information Systems, Mass Communications, Mathematics, Mathematics/Physics, Modern Languages, Music, Political Science, Psychology, Religion/Philosophy, Science, Social Sciences, Social Work, Spanish, Special Education, Speech/Drama.

**Distribution of degrees:** The majors with the highest enrollment are business, education, and science; religion/philosophy, art, and history have the lowest.

**Requirements:** General education requirement.

**Academic regulations:** Freshmen must maintain minimum 1.7 GPA; sophomores, 1.8 GPA; juniors, 1.9 GPA; seniors, 2.0 GPA.

**Special:** Minors offered in most majors and in physics and recreation; numerous career minors offered. Distributive major; student designs program with supervising faculty committee. Academic and Cultural Event Series required for graduation. Self-designed majors. Double majors. Dual degrees. Independent study. Accelerated study. Pass/fail grading option. Internships. Preprofessional programs in law, medicine, veterinary science, pharmacy, dentistry, theology, optometry, chiropractic, engineering, mortuary science, osteopathy, and podiatry. 3-2 engineering program with Washington U. Off-campus or foreign study for semester, year, or summer. Teacher certification in elementary, secondary, and special education. Certification in specific subject areas. Exchange programs abroad in Japan (Hokusei Gakuen Coll) and Taiwan (Taipei Language Inst). Study abroad in China, Korea, Mexico, and European countries. Student teaching in England.

**Honors:** Honors program. Honor societies.

**Academic Assistance:** Nonremedial tutoring.

**ADMISSIONS. Academic basis for candidate selection** (in order of priority): Secondary school record, standardized test scores, school's recommendation, class rank.

**Nonacademic basis for candidate selection:** Particular talent or ability is emphasized. Extracurricular participation is important. Character and personality, geographical distribution, and alumni/ae relationship are considered.

**Requirements:** Graduation from secondary school is required; GED is accepted. 14 units and the following program of study are recommended: 4 units of English, 3 units of math, 3 units of science, 2 units of foreign language, 2 units of social studies. Minimum composite ACT score of 21, rank in top half of secondary school class, and minimum 2.8 GPA recommended. Audition required of drama and music program applicants and talent scholarships applicants. Portfolio required of art program applicants. ACT is required; SAT may be substituted. Campus visit and interview recommended. Off-campus interviews available with an admissions representative.

**Procedure:** Take SAT or ACT by February of 12th year. Visit college for interview by April 1 of 12th year. Suggest filing application by February 1. Application deadline is May 1. Notification of admission on rolling basis. No set date by which applicant must accept offer. $50 tuition deposit, refundable until May 1. $100 room deposit, refundable until May 1. Freshmen accepted for terms other than fall.

**Special programs:** Admission may be deferred one semester. Credit and/or placement may be granted through CEEB Advanced Placement exams for scores of 4 or higher. Credit and/or placement may be granted through CLEP general and subject exams. Credit may be granted through military and life experience. Early decision program. In fall 1993, 350 applied for early decision and 300 were accepted. Deadline for applying for early decision is January 15. Early entrance/early admission program. Concurrent enrollment program.

**Transfer students:** Transfer students accepted for terms other than fall. In fall 1993, 18% of all new students were transfers into all classes. 133 transfer applications were received, 107 were accepted. Application deadline is May 1 for fall; January 30 for spring. Minimum 2.5 GPA recommended. Lowest course grade accepted is "C." Maximum number of transferable credits is 98 semester hours. At least 30 semester hours must be completed at the college to receive degree.

**Admissions contact:** Joanne Loonan, M.A., Director of Admissions. 712 749-2235, 800 383-9600.

**FINANCIAL AID. Available aid:** Pell grants, SEOG, state scholarships and grants, school scholarships and grants, private scholarships and grants, academic merit scholarships, and aid for undergraduate foreign students. Perkins Loans (NDSL), PLUS, Stafford Loans (GSL), school loans, private loans, and SLS. Knight Tuition Plans and deferred payment plan.

**Financial aid statistics:** 18% of aid is not need-based. In 1993-94, 98% of all undergraduate applicants received aid; 98% of freshman applicants. Average amounts of aid awarded freshmen: Scholarships and grants, $8,658; loans, $3,544.

**Supporting data/closing dates:** FAFSA: Priority filing date is April 20. Notification of awards on rolling basis.

**Financial aid contact:** Leanne Valentine, Director of Financial Aid. 712 749-2164, 800 383-2821.

# Central College

**Pella, IA 50219** **515 628-9000**

**1994-95 Costs.** Tuition: $10,938. Room: $1,638. Board: $2,022. Fees, books, misc. academic expenses (school's estimate): $791.

**Enrollment.** Undergraduates: 604 men, 751 women (full-time). Freshman class: 1,293 applicants, 1,123 accepted, 400 enrolled.

**Test score averages/ranges.** Average ACT scores: 24 English, 23 math, 24 composite. Range of ACT scores of middle 50%: 20-27 composite.

**Faculty.** 81 full-time; 50 part-time. 86% of faculty holds highest degree in specific field. Student/faculty ratio: 14 to 1.

**Selectivity rating.** Competitive.

**PROFILE.** Central is a church-affliated, liberal arts college. The modern campus is located in Pella, 45 miles southeast of Des Moines.

**Accreditation:** NCACS. Professionally accredited by the National Association of Schools of Music.

**Religious orientation:** Central College is affiliated with the Reformed Church in America; one term of religion required.

**Library:** Collections totaling over 170,500 volumes, 940 periodical subscriptions, and 32,500 microform items.

**Special facilities/museums:** Art gallery, center for communication and theatre, music center, language lab, glass-blowing studio.

**Athletic facilities:** Athletic complex, gymnasium, field house, stadium, racquetball and tennis courts, tracks, weight training area, athletic fields, batting cages, golf driving range.

**STUDENT BODY. Undergraduate profile:** 79% are state residents; 12% are transfers. 2% Asian-American, 1% Black, 2% Hispanic, 90% White, 5% Other. Average age of undergraduates is 20.

**Freshman profile:** 18% of accepted applicants took SAT; 92% took ACT. 97% of freshmen come from public schools.

**Undergraduate achievement:** 82% of fall 1992 freshmen returned for fall 1993 term. 61% of entering class graduated. 16% of students who completed a degree program immediately went on to graduate study.

**Foreign students:** 62 students are from out of the country. Countries represented include Austria, China, France, Japan, Mexico, and Spain; 18 in all.

**PROGRAMS OF STUDY. Degrees:** B.A.

**Majors:** Accounting, Art, Biology, Business Management, Chemistry, Communication/Theatre, Computer/Information Sciences, Economics, Elementary Education, English, Environmental Studies, French, General Studies, German, History, International Business Management, International Studies, Latin American Studies, Linguistics, Mathematics/Computer Science, Music, Music Education, Philosophy, Physical Education, Physics, Political Science/Government, Psychology, Recreation, Religion, Sociology, Spanish, Systems Management, Urban Studies, Western European Studies.

**Distribution of degrees:** The majors with the highest enrollment are management, education, and foreign languages; religion, urban studies, and interdisciplinary have the lowest.

**Requirements:** General education requirement.

**Academic regulations:** Freshmen must maintain minimum 1.70 GPA; sophomores, 1.80 GPA; juniors, 2.00 GPA; seniors, 2.00 GPA.

**Special:** Minors offered in all majors. Student participation in faculty research projects encouraged. Self-designed majors. Double majors. Independent study. Pass/fail grading option. Internships. Preprofessional programs in law, medicine, veterinary science, pharmacy, dentistry, theology, optometry, health science, occupational therapy, physical therapy, engineering, and architecture. 3-2 engineering and occupational therapy program and 3-4 architecture program with Washington U. Washington Semester. Chicago Metro Program. Teacher certification in early childhood, elementary, and secondary education. Certification in specific subject areas. Study abroad in Austria, China, England, France, Mexico, the Netherlands, Spain, and Wales.

**Honors:** Honors program. Honor societies.

**Academic Assistance:** Remedial reading, writing, math, and study skills. Nonremedial tutoring.

**STUDENT LIFE. Housing:** All unmarried students under age 21 must live on campus unless living near campus with relatives. Coed, women's, and men's dorms. Sorority and fraternity housing. On-campus married-student housing. Coed townhouses. 96% of students live in college housing.

**Services and counseling/handicapped student services:** Placement services. Health service. Personal counseling. Career and academic guidance services. Religious counseling. Physically disabled student services. Learning disabled services. Notetaking services. Tape recorders. Tutors. Reader services for the blind.

**Campus organizations:** Undergraduate student government. Student newspaper (Ray, published once/week). Literary magazine. Yearbook. Radio station. Orchestra, marching band, jazz ensemble, wind symphony, a cappella choir, chamber singers, drama group, speech teams, speaking groups, Association of Women Students, dorm councils, Activity Board, Amnesty International, Students Concerned about the Environment, athletic, departmental, service, and special-interest groups, 56 organizations in all. Four fraternities, all with chapter houses; two sororities, all with chapter houses. 7% of men join a fraternity. 4% of women join a sorority.

**Religious organizations:** Fellowship of Christian Athletes, Campus Ministries, Action, Intervarsity Christian Fellowship.

**Minority/foreign student organizations:** Coalition for a Multicultural Campus. International Student Association.

**ATHLETICS. Physical education requirements:** None.

**Intercollegiate competition:** 30% of students participate. Baseball (M), basketball (M,W), cheerleading (M,W), cross-country (M,W), football (M), golf (M,W), soccer (M), softball (W), tennis (M,W), track and field (indoor) (M,W), track and field (outdoor) (M,W), volleyball (W), wrestling (M). Member of Iowa Intercollegiate Athletic Conference, NCAA Division III.
**Intramural and club sports:** 74% of students participate. Intramural archery, badminton, basketball, bowling, canoeing, flag football, racquetball, softball, track, volleyball, walleyball. Men's club rugby, soccer. Women's club soccer.
**ADMISSIONS. Academic basis for candidate selection** (in order of priority): Secondary school record, class rank, standardized test scores, school's recommendation, essay.
**Nonacademic basis for candidate selection:** Extracurricular participation is emphasized. Character and personality, particular talent or ability, and geographical distribution are important. Alumni/ae relationship is considered.
**Requirements:** Graduation from secondary school is required; GED is accepted. 15 units required and the following program of study recommended: 4 units of English, 3 units of math, 2 units of science, 2 units of foreign language, 3 units of social sstudies, 2 units of history. Minimum composite ACT score of 20, rank in top half of secondary school class, and minimum 2.75 GPA recommended. Guided Studies program for applicants not normally admissible. ACT is required; SAT may be substituted. ACH recommended. Campus visit and interview recommended. Off-campus interviews available with an admissions representative.
**Procedure:** Take SAT or ACT by January of 12th year. Visit college for interview by March 1 of 12th year. Suggest filing application by January 1. Notification of admission on rolling basis. Reply is required within 30 days of acceptance. $50 tuition deposit, refundable until May 1. $50 room deposit, refundable until May 1. Freshmen accepted for terms other than fall.
**Special programs:** Admission may be deferred one year. Credit and/or placement may be granted through CEEB Advanced Placement exams for scores of 3 or higher. Credit and/or placement may be granted through CLEP subject exams. Credit and placement may be granted through challenge exams. Concurrent enrollment program.
**Transfer students:** Transfer students accepted for terms other than fall. In fall 1993, 12% of all new students were transfers into all classes. 105 transfer applications were received, 76 were accepted. Application deadline is September 1 for fall; January 1 for spring. Minimum 3.0 GPA recommended. Lowest course grade accepted is "C." Maximum number of transferable credits is 100 quarter hours. At least 45 quarter hours must be completed at the college to receive degree.
**Admissions contact:** Eric Sickler, Vice President for Admissions and Marketing. 800 458-5503.
**FINANCIAL AID. Available aid:** Pell grants, SEOG, state scholarships and grants, school scholarships and grants, private scholarships and grants, academic merit scholarships, and aid for undergraduate foreign students. Perkins Loans (NDSL), PLUS, Stafford Loans (GSL), school loans, private loans, and SLS. AMS. Installment Plan.
**Financial aid statistics:** 51% of aid is not need-based. In 1993-94, 87% of all undergraduate applicants received aid; 97% of freshman applicants. Average amounts of aid awarded freshmen: Scholarships and grants, $7,239; loans, $2,582.
**Supporting data/closing dates:** FAFSA/FAF/FFS: Accepted on rolling basis. School's own aid application: Priority filing date is January 1; accepted on rolling basis. Notification of awards begins March 1.
**Financial aid contact:** Jean VanderWert, Director of Student Financial Assistance. 515 628-5268.
**STUDENT EMPLOYMENT.** College Work/Study Program. Institutional employment. 86% of full-time undergraduates work on campus during school year. Students may expect to earn an average of $900 during school year. Off-campus part-time employment opportunities rated "good."
**COMPUTER FACILITIES.** 192 IBM/IBM-compatible and Macintosh/Apple microcomputers. Students may access AT&T, Digital minicomputer/mainframe systems, Internet. Client/LAN operating systems include Apple/Macintosh, DOS, UNIX/XENIX/AIX, DEC, LocalTalk/AppleTalk, Novell. Computer languages and software packages include ADA, BASIC, C, COBOL, FORTRAN, LISP, MINITAB, Modula 2, Pascal, Prolog, SPSS; database, spreadsheet, statistical, word processing packages. Computer facilities are available to all students.
**Fees:** None.
**Hours:** 7 AM-11 PM daily.
**GRADUATE CAREER DATA.** Graduate school percentages: 8% enter law school. 23% enter medical school. 2% enter dental school. 4% enter graduate business programs. 13% enter graduate arts and sciences programs. 2% enter theological school/seminary. Highest graduate school enrollments: Drake U, Iowa State U, U of Iowa, U of Kansas. 38% of graduates choose careers in business and industry. Companies and businesses that hire graduates: Principal Financial, FDIC, Pella Corporation.
**PROMINENT ALUMNI/AE.** Steve Bell, anchor, USA network; Harry Smith, co-host, *CBS This Morning;* Dick Shultz, former executive director, NCAA.

## Clarke College

**Dubuque, IA 52001-3198 — 319 588-6300**

**1994-95 Costs.** Tuition: $10,740. Room: $1,838. Board: $1,838. Fees, books, misc. academic expenses (school's estimate): $575.
**Enrollment.** Undergraduates: 192 men, 412 women (full-time). Freshman class: 460 applicants, 340 accepted, 167 enrolled. Graduate enrollment: 1 man, 25 women.
**Test score averages/ranges.** Range of ACT scores of middle 50%: 21-26 composite.
**Faculty.** 57 full-time; 19 part-time. 68% of faculty holds highest degree in specific field. Student/faculty ratio: 12 to 1.
**Selectivity rating.** Less competitive.

**PROFILE.** Clarke is a church-affiliated, liberal arts college. Founded as a women's academy in 1843, it adopted coeducation in 1979. Its 50-acre campus is located in Dubuque.
**Accreditation:** NCACS. Professionally accredited by the Council on Social Work Education, the National Association of Schools of Music, the National Council for Accreditation of Teacher Education, the National League for Nursing.
**Religious orientation:** Clarke College is affiliated with the Roman Catholic Church; two semesters of religion required.
**Library:** Collections totaling over 102,216 volumes, 684 periodical subscriptions, and 8,000 microform items.
**Special facilities/museums:** Art gallery, computer classrooms for math, biology, and computer science, computer-interfaced chemistry lab, electron microscope, music performance hall.
**Athletic facilities:** Gymnasium, field house, swimming pool, weight room, baseball, soccer, and softball fields, track, sand volleyball, tennis, and volleyball courts, fitness trail.

**STUDENT BODY. Undergraduate profile:** 47% are state residents; 27% are transfers. .5% Asian-American, 5% Black, 2% Hispanic, .5% Native American, 92% White. Average age of undergraduates is 23.
**Freshman profile:** 2% of freshmen who took ACT scored 30 or over on composite; 38% scored 24 or over on composite; 93% scored 18 or over on composite; 99% scored 12 or over on composite. 99% of accepted applicants took ACT. 69% of freshmen come from public schools.
**Undergraduate achievement:** 79% of fall 1992 freshmen returned for fall 1993 term. 49% of entering class graduated. 10% of students who completed a degree program immediately went on to graduate study.
**Foreign students:** 13 students are from out of the country. Countries represented include Argentina, Columbia, Japan, Mexico, and Taiwan; six in all.

**PROGRAMS OF STUDY. Degrees:** B.A., B.F.A., B.S.
**Majors:** Accounting, Advertising, Art, Art History, Biochemistry, Biology, Business Administration, Chemistry, Communication, Computer Information/Management Information Systems, Computer Science, Drama/Speech, Education, English, French, German, History, International Business, Marketing, Mathematics, Music, Musical Theatre, Nursing, Peace/Justice, Philosophy, Physical Education, Physical Therapy/Human Biology, Political Science, Psychology, Religious Studies, Sociology, Spanish, Special Education, Studio Art.
**Distribution of degrees:** The majors with the highest enrollment are business administration, accounting, and computer science; philosophy, French, and Spanish have the lowest.
**Requirements:** General education requirement.
**Academic regulations:** Freshmen must maintain minimum 1.8 GPA; sophomores, juniors, seniors, 2.0 GPA.
**Special:** Minors offered in all majors except nursing, education, and physical therapy. Associate's degrees offered. Self-designed majors. Double majors. Dual degrees. Independent study. Accelerated study. Pass/fail grading option. Internships. Cooperative education programs. Graduate school at which undergraduates may take graduate-level courses. Preprofessional programs in law, medicine, veterinary science, pharmacy, dentistry, theology, and optometry. 3-2 engineering program with U of Southern California and Washington U. Medical technology program with Mercy Hospital (Des Moines). Member of Tri-College Cooperative Effort and Mid-America Catholic Colleges (MACC). Teacher certification in early childhood, elementary, secondary, and special education. Certification in specific subject areas. Study abroad in England, Italy, Mexico, and Spain.
**Honors:** Honors program. Honor societies.
**Academic Assistance:** Remedial reading, writing, math, and study skills. Nonremedial tutoring.

**ADMISSIONS. Academic basis for candidate selection** (in order of priority): Secondary school record, standardized test scores, essay, school's recommendation, class rank.
**Requirements:** Graduation from secondary school is recommended; GED is accepted. 18 units and the following program of study are required: 4 units of English, 3 units of math, 2 units of lab science, 2 units of foreign language, 2 units of social studies, 5 units of academic electives. Units in social studies should include history. Minimum composite ACT score of 21 (combined SAT score of 910), rank in top half of secondary school class, and minimum 2.0 GPA required. Conditional admission possible for applicants not meeting standard requirements. ACT is required; SAT may be substituted. Campus visit and interview recommended. Off-campus interviews available with an admissions representative.
**Procedure:** Take SAT or ACT by June of 12th year. Visit college for interview by June of 12th year. Suggest filing application by March 15 (January 15 for physical therapy program applicants). Application deadline is August 15. Notification of admission on rolling basis. No set date by which most applicants must accept offer; applicants to physical therapy program must accept offer within two weeks of notification. $150 tuition deposit, refundable until May 1. $150 room deposit, refundable until May 1. Freshmen accepted for terms other than fall.
**Special programs:** Admission may be deferred one year. Credit and/or placement may be granted through CEEB Advanced Placement exams for scores of 3 or higher. Credit and/or placement may be granted through CLEP general and subject exams. Credit and placement may be granted through ACT PEP exams, and military and life experience. Early entrance/early admission program. Concurrent enrollment program.
**Transfer students:** Transfer students accepted for terms other than fall. In fall 1993, 27% of all new students were transfers into all classes. 170 transfer applications were received, 142 were accepted. Application deadline is August 15 for fall; January 10 for spring. Minimum 2.0 GPA required. Lowest course grade accepted is "C." Maximum number of transferable credits is 64 semester hours from a two-year school and 90 semester hours from a four-year school. At least 34 semester hours must be completed at the college to receive degree.
**Admissions contact:** Bobbe Ames, Vice President for Institutional Marketing/Recruitment. 319 588-6316, 800 383-2345.

**FINANCIAL AID. Available aid:** Pell grants, SEOG, state scholarships and grants, school scholarships and grants, private scholarships and grants, academic merit scholarships, and aid for undergraduate foreign students. Perkins Loans (NDSL), PLUS, Stafford Loans (GSL), NSL, and SLS. Family tuition reduction.

**Financial aid statistics:** 20% of aid is not need-based. In 1993-94, 97% of all undergraduate applicants received aid; 96% of freshman applicants. Average amounts of aid awarded freshmen: Scholarships and grants, $5,619.
**Supporting data/closing dates:** FAFSA: Priority filing date is March 15. Notification of awards on rolling basis.
**Financial aid contact:** Kelly Funk, M.A., Director of Financial Aid. 319 588-6327.

# Coe College

**Cedar Rapids, IA 52402** **319 399-8000**

**1994-95 Costs.** Tuition: $13,925. Room: $1,990. Board: $2,400. Fees, books, misc. academic expenses (school's estimate): $625.
**Enrollment.** Undergraduates: 513 men, 614 women (full-time). Freshman class: 1,006 applicants, 742 accepted, 275 enrolled. Graduate enrollment: 8 men, 14 women.
**Test score averages/ranges.** Average SAT scores: 500 verbal, 560 math. Range of SAT scores of middle 50%: 450-560 verbal, 490-590 math. Average ACT scores: 25 composite. Range of ACT scores of middle 50%: 23-27 composite.
**Faculty.** 83 full-time; 31 part-time. 85% of faculty holds highest degree in specific field. Student/faculty ratio: 13 to 1.
**Selectivity rating.** Competitive.

**PROFILE.** Coe, founded in 1851, is a church-affiliated, liberal arts college. Its campus is located a mile from downtown Cedar Rapids.

**Accreditation:** NCACS. Professionally accredited by the National Association of Schools of Music, the National League for Nursing.
**Religious orientation:** Coe College is affiliated with the United Presbyterian Church; no religious requirements.
**Library:** Collections totaling over 180,448 volumes, 870 periodical subscriptions, and 35,392 microform items.
**Special facilities/museums:** Ornithological museum, foreign language computer lab, writing lab, theatre, greenhouse, planetarium, electron microscope, infrared spectrometer.
**Athletic facilities:** Field house, stadium, football, intramural, and softball fields, tracks, basketball, racquetball, squash, tennis, and volleyball courts, swimming pool, sauna, aerobics and weight rooms.

**STUDENT BODY. Undergraduate profile:** 58% are state residents; 22% are transfers. 2% Asian-American, 3% Black, 2% Hispanic, 1% Native American, 87% White, 5% Other. Average age of undergraduates is 21.
**Freshman profile:** 11% of freshmen who took SAT scored 700 or over on math; 14% scored 600 or over on verbal, 36% scored 600 or over on math; 52% scored 500 or over on verbal, 72% scored 500 or over on math; 92% scored 400 or over on verbal, 96% scored 400 or over on math; 100% scored 300 or over on verbal, 100% scored 300 or over on math. 7% of freshmen who took ACT scored 30 or over on composite; 51% scored 24 or over on composite; 98% scored 18 or over on composite; 100% scored 12 or over on composite. 27% of accepted applicants took SAT; 97% took ACT. 85% of freshmen come from public schools.
**Undergraduate achievement:** 82% of fall 1992 freshmen returned for fall 1993 term. 68% of entering class graduated. 26% of students who completed a degree program immediately went on to graduate study.
**Foreign students:** 66 students are from out of the country. Countries represented include China, India, Japan, Kenya, Malaysia, and Pakistan; 20 in all.

**PROGRAMS OF STUDY. Degrees:** B.A., B.Mus., B.S.Nurs.
**Majors:** Accounting, Afro-American Studies, American Studies, Art, Asian Studies, Biology, Business Administration/Management, Chemistry, Computer/Information Sciences, Economics, Elementary Education, English, French, General Science, German, History, Humanities, Interdisciplinary Studies, Literature, Mathematics, Music, Music Performance, Music Theory/Composition, Nursing, Philosophy, Philosophy/Religion, Physical Education, Physics, Political Science/Government, Psychology, Religion, Secondary Education, Sociology, Spanish, Theatre Arts.
**Distribution of degrees:** The majors with the highest enrollment are economics, psychology, and biology; philosophy and religion have the lowest.
**Requirements:** General education requirement.
**Academic regulations:** Minimum 2.0 GPA must be maintained.
**Special:** Program in computer applications. Three-year degree program for exceptional students begins in freshman year. Community service certificate program. Three- and five-year programs in allied health sciences. Self-designed majors. Double majors. Dual degrees. Independent study. Accelerated study. Pass/fail grading option. Internships. Cooperative education programs. Preprofessional programs in law, medicine, veterinary science, pharmacy, dentistry, and engineering. 3-1 medical technology program. 3-2 engineering program and 3-4 architecture program with Washington U. 3-2 and 3-1 social service administration programs with U of Chicago. 3-2 occupational therapy program with Washington U. Member of Associated Colleges of the Midwest and National Association of Independent Colleges. Washington Semester. New York Semester. Interim exchange programs. Cross-registration programs with U of Iowa and Mount Mercy Coll. Teacher certification in elementary and secondary education. Certification in specific subject areas. Study abroad in China, Costa Rica, England, India, Italy, Japan, Latin American countries, the former Soviet Republics, and Zimbabwe. ROTC at U of Iowa.
**Honors:** Phi Beta Kappa. Honors program. Honor societies.
**Academic Assistance:** Nonremedial tutoring.

**STUDENT LIFE. Housing:** All unmarried students under age 21 must live on campus unless living near campus with relatives. Coed, women's, and men's dorms. Fraternity housing. School-owned/operated apartments. 80% of students live in college housing.
**Social atmosphere:** Hot spots on and off campus include the Pub, Denny's, Leonardo's, the Sip'n Stir, the Maid Rite, Dows Fine Arts Center, the Lambda Chi Alpha Chapter Room, and 7th Murray Lobby. Students groups who influence campus life include Greeks, Cosmos, athletes, and Senate. Popular social events include Flunk Day, Homecoming, football events, movie night, dances, and Block Party.
**Services and counseling/handicapped student services:** Placement services. Health service. Writing center. Counseling services for older students. Personal and psychological counseling. Career and academic guidance services. Religious counseling. Physically disabled student services. Learning disabled services. Notetaking services. Tutors. Reader services for the blind.
**Campus organizations:** Undergraduate student government. Student newspaper (Cosmos, published once/week). Literary magazine. Yearbook. Affiliate artist program, chamber orchestra, city orchestra, choral and instrumental ensembles, several bands, a cappella choir, varsity lettermen group, volunteer bureau, Student Activities Committee, departmental groups, 60 organizations in all. Four fraternities, two chapter houses; three sororities, no chapter houses. 25% of men join a fraternity. 25% of women join a sorority.
**Religious organizations:** Catholic Student Organization, Shalom.
**Minority/foreign student organizations:** Black literary publication, Black Self-Education Organization. International Club.

**ATHLETICS. Physical education requirements:** None.
**Intercollegiate competition:** 30% of students participate. Baseball (M), basketball (M,W), cheerleading (W), cross-country (M,W), diving (M,W), football (M), golf (M,W), soccer (M,W), softball (W), swimming (M,W), tennis (M,W), track (indoor) (M,W), track (outdoor) (M,W), track and field (indoor) (M,W), track and field (outdoor) (M,W), volleyball (W), wrestling (M). Member of Midwest Athletic Conference for Women, Midwest Collegiate Athletic Conference, NCAA Division III.
**Intramural and club sports:** 40% of students participate. Intramural basketball, football, golf, racquetball, soccer, softball, swimming, tennis, volleyball, wrestling.

**ADMISSIONS. Academic basis for candidate selection** (in order of priority): Secondary school record, standardized test scores, class rank, school's recommendation, essay.
**Nonacademic basis for candidate selection:** Character and personality and extracurricular participation are emphasized. Particular talent or ability is important. Alumni/ae relationship is considered.
**Requirements:** Graduation from secondary school is required; GED is accepted. 18 units and the following program of study are recommended: 4 units of English, 3 units of math, 2 units of science including 1 unit of lab, 2 units of foreign language, 2 units of social studies, 2 units of history, 3 units of electives. Minimum composite ACT score of 20, rank in top two-fifths of secondary school class, and minimum 2.6 GPA recommended. Portfolio or audition required of scholarship applicants. Conditional admission possible for applicants not meeting standard requirements. SAT or ACT is required. PSAT is recommended. Campus visit and interview recommended. Off-campus interviews available with admissions and alumni representatives.
**Procedure:** Take SAT or ACT by December of 12th year. Visit college for interview by May 1 of 12th year. Suggest filing application by December 1; no deadline. Notification of admission on rolling basis. Reply is required by May 1. $75 nonrefundable tuition deposit. $75 nonrefundable room deposit. Freshmen accepted for terms other than fall.
**Special programs:** Admission may be deferred two years. Credit and/or placement may be granted through CEEB Advanced Placement exams for scores of 4 or higher. Credit and/or placement may be granted through CLEP subject exams, ACT PEP exams, and military experience. Early decision program. In fall 1993, 22 applied for early decision and 20 were accepted. Deadline for applying for early decision is December 1. Early entrance/early admission program.
**Transfer students:** Transfer students accepted for terms other than fall. In fall 1993, 22% of all new students were transfers into all classes. 183 transfer applications were received, 125 were accepted. Application deadline is rolling for fall; rolling for spring. Minimum 2.5 GPA required. Lowest course grade accepted is "C." Maximum number of transferable credits is 27 course credits. At least nine course credits must be completed at the college to receive degree.
**Admissions contact:** Michael White, M.A., Dean of Admissions and Financial Aid. 319 399-8500.

**FINANCIAL AID. Available aid:** Pell grants, SEOG, state scholarships and grants, school scholarships and grants, private scholarships and grants, ROTC scholarships, academic merit scholarships, and aid for undergraduate foreign students. Perkins Loans (NDSL), PLUS, Stafford Loans (GSL), school loans, and SLS. Institutional monthly payment plan.
**Financial aid statistics:** 20% of aid is not need-based. In 1993-94, 89% of all undergraduate applicants received aid; 84% of freshman applicants. Average amounts of aid awarded freshmen: Scholarships and grants, $8,470; loans, $3,375.
**Supporting data/closing dates:** FAFSA: Priority filing date is March 1. FAF/FFS: Accepted on rolling basis. School's own aid application: Priority filing date is March 1. Income tax forms: Priority filing date is March 1; accepted on rolling basis. Notification of awards on rolling basis.
**Financial aid contact:** Brenda Buzynski, Director of Financial Aid. 319 399-8540.

**STUDENT EMPLOYMENT.** College Work/Study Program. Institutional employment. 47% of full-time undergraduates work on campus during school year. Students may expect to earn an average of $1,100 during school year. Off-campus part-time employment opportunities rated "excellent."

**COMPUTER FACILITIES.** 207 IBM/IBM-compatible, Macintosh/Apple, and RISC-/UNIX-based microcomputers; 60 are networked. Client/LAN operating systems include Apple/Macintosh, DOS, UNIX/XENIX/AIX, LocalTalk/AppleTalk, Novell. Computer languages and software packages include dBASE, Fox pro, Lotus, MINITAB, Pascal, Quattro Pro, SAS, SPSS, W, WordPerfect. Computer facilities are available to all students.
**Fees:** Computer fee is included in tuition/fees.
**Hours:** 8 AM-1 AM (M-Th); 8 AM-5 PM (F); noon-6 PM (Sa); noon-1 AM (Su).

**GRADUATE CAREER DATA.** Graduate school percentages: 5% enter law school. 2% enter medical school. 1% enter dental school. 6% enter graduate business programs. 11% enter graduate arts and sciences programs. 1% enter theological school/seminary. Highest graduate school enrollments: Brown U, Creighton U, U of Iowa, U of Kansas. 66% of graduates choose careers in business and industry. Companies and businesses that hire graduates: Aegon USA, Quaker Oats, school districts.

**PROMINENT ALUMNI/AE.** Marv Levy, head coach, Buffalo Bills; Theodore Miller, editor, *Kiplinger's Magazine;* David Jones, vice president and chief economist, Aubrey Lonston & Co.

# Cornell College

**Mount Vernon, IA 52314 319 895-4000**

**1994-95 Costs.** Tuition: $15,248. Room: $1,978. Board: $2,345. Fees, books, misc. academic expenses (school's estimate): $625.
**Enrollment.** Undergraduates: 482 men, 668 women (full-time). Freshman class: 1,603 applicants, 1,370 accepted, 404 enrolled.
**Test score averages/ranges.** Average SAT scores: 520 verbal, 560 math. Range of SAT scores of middle 50%: 450-580 verbal, 490-630 math. Average ACT scores: 25 composite. Range of ACT scores of middle 50%: 23-28 composite.
**Faculty.** 75 full-time; 50 part-time. 76% of faculty holds doctoral degree. Student/faculty ratio: 14 to 1.
**Selectivity rating.** Competitive.

**PROFILE.** Cornell, founded in 1853, is a private, liberal arts college. Its 110-acre campus is located in the village of Mount Vernon, 10 miles east of Cedar Rapids. The campus, containing several 19th- and early 20th-century buildings, is listed with the National Register of Historic Places.

**Accreditation:** NCACS. Professionally accredited by the National Association of Schools of Music, the National Council for Accreditation of Teacher Education.
**Religious orientation:** Cornell College is affiliated with the Methodist Church; no religious requirements.
**Library:** Collections totaling over 181,500 volumes, 573 periodical subscriptions, and 127,000 microform items.
**Special facilities/museums:** Geology center and museum.
**Athletic facilities:** Gymnasium, field house, basketball, handball, racquetball, tennis, and volleyball courts, weight rooms, tracks, baseball, soccer, and softball fields, swimming pool, football stadium.

**STUDENT BODY. Undergraduate profile:** 27% are state residents; 5% are transfers. 2% Asian-American, 3% Black, 1% Hispanic, 1% Native American, 91% White, 2% Other. Average age of undergraduates is 19.
**Freshman profile:** 4% of freshmen who took SAT scored 700 or over on verbal, 8% scored 700 or over on math; 24% scored 600 or over on verbal, 30% scored 600 or over on math; 58% scored 500 or over on verbal, 75% scored 500 or over on math; 90% scored 400 or over on verbal, 97% scored 400 or over on math; 100% scored 300 or over on verbal, 100% scored 300 or over on math. 13% of freshmen who took ACT scored 30 or over on composite; 72% scored 24 or over on composite; 98% scored 18 or over on composite; 100% scored 12 or over on composite. 40% of accepted applicants took SAT; 92% took ACT. 87% of freshmen come from public schools.
**Undergraduate achievement:** 75% of fall 1992 freshmen returned for fall 1993 term. 65% of entering class graduated. 35% of students who completed a degree program immediately went on to graduate study.
**Foreign students:** 24 students are from out of the country. Countries represented include Brazil, India, Japan, Korea, Malaysia, and Thailand; 16 in all.

**PROGRAMS OF STUDY. Degrees:** B.A., B.Mus., B.Phil., B.Spec.Studies.
**Majors:** Art, Biochemistry/Molecular Biology, Biology, Chemistry, Classical Studies, Computer Science, Economics/Business, Education, Elementary Education, English, Environmental Studies, French, Geology, German, Health/Physical Education, History, International Business, International Relations, Latin American Studies, Mathematics, Medieval/Renaissance Studies, Music, Origins of Behavior, Philosophy, Physics, Politics, Psychology, Religion, Russian, Russian Studies, Secondary Education, Sociology, Sociology/Anthropology, Spanish, Theatre/Communication Studies, Women's Studies.
**Distribution of degrees:** The majors with the highest enrollment are English, economics/business, and psychology; medieval/renaissance studies, Latin American studies, and origins of behavior have the lowest.
**Academic regulations:** Minimum 2.0 GPA must be maintained.
**Special:** Program in ethnic studies. Self-designed majors. Double majors. Independent study. Accelerated study. Pass/fail grading option. Internships. Cooperative education programs. Preprofessional programs in law, medicine, veterinary science, and dentistry. Cooperative nursing and allied health sciences programs with Rush U. Combined degree program in medical technology with two hospitals in Cedar Rapids. 3-4 architecture program with Washington U. Five-year M.B.A. program with U of Iowa. 3-2 forestry and environmental studies programs with Duke U and U of Michigan. 3-2 engineering and occupational therapy programs with Washington U. 3-2 social service administration program with U of Chicago. Member of Associated Colleges of the Midwest. Washington Semester. Exchange program with Fisk U. Teacher certification in elementary and secondary education. Certification in specific subject areas. Study abroad in the Bahamas, Central American countries, East Asian countries, England, India, Italy, Mexico, Puerto Rico, the former Soviet Republics. Experiment in International Living for upperclass students.
**Honors:** Phi Beta Kappa. Honor societies.
**Academic Assistance:** Nonremedial tutoring.

**STUDENT LIFE. Housing:** All unmarried students under age 21 must live on campus unless living near campus with relatives. Coed, women's, and men's dorms. School-owned/operated apartments. Off-campus privately-owned housing. 93% of students live in college housing.
**Social atmosphere:** Favorite gathering spots include the Ratt, the commons, and bars. Groups which influence student life include the media, Greeks, and multicultural groups. Popular events include football games, homecoming, and convocations. There are limited off-campus events and transportation, according to the editor of the student newspaper.
**Services and counseling/handicapped student services:** Placement services. Health service. Counseling services for minority students. Birth control, personal, and psychological counseling. Career and academic guidance services. Religious counseling. Physically disabled student services. Learning disabled services. Notetaking services. Tape recorders. Tutors. Reader services for the blind.
**Campus organizations:** Undergraduate student government. Student newspaper (Cornellian, published three times/month). Literary magazine. Yearbook. Radio station. Band, orchestra, oratorio society, instrumental and vocal ensembles, choir, Commons Union Board, theatre, speech groups, debating, writers club, modern dance group, PIRG, departmental and special-interest groups, 60 organizations in all. Seven fraternities, no chapter houses; six sororities, no chapter houses. 35% of men join a fraternity. 35% of women join a sorority.
**Religious organizations:** Fellowship of Christian Athletes, Intervarsity Christian Fellowship, Religious Life Council.
**Minority/foreign student organizations:** Black Awareness Cultural Organization, Multicultural Task Force, Hispanic Student Organization, Asian-American Student Organization. International Club.

**ATHLETICS. Physical education requirements:** One term of physical education required.
**Intercollegiate competition:** 35% of students participate. Baseball (M), basketball (M,W), cross-country (M,W), diving (M,W), football (M), golf (M), soccer (M,W), softball (W), swimming (M,W), tennis (M,W), track (indoor) (M,W), track (outdoor) (M,W), track and field (indoor) (M,W), track and field (outdoor) (M,W), volleyball (W), wrestling (M). Member of Midwest Athletic Conference for Women, Midwest Collegiate Athletic Conference, NCAA Division III.
**Intramural and club sports:** 75% of students participate. Intramural badminton, basketball, bowling, flag football, frisbee golf, golf, inner-tube water polo, pool, racquetball, softball, table tennis, tennis, track, volleyball, walleyball, wrestling. Men's club ice hockey, volleyball.

**ADMISSIONS. Academic basis for candidate selection** (in order of priority): Secondary school record, class rank, school's recommendation, essay, standardized test scores.
**Nonacademic basis for candidate selection:** Character and personality, extracurricular participation, particular talent or ability, and alumni/ae relationship are important.
**Requirements:** Graduation from secondary school is required; GED is accepted. 15 units and the following program of study are recommended: 4 units of English, 3 units of math, 3 units of science, 2 units of foreign language, 3 units of social studies. Minimum composite ACT score of 20 (minimum combined SAT score of 820), rank in top half of secondary school class, and minimum 2.6 GPA recommended. Conditional admission possible for applicants not meeting standard requirements. SAT or ACT is required. Campus visit and interview recommended. Off-campus interviews available with an admissions representative.
**Procedure:** Take SAT or ACT by January of 12th year. Suggest filing application by March 1; no deadline. Notification of admission by April 1. Reply is required by May 1. $300 nonrefundable tuition deposit. Freshmen accepted for fall terms only.
**Special programs:** Admission may be deferred one year. Credit and/or placement may be granted through CEEB Advanced Placement exams for scores of 3 or higher. Credit and/or placement may be granted through CLEP general and subject exams. Credit may be granted through life experience. Credit and placement may be granted through challenge exams. Early decision program. In fall 1993, 388 applied for early decision and 355 were accepted. Deadline for applying for early decision is December 1. Early entrance/early admission program.
**Transfer students:** Transfer students accepted for terms other than fall. In fall 1993, 5% of all new students were transfers into all classes. 64 transfer applications were received, 41 were accepted. Application deadline is March 1 for fall; November 15 for spring. Minimum 3.0 GPA recommended. Lowest course grade accepted is "C." Maximum number of transferable credits is 96 semester hours. At least 32 semester hours must be completed at the college to receive degree.
**Admissions contact:** Kevin Crockett, Dean of Admissions and Enrollment Management. 800 747-1112.

**FINANCIAL AID. Available aid:** Pell grants, SEOG, state scholarships and grants, school scholarships and grants, private scholarships and grants, academic merit scholarships, aid for undergraduate foreign students, and United Negro College Fund. Perkins Loans (NDSL), PLUS, Stafford Loans (GSL), state loans, school loans, and SLS.
**Financial aid statistics:** 32% of aid is not need-based. In 1993-94, 80% of all undergraduate applicants received aid; 80% of freshman applicants. Average amounts of aid awarded freshmen: Scholarships and grants, $9,000; loans, $3,125.
**Supporting data/closing dates:** FAFSA: Priority filing date is March 1. School's own aid application: Priority filing date is March 1. Income tax forms: Deadline is March 1. Notification of awards begins March 1.
**Financial aid contact:** Julie Junker, Director of Financial Aid. 800 747-1112.

**STUDENT EMPLOYMENT.** College Work/Study Program. Institutional employment. 60% of full-time undergraduates work on campus during school year. Students may expect to earn an average of $1,200 during school year. Off-campus part-time employment opportunities rated "fair."

**COMPUTER FACILITIES.** 175 IBM/IBM-compatible and Macintosh/Apple microcomputers; all are networked. Students may access Digital, Hewlett-Packard minicomputer/mainframe systems, Internet. Residence halls may be equipped with stand-alone microcomputers. Client/LAN operating systems include Apple/Macintosh, DOS, UNIX/XENIX/AIX. 25 major computer languages and software packages available. Computer facilities are available to all students.
**Fees:** Computer fee is included in tuition/fees.
**Hours:** 7 AM-11 PM; 7 AM-1 AM during finals week.

**PROMINENT ALUMNI/AE.** Dr. Campbell McConnell, economics professor, U of Nebraska; David Klaus, economist and educator, World Bank; Richard P. Small, former president, Checker Oil; David Hilmers, astronaut, NASA Space Shuttle Program.

## Dordt College

**Sioux Center, IA 51250** **712 722-3771**

**1993-94 Costs.** Tuition: $9,250. Room & board: $2,440. Fees, books, misc. academic expenses (school's estimate): $680.
**Enrollment.** Undergraduates: 511 men, 537 women (full-time). Freshman class: 604 applicants, 562 accepted, 325 enrolled.
**Test score averages/ranges.** Average ACT scores: 23 composite.
**Faculty.** 72 full-time; 18 part-time. 60% of faculty holds doctoral degree. Student/faculty ratio: 14 to 1.
**Selectivity rating.** Less competitive.

**PROFILE.** Dordt, founded in 1955, is a church-affiliated college. Its 45-acre campus is located in Sioux Center, in Northwest Iowa.

**Accreditation:** NCACS.
**Religious orientation:** Dordt College is affiliated with the Christian Reformed Church; one semester of theology and an additional semester of theology or philosophy required.
**Library:** Collections totaling over 185,000 volumes, 489 periodical subscriptions, and 3,616 microform items.
**Special facilities/museums:** Language lab, access to observatories.
**Athletic facilities:** Swimming pool, gymnasium, track, baseball and softball fields, exercise and weight rooms, racquetball courts.

**STUDENT BODY. Undergraduate profile:** 38% are state residents; 4% are transfers. 3% Asian-American, 1% Black, 1% Hispanic, 93% White, 2% Other. Average age of undergraduates is 22.
**Freshman profile:** 90% of accepted applicants took ACT. 40% of freshmen come from public schools.
**Undergraduate achievement:** 85% of fall 1992 freshmen returned for fall 1993 term. 56% of entering class graduated. 17% of students who completed a degree program immediately went on to graduate study.
**Foreign students:** 164 students are from out of the country. Countries represented include Australia, Canada, Mexico, the Netherlands, Nigeria, and Sierra Leone; eight in all.

**PROGRAMS OF STUDY. Degrees:** B.A., B.S., B.Soc.Work.
**Majors:** Accounting, Agriculture, Agriculture/Business, Art, Biology, Business Administration, Business Education, Chemical Engineering, Chemistry, Classical Studies, Communication, Computer Science, Dutch, Electrical Engineering, Elementary Education, Engineering Science, English, German, History, Individual Studies, Mathematics, Mechanical Engineering, Music, Natural Science, Philosophy, Physical Education, Physics, Political Science, Psychology, Social Sciences, Social Work, Sociology, Spanish, Speech, Theatre Arts, Theology.
**Distribution of degrees:** The majors with the highest enrollment are education, business, and social work; philosophy has the lowest.
**Requirements:** General education requirement.
**Academic regulations:** Freshmen must maintain minimum 1.85 GPA; sophomores, juniors, seniors, 2.0 GPA.
**Special:** Minor offered in church music. Courses offered in economics, geography, Greek, Hebrew, Latin, library science, linguistics, physical science, and reading. Associate's degrees offered. Independent study. Pass/fail grading option. Graduate school at which undergraduates may take graduate-level courses. Preprofessional programs in law, medicine, veterinary science, pharmacy, dentistry, allied health, and seminary studies. Combined transfer programs may be arranged in dentistry, law, and medicine. First year of four-year nursing program (B.A. or R.N.) offered. 3-1 medical technology program. Member of Colleges of Mid-America Consortium. American Studies Program (Washington, D.C.), AuSable Inst of Environmental Studies Program (Michigan). Exchange programs with Illinois and Washington schools. Teacher certification in elementary and secondary education. Study abroad in Costa Rica, Germany, Mexico, the Netherlands, Russia, and Spain.
**Academic Assistance:** Remedial study skills. Nonremedial tutoring.

**ADMISSIONS. Academic basis for candidate selection** (in order of priority): Secondary school record, class rank, standardized test scores, school's recommendation, essay.
**Nonacademic basis for candidate selection:** Extracurricular participation, particular talent or ability, geographical distribution, and alumni/ae relationship are considered.
**Requirements:** Graduation from secondary school is required; GED is accepted. 18 units and the following program of study are required: 3 units of English, 2 units of math, 2 units of science, 2 units of foreign language, 2 units of social studies, 1 unit of history, 6 units of academic electives. Minimum composite ACT score of 20, rank in top half of secondary school class, and minimum 2.0 GPA required. Conditional admission possible for applicants not meeting standard requirements. ACT is required. Campus visit recommended.
**Procedure:** Take ACT by June of 12th year. Suggest filing application by April 15. Application deadline is August 30. Notification of admission on rolling basis. Reply is required by May 1 or within 21 days of acceptance. $100 tuition deposit, refundable until May 1. Freshmen accepted for terms other than fall.
**Special programs:** Credit and/or placement may be granted through CEEB Advanced Placement exams for scores of 3 or higher. Credit and/or placement may be granted through CLEP general and subject exams. Early entrance/early admission program. Concurrent enrollment program.
**Transfer students:** Transfer students accepted for terms other than fall. In fall 1993, 4% of all new students were transfers into all classes. 58 transfer applications were received, 45 were accepted. Application deadline is August 1 for fall; December 1 for spring. Minimum 2.0 GPA required. Lowest course grade accepted is "D." Maximum number of transferable credits is 60 semester hours. At least 60 semester hours must be completed at the college to receive degree.
**Admissions contact:** Quentin Van Essen, M.A., Director of Admissions. 712 722-6080.

**FINANCIAL AID. Available aid:** Pell grants, SEOG, state scholarships and grants, school scholarships and grants, private scholarships and grants, academic merit scholarships, and aid for undergraduate foreign students. Perkins Loans (NDSL), PLUS, Stafford Loans (GSL), school loans, private loans, and SLS. Deferred payment plan.
**Financial aid statistics:** In 1993-94, 99% of all undergraduate applicants received aid; 98% of freshman applicants. Average amounts of aid awarded freshmen: Loans, $2,200.
**Supporting data/closing dates:** FAFSA/FAF/FFS. School's own aid application: Priority filing date is April 15. State aid form: Priority filing date is April 15. Notification of awards on rolling basis.
**Financial aid contact:** Mike Epema, Director of Financial Aid. 712 722-6080.

## Drake University

**Des Moines, IA 50311** **515 271-2011**

**1994-95 Costs.** Tuition: $13,420. Room: $2,340. Board: $2,180. Fees, books, misc. academic expenses (school's estimate): $550.
**Enrollment.** Undergraduates: 1,486 men, 1,983 women (full-time). Freshman class: 2,804 applicants, 2,574 accepted, 832 enrolled. Graduate enrollment: 965 men, 1,108 women.
**Test score averages/ranges.** Average SAT scores: 499 verbal, 548 math. Range of SAT scores of middle 50%: 430-550 verbal, 470-610 math. Average ACT scores: 25 English, 24 math, 25 composite. Range of ACT scores of middle 50%: 22-28 English, 21-27 math.
**Faculty.** 278 full-time. 93% of faculty holds highest degree in specific field. Student/faculty ratio: 16 to 1.
**Selectivity rating.** Competitive.

**PROFILE.** Drake, founded in 1881, is a private university. Programs are offered through the Colleges of Arts and Sciences, Business and Public Administration, and Pharmacy and Health Sciences and the Schools of Education, Journalism and Mass Communication, and Law. Its 120-acre campus is located in Des Moines.

**Accreditation:** NCACS. Professionally accredited by the Accrediting Council on Education in Journalism and Mass Communication, the American Assembly of Collegiate Schools of Business, the American Bar Association, the American Council on Pharmaceutical Education, the Association of American Law Schools, the National Association of Schools of Music, the National League for Nursing.
**Religious orientation:** Drake University is nonsectarian; no religious requirements.
**Library:** Collections totaling over 540,000 volumes, 2,400 periodical subscriptions, and 600,000 microform items.
**Special facilities/museums:** Language lab, observatory, media service center.
**Athletic facilities:** Gymnasiums, field house, swimming pool, aerobics, combative sports, and weight rooms, stadium, tracks, badminton, basketball, handball, racquetball, tennis, and volleyball courts, football, intramural, soccer, and softball fields.

**STUDENT BODY. Undergraduate profile:** 40% are state residents; 30% are transfers. 3% Asian-American, 5% Black, 1% Hispanic, 1% Native American, 85% White, 5% Foreign national. Average age of undergraduates is 20.
**Freshman profile:** 8% of freshmen who took SAT scored 700 or over on verbal, 1% scored 700 or over on math; 26% scored 600 or over on verbal, 11% scored 600 or over on math; 65% scored 500 or over on verbal, 44% scored 500 or over on math; 89% scored 400 or over on verbal, 86% scored 400 or over on math; 99% scored 300 or over on verbal, 100% scored 300 or over on math. 13% of freshmen who took ACT scored 30 or over on English, 14% scored 30 or over on math, 14% scored 30 or over on composite; 66% scored 24 or over on English, 57% scored 24 or over on math, 66% scored 24 or over on composite; 96% scored 18 or over on English, 96% scored 18 or over on math, 99% scored 18 or over on composite; 100% scored 12 or over on English, 100% scored 12 or over on math, 100% scored 12 or over on composite. 8% of accepted applicants took SAT; 92% took ACT. 85% of freshmen come from public schools.
**Undergraduate achievement:** 80% of fall 1992 freshmen returned for fall 1993 term. 62% of entering class graduated. 13% of students who completed a degree program immediately went on to graduate study.
**Foreign students:** 105 students are from out of the country. Countries represented include India, Japan, Singapore, Spain, Taiwan, and Thailand; 45 in all.

**PROGRAMS OF STUDY. Degrees:** B.A., B.A.Journ., B.Art, B.Art Ed., B.F.A., B.Mus., B.Mus.Ed., B.S., B.S.Bus.Admin., B.S.Nurs., B.S.Pharm.
**Majors:** Accounting, Accounting/Actuarial Science, Actuarial Science, Advertising, Art, Art Education, Art History, Astronomy, Biology, Broadcast News, Broadcast Sales/Management, Chemistry, Church Music, Commercial Art/Graphic Design, Computer Information Systems, Computer Science, Early Childhood Education, Earth Science, Economics, Economics/Business Administration, Elementary Education, English, Environmental Science, Finance, Foreign Language, French, General Business, Geography, German, History, Insurance, Interior Design, International Business, International Relations, Journalism Teaching, Latin American Studies, Magazines, Management, Marine Science, Marketing, Mathematics, Media Graphics, Medical Technology, Military Science, Music, Music Business, Music Composition, Music Education, Music History, Music Theater, News/Editorial, Nursing, Painting/Drawing, Pharmacy, Philosophy, Physics, Physics/Engineering, Piano Pedagogy, Political Science, Pre-Law, Printmaking, Psychology, Public Administration, Public Relations, Radio/Television, Religion, Sculpture, Secondary Education, Sociology, Spanish, Speech Communication, Theatre Arts, Theatre Arts Education.
**Distribution of degrees:** The majors with the highest enrollment are pharmacy, marketing/management, and psychology; Spanish and religion have the lowest.
**Requirements:** General education requirement.
**Academic regulations:** Minimum 2.0 GPA must be maintained.
**Special:** Minors offered in numerous fields. Advertising major has management track and creative track options; radio/television major has management track and production track options. Self-designed majors. Double majors. Dual degrees. Independent study. Accelerated study. Pass/fail grading option. Internships. Graduate school at which undergraduates may take graduate-level courses. Preprofessional programs in law, medicine, veterinary science, dentistry, theology, optometry, engineering, physical therapy, and social work.

2-2 marine science program with Southampton Campus of Long Island U. 3-1 medical technology programs with Iowa Methodist Medical Center, Mercy Medical Center, and St. Luke's Methodist Hospital. 3-2 engineering programs with Cornell U and Washington U. Five-year pharmacy program, with B.S./M.B.A. option. Combined pharmacy/law program. 3-3 journalism/law program. Member of Des Moines Area Consortium of Higher Education. Washington Semester, UN Semester, and Sea Semester. Teacher certification in early childhood, elementary, and secondary education. Certification in specific subject areas. Member of International Student Exchange Program (ISEP). Campus Afloat world cruise program. ROTC. AFROTC at Iowa State U.
**Honors:** Phi Beta Kappa. Honors program. Honor societies.
**Academic Assistance:** Nonremedial tutoring.

**STUDENT LIFE. Housing:** All freshmen and sophomores within two years of secondary school must live on campus. Coed dorms. Sorority and fraternity housing. School-owned/operated apartments. Off-campus privately-owned housing. On-campus married-student housing. 53% of students live in college housing.
**Services and counseling/handicapped student services:** Placement services. Health service. Counseling services for minority, military, veteran, and older students. Birth control, personal, and psychological counseling. Career and academic guidance services. Religious counseling. Physically disabled student services. Learning disabled services. Tape recorders. Tutors. Reader services for the blind.
**Campus organizations:** Undergraduate student government. Student newspaper (Times-Delphic, published twice/week). Literary magazine. Yearbook. Radio and TV stations. Choir, opera workshop, concert band, orchestra, theatre, volunteer opportunities, academic, athletic, professional, and special-interest groups, 140 organizations in all. 11 fraternities, nine chapter houses; 10 sororities, six chapter houses. 29% of men join a fraternity. 31% of women join a sorority.
**Religious organizations:** Baptist Student Union, Bureau for Jewish Living (Hillel), Campus Crusade for Christ, Christian Science Organization, Fellowship of Christian Athletes, Intervarsity Christian Fellowship, Navigators, Newman Community, REACHOUT, United Ministries, Wesley Foundation, Catholic, Episcopalian, and Lutheran groups.
**Minority/foreign student organizations:** Association of Black Journalists, Black Law Student Association, Black Student Organization, La Fuerza Latina, Los Estudiantes, Black Greek Council, Society for Minorities in the Arts. International Student Organization, Malaysian student group.

**ATHLETICS. Physical education requirements:** None.
**Intercollegiate competition:** 6% of students participate. Basketball (M,W), cross-country (M,W), football (M), golf (M), soccer (M), softball (W), tennis (M,W), track (indoor) (M,W), track (outdoor) (M,W), track and field (indoor) (M,W), track and field (outdoor) (M,W), volleyball (W), wrestling (M). Member of Gateway Conference, Missouri Valley Athletic Conference, NCAA Division I, NCAA Division III for football, WAC (wrestling).
**Intramural and club sports:** 60% of students participate. Intramural aerobics, badminton, basketball, billiards, flag football, floor hockey, golf, horsemanship, indoor soccer, indoor track, martial arts, racquetball, softball, swimming, table tennis, tennis, volleyball, water aerobics, Wiffle ball. Men's club baseball, crew, ice hockey, lacrosse, martial arts, rugby, swimming, volleyball. Women's club crew, martial arts, soccer, swimming.

**ADMISSIONS. Academic basis for candidate selection** (in order of priority): Secondary school record, class rank, standardized test scores, school's recommendation, essay.
**Nonacademic basis for candidate selection:** Character and personality are emphasized. Extracurricular participation, particular talent or ability, and alumni/ae relationship are considered.
**Requirements:** Graduation from secondary school is required; GED is accepted. 16 units required and the following program of study recommended: 4 units of English, 2 units of math, 2 units of science, 2 units of foreign language, 2 units of social studies, 2 units of history. R.N. required of nursing program applicants. SAT or ACT is required. Campus visit and interview recommended. Off-campus interviews available with admissions and alumni representatives.
**Procedure:** Take SAT or ACT by December of 12th year. Visit college for interview by December of 12th year. Notification of admission on rolling basis beginning November 1. Reply is required by May 1. $125 nonrefundable tuition deposit. $100 room deposit, refundable until May 1. Freshmen accepted for terms other than fall.
**Special programs:** Admission may be deferred one year. Credit and/or placement may be granted through CEEB Advanced Placement exams for scores of 3 or higher. Credit and/or placement may be granted through CLEP general and subject exams. Credit may be granted through ACT PEP and DANTES exams, and military and life experience. Credit and placement may be granted through challenge exams. Early entrance/early admission program. Concurrent enrollment program.
**Transfer students:** Transfer students accepted for terms other than fall. In fall 1993, 30% of all new students were transfers into all classes. 875 transfer applications were received, 604 were accepted. Application deadline is August 1 (December 1 and February 1 for pharmacy) for fall; December 1 for spring. Minimum 3.0 GPA required of pharmacy program applicants; 2.0 GPA required of all others. Lowest course grade accepted is "C." Maximum number of transferable credits is 66 semester hours from a two-year school and 94 semester hours from a four-year school. At least 30 semester hours must be completed at the university to receive degree.
**Admissions contact:** Thomas F. Willoughby, M.A., Director of Admission. 515 271-3181.

**FINANCIAL AID. Available aid:** Pell grants, SEOG, state scholarships and grants, school scholarships and grants, private scholarships and grants, ROTC scholarships, academic merit scholarships, athletic scholarships, and aid for undergraduate foreign students. Perkins Loans (NDSL), PLUS, Stafford Loans (GSL), Health Professions Loans, state loans, school loans, and SLS. Knight Tuition Plans, AMS, and Tuition Management Systems. Guaranteed Cost Plan
**Financial aid statistics:** 40% of aid is not need-based. In 1993-94, 80% of all undergraduate applicants received aid; 85% of freshman applicants. Average amounts of aid awarded freshmen: Scholarships and grants, $7,640; loans, $3,670.
**Supporting data/closing dates:** FAFSA: Priority filing date is March 1. Notification of awards begins March 1.
**Financial aid contact:** John C. Parker, Ph.D., Director of Student Financial Planning. 515 271-2905.

**STUDENT EMPLOYMENT.** College Work/Study Program. Institutional employment. 30% of full-time undergraduates work on campus during school year. Students may expect to earn an average of $1,000 during school year. Off-campus part-time employment opportunities rated "good."
**COMPUTER FACILITIES.** 900 IBM/IBM-compatible and Macintosh/Apple microcomputers; all are networked. Students may access Digital minicomputer/mainframe systems, Internet. Residence halls may be equipped with networked microcomputers. Client/LAN operating systems include Apple/Macintosh, DOS, UNIX/XENIX/AIX, LocalTalk/AppleTalk. Computer languages and software packages include BASIC, BMDP, C, COBOL, Excel, FORTRAN, Kermit, LISP, MacPaint, Microsoft Word, PageMaker, Pascal, SAS, SPSS. Computer facilities are available to all students.
**Fees:** Computer fee is included in tuition/fees.
**Hours:** 8 AM-11 PM (M-F); reduced hours on weekends.
**GRADUATE CAREER DATA.** Graduate school percentages: 4% enter law school. 3% enter medical school. 1% enter dental school. 4% enter graduate business programs. 8% enter graduate arts and sciences programs. Highest graduate school enrollments: U of Illinois, U of Iowa, Northwestern U. 65% of graduates choose careers in business and industry. Companies and businesses that hire graduates: Arthur Andersen, Coca-Cola, Deere & Co., Honeywell-Bull, Hormel, IBM, various school districts.
**PROMINENT ALUMNI/AE.** Terry Branstad, governor, Iowa; Frances Bartlett Kinne, former president, Jacksonville U; Kenneth Macke, chairperson and CEO, Dayton Hudson Co.; Sherrill Milnes, leading baritone, Metropolitan Opera.

# Faith Baptist Bible College and Seminary

**Ankeny, IA 50021** **515 964-0601**

**1993-94 Costs.** Tuition: $4,620. Room & board: $3,038. Fees, books, misc. academic expenses (school's estimate): $892.
**Enrollment.** Undergraduates: 95 men, 100 women (full-time). Freshman class: 152 applicants, 129 accepted, 94 enrolled. Graduate enrollment: 23 men, 3 women.
**Test score averages/ranges.** Average ACT scores: 19 composite.
**Faculty.** 11 full-time; 14 part-time. 45% of faculty holds doctoral degree. Student/faculty ratio: 10 to 1.
**Selectivity rating.** Less competitive.

**PROFILE.** Faith Baptist Bible, founded in 1921, is a church-affiliated college. Its 52-acre campus is located in Ankeny, six miles from Des Moines.

**Accreditation:** AABC.
**Religious orientation:** Faith Baptist Bible College and Seminary is affiliated with the Baptist Church (General Association of Regular Baptist Churches); no religious requirements.
**Library:** Collections totaling over 54,200 volumes, 566 periodical subscriptions and 502 microform items.
**Athletic facilities:** Gymnasium, soccer and softball fields, basketball, tennis, and volleyball courts, weight room.
**STUDENT BODY. Undergraduate profile:** 48% are state residents. 2% Asian-American, 1% Black, 1% Hispanic, 1% Native American, 95% White. Average age of undergraduates is 20.
**Freshman profile:** 3% of accepted applicants took SAT; 97% took ACT. 60% of freshmen come from public schools.
**Undergraduate achievement:** 59% of fall 1991 freshmen returned for fall 1992 term. 53% of entering class graduated. 5% of students who completed a degree program immediately went on to graduate study.
**PROGRAMS OF STUDY. Degrees:** B.A., B.S.
**Majors:** Assistant Pastor, Bible/Theology, Christian Education, Christian School Education, Missions/Church Planting, Music Ministry, Pastoral Training.
**Distribution of degrees:** The majors with the highest enrollment are Christian school education, Bible/theology, and missions/church planting; assistant pastor and music ministry have the lowest.
**Requirements:** General education requirement.
**Special:** Minors offered in counseling, missions, music, and youth. Associate's degrees offered. Double majors. Internships. Graduate school at which undergraduates may take graduate-level courses. Teacher certification in elementary education. Certification in specific subject areas.
**Honors:** Honor societies.
**ADMISSIONS. Academic basis for candidate selection** (in order of priority): Secondary school record, standardized test scores, school's recommendation, class rank.
**Nonacademic basis for candidate selection:** Character and personality are emphasized.
**Requirements:** Graduation from secondary school is required; GED is accepted. No specific distribution of secondary school units required. ACT is required; SAT may be substituted. Campus visit and interview recommended. No off-campus interviews.
**Procedure:** Take SAT or ACT by June of 12th year. Application deadline is August 15. Notification of admission on rolling basis. $100 refundable tuition deposit. $25 refundable room deposit. Freshmen accepted for terms other than fall.
**Special programs:** Admission may be deferred one year. Credit may be granted through CEEB Advanced Placement exams, CLEP general and subject exams, and challenge exams.
**Transfer students:** Transfer students accepted for terms other than fall. In fall 1992, 28 transfer applications were received, 22 were accepted. Application deadline is August 1 for fall; January 1 for spring. Minimum 2.0 GPA recommended. Lowest course grade accepted is "C." At least 24 semester hours must be completed at the college to receive degree.
**Admissions contact:** Jeff Newman, M.A., Director of Admissions and Financial Aid. 800 352-0147.

**FINANCIAL AID. Available aid:** Pell grants, state scholarships and grants, school scholarships and grants, private scholarships, and academic merit scholarships. PLUS, Stafford Loans (GSL), private loans, and SLS. AMS and deferred payment plan.
**Financial aid statistics:** 12% of aid is not need-based. In 1992-93, 92% of all undergraduate applicants received aid; 91% of freshman applicants. Average amounts of aid awarded freshmen: Scholarships and grants, $2,428; loans, $2,208.
**Supporting data/closing dates:** FAFSA/FAF/FFS: Priority filing date is April 15. Notification of awards on rolling basis.
**Financial aid contact:** Jeff Newman, M.A., Director of Admissions and Financial Aid. 515 964-0601, extension 248.

## Graceland College

**Lamoni, IA 50140** **515 784-5000**

**1994-95 Costs.** Tuition: $9,100. Room: $1,130. Board: $1,970 Fees, books, misc. academic expenses (school's estimate): $650.
**Enrollment.** Undergraduates: 483 men, 513 women (full-time). Freshman class: 564 applicants, 422 accepted, 248 enrolled.
**Test score averages/ranges.** Average SAT scores: 447 verbal, 502 math. Range of SAT scores of middle 50%: 300-520 verbal, 440-590 math. Average ACT scores: 22 composite. Range of ACT scores of middle 50%: 19-24 composite.
**Faculty.** 70 full-time; 11 part-time. 54% of faculty holds doctoral degree. Student/faculty ratio: 15 to 1.
**Selectivity rating.** Less competitive.

**PROFILE.** Graceland, founded in 1895 is a church-affiliated college. Its 169-acre campus is located in Lamoni, on the Missouri border, 75 miles south of Des Moines.

**Accreditation:** NCACS. Professionally accredited by the National Council for Accreditation of Teacher Education, the National League for Nursing.
**Religious orientation:** Graceland College is affiliated with the Reorganized Church of Jesus Christ of Latter-Day Saints; no religious requirements.
**Library:** Collections totaling over 110,559 volumes, 697 periodical subscriptions, and 3,774 microform items.
**Special facilities/museums:** Electron microscope.
**Athletic facilities:** Physical education center, sports complex.

**STUDENT BODY. Undergraduate profile:** 31% are state residents; 32% are transfers. 1% Asian-American, 4% Black, 2% Hispanic, 1% Native American, 82% White, 10% Other. Average age of undergraduates is 22.
**Freshman profile:** 2% of freshmen who took SAT scored 700 or over on math; 9% scored 600 or over on verbal, 18% scored 600 or over on math; 32% scored 500 or over on verbal, 50% scored 500 or over on math; 72% scored 400 or over on verbal, 87% scored 400 or over on math; 93% scored 300 or over on verbal, 96% scored 300 or over on math. 23% of accepted applicants took SAT; 77% took ACT.
**Undergraduate achievement:** 78% of fall 1992 freshmen returned for fall 1993 term. 26% of entering class graduated. 10% of students who completed a degree program immediately went on to graduate study.
**Foreign students:** 106 students are from out of the country. Countries represented include Bulgaria, Canada, Hungary, India, Japan, and Taiwan; 21 in all.

**PROGRAMS OF STUDY. Degrees:** B.A., B.S., B.S.Nurs.
**Majors:** Accounting, Addiction Studies, Art, Basic Sciences, Biology, Business Administration, Chemistry, Commercial Design, Communications, Computer Engineering, Computer Information Systems, Computer Science, Economics, Elementary Education, English, French, German, Health, History, International Studies, Liberal Studies, Mathematics, Medical Technology, Music, Music Education, Nursing, Physical Education, Physical Sciences, Psychology, Publications Design, Recreation, Religion, Social Studies, Sociology, Spanish, Speech, Studio Art, Theatre.
**Distribution of degrees:** The majors with the highest enrollment are nursing, business administration, and education; computer engineering, German, and Spanish have the lowest.
**Requirements:** General education requirement.
**Academic regulations:** Freshmen must maintain minimum 1.7 GPA; sophomores, juniors, seniors, 2.0 GPA.
**Special:** Minors offered in most majors. Courses offered in Japanese and peace studies. Junior and senior years of nursing program spent at Education Center (Independence, Mo.). Outreach program for R.N.'s seeking completion of B.S.N. includes home-study component. Home-study program in addiction studies, including residencies. Self-designed majors. Double majors. Dual degrees. Independent study. Pass/fail grading option. Internships. Preprofessional programs in law, medicine, and dentistry. Exchange program with Park Coll. Teacher certification in early childhood, elementary, and secondary education. Certification in specific subject areas. Exchange programs abroad in Bulgaria (U of Sofia), Hungary (ELTE U), Taiwan (China Junior Coll of Tech), and the Ukraine (Kiev Inst of Trade and Economics). Study abroad also in Austria, France, Germany, Japan, Mexico, and Spain.
**Honors:** Honors program. Honor societies.
**Academic Assistance:** Nonremedial tutoring.

**ADMISSIONS. Academic basis for candidate selection** (in order of priority): Standardized test scores, class rank, secondary school record, school's recommendation.
**Nonacademic basis for candidate selection:** Extracurricular participation is emphasized. Character and personality are important. Particular talent or ability is considered.
**Requirements:** Graduation from secondary school is required; GED is accepted. 16 units and the following program of study are recommended: 3 units of English, 2 units of math, 2 units of science, 2 units of foreign language, 2 units of social studies. Minimum combined SAT score of 840 (composite ACT score of 21), rank in top half of secondary school class, and minimum 2.0 GPA required. Conditional admission possible for applicants not meeting standard requirements. SAT or ACT is required. Campus visit recommended. Off-campus interviews available with an admissions representative.
**Procedure:** Take SAT or ACT by December of 12th year. Application deadline is August 15. Notification of admission on rolling basis. Reply is required by registration. $80 tuition deposit, refundable until June 1. Freshmen accepted for terms other than fall.
**Special programs:** Admission may be deferred indefinitely. Credit and/or placement may be granted through CEEB Advanced Placement exams for scores of 3 or higher. Credit and/or placement may be granted through CLEP general exams. Placement may be granted through CLEP subject exams. Credit may be granted through military and life experience. Concurrent enrollment program.
**Transfer students:** Transfer students accepted for terms other than fall. In fall 1993, 32% of all new students were transfers into all classes. 354 transfer applications were received, 235 were accepted. Application deadline is August 15. Minimum 2.0 GPA required. Lowest course grade accepted is "D." Maximum number of transferable credits is 75 semester hours. At least 53 semester hours must be completed at the college to receive degree.
**Admissions contact:** Bonita A. Booth, M.A., Dean of Admissions. 515 784-5196, 800 638-0053, 800 346-9208.

**FINANCIAL AID. Available aid:** Pell grants, SEOG, state scholarships and grants, school scholarships and grants, private scholarships, academic merit scholarships, athletic scholarships, and aid for undergraduate foreign students. Perkins Loans (NDSL), PLUS, Stafford Loans (GSL), school loans, and SLS. Deferred payment plan.
**Financial aid statistics:** 46% of aid is not need-based. In 1993-94, 97% of all undergraduate applicants received aid; 98% of freshman applicants. Average amounts of aid awarded freshmen: Scholarships and grants, $6,050; loans, $3,453.
**Supporting data/closing dates:** FAFSA/FFS: Accepted on rolling basis. Notification of awards on rolling basis.
**Financial aid contact:** Nancy B. Wolff, M.S., Director of Student Finance. 515 784-5136.

## Grand View College

**Des Moines, IA 50316** **515 263-2800**

**1993-94 Costs.** Tuition: $9,820. Room & board: $3,260. Fees, books, misc. academic expenses (school's estimate): $450.
**Enrollment.** Undergraduates: 365 men, 653 women (full-time). Freshman class: 423 applicants, 398 accepted, 183 enrolled.
**Test score averages/ranges.** Average ACT scores: 20 composite.
**Faculty.** 75 full-time; 57 part-time. 35% of faculty holds doctoral degree. Student/faculty ratio: 17 to 1.
**Selectivity rating.** Less competitive.

**PROFILE.** Grand View, founded in 1896, is a church-affiliated college. Programs are offered through the Divisions of Humanities, Natural Sciences, Nursing, and Social Sciences. Its 25-acre campus is located in Des Moines.

**Accreditation:** NCACS. Professionally accredited by the National League for Nursing.
**Religious orientation:** Grand View College is affiliated with the Evangelical Lutheran Church in America; two courses of religion required.
**Library:** Collections totaling over 100,000 volumes, 715 periodical subscriptions, and 35,000 microform items.
**Athletic facilities:** Gymnasium, tennis courts, baseball, intramural, and soccer fields, weight room.

**STUDENT BODY. Undergraduate profile:** 97% are state residents; 48% are transfers. 2% Asian-American, 5% Black, 1% Hispanic, 1% Native American, 91% White. Average age of undergraduates is 24.
**Freshman profile:** 1% of accepted applicants took SAT; 88% took ACT. 91% of freshmen come from public schools.
**Undergraduate achievement:** 54% of fall 1992 freshmen returned for fall 1993 term. 18% of entering class graduated.
**Foreign students:** 16 students are from out of the country. Countries represented include Japan, Korea, Namibia, and Saudi Arabia; 14 in all.

**PROGRAMS OF STUDY. Degrees:** B.A., B.S.Nurs.
**Majors:** Accounting, Applied Computer Science, Art Education, Biology, Business Administration, Commercial Art, Creative/Performing Arts, Criminal Justice, Education, Elementary Education, English, General Social Sciences, Human Behavior, Human Services, Humanities, Individualized Major, Journalism, Mass Communication, Mathematics, Nursing, Pre-Law, Pre-Medicine/Allied Health Fields, Radio/Television, Religion, Secondary Education, Visual Arts.
**Distribution of degrees:** The majors with the highest enrollment are business administration, nursing, and elementary education; humanities, computer science, and religion have the lowest.
**Requirements:** General education requirement.
**Academic regulations:** Freshmen must maintain minimum 1.5 GPA; sophomores, 1.8 GPA; juniors, 1.9 GPA; seniors, 2.0 GPA. Minimum 2.2 GPA required in major.
**Special:** Courses offered in geography, physical science, pre-engineering, and theatre arts. Associate's degrees offered. Self-designed majors. Double majors. Independent study. Accelerated study. Pass/fail grading option. Internships. Graduate school at which undergraduates may take graduate-level courses. Preprofessional programs in law, medicine, dentistry, and theology. Five-year bachelor's/master's hospital and health administration program with U of Iowa. Cross-registration with Des Moines Area Community Coll and Drake Coll. Courses may be taken at Des Moines Art Center. Washington Semester. Teacher certification in elementary and secondary education. Certification in specific subject areas. ROTC at Drake U. AFROTC at Iowa State U.
**Honors:** Honors program.
**Academic Assistance:** Remedial reading, writing, math, and study skills. Nonremedial tutoring.

**ADMISSIONS. Academic basis for candidate selection** (in order of priority): Secondary school record, standardized test scores, class rank, school's recommendation.
**Nonacademic basis for candidate selection:** Character and personality, extracurricular participation, and particular talent or ability are considered.

**Requirements:** Graduation from secondary school is required; GED is accepted. 17 units and the following program of study are required: 4 units of English, 3 units of math, 3 units of science, 2 units of foreign language, 3 units of social studies, 2 units of history. Minimum composite ACT score of 16, rank in top half of secondary school class, and minimum 2.0 GPA recommended. ACT is required; SAT may be substituted. Campus visit and interview recommended. Off-campus interviews available with an admissions representative.
**Procedure:** Application deadline is September 1. Notification of admission on rolling basis. $100 tuition deposit, refundable until June 1. $100 room deposit, refundable until June 1. Freshmen accepted for terms other than fall.
**Special programs:** Credit and/or placement may be granted through CEEB Advanced Placement exams for scores of 3 or higher. Credit and/or placement may be granted through CLEP subject exams. Credit and placement may be granted through ACT PEP and challenge exams, and military and life experience. Concurrent enrollment program.
**Transfer students:** Transfer students accepted for terms other than fall. In fall 1993, 48% of all new students were transfers into all classes. 384 transfer applications were received, 344 were accepted. Application deadline is September 1 for fall; January 1 for spring. Minimum 2.0 GPA recommended. Lowest course grade accepted is "D." Maximum number of transferable credits is 66 semester hours from a two-year school and 92 semester hours from a four-year school. At least 30 semester hours must be completed at the college to receive degree.
**Admissions contact:** Lori Hanson, M.A., Director of Admissions. 515 263-2810.

**FINANCIAL AID. Available aid:** Pell grants, SEOG, state scholarships and grants, school scholarships and grants, private scholarships, academic merit scholarships, athletic scholarships, and aid for undergraduate foreign students. Perkins Loans (NDSL), PLUS, Stafford Loans (GSL), state loans, and SLS. Tuition Plan Inc., EFI Fund Management, Tuition Management Systems, and deferred payment plan.
**Financial aid statistics:** In 1993-94, 100% of all undergraduate applicants received aid. Average amounts of aid awarded freshmen: Scholarships and grants, $2,480; loans, $500.
**Supporting data/closing dates:** FAFSA: Priority filing date is April 1. Notification of awards on rolling basis.
**Financial aid contact:** Patrick Olson, M.A., Director of Financial Aid. 515 263-2820.

## Grinnell College

**Grinnell, IA 50112 — 515 269-4000**

**1994-95 Costs.** Tuition: $15,688. Room: $2,120. Board: $2,498. Fees, books, misc. academic expenses (school's estimate): $774.
**Enrollment.** Undergraduates: 626 men, 696 women (full-time). Freshman class: 1,861 applicants, 1,389 accepted, 432 enrolled.
**Test score averages/ranges.** Average SAT scores: 602 verbal, 642 math. Range of SAT scores of middle 50%: 560-650 verbal, 590-690 math. Average ACT scores: 29 composite. Range of ACT scores of middle 50%: 27-30 composite.
**Faculty.** 139 full-time; 11 part-time. 96% of faculty holds highest degree in specific field. Student/faculty ratio: 10 to 1.
**Selectivity rating.** Highly competitive.

**PROFILE.** Grinnell, founded in 1846, is a private, liberal arts college. Its 90-acre campus is located in Grinnell, 55 miles east of Des Moines.

**Accreditation:** NCACS. Professionally accredited by the National Council for Accreditation of Teacher Education.
**Religious orientation:** Grinnell College is nonsectarian; no religious requirements.
**Library:** Collections totaling over 352,555 volumes, 2,452 periodical subscriptions, and 6,005 microform items.
**Special facilities/museums:** Art galleries, language lab, nuclear magnetic resonance spectrometer, electron microscope, 24-inch reflecting telescope, 365-acre environmental research area.
**Athletic facilities:** Physical education complex, swimming pool, track, basketball, handball, racquetball, squash, and tennis courts, weight room, saunas, gymnasium, playing fields.

**STUDENT BODY. Undergraduate profile:** 23% are state residents; 10% are transfers. 4% Asian-American, 4% Black, 2% Hispanic, 79% White, 11% Other. Average age of undergraduates is 20.
**Freshman profile:** 12% of freshmen who took SAT scored 700 or over on verbal, 27% scored 700 or over on math; 56% scored 600 or over on verbal, 75% scored 600 or over on math; 92% scored 500 or over on verbal, 96% scored 500 or over on math; 98% scored 400 or over on verbal, 99% scored 400 or over on math; 100% scored 300 or over on verbal, 100% scored 300 or over on math. 85% of accepted applicants took SAT; 54% took ACT. 75% of freshmen come from public schools.
**Undergraduate achievement:** 88% of fall 1992 freshmen returned for fall 1993 term. 75% of entering class graduated. 30% of students who completed a degree program immediately went on to graduate study.
**Foreign students:** 144 students are from out of the country. Countries represented include China, Greece, India, Japan, Mexico, and Russia; 42 in all.

**PROGRAMS OF STUDY. Degrees:** B.A.
**Majors:** American Studies, Anthropology, Art, Biology, Chemistry, Chinese, Classics, Computer Science, Economics, English, French, General Science, German, History, Mathematics, Music, Philosophy, Physics, Political Science, Psychology, Religious Studies, Russian, Sociology, Spanish, Theatre.
**Distribution of degrees:** The majors with the highest enrollment are history, political science, and English; general science, German, and Chinese have the lowest.
**Requirements:** General education requirement.
**Academic regulations:** Freshmen must maintain minimum 1.8 GPA; sophomores, juniors, seniors, 2.0 GPA.
**Special:** Interdisciplinary concentrations in Afro-American, Chinese, environmental, gender/women's, Latin American, linguistic, regional/community, Russian/Eastern European, technology, and Western European studies. Self-designed majors. Double majors. Independent study. Accelerated study. Pass/fail grading option. Internships. Preprofessional programs in law, medicine, veterinary science, pharmacy, dentistry, optometry, and nursing. 3-2 engineering programs with Caltech, Columbia U, Rensselaer Polytech Inst, and Washington U. 3-3 law program with Columbia U. 3-4 architecture program with Washington U. Students may earn Grinnell degree after three years of undergraduate study and one year of professional school. Associated Colleges of the Midwest. Newberry Library Program in the Humanities (Illinois). Oak Ridge Science Semester (Tennessee). Wilderness Field Station Program (Minnesota). Other semester-away programs available. Exchange programs with Howard U and Spelman Coll. Teacher certification in elementary and secondary education. Exchange program abroad in Japan (Waseda U). Study abroad also in Austria, Bolivia, Brazil, China, Costa Rica, the Czech Republic, Ecuador, Egypt, England, France, Germany, Greece, Hungary, India, Israel, Italy, Kenya, Nepal, Norway, Scotland, Slovakia, the former Soviet Republics, Spain, Switzerland, Taiwan, Tanzania, the former Yugoslav Republics, and Zimbabwe.
**Honors:** Phi Beta Kappa. Honor societies.
**Academic Assistance:** Nonremedial tutoring.

**STUDENT LIFE. Housing:** All unmarried freshmen and sophomores must live on campus unless living with family. Coed dorms. Off-campus privately-owned housing. College-owned houses. 86% of students live in college housing.
**Social atmosphere:** According to the editor of the student newspaper, since the town is small with a population under 10,000, all of the social-cultural life is on campus. The college provides programming such as bands, dance troupes, films, and orchestras. Groups influencing social life include several political groups and women's groups and the Grinnell Lesbian-Gay Alliance, all of which are very vocal. There are no fraternities, and religion is low-key. On campus, students like to hang out at the Forum, and off campus they head for the Bar.
**Services and counseling/handicapped student services:** Placement services. Health service. Counseling services for minority students. Birth control, personal, and psychological counseling. Career and academic guidance services. Religious counseling. Physically disabled student services. Learning disabled services. Notetaking services. Tape recorders. Tutors. Reader services for the blind.
**Campus organizations:** Undergraduate student government. Student newspaper (Scarlet and Black, published once/week). Literary magazine. Yearbook. Radio station. Choir, orchestra, choral society, gospel choir, marimba ensemble, dance group, international folk dance group, women's group, Outdoor Recreation Program, PIRG, student publications, Proteus, athletic, departmental, service, and special-interest groups, 105 organizations in all.
**Religious organizations:** Chalutzim, Christian Fellowship, Christian Science Organization, Fellowship of Christian Athletes, Friends Worship Group, Roman Catholic Students Group, Unitarian-Universalist Fellowship.
**Minority/foreign student organizations:** Multiethnic Coalition, Concerned Black Students, Black Women's Support Group, Black Men's Support Group, Native American Interest Group, Asian American Students in Alliance, Student Organization of Latinas/os. International Student Organization.

**ATHLETICS. Physical education requirements:** None.
**Intercollegiate competition:** 45% of students participate. Basketball (M,W), cross-country (M,W), diving (M,W), football (M,W), golf (M), soccer (M,W), softball (W), swimming (M,W), track and field (indoor) (M,W), track and field (outdoor) (M,W), volleyball (W). Member of Midwest Athletic Conference for Women, Midwest Collegiate Athletic Conference, NCAA Division III.
**Intramural and club sports:** 35% of students participate. Intramural basketball, racquetball, soccer, softball, ultimate frisbee, volleyball. Men's club fencing, lacrosse, rugby, ultimate frisbee, volleyball, water polo. Women's club fencing, lacrosse, rugby, ultimate frisbee, water polo.

**ADMISSIONS. Academic basis for candidate selection** (in order of priority): Secondary school record, class rank, standardized test scores, school's recommendation, essay.
**Nonacademic basis for candidate selection:** Character and personality, extracurricular participation, and particular talent or ability are emphasized. Geographical distribution and alumni/ae relationship are considered.
**Requirements:** Graduation from secondary school is required; GED is accepted. 16 units and the following program of study are required: 4 units of English, 3 units of math. SAT or ACT is required. Campus visit and interview recommended. Off-campus interviews available with admissions and alumni representatives.
**Procedure:** Take SAT or ACT by December of 12th year. Visit college for interview by February 1 of 12th year. Suggest filing application by February 1; no deadline. Notification of admission by April 1. Reply is required by May 1. $100 nonrefundable tuition deposit. Freshmen accepted for fall terms only.
**Special programs:** Admission may be deferred one year. Credit may be granted through CEEB Advanced Placement for scores of 3 or higher in sciences, 4 or higher in humanities and social studies. Placement may be granted through challenge exams. Early decision program. In fall 1993, 147 applied for early decision and 108 were accepted. Deadline for applying for early decision is November 20. Early entrance/early admission program.
**Transfer students:** Transfer students accepted for terms other than fall. In fall 1993, 10% of all new students were transfers into all classes. 174 transfer applications were received, 138 were accepted. Application deadline is May 1 for fall; December 15 for spring. Minimum 3.0 GPA recommended. Lowest course grade accepted is "C." Maximum number of transferable credits is 62 semester hours. At least 62 semester hours must be completed at the college to receive degree.
**Admissions contact:** Vincent Cuseo, M.A., Director of Admission. 515 269-3600.

**FINANCIAL AID. Available aid:** Pell grants, SEOG, state scholarships and grants, school scholarships and grants, academic merit scholarships, and aid for undergraduate foreign students. Perkins Loans (NDSL), PLUS, Stafford Loans (GSL), school loans, and SLS. AMS. Cost Stabilization Plan.
**Financial aid statistics:** 13% of aid is not need-based. In 1993-94, 95% of all undergraduate applicants received aid; 96% of freshman applicants. Average amounts of aid awarded freshmen: Scholarships and grants, $10,245; loans, $3,583.
**Supporting data/closing dates:** FAFSA: Priority filing date is February 1. School's own aid application: Priority filing date is February 1. Notification of awards begins April 1.

**Financial aid contact:** Arnold Woods, Director of Student Financial Aid. 515 269-3250.

**STUDENT EMPLOYMENT.** College Work/Study Program. Institutional employment. 49% of full-time undergraduates work on campus during school year. Students may expect to earn an average of $1,000 during school year. Off-campus part-time employment opportunities rated "fair."

**COMPUTER FACILITIES.** 365 IBM/IBM-compatible, Macintosh/Apple, and RISC-/UNIX-based microcomputers; 229 are networked. Students may access Digital, IBM, SUN minicomputer/mainframe systems, BITNET, Internet. Residence halls may be equipped with networked microcomputers, networked terminals. Client/LAN operating systems include Apple/Macintosh, DOS, UNIX/XENIX/AIX, DEC, LocalTalk/AppleTalk, Novell. Computer languages and software packages include BASIC, C, Excel, FORTRAN, LISP, MINITAB, Microsoft Word, Pascal, SAS, SPSS, WordPerfect; 80 in all. Computer facilities are available to all students.

**Fees:** None.

**Hours:** 24 hours.

**GRADUATE CAREER DATA.** Highest graduate school enrollments: U of California, U of Chicago, U of Illinois, Indiana U, U of Iowa, Iowa State U, U of Minnesota, Ohio State U, Stanford U, U of Washington, Washington U, U of Wisconsin. 12% of graduates choose careers in business and industry.

**PROMINENT ALUMNI/AE.** Michael Schulhof, president, Sony-USA; Peter Coyote, actor; Andrew Cooper, president, Burson-Marsteller; Edward Hirsch, poet; Tom Cech, Nobel Prize-winning chemist; Amy Clampitt, poet.

# Iowa State University

**Ames, IA 50011-2010** **515 294-4111**

**1994-95 Costs.** Tuition: $2,291 (state residents), $7,551 (out-of-state). Room & board: $3,104. Fees, books, misc. academic expenses (school's estimate): $800.

**Enrollment.** Undergraduates: 11,175 men, 7,867 women (full-time). Freshman class: 8,427 applicants, 7,424 accepted, 3,441 enrolled. Graduate enrollment: 2,756 men, 1,727 women.

**Test score averages/ranges.** Range of SAT scores of middle 50%: 380-460 verbal, 530-640 math. Range of ACT scores of middle 50%: 22-27 composite.

**Faculty.** 1,590 full-time; 169 part-time. 76% of faculty holds doctoral degree. Student/faculty ratio: 19 to 1.

**Selectivity rating.** Competitive.

**PROFILE.** Iowa State, founded in 1858, is a public, land-grant university. Programs are offered through the Colleges of Agriculture, Business Administration, Design, Education, Engineering, Family and Consumer Sciences, Sciences and Humanities, and Veterinary Medicine and the Graduate College. Its 1,736-acre campus is located in Ames, 30 miles north of Des Moines.

**Accreditation:** NCACS. Professionally accredited by the Accreditation Board for Engineering and Technology, the Accrediting Council on Education in Journalism and Mass Communication, the American Assembly of Collegiate Schools of Business, the American Dietetic Association, the American Psychological Association, the American Society of Landscape Architects, the American Veterinary Medical Association, the Council on Social Work Education, the Foundation for Interior Design Education Research, the National Architecture Accrediting Board, the National Association of Schools of Music, the Society of American Foresters.

**Religious orientation:** Iowa State University is nonsectarian; no religious requirements.

**Library:** Collections totaling over 1,900,000 volumes, 21,723 periodical subscriptions, and 2,471,564 microform items.

**Special facilities/museums:** Art museum, observatory, numerous institutes, research centers, service agencies.

**Athletic facilities:** Athletic hall, gymnasium, physical education building, intramural fields, recreation/athletic center, tennis courts, athletic fields, swimming pool, track.

**STUDENT BODY. Undergraduate profile:** 76% are state residents; 33% are transfers. 2% Asian-American, 3.4% Black, 1.4% Hispanic, 87.1% White, 6.1% Other. Average age of undergraduates is 22.

**Freshman profile:** 1% of freshmen who took SAT scored 700 or over on verbal, 12% scored 700 or over on math; 12% scored 600 or over on verbal, 36% scored 600 or over on math; 36% scored 500 or over on verbal, 65% scored 500 or over on math; 71% scored 400 or over on verbal, 86% scored 400 or over on math; 91% scored 300 or over on verbal, 97% scored 300 or over on math. 10% of freshmen who took ACT scored 30 or over on composite; 57% scored 24 or over on composite; 97% scored 18 or over on composite; 100% scored 12 or over on composite. 9% of accepted applicants took SAT; 91% took ACT. 92% of freshmen come from public schools.

**Undergraduate achievement:** 83% of fall 1992 freshmen returned for fall 1993 term. 18% of students who completed a degree program immediately went on to graduate study.

**Foreign students:** 1,218 students are from out of the country. Countries represented include Hong Kong, Indonesia, Japan, Malaysia, South Korea, and Taiwan; 91 in all.

**PROGRAMS OF STUDY. Degrees:** B.A., B.Arch., B.F.A., B.Land.Arch., B.Lib.Studies, B.Mus., B.S.

**Majors:** Accounting, Advertising, Aerospace Engineering, Agricultural Biochemistry, Agricultural Business, Agricultural Education, Agricultural Engineering, Agricultural Extension Education, Agricultural Studies, Agricultural Systems Technology, Agronomy, Animal Ecology, Animal Science, Anthropology, Apparel Merchandising/Design/Production, Architecture, Art/Design, Biochemistry, Biological/Pre-Medical Illustration, Biology, Biophysics, Botany, Ceramic Engineering, Chemical Engineering, Chemistry, Child/Family Services, Civil Engineering, Community Health Education, Community/Regional Planning, Computer Engineering, Computer Science, Construction Engineering, Dairy Science, Dietetics, Early Childhood Education, Earth Science, Economics, Electrical Engineering, Elementary Education, Engineering Operations, Engineering Science, English, Entomology, Environmental Studies, Family/Consumer Sciences Education, Family Resource Management/Consumer Science, Finance, Fisheries/Wildlife Biology, Food Science, Forestry, French, Genetics, Geology, German, Graphic Design, History, Horticulture, Hotel/Restaurant/Institution Management, Housing/the Near Environment, Industrial Education/Technology, Industrial Engineering, Interdisciplinary Major, Interior Design, International Agriculture, International Studies, Journalism/Mass Communications, Landscape Architecture, Liberal Studies, Linguistics, Management, Management Information Systems, Marketing, Mathematics, Mechanical Engineering, Metallurgical Engineering, Meteorology, Microbiology, Music, Naval Science, Nutritional Science, Pest Management, Philosophy, Physical Education, Physics, Plant Health/Protection, Political Science, Professional Agriculture, Psychology, Public Service/Administration in Agriculture, Religious Studies, Russian, Secondary Education, Seed Science, Social Work, Sociology, Spanish, Speech Communication, Statistics, Studies in Family/Consumer Sciences, Teaching Pre-Kindergarten/Kindergarten Children, Transportation/Logistics, Zoology.

**Distribution of degrees:** The majors with the highest enrollment are elementary education, psychology, and management; Russian, food service management, and biophysics/earth science/naval science have the lowest.

**Academic regulations:** Seniors must maintain minimum 2.0 GPA.

**Special:** Minors offered in agriculture, business, design, education, family/consumer sciences, and interdisciplinary studies. Lakeside and Gulf Coast Research Labs. Summer enrichment program. Intensive English orientation program. Field camps in archaeology, forestry, geology, and liberal arts/sciences. Self-designed majors. Double majors. Dual degrees. Independent study. Accelerated study. Pass/fail grading option. Internships. Cooperative education programs. Graduate school at which undergraduates may take graduate-level courses. Preprofessional programs in law, medicine, veterinary science, pharmacy, dentistry, theology, optometry, clinical lab science, cytotechnology, dental hygiene, hospital/health administration, library/information sciences, medical record administration, medical technology, nuclear medicine technology, nursing, occupational therapy, physical therapy, physician assistant, podiatry, and speech-language pathology/audiology. 2-2-1/2 nursing program with U of Iowa. 3-1 cytotechnology program with U of Wisconsin. 3-2 occupational therapy program with Washington U. Washington Semester. Traveling Scholars program. Other semester-away programs for agriculture, architecture, civil engineering, and journalism students. Exchange programs with U of Iowa and U of Northern Iowa. Teacher certification in early childhood, elementary, secondary, and special education. Certification in specific subject areas. Study abroad in Austria, England, France, Germany, Korea, Mexico, New Zealand, Scotland, Spain, Switzerland, and Wales. ROTC, NROTC, and AFROTC.

**Honors:** Phi Beta Kappa. Honors program. Honor societies.

**Academic Assistance:** Nonremedial tutoring.

**STUDENT LIFE. Housing:** Coed, women's, and men's dorms. Sorority and fraternity housing. Off-campus privately-owned housing. 52% of students live in college housing.

**Social atmosphere:** "The variety of social and cultural events in Ames far exceeds that of most towns its size," reports the student newspaper. "There is also opportunity for other events in the Des Moines area just 30 minutes away. There is something for everyone in Ames and at ISU." Popular gathering spots for students include the Maintenance Shop, Beamers, People's, The Cave, Top of the Town, and Dugan's Deli. Greeks, Residence Hall Association, athletic clubs, arts groups, and Hilton events are influential in campus life. VEISHEA, Homecoming, concerts, ISU theatre, basketball and football games are among the year's favorite events.

**Services and counseling/handicapped student services:** Placement services. Health service. Women's center. Counseling services for minority, military, veteran, and older students. Birth control, personal, and psychological counseling. Career and academic guidance services. Physically disabled student services. Learning disabled services. Notetaking services. Tape recorders. Tutors. Reader services for the blind.

**Campus organizations:** Undergraduate student government. Student newspaper (Iowa State Daily). Literary magazine. Yearbook. Radio and TV stations. Marching band, Cardinal Keynotes, ballroom dance club, magazines, many other musical, cultural, academic, departmental, social, and political groups, 500 organizations in all. 32 fraternities, all with chapter houses; 15 sororities, all with chapter houses. 17% of men join a fraternity. 16% of women join a sorority.

**Religious organizations:** Bahai Club, Campus Crusade for Christ, Hillel, International Christian Fellowship, Lutheran Student Movement, Wesley Foundation, other religious groups.

**Minority/foreign student organizations:** Black Student Alliance, Hispanic-American Student Union, Society of Hispanic Professional Engineers, United Native American Association. African Student Association, many other foreign student groups.

**ATHLETICS. Physical education requirements:** None.

**Intercollegiate competition:** 2% of students participate. Baseball (M), basketball (M,W), cross-country (M,W), diving (M,W), football (M), golf (M,W), gymnastics (M,W), softball (W), swimming (M,W), tennis (M,W), track and field (indoor) (M,W), track and field (outdoor) (M,W), volleyball (W), wrestling (M). Member of Big 8 Conference, NCAA Division I.

**Intramural and club sports:** 70% of students participate. Intramural arena football, badminton, basketball, billiards, broomball, curling, fitness event, flag football, free-throw shooting, golf, ice hockey, inner-tube water basketball, miniature golf, pickleball, racquetball, ragball, soccer, softball, table tennis, tennis, ultimate frisbee, volleyball, walleyball, water volleyball, wrestling. Men's club badminton, ballroom dance, bowling, boxing, cycling, fencing, flying, horsemanship, ice hockey, kayak, lacrosse, martial arts, Nordic skiing, racquetball, rifle/pistol, rodeo, rugby, sailing, scuba, sky diving, soccer, table tennis, trap/skeet shooting, volleyball, water polo, water skiing, weight lifting. Women's club badminton, ballroom dance, bowling, cycling, fencing, flying, horsemanship, kayak, martial arts, Nordic skiing, racquetball, rifle/pistol, rodeo, rugby, sailing, scuba, sky diving, soccer, table tennis, trap/skeet shooting, volleyball, water polo, water skiing, weight lifting.

**ADMISSIONS. Academic basis for candidate selection** (in order of priority): Class rank, secondary school record, standardized test scores, school's recommendation.

**Nonacademic basis for candidate selection:** Particular talent or ability is considered.

**Requirements:** Graduation from secondary school is required; GED is accepted. 12 units and the following program of study are required: 4 units of English, 3 units of math, 3 units of science, 2 units of social studies. Rank in top half of secondary school class required. An additional unit of social studies and two units of a single foreign language required of ap-

plicants to College of Liberal Arts and Sciences. ACT is required; SAT may be substituted. Campus visit recommended. No off-campus interviews.
**Procedure:** Take SAT or ACT by October of 12th year. Application deadline is August 19. Notification of admission on rolling basis. $100 room deposit, refundable depending on date. Freshmen accepted for terms other than fall.
**Special programs:** Admission may be deferred one year. Credit and/or placement may be granted through CEEB Advanced Placement exams for scores of 3 or higher. Credit may be granted through CLEP general exams, DANTES exams, and military experience. Credit and/or placement may be granted through CLEP subject exams. Credit and placement may be granted through challenge exams. Concurrent enrollment program.
**Transfer students:** Transfer students accepted for terms other than fall. In fall 1993, 33% of all new students were transfers into all classes. 3,729 transfer applications were received, 2,449 were accepted. Application deadline is August 19 for fall; January 13 for spring. Minimum 2.0 GPA required. Lowest course grade accepted is "D." Maximum number of transferable credits is 65 semester hours. Transfer students must complete the last 32 semester hours at the university to receive degree.
**Admissions contact:** Karsten Smedal, M.S., Director of Admissions. 515 294-5836.

**FINANCIAL AID. Available aid:** Pell grants, SEOG, state scholarships and grants, school scholarships and grants, private scholarships and grants, ROTC scholarships, academic merit scholarships, athletic scholarships, and aid for undergraduate foreign students. Perkins Loans (NDSL), PLUS, Stafford Loans (GSL), Health Professions Loans, school loans, private loans, and SLS. Tuition Management Systems and deferred payment plan.
**Financial aid statistics:** 39% of aid is not need-based. In 1993-94, 75% of all undergraduate applicants received aid; 64% of freshman applicants. Average amounts of aid awarded freshmen: Scholarships and grants, $1,720; loans, $2,407.
**Supporting data/closing dates:** FAFSA: Priority filing date is March 1; accepted on rolling basis. Notification of awards begins April 1.
**Financial aid contact:** Earl E. Dowling, M.A., Director of Student Financial Aid. 515 294-2223.

**STUDENT EMPLOYMENT.** College Work/Study Program. Institutional employment. 15% of full-time undergraduates work on campus during school year. Students may expect to earn an average of $1,835 during school year. Off-campus part-time employment opportunities rated "good."

**COMPUTER FACILITIES.** 1,500 IBM/IBM-compatible, Macintosh/Apple, and RISC-/UNIX-based microcomputers; 1,350 are networked. Students may access AT&T, Digital, Hewlett-Packard, IBM, SUN minicomputer/mainframe systems, BITNET, Internet, CompuServe. Residence halls may be equipped with networked microcomputers, networked terminals. Client/LAN operating systems include Apple/Macintosh, DOS, OS/2, UNIX/XENIX/AIX, Windows NT, X-windows, Artisoft, DEC, LocalTalk/AppleTalk, Microsoft, Novell. Computer languages and software packages include Autocad, C, COBOL, DECwrite, Excel, FORTRAN, GPSS, Interleaf, Lotus 1-2-3, Microsoft Word, OPS-5, Oracle, Pascal, SAS, Script, Spires, SPSS, TEX, WordPerfect, Xess; 100 in all. Computer facilities are available to all students.
**Fees:** $40 computer fee per semester.
**Hours:** Designated by department; several 24-hours sites.

**GRADUATE CAREER DATA.** Graduate school percentages: 1% enter law school. 1% enter medical school. 1% enter dental school. 2% enter graduate business programs. 12% enter graduate arts and sciences programs. Highest graduate school enrollments: Drake U, Iowa State U, U of Iowa. 47% of graduates choose careers in business and industry. Companies and businesses that hire graduates: Anderson Consulting, Cargill, Principal Financial Group.

**PROMINENT ALUMNI/AE.** Tom Harkin, U.S. Senator; Susan Beckett, vice president for business affairs, NBC; Jerry Junkins, president/CEO, Texas Instruments.

## Iowa Wesleyan College

**Mount Pleasant, IA 52641** 319 385-8021

**1994-95 Costs.** Tuition: $10,400. Room: $1,575. Board: $1,975. Fees, books, misc. academic expenses (school's estimate): $500.
**Enrollment.** Undergraduates: 242 men, 266 women (full-time). Freshman class: 432 applicants, 254 accepted, 77 enrolled.
**Test score averages/ranges.** Average ACT scores: 20 composite. Range of ACT scores of middle 50%: 18-22 composite.
**Faculty.** 41 full-time; 16 part-time. 35% of faculty holds doctoral degree. Student/faculty ratio: 14 to 1.
**Selectivity rating.** Competitive.

**PROFILE.** Iowa Wesleyan, founded in 1842, is a church-affiliated college. Programs are offered through the Divisions of Business, Education, Fine Arts, Human Studies, Language and Literature, Nursing, and Science. Its 60-acre campus is located in the town of Mount Pleasant, 28 miles west of Burlington.

**Accreditation:** NCACS. Professionally accredited by the National League for Nursing.
**Religious orientation:** Iowa Wesleyan College is affiliated with the United Methodist Church; one semester of religion/theology required.
**Library:** Collections totaling over 108,395 volumes and 600 periodical subscriptions.
**Special facilities/museums:** Art gallery, biological environment chamber.
**Athletic facilities:** Gymnasium, weight room, baseball, football, intramural, and softball fields, track.

**STUDENT BODY. Undergraduate profile:** 65% are state residents; 46% are transfers. 1% Asian-American, 5% Black, 1% Hispanic, 88% White, 5% Other.
**Freshman profile:** 10% of accepted applicants took SAT; 90% took ACT. 90% of freshmen come from public schools.
**Undergraduate achievement:** 46% of fall 1992 freshmen returned for fall 1993 term. 21% of entering class graduated. 6% of students who completed a degree program immediately went on to graduate study.
**Foreign students:** 47 students are from out of the country. Countries represented include Canada, Indonesia, Japan, Malaysia, and Taiwan; nine in all.

**PROGRAMS OF STUDY. Degrees:** B.A., B.Gen.Studies, B.Mus.Ed., B.S., B.S.Nurs.
**Majors:** Accounting, Art, Biology, Biology/Forestry Option, Business Administration, Business/Computer Science, Chemistry, Communications, Computer Science, Criminal Justice, Early Childhood Education, Elementary Education, English, Life Sciences, Mathematics, Music, Nursing, Physical Education, Psychology, Sociology.
**Distribution of degrees:** The majors with the highest enrollment are business administration, elementary education, and nursing; chemistry has the lowest.
**Requirements:** General education requirement.
**Academic regulations:** Minimum 2.0 GPA must be maintained.
**Special:** Minors offered in most majors and in approximately 15 other fields. Continuing education program offers general studies degree. Center for Participative Learning grants academic credit for required service project. Self-designed majors. Double majors. Dual degrees. Independent study. Pass/fail grading option. Internships. Cooperative education programs. Graduate school at which undergraduates may take graduate-level courses. Preprofessional programs in law, medicine, veterinary science, pharmacy, dentistry, theology, optometry, engineering, forestry, and physical therapy. 3-1 medical technology program with St. Luke's Hospital at Cedar Rapids. Other 3-1 programs may be arranged with professional schools. Accelerated admission possible to U of Iowa's M.B.A. program. 3-2 B.S./M.S. forestry programs with Duke U and Iowa State U. Legislative internship program. Teacher certification in early childhood, elementary, and secondary education. Certification in specific subject areas. Study abroad in Japan and Mexico.
**Honors:** Honor societies.
**Academic Assistance:** Remedial reading, writing, math, and study skills. Nonremedial tutoring.

**ADMISSIONS. Academic basis for candidate selection** (in order of priority): Class rank, standardized test scores, secondary school record, essay, school's recommendation.
**Nonacademic basis for candidate selection:** Character and personality and particular talent or ability are important. Extracurricular participation is considered.
**Requirements:** Graduation from secondary school is required; GED is accepted. 15 units and the following program of study are recommended: 4 units of English, 2 units of math, 2 units of science, 2 units of social studies, 3 units of history, 2 units of electives. Minimum composite ACT score of 19 (combined SAT score of 700) and rank in top three-fifths of secondary school class required. Conditional admission possible for applicants not meeting standard requirements. ACT is required; SAT may be substituted. Campus visit recommended. No off-campus interviews.
**Procedure:** Take SAT or ACT by October of 12th year. Visit college for interview by December of 12th year. Notification of admission on rolling basis. Reply is required within 30 days of notification. $75 tuition deposit, refundable until May 15. $25 room deposit, refundable until May 15. Freshmen accepted for terms other than fall.
**Special programs:** Credit and/or placement may be granted through CEEB Advanced Placement exams for scores of 4 or higher. Credit may be granted through CLEP general and subject exams, and life experience. Placement may be granted through challenge exams.
**Transfer students:** Transfer students accepted for terms other than fall. In fall 1993, 46% of all new students were transfers into all classes. 195 transfer applications were received, 132 were accepted. Application deadline is rolling for fall; rolling for spring. Minimum 2.0 GPA required. Lowest course grade accepted is "D." Maximum number of transferable credits is 64 semester hours from a two-year school and 94 semester hours from a four-year school. At least 30 semester hours must be completed at the college to receive degree.
**Admissions contact:** Karen J. Conrad, Director of Admissions. 319 385-6231.

**FINANCIAL AID. Available aid:** Pell grants, SEOG, state scholarships and grants, school scholarships and grants, private scholarships and grants, academic merit scholarships, athletic scholarships, and aid for undergraduate foreign students. Perkins Loans (NDSL), PLUS, Stafford Loans (GSL), and SLS. Tuition Plan Inc. and AMS.
**Financial aid statistics:** 5% of aid is not need-based. In 1993-94, 90% of all undergraduate applicants received aid; 92% of freshman applicants. Average amounts of aid awarded freshmen: Scholarships and grants, $7,000; loans, $2,625.
**Supporting data/closing dates:** FAFSA/FAF/FFS. State aid form: Deadline is April 20. Notification of awards on rolling basis.
**Financial aid contact:** Phyllis Fricke, Director of Financial Aid. 319 385-6242.

## Loras College

**Dubuque, IA 52001** 319 588-7100

**1993-94 Costs.** Tuition: $10,580. Room & board: $3,660. Fees, books, misc. academic expenses (school's estimate): $450.
**Enrollment.** Undergraduates: 828 men, 835 women (full-time). Freshman class: 1,641 applicants, 1,283 accepted, 621 enrolled. Graduate enrollment: 26 men, 55 women.
**Test score averages/ranges.** Average SAT scores: 374 verbal, 466 math. Average ACT scores: 22 composite. Range of ACT scores of middle 50%: 19-24 composite.
**Faculty.** 115 full-time; 15 part-time. 60% of faculty holds doctoral degree. Student/faculty ratio: 13 to 1.
**Selectivity rating.** Less competitive.

**PROFILE.** Loras is a church-affiliated, liberal arts college. Founded as a seminary for men in 1839, it adopted coeducation in 1971. Programs are offered through the undergraduate college and graduate division. Its 60-acre campus is located in a residential area of Dubuque, on the borders of Wisconsin, Illinois, and Iowa.

**Accreditation:** NCACS. Professionally accredited by the Council on Social Work Education, the National Council for Accreditation of Teacher Education.
**Religious orientation:** Loras College is affiliated with the Roman Catholic Church (Archdiocese of Dubuque); 12 semester hours of theology/philosophy required.
**Library:** Collections totaling over 250,000 volumes, and 1,100 periodical subscriptions.
**Special facilities/museums:** Language lab.

**Athletic facilities:** Gymnasium, field house, swimming pool, basketball and volleyball courts, tracks, baseball, football, soccer, and softball fields, wrestling room.

**STUDENT BODY. Undergraduate profile:** 50% are state residents; 15% are transfers. 2% Black, 95% White, 3% Other. Average age of undergraduates is 20.

**Freshman profile:** 4% of freshmen who took ACT scored 30 or over on English, 14% scored 30 or over on math, 10% scored 30 or over on composite; 39% scored 24 or over on English, 53% scored 24 or over on math, 44% scored 24 or over on composite; 97% scored 18 or over on English, 88% scored 18 or over on math, 92% scored 18 or over on composite; 100% scored 12 or over on English, 100% scored 12 or over on math, 100% scored 12 or over on composite. 95% of accepted applicants took ACT. 55% of freshmen come from public schools.

**Undergraduate achievement:** 85% of fall 1992 freshmen returned for fall 1993 term. 55% of entering class graduated. 15% of students who completed a degree program immediately went on to graduate study.

**Foreign students:** 12 countries represented in all.

**PROGRAMS OF STUDY. Degrees:** B.A., B.Mus., B.S.

**Majors:** Accounting, Art, Art Education, Biology, Business, Chemistry, Classical Studies, Computer Science, Economics, Education, Elementary Education, English, Finance, French, German, Gerontology, History, Human Resource Management, International Studies, Journalism, Mathematics, Mathematics/Computer Studies, Medical Technology, Modern Languages, Music, Parish Ministry, Philosophy, Physical Education, Physics, Political Science, Psychology, Public Address, Public Relations, Radio/Television, Religious Studies, Secondary Education, Social Work, Sociology, Spanish, Special Education, Speech/Dramatic Arts Education.

**Distribution of degrees:** The majors with the highest enrollment are accounting, English, and psychology; music, art, and classical studies have the lowest.

**Requirements:** General education requirement.

**Academic regulations:** Minimum 2.0 GPA required for graduation.

**Special:** Associate's degrees offered. Self-designed majors. Double majors. Independent study. Pass/fail grading option. Internships. Graduate school at which undergraduates may take graduate-level courses. Preprofessional programs in law, medicine, veterinary science, pharmacy, dentistry, theology, optometry, engineering, and physical therapy. 2-2 nursing program with U of Iowa. 3-1 medical technology programs with many schools and hospitals. 3-2 engineering programs with Iowa State U, U of Iowa, U of Notre Dame, and others. Member of Tri-State Cooperative. Cross-registration with Clarke Coll and U of Dubuque. Teacher certification in early childhood, elementary, secondary, and special education. Study abroad possible.

**Honors:** Honors program. Honor societies.

**Academic Assistance:** Remedial writing and math. Nonremedial tutoring.

**STUDENT LIFE. Housing:** Freshmen, sophomores, and juniors must live on campus unless living with family. Coed, women's, and men's dorms. School-owned/operated apartments. 55% of students live in college housing.

**Social atmosphere:** Popular gathering spots include the student center, the Kennedy Mall, and the college bars. Among the most influential campus groups are athletes, Greeks, the Campus Ministry, the Campus Activities Board, and the newspaper staff. Students enjoy sporting events and activities planned by the College Activities Board. "Loras College helps students develop a rich Christian background while academically challenging them," observes the editor of the school newspaper. Dubuque, he also notes, has little to offer either socially or culturally.

**Services and counseling/handicapped student services:** Placement services. Health service. Counseling services for minority students. Personal and psychological counseling. Career and academic guidance services. Religious counseling. Physically disabled student services. Learning disabled program/services. Notetaking services. Tape recorders. Reader services for the blind.

**Campus organizations:** Undergraduate student government. Student newspaper (Lorian, published once/week). Literary magazine. Yearbook. Radio station. Stage and concert bands, brass and other choirs, athletic, departmental, service, and special-interest groups. Six fraternities, no chapter houses; five sororities, no chapter houses.

**Religious organizations:** Campus Ministry, Religious Life Council.

**ATHLETICS. Physical education requirements:** None.

**Intercollegiate competition:** 31% of students participate. Baseball (M), basketball (M,W), cheerleading (W), cross-country (M,W), diving (M,W), football (M), golf (M,W), soccer (M), softball (W), swimming (M,W), tennis (M,W), track (indoor) (M,W), track (outdoor) (M,W), track and field (indoor) (M,W), track and field (outdoor) (M,W), volleyball (W), wrestling (M). Member of Iowa Intercollegiate Athletic Conference, NCAA Division III.

**Intramural and club sports:** 80% of students participate. Men's club ice hockey, volleyball. Women's club soccer.

**ADMISSIONS. Academic basis for candidate selection** (in order of priority): Class rank, secondary school record, standardized test scores, school's recommendation, essay.

**Nonacademic basis for candidate selection:** Character and personality and alumni/ae relationship are considered.

**Requirements:** Graduation from secondary school is required; GED is accepted. 16 units and the following program of study are recommended: 4 units of English, 3 units of math, 3 units of science, 2 units of foreign language, 3 units of social studies, 2 units of history. Minimum composite ACT score of 20 and rank in top half of secondary school class recommended. SAT or ACT is required. PSAT is recommended. Campus visit and interview recommended. Off-campus interviews available with an admissions representative.

**Procedure:** Take SAT or ACT by February of 12th year. Visit college for interview by February of 12th year. Notification of admission on rolling basis. Reply is required within 60 days of notification. $45 tuition deposit, refundable until May 1. $40 room deposit, refundable until May 1. Freshmen accepted for terms other than fall.

**Special programs:** Admission may be deferred one year. Credit and/or placement may be granted through CEEB Advanced Placement exams for scores of 3 or higher. Credit may be granted through CLEP general and subject exams. Credit and placement may be granted through life experience. Concurrent enrollment program.

**Transfer students:** Transfer students accepted for terms other than fall. In fall 1993, 15% of all new students were transfers into all classes. 146 transfer applications were received, 126 were accepted. Application deadline is rolling for fall; rolling for spring. Minimum 2.0 GPA required. Lowest course grade accepted is "D." At least 30 semester hours must be completed at the college to receive degree.

**Admissions contact:** Kelly Myers, Director of Admissions. 319 588-7236.

**FINANCIAL AID. Available aid:** Pell grants, SEOG, state scholarships and grants, school scholarships and grants, private scholarships, academic merit scholarships, and aid for undergraduate foreign students. Perkins Loans (NDSL), PLUS, Stafford Loans (GSL), state loans, and SLS.

**Financial aid statistics:** In 1993-94, 82% of all undergraduate applicants received aid; 80% of freshman applicants. Average amounts of aid awarded freshmen: Scholarships and grants, $5,521; loans, $2,167.

**Supporting data/closing dates:** FAFSA: Priority filing date is April 15. Notification of awards on rolling basis.

**Financial aid contact:** Charles McCormick, Director of Financial Aid. 319 588-7166.

**STUDENT EMPLOYMENT.** College Work/Study Program. Institutional employment. 60% of full-time undergraduates work on campus during school year. Students may expect to earn an average of $1,200 during school year. Off-campus part-time employment opportunities rated "good."

**COMPUTER FACILITIES.** 80 IBM/IBM-compatible and Macintosh/Apple microcomputers; all are networked. Students may access IBM minicomputer/mainframe systems, BITNET, Internet, CompuServe. Residence halls may be equipped with modems. Client/LAN operating systems include Apple/Macintosh, DOS, UNIX/XENIX/AIX, X-windows, LocalTalk/AppleTalk, Novell. Computer facilities are available to all students.

**Fees:** None.

**Hours:** 8 AM-midn.

**GRADUATE CAREER DATA.** Graduate school percentages: 5% enter law school. 5% enter medical school. 5% enter graduate business programs.

# Luther College

**Decorah, IA 52101** **319 387-2000**

**1994-95 Costs.** Tuition: $13,240. Room: $1,710. Board: $1,850. Fees, books, misc. academic expenses (school's estimate): $505.

**Enrollment.** Undergraduates: 921 men, 1,348 women (full-time). Freshman class: 1,549 applicants, 1,392 accepted, 587 enrolled.

**Test score averages/ranges.** Average SAT scores: 520 verbal, 590 math. Range of SAT scores of middle 50%: 460-580 verbal, 520-650 math. Average ACT scores: 25 composite. Range of ACT scores of middle 50%: 23-28 composite.

**Faculty.** 150 full-time; 43 part-time. 85% of faculty holds highest degree in specific field. Student/faculty ratio: 13 to 1.

**Selectivity rating.** More competitive.

**PROFILE.** Luther is a church-affiliated, liberal arts college. Founded as a college for men in 1861, it adopted coeducation in 1936. Its 800-acre campus is located in Decorah, 15 miles south of the Minnesota border.

**Accreditation:** NCACS. Professionally accredited by the Council on Social Work Education, the National Association of Schools of Music, the National Council for Accreditation of Teacher Education, the National League for Nursing.

**Religious orientation:** Luther College is affiliated with the Evangelical Lutheran Church in America; three semesters of religion required.

**Library:** Collections totaling over 291,500 volumes, 1,580 periodical subscriptions, and 17,000 microform items.

**Special facilities/museums:** Natural history museum, Norwegian-American museum, five art galleries, planetarium, live animal center, archaeological research center, computer music lab, two electron microscopes.

**Athletic facilities:** Gymnasiums, field house, basketball, racquetball, tennis, and volleyball courts, weight and wrestling rooms, swimming pool, stadium, baseball, football, intramural, rugby, soccer, and softball fields, fitness trail, cross-country trail, tracks, batting cages, dance studio.

**STUDENT BODY. Undergraduate profile:** 39% are state residents; 3% are transfers. 3% Asian-American, 1% Black, 1% Hispanic, 92% White, 3% Other. Average age of undergraduates is 21.

**Freshman profile:** 2% of freshmen who took SAT scored 700 or over on verbal, 13% scored 700 or over on math; 21% scored 600 or over on verbal, 49% scored 600 or over on math; 64% scored 500 or over on verbal, 86% scored 500 or over on math; 92% scored 400 or over on verbal, 96% scored 400 or over on math; 99% scored 300 or over on verbal, 100% scored 300 or over on math. 22% of accepted applicants took SAT; 94% took ACT. 90% of freshmen come from public schools.

**Undergraduate achievement:** 88% of fall 1992 freshmen returned for fall 1993 term. 67% of entering class graduated. 21% of students who completed a degree program immediately went on to graduate study.

**Foreign students:** 141 students are from out of the country. Countries represented include the Bahamas, Cyprus, India, Malta, Nepal, and Norway.

**PROGRAMS OF STUDY. Degrees:** B.A.

**Majors:** Accounting, Africana Studies, Anthropology, Art, Biology, Chemistry, Classical Studies, Computer Science, Economics, Elementary Education, English, French, German, Greek, Health Education, History, Latin, Management, Management Information Systems, Mathematics, Museum Studies, Music, Nursing, Philosophy, Physical Education/Health, Physics, Political Science, Psychobiology, Psychology, Public Communication, Religion, Scandinavian Studies, Social Work, Sociology, Sociology/Politics, Spanish, Theatre, Theatre/Dance.

**Distribution of degrees:** The majors with the highest enrollment are biology, management, and psychology; Greek, Latin, and Africana studies have the lowest.

**Requirements:** General education requirement.

**Academic regulations:** Freshmen must maintain minimum 1.75 GPA; sophomores, 1.84 GPA; juniors, 1.91 GPA; seniors, 1.96 GPA.

**Special:** Minors offered in most majors. Latin American studies, museum studies, Russian studies and social science field programs. Special January Term Programs. Courses offered in Hebrew and linguistics. Self-designed majors. Double majors. Independent study. Pass/fail grading option. Internships. Graduate school at which undergraduates may take graduate-level courses. Preprofessional programs in law, medicine, veterinary science, pharmacy, dentistry, optometry, medical technology, physical therapy, cytotechnology, and occupational therapy. 3-2 engineering programs with U of Minnesota and Washington U. 3-2 forestry and environmental studies program with Duke U. 3-2 occupational therapy program with Boston U. Washington Semester. Iowa legislative internships. Teacher certification in elementary, secondary, and special education. Study abroad in China, England, Germany, Hong Kong, Japan, Malaysia, Malta, Norway, Spain, Tanzania, and other countries.
**Honors:** Phi Beta Kappa. Honors program.
**Academic Assistance:** Nonremedial tutoring.

**STUDENT LIFE. Housing:** Students must live on campus unless granted permission otherwise. Coed dorms. Off-campus privately-owned housing. On-campus married-student housing. 85% of students live in college housing.
**Services and counseling/handicapped student services:** Placement services. Health service. Counseling services for minority students. Birth control, personal, and psychological counseling. Career and academic guidance services. Religious counseling. Physically disabled student services. Learning disabled services. Notetaking services. Tape recorders. Tutors. Reader services for the blind.
**Campus organizations:** Undergraduate student government. Student newspaper (Chips, published once/week). Literary magazine. Yearbook. Radio station. Brass choir, dance ensembles, choirs, jazz band, touring band, orchestra, Community Assembly, Student Caucus, 72 organizations in all. Five fraternities, no chapter houses; six sororities, no chapter houses. 7% of men join a fraternity. 9% of women join a sorority.
**Religious organizations:** Student Congregation, Fellowship of Christian Athletes, Gathering.
**Minority/foreign student organizations:** Black Student Union, Asian Student Association. International Student Association.

**ATHLETICS. Physical education requirements:** Two semesters of physical education required.
**Intercollegiate competition:** 21% of students participate. Baseball (M), basketball (M,W), cross-country (M,W), diving (M,W), football (M), golf (M,W), soccer (M,W), softball (W), swimming (M,W), tennis (M,W), track and field (indoor) (M,W), track and field (outdoor) (M,W), volleyball (W), wrestling (M). Member of Iowa Intercollegiate Athletic Conference, NCAA Division III.
**Intramural and club sports:** 70% of students participate. Intramural aerobics, badminton, basketball, bowling, broomball, cross-country, flag football, floor hockey, free throw, golf, Nordic skiing, oofball, pool, racquetball, rock climbing, softball, swimming, table tennis, track and field, tug-of-war, ultimate frisbee, volleyball, weight lifting, wellness program, wrestling. Men's club cycling, fencing, martial arts, rugby, volleyball. Women's club cycling, fencing, martial arts, rugby.

**ADMISSIONS. Academic basis for candidate selection** (in order of priority): Class rank, standardized test scores, secondary school record, school's recommendation, essay.
**Nonacademic basis for candidate selection:** Character and personality, extracurricular participation, particular talent or ability, and geographical distribution are considered.
**Requirements:** Graduation from secondary school is recommended; GED is accepted. 15 units and the following program of study are recommended: 4 units of English, 3 units of math, 2 units of science, 3 units of social studies. Minimum composite ACT score of 21 (combined SAT score of 860), rank in top half of secondary school class, and minimum 2.5 GPA required. ACT is required; SAT may be substituted. Campus visit and interview recommended. Off-campus interviews available with admissions and alumni representatives.
**Procedure:** Take SAT or ACT by March of 12th year. Visit college for interview by March of 12th year. Suggest filing application by March 1. Application deadline is August 1. Notification of admission on rolling basis. $200 nonrefundable tuition deposit. Freshmen accepted for terms other than fall.
**Special programs:** Admission may be deferred one year. Credit and/or placement may be granted through CEEB Advanced Placement exams. Placement may be granted through CLEP general exams. Credit and/or placement may be granted through CLEP subject exams. Credit and placement may be granted through challenge exams. Early entrance/early admission program. Concurrent enrollment program.
**Transfer students:** Transfer students accepted for terms other than fall. In fall 1993, 3% of all new students were transfers into all classes. 182 transfer applications were received, 141 were accepted. Application deadline is March 1. Minimum 2.5 GPA required. Lowest course grade accepted is "C." Maximum number of transferable credits is 64 semester hours. At least 32 semester hours must be completed at the college to receive degree.
**Admissions contact:** David L. Sallee, Ph.D., Dean for Enrollment Management. 319 387-1287.

**FINANCIAL AID. Available aid:** Pell grants, SEOG, state scholarships and grants, school scholarships and grants, private scholarships and grants, academic merit scholarships, and aid for undergraduate foreign students. Perkins Loans (NDSL), PLUS, Stafford Loans (GSL), state loans, school loans, and SLS. Guaranteed tuition.
**Financial aid statistics:** 35% of aid is not need-based. In 1993-94, 98% of all undergraduate applicants received aid; 98% of freshman applicants. Average amounts of aid awarded freshmen: Scholarships and grants, $2,000; loans, $2,100.
**Supporting data/closing dates:** FAFSA/FAF/FFS: Deadline is March 1. Income tax forms: Deadline is March 1. Notification of awards on rolling basis.
**Financial aid contact:** Sally J. Harris, M.S., Director of Student Financial Planning. 319 387-1018.

**STUDENT EMPLOYMENT.** College Work/Study Program. Institutional employment. 64% of full-time undergraduates work on campus during school year. Students may expect to earn an average of $1,200 during school year. Off-campus part-time employment opportunities rated "good."

**COMPUTER FACILITIES.** 250 IBM/IBM-compatible and Macintosh/Apple microcomputers; 100 are networked. Students may access Hewlett-Packard, IBM minicomputer/mainframe systems, Internet. Residence halls may be equipped with networked terminals, modems. Client/LAN operating systems include Apple/Macintosh, DOS, UNIX/XENIX/AIX, X-windows, Artisoft, LocalTalk/AppleTalk, Novell. Computer languages and software packages include BASIC, COBOL, dBASE IV Procomm, FORTRAN, Excel, Lotus 1-2-3, Microsoft Word, Modula 2, Pascal, SYSTAT. Computer facilities are available to all students.
**Fees:** None.
**Hours:** 8 AM-12 midn.

**GRADUATE CAREER DATA.** Graduate school percentages: 2% enter law school. 5% enter medical school. 2% enter graduate business programs. 11% enter graduate arts and sciences programs. 1% enter theological school/seminary. Highest graduate school enrollments: U of Iowa. 30% of graduates choose careers in business and industry. Companies and businesses that hire graduates: Cargill, Carlson Co., IBM, Lutheran Brotherhood, Mayo Clinic, Principal Financial Group.

**PROMINENT ALUMNI/AE.** Jim Nussell, U.S. congressman; Dr. David Larsen, editor, Mayo Medical Guide; Dr. Michael Osterholm, Minnesota state epidemiologist.

# Maharishi International University

**Fairfield, IA 52556-2091** **515 472-5031**

**1993-94 Costs.** Tuition: $10,736. Room & board: $2,760. Fees, books, misc. academic expenses (school's estimate): $570.
**Enrollment.** Undergraduates: 181 men, 170 women (full-time). Freshman class: 157 applicants, 99 accepted, 60 enrolled. Graduate enrollment: 130 men, 120 women.
**Test score averages/ranges.** Average SAT scores: 498 verbal, 533 math. Average ACT scores: 23 English, 18 math, 21 composite.
**Faculty.** 102 full-time; 20 part-time. 66% of faculty holds highest degree in specific field. Student/faculty ratio: 5 to 1.
**Selectivity rating.** Less competitive.

**PROFILE.** Maharishi International, founded in 1971, is a private university. Programs are offered through the Colleges of Arts and Sciences, Continuing Education and International Programs, Natural Law, and the Science of the Creative Intelligence; the Graduate School; the Institutes for Ayur-Vedic Studies and World Leadership; and the School of the Age of Enlightenment. Its 262-acre campus is located in Fairfield, 125 miles southeast of Des Moines.
**Accreditation:** NCACS.
**Religious orientation:** Maharishi International University is nonsectarian; Transcendental Meditation (TM) practice required twice/day.
**Library:** Collections totaling over 144,000 volumes, 1,438 periodical subscriptions, and 49,374 microform items.
**Special facilities/museums:** Art gallery, scanning electron microscope, real-time cell-imaging computer system, DNA synthesizer, TM facilities.
**Athletic facilities:** Indoor tennis courts, outdoor swimming pool, soccer stadium and track, gymnasium, recreation center.

**STUDENT BODY. Undergraduate profile:** 20% are state residents; 11% are transfers. 2% Asian-American, 2% Black, 2% Hispanic, 1% Native American, 36% White, 57% Foreign. Average age of undergraduates is 26.
**Freshman profile:** 3% of freshmen who took SAT scored 600 or over on verbal, 5% scored 600 or over on math; 8% scored 500 or over on verbal, 10% scored 500 or over on math; 13% scored 400 or over on verbal, 13% scored 400 or over on math; 16% scored 300 or over on verbal, 16% scored 300 or over on math. 3% of freshmen who took ACT scored 30 or over on English; 16% scored 24 or over on English, 5% scored 24 or over on math, 10% scored 24 or over on composite; 21% scored 18 or over on English, 13% scored 18 or over on math, 18% scored 18 or over on composite; 29% scored 12 or over on English, 28% scored 12 or over on math, 23% scored 12 or over on composite; 26% scored 6 or over on composite. Majority of accepted applicants took ACT. 98% of freshmen come from public schools.
**Undergraduate achievement:** 56% of fall 1992 freshmen returned for fall 1993 term. 48% of entering class graduated.
**Foreign students:** 216 students are from out of the country. Countries represented include Canada, Colombia, England, Germany, Hungary, and the former Yugoslav Republics; 69 in all.

**PROGRAMS OF STUDY. Degrees:** B.A., B.F.A., B.S.
**Majors:** Art, Biochemistry, Biology, Business Administration, Chemistry, Computer Science, Electronic Engineering, Electronics, Fine Art, Government, Literature, Maharishi Ayur-Ved, Mathematics, Mechanical Engineering, Physics, Psychology, Science of Creative Intelligence.
**Distribution of degrees:** The majors with the highest enrollment are business administration, literature, and art; chemistry, biochemistry, and mathematics have the lowest.
**Requirements:** General education requirement.
**Academic regulations:** Freshmen must maintain minimum 2.0 GPA; sophomores, juniors, seniors, 2.5 GPA.
**Special:** Minors offered in many majors and in education, French, music, Sanskrit, Spanish, sports science/exercise. The Maharishi "unified field-based integrated system" of education combines the intellectual understanding of the "unified field" developed by modern science with the direct experience of this field through the practice of the Maharishi technology. Program involves daily practice of Transcendental Meditation (TM) and TM-Sidhi program. Associate's degrees offered. Double majors. Independent study. Internships. Graduate school at which undergraduates may take graduate-level courses. Certification in specific subject areas. Study abroad in Canada, France, and Mexico.
**Honors:** Honors program.
**Academic Assistance:** Remedial reading, writing, math, and study skills. Nonremedial tutoring.

**ADMISSIONS. Academic basis for candidate selection** (in order of priority): School's recommendation, secondary school record, essay, class rank, standardized test scores.

**Nonacademic basis for candidate selection:** Character and personality are emphasized. Extracurricular participation and particular talent or ability are considered.
**Requirements:** Graduation from secondary school is required; GED is accepted. No specific distribution of secondary school units required. Minimum 2.5 GPA required. Conditional admission possible for applicants not meeting standard requirements. SAT or ACT is recommended. Campus visit and interview recommended. Off-campus interviews available with admissions and alumni representatives.
**Procedure:** Application deadlines are August 1 for fall, January 1 for spring. Notification of admission on rolling basis beginning April 15. $150 nonrefundable tuition deposit. Freshmen accepted for terms other than fall.
**Special programs:** Admission may be deferred one semester. Credit and/or placement may be granted through CEEB Advanced Placement exams for scores of 3 or higher. Credit and/or placement may be granted through CLEP general and subject exams. Placement may be granted through challenge exams.
**Transfer students:** Transfer students accepted for terms other than fall. In fall 1993, 11% of all new students were transfers into all classes. Application deadline is August 1 for fall; January 1 for spring. Minimum 2.5 GPA required. Lowest course grade accepted is "C." Maximum number of transferable credits is 100 semester hours. At least 60 semester hours must be completed at the university to receive degree.
**Admissions contact:** Harry Bright, Director of Admissions. 515 472-1166.

**FINANCIAL AID. Available aid:** Pell grants, SEOG, state grants, school scholarships, private scholarships, academic merit scholarships, and aid for undergraduate foreign students. Perkins Loans (NDSL), PLUS, Stafford Loans (GSL), and SLS. Deferred payment plan.
**Financial aid statistics:** 1% of aid is not need-based. In 1993-94, 96% of all undergraduate applicants received aid; 65% of freshman applicants. Average amounts of aid awarded freshmen: Scholarships and grants, $6,223; loans, $5,295.
**Supporting data/closing dates:** FAFSA/FAF: Priority filing date is April 15; deadline is July 15. School's own aid application: Priority filing date is April 15; deadline is July 15. State aid form: Deadline is April 15. Notification of awards on rolling basis.
**Financial aid contact:** Jean Symington, M.A., Director of Financial Aid. 515 472-1156.

# Morningside College

**Sioux City, IA 51106 — 712 274-5000**

**1994-95 Costs.** Tuition: $10,520. Room & board: $3,678. Fees, books, misc. academic expenses (school's estimate): $666.
**Enrollment.** Undergraduates: 405 men, 547 women (full-time). Freshman class: 586 applicants, 533 accepted, 239 enrolled. Graduate enrollment: 25 men, 86 women.
**Test score averages/ranges.** Average SAT scores: 455 verbal, 496 math. Range of SAT scores of middle 50%: 370-550 verbal, 440-590 math. Average ACT scores: 22 English, 21 math, 22 composite. Range of ACT scores of middle 50%: 19-25 English, 18-25 math.
**Faculty.** 66 full-time; 58 part-time. 64% of faculty holds highest degree in specific field. Student/faculty ratio: 15 to 1.
**Selectivity rating.** Less competitive.

**PROFILE.** Morningside, founded in 1894, is a church-affiliated, private, liberal arts college. Its 25-acre campus, which contains both modern and traditional architecture, is located in Sioux City.

**Accreditation:** NCACS. Professionally accredited by the National Association of Schools of Music, the National Council for Accreditation of Teacher Education, the National League for Nursing.
**Religious orientation:** Morningside College is affiliated with the United Methodist Church; three semester hours of theology or religion required of B.A. students.
**Library:** Collections totaling over 115,669 volumes, 797 periodical subscriptions, and 133,552 microform items.
**Special facilities/museums:** Observatory, biology research station, health center.
**Athletic facilities:** Health/physical education/recreation center.

**STUDENT BODY. Undergraduate profile:** 78% are state residents; 27% are transfers. 4% Asian-American, 3% Black, 1% Hispanic, 1% Native American, 89% White, 2% Other. Average age of undergraduates is 20.
**Freshman profile:** 7% of freshmen who took SAT scored 700 or over on verbal, 7% scored 700 or over on math; 14% scored 600 or over on verbal, 20% scored 600 or over on math; 34% scored 500 or over on verbal, 40% scored 500 or over on math; 60% scored 400 or over on verbal, 93% scored 400 or over on math; 100% scored 300 or over on verbal, 100% scored 300 or over on math. 4% of freshmen who took ACT scored 30 or over on English, 3% scored 30 or over on math, 5% scored 30 or over on composite; 35% scored 24 or over on English, 26% scored 24 or over on math, 34% scored 24 or over on composite; 84% scored 18 or over on English, 77% scored 18 or over on math, 91% scored 18 or over on composite; 99% scored 12 or over on English, 100% scored 12 or over on math, 100% scored 12 or over on composite; 100% scored 6 or over on English. Majority of accepted applicants took ACT. 95% of freshmen come from public schools.
**Undergraduate achievement:** 69% of fall 1992 freshmen returned for fall 1993 term. 39% of entering class graduated. 18% of students who completed a degree program immediately went on to graduate study.
**Foreign students:** 36 students are from out of the country. Countries represented include China, Ivory Coast, Japan, and Taiwan; 10 in all.

**PROGRAMS OF STUDY. Degrees:** B.A., B.Mus., B.Mus.Ed., B.S., B.S.Nurs.
**Majors:** Accounting, Agribusiness, Art, Biology, Biopsychology, Business Administration, Business Education, Chemistry, Computer Science, Corporate Communications, Criminal Justice, Drama, Early Childhood Education, Economics, Elementary Education, Engineering Physics, English, French, Graphic Arts, History, Humanities, Indian Studies, Industrial Psychology, Mass Communications, Mathematics, Music, Music Education, Natural Science, Nursing, Office Administration, Philosophy, Photography, Physical Education, Physics, Political Science, Pre-Chiropractic, Pre-Engineering, Pre-Forestry, Pre-Law Studies, Pre-Medicine, Pre-Optometry, Pre-Pharmacy, Pre-Physical Therapy, Pre-Veterinary Medicine, Psychology, Recreation Management, Religion/Philosophy, Religious Studies, Social Sciences, Sociology, Spanish, Special Education, Speech/Drama, Tribal Management.
**Distribution of degrees:** The majors with the highest enrollment are business administration, education, and nursing; liberal arts and engineering have the lowest.
**Requirements:** General education requirement.
**Academic regulations:** Minimum 2.0 GPA must be maintained.
**Special:** Minors offered in all majors except nursing. Associate's degrees offered. Self-designed majors. Double majors. Independent study. Accelerated study. Pass/fail grading option. Internships. Cooperative education programs. Graduate school at which undergraduates may take graduate-level courses. Preprofessional programs in law, medicine, veterinary science, pharmacy, dentistry, theology, optometry, chiropractic, engineering, and physical therapy. Combined-degree engineering programs with U of Iowa, Iowa State U, South Dakota State U, and Washington U. Combined-degree fashion merchandising, hotel/restaurant management, and nutritional science programs with Iowa State U. Washington Semester and UN Semester. Exchange program with Drew U. Teacher certification in early childhood, elementary, secondary, and special education. Certification in specific subject areas. Exchange programs abroad in England (Edge Hill Coll, Oxford U) and Japan (Kansai Gadai U). Study abroad also in Austria, France, Germany, Israel, Mexico, and Spain.
**Honors:** Honors program. Honor societies.
**Academic Assistance:** Remedial reading, writing, math, and study skills. Nonremedial tutoring.

**ADMISSIONS. Academic basis for candidate selection** (in order of priority): Secondary school record, standardized test scores, class rank, school's recommendation, essay.
**Nonacademic basis for candidate selection:** Particular talent or ability and alumni/ae relationship are emphasized. Character and personality and extracurricular participation are important.
**Requirements:** Graduation from secondary school is recommended; GED is accepted. 16 units required and the following program of study recommended: 3 units of English, 3 units of math, 2 units of foreign language, 3 units of social studies, 2 units of history. Minimum composite ACT score of 20, rank in top half of secondary school class, and minimum 2.5 GPA recommended. Application to nursing program is made following successful completion of freshman year. Portfolio required of art program applicants. Audition required of music program applicants. Conditional admission possible for applicants not meeting standard requirements. Program for Native American applicants. ACT is required; SAT may be substituted. Campus visit and interview recommended. Off-campus interviews available with admissions and alumni representatives.
**Procedure:** Take SAT or ACT by December of 12th year. Visit college for interview by February of 12th year. Suggest filing application by December. Notification of admission on rolling basis. Reply is required by May 1. $100 tuition deposit, refundable until May 1. Freshmen accepted for terms other than fall.
**Special programs:** Credit and/or placement may be granted through CEEB Advanced Placement exams and CLEP general and subject exams. Credit and placement may be granted through challenge exams, and military and life experience. Concurrent enrollment program.
**Transfer students:** Transfer students accepted for terms other than fall. In fall 1993, 27% of all new students were transfers into all classes. 132 transfer applications were received, 131 were accepted. Application deadline is rolling for fall; rolling for spring. Minimum 2.0 GPA required. Lowest course grade accepted is "C." Maximum number of transferable credits is 94 semester hours. At least 30 semester hours must be completed at the college to receive degree.
**Admissions contact:** Lora Vander Zwaag, M.A., Director of Admissions. 712 274-5111.

**FINANCIAL AID. Available aid:** Pell grants, SEOG, state scholarships and grants, school scholarships and grants, private scholarships, academic merit scholarships, athletic scholarships, and aid for undergraduate foreign students. Perkins Loans (NDSL), PLUS, Stafford Loans (GSL), school loans, private loans, and SLS.
**Financial aid statistics:** 35% of aid is not need-based. In 1993-94, 71% of all undergraduate applicants received aid; 95% of freshman applicants. Average amounts of aid awarded freshmen: Scholarships and grants, $7,290; loans, $2,918.
**Supporting data/closing dates:** FAFSA: Priority filing date is March 1; accepted on rolling basis.
**Financial aid contact:** Alice Villone, M.B.A., Director of Financial Aid. 712 274-5159.

# Mount Mercy College

**Cedar Rapids, IA 52402-4798 — 319 363-8213**

**1993-94 Costs.** Tuition: $9,800. Room & board: $3,330. Fees, books, misc. academic expenses (school's estimate): $600.
**Enrollment.** Undergraduates: 206 men, 600 women (full-time). Freshman class: 386 applicants, 331 accepted, 165 enrolled.
**Test score averages/ranges.** Average ACT scores: 23 English, 22 math, 23 composite. Range of ACT scores of middle 50%: 20-25 English, 20-25 math.
**Faculty.** 65 full-time; 36 part-time. 28% of faculty holds doctoral degree. Student/faculty ratio: 13 to 1.
**Selectivity rating.** Less competitive.

**PROFILE.** Mount Mercy, founded in 1928, is a private, church-affiliated, liberal arts college. Its 30-acre campus is located in Cedar Rapids.

**Accreditation:** NCACS. Professionally accredited by the Council on Social Work Education, the National League for Nursing.
**Religious orientation:** Mount Mercy College is affiliated with the Roman Catholic Church (Sisters of Mercy); one semester of religion required.
**Library:** Collections totaling over 91,678 volumes, 625 periodical subscriptions, and 1,278 microform items.

**Athletic facilities:** Gymnasium, field house, weight room, basketball, racquetball, tennis, and volleyball courts, baseball, softball, and soccer fields.

**STUDENT BODY. Undergraduate profile:** 94% are state residents; 56% are transfers. 1% Asian-American, 1% Black, 2% Hispanic, 2% Native American, 94% White. Average age of undergraduates is 21.

**Freshman profile:** 2% of accepted applicants took SAT; 98% took ACT. 90% of freshmen come from public schools.

**Undergraduate achievement:** 70% of fall 1992 freshmen returned for fall 1993 term. 49% of entering class graduated. 6% of students who completed a degree program immediately went on to graduate study.

**Foreign students:** 15 students are from out of the country. Countries represented include China and the Czech Republic/Slovakia; seven in all.

**PROGRAMS OF STUDY. Degrees:** B.A., B.Appl.Arts, B.Appl.Sci., B.Bus.Admin., B.S.

**Majors:** Accounting, Administrative Management, Art, Biology, Business Education, Computer Science, Criminal Justice, Elementary Education, English, Interdisciplinary Major, Marketing, Mathematics, Medical Technology, Music, Music Education, Nursing, Political Science, Psychology, Public Relations, Religion, Social Work, Sociology, Speech/Drama.

**Distribution of degrees:** The majors with the highest enrollment are administrative management, education, and nursing; religious studies, speech/drama, and music have the lowest.

**Requirements:** General education requirement.

**Academic regulations:** Minimum 2.0 GPA must be maintained.

**Special:** Minors offered in chemistry, communication, and economics. Self-designed majors. Double majors. Independent study. Pass/fail grading option. Internships. Graduate school at which undergraduates may take graduate-level courses. Preprofessional programs in law, medicine, veterinary science, pharmacy, dentistry, theology, and optometry. Teacher certification in early childhood, elementary, and secondary education. Certification in specific subject areas. Exchange program abroad in the Czech Republic.

**Honors:** Phi Beta Kappa. Honors program. Honor societies.

**Academic Assistance:** Remedial reading, writing, and math. Nonremedial tutoring.

**ADMISSIONS. Academic basis for candidate selection** (in order of priority): Secondary school record, class rank, essay, school's recommendation, standardized test scores.

**Nonacademic basis for candidate selection:** Character and personality, extracurricular participation, particular talent or ability, geographical distribution, and alumni/ae relationship are considered.

**Requirements:** Graduation from secondary school is required; GED is accepted. 17 units and the following program of study are recommended: 4 units of English, 4 units of math, 3 units of science, 2 units of foreign language, 2 units of social studies, 2 units of history. Minimum composite ACT score of 19, rank in top half of secondary school class, and minimum 2.5 GPA required. SAT or ACT is required. PSAT is recommended. Campus visit and interview recommended. Off-campus interviews available with an admissions representative.

**Procedure:** Take SAT or ACT by October of 12th year. Visit college for interview by April of 12th year. Suggest filing application by March 1. Application deadline is August 15. Notification of admission on rolling basis. Reply is required by May 1. $200 nonrefundable tuition deposit. $50 nonrefundable room deposit. Freshmen accepted for terms other than fall.

**Special programs:** Admission may be deferred one year. Credit and/or placement may be granted through CEEB Advanced Placement exams for scores of 3 or higher. Credit and/or placement may be granted through CLEP general and subject exams. Credit and placement may be granted through ACT PEP and challenge exams, and life experience. Early entrance/early admission program.

**Transfer students:** Transfer students accepted for terms other than fall. In fall 1993, 56% of all new students were transfers into all classes. 374 transfer applications were received, 284 were accepted. Application deadline is August 15 for fall; January 15 for spring. Minimum 2.5 GPA required. Lowest course grade accepted is "D." Maximum number of transferable credits is 63 semester hours. At least 30 semester hours must be completed at the college to receive degree.

**Admissions contact:** Larry Erenberger, Vice President for Enrollment Management. 319 363-8213, extension 221.

**FINANCIAL AID. Available aid:** Pell grants, SEOG, state scholarships and grants, school scholarships and grants, private scholarships and grants, and academic merit scholarships. Perkins Loans (NDSL), Stafford Loans (GSL), NSL, state loans, school loans, and SLS.

**Financial aid statistics:** 10% of aid is not need-based. In 1993-94, 85% of all undergraduate applicants received aid; 85% of freshman applicants. Average amounts of aid awarded freshmen: Scholarships and grants, $3,200; loans, $3,000.

**Supporting data/closing dates:** FAFSA/FAF/FFS: Priority filing date is March 1. Notification of awards on rolling basis.

**Financial aid contact:** Jacqueline Kennedy, Director of Financial Aid. 319 363-8213, extension 251.

## Mount St. Clare College

**Clinton, IA 52732** — **319 242-4023**

**1993-94 Costs.** Tuition: $9,200. Room: $1,610. Board: $1,990. Fees, books, misc. academic expenses (school's estimate): $750.

**Enrollment.** Undergraduates: 143 men, 221 women (full-time). Freshman class: 415 applicants, 415 accepted, 171 enrolled.

**Test score averages/ranges.** Average ACT scores: 20 English, 18 math, 20 composite. Range of ACT scores of middle 50%: 19-21 English, 17-20 math.

**Faculty.** 19 full-time; 26 part-time. 22% of faculty holds doctoral degree. Student/faculty ratio: 10 to 1.

**Selectivity rating.** Noncompetitive.

**PROFILE.** Mount St. Clare, founded in 1895, is a private, church-affiliated, liberal arts college. Its 33-acre campus is located in Clinton, 40 miles north of Moline.

**Accreditation:** NCACS.

**Religious orientation:** Mount St. Clare College is an interdenominational Christian school; two semesters of theology required.

**Library:** Collections totaling over 67,000 volumes, 400 periodical subscriptions, and 2,500 microform items.

**Special facilities/museums:** On-campus preschool for early childhood, elementary, and secondary education majors.

**Athletic facilities:** Gymnasium, soccer and softball fields, tennis courts.

**STUDENT BODY. Undergraduate profile:** 70% are state residents; 42% are transfers. 1% Asian-American, 7% Black, 2% Hispanic, 1% Native American, 89% White. Average age of undergraduates is 19.

**Freshman profile:** 100% of accepted applicants took ACT. 75% of freshmen come from public schools.

**Undergraduate achievement:** 53% of fall 1992 freshmen returned for fall 1993 term. 30% of entering class graduated.

**Foreign students:** 16 students are from out of the country. Countries represented include the Bahamas, China, France, Germany, Japan, and South Korea; seven in all.

**PROGRAMS OF STUDY. Degrees:** B.A.

**Majors:** Accounting, Business Administration, Computer Information Systems, Cytotechnology, Elementary Education, General Studies, Liberal Arts, Social Science.

**Distribution of degrees:** The majors with the highest enrollment are liberal arts, business administration, and accounting; computer information systems have the lowest.

**Requirements:** General education requirement.

**Academic regulations:** Minimum 2.0 GPA must be maintained.

**Special:** Minors offered in some majors. Associate's degrees offered. Double majors. Graduate school at which undergraduates may take graduate-level courses. Preprofessional programs in law, medicine, veterinary science, pharmacy, dentistry, and physical therapy. Teacher certification in early childhood education.

**Honors:** Phi Beta Kappa.

**Academic Assistance:** Remedial reading, writing, math, and study skills. Nonremedial tutoring.

**ADMISSIONS. Academic basis for candidate selection** (in order of priority): Standardized test scores, secondary school record, school's recommendation, class rank, essay.

**Nonacademic basis for candidate selection:** Character and personality and extracurricular participation are important. Particular talent or ability and alumni/ae relationship are considered.

**Requirements:** Graduation from secondary school is recommended; GED is accepted. No specific distribution of secondary school units required. Foreign language and history units are recommended. Minimum composite ACT score of 17, rank in top half of secondary school class, or minimum 2.0 GPA required. Conditional admission possible for applicants not meeting standard requirements. Bridges program. ACT is required; SAT may be substituted. PSAT is recommended. Campus visit and interview recommended. Off-campus interviews available with an admissions representative.

**Procedure:** Suggest filing application by April 1. Application deadline is August 15. Notification of admission on rolling basis. Reply is required by August 15. $125 tuition deposit, refundable until April 30. $100 room deposit, refundable until August 15. Freshmen accepted for terms other than fall.

**Special programs:** Admission may be deferred one year. Credit and/or placement may be granted through CEEB Advanced Placement exams for scores of 3 or higher. Credit and/or placement may be granted through CLEP general and subject exams. Credit and placement may be granted through Regents College and DANTES exams, and military experience. Early entrance/early admission program. Concurrent enrollment program.

**Transfer students:** Transfer students accepted for terms other than fall. In fall 1993, 42% of all new students were transfers into all classes. 91 transfer applications were received, 91 were accepted. Application deadline is rolling for fall; rolling for spring. Minimum 2.0 GPA required. Lowest course grade accepted is "C." Maximum number of transferable credits is 64 semester hours from a two-year school and 90 semester hours from a four-year school. At least 30 semester hours must be completed at the college to receive degree.

**Admissions contact:** Waunita Sullivan, Director of Enrollment. 319 242-4153.

**FINANCIAL AID. Available aid:** Pell grants, SEOG, state scholarships and grants, school scholarships and grants, private scholarships and grants, academic merit scholarships, and athletic scholarships. Perkins Loans (NDSL), PLUS, state loans, and SLS. Tuition Plan Inc.

**Supporting data/closing dates:** FAFSA/FAF/FFS: Priority filing date is April 1; deadline is August 1. Income tax forms: Priority filing date is April 1; deadline is August 1. Notification of awards begins March 1.

**Financial aid contact:** Lisa K. Erling, Director of Financial Aid. 319 242-4023, ext. 18.

## Northwestern College

**Orange City, IA 51041** — **712 737-7000**

**1994-95 Costs.** Tuition: $9,900. Room & board: $3,075. Fees, books, misc. academic expenses (school's estimate): $300.

**Enrollment.** Undergraduates: 452 men, 588 women (full-time). Freshman class: 840 applicants, 764 accepted, 356 enrolled. Graduate enrollment: 1 man, 16 women.

**Test score averages/ranges.** Average ACT scores: 23 composite. Range of ACT scores of middle 50%: 21-24 composite.

**Faculty.** 60 full-time; 25 part-time. 70% of faculty holds doctoral degree. Student/faculty ratio: 16 to 1.

**Selectivity rating.** Less competitive.

**PROFILE.** Northwestern, founded in 1882, is a private, church-affiliated, liberal arts college. Its 51-acre campus is located in Orange City, 40 miles north of Sioux City.

**Accreditation:** NCACS. Professionally accredited by the Council on Social Work Education, the National Council for Accreditation of Teacher Education.

**Religious orientation:** Northwestern College is affiliated with the Reformed Church in America; eight semester hours of religion required.
**Library:** Collections totaling over 90,000 volumes, 550 periodical subscriptions, and 3,200 microform items.
**Special facilities/museums:** Language lab.
**Athletic facilities:** Gymnasium, basketball, racquetball, and tennis courts, weight room, track.

**STUDENT BODY. Undergraduate profile:** 70% are state residents; 14% are transfers. 5% Asian-American, 1% Black, 94% White. Average age of undergraduates is 20.
**Freshman profile:** 2% of accepted applicants took SAT; 98% took ACT. 85% of freshmen come from public schools.
**Undergraduate achievement:** 88% of fall 1992 freshmen returned for fall 1993 term. 51% of entering class graduated. 15% of students who completed a degree program immediately went on to graduate study.
**Foreign students:** 61 students are from out of the country. Countries represented include Bahrain, Canada, China, India, Japan, and Taiwan; 17 in all.

**PROGRAMS OF STUDY. Degrees:** B.A.
**Majors:** Accounting, Art, Athletic Training, Biology, Biology/Health Professions, Business Administration/Management, Business Education, Chemistry, Christian Education, Communications, Computer/Information Sciences, Economics, Elementary Education, English, French, History, Humanities, Mathematics, Medical Technology, Music, Philosophy, Physical Education, Political Science/Government, Psychology, Recreation, Religion, Social Work, Sociology, Spanish, Theatre, Theatre/Speech.
**Distribution of degrees:** The majors with the highest enrollment are elementary education, business administration, and biology; philosophy, humanities, and art have the lowest.
**Requirements:** General education requirement.
**Academic regulations:** Freshmen must maintain minimum 1.7 GPA; sophomores, juniors, seniors, 2.0 GPA.
**Special:** Minors offered in most majors. Career concentrations in agribusiness, Christian theatre ministries, conservation of natural resources, criminal justice, financial management, general management, marketing, mission service, public administration, and vocational rehabilitation. Courses offered in Dutch, general studies, geography, and Greek. In junior year, students engage in cross-cultural experience, either through classwork or off-campus activities. Associate's degrees offered. Self-designed majors. Double majors. Independent study. Accelerated study. Pass/fail grading option. Internships. Cooperative education programs. Graduate school at which undergraduates may take graduate-level courses. Preprofessional programs in law, medicine, veterinary science, pharmacy, dentistry, theology, chiropractic, engineering, mortuary science, music performance, nuclear medical technology, and physical therapy. 3-2 engineering program with Washington U. 3-1 medical technology program. Member of Colleges of Mid-America and Christian College Coalition. American Studies Program (Washington, D.C.). AuSable Inst of Environmental Studies Program (Michigan). Los Angeles Film Studies Semester. Urban Studies Program (Chicago). Teacher certification in early childhood, elementary, secondary, and special education. Study abroad in France, Mexico, the Netherlands, and Spain.
**Honors:** Honors program. Honor societies.
**Academic Assistance:** Remedial reading, writing, math, and study skills. Nonremedial tutoring.

**STUDENT LIFE. Housing:** All unmarried students under age 21 must live on campus unless living near campus with relatives. Women's and men's dorms. School-owned/operated apartments. Off-campus privately-owned housing. 82% of students live in college housing.
**Social atmosphere:** The student newspaper reports, "Every weekend there is at least one thing to do on campus thanks to the Student Activities Board which organizes dances, concerts, and weekend retreats." Other influential organizations are athletics and the Student Ministries Board. Some favorite gathering spots on campus are the RSC Student Center, the Firelite cafe, and dorm lounges. Popular campus events include Homecoming, theatre performances, Springfest, and Parents Weekend.
**Services and counseling/handicapped student services:** Placement services. Health service. Counseling services for older students. Personal and psychological counseling. Career and academic guidance services. Religious counseling. Physically disabled student services. Learning disabled services. Notetaking services. Reader services for the blind.
**Campus organizations:** Undergraduate student government. Student newspaper (Beacon, published once/week). Literary magazine. Yearbook. Radio and TV stations. A cappella choir, jazz band, Art Student League, drama ministries ensemble, 30 organizations in all.
**Religious organizations:** Campus Ministries, Fellowship of Christian Athletes, Summer of Service, Community Impact, Global Ministries.
**Minority/foreign student organizations:** Black Student Union. International Club.

**ATHLETICS. Physical education requirements:** Two semester hours of physical education required.
**Intercollegiate competition:** 35% of students participate. Baseball (M), basketball (M,W), cheerleading (M,W), cross-country (M,W), football (M), golf (M,W), softball (W), tennis (M,W), track (indoor) (M,W), track (outdoor) (M,W), track and field (indoor) (M,W), track and field (outdoor) (M,W), volleyball (W), wrestling (M). Member of NAIA, Nebraska-Iowa Athletic Conference.
**Intramural and club sports:** 60% of students participate. Intramural badminton, basketball, bowling, darts, eightball, flag football, football, frisbee golf, golf, handball, hot-shot basketball, pickleball, pool, snooker, table tennis, tennis, volleyball, walleyball. Men's club soccer. Women's club soccer.

**ADMISSIONS. Academic basis for candidate selection** (in order of priority): Class rank, standardized test scores, secondary school record, school's recommendation.
**Nonacademic basis for candidate selection:** Character and personality, geographical distribution, and alumni/ae relationship are considered.
**Requirements:** Graduation from secondary school is required; GED is accepted. 15 units and the following program of study are recommended: 4 units of English, 3 units of math, 2 units of science, 1 unit of foreign language, 3 units of social studies. Minimum composite ACT score of 18, rank in top three-quarters of secondary school class, and minimum 2.0 GPA required. Conditional admission possible for applicants not meeting standard requirements. ACT is required; SAT may be substituted. Campus visit and interview recommended. Off-campus interviews available with an admissions representative.
**Procedure:** Take SAT or ACT by fall of 12th year. Application deadline is August 15. Notification of admission on rolling basis. Reply is required by May 1. $100 tuition deposit, refundable until May 1. Freshmen accepted for terms other than fall.
**Special programs:** Admission may be deferred two years. Credit and/or placement may be granted through CEEB Advanced Placement exams for scores of 3 or higher. Credit may be granted through CLEP subject exams. Credit and placement may be granted through challenge exams.
**Transfer students:** Transfer students accepted for terms other than fall. In fall 1993, 14% of all new students were transfers into all classes. 96 transfer applications were received, 81 were accepted. Application deadline is August 15 for fall; January 1 for spring. Minimum 2.0 GPA recommended. Lowest course grade accepted is "D-." Maximum number of transferable credits is 62 semester hours from a two-year school and 94 semester hours from a four-year school. At least 30 semester hours must be completed at the college to receive degree.
**Admissions contact:** Ronald K. DeJong, Director of Admissions. 712 737-7130.

**FINANCIAL AID. Available aid:** Pell grants, SEOG, state scholarships and grants, school scholarships and grants, private scholarships and grants, academic merit scholarships, athletic scholarships, and aid for undergraduate foreign students. Perkins Loans (NDSL), PLUS, Stafford Loans (GSL), state loans, school loans, and SLS. Family tuition reduction. Monthly payment plan.
**Financial aid statistics:** 30% of aid is not need-based. In 1993-94, 100% of all undergraduate applicants received aid. Average amounts of aid awarded freshmen: Scholarships and grants, $1,600; loans, $2,400.
**Supporting data/closing dates:** FAFSA/FAF/FFS: Priority filing date is April 1. School's own aid application: Priority filing date is April 1. State aid form: Deadline is April 20. Notification of awards begins March 1.
**Financial aid contact:** Carol Bogaard, Director of Financial Aid. 712 737-7131.

**STUDENT EMPLOYMENT.** College Work/Study Program. Institutional employment. 52% of full-time undergraduates work on campus during school year. Students may expect to earn an average of $650 during school year. Off-campus part-time employment opportunities rated "fair."

**COMPUTER FACILITIES.** 150 IBM/IBM-compatible and Macintosh/Apple microcomputers; all are networked. Students may access Digital minicomputer/mainframe systems. Residence halls may be equipped with networked microcomputers. Client/LAN operating systems include Apple/Macintosh, DOS, UNIX/XENIX/AIX, Windows NT, X-windows, DEC, LocalTalk/AppleTalk, Microsoft, Novell. Computer languages and software packages include Assembly, BASIC, C, COBOL, Eric, FORTRAN, Harvard Graphics, Lotus 1-2-3, Microsoft Word, PageMaker, Pascal; 50 in all. Computer facilities are available to all students.
**Fees:** Computer fee is included in tuition/fees.

**GRADUATE CAREER DATA.** Graduate school percentages: 1% enter law school. 4% enter medical school. 3% enter graduate business programs. 7% enter theological school/seminary. Highest graduate school enrollments: Fuller Theological Seminary, U of Iowa, Iowa State U, Northwestern U, Western Theological Seminary. 34% of graduates choose careers in business and industry. Companies and businesses that hire graduates: IBM, General Dynamics, Citibank.

**PROMINENT ALUMNI/AE.** Richard Mouw, author and provost, Fuller Theological Seminary; Arie Brouwer, former general secretary, National Council of Churches; Robert Muilenburg, executive director, U of Washington Hospitals; Alfred Popma, M.D., founder, Mountain States Tumor Institute.

# St. Ambrose University

**Davenport, IA 52803** **319 383-8800**

**1994-95 Costs.** Tuition: $10,450. Room: $1,710. Board: $2,310. Fees, books, misc. academic expenses (school's estimate): $425.
**Enrollment.** Undergraduates: 594 men, 755 women (full-time). Freshman class: 809 applicants, 647 accepted, 279 enrolled. Graduate enrollment: 454 men, 301 women.
**Test score averages/ranges.** Average ACT scores: 21 composite.
**Faculty.** 72 full-time; 101 part-time. 72% of faculty holds doctoral degree. Student/faculty ratio: 15 to 1.
**Selectivity rating.** Less competitive.

**PROFILE.** St. Ambrose is a church-affiliated, liberal arts college. Founded in 1882, it adopted coeducation in 1968. Its four-acre campus is located in Davenport, 80 miles southeast of Cedar Rapids.

**Accreditation:** NCACS. Professionally accredited by the American Medical Association (CAHEA).
**Religious orientation:** St. Ambrose University is affiliated with the Roman Catholic Church; 12 semester hours of theology required.
**Library:** Collections totaling over 130,000 volumes, 750 periodical subscriptions and 350 microform items.
**Special facilities/museums:** Art gallery, observatory, language lab.
**Athletic facilities:** Racquetball courts, batting cage, workout area, track, weight rooms, field house, athletic field, swimming pool.

**STUDENT BODY. Undergraduate profile:** 70% are state residents; 35% are transfers. 1% Asian-American, 4% Black, 2% Hispanic, 93% White. Average age of undergraduates is 22.
**Freshman profile:** 100% of accepted applicants took ACT. 55% of freshmen come from public schools.
**Undergraduate achievement:** 88% of fall 1992 freshmen returned for fall 1993 term. 68% of entering class graduated. 12% of students who completed a degree program immediately went on to graduate study.

**Foreign students:** 12 students are from out of the country. Countries represented include Argentina, Brazil, China, Nigeria, Panama, and the Philippines; eight in all.

**PROGRAMS OF STUDY. Degrees:** B.A., B.Ed., B.Elect.Studies, B.Indust.Eng., B.S.

**Majors:** Accounting, Art, Biology, Business Administration, Chemistry, Classical/Modern Languages, Computer Science, Criminal Justice, Criminalistics, Criminology, Economics, Education, Elementary Education, English, History, Industrial Engineering, Management Science/Statistics, Mass Communications, Mathematics, Mathematics Education, Music, Music Education, Natural Science, Occupational Therapy, Philosophy, Physical Education/Recreation, Physics, Political Science, Psychology, Public Administration, Sociology, Speech/Theatre, Theology.

**Distribution of degrees:** The majors with the highest enrollment are business administration, accounting, and mass communications; philosophy, theology, and computer science have the lowest.

**Requirements:** General education requirement.

**Academic regulations:** Minimum 2.0 GPA must be maintained.

**Special:** Minors offered in many majors and in geography and women's studies. Special studies majors develop own programs with advisers. Courses offered in acoustics, astronomy, coaching, French, geology, German, Greek, Italian, Latin, Russian, and Spanish. Self-designed majors. Double majors. Independent study. Pass/fail grading option. Internships. Cooperative education programs. Graduate school at which undergraduates may take graduate-level courses. Preprofessional programs in law, medicine, veterinary science, pharmacy, dentistry, chiropractic, engineering, and meteorology. Member of Midwest International Studies; exchange possible. Teacher certification in early childhood, elementary, secondary, and special education. Certification in specific subject areas. Study abroad in Austria, England, France, Mexico, and Spain. ROTC, NROTC, and AFROTC at U of Iowa.

**Honors:** Phi Beta Kappa. Honors program. Honor societies.

**Academic Assistance:** Remedial reading, writing, math, and study skills. Nonremedial tutoring.

**STUDENT LIFE. Housing:** All freshmen and sophomores must live on campus unless living with family. Coed, women's, and men's dorms. School-owned/operated apartments. Townhouses. 50% of students live in college housing.

**Social atmosphere:** Favorite hangouts include Rookie's Sports Bar, Stickman's, and Rock Island Brewing Co. Black Student Union, Student Alumni Association, and Ambrosians for Peace and Justice have widespread influence on student life. Popular social events include Turk Fest, which is a fundraising effort to raise money for food for the poor, and Woodstock, which is a reenactment of the 1960s music festival. "There seems to be a general sense of family and community on campus," reports the editor of the student newspaper.

**Services and counseling/handicapped student services:** Placement services. Health service. Day care. Counseling services for minority, veteran, and older students. Personal and psychological counseling. Career and academic guidance services. Religious counseling. Physically disabled student services. Learning disabled program/services. Notetaking services. Tape recorders. Tutors. Reader services for the blind.

**Campus organizations:** Undergraduate student government. Student newspaper (the Buzz on Campus, published once/two weeks). Literary magazine. Radio and TV stations. Band, chorus, veterans club, Big Brothers/Big Sisters, Young Democrats, College Republicans, athletic, departmental, and special-interest groups, 10 organizations in all. 6% of men join a fraternity. 6% of women join a sorority.

**Religious organizations:** Ambrosians for Peace, Campus Ministry.

**Minority/foreign student organizations:** AOH, Hispanic Union, Multicultural Club, Black Student Union.

**ATHLETICS. Physical education requirements:** Two semesters of physical education required.

**Intercollegiate competition:** 25% of students participate. Baseball (M), basketball (M,W), cheerleading (M,W), cross-country (M,W), football (M), golf (M,W), soccer (M), softball (W), tennis (M,W), track (indoor) (M,W), track (outdoor) (M,W), track and field (indoor) (M,W), track and field (outdoor) (M,W), volleyball (W). Member of Midwest Classic Conference, NAIA.

**Intramural and club sports:** 36% of students participate. Intramural aerobics, archery, badminton, basketball, bowling, football, free throw, frisbee golf, golf, hooverball, innertube water race, miniature golf, roller skating, sand golf, softball, table tennis, tennis, track and field, triathlon, volleyball, walleyball, water aerobics, water basketball, water volleyball, weight lifting.

**ADMISSIONS. Academic basis for candidate selection** (in order of priority): Secondary school record, standardized test scores, class rank, school's recommendation.

**Nonacademic basis for candidate selection:** Character and personality, extracurricular participation, particular talent or ability, and alumni/ae relationship are considered.

**Requirements:** Graduation from secondary school is required; GED is accepted. 16 units and the following program of study are required: 4 units of English, 2 units of math, 2 units of lab science, 1 unit of foreign language, 2 units of social studies, 1 unit of history, 4 units of academic electives. Minimum composite ACT score of 20 (combined SAT score of 780), rank in top half of secondary school class, and minimum 2.5 GPA required. Conditional admission possible for applicants not meeting standard requirements. ACT is required; SAT may be substituted. Campus visit and interview recommended. No off-campus interviews.

**Procedure:** Take SAT or ACT by October of 12th year. Notification of admission on rolling basis. Reply is required by date specified in letter of acceptance. $50 nonrefundable tuition deposit. $100 room deposit, refundable until July 1. Freshmen accepted for terms other than fall.

**Special programs:** Admission may be deferred one semester. Credit may be granted through CEEB Advanced Placement for scores of 3 or higher. Credit may be granted through CLEP general and subject exams. Placement may be granted through challenge exams and military and life experience. Credit and placement may be granted through DANTES exams. Concurrent enrollment program.

**Transfer students:** Transfer students accepted for terms other than fall. In fall 1993, 35% of all new students were transfers into all classes. 332 transfer applications were received, 290 were accepted. Application deadline is rolling for fall; rolling for spring. Minimum 2.0 GPA required. Lowest course grade accepted is "C." Maximum number of transferable credits is 60 semester hours from a two-year school and 90 semester hours from a four-year school. At least 30 semester hours must be completed at the university to receive degree.

**Admissions contact:** Patrick O'Connor, M.A., Dean of Admissions. 800 383-2627, 319 383-8888.

**FINANCIAL AID. Available aid:** Pell grants, SEOG, state scholarships and grants, school scholarships and grants, private scholarships and grants, academic merit scholarships, and athletic scholarships. Perkins Loans (NDSL), PLUS, Stafford Loans (GSL), and SLS. Tuition Plan Inc. and AMS.

**Financial aid statistics:** 40% of aid is not need-based. In 1993-94, 96% of all undergraduate applicants received aid; 98% of freshman applicants. Average amounts of aid awarded freshmen: Scholarships and grants, $3,000; loans, $2,625.

**Supporting data/closing dates:** FAFSA/FFS: Priority filing date is March 15; accepted on rolling basis. School's own aid application: Priority filing date is March 15; accepted on rolling basis. State aid form: Priority filing date is March 15. Notification of awards on rolling basis.

**Financial aid contact:** Rita O'Connor, M.S., Director of Financial Aid. 319 383-8885.

**STUDENT EMPLOYMENT.** College Work/Study Program. Institutional employment. 30% of full-time undergraduates work on campus during school year. Students may expect to earn an average of $1,700 during school year. Off-campus part-time employment opportunities rated "good."

**COMPUTER FACILITIES.** 75 IBM/IBM-compatible and Macintosh/Apple microcomputers. Students may access Digital, IBM minicomputer/mainframe systems, Internet. Client/LAN operating systems include Apple/Macintosh, DOS, DEC, LocalTalk/AppleTalk, Microsoft. Computer languages and software packages include Assembler, BASIC, COBOL, dBASE, FORTRAN, Lotus 1-2-3, Pascal, PC-Write, PFS, SuperCalc, WordStar, Write. Computer facilities are available to all students.

**Fees:** None.

**Hours:** 8 AM-10 PM (M-Sa).

**GRADUATE CAREER DATA.** Graduate school percentages: 5% enter law school. 2% enter medical school. 6% enter graduate business programs. 2% enter graduate arts and sciences programs. Highest graduate school enrollments: U of Illinois, U of Iowa. 70% of graduates choose careers in business and industry. Companies and businesses that hire graduates: Arthur Andersen, Boeing, IBM, John Deere, IBM, U.S. government.

# Simpson College

**Indianola, IA 50125** **515 961-6251**

**1993-94 Costs.** Tuition: $10,720. Room: $1,770. Board: $2,040. Fees, books, misc. academic expenses (school's estimate): $655.

**Enrollment.** Undergraduates: 538 men, 578 women (full-time). Freshman class: 1,016 applicants, 872 accepted, 300 enrolled.

**Test score averages/ranges.** Range of ACT scores of middle 50%: 22-27 composite.

**Faculty.** 70 full-time; 76 part-time. 74% of faculty holds highest degree in specific field. Student/faculty ratio: 13 to 1.

**Selectivity rating.** Competitive.

**PROFILE.** Simpson, founded in 1860, is a private, church-affiliated, liberal arts college. Programs are offered through the Divisions of Education, Fine Arts, Humanities, Natural Sciences, and Social Sciences. Its 63-acre campus is located in Indianola, 12 miles from Des Moines.

**Accreditation:** NCACS. Professionally accredited by the National Association of Schools of Music, the National Council for Accreditation of Teacher Education.

**Religious orientation:** Simpson College is affiliated with the United Methodist Church; no religious requirements.

**Library:** Collections totaling over 152,499 volumes, 592 periodical subscriptions, and 12,675 microform items.

**Athletic facilities:** Gymnasium, field house, swimming pool, fitness and weight rooms, sauna, tracks, basketball, tennis, and volleyball courts, baseball, intramural, and softball fields.

**STUDENT BODY. Undergraduate profile:** 97% are state residents; 17% are transfers. 1.3% Asian-American, 1.2% Black, .8% Hispanic, .2% Native American, 96.5% White. Average age of undergraduates is 21.

**Freshman profile:** Majority of accepted applicants took ACT. 96% of freshmen come from public schools.

**Undergraduate achievement:** 78% of fall 1992 freshmen returned for fall 1993 term. 55% of entering class graduated. 18% of students who completed a degree program went on to graduate study within one year.

**Foreign students:** Three students are from out of the country. Three countries represented in all.

**PROGRAMS OF STUDY. Degrees:** B.A., B.Mus.

**Majors:** Accounting, Art, Art/Design, Biology, Chemistry, Communication, Computer Science, Criminal Justice, Economics, Elementary Education, English, Environmental Studies, French, German, History, International Management, International Relations, Management, Mathematics, Music, Music Education, Music Performance, Philosophy, Physical Education, Political Science, Psychology, Religion, Sociology, Spanish, Sports Administration, Theatre Arts.

**Distribution of degrees:** The majors with the highest enrollment are management, accounting, and education; religion, art, and international relations have the lowest.

**Requirements:** General education requirement.

**Academic regulations:** Freshmen must maintain minimum 1.8 GPA; sophomores, 1.9 GPA; juniors, 2.0 GPA; seniors, 2.0 GPA.

**Special:** Minors offered in most majors. Self-designed majors. Double majors. Independent study. Pass/fail grading option. Internships. Cooperative education programs. Graduate school at which undergraduates may take graduate-level courses. Preprofessional programs in law, medicine, veterinary science, pharmacy, dentistry, theology, and optometry.

2-2 pre-nursing program with U of Iowa. 3-1 medical technology program with Iowa Methodist Hospital. 3-2 pre-engineering program with Washington U. Member of Iowa Private College Placement Consortium. Washington Semester and UN Semester. International Program. Exchange programs with American U, Des Moines Area Comm Coll, Drew U, Grand View Coll, Iowa Coll of Nursing, New York U, Ottuwa Sch of Medical Tech, Union Coll, and Washington U. Teacher certification in early childhood, elementary, and secondary education. Certification in specific subject areas. Study abroad in Austria, China, England, France, Germany, Italy, Mexico, and Spain.
**Honors:** Honors program. Honor societies.
**Academic Assistance:** Nonremedial tutoring.

**STUDENT LIFE. Housing:** All unmarried students under age 23 must live on campus unless living with relatives. Coed, women's, and men's dorms. Sorority and fraternity housing. School-owned/operated apartments. Theme houses. 82% of students live in college housing.
**Services and counseling/handicapped student services:** Placement services. Health service. Counseling services for minority students. Personal counseling. Career and academic guidance services. Religious counseling. Physically disabled student services. Learning disabled services. Tutors.
**Campus organizations:** Undergraduate student government. Student newspaper (Simpsonian, published once/week). Literary magazine. Yearbook. Brass quintet, concert band and choir, jazz ensemble, opera musical theatre, festival chorus, jazz workshop, madrigal singers, theatre, College Activities Board, Amnesty International, Habitat for Humanity, departmental groups, 81 organizations in all. Four fraternities, all with chapter houses; four sororities, all with chapter houses. 36% of men join a fraternity. 36% of women join a sorority.
**Religious organizations:** Fellowship of Christian Athletes, Religious Life Council, Scripture and Supper, SERVE.
**Minority/foreign student organizations:** Concerned Multicultural Students.

**ATHLETICS. Physical education requirements:** None.
**Intercollegiate competition:** 40% of students participate. Baseball (M), basketball (M,W), cross-country (M,W), football (M), golf (M,W), softball (W), tennis (M,W), track and field (indoor) (M,W), track and field (outdoor) (M,W), volleyball (W), wrestling (M). Member of Iowa Intercollegiate Athletic Conference, NCAA Division III.
**Intramural and club sports:** 60% of students participate. Intramural basketball, flag football, floor hockey, sand volleyball, softball, volleyball, wrestling. Men's club soccer.

**ADMISSIONS. Academic basis for candidate selection** (in order of priority): Secondary school record, standardized test scores, class rank, school's recommendation.
**Nonacademic basis for candidate selection:** Character and personality and extracurricular participation are important. Particular talent or ability, geographical distribution, and alumni/ae relationship are considered.
**Requirements:** Graduation from secondary school is recommended; GED is accepted. 14 units and the following program of study are recommended: 4 units of English, 3 units of math, 2 units of science, 3 units of foreign language, 2 units of social studies. Rank in top half of secondary school class required; minimum composite ACT score of 20 recommended. Audition required of music and theatre program applicants. Portfolio required of art program applicants. ACT is required; SAT may be substituted. PSAT is recommended. Campus visit and interview recommended. Off-campus interviews available with an admissions representative.
**Procedure:** Take SAT or ACT by February of 12th year. Visit college for interview by March of 12th year. Application deadline is August 15. Notification of admission on rolling basis. Reply is required prior to enrollment. $200 room deposit, refundable until May 1. Freshmen accepted for terms other than fall.
**Special programs:** Admission may be deferred two years. Credit and/or placement may be granted through CEEB Advanced Placement exams for scores of 3 or higher. Credit may be granted through CLEP general and subject exams. Credit and placement may be granted through challenge exams. Early entrance/early admission program. Concurrent enrollment program.
**Transfer students:** Transfer students accepted for terms other than fall. In fall 1993, 17% of all new students were transfers into all classes. 116 transfer applications were received, 100 were accepted. Application deadline is August 15 for fall; January 5 for spring. Minimum 2.5 GPA recommended. Lowest course grade accepted is "C." Maximum number of transferable credits is 96 semester hours. At least 32 semester hours must be completed at the college to receive degree.
**Admissions contact:** John A. Kellogg, M.A., Vice President for Enrollment and Planning. 515 961-1624.

**FINANCIAL AID. Available aid:** Pell grants, SEOG, state scholarships and grants, school scholarships and grants, private scholarships and grants, and academic merit scholarships. Perkins Loans (NDSL), PLUS, Stafford Loans (GSL), state loans, school loans, private loans, and SLS. AMS and Tuition Management Systems.
**Financial aid statistics:** 20% of aid is not need-based. In 1993-94, 94% of all undergraduate applicants received aid; 97% of freshman applicants. Average amounts of aid awarded freshmen: Scholarships and grants, $8,297; loans, $2,221.
**Supporting data/closing dates:** FAFSA: Priority filing date is April 20. School's own aid application: Priority filing date is April 20. Notification of awards on rolling basis.
**Financial aid contact:** Debbie Barger, M.A., Director of Financial Aid. 515 961-1630.

**STUDENT EMPLOYMENT.** College Work/Study Program. Institutional employment. 49% of full-time undergraduates work on campus during school year. Students may expect to earn an average of $720 during school year. Off-campus part-time employment opportunities rated "good."

**COMPUTER FACILITIES.** 200 IBM/IBM-compatible and Macintosh/Apple microcomputers; 60 are networked. Students may access Digital minicomputer/mainframe systems. Computer languages and software packages include BASIC, C, Excel, FORTRAN, Lotus 1-2-3, Pascal, WordPerfect; 15 in all. Computer facilities are available to all students.
**Fees:** Computer fee is included in tuition/fees.
**Hours:** 8 AM-11 PM.

**GRADUATE CAREER DATA.** Graduate school percentages: 2% enter law school. 3% enter medical school. 1% enter dental school. 2% enter graduate business programs. 10% enter graduate arts and sciences programs. Highest graduate school enrollments: Drake U, Iowa State U, U of Iowa, Northwestern U, U of Osteopathic Medicine and Health Services. Companies and businesses that hire graduates: Ernst & Whitney, McGladrey Pullen, Pete-Marwick, Principal Financial Group.

**PROMINENT ALUMNI/AE.** George Washington Carver, scientist, agricultural chemist.

# Teikyo Marycrest University

**Davenport, IA 52804-4096** **319 326-9512**

**1994-95 Costs.** Tuition: $9,980. Room: $1,500. Board: $2,140. Fees, books, misc. academic expenses (school's estimate): $710.
**Enrollment.** Undergraduates: 216 men, 446 women (full-time). Freshman class: 252 applicants, 243 accepted, 90 enrolled. Graduate enrollment: 39 men, 128 women.
**Test score averages/ranges.** Average ACT scores: 21 composite. Range of ACT scores of middle 50%: 18-23 composite.
**Faculty.** 54 full-time; 20 part-time. 30% of faculty holds doctoral degree. Student/faculty ratio: 15 to 1.
**Selectivity rating.** Noncompetitive.

**PROFILE.** Teikyo Marycrest is a private, church-affiliated, liberal arts college. Founded as a women's college in 1939, it adopted coeducation in 1969, and in 1991, its name was changed from Marycrest College. Its 30-acre campus is located in Davenport.

**Accreditation:** NCACS. Professionally accredited by the Council on Social Work Education, the National League for Nursing.
**Religious orientation:** Teikyo Marycrest University is nonsectarian; no religious requirements.
**Library:** Collections totaling over 106,000 volumes, 545 periodical subscriptions, and 16,800 microform items.
**Athletic facilities:** Basketball, volleyball courts, student activity center, baseball, soccer, softball areas, jogging area, aerobic dance, martial arts, weight rooms.

**STUDENT BODY. Undergraduate profile:** 60% are state residents; 62% are transfers. 7% Asian-American, 5% Black, 3% Hispanic, 85% White. Average age of undergraduates is 28.
**Freshman profile:** Majority of accepted applicants took ACT.
**Undergraduate achievement:** 69% of fall 1991 freshmen returned for fall 1992 term. 35% of entering class graduated.
**Foreign students:** 50 students are from out of the country. Countries represented include China, India, Japan, and Pakistan; 13 in all.

**PROGRAMS OF STUDY. Degrees:** B.A., B.S., B.S.Nurs.
**Majors:** Accounting, American Language/Culture, Art, Biology, Business Administration, Business Management, Chemistry/Biology, Communications, Computer Graphics, Computer Science, Early Childhood Education, Education, Elementary Education, English, Environmental Management, Finance, Foods/Nutrition, Global Studies, History, International Business, Management, Mathematics, Nursing, Performing Arts, Pre-Law, Pre-Medicine, Psychology, Social/Behavioral Science, Social Work, Special Studies, Theatre Arts.
**Distribution of degrees:** The majors with the highest enrollment are business administration, nursing, and elementary education; foods/nutrition and theatre arts have the lowest.
**Requirements:** General education requirement.
**Academic regulations:** Freshmen must maintain minimum 1.75 GPA; sophomores, juniors, seniors, 2.0 GPA.
**Special:** Minors offered in some majors and in French, philosophy, religious studies, and Spanish. Associate's degrees offered. Self-designed majors. Double majors. Independent study. Pass/fail grading option. Internships. Cooperative education programs. Graduate school at which undergraduates may take graduate-level courses. Preprofessional programs in law, medicine, veterinary science, and dentistry. Special affiliation with Teikyo Westmar U. Teacher certification in early childhood, elementary, and secondary education. Certification in specific subject areas. Study abroad in England, Germany, Japan, and the Netherlands.
**Academic Assistance:** Remedial writing, math, and study skills. Nonremedial tutoring.

**ADMISSIONS. Academic basis for candidate selection** (in order of priority): Secondary school record, standardized test scores, class rank, school's recommendation.
**Nonacademic basis for candidate selection:** Character and personality, extracurricular participation, and particular talent or ability are considered.
**Requirements:** Graduation from secondary school is recommended; GED is accepted. 16 units and the following program of study are recommended: 4 units of English, 3 units of math, 2 units of science, 3 units of foreign language, 2 units of social studies, 2 units of history. Minimum composite ACT score of 18 and minimum 2.0 GPA required; rank in top half of secondary school class recommended. Chemistry and biology recommended of nursing and dietetics program applicants. Portfolio recommended of art program applicants. Audition recommended of performing arts program applicants. Conditional admission possible for applicants not meeting standard requirements. ACT is required; SAT may be substituted. Campus visit and interview recommended. Off-campus interviews available with admissions and alumni representatives.
**Procedure:** Notification of admission on rolling basis. $100 tuition deposit, refundable until June 1. $100 room deposit, refundable until June 1. Freshmen accepted for terms other than fall.
**Special programs:** Admission may be deferred one year. Credit and/or placement may be granted through CEEB Advanced Placement exams. Credit and/or placement may be granted through CLEP general and subject exams. Credit and placement may be granted through ACT PEP, DANTES, and challenge exams, and military and life experience. Concurrent enrollment program.
**Transfer students:** Transfer students accepted for terms other than fall. In fall 1992, 62% of all new students were transfers into all classes. 219 transfer applications were received, 216 were accepted. Application deadline is rolling for fall; rolling for spring. Minimum 2.0 GPA required. Lowest course grade accepted is "D." Maximum number of transfer-

able credits is 66 semester hours from a two-year school and 90 semester hours from a four-year school. At least 30 semester hours must be completed at the university to receive degree.
**Admissions contact:** Suellen Ofe, M.A., Associate Vice President for Enrollment Management. 319 326-9225.

**FINANCIAL AID. Available aid:** Pell grants, SEOG, state scholarships and grants, school scholarships and grants, private scholarships and grants, academic merit scholarships, athletic scholarships, and aid for undergraduate foreign students. Perkins Loans (NDSL), PLUS, Stafford Loans (GSL), and SLS. Tuition Plan Inc., AMS, deferred payment plan, and family tuition reduction.
**Financial aid statistics:** 10% of aid is not need-based. In 1992-93, 80% of all undergraduate applicants received aid; 80% of freshman applicants. Average amounts of aid awarded freshmen: Loans, $2,007.
**Supporting data/closing dates:** School's own aid application: Priority filing date is April 1; accepted on rolling basis. Notification of awards begins March 1.
**Financial aid contact:** Betty Albrecht, Director of Financial Aid. 319 326-9590.

# Teikyo Westmar University

**LeMars, IA 51031 800 352-4634**

**1994-95 Costs.** Tuition: $12,000. Room & board: $3,640. Fees, books, misc. academic expenses (school's estimate): $2,520.
**Enrollment.** Undergraduates: 402 men, 209 women (full-time). Freshman class: 451 applicants, 306 accepted, 123 enrolled.
**Test score averages/ranges.** Range of ACT scores of middle 50%: 19-25 English, 16-26 math.
**Faculty.** 39 full-time; 41 part-time. 60% of faculty holds doctoral degree. Student/faculty ratio: 16 to 1.
**Selectivity rating.** Less competitive.

**PROFILE.** Teikyo Westmar is a liberal arts university. It was founded in 1890, and in 1990 its name was changed from Westmar College. Its 62-acre campus is located in LeMars, in western Iowa, 25 miles northeast of Sioux City.

**Accreditation:** NCACS.
**Religious orientation:** Teikyo Westmar University is nonsectarian; one semester of religion required.
**Library:** Collections totaling over 100,961 volumes, 510 periodical subscriptions, and 6,373 microform items.
**Athletic facilities:** Gymnasium, weight room, baseball, football practice, and soccer fields, community football stadium, arena, track, community softball field, weight and wrestling rooms.

**STUDENT BODY. Undergraduate profile:** 39% are state residents; 38% are transfers. 1% Asian-American, 5% Black, 2% Hispanic, 52% White, 40% Foreign. Average age of undergraduates is 23.
**Freshman profile:** Majority of accepted applicants took ACT.
**Undergraduate achievement:** 66% of fall 1992 freshmen returned for fall 1993 term. 32% of entering class graduated. 5% of students who completed a degree program immediately went on to graduate study.
**Foreign students:** 11 students are from out of the country. Countries represented include the Dominica Republic, India, Japan, Spain, the United Kingdom, and Zaire; 11 in all.

**PROGRAMS OF STUDY. Degrees:** B.A., B.Appl.Sci., B.M.Ed.
**Majors:** Accounting, Biology, Business Administration, Computer Science, Cultural Science, Dance, Economics, Elementary Education, English, German, History, Human Services, International Business, International Communication, International Cultural Communications, Japanese, Mass Communications, Mathematics, Music, Music Education, Natural Science, Philosophy, Physical Education, Psychology, Religion, Secondary Education, Sociology, Speech Communication, Speech/Dramatic Arts, Theatre Arts.
**Distribution of degrees:** The majors with the highest enrollment are elementary education and human services; German and sociology have the lowest.
**Requirements:** General education requirement.
**Academic regulations:** Freshmen must maintain minimum 1.5 GPA; sophomores, 2.0 GPA; juniors, 1.75 GPA; seniors, 2.0 GPA.
**Special:** Minors offered in art, chemistry, dramatic arts, finance, management, marketing, and speech communication. Marine biology program. Research with Gulf Coast Research Lab (Mississippi). Science trips in the U.S. and Caribbean. Self-designed majors. Double majors. Internships. Graduate school at which undergraduates may take graduate-level courses. Preprofessional programs in medicine and medical technology. Member of Higher Education Consortium for Urban Affairs. Teacher certification in elementary and secondary education. Exchange programs abroad in Germany (Phillips U), Japan (Teikyo U), and the Netherlands (Teikyo U).
**Academic Assistance:** Remedial writing and math. Nonremedial tutoring.

**ADMISSIONS. Academic basis for candidate selection** (in order of priority): Secondary school record, class rank, standardized test scores, school's recommendation, essay.
**Nonacademic basis for candidate selection:** Character and personality, extracurricular participation, particular talent or ability, and alumni/ae relationship are considered.
**Requirements:** Graduation from secondary school is required; GED is accepted. 15 units and the following program of study are recommended: 4 units of English, 4 units of math, 3 units of science, 2 units of foreign language, 2 units of social studies. Two of three required: minimum composite ACT score of 20 (or combined SAT score of 750), rank in top half of secondary school class, minimum 2.3 GPA. Audition required of music program applicants. ACT is required; SAT may be substituted. Campus visit and interview recommended. Off-campus interviews available with an admissions representative.
**Procedure:** Take SAT or ACT by spring of 12th year. Notification of admission on rolling basis. Reply is required by May 1. $200 tuition deposit, refundable until May 1. $100 room deposit, refundable until May 1. Freshmen accepted for terms other than fall.
**Special programs:** Admission may be deferred three semesters. Credit and/or placement may be granted through CEEB Advanced Placement exams for scores of 4 or higher. Credit may be granted through CLEP general and subject exams, DANTES and challenge exams, and military and life experience. Early entrance/early admission program. Concurrent enrollment program.
**Transfer students:** Transfer students accepted for terms other than fall. In fall 1993, 38% of all new students were transfers into all classes. 128 transfer applications were received, 76 were accepted. Application deadline is September 1 for fall; January 10 for spring. Minimum 2.3 GPA required. Lowest course grade accepted is "C-." Maximum number of transferable credits is 64 semester hours. At least 30 semester hours must be completed at the university to receive degree.
**Admissions contact:** Richard Phillips, M.S., Vice President of Enrollment Management. 712 546-2070.

**FINANCIAL AID. Available aid:** Pell grants, SEOG, state scholarships and grants, school scholarships and grants, private scholarships and grants, academic merit scholarships, athletic scholarships, and aid for undergraduate foreign students. Perkins Loans (NDSL), PLUS, Stafford Loans (GSL), school loans, private loans, and SLS. School's payment plan.
**Financial aid statistics:** 35% of aid is not need-based. In 1993-94, 100% of all undergraduate applicants received aid. Average amounts of aid awarded freshmen: Scholarships and grants, $6,100; loans, $2,600.
**Supporting data/closing dates:** FAFSA: Priority filing date is April 1. Notification of awards on rolling basis.
**Financial aid contact:** Dennis Mertes, Director of Financial Aid. 712 546-2066.

# University of Dubuque, College of Liberal Arts

**Dubuque, IA 52001 319 589-3000**

**1993-94 Costs.** Tuition: $10,430. Room: $1,775. Board: $1,845. Fees, books, misc. academic expenses (school's estimate): $500.
**Enrollment.** Undergraduates: 359 men, 332 women (full-time). Freshman class: 958 applicants, 707 accepted, 310 enrolled. Graduate enrollment: 252 men, 132 women.
**Test score averages/ranges.** Average SAT scores: 460 verbal, 450 math. Average ACT scores: 23 composite.
**Faculty.** 53 full-time; 29 part-time. 72% of faculty holds doctoral degree. Student/faculty ratio: 15 to 1.
**Selectivity rating.** Less competitive.

**PROFILE.** The University of Dubuque, is a church-affiliated, liberal arts college and theological seminary. Founded as a school for prospective pastors in 1852, the College of Liberal Arts was added several years later. Its 56-acre campus is located in a residential area of Dubuque.

**Accreditation:** NCACS. Professionally accredited by the Council on Social Work Education, the National Council for Accreditation of Teacher Education, the National League for Nursing.
**Religious orientation:** University of Dubuque, College of Liberal Arts is affiliated with the Presbyterian Church USA; no religious requirements.
**Library:** Collections totaling over 166,000 volumes, 1,200 periodical subscriptions, and 25,000 microform items.
**Special facilities/museums:** Art gallery, language labs, electron microscope.
**Athletic facilities:** Baseball, football, soccer, softball fields, gymnasiums, racquetball and tennis courts, sports center, swimming pool, track, and weight room.

**STUDENT BODY. Undergraduate profile:** 40% are state residents. 1% Asian-American, 4% Black, 1% Hispanic, 1% Native American, 78% White, 15% Other. Average age of undergraduates is 25.
**Freshman profile:** 4% of freshmen who took SAT scored 600 or over on verbal, 4% scored 600 or over on math; 31% scored 500 or over on verbal, 31% scored 500 or over on math; 83% scored 400 or over on verbal, 70% scored 400 or over on math; 100% scored 300 or over on verbal, 96% scored 300 or over on math. 29% of freshmen who took ACT scored 24 or over on composite; 91% scored 18 or over on composite; 100% scored 12 or over on composite. 11% of accepted applicants took SAT; 89% took ACT. 92% of freshmen come from public schools.
**Undergraduate achievement:** 65% of fall 1991 freshmen returned for fall 1992 term. 48% of entering class graduated. 14% of students who completed a degree program went on to graduate study within one year.
**Foreign students:** 141 students are from out of the country. Countries represented include Barbados, China, Hong Kong, Japan, Taiwan, and United Arab Emirates; 23 in all.

**PROGRAMS OF STUDY. Degrees:** B.A., B.Bus.Admin., B.S., B.S.Nurs.
**Majors:** Accounting, Aviation Management, Biology, Business Administration/Management, Chemistry, Computer/Information Sciences, Early Childhood Education, Earth Science, Economics, Education, Elementary Education, English, Environmental Science, Flight Operations, Foreign Language, General Science, History, International Studies, Marketing, Mathematics, Music, Music Education, Nursing, Physical Education, Physics, Political Science/Government, Pre-Law, Pre-Medicine, Psychology, Social Work, Sociology, Spanish, Special Administration, Special Education, Speech.
**Distribution of degrees:** The majors with the highest enrollment are business administration, flight operations, and education; Spanish, physics, and history have the lowest.
**Requirements:** General education requirement.
**Academic regulations:** Minimum 2.0 GPA must be maintained.
**Special:** Minors offered in all majors. Interdepartmental courses. Aviation flight operations and management program. B.S. degree program for nurses includes two years at Dubuque U with satisfactory completion of diploma nursing program. One year of credit from accredited dental, medical, law, or veterinary school may be applied toward bachelor's degree. Associate's degrees offered. Self-designed majors. Double majors. Independent study. Accelerated study. Internships. Graduate school at which undergraduates may

take graduate-level courses. Preprofessional programs in law and medicine. 3-3 M.Div. program. Member of Higher Education Consortium for Urban Affairs and Tri-College Cooperative Program; cross-registration possible. Semester-away programs. Teacher certification in early childhood, elementary, secondary, and special education. Certification in specific subject areas. Study abroad in Colombia, Ecuador, Mexico, and Norway.
**Honors:** Honor societies.
**Academic Assistance:** Remedial reading, writing, math, and study skills. Nonremedial tutoring.

**ADMISSIONS. Academic basis for candidate selection** (in order of priority): Secondary school record, standardized test scores, school's recommendation, class rank, essay.
**Nonacademic basis for candidate selection:** Extracurricular participation is emphasized. Character and personality and particular talent or ability are important. Alumni/ae relationship is considered.
**Requirements:** Graduation from secondary school is required; GED is accepted. 15 units and the following program of study are required: 4 units of English, 3 units of math, 3 units of social studies. Minimum composite ACT score of 18 and rank in top half of secondary school class required. Audition required of music program applicants. R.N. required of nursing program applicants. Academic program for applicants not normally admissible; developmental courses are required. ACT is required; SAT may be substituted. PSAT is recommended. Campus visit and interview recommended. Off-campus interviews available with admissions and alumni representatives.
**Procedure:** Take SAT or ACT by April of 12th year. Visit college for interview by April of 12th year. Notification of admission on rolling basis. $50 tuition deposit, refundable until May 1. $50 room deposit, refundable until May 1. Freshmen accepted for terms other than fall.
**Special programs:** Admission may be deferred one year. Credit may be granted through CEEB Advanced Placement for scores of 3 or higher. Credit and/or placement may be granted through CLEP general and subject exams. Credit may be granted through military and life experience. Credit and placement may be granted through challenge exams. Concurrent enrollment program.
**Transfer students:** Transfer students accepted for terms other than fall. Application deadline is rolling for fall; rolling for spring. Minimum 2.0 GPA required. Lowest course grade accepted is "D." Maximum number of transferable credits is 64 semester hours from a two-year school and 90 semester hours from a four-year school. At least 30 semester hours must be completed at the university to receive degree.
**Admissions contact:** Christine Chapin-Tilton, M.A., Director of Undergraduate Admission. 319 589-3200.

**FINANCIAL AID. Available aid:** Pell grants, SEOG, state scholarships and grants, school scholarships and grants, private scholarships and grants, and academic merit scholarships. Perkins Loans (NDSL), PLUS, Stafford Loans (GSL), state loans, school loans, private loans, and SLS. AMS, deferred payment plan, and family tuition reduction.
**Financial aid statistics:** In 1992-93, 80% of all undergraduate applicants received aid; 80% of freshman applicants. Average amounts of aid awarded freshmen: Scholarships and grants, $4,500; loans, $4,500.
**Supporting data/closing dates:** School's own aid application: Priority filing date is April 1; accepted on rolling basis. Income tax forms: Priority filing date is April 1; accepted on rolling basis. Notification of awards on rolling basis.
**Financial aid contact:** Carol Scherrman, M.A., Director of Financial Aid. 319 589-3170.

# University of Iowa

**Iowa City, IA 52242-1396 319 335-3500**

**1993-94 Costs.** Tuition: $2,192 (state residents), $7,580 (out-of-state). Room & board: $3,306. Fees, books, misc. academic expenses (school's estimate): $770.
**Enrollment.** Undergraduates: 7,652 men, 8,125 women (full-time). Freshman class: 8,870 applicants, 7,712 accepted, 3,253 enrolled. Graduate enrollment: 3,233 men, 3,270 women.
**Test score averages/ranges.** Range of ACT scores of middle 50%: 22-27 composite.
**Faculty.** 1,674 full-time; 55 part-time. 98% of faculty holds highest degree in specific field. Student/faculty ratio: 16 to 1.
**Selectivity rating.** Competitive.

**PROFILE.** The University of Iowa, founded in 1847, is a public, comprehensive institution. Its 1,880-acre campus is located on the Iowa River in Iowa City, 25 miles from Cedar Rapids.

**Accreditation:** NCACS. Professionally accredited by the American Assembly of Collegiate Schools of Business, the American Bar Association, the American Council on Pharmaceutical Education, the American Dental Association, the American Medical Association (CAHEA), the National Council for Accreditation of Teacher Education, the National League for Nursing.
**Religious orientation:** University of Iowa is nonsectarian; no religious requirements.
**Library:** Collections totaling over 3,253,141 volumes, 33,112 periodical subscriptions, and 3,557,405 microform items.
**Special facilities/museums:** Art and natural history museums, newspaper production lab, TV lab, survey research facilities, electron microscope, laser facility.
**Athletic facilities:** Indoor practice facility, field house, arena, softball fields, golf course, recreation building, tennis center, track.

**STUDENT BODY. Undergraduate profile:** 71% are state residents; 29% are transfers. 3% Asian-American, 2% Black, 2% Hispanic, 90% White, 3% Other. Average age of undergraduates is 21.
**Freshman profile:** 10% of freshmen who took ACT scored 30 or over on composite; 57% scored 24 or over on composite; 98% scored 18 or over on composite; 100% scored 12 or over on composite. 19% of accepted applicants took SAT; 92% took ACT. 88% of freshmen come from public schools.
**Undergraduate achievement:** 89% of fall 1991 freshmen returned for fall 1992 term. 29% of entering class graduated.
**Foreign students:** 513 students are from out of the country. Countries represented include China, Hong Kong, Japan, Korea, Malaysia, and Taiwan; 56 in all.

**PROGRAMS OF STUDY. Degrees:** B.A., B.Bus.Admin., B.F.A., B.Lib.Studies, B.Mus., B.S., B.S.Eng., B.S.Nurs., B.S.Pharm.
**Majors:** Accounting, Actuarial Sciences, American Studies, Ancient Civilization, Anthropology, Art, Asian Languages/Literatures, Asian Studies, Astronomy, Biochemistry, Biology, Biomedical Engineering, Botany, Broadcasting/Film, Business Administration, Chemical/Materials Engineering, Chemistry, Civil/Environmental Engineering, Classics, Communication Studies, Comparative Literature, Computer Science, Dance, Early Childhood Education, Economics, Electrical/Computer Engineering, Elementary Education, Engineering, English, Exercise Science, Finance, French, Geography, Geology, German, Greek, Health Occupations Education, History, Industrial/Management Engineering, Industrial Relations/Human Resources, Interdisciplinary Studies, Italian, Journalism/Mass Communications, Latin, Leisure Studies, Liberal Studies, Linguistics, Literature/Science/Arts, Management Science, Marketing, Mathematical Sciences, Mathematics, Mechanical Engineering, Medical Technology, Microbiology, Music, Music Therapy, Nuclear Medical Technology, Nursing, Pharmacy, Philosophy, Physical Education, Physician Assistant, Physics, Political Science, Portuguese, Psychology, Religion, Russian, Russian/East European/Eurasian Studies, Science Education, Secondary Education, Social Studies, Social Work, Sociology, Spanish, Speech/Hearing Sciences, Statistics, Theatre Arts.
**Distribution of degrees:** The majors with the highest enrollment are business administration, communication studies, and engineering; Portuguese, Latin, and astronomy have the lowest.
**Requirements:** General education requirement.
**Academic regulations:** Freshmen must maintain minimum 1.7 GPA; sophomores, 1.85 GPA; juniors, 2.0 GPA; seniors, 2.0 GPA.
**Special:** Minors offered. Self-designed majors. Double majors. Dual degrees. Independent study. Accelerated study. Pass/fail grading option. Internships. Cooperative education programs. Graduate school at which undergraduates may take graduate-level courses. Preprofessional programs in law, medicine, veterinary science, dentistry, optometry, chiropractic, mortuary science, nursing, physical therapy, and podiatry. 3-1 early admission programs in dentistry, medicine, and medical technology. 3-2 B.S./M.S. physician assistant program. Combined degree programs including liberal arts with both engineering and medicine. Member of Committee for Institutional Cooperation. Exchange programs with Iowa State U and U of Northern Iowa. Teacher certification in early childhood, elementary, secondary, and special education. Member of International Student Exchange Program (ISEP). Study abroad in 29 countries. ROTC and AFROTC.
**Honors:** Phi Beta Kappa. Honors program.
**Academic Assistance:** Remedial reading, writing, math, and study skills. Nonremedial tutoring.

**STUDENT LIFE. Housing:** Students may live on or off campus. Coed dorms. Sorority and fraternity housing. School-owned/operated apartments. Language houses. 29% of students live in college housing.
**Social atmosphere:** The student newspaper reports, "Iowa is a clean campus with much to do. Pretty serious academics, fun social life. Great weekend sports and activities. Greeks are strong but not dominant. Dorm activities are big. There are many student organizations, professional societies, sports, and activities. People go to Schaefer Hall to study, to Great Midwestern Ice Cream for sweets and coffee, to Iowa Memorial Union to meet people, and to Joe's Place (journalists) and the field house (freshmen)."
**Services and counseling/handicapped student services:** Placement services. Health service. Women's center. Counseling services for minority, veteran, and older students. Birth control, personal, and psychological counseling. Career and academic guidance services. Physically disabled student services. Learning disabled services. Notetaking services. Tape recorders. Reader services for the blind.
**Campus organizations:** Undergraduate student government. Student newspaper (Daily Iowan). Literary magazine. Yearbook. Bands, choruses, orchestra, theatre, debating, public speaking, 370 organizations in all. 27 fraternities, 23 chapter houses; 20 sororities, 16 chapter houses. 15% of men join a fraternity. 17% of women join a sorority.
**Religious organizations:** Numerous religious groups.
**Minority/foreign student organizations:** Black Journalist Association, Black Social Workers, Black Student Union, Black Students in Engineering, Chicano/Indian American Union, Latin American Student Association, science/M.D. minority organization. Numerous foreign student groups.

**ATHLETICS. Physical education requirements:** Four semester hours of physical education required.
**Intercollegiate competition:** 3% of students participate. Baseball (M), basketball (M,W), cross-country (M,W), diving (M,W), field hockey (W), football (M), golf (M,W), gymnastics (M,W), softball (W), swimming (M,W), tennis (M,W), track (indoor) (M,W), track (outdoor) (M,W), track and field (indoor) (M,W), track and field (outdoor) (M,W), volleyball (W), wrestling (M). Member of Big 10 Conference, NCAA Division I.
**Intramural and club sports:** 33% of students participate. Intramural badminton, basketball, bowling, foul shooting, flag football, golf, home run derby, inner-tube water polo, softball, swimming, table tennis, tennis, three-point contest, trap shooting, turkey trot, volleyball, walleyball, wrestling. Men's club bowling, crew, fencing, lacrosse, rugby, sailing, soccer, volleyball, water polo. Women's club bowling, crew, fencing, rugby, sailing, water polo.

**ADMISSIONS. Academic basis for candidate selection** (in order of priority): Class rank, secondary school record, standardized test scores, school's recommendation.
**Nonacademic basis for candidate selection:** Particular talent or ability is emphasized. Character and personality, extracurricular participation, and alumni/ae relationship are considered.
**Requirements:** Graduation from secondary school is required; GED is accepted. 15 units and the following program of study are required: 4 units of English, 3 units of math, 3 units of science, 2 units of foreign language, 3 units of social studies. Art and music courses recommended. Rank in top half of secondary school class required of in-state applicants; rank in top 30% of secondary school class required of out-of-state applicants; admissions index based on class rank and ACT or SAT scores used for all applicants who do not meet these requirements. Specific requirements for each college. Portfolio required of art program applicants. Audition required of music program applicants. EOP for applicants not normally admissible. Conditional admission possible for applicants not meeting standard

requirements. SAT or ACT is required. Campus visit and interview recommended. No off-campus interviews.
**Procedure:** Take SAT or ACT by September of 12th year. Visit college for interview by October of 12th year. Notification of admission on rolling basis. No set date by which applicants must accept offer. $50 room deposit, refundable within 10 days of receiving room assignment. Freshmen accepted for terms other than fall.
**Special programs:** Admission may be deferred one year. Credit and/or placement may be granted through CEEB Advanced Placement exams for scores of 3 or higher. Credit may be granted through CLEP general and subject exams, and DANTES exams. Placement may be granted through challenge exams. Credit and placement may be granted through ACT PEP exams. Concurrent enrollment program.
**Transfer students:** Transfer students accepted for terms other than fall. In fall 1992, 29% of all new students were transfers into all classes. 3,303 transfer applications were received, 2,310 were accepted. Application deadline is May 15 for fall; November 15 for spring. Minimum 2.25 GPA required. Lowest course grade accepted is "D." Maximum number of transferable credits is 62 semester hours. At least 30 semester hours must be completed at the university to receive degree.
**Admissions contact:** Michael Barron, M.A., Director of Admissions. 319 335-3847.

**FINANCIAL AID. Available aid:** Pell grants, SEOG, Federal Nursing Student Scholarships, state scholarships and grants, school scholarships and grants, private scholarships and grants, ROTC scholarships, academic merit scholarships, and athletic scholarships. Perkins Loans (NDSL), PLUS, Stafford Loans (GSL), NSL, Health Professions Loans, school loans, private loans, and SLS. Tuition Management Systems. Institutional payment plan.
**Financial aid statistics:** 25% of aid is not need-based.
**Supporting data/closing dates:** FAFSA: Accepted on rolling basis. School's own aid application: Accepted on rolling basis. Income tax forms: Accepted on rolling basis. Notification of awards on rolling basis.
**Financial aid contact:** Mark Warner, M.A., Director of Financial Aid. 319 335-1450.

**STUDENT EMPLOYMENT.** College Work/Study Program. Institutional employment. 53% of full-time undergraduates work on campus during school year. Students may expect to earn an average of $2,400 during school year. Off-campus part-time employment opportunities rated "excellent."

**COMPUTER FACILITIES.** 744 IBM/IBM-compatible and Macintosh/Apple microcomputers; all are networked. Students may access Digital, IBM minicomputer/mainframe systems, BITNET, Internet. Residence halls may be equipped with stand-alone microcomputers, networked microcomputers, networked terminals. Client/LAN operating systems include Apple/Macintosh, Novell. Computer languages and software packages include BASIC, C, COBOL, Excel, FORTRAN, Lotus 1-2-3, Microsoft Word, MYSTAT, PageMaker, Pascal, Super Paint, WordPerfect, Write Now. Computer facilities are available to all students.
**Fees:** $60 computer fee per semester.
**Hours:** 24 hours (main computer center); 8 AM-1 AM (most other facilities).

**GRADUATE CAREER DATA.** Highest graduate school enrollments: U of Iowa. Companies and businesses that hire graduates: AMOCO, Arthur Andersen, Baxter Healthcare, Ford, General Electric, Maytag, McGladrey & Pullen, Principal Financial.

**PROMINENT ALUMNI/AE.** George H. Gallup, founder, American Institute of Public Opinion; Flannery O'Connor, author; Dr. James A. Van Allen, space physicist.

# University of Northern Iowa

**Cedar Falls, IA 50614-0033 319 273-2311**

**1994-95 Costs.** Tuition: $2,295 (state residents), $5,937 (out-of-state). Room & board: $2,785. Fees, books, misc. academic expenses (school's estimate): $710.
**Enrollment.** Undergraduates: 4,448 men, 5,697 women (full-time). Freshman class: 3,808 applicants, 3,379 accepted, 1,853 enrolled. Graduate enrollment: 479 men, 771 women.
**Test score averages/ranges.** Average ACT scores: 23 composite. Range of ACT scores of middle 50%: 21-26 composite.
**Faculty.** 699 full-time; 142 part-time. 60% of faculty holds doctoral degree. Student/faculty ratio: 15 to 1.
**Selectivity rating.** Less competitive.

**PROFILE.** The University of Northern Iowa, founded in 1876, is a public, comprehensive institution. Programs are offered through the Colleges of Education, Humanities and Fine Arts, Natural Sciences, and Social and Behavioral Sciences and the School of Business. Its 996-acre campus is located in Cedar Falls, seven miles from Waterloo.

**Accreditation:** NCACS. Professionally accredited by the American Council for Construction Education, the American Dietetic Association, the American Home Economics Association, the American Speech-Language-Hearing Association, the Association of Collegiate Business Schools and Programs, the Council on Social Work Education, the National Association of Schools of Art and Design, the National Association of Schools of Music, the National Recreation and Park Association.
**Religious orientation:** University of Northern Iowa is nonsectarian; no religious requirements.
**Library:** Collections totaling over 738,878 volumes, 3,037 periodical subscriptions, and 618,357 microform items.
**Special facilities/museums:** Natural history museum, art gallery, greenhouse and biological preserves, lakeside biology lab and field lab for conservation problems, educational media center, curriculum lab, on-campus school for student teachers, NASA Regional Teacher Resource Center, speech and hearing clinic, small business development center, Iowa waste reduction center, center for applied research in metal casting.
**Athletic facilities:** Gymnasiums, physical education center, dome, playing fields, golf range, racquetball and tennis courts, swimming pool.

**STUDENT BODY. Undergraduate profile:** 96% are state residents; 32% are transfers. 1% Asian-American, 2% Black, 1% Hispanic, .1% Native American, 95% White, .9% Foreign students. Average age of undergraduates is 21.
**Freshman profile:** 4% of freshmen who took ACT scored 30 or over on composite; 42% scored 24 or over on composite; 96% scored 18 or over on composite; 100% scored 12 or over on composite. 98% of accepted applicants took ACT.
**Undergraduate achievement:** 81% of fall 1992 freshmen returned for fall 1993 term. 25% of entering class graduated. 12% of students who completed a degree program immediately went on to graduate study.
**Foreign students:** 113 students are from out of the country. Countries represented include Austria, Hong Kong, Japan, Malaysia, Russia, and Taiwan; 62 in all.

**PROGRAMS OF STUDY. Degrees:** B.A., B.A.Lib.Arts, B.A.Teach., B.F.A., B.Lib.Studies, B.Mus., B.S., B.Tech.
**Majors:** Accounting, Administrative Management, American Studies, Anthropology, Applied Physics, Art, Asian Studies, Biology, Biotechnology, Broadcast Journalism, Business Education, Chemistry, Chemistry/Marketing, Clothing/Textiles, Communication, Communication Disorders, Communications/Electronic Media, Community Health Education, Community Recreation, Computer Information Systems, Computer Science, Construction Technology, Criminology, Design/Human Environment, Dietetics, Early Childhood Education, Earth Science, Economics, Electromechanical Systems, Elementary Education, English, Environmental/Conservation Education, European Studies, Family Services, Finance, Food/Nutrition, French, General Studies, Geography, Geology, German, Graphic Communication, Health Administration, Health Education, History, Humanities, Individual Studies, Industrial Arts Education, Industrial Technology, Industry, Junior High School Education, Junior High School Science, Latin American Studies, Management, Management Information Systems, Manufacturing Technology, Marketing, Mathematics, Modern Languages, Music, Music Education, Music Performance, Music Theory/Composition, Natural History Interpretation, Philosophy, Philosophy/Religion, Physical Education, Physical Education/Health, Physics, Political Science, Psychology, Public Administration, Public Relations, Religion, Russian Area Studies, Safety Education, Science, Sciences, Social Science Education, Social Work, Sociology, Spanish, Special Education, Speech/Language Pathology, Teacher Education, Teaching English to Speakers of Other Languages, Technology Education, Theatre.
**Distribution of degrees:** The majors with the highest enrollment are elementary education, accounting, and general studies; European studies, Asian studies, and Latin American studies have the lowest.
**Requirements:** General education requirement.
**Academic regulations:** Minimum 2.0 GPA must be maintained.
**Special:** Minors offered in some majors. College GPA must be established before declaration of business, education, or social work area major. Credit possible for marching band participation. Self-designed majors. Double majors. Dual degrees. Independent study. Pass/fail grading option. Internships. Cooperative education programs. Graduate school at which undergraduates may take graduate-level courses. Preprofessional programs in law, medicine, veterinary science, pharmacy, dentistry, theology, optometry, cytotechnology, engineering, medical technology, mortuary science, nursing, osteopathy, physical therapy, and podiatry. 3-1 program in cytotechnology with Mayo Sch of Health Related Sciences. 3-1 program in medical technology with Covenant Medical Center. Two-year cooperative nursing program with U of Iowa. Cooperative nursing program with Allen Coll of Nursing. Washington Semester. Member of National Student Exchange (NSE). Regents Universities exchange programs with Iowa State U and U of Iowa. Teacher certification in early childhood, elementary, secondary, special education, and bilingual/bicultural education. Certification in specific subject areas. Study abroad in Austria, Chile, China, Denmark, Finland, France, Germany, Japan, Mexico, Nigeria, Russia, and Spain. ROTC.
**Honors:** Honors program. Honor societies.
**Academic Assistance:** Remedial reading, writing, and math. Nonremedial tutoring.

**STUDENT LIFE. Housing:** Students may live on or off campus. Coed, women's, and men's dorms. On-campus married-student housing. 39% of students live in college housing.
**Social atmosphere:** Popular campus activities include the annual Delta Upsilon Halloween Party, the Christmas Variety Show, Panther football games, wrestling matches, the artists' series, the chamber series, Theatre UNI, the UNI Jazz Band, and the Tuba Boys. Favorite student gathering spots include Maucker Union, the UNI Dome, the Hill (bars and eating establishments), the library, the newspaper office, Fourth and Main, Spinner's, and Shagnasty's.
**Services and counseling/handicapped student services:** Placement services. Health service. Day care. Counseling services for minority, military, veteran, and older students. Birth control, personal, and psychological counseling. Career and academic guidance services. Physically disabled student services. Notetaking services. Tape recorders. Tutors. Reader services for the blind.
**Campus organizations:** Undergraduate student government. Student newspaper (Northern Iowan, published twice/week). Literary magazine. Yearbook. Radio station. Orchestra, wind ensemble, marching band, women's chorus, men's glee club, gospel choir, International Dance Theatre, Conservation Club, English Club, R.U.N.(promotes handicap awareness), TESOL/Linguistics Club, special-interest groups, 180 organizations in all. Seven fraternities, all with chapter houses; four sororities, all with chapter houses. 6% of men join a fraternity. 4% of women join a sorority.
**Religious organizations:** Baptist Student Union, Campus Bible Fellowship, Campus Crusade for Christ, Catholic Student Association, Christ for UNI, other religious groups.
**Minority/foreign student organizations:** Ethnic Minority Student Association, Ladies of Twenty Pearls. International Student Association.

**ATHLETICS. Physical education requirements:** Three semester hours of physical education required.
**Intercollegiate competition:** 4% of students participate. Baseball (M), basketball (M,W), cheerleading (M,W), cross-country (M,W), diving (M,W), football (M), golf (M,W), softball (W), swimming (M,W), tennis (M,W), track (indoor) (M,W), track (outdoor) (M,W), track and field (indoor) (M,W), track and field (outdoor) (M,W), volleyball (W), wrestling (M). Member of Central Collegiate Conference, Gateway Football Conference, Missouri Valley Conference, NCAA Division I, NCAA Division I-AA for football.
**Intramural and club sports:** 64% of students participate. Intramural badminton, basketball, bench press, bowling, flag football, free throw, fun run, golf, indoor track, slow-pitch

softball, softball, swimming, table tennis, tennis, track, triathlon, volleyball, wrestling. Men's club bowling, ice hockey, racquetball, soccer, tae kwon do, triathlon, volleyball. Women's club bowling, racquetball, soccer, tae kwon do, triathlon, volleyball.

**ADMISSIONS. Academic basis for candidate selection** (in order of priority): Secondary school record, class rank, standardized test scores, school's recommendation.
**Nonacademic basis for candidate selection:** Character and personality, extracurricular participation, particular talent or ability, geographical distribution, and alumni/ae relationship are considered.
**Requirements:** Graduation from secondary school is required; GED is accepted. 15 units and the following program of study are required: 4 units of English, 3 units of math, 3 units of science including 1 unit of lab, 3 units of social studies, 2 units of academic electives. English should include 1 unit of composition; math should include 1 unit of algebra. Electives must be selected from listed required subject areas or from foreign language or humanities. Rank in top half of secondary school class required of in-state applicants; rank in top third of secondary school class required of out-of-state applicants. Portfolio required of art program applicants. Audition required of music program applicants. Conditional admission possible for applicants not meeting standard requirements. ACT is required; SAT may be substituted. Campus visit and interview recommended. Off-campus interviews available with admissions and alumni representatives.
**Procedure:** Take SAT or ACT by August following 12th year. Application deadline is August 15. Notification of admission on rolling basis. $30 room deposit, refundable until July 15. Freshmen accepted for terms other than fall.
**Special programs:** Admission may be deferred one year. Credit and/or placement may be granted through CEEB Advanced Placement exams for scores of 3 or higher. Credit may be granted through CLEP general and subject exams, DANTES and challenge exams, and military experience. Concurrent enrollment program.
**Transfer students:** Transfer students accepted for terms other than fall. In fall 1993, 32% of all new students were transfers into all classes. 1,428 transfer applications were received, 1,314 were accepted. Application deadline is August 15 for fall; December 15 for spring. Minimum 2.5 GPA required for 24-41 semester hours; 2.25 GPA for 42-59 hours; 2.0 GPA for 60 or more hours. Lowest course grade accepted is "D-." Maximum number of transferable credits is 65 semester hours. At least 32 semester hours must be completed at the university to receive degree.
**Admissions contact:** Clark Elmer, M.A., Director of Admissions. 319 273-2281, 800 772-2037.

**FINANCIAL AID. Available aid:** Pell grants, SEOG, state scholarships and grants, school scholarships and grants, private scholarships, ROTC scholarships, academic merit scholarships, and athletic scholarships. Perkins Loans (NDSL), PLUS, Stafford Loans (GSL), and SLS. Deferred payment plan.
**Financial aid statistics:** In 1993-94, 81% of all undergraduate applicants received aid; 82% of freshman applicants. Average amounts of aid awarded freshmen: Scholarships and grants, $2,052; loans, $2,802.
**Supporting data/closing dates:** FAFSA: Accepted on rolling basis.
**Financial aid contact:** Roland Carrillo, M.A., Director of Financial Aid. 319 273-2700, 800 772-2736.

**STUDENT EMPLOYMENT.** College Work/Study Program. Institutional employment. 23% of full-time undergraduates work on campus during school year. Students may expect to earn an average of $1,800 during school year. Off-campus part-time employment opportunities rated "good."

**COMPUTER FACILITIES.** 600 IBM/IBM-compatible, Macintosh/Apple, and RISC-/UNIX-based microcomputers; all are networked. Students may access Digital, SUN minicomputer/mainframe systems, BITNET, Internet, CompuServe. Residence halls may be equipped with networked microcomputers, networked terminals, modems. Client/LAN operating systems include Apple/Macintosh, DOS, UNIX/XENIX/AIX, LocalTalk/AppleTalk, Novell. Computer languages and software packages include Ada, APL, BASIC, C, C++, COBOL, dBase, FORTRAN, Harvard Business Graphics, Lotus 1-2-3, Macro, MINITAB, Paradox, Quattro Pro, SAS, SPSS-X, VAX MAIL, VAX NOTES, WordPerfect. Computer facilities are available to all students.
**Fees:** $40 computer fee per semester.
**Hours:** One 24-hour lab; network available 24 hours per day.

**GRADUATE CAREER DATA.** Graduate school percentages: 1% enter law school. 1% enter medical school. 1% enter graduate business programs. 4% enter graduate arts and sciences programs. Highest graduate school enrollments: Drake U, Iowa State U, U of Iowa, U of Northern Iowa. 50% of graduates choose careers in business and industry. Companies and businesses that hire graduates: Maytag, Principal Financial Group, McGladrey and Pullen.

## Vennard College

**University Park, IA 52595 — 515 673-8391**

**1993-94 Costs.** Tuition: $5,148. Room: $730. Board: $1,942. Fees, books, misc. academic expenses (school's estimate): $846.
**Enrollment.** Undergraduates: 70 men, 68 women (full-time). Freshman class: 279 applicants, 150 accepted, 77 enrolled. Graduate enrollment: 74 men, 75 women.
**Test score averages/ranges.** Average SAT scores: 403 verbal, 423 math. Average ACT scores: 18 composite.
**Faculty.** 11 full-time; 6 part-time. 29% of faculty holds doctoral degree. Student/faculty ratio: 10 to 1.
**Selectivity rating.** Less competitive.

**PROFILE.** Vennard, founded in Chicago in 1910, is a multipurpose college with religious orientation. Its 75-acre campus is located in Vennard, just outside Oskalooska, 60 miles southeast of Des Moines.

**Accreditation:** AABC.
**Religious orientation:** Vennard College is an interdenominational Christian school; eight semesters of religion/theology required.
**Athletic facilities:** Gymnasium, soccer and softball fields.

**STUDENT BODY. Undergraduate profile:** 40% are state residents; 16% are transfers. 99% White, 1% Other. Average age of undergraduates is 20.
**Freshman profile:** 67% of freshmen who took SAT scored 400 or over on verbal, 100% scored 400 or over on math; 100% scored 300 or over on verbal. 7% of accepted applicants took SAT; 74% took ACT.
**Undergraduate achievement:** 80% of fall 1991 freshmen returned for fall 1992 term. 14% of entering class graduated. 30% of students who completed a degree program went on to graduate study within five years.
**Foreign students:** Three students are from out of the country. Countries represented include Japan, Kenya, and Korea.

**PROGRAMS OF STUDY. Degrees:** B.A., B.Mus., Theol.B.
**Majors:** Bible/Theology, Business Management, Christian Education, Elementary Education, Missions, Music Performance, Musical Composition, Nursing, Office Administration, Pastoral Ministries, Pre-Seminary Studies, Psychology/Human Relations, Sacred Music, Social Science.
**Distribution of degrees:** The majors with the highest enrollment are pastoral ministries and missions; sacred music and Christian education have the lowest.
**Requirements:** General education requirement.
**Special:** Double majors. Internships. Cooperative education programs. Graduate school at which undergraduates may take graduate-level courses. 2-2 Salvation Army officer training program. 3-2 nursing program with Indian Hills Community Coll. 4-1 elementary education program with William Penn Coll. Teacher certification in elementary and secondary education.
**Academic Assistance:** Nonremedial tutoring.

**ADMISSIONS. Academic basis for candidate selection** (in order of priority): Secondary school record, standardized test scores, school's recommendation, class rank, essay.
**Nonacademic basis for candidate selection:** Character and personality are emphasized. Particular talent or ability and alumni/ae relationship are considered. Christian commitment and pastor's reference are considered.
**Requirements:** Graduation from secondary school is recommended; GED is accepted. No specific distribution of secondary school units required. Personal account of Christian experience, pastor's reference and two additional references, and minimum 2.0 GPA required. Conditional admission possible for applicants not meeting standard requirements. ACT is required. Campus visit and interview recommended. Off-campus interviews available with an admissions representative.
**Procedure:** Notification of admission on rolling basis. $50 tuition deposit, refundable before May 30. $50 refundable room deposit. Freshmen accepted for terms other than fall.
**Special programs:** Admission may be deferred. Credit and/or placement may be granted through CLEP general and subject exams. Credit and placement may be granted through challenge exams.
**Transfer students:** Transfer students accepted for terms other than fall. In fall 1992, 16% of all new students were transfers into all classes. 15 transfer applications were received, 10 were accepted. Minimum 2.0 GPA required. Lowest course grade accepted is "C." At least 24 semester hours must be completed at the college to receive degree.
**Admissions contact:** Mark Becker, Director of Admissions. 515 673-8391, extension 217.

**FINANCIAL AID. Available aid:** Pell grants, SEOG, school scholarships and grants, private scholarships and grants, academic merit scholarships, and aid for undergraduate foreign students. Perkins Loans (NDSL), PLUS, Stafford Loans (GSL), school loans, and SLS. Family tuition reduction. Institutional payment plan.
**Financial aid statistics:** Average amounts of aid awarded freshmen: Loans, $2,103.
**Supporting data/closing dates:** FAFSA/FAF/FFS: Accepted on rolling basis. Notification of awards on rolling basis.
**Financial aid contact:** Kay Paden, Director of Financial Aid. 515 673-8391, extension 213.

## Wartburg College

**Waverly, IA 50677 — 319 352-8200**

**1994-95 Costs.** Tuition: $11,600. Room: $1,760. Board: $1,940. Fees, books, misc. academic expenses (school's estimate): $520.
**Enrollment.** Undergraduates: 584 men, 711 women (full-time). Freshman class: 1,145 applicants, 1,074 accepted, 413 enrolled.
**Test score averages/ranges.** Average SAT scores: 478 verbal, 557 math. Range of SAT scores of middle 50%: 410-520 verbal, 500-640 math. Average ACT scores: 24 English, 23 math, 24 composite. Range of ACT scores of middle 50%: 20-27 English, 20-25 math.
**Faculty.** 92 full-time; 49 part-time. 87% of faculty holds highest degree in specific field. Student/faculty ratio: 14 to 1.
**Selectivity rating.** Competitive.

**PROFILE.** Wartburg, founded in 1852, is a church-affiliated, liberal arts college. Its 83-acre campus is located in Waverly, 15 miles north of Cedar Falls.

**Accreditation:** NCACS. Professionally accredited by the Council on Social Work Education, the National Association of Schools of Music, the National Council for Accreditation of Teacher Education.
**Religious orientation:** Wartburg College is affiliated with the Evangelical Lutheran Church in America; three semester hours of religion required.
**Library:** Collections totaling over 140,000 volumes, 725 periodical subscriptions, and 5,816 microform items.
**Special facilities/museums:** International museum, art gallery, fine arts center, institute for leadership education, planetarium, prairie preserve.

**Athletic facilities:** Racquetball and squash courts, volleyball courts, indoor and outdoor tracks, field house, gymnasium, football field.

**STUDENT BODY. Undergraduate profile:** 76% are state residents; 17% are transfers. 1% Asian-American, 3% Black, 1% Hispanic, 89% White, 6% Other. Average age of undergraduates is 20.
**Freshman profile:** 11% of freshmen who took SAT scored 700 or over on math; 11% scored 600 or over on verbal, 47% scored 600 or over on math; 50% scored 500 or over on verbal, 75% scored 500 or over on math; 81% scored 400 or over on verbal, 86% scored 400 or over on math; 95% scored 300 or over on verbal, 100% scored 300 or over on math. 6% of freshmen who took ACT scored 30 or over on English, 6% scored 30 or over on math, 8% scored 30 or over on composite; 48% scored 24 or over on English, 41% scored 24 or over on math, 49% scored 24 or over on composite; 85% scored 18 or over on English, 87% scored 18 or over on math, 95% scored 18 or over on composite; 99% scored 12 or over on English, 100% scored 12 or over on math, 100% scored 12 or over on composite; 100% scored 6 or over on English. 9% of accepted applicants took SAT; 90% took ACT.
**Undergraduate achievement:** 77% of fall 1992 freshmen returned for fall 1993 term. 54% of entering class graduated. 19% of students who completed a degree program immediately went on to graduate study.
**Foreign students:** 65 students are from out of the country. Countries represented include Indonesia, Japan, Malaysia, Namibia, Singapore, and Tanzania; 23 in all.

**PROGRAMS OF STUDY. Degrees:** B.A., B.Appl.Arts, B.Appl.Sci., B.Mus., B.Mus.Ed.
**Majors:** Accounting, Applied Music, Art, Biology, Business Administration, Chemistry, Communication Arts, Computer Information Systems, Computer Science, Economics, Elementary Education, English, Fitness Management, French, French Studies, German, German Studies, History, Law Enforcement, Mathematics, Music Education, Music Performance, Music Theory, Music Therapy, Philosophy, Physical Education, Physics, Political Science, Pre-Agriculture, Pre-Engineering, Pre-Occupational Therapy, Pre-Physical Therapy, Psychology, Recreation, Religion, Secondary Education, Security Administration, Social Work, Sociology, Spanish, Spanish Studies, Visual Arts Management.
**Distribution of degrees:** The majors with the highest enrollment are business administration, teacher education, and biology; philosophy, physics, and religion have the lowest.
**Requirements:** General education requirement.
**Academic regulations:** Freshmen must maintain minimum 1.6 GPA; sophomores, 1.8 GPA; juniors, 2.0 GPA; seniors, 2.0 GPA.
**Special:** Minors offered in all majors and in environmental and women's studies. Intercultural Certification Program. Leadership Education Program. Self-designed majors. Double majors. Dual degrees. Independent study. Pass/fail grading option. Internships. Cooperative education programs. Graduate school at which undergraduates may take graduate-level courses. Preprofessional programs in pharmacy, dentistry, optometry, architecture, engineering, occupational therapy, and physical therapy. 2-2 nursing program with Allen Coll and U of Iowa. 3-1 occupational therapy programs with Boston U and Washington U. 3-1 or 3-2 public health education program with U of South Florida. 3-2 engineering programs with U of Illinois at Urbana-Champaign, Iowa State U, U of Iowa, and Washington U. 3-2 physical therapy program with Mayo Clinic (Minn.). Washington Semester. Wartburg West program (Denver). Teacher certification in early childhood, elementary, and secondary education. Certification in specific subject areas. Exchange programs abroad in Germany (Bonn U, Jena U) and Japan (International Christian U). Study abroad also in Australia, Chile, China, England, France, Guyana, Jamaica, Mexico, Namibia, Palestine, the Philippines, Spain, and Tanzania.
**Honors:** Honor societies.
**Academic Assistance:** Remedial reading, writing, math, and study skills. Nonremedial tutoring.

**STUDENT LIFE. Housing:** All unmarried students under age 24 without dependents must live on campus. Coed, women's, and men's dorms. 76% of students live in college housing.
**Social atmosphere:** The student newspaper reports, "Opportunities are available for almost any type of social life. It remains the student's decision whether to participate and what to participate in." Influential groups on campus include the football players, Student Senate, Student Activities Committee, the Choir, and the Orientation Group Leaders (OGL's). Favorite college events are the Artist Series, Homecoming, sports events rivalries, and various holiday celebrations. On campus, students hang out at Buhr Lounge, the cafeteria, P.E. complex, dorm lounges, and rec rooms. Off campus, popular spots are Kohlmann Park, the Other Place, Joe's Nighthawk, Outfly Grounds, and Hardee's.
**Services and counseling/handicapped student services:** Placement services. Health service. Counseling services for minority and veteran students. Personal and psychological counseling. Career and academic guidance services. Religious counseling. Physically disabled student services. Learning disabled services. Tutors. Reader services for the blind.
**Campus organizations:** Undergraduate student government. Student newspaper (Trumpet, published once/week). Literary magazine. Yearbook. Radio and TV stations. Castle Singers, choirs, bands, chamber orchestra, Wartburg Players, speech team, student activities committee, Tae Kwon Do club, Students for Peace and Justice, Habitat for Humanity, Young Democrats, Young Republicans, Womyn of Wartburg, service and special-interest groups, departmental clubs, 74 organizations in all.
**Religious organizations:** Campus Crusade for Christ, Catholic Knights, Christ's Jesters, Faith Alive, Faith and Fellowship, Fellowship of Christian Athletes, Spiritsong.
**Minority/foreign student organizations:** Cultural Awareness Organization. International Club.

**ATHLETICS. Physical education requirements:** One semester hour of physical education required.
**Intercollegiate competition:** 9% of students participate. Baseball (M), basketball (M,W), cross-country (M,W), football (M), golf (M,W), soccer (M), softball (W), tennis (M,W), track (M,W), volleyball (W), wrestling (M). Member of Iowa Intercollegiate Athletic Conference, NCAA Division III.
**Intramural and club sports:** 3% of students participate. Intramural badminton, basketball, bowling, cross-country, golf, pool, softball, tennis, touch football, track, volleyball, wrestling.

**ADMISSIONS. Academic basis for candidate selection** (in order of priority): Secondary school record, class rank, standardized test scores, school's recommendation.
**Nonacademic basis for candidate selection:** Alumni/ae relationship is important. Character and personality, extracurricular participation, particular talent or ability, and geographical distribution are considered.
**Requirements:** Graduation from secondary school is required; GED is accepted. 14 units and the following program of study are recommended: 4 units of English, 3 units of math, 3 units of science, 2 units of foreign language, 2 units of social studies. Minimum composite ACT score of 19, rank in top half of secondary school class, and minimum 2.5 GPA recommended. SAT or ACT is required. Campus visit and interview recommended. Off-campus interviews available with an admissions representative.
**Procedure:** Take SAT or ACT by October of 12th year. Visit college for interview by April of 12th year. Suggest filing application by December 1. Application deadline is May 1. Notification of admission on rolling basis. $100 nonrefundable tuition deposit. $100 nonrefundable room deposit. Freshmen accepted for terms other than fall.
**Special programs:** Admission may be deferred one year. Credit and/or placement may be granted through CEEB Advanced Placement exams for scores of 3 or higher. Credit and/or placement may be granted through CLEP general and subject exams. Credit and placement may be granted through challenge exams, and military and life experience. Early entrance/early admission program. Concurrent enrollment program.
**Transfer students:** Transfer students accepted for terms other than fall. In fall 1993, 17% of all new students were transfers into all classes. 150 transfer applications were received, 119 were accepted. Application deadline is December for fall; May for spring. Minimum 2.0 GPA required. Lowest course grade accepted is "C." Maximum number of transferable credits is 78 semester hours from a two-year school and 103 semester hours from a four-year school. At least 25 semester hours must be completed at the college to receive degree.
**Admissions contact:** Deanndrea Katko-Roquet, Director of Admissions. 319 352-8264, 800 772-2085.

**FINANCIAL AID. Available aid:** Pell grants, SEOG, state scholarships and grants, school scholarships and grants, private scholarships and grants, academic merit scholarships, and aid for undergraduate foreign students. Perkins Loans (NDSL), PLUS, Stafford Loans (GSL), school loans, private loans, and SLS. Tuition Plan Inc. and AMS. Local bank payment plan.
**Financial aid statistics:** 21% of aid is not need-based. In 1993-94, 97% of all undergraduate applicants received aid; 90% of freshman applicants. Average amounts of aid awarded freshmen: Scholarships and grants, $6,113; loans, $3,138.
**Supporting data/closing dates:** FAFSA/FAF/FFS: Priority filing date is March 1. Notification of awards on rolling basis.
**Financial aid contact:** Jamie Hightower, Director of Financial Aid. 319 352-8262.

**STUDENT EMPLOYMENT.** College Work/Study Program. Institutional employment. 55% of full-time undergraduates work on campus during school year. Students may expect to earn an average of $900 during school year. Off-campus part-time employment opportunities rated "good."

**COMPUTER FACILITIES.** 225 IBM/IBM-compatible and Macintosh/Apple microcomputers; all are networked. Students may access Digital minicomputer/mainframe systems, Internet. Client/LAN operating systems include Apple/Macintosh, DOS, LocalTalk/AppleTalk, Novell. 70 major computer languages and software packages available. Computer facilities are available to all students.
**Fees:** None.
**Hours:** 24 hours.

**GRADUATE CAREER DATA.** Highest graduate school enrollments: U of Iowa. 56% of graduates choose careers in business and industry. Companies and businesses that hire graduates: Principal Financial Group.

**PROMINENT ALUMNI/AE.** Dr. Delbert H. Meyer, inventor of polyester and director of exploratory research, Amoco Chemical Co.; Dr. Noel Florendo, pathologist; Rev. Martin J. Heinecken, retired professor of theology.

# William Penn College

**Oskaloosa, IA 52577** **515 673-1001**

**1993-94 Costs.** Tuition: $10,000. Room & board: $3,110. Fees, books, misc. academic expenses (school's estimate): $785.
**Enrollment.** Undergraduates: 317 men, 316 women (full-time). Freshman class: 344 applicants, 284 accepted, 133 enrolled.
**Test score averages/ranges.** Average ACT scores: 20 composite.
**Faculty.** 42 full-time; 12 part-time. 50% of faculty holds doctoral degree. Student/faculty ratio: 13 to 1.
**Selectivity rating.** Less competitive.

**PROFILE.** William Penn, founded in 1873, is a church-affiliated college. Its 40-acre campus is located in Oskaloosa, 60 miles southeast of Des Moines.

**Accreditation:** NCACS.
**Religious orientation:** William Penn College is affiliated with the Society of Friends; five semester hours of religion required.
**Library:** Collections totaling over 80,000 volumes, 400 periodical subscriptions, and 2,000 microform items.
**Athletic facilities:** Gymnasiums, tennis courts, track, baseball, football, intramural, and softball fields, weight room, YMCA.

**STUDENT BODY. Undergraduate profile:** 80% are state residents; 44% are transfers. 2% Asian-American, 6% Black, 2% Hispanic, 89% White, 1% Other. Average age of undergraduates is 20.
**Freshman profile:** 1% of accepted applicants took SAT; 76% took ACT. 96% of freshmen come from public schools.
**Undergraduate achievement:** 60% of fall 1992 freshmen returned for fall 1993 term. 40% of entering class graduated.
**Foreign students:** Countries represented include China, Honduras, Japan, Jordan, Kenya, and Korea.

**PROGRAMS OF STUDY. Degrees:** B.A.

**Majors:** Accounting, Applied Computer Science, Art, Biology, Biology Education, Business Education, Business Management, Chemistry, Chemistry Education, Communication Arts, Computer Analytical Systems, Computer Information Systems, Elementary Education, Engineering, English, English Education, Health Education, History, History Education, Home Economics, Human Relations, Human Resources Management, Industrial Technology, Industrial Technology Education, Information Systems Management, Interior Design, Mathematics, Mathematics Education, Music, Music Education, Natural Science, Natural Science Education, Operations Management, Physical Education, Political Science, Pre-Mortuary Science, Pre-Physical Therapy, Pre-Professional Biology, Recreation, Religion, Safety/Driver Education, Secondary Education, Social Science, Social Studies Education, Sociology, Sports Administration.
**Distribution of degrees:** The majors with the highest enrollment are elementary education, business management, and industrial technology; interior design, natural science, and political science have the lowest.
**Requirements:** General education requirement.
**Special:** Minors offered in anthropology, drama/speech, English, French, industrial arts/technology, philosophy, psychology, and Spanish. Double majors. Dual degrees. Independent study. Accelerated study. Pass/fail grading option. Internships. Graduate school at which undergraduates may take graduate-level courses. Preprofessional programs in law, medicine, dentistry, theology, optometry, agriculture, engineering, journalism, medical technology, nursing, physical therapy, and social welfare. Cooperative majors with Indian Hills Comm Coll. Washington Semester. Teacher certification in early childhood, elementary, secondary, and special education. Exchange programs abroad in Korea (Kyung Won U) and Ukraine (Cherkassy Inst).
**Academic Assistance:** Remedial writing, math, and study skills.

**ADMISSIONS. Academic basis for candidate selection** (in order of priority): Class rank, standardized test scores, secondary school record, school's recommendation, essay.
**Nonacademic basis for candidate selection:** Character and personality are emphasized. Particular talent or ability and alumni/ae relationship are considered.
**Requirements:** Graduation from secondary school is required; GED is accepted. 15 units and the following program of study are recommended: 3 units of English, 2 units of math, 2 units of science, 2 units of foreign language, 2 units of social studies, 2 units of history, 2 units of electives. Conditional admission possible for applicants not meeting standard requirements. SAT or ACT is required. PSAT is recommended. Campus visit and interview recommended. Off-campus interviews available with an admissions representative.
**Procedure:** Take SAT or ACT by August 1 of 12th year. Visit college for interview by August 15 of 12th year. Suggest filing application by May 1. Application deadline is August 1. Notification of admission on rolling basis. Reply is required within 30 days of acceptance. $100 tuition deposit, refundable until April 15. Freshmen accepted for terms other than fall.
**Special programs:** Admission may be deferred one year. Credit may be granted through CEEB Advanced Placement for scores of 3 or higher. Credit may be granted through CLEP general and subject exams. Early decision program. Early entrance/early admission program. Concurrent enrollment program.
**Transfer students:** Transfer students accepted for terms other than fall. In fall 1993, 44% of all new students were transfers into all classes. 246 transfer applications were received, 189 were accepted. Application deadline is August 1 for fall; January 1 for spring. Minimum 2.0 GPA required. Lowest course grade accepted is "C." Maximum number of transferable credits is 64 semester hours from a two-year school and 94 semester hours from a four-year school. At least 30 semester hours must be completed at the college to receive degree.
**Admissions contact:** Eric Otto, Director of Admissions. 515 673-1012.

**FINANCIAL AID. Available aid:** Pell grants, SEOG, state scholarships and grants, school scholarships and grants, private scholarships and grants, academic merit scholarships, and aid for undergraduate foreign students. Perkins Loans (NDSL), PLUS, Stafford Loans (GSL), private loans, and SLS. SLUS. AMS.
**Financial aid statistics:** 2% of aid is not need-based. In 1993-94, 100% of all undergraduate applicants received aid. Average amounts of aid awarded freshmen: Scholarships and grants, $2,300; loans, $2,500.
**Supporting data/closing dates:** FAFSA/FAF/FFS: Deadline is April 15. Notification of awards on rolling basis.
**Financial aid contact:** Nancy Ferguson, Director of Financial Aid. 515 673-1060.

# Kansas

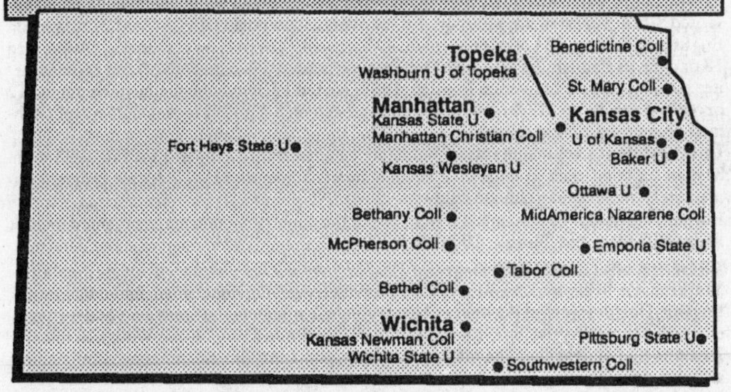


## Baker University

**Baldwin City, KS 66006** 913 594-6451

**1993-94 Costs.** Tuition: $7,990. Room & board: $4,050. Fees, books, misc. academic expenses (school's estimate): $640.
**Enrollment.** Undergraduates: 378 men, 457 women (full-time). Freshman class: 602 applicants, 483 accepted, 206 enrolled.
**Test score averages/ranges.** Average ACT scores: 22 composite.
**Faculty.** 63 full-time; 20 part-time. 57% of faculty holds doctoral degree. Student/faculty ratio: 14 to 1.
**Selectivity rating.** Less competitive.

**PROFILE.** Baker, founded in 1858, is a church-affiliated, liberal arts university. Its 54-acre campus is located in Baldwin City, 40 miles southwest of Kansas City.

**Accreditation:** NCACS. Professionally accredited by the National Council for Accreditation of Teacher Education.
**Religious orientation:** Baker University is affiliated with the United Methodist Church; one semester of religion/theology required.
**Library:** Collections totaling over 64,000 volumes, 327 periodical subscriptions, and 3,000 microform items.
**Special facilities/museums:** Historical museum, language lab.
**Athletic facilities:** Gymnasiums, track, aerobics and weight rooms, racquetball, tennis, and volleyball courts, baseball, soccer, and softball fields, golf course.
**STUDENT BODY. Undergraduate profile:** 60% are state residents; 20% are transfers. 1% Asian-American, 4% Black, 2% Hispanic, 89% White, 4% Other. Average age of undergraduates is 19.
**Freshman profile:** 6% of accepted applicants took SAT; 94% took ACT. 95% of freshmen come from public schools.
**Undergraduate achievement:** 80% of fall 1992 freshmen returned for fall 1993 term. 43% of entering class graduated. 19% of students who completed a degree program immediately went on to graduate study.
**Foreign students:** 42 students are from out of the country. Countries represented include England, Japan, and Taiwan; nine in all.
**PROGRAMS OF STUDY. Degrees:** B.A., B.Mus., B.Mus.Ed., B.S.
**Majors:** Accounting, Art Education, Art History, Biology, Business, Chemistry, Computer Information Systems, Computer Science, Economics, Education, Elementary Education, Engineering/Liberal Arts, English, Environmental Chemistry, Environmental Technology and Management, Fashion Merchandising, Forestry/Liberal Arts, French, German, History, International Business, Mass Communications, Mathematics, Medical Technology, Music, Music Education, Music Therapy, Nursing, Philosophy, Physical Education, Physics, Political Science, Psychology, Religion, Sociology, Spanish, Speech Communication, Studio Art, Theatre, Wildlife Biology.
**Distribution of degrees:** The majors with the highest enrollment are business, psychology, and biology; theatre and philosophy have the lowest.
**Requirements:** General education requirement.
**Academic regulations:** Minimum 2.0 GPA must be maintained.
**Special:** Double majors. Dual degrees. Independent study. Pass/fail grading option. Internships. Cooperative education programs in medical technology and nursing. Preprofessional programs in law, medicine, veterinary science, pharmacy, dentistry, social welfare, and theology. 3-2 forestry program with Duke U. 3-2 pre-engineering program with Washington U. Member of Kansas City Regional Council of Higher Education. Teacher certification in elementary and secondary education. Certification in specific subject areas. Study abroad in England, France, Germany, Greece, and Spain. ROTC and AFROTC at U of Kansas.
**Honors:** Honors program. Honor societies.
**Academic Assistance:** Remedial writing, math, and study skills. Nonremedial tutoring.
**ADMISSIONS. Academic basis for candidate selection** (in order of priority): Secondary school record, standardized test scores, school's recommendation, class rank.
**Nonacademic basis for candidate selection:** Extracurricular participation and particular talent or ability are considered.
**Requirements:** Graduation from secondary school is required; GED is accepted. No specific distribution of secondary school units required. Minimum composite ACT score of 19 and a minimum 2.7 GPA required. Conditional admission possible for applicants not meeting standard requirements. ACT is required; SAT may be substituted. Campus visit and interview recommended. No off-campus interviews.
**Procedure:** Take SAT or ACT by May of 12th year. Visit college for interview by August 1 of 12th year. Notification of admission on rolling basis. $50 tuition deposit, refundable until June 1. $50 room deposit, refundable until June 1. Freshmen accepted for terms other than fall.
**Special programs:** Admission may be deferred on conditional basis. Credit and/or placement may be granted through CEEB Advanced Placement exams for scores of 3 or higher. Credit and/or placement may be granted through CLEP general and subject exams. Placement may be granted through challenge exams. Credit and placement may be granted through military and life experience. Early decision program. In fall 1993, three applied for early decision and one was accepted. Concurrent enrollment program.
**Transfer students:** Transfer students accepted for terms other than fall. In fall 1993, 20% of all new students were transfers into all classes. 105 transfer applications were received, 61 were accepted. Application deadline is rolling for fall; rolling for spring. Minimum 2.5 GPA required. Lowest course grade accepted is "C." At least 31 semester hours must be completed at the university to receive degree.
**Admissions contact:** John Haynes, Director of Admissions. 800 873-4282.
**FINANCIAL AID. Available aid:** Pell grants, SEOG, state scholarships and grants, school scholarships and grants, private scholarships, academic merit scholarships, athletic scholarships, and aid for undergraduate foreign students. Perkins Loans (NDSL), PLUS, Stafford Loans (GSL), and SLS. Deferred payment plan. 10-month and six-month payment plans.
**Financial aid statistics:** 45% of aid is not need-based. In 1993-94, 98% of all undergraduate applicants received aid; 95% of freshman applicants. Average amounts of aid awarded freshmen: Scholarships and grants, $4,536; loans, $4,401.
**Supporting data/closing dates:** FAFSA: Priority filing date is March 1; accepted on rolling basis. School's own aid application: Priority filing date is March 1. Income tax forms: Priority filing date is March 1. Notification of awards begins March.
**Financial aid contact:** Jeanne Mott, M.S., Director of Financial Aid. 913 594-6451, extension 595.

## Benedictine College

**Atchison, KS 66002** 913 367-5340

**1994-95 Costs.** Tuition: $9,550. Room & board: $3,830-4,050. Fees, books, misc. academic expenses (school's estimate): $660.
**Enrollment.** Undergraduates: 420 men, 314 women (full-time). Freshman class: 567 applicants, 556 accepted, 222 enrolled. Graduate enrollment: 4 men, 7 women.
**Test score averages/ranges.** Average SAT scores: 435 verbal, 560 math. Range of SAT scores of middle 50%: 430-510 verbal, 450-550 math. Average ACT scores: 22 composite.
**Faculty.** 56 full-time; 27 part-time. 54% of faculty holds doctoral degree. Student/faculty ratio: 13 to 1.
**Selectivity rating.** Less competitive.

**PROFILE.** Benedictine is a church-affiliated, liberal arts college. It is the product of the 1971 merger of St. Benedict's Abbey (founded in 1859) and St. Scholastica's Academy (founded in 1924); coeducation was adopted in 1971. Its two campuses of 200 acres are located a mile and a half apart, in a residential area of Atchison, 60 miles from Kansas City. Campus architecture includes Tudor-Gothic and modern styles.

**Accreditation:** NCACS. Professionally accredited by the National Association of Schools of Music, the National Council for Accreditation of Teacher Education.
**Religious orientation:** Benedictine College is affiliated with the Roman Catholic Church (Benedictine Order); three semesters of religion required.
**Library:** Collections totaling over 310,000 volumes, 625 periodical subscriptions, and 16,292 microform items.
**Special facilities/museums:** Language and special education labs.
**Athletic facilities:** Gymnasiums, baseball, football, soccer, and softball fields, swimming pool, batting cages, basketball, racquetball, tennis, and volleyball courts, weight room, fitness center.
**STUDENT BODY. Undergraduate profile:** 38% are state residents; 16% are transfers. 1% Asian-American, 2% Black, 3% Hispanic, 1% Native American, 90% White, 3% Other. Average age of undergraduates is 20.
**Freshman profile:** 4% of freshmen who took ACT scored 30 or over on composite; 37% scored 24 or over on composite; 91% scored 18 or over on composite; 100% scored 12 or over on composite. Majority of accepted applicants took ACT. 32% of freshmen come from public schools.
**Undergraduate achievement:** 61% of fall 1992 freshmen returned for fall 1993 term. 38% of entering class graduated. 17% of students who completed a degree program immediately went on to graduate study.
**Foreign students:** 34 students are from out of the country. Countries represented include China, Ethiopia, Japan, Sweden, Taiwan, and U.S. Virgin Islands.
**PROGRAMS OF STUDY. Degrees:** B.A., B.Mus.Ed.
**Majors:** Accounting, Astronomy, Biochemistry, Biology, Business Administration, Chemistry, Computer Information Systems, Computer Science, Economics, Elementary Education, English, French, Health Care Administration, History, Journalism, Latin, Liberal Studies, Mathematics, Music, Music Education, Music Marketing, Natural Science, Philosophy, Physical Education, Physics, Political Science, Psychology, Religious Studies, Social Science, Sociology, Spanish, Special Education, Theatre Arts, Theatre Arts Management, Youth Ministries.
**Distribution of degrees:** The majors with the highest enrollment are business administration, sociology, and English; special education, liberal studies, and astronomy have the lowest.
**Requirements:** General education requirement.
**Academic regulations:** Freshmen must maintain minimum 1.8 GPA; sophomores, juniors, seniors, 2.0 GPA.

**Special:** Minors offered in all majors and in art, Greek, and secondary education. Associate's degrees offered. Self-designed majors. Double majors. Independent study. Pass/fail grading option. Internships. Graduate school at which undergraduates may take graduate-level courses. 3-1 medical technology program with four area schools. 3-2 engineering program with Washington U and several other institutions. 3-2 occupational therapy program with Washington U. Member of Kansas City Regional Council for Higher Education (KCRCHE); cross-registration possible. Teacher certification in elementary, secondary, and special education. Certification in specific subject areas. Exchange program abroad in Mexico (Inst Ideal). Study abroad in England, France, Germany, the Netherlands, Spain, and Wales. ROTC.
**Honors:** Honors program. Honor societies.
**Academic Assistance:** Remedial reading, writing, math, and study skills. Nonremedial tutoring.

**ADMISSIONS. Academic basis for candidate selection** (in order of priority): Secondary school record, class rank, standardized test scores, school's recommendation, essay.
**Nonacademic basis for candidate selection:** Character and personality are emphasized. Extracurricular participation, particular talent or ability, and alumni/ae relationship are important.
**Requirements:** Graduation from secondary school is recommended; GED is accepted. 16 units and the following program of study are required: 2 units of science, 2 units of social studies, 1 unit of history, 2 units of electives. Minimum composite ACT score of 18 (combined SAT score of 730) and rank in top half of secondary school class or minimum 2.0 GPA required. Audition required of music program applicants. Conditional admission possible for applicants not meeting standard requirements. ACT is required; SAT may be substituted. Campus visit and interview recommended. Off-campus interviews available with an admissions representative.
**Procedure:** Take SAT or ACT by June of 12th year. Visit college for interview by August 1 of 12th year. Suggest filing application by May 1. Application deadline is August 1. Notification of admission on rolling basis. Reply is required by May 1 or within four weeks of acceptance. $100 tuition deposit, refundable until May 1. Freshmen accepted for terms other than fall.
**Special programs:** Admission may be deferred one year. Credit and/or placement may be granted through CEEB Advanced Placement exams for scores of 3 or higher. Credit and/or placement may be granted through CLEP general and subject exams. Credit and placement may be granted through Regents College, ACT PEP, DANTES, and challenge exams, and military experience. Early entrance/early admission program. Concurrent enrollment program.
**Transfer students:** Transfer students accepted for terms other than fall. In fall 1993, 16% of all new students were transfers into all classes. 138 transfer applications were received, 134 were accepted. Application deadline is August 1 for fall; December 1 for spring. Minimum 2.0 GPA required. Lowest course grade accepted is "C." Maximum number of transferable credits is 64 semester hours. At least 30 semester hours must be completed at the college to receive degree.
**Admissions contact:** James Hoffman, M.A., Director of Admissions. 913 367-5340, extension 2474.

**FINANCIAL AID. Available aid:** Pell grants, SEOG, state scholarships and grants, school scholarships and grants, private scholarships, ROTC scholarships, academic merit scholarships, and athletic scholarships. Ethnic minority incentive award. Perkins Loans (NDSL), PLUS, Stafford Loans (GSL), private loans, and SLS. Tuition Plan Inc., AMS, EFI Fund Management, Tuition Management Systems, and deferred payment plan.
**Financial aid statistics:** 5% of aid is not need-based. In 1993-94, 92% of all undergraduate applicants received aid; 92% of freshman applicants. Average amounts of aid awarded freshmen: Scholarships and grants, $6,100; loans, $4,000.
**Supporting data/closing dates:** FAFSA/FAF/FFS: Priority filing date is March 1; deadline is July 15. School's own aid application: Accepted on rolling basis. State aid form: Priority filing date is March 1; accepted on rolling basis. Income tax forms: Accepted on rolling basis. Notification of awards on rolling basis.
**Financial aid contact:** Gilbert Estrada, Director of Financial Aid. 913 367-5340, extension 2484.

## Bethany College

**Lindsborg, KS 67456-1897 — 913 227-3311**

**1993-94 Costs.** Tuition: $8,000. Room & board: $3,225. Fees, books, misc. academic expenses (school's estimate): $480.
**Enrollment.** Undergraduates: 381 men, 325 women (full-time). Freshman class: 878 applicants, 821 accepted, 200 enrolled.
**Test score averages/ranges.** Average ACT scores: 23 English, 22 math, 23 composite. Range of ACT scores of middle 50%: 20-26 English, 19-26 math.
**Faculty.** 49 full-time; 29 part-time. 60% of faculty holds doctoral degree. Student/faculty ratio: 13 to 1.
**Selectivity rating.** Less competitive.

**PROFILE.** Bethany, founded in 1881, is a church-affiliated, liberal arts college. Its 40-acre campus is located in Lindsborg, 15 miles south of Salina.

**Accreditation:** NCACS. Professionally accredited by the Council on Social Work Education, the National Association of Schools of Music, the National Council for Accreditation of Teacher Education.
**Religious orientation:** Bethany College is an interdenominational Christian school; two semesters of religion required.
**Library:** Collections totaling over 109,853 volumes, 600 periodical subscriptions, and 31,678 microform items.
**Special facilities/museums:** Art gallery.
**Athletic facilities:** Gymnasium, baseball, football, and softball fields, basketball and tennis courts, track.

**STUDENT BODY. Undergraduate profile:** 67% are state residents; 11% are transfers. 2% Asian-American, 4% Black, 3% Hispanic, 1% Native American, 87% White, 3% Other. Average age of undergraduates is 20.
**Freshman profile:** 4% of freshmen who took ACT scored 30 or over on English, 5% scored 30 or over on math, 5% scored 30 or over on composite; 43% scored 24 or over on English, 31% scored 24 or over on math, 39% scored 24 or over on composite; 84% scored 18 or over on English, 82% scored 18 or over on math, 93% scored 18 or over on composite; 100% scored 12 or over on English, 100% scored 12 or over on math, 100% scored 12 or over on composite. 18% of accepted applicants took SAT; 72% took ACT. 96% of freshmen come from public schools.
**Undergraduate achievement:** 77% of fall 1992 freshmen returned for fall 1993 term. 31% of entering class graduated. 15% of students who completed a degree program immediately went on to graduate study.
**Foreign students:** 12 students are from out of the country. Countries represented include Brazil, Sweden, and Taiwan; 10 in all.

**PROGRAMS OF STUDY. Degrees:** B.A.
**Majors:** Art, Biology, Chemistry, Computer Science, Economics/Business, Education, English, Health/Physical Education, History/Political Science, Information Systems, Mathematics, Music, Psychology, Recreation, Religion/Philosophy, Social Work, Sociology.
**Distribution of degrees:** The majors with the highest enrollment are economics/business and education.
**Requirements:** General education requirement.
**Academic regulations:** Freshmen must maintain minimum 1.7 GPA; sophomores, juniors, seniors, 2.0 GPA.
**Special:** Minors offered in some majors and in administration of justice, information science, sacred music, and theatre. Majors in foreign language, physics, and theatre can be arranged on contract basis. Self-designed majors. Dual degrees. Independent study. Internships. Cooperative education programs. Preprofessional programs in law, medicine, pharmacy, dentistry, theology, and optometry. 3-2 engineering program with Wichita State U. Member of Associated Colleges of Central Kansas. Washington Semester. Teacher certification in elementary, secondary, and special education. Certification in specific subject areas.
**Academic Assistance:** Remedial reading, writing, math, and study skills. Nonremedial tutoring.

**ADMISSIONS. Academic basis for candidate selection** (in order of priority): Secondary school record, standardized test scores, class rank, school's recommendation, essay.
**Nonacademic basis for candidate selection:** Extracurricular participation is emphasized. Character and personality are considered.
**Requirements:** Graduation from secondary school is required; GED is accepted. 13 units and the following program of study are recommended: 4 units of English, 3 units of math, 2 units of science, 1 unit of foreign language, 3 units of social studies. Minimum composite ACT score of 19, rank in top half of secondary school class, and minimum 2.5 GPA recommended. Portfolio required of art program applicants. Audition required of music program applicants. SAT or ACT is required. Campus visit and interview recommended. Off-campus interviews available with an admissions representative.
**Procedure:** Take SAT or ACT by June of 12th year. Visit college for interview by March of 12th year. Notification of admission on rolling basis. No set date by which applicants must accept offer. $100 tuition deposit, refundable until June 1. Freshmen accepted for terms other than fall.
**Special programs:** Credit may be granted through CEEB Advanced Placement for scores of 3 or higher. Credit may be granted through CLEP general and subject exams, and military experience. Early entrance/early admission program. Concurrent enrollment program.
**Transfer students:** Transfer students accepted for terms other than fall. In fall 1993, 11% of all new students were transfers into all classes. 188 transfer applications were received, 121 were accepted. Application deadline is August 1 for fall; January 1 for spring. Minimum 2.3 GPA recommended. Lowest course grade accepted is "D." Maximum number of transferable credits is 64 semester hours. At least 32 semester hours must be completed at the college to receive degree.
**Admissions contact:** Louise Cummings-Simmons, Dean of Admissions and Financial Aid. 913 227-3311, extension 113.

**FINANCIAL AID. Available aid:** Pell grants, SEOG, state scholarships and grants, school scholarships and grants, private scholarships and grants, academic merit scholarships, athletic scholarships, and aid for undergraduate foreign students. Perkins Loans (NDSL), PLUS, Stafford Loans (GSL), and SLS. AMS. Institutional payment plan.
**Financial aid statistics:** 34% of aid is not need-based. In 1993-94, 97% of all undergraduate applicants received aid; 97% of freshman applicants. Average amounts of aid awarded freshmen: Scholarships and grants, $4,040; loans, $3,750.
**Supporting data/closing dates:** FAFSA: Priority filing date is March 15. Income tax forms: Priority filing date is January 15; accepted on rolling basis. Notification of awards on rolling basis.
**Financial aid contact:** Jayne Norlin, M.A., Director of Financial Aid. 913 227-3311, extension 248.

## Bethel College

**North Newton, KS 67117 — 316 283-2500**

**1994-95 Costs.** Tuition: $8,540. Room: $1,620. Board: $1,960. Fees, books, misc. academic expenses (school's estimate): $700.
**Enrollment.** Undergraduates: 234 men, 303 women (full-time). Freshman class: 202 applicants, 184 accepted, 123 enrolled.
**Test score averages/ranges.** Average ACT scores: 23 composite.
**Faculty.** 54 full-time; 29 part-time. 80% of faculty holds highest degree in specific field. Student/faculty ratio: 13 to 1.
**Selectivity rating.** Less competitive.

**PROFILE.** Bethel, founded in 1887, is a church-affiliated, liberal arts college. Its 47-acre campus is located North Newtown, in the agricultural and industrial region of south-central Kansas.

**Accreditation:** NCACS. Professionally accredited by the Council on Social Work Education, the National League for Nursing.

**Religious orientation:** Bethel College is affiliated with the Mennonite Church; seven credit hours of religion required.

**Library:** Collections totaling over 120,500 volumes, 750 periodical subscriptions, and 2,800 microform items.

**Special facilities/museums:** Art gallery, natural history and Midwestern/Kansas history museums, natural history preservation for biological studies, radio station, TV lab.

**Athletic facilities:** Gymnasiums, soccer field, tennis courts, track, weight room.

**STUDENT BODY. Undergraduate profile:** 70% are state residents; 37% are transfers. 1% Asian-American, 4% Black, 2% Hispanic, 1% Native American, 89% White, 3% Other. Average age of undergraduates is 20.

**Freshman profile:** 5% of accepted applicants took SAT; 95% took ACT. 99% of freshmen come from public schools.

**Undergraduate achievement:** 78% of fall 1992 freshmen returned for fall 1993 term. 8% of students who completed a degree program immediately went on to graduate study.

**Foreign students:** 28 students are from out of the country. Countries represented include China, Germany, India, Japan, Mexico, and Spain; nine in all.

**PROGRAMS OF STUDY. Degrees:** B.A., B.S.

**Majors:** Accounting, Art, Bible/Religion, Biology, Business Administration, Chemistry/Physics, Communication Arts, Elementary Education, English, Fine Arts, German, Global Studies, Health Management/Human Ecology, History, Mathematics, Music, Nursing, Psychology, Social Science, Social Work.

**Distribution of degrees:** The majors with the highest enrollment are nursing, elementary education, and business; communication arts and social sciences have the lowest.

**Requirements:** General education requirement.

**Academic regulations:** Minimum 2.0 GPA must be maintained.

**Special:** Minors offered in some majors and in computer science, early childhood education, economics, environmental studies, international development, mass media, peace studies, pre-medicine, pre-law, pre-engineering, pre-ministry, philosophy, physics, political science, sociology, Spanish, and theatre arts. Double majors. Dual degrees. Independent study. Accelerated study. Pass/fail grading option. Internships. Cooperative education programs. Preprofessional programs in law, medicine, and theology. 3-2 engineering program with Kansas State U. Member of Associated Colleges of Central Kansas. Washington Semester. Urban Studies Program (Chicago). Teacher certification in early childhood, elementary, secondary, and special education. Certification in specific subject areas. Exchange program abroad in Germany. Study abroad also in China, England, Japan, Mexico, and Spain.

**Academic Assistance:** Remedial reading, writing, math, and study skills. Nonremedial tutoring.

**ADMISSIONS. Academic basis for candidate selection** (in order of priority): Secondary school record, standardized test scores, class rank, school's recommendation.

**Nonacademic basis for candidate selection:** Character and personality and extracurricular participation are important. Particular talent or ability, geographical distribution, and alumni/ae relationship are considered.

**Requirements:** Graduation from secondary school is required; GED is accepted. No specific distribution of secondary school units required. Minimum composite ACT score of 19 (combined SAT score of 770) and rank in top third of secondary school class required. Conditional admission possible for applicants not meeting standard requirements. SAT or ACT is required. Campus visit and interview recommended. Off-campus interviews available with an admissions representative.

**Procedure:** Take SAT or ACT by fall of 12th year. Visit college for interview by June 1 of 12th year. Suggest filing application by December 1. Application deadline is August 15. Notification of admission on rolling basis. Reply is required by August 15. $100 tuition deposit, refundable until May 1. Freshmen accepted for terms other than fall.

**Special programs:** Admission may be deferred one year. Credit may be granted through CEEB Advanced Placement for scores of 4 or higher. Credit may be granted through CLEP general and subject exams, challenge exams, and life experience. Early entrance/early admission program. Concurrent enrollment program.

**Transfer students:** Transfer students accepted for terms other than fall. In fall 1993, 37% of all new students were transfers into all classes. 146 transfer applications were received, 137 were accepted. Application deadline is August 15 for fall; January 15 for spring. Minimum 2.0 GPA required. SAT or ACT scores required of transfer applicants under age 25. Lowest course grade accepted is "D." Maximum number of transferable credits is 94 credit hours. At least 30 credit hours must be completed at the college to receive degree.

**Admissions contact:** Michael Lamb, Director of Admissions. 800 522-1887.

**FINANCIAL AID. Available aid:** Pell grants, SEOG, Federal Nursing Student Scholarships, state scholarships and grants, school scholarships and grants, academic merit scholarships, athletic scholarships, and aid for undergraduate foreign students. Perkins Loans (NDSL), PLUS, Stafford Loans (GSL), NSL, and SLS. AMS.

**Financial aid statistics:** 26% of aid is not need-based. In 1993-94, 98% of all undergraduate applicants received aid; 98% of freshman applicants. Average amounts of aid awarded freshmen: Scholarships and grants, $2,450; loans, $1,500.

**Supporting data/closing dates:** FAFSA: Priority filing date is March 1. Notification of awards on rolling basis.

**Financial aid contact:** Dick Koontz, Director of Financial Aid. 800 522-1887.

# Emporia State University

**Emporia, KS 66801 — 316 341-1200**

**1993-94 Costs.** Tuition: $1,685 (state residents), $4,737 (out-of-state). Room & board: $2,955. Fees, books, misc. academic expenses (school's estimate): $350.

**Enrollment.** Undergraduates: 1,720 men, 2,178 women (full-time). Freshman class: 1,041 applicants, 1,041 accepted, 743 enrolled. Graduate enrollment: 462 men, 1,068 women.

**Test score averages/ranges.** N/A.

**Faculty.** 234 full-time; 52 part-time. 68% of faculty holds doctoral degree. Student/faculty ratio: 19 to 1.

**Selectivity rating.** Noncompetitive.

**PROFILE.** Emporia State, founded as a Normal school in 1863, is a public university. Programs are now offered through the Teachers College; the College of Liberal Arts and Sciences; and the Schools of Business, Graduate and Professional Studies, and Library and Information Management. Its 200-acre campus is located in Emporia, 55 miles from Topeka.

**Accreditation:** NCACS. Professionally accredited by the American Library Association, the Council on Rehabilitation Education, the National Association of Schools of Music, the National Council for Accreditation of Teacher Education.

**Religious orientation:** Emporia State University is nonsectarian; no religious requirements.

**Library:** Collections totaling over 708,448 volumes, 1,665 periodical subscriptions, and 957,522 microform items.

**Special facilities/museums:** Art gallery, geology and natural history museums, on-campus elementary school, Great Plains study center, planetarium.

**Athletic facilities:** Gymnasiums, racquetball courts, weight rooms, swimming pools, dance studio, fitness trail, soccer and softball fields, track.

**STUDENT BODY. Undergraduate profile:** 92% are state residents. 1% Asian-American, 3% Black, 2% Hispanic, 90% White, 4% Other. Average age of undergraduates is 23.

**Freshman profile:** 88% of accepted applicants took ACT. 90% of freshmen come from public schools.

**Undergraduate achievement:** 15% of students who completed a degree program went on to graduate study within one year.

**Foreign students:** 120 students are from out of the country. Countries represented include China, Japan, South Korea, Taiwan, and Thailand; 58 in all.

**PROGRAMS OF STUDY. Degrees:** B.A., B.F.A., B.Gen.Studies, B.Mus., B.Mus.Ed., B.S., B.S.Bus., B.S.Ed., B.S.Med.Tech., B.S.Nurs.

**Majors:** Accounting, Art, Biology, Business Administration, Business Education, Chemistry, Communication, Computer Information Systems, Computer Science, Dramatic Arts, Earth Science, Economics, Elementary Education, English, Finance, Foreign Languages, General Studies, Geography, Health Education, History, Management, Marketing, Mathematics, Medical Technology, Music, Music Education, Nursing, Office Services, Office Systems Management, Physical Education, Physical Science, Physics, Political Science, Psychology, Recreation, Rehabilitation Services Education, Social Science, Sociology, Speech Communication.

**Distribution of degrees:** The majors with the highest enrollment are elementary education, business administration, and psychology; physics, music, and foreign languages have the lowest.

**Requirements:** General education requirement.

**Academic regulations:** Freshmen must maintain minimum 1.7 GPA; sophomores, 1.8 GPA; juniors, 2.0 GPA; seniors, 2.0 GPA.

**Special:** Minors offered in many majors and in coaching, creative writing, family sciences, health, philosophy, and public affairs. Associate's degrees offered. Double majors. Dual degrees. Independent study. Pass/fail grading option. Internships. Cooperative education programs. Graduate school at which undergraduates may take graduate-level courses. Preprofessional programs in law, medicine, veterinary science, pharmacy, dentistry, optometry, agriculture, journalism, osteopathy, and social work. 2-2 and 3-2 engineering programs with Kansas State U and U of Kansas. Teacher certification in early childhood, elementary, secondary, special education, vo-tech, and bilingual/bicultural education. Certification in specific subject areas. Exchange program abroad in Latvia (U of Latvia). ROTC.

**Honors:** Honors program. Honor societies.

**Academic Assistance:** Remedial reading, writing, math, and study skills. Nonremedial tutoring.

**STUDENT LIFE. Housing:** All unmarried freshmen must live on campus unless living with family. Coed, women's, and men's dorms. Sorority and fraternity housing. School-owned/operated apartments. 23% of students live in college housing.

**Social atmosphere:** The student newspaper reports, "ESU is very much into small groups congregating. But sports events are popular." Other popular events include Flintstock, an outside concert featuring three bands; La Vit Set, an "annual small-change carnival"; and the annual musical production. Students gather at the union, the snack bar, on the lawns of residence halls, and at local bars off campus. Greeks have a strong influence on campus.

**Services and counseling/handicapped student services:** Placement services. Health service. Women's center. Day care. Counseling services for minority, veteran, and older students. Birth control, personal, and psychological counseling. Career and academic guidance services. Religious counseling. Physically disabled student services. Learning disabled services. Notetaking services. Tape recorders. Tutors. Reader services for the blind.

**Campus organizations:** Undergraduate student government. Student newspaper (Bulletin, published once/week). Literary magazine. Yearbook. A cappella choir, madrigal sing-

ers, men's chorale, symphonic choir, Treble Clef choir, orchestra bands, drama group, debating, Residence Hall Association, Union Activities Council, 148 organizations in all. Seven fraternities, five chapter houses; four sororities, three chapter houses. 17% of men join a fraternity. 13% of women join a sorority.
**Religious organizations:** Intervarsity Christian Fellowship, ICTHUS, Baptist, Catholic, Church of Christ, Latter-Day Saints, Lutheran, Nazarene, and United Methodist groups.
**Minority/foreign student organizations:** Black Student Union, Hispanic-American Leadership Organization, Native American Association. International Club, African, Arab, Chinese, and Korean groups.

**ATHLETICS. Physical education requirements:** Two semesters of physical education required.
**Intercollegiate competition:** 8% of students participate. Baseball (M), basketball (M,W), cheerleading (M,W), cross-country (M,W), football (M), golf (M), softball (W), tennis (M,W), track (indoor) (M,W), track (outdoor) (M,W), track and field (indoor) (M,W), track and field (outdoor) (M,W), volleyball (W). Member of Mid-America Intercollegiate Athletic Association, NCAA Division II.
**Intramural and club sports:** 60% of students participate. Intramural aerobics, badminton, basketball, bowling, flag football, power lifting, racquetball, softball, swimming, table tennis, tennis, volleyball, walleyball. Men's club bowling, racquetball, rugby, running, soccer. Women's club bowling, racquetball, running.

**ADMISSIONS.**
**Requirements:** Graduation from secondary school is required; GED is accepted. No specific distribution of secondary school units required. Open admission for graduates of accredited in-state secondary schools; minimum composite ACT score of 19, rank in top half of secondary school class, or minimum 3.0 GPA required of out-of-state applicants. Conditional admission possible for applicants not meeting standard requirements. ACT is required; SAT may be substituted. Campus visit recommended. No off-campus interviews.
**Procedure:** Notification of admission on rolling basis. No set date by which applicants must accept offer. $35 nonrefundable room deposit. Freshmen accepted for terms other than fall.
**Special programs:** Admission may be deferred one year. Credit and/or placement may be granted through CEEB Advanced Placement exams for scores of 4 or higher. Credit may be granted through CLEP general and subject exams. Credit and placement may be granted through challenge exams. Concurrent enrollment program.
**Transfer students:** Transfer students accepted for terms other than fall. Minimum 2.0 GPA recommended. Lowest course grade accepted is "D." At least 30 semester hours must be completed at the university to receive degree.
**Admissions contact:** Barbara Tarter, Ph.D., Director of Admissions. 316 341-5465.

**FINANCIAL AID. Available aid:** Pell grants, SEOG, state scholarships and grants, school scholarships, private scholarships, ROTC scholarships, academic merit scholarships, and athletic scholarships. Perkins Loans (NDSL), PLUS, Stafford Loans (GSL), and SLS. Deferred payment plan.
**Financial aid statistics:** In 1993-94, 70% of all undergraduate applicants received aid; 75% of freshman applicants. Average amounts of aid awarded freshmen: Scholarships and grants, $300; loans, $2,200.
**Supporting data/closing dates:** FAFSA/FAF/FFS: Priority filing date is February 15. Notification of awards on rolling basis.
**Financial aid contact:** Wilma Kasnic, M.S., Director of Financial Aid. 316 341-5457.

**STUDENT EMPLOYMENT.** College Work/Study Program. Institutional employment. 43% of full-time undergraduates work on campus during school year. Students may expect to earn an average of $2,300 during school year. Off-campus part-time employment opportunities rated "excellent."

**COMPUTER FACILITIES.** 696 IBM/IBM-compatible and Macintosh/Apple microcomputers; 20 are networked. Students may access IBM minicomputer/mainframe systems, BITNET. Residence halls may be equipped with stand-alone microcomputers. Computer languages and software packages include Lotus 1-2-3, WordPerfect. Computer facilities are available to all students.
**Fees:** None.

**GRADUATE CAREER DATA.** Graduate school percentages: 1% enter law school. 1% enter medical school. 1% enter dental school. 3% enter graduate business programs. 6% enter graduate arts and sciences programs. 1% enter theological school/seminary. Highest graduate school enrollments: Emporia State U, Kansas State U, U of Kansas. 56% of graduates choose careers in business and industry. Companies and businesses that hire graduates: Koch Industries, State Farm Insurance, Wal-Mart

# Fort Hays State University

**Hays, KS 67601-4099** **913 628-4000**

**1993-94 Costs.** Tuition: $1,296 (state residents), $4,349 (out-of-state). Room & board: $2,972. Fees, books, misc. academic expenses (school's estimate): $414.
**Enrollment.** Undergraduates: 1,759 men, 1,881 women (full-time). Freshman class: 806 enrolled. Graduate enrollment: 394 men, 863 women.
**Test score averages/ranges.** Average ACT scores: 20 English, 19 math, 20 composite.
**Faculty.** 232 full-time; 17 part-time. 57% of faculty holds highest degree in specific field.
**Selectivity rating.** Noncompetitive.

**PROFILE.** Fort Hays, founded in 1902, is a public university of the liberal and applied arts. Programs are offered through the Schools of Arts and Sciences, Business, Education, and Nursing. Its 200-acre campus, part of a former military reservation, is located in Hays, in central Kansas.

**Accreditation:** NCACS. Professionally accredited by the American Medical Association (CAHEA), the American Speech-Language-Hearing Association, the National Council for Accreditation of Teacher Education, the National League for Nursing.
**Religious orientation:** Fort Hays State University is nonsectarian; no religious requirements.
**Library:** Collections totaling over 510,665 volumes, 2,300 periodical subscriptions, and 217,997 microform items.
**Special facilities/museums:** Museums of paleontology, natural history, archaeology/ethnology, history/pioneers, geology, botany, and zoology, visual arts and media center, farm, NMR gas analyzer, telescope (HG).
**Athletic facilities:** Gymnasiums, coliseum, weight rooms, racquetball courts, swimming pool, football field, softball diamonds, tracks.

**STUDENT BODY. Undergraduate profile:** 90% are state residents; 32% are transfers. 2% Asian-American, 1% Black, 1% Hispanic, 1% Native American, 94% White, 1% Other. Average age of undergraduates is 23.
**Freshman profile:** 99% of accepted applicants took ACT.
**Undergraduate achievement:** 34% of fall 1991 freshmen returned for fall 1992 term. 18% of entering class graduated.
**Foreign students:** 24 students are from out of the country. 25 countries represented in all.

**PROGRAMS OF STUDY. Degrees:** B.A., B.Bus.Admin., B.F.A., B.Gen.Studies, B.Mus.
**Majors:** Accounting, Agribusiness, Agriculture, Art, Art Education, Biology, Biology/Medical Technology, Business Communications, Business Education, Chemistry, Communication, Communication/Communication Disorders, Communication/Journalism, Communication/Public Relations, Computer Information Systems, Economics, Elementary Education, English, Finance, Foreign Language, General Science, General Studies, Geology, History, Home Economics, Industrial Education, Management, Marketing, Mathematics, Music, Music Education, Music Performance, Music Theory/Composition, Nursing, Office Administration, Philosophy, Physical Education, Physical Sciences, Physics, Political Science, Psychology, Sociology.
**Requirements:** General education requirement.
**Special:** Concentrations offered. Associate's degrees offered. Self-designed majors. Double majors. Internships. Graduate school at which undergraduates may take graduate-level courses. Preprofessional programs in law, medicine, veterinary science, pharmacy, dentistry, theology, optometry, engineering, forestry, osteopathy, physical therapy, and public administration. 3-1 programs in allied health, dentistry, and engineering. Cooperative social work program with Kansas State U. Specialist degree in counseling. Study-away executive summer program. Member of National Student Exchange (NSE). Teacher certification in early childhood, elementary, secondary, and special education. Member of International Student Exchange Program (ISEP). ROTC.
**Honors:** Honors program.
**Academic Assistance:** Nonremedial tutoring.

**STUDENT LIFE. Housing:** All unmarried freshmen and some athletes must live on campus unless living with family. Coed, women's, and men's dorms. Sorority and fraternity housing. School-owned/operated apartments. On-campus married-student housing. 20% of students live in college housing.
**Social atmosphere:** The student newspaper reports, "This is a small college which nevertheless offers endless opportunities for involvement. A strong alcohol awareness group (BACCHUS) tries to offer alternatives to drinking. The school is known for its personal touch, its personal atmosphere in and out of the classroom. Lots of socializing, hardly any anonymity. Oktoberfest and Homecoming, traditionally on the same weekend, are the absolute highlight of the year. Students get off class, other students from all over Kansas come to have a good time. A strong Volga-German heritage is always present. Athletics contribute to campus life, as can be seen in the high turnout at basketball and football games."
**Services and counseling/handicapped student services:** Placement services. Health service. Day care. Diagnostic testing service. Counseling services for minority, veteran, and older students. Birth control, personal, and psychological counseling. Career and academic guidance services. Religious counseling. Physically disabled student services. Notetaking services. Reader services for the blind.
**Campus organizations:** Undergraduate student government. Student newspaper (University Leader, published twice/week). Yearbook. Radio and TV stations. Bands, choirs, orchestras, ensembles, debating, political, social, and special-interest groups. Five fraternities, all with chapter houses; three sororities, all with chapter houses. 8% of men join a fraternity. 4% of women join a sorority.
**Religious organizations:** Baptist Campus Center, Campus Bible Fellowship, Catholic Campus Center, Ecumenical Christian Ministries, Intervarsity Christian Fellowship, Bahai Club, BASIC.
**Minority/foreign student organizations:** Black Student Union, Disabled Student Organization, Nontraditional Students. International Student Union.

**ATHLETICS. Physical education requirements:** Four semesters of physical education required.
**Intercollegiate competition:** 8% of students participate. Baseball (M), basketball (M,W), cheerleading (M,W), cross-country (M,W), football (M), golf (M), tennis (W), track (indoor) (M,W), track (outdoor) (M,W), track and field (indoor) (M,W), track and field (outdoor) (M,W), volleyball (W), wrestling (M). Member of NCAA Division II, Rocky Mountain Athletic Conference.
**Intramural and club sports:** 60% of students participate. Intramural archery, badminton, basketball, basketball golf, billiards, bowling, cross-country, diving, free-throw, frisbee golf, golf, horseshoes, hot-shot basketball, Hula Hoop golf, inner-tube water polo, pickleball, racquetball, skeet and trap shooting, soccer, softball, swimming, table tennis, team handball, tennis, touch football, track and field, triathlon, volleyball, walleyball, water volleyball, Wiffle ball. Men's club rodeo.

**ADMISSIONS.**
**Requirements:** Graduation from secondary school is required; GED is accepted. No specific distribution of secondary school units required. Open admissions policy. Minimum 2.5 GPA recommended of out-of-state applicants. 3 units of mathematics (including algebra, geometry, and trigonometry), 1 unit of physics, and 1 unit of chemistry recommended of pre-engineering program applicants. Separate application required of nursing program applicants. Special requirements for teacher education program. Applicants not normally admissible may enroll on nondegree basis and apply for regular admission later. ACT is recommended. Campus visit recommended. Off-campus interviews available with an admissions representative.

**Procedure:** Take SAT or ACT by July of 12th year. Notification of admission by early August. No set date by which applicants must accept offer. $25 nonrefundable room deposit. Freshmen accepted for terms other than fall.
**Special programs:** Admission may be deferred one year. Credit and/or placement may be granted through CEEB Advanced Placement exams for scores of 3 or higher. Credit and/or placement may be granted through CLEP general and subject exams. Credit and placement may be granted through ACT PEP and challenge exams. Early entrance/early admission program. Concurrent enrollment program.
**Transfer students:** Transfer students accepted for terms other than fall. In fall 1992, 32% of all new students were transfers into all classes. Minimum 2.0 GPA required. All requirements depend on number of credits accepted through community college agreement program.
**Admissions contact:** Pat Mahon, M.S., Director of Admissions. 913 628-4222.

**FINANCIAL AID. Available aid:** Pell grants, SEOG, state scholarships, school scholarships, private scholarships, ROTC scholarships, academic merit scholarships, and athletic scholarships. Perkins Loans (NDSL), PLUS, Stafford Loans (GSL), school loans, and SLS.
**Financial aid statistics:** Average amounts of aid awarded freshmen: Scholarships and grants, $700.
**Supporting data/closing dates:** FAFSA/FFS: Priority filing date is March 10. School's own aid application: Accepted on rolling basis. Notification of awards on rolling basis.
**Financial aid contact:** Karl Metzger, M.S., Director of Student Financial Aid. 913 628-4408.

**STUDENT EMPLOYMENT.** College Work/Study Program. Institutional employment. 47% of full-time undergraduates work on campus during school year. Students may expect to earn an average of $1,525 during school year. Off-campus part-time employment opportunities rated "good."

**COMPUTER FACILITIES.** 183 IBM/IBM-compatible and Macintosh/Apple microcomputers. Students may access AT&T, IBM minicomputer/mainframe systems. Residence halls may be equipped with networked terminals. Computer languages and software packages include Assembler, C, COBOL, dBASE, FORTRAN, Lotus 1-2-3, PC-File, Pascal, Smart Writer's Workbench, SuperCalc, WordPerfect, WordStar. Computer facilities are available to all students.
**Fees:** None.
**Hours:** 24 hours.

**GRADUATE CAREER DATA.** Highest graduate school enrollments: Kansas State U, U of Kansas, Washburn U. Companies and businesses that hire graduates: Boeing, Conoco, Federal Deposit Insurance Corporation, Koch Industries, Phillips.

**PROMINENT ALUMNI/AE.** Mike Hayden, governor of Kansas; Robert E. Schmidt, communications; Omar Voss, retired vice-president, International Harvester; Gerald W. Tomanek, president emeritus, Fort Hays State U; George Omer, surgeon, U of New Mexico Medical School.

## Kansas Newman College

**Wichita, KS 67213** **316 942-4291**

**1993-94 Costs.** Tuition: $7,380. Room: $1,394. Board: $1,850. Fees, books, misc. academic expenses (school's estimate): $500.
**Enrollment.** Undergraduates: 215 men, 557 women (full-time). Freshman class: 151 applicants, 132 accepted, 72 enrolled.
**Test score averages/ranges.** Average ACT scores: 21 English, 21 math, 21 composite. Range of ACT scores of middle 50%: 12-31 English, 10-33 math.
**Faculty.** 39% of faculty holds doctoral degree. Student/faculty ratio: 14 to 1.
**Selectivity rating.** Less competitive.

**PROFILE.** Kansas Newman is a church-affiliated, liberal arts college. It was founded as a junior college for women in 1933, reorganized as a four-year college in 1952, and adopted coeducation in 1965. Its 51-acre campus is located in southwest Wichita, 10 minutes from the downtown area and the airport.

**Accreditation:** NCACS. Professionally accredited by the National League for Nursing.
**Religious orientation:** Kansas Newman College is affiliated with the Roman Catholic Church; two semesters of theology required.
**Library:** Collections totaling over 85,000 volumes and 450 periodical subscriptions.
**Special facilities/museums:** Planetarium.
**Athletic facilities:** Gymnasium, weight room, baseball and soccer field, golf course, basketball and volleyball courts.

**STUDENT BODY. Undergraduate profile:** 86% are state residents; 67% are transfers. 1% Asian-American, 5% Black, 5% Hispanic, 1% Native American, 86% White, 2% Other. Average age of undergraduates is 27.
**Freshman profile:** 5% of freshmen who took ACT scored 30 or over on English, 5% scored 30 or over on math, 1% scored 30 or over on composite; 26% scored 24 or over on English, 25% scored 24 or over on math, 24% scored 24 or over on composite; 82% scored 18 or over on English, 74% scored 18 or over on math, 80% scored 18 or over on composite; 100% scored 12 or over on English, 99% scored 12 or over on math, 100% scored 12 or over on composite; 100% scored 6 or over on math. 1% of accepted applicants took SAT; 40% took ACT.
**Undergraduate achievement:** 63% of fall 1991 freshmen returned for fall 1992 term. 25% of entering class graduated.
**Foreign students:** 24 students are from out of the country. Nine countries represented in all.

**PROGRAMS OF STUDY. Degrees:** B.A., B.S., B.S.Nurs.
**Majors:** Accounting, Addiction Counseling, Biology, Business Administration, Business Management, Chemistry, Communication, Computer Information Systems, Cytotechnology, Elementary Education, English, Fine Arts, Fitness Management, Graphic Design, Health/Physical Education, Health Sciences, History, Marketing, Mathematics, Medical Technology, Nuclear Medical Technology, Nursing, Occupational Therapy, Pastoral Ministry, Physical Education, Psychology, Secondary Education, Sociology, Sonography, Statistics, Theology, Total Quality Management.
**Distribution of degrees:** The majors with the highest enrollment are business management, business administration, and elementary education; graphic design, English, and chemistry have the lowest.
**Requirements:** General education requirement.
**Academic regulations:** Freshmen must maintain minimum 1.8 GPA; sophomores, 1.8 GPA; juniors, 2.0 GPA; seniors, 2.0 GPA.
**Special:** Minors offered. Associate's degrees offered. Double majors. Dual degrees. Independent study. Accelerated study. Internships. Cooperative education programs. Preprofessional programs in law, medicine, veterinary science, pharmacy, dentistry, and optometry. Combined-degree physical therapy programs with Boston Coll and Washington U. Member of Kansas Independent Colleges. Teacher certification in elementary and secondary education.
**Academic Assistance:** Remedial reading, writing, math, and study skills. Nonremedial tutoring.

**ADMISSIONS. Academic basis for candidate selection** (in order of priority): Secondary school record, standardized test scores, class rank.
**Nonacademic basis for candidate selection:** Alumni/ae relationship is important. Character and personality, extracurricular participation, and particular talent or ability are considered.
**Requirements:** Graduation from secondary school is required; GED is accepted. 21 units and the following program of study are recommended: 4 units of English, 2.5 units of math, 2 units of science, 2.5 units of social studies. Minimum composite ACT score of 18 and minimum 2.0 GPA required. Additional application required of nursing, occupational therapy, and sonography program applicants. Conditional admission possible for applicants not meeting standard requirements. ACT is required; SAT may be substituted. Campus visit and interview recommended. Off-campus interviews available with admissions and alumni representatives.
**Procedure:** Take SAT or ACT by December of 12th year. Visit college for interview by April of 12th year. Suggest filing application by April. Application deadline is July. Notification of admission on rolling basis. Reply is required by August 1. $50 tuition deposit, refundable until August 1. $50 nonrefundable room deposit. Freshmen accepted for terms other than fall.
**Special programs:** Admission may be deferred two years. Credit may be granted through CEEB Advanced Placement for scores of 3 or higher. Credit and/or placement may be granted through CLEP general and subject exams. Credit and placement may be granted through Regents College, ACT PEP, DANTES, and challenge exams, and military and life experience. Early entrance/early admission program. Concurrent enrollment program.
**Transfer students:** Transfer students accepted for terms other than fall. In fall 1992, 67% of all new students were transfers into all classes. 300 transfer applications were received, 251 were accepted. Application deadline is rolling for fall; rolling for spring. Minimum 2.0 GPA recommended. Lowest course grade accepted is "D." At least 30 semester hours must be completed at the college to receive degree.
**Admissions contact:** Ken R. Rasp, M.A., Dean of Admissions. 316 942-4291, extension 144.

**FINANCIAL AID. Available aid:** Pell grants, SEOG, state scholarships and grants, school scholarships and grants, private scholarships and grants, and athletic scholarships. Perkins Loans (NDSL), PLUS, Stafford Loans (GSL), and SLS. AMS and deferred payment plan.
**Financial aid statistics:** 15% of aid is not need-based. In 1992-93, 98% of all undergraduate applicants received aid; 93% of freshman applicants. Average amounts of aid awarded freshmen: Scholarships and grants, $2,000; loans, $2,281.
**Supporting data/closing dates:** FAFSA/FAF/FFS: Accepted on rolling basis; deadline is March 15. School's own aid application: Priority filing date is March 5. State aid form: Priority filing date is March 15. Notification of awards on rolling basis.
**Financial aid contact:** Dixie Balman, Director of Financial Aid. 316 942-4291, extension 103.

## Kansas State University

**Manhattan, KS 66506** **913 532-6318**

**1994-95 Costs.** Tuition: $1,710 (state residents), $6,990 (out-of-state). Room & board: $3,120. Fees, books, misc. academic expenses (school's estimate): $900.
**Enrollment.** Undergraduates: 8,083 men, 6,831 women (full-time). Freshman class: 5,880 applicants, 4,075 accepted, 2,833 enrolled. Graduate enrollment: 1,880 men, 1,735 women.
**Test score averages/ranges.** Average ACT scores: 22 English, 22 math, 22 composite. Range of ACT scores of middle 50%: 18-25 English, 18-25 math.
**Faculty.** 1,191 full-time. 79% of faculty holds doctoral degree. Student/faculty ratio: 16 to 1.
**Selectivity rating.** Less competitive.

**PROFILE.** Kansas State, founded as a land-grant institution in 1863, is a public, comprehensive university. Programs are offered through the Colleges of Agriculture, Architecture and Design, Arts and Sciences, Business Administration, Education, Engineering, and Human Ecology and the Graduate School. Its 664-acre campus is located in northern Manhattan, close to both business and residential areas. Campus buildings are constructed with native limestone.

**Accreditation:** NCACS. Professionally accredited by the Accreditation Board for Engineering and Technology, the American Assembly of Collegiate Schools of Business, the American Council for Construction Education, the American Dietetic Association, the American Home Economics Association, the Council on Social Work Education, the Foundation for Interior Design Education Research, the National Association of Schools of Music, the National Council for Accreditation of Teacher Education, the National Recreation and Park Association.

**Religious orientation:** Kansas State University is nonsectarian; no religious requirements.
**Library:** Collections totaling over 1,276,462 volumes, 9,607 periodical subscriptions, and 2,371,205 microform items.
**Special facilities/museums:** South Asian area study center, education communications center, center for cancer research, planetarium, nuclear reactor/accelerator.
**Athletic facilities:** Field house, gymnasium, stadium, recreation complex, handball courts, natatorium, track, coliseum, baseball field.

**STUDENT BODY. Undergraduate profile:** 87% are state residents; 43% are transfers. 2% Asian-American, 4% Black, 2% Hispanic, .5% Native American, 90% White, 1.5% Other. Average age of undergraduates is 20.
**Freshman profile:** 95% of accepted applicants took ACT. 89% of freshmen come from public schools.
**Undergraduate achievement:** 75% of fall 1992 freshmen returned for fall 1993 term. 20% of entering class graduated.
**Foreign students:** 1,200 students are from out of the country. Countries represented include China, Costa Rica, India, Korea, Pakistan, and Taiwan; 96 in all.

**PROGRAMS OF STUDY. Degrees:** B.A., B.F.A., B.Land.Arch., B.Mus., B.S., B.S.Mus.Ed.
**Majors:** Accounting, Agribusiness, Agricultural Economics, Agricultural Engineering, Agricultural Journalism, Agricultural Technology Management, Agronomy, Animal Science/Industry, Anthropology, Apparel Design, Apparel/Textile Marketing, Architectural Engineering, Architecture, Art, Bakery Science/Management, Biochemistry, Biology, Business Administration, Chemical Engineering, Chemical Science, Chemistry, Civil Engineering, Community Health/Nutrition, Computer Engineering, Computer Science, Construction Science/Management, Dietetics, Early Childhood Education, Economics, Electrical Engineering, Elementary Education, English, Family/Consumer Economics, Feed Science/Management, Finance, Fisheries/Wildlife Biology, Food Science, Food Science/Industry, Geography, Geology, Geophysics, History, Horticultural Therapy, Horticulture, Hotel/Restaurant Management, Human Development/Family Studies, Human Ecology, Human Ecology/Mass Communication, Humanities, Industrial Engineering, Information Systems, Interior Architecture, Interior Design, Journalism/Mass Communications, Kinesiology, Landscape Architecture, Life Sciences, Management, Marketing, Mathematics, Mechanical Engineering, Medical Technology, Microbiology, Milling Science/Management, Modern Languages, Music, Music Education, Nuclear Engineering, Nutrition/Exercise Science, Park Resource Management, Philosophy, Physical Science, Physics, Political Science, Pre-Dentistry, Pre-Medicine, Pre-Veterinary Medicine, Psychology, Radio/Television, Secondary Education, Social Science, Social Work, Sociology, Speech, Speech Pathology/Audiology, Statistics, Textiles, Theatre.
**Distribution of degrees:** The majors with the highest enrollment are journalism, mechanical engineering, and elementary education.
**Requirements:** General education requirement.
**Academic regulations:** Minimum 2.0 GPA must be maintained.
**Special:** Associate's degrees offered. Double majors. Dual degrees. Independent study. Accelerated study. Pass/fail grading option. Internships. Cooperative education programs. Graduate school at which undergraduates may take graduate-level courses. Preprofessional programs in law, medicine, veterinary science, pharmacy, dentistry, and optometry. Teacher certification in early childhood, elementary, secondary, and special education. Certification in specific subject areas. Study abroad in over 100 countries. ROTC and AFROTC.
**Honors:** Phi Beta Kappa. Honors program.
**Academic Assistance:** Remedial reading, writing, math, and study skills. Nonremedial tutoring.

**STUDENT LIFE. Housing:** Students may live on or off campus. Coed, women's, and men's dorms. Sorority and fraternity housing. School-owned/operated apartments. Both on-campus and off-campus married-student housing. 16% of students live in college housing.
**Social atmosphere:** According to the student newspaper, "Social and cultural life is not limited by the Puritan values that are associated with Kansas. Kansas State is truly a liberal arts and sciences university." Popular spots where students hang out are the Union Building, the Last Chance Bar and Saloon, the Rock-a-Belly Deli, the rocks at Turtle Creek, and the Hibatchi Hut. Athletes, Greeks, the Student Senate, and the Board of Regents are influential groups on campus. Football and basketball games, mud volleyball tournaments, Homecoming, and Parents Weekend are among the year's favorite events.
**Services and counseling/handicapped student services:** Placement services. Health service. Women's center. Day care. Counseling services for minority, military, veteran, and older students. Birth control, personal, and psychological counseling. Career and academic guidance services. Religious counseling. Physically disabled student services. Learning disabled services. Notetaking services. Tape recorders. Tutors. Reader services for the blind.
**Campus organizations:** Undergraduate student government. Student newspaper (Collegian, published five days/week). Literary magazine. Yearbook. Radio and TV stations. A cappella choir, glee club, madrigal ensemble, bands, ensembles, orchestra, theatre, debating, Union Governing Board, Program Council, recreation club, athletic and departmental groups, political groups, 340 organizations in all. 26 fraternities, 25 chapter houses; 12 sororities, all with chapter houses. 20% of men join a fraternity. 21% of women join a sorority.
**Religious organizations:** Bahai Club, Baptist Student Union, Buddhist Student Association, Campus Crusade for Christ, Christian Science Organization, Eckankar Campus Society.
**Minority/foreign student organizations:** Black Student Union, United Black Voices, Brothers for Progress, Puerto Rican Student Organization, Hispanic Professional Engineers, Mexican-American Council, American Indian Sciences Society. International Club, African, Iraqi, and Korean groups.

**ATHLETICS. Physical education requirements:** One semester of physical education required.
**Intercollegiate competition:** 2% of students participate. Baseball (M), basketball (M,W), cheerleading (M,W), cross-country (M,W), football (M), golf (M,W), tennis (W), track and field (indoor) (M,W), track and field (outdoor) (M,W), volleyball (W). Member of Big Eight Conference, College Football Association, NCAA Division I, NCAA Division I-A for football.
**Intramural and club sports:** 78% of students participate. Intramural arm wrestling, badminton, basketball, bench press, bowling, cross-country, flag football, golf, handball, horseshoes, inner-tube water polo, putt-putt golf, racquetball, soccer, softball, squash, swimming, table tennis, tennis, track, volleyball, walleyball, weight lifting. Men's club bowling, crew, fencing, gymnastics, horsemanship, lacrosse, martial arts, parachuting, rodeo, rugby, sailing, soccer, tennis, triathlon, water skiing. Women's club bowling, crew, fencing, gymnastics, horsemanship, martial arts, parachuting, rodeo, rugby, sailing, soccer, tennis, triathlon, water skiing.

**ADMISSIONS. Academic basis for candidate selection** (in order of priority): Secondary school record, standardized test scores, class rank.
**Requirements:** Graduation from secondary school is required; GED is accepted. No specific distribution of secondary school units required. Architecture program applicants must meet selective criteria. ACT is required; SAT may be substituted. PSAT is recommended. Campus visit recommended. No off-campus interviews.
**Procedure:** Take SAT or ACT by December 30 of 12th year. Visit college for interview by April of 12th year. Notification of admission on rolling basis. No set date by which applicants must accept offer. $395 room deposit, refundable until July 1. Freshmen accepted for terms other than fall.
**Special programs:** Credit and/or placement may be granted through CEEB Advanced Placement exams for scores of 3 or higher. Credit may be granted through CLEP general exams, ACT PEP and DANTES exams, and military experience. Credit and/or placement may be granted through CLEP subject exams. Credit and placement may be granted through challenge exams. Concurrent enrollment program.
**Transfer students:** Transfer students accepted for terms other than fall. In fall 1993, 43% of all new students were transfers into all classes. 2,789 transfer applications were received, 2,214 were accepted. Application deadline is rolling for fall; rolling for spring. Minimum 2.0 GPA required. Lowest course grade accepted is "D." At least 30 semester hours must be completed at the university to receive degree.
**Admissions contact:** Richard N. Elkins, M.S., Director of Admissions. 913 532-6250.

**FINANCIAL AID. Available aid:** Pell grants, SEOG, state scholarships and grants, school scholarships and grants, private scholarships and grants, ROTC scholarships, academic merit scholarships, athletic scholarships, and aid for undergraduate foreign students. Perkins Loans (NDSL), PLUS, Stafford Loans (GSL), Health Professions Loans, school loans, private loans, and SLS. Deferred payment plan.
**Financial aid statistics:** 18% of aid is not need-based. In 1993-94, 70% of all undergraduate applicants received aid; 70% of freshman applicants. Average amounts of aid awarded freshmen: Scholarships and grants, $950; loans, $2,200.
**Supporting data/closing dates:** FAFSA: Priority filing date is March 15. School's own aid application: Deadline is February 1. Income tax forms: Accepted on rolling basis. Notification of awards on rolling basis.
**Financial aid contact:** Larry Moeder, M.S., Director of Student Financial Assistance. 913 532-6420.

**STUDENT EMPLOYMENT.** College Work/Study Program. Institutional employment. 21% of full-time undergraduates work on campus during school year. Off-campus part-time employment opportunities rated "good."

**COMPUTER FACILITIES.** 400 IBM/IBM-compatible and Macintosh/Apple microcomputers; 300 are networked. Students may access IBM minicomputer/mainframe systems, BITNET, Internet. Residence halls may be equipped with networked microcomputers, networked terminals. Client/LAN operating systems include Apple/Macintosh, DOS, UNIX/XENIX/AIX, Novell. Computer languages and software packages include Assembly, C, C+, COBOL, dBASE, FORTRAN, Framemaker, ImSL, Lotus 1-2-3, Pascal, SAS, SPSS-X, Turbo Pascal, USENET News, WordPerfect; 35 in all. Computer facilities are available to all students.
**Fees:** None.
**Hours:** 24 hours.

**GRADUATE CAREER DATA.** Companies and businesses that hire graduates: AT&T, Arthur Andersen, Boeing, Cargill, Con Agra, Conoco, General Mills, Hallmark, Phillips 66, Signal.

**PROMINENT ALUMNI/AE.** John Rhodes, former minority leader, U.S. House of Representatives; Marlin Fitzwater, presidential spokesperson, Bush Administration; Alfred Schroeder, chief justice, Kansas Supreme Court; Mel Harris, president, Paramount Television; Mike Hayden, governor, Kansas; Gordon Jump, actor; Mitch Richmond, professional basketball player, Sacramento Kings.

# Kansas Wesleyan University

**Salina, KS 67401** — **913 827-5541**

**1994-95 Costs.** Tuition: $8,400. Room & board: $3,250. Fees, books, misc. academic expenses (school's estimate): $420.

**Enrollment.** Undergraduates: 269 men, 231 women (full-time). Freshman class: 497 applicants, 261 accepted, 134 enrolled.

**Test score averages/ranges.** Average ACT scores: 20 English, 19 math, 21 composite. Range of ACT scores of middle 50%: 19-26 composite.

**Faculty.** 35 full-time; 8 part-time. 65% of faculty holds doctoral degree. Student/faculty ratio: 14 to 1.

**Selectivity rating.** Less competitive.

**PROFILE.** Kansas Wesleyan, founded in 1886, is a church-affiliated, liberal arts university. Its 27-acre campus is located in Salina.

**Accreditation:** CCA-ACICS, NCACS.
**Religious orientation:** Kansas Wesleyan University is affiliated with the United Methodist Church; one semester of religion required.
**Library:** Collections totaling over 82,000 volumes, 411 periodical subscriptions and 193 microform items.

**Special facilities/museums:** Art gallery, Casegrain telescope.
**Athletic facilities:** Athletic fields, gymnasium, tennis courts, track, weight room.

**STUDENT BODY. Undergraduate profile:** 1% Asian-American, 4% Black, 1% Hispanic, 1% Native American, 88% White, 5% Other. Average age of undergraduates is 24.
**Freshman profile:** 98% of freshmen come from public schools.
**Undergraduate achievement:** 90% of fall 1991 freshmen returned for fall 1992 term.
**Foreign students:** 13 students are from out of the country. Countries represented include Bosnia, India, and Malaysia.

**PROGRAMS OF STUDY. Degrees:** B.A., B.S.
**Majors:** Accounting, Arts Management, Business Management, Chemistry, Communication Arts, Computer Science, Criminal Justice, Education, Elementary Education, English, History, Mathematics, Music, Physics, Psychology, Religion, Secondary Education, Sociology, Spanish, Special Education, Speech, Theatre/Drama.
**Distribution of degrees:** The majors with the highest enrollment are business administration, computer science, and education.
**Requirements:** General education requirement.
**Academic regulations:** Freshmen must maintain minimum 1.7 GPA; sophomores, 1.8 GPA; juniors, 1.9 GPA; seniors, 2.0 GPA.
**Special:** Associate's degrees offered. Self-designed majors. Double majors. Dual degrees. Independent study. Pass/fail grading option. Internships. Preprofessional programs in law, medicine, veterinary science, pharmacy, dentistry, theology, optometry, agriculture, chiropractic, cytotechnology, engineering, mortuary science, occupational therapy, physical therapy, podiatry, and respiratory therapy. 3-2 and 4-2 engineering programs with Columbia U and Washington U. Member of Associated Colleges of Central Kansas. Teacher certification in early childhood, elementary, secondary, and special education.
**Honors:** Honor societies.
**Academic Assistance:** Nonremedial tutoring.

**ADMISSIONS. Academic basis for candidate selection** (in order of priority): Standardized test scores, secondary school record, class rank, essay, school's recommendation.
**Nonacademic basis for candidate selection:** Character and personality, extracurricular participation, and particular talent or ability are important. Geographical distribution and alumni/ae relationship are considered.
**Requirements:** Graduation from secondary school is required; GED is accepted. No specific distribution of secondary school units required. Minimum composite ACT score of 18 (combined SAT score of 700) and rank in top half of secondary school class or minimum 2.5 GPA required. Portfolio required of art program scholarships applicants. Audition required of music program scholarships applicants. Conditional admission possible for applicants not meeting standard requirements. ACT is required; SAT may be substituted. PSAT is recommended. Campus visit and interview recommended. No off-campus interviews.
**Procedure:** Take SAT or ACT by April of 12th year. Visit college for interview by May of 12th year. Suggest filing application by March 1. Application deadline is April 1. Notification of admission on rolling basis. Reply is recommended by May 1. $100 refundable tuition deposit. Freshmen accepted for terms other than fall.
**Special programs:** Admission may be deferred one year. Credit and/or placement may be granted through CEEB Advanced Placement exams for scores of 3 or higher. Credit may be granted through CLEP general and subject exams, challenge exams, and military and life experience. Concurrent enrollment program.
**Transfer students:** Transfer students accepted for terms other than fall. In fall 1992, 75 transfer applications were received, 74 were accepted. Application deadline is August 1 for fall; December 15 for spring. Minimum 2.0 GPA required. Lowest course grade accepted is "C." At least 63 semester hours must be completed at the university to receive degree.
**Admissions contact:** Valerie D. Robinson, M.P.P.M., Director of Admissions. 913 827-5541, extension 307.

**FINANCIAL AID. Available aid:** Pell grants, SEOG, Federal Nursing Student Scholarships, state scholarships and grants, school scholarships and grants, private scholarships and grants, academic merit scholarships, and athletic scholarships. Perkins Loans (NDSL), PLUS, Stafford Loans (GSL), NSL, and SLS. AMS, deferred payment plan, and family tuition reduction.
**Financial aid statistics:** 14% of aid is not need-based. In 1992-93, 96% of all undergraduate applicants received aid; 100% of freshman applicants. Average amounts of aid awarded freshmen: Scholarships and grants, $4,539; loans, $4,450.
**Supporting data/closing dates:** FAFSA/FAF/FFS: Priority filing date is March 1; deadline is April 1. School's own aid application: Accepted on rolling basis.
**Financial aid contact:** Glenna Alexander, Director of Financial Aid. 913 827-5541, extension 217.

## Manhattan Christian College

**Manhattan, KS 66502** **913 539-3571**

**1994-95 Costs.** Tuition: $4,300. Room & board: $2,806. Fees, books, misc. academic expenses (school's estimate): $1,925.
**Enrollment.** Undergraduates: 97 men, 92 women (full-time). Freshman class: 183 applicants, 136 accepted, 116 enrolled.
**Test score averages/ranges.** Average ACT scores: 22 composite.
**Faculty.** 13 full-time; 6 part-time. 15% of faculty holds doctoral degree. Student/faculty ratio: 14 to 1.
**Selectivity rating.** Less competitive.

**PROFILE.** Manhattan Christian, founded in 1927, is a church-affiliated college. Its 30-acre campus is located in Manhattan, 60 miles from Topeka.

**Accreditation:** AABC.
**Religious orientation:** Manhattan Christian College is affiliated with the Independent Christian Church; eight semesters of religion/theology required.
**Library:** Collections totaling over 20,000 volumes, 50 periodical subscriptions and 25 microform items.
**Athletic facilities:** Swimming pool, basketball, handball, racquetball, sand volleyball, and tennis courts, softball field.

**STUDENT BODY. Undergraduate profile:** 62% are state residents; 84% are transfers. 2% Asian-American, 5% Black, 1% Hispanic, 1% Native American, 90% White, 1% Other. Average age of undergraduates is 20.
**Freshman profile:** 9% of accepted applicants took SAT; 91% took ACT. 97% of freshmen come from public schools.
**Undergraduate achievement:** 76% of fall 1992 freshmen returned for fall 1993 term. 32% of entering class graduated. 3% of students who completed a degree program immediately went on to graduate study.
**Foreign students:** Eight students are from out of the country. Countries represented include China, Ethiopia, and Korea.

**PROGRAMS OF STUDY. Degrees:** B.A., B.S.
**Majors:** Christian Education, Christian Ministries, Christian Service, Church Music, Missions.
**Requirements:** General education requirement.
**Academic regulations:** Freshmen must maintain minimum 1.75 GPA; sophomores, 1.85 GPA; juniors, 2.0 GPA; seniors, 2.0 GPA.
**Special:** Minors offered in most majors and in youth ministry. Dual degrees. Internships. Cooperative education programs. Preprofessional programs in medicine, veterinary science, dentistry, theology, and physical therapy. Dual-degree and cooperative education programs with Kansas State U. Exchange program abroad in England (Springdale Coll).
**Honors:** Honor societies.

**ADMISSIONS. Academic basis for candidate selection** (in order of priority): Secondary school record, standardized test scores, school's recommendation, class rank.
**Nonacademic basis for candidate selection:** Character and personality are emphasized. Extracurricular participation and particular talent or ability are considered.
**Requirements:** Graduation from secondary school is required; GED is accepted. No specific distribution of secondary school units required. Minimum 2.0 GPA recommended. ACT is required; SAT may be substituted. Campus visit and interview recommended. Off-campus interviews available with an admissions representative.
**Procedure:** Take SAT or ACT by March of 12th year. Notification of admission on rolling basis. No set date by which applicants must accept offer. $75 room deposit, refundable until July 15. Freshmen accepted for terms other than fall.
**Special programs:** Credit may be granted through CLEP general and subject exams.
**Transfer students:** Transfer students accepted for terms other than fall. In fall 1993, 84% of all new students were transfers into all classes. 27 transfer applications were received, 24 were accepted. Application deadline is rolling for fall; rolling for spring. Minimum 1.75 GPA required. Lowest course grade accepted is "C." Maximum number of transferable credits is 60 semester hours. At least 30 semester hours must be completed at the college to receive degree.
**Admissions contact:** John Poulson, Vice President of Admissions. 913 539-3571, extension 32.

**FINANCIAL AID. Available aid:** Pell grants, SEOG, state scholarships, school scholarships, and private scholarships and grants. Perkins Loans (NDSL), PLUS, Stafford Loans (GSL), and school loans.
**Financial aid statistics:** 37% of aid is not need-based. In 1993-94, 81% of all undergraduate applicants received aid; 64% of freshman applicants. Average amounts of aid awarded freshmen: Scholarships and grants, $300.
**Supporting data/closing dates:** FAFSA/FAF/FFS: Accepted on rolling basis. School's own aid application: Priority filing date is March 1. Notification of awards on rolling basis.
**Financial aid contact:** Margaret Cook, Director of Financial Aid.

## McPherson College

**McPherson, KS 67460** **316 241-0731**

**1994-95 Costs.** Tuition: $7,950. Room & board: $3,750. Fees, books, misc. academic expenses (school's estimate): $710.
**Enrollment.** Undergraduates: 182 men, 157 women (full-time). Freshman class: 420 applicants, 293 accepted, 95 enrolled.
**Test score averages/ranges.** Average ACT scores: 21 composite.
**Faculty.** 37 full-time; 12 part-time. 55% of faculty holds doctoral degree. Student/faculty ratio: 12 to 1.
**Selectivity rating.** Competitive.

**PROFILE.** McPherson, founded in 1888, is a private, church-affiliated, liberal arts college. Programs are offered in the Divisions of Humanities, Natural Science, Social Sciences, and Applied Arts. Its 23-acre campus is located in McPherson, 60 miles north of Witchita.

**Accreditation:** NCACS.
**Religious orientation:** McPherson College is affiliated with the Church of the Brethren; three semester hours of religion required.
**Library:** Collections totaling over 63,900 volumes, 420 periodical subscriptions, and 31,220 microform items.
**Special facilities/museums:** Natural history museum.
**Athletic facilities:** Gymnasiums, basketball, racquetball, tennis, and volleyball courts, athletic fields, weight room, tracks, dance studio.

**STUDENT BODY. Undergraduate profile:** 64% are state residents; 29% are transfers. 1% Asian-American, 4% Black, 2% Hispanic, 1% Native American, 87% White, 5% Other. Average age of undergraduates is 21.
**Freshman profile:** 1% of freshmen who took ACT scored 30 or over on composite; 29% scored 24 or over on composite; 86% scored 18 or over on composite; 100% scored 12 or over on composite. 5% of accepted applicants took SAT; 95% took ACT. 99% of freshmen come from public schools.

**Undergraduate achievement:** 76% of fall 1992 freshmen returned for fall 1993 term. 39% of entering class graduated.
**Foreign students:** 22 students are from out of the country. Countries represented include China, England, France, Germany, Japan, and Spain; 10 in all.

**PROGRAMS OF STUDY. Degrees:** B.A., B.S.
**Majors:** Accounting, Agricultural Science, Art, Biology, Business Administration, Chemistry, Computer Science, Early Childhood, Economics/Business Administration, Education, English, German, History, Interior Design, Mathematics, Music, Philosophy/Religion, Physical Education/Health, Psychology, Sociology, Spanish, Special Education, Speech/Theatre.
**Distribution of degrees:** The majors with the highest enrollment are business administration, education, and biology; speech/theatre and interior design have the lowest.
**Requirements:** General education requirement.
**Special:** Minors offered in music and history. Associate's degrees offered. Self-designed majors. Double majors. Independent study. Pass/fail grading option. Internships. Cooperative education programs. Preprofessional programs in law, medicine, veterinary science, pharmacy, and dentistry. Member of Associated Colleges of Central Kansas. January Interterm with other colleges with 4-1-4 calendars. Teacher certification in early childhood, elementary, secondary, and special education. Certification in specific subject areas. Study abroad in China, Ecuador, England, France, Germany, Greece, Japan, and Spain.
**Academic Assistance:** Remedial study skills.

**STUDENT LIFE. Housing:** All unmarried students under age 23 must live on campus unless living with family. Coed, women's, and men's dorms. On-campus married-student housing. 81% of students live in college housing.
**Social atmosphere:** According to editor of the student newspaper, "McPherson is a fun and friendly place." Students enjoy going to basketball and football games and track meets. Popular events are dances and graduation. Most influential groups are the Student Activity Board and the Student Council. Favorite gathering spots on campus are the Student Union, Sports Center, and the dorms.
**Services and counseling/handicapped student services:** Placement services. Health service. Counseling services for minority students. Personal counseling. Career and academic guidance services. Learning disabled services.
**Campus organizations:** Undergraduate student government. Student newspaper (Spectator, published once/two weeks). Yearbook. Band, choir, drama productions, cheerleaders, debating, academic and special-interest groups, 27 organizations in all.
**Religious organizations:** Oasis, Brethren Identity Group, Christian Vocations Club, Peace Awareness, Bible study groups.
**Minority/foreign student organizations:** Intercultural Forum. International Student Organization, Germany Club, Spanish Circle.

**ATHLETICS. Physical education requirements:** None.
**Intercollegiate competition:** 30% of students participate. Basketball (M,W), cross-country (M,W), football (M), golf (M,W), soccer (M,W), tennis (M,W), track and field (indoor) (M,W), track and field (outdoor) (M,W), volleyball (W). Member of Kansas Collegiate Athletic Conference, NAIA.
**Intramural and club sports:** 60% of students participate. Intramural basketball, billiards, flag football, soccer, softball, table tennis, volleyball. Women's club cheerleading.

**ADMISSIONS. Academic basis for candidate selection** (in order of priority): Secondary school record, class rank, standardized test scores, school's recommendation.
**Nonacademic basis for candidate selection:** Character and personality are important.
**Requirements:** Graduation from secondary school is recommended; GED is accepted. No specific distribution of secondary school units required. Minimum composite ACT score of 19, rank in top third of secondary school class, and minimum 2.25 GPA required. Conditional admission possible for applicants not meeting standard requirements. ACT is required. Campus visit and interview recommended. Off-campus interviews available with an admissions representative.
**Procedure:** Take ACT by June of 12th year. Suggest filing application by fall; no deadline. Notification of admission on rolling basis. Reply is required within four weeks of acceptance. $100 nonrefundable tuition deposit. $50 refundable room deposit. Freshmen accepted for terms other than fall.
**Special programs:** Admission may be deferred. Credit may be granted through CEEB Advanced Placement for scores of 3 or higher. Credit may be granted through CLEP general and subject exams, ACT PEP exams, and military experience. Credit and placement may be granted through challenge exams. Concurrent enrollment program.
**Transfer students:** Transfer students accepted for terms other than fall. In fall 1993, 29% of all new students were transfers into all classes. 123 transfer applications were received, 82 were accepted. Application deadline is August 15 for fall; January 15 for spring. Minimum 2.25 GPA recommended. Lowest course grade accepted is "C." Maximum number of transferable credits is 64 semester hours. At least 32 semester hours must be completed at the college to receive degree.
**Admissions contact:** Frederick A. Schmidt, Jr., Director of Admissions.

**FINANCIAL AID. Available aid:** Pell grants, SEOG, state scholarships and grants, school scholarships and grants, private scholarships, academic merit scholarships, and athletic scholarships. Perkins Loans (NDSL), PLUS, Stafford Loans (GSL), state loans, school loans, private loans, and SLS. Tuition Plan Inc. and AMS.
**Financial aid statistics:** 15% of aid is not need-based. In 1993-94, 95% of all undergraduate applicants received aid; 95% of freshman applicants.
**Supporting data/closing dates:** FAFSA: Priority filing date is March 1. State aid form: Deadline is March 28. Notification of awards on rolling basis.
**Financial aid contact:** John M. Hoffman, M.Th., Director of Financial Aid.

**STUDENT EMPLOYMENT.** College Work/Study Program. Institutional employment. Off-campus part-time employment opportunities rated "good."

**COMPUTER FACILITIES.** 30 IBM/IBM-compatible and Macintosh/Apple microcomputers. Students may access minicomputer/mainframe systems. Residence halls may be equipped with stand-alone microcomputers. Computer languages and software packages include Assembly, C, COBOL, FORTRAN, LISP, LOGO, MYSTAT, Pascal, SNOBOL; spreadsheet, word processing, other software programs. Computer facilities are available to all students.
**Hours:** 7 AM-10 PM (M-Th); 7 AM-5 PM (F); 2 PM-5 PM (Sa); 2 PM-10 PM (Su).

# MidAmerica Nazarene College

**Olathe, KS 66062-1899** **913 782-3750**

**1993-94 Costs.** Tuition: $6,270. Room & board: $3,542. Fees, books, misc. academic expenses (school's estimate): $996.
**Enrollment.** Undergraduates: 495 men, 645 women (full-time). Freshman class: 321 applicants, 321 accepted, 214 enrolled. Graduate enrollment: 122.
**Test score averages/ranges.** N/A.
**Faculty.** 35% of faculty holds doctoral degree. Student/faculty ratio: 20 to 1.
**Selectivity rating.** N/A.

**PROFILE.** MidAmerica Nazarene, founded in 1968, is a church-affiliated, liberal arts college. Its 112-acre campus is located in Olathe, 15 miles south of downtown Kansas City.

**Accreditation:** NCACS. Professionally accredited by the National Association of Schools of Music, the National League for Nursing.
**Religious orientation:** MidAmerica Nazarene College is affiliated with the Church of the Nazarene; Six semester hours of religion required.
**Library:** Collections totaling over 79,297 volumes, 18,000 periodical subscriptions, and 130,462 microform items.
**Athletic facilities:** Gymnasium, track, weight room, sand volleyball court, baseball, football, soccer, and softball fields.

**STUDENT BODY. Undergraduate profile:** 64% are state residents; 41% are transfers. 1% Asian-American, 3% Black, 1% Hispanic, 82% White, 13% Other. Average age of undergraduates is 30.
**Freshman profile:** Majority of accepted applicants took ACT.
**Undergraduate achievement:** 66% of fall 1991 freshmen returned for fall 1992 term.
**Foreign students:** 38 students are from out of the country. Countries represented include Ethiopia and Kenya; 36 in all.

**PROGRAMS OF STUDY. Degrees:** B.A., B.S.Nurs.
**Majors:** Accounting, Agribusiness, Athletic Training, Biology, Business Administration, Chemistry, Christian Education, Church Music, Communication, Computer Science, Early Childhood Education, Elementary/Christian Education, Elementary Education, English, History, International Agribusiness, Mathematics, Modern Languages, Music, Music Performance, Nursing, Physical Education, Physics, Psychology, Public Relations, Religion, Spanish.
**Distribution of degrees:** The majors with the highest enrollment are elementary education and business administration.
**Requirements:** General education requirement.
**Academic regulations:** Minimum 2.0 GPA must be maintained.
**Special:** Minors offered. Urban Ministry Program. Associate's degrees offered. Double majors. Accelerated study. Preprofessional programs in law and medicine. American Studies Program (Washington, D.C.). Member of Kansas City Regional Council for Higher Education (KCRCHE); cross-registration possible. Teacher certification in early childhood, elementary, and secondary education. ROTC and AFROTC at U of Kansas.
**Academic Assistance:** Remedial reading, writing, math, and study skills.

**ADMISSIONS. Academic basis for candidate selection** (in order of priority): Standardized test scores, secondary school record, class rank, school's recommendation.
**Nonacademic basis for candidate selection:** Character and personality and particular talent or ability are important. Extracurricular participation and alumni/ae relationship are considered.
**Requirements:** Graduation from secondary school is recommended; GED is accepted. No specific distribution of secondary school units required. Minimum composite ACT score of 18 (combined SAT score of 680) required. R.N. required of nursing program applicants. Conditional admission possible for applicants not meeting standard requirements. ACT is required; SAT may be substituted. Campus visit and interview recommended. Off-campus interviews available with an admissions representative.
**Procedure:** Take SAT or ACT by June of 12th year. Visit college for interview by August of 12th year. Suggest filing application by March 1. Application deadline is September 1. Notification of admission on rolling basis. No set date by which applicants must accept offer. $50 tuition deposit, refundable until two weeks before beginning of term. $75 room deposit, refundable until two weeks before beginning of term. Freshmen accepted for terms other than fall.
**Special programs:** Admission may be deferred. Credit may be granted through CEEB Advanced Placement for scores of 3 or higher. Credit may be granted through CLEP general and subject exams, DANTES and challenge exams, and military and life experience. Early entrance/early admission program. Concurrent enrollment program.
**Transfer students:** Transfer students accepted for terms other than fall. In fall 1992, 41% of all new students were transfers into all classes. Application deadline is September 1 for fall; January 1 for spring. Minimum 2.0 GPA required. Lowest course grade accepted is "D." At least 30 semester hours must be completed at the college to receive degree.
**Admissions contact:** Dennis Troyer, Director of Admissions. 913 782-3750, extension 481.

**FINANCIAL AID. Available aid:** Pell grants, SEOG, state scholarships and grants, school scholarships and grants, private scholarships and grants, ROTC scholarships, academic merit scholarships, and athletic scholarships. Perkins Loans (NDSL), PLUS, Stafford Loans (GSL), and SLS. Deferred payment plan.
**Financial aid statistics:** In 1992-93, 87% of all undergraduate applicants received aid.
**Supporting data/closing dates:** FAFSA/FAF/FFS: Priority filing date is March 1. School's own aid application: Priority filing date is March 1. State aid form: Priority filing date is March 1. Income tax forms: Priority filing date is March 1. Notification of awards on rolling basis.
**Financial aid contact:** Sharon Williams, Director of Financial Aid. 913 782-3750, extension 228.

## Ottawa University

**Ottawa, KS 66067** **913 242-5200**

**1994-95 Costs.** Tuition: $7,590. Room: $1,380. Board: $2,020. Fees, books, misc. academic expenses (school's estimate): $440.
**Enrollment.** Undergraduates: 299 men, 239 women (full-time). Freshman class: 881 applicants, 571 accepted, 256 enrolled. Graduate enrollment: 320 men, 254 women.
**Test score averages/ranges.** Average ACT scores: 21 composite.
**Faculty.** 34 full-time; 16 part-time. 42% of faculty holds doctoral degree. Student/faculty ratio: 15 to 1.
**Selectivity rating.** Competitive.

**PROFILE.** Ottawa University, founded in 1865, is a church-affiliated university. Programs are offered in the Divisions of Arts and Humanities, Natural Sciences, and Social and Behavioral Sciences. Its 60-acre campus is located in Ottawa, 50 miles west of Kansas City.

**Accreditation:** NCACS.
**Religious orientation:** Ottawa University is affiliated with the American Baptist Church; one semester of religion required.
**Library:** Collections totaling over 85,000 volumes, 377 periodical subscriptions, and 4,542 microform items.
**Special facilities/museums:** Art museum.
**Athletic facilities:** Athletic field, field house, track, wellness center, indoor swimming pool, weight room.
**STUDENT BODY. Undergraduate profile:** 66% are state residents; 19% are transfers. 1% Asian-American, 7% Black, 2% Hispanic, 2% Native American, 76% White, 12% Other. Average age of undergraduates is 22.
**Freshman profile:** 23% of freshmen who took ACT scored 24 or over on composite; 81% scored 18 or over on composite; 98% scored 12 or over on composite. Majority of accepted applicants took ACT.
**Undergraduate achievement:** 82% of fall 1992 freshmen returned for fall 1993 term. 23% of students who completed a degree program immediately went on to graduate study.
**Foreign students:** 51 students are from out of the country. Countries represented include China, Hong Kong, Indonesia, Japan, and Taiwan; 14 in all.
**PROGRAMS OF STUDY. Degrees:** B.A.
**Majors:** Accounting, Art, Arts Management, Biology, Business Administration/Management, Chemistry, Communications, Computer Information Systems, Criminal Justice, Economics, Education, Elementary Education, English, Health Facilities Management, History/Political Science, Human Services, Humanities, Individualized Major Program, Mathematics, Middle School Education, Music/Vocal/Instrumental, Personnel Administration, Physical Education/Health, Pre-Dentistry, Pre-Engineering, Pre-Law, Pre-Medicine, Pre-Nursing, Pre-Pharmacy Studies, Pre-Physical Therapy, Psychology, Public Relations, Recreational Leadership, Religion, Secondary Education, Sociology, Speech/Drama.
**Distribution of degrees:** The majors with the highest enrollment are business, communications, and education; religion, English, and psychology have the lowest.
**Requirements:** General education requirement.
**Academic regulations:** Minimum 2.0 GPA must be maintained.
**Special:** Dual degrees. Independent study. Preprofessional programs in law, medicine, veterinary science, and dentistry. 3-1 medical technology program with Providence St. Margaret Health Center (Kansas City, Kans.). 3-1 agronomy/physical science and agronomy/business administration programs with Kansas State U. 3-2 engineering program with Kansas State U. Teacher certification in elementary and secondary education.
**Honors:** Honor societies.
**Academic Assistance:** Remedial reading, writing, and math. Nonremedial tutoring.
**ADMISSIONS. Academic basis for candidate selection** (in order of priority): Secondary school record, class rank, standardized test scores, school's recommendation.
**Nonacademic basis for candidate selection:** Character and personality, extracurricular participation, particular talent or ability, and alumni/ae relationship are considered.
**Requirements:** Graduation from secondary school is recommended; GED is accepted. No specific distribution of secondary school units required. Minimum composite ACT score of 17, rank in top half of secondary school class, and minimum 2.0 GPA required. Conditional admission possible for applicants not meeting standard requirements. SAT or ACT is required. Campus visit recommended. Off-campus interviews available with admissions and alumni representatives.
**Procedure:** Notification of admission on rolling basis. No set date by which applicants must accept offer. $100 tuition deposit, refundable until July 1. Freshmen accepted for terms other than fall.
**Special programs:** Admission may be deferred. Credit and/or placement may be granted through CEEB Advanced Placement exams for scores of 3 or higher. Credit and/or placement may be granted through CLEP general exams. Credit may be granted through CLEP subject exams. Early entrance/early admission program. Concurrent enrollment program.
**Transfer students:** Transfer students accepted for terms other than fall. In fall 1993, 19% of all new students were transfers into all classes. 194 transfer applications were received, 125 were accepted. Application deadline is rolling for fall; rolling for spring. Minimum 2.0 GPA required. Lowest course grade accepted is "D." Maximum number of transferable credits is 62 semester hours. At least 30 semester hours must be completed at the university to receive degree.
**Admissions contact:** Tim Adams, Director of Admissions. 913 242-5200, extension 5555.
**FINANCIAL AID. Available aid:** Pell grants, SEOG, state scholarships and grants, school scholarships and grants, private scholarships and grants, academic merit scholarships, athletic scholarships, and aid for undergraduate foreign students. Perkins Loans (NDSL), PLUS, Stafford Loans (GSL), and SLS. Tuition Plan Inc. and AMS.
**Financial aid statistics:** 50% of aid is not need-based. In 1993-94, 95% of all undergraduate applicants received aid; 98% of freshman applicants. Average amounts of aid awarded freshmen: Scholarships and grants, $1,500; loans, $2,200.
**Supporting data/closing dates:** FAFSA/FAF/FFS: Priority filing date is February 1; deadline is September 1. School's own aid application: Priority filing date is February 1; accepted on rolling basis; deadline is August 1. State aid form: Priority filing date is February 1; deadline is May 1. Income tax forms: Priority filing date is April 1; deadline is May 1. Notification of awards on rolling basis.
**Financial aid contact:** Ronald C. Yingling, Financial Aid Administrator. 913 242-5200, extension 5571.

## Pittsburg State University

**Pittsburg, KS 66762** **316 231-7000**

**1994-95 Costs.** Tuition: $1,664 (state residents), $4,798 (out-of-state). Room & board: $2,814. Fees, books, misc. academic expenses (school's estimate): $1,900.
**Enrollment.** Undergraduates: 2,311 men, 2,180 women (full-time). Freshman class: 1,419 applicants, 1,313 accepted, 813 enrolled. Graduate enrollment: 503 men, 884 women.
**Test score averages/ranges.** Average ACT scores: 20 English, 20 math, 21 composite.
**Faculty.** 250 full-time; 45 part-time. 63% of faculty holds doctoral degree. Student/faculty ratio: 23 to 1.
**Selectivity rating.** Less competitive.

**PROFILE.** Pittsburg State, founded in 1903, is a public, comprehensive university. Programs are offered through the College of Arts and Sciences, the School of Technology and Applied Science, and the Gladys A. Kelce School of Business and Economics. Its 125-acre campus is located in Pittsburg, south of Kansas City.
**Accreditation:** NCACS. Professionally accredited by the Accreditation Board for Engineering and Technology, the National Association of Schools of Music, the National Council for Accreditation of Teacher Education, the National League for Nursing.
**Religious orientation:** Pittsburg State University is nonsectarian; no religious requirements.
**Library:** Collections totaling over 290,798 volumes, 1,368 periodical subscriptions, and 16,718 microform items.
**Special facilities/museums:** Planetarium, observatory.
**Athletic facilities:** Physical education building with swimming pool, indoor track, weight rooms, and racquetball, basketball, and volleyball courts; gymnasium, tennis courts.
**STUDENT BODY. Undergraduate profile:** 78% are state residents; 47% are transfers. 2% Asian-American, 2% Black, 1% Hispanic, 2% Native American, 76% White, 17% Other. Average age of undergraduates is 23.
**Freshman profile:** Majority of accepted applicants took ACT. 86% of freshmen come from public schools.
**Undergraduate achievement:** 70% of fall 1992 freshmen returned for fall 1993 term. 39% of entering class graduated. 25% of students who completed a degree program went on to graduate study within five years.
**Foreign students:** 381 students are from out of the country. Countries represented include China, Indonesia, Japan, Malaysia, Taiwan, and Thailand; 42 in all.
**PROGRAMS OF STUDY. Degrees:** B.A., B.Bus.Admin., B.F.A., B.Gen.Studies, B.Mus., B.Mus.Ed., B.S., B.S.Bus.Admin., B.S.Ed., B.S.Eng.Tech., B.S.Med.Tech., B.S.Nurs., B.S.Tech., B.S.Voc.Tech.Ed.
**Majors:** Accounting, Art, Art Education, Art Therapy, Automotive Technology, Biology, Biology Teaching, Business Administration, Chemistry, Chemistry Teaching, Commercial Graphic Art/Design, Communication, Computer Science, Construction Management, Construction Technology, Economics, Electronic Sales/Management, Elementary Education, English, Environmental Studies, Finance, French, General Science, Geography, History, Home Economics, Industrial Administration, Industrial Arts Education, Information Systems, Manufacturing Production Technology, Marketing, Mathematics, Mechanical Design, Medical Technology, Music, Nursing, Physical Education, Physical Sciences, Physics, Plastics Technology, Political Science, Pre-Dental, Pre-Law, Pre-Medical, Printing/Management, Printing Technology, Psychology, Recreation, Social Sciences, Social Work, Spanish, Speech, Vocational-Technical Education, Wood Technology.
**Distribution of degrees:** The majors with the highest enrollment are business administration, engineering technology, and nursing; foreign language, economics, and home economics have the lowest.
**Requirements:** General education requirement.
**Academic regulations:** Minimum 2.0 GPA must be maintained.
**Special:** Certificate programs offered. Double majors. Dual degrees. Independent study. Accelerated study. Pass/fail grading option. Internships. Cooperative education programs. Graduate school at which undergraduates may take graduate-level courses. Preprofessional programs in law, medicine, pharmacy, dentistry, optometry, engineering, forestry, and physical therapy. 3-2 chemistry/chemical engineering, chemistry/nuclear engineering, and physics/nuclear engineering programs with Kansas State U. Member of Southeast Kansas Higher Education Consortium and Midwestern Higher Education Commission. Teacher certification in early childhood, elementary, secondary, and special education. Certification in specific subject areas. Study abroad in 42 countries. ROTC.
**Honors:** Phi Beta Kappa. Honors program.
**Academic Assistance:** Remedial reading, writing, math, and study skills. Nonremedial tutoring.
**STUDENT LIFE. Housing:** All unmarried, nonveteran freshmen under age 22 and living beyond a 50-mile radius must live on campus unless living with family. Coed, women's, and men's dorms. Sorority and fraternity housing. On-campus married-student housing. Off-campus housing. 18% of students live in college housing.
**Social atmosphere:** Students gather on campus at the student union and fraternity houses. Off campus, students head for Lewski's, Hollywoods 21, and other local bars. The student government, student publications, Greeks, and athletes have a widespread influence on campus life. Popular events include football games, Homecoming, Greek Week, international

student events, theatre events, and shows by visiting comedians. "PSU has a larger-than-average international student population, verging on 10%. Exposure to Asian and Baltic cultures is a unique experience. Pittsburg has a small-town feel and inexpensive housing. But Kansas City, Tulsa, Little Rock, and Wichita are all within a few hours' drive," reports the student newspaper.

**Services and counseling/handicapped student services:** Placement services. Health service. Counseling services for minority, military, veteran, and older students. Birth control, personal, and psychological counseling. Career and academic guidance services. Physically disabled student services. Learning disabled services. Notetaking services. Tape recorders. Tutors. Reader services for the blind.

**Campus organizations:** Undergraduate student government. Student newspaper (Collegio, published once/week). Literary magazine. Yearbook. Radio and TV stations. Choir, 100 organizations in all. Seven fraternities, five chapter houses; three sororities, all with chapter houses. 11% of men join a fraternity. 4% of women join a sorority.

**Religious organizations:** American Baptist Campus Ministry, Baptist Student Union, Campus Christians, Lutheran Student Association, other religious groups.

**Minority/foreign student organizations:** Minority Student Association, Black Student Association. International Student Association, Chinese, Japanese, Korean, Malaysian, and Nigerian groups.

**ATHLETICS. Physical education requirements:** One semester of physical education required.

**Intercollegiate competition:** 6% of students participate. Baseball (M), basketball (M,W), cheerleading (M,W), cross-country (M,W), football (M,W), golf (M,W), softball (W), track (M,W), track (indoor) (M,W), track (outdoor) (M,W), track and field (indoor) (M,W), track and field (outdoor) (M,W), volleyball (W). Member of MIAA, NCAA Division II.

**Intramural and club sports:** Intramural archery, badminton, baseball, basketball, cross-country, diving, football, racquetball, rugby, softball, swimming, tennis, track and field, volleyball, wrestling. Men's club rugby.

**ADMISSIONS. Academic basis for candidate selection** (in order of priority): Secondary school record, class rank, standardized test scores.

**Requirements:** Graduation from secondary school is required; GED is accepted. 15 units and the following program of study are recommended: 4 units of English, 3 units of math, 3 units of science, 2 units of foreign language, 3 units of social studies. Open admissions policy for in-state applicants. Rank in top half of secondary school class and minimum 2.0 GPA required of out-of-state applicants. Admissions requirements vary for nursing, education, business, and social work programs and for honors college. ACT is required. Campus visit and interview recommended. Off-campus interviews available with an admissions representative.

**Procedure:** Take ACT by May 1 of 12th year. Visit college for interview by August 1 of 12th year. Suggest filing application by March 15. Notification of admission on rolling basis. Reply is required by August 15. $200 room deposit, refundable until August 11. Freshmen accepted for terms other than fall.

**Special programs:** Admission may be deferred indefinitely. Credit and/or placement may be granted through CEEB Advanced Placement exams for scores of 3 or higher. Credit may be granted through CLEP general exams. Credit and/or placement may be granted through CLEP subject exams. Placement may be granted through ACT PEP and DANTES exams. Credit and placement may be granted through challenge exams and military experience. Concurrent enrollment program.

**Transfer students:** Transfer students accepted for terms other than fall. In fall 1993, 47% of all new students were transfers into all classes. 1,026 transfer applications were received, 842 were accepted. Application deadline is rolling for fall; rolling for spring. Minimum 2.0 GPA required. Lowest course grade accepted is "D." Maximum number of transferable credits is 64 semester hours. At least 30 semester hours must be completed at the university to receive degree.

**Admissions contact:** James Taylor, Ph.D., Director of Enrollment Services. 316 235-4250, 800 854-PITT.

**FINANCIAL AID. Available aid:** Pell grants, SEOG, state scholarships and grants, school scholarships, private scholarships, ROTC scholarships, academic merit scholarships, athletic scholarships, and aid for undergraduate foreign students. Perkins Loans (NDSL), PLUS, Stafford Loans (GSL), NSL, school loans, and SLS. Deferred payment plan.

**Financial aid statistics:** In 1993-94, 88% of all undergraduate applicants received aid; 92% of freshman applicants. Average amounts of aid awarded freshmen: Scholarships and grants, $1,768; loans, $2,354.

**Supporting data/closing dates:** FAFSA/FAF/FFS: Priority filing date is March 15. Notification of awards begins April 1.

**Financial aid contact:** Ronald G. Hopkins, M.Ed., Director of Financial Aid. 316 235-4240, 800 854-PITT.

**STUDENT EMPLOYMENT.** College Work/Study Program. Institutional employment. 22% of full-time undergraduates work on campus during school year. Students may expect to earn an average of $1,500 during school year. Off-campus part-time employment opportunities rated "good."

**COMPUTER FACILITIES.** 125 IBM/IBM-compatible and Macintosh/Apple microcomputers; 100 are networked. Students may access Prime minicomputer/mainframe systems, BITNET, Internet. Residence halls may be equipped with stand-alone microcomputers, networked microcomputers. Computer languages and software packages include COBOL, FORTRAN, GW-BASIC, Quick BASIC, Macro Assembler, Quick C, Turbo Pascal; 100 in all. Computer facilities are available to all students.

**Fees:** Computer fee is included in tuition/fees.

**Hours:** 8 AM-11 PM.

**GRADUATE CAREER DATA.** Graduate school percentages: 2% enter law school. 1% enter medical school. 1% enter dental school. 10% enter graduate business programs. 10% enter graduate arts and sciences programs. 1% enter theological school/seminary. Highest graduate school enrollments: Pittsburg State U, Kansas State U, U of Kansas, Washburn U. 80% of graduates choose careers in business and industry. Companies and businesses that hire graduates: Electronic Data Systems, Phillips Petroleum, Koch Industries.

**PROMINENT ALUMNI/AE.** O. Gene Bicknell, founder and CEO, National Pizza Co.; Ted Watts, sports illustrator; Wayland Gregory, developer of NASA shield; James England, provost, Swarthmore Coll.

# Saint Mary College

**Leavenworth, KS 66048-5082 913 682-5151**

**1993-94 Costs.** Tuition: $7,300. Room & board: $3,700. Fees, books, misc. academic expenses (school's estimate): $450.

**Enrollment.** Undergraduates: 140 men, 299 women (full-time). Freshman class: 273 applicants, 269 accepted, 103 enrolled. Graduate enrollment: 7 men, 14 women.

**Test score averages/ranges.** Average ACT scores: 21 composite.

**Faculty.** 40 full-time; 73 part-time. 48% of faculty holds highest degree in specific field. Student/faculty ratio: 11 to 1.

**Selectivity rating.** Competitive.

**PROFILE.** Saint Mary, founded in 1923, is a private, church-affiliated, liberal arts college for women. Its 200-acre campus, including several buildings from the 19th and early 20th centuries, is located in Leavenworth, 30 miles north of Kansas City.

**Accreditation:** NCACS. Professionally accredited by the National Council for Accreditation of Teacher Education, the National League for Nursing.

**Religious orientation:** Saint Mary College is affiliated with the Roman Catholic Church; two semesters of religion/theology required.

**Library:** Collections totaling over 119,300 volumes, 445 periodical subscriptions and 772 microform items.

**Athletic facilities:** Gymnasium, exercise rooms, swimming pool, racquetball and tennis courts, cross-country course, soccer and softball fields, indoor track, weight room.

**STUDENT BODY. Undergraduate profile:** 65% are state residents; 35% are transfers. 1% Asian-American, 18% Black, 4% Hispanic, 3% Native American, 63% White, 11% Other.

**Freshman profile:** Majority of accepted applicants took ACT.

**Undergraduate achievement:** 65% of fall 1992 freshmen returned for fall 1993 term. 28% of entering class graduated. 10% of students who completed a degree program immediately went on to graduate study.

**Foreign students:** 25 students are from out of the country. Countries represented include Bulgaria, Japan, Korea, Mexico, Pacific islands, and Thailand; nine in all.

**PROGRAMS OF STUDY. Degrees:** B.A., B.Mus., B.S.

**Majors:** Accounting, Art, Biology, Business, Chemistry, Computer Science, Drama, Elementary Education, English, History, Human Services, Mathematics, Medical Technology, Music, Political Science, Psychology, Public Affairs, Sociology, Spanish, Theology.

**Distribution of degrees:** The majors with the highest enrollment are elementary education, business, and human services; music and Spanish have the lowest.

**Requirements:** General education requirement.

**Academic regulations:** Minimum 2.0 GPA required for graduation.

**Special:** Minors offered in all majors and in dance, economics, French, organizational management, philosophy, and speech. Organizational Leadership Program. Women as Managers and Formation for Youth Ministry certificate programs. Associate's degrees offered. Double majors. Pass/fail grading option. Internships. Preprofessional programs in law, medicine, pharmacy, dentistry, and nursing. 2-2 accounting, business, computer science, and public affairs programs with Donnelly Coll. Member of Kansas City Regional Council for Higher Education (KCRCHE). Semester-away programs available. Exchange program with U of Kansas. Teacher certification in early childhood, elementary, and secondary education. Exchange program abroad in Japan (Sophia U). ROTC.

**Honors:** Honors program.

**Academic Assistance:** Remedial reading, writing, math, and study skills. Nonremedial tutoring.

**ADMISSIONS. Academic basis for candidate selection** (in order of priority): Secondary school record, standardized test scores, class rank, school's recommendation.

**Nonacademic basis for candidate selection:** Character and personality are considered.

**Requirements:** Graduation from secondary school is required; GED is accepted. 16 units required and the following program of study recommended: 4 units of English, 2 units of math, 1 unit of science, 2 units of foreign language, 2 units of social studies, 5 units of electives. Minimum composite ACT score of 19, rank in top third of secondary school class, and minimum 2.5 GPA recommended. Conditional admission possible for applicants not meeting standard requirements. ACT is required; SAT may be substituted. Campus visit recommended. Off-campus interviews available with admissions and alumni representatives.

**Procedure:** Take SAT or ACT by January of 12th year. Visit college for interview by February of 12th year. Application deadline is August. Notification of admission on rolling basis. Reply is required by May 1. $50 tuition deposit, refundable until May 1. $50 room deposit, refundable until May 1. Freshmen accepted for terms other than fall.

**Special programs:** Admission may be deferred one year. Credit and/or placement may be granted through CEEB Advanced Placement exams for scores of 3 or higher. Credit may be granted through CLEP general and subject exams, ACT PEP, DANTES, and challenge exams, and military and life experience. Concurrent enrollment program.

**Transfer students:** Transfer students accepted for terms other than fall. In fall 1993, 35% of all new students were transfers into all classes. 103 transfer applications were received, 50 were accepted. Application deadline is August 15 for fall; January 5 for spring. Minimum 2.0 GPA required. Lowest course grade accepted is "C." Maximum number of transferable credits is 64 semester hours from a two-year school and 90 semester hours from a four-year school. At least 30 semester hours must be completed at the college to receive degree.

**Admissions contact:** Domenic Teti, M.A., Director of Admissions. 800 752-7043.

**FINANCIAL AID. Available aid:** Pell grants, SEOG, state scholarships and grants, school scholarships, ROTC scholarships, academic merit scholarships, and athletic schol-

arships. Perkins Loans (NDSL), PLUS, Stafford Loans (GSL), and SLS. Deferred payment plan and family tuition reduction. Institutional payment plan.
**Financial aid statistics:** 15% of aid is not need-based. In 1993-94, 85% of all undergraduate applicants received aid; 80% of freshman applicants. Average amounts of aid awarded freshmen: Scholarships and grants, $6,627; loans, $2,500.
**Supporting data/closing dates:** FAFSA: Priority filing date is March 15. State aid form: Priority filing date is March 15. Notification of awards on rolling basis.
**Financial aid contact:** Judy Wiedower, M.A., Director of Financial Aid. 800 752-7043.

## Southwestern College

**Winfield, KS 67156 316 221-4150**

**1994-95 Costs.** Tuition: $7,200. Room: $1,500. Board: $2,032. Fees, books, misc. academic expenses (school's estimate): $500.
**Enrollment.** Undergraduates: 275 men, 302 women (full-time). Freshman class: 188 applicants, 115 accepted, 106 enrolled. Graduate enrollment: 6 men, 20 women.
**Test score averages/ranges.** Average SAT scores: 398 verbal, 437 math. Average ACT scores: 22 composite.
**Faculty.** 51 full-time; 28 part-time. 48% of faculty holds doctoral degree. Student/faculty ratio: 12 to 1.
**Selectivity rating.** Competitive.

**PROFILE.** Southwestern, founded in 1885, is a private, church-affiliated college. Programs are offered in the Divisions of Business and Economics, Education, Fine Arts, Humanities, Natural Science, and Social Science. Its 70-acre campus is located in Winfield, 45 miles from Wichita.

**Accreditation:** NCACS. Professionally accredited by the Council on Social Work Education, the National Association of Schools of Music, the National League for Nursing.
**Religious orientation:** Southwestern College is affiliated with the United Methodist Church; no religious requirements.
**Library:** Collections totaling over 125,000 volumes, 500 periodical subscriptions, and 6,500 microform items.
**Athletic facilities:** Field house, physical education building, swimming pool, weight room, track, sand volleyball and tennis courts, football and soccer fields, gymnasiums.
**STUDENT BODY. Undergraduate profile:** 81% are state residents; 60% are transfers. 1% Asian-American, 7% Black, 3% Hispanic, 2% Native American, 86% White, 1% Other. Average age of undergraduates is 23.
**Freshman profile:** 7% of freshmen who took SAT scored 600 or over on verbal, 13% scored 600 or over on math; 20% scored 500 or over on verbal, 33% scored 500 or over on math; 47% scored 400 or over on verbal, 46% scored 400 or over on math; 87% scored 300 or over on verbal, 93% scored 300 or over on math. 6% of accepted applicants took SAT; 9% took ACT. 99% of freshmen come from public schools.
**Undergraduate achievement:** 56% of fall 1992 freshmen returned for fall 1993 term. 19% of entering class graduated.
**Foreign students:** Eight students are from out of the country. Countries represented include Argentina, Japan, Norway, and Spain.
**PROGRAMS OF STUDY. Degrees:** B.A., B.Bus.Admin., B.Gen.Studies, B.Mus., B.Phil., B.S., B.S.Nurs., B.Soc.Work.
**Majors:** Accounting, Biochemistry, Biology/Marine Biology, Business Administration, Business/Computer Information Systems, Business Education, Chemistry, Comprehensive Social Studies Education, Computer Science, Computer Science Education, Elementary Education, Emergency Mobile Intensive Care Technology, English, French Education, Health/Physical Education/Recreation, History, Human Resources, Mass Communication/Film, Modern Languages, Music, Music/Drama, Music Education, Nursing, Philosophy/Religion, Physical Science Education, Physics, Psychology, Social Work, Speech, Theatre Arts.
**Distribution of degrees:** The majors with the highest enrollment are nursing, elementary education, and biology.
**Requirements:** General education requirement.
**Academic regulations:** Minimum 2.0 GPA must be maintained.
**Special:** Minors offered in some majors and in art, environmental studies, journalism, political science, and Spanish. Self-designed majors. Double majors. Dual degrees. Independent study. Pass/fail grading option. Internships. Cooperative education programs. Preprofessional programs in law, medicine, veterinary science, pharmacy, dentistry, theology, and optometry. 3-2 engineering program with Washington U. Urban Education Program (Kansas City), Urban Studies Program (Chicago). Exchange program with Cowley County Comm Coll. Teacher certification in elementary and secondary education. Certification in specific subject areas. Exchange program abroad in Japan (International Christian U). Study abroad also in England, France, Germany, and Italy.
**Honors:** Honor societies.
**Academic Assistance:** Remedial reading, writing, math, and study skills. Nonremedial tutoring.
**ADMISSIONS. Academic basis for candidate selection** (in order of priority): Secondary school record, standardized test scores, class rank, essay, school's recommendation.
**Nonacademic basis for candidate selection:** Character and personality, extracurricular participation, particular talent or ability, and alumni/ae relationship are considered.
**Requirements:** Graduation from secondary school is required; GED is accepted. No specific distribution of secondary school units required. Minimum composite ACT score of 18, rank in top half of secondary school class, and minimum 2.0 GPA required. Audition required of music program applicants. SAT or ACT is required. Campus visit and interview recommended. Off-campus interviews available with an admissions representative.
**Procedure:** Take SAT or ACT by May of 12th year. Visit college for interview by April 15 of 12th year. Suggest filing application by February 1. Application deadline is August 1. Notification of admission on rolling basis. $50 tuition deposit, refundable until July 1. $100 room deposit, refundable until July 1. Freshmen accepted for terms other than fall.
**Special programs:** Credit and/or placement may be granted through CEEB Advanced Placement exams for scores of 4 or higher. Credit and/or placement may be granted through CLEP general and subject exams. Credit may be granted through military and life experience. Credit and placement may be granted through ACT PEP, DANTES, and challenge exams. Early entrance/early admission program. Concurrent enrollment program.
**Transfer students:** Transfer students accepted for terms other than fall. In fall 1993, 60% of all new students were transfers into all classes. 190 transfer applications were received, 144 were accepted. Application deadline is August 1 for fall; rolling for spring. Minimum 2.0 GPA required. Maximum number of transferable credits is 64 semester hours. At least 30 semester hours must be completed at the college to receive degree.
**Admissions contact:** Douglas M. Mason, M.In.Ed., Director of Admissions. 316 221-8236, 800 846-1543.
**FINANCIAL AID. Available aid:** Pell grants, SEOG, state scholarships and grants, school scholarships and grants, private scholarships, academic merit scholarships, and athletic scholarships. Perkins Loans (NDSL), PLUS, Stafford Loans (GSL), school loans, and SLS. Deferred payment plan and family tuition reduction.
**Financial aid statistics:** 28% of aid is not need-based. In 1993-94, 99% of all undergraduate applicants received aid; 92% of freshman applicants. Average amounts of aid awarded freshmen: Scholarships and grants, $1,089; loans, $2,916.
**Supporting data/closing dates:** FAFSA/FAF/FFS: Priority filing date is March 15; deadline is August 1. Income tax forms: Priority filing date is March 15; accepted on rolling basis. Notification of awards on rolling basis.
**Financial aid contact:** Margaret Robinson, Director of Financial Aid. 316 221-8215.

## Tabor College

**Hillsboro, KS 67063 316 947-3121**

**1994-95 Costs.** Tuition: $8,480. Room: $1,420. Board: $2,100. Fees, books, misc. academic expenses (school's estimate): $700.
**Enrollment.** Undergraduates: 247 men, 167 women (full-time). Freshman class: 254 applicants, 148 accepted, 148 enrolled.
**Test score averages/ranges.** Average ACT scores: 22 composite.
**Faculty.** 33 full-time; 21 part-time. 70% of faculty holds highest degree in specific field. Student/faculty ratio: 16 to 1.
**Selectivity rating.** Competitive.

**PROFILE.** Tabor, founded in 1908, is a private, church-affiliated, liberal arts college. Its 26-acre campus is located in Hillsboro, 50 miles north of Wichita.

**Accreditation:** NCACS. Professionally accredited by the Council on Social Work Education, the National Association of Schools of Music.
**Religious orientation:** Tabor College is affiliated with the Mennonite Brethren Church; three semesters of religion/theology required.
**Library:** Collections totaling over 70,000 volumes, 450 periodical subscriptions, and 2,000 microform items.
**Special facilities/museums:** Center for Mennonite studies.
**Athletic facilities:** All-weather lighted tennis courts, baseball diamond, playing fields, track and football field.
**STUDENT BODY. Undergraduate profile:** 54% are state residents; 22% are transfers. 4% Black, 3% Hispanic, 1% Native American, 92% White. Average age of undergraduates is 20.
**Freshman profile:** 14% of accepted applicants took SAT; 86% took ACT.
**Undergraduate achievement:** 57% of fall 1991 freshmen returned for fall 1992 term.
**Foreign students:** 10 students are from out of the country. Countries represented include Japan, Taiwan, and Zambia; eight in all.
**PROGRAMS OF STUDY. Degrees:** B.A.
**Majors:** Accounting, Agribusiness, Applied Mathematics, Biblical/Religious Studies, Biology, Biology Education, Business Administration/Economics, Business Administration/Economics Education, Chemistry, Chemistry Education, Church Education, Church Music, Communications, Computer Science, Contemporary Church Ministries, Cross-Cultural Studies, Elementary Education, English, Environmental Biology, Executive Office Administration, Health/Physical Education, Health Science, History, Human Services, Humanities, Instrumental Music, Instrumental/Vocal Music, International Studies, Legal Office Administration, Mathematics, Mathematics Education, Medical Office Administration, Medical Technology, Music, Music Business, Natural/Mathematical Sciences, Office Administration, Psychology, Recreation, Secondary Education, Social Science, Social Work, Sociology, Speech/Drama, Teacher Education, Vocal Music.
**Distribution of degrees:** The majors with the highest enrollment are elementary education, business administration, and church ministries; accounting and international studies have the lowest.
**Requirements:** General education requirement.
**Special:** Associate's degrees offered. Self-designed majors. Double majors. Independent study. Accelerated study. Pass/fail grading option. Internships. Preprofessional programs in law, medicine, veterinary science, dentistry, and optometry. Member of Associated Colleges of Central Kansas and Christian College Coalition; exchange possible. Exchange programs with other 4-1-4 colleges. Teacher certification in early childhood, elementary, secondary, and special education. Certification in specific subject areas. Exchange program abroad in the former Soviet Republics. Study abroad also in other countries.
**Academic Assistance:** Remedial reading, writing, math, and study skills. Nonremedial tutoring.
**ADMISSIONS. Academic basis for candidate selection** (in order of priority): Standardized test scores, secondary school record, school's recommendation, class rank, essay.
**Nonacademic basis for candidate selection:** Character and personality are emphasized. Extracurricular participation is important. Particular talent or ability and alumni/ae relationship are considered.
**Requirements:** Graduation from secondary school is required; GED is accepted. No specific distribution of secondary school units required. Minimum composite ACT score of 18 and rank in top half of secondary school class required; minimum 2.5 GPA recommended.

ACT is required; SAT may be substituted. Campus visit and interview recommended. Off-campus interviews available with an admissions representative.
**Procedure:** Take SAT or ACT by June of 12th year. Visit college for interview by May of 12th year. Suggest filing application by March 15. Application deadline is July 15. Notification of admission on rolling basis. Reply is required by August 15. $100 tuition deposit, refundable partially. $50 refundable room deposit. Freshmen accepted for terms other than fall.
**Special programs:** Admission may be deferred one year. Credit and/or placement may be granted through CEEB Advanced Placement exams for scores of 3 or higher. Credit may be granted through CLEP general and subject exams, challenge exams, and military and life experience. Early decision program. Deadline for applying for early decision is June 30. Concurrent enrollment program.
**Transfer students:** Transfer students accepted for terms other than fall. In fall 1992, 22% of all new students were transfers into all classes. 58 transfer applications were received, 34 were accepted. Application deadline is August 1 for fall; December 1 for spring. Minimum 2.0 GPA recommended. Lowest course grade accepted is "C." Maximum number of transferable credits is 64 semester hours. At least 30 semester hours must be completed at the college to receive degree.
**Admissions contact:** Glenn Lygrisse, M.Ed., Vice President for Enrollment Management. 800 822-6799.

**FINANCIAL AID. Available aid:** Pell grants, SEOG, state scholarships and grants, school scholarships and grants, private scholarships, academic merit scholarships, athletic scholarships, and aid for undergraduate foreign students. Church match scholarships. Perkins Loans (NDSL), PLUS, Stafford Loans (GSL), and SLS. Tuition Plan Inc. and AMS. Institutional Plan.
**Financial aid statistics:** 15% of aid is not need-based. In 1992-93, 100% of all undergraduate applicants received aid. Average amounts of aid awarded freshmen: Scholarships and grants, $2,850; loans, $2,300.
**Supporting data/closing dates:** FAFSA/FFS: Priority filing date is March 1. Income tax forms: Accepted on rolling basis. Notification of awards on rolling basis.
**Financial aid contact:** Barbara Godsey, Director of Student Finances. 800 822-6799.

# University of Kansas

**Lawrence, KS 66045 — 913 864-2700**

**1994-95 Costs.** Tuition: $1,714 (state residents), $6,994 (out-of-state). Room & board: $3,384. Fees, books, misc. academic expenses (school's estimate): $1,086.
**Enrollment.** Undergraduates: 8,970 men, 8,910 women (full-time). Freshman class: 8,579 applicants, 5,561 accepted, 3,681 enrolled. Graduate enrollment: 4,371 men, 4,938 women.
**Test score averages/ranges.** Average ACT scores: 23 English, 22 math, 23 composite. Range of ACT scores of middle 50%: 19-26 English, 19-25 math.
**Faculty.** 1,078 full-time; 234 part-time. 96% of faculty holds highest degree in specific field. Student/faculty ratio: 16 to 1.
**Selectivity rating.** Competitive.

**PROFILE.** The University of Kansas, founded in 1866, is a public, comprehensive institution. Programs are offered through the College of Liberal Arts and Sciences; the Graduate School; and the Schools of Architecture and Urban Design, Business, Education, Engineering, Fine Arts, Journalism, Law, Medicine, Nursing, Pharmacy, and Social Welfare. Its 1,000-acre campus is located in a residential area of Lawrence.

**Accreditation:** NCACS. Professionally accredited by the Accreditation Board for Engineering and Technology, the Accrediting Council on Education in Journalism and Mass Communication, the American Assembly of Collegiate Schools of Business, the American Council on Pharmaceutical Education, the American Medical Association (CAHEA), the American Psychological Association, the Council on Social Work Education, the National Architecture Accrediting Board, the National Association of Schools of Art and Design, the National Association of Schools of Music, the National Council for Accreditation of Teacher Education, the National League for Nursing.
**Religious orientation:** University of Kansas is nonsectarian; no religious requirements.
**Library:** Collections totaling over 3,200,000 volumes, 33,047 periodical subscriptions, and 2,700,000 microform items.
**Special facilities/museums:** Performing arts center, museums of art, anthropology, entomology, invertebrate paleontology, and natural history, film studio, 464-bed hospital for clinical learning, herbarium, space technology center, observatory, laser lab.
**Athletic facilities:** Gymnasium, sports pavilion, strength center, swimming pool, baseball and softball fields, handball and tennis courts, tracks, field house, stadium.

**STUDENT BODY. Undergraduate profile:** 69% are state residents; 28% are transfers. 3% Asian-American, 3% Black, 2% Hispanic, 1% Native American, 83% White, 8% Unknown and foreign. Average age of undergraduates is 22.
**Freshman profile:** 6% of freshmen who took ACT scored 30 or over on English, 8% scored 30 or over on math, 8% scored 30 or over on composite; 45% scored 24 or over on English, 40% scored 24 or over on math, 47% scored 24 or over on composite; 89% scored 18 or over on English, 85% scored 18 or over on math, 94% scored 18 or over on composite; 100% scored 12 or over on English, 100% scored 12 or over on math, 100% scored 12 or over on composite. 88% of accepted applicants took ACT.
**Undergraduate achievement:** 80% of fall 1992 freshmen returned for fall 1993 term. 25% of entering class graduated.
**Foreign students:** 789 students are from out of the country. Countries represented include China, India, Japan, Malaysia, South Korea, and Taiwan; 112 in all.

**PROGRAMS OF STUDY. Degrees:** B.A., B.Arch., B.Art Ed., B.F.A., B.Gen.Studies, B.Mus., B.Mus.Ed., B.S., B.S.Bus., B.S.Ed., B.S.Journ., B.S.Nurs., B.S.Pharm., B.Soc.Work.
**Majors:** Accounting, Advertising, Aerospace Engineering, African-American Studies, African Studies, American Studies, Anthropology, Applied Music, Architectural Engineering, Architectural Studies, Architecture, Astronomy, Atmospheric Sciences, Biochemistry, Biology, Business Administration, Cellular Biology, Ceramics, Chemical Engineering, Chemistry, Chinese, Civil Engineering, Classical Antiquity, Classical Languages, Cognitive Psychology, Communication Disorders, Comparative Literature, Computer Engineering, Computer Science, Cytotechnology, Dance, Design, Developmental/Child Psychology, East Asian Languages/Cultures, Economics, Electrical Engineering, Elementary Education, Engineering Physics, English, Environmental Studies, French, Genetics, Geography, Geology, Germanic Languages/Literatures, Health Education, Health Information Management, History, History of Art, Human Biology, Humanities, Industrial Design, Instrumental Music, Interior Design, Italian, Japanese, Latin American Studies, Liberal Studies, Linguistics, Mathematics, Mechanical Engineering, Medical Technology, Metalsmithing/Jewelry, Microbiology, Music Education, Music History, Music Theory/Composition, Music Therapy, News, Nursing, Occupational Therapy, Organismal Biology, Painting, Petroleum Engineering, Pharmacy, Philosophy, Photojournalism, Physical Education, Physics, Political Science, Printmaking, Psychology, Radio/Television/Magazine, Religious Studies, Respiratory Care, Russian, Sculpture, Secondary Education, Social Work, Sociology, Soviet/East European Studies, Spanish, Speech, Sport Science, Systematics/Ecology, Textile Design, Theatre Design, Theatre/Film, Visual Arts Education, Visual Communications, Vocal Music, Women's Studies.
**Distribution of degrees:** The majors with the highest enrollment are journalism, business, and speech; engineering physics, Italian, and art teacher education have the lowest.
**Academic regulations:** Freshmen must maintain minimum 1.4 GPA; sophomores, 1.8 GPA; juniors, 2.0 GPA; seniors, 2.0 GPA.
**Special:** Self-designed majors. Double majors. Dual degrees. Independent study. Pass/fail grading option. Internships. Cooperative education programs. Graduate school at which undergraduates may take graduate-level courses. Preprofessional programs in law, medicine, and dentistry. Washington Semester. Teacher certification in elementary, secondary, and special education. Certification in specific subject areas. Study abroad in over 50 countries. ROTC, NROTC, and AFROTC.
**Honors:** Phi Beta Kappa. Honors program. Honor societies.
**Academic Assistance:** Remedial math. Nonremedial tutoring.

**STUDENT LIFE. Housing:** Students may live on or off campus. Coed, women's, and men's dorms. Sorority and fraternity housing. School-owned/operated apartments. Off-campus privately-owned housing. Both on-campus and off-campus married-student housing. Private dorms, scholarship halls. 20% of students live in college housing.
**Services and counseling/handicapped student services:** Placement services. Health service. Women's center. Day care. Counseling services for minority, military, veteran, and older students. Birth control, personal, and psychological counseling. Career and academic guidance services. Physically disabled student services. Learning disabled services. Notetaking services. Tape recorders. Tutors. Reader services for the blind.
**Campus organizations:** Undergraduate student government. Student newspaper (University Daily Kansan). Literary magazine. Yearbook. Radio and TV stations. Departmental clubs, musical groups, career and professional groups, community service groups, language groups, hobby clubs, forensics, political groups, environmental, cultural, governmental, and sports clubs, other special-interest groups, 300 organizations in all. 28 fraternities, 25 chapter houses; 19 sororities, 14 chapter houses. 20% of men join a fraternity. 25% of women join a sorority.
**Religious organizations:** Numerous religious groups.
**Minority/foreign student organizations:** Numerous minority student groups. African, Chinese, Indian, Indonesian, Korean, Malaysian, Pakistani, Palestinian, Taiwanese, Vietnamese, and other foreign student groups.

**ATHLETICS. Physical education requirements:** None.
**Intercollegiate competition:** 2% of students participate. Baseball (M), basketball (M,W), cheerleading (M,W), cross-country (M,W), diving (M,W), football (M), golf (M,W), softball (W), swimming (M,W), tennis (M,W), track and field (indoor) (M,W), track and field (outdoor) (M,W), volleyball (W). Member of Big Eight Conference, NCAA Division I-A.
**Intramural and club sports:** 25% of students participate. Intramural badminton, basketball, floor hockey, football, racquetball, soccer, softball, tennis, volleyball, wrestling. Men's club bowling, crew, fencing, horsemanship, ice hockey, lacrosse, martial arts, racquetball, rugby, sailing, soccer, squash, ultimate frisbee, volleyball, water skiing. Women's club bowling, crew, fencing, horsemanship, lacrosse, sailing, soccer, squash, ultimate frisbee, water skiing.

**ADMISSIONS. Academic basis for candidate selection** (in order of priority): Secondary school record, standardized test scores, class rank, school's recommendation.
**Nonacademic basis for candidate selection:** Particular talent or ability is considered.
**Requirements:** Graduation from secondary school is required; GED is accepted. No specific distribution of secondary school units required. Open admission for in-state applicants who are graduates of accredited secondary schools. Minimum composite ACT score of 24 (combined SAT score of 990) and minimum 2.0 GPA required of out-of-state applicants. Audition required of music performance program applicants. Portfolio required of design program applicants. Conditional admission possible for applicants not meeting standard requirements. SAT or ACT is required. Campus visit and interview recommended. No off-campus interviews.
**Procedure:** Take SAT or ACT by February of 12th year. Application deadlines are February 1 (out-of-state) and April 1 (state residents). Notification of admission on rolling basis. Reply is required prior to beginning of term. $25 nonrefundable room deposit. Freshmen accepted for terms other than fall.
**Special programs:** Credit and/or placement may be granted through CEEB Advanced Placement exams. Credit and/or placement may be granted through CLEP general and subject exams. Credit and placement may be granted through challenge exams. Early entrance/early admission program. Concurrent enrollment program.
**Transfer students:** Transfer students accepted for terms other than fall. In fall 1993, 28% of all new students were transfers into all classes. 3,575 transfer applications were received, 2,338 were accepted. Application deadline is February 1 for fall; December 1 for spring. Minimum 2.5 GPA required. Lowest course grade accepted is "C." At least 30 semester hours must be completed at the university to receive degree.
**Admissions contact:** Deborah Castrop, M.A., Director of Admissions. 913 864-3911.

**FINANCIAL AID. Available aid:** Pell grants, SEOG, state scholarships, school scholarships, private scholarships and grants, ROTC scholarships, academic merit scholarships, and athletic scholarships. Perkins Loans (NDSL), PLUS, Stafford Loans (GSL), Health Professions Loans, and SLS. Deferred payment plan. Credit card payment plan.

**Financial aid statistics:** In 1993-94, 100% of all undergraduate applicants received aid. Average amounts of aid awarded freshmen: Scholarships and grants, $1,000; loans, $2,530.
**Supporting data/closing dates:** State aid form: Deadline is March 15. Notification of awards begins May 1.
**Financial aid contact:** Diane Del Buono, J.D., Director of Financial Aid. 913 864-4700.

**STUDENT EMPLOYMENT.** College Work/Study Program. Institutional employment. 15% of full-time undergraduates work on campus during school year. Students may expect to earn an average of $2,300 during school year. Off-campus part-time employment opportunities rated "good."

**COMPUTER FACILITIES.** 550 IBM/IBM-compatible and Macintosh/Apple microcomputers; 400 are networked. Students may access Digital, IBM, SUN minicomputer/mainframe systems, Internet. Residence halls may be equipped with stand-alone microcomputers, networked microcomputers, networked terminals, modems. Client/LAN operating systems include Apple/Macintosh, DOS, DEC, LocalTalk/AppleTalk, Novell. Computer languages and software packages include Assembler, BASIC, BMDP, C, COBOL, FORTRAN, ImSL, LISP, MINITAB, Pascal, SPSS-X; 100 in all. Computer facilities are available to all students.
**Fees:** None.
**Hours:** 24 hours.

**GRADUATE CAREER DATA.** Highest graduate school enrollments: U of Kansas.

**PROMINENT ALUMNI/AE.** William Allen White, Pulitzer Prize-winning editor; William Inge, playwright; Robert Dole, U.S. senator; Steve Hawley, Ron Evans, and Joe Engle, astronauts; Wilt Chamberlain, Gale Sayers, and Lynette Woodard, athletes; Elmer V. McCollum, scientist; Don Johnson, Buddy Rogers, and Mandy Patinkin, actors.

## Washburn University of Topeka

**Topeka, KS 66621** **913 231-1010**

**1993-94 Costs.** Tuition: $2,642 (state residents), $4,562 (out-of-state). Room & board: $3,100. Fees, books, misc. academic expenses (school's estimate): $450.
**Enrollment.** Undergraduates: 1,309 men, 1,848 women (full-time). Freshman class: 1,400 applicants, 96 accepted, 840 enrolled. Graduate enrollment: 362 men, 350 women.
**Test score averages/ranges.** Average ACT scores: 22 composite.
**Faculty.** 245 full-time; 175 part-time. 75% of faculty holds doctoral degree. Student/faculty ratio: 17 to 1.
**Selectivity rating.** Competitive.

**PROFILE.** Washburn, founded in 1865, is a public, comprehensive university. Programs are offered through the College of Arts and Sciences and the Schools of Applied and Continuing Education, Business, and Nursing. Its 160-acre campus is located in the center of Topeka.

**Accreditation:** NCACS. Professionally accredited by the American Assembly of Collegiate Schools of Business, the American Bar Association, the American Psychological Association, the Council on Social Work Education, the National Association of Schools of Art and Design, the National League for Nursing.
**Religious orientation:** Washburn University of Topeka is nonsectarian; no religious requirements.
**Library:** Collections totaling over 500,000 volumes, 1,500 periodical subscriptions, and 100,000 microform items.
**Special facilities/museums:** Art museum, language lab.
**Athletic facilities:** Swimming pool, weight room, basketball and tennis courts, tracks, baseball and softball fields.

**STUDENT BODY. Undergraduate profile:** 95% are state residents; 40% are transfers. 3% Asian-American, 6% Black, 4% Hispanic, 1% Native American, 82% White, 4% Other. Average age of undergraduates is 22.
**Freshman profile:** 75% of accepted applicants took ACT.
**Undergraduate achievement:** 55% of fall 1992 freshmen returned for fall 1993 term. 15% of students who completed a degree program immediately went on to graduate study.
**Foreign students:** 108 students are from out of the country. Countries represented include Bangladesh, China, Japan, Korea, Malaysia, and Thailand; 47 in all.

**PROGRAMS OF STUDY. Degrees:** B.A., B.A.S., B.Bus.Admin., B.Ed., B.F.A., B.Gen.Studies, B.Mus., B.S., B.S.Crim.Just., B.S.Nurs., B.Soc.Work.
**Majors:** Accounting, American Citizenship, Anthropology, Applied Music, Art, Biology, Chemistry, Communication Arts, Computer Information Systems, Corrections, Criminal Justice, Economics, Education, Elementary Education, Engineering, English, Finance, French, General Business, General Studies, German, Health Education, History, Home Economics, Journalism, Management, Marketing, Mathematics, Medical Technology, Music, Music Education, Nursing, Philosophy, Physical Education, Physics/Astronomy, Political Science, Psychology, Radio/Television, Recreation, Religious Studies, Secondary Education, Social Work, Sociology, Spanish, Speech, Theatre.
**Distribution of degrees:** The majors with the highest enrollment are business, nursing, and education; chemistry and mathematics have the lowest.
**Requirements:** General education requirement.
**Special:** Associate's degrees offered. Self-designed majors. Double majors. Dual degrees. Independent study. Pass/fail grading option. Internships. Graduate school at which undergraduates may take graduate-level courses. Preprofessional programs in law, medicine, dentistry, and optometry. Teacher certification in early childhood, elementary, secondary, and special education. Study abroad in Denmark, Japan, and the Netherlands. ROTC. AFROTC at U of Kansas.
**Honors:** Honors program.
**Academic Assistance:** Nonremedial tutoring.

**STUDENT LIFE. Housing:** Students may live on or off campus. Coed dorms. Sorority and fraternity housing. Off-campus privately-owned housing. On-campus married-student housing. 8% of students live in college housing.
**Social atmosphere:** Popular on-campus events include basketball and football games, Sneakers Night, and Homecoming. Among influential student groups are student government and Alpha Delta fraternity. On campus, students gather at the union and the library. Favorite off-campus spots include College Hill Bar, Pryor's Pub, Quincy MaGoo's, Pore Richard's, and The Great Wall.
**Services and counseling/handicapped student services:** Placement services. Health service. Counseling services for minority, military, veteran, and older students. Personal and psychological counseling. Career and academic guidance services. Physically disabled student services. Learning disabled program/services. Notetaking services. Tape recorders. Tutors. Reader services for the blind.
**Campus organizations:** Undergraduate student government. Student newspaper (Review, published once/week). Yearbook. TV station. Symphonette, orchestra, band, ensembles, Washburn Singers, choirs, debating, Washburn Players, activities board, judo and modern dance clubs, College Republicans, Young Democrats, departmental groups, 70 organizations in all. Four fraternities, all with chapter houses; four sororities, all with chapter houses. 5% of men join a fraternity. 5% of women join a sorority.
**Religious organizations:** Campus Catholic Center, Ecumenical Christian Ministries, Fellowship of Christian Athletes.
**Minority/foreign student organizations:** BALSA, Black Student Alliance, Latin American Student Service. International Student Club.

**ATHLETICS. Physical education requirements:** Two semesters of physical education required.
**Intercollegiate competition:** 5% of students participate. Baseball (M), basketball (M,W), cheerleading (M,W), football (M), golf (M), softball (W), tennis (M,W), volleyball (W). Member of MIAA, NCAA Division II.
**Intramural and club sports:** Intramural basketball, flag football, volleyball. Men's club crew, soccer, volleyball, weight lifting. Women's club crew.

**ADMISSIONS. Academic basis for candidate selection** (in order of priority): Secondary school record, standardized test scores.
**Requirements:** Graduation from secondary school is required; GED is accepted. No specific distribution of secondary school units required. Minimum 2.0 GPA required of out-of-state applicants. ACT is recommended; SAT may be substituted. Campus visit recommended. Off-campus interviews available with an admissions representative.
**Procedure:** Take SAT or ACT by November of 12th year. Visit college for interview by January of 12th year. Suggest filing application by January. Application deadline is July. Notification of admission on rolling basis. No set date by which applicants must accept offer. $100 room deposit, refundable until August 1. Freshmen accepted for terms other than fall.
**Special programs:** Admission may be deferred one year. Credit and/or placement may be granted through CEEB Advanced Placement exams for scores of 3 or higher. Credit may be granted through CLEP general exams, DANTES exams, and military experience. Credit and placement may be granted through ACT PEP and challenge exams. Concurrent enrollment program.
**Transfer students:** Transfer students accepted for terms other than fall. In fall 1993, 40% of all new students were transfers into all classes. 842 transfer applications were received, 812 were accepted. Application deadline is July 1 for fall; December 1 for spring. Minimum 2.0 GPA recommended. Lowest course grade accepted is "D." Maximum number of transferable credits is 64 semester hours from a two-year school and 94 semester hours from a four-year school. At least 30 semester hours must be completed at the university to receive degree.
**Admissions contact:** Greg Gomez, III, Ed.D., Director of Admissions Process. 913 231-1010, extension 1625.

**FINANCIAL AID. Available aid:** Pell grants, SEOG, state scholarships, school scholarships and grants, private scholarships and grants, ROTC scholarships, academic merit scholarships, athletic scholarships, and aid for undergraduate foreign students. Perkins Loans (NDSL), PLUS, Stafford Loans (GSL), and SLS. Deferred payment plan.
**Supporting data/closing dates:** FAFSA/FAF/FFS: Priority filing date is March 15. School's own aid application: Priority filing date is March 15. Notification of awards begins April 1.
**Financial aid contact:** Joe McGreevy, M.S., Director of Financial Aid. 913 231-1010, extension 1451.

**STUDENT EMPLOYMENT.** College Work/Study Program. Institutional employment. 65% of full-time undergraduates work on campus during school year. Students may expect to earn an average of $1,800 during school year. Off-campus part-time employment opportunities rated "excellent."

**COMPUTER FACILITIES.** IBM/IBM-compatible and Macintosh/Apple microcomputers. Students may access IBM, Prime minicomputer/mainframe systems. Computer languages and software packages include BMDP, COBOL, FORTRAN, Info, LISP, MINITAB, Oracle, Pascal, Prolog, RPG, SAS, SPSS-X. Computer facilities are available to all students.
**Fees:** None.

**GRADUATE CAREER DATA.** Highest graduate school enrollments: Kansas State U. 40% of graduates choose careers in business and industry. Companies and businesses that hire graduates: Blue Cross/Blue Shield, Fleming, Internal Revenue Service, Koch Industries, Main Hurdman, Mize Houser and Co., Southwestern Bell, State of Kansas.

**PROMINENT ALUMNI/AE.** Robert Dole, U.S. senator, Kansas; Georgia Neese Gray, first woman treasurer of the U.S.; Dr. Earl Sutherland, Nobel Laureate in medicine; Joe Morris, vice-president and chief counsel, Shell Oil.

# Wichita State University

**Wichita, KS 67260-0113 316 689-3456**

**1993-94 Costs.** Tuition: $1,995 (state residents), $6,501 (out-of-state). Room & board: $3,005. Fees, books, misc. academic expenses (school's estimate): $276.
**Enrollment.** Undergraduates: 4,811 men, 5,233 women (full-time). Freshman class: 2,901 applicants, 2,236 accepted, 1,200 enrolled. Graduate enrollment: 1,266 men, 1,611 women.
**Test score averages/ranges.** Average ACT scores: 21 English, 20 math, 21 composite.
**Faculty.** 467 full-time; 20 part-time. 87% of faculty holds doctoral degree. Student/faculty ratio: 15 to 1.
**Selectivity rating.** Less competitive.

**PROFILE.** Wichita State is a public, comprehensive university. Founded in 1895 as a private college, it joined the state system of higher education in 1964. Programs are offered through the Colleges of Education, Engineering, Fine Arts, Health Professions, and Liberal Arts and Sciences; the Graduate School; the School of Business; and University College. Its 330-acre, urban campus is located in Wichita.

**Accreditation:** NCACS. Professionally accredited by the Accreditation Board for Engineering and Technology, the American Assembly of Collegiate Schools of Business, the American Bar Association, the American Dental Association, the American Medical Association (CAHEA), the American Physical Therapy Association, the American Speech-Language-Hearing Association, the Committee on Allied Health Education and Accreditation, the Council on Social Work Education, the National Association of Schools of Dance, the National Association of Schools of Music, the National Council for Accreditation of Teacher Education, the National League for Nursing.
**Religious orientation:** Wichita State University is nonsectarian; no religious requirements.
**Library:** Collections totaling over 926,440 volumes, 4,103 periodical subscriptions, and 830,024 microform items.
**Special facilities/museums:** Art museum, performance hall, media resource center, institute of aviation research, institute of logopedics, supersonic wind tunnels.
**Athletic facilities:** Gymnasiums, basketball, handball, racquetball, tennis, and volleyball courts, swimming pool, fitness and weight rooms, bowling lanes, multipurpose athletic center.

**STUDENT BODY. Undergraduate profile:** 86% are state residents; 35% are transfers. 2.8% Asian-American, 5.4% Black, 2.8% Hispanic, .8% Native American, 76.6% White, 11.6% Other. Average age of undergraduates is 29.
**Freshman profile:** 59% of accepted applicants took ACT.
**Undergraduate achievement:** 15% of fall 1992 freshmen returned for fall 1993 term. 54% of students who completed a degree program went on to graduate study within one year.
**Foreign students:** 899 students are from out of the country. Countries represented include Indonesia, Japan, Korea, Malaysia, Pakistan, and Taiwan; 73 in all.

**PROGRAMS OF STUDY. Degrees:** B.A., B.Art Ed., B.Bus.Admin., B.F.A., B.Gen.Studies, B.Hlth.Sci., B.Mus., B.Mus.Ed., B.S., B.S.Aero.Eng., B.S.Elec.Eng., B.S.Indust.Eng., B.S.Mech.Eng., B.S.Nurs.
**Majors:** Accounting, Aeronautical Engineering, American Studies, Anthropology, Art, Art Education, Art History, Aviation Management, Biology, Business, Business Administration, Business Management, Business Marketing Management, Chemistry, Communications, Computer Science, Criminal Justice Studies, Dance, Economics, Educational Administration, Educational Psychology, Electrical Engineering, Elementary Education, English, Entrepreneurship, Finance, Fine Arts, French, General Studies, Geology, German, Gerontology, Graphic Design, Health/Medical Administration, Health Systems/Health Services Administration, History, Human Resources Management, Industrial Engineering, International Business, Latin, Marketing, Mathematics, Mechanical Engineering, Medical Records Administration, Medical Technologies, Minority Studies, Music, Music Composition, Music Education, Music Performance, Music Theory, Nursing, Philosophy, Physical Education, Physician's Assistant, Physics, Political Science, Production Management, Psychology, Real Estate, Secondary Education, Social Work, Sociology, Spanish, Speech Pathology/Audiology, Student Counseling/Personnel Services, Studio Arts, Visual/Performing Arts, Women's Studies.
**Distribution of degrees:** The majors with the highest enrollment are liberal arts/science, business administration, and health professions; American studies, Latin, and chemistry have the lowest.
**Requirements:** General education requirement.
**Special:** Minors offered. Associate's degrees offered. Double majors. Dual degrees. Independent study. Accelerated study. Pass/fail grading option. Internships. Cooperative education programs. Graduate school at which undergraduates may take graduate-level courses. Preprofessional programs in law, medicine, veterinary science, pharmacy, dentistry, optometry, podiatry, and physical therapy. Combined bachelor's/master's programs in accounting and engineering. Teacher certification in early childhood, elementary, secondary, and special education. Certification in specific subject areas. Study abroad in England, France, Germany, Italy, Mexico, and Spain.
**Honors:** Phi Beta Kappa. Honors program.
**Academic Assistance:** Remedial reading, writing, math, and study skills. Nonremedial tutoring.

**STUDENT LIFE. Housing:** All unmarried freshmen must live on campus unless living with family within a 30-mile radius. Coed, women's, and men's dorms. Sorority and fraternity housing. Off-campus privately-owned housing. 3% of students live in college housing.
**Social atmosphere:** "The average age of students at WSU is 28," reports the student newspaper. "It is an urban school full of nontraditional students, thus making no groups dominant." Basketball games are among the popular events at WSU. "The football program was recently dropped, partially due to poor attendance." Favorite on-campus meeting places include the campus activities center, Copperfield's, and the Union Pub. Off campus, students frequent Kirby's Bar.
**Services and counseling/handicapped student services:** Placement services. Health service. Women's center. Day care. Counseling services for minority, military, veteran, and older students. Birth control, personal, and psychological counseling. Career and academic guidance services. Religious counseling. Physically disabled student services. Learning disabled services. Notetaking services. Reader services for the blind.
**Campus organizations:** Undergraduate student government. Student newspaper (Sunflower, published three times/week). Literary magazine. Radio and TV stations. Orchestra, choir, jazz ensemble, opera groups, experimental theatre, Orchesis, debating, political, service, and special-interest groups, 195 organizations in all. 12 fraternities, eight chapter houses; eight sororities, four chapter houses. 2% of men join a fraternity. 2% of women join a sorority.
**Religious organizations:** 9 religious groups.
**Minority/foreign student organizations:** 17 minority student groups. 14 foreign student groups.

**ATHLETICS. Physical education requirements:** None.
**Intercollegiate competition:** 8% of students participate. Baseball (M), basketball (M,W), cheerleading (M,W), cross-country (M,W), golf (M,W), softball (W), tennis (M,W), track (indoor) (M,W), track (outdoor) (M,W), track and field (indoor) (M,W), track and field (outdoor) (M,W), volleyball (W). Member of Missouri Valley Athletic Conference, NCAA Division I.
**Intramural and club sports:** 3% of students participate. Intramural badminton, basketball, flag football, free-throw shooting, golf, homerun contest, hot-shot basketball, racquetball, soccer, softball, swimming, tennis, volleyball. Men's club bowling, crew, lacrosse, martial arts, racquetball, scuba, sky diving, soccer, swimming, wrestling. Women's club bowling, crew, martial arts, racquetball, scuba, sky diving, soccer, swimming.

**ADMISSIONS. Academic basis for candidate selection** (in order of priority): Secondary school record, standardized test scores.
**Requirements:** Graduation from secondary school is required; GED is accepted. No specific distribution of secondary school units required. Open admission for in-state applicants who are graduates of accredited secondary schools. Minimum composite ACT score of 21, rank in top half of secondary school class, or minimum 2.0 GPA required of out-of-state applicants. Additional units in English, speech, math, and science required of engineering program applicants. Additional units in English, speech, and algebra, and minimum 2.5 GPA required of business program applicants. Conditional admission possible for applicants not meeting standard requirements. ACT is required; SAT may be substituted. Off-campus interviews available with an admissions representative.
**Procedure:** Take SAT or ACT by fall of 12th year. Suggest filing application by March 15. Application deadline is September 1. Notification of admission on rolling basis. $100 nonrefundable room deposit. Freshmen accepted for terms other than fall.
**Special programs:** Admission may be deferred one year. Credit and/or placement may be granted through CEEB Advanced Placement exams for scores of 3 or higher. Credit and/or placement may be granted through CLEP general and subject exams. Credit may be granted through DANTES and challenge exams. Credit and placement may be granted through ACT PEP exams. Early entrance/early admission program. Concurrent enrollment program.
**Transfer students:** Transfer students accepted for terms other than fall. In fall 1993, 35% of all new students were transfers into all classes. 1,834 transfer applications were received, 1,462 were accepted. Minimum 2.0 GPA required. Lowest course grade accepted is "D." At least 30 semester hours must be completed at the university to receive degree.
**Admissions contact:** Rita Abent, Director of Admissions. 316 689-3085, 800 362-2594.

**FINANCIAL AID. Available aid:** Pell grants, SEOG, Federal Nursing Student Scholarships, state scholarships, school scholarships, private scholarships, academic merit scholarships, and athletic scholarships. Perkins Loans (NDSL), PLUS, Stafford Loans (GSL), school loans, and SLS. AMS.
**Financial aid statistics:** 40% of aid is not need-based. In 1993-94, 60% of all undergraduate applicants received aid; 40% of freshman applicants. Average amounts of aid awarded freshmen: Scholarships and grants, $556; loans, $805.
**Supporting data/closing dates:** FAFSA: Priority filing date is March 15. Notification of awards on rolling basis.
**Financial aid contact:** Larry Rector, Director of Financial Aid. 316 689-3430, 800 522-2978.

**STUDENT EMPLOYMENT.** College Work/Study Program. Institutional employment. 6% of full-time undergraduates work on campus during school year. Students may expect to earn an average of $1,700 during school year. Off-campus part-time employment opportunities rated "excellent."

**COMPUTER FACILITIES.** 2,600 IBM/IBM-compatible and Macintosh/Apple microcomputers; 600 are networked. Students may access Digital, IBM minicomputer/mainframe systems, BITNET, Internet. Residence halls may be equipped with stand-alone microcomputers, modems. Client/LAN operating systems include Apple/Macintosh, DOS, DEC. Computer languages and software packages include dBASE, Lotus 1-2-3, WordPerfect. Computer facilities are available to all students.
**Fees:** None.
**Hours:** 18 hours/day.

**GRADUATE CAREER DATA.** Companies and businesses that hire graduates: Koch Industries, Wichita public schools.

**PROMINENT ALUMNI/AE.** Barbara Uehling, chancellor, UC Santa Barbara; Samuel Ramey, Metropolitan Opera; Frank and Daniel Carney, co-founders, Pizza Hut; Thomas Devlin, chairperson, Rent-A-Center; Garner Shriver, former congressman; Bill Parcels, NFL coach.

# Kentucky

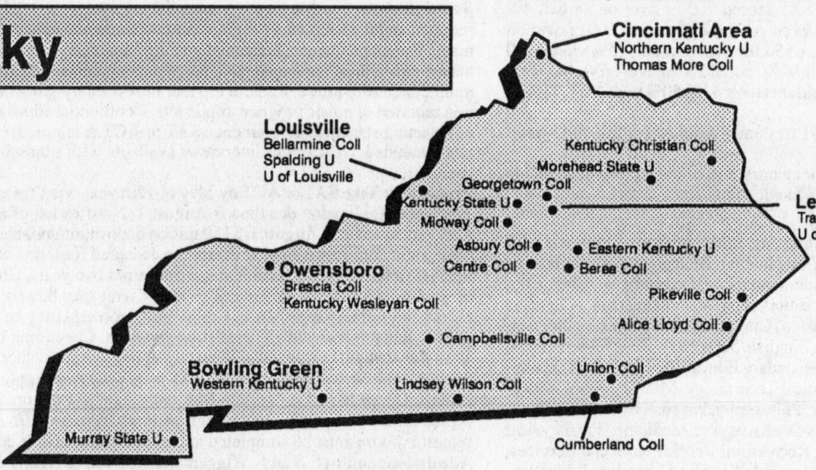


## Alice Lloyd College

**Pippa Passes, KY 41844** **606 368-2101**

**1993-94 Costs.** No tuition for students from the 76 Mountain counties (located in Ky., Ohio, Tenn., Va., and W.Va.). Tuition for students outside this area is $3,500 per academic year. Room: $1,100. Board: $1,380. Fees, books, misc. academic expenses (school's estimate): $1,040.
**Enrollment.** Undergraduates: 208 men, 338 women (full-time). Freshman class: 1,174 applicants, 610 accepted, 208 enrolled.
**Test score averages/ranges.** Average SAT scores: 450 verbal, 425 math. Range of SAT scores of middle 50%: 380-490 verbal, 360-470 math. Average ACT scores: 21 English, 20 math, 21 composite. Range of ACT scores of middle 50%: 18-24 English, 17-22 math.
**Faculty.** 27 full-time; 5 part-time. 60% of faculty holds highest degree in specific field. Student/faculty ratio: 17 to 1.
**Selectivity rating.** Noncompetitive.

**PROFILE.** Alice Lloyd, founded in 1923, is a private, liberal arts college. The 256-acre campus is in rural Pippa Passes, 150 miles southeast of Lexington.

**Accreditation:** SACS.
**Religious orientation:** Alice Lloyd College is nonsectarian; no religious requirements.
**Library:** Collections totaling over 60,000 volumes, 300 periodical subscriptions, and 3,000 microform items.
**Special facilities/museums:** Photographic archives, oral history museum, Appalachian collection, on-campus day care center, kindergarten, elementary, and secondary school.
**Athletic facilities:** Gymnasiums, baseball and softball fields, swimming pool, tennis courts, recreation rooms.
**STUDENT BODY. Undergraduate profile:** 80% are state residents; 10% are transfers. 1% Black, 99% White. Average age of undergraduates is 24.
**Freshman profile:** 5% of freshmen who took SAT scored 600 or over on verbal, 5% scored 600 or over on math; 20% scored 500 or over on verbal, 18% scored 500 or over on math; 95% scored 400 or over on verbal, 95% scored 400 or over on math; 100% scored 300 or over on verbal, 100% scored 300 or over on math. 5% of freshmen who took ACT scored 30 or over on English, 5% scored 30 or over on math, 5% scored 30 or over on composite; 40% scored 24 or over on English, 35% scored 24 or over on math, 38% scored 24 or over on composite; 95% scored 18 or over on English, 85% scored 18 or over on math, 91% scored 18 or over on composite; 100% scored 12 or over on English, 100% scored 12 or over on math, 100% scored 12 or over on composite. 5% of accepted applicants took SAT; 95% took ACT. 99% of freshmen come from public schools.
**Undergraduate achievement:** 49% of fall 1991 freshmen returned for fall 1992 term. 85% of students who completed a degree program went on to graduate study.
**Foreign students:** Eight students are from out of the country. Countries represented include Ethiopia, Honduras, India, Jamaica, and Uganda; five in all.
**PROGRAMS OF STUDY. Degrees:** B.A., B.S.
**Majors:** Accounting, Biology, Biology/Secondary Education, Business, Early Elementary Education, English, English/Secondary Education, History, Math and Physical Sciences/Secondary Education, Middle School Education, Physical Education, Science/Secondary Education, Social Studies/Secondary Education.
**Distribution of degrees:** The majors with the highest enrollment are early elementary education and middle school education; secondary education, biology, and history have the lowest.
**Requirements:** General education requirement.
**Academic regulations:** Minimum 2.00 GPA must be maintained.
**Special:** Required work-study program enables students to help pay for their own education while learning leadership skills, self-discipline, and self-reliance. Preprofessional programs in law, medicine, pharmacy, dentistry, optometry, and physical therapy. Member of Council of Independent Colleges (Tuition Exchange Program). Teacher certification in elementary and secondary education.
**Academic Assistance:** Remedial reading, writing, math, and study skills. Nonremedial tutoring.
**ADMISSIONS. Academic basis for candidate selection** (in order of priority): Secondary school record, standardized test scores, class rank, school's recommendation, essay.
**Nonacademic basis for candidate selection:** Character and personality, extracurricular participation, and particular talent or ability are emphasized. Geographical distribution is considered.
**Requirements:** Graduation from secondary school is recommended; GED is accepted. 14 units and the following program of study are required: 4 units of English, 2 units of math, 2 units of lab science, 3 units of social studies, 1 unit of history. Minimum composite ACT score of 16 (SAT scores of 350 in both verbal and math), rank in top three-fifths of secondary school class, and minimum 2.25 GPA required. Minimum 2.5 GPA required of education program applicants. ACT is required; SAT may be substituted. Campus visit and interview recommended. Off-campus interviews available with an admissions representative.
**Procedure:** Take SAT or ACT by June of 12th year. Suggest filing application by May 1; no deadline. Notification of admission on rolling basis. No set date by which applicants must accept offer. $50 nonrefundable room deposit. Freshmen accepted for terms other than fall.
**Special programs:** Credit and/or placement may be granted through CEEB Advanced Placement exams for scores of 4 or higher. Credit and/or placement may be granted through CLEP general and subject exams. Credit and placement may be granted through ACT PEP exams.
**Transfer students:** Transfer students accepted for terms other than fall. In fall 1992, 10% of all new students were transfers into all classes. 60 transfer applications were received, 40 were accepted. Application deadline is August 1 for fall; December 1 for spring. Minimum 2.0 GPA required. Lowest course grade accepted is "C." Maximum number of transferable credits is 64 semester hours. At least 30 semester hours must be completed at the college to receive degree.
**Admissions contact:** Bill Melton, M.S., Director of Admissions. 606 368-2101, extension 4404.
**FINANCIAL AID. Available aid:** Pell grants, SEOG, state grants, school scholarships and grants, private scholarships and grants, academic merit scholarships, athletic scholarships, and aid for undergraduate foreign students. Perkins Loans (NDSL), PLUS, Stafford Loans (GSL), state loans, private loans, and SLS. Deferred payment plan.
**Supporting data/closing dates:** FAFSA/FAF/FFS: Accepted on rolling basis. Notification of awards on rolling basis.
**Financial aid contact:** Nancy M. Melton, M.A., Director of Financial Aid. 606 368-2101, extension 4801.

## Asbury College

**Wilmore, KY 40390** **606 858-3511**

**1993-94 Costs.** Tuition: $8,322. Room: $1,166. Board: $1,494. Fees, books, misc. academic expenses (school's estimate): $623.
**Enrollment.** Undergraduates: 484 men, 589 women (full-time). Freshman class: 638 applicants, 485 accepted, 376 enrolled.
**Test score averages/ranges.** Average SAT scores: 950 combined. Range of SAT scores of middle 50%: 800-1050 combined. Average ACT scores: 23 composite. Range of ACT scores of middle 50%: 21-25 composite.
**Faculty.** 78 full-time; 40 part-time. 71% of faculty holds highest degree in specific field. Student/faculty ratio: 14 to 1.
**Selectivity rating.** Less competitive.

**PROFILE.** Asbury, founded in 1890, is a liberal arts college with religious emphasis. Its 400-acre campus is located in Wilmore, 15 miles from Lexington.

**Accreditation:** SACS. Professionally accredited by the National Association of Schools of Music.
**Religious orientation:** Asbury College is a nondenominational Christian school; nine semester hours of religion required.
**Library:** Collections totaling over 146,972 volumes, 599 periodical subscriptions, and 10,059 microform items.
**Special facilities/museums:** Art gallery.
**Athletic facilities:** Gymnasiums, baseball, soccer, and softball fields, three-hole golf course, weight room, swimming pool, indoor running track, racquetball courts, diving boards.
**STUDENT BODY. Undergraduate profile:** 23% are state residents. 1% Asian-American, 1% Black, 1% Hispanic, 94% White, 3% Other. Average age of undergraduates is 21.

**Freshman profile:** 1% of freshmen who took SAT scored 700 or over on verbal, 4% scored 700 or over on math; 9% scored 600 or over on verbal, 20% scored 600 or over on math; 36% scored 500 or over on verbal, 46% scored 500 or over on math; 75% scored 400 or over on verbal, 86% scored 400 or over on math; 99% scored 300 or over on verbal, 99% scored 300 or over on math. 47% of accepted applicants took SAT; 50% took ACT. 71% of freshmen come from public schools.
**Undergraduate achievement:** 74% of fall 1991 freshmen returned for fall 1992 term. 76% of entering class graduated.
**Foreign students:** 36 students are from out of the country. Countries represented include Canada, Japan, Kenya, Romania, and Russia; 16 in all.

**PROGRAMS OF STUDY. Degrees:** B.A., B.S.
**Majors:** Ancient Languages, Applied Mathematics, Art, Bible, Biology, Biology/Health Science, Biology/Medical Technology, Biology/Pre-Nursing, Biology/Secondary Education, Broadcast Communication, Business Administration/Management, Chemistry, Chemistry/Biology, Chemistry/Secondary Education, Christian Ministries, Christian Ministries/Journalism, Christian Ministries/Mission, Computer Science, Computer Science/Business, Elementary Education, English, English/Secondary Education, French, French/Secondary Education, History, History/Secondary Education, Journalism, Mathematics, Mathematics/Secondary Education, Medical Technology, Middle School Education, Missions, Music, Music Education, Nursing, Philosophy, Physical Education, Physical Education Teaching, Physical Science, Pre-Dentistry, Pre-Medicine, Pre-Physical Therapy, Pre-Veterinary Medicine, Psychology, Recreation, Recreation/Social Services, Social Studies Secondary Education, Sociology, Spanish, Spanish/Secondary Education, Speech Communication.
**Distribution of degrees:** The majors with the highest enrollment are education, business, and bible; computer science, philosophy, and French have the lowest.
**Requirements:** General education requirement.
**Academic regulations:** Minimum 2.0 GPA must be maintained.
**Special:** Minors offered in some majors and in accounting, art history, coaching, economics and physics, and theatre arts. Double majors. Dual degrees. Independent study. Pass/fail grading option. Internships. Preprofessional programs in medicine, veterinary science, dentistry, and physical therapy. 3-1 medical technology programs with U of Louisville, Daemon Coll, and Methodist Hospital (Pikeville). 3-2 engineering and nursing programs with U of Kentucky. Member of Christian College Consortium. American Studies Program (Washington, D.C.), Wesleyan Urban Coalition (Chicago). Member of Christian College Coalition Visitors Program. Teacher certification in elementary and secondary education. Certification in specific subject areas. Exchange programs abroad in Bolivia (Evangelical U) and Kenya (Highlands Bible Coll). Study abroad also in the United Kingdom, France, and Latin American countries.
**Honors:** Honor societies.
**Academic Assistance:** Remedial reading, writing, math, and study skills. Nonremedial tutoring.

**STUDENT LIFE. Housing:** All students under age 23 must live on campus unless living with family. Women's and men's dorms. Off-campus privately-owned housing. On-campus married-student housing. Government-subsidized housing. Seminary housing. 84% of students live in college housing.
**Social atmosphere:** The Grille (student center and restaurant), the Luce Center sports complex, and several student centers run by religious organizations are popular on-campus gathering places. Off-campus hot spots include Applebee's, Hardee's, and dollar movie houses. Influential groups include Christian Service Association, Community Involvement, Foreign Missions Council, Fellowship of Christian Athletes, Salvation Army Student Fellowship, WGM, OMS, SGA, student broadcasters, and musical performers. Popular events on campus include homecoming, movie marathons, TWIRP week (girls ask guys out), artist series, sporting events, Christmas tree lighting, and Missions and Holiness conference. According to the editor of the student newspaper, "Asbury is known for its friendly students and faculty; campus events are designed to create strong bonds within the community. The religious atmosphere is not stifling: Asburians know how to have "good, clean" fun, whether it's watching the wrestling society in action or just hanging out in Lexington area shops and restaurants."
**Services and counseling/handicapped student services:** Placement services. Health service. Counseling services for minority, military, veteran, and older students. Birth control, personal, and psychological counseling. Career and academic guidance services. Physically disabled student services. Learning disabled program/services. Tape recorders. Tutors.
**Campus organizations:** Undergraduate student government. Student newspaper (Collegian, published once/week). Literary magazine. Yearbook. Radio and TV stations. Concert band and choir, chess club, art club, speech and drama clubs, English, French, and Spanish clubs, psychology and social services clubs, community tutorial service, intramural council, Asburians for Life, Missionary Kid Fellowship, Student Music Educators, Young Democrats, Young Republicans, Married Student Fellowship, science club, 35 organizations in all.
**Religious organizations:** Alliance Student Fellowship, Christian Service Association, Christians in Action, Fellowship of Christian Athletes, Foreign Missions Council, Salvation Army Student Fellowship, WGM Student Involvement, OMS International, Religious Broadcasters.
**Minority/foreign student organizations:** BASIC. International Student Fellowship.

**ATHLETICS. Physical education requirements:** Three semester hours of physical education required.
**Intercollegiate competition:** 10% of students participate. Baseball (M), basketball (M,W), cross-country (M,W), soccer (M), softball (W), swimming (M,W), tennis (M,W), volleyball (W). Member of Kentucky Women's Intercollegiate Conference, NAIA, NCCAA.
**Intramural and club sports:** 60% of students participate. Intramural basketball, flag football, floor hockey, indoor soccer, soccer, softball, Wiffle ball.

**ADMISSIONS. Academic basis for candidate selection** (in order of priority): Secondary school record, standardized test scores, school's recommendation, class rank, essay.
**Nonacademic basis for candidate selection:** Character and personality and extracurricular participation are emphasized. Particular talent or ability, geographical distribution, and alumni/ae relationship are considered.
**Requirements:** Graduation from secondary school is required; GED is accepted. 15 units required and the following program of study recommended: 4 units of English, 3 units of math, 2 units of science, 2 units of foreign language, 2 units of social studies, 1 unit of history. Minimum combined SAT score of 830 (composite ACT score of 20) and minimum 2.0 GPA required. Rank in top half of secondary school class recommended. Audition required of music program applicants. Conditional admission possible for applicants not meeting standard requirements. SAT or ACT is required. Campus visit and interview recommended. Off-campus interviews available with admissions and alumni representatives.
**Procedure:** Take SAT or ACT by May of 12th year. Visit college for interview by July of 12th year. Application deadline is August 1. Notification of admission on rolling basis. Reply is required by August 1. $150 tuition deposit, refundable until May 1. $25 room deposit, refundable until June 1. Freshmen accepted for terms other than fall.
**Special programs:** Admission may be deferred two years. Credit and/or placement may be granted through CLEP general exams. Credit may be granted through CLEP subject exams and military experience. Credit and placement may be granted through challenge exams. Early entrance/early admission program. Concurrent enrollment program.
**Transfer students:** Transfer students accepted for terms other than fall. In fall 1992, 206 transfer applications were received, 135 were accepted. Application deadline is August 1 for fall; December 15 for spring. Minimum 2.0 GPA required. Lowest course grade accepted is "C." Maximum number of transferable credits is 75 semester hours. At least 49 semester hours must be completed at the college to receive degree.
**Admissions contact:** Stan F. Wiggam, M.S., Dean of Admissions. 606 858-3511, extension 2142.

**FINANCIAL AID. Available aid:** Pell grants, SEOG, state scholarships and grants, school scholarships and grants, private scholarships and grants, and academic merit scholarships. Perkins Loans (NDSL), PLUS, Stafford Loans (GSL), state loans, school loans, and SLS. Knight Tuition Plans, deferred payment plan, and family tuition reduction. Institutional ten-month payment plan.
**Financial aid statistics:** 9% of aid is not need-based. In 1992-93, 94% of all undergraduate applicants received aid; 97% of freshman applicants. Average amounts of aid awarded freshmen: Scholarships and grants, $3,012; loans, $3,298.
**Supporting data/closing dates:** FAFSA/FAF/FFS: Priority filing date is March 15. School's own aid application: Priority filing date is March 15. Notification of awards begins April 1.
**Financial aid contact:** Troy R. Martin, M.B.A., Financial Aid Director. 606 858-3511, extension 2195.

**STUDENT EMPLOYMENT.** College Work/Study Program. Institutional employment. 47% of full-time undergraduates work on campus during school year. Students may expect to earn an average of $1,000 during school year. Off-campus part-time employment opportunities rated "fair."

**COMPUTER FACILITIES.** 53 IBM/IBM-compatible and Macintosh/Apple microcomputers; 32 are networked. Students may access AT&T minicomputer/mainframe systems. Computer languages and software packages include BASIC, C, COBOL, FORTRAN, FoxBase, Harvard Graphics, LOGO, Lotus 1-2-3, MINITAB, PageMaker, Pascal, SPSS, WordPerfect, Windows. Computer facilities are available to all students.
**Fees:** None.
**Hours:** 8 AM-11 PM.

**GRADUATE CAREER DATA.** Highest graduate school enrollments: Asbury Theological Seminary, Emory U, Georgia State U, U of Kentucky, U of Louisville. Companies and businesses that hire graduates: Business firms, churches, colleges, mission agencies, schools, and social service agencies.

**PROMINENT ALUMNI/AE.** Bishop J. Waskom Pickett, missionary and churchman; Dr. Carl Fliermans, scientist, epidemiologist and biochemist; Dr. David Seamands, author, professor and churchman.

# Bellarmine College

**Louisville, KY 40205** **502 452-8211**

**1994-95 Costs.** Tuition: $8,840. Room: $1,950. Board: $2,500. Fees, books, misc. academic expenses (school's estimate): $700.
**Enrollment.** Undergraduates: 489 men, 709 women (full-time). Freshman class: 808 applicants, 711 accepted, 310 enrolled. Graduate enrollment: 201 men, 334 women.
**Test score averages/ranges.** Average SAT scores: 474 verbal, 515 math. Range of SAT scores of middle 50%: 410-530 verbal, 460-580 math. Average ACT scores: 23 English, 22 math, 23 composite. Range of ACT scores of middle 50%: 20-26 composite.
**Faculty.** 89 full-time; 83 part-time. 82% of faculty holds doctoral degree. Student/faculty ratio: 13 to 1.
**Selectivity rating.** Less competitive.

**PROFILE.** Bellarmine is a church-affiliated, liberal arts college. Founded as a college for men in 1950, it adopted coeducation when it merged with Ursuline College in 1968. Its 115-acre campus is located in Louisville.

**Accreditation:** SACS. Professionally accredited by the National League for Nursing.
**Religious orientation:** Bellarmine College is affiliated with the Roman Catholic Church; three semesters of theology required.
**Library:** Collections totaling over 115,000 volumes, and 1,900 periodical subscriptions.
**Special facilities/museums:** Art gallery.
**Athletic facilities:** Gymnasium, basketball, sand volleyball, and tennis courts, golf course, baseball, field hockey, soccer, and softball fields, free weight, Nautilus, and Universal rooms.

**STUDENT BODY. Undergraduate profile:** 79% are state residents; 10% are transfers. 1% Asian-American, 2% Black, 1% Hispanic, 95% White, 1% Other. Average age of undergraduates is 20.
**Freshman profile:** 3% of freshmen who took SAT scored 700 or over on math; 12% scored 600 or over on verbal, 21% scored 600 or over on math; 41% scored 500 or over on

verbal, 63% scored 500 or over on math; 84% scored 400 or over on verbal, 89% scored 400 or over on math; 100% scored 300 or over on verbal, 100% scored 300 or over on math. 43% of accepted applicants took SAT; 92% took ACT. 43% of freshmen come from public schools.
**Undergraduate achievement:** 75% of fall 1992 freshmen returned for fall 1993 term. 55% of entering class graduated. 20% of students who completed a degree program immediately went on to graduate study.
**Foreign students:** 16 students are from out of the country. Countries represented include Bahamas, Canada, England, and India; 11 in all.

**PROGRAMS OF STUDY. Degrees:** B.A., B.S., B.S.Nurs.
**Majors:** Accounting, Art, Biology, Business Administration, Chemistry, Communication, Computer Engineering, Computer Science, Economics, Elementary Education, English, Health Administration, History, Learning/Behavior Disorders, Mathematics, Mathematics/Actuarial Science, Middle School Education, Music, Nursing, Philosophy, Political Science, Psychology, Secondary Education, Sociology, Special Education, Theology.
**Distribution of degrees:** The majors with the highest enrollment are business administration, accounting, and nursing; philosophy, theology, and sociology have the lowest.
**Requirements:** General education requirement.
**Academic regulations:** Minimum 2.00 GPA must be maintained.
**Special:** Minors offered in all majors except elementary education, nursing, and middle school education. Double majors. Dual degrees. Independent study. Pass/fail grading option. Internships. Graduate school at which undergraduates may take graduate-level courses. Preprofessional programs in law, medicine, veterinary science, pharmacy, and dentistry. 2-2 nursing program. B.A./M.B.A. program. Pre-engineering program with U of Kentucky and U of Detroit Mercy. Member of Kentuckiana Metroversity; exchange possible. Exchange programs with Indiana U Southeast, Jefferson Comm Coll, Louisville Presbyterian Seminary, U of Louisville, Southern Baptist Theological Seminary, and Spalding U. Teacher certification in elementary, secondary, and special education. Certification in specific subject areas. Study abroad in the Bahamas and in the Czech Republic. Member of International Student Exchange Program (ISEP). ROTC and AFROTC at U of Louisville.
**Honors:** Honors program. Honor societies.
**Academic Assistance:** Remedial study skills. Nonremedial tutoring.

**STUDENT LIFE. Housing:** All out-of-town unmarried freshmen and sophomores must live on campus unless living with family. Coed, women's, and men's dorms. 33% of students live in college housing.
**Social atmosphere:** According to the editor of the student newspaper, "Bellarmine is a small private college that is a warm and friendly community." Students meet in the cafeteria on campus and at Shananigans Pub off campus. Among popular events of the school year are basketball and soccer games and the dances that follow, the Halloween Dance held on the Belle of Louisville, Derby Week's "Chow Wagon," and on-campus concerts.
**Services and counseling/handicapped student services:** Placement services. Health service. Counseling services for older students. Personal and psychological counseling. Career and academic guidance services. Religious counseling. Physically disabled student services. Notetaking services. Tutors.
**Campus organizations:** Undergraduate student government. Student newspaper (Concord, published once/week). Literary magazine. Yearbook. Pep band, chorus, debating, drama group, Rotoract, service and special-interest groups, 40 organizations in all. One fraternity, no chapter house.
**Religious organizations:** Campus Ministry, Fellowship of Christian Athletes.
**Minority/foreign student organizations:** UNITY.

**ATHLETICS. Physical education requirements:** None.
**Intercollegiate competition:** 25% of students participate. Baseball (M), basketball (M,W), cheerleading (M,W), cross-country (M,W), field hockey (W), golf (M,W), soccer (M,W), softball (W), tennis (M,W), track (indoor) (M,W), track (outdoor) (M,W), track and field (indoor) (M,W), track and field (outdoor) (M,W), volleyball (W). Member of Great Lakes Valley Conference, Kentucky Women's Intercollegiate Conference, NCAA Division II.
**Intramural and club sports:** 65% of students participate. Intramural basketball, flashball, free throw, golf, martial arts, pool, softball, table tennis, tennis, volleyball, weight lifting. Men's club crew, volleyball.

**ADMISSIONS. Academic basis for candidate selection** (in order of priority): Secondary school record, class rank, standardized test scores, school's recommendation, essay.
**Nonacademic basis for candidate selection:** Extracurricular participation is emphasized. Character and personality, particular talent or ability, geographical distribution, and alumni/ae relationship are considered.
**Requirements:** Graduation from secondary school is recommended; GED is accepted. No specific distribution of secondary school units required. Minimum combined SAT score of 900 (composite ACT score of 21), rank in top half of secondary school class, and minimum 2.5 GPA recommended. Audition required of music program applicants. Conditional admission possible for applicants not meeting standard requirements. SAT or ACT is required. Campus visit and interview recommended. Off-campus interviews available with an admissions representative.
**Procedure:** Take SAT or ACT by December of 12th year. Visit college for interview by fall of 12th year. Suggest filing application by February 1; no deadline. Notification of admission on rolling basis. Reply is required by May 1. $50 tuition deposit, refundable until May 15. $200 room deposit, refundable until August 1. Freshmen accepted for terms other than fall.
**Special programs:** Admission may be deferred one year. Credit and/or placement may be granted through CEEB Advanced Placement exams for scores of 3 or higher. Credit may be granted through CLEP general and subject exams, Regents College, ACT PEP, DANTES, and challenge exams, and military and life experience. Early entrance/early admission program. Concurrent enrollment program.
**Transfer students:** Transfer students accepted for terms other than fall. In fall 1993, 10% of all new students were transfers into all classes. 263 transfer applications were received, 237 were accepted. Application deadline is rolling for fall; rolling for spring. Minimum 2.0 GPA required. Lowest course grade accepted is "D." Maximum number of transferable credits is 90 semester hours. At least 36 semester hours must be completed at the college to receive degree.
**Admissions contact:** R. Edwin Wilkes, Ed.M., Dean of Admissions and Financial. 502 452-8131, 800 274-4723.

**FINANCIAL AID. Available aid:** Pell grants, SEOG, state scholarships and grants, school scholarships and grants, private scholarships and grants, ROTC scholarships, academic merit scholarships, athletic scholarships, aid for undergraduate foreign students, and United Negro College Fund. Perkins Loans (NDSL), PLUS, Stafford Loans (GSL), school loans, private loans, and SLS. Loans available to nursing students through area hospitals. Tuition Plan Inc., Knight Tuition Plans, AMS, and deferred payment plan.
**Financial aid statistics:** 40% of aid is not need-based. In 1993-94, 99% of all undergraduate applicants received aid; 99% of freshman applicants. Average amounts of aid awarded freshmen: Scholarships and grants, $4,180; loans, $2,711.
**Supporting data/closing dates:** FAFSA: Priority filing date is March 15. Notification of awards on rolling basis.
**Financial aid contact:** Mike Petter, Director of Financial Aid. 502 452-8131, 800 274-4723.

**STUDENT EMPLOYMENT.** College Work/Study Program. Institutional employment. 18% of full-time undergraduates work on campus during school year. Students may expect to earn an average of $2,250 during school year. Off-campus part-time employment opportunities rated "excellent."

**COMPUTER FACILITIES.** 80 IBM/IBM-compatible, Macintosh/Apple, and RISC-/UNIX-based microcomputers; 20 are networked. Students may access IBM minicomputer/mainframe systems, BITNET, Internet. Residence halls may be equipped with stand-alone microcomputers. Client/LAN operating systems include Apple/Macintosh, DOS, UNIX/XENIX/AIX, Windows NT, Novell. Computer languages and software packages include BASIC, C, C++, COBOL, dBASE, Derive, FORTRAN, J SETL, Linear Kit, LISP, Lotus, Pascal, Prolog, SPSS, WordPerfect, WordStar. Computer facilities are available to all students.
**Fees:** $42 computer fee per course.
**Hours:** 8 AM-midn.

**GRADUATE CAREER DATA.** Graduate school percentages: 6% enter law school. 5% enter medical school. 2% enter dental school. 9% enter graduate business programs. 6% enter graduate arts and sciences programs. Highest graduate school enrollments: U of Kentucky, U of Louisville. 40% of graduates choose careers in business and industry. Companies and businesses that hire graduates: Big Six accounting firms, Blue Cross & Blue Shield, Capital Holding, Cotten Allen, General Electric, Jefferson county schools, KFC, Louisville Gas & Electric, Monroe-Shine.

**PROMINENT ALUMNI/AE.** John MacLeod, basketball coach, U of Notre Dame; Brigadier General William Donahue, US Air Force.

# Berea College

**Berea, KY 40404** **606 986-9341**

**1994-95 Costs.** Tuition: None. Room: $1,355. Board: $1,479. Fees, books, misc. academic expenses (school's estimate): $638.
**Enrollment.** Undergraduates: 690 men, 850 women (full-time). Freshman class: 1,836 applicants, 599 accepted, 455 enrolled.
**Test score averages/ranges.** Average SAT scores: 465 verbal, 514 math. Average ACT scores: 22 composite. Range of ACT scores of middle 50%: 19-24 composite.
**Faculty.** 112 full-time; 16 part-time. 81% of faculty holds highest degree in specific field. Student/faculty ratio: 13 to 1.
**Selectivity rating.** Competitive.

**PROFILE.** Berea, founded in 1855, is a college with religious orientation. Its 140-acre campus is located in Berea, 40 miles south of Lexington.
**Accreditation:** SACS. Professionally accredited by the American Dietetic Association, the National Council for Accreditation of Teacher Education, the National League for Nursing.
**Religious orientation:** Berea College is a nondenominational Christian school; one term of religion required.
**Library:** Collections totaling over 288,116 volumes, 1,583 periodical subscriptions, and 83,450 microform items.
**Special facilities/museums:** Appalachian and geology museums, nursery school lab for child psychology and development majors, language labs, 1,100-acre farm, planetarium with observatory and 16-inch telescope.
**Athletic facilities:** Gymnasium, basketball, handball, racquetball, squash, and tennis courts, dance studio, baseball, intramural, soccer, and softball fields, weight room.

**STUDENT BODY. Undergraduate profile:** 49% are state residents; 10% are transfers. 1% Asian-American, 9% Black, 83% White, 7% Other. Average age of undergraduates is 20.
**Freshman profile:** 2% of freshmen who took SAT scored 700 or over on math; 8% scored 600 or over on verbal, 23% scored 600 or over on math; 37% scored 500 or over on verbal, 57% scored 500 or over on math; 76% scored 400 or over on verbal, 85% scored 400 or over on math; 98% scored 300 or over on verbal, 99% scored 300 or over on math. 25% of accepted applicants took SAT; 87% took ACT. 93% of freshmen come from public schools.
**Undergraduate achievement:** 73% of fall 1992 freshmen returned for fall 1993 term.
**Foreign students:** 104 students are from out of the country. Countries represented include China, Greece, India, Kenya, Liberia, and Tibet; 52 in all.

**PROGRAMS OF STUDY. Degrees:** B.A., B.S.
**Majors:** Agriculture, Art, Biology, Business Administration, Chemistry, Child Development, Child/Family Studies, Classical Languages, Dietetics, Economics, Education, English, French, German, History, Hotel Management, Mathematics, Music, Nursing, Philosophy, Physical Education, Physics, Political Science, Psychology, Religion, Sociology, Spanish, Technology/Industrial Arts, Theatre.

**Distribution of degrees:** The majors with the highest enrollment are business administration, English, and child development; religion, theatre, and philosophy have the lowest.
**Requirements:** General education requirement.
**Academic regulations:** Freshmen must maintain minimum 1.67 GPA; sophomores, juniors, seniors, 2.0 GPA.
**Special:** Minors offered in some majors and in computer science, health, Appalachian, black, Latin, and women's studies. Area major in elementary education. Courses offered in computer science, geography, geology, library science, and speech. Student work program is integral part of college curriculum. Self-designed majors. Double majors. Dual degrees. Independent study. Internships. Preprofessional programs in law, medicine, and veterinary science. 3-2 engineering programs with Washington U. Exchange program with 12 to 15 private colleges during January short term. Teacher certification in early childhood, elementary, and secondary education. Certification in specific subject areas. Exchange program abroad in Japan (Kansai Gaidai U). Study abroad also in Austria, France, Germany, Italy, and Spain.
**Honors:** Honor societies.
**Academic Assistance:** Remedial reading, writing, math, and study skills. Nonremedial tutoring.

**STUDENT LIFE. Housing:** All unmarried students under age 25 must live on campus unless living with family. Women's and men's dorms. On-campus married-student housing. Single-parent housing. 85% of students live in college housing.
**Social atmosphere:** According to the editor of the student newspaper, "Students could do much more, but many have a hard time with a small and simple college town." Popular gathering spots on campus include "The Wall" in front of the college post office and the student center snack bar. Off-campus destinations may include Papaleno's Restaurant, Hardee's, People's Restaurant, Mario's Pizza, and the bars north of Richmond. Basketball and baseball players are influential. Students also enjoy Campus Activity dances.
**Services and counseling/handicapped student services:** Placement services. Health service. Women's center. Day care. Counseling services for minority, veteran, and older students. Birth control, personal, and psychological counseling. Career and academic guidance services. Religious counseling. Physically disabled student services. Notetaking services. Reader services for the blind.
**Campus organizations:** Undergraduate student government. Student newspaper (Pinnacle, published twice/month). Literary magazine. Yearbook. Berea Players, Country Dancers, musical groups, Agricultural Union, Harmonia Society, Mountain Day, Habitat for Humanity, debating, law forum, People Who Care, departmental, service, and special-interest groups, 86 organizations in all.
**Religious organizations:** Baptist Student Union, Fellowship of Christian Athletes, Intervarsity Christian Fellowship, Newman Club, Campus Christian Council, Christian Vocations, Collegiate Fellowship.
**Minority/foreign student organizations:** Black Ensemble, Black Student Union, African Student Association, black student literary magazine. Cosmopolitan Club.

**ATHLETICS. Physical education requirements:** Three terms of physical education required.
**Intercollegiate competition:** 25% of students participate. Baseball (M), basketball (M,W), cross-country (M,W), field hockey (W), golf (M), soccer (M), softball (W), swimming (M,W), tennis (M,W), track and field (M,W), volleyball (W). Member of Kentucky Intercollegiate Athletic Conference, NAIA, NCAA Division III, WIAC.
**Intramural and club sports:** 50% of students participate. Intramural basketball, flag football, racquetball, soccer, softball, volleyball.

**ADMISSIONS. Academic basis for candidate selection** (in order of priority): Class rank, secondary school record, standardized test scores, essay, school's recommendation.
**Nonacademic basis for candidate selection:** Only applicants demonstrating financial need may be enrolled. Character and personality, extracurricular participation, and geographical distribution are emphasized. Particular talent or ability is considered.
**Requirements:** Graduation from secondary school is required; GED is accepted. 20 units and the following program of study are recommended: 4 units of English, 3 units of math, 2 units of science, 1 unit of social studies, 1 unit of history, 9 units of electives. Foreign language units are highly desirable. Minimum SAT verbal score of 350 (composite ACT score of 17) and rank in top three-fifths of secondary school class required. SAT or ACT is required. Campus visit and interview recommended. Off-campus interviews available with admissions and alumni representatives.
**Procedure:** Take SAT or ACT by December of 12th year. Visit college for interview by February of 12th year. Suggest filing application by February 1. Notification of admission on rolling basis. Reply is required by June 15. $50 general deposit refundable until August 1. Freshmen accepted for terms other than fall.
**Special programs:** Credit may be granted through CEEB Advanced Placement for scores of 3 or higher. Credit and/or placement may be granted through CLEP subject exams. Early entrance/early admission program.
**Transfer students:** Transfer students accepted for terms other than fall. In fall 1993, 10% of all new students were transfers into all classes. 230 transfer applications were received, 65 were accepted. Application deadline is rolling for fall; rolling for spring. Minimum 2.0 GPA required. Lowest course grade accepted is "C." Maximum number of transferable credits is 24 credits. At least eight of last 11 course credits must be completed at the college to receive degree.
**Admissions contact:** John S. Cook, M.A., Director of Admissions. 606 986-9341, extension 5083.

**FINANCIAL AID. Available aid:** Pell grants, SEOG, state scholarships and grants, school scholarships and grants, private scholarships and grants, and aid for undergraduate foreign students. Perkins Loans (NDSL), Stafford Loans (GSL), school loans, and SLS. Deferred payment plan.
**Financial aid statistics:** In 1993-94, 100% of all undergraduate applicants received aid; 100% of freshman applicants. Average amounts of aid awarded freshmen: Scholarships and grants, $14,383; loans, $325.
**Supporting data/closing dates:** FAFSA: Priority filing date is February 15. Notification of awards begins May 1.
**Financial aid contact:** Hazel Wehrle, Associate Dean, Student Financial Services. 606 986-9341, extension 5311.

**STUDENT EMPLOYMENT.** College Work/Study Program. Institutional employment. All students are required to work at least ten hours per week in student labor program. Students may expect to earn an average of $1,000 during school year. Off-campus part-time employment opportunities rated "poor."

**COMPUTER FACILITIES.** 165 IBM/IBM-compatible and Macintosh/Apple microcomputers; all are networked. Students may access Prime minicomputer/mainframe systems. Residence halls may be equipped with networked microcomputers. Client/LAN operating systems include Apple/Macintosh. Computer languages and software packages include BASIC, Claris CAD, COBOL, Excel, FORTRAN, INFO, Lotus 1-2-3, Maple, MS-Word, MS-Works, Pascal; database, spreadsheet, word processing software; 50 in all. Computer facilities are available to all students.
**Fees:** None.
**Hours:** 24 hours.

**PROMINENT ALUMNI/AE.** Juanita Kreps, former Secretary of Commerce; Robert Parks, president, Iowa State U; Thomas Kim, president, McMurray College.

# Brescia College

**Owensboro, KY 42301-3023** **502 685-3131**

**1994-95 Costs.** Tuition: $7,500. Room & board: $3,200. Fees, books, misc. academic expenses (school's estimate): $725.
**Enrollment.** Undergraduates: 168 men, 284 women (full-time). Freshman class: 307 applicants, 260 accepted, 99 enrolled.
**Test score averages/ranges.** Average ACT scores: 22 English, 21 math, 22 composite.
**Faculty.** 41 full-time; 30 part-time. 34% of faculty holds highest degree in specific field. Student/faculty ratio: 14 to 1.
**Selectivity rating.** Less competitive.

**PROFILE.** Brescia, founded in 1950, is a church-affiliated, liberal arts college. Its campus is located near downtown Owensboro, 125 miles west of Louisville.

**Accreditation:** SACS.
**Religious orientation:** Brescia College is affiliated with the Roman Catholic Church; no religious requirements.
**Library:** Collections totaling over 109,129 volumes, 429 periodical subscriptions, and 254,081 microform items.
**Special facilities/museums:** Greenhouse, observatory, darkroom facilities including color labs and lighting studio.
**Athletic facilities:** Gymnasium, racquetball court, weight room.

**STUDENT BODY. Undergraduate profile:** 1% Asian-American, 2% Black, 1% Hispanic, 1% Native American, 94% White, 1% Other. Average age of undergraduates is 23.
**Freshman profile:** 4% of freshmen who took ACT scored 30 or over on English, 1% scored 30 or over on composite; 32% scored 24 or over on English, 21% scored 24 or over on math, 24% scored 24 or over on composite; 65% scored 18 or over on English, 56% scored 18 or over on math, 65% scored 18 or over on composite; 75% scored 12 or over on English, 75% scored 12 or over on math, 76% scored 12 or over on composite; 76% scored 6 or over on English, 76% scored 6 or over on math. Majority of accepted applicants took ACT. 84% of freshmen come from public schools.
**Undergraduate achievement:** 67% of fall 1992 freshmen returned for fall 1993 term. 33% of entering class graduated. 25% of students who completed a degree program went on to graduate study.
**Foreign students:** Countries represented include Canada and Cyprus; four in all.

**PROGRAMS OF STUDY. Degrees:** B.A., B.S.
**Majors:** Accounting, Art, Art Education, Biology, Business, Chemistry, Communication Sciences/Disorders, Elementary Education, English, General Studies, Graphic Design, History, Human Resource Development, Mathematics, Medical Technology, Ministry Formation, Psychology, Religious Studies, Science, Secondary Education, Social Sciences, Social Work, Sociology, Special Education.
**Distribution of degrees:** The majors with the highest enrollment are education, business, and accounting.
**Requirements:** General education requirement.
**Academic regulations:** Freshmen must maintain minimum 1.5 GPA; sophomores, 1.65 GPA; juniors, 1.75 GPA; seniors, 2.0 GPA.
**Special:** Optional minors offered in some majors and in computer studies, economics, and political science. Several concentrations available in art and business. Self-designed majors. Double majors. Independent study. Pass/fail grading option. Internships. Cooperative education programs. Preprofessional programs in law, medicine, veterinary science, pharmacy, dentistry, theology, optometry, art therapy, and communication sciences/disorders. 2-2 engineering program with U of Kentucky. 3-3 nursing program with Case Western U. Teacher certification in early childhood, elementary, secondary, and special education.
**Honors:** Honors program. Honor societies.
**Academic Assistance:** Remedial reading, writing, math, and study skills. Nonremedial tutoring.

**ADMISSIONS. Academic basis for candidate selection** (in order of priority): Secondary school record, standardized test scores, class rank, school's recommendation, essay.
**Nonacademic basis for candidate selection:** Character and personality are important. Extracurricular participation, particular talent or ability, and alumni/ae relationship are considered.
**Requirements:** Graduation from secondary school is required; GED is accepted. 16 units and the following program of study are recommended: 4 units of English, 3 units of math, 2 units of science, 2 units of social studies. Rank in top third of secondary school class and minimum 2.0 GPA required. Consideration on basis of recommendations and supplemental information for applicants not meeting standard requirements. Test of Potential in College (TOPIC) for applicants beyond traditional age. ACT is required; SAT may be substituted. Campus visit and interview recommended. Off-campus interviews available with an admissions representative.

**Procedure:** Take SAT or ACT by December of 12th year. (Students applying more than one year after secondary school graduation are not required to submit test scores.) Visit college for interview by February of 12th year. Notification of admission on rolling basis. $25 room deposit, refundable until June 1. Freshmen accepted for terms other than fall.
**Special programs:** Admission may be deferred. Credit and/or placement may be granted through CEEB Advanced Placement exams for scores of 3 or higher. Credit and/or placement may be granted through CLEP general and subject exams. Credit and placement may be granted through DANTES and challenge exams, and military and life experience. Concurrent enrollment program.
**Transfer students:** Transfer students accepted for terms other than fall. In fall 1993, 144 transfer applications were received, 114 were accepted. Application deadline is rolling for fall; rolling for spring. Minimum 2.0 GPA recommended. Lowest course grade accepted is "C." Maximum number of transferable credits is 67 semester hours. At least 42 semester hours must be completed at the college to receive degree.
**Admissions contact:** Thomas G. Green, Director of Admissions. 502 686-4241.

**FINANCIAL AID. Available aid:** Pell grants, SEOG, state scholarships and grants, school scholarships and grants, academic merit scholarships, and athletic scholarships. Perkins Loans (NDSL), PLUS, Stafford Loans (GSL), state loans, school loans, and private loans. Deferred payment plan and guaranteed tuition.
**Financial aid statistics:** 35% of aid is not need-based. In 1992-93, 71% of all undergraduate applicants received aid; 99% of freshman applicants.
**Supporting data/closing dates:** FAFSA/FAF/FFS: Priority filing date is April 1. State aid form: Priority filing date is April 1. Notification of awards on rolling basis.
**Financial aid contact:** Vivian Pearson, Director of Financial Aid. 502 686-4290.

## Campbellsville College

**Campbellsville, KY 42718** **502 465-8158**

**1994-95 Costs.** Tuition: $6,060. Room: $1,220. Board: $1,850. Fees, books, misc. academic expenses (school's estimate): $600.
**Enrollment.** Undergraduates: 280 men, 342 women (full-time). Freshman class: 634 applicants, 440 accepted, 213 enrolled. Graduate enrollment: 31.
**Test score averages/ranges.** Average ACT scores: 20 composite.
**Faculty.** 47 full-time; 26 part-time. 59% of faculty holds highest degree in specific field. Student/faculty ratio: 15 to 1.
**Selectivity rating.** Competitive.

**PROFILE.** Campbellsville, founded in 1906, is a church-affiliated college of the liberal arts and sciences. Its 35-acre campus is located in Campbellsville, 80 miles from Louisville and Lexington.

**Accreditation:** SACS. Professionally accredited by the National Association of Schools of Music.
**Religious orientation:** Campbellsville College is affiliated with the Southern Baptist Church (Kentucky Baptist Convention); two semesters of religion required.
**Library:** Collections totaling over 108,000 volumes, 500 periodical subscriptions, and 8,000 microform items. 2,000–volume children's library.
**Athletic facilities:** Gymnasiums, swimming pool, baseball, football, and soccer fields, weight rooms.

**STUDENT BODY. Undergraduate profile:** 92% are state residents; 29% are transfers. 1% Asian-American, 8% Black, 1% Hispanic, 2% Native American, 88% White. Average age of undergraduates is 21.
**Freshman profile:** 5% of freshmen who took ACT scored 30 or over on composite; 30% scored 24 or over on composite; 56% scored 18 or over on composite; 98% scored 12 or over on composite; 100% scored 6 or over on composite. 98% of freshmen come from public schools.
**Undergraduate achievement:** 69% of fall 1991 freshmen returned for fall 1992 term. 33% of entering class graduated. 65% of students who completed a degree program went on to graduate study within five years.
**Foreign students:** 15 students are from out of the country. Five countries represented in all.

**PROGRAMS OF STUDY. Degrees:** B.A., B.Mus., B.S., B.S.Med.Tech.
**Majors:** Accounting, Art, Biology, Business Administration, Chemistry, Christian Studies, Church Music, Church Recreation, Communications, Computer Information Systems, Economics, Elementary Education, English, History, Mathematics, Medical Technology, Middle Grades Education, Music, Music Education, Office Management, Organizational Administration, Physical Education, Political Science, Psychology, Religious Education, Science, Social Studies, Sociology.
**Distribution of degrees:** The majors with the highest enrollment are elementary education, business administration, and computer information systems; Christian studies and church recreation have the lowest.
**Requirements:** General education requirement.
**Special:** Minors offered in most majors and in athletic coaching, criminal justice, data processing, drama, health, and journalism. Required Correlated Studies Program. GRE required of all graduating seniors. Associate's degrees offered. Double majors. Dual degrees. Independent study. Internships. Graduate school at which undergraduates may take graduate-level courses. Preprofessional programs in law, medicine, veterinary science, pharmacy, dentistry, theology, engineering, nursing, and physical therapy. 3-1 programs with medical and dental schools. 3-2 engineering program with U of Kentucky. Member of consortium with Western Kentucky U. Washington Semester. Teacher certification in early childhood, elementary, and secondary education. Study abroad in England, France, and Israel.
**Honors:** Honors program.
**Academic Assistance:** Remedial reading, math, and study skills.

**ADMISSIONS. Academic basis for candidate selection** (in order of priority): Secondary school record, standardized test scores, class rank, essay, school's recommendation.
**Nonacademic basis for candidate selection:** Character and personality are emphasized. Extracurricular participation is important. Particular talent or ability and alumni/ae relationship are considered.
**Requirements:** Graduation from secondary school is required; GED is accepted. 20 units and the following program of study are recommended: 4 units of English, 3 units of math, 3 units of science, 1 unit of foreign language, 2 units of social studies, 2 units of history, 3 units of electives. Minimum composite ACT score of 19 (combined SAT score of 720) and minimum 2.0 GPA recommended. ACT is required; SAT may be substituted. Campus visit and interview recommended. Off-campus interviews available with an admissions representative.
**Procedure:** Take SAT or ACT by February of 12th year. Visit college for interview by March of 12th year. Suggest filing application by January. Application deadline is August. Notification of admission on rolling basis. $50 tuition deposit, refundable until May 1. $60 room deposit, refundable until May 1. Freshmen accepted for terms other than fall.
**Special programs:** Admission may be deferred one year. Credit and/or placement may be granted through CEEB Advanced Placement exams for scores of 4 or higher. Credit and/or placement may be granted through CLEP general and subject exams. Credit and placement may be granted through DANTES exams, and military and life experience. Concurrent enrollment program.
**Transfer students:** Transfer students accepted for terms other than fall. In fall 1992, 29% of all new students were transfers into all classes. 95 transfer applications were received, 87 were accepted. Application deadline is rolling for fall; rolling for spring. Minimum 2.0 GPA required. Lowest course grade accepted is "D."
**Admissions contact:** R. Trent Argo, Director of Admission. 502 789-5220.

**FINANCIAL AID. Available aid:** Pell grants, SEOG, state scholarships and grants, school scholarships and grants, private scholarships and grants, academic merit scholarships, athletic scholarships, and aid for undergraduate foreign students. Church-related scholarships and grants. Perkins Loans (NDSL), PLUS, Stafford Loans (GSL), state loans, school loans, and private loans. Tuition Plan Inc. and deferred payment plan.
**Supporting data/closing dates:** FAFSA/FAF: Priority filing date is April 1. School's own aid application: Priority filing date is April 1. Notification of awards on rolling basis.
**Financial aid contact:** Paul Demeron, M.A., Director of Financial Aid. 502 789-5013.

## Centre College

**Danville, KY 40422** **606 238-5200**

**1994-95 Costs.** Tuition: $11,850. Room: $2,150. Board: $1,990-$2,120. Fees, books, misc. academic expenses (school's estimate): $980.
**Enrollment.** Undergraduates: 493 men, 459 women (full-time). Freshman class: 1,010 applicants, 880 accepted, 282 enrolled.
**Test score averages/ranges.** Average SAT scores: 1120 combined. Range of SAT scores of middle 50%: 480-600 verbal, 550-650 math. Average ACT scores: 27 composite. Range of ACT scores of middle 50%: 25-29 composite.
**Faculty.** 87 full-time; 7 part-time. 87% of faculty holds highest degree in specific field. Student/faculty ratio: 11 to 1.
**Selectivity rating.** Highly competitive.

**PROFILE.** Centre, founded in 1820, is a private, liberal arts college. Its 75-acre campus, containing architecture of the Greek Revival style, is located in Danville, 35 miles from Lexington.

**Accreditation:** SACS.
**Religious orientation:** Centre College is nonsectarian; no religious requirements.
**Library:** Collections totaling over 250,000 volumes, 750 periodical subscriptions, and 30,000 microform items.
**Special facilities/museums:** Arts center, physical science and math facility, electron microscope, visible and infrared mass spectroscopy equipment.
**Athletic facilities:** Gymnasiums, basketball, racquetball, tennis, and volleyball courts, track, football stadium, baseball, field hockey, football, intramural, soccer, and softball fields, weight room, training room.

**STUDENT BODY. Undergraduate profile:** 65% are state residents; 5% are transfers. 2% Asian-American, 3% Black, 1% Hispanic, 94% White. Average age of undergraduates is 20.
**Freshman profile:** 18% of freshmen who took ACT scored 30 or over on composite; 79% scored 24 or over on composite; 100% scored 18 or over on composite. 62% of accepted applicants took SAT; 88% took ACT. 80% of freshmen come from public schools.
**Undergraduate achievement:** 87% of fall 1992 freshmen returned for fall 1993 term. 76% of entering class graduated. 37% of students who completed a degree program immediately went on to graduate study.
**Foreign students:** Five students are from out of the country. Five countries represented in all.

**PROGRAMS OF STUDY. Degrees:** B.A., B.S.
**Majors:** Anthropology/Sociology, Art, Biochemistry/Molecular Biology, Biology, Chemical Physics, Chemistry, Computer Science, Dramatic Arts, Economics, Elementary Education, English, French, German, Government, History, International Relations, Mathematics, Music, Philosophy, Physics, Psychobiology, Psychology, Religion, Sociology/Anthropology, Spanish.
**Distribution of degrees:** The majors with the highest enrollment are economics, English, and history; philosophy, German, and music have the lowest.
**Requirements:** General education requirement.
**Academic regulations:** Freshmen must maintain minimum 1.65 GPA; sophomores, 1.9 GPA; juniors, 2.0 GPA; seniors, 2.0 GPA.
**Special:** Minors offered in most majors and in classics. Courses offered in creative writing, journalism, and speech. Freshmen required to take integrative humanities course (two terms). Self-designed majors. Double majors. Independent study. Pass/fail grading option. Internships. Preprofessional programs in law and medicine. 3-2 engineering programs with Columbia U, Georgia Tech, U of Kentucky, Vanderbilt U, and Washington U. Member of Associated Colleges of the South. Teacher certification in elementary and

secondary education. Certification in specific subject areas. Study abroad in England, France, and Mexico. ROTC.
**Honors:** Phi Beta Kappa. Honor societies.
**Academic Assistance:** Remedial study skills. Nonremedial tutoring.

**ADMISSIONS. Academic basis for candidate selection** (in order of priority): Secondary school record, class rank, school's recommendation, standardized test scores, essay.
**Nonacademic basis for candidate selection:** Character and personality, extracurricular participation, and particular talent or ability are important. Geographical distribution and alumni/ae relationship are considered.
**Requirements:** Graduation from secondary school is required; GED is accepted. 14 units and the following program of study are required: 4 units of English, 4 units of math, 2 units of lab science, 2 units of social studies. SAT or ACT is required. Campus visit and interview recommended. Off-campus interviews available with an admissions representative.
**Procedure:** Take SAT or ACT by December of 12th year. Visit college for interview by March 1 of 12th year. Application deadline is February 1. Notification of admission by March 15. Reply is required by May 1. $250 tuition deposit, refundable until May 1. Freshmen accepted for terms other than fall.
**Special programs:** Admission may be deferred two years. Credit and/or placement may be granted through CEEB Advanced Placement exams for scores of 4 or higher. Credit may be granted through CLEP general exams. Placement may be granted through challenge exams. Early decision program. Deadline for applying for early decision is November 15.
**Transfer students:** Transfer students accepted for terms other than fall. In fall 1993, 5% of all new students were transfers into all classes. 20 transfer applications were received, 16 were accepted. Application deadline is July 15 for fall; December 15 for spring. Minimum 2.5 GPA recommended. Lowest course grade accepted is "C." Both secondary school and college transcripts required for transfer applicants with fewer than two years of college credit. Maximum number of transferable credits is 70 semester hours. At least 45 semester hours must be completed at the college to receive degree.
**Admissions contact:** John W. Rogers, M.A., Director of Admission. 606 238-5350, 800 423-6236.

**FINANCIAL AID. Available aid:** Pell grants, SEOG, state scholarships and grants, school scholarships and grants, private scholarships, ROTC scholarships, and academic merit scholarships. Perkins Loans (NDSL), PLUS, Stafford Loans (GSL), school loans, private loans, and SLS. College payment plans.
**Financial aid statistics:** 24% of aid is not need-based. In 1993-94, 96% of all undergraduate applicants received aid; 94% of freshman applicants. Average amounts of aid awarded freshmen: Scholarships and grants, $6,900; loans, $1,900.
**Supporting data/closing dates:** FAFSA/FAF/FFS: Deadline is March 15. School's own aid application: Deadline is March 15. Income tax forms: Deadline is March 15. Notification of awards begins March 15.
**Financial aid contact:** Elaine Larson, M.A., Director of Financial Aid. 606 238-5365.

# Cumberland College

**Williamsburg, KY 40769 — 606 549-2200**

**1994-95 Costs.** Tuition: $6,598. Room & board: $3,526. Fees, books, misc. academic expenses (school's estimate): $532.
**Enrollment.** Undergraduates: 601 men, 705 women (full-time). Freshman class: 995 applicants, 789 accepted, 398 enrolled. Graduate enrollment: 18 men, 72 women.
**Test score averages/ranges.** Average SAT scores: 420 verbal, 470 math. Range of SAT scores of middle 50%: 360-480 verbal, 410-540 math. Average ACT scores: 22 English, 20 math, 21 composite. Range of ACT scores of middle 50%: 19-24 English, 17-23 math.
**Faculty.** 100 full-time; 7 part-time. 49% of faculty holds doctoral degree. Student/faculty ratio: 15 to 1.
**Selectivity rating.** Competitive.

**PROFILE.** Cumberland, founded in 1889, is a church-affiliated, liberal arts college. Its 30-acre campus is located in Williamsburg, 70 miles north of Knoxville, Tenn.

**Accreditation:** SACS. Professionally accredited by the National Association of Schools of Music.
**Religious orientation:** Cumberland College is affiliated with the Kentucky Baptist Convention; two semesters of religion required.
**Library:** Collections totaling over 160,000 volumes, 1,469 periodical subscriptions, and 575,000 microform items.
**Special facilities/museums:** Natural history and student art museums.
**Athletic facilities:** Gymnasiums, baseball and football fields, football stadium, track, tennis courts.

**STUDENT BODY. Undergraduate profile:** 52% are state residents; 16% are transfers. .5% Asian-American, 6% Black, 1% Hispanic, .5% Native American, 91% White, 1% Other. Average age of undergraduates is 20.
**Freshman profile:** 24% of accepted applicants took SAT; 76% took ACT. 98% of freshmen come from public schools.
**Undergraduate achievement:** 65% of fall 1992 freshmen returned for fall 1993 term. 35% of entering class graduated. 15% of students who completed a degree program immediately went on to graduate study.
**Foreign students:** 30 students are from out of the country. Countries represented include China, Ethiopia, India, Japan, Malaysia, and Thailand; 18 in all.

**PROGRAMS OF STUDY. Degrees:** B.A., B.Gen.Studies, B.S., B.S.Mus.
**Majors:** Art, Biology, Business Administration, Chemistry, Communications/Theatre Arts, Computer Information Systems, Elementary Education, English, Health, History, History/Political Science, Mathematics, Medical Technology, Movement/Leisure Studies, Music, Physics, Political Science, Psychology, Religion, Sociology, Special Education.
**Distribution of degrees:** The majors with the highest enrollment are business administration, elementary education, and computer information systems; sociology and communications/theatre arts have the lowest.
**Requirements:** General education requirement.
**Academic regulations:** Freshmen must maintain minimum 1.6 GPA; sophomores, 1.8 GPA; juniors, 2.0 GPA; seniors, 2.0 GPA.
**Special:** Minors offered in most majors and in biblical languages, early elementary and special education (nonteaching), French, geography, philosophy, physical education, social work, and Spanish. Credit possible for correspondence work. Courses offered in general science, Greek, and Hebrew. Double majors. Dual degrees. Independent study. Cooperative education programs. Graduate school at which undergraduates may take graduate-level courses. Preprofessional programs in law, medicine, veterinary science, pharmacy, dentistry, optometry, and engineering. 3-2 nursing programs with Carson-Newman Coll and Eastern Kentucky U. 3-2 engineering program with any offering institution. Teacher certification in early childhood, elementary, secondary, and special education. Certification in specific subject areas. Study abroad in China and England. ROTC.
**Honors:** Honors program. Honor societies.
**Academic Assistance:** Remedial reading, writing, math, and study skills. Nonremedial tutoring.

**STUDENT LIFE. Housing:** All freshmen must live on campus. Women's and men's dorms. Off-campus privately-owned housing. 59% of students live in college housing.
**Social atmosphere:** According to the editor of the student newspaper, "The social life is varied and ranges from extremely religious to pro-parties (socially). Culturally, there are various opportunities on-campus (plays, concerts, etc.), but little off campus." Influential groups on campus include the Baptist Student Union, Fellowship of Christian Athletes, the ball teams, and the various departmental organizations. Popular events are Mock Rack, Hanging of the Green, and rivalry football and basketball games. Students like to gather at the campus Grill, Student Center, the library, Boswell Park, and dorm lobbies. Off campus, they head for Deli Mart, Ivey's, and Cumberland Falls Park.
**Services and counseling/handicapped student services:** Placement services. Health service. Counseling services for minority and veteran students. Personal and psychological counseling. Career and academic guidance services. Religious counseling. Learning disabled services.
**Campus organizations:** Undergraduate student government. Yearbook. TV station. Brass and woodwind quintets, choir, chorale, concert band, jazz workshop, percussion ensemble, orchestra, theatre, Student Union, Student Artists Collective, Campus Activity Board, Outdoor Adventures Club, departmental and special-interest groups, 45 organizations in all.
**Religious organizations:** Appalachian Ministries, Baptist Student Union, Bread for the World, Fellowship of Christian Athletes, Mountain Outreach.
**Minority/foreign student organizations:** Black Student Union. Foreign Student Organization, International Club.

**ATHLETICS. Physical education requirements:** Two semesters of physical education required.
**Intercollegiate competition:** 20% of students participate. Baseball (M), basketball (M,W), cheerleading (M,W), cross-country (M,W), golf (M,W), soccer (M,W), softball (W), swimming (M,W), tennis (M,W), track (indoor) (M,W), track (outdoor) (M,W), track and field (indoor) (M,W), track and field (outdoor) (M,W), volleyball (W). Member of KAIC, NAIA.
**Intramural and club sports:** 50% of students participate. Intramural badminton, basketball, judo, softball, table tennis, tennis, touch football, volleyball.

**ADMISSIONS. Academic basis for candidate selection** (in order of priority): Secondary school record, standardized test scores, class rank, school's recommendation, essay.
**Nonacademic basis for candidate selection:** Character and personality, extracurricular participation, and particular talent or ability are considered.
**Requirements:** Graduation from secondary school is required; GED is accepted. No specific distribution of secondary school units required. Minimum combined SAT score of 650 (composite ACT score of 16), rank in top half of secondary class, and minimum 2.0 GPA required. Conditional admission possible for applicants not meeting standard requirements. SAT or ACT is required. Campus visit recommended. Off-campus interviews available with an admissions representative. No off-campus interviews.
**Procedure:** Take SAT or ACT by June of 12th year. Suggest filing application by March 1. Application deadline is August 1. Notification of admission on rolling basis. Reply is required by August 1. $75 tuition deposit, refundable until May 1. Freshmen accepted for terms other than fall.
**Special programs:** Admission may be deferred one year. Credit and/or placement may be granted through CLEP general and subject exams. Credit may be granted through life experience. Credit and placement may be granted through military experience.
**Transfer students:** Transfer students accepted for terms other than fall. In fall 1993, 16% of all new students were transfers into all classes. 185 transfer applications were received, 113 were accepted. Application deadline is August 15 for fall; January 6 for spring. Minimum 2.0 GPA required. Lowest course grade accepted is "C." Maximum number of transferable credits is 67 semester hours from a two-year school and 92 semester hours from a four-year school. At least 30 semester hours must be completed at the college to receive degree.
**Admissions contact:** Erica Harris, Senior Admissions Counselor. 606 549-2200, extension 4248, 800 343-1609.

**FINANCIAL AID. Available aid:** Pell grants, SEOG, state scholarships and grants, school scholarships and grants, private scholarships and grants, academic merit scholarships, athletic scholarships, and aid for undergraduate foreign students. Perkins Loans (NDSL), PLUS, Stafford Loans (GSL), school loans, private loans, and SLS. Deferred payment plan.
**Financial aid statistics:** 34% of aid is not need-based. In 1993-94, 85% of all undergraduate applicants received aid; 90% of freshman applicants. Average amounts of aid awarded freshmen: Scholarships and grants, $4,300; loans, $3,200.
**Supporting data/closing dates:** FAFSA: Priority filing date is March 1. Notification of awards on rolling basis.
**Financial aid contact:** Jack Stanfill, Director of Financial Aid. 606 549-2200, extension 4220, 800 532-0828.

**STUDENT EMPLOYMENT.** College Work/Study Program. Institutional employment. 36% of full-time undergraduates work on campus during school year. Students may expect to earn an average of $1,640 during school year. Off-campus part-time employment opportunities rated "good."

**COMPUTER FACILITIES.** 100 IBM/IBM-compatible, Macintosh/Apple, and RISC-/UNIX-based microcomputers; 75 are networked. Students may access AT&T, IBM minicomputer/mainframe systems. Residence halls may be equipped with stand-alone microcomputers, networked microcomputers. Client/LAN operating systems include DOS, UNIX/XENIX/AIX, Novell. Computer languages and software packages include C, COBOL, FORTRAN, Lotus 1-2-3, Pascal, Phase 3, WordPerfect; 25 in all. Computer facilities are available to all students.
**Fees:** None.
**Hours:** 8 AM-9 PM (M-Th); 8 AM-5 PM (F).

**GRADUATE CAREER DATA.** Graduate school percentages: 2% enter law school. 6% enter medical school. 2% enter dental school. 4% enter graduate business programs. 8% enter graduate arts and sciences programs. 3% enter theological school/seminary. Highest graduate school enrollments: Duke U, Eastern Kentucky U, U of Kentucky, U of Louisville, U of Michigan, U of North Carolina, Vanderbilt U. 60% of graduates choose careers in business and industry. Companies and businesses that hire graduates: Belk's, Biggs, CompCare, electronic data firms, federal government, Fruit-of-the-Loom, Humana Hospital, Procter & Gamble, Rollins, State Farm Insurance.

**PROMINENT ALUMNI/AE.** Bert Combs, former governor, Kentucky; Betty Siegel, president, Kennesaw Coll; Arliss Roaden, director of higher education, Tennessee; Howard Bozer, director of higher education, South Carolina.

## Eastern Kentucky University

**Richmond, KY 40475-3101 606 622-1000**

**1993-94 Costs.** Tuition: $1,700 (state residents), $4,700 (out-of-state). Room: $1,236. Board: $1,720. Fees, books, misc. academic expenses (school's estimate): $600.
**Enrollment.** Undergraduates: 5,022 men, 6,612 women (full-time). Freshman class: 5,405 applicants, 5,130 accepted, 2,499 enrolled. Graduate enrollment: 602 men, 1,342 women.
**Test score averages/ranges.** Average ACT scores: 19 composite.
**Faculty.** 610 full-time; 219 part-time. 65% of faculty holds doctoral degree. Student/faculty ratio: 23 to 1.
**Selectivity rating.** Noncompetitive.

**PROFILE.** Eastern Kentucky, founded in 1906, is public university. Programs are offered through the Colleges of Applied Arts and Technology; Applied Health and Nursing; Arts and Humanities; Business; Education; Health, Physical Education, Recreation, and Athletics; Law Enforcement; Natural and Mathematical Sciences; and Social and Behavioral Sciences and the Graduate School. Its 350-acre campus is located in Richmond, 30 miles from Lexington.

**Accreditation:** SACS. Professionally accredited by the American Dietetic Association, the American Medical Association (CAHEA), the American Speech-Language-Hearing Association, the Council on Social Work Education, the Foundation for Interior Design Education Research, the National Association of Schools of Music, the National Association of Schools of Public Affairs and Administration, the National Council for Accreditation of Teacher Education, the National League for Nursing, the National Recreation and Park Association.
**Religious orientation:** Eastern Kentucky University is nonsectarian; no religious requirements.
**Library:** Collections totaling over 845,977 volumes, 4,070 periodical subscriptions, and 1,800,732 microform items.
**Special facilities/museums:** Planetarium, model lab school.
**Athletic facilities:** Gymnasium, basketball, racquetball, and tennis courts, golf course, baseball, football, and softball fields, swimming pools.

**STUDENT BODY. Undergraduate profile:** 92% are state residents; 8% are transfers. 1% Asian-American, 5% Black, 93% White, 1% Other. Average age of undergraduates is 21.
**Freshman profile:** Majority of accepted applicants took ACT.
**Undergraduate achievement:** 7% of fall 1991 freshmen returned for fall 1992 term. 25% of entering class graduated.
**Foreign students:** 135 students are from out of the country. Countries represented include Cameroon, Hong Kong, Malaysia, and Saudi Arabia; 43 in all.

**PROGRAMS OF STUDY. Degrees:** B.A., B.Bus.Admin., B.F.A., B.Indiv.Studies, B.Mus., B.Mus.Ed., B.S., B.S.Nurs., B.Soc.Work
**Majors:** Accounting, Administrative Communication/Services, Agricultural, Anthropology, Art, Art Education, Aviation Administration, Biology, Broadcasting, Business, Business Economics, Business Education, Chemistry, Child Care/Family Studies, Clothing Construction/Design, Communication Disorders/Hearing Impaired, Community Health, Computer Information Systems, Computer Science, Construction Technology, Corrections/Administration of Justice, Corrections/Juvenile Services, Earth Sciences, Economics, Elementary Education, English, Environmental Health Science, Environmental Resources, Fashion Merchandising, Finance, Fire/Safety Engineering Technology, Fisheries Management, Food Services Administration, Forensic Science, French, General Dietetics, General Home Economics, Geography, Geology, German, Health Care Administration, Health Education/School Health, History, Home Economics Education, Horticulture Therapy, Individualized Studies, Industrial Arts Education, Industrial Technology, Insurance Management, Interior Design, Journalism, Marketing, Mathematics, Medical Records Administration, Medical Technology, Microbiology, Music, Music Education, Music Merchandising, Nursing, Occupational Therapy, Office Administration, Paralegal Science, Performing Arts, Philosophy, Physical Education, Physics, Police Administration, Political Science, Psychology, Public Relations, Real Estate, Recreation/Park Administration, Religion, Security/Loss Prevention, Social Work, Sociology, Spanish, Special Education, Speech Communication Studies, Statistics, Technical Agriculture, Technical Education, Technical Horticulture, Theatre Arts, Transportation/Physical Distribution Management, Vocational Industrial Education, Wildlife Management.
**Distribution of degrees:** The majors with the highest enrollment are education, business, and nursing; arts/humanities and social behavior sciences have the lowest.
**Requirements:** General education requirement.
**Academic regulations:** Minimum 2.00 GPA must be maintained.
**Special:** Minors offered in many majors and in over 60 areas of specialization. Police administration program. Double majors. Dual degrees. Independent study. Pass/fail grading option. Internships. Cooperative education programs. Graduate school at which undergraduates may take graduate-level courses. Preprofessional programs in law, medicine, veterinary science, pharmacy, dentistry, theology, and optometry. 2-2 and 3-2 engineering programs with Auburn U, Georgia Tech, and U of Kentucky. 3-2 preveterinary medicine programs with Auburn U and Tuskegee U. Teacher certification in early childhood, elementary, secondary, special education, vo-tech, and bilingual/bicultural education. ROTC and AFROTC.
**Honors:** Phi Beta Kappa. Honors program. Honor societies.
**Academic Assistance:** Remedial reading, writing, and math. Nonremedial tutoring.

**STUDENT LIFE. Housing:** All unmarried students under age 21 must live on campus unless living near campus with relatives. Coed, women's, and men's dorms. On-campus married-student housing. 50% of students live in college housing.
**Social atmosphere:** The student newspaper reports, "Eastern has always been a 'suitcase college.' Many students live in nearby counties and go home in droves on Fridays to Mom and Dad, girlfriend or boyfriend, jobs, etc. Greeks comprise only 15 percent or so of the student body, but they are very visible. The Baptist Student Union is also very active here. Student attendance is poor at sporting events (football games are the biggest draw). The Theater Department's plays are often popular, as are hanging of the greens and the Madrigal Dinners (held in December). Various Greek events held annually are well attended by Greeks."
**Services and counseling/handicapped student services:** Placement services. Health service. Counseling services for minority, military, veteran, and older students. Birth control, personal, and psychological counseling. Career and academic guidance services. Religious counseling. Physically disabled student services. Learning disabled services. Notetaking services. Tape recorders. Tutors. Reader services for the blind.
**Campus organizations:** Undergraduate student government. Student newspaper (Eastern Progress, published once/week). Yearbook. Radio station. University Players, accounting club, Space Force, departmental and special-interest groups. 16 fraternities, two chapter houses; 12 sororities, no chapter houses. 13% of men join a fraternity. 15% of women join a sorority.
**Religious organizations:** Baptist Student Center, Fellowship of Christian Athletes, Methodist Student Center, Newman Center, Americans for Biblical Government, Campus Crusade, Christian Student Fellowship.
**Minority/foreign student organizations:** Black Student Union, Office of Minority Affairs, Asian Student Organization, Kappa Alpha Psi, Alpha Phi Alpha, Phi Beta Sigma, other minority groups. International Student Association.

**ATHLETICS. Physical education requirements:** Two semesters of physical education required.
**Intercollegiate competition:** 4% of students participate. Baseball (M), basketball (M,W), cheerleading (M,W), cross-country (M,W), football (M), golf (M,W), softball (W), tennis (M,W), track and field (indoor) (M,W), track and field (outdoor) (M,W), volleyball (W). Member of NCAA Division I, NCAA Division I-AA for football, Ohio Valley Athletic Conference.
**Intramural and club sports:** 40% of students participate. Intramural aerobics, basketball, camping, canoeing, golf, flag football, hiking, racquetball, rafting, softball, tennis, volleyball, weight lifting. Men's club judo, lacrosse, rugby, soccer, volleyball. Women's club judo, lacrosse, rugby, soccer, volleyball.

**ADMISSIONS. Academic basis for candidate selection** (in order of priority): Class rank, standardized test scores, secondary school record, school's recommendation, essay.
**Requirements:** Graduation from secondary school is required; GED is accepted. 20 units and the following program of study are required: 4 units of English, 3 units of math, 2 units of science including 1 unit of lab, 1 unit of social studies, 1 unit of history, 9 units of electives. Minimum composite ACT score of 21 (combined SAT score of 870), rank in top half of secondary school class, and minimum 2.5 GPA required of out-of-state applicants. Higher requirements for allied health, nursing, and business programs. Conditional admission possible for applicants not meeting standard requirements. ACT is required. Campus visit recommended. No off-campus interviews.
**Procedure:** Take ACT by January of 12th year. Notification of admission on rolling basis. No set date by which applicants must accept offer. $100 room deposit, refundable until July 15. Freshmen accepted for terms other than fall.
**Special programs:** Admission may be deferred one year. Applicants may be admitted without ACT, but are required to enroll in summer session prior to entrance for at least six hours of credit, including English composition, and attain a minimum 2.0 GPA. Credit and/or placement may be granted through CEEB Advanced Placement exams for scores of 3 or higher. Credit may be granted through CLEP general and subject exams, ACT PEP, DANTES, and challenge exams, and military experience. Early entrance/early admission program. Concurrent enrollment program.
**Transfer students:** Transfer students accepted for terms other than fall. In fall 1992, 8% of all new students were transfers into all classes. 1,387 transfer applications were received, 1,347 were accepted. Minimum 2.0 GPA required. Lowest course grade accepted is "D." At least 30 semester hours must be completed at the university to receive degree.
**Admissions contact:** James L. Grigsby, M.A., Director of Admissions. 606 622-2106.

**FINANCIAL AID. Available aid:** Pell grants, state grants, school scholarships and grants, ROTC scholarships, academic merit scholarships, and athletic scholarships. Perkins Loans (NDSL), Stafford Loans (GSL), and state loans. Deferred payment plan.
**Financial aid statistics:** In 1992-93, 71% of all undergraduate applicants received aid. Average amounts of aid awarded freshmen: Scholarships and grants, $750.
**Supporting data/closing dates:** FAFSA/FAF/FFS: Priority filing date is April 1. School's own aid application: Priority filing date is April 1. Income tax forms: Priority filing date is April 1. Notification of awards on rolling basis.
**Financial aid contact:** Herbert S. Vesico, M.A., Director of Financial Aid. 606 622-2361.

**STUDENT EMPLOYMENT.** College Work/Study Program. Institutional employment. 12% of full-time undergraduates work on campus during school year. Students may expect to earn an average of $800 during school year. Off-campus part-time employment opportunities rated "good."

**COMPUTER FACILITIES.** 350 IBM/IBM-compatible and Macintosh/Apple microcomputers. Students may access Digital minicomputer/mainframe systems, BITNET, Internet, CompuServe. Residence halls may be equipped with networked terminals. Computer languages and software packages include BASIC, C, COBOL, dBASE, Lotus 1-2-3, Pascal, RPG, SAS, SPSS-X, WordPerfect; 70 in all. Computer facilities are available to all students.
**Fees:** None.
**Hours:** 24 hours.

**PROMINENT ALUMNI/AE.** Karl D. Bays, chairperson of the board, Baxter Travenol Labs; Lee Majors, actor; Guy Doug Johnston, publisher, *Vanity Fair.*

# Georgetown College

**Georgetown, KY 40324-1696 502 863-8000**

**1994-95 Costs.** Tuition: $8,000 (state residents), $8,100 (out-of-state). Room: $1,975. Board: $1,975. Fees, books, misc. academic expenses (school's estimate): $600.
**Enrollment.** Undergraduates: 499 men, 564 women (full-time). Freshman class: 727 applicants, 693 accepted, 286 enrolled. Graduate enrollment: 44 men, 227 women.
**Test score averages/ranges.** Average ACT scores: 23 composite. Range of ACT scores of middle 50%: 20-26 composite.
**Faculty.** 73 full-time; 32 part-time. 72% of faculty holds doctoral degree. Student/faculty ratio: 15 to 1.
**Selectivity rating.** Less competitive.

**PROFILE.** Georgetown College, founded in 1829, is a church-affiliated, liberal arts institution. Its 52-acre campus is located in Kentucky's Bluegrass region. The Colonial-style campus includes three antebellum buildings.

**Accreditation:** SACS.
**Religious orientation:** Georgetown College is affiliated with the Southern Baptist Church; two semesters of religion required.
**Library:** Collections totaling over 125,707 volumes, 987 periodical subscriptions, and 106,159 microform items.
**Special facilities/museums:** Planetarium.
**Athletic facilities:** Gymnasium.

**STUDENT BODY. Undergraduate profile:** 80% are state residents; 8% are transfers. 1% Asian-American, 3% Black, 96% White. Average age of undergraduates is 20.
**Freshman profile:** 3% of freshmen who took ACT scored 30 or over on composite; 32% scored 24 or over on composite; 90% scored 18 or over on composite; 99% scored 12 or over on composite. 10% of accepted applicants took SAT; 99% took ACT. 92% of freshmen come from public schools.
**Undergraduate achievement:** 71% of fall 1992 freshmen returned for fall 1993 term. 31% of entering class graduated.
**Foreign students:** 22 students are from out of the country. Countries represented include Canada, China, France, Japan, Kenya, and Nigeria; 12 in all.

**PROGRAMS OF STUDY. Degrees:** B.A., B.Med.Tech., B.Mus., B.Mus.Ed., B.S., B.S.Nurs.
**Majors:** Accounting, American Studies, Area Studies, Art, Biological Sciences, Business Administration/Communications, Business Administration/Ethics, Chemistry, Church Music, Communication Arts, Computer Science, Economics, Elementary Education, Engineering Arts, English, Environmental Science, European Studies, Finance, French, German, Health/Physical Education/Recreation, History, International Management, Management, Management Information Systems, Marketing, Mathematics/Computers, Medical Technology, Music, Music Education, Nursing Arts, Philosophy, Physics, Political Science, Psychology, Religion, Sociology, Spanish.
**Distribution of degrees:** The majors with the highest enrollment are marketing/finance, education, and English; art, music, and physics have the lowest.
**Requirements:** General education requirement.
**Academic regulations:** Freshmen must maintain minimum 1.7 GPA; sophomores, 1.9 GPA; juniors, 2.0 GPA; seniors, 2.0 GPA.
**Special:** Minors offered include youth ministries, child development, and family studies. Courses offered in geography, geology, Greek, Hebrew, and social science. Seniors take comprehensive exams in major department. Self-designed majors. Double majors. Dual degrees. Independent study. Pass/fail grading option. Internships. Preprofessional programs in law, medicine, veterinary science, pharmacy, dentistry, theology, and optometry. 3-2 engineering programs with Georgia Tech, U of Kentucky, and Washington U. 3-2 nursing program with U of Kentucky. Teacher certification in elementary and secondary education. Study in France (U of Caen) for French majors; other study-abroad options in England, Germany, and Spain. ROTC and AFROTC at U of Kentucky.
**Honors:** Honors program.
**Academic Assistance:** Remedial writing and study skills. Nonremedial tutoring.

**STUDENT LIFE. Housing:** All unmarried students under age 21 must live on campus unless living near campus with relatives. Women's and men's dorms. 90% of students live in college housing.
**Social atmosphere:** On campus, students gather at The Grille. Off campus, students head for Sam's Truck Stop and Richmond nightclubs. Greeks and athletes are influential on campus. Homecoming, the Greek-sponsored volleyball tournament, and Watermelon Bust are popular annual events. According to the student newspaper, Georgetown College is small and community-oriented but sometimes quiet on weekends: "This is a go-home-on-the-weekends campus. The administration is constantly trying new ways to keep students here on weekends."
**Services and counseling/handicapped student services:** Placement services. Health service. Personal and psychological counseling. Career and academic guidance services. Religious counseling. Physically disabled student services. Tutors.
**Campus organizations:** Undergraduate student government. Student newspaper (Georgetonian, published once/week). Literary magazine. Yearbook. Radio station. A cappella choir, oratorio chorus, band, student theatre, Young Democrats, College Republicans, Student Foundation, Environmental Action Group, Maskrafters, 20 organizations in all. Five fraternities, all with chapter houses; three sororities, all with chapter houses. 40% of men join a fraternity. 30% of women join a sorority.
**Religious organizations:** Baptist Student Union, Fellowship of Christian Athletes.
**Minority/foreign student organizations:** Afro-American Fellowship.

**ATHLETICS. Physical education requirements:** Two semesters of physical education required.
**Intercollegiate competition:** 7% of students participate. Baseball (M), basketball (M,W), cross-country (M,W), football (M), golf (M), soccer (M), softball (W), tennis (M,W), volleyball (W). Member of Kentucky Intercollegiate Athletic Conference, Mid South Football Conference.
**Intramural and club sports:** 2% of students participate.

**ADMISSIONS. Academic basis for candidate selection** (in order of priority): Secondary school record, standardized test scores, class rank, essay, school's recommendation.
**Nonacademic basis for candidate selection:** Character and personality, extracurricular participation, and particular talent or ability are important. Alumni/ae relationship is considered.
**Requirements:** Graduation from secondary school is required; GED is accepted. 20 units and the following program of study are required: 4 units of English, 2 units of math, 2 units of science, 2 units of foreign language, 2 units of social studies. Minimum composite ACT score of 20, rank in top half of secondary school class, and minimum 2.7 GPA required. Restricted admissions program for applicants not normally admissible. ACT is required; SAT may be substituted. Campus visit and interview recommended. No off-campus interviews.
**Procedure:** Take SAT or ACT by March of 12th year. Visit college for interview by May 1 of 12th year. Suggest filing application by June 1. Application deadline is August 1. Notification of admission on rolling basis. Reply is required by May 1. $125 tuition deposit, refundable until May 1. Freshmen accepted for terms other than fall.
**Special programs:** Credit and/or placement may be granted through CEEB Advanced Placement exams for scores of 3 or higher. Credit may be granted through CLEP subject exams.
**Transfer students:** Transfer students accepted for terms other than fall. In fall 1993, 8% of all new students were transfers into all classes. 72 transfer applications were received, 47 were accepted. Application deadline is August 1 for fall; January 5 for spring. Minimum 2.0 GPA required. Lowest course grade accepted is "C." Maximum number of transferable credits is 66 semester hours from a two-year school and 98 semester hours from a four-year school. At least 30 semester hours must be completed at the college to receive degree.
**Admissions contact:** Garvel R. Kindrick, Director of Admissions. 800 788-9985.

**FINANCIAL AID. Available aid:** Pell grants, SEOG, state grants, school scholarships and grants, private scholarships and grants, ROTC scholarships, academic merit scholarships, and athletic scholarships. Perkins Loans (NDSL), PLUS, Stafford Loans (GSL), school loans, and SLS. Tuition Plan Inc. and deferred payment plan.
**Financial aid statistics:** 51% of aid is not need-based. In 1993-94, 95% of all undergraduate applicants received aid; 90% of freshman applicants. Average amounts of aid awarded freshmen: Scholarships and grants, $2,200; loans, $2,000.
**Supporting data/closing dates:** FAFSA/FAF: Priority filing date is February 1. School's own aid application: Priority filing date is February 1. Notification of awards begins April 1.
**Financial aid contact:** Debra Covert, Director of Financial Aid. 502 863-8027.

**STUDENT EMPLOYMENT.** College Work/Study Program. Institutional employment. 27% of full-time undergraduates work on campus during school year. Students may expect to earn an average of $1,200 during school year. Off-campus part-time employment opportunities rated "good."

**COMPUTER FACILITIES.** 45 IBM/IBM-compatible microcomputers; 21 are networked. Students may access Hewlett-Packard minicomputer/mainframe systems. Client/LAN operating systems include Apple/Macintosh, DOS, UNIX/XENIX/AIX, Novell. Computer languages and software packages include BASIC, C, COBOL, FORTRAN, Lotus 1-2-3, Turbo Pascal, WordPerfect; 15 in all. Computer facilities are available to all students.
**Fees:** Computer fee is included in tuition/fees.

**GRADUATE CAREER DATA.** Highest graduate school enrollments: U of Kentucky, U of Louisville, Vanderbilt U.

**PROMINENT ALUMNI/AE.** Gary Bauer, chief domestic adviser, Reagan Administration; Robert Bratcher, translator of the *Good News Bible;* Ron Meredith, federal district court judge.

# Kentucky Christian College

**Grayson, KY 41143-1199 606 474-6613**

**1994-95 Costs.** Tuition: $4,640. Room & board: $3,520. Fees, books, misc. academic expenses (school's estimate): $600.
**Enrollment.** Undergraduates: 240 men, 231 women (full-time). Freshman class: 246 applicants, 217 accepted, 166 enrolled.
**Test score averages/ranges.** Average SAT scores: 854 combined. Average ACT scores: 20 composite.
**Faculty.** 27 full-time; 10 part-time. 45% of faculty holds doctoral degree. Student/faculty ratio: 16 to 1.
**Selectivity rating.** Competitive.

**PROFILE.** Kentucky Christian, founded in 1919, is a church-affiliated college. Its 121-acre campus is located in the Appalachian foothills of eastern Kentucky.

**Accreditation:** AABC, SACS.
**Religious orientation:** Kentucky Christian College is affiliated with the Church of Christ/Christian Church; 30 semester hours of religion/theology required.
**Library:** Collections totaling over 73,987 volumes, 268 periodical subscriptions and 22 microform items.
**Athletic facilities:** Gymnasium, baseball and soccer fields.

**STUDENT BODY. Undergraduate profile:** 62% are state residents; 27% are transfers. 1% Asian-American, 1% Black, 98% White. Average age of undergraduates is 22.
**Freshman profile:** 94% of accepted applicants took ACT.
**Undergraduate achievement:** 75% of fall 1991 freshmen returned for fall 1992 term. 55% of entering class graduated.
**Foreign students:** Six students are from out of the country. Countries represented include Haiti, India, and Mexico; three in all.

**PROGRAMS OF STUDY. Degrees:** B.A., B.S.
**Majors:** Business Administration, Christian Ministry, Music, Psychology, Social Work, Teacher Education.
**Distribution of degrees:** The majors with the highest enrollment are Christian ministry, teacher education, and business administration.
**Requirements:** General education requirement.
**Academic regulations:** Freshmen must maintain minimum 1.85 GPA; sophomores, juniors, seniors, 2.0 GPA.
**Special:** At least one major and one minor required; every student majors in Bible as well as in one additional major or minor. Minors offered in business, Christian education, communications, history, missions, new church evangelism, pastoral counseling, psychology, secretarial science, social welfare, and youth ministry. Associate's degrees offered. Teacher certification in elementary and secondary education.
**Academic Assistance:** Remedial reading, writing, and math. Nonremedial tutoring.

**ADMISSIONS. Academic basis for candidate selection** (in order of priority): Standardized test scores, secondary school record, class rank, school's recommendation, essay.
**Nonacademic basis for candidate selection:** Character and personality and particular talent or ability are emphasized. Extracurricular participation is considered.
**Requirements:** Graduation from secondary school is required; GED is accepted. No specific distribution of secondary school units required. Minimum composite ACT score of 17 and minimum 2.0 GPA recommended. ACT is required; SAT may be substituted. Campus visit and interview recommended. Off-campus interviews available with admissions and alumni representatives.
**Procedure:** Suggest filing application by August 1; no deadline. Notification of admission on rolling basis. No set date by which applicants must accept offer. $100 nonrefundable room deposit. Freshmen accepted for terms other than fall.
**Special programs:** Admission may be deferred one year. Credit may be granted through CEEB Advanced Placement for scores of 4 or higher. Credit may be granted through CLEP general and subject exams, and military experience.
**Transfer students:** Transfer students accepted for terms other than fall. In fall 1992, 27% of all new students were transfers into all classes. Application deadline is August 1. Minimum 2.0 GPA recommended. Lowest course grade accepted is "C." At least 32 semester hours must be completed at the college to receive degree.
**Admissions contact:** Sandra Deakins, Director of Admissions. 606 474-3266.

**FINANCIAL AID. Available aid:** Pell grants, SEOG, state scholarships and grants, school scholarships and grants, private scholarships and grants, and academic merit scholarships. Perkins Loans (NDSL), PLUS, Stafford Loans (GSL), private loans, and SLS. University payment plan.
**Financial aid statistics:** 20% of aid is not need-based. In 1992-93, 92% of all freshman applicants received aid. Average amounts of aid awarded freshmen: Scholarships and grants, $3,428; loans, $2,625.
**Supporting data/closing dates:** FAFSA/FAF/FFS: Priority filing date is April 1; accepted on rolling basis. School's own aid application: Priority filing date is April 1; accepted on rolling basis. State aid form: Priority filing date is April 1. Notification of awards on rolling basis.
**Financial aid contact:** Jennie Bender, Director of Financial Aid. 606 474-3226.

# Kentucky State University

**Frankfort, KY 40601 — 502 227-6000**

**1994-95 Costs.** Tuition: $1,500 (state residents), $4,500 (out-of-state). Room: $1,226. Board: $1,456. Fees, books, misc. academic expenses (school's estimate): $900.
**Enrollment.** Undergraduates: 1,630 (full-time). Graduate enrollment: 80.
**Test score averages/ranges.** N/A.
**Faculty.** 123 full-time; 35 part-time. 55% of faculty holds doctoral degree. Student/faculty ratio: 12 to 1.
**Selectivity rating.** N/A.

**PROFILE.** Kentucky State, founded in 1886, is a public university of liberal studies. Programs are offered through the Colleges of Applied Sciences, Arts and Sciences, and Leadership Studies; the Community College; the Graduate Center/the School of Public Affairs; and the School of Business. Its 309-acre campus is located in Frankfort, 25 miles from Lexington.

**Accreditation:** SACS. Professionally accredited by the Council on Social Work Education, the National Association of Schools of Music, the National Council for Accreditation of Teacher Education, the National League for Nursing.
**Religious orientation:** Kentucky State University is nonsectarian; Students are encouraged to attend convocations.
**Library:** Collections totaling over 300,000 volumes.
**Special facilities/museums:** Art gallery, school for early childhood education, nutrition lab, agriculture research building, research farm, fish hatchery, electron microscope.
**Athletic facilities:** Gymnasium, tennis courts, weight room, track, baseball and football stadiums, intramural field, swimming pool.

**STUDENT BODY. Undergraduate profile:** 83% are state residents; 7% are transfers. 44% Black, 56% White. Average age of undergraduates is 25.
**Undergraduate achievement:** 62% of fall 1992 freshmen returned for fall 1993 term. 22% of entering class graduated. 10% of students who completed a degree program went on to graduate study within five years.
**Foreign students:** 19 students are from out of the country. Countries represented include India, Kenya, Nigeria, and Thailand.

**PROGRAMS OF STUDY. Degrees:** B.A., B.Mus., B.S.
**Majors:** Accounting, Applied Mathematics/Engineering, Art Education, Biology, Biology Education, Business Administration, Chemistry, Child Development/Family Relations, Computer Science, Criminal Justice, Early Elementary Education, Economics, English, English Education, History, History Education, Liberal Studies, Management, Marketing, Mathematics, Mathematics Education, Medical Technology, Microcomputers, Music Education, Music Performance, Physical Education, Political Science, Psychology, Public Administration, Social Studies Education, Social Work, Sociology, Studio Art, Textiles/Clothing/Merchandising.
**Distribution of degrees:** The majors with the highest enrollment are business administration, computer science, and criminal justice.
**Requirements:** General education requirement.
**Special:** Minors offered in many majors and in African-American studies, athletic training, fashion merchandising, finance, French, gerontology, philosophy, physics, recreation, Spanish, speech/theatre, and sports management. Associate's degrees offered. Self-designed majors. Dual degrees. Independent study. Pass/fail grading option. Internships. Cooperative education programs. Preprofessional programs in law, medicine, veterinary science, pharmacy, dentistry, optometry, community health, cytotechnology, engineering, medical technology, and physical therapy. Dual-degree engineering programs with U of Kentucky and U of Maryland. Member of Kentucky Educational Television consortium. Exchange program with Berea Coll. Teacher certification in elementary and secondary education. Certification in specific subject areas. Exchange programs abroad in England (Oxford U, U of London). ROTC. AFROTC at U of Kentucky.
**Honors:** Honors program.
**Academic Assistance:** Remedial reading, writing, math, and study skills. Nonremedial tutoring.

**STUDENT LIFE. Housing:** All unmarried, nonveteran students under age 21 must live on campus unless living with family. Women's and men's dorms. School-owned/operated apartments. 57% of students live in college housing.
**Services and counseling/handicapped student services:** Placement services. Health service. Counseling services for minority, military, and veteran students. Birth control, personal, and psychological counseling. Career and academic guidance services. Physically disabled student services.
**Campus organizations:** Undergraduate student government. Student newspaper (Thorobred News). Literary magazine. Yearbook. Jazz ensemble, Kentucky Players, intercollegiate debating, departmental and special-interest groups. Four fraternities, no chapter houses; four sororities, no chapter houses.
**Religious organizations:** Bahai Club, Baptist Student Union, Wesley Foundation.
**Minority/foreign student organizations:** Black Student Union. International Student Association.

**ATHLETICS. Physical education requirements:** Two semester hours of physical education required.
**Intercollegiate competition:** 10% of students participate. Baseball (M), basketball (M,W), cross-country (M,W), football (M), golf (M), softball (W), tennis (M,W), track (indoor) (M,W), track (outdoor) (M,W), track and field (indoor) (M,W), track and field (outdoor) (M,W), volleyball (W). Member of Great Lakes Valley Conference, NCAA Division II.
**Intramural and club sports:** 70% of students participate. Intramural basketball, softball, tennis, touch football, volleyball. Women's club cheerleading.

**ADMISSIONS. Academic basis for candidate selection** (in order of priority): Secondary school record, standardized test scores.
**Requirements:** Graduation from secondary school is required; GED is accepted. 21 units and the following program of study are required: 4 units of English, 3 units of math, 2 units of science, 1 unit of social studies, 1 unit of history, 8 units of electives. Minimum combined SAT score of 720 (composite ACT score of 18) and minimum 2.5 GPA required. ACT is required; SAT may be substituted. Campus visit recommended. No off-campus interviews.
**Procedure:** Take SAT or ACT by October of 12th year. Notification of admission on rolling basis. $85 room deposit, refundable until August 1. Freshmen accepted for terms other than fall.
**Special programs:** Credit and/or placement may be granted through CEEB Advanced Placement exams for scores of 3 or higher. Credit may be granted through CLEP general and subject exams. Credit and placement may be granted through ACT PEP and DANTES exams, and military and life experience. Early entrance/early admission program. Concurrent enrollment program.
**Transfer students:** Transfer students accepted for terms other than fall. In fall 1993, 7% of all new students were transfers into all classes. 297 transfer applications were received, 177 were accepted. Lowest course grade accepted is "C." Maximum number of transferable credits is 65 semester hours. At least 32 semester hours must be completed at the university to receive degree.
**Admissions contact:** Lyman R. Dale, M.S., Director of Records, Registration, and Admissions. 502 227-6813, 800 633-9415 (in-state), 800 325-1716 (out-of-state).

**FINANCIAL AID. Available aid:** Pell grants, SEOG, state grants, school scholarships, private scholarships and grants, academic merit scholarships, and athletic scholarships. SSIG. Perkins Loans (NDSL), PLUS, Stafford Loans (GSL), and SLS. Tuition Management Systems and deferred payment plan.

**Financial aid statistics:** 5% of aid is not need-based. In 1993-94, 85% of all undergraduate applicants received aid; 75% of freshman applicants. Average amounts of aid awarded freshmen: Scholarships and grants, $2,216; loans, $1,800.
**Supporting data/closing dates:** FAFSA/FAF/FFS: Priority filing date is April 15; deadline is in May. Notification of awards on rolling basis.
**Financial aid contact:** Carmella Conner, M.S.Ed., Director of Financial Aid. 502 227-5960.

**STUDENT EMPLOYMENT.** College Work/Study Program. Institutional employment. 32% of full-time undergraduates work on campus during school year. Students may expect to earn an average of $1,000 during school year. Off-campus part-time employment opportunities rated "good."

**COMPUTER FACILITIES.** 50 IBM/IBM-compatible and Macintosh/Apple microcomputers. Students may access IBM minicomputer/mainframe systems. Residence halls may be equipped with networked terminals, modems. Computer languages and software packages include Assembler, BASIC, COBOL, FORTRAN, Pascal, RPG; database, spreadsheet, word processing packages. Computer facilities are available to all students.
**Fees:** $10 computer fee per semester.
**Hours:** 8 AM-9 PM (M-F); 10 AM-4 PM (Sa).

**GRADUATE CAREER DATA.** Highest graduate school enrollments: Jackson State U, U of Kentucky, U of Louisville. 47% of graduates choose careers in business and industry. Companies and businesses that hire graduates: Ashland Oil, AT&T, Darcom, Department of Defense, Humana, Internal Revenue Service, Kroger, McDonnell Douglas.

**PROMINENT ALUMNI/AE.** Patricia Russel McCloud, attorney; Moneta Sleet, Pulitzer prize-winning photographer; Dr. Bailus Walker, Jr., Commissioner of Public Health, Massachusetts; Harrison B. Wilson, president, Norfolk State U; George Wilson, secretary, Corrections Cabinet, Kentucky.

# Kentucky Wesleyan College

**Owensboro, KY 42302-1039** **502 926-3111**

**1993-94 Costs.** Tuition: $7,400. Room & board: $3,950. Fees, books, misc. academic expenses (school's estimate): $650.
**Enrollment.** Undergraduates: 313 men, 349 women (full-time). Freshman class: 584 applicants, 497 accepted, 179 enrolled.
**Test score averages/ranges.** Average SAT scores: 420 verbal, 470 math. Average ACT scores: 22 English, 21 math, 22 composite.
**Faculty.** 51 full-time; 31 part-time. 60% of faculty holds doctoral degree. Student/faculty ratio: 9 to 1.
**Selectivity rating.** Less competitive.

**PROFILE.** Kentucky Wesleyan, founded in 1858, is a church-affiliated, liberal arts college. Its 62-acre campus is located in Owensboro, 100 miles from Louisville.

**Accreditation:** SACS. Professionally accredited by the National League for Nursing.
**Religious orientation:** Kentucky Wesleyan College is affiliated with the United Methodist Church; two semesters of religion required.
**Library:** Collections totaling over 93,940 volumes, 450 periodical subscriptions and 347 microform items.
**Special facilities/museums:** FM radio station.
**Athletic facilities:** Recreation center, basketball, racquetball, tennis, and volleyball courts, baseball, football, soccer, and softball fields, fitness and weight rooms, sauna, gymnasiums.

**STUDENT BODY. Undergraduate profile:** 78% are state residents; 34% are transfers. 3% Black, 97% White. Average age of undergraduates is 21.
**Freshman profile:** 2% of freshmen who took SAT scored 700 or over on math; 2% scored 600 or over on verbal, 4% scored 600 or over on math; 20% scored 500 or over on verbal, 37% scored 500 or over on math; 61% scored 400 or over on verbal, 80% scored 400 or over on math; 98% scored 300 or over on verbal, 96% scored 300 or over on math. 2% of freshmen who took ACT scored 30 or over on composite; 35% scored 24 or over on composite; 92% scored 18 or over on composite; 100% scored 12 or over on composite. 9% of accepted applicants took SAT; 79% took ACT. 89% of freshmen come from public schools.
**Undergraduate achievement:** 60% of fall 1992 freshmen returned for fall 1993 term. 45% of entering class graduated. 53% of students who completed a degree program immediately went on to graduate study.
**Foreign students:** Nine students are from out of the country. Countries represented include Japan; five in all.

**PROGRAMS OF STUDY. Degrees:** B.A., B.Mus., B.Mus.Ed., B.S., B.S.Nurs.
**Majors:** Accounting, Art, Art Education, Biology, Business Administration, Chemistry, Computer Science, Criminal Justice, Education, Engineering, English, History, Human Resources Administration, Interdisciplinary Studies, Mass Communications, Mathematics, Modern Languages, Music Education, Music Performance, Nursing, Physical Education, Physics, Political Science, Psychology, Religion/Philosophy, Secondary Education, Sociology, Speech/Theatre.
**Distribution of degrees:** The majors with the highest enrollment are criminal justice, education, and business administration; modern languages, speech/theatre, and physics have the lowest.
**Requirements:** General education requirement.
**Academic regulations:** Freshmen must maintain minimum 1.6 GPA; sophomores, 1.8 GPA; juniors, 2.0 GPA; seniors, 2.0 GPA.
**Special:** Minors offered in most majors. Associate's degrees offered. Self-designed majors. Double majors. Dual degrees. Independent study. Internships. Preprofessional programs in law, medicine, veterinary science, pharmacy, dentistry, theology, optometry, physical therapy, and Christian ministries. 3-2 engineering programs with Auburn U and U of Kentucky. Teacher certification in elementary and secondary education. Certification in specific subject areas. Study abroad in England (Harlaxton Coll) and other countries.
**Honors:** Honor societies.
**Academic Assistance:** Remedial study skills. Nonremedial tutoring.

**ADMISSIONS. Academic basis for candidate selection** (in order of priority): Secondary school record, standardized test scores, class rank, school's recommendation, essay.
**Nonacademic basis for candidate selection:** Character and personality, extracurricular participation, particular talent or ability, and alumni/ae relationship are considered.
**Requirements:** Graduation from secondary school is required; GED is accepted. 14 units and the following program of study are required: 4 units of English, 3 units of math, 3 units of science, 2 units of social studies, 2 units of electives. Minimum composite ACT score of 19 (combined SAT score of 800) and minimum 2.25 GPA required in college prep curriculum. Portfolio required of art program applicants. Audition required of music program applicants. Conditional admission possible for applicants not meeting standard requirements. SAT or ACT is required. Campus visit and interview recommended. No off-campus interviews.
**Procedure:** Application deadline is August 28. Notification of admission on rolling basis. No set date by which applicants must accept offer. $100 tuition deposit, refundable until May 1. $100 room deposit, refundable until May 1. Freshmen accepted for terms other than fall.
**Special programs:** Admission may be deferred one year. Credit and/or placement may be granted through CEEB Advanced Placement exams for scores of 3 or higher. Credit and/or placement may be granted through CLEP general and subject exams. Credit may be granted through DANTES exams and military experience. Credit and placement may be granted through challenge exams. Early entrance/early admission program. Concurrent enrollment program.
**Transfer students:** Transfer students accepted for terms other than fall. In fall 1993, 34% of all new students were transfers into all classes. 149 transfer applications were received, 147 were accepted. Application deadline is rolling for fall; rolling for spring. Minimum 2.25 GPA required. Lowest course grade accepted is "C." Maximum number of transferable credits is 64 semester hours from a two-year school and 96 semester hours from a four-year school. At least 32 semester hours must be completed at the college to receive degree.
**Admissions contact:** Gloria Smith Kunik, Director of Enrollment Services. 502 926-3111, extension 143.

**FINANCIAL AID. Available aid:** Pell grants, SEOG, Federal Nursing Student Scholarships, state scholarships and grants, school scholarships and grants, private scholarships and grants, academic merit scholarships, and athletic scholarships. Perkins Loans (NDSL), PLUS, Stafford Loans (GSL), private loans, and SLS. Knight Tuition Plans and deferred payment plan. Institutional payment plan.
**Financial aid statistics:** 69% of aid is not need-based. In 1993-94, 99% of all undergraduate applicants received aid; 95% of freshman applicants. Average amounts of aid awarded freshmen: Scholarships and grants, $4,736; loans, $2,600.
**Supporting data/closing dates:** FAFSA: Priority filing date is March 1. School's own aid application: Priority filing date is March 1. Notification of awards on rolling basis.
**Financial aid contact:** Lena C. Terry, Director of Financial Aid. 502 926-3111, extension 113.

# Lindsey Wilson College

**Columbia, KY 42728** **502 384-2126**

**1993-94 Costs.** Tuition: $6,080. Room: $1,340. Board: $2,110. Fees, books, misc. academic expenses (school's estimate): $350.
**Enrollment.** Undergraduates: 493 men, 513 women (full-time). Freshman class: 1,089 applicants, 865 accepted, 382 enrolled.
**Test score averages/ranges.** Average ACT scores: 19 composite.
**Faculty.** Student/faculty ratio: 18 to 1.
**Selectivity rating.** Less competitive.

**PROFILE.** Lindsey Wilson is a church-affiliated college. Founded as a preparatory school in 1903, it became a four-year college in 1986. Its 70-acre campus is located in Columbia, 100 miles from Lexington, Louisville, and Nashville.

**Accreditation:** SACS.
**Religious orientation:** Lindsey Wilson College is a nondenominational Christian school; one semester of religion required.
**Library:** Collections totaling over 62,164 volumes, 1,350 periodical subscriptions, and 227,812 microform items.
**Athletic facilities:** Fitness and sports centers.

**STUDENT BODY. Undergraduate profile:** 94% are state residents. 1% Asian-American, 8% Black, 1% Hispanic, 89% White, 1% Other. Average age of undergraduates is 24.
**Freshman profile:** 10% of accepted applicants took SAT; 90% took ACT. 90% of freshmen come from public schools.
**Undergraduate achievement:** 49% of fall 1992 freshmen returned for fall 1993 term. 16% of entering class graduated.
**Foreign students:** Countries represented include African countries, India, Japan, and the United Kingdom; six in all.

**PROGRAMS OF STUDY. Degrees:** B.A.
**Majors:** Accounting, Biology, Business Administration, Elementary Education, English, History, Human Services, Liberal Arts.
**Distribution of degrees:** The majors with the highest enrollment are elementary education, business administration, and human services; history and accounting have the lowest.
**Requirements:** General education requirement.
**Academic regulations:** Freshmen must maintain minimum 1.25 GPA.
**Special:** Minors offered in all majors. Associate's degrees offered. Double majors. Independent study. Pass/fail grading option. Internships. Cooperative education programs.

Preprofessional programs in law, medicine, pharmacy, and physical therapy. 2-2 agriculture program with U of Kentucky. Teacher certification in elementary and secondary education. Certification in specific subject areas.
**Academic Assistance:** Remedial reading, writing, math, and study skills. Nonremedial tutoring.

**ADMISSIONS. Academic basis for candidate selection** (in order of priority): School's recommendation, secondary school record, essay, standardized test scores, class rank.
**Nonacademic basis for candidate selection:** Particular talent or ability is emphasized. Character and personality and extracurricular participation are important. Geographical distribution and alumni/ae relationship are considered.
**Requirements:** Graduation from secondary school is recommended; GED is accepted. No specific distribution of secondary school units required. ACT is recommended. Campus visit and interview recommended. Off-campus interviews available with admissions and alumni representatives.
**Procedure:** Take SAT or ACT by June of 12th year. Visit college for interview by August of 12th year. Notification of admission on rolling basis. No set date by which applicants must accept offer. $40 room deposit, refundable until three weeks after beginning of term. Freshmen accepted for terms other than fall.
**Special programs:** Placement may be granted through CEEB Advanced Placement exams for scores of 3 or higher. Credit and/or placement may be granted through CLEP general and subject exams. Placement may be granted through challenge exams.
**Transfer students:** Transfer students accepted for terms other than fall. Lowest course grade accepted is "D."
**Admissions contact:** Kevin Thompson, M.A., Director of Admissions. 800 264-0138.

**FINANCIAL AID. Available aid:** Pell grants, SEOG, state scholarships and grants, school scholarships, private scholarships and grants, academic merit scholarships, athletic scholarships, and aid for undergraduate foreign students. Perkins Loans (NDSL), PLUS, Stafford Loans (GSL), school loans, private loans, and SLS. Payment plan may be individually arranged.
**Financial aid statistics:** In 1993-94, 95% of all undergraduate applicants received aid; 95% of freshman applicants. Average amounts of aid awarded freshmen: Scholarships and grants, $1,000; loans, $2,625.
**Supporting data/closing dates:** FAFSA/FAF: Accepted on rolling basis. School's own aid application: Accepted on rolling basis. State aid form: Priority filing date is April 15; deadline is June 30. Income tax forms: Accepted on rolling basis. Notification of awards on rolling basis.
**Financial aid contact:** Marilyn Radford, Director of Financial Aid. 502 384-8022.

# Midway College

**Midway, KY 40347-1120 — 606 846-4421**

**1994-95 Costs.** Tuition: $7,300. Room & board: $4,050. Fees, books, misc. academic expenses (school's estimate): $60.
**Enrollment.** Undergraduates: 6 men, 520 women (full-time). Freshman class: 717 applicants, 545 accepted, 393 enrolled.
**Test score averages/ranges.** Average ACT scores: 20 composite. Range of ACT scores of middle 50%: 16-22 composite.
**Faculty.** 38 full-time; 39 part-time. 33% of faculty holds doctoral degree. Student/faculty ratio: 12 to 1.
**Selectivity rating.** Less competitive.

**PROFILE.** Midway, founded in 1847, is a private, church-affiliated, liberal arts college. Its 105-acre campus is in Midway, 12 miles from Lexington.

**Accreditation:** SACS. Professionally accredited by the American Bar Association, the National League for Nursing.
**Religious orientation:** Midway College is affiliated with the Disciples of Christ; one semester of religion/theology required.
**Library:** Collections totaling over 34,500 volumes, 344 periodical subscriptions, and 5,769 microform items.
**Special facilities/museums:** Early childhood education center on campus.
**Athletic facilities:** Gymnasium, tennis courts, riding arena, weight room, soccer and softball fields.

**STUDENT BODY. Undergraduate profile:** 81% are state residents; 36% are transfers. 3% Asian-American, 7% Black, 89% White, 1% Other. Average age of undergraduates is 20.
**Freshman profile:** 15% of freshmen who took ACT scored 24 or over on composite; 69% scored 18 or over on composite; 98% scored 12 or over on composite; 100% scored 6 or over on composite.
**Undergraduate achievement:** 85% of fall 1992 freshmen returned for fall 1993 term. 36% of entering class graduated.
**Foreign students:** 10 students are from out of the country. Countries represented include Canada, Ethiopia, Hong Kong, Japan, and Malaysia; seven in all.

**PROGRAMS OF STUDY. Degrees:** B.A., B.S.
**Majors:** Accounting, Business Administration, Equine Studies, Liberal Studies, Nursing, Paralegal Studies, Teacher Education.
**Distribution of degrees:** The majors with the highest enrollment are business administration and nursing.
**Requirements:** General education requirement.
**Academic regulations:** Freshmen must maintain minimum 1.85 GPA; sophomores, juniors, seniors, 2.0 GPA.
**Special:** Associate's degrees offered. Double majors. Dual degrees. Pass/fail grading option. Internships. Preprofessional programs in law, medicine, veterinary science, pharmacy, dentistry, and theology. Teacher certification in early childhood and elementary education. Certification in specific subject areas.
**Honors:** Phi Beta Kappa. Honor societies.

**Academic Assistance:** Remedial reading, writing, and math. Nonremedial tutoring.

**ADMISSIONS. Academic basis for candidate selection** (in order of priority): Secondary school record, standardized test scores.
**Nonacademic basis for candidate selection:** Particular talent or ability is considered.
**Requirements:** Graduation from secondary school is required; GED is accepted. 18 units and the following program of study are required: 4 units of English, 2 units of math, 2 units of science, 3 units of social studies. Minimum composite ACT score of 18 (combined SAT score of 690) and minimum 2.2 GPA required. Minimum 3.0 GPA, minimum composite ACT score of 20, and interview required of applicants to nursing, paralegal, and teacher education programs. R.N. required of nursing program applicants. Conditional admission possible for applicants not meeting standard requirements. SAT or ACT is required. Campus visit recommended. No off-campus interviews.
**Procedure:** Suggest filing application by April 1. Application deadline is August 1. Notification of admission on rolling basis. $50 tuition deposit, refundable until May 1. $25 room deposit, refundable until May 1. Freshmen accepted for terms other than fall.
**Special programs:** Admission may be deferred. Credit and/or placement may be granted through CEEB Advanced Placement exams for scores of 3 or higher. Credit and/or placement may be granted through CLEP general and subject exams. Placement may be granted through challenge exams. Concurrent enrollment program.
**Transfer students:** Transfer students accepted for terms other than fall. In fall 1993, 36% of all new students were transfers into all classes. Minimum 2.0 GPA required. Lowest course grade accepted is "C." Maximum number of transferable credits is 90 semester hours.
**Admissions contact:** Carl Rollins, Director of Admissions. 800 755-0031, 606 846-5346.

**FINANCIAL AID. Available aid:** Pell grants, SEOG, state grants, school scholarships and grants, academic merit scholarships, athletic scholarships, and aid for undergraduate foreign students. Kentucky Higher Education Assistance Grant. Perkins Loans (NDSL), PLUS, Stafford Loans (GSL), and school loans. Tuition Plan Inc. and Tuition Management Systems. School's own payment plan.
**Financial aid statistics:** In 1993-94, 87% of all undergraduate applicants received aid.
**Supporting data/closing dates:** FAFSA/FAF: Accepted on rolling basis. Notification of awards on rolling basis.
**Financial aid contact:** Laura Keown, Director of Financial Aid. 606 846-5410.

# Morehead State University

**Morehead, KY 40351 — 606 783-2221**

**1994-95 Costs.** Tuition: $1,770 (state residents), $4,770 (out-of-state). Room & board: $2,800. Fees, books, misc. academic expenses (school's estimate): $610.
**Enrollment.** Undergraduates: 2,765 men, 3,546 women (full-time). Freshman class: 2,825 applicants, 2,495 accepted, 1,296 enrolled. Graduate enrollment: 484 men, 1,128 women.
**Test score averages/ranges.** Average ACT scores: 20 English, 19 math, 20 composite.
**Faculty.** 336 full-time. 59% of faculty holds highest degree in specific field.
**Selectivity rating.** Less competitive.

**PROFILE.** Morehead State, founded in 1922, is a comprehensive, public, liberal arts university. Programs are offered through the Schools of Applied Sciences and Technology, Business and Economics, Education, Humanities, Sciences and Mathematics, and Social Sciences. Its 809-acre campus is located in Morehead, 57 miles east of Lexington.

**Accreditation:** SACS. Professionally accredited by the American Dietetic Association, the American Veterinary Medical Association, the Council on Social Work Education, the National Association of Schools of Music, the National Council for Accreditation of Teacher Education, the National League for Nursing.
**Religious orientation:** Morehead State University is nonsectarian; no religious requirements.
**Library:** Collections totaling over 378,618 volumes, 2,037 periodical subscriptions, and 623,477 microform items.
**Special facilities/museums:** Appalachian folk art museum, moonlight school, natural biological/ecological habitat site, observatory, electron microscope.
**Athletic facilities:** Gymnasiums, baseball, football, and soccer fields, basketball, tennis, and volleyball courts, track, swimming pool, golf course, arena.

**STUDENT BODY. Undergraduate profile:** 85% are state residents. 1% Asian-American, 3% Black, 1% Hispanic, 95% White. Average age of undergraduates is 22.
**Freshman profile:** Majority of accepted applicants took ACT.
**Foreign students:** Countries represented include India, Japan, Malaysia, and Taiwan

**PROGRAMS OF STUDY. Degrees:** A.B., B.Bus.Admin., B.M., B.Mus.Ed., B.S., B.S.Nurs., B.Soc.Work, B.Univ.Studies.
**Majors:** Accounting, Agriculture, Art, Basic Business, Biology, Chemistry, Communications, Data Processing, Dietetics, Earth Science, Economics, Elementary Education, English, Environmental Sciences, Finance, French, Geography, Geology, Government, Health, History, Home Economics, Hotel/Restaurant/Institutional Management, Industrial Education, Industrial Technology, Interior Design, Journalism, Management, Marketing, Mathematics, Mathematics/Computer Programming, Medical Technology, Music, Music Education, Nursing, Paralegal Studies, Philosophy, Physical Education, Physics, Psychology, Radio/Television, Real Estate, Recreation, Secondary Education/Science, Social Science, Social Work, Sociology, Spanish, Special Education, Speech, Speech/Theatre, Textiles/Clothing, Theatre, University Studies, Veterinary Technology, Vocational Agriculture Education.
**Distribution of degrees:** The majors with the highest enrollment are elementary education, university studies, and accounting.
**Requirements:** General education requirement.
**Academic regulations:** Freshmen must maintain minimum 1.7 GPA; sophomores, 1.8 GPA; juniors, 1.9 GPA; seniors, 2.0 GPA.
**Special:** Minors offered in many majors and in approximately 15 other fields. Courses offered in Latin, religious studies, and Russian. Robotics program. Associate's degrees of-

fered. Self-designed majors. Dual degrees. Graduate school at which undergraduates may take graduate-level courses. Preprofessional programs in law, medicine, veterinary science, pharmacy, dentistry, optometry, chiropractic, engineering, forestry, and physical therapy. 2-2 and 3-2 engineering programs with Auburn U and U of Kentucky. Member of Appalachian Regional Consortium. Kentucky Legislature Intern Program in even-numbered years. Exchange program with Pikeville Coll. Teacher certification in early childhood, elementary, secondary, special education, and vo-tech education. Study abroad in England, France, and Spain. ROTC.
**Honors:** Honors program.
**Academic Assistance:** Remedial math and study skills. Nonremedial tutoring.

**STUDENT LIFE. Housing:** All unmarried freshmen must live on campus unless living with family. Coed, women's, and men's dorms. School-owned/operated apartments. Both on-campus and off-campus married-student housing. 58% of students live in college housing.
**Social atmosphere:** Morehead is a suitcase college where everyone goes away for the weekend. On-campus activities revolve around club gatherings and the student center on campus. Students head for Hardee's, the Baptist Student Union, the Wesley Foundation, and various bars and night spots off campus. With a diverse campus of almost 100 student organizations, no one group dominates student social life. Students enjoy the school's theatre productions, Homecoming, concerts, and sports, especially football and basketball.
**Services and counseling/handicapped student services:** Placement services. Health service. Counseling services for minority, military, veteran, and older students. Personal counseling. Career and academic guidance services. Religious counseling. Physically disabled student services. Learning disabled services. Tape recorders. Reader services for the blind.
**Campus organizations:** Undergraduate student government. Student newspaper (Trail Blazer, published once/week). Literary magazine. Yearbook. Radio and TV stations. 86 registered organizations. 14 fraternities, seven sororities. 20% of men join a fraternity. 18% of women join a sorority.
**Religious organizations:** Baptist Student Union, Campus Crusade for Christ, Chi Alpha, Christian Student Fellowship, Fellowship of Christian Athletes, Mormon Association, Muslim Student Association, Newman Catholic Student Center, Wesley Foundation.
**Minority/foreign student organizations:** Black Coalition, Black Gospel Ensemble. Cosmopolitan Club, Malaysian Student Organization.

**ATHLETICS. Physical education requirements:** Two semesters of physical education required.
**Intercollegiate competition:** 5% of students participate. Baseball (M), basketball (M,W), cheerleading (M,W), cross-country (M,W), diving (M,W), football (M), golf (M), riflery (M,W), softball (W), swimming (M,W), tennis (M,W), track (indoor) (M,W), track (outdoor) (M,W), volleyball (W). Member of NCAA Division I, NCAA Division I-AA for football, Ohio Valley Conference.
**Intramural and club sports:** Men's club bowling, soccer. Women's club bowling.

**ADMISSIONS. Academic basis for candidate selection** (in order of priority): Secondary school record, standardized test scores.
**Nonacademic basis for candidate selection:** Character and personality, extracurricular participation, and alumni/ae relationship are important.
**Requirements:** Graduation from secondary school is required; GED is accepted. 20 units and the following program of study are required: 4 units of English, 3 units of math, 2 units of science including 1 unit of lab, 2 units of social studies, 9 units of electives. Additional admissions requirements vary by department. Conditional admission possible for applicants not meeting standard requirements. ACT is required; SAT may be substituted. Campus visit and interview recommended. No off-campus interviews.
**Procedure:** Take SAT or ACT by December of 12th year. Visit college for interview by November of 12th year. Notification of admission on rolling basis. No set date by which applicants must accept offer. $75 room deposit, refundable until July 1. Freshmen accepted for terms other than fall.
**Special programs:** Admission may be deferred one semester. Credit and/or placement may be granted through CEEB Advanced Placement exams for scores of 3 or higher. Credit and/or placement may be granted through CLEP general exams. Credit may be granted through CLEP subject exams and DANTES exams. Credit and placement may be granted through challenge exams. Early entrance/early admission program. Concurrent enrollment program.
**Transfer students:** Transfer students accepted for terms other than fall. In fall 1993, 1,069 transfer applications were received, 885 were accepted. Application deadline is rolling for fall; rolling for spring. Minimum 2.0 GPA required. Lowest course grade accepted is "C."
**Admissions contact:** Charlie Myers, M.Ed., Director of Admissions. 606 783-2000.

**FINANCIAL AID. Available aid:** Pell grants, SEOG, Federal Nursing Student Scholarships, state grants, school scholarships, private scholarships and grants, ROTC scholarships, academic merit scholarships, athletic scholarships, and aid for undergraduate foreign students. Perkins Loans (NDSL), PLUS, Stafford Loans (GSL), and SLS. Deferred payment plan. Installment payment plan.
**Financial aid statistics:** 20% of aid is not need-based. In 1993-94, 80% of all undergraduate applicants received aid; 75% of freshman applicants. Average amounts of aid awarded freshmen: Scholarships and grants, $1,850; loans, $2,000.
**Supporting data/closing dates:** FAFSA: Priority filing date is April 1. School's own aid application: Priority filing date is April 1. Notification of awards on rolling basis.
**Financial aid contact:** Tim Rhodes, M.B.A., Director of Financial Aid. 606 783-2011.

**STUDENT EMPLOYMENT.** College Work/Study Program. Institutional employment. 24% of full-time undergraduates work on campus during school year. Students may expect to earn an average of $1,300 during school year. Off-campus part-time employment opportunities rated "fair."

**COMPUTER FACILITIES.** 600 IBM/IBM-compatible and Macintosh/Apple microcomputers; 400 are networked. Students may access Hewlett-Packard minicomputer/mainframe systems, Internet. Residence halls may be equipped with networked microcomputers. Client/LAN operating systems include Apple/Macintosh, DOS, Novell. Computer languages and software packages include BMDP, FORTRAN, MINITAB, Pascal, Pilot, Primeword, SAS, Script, SPSS, SPSS-X. Computer facilities are available to all students.
**Fees:** $20 computer fee per semester.

**GRADUATE CAREER DATA.** Companies and businesses that hire graduates: Armco Steel, Ashland Oil, IBM, Kentucky school system.

**PROMINENT ALUMNI/AE.** Phil Simms, quarterback, New York Giants; Terry McBrayer, lawyer and state legislator, Kentucky; Gary Cox, executive director, Kentucky Council on Higher Education.

# Murray State University

**Murray, KY 42071** **800 272-4678**

**1994-95 Costs.** Tuition: $1,600 (state residents), $4,640 (out-of-state). Room & board: $2,922. Fees, books, misc. academic expenses (school's estimate): $660.
**Enrollment.** Undergraduates: 2,847 men, 3,121 women (full-time). Freshman class: 2,288 applicants, 1,938 accepted, 1,197 enrolled. Graduate enrollment: 438 men, 759 women.
**Test score averages/ranges.** Average ACT scores: 23 English, 21 math, 22 composite.
**Faculty.** 347 full-time; 18 part-time. 78% of faculty holds doctoral degree. Student/faculty ratio: 18 to 1.
**Selectivity rating.** Less competitive.

**PROFILE.** Murray State, founded in 1922, is a public, comprehensive university. Programs are offered through the Colleges of Business and Public Affairs, Education, Fine Arts and Communication, Humanistic Studies, Industry Technology, and Science and the Department of Library Science. Its 350-acre campus is located in Murray.

**Accreditation:** SACS. Professionally accredited by the Accreditation Board for Engineering and Technology, the Accrediting Council on Education in Journalism and Mass Communication, the American Assembly of Collegiate Schools of Business, the American Dietetic Association, the American Speech-Language-Hearing Association, the American Veterinary Medical Association, the Council on Social Work Education, the National Association of Schools of Music, the National Council for Accreditation of Teacher Education, the National League for Nursing.
**Religious orientation:** Murray State University is nonsectarian; no religious requirements.
**Library:** Collections totaling over 460,000 volumes, and 2,500 periodical subscriptions.
**Special facilities/museums:** Biological station, agricultural lab farms, language lab.

**STUDENT BODY. Undergraduate profile:** 76% are state residents; 32% are transfers. 5% Black, 92% White, 3% Other. Average age of undergraduates is 21.
**Freshman profile:** 8% of freshmen who took ACT scored 30 or over on English, 3% scored 30 or over on math, 3% scored 30 or over on composite; 44% scored 24 or over on English, 23% scored 24 or over on math, 32% scored 24 or over on composite; 90% scored 18 or over on English, 77% scored 18 or over on math, 95% scored 18 or over on composite; 100% scored 12 or over on English, 100% scored 12 or over on math, 100% scored 12 or over on composite. 20% of accepted applicants took SAT; 100% took ACT. 85% of freshmen come from public schools.
**Undergraduate achievement:** 68% of fall 1992 freshmen returned for fall 1993 term. 35% of entering class graduated.
**Foreign students:** 77 students are from out of the country. Countries represented include Canada, China, Germany, Japan, Korea, and Malaysia; 46 in all.

**PROGRAMS OF STUDY. Degrees:** B.A., B.A.Bus., B.F.A., B.Info.Sys., B.Mus., B.Mus.Ed., B.S., B.S.Agri., B.S.Bus., B.S.Home Econ., B.S.Nurs., B.S.Voc.Tech.Ed.
**Majors:** Accounting, Agriculture, Art, Biological Science, Business Administration, Business Education, Chemistry, Child Development, Civil Engineering, Clothing/Textiles/Fashion, Communication Disorders, Communications, Computer Science, Computer Systems Management, Constuction Technology, Consumer Affairs, Criminal Justice, Distributive Education, Earth Science, Economics, Electrical Engineering, Elementary Education, Engineering Physics, English, Family/Consumer Studies, Family Services, Finance, Food/Nutrition/Dietetics, French, Geography, Geology, German, History, Home Economics, Industrial Arts Education, Journalism, Library Science, Management, Manufacturing Engineering Technology, Marketing, Mathematics, Medical Technology, Middle School Education, Mine Management, Music, Music Education, Music Performance, Music Theory/Composition, Nursing, Occupational Safety/Health, Office Administration, Organizational Communication, Philosophy, Physical Education, Physics, Political Science, Printing Management, Psychology, Public Administration, Radio/TV, Real Estate, Recreational/Leisure Studies, Rehabilitation Services, Secondary Education, Social Work, Sociology, Spanish, Speech/Theatre, Trainable Mentally Retarded, Vocational Education, Vocational-Technical Education.
**Distribution of degrees:** The majors with the highest enrollment are business, education, and journalism; library science and philosophy have the lowest.
**Requirements:** General education requirement.
**Academic regulations:** Minimum 2.0 GPA must be maintained.
**Special:** Area of concentration or a major and minor required. Minors offered in many majors and in advertising, anthropology, athletic coaching, child studies, computer data processing, early childhood education, equine science, paralegal studies, religious studies, retail merchandising, secretarial science, and social gerontology. Interdisciplinary studies. Associate's degrees offered. Double majors. Independent study. Internships. Cooperative education programs. Preprofessional programs in law, medicine, veterinary science, pharmacy, dentistry, and optometry. Sea Semester. Member of National Student Exchange (NSE). Teacher certification in early childhood, elementary, secondary, special education, and vo-tech education. Certification in specific subject areas. Study abroad in numerous countries. ROTC.
**Honors:** Phi Beta Kappa. Honors program. Honor societies.
**Academic Assistance:** Remedial reading, writing, math, and study skills. Nonremedial tutoring.

**STUDENT LIFE. Housing:** Students from some counties in Illinois, Indiana, Missouri, and Tennessee who accept out-of-state waivers must live on campus. Coed, women's, and

men's dorms. Sorority and fraternity housing. Off-campus privately-owned housing. On-campus married-student housing. 50% of students live in college housing.
**Services and counseling/handicapped student services:** Placement services. Health service. Women's center. Testing center. Learning center. Counseling services for minority, military, veteran, and older students. Birth control, personal, and psychological counseling. Career and academic guidance services. Learning disabled program/services.
**Campus organizations:** Undergraduate student government. Student newspaper. Yearbook. Radio and TV stations. Brass choir, ensembles, chamber singers, choir, chorus, concert and marching bands, string and woodwind quintets, opera workshop, orchestra, symphonic band, wind sinfonietta, intercollegiate debating, interpretive activities groups, departmental, political, and special-interest groups, 168 organizations in all. 16 fraternities, 10 chapter houses; nine sororities, six chapter houses. 32% of men join a fraternity. 34% of women join a sorority.
**Religious organizations:** Several religious groups.

**ATHLETICS. Physical education requirements:** None.
**Intercollegiate competition:** 1% of students participate. Baseball (M), basketball (M,W), cross-country (W), football (M), golf (M), riflery (M,W), tennis (M,W), track (M), track and field (W), volleyball (W). Member of Kentucky Women's Intercollegiate Conference, NCAA Division I, NCAA Division I-AA for football, Ohio Valley Conference.

**ADMISSIONS. Academic basis for candidate selection** (in order of priority): Class rank, standardized test scores, secondary school record, school's recommendation.
**Nonacademic basis for candidate selection:** Extracurricular participation, particular talent or ability, and alumni/ae relationship are emphasized.
**Requirements:** Graduation from secondary school is required; GED is accepted. 20 units and the following program of study are required: 4 units of English, 3 units of math, 2 units of lab science, 2 units of social studies, 1 unit of history. College preparatory curriculum required of all students. Minimum composite ACT score of 20 and rank in top half of secondary school class required of in-state applicants. Minimum composite ACT score of 21 and rank in top third of secondary school class required of out-of-state applicants. Portfolio required of art program applicants. Audition required of music program applicants. ACT is required. Campus visit and interview recommended. Off-campus interviews available with an admissions representative.
**Procedure:** Take ACT by December of 12th year. Visit college for interview by May 1 of 12th year. Application deadline is August 1. Notification of admission on rolling basis. No set date by which applicants must accept offer. $75 room deposit, refundable until July 1. Freshmen accepted for terms other than fall.
**Special programs:** Admission may be deferred. Credit may be granted through CEEB Advanced Placement for scores of 3 or higher. Credit may be granted through CLEP general and subject exams, challenge exams, and military and life experience.
**Transfer students:** Transfer students accepted for terms other than fall. In fall 1993, 32% of all new students were transfers into all classes. Application deadline is August 1 for fall; December 1 for spring. SAT/ACT scores required of transfer applicants with fewer than 24 semester hours. Both secondary school and college transcripts required for transfer applicants with fewer than 24 semester hours. Minimum 2.0 GPA required. Lowest course grade accepted is "D." Maximum number of transferable credits is 67 semester hours. 24 of the last 36 semester hours must be completed at the university to receive degree.
**Admissions contact:** Phil Bryan, M.S., Dean of Admissions and Registrar. 800 272-4678, 502 762-2896.

**FINANCIAL AID. Available aid:** Pell grants, SEOG, state scholarships and grants, school scholarships, private scholarships, ROTC scholarships, academic merit scholarships, and athletic scholarships. Perkins Loans (NDSL), PLUS, Stafford Loans (GSL), NSL, state loans, school loans, and SLS. Deferred payment plan. Monthly payment plan.
**Financial aid statistics:** 24% of aid is not need-based. In 1993-94, 63% of all undergraduate applicants received aid; 50% of freshman applicants. Average amounts of aid awarded freshmen: Scholarships and grants, $1,300; loans, $2,000.
**Supporting data/closing dates:** FAFSA: Priority filing date is April 1; accepted on rolling basis. School's own aid application: Priority filing date is April 1; accepted on rolling basis. Notification of awards on rolling basis.
**Financial aid contact:** John McDougal, M.S., Director of Financial Aid. 502 762-2546, 800 272-4678.

**STUDENT EMPLOYMENT.** College Work/Study Program. Institutional employment. 18% of full-time undergraduates work on campus during school year. Students may expect to earn an average of $1,200 during school year. Off-campus part-time employment opportunities rated "good."

**COMPUTER FACILITIES.** 225 IBM/IBM-compatible and Macintosh/Apple microcomputers. Students may access IBM minicomputer/mainframe systems, BITNET, Internet. Residence halls may be equipped with stand-alone microcomputers, networked terminals. Client/LAN operating systems include Apple/Macintosh, DOS, OS/2, Windows NT. Computer facilities are available to all students.
**Fees:** None.

# Northern Kentucky University

**Highland Heights, KY 41099-7010 — 606 572-5100**

**1993-94 Costs.** Tuition: $1,720 (state residents), $4,720 (out-of-state). Room & board: $2,950-$3,240. Fees, books, misc. academic expenses (school's estimate): $500.
**Enrollment.** Undergraduates: 2,716 men, 3,116 women (full-time). Freshman class: 2,384 applicants, 2,384 accepted, 1,636 enrolled. Graduate enrollment: 191 men, 461 women.
**Test score averages/ranges.** Average ACT scores: 20 composite.
**Faculty.** 368 full-time; 241 part-time. 62% of faculty holds doctoral degree. Student/faculty ratio: 15 to 1.
**Selectivity rating.** Noncompetitive.

**PROFILE.** Northern Kentucky, founded in 1968, is a public university. Programs are offered through the Colleges of Arts and Sciences, Business, and Professional Studies and the Salmon P. Chase College of Law. Its 300-acre campus is located in Highland Heights, seven miles southeast of Cincinnati.

**Accreditation:** SACS. Professionally accredited by the American Bar Association, the American Medical Association (CAHEA), the Association of American Law Schools, the Council on Social Work Education, the National League for Nursing.
**Religious orientation:** Northern Kentucky University is nonsectarian; no religious requirements.
**Library:** Collections totaling over 236,879 volumes, 1,564 periodical subscriptions, and 606,167 microform items.
**Special facilities/museums:** Art gallery, anthropology, biology, and geology museums, research/technical center, two electron microscopes.
**Athletic facilities:** Gymnasium, track, swimming pool, weight room, badminton, basketball, racquetball, tennis, and volleyball courts, baseball, soccer, and softball fields.

**STUDENT BODY. Undergraduate profile:** 78% are state residents; 24% are transfers. 2% Black, 97% White, 1% Other. Average age of undergraduates is 25.
**Freshman profile:** 100% of accepted applicants took ACT.
**Foreign students:** 145 students are from out of the country. Countries represented include Bangladesh, India, Japan, Jordan, Pakistan, and Thailand; 47 in all.

**PROGRAMS OF STUDY. Degrees:** B.A., B.F.A., B.Mus., B.Mus.Ed., B.S., B.S.Nurs., B.Soc.Work.
**Majors:** Accounting, Anthropology, Applied Sociology/Anthropology, Art, Art Education, Biology, Business Education, Chemistry, Computer Science, Economics, Electrical Engineering Technology, Elementary Education, English, Finance, French, Geography, Geology, Graphic Design, History, Industrial Education/Technology, Information Systems, International Studies, Journalism, Justice Studies, Labor Relations/Industrial Relations, Management, Manufacturing Engineering Technology, Marketing, Mathematics, Mathematics/Physical Science, Mental Health/Human Services, Middle Grades Education, Music, Music Education, Nursing, Office Systems Technology, Philosophy, Physical Education, Physics, Political Science, Psychology, Public Administration, Radio/Television, Radiologic Technology, Science, Secondary Education, Social Studies, Social Work, Sociology, Spanish, Speech, Speech/Theatre Arts, Theatre Arts.
**Distribution of degrees:** The majors with the highest enrollment are elementary education, marketing, and management; geology and philosophy have the lowest.
**Requirements:** General education requirement.
**Academic regulations:** Freshmen must maintain minimum 1.89 GPA; sophomores, 1.89 GPA; juniors, 2.0 GPA; seniors, 2.0 GPA.
**Special:** Minors offered in all majors and in applied physics, archaeology, business administration, Latin American studies, legal studies, religious studies, and urban studies. Associate's degrees offered. Self-designed majors. Double majors. Independent study. Pass/fail grading option. Internships. Cooperative education programs. Graduate school at which undergraduates may take graduate-level courses. Preprofessional programs in law, medicine, veterinary science, pharmacy, dentistry, optometry, engineering, forestry, medical technology, physical therapy, and wildlife management. 3-2 engineering program with U of Kentucky. Member of Greater Cincinnati Consortium of Colleges and Universities and of Southwestern Ohio Council on Higher Education. Teacher certification in elementary and secondary education. Study abroad in Austria, England, France, Germany, Ireland, Italy, Scotland, Spain, and Wales. ROTC. AFROTC at U of Cincinnati.
**Honors:** Honors program.
**Academic Assistance:** Remedial math. Nonremedial tutoring.

**STUDENT LIFE. Housing:** Coed dorms. 6% of students live in college housing.
**Social atmosphere:** On campus, students gather at the cafeteria, the Box, and the University Center; off campus, the Skyline Tavern is a popular gathering spot. "Greeks are involved in almost every aspect of campus life," reports the editor of the student newspaper. Other influential groups on campus include the Black Women's Organization, the African American Affairs Office, the Newman Center, the Baptist Student Union, and Residence Hall Students. Among the most popular on-campus social events are Homecoming, the Norse Leadership Society Retreat, Martin Luther King, Jr. Day Celebration, and Greek Week. Also popular are the Thursday night spaghetti dinners at the Newman Center and soccer, volleyball, and basketball games. "On-campus life is getting better because of the new Residence Halls, but many people still leave campus and don't hang out there a lot. Students frequently go to Cincinnati to the bars and to the ballet; it's a very diverse group."
**Services and counseling/handicapped student services:** Placement services. Health service. Women's center. Day care. Educational Media Services. Counseling services for minority, military, veteran, and older students. Birth control, personal, and psychological counseling. Career and academic guidance services. Religious counseling. Physically disabled student services. Learning disabled services. Notetaking services. Tape recorders. Tutors.
**Campus organizations:** Undergraduate student government. Student newspaper (Northerner, published once/week). Radio and TV stations. Choir, chamber singers, debating, Judicial Council, varsity club, peer support group, Young Democrats, Campus Republicans, Panhellenic Council, Interfraternity Council, departmental groups, special-interest groups, 56 organizations in all. Six fraternities, no chapter houses; four sororities, no chapter houses. 3% of men join a fraternity. 3% of women join a sorority.
**Religious organizations:** Baptist Student Union, Wesley Foundation, Christian Student Fellowship, Newman Center, Campus Advance.
**Minority/foreign student organizations:** Black United Students, Black Women's Organization, Rebuilders of African Humanity. International Student Union.

**ATHLETICS. Physical education requirements:** None.
**Intercollegiate competition:** 1% of students participate. Baseball (M), basketball (M,W), cheerleading (M,W), cross-country (M,W), golf (M), soccer (M), softball (W), tennis (M,W), volleyball (W). Member of Great Lakes Valley Conference, NCAA Division II.
**Intramural and club sports:** 20% of students participate. Intramural basketball, camping, cycling, dancercize, flag football, inner-tube water polo, racquetball, skiing, soccer, softball, swimming, tennis, triathlon, volleyball, walleyball. Men's club rugby. Women's club soccer.

**ADMISSIONS. Academic basis for candidate selection** (in order of priority): Secondary school record, standardized test scores, class rank, school's recommendation.

**Nonacademic basis for candidate selection:** Particular talent or ability is considered.
**Requirements:** Graduation from secondary school is recommended; GED is accepted. 20 units and the following program of study are required: 4 units of English, 3 units of math, 2 units of lab science, 2 units of foreign language, 2 units of social studies, 7 units of academic electives. ACT score in the top 50th percentile and rank in top half of secondary school class (or demonstration of academic ability in some other manner) recommended of out-of-state applicants. Different entrance requirements and selective admission for nursing and radiologic technology program applicants. ACT is required. Campus visit recommended. No off-campus interviews.
**Procedure:** Take ACT by October of 12th year. Visit college for interview by October of 12th year. Suggest filing application by May 1. Application deadline is August 26. Notification of admission on rolling basis. $100 room deposit, refundable until August 31. Freshmen accepted for terms other than fall.
**Special programs:** Credit and/or placement may be granted through CEEB Advanced Placement exams for scores of 2 or higher. Credit may be granted through CLEP general and subject exams. Credit and placement may be granted through ACT PEP, DANTES, and challenge exams and military and life experience. Early entrance/early admission program. Concurrent enrollment program.
**Transfer students:** Transfer students accepted for terms other than fall. In fall 1992, 24% of all new students were transfers into all classes. 926 transfer applications were received, 925 were accepted. Application deadline is May 1 for fall; November 1 for spring. Minimum 2.0 GPA required. Lowest course grade accepted is "C." At least 90 semester hours must be completed at the university to receive degree.
**Admissions contact:** Gregory Stewart, Ph.D., Director of Admissions. 606 572-5220.

**FINANCIAL AID. Available aid:** Pell grants, SEOG, state grants, school scholarships, ROTC scholarships, and athletic scholarships. Perkins Loans (NDSL), PLUS, Stafford Loans (GSL), private loans, and SLS. Deferred payment plan. Institutional tuition installment plan.
**Financial aid statistics:** 35% of aid is not need-based. In 1992-93, 40% of all undergraduate applicants received aid; 11% of freshman applicants. Average amounts of aid awarded freshmen: Scholarships and grants, $1,560; loans, $2,100.
**Supporting data/closing dates:** FAFSA: Priority filing date is in April. School's own aid application: Priority filing date is April. Notification of awards on rolling basis.
**Financial aid contact:** Robert Sprague, M.A., Director of Financial Aid. 606 572-5143.

**STUDENT EMPLOYMENT.** College Work/Study Program. Institutional employment. 10% of full-time undergraduates work on campus during school year. Students may expect to earn an average of $2,423 during school year. Off-campus part-time employment opportunities rated "excellent."

**COMPUTER FACILITIES.** 100 Macintosh/Apple microcomputers; 55 are networked. Students may access Digital minicomputer/mainframe systems. Residence halls may be equipped with stand-alone microcomputers, networked terminals. Computer languages and software packages include dBASE, Lotus 1-2-3, Microsoft Word, Quattro, WordPerfect; 10 in all. Computer facilities are available to all students.
**Fees:** None.
**Hours:** 8:30 AM-11:30 PM (M-Th); 8:30 AM-5 PM (F); 10 AM-4 PM (Sa); noon-6 PM (Su).

**GRADUATE CAREER DATA.** Companies and businesses that hire graduates: AT&T, Cincinnati Bell, P&G, Structural Dynamics.

**PROMINENT ALUMNI/AE.** Sandra Gubser, secretary of cabinet for work force development, state of Kentucky; Dr. Joseph Beechem, assistant professor of molecular biology, physiology, and biophysics, Vanderbilt U.

# Pikeville College

**Pikeville, KY 41501** **606 432-9200**

**1993-94 Costs.** Tuition: $5,500. Room & board: $3,000. Fees, books, misc. academic expenses (school's estimate): $900.
**Enrollment.** Undergraduates: 241 men, 560 women (full-time). Freshman class: 1,185 applicants, 675 accepted, 375 enrolled.
**Test score averages/ranges.** Average ACT scores: 20 English, 19 math, 20 composite.
**Faculty.** 54 full-time; 6 part-time. 46% of faculty holds doctoral degree. Student/faculty ratio: 16 to 1.
**Selectivity rating.** Less competitive.

**PROFILE.** Pikeville, founded in 1889, is a private, church-affiliated, liberal arts college. Its 20-acre campus is located in Pikeville, in eastern Kentucky.

**Accreditation:** SACS.
**Religious orientation:** Pikeville College is affiliated with the Presbyterian Church USA; six semesters of religion/theology required.
**Library:** Collections totaling over 90,000 volumes, 470 periodical subscriptions, and 14,500 microform items.
**Special facilities/museums:** Simulated hospital ward.
**Athletic facilities:** Gymnasium, tennis courts, city tennis courts and running track, swimming pool, outdoor basketball court, baseball and softball field.

**STUDENT BODY. Undergraduate profile:** 90% are state residents; 33% are transfers. 1% Black, 99% White. Average age of undergraduates is 24.
**Freshman profile:** 4% of freshmen who took ACT scored 30 or over on English, 1% scored 30 or over on math, 1% scored 30 or over on composite; 19% scored 24 or over on English, 6% scored 24 or over on math, 8% scored 24 or over on composite; 94% scored 18 or over on English, 71% scored 18 or over on math, 78% scored 18 or over on composite; 100% scored 12 or over on English, 96% scored 12 or over on math, 98% scored 12 or over on composite; 100% scored 6 or over on math, 100% scored 6 or over on composite. 70% of accepted applicants took ACT. 100% of freshmen come from public schools.
**Undergraduate achievement:** 69% of fall 1992 freshmen returned for fall 1993 term. 45% of entering class graduated. 1% of students who completed a degree program immediately went on to graduate study.
**Foreign students:** Countries represented include Nigeria.

**PROGRAMS OF STUDY. Degrees:** B.A., B.Bus.Admin., B.S.
**Majors:** Art, Biology, Business Education, Chemistry, Computer/Information Sciences, Elementary Education, General Business, History, Human Services, Mathematics, Medical Technology, Office Administration, Psychology, Secondary Education, Special Education.
**Distribution of degrees:** The majors with the highest enrollment are education and business.
**Requirements:** General education requirement.
**Academic regulations:** Minimum 2.0 GPA must be maintained.
**Special:** Medical technology majors apply at end of junior year for fourth-year lab work. Associate's degrees offered. Double majors. Dual degrees. Independent study. Pass/fail grading option. Internships. Member of Appalachian Consortium. Teacher certification in early childhood, elementary, secondary, and special education. Certification in specific subject areas.
**Academic Assistance:** Remedial reading, writing, math, and study skills. Nonremedial tutoring.

**ADMISSIONS. Academic basis for candidate selection** (in order of priority): Secondary school record, standardized test scores, school's recommendation, class rank.
**Nonacademic basis for candidate selection:** Character and personality, extracurricular participation, particular talent or ability, and alumni/ae relationship are considered.
**Requirements:** Graduation from secondary school is recommended; GED is accepted. 19 units and the following program of study are recommended: 4 units of English, 2 units of math, 2 units of science, 2 units of social studies. Foreign language study recommended. Minimum composite ACT score of 17 and separate application required of nursing program applicants; previous medical training recommended. Conditional admission possible for applicants not meeting standard requirements. Special Services Unit for applicants not normally admissible. ACT is required; SAT may be substituted. Admissions interview recommended. Off-campus interviews available with an admissions representative.
**Procedure:** Take SAT or ACT by February of 12th year. Application deadline is September 7. Notification of admission on rolling basis. $50 refundable room deposit. Freshmen accepted for terms other than fall.
**Special programs:** Admission may be deferred. Credit and/or placement may be granted through CEEB Advanced Placement exams. Credit and/or placement may be granted through CLEP general and subject exams. Early entrance/early admission program. Concurrent enrollment program.
**Transfer students:** Transfer students accepted for terms other than fall. In fall 1993, 33% of all new students were transfers into all classes. 110 transfer applications were received, 125 were accepted. Lowest course grade accepted is "C."
**Admissions contact:** John W. Sanders, Ed.D., Director of Admissions. 606 432-9322, 606 432-9382.

**FINANCIAL AID. Available aid:** Pell grants, SEOG, state scholarships and grants, school scholarships and grants, private scholarships and grants, academic merit scholarships, and athletic scholarships. Perkins Loans (NDSL), PLUS, Stafford Loans (GSL), NSL, state loans, school loans, private loans, and SLS. Deferred payment plan.
**Financial aid statistics:** In 1993-94, 85% of all freshman applicants received aid. Average amounts of aid awarded freshmen: Scholarships and grants, $2,000.
**Supporting data/closing dates:** FAFSA/FAF: Priority filing date is March 15. School's own aid application: Priority filing date is March 15. Notification of awards on rolling basis.
**Financial aid contact:** Bobby G. Price, Coordinator of Financial Aid. 606 432-9382.

# Spalding University

**Louisville, KY 40203** **502 585-9911**

**1994-95 Costs.** Tuition: $8,400. Room & board: $2,800. Fees, books, misc. academic expenses (school's estimate): $496.
**Enrollment.** Undergraduates: 70 men, 519 women (full-time). Freshman class: 278 applicants, 216 accepted, 96 enrolled. Graduate enrollment: 95 men, 274 women.
**Test score averages/ranges.** Average ACT scores: 20 composite.
**Faculty.** 61 full-time; 30 part-time. 60% of faculty holds doctoral degree. Student/faculty ratio: 18 to 1.
**Selectivity rating.** Competitive.

**PROFILE.** Spalding, founded in 1814, is a church-affiliated university of liberal arts and sciences. Its six-acre campus is located in downtown Louisville.

**Accreditation:** SACS. Professionally accredited by the American Dietetic Association, the Council on Social Work Education, the National Council for Accreditation of Teacher Education, the National League for Nursing.
**Religious orientation:** Spalding University is an interdenominational Christian school; two semesters of theology required.
**Library:** Collections totaling over 154,555 volumes, 403 periodical subscriptions, and 13,382 microform items.
**Special facilities/museums:** Art museum, on-campus preschool, radio and recording studios.
**Athletic facilities:** Gymnasium, weight rooms, exercise room.

**STUDENT BODY. Undergraduate profile:** 90% are state residents; 50% are transfers. 1% Asian-American, 8% Black, 89% White, 2% Other. Average age of undergraduates is 28.
**Freshman profile:** 11% of freshmen who took SAT scored 600 or over on math; 33% scored 500 or over on math; 56% scored 400 or over on verbal, 78% scored 400 or over on

math; 78% scored 300 or over on verbal, 100% scored 300 or over on math. Majority of accepted applicants took ACT. 80% of freshmen come from public schools.
**Undergraduate achievement:** 79% of fall 1992 freshmen returned for fall 1993 term. 55% of entering class graduated. 30% of students who completed a degree program went on to graduate study within 10 years.
**Foreign students:** 10 students are from out of the country. Countries represented include Germany, India, Japan, Trinidad, the United Kingdom, and the former Yugoslav Republics; six in all.

**PROGRAMS OF STUDY. Degrees:** B.A., B.S., B.S.Nurs.
**Majors:** Art, Biology, Business Administration, Chemistry, Communications, Dietetics, Education, English, History, Information Systems, Liberal Studies, Library Science, Mathematics, Nursing, Pastoral Ministry, Philosophy, Religious Studies, Social Sciences, Social Work, Sociology, Special Education.
**Distribution of degrees:** The majors with the highest enrollment are nursing, education, and business administration; chemistry, mathematics, and religious studies have the lowest.
**Requirements:** General education requirement.
**Academic regulations:** Minimum 2.0 GPA must be maintained.
**Special:** Minors offered in all majors. Associate's degrees offered. Self-designed majors. Double majors. Independent study. Accelerated study. Pass/fail grading option. Internships. Graduate school at which undergraduates may take graduate-level courses. Preprofessional programs in law, medicine, veterinary science, and dentistry. Member of Kentuckiana Metroversity Consortium; exchange possible. Teacher certification in early childhood, elementary, secondary, and special education. Certification in specific subject areas. Junior Year Abroad. ROTC at U of Louisville. AFROTC at Indiana U Southeast.
**Honors:** Honor societies.
**Academic Assistance:** Remedial reading, writing, and math. Nonremedial tutoring.

**ADMISSIONS. Academic basis for candidate selection** (in order of priority): Secondary school record, standardized test scores, class rank, school's recommendation.
**Nonacademic basis for candidate selection:** Particular talent or ability is important. Character and personality, extracurricular participation, and alumni/ae relationship are considered.
**Requirements:** Graduation from secondary school is recommended; GED is accepted. 16 units and the following program of study are recommended: 4 units of English, 2 units of math, 2 units of science, 2 units of foreign language, 2 units of social studies. Minimum composite ACT score of 18 (combined SAT score of 800), rank in top half of secondary school class, and minimum 2.0 GPA required. R.N.'s required of nursing program applicants to Weekend Coll. Conditional admission possible for applicants not meeting standard requirements. SAT or ACT is recommended. Campus visit and interview recommended. Off-campus interviews available with an admissions representative.
**Procedure:** Take SAT or ACT by August 1 of 12th year. Visit college for interview by August 1 of 12th year. Suggest filing application by March 1. Application deadline is August 15. Notification of admission on rolling basis. $50 tuition deposit, refundable until June 1. $100 refundable room deposit. Freshmen accepted for terms other than fall.
**Special programs:** Admission may be deferred one year. Credit and/or placement may be granted through CEEB Advanced Placement exams for scores of 3 or higher. Credit and/or placement may be granted through CLEP general exams. Credit may be granted through CLEP subject exams, challenge exams, and life experience. Credit and placement may be granted through military experience. Concurrent enrollment program.
**Transfer students:** Transfer students accepted for terms other than fall. In fall 1993, 50% of all new students were transfers into all classes. 359 transfer applications were received, 219 were accepted. Application deadline is August 15 for fall; December 31 for spring. Minimum 2.5 GPA recommended. Lowest course grade accepted is "C." Maximum number of transferable credits is 64 semester hours. At least 32 semester hours must be completed at the university to receive degree.
**Admissions contact:** Dorothy Allen, Director of Admissions. 502 585-7111.

**FINANCIAL AID. Available aid:** Pell grants, SEOG, state grants, school scholarships and grants, private scholarships, ROTC scholarships, and academic merit scholarships. Perkins Loans (NDSL), PLUS, Stafford Loans (GSL), NSL, state loans, school loans, and SLS.
**Financial aid statistics:** 10% of aid is not need-based. In 1993-94, 92% of all undergraduate applicants received aid; 84% of freshman applicants. Average amounts of aid awarded freshmen: Scholarships and grants, $2,578; loans, $3,701.
**Supporting data/closing dates:** FAFSA/FAF/FFS: Priority filing date is March 15. School's own aid application: Priority filing date is March 15. Notification of awards on rolling basis.
**Financial aid contact:** Elinor Starr, M.S., Director of Financial Aid. 502 585-9911, extension 241.

# Thomas More College

**Crestview Hills, KY 41017 — 606 341-5800**

**1993-94 Costs.** Tuition: $9,072. Room & board: $3,780. Fees, books, misc. academic expenses (school's estimate): $610.
**Enrollment.** Undergraduates: 399 men, 412 women (full-time). Freshman class: 835 applicants, 605 accepted, 286 enrolled.
**Test score averages/ranges.** Average SAT scores: 450 verbal, 550 math. Average ACT scores: 21 composite.
**Faculty.** 68 full-time; 42 part-time. 55% of faculty holds highest degree in specific field. Student/faculty ratio: 12 to 1.
**Selectivity rating.** Competitive.

**PROFILE.** Thomas More, founded in 1921, is a church-affiliated college. Its 320-acre campus is located in Crestview Hills, eight miles south of Cincinnati.
**Accreditation:** SACS. Professionally accredited by the Council on Social Work Education, the National League for Nursing.
**Religious orientation:** Thomas More College is affiliated with the Roman Catholic Church; nine semester hours of theology required.
**Library:** Collections totaling over 120,000 volumes, 500 periodical subscriptions, and 2,755 microform items.
**Special facilities/museums:** Art gallery, X-ray diffraction machine, research-grade electromagnets, research facility.
**Athletic facilities:** Gymnasium, basketball and volleyball courts, track, baseball and soccer fields, weight room, athletic center.

**STUDENT BODY. Undergraduate profile:** 62% are state residents. 1% Asian-American, 5% Black, 1% Hispanic, 1% Native American, 88% White, 4% Other. Average age of undergraduates is 20.
**Freshman profile:** 17% of accepted applicants took SAT; 70% took ACT. 67% of freshmen come from public schools.
**Undergraduate achievement:** 64% of fall 1992 freshmen returned for fall 1993 term. 55% of entering class graduated. 30% of students who completed a degree program immediately went on to graduate study.
**Foreign students:** 15 students are from out of the country. Countries represented include China, Germany, Hong Kong, Peru, Poland, and Thailand; six in all.

**PROGRAMS OF STUDY. Degrees:** B.A., B.Elect.Studies, B.S., B.S.Nurs.
**Majors:** Accountancy, Art, Biology, Business Administration, Chemistry, Computer Information Systems, Computer Science, Criminal Justice, Drama, Economics, Education, English, Fine Arts, History, International Studies, Mathematics, Medical Technology, Nursing, Philosophy, Physics, Psychology, Sociology, Speech Communications, Theology.
**Distribution of degrees:** The majors with the highest enrollment are business administration, accounting, and nursing; art and mathematics have the lowest.
**Requirements:** General education requirement.
**Academic regulations:** Freshmen must maintain minimum 1.75 GPA; sophomores, juniors, seniors, 2.0 GPA.
**Special:** Minors offered in some majors. Courses offered in dance, French, German, health and physical education, music, Russian, Spanish, and speech. Certificate program. 55-60% of student's program may be spent in major field of study, including practical experience and electives. Associate's degrees offered. Self-designed majors. Double majors. Independent study. Internships. Cooperative education programs. Preprofessional programs in law, medicine, veterinary science, pharmacy, dentistry, and optometry. 3-2 engineering programs with several institutions. Member of Greater Cincinnati Consortium of Colleges and Universities; cross registration possible. Teacher certification in elementary and secondary education. Certification in specific subject areas. Study abroad in England and Japan. ROTC at Northern Kentucky U. AFROTC at U of Cincinnati.
**Honors:** Honors program. Honor societies.
**Academic Assistance:** Remedial reading, writing, math, and study skills. Nonremedial tutoring.

**ADMISSIONS. Academic basis for candidate selection** (in order of priority): Secondary school record, standardized test scores, class rank, school's recommendation.
**Nonacademic basis for candidate selection:** Character and personality, extracurricular participation, and particular talent or ability are important. Alumni/ae relationship is considered.
**Requirements:** Graduation from secondary school is required; GED is accepted. 16 units required and the following program of study recommended: 4 units of English, 2 units of math, 2 units of science, 2 units of foreign language, 2 units of social studies. Minimum composite ACT score of 20 (combined SAT score of 900), rank in top half of secondary school class, and minimum grade average of 80 required. Conditional admission possible for applicants not meeting standard requirements. SAT or ACT is required. Campus visit and interview recommended. Off-campus interviews available with an admissions representative.
**Procedure:** Take SAT or ACT by February of 12th year. Visit college for interview by August of 12th year. Suggest filing application by March 1. Application deadline is August 15. Notification of admission on rolling basis. Reply is required by August 15. $50 tuition and $50 room deposit, both refundable until May 1. Freshmen accepted for terms other than fall.
**Special programs:** Admission may be deferred one year. Credit and/or placement may be granted through CEEB Advanced Placement exams for scores of 3 or higher. Credit and/or placement may be granted through CLEP general and subject exams. Credit and placement may be granted through challenge exams, and military and life experience. Concurrent enrollment program.
**Transfer students:** Transfer students accepted for terms other than fall. In fall 1991, 100 transfer applications were received, 86 were accepted. Application deadline is August 15 for fall; December 15 for spring. Minimum 2.0 GPA recommended. Lowest course grade accepted is "C." Maximum number of transferable credits is 90 semester hours. At least 38 semester hours must be completed at the college to receive degree.
**Admissions contact:** Victoria Thompson-Campbell, M.A., Director of Admissions. 606 344-3332.

**FINANCIAL AID. Available aid:** Pell grants, SEOG, state grants, school scholarships and grants, private scholarships and grants, ROTC scholarships, and academic merit scholarships. Perkins Loans (NDSL), PLUS, and Stafford Loans (GSL). AMS.
**Financial aid statistics:** In 1993-94, 70% of all undergraduate applicants received aid; 68% of freshman applicants. Average amounts of aid awarded freshmen: Scholarships and grants, $3,000; loans, $1,817.
**Supporting data/closing dates:** FAFSA/FAF/FFS: Priority filing date is March 1; accepted on rolling basis. School's own aid application: Priority filing date is March 1; accepted on rolling basis. State aid form: Priority filing date is March 1; accepted on rolling basis. Notification of awards on rolling basis.
**Financial aid contact:** Victoria Holloman Walker, Director of Financial Aid. 606 344-3331.

# Transylvania University

**Lexington, KY 40508-1797 606 233-8300**

**1993-94 Costs.** Tuition: $10,240. Room & board: $4,300. Fees, books, misc. academic expenses (school's estimate): $930.
**Enrollment.** Undergraduates: 372 men, 495 women (full-time). Freshman class: 759 applicants, 729 accepted, 244 enrolled.
**Test score averages/ranges.** Average SAT scores: 532 verbal, 564 math. Range of SAT scores of middle 50%: 460-610 verbal, 500-650 math. Average ACT scores: 27 English, 25 math, 26 composite. Range of ACT scores of middle 50%: 23-29 composite.
**Faculty.** 64 full-time; 24 part-time. 90% of faculty holds highest degree in specific field. Student/faculty ratio: 12 to 1.
**Selectivity rating.** Highly competitive.

**PROFILE.** Transylvania, founded in 1780, is a church-affiliated, liberal arts university. Its 33-acre campus is located several blocks from downtown Lexington. One of its oldest buildings, in the Greek Revival style and dating from 1833, is a National Historic Landmark.

**Accreditation:** SACS.
**Religious orientation:** Transylvania University is affiliated with the Disciples of Christ; no religious requirements.
**Library:** Collections totaling over 130,000 volumes, 580 periodical subscriptions and 64 microform items.
**Special facilities/museums:** Art gallery, museum of early scientific apparatus, medical museum, language lab, transmission electron microscope.
**Athletic facilities:** Athletic complex, athletic field, campus center, gymnasium.

**STUDENT BODY. Undergraduate profile:** 79% are state residents; 10% are transfers. 2% Asian-American, 2% Black, 1% Hispanic, 94% White, 1% Other. Average age of undergraduates is 19.
**Freshman profile:** 6% of freshmen who took SAT scored 700 or over on verbal, 11% scored 700 or over on math; 28% scored 600 or over on verbal, 40% scored 600 or over on math; 63% scored 500 or over on verbal, 76% scored 500 or over on math; 93% scored 400 or over on verbal, 96% scored 400 or over on math; 100% scored 300 or over on verbal, 100% scored 300 or over on math. 24% of freshmen who took ACT scored 30 or over on composite; 73% scored 24 or over on composite; 99% scored 18 or over on composite; 100% scored 12 or over on composite. 65% of accepted applicants took SAT; 90% took ACT. 91% of freshmen come from public schools.
**Undergraduate achievement:** 82% of fall 1992 freshmen returned for fall 1993 term. 62% of entering class graduated. 35% of students who completed a degree program immediately went on to graduate study.
**Foreign students:** Three students are from out of the country. Three countries represented in all.

**PROGRAMS OF STUDY. Degrees:** B.A.
**Majors:** Art, Biology, Business Administration, Chemistry, Computer Science, Drama, Economics, Education, English, French, History, Mathematics, Music, Philosophy, Physical Education, Physics, Political Science, Psychology, Religion, Sociology, Sociology/Anthropology, Spanish.
**Distribution of degrees:** The majors with the highest enrollment are business administration, biology, and psychology; French and Spanish have the lowest.
**Requirements:** General education requirement.
**Academic regulations:** Freshmen must maintain minimum 1.75 GPA; sophomores, 1.85 GPA; juniors, 2.0 GPA; seniors, 2.0 GPA.
**Special:** Minors offered in some majors and in anthropology, communications, German, environmental studies, European studies, health education, international affairs, multicultural studies, studio art, teaching English, and women's studies. Seminars and honors work in all majors. Self-designed majors. Double majors. Pass/fail grading option. Internships. Preprofessional programs in law, medicine, veterinary science, pharmacy, dentistry, theology, and engineering. 3-2 engineering programs with U of Kentucky and Washington U. Member of May Term Consortium, Kentucky Institute for International Studies, and Indiana Consortium for International Programs. Washington Semester. Teacher certification in elementary and secondary education. Certification in specific subject areas. Study abroad in Austria, France, Germany, Italy, Mexico, Spain, the former Soviet Republics, and the United Kingdom. ROTC and AFROTC at U of Kentucky.
**Honors:** Honor societies.
**Academic Assistance:** Remedial reading and writing. Nonremedial tutoring.
**ADMISSIONS. Academic basis for candidate selection** (in order of priority): Secondary school record, standardized test scores, school's recommendation, class rank, essay.
**Nonacademic basis for candidate selection:** Extracurricular participation is emphasized. Character and personality and particular talent or ability are important. Alumni/ae relationship is considered.
**Requirements:** Graduation from secondary school is required; GED is accepted. 13 units and the following program of study are required: 4 units of English, 3 units of math, 2 units of science, 2 units of social studies, 1 unit of history. 1 unit of foreign language recommended. Minimum combined SAT score of 840 (composite ACT score of 21), rank in top half of secondary school class, and minimum 2.25 GPA required. Portfolio required of art scholarship applicants. Audition required of music scholarship applicants. Conditional admission possible for applicants not meeting standard requirements. SAT or ACT is required. Campus visit and interview recommended. Off-campus interviews available with admissions and alumni representatives.
**Procedure:** Take SAT or ACT by December of 12th year. Visit college for interview by March 15 of 12th year. Suggest filing application by March 15. Application deadline is June 1. Notification of admission on rolling basis. Reply is required by July 1. $125 tuition deposit, partially refundable until May 1. $75 room deposit, refundable until August 15. Freshmen accepted for terms other than fall.
**Special programs:** Admission may be deferred one year. Credit and/or placement may be granted through CEEB Advanced Placement exams for scores of 4 or higher. Credit and/or placement may be granted through CLEP general and subject exams. Early decision program. In fall 1993, 24 applied for early decision and 23 were accepted. Deadline for applying for early decision is November 1. Early entrance/early admission program.
**Transfer students:** Transfer students accepted for terms other than fall. In fall 1993, 10% of all new students were transfers into all classes. 51 transfer applications were received, 41 were accepted. Application deadline is March 15 for fall; November 1 for spring. Minimum 2.25 GPA required. Lowest course grade accepted is "C." Maximum number of transferable credits is 18 course units. At least 18 course units must be completed at the university to receive degree.
**Admissions contact:** Thomas Nowack, M.S., Director of Enrollment Management. 606 233-8242, 800 872-6798.

**FINANCIAL AID. Available aid:** Pell grants, SEOG, state scholarships and grants, school scholarships and grants, private scholarships and grants, ROTC scholarships, academic merit scholarships, and athletic scholarships. Perkins Loans (NDSL), PLUS, Stafford Loans (GSL), school loans, and SLS. Deferred payment plan.
**Financial aid statistics:** 63% of aid is not need-based. In 1993-94, 98% of all undergraduate applicants received aid; 98% of freshman applicants. Average amounts of aid awarded freshmen: Scholarships and grants, $6,013; loans, $2,199.
**Supporting data/closing dates:** FAFSA/FAF: Priority filing date is March 15; deadline is July 1. Income tax forms: Priority filing date is April 1; deadline is September 1. Notification of awards on rolling basis.
**Financial aid contact:** Peggy C. Fain, M.S., Director of Financial Aid. 606 233-8239.

# Union College

**Barbourville, KY 40906 606 546-4151**

**1994-95 Costs.** Tuition: $7,800. Room & board: $2,950. Fees, books, misc. academic expenses (school's estimate): $550.
**Enrollment.** Undergraduates: 346 men, 294 women (full-time). Freshman class: 484 applicants, 384 accepted, 175 enrolled. Graduate enrollment: 83 men, 210 women.
**Test score averages/ranges.** Average SAT scores: 400 verbal, 440 math. Range of SAT scores of middle 50%: 390-430 verbal, 410-440 math. Average ACT scores: 19 English, 19 math, 20 composite. Range of ACT scores of middle 50%: 17-21 English, 17-21 math.
**Faculty.** 54 full-time; 16 part-time. 66% of faculty holds doctoral degree. Student/faculty ratio: 13 to 1.
**Selectivity rating.** Less competitive.

**PROFILE.** Union, founded in 1879, is a private, church-affiliated college. Its 101-acre campus is located in Barbourville, 95 miles southeast of Lexington.

**Accreditation:** SACS.
**Religious orientation:** Union College is an interdenominational Christian school; two semesters of religion required.
**Library:** Collections totaling over 88,500 volumes, 440 periodical subscriptions and 430 microform items.
**Special facilities/museums:** Lincoln Library collection, U.S. government depository.
**Athletic facilities:** Gymnasium, basketball, beach volleyball, and tennis courts, baseball, football, and soccer fields, swimming pool, track, training and weight rooms.

**STUDENT BODY. Undergraduate profile:** 66% are state residents; 30% are transfers. 8% Black, 1% Hispanic, 1% Native American, 90% White. Average age of undergraduates is 25.
**Freshman profile:** 1% of freshmen who took SAT scored 700 or over on math; 2% scored 600 or over on verbal, 5% scored 600 or over on math; 9% scored 500 or over on verbal, 24% scored 500 or over on math; 62% scored 400 or over on verbal, 66% scored 400 or over on math; 100% scored 300 or over on verbal, 99% scored 300 or over on math. 4% of freshmen who took ACT scored 30 or over on English, 1% scored 30 or over on math, 2% scored 30 or over on composite; 27% scored 24 or over on English, 20% scored 24 or over on math, 23% scored 24 or over on composite; 56% scored 18 or over on English, 46% scored 18 or over on math, 50% scored 18 or over on composite; 100% scored 12 or over on English, 100% scored 12 or over on math, 100% scored 12 or over on composite. 11% of accepted applicants took SAT; 86% took ACT. 91% of freshmen come from public schools.
**Undergraduate achievement:** 61% of fall 1992 freshmen returned for fall 1993 term. 48% of entering class graduated. 13% of students who completed a degree program immediately went on to graduate study.
**Foreign students:** Nine students are from out of the country. Countries represented include Brazil, Canada, Ghana, and Japan; five in all.

**PROGRAMS OF STUDY. Degrees:** B.A., B.Mus., B.Mus.Ed., B.S.
**Majors:** Accounting, Biology, Business Administration, Business Education, Chemistry, Christian Education, Church Music, Computer/Information Sciences, Criminal Justice, Drama, Early Elementary Education, English, History, Journalism, Mathematics, Medical Technology, Middle Grades Education, Music, Music Business, Music Education, Music Performance, Office Administration, Philosophy/Religion, Physical Education, Physics, Psychology, Religion, Science Education, Secondary Education, Sociology, Special Education, Sports Management.
**Distribution of degrees:** The majors with the highest enrollment are education, business administration/sociology, and psychology; physics, office administration, and science education have the lowest.
**Requirements:** General education requirement.
**Academic regulations:** Freshmen must maintain minimum 1.80 GPA; sophomores, 1.90 GPA; juniors, 2.00 GPA; seniors, 2.00 GPA.

**Special:** Minors offered in accounting, athletic training, business administration, computer information systems, environmental studies, and marketing. Associate's degrees offered. Double majors. Dual degrees. Independent study. Accelerated study. Internships. Cooperative education programs. Graduate school at which undergraduates may take graduate-level courses. Preprofessional programs in law, medicine, veterinary science, pharmacy, dentistry, theology, optometry, and physical therapy. 3-2 engineering program with U of Kentucky. 3-2 physical therapy program with U of Louisville. Appalachian Semester (Kentucky). Teacher certification in early childhood, elementary, secondary, and special education. Certification in specific subject areas. Member of Kentucky Institute of International Studies (KIIS). Study abroad summer programs in Austria, England, France, Germany, Italy, Mexico, and Spain. ROTC.

**Honors:** Honors program. Honor societies.

**Academic Assistance:** Remedial reading, writing, math, and study skills. Nonremedial tutoring.

**ADMISSIONS. Academic basis for candidate selection** (in order of priority): Secondary school record, class rank, standardized test scores, school's recommendation.

**Nonacademic basis for candidate selection:** Particular talent or ability and geographical distribution are emphasized. Extracurricular participation and alumni/ae relationship are important. Character and personality are considered.

**Requirements:** Graduation from secondary school is required; GED is accepted. 20 units and the following program of study are required: 4 units of English, 3 units of math, 1 unit of lab science, 1 unit of social studies, 2 units of history, 8 units of academic electives. Minimum combined SAT score of 750 (composite ACT score of 17), rank in top three-fifths of secondary school class, and minimum 2.0 GPA required. Minimum 2.5 GPA and satisfactory score on competency test required of teacher education program applicants. Audition required of music program applicants. EOP and HEOP for applicants not normally admissible. Conditional admission possible for applicants not meeting standard requirements. ACT is required; SAT may be substituted. ACH recommended. Campus visit and interview recommended. Off-campus interviews available with an admissions representative.

**Procedure:** Take SAT or ACT by June of 12th year. Take ACH by June of 12th year. Visit college for interview by August 15 of 12th year. Suggest filing application by June 1. Application deadline is August 1. Notification of admission on rolling basis. Reply is required by May 15. $50 tuition deposit, refundable until August 1. $50 room deposit, refundable until September 1. Freshmen accepted for terms other than fall.

**Special programs:** Admission may be deferred one semester. Credit and/or placement may be granted through CEEB Advanced Placement exams for scores of 3 or higher. Credit may be granted through CLEP general exams, DANTES and challenge exams, and military experience. Credit and/or placement may be granted through CLEP subject exams. Credit and placement may be granted through ACT PEP exams and life experience. Early entrance/early admission program. Concurrent enrollment program.

**Transfer students:** Transfer students accepted for terms other than fall. In fall 1993, 30% of all new students were transfers into all classes. 158 transfer applications were received, 126 were accepted. Application deadline is August 15 for fall; January 5 for spring. Minimum 2.0 GPA required. Lowest course grade accepted is "C." Maximum number of transferable credits is 67 semester hours. At least 30 semester hours must be completed at the college to receive degree.

**Admissions contact:** Donald Hapward, M.A., Dean of Admissions. 800 489-8646.

**FINANCIAL AID. Available aid:** Pell grants, SEOG, state scholarships and grants, school scholarships and grants, private scholarships and grants, academic merit scholarships, athletic scholarships, and aid for undergraduate foreign students. Perkins Loans (NDSL), PLUS, Stafford Loans (GSL), school loans, and SLS. Installment plan.

**Financial aid statistics:** 18% of aid is not need-based. In 1993-94, 89% of all undergraduate applicants received aid; 85% of freshman applicants. Average amounts of aid awarded freshmen: Scholarships and grants, $1,565; loans, $1,852.

**Supporting data/closing dates:** FAFSA/FAF: Priority filing date is March 15. State aid form: Priority filing date is February 15. Income tax forms: Priority filing date is April 15. Notification of awards on rolling basis.

**Financial aid contact:** Debra Smith, Director of Financial Aid. 606 546-4151.

**STUDENT EMPLOYMENT.** College Work/Study Program. 33% of full-time undergraduates work on campus during school year. Students may expect to earn an average of $1,008 during school year. Off-campus part-time employment opportunities rated "good."

**COMPUTER FACILITIES.** 54 IBM/IBM-compatible and Macintosh/Apple microcomputers; 24 are networked. Students may access AT&T minicomputer/mainframe systems. Computer languages and software packages include BASIC, C, dBASE, FORTRAN, Lotus 1-2-3, Pascal, RPG, WordPerfect, WordStar. Computer facilities are available to all students.

**Fees:** $5 computer fee per semester.

**Hours:** 8 AM-10 PM (M-F); 1 PM-4 PM (Sa-Sun).

**GRADUATE CAREER DATA.** Graduate school percentages: 3% enter law school. 4% enter medical school. 1% enter dental school. 9% enter graduate business programs. 6% enter graduate arts and sciences programs. 2% enter theological school/seminary. Highest graduate school enrollments: U of Cincinnati, U of Kentucky, U of Louisville, U of Tennessee. 26% of graduates choose careers in business and industry. Companies and businesses that hire graduates: Internal Revenue Service, Tremco Manufacturing, area school systems.

**PROMINENT ALUMNI/AE.** Phillip A. Sharp, Ph.D., winner, 1993 Nobel Prize for medicine; Marcetta Y. Darensbourg, Ph.D., chemistry professor, Texas A & M University; Albert Capwood, editor, *Dayton Daily News*; Dr. Mary Pauline Fox, Pike County, KY health director.

# University of Kentucky

**Lexington, KY 40506** **606 257-9000**

**1993-94 Costs.** Tuition: $1,960 (state residents), $5,880 (out-of-state). Room & board: $2,952. Fees, books, misc. academic expenses (school's estimate): $768.

**Enrollment.** Undergraduates: 7,421 men, 7,324 women (full-time). Freshman class: 6,960 applicants, 5,265 accepted, 2,567 enrolled. Graduate enrollment: 3,408 men, 2,704 women.

**Test score averages/ranges.** Average SAT scores: 1017 combined. Average ACT scores: 24 composite. Range of ACT scores of middle 50%: 22-28 composite.

**Faculty.** 1,658 full-time; 423 part-time. 95% of faculty holds doctoral degree. Student/faculty ratio: 16 to 1.

**Selectivity rating.** Competitive.

**PROFILE.** The University of Kentucky, founded in 1865, is a public, comprehensive university. Programs are offered through the Colleges of Agriculture, Allied Health Professions, Architecture, Arts and Sciences, Business and Economics, Dentistry, Education, Engineering, Fine Arts, Home Economics, Law, Library and Information Science, Medicine, Nursing, Pharmacy, and Social Professions and the Graduate School. Its 716-acre campus is located in Lexington, 75 miles from Cincinnati.

**Accreditation:** SACS. Professionally accredited by the Accreditation Board for Engineering and Technology, the Accrediting Council on Education in Journalism and Mass Communication, the American Assembly of Collegiate Schools of Business, the American Bar Association, the American Council on Pharmaceutical Education, the American Dental Association, the American Dietetic Association, the American Home Economics Association, the American Library Association, the American Medical Association (CAHEA), the American Physical Therapy Association, the American Society of Landscape Architects, the Association of American Law Schools, the Council on Social Work Education, the Foundation for Interior Design Education Research, the Liaison Committee on Medical Education, the National Architecture Accrediting Board, the National Association of Schools of Art and Design, the National Association of Schools of Music, the National Council for Accreditation of Teacher Education, the National League for Nursing, the Society of American Foresters.

**Religious orientation:** University of Kentucky is nonsectarian; no religious requirements.

**Library:** Collections totaling over 2,212,083 volumes, 27,902 periodical subscriptions, and 4,802,822 microform items.

**Special facilities/museums:** Anthropology and art museums, center for the humanities, centers for equine research, cancer research, and robotics, pharmacy manufacturing lab.

**Athletic facilities:** Indoor field house, gymnasiums, swimming pools, coliseum, stadium, tracks, aerobic and weight rooms, intramural, rugby, soccer fields, fitness course, badminton, basketball, handball, racquetball, squash, tennis, and volleyball courts.

**STUDENT BODY. Undergraduate profile:** 82% are state residents. 1% Asian-American, 5% Black, 1% Hispanic, 89% White, 4% Other. Average age of undergraduates is 20.

**Freshman profile:** 10% of accepted applicants took SAT; 90% took ACT.

**Undergraduate achievement:** 78% of fall 1991 freshmen returned for fall 1992 term. 18% of entering class graduated.

**Foreign students:** 600 students are from out of the country. Countries represented include China, India, Indonesia, Japan, Malaysia, and Taiwan; 95 in all.

**PROGRAMS OF STUDY. Degrees:** B.A., B.Arch., B.Bus.Admin., B.F.A., B.Hlth.Sci., B.Mus., B.Mus.Ed., B.S., B.S.Nurs., B.S.Pharm.

**Majors:** Accounting, Advertising, Agricultural Economics, Agricultural Education, Agricultural Engineering, Agriculture/Individual Curriculum, Agronomy, Animal Science, Anthropology, Architecture, Art Education, Art History, Art Studio, Arts Administration, Biology, Botany, Business Education, Chemical Engineering, Chemistry, Civil Engineering, Classics, Clinical Lab Science, Communications, Communications Disorders, Computer Science, Decision Science/Information Systems, Distributive Education, Dramatics/Speech Education, Economics, Electrical Engineering, Elementary Education, English, English Education, Entomology, Family Resource Management/Consumer Studies, Finance, Food Science, Foreign Language Education, Forestry, French, Geography, Geology, German, Health Administration, Health Occupations, Health/Safety Education, Health Science Education, History, Home Economics Education, Horticulture, Housing/Interior Design, Individual/Family Development, Individualized Studies, Industrial/Technical Education, Italian, Journalism, Landscape Architecture, Latin American Studies, Learning/Behavior Disorders, Linguistics, Management, Marketing, Materials Engineering, Mathematical Sciences, Mathematics, Mathematics Education, Mechanical Engineering, Merchandising/Apparel/Textiles, Microbiology, Middle School Education, Mining Engineering, Music, Music Education, Music Performance, Nursing, Nutrition/Food Science, Pharmacy, Philosophy, Physical Education, Physical Therapy, Physician Assistant Studies, Physics, Political Science, Production Agriculture, Psychology, Radiological Health Science, Recreation, Restaurant Management, Russian/Eastern Studies, School Media/Librarian, Science Education, Social Studies Education, Social Work, Sociology, Spanish, Special Education, Speech Education, Teacher Education, Telecommunications, Theatre, Topical Major, Zoology.

**Distribution of degrees:** The majors with the highest enrollment are accounting, marketing, and finance.

**Requirements:** General education requirement.

**Special:** Credit offered for televised courses and Experimental Education Program. Self-designed majors. Double majors. Dual degrees. Independent study. Accelerated study. Pass/fail grading option. Internships. Cooperative education programs. Graduate school at which undergraduates may take graduate-level courses. Preprofessional programs in law, medicine, veterinary science, pharmacy, dentistry, optometry, and physical therapy. 3-2 engineering program. Member of Academic Common Market. Teacher certification in early childhood, elementary, secondary, and special education. Certification in specific subject areas. Member of International Student Exchange Program (ISEP). Study abroad

also in Costa Rica, England, France, Germany, Italy, Mexico, and Spain. ROTC and AFROTC.
**Honors:** Phi Beta Kappa. Honors program.
**Academic Assistance:** Remedial writing, math, and study skills. Nonremedial tutoring.

**STUDENT LIFE. Housing:** Coed, women's, and men's dorms. Sorority and fraternity housing. School-owned/operated apartments. On-campus married-student housing. 25% of students live in college housing.
**Social atmosphere:** The student newspaper reports that the most popular events of the year at UK are the Wildcats basketball games, UK theatre productions, and concerts presented through the year. On campus, students meet at the pizza parlor. Favorite off-campus nightspots include the Bearded Seale and Rick's, local pubs with darts, trivia contests, and live bands.
**Services and counseling/handicapped student services:** Placement services. Health service. Women's center. Counseling services for minority, military, and older students. Personal and psychological counseling. Career and academic guidance services. Physically disabled student services. Learning disabled services. Notetaking services. Tape recorders. Tutors. Reader services for the blind.
**Campus organizations:** Undergraduate student government. Student newspaper (Kentucky Kernal, published once/day). Yearbook. Radio station. Chorus, glee club, marching band, symphonic band and orchestra, opera workshop, modern dance club, theatre, debating, departmental, political, and special-interest groups, 254 organizations in all. 23 fraternities, 15 chapter houses; 16 sororities, 13 chapter houses. 20% of men join a fraternity. 20% of women join a sorority.
**Religious organizations:** Bahai Association, Baptist Student Union, Bible Study Group, Campus Crusade for Christ, Christian Student Fellowship, Collegiate Women for Christ, many other religious groups.
**Minority/foreign student organizations:** Black Student Union, Black Voices, minority fraternities/sororities. International Student Center.

**ATHLETICS. Physical education requirements:** None.
**Intercollegiate competition:** 3% of students participate. Baseball (M), basketball (M,W), cheerleading (M,W), cross-country (M,W), diving (M,W), football (M), golf (M,W), gymnastics (W), riflery (M,W), soccer (M,W), swimming (M,W), tennis (M,W), track and field (indoor) (M,W), track and field (outdoor) (M,W), volleyball (W). Member of NCAA Division I, NCAA Division I-A for football, Southeastern Conference.
**Intramural and club sports:** 10% of students participate. Intramural badminton, basketball, fencing, football, golf, gymnastics, racquetball, soccer, softball, swimming, table tennis, tennis, track, volleyball. Men's club cycling, disabled basketball, fencing, handball, horsemanship, ice hockey, lacrosse, martial arts, racquetball, rugby, ultimate frisbee, volleyball, water skiing. Women's club cycling, fencing, handball, horsemanship, racquetball, soccer, softball, ultimate frisbee, water skiing.

**ADMISSIONS. Academic basis for candidate selection** (in order of priority): Secondary school record, standardized test scores.
**Nonacademic basis for candidate selection:** Extracurricular participation, particular talent or ability, and geographical distribution are considered.
**Requirements:** Graduation from secondary school is required; GED is accepted. 12 units and the following program of study are required: 4 units of English, 3 units of math, 2 units of science including 1 unit of lab, 1 unit of social studies, 1 unit of history. Minimum composite ACT score of 18 and minimum 2.0 GPA required for initial consideration. Tests required of architecture program applicants. Audition required of music program applicants. EOP and HEOP for applicants not normally admissible. ACT is required; SAT may be substituted. Campus visit recommended. No off-campus interviews.
**Procedure:** Take SAT or ACT by April of 12th year. Application deadline is June 1. Notification of admission on rolling basis. $100 room deposit, refundable until August 1. Freshmen accepted for terms other than fall.
**Special programs:** Credit and/or placement may be granted through CLEP general and subject exams. Credit and placement may be granted through challenge exams. Concurrent enrollment program.
**Transfer students:** Transfer students accepted for terms other than fall. Application deadline is June 1 for fall; October 15 for spring. Minimum 2.0 GPA required. Lowest course grade accepted is "D." Maximum number of transferable credits is 67 semester hours from a two-year school and 90 semester hours from a four-year school. At least 30 semester hours must be completed at the university to receive degree.
**Admissions contact:** Joseph L. Fink III, J.D., Director of Admissions. 606 257-2000.

**FINANCIAL AID. Available aid:** Pell grants, SEOG, state grants, school scholarships, private scholarships, ROTC scholarships, academic merit scholarships, athletic scholarships, and United Negro College Fund. Perkins Loans (NDSL), PLUS, Stafford Loans (GSL), NSL, Health Professions Loans, state loans, and SLS.
**Financial aid statistics:** Average amounts of aid awarded freshmen: Scholarships and grants, $1,800; loans, $2,625.
**Supporting data/closing dates:** FAFSA/FAF: Priority filing date is April 1; accepted on rolling basis. Notification of awards on rolling basis.
**Financial aid contact:** Robert Halsey, M.A., Director of Financial Aid. 606 257-3172.

**STUDENT EMPLOYMENT.** College Work/Study Program. Institutional employment. 72% of full-time undergraduates work on campus during school year. Off-campus part-time employment opportunities rated "excellent."

**COMPUTER FACILITIES.** 400 IBM/IBM-compatible and Macintosh/Apple microcomputers. Students may access Prime minicomputer/mainframe systems. Residence halls may be equipped with stand-alone microcomputers, networked terminals. Computer languages and software packages include MINITAB, SAS, SPSS; graphics, spreadsheet packages. Computer facilities are available to all students.
**Fees:** $40 computer fee per semester.
**Hours:** 24 hours.

**GRADUATE CAREER DATA.** Companies and businesses that hire graduates: General Electric, LexMark, Procter & Gamble.

**PROMINENT ALUMNI/AE.** Story Musgrave, astronaut; Thomas H. Morgan, Nobel Prize winner; Martha Layne Collins, governor of Kentucky; Steve Breshear, lieutenant governor of Kentucky; John Gaines, horseman.

# University of Louisville

**Louisville, KY 40292 — 800 334-8635**

**1993-94 Costs.** Tuition: $1,880 (state residents), $5,240 (out-of-state). Room & board: $3,468. Fees, books, misc. academic expenses (school's estimate): $430.
**Enrollment.** Undergraduates: 5,085 men, 5,333 women (full-time). Freshman class: 4,778 applicants, 3,074 accepted, 1,841 enrolled. Graduate enrollment: 694 men, 732 women.
**Test score averages/ranges.** Average ACT scores: 19 English, 20 math, 19 composite.
**Faculty.** 866 full-time; 267 part-time. 58% of faculty holds doctoral degree. Student/faculty ratio: 19 to 1.
**Selectivity rating.** Less competitive.

**PROFILE.** The University of Louisville, founded in 1778, is a public, comprehensive institution. Programs are offered through the Colleges of Arts and Sciences and Urban and Public Affairs; the Division of Allied Health; the Schools of Business, Dentistry, Education, Law, Medicine, Music, and Nursing; and the Speed Scientific School. Its 140-acre campus is located in Louisville.

**Accreditation:** SACS. Professionally accredited by the Accreditation Board for Engineering and Technology, the American Assembly of Collegiate Schools of Business, the Council on Social Work Education, the National Association of Schools of Music, the National Council for Accreditation of Teacher Education, the National League for Nursing.
**Religious orientation:** University of Louisville is nonsectarian; no religious requirements.
**Library:** Collections totaling over 1,165,617 volumes, 11,816 periodical subscriptions, and 894,909 microform items.
**Special facilities/museums:** Natural history and art museums, planetarium, numerous institutes and centers.
**Athletic facilities:** Swimming and diving pools, baseball, field hockey, football, and soccer fields, basketball, tennis, and volleyball courts.

**STUDENT BODY. Undergraduate profile:** 93% are state residents. 3% Asian-American, 10% Black, 1% Hispanic, 1% Native American, 83% White, 2% Other. Average age of undergraduates is 27.
**Freshman profile:** Majority of accepted applicants took ACT.
**Undergraduate achievement:** 43% of fall 1992 freshmen returned for fall 1993 term. 40% of entering class graduated.
**Foreign students:** 424 students are from out of the country.

**PROGRAMS OF STUDY. Degrees:** B.A., B.F.A., B.Hlth.Sci., B.Mus., B.Mus.Ed., B.S., B.S.Admin., B.S.Econ., B.S.Nurs.
**Majors:** Accounting, American Studies, Anthropology, Art, Art History, Biology, Botany, Chemical Engineering, Chemistry, Chemistry/Business, Civil Engineering, Clinical Laboratory Sciences, Computer Information Systems, Correctional Administration, Counseling/Guidance, Cytotechnology, Early Elementary Education, Economics, Electrical Engineering, Engineering Mathematics/Computer Science, English, Equine Administration, Finance, Fine Arts/Interior Design, Foods/Nutrition, French, Geography, Geology, German, Health Occupations Education, History, Humanities, Industrial Engineering, Liberal Studies, Linguistics, Management, Management/Decision Information Systems, Management/Personnel/Industrial Relations, Marketing, Mathematics, Mechanical Engineering, Middle School Education, Music/Band, Music Education/Instrumental, Music Education/Vocal, Music/Guitar, Music History, Music/Orchestral Instrument, Music/Organ, Music/Piano, Music/Piano Pedagogy, Music/Voice, Nuclear Medicine Technology, Nursing, Occupational Education, Pan-African Studies, Philosophy, Physical Education, Physical Therapy, Physics, Police Administration, Political Science, Psychology, Respiratory Therapy, Russian, Science, Science/Dental, Science/Dental Hygiene, Science/Medical, Sociology, Sociology/Social Work, Soviet Area Studies, Spanish, Theatre Arts, Theory/Composition, Urban Affairs, Zoology.
**Distribution of degrees:** The majors with the highest enrollment are business and education; nursing has the lowest.
**Requirements:** General education requirement.
**Special:** Associate's degrees offered. Dual degrees. Accelerated study. Pass/fail grading option. Internships. Cooperative education programs. Preprofessional programs in law, medicine, veterinary science, pharmacy, dentistry, and optometry. Teacher certification in early childhood, elementary, secondary, special education, and vo-tech education. Study abroad in France, Germany, Japan, Latin American countries, and other countries. ROTC and AFROTC.
**Honors:** Honors program.
**Academic Assistance:** Remedial reading, writing, math, and study skills. Nonremedial tutoring.

**STUDENT LIFE. Housing:** Students may live on or off campus. Coed dorms. Sorority and fraternity housing. School-owned/operated apartments. Both on-campus and off-campus married-student housing. 8% of students live in college housing.
**Services and counseling/handicapped student services:** Placement services. Health service. Women's center. Day care. Counseling services for minority, military, veteran, and older students. Birth control, personal, and psychological counseling. Career and academic guidance services. Religious counseling. Physically disabled student services. Learning disabled services. Notetaking services. Tape recorders. Tutors.
**Campus organizations:** Undergraduate student government. Student newspaper (Cardinal). Radio station. Orchestra, marching and concert bands, repertory company, service and special-interest groups. 14 fraternities, three chapter houses; 10 sororities, three chapter houses.
**Religious organizations:** Baptist and other Protestant groups, Catholic group, Hillel.
**Minority/foreign student organizations:** Minority Services, black law and engineering student groups. International student center.

**ATHLETICS. Physical education requirements:** Two semesters of physical education required.

**Intercollegiate competition:** Baseball (M), basketball (M,W), cheerleading (M,W), cross-country (M,W), diving (M,W), field hockey (W), football (M), golf (M), soccer (M,W), swimming (M,W), tennis (M,W), track and field (indoor) (M,W), track and field (outdoor) (M,W), volleyball (W). Member of Metro Conference, NCAA Division I, NCAA Division I-A for football, NSCAA.
**Intramural and club sports:** 6% of students participate. Intramural basketball, bowling, canoeing, flag football, free throw, horse shoes, putt-putt golf, racquetball, running, soccer, softball, table tennis, tennis, tug-of-war, turkey trot, volleyball, walleyball. Women's club diving.

**ADMISSIONS. Academic basis for candidate selection** (in order of priority): Secondary school record, standardized test scores, class rank.
**Nonacademic basis for candidate selection:** Character and personality, extracurricular participation, and particular talent or ability are considered.
**Requirements:** Graduation from secondary school is required; GED is accepted. 20 units and the following program of study are required: 4 units of English, 3 units of math, 2 units of lab science, 2 units of social studies, 2 units of history, 7 units of academic electives. Minimum composite ACT score of 20, rank in top half of secondary school class, or minimum 2.5 GPA required. Physics and chemistry, 4 units of math, and minimum 3.0 GPA required of engineering program applicants. Audition required of music program applicants. R.N. required of nursing program applicants. Conditional admission possible for applicants not meeting standard requirements. ACT is required; SAT may be substituted. Campus visit and interview recommended. No off-campus interviews.
**Procedure:** Take SAT or ACT by October of 12th year. Notification of admission on rolling basis. No set date by which applicants must accept offer. $50 room deposit, refundable until July 1. Freshmen accepted for terms other than fall.
**Special programs:** Credit and/or placement may be granted through CEEB Advanced Placement exams. Credit and/or placement may be granted through CLEP general and subject exams. Credit may be granted through military and life experience. Credit and placement may be granted through challenge exams. Concurrent enrollment program.
**Transfer students:** Transfer students accepted for terms other than fall. Application deadline is rolling for fall; rolling for spring. Minimum 2.0 GPA required. Lowest course grade accepted is "C." Maximum number of transferable credits is 62 semester hours. At least 30 semester hours must be completed at the university to receive degree.
**Admissions contact:** Robert Parrent, Ed.D., Director of Admissions. 502 852-6531.

**FINANCIAL AID. Available aid:** Pell grants, SEOG, Federal Nursing Student Scholarships, state scholarships and grants, school scholarships, private scholarships and grants, ROTC scholarships, academic merit scholarships, and athletic scholarships. Perkins Loans (NDSL), PLUS, Stafford Loans (GSL), NSL, Health Professions Loans, state loans, school loans, private loans, and SLS. Tuition Plan Inc., Education Plan Inc., deferred payment plan, and guaranteed tuition.
**Financial aid statistics:** 35% of aid is not need-based. Average amounts of aid awarded freshmen: Scholarships and grants, $800.
**Supporting data/closing dates:** FAFSA/FAF: Priority filing date is April 15; accepted on rolling basis. School's own aid application: Priority filing date is April 15; accepted on rolling basis. Notification of awards on rolling basis.
**Financial aid contact:** Blake Tanner, M.A., Director of Financial Aid. 502 852-5511.

**STUDENT EMPLOYMENT.** College Work/Study Program. Off-campus part-time employment opportunities rated "good."

**COMPUTER FACILITIES.** IBM/IBM-compatible and Macintosh/Apple microcomputers. Residence halls may be equipped with networked microcomputers, modems. Computer facilities are available to all students.
**Fees:** None.

**PROMINENT ALUMNI/AE.** Christopher Dodd, U.S. senator, Connecticut; Mitch McConnell, U.S. senator, Kentucky; Johnny Unitas, quarterback.

# Western Kentucky University

**Bowling Green, KY 42101 — 502 745-0111**

**1994-95 Costs.** Tuition: $1,580 (state residents), $4,740 (out-of-state). Room & board: $3,162. Fees, books, misc. academic expenses (school's estimate): $704.
**Enrollment.** Undergraduates: 4,678 men, 5,616 women (full-time). Freshman class: 4,441 applicants, 3,260 accepted, 2,257 enrolled. Graduate enrollment: 550 men, 1,517 women.
**Test score averages/ranges.** Average ACT scores: 21 composite. Range of ACT scores of middle 50%: 18-23 composite.
**Faculty.** 552 full-time; 217 part-time. 67% of faculty holds doctoral degree. Student/faculty ratio: 19 to 1.
**Selectivity rating.** Less competitive.

**PROFILE.** Western Kentucky is a public, comprehensive university. Founded as a state Normal school in 1906, it gained university status in 1966. Programs are offered through the Colleges of Arts, Humanities, and Social Sciences; Business Administration; Education and Behavioral Sciences; and Science, Technology, and Health; the Community College; the Evening and Weekend Division; and the Graduate School. Its 200-acre main campus and 785-acre university farm are located in Bowling Green, 65 miles north of Nashville.

**Accreditation:** SACS.
**Religious orientation:** Western Kentucky University is nonsectarian; no religious requirements.
**Library:** Collections totaling over 837,898 volumes, 6,296 periodical subscriptions, and 1,284,395 microform items.
**Special facilities/museums:** Kentucky museum, university farm, plantetarium.
**Athletic facilities:** Gymnasium, football, rugby, soccer, and softball fields, arena, stadium.

**STUDENT BODY. Undergraduate profile:** 79% are state residents; 29% are transfers. 1% Asian-American, 6% Black, 1% Hispanic, 92% White. Average age of undergraduates is 23.
**Freshman profile:** 90% of accepted applicants took ACT.
**Undergraduate achievement:** 65% of fall 1992 freshmen returned for fall 1993 term. 10% of entering class graduated.
**Foreign students:** 89 students are from out of the country. Countries represented include Bangladesh, Canada, China, Japan, Kuwait, and South Africa; 34 in all.

**PROGRAMS OF STUDY. Degrees:** B.A., B.F.A., B.Mus., B.S., B.S.Nurs.
**Majors:** Accounting, Advertising, Agriculture, Allied Health Education, Anthropology, Area Studies, Art, Art Education, Biochemistry, Biology, Broadcasting, Business Economics, Business Education, Chemistry, Civil Engineering Technology, Commercial Art, Community Health, Computer/Information Sciences, Corporate/Organizational Communications, Dental Hygiene, Dietetics/Institutional Administration, Earth Science, Economics, Electrical Engineering Technology, Elementary Education, English, English/Allied Language Arts, Environmental Science, Exceptional Children, Finance, French, General Science, General Studies, Geography, Geology, German, Government, Health Care Administration, Health Education, Health Occupation/Teacher Education, History, History/Government, Home Economics Education, Hotel/Motel Management, Industrial Arts Education, Industrial Technology, Information Systems, Institution Administration, Interior Design, Journalism, Learning/Behavior Disabled, Library Science, Management, Marketing, Mass Communications, Mathematics, Mathematics/Physical Science, Mechanical Engineering Technology, Medical Technology, Middle Grades Education, Music, Music Education, Music History/Literature, Music Performance, Music Theory/Composition, Nursing, Performing Arts, Philosophy, Philosophy/Religion, Photojournalism, Physical Education, Physics, Psychology, Public Relations, Recombinant Genetics, Recreation, Religious Studies, Restaurant Management, Social Studies, Sociology, Spanish, Speech, Speech/Communication Disabled, Speech/Theatre, Textiles/Clothing, Theatre, Trainable Mentally Handicapped, Vocational Industrial/Technical Teacher Education.
**Distribution of degrees:** The majors with the highest enrollment are elementary education, general studies, and psychology.
**Requirements:** General education requirement.
**Academic regulations:** Freshmen must maintain minimum 1.7 GPA; sophomores, 1.8 GPA; juniors, 2.0 GPA; seniors, 2.0 GPA.
**Special:** Minors offered in most majors. Certificate programs available. Associate's degrees offered. Self-designed majors. Double majors. Dual degrees. Independent study. Accelerated study. Internships. Cooperative education programs. Graduate school at which undergraduates may take graduate-level courses. Preprofessional programs in law, medicine, veterinary science, pharmacy, dentistry, theology, optometry, and engineering. 2-2 engineering program with U of Missouri. 3-1 medical technology program. 3-2 engineering physics program. Teacher certification in early childhood, elementary, secondary, and special education. Exchange programs abroad in Colombia (Corporacion Internacional and Colegio Santa Francisca Romana), Chile (U of Southern Chili), and Japan (Kansasi U of Foreign Studies). Study abroad also in Austria, Belgium, Costa Rica, England, France, Guatemala, Italy, and Spain. ROTC. AFROTC at Tennessee State U.
**Honors:** Honors program. Honor societies.
**Academic Assistance:** Remedial reading, writing, math, and study skills. Nonremedial tutoring.

**STUDENT LIFE. Housing:** All freshmen must live on campus. Coed, women's, and men's dorms. Sorority and fraternity housing. Off-campus privately-owned housing. 28% of students live in college housing.
**Social atmosphere:** The student newspaper reports, "It seems that people gather at students' apartments or houses rather than at a bar or or restaurant. Student life is very diverse. There doesn't seem to be one popular place everyone goes to all of the time." Various places where students gather are the Garrett Center, the DUC Student Center, O'Charley's Restaurant, Marian's, Cutters, and Picasso's. Popular organizations on campus are Greeks, Student Government, Baptist Student Union, United Student Activists, and the Black Student Alliance. Some of the favorite events during the school year are Homecoming, football games, Banshee tournament and party, and plays by the theatre department.
**Services and counseling/handicapped student services:** Placement services. Health service. Day care. Counseling services for minority, veteran, and older students. Birth control, personal, and psychological counseling. Career and academic guidance services. Physically disabled student services. Learning disabled services. Notetaking services.
**Campus organizations:** Undergraduate student government. Student newspaper (College Heights Herald, published twice/week). Literary magazine. Yearbook. Radio and TV stations. Frisbee team, Speculative Fiction Club, political and service groups, departmental groups, professional groups, special-interest groups, 168 organizations in all. 15 fraternities, 11 chapter houses; 10 sororities, four chapter houses. 12% of men join a fraternity. 13% of women join a sorority.
**Religious organizations:** Western Religious Council, Campus Crusade for Christ, Fellowship of Christian Athletes, Navigators.
**Minority/foreign student organizations:** United Black Students, Black Scholastic Achievers, Afro-American Players. International Student Committee.

**ATHLETICS. Physical education requirements:** Two to three hours of physical development (physical education, military science, or nutrition) required.
**Intercollegiate competition:** 2% of students participate. Baseball (M), basketball (M,W), cross-country (M,W), football (M), golf (M,W), soccer (M), swimming (M), tennis (M,W), track and field (indoor) (M,W), track and field (outdoor) (M,W), volleyball (W). Member of NCAA Division I, NCAA Division I-AA for football, Sun Belt Conference.
**Intramural and club sports:** 44% of students participate. Intramural basketball, bowling, flag football, free throw, golf, horseshoes, racquetball, softball, swimming, tennis, triathlon, turkey trot, volleyball, wallyball, weight lifting, Wiffle ball, wrestling. Men's club fencing, rugby, soccer. Women's club fencing.

**ADMISSIONS. Academic basis for candidate selection** (in order of priority): Standardized test scores, secondary school record, school's recommendation, class rank.
**Nonacademic basis for candidate selection:** Character and personality, extracurricular participation, and particular talent or ability are considered.
**Requirements:** Graduation from secondary school is recommended; GED is accepted. 20 units and the following program of study are required: 4 units of English, 3 units of math, 2 units of science including 1 unit of lab, 2 units of social studies. Minimum composite ACT

score of 17 and minimum 2.2 GPA required of in-state applicants; minimum composite ACT score of 19 and minimum 2.2 GPA required of out-of-state applicants. Admittance to department (in addition to university) required of dental hygiene and nursing program applicants. Conditional admission possible for applicants not meeting standard requirements. ACT is required. Campus visit recommended.

**Procedure:** Take ACT by December of 12th year. Visit college for interview by December 31 of 12th year. Suggest filing application by November; no deadline. Notification of admission on rolling basis. Reply is required by August 1. $100 tuition deposit, refundable until August 1. $75 room deposit, refundable until August 1. Freshmen accepted for terms other than fall.

**Special programs:** Admission may be deferred one semester. Credit and/or placement may be granted through CEEB Advanced Placement exams for scores of 3 or higher. Credit and/or placement may be granted through CLEP general and subject exams. Credit may be granted through military experience. Credit and placement may be granted through challenge exams. Early entrance/early admission program. Concurrent enrollment program.

**Transfer students:** Transfer students accepted for terms other than fall. In fall 1993, 29% of all new students were transfers into all classes. Application deadline is June 1 (out-of-state), August 1 (in-state) for fall; November 1 (out-of-state), December 1 (in-state) for spring. Minimum 2.0 GPA required. Lowest course grade accepted is "C."

**Admissions contact:** Cheryl Chambless, Ed.D., Director of Admissions. 502 745-2551.

**FINANCIAL AID. Available aid:** Pell grants, SEOG, state scholarships and grants, school scholarships, and private scholarships. Perkins Loans (NDSL), PLUS, Stafford Loans (GSL), private loans, and SLS.

**Financial aid statistics:** 25% of aid is not need-based. In 1993-94, 85% of all undergraduate applicants received aid; 85% of freshman applicants. Average amounts of aid awarded freshmen: Scholarships and grants, $1,725; loans, $2,625.

**Supporting data/closing dates:** FAFSA: Priority filing date is May 1. School's own aid application: Priority filing date is May 1. Notification of awards begins June 1.

**Financial aid contact:** Marilyn Clark, M.A.E., Director of Financial Aid. 502 745-2755.

**STUDENT EMPLOYMENT.** College Work/Study Program. Institutional employment. 11% of full-time undergraduates work on campus during school year. Students may expect to earn an average of $2,000 during school year. Off-campus part-time employment opportunities rated "good."

**COMPUTER FACILITIES.** 500 IBM/IBM-compatible, Macintosh/Apple, and RISC-/UNIX-based microcomputers; all are networked. Students may access Digital, IBM minicomputer/mainframe systems, BITNET, Internet. Residence halls may be equipped with stand-alone microcomputers, networked microcomputers. Client/LAN operating systems include UNIX/XENIX/AIX, Windows NT, Novell. Computer languages and software packages include all standard and many special-purpose languages; numerous data management, graphics, simulation, spreadsheet, statistical, word processing packages. Computer facilities are available to all students.

**Fees:** $10 computer fee per semester; included in tuition/fees.

**Hours:** 8 AM-2 AM (M-Th); 8 AM-5 PM (F-Sa); 2 PM-2 AM (Su); 24-hour access to multi-user systems.

# Louisiana

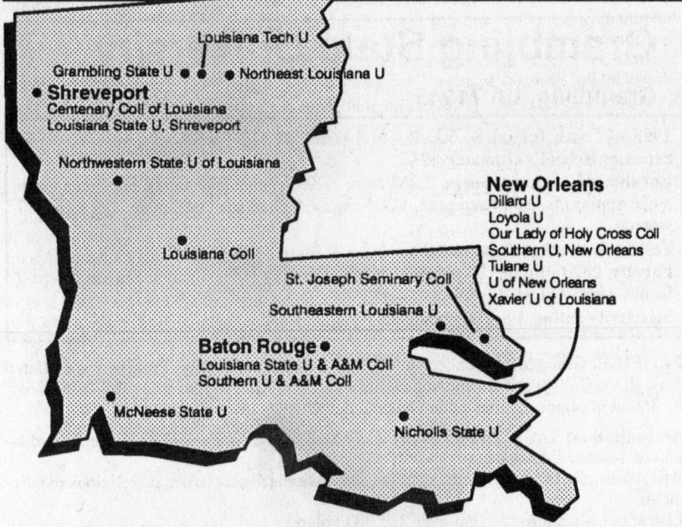


## Centenary College of Louisiana

**Shreveport, LA 71104** **318 869-5100**

**1994-95 Costs.** Tuition: $8,950. Room: $1,475. Board: $2,020. Fees, books, misc. academic expenses (school's estimate): $856.
**Enrollment.** Undergraduates: 345 men, 430 women (full-time). Freshman class: 495 applicants, 434 accepted, 210 enrolled. Graduate enrollment: 88 men, 67 women.
**Test score averages/ranges.** Average SAT scores: 500 verbal, 550 math. Average ACT scores: 25 composite.
**Faculty.** 64 full-time; 36 part-time. 92% of faculty holds doctoral degree. Student/faculty ratio: 11 to 1.
**Selectivity rating.** Competitive.

**PROFILE.** Centenary, founded in 1825, is a church-affiliated, liberal arts college. Its 65-acre campus is located two miles from downtown Shreveport, in northwest Louisiana. Campus architecture is primarily Georgian style.

**Accreditation:** SACS. Professionally accredited by the National Association of Schools of Music.
**Religious orientation:** Centenary College of Louisiana is affiliated with the Methodist Church; one semester of religion required.
**Library:** Collections totaling over 175,000 volumes, 901 periodical subscriptions, and 269,000 microform items.
**Special facilities/museums:** Art museum, art studios, theatre, performance and practice organs, piano lab, language lab.
**Athletic facilities:** Gymnasium, weight rooms, basketball, handball, racquetball, and tennis courts, baseball, soccer, and softball fields.
**STUDENT BODY. Undergraduate profile:** 60% are state residents; 22% are transfers. 2% Asian-American, 5.5% Black, 2% Hispanic, .5% Native American, 86% White, 4% Other. Average age of undergraduates is 20.
**Freshman profile:** 2% of freshmen who took SAT scored 700 or over on verbal, 1% scored 700 or over on math; 16% scored 600 or over on verbal, 33% scored 600 or over on math; 53% scored 500 or over on verbal, 67% scored 500 or over on math; 89% scored 400 or over on verbal, 91% scored 400 or over on math; 100% scored 300 or over on verbal, 99% scored 300 or over on math. 15% of freshmen who took ACT scored 30 or over on English, 6% scored 30 or over on math, 8% scored 30 or over on composite; 65% scored 24 or over on English, 43% scored 24 or over on math, 53% scored 24 or over on composite; 96% scored 18 or over on English, 90% scored 18 or over on math, 98% scored 18 or over on composite; 100% scored 12 or over on English, 100% scored 12 or over on math, 100% scored 12 or over on composite. 53% of accepted applicants took SAT; 84% took ACT.
**Undergraduate achievement:** 40% of entering class graduated. 27% of students who completed a degree program immediately went on to graduate study.
**Foreign students:** Countries represented include Bosnia, England, Singapore, and Taiwan.
**PROGRAMS OF STUDY. Degrees:** B.A., B.Mus., B.S.
**Majors:** Accounting, Art, Biochemistry, Biology, Biophysics, Business, Chemistry, Christian Education, Dance, Economics, Education, Elementary Education, English, Foreign Languages, French, Geology, History, Kindergarten Education, Liberal Arts, Mathematics, Music, Music Education, Music Performance, Philosophy, Physical Education, Physics, Political Science, Psychology, Religion, Sacred Music, Secondary Education, Sociology, Spanish, Speech, Theatre.
**Distribution of degrees:** The majors with the highest enrollment are business, education, and psychology; art, history, and chemistry have the lowest.
**Requirements:** General education requirement.
**Academic regulations:** Minimum 2.0 GPA must be maintained.
**Special:** Minors offered in many majors and in communications. Programs offered in business/Spanish and in professional church careers (Christian education, sacred music, preseminary) for students of all denominations. Courses offered in German, Greek, and Latin. Double majors. Dual degrees. Independent study. Pass/fail grading option. Internships. Graduate school at which undergraduates may take graduate-level courses. Preprofessional programs in law, medicine, veterinary science, pharmacy, and dentistry. 3-1 medicine and medical technology programs. 3-2 engineering programs with U of Arkansas, Case Western Reserve U, Columbia U, Louisiana Tech U, Southern Methodist U, Texas A&M U, Tulane U, and Washington U. Five-year B.A./B.S. program in math/computer science with Southern Methodist U. Member of Associated Colleges of the South. Washington Semester. Oak Ridge Science Semester (Tennessee). Teacher certification in early childhood, elementary, and secondary education. Certification in specific subject areas. Study abroad in Denmark, England, France, and Japan. ROTC at Louisiana State U at Shreveport.
**Honors:** Honors program. Honor societies.

**ADMISSIONS. Academic basis for candidate selection** (in order of priority): Secondary school record, standardized test scores, class rank, essay, school's recommendation.
**Nonacademic basis for candidate selection:** Character and personality are emphasized. Extracurricular participation and particular talent or ability are important. Alumni/ae relationship is considered.
**Requirements:** Graduation from secondary school is required; GED is accepted. No specific distribution of secondary school units required. Minimum composite ACT score of 22 (combined SAT score of 930) and minimum 2.5 GPA required. Audition required of music program applicants. SAT or ACT is required. Campus visit recommended. Off-campus interviews available with an admissions representative.
**Procedure:** Take SAT or ACT by December of 12th year. Visit college for interview by February of 12th year. Suggest filing application by February 15. Application deadline is May 1. Notification of admission on rolling basis. Reply is required by May 31. $100 tuition deposit, refundable until May 1. $60 room deposit, refundable until May 1. Freshmen accepted for terms other than fall.
**Special programs:** Admission may be deferred one year. Credit and/or placement may be granted through CEEB Advanced Placement exams for scores of 3 or higher. Credit may be granted through CLEP general exams and military experience. Credit and/or placement may be granted through CLEP subject exams. Placement may be granted through challenge exams. Early entrance/early admission program. Concurrent enrollment program.
**Transfer students:** Transfer students accepted for terms other than fall. In fall 1993, 22% of all new students were transfers into all classes. 88 transfer applications were received, 60 were accepted. Application deadline is May 1 for fall; December 1 for spring. Minimum 2.5 GPA required. Lowest course grade accepted is "C-." Maximum number of transferable credits is 60 semester hours from a two-year school and 85 semester hours from a four-year school. At least 30 semester hours must be completed at the college to receive degree.
**Admissions contact:** Dorothy Bird Gwin, M.S., Ed.D., Dean of Enrollment Management. 318 869-5131.

**FINANCIAL AID. Available aid:** Pell grants, SEOG, state scholarships and grants, school scholarships and grants, private scholarships and grants, ROTC scholarships, academic merit scholarships, and athletic scholarships. Perkins Loans (NDSL), PLUS, Stafford Loans (GSL), state loans, private loans, and SLS. Tuition Plan Inc., deferred payment plan, and guaranteed tuition.
**Financial aid statistics:** 65% of aid is not need-based. In 1993-94, 82% of all undergraduate applicants received aid; 84% of freshman applicants. Average amounts of aid awarded freshmen: Scholarships and grants, $5,450; loans, $2,470.
**Supporting data/closing dates:** School's own aid application: Priority filing date is January 15; accepted on rolling basis. State aid form: Accepted on rolling basis. Income tax forms: Priority filing date is April 15. Notification of awards begins April 15.
**Financial aid contact:** Mary Sue Rix, M.A., Director of Financial Aid. 318 869-5137.

## Dillard University

**New Orleans, LA 70122** **504 283-8822**

**1993-94 Costs.** Tuition: $6,400. Room & board: $3,505. Fees, books, misc. academic expenses (school's estimate): $450.
**Enrollment.** Undergraduates: 337 men, 1,207 women (full-time). Freshman class: 1,998 applicants, 1,376 accepted, 581 enrolled.
**Test score averages/ranges.** Average SAT scores: 900 combined. Average ACT scores: 19 composite.
**Faculty.** 112 full-time; 11 part-time. 63% of faculty holds doctoral degree. Student/faculty ratio: 15 to 1.
**Selectivity rating.** Less competitive.

**PROFILE.** Dillard, a church-affiliated, liberal arts university, was formed through the 1930 merger of New Orleans University and Straight College. Programs are offered through the Divisions of Business Administration, Education, Humanities, Natural Sciences, Nursing, and Social Sciences. Its 35-acre campus is located in a residential section of New Orleans. Campus architecture is predominantly neo-classical in style.

**Accreditation:** SACS. Professionally accredited by the National Association of Schools of Music, the National League for Nursing.
**Religious orientation:** Dillard University is an interdenominational Christian school; no religious requirements.
**Library:** Collections totaling over 144,000 volumes and 682 periodical subscriptions.
**STUDENT BODY. Undergraduate profile:** 38% are state residents; 26% are transfers. .1% Asian-American, 97% Black, 2% White, .9% Other.
**Freshman profile:** Majority of accepted applicants took ACT. 61% of freshmen come from public schools.

**Undergraduate achievement:** 86% of fall 1992 freshmen returned for fall 1993 term. 79% of entering class graduated. 41% of students who completed a degree program went on to graduate study within five years.
**Foreign students:** 12 students are from out of the country. Countries represented include Canada, Ghana, Greece, Nigeria, South Africa, and Spain.

**PROGRAMS OF STUDY. Degrees:** B.A., B.S., B.S.Nurs.
**Majors:** Art, Biology, Business Administration/Accounting, Chemistry, Computer Science, Criminal Justice, Drama, Early Childhood Education, Economics, Elementary Education, English, Foreign Languages, French, Health/Physical Education, History, Japanese Studies, Mass Communications, Mathematics, Music, Nursing, Philosophy, Physics, Political Science, Pre-Engineering, Psychology, Public Health, Religion, Secondary Education, Social Welfare, Sociology/Anthropology, Spanish, Special Education, Speech, Urban Studies.
**Distribution of degrees:** The majors with the highest enrollment are business administration/accounting, pre-engineering, and mass communications; physics, mathematics, and secondary education have the lowest.
**Requirements:** General education requirement.
**Academic regulations:** Minimum 2.00 GPA must be maintained.
**Special:** Dual degrees. Independent study. Internships. Graduate school at which undergraduates may take graduate-level courses. Preprofessional programs in law, medicine, veterinary science, pharmacy, dentistry, and optometry. 3-2 program in engineering. Teacher certification in early childhood, elementary, secondary, and special education. ROTC. AFROTC at Tulane U.
**Honors:** Honors program. Honor societies.
**Academic Assistance:** Remedial reading, writing, math, and study skills. Nonremedial tutoring.

**STUDENT LIFE. Housing:** Women's and men's dorms. School-owned/operated apartments. 49% of students live in college housing.
**Social atmosphere:** The student newspaper reports, "The students at Dillard are highly pleased with the university's efforts to provide highly outstanding social and cultural events. Often celebrities (such as Lou Rawls and Isaac Hayes) and others from radio and television visit the campus." Influential groups on campus include the various Greek organizations and the Bible Study Group. Favorite off-campus destinations include MPG's and the French Quarter.
**Services and counseling/handicapped student services:** Placement services. Health service. Personal counseling. Career and academic guidance services.
**Campus organizations:** Undergraduate student government. Student newspaper (Courtbouillon). Yearbook. Radio station. Choir, band, drama group, athletic, departmental, political, and service groups. Eight fraternities, no chapter houses; eight sororities, no chapter houses. 30% of men join a fraternity. 26% of women join a sorority.
**Religious organizations:** Bible Study Group, gospel choir.

**ATHLETICS. Physical education requirements:** Four semesters of physical education required.
**Intercollegiate competition:** Basketball (M,W).

**ADMISSIONS. Academic basis for candidate selection** (in order of priority): Secondary school record, school's recommendation, standardized test scores, class rank, essay.
**Nonacademic basis for candidate selection:** Character and personality are important. Extracurricular participation, particular talent or ability, and alumni/ae relationship are considered.
**Requirements:** Graduation from secondary school is recommended; GED is accepted. 18 units and the following program of study are required: 4 units of English, 3 units of math, 3 units of lab science, 2 units of social studies, 6 units of electives including 4 units of academic electives. Biology and chemistry required of nursing program applicants. Audition required of music program applicants. SAT or ACT is required. Campus visit and interview recommended. No off-campus interviews.
**Procedure:** Take SAT or ACT by December of 12th year. Application deadline is July 1. Notification of admission on rolling basis. Reply is required within two weeks of acceptance. $50 nonrefundable tuition deposit. $100 nonrefundable room deposit. Freshmen accepted for terms other than fall.
**Special programs:** Credit and/or placement may be granted through CEEB Advanced Placement exams for scores of 3 or higher. Credit and/or placement may be granted through CLEP general and subject exams. Credit may be granted through DANTES and challenge exams. Early entrance/early admission program. Concurrent enrollment program.
**Transfer students:** Transfer students accepted for terms other than fall. In fall 1993, 26% of all new students were transfers into all classes. 68 transfer applications were received, 42 were accepted. Application deadline is July 1 for fall; December 1 for spring. Minimum 2.0 GPA required. Lowest course grade accepted is "C." Maximum number of transferable credits is 60 semester hours. At least 60 semester hours must be completed at the university to receive degree.
**Admissions contact:** Vernese B. O'Neal, M.S., Director of Admissions. 504 286-4670.

**FINANCIAL AID. Available aid:** Pell grants. Perkins Loans (NDSL), Stafford Loans (GSL), and NSL. AMS and deferred payment plan.
**Financial aid statistics:** In 1993-94, 82% of all undergraduate applicants received aid. Average amounts of aid awarded freshmen: Loans, $2,500.
**Supporting data/closing dates:** FAFSA/FAF/FFS: Deadline is June 1. School's own aid application: Deadline is June 1. Notification of awards on rolling basis.
**Financial aid contact:** Rosie C. Toney, Director of Financial Aid. 504 286-4677.

**STUDENT EMPLOYMENT.** College Work/Study Program. 48% of full-time undergraduates work on campus during school year. Students may expect to earn an average of $2,000 during school year. Off-campus part-time employment opportunities rated "excellent."

**COMPUTER FACILITIES.** 70 IBM/IBM-compatible and Macintosh/Apple microcomputers. Students may access IBM minicomputer/mainframe systems. Client/LAN operating systems include Apple/Macintosh, DOS, Windows NT. Computer facilities are available to all students.
**Fees:** Computer fee is included in tuition/fees.
**Hours:** 8 AM-5 PM daily.

**GRADUATE CAREER DATA.** Highest graduate school enrollments: Columbia U, U of New Orleans. Companies and businesses that hire graduates: Cargill, AETNA.
**PROMINENT ALUMNI/AE.** Rheta Dumas, Dean of Nursing, U of Michigan; D. Mitchell Spelman, Dean, Harvard Medical School; Bishop Alfred Norris, Texas/New Mexico.

# Grambling State University

**Grambling, LA 71245** **318 274-2000**

**1993-94 Costs.** Tuition: $1,600. Room & board: $2,612. Fees, books, misc. academic expenses (school's estimate): $938.
**Enrollment.** Undergraduates: 2,268 men, 3,299 women (full-time). Freshman class: 3,626 applicants, 2,584 accepted, 1,304 enrolled. Graduate enrollment: 172 men, 417 women.
**Test score averages/ranges.** N/A.
**Faculty.** 262 full-time; 20 part-time. 50% of faculty holds doctoral degree. Student/faculty ratio: 21 to 1.
**Selectivity rating.** Less competitive.

**PROFILE.** Grambling, founded in 1901, is a public university. Programs are offered through the Colleges of Business, Education, Liberal Arts, and Sciences and Technology. Its 360-acre campus is located in Grambling, 36 miles from Monroe.

**Accreditation:** SACS. Professionally accredited by the National Council for Accreditation of Teacher Education.
**Religious orientation:** Grambling State University is nonsectarian; no religious requirements.
**Library:** Collections totaling over 227,000 volumes.
**Special facilities/museums:** Audio-visual and TV center, lab schools.
**STUDENT BODY. Undergraduate profile:** 57% are state residents; 23% are transfers. 98% Black, 1% White, 1% Other. Average age of undergraduates is 20.
**Foreign students:** 103 students are from out of the country. Countries represented include India, Mexico, and Nigeria; 21 in all.
**PROGRAMS OF STUDY. Degrees:** B.A., B.Pub.Admin., B.S., B.Soc.Work.
**Majors:** Accounting, Afro-American Study, Air Conditioning/Refrigeration Technology, Anthropology, Applied Mathematics, Applied Music, Art, Art Education, Automotive Technology, Biology, Biology Education, Building Construction Technology, Building Technology, Business Administration, Business Education, Cardiopulmonary Science, Chemistry, Chemistry Education, Computer Science, Criminal Justice, Cytotechnology, Dietetics, Drafting Technology, Early Childhood Education, Electrical Technology, Electronics Technology, Elementary Education, English, English Education, French, French Education, Geography, Health/Physical Education, History, Home Economics Education, Industrial Arts Education, Industrial Technology, Information Systems, Institutional Management, Institutional Management/Production, Journalism, Management, Marketing, Mathematics, Mathematics Education, Medical Technology, Metal Technology, Music, Music Education, Music Theory, Occupational Therapy, Philosophy, Physical Therapy, Physics, Political Science, Psychology, Public Administration, Radio/Television, Recreation, Rehabilitative Counseling, Secondary Education, Social Science, Social Science Education, Sociology, Spanish, Spanish Education, Special Education, Speech/Language/Hearing Specialist, Speech Pathology, Theatre, Theatre Education, Urban Studies.
**Distribution of degrees:** The majors with the highest enrollment are business administration and criminal justice.
**Requirements:** General education requirement.
**Special:** Double majors. Independent study. Pass/fail grading option. Internships. Cooperative education programs. Graduate school at which undergraduates may take graduate-level courses. Preprofessional programs in law, medicine, veterinary science, dentistry, and engineering. Cooperative program with Louisiana Tech U; agriculture departments share facilities and staff. Teacher certification in early childhood, elementary, secondary, and special education. Study abroad in India and Japan. ROTC and AFROTC.
**Honors:** Phi Beta Kappa. Honors program.
**Academic Assistance:** Remedial reading, writing, math, and study skills.
**STUDENT LIFE. Housing:** Freshmen must live on campus if space is available unless living with family. Women's and men's dorms. 40% of students live in college housing.
**Social atmosphere:** Students meet at the student union and the Renaissance. Greeks and Voice of Faith, a religious group, influence life on campus. Football games, Homecoming, Springfest, and job fairs are popular events on campus. "Campus life at Grambling prepares you for a real world full of different people," comments the student newspaper.
**Services and counseling/handicapped student services:** Placement services. Health service. Communicative Study and Skills Center. Counseling services for veteran students. Birth control and personal counseling. Career and academic guidance services.
**Campus organizations:** Undergraduate student government. Student newspaper (Gramblinite, published once/week). Yearbook. Radio and TV stations. Choir, women's choral, orchestra, string ensemble, opera workshop, several bands, Student Activities Committee, Debating Symposium, Little Theatre Guild, Associated Women Students, Men's Dormitory Council, athletic groups, special-interest groups. Four fraternities, no chapter houses; five sororities, no chapter houses. 5% of men join a fraternity. 5% of women join a sorority.
**Religious organizations:** Some religious groups.
**ATHLETICS. Physical education requirements:** Four semesters of physical education required.
**Intercollegiate competition:** Baseball (M), basketball (M,W), football (M), golf (M), tennis (M,W), track and field (M,W), volleyball (W). Member of NCAA Division I, NCAA Division I-AA for football, Southwestern Athletic Conference.
**ADMISSIONS. Academic basis for candidate selection** (in order of priority): Secondary school record, standardized test scores.
**Nonacademic basis for candidate selection:** Character and personality, particular talent or ability, and alumni/ae relationship are important. Extracurricular participation is considered.

**Requirements:** Graduation from secondary school is required; GED is accepted. 23 units and the following program of study are required: 3 units of English, 3 units of math, 2 units of science, 2 units of social studies, 2 units of history, 11 units of electives. Minimum 2.0 GPA required of out-of-state applicants; minimum composite ACT score of 16 recommended. Conditional admission possible for applicants not meeting standard requirements. ACT is required; SAT may be substituted. No off-campus interviews.
**Procedure:** Take SAT or ACT by January of 12th year. Application deadline is July 15. Notification of admission on rolling basis. Applicant must accept offer by registration. $50 refundable room deposit. Freshmen accepted for terms other than fall.
**Special programs:** Admission may be deferred one year. Credit may be granted through military experience. Early entrance/early admission program. Concurrent enrollment program.
**Transfer students:** Transfer students accepted for terms other than fall. In fall 1991, 23% of all new students were transfers into all classes. 742 transfer applications were received, 501 were accepted. Application deadline is July 15 for fall; November 30 for spring. Minimum 2.0 GPA recommended. Lowest course grade accepted is "C." Maximum number of transferable credits is 90 semester hours. At least 30 semester hours must be completed at the university to receive degree.
**Admissions contact:** Karen Lewis, M.B.A., Director of Admissions. 318 274-2435.
**FINANCIAL AID. Available aid:** Pell grants, SEOG, state grants, school scholarships, private grants, academic merit scholarships, and athletic scholarships. Perkins Loans (NDSL), PLUS, Stafford Loans (GSL), NSL, state loans, and SLS.
**Supporting data/closing dates:** School's own aid application: Deadline is June 15.
**Financial aid contact:** Cynthia Burks, M.B.A., Director of Financial Aid. 318 274-2334.
**STUDENT EMPLOYMENT.** College Work/Study Program. 40% of full-time undergraduates work on campus during school year. Students may expect to earn an average of $460 during school year. Off-campus part-time employment opportunities rated "good."
**GRADUATE CAREER DATA.** 50% of graduates choose careers in business and industry. Companies and businesses that hire graduates: IBM.

# Louisiana College

**Pineville, LA 71360 — 318 487-7011**

**1994-95 Costs.** Tuition: $4,950. Room & board: $3,000. Fees, books, misc. academic expenses (school's estimate): $622.
**Enrollment.** Undergraduates: 331 men, 581 women (full-time). Freshman class: 1,746 applicants, 849 accepted, 221 enrolled.
**Test score averages/ranges.** Average ACT scores: 21 composite.
**Faculty.** 69 full-time; 6 part-time. 63% of faculty holds doctoral degree. Student/faculty ratio: 16 to 1.
**Selectivity rating.** Competitive.

**PROFILE.** Louisiana College, founded in 1906, is a church-affiliated college. Its 81-acre campus is located in Pineville, 10 miles from Alexandria. Alexandria Hall, a campus focal point, is listed in the National Register of Historic Places.

**Accreditation:** SACS. Professionally accredited by the Council on Social Work Education, the National Association of Schools of Music, the National Council for Accreditation of Teacher Education, the National League for Nursing. Numerous professional accreditations.
**Religious orientation:** Louisiana College is affiliated with the Southern Baptist Church; six semester hours of religion required.
**Library:** Collections totaling over 125,000 volumes, 551 periodical subscriptions and 62 microform items.
**Special facilities/museums:** Historical museum, language lab.
**Athletic facilities:** Gymnasiums, swimming pool, tennis courts, football and softball fields, fitness lab, local golf course.
**STUDENT BODY. Undergraduate profile:** 95% are state residents; 21% are transfers. 1% Asian-American, 7% Black, 1% Hispanic, 1% Native American, 89% White, 1% Other. Average age of undergraduates is 23.
**Freshman profile:** 5% of freshmen who took ACT scored 30 or over on composite; 37% scored 24 or over on composite; 100% scored 18 or over on composite. Majority of accepted applicants took ACT. 80% of freshmen come from public schools.
**Undergraduate achievement:** 70% of fall 1992 freshmen returned for fall 1993 term. 50% of students who completed a degree program went on to graduate study within five years.
**Foreign students:** 10 students are from out of the country. Countries represented include Brazil, China, India, Pakistan, the former Yugoslav Republics, and Zimbabwe.
**PROGRAMS OF STUDY. Degrees:** B.A., B.Gen.Studies, B.Mus., B.S., B.S.Nurs.
**Majors:** Art, Art Education, Biology, Business Administration, Business Education, Chemistry, Church Music, Communication Arts, Criminal Justice, Elementary Education, English, English Education, Family Life Studies, Fitness/Wellness Management, French, French Education, Health/Physical Education, History, Journalism, Kindergarten/Lower Elementary Education, Languages, Mathematical Computing, Mathematics, Mathematics Education, Media Communications, Medical Technology, Music Education, Music/Organ/Piano/Voice, Nursing, Office Administration, Philosophy/Religion, Pre-Music Therapy, Pre-Law, Pre-Medical, Pre-Veterinary, Psychology, Public Administration, Religion, Religious Education, Science Education, Social Studies Education, Social Work, Sociology, Special Education, Speech, Speech Education, Theatre Arts.
**Distribution of degrees:** The majors with the highest enrollment are nursing, business, and education; art, chemistry, and communication arts have the lowest.
**Requirements:** General education requirement.
**Academic regulations:** Freshmen must maintain minimum 1.5 GPA; sophomores, 1.75 GPA; juniors, 2.0 GPA; seniors, 2.0 GPA.
**Special:** Minors offered in several majors and in accounting, business management, computer science, economics, finance, French, general business, political science, and Spanish. Concentrations in many majors. Courses offered in geography, Greek, and physics. Interdisciplinary Studies Program. External degree program leads to Bachelor of General Studies. Associate's degrees offered. Double majors. Pass/fail grading option. Graduate school at which undergraduates may take graduate-level courses. Preprofessional programs in law, medicine, veterinary science, pharmacy, dentistry, optometry, architecture, engineering, music, occupational therapy, and physical therapy. Member of Cooperative Services International Education Consortium (CSIEC) and Louisiana Universities Marine Consortium. Teacher certification in elementary, secondary, and special education. CSIEC program in China teaching conversational English. Study abroad also possible in England through Overseas Program.
**Honors:** Honor societies.
**Academic Assistance:** Remedial reading and math. Nonremedial tutoring.
**ADMISSIONS. Academic basis for candidate selection** (in order of priority): Standardized test scores, secondary school record, class rank, school's recommendation.
**Nonacademic basis for candidate selection:** Character and personality are emphasized. Particular talent or ability is important. Extracurricular participation and alumni/ae relationship are considered.
**Requirements:** Graduation from secondary school is required; GED is accepted. 17 units and the following program of study are required: 4 units of English, 3 units of math, 3 units of science, 3 units of social studies. Minimum composite ACT score of 20 (or SAT equivalent), rank in top half of secondary school class, and minimum 2.0 GPA required. Audition required of music program applicants. Conditional admission possible for applicants not meeting standard requirements. ACT is required; SAT may be substituted. Campus visit and interview recommended. Off-campus interviews available with admissions and alumni representatives.
**Procedure:** Take SAT or ACT by October of 12th year. Visit college for interview by January of 12th year. Suggest filing application by January 1. Application deadline is August 15. Notification of admission on rolling basis. $50 nonrefundable room deposit. Freshmen accepted for terms other than fall.
**Special programs:** Admission may be deferred one semester. Credit and/or placement may be granted through CLEP general and subject exams. Credit may be granted through military experience. Early decision program. Deadline for applying for early decision is August 15. Early entrance/early admission program. Concurrent enrollment program.
**Transfer students:** Transfer students accepted for terms other than fall. In fall 1993, 21% of all new students were transfers into all classes. 195 transfer applications were received, 134 were accepted. Application deadline is August 15 for fall; January 5 for spring. College transcripts required of all applicants. Minimum 2.0 GPA required. Lowest course grade accepted is "C." At least 30 semester hours must be completed at the college to receive degree.
**Admissions contact:** George Justice, J.D., M.Div., Director of Admissions. 318 487-7259.
**FINANCIAL AID. Available aid:** Pell grants, SEOG, state grants, school scholarships, private scholarships, academic merit scholarships, and athletic scholarships. Discretionary Awards. Perkins Loans (NDSL), PLUS, Stafford Loans (GSL), private loans, and SLS. AMS and deferred payment plan.
**Financial aid statistics:** Average amounts of aid awarded freshmen: Scholarships and grants, $600.
**Supporting data/closing dates:** FAFSA/FFS: Priority filing date is May 1; accepted on rolling basis. State aid form: Accepted on rolling basis. Income tax forms: Accepted on rolling basis. Notification of awards begins June 15.
**Financial aid contact:** Craig Poleman, M.A., Director of Financial Aid. 318 487-7396.

# Louisiana State University and Agricultural and Mechanical College

**Baton Rouge, LA 70803-2750 — 504 388-3202**

**1992-93 Costs.** Tuition: $2,373 (state residents), $5,473 (out-of-state). Room & board: $2,900. Fees, books, misc. academic expenses (school's estimate): $2,120.
**Enrollment.** Undergraduates: 8,694 men, 8,621 women (full-time). Freshman class: 6,772 applicants, 5,331 accepted, 3,363 enrolled. Graduate enrollment: 2,954 men, 2,452 women.
**Test score averages/ranges.** Average ACT scores: 24 English, 23 math, 23 composite. Range of ACT scores of middle 50%: 20-27 English, 19-25 math.
**Faculty.** 1,399 full-time; 88 part-time. 77% of faculty holds doctoral degree. Student/faculty ratio: 18 to 1.
**Selectivity rating.** Less competitive.

**PROFILE.** Louisiana State University and Agricultural and Mechanical College, founded in 1860, is a public, comprehensive, land-grant university. Undergraduate programs are offered through the Colleges of Agriculture, Arts and Sciences, Basic Studies, Business Administration, Design, Education, and Engineering; the General College; the Junior Division; and the School of Music. Graduate programs are offered through the Graduate School; the Schools of Library and Information Science, Social Welfare, and Veterinary Medicine; and the Center for Wetland Resources. Its 1,944-acre campus is located in Baton Rouge.

**Accreditation:** SACS. Professionally accredited by the Accreditation Board for Engineering and Technology, the Accrediting Council on Education in Journalism and Mass Communication, the American Assembly of Collegiate Schools of Business, the American Council for Construction Education, the American Dietetic Association, the American Home Economics Association, the American Psychological Association, the American Society of Landscape Architects, the Foundation for Interior Design Education Research, the National Architecture Accrediting Board, the National Association of Schools of Art and Design, the National Association of Schools of Music, the National Council for Accreditation of Teacher Education, the Society of American Foresters.

**Religious orientation:** Louisiana State University and Agricultural and Mechanical College is nonsectarian; no religious requirements.
**Library:** Collections totaling over 2,654,485 volumes, 20,233 periodical subscriptions, and 3,923,432 microform items.
**Special facilities/museums:** Art museum, natural science and rural life museums, herbariums, on-campus elementary school, geoscience and mycological museums, electron microscope, nuclear science center.
**Athletic facilities:** Field house, tennis courts, track stadium, natatorium.

**STUDENT BODY. Undergraduate profile:** 90% are state residents; 26% are transfers. 3% Asian-American, 8% Black, 2% Hispanic, 84% White, 3% Other. Average age of undergraduates is 21.
**Freshman profile:** 93% of accepted applicants took ACT.
**Undergraduate achievement:** 76% of fall 1991 freshmen returned for fall 1992 term. 15% of entering class graduated. 19% of students who completed a degree program immediately went on to graduate study.
**Foreign students:** 394 students are from out of the country. Countries represented include Canada, China, Honduras, India, Korea, and the United Kingdom; 101 in all.

**PROGRAMS OF STUDY. Degrees:** B.A., B.A.Mass Comm., B.Arch., B.Crim.Just., B.F.A., B.Gen.Studies, B.Inter.Design, B.Land.Arch., B.Mus., B.Mus.Ed., B.S., B.S.Bio./Agri.Eng., B.S.Chem.Eng., B.S.Civil Eng., B.S.Constr., B.S.Elec.Eng., B.S.Forestry, B.S.Geol., B.S.Indust.Eng., B.S.Mech.Eng., B.S.Petrol.Eng.
**Majors:** Accounting, Advertising, Agricultural Business, Agronomic Systems, Animal Systems, Anthropology, Architecture, Art Education, Arts/Sciences/Pre-Dental, Arts/Sciences/Pre-Medical, Biochemistry, Biological/Agricultural Engineering, Botany, Broadcasting, Business/Public Administration, Chemical Engineering, Chemistry, Civil Engineering, Commercial Banking, Communications Disorders, Computer Science, Construction, Crafts/Ceramics, Criminal Justice, Dietetics, Economics, Electrical Engineering, Electrical Engineering/Computer Engineering, Elementary Education, English, Environmental Management Systems, Family/Child/Consumer Sciences, Family Life/Environment, Finance, Food/Nutrition, Food/Resource Economics, Food Systems, Forestry, French, General Business Administration, General Studies, Geography, Geology, German, Graphic Design, History, Horticultural Systems, Horticulture, Industrial Engineering, Industrial Technology, Instrumental Music, Interior Design, International Trade/Finance, Italian, Journalism, Keyboard Performance, Kinesiology, Landscape Architecture, Latin, Liberal Arts, Management, Marketing, Mathematics, Mechanical Engineering, Merchandising, Microbiology, Music Composition, Music Education, News/Editorial, Painting/Drawing, Petroleum Engineering, Petroleum Land Management, Philosophy, Physics, Political Science, Printmaking, Psychology, Quantitative Business Analysis, Real Estate, Religious Studies, Risk/Insurance, Rural Sociology, Russian, Russian Area Studies, Sacred Music, Sculpture, Secondary Education, Sociology, Soil Science, Spanish, Special Education, Speech, Speech Communication, Speech/Language/Hearing Specialist, Textiles/Clothing, Theatre, Vocational Agricultural Education, Vocational Business Education, Vocational Education, Vocational Education/Industrial Arts Tech. Education, Vocational Home Economics Education, Voice, Wildlife/Fisheries Management, Zoology.
**Distribution of degrees:** The majors with the highest enrollment are general studies, psychology, and accounting; sculpture, printmaking, and forestry have the lowest.
**Requirements:** General education requirement.
**Academic regulations:** Minimum 2.0 GPA must be maintained.
**Special:** Minors offered in many majors and in agronomy, art history, ceramics, classical civilization, Greek, jewelry/metalsmithing, linguistics, mass communication, photography, and physiology. Double majors. Independent study. Pass/fail grading option. Internships. Cooperative education programs. Graduate school at which undergraduates may take graduate-level courses. Preprofessional programs in law, medicine, veterinary science, pharmacy, dentistry, optometry, and specialized medical fields. Member of Louisiana Universities Marine Consortium, Oak Ridge Associated Universities, and Organization for Tropical Studies. Exchange program with Southern U and A&M Coll. Teacher certification in elementary, secondary, special education, and vo-tech education. Certification in specific subject areas. Study abroad in England, France, Germany, Honduras, Italy, Japan, Mexico, and Spain. ROTC and AFROTC. NROTC at Southern U and A&M Coll.
**Honors:** Phi Beta Kappa. Honors program. Honor societies.
**Academic Assistance:** Remedial reading, writing, math, and study skills. Nonremedial tutoring.

**STUDENT LIFE. Housing:** Students may live on or off campus. Women's and men's dorms. Sorority and fraternity housing. School-owned/operated apartments. On-campus married-student housing. 22% of students live in college housing.
**Services and counseling/handicapped student services:** Placement services. Health service. Counseling services for minority, military, veteran, and older students. Personal counseling. Career and academic guidance services. Physically disabled student services. Learning disabled program/services. Notetaking services. Tutors. Reader services for the blind.
**Campus organizations:** Undergraduate student government. Student newspaper (Reveille, published four times/week). Radio and TV stations. A cappella choir, chorus, opera chorus, band, orchestra, Louisiana Players Guild, Summer Arts Festival, Block and Bridle Club, Angel Flight, Circle K, College Democrats, College Republicans, Progressive Student Network, 223 organizations in all. 27 fraternities, 22 chapter houses; 16 sororities, 12 chapter houses. 14% of men join a fraternity. 15% of women join a sorority.
**Religious organizations:** Adventists, Campus Christian Outreach, Campus Crusade for Christ, Catholic Student Center, Chi Alpha Christian Fellowship, Consuming Fires Ministries, Hillel, Living Waters Fellowship, Muslim Student Association, Young Life, various Protestant denominational groups.
**Minority/foreign student organizations:** National Society of Black Engineers, Society of Women Engineers. International Student Association, African, Brazilian, Caribbean, Chinese, Filipino, Indian, Indonesia, Mexican, Nigerian, Palestinian, Turkish, Vietnamese, and other foreign student groups.

**ATHLETICS. Physical education requirements:** None.
**Intercollegiate competition:** 1% of students participate. Baseball (M), basketball (M,W), cross-country (M,W), diving (M,W), football (M), golf (M,W), gymnastics (W), swimming (M,W), tennis (M,W), track (indoor) (M,W), track (outdoor) (M,W), track and field (indoor) (M,W), track and field (outdoor) (M,W), volleyball (W). Member of NCAA Division I, Southeastern Conference.
**Intramural and club sports:** Intramural archery, basketball, bowling, cycling, fencing, flag football, floor hockey, golf, lacrosse, martial arts, racquetball, rugby, sailing, soccer, softball, swimming, table tennis, tennis, volleyball, water polo, water skiing, weight lifting, wrestling.

**ADMISSIONS. Academic basis for candidate selection** (in order of priority): Secondary school record, standardized test scores.
**Nonacademic basis for candidate selection:** Extracurricular participation and particular talent or ability are considered.
**Requirements:** Graduation from secondary school is required; GED is accepted. 17.5 units and the following program of study are required: 4 units of English, 3 units of math, 3 units of science, 2 units of foreign language, 3 units of social studies, 2.5 units of academic electives. Minimum 2.0 GPA required. Portfolio required of art program applicants. Audition required of music program applicants. ACT is required; SAT may be substituted. Campus visit recommended.
**Procedure:** Take SAT or ACT by fall of 12th year. Application deadline is July 1. Notification of admission on rolling basis. No set date by which applicants must accept offer. $75 room deposit, partially refundable until July 1. Freshmen accepted for terms other than fall.
**Special programs:** Credit may be granted through CEEB Advanced Placement for scores of 3 or higher. Credit may be granted through CLEP subject exams and military experience. Credit and placement may be granted through challenge exams. Early entrance/early admission program. Concurrent enrollment program.
**Transfer students:** Transfer students accepted for terms other than fall. In fall 1992, 26% of all new students were transfers into all classes. 2,084 transfer applications were received, 1,468 were accepted. Application deadline is July 1 for fall; December 1 for spring. Minimum 2.0 GPA required. At least 30 semester hours must be completed at the university to receive degree.
**Admissions contact:** Lisa Harris, Director of Admissions. 504 388-1175.

**FINANCIAL AID. Available aid:** Pell grants, SEOG, state scholarships and grants, school scholarships, ROTC scholarships, academic merit scholarships, and athletic scholarships. PLUS, Stafford Loans (GSL), state loans, and SLS. Tuition Plan Inc., AMS, and deferred payment plan. Payment plan for Perkins Loan.
**Financial aid statistics:** 43% of aid is not need-based. In 1992-93, 99% of all undergraduate applicants received aid; 99% of freshman applicants. Average amounts of aid awarded freshmen: Scholarships and grants, $933; loans, $2,093.
**Supporting data/closing dates:** FAFSA/FFS: Accepted on rolling basis. School's own aid application: Accepted on rolling basis. Notification of awards on rolling basis.
**Financial aid contact:** Esther Hill, Director of Financial Aid. 504 388-3103.

**STUDENT EMPLOYMENT.** College Work/Study Program. Institutional employment. 23% of full-time undergraduates work on campus during school year. Students may expect to earn an average of $1,634 during school year. Off-campus part-time employment opportunities rated "excellent."

**COMPUTER FACILITIES.** 2,000 IBM/IBM-compatible and Macintosh/Apple microcomputers; 1,500 are networked. Students may access Digital, IBM minicomputer/mainframe systems, BITNET, Internet. Residence halls may be equipped with networked terminals. Client/LAN operating systems include OS/2. Computer languages and software packages include ACF2, Assembler, dBASE, C, CICS, COBOL, FORTRAN, ISPF, JCL, LISP, Maple, Pascal, SAS, TSO, VM/CMS, VSAM; 300 in all. Computer facilities are available to all students.
**Fees:** None.
**Hours:** 8 AM-11 PM daily.

**GRADUATE CAREER DATA.** 51% of graduates choose careers in business and industry. Companies and businesses that hire graduates: Arthur Andersen, Dow Chemical, East Baton Rouge School Board, Exxon, Hibernia Bank, Maison Blanche.

**PROMINENT ALUMNI/AE.** William Conti, Academy Award-winning composer; Loderick Cook, president and CEO, Atlantic Richfield Co.; John P. Paborde, CEO, Tidewater, Inc.; Russell Long, former U.S. senator; John Breaux, U.S. senator; Hubert Humphrey, former U.S. senator and vice-president; Abe Mickal, M.D., chairperson, Department of OB/GYN, Louisiana State U Medical Sch; Henry Goodrich, president, Goodrich Oil; Robert Chinn, president, Control Data Caribbean Basin.

# Louisiana State University in Shreveport

**Shreveport, LA 71115** 318 797-5000

**1994-95 Costs.** Tuition: $2,060 (state residents), $4,990 (out-of-state). Room: $1,620. Fees, books, misc. academic expenses (school's estimate): $730.
**Enrollment.** Undergraduates: 1,066 men, 1,347 women (full-time). Freshman class: 618 applicants, 615 accepted, 436 enrolled. Graduate enrollment: 165 men, 305 women.
**Test score averages/ranges.** Range of ACT scores of middle 50%: 18-24 English, 18-23 math.
**Faculty.** 153 full-time; 24 part-time. 78% of faculty holds doctoral degree. Student/faculty ratio: 21 to 1.
**Selectivity rating.** Noncompetitive.

**PROFILE.** Louisiana State University in Shreveport, founded in 1965, is a public, comprehensive institution. Its 200-acre campus is located in Shreveport.

**Accreditation:** SACS. Professionally accredited by the American Assembly of Collegiate Schools of Business, the National Council for Accreditation of Teacher Education.
**Religious orientation:** Louisiana State University in Shreveport is nonsectarian; no religious requirements.

**Library:** Collections totaling over 225,386 volumes, 2,207 periodical subscriptions, and 229,750 microform items.
**Special facilities/museums:** Art center, life science museum, pioneer heritage center.
**Athletic facilities:** Swimming pool, indoor track, badminton, basketball, racquetball, tennis, and volleyball courts, baseball, football, soccer, and softball fields, weight room.

**STUDENT BODY. Undergraduate profile:** 99% are state residents; 49% are transfers. 2% Asian-American, 14% Black, 1% Hispanic, 1% Native American, 82% White. Average age of undergraduates is 23.
**Freshman profile:** 4% of freshmen who took ACT scored 30 or over on English, 1% scored 30 or over on math; 30% scored 24 or over on English, 8% scored 24 or over on math, 18% scored 24 or over on composite; 75% scored 18 or over on English, 57% scored 18 or over on math, 70% scored 18 or over on composite; 99% scored 12 or over on English, 98% scored 12 or over on math, 98% scored 12 or over on composite; 100% scored 6 or over on English, 100% scored 6 or over on math, 100% scored 6 or over on composite. Majority of accepted applicants took ACT. 90% of freshmen come from public schools.
**Undergraduate achievement:** 46% of fall 1992 freshmen returned for fall 1993 term. 8% of students who completed a degree program went on to graduate study within one year.
**Foreign students:** Nine students are from out of the country. Countries represented include Thailand; seven in all.

**PROGRAMS OF STUDY. Degrees:** B.A., B.Crim.Just., B.Gen.Studies, B.S.
**Majors:** Accounting, Art Education, Biochemistry, Biological Sciences, Chemistry, Communication, Computer Science, Economics, Education, Finance, Fine Arts, Foreign Language, French, General Business, Geography, Health/Physical Education, History, Journalism, Management/Administration, Marketing, Mathematics, Medical Technology, Physics, Political Science, Psychology, Public Administration, Public Relations, Social Sciences, Sociology, Spanish, Speech, Speech/Hearing Therapy, Speech Pathology.
**Distribution of degrees:** The majors with the highest enrollment are accounting, elementary education, and computer science.
**Requirements:** General education requirement.
**Academic regulations:** Minimum 2.0 GPA must be maintained.
**Special:** Minors offered in business administration, communication/information processing skills, international studies, and urban studies. Courses offered in agriculture, anthropology, astronomy, library science, philosophy, and social welfare. Double majors. Independent study. Pass/fail grading option. Internships. Cooperative education programs. Graduate school at which undergraduates may take graduate-level courses. Preprofessional programs in law, medicine, veterinary science, pharmacy, dentistry, animal science, cardiopulmonary science, forestry/wildlife, nursing, occupational therapy, physical therapy, radiological technology, rehabilitation counseling, respiratory therapy, and social welfare. 2-2 engineering program with Louisiana Tech. Combined social work program with Grambling State U. Washington Semester. Teacher certification in early childhood, elementary, secondary, and special education. Certification in specific subject areas. Study abroad in England and in other countries. ROTC.
**Honors:** Honor societies.
**Academic Assistance:** Remedial reading and math. Nonremedial tutoring.

**STUDENT LIFE. Housing:** Five percent of students live in privately-owned/operated residence facilities on campus property.
**Social atmosphere:** The student newspapers reports, "We're a small, commuter campus, so most students work part-time to help pay tuition. Because of this, many students have been unwilling to attend campus functions, especially at night. But our newly formed Division III sports program is helping to eliminate this problem." Popular gathering spots include the Student Recreational Center and local sports bars. Greeks, various Christian groups, and athletes are influential on campus. Favorite campus events include Greek Rush, Fallfest, and Spring Fling.
**Services and counseling/handicapped student services:** Placement services. Counseling services for minority, military, and veteran students. Personal and psychological counseling. Career and academic guidance services. Physically disabled student services. Notetaking services. Tape recorders. Tutors. Reader services for the blind.
**Campus organizations:** Undergraduate student government. Student newspaper (Almagest, published once/week). Literary magazine. Chorale ensemble, Love Alive, Rangers, Rotaract, 47 organizations in all. Two fraternities, no chapter houses; three sororities, no chapter houses. 5% of men join a fraternity. 6% of women join a sorority.
**Religious organizations:** Baptist Student Union, Catholic Student Union, Mainstream.
**Minority/foreign student organizations:** Colleagues. SPICE (international culture group).

**ATHLETICS. Physical education requirements:** Physical education requirements vary by major.
**Intercollegiate competition:** 4% of students participate. Baseball (M), basketball (M,W), cheerleading (M,W), cross-country (W), golf (M), soccer (M), tennis (M,W), volleyball (W). Member of NAIA.
**Intramural and club sports:** 6% of students participate. Intramural badminton, basketball, flag football, inner-tube water polo, racquetball, softball, swimming, tennis, volleyball. Men's club water skiing, weight lifting. Women's club water skiing, weight lifting.

**ADMISSIONS. Academic basis for candidate selection** (in order of priority): Secondary school record, standardized test scores.
**Requirements:** Graduation from secondary school is required; GED is accepted. 18 units and the following program of study are recommended: 4 units of English, 3 units of math, 3 units of science, 2 units of foreign language, 3 units of social studies. Minimum composite ACT score of 19 or minimum 2.4 GPA recommended. ACT is required. Campus visit recommended. No off-campus interviews.
**Procedure:** Take ACT by December of 12th year. Suggest filing application by February. Application deadline is August 5. Notification of admission on rolling basis. No set date by which applicants must accept offer. Freshmen accepted for terms other than fall.
**Special programs:** Credit may be granted through CEEB Advanced Placement for scores of 3 or higher. Credit may be granted through CLEP general and subject exams, DANTES and challenge exams. Early entrance/early admission program. Concurrent enrollment program.
**Transfer students:** Transfer students accepted for terms other than fall. In fall 1993, 49% of all new students were transfers into all classes. Application deadline is August 5 for fall; December 15 for spring. Minimum 2.0 GPA recommended. Lowest course grade accepted is "D." Maximum number of transferable semester hours from two-year schools is no more than half of those required for bachelor's degree. At least 30 semester hours must be completed at the university to receive degree.
**Admissions contact:** Kathleen G. Plante, M.A., Registrar and Director of Admissions. 318 797-5061.

**FINANCIAL AID. Available aid:** Pell grants, SEOG, state scholarships and grants, school scholarships, private scholarships, ROTC scholarships, and academic merit scholarships. PLUS, Stafford Loans (GSL), and SLS.
**Financial aid statistics:** In 1993-94, 75% of all undergraduate applicants received aid; 28% of freshman applicants.
**Supporting data/closing dates:** FAFSA. Notification of awards on rolling basis.
**Financial aid contact:** Edgar L. Chase, Director of Financial Aid. 318 797-5363.

**STUDENT EMPLOYMENT.** College Work/Study Program. Institutional employment. 15% of full-time undergraduates work on campus during school year. Students may expect to earn an average of $2,000 during school year. Off-campus part-time employment opportunities rated "good."

**COMPUTER FACILITIES.** 150 IBM/IBM-compatible and Macintosh/Apple microcomputers; 24 are networked. Students may access IBM minicomputer/mainframe systems, BITNET, Internet. Client/LAN operating systems include DOS, UNIX/XENIX/AIX, Artisoft. Computer languages and software packages include First Choice. Computer facilities are available to all students.
**Fees:** None.
**Hours:** 9 AM-9 PM.

**GRADUATE CAREER DATA.** Highest graduate school enrollments: Law and Medical Schools at Louisiana State U at Shreveport, Louisiana Tech. 32% of graduates choose careers in business and industry.

# Louisiana Tech University

**Ruston, LA 71272** — **318 257-0211**

**1994-95 Costs.** Tuition: $2,169 (state residents), $3,624 (out-of-state). Room: $1,245. Board: $1,080. Fees, books, misc. academic expenses (school's estimate): $618.
**Enrollment.** Undergraduates: 3,736 men, 2,984 women (full-time). Freshman class: 2,397 applicants, 2,144 accepted, 1,525 enrolled. Graduate enrollment: 653 men, 846 women.
**Test score averages/ranges.** Average ACT scores: 22 English, 21 math, 22 composite.
**Faculty.** 389 full-time; 66 part-time. 66% of faculty holds doctoral degree. Student/faculty ratio: 22 to 1.
**Selectivity rating.** Less competitive.

**PROFILE.** Louisiana Tech, founded in 1894, is a public, comprehensive university. Programs are offered through the Colleges of Administration and Business, Arts and Sciences, Education, Engineering, Home Economics, and Life Sciences. Its 235-acre campus is located in Ruston, 30 miles west of Monroe.

**Accreditation:** SACS. Professionally accredited by the Accreditation Board for Engineering and Technology, the American Assembly of Collegiate Schools of Business, the American Dietetic Association, the American Home Economics Association, the American Speech-Language-Hearing Association, the National Architecture Accrediting Board, the National Association of Schools of Art and Design, the National Association of Schools of Music, the National Council for Accreditation of Teacher Education, the National League for Nursing, the Society of American Foresters.
**Religious orientation:** Louisiana Tech University is nonsectarian; no religious requirements.
**Library:** Collections totaling over 349,780 volumes, 2,627 periodical subscriptions, and 481,555 microform items.
**Special facilities/museums:** Art gallery, natural history museum, on-campus elementary school, arboretum, planetarium, center for rehabilitation science and biomedical engineering, institute for microengineering, water resources center.
**Athletic facilities:** Intramural center, natatorium, basketball, handball, tennis, and volleyball courts, bowling lanes, gymnastics facilities, golf course, weight room, track, baseball, football, soccer, and softball fields.

**STUDENT BODY. Undergraduate profile:** 87% are state residents; 23% are transfers. 1% Asian-American, 14% Black, 1% Hispanic, 80% White, 4% Other. Average age of undergraduates is 21.
**Freshman profile:** 5% of freshmen who took ACT scored 30 or over on composite; 35% scored 24 or over on composite; 86% scored 18 or over on composite; 100% scored 12 or over on composite. 90% of accepted applicants took ACT. 80% of freshmen come from public schools.
**Undergraduate achievement:** 70% of fall 1992 freshmen returned for fall 1993 term. 20% of entering class graduated. 30% of students who completed a degree program went on to graduate study.
**Foreign students:** 151 students are from out of the country. Countries represented include India, Japan, Jordan, Mexico, Saudia Arabia, and Syria; 42 in all.

**PROGRAMS OF STUDY. Degrees:** B.A., B.Arch., B.F.A., B.Gen.Studies, B.S.
**Majors:** Accounting, Agricultural Business, Agricultural Education, Animal Science, Apparel/Textiles Merchandising, Architecture, Art Education, Biomedical Engineering, Botany, Business Analysis, Business Economics, Business Education, Business Management/Entrepreneurship, Chemical Engineering, Chemistry, Child Life/Family Studies, Civil Engineering, Computer Engineering, Construction Engineering Technology, Consumer Affairs, Electrical Engineering, Electrical Engineering Technology, Elementary/Early Childhood Education, Elementary Education, Elementary Library Science, English, English Education, Food Services, Forestry, Forestry/Business, Forestry/Recreation, Forestry/Wildlife, French, French Education, General Business Administration, General Studies, Geography, Geology, Graphic Design, Health/Physical Education, Health/Physical Education/Recreation, History, Human Ecology/Home Economics Education, Human Resources Management, Industrial Engineering, Interior Design, Journalism, Manage-

ment Information Systems, Management/Pre-Law, Marketing, Mathematics, Mathematics Education, Mechanical Engineering, Medical Record Administration, Medical Record Technology, Medical Technology, Microbiology/Bacteriology, Music, Music Education, Nursing, Nutrition/Dietetics, Petroleum Engineering, Photography, Physics, Plant Science, Political Science, Pre-Law, Pre-Social Welfare, Pre-Speech Language Pathology, Production Operations Management, Professional Aviation, Psychology, Science Education, Social Studies Education, Sociology, Spanish, Special Education/Mild/Moderate, Special Education/Pre-School, Special Education/Severe/Profound, Speech, Speech Education, Speech/Language/Hearing Therapy, Studio Arts, Technical Writing, Wildlife Conservation, Wood Utilization, Zoology.
**Distribution of degrees:** The majors with the highest enrollment are business management/entrepreneurship, engineering, and education; chemistry, photography, and foreign language have the lowest.
**Requirements:** General education requirement.
**Academic regulations:** Minimum 2.0 GPA required for graduation.
**Special:** Minors offered in many majors. Several concentrations offered in plant science. Courses offered in archaeology, counseling, German, Italian, philosophy, Portuguese, and Russian. Associate's degrees offered. Dual degrees. Independent study. Accelerated study. Pass/fail grading option. Internships. Cooperative education programs. Preprofessional programs in law, medicine, veterinary science, pharmacy, dentistry, and optometry. Exchange program with Grambling State U. Teacher certification in early childhood, elementary, secondary, and special education. Certification in specific subject areas. Study abroad in Italy and Mexico. ROTC and AFROTC.
**Honors:** Phi Beta Kappa. Honors program. Honor societies.
**Academic Assistance:** Remedial reading, writing, math, and study skills.

**STUDENT LIFE. Housing:** All unmarried students under age 21 must live on campus unless living near campus with relatives. Women's and men's dorms. 35% of students live in college housing.
**Social atmosphere:** Influential groups on campus include Greeks, Christian groups, athletes, theatre groups, and the radio station, according to the student newspaper. Students gather at the student center, the quad, the sports center, and local bars. Homecoming, Spring Fling, and sporting events are among the most popular events of the school year.
**Services and counseling/handicapped student services:** Placement services. Health service. Counseling services for minority, military, and veteran students. Personal and psychological counseling. Career and academic guidance services. Religious counseling.
**Campus organizations:** Undergraduate student government. Student newspaper (Tech Talk, published once/week). Yearbook. Numerous honor societies. Radio station. Orchestra, gospel choir, debating and public speaking groups, 124 organizations in all. 11 fraternities, all with chapter houses; five sororities, all with chapter houses. 9% of men join a fraternity. 12% of women join a sorority.
**Religious organizations:** Major denominational groups.
**Minority/foreign student organizations:** NAACP, Society of Black Engineers. International Student Association, Indian and Muslim groups.

**ATHLETICS. Physical education requirements:** None.
**Intercollegiate competition:** 3% of students participate. Baseball (M), basketball (M,W), cross-country (M,W), football (M), golf (M), softball (W), tennis (W), track and field (indoor) (M,W), track and field (outdoor) (M,W), volleyball (W). Member of Big West Conference for football, NCAA Division I-A, Sun Belt Conference.
**Intramural and club sports:** 25% of students participate. Intramural badminton, basketball, bowling, golf, racquetball, soccer, softball, table tennis, tennis, touch football, track. Men's club aviation, cheerleading, cycling, karate, racquetball, rugby, soccer, water skiing, weight lifting. Women's club aviation, cheerleading, karate, water skiing, weight lifting.

**ADMISSIONS. Academic basis for candidate selection** (in order of priority): Secondary school record, class rank, standardized test scores.
**Requirements:** Graduation from secondary school is required; GED is accepted. 17.5 units and the following program of study are required: 4 units of English, 3 units of math, 3 units of science including 1 unit of lab, 2 units of social studies, 1 unit of history, 4.5 units of electives. Minimum composite ACT score of 22, minimum combined SAT score of 920, rank in top half of secondary school class, or minimum 2.0 GPA in core courses required. Conditional admission possible for applicants not meeting standard requirements. Summer program for applicants not meeting standard requirements. ACT is required; SAT may be substituted. Off-campus interviews available with admissions and alumni representatives.
**Procedure:** Take SAT or ACT by April of 12th year. Application deadline is August 15. Notification of admission on rolling basis. No set date by which applicants must accept offer. $50 room deposit, refundable until 45 days prior to beginning of term. Freshmen accepted for terms other than fall.
**Special programs:** Admission may be deferred. Credit and/or placement may be granted through CEEB Advanced Placement exams for scores of 3 or higher. Credit may be granted through CLEP subject exams, DANTES and challenge exams. Early entrance/early admission program. Concurrent enrollment program.
**Transfer students:** Transfer students accepted for terms other than fall. In fall 1993, 23% of all new students were transfers into all classes. 739 transfer applications were received, 623 were accepted. Application deadline is August 15 for fall; November 10 for winter; February 15 for spring. Minimum 2.0 GPA required. Lowest course grade accepted is "D." Maximum number of transferable credits is 68 semester hours from a two-year school and 90 semester hours from a four-year school. At least 30 semester hours must be completed at the university to receive degree.
**Admissions contact:** Karen Akin, Director of Admissions. 318 257-3036.

**FINANCIAL AID. Available aid:** Pell grants, SEOG, state scholarships and grants, school scholarships, private scholarships, ROTC scholarships, academic merit scholarships, and athletic scholarships. Perkins Loans (NDSL), PLUS, Stafford Loans (GSL), and SLS. Tuition Plan Inc.
**Financial aid statistics:** 30% of aid is not need-based. In 1993-94, 95% of all undergraduate applicants received aid; 95% of freshman applicants. Average amounts of aid awarded freshmen: Scholarships and grants, $1,500; loans, $1,300.
**Supporting data/closing dates:** FAFSA: Priority filing date is April 1; deadline is June 1. FAF/FFS: Accepted on rolling basis. School's own aid application: Priority filing date is April 1; accepted on rolling basis; deadline is June 1. Notification of awards begins April 1.
**Financial aid contact:** Etienna R. Winzer, M.B.A., Director of Financial Aid. 318 257-2641.

**STUDENT EMPLOYMENT.** College Work/Study Program. Institutional employment. 22% of full-time undergraduates work on campus during school year. Students may expect to earn an average of $1,800 during school year. Off-campus part-time employment opportunities rated "good."

**COMPUTER FACILITIES.** 1,000 IBM/IBM-compatible and Macintosh/Apple microcomputers; 500 are networked. Students may access IBM minicomputer/mainframe systems, BITNET, Internet. Residence halls may be equipped with stand-alone microcomputers, networked microcomputers, networked terminals, modems. Computer languages and software packages include C, COBOL, FORTRAN, MASTRAN, PL1, SAS, SPSS, simulation languages. Computer facilities are available to all students.
**Fees:** None.
**Hours:** 24 hours, seven days a week.

**GRADUATE CAREER DATA.** Companies and businesses that hire graduates: Arthur Andersen, Chevron, International Paper.

**PROMINENT ALUMNI/AE.** James Lee, CEO, Gulf Oil; Gen. R.E. Hearne, U.S. Air Force; Dr. John Palmer, dean, Yale U; Lawson Swenigen, CEO, Commercial Union Ins.

# Loyola University

**New Orleans, LA 70118** **504 865-2011**

**1993-94 Costs.** Tuition: $10,400. Room: $2,890. Board: $2,300. Fees, books, misc. academic expenses (school's estimate): $825.
**Enrollment.** Undergraduates: 1,141 men, 1,506 women (full-time). Freshman class: 1,696 applicants, 1,424 accepted, 661 enrolled. Graduate enrollment: 703 men, 694 women.
**Test score averages/ranges.** Average SAT scores: 510 verbal, 540 math. Range of SAT scores of middle 50%: 450-560 verbal, 470-570 math. Average ACT scores: 25 composite. Range of ACT scores of middle 50%: 23-27 composite.
**Faculty.** 240 full-time; 151 part-time. 86% of faculty holds highest degree in specific field. Student/faculty ratio: 15 to 1.
**Selectivity rating.** Competitive.

**PROFILE.** Loyola, founded in 1912, is a church-affiliated university. Programs are offered through the Colleges of Arts and Sciences and Music; City College; the Joseph A. Butt, S.J. College of Business Administration; and the School of Law. Its 23-acre campus is located in a residential section of New Orleans. Campus architecture includes Tudor, Gothic and modern styles.

**Accreditation:** SACS. Professionally accredited by the National Association of Schools of Music, the National Council for Accreditation of Teacher Education, the National League for Nursing.
**Religious orientation:** Loyola University is affiliated with the Roman Catholic Church (Society of Jesus); three semesters of religion required.
**Library:** Collections totaling over 206,577 volumes, 1,834 periodical subscriptions, and 253,094 microform items.
**Special facilities/museums:** Art gallery, electron microscope.
**Athletic facilities:** Swimming pool, weight rooms, track, aerobics room, badminton, basketball, racquetball, tennis, and volleyball courts.

**STUDENT BODY. Undergraduate profile:** 55% are state residents; 24% are transfers. 2% Asian-American, 11% Black, 9% Hispanic, 1% Native American, 72% White, 5% Other. Average age of undergraduates is 20.
**Freshman profile:** 1% of freshmen who took SAT scored 700 or over on verbal, 1% scored 700 or over on math; 12% scored 600 or over on verbal, 17% scored 600 or over on math; 53% scored 500 or over on verbal, 69% scored 500 or over on math; 100% scored 400 or over on verbal, 100% scored 400 or over on math. 40% of accepted applicants took SAT; 49% took ACT. 38% of freshmen come from public schools.
**Undergraduate achievement:** 78% of fall 1991 freshmen returned for fall 1992 term.
**Foreign students:** Countries represented include El Salvador, Honduras, Japan, Panama, South American countries, and Spain.

**PROGRAMS OF STUDY. Degrees:** B.A., B.A.Mus., B.Bus.Admin., B.Mus., B.Mus.Ed., B.Mus.Ther., B.S.
**Majors:** Accounting, Biology, Chemistry, Communication, Computer Information Processing, Computer Science, Drama, Economics, Education, Elementary Education, English, Finance, French, General Business, German, Graphics, Greek/Latin, Harpsichord, History, Instrumental Music, International Business, Jazz Studies, Management, Marketing, Mathematics, Music Education, Music Theory/Composition, Music Therapy, Organ, Philosophy, Physical Education, Physics, Piano, Piano Pedagogy, Political Science, Psychology, Public Administration, Religious Studies, Russian, Sacred Music, Secondary Education, Social Work, Sociology, Spanish, Visual Arts, Voice.
**Distribution of degrees:** The majors with the highest enrollment are business management, communication, and social sciences; languages have the lowest.
**Requirements:** General education requirement.
**Special:** Self-designed majors. Double majors. Dual degrees. Independent study. Accelerated study. Pass/fail grading option. Internships. Graduate school at which undergraduates may take graduate-level courses. Preprofessional programs in law, medicine, pharmacy, dentistry, and engineering. 3-2 engineering program with U of New Orleans. Member of New Orleans Consortium. Teacher certification in early childhood, elementary, and secondary education. Study abroad in Italy and Mexico. ROTC, NROTC, and AFROTC at Tulane U.

Honors: Honors program.
**Academic Assistance:** Nonremedial tutoring.

**STUDENT LIFE. Housing:** All freshmen must live on campus. Coed, women's, and men's dorms. 21% of students live in college housing.
**Social atmosphere:** "Social and cultural life at Loyola is greatly influenced by our unique city," reports the student newspaper. Greeks and the University Programming Board influence student social life. Student activities on campus revolve around The Danna Center, the quad, and the recreational sports complex. Off campus, students frequent T.J. Quill's, Bruno's, and Borsodi's. Students enjoy New Orleans Saints' football games and Mardi Gras.
**Services and counseling/handicapped student services:** Placement services. Health service. Day care. Counseling services for older students. Personal and psychological counseling. Career and academic guidance services. Learning disabled services.
**Campus organizations:** Undergraduate student government. Student newspaper (Loyola Maroon, published once/week). Literary magazine. Yearbook. Radio and TV stations. Chorale, jazz band, chamber orchestra, symphony orchestra, music workshops, Lower Depths Theatre, ballet, Model UN, Amnesty International. Five fraternities, no chapter houses; five sororities, no chapter houses. 7% of men join a fraternity. 12% of women join a sorority.
**Religious organizations:** Campus Ministry, Community Action Program.
**Minority/foreign student organizations:** Black Student Union. International Student Association, International Student Affairs.

**ATHLETICS. Physical education requirements:** None.
**Intercollegiate competition:** 5% of students participate. Baseball (M), basketball (M), cheerleading (M,W), cycling (M,W), sailing (M,W), soccer (W). Member of Gulf Coast Athletic Conference, NAIA.
**Intramural and club sports:** 80% of students participate. Intramural aerobics, basketball, cycling, flag football, floor hockey, racquetball, soccer, softball, swimming, table tennis, tennis, volleyball, walleyball, weight lifting. Men's club cheerleading, cycling, crew, martial arts, rugby, sailing, soccer, swimming, volleyball. Women's club cheerleading, crew, cycling, dance, martial arts, sailing, soccer, swimming.

**ADMISSIONS. Academic basis for candidate selection** (in order of priority): Secondary school record, standardized test scores, essay, school's recommendation, class rank.
**Nonacademic basis for candidate selection:** Extracurricular participation is emphasized. Character and personality and particular talent or ability are important. Alumni/ae relationship is considered.
**Requirements:** Graduation from secondary school is required; GED is accepted. 17 units and the following program of study are required: 4 units of English, 3 units of math, 2 units of science, 2 units of social studies, 6 units of academic electives. Portfolio required of art program applicants. Audition required of music program applicants. R.N. required of nursing program applicants. Conditional admission possible for applicants not meeting standard requirements. SAT or ACT is required. Campus visit and interview recommended. Off-campus interviews available with admissions and alumni representatives.
**Procedure:** Take SAT or ACT by October of 12th year. Visit college for interview by December of 12th year. Suggest filing application by March 1; no deadline. Notification of admission on rolling basis. $100 tuition deposit, half refundable until July 1. $100 nonrefundable room deposit. Freshmen accepted for terms other than fall.
**Special programs:** Admission may be deferred. Credit and/or placement may be granted through CEEB Advanced Placement exams for scores of 4 or higher. Credit and/or placement may be granted through CLEP general and subject exams. Credit and placement may be granted through challenge exams, and military and life experience. Early entrance/early admission program. Concurrent enrollment program.
**Transfer students:** Transfer students accepted for terms other than fall. In fall 1992, 24% of all new students were transfers into all classes. 588 transfer applications were received, 484 were accepted. Application deadline is August 1 for fall; December 15 for spring. Minimum 2.25 GPA required. Lowest course grade accepted is "C." Maximum number of transferable semester hours is 64 from two-year schools; varies from four-year schools. At least 30 semester hours must be completed at the university to receive degree.
**Admissions contact:** Nan Massingill, M.Ed., Director of Admissions. 504 865-3240, 800 4-LOYOLA.

**FINANCIAL AID. Available aid:** Pell grants, SEOG, state grants, school grants, private scholarships and grants, and academic merit scholarships. Perkins Loans (NDSL), PLUS, Stafford Loans (GSL), and private loans. EFI Fund Management.
**Financial aid statistics:** 56% of aid is not need-based. In 1992-93, 68% of all undergraduate applicants received aid; 50% of freshman applicants. Average amounts of aid awarded freshmen: Loans, $2,300.
**Supporting data/closing dates:** FAFSA/FAF: Priority filing date is May 1.
**Financial aid contact:** Edward P. Seybold, Jr., J.D., Director of Financial Aid. 504 865-3231.

**STUDENT EMPLOYMENT.** College Work/Study Program. Institutional employment. 30% of full-time undergraduates work on campus during school year. Students may expect to earn an average of $1,350 during school year. Off-campus part-time employment opportunities rated "excellent."

**COMPUTER FACILITIES.** 258 IBM/IBM-compatible and Macintosh/Apple microcomputers. Students may access Digital, Hewlett-Packard, IBM minicomputer/mainframe systems. Computer languages and software packages include BASIC, COBOL, FORTRAN, Microsoft Works, Pascal; 100 in all. Some computers restricted to special programs.
**Fees:** None.
**Hours:** 7 AM-midn.; dormitory labs until 2 AM.

**PROMINENT ALUMNI/AE.** Moon Landrieu, former mayor of New Orleans and HUD secretary during Carter administration; Charles Zewe, reporter, CBS; Sean O'Keefe, secretary of the Navy.

# McNeese State University

**Lake Charles, LA 70609-2495** **318 475-5000**

**1994-95 Costs.** Tuition: $1,953 (state residents), $4,163 (out-of-state). Room & board: $2,590. Fees, books, misc. academic expenses (school's estimate): $600.
**Enrollment.** Undergraduates: 2,654 men, 3,367 women (full-time). Freshman class: 2,110 applicants, 2,098 accepted, 1,518 enrolled. Graduate enrollment: 367 men, 689 women.
**Test score averages/ranges.** Average ACT scores: 19 English, 18 math, 19 composite. Range of ACT scores of middle 50%: 16-22 English, 15-21 math.
**Faculty.** 297 full-time. 52% of faculty holds doctoral degree.
**Selectivity rating.** Noncompetitive.

**PROFILE.** McNeese State is a public, comprehensive university. Founded as a two-year division of Louisiana State University in 1918, it gained university status in 1970. Programs are offered through the Colleges of Business, Education, Engineering and Technology, Liberal Arts, and Science; the Graduate School; the Office of Community Services; and the Division of Basic Studies. Its 99-acre campus is located in Lake Charles, 80 miles west of New Orleans.

**Accreditation:** SACS. Professionally accredited by the Accreditation Board for Engineering and Technology, the American Assembly of Collegiate Schools of Business, the American Medical Association (CAHEA), the National Association of Schools of Music, the National Council for Accreditation of Teacher Education, the National League for Nursing.
**Religious orientation:** McNeese State University is nonsectarian; no religious requirements.
**Library:** Collections totaling over 429,093 volumes, 1,557 periodical subscriptions, and 543,962 microform items.
**Special facilities/museums:** Vertebrate museum, art gallery, planetarium.
**Athletic facilities:** Football stadium, basketball pavilion, tracks, baseball and softball fields, tennis and volleyball courts.

**STUDENT BODY. Undergraduate profile:** 96% are state residents; 18% are transfers. 1% Asian-American, 14% Black, 1% Hispanic, 83% White, 1% Other. Average age of undergraduates is 23.
**Freshman profile:** Majority of accepted applicants took ACT.
**Undergraduate achievement:** 55% of fall 1992 freshmen returned for fall 1993 term. 10% of entering class graduated.
**Foreign students:** 90 students are from out of the country. Countries represented include China, Honduras, India, Mexico, Taiwan, and Thailand; 32 in all.

**PROGRAMS OF STUDY. Degrees:** B.A., B.Mus., B.Mus.Ed., B.S., B.S.Nurs.
**Majors:** Accounting, Agricultural Business, Animal Science, Art, Art Education, Biological Sciences, Biology Education, Business Education, Chemical Engineering, Chemistry, Chemistry Education, Civil Engineering, Computer Sciences, Criminal Justice, Early Childhood Education, Electrical/Electronics Technology, Electrical Engineering, Elementary Education, English, English Education, Environmental Sciences, Finance, Foreign Language Education, French, General Administration, General Agriculture, Geology, Government, Health/Physical Education, History, Home Economics, Liberal Studies, Management, Marketing, Mass Communication, Mathematics, Mathematics Education, Mechanical Engineering, Medical Technology, Music Education, Music Performance, Nursing, Office Systems, Physics, Physics Education, Pre-Dentistry, Pre-Medicine, Psychology, Psychology Education, Radiologic Technology, Social Studies Education, Sociology, Spanish, Special Education, Speech, Speech Education, Theatre Arts, Vocational Home Economics Education, Wildlife Management.
**Distribution of degrees:** The majors with the highest enrollment are nursing, elementary education, and early childhood education; mathematics and physics have the lowest.
**Requirements:** General education requirement.
**Academic regulations:** Minimum 2.0 GPA must be maintained.
**Special:** Associate's degrees offered. Double majors. Internships. Cooperative education programs. Graduate school at which undergraduates may take graduate-level courses. Preprofessional programs in law, medicine, and dentistry. Member of Intercollegiate Consortium for an M.S. in Nursing. Teacher certification in early childhood, elementary, secondary, special education, vo-tech, and bilingual/bicultural education. Certification in specific subject areas. ROTC.
**Honors:** Honor societies.
**Academic Assistance:** Remedial reading, math, and study skills.

**STUDENT LIFE. Housing:** All unmarried full-time freshmen must live on campus unless living with family. Coed, women's, and men's dorms. Sorority and fraternity housing. On-campus married-student housing. 10% of students live in college housing.
**Services and counseling/handicapped student services:** Placement services. Health service. Day care. Personal and psychological counseling. Career and academic guidance services. Physically disabled student services. Learning disabled services. Notetaking services. Tape recorders. Tutors. Reader services for the blind.
**Campus organizations:** Undergraduate student government. Student newspaper (Contraband, published once/week). Literary magazine. Yearbook. Band, chorus, orchestra ensembles, drama group, musical theatre, debating, academic and athletic groups, 75 organizations in all. Eight fraternities, four chapter houses; six sororities, three chapter houses. 5% of men join a fraternity. 5% of women join a sorority.
**Religious organizations:** Baptist Student Union, Newman Club, Fellowship of Christian Athletes, Wesley Foundation.
**Minority/foreign student organizations:** NAACP. International Student Association.

**ATHLETICS. Physical education requirements:** Two semesters of physical education required.

**Intercollegiate competition:** Baseball (M,W), basketball (M,W), cross-country (M,W), football (M), golf (M), softball (W), track (indoor) (M,W), track (outdoor) (M,W), track and field (indoor) (M,W), track and field (outdoor) (M,W), volleyball (W). Member of NCAA Division I, NCAA Division I-AA for football, Southland Conference.
**Intramural and club sports:** Intramural badminton, basketball, football, handball, soccer, softball, track, volleyball.

**ADMISSIONS. Academic basis for candidate selection** (in order of priority): Secondary school record, class rank, standardized test scores.
**Requirements:** Graduation from secondary school is recommended; GED is accepted. No specific distribution of secondary school units required. Minimum 2.0 GPA required. ACT is required. No off-campus interviews.
**Procedure:** Take ACT by October of 12th year. Suggest filing application by April; application deadline is 30 days prior to beginning of semester. Notification of admission on rolling basis. $75 refundable room deposit. Freshmen accepted for terms other than fall.
**Special programs:** Credit and/or placement may be granted through CEEB Advanced Placement exams for scores of 2 or higher. Credit may be granted through CLEP subject exams, ACT PEP and challenge exams, and military experience. Early entrance/early admission program. Concurrent enrollment program.
**Transfer students:** Transfer students accepted for terms other than fall. In fall 1993, 18% of all new students were transfers into all classes. 723 transfer applications were received, 707 were accepted. Application deadline is rolling for fall; rolling for spring. Minimum 2.0 GPA required. Lowest course grade accepted is "C." SAT/ACT scores required of applicants who have not successfully completed Freshman English and math. At least 30 semester hours must be completed at the university to receive degree.
**Admissions contact:** Kathy Bond, M.Ed., Director of Admissions. 318 475-5146.

**FINANCIAL AID. Available aid:** Pell grants, SEOG, Federal Nursing Student Scholarships, state scholarships and grants, school scholarships, private scholarships, ROTC scholarships, academic merit scholarships, athletic scholarships, and aid for undergraduate foreign students. Perkins Loans (NDSL), PLUS, Stafford Loans (GSL), school loans, private loans, and SLS. Deferred payment plan.
**Financial aid statistics:** 41% of aid is not need-based. In 1993-94, 55% of all undergraduate applicants received aid; 48% of freshman applicants. Average amounts of aid awarded freshmen: Scholarships and grants, $1,100; loans, $1,800.
**Supporting data/closing dates:** FAFSA/FFS: Priority filing date is May 1; accepted on rolling basis. School's own aid application: Priority filing date is May 1; accepted on rolling basis. Income tax forms: Priority filing date is May 1; accepted on rolling basis. Notification of awards on rolling basis.
**Financial aid contact:** Mary Kay Eason, M.B.A., Director of Financial Aid. 318 475-5065.

**STUDENT EMPLOYMENT.** College Work/Study Program. Institutional employment. 8% of full-time undergraduates work on campus during school year. Students may expect to earn an average of $1,360 during school year. Off-campus part-time employment opportunities rated "good."

**COMPUTER FACILITIES.** IBM/IBM-compatible and Macintosh/Apple microcomputers. Students may access IBM minicomputer/mainframe systems. Computer languages and software packages include dBASE, Lotus 1-2-3, SAS, SPSS, VP-Planner, WordPerfect. Computer facilities are restricted to students in courses requiring use.
**Fees:** None.

# Nicholls State University

**Thibodaux, LA 70310** — **504 446-8111**

**1994-95 Costs.** Tuition: $1,980 (state residents), $4,572 (out-of-state). Room & board: $2,550. Fees, books, misc. academic expenses (school's estimate): $600.
**Enrollment.** Undergraduates: 2,060 men, 2,861 women (full-time). Freshman class: 3,679 applicants, 3,589 accepted, 2,454 enrolled. Graduate enrollment: 240 men, 577 women.
**Test score averages/ranges.** Average ACT scores: 19 English, 18 math, 19 composite. Range of ACT scores of middle 50%: 16-21 English, 15-20 math.
**Faculty.** 267 full-time; 3 part-time. 54% of faculty holds doctoral degree. Student/faculty ratio: 22 to 1.
**Selectivity rating.** Noncompetitive.

**PROFILE.** Nicholls State, founded in 1948, is a public, comprehensive university. Programs are offered through the Colleges of Business Administration, Education, Liberal Arts, Life Sciences and Technology, and Sciences; the University College; and the Graduate School. Its 210-acre campus, formerly part of the historic Acadia Plantation, is located within the Mississippi River Valley, in Thibodaux.

**Accreditation:** SACS. Professionally accredited by the American Assembly of Collegiate Schools of Business, the American Medical Association (CAHEA), the National Association of Schools of Music, the National Council for Accreditation of Teacher Education, the National League for Nursing.
**Religious orientation:** Nicholls State University is nonsectarian; no religious requirements.
**Library:** Collections totaling over 278,386 volumes, 1,815 periodical subscriptions, and 754,219 microform items.
**Athletic facilities:** Gymnasiums, weight room, racquetball and tennis courts, stadium.

**STUDENT BODY. Undergraduate profile:** 98% are state residents; 4% are transfers. 1% Asian-American, 12% Black, 2% Hispanic, 1% Native American, 84% White. Average age of undergraduates is 23.
**Freshman profile:** 1% of freshmen who took ACT scored 30 or over on composite; 10% scored 24 or over on composite; 62% scored 18 or over on composite; 100% scored 12 or over on composite. 100% of accepted applicants took ACT. 81% of freshmen come from public schools.
**Undergraduate achievement:** 61% of fall 1992 freshmen returned for fall 1993 term. 13% of entering class graduated.
**Foreign students:** 91 students are from out of the country. Countries represented include Brazil, Canada, France, Indonesia, Taiwan, and Thailand; 34 in all.

**PROGRAMS OF STUDY. Degrees:** B.A., B.Gen.Studies, B.Mus., B.Mus.Ed., B.S., B.S.Nurs.
**Majors:** Accounting, Aeronautical Science, Agribusiness, Apparel Merchandising/Retail Management, Art, Art Education, Biology, Business Administration, Business Administration/Pre-Law, Business Education, Chemistry, Chemistry Interdisciplinary, Chemistry/Pre-Dentistry, Chemistry/Pre-Medicine, Civil Engineering Technology, Communicative Disorders, Computer Science, Dietetics, Economics, Electrical Engineering Technology, Elementary Education, Engineering Technology, English, English Education, Finance, Floricultural Technology, Foreign Language Education, French, General Business, General Home Economics, General Studies, Geography, Geology, Government, Health/Physical Education, History, Instrumental Music Education, Kindergarten Education, Legal Assistant Studies, Management, Marketing, Mass Communications, Mathematics, Mathematics Education, Mechanical Engineering Technology, Nursing, Office Information Systems, Petroleum Engineering Technology, Petroleum Services, Piano Performance, Pre-Agricultural Engineering, Pre-Engineering, Pre-Medical Technology, Pre-Occupational Therapy, Pre-Pharmacy, Pre-Physical Therapy, Pre-Veterinary Medicine, Pre-Cardiopulmonary Science, Psychology, Respiratory Therapy Technology, Science Education, Social Studies Education, Sociology, Special Education, Vocal Music Education, Vocational Home Economics.
**Distribution of degrees:** The majors with the highest enrollment are education, nursing, and general studies; agriculture, foreign language, and music have the lowest.
**Requirements:** General education requirement.
**Academic regulations:** Minimum 2.0 GPA must be maintained.
**Special:** Minors offered in many majors. Courses offered in astronomy, German, Greek, Japanese, Latin, philosophy, and Spanish. Associate's degrees offered. Double majors. Dual degrees. Internships. Cooperative education programs. Graduate school at which undergraduates may take graduate-level courses. Preprofessional programs in law, medicine, veterinary science, pharmacy, dentistry, occupational therapy, pharmacy, physical therapy, and cardiopulmonary science. Member of LUMCON. Teacher certification in early childhood, elementary, secondary, and special education. Study abroad in Europe.
**Honors:** Honors program.
**Academic Assistance:** Remedial reading, writing, math, and study skills. Nonremedial tutoring.

**STUDENT LIFE. Housing:** All unmarried students under age 21 must live on campus unless living near campus with relatives. Coed, women's, and men's dorms. On-campus married-student housing. 12% of students live in college housing.
**Social atmosphere:** The student newspaper reports, "Spring is a time of great weather, good times, and the only worry is how to decide what to do in your spare time." Popular events at Nicholls State are Crawfish Day, consisting of "boiled crawfish, bands, amusement rides," and football, baseball, and basketball games. In the fall, students look forward to Career Day. The Greeks are active, as is the Aquinas Catholic Student Center and the Student Union. Favorite off-campus gathering spots include local night clubs such as The Iron Horse, The Retreat, Bayouside on Bayou Lafourche, Flannigan's, Rox's Bar, and Renee's Bar.
**Services and counseling/handicapped student services:** Placement services. Health service. Women's center. Day care. Counseling services for minority, veteran, and older students. Birth control, personal, and psychological counseling. Career and academic guidance services. Religious counseling. Physically disabled student services. Learning disabled services. Notetaking services. Tape recorders. Tutors. Reader services for the blind.
**Campus organizations:** Undergraduate student government. Student newspaper (Nicholls Worth, published once/week). Literary magazine. Yearbook. Radio and TV stations. Band, Chamber Singers, drama group, Fashion Incorporated, Flying Colonels, Student Programming Association, BACCHUS, Circle K, Rotaract, College Republicans, College Democrats, diving and ski clubs, departmental groups, Society for the Advancement of Global Equality, Support for the Handicapped Association, 80 organizations in all. 10 fraternities, one chapter house; six sororities, no chapter houses. 8% of men join a fraternity. 4% of women join a sorority.
**Religious organizations:** Fellowship of Christian Athletes, Baptist Student Union, Catholic student group, Chi Alpha, United Campus Ministry.
**Minority/foreign student organizations:** African-American Voices, other minority groups. International Student Association.

**ATHLETICS. Physical education requirements:** Two semesters of physical education required.
**Intercollegiate competition:** 10% of students participate. Baseball (M), basketball (M,W), cross-country (M,W), football (M), golf (M), softball (W), tennis (W), track (indoor) (M,W), track (outdoor) (M,W), track and field (M,W), track and field (indoor) (M,W), volleyball (W). Member of NCAA Division I, NCAA Division I-AA for football, Southland Conference.
**Intramural and club sports:** 7% of students participate. Intramural basketball, bowling, football, golf, softball, tennis, volleyball.

**ADMISSIONS. Academic basis for candidate selection** (in order of priority): Secondary school record, standardized test scores.
**Requirements:** Graduation from secondary school is required; GED is accepted. No specific distribution of secondary school units required. Open admission for graduates of approved in-state secondary schools. Entrance exams possible for applicants not meeting standard requirements. ACT is required. Campus visit recommended.
**Procedure:** Suggest filing application by August 1; no deadline. Notification of admission on rolling basis. No set date by which applicants must accept offer. $50 refundable room deposit. Freshmen accepted for terms other than fall.
**Special programs:** Credit may be granted through CEEB Advanced Placement for scores of 3 or higher. Credit may be granted through CLEP subject exams, challenge exams, and military experience. Early entrance/early admission program. Concurrent enrollment program.

**Transfer students:** Transfer students accepted for terms other than fall. In fall 1993, 4% of all new students were transfers into all classes. 612 transfer applications were received, 561 were accepted. Application deadline is rolling for fall; rolling for spring. Minimum 1.4 GPA recommended. All credits may be transferred. At least 30 semester hours must be completed at the university to receive degree.
**Admissions contact:** Bernadette F. Dugas-Chauvin, M.Ed., Director of Admissions Information. 504 448-4145.

**FINANCIAL AID. Available aid:** Pell grants, SEOG, state scholarships and grants, school scholarships, private scholarships, academic merit scholarships, and athletic scholarships. Perkins Loans (NDSL), PLUS, Stafford Loans (GSL), and SLS.
**Financial aid statistics:** 61% of aid is not need-based. In 1993-94, 68% of all undergraduate applicants received aid; 26% of freshman applicants. Average amounts of aid awarded freshmen: Scholarships and grants, $2,100; loans, $2,500.
**Supporting data/closing dates:** FAFSA: Priority filing date is March 25. Notification of awards on rolling basis.
**Financial aid contact:** Allison A. Kleinpeter, Director of Financial Aid. 504 448-4047.

**STUDENT EMPLOYMENT.** College Work/Study Program. Institutional employment. 11% of full-time undergraduates work on campus during school year. Students may expect to earn an average of $1,387 during school year. Off-campus part-time employment opportunities rated "fair."

**COMPUTER FACILITIES.** 956 IBM/IBM-compatible, Macintosh/Apple, and RISC-/UNIX-based microcomputers; 85 are networked. Students may access Digital, IBM, UNISYS minicomputer/mainframe systems. Residence halls may be equipped with stand-alone microcomputers, networked microcomputers. Client/LAN operating systems include Apple/Macintosh, DOS, UNIX/XENIX/AIX, Novell. Computer languages and software packages include Lotus 1-2-3, MINITAB, SSPS, SMART, WordPerfect. Computer use restricted to students enrolled in computer courses.
**Fees:** None.
**Hours:** 24 hours for some computers.

# Northeast Louisiana University

**Monroe, LA 71209 — 318 342-1000**

**1993-94 Costs.** Tuition: $1,536 (state residents), $1,584 (out-of-state). Room & board: $1,980. Fees, books, misc. academic expenses (school's estimate): $882.
**Enrollment.** Undergraduates: 3,699 men, 5,013 women (full-time). Freshman class: 2,843 applicants, 2,843 accepted, 1,885 enrolled. Graduate enrollment: 373 men, 742 women.
**Test score averages/ranges.** Average ACT scores: 19 English, 18 math, 19 composite. Range of ACT scores of middle 50%: 16-23 English, 15-20 math.
**Faculty.** 464 full-time; 63 part-time. 52% of faculty holds doctoral degree. Student/faculty ratio: 20 to 1.
**Selectivity rating.** Noncompetitive.

**PROFILE.** Northeast Louisiana is a public, comprehensive university. Founded as a two-year college in 1931, it became a state college in 1939, and gained university status in 1970. Programs are offered through the Colleges of Business Administration, Education, Liberal Arts, Pharmacy and Health Sciences, and Pure and Applied Sciences. Its 227-acre campus is located in Monroe.

**Accreditation:** SACS. Professionally accredited by the Accrediting Bureau of Health Education Schools, the American Home Economics Association, the Council on Social Work Education, the National Association of Schools of Music, the National League for Nursing.
**Religious orientation:** Northeast Louisiana University is nonsectarian; no religious requirements.
**Library:** Collections totaling over 524,143 volumes, 2,918 periodical subscriptions, and 467,923 microform items.
**Special facilities/museums:** Agricultural farm lab, soil/plant analysis lab, climate research center, herbarium, biology/geology summer field camp, pre-school child lab, educational media center, cancer research center.
**Athletic facilities:** Activity center, gymnasium, natatorium, coliseum, stadiums, track, baseball and football fields, basketball, tennis, and volleyball courts.

**STUDENT BODY. Undergraduate profile:** 93% are state residents; 29% are transfers. 2% Asian-American, 18% Black, 78% White, 2% Other. Average age of undergraduates is 22.
**Freshman profile:** 89% of accepted applicants took ACT.
**Undergraduate achievement:** 66% of fall 1991 freshmen returned for fall 1992 term. 7% of entering class graduated.
**Foreign students:** 127 students are from out of the country. Countries represented include Bangladesh, Canada, China, France, Hong Kong, and Malaysia; 37 in all.

**PROGRAMS OF STUDY. Degrees:** B.A., B.Bus.Admin., B.F.A., B.Gen.Studies, B.Mus., B.Mus.Ed., B.S.
**Majors:** Accounting, Agribusiness, Agricultural Aviation, Air Traffic Management, Air Transportation, Art, Art Education, Atmospheric Sciences, Aviation, Biology, Business Education, Business/Office Education, Chemistry, Communicative Disorders, Computer/Information Sciences, Computer Information Systems, Construction, Criminal Justice, Dental Hygiene, Early Childhood Education, Earth Science, Economics, Elementary Education, English, English Education, Family Life/Child Development, Fashion Merchandising, Finance/Commercial Banking, Foreign Language, Foreign Language Education, French, General Business, General Studies, Geography, Geology, Geophysics, Government, Handicapped Education, History, Home Economics, Home Economics Education, Industrial Management, Instrumental/Vocal Music, Insurance/Real Estate, Interior Design, Journalism, Legal Studies, Management, Marketing, Mathematics, Medical Technology, Mildly/Moderately Handicapped, Music, Music Education, Nursing, Occupational Therapy, Office Information Systems Management, Orchestral/Band Instruments, Pharmacy, Physical Education, Physics, Pre-School Handicapped, Psychology, Radio/Television/Film, Radiologic Technology, School Library Science, School Library Science/Secondary Education, Science Education, Social Work, Sociology, Spanish, Special Education/Pre-School, Speech Education, Vocal Education, Zoology.
**Distribution of degrees:** The majors with the highest enrollment are pharmacy, elementary education, and general studies; industrial management, agricultural aviation, and geology have the lowest.
**Requirements:** General education requirement.
**Academic regulations:** Minimum 1.6 GPA must be maintained.
**Special:** Associate's degrees offered. Double majors. Accelerated study. Graduate school at which undergraduates may take graduate-level courses. Preprofessional programs in law, medicine, and dentistry. Teacher certification in early childhood, elementary, secondary, and special education. Study abroad in France. ROTC.
**Honors:** Honors program.
**Academic Assistance:** Remedial math.

**STUDENT LIFE. Housing:** All unmarried students under age 21 must live on campus unless living near campus with relatives. Coed, women's, and men's dorms. 25% of students live in college housing.
**Services and counseling/handicapped student services:** Placement services. Health service. Day care. Counseling services for minority, military, veteran, and older students. Personal counseling. Career and academic guidance services. Physically disabled student services. Notetaking services. Tape recorders. Reader services for the blind.
**Campus organizations:** Undergraduate student government. Student newspaper (Pow Wow, published once/week). Literary magazine. Yearbook. Radio station. Brass, jazz, and woodwind ensembles, concert choir, chorale, concert, marching, and symphonic bands, orchestra, drama groups, Miss NLU Pageant, Residence Hall Council, Union board, academic and professional groups, 146 organizations in all. Seven fraternities, no chapter houses; eight sororities, no chapter houses. 5% of men join a fraternity. 5% of women join a sorority.
**Religious organizations:** Baptist Student Union, Catholic Student Association, Christian United Fellowship, Church of Christ Student Center, Epsicopal Student Fellowship, Northeast United Campus Ministries, Wesley Foundation, other religious groups.
**Minority/foreign student organizations:** Alpha Kappa Alpha, Alpha Phi Alpha, Black Caucus Association, Delta Sigma Theta, Members of Minority Distinction, Omega Psi Phi, Phi Beta Sigma. Rabitah Al-Tulab International, Chinese, Hong Kong, Indian, Malaysian, and Thai groups.

**ATHLETICS. Physical education requirements:** None.
**Intercollegiate competition:** 3% of students participate. Baseball (M), basketball (M,W), cheerleading (M,W), cross-country (M,W), diving (M), football (M), golf (M), softball (W), swimming (M), tennis (M,W), track (indoor) (M,W), track (outdoor) (M,W), track and field (indoor) (M,W), track and field (outdoor) (M,W), volleyball (W). Member of NCAA Division I, NCAA Division I-A for football, Southland Conference.
**Intramural and club sports:** 35% of students participate. Intramural archery, badminton, basketball, bowling, cross-country, flag football, golf, horseshoes, karate, pool, softball, swimming, tennis, track, triathlon, volleyball, water skiing. Men's club water skiing. Women's club water skiing.

**ADMISSIONS.**
**Requirements:** Graduation from secondary school is required; GED is accepted. No specific distribution of secondary school units required. Special admissions requirements for teacher education, pharmacy, dental hygiene, nursing, occupational therapy, and radiologic technology program applicants. Conditional admission possible for applicants not meeting standard requirements. Special Nondegree Academic Program (SNAP) for applicants not meeting standard requirements. ACT is required. Campus visit recommended. No off-campus interviews.
**Procedure:** Take ACT by April of 12th year. Notification of admission on rolling basis. No set date by which applicants must accept offer. $50 room deposit, refundable until 45 days prior to beginning of term. Freshmen accepted for terms other than fall.
**Special programs:** Credit may be granted through CLEP subject exams and military experience. Early entrance/early admission program. Concurrent enrollment program.
**Transfer students:** Transfer students accepted for terms other than fall. In fall 1992, 29% of all new students were transfers into all classes. Lowest course grade accepted is "D." At least 30 semester hours must be completed at the university to receive degree.
**Admissions contact:** James Robertson, Jr., Ph.D., Director of Admissions. 318 342-5252.

**FINANCIAL AID. Available aid:** Pell grants, SEOG, state scholarships and grants, school scholarships, private scholarships, ROTC scholarships, academic merit scholarships, athletic scholarships, and United Negro College Fund. Perkins Loans (NDSL), PLUS, Stafford Loans (GSL), Health Professions Loans, state loans, and SLS.
**Financial aid statistics:** In 1992-93, 75% of all undergraduate applicants received aid; 65% of freshman applicants. Average amounts of aid awarded freshmen: Scholarships and grants, $750; loans, $1,000.
**Supporting data/closing dates:** School's own aid application: Priority filing date is April 1. Notification of awards begins June 1.
**Financial aid contact:** R. Keith Joiner, M.B.A., Director of Financial Aid. 318 342-5320.

**STUDENT EMPLOYMENT.** College Work/Study Program. Institutional employment. 10% of full-time undergraduates work on campus during school year. Students may expect to earn an average of $1,000 during school year. Off-campus part-time employment opportunities rated "good."

**COMPUTER FACILITIES.** 241 IBM/IBM-compatible and Macintosh/Apple microcomputers; 105 are networked. Students may access Digital, IBM minicomputer/mainframe systems. Computer languages and software packages include Ada, BASIC, COBOL, DataTrieve, dBASE, First Choice, FORTRAN, ImSL, Lotus 1-2-3, Pascal, PL/1, RDB, SAS, SPSS-X, WordPerfect.
**Fees:** None.
**Hours:** 7 AM-midn. for multi-user computer system.

**PROMINENT ALUMNI/AE.** Quinn Beker, surgeon general, U.S. Army; Harry Walker, brigadier general, U.S. Army; Calvin Natt, professional basketball player; Chuck Finley, professional baseball player; Bubby Brister, professional football player; Jack Blitch, executive director for Walt Disney Imagineering, Florida/California.

## Northwestern State University of Louisiana

**Natchitoches, LA 71497** **318 357-6361**

**1992-93 Costs.** Tuition: $1,580 (state residents), $3,380 (out-of-state). Room: $980-$1,640. Board: $1,174. Fees, books, misc. academic expenses (school's estimate): $690.
**Enrollment.** Undergraduates: 2,292 men, 3,450 women (full-time). Freshman class: 2,945 applicants, 2,671 accepted. Graduate enrollment: 145 men, 521 women.
**Test score averages/ranges.** Average ACT scores: 20 English, 18 math, 19 composite.
**Faculty.** 211 full-time; 40 part-time. 59% of faculty holds doctoral degree. Student/faculty ratio: 35 to 1.
**Selectivity rating.** Less competitive.

**PROFILE.** Northwestern State is a public, liberal arts university. Founded in 1884, it adopted coeducation in 1920. Programs are offered through the Divisions of Business, Education, and Nursing and the Departments of Creative and Performing Arts; General Studies; Health, Physical Education, and Recreation; Language and Communication; Life Sciences; Mathematical and Physical Sciences; Military Science; Nursing; and Social Sciences. Its 950-acre campus is located in Natchitoches.

**Accreditation:** SACS. Professionally accredited by the Council on Social Work Education, the National Association of Schools of Music, the National Council for Accreditation of Teacher Education, the National League for Nursing.
**Religious orientation:** Northwestern State University of Louisiana is nonsectarian; no religious requirements.
**Library:** Collections totaling over 296,694 volumes, 1,834 periodical subscriptions, and 598,390 microform items.
**Special facilities/museums:** Natural history museum, museum of the history of Louisiana education, language lab, teacher education center, lab school.
**Athletic facilities:** Basketball and tennis courts, track, cross-country path, baseball, football, soccer, and softball fields, swimming pools, golf course.

**STUDENT BODY. Undergraduate profile:** 93% are state residents; 31% are transfers. 1% Asian-American, 21% Black, 2% Hispanic, 1% Native American, 73% White, 2% Other. Average age of undergraduates is 24.
**Freshman profile:** 2% of freshmen who took ACT scored 30 or over on English, 1% scored 30 or over on math, 1% scored 30 or over on composite; 16% scored 24 or over on English, 7% scored 24 or over on math, 12% scored 24 or over on composite; 43% scored 18 or over on English, 35% scored 18 or over on math, 43% scored 18 or over on composite; 64% scored 12 or over on English, 65% scored 12 or over on math, 66% scored 12 or over on composite; 66% scored 6 or over on English, 66% scored 6 or over on math, 67% scored 6 or over on composite. 88% of accepted applicants took ACT.
**Undergraduate achievement:** 55% of fall 1992 freshmen returned for fall 1993 term. 36% of entering class graduated.
**Foreign students:** 42 students are from out of the country. Countries represented include China, England, India, and the former Yugoslav Republics; 17 in all.

**PROGRAMS OF STUDY. Degrees:** B.A., B.Ed., B.M., B.Med., B.Mus., B.S., B.S.Nurs.
**Majors:** Accounting, Advertising Design, Anthropology, Art, Art Education, Aviation Science, Biology Education, Business Administration, Business/Office Education, Chemistry, Computer/Information Systems, Dance, Distributive/Business Education, Early Childhood Education, Electronics Engineering Technology, Elementary Education, English, English Education, General Studies, Geology, Health/Safety/Physical Education, History, Home Economics, Industrial Arts Education, Industrial Technology, Industrial Technology/Management, Instrumental Music, Journalism, Mathematics, Mathematics/Computer Science, Mathematics Education, Medical Technology, Microbiology, Military Science, Music, Music Education, Music Performance, Nursing, Office Administration/Word Processing, Photography, Physics, Political Science/Government, Pre-Dentistry, Pre-Law Business/Political Science, Pre-Medicine Chemistry/Microbiology/Zoology, Psychology, Radiologic Technology, Recreation, Science Education, Secretarial Administration, Social Science Education, Social Sciences, Social Work, Sociology, Special Education/Mild/Moderate, Special Education/Severe/Profound, Speech/Theatre, Vocal Music, Vocal with Piano, Vocational Home Economics, Wildlife Management.
**Distribution of degrees:** The majors with the highest enrollment are business administration, nursing, and education; microbiology and computer technology have the lowest.
**Requirements:** General education requirement.
**Academic regulations:** Freshmen must maintain minimum 1.50 GPA; sophomores, juniors, seniors, 2.0 GPA.
**Special:** College of Nursing maintains clinical campus in Shreveport for study in junior and senior years. Double majors. Pass/fail grading option. Internships. Graduate school at which undergraduates may take graduate-level courses. Preprofessional programs in law and medicine. Teacher certification in early childhood, elementary, secondary, and special education. Certification in specific subject areas. Study abroad in England and Wales. ROTC.
**Honors:** Honors program. Honor societies.
**Academic Assistance:** Remedial reading, writing, and math.

**STUDENT LIFE. Housing:** Freshmen must live on campus. Women's and men's dorms. Fraternity housing. Off-campus privately-owned housing. On-campus married-student housing. 33% of students live in college housing.
**Social atmosphere:** The most socially influential groups on campus, according to the student newspaper, are Kappa Sigma and Kappa Alpha fraternities, Phi Mu sorority, and the Baptist Student Union. Students frequent the campus student union and, off campus, Sassy's, Student Body, and Yesterday's. The most popular events of the year are the state fair, Homecoming, and the Natchitoches Christmas Festival. "The Natchitoches Christmas is considered the Mardi Gras of North Louisiana."
**Services and counseling/handicapped student services:** Placement services. Health service. Day care. Counseling services for veteran and older students.
**Campus organizations:** Undergraduate student government. Student newspaper (Current Sauce, published once/week). Literary magazine. Yearbook. Radio station. Band, symphony orchestra, Davis Players, athletic and departmental groups, service and social groups, special-interest groups. Eight fraternities, all with chapter houses; 12 sororities, nine chapter houses. 26% of men join a fraternity. 20% of women join a sorority.
**Religious organizations:** Baptist Student Union, Fellowship of Christian Athletes, Holy Cross, Pentecostal Fellowship, Wesley Fellowship.

**ATHLETICS. Physical education requirements:** Six semester hours of physical education required.
**Intercollegiate competition:** 6% of students participate. Baseball (M), basketball (M,W), cheerleading (M,W), cross-country (M,W), football (M), golf (M), softball (W), tennis (W), track (indoor) (M,W), track (outdoor) (M,W), track and field (indoor) (M,W), track and field (outdoor) (M,W), volleyball (W). Member of NCAA Division I, NCAA Division I-AA for football, Southland Athletic Conference.
**Intramural and club sports:** 80% of students participate. Intramural basketball, bowling, football, golf, racquetball, rowing, soccer, softball, swimming, tennis, track, volleyball. Men's club rodeo, rowing, soccer. Women's club rodeo, rowing.

**ADMISSIONS.**
**Requirements:** Graduation from secondary school is required; GED is accepted. 20 units and the following program of study are required: 4 units of English, 3 units of math, 2 units of science including 1 unit of lab, 1 unit of social studies, 1 unit of history, 5 units of electives including 3 units of academic electives. ACT is required. Campus visit and interview recommended. Off-campus interviews available with an admissions representative.
**Procedure:** Take ACT by April of 12th year. Visit college for interview by May of 12th year. Suggest filing application by April 1. Application deadline is August 1. Notification of admission on rolling basis. $50 room deposit, refundable until August 1. Freshmen accepted for terms other than fall.
**Special programs:** Credit and/or placement may be granted through CEEB Advanced Placement exams for scores of 3 or higher. Credit may be granted through CLEP general and subject exams, challenge exams, and military and life experience. Early entrance/early admission program. Concurrent enrollment program.
**Transfer students:** Transfer students accepted for terms other than fall. In fall 1993, 31% of all new students were transfers into all classes. 1,368 transfer applications were received, 1,044 were accepted. Application deadline is August 1 for fall; December 1 for spring. Minimum 2.0 GPA required. Lowest course grade accepted is "C." At least 60 semester hours must be completed at the university to receive degree.
**Admissions contact:** Marsha Zulick, M.A., Director of Admissions. 318 357-4503.

**FINANCIAL AID. Available aid:** Pell grants, SEOG, state scholarships and grants, school scholarships, private scholarships, academic merit scholarships, athletic scholarships, and aid for undergraduate foreign students. Perkins Loans (NDSL), PLUS, Stafford Loans (GSL), NSL, and school loans. Deferred payment plan.
**Financial aid statistics:** 41% of aid is not need-based. Average amounts of aid awarded freshmen: Scholarships and grants, $900.
**Supporting data/closing dates:** FAFSA/FFS: Priority filing date is April 1.
**Financial aid contact:** Gil Gilson, M.S., Director of Financial Aid. 318 357-5961.

**STUDENT EMPLOYMENT.** College Work/Study Program. Institutional employment. 33% of full-time undergraduates work on campus during school year. Students may expect to earn an average of $1,050 during school year. Off-campus part-time employment opportunities rated "fair."

**COMPUTER FACILITIES.** 327 IBM/IBM-compatible and Macintosh/Apple microcomputers; 45 are networked. Residence halls may be equipped with stand-alone microcomputers, modems. Client/LAN operating systems include Apple/Macintosh, OS/2, Windows NT. Computer facilities are available to all students.
**Fees:** None.
**Hours:** 24 hours.

**GRADUATE CAREER DATA.** Companies and businesses that hire graduates: IBM; banks, hospitals, nursing homes, schools.

## Our Lady of Holy Cross College

**New Orleans, LA 70131-7399** **504 394-7744**

**1992-93 Costs.** Tuition: $4,500. Housing: None. Fees, books, misc. academic expenses (school's estimate): $300.
**Enrollment.** Undergraduates: 256 men, 403 women (full-time). Freshman class: 577 applicants, 297 enrolled. Graduate enrollment: 40 men, 20 women.
**Test score averages/ranges.** N/A.
**Faculty.** 31 full-time; 68 part-time. 52% of faculty holds doctoral degree. Student/faculty ratio: 15 to 1.
**Selectivity rating.** N/A.

**PROFILE.** Our Lady of Holy Cross is a church-affiliated, liberal arts college. Founded in 1960, it adopted coeducation in 1967. Its 40-acre campus is in a suburban section of New Orleans.

**Accreditation:** SACS.
**Religious orientation:** Our Lady of Holy Cross College is affiliated with the Roman Catholic Church; one semester of religion/theology required.
**Library:** Collections totaling over 56,667 volumes, 410 periodical subscriptions, and 136,015 microform items.

**STUDENT BODY. Undergraduate profile:** 2% Asian-American, 14% Black, 5% Hispanic, 77% White, 2% Other. Average age of undergraduates is 19.
**Undergraduate achievement:** 80% of fall 1992 freshmen returned for fall 1993 term.

**PROGRAMS OF STUDY. Degrees:** B.A., B.S.

**Majors:** Allied Health, Applied Behavioral Science, Biology, Business Administration/Management, Business Economics, Business Education, Business/Management, Curriculum/Instruction, Education, Educational Administration, Elementary Education, English Education, Health Sciences, History, Library Science, Mathematics Education, Nursing, Physical Education, Reading Education, Respiratory Therapy, Science Education, Secondary Education, Social Science Education, Supervision, Teacher Aide.
**Distribution of degrees:** The majors with the highest enrollment are education, nursing, and business.
**Requirements:** General education requirement.
**Special:** Graduate school at which undergraduates may take graduate-level courses. 3-2 social and marriage/family counseling programs. Teacher certification in elementary and secondary education. Study abroad in France. ROTC at U of New Orleans.

**ADMISSIONS. Academic basis for candidate selection** (in order of priority): Secondary school record, class rank, school's recommendation, standardized test scores.
**Requirements:** Graduation from secondary school is recommended; GED is accepted. 24 units required. Student Support Services for applicants not normally admissible. ACT is required; SAT may be substituted. Campus visit recommended. No off-campus interviews.
**Procedure:** Take SAT or ACT by spring of 12th year. Notification of admission on rolling basis. No set date by which applicants must accept offer. Freshmen accepted for terms other than fall.
**Special programs:** Credit and/or placement may be granted through CLEP subject exams. Credit and placement may be granted through ACT PEP and challenge exams. Concurrent enrollment program.
**Transfer students:** Transfer students accepted for terms other than fall. Lowest course grade accepted is "C-."
**Admissions contact:** Matthew Alonzo, M.A., Director of Admissions and Student Affairs. 504 394-7744, extension 126.

**FINANCIAL AID. Available aid:** Pell grants, SEOG, state grants, school scholarships, private scholarships, and academic merit scholarships. Perkins Loans (NDSL), PLUS, Stafford Loans (GSL), NSL, private loans, and SLS.
**Financial aid statistics:** Average amounts of aid awarded freshmen: Loans, $2,625.
**Supporting data/closing dates:** FAFSA/FAF/FFS: Priority filing date is June 1. School's own aid application: Priority filing date is June 1. Notification of awards begins July 1.
**Financial aid contact:** Frank Candalisa, Director of Financial Aid. 504 394-7744, extension 111.

## Saint Joseph Seminary College

**St. Benedict, LA 70457** 504 892-1800

**1994-95 Costs.** Tuition: $5,400. Room: $1,950. Board: $2,250. Fees, books, misc. academic expenses (school's estimate): $670.
**Enrollment.** 60 men (full-time). Freshman class: 24 applicants, 23 accepted, 22 enrolled.
**Test score averages/ranges.** Average ACT scores: 18 English, 18 math, 20 composite.
**Faculty.** 2 full-time; 27 part-time. 40% of faculty holds doctoral degree. Student/faculty ratio: 2 to 1.
**Selectivity rating.** Less competitive.

**PROFILE.** Saint Joseph Seminary, founded in 1891, is a private, church-affiliated, liberal arts college. Its 1,200-acre campus is located in Covington, 40 miles from New Orleans.

**Accreditation:** SACS.
**Religious orientation:** Saint Joseph Seminary College is affiliated with the Roman Catholic Church; 12 semesters of religion required.
**Library:** Collections totaling over 62,672 volumes, 157 periodical subscriptions, and 1,806 microform items.
**Athletic facilities:** Gymnasium with weight room, football and baseball fields, swimming pool, racquetball/handball and tennis courts.

**STUDENT BODY. Undergraduate profile:** 68% are state residents; 55% are transfers. 22% Asian-American, 3% Black, 75% White. Average age of undergraduates is 23.
**Freshman profile:** 13% of freshmen who took ACT scored 24 or over on English, 13% scored 24 or over on math, 38% scored 24 or over on composite; 63% scored 18 or over on English, 51% scored 18 or over on math, 51% scored 18 or over on composite; 76% scored 12 or over on English, 100% scored 12 or over on math, 100% scored 12 or over on composite; 100% scored 6 or over on English. 100% of accepted applicants took ACT. 63% of freshmen come from public schools.
**Undergraduate achievement:** 88% of fall 1991 freshmen returned for fall 1992 term.

**PROGRAMS OF STUDY. Degrees:** B.A.
**Majors:** Liberal Arts.
**Requirements:** General education requirement.
**Academic regulations:** Minimum 2.0 GPA must be maintained.
**Special:** Accelerated study. Preprofessional programs in theology.
**Academic Assistance:** Remedial reading, writing, and study skills.

**ADMISSIONS. Academic basis for candidate selection** (in order of priority): Sponsorship letter, essay, standardized test scores, secondary school record.
**Nonacademic basis for candidate selection:** Character and personality are important.
**Requirements:** Graduation from secondary school is required; GED is accepted. 17 units and the following program of study are required: 3 units of English, 2 units of math, 2 units of science, 2 units of foreign language, 1 unit of history, 7 units of academic electives. Academic probation for applicants not normally admissible. ACT is required. Campus visit and interview recommended. Off-campus interviews available with an admissions representative.
**Procedure:** Take ACT by January of 12th year. Notification of admission on rolling basis. Freshmen accepted for terms other than fall.
**Special programs:** Admission may be deferred indefinitely. Credit may be granted through CEEB Advanced Placement, CLEP subject exams, DANTES and challenge exams, and military and life experience. Credit and/or placement may be granted through CLEP general exams. Concurrent enrollment program.
**Transfer students:** Transfer students accepted for terms other than fall. In fall 1993, 55% of all new students were transfers into all classes. 12 transfer applications were received, 12 were accepted. Application deadline is rolling for fall; rolling for spring. Minimum 2.0 GPA required. Lowest course grade accepted is "C." Maximum number of transferable credits is 102 semester hours. At least 30 semester hours must be completed at the college to receive degree.
**Admissions contact:** Thomas A. Siegrist, M.Ed., Ed.S., Director of Admissions. 504 892-1800.

**FINANCIAL AID. Available aid:** Pell grants, SEOG, state grants, private scholarships, and academic merit scholarships. Perkins Loans (NDSL), PLUS, Stafford Loans (GSL), and SLS. Deferred payment plan.
**Financial aid statistics:** In 1993-94, 100% of all undergraduate applicants received aid; 50% of freshman applicants. Average amounts of aid awarded freshmen: Scholarships and grants, $2,600; loans, $2,000.
**Supporting data/closing dates:** FAFSA. Notification of awards on rolling basis.
**Financial aid contact:** Winnie Haydel, Director of Financial Aid. 504 892-1800.

## Southeastern Louisiana University

**Hammond, LA 70402** 504 549-2000

**1994-95 Costs.** Tuition: $1,910 (state residents), $3,854 (out-of-state). Room: $1,030-$1,900. Board: $1,200-$1,360. Fees, books, misc. academic expenses (school's estimate): $120.
**Enrollment.** Undergraduates: 3,900 men, 5,883 women (full-time). Freshman class: 3,247 applicants, 3,149 accepted, 2,306 enrolled. Graduate enrollment: 297 men, 965 women.
**Test score averages/ranges.** Average ACT scores: 19 English, 18 math, 19 composite.
**Faculty.** 415 full-time; 130 part-time. 63% of faculty holds highest degree in specific field. Student/faculty ratio: 24 to 1.
**Selectivity rating.** Noncompetitive.

**PROFILE.** Southeastern Louisiana, founded in 1925, is a public, comprehensive university. Programs are offered through the Colleges of Arts and Sciences, Business, and Education; the School of Nursing; and the Graduate School. Its 365-acre campus is located in Hammond.

**Accreditation:** SACS. Professionally accredited by the American Assembly of Collegiate Schools of Business, the Council on Social Work Education, the National Association of Schools of Music, the National Council for Accreditation of Teacher Education, the National League for Nursing.
**Religious orientation:** Southeastern Louisiana University is nonsectarian; no religious requirements.
**Library:** Collections totaling over 310,000 volumes, 2,200 periodical subscriptions, and 491,929 microform items.
**Special facilities/museums:** On-campus elementary school.
**Athletic facilities:** Gymnasiums, basketball arena, football stadium, track, baseball, rugby, and softball fields, tennis courts, weight rooms, swimming pool.

**STUDENT BODY. Undergraduate profile:** 96% are state residents; 15% are transfers. 1% Asian-American, 7% Black, 1% Hispanic, 1% Native American, 90% White. Average age of undergraduates is 23.
**Freshman profile:** 99% of accepted applicants took ACT.
**Undergraduate achievement:** 50% of fall 1992 freshmen returned for fall 1993 term. 30% of entering class graduated.
**Foreign students:** 48 students are from out of the country. Countries represented include Germany, Japan, Kuwait, Lebanon, Malaysia, and Sweden; 32 in all.

**PROGRAMS OF STUDY. Degrees:** B.A., B.Gen.Studies, B.Mus., B.Mus.Ed., B.S.
**Majors:** Accounting, Art, Art Education, Band Instrument, Biochemistry, Biology, Biology Education, Botany, Business Administration, Business Education, Chemistry, Communication, Computer Science, Criminal Justice, Early Childhood Education, Economics, Elementary Education, Elementary/Secondary School Music, English, English/Journalism, Executive Secretary, Fashion Merchandising, Finance, French, French Education, Geography, Government, Health/Safety/Physical Education/Coaching, History, Home Economics, Home Economics Education, Industrial Arts Education, Industrial Technology, Liberal Arts Studies, Marketing, Mathematics, Microbiology, Music, Music Education, Nursing, Office Administration, Office Management, Orchestral Instrument, Physics, Piano, Plant Sciences, Political Science/Government, Psychology, Shorthand, Social Studies, Social Work, Sociology, Spanish, Spanish Education, Speech Correction, Speech Education, Teaching the Emotionally Disturbed/Maladjusted, Teaching the Mentally Retarded, Typing, Voice, Zoology.
**Distribution of degrees:** The majors with the highest enrollment are business, education, and nursing.
**Requirements:** General education requirement.
**Academic regulations:** Minimum 2.0 GPA required for graduation.
**Special:** Minors offered in all majors. Associate's degrees offered. Double majors. Dual degrees. Cooperative education programs. Graduate school at which undergraduates may take graduate-level courses. Preprofessional programs in law, medicine, pharmacy, dentistry, optometry, engineering, journalism, and physical therapy. Combined-degree program in psychology with Louisiana State U. Teacher certification in early childhood, elementary, secondary, and special education. Study abroad in Mexico. ROTC.
**Honors:** Honors program.
**Academic Assistance:** Remedial reading, writing, math, and study skills. Nonremedial tutoring.

**STUDENT LIFE. Housing:** All unmarried students must live on campus. Coed, women's, and men's dorms. Fraternity housing. School-owned/operated apartments. On-campus married-student housing. 30% of students live in college housing.
**Social atmosphere:** Southeastern's student social life is greatly influenced by the Greeks. Students gather at The Lion's Den and the Student Union on campus and at Starz, Brady's, The Beach Club, and the Hammond Square Mall off campus. Homecoming and the October Arts Festival highlight the school year.
**Services and counseling/handicapped student services:** Placement services. Health service. Counseling services for veteran and older students. Personal and psychological counseling. Career and academic guidance services.
**Campus organizations:** Undergraduate student government. Student newspaper (Lion's Roar, published once/week). Literary magazine. Yearbook. Radio station. Choral groups, concert and marching bands, orchestra, jazz ensemble, musical theatre troupe, drama club, debating, cinema program, 109 organizations in all. 10 fraternities, four chapter houses; eight sororities, no chapter houses. 5% of men join a fraternity. 5% of women join a sorority.

**ATHLETICS. Physical education requirements:** Physical education requirements vary with program.
**Intercollegiate competition:** 2% of students participate. Baseball (M), basketball (M,W), cross-country (M,W), golf (M), softball (W), tennis (M,W), track (indoor) (M,W), track (outdoor) (M,W), track and field (indoor) (M,W), track and field (outdoor) (M,W), volleyball (W). Member of NCAA Division I, Trans America Athletic Conference.
**Intramural and club sports:** 38% of students participate. Intramural badminton, basketball, bowling, darts, field goal kick, flag football, floor hockey, free throw, horseshoes, pickleball, pool, racquetball, shuffleboard, soccer, softball, table tennis, tennis, volleyball. Men's club rugby, soccer.

**ADMISSIONS. Academic basis for candidate selection** (in order of priority): Secondary school record.
**Requirements:** Graduation from secondary school is required; GED is accepted. 24 units and the following program of study are recommended: 4 units of English, 3 units of math, 3 units of science, 2 units of foreign language, 3 units of social studies, 2 units of history, 7 units of electives. Audition recommended of music program applicants. Developmental Education Program for applicants not normally admissible. ACT is required; SAT may be substituted. Campus visit recommended. No off-campus interviews.
**Procedure:** Take SAT or ACT by February of 12th year. Application deadline is July 15. Notification of admission on rolling basis. Reply is required by last day of late registration. $100 nonrefundable room deposit. Freshmen accepted for terms other than fall.
**Special programs:** Admission may be deferred. Credit may be granted through CEEB Advanced Placement for scores of 3 or higher. Credit may be granted through CLEP general and subject exams, ACT PEP and challenge exams, and military experience. Early entrance/early admission program. Concurrent enrollment program.
**Transfer students:** Transfer students accepted for terms other than fall. In fall 1993, 15% of all new students were transfers into all classes. 1,131 transfer applications were received, 1,125 were accepted. Application deadline is July 15 for fall; December 1 for spring. Minimum 2.0 GPA recommended. Lowest course grade accepted is "D." Maximum number of transferable credits is 68 semester hours. At least 30 semester hours must be completed at the university to receive degree.
**Admissions contact:** Stephen Soutullo, M.Ed., Director of Enrollment Services. 504 549-2123, 800 222-7358 (in-state).

**FINANCIAL AID. Available aid:** Pell grants, SEOG, state scholarships and grants, private scholarships, ROTC scholarships, academic merit scholarships, athletic scholarships, and aid for undergraduate foreign students. Perkins Loans (NDSL), PLUS, Stafford Loans (GSL), and SLS.
**Financial aid statistics:** In 1993-94, 55% of all undergraduate applicants received aid; 55% of freshman applicants. Average amounts of aid awarded freshmen: Scholarships and grants, $3,300; loans, $1,750.
**Supporting data/closing dates:** FAFSA/FAF: Priority filing date is May 1. Notification of awards on rolling basis.

**STUDENT EMPLOYMENT.** College Work/Study Program. Institutional employment. 6% of full-time undergraduates work on campus during school year. Off-campus part-time employment opportunities rated "fair."

**COMPUTER FACILITIES.** 300 IBM/IBM-compatible and Macintosh/Apple microcomputers; all are networked. Students may access Digital minicomputer/mainframe systems, Internet. Residence halls may be equipped with networked microcomputers, networked terminals. Client/LAN operating systems include Apple/Macintosh, DOS, UNIX/XENIX/AIX, Windows NT, DEC. Computer languages and software packages include APL, ARES, BASIC, BMDP, C, COBOL, Edit, FORTRAN, GMAP, LISP, Pascal, PL/6, RPG II, SLAM, SPITBOL, SPSS-X. Computer facilities are available to all students.
**Fees:** None.
**Hours:** 8 AM-midn.

**GRADUATE CAREER DATA.** Companies and businesses that hire graduates: FAA, FBI, Internal Revenue Service, K mart, Shell Oil, Wal-Mart.

# Southern University at New Orleans

**New Orleans, LA 70126** **504 286-5314**

**1994-95 Costs.** Tuition: $1,656 (state residents), $3,206 (out-of-state). Housing: None. Fees, books, misc. academic expenses (school's estimate): $800.
**Enrollment.** Undergraduates: 1,100 men, 2,200 women (full-time). Freshman class: 950 applicants, 950 accepted, 530 enrolled. Graduate enrollment: 40 men, 160 women.
**Test score averages/ranges.** N/A.
**Faculty.** 126 full-time. 60% of faculty holds doctoral degree.
**Selectivity rating.** N/A.

**PROFILE.** Southern University, founded in 1956, is a public, comprehensive institution. Programs are offered through the Divisions of Business, Education, Humanities, Science, and Social Science. Its 17-acre campus is located in a residential secion of New Orleans.

**Accreditation:** SACS. Professionally accredited by the Council on Social Work Education.
**Religious orientation:** Southern University at New Orleans is nonsectarian; no religious requirements.

**STUDENT BODY. Undergraduate profile:** 1% Asian-American, 89% Black, 1% Hispanic, 6% White, 3% Other.
**Freshman profile:** 99% of accepted applicants took ACT. 98% of freshmen come from public schools.
**Foreign students:** 70 students are from out of the country. Nine countries represented in all.

**PROGRAMS OF STUDY. Degrees:** B.A., B.S.
**Majors:** Accounting, Art, Biology, Business Administration, Chemistry, Economics, Elementary Education, English, French, Health/Physical Education, History, Mathematics, Office Administration, Physics, Political Science, Psychology, Secondary Education, Social Work, Sociology, Spanish.
**Special:** Minors offered in most majors and in finance, management, and marketing. Freshmen remain under jurisdiction of Division of Freshman Studies until 31 semester hour credits have been earned. Primary emphasis in education placed on preparing inner-city school teachers. Associate's degrees offered. Double majors. Dual degrees. Cooperative education programs. Graduate school at which undergraduates may take graduate-level courses. Preprofessional programs in medicine, veterinary science, pharmacy, optometry, allied health, engineering, medical technology, and nursing. 3-1 medical technology program. Cross-registration with U of New Orleans and Delgado Junior Coll. Teacher certification in elementary and secondary education. ROTC.
**Honors:** Honors program.

**STUDENT LIFE. Housing:** Commuter campus; no student housing.
**Services and counseling/handicapped student services:** Placement services. Health service. Testing center. Personal counseling. Career and academic guidance services. Learning disabled services.
**Campus organizations:** Undergraduate student government. Lyceum Committee, academic groups, special-interest groups. Four fraternities, no chapter houses; four sororities, no chapter houses. 10% of men join a fraternity. 12% of women join a sorority.
**Religious organizations:** Denominational religious groups.

**ATHLETICS. Physical education requirements:** Four hours of health/physical education required.

**ADMISSIONS. Academic basis for candidate selection** (in order of priority): Standardized test scores, secondary school record.
**Requirements:** Graduation from secondary school is required; GED is accepted. No specific distribution of secondary school units required. Program should include English, math, science, social studies, and physical education. ACT is required. No off-campus interviews.
**Procedure:** Take ACT by fall of 12th year. Notification of admission on rolling basis. No set date by which applicant must accept offer; no advance deposits required. Freshmen accepted for terms other than fall.
**Special programs:** Credit may be granted through CEEB Advanced Placement. Credit may be granted through CLEP general and subject exams, DANTES and challenge exams, and military experience. Early entrance/early admission program. Concurrent enrollment program.
**Transfer students:** Transfer students accepted for terms other than fall. Application deadline is 30 days prior to registration for fall; 30 days prior to registration for spring. Lowest course grade accepted is "C." Maximum number of transferable credits is 93 semester hours.
**Admissions contact:** Melvin L. Hodges, Director of Admissions.

**FINANCIAL AID. Available aid:** Pell grants, SEOG, and aid for undergraduate foreign students. Legislative scholarships. Stafford Loans (GSL).
**Supporting data/closing dates:** FAFSA: Priority filing dates are April 1, October 1; accepted on rolling basis. Verification Form: Priority filing dates are April 1, October 1.
**Financial aid contact:** Gerald Williams, Director of Financial Aid.

**STUDENT EMPLOYMENT.** College Work/Study Program.

# Tulane University

**New Orleans, LA 70118** **504 865-5000**

**1994-95 Costs.** Tuition: $18,500. Room & board: $5,780. Fees, books, misc. academic expenses (school's estimate): $610.
**Enrollment.** Undergraduates: 2,540 men, 2,406 women (full-time). Freshman class: 7,033 applicants, 5,125 accepted, 1,223 enrolled. Graduate enrollment: 2,662 men, 2,066 women.
**Test score averages/ranges.** Average SAT scores: 556 verbal, 612 math. Range of SAT scores of middle 50%: 490-616 verbal, 560-670 math.
**Faculty.** 485 full-time; 230 part-time. 98% of faculty holds doctoral degree. Student/faculty ratio: 13 to 1.
**Selectivity rating.** Highly competitive.

**PROFILE.** Tulane is a private, comprehensive university. Founded in 1834, it adopted coeducation in 1886. Programs are offered in the College of Arts and Sciences, Newcombe College, and the Schools of Engineering and Architecture. Its 110-acre campus is located five miles from downtown New Orleans.

**Accreditation:** SACS. Professionally accredited by the Accreditation Board for Engineering and Technology, the Accrediting Commission on Education for Health Services Administration, the American Assembly of Collegiate Schools of Business, the American Bar Association, the American Medical Association (CAHEA), the Association of Ameri-

can Law Schools, the Computing Sciences Accreditation Board, the Council on Education for Public Health, the Council on Social Work Education, the Liaison Committee on Medical Education, the National Architecture Accrediting Board.
**Religious orientation:** Tulane University is nonsectarian; no religious requirements.
**Library:** Collections totaling over 1,946,312 volumes, 17,292 periodical subscriptions, and 2,114,185 microform items.
**Special facilities/museums:** Art gallery, jazz and architecture archives, Louisiana collection of historical materials, language labs, research facilities and research centers covering many areas. Coordinated (scientific interdisciplinary) research instrumentation facility.
**Athletic facilities:** Recreational center, swimming pool, basketball, racquetball, and volleyball courts, sports center, training, and weight rooms, athletic fields.

**STUDENT BODY. Undergraduate profile:** 20% are state residents. 3.9% Asian-American, 9.8% Black, 5.7% Hispanic, .3% Native American, 80% White, .3% Other. Average age of undergraduates is 20.
**Freshman profile:** 6% of freshmen who took SAT scored 700 or over on verbal, 17% scored 700 or over on math; 32% scored 600 or over on verbal, 57% scored 600 or over on math; 72% scored 500 or over on verbal, 92% scored 500 or over on math; 98% scored 400 or over on verbal, 99% scored 400 or over on math; 100% scored 300 or over on verbal, 100% scored 300 or over on math. Majority of accepted applicants took SAT. 55% of freshmen come from public schools.
**Undergraduate achievement:** 85% of fall 1992 freshmen returned for fall 1993 term. 65% of entering class graduated. 80% of students who completed a degree program went on to graduate study.
**Foreign students:** 254 students are from out of the country. Countries represented include Bolivia, Costa Rica, India, and Saudi Arabia; 60 in all.

**PROGRAMS OF STUDY. Degrees:** B.A., B.Arch., B.F.A., B.Gen.Studies, B.S., B.S.Eng., B.S.Mgmt.
**Majors:** American Studies, Anthropology, Architecture, Art/Biology, Art History/Appreciation, Asian Studies, Bioengineering/Biomedical Engineering, Biological Chemistry, Cell/Molecular Biology, Chemical Engineering, Chemistry, Civil Engineering, Classical Studies, Cognitive Studies, Communication, Computer Engineering, Computer/Information Sciences, Computer Science, Earth Science, Ecology/Evolution/Organismal Biology, Economics, Education/Psychology, Electrical Engineering, English, Environmental Engineering, Environmental Studies, Exercise Science, French, Geology, German, Greek, Greek/Latin, History, Italian, Jewish Studies, Latin, Latin American Studies, Linguistics, Management, Mathematical Economics, Mathematics, Mechanical Engineering, Media Arts, Medieval Studies, Music, Philosophy, Physics, Political Economy, Political Science/Government, Political Science/International Relations, Psychology, Russian, Russian/Soviet Studies, Sociology, Spanish/Portuguese, Sports Management, Studio Art, Theatre, Women's Studies.
**Distribution of degrees:** The majors with the highest enrollment are biology, English, and psychology; Jewish studies, Italian, and medieval studies have the lowest.
**Requirements:** General education requirement.
**Special:** Minors offered in many majors and in African diaspora studies, art studio, dance, and pharmacology. Tulane U Scholars, Honors Program, honors sections, interdepartmental honor colloquia, and honor societies available. Early admission to Tulane Medical Sch. Multiple interdisciplinary studies. Associate's degrees offered. Self-designed majors. Double majors. Dual degrees. Independent study. Accelerated study. Pass/fail grading option. Internships. Graduate school at which undergraduates may take graduate-level courses. Joint degrees offered in business, law, medicine, public health and tropical medicine, and social work. 3-3 B.A. or B.S./J.D. program. 3-4 B.A. or B.S./M.D. program. 3-2 B.A. or B.S./M.B.A. program with Tulane's Freeman Sch of Business. 3-2 engineering program with Loyola U. Member of the Southern Consortium. Washington Semester. Teacher certification in early childhood, elementary, secondary, and special education. Certification in specific subject areas. Junior Year Abroad in France, Germany, Ireland, Israel, Italy, Spain, and the United Kingdom. Summer abroad programs in geology and theatre. Summer abroad also offered in Athens and Rome. Short term study abroad programs are offered in the Czech Republic, Ghana, Hungary, Japan, Poland, Slovakia, and Taiwan. ROTC, NROTC, and AFROTC.
**Honors:** Phi Beta Kappa. Honors program. Honor societies.
**Academic Assistance:** Remedial study skills. Nonremedial tutoring.

**STUDENT LIFE. Housing:** All freshmen must live on campus. Coed and women's dorms. Sorority and fraternity housing. School-owned/operated apartments. Off-campus privately-owned housing. 48% of students live in college housing.
**Social atmosphere:** According to the editor of the student newspaper, students at Tulane "party a lot–most likely too much." Greeks and ROTC are influential groups on campus. Popular events include the LSU football game, Homecoming, and TGIF's (weekly quad parties, including bands). On campus, students tend to gather at the library, Pocket Park, and Reily Student Recreation Center. Off campus, they head for The Book and the Rendon Inn.
**Services and counseling/handicapped student services:** Placement services. Health service. Women's center. Day care. Educational Resource Center; supplemental instruction, study skills workshops, study groups, summer program. Counseling services for minority, military, and older students. Birth control, personal, and psychological counseling. Career and academic guidance services. Physically disabled student services. Learning disabled services. Reader services for the blind.
**Campus organizations:** Undergraduate student government. Student newspaper (Tulane Hullabaloo, published once/week). Literary magazine. Yearbook. Radio and TV stations. Drama Club, cheerleaders, literary society, speech and debate society, Amnesty International, College Democrats, College Republicans, BACCHUS, AIDS prevention group, Circle K, several community action groups, Gay and Lesbian Association, Kafka Circle, Objectivists, Town Student Association, Celebrate Difference, Green Club, Peace in Central America Movement, engineering, business, and other departmental groups, 200 organizations in all. 17 fraternities, 14 chapter houses; eight sororities, seven chapter houses. 32% of men join a fraternity. 35% of women join a sorority.
**Religious organizations:** Baptist Student Union, B'nai B'rith Hillel, Catholic Center, Chabad House, Eastern Orthodox Ministry, Intervarsity Christian Fellowship, Lutheran Campus Ministry, Christian Science, Episcopal, Muslim, Presbyterian, and United Methodist groups.
**Minority/foreign student organizations:** Coalition Against Racism, African-American Congress, Black Engineers, Black Lawyers, Asian-American Congress, Black MBA Association, National Organization of Minority Architecture Students. International Student Organization, African, Asian, Caribbean, Chinese, Indian, Israeli, Latin American, Mexican, Taiwanese, and Vietnamese groups.

**ATHLETICS. Physical education requirements:** None.
**Intercollegiate competition:** 8% of students participate. Baseball (M), basketball (M,W), cross-country (M,W), football (M), golf (M,W), tennis (M,W), track (indoor) (M,W), track (outdoor) (M,W), track and field (indoor) (M,W), track and field (outdoor) (M,W), volleyball (W). Member of Metro Athletic Conference, NCAA Division I.
**Intramural and club sports:** Intramural basketball, flag football, inner-tube water polo, soccer, tennis, volleyball, Wiffle ball.

**ADMISSIONS. Academic basis for candidate selection** (in order of priority): Secondary school record, class rank, standardized test scores, school's recommendation, essay.
**Nonacademic basis for candidate selection:** Extracurricular participation is emphasized. Character and personality and alumni/ae relationship are important. Particular talent or ability is considered.
**Requirements:** Graduation from secondary school is recommended; GED is accepted. 15 units and the following program of study are recommended: 4 units of English, 3 units of math, 3 units of science, 3 units of foreign language, 2 units of social studies. Strong college-preparatory program emphasized; English should include extensive reading and writing; math should include algebra, geometry, trigonometry, and calculus or other more advanced courses; 3 or 4 years of a single foreign language preferred over 2 years each of 2 languages; social studies should emphasize history. Even if academic requirements are met in first three years of secondary school, final year should include at least 4 college-preparatory subjects. SAT or ACT is required. ACH recommended. Campus visit recommended. Off-campus interviews available with an alumni representative.
**Procedure:** Take SAT or ACT by November of 12th year. Take ACH by December of 12th year. Application deadline is January 15. Notification of admission by April 15. Reply is required by May 1. $150 tuition deposit, refundable until May 1. $150 room deposit, refundable until May 1. Freshmen accepted for terms other than fall.
**Special programs:** Admission may be deferred one year. Credit and/or placement may be granted through CEEB Advanced Placement exams for scores of 4 or higher. Placement may be granted through challenge exams. Early entrance/early admission program. Concurrent enrollment program.
**Transfer students:** Transfer students accepted for terms other than fall. In fall 1993, 450 transfer applications were received, 299 were accepted. Application deadline is July 1 for fall; November 15 for spring. Minimum 3.0 GPA required. Lowest course grade accepted is "C." At least 64 semester hours must be completed at the university to receive degree.
**Admissions contact:** Richard Whiteside, Ph.D., Dean of Admission and Enrollment Management. 504 865-5731.

**FINANCIAL AID. Available aid:** Pell grants, SEOG, state grants, school scholarships, ROTC scholarships, academic merit scholarships, athletic scholarships, and aid for undergraduate foreign students. Perkins Loans (NDSL), PLUS, Stafford Loans (GSL), private loans, and SLS. AMS and guaranteed tuition.
**Financial aid statistics:** 20% of aid is not need-based. In 1993-94, 92% of all undergraduate applicants received aid; 87% of freshman applicants. Average amounts of aid awarded freshmen: Scholarships and grants, $13,050; loans, $2,600.
**Supporting data/closing dates:** FAFSA/FAF: Priority filing date is March 1. Notification of awards on rolling basis.
**Financial aid contact:** Elaine Rivera, Director of Financial Aid. 504 865-5723.

**STUDENT EMPLOYMENT.** College Work/Study Program. Institutional employment. 25% of full-time undergraduates work on campus during school year. Students may expect to earn an average of $1,300 during school year. Off-campus part-time employment opportunities rated "fair."

**COMPUTER FACILITIES.** 350 IBM/IBM-compatible, Macintosh/Apple, and RISC-/UNIX-based microcomputers; 200 are networked. Students may access Digital, IBM, Pyramid, SUN minicomputer/mainframe systems, Internet. Residence halls may be equipped with stand-alone microcomputers. Client/LAN operating systems include Apple/Macintosh, DOS, UNIX/XENIX/AIX, X-windows, DEC, LocalTalk/AppleTalk, Novell. Computer languages and software packages include Abaqus, Assembler, BASIC, BMDP, C, COBOL, Data Explorer, FORTRAN, IMSL, Mathematica, Matlab, MINITAB, Nastran, Pascal, SAS, SPSS-X, TSP. Computer facilities are available to all students.
**Fees:** None.
**Hours:** 24 hours, (RISC cluster); 8:30 AM-11 PM (M-Su), (microcomputers).

**GRADUATE CAREER DATA.** Graduate school percentages: 16% enter law school. 9% enter medical school. 7% enter graduate business programs. 13% enter graduate arts and sciences programs. Highest graduate school enrollments: UC Berkeley, Emory U, Georgetown U, Harvard U, Johns Hopkins U, Louisiana State U, Loyola U of Chicago, Ohio State U, Northwestern U, Stanford U, U of Texas, Tufts U, Tulane U, Vanderbilt U, U of Virginia, U of Wisconsin, Yale U. 35% of graduates choose careers in business and industry. Companies and businesses that hire graduates: Arthur Andersen, Bell-Northern Research, KPMG Peat Marwick, Peace Corps, Shell Oil.

**PROMINENT ALUMNI/AE.** Howard K. Smith, news commentator; Newt Gingrich, Republican congressional whip; David Treen, former governor and U.S. representative; Lindy Boggs and Hale Boggs, former U.S. representatives; Sidney Barthelemy, former mayor of New Orleans; Shirley Ann Grau, Pulitzer Prize-winning author; John Kennedy Toole, Pulitzer Prize-winning author; Robert Harling, playwright, *Steel Magnolias;* Dr. Michael DeBakey, surgeon; John Minor Wisdom, U.S. Appeals Court judge.

# University of New Orleans

**New Orleans, LA 70148** **504 286-6000**

**1993-94 Costs.** Tuition: $2,362 (state residents), $5,154 (out-of-state). Room & board: $3,476. Fees, books, misc. academic expenses (school's estimate): $700.
**Enrollment.** Undergraduates: 3,761 men, 4,397 women (full-time). Freshman class: 2,406 applicants, 2,139 accepted, 1,501 enrolled. Graduate enrollment: 1,652 men, 2,117 women.
**Test score averages/ranges.** Average ACT scores: 21 English, 20 math, 21 composite. Range of ACT scores of middle 50%: 17-19 English, 17-22 math.
**Faculty.** 557 full-time; 262 part-time. 76% of faculty holds doctoral degree. Student/faculty ratio: 20 to 1.
**Selectivity rating.** Less competitive.

**PROFILE.** The University of New Orleans, founded in 1958, is a public institution. Programs are offered through the Colleges of Business Administration, Education, Engineering, Liberal Arts, Sciences, and Urban and Regional Studies; the Metropolitan College; and the Graduate School. Its 195-acre campus is located in a residential section of New Orleans.

**Accreditation:** SACS. Professionally accredited by the Accreditation Board for Engineering and Technology, the American Assembly of Collegiate Schools of Business, the National Association of Schools of Art and Design, the National Association of Schools of Music, the National Council for Accreditation of Teacher Education.
**Religious orientation:** University of New Orleans is nonsectarian; no religious requirements.
**Library:** Collections totaling over 591,545 volumes, 3,009 periodical subscriptions, and 1,856,260 microform items.
**Special facilities/museums:** Performing arts center, audio-visual center, learning resources center, TV studio, electronic lab, Eisenhower center, engineering building.
**Athletic facilities:** Indoor swimming pool and sauna, tennis courts, track, baseball diamond, handball/racquetball courts, golf course, weight room, basketball court, stadium, sports center.

**STUDENT BODY. Undergraduate profile:** 93% are state residents; 35% are transfers. 4% Asian-American, 14% Black, 6% Hispanic, 1% Native American, 73% White, 2% Other. Average age of undergraduates is 23.
**Freshman profile:** 2% of freshmen who took ACT scored 30 or over on English, 1% scored 30 or over on math, 1% scored 30 or over on composite; 26% scored 24 or over on English, 15% scored 24 or over on math, 20% scored 24 or over on composite; 74% scored 18 or over on English, 68% scored 18 or over on math, 79% scored 18 or over on composite; 99% scored 12 or over on English, 100% scored 12 or over on math, 100% scored 12 or over on composite; 100% scored 6 or over on English. 80% of accepted applicants took ACT. 66% of freshmen come from public schools.
**Foreign students:** 214 students are from out of the country. Countries represented include Japan, Norway, Pakistan, Saudi Arabia, Sweden, and United Kingdom; 62 in all.

**PROGRAMS OF STUDY. Degrees:** B.A., B.Gen.Studies, B.S.
**Majors:** Accounting, Anthropology, Biological Sciences, Business Education, Chemistry, Civil Engineering, Computer Science, Drama, Drama/Communications, Economics, Electrical Engineering, Elementary Education, English, Finance, Fine Arts, French, General Business Administration, Geography, Geology, Geophysics, Health/Physical Education, History, Hotel/Restaurant/Tourism Administration, Management, Marketing, Mathematics, Mechanical Engineering, Medical Technology, Music, Music Education, Naval Architecture/Marine Engineering, Philosophy, Physics, Political Science, Psychology, Science Education, Secondary Education, Sociology, Spanish, Speech Education.
**Distribution of degrees:** The majors with the highest enrollment are general studies, elementary education, and business administration; physics and science education have the lowest.
**Requirements:** General education requirement.
**Academic regulations:** Minimum 2.0 GPA must be maintained.
**Special:** Courses offered in Greek, Italian, Russian, and speech. Double majors. Dual degrees. Pass/fail grading option. Internships. Cooperative education programs. Graduate school at which undergraduates may take graduate-level courses. Preprofessional programs in medicine, veterinary science, pharmacy, and dentistry. 2-2 nursing program with Louisiana State U. 3-1 medical technology program with Louisiana State U Medical Center. Two-year transfer programs in inhalation therapy and physical therapy. Three-year transfer programs in dentistry, law, and medicine may be arranged. 3-2 engineering program. Cross-registration with Delgado Comm Coll and Southern U at New Orleans. Washington Semester. Teacher certification in early childhood, elementary, secondary, and special education. Exchange programs abroad in Austria (U of Innsbruck) and France (U of Orleans). ROTC and AFROTC at Tulane U.
**Honors:** Honors program. Honor societies.
**Academic Assistance:** Remedial reading, writing, and math. Nonremedial tutoring.

**STUDENT LIFE. Housing:** Students may live on or off campus. Coed, women's, and men's dorms. On-campus married-student housing. 5% of students live in college housing.
**Social atmosphere:** The editor of the student newspaper reports, "The campus bar has bands on the weekends, and a Jazz Night every other Wednesday. We are in New Orleans, so there are dozens of social and cultural activities going on all the time, such as Mardi Gras, the French Quarter Festival, Art for Art's Sake, and Jazz Fest." The French Quarter is just a 20 minute bus ride away. Most influential groups are the International Student Organization, Amnesty International, GALA, and Greeks. Favorite yearly events are International Evening (food, music, poetry, dance from over 12 countries), Madrigal Dinner/Performance, Fallfest, Aprilfest and Homecoming. Popular student gathering spots are the Sandbar (on-campus bar), the University Center (where the fraternities and sororities hangout), and the Quarter.
**Services and counseling/handicapped student services:** Placement services. Health service. Women's center. Day care. Counseling services for minority and older students. Birth control, personal, and psychological counseling. Career and academic guidance services. Religious counseling. Physically disabled student services. Learning disabled services. Notetaking services. Tape recorders. Tutors. Reader services for the blind.
**Campus organizations:** Undergraduate student government. Student newspaper (Driftwood, published once/week). Literary magazine. Yearbook. College Life, Circle K, UNO Ambassadors, musical and drama groups, political groups, service and special-interest groups, 120 organizations in all. 10 fraternities, one chapter house; seven sororities, no chapter houses. 5% of men join a fraternity. 5% of women join a sorority.
**Religious organizations:** Bahai Club, Baptist Student Union, Catholic Hispanic group, Muslim Student Association, Chi Alpha, Intervarsity Christian Fellowship, Crossroads Campus Ministry, Newman Club, Upreach Outreach.
**Minority/foreign student organizations:** NAACP, African-American Business Society, National Society of Black Engineers. International Student Organization, Chinese, Indian, Latin American, and Vietnamese groups.

**ATHLETICS. Physical education requirements:** None.
**Intercollegiate competition:** Baseball (M), basketball (M,W), cross-country (M,W), diving (W), golf (M), softball (W), swimming (W), tennis (W), track and field (W), volleyball (W). Member of ASAC, NCAA Division I.
**Intramural and club sports:** Intramural badminton, flag football, floor hockey, free throw, golf, H.O.R.S.E., punt-pass-kick, racquetball, soccer, softball, tennis, turkey trot, volleyball, wrestling.

**ADMISSIONS. Academic basis for candidate selection** (in order of priority): Standardized test scores, secondary school record.
**Nonacademic basis for candidate selection:** Character and personality, extracurricular participation, particular talent or ability, and alumni/ae relationship are considered.
**Requirements:** Graduation from secondary school is required; GED is accepted. 17.5 units and the following program of study are required: 4 units of English, 3 units of math, 3 units of science, 2 units of foreign language, 2 units of social studies, 1 unit of history, .5 units of computer science, 2 units of electives. Minimum composite ACT score of 20 (combined SAT score of 810) or minimum 2.0 GPA required. Portfolio required of art program applicants. Audition required of music program applicants. College Life Development and Tutorial Program for applicants not normally admissible (minimum composite ACT score of 15 or combined SAT score of 630). ACT is required; SAT may be substituted. Campus visit recommended. Off-campus interviews available with admissions and alumni representatives.
**Procedure:** Take SAT or ACT by April of 12th year. Suggest filing application by July 1. Application deadline is August 15. Notification of admission on rolling basis. No set date by which applicants must accept offer. $200 nonrefundable room deposit. Freshmen accepted for terms other than fall.
**Special programs:** Admission may be deferred one year. Credit may be granted through CEEB Advanced Placement for scores of 3 or higher. Credit may be granted through CLEP subject exams and military experience. Credit and placement may be granted through challenge exams. Early entrance/early admission program. Concurrent enrollment program.
**Transfer students:** Transfer students accepted for terms other than fall. In fall 1993, 35% of all new students were transfers into all classes. 1,827 transfer applications were received, 1,443 were accepted. Application deadline is August 15 for fall; January 10 for spring. Minimum 2.0 GPA required. Lowest course grade accepted is "D." Maximum number of transferable credits is 64 semester hours from a two-year school and 98 semester hours from a four-year school. At least 30 semester hours must be completed at the university to receive degree.
**Admissions contact:** Roslyn S. Sheley, M.A., Associate Director of Admissions and Special Programs. 504 286-6595.

**FINANCIAL AID. Available aid:** Pell grants, SEOG, Federal Nursing Student Scholarships, state scholarships and grants, school scholarships, private scholarships, academic merit scholarships, athletic scholarships, and aid for undergraduate foreign students. Perkins Loans (NDSL), PLUS, Stafford Loans (GSL), state loans, and SLS. Deferred payment plan.
**Financial aid statistics:** 10% of aid is not need-based. In 1993-94, 88% of all undergraduate applicants received aid; 93% of freshman applicants. Average amounts of aid awarded freshmen: Scholarships and grants, $3,500; loans, $2,500.
**Supporting data/closing dates:** FAFSA/FFS: Priority filing date is May 1. State aid form: Deadline is April 1. Notification of awards begins April 15.
**Financial aid contact:** Avon Dennis, M.B.A., Director of Financial Aid. 504 286-6603.

**STUDENT EMPLOYMENT.** College Work/Study Program. Institutional employment. 20% of full-time undergraduates work on campus during school year. Students may expect to earn an average of $2,800 during school year. Freshmen are discouraged from working during their first term. Off-campus part-time employment opportunities rated "excellent."

**COMPUTER FACILITIES.** 1,084 IBM/IBM-compatible and Macintosh/Apple microcomputers; 296 are networked. Students may access Digital, IBM, SUN minicomputer/mainframe systems, Internet. Client/LAN operating systems include Apple/Macintosh, DOS, UNIX/XENIX/AIX, X-windows, Novell. Computer languages and software packages include Ada, BASIC, C, COBOL, FORTRAN, FreeHand, LISP, Macro 32, Pascal, PageMaker, SAS, SPSS; 70 in all. Computer facilities are available to all students.
**Fees:** Computer fee is included in tuition/fees.
**Hours:** 8 AM-midn.

**GRADUATE CAREER DATA.** Companies and businesses that hire graduates: Bell South, First NBC New Orleans, KPMG Peat Marwick.

**PROMINENT ALUMNI/AE.** Mike Kettenring, president and general manager, Gillett Broadcasting of Tennessee (WSMV); Melinda Schwegmann, lieutenant governor, Louisiana; Dr. Reuben Arminana, president, Sonoma State U.

# Xavier University of Louisiana

New Orleans, LA 70125 504 486-7411

**1994-95 Costs.** Tuition: $6,900. Room & board: $4,000. Fees, books, misc. academic expenses (school's estimate): $800.
**Enrollment.** Undergraduates: 889 men, 1,804 women (full-time). Freshman class: 2,398 applicants, 1,915 accepted, 695 enrolled. Graduate enrollment: 112 men, 320 women.
**Test score averages/ranges.** Average SAT scores: 438 verbal, 469 math. Range of SAT scores of middle 50%: 820-1000 combined. Average ACT scores: 21 English, 20 math, 21 composite. Range of ACT scores of middle 50%: 19-21 composite.
**Faculty.** 208 full-time; 47 part-time. 72% of faculty holds doctoral degree. Student/faculty ratio: 19 to 1.
**Selectivity rating.** Competitive.

**PROFILE.** Xavier, founded in 1925, is a church-affiliated, liberal arts university. Its 29-acre, urban campus is located in New Orleans.

**Accreditation:** SACS. Professionally accredited by the American Council on Pharmaceutical Education, the National Association of Schools of Music.
**Religious orientation:** Xavier University of Louisiana is affiliated with the Roman Catholic Church; two semesters of theology required.
**Library:** Collections totaling over 113,000 volumes, 1,200 periodical subscriptions, and 70,000 microform items.
**Athletic facilities:** Gymnasium, tennis courts, swimming pool.
**STUDENT BODY. Undergraduate profile:** 63% are state residents. 2% Asian-American, 94% Black, 2% White, 1% Foreign. Average age of undergraduates is 22.
**Freshman profile:** 3% of freshmen who took SAT scored 600 or over on verbal, 7% scored 600 or over on math; 23% scored 500 or over on verbal, 37% scored 500 or over on math; 62% scored 400 or over on verbal, 73% scored 400 or over on math; 92% scored 300 or over on verbal, 96% scored 300 or over on math. 36% of accepted applicants took SAT; 87% took ACT. 70% of freshmen come from public schools.
**Undergraduate achievement:** 79% of fall 1992 freshmen returned for fall 1993 term. 20% of entering class graduated. 37% of students who completed a degree program immediately went on to graduate study.
**Foreign students:** 80 students are from out of the country. Countries represented include the Bahamas, Ghana, India, Nigeria, South Africa, and Vietnam.
**PROGRAMS OF STUDY. Degrees:** B.A., B.Mus., B.S.
**Majors:** Accounting, Art, Art Education, Biochemistry, Biology, Business Administration, Chemistry, Computer Information Systems, Computer Science, Early Childhood Education, Economics, Elementary Education, English, English Education, French, German, Health/Physical Education, History, Mass Communications, Mathematics, Mathematics Education, Microbiology, Music, Music Education, Music Performance, Philosophy, Physics, Political Science, Psychology, Science Education, Social Studies Education, Sociology, Spanish, Special Education, Speech Pathology, Speech Pathology Education, Statistics, Theology.
**Distribution of degrees:** The majors with the highest enrollment are pharmacy, theology, and philosophy; languages, history, and art have the lowest.
**Requirements:** General education requirement.
**Academic regulations:** Minimum 2.0 GPA must be maintained.
**Special:** Minors offered in most majors and in analytical research, languages, and public administration. Comprehensive exams required for graduation. Double majors. Dual degrees. Independent study. Accelerated study. Internships. Cooperative education programs. Graduate school at which undergraduates may take graduate-level courses. Preprofessional programs in law, medicine, veterinary science, pharmacy, dentistry, theology, and optometry. 3-1 medical and dental programs with Louisiana State U Medical School and many participating medical schools. Statistics/biometrics program with Louisiana State U Medical Sch. 3-2 engineering programs with U of Detroit, Georgia Tech, U of Maryland, Morgan State U, U of New Orleans, Southern U, Tulane U, and U of Wisconsin. 3-2 M.B.A. program with Tulane U. 3-3 law program. Member of New Orleans Consortium. Exchange program with St. Michael's Coll and Notre Dame U. Teacher certification in early childhood, elementary, secondary, and special education. Certification in specific subject areas. ROTC, NROTC, and AFROTC at Tulane U.
**Honors:** Honors program. Honor societies.
**Academic Assistance:** Remedial reading, writing, math, and study skills. Nonremedial tutoring.
**STUDENT LIFE. Housing:** Students may live on or off campus. Women's and men's dorms. 27% of students live in college housing.
**Services and counseling/handicapped student services:** Placement services. Health service. Counseling services for minority, veteran, and older students. Birth control, personal, and psychological counseling. Career and academic guidance services. Religious counseling. Learning disabled services.
**Campus organizations:** Undergraduate student government. Student newspaper (Xavier Herald, published twice/month). Yearbook. TV station. University Chorus, jazz and symphonic bands, Big Brothers/Big Sisters, MAX, Panhellenic Council, dormitory councils, 59 organizations in all. Two fraternities, no chapter houses; four sororities, no chapter houses. 5% of men join a fraternity. 20% of women join a sorority.
**Religious organizations:** Peer Ministers, Campus Ministry, Legion of Mary, Christian Life Community, Retreat Team, Bible study and prayer groups.
**Minority/foreign student organizations:** NAACP, AWARE (African-Americans with Responsibility to Enlighten), National Association of Black Accountants, National Organization of Black Chemists, National Society of Black Engineers. International Student Club.
**ATHLETICS. Physical education requirements:** One semester of physical education required.
**Intercollegiate competition:** 6% of students participate. Basketball (M,W), cheerleading (M,W). Member of Gulf Coast Athletic Conference, NAIA.
**Intramural and club sports:** 20% of students participate. Intramural archery, flag football, pool, softball, table tennis, tennis, track, volleyball. Men's club basketball, flag football. Women's club volleyball.
**ADMISSIONS. Academic basis for candidate selection** (in order of priority): Secondary school record, standardized test scores, class rank, school's recommendation, essay.
**Nonacademic basis for candidate selection:** Character and personality are important. Extracurricular participation and particular talent or ability are considered.
**Requirements:** Graduation from secondary school is required; GED is accepted. 18 units and the following program of study are required: 4 units of English, 2 units of math, 1 unit of lab science, 1 unit of social studies, 10 units of academic electives. Additional units in math, social studies, and foreign language recommended. Minimum composite ACT score of 16 and minimum 2.0 GPA required. Portfolio required of art program applicants. Audition required of music program applicants. Limited admission consideration for applicants not meeting standard requirements. SAT or ACT is required. Campus visit and interview recommended. No off-campus interviews.
**Procedure:** Take SAT or ACT by January of 12th year. Suggest filing application by October. Application deadline is March 1. Notification of admission by April 1. Reply is required by May 1. $20 nonrefundable tuition deposit. $100 room deposit, refundable until one month before beginning of semester. Freshmen accepted for terms other than fall.
**Special programs:** Admission may be deferred one year. Credit and/or placement may be granted through CEEB Advanced Placement exams for scores of 3 or higher. Credit and/or placement may be granted through CLEP subject exams. Credit and placement may be granted through challenge exams. Early decision program. In fall 1993, 400 applied for early decision and 400 were accepted. Deadline for applying for early decision is March 1. Concurrent enrollment program.
**Transfer students:** Transfer students accepted for terms other than fall. In fall 1993, 328 transfer applications were received, 285 were accepted. Application deadline is June 15 for fall; December 1 for spring. Minimum 2.0 GPA required. Lowest course grade accepted is "C." Maximum number of transferable credits is 62 semester hours from a two-year school and 98 semester hours from a four-year school. At least 30 semester hours must be completed at the university to receive degree.
**Admissions contact:** Winston D. Brown, M.A., Director of Admissions. 504 483-7388.
**FINANCIAL AID. Available aid:** Pell grants, SEOG, state scholarships, school scholarships, private scholarships, ROTC scholarships, academic merit scholarships, athletic scholarships, and United Negro College Fund. Perkins Loans (NDSL), PLUS, Stafford Loans (GSL), Health Professions Loans, private loans, and SLS. Deferred payment plan and family tuition reduction.
**Financial aid statistics:** 46% of aid is not need-based. In 1993-94, 98% of all undergraduate applicants received aid; 97% of freshman applicants. Average amounts of aid awarded freshmen: Scholarships and grants, $4,097; loans, $3,291.
**Supporting data/closing dates:** FAFSA/FAF/FFS: Priority filing date is May 1; accepted on rolling basis. School's own aid application: Priority filing date is May 1; accepted on rolling basis. Notification of awards begins June 15.
**Financial aid contact:** Mildred Higgins, Director of Financial Aid. 504 482-2801.
**STUDENT EMPLOYMENT.** College Work/Study Program. Institutional employment. 24% of full-time undergraduates work on campus during school year. Students may expect to earn an average of $1,000 during school year. Off-campus part-time employment opportunities rated "fair."
**COMPUTER FACILITIES.** 136 IBM/IBM-compatible microcomputers; 62 are networked. Students may access AT&T, Hewlett-Packard minicomputer/mainframe systems. Computer languages and software packages include BASIC, C, dBASE, FORTRAN, Lotus 1-2-3, Pascal, Quattro, Word. Computer facilities are available to all students.
**Fees:** Computer fee is included in tuition/fees.
**Hours:** 8:30 AM-8:30 PM.
**GRADUATE CAREER DATA.** Graduate school percentages: 2% enter law school. 1% enter graduate business programs. 16% enter graduate arts and sciences programs. 18% enter medical/dental schools. Highest graduate school enrollments: Harvard U, Louisiana State U, Meharry Medical Coll, U of Mississippi, U of Notre Dame, Texas Southern U, Tulane U. Companies and businesses that hire graduates: AT&T, Champion International, Environmental Protection Agency, IBM, Polaroid, Shell Oil, State Farm Insurance, local schools.
**PROMINENT ALUMNI/AE.** Dr. Claude H. Organ, Jr., chairperson, American Board of Surgery; Ernst Morial, mayor, New Orleans; Annabell Bernard, soprano; Dr. Milton Gordon, president, California State U at Fullerton; Mary Nunson Runge, first black president, American Pharmaceutical Association; Gen. Bernard Randolph, U.S. Air Force (retired); John T. Scott, sculptor.

# Maine

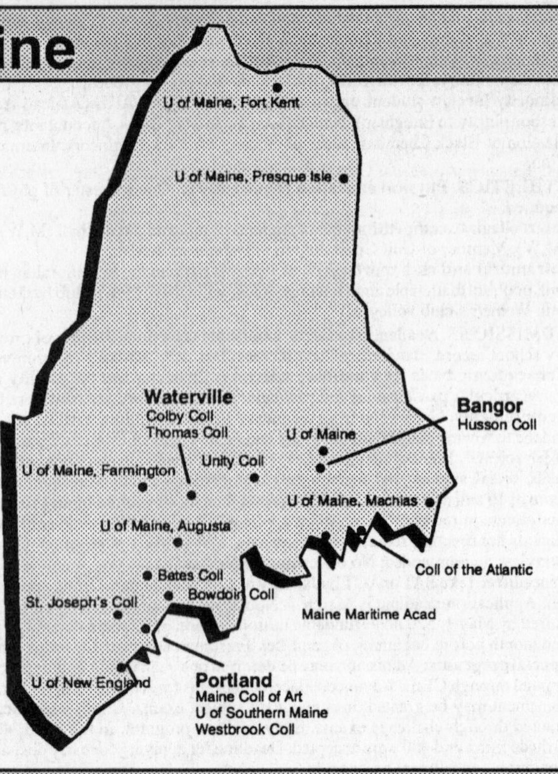


## Bates College

**Lewiston, ME 04240** **207 786-6255**

**1994-95 Costs.** Tuition, room, and board: $25,180 per year. Fees, books, misc. academic expenses (school's estimate): $650.
**Enrollment.** Undergraduates: 745 men, 854 women (full-time). Freshman class: 3,600 applicants, 1,592 accepted, 577 enrolled.
**Test score averages/ranges.** Range of SAT scores of middle 50%: 540-630 verbal, 590-690 math.
**Faculty.** 151 full-time; 14 part-time. 96% of faculty holds highest degree in specific field. Student/faculty ratio: 11 to 1.
**Selectivity rating.** Highly competitive.

**PROFILE.** Bates, founded in 1855, is a private, liberal arts college. Its 109-acre campus is located in Lewiston, 35 miles northeast of Portland.
**Accreditation:** NEASC.
**Religious orientation:** Bates College is nonsectarian; no religious requirements.
**Library:** Collections totaling over 563,123 volumes, 1,841 periodical subscriptions, and 264,781 microform items.
**Special facilities/museums:** Art gallery, Edmund S. Muskie Archives, language labs, planetarium, 600-acre conservation area on seacoast for environmental studies, scanning electron microscope.
**Athletic facilities:** Swimming pool, tracks, basketball, racquetball, squash, and tennis courts, dance studio, free weight and Nautilus rooms, field house, athletic fields, rock-climbing wall, boat house and dock.
**STUDENT BODY. Undergraduate profile:** 13% are state residents. 3% Asian-American, 3% Black, 1% Hispanic, 87% White, 6% Other. Average age of undergraduates is 20.
**Freshman profile:** 4% of freshmen who took SAT scored 700 or over on verbal, 19% scored 700 or over on math; 44% scored 600 or over on verbal, 75% scored 600 or over on math; 96% scored 500 or over on verbal, 99% scored 500 or over on math; 100% scored 400 or over on verbal, 100% scored 400 or over on math. Majority of accepted applicants took SAT. 65% of freshmen come from public schools.
**Undergraduate achievement:** 96% of fall 1992 freshmen returned for fall 1993 term. 81% of entering class graduated. 55% of students who completed a degree program went on to graduate study.
**Foreign students:** 52 students are from out of the country. Countries represented include Canada, England, India, Japan, Pakistan, and Turkey; 30 in all.
**PROGRAMS OF STUDY. Degrees:** B.A., B.S.
**Majors:** African-American Studies, American Cultural Studies, Anthropology, Art, Biochemistry, Biology, Chemistry, Classic/Medieval Studies, East Asian Languages/Cultures, Economics, English, French, Geology, German, History, Mathematics, Music, Philosophy, Physics, Political Science, Psychology, Religion, Rhetoric, Russian, Sociology, Spanish, Theatre Arts, Women's Studies.
**Distribution of degrees:** The majors with the highest enrollment are political science, psychology, and English; music and American cultural studies have the lowest.
**Requirements:** General education requirement.
**Academic regulations:** Minimum 2.0 GPA required for graduation.
**Special:** Secondary concentrations offered in computer studies and foreign languages. Courses offered in astronomy, dance, education, Latin, physical education, and social studies. Interdisciplinary freshman seminars. Self-designed majors. Double majors. Dual degrees. Independent study. Accelerated study. Internships. 3-2 engineering programs with Case Western Reserve U, Columbia U, Dartmouth Coll, Rensselaer Polytech Inst, Washington U (Missouri). Washington Semester and Sea Semester. Mystic Seaport Semester at Williams Coll. Exchange programs with McGill U and Washington and Lee U. Teacher certification in secondary education. Study abroad in Australia, Austria, China, Ecuador, France, Germany, Israel, Italy, Japan, Kenya, Mexico, Nepal, the Netherlands, Nigeria, Russia, Spain, Sri Lanka, Switzerland, and the United Kingdom.
**Honors:** Phi Beta Kappa. Honors program.
**Academic Assistance:** Remedial writing. Nonremedial tutoring.
**STUDENT LIFE. Housing:** All first-year students must live on campus. Coed, women's, and men's dorms. Off-campus privately-owned housing. 93% of students live in college housing.
**Social atmosphere:** The Den and Chase Hall are popular on-campus gathering spots. Hot off-campus spots include the Goose, Nothing But the Blues, and Austin's Cafe. The Outing Club is influential in student life. Triad (semi-formal party sponsored by AMANDLA!, an African-American organization), President's Gala, concerts, and Back-to-Bates football game are eagerly anticipated social/sporting events. "Social life is very centered on campus because over 90 percent of students live on campus," reports the editor of the student newspaper. "The social scene can get repetitive, but there are also cultural events that are well attended, like contradances and films."
**Services and counseling/handicapped student services:** Placement services. Health service. Women's center. Counseling services for minority, veteran, and older students. Birth control, personal, and psychological counseling. Career and academic guidance services. Religious counseling. Physically disabled student services. Learning disabled services. Notetaking services. Tape recorders. Tutors. Reader services for the blind.
**Campus organizations:** Undergraduate student government. Student newspaper (Bates Student, published once/week). Literary magazine. Yearbook. Radio and TV stations. Amnesty International, choral society, band, modern dance company, drama group, debating, film board, outing club, community activities, Big Brothers/Big Sisters, social events club, political groups, language clubs, photography club, 72 organizations in all.
**Religious organizations:** Christian Fellowship, Hillel, Newman Club, Friends Meeting, Jewish Cultural Community.
**Minority/foreign student organizations:** Asian Society, Solidaridad Latina, AMANDLA!. International Student Club.
**ATHLETICS. Physical education requirements:** Two semesters of physical education required.
**Intercollegiate competition:** 66% of students participate. Alpine skiing (M,W), baseball (M), basketball (M,W), cross-country (M,W), diving (M,W), field hockey (W), football (M), golf (M,W), lacrosse (M,W), Nordic skiing (M,W), soccer (M,W), softball (W), squash (M,W), swimming (M,W), tennis (M,W), track (indoor) (M,W), track (outdoor) (M,W), track and field (indoor) (M,W), track and field (outdoor) (M,W), volleyball (W). Member of ECAC, MAIAW, NAIA, NCAA Division III, NESCAC.
**Intramural and club sports:** 85% of students participate. Intramural basketball, innertube water polo, road races, soccer, softball, squash, swimming, tennis, volleyball. Men's club Crew, badminton, fencing, ice hockey, rugby, sailing, ultimate frisbee, volleyball, water polo. Women's club crew, ice hockey, rugby, sailing, ultimate frisbee, water polo.
**ADMISSIONS. Academic basis for candidate selection** (in order of priority): Secondary school record, class rank, essay, school's recommendation.
**Nonacademic basis for candidate selection:** Extracurricular participation and particular talent or ability are emphasized. Geographical distribution is important. Character and personality and alumni/ae relationship are considered.
**Requirements:** Graduation from secondary school is recommended; GED is not accepted. No specific distribution of secondary school units required. SAT, ACT, and CEEB Achievement Tests are optional. Campus visit and interview recommended. Off-campus interviews available with admissions and alumni representatives.
**Procedure:** Visit college for interview by January 31 of 12th year. Application deadline is February 1. Notification of admission by April 3. Reply is required by May 1. $200 nonrefundable tuition deposit. Freshmen accepted for terms other than fall.
**Special programs:** Admission may be deferred one year. Credit and/or placement may be granted through CEEB Advanced Placement exams for scores of 4 or higher. Early decision program. In fall 1993, 333 applied for early decision and 219 were accepted. Deadline for applying for early decision is December 1 and January 1. Early entrance/early admission program. Concurrent enrollment program.
**Transfer students:** Transfer students accepted for terms other than fall. In fall 1993, 139 transfer applications were received, 51 were accepted. Application deadline is February 1 for fall; November 15 for spring. Minimum 3.0 GPA recommended. Lowest course grade accepted is "C." Maximum number of transferable credits is the equivalent of two years of course work. At least two years must be completed at the college to receive degree.
**Admissions contact:** William C. Hiss, Ph.D., Dean of Admissions. 207 786-6000.
**FINANCIAL AID. Available aid:** Pell grants, SEOG, state scholarships and grants, school scholarships and grants, private scholarships and grants, and aid for undergraduate foreign students. Perkins Loans (NDSL), PLUS, Stafford Loans (GSL), state loans, school loans, private loans, and SLS. Knight Tuition Plans, AMS, and Tuition Management Systems.
**Financial aid statistics:** In 1993-94, 88% of all undergraduate applicants received aid; 87% of freshman applicants. Average amounts of aid awarded freshmen: Scholarships and grants, $12,400; loans, $3,564.
**Supporting data/closing dates:** FAFSA: Deadline is February 11. School's own aid application: Deadline is February 11. Income tax forms: Deadline is February 11. Divorced/Separated Statement; Business Supplements: Deadline is February 11. Notification of awards begins April 3.
**Financial aid contact:** Leigh P. Campbell, Director of Financial Aid. 207 786-6060.
**STUDENT EMPLOYMENT.** College Work/Study Program. Institutional employment. 47% of full-time undergraduates work on campus during school year. Students may expect to earn an average of $1,300 during school year. Off-campus part-time employment opportunities rated "good."
**COMPUTER FACILITIES.** 275 IBM/IBM-compatible, Macintosh/Apple, and RISC-/UNIX-based microcomputers; 240 are networked. Students may access Digital minicomputer/mainframe systems, Internet. Client/LAN operating systems include Apple/Macintosh,

DOS, UNIX/XENIX/AIX, X-windows, Banyan, LocalTalk/AppleTalk. Computer languages and software packages include Assembly, BASIC, C, COBOL, Draw Perfect, FORTRAN, LISP, Lotus, MACSOLVE, MINITAB, Pascal, PCSOLVE, PL/1, SPSSPC, SPSS-X, TSP, WordPerfect. Computer facilities are available to all students.
**Fees:** None.
**Hours:** 24 hours.

**GRADUATE CAREER DATA.** 31% of graduates choose careers in business and industry.

**PROMINENT ALUMNI/AE.** Edmund S. Muskie, statesman; Bryant Gumbel, television co-host; Benjamin E. Mays, educator.

# Bowdoin College

**Brunswick, ME 04011** **207 725-3000**

**1994-95 Costs.** Tuition: $19,030. Room: $2,620. Board: $3,265. Fees, books, misc. academic expenses (school's estimate): $960.
**Enrollment.** Undergraduates: 749 men, 741 women (full-time). Freshman class: 3,356 applicants, 1,019 accepted, 418 enrolled.
**Test score averages/ranges.** Average SAT scores: 580 verbal, 640 math. Range of SAT scores of middle 50%: 540-640 verbal, 590-690 math.
**Faculty.** 112 full-time; 65 part-time. 90% of faculty holds highest degree in specific field. Student/faculty ratio: 12 to 1.
**Selectivity rating.** Most competitive.

**PROFILE.** Bowdoin, founded in 1794, is a private, liberal arts college. Its 110-acre campus is located in Brunswick, 25 miles northeast of Portland. Historic buildings on campus include its faculty building, which dates from 1802 and is a Registered Historical Landmark.

**Accreditation:** NEASC.
**Religious orientation:** Bowdoin College is nonsectarian; no religious requirements.
**Library:** Collections totaling over 815,314 volumes, 2,055 periodical subscriptions, and 329,677 microform items.
**Special facilities/museums:** Art museum, arctic museum, coastal marine biology and ornithology research facilities.
**Athletic facilities:** Gymnasiums, field house, swimming pool, squash and tennis courts, dance studio, weight facilities, aerobics room, hockey rink, football, baseball, soccer, and lacrosse fields, track facilities, cross-country ski trails.

**STUDENT BODY. Undergraduate profile:** 15% are state residents; 2% are transfers. 7% Asian-American, 3% Black, 3% Hispanic, 1% Native American, 84% White, 2% Other. Average age of undergraduates is 20.
**Freshman profile:** 2% of freshmen who took SAT scored 700 or over on verbal, 19% scored 700 or over on math; 29% scored 600 or over on verbal, 53% scored 600 or over on math; 65% scored 500 or over on verbal, 74% scored 500 or over on math; 76% scored 400 or over on verbal, 77% scored 400 or over on math; 78% scored 300 or over on verbal. 77% of accepted applicants took SAT. 54% of freshmen come from public schools.
**Undergraduate achievement:** 95% of fall 1992 freshmen returned for fall 1993 term. 85% of entering class graduated. 18% of students who completed a degree program immediately went on to graduate study.
**Foreign students:** 55 students are from out of the country. Countries represented include Canada, England, Germany, Japan, and Pakistan; 25 in all.

**PROGRAMS OF STUDY. Degrees:** A.B.
**Majors:** Afro-American Studies, Anthropology, Art History, Asian Studies, Biochemistry, Biology, Chemistry, Classics, Classics/Archaeology, Computer Science, Economics, English, Environmental Studies, French, Geology, German, Government/Legal Studies, History, Mathematics, Music, Neuroscience, Philosophy, Physics, Physics/Astronomy, Psychology, Religion, Romance Languages, Russian, Sociology, Spanish, Studio Art.
**Distribution of degrees:** The majors with the highest enrollment are government/legal studies, history, and English; psychobiology has the lowest.
**Requirements:** General education requirement.
**Special:** Minors offered in all majors and in dance, education, Greek, Italian, Latin, Latin American studies, and women's studies. Self-designed majors. Double majors. Independent study. Accelerated study. Pass/fail grading option. Internships. Preprofessional programs in law and medicine. 3-2 engineering programs with Caltech and Columbia U. 3-2 law program with Columbia U. Washington Semester and Sea Semester. National Theatre Institute Semester (Connecticut). Williams-Mystic Seaport Semester (Connecticut). Member of Twelve College Exchange Program. Teacher certification in secondary education. Certification in specific subject areas. Exchange program abroad in Ecuador (Escuela Superior Polytecnica del Litoral). Study abroad also in China, India, Italy, Japan, Sri Lanka, Sweden, and several other countries. ROTC, NROTC, and AFROTC at U of Maine.
**Honors:** Phi Beta Kappa.
**Academic Assistance:** Nonremedial tutoring.

**STUDENT LIFE. Housing:** All first-year students must live on campus. Coed dorms. Fraternity housing. School-owned/operated apartments. 86% of students live in college housing.
**Social atmosphere:** Favorite gathering spots include the Pub, the Game Room, and fraternity houses. Greeks and sport teams influence student life. Favorite events include May Day, Winter Ball, Homecoming, Charity Ball, hockey games, and Rush Week.
**Services and counseling/handicapped student services:** Placement services. Health service. Women's center. Day care. Counseling services for minority and older students. Birth control, personal, and psychological counseling. Career and academic guidance services. Physically disabled student services. Learning disabled services. Notetaking services. Tape recorders. Tutors. Reader services for the blind.
**Campus organizations:** Undergraduate student government. Student newspaper (Orient, published once/week). Literary magazine. Yearbook. Radio station. Chorale, chamber choir, community orchestra, wind ensemble, marching and jazz bands, dance group, Big Brothers/Big Sisters, Amnesty International, literary society, women's association, College Republicans, Young Democrats, outing club, service and special-interest groups, 56 organizations in all. Eight coed fraternities, all with chapter houses. 43% of men and women join a fraternity.
**Religious organizations:** Canterbury Club, Christian Fellowship, Jewish Organization, Newman Apostolate.
**Minority/foreign student organizations:** African-American Society, Asian Interest Group, Latin American Student Organization. International Club.

**ATHLETICS. Physical education requirements:** None.
**Intercollegiate competition:** 70% of students participate. Alpine skiing (M,W), baseball (M), basketball (M,W), cross-country (M,W), diving (M,W), field hockey (W), football (M), golf (M,W), ice hockey (M,W), lacrosse (M,W), Nordic skiing (M,W), sailing (M,W), soccer (M,W), softball (W), squash (M,W), swimming (M,W), tennis (M,W), track (indoor) (M,W), track (outdoor) (M,W), track and field (indoor) (M,W), track and field (outdoor) (M,W), volleyball (W). Member of CBB, ECAC III, MAIAW, NCAA Division III, NESCAC.
**Intramural and club sports:** 50% of students participate. Intramural football, ice hockey, softball, tennis, triathlon, ultimate frisbee, volleyball, water basketball. Men's club crew, rugby, water polo, ultimate frisbee. Women's club crew, water polo, rugby, ultimate frisbee.

**ADMISSIONS. Academic basis for candidate selection** (in order of priority): Secondary school record, class rank, school's recommendation, essay, standardized test scores.
**Nonacademic basis for candidate selection:** Character and personality, extracurricular participation, and particular talent or ability are important. Geographical distribution and alumni/ae relationship are considered.
**Requirements:** Graduation from secondary school is recommended; GED is accepted. No specific distribution of secondary school units required. SAT or ACT scores not required until matriculation; may be submitted with application if student wishes them to be considered. Rank in top tenth of secondary school class and minimum 3.5 GPA recommended. Portfolio recommended of art program applicants. Sample or tape recommended of music program applicants. Campus visit and interview recommended. Off-campus interviews available with an alumni representative.
**Procedure:** Take SAT or ACT by January of 12th year. Visit college for interview by January 15 of 12th year. Application deadline is January 15. Acceptance notification by early April. Reply is required by May 1. $300 nonrefundable tuition deposit. Freshmen accepted for fall terms only.
**Special programs:** Admission may be deferred one year. Credit and/or placement may be granted through CEEB Advanced Placement exams for scores of 4 or higher. Placement may be granted through challenge exams. Early decision program. In fall 1993, 450 applied for early decision and 176 were accepted. Deadline for applying for early decision is November 15.
**Transfer students:** Transfer students accepted for terms other than fall. In fall 1993, 2% of all new students were transfers into all classes. 123 transfer applications were received, 14 were accepted. Application deadline is April 15 for fall; November 15 for spring. Minimum 3.0 GPA recommended. Lowest course grade accepted is "C." Maximum number of transferable credits is 4 semesters. At least 4 semesters must be completed at the college to receive degree.
**Admissions contact:** Richard E. Steele, Ph.D., Dean of Admissions. 207 725-3100.

**FINANCIAL AID. Available aid:** Pell grants, SEOG, state scholarships and grants, school scholarships and grants, private scholarships and grants, and aid for undergraduate foreign students. Perkins Loans (NDSL), PLUS, Stafford Loans (GSL), state loans, school loans, and private loans. Tuition Plan Inc., Knight Tuition Plans, AMS, and Tuition Management Systems.
**Financial aid statistics:** In 1992-93, 79% of all undergraduate applicants received aid; 79% of freshman applicants. Average amounts of aid awarded freshmen: Scholarships and grants, $13,400; loans, $2,900.
**Supporting data/closing dates:** FAFSA/FAF: Deadline is March 1. School's own aid application: Priority filing date is December 1; deadline is March 1. Income tax forms: Priority filing date is March 1; accepted on rolling basis. Notification of awards begins April 5.
**Financial aid contact:** Walter H. Moulton, Director of Financial Aid. 207 725-3273.

**STUDENT EMPLOYMENT.** College Work/Study Program. Institutional employment. 54% of full-time undergraduates work on campus during school year. Students may expect to earn an average of $1,100 during school year. Freshmen are discouraged from working during their first term. Off-campus part-time employment opportunities rated "fair."

**COMPUTER FACILITIES.** 90 IBM/IBM-compatible and Macintosh/Apple microcomputers; all are networked. Students may access Digital minicomputer/mainframe systems, Internet. Client/LAN operating systems include Apple/Macintosh, DOS, UNIX/XENIX/AIX, X-windows, DEC, LocalTalk/AppleTalk. Computer languages and software packages include BASIC, BMDP, C, dBASE, FORTRAN, ISP, LISP, Lotus 1-2-3, Macsyma, MINITAB, Modula 2, Pascal, Pro-Matlab, SPSS, Stella, TEX, VAXCalc, TSP, WordPerfect. Computer facilities are available to all students.
**Fees:** None.
**Hours:** 8:30 AM-midn. (M-Th); 9 AM-5 PM (F); noon-midn (Sa, Su).

**GRADUATE CAREER DATA.** Graduate school percentages: 9% enter law school. 14% enter medical school. 14% enter graduate business programs. 24% enter graduate arts and sciences programs. Highest graduate school enrollments: Boston Coll, Columbia U, Dartmouth Coll, Harvard U, Tufts U, U of Maine. 35% of graduates choose careers in business and industry. Companies and businesses that hire graduates: Chubb Group, Deloitte & Touche, First Boston, Goldman Sachs, Hannaford Bros., ICF, UNUM Insurance.

**PROMINENT ALUMNI/AE.** Franklin Pierce, 14th president of the U.S.; Nathaniel Hawthorne, author; Admiral Robert Peary and Commander Donald B. MacMillan, Arctic explorers; Henry Wadsworth Longfellow, poet; Joan Benoit Samuelson, Olympic marathon runner; William Cohen and George Mitchell, U.S. senators.

# Colby College

Waterville, ME 04901 207 872-3000

**1994-95 Costs.** Tuition: $18,930. Room: $2,890. Board: $2,700. Fees, books, misc. academic expenses (school's estimate): $1,400.
**Enrollment.** Undergraduates: 810 men, 910 women (full-time). Freshman class: 3,024 applicants, 1,366 accepted, 475 enrolled.
**Test score averages/ranges.** Average SAT scores: 580 verbal, 620 math. Range of SAT scores of middle 50%: 520-610 verbal, 570-660 math. Average ACT scores: 27 composite. Range of ACT scores of middle 50%: 25-29 composite.
**Faculty.** 98% of faculty holds highest degree in specific field. Student/faculty ratio: 10 to 1.
**Selectivity rating.** Highly competitive.

**PROFILE.** Colby, founded in 1813, is a private, liberal arts college. Its 714-acre Mayflower Hill campus is located one mile from downtown Waterville, 75 miles north of Portland.

**Accreditation:** NEASC.
**Religious orientation:** Colby College is nonsectarian; no religious requirements.
**Library:** Collections totaling over 467,195 volumes, 2,135 periodical subscriptions, and 255,700 microform items.
**Special facilities/museums:** Art museum, arboretum, campus video information network, computer music studio, electron microscopes, greenhouse, language lab, observatory, satellite dish for foreign language broadcasts, numerous scientific analytical instruments.
**Athletic facilities:** Gymnasium, swimming pool, ice rink, Nautilus and weight rooms, baseball, field hockey, football, lacrosse, and soccer fields, track, basketball, squash, and tennis courts, saunas.

**STUDENT BODY. Undergraduate profile:** 12% are state residents; 5% are transfers. 3% Asian-American, 2% Black, 2% Hispanic, 91% White, 2% International. Average age of undergraduates is 20.
**Freshman profile:** 95% of accepted applicants took SAT; 14% took ACT. 63% of freshmen come from public schools.
**Undergraduate achievement:** 96% of fall 1992 freshmen returned for fall 1993 term. 84% of entering class graduated. 15% of students who completed a degree program immediately went on to graduate study.
**Foreign students:** 94 students are from out of the country. Countries represented include Canada, France, Germany, India, Japan, and the United Kingdom; 42 in all.

**PROGRAMS OF STUDY. Degrees:** A.B.
**Majors:** Administrative Science, Administrative Science/Quantitative Methods, American Studies, Anthropology, Art, Biology, Biology/Environmental Science, Chemistry, Chemistry/Biochemistry, Chemistry/Environmental Science, Classics, Classics/English, Classics/Philosophy, East Asian Studies, Economics, Economics/Mathematics, English, French, Geology, Geology/Biology, Geology/Chemistry, Geology/Environmental Science, German, Government, History, International Studies, Mathematics, Mathematics/Computer Science, Music, Performing Arts, Philosophy, Philosophy/Mathematics, Philosophy/Religion, Physics, Psychology, Psychology/Mathematics, Religion, Russian, Sociology, Spanish.
**Distribution of degrees:** The majors with the highest enrollment are government, English, and biology.
**Requirements:** General education requirement.
**Academic regulations:** Minimum 2.0 GPA must be maintained.
**Special:** Minors offered in most majors and in African/American studies, applied mathematics/quantitative analysis, classical civilization, computer science, creative writing, education, environmental studies, Japanese, public policy, Russian language/literature, science/technology studies, and women's studies. Self-designed majors. Double majors. Dual degrees. Independent study. Pass/fail grading option. Internships. Graduate school at which undergraduates may take graduate-level courses. Preprofessional advisory committees for dentistry, engineering, law, medicine, and veterinary medicine. 3-2 engineering programs with Case Western Reserve U, Dartmouth College, and U of Rochester. Washington Semester. Williams-Mystic Maritime Studies Program (Connecticut), School for Field Studies, Sea Semester at Woods Hole, Mass. Exchange programs with Claremont McKenna Coll, Howard U, Pitzer Coll, Pomona Coll, and Scripps Coll. Teacher certification in secondary education. Exchange programs abroad in England (Manchester Coll Oxford), France (U Caen), Ireland (U Coll Cork), and Spain (U Salamanaca). Study abroad also in England, France, Japan, Mexico, Russia, and the former Soviet Republics. Two-thirds of all Colby students have some foreign study experience. ROTC at U of Maine.
**Honors:** Phi Beta Kappa. Honors program. Honor societies.
**Academic Assistance:** Nonremedial tutoring.

**STUDENT LIFE. Housing:** All freshmen must live on campus unless living with family. Coed dorms. Off-campus privately-owned housing. 93% of students live in college housing.
**Social atmosphere:** Favorite on-campus gathering spots include The Spa, and The Street of the Library. Off-campus students gather at You Know Whose Pub, Safari Bar, Champions, and Big G's. Student government, athletes and off-campus residents are influential groups on campus. Favorite events are Foss Arts, the Foss Skalloween Party, the Bowdoin vs. Colby hockey game, and the Last Day of Loudness. The student newspaper reports "Since Colby abolished fraternities in 1984, the college has been in a social transition, attempting to establish another center of social and cultural life. The student government system has somewhat filled this role, but there is a definite trend developing where students are going off-campus instead of staying on campus at college-sponsored events."
**Services and counseling/handicapped student services:** Placement services. Health service. Women's center. Counseling services for minority, military, veteran, and older students. Birth control, personal, and psychological counseling. Career and academic guidance services. Religious counseling. Physically disabled student services. Learning disabled services. Notetaking services. Tape recorders. Tutors. Reader services for the blind.
**Campus organizations:** Undergraduate student government. Student newspaper (Echo, published once/week). Literary magazine. Yearbook. Radio station. Bands, informal singing groups, concert and chapel choirs, orchestra, glee club, drama groups, outing club, women's committee, intercollegiate public speaking, volunteer opportunities, 90 organizations in all.
**Religious organizations:** Hillel, Christian Fellowship, Newman Council, interdenominational committee.
**Minority/foreign student organizations:** Asian-American Student Coalition, Asian Cultural Society, Student Organization for Black and Hispanic Unity. International Club.

**ATHLETICS. Physical education requirements:** Two semesters of physical education required.
**Intercollegiate competition:** 33% of students participate. Alpine skiing (M,W), baseball (M), basketball (M,W), cross-country (M,W), field hockey (W), football (M), golf (M,W), ice hockey (M,W), lacrosse (M,W), Nordic skiing (M,W), soccer (M,W), softball (W), squash (M,W), swimming (M,W), tennis (M,W), volleyball (W). Member of ECAC, NCAA Division I for Alpine and Nordic skiing, NCAA Division III, NESCAC.
**Intramural and club sports:** 65% of students participate. Intramural basketball, field hockey, ice hockey, soccer, softball, touch football, volleyball. Men's club crew, cycling, fencing, rugby, sailing, volleyball, water polo. Women's club crew, cycling, fencing, rugby, sailing, water polo.

**ADMISSIONS. Academic basis for candidate selection** (in order of priority): Secondary school record, school's recommendation, class rank, standardized test scores, essay.
**Nonacademic basis for candidate selection:** Character and personality and extracurricular participation are emphasized. Particular talent or ability is important. Geographical distribution and alumni/ae relationship are considered.
**Requirements:** Graduation from secondary school is recommended; GED is accepted. 16 units and the following program of study are recommended: 4 units of English, 3 units of math, 2 units of lab science, 3 units of foreign language, 2 units of social studies, 2 units of electives. SAT or ACT is required. ACH recommended. Campus visit and interview recommended. Off-campus interviews available with admissions and alumni representatives.
**Procedure:** Take SAT or ACT by January 31 of 12th year. Visit college for interview by January 15 of 12th year. Application deadline is January 15. Notification of admission by April. Reply is required by May 1. $200 nonrefundable tuition deposit. Freshmen accepted for terms other than fall.
**Special programs:** Admission may be deferred one year. Credit and/or placement may be granted through CEEB Advanced Placement exams for scores of 4 or higher. Credit and placement may be granted through challenge exams. Early decision program. In fall 1993, 260 applied for early decision and 129 were accepted. Deadline for applying for early decision is November 15 and January 1. Early entrance/early admission program.
**Transfer students:** Transfer students accepted for terms other than fall. In fall 1993, 5% of all new students were transfers into all classes. 176 transfer applications were received, 47 were accepted. Application deadline is December 1 for fall; March 15 for spring. Minimum 3.0 GPA recommended. Lowest course grade accepted is "C." Maximum number of transferable credits is 60 semester hours. At least 60 semester hours must be completed at the college to receive degree.
**Admissions contact:** Parker J. Beverage, M.A., Dean of Admissions. 207 872-3168.

**FINANCIAL AID. Available aid:** Pell grants, SEOG, state scholarships and grants, school grants, private scholarships and grants, ROTC scholarships, and aid for undergraduate foreign students. Perkins Loans (NDSL), PLUS, Stafford Loans (GSL), state loans, school loans, and SLS. Knight Tuition Plans and AMS.
**Financial aid statistics:** In 1993-94, 86% of all undergraduate applicants received aid; 78% of freshman applicants. Average amounts of aid awarded freshmen: Scholarships and grants, $12,158; loans, $2,069.
**Supporting data/closing dates:** FAFSA/FAF: Deadline is February 1. School's own aid application: Priority filing date is February 1; deadline is March 1. Income tax forms: Priority filing date is February 1. Divorced/Separated Parents Statement: Priority filing date is February 1. Notification of awards begins April 1.
**Financial aid contact:** Lucia W. Whittelsey, Director of Financial Aid. 207 872-3379.

**STUDENT EMPLOYMENT.** College Work/Study Program. Institutional employment. 65% of full-time undergraduates work on campus during school year. Students may expect to earn an average of $1,450 during school year. Off-campus part-time employment opportunities rated "fair."

**COMPUTER FACILITIES.** 122 Macintosh/Apple and RISC-/UNIX-based microcomputers; all are networked. Students may access Digital minicomputer/mainframe systems, Internet. Client/LAN operating systems include Apple/Macintosh, UNIX/XENIX/AIX, X-windows. Computer languages and software packages include Apple Macintosh software library, APL, BASIC, C, Cricketgraph, Excel, FORTRAN, LISP, LOGO, PageMaker, Pascal, SPSS-X, Statview Systat; 450 in all. Computer facilities are available to all students.
**Fees:** None.
**Hours:** 8 AM-5 AM.

**GRADUATE CAREER DATA.** Graduate school percentages: 5% enter law school. 5% enter medical school. 1% enter dental school. 4% enter graduate business programs. 35% enter graduate arts and sciences programs. 1% enter theological school/seminary. Highest graduate school enrollments: Babson Coll, Boston Coll, Boston U, Duke U, George Washington U, U of Maine, U of Vermont. 60% of graduates choose careers in business and industry. Companies and businesses that hire graduates: Fleet National Bank, Hannaford Bros., Jackson Labs, Peace Corps, Shawmut Corp, UNUM, Teach for America.

**PROMINENT ALUMNI/AE.** Elijah Lovejoy, 19th century abolitionist; Charles Angwenye, CEO, National Bank of Kenya; Jan Volk, general manager, Boston Celtics; Robert Parker, author; Lawrence Pugh, chairman, VF Corp., Robert Gelbard, U.S. ambassador to Bolivia; Doris Kearns Goodwin, author, *The Kennedys and Fitzgeralds*.

# College of the Atlantic

**Bar Harbor, ME 04609 207 288-5015**

**1993-94 Costs.** Tuition: $13,161. Room: $2,460. Board: $1,400. Fees, books, misc. academic expenses (school's estimate): $576.
**Enrollment.** Undergraduates: 85 men, 120 women (full-time). Freshman class: 164 applicants, 119 accepted, 34 enrolled. Graduate enrollment: 2 men, 1 woman.
**Test score averages/ranges.** Average SAT scores: 563 verbal, 564 math. Range of SAT scores of middle 50%: 510-590 verbal, 500-590 math.
**Faculty.** 18 full-time; 12 part-time. 80% of faculty holds doctoral degree. Student/faculty ratio: 10 to 1.
**Selectivity rating.** More competitive.

**PROFILE.** The College of the Atlantic, founded in 1969, is a private institution that offers a single degree program in human ecology. Its 25-acre campus is located in coastal Bar Harbor, 45 miles from Bangor.

**Accreditation:** NEASC.
**Religious orientation:** College of the Atlantic is nonsectarian; no religious requirements.
**Library:** Collections totaling over 30,000 volumes, 378 periodical subscriptions and 30 microform items.
**Special facilities/museums:** Natural history museum, pottery studio, greenhouse, geographical information systems lab.
**Athletic facilities:** Canoes, sailboat, camping gear, membership at YMCA.

**STUDENT BODY. Undergraduate profile:** 21% are state residents; 46% are transfers. 1% Asian-American, 2% Hispanic, 97% White. Average age of undergraduates is 21.
**Freshman profile:** 2% of freshmen who took SAT scored 700 or over on verbal, 2% scored 700 or over on math; 22% scored 600 or over on verbal, 22% scored 600 or over on math; 91% scored 500 or over on verbal, 74% scored 500 or over on math; 100% scored 400 or over on verbal, 100% scored 400 or over on math. 66% of accepted applicants took SAT; 10% took ACT. 48% of freshmen come from public schools.
**Undergraduate achievement:** 88% of fall 1992 freshmen returned for fall 1993 term. 51% of entering class graduated. 50% of students who completed a degree program went on to graduate study within five years.
**Foreign students:** 12 students are from out of the country. Countries represented include Canada, Croatia, England, Finland, Germany, and Japan; nine in all.

**PROGRAMS OF STUDY. Degrees:** B.A.
**Majors:** Environmental Studies, Human Ecology/Environmental Studies.
**Distribution of degrees:** The major with the highest enrollment is human ecology.
**Requirements:** General education requirement.
**Special:** Areas of study include creative arts, culture/consciousness, education, environmental/biological science, environmental design, marine studies, public policy, and writing. Self-designed majors. Independent study. Pass/fail grading option. Internships. Graduate school at which undergraduates may take graduate-level courses. Exchange program with U of Maine. Teacher certification in elementary and secondary education. Certification in specific subject areas. Study abroad in the Czech Republic (Palacky U).
**Academic Assistance:** Remedial writing. Nonremedial tutoring.

**ADMISSIONS. Academic basis for candidate selection** (in order of priority): Secondary school record, essay, school's recommendation, class rank, standardized test scores.
**Nonacademic basis for candidate selection:** Character and personality are emphasized. Extracurricular participation is important. Particular talent or ability, geographical distribution, and alumni/ae relationship are considered.
**Requirements:** Graduation from secondary school is required; GED is accepted. 16 units and the following program of study are recommended: 4 units of English, 4 units of math, 3 units of science including 2 units of lab, 2 units of foreign language, 1 unit of social studies, 2 units of history, 1 unit of electives. Rank in top half of secondary school class or minimum 3.0 GPA recommended. SAT or ACT is recommended. Campus visit and interview recommended. Off-campus interviews available with admissions and alumni representatives.
**Procedure:** Take SAT or ACT by December 1 of 12th year. Visit college for interview by December 1 of 12th year. Suggest filing application by March 1; no deadline. Notification of admission on rolling basis. Reply is required by May 1 or within 30 days of acceptance. $200 nonrefundable tuition deposit. $100 nonrefundable room deposit. Freshmen accepted for terms other than fall.
**Special programs:** Admission may be deferred one year. Credit may be granted through CEEB Advanced Placement for scores of 3 or higher. Credit may be granted through CLEP general and subject exams. Early decision program. Deadline for applying for early decision is December 1.
**Transfer students:** Transfer students accepted for terms other than fall. In fall 1993, 46% of all new students were transfers into all classes. 77 transfer applications were received, 57 were accepted. Application deadline is May 1 for fall; February 15 for spring. Minimum 3.0 GPA recommended. Lowest course grade accepted is "C." Maximum number of transferable credits is 60 semester hours. At least 60 semester hours must be completed at the college to receive degree.
**Admissions contact:** Steve Thomas, M.A., Director of Admission/Student Services. 207 288-5015, extension 230.

**FINANCIAL AID. Available aid:** Pell grants, SEOG, state scholarships and grants, school scholarships and grants, private scholarships and grants, academic merit scholarships, and aid for undergraduate foreign students. Perkins Loans (NDSL), PLUS, Stafford Loans (GSL), state loans, school loans, private loans, and SLS. Knight Tuition Plans, AMS, Tuition Management Systems, and deferred payment plan.
**Financial aid statistics:** 5% of aid is not need-based. In 1993-94, 59% of all undergraduate applicants received aid; 61% of freshman applicants. Average amounts of aid awarded freshmen: Scholarships and grants, $5,880; loans, $2,625.
**Supporting data/closing dates:** FAFSA: Priority filing date is February 15; accepted on rolling basis. School's own aid application: Priority filing date is February 15; accepted on rolling basis. Income tax forms: Accepted on rolling basis. Notification of awards on rolling basis.
**Financial aid contact:** Steve Thomas, M.A., Director of Admission/Student Services. 207 288-5015, extension 232.

# Husson College

**Bangor, ME 04401 207 941-7000**

**1994-95 Costs.** Tuition: $7,800. Room & board: $4,000. Fees, books, misc. academic expenses (school's estimate): $590.
**Enrollment.** Undergraduates: 348 men, 587 women (full-time). Freshman class: 706 applicants, 633 accepted, 361 enrolled. Graduate enrollment: 124 men, 126 women.
**Test score averages/ranges.** Average SAT scores: 383 verbal, 435 math.
**Faculty.** 49 full-time; 27 part-time. 31% of faculty holds doctoral degree. Student/faculty ratio: 20 to 1.
**Selectivity rating.** Less competitive.

**PROFILE.** Husson, founded in 1898, is a private college. Its 170-acre campus is located in Bangor.

**Accreditation:** NEASC. Professionally accredited by the National League for Nursing.
**Religious orientation:** Husson College is nonsectarian; no religious requirements.
**Library:** Collections totaling over 34,500 volumes, 387 periodical subscriptions, and 5,168 microform items.
**Athletic facilities:** Gymnasium, swimming pool, basketball, racquetball, and tennis courts, weight room, exercise rooms, softball and baseball fields.

**STUDENT BODY. Undergraduate profile:** 88% are state residents; 24% are transfers. 2% Asian-American, 2% Black, .5% Hispanic, .5% Native American, 93% White, 2% Other. Average age of undergraduates is 24.
**Freshman profile:** 5% of freshmen who took SAT scored 600 or over on math; 6% scored 500 or over on verbal, 27% scored 500 or over on math; 42% scored 400 or over on verbal, 63% scored 400 or over on math; 88% scored 300 or over on verbal, 96% scored 300 or over on math. 85% of accepted applicants took SAT. 90% of freshmen come from public schools.
**Undergraduate achievement:** 66% of fall 1992 freshmen returned for fall 1993 term. 2% of students who completed a degree program immediately went on to graduate study.
**Foreign students:** 30 students are from out of the country. Countries represented include Canada, China, Greece, Japan, Korea, and Saudi Arabia; nine in all.

**PROGRAMS OF STUDY. Degrees:** B.S., B.S.Nurs.
**Majors:** Accounting, Business Administration/Management, Business Teacher Education, Court/Conference Reporting, Executive Administration, Financial Management, Management, Management Accounting, Management Accounting/Management Information Systems, Management Information Systems, Marketing, Nursing, Office Management, Office Management/Secretarial Studies, Public Accounting, Public Accounting/Management Information Systems, Sports Management.
**Distribution of degrees:** The majors with the highest enrollment are business administration, nursing, and accounting; management information systems and business teacher education have the lowest.
**Requirements:** General education requirement.
**Academic regulations:** Minimum 2.00 GPA must be maintained.
**Special:** Minors offered in behavioral science, English, and psychology. Executive administration major has options in shorthand, management, accounting, and management information systems. Courses offered in anatomy/physiology, biology, business communications, debate, English, ethics, French, government, history, international relations, mathematics, philosophy, physical science, psychology, sociology, and Spanish. Associate's degrees offered. Independent study. Internships. Cooperative education programs. Graduate school at which undergraduates may take graduate-level courses. 2-2 programs in accounting and computer information systems. Member of Downeast Consortium. Teacher certification in secondary education. Certification in specific subject areas. ROTC and NROTC at U of Maine.
**Academic Assistance:** Remedial reading, writing, math, and study skills. Nonremedial tutoring.

**ADMISSIONS. Academic basis for candidate selection** (in order of priority): Secondary school record, class rank, standardized test scores, school's recommendation, essay.
**Nonacademic basis for candidate selection:** Character and personality are important. Extracurricular participation and alumni/ae relationship are considered.
**Requirements:** Graduation from secondary school is recommended; GED is accepted. 16 units and the following program of study are recommended: 4 units of English, 2 units of math, 2 units of science, 1 unit of social studies, 1 unit of history. Conditional admission possible for applicants not meeting standard requirements. SAT is required; ACT may be substituted. Campus visit and interview recommended. No off-campus interviews.
**Procedure:** Notification of admission on rolling basis. Reply is required by May 1. $125 tuition deposit, refundable until May 1 $50 refundable room deposit. Freshmen accepted for terms other than fall.
**Special programs:** Admission may be deferred. Credit and/or placement may be granted through CEEB Advanced Placement exams for scores of 2 or higher. Credit and/or placement may be granted through CLEP general and subject exams. Early decision program. In fall 1993, 10 applied for early decision and 10 were accepted. Deadline for applying for early decision is December 15. Early entrance/early admission program. Concurrent enrollment program.
**Transfer students:** Transfer students accepted for terms other than fall. In fall 1993, 24% of all new students were transfers into all classes. 106 transfer applications were received, 106 were accepted. Application deadline is rolling for fall; rolling for spring. Minimum 2.0 GPA required. Lowest course grade accepted is "C." Maximum number of transferable credits is 90 semester hours. At least 30 semester hours must be completed at the college to receive degree.

**Admissions contact:** Jane Goodwin, Director of Admissions. 207 941-7100.

**FINANCIAL AID. Available aid:** Pell grants, SEOG, Federal Nursing Student Scholarships, state scholarships and grants, school scholarships and grants, private scholarships and grants, ROTC scholarships, academic merit scholarships, and athletic scholarships. Perkins Loans (NDSL), PLUS, Stafford Loans (GSL), NSL, state loans, and SLS. Protected payment plan through college.
**Financial aid statistics:** 10% of aid is not need-based. In 1993-94, 85% of all undergraduate applicants received aid; 94% of freshman applicants. Average amounts of aid awarded freshmen: Scholarships and grants, $6,723; loans, $2,625.
**Supporting data/closing dates:** FAFSA/FAF/FFS: Accepted on rolling basis. School's own aid application: Accepted on rolling basis. Notification of awards on rolling basis.
**Financial aid contact:** Robert Caswell, Director of Financial Aid. 207 941-7156.

## Maine College of Art

**Portland, ME 04101** 207 775-3052

**1994-95 Costs.** Tuition: $11,200. Room & board: $4,990. Fees, books, misc. academic expenses (school's estimate): $1,045.
**Enrollment.** Undergraduates: 110 men, 166 women (full-time).
**Test score averages/ranges.** Average SAT scores: 450 verbal, 450 math. Range of SAT scores of middle 50%: 450-510 verbal, 440-500 math.
**Faculty.** 18 full-time; 27 part-time. 67% of faculty holds highest degree in specific field. Student/faculty ratio: 6 to 1.
**Selectivity rating.** Less competitive.

**PROFILE.** The Maine College of Art (formerly Portland School of Art), founded in 1882, is a private institution of the arts. The campus is located in Portland, 100 miles north of Boston.

**Accreditation:** NEASC. Professionally accredited by the National Association of Schools of Art and Design.
**Religious orientation:** Maine College of Art is nonsectarian; no religious requirements.
**Library:** Collections totaling over 16,361 volumes and 114 periodical subscriptions.
**Special facilities/museums:** Art and photography galleries.
**Athletic facilities:** Basketball courts; nearby YMCA offers swimming privileges.

**STUDENT BODY. Undergraduate profile:** 51% are state residents. 99% White, 1% Other. Average age of undergraduates is 24.
**Freshman profile:** 98% of accepted applicants took SAT.
**Undergraduate achievement:** 60% of fall 1992 freshmen returned for fall 1993 term. 34% of entering class graduated.

**PROGRAMS OF STUDY. Degrees:** B.F.A.
**Majors:** Ceramics, Graphic Design, Jewelry/Metalsmithing, Painting, Photography, Printmaking, Sculpture.
**Requirements:** General education requirement.
**Academic regulations:** Minimum 2.0 GPA must be maintained.
**Special:** Independent study. Pass/fail grading option. Internships. Cooperative education programs. Graduate school at which undergraduates may take graduate-level courses. Member of Southern Maine Admissions Consortium, Art Student League (New York), Association of Independent Colleges of Art & Design (AICAD). Photography winter session in France. Study abroad possible.
**Honors:** Honor societies.
**Academic Assistance:** Remedial writing.

**ADMISSIONS. Academic basis for candidate selection** (in order of priority): Secondary school record, class rank, essay, school's recommendation, standardized test scores.
**Nonacademic basis for candidate selection:** Particular talent or ability is emphasized. Character and personality and extracurricular participation are important.
**Requirements:** Graduation from secondary school is recommended; GED is accepted. 16 units and the following program of study are recommended: 4 units of English, 3 units of math, 2 units of science, 2 units of foreign language, 2 units of social studies, 3 units of electives. Portfolio required of all applicants. SAT is required. Campus visit and interview recommended. Off-campus interviews available with an admissions representative.
**Procedure:** Take SAT by December of 12th year. Visit college for interview by March 1 of 12th year. Notification of admission on rolling basis. Reply is required by May 1. $150 tuition deposit, refundable until May 1. $200 nonrefundable room deposit. Freshmen accepted for fall terms only.
**Special programs:** Admission may be deferred one year. Credit and/or placement may be granted through CEEB Advanced Placement exams. Early entrance/early admission program. Concurrent enrollment program.
**Transfer students:** Transfer students accepted for terms other than fall. Application deadline is rolling for fall; rolling for spring. Lowest course grade accepted is "C." Maximum number of transferable credits is 67 semester hours. At least 67 semester hours must be completed at the college to receive degree.
**Admissions contact:** Elizabeth Shea, Director of Admissions.

**FINANCIAL AID. Available aid:** Pell grants, SEOG, state scholarships and grants, school scholarships and grants, private scholarships and grants, academic merit scholarships, and aid for undergraduate foreign students. Perkins Loans (NDSL), PLUS, Stafford Loans (GSL), private loans, and SLS. AMS and Tuition Management Systems. School's own payment plan.
**Financial aid statistics:** 5% of aid is not need-based. In 1993-94, 95% of all undergraduate applicants received aid; 97% of freshman applicants. Average amounts of aid awarded freshmen: Scholarships and grants, $3,682; loans, $2,625.
**Supporting data/closing dates:** FAFSA/FAF: Priority filing date is March 1. School's own aid application. Income tax forms: Accepted on rolling basis. Notification of awards on rolling basis.
**Financial aid contact:** Martha Johnston-Farr, Director of Financial Aid. 207 775-3052.

## Maine Maritime Academy

**Castine, ME 04420** 207 326-4311

**1994-95 Costs.** Tuition: $3,880 (state residents), $6,930 (out-of-state). Room & board: $4,550. Fees, books, misc. academic expenses (school's estimate): $1,280.
**Enrollment.** Undergraduates: 645 men, 45 women (full-time). Freshman class: 650 applicants, 475 accepted, 205 enrolled. 60 men.
**Test score averages/ranges.** N/A.
**Faculty.** 45 full-time; 15 part-time. 13% of faculty holds doctoral degree. Student/faculty ratio: 12 to 1.
**Selectivity rating.** N/A.

**PROFILE.** The Maine Maritime Academy is a public academy. Founded in 1941, it adopted coeducation in 1974. Its 35-acre campus is located in Castine, 38 miles south of Bangor.

**Accreditation:** NEASC.
**Religious orientation:** Maine Maritime Academy is nonsectarian; no religious requirements.
**Library:** Collections totaling over 72,000 volumes, 900 periodical subscriptions, and 168,000 microform items.
**Special facilities/museums:** Visual deck simulator, power generation simulator, 100 vessels.
**Athletic facilities:** Gymnasium, field house, swimming pool, soccer and football fields, waterfront for sailing, racquetball, squash, and tennis courts, golf course, weight rooms.

**STUDENT BODY. Undergraduate profile:** 60% are state residents; 9% are transfers. 1% Asian-American, 1% Black, 1% Native American, 95% White, 2% Other. Average age of undergraduates is 22.
**Undergraduate achievement:** 80% of fall 1992 freshmen returned for fall 1993 term. 67% of entering class graduated. 1% of students who completed a degree program immediately went on to graduate study.
**Foreign students:** Countries represented include Canada, Liberia, Panama, and Saudi Arabia.

**PROGRAMS OF STUDY. Degrees:** B.S.
**Majors:** Marine Engineering, Marine Transportation, Nautical Science, Ocean Studies, Power Engineering Technology.
**Requirements:** General education requirement.
**Academic regulations:** Freshmen must maintain minimum 1.8 GPA; sophomores, juniors, seniors 2.0 GPA.
**Special:** Minors offered in humanities, industrial power plant management, marina management, naval architecture, naval science, nuclear power, oceanography, and small vessel operations. Associate's degrees offered. Internships. Cooperative education programs. Member of Downeast Consortium of Maine Colleges. Sea Semester. NROTC.
**Academic Assistance:** Remedial writing, math, and study skills. Nonremedial tutoring.

**ADMISSIONS. Academic basis for candidate selection** (in order of priority): Secondary school record, class rank, standardized test scores, school's recommendation, essay.
**Nonacademic basis for candidate selection:** Character and personality are important. Extracurricular participation, particular talent or ability, and alumni/ae relationship are considered.
**Requirements:** Graduation from secondary school is recommended; GED is accepted. No specific distribution of secondary school units required. SAT or ACT is required. Campus visit and interview recommended. Off-campus interviews available with an admissions representative.
**Procedure:** Take SAT or ACT by December of 12th year. Visit college for interview by December of 12th year. Application deadline is July 1. Notification of admission on rolling basis. Reply is required by May 1. $100 nonrefundable tuition deposit. Freshmen accepted for fall terms only.
**Special programs:** Admission may be deferred one year. Credit may be granted through CEEB Advanced Placement for scores of 3 or higher.
**Transfer students:** Transfer students accepted for terms other than fall. In fall 1993, 9% of all new students were transfers into all classes. Application deadline is July 1 for fall; October 1 for spring. Minimum 2.0 GPA required. Lowest course grade accepted is "C." Maximum number of transferable credits is 115 semester hours.
**Admissions contact:** Daniel J. Jones, Director of Admissions. 207 326-4311, extensions 206, 215, 373.

**FINANCIAL AID. Available aid:** Pell grants, SEOG, private scholarships, and ROTC scholarships. Perkins Loans (NDSL), PLUS, Stafford Loans (GSL), school loans, and SLS. Knight Tuition Plans.
**Financial aid statistics:** Average amounts of aid awarded freshmen: Scholarships and grants, $2,300.
**Supporting data/closing dates:** FAFSA: Priority filing date is April 15. Notification of awards on rolling basis.
**Financial aid contact:** Mary Beth Sommers, Director of Financial Aid. 207 326-4311, extensions 207, 339.

## Saint Joseph's College

Windham, ME 04062-1198 207 892-6766

**1994-95 Costs.** Tuition: $9,985. Room & board: $5,180. Fees, books, misc. academic expenses (school's estimate): $795.
**Enrollment.** Undergraduates: 257 men, 459 women (full-time). Freshman class: 833 applicants, 682 accepted, 217 enrolled.
**Test score averages/ranges.** Average SAT scores: 420 verbal, 460 math.
**Faculty.** 45 full-time; 47 part-time. 54% of faculty holds doctoral degree. Student/faculty ratio: 17 to 1.
**Selectivity rating.** Less competitive.

**PROFILE.** Saint Joseph's is a church-affiliated, liberal arts college. Founded in 1912 for women only, it adopted coeducation in 1970. Its 285-acre campus is located in Windham, 16 miles northwest of Portland.

**Accreditation:** NEASC. Professionally accredited by the National League for Nursing. Numerous professional accreditations.
**Religious orientation:** Saint Joseph's College is affiliated with the Roman Catholic Church; two semesters of religion required.
**Library:** Collections totaling over 73,697 volumes, 497 periodical subscriptions, and 3,187 microform items.
**Special facilities/museums:** TV studio, Celeston-14 telescope.
**Athletic facilities:** Gymnasium, dance, exercise, and weight rooms, baseball and softball field, cross-country running and ski trails, 2,000-foot private beach on Sebago Lake.
**STUDENT BODY. Undergraduate profile:** 50% are state residents; 20% are transfers. 1% Asian-American, 1% Black, 98% White. Average age of undergraduates is 20.
**Freshman profile:** 1% of freshmen who took SAT scored 700 or over on math; 1% scored 600 or over on verbal, 7% scored 600 or over on math; 17% scored 500 or over on verbal, 35% scored 500 or over on math; 63% scored 400 or over on verbal, 73% scored 400 or over on math; 100% scored 300 or over on verbal, 100% scored 300 or over on math. 100% of accepted applicants took SAT. 86% of freshmen come from public schools.
**Undergraduate achievement:** 76% of fall 1992 freshmen returned for fall 1993 term. 62% of entering class graduated. 20% of students who completed a degree program immediately went on to graduate study.
**Foreign students:** Six students are from out of the country. Countries represented include Austria, the Bahamas, Canada, China, France, and Italy.
**PROGRAMS OF STUDY. Degrees:** B.A., B.S
**Majors:** Biology, Business Administration, Communications, Elementary Education, English, Environmental Science, History, Mathematics, Natural Science, Nursing, Philosophy, Physical Education, Pre-Pharmacy, Psychology, Radiologic Technology, Religious Studies, Secondary Education, Sociology.
**Distribution of degrees:** The majors with the highest enrollment are nursing, business administration, and elementary education; religious studies, natural science, and philosophy have the lowest.
**Requirements:** General education requirement.
**Academic regulations:** Freshmen must maintain minimum 1.75 GPA; sophomores, juniors, seniors 2.00 GPA.
**Special:** Minors offered in all majors and in art, chemistry, computer systems administration, journalism, and political science. Concentrations offered in accounting, international business, management, and marketing. Associate's degrees offered. Double majors. Independent study. Accelerated study. Pass/fail grading option. Internships. Graduate school at which undergraduates may take graduate-level courses. Preprofessional programs in law, medicine, veterinary science, pharmacy, and dentistry. 2-3 pharmacy program with Massachusetts Coll of Pharmacy. Member of Greater Portland Alliance. Teacher certification in elementary and secondary education. Certification in specific subject areas. Exchange program abroad in Canada. Study abroad also in numerous other countries. ROTC.
**Honors:** Honors program. Honor societies.
**Academic Assistance:** Remedial reading, writing, math, and study skills. Nonremedial tutoring.
**ADMISSIONS. Academic basis for candidate selection** (in order of priority): Secondary school record, class rank, standardized test scores, school's recommendation, essay.
**Nonacademic basis for candidate selection:** Character and personality are emphasized. Extracurricular participation and particular talent or ability are important. Geographical distribution and alumni/ae relationship are considered.
**Requirements:** Graduation from secondary school is required; GED is accepted. 18 units and the following program of study are required: 4 units of English, 2 units of math, 2 units of social studies, 8 units of electives. Minimum combined SAT score of 740 recommended. Lab biology and chemistry required of nursing and science program applicants. SAT is required; ACT may be substituted. PSAT is required. ACH required. Campus visit and interview recommended. No off-campus interviews.
**Procedure:** Take SAT or ACT by January of 12th year. Take ACH by January of 12th year. Visit college for interview by March 14 of 12th year. Suggest filing application by March 1. Application deadline is June 1. Notification of admission on rolling basis. Reply is required by May 1. $100 tuition deposit, refundable until May 1. Freshmen accepted for terms other than fall.
**Special programs:** Admission may be deferred one year. Credit and/or placement may be granted through CEEB Advanced Placement exams for scores of 3 or higher. Credit and/or placement may be granted through CLEP subject exams. Early entrance/early admission program.
**Transfer students:** Transfer students accepted for terms other than fall. In fall 1993, 20% of all new students were transfers into all classes. 143 transfer applications were received, 117 were accepted. Application deadline is July 1 for fall; December 1 for spring. Minimum 2.0 GPA recommended. Lowest course grade accepted is "C." Maximum number of transferable credits is 96 semester hours. At least 32 semester hours must be completed at the college to receive degree.
**Admissions contact:** Fredric V. Stone, M.A., Director of Admissions. 800 338-7057, extension 1740.
**FINANCIAL AID. Available aid:** Pell grants, SEOG, state scholarships and grants, school scholarships and grants, private scholarships and grants, ROTC scholarships, academic merit scholarships, and aid for undergraduate foreign students. Perkins Loans (NDSL), PLUS, Stafford Loans (GSL), NSL, state loans, private loans, and SLS. Tuition Plan Inc., AMS, Tuition Management Systems, and family tuition reduction.
**Financial aid statistics:** 10% of aid is not need-based. In 1993-94, 93% of all undergraduate applicants received aid; 92% of freshman applicants. Average amounts of aid awarded freshmen: Scholarships and grants, $3,150; loans, $2,860.
**Supporting data/closing dates:** FAFSA/FAF: Priority filing date is March 14. Income tax forms: Accepted on rolling basis. Notification of awards begins April 1.
**Financial aid contact:** Andrea Cross, M.A., Director of Financial Aid. 800 338-7057, extension 1761.

## Thomas College

Waterville, ME 04901-9986 207 873-0771

**1994-95 Costs.** Tuition: $9,195. Room & board: $4,650. Fees, books, misc. academic expenses (school's estimate): $855.
**Enrollment.** Undergraduates: 191 men, 253 women (full-time). Freshman class: 354 applicants, 312 accepted, 140 enrolled. Graduate enrollment: 125 men, 79 women.
**Test score averages/ranges.** Average SAT scores: 370 verbal, 470 math. Range of SAT scores of middle 50%: 350-440 verbal, 400-510 math.
**Faculty.** 18 full-time; 6 part-time. 33% of faculty holds doctoral degree. Student/faculty ratio: 20 to 1.
**Selectivity rating.** Competitive.

**PROFILE.** Thomas, founded in 1894, is a private college of business. Its 70-acre campus is located two miles outside of Waterville.

**Accreditation:** NEASC.
**Religious orientation:** Thomas College is nonsectarian; no religious requirements.
**Library:** Collections totaling over 25,000 volumes and 250 periodical subscriptions.
**Athletic facilities:** Gymnasium, athletic field, basketball courts, weight and fitness room.
**STUDENT BODY. Undergraduate profile:** 91% are state residents; 11% are transfers. 1% Asian-American, 1% Black, 98% White. Average age of undergraduates is 20.
**Freshman profile:** Majority of accepted applicants took SAT. 98% of freshmen come from public schools.
**Undergraduate achievement:** 80% of fall 1992 freshmen returned for fall 1993 term. 66% of entering class graduated. 6% of students who completed a degree program went on to graduate study within three years.
**Foreign students:** Five students are from out of the country. Countries represented include Bermuda, Brazil, England, and Japan.
**PROGRAMS OF STUDY. Degrees:** B.S.
**Majors:** Accounting, Accounting Information Systems, Business Teacher Education, Computer Information Systems, Finance/Economics, Management, Management Information Systems, Marketing Information Systems, Marketing Management, Mathematics/Computer Information Systems Teacher Education, Retailing Management.
**Distribution of degrees:** The majors with the highest enrollment are accounting, marketing management, and management; finance/economics, retail management, and computer information systems have the lowest.
**Requirements:** General education requirement.
**Academic regulations:** Minimum 2.00 GPA must be maintained.
**Special:** Minors offered in some majors and in international studies, marketing, and retailing. Associate's degrees offered. Independent study. Internships. Cooperative education programs. Graduate school at which undergraduates may take graduate-level courses. Five-year accounting or computer information systems/M.B.A. programs. Teacher certification in secondary education. Certification in specific subject areas. Exchange program abroad in Canada. ROTC at U of Maine.
**Honors:** Honor societies.
**Academic Assistance:** Nonremedial tutoring.
**ADMISSIONS. Academic basis for candidate selection** (in order of priority): Secondary school record, school's recommendation, standardized test scores, class rank, essay.
**Nonacademic basis for candidate selection:** Extracurricular participation is important. Character and personality, particular talent or ability, and alumni/ae relationship are considered.
**Requirements:** Graduation from secondary school is required; GED is accepted. 19 units and the following program of study are recommended: 4 units of English, 3 units of math, 2 units of science, 2 units of foreign language, 1 unit of social studies, 2 units of history, 5 units of electives. Minimum combined SAT score of 750, rank in top half of secondary school class, and minimum 2.0 GPA recommended. SAT or ACT is required. PSAT is recommended. Campus visit and interview recommended.
**Procedure:** Notification of admission on rolling basis. $100 tuition deposit, refundable until May 1. $50 room deposit, refundable until May 1. Freshmen accepted for terms other than fall.
**Special programs:** Admission may be deferred two years. Credit may be granted through CLEP general and subject exams. Early entrance/early admission program. Concurrent enrollment program.
**Transfer students:** Transfer students accepted for terms other than fall. In fall 1993, 11% of all new students were transfers into all classes. 18 transfer applications were received, 16 were accepted. Application deadline is September for fall; January for spring. Minimum 2.1 GPA recommended. Lowest course grade accepted is "C." Maximum number of transferable credits is 30 semester hours from a two-year school and 90 semester hours from a four-year school. At least 30 semester hours must be completed at the college to receive degree.
**Admissions contact:** Susan Potter, Director of Admissions. 207 877-0101.

**FINANCIAL AID. Available aid:** Pell grants, SEOG, state scholarships and grants, school scholarships and grants, private scholarships and grants, ROTC scholarships, academic merit scholarships, and athletic scholarships. Perkins Loans (NDSL), PLUS, Stafford Loans (GSL), school loans, private loans, and SLS. Tuition Plan Inc., Knight Tuition Plans, AMS, and Tuition Management Systems.
**Financial aid statistics:** 11% of aid is not need-based. In 1993-94, 100% of all undergraduate applicants received aid. Average amounts of aid awarded freshmen: Scholarships and grants, $3,860; loans, $2,550.
**Supporting data/closing dates:** FAFSA: Priority filing date is February 1. Income tax forms: Priority filing date is April 30. Notification of awards begins March 18.
**Financial aid contact:** Lisa Vashon, Director of Financial Aid. 207 877-0112.

# Unity College

**Unity, ME 04988-0532 — 207 948-3131**

**1994-95 Costs.** Tuition: $8,750 (state residents), $9,550 (out-of-state). Room & board: $4,750. Fees, books, misc. academic expenses (school's estimate): $825.
**Enrollment.** Undergraduates: 348 men, 122 women (full-time). Freshman class: 425 applicants, 407 accepted, 173 enrolled.
**Test score averages/ranges.** Average SAT scores: 450 verbal, 490 math.
**Faculty.** 31 full-time; 27 part-time. 56% of faculty holds doctoral degree. Student/faculty ratio: 14 to 1.
**Selectivity rating.** Less competitive.

**PROFILE.** Unity, founded in 1965, is a private, multipurpose college. Its 185-acre campus is located in Unity, 18 miles east of Waterville.

**Accreditation:** NEASC.
**Religious orientation:** Unity College is nonsectarian; no religious requirements.
**Library:** Collections totaling over 40,000 volumes and 651 periodical subscriptions.
**Special facilities/museums:** Art gallery, Indian museum, wetlands research area.
**Athletic facilities:** Gymnasium, weight room, cross-country skiing and running trails, climbing wall, lacrosse, softball, and soccer fields.
**STUDENT BODY. Undergraduate profile:** 22% are state residents; 25% are transfers. 93% White, 7% Other. Average age of undergraduates is 19.
**Freshman profile:** 97% of freshmen come from public schools.
**Undergraduate achievement:** 12% of students who completed a degree program immediately went on to graduate study.
**Foreign students:** Nine students are from out of the country. Countries represented include Austria, Canada, Japan, and Turkey.
**PROGRAMS OF STUDY. Degrees:** B.A., B.S.
**Majors:** Aquaculture, Arboriculture, Conservation Law Enforcement, Ecology, Environmental Education, Environmental Policy, Fisheries, Forestry, Interdisciplinary Studies, Land Use Planning, Outdoor Recreation, Park Management, Pre-Law, Self-Designed Majors, Wildlife.
**Distribution of degrees:** The majors with the highest enrollment are conservation law enforcement, outdoor recreation, and wildlife.
**Requirements:** General education requirement.
**Academic regulations:** Freshmen must maintain minimum 1.50 GPA; sophomores, 1.70 GPA; juniors, 2.00 GPA; seniors, 2.00 GPA.
**Special:** Associate's degrees offered. Self-designed majors. Dual degrees. Independent study. Accelerated study. Internships. Cooperative education programs. Preprofessional programs in law. Washington Semester. Study abroad possible. ROTC at U of Maine at Orono.
**Academic Assistance:** Remedial reading, writing, math, and study skills. Nonremedial tutoring.
**ADMISSIONS. Academic basis for candidate selection** (in order of priority): Secondary school record, class rank, school's recommendation, essay, standardized test scores.
**Nonacademic basis for candidate selection:** Character and personality are emphasized. Extracurricular participation is important.
**Requirements:** Graduation from secondary school is required; GED is accepted. 16 units and the following program of study are required: 4 units of English, 2 units of math, 3 units of science including 2 units of lab, 2 units of social studies, 1 unit of history, 2 units of academic electives. Minimum combined SAT score of 900, rank in top three-fifths of secondary school class, and minimum 2.0 GPA recommended. Conditional admission possible for applicants not meeting standard requirements. SAT is recommended. PSAT is recommended. Campus visit and interview recommended. Off-campus interviews available with an admissions representative.
**Procedure:** Take SAT or ACT by fall of 12th year. Visit college for interview by spring of 12th year. Notification of admission on rolling basis. Reply is required by May 1. $50 nonrefundable tuition deposit. $100 nonrefundable room deposit. Freshmen accepted for terms other than fall.
**Special programs:** Admission may be deferred. Credit and/or placement may be granted through CEEB Advanced Placement exams for scores of 3 or higher. Credit and/or placement may be granted through CLEP general and subject exams. Credit and placement may be granted through military and life experience. Early entrance/early admission program. Concurrent enrollment program.
**Transfer students:** Transfer students accepted for terms other than fall. In fall 1992, 25% of all new students were transfers into all classes. 38 transfer applications were received, 38 were accepted. Application deadline is rolling for fall; rolling for spring. Minimum 2.0 GPA required. Lowest course grade accepted is "C-." Maximum number of transferable credits is 60 semester hours. At least 60 semester hours must be completed at the college to receive degree.
**Admissions contact:** John M.B. Craig, Ed.D., Dean for Admissions. 207 948-3131, extension 228.
**FINANCIAL AID. Available aid:** Pell grants, SEOG, state scholarships and grants, school scholarships and grants, private scholarships, academic merit scholarships, and athletic scholarships. Perkins Loans (NDSL), PLUS, Stafford Loans (GSL), state loans, and SLS. Tuition Plan Inc., AMS, and guaranteed tuition. Installment Plan.
**Financial aid statistics:** In 1993-94, 86% of all undergraduate applicants received aid; 84% of freshman applicants. Average amounts of aid awarded freshmen: Scholarships and grants, $3,017.
**Supporting data/closing dates:** FAFSA/FAF: Priority filing date is April 15. School's own aid application: Priority filing date is April 15. State aid form: Priority filing date is April 15. Income tax forms: Priority filing date is April 15. Notification of awards on rolling basis.
**Financial aid contact:** Rand Newell, Director of Financial Aid. 207 948-3131, extension 200.

# University of Maine

**Orono, ME 04469 — 207 581-1110**

**1994-95 Costs.** Tuition: $3,250 (state residents), $8,375 (out-of-state). Room & board: $4,600. Fees, books, misc. academic expenses (school's estimate): $500.
**Enrollment.** Undergraduates: 4,556 men, 3,960 women (full-time). Freshman class: 5,205 applicants, 4,361 accepted, 2,353 enrolled. Graduate enrollment: 943 men, 1,133 women.
**Test score averages/ranges.** Range of SAT scores of middle 50%: 410-510 verbal, 460-580 math.
**Faculty.** 64% of faculty holds doctoral degree. Student/faculty ratio: 16 to 1.
**Selectivity rating.** Less competitive.

**PROFILE.** The University of Maine, founded in 1865, is a public, land-grant institution. Programs are offered through the Colleges of Applied Sciences and Agriculture, Arts and Humanities, Business Administration, Education, Engineering and Technology, Forest Resources, Sciences, and Social and Behavioral Sciences. Its 3,298-acre main campus is located in Orono, eight miles north of Bangor.
**Accreditation:** NEASC. Professionally accredited by the Accreditation Board for Engineering and Technology, the American Assembly of Collegiate Schools of Business, the American Dental Association, the American Home Economics Association, the American Medical Association (CAHEA), the American Psychological Association, the American Veterinary Medical Association, the Council on Social Work Education, the National Association of Schools of Art and Design, the National Association of Schools of Music, the National Council for Accreditation of Teacher Education, the Society of American Foresters.
**Religious orientation:** University of Maine is nonsectarian; no religious requirements.
**Library:** Collections totaling over 732,000 volumes, 6,900 periodical subscriptions, and 1,200,000 microform items.
**Special facilities/museums:** Anthropology museum, folklore and oral history museum, art museum, Canadian-American center, social sciences research institute, exceptional child research lab, preschool, experimental farms, land/water resources center, center for marine studies, planetarium/observatory, two electron microscopes.
**Athletic facilities:** Gymnasium, swimming pool, baseball and intramural fields, racquetball, squash, and tennis courts, weight rooms, ice skating rink, field house, tracks, cross-country trails.
**STUDENT BODY. Undergraduate profile:** 81% are state residents. 1% Asian-American, 1% Black, 1% Native American, 97% White. Average age of undergraduates is 20.
**Freshman profile:** 98% of accepted applicants took SAT.
**Foreign students:** 200 students are from out of the country. Countries represented include Canada and Japan; 60 in all.
**PROGRAMS OF STUDY. Degrees:** B.A., B.S.
**Majors:** Accounting, Agribusiness Administration, Agribusiness/Resource Economics, Animal/Veterinary Sciences, Anthropology, Art, Art Education, Art History, Biochemistry, Biology, Bioresource Engineering, Botany, Broadcasting, Business Administration, Chemical Engineering, Chemistry, Child Development/Family Relations, Civil Engineering, Computer Engineering, Computer Science, Construction Management Technology, Economics, Electrical Engineering, Electrical Engineering Technology, Elementary Education, Engineering Physics, English, Finance, Food Science, Foreign Languages/Classics, Forest Engineering, Forestry, French, Geological Sciences, German, Health/Family Life Education, History, Hotel/Restaurant/Tourism Administration, Human Nutrition/Foods, International Affairs, Journalism, Landscape Horticulture, Latin, Management, Management Information Systems, Marketing, Mathematics, Mechanical Engineering, Mechanical Engineering Technology, Medical Technology, Merchandising/Consumer Resources, Microbiology, Modern Languages, Molecular/Cellular Biology, Music, Natural Resources, Nursing, Philosophy, Physical Education/Recreation, Physics, Political Science, Production/Processing Technology, Psychology, Public Management, Pulp/Paper Technology, Recreation/Parks Management, Romance Languages, Secondary Education, Social Work, Sociology, Spanish, Speech Communication, Surveying Engineering, Sustainable Agriculture, Theatre, Wildlife Management, Wood Technology, Zoology.
**Distribution of degrees:** The majors with the highest enrollment are business administration, education, and mechanical engineering; Romance languages, food science, and music education have the lowest.
**Academic regulations:** Freshmen must maintain minimum 1.7 GPA; sophomores, 1.8 GPA; juniors, 1.9 GPA; seniors, 2.0 GPA.
**Special:** Minors offered by some colleges. Associate's degrees offered. Double majors. Dual degrees. Independent study. Pass/fail grading option. Internships. Cooperative education programs. Graduate school at which undergraduates may take graduate-level courses. Preprofessional programs in medicine, veterinary science, and dentistry. Cross-registration with Bangor Theological Seminary. Washington Semester. National Student Exchange. Teacher certification in early childhood, elementary, and secondary education. Study abroad in Australia, Austria, Brazil, Canada, France, Germany, Greece, Ireland, and Spain. ROTC, NROTC, and AFROTC.
**Honors:** Phi Beta Kappa. Honors program. Honor societies.
**Academic Assistance:** Remedial writing, math, and study skills. Nonremedial tutoring.

**STUDENT LIFE. Housing:** All traditional first-year students must live on campus. Coed, women's, and men's dorms. School-owned/operated apartments. 40% of students live in college housing.
**Social atmosphere:** The student newspaper reports, "On-campus activities are limited by the control of drinking and noise in residence halls and officially sanctioned activities. However, off-campus parties are abundant." Popular spots on campus are the Bear's Den, Damn Yankee, and Fogler Library. Students tend to gather off campus at Pat's Pizza, Geddy's Pub, Marguarita's Pub, El Cheepo's, and the Penny Post. Prominent groups on campus include Greeks, athletes, student government, the Union Board, and the Maine Center for the Arts. Bumstock, Homecoming, and sporting events are among the favorite events during the year.
**Services and counseling/handicapped student services:** Placement services. Health service. Women's center. Day care. Counseling services for minority, military, veteran, and older students. Birth control, personal, and psychological counseling. Career and academic guidance services. Religious counseling. Physically disabled student services. Learning disabled services. Tutors.
**Campus organizations:** Undergraduate student government. Student newspaper (Maine Campus, published twice/week). Literary magazine. Yearbook. Radio and TV stations. Concert and symphonic bands, varsity and pep bands, orchestra, ensembles, chorus, women's glee club, Oratorio Society, opera workshop, debating, Maine Masque Theatre, dance club, illustrated magazines, 130 organizations in all. 12 fraternities, all with chapter houses; seven sororities, no chapter houses. 6% of men join a fraternity. 4% of women join a sorority.
**Religious organizations:** B'nai B'rith, Campus Crusade for Christ, Canterbury Club, Intervarsity Christian Fellowship, Christian Association, Newman Club, Orono Friends, Orthodox Christian Fellowship, Navigators.
**Minority/foreign student organizations:** African-American group, Indians at Maine.

**ATHLETICS. Physical education requirements:** None.
**Intercollegiate competition:** 8% of students participate. Baseball (M), basketball (M,W), cross-country (M,W), diving (M,W), field hockey (W), football (M), golf (M), ice hockey (M), soccer (M,W), softball (W), swimming (M,W), tennis (W), track (indoor) (M,W), track (outdoor) (M,W), track and field (indoor) (M,W), track and field (outdoor) (M,W). Member of ECAC, Hockey East, NCAA Division I, NCAA Division I-AA for football, North Atlantic Conference, Yankee Conference.
**Intramural and club sports:** 67% of students participate. Intramural aerobics, badminton, basketball, billiards, bowling, broomball, cross-country, cycling, flag football, floor hockey, golf, Nordic skiing, polo, racquetball, soccer, softball, squash, swimming, tennis, track, volleyball, weight lifting. Men's club basketball, cheerleading, golf, soccer, softball, swimming, tennis, volleyball, water polo, weight lifting. Women's club basketball, cheerleading, ice hockey, soccer, volleyball, water polo, weight lifting.

**ADMISSIONS. Academic basis for candidate selection** (in order of priority): Secondary school record, class rank, standardized test scores, school's recommendation, essay.
**Nonacademic basis for candidate selection:** Extracurricular participation and geographical distribution are important. Character and personality, particular talent or ability, and alumni/ae relationship are considered.
**Requirements:** Graduation from secondary school is required; GED is accepted. 16 units and the following program of study are required: 4 units of English, 3 units of math, 2 units of lab science, 2 units of foreign language, 1 unit of social studies, 1 unit of history, 6 units of electives. Minimum combined SAT score of 900, rank in top half of secondary school class, and minimum 2.5 GPA recommended. Audition required of music program applicants. Onward Special Services Program for applicants not normally admissible. SAT is required; ACT may be substituted. Campus visit and interview recommended. Off-campus interviews available with an alumni representative.
**Procedure:** Take SAT or ACT by January of 12th year. Visit college for interview by January of 12th year. Suggest filing application by December 1. Application deadline is February 1. Notification of admission on rolling basis. Reply is required by May 1. $150 nonrefundable tuition deposit. $50 nonrefundable room deposit. Freshmen accepted for terms other than fall.
**Special programs:** Admission may be deferred one year. Credit and/or placement may be granted through CEEB Advanced Placement exams. Credit may be granted through CLEP general and subject exams. Early entrance/early admission program.
**Transfer students:** Transfer students accepted for terms other than fall. Application deadline is June 1 for fall; December 1 for spring. Minimum 2.0 GPA required. Lowest course grade accepted is "C." At least 30 credits must be completed at the university to receive degree.
**Admissions contact:** William J. Munsey, M.Ed., Director of Admissions. 207 581-1561.

**FINANCIAL AID. Available aid:** Pell grants, SEOG, state scholarships and grants, school scholarships and grants, private scholarships and grants, ROTC scholarships, academic merit scholarships, athletic scholarships, and aid for undergraduate foreign students. Perkins Loans (NDSL), PLUS, Stafford Loans (GSL), school loans, private loans, and SLS. Deferred payment plan.
**Financial aid statistics:** 40% of aid is not need-based.
**Supporting data/closing dates:** FAFSA/FAF: Priority filing date is March 1. Income tax forms: Priority filing date is April 20. Notification of awards begins April 1.
**Financial aid contact:** Peggy Crawford, M.Ed., Director of Financial Aid. 207 581-1324.

**STUDENT EMPLOYMENT.** College Work/Study Program. Institutional employment. 25% of full-time undergraduates work on campus during school year. Students may expect to earn an average of $1,100 during school year. Off-campus part-time employment opportunities rated "good."

**COMPUTER FACILITIES.** 250 IBM/IBM-compatible and Macintosh/Apple microcomputers. Students may access IBM minicomputer/mainframe systems. Residence halls may be equipped with stand-alone microcomputers, networked microcomputers. Computer languages and software packages include Assembler, BASIC, COBOL, FORTRAN, Natural, NOMAD, Oracle, PL/1, SAS, SPSS. Computer facilities are available to all students.
**Fees:** $3 computer fee per semester.
**Hours:** 24 hours.

**GRADUATE CAREER DATA.** Highest graduate school enrollments: Boston Coll, Cornell U, Rensselaer Polytech Inst, U of Maine, U of Wisconsin. 65% of graduates choose careers in business and industry. Companies and businesses that hire graduates: Raytheon, Bath Iron Works, Liberty Mutual.

**PROMINENT ALUMNI/AE.** W.T. Grant, former undersecretary, U.S. Navy; Colby Chandler, CEO, Eastman Kodak; Stephanie Cole, vice president, New England Life Insurance; Stephen King, author; Bernard Lown, cardiologist and Nobel prize-winner.

# University of Maine at Augusta

**Augusta, ME 04330-9410** **207 621-3000**

**1994-95 Costs.** Tuition: $2,550 (state residents), $6,210 (out-of-state). Housing: None. Fees, books, misc. academic expenses (school's estimate): $635.
**Enrollment.** Undergraduates: 412 men, 525 women (full-time). Freshman class: 2,193 applicants, 1,692 accepted, 1,128 enrolled. Graduate enrollment: 5 men, 1 woman.
**Test score averages/ranges.** Average SAT scores: 390 verbal, 413 math. Range of SAT scores of middle 50%: 300-500 verbal, 300-500 math.
**Faculty.** 64 full-time; 108 part-time. 22% of faculty holds doctoral degree. Student/faculty ratio: 24 to 1.
**Selectivity rating.** Less competitive.

**PROFILE.** U Maine at Augusta, founded in 1965, is a public university. Programs are offered through the College of Arts and Sciences and the Divisions of Business and Governmental Science and Nursing Education. Its 165-acre campus is located in Augusta, 50 miles northeast of Portland.

**Accreditation:** NEASC. Professionally accredited by the American Medical Association (CAHEA), the National League for Nursing.
**Religious orientation:** University of Maine at Augusta is nonsectarian; no religious requirements.
**Library:** Collections totaling over 42,000 volumes, 800 periodical subscriptions and 400 microform items.
**Special facilities/museums:** Art gallery, interactive TV system.
**Athletic facilities:** Gymnasium, basketball and racquetball courts, weight room, athletic fields.

**STUDENT BODY. Undergraduate profile:** 99% are state residents. 26% are transfers. 1% Asian-American, 1% Black, 1% Hispanic, 97% White. Average age of undergraduates is 32.
**Freshman profile:** 1% of freshmen who took SAT scored 600 or over on verbal, 3% scored 600 or over on math; 13% scored 500 or over on verbal, 24% scored 500 or over on math; 46% scored 400 or over on verbal, 51% scored 400 or over on math; 84% scored 300 or over on verbal, 90% scored 300 or over on math. 40% of accepted applicants took SAT. 99% of freshmen come from public schools.
**Undergraduate achievement:** 60% of fall 1992 freshmen returned for fall 1993 term. 40% of entering class graduated.
**Foreign students:** 10 students are from out of the country. Countries represented include Canada, France, Lebanon, Mexico, the United Kingdom, and Uruguay; eight in all.

**PROGRAMS OF STUDY. Degrees:** B.A., B.Mus., B.S.
**Majors:** Business Administration, Jazz/Contemporary Music, Liberal Arts.
**Distribution of degrees:** The major with the highest enrollment is business administration; music has the lowest.
**Requirements:** General education requirement.
**Academic regulations:** Minimum 2.0 GPA required for graduation.
**Special:** Associate's degrees offered. Independent study. Pass/fail grading option. Internships. Cooperative education programs. Member of consortium with U of Maine system; exchange possible.
**Honors:** Honors program. Honor societies.
**Academic Assistance:** Remedial reading, writing, math, and study skills.

**ADMISSIONS. Academic basis for candidate selection** (in order of priority): Secondary school record, class rank.
**Requirements:** Graduation from secondary school is required; GED is accepted. No specific distribution of secondary school units required. Audition required of music program applicants. SAT is recommended. Campus visit recommended. No off-campus interviews.
**Procedure:** Take SAT or ACT by June 1 of 12th year. Notification of admission on rolling basis. Reply is required by May 1 or within two weeks of acceptance. $25 tuition deposit, refundable until May 1. Freshmen accepted for terms other than fall.
**Special programs:** Admission may be deferred one year. Credit may be granted through CEEB Advanced Placement for scores of 5 or higher. Credit may be granted through CLEP subject exams and DANTES exams. Credit and placement may be granted through challenge exams and military and life experience. Early decision program. In fall 1993, one applied for early decision and one was accepted. Deadline for applying for early decision is November 1. Early entrance/early admission program.
**Transfer students:** Transfer students accepted for terms other than fall. In fall 1993, 26% of all new students were transfers into all classes. 459 transfer applications were received, 352 were accepted. Application deadline is rolling for fall; rolling for spring. Minimum 2.0 GPA required. Lowest course grade accepted is "C." Maximum number of transferable credits is 45 semester hours from a two-year school and 90 semester hours from a four-year school. At least 27 semester hours must be completed at the university to receive degree.

**FINANCIAL AID. Available aid:** Pell grants, SEOG, Federal Nursing Student Scholarships, state grants, and school grants. Perkins Loans (NDSL), PLUS, Stafford Loans (GSL), NSL, and SLS. University payment plan.
**Financial aid statistics:** In 1993-94, 83% of all undergraduate applicants received aid; 82% of freshman applicants. Average amounts of aid awarded freshmen: Scholarships and grants, $2,400.

**Supporting data/closing dates:** Income tax forms: Priority filing date is April 1; accepted on rolling basis. Notification of awards on rolling basis.
**Financial aid contact:** Keith P. DuBois, M.P.A., Director of Financial Aid. 207 621-3165.

# University of Maine at Farmington

**Farmington, ME 04938** **207 778-7000**

**1994-95 Costs.** Tuition: $2,790 (state residents), $6,810 (out-of-state). Room & board: $4,070. Fees, books, misc. academic expenses (school's estimate): $690.
**Enrollment.** Undergraduates: 589 men, 1,287 women (full-time). Freshman class: 1,200 applicants, 840 accepted, 455 enrolled.
**Test score averages/ranges.** Average SAT scores: 447 verbal, 463 math.
**Faculty.** 114 full-time; 34 part-time. 73% of faculty holds doctoral degree. Student/faculty ratio: 16 to 1.
**Selectivity rating.** Less competitive.

**PROFILE.** U Maine at Farmington, founded in 1864, is a public university. Its 31-acre campus is located in Farmington, 30 miles northwest of Augusta.

**Accreditation:** NEASC. Professionally accredited by the National Council for Accreditation of Teacher Education.
**Religious orientation:** University of Maine at Farmington is nonsectarian; no religious requirements.
**Library:** Collections totaling over 106,877 volumes, 794 periodical subscriptions, and 52,201 microform items.
**Special facilities/museums:** Art gallery.
**Athletic facilities:** Gymnasium, track, swimming pool, weight room.

**STUDENT BODY. Undergraduate profile:** 89% are state residents; 6% are transfers. 99% White, 1% Other. Average age of undergraduates is 24.
**Freshman profile:** Majority of accepted applicants took SAT. 87% of freshmen come from public schools.
**Undergraduate achievement:** 70% of fall 1991 freshmen returned for fall 1992 term. 14% of students who completed a degree program immediately went on to graduate study.
**Foreign students:** 24 students are from out of the country. Countries represented include France, Gambia, India, Japan, Sri Lanka, and the former Yugoslav Republics; 18 in all.

**PROGRAMS OF STUDY. Degrees:** B.A., B.F.A., B.S.
**Majors:** Biology, Business/Economics, Community Health Education, Creative Writing, Early Childhood Education, Early Childhood Special Education, Economics/Business, Elementary Education, English, Environmental Sciences, General Studies, Geography, Geology/Chemistry, Geology/Geography, History, International Studies, Mathematics, Mathematics/Computer Science, Music/Arts, Political Science/Social Science, Psychology, Rehabilitation Services, School Health Education, Secondary Education, Sociology/Anthropology, Special Education, Theatre/Arts, Visual Arts/Performing Arts.
**Distribution of degrees:** The majors with the highest enrollment are elementary education, psychology, and community health education.
**Requirements:** General education requirement.
**Academic regulations:** Minimum 2.0 GPA must be maintained.
**Special:** Minors offered in many majors and in art, government, philosophy, and physics. French Immersion Program. Associate's degrees offered. Self-designed majors. Independent study. Pass/fail grading option. Internships. Graduate school at which undergraduates may take graduate-level courses. Preprofessional programs in law, medicine, veterinary science, and dentistry. Consortium Program with U of Maine at Augusta and Vocational Technical Institutes at Auburn and Waterville. Member of Southern Maine Admissions Consortium. Member of National Student Exchange (NSE). Teacher certification in elementary, secondary, and special education. Certification in specific subject areas. Exchange programs abroad in China (Beijing Polytech U), Denmark (U of Copenhagen), England (Oxford Polytech U), France, Ireland (U of Galway), and Scotland (Sterling U). Study abroad also in Canada.
**Honors:** Honors program. Honor societies.
**Academic Assistance:** Remedial reading, writing, math, and study skills. Nonremedial tutoring.

**STUDENT LIFE. Housing:** Students may live on or off campus. Coed and women's dorms. 39% of students live in college housing.
**Services and counseling/handicapped student services:** Placement services. Health service. Counseling services for older students. Birth control, personal, and psychological counseling. Career and academic guidance services. Physically disabled student services. Learning disabled services. Notetaking services. Tape recorders. Tutors. Reader services for the blind.
**Campus organizations:** Undergraduate student government. Student newspaper (Mainestream, published three times/month). Literary magazine. Yearbook. Radio station. Chorus, orchestra, band, dance and drama groups, Amnesty International, Women's Alliance for New Awareness, Gay and Straight People's Alliance, Commuter Council, Human Service Awareness, Literary Guild, Psychological Wednesday Society, Student Alcohol Educators, Environmental/Political Awareness, cheerleading, special-interest groups, 41 organizations in all.
**Religious organizations:** Intervarsity Christian Fellowship.
**Minority/foreign student organizations:** International Club.

**ATHLETICS. Physical education requirements:** One semester of physical education required.
**Intercollegiate competition:** 10% of students participate. Baseball (M), basketball (M,W), cheerleading (W), field hockey (W), golf (M), soccer (M,W), softball (W), volleyball (W). Member of Maine Association of Intercollegiate Athletics for Women, Maine Athletic Conference, NAIA.
**Intramural and club sports:** 20% of students participate. Intramural basketball, bowling, flag football, floor hockey, golf, ice hockey, indoor soccer, lacrosse, softball, ultimate frisbee, volleyball. Men's club ice hockey, lacrosse, rugby. Women's club lacrosse, rugby.

**ADMISSIONS. Academic basis for candidate selection** (in order of priority): Secondary school record, class rank, school's recommendation.
**Nonacademic basis for candidate selection:** Geographical distribution is emphasized. Extracurricular participation, particular talent or ability, and alumni/ae relationship are important. Character and personality are considered.
**Requirements:** Graduation from secondary school is required; GED is accepted. 14 units and the following program of study are required: 4 units of English, 3 units of math, 2 units of lab science, 2 units of foreign language, 1 unit of history. Rank in top half of secondary school class and minimum 2.0 GPA required. Program of Basic Studies for applicants not normally admissible. Campus visit and interview recommended. No off-campus interviews.
**Procedure:** Suggest filing application by December 15; no deadline. Notification of admission on rolling basis. Reply is required by May 1. $100 tuition deposit, refundable until May 1. $50 room deposit, refundable until May 1. Freshmen accepted for terms other than fall.
**Special programs:** Admission may be deferred one year. Credit may be granted through CEEB Advanced Placement for scores of 3 or higher. Credit may be granted through CLEP subject exams and military experience. Credit and placement may be granted through challenge exams. Early action program. Deadline for applying for early action is December 15. Early entrance/early admission program. Concurrent enrollment program.
**Transfer students:** Transfer students accepted for terms other than fall. In fall 1992, 6% of all new students were transfers into all classes. 319 transfer applications were received, 149 were accepted. Application deadline is rolling for fall; rolling for spring. Minimum 2.0 GPA required. Lowest course grade accepted is "C." Number of transferable credits is unlimited. At least 30 semester hours must be completed at the university to receive degree.
**Admissions contact:** J. Anthony McLaughlin, M.A.T., Director of Admissions. 207 778-7050.

**FINANCIAL AID. Available aid:** Pell grants, SEOG, state scholarships and grants, school scholarships and grants, private scholarships, academic merit scholarships, and aid for undergraduate foreign students. Native American scholarships and waivers. Perkins Loans (NDSL), PLUS, Stafford Loans (GSL), state loans, and SLS. AMS and deferred payment plan.
**Financial aid statistics:** 15% of aid is not need-based. In 1992-93, 65% of all undergraduate applicants received aid; 65% of freshman applicants. Average amounts of aid awarded freshmen: Scholarships and grants, $1,500; loans, $1,500.
**Supporting data/closing dates:** FAFSA: Priority filing date is February 15. FAF/FFS: Priority filing date is February 15; accepted on rolling basis. School's own aid application: Priority filing date is March 15; accepted on rolling basis. Income tax forms: Priority filing date is March 15; accepted on rolling basis. Notification of awards begins March 15.
**Financial aid contact:** Ronald P. Milliken, Director of Financial Aid. 207 778-7100.

**STUDENT EMPLOYMENT.** College Work/Study Program. Institutional employment. 25% of full-time undergraduates work on campus during school year. Students may expect to earn an average of $900 during school year. Off-campus part-time employment opportunities rated "fair."

**COMPUTER FACILITIES.** 105 IBM/IBM-compatible and Macintosh/Apple microcomputers; 70 are networked. Students may access IBM, SUN minicomputer/mainframe systems, BITNET, Internet. Computer languages and software packages include BASIC, C, FORTRAN, Pascal; 2,000 in all. Computer facilities are available to all students.
**Fees:** $60 computer fee per year.
**Hours:** 24 hours.

**GRADUATE CAREER DATA.** Graduate school percentages: 2% enter law school. 1% enter medical school. 1% enter dental school. 1% enter graduate business programs. 8% enter graduate arts and sciences programs. Highest graduate school enrollments: Syracuse U, U of Maine, U of New England, U of New Hampshire, U of Southern Maine. 25% of graduates choose careers in business and industry. Companies and businesses that hire graduates: Insurance, manufacturing, and technical companies.

**PROMINENT ALUMNI/AE.** Kirsten Scarcelli, CEO, Kirsten Scarcelli Co.; Melanie Arsenault, employee relations representative, L.L. Bean; Jane Chee, owner and CEO, Global Seafood.

# University of Maine at Fort Kent

**Fort Kent, ME 04743** **207 834-3162**

**1994-95 Costs.** Tuition: $2,610 (state residents), $6,360 (out-of-state). Room & board: $3,545. Fees, books, misc. academic expenses (school's estimate): $550.
**Enrollment.** Undergraduates: 207 men, 248 women (full-time). Freshman class: 202 applicants, 146 accepted, 93 enrolled.
**Test score averages/ranges.** Average SAT scores: 396 verbal, 438 math. Range of SAT scores of middle 50%: 340-460 verbal, 360-510 math.
**Faculty.** 32 full-time; 1 part-time. 56% of faculty holds doctoral degree. Student/faculty ratio: 14 to 1.
**Selectivity rating.** Competitive.

**PROFILE.** U Maine at Fort Kent, founded in 1878, is a public university. Its 52-acre campus is located in Fort Kent, in northern Maine.

**Accreditation:** NEASC. Professionally accredited by the National League for Nursing.
**Religious orientation:** University of Maine at Fort Kent is nonsectarian; no religious requirements.
**Library:** Collections totaling over 60,000 volumes, 300 periodical subscriptions, and 4,836 microform items.
**Special facilities/museums:** Acadian archives, interactive television center, biological park, greenhouse.

**Athletic facilities:** Weight room, racquetball courts, soccer and practice fields, arena, ski slope.

**STUDENT BODY. Undergraduate profile:** 76% are state residents; 52% are transfers. 1% Asian-American, 1% Black, 1% Native American, 97% White. Average age of undergraduates is 26.

**Freshman profile:** 1% of freshmen who took SAT scored 700 or over on math; 1% scored 600 or over on verbal, 3% scored 600 or over on math; 6% scored 500 or over on verbal, 11% scored 500 or over on math; 17% scored 400 or over on verbal, 19% scored 400 or over on math; 30% scored 300 or over on verbal, 31% scored 300 or over on math. 32% of accepted applicants took SAT. 100% of freshmen come from public schools.

**Undergraduate achievement:** 62% of fall 1992 freshmen returned for fall 1993 term. 35% of entering class graduated. 10% of students who completed a degree program immediately went on to graduate study.

**PROGRAMS OF STUDY. Degrees:** B.A., B.S., B.Univ.Studies.

**Majors:** Behavioral Science, Bilingual/Bicultural Studies, Biology, Business/Management, Computer Applications, Education, Elementary Education, English, Environmental Studies, French, History, Junior High Education, Mathematics/Science, Multidisciplinary Study, Nursing, Science, Social Sciences, University Studies.

**Distribution of degrees:** The majors with the highest enrollment are education, English, and behavioral science; bicultural studies and French have the lowest.

**Requirements:** General education requirement.

**Academic regulations:** Freshmen must maintain minimum 1.25 GPA; sophomores, 1.75 GPA; juniors, 2.00 GPA; seniors, 2.00 GPA.

**Special:** Minors offered in some majors and in art, computer science, mathematics, music, and theatre. Associate's degrees offered. Self-designed majors. Double majors. Independent study. Pass/fail grading option. Internships. Teacher certification in elementary education. Exchange program abroad in Canada (Centre U Saint-Louis Maillet). Study abroad also in several other countries.

**Honors:** Honors program. Honor societies.

**Academic Assistance:** Remedial reading, writing, math, and study skills. Nonremedial tutoring.

**ADMISSIONS. Academic basis for candidate selection** (in order of priority): Secondary school record, class rank, standardized test scores, school's recommendation, essay.

**Nonacademic basis for candidate selection:** Character and personality, extracurricular participation, and particular talent or ability are considered.

**Requirements:** Graduation from secondary school is required; GED is accepted. No specific distribution of secondary school units required. Minimum combined SAT score of 720, rank in top half of secondary school class, and minimum 2.0 GPA recommended. Conditional admission possible for applicants not meeting standard requirements. SAT is required; ACT may be substituted. Campus visit and interview recommended. No off-campus interviews.

**Procedure:** Application deadline is August 15. Notification of admission on rolling basis. Reply is required by May 1 or within 30 days of acceptance. $25 tuition deposit, refundable until May 1. $50 room deposit, refundable until May 1. Freshmen accepted for terms other than fall.

**Special programs:** Admission may be deferred. Credit and/or placement may be granted through CEEB Advanced Placement exams for scores of 3 or higher. Credit and/or placement may be granted through CLEP general and subject exams. Credit and placement may be granted through ACT PEP, DANTES, and challenge exams, and military and life experience. Early decision program. Deadline for applying for early decision is December 1. Early entrance/early admission program. Concurrent enrollment program.

**Transfer students:** Transfer students accepted for terms other than fall. In fall 1993, 52% of all new students were transfers into all classes. 180 transfer applications were received, 127 were accepted. Application deadline is August 15 for fall; January 4 for spring. Minimum 2.0 GPA recommended. Lowest course grade accepted is "D." At least 30 semester hours must be completed at the university to receive degree.

**Admissions contact:** Jerry Nadeau, Director of Admissions. 207 834-3162, extension 135.

**FINANCIAL AID. Available aid:** Pell grants, SEOG, state scholarships, school scholarships, and private scholarships. Perkins Loans (NDSL), PLUS, Stafford Loans (GSL), state loans, and SLS. AMS and EFI Fund Management.

**Financial aid statistics:** 5% of aid is not need-based. In 1993-94, 90% of all undergraduate applicants received aid; 90% of freshman applicants. Average amounts of aid awarded freshmen: Scholarships and grants, $2,350; loans, $1,100.

**Supporting data/closing dates:** FAFSA/FAF: Priority filing date is April 1. School's own aid application: Priority filing date is April 1. Income tax forms: Priority filing date is April 1. Notification of awards on rolling basis.

**Financial aid contact:** John Murphy, Acting Director of Financial Aid. 207 834-3162, extension 128.

# University of Maine at Machias

**Machias, ME 04654** — **207 255-3313**

**1993-94 Costs.** Tuition: $2,610 (state residents), $6,360 (out-of-state). Room & board: $3,560. Fees, books, misc. academic expenses (school's estimate): $775.

**Enrollment.** Undergraduates: 225 men, 408 women (full-time). Freshman class: 441 applicants, 369 accepted, 172 enrolled.

**Test score averages/ranges.** N/A.

**Faculty.** 39 full-time; 22 part-time. Student/faculty ratio: 16 to 1.

**Selectivity rating.** Less competitive.

**PROFILE.** U Maine at Machias, founded in 1909, is a public university. Its 42-acre campus is located in Machias, 60 miles north of Ellsworth.

**Accreditation:** NEASC. Professionally accredited by the National Recreation and Park Association.

**Religious orientation:** University of Maine at Machias is nonsectarian; no religious requirements.

**Library:** Collections totaling over 73,155 volumes, 455 periodical subscriptions, and 4,165 microform items.

**Athletic facilities:** Gymnasium, racquetball/handball courts, weight room, archery, wrestling facilities.

**STUDENT BODY. Undergraduate profile:** 76% are state residents; 40% are transfers. 1% Black, 2% Native American, 97% White. Average age of undergraduates is 21.

**Freshman profile:** 9% of freshmen who took SAT scored 600 or over on verbal, 11% scored 600 or over on math; 28% scored 500 or over on verbal, 28% scored 500 or over on math; 76% scored 400 or over on verbal, 79% scored 400 or over on math; 100% scored 300 or over on verbal, 100% scored 300 or over on math. 70% of accepted applicants took SAT. 98% of freshmen come from public schools.

**Undergraduate achievement:** 68% of fall 1992 freshmen returned for fall 1993 term.

**Foreign students:** 81 students are from out of the country. Countries represented include Canada, Central African Republic, Germany, Malawi, Nepal, and the United Kingdom; 16 in all.

**PROGRAMS OF STUDY. Degrees:** B.A., B.S.

**Majors:** Accounting, Behavioral Science, Biology, Business Administration, Business Teacher Education, Early Childhood Education, Elementary Education, English, Environmental Studies, History, Management, Marketing, Recreation Management, Secondary Education/Biology, Secondary Education/Business, Secondary Education/English, Secondary Education/History.

**Distribution of degrees:** The majors with the highest enrollment are business administration, elementary education, and recreation.

**Requirements:** General education requirement.

**Academic regulations:** Minimum 2.0 GPA required for graduation.

**Special:** Minors offered in some majors and in art, chemistry, computer applications, music, quantitative skills, real estate, and social science. Associate's degrees offered. Self-designed majors. Double majors. Independent study. Accelerated study. Internships. Cooperative education programs. 2-2 community health education program with U of Maine at Farmington. Member of Down East Consortium. Teacher certification in early childhood, elementary, and secondary education.

**Honors:** Honors program.

**Academic Assistance:** Nonremedial tutoring.

**ADMISSIONS. Academic basis for candidate selection** (in order of priority): Secondary school record, class rank, school's recommendation, standardized test scores, essay.

**Nonacademic basis for candidate selection:** Character and personality and particular talent or ability are important. Extracurricular participation is considered.

**Requirements:** Graduation from secondary school is required; GED is accepted. 4 units and the following program of study are required: 4 units of English. Minimum SAT scores of 450 in both verbal and math, rank in top half of secondary school class, and minimum 2.6 GPA required. SAT is required; ACT may be substituted. Campus visit and interview recommended. Off-campus interviews available with an admissions representative.

**Procedure:** Take SAT or ACT by June of 12th year. Suggest filing application by December; no deadline. Notification of admission on rolling basis. No set date by which applicants must accept offer. $25 tuition deposit, refundable until May 1. $75 room deposit, refundable until May 1. Freshmen accepted for terms other than fall.

**Special programs:** Admission may be deferred one year. Credit may be granted through CLEP subject exams and Regents College exams. Credit and placement may be granted through DANTES and challenge exams and military and life experience. Early entrance/early admission program. Concurrent enrollment program.

**Transfer students:** Transfer students accepted for terms other than fall. In fall 1993, 40% of all new students were transfers into all classes. Application deadline is rolling for fall; rolling for spring. Minimum 2.0 GPA required. Lowest course grade accepted is "C." At least 30 semester hours must be completed at the university to receive degree.

**Admissions contact:** Dave Baldwin, Director of Admissions. 207 255-3313, extensions 318, 339.

**FINANCIAL AID. Available aid:** Pell grants, SEOG, state scholarships and grants, private scholarships and grants, and academic merit scholarships. Perkins Loans (NDSL), PLUS, Stafford Loans (GSL), state loans, school loans, and SLS. AMS.

**Financial aid statistics:** In 1993-94, 65% of all undergraduate applicants received aid; 65% of freshman applicants. Average amounts of aid awarded freshmen: Scholarships and grants, $1,500; loans, $2,000.

**Supporting data/closing dates:** FAFSA: Accepted on rolling basis. FAF: Priority filing date is March 1; accepted on rolling basis. Income tax forms: Accepted on rolling basis. Notification of awards on rolling basis.

**Financial aid contact:** Stephanie Armstrong, Director of Financial Aid. 207 255-3313, extension 203.

# University of Maine at Presque Isle

**Presque Isle, ME 04769** — **207 764-0311**

**1993-94 Costs.** Tuition: $2,610 (state residents), $6,360 (out-of-state). Room & board: $3,494. Fees, books, misc. academic expenses (school's estimate): $650.

**Enrollment.** Undergraduates: 430 men, 544 women (full-time). Freshman class: 523 applicants, 378 accepted, 234 enrolled.

**Test score averages/ranges.** Average SAT scores: 812 combined.

**Faculty.** 67 full-time; 37 part-time. Student/faculty ratio: 13 to 1.

**Selectivity rating.** Less competitive.

**PROFILE.** U Maine Presque Isle, founded in 1903, is a public, comprehensive university. Programs are offered through the Divisions of Education/Health, Physical Education, and Recreation; Humanities; Mathematics-Science; and Social Science. Its 150-acre campus is located in Presque Isle, north of Bangor.

**Accreditation:** NEASC.
**Religious orientation:** University of Maine at Presque Isle is nonsectarian; no religious requirements.
**Library:** Collections totaling over 116,700 volumes, 930 periodical subscriptions, and 4,200 microform items.
**Special facilities/museums:** Natural history museum, language lab, interactive TV.
**Athletic facilities:** Gymnasiums, weight room, aerobics studio, basketball and tennis courts, wrestling room, athletic fields.

**STUDENT BODY. Undergraduate profile:** 97% are state residents; 40% are transfers. 2% Black, 89% White, 9% Other. Average age of undergraduates is 28.
**Freshman profile:** Majority of accepted applicants took SAT. 97% of freshmen come from public schools.
**Undergraduate achievement:** 60% of fall 1992 freshmen returned for fall 1993 term. 60% of entering class graduated.
**Foreign students:** 261 students are from out of the country. Countries represented include Australia, Canada, Japan, Napal, Sweden, and the former Yugoslav Republics.

**PROGRAMS OF STUDY. Degrees:** B.A., B.F.A., B.Lib.Studies, B.S., B.Soc.Work.
**Majors:** Accounting, Art, Athletic Training, Behavioral Science, Biology, Business/Management, Criminal Justice, Elementary Education, English, Environmental Studies, French, Geological/Environmental Science, Health Education, Health/Physical Education/Recreation, History, Humanities, Industrial Technology, Mathematics, Park Law, Parks/Recreation, Political Science/Government, Psychology, Recreation/Leisure Services, Secondary Education, Social Sciences, Social Work, Sociology, Speech Communication.
**Distribution of degrees:** The majors with the highest enrollment are education, business, and behavioral science; industrial technology, political science, and English/speech have the lowest.
**Requirements:** General education requirement.
**Academic regulations:** Freshmen must maintain minimum 1.6 GPA; sophomores, 1.8 GPA; juniors, 2.0 GPA; seniors, 2.0 GPA.
**Special:** Minors offered in most majors and in geology, music, Soviet area studies, and teaching exceptional children. Associate's degrees offered. Self-designed majors. Double majors. Independent study. Accelerated study. Pass/fail grading option. Internships. Graduate school at which undergraduates may take graduate-level courses. Two-year transfer programs with U of Maine in agricultural mechanization, animal/veterinary science, biology, child development, engineering, food/nutrition, forest engineering, forest management, geology, plant/soil science, and wildlife management. Two-year transfer program with U of Southern Maine in nursing. Teacher certification in early childhood, elementary, and secondary education. Member of New England/Quebec Student Exchange Program. Study abroad in England, France, and Ireland.
**Honors:** Honors program.
**Academic Assistance:** Remedial reading, writing, and math. Nonremedial tutoring.

**ADMISSIONS. Academic basis for candidate selection** (in order of priority): Secondary school record, class rank, school's recommendation, essay, standardized test scores.
**Nonacademic basis for candidate selection:** Character and personality are important. Extracurricular participation is considered.
**Requirements:** Graduation from secondary school is required; GED is accepted. No specific distribution of secondary school units required. Rank in top half of secondary school class required; minimum combined SAT score of 850 and minimum 2.0 GPA recommended. Conditional admission possible for applicants not meeting standard requirements. SAT is required. PSAT is recommended. ACH recommended. Campus visit and interview recommended. Off-campus interviews available with an admissions representative.
**Procedure:** Application deadline is August 19. Notification of admission on rolling basis. Reply is required by May 1. $50 tuition deposit, refundable until May 1. $50 nonrefundable room deposit. Freshmen accepted for terms other than fall.
**Special programs:** Admission may be deferred one year. Credit and/or placement may be granted through CEEB Advanced Placement exams for scores of 4 or higher. Credit may be granted through CLEP general and subject exams. Credit and placement may be granted through ACT PEP, DANTES, and challenge exams and military and life experience. Early decision program.
**Transfer students:** Transfer students accepted for terms other than fall. In fall 1993, 40% of all new students were transfers into all classes. 249 transfer applications were received, 191 were accepted. Application deadline is August 6 for fall; January 8 for spring. Minimum 2.0 GPA required. Lowest course grade accepted is "C-." Maximum number of transferable credits is 90 semester hours. At least 30 semester hours must be completed at the university to receive degree.
**Admissions contact:** Gerald K. Wuori, Ph.D., Director of Admissions. 207 764-0311, extension 385.

**FINANCIAL AID. Available aid:** Pell grants, SEOG, state scholarships and grants, school scholarships, private scholarships, academic merit scholarships, and athletic scholarships. Perkins Loans (NDSL), PLUS, Stafford Loans (GSL), state loans, and school loans. AMS.
**Financial aid statistics:** In 1993-94, 80% of all undergraduate applicants received aid. Average amounts of aid awarded freshmen: Scholarships and grants, $3,264; loans, $800.
**Supporting data/closing dates:** FAFSA/FAF: Accepted on rolling basis. School's own aid application: Accepted on rolling basis. Income tax forms: Accepted on rolling basis. W-2: Accepted on rolling basis. Notification of awards on rolling basis.
**Financial aid contact:** Barbara Bridges, Director of Financial Aid. 207 764-0311, extension 212.

# University of New England

**Biddeford, ME 04005** **207 283-0171**

**1993-94 Costs.** Tuition: $10,700. Room & board: $4,850. Fees, books, misc. academic expenses (school's estimate): $1,000.
**Enrollment.** Undergraduates: 238 men, 582 women (full-time). Freshman class: 978 applicants, 833 accepted, 314 enrolled. Graduate enrollment: 288 men, 322 women.
**Test score averages/ranges.** Average SAT scores: 430 verbal, 460 math. Range of SAT scores of middle 50%: 370-470 verbal, 410-530 math.
**Faculty.** 73 full-time; 36 part-time. 75% of faculty holds doctoral degree. Student/faculty ratio: 14 to 1.
**Selectivity rating.** Competitive.

**PROFILE.** The University of New England, founded in 1939, is a private, liberal arts institution. Programs are offered through the Colleges of Arts and Sciences and Osteopathic Medicine. Its 120-acre campus is located in Biddeford, 18 miles south of Portland.

**Accreditation:** NEASC. Professionally accredited by the American Osteopathic Association, the American Physical Therapy Association, the National League for Nursing.
**Religious orientation:** University of New England is nonsectarian; no religious requirements.
**Library:** Collections totaling over 94,000 volumes, 750 periodical subscriptions, and 6,500 microform items.
**Special facilities/museums:** Community medical clinic.
**Athletic facilities:** Indoor track, gymnasium, racquetball courts, swimming pool, weight room, lacrosse, soccer, and softball fields.

**STUDENT BODY. Undergraduate profile:** 50% are state residents; 17% are transfers. 1% Asian-American, 1% Black, 98% White. Average age of undergraduates is 22.
**Freshman profile:** 1% of freshmen who took SAT scored 700 or over on math; 3% scored 600 or over on verbal, 9% scored 600 or over on math; 20% scored 500 or over on verbal, 38% scored 500 or over on math; 62% scored 400 or over on verbal, 75% scored 400 or over on math; 99% scored 300 or over on verbal, 98% scored 300 or over on math. 88% of accepted applicants took SAT.
**Undergraduate achievement:** 77% of fall 1992 freshmen returned for fall 1993 term. 58% of entering class graduated.
**Foreign students:** Four students are from out of the country. Countries represented include Canada, Japan, and Mexico.

**PROGRAMS OF STUDY. Degrees:** B.A., B.S.
**Majors:** Biology, Business Management, Education, Elementary Education, Environmental Science/Studies, Health Services Management, Laboratory Science, Liberal Studies, Marine Biology, Medical Biology, Medical Technology, Occupational Therapy, Physical Therapy, Pre-Pharmacy, Psychology, Science Education, Sports/Fitness Management.
**Distribution of degrees:** The majors with the highest enrollment are physical therapy, occupational therapy, and medical biology; medical technology, health services management, and liberal studies have the lowest.
**Requirements:** General education requirement.
**Academic regulations:** Freshmen must maintain minimum 1.7 GPA; sophomores, 1.8 GPA; juniors, 1.9 GPA; seniors, 2.0 GPA.
**Special:** Minors offered in most majors. Associate's degrees offered. Self-designed majors. Double majors. Independent study. Internships. Graduate school at which undergraduates may take graduate-level courses. Preprofessional programs in medicine, veterinary science, and dentistry. 3-4 medical program. 2-3 pharmacy program with Massachusetts Coll of Pharmacy. Member of Southern Maine Admissions Consortium. Teacher certification in elementary and secondary education. Study abroad possible.
**Honors:** Honor societies.
**Academic Assistance:** Remedial reading, writing, math, and study skills. Nonremedial tutoring.

**ADMISSIONS. Academic basis for candidate selection** (in order of priority): Secondary school record, school's recommendation, class rank, standardized test scores.
**Nonacademic basis for candidate selection:** Character and personality, extracurricular participation, and particular talent or ability are important. Geographical distribution and alumni/ae relationship are considered.
**Requirements:** Graduation from secondary school is required; GED is accepted. 18 units and the following program of study are recommended: 3 units of science, 2 units of foreign language, 3 units of social studies, 3 units of history. Conditional admission possible for applicants not meeting standard requirements. SAT is required; ACT may be substituted. Campus visit and interview recommended. Off-campus interviews available with an admissions representative.
**Procedure:** Take SAT or ACT by December of 12th year. Visit college for interview by March of 12th year. Notification of admission on rolling basis. Reply is required by May 1. $100 tuition deposit, refundable until May 1. $50 nonrefundable room deposit. Freshmen accepted for terms other than fall.
**Special programs:** Admission may be deferred one year. Credit may be granted through CEEB Advanced Placement for scores of 3 or higher. Credit may be granted through CLEP general and subject exams, and challenge exams. Early decision program. Deadline for applying for early decision is November 15. Early entrance/early admission program. Concurrent enrollment program.
**Transfer students:** Transfer students accepted for terms other than fall. In fall 1993, 17% of all new students were transfers into all classes. 80 transfer applications were received, 62 were accepted. Application deadline is rolling for fall; rolling for spring. Minimum 2.5 GPA recommended. Lowest course grade accepted is "C." Maximum number of transferable credits is 66 semester hours from a two-year school and 96 semester hours from a four-year school.

**Admissions contact:** Patricia Cribby, Dean of Admissions and Enrollment Management. 207 283-0171, extension 297.

**FINANCIAL AID. Available aid:** Pell grants, SEOG, state scholarships and grants, school scholarships and grants, private scholarships and grants, ROTC scholarships, academic merit scholarships, and athletic scholarships. Perkins Loans (NDSL), PLUS, Stafford Loans (GSL), NSL, state loans, school loans, private loans, and SLS. Tuition Plan Inc., AMS, and Tuition Management Systems.

**Financial aid statistics:** 30% of aid is not need-based. In 1993-94, 88% of all undergraduate applicants received aid; 85% of freshman applicants. Average amounts of aid awarded freshmen: Scholarships and grants, $1,250; loans, $4,125.

**Supporting data/closing dates:** FAFSA: Priority filing date is April 1. Notification of awards on rolling basis.

**Financial aid contact:** Daniel Pinch, Director of Financial Aid. 207 283-0171, extension 342.

# University of Southern Maine

**Portland, ME 04103 — 207 780-4141**

**1993-94 Costs.** Tuition: $2,880 (state residents), $8,160 (out-of-state). Room & board: $4,219. Fees, books, misc. academic expenses (school's estimate): $700.

**Enrollment.** Undergraduates: 2,145 men, 2,689 women (full-time). Freshman class: 2,358 applicants, 1,814 accepted, 889 enrolled. Graduate enrollment: 581 men, 1,205 women.

**Test score averages/ranges.** Average SAT scores: 456 verbal, 501 math. Range of SAT scores of middle 50%: 410-510 verbal, 440-550 math.

**Faculty.** 329 full-time; 245 part-time. Student/faculty ratio: 15 to 1.

**Selectivity rating.** Less competitive.

**PROFILE.** The University of Southern Maine, founded in 1878, is a public, comprehensive institution. Programs are offered through the College of Arts and Sciences and the Schools of Applied Science, Business and Economics, and Nursing. Its 120-acre campus is located in Portland, 50 miles north of Portsmouth, N.H.

**Accreditation:** NEASC. Professionally accredited by the Council on Social Work Education, the National Association of Schools of Art and Design, the National Association of Schools of Music, the National Council for Accreditation of Teacher Education, the National League for Nursing.

**Religious orientation:** University of Southern Maine is nonsectarian; no religious requirements.

**Library:** Collections totaling over 335,618 volumes, 2,475 periodical subscriptions, and 915,216 microform items.

**Special facilities/museums:** Art gallery, anthropology museum, language and writing labs, planetarium.

**Athletic facilities:** Gymnasiums, weight rooms, basketball, racquetball, squash, and tennis courts, cross-country ski trails, baseball, field hockey, soccer, and softball fields, track.

**STUDENT BODY. Undergraduate profile:** 94% are state residents; 47% are transfers. 99% White, 1% Other. Average age of undergraduates is 21.

**Freshman profile:** 1% of freshmen who took SAT scored 700 or over on verbal, 1% scored 700 or over on math; 4% scored 600 or over on verbal, 13% scored 600 or over on math; 26% scored 500 or over on verbal, 50% scored 500 or over on math; 81% scored 400 or over on verbal, 92% scored 400 or over on math; 100% scored 300 or over on verbal, 100% scored 300 or over on math. 92% of accepted applicants took SAT.

**Foreign students:** 54 students are from out of the country. Countries represented include China, European countries, India, Japan, and South American countries; 25 in all.

**PROGRAMS OF STUDY. Degrees:** B.A., B.F.A., B.Mus., B.S.

**Majors:** Accounting, Applied Chemistry, Art, Biology, Business Administration, Chemistry, Communication, Computer Science, Criminology, Economics, Electrical Engineering, English, French, Geography/Anthropology, Geology, History, Industrial Technology, Industry/Technology, Linguistics, Management/Organizational Studies, Mathematics, Music, Music Education, Music Performance, Nursing, Philosophy, Physics, Political Science, Psychology, Self-Designed Major, Social/Behavioral Sciences, Social Work, Sociology, Technology Education, Theatre, Therapeutic Recreation, Vocational/Occupational Education, Vocational Technology, Women's Studies.

**Distribution of degrees:** The majors with the highest enrollment are business administration, psychology, and criminology; computer science, mathematics, and physical sciences have the lowest.

**Requirements:** General education requirement.

**Academic regulations:** Freshmen must maintain minimum 1.70 GPA; sophomores, 1.80 GPA; juniors, 1.90 GPA; seniors, 2.00 GPA.

**Special:** Minors offered in many majors and in art history, classics, German, and Spanish. Associate's degrees offered. Self-designed majors. Double majors. Independent study. Pass/fail grading option. Internships. Graduate school at which undergraduates may take graduate-level courses. Preprofessional programs in medicine, veterinary science, and dentistry. One-year engineering program leads to transfer to U of Maine; two-year transfer program in engineering physics. Member of Southern Maine Admissions Consortium. Washington Semester. Member of National Student Exchange (NSE). Teacher certification in vo-tech education. Exchange programs abroad in England, France, Ireland, and the Netherlands. ROTC at U of New Hampshire.

**Honors:** Honors program. Honor societies.

**Academic Assistance:** Remedial reading, writing, math, and study skills. Nonremedial tutoring.

**STUDENT LIFE. Housing:** Students may live on or off campus. Coed dorms. 14% of students live in college housing.

**Social atmosphere:** The student newspaper reports, "Students on the Portland campus are largely nontraditional, ranging in age from mid-twenties on up. The popular gathering spots are the bars in the Old Port. Students on the Gorham campus are dorm rats, and they hang out at frat parties." The university has a large population of commuter students who tend not to participate in campus activities. In the Old Port district of Portland, students frequent Dewey's, Moose Alley, Squire Morgan's, and Hu Shang's. Near campus, the Rustic is a popular spot.

**Services and counseling/handicapped student services:** Health service. Women's center. Day care. Counseling services for minority, military, veteran, and older students. Birth control, personal, and psychological counseling. Career and academic guidance services. Religious counseling. Physically disabled student services. Learning disabled services. Notetaking services. Tape recorders. Tutors. Reader services for the blind.

**Campus organizations:** Undergraduate student government. Student newspaper (Free Press, published once/week). Radio and TV stations. Chamber singers, chorale, chamber orchestra, jazz ensemble, wind ensemble, concert band, performing arts ensemble, films committee, outing and ski clubs, public interest group, Women's Forum, Gay and Lesbian Alliance, academic, athletic, and special-interest groups, 66 organizations in all. Six fraternities, four chapter houses; four sororities, no chapter houses.

**Religious organizations:** Latter-Day Saints Student Association, Campus Ministry, Intervarsity Christian Fellowship.

**Minority/foreign student organizations:** Minority Student Affairs. International Student Organization.

**ATHLETICS. Physical education requirements:** None.

**Intercollegiate competition:** 3% of students participate. Baseball (M), basketball (M,W), cross-country (M,W), field hockey (W), ice hockey (M), soccer (M,W), softball (W), tennis (M,W), track (indoor) (W), track (outdoor) (W). Member of ECAC, Little East Conference, Maine Association of Intercollegiate Athletics for Women, NCAA Division III.

**Intramural and club sports:** 8% of students participate. Intramural basketball, flag football, soccer, softball, volleyball, walleyball. Men's club lacrosse.

**ADMISSIONS. Academic basis for candidate selection** (in order of priority): Secondary school record, standardized test scores, class rank, essay, school's recommendation.

**Nonacademic basis for candidate selection:** Character and personality are emphasized. Particular talent or ability is important. Extracurricular participation is considered.

**Requirements:** Graduation from secondary school is required; GED is accepted. 13 units and the following program of study are required: 4 units of English, 3 units of math, 2 units of lab science, 2 units of foreign language, 2 units of social studies. 4 units of math required of math applicants. 3 units of foreign language required of language program applicants; optional in Schools of Applied Science, Business, and Nursing. 3 units of lab science required of biology and pre-medicine program applicants. Courses in art, industrial arts/technology, and music recommended of applicants to each of those programs. Interviews required of industrial technology program applicants. Audition required of music program applicants. Conditional admission possible for applicants not meeting standard requirements. SAT is required; ACT may be substituted. Campus visit and interview recommended. No off-campus interviews.

**Procedure:** Take SAT or ACT by November of 12th year. Suggest filing application by February 1. Application deadline is July 15. Notification of admission on rolling basis. Reply is required by May 1. $100 tuition deposit, refundable until May 1. $75 room deposit, refundable until May 1. Freshmen accepted for terms other than fall.

**Special programs:** Credit may be granted through CEEB Advanced Placement for scores of 3 or higher. Credit may be granted through CLEP general and subject exams, DANTES exams, and military and life experience. Credit and placement may be granted through challenge exams. Early entrance/early admission program. Concurrent enrollment program.

**Transfer students:** Transfer students accepted for terms other than fall. In fall 1992, 47% of all new students were transfers into all classes. 1,397 transfer applications were received, 1,107 were accepted. Application deadline is July 15 for fall; November 15 for spring. Minimum 2.0 GPA required. Lowest course grade accepted is "C-." At least 30 semester hours must be completed at the university to receive degree.

**Admissions contact:** Dan Palubniak, M.Ed., Director of Admissions. 207 780-5670.

**FINANCIAL AID. Available aid:** Pell grants, SEOG, state scholarships, school scholarships, private scholarships and grants, and academic merit scholarships. Perkins Loans (NDSL), PLUS, Stafford Loans (GSL), NSL, school loans, private loans, and SLS.

**Financial aid statistics:** In 1992-93, 65% of all undergraduate applicants received aid; 64% of freshman applicants. Average amounts of aid awarded freshmen: Scholarships and grants, $2,400; loans, $2,250.

**Supporting data/closing dates:** FAFSA/FAF: Priority filing date is March 1. Income tax forms: Priority filing date is March 30. Notification of awards on rolling basis.

**Financial aid contact:** Susan M. Roberts, M.S., Special Assistant to the Vice President for Student Affairs. 207 780-5250.

**STUDENT EMPLOYMENT.** College Work/Study Program. Institutional employment. 20% of full-time undergraduates work on campus during school year. Students may expect to earn an average of $1,500 during school year. Off-campus part-time employment opportunities rated "good."

**COMPUTER FACILITIES.** 250 IBM/IBM-compatible and Macintosh/Apple microcomputers; all are networked. Students may access Digital, IBM minicomputer/mainframe systems, BITNET, Internet. Residence halls may be equipped with networked microcomputers. Computer languages and software packages include BASIC, C, COBOL, FORTRAN, LISP, R:BASE, Smart, Systat, Turbo Pascal, WordStar. Computer facilities are available to all students.

**Fees:** None.

**Hours:** 7:30 AM-1 AM.

# Westbrook College

**Portland, ME 04103** 207 797-7261

**1993-94 Costs.** Tuition: $11,000. Room & board: $4,900. Fees, books, misc. academic expenses (school's estimate): $550.
**Enrollment.** Undergraduates: 54 men, 246 women (full-time). Freshman class: 249 applicants, 181 accepted, 72 enrolled.
**Test score averages/ranges.** Average SAT scores: 406 verbal, 438 math. Range of SAT scores of middle 50%: 800-950 combined. Average ACT scores: 22 composite.
**Faculty.** 33 full-time; 15 part-time. 40% of faculty holds highest degree in specific field. Student/faculty ratio: 10 to 1.
**Selectivity rating.** Competitive.

**PROFILE.** Westbrook is a private college. Founded in 1831, it became coeducational in 1973. Its 50-acre campus is located in a residential section of Portland.

**Accreditation:** NEASC. Professionally accredited by the American Dental Association, the National League for Nursing.
**Religious orientation:** Westbrook College is nonsectarian; no religious requirements.
**Library:** Collections totaling over 53,271 volumes, 596 periodical subscriptions, and 2,310 microform items.
**Special facilities/museums:** Art gallery, preschool lab center, dental hygiene clinic.
**Athletic facilities:** Gymnasium, field house, basketball and tennis courts, dance and weight rooms, athletic field.

**STUDENT BODY. Undergraduate profile:** 72% are state residents; 36% are transfers. 1% Asian-American, .3% Black, .3% Hispanic, 98% White, .4% Other. Average age of undergraduates is 20.
**Freshman profile:** 1% of freshmen who took SAT scored 700 or over on verbal; 1% scored 600 or over on math; 5% scored 500 or over on verbal, 12% scored 500 or over on math; 32% scored 400 or over on verbal, 51% scored 400 or over on math; 68% scored 300 or over on verbal, 73% scored 300 or over on math. 77% of accepted applicants took SAT.
**Undergraduate achievement:** 65% of fall 1992 freshmen returned for fall 1993 term.
**Foreign students:** Nine students are from out of the country. Countries represented include Canada.

**PROGRAMS OF STUDY. Degrees:** B.A., B.S.
**Majors:** American Studies, Business Management, Dental Hygiene, Early Childhood Education, English, Human Development, Individualized Major, Medical Technology, Nursing, Psychology.
**Distribution of degrees:** The majors with the highest enrollment are business management, nursing, and medical technology; dental hygiene have the lowest.
**Requirements:** General education requirement.
**Academic regulations:** Freshmen must maintain minimum 1.90 GPA; sophomores, juniors, seniors, 2.00 GPA.
**Special:** Minors offered in some majors and in health science and individualized career focus. Associate's degrees offered. Self-designed majors. Internships. Cooperative education programs. Preprofessional programs in law, medicine, and dentistry.
**Honors:** Honors program. Honor societies.
**Academic Assistance:** Remedial reading, writing, math, and study skills. Nonremedial tutoring.

**ADMISSIONS. Academic basis for candidate selection** (in order of priority): Secondary school record, class rank, standardized test scores, essay, school's recommendation.
**Nonacademic basis for candidate selection:** Character and personality and extracurricular participation are important. Particular talent or ability, geographical distribution, and alumni/ae relationship are considered.
**Requirements:** Graduation from secondary school is required; GED is accepted. 12 units and the following program of study are required: 4 units of English, 3 units of math, 2 units of science including 1 unit of lab, 1 unit of social studies, 1 unit of history, 1 unit of academic electives. Minimum combined SAT score of 800, rank in top third of secondary school class, and minimum 2.5 GPA recommended. 2 years of college-preparatory biology and chemistry (both with lab) and math required of health sciences program applicants. Conditional admission possible for applicants not meeting standard requirements. Campus visit and interview recommended. Off-campus interviews available with admissions and alumni representatives.
**Procedure:** Take SAT or ACT by November of 12th year. Visit college for interview by April of 12th year. Suggest filing application by February 1. Application deadline is August 1. Notification of admission on rolling basis. Reply is required by May. $100 tuition deposit, refundable until May $50 room deposit, refundable until May. Freshmen accepted for terms other than fall.
**Special programs:** Admission may be deferred one year. Credit may be granted through CEEB Advanced Placement for scores of 3 or higher. Credit may be granted through CLEP subject exams, DANTES and challenge exams. Early entrance/early admission program.
**Transfer students:** Transfer students accepted for terms other than fall. In fall 1993, 36% of all new students were transfers into all classes. 92 transfer applications were received, 74 were accepted. Application deadline is August for fall; December for spring. Minimum 2.5 GPA recommended. Lowest course grade accepted is "C." Maximum number of transferable credits is 60 semester hours. At least 60 semester hours must be completed at the college to receive degree.
**Admissions contact:** David D. Anthony, M.A., Director of Admissions. 207 797-7261, extension 225.

**FINANCIAL AID. Available aid:** Pell grants, SEOG, state scholarships and grants, and school scholarships and grants. Perkins Loans (NDSL), PLUS, Stafford Loans (GSL), NSL, and SLS. Knight Tuition Plans, AMS, and Tuition Management Systems.
**Financial aid statistics:** In 1993-94, 95% of all undergraduate applicants received aid; 94% of freshman applicants. Average amounts of aid awarded freshmen: Scholarships and grants, $4,100; loans, $3,200.
**Supporting data/closing dates:** FAFSA/FAF: Priority filing date is March 15. School's own aid application: Priority filing date is May 1. State aid form: Priority filing date is May 1. Income tax forms: Priority filing date is May 1. Notification of awards on rolling basis.
**Financial aid contact:** Lisa Connor, Director of Financial Aid. 207 797-7261, extension 216.

# Maryland

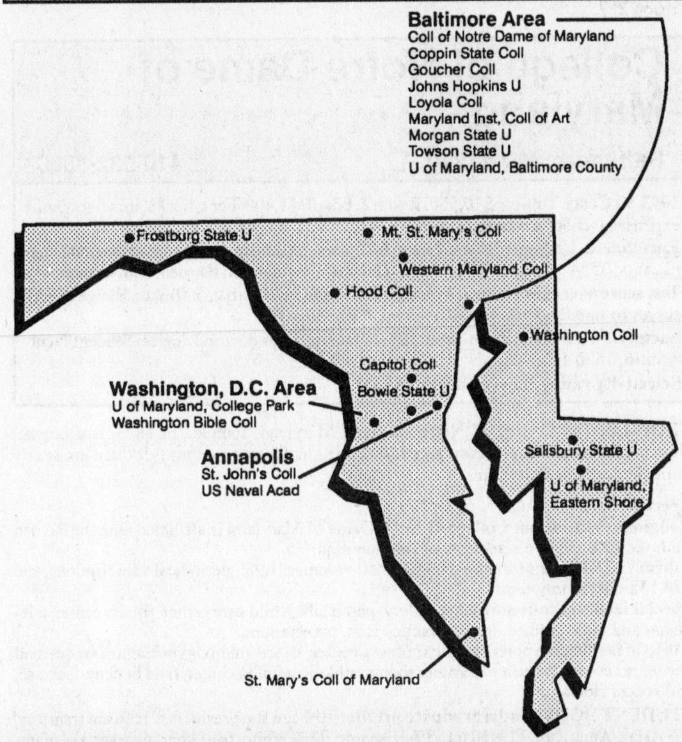


## Bowie State University

**Bowie, MD 20715** 301 464-3000

**1993-94 Costs.** Tuition: $2,736 (state residents), $5,128 (out-of-state). Room & board: $3,818. Fees, books, misc. academic expenses (school's estimate): $1,234.
**Enrollment.** Undergraduates: 890 men, 1,289 women (full-time). Freshman class: 1,732 applicants, 902 accepted, 414 enrolled. Graduate enrollment: 625 men, 1,053 women.
**Test score averages/ranges.** Average SAT scores: 355 verbal, 376 math.
**Faculty.** 126 full-time; 93 part-time. Student/faculty ratio: 22 to 1.
**Selectivity rating.** Less competitive.

**PROFILE.** Bowie State, founded in 1865, is a public university of liberal arts and technology studies. Programs are offered through the Departments of Behavioral Sciences and Human Services; Business, Economics, and Public Administration; Communications; Education and Physical Education; History, Politics, and International Studies; Humanities and Fine Arts; Military Science; Natural Sciences, Mathematics, and Computer Science; and Nursing. Its 267-acre campus is located in Bowie, 22 miles from Washington, D.C.

**Accreditation:** MSACS. Professionally accredited by the Council on Social Work Education, the National Council for Accreditation of Teacher Education.
**Religious orientation:** Bowie State University is nonsectarian; no religious requirements.
**Library:** Collections totaling over 255,282 volumes, 1,287 periodical subscriptions, and 598,007 microform items.
**Special facilities/museums:** Science and math labs with state-of-the-art equipment, computer academy.
**Athletic facilities:** Gymnasium, fitness, Universal, and weight rooms, swimming pool, basketball, racquetball, and volleyball courts, baseball, soccer, and softball fields, track.

**STUDENT BODY. Undergraduate profile:** 86% are state residents. 1% Asian-American, 78% Black, 1% Hispanic, 17% White, 3% Other. Average age of undergraduates is 22.
**Freshman profile:** 2% of freshmen who took SAT scored 600 or over on math; 1% scored 500 or over on verbal, 6% scored 500 or over on math; 22% scored 400 or over on verbal, 40% scored 400 or over on math; 84% scored 300 or over on verbal, 95% scored 300 or over on math. 92% of accepted applicants took SAT.
**Undergraduate achievement:** 70% of fall 1992 freshmen returned for fall 1993 term.
**Foreign students:** 49 students are from out of the country. Countries represented include Cameroon, China, India, and Nigeria; 48 in all.

**PROGRAMS OF STUDY. Degrees:** B.A., B.S., B.S.Ed., B.S.Nurs.
**Majors:** Biology, Business Administration, Communications Media, Computer Science, Early Childhood, Elementary Education, Engineering, English, English Education, History, History Education, International Studies, Mathematics, Mathematics Education, Nursing, Political Science, Psychology, Science Education, Social Work Education, Sociology/Anthropology, Technology.
**Distribution of degrees:** The majors with the highest enrollment are business administration, communications media, and elementary education; science education has the lowest.
**Requirements:** General education requirement.
**Academic regulations:** Freshmen must maintain minimum 1.7 GPA; sophomores, 1.9 GPA; juniors, 2.0 GPA; seniors, 2,0 GPA.
**Special:** Minors offered in some majors and in approximately 15 other fields including Hispanic culture and literature of the Third World. Double majors. Dual degrees. Independent study. Pass/fail grading option. Internships. Cooperative education programs. Preprofessional programs in law, medicine, and dentistry. Dual-degree programs in dentistry with Maryland Dental Sch and in engineering with George Washington U, Morgan State U, and U of Maryland at College Park. Teacher certification in early childhood, elementary, secondary, and special education. Certification in specific subject areas. ROTC. AFROTC at U of Maryland at College Park.
**Honors:** Phi Beta Kappa. Honors program. Honor societies.
**Academic Assistance:** Remedial reading, writing, math, and study skills. Nonremedial tutoring.

**STUDENT LIFE. Housing:** Students may live on or off campus. Women's and men's dorms. School-owned/operated apartments. 18% of students live in college housing.
**Social atmosphere:** According to the student newspaper, "Bowie State has an extremely friendly, small, family-like atmosphere which has numerous cultural events and monthly speakers." Popular gathering spots for students include the Wiseman College Center, the Thurgood Marshall Library, Chapter Three Nightclub, and Baltimore Harbor. Greeks, Good Brothers, and Public Relations Student Society are influential organizations on campus. Homecoming, the Coronation of Miss BSU, and Bowiefest are among the year's favorite events.
**Services and counseling/handicapped student services:** Placement services. Health service. Counseling services for minority, military, veteran, and older students. Birth control, personal, and psychological counseling. Career and academic guidance services. Religious counseling. Learning disabled services.
**Campus organizations:** Undergraduate student government. Student newspaper (Spectrum, published four times/semester). Literary magazine. Yearbook. Radio and TV stations. Jazz ensemble, marching and pep bands, University Singers, gospel choir, departmental clubs, 40 organizations in all. Four fraternities, no chapter houses; four sororities, no chapter houses. 25% of men join a fraternity. 18% of women join a sorority.
**Religious organizations:** Campus Christian Fellowship.
**Minority/foreign student organizations:** International Student Association.

**ATHLETICS. Physical education requirements:** Two semesters of physical education required.
**Intercollegiate competition:** 13% of students participate. Baseball (M), basketball (M,W), cheerleading (M,W), cross-country (M,W), football (M), golf (M,W), softball (W), tennis (M,W), track (indoor) (M,W), track (outdoor) (M,W), volleyball (W). Member of CIAA, NCAA Division II.
**Intramural and club sports:** 52% of students participate. Intramural basketball, flag football, softball, swimming, volleyball. Men's club soccer. Women's club soccer.

**ADMISSIONS. Academic basis for candidate selection** (in order of priority): Secondary school record, standardized test scores, school's recommendation.
**Nonacademic basis for candidate selection:** Character and personality, extracurricular participation, particular talent or ability, geographical distribution, and alumni/ae relationship are considered.
**Requirements:** Graduation from secondary school is required; GED is accepted. 20 units and the following program of study are required: 4 units of English, 3 units of math, 2 units of lab science, 2 units of foreign language, 3 units of social studies, 6 units of academic electives. Minimum combined SAT score of 700 and minimum 2.0 GPA required of in-state applicants; minimum combined SAT score of 800 and minimum 2.5 GPA required of out-of-state applicants. R.N. required of nursing program applicants. Summer Emerging Scholars program. SAT or ACT is required. Campus visit recommended. No off-campus interviews.
**Procedure:** Take SAT or ACT by December of 12th year. Visit college for interview by April 1 of 12th year. Suggest filing application by January 1. Application deadline is April 1. Notification of admission on rolling basis. $50 nonrefundable tuition deposit. $50 nonrefundable room deposit. Freshmen accepted for terms other than fall.
**Special programs:** Admission may be deferred one semester. Credit and/or placement may be granted through CEEB Advanced Placement exams for scores of 3 or higher. Credit may be granted through CLEP general and subject exams, military and life experience. Credit and placement may be granted through ACT PEP, DANTES, and challenge exams. Early decision program. Deadline for applying for early decision is November 1. Concurrent enrollment program.
**Transfer students:** Transfer students accepted for terms other than fall. In fall 1993, 664 transfer applications were received, 560 were accepted. Application deadline is May 1 for fall; November 1 for spring. Minimum 2.0 GPA required. Lowest course grade accepted is "C." Maximum number of transferable credits is 70 semester hours from a two-year school and 90 semester hours from a four-year school. At least 30 semester hours must be completed at the university to receive degree.
**Admissions contact:** Lawrence A. Waters, Ph.D., Director of Admissions, Records, and Registration. 301 464-6570.

**FINANCIAL AID. Available aid:** Pell grants, SEOG, state scholarships and grants, school scholarships and grants, private scholarships and grants, ROTC scholarships, academic merit scholarships, and athletic scholarships. Perkins Loans (NDSL), PLUS, Stafford Loans (GSL), and SLS. AMS and deferred payment plan.
**Financial aid statistics:** 31% of aid is not need-based.
**Supporting data/closing dates:** FAFSA/FAF: Priority filing date is June 1. School's own aid application: Priority filing date is June 1. Student Aid Report: Priority filing date is June 1. Notification of awards begins June 1.
**Financial aid contact:** Donald Kiah, M.Ed., Director of Financial Aid. 301 464-6544.

**STUDENT EMPLOYMENT.** College Work/Study Program. Institutional employment. 30% of full-time undergraduates work on campus during school year. Students may expect to earn an average of $1,000 during school year. Off-campus part-time employment opportunities rated "good."

**COMPUTER FACILITIES.** 55 IBM/IBM-compatible and Macintosh/Apple microcomputers; 20 are networked. Students may access Digital minicomputer/mainframe systems, BITNET, Internet. Client/LAN operating systems include Novell. Computer languages and software packages include BASIC, COBOL, FORTRAN, Lotus 1-2-3,

Paradox, Pascal, SPSS, Ventura, WordPerfect; 22 in all. Computer facilities are available to all students.
**Fees:** Computer fee is included in tuition/fees.
**Hours:** 8 AM-10 PM (M-Th); 8 AM-5 PM (F); 10 AM-5 PM (Sa-Su).

**GRADUATE CAREER DATA.** Highest graduate school enrollments: Bowie State U. Companies and businesses that hire graduates: Giant Food, government agencies, IBM, NASA contractors, Xerox.

**PROMINENT ALUMNI/AE.** Christa McAuliffe, teacher selected for Challenger spaceflight; William Missouri, Prince George's County judge; Dr. Roland Smith, assistant to president of Notre Dame U.

# Capitol College

**Laurel, MD 20708** **301 953-0060**

**1994-95 Costs.** Tuition: $8,400. Room: $2,800. Fees, books, misc. academic expenses (school's estimate): $360.
**Enrollment.** Undergraduates: 248 men, 34 women (full-time). Freshman class: 100 applicants, 90 accepted, 35 enrolled. Graduate enrollment: 64 men, 30 women.
**Test score averages/ranges.** Average SAT scores: 400 verbal, 450 math.
**Faculty.** 20 full-time; 28 part-time. 10% of faculty holds doctoral degree. Student/faculty ratio: 14 to 1.
**Selectivity rating.** Less competitive.

**PROFILE.** Capitol, founded in 1964, is a private college of engineering studies. Its 52-acre campus is located in Laurel, 20 miles from Washington, D.C.

**Accreditation:** MSACS. Professionally accredited by the Accreditation Board for Engineering and Technology.
**Religious orientation:** Capitol College is nonsectarian; no religious requirements.
**Library:** Collections totaling over 10,000 volumes and 100 periodical subscriptions.
**Special facilities/museums:** Electronics labs, telecommunications hall.
**Athletic facilities:** Athletic field, basketball and volleyball courts.

**STUDENT BODY. Undergraduate profile:** 85% are state residents; 60% are transfers. 8% Asian-American, 23% Black, 3% Hispanic, 1% Native American, 60% White, 5% Other. Average age of undergraduates is 24.
**Freshman profile:** 99% of accepted applicants took SAT. 85% of freshmen come from public schools.
**Undergraduate achievement:** 60% of fall 1992 freshmen returned for fall 1993 term. 33% of entering class graduated.
**Foreign students:** 26 students are from out of the country. Countries represented include Cameroon, China, Ghana, and Saudi Arabia; 16 in all.

**PROGRAMS OF STUDY. Degrees:** B.S.
**Majors:** Computer Engineering Technology, Electrical Engineering, Electronics Engineering Technology, Management of Telecommunications Systems, Systems Management, Telecommunications Engineering Technology.
**Distribution of degrees:** The majors with the highest enrollment are electronics engineering, computer engineering, and electrical engineering.
**Requirements:** General education requirement.
**Special:** Associate's degrees offered. Double majors. Dual degrees. Independent study. Accelerated study. Internships. Cooperative education programs. ROTC at Bowie State U.
**Honors:** Honors program. Honor societies.
**Academic Assistance:** Remedial writing and math.

**ADMISSIONS. Academic basis for candidate selection** (in order of priority): Secondary school record, class rank, school's recommendation, essay, standardized test scores.
**Nonacademic basis for candidate selection:** Character and personality and particular talent or ability are important. Extracurricular participation and alumni/ae relationship are considered.
**Requirements:** Graduation from secondary school is required; GED is accepted. 21 units and the following program of study are required: 4 units of English, 3 units of math, 2 units of lab science, 2 units of foreign language, 4 units of social studies, 2 units of history, 4 units of academic electives. Minimum combined SAT score of 900 and minimum 2.5 GPA recommended. 4 units of math, including 1 unit beyond algebra II, and 3 units of lab science recommended of engineering program applicants. SAT is required; ACT may be substituted. Campus visit and interview recommended.
**Procedure:** Take SAT or ACT by October of 12th year. Visit college for interview by March 30 of 12th year. Suggest filing application by March 1; no deadline. Notification of admission on rolling basis. $150 nonrefundable tuition deposit. $150 nonrefundable room deposit. Freshmen accepted for terms other than fall.
**Special programs:** Admission may be deferred one year. Credit and/or placement may be granted through CEEB Advanced Placement exams for scores of 3 or higher. Credit and/or placement may be granted through CLEP general and subject exams. Credit and placement may be granted through Regents College, ACT PEP, DANTES, and challenge exams and military experience. Concurrent enrollment program.
**Transfer students:** Transfer students accepted for terms other than fall. In fall 1993, 60% of all new students were transfers into all classes. 85 transfer applications were received, 85 were accepted. Application deadline is rolling for fall; rolling for spring. Minimum 2.0 GPA recommended. Lowest course grade accepted is "C." Maximum number of transferable credits is 70 semester hours. At least 40 semester hours must be completed at the college to receive degree.
**Admissions contact:** Anthony G. Miller, Director of Admissions. 301 953-3200.

**FINANCIAL AID. Available aid:** Pell grants, SEOG, state scholarships and grants, school scholarships and grants, and private scholarships and grants. Perkins Loans (NDSL), PLUS, Stafford Loans (GSL), private loans, and SLS. AMS and EFI Fund Management.
**Financial aid statistics:** In 1993-94, 53% of all undergraduate applicants received aid.
**Supporting data/closing dates:** FAFSA/FAF/FFS. State aid form: Priority filing date is March 1. Income tax forms: Accepted on rolling basis. Notification of awards on rolling basis.
**Financial aid contact:** Sheila Sauls-White, Director of Financial Aid. 301 953-3200, extension 257.

# College of Notre Dame of Maryland

**Baltimore, MD 21210** **410 532-5360**

**1993-94 Costs.** Tuition: $10,550. Room & board: $5,400. Fees, books, misc. academic expenses (school's estimate): $550.
**Enrollment.** Undergraduates: 2 men, 665 women (full-time). Freshman class: 457 applicants, 356 accepted, 177 enrolled. Graduate enrollment: 54 men, 369 women.
**Test score averages/ranges.** Average SAT scores: 470 verbal, 500 math. Range of SAT scores of middle 50%: 410-540 verbal, 440-580 math.
**Faculty.** 76 full-time; 8 part-time. 58% of faculty holds doctoral degree. Student/faculty ratio: 15 to 1.
**Selectivity rating.** Less competitive.

**PROFILE.** The College of Notre Dame of Maryland, founded in 1873, is a private, church-affiliated, liberal arts college for women. Its 58-acre campus is located inside city limits in northern Baltimore.

**Accreditation:** MSACS.
**Religious orientation:** College of Notre Dame of Maryland is affiliated with the Roman Catholic Church; two semesters of religion required.
**Library:** Collections totaling over 277,450 volumes, 1,983 periodical subscriptions, and 378,138 microform items.
**Special facilities/museums:** Art gallery, photo labs, child care center, fitness center, television and radio studios, music practice labs, planetarium.
**Athletic facilities:** Sports complex, fitness center, dance studio, gymnasium, racquetball and tennis courts, game and seminar rooms, athletic training center, field hockey, lacrosse, and soccer fields.

**STUDENT BODY. Undergraduate profile:** 70% are state residents; 16% are transfers. 6% Asian-American, 12% Black, 3% Hispanic, 73% White, 6% Other. Average age of undergraduates is 19.
**Freshman profile:** 1% of freshmen who took SAT scored 700 or over on verbal, 1% scored 700 or over on math; 11% scored 600 or over on verbal, 18% scored 600 or over on math; 35% scored 500 or over on verbal, 50% scored 500 or over on math; 77% scored 400 or over on verbal, 87% scored 400 or over on math; 97% scored 300 or over on verbal, 98% scored 300 or over on math. 98% of accepted applicants took SAT; 8% took ACT. 59% of freshmen come from public schools.
**Undergraduate achievement:** 84% of fall 1992 freshmen returned for fall 1993 term. 54% of entering class graduated. 15% of students who completed a degree program immediately went on to graduate study.
**Foreign students:** 11 students are from out of the country. Countries represented include Japan, Korea, Nigeria, Panama, Sierra Leone, and Turkey.

**PROGRAMS OF STUDY. Degrees:** B.A., B.S., B.S.Nurs.
**Majors:** Art, Biology, Business, Chemistry, Classical Studies, Communication Arts, Computer Information Systems, Computer Science, Economics, Education, Engineering, English, History, Interdisciplinary Studies, International Studies, Liberal Arts, Mathematics, Modern Foreign Languages, Music, Nursing, Physics, Political Science, Psychology, Religious Studies.
**Distribution of degrees:** The majors with the highest enrollment are business, communication arts, and education; economics, physics, and computer science have the lowest.
**Requirements:** General education requirement.
**Academic regulations:** Minimum 2.0 GPA must be maintained.
**Special:** Minors offered in all majors and in special education and philosophy. Bachelor's degrees for weekend nursing program. Four-week January Winterim offers opportunity for independent study, study trips, or internships. Self-designed majors. Double majors. Dual degrees. Independent study. Accelerated study. Pass/fail grading option. Internships. Preprofessional programs in law, medicine, veterinary science, pharmacy, and dentistry. 3-2 engineering programs with U of Maryland and Johns Hopkins U. 3-2 B.A./B.S. nursing program with Johns Hopkins U. Cross-registration with Coppin State Coll, Goucher Coll, Johns Hopkins U, Loyola U, Maryland Inst of Art, Morgan State U, and Towson State U. Teacher certification in early childhood, elementary, secondary, and special education. Certification in specific subject areas. Study abroad in numerous countries. ROTC at Loyola Coll.
**Honors:** Honors program.
**Academic Assistance:** Nonremedial tutoring.

**ADMISSIONS. Academic basis for candidate selection** (in order of priority): Secondary school record, standardized test scores, school's recommendation, essay, class rank.
**Nonacademic basis for candidate selection:** Extracurricular participation and particular talent or ability are emphasized. Alumni/ae relationship is important. Character and personality and geographical distribution are considered.
**Requirements:** Graduation from secondary school is required; GED is not accepted. 18 units and the following program of study are required: 4 units of English, 3 units of math, 2 units of science, 3 units of foreign language, 2 units of history, 4 units of electives. Minimum composite SAT score of 800, minimum 2.5 GPA for college preparatory courses, and strong recommendations required. R.N. required of nursing program applicants. SAT is required; ACT may be substituted. PSAT is recommended. Campus visit and interview recommended. No off-campus interviews.
**Procedure:** Take SAT or ACT by December of 12th year. Visit college for interview by February 15 of 12th year. Suggest filing application by February 15; no deadline. Notification of admission on rolling basis. Reply is required by May 1. $100 nonrefundable

tuition deposit. $100 nonrefundable room deposit. Freshmen accepted for terms other than fall.
**Special programs:** Admission may be deferred one year. Credit and/or placement may be granted through CEEB Advanced Placement exams for scores of 3 or higher. Early decision program. Deadline for applying for early decision is November 15. Early entrance/early admission program.
**Transfer students:** Transfer students accepted for terms other than fall. In fall 1993, 16% of all new students were transfers into all classes. 74 transfer applications were received, 58 were accepted. Application deadline is June 30 for fall; December 15 for spring. Minimum 2.5 GPA required. Lowest course grade accepted is "C." Maximum number of transferable credits is 64 semester hours from a two-year school and 68 semester hours from a four-year school. At least 60 semester hours must be completed at the college to receive degree.
**Admissions contact:** Terry Boer, M.Ed., Director of Admissions/Enrollment Management. 800 435-0300, 410 532-5330.

**FINANCIAL AID. Available aid:** Pell grants, SEOG, state scholarships and grants, school scholarships and grants, private scholarships and grants, ROTC scholarships, and academic merit scholarships. Perkins Loans (NDSL), PLUS, Stafford Loans (GSL), private loans, and SLS. Knight Tuition Plans, AMS, and family tuition reduction.
**Financial aid statistics:** 40% of aid is not need-based. In 1993-94, 95% of all undergraduate applicants received aid; 100% of freshman applicants. Average amounts of aid awarded freshmen: Scholarships and grants, $7,909; loans, $2,625.
**Supporting data/closing dates:** FAFSA/FAF: Priority filing date is February 15. State aid form: Priority filing date is February 15. Income tax forms: Priority filing date is February 15. Notification of awards begins April 1.
**Financial aid contact:** Robin Sullivan, M.A., Director of Financial Aid. 800 435-0300, 410 532-5369.

# Coppin State College

**Baltimore, MD 21216** **410 383-4500**

**1993-94 Costs.** Tuition: $1,852 (state residents), $3,924 (out-of-state). Room & board: $4,540. Fees, books, misc. academic expenses (school's estimate): $1,253.
**Enrollment.** Undergraduates: 869 men, 1,293 women (full-time). Freshman class: 1,689 applicants, 1,232 accepted, 520 enrolled. Graduate enrollment: 102 men, 249 women.
**Test score averages/ranges.** Average SAT scores: 376 verbal, 411 math. Average ACT scores: 19 English, 21 math, 20 composite.
**Faculty.** 102 full-time; 91 part-time. 85% of faculty holds doctoral degree. Student/faculty ratio: 25 to 1.
**Selectivity rating.** Less competitive.

**PROFILE.** Coppin State, founded in 1900, is a public college. Programs are offered through the Divisions of Arts and Sciences, Continuing Education, Education, and Nursing. Its 38-acre campus is located in Baltimore.

**Accreditation:** MSACS. Professionally accredited by the National Council for Accreditation of Teacher Education.
**Religious orientation:** Coppin State College is nonsectarian; no religious requirements.
**Library:** Collections totaling over 134,983 volumes, 665 periodical subscriptions, and 231,573 microform items.
**Special facilities/museums:** Language lab, school of special education, TV studio.
**Athletic facilities:** Gymnasium, training, weight, and wrestling rooms, dance studio, basketball, handball, racquetball, tennis, and volleyball courts, swimming pool, track, baseball and other athletic fields.

**STUDENT BODY. Undergraduate profile:** 93% are state residents; 36% are transfers. 2% Asian-American, 92% Black, 1% Native American, 5% White. Average age of undergraduates is 25.
**Freshman profile:** 98% of accepted applicants took SAT; 2% took ACT. 85% of freshmen come from public schools.
**Undergraduate achievement:** 80% of fall 1992 freshmen returned for fall 1993 term. 60% of entering class graduated. 25% of students who completed a degree program went on to graduate study within five years.
**Foreign students:** 58 students are from out of the country. Countries represented include Canada, India, Japan, Liberia, Thailand, and Trinidad/Tobago; 19 in all.

**PROGRAMS OF STUDY. Degrees:** B.A., B.S.
**Majors:** Adapted Physical Education, Biology, Chemistry, Computer Science, Criminal Justice, Early Childhood Education, Elementary Education, English, General Science/Chemistry, History, Management Science, Mathematics, Nursing, Philosophy, Psychology, Social Science/Social Work, Social Sciences, Special Education.
**Distribution of degrees:** The majors with the highest enrollment are management science, psychology, and nursing; history, philosophy, and chemistry have the lowest.
**Requirements:** General education requirement.
**Academic regulations:** Freshmen must maintain minimum 1.2 GPA; sophomores, 1.6 GPA; juniors, 1.8 GPA; seniors, 2.0 GPA.
**Special:** Courses offered in African-American studies, art, economics, French, geography, international studies, journalism, Latin, linguistics, mass communications, music, physical science, physics, political science, Spanish, speech/theatre, and urban recreation. Undergraduate Record Exam required except of students eligible for major exam/professional school entrance exam. Double majors. Dual degrees. Internships. Cooperative education programs. Graduate school at which undergraduates may take graduate-level courses. Cooperative social work program with U of Maryland at Baltimore County. Dual-degree programs in chemistry/engineering, general science/engineering, math/engineering, pre-dental/general science, and pre-pharmacy/general science with U of Maryland. Pre-physical therapy program with U of Maryland. Member of consortium with Bowie State U, Frostburg State U, Salisbury State U, Towson State U, and U of Maryland at Baltimore, Baltimore County, College Park, and Eastern Shore. Teacher certification in elementary, secondary, and special education. ROTC at Morgan State U.
**Honors:** Honors program. Honor societies.
**Academic Assistance:** Remedial reading and math. Nonremedial tutoring.

**STUDENT LIFE. Housing:** Students may live on or off campus. Coed dorms.
**Social atmosphere:** "There is incredible love and bonding on this campus," reports the student newspaper. "Students are involved in campus activity. In the past one could say there was no student support but not anymore. There are not enough activities for students to support." Popular on-campus gathering spots include Tawes Center, the fireside lounge, quiet lounge, the game room, and the Student Government office. Greeks, the basketball team, and Student Government are influential groups on campus. Favorite events during the school year are Christmas parties, the spring play, basketball games, Homecoming, and jazz concerts.
**Services and counseling/handicapped student services:** Placement services. Health service. Counseling services for minority and veteran students. Personal counseling. Career and academic guidance services. Physically disabled student services. Learning disabled services. Reader services for the blind.
**Campus organizations:** Undergraduate student government. Student newspaper (Courier, published twice/semester). Yearbook. TV station. Gospel choir, Coppin Dancers, Coppin Players, College Democrats, Democrats of America, Women's Symposium, professional and departmental groups, 20 organizations in all. 12 fraternities, no chapter houses; 12 sororities, no chapter houses.
**Religious organizations:** Alpha Nu Omega.
**Minority/foreign student organizations:** African-American Student Society, Association of Black Journalists. Korean Student Club.

**ATHLETICS. Physical education requirements:** One semester of physical education required.
**Intercollegiate competition:** 7% of students participate. Baseball (M), basketball (M,W), cheerleading (W), cross-country (M,W), diving (M,W), softball (W), swimming (M,W), tennis (M,W), track (indoor) (M,W), track (outdoor) (M,W), track and field (indoor) (M,W), track and field (outdoor) (M,W), volleyball (W), wrestling (M). Member of Mid-Eastern Athletic Conference, NCAA Division I.
**Intramural and club sports:** 5% of students participate. Intramural basketball, volleyball.

**ADMISSIONS. Academic basis for candidate selection** (in order of priority): Secondary school record, standardized test scores, school's recommendation, class rank, essay.
**Nonacademic basis for candidate selection:** Character and personality, extracurricular participation, geographical distribution, and alumni/ae relationship are considered.
**Requirements:** Graduation from secondary school is required; GED is accepted. No specific distribution of secondary school units required. Minimum composite ACT score of 19 (combined SAT score of 730) and minimum 2.3 GPA required. Separate application required of nursing program applicants. Non-degree-seeking students ineligible for financial aid. SAT is required; ACT may be substituted. Campus visit and interview recommended. Off-campus interviews available with an admissions representative.
**Procedure:** Take SAT or ACT by March of 12th year. Suggest filing application by January 15. Application deadline is July 15. Notification of admission on rolling basis. No set date by which applicants must accept offer. $25 nonrefundable tuition deposit. $100 refundable room deposit. Freshmen accepted for terms other than fall.
**Special programs:** Admission may be deferred one year. Credit may be granted through CEEB Advanced Placement for scores of 3 or higher. Credit and/or placement may be granted through CLEP general exams. Credit may be granted through CLEP subject exams. Placement may be granted through military experience. Credit and placement may be granted through challenge exams. Early decision program. In fall 1993, 152 applied for early decision and 65 were accepted. Deadline for applying for early decision is January 15. Concurrent enrollment program.
**Transfer students:** Transfer students accepted for terms other than fall. In fall 1993, 36% of all new students were transfers into all classes. 751 transfer applications were received, 541 were accepted. Application deadline is July 15 for fall; December 15 for spring. Minimum 2.0 GPA required. Lowest course grade accepted is "D." Maximum number of transferable credits is 70 semester hours from a two-year school and 90 semester hours from a four-year school. At least 30 semester hours must be completed at the college to receive degree.
**Admissions contact:** Allen D. Mosley, M.S., Director of Admissions. 410 383-5990.

**FINANCIAL AID. Available aid:** Pell grants, SEOG, state scholarships, school scholarships and grants, private scholarships and grants, academic merit scholarships, and athletic scholarships. Perkins Loans (NDSL), PLUS, Stafford Loans (GSL), and SLS. Deferred payment plan.
**Financial aid statistics:** 12% of aid is not need-based. In 1993-94, 86% of all undergraduate applicants received aid; 85% of freshman applicants. Average amounts of aid awarded freshmen: Scholarships and grants, $1,680; loans, $1,500.
**Supporting data/closing dates:** FAFSA/FAF/FFS: Priority filing date is May 3; deadline is July 15. School's own aid application: Priority filing date is May 3; deadline is July 15. State aid form: Priority filing date is January 2; deadline is March 1. Notification of awards on rolling basis.
**Financial aid contact:** Ron Smith, M.S., Director of Financial Aid. 410 383-5930.

**STUDENT EMPLOYMENT.** College Work/Study Program. Institutional employment. 40% of full-time undergraduates work on campus during school year. Students may expect to earn an average of $2,500 during school year. Off-campus part-time employment opportunities rated "excellent."

**COMPUTER FACILITIES.** 130 IBM/IBM-compatible and Macintosh/Apple microcomputers. Computer languages and software packages include Ada, APL, BASIC, C, COBOL, dBASE, FORTRAN, LISP, Lotus 1-2-3, Pascal, Prolog, Small Talk, WordPerfect. Computer facilities are available to all students.
**Fees:** None.

**GRADUATE CAREER DATA.** Highest graduate school enrollments: Johns Hopkins U, U of Maryland at Baltimore County.

**PROMINENT ALUMNI/AE.** Bishop Robinson, commissioner, Baltimore City Police; Milton Allen, state supreme court justice; Vondalu Clark, assistant superintendent, Baltimore Public Schools; Dr. Patricia Schmoke, optometrist; Quentin Lawson, vice-chairperson, Maryland Commission of Higher Education.

# Frostburg State University

**Frostburg, MD 21532** **301 689-4000**

**1994-95 Costs.** Tuition: $2,849 (state residents), $6,528 (out-of-state). Room & board: $4,400. Fees, books, misc. academic expenses (school's estimate): $1,206.
**Enrollment.** Undergraduates: 2,123 men, 2,039 women (full-time). Freshman class: 3,014 applicants, 2,243 accepted, 942 enrolled. Graduate enrollment: 340 men, 438 women.
**Test score averages/ranges.** Average SAT scores: 426 verbal, 476 math. Range of SAT scores of middle 50%: 800-1049 combined.
**Faculty.** 234 full-time; 71 part-time. 67% of faculty holds doctoral degree. Student/faculty ratio: 18 to 1.
**Selectivity rating.** Less competitive.

**PROFILE.** Frostburg State, founded in 1898, is a public, comprehensive university. Its 150-acre campus is located in Frostburg, 100 miles southeast of Pittsburgh.

**Accreditation:** MSACS.
**Religious orientation:** Frostburg State University is nonsectarian; no religious requirements.
**Library:** Collections totaling over 221,005 volumes, 1,291 periodical subscriptions, and 154,604 microform items.
**Special facilities/museums:** Art gallery, planetarium, electron microscope.
**Athletic facilities:** Gymnasium, baseball, field hockey, football, lacrosse, and soccer field, weight room, racquetball, squash, and tennis courts, swimming pool, track.
**STUDENT BODY. Undergraduate profile:** 87% are state residents; 35% are transfers. 1% Asian-American, 8% Black, 1% Hispanic, 89% White, 1% Other. Average age of undergraduates is 20.
**Freshman profile:** 1% of freshmen who took SAT scored 700 or over on math; 2% scored 600 or over on verbal, 11% scored 600 or over on math; 16% scored 500 or over on verbal, 42% scored 500 or over on math; 68% scored 400 or over on verbal, 82% scored 400 or over on math; 97% scored 300 or over on verbal, 98% scored 300 or over on math. Majority of accepted applicants took SAT.
**Undergraduate achievement:** 78% of fall 1992 freshmen returned for fall 1993 term.
**Foreign students:** 32 students are from out of the country. Countries represented include China, Hong Kong, India, Japan, Trinidad, and Zimbabwe; 12 in all.
**PROGRAMS OF STUDY. Degrees:** B.A., B.F.A., B.S.
**Majors:** Accounting, Actuarial Science, Art, Biology, Business Administration, Business Education, Chemistry, Computer Science, Economics, Elementary/Early Childhood Education, Elementary/Middle School Education, English, Environmental Analysis/Planning, Fine Arts, Foreign Language/Literature, General Science, Geography, Graphic Design, Health/Physical Education, History, International Studies, Justice Studies, Mass Communication, Mathematics, Music, Philosophy, Physics, Political Science, Psychology, Recreation, Social Science, Social Work, Sociology, Speech Communication/Theatre, Visual Arts, Wildlife/Fisheries Management.
**Distribution of degrees:** The majors with the highest enrollment are business administration, early childhood education, and psychology; fine arts, music, and chemistry have the lowest.
**Requirements:** General education requirement.
**Academic regulations:** Minimum 2.0 GPA must be maintained.
**Special:** Minors offered in most majors and in art history, dance, public relations, and women's studies. Double majors. Dual degrees. Independent study. Accelerated study. Pass/fail grading option. Internships. Cooperative education programs. Graduate school at which undergraduates may take graduate-level courses. Preprofessional programs in law, medicine, veterinary science, dentistry, and optometry. 3-2 engineering program with U of Maryland College Park. 3-2 pharmacy program with U of Maryland Baltimore. 3-3 bachelors/J.D. program with U of Baltimore Sch of Law. Member of International Studies Association of University of Maryland System. Teacher certification in early childhood, elementary, and secondary education. Certification in specific subject areas. Member of International Studies Association. Study abroad in Ireland. ROTC.
**Honors:** Honors program. Honor societies.
**Academic Assistance:** Remedial reading, writing, math, and study skills. Nonremedial tutoring.
**STUDENT LIFE. Housing:** Students may live on or off campus. Coed, women's, and men's dorms. 40% of students live in college housing.
**Social atmosphere:** Gandalf's is a popular gathering-spot for Frostburg State students. Greeks, the student government, and the Noble Order of the Unicorn (role-playing group) are influential on campus social life. Highlights of the school year include Homecoming and dances. "This is a friendly school," according to the editor of the student newspaper. "It's small, yet public, and many people go here because it's affordable. A brand-new multi-million dollar performing arts center has just been completed."
**Services and counseling/handicapped student services:** Placement services. Health service. Women's center. Day care. Counseling services for minority, military, veteran, and older students. Birth control, personal, and psychological counseling. Career and academic guidance services. Religious counseling. Physically disabled student services. Learning disabled program/services. Notetaking services. Tape recorders. Tutors. Reader services for the blind.
**Campus organizations:** Undergraduate student government. Student newspaper (Bottom Line, published once/week). Literary magazine. Radio station. Choral union, brass choir, wind symphony, orchestra, concert and marching bands, jazz ensemble, debating, drama group, Campus Activities Board, Honors Student Association, Residence Hall Association, outdoor club, academic, service, and special-interest groups, 96 organizations in all. Eight fraternities, no chapter houses; six sororities, no chapter houses. 12% of men join a fraternity. 10% of women join a sorority.
**Religious organizations:** Baptist Student Union, Fellowship of Christian Athletes, United Campus Ministry, Chi-Alpha, Christian Fellowship, Hillel.
**Minority/foreign student organizations:** Black Student Alliance, Gospel Voices, Imagination.
**ATHLETICS. Physical education requirements:** One semester of physical education required.
**Intercollegiate competition:** 8% of students participate. Baseball (M), basketball (M,W), cross-country (M,W), diving (M,W), field hockey (W), football (M), lacrosse (W), soccer (M), swimming (M,W), tennis (M,W), track (indoor) (M,W), track (outdoor) (M,W), track and field (indoor) (M,W), track and field (outdoor) (M,W). Member of Eastern States Athletic Conference, ECAC, NCAA Division III.
**Intramural and club sports:** Intramural basketball, flag football, raquetball, soccer, softball, squash, tennis, volleyball. Men's club karate, lacrosse, rugby, volleyball. Women's club karate, rugby, soccer, softball.
**ADMISSIONS. Academic basis for candidate selection** (in order of priority): Secondary school record, standardized test scores, school's recommendation.
**Nonacademic basis for candidate selection:** Character and personality and particular talent or ability are considered.
**Requirements:** Graduation from secondary school is recommended; GED is accepted. 14 units and the following program of study are required: 4 units of English, 3 units of math, 2 units of lab science, 2 units of foreign language, 3 units of social studies. Minimum combined SAT score of 920 and minimum 2.7 GPA recommended. SAT is required; ACT may be substituted. Campus visit and interview recommended. No off-campus interviews.
**Procedure:** Notification of admission on rolling basis. Reply is required by April 1. $100 nonrefundable tuition deposit. Freshmen accepted for terms other than fall.
**Special programs:** Credit and/or placement may be granted through CEEB Advanced Placement exams for scores of 3 or higher. Credit and/or placement may be granted through CLEP general and subject exams. Credit and placement may be granted through challenge exams. Concurrent enrollment program.
**Transfer students:** Transfer students accepted for terms other than fall. In fall 1993, 35% of all new students were transfers into all classes. 962 transfer applications were received, 705 were accepted. Application deadline is August 1 for fall; December 1 for spring. Minimum 2.0 GPA required. Lowest course grade accepted is "C." Maximum number of transferable credits is 70 semester hours. At least 30 semester hours must be completed at the university to receive degree.
**Admissions contact:** David L. Sanford, M.Ed., Dean of Admissions. 301 689-4201.
**FINANCIAL AID. Available aid:** Pell grants, SEOG, state scholarships and grants, school scholarships, private scholarships, ROTC scholarships, and academic merit scholarships. Perkins Loans (NDSL), PLUS, Stafford Loans (GSL), school loans, and SLS. AMS and deferred payment plan.
**Financial aid statistics:** 30% of aid is not need-based. In 1993-94, 65% of all undergraduate applicants received aid; 65% of freshman applicants. Average amounts of aid awarded freshmen: Scholarships and grants, $1,200; loans, $2,000.
**Supporting data/closing dates:** FAFSA: Priority filing date is April 1. Income tax forms: Accepted on rolling basis. Notification of awards begins May 15.
**Financial aid contact:** Katherine M. Kutler, M.Ed., Director of Financial Aid. 301 689-4301.
**STUDENT EMPLOYMENT.** College Work/Study Program. Institutional employment. 40% of full-time undergraduates work on campus during school year. Students may expect to earn an average of $800 during school year. Off-campus part-time employment opportunities rated "poor."
**COMPUTER FACILITIES.** 160 IBM/IBM-compatible, Macintosh/Apple, and RISC-/UNIX-based microcomputers; all are networked. Students may access Digital, SUN minicomputer/mainframe systems, BITNET, Internet. Residence halls may be equipped with stand-alone microcomputers. Client/LAN operating systems include Apple/Macintosh, DOS, UNIX/XENIX/AIX, LocalTalk/AppleTalk, Novell. Computer languages and software packages include Assembly, BASIC, C, COBOL, Excel, FileMaker Pro, FORTRAN, FoxPro, LISP, LOGO, Lotus 1-2-3, Oracle, Pascal, PL/1, Prolog, QuattroPro Works, SAS, SPSS, Word, WordPerfect, WordStar; 45 in all. Computer facilities are available to all students.
**Fees:** None.
**Hours:** 150 hours/week.
**GRADUATE CAREER DATA.** Companies and businesses that hire graduates: Computer Sciences Corp., Defense Mapping Agency, Hercules/Allegany Ballistics Laboratory, IBM, Kelly-Springfield, Marriott, Martin Marietta, Potomac Edison, U.S. Postal Service, educational institutions.
**PROMINENT ALUMNI/AE.** Donald Hutchinson, president, Maryland Economic Growth Associates/Maryland Chamber of Commerce; Michael Owen, vice president of circulation, Time-Life, Inc.; David Mahoney, vice president of consumer division, Phillips Publishing Company.

# Goucher College

**Baltimore, MD 21204** **410 337-6000**

**1993-94 Costs.** Tuition: $14,300. Room & board: $5,895. Fees, books, misc. academic expenses (school's estimate): $725.
**Enrollment.** Undergraduates: 266 men, 584 women (full-time). Freshman class: 1,151 applicants, 813 accepted, 245 enrolled. Graduate enrollment: 5 men, 66 women.
**Test score averages/ranges.** Average SAT scores: 539 verbal, 572 math. Range of SAT scores of middle 50%: 470-610 verbal, 510-630 math.
**Faculty.** 77 full-time; 56 part-time. 85% of faculty holds doctoral degree. Student/faculty ratio: 9 to 1.
**Selectivity rating.** More competitive.

**PROFILE.** Goucher is a private, liberal arts college. Founded as a college for women in 1885, it adopted coeducation in 1987. Its 287-acre campus is located in Towson, eight miles north of the center of Baltimore.

**Accreditation:** MSACS.

**Religious orientation:** Goucher College is nonsectarian; no religious requirements.
**Library:** Collections totaling over 269,262 volumes, 1,114 periodical subscriptions, and 58,419 microform items.
**Special facilities/museums:** Centers for computers, politics, sociological studies, technology and media, sports and recreation.
**Athletic facilities:** Gymnasium, racquetball, squash, and tennis courts, weight room, athletic fields, recreation center, swimming pool, dance studios, riding ring, wellness laboratory.

**STUDENT BODY. Undergraduate profile:** 46% are state residents; 14% are transfers. 4% Asian-American, 6% Black, 3% Hispanic, 83% White, 4% Other. Average age of undergraduates is 21.
**Freshman profile:** 4% of freshmen who took SAT scored 700 or over on verbal, 9% scored 700 or over on math; 19% scored 600 or over on verbal, 27% scored 600 or over on math; 52% scored 500 or over on verbal, 68% scored 500 or over on math; 100% scored 400 or over on verbal, 100% scored 400 or over on math. 100% of accepted applicants took SAT. 60% of freshmen come from public schools.
**Undergraduate achievement:** 89% of fall 1992 freshmen returned for fall 1993 term. 75% of entering class graduated. 80% of students who completed a degree program went on to graduate study within five years.
**Foreign students:** 10 students are from out of the country. Countries represented include Canada, Colombia, Japan, the Philippines, Thailand, and the United Kingdom; nine in all.

**PROGRAMS OF STUDY. Degrees:** B.A.
**Majors:** American Studies, Applied Art, Applied Mathematics, Art, Art Education, Art/History, Arts Administration, Behavioral Sciences, Biochemistry, Biological Sciences, Biomedical Sciences, Black Studies, Business Administration, Business Economics, Cell Biology, Chemistry, Cognitive Studies, Communication, Computer Programming, Computer Science, Creative Writing, Dance, Dance Therapy, Economics, Education, Elementary Education, English, Environmental Biology, European Studies, Evolutionary Biology, Experimental Psychology, French, German, Historic Preservation, History, International Studies, Latin American Studies, Liberal/General Studies, Marine Biology, Mathematics, Microbiology, Modern Language, Molecular Biology, Music, Music History, Philosophy, Physics, Political Science, Pre-Dentistry, Pre-Law, Pre-Medicine, Pre-Veterinary Medicine, Psychology, Public Affairs, Radio/Television, Religion, Romance Languages, Russian, Social Science, Social Work, Sociology/Anthropology, Spanish, Special Education, Studio Art, Theatre, Voice, Wind/Percussion Instruments, Women's Studies.
**Distribution of degrees:** The majors with the highest enrollment are English, psychology, and education; area studies, cognitive studies, and European studies have the lowest.
**Requirements:** General education requirement.
**Academic regulations:** Freshmen must maintain minimum 1.7 GPA; sophomores, 1.9 GPA; juniors, 2.0 GPA; seniors, 2.0 GPA.
**Special:** Minors offered in all majors. Self-designed majors. Double majors. Independent study. Pass/fail grading option. Internships. Preprofessional programs in law, medicine, veterinary science, and dentistry. Exchange programs with Johns Hopkins U and other schools in the Baltimore and Washington, D.C. vicinity. Teacher certification in elementary, secondary, and special education. Certification in specific subject areas. Exchange programs abroad in England (U of Exeter), France (Sorbonne), Spain (U of Salamanca), the Ukraine (U of Odessa), Germany, and Spain.
**Honors:** Honors program. Honor societies.
**Academic Assistance:** Remedial reading, writing, math, and study skills. Nonremedial tutoring.

**ADMISSIONS. Academic basis for candidate selection** (in order of priority): Secondary school record, essay, school's recommendation, class rank, standardized test scores.
**Nonacademic basis for candidate selection:** Extracurricular participation is important. Character and personality, particular talent or ability, and alumni/ae relationship are considered.
**Requirements:** Graduation from secondary school is required; GED is accepted. 15 units and the following program of study are required: 4 units of English, 3 units of math, 2 units of lab science, 2 units of foreign language, 2 units of social studies. SAT or ACT is required. PSAT is recommended. ACH recommended. Campus visit and interview recommended. Off-campus interviews available with admissions and alumni representatives.
**Procedure:** Take SAT or ACT by January of 12th year. Take ACH by January of 12th year. Visit college for interview by February of 12th year. Application deadline is February 1. Notification of admission by April 1. Reply is required by May 1. $500 tuition deposit, refundable until May 1. $100 room deposit, refundable until May 1. Freshmen accepted for terms other than fall.
**Special programs:** Admission may be deferred two years. Credit and/or placement may be granted through CEEB Advanced Placement exams for scores of 4 or higher. Credit and/or placement may be granted through CLEP subject exams. Early decision program. In fall 1993, 20 applied for early decision and 17 were accepted. Deadline for applying for early decision is November 15. Early entrance/early admission program.
**Transfer students:** Transfer students accepted for terms other than fall. In fall 1993, 14% of all new students were transfers into all classes. 99 transfer applications were received, 80 were accepted. Application deadline is April 1 for fall; December 15 for spring. Minimum 2.5 GPA recommended. Lowest course grade accepted is "C." Maximum number of transferable credits is 60 semester hours. At least 60 semester hours must be completed at the college to receive degree.
**Admissions contact:** Elise Seraydarian, B.A., Director of Admissions. 410 337-6100.

**FINANCIAL AID. Available aid:** Pell grants, SEOG, state scholarships and grants, school scholarships and grants, private scholarships, and academic merit scholarships. Perkins Loans (NDSL), PLUS, Stafford Loans (GSL), state loans, school loans, private loans, and SLS. AMS.
**Financial aid statistics:** 42% of aid is not need-based. In 1993-94, 87% of all freshman applicants received aid. Average amounts of aid awarded freshmen: Scholarships and grants, $13,000; loans, $2,700.
**Supporting data/closing dates:** FAFSA/FAF: Priority filing date is February 15. School's own aid application: Priority filing date is February 15. State aid form: Priority filing date is February 15; deadline is March 1. Income tax forms: Priority filing date is February 15; accepted on rolling basis. Notification of awards begins April 1.
**Financial aid contact:** Faye W. Perry, M.B.A., Director of Financial Aid. 410 337-6141.

# Hood College

**Frederick, MD 21701-8575** **301 696-3400**

**1994-95 Costs.** Tuition: $13,960. Room: $3,266. Board: $2,774. Fees, books, misc. academic expenses (school's estimate): $150.
**Enrollment.** Undergraduates: 38 men, 671 women (full-time). Freshman class: 570 applicants, 450 accepted, 150 enrolled. Graduate enrollment: 343 men, 628 women.
**Test score averages/ranges.** Range of SAT scores of middle 50%: 440-560 verbal, 470-600 math.
**Faculty.** 76 full-time; 17 part-time. 84% of faculty holds doctoral degree. Student/faculty ratio: 13 to 1.
**Selectivity rating.** Competitive.

**PROFILE.** Hood, founded in 1893, is a church-affiliated college. Although it is predominantly a college for women, men have been admitted as commuting students since 1971. Its 100-acre campus is located in downtown Frederick, 45 miles north of Washington, D.C. Campus architecture is Georgian in style.
**Accreditation:** MSACS. Professionally accredited by the American Dietetic Association, the American Home Economics Association, the American Medical Association (CAHEA), the Council on Social Work Education.
**Religious orientation:** Hood College is affiliated with the United Church of Christ; no religious requirements.
**Library:** Collections totaling over 228,000 volumes, 900 periodical subscriptions, and 60,000 microform items.
**Special facilities/museums:** Art gallery, child development lab, language lab, observatory, solar-heated home economics management house.
**Athletic facilities:** Gymnasium, aerobics and weight rooms, dance studio, swimming pools, tennis and volleyball courts, archery range, field hockey, lacrosse, and softball fields, fitness course.

**STUDENT BODY. Undergraduate profile:** 58% are state residents; 5% are transfers. 2% Asian-American, 17% Black, 3% Hispanic, 67% White, 11% International. Average age of undergraduates is 20.
**Freshman profile:** 1% of freshmen who took SAT scored 700 or over on math; 10% scored 600 or over on verbal, 20% scored 600 or over on math; 47% scored 500 or over on verbal, 59% scored 500 or over on math; 100% scored 400 or over on verbal, 100% scored 400 or over on math. 97% of accepted applicants took SAT; 7% took ACT. 80% of freshmen come from public schools.
**Undergraduate achievement:** 82% of fall 1992 freshmen returned for fall 1993 term. 65% of entering class graduated. 30% of students who completed a degree program went on to graduate study within two years.
**Foreign students:** 47 students are from out of the country. Countries represented include Bulgaria, India, Japan, Kenya, Malaysia, and Panama; 26 in all.

**PROGRAMS OF STUDY. Degrees:** B.A., B.Bus.Admin., B.S.
**Majors:** Art, Biochemistry, Biology, Chemistry, Communication Arts, Early Childhood Education, Economics, English, Environmental Studies, French, German, History, Information/Computer Science, Interior Design, Latin American Studies, Law/Society, Management, Mathematics, Medical Technology, Nutrition, Philosophy, Political Science, Psychobiology, Psychology, Religion, Religion/Philosophy, Retailing, Social Work, Sociology, Spanish, Special Education.
**Distribution of degrees:** The majors with the highest enrollment are management, biology, and education; German and philosophy have the lowest.
**Requirements:** General education requirement.
**Academic regulations:** Minimum 2.0 GPA must be maintained.
**Special:** Minors and concentrations offered in some majors and in over 25 other fields. Self-designed majors. Double majors. Independent study. Pass/fail grading option. Internships. Graduate school at which undergraduates may take graduate-level courses. Preprofessional programs in law, medicine, veterinary science, and dentistry. 3-2 engineering program with George Washington U. Member of Duke U Marine Sciences Education Consortium. Washington Semester. Teacher certification in early childhood, secondary, and special education. Certification in specific subject areas. Study abroad in the Dominican Republic, France, and Spain. ROTC at Western Maryland Coll.
**Honors:** Honors program. Honor societies.
**Academic Assistance:** Remedial reading, writing, math, and study skills. Nonremedial tutoring.

**ADMISSIONS. Academic basis for candidate selection** (in order of priority): Secondary school record, essay, class rank, standardized test scores, school's recommendation.
**Nonacademic basis for candidate selection:** Character and personality, extracurricular participation, particular talent or ability, and alumnae relationship are considered.
**Requirements:** Graduation from secondary school is required; GED is accepted. No specific distribution of secondary school units required. Minimum of 16 academic units in English, math, natural sciences, foreign language, and social sciences required. Conditional admission possible for applicants not meeting standard requirements. SAT is required; ACT may be substituted. Campus visit and interview recommended. No off-campus interviews.
**Procedure:** Take SAT or ACT by November of 12th year. Visit college for interview by February of 12th year. Suggest filing application by January 31. Application deadline is March 31. Notification of admission by April 15. Reply is required by May 1. $250 deposit required of resident students, $100 of commuters; refundable until May 1. Freshmen accepted for terms other than fall.
**Special programs:** Admission may be deferred one year. Credit and/or placement may be granted through CEEB Advanced Placement exams for scores of 3 or higher. Credit and/or placement may be granted through CLEP subject exams. Credit and placement may be granted through challenge exams and life experience. Early entrance/early admission program. Concurrent enrollment program.
**Transfer students:** Transfer students accepted for terms other than fall. In fall 1993, 5% of all new students were transfers into all classes. 93 transfer applications were received, 81

were accepted. Application deadline is March 31 for fall; December 31 for spring. Minimum 2.5 GPA recommended. Lowest course grade accepted is "C." Maximum number of transferable credits is 70 semester hours. At least 30 semester hours must be completed at the college to receive degree.

**Admissions contact:** Nancy Gillece, Director of Admissions. 800 922-1599.

**FINANCIAL AID. Available aid:** Pell grants, SEOG, state scholarships and grants, school scholarships and grants, private scholarships and grants, academic merit scholarships, and aid for undergraduate foreign students. Perkins Loans (NDSL), PLUS, Stafford Loans (GSL), private loans, and SLS. Tuition Plan Inc., Knight Tuition Plans, AMS, EFI Fund Management, and family tuition reduction. Prepaid tuition plan.

**Financial aid statistics:** 32% of aid is not need-based. In 1993-94, 90% of all undergraduate applicants received aid; 90% of freshman applicants. Average amounts of aid awarded freshmen: Scholarships and grants, $10,000; loans, $2,600.

**Supporting data/closing dates:** FAFSA/FAF/FFS: Priority filing date is March 31. School's own aid application: Priority filing date is May 1. State aid form: Priority filing date is March 1. Income tax forms: Priority filing date is May 1. Notification of awards on rolling basis.

**Financial aid contact:** Richelle Emerick, M.A., Director of Financial Aid. 301 696-3411.

# The Johns Hopkins University

**Baltimore, MD 21218** **410 516-8000**

**1994-95 Costs.** Tuition: $18,800. Room: $3,815. Board: $2,925. Fees, books, misc. academic expenses (school's estimate): $500.

**Enrollment.** Undergraduates: 2,092 men, 1,244 women (full-time). Freshman class: 8,474 applicants, 3,436 accepted, 906 enrolled. Graduate enrollment: 839 men, 484 women.

**Test score averages/ranges.** Average SAT scores: 606 verbal, 686 math. Range of SAT scores of middle 50%: 560-660 verbal, 640-740 math. Average ACT scores: 30 composite.

**Faculty.** 355 full-time; 135 part-time. 99% of faculty holds doctoral degree. Student/faculty ratio: 10 to 1.

**Selectivity rating.** Most competitive.

**PROFILE.** Johns Hopkins, founded in 1876, is a private university. Programs are offered through the Schools of Advanced International Studies, Arts and Sciences, Hygiene and Public Health, and Medicine; the G.W.C. Whiting School of Engineering; the Peabody Conservatory of Music; and the Evening College. Its 140-acre campus is located in a residential area of northern Baltimore.

**Accreditation:** MSACS. Professionally accredited by the Accreditation Board for Engineering and Technology.

**Religious orientation:** The Johns Hopkins University is nonsectarian; no religious requirements.

**Library:** Collections totaling over 2,900,000 volumes, 20,677 periodical subscriptions, and 1,600,000 microform items.

**Special facilities/museums:** Baltimore Museum of Art on campus, art gallery, electron microscope, space telescope institute, four major research centers, undergraduate physics research building.

**Athletic facilities:** Gymnasiums, dance, fencing, weight, and wrestling rooms, astroturf, baseball, intramural, and practice fields, sauna, swimming pool, diving area, basketball, handball, and squash courts.

**STUDENT BODY. Undergraduate profile:** 14% are state residents; 5% are transfers. 23% Asian-American, 5% Black, 2% Hispanic, 67% White, 3% Other. Average age of undergraduates is 20.

**Freshman profile:** 15% of freshmen who took SAT scored 700 or over on verbal, 49% scored 700 or over on math; 70% scored 600 or over on verbal, 90% scored 600 or over on math; 95% scored 500 or over on verbal, 100% scored 500 or over on math; 100% scored 400 or over on verbal. 55% of freshmen who took ACT scored 30 or over on composite; 100% scored 24 or over on composite. 99% of accepted applicants took SAT; 6% took ACT. 59% of freshmen come from public schools.

**Undergraduate achievement:** 94% of fall 1992 freshmen returned for fall 1993 term. 82% of entering class graduated. 65% of students who completed a degree program went on to graduate study within one year.

**Foreign students:** 142 students are from out of the country. Countries represented include China, France, Germany, India, Japan, and Taiwan; 32 in all.

**PROGRAMS OF STUDY. Degrees:** B.A., B.S.

**Majors:** Anthropology, Behavioral Biology, Biology, Biomedical Engineering, Biophysics, Chemical Engineering, Chemistry, Civil Engineering, Classics, Cognitive Sciences, Computer Engineering, Computer Science, Earth/Planetary Sciences, Economics, Electrical Engineering, Engineering, English, Environmental Earth Science, French, Geography/Environmental Engineering, Geology, Geophysics, German, History, History of Art, History of Science, Humanistic Studies, International Studies, Italian/Hispanic Studies, Latin American Studies, Materials Science/Engineering, Mathematical Sciences, Mathematics, Mechanical Engineering/Engineering Mechanics, Medicine/Technology, Music, Natural Sciences, Near Eastern Studies, Philosophy, Physics/Astronomy, Political Science, Psychology, Public Health, Social/Behavioral Sciences, Sociology, Writing Seminars.

**Distribution of degrees:** The majors with the highest enrollment are biology, international studies, and biomedical engineering; German, earth/planetary sciences, and French have the lowest.

**Academic regulations:** Freshmen must maintain minimum 2.0 GPA; sophomores, 2.0 GPA; juniors, 2.0 GPA; seniors, 2.0 GPA.

**Special:** Minors offered in many majors and in Greek, Italian, Latin, multicultural studies, Russian, and women's studies. Courses offerd in public health, oceanography, and statistics. Interdepartmental liberal arts major and urban studies program. Area majors (student-designed, interdisciplinary) in behavioral biology, humanistic studies, natural sciences, quantitative studies, and social and behavioral sciences. Opportunities in many departments for early entrance into independent research or advanced courses. Curriculum oriented toward postgraduate education in either professional or graduate schools. Self-designed majors. Double majors. Dual degrees. Independent study. Pass/fail grading option. Internships. Cooperative education programs. Graduate school at which undergraduates may take graduate-level courses. Preprofessional programs in law, medicine, veterinary science, and dentistry. Flex-Med program with Johns Hopkins Medical Sch; five-year B.A./Ph.D. program in psychology. Five-year B.A./M.A. program with Johns Hopkins Sch of Advanced International Studies. Five-year B.S./M.S. engineering programs. Member of COFHE, AAU, and UAA. Teacher certification in secondary education. Study abroad in all countries, including one-year program in Italy (Johns Hopkins Bologna Center). ROTC. AFROTC at U of Maryland at College Park.

**Honors:** Phi Beta Kappa. Honors program. Honor societies.

**Academic Assistance:** Remedial study skills. Nonremedial tutoring.

**STUDENT LIFE. Housing:** All freshmen and sophomores must live on campus unless living with family. Coed, women's, and men's dorms. Sorority and fraternity housing. School-owned/operated apartments. Off-campus privately-owned housing. 81% of students live in college housing.

**Social atmosphere:** The social atmosphere on campus is "somewhat dim, but present," reports the student newspaper. Greeks and lacrosse enthusiasts exert widespread influence on the campus. On campus, students gather at the undergraduate library ("The Hut"). P.J.'s Pub is the popular off-campus spot. Fiji Islander, lacrosse games, and the Phi Psi 500 are popular campus events.

**Services and counseling/handicapped student services:** Placement services. Health service. Counseling services for minority, military, and veteran students. Personal and psychological counseling. Career and academic guidance services. Religious counseling. Physically disabled student services. Learning disabled services. Tutors.

**Campus organizations:** Undergraduate student government. Student newspaper (Hopkins Newsletter and Hopkins Standard, published once/week). Literary magazine. Yearbook. Radio station. Gospel choir, band, orchestra, Hopkins Symphony, Barnstormers, debating, Amnesty International, Students for Environmental Action, bicycle and outdoor clubs, 80 organizations in all. 13 fraternities, eight chapter houses; five sororities, one chapter house. 30% of men join a fraternity. 25% of women join a sorority.

**Religious organizations:** Catholic Community, Christian Fellowship, Jewish Student Organization.

**Minority/foreign student organizations:** Black Student Union, InterAsian Council, OLE (Organization Latino Estudentes). International club, Caribbean, Chinese, Hellenic, Indian, Japanese, Korean, Middle Eastern, Russian, Scandinavian, and Spanish student groups.

**ATHLETICS. Physical education requirements:** None.

**Intercollegiate competition:** 25% of students participate. Baseball (M), basketball (M,W), crew (M,W), cross-country (M,W), diving (M,W), fencing (M,W), field hockey (W), football (M), golf (M), lacrosse (M,W), riflery (M,W), soccer (M,W), squash (W), swimming (M,W), tennis (M,W), track and field (outdoor) (M,W), volleyball (W), water polo (M,W), wrestling (M). Member of Centennial Conference, NCAA Division I for men's lacrosse, NCAA Division III, University Athletic Association.

**Intramural and club sports:** 25% of students participate. Intramural badminton, basketball, billiards, cycling, flag football, floor hockey, foosball, lacrosse, racquetball, road racing, soccer, softball, squash, swimming, table tennis, tennis, track and field, ultimate frisbee, volleyball, wrestling. Men's club ice hockey, indoor track, martial arts, rugby, sailing, ultimate frisbee, volleyball. Women's club cheerleading, indoor track, martial arts, sailing, soccer, ultimate frisbee.

**ADMISSIONS. Academic basis for candidate selection** (in order of priority): Secondary school record, standardized test scores, class rank, school's recommendation, essay.

**Nonacademic basis for candidate selection:** Character and personality and extracurricular participation are important. Particular talent or ability, geographical distribution, and alumni/ae relationship are considered.

**Requirements:** Graduation from secondary school is recommended; GED is accepted. No specific distribution of secondary school units required. SAT is required; ACT may be substituted. PSAT is recommended. ACH required. Campus visit and interview recommended. Off-campus interviews available with admissions and alumni representatives.

**Procedure:** Take SAT or ACT by January of 12th year. Take ACH by January of 12th year. Visit college for interview by March 1 of 12th year. Application deadline is January 1. Notification of admission by April 1. Reply is required by May 1. $400 nonrefundable tuition deposit. $100 nonrefundable room deposit. Freshmen accepted for fall terms only.

**Special programs:** Admission may be deferred two years. Credit and/or placement may be granted through CEEB Advanced Placement exams for scores of 4 or higher. Placement may be granted through ACT PEP and challenge exams. Early decision program. In fall 1993, 529 applied for early decision and 246 were accepted. Deadline for applying for early decision is November 1. Early entrance/early admission program. Concurrent enrollment program.

**Transfer students:** Transfer students accepted for terms other than fall. In fall 1993, 5% of all new students were transfers into all classes. 332 transfer applications were received, 103 were accepted. Application deadline is May 1 for fall; November 1 for spring. Minimum 3.0 GPA required. Lowest course grade accepted is "C." Maximum number of transferable credits is 60 semester hours. At least 60 semester hours must be completed at the university to receive degree.

**Admissions contact:** Richard M. Fuller, M.A., Director of Admissions. 410 516-8171.

**FINANCIAL AID. Available aid:** Pell grants, SEOG, state scholarships and grants, school scholarships and grants, private scholarships and grants, ROTC scholarships, academic merit scholarships, and athletic scholarships. Perkins Loans (NDSL), PLUS, Stafford Loans (GSL), school loans, and SLS. Knight Tuition Plans, AMS, and guaranteed tuition.

**Financial aid statistics:** 7% of aid is not need-based. In 1993-94, 80% of all undergraduate applicants received aid; 68% of freshman applicants. Average amounts of aid awarded freshmen: Scholarships and grants, $11,700; loans, $3,500.

**Supporting data/closing dates:** FAFSA: Priority filing date is February 1. School's own aid application: Deadline is January 15. Income tax forms: Deadline is January 15. Notification of awards begins April 1.

**Financial aid contact:** Ellen Frishberg, Ed.S., Director of Financial Aid. 410 516-8028.

**STUDENT EMPLOYMENT.** College Work/Study Program. Institutional employment. 50% of full-time undergraduates work on campus during school year. Students may ex-

pect to earn an average of $1,700 during school year. Off-campus part-time employment opportunities rated "good."

**COMPUTER FACILITIES.** 150 IBM/IBM-compatible, Macintosh/Apple, and RISC-/UNIX-based microcomputers; all are networked. Students may access Cray, Digital, IBM, SUN minicomputer/mainframe systems, BITNET, Internet. Residence halls may be equipped with networked terminals, modems. Client/LAN operating systems include Apple/Macintosh, DOS, OS/2, UNIX/XENIX/AIX, Windows NT, DEC, Microsoft, Novell. Computer languages and software packages include BASIC, C, COBOL, FORTRAN, Lisp, MINITAB, Pascal, SAS, SPSS-X, WordPerfect; mathematical modeling, text editing, word processing programs; 210 in all. Computer facilities are available to all students.
**Fees:** None.
**Hours:** 24 hours.

**GRADUATE CAREER DATA.** Graduate school percentages: 10% enter law school. 25% enter medical school. 7% enter graduate business programs. 17% enter graduate arts and sciences programs. Highest graduate school enrollments: Harvard U, Johns Hopkins U, Stanford U. 50% of graduates choose careers in business and industry. Companies and businesses that hire graduates: Arthur Andersen, General Electric, U.S. government.

**PROMINENT ALUMNI/AE.** Woodrow Wilson, 28th President of the U.S.; Benjamin J. Civiletti, former U.S. attorney general; Russell Baker, columnist, *New York Times*, and host, *Masterpiece Theatre*; Dr. Donald A. Henderson, responsible for the eradication of smallpox; Donald Grant, president, CBS Entertainment; John Barth, novelist.

# Loyola College

**Baltimore, MD 21210-2699 — 410 617-2000**

**1994-95 Costs.** Tuition: $12,990. Room & board: $6,300-$6,530. Fees, books, misc. academic expenses (school's estimate): $970.
**Enrollment.** Undergraduates: 1,286 men, 1,724 women (full-time). Freshman class: 4,077 applicants, 3,137 accepted, 751 enrolled.
**Test score averages/ranges.** Average SAT scores: 507 verbal, 563 math.
**Faculty.** 220 full-time; 186 part-time. 87% of faculty holds highest degree in specific field. Student/faculty ratio: 14 to 1.
**Selectivity rating.** Competitive.

**PROFILE.** Loyola is a church-affiliated, liberal arts college. Founded as a women's college in 1852, it adopted coeducation in 1971. Programs are offered through the College of Arts and Sciences and the School of Business and Management. Its 63-acre campus is located in a residential area of Baltimore.

**Accreditation:** MSACS. Professionally accredited by the American Assembly of Collegiate Schools of Business.
**Religious orientation:** Loyola College is affiliated with the Roman Catholic Church; two semesters of theology required.
**Library:** Collections totaling over 287,000 volumes, 2,000 periodical subscriptions, and 350,000 microform items.
**Special facilities/museums:** Art gallery, advanced biology lab, humanities building, speech pathology lab and audiology center.
**Athletic facilities:** Basketball, racquetball, squash, tennis, and volleyball courts, swimming pool, training, weight, and wrestling rooms, playing fields, arena.

**STUDENT BODY. Undergraduate profile:** 35% are state residents; 21% are transfers. 4% Asian-American, 3% Black, 2% Hispanic, 1% Native American, 90% White. Average age of undergraduates is 20.
**Freshman profile:** 1% of freshmen who took SAT scored 700 or over on verbal, 7% scored 700 or over on math; 14% scored 600 or over on verbal, 34% scored 600 or over on math; 53% scored 500 or over on verbal, 80% scored 500 or over on math; 94% scored 400 or over on verbal, 98% scored 400 or over on math; 100% scored 300 or over on verbal, 100% scored 300 or over on math. 100% of accepted applicants took SAT. 51% of freshmen come from public schools.
**Undergraduate achievement:** 91% of fall 1992 freshmen returned for fall 1993 term. 76% of entering class graduated. 30% of students who completed a degree program went on to graduate study within five years.
**Foreign students:** 11 students are from out of the country. Eight countries represented in all.

**PROGRAMS OF STUDY. Degrees:** B.A., B.Bus.Admin., B.S.
**Majors:** Accounting, Biology, Business Economics, Chemistry, Classics, Communications, Computer Science, Economics, Education, Engineering Sciences, English, Finance, Fine Arts, French, General Business, German, History, International Business, Management, Management Information Systems, Marketing, Mathematics, Philosophy, Physics, Political Science, Psychology, Sociology, Spanish, Speech Pathology, Theology, Writing/Media.
**Distribution of degrees:** The majors with the highest enrollment are business, communications, and biology; classics and theology have the lowest.
**Requirements:** General education requirement.
**Special:** Minors offered in most academic departments. Interdisciplinary programs offered in ethics and society and in gender studies. Self-designed majors. Double majors. Dual degrees. Independent study. Accelerated study. Internships. Graduate school at which undergraduates may take graduate-level courses. Preprofessional programs in law, medicine, veterinary science, dentistry, and theology. 3-1 medical technology program with Sch of Medical Tech at Mercy Hospital. 3-4 dentistry program with Georgetown U Dental Sch. Five-year speech pathology/audiology program. 3-2 education program leads to bachelor's and master's degrees. Courses may be taken at Coll of Notre Dame of Maryland, Goucher Coll, Johns Hopkins U, Maryland Inst Coll of Art, Morgan State U, and Towson State U. Qualified music students may take courses at the Peabody Conservatory. Teacher certification in elementary, secondary, and special education. Study abroad in numerous countries. ROTC. AFROTC at U of Maryland.
**Honors:** Honors program. Honor societies.
**Academic Assistance:** Remedial reading, writing, math, and study skills. Nonremedial tutoring.

**STUDENT LIFE. Housing:** All freshmen must live on campus unless living with family. Coed, women's, and men's dorms. School-owned/operated apartments. 70% of students live in college housing.
**Services and counseling/handicapped student services:** Placement services. Health service. Counseling services for minority students. Personal and psychological counseling. Career and academic guidance services. Religious counseling. Physically disabled student services. Learning disabled services.
**Campus organizations:** Undergraduate student government. Student newspaper (Greyhound, published biweekly). Literary magazine. Yearbook. Radio station. Concert choir, music ensembles, folk groups, Commuter Students Association, Loyola Dramatic Players, Student Government Association, Resident Affairs Council, debating, special-interest clubs, volunteer groups, 50 organizations in all.
**Religious organizations:** Campus Ministries, Interfaith Association.
**Minority/foreign student organizations:** Black Student Association. Foreign Student Association, Korean Student Association.

**ATHLETICS. Physical education requirements:** None.
**Intercollegiate competition:** 9% of students participate. Basketball (M,W), cheerleading (W), cross-country (M,W), diving (M,W), golf (M), lacrosse (M,W), soccer (M,W), swimming (M,W), tennis (M,W), volleyball (W). Member of ECAC, Metro Atlantic Athletic Conference, NCAA Division I, South Atlantic Field Hockey/Lacrosse Conference.
**Intramural and club sports:** 80% of students participate. Intramural badminton, basketball, flag football, floor hockey, ice hockey, indoor hockey, indoor soccer, soccer, softball, squash, tennis, volleyball, walleyball. Men's club baseball, crew, ice hockey, indoor track, lacrosse, rugby, sailing, track, volleyball. Women's club crew, field hockey, indoor track, lacrosse, sailing, track.

**ADMISSIONS. Academic basis for candidate selection** (in order of priority): Secondary school record, standardized test scores, class rank, essay, school's recommendation.
**Nonacademic basis for candidate selection:** Extracurricular participation is important. Character and personality, particular talent or ability, and alumni/ae relationship are considered.
**Requirements:** Graduation from secondary school is required; GED is not accepted. 16 units and the following program of study are recommended: 4 units of English, 3 units of math, 2 units of science, 2 units of foreign language, 2 units of history. No more than 3 commercial, industrial, or technical subjects may be counted. Combined SAT score of 1000 with at least 500 in both verbal and math, rank in top fifth of secondary school class, and 3.0 GPA recommended. SAT is required. Campus visit and interview recommended. No off-campus interviews.
**Procedure:** Take SAT by December of 12th year. Suggest filing application by December 31. Application deadline is February 1. Notification of admission by April 15. Reply is required as early as possible. $100 nonrefundable tuition deposit. $500 nonrefundable room deposit. Freshmen accepted for terms other than fall.
**Special programs:** Admission may be deferred. Credit may be granted through CEEB Advanced Placement for scores of 3 or higher. Early entrance/early admission program. Concurrent enrollment program.
**Transfer students:** Transfer students accepted for terms other than fall. In fall 1992, 21% of all new students were transfers into all classes. 65 transfer applications were received. Application deadline is August 1 for fall; December 15 for spring. Minimum 2.5 GPA required. Lowest course grade accepted is "C." Maximum number of transferable credits is 60 semester hours. At least 60 semester hours must be completed at the college to receive degree.
**Admissions contact:** William J. Bossemeyer III, M.B.A., M.Ed., Director of Admissions. 410 617-2252, 800 221-9107 ext 2252.

**FINANCIAL AID. Available aid:** Pell grants, SEOG, state scholarships and grants, school scholarships and grants, private scholarships and grants, ROTC scholarships, academic merit scholarships, and athletic scholarships. Perkins Loans (NDSL), PLUS, Stafford Loans (GSL), private loans, and SLS. Knight Tuition Plans, AMS, EFI Fund Management, and family tuition reduction.
**Financial aid statistics:** 40% of aid is not need-based. Average amounts of aid awarded freshmen: Scholarships and grants, $5,800; loans, $3,000.
**Supporting data/closing dates:** FAFSA/FAF: Deadline is March 1. School's own aid application: Deadline is March 1. Notification of awards begins April 15.
**Financial aid contact:** Mark Lindenmeyer, M.B.A., Director of Financial Aid. 410 617-2000, extension 2343, 800 221-9107.

**STUDENT EMPLOYMENT.** College Work/Study Program. Institutional employment. 15% of full-time undergraduates work on campus during school year. Students may expect to earn an average of $1,200 during school year. Freshmen are discouraged from working during their first term. Off-campus part-time employment opportunities rated "excellent."

**COMPUTER FACILITIES.** 220 IBM/IBM-compatible and Macintosh/Apple microcomputers. Students may access Digital minicomputer/mainframe systems, Internet. Residence halls may be equipped with networked microcomputers. Computer languages and software packages include Assembler, BASIC, C, COBOL, FORTRAN, LISP, Pascal, Prolog; graphics, spreadsheet, statistical, word processing packages. Computer facilities are available to all students.
**Fees:** None.
**Hours:** 24 hours at some computer labs.

**GRADUATE CAREER DATA.** Highest graduate school enrollments: Georgetown U, Johns Hopkins U, U of Maryland. 77% of graduates choose careers in business and industry. Companies and businesses that hire graduates: Big Six accounting firms.

**PROMINENT ALUMNI/AE.** Jim McKay, broadcaster, "ABC Wide World of Sports"; Tom Clancy, author.

# Maryland Institute, College of Art

**Baltimore, MD 21217** **410 669-9200**

**1993-94 Costs.** Tuition: $12,960. Room: $3,980. Board: $1,440. Fees, books, misc. academic expenses (school's estimate): $1,320.
**Enrollment.** Undergraduates: 356 men, 436 women (full-time). Freshman class: 629 applicants, 399 accepted, 186 enrolled. Graduate enrollment: 39 men, 36 women.
**Test score averages/ranges.** N/A.
**Faculty.** 68 full-time; 78 part-time. 72% of faculty holds highest degree in specific field. Student/faculty ratio: 11 to 1.
**Selectivity rating.** N/A.

**PROFILE.** Maryland Institute, College of Art, founded in 1826, is a private college. Its campus is located in downtown Baltimore. Campus architecture is in the Italian Renaissance style.

**Accreditation:** MSACS. Professionally accredited by the National Association of Schools of Art and Design.
**Religious orientation:** Maryland Institute, College of Art is nonsectarian; no religious requirements.
**Library:** Collections totaling over 50,000 volumes and 200 periodical subscriptions. 70,000 color slides also available.
**Special facilities/museums:** Exhibition galleries; over 60 exhibitions featured each year.
**STUDENT BODY. Undergraduate profile:** 37% are state residents; 27% are transfers. 7% Asian-American, 5% Black, 2% Hispanic, 1% Native American, 78% White, 7% Other. Average age of undergraduates is 19.
**Freshman profile:** Majority of accepted applicants took SAT.
**Undergraduate achievement:** 77% of fall 1992 freshmen returned for fall 1993 term. 50% of entering class graduated. 36% of students who completed a degree program went on to graduate study within four years.
**Foreign students:** 48 students are from out of the country. Countries represented include Canada, England, India, Japan, Korea, and Switzerland; 36 in all.
**PROGRAMS OF STUDY. Degrees:** B.F.A.
**Majors:** Ceramics, Drawing, General Fine Arts, Graphic Design/Illustration, Interior Design/Architecture, Painting, Photography, Printmaking, Sculpture.
**Distribution of degrees:** The majors with the highest enrollment are general fine arts and painting.
**Academic regulations:** Sophomores must maintain minimum 2.0 GPA; juniors, 2.0 GPA; seniors, 2.0 GPA.
**Special:** Minors offered in creative writing and art history. New York Studio Program available. Self-designed majors. Double majors. Dual degrees. Independent study. Internships. Five-year B.F.A./M.A.Teach. program. Member of East Coast Art Schools. Exchange programs with Goucher Coll, Johns Hopkins U, Peabody Conservatory of Music, U of Baltimore, and other professional art colleges. Teacher certification in elementary, and secondary education. Study abroad in Canada, England, France, Greece, Italy, Japan, and Scotland.
**Honors:** Honors program.
**Academic Assistance:** Remedial writing.
**ADMISSIONS. Academic basis for candidate selection** (in order of priority): Portfolio, class rank, essay, standardized test scores.
**Nonacademic basis for candidate selection:** Particular talent or ability is emphasized. Character and personality are important. Extracurricular participation is considered.
**Requirements:** Graduation from secondary school is required; GED is accepted. No specific distribution of secondary school units required. Portfolio of 12 to 20 pieces, including three drawings, required. Samples of drawing from observation (rather than from the imagination or copies of photographs) strongly recommended; other pieces should represent best and most recent work. SAT or ACT is required. Campus visit and interview recommended. Off-campus interviews available with an admissions representative.
**Procedure:** Take SAT or ACT by December 15 of 12th year; those who are unable to do so before entrance may take SAT during first week on campus. Visit college for interview by May 1 of 12th year. Suggest filing application as early as possible after September 1 of 12th year. Portfolio may be submitted during visit, at portfolio days in various cities, or by sending slides. Application deadline is June 1. Notification of admission on rolling basis. Reply is required by May 1 or within 3 weeks of acceptance, whichever is later. $300 nonrefundable tuition deposit. $550 room deposit, partially refundable. Freshmen accepted for terms other than fall.
**Special programs:** Admission may be deferred one year. Credit and/or placement may be granted through CEEB Advanced Placement exams for scores of 4 or higher. Credit and/or placement may be granted through CLEP general and subject exams. Placement may be granted through challenge exams. Credit and placement may be granted through life experience. Early decision program. In fall 1993, 25 applied for early decision and 12 were accepted. Deadline for applying for early decision is November 15. Early entrance/early admission program. Concurrent enrollment program.
**Transfer students:** Transfer students accepted for terms other than fall. In fall 1993, 27% of all new students were transfers into all classes. 212 transfer applications were received, 133 were accepted. Application deadline is April 1 for fall; December 1 for spring. Lowest course grade accepted is "C." Maximum number of transferable credits is 63 semester hours. At least 63 semester hours must be completed at the college to receive degree.
**Admissions contact:** Theresa Lynch Bedoya, Vice President for Admissions and Financial Aid. 410 225-2222.
**FINANCIAL AID. Available aid:** Pell grants, SEOG, state scholarships and grants, school scholarships and grants, and private scholarships and grants. $1,500 art scholarships awarded to 10 incoming freshmen; $300,000 in art and academic scholarships awarded through annual competition. Perkins Loans (NDSL), PLUS, and Stafford Loans (GSL). Tuition Plan Inc. and Knight Tuition Plans. Monthly payment plans.
**Financial aid statistics:** 36% of aid is not need-based. In 1993-94, 67% of all undergraduate applicants received aid; 100% of freshman applicants.
**Supporting data/closing dates:** FAFSA: Priority filing date is March 15. FAF: Deadline is March 1. School's own aid application: Priority filing date is March 15. State aid form: Deadline is February 15. Income tax forms: Priority filing date is March 15. Notification of awards on rolling basis.
**Financial aid contact:** Diane Prengaman, Director of Financial Aid. 410 225-2285.

# Morgan State University

**Baltimore, MD 21239** **410 319-3333**

**1993-94 Costs.** Tuition: $1,848 (state residents), $4,384 (out-of-state). Room: $2,960. Board: $1,820. Fees, books, misc. academic expenses (school's estimate): $1,278.
**Enrollment.** Freshman class: 5,735 applicants, 2,881 accepted, 1,400 enrolled.
**Test score averages/ranges.** Average SAT scores: 405 verbal, 441 math.
**Faculty.** 209 full-time; 80 part-time. 80% of faculty holds doctoral degree. Student/faculty ratio: 18 to 1.
**Selectivity rating.** Less competitive.

**PROFILE.** Morgan State, founded in 1867, is a public, comprehensive university. Programs are offered through the College of Arts and Sciences and the Schools of Business and Management, Education and Urban Studies, Engineering, and Graduate Studies. Its 122-acre campus is located in Baltimore, 37 miles north of Washington, D.C.
**Accreditation:** MSACS. Professionally accredited by the Accreditation Board for Engineering and Technology, the American Medical Association (CAHEA), the Council on Social Work Education, the National Association of Schools of Art and Design, the National Association of Schools of Music, the National Council for Accreditation of Teacher Education.
**Religious orientation:** Morgan State University is nonsectarian; no religious requirements.
**Library:** Collections totaling over 270,778 volumes, 2,003 periodical subscriptions, and 297,913 microform items.
**Special facilities/museums:** African-American collection, new science complex and school of engineering.
**Athletic facilities:** Field house, athletic center, gymnasium, stadium.
**STUDENT BODY. Undergraduate profile:** 60% are state residents; 14% are transfers. 92% Black, 4% White, 4% Other.
**Freshman profile:** Majority of accepted applicants took SAT.
**Undergraduate achievement:** 76% of fall 1991 freshmen returned for fall 1992 term.
**Foreign students:** 61 students are from out of the country. Countries represented include China, Korea, Nigeria, Trinidad, and the Virgin Islands; 48 in all.
**PROGRAMS OF STUDY. Degrees:** B.A., B.S.
**Majors:** Accounting, African-American Studies, Biology, Business Administration, Business Education, Chemistry, Civil Engineering, Computer Science, Economics, Electrical Engineering, Elementary Education, Engineering Physics, English, Fine Arts, French, Gerontology, Health Education, History, Human Ecology/Home Economics, Industrial Engineering, Information Sciences/Systems, Management, Marketing, Medical Technology, Mental Health, Music, Philosophy, Physical Education, Physics, Political Science, Psychology, Religious Studies, Social Work, Sociology, Spanish, Speech Communication, Telecommunication, Theatre Arts.
**Distribution of degrees:** The majors with the highest enrollment are business administration, accounting, and telecommunication; mental health has the lowest.
**Requirements:** General education requirement.
**Academic regulations:** Minimum 2.0 GPA must be maintained.
**Special:** Minors offered in food and nutrition. Dual degrees. Internships. Graduate school at which undergraduates may take graduate-level courses. Preprofessional programs in law, medicine, pharmacy, and dentistry. 2-3 pharmacy honors program with U of Maryland. 3-4 predental and premedical programs with U of Maryland. Member of Historically Black Colleges and Universities. Cross-registration with U of Baltimore, Bowie State U, Coppin State Coll, Frostburg State Coll, U of Maryland, and Salisbury State Coll. Other cooperative programs with Goucher Coll, Johns Hopkins U, Loyola Coll, Coll of Notre Dame of Maryland, and Towson State U. Teacher certification in elementary and secondary education. Certification in specific subject areas. ROTC.
**Honors:** Honors program.
**Academic Assistance:** Remedial reading, writing, math, and study skills. Nonremedial tutoring.
**STUDENT LIFE. Housing:** Students may live on or off campus. Coed, women's, and men's dorms. School-owned/operated apartments. 30% of students live in college housing.
**Social atmosphere:** The student newspaper reports that favorite gathering spots for students include The Bridge, McKeldin Center, and The Canteen. Greeks, the Christian Center, and Alpha Nu Omega Christian fraternity/sorority are influential organizations on campus. Homecoming and basketball games are popular events during the school year.
**Services and counseling/handicapped student services:** Health service. Counseling services for minority and veteran students. Personal counseling. Career and academic guidance services. Physically disabled student services. Tutors.
**Campus organizations:** Undergraduate student government. Student newspaper (Spokesman, published twice/week). Yearbook. Radio station. Choir, Morgan Singers, marching band, symphonic band, symphony orchestra, drama group, dance club, Social Work Student Organization, American Marketing Association, Art Association, Commerce Club, departmental and special-interest groups, 25 organizations in all. Four fraternities, no chapter houses; four sororities, no chapter houses.
**Religious organizations:** Abundant Life Prayer Group, Apostolic Club, Baptist Club, Canterbury Club, Christian Center.
**Minority/foreign student organizations:** International Student Association.

**ATHLETICS. Physical education requirements:** Two semesters of physical education required.
**Intercollegiate competition:** 3% of students participate. Basketball (M,W), cheerleading (M,W), cross-country (M,W), football (M), softball (W), tennis (M,W), track (indoor) (W), track and field (M,W), volleyball (W), wrestling (M). Member of ECAC, Mid-Eastern Athletic Conference, NCAA Division I-AA.
**Intramural and club sports:** 5% of students participate. Intramural aerobics, basketball, football, weight lifting.

**ADMISSIONS. Academic basis for candidate selection** (in order of priority): Standardized test scores, secondary school record.
**Nonacademic basis for candidate selection:** Character and personality, extracurricular participation, and particular talent or ability are important. Alumni/ae relationship is considered.
**Requirements:** Graduation from secondary school is required; GED is accepted. No specific distribution of secondary school units required. Minimum combined SAT score of 750 (composite ACT score of 18) and minimum 2.5 GPA required. Audition required of music program applicants. "Connect" program with selected community colleges. SAT or ACT is required. Campus visit and interview recommended. No off-campus interviews.
**Procedure:** Take SAT or ACT by December of 12th year. Visit college for interview by February of 12th year. Suggest filing application by April 15. Application deadline is July 15. Notification of admission on rolling basis. Reply is required by May 1 or within 30 days of notification. $50 refundable tuition deposit. $100 refundable room deposit. Freshmen accepted for terms other than fall.
**Special programs:** Admission may be deferred one year. Credit may be granted through CEEB Advanced Placement exams and CLEP general and subject exams. Early decision program. Early entrance/early admission program. Concurrent enrollment program.
**Transfer students:** Transfer students accepted for terms other than fall. In fall 1993, 14% of all new students were transfers into all classes. 952 transfer applications were received, 536 were accepted. Application deadline is April 15 for fall; December 1 for spring. Minimum 2.0 GPA required. Lowest course grade accepted is "C." Maximum number of transferable credits is 70 semester hours. At least 30 semester hours must be completed at the university to receive degree.
**Admissions contact:** Chelseia Harold Miller, M.P.A., Director of Admissions amd Recruitment. 410 319-3000.

**FINANCIAL AID. Available aid:** Pell grants, SEOG, state scholarships and grants, school scholarships and grants, private scholarships, ROTC scholarships, academic merit scholarships, athletic scholarships, and United Negro College Fund. Other race-based grants. Perkins Loans (NDSL), PLUS, Stafford Loans (GSL), state loans, and school loans. AMS and deferred payment plan.
**Financial aid statistics:** In 1993-94, 80% of all undergraduate applicants received aid; 80% of freshman applicants.
**Supporting data/closing dates:** FAFSA/FAF/FFS: Priority filing date is April 1. School's own aid application: Priority filing date is April 1. Income tax forms: Priority filing date is April 1. Notification of awards on rolling basis.
**Financial aid contact:** Reginald Cureton, M.S., Director of Financial Aid. 410 319-3170.

**STUDENT EMPLOYMENT.** College Work/Study Program. Institutional employment. Students may expect to earn an average of $2,000 during school year. Off-campus part-time employment opportunities rated "good."

**COMPUTER FACILITIES.** IBM/IBM-compatible and Macintosh/Apple microcomputers. Students may access Digital minicomputer/mainframe systems. Client/LAN operating systems include DOS, Windows NT. Computer languages and software packages include Ada, BMDP, C, COBOL, FORTRAN, SPSS; 35 in all. Some microcomputers are restricted to departmental use.
**Fees:** None.
**Hours:** 9 AM-10 PM (M-F); 9 AM-4 PM (Sa).

**GRADUATE CAREER DATA.** Highest graduate school enrollments: Howard U, U of Maryland, Morgan State U. 60% of graduates choose careers in business and industry. Companies and businesses that hire graduates: Allstate, Citicorp, Ford, Maryland National Bank, Social Security Administration, Westinghouse.

**PROMINENT ALUMNI/AE.** Darren J. Mitchell, former U.S. congressman; Kweisi Mfume, U.S. congressman; Joe Black, vice-president, Greyhound; Yvonne Kennedy, president, S.D. Bishop Junior College; Wilson Goode, mayor, Philadelphia; Earl Graves, publisher, *Black Enterprise* magazine.

# Mount Saint Mary's College

**Emmitsburg, MD 21727 — 301 447-6122**

**1994-95 Costs.** Tuition: $12,850. Room: $3,100. Board: $3,100. Fees, books, misc. academic expenses (school's estimate): $550.
**Enrollment.** Undergraduates: 588 men, 655 women (full-time). Freshman class: 1,321 applicants, 1,159 accepted, 328 enrolled. Graduate enrollment: 302 men, 113 women.
**Test score averages/ranges.** Average SAT scores: 460 verbal, 510 math. Range of SAT scores of middle 50%: 400-510 verbal, 440-570 math.
**Faculty.** 92 full-time; 40 part-time. 84% of faculty holds highest degree in specific field. Student/faculty ratio: 14 to 1.
**Selectivity rating.** Less competitive.

**PROFILE.** Mount Saint Mary's, founded in 1808, is the oldest private, Catholic college in the U.S. Programs are offered through the Departments of Business and Economics, Education, English, Foreign Languages, Government and International Studies, History, Mathematics and Computer Science, Philosophy, Psychology, Science, Sociology, Theology, and Visual and Performing Arts. Its 1,400-acre campus is located in Emmitsburg, 12 miles south of Gettysburg, Pa.

**Accreditation:** MSACS.
**Religious orientation:** Mount Saint Mary's College is affiliated with the Roman Catholic Church; two semesters of theology required.
**Library:** Collections totaling over 185,000 volumes, 935 periodical subscriptions, and 14,000 microform items.
**Special facilities/museums:** Historical art collection reflecting Catholic history in America.
**Athletic facilities:** Athletic center, basketball, racquetball, tennis, and volleyball courts, tracks, playing fields, swimming pool, aerobics and weight rooms, field house.

**STUDENT BODY. Undergraduate profile:** 46% are state residents; 10% are transfers. 2% Asian-American, 6% Black, 2% Hispanic, 90% White. Average age of undergraduates is 20.
**Freshman profile:** 2% of freshmen who took SAT scored 700 or over on math; 8% scored 600 or over on verbal, 14% scored 600 or over on math; 31% scored 500 or over on verbal, 55% scored 500 or over on math; 74% scored 400 or over on verbal, 89% scored 400 or over on math; 98% scored 300 or over on verbal, 99% scored 300 or over on math. 99% of accepted applicants took SAT. 44% of freshmen come from public schools.
**Undergraduate achievement:** 82% of fall 1992 freshmen returned for fall 1993 term. 63% of entering class graduated. 20% of students who completed a degree program went on to graduate study within one year.
**Foreign students:** 20 students are from out of the country. Countries represented include Ecuador, England, Kenya, and Spain; 15 in all.

**PROGRAMS OF STUDY. Degrees:** B.A., B.S.
**Majors:** Accounting, American Culture, Art, Biochemistry, Biology, Biopsychology, Business/Finance, Chemistry, Classical Studies, Economics, Elementary Education, English, English/Secondary Education, Foreign Language, French, German, History, International Studies, Mathematics, Music, Philosophy, Political Science, Psychology, Rhetoric/Writing, Social Studies Education, Sociology, Spanish, Theatre, Theology.
**Distribution of degrees:** The majors with the highest enrollment are business/finance, sociology, and accounting; French, philosophy, and Spanish have the lowest.
**Requirements:** General education requirement.
**Academic regulations:** Freshmen must maintain minimum 1.6 GPA; sophomores, 1.8 GPA; juniors, 2.0 GPA; seniors, 2.0 GPA.
**Special:** Minors offered in most majors and in computer science, Latin American studies. Formal area of concentration offered in criminal justice, marketing, and religious education. Self-designed majors. Double majors. Dual degrees. Independent study. Accelerated study. Pass/fail grading option. Internships. Cooperative education programs. Preprofessional programs in law, medicine, dentistry, and theology. 3-2 computer science engineering program with Catholic U. 3-2 nursing program with Johns Hopkins U. Internships. Exchange program with Frederick Comm Coll. Teacher certification in elementary and secondary education. Study abroad in England, France, Italy, and Spain. ROTC.
**Honors:** Honors program. Honor societies.
**Academic Assistance:** Remedial reading, writing, math, and study skills. Nonremedial tutoring.

**STUDENT LIFE. Housing:** Freshmen must live on campus. Coed dorms. School-owned/operated apartments. 86% of students live in college housing.
**Social atmosphere:** The student newspaper describes Mount Saint Mary's as a small college with a strong sense of unity. The Student Government Association, the Student Union Board, the Campus Ministry, and the yearbook staff are influential in student social life. Students frequent High Rock, The Bridge, and Cunningham Falls. Popular events include basketball games, class socials, and small parties.
**Services and counseling/handicapped student services:** Placement services. Health service. Chaplain, faculty priests. Counseling services for minority, military, veteran, and older students. Personal and psychological counseling. Career and academic guidance services. Religious counseling. Physically disabled student services. Notetaking services. Tape recorders. Tutors. Reader services for the blind.
**Campus organizations:** Undergraduate student government. Student newspaper (Mountain Echo, published once/two weeks). Literary magazine. Yearbook. Radio and TV stations. Mount Singers, Drama Society, departmental groups, special-interest groups, 70 organizations in all.
**Religious organizations:** Campus Ministry, Pax Christi.
**Minority/foreign student organizations:** Heritage. International Student Association.

**ATHLETICS. Physical education requirements:** None.
**Intercollegiate competition:** 25% of students participate. Baseball (M), basketball (M,W), cross-country (M,W), golf (M), lacrosse (M), soccer (M,W), softball (W), tennis (M,W), track and field (indoor) (M,W), track and field (outdoor) (M,W). Member of ECAC, NCAA Division I, Northeast Conference.
**Intramural and club sports:** 65% of students participate. Intramural badminton, basketball, football, horseshoes, racquetball, running, softball, swimming, tennis, volleyball, walleyball, Wiffle ball. Men's club cheerleading, choi kwang do, karate, rugby. Women's club cheerleading, choi kwang do, karate, lacrosse.

**ADMISSIONS. Academic basis for candidate selection** (in order of priority): Secondary school record, class rank, standardized test scores, school's recommendation, essay.
**Nonacademic basis for candidate selection:** Character and personality, extracurricular participation, particular talent or ability, and alumni/ae relationship are considered.
**Requirements:** Graduation from secondary school is required; GED is accepted. 16 units and the following program of study are required: 4 units of English, 3 units of math, 3 units of science including 2 units of lab, 2 units of foreign language, 3 units of social studies, 1 unit of academic electives. SAT is required; ACT may be substituted. Campus visit and interview recommended. Off-campus interviews available with admissions and alumni representatives.
**Procedure:** Take SAT or ACT by January of 12th year. Visit college for interview by March 1 of 12th year. Application deadline is March 1. Notification of admission by April 1. Reply is required by May 1 or within two weeks of acceptance if after April 15. $500 tuition deposit, refundable until May 1. $150 of tuition deposit refundable at graduation. Freshmen accepted for terms other than fall.
**Special programs:** Admission may be deferred 1 semester or 1 year. Credit and/or placement may be granted through CEEB Advanced Placement exams for scores of 3 or higher. Credit and/or placement may be granted through CLEP general exams. Credit may be granted through CLEP subject exams and DANTES exams. Early decision program. In fall 1993, 220 applied for early decision and 190 were accepted. Deadline for applying for

early decision is December 1. Early entrance/early admission program. Concurrent enrollment program.
**Transfer students:** Transfer students accepted for terms other than fall. In fall 1993, 10% of all new students were transfers into all classes. 121 transfer applications were received, 83 were accepted. Application deadline is June 1 for fall; December 1 for spring. Minimum 2.5 GPA recommended. Lowest course grade accepted is "C." Maximum number of transferable credits is 60 semester hours from a two-year school and 90 semester hours from a four-year school. At least 30 semester hours must be completed at the college to receive degree.
**Admissions contact:** Michael Kennedy, Director of Admissions. 301 447-5214.

**FINANCIAL AID. Available aid:** Pell grants, SEOG, state scholarships and grants, school scholarships and grants, private scholarships and grants, ROTC scholarships, academic merit scholarships, athletic scholarships, and aid for undergraduate foreign students. Minority scholarships. Perkins Loans (NDSL), PLUS, Stafford Loans (GSL), state loans, school loans, private loans, and SLS. Deferred payment plan and family tuition reduction.
**Financial aid statistics:** In 1993-94, 93% of all undergraduate applicants received aid; 96% of freshman applicants. Average amounts of aid awarded freshmen: Scholarships and grants, $5,863; loans, $2,825.
**Supporting data/closing dates:** FAFSA/FAF: Priority filing date is March 15. Notification of awards on rolling basis.
**Financial aid contact:** Joseph P. Zanella, Director of Financial Aid. 301 447-5207.

**STUDENT EMPLOYMENT.** College Work/Study Program. Institutional employment. 28% of full-time undergraduates work on campus during school year. Students may expect to earn an average of $1,200 during school year. Off-campus part-time employment opportunities rated "fair."

**COMPUTER FACILITIES.** 65 IBM/IBM-compatible and Macintosh/Apple microcomputers; 20 are networked. Students may access Prime, SUN minicomputer/mainframe systems, Internet. Client/LAN operating systems include Apple/Macintosh, DOS, UNIX/XENIX/AIX, Novell. Computer languages and software packages include BASIC, COBOL, FORTRAN, LISP, Pascal, SPSS. Computer facilities are available to all students.
**Fees:** None.
**Hours:** 24 hours.

**GRADUATE CAREER DATA.** Graduate school percentages: 3% enter law school. 3% enter medical school. 8% enter graduate business programs. 5% enter graduate arts and sciences programs. Highest graduate school enrollments: George Washington U, Georgetown U, U of Maryland. 58% of graduates choose careers in business and industry. Companies and businesses that hire graduates: Big Six accounting firms, Citicorp, IBM.

**PROMINENT ALUMNI/AE.** Susan O'Malley, president, Washington Bullets; Dr. William Magee, partner, Plastic Surgery Assoc., co-founder of Operation Smile International; Matt McHugh, chief counsel to president of World Bank, former congressman.

## St. John's College

**Annapolis, MD 21404** **410 263-2371**

**1994-95 Costs.** Tuition: $17,430. Room & board: $5,720. Fees, books, misc. academic expenses (school's estimate): $475.
**Enrollment.** Undergraduates: 223 men, 170 women (full-time). Freshman class: 323 applicants, 78 accepted, 122 enrolled. Graduate enrollment: 60 men, 5 women.
**Test score averages/ranges.** Range of SAT scores of middle 50%: 580-680 verbal, 530-660 math.
**Faculty.** 60 full-time; 7 part-time. 57% of faculty holds doctoral degree. Student/faculty ratio: 8 to 1.
**Selectivity rating.** Highly competitive.

**PROFILE.** St. John's, founded in 1696, is a private, liberal arts college. At the core of St. John's curriculum is a list of "great books." Its 36-acre campus is located in Annapolis, 32 miles from Washington, D.C.

**Accreditation:** MSACS.
**Religious orientation:** St. John's College is nonsectarian; no religious requirements.
**Library:** Collections totaling over 93,684 volumes, 120 periodical subscriptions, and 1,414 microform items.
**Special facilities/museums:** Art gallery, planetarium.
**Athletic facilities:** Gymnasium, tennis court, athletic fields, weight room, boat house.

**STUDENT BODY. Undergraduate profile:** 15% are state residents; 17% are transfers. 5% Asian-American, 2% Black, 2% Hispanic, 89% White, 2% Other. Average age of undergraduates is 21.
**Freshman profile:** 16% of freshmen who took SAT scored 700 or over on verbal, 12% scored 700 or over on math; 62% scored 600 or over on verbal, 45% scored 600 or over on math; 82% scored 500 or over on verbal, 75% scored 500 or over on math; 89% scored 400 or over on verbal, 87% scored 400 or over on math; 89% scored 300 or over on math. 89% of accepted applicants took SAT. 63% of freshmen come from public schools.
**Undergraduate achievement:** 83% of fall 1992 freshmen returned for fall 1993 term. 50% of entering class graduated. 20% of students who completed a degree program immediately went on to graduate study.
**Foreign students:** Six students are from out of the country. Countries represented include Bulgaria, Canada, China, and India; six in all.

**PROGRAMS OF STUDY. Degrees:** B.A.Lib.Arts
**Requirements:** General education requirement.
**Academic regulations:** Minimum 2.0 GPA must be maintained.
**Special:** All students take Great Books Program. Students and faculty at St. John's work together in small discussion classes without lecture courses, written finals, or emphasis on grades. The program is a rigorous interdisciplinary curriculum based on great books: literature, mathematics, philosophy, theology, science, political theory, music, history, and economics. Preprofessional programs in law. Students may spend one or more years at college's Santa Fe campus.
**Academic Assistance:** Nonremedial tutoring.

**ADMISSIONS. Academic basis for candidate selection** (in order of priority): Essay, secondary school record, school's recommendation, class rank, standardized test scores.
**Nonacademic basis for candidate selection:** Character and personality are emphasized. Extracurricular participation is important. Particular talent or ability and alumni/ae relationship are considered.
**Requirements:** Graduation from secondary school is required; GED is accepted. No specific distribution of secondary school units required. 2 units of algebra, 1 unit of geometry, and 2 units of a single language recommended. No standarized test or minimum GPA required. Conditional admission possible for applicants not meeting standard requirements. SAT or ACT is recommended. Campus visit and interview recommended. Off-campus interviews available with admissions and alumni representatives.
**Procedure:** Take SAT or ACT by fall of 12th year. Visit college for interview by April of 12th year. Suggest filing application by March 1; no deadline. Acceptance notification within two weeks of receipt of all credentials. Reply is required by May 1. $250 nonrefundable tuition deposit. Freshmen accepted for terms other than fall.
**Special programs:** Admission may be deferred one year. Early entrance/early admission program.
**Transfer students:** Transfer students accepted for terms other than fall. In fall 1993, 17% of all new students were transfers into all classes. 26 transfer applications were received, 24 were accepted. Application deadline for fall is March 1 (preferred); November 1 (preferred) for spring. At least 132 semester units must be completed at the college to receive degree.
**Admissions contact:** John Christensen, Ph.D., Director of Admissions. 800 727-9238.

**FINANCIAL AID. Available aid:** Pell grants, SEOG, state scholarships and grants, school grants, and aid for undergraduate foreign students. Perkins Loans (NDSL), PLUS, Stafford Loans (GSL), school loans, and SLS. AMS and guaranteed tuition.
**Financial aid statistics:** In 1993-94, 78% of all undergraduate applicants received aid; 85% of freshman applicants. Average amounts of aid awarded freshmen: Scholarships and grants, $10,700; loans, $2,625.
**Supporting data/closing dates:** FAFSA/FAF: Priority filing date is February 15; accepted on rolling basis. School's own aid application: Priority filing date is February 15; accepted on rolling basis. State aid form: Priority filing date is February 15; accepted on rolling basis. Income tax forms: Accepted on rolling basis. Notification of awards on rolling basis.
**Financial aid contact:** Caroline Christensen, M.A., Director of Financial Aid. 410 263-2371, extension 203.

## St. Mary's College of Maryland

**St. Mary's City, MD 20686** **301 862-0200**

**1994-95 Costs.** Tuition: $4,000 (state residents), $6,500 (out-of-state). Room & board: $4,730. Fees, books, misc. academic expenses (school's estimate): $1,415.
**Enrollment.** Undergraduates: 601 men, 714 women (full-time). Freshman class: 1,340 applicants, 695 accepted, 286 enrolled.
**Test score averages/ranges.** Average SAT scores: 579 verbal, 615 math. Range of SAT scores of middle 50%: 530-630 verbal, 570-670 math.
**Faculty.** 103 full-time; 55 part-time. 97% of faculty holds highest degree in specific field. Student/faculty ratio: 14 to 1.
**Selectivity rating.** Highly competitive.

**PROFILE.** St. Mary's College of Maryland, founded in 1840, is a public, liberal arts college. Programs are offered through the Divisions of Arts and Letters, History and Social Science, Human Development, and Natural Science and Mathematics. Its 275-acre campus is located in St. Mary's City, 70 miles north of Washington, D.C.

**Accreditation:** MSACS. Professionally accredited by the National Association of Schools of Music.
**Religious orientation:** St. Mary's College of Maryland is nonsectarian; no religious requirements.
**Library:** Collections totaling over 141,395 volumes, 1,452 periodical subscriptions, and 31,965 microform items.
**Special facilities/museums:** Art gallery, historic state house of early Maryland settlers, electron microscope, marine research vessel, freshwater and saltwater research tanks.
**Athletic facilities:** Gymnasiums, swimming pools, track, weight room, tennis courts, athletic fields.

**STUDENT BODY. Undergraduate profile:** 84% are state residents; 19% are transfers. 5% Asian-American, 9% Black, 2% Hispanic, 84% White. Average age of undergraduates is 21.
**Freshman profile:** 5% of freshmen who took SAT scored 700 or over on verbal, 12% scored 700 or over on math; 47% scored 600 or over on verbal, 64% scored 600 or over on math; 86% scored 500 or over on verbal, 92% scored 500 or over on math; 97% scored 400 or over on verbal, 99% scored 400 or over on math; 100% scored 300 or over on verbal, 100% scored 300 or over on math. 91% of accepted applicants took SAT. 79% of freshmen come from public schools.
**Undergraduate achievement:** 88% of fall 1992 freshmen returned for fall 1993 term. 57% of entering class graduated. 39% of students who completed a degree program went on to graduate study within one year.
**Foreign students:** 47 students are from out of the country. Countries represented include Canada, England, Germany, Japan, Korea, and the Netherlands; 24 in all.

**PROGRAMS OF STUDY. Degrees:** B.A.
**Majors:** Anthropology/Sociology, Art, Biology, Chemistry, Dramatic Arts, Economics, English, Foreign Language, History, Human Development, Mathematics, Music, Natural

Science, Philosophy, Physics, Political Science, Psychology, Public Policy Studies, Student-Designed Major.
**Distribution of degrees:** The majors with the highest enrollment are economics, psychology, and biology; natural science, chemistry, and physics have the lowest.
**Requirements:** General education requirement.
**Academic regulations:** Minimum 2.0 GPA must be maintained.
**Special:** Courses offered in astronomy, Chinese, computer science, French, geology, German, physics, sociology, and Spanish. Students may assist in professorial research and participate in archaeological digs. Self-designed majors. Double majors. Independent study. Pass/fail grading option. Internships. Preprofessional programs in medicine, veterinary science, pharmacy, dentistry, and optometry. Exchange program with Johns Hopkins U. Exchange program abroad in Germany (Heidelberg U). Study abroad also in China, Costa Rica, England, and France.
**Honors:** Honors program. Honor societies.
**Academic Assistance:** Remedial study skills. Nonremedial tutoring.

**STUDENT LIFE. Housing:** Students may live on or off campus. Coed, women's, and men's dorms. School-owned/operated apartments. 71% of students live in college housing.
**Social atmosphere:** The student newspaper reports that different groups influence social life at different times of the year; for example, the rugby club in the fall and the crew club in the spring. On campus, students gather in the library, the townhouses, and the Student Center. Students frequent The Green Door, and Pizza Hut off campus. Popular school-year events include Waterfront Day, the Holiday Formal, and rugby parties.
**Services and counseling/handicapped student services:** Placement services. Health service. Counseling services for minority, veteran, and older students. Birth control, personal, and psychological counseling. Career and academic guidance services. Physically disabled student services. Notetaking services. Tape recorders. Tutors. Reader services for the blind.
**Campus organizations:** Undergraduate student government. Student newspaper (Point News, published once/week). Literary magazine. Yearbook. Radio and TV stations. Coffeehouse, film and TV/video clubs, Fine Arts Committee, biology, philosophy, and psychology clubs, Dormitory Councils, Speakers Committee, Amnesty International, Avatar, BACCHUS, Coalition for Global Responsibility, College Republicans, For Goodness' Sake, Students Against Drunk Driving, chess, outdoor, and science fiction clubs, 62 organizations in all.
**Religious organizations:** Christian Fellowship, Hillel.
**Minority/foreign student organizations:** Black Student Union. International Spectrum.

**ATHLETICS. Physical education requirements:** None.
**Intercollegiate competition:** 25% of students participate. Baseball (M), basketball (M,W), lacrosse (M,W), sailing (M,W), soccer (M,W), tennis (M,W), volleyball (W). Member of Capital Athletic Conference, NCAA Division III.
**Intramural and club sports:** 50% of students participate. Intramural basketball, flag football, indoor lacrosse, indoor soccer, inner-tube water polo, sailing, volleyball. Men's club rugby, ultimate frisbee. Women's club field hockey, ultimate frisbee.

**ADMISSIONS. Academic basis for candidate selection** (in order of priority): Secondary school record, essay, school's recommendation, class rank, standardized test scores.
**Nonacademic basis for candidate selection:** Particular talent or ability is important. Character and personality, extracurricular participation, geographical distribution, and alumni/ae relationship are considered.
**Requirements:** Graduation from secondary school is required; GED is accepted. 22 units and the following program of study are required: 4 units of English, 3 units of math, 3 units of science including 2 units of lab, 2 units of foreign language, 3 units of social studies, 7 units of electives including 5 units of academic electives. Minimum combined SAT score of 1050 and rank in top half of secondary school class recommended. Minimum 2.5 GPA required. Conditional admission possible for applicants not meeting standard requirements. SAT is required; ACT may be substituted. ACH recommended. Campus visit and interview recommended. No off-campus interviews.
**Procedure:** Take SAT or ACT by November of 12th year. Take ACH by November of 12th year. Visit college for interview by December of 12th year. Suggest filing application by December 1. Application deadline is January 15. Notification of admission by April 1. Reply is required by May 1. $100 nonrefundable tuition deposit required for commuters only. $300 nonrefundable room deposit. Freshmen accepted for terms other than fall.
**Special programs:** Credit may be granted through CEEB Advanced Placement for scores of 4 or higher. Credit and/or placement may be granted through CLEP general and subject exams. Credit and placement may be granted through Regents College and DANTES exams. Early decision program. In fall 1993, 286 applied for early decision and 129 were accepted. Deadline for applying for early decision is December 1 and January 15. Early entrance/early admission program. Concurrent enrollment program.
**Transfer students:** Transfer students accepted for terms other than fall. In fall 1993, 19% of all new students were transfers into all classes. 273 transfer applications were received, 107 were accepted. Application deadline is January 15 for fall; November 1 for spring. Minimum 2.5 GPA recommended. Lowest course grade accepted is "C." Maximum number of transferable credits is 70 semester hours from a two-year school and 90 semester hours from a four-year school. At least 38 semester hours must be completed at the college to receive degree.
**Admissions contact:** Richard J. Edgar, Director of Admissions. 301 862-0292, 800 492-7181.

**FINANCIAL AID. Available aid:** Pell grants, SEOG, state scholarships, school scholarships and grants, private scholarships and grants, and academic merit scholarships. Perkins Loans (NDSL), PLUS, Stafford Loans (GSL), state loans, school loans, and SLS.
**Financial aid statistics:** 55% of aid is not need-based. In 1993-94, 65% of all undergraduate applicants received aid; 65% of freshman applicants. Average amounts of aid awarded freshmen: Scholarships and grants, $2,900; loans, $4,000.
**Supporting data/closing dates:** FAFSA/FAF: Priority filing date is March 1. Notification of awards begins April 1.
**Financial aid contact:** George T. Bachman, M.Ed., Director of Financial Aid. 301 862-0300, 800 492-7181.

**STUDENT EMPLOYMENT.** College Work/Study Program. Institutional employment. 23% of full-time undergraduates work on campus during school year. Students may expect to earn an average of $800 during school year. Off-campus part-time employment opportunities rated "good."

**COMPUTER FACILITIES.** 134 IBM/IBM-compatible, Macintosh/Apple, and RISC-/UNIX-based microcomputers; all are networked. Students may access Digital minicomputer/mainframe systems, Internet. Client/LAN operating systems include Apple/Macintosh, DOS, UNIX/XENIX/AIX, Novell. Computer languages and software packages include ADA, Assembler, BASIC, COBOL, dBase, FORTRAN, Paradox, Pascal, Quattro-Pro, SPSS, Turbo C++, Turbo Pascal, WordStar; 30 in all. Computer facilities are available to all students.
**Fees:** Computer fee is included in tuition/fees.
**Hours:** 8:30 AM-11 PM (M-Th); 8:30 AM-9 PM (F); 1 PM-9 PM (Sa); 1 PM-11 PM (Su).

**GRADUATE CAREER DATA.** Graduate school percentages: 2% enter law school. 4% enter graduate business programs. 33% enter graduate arts and sciences programs. Highest graduate school enrollments: Johns Hopkins U, U of Maryland. 43% of graduates choose careers in business and industry.

**PROMINENT ALUMNI/AE.** Scott Steele, Olympic silver-medal winner in sailboarding; David Bower, aquaculture pioneer and entrepreneur; Ruth Hudicek, founder, Chrysalis House.

# Salisbury State University

**Salisbury, MD 21801** **410 543-6000**

**1994-95 Costs.** Tuition: $2,328 (state residents), $5,130 (out-of-state). Room & board: $4,690. Fees, books, misc. academic expenses (school's estimate): $1,266.
**Enrollment.** Undergraduates: 1,965 men, 2,331 women (full-time). Freshman class: 4,216 applicants, 2,290 accepted, 687 enrolled. Graduate enrollment: 193 men, 440 women.
**Test score averages/ranges.** Average SAT scores: 491 verbal, 554 math. Range of SAT scores of middle 50%: 440-540 verbal, 520-620 math. Average ACT scores: 24 composite. Range of ACT scores of middle 50%: 21-24 composite.
**Faculty.** 240 full-time; 93 part-time. 80% of faculty holds doctoral degree. Student/faculty ratio: 16 to 1.
**Selectivity rating.** More competitive.

**PROFILE.** Salisbury State, founded in 1925, is a public university. Programs are offered through the Schools of Business, Liberal Arts, Nursing and Health Sciences, Professional Studies, and Science. Its 140-acre campus is located in Salisbury, 90 miles south of Annapolis.

**Accreditation:** MSACS. Professionally accredited by the American Medical Association (CAHEA), the Council on Social Work Education, the National League for Nursing.
**Religious orientation:** Salisbury State University is nonsectarian; no religious requirements.
**Library:** Collections totaling over 254,000 volumes, 1,800 periodical subscriptions, and 600,000 microform items.
**Special facilities/museums:** Arboretum.
**Athletic facilities:** Gymnasiums, natatorium, field house, Nautilus and weight rooms, stadium, baseball, football, intramural, practice, and softball fields, tracks, basketball, handball, racquetball, and tennis courts.

**STUDENT BODY. Undergraduate profile:** 75% are state residents; 41% are transfers. 1% Asian-American, 6% Black, 1% Hispanic, 91% White, 1% Other. Average age of undergraduates is 20.
**Freshman profile:** 1% of freshmen who took SAT scored 700 or over on verbal, 3% scored 700 or over on math; 9% scored 600 or over on verbal, 28% scored 600 or over on math; 45% scored 500 or over on verbal, 82% scored 500 or over on math; 95% scored 400 or over on verbal, 99% scored 400 or over on math; 100% scored 300 or over on verbal, 100% scored 300 or over on math. 100% of accepted applicants took SAT; 5% took ACT. 75% of freshmen come from public schools.
**Undergraduate achievement:** 83% of fall 1992 freshmen returned for fall 1993 term. 39% of entering class graduated. 26% of students who completed a degree program immediately went on to graduate study.
**Foreign students:** 23 students are from out of the country. Countries represented include China, Ghana, Taiwan, Tanzania, and the United Kingdom; 16 in all.

**PROGRAMS OF STUDY. Degrees:** B.A., B.F.A., B.S., B.S.Nurs., B.Soc.Work.
**Majors:** Accounting, Art, Biology, Business Administration, Chemistry, Communication Arts, Economics, Elementary Education, English, Environmental Health, Environmental/Marine Science, Fine Arts, French, Geography/Regional Planning, History, Liberal Studies, Management Information Systems, Mathematics, Medical Technology, Music, Nursing, Philosophy, Physical Education, Physical Sciences, Physics, Physics/Micro-electronics, Political Science, Psychology, Respiratory Therapy, Social Work, Sociology, Spanish.
**Distribution of degrees:** The majors with the highest enrollment are business administration, elementary education, and biology; French and Spanish have the lowest.
**Requirements:** General education requirement.
**Academic regulations:** Minimum 2.0 GPA required for graduation.
**Special:** Minors offered in some majors and in American studies, anthropology, comparative literature, gerontology, marketing management, and planning. Interdisciplinary programs in American studies, earth sciences, European studies, Latin American studies, and urban affairs. Courses in German and statistics. Self-designed majors. Double majors. Dual degrees. Independent study. Accelerated study. Pass/fail grading option. Internships. Cooperative education programs. Graduate school at which undergraduates may take graduate-level courses. Preprofessional programs in law, medicine, veterinary science, pharmacy, dentistry, optometry, physical therapy, and podiatry. 3-2 engineering programs with U of Maryland at College Park, Old Dominion U, and Widener U. Annapolis Semester (state legislature). Credit exchange programs with U of Maryland system institutions. Teacher certification in early childhood, elementary, and secondary education. Certification in specific subject areas. Study abroad in Western Europe. ROTC.

**Honors:** Honors program. Honor societies.
**Academic Assistance:** Remedial reading, writing, math, and study skills. Nonremedial tutoring.

**STUDENT LIFE. Housing:** Students may live on or off campus. Coed, women's, and men's dorms. School-owned/operated apartments. Honors House, International Student House. 60% of students live in college housing.
**Social atmosphere:** The student newspaper reports, "Most social and weekend activities are centered around small groups of friends. Very few campus activities are organized with the exception of the dances and military functions." Greeks and athletes are influential, and popular events include the Homecoming game and dance, the Spring Formal, Derby Days (sponsored by the student radio station), the Military Ball, and ROTC Dining In. Off campus, students like to go to Ocean City, a resort town with several nightclubs.
**Services and counseling/handicapped student services:** Placement services. Health service. Women's center. Counseling services for minority, veteran, and older students. Birth control, personal, and psychological counseling. Career and academic guidance services. Physically disabled student services. Learning disabled services. Notetaking services. Tape recorders. Reader services for the blind.
**Campus organizations:** Undergraduate student government. Student newspaper (Flyer, published four times/semester). Literary magazine. Yearbook. Radio station. Symphony orchestra, concert and gospel choirs, concert band, jazz band, dance company, student theatre organization, sign language club, PROUD (disabled students group). Six fraternities, no chapter houses; four sororities, no chapter houses. 7% of men join a fraternity. 8% of women join a sorority.
**Religious organizations:** Baptist Student Ministries, Campus Crusade for Christ, Chi Alpha Christian Fellowship, Latter-Day Saints Student Association, Newman Club.
**Minority/foreign student organizations:** Union of African Americans, NAACP, African-American Historical and Philosophical Society. International Student Organization.

**ATHLETICS. Physical education requirements:** One semester of physical education required.
**Intercollegiate competition:** 12% of students participate. Baseball (M), basketball (M,W), cheerleading (M,W), cross-country (M,W), field hockey (W), football (M), lacrosse (M,W), soccer (M,W), softball (W), swimming (M,W), tennis (M,W), track and field (outdoor) (M,W), volleyball (W). Member of Capital Athletic Conference, ECAC, Mason/Dixon Conference, NCAA Division III.
**Intramural and club sports:** 30% of students participate. Intramural aerobics, basketball, billiards, box lacrosse, flag football, floor hockey, free throw, racquetball, soccer, softball, table tennis, tennis, turkey trot, ultimate frisbee, volleyball, walleyball, water polo. Men's club cycling, diving, floor hockey, ice hockey, martial arts, outdoor club, rugby, sailing, swimming, weight lifting. Women's club cycling, martial arts, outdoor club, sailing, soccer, weight lifting.

**ADMISSIONS. Academic basis for candidate selection** (in order of priority): Secondary school record, standardized test scores, class rank, school's recommendation, essay.
**Nonacademic basis for candidate selection:** Extracurricular participation, particular talent or ability, geographical distribution, and alumni/ae relationship are considered.
**Requirements:** Graduation from secondary school is required; GED is accepted. 18 units and the following program of study are required: 4 units of English, 3 units of math, 2 units of lab science, 2 units of foreign language, 2 units of social studies, 1 unit of history, 2 units of academic electives. Minimum combined SAT score of 900, rank in top half of secondary school class, and minimum 2.5 GPA preferred. Portfolio required of art program applicants. Audition required of music program applicants. SAT is required. ACT is recommended. Campus visit and interview recommended. No off-campus interviews.
**Procedure:** Take SAT by December of 12th year. Visit college for interview by February of 12th year. Suggest filing application by January 15. Application deadline is March 15. Notification of admission by March 15. Reply is required by May 1. $200 nonrefundable tuition deposit. $175 room deposit, refundable until June 1. Freshmen accepted for terms other than fall.
**Special programs:** Credit and/or placement may be granted through CEEB Advanced Placement exams for scores of 3 or higher. Credit and/or placement may be granted through CLEP general and subject exams. Credit may be granted through military experience. Credit and placement may be granted through ACT PEP, DANTES, and challenge exams. Early decision program. Deadline for applying for early decision is December 15. Early entrance/early admission program. Concurrent enrollment program.
**Transfer students:** Transfer students accepted for terms other than fall. In fall 1993, 41% of all new students were transfers into all classes. 1,112 transfer applications were received, 856 were accepted. Application deadline is May 1 for fall; January 1 for spring. Minimum 2.0 GPA required. Lowest course grade accepted is "C." Maximum number of transferable credits is 64 semester hours from a two-year school and 90 semester hours from a four-year school. At least 30 semester hours must be completed at the university to receive degree.
**Admissions contact:** Jane H. Dane, M.Ed., Dean of Admissions. 410 543-6161.

**FINANCIAL AID. Available aid:** Pell grants, SEOG, state scholarships and grants, school scholarships and grants, private scholarships and grants, ROTC scholarships, and academic merit scholarships. Perkins Loans (NDSL), PLUS, and SLS.
**Financial aid statistics:** 40% of aid is not need-based. In 1993-94, 50% of all undergraduate applicants received aid; 40% of freshman applicants. Average amounts of aid awarded freshmen: Scholarships and grants, $1,250; loans, $1,200.
**Supporting data/closing dates:** FAFSA/FAF: Priority filing date is March 1. State aid form. Notification of awards begins April 1.
**Financial aid contact:** Beverly Horner, M.Ed., Director of Financial Aid. 410 543-6165.

**STUDENT EMPLOYMENT.** College Work/Study Program. Institutional employment. 30% of full-time undergraduates work on campus during school year. Students may expect to earn an average of $1,500 during school year. Off-campus part-time employment opportunities rated "good."

**COMPUTER FACILITIES.** 125 IBM/IBM-compatible, Macintosh/Apple, and RISC-/UNIX-based microcomputers; all are networked. Students may access Digital minicomputer/mainframe systems, BITNET, Internet. Client/LAN operating systems include Apple/Macintosh, DOS, UNIX/XENIX/AIX, DEC, LocalTalk/AppleTalk, Microsoft. Computer languages and software packages include BASIC, C, COBOL, dBASE III, dBASE IV, FORTRAN, Hyper Card, Lotus 1-2-3, Mathematica, PageMaker, Pascal, Quatro Pro, Paradox, SPSS-X, Turbo C, Turbo Pascal, 20/20, WordPerfect; 100 in all. Computer facilities are available to all students.
**Fees:** None.
**Hours:** 8 AM-midn.; 24 hours for modem use.

**GRADUATE CAREER DATA.** Graduate school percentages: 1% enter law school. 5% enter medical school. 7% enter graduate business programs. 3% enter graduate arts and sciences programs. Highest graduate school enrollments: U of Baltimore, U of Delaware, U of Maryland, Salisbury State U. 60% of graduates choose careers in business and industry. Companies and businesses that hire graduates: Federal government, hospitals, Perdue Farms, hospitals.

**PROMINENT ALUMNI/AE.** Frank Perdue, Perdue Farms; Diane P. Bradley, international and professional staffing at Walt Disney World; Joe Bernard, owner, Mrs. Iries Potato Chips & Wye River.

# Towson State University

**Towson, MD 21204-7097** **410 830-2000**

**1994-95 Costs.** Tuition: $2,166 (state residents), $5,166 (out-of-state). Room & board: $4,480. Fees, books, misc. academic expenses (school's estimate): $1,451.
**Enrollment.** Undergraduates: 3,787 men, 5,460 women (full-time). Freshman class: 6,151 applicants, 3,831 accepted, 1,278 enrolled. Graduate enrollment: 431 men, 1,434 women.
**Test score averages/ranges.** Average SAT scores: 467 verbal, 516 math. Range of SAT scores of middle 50%: 420-510 verbal, 470-560 math.
**Faculty.** 481 full-time; 422 part-time. 74% of faculty holds doctoral degree. Student/faculty ratio: 17 to 1.
**Selectivity rating.** Less competitive.

**PROFILE.** Towson State, founded in 1866, is a public university. Programs are offered through the Colleges of Allied Health Sciences and Physical Education, Continuing Studies, Education, Fine Arts and Communication, Liberal Arts, and Natural and Mathematical Sciences; the School of Business and Economics; and the Graduate School. Its 306-acre campus is located in Towson, five miles from downtown Baltimore.
**Accreditation:** MSACS. Professionally accredited by the American Assembly of Collegiate Schools of Business, the American Medical Association (CAHEA), the American Speech-Language-Hearing Association, the National Association of Schools of Music, the National Council for Accreditation of Teacher Education, the National League for Nursing.
**Religious orientation:** Towson State University is nonsectarian; no religious requirements.
**Library:** Collections totaling over 504,606 volumes, 2,080 periodical subscriptions, and 661,101 microform items.
**Special facilities/museums:** Art galleries, animal museum, Asian art collection, elementary school, media center, speech/language clinic, planetarium/observatory, herbarium, electron microscope, argon laser.
**Athletic facilities:** Gymnasiums, fitness center, weight room, basketball, racquetball, squash, and tennis courts, track, swimming pool, fitness trail, athletic fields, par course.

**STUDENT BODY. Undergraduate profile:** 85% are state residents; 52% are transfers. 3% Asian-American, 9% Black, 1% Hispanic, 85% White, 2% Other. Average age of undergraduates is 23.
**Freshman profile:** 1% of freshmen who took SAT scored 700 or over on math; 4% scored 600 or over on verbal, 13% scored 600 or over on math; 32% scored 500 or over on verbal, 57% scored 500 or over on math; 89% scored 400 or over on verbal, 93% scored 400 or over on math; 98% scored 300 or over on verbal, 97% scored 300 or over on math. Majority of accepted applicants took SAT. 65% of freshmen come from public schools.
**Undergraduate achievement:** 82% of fall 1992 freshmen returned for fall 1993 term.
**Foreign students:** 238 students are from out of the country. Countries represented include China, Germany, Indonesia, Japan, Korea, and United Kingdom; 53 in all.

**PROGRAMS OF STUDY. Degrees:** B.A., B.F.A., B.S.
**Majors:** Accounting, Art, Art Education, Biology, Business Administration, Chemistry, Communication Studies, Computer Science, Dance, Early Childhood Education, Economics, Elementary Education, English, French, General Education, Geography, German, Health Science, History, Interdisciplinary Studies, International Studies, Mass Communication, Mathematics, Medical Technology, Music, Music Education, Natural Science, Nursing, Occupational Therapy, Philosophy, Physical Education, Physics, Political Science, Psychology, Social Sciences, Sociology, Spanish, Speech Pathology/Audiology, Theater Arts, Women's Studies.
**Distribution of degrees:** The majors with the highest enrollment are business administration, mass communication, and elementary education; French and German have the lowest.
**Requirements:** General education requirement.
**Academic regulations:** Freshmen must maintain minimum 1.5 GPA; sophomores, 1.75 GPA; juniors, 2.0 GPA; seniors, 2.0 GPA.
**Special:** Minors offered in all majors and in anthropology. Second-degree program. Several thematic options within general studies major. Clinical concentration program leads to B.S. in psychology and certificate in mental health. Certificate program in cartography. Elder-hostel Program. Television courses. Self-designed majors. Double majors. Dual degrees. Independent study. Accelerated study. Pass/fail grading option. Internships. Cooperative education programs. Graduate school at which undergraduates may take graduate-level courses. Preprofessional programs in law, medicine, veterinary science, pharmacy, and dentistry. 3-1 medical technology program. 3-2 engineering program with U of Maryland at College Park. Member of consortium with U of Maryland system; cross-registration possible. Member of National Student Exchange (NSE). Teacher certification in early childhood, elementary, secondary, and special education. Certification in specific subject areas. Member of International Student Exchange Program (ISEP). Study abroad in Belgium, England, Germany, Italy, Japan, Russia, and other countries. ROTC at Loyola Coll. AFROTC at U of Maryland at College Park.
**Honors:** Phi Beta Kappa. Honors program. Honor societies.

**Academic Assistance:** Remedial reading, writing, math, and study skills. Nonremedial tutoring.

**STUDENT LIFE. Housing:** Students may live on or off campus. Coed dorms. School-owned/operated apartments. On-campus married-student housing. 19% of students live in college housing.
**Social atmosphere:** Students gather at The Ratt on campus for food, music, and entertainment. Off campus, students head for local bars such as Kelly's, Gator's Pub, Poor Richard's Saloon, and Fell's Point. Greeks, athletes, and the student newspaper are influential on campus. Favorite events include Homecoming, the Towson State vs. Johns Hopkins lacrosse game, and the Towsontown Festival. "The social life at TSU focuses on the many bars and pubs in the Baltimore area. Apathy runs rampant on campus, so people like to do things off campus," comments the student newspaper.
**Services and counseling/handicapped student services:** Placement services. Health service. Women's center. Day care. Counseling services for minority, military, veteran, and older students. Birth control, personal, and psychological counseling. Career and academic guidance services. Religious counseling. Physically disabled student services. Learning disabled services. Notetaking services. Tutors. Reader services for the blind.
**Campus organizations:** Undergraduate student government. Student newspaper (Towerlight, published once/week). Literary magazine. Yearbook. Radio and TV stations. Marching band, music ensembles, pep band, orchestra, jazz band, drama, choral groups, concert band, dance company, Outdoor Adventures Unlimited, Circle K, women's center, Democrat/Republican groups, Student Government Association, 105 organizations in all. 18 fraternities, no chapter houses; 13 sororities, no chapter houses. 11% of men join a fraternity. 10% of women join a sorority.
**Religious organizations:** Baptist Campus Ministry, Campus Crusade for Christ, Episcopalian group, University Christian Outreach, Jewish Student Association, Lutheran Student Movement, Newman Club.
**Minority/foreign student organizations:** Black Student Union, Brotherhood, NAACP, SAGE Program, Jewish Student Union. International Club, Asian, Hispanic, and Korean groups.

**ATHLETICS. Physical education requirements:** One credit hour of physical education required.
**Intercollegiate competition:** 5% of students participate. Baseball (M), basketball (M,W), cheerleading (M,W), cross-country (M,W), diving (M,W), field hockey (W), football (M), golf (M), gymnastics (W), lacrosse (M,W), soccer (M,W), softball (W), swimming (M,W), tennis (M,W), track (outdoor) (M,W), track and field (outdoor) (M,W), volleyball (W). Member of Big South Conference, ECAC, NCAA Division I, NCAA Division I-AA for football.
**Intramural and club sports:** 20% of students participate. Intramural badminton, basketball, bowling, flag football, floor hockey, ice hockey, indoor soccer, karate, rugby, softball, ultimate frisbee, volleyball, water polo, weight lifting. Men's club basketball, bowling, flag football, ice hockey, martial arts, racquetball, rugby, softball, squash, ultimate frisbee, volleyball, water polo, weight lifting, wrestling. Women's club basketball, bowling, flag football, martial arts, racquetball, rugby, softball, squash, ultimate frisbee, water polo, weight lifting.

**ADMISSIONS. Academic basis for candidate selection** (in order of priority): Secondary school record, school's recommendation, standardized test scores.
**Nonacademic basis for candidate selection:** Extracurricular participation, particular talent or ability, geographical distribution, and alumni/ae relationship are considered.
**Requirements:** Graduation from secondary school is required; GED is accepted. 20 units and the following program of study are required: 4 units of English, 3 units of math, 2 units of lab science, 2 units of foreign language, 3 units of social studies, 6 units of electives. Minimum combined SAT score of 850 and minimum 2.0 GPA required; minimum combined SAT score of 1000 and minimum 2.5 GPA recommended. Audition required of dance and music program applicants. Developmental testing and remedial course work possible for applicants not normally admissible. SAT is required; ACT may be substituted. Campus visit recommended. No off-campus interviews.
**Procedure:** Take SAT or ACT by November of 12th year. Suggest filing application by October 1. Application deadline is March 1. Notification of admission on rolling basis. Reply is required by May 1. $200 nonrefundable enrollment fee. $200 nonrefundable room deposit. Freshmen accepted for terms other than fall.
**Special programs:** Credit and/or placement may be granted through CEEB Advanced Placement exams. Credit and/or placement may be granted through CLEP general and subject exams. Credit and placement may be granted through ACT PEP, DANTES, and challenge exams, and military and life experience. Early entrance/early admission program.
**Transfer students:** Transfer students accepted for terms other than fall. In fall 1993, 52% of all new students were transfers into all classes. 3,101 transfer applications were received, 2,478 were accepted. Application deadline is March 1 for fall; December 1 for spring. Minimum 2.0 GPA required. Lowest course grade accepted is "D." Maximum number of transferable credits is 90 semester hours. At least 30 semester hours must be completed at the university to receive degree.
**Admissions contact:** Angel Jackson, Acting Director of Admissions. 410 830-2112, 800 CALL-TSU.

**FINANCIAL AID. Available aid:** Pell grants, SEOG, state scholarships, school scholarships and grants, private scholarships, ROTC scholarships, academic merit scholarships, athletic scholarships, aid for undergraduate foreign students, and United Negro College Fund. Perkins Loans (NDSL), PLUS, Stafford Loans (GSL), private loans, and SLS. AMS.
**Financial aid statistics:** 30% of aid is not need-based. In 1992-93, 83% of all undergraduate applicants received aid.
**Supporting data/closing dates:** FAFSA: Priority filing date is March 15. FAF: Priority filing date is March 15; accepted on rolling basis. FFS: Accepted on rolling basis; deadline is March 1. School's own aid application: Priority filing date is March 15. Income tax forms: Priority filing date is March 15; accepted on rolling basis. Financial aid transcripts: Priority filing date is March 15; accepted on rolling basis. Notification of awards begins April 15.
**Financial aid contact:** Marilyn Leuthold, M.L.A., M.A.S., Director of Financial Aid. 410 830-2061.

**STUDENT EMPLOYMENT.** College Work/Study Program. Institutional employment. 12% of full-time undergraduates work on campus during school year. Students may expect to earn an average of $1,750 during school year. Off-campus part-time employment opportunities rated "good."

**COMPUTER FACILITIES.** 500 IBM/IBM-compatible and Macintosh/Apple microcomputers; 100 are networked. Students may access Digital minicomputer/mainframe systems, BITNET, Internet. Client/LAN operating systems include Apple/Macintosh. Computer languages and software packages include Ada, BASIC, C, C++, COBOL, FORTRAN, Lotus 1-2-3, Pascal, PageMaker, SAS, SPSS, WordPerfect. Computer facilities are available to all students.
**Fees:** $70 computer fee per year; included in tuition/fees.
**Hours:** 24 hours access.

**GRADUATE CAREER DATA.** 10% of graduates choose careers in business and industry. Companies and businesses that hire graduates: Accounting firms, public and private school systems, sales companies, insurance companies, advertising and marketing firms.

**PROMINENT ALUMNI/AE.** John Schuerholz, general manager, Atlanta Braves; Robert Ward, author, screenwriter, television producer; John Glover, actor; Dr. Nancy Grasmick, Maryland state superintendent of schools.

# United States Naval Academy

**Annapolis, MD 21402-5018** **410 267-6100**

**1994-95 Costs.** Tuition: None.
**Enrollment.** Undergraduates: 3,615 men, 512 women (full-time). Freshman class: 12,135 applicants, 1,483 accepted, 1,182 enrolled.
**Test score averages/ranges.** Average SAT scores: 568 verbal, 663 math. Range of SAT scores of middle 50%: 530-620 verbal, 630-710 math.
**Faculty.** 567 full-time; 32 part-time. 89% of faculty holds doctoral degree. Student/faculty ratio: 7 to 1.
**Selectivity rating.** Highly competitive.

**PROFILE.** The U.S. Naval Academy is a public service academy. Founded in 1845, it adopted coeducation in 1976. Its 338-acre campus is located in Annapolis, 30 miles southeast of Baltimore and 33 miles east of Washington, D.C.

**Accreditation:** MSACS. Professionally accredited by the Accreditation Board for Engineering and Technology.
**Religious orientation:** United States Naval Academy is nonsectarian; no religious requirements.
**Library:** Collections totaling over 750,000 volumes, 1,987 periodical subscriptions, and 75,000 microform items.
**Special facilities/museums:** Naval history museum, naval institute, propulsion lab, subsonic and supersonic wind tunnels, flight simulator, subcritical nuclear reactor, 120/380-foot tow tanks, satellite dish, coastal chamber facilities, extensive fleet of small craft (power and sail), oceanographic research vessel.
**Athletic facilities:** Gymnasiums, swimming pools, tracks, basketball, handball, racquetball, squash, and tennis courts, bowling lanes, rifle and pistol ranges, golf course, sailing vessels, athletic and baseball fields, field house, ice rink, boxing, fencing, training, weight, and wrestling rooms, boat house, rowing tank.

**STUDENT BODY. Undergraduate profile:** 2% are state residents. 4.5% Asian-American, 7.5% Black, 6.5% Hispanic, 1% Native American, 80.5% White. Average age of undergraduates is 19.
**Freshman profile:** 6% of freshmen who took SAT scored 700 or over on verbal, 36% scored 700 or over on math; 35% scored 600 or over on verbal, 87% scored 600 or over on math; 83% scored 500 or over on verbal, 98% scored 500 or over on math; 100% scored 400 or over on verbal, 100% scored 400 or over on math. 6% of freshmen who took ACT scored 30 or over on English, 52% scored 30 or over on math; 51% scored 24 or over on English, 96% scored 24 or over on math; 96% scored 18 or over on English, 100% scored 18 or over on math; 100% scored 12 or over on English. 65% of accepted applicants took SAT; 35% took ACT. 66% of freshmen come from public schools.
**Undergraduate achievement:** 88% of fall 1992 freshmen returned for fall 1993 term. 77% of entering class graduated.
**Foreign students:** 39 students are from out of the country. Countries represented include Egypt, Honduras, Korea, Nigeria, the Philippines, and Singapore; 21 in all.

**PROGRAMS OF STUDY. Degrees:** B.S.
**Majors:** Aerospace Engineering, Chemistry, Computer Science, Economics, Electrical Engineering, English, General Engineering, General Science, History, Marine Engineering, Mathematics, Mechanical Engineering, Naval Architecture, Ocean Engineering, Oceanography, Physics, Political Science, Systems Engineering.
**Distribution of degrees:** The majors with the highest enrollment are political science, aerospace engineering, and oceanography; marine engineering, chemistry, and electrical engineering have the lowest.
**Requirements:** General education requirement.
**Academic regulations:** Minimum 2.0 GPA must be maintained.
**Special:** Courses offered in Chinese, French, German, leadership and law, Russian, seamanship and navigation, and Spanish. Double majors. Independent study. Accelerated study. Graduate school at which undergraduates may take graduate-level courses. Preprofessional programs in medicine. Plebe summer includes instruction in seamanship, navigation, signaling, infantry drill, firing a .45 calibre pistol, sailing Navy yawls, and a physical conditioning program. Third Class summer is six to eight weeks of training at sea with the Fleet. Second Class summer includes familiarization training in the warfare specialities of the Navy and Marine Corps: submarine service, combat systems training, flight indoctrination, techniques of vertical envelopment and amphibious assault. During First Class summer, the midshipmen go to sea for training and perform the duties of junior officers; some participate in the training and indoctrination of the new plebe class. Upon graduation, every midshipman is commissioned as an Ensign in the U.S. Navy or a Second

Lieutenant in the Marine Corps and must serve six years on active duty. Exchange programs with interservice academy.
**Honors:** Phi Beta Kappa. Honors program. Honor societies.
**Academic Assistance:** Remedial writing and study skills.
**STUDENT LIFE. Housing:** All midshipmen must live on campus. Coed dorms. 100% of students live in college housing.
**Services and counseling/handicapped student services:** Personal counseling. Academic guidance services. Religious counseling.
**Campus organizations:** Undergraduate student government. Student newspaper (Log, published once/four or six weeks). Yearbook. Radio station. Choirs, bands, Drum and Bugle Corps, athletic and professional groups, archery, art/printing, computer, photography, and sports clubs, Women's Professional Association, Yard Patrol Squadron, Foreign Affairs Conference, 73 organizations in all.
**Religious organizations:** Baptist Student Union, Catholic Club, Fellowship of Christian Athletes, Jewish Club, Latter-Day Saints Association.
**Minority/foreign student organizations:** Black Studies Club, Filipino-American Club, Latin American Club.
**ATHLETICS. Physical education requirements:** Eight semesters of physical education required.
**Intercollegiate competition:** 40% of students participate. Baseball (M), basketball (M,W), crew (M,W), cross-country (M,W), diving (M,W), football (M), golf (M), gymnastics (M), lacrosse (M), lightweight football (M), pistol (M), riflery (M,W), sailing (M,W), soccer (M,W), squash (M), swimming (M,W), tennis (M), track (indoor) (M,W), track (outdoor) (M,W), track and field (indoor) (M,W), track and field (outdoor) (M,W), volleyball (W), water polo (M), wrestling (M). Member of ECAC, NCAA Division I, Patriot League.
**Intramural and club sports:** 60% of students participate. Intramural basketball, boxing, cross-country, disc football, fencing, fieldball, football, golf, powerlifting, racquetball, sailing, soccer, softball, swimming, team handball, tennis, touch football, volleyball, water polo. Men's club boxing, cycling, ice hockey, martial arts, powerlifting, rugby. Women's club cycling, lacrosse, martial arts, powerlifting, softball, tennis.
**ADMISSIONS. Academic basis for candidate selection** (in order of priority): Class rank, secondary school record, standardized test scores, school's recommendation, essay.
**Nonacademic basis for candidate selection:** Character and personality, extracurricular participation, and geographical distribution are emphasized. Particular talent or ability and alumni/ae relationship are important.
**Requirements:** Graduation from secondary school is recommended; GED is accepted. 13 units and the following program of study are recommended: 4 units of English, 4 units of math, 4 units of science, 2 units of foreign language, 1 unit of history. Applicants must be minimum age 17 and not yet age 22 on July 1 of year of admission and unmarried U.S. citizens (except for limited quota of foreign students) and have no parental obligations or responsibilities. Highly competitive admissions process. Minimum SAT scores of 520 verbal, 600 math and rank in top fifth of secondary school class recommended. Strict medical qualifications required of Navy and Marine Corps applicants for commissioning standards upon graduation. Naval Academy Preparatory School in Newport, R.I., for highly qualified nominees who do not obtain appointment; school offers one-year training program to prepare students for entry into the Naval Academy. SAT is required; ACT may be substituted. PSAT is recommended. Campus visit recommended. Off-campus interviews available with an alumni representative.
**Procedure:** Submit service academy's Precandidate Questionnaire in spring of 11th year. Seek nomination in spring of 11th year. Applicants advised to seek nominations from as many sources as possible. Take SAT or ACT by January of 12th year. Application deadline is March 1. Notification of admission on rolling basis. Reply is required by May 1. Freshmen accepted for fall terms only.
**Transfer students:** Transfer students accepted for fall term. Application deadline is March 1.
**Admissions contact:** Capt. John Renard, USN (Ret.), Dean of Admissions. 410 267-4361.
**COMPUTER FACILITIES.** 4,500 IBM/IBM-compatible microcomputers; all are networked. Students may access Bull minicomputer/mainframe systems. Residence halls may be equipped with networked microcomputers. Client/LAN operating systems include DOS. Computer languages and software packages include Ada, BASIC, Pascal. Computer facilities are available to all students.
**GRADUATE CAREER DATA.** Graduate school percentages: 1% enter medical school.
**PROMINENT ALUMNI/AE.** Alan B. Shepard and Bruce McCandless, astronauts; Jimmy Carter, former U.S. President; John McCain, U.S. senator, Arizona; Adm. William Crowe, former chairperson, Joint Chiefs of Staff; David Robinson, NBA basketball player; Napoleon McCallum, NFL football player.

## University of Maryland Baltimore County

**Baltimore, MD 21228** — **410 455-1000**

**1993-94 Costs.** Tuition: $3,338 (state residents), $8,594 (out-of-state). Room: $2,278. Board: $1,930. Fees, books, misc. academic expenses (school's estimate): $470.
**Enrollment.** Undergraduates: 3,303 men, 3,173 women (full-time). Freshman class: 4,269 applicants, 2,594 accepted, 985 enrolled. Graduate enrollment: 797 men, 802 women.
**Test score averages/ranges.** Average SAT scores: 505 verbal, 578 math. Range of SAT scores of middle 50%: 440-560 verbal, 510-640 math. Average ACT scores: 23 English, 23 math, 23 composite. Range of ACT scores of middle 50%: 20-26 English, 20-25 math.
**Faculty.** 384 full-time; 239 part-time. 85% of faculty holds highest degree in specific field. Student/faculty ratio: 15 to 1.
**Selectivity rating.** Competitive.

**PROFILE.** U Maryland, Baltimore County, founded in 1963, is a public, comprehensive institution. Its 1,539-acre campus is located six miles from downtown Baltimore.

**Accreditation:** MSACS. Professionally accredited by the Accreditation Board for Engineering and Technology, the Council on Social Work Education, the National League for Nursing.
**Religious orientation:** University of Maryland Baltimore County is nonsectarian; no religious requirements.
**Library:** Collections totaling over 550,000 volumes, 4,114 periodical subscriptions, and 787,373 microform items.
**Special facilities/museums:** Art gallery, dance studio, photographic collection, science fiction collection, computer laboratories, research greenhouse, geography laboratory, molecular biology laboratory, electron microscopic facility, research-grade lasers, spectrometers, various testing devices.
**Athletic facilities:** Field house, natatorium, gymnasiums, stadium, basketball and tennis courts, athletic, baseball, and softball fields, track, fitness trails, Nautilus and weight rooms, cross-country course.
**STUDENT BODY. Undergraduate profile:** 96% are state residents; 48% are transfers. 10% Asian-American, 14% Black, 2% Hispanic, 72% White, 2% Other. Average age of undergraduates is 22.
**Freshman profile:** 1% of freshmen who took SAT scored 700 or over on verbal, 9% scored 700 or over on math; 10% scored 600 or over on verbal, 37% scored 600 or over on math; 49% scored 500 or over on verbal, 76% scored 500 or over on math; 78% scored 400 or over on verbal, 92% scored 400 or over on math; 92% scored 300 or over on verbal, 94% scored 300 or over on math. 95% of accepted applicants took SAT; 4% took ACT. 83% of freshmen come from public schools.
**Undergraduate achievement:** 83% of fall 1992 freshmen returned for fall 1993 term. 17% of entering class graduated. 32% of students who completed a degree program went on to graduate study within one year.
**Foreign students:** 158 students are from out of the country. Countries represented include Canada, China, Hong Kong, India, Iran, and Taiwan; 56 in all.
**PROGRAMS OF STUDY. Degrees:** B.A., B.S., B.S.Eng., B.S.Nurs.
**Majors:** African-American Studies, American Studies, Ancient Studies, Applied Mathematics, Biochemistry/Molecular Biology, Biological Chemistry, Biological Sciences, Biopsychology, Chemical Engineering, Chemistry, Computer Science, Dance, Developmental Psychology, Economics, Emergency Health Services, Engineering, English, French, Geography, German, Health Science/Policy, History, Information Systems Management, Interdisciplinary Studies, Language/Literary Studies, Linguistics, Mathematics, Mathematics/Secondary Education, Mechanical Engineering, Modern Languages/Linguistics, Music, Nursing, Paramedic, Philosophy, Photography, Physics, Political Science, Probability/Statistics, Russian, Social Work, Sociology, Spanish, Theatre, Theoretical/Experimental Psychology, Visual Arts, Visual/Performing Arts.
**Distribution of degrees:** The majors with the highest enrollment are psychology, information systems management, and computer science; ancient studies, physics, and African-American studies have the lowest.
**Requirements:** General education requirement.
**Academic regulations:** Minimum 2.0 GPA must be maintained.
**Special:** Minors offered in some majors and in anthropology, applied politics, art history, computer art, international affairs, Judaic studies, political thought, public administration, religious studies, social welfare, women's studies, and writing. African-American studies major includes Africa, African diaspora, and community involvement options. Programs in administrative science and in comparative and world literature. Certificates offered in music, including ethnomusicology. Self-designed majors. Double majors. Independent study. Accelerated study. Pass/fail grading option. Internships. Cooperative education programs. Graduate school at which undergraduates may take graduate-level courses. Preprofessional programs in law, medicine, veterinary science, dentistry, and optometry. Combined degree programs include B.S./M.S. in biochemistry, chemistry, and math, B.A./M.A. in history, sociology, and interdisciplinary studies, and B.A./M.P.S. in political science. Teacher certification in early childhood, elementary, and secondary education. Certification in specific subject areas. Study abroad in Chile, England, and Mexico. ROTC at Johns Hopkins U. AFROTC at U of Maryland at College Park.
**Honors:** Honors program. Honor societies.
**Academic Assistance:** Remedial reading, writing, and math. Nonremedial tutoring.
**STUDENT LIFE. Housing:** Students may live on or off campus. Coed dorms. School-owned/operated apartments. 23% of students live in college housing.
**Social atmosphere:** According to the student newspaper, "The University Center is our student union and is the only real on-campus gathering spot aside from the commuter cafeteria. Off campus, students gather at the Double-T Diner, Arbutus Hardee's and Loui's Bookstore Cafe. Popular events include basketball games, Quadmania (a spring festival), the homecoming lacrosse game, and specialty night at the dining hall. Greeks, the Black Student Union, and the Progressive Action Committee are influential on campus. Weeknights are more lively than weekends, but social/cultural life is growing by leaps and bounds every year."
**Services and counseling/handicapped student services:** Placement services. Health service. Women's center. Counseling services for minority, veteran, and older students. Birth control, personal, and psychological counseling. Career and academic guidance services. Religious counseling. Physically disabled student services. Learning disabled services. Notetaking services. Tape recorders. Tutors. Reader services for the blind.
**Campus organizations:** Undergraduate student government. Student newspaper (Retriever, published once/week). Literary magazine. Radio station. Choral groups, orchestra, jazz ensemble, pep band, debating, public speaking, and drama groups, Women's Union, Philosophers Anonymous, pre-law and pre-med societies, service and special-interest groups, 88 organizations in all. 12 fraternities, no chapter houses; eight sororities, no chapter houses. 8% of men join a fraternity. 7% of women join a sorority.
**Religious organizations:** Baptist Campus Ministry, Campus Crusade for Christ, Intervarsity Christian Fellowship, Islamic Society, Jewish Student Union, Korean Student Ministry, Newman Club, Sons of Light Christian Fellowship.
**Minority/foreign student organizations:** Black Student Union, Black Visions, Society of Black Engineers. International Student Association, Chinese, Indian, Korean, Russian, Singapore, and Vietnamese student groups.

**ATHLETICS. Physical education requirements:** Two semesters of physical education required.
**Intercollegiate competition:** 10% of students participate. Baseball (M), basketball (M,W), cheerleading (M,W), cross-country (M,W), diving (M,W), golf (M), lacrosse (M,W), soccer (M,W), softball (W), swimming (M,W), tennis (M,W), track (indoor) (M,W), track (outdoor) (M,W), track and field (indoor) (M,W), track and field (outdoor) (M,W), volleyball (W). Member of Big South Conference, ECAC, NCAA Division I.
**Intramural and club sports:** 30% of students participate. Intramural aerobics, badminton, basketball, beach volleyball, flag football, floor hockey, football, foul shooting, grass volleyball, indoor soccer, inner-tube water polo, running, slam dunk contest, soccer, softball, team handball, tennis, turkey trot, volleyball. Men's club crew, ice hockey, rugby, volleyball. Women's club crew, rugby.

**ADMISSIONS. Academic basis for candidate selection** (in order of priority): Secondary school record, standardized test scores, class rank, school's recommendation, essay.
**Nonacademic basis for candidate selection:** Character and personality, extracurricular participation, and particular talent or ability are considered.
**Requirements:** Graduation from secondary school is required; GED is accepted. 20 units and the following program of study are required: 4 units of English, 3 units of math, 2 units of lab science, 2 units of foreign language, 3 units of social studies. Minimum combined SAT score of 1100 (math score of 580) or 3.0 GPA required of engineering program applicants. SAT or ACT is required. Campus visit recommended. No off-campus interviews.
**Procedure:** Take SAT or ACT by January of 12th year. Suggest filing application by December 1. Application deadline is May 1. Notification of admission is sent following review dates in early December, February, and April. Reply is required by May 1. $100 nonrefundable tuition deposit. $100 room deposit, fully refundable until June 1; partially refundable thereafter. Freshmen accepted for terms other than fall.
**Special programs:** Admission may be deferred one semester. Credit and/or placement may be granted through CEEB Advanced Placement exams for scores of 3 or higher. Credit and/or placement may be granted through CLEP general and subject exams. Credit and placement may be granted through challenge exams. Early entrance/early admission program. Concurrent enrollment program.
**Transfer students:** Transfer students accepted for terms other than fall. In fall 1993, 48% of all new students were transfers into all classes. 2,371 transfer applications were received, 1,965 were accepted. Application deadline is July 1 for fall; December 1 for spring. Minimum 2.0 GPA required. Lowest course grade accepted is "C." Maximum number of transferable credits is 60 semester hours from a two-year school and 90 semester hours from a four-year school. At least 30 semester hours must be completed at the university to receive degree.
**Admissions contact:** Mindy Hand, Ed.M., Director of Admissions. 410 455-2291.

**FINANCIAL AID. Available aid:** Pell grants, SEOG, state scholarships and grants, school scholarships and grants, private scholarships and grants, ROTC scholarships, academic merit scholarships, and athletic scholarships. PLUS, Stafford Loans (GSL), school loans, private loans, and SLS. Tuition Plan Inc. and deferred payment plan.
**Financial aid statistics:** 57% of aid is not need-based. In 1993, 42% of all undergraduate applicants received aid; 38% of freshman applicants. Average amounts of aid awarded freshmen: Scholarships and grants, $1,502; loans, $2,663.
**Supporting data/closing dates:** FAFSA: Priority filing date is March 1. Notification of awards on rolling basis.
**Financial aid contact:** Thomas R. Taylor, Director of Financial Aid. 410 455-2387.

**STUDENT EMPLOYMENT.** College Work/Study Program. Institutional employment. 24% of full-time undergraduates work on campus during school year. Students may expect to earn an average of $990 during school year. Off-campus part-time employment opportunities rated "good."

**COMPUTER FACILITIES.** 400 IBM/IBM-compatible and Macintosh/Apple microcomputers; all are networked. Students may access Digital minicomputer/mainframe systems, BITNET, Internet. Residence halls may be equipped with stand-alone microcomputers, networked microcomputers, networked terminals, modems. Client/LAN operating systems include Apple/Macintosh, DOS, UNIX/XENIX/AIX, X-windows, LocalTalk/AppleTalk, Novell. Computer languages and software packages include Ada, BASIC, C, C++, COBOL, dBASE, GKS, ImSL, Kermit, LISP, Lotus 1-2-3, MAPLE, MATLAB, MINITAB, Pascal, Prolog, Shazam, SimScript, SAS, SPSS-X, TSP, WordPerfect; 50 in all. Computer facilities are available to all students.
**Hours:** 24 hours.

**GRADUATE CAREER DATA.** Graduate school percentages: 2% enter law school. 3% enter medical school. 2% enter graduate business programs. 25% enter graduate arts and sciences programs.

**PROMINENT ALUMNI/AE.** Peggy Sutherland, Grammy award winner for visual graphics; Lynette Young, chief of staff, Baltimore mayor's office; Nathan Chapman, CEO, Chapman Company.

# University of Maryland at College Park

**College Park, MD 20742** — **301 405-1000**

**1994-95 Costs.** Tuition: $2,919 (state residents), $8,723 (out-of-state). Room: $2,899. Board: $2,247. Fees, books, misc. academic expenses (school's estimate): $1,111.
**Enrollment.** Undergraduates: 10,070 men, 9,270 women (full-time). Freshman class: 14,292 applicants, 10,315 accepted, 3,409 enrolled. Graduate enrollment: 4,743 men, 4,367 women.
**Test score averages/ranges.** Average SAT scores: 501 verbal, 584 math. Range of SAT scores of middle 50%: 440-550 verbal, 530-640 math.
**Faculty.** 1,205 full-time; 376 part-time. 93% of faculty holds highest degree in specific field. Student/faculty ratio: 13 to 1.
**Selectivity rating.** Competitive.

**PROFILE.** U Maryland, College Park, founded in 1859, is a public institution. Programs are offered through the Colleges of Agriculture; Arts and Humanities; Behavioral and Social Sciences; Business and Management; Computer, Mathematical, and Physical Sciences; Education; Engineering; Human Ecology; Journalism; Library and Information Services; Life Sciences; and Physical Education, Health, and Recreation and the School of Architecture. Its 1,539-acre campus is located in College Park, nine miles from Washington, D.C.

**Accreditation:** MSACS. Professionally accredited by the American Assembly of Collegiate Schools of Business, the American Library Association, the National Council for Accreditation of Teacher Education. Numerous professional accreditations.
**Religious orientation:** University of Maryland at College Park is nonsectarian; no religious requirements.
**Library:** Collections totaling over 2,231,552 volumes, 19,433 periodical subscriptions, and 4,796,258 microform items.
**Special facilities/museums:** Aerospace buoyancy lab, art gallery, international piano archives, center for architectural design and research, model nuclear reactor, wind tunnel.
**Athletic facilities:** Recreation and fitness centers, athletic fields, basketball, racquetball, squash, and tennis courts, weight rooms, swimming pool, track, gymnasiums.

**STUDENT BODY. Undergraduate profile:** 77% are state residents; 45% are transfers. 14% Asian-American, 12% Black, 4% Hispanic, 1% Native American, 66% White, 3% Other. Average age of undergraduates is 21.
**Freshman profile:** 2% of freshmen who took SAT scored 700 or over on verbal, 11% scored 700 or over on math; 14% scored 600 or over on verbal, 44% scored 600 or over on math; 51% scored 500 or over on verbal, 85% scored 500 or over on math; 91% scored 400 or over on verbal, 98% scored 400 or over on math; 99% scored 300 or over on verbal, 100% scored 300 or over on math. Majority of accepted applicants took SAT. 80% of freshmen come from public schools.
**Undergraduate achievement:** 84% of fall 1992 freshmen returned for fall 1993 term. 30% of entering class graduated. 31% of students who completed a degree program went on to graduate study within one year.
**Foreign students:** 823 students are from out of the country. Countries represented include China, England, Germany, Hong Kong, India, and Korea; 106 in all.

**PROGRAMS OF STUDY. Degrees:** B.A., B.Arch., B.Lib.Arts, B.Mus., B.S.
**Majors:** Accounting, Aerospace Engineering, Afro-American Studies, Agricultural Chemistry, Agricultural Engineering, Agricultural/Extension Education, Agricultural/Resource Economics, Agriculture, Agronomy, American Studies, Animal Sciences, Anthropology, Architecture, Art, Art History, Astronomy, Biological Sciences, Botany, Chemical/Nuclear Engineering, Chemistry/Biochemistry, Chinese, Civil Engineering, Classical Languages/Literature, Community Studies, Comparative Literature, Computer Science, Consumer Economics, Criminal Justice/Criminology, Dance, Decision/Information Sciences, Dietetics, Early Childhood Education, Economics, Electrical Engineering, Elementary Education, Engineering, English, Entomology, Family/Community Development, Finance, Fire Protection Engineering, Food Science, Foodservice Administration, French/Italian Languages/Literature, General Business, Geography, Geology, Germanic/Slavic Languages/Literature, Government/Politics, Health Education, Hearing/Speech Science, Hearing/Speech Sciences, History, Horticulture, Individual Studies, Industrial/Technical/Occupational Education, Japanese, Jewish Studies, Journalism, Kinesiological Sciences, Landscape Architecture, Linguistics, Management/Organization, Management Science/Statistics, Marketing, Mathematics, Mechanical Engineering, Microbiology, Music, Natural Resource Management, Personnel/Labor Relations, Philosophy, Physical Education, Physical Sciences, Physics, Production Management, Psychology, Recreation, Romance Languages, Russian Area Studies, Secondary Education, Sociology, Spanish/Portuguese Languages/Literature, Special Education, Speech, Transportation/Business/Public Policy, Women's Studies, Zoology.
**Distribution of degrees:** The majors with the highest enrollment are computer science, electrical engineering, and accounting; Jewish studies, Afro-American studies, and community studies have the lowest.
**Requirements:** General education requirement.
**Academic regulations:** Minimum 2.0 GPA must be maintained.
**Special:** Certificates in African-American studies, East Asian studies, liberal arts in business, national security studies, public management, social sciences, and women's studies. Self-designed majors. Double majors. Independent study. Pass/fail grading option. Internships. Cooperative education programs. Graduate school at which undergraduates may take graduate-level courses. Preprofessional programs in law, medicine, veterinary science, pharmacy, dentistry, and optometry. Binary programs with Schools of Dentistry, Law, and Medicine. Cooperative engineering program. Combined degrees in business/law, library science/history, library science/geography, M.A.A./M.S. in business management. Member of Consortium of Universities of the Washington Metropolitan Area. Exchange programs with U of Michigan and U of Virginia. Teacher certification in early childhood, elementary, secondary, special education, and vo-tech education. Certification in specific subject areas. Study abroad in Brazil, Denmark, England, France, Germany, Israel, and Mexico. AFROTC.
**Honors:** Phi Beta Kappa. Honors program. Honor societies.
**Academic Assistance:** Remedial reading, writing, math, and study skills. Nonremedial tutoring.

**STUDENT LIFE. Housing:** Students may live on or off campus. Coed, women's, and men's dorms. Sorority and fraternity housing. School-owned/operated apartments. Off-campus married-student housing. 33% of students live in college housing.
**Social atmosphere:** Students gather on campus at the McKeldin Mall reflecting pool and at Student Union restaurants. Off campus, students frequent the Vous and the Santa Fe Cafe. According to the student newspaper, Greeks are influential on campus social life, though their influence is waning as more students look to Washington, D.C. for entertainment. Among the most popular events of the year are Art Attack, Rush Week, and the annual job fair.
**Services and counseling/handicapped student services:** Placement services. Health service. Women's center. Day care. Returning student program, computer training. Counseling services for minority, military, veteran, and older students. Birth control, personal, and psychological counseling. Career and academic guidance services. Religious counseling.

Physically disabled student services. Learning disabled services. Notetaking services. Tape recorders. Tutors.
**Campus organizations:** Undergraduate student government. Student newspaper (Diamondback, published once/day). Literary magazine. Yearbook. Radio station. Pep bands, glee clubs, chorus, marching and symphonic bands, orchestra ensembles, chapel and gospel choirs, theatre, chess, photo, amateur radio, and debating clubs, humor and art magazines, black and Jewish newspapers, departmental, service, and special-interest groups, 250 organizations in all. 30 fraternities, 21 chapter houses; 20 sororities, 16 chapter houses. 15% of men join a fraternity. 15% of women join a sorority.
**Religious organizations:** Bahai Club, Jewish Student Union, Muslim Student Union, Black Ministry, United Campus Ministry.
**Minority/foreign student organizations:** Black Business Society, Black Engineering Society, Black Explosion Newspaper, Black Prelaw Society, Black Science Society, Black Student Athletes Council, Black Student Union, NAACP, Black Coalition, Hispanic Student Union, Minority Computer Science Society, National Association of Black Journalists, Native American Student Union, Shades of Harlem, Thurgood Marshall Pre-Law Society. International Student Council, Chinese, Filipino, Japanese, and Nyumburu cultural groups, African, Bangladeshi, Caribbean, Chinese, Indian, Israeli, Korean, Pakistani, and Vietnamese student associations, several other groups.

**ATHLETICS. Physical education requirements:** None.
**Intercollegiate competition:** 1% of students participate. Baseball (M), basketball (M,W), cross-country (M,W), diving (M,W), field hockey (W), football (M), golf (M), gymnastics (W), lacrosse (M,W), soccer (M,W), swimming (M,W), tennis (M,W), track and field (indoor) (M,W), track and field (outdoor) (M,W), volleyball (W), wrestling (M). Member of Atlantic Coast Conference, ECAC, NCAA Division I.
**Intramural and club sports:** 48% of students participate. Intramural badminton, basketball, billiards, bowling, cross-country, golf, flag football, horseshoes, inner-tube water polo, racquetball, soccer, softball, table tennis, tennis, ultimate frisbee, volleyball, weight lifting, wrestling. Men's club badminton, bowling, equestrian sports, fencing, ice hockey, lacrosse, martial arts, racquetball, rugby, sailing, squash, table tennis, volleyball, water polo, weight lifting, wrestling. Women's club bowling, fencing, lacrosse, sailing, softball, squash, water polo.

**ADMISSIONS. Academic basis for candidate selection** (in order of priority): Secondary school record, standardized test scores, class rank, school's recommendation, essay.
**Nonacademic basis for candidate selection:** Character and personality, extracurricular participation, particular talent or ability, geographical distribution, and alumni/ae relationship are considered.
**Requirements:** Graduation from secondary school is required; GED is accepted. 20 units and the following program of study are recommended: 4 units of English, 3 units of math, 2 units of science, 2 units of foreign language, 3 units of social studies, 6 units of electives. Portfolio required of architecture, art, and design program applicants. Audition required of music program applicants. SAT or ACT is required. Campus visit recommended. No off-campus interviews.
**Procedure:** Take SAT or ACT by November of 12th year. Suggest filing application by December 1. Application deadline is April 30. Notification of admission on rolling basis. Reply is required by May 1. $100 tuition deposit, refundable until May 1. Freshmen accepted for terms other than fall.
**Special programs:** Credit and/or placement may be granted through CEEB Advanced Placement exams for scores of 3 or higher. Credit may be granted through CLEP general and subject exams. Placement may be granted through challenge exams. Credit and placement may be granted through military and life experience. Concurrent enrollment program.
**Transfer students:** Transfer students accepted for terms other than fall. In fall 1993, 45% of all new students were transfers into all classes. 5,491 transfer applications were received, 4,180 were accepted. Application deadline is July 1 for fall; December 1 for spring. Minimum 2.5 GPA. Lowest course grade accepted is "C." Maximum number of transferable credits is 60 semester hours from a two-year school and 90 semester hours from a four-year school. At least 120 semester hours must be completed at the university to receive degree; 132 semester hours required for engineering majors.
**Admissions contact:** Linda Clement, Ph.D., Director of Undergraduate Admissions. 301 314-8385.

**FINANCIAL AID. Available aid:** Pell grants, SEOG, state scholarships and grants, school scholarships and grants, private scholarships and grants, academic merit scholarships, and athletic scholarships. Perkins Loans (NDSL), PLUS, Stafford Loans (GSL), and SLS. Tuition Plan Inc., Education Plan Inc., and deferred payment plan.
**Financial aid statistics:** 47% of aid is not need-based. In 1993-94, 84% of all undergraduate applicants received aid; 77% of freshman applicants. Average amounts of aid awarded freshmen: Scholarships and grants, $1,533; loans, $2,155.
**Supporting data/closing dates:** FAFSA: Priority filing date is February 15; accepted on rolling basis. Notification of awards begins in early April.
**Financial aid contact:** William McLean, Acting Director of Financial Aid. 301 314-8313.

**STUDENT EMPLOYMENT.** College Work/Study Program. Institutional employment. 41% of full-time undergraduates work on campus during school year. Students may expect to earn an average of $1,200 during school year. Off-campus part-time employment opportunities rated "excellent."

**COMPUTER FACILITIES.** 1,500 IBM/IBM-compatible and Macintosh/Apple microcomputers; all are networked. Students may access AT&T, Cray, Digital, IBM minicomputer/mainframe systems, BITNET, Internet. Residence halls may be equipped with stand-alone microcomputers, networked microcomputers. Client/LAN operating systems include Apple/Macintosh, DOS, OS/2, UNIX/XENIX/AIX, Windows NT, X-windows, LocalTalk/AppleTalk, Novell. Computer languages and software packages include BASIC, Borland, Excel, FORTRAN, Lotus, Paradox, Pascal, Quattro Pro, SAS, Turbo C, Turbo Pascal, WordPerfect; 102 in all. Computer facilities are available to all students.
**Fees:** None.
**Hours:** 24 hours.

**GRADUATE CAREER DATA.** Graduate school percentages: 4% enter law school. 2% enter medical school. 4% enter graduate business programs. 12% enter graduate arts and sciences programs. Highest graduate school enrollments: George Washington U, U of Baltimore, U of Maryland at Baltimore and College Park. 60% of graduates choose careers in business and industry. Companies and businesses that hire graduates: Big Six accounting firms, IBM, Westinghouse, National Institute of Health, U.S. government agencies.

**PROMINENT ALUMNI/AE.** Connie Chung, co-anchor, CBS Nighly News; Herbert Hauptman, Nobel Prize-winning physicist; Jim Henson, creator of the Muppets; Boomer Esiason, quarterback, New York Jets; Tom McMillen and Steny Hoyer, U.S. congressmen; Charles Schultz, former chairperson, President's Council of Economics Advisors; Jon Franklin, Pulitzer Prize-winner.

# University of Maryland Eastern Shore

**Princess Anne, MD 21853** **410 651-2200**

**1994-95 Costs.** Tuition: $2,674 (state residents), $7,493 (out-of-state). Room & board: $3,580. Fees, books, misc. academic expenses (school's estimate): $1,100.
**Enrollment.** Undergraduates: 1,041 men, 1,080 women (full-time). Freshman class: 2,396 applicants, 1,374 accepted, 524 enrolled. Graduate enrollment: 107 men, 118 women.
**Test score averages/ranges.** Average SAT scores: 368 verbal, 400 math.
**Faculty.** 145 full-time; 75 part-time. 80% of faculty holds doctoral degree. Student/faculty ratio: 25 to 1.
**Selectivity rating.** Less competitive.

**PROFILE.** U Maryland, Eastern Shore is a public, multipurpose institution. It was founded in 1886, became a state college in 1948, and gained university status in 1970. Programs are offered through the Schools of Agricultural Sciences, Arts and Sciences, and Professional Studies. Its 540-acre campus is located in Princess Anne, 15 miles from Salisbury.

**Accreditation:** MSACS.
**Religious orientation:** University of Maryland Eastern Shore is nonsectarian; no religious requirements.
**Library:** Collections totaling over 150,000 volumes, 1,260 periodical subscriptions, and 143,000 microform items.
**Special facilities/museums:** Art museum, performing arts center, college farm, academic center.
**Athletic facilities:** Gymnasium, swimming pool, tennis courts, track, playing fields, stadium.

**STUDENT BODY. Undergraduate profile:** 80% are state residents; 24% are transfers. 1% Asian-American, 74% Black, 1% Hispanic, 21% White, 3% Other. Average age of undergraduates is 22.
**Freshman profile:** 1% of freshmen who took SAT scored 700 or over on math; 1% scored 600 or over on verbal, 3% scored 600 or over on math; 8% scored 500 or over on verbal, 15% scored 500 or over on math; 38% scored 400 or over on verbal, 49% scored 400 or over on math; 80% scored 300 or over on verbal, 87% scored 300 or over on math. 95% of accepted applicants took SAT; 5% took ACT. 90% of freshmen come from public schools.
**Undergraduate achievement:** 71% of fall 1992 freshmen returned for fall 1993 term. 30% of entering class graduated.
**Foreign students:** 92 students are from out of the country. Countries represented include Bermuda, Cameroon, Ethiopia, Jamaica, Liberia, and Zambia; 50 in all.

**PROGRAMS OF STUDY. Degrees:** B.A., B.Gen.Studies, B.S.
**Majors:** Accounting, Agribusiness, Agricultural Education, Agriculture, Airway Science, Art Education, Biology, Biology Education, Business Administration, Business Education, Chemistry, Computer Science, Construction Management Technology, Criminal Justice, Dietetics, Electrical/Electronics Engineering, Elementary/Special Education, English, Environmental Science, Fashion Merchandising, Fine Arts, Home Economics, Hotel/Restaurant Management, Industrial Arts Education, Mathematics, Music Education, Nutrition, Physical Education, Poultry Technology/Management, Rehabilitation Services, Social Sciences, Sociology.
**Distribution of degrees:** The majors with the highest enrollment are business, natural sciences, and liberal arts; fine arts have the lowest.
**Requirements:** General education requirement.
**Academic regulations:** Minimum 2.0 GPA required for graduation.
**Special:** Minors offered in many majors and in economics, French, German, physics, and political science. Courses offered in geography, philosophy, photography, psychology, Russian, and Spanish. General agriculture students may concentrate in agribusiness, agriscience, animal science, conservation, food and dairy processing, forestry, mechanization, plant science, poultry husbandry, or veterinary science. Department of Experimental Studies offers numerous workshops, institutes, and programs. Center for Interdisciplinary studies. Honors program with preprofessional tracks in allied health fields, community planning, dentistry, law, medicine, nursing, pharmancy, and social work guarantees admission into corresponding professional school of U of Maryland. Self-designed majors. Double majors. Dual degrees. Independent study. Accelerated study. Pass/fail grading option. Internships. Cooperative education programs. Graduate school at which undergraduates may take graduate-level courses. Preprofessional programs in law, medicine, veterinary science, pharmacy, and dentistry. 2-2 engineering program and numerous one-year transfer programs with U of Maryland at College Park. 3-1 medical technology program. Cross-registration with Salisbury State U. Hotel/restaurant management semester, NASA program, study possible at Wallops Island, Va., other off-campus study opportunities in marine research. Teacher certification in elementary, secondary, and special education. ROTC at Salisbury State U.
**Honors:** Honors program.
**Academic Assistance:** Remedial reading, writing, math, and study skills. Nonremedial tutoring.

**STUDENT LIFE. Housing:** Students may live on or off campus. Coed, women's, and men's dorms. School-owned/operated apartments. Hospitality House for hotel majors. 55% of students live in college housing.

**Social atmosphere:** The student newspaper reports that the Greeks and the Student Government Association are among the groups that influence student social life. Stepshows (Greeks), parties, and basketball games are popular events during the school year. On campus, students gather in the cafeteria and the Student Development Center.
**Services and counseling/handicapped student services:** Placement services. Health service. Counseling services for military and veteran students. Birth control, personal, and psychological counseling. Career and academic guidance services. Learning disabled program/services.
**Campus organizations:** Undergraduate student government. Student newspaper (Hawk Flyer, published once/quarter). Yearbook. Radio station. Future Agriculturalists of America, Veteran's Tutorial Program, drama club, music and athletic groups, departmental and service groups, special-interest groups. Five fraternities, no chapter houses; four sororities, no chapter houses. 20% of men join a fraternity. 30% of women join a sorority.
**Minority/foreign student organizations:** Black Awareness Movement, NAACP. International Student Organization, Caribbean Club.

**ATHLETICS. Physical education requirements:** Three semesters of physical education required.
**Intercollegiate competition:** 8% of students participate. Baseball (M), basketball (M,W), cheerleading (M,W), cross-country (M,W), soccer (M), softball (W), tennis (M,W), track (indoor) (M,W), track (outdoor) (M,W), track and field (indoor) (M,W), track and field (outdoor) (M,W), volleyball (W). Member of Mid Eastern Athletic Conference, NCAA Division I.
**Intramural and club sports:** 12% of students participate. Intramural basketball, flag football, softball, swimming, tennis, volleyball.

**ADMISSIONS. Academic basis for candidate selection** (in order of priority): Secondary school record, class rank, standardized test scores, school's recommendation, essay.
**Nonacademic basis for candidate selection:** Particular talent or ability is emphasized. Character and personality, extracurricular participation, and alumni/ae relationship are important.
**Requirements:** Graduation from secondary school is required; GED is accepted. 20 units and the following program of study are required: 4 units of English, 2 units of math, 3 units of science including 2 units of lab, 2 units of foreign language, 3 units of social studies, 4 units of electives. Minimum 2.25 GPA and combined SAT score of 750 recommended. In-state applicants who have secondary school diploma and have "C" average may be admitted on basis of predictive index weighing GPA and SAT scores. Recommendations and interviews required of physical therapy program applicants. Specific requirements for music and engineering program applicants. General Curriculum Program required for applicants not normally admissible; summer program required. SAT or ACT is required. Campus visit and interview recommended. Off-campus interviews available with admissions and alumni representatives.
**Procedure:** Take SAT or ACT by April of 12th year. Visit college for interview by April 20 of 12th year. Suggest filing application by April. Application deadline is May. Notification of admission on rolling basis. Reply is required by May 1. $25 tuition deposit, refundable until June 1. $100 room deposit, refundable until June 1. Freshmen accepted for terms other than fall.
**Special programs:** Admission may be deferred one year. Credit may be granted through CEEB Advanced Placement. Credit and/or placement may be granted through CLEP general and subject exams. Early decision program. In fall 1993, 20 applied for early decision and 10 were accepted. Deadline for applying for early decision is April. Early entrance/early admission program. Concurrent enrollment program.
**Transfer students:** Transfer students accepted for terms other than fall. In fall 1993, 24% of all new students were transfers into all classes. 250 transfer applications were received, 254 were accepted. Application deadline is April for fall; December for spring. Minimum 2.0 GPA required. Lowest course grade accepted is "C." Maximum number of transferable credits is 60 semester hours. At least 30 semester hours must be completed at the university to receive degree.
**Admissions contact:** Rochell Peoples, Ed.D., Director of Admissions and Registrations. 410 651-6410.

**FINANCIAL AID. Available aid:** Pell grants, SEOG, state scholarships and grants, school scholarships and grants, private scholarships and grants, academic merit scholarships, and athletic scholarships. Perkins Loans (NDSL), PLUS, Stafford Loans (GSL), school loans, and SLS. Tuition Plan Inc. and AMS.
**Financial aid statistics:** In 1993-94, 85% of all undergraduate applicants received aid; 89% of freshman applicants. Average amounts of aid awarded freshmen: Loans, $1,500.
**Supporting data/closing dates:** FAFSA/FAF/FFS: Priority filing date is April 15. Notification of awards begins in April.
**Financial aid contact:** Dorothy Body, M.A., Director of Financial Aid. 410 651-6172.

**STUDENT EMPLOYMENT.** College Work/Study Program. Institutional employment. 30% of full-time undergraduates work on campus during school year. Students may expect to earn an average of $800 during school year. Freshmen are discouraged from working during their first term. Off-campus part-time employment opportunities rated "fair."

**COMPUTER FACILITIES.** 80 IBM/IBM-compatible microcomputers. Residence halls may be equipped with modems. Computer languages and software packages include BASIC, COBOL, FORTRAN, Pascal. Computer facilities are available to all students.

## Washington Bible College

**Lanham, MD 20706** — **301 552-1400**

**1994-95 Costs.** Tuition: $5,550. Room: $1,500. Board: $1,990. Fees, books, misc. academic expenses (school's estimate): $478.
**Enrollment.** Undergraduates: 75 men, 74 women (full-time). Freshman class: 175 applicants, 108 accepted, 95 enrolled. Graduate enrollment: 12 men, 16 women.
**Test score averages/ranges.** N/A.
**Faculty.** 16 full-time; 21 part-time. 19% of faculty holds doctoral degree. Student/faculty ratio: 15 to 1.
**Selectivity rating.** N/A.

**PROFILE.** Washington Bible College, founded in 1938, is a college with religious orientation. Its 63-acre campus is located in Lanham, 10 miles from Washington, D.C.
**Accreditation:** AABC.
**Religious orientation:** Washington Bible College is a nondenominational Christian school; eight semesters of theology required.
**Library:** Collections totaling over 50,000 volumes, 1,827 periodical subscriptions, and 1,695 microform items.
**Athletic facilities:** Gymnasium, baseball, soccer, and softball fields.

**STUDENT BODY. Undergraduate profile:** 61% are state residents; 7% are transfers. 8% Asian-American, 46% Black, 1% Hispanic, 37% White, 8% Other.
**Foreign students:** 28 students are from out of the country. Countries represented include Canada, Haiti, Kenya, Korea, South Africa, and Trinidad/Tobago; 12 in all.

**PROGRAMS OF STUDY. Degrees:** B.A.
**Majors:** Bible/Theology, Elementary Education, Music.
**Requirements:** General education requirement.
**Special:** Minors offered in Christian education, counseling, journalism, missions, music, pastoral ministries, sports and recreation administration, and urban ministries. Associate's degrees offered. Double majors. Internships. Graduate school at which undergraduates may take graduate-level courses. Preprofessional programs in theology. Teacher certification in early childhood and elementary education.

**ADMISSIONS. Academic basis for candidate selection** (in order of priority): Essay, secondary school record, school's recommendation, standardized test scores, class rank.
**Nonacademic basis for candidate selection:** Character and personality are emphasized.
**Requirements:** Graduation from secondary school is required; GED is accepted. 15 units and the following program of study are required: 4 units of English, 2 units of math, 2 units of science, 2 units of social studies, 5 units of academic electives. Minimum SAT scores of 450 in both verbal and math and minimum 2.0 GPA recommended. Audition required of music program applicants. SAT or ACT is required. Campus visit and interview recommended. Off-campus interviews available with admissions and alumni representatives.
**Procedure:** Take SAT or ACT by June of 12th year. Suggest filing application by July 1. Notification of admission by August 15. $50 nonrefundable tuition deposit. $100 nonrefundable room deposit. Freshmen accepted for terms other than fall.
**Special programs:** Admission may be deferred one year. Credit may be granted through CEEB Advanced Placement for scores of 3 or higher. Credit and/or placement may be granted through CLEP general and subject exams. Credit may be granted through DANTES exams and military experience. Early decision program. Early entrance/early admission program. Concurrent enrollment program.
**Transfer students:** Transfer students accepted for terms other than fall. In fall 1992, 7% of all new students were transfers into all classes. Minimum 2.0 GPA required. Lowest course grade accepted is "C." Maximum number of transferable credits is 98 semester hours. At least 30 semester hours must be completed at the college to receive degree.
**Admissions contact:** Stephen Salvas, Director of Admissions. 301 552-1400, extensions 212, 280.

**FINANCIAL AID. Available aid:** Pell grants, SEOG, state scholarships, academic merit scholarships, aid for undergraduate foreign students, and United Negro College Fund. Leadership Scholarships. PLUS, Stafford Loans (GSL), and SLS. Deferred payment plan.
**Financial aid statistics:** Average amounts of aid awarded freshmen: Scholarships and grants, $2,500.
**Supporting data/closing dates:** FAFSA/FAF: Accepted on rolling basis. School's own aid application: Accepted on rolling basis. Income tax forms: Accepted on rolling basis. Notification of awards on rolling basis.
**Financial aid contact:** Darrell Dehaven, M.A.R., Director of Financial Aid. 301 552-1400, extension 222.

## Washington College

**Chestertown, MD 21620** — **410 778-2800**

**1993-94 Costs.** Tuition: $13,952. Room & board: $5,318. Fees, books, misc. academic expenses (school's estimate): $500.
**Enrollment.** Undergraduates: 374 men, 438 women (full-time). Freshman class: 1,209 applicants, 942 accepted, 214 enrolled. Graduate enrollment: 10 men, 25 women.
**Test score averages/ranges.** Average SAT scores: 473 verbal, 507 math. Range of SAT scores of middle 50%: 420-560 verbal, 430-570 math.
**Faculty.** 63 full-time; 21 part-time. 85% of faculty holds doctoral degree. Student/faculty ratio: 12 to 1.
**Selectivity rating.** Less competitive.

**PROFILE.** Washington College, founded in 1782, is a private, liberal arts college. Its 104-acre campus is located in Chestertown on Maryland's Eastern Shore, 75 miles from Baltimore.

**Accreditation:** MSACS.
**Religious orientation:** Washington College is nonsectarian; no religious requirements.
**Library:** Collections totaling over 201,576 volumes, 801 periodical subscriptions, and 159,270 microform items.
**Special facilities/museums:** Language lab, computer classroom.
**Athletic facilities:** Gymnasium, basketball, paddle tennis, racquetball, squash, and tennis courts, aerobics, conditioning and weight rooms, track, baseball, lacrosse, soccer, and softball fields, field house, swimming pool, dance studio, wellness center.

**STUDENT BODY. Undergraduate profile:** 47% are state residents; 11% are transfers. 2% Asian-American, 6% Black, 2% Hispanic, 90% White. Average age of undergraduates is 20.
**Freshman profile:** 2% of freshmen who took SAT scored 700 or over on verbal, 2% scored 700 or over on math; 16% scored 600 or over on verbal, 23% scored 600 or over on math; 44% scored 500 or over on verbal, 61% scored 500 or over on math; 86% scored 400 or over on verbal, 89% scored 400 or over on math; 100% scored 300 or over on verbal,

100% scored 300 or over on math. 99% of accepted applicants took SAT. 66% of freshmen come from public schools.
**Undergraduate achievement:** 82% of fall 1992 freshmen returned for fall 1993 term. 53% of entering class graduated. 15% of students who completed a degree program immediately went on to graduate study.
**Foreign students:** 33 students are from out of the country. Countries represented include France, Germany, Mexico, South Africa, and the United Kingdom; 23 in all.
**PROGRAMS OF STUDY. Degrees:** B.A., B.S.
**Majors:** American Studies, Art, Biology, Business Management, Chemistry, Dramatic Arts, Economics, English, French, German, History, Humanities, International Studies, Mathematics/Computer Science, Music, Philosophy, Physics, Political Science, Psychology, Sociology, Spanish.
**Distribution of degrees:** The majors with the highest enrollment are English, business, and psychology.
**Requirements:** General education requirement.
**Academic regulations:** Freshmen must maintain minimum 1.85 GPA; sophomores, juniors, seniors, 2.0 GPA.
**Special:** Minors offered in all disciplines. Courses offered in education, religion, and world literature. Creative writing program. Self-designed majors. Double majors. Dual degrees. Independent study. Pass/fail grading option. Internships. Graduate school at which undergraduates may take graduate-level courses. Preprofessional programs in law, medicine, engineering, and nursing. 3-2 engineering program with U of Maryland. 3-2 nursing program with Johns Hopkins U. Washington Semester. Teacher certification in secondary education. Certification in specific subject areas. Study abroad in the United Kingdom and other European countries.
**Honors:** Honors program. Honor societies.
**Academic Assistance:** Remedial reading, writing, math, and study skills. Nonremedial tutoring.
**ADMISSIONS. Academic basis for candidate selection** (in order of priority): Secondary school record, class rank, school's recommendation, standardized test scores, essay.
**Nonacademic basis for candidate selection:** Character and personality are emphasized. Extracurricular participation, particular talent or ability, geographical distribution, and alumni/ae relationship are considered.
**Requirements:** Graduation from secondary school is recommended; GED is accepted. 16 units and the following program of study are required: 4 units of English, 3 units of math, 3 units of science including 2 units of lab, 2 units of foreign language, 2 units of social studies, 2 units of history. Minimum combined SAT score of 900, rank in top half of secondary school class, and minimum 2.75 GPA recommended. SAT is required; ACT may be substituted. Campus visit and interview recommended. Off-campus interviews available with an alumni representative.
**Procedure:** Take SAT by May of 11th year. Visit college for interview by December of 12th year. Suggest filing application by February 15. Application deadline is June 1. Acceptance notification biweekly from January 30 to April 1. Reply is required by May 1. $300 tuition deposit, refundable until May 1. $200 room deposit, refundable until May 1. Freshmen accepted for terms other than fall.
**Special programs:** Admission may be deferred one year. Credit and/or placement may be granted through CEEB Advanced Placement exams for scores of 3 or higher. Credit and/or placement may be granted through CLEP general and subject exams. Placement may be granted through challenge exams. Early decision program. In fall 1993, 60 applied for early decision and 45 were accepted. Deadline for applying for early decision is December 1. Early entrance/early admission program. Concurrent enrollment program.
**Transfer students:** Transfer students accepted for terms other than fall. In fall 1993, 11% of all new students were transfers into all classes. 76 transfer applications were received, 48 were accepted. Application deadline is July 15 for fall; December 15 for spring. Minimum 2.5 GPA recommended. Lowest course grade accepted is "C." Maximum number of transferable credits is 96 semester hours. At least 32 semester hours must be completed at the college to receive degree.
**Admissions contact:** Kevin R. Coveney, M.S., Vice President for Admissions. 410 778-7700.
**FINANCIAL AID. Available aid:** Pell grants, SEOG, state scholarships and grants, school scholarships and grants, private scholarships and grants, academic merit scholarships, and aid for undergraduate foreign students. Perkins Loans (NDSL), PLUS, Stafford Loans (GSL), school loans, and SLS. Knight Tuition Plans and AMS.
**Financial aid statistics:** 10% of aid is not need-based. In 1993-94, 71% of all undergraduate applicants received aid; 70% of freshman applicants. Average amounts of aid awarded freshmen: Scholarships and grants, $9,600; loans, $2,625.
**Supporting data/closing dates:** FAFSA: Priority filing date is February 15. FAF: Priority filing date is February 15; accepted on rolling basis. Income tax forms: Priority filing date is March 1; accepted on rolling basis. Notification of awards on rolling basis.
**Financial aid contact:** Jean M. Narcum, Director of Financial Aid. 410 778-7214.

# Western Maryland College

**Westminster, MD 21157 — 410 848-7000**

**1994-95 Costs.** Tuition: $14,510. Room & board: $5,240. Fees, books, misc. academic expenses (school's estimate): $500.
**Enrollment.** Undergraduates: 519 men, 599 women (full-time). Freshman class: 1,205 applicants, 984 accepted, 261 enrolled. Graduate enrollment: 150 men, 966 women.
**Test score averages/ranges.** Average SAT scores: 484 verbal, 527 math. Range of SAT scores of middle 50%: 470-480 verbal, 520-530 math.
**Faculty.** 83 full-time; 45 part-time. 82% of faculty holds doctoral degree. Student/faculty ratio: 13 to 1.
**Selectivity rating.** Competitive.

**PROFILE.** Western Maryland, founded in 1867, is a private, liberal arts college. Its 160-acre campus is located in Westminster, 31 miles northwest of Baltimore.
**Accreditation:** MSACS. Professionally accredited by the Council on Social Work Education, the National Association of Schools of Music.
**Religious orientation:** Western Maryland College is nonsectarian; no religious requirements.
**Library:** Collections totaling over 173,000 volumes, 910 periodical subscriptions, and 8,500 microform items.
**Special facilities/museums:** Language and physiology labs, electron microscope, math spectrometer.
**Athletic facilities:** Gymnasiums, swimming pool, racquetball, squash, and tennis courts, golf course, weight room, athletic fields.
**STUDENT BODY. Undergraduate profile:** 58% are state residents; 22% are transfers. 1% Asian-American, 5% Black, 1% Hispanic, 1% Native American, 88% White, 4% Other. Average age of undergraduates is 20.
**Freshman profile:** 11% of freshmen who took SAT scored 600 or over on verbal, 19% scored 600 or over on math; 40% scored 500 or over on verbal, 61% scored 500 or over on math; 85% scored 400 or over on verbal, 93% scored 400 or over on math; 100% scored 300 or over on verbal, 100% scored 300 or over on math. Majority of accepted applicants took SAT.
**Undergraduate achievement:** 80% of fall 1992 freshmen returned for fall 1993 term. 57% of entering class graduated. 22% of students who completed a degree program went on to graduate study within one year.
**Foreign students:** 11 students are from out of the country. Countries represented include China, Ethiopia, India, Japan, Malaysia, and Sri Lanka; eight in all.
**PROGRAMS OF STUDY. Degrees:** B.A.
**Majors:** American Studies, Art, Biology, Business Administration, Chemistry, Communications, Economics, English, French, German, History, Mathematics, Music, Philosophy, Physical Education, Physics, Political Science, Psychology, Religious Studies, Social Work, Sociology, Spanish, Theatre Arts.
**Distribution of degrees:** The majors with the highest enrollment are English, psychology, and biology; French, German, and American studies have the lowest.
**Requirements:** General education requirement.
**Academic regulations:** Freshmen must maintain minimum 1.5 GPA; sophomores, 1.7 GPA; juniors, 1.9 GPA; seniors, 2.0 GPA.
**Special:** Minors offered in most majors and in accounting, aquatics, art history, athletic training, classics, comparative literature, cross-cultural studies, elementary education, English literature, Japanese civilization, outdoor education, secondary education, sports coaching, sports communication, studio art, writing, and women's studies. Courses offered in astronomy, education of the deaf, general science, military science, Russian, and statistics. Certificate in social work. Self-designed majors. Double majors. Dual degrees. Independent study. Pass/fail grading option. Internships. Cooperative education programs. Graduate school at which undergraduates may take graduate-level courses. Preprofessional programs in law, medicine, veterinary science, pharmacy, dentistry, museum studies, nursing, occupational therapy, physical therapy, and podiatry. 3-2 forestry and environmental studies program with Duke U. 3-2 engineering programs with U of Maryland and Washington U. 3-2 occupational therapy programs with Boston U and Washington U. 3-2 physical therapy program with U of Maryland. Washington Semester and UN Semester. Appalachian Semester (Kentucky). Teacher certification in elementary, secondary, and special education. Certification in specific subject areas. Exchange program abroad in Japan (Nagasaki Wesleyan Junior Coll). Study abroad also in Australia, Austria, Belgium, China, Denmark, England, France, Germany, Israel, Italy, Mexico, Spain, and Wales. ROTC. AFROTC at U of Maryland at College Park.
**Honors:** Phi Beta Kappa. Honors program. Honor societies.
**Academic Assistance:** Remedial writing, math, and study skills. Nonremedial tutoring.
**STUDENT LIFE. Housing:** All full-time freshmen, sophomores, and juniors must live on campus unless living with family. Coed, women's, and men's dorms. Sorority and fraternity housing. School-owned/operated apartments. Off-campus privately-owned housing. 82% of students live in college housing.
**Social atmosphere:** On campus, students gather at Gazebo, Harvey Stone Park, Upper Decker, and the Game Room. Popular off-campus haunts include Ernie's, Westminster Inn, Champs, and Maggie's. Influential groups on campus include Greeks, Christian Fellowship, CAPBoard, the football team, BACCHUS, SEAC, Residence Life, and the International Club. Popular social events include home football games, off-campus parties, Welcome Back Weekend, Spring Fling, homecoming, and Parent's Weekend. The editor of the student newspaper observes that because the campus is small, it is possible to get to know just about everyone. "And the campus is beautiful, with beautiful sunsets over the hill."
**Services and counseling/handicapped student services:** Placement services. Health service. Counseling services for minority, military, veteran, and older students. Birth control, personal, and psychological counseling. Career and academic guidance services. Religious counseling. Physically disabled student services. Learning disabled services. Notetaking services. Tape recorders. Tutors. Reader services for the blind.
**Campus organizations:** Undergraduate student government. Student newspaper (Phoenix, published once/two weeks). Literary magazine. Yearbook. Radio and TV stations. Band, choir, equestrian club, Amnesty International, Lesbian and Gay Alliance, Women Making Choices, departmental clubs, service and political organizations, environment group, 91 organizations in all. Five fraternities, no chapter houses; four sororities, no chapter houses. 35% of men join a fraternity. 35% of women join a sorority.
**Religious organizations:** Bahai Club, Catholic Campus Ministry, Chapel Committee, Jewish Student Union, Christian Fellowship, Christian Athletes, DOJO, FEN.
**Minority/foreign student organizations:** Minority Student Association. International Student Association.
**ATHLETICS. Physical education requirements:** Two semesters of physical education required.
**Intercollegiate competition:** 35% of students participate. Baseball (M), basketball (M,W), cross-country (M,W), field hockey (W), football (M), golf (M), lacrosse (M,W), soccer (M,W), softball (W), swimming (M,W), tennis (M,W), track (indoor) (M,W), track and field (outdoor) (M,W), volleyball (W), wrestling (M). Member of Centennial Conference, NCAA Division III.
**Intramural and club sports:** 75% of students participate. Intramural badminton, basketball, golf, soccer, softball, swimming, table tennis, tennis, touch football, volleyball.

**ADMISSIONS. Academic basis for candidate selection** (in order of priority): Secondary school record, class rank, essay, school's recommendation, standardized test scores. **Nonacademic basis for candidate selection:** Extracurricular participation and particular talent or ability are important. Character and personality are considered.
**Requirements:** Graduation from secondary school is required; GED is accepted. 16 units and the following program of study are required: 4 units of English, 3 units of math, 2 units of lab science, 2 units of foreign language, 3 units of social studies. Minimum combined SAT score of 900 and minimum 2.5 GPA required. Freshmen Success program for applicants not normally admissible. SAT or ACT is required. Campus visit and interview recommended. Off-campus interviews available with an admissions representative.
**Procedure:** Take SAT or ACT by November of 12th year. Visit college for interview by January 1 of 12th year. Suggest filing application by February 1. Application deadline is March 15. Notification of admission by April 1. Reply is required by May 1. $200 nonrefundable tuition deposit. $100 nonrefundable room deposit. Freshmen accepted for terms other than fall.
**Special programs:** Admission may be deferred one year. Credit and/or placement may be granted through CEEB Advanced Placement exams for scores of 3 or higher. Credit and/or placement may be granted through CLEP subject exams. Credit may be granted through military experience. Credit and placement may be granted through life experience. Early decision program. In fall 1993, 41 applied for early decision and 31 were accepted. Deadline for applying for early decision is December 1. Early entrance/early admission program. Concurrent enrollment program.
**Transfer students:** Transfer students accepted for terms other than fall. In fall 1993, 22% of all new students were transfers into all classes. 160 transfer applications were received, 116 were accepted. Application deadline is August 1 for fall; January 15 for spring. Minimum 2.0 GPA required. Lowest course grade accepted is "C." Maximum number of transferable credits is 64 semester hours from a two-year school and 90 semester hours from a four-year school. At least 30 semester hours must be completed at the college to receive degree.
**Admissions contact:** Martha O'Connell, M.Ed., Director of Admissions. 410 857-2230, 800 638-5005.

**FINANCIAL AID. Available aid:** Pell grants, SEOG, state scholarships and grants, school scholarships and grants, private scholarships and grants, ROTC scholarships, academic merit scholarships, and aid for undergraduate foreign students. Perkins Loans (NDSL), PLUS, Stafford Loans (GSL), private loans, and SLS. Knight Tuition Plans, deferred payment plan, and family tuition reduction. School's own monthly tuition payment plan.
**Financial aid statistics:** 37% of aid is not need-based. In 1993-94, 95% of all undergraduate applicants received aid; 95% of freshman applicants. Average amounts of aid awarded freshmen: Scholarships and grants, $8,640; loans, $3,600.
**Supporting data/closing dates:** FAFSA/FAF/FFS: Priority filing date is March 1. School's own aid application: Priority filing date is March 1. Income tax forms: Priority filing date is March 1. Notification of awards on rolling basis.
**Financial aid contact:** Eva Hess, M.Ed., Director of Financial Aid. 410 857-2233.

**STUDENT EMPLOYMENT.** College Work/Study Program. Institutional employment. 33% of full-time undergraduates work on campus during school year. Students may expect to earn an average of $800 during school year. Off-campus part-time employment opportunities rated "good."

**COMPUTER FACILITIES.** 160 IBM/IBM-compatible, Macintosh/Apple, and RISC-/UNIX-based microcomputers; 67 are networked. Client/LAN operating systems include Apple/Macintosh, DOS, UNIX/XENIX/AIX, LocalTalk/AppleTalk. Computer languages and software packages include BASIC, FORTRAN, Hypercard, Lotus 1-2-3, Pascal, SPSS-X, SuperPaint, Word, WordPerfect, Works, Write Now. Computer facilities are available to all students.
**Fees:** None.
**Hours:** 8:30 AM-midn.

**GRADUATE CAREER DATA.** Graduate school percentages: 2% enter law school. 3% enter medical school. 1% enter dental school. 4% enter graduate business programs. 14% enter graduate arts and sciences programs. Highest graduate school enrollments: Brown U, Johns Hopkins U, MIT, Stanford U, U of Maryland. 71% of graduates choose careers in business and industry. Companies and businesses that hire graduates: Biowhittaker, Black & Decker, Kennedy Kreiger Inst., Marriott, MCI, T. Rowe Price, USF&G, Westinghouse.

**PROMINENT ALUMNI/AE.** David Marine, discoverer of iodine treatment for goiter; Bessie Grambrill, first woman to receive tenure from major university in a profession other than nursing (Yale); George Gipe, Hollywood screenwriter, *Gremlins*; Dr. Joseph McDade, discoverer of organism causing Legionnaires' disease; Arthur Broll, president, PepsiCo.

# Massachusetts

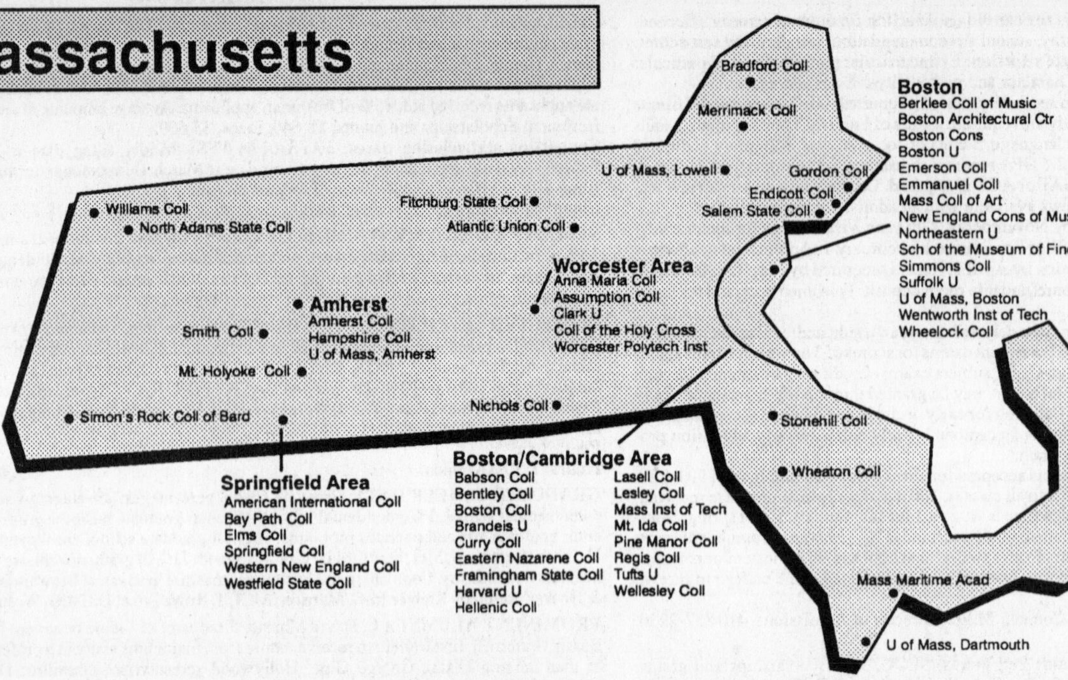


## American International College

**Springfield, MA 01109** **413 737-7000**

**1994-95 Costs.** Tuition: $9,280. Room & board: $4,770. Fees, books, misc. academic expenses (school's estimate): $750.
**Enrollment.** Undergraduates: 496 men, 522 women (full-time). Freshman class: 1,420 applicants, 1,093 accepted, 223 enrolled. Graduate enrollment: 164 men, 312 women.
**Test score averages/ranges.** Average SAT scores: 424 verbal, 460 math. Range of SAT scores of middle 50%: 350-480 verbal, 380-490 math.
**Faculty.** 74 full-time; 48 part-time. 54% of faculty holds doctoral degree. Student/faculty ratio: 15 to 1.
**Selectivity rating.** Less competitive.

**PROFILE.** American International, founded in 1885, is a private college of liberal arts and professional education. Programs are offered through the Division of Nursing and the Schools of Arts and Sciences, Business Administration, and Psychology and Education. Its 58-acre campus is located in Springfield, 90 miles west of Boston.

**Accreditation:** NEASC. Professionally accredited by the National League for Nursing.
**Religious orientation:** American International College is nonsectarian; no religious requirements.
**Library:** Collections totaling over 118,000 volumes, 390 periodical subscriptions, and 83,700 microform items.
**Special facilities/museums:** Centers for human technology, cultural arts, and child development.
**Athletic facilities:** Gymnasium, fitness center.

**STUDENT BODY. Undergraduate profile:** 59% are state residents; 33% are transfers. 1% Asian-American, 13% Black, 4% Hispanic, 79% White, 3% Other. Average age of undergraduates is 23.
**Freshman profile:** 1% of freshmen who took SAT scored 700 or over on verbal, 1% scored 700 or over on math; 3% scored 600 or over on verbal, 2% scored 600 or over on math; 32% scored 500 or over on verbal, 35% scored 500 or over on math; 75% scored 400 or over on verbal, 80% scored 400 or over on math; 98% scored 300 or over on verbal, 99% scored 300 or over on math. 97% of accepted applicants took SAT. 62% of freshmen come from public schools.
**Undergraduate achievement:** 82% of fall 1992 freshmen returned for fall 1993 term. 60% of entering class graduated. 21% of students who completed a degree program went on to graduate study.
**Foreign students:** 80 students are from out of the country. Countries represented include Bermuda, Canada, China, Greece, Japan, and Singapore; 24 in all.

**PROGRAMS OF STUDY. Degrees:** B.A., B.S., B.S.Bus.Admin., B.S.Nurs.
**Majors:** Accounting, American Studies, Biochemistry, Biology, Business Education, Business Studies, Chemistry, Communications, Criminal Justice, Economics, Elementary Education, English, Finance, General Business, History, Human Services, Interdepartmental Science, International Business, Liberal/General Studies, Management, Management Information Systems, Marketing, Mathematics, Medical Technology, Nursing, Personnel Management, Philosophy, Political Science/Government, Pre-Physical Therapy, Psychology, Public Administration, Secondary Education, Sociology, Spanish, Special Education.
**Distribution of degrees:** The majors with the highest enrollment are accounting, criminal justice, and elementary education; philosophy, medical technology, and biochemistry have the lowest.
**Requirements:** General education requirement.
**Academic regulations:** Minimum 2.0 GPA must be maintained.
**Special:** Minors offered in many majors and in journalism. Coaching certificate program. Courses offered in data processing, fine arts, Italian, law, music, and secretarial science; courses also offered through college's Center for Human Relations and Community Affairs, which focuses on solutions to a variety of human resource development problems in public- and private-sector organizations. Associate's degrees offered. Double majors. Independent study. Accelerated study. Internships. Graduate school at which undergraduates may take graduate-level courses. Preprofessional programs in law, medicine, veterinary science, dentistry, optometry, physical therapy, and podiatry. 4-1 bachelor's/M.B.A. program. Member of Cooperating Colleges of Greater Springfield; cross-registration possible. Washington Semester. Teacher certification in early childhood, elementary, secondary, and special education. Certification in specific subject areas. Study abroad in Belgium, England, France, Ireland, Italy, and Spain. ROTC and AFROTC at Western New England Coll.
**Honors:** Honors program. Honor societies.
**Academic Assistance:** Remedial writing, math, and study skills. Nonremedial tutoring.

**STUDENT LIFE. Housing:** All freshmen must live on campus unless living with family. Coed, women's, and men's dorms. 57% of students live in college housing.
**Services and counseling/handicapped student services:** Health service. Counseling services for minority and older students. Birth control, personal, and psychological counseling. Career and academic guidance services. Religious counseling. Physically disabled student services. Learning disabled program/services. Tape recorders. Tutors. Reader services for the blind.
**Campus organizations:** Undergraduate student government. Student newspaper (Yellow Jacket, published twice/month). Literary magazine. Yearbook. Radio station. Chorale, dance and drama groups, outdoor club, Model Congress, SADD, equestrian sports club, international business and marketing clubs, women's organization, 40 organizations in all. Seven fraternities, no chapter houses; eight sororities, no chapter houses. 8% of men join a fraternity. 9% of women join a sorority.
**Religious organizations:** Hillel, Newman Club, United Protestant Fellowship.
**Minority/foreign student organizations:** PRIDE, BUZZARDS. International Club.

**ATHLETICS. Physical education requirements:** Four semesters of physical education required.
**Intercollegiate competition:** 28% of students participate. Baseball (M), basketball (M,W), football (M), golf (M), ice hockey (M), lacrosse (M), soccer (M,W), softball (W), tennis (M,W), volleyball (W), wrestling (M). Member of ECAC, NCAA Division II, NECAC, Northeast 10.
**Intramural and club sports:** 25% of students participate. Intramural basketball, flag football, softball, volleyball.

**ADMISSIONS. Academic basis for candidate selection** (in order of priority): Secondary school record, class rank, school's recommendation, standardized test scores, essay.
**Nonacademic basis for candidate selection:** Character and personality, extracurricular participation, particular talent or ability, geographical distribution, and alumni/ae relationship are considered.
**Requirements:** Graduation from secondary school is required; GED is accepted. 16 units and the following program of study are required: 4 units of English, 2 units of math, 2 units of science including 1 unit of lab, 1 unit of social studies, 1 unit of history, 5 units of academic electives. 1 unit of chemistry required of nursing program applicants. Conditional admission possible for applicants not meeting standard requirements. SAT is required; ACT may be substituted. Campus visit and interview recommended. Off-campus interviews available with an admissions representative.
**Procedure:** Take SAT or ACT by April 1 of 12th year. Suggest filing application by March 1; no deadline. Notification of admission on rolling basis. Reply is required by May 1. $100 tuition deposit, refundable until May 1. $100 room deposit, refundable until May 1. Freshmen accepted for terms other than fall.

**Special programs:** Admission may be deferred one year. Credit and/or placement may be granted through CEEB Advanced Placement exams for scores of 3 or higher. Credit and/or placement may be granted through CLEP general and subject exams. Credit and placement may be granted through Regents College, ACT PEP, and DANTES exams. Early decision program. In fall 1993, 30 applied for early decision and 19 were accepted. Deadline for applying for early decision is November 15. Early entrance/early admission program. Concurrent enrollment program.
**Transfer students:** Transfer students accepted for terms other than fall. In fall 1993, 33% of all new students were transfers into all classes. 348 transfer applications were received, 284 were accepted. Application deadline is rolling for fall; rolling for spring. Minimum 2.0 GPA required. Lowest course grade accepted is "C." Maximum number of transferable credits is 75 semester hours from a two-year school and 90 semester hours from a four-year school. At least 30 semester hours must be completed at the college to receive degree.
**Admissions contact:** Peter J. Miller, Dean of Admissions. 413 747-6201.

**FINANCIAL AID. Available aid:** Pell grants, SEOG, state scholarships and grants, school scholarships and grants, private scholarships and grants, ROTC scholarships, academic merit scholarships, and athletic scholarships. Perkins Loans (NDSL), PLUS, Stafford Loans (GSL), NSL, Health Professions Loans, school loans, private loans, and SLS. Deferred payment plan.
**Financial aid statistics:** 18% of aid is not need-based. In 1993-94, 69% of all undergraduate applicants received aid; 63% of freshman applicants. Average amounts of aid awarded freshmen: Scholarships and grants, $2,950; loans, $2,625.
**Supporting data/closing dates:** FAFSA: Priority filing date is April 1. School's own aid application: Priority filing date is April 1; accepted on rolling basis. Income tax forms. Notification of awards begins March 1.
**Financial aid contact:** Lee Sirois, Ed.D., Director of Financial Aid. 413 747-6259.

**STUDENT EMPLOYMENT.** College Work/Study Program. Institutional employment. 53% of full-time undergraduates work on campus during school year. Students may expect to earn an average of $1,095 during school year. Off-campus part-time employment opportunities rated "good."

**COMPUTER FACILITIES.** 48 IBM/IBM-compatible microcomputers; all are networked. Students may access Digital minicomputer/mainframe systems. Client/LAN operating systems include Apple/Macintosh, DOS, Windows NT, Novell. Computer languages and software packages include BASIC, C, COBOL, dBASE, FORTRAN, Lotus 1-2-3, Pascal, word processing packages. Computer facilities are available to all students.
**Fees:** $25 computer fee per semester; included in tuition/fees.
**Hours:** 80 hours/week.

**GRADUATE CAREER DATA.** Graduate school percentages: 3% enter law school. 1% enter medical school. 2% enter dental school. 10% enter graduate business programs. 7% enter graduate arts and sciences programs. Highest graduate school enrollments: American International Coll, U of Massachusetts, Western New England Coll. 40% of graduates choose careers in business and industry.

**PROMINENT ALUMNI/AE.** Richard Neal, U.S. congressman; Dr. Gerald Desforges, first open-heart surgeon; James S. Morrison, vice-president and general sales manager, Arco.

# Amherst College

**Amherst, MA 01002** **413 542-2000**

**1994-95 Costs.** Tuition: $18,880. Room & board: $5,000. Fees, books, misc. academic expenses (school's estimate): $932.
**Enrollment.** Undergraduates: 888 men, 697 women (full-time). Freshman class: 4,302 applicants, 991 accepted, 421 enrolled.
**Test score averages/ranges.** Average SAT scores: 639 verbal, 684 math. Average ACT scores: 29 composite.
**Faculty.** 153 full-time; 3 part-time. 77% of faculty holds highest degree in specific field. Student/faculty ratio: 9 to 1.
**Selectivity rating.** Most competitive.

**PROFILE.** Amherst is a private, liberal arts college. Founded in 1821 as an educational institution for men, it began admitting women in 1975. Its 970-acre campus is located close to the center of Amherst, 55 miles west of Worcester.

**Accreditation:** NEASC.
**Religious orientation:** Amherst College is nonsectarian; no religious requirements.
**Library:** Collections totaling over 760,457 volumes, 4,357 periodical subscriptions, and 402,352 microform items.
**Special facilities/museums:** Art, natural history, geology, natural science museums; language labs; observatory.
**Athletic facilities:** Gymnasium, field house, weight rooms, swimming pools, basketball, squash, and tennis courts, ice rink, athletic fields.

**STUDENT BODY. Undergraduate profile:** 15% are state residents; 3% are transfers. 11% Asian-American, 7% Black, 8% Hispanic, 64% White, 10% Other. Average age of undergraduates is 19.
**Freshman profile:** 24% of freshmen who took SAT scored 700 or over on verbal, 51% scored 700 or over on math; 75% scored 600 or over on verbal, 86% scored 600 or over on math; 95% scored 500 or over on verbal, 99% scored 500 or over on math; 100% scored 400 or over on verbal, 100% scored 400 or over on math. 90% of accepted applicants took SAT; 10% took ACT. 59% of freshmen come from public schools.
**Undergraduate achievement:** 98% of fall 1992 freshmen returned for fall 1993 term. 97% of entering class graduated. 30% of students who completed a degree program went on to graduate study within one year.
**Foreign students:** 51 students are from out of the country. Countries represented include Canada, China, England, India, Japan, and Korea; 29 in all.

**PROGRAMS OF STUDY. Degrees:** B.A.
**Majors:** American Studies, Anthropology, Asian Studies, Astronomy, Biology, Black Studies, Chemistry, Classics, Economics, English, European Studies, Fine Arts, French, Geology, German, Greek, History, Independent Scholar, Interdisciplinary Studies, Latin, Law/Jurisprudence/Social Thought, Mathematics/Computers, Music, Neurosciences, Philosophy, Physics, Political Science, Psychology, Religion, Romance Languages, Russian, Sociology, Spanish, Theatre/Dance, Women's/Gender Studies.
**Distribution of degrees:** The majors with the highest enrollment are English, political science, and economics; women's/gender studies, black studies, and computer science have the lowest.
**Special:** Latin American studies and interdepartmental majors may be arranged. Interdisciplinary colloquia for upperclass students. Special topics courses. Field study may be undertaken for one or two semesters. Self-designed majors. Double majors. Independent study. Pass/fail grading option. Internships. Preprofessional programs in law, medicine, veterinary science, and dentistry. Member of Five College Cooperation; cross-registration possible. National Theatre Institute Semester (Connecticut). Williams-Mystic Seaport Semester (Connecticut). Member of Twelve College Exchange Program. Exchange programs abroad in Japan and Germany. Study abroad also in Australia, China, Colombia, Costa Rica, Ecuador, Egypt, England, France, India, Ireland, Israel, Italy, Kenya, Scotland, Senegal, Spain, and other countries.
**Honors:** Phi Beta Kappa. Honors program. Honor societies.
**Academic Assistance:** Remedial writing. Nonremedial tutoring.

**STUDENT LIFE. Housing:** Coed dorms. Off-campus privately-owned housing. Off-campus married-student housing. 98% of students live in college housing.
**Social atmosphere:** Students gather at the campus center and at Antonio's, a local pizza parlor. Athletes and theme houses (similar to Greek organizations) are influential on campus. Theme parties, the Casino Dance, Williams Weekend, Homecoming, and the Fall and Spring Weekends are popular campus events. According to the student newspaper, "Almost anyone can find something to do, whether it's a movie, lecture, or party. The other four colleges in the area help the local cultural and social life, also."
**Services and counseling/handicapped student services:** Placement services. Health service. Women's center. Day care. Counseling services for minority and older students. Birth control, personal, and psychological counseling. Career and academic guidance services. Religious counseling. Physically disabled student services. Notetaking services. Tape recorders. Tutors. Reader services for the blind.
**Campus organizations:** Undergraduate student government. Student newspaper (Amherst Student, published once/week). Literary magazine. Yearbook. Radio station. Glee club, choir, octet, choruses, intercollegiate orchestra, debating, drama group, social center, Oxfam, Outreach, outing club, Adopt-A-Grandparent, Beyond War, departmental groups, special-interest groups, 100 organizations in all.
**Religious organizations:** Christian Association, Hillel, Insight, Newman Club.
**Minority/foreign student organizations:** Asian Student Association, Black Student Union, Black Business Association, La Causa, Straight Ahead. Foreign Affairs Society.

**ATHLETICS. Physical education requirements:** None.
**Intercollegiate competition:** 42% of students participate. Baseball (M), basketball (M,W), cross-country (M,W), diving (M,W), field hockey (W), football (M), golf (M,W), ice hockey (M), lacrosse (M,W), soccer (M,W), squash (M,W), swimming (M,W), tennis (M,W), track (indoor) (M,W), track (outdoor) (M,W), track and field (indoor) (M,W), volleyball (W). Member of NCAA Division III, NESCAC.
**Intramural and club sports:** 70% of students participate. Intramural basketball, broomball, golf, racquetball, soccer, softball, squash, tennis, touch football, volleyball. Men's club badminton, crew, cycling, equestrian sports, fencing, karate, rugby, sailing, skiing, ultimate frisbee, volleyball, water polo. Women's club badminton, crew, cycling, equestrian sports, fencing, ice hockey, karate, rugby, sailing, skiing, ultimate frisbee, water polo.

**ADMISSIONS. Academic basis for candidate selection** (in order of priority): Secondary school record, essay, school's recommendation, class rank, standardized test scores.
**Nonacademic basis for candidate selection:** Character and personality, extracurricular participation, and particular talent or ability are important. Geographical distribution and alumni/ae relationship are considered.
**Requirements:** Graduation from secondary school is required; GED is accepted. 16 units and the following program of study are recommended: 4 units of English, 4 units of math, 3 units of science, 4 units of foreign language, 2 units of social studies, 2 units of history. Rank in top tenth of secondary school class recommended. SAT or ACT is required. ACH required. Campus visit recommended. Off-campus interviews available with an alumni representative.
**Procedure:** Take SAT or ACT by December of 12th year. Take ACH by December of 12th year. Application deadline is December 31. Acceptance notification by early April. Reply is required by May 1. $200 nonrefundable tuition deposit. Freshmen accepted for fall term only.
**Special programs:** Admission may be deferred one year. Placement may be granted through CEEB Advanced Placement exams for scores of 5 or higher. Placement may be granted through challenge exams. Early decision program. In fall 1993, 360 applied for early decision and 136 were accepted. Deadline for applying for early decision is November 15.
**Transfer students:** Transfer students accepted for terms other than fall. In fall 1993, 3% of all new students were transfers into all classes. 198 transfer applications were received, 19 were accepted. Application deadline is February 1 for fall; November 1 for spring. Minimum 3.0 GPA recommended. Lowest course grade accepted is "C." Maximum number of transferable credits is 16 credits. At least 16 credits must be completed at the college to receive degree.
**Admissions contact:** Jane E. Reynolds, Ed.M., Director of Admissions. 413 542-2328.

**FINANCIAL AID. Available aid:** Pell grants, school grants, and aid for undergraduate foreign students. Perkins Loans (NDSL), PLUS, Stafford Loans (GSL), state loans, school loans, and private loans. Knight Tuition Plans.
**Financial aid statistics:** Average amounts of aid awarded freshmen: Scholarships and grants, $13,314; loans, $2,772.
**Supporting data/closing dates:** FAFSA/FAF/FFS: Priority filing date is February 1. School's own aid application: Deadline is February 1. Notification of awards begins April.
**Financial aid contact:** Joe Paul Case, Dean of Financial Aid. 413 542-2296.

**STUDENT EMPLOYMENT.** College Work/Study Program. Institutional employment. 68% of full-time undergraduates work on campus during school year. Students may expect to earn an average of $748 during school year. Off-campus part-time employment opportunities rated "fair."

**COMPUTER FACILITIES.** 75 IBM/IBM-compatible microcomputers; all are networked. Students may access Digital minicomputer/mainframe systems, BITNET. Residence halls may be equipped with modems. Computer languages and software packages include APL, AQD, BASIC, C, Excel, FORTRAN, KERMIT, LISP, Lotus 1-2-3, Pascal, RS/1, SAS, SPSS-X, WordPerfect. Computer facilities are available to all students.
**Fees:** None.

**GRADUATE CAREER DATA.** Highest graduate school enrollments: Columbia U, Harvard U, New York U, Stanford U, U of Chicago, Yale U.

**PROMINENT ALUMNI/AE.** Charles Hamilton Houston, legal counsel, NAACP; Calvin Coolidge, 30th president of the U.S.; Richard P. Wilbur, Pulitzer Prize-winning poet; Harold Varmus, Nobel Prize winner in medicine; Daniel Bliss, founder, American U of Beirut; Henry Ward Beecher, 19th century preacher and orator.

# Anna Maria College

**Paxton, MA 01612** **508 849-3300**

**1994-95 Costs.** Tuition: $10,800. Room & board: $4,835. Fees, books, misc. academic expenses (school's estimate): $926.

**Enrollment.** Undergraduates: 134 men, 335 women (full-time). Freshman class: 337 applicants, 271 accepted, 91 enrolled.

**Test score averages/ranges.** Average SAT scores: 410 verbal, 420 math.

**Faculty.** 35 full-time; 45 part-time. 44% of faculty holds doctoral degree. Student/faculty ratio: 16 to 1.

**Selectivity rating.** Less competitive.

**PROFILE.** Anna Maria is a church-affiliated, liberal arts college. Founded in 1946 as a college for women, it began admitting men in 1973. Its 180-acre campus is set on the grounds of a 19th century estate, eight miles from Worcester.

**Accreditation:** NEASC. Professionally accredited by the American Bar Association, the American Medical Association (CAHEA), the Council on Social Work Education, the National League for Nursing.
**Religious orientation:** Anna Maria College is affiliated with the Roman Catholic Church; two semesters of religion required.
**Library:** Collections totaling over 68,000 volumes, 402 periodical subscriptions, and 1,420 microform items.
**Athletic facilities:** Gymnasium, weight room, baseball, field hockey, soccer, and softball fields, fitness trail.
**STUDENT BODY. Undergraduate profile:** 82% are state residents; 36% are transfers. 5% Asian-American, 5% Black, 2% Hispanic, 88% White. Average age of undergraduates is 22.
**Freshman profile:** 4% of freshmen who took SAT scored 600 or over on math; 9% scored 500 or over on verbal, 17% scored 500 or over on math; 49% scored 400 or over on verbal, 44% scored 400 or over on math; 94% scored 300 or over on verbal, 88% scored 300 or over on math. 95% of accepted applicants took SAT; 1% took ACT. 70% of freshmen come from public schools.
**Undergraduate achievement:** 92% of fall 1992 freshmen returned for fall 1993 term. 83% of entering class graduated. 32% of students who completed a degree program went on to graduate study within five years.
**Foreign students:** 25 students are from out of the country. Countries represented include Burundi, China, and Japan; seven in all.
**PROGRAMS OF STUDY. Degrees:** B.A., B.Bus.Admin., B.F.A., B.Mus., B.S.
**Majors:** Accounting, Art Education, Art Therapy, Computer Science, Criminal Justice, Early Childhood Education, Elementary Education, English, Finance, Liberal Studies, Management, Marketing, Medical Technology, Music, Music Education, Music Performance, Music Therapy, Paralegal, Pre-Dentistry, Pre-Law, Pre-Medicine, Psychology, Social Relations, Social Work, Spanish, Studio Art.
**Distribution of degrees:** The majors with the highest enrollment are education, business, and psychology; medical technology, studio art, and Spanish have the lowest.
**Requirements:** General education requirement.
**Academic regulations:** Minimum 2.0 GPA must be maintained.
**Special:** Minors offered in interior design, medical science, environmental health, and religious studies. Associate's degrees offered. Self-designed majors. Double majors. Dual degrees. Independent study. Accelerated study. Pass/fail grading option. Internships. Graduate school at which undergraduates may take graduate-level courses. Preprofessional programs in law, medicine, veterinary science, and dentistry. 3-2 engineering program with Worcester Polytech Inst. Member of Worcester Consortium for Higher Education. Washington Semester. Exchange program with Holy Names Coll. Teacher certification in early childhood, elementary, and secondary education. Study abroad in Canada, Mexico, and European countries. ROTC at Worcester State Coll. NROTC at Coll of the Holy Cross. AFROTC at Worcester Polytech Inst.
**Honors:** Honors program. Honor societies.
**Academic Assistance:** Remedial reading, writing, math, and study skills. Nonremedial tutoring.
**ADMISSIONS. Academic basis for candidate selection** (in order of priority): Secondary school record, essay, class rank, school's recommendation, standardized test scores.
**Nonacademic basis for candidate selection:** Extracurricular participation is emphasized. Character and personality and particular talent or ability are important. Alumni/ae relationship is considered.
**Requirements:** Graduation from secondary school is required; GED is accepted. 16 units and the following program of study are required: 4 units of English, 2 units of math, 2 units of science including 1 unit of lab, 2 units of social studies, 2 units of history, 2 units of academic electives. Rank in top half of secondary school class and minimum 2.50 GPA recommended. Portfolio required of art program applicants. Audition required of music program applicants. R.N. required of nursing program applicants. SAT is required; ACT may be substituted. Campus visit and interview recommended. Off-campus interviews available with an admissions representative.
**Procedure:** Take SAT or ACT by June of 12th year. Visit college for interview by June of 12th year. Suggest filing application by June 1; no deadline. Notification of admission on rolling basis. Reply is required by May 1 or within 30 days of acceptance. $100 nonrefundable tuition deposit. $100 room deposit, refundable until May 1. Freshmen accepted for terms other than fall.
**Special programs:** Admission may be deferred one year. Credit and/or placement may be granted through CEEB Advanced Placement exams for scores of 3 or higher. Credit and/or placement may be granted through CLEP general and subject exams. Credit and placement may be granted through Regents College, ACT PEP, DANTES, and challenge exams, and military and life experience. Early decision program. In fall 1993, two applied for early decision and two were accepted. Deadline for applying for early decision is November 1. Early entrance/early admission program. Concurrent enrollment program.
**Transfer students:** Transfer students accepted for terms other than fall. In fall 1993, 36% of all new students were transfers into all classes. 77 transfer applications were received, 62 were accepted. Application deadline is September 15 for fall; January 15 for spring. Minimum 2.2 GPA required. Lowest course grade accepted is "C." Maximum number of transferable credits is 75 semester hours. At least 45 semester hours must be completed at the college to receive degree.
**Admissions contact:** John F. Wilbur, Ph.D., Associate Director of Enrollment Management/Director of Admissions. 508 849-3360.
**FINANCIAL AID. Available aid:** Pell grants, SEOG, state scholarships and grants, school scholarships and grants, private scholarships and grants, ROTC scholarships, academic merit scholarships, and aid for undergraduate foreign students. Perkins Loans (NDSL), PLUS, Stafford Loans (GSL), state loans, private loans, and SLS. AMS, Tuition Management Systems, deferred payment plan, and family tuition reduction.
**Financial aid statistics:** 20% of aid is not need-based. In 1993-94, 86% of all undergraduate applicants received aid; 82% of freshman applicants. Average amounts of aid awarded freshmen: Scholarships and grants, $5,500; loans, $2,227.
**Supporting data/closing dates:** FAFSA/FAF. School's own aid application. Income tax forms. Notification of awards begins April 1.
**Financial aid contact:** Christine Wilson, M.A., Director of Financial Aid. 508 849-3366.

# Assumption College

**Worcester, MA 01615-0005** **508 752-5615**

**1994-95 Costs.** Tuition: $12,000. Room & board: $5,520–5,820. Fees, books, misc. academic expenses (school's estimate): $620.

**Enrollment.** Undergraduates: 665 men, 1,033 women (full-time). Freshman class: 2,250 applicants, 1,700 accepted, 454 enrolled. Graduate enrollment: 117 men, 220 women.

**Test score averages/ranges.** Range of SAT scores of middle 50%: 400-500 verbal, 430-530 math.

**Faculty.** 115 full-time; 60 part-time. 95% of faculty holds highest degree in specific field. Student/faculty ratio: 16 to 1.

**Selectivity rating.** Less competitive.

**PROFILE.** Assumption, founded in 1904, is a church-affiliated, liberal arts college. Its 150-acre campus is located in Worcester, approximately three miles from the center of the city.

**Accreditation:** NEASC.
**Religious orientation:** Assumption College is affiliated with the Roman Catholic Church (the Assumptionists); no religious requirements.
**Library:** Collections totaling over 188,837 volumes, 1,198 periodical subscriptions, and 3,236 microform items.
**Special facilities/museums:** French Institute museum, religious studies institute, social and rehabilitation services institute, language lab, media center.
**Athletic facilities:** Gymnasium, baseball, football, and softball fields, tracks, recreation center, basketball, racquetball, and tennis courts, swimming pool.
**STUDENT BODY. Undergraduate profile:** 50% are state residents; 12% are transfers. 1% Asian-American, 1% Black, 1% Hispanic, 97% White. Average age of undergraduates is 20.
**Freshman profile:** Majority of accepted applicants took SAT. 60% of freshmen come from public schools.
**Foreign students:** 21 students are from out of the country. Countries represented include Canada, France, Iceland, Japan, Puerto Rico, and Uganda; 11 in all.
**PROGRAMS OF STUDY. Degrees:** A.B.
**Majors:** Accounting, Biology, Chemistry, Computer Science, Economics, Economics/Business, English, Foreign Affairs, Foreign Languages, French, History, Management, Marketing, Mathematics, Natural Science, Philosophy, Politics, Psychology, Religious Studies, Social/Rehabilitation Services, Sociology, Spanish, Theology.
**Distribution of degrees:** The majors with the highest enrollment are business, English, and psychology; foreign language, sociology, and religious studies have the lowest.
**Requirements:** General education requirement.
**Academic regulations:** Minimum 2.0 GPA required for graduation.
**Special:** Minors offered in most majors and in classics, comparative literature, education, fine arts, French studies, geography, Latin American studies, linguistics, and theatre arts. Courses offered in German, Greek, Italian, physics, and Russian. Community studies, Native American studies, and Third World studies programs. Self-designed majors. Double majors. Independent study. Accelerated study. Internships. Cooperative education programs. Graduate school at which undergraduates may take graduate-level courses. Preprofessional programs in law, medicine, and dentistry. 3-1 medical technology program. 3-2 engineering program with Worcester Polytech Inst. Member of Worcester Consortium of Higher Education; cross-registration possible. Washington Semester. Teacher certification

in elementary and secondary education. Exchange programs abroad in Ireland and Italy. Study abroad also in numerous other countries. ROTC and NROTC at Worcester Polytech Inst. AFROTC at Coll of the Holy Cross.
**Honors:** Honors program. Honor societies.
**Academic Assistance:** Nonremedial tutoring.

**STUDENT LIFE. Housing:** Students may live on or off campus. Coed, women's, and men's dorms. School-owned/operated apartments. Language and substance-free housing. 90% of students live in college housing.
**Social atmosphere:** The student newspaper reports, "Social events are held on campus most every weekend. Students are friendly, though very conservative. The student body, for the most part, is a very homogeneous group. The city of Worcester provides a number of social and cultural opportunities." On campus students gather at the Student Center and the Junction; off campus they hang out at the Lietrim Pub, Kasey's Pub, Coffee Kingdom, and the Firehouse Cafe. Some of the prominent groups on campus include Student Government, the Campus Ministry, and the Senior Class. Club 21, Sibling Weekend, Senior Week, the Coffeehouse Series, and the Last Six Weeks program are among the year's favorite events.
**Services and counseling/handicapped student services:** Placement services. Health service. Counseling services for minority, military, veteran, and older students. Personal and psychological counseling. Career and academic guidance services. Physically disabled student services.
**Campus organizations:** Undergraduate student government. Student newspaper (Le Provocateur, published twice/week). Literary magazine. Yearbook. Radio station. Glee club, Renaissance Singers, drama group, lectures, films, 41 organizations in all.
**Religious organizations:** Campus Ministry, Communitas, Ecumenical Institute.

**ATHLETICS. Physical education requirements:** None.
**Intercollegiate competition:** 40% of students participate. Baseball (M), basketball (M,W), crew (M,W), cross-country (M,W), field hockey (W), football (M), golf (M), ice hockey (M), lacrosse (M), soccer (M,W), softball (W), tennis (M,W), volleyball (W). Member of Eastern Collegiate Football Conference, National Rowing Association, NCAA Division II, New England Intercollegiate Golf Association, Northeast Ten Conference, Pilgrim Lacrosse League.
**Intramural and club sports:** 80% of students participate. Intramural aerobics, basketball, fitness and weight training, floor hockey, indoor soccer, softball, racquetball, volleyball, walleyball, water polo. Men's club cheerleading. Women's club cheerleading.

**ADMISSIONS. Academic basis for candidate selection** (in order of priority): Secondary school record, class rank, standardized test scores, school's recommendation.
**Nonacademic basis for candidate selection:** Character and personality are emphasized. Alumni/ae relationship is important. Extracurricular participation, particular talent or ability, and geographical distribution are considered.
**Requirements:** Graduation from secondary school is required; GED is accepted. 15 units and the following program of study are required: 4 units of English, 2 units of math, 1 unit of science, 2 units of foreign language, 1 unit of history, 5 units of academic electives. SAT or ACT is required. ACH recommended. Campus visit and interview recommended. No off-campus interviews.
**Procedure:** Take SAT or ACT by January of 12th year. Suggest filing application by fall. Application deadline is March 1. Acceptance notification within three weeks of receipt of application. Reply is required by May 1. $200 nonrefundable tuition deposit. Freshmen accepted for terms other than fall.
**Special programs:** Admission may be deferred one semester. Credit and/or placement may be granted through CEEB Advanced Placement exams for scores of 3 or higher. Credit and/or placement may be granted through CLEP general and subject exams. Placement may be granted through challenge exams. Credit and placement may be granted through military and life experience. Early decision program. In fall 1992, 16 applied for early decision and six were accepted. Deadline for applying for early decision is November 1. Early entrance/early admission program.
**Transfer students:** Transfer students accepted for terms other than fall. In fall 1992, 12% of all new students were transfers into all classes. 220 transfer applications were received, 174 were accepted. Application deadline is August 1 for fall; December 1 for spring. Minimum 2.5 GPA required. Lowest course grade accepted is "C." At least 60 semester hours must be completed at the college to receive degree.
**Admissions contact:** Thomas E. Dunn, Director of Admissions. 508 752-5615, extension 285.

**FINANCIAL AID. Available aid:** Pell grants, SEOG, state scholarships, school scholarships and grants, private scholarships, ROTC scholarships, and athletic scholarships. Perkins Loans (NDSL), PLUS, Stafford Loans (GSL), state loans, and SLS. Tuition Plan Inc. and Education Plan Inc.
**Financial aid statistics:** Average amounts of aid awarded freshmen: Scholarships and grants, $4,500.
**Supporting data/closing dates:** FAFSA/FAF: Deadline is February 1. Income tax forms: Deadline is February 1.
**Financial aid contact:** Lynn Stanovich, Director of Financial Aid. 508 752-5615, extension 158.

**STUDENT EMPLOYMENT.** College Work/Study Program. Institutional employment. 25% of full-time undergraduates work on campus during school year. Students may expect to earn an average of $1,100 during school year. Off-campus part-time employment opportunities rated "excellent."

**COMPUTER FACILITIES.** 75 IBM/IBM-compatible and Macintosh/Apple microcomputers; 5 are networked. Students may access Digital minicomputer/mainframe systems. Client/LAN operating systems include Novell. Computer languages and software packages include BASIC, C, COBOL, dBASE III+, FORTRAN, LISP, Lotus 1-2-3, MINITAB, Pascal, Prolog, SPSS-X, WordPerfect. Computer facilities are available to all students.
**Fees:** None.
**Hours:** 7 AM-2 AM, except Friday and Saturday evenings.

# Atlantic Union College

**South Lancaster, MA 01561** **508 368-2000**

**1994-95 Costs.** Tuition: $10,600. Room & board: $3,600. Fees, books, misc. academic expenses (school's estimate): $1,100.
**Enrollment.** Undergraduates: 279 men, 305 women (full-time). Freshman class: 763 applicants, 268 accepted, 120 enrolled. Graduate enrollment: 37 men, 41 women.
**Test score averages/ranges.** Average ACT scores: 21 composite.
**Faculty.** 51 full-time; 36 part-time. Student/faculty ratio: 12 to 1.
**Selectivity rating.** Less competitive.

**PROFILE.** Atlantic Union, founded in 1882 is a church-affiliated, liberal arts college. Its 330-acre campus is located in South Lancaster, 49 miles west of Boston.

**Accreditation:** NEASC. Professionally accredited by the Council on Social Work Education, the National Council for Accreditation of Teacher Education, the National League for Nursing.
**Religious orientation:** Atlantic Union College is affiliated with the Seventh-day Adventist Church; 12 semester hours of religion/theology required.
**Library:** Collections totaling over 110,150 volumes, 771 periodical subscriptions, and 8,867 microform items.
**Special facilities/museums:** Art gallery, music conservatory, demonstration high school and elementary school near campus.
**Athletic facilities:** Gymnasium, swimming pool, field house, weight room, basketball, racquetball, tennis, and volleyball courts, athletic field.

**STUDENT BODY. Undergraduate profile:** 52% are state residents. 7% Asian-American, 28% Black, 21% Hispanic, 37% White, 7% Other.
**Freshman profile:** Majority of accepted applicants took ACT.
**Undergraduate achievement:** 17% of entering class graduated.

**PROGRAMS OF STUDY. Degrees:** B.A., B.Mus., B.S.
**Majors:** Accounting, Art, Biochemistry, Biology, Business Administration, Business Education, Chemistry, Computer Information Systems, Computer Science, Early Childhood Education, Elementary Education, English, French, History, Interior Design, Life Sciences, Mathematics, Medical Technology, Music, Natural Sciences, Nursing, Office Management, Personal Ministries, Physical Education, Psychology, Religion, Social Work, Spanish, Theology.
**Distribution of degrees:** The majors with the highest enrollment are business administration, nursing, and psychology; physical education, religion, and music have the lowest.
**Requirements:** General education requirement.
**Academic regulations:** Minimum 2.0 GPA must be maintained.
**Special:** Minors offered in some majors and in biblical languages, communications, composition/journalism, criminal justice, economics, German, political science, secondary education, sociology, and women's studies. Associate's degrees offered. Double majors. Independent study. Pass/fail grading option. Internships. Cooperative education programs. Preprofessional programs in law, medicine, veterinary science, pharmacy, dentistry, and optometry. 1-3 engineering program with Walla Walla Coll. Preprofessional programs in dental hygiene, occupational therapy, physical therapy, radiologic technology, and respiratory therapy with Loma Linda U. Teacher certification in early childhood, elementary, and secondary education. Certification in specific subject areas. Exchange programs abroad in Austria, France, and Spain.
**Honors:** Honors program. Honor societies.
**Academic Assistance:** Remedial reading, writing, math, and study skills. Nonremedial tutoring.

**ADMISSIONS. Academic basis for candidate selection** (in order of priority): School's recommendation, secondary school record, class rank, standardized test scores.
**Nonacademic basis for candidate selection:** Character and personality are emphasized. Extracurricular participation is important. Particular talent or ability and alumni/ae relationship are considered.
**Requirements:** Graduation from secondary school is required; GED is accepted. No specific distribution of secondary school units required. 1/2 unit of computer science required; 1/2 unit of music or visual arts recommended. Minimum composite ACT score of 17 and minimum 2.0 GPA required. ACT is required; SAT may be substituted. Admissions interview recommended. Off-campus interviews available with an admissions representative.
**Procedure:** Take SAT or ACT by June of 12th year. Suggest filing application by February 1. Application deadline is August 1. Notification of admission on rolling basis. No set date by which applicant must accept offer. $100 tuition deposit, refundable if requested in writing. Freshmen accepted for terms other than fall.
**Special programs:** Credit may be granted through CLEP general and subject exams and challenge exams.
**Transfer students:** Transfer students accepted for terms other than fall. Application deadline is August 1 for fall; January 2 for spring. Minimum 2.0 GPA required. Lowest course grade accepted is "C." Maximum number of transferable credits is 72 semester hours. At least 30 semester hours must be completed at the college to receive degree.
**Admissions contact:** James Norcliffe, M.A., Director of Admissions. 508 368-2235.

**FINANCIAL AID. Available aid:** Pell grants, SEOG, state scholarships and grants, school scholarships and grants, private scholarships and grants, academic merit scholarships, athletic scholarships, and aid for undergraduate foreign students. Perkins Loans (NDSL), PLUS, Stafford Loans (GSL), NSL, state loans, school loans, and SLS. Tuition Plan Inc., Knight Tuition Plans, AMS, deferred payment plan, family tuition reduction, and guaranteed tuition.
**Financial aid statistics:** 30% of aid is not need-based. In 1993-94, 90% of all undergraduate applicants received aid; 90% of freshman applicants. Average amounts of aid awarded freshmen: Scholarships and grants, $1,500; loans, $2,600.

**Supporting data/closing dates:** FAFSA/FFS: Priority filing date is April 15. School's own aid application: Priority filing date is April 15. State aid form: Priority filing date is April 15. Income tax forms: Priority filing date is May 1. Notification of awards on rolling basis.

**Financial aid contact:** William Deitemeyer, M.B.A., Director of Financial Aid. 508 368-2280.

# Babson College

**Babson Park, MA 02157-0310** **617 235-1200**

**1994-95 Costs.** Tuition: $16,600. Room: $4,490. Board: $2,495. Fees, books, misc. academic expenses (school's estimate): $1,160.

**Enrollment.** Undergraduates: 1,065 men, 615 women (full-time). Freshman class: 2,007 applicants, 1,137 accepted, 412 enrolled. Graduate enrollment: 969 men, 586 women.

**Test score averages/ranges.** Range of SAT scores of middle 50%: 430-530 verbal, 520-630 math.

**Faculty.** 114 full-time; 36 part-time. 93% of faculty holds doctoral degree. Student/faculty ratio: 17 to 1.

**Selectivity rating.** More competitive.

**PROFILE.** Babson, founded in 1919, is a private college of business administration and management. Its 450-acre campus is located in Wellesley, 12 miles from Boston.

**Accreditation:** NEASC. Professionally accredited by the American Assembly of Collegiate Schools of Business.

**Religious orientation:** Babson College is nonsectarian; no religious requirements.

**Library:** Collections totaling over 110,342 volumes, 1,482 periodical subscriptions, and 345,588 microform items.

**Special facilities/museums:** Sir Isaac Newton Collection, archives, museum, globe and relief map, management lab.

**Athletic facilities:** Gymnasium, field house, track, swimming pool, weight rooms, dance studio, basketball, racquetball, squash, tennis, and volleyball courts, athletic fields, ice rink, sauna, batting cage, fitness center.

**STUDENT BODY. Undergraduate profile:** 41% are state residents; 15% are transfers. 6% Asian-American, 2% Black, 3% Hispanic, 61% White, 28% International. Average age of undergraduates is 20.

**Freshman profile:** 7% of freshmen who took SAT scored 700 or over on math; 7% scored 600 or over on verbal, 41% scored 600 or over on math; 45% scored 500 or over on verbal, 85% scored 500 or over on math; 91% scored 400 or over on verbal, 99% scored 400 or over on math; 100% scored 300 or over on verbal, 100% scored 300 or over on math. 99% of accepted applicants took SAT; 1% took ACT. 53% of freshmen come from public schools.

**Undergraduate achievement:** 91% of fall 1992 freshmen returned for fall 1993 term. 76% of entering class graduated. 4% of students who completed a degree program immediately went on to graduate study.

**Foreign students:** 344 students are from out of the country. Countries represented include India, the Netherlands, Peru, Turkey, the United Kingdom, and Venezuela; 58 in all.

**PROGRAMS OF STUDY. Degrees:** B.S.Mgmt.

**Majors:** Accounting, American Studies, Communication, Economics, Entrepreneurial Studies, Entrepreneurial Studies/Business Law, Entrepreneurial Studies/Economics, Entrepreneurial Studies/Marketing, Finance, Finance/Investments, International Business Studies, Investments, Management, Management Information Systems, Marketing, Quantitative Methods, Quantitative Methods/Economics, Quantitative Methods/Finance, Quantitative Methods/Investments, Quantitative Methods/Marketing, Society/Technology.

**Distribution of degrees:** The majors with the highest enrollment are marketing, accounting, and finance; quantitative methods/investments, quantitative methods/marketing, and accounting/management information systems have the lowest.

**Requirements:** General education requirement.

**Academic regulations:** Freshmen must maintain minimum 1.58 GPA; sophomores, 1.75 GPA; juniors, 1.92 GPA; seniors, 2.0 GPA.

**Special:** Liberal arts concentrations include the classical tradition, creative arts, history, human behavior, language/culture, literature, philosophy, science/technology/society, and sociology. Self-designed majors. Double majors. Independent study. Internships. Preprofessional programs in law and business management. Cross-registration with Brandeis U, Pine Manor Coll, Regis Coll, and Wellesley Coll. Study abroad in England, Ireland, and Scotland; also possible through other institutions' exchange programs. ROTC at Boston U.

**Honors:** Honors program. Honor societies.

**STUDENT LIFE. Housing:** Freshmen must live on campus unless living with family within 25 miles of campus. Coed dorms. Sorority and fraternity housing. On-campus married-student housing. Single-sex floors and wings for women. 82% of students live in college housing.

**Social atmosphere:** According to the student newspaper, "Babson used to be known for a good social life, but now with changing laws and administration most parties are smaller and stay in individual rooms." Spring Weekend is popular at Babson. "Well-known bands play and the atmosphere of the weekend is total enjoyment and relaxation before finals." Hockey is also popular. "Babson made the division finals the last four years, and won in 1984." Students frequent the bars, restaurants, and clubs in Boston and the local area.

**Services and counseling/handicapped student services:** Placement services. Health service. Counseling services for minority students. Birth control, personal, and psychological counseling. Career and academic guidance services.

**Campus organizations:** Undergraduate student government. Student newspaper (Babson Free Press, published once/week). Yearbook. Jazz band, dance ensemble, vocal groups, Babson Players, management society, activities board, prelaw society, judicial court, film society, outing club, women's organization, Babson Association of College Entrepreneurs, Circle K, Academy of Accountancy, Gay and Lesbian Alliance, Republican Club, commuter student group, 60 organizations in all. Four fraternities, no chapter houses; two sororities, no chapter houses. 10% of men join a fraternity. 8% of women join a sorority.

**Religious organizations:** Hillel, Babson Christian Fellowship.

**Minority/foreign student organizations:** Asian Student Association, African Cultural Society. International Student Organization, European Connection, Latin Forum, MBA Latin Forum, Eastern European Association.

**ATHLETICS. Physical education requirements:** Two credits of physical education required.

**Intercollegiate competition:** 23% of students participate. Alpine skiing (M,W), baseball (M), basketball (M,W), cross-country (M,W), diving (M,W), field hockey (W), golf (M), ice hockey (M), lacrosse (M,W), softball (W), squash (M), swimming (M,W), tennis (M,W), volleyball (W). Member of CAC, ECAC, NCAA Division III, NCSA, New 8 Athletic Conference, NEWB.

**Intramural and club sports:** 85% of students participate. Intramural basketball, flag football, floor hockey, frisbee golf, ice hockey, soccer, tennis, volleyball, water polo, Wiffle ball. Men's club rugby, sailing, indoor track, outdoor track, ultimate frisbee, volleyball, water polo. Women's club sailing, indoor track, outdoor track.

**ADMISSIONS. Academic basis for candidate selection** (in order of priority): Secondary school record, class rank, standardized test scores, essay, school's recommendation.

**Nonacademic basis for candidate selection:** Extracurricular participation is emphasized. Character and personality and particular talent or ability are important. Geographical distribution and alumni/ae relationship are considered.

**Requirements:** Graduation from secondary school is required; GED is accepted. 16 units and the following program of study are required: 4 units of English, 3 units of math, 1 unit of lab science, 2 units of social studies. SAT is required; ACT may be substituted. ACH required. Campus visit and interview recommended. Off-campus interviews available with an alumni representative.

**Procedure:** Take SAT or ACT by February 1 of 12th year. Take ACH by June 1 of 12th year. Visit college for interview by February 1 of 12th year. Application deadline is February 1. Notification of admission by April 1. Reply is required by May 1. $250 nonrefundable tuition deposit. $250 refundable room deposit. Freshmen accepted for terms other than fall.

**Special programs:** Admission may be deferred one year. Credit and/or placement may be granted through CEEB Advanced Placement exams for scores of 3 or higher. Credit and/or placement may be granted through CLEP general and subject exams. Credit may be granted through life experience. Credit and placement may be granted through challenge exams. Early action program. In fall 1993, 93 applied for early action and 69 were accepted. Deadline for applying for early action is December 1.

**Transfer students:** Transfer students accepted for terms other than fall. In fall 1993, 15% of all new students were transfers into all classes. 241 transfer applications were received, 128 were accepted. Application deadline is April 1 for fall; November 1 for spring. Minimum 3.0 GPA. Lowest course grade accepted is "C." Maximum number of transferable credits is 64 semester hours. At least 64 semester hours must be completed at the college to receive degree.

**Admissions contact:** Charles S. Nolan, Ph.D., Dean of Admissions. 800 488-3696, 617 239-5522.

**FINANCIAL AID. Available aid:** Pell grants, SEOG, state scholarships and grants, school scholarships and grants, and academic merit scholarships. Perkins Loans (NDSL), PLUS, Stafford Loans (GSL), state loans, and SLS. Knight Tuition Plans and AMS. Educational Resources Institute Tuition Payment Plan.

**Financial aid statistics:** 4% of aid is not need-based. In 1993-94, 97% of all undergraduate applicants received aid; 93% of freshman applicants. Average amounts of aid awarded freshmen: Scholarships and grants, $8,094; loans, $2,883.

**Supporting data/closing dates:** FAFSA/FAF: Deadline is February 1. Income tax forms: Deadline is June 15. Notification of awards begins April 1.

**Financial aid contact:** Melissa Shaak, Director of Financial Aid. 617 239-4219.

**STUDENT EMPLOYMENT.** College Work/Study Program. Institutional employment. 35% of full-time undergraduates work on campus during school year. Students may expect to earn an average of $1,200 during school year. Off-campus part-time employment opportunities rated "fair."

**COMPUTER FACILITIES.** 250 IBM/IBM-compatible and Macintosh/Apple microcomputers; 50 are networked. Students may access Digital minicomputer/mainframe systems, BITNET, Internet. Residence halls may be equipped with modems. Client/LAN operating systems include Apple/Macintosh, DOS, UNIX/XENIX/AIX, Windows NT, Banyan, LocalTalk/AppleTalk. Computer languages and software packages include BASIC, BoxPro, COBOL, Harvard Graphics, Lotus 1-2-3, Microsoft Excel, Microsoft Word, MINITAB, Power Point, Select, Word for Windows; other software, ranging from simple linear programs to sophisticated statistical and financial modeling packages; 20 in all. Computer facilities are available to all students.

**Hours:** 24 hours.

**GRADUATE CAREER DATA.** 90% of graduates choose careers in business and industry. Companies and businesses that hire graduates: Accounting firms, commerical and investment banks, retail firms.

**PROMINENT ALUMNI/AE.** Roger Enrico, chairman/CEO, Frito-Lay, Inc.; Robert Weissman, president/COO, Dunn & Bradstreet; Arthur Blank, president/COO, The Home Depot.

# Bay Path College

**Longmeadow, MA 01106 413 567-0621**

**1994-95 Costs.** Tuition: $9,600. Room & board: $6,100. Fees, books, misc. academic expenses (school's estimate): $600.
**Enrollment.** 485 women (full-time). Freshman class: 660 applicants, 589 accepted, 218 enrolled.
**Test score averages/ranges.** N/A.
**Faculty.** 20 full-time; 23 part-time. 37% of faculty holds highest degree in specific field. Student/faculty ratio: 23 to 1.
**Selectivity rating.** Less competitive.

**PROFILE.** Bay Path, founded in 1897, is a private, liberal arts college for women. Its 27-acre campus is located in the town of Longmeadow, three miles from Springfield.

**Accreditation:** NEASC. Professionally accredited by the American Bar Association.
**Religious orientation:** Bay Path College is nonsectarian; no religious requirements.
**Library:** Collections totaling over 35,582 volumes, 283 periodical subscriptions, and 2,444 microform items.
**Special facilities/museums:** On-campus preschool.
**Athletic facilities:** Physical fitness center.

**STUDENT BODY. Undergraduate profile:** 55% are state residents; 6% are transfers. 1% Asian-American, 5% Black, 3% Hispanic, 83% White, 8% Other. Average age of undergraduates is 19.
**Freshman profile:** 2% of freshmen who took SAT scored 600 or over on verbal; 8% scored 500 or over on verbal, 11% scored 500 or over on math; 31% scored 400 or over on verbal, 42% scored 400 or over on math; 82% scored 300 or over on verbal, 81% scored 300 or over on math. Majority of accepted applicants took SAT. 93% of freshmen come from public schools.
**Undergraduate achievement:** 84% of fall 1992 freshmen returned for fall 1993 term. 84% of entering class graduated. 45% of students who completed a degree program immediately went on to graduate study.
**Foreign students:** 33 students are from out of the country. Countries represented include Indonesia, Japan, Mexico, Singapore, and Thailand; eight in all.

**PROGRAMS OF STUDY. Degrees:** B.A., B.S.
**Majors:** Business, Business/Accounting, Legal Studies, Psychology, Psychology/Criminal Justice, Psychology/Early Childhood Education.
**Distribution of degrees:** The majors with the highest enrollment are business, psychology, and legal studies.
**Requirements:** General education requirement.
**Academic regulations:** Freshmen must maintain minimum 1.9 GPA; sophomores, 1.9 GPA; juniors, 2.0 GPA; seniors, 2.0 GPA.
**Special:** Associate's degrees offered. Independent study. Internships. Cooperative education programs. Member of Cooperating Colleges of Greater Springfield; exchange possible. Teacher certification in early childhood education. ROTC at Western New England Coll.
**Honors:** Honor societies.
**Academic Assistance:** Remedial writing, math, and study skills. Nonremedial tutoring.

**ADMISSIONS. Academic basis for candidate selection** (in order of priority): Secondary school record, school's recommendation, class rank, standardized test scores.
**Nonacademic basis for candidate selection:** Character and personality, extracurricular participation, particular talent or ability, and geographical distribution are considered.
**Requirements:** Graduation from secondary school is required; GED is accepted. No specific distribution of secondary school units required. Minimum combined SAT score of 700, rank in top fifth of secondary school class, and minimum 2.0 GPA required; higher test scores and rank recommended. Conditional admission possible for applicants not meeting standard requirements. SAT or ACT is required. Campus visit and interview required. Off-campus interviews available with an admissions representative.
**Procedure:** Take SAT or ACT by November of 12th year. Take ACH by November of 12th year. Visit college for interview by February of 12th year. Notification of admission on rolling basis. Reply required within 30 days of acceptance. $200 nonrefundable tuition deposit. $100 nonrefundable room deposit. Freshmen accepted for terms other than fall.
**Special programs:** Admission may be deferred two years. Credit may be granted through CEEB Advanced Placement for scores of 3 or higher. Credit may be granted through CLEP general and subject exams and Regents College exams. Placement may be granted through challenge exams. Early decision program. In fall 1993, 38 applied for early decision and 31 were accepted. Deadline for applying for early decision is November 15. Early entrance/early admission program.
**Transfer students:** Transfer students accepted for terms other than fall. In fall 1993, 6% of all new students were transfers into all classes. 34 transfer applications were received, 33 were accepted. Application deadline is rolling for fall; rolling for spring. Minimum 2.0 GPA recommended. Lowest course grade accepted is "C-." Maximum number of transferable credits is 90 semester hours. At least 30 semester hours must be completed at the college to receive degree.
**Admissions contact:** Paula DesRoberts, M.B.A., Dean of Admissions and Advancement. 413 567-0621, extension 331.

**FINANCIAL AID. Available aid:** Pell grants, SEOG, state scholarships and grants, school scholarships and grants, private scholarships and grants, and academic merit scholarships. Perkins Loans (NDSL), PLUS, Stafford Loans (GSL), state loans, private loans, and SLS. Tuition Management Systems and family tuition reduction.
**Financial aid statistics:** 10% of aid is not need-based. In 1993-94, 100% of all undergraduate applicants received aid. Average amounts of aid awarded freshmen: Scholarships and grants, $3,600; loans, $3,200.
**Supporting data/closing dates:** FAFSA/FAF/FFS: Accepted on rolling basis. State aid form. Income tax forms: Accepted on rolling basis. Notification of awards on rolling basis.
**Financial aid contact:** Edward Ciosek, M.Ed., Director of Financial Aid. 413 567-0621, extension 345.

# Bentley College

**Waltham, MA 02154-4705 617 891-2000**

**1994-95 Costs.** Tuition: $13,800. Room & board: $5,510. Fees, books, misc. academic expenses (school's estimate): $695.
**Enrollment.** Undergraduates: 1,861 men, 1,438 women (full-time). Freshman class: 3,100 applicants, 2,109 accepted, 789 enrolled. Graduate enrollment: 1,241 men, 947 women.
**Test score averages/ranges.** Range of SAT scores of middle 50%: 410-490 verbal, 480-590 math.
**Faculty.** 203 full-time; 171 part-time. 89% of faculty holds doctoral degree. Student/faculty ratio: 20 to 1.
**Selectivity rating.** Less competitive.

**PROFILE.** Bentley College, founded in 1917, is a private college of business and liberal arts. Its 110-acre campus is located in Waltham, nine miles from Boston.

**Accreditation:** NEASC. Professionally accredited by the American Assembly of Collegiate Schools of Business.
**Religious orientation:** Bentley College is nonsectarian; no religious requirements.
**Library:** Collections totaling over 190,000 volumes, 2,590 periodical subscriptions, and 215,000 microform items.
**Special facilities/museums:** Small-business resource center, observatory.
**Athletic facilities:** Gymnasium, swimming pool, baseball, football/soccer, and intramural fields, tennis courts.

**STUDENT BODY. Undergraduate profile:** 56% are state residents; 23% are transfers. 5% Asian-American, 3% Black, 3% Hispanic, 72% White, 17% Other. Average age of undergraduates is 20.
**Freshman profile:** 3% of freshmen who took SAT scored 700 or over on math; 2% scored 600 or over on verbal, 26% scored 600 or over on math; 23% scored 500 or over on verbal, 74% scored 500 or over on math; 79% scored 400 or over on verbal, 98% scored 400 or over on math; 94% scored 300 or over on verbal, 100% scored 300 or over on math. 80% of accepted applicants took SAT. 67% of freshmen come from public schools.
**Undergraduate achievement:** 87% of fall 1991 freshmen returned for fall 1992 term. 62% of entering class graduated. 6% of students who completed a degree program immediately went on to graduate study.
**Foreign students:** 270 students are from out of the country. Countries represented include Colombia, India, Japan, Panama, Peru, and Spain; 66 in all.

**PROGRAMS OF STUDY. Degrees:** B.A., B.S.
**Majors:** Accountancy, Business Communications, Business Economics, Computer Information Systems, Economics/Finance, English, Finance, History, International Culture/Economy, Liberal Arts, Management, Marketing, Mathematical Sciences, Philosophy.
**Distribution of degrees:** The majors with the highest enrollment are accountancy, marketing, and finance.
**Requirements:** General education requirement.
**Academic regulations:** Freshmen must maintain minimum 1.7 GPA; sophomores, 1.9 GPA; juniors, 2.0 GPA; seniors, 2.0 GPA.
**Special:** Minors offered. Business Ethics Conference. Service Learning Program. Self-designed majors. Dual degrees. Independent study. Accelerated study. Internships. Graduate school at which undergraduates may take graduate-level courses. Preprofessional programs in law. Five-year B.A./M.B.A. program and B.A./M.S.Acct. program. Exchange programs with Brandeis U and Regis Coll. Study abroad in Australia, Belgium, England, France, Japan, and Mexico. ROTC. AFROTC at U of Massachusetts at Lowell.
**Honors:** Honors program. Honor societies.
**Academic Assistance:** Remedial reading, writing, math, and study skills. Nonremedial tutoring.

**STUDENT LIFE. Housing:** Students may live on or off campus. Coed dorms. School-owned/operated apartments. 80% of students live in college housing.
**Social atmosphere:** On campus, students enjoy the Pub and the lower cafe. Off campus, Harvard Square, Bambino's, and downtown Boston are popular hangouts. Groups with a considerable influence on campus life include Greeks, athletes, student government, and BACCHUS. Among the most popular events of the school year are Homecoming, Monte Carlo Night, Spring Weekend, and the numerous concerts, sports events, and Greek-sponsored activities. According to the student newspaper, there's always a lot of activity on campus. Students also have easy access to Boston and its diverse cultural life.
**Services and counseling/handicapped student services:** Placement services. Health service. Counseling services for minority students. Birth control, personal, and psychological counseling. Career and academic guidance services. Religious counseling. Learning disabled services.
**Campus organizations:** Undergraduate student government. Student newspaper (Vanguard, published once/week). Literary magazine. Yearbook. Radio station. Chorus, jazz band, debating, drama group, creative and performing arts groups, Circle K, service groups, 74 organizations in all. Seven fraternities, no chapter houses; six sororities, no chapter houses.
**Religious organizations:** Protestant Student Organization, Catholic Student Organization, Hillel.
**Minority/foreign student organizations:** Black United Body, La Cultura Latina. International Club, Armenian Club, Asian Club.

**ATHLETICS. Physical education requirements:** One semester of physical education required.
**Intercollegiate competition:** 10% of students participate. Baseball (M), basketball (M,W), cross-country (M,W), field hockey (W), football (M), golf (M), ice hockey (M), lacrosse (M), soccer (M,W), softball (W), tennis (M,W), track and field (indoor) (M,W), track and field (outdoor) (M,W), volleyball (W). Member of Eastern Collegiate Football Conference, ECAC, NCAA Division II, Northeast-10.

**Intramural and club sports:** 20% of students participate. Intramural basketball, flag football, floor hockey, racquetball, soccer, volleyball. Men's club swimming. Women's club swimming.

**ADMISSIONS. Academic basis for candidate selection** (in order of priority): Secondary school record, class rank, standardized test scores, school's recommendation, essay.
**Nonacademic basis for candidate selection:** Character and personality, extracurricular participation, particular talent or ability, and geographical distribution are important. Alumni/ae relationship is considered.
**Requirements:** Graduation from secondary school is required; GED is accepted. 16 units and the following program of study are recommended: 4 units of English, 4 units of math, 1 unit of science, 2 units of foreign language, 2 units of social studies, 3 units of electives. SAT, ACT, or three ACH (math, English, and one of applicant's choice) required. Campus visit and interview recommended. Off-campus interviews available with admissions and alumni representatives.
**Procedure:** Take SAT or ACT by January of 12th year. Visit college for interview by February 1 of 12th year. Application deadline is February 15. Notification of admission by April 1. Reply is required by May 1. $100 nonrefundable tuition deposit. $200 room deposit, refundable until May 1. Freshmen accepted for terms other than fall.
**Special programs:** Admission may be deferred one year. Credit and/or placement may be granted through CEEB Advanced Placement exams for scores of 3 or higher. Credit and/or placement may be granted through CLEP general and subject exams. Credit and placement may be granted through DANTES and challenge exams. Early decision program. In fall 1992, 127 applied for early decision and 91 were accepted. Deadline for applying for early decision is December 1. Early entrance/early admission program.
**Transfer students:** Transfer students accepted for terms other than fall. In fall 1992, 23% of all new students were transfers into all classes. 567 transfer applications were received, 373 were accepted. Application deadline is May 15 for fall; December 1 for spring. Minimum 2.5 GPA required. Lowest course grade accepted is "C-." Maximum number of transferable credits is 75 semester hours. At least 45 semester hours must be completed at the college to receive degree.
**Admissions contact:** Director of Admissions. 617 891-2244, 800 523-2354.

**FINANCIAL AID. Available aid:** Pell grants, SEOG, state scholarships and grants, school scholarships and grants, private scholarships and grants, ROTC scholarships, academic merit scholarships, and athletic scholarships. Service Learning scholarships. Perkins Loans (NDSL), PLUS, Stafford Loans (GSL), state loans, school loans, private loans, and SLS. Tuition Plan Inc., Knight Tuition Plans, and AMS.
**Financial aid statistics:** 21% of aid is not need-based. In 1992-93, 91% of all undergraduate applicants received aid; 88% of freshman applicants. Average amounts of aid awarded freshmen: Scholarships and grants, $7,593; loans, $3,100.
**Supporting data/closing dates:** FAFSA/FAF/FFS: Priority filing date is February 15. Income tax forms: Priority filing date is May 1. Notification of awards begins April 1.
**Financial aid contact:** Marilyn Molnar, Director of Financial Aid. 617 891-3441.

**STUDENT EMPLOYMENT.** College Work/Study Program. Institutional employment. 26% of full-time undergraduates work on campus during school year. Students may expect to earn an average of $2,000 during school year. Off-campus part-time employment opportunities rated "excellent."

**COMPUTER FACILITIES.** 3,000 IBM/IBM-compatible and Macintosh/Apple microcomputers. Students may access Digital minicomputer/mainframe systems, BITNET. Residence halls may be equipped with networked microcomputers, networked terminals, modems. Client/LAN operating systems include Apple/Macintosh. Computer languages and software packages include Assembler, BASIC, BIZPLAN, COBOL, CompuStat, FOREX, FORTRAN, IFPS, LINDO, LISP, Lotus 1-2-3, MINITAB, OPS-5, Oracle, Pascal, PROCOMM Plus, Prolog, RDB, SAS, SPSS-X, 20/20, WordPerfect. Computer facilities are available to all students.
**Fees:** $250 computer fee per semester.
**Hours:** 24 hours.

**GRADUATE CAREER DATA.** Graduate school percentages: 1% enter law school. 5% enter graduate business programs. Highest graduate school enrollments: Bentley Coll. 85% of graduates choose careers in business and industry. Companies and businesses that hire graduates: Arthur Andersen, The Boston Company, Coopers & Lybrand, Digital Equipment Corp., Jordan Marsh, Raytheon.

# Berklee College of Music

**Boston, MA 02215-3693** **617 266-1400**

**1994-95 Costs.** Tuition: $11,550. Room & board: $6,990. Fees, books, misc. academic expenses (school's estimate): $450.
**Enrollment.** Undergraduates: 1,850 men, 382 women (full-time). Freshman class: 1,975 applicants, 1,516 accepted, 712 enrolled.
**Test score averages/ranges.** N/A.
**Faculty.** 138 full-time; 142 part-time. 11% of faculty holds doctoral degree. Student/faculty ratio: 8 to 1.
**Selectivity rating.** N/A.

**PROFILE.** Berklee, founded in 1945, is a private college. Its urban campus is located in Boston's Back Bay area.

**Accreditation:** NEASC.
**Religious orientation:** Berklee College of Music is nonsectarian; no religious requirements.
**Library:** Collections totaling over 34,982 volumes, 51 periodical subscriptions, and 3,303 microform items.
**Special facilities/museums:** Ensemble library, 10 professional recording studios, film scoring and editing studio, analog and digital music synthesis labs, 1,200-seat performance center, learning center.
**Athletic facilities:** Discount memberships available at nearby YMCA/YWCA.

**STUDENT BODY. Undergraduate profile:** 57% are state residents. Average age of undergraduates is 22.
**Undergraduate achievement:** 67% of fall 1992 freshmen returned for fall 1993 term.
**Foreign students:** 700 students are from out of the country. Countries represented include Canada, Japan, and European, Middle Eastern, and South American countries; 70 in all.

**PROGRAMS OF STUDY. Degrees:** B.Mus.
**Majors:** Arranging, Composition, Film Scoring, Jazz Composition/Arranging, Music Business/Management, Music Education, Music Production/Engineering, Music Synthesis, Performance, Professional Music, Songwriting.
**Distribution of degrees:** The majors with the highest enrollment are professional music, music production/engineering, and performance; composition, arranging, and jazz composition have the lowest.
**Requirements:** General education requirement.
**Academic regulations:** Minimum 2.0 GPA must be maintained.
**Special:** Dual degrees. Accelerated study. Member of Pro-Arts Consortium. Exchange programs with Boston Architectural Center, Boston Conservatory, Emerson Coll, Massachusetts Coll of Art, MFA Museum Sch. Teacher certification in elementary and secondary education. Certification in specific subject areas. Exchange program abroad in the Netherlands (Rotterdam Conservatory).
**Academic Assistance:** Nonremedial tutoring.

**STUDENT LIFE. Housing:** Students may live on or off campus. Coed dorms. Off-campus privately-owned housing. 33% of students live in college housing.
**Social atmosphere:** Students at Berklee enjoy all of Boston as their campus, and music is their life. They are absorbed in being performers, composers, arrangers, producers, and engineers. Students enjoy gathering in the Dining Hall on campus. Off campus they head for Crossroads, Maxwell Jump, The Ratt, and The Centrum. There are no really prominent school groups which have a social influence, but students attend International Folk Music Night, Singer Showcase, and celebrate Black History Month.
**Services and counseling/handicapped student services:** Counseling services for minority students. Personal counseling. Career and academic guidance services. Physically disabled student services. Learning disabled services. Tape recorders. Reader services for the blind.
**Campus organizations:** Society of Screen Composers, International Trombone Association, drama and chess clubs, songwriters forum, 45 organizations in all.
**Religious organizations:** Christian Fellowship, Buddhist Club, Jewish Organization.
**Minority/foreign student organizations:** Black Student Union, Women's Network, BUGLE (Gay/Lesbian student group). International Student Club, Brazilian, Canadian, Japanese, and other foreign groups.

**ATHLETICS. Physical education requirements:** None.

**ADMISSIONS. Academic basis for candidate selection** (in order of priority): Secondary school record, school's recommendation, essay, class rank, standardized test scores.
**Nonacademic basis for candidate selection:** Extracurricular participation and particular talent or ability are emphasized. Character and personality and alumni/ae relationship are considered.
**Requirements:** Graduation from secondary school is required; GED is accepted. 16 units and the following program of study are required: 4 units of English, 1 unit of math, 1 unit of lab science, 2 units of social studies, 8 units of academic electives. No more than 3 units of nonacademic electives are recommended. Minimum of two years of musical study and/or significant experience in some phase of music required of applicants. Special application and interview required of music production and engineering program applicants. SAT or ACT is required. Campus visit and interview recommended. Off-campus interviews available with admissions and alumni representatives.
**Procedure:** Suggest filing application by February 1; no deadline. Notification of admission on rolling basis. $250 nonrefundable tuition deposit. $200 nonrefundable room deposit. Freshmen accepted for terms other than fall.
**Special programs:** Admission may be deferred two years. Credit may be granted through CEEB Advanced Placement for scores of 3 or higher. Credit and/or placement may be granted through CLEP general and subject exams. Credit may be granted through challenge exams.
**Transfer students:** Transfer students accepted for terms other than fall. Application deadline is rolling for fall; rolling for spring. Lowest course grade accepted is "C." Maximum number of transferable credits is 52 semester hours. At least 60 semester hours must be completed at the college to receive degree.
**Admissions contact:** Steven Lipman, Assistant Dean of Students/Director of Admissions. 800 421-0084, 617 266-1400, extensions 221, 222, 223.

**FINANCIAL AID. Available aid:** Pell grants, SEOG, state scholarships and grants, school scholarships and grants, private scholarships, and aid for undergraduate foreign students. Merit Scholarships. Perkins Loans (NDSL), PLUS, Stafford Loans (GSL), private loans, and SLS. Knight Tuition Plans and Tuition Management Systems. Extended repayment plan.
**Supporting data/closing dates:** FAFSA/FAF: Priority filing date is March 31. School's own aid application: Priority filing date is May 1. State aid form: Accepted on rolling basis. Income tax forms: Priority filing date is May 1. Notification of awards on rolling basis.
**Financial aid contact:** Pam Gilligan, Director of Financial Aid. 617 266-1400, extension 274.

**STUDENT EMPLOYMENT.** College Work/Study Program. Institutional employment. 6% of full-time undergraduates work on campus during school year. Students may expect to earn an average of $2,500 during school year. Freshmen are discouraged from working during their first term. Off-campus part-time employment opportunities rated "good."

**PROMINENT ALUMNI/AE.** Quincy Jones, producer; Branford Marsalis, saxophonist; Steve Smith, percussionist with Journey, leads Vital Information; Jan Hammer, composer of "Miami Vice" theme; Gary Burton, vibist and Berklee Dean of Curriculum.

## Boston Architectural Center

**Boston, MA 02115** 617 536-3170

**1993-94 Costs.** Tuition: $3,264. Housing: None. Fees, books, misc. academic expenses (school's estimate): $1,488.
**Enrollment.** Undergraduates: 425 men, 113 women (full-time). Freshman class: 286 applicants, 256 accepted, 141 enrolled.
**Test score averages/ranges.** N/A.
**Faculty.** 181 part-time. 3% of faculty holds doctoral degree.
**Selectivity rating.** N/A.

**PROFILE.** The Boston Architectural Center, founded in 1889, is a private institution. The center's facilities are located in Boston's Back Bay.

**Accreditation:** NEASC. Professionally accredited by the National Architecture Accrediting Board.
**Religious orientation:** Boston Architectural Center is nonsectarian; no religious requirements.
**Library:** Collections totaling over 23,000 volumes, and 1,400 periodical subscriptions.
**Special facilities/museums:** Gallery, studio space.
**STUDENT BODY. Undergraduate profile:** 60% are state residents; 65% are transfers. 2% Asian-American, 1% Black, 3% Hispanic, 93% White, 1% Other. Average age of undergraduates is 27.
**Undergraduate achievement:** 70% of fall 1992 freshmen returned for fall 1993 term.
**PROGRAMS OF STUDY. Degrees:** B.Arch., B.Inter.Design.
**Majors:** Architecture, Interior Design.
**Requirements:** General education requirement.
**Academic regulations:** Minimum 2.5 GPA must be maintained.
**Special:** Independent study. Accelerated study. Internships. Cooperative education programs. Member of Pro Arts Consortium.
**Academic Assistance:** Nonremedial tutoring.
**ADMISSIONS.**
**Requirements:** Graduation from secondary school is required; GED is accepted. No specific distribution of secondary school units required. Open admissions policy. Campus visit recommended. No off-campus interviews.
**Procedure:** Notification of admission on rolling basis. No set date by which applicants must accept offer. $125 nonrefundable tuition deposit. Freshmen accepted for terms other than fall.
**Special programs:** Credit and/or placement may be granted through CEEB Advanced Placement exams for scores of 4 or higher. Placement may be granted through CLEP general exams. Credit and/or placement may be granted through CLEP subject exams. Placement may be granted through challenge exams and life experience. Credit and placement may be granted through military experience.
**Transfer students:** Transfer students accepted for terms other than fall. In fall 1993, 65% of all new students were transfers into all classes. Application deadline is rolling for fall; rolling for spring. Lowest course grade accepted is "C." Maximum number of transferable credits is 66 semester hours. At least 57 semester hours must be completed at the institute to receive degree.
**Admissions contact:** Ellen M. Driscoll, Admissions Coordinator. 617 536-3170.
**FINANCIAL AID. Available aid:** Pell grants, state scholarships and grants, school scholarships, private scholarships, and academic merit scholarships. PLUS, Stafford Loans (GSL), state loans, private loans, and SLS. AMS.
**Financial aid statistics:** In 1993-94, 81% of all undergraduate applicants received aid; 75% of freshman applicants. Average amounts of aid awarded freshmen: Scholarships and grants, $1,281; loans, $3,031.
**Supporting data/closing dates:** FAFSA: Accepted on rolling basis. School's own aid application: Accepted on rolling basis. Income tax forms: Accepted on rolling basis. Notification of awards on rolling basis.
**Financial aid contact:** Ilene Coddon, Financial Aid Officer. 617 536-3170.

## Boston College

**Chestnut Hill, MA 02167** 617 552-8000

**1994-95 Costs.** Tuition: $16,640. Room: $3,830. Board: $3,130. Fees, books, misc. academic expenses (school's estimate): $948.
**Enrollment.** Undergraduates: 4,182 men, 4,625 women (full-time). Freshman class: 13,112 applicants, 6,179 accepted, 2,154 enrolled. Graduate enrollment: 1,855 men, 2,442 women.
**Test score averages/ranges.** Range of SAT scores of middle 50%: 520-610 verbal, 600-690 math.
**Faculty.** 591 full-time; 376 part-time. 95% of faculty holds highest degree in specific field. Student/faculty ratio: 15 to 1.
**Selectivity rating.** Highly competitive.

**PROFILE.** Boston College, founded in 1863, is a church-affiliated, liberal arts institution. Programs are offered through the Schools of Arts and Sciences, Education, Management, and Nursing. Its 240-acre campus is located in Chestnut Hill, overlooking the city of Boston.

**Accreditation:** NEASC. Professionally accredited by the American Assembly of Collegiate Schools of Business, the American Bar Association, the American Psychological Association, the Association of American Law Schools, the Council on Social Work Education, the National League for Nursing.
**Religious orientation:** Boston College is affiliated with the Roman Catholic Church (Society of Jesus); two semesters of religion required.
**Library:** Collections totaling over 1,322,380 volumes, 14,619 periodical subscriptions, and 2,282,582 microform items.
**Special facilities/museums:** Art museum, theatre arts center, on-campus school for multi-handicapped students, observatory, state-of-the-art science facilities.
**Athletic facilities:** Sports center, recreation complex, stadium, athletic fields, ice rink, gymnasium, training and weight rooms, swimming pool, track, handball, volleyball, and tennis courts.
**STUDENT BODY. Undergraduate profile:** 31% are state residents; 3% are transfers. 7% Asian-American, 3% Black, 5% Hispanic, 78% White, 7% Other. Average age of undergraduates is 20.
**Freshman profile:** 2% of freshmen who took SAT scored 700 or over on verbal, 21% scored 700 or over on math; 34% scored 600 or over on verbal, 75% scored 600 or over on math; 83% scored 500 or over on verbal, 98% scored 500 or over on math; 98% scored 400 or over on verbal, 100% scored 400 or over on math; 100% scored 300 or over on verbal. 97% of accepted applicants took SAT; 3% took ACT. 58% of freshmen come from public schools.
**Undergraduate achievement:** 93% of fall 1992 freshmen returned for fall 1993 term. 29% of students who completed a degree program immediately went on to graduate study.
**Foreign students:** 318 students are from out of the country. Countries represented include Greece, Indonesia, Japan, Korea, Spain, and the United Kingdom; 63 in all.
**PROGRAMS OF STUDY. Degrees:** A.B., B.S.
**Majors:** Accounting, Art History, Biochemistry, Biology, Chemistry, Classical Civilization, Classics, Communication, Computer Science, Early Childhood, Economics, Elementary Education, Elementary/Intense Special Needs, Elementary/Moderate Special Needs, English, Environmental Geosciences, Finance, General Management, Geology, Geophysics, Germanic Studies, Greek, History, Human Development, Human Resources Management, Information Systems, Latin, Linguistics, Management Economics/Operations Research, Marketing, Mathematics, Music, Nursing, Operations/Strategic Management, Philosophy, Physics, Political Science, Psychology, Romance Languages/French, Romance Languages/Italian, Romance Languages/Spanish, Russian, Secondary Education, Slavic Studies, Sociology, Studio Art, Theatre Arts, Theology.
**Distribution of degrees:** The majors with the highest enrollment are English, finance, and political science; linguistics and geophysics/seismology have the lowest.
**Requirements:** General education requirement.
**Academic regulations:** Minimum 1.67 GPA required for graduation.
**Special:** Minors offered in American, Asian, biblical, black, film, Germanic, international, Irish, Italian, medieval, Middle Eastern, modern Greek, and Russian/East European studies and in church history, cognitive science, computer science, faith/peace/justice, general education, secondary education, and women's studies. PULSE program combines study of philosophy or theology with community-based field work. Self-designed majors. Double majors. Dual degrees. Independent study. Accelerated study. Pass/fail grading option. Internships. Graduate school at which undergraduates may take graduate-level courses. Preprofessional programs in law, medicine, and dentistry. 3-2 B.A./M.Ed. education program. 3-2 B.S./M.S. nursing program. 3-2 B.A./M.S.W. program. 3-2 B.A./M.A. arts and sciences program. Combined engineering program with Boston U. Member of library and theological consortiums. Cross-registration with six area schools. Washington Semester. Exchange program with American U. Teacher certification in early childhood, elementary, secondary, and special education. Certification in specific subject areas. Exchange programs abroad in Belgium (Inst for European Affairs), Ireland (U Coll and Abbey Theatre), Japan (Sophia U), and Scotland (U of Glasgow). Study abroad also in Australia, Austria, China, England, France, Germany, Greece, Italy, Switzerland, and other countries. ROTC at Northeastern U. NROTC at Boston U (nursing students only). AFROTC at Boston U.
**Honors:** Phi Beta Kappa. Honors program. Honor societies.
**Academic Assistance:** Nonremedial tutoring.
**STUDENT LIFE. Housing:** Students may live on or off campus. Coed and women's dorms. 74% of students live in college housing.
**Social atmosphere:** According to the student newspaper, "Students are very social–many live off campus junior year, which helps to expand social circles." Students gather off campus at Mary Ann's, a bar in nearby Cleveland Circle, and The Rat, a social bar for those over 21, on Thursday nights. Although there are no groups on campus with special influence, athletics and athletes are prominent. Favorite events of the year include football and hockey games (especially the Beanpot) and the Middle March Ball, which is nationally ranked.
**Services and counseling/handicapped student services:** Placement services. Health service. Women's center. Day care. Counseling services for minority students. Personal and psychological counseling. Career and academic guidance services. Religious counseling. Physically disabled student services. Learning disabled services. Tape recorders. Tutors. Reader services for the blind.
**Campus organizations:** Undergraduate student government. Student newspaper (Heights, published once/week). Literary magazine. Yearbook. Radio and TV stations. Chorale, Musical Guild, orchestra, flute choir, debating, drama groups, dance ensemble, Model UN, Amnesty International, World Hunger Committee, academic, political, and special-interest groups, 150 organizations in all.
**Religious organizations:** Baptist Campus Ministries, Intervarsity Christian Fellowship, Liturgy Arts Group, Salt and Light Company, St. Thomas More Society.
**Minority/foreign student organizations:** Black Student Forum, NAACP. International Club, Armenian, Asian, Caribbean, Chinese, Filipino, Indian, Irish, Japanese, Korean, Latin American, Middle Eastern, Vietnamese, and other foreign student groups.
**ATHLETICS. Physical education requirements:** None.
**Intercollegiate competition:** 10% of students participate. Alpine skiing (M,W), baseball (M), basketball (M,W), cheerleading (M,W), cross-country (M,W), diving (M,W), fencing (M,W), field hockey (W), football (M), golf (M,W), ice hockey (M), lacrosse (M,W), sailing (M,W), soccer (M,W), softball (W), swimming (M,W), tennis (M,W), track (indoor) (M,W), track (outdoor) (M,W), track and field (indoor) (M,W), track and field (outdoor) (M,W), volleyball (W), water polo (M), wrestling (M). Member of Big East Conference, ECAC, Greater Boston League, Hockey East Conference, NCAA Division I, NCAA Division I-A for football.

**Intramural and club sports:** 50% of students participate. Intramural basketball, football, racquetball, softball, squash, tennis, volleyball. Men's club crew, rugby, ultimate frisbee, volleyball. Women's club crew, rugby.

**ADMISSIONS. Academic basis for candidate selection** (in order of priority): Secondary school record, standardized test scores, class rank, school's recommendation, essay.

**Nonacademic basis for candidate selection:** Character and personality and particular talent or ability are emphasized. Extracurricular participation, geographical distribution, and alumni/ae relationship are important.

**Requirements:** Graduation from secondary school is required; GED is accepted. 20 units and the following program of study are recommended: 4 units of English, 4 units of math, 3 units of science including 2 units of lab, 4 units of foreign language, 2 units of social studies, 1 unit of history, 2 units of academic electives. 2 units of lab science including chemistry required of nursing program applicants. 4 units of college-preparatory math strongly recommended of School of Management applicants. SAT or ACT is required. PSAT is recommended. ACH required. Campus visit and interview recommended. Off-campus interviews available with an alumni representative.

**Procedure:** Take SAT or ACT by January of 12th year. Take ACH by January of 12th year. Visit college for interview by December of 12th year. Application deadlines are January 10 for preliminary application, January 25 for secondary application. Notification of admission by April 15. Reply is required by May 1. $200 nonrefundable tuition deposit. $200 room deposit, refundable until July 15. Freshmen accepted for terms other than fall.

**Special programs:** Admission may be deferred two years. Placement may be granted through CEEB Advanced Placement exams for scores of 4 or higher. Early action program. In fall 1993, 2,158 applied for early action and 1,075 were accepted. Deadline for applying for early action is November 1. Early entrance/early admission program.

**Transfer students:** Transfer students accepted for terms other than fall. In fall 1993, 3% of all new students were transfers into all classes. 1,599 transfer applications were received, 535 were accepted. Application deadline is May 1 for fall; November 1 for spring. Minimum 2.5 GPA recommended. Lowest course grade accepted is "C-." Maximum number of transferable credits is 60 semester hours. At least 54 semester hours must be completed at the college to receive degree.

**Admissions contact:** John L. Mahoney, Jr., M.A.T., Director of Admissions. 617 552-3100.

**FINANCIAL AID. Available aid:** Pell grants, SEOG, Federal Nursing Student Scholarships, state scholarships and grants, school scholarships and grants, private scholarships and grants, ROTC scholarships, academic merit scholarships, and athletic scholarships. Perkins Loans (NDSL), PLUS, Stafford Loans (GSL), NSL, state loans, and SLS. Tuition Plan Inc., Education Plan Inc., and guaranteed tuition.

**Financial aid statistics:** 11% of aid is not need-based. In 1992-93, 86% of all undergraduate applicants received aid; 80% of freshman applicants. Average amounts of aid awarded freshmen: Scholarships and grants, $8,650; loans, $3,200.

**Supporting data/closing dates:** FAFSA/FAF/FFS: Priority filing date is February 1. School's own aid application: Priority filing date is February 1. Notification of awards begins April 1.

**Financial aid contact:** Mary McGranahan, Acting Director of Financial Aid. 617 552-3320.

**STUDENT EMPLOYMENT.** College Work/Study Program. Institutional employment. 17% of full-time undergraduates work on campus during school year. Students may expect to earn an average of $2,000 during school year. Off-campus part-time employment opportunities rated "good."

**COMPUTER FACILITIES.** 200 IBM/IBM-compatible and Macintosh/Apple microcomputers; all are networked. Students may access Digital, IBM minicomputer/mainframe systems, BITNET, Internet. Client/LAN operating systems include Apple/Macintosh, DOS, UNIX/XENIX/AIX, DEC, LocalTalk/AppleTalk. Computer languages and software packages include Assembler, BASIC, COBOL, Excel, FORTRAN, LISP, Lotus 1-2-3, MacWrite, Microsoft Word, Pascal, SuperPaint; 50 in all. Computer facilities are available to all students.

**Fees:** Computer fee is included in tuition/fees.

**Hours:** 113 hours/week (main computer center).

**GRADUATE CAREER DATA.** Graduate school percentages: 8% enter law school. 2% enter medical school. 2% enter dental school. 4% enter graduate business programs. 11% enter graduate arts and sciences programs. Highest graduate school enrollments: Boston Coll, Boston U, Columbia U, Georgetown U, Tufts U. 62% of graduates choose careers in business and industry. Companies and businesses that hire graduates: Arthur Andersen, Ernst & Young, General Electric, Procter & Gamble.

**PROMINENT ALUMNI/AE.** John F. Kerry, U.S. senator, Massachusetts; Warren Rudman, former U.S. senator, New Hampshire; Thomas P. O'Neill, Jr., former speaker, U.S. House of Representatives; Peter S. Lynch, former managing director, Fidelity Management; Roberta Hazard, rear admiral, U.S. Navy; Sr. Catherine McNamee, president, National Catholic Education Association; John Guiggio, former president, *Boston Globe*.

# The Boston Conservatory

**Boston, MA 02215** — **617 536-6340**

**1993-94 Costs.** Tuition: $11,400. Room & board: $5,925. Fees, books, misc. academic expenses (school's estimate): $225.

**Enrollment.** Undergraduates: 311 (full-time). Freshman class: 283 applicants, 164 accepted, 93 enrolled. Graduate enrollment: 115.

**Test score averages/ranges.** Average SAT scores: 472 verbal, 454 math.

**Faculty.** 40 full-time; 55 part-time. 5% of faculty holds doctoral degree. Student/faculty ratio: 5 to 1.

**Selectivity rating.** Less competitive.

**PROFILE.** The Boston Conservatory, founded in 1867, is a private institution. Its facilities are located in Boston's Fenway section, not far from Symphony Hall, home of the Boston Symphony Orchestra.

**Accreditation:** NEASC. Professionally accredited by the National Association of Schools of Music.

**Religious orientation:** The Boston Conservatory is nonsectarian; no religious requirements.

**Library:** Collections totaling over 40,000 volumes, and 1,500 periodical subscriptions.

**STUDENT BODY. Undergraduate profile:** 15% are state residents; 33% are transfers. Average age of undergraduates is 20.

**Freshman profile:** Majority of accepted applicants took SAT.

**Undergraduate achievement:** 85% of fall 1992 freshmen returned for fall 1993 term. 55% of entering class graduated.

**Foreign students:** Countries represented include Australia, Hong Kong, Japan, Korea, New Zealand, and Taiwan; 29 in all.

**PROGRAMS OF STUDY. Degrees:** B.F.A., B.Mus.

**Majors:** Dance, Music Composition, Music Education, Music Performance, Musical Theatre, Opera.

**Distribution of degrees:** The majors with the highest enrollment are music, musical theatre, and dance.

**Special:** Double majors. Graduate school at which undergraduates may take graduate-level courses. Teacher certification in music education. Member of Pro Arts Consortium. Certification in specific subject areas.

**Honors:** Honor societies.

**ADMISSIONS. Academic basis for candidate selection** (in order of priority): Secondary school record, standardized test scores, essay, school's recommendation.

**Nonacademic basis for candidate selection:** Extracurricular participation and particular talent or ability are emphasized. Character and personality and alumni/ae relationship are considered.

**Requirements:** Graduation from secondary school is required; GED is accepted. 16 units and the following program of study are recommended: 4 units of English, 2 units of math, 2 units of science, 3 units of foreign language, 4 units of social studies, 4 units of electives. Minimum combined SAT score of 950 (composite ACT score of 23) and minimum 2.7 GPA required. Audition required of all applicants. SAT or ACT is recommended. Campus visit recommended. Off-campus interviews available with an admissions representative.

**Procedure:** Suggest filing application by March 1. Application deadline is June 1. Notification of admission on rolling basis. Reply is required by May 1. $500 nonrefundable tuition deposit. $250 nonrefundable room deposit. Freshmen accepted for fall term only.

**Special programs:** Admission may be deferred one year. Credit and/or placement may be granted through CEEB Advanced Placement exams for scores of 3 or higher. Credit and/or placement may be granted through CLEP general and subject exams. Credit and placement may be granted through life experience. Early decision program. Deadline for applying for early decision is November 1. Early entrance/early admission program.

**Transfer students:** Transfer students accepted for terms other than fall. In fall 1993, 33% of all new students were transfers into all classes. 129 transfer applications were received, 72 were accepted. Application deadline is June 1 for fall; November 1 for spring. Audition required of all transfers. Minimum 2.0 GPA required. Lowest course grade accepted is "C." Maximum number of transferable credits is 75 semester hours. At least 50 semester hours must be completed at the conservatory to receive degree.

**Admissions contact:** Allison Ball, M.M., Director of Enrollment Management. 617 536-6340, extension 15.

**FINANCIAL AID. Available aid:** Pell grants, SEOG, and school scholarships. Perkins Loans (NDSL), PLUS, Stafford Loans (GSL), and SLS. Tuition Plan Inc.

**Supporting data/closing dates:** FAFSA/FAF: Deadline is March 1. School's own aid application: Deadline is March 1. Notification of awards begins April 1.

**Financial aid contact:** James Bynum, Director of Financial Aid. 617 536-6340, ext. 20.

# Boston University

**Boston, MA 02215** — **617 353-2000**

**1993-94 Costs.** Tuition: $18,420. Room & board: $6,810. Fees, books, misc. academic expenses (school's estimate): $745.

**Enrollment.** Undergraduates: 6,392 men, 7,537 women (full-time). Freshman class: 20,192 applicants, 13,007 accepted, 3,810 enrolled. Graduate enrollment: 5,203 men, 5,343 women.

**Test score averages/ranges.** Average SAT scores: 548 verbal, 599 math. Range of SAT scores of middle 50%: 500-600 verbal, 550-650 math. Average ACT scores: 26 composite. Range of ACT scores of middle 50%: 24-29 composite.

**Faculty.** 1,018 full-time; 566 part-time. 82% of faculty holds highest degree in specific field. Student/faculty ratio: 14 to 1.

**Selectivity rating.** Highly competitive.

**PROFILE.** Boston University, founded in 1839, is a private institution. Programs are offered through the Colleges of Basic Studies, Communication, Engineering, and Liberal Arts; the Schools of the Arts, Education, Law, Management, Medicine, Public Health, Social Work, and Theology; the Metropolitan College; the Sargent College of Allied Health Professions; the Goldman School of Graduate Dentistry; and the Graduate School. Its 110-acre campus is located on the Charles River in downtown Boston.

**Accreditation:** NEASC. Professionally accredited by the Accreditation Board for Engineering and Technology, the American Assembly of Collegiate Schools of Business, the American Medical Association (CAHEA), the American Physical Therapy Association, the American Psychological Association, the National Association of Schools of Music, the National Council for Accreditation of Teacher Education.

**Religious orientation:** Boston University is nonsectarian; no religious requirements.

**Library:** Collections totaling over 1,896,000 volumes, 28,512 periodical subscriptions, and 3,208,000 microform items.

**Special facilities/museums:** Art galleries, professional theatre, preschool, planetarium, hotel and culinary center, science and engineering complex, institute for accounting research, center for adaptive systems, African studies center, athletic center, national center for America's founding documents, center for archeological studies, arthritis center,

Asian management center, center for banking law studies, biomedical engineering research center, cancer research center, cardiovascular institute, institute for the study of conflict, ideology, and policy, center for defense journalism, center for English language and orientation programs, center for the advancement of ethics and character, national research center on families, communities, schools and children's learning, health policy institute, James Joyce research center, center for remote sensing.
**Athletic facilities:** Gymnasiums, ice rink, dance studios, fitness and weight rooms, swimming pool, saunas, tracks, basketball and tennis courts, athletic fields, boathouse.

**STUDENT BODY. Undergraduate profile:** 27% are state residents; 13% are transfers. 14.7% Asian-American, 4.1% Black, 6% Hispanic, .3% Native American, 72% White, 2.9% Other. Average age of undergraduates is 21.
**Freshman profile:** 3% of freshmen who took SAT scored 700 or over on verbal, 13% scored 700 or over on math; 28% scored 600 or over on verbal, 52% scored 600 or over on math; 74% scored 500 or over on verbal, 90% scored 500 or over on math; 98% scored 400 or over on verbal, 99% scored 400 or over on math; 100% scored 300 or over on verbal, 100% scored 300 or over on math. 97% of accepted applicants took SAT; 18% took ACT. 68% of freshmen come from public schools.
**Undergraduate achievement:** 82% of fall 1992 freshmen returned for fall 1993 term. 71% of entering class graduated.
**Foreign students:** 1,752 students are from out of the country. Countries represented include Brazil, Greece, Hong Kong, Japan, Pakistan, and Spain; 129 in all.

**PROGRAMS OF STUDY. Degrees:** B.A., B.F.A., B.Lib.Studies, B.Mus., B.S.
**Majors:** Accounting, Acting, Advertising, Aerospace, African Studies, American History/Civilization, American Studies, Anthropology, Applied Science, Archaeological Studies, Art Education, Art History, Astronomy, Astronomy/Physics, Athletic Training, Bilingual Education, Biochemistry/Molecular Biology, Biology, Biomedical Engineering, Biomedical Laboratory/Clinical Sciences, Broadcast Journalism, Broadcasting/Film, Business Administration, Chemistry, Chemistry Teaching, Childhood Education, Classical Civilization, Classical Languages/Literature, Classics/Religion, Clinical Exercise Physiology, Collaborative Piano, Communication Disorders, Communications, Computer Engineering, Computer Science, Costume Design, Deaf Education, Deaf Studies, Dental Technology, Directing, Drawing, Early Childhood Education, East Asian Studies, Economics, Economics/Mathematics, Electrical Engineering, Engineering Management, English, English Education, Environmental Analysis/Policy, Environmental Geology, Environmental Science, European Literature/French, European Literature/German, European Literature/Italian, European Literature/Russian, European Literature/Spanish, Finance, French/Continental European Literatures, French Language/Literature, General Engineering, Geography, Geology, German/Continental Literatures, German Language/Literature, German Studies, Graphic Design, Greek Language/Literature/Ancient, Health/Fitness Education, Health Studies, Hispanic/Continental Literatures, Hispanic Language/Literature, History, History/Literature of Music, History/Social Sciences, Hotel/Food Service Administration, Human Movement Education, Human Physiology, Independent Concentration, Interdisciplinary Italian Studies, Interdisciplinary Studies, Interdisciplinary Study, International Management, International Relations, Italian, Italian/Continental Literatures, Journalism, Latin American Studies, Latin Language/Literature, Leisure Education, Liberal Studies, Lighting Design, Linguistics, Luso-Brazilian Language/Literature, Management Information Systems, Management Studies, Manufacturing Engineering, Marine Science, Marketing, Mass Communication/Public Relations, Mathematical Astronomy, Mathematics, Mathematics/Computer Science, Mathematics Education, Mathematics/Mathematics Education, Mathematics/Philosophy, Mechanical Engineering, Medical Bacteriology, Modern Foreign Language Education, Modern Greek Studies, Music, Music Composition, Music Education, Music Performance, Music Theory, Occupational Therapy, Operations Management, Organizational Behavior, Painting, Paralegal Studies, Philosophy, Philosophy/Anthropology, Philosophy/Physics, Philosophy/Political Science, Philosophy/Psychology, Philosophy/Religion, Photojournalism, Physical Therapy, Physics, Planetary/Space Sciences, Political Science, Pre-Dentistry, Pre-Law, Pre-Medicine, Psychology, Rehabilitation/Human Services, Religion, Russian/East European Studies, Russian Language/Literature, Scene Design, Science Education, Sculpture, Social Studies Education, Social Work, Sociology, Special Education, Stage Management, Systems Engineering, Technical Production, Theatre Education, Theatre Production, Theatre Studies, Urban Affairs, Urban Studies/Public Policy, Visual Studies.
**Distribution of degrees:** The majors with the highest enrollment are management, communications, and psychology; East Asian studies, linguistics, and foreign language education have the lowest.
**Requirements:** General education requirement.
**Special:** Hundreds of minors offered. Self-designed majors. Double majors. Dual degrees. Independent study. Accelerated study. Pass/fail grading option. Internships. Cooperative education programs. Graduate school at which undergraduates may take graduate-level courses. Preprofessional programs in law, medicine, and dentistry. Seven-year medical program with Boston U Sch of Medicine. Seven-year liberal arts/dental education program with Boston U Sch of Graduate Dentistry. Accelerated BS/MS in engineering. 5 year BS/MS program in physical therapy. BA/MA programs in American studies, anthropology, astronomy/physics, biology, biotechnology, chemistry, classical studies, computer science, economics, English, french language/literature, geography, geology, hispanic language/literature, history, math/statistic, philosphy, physics, political science, religion, and sociology. Cross-registration with Boston Coll, Brandeis U, Hebrew Coll, and Tufts U. Washington Semester and Sea Semester. Teacher certification in early childhood, elementary, secondary, special education, and bilingual/bicultural education. Certification in specific subject areas. Member of International Student Exchange Program (ISEP). Study abroad in Australia, China, the Czech Republic, England, France, Greece, Hungary, Israel, Italy, Niger, Poland, Spain, and Russia. ROTC, NROTC, and AFROTC.
**Honors:** Phi Beta Kappa. Honors program. Honor societies.
**Academic Assistance:** Nonremedial tutoring.

**STUDENT LIFE. Housing:** All freshmen must live on campus. Coed, women's, and men's dorms. School-owned/operated apartments. 55% of students live in college housing.
**Services and counseling/handicapped student services:** Placement services. Health service. Day care. Counseling services for minority and military students. Birth control, personal, and psychological counseling. Career and academic guidance services. Religious counseling. Physically disabled student services. Learning disabled services. Notetaking services. Tape recorders. Tutors. Reader services for the blind.
**Campus organizations:** Undergraduate student government. Student newspaper (Daily Free Press). Literary magazine. Yearbook. Radio and TV stations. Marching, concert, and jazz bands, gospel, choral and opera groups, orchestra, musical drama and dance groups, drama and film clubs, political and social service groups, over 300 organizations in all. Seven fraternities, no chapter houses; nine sororities, no chapter houses. 5% of men join a fraternity. 8% of women join a sorority.
**Religious organizations:** Bahai Club, Beth Sarskakin Messianic Group, Christian Science Organization, Divine Light Club, Hillel Association, Islamic Society, Navigators, New Covenant Fellowship, Newman House, Seekers Christian Fellowship, The League, Campus Crusade for Christ, Chabad Jewish Student Organization, Latter-Day Saint Student Association.
**Minority/foreign student organizations:** Black Drama Collective, Hispanic-American Law Association, Los Amigos, Minorities in Communication, Minority Engineers Society, Latinos Unidos, UMOJA, Black Theatre Organization. International Student Club, African, Arab, Asian, Armenian, Caribbean, Chinese, European, Filipino, French, German, Hellenic, Hong Kong, Indian, Indonesian, Japanese, Korean, Latin American, Persian, Puerto Rican, Russian, Scandinavian, Singaporean, Thai, Turkish, and Vietnamese groups.

**ATHLETICS. Physical education requirements:** None.
**Intercollegiate competition:** 10% of students participate. Baseball (M), basketball (M,W), crew (M,W), cross-country (M,W), diving (M,W), field hockey (W), football (M), golf (M), ice hockey (M), soccer (M), softball (W), swimming (M,W), tennis (M,W), track (indoor) (M,W), track (outdoor) (M,W), track and field (indoor) (M,W), track and field (outdoor) (M,W), wrestling (M). Member of ECAC, Hockey East, NCAA Division I, NCAA Division I-AA for football, North Atlantic Conference, Yankee Conference.
**Intramural and club sports:** 30% of students participate. Intramural basketball, flag football, floor hockey, ice broomball, ice hockey, indoor soccer, inner-tube water polo, soccer, softball, tennis, volleyball. Men's club Alpine skiing, cheerleading, fencing, gymnastics, horsemanship, lacrosse, martial arts, rugby, sailing, softball, ultimate frisbee, volleyball. Women's club Alpine skiing, cheerleading, fencing, gymnastics, horsemanship, ice hockey, lacrosse, martial arts, sailing, soccer, ultimate frisbee, volleyball.

**ADMISSIONS. Academic basis for candidate selection** (in order of priority): Secondary school record, class rank, school's recommendation, standardized test scores, essay.
**Nonacademic basis for candidate selection:** Particular talent or ability is important. Character and personality, extracurricular participation, and alumni/ae relationship are considered.
**Requirements:** Graduation from secondary school is required; GED is accepted. 18 units and the following program of study are required: 4 units of English, 4 units of math, 4 units of science including 3 units of lab, 2 units of foreign language, 4 units of social studies. SAT or ACT is required. ACH required. ACH in chemistry, English, and math required of applicants to accelerated medical and dental programs; ACH in a foreign language recommended. ACH in English and math required of applicants to University Professors Program; ACH in a foreign language recommended. ACH in English with essay recommended of applicants to College of Communications. Audition required of music and theatre performance program applicants. Portfolio required of visual arts program applicants. Interviews required of finalists for the Accelerated Medical and Dental Programs and all applicants for the Sch for the Arts, Theatre Division (stage management, design, and technical program). Campus visit recommended. Off-campus interviews available with admissions and alumni representatives.
**Procedure:** Take SAT or ACT by December of 12th year. Take ACH by December of 12th year. Visit college for interview by February of 12th year. Suggest filing application by January 15; no deadline. Notification of admission is sent beginning mid-March through April 15 for those applicants who met the January 15 priority filing date. Reply is required by May 1. $200 nonrefundable tuition deposit. $200 nonrefundable room deposit. Freshmen accepted for terms other than fall.
**Special programs:** Admission may be deferred one year. Credit and/or placement may be granted through CEEB Advanced Placement exams for scores of 3 or higher. Placement may be granted through CLEP general exams. Credit and/or placement may be granted through CLEP subject exams. Early decision program. In fall 1993, 376 applied for early decision and 230 were accepted. Deadline for applying for early decision is November 15. Early entrance/early admission program.
**Transfer students:** Transfer students accepted for terms other than fall. In fall 1993, 13% of all new students were transfers into all classes. 2,328 transfer applications were received, 1,492 were accepted. Application deadline is May 1 for fall; November 15 for spring. SAT/ACT scores recommended of all transfer applicants. Minimum 2.7 GPA recommended. Lowest course grade accepted is "C-." Maximum number of transferable credits is 80 semester hours.
**Admissions contact:** Thomas Rajala, M.Ed., Director of Admissions. 617 353-2300.

**FINANCIAL AID. Available aid:** Pell grants, SEOG, state scholarships and grants, school scholarships and grants, private scholarships and grants, ROTC scholarships, academic merit scholarships, and athletic scholarships. Music, theatre, and visual arts scholarships. Perkins Loans (NDSL), PLUS, Stafford Loans (GSL), state loans, private loans, and SLS. Mass Plan. AMS. Pre-paid Tuition Plan.
**Financial aid statistics:** 20% of aid is not need-based. In 1993-94, 96% of all undergraduate applicants received aid; 96% of freshman applicants. Average amounts of aid awarded freshmen: Scholarships and grants, $12,469; loans, $3,400.
**Supporting data/closing dates:** FAFSA/FAF: Priority filing date is March 1. State aid form: Priority filing date is March 1. Income tax forms: Priority filing date is April 22. Notification of awards begins mid-March.
**Financial aid contact:** Barbara Tornow, M.A., Director of Financial Aid. 617 353-2965.

**STUDENT EMPLOYMENT.** College Work/Study Program. Institutional employment. 25% of full-time undergraduates work on campus during school year. Students may expect to earn an average of $1,500 during school year. Off-campus part-time employment opportunities rated "excellent."

**COMPUTER FACILITIES.** 300 IBM/IBM-compatible and Macintosh/Apple microcomputers; 2,000 are networked. Students may access Digital, IBM, SUN minicomputer/mainframe systems, BITNET, Internet, NearNet. Residence halls may be equipped with

stand-alone microcomputers, networked microcomputers, networked terminals, modems. Client/LAN operating systems include Apple/Macintosh, DOS, UNIX/XENIX/AIX, Windows NT, X-windows, LocalTalk/AppleTalk, Novell. Computer languages and software packages include Ada, Aldus PageMaker, Aldus Persuasion, BMDP, C, C+, COBOL, Emacs, ESSL, Excel, FORTRAN, FrameMaker, IMSL, Interleaf, Island Draw, Island Paint, Island Write, LaTex, Lisp, Lotus 1-2-3, Mathematica, MINITAB, NAG, Pascal, SAS, SPSS, TSP, Tex, Wingz, Word ; 40 in all. Computer facilities are available to all students.
**Fees:** None.
**Hours:** 24 hours.
**PROMINENT ALUMNI/AE.** Martin Luther King, Jr., civil rights leader; Geena Davis and Alfre Woodard, actresses; Nicolas Gage, author; Nina Totenberg, correspondent, National Public Radio; Barbara Jordan, former U.S. congresswoman.

# Bradford College

**Bradford, MA 01835 — 508 372-7161**

**1994-95 Costs.** Tuition: $14,080. Room & board: $6,270. Fees, books, misc. academic expenses (school's estimate): $500.
**Enrollment.** Undergraduates: 200 men, 319 women (full-time). Freshman class: 926 applicants, 715 accepted, 186 enrolled.
**Test score averages/ranges.** N/A.
**Faculty.** 36 full-time; 26 part-time. 85% of faculty holds doctoral degree. Student/faculty ratio: 12 to 1.
**Selectivity rating.** N/A.

**PROFILE.** Bradford, founded in 1803, is a private, liberal arts college. Its 70-acre campus is located in Bradford, 35 miles north of Boston.

**Accreditation:** NEASC.
**Religious orientation:** Bradford College is nonsectarian; no religious requirements.
**Library:** Collections totaling over 60,000 volumes, 251 periodical subscriptions, and 22,976 microform items.
**Athletic facilities:** Gymnasium, lacrosse, soccer, and softball fields, weight room, swimming pool, basketball, volleyball courts.
**STUDENT BODY. Undergraduate profile:** 45% are state residents; 29% are transfers. 7% Asian-American, 7% Black, 6% Hispanic, 78% White, 2% Other. Average age of undergraduates is 20.
**Freshman profile:** 85% of freshmen come from public schools.
**Undergraduate achievement:** 75% of fall 1992 freshmen returned for fall 1993 term. 43% of entering class graduated. 30% of students who completed a degree program went on to graduate study within five years.
**Foreign students:** 50 students are from out of the country. Countries represented include Japan and Korea; 30 in all.
**PROGRAMS OF STUDY. Degrees:** B.A.
**Majors:** Creative Arts, Human Studies, Humanities, Individual Studies, Management, Natural Science/Mathematics.
**Distribution of degrees:** The majors with the highest enrollment are humanities, creative arts, and human studies; natural science/mathematics have the lowest.
**Requirements:** General education requirement.
**Academic regulations:** Freshmen must maintain minimum 1.5 GPA; sophomores, 1.7 GPA; juniors, 1.9 GPA; seniors, 2.0 GPA.
**Special:** Minors offered. Self-designed majors. Double majors. Independent study. Pass/fail grading option. Internships. Preprofessional programs in law, medicine, veterinary science, pharmacy, dentistry, and optometry. Member of Northeast Consortium of Colleges and Universities in Massachusetts; exchange possible. Member of Massachusetts Bay Consortium and Council on International Education Exchange. Washington Semester and Sea Semester. National Theatre Institute Semester (Connecticut). Teacher certification in elementary education. Study abroad in Australia, China, England, France, Japan, Mexico, the Netherlands, and other countries.
**Honors:** Honors program.
**Academic Assistance:** Remedial reading, writing, math, and study skills. Nonremedial tutoring.
**ADMISSIONS. Academic basis for candidate selection** (in order of priority): Secondary school record, class rank, school's recommendation, essay, standardized test scores.
**Nonacademic basis for candidate selection:** Character and personality, extracurricular participation, and particular talent or ability are important. Geographical distribution and alumni/ae relationship are considered.
**Requirements:** Graduation from secondary school is required; GED is accepted. 18 units and the following program of study are required: 4 units of English, 3 units of math, 2 units of lab science, 2 units of foreign language, 2 units of social studies, 2 units of history. Minimum 2.0 GPA required. Portfolio required of art program applicants. SAT or ACT is recommended. Campus visit and interview recommended. Off-campus interviews available with an admissions representative.
**Procedure:** Take SAT or ACT by December of 12th year. Visit college for interview by May of 12th year. Notification of admission on rolling basis. Reply is required by May 1. $100 tuition deposit, refundable until May 1. $150 room deposit, refundable until May 1. Freshmen accepted for terms other than fall.
**Special programs:** Admission may be deferred one year. Credit and/or placement may be granted through CEEB Advanced Placement exams for scores of 3 or higher. Credit and/or placement may be granted through CLEP general and subject exams.
**Transfer students:** Transfer students accepted for terms other than fall. In fall 1993, 29% of all new students were transfers into all classes. 131 transfer applications were received, 87 were accepted. Application deadline is rolling for fall; rolling for spring. Minimum 2.0 GPA required. Lowest course grade accepted is "C." Maximum number of transferable credits is 66 semester hours from a two-year school and 75 semester hours from a four-year school. At least 46 semester hours must be completed at the college to receive degree.
**Admissions contact:** William R. Dunfey, M.Ed., M.A., Dean of Admissions. 508 372-7161, extension 271.
**FINANCIAL AID. Available aid:** Pell grants, SEOG, state scholarships and grants, school scholarships and grants, private scholarships and grants, and academic merit scholarships. Perkins Loans (NDSL), PLUS, Stafford Loans (GSL), state loans, and SLS. Knight Tuition Plans and AMS.
**Financial aid statistics:** 30% of aid is not need-based. In 1993-94, 76% of all undergraduate applicants received aid; 76% of freshman applicants. Average amounts of aid awarded freshmen: Loans, $2,625.
**Supporting data/closing dates:** FAFSA/FAF/FFS: Priority filing date is February 15. School's own aid application: Priority filing date is February 15. Income tax forms: Deadline is April 15. Notification of awards begins March 1.
**Financial aid contact:** Edwinia Middleton, Director of Financial Aid. 508 372-7161.

# Brandeis University

**Waltham, MA 02254-9110 — 617 736-2000**

**1994-95 Costs.** Tuition: $19,380. Room: $3,500. Board: $3,250. Fees, books, misc. academic expenses (school's estimate): $860.
**Enrollment.** Undergraduates: 1,312 men, 1,507 women (full-time). Freshman class: 4,186 applicants, 2,776 accepted, 740 enrolled. Graduate enrollment: 506 men, 551 women.
**Test score averages/ranges.** Range of SAT scores of middle 50%: 530-640 verbal, 570-690 math.
**Faculty.** 341 full-time; 126 part-time. 90% of faculty holds highest degree in specific field. Student/faculty ratio: 8 to 1.
**Selectivity rating.** Most competitive.

**PROFILE.** Brandeis, founded in 1948, is a private, liberal arts university. Programs are offered through the Schools of Creative Arts, Humanities, Science, and Social Science; the Graduate School of Arts and Sciences; Rosenstiel Basic Medical Sciences Research Center; and Florence Heller Graduate School for Advanced Studies in Social Welfare. Its 235-acre campus is located in Waltham, 10 miles west of Boston.

**Accreditation:** NEASC.
**Religious orientation:** Brandeis University is nonsectarian; no religious requirements.
**Library:** Collections totaling over 939,000 volumes, 7,104 periodical subscriptions, and 826,737 microform items.
**Special facilities/museums:** Art museum, multicultural library, intercultural center, theatre arts complex, language lab, American Jewish Historical Society headquarters, spatial orientation lab, basic medical sciences research center.
**Athletic facilities:** Sports center, gymnasium, swimming pool, basketball, squash and tennis courts, exercise, fencing, Nautilus, sauna, steam, training, and weight rooms, track, baseball, intramural, practice, soccer, and softball fields, cross-country/fitness course.
**STUDENT BODY. Undergraduate profile:** 25% are state residents; 12% are transfers. 9% Asian-American, 4% Black, 3% Hispanic, 84% White. Average age of undergraduates is 20.
**Freshman profile:** Majority of accepted applicants took SAT. 72% of freshmen come from public schools.
**Undergraduate achievement:** 89% of fall 1992 freshmen returned for fall 1993 term. 78% of entering class graduated. 40% of students who completed a degree program immediately went on to graduate study.
**Foreign students:** 133 students are from out of the country. Countries represented include Austria, Canada, China, Germany, Israel, and Japan; 57 in all.
**PROGRAMS OF STUDY. Degrees:** B.A.
**Majors:** African/Afro-American Studies, American Studies, Anthropology, Biochemistry, Biology, Chemistry, Classical Studies, Comparative Literature, Computer Science, Economics, English/American Literature, European Cultural Studies, Fine Arts, French Language/Literature, General Science, German Language/Literature, History, History of Ideas, Latin American Studies, Linguistics/Cognitive Science, Mathematics, Music, Near Eastern/Judaic Studies, Neuroscience, Philosophy, Physics, Politics, Psychology, Russian Language/Literature, Sociology, Spanish Language/Literature, Theatre Arts.
**Distribution of degrees:** The majors with the highest enrollment are psychology, politics, and English.
**Requirements:** General education requirement.
**Special:** Minors offered in many majors and in art history and managerial/business economics. Interdisciplinary programs in East Asian, education, international, Islamic/Middle Eastern, Italian, journalism, Latin American, legal, medieval, peace, Russian/East European, and women's studies. Mt. Sinai Humanities and Medicine Program grants admission to Mt. Sinai Medical School at end of freshman year. Self-designed majors. Double majors. Dual degrees. Independent study. Pass/fail grading option. Internships. Graduate school at which undergraduates may take graduate-level courses. Preprofessional programs in law, medicine, veterinary science, and dentistry. Four-year combined B.A./M.A. programs in biochemistry, biology, chemistry, history, mathematics, and physics. Five-year combined B.A./M.A. programs in computer science, international economics and finance, Near Eastern and Judaic studies, and theatre arts. Cross-registration with Babson Coll, Bentley Coll, Boston Coll, Boston U, Tufts U, and Wellesley Coll; seminars at Boston Museum of Fine Arts and through Massachusetts Bay Marine Studies Consortium. Teacher certification in early childhood, elementary, and secondary education. Study abroad in over 30 countries. ROTC and AFROTC at Boston U.
**Honors:** Phi Beta Kappa.
**Academic Assistance:** Remedial reading, writing, math, and study skills. Nonremedial tutoring.
**STUDENT LIFE. Housing:** Students may live on or off campus. Coed dorms. Off-campus privately-owned housing. 91% of students live in college housing.
**Social atmosphere:** The student newspaper reports, "Brandeis has an amazing cultural life with theatre, music, and bands, but the parties are small, few, and far between." There are no fraternities at Brandeis; social events are organized by Student Events (SE). SE is

the most influential group on campus. Bronstein Weekend and Homecoming are the most popular social events. Students gather at the library, Chumley's, and the Stein.
**Services and counseling/handicapped student services:** Placement services. Health service. Day care. Counseling services for minority and older students. Birth control, personal, and psychological counseling. Career and academic guidance services. Religious counseling. Physically disabled student services. Learning disabled services. Tutors.
**Campus organizations:** Undergraduate student government. Student newspaper (Justice, published once/week). Literary magazine. Yearbook. Radio and TV stations. Chorus, gospel choir, orchestra, bands, debating, drama group, comedy troupe, Israeli dance troupe, modern dance, Gilbert and Sullivan Society, Gay Alliance, Amnesty International, Women's Coalition, outdoor and mountain club, photography club, Model UN, departmental and special-interest groups, 130 organizations in all.
**Religious organizations:** Catholic Student Organization, Christian Fellowship, Hillel, Interfaith Group, King's Fellowship.
**Minority/foreign student organizations:** African-American, Asian-American, Hispanic, and Korean groups. Friendship International.

**ATHLETICS. Physical education requirements:** Two semesters of physical education required.
**Intercollegiate competition:** 10% of students participate. Baseball (M), basketball (M,W), cross-country (M,W), diving (M,W), fencing (M,W), golf (M), sailing (M,W), soccer (M,W), softball (W), swimming (M,W), tennis (M,W), track (indoor) (M,W), track (outdoor) (M,W), track and field (M,W), volleyball (W). Member of Eastern College Athletic Conference, Greater Boston League, MAIAW, NCAA Division III, New England Women's Eight, University Athletic Association.
**Intramural and club sports:** 25% of students participate. Intramural basketball, cross-country, floor hockey, golf, softball, squash, tennis, touch football, volleyball. Men's club crew, curling, equestrian sports, golf, ice hockey, judo, rugby, soccer, tae kwon do, volleyball, water polo, weight lifting, wrestling. Women's club crew, curling, equestrian sports, golf, ice hockey, judo, rugby, soccer, tae kwon do, volleyball, water polo, weight lifting, wrestling.

**ADMISSIONS. Academic basis for candidate selection** (in order of priority): Secondary school record, class rank, school's recommendation, standardized test scores, essay.
**Nonacademic basis for candidate selection:** Character and personality, extracurricular participation, and particular talent or ability are emphasized. Alumni/ae relationship is considered.
**Requirements:** Graduation from secondary school is recommended; GED is accepted. No specific distribution of secondary school units required. SAT or ACT is required. ACH required. Campus visit and interview recommended. Off-campus interviews available with an alumni representative.
**Procedure:** Take SAT or ACT by January of 12th year. Take ACH by January of 12th year. Visit college for interview by February of 12th year. Application deadlines are January 1 for Part I and February 1 for Part II. Notification of admission by April 15. Reply is required by May 1. $300 nonrefundable tuition deposit. $200 room deposit, refundable until July 1. Freshmen accepted for terms other than fall.
**Special programs:** Admission may be deferred one year. Credit and/or placement may be granted through CEEB Advanced Placement exams. Placement may be granted through challenge exams. Early decision program. In fall 1993, 167 applied for early decision and 112 were accepted. Deadline for applying for early decision is January 1. Early entrance/early admission program.
**Transfer students:** Transfer students accepted for terms other than fall. In fall 1993, 12% of all new students were transfers into all classes. 270 transfer applications were received, 174 were accepted. Application deadline is April 1 for fall; December 1 for spring. Minimum 3.0 GPA recommended. Lowest course grade accepted is "C-." At least 16 courses must be completed at the university to receive degree.
**Admissions contact:** Michael N. Kalafatas, M.A.T., Director of Admissions. 617 736-3500, 800 622-0622 (out-of-state).

**FINANCIAL AID. Available aid:** Pell grants, SEOG, state scholarships and grants, school scholarships and grants, and academic merit scholarships. Perkins Loans (NDSL), PLUS, Stafford Loans (GSL), school loans, and SLS. Knight Tuition Plans.
**Financial aid statistics:** 7% of aid is not need-based. In 1993-94, 100% of all undergraduate applicants received aid. Average amounts of aid awarded freshmen: Scholarships and grants, $13,600; loans, $3,500.
**Supporting data/closing dates:** FAFSA/FAF: Priority filing date is February 15. School's own aid application: Priority filing date is February 15; deadline is February 15. Income tax forms: Deadline is February 15. Notification of awards begins April 1.
**Financial aid contact:** Lynda Watson, M.B.A., Director of Financial Aid. 617 736-3700.

**STUDENT EMPLOYMENT.** College Work/Study Program. Institutional employment. 45% of full-time undergraduates work on campus during school year. Students may expect to earn an average of $1,150 during school year. Off-campus part-time employment opportunities rated "good."

**COMPUTER FACILITIES.** 77 IBM/IBM-compatible and Macintosh/Apple microcomputers; 62 are networked. Students may access Digital minicomputer/mainframe systems, BITNET, Internet. Client/LAN operating systems include Apple/Macintosh, DOS, LocalTalk/AppleTalk. Computer languages and software packages include Ada, BASIC, C, FORTRAN, Hypercard, LISP, Lotus 1-2-3, Microsoft Word, Pascal, Prolog, SCHEME, SAS, SPSS, WordPerfect. Computer facilities are available to all students.
**Fees:** None.
**Hours:** Most microcomputers available 15 hours/day; some available 24 hours.

**GRADUATE CAREER DATA.** Graduate school percentages: 15% enter law school. 8% enter medical school. 3% enter graduate business programs. 10% enter graduate arts and sciences programs. Highest graduate school enrollments: Albert Einstein Coll of Medicine, Columbia U, Harvard U, MIT, New York U, Tufts U, U of Chicago, U of Pennsylvania. Companies and businesses that hire graduates: BBDO Worldwide, Coopers & Lybrand, Digital Equipment Corp., Fidelity Investments, Grey Advertising, Macy's, Merrill Lynch, Teach for America.

**PROMINENT ALUMNI/AE.** Marshall Herscovitz, television producer, co-creator of *thirtysomething;* Thomas Friedman, chief diplomatic correspondent, *New York Times*; Barbara Dortch, Massachusetts Superior Court judge.

# Clark University

**Worcester, MA 01610-1477 508 793-7711**

**1994-95 Costs.** Tuition: $17,500. Room: $2,200. Board: $2,000. Fees, books, misc. academic expenses (school's estimate): $940.
**Enrollment.** Undergraduates: 809 men, 1,090 women (full-time). Freshman class: 2,886 applicants, 2,059 accepted, 457 enrolled. Graduate enrollment: 359 men, 336 women.
**Test score averages/ranges.** Range of SAT scores of middle 50%: 470-570 verbal, 510-620 math.
**Faculty.** 180 full-time; 82 part-time. 98% of faculty holds doctoral degree. Student/faculty ratio: 11 to 1.
**Selectivity rating.** Competitive.

**PROFILE.** Clark, founded in 1887, is a private, liberal arts university. Its 50-acre campus is located in Worcester, 40 miles west of Boston.

**Accreditation:** NEASC. Professionally accredited by the Accrediting Commission on Education for Health Services Administration, the American Assembly of Collegiate Schools of Business, the American Psychological Association.
**Religious orientation:** Clark University is nonsectarian; no religious requirements.
**Library:** Collections totaling over 519,000 volumes, and 1,883 periodical subscriptions.
**Special facilities/museums:** Galleries, theatres, Robert H. Goddard historical exhibition, rare book room, craft center, music center, map library, arboretum, herbarium, extensive darkroom facilities, satellite dish for international program reception, electron microscope, nuclear magnetic resonance spectrometer.
**Athletic facilities:** Gymnasium, badminton, basketball, racquetball, squash, tennis, and volleyball courts, swimming pool, dance, martial arts, training, and weight rooms, baseball, field hockey, lacrosse, and soccer fields, boathouse.

**STUDENT BODY. Undergraduate profile:** 32% are state residents; 14% are transfers. 4% Asian-American, 2% Black, 2% Hispanic, 63% White, 29% Other. Average age of undergraduates is 20.
**Freshman profile:** 92% of accepted applicants took SAT; 5% took ACT. 67% of freshmen come from public schools.
**Undergraduate achievement:** 85% of fall 1992 freshmen returned for fall 1993 term. 64% of entering class graduated. 70% of students who completed a degree program went on to graduate study within 10 years.
**Foreign students:** 93 students are from out of the country. Countries represented include India, Japan, Pakistan, South Korea, Turkey, and the United Kingdom; 43 in all.

**PROGRAMS OF STUDY. Degrees:** B.A.
**Majors:** Ancient Civilization, Art, Art History, Biochemistry/Molecular Biology, Biology, Business Administration/Management, Business Management, Chemistry, Comparative Literature, Computer Science, Ecology/Environmental Engineering, Economics, Energy Conservation/Use of Technology, English, English Literature, Environment/Technology/Society, Fine Arts, Foreign Languages/Literatures, French, Geography, German, Government/International Relations, History, Individual Majors, International Development, International Development/Social Change, Mathematics, Molecular Biology, Music, Philosophy, Physics, Political Science/Government, Psychology, Romance Languages, Screen Studies, Self-Designed Majors, Sociology, Spanish, Studio Art, Theatre Arts.
**Distribution of degrees:** The majors with the highest enrollment are psychology, government/international relations, and sociology; German, physics, and music have the lowest.
**Requirements:** General education requirement.
**Academic regulations:** Minimum 2.0 GPA required for graduation.
**Special:** Minors offered in some majors. Concentrations offered in Asian studies, communication studies, cultural identities and global processes, environmental studies, ethics/public policy, Jewish studies, neuroscience, peace studies, race/ethnic relations, and women's studies. Self-designed majors. Double majors. Dual degrees. Independent study. Accelerated study. Pass/fail grading option. Internships. Graduate school at which undergraduates may take graduate-level courses. Preprofessional programs in law, medicine, veterinary science, and dentistry. 3-2 engineering program with Columbia U. Five-year B.A./M.A. programs in environment, technology, and society/international development/social change. Five-year B.A./M.B.A. program. Seven-year B.A./Ph.D. program in geography. Member of Worcester Consortium for Higher Education; cross-registration possible. Washington Semester. Exchange program with Howard U. Teacher certification in elementary education. Exchange programs abroad in France (U of Bourgogne), Germany (U of Trier), Great Britain (U of East Anglia, U of Stirling, U of Sussex, London Sch of Economics and Political Science), Israel, Japan (Kansai Gadai U), and Spain (Tandem Sch and U of Seville). Study abroad also in Australia, Bermuda, the Caribbean, Costa Rica, Kenya, Luxembourg, and Mexico. ROTC at Worcester Polytech Inst. AFROTC at Coll of the Holy Cross.
**Honors:** Phi Beta Kappa. Honors program. Honor societies.
**Academic Assistance:** Remedial writing, math, and study skills.

**STUDENT LIFE. Housing:** All first-year students are expected to live on campus unless living with family. Coed and women's dorms. School-owned/operated apartments. 67% of students live in college housing.
**Social atmosphere:** "The school does a good job of creating a self-contained atmosphere," reports the student newspaper. "Whereas some schools cannot keep students on campus for entertainment, Clark can't get them off." Students tend to congregate at The Pub, The Kneller, Moynihan's, and the Blarney Stone. The Students Activities Board and the Pub Entertainment Committee are influential organizations on campus. Basketball games, weekly bands, dances, and Spree Day are among the favorite events of the school year.
**Services and counseling/handicapped student services:** Placement services. Health service. Women's center. Counseling services for minority, military, veteran, and older students. Birth control, personal, and psychological counseling. Career and academic guidance services. Religious counseling. Physically disabled student services. Learning

disabled program/services. Notetaking services. Tape recorders. Tutors. Reader services for the blind.
**Campus organizations:** Undergraduate student government. Student newspaper (Scarlet, published once/two weeks). Literary magazine. Yearbook. Radio and TV stations. Concert choir, a cappella singing group, dance group, Players Society, debating, film society, Model UN, Amnesty International, Young Democrats, Campus Republicans, Big Brothers/Big Sisters, Bisexual/Lesbian/Gay Alliance, academic, athletic, service, and special-interest groups, 80 organizations in all.
**Religious organizations:** Baptist Student Union, Christian Fellowship, Catholic Student Association, Protestant Campus Ministry, Hillel, Muslim Student Organization.
**Minority/foreign student organizations:** Asian Society, Black Student Union, Latin American Student Organization. International Student Association, Caribbean African Student Association, African, and Armenian groups.

**ATHLETICS. Physical education requirements:** None.
**Intercollegiate competition:** 15% of students participate. Baseball (M), basketball (M,W), crew (M,W), cross-country (M,W), diving (M,W), field hockey (W), lacrosse (M), soccer (M,W), softball (W), swimming (M,W), tennis (M,W), volleyball (W). Member of Constitution Conference, ECAC, NCAA (No division specified), NCAA Division III.
**Intramural and club sports:** 50% of students participate. Intramural badminton, basketball, bowling, touch football, racquetball, soccer, softball, squash, table tennis, volleyball, walleyball, water basketball, Wiffle ball. Men's club ice hockey, rugby. Women's club equestrian sports, lacrosse, rugby.

**ADMISSIONS. Academic basis for candidate selection** (in order of priority): Secondary school record, class rank, standardized test scores, school's recommendation, essay.
**Nonacademic basis for candidate selection:** Character and personality, extracurricular participation, and particular talent or ability are important. Geographical distribution and alumni/ae relationship are considered.
**Requirements:** Graduation from secondary school is required; GED is accepted. 16 units and the following program of study are recommended: 4 units of English, 3 units of math, 3 units of science, 2 units of foreign language, 2 units of social studies. SAT or ACT is required. ACH required. Campus visit and interview recommended. Off-campus interviews available with admissions and alumni representatives.
**Procedure:** Take SAT or ACT by November of 12th year. Take ACH by December of 12th year. Visit college for interview by March 15 of 12th year. Suggest filing application by January. Application deadline is February 15. Notification of admission by April 1. Reply is required by May 1. $300 nonrefundable tuition deposit. $100 nonrefundable room deposit. Freshmen accepted for terms other than fall.
**Special programs:** Admission may be deferred one year. Credit and/or placement may be granted through CEEB Advanced Placement exams for scores of 4 or higher. Early decision program. In fall 1993, 58 applied for early decision and 54 were accepted. Deadline for applying for early decision is December 1 and January 1.
**Transfer students:** Transfer students accepted for terms other than fall. In fall 1993, 14% of all new students were transfers into all classes. 332 transfer applications were received, 206 were accepted. Application deadline is April 15 for fall; November 15 for spring. Minimum 2.8 GPA recommended. Lowest course grade accepted is "C-." Maximum number of transferable credits is 16 units (eight units/year). At least 16 units must be completed at the university to receive degree.
**Admissions contact:** Richard W. Pierson, M.A., Dean of Admissions. 508 793-7431, 800-GO-CLARK.

**FINANCIAL AID. Available aid:** Pell grants, SEOG, state scholarships and grants, school scholarships and grants, private scholarships and grants, ROTC scholarships, academic merit scholarships, and aid for undergraduate foreign students. Perkins Loans (NDSL), PLUS, Stafford Loans (GSL), state loans, school loans, private loans, and SLS. Mass Plan. Tuition Plan Inc., Knight Tuition Plans, AMS, deferred payment plan, and guaranteed tuition. Mastercard/Visa/Discover.
**Financial aid statistics:** 3% of aid is not need-based. In 1993-94, 92% of all undergraduate applicants received aid; 87% of freshman applicants. Average amounts of aid awarded freshmen: Scholarships and grants, $11,066; loans, $3,100.
**Supporting data/closing dates:** FAFSA: Priority filing date is February 15. FAF/FFS: Priority filing date is February 1. Income tax forms: Priority filing date is June 1. Notification of awards begins April 1.
**Financial aid contact:** Peter M. Giumette, Director of Financial Aid. 508 793-7478.

**STUDENT EMPLOYMENT.** College Work/Study Program. Institutional employment. 36% of full-time undergraduates work on campus during school year. Students may expect to earn an average of $1,300 during school year. Off-campus part-time employment opportunities rated "good."

**COMPUTER FACILITIES.** 100 IBM/IBM-compatible and Macintosh/Apple microcomputers; all are networked. Students may access Digital minicomputer/mainframe systems, BITNET, Internet. Client/LAN operating systems include Apple/Macintosh, DOS, UNIX/XENIX/AIX, X-windows, DEC, LocalTalk/AppleTalk. Computer languages and software packages include BASIC, BMDP, C, Canvas, Cricket Graph, dBASE III, Excel, FORTRAN, Hyper Card, LISP, Lotus 1-2-3, MFoxbase, MINITAB, PageMaker, Pascal, SAS, SPSS-X, SuperPaint, TSP, Word, WordPerfect; 25 in all. Computer facilities are available to all students.
**Fees:** None.
**Hours:** 18 hours/day, seven days/week in labs; computer system available 24 hrs.

**GRADUATE CAREER DATA.** Graduate school percentages: 4% enter law school. 6% enter graduate business programs. 3% enter medical/dental programs. 9% enter graduate arts and sciences programs. Highest graduate school enrollments: Boston U, Brown U, Columbia U, Cornell U, Georgetown U, Harvard U, MIT, New York U, Tufts U, U of Chicago, U of Pennsylvania. 50% of graduates choose careers in business and industry. Companies and businesses that hire graduates: Chase Manhattan Bank, Solomon Brothers, Metropolitan Life Insurance, KPMG Peat Marwick, Citibank.

**PROMINENT ALUMNI/AE.** Ben Bagdikian, Pulitzer prize-winning journalist and former dean of UC Berkeley Graduate Sch of Journalism; Robert Atwood, editor and publisher, *Anchorage Times;* Marcia Savage, president, Manhattanville Coll; Ron Kessler, investigative reporter and author; William Finklestein, producer, *L.A. Law;* John Heard, actor; Jacob Hiatt, philanthropist.

# College of the Holy Cross

**Worcester, MA 01610-2395 508 793-2011**

**1994-95 Costs.** Tuition: $18,000. Room & board: $6,300. Fees, books, misc. academic expenses (school's estimate): $755.
**Enrollment.** Undergraduates: 1,281 men, 1,394 women (full-time). Freshman class: 2,994 applicants, 1,691 accepted, 659 enrolled.
**Test score averages/ranges.** Average SAT scores: 573 verbal, 627 math. Range of SAT scores of middle 50%: 550-650 verbal, 570-670 math.
**Faculty.** 212 full-time; 69 part-time. 90% of faculty holds doctoral degree. Student/faculty ratio: 13 to 1.
**Selectivity rating.** Most competitive.

**PROFILE.** Holy Cross is a church-affiliated, liberal arts college. Founded in 1843, it adopted coeducation in 1972. Its 174-acre campus is located in a residential area of Worcester, 45 miles west of Boston.

**Accreditation:** NEASC.
**Religious orientation:** College of the Holy Cross is affiliated with the Roman Catholic Church (Society of Jesus); one semester of religion required.
**Library:** Collections totaling over 484,438 volumes, 2,600 periodical subscriptions, and 20,000 microform items.
**Special facilities/museums:** Art gallery, Taylor and Boody tracker organ, greenhouse, electron microscope, facilities for aquatic research, music hall.
**Athletic facilities:** Gymnasium, field house, baseball, field hockey, football, lacrosse, soccer, and softball fields, tracks, crew tank, ice rink, swimming pool, basketball, racquetball, squash, tennis, and volleyball courts, aerobics and weight rooms, fitness center.

**STUDENT BODY. Undergraduate profile:** 39% are state residents; 2% are transfers. 2.3% Asian-American, 2.7% Black, 2.5% Hispanic, .5% Native American, 92% White. Average age of undergraduates is 20.
**Freshman profile:** 3% of freshmen who took SAT scored 700 or over on verbal, 17% scored 700 or over on math; 37% scored 600 or over on verbal, 68% scored 600 or over on math; 89% scored 500 or over on verbal, 97% scored 500 or over on math; 98% scored 400 or over on verbal, 99% scored 400 or over on math; 99% scored 300 or over on verbal, 100% scored 300 or over on math. 99% of accepted applicants took SAT. 50% of freshmen come from public schools.
**Undergraduate achievement:** 99% of fall 1992 freshmen returned for fall 1993 term. 98% of entering class graduated. 30% of students who completed a degree program immediately went on to graduate study.
**Foreign students:** 13 students are from out of the country. Countries represented include Canada and England; 12 in all.

**PROGRAMS OF STUDY. Degrees:** B.A.
**Majors:** Biology, Chemistry, Classics, Economics, Economics/Accounting, English, French, German, History, Mathematics, Music, Philosophy, Physics, Political Science, Psychology, Religious Studies, Russian, Russian Studies, Sociology/Anthropology, Spanish, Studies in European Literature, Theatre, Visual Arts.
**Distribution of degrees:** The majors with the highest enrollment are English, economics, and biology; music, Russian, and theatre have the lowest.
**Requirements:** General education requirement.
**Academic regulations:** Freshmen must maintain minimum 1.75 GPA; sophomores, juniors, seniors, 2.0 GPA.
**Special:** Courses offered in education, Chinese, Italian, and Japanese. Interdisciplinary concentrations in peace/conflict studies, psychobiology, and African-American, Asian, Latin-American, Middle Eastern, Russian, and women's studies. Optional First-Year Program for interested students. Center for Experimental Studies offers nontraditional programs, internships, and multidisciplinary majors. Self-designed majors. Double majors. Independent study. Accelerated study. Pass/fail grading option. Internships. Preprofessional programs in medicine and dentistry. 3-2 engineering programs with Columbia U, Dartmouth Coll, and Washington U. 4-1 B.A./M.B.A. with Clark U. Member of Worcester Consortium for Higher Education. Washington Semester and Sea Semester. Study abroad in Australia, Austria, China, England, France, Germany, Greece, Ireland, Italy, Japan, Mexico, the former Soviet Republics, and Spain. NROTC. ROTC and AFROTC at Worcester Polytech Inst.
**Honors:** Phi Beta Kappa. Honors program. Honor societies.
**Academic Assistance:** Nonremedial tutoring.

**STUDENT LIFE. Housing:** Students may live on or off campus. Coed dorms. Fit For Life dorms. 87% of students live in college housing.
**Services and counseling/handicapped student services:** Placement services. Health service. Women's center. Counseling services for minority students. Personal and psychological counseling. Career and academic guidance services. Religious counseling.
**Campus organizations:** Undergraduate student government. Student newspaper (Crusader, published once/week). Literary magazine. Yearbook. Radio station. Jazz ensemble, choir, marching and dance bands, drama group, debating, philosophy society, chess club, Alternative College Theatre, urban development program, Green Earth Restoration Project, Coalition on Homelessness and Housing, professional, service, and special-interest groups, 75 organizations in all.
**Religious organizations:** Committee for Campus Ministry, Christian Leadership Program, Lay Ministry, Pax Christi, CCD teachers, Prison Ministry.
**Minority/foreign student organizations:** Black Student Union, Asian Student Union, Latin American Student Organization, Multicultural Awareness Club, Multicultural Society. International Student Union.

**ATHLETICS. Physical education requirements:** None.
**Intercollegiate competition:** 25% of students participate. Baseball (M), basketball (M,W), cheerleading (M,W), crew (M,W), cross-country (M,W), diving (M,W), field hockey (W), football (M), golf (M), ice hockey (M), lacrosse (M,W), soccer (M,W), softball (W), swimming (M,W), tennis (M,W), track (indoor) (M,W), track (outdoor) (M,W),

track and field (indoor) (M,W), track and field (outdoor) (M,W), volleyball (W). Member of ECAC, NCAA Division I, Patriot League.

**Intramural and club sports:** 50% of students participate. Intramural basketball, football, rugby, sailing, skiing, volleyball. Men's club rugby, sailing, volleyball. Women's club rugby, sailing, ice hockey.

**ADMISSIONS. Academic basis for candidate selection** (in order of priority): Secondary school record, class rank, standardized test scores, school's recommendation, essay.

**Nonacademic basis for candidate selection:** Character and personality and particular talent or ability are emphasized. Extracurricular participation, geographical distribution, and alumni/ae relationship are important.

**Requirements:** Graduation from secondary school is required; GED is accepted. 22 units and the following program of study are recommended: 4 units of English, 4 units of math, 4 units of science, 4 units of foreign language, 3 units of social studies, 3 units of history. SAT is required. ACH required. Campus visit and interview recommended. Off-campus interviews available with admissions and alumni representatives.

**Procedure:** Take SAT by January of 12th year. Take ACH by January of 12th year. Visit college for interview by January 31 of 12th year. Application deadline is February 1. Notification of admission by April 1. Reply is required by May 1. $200 nonrefundable tuition deposit. Freshmen accepted for terms other than fall.

**Special programs:** Admission may be deferred one year. Credit and/or placement may be granted through CEEB Advanced Placement exams for scores of 4 or higher. Early decision program. In fall 1993, 267 applied for early decision and 126 were accepted. Deadline for applying for early decision is November 1 and January 15. Early entrance/early admission program.

**Transfer students:** Transfer students accepted for terms other than fall. In fall 1993, 2% of all new students were transfers into all classes. 57 transfer applications were received, 22 were accepted. Application deadline is May 1 for fall; December 1 for spring. Minimum 3.3 GPA recommended. Lowest course grade accepted is "C." Maximum number of transferable credits is 64 semester hours. At least 64 semester hours must be completed at the college to receive degree.

**Admissions contact:** William R. Mason, Director of Admissions. 508 793-2443.

**FINANCIAL AID. Available aid:** Pell grants, SEOG, state scholarships, school scholarships, and ROTC scholarships. Perkins Loans (NDSL), PLUS, Stafford Loans (GSL), and private loans. Knight Tuition Plans and AMS.

**Financial aid statistics:** 1% of aid is not need-based. In 1993-94, 57% of all undergraduate applicants received aid; 59% of freshman applicants. Average amounts of aid awarded freshmen: Scholarships and grants, $10,710; loans, $3,297.

**Supporting data/closing dates:** FAFSA/FAF: Priority filing date is February 1. Notification of awards begins April 1.

**Financial aid contact:** Francis H. Delaney, Jr., Ed.D., Director of Financial Aid. 508 793-2265.

**STUDENT EMPLOYMENT.** College Work/Study Program. Institutional employment. 46% of full-time undergraduates work on campus during school year. Students may expect to earn an average of $1,200 during school year. Off-campus part-time employment opportunities rated "fair."

**COMPUTER FACILITIES.** 130 IBM/IBM-compatible, Macintosh/Apple, and RISC-/UNIX-based microcomputers; 65 are networked. Students may access Digital minicomputer/mainframe systems, BITNET, Internet. Client/LAN operating systems include Apple/Macintosh, DOS, UNIX/XENIX/AIX, Windows NT, X-windows, DEC, LocalTalk/AppleTalk. Computer languages and software packages include BASIC, C, FORTRAN, LISP, Lotus 1-2-3, Microsoft Word, Pascal, SPSS-X, Turbo Pascal; 50 in all. Computer facilities are available to all students.

**Fees:** None.

**Hours:** 24 hours.

**GRADUATE CAREER DATA.** Graduate school percentages: 32% enter law school. 18% enter medical school. 7% enter graduate business programs. 31% enter graduate arts and sciences programs. Highest graduate school enrollments: Boston Coll, Boston U, Columbia U, Fordham U, George Washington U, Georgetown U, Harvard U, U of Connecticut, U of North Carolina, U of Notre Dame. 59% of graduates choose careers in business and industry. Companies and businesses that hire graduates: Arthur Andersen, Prudential, Travelers.

**PROMINENT ALUMNI/AE.** Robert Casey, governor of Pennsylvania; Anthony Fauci, head of Infectious Diseases Division, National Institutes of Health; Clarence Thomas, justice, U.S. Supreme Court; John Hamill, president, Shawmut Corp.; James Burke, retired chairperson and CEO, Johnson & Johnson; Robert Wright, president and CEO, NBC; Dr. Joseph Murray, Nobel Prize winner.

## Curry College

**Milton, MA 02186 — 617 333-0500**

**1994-95 Costs.** Tuition: $13,100. Room & board: $5,200. Fees, books, misc. academic expenses (school's estimate): $1,075.

**Enrollment.** Undergraduates: 430 men, 461 women (full-time). Freshman class: 1,224 applicants, 937 accepted, 283 enrolled. Graduate enrollment: 3 men, 23 women.

**Test score averages/ranges.** Average SAT scores: 390 verbal, 400 math.

**Faculty.** 68 full-time; 80 part-time. 67% of faculty holds highest degree in specific field. Student/faculty ratio: 12 to 1.

**Selectivity rating.** Less competitive.

**PROFILE.** Curry, founded in 1879, is a private, career-oriented, liberal arts institution. Its 120-campus is located in Milton, seven miles from downtown Boston.

**Accreditation:** NEASC. Professionally accredited by the National League for Nursing.

**Religious orientation:** Curry College is nonsectarian; no religious requirements.

**Library:** Collections totaling over 110,000 volumes, 650 periodical subscriptions, and 10,000 microform items.

**Special facilities/museums:** On-campus preschool, nursing lab, psychology lab.

**Athletic facilities:** Gymnasium, football, baseball, soccer, lacrosse, and softball fields, basketball, volleyball, handball, and tennis courts, weight lifting and wrestling facilities, outdoor swimming pool, cross-country and fitness trail.

**STUDENT BODY. Undergraduate profile:** 59% are state residents; 26% are transfers. 2% Asian-American, 4% Black, 1% Hispanic, 89% White, 4% Other. Average age of undergraduates is 20.

**Freshman profile:** 1% of freshmen who took SAT scored 600 or over on math; 5% scored 500 or over on verbal, 9% scored 500 or over on math; 33% scored 400 or over on verbal, 44% scored 400 or over on math; 90% scored 300 or over on verbal, 94% scored 300 or over on math.

**Undergraduate achievement:** 70% of fall 1992 freshmen returned for fall 1993 term. 44% of entering class graduated.

**Foreign students:** 36 students are from out of the country. Countries represented include China, Italy, Japan, Mexico, the Netherlands, and Thailand; 19 in all.

**PROGRAMS OF STUDY. Degrees:** B.A., B.S.

**Majors:** Biology, Business Management, Chemistry, Communication, Education, English, Fine/Applied Arts, Justice Studies, Nursing, Philosophy, Physics, Politics/History, Psychology, Sociology.

**Distribution of degrees:** The majors with the highest enrollment are business management, communication, and education; philosophy, chemistry, and physics have the lowest.

**Requirements:** General education requirement.

**Academic regulations:** Minimum 2.0 GPA must be maintained.

**Special:** Minors offered in all majors (except nursing) and in applied computing, dance, environmental studies, film studies, music, photography, religion, Spanish, women's studies, and writing. Self-designed majors. Double majors. Independent study. Accelerated study. Pass/fail grading option. Internships. Preprofessional programs in law, medicine, and dentistry. Member of Southeastern Massachusetts Counselors' Consortium. Teacher certification in elementary education. Study abroad possible. ROTC at Suffolk U.

**Honors:** Honors program. Honor societies.

**Academic Assistance:** Remedial reading, writing, math, and study skills. Nonremedial tutoring.

**ADMISSIONS. Academic basis for candidate selection** (in order of priority): Secondary school record, school's recommendation, essay, class rank, standardized test scores.

**Nonacademic basis for candidate selection:** Character and personality and extracurricular participation are emphasized. Particular talent or ability and geographical distribution are important. Alumni/ae relationship is considered.

**Requirements:** Graduation from secondary school is required; GED is accepted. 16 units and the following program of study are required: 4 units of English, 3 units of math, 2 units of science including 1 unit of lab, 2 units of foreign language, 2 units of social studies, 2 units of history, 1 unit of academic electives. Minimum SAT scores of 400 in both verbal and math, rank in top half of secondary school class, and minimum 2.0 GPA recommended. Biology and chemistry, both with labs, required of nursing program applicants. SAT is required; ACT may be substituted. Campus visit and interview recommended. No off-campus interviews.

**Procedure:** Take SAT or ACT by February of 12th year. Visit college for interview by March of 12th year. Application deadline is April 1. Acceptance notification on rolling basis beginning January 15. Reply is required by May 1. $200 tuition deposit, refundable until May 1. $100 room deposit, refundable until May 1. Freshmen accepted for terms other than fall.

**Special programs:** Admission may be deferred one year. Credit and/or placement may be granted through CEEB Advanced Placement exams for scores of 3 or higher. Credit and/or placement may be granted through CLEP general and subject exams. Credit may be granted through ACT PEP exams and military and life experience. Credit and placement may be granted through challenge exams. Early decision program. In fall 1993, 10 applied for early decision and 7 were accepted. Deadline for applying for early decision is December 1. Early entrance/early admission program.

**Transfer students:** Transfer students accepted for terms other than fall. In fall 1993, 26% of all new students were transfers into all classes. 318 transfer applications were received, 235 were accepted. Application deadline is July 1 (priority) for fall; December 1 for spring. Minimum 2.0 GPA required. Lowest course grade accepted is "C-." Maximum number of transferable credits is 90 semester hours. At least 30 semester hours must be completed at the college to receive degree.

**Admissions contact:** Janet Cromie Kelly, M.S., Dean of Admissions. 617 333-0500, extensions 2210, 2211.

**FINANCIAL AID. Available aid:** Pell grants, SEOG, state scholarships and grants, and school scholarships and grants. Perkins Loans (NDSL), PLUS, Stafford Loans (GSL), state loans, and SLS. Tuition Plan Inc., Knight Tuition Plans, and AMS. TERI.

**Financial aid statistics:** In 1993-94, 90% of all undergraduate applicants received aid; 52% of freshman applicants. Average amounts of aid awarded freshmen: Scholarships and grants, $4,000; loans, $2,596.

**Supporting data/closing dates:** FAFSA/FAF/FFS: Priority filing date is March 15. School's own aid application: Priority filing date is March 15. Income tax forms: Accepted on rolling basis. Notification of awards on rolling basis.

**Financial aid contact:** Maureen F. Lynch, Director of Financial Aid. 617 333-0500, extension 2146.

## Eastern Nazarene College

**Quincy, MA 02170** 617 773-6350

**1994-95 Costs.** Tuition: $8,770. Room & board: $3,500. Fees, books, misc. academic expenses (school's estimate): $1,040.
**Enrollment.** Undergraduates: 562 (full-time). Freshman class: 516 applicants, 409 accepted, 200 enrolled. Graduate enrollment: 105.
**Test score averages/ranges.** Average SAT scores: 468 verbal, 512 math. Range of SAT scores of middle 50%: 410-530 verbal, 440-580 math.
**Faculty.** 51 full-time; 15 part-time. 59% of faculty holds doctoral degree. Student/faculty ratio: 13 to 1.
**Selectivity rating.** Less competitive.

**PROFILE.** Eastern Nazarene, founded in 1918, is a church-affiliated, liberal arts college. Its 15-acre campus is located in Quincy, a suburb of Boston.

**Accreditation:** NEASC. Professionally accredited by the Council on Social Work Education.
**Religious orientation:** Eastern Nazarene College is affiliated with the Church of the Nazarene; eight credit hours of religion required.
**Library:** Collections totaling over 121,050 volumes and 545 periodical subscriptions.
**Special facilities/museums:** On-campus preschool.
**Athletic facilities:** Gymnasium, baseball, soccer, and softball fields, training and weight rooms, tennis courts, batting cage.
**STUDENT BODY. Undergraduate profile:** 34% are state residents; 14% are transfers. 4% Asian-American, 5% Black, 1% Hispanic, 88% White, 2% Other.
**Freshman profile:** 1% of freshmen who took SAT scored 700 or over on math; 11% scored 600 or over on verbal, 18% scored 600 or over on math; 33% scored 500 or over on verbal, 54% scored 500 or over on math; 79% scored 400 or over on verbal, 90% scored 400 or over on math; 100% scored 300 or over on verbal, 100% scored 300 or over on math. 87% of accepted applicants took SAT; 5% took ACT.
**Undergraduate achievement:** 69% of fall 1992 freshmen returned for fall 1993 term. 41% of entering class graduated.
**Foreign students:** 32 students are from out of the country. Countries represented include Canada and Kenya; 23 in all.
**PROGRAMS OF STUDY. Degrees:** B.A., B.S.
**Majors:** Biology, Business Administration, Chemistry, Church Music, Communication Arts, Computer Engineering, Computer/Information Sciences, Education, Engineering, Engineering Physics, English, French, General Science, History, Mathematics, Music, Music Education, Music Performance, Physical Education, Physics, Psychology, Religion, Social Studies, Social Work, Sociology, Spanish, Sports Therapy, Youth Ministry.
**Distribution of degrees:** The majors with the highest enrollment are business administration, educataion, and psychology; church music, physics, and chemistry have the lowest.
**Requirements:** General education requirement.
**Academic regulations:** Freshmen must maintain minimum 1.7 GPA; sophomores, 1.8 GPA; juniors, 1.9 GPA; seniors, 2.0 GPA.
**Special:** Associate's degrees offered. Self-designed majors. Double majors. Dual degrees. Independent study. Accelerated study. Pass/fail grading option. Internships. Cooperative education programs. Graduate school at which undergraduates may take graduate-level courses. Preprofessional programs in law, medicine, veterinary science, pharmacy, dentistry, theology, optometry, ministerial studies, psychology, speech/language pathology, and engineering. 2-3 pharmacy program with Massachusetts Coll of Pharmacy and Allied Health Sciences. 3-2 engineering program with Boston U. Member of Christian College Coalition; semester-away study possible. Washington Semester. Teacher certification in early childhood, elementary, secondary, and special education. Certification in specific subject areas. Study abroad in Belize and European countries.
**Honors:** Honor societies.
**Academic Assistance:** Remedial reading, writing, math, and study skills. Nonremedial tutoring.
**ADMISSIONS. Academic basis for candidate selection** (in order of priority): Secondary school record, standardized test scores, class rank, school's recommendation, essay.
**Nonacademic basis for candidate selection:** Character and personality and alumni/ae relationship are considered.
**Requirements:** Graduation from secondary school is required; GED is accepted. 16 units and the following program of study are recommended: 4 units of English, 2 units of math, 1 unit of science, 2 units of foreign language, 1 unit of social studies, 1 unit of history. Minimum combined SAT score of 700, rank in top half of secondary school class, and minimum 2.0 GPA recommended. Minimum of 1.5 units of algebra, 2 units of modern foreign language, and as many additional math and lab science courses as possible recommended of math program applicants. Audition required of music program applicants. Conditional admission possible for applicants not meeting standard requirements. SAT is required; ACT may be substituted. Campus visit and interview recommended. Off-campus interviews available with an admissions representative.
**Procedure:** Take SAT or ACT by January of 12th year. Visit college for interview by March of 12th year. Suggest filing application by March 1. Application deadline is August 1. Notification of admission on rolling basis. Reply is required by May 1. $250 nonrefundable tuition deposit. Freshmen accepted for terms other than fall.
**Special programs:** Admission may be deferred three years. Credit and/or placement may be granted through CEEB Advanced Placement exams for scores of 4 or higher. Credit and/or placement may be granted through CLEP general and subject exams. Early entrance/early admission program. Concurrent enrollment program.
**Transfer students:** Transfer students accepted for terms other than fall. In fall 1993, 14% of all new students were transfers into all classes. 97 transfer applications were received, 67 were accepted. Application deadline is August 1 for fall; January 1 for spring. Minimum 2.0 GPA recommended. Lowest course grade accepted is "C-." Maximum number of transferable credits is 96 semester hours. At least 34 semester hours must be completed at the college to receive degree.
**Admissions contact:** D. William Nichols, M.A., Executive Director of Enrollment Management. 617 773-2373, 800 88 ENC88.
**FINANCIAL AID. Available aid:** Pell grants, SEOG, state scholarships and grants, school scholarships and grants, private scholarships and grants, and academic merit scholarships. Perkins Loans (NDSL), PLUS, Stafford Loans (GSL), school loans, and SLS. AMS and Tuition Management Systems.
**Financial aid statistics:** 25% of aid is not need-based. In 1993-94, 80% of all undergraduate applicants received aid; 80% of freshman applicants. Average amounts of aid awarded freshmen: Scholarships and grants, $500; loans, $2,625.
**Supporting data/closing dates:** FAFSA: Priority filing date is March 1. FFS: Priority filing date is March 1; accepted on rolling basis. School's own aid application: Priority filing date is March 1; accepted on rolling basis. State aid form: Priority filing date is March 1; accepted on rolling basis. Income tax forms: Priority filing date is March 1; accepted on rolling basis. Notification of awards on rolling basis.
**Financial aid contact:** Patricia Trout, Director of Financial Aid. 617 773-6350.

## Elms College (College of Our Lady of the Elms)

**Chicopee, MA 01013** 413 594-2761

**1994-95 Costs.** Tuition: $11,400. Room & board: $4,765. Fees, books, misc. academic expenses (school's estimate): $850.
**Enrollment.** 600 women (full-time). Freshman class: 330 applicants, 301 accepted, 112 enrolled. Graduate enrollment: 2 men, 170 women.
**Test score averages/ranges.** Average SAT scores: 440 verbal, 420 math.
**Faculty.** 44 full-time; 35 part-time. 70% of faculty holds highest degree in specific field. Student/faculty ratio: 14 to 1.
**Selectivity rating.** Competitive.

**PROFILE.** Elms, founded in 1928, is a church-affiliated, liberal arts college for women. The Chicopee campus is located in the Pioneer Valley, two miles from Springfield.
**Accreditation:** NEASC. Professionally accredited by the American Bar Association, the Council on Social Work Education, the National League for Nursing.
**Religious orientation:** Elms College (College of Our Lady of the Elms) is affiliated with the Roman Catholic Church (Sisters of Saint Joseph); one semester of religion required.
**Library:** Collections totaling over 92,735 volumes, 717 periodical subscriptions, and 73,404 microform items.
**Special facilities/museums:** Art gallery, rare book gallery with Edward Bellamy Collection of rare manuscripts.
**Athletic facilities:** Gymnasium, weight room, fitness center, track, field hockey, lacrosse, soccer, and softball fields.
**STUDENT BODY. Undergraduate profile:** 47% are state residents; 20% are transfers. 3% Asian-American, 9% Black, 11% Hispanic, 72% White, 5% Other. Average age of undergraduates is 20.
**Freshman profile:** 100% of accepted applicants took SAT. 60% of freshmen come from public schools.
**Undergraduate achievement:** 80% of fall 1991 freshmen returned for fall 1992 term. 65% of entering class graduated. 25% of students who completed a degree program immediately went on to graduate study.
**Foreign students:** 44 students are from out of the country. Countries represented include Estonia, France, India, Ireland, Japan, and Sri Lanka; 14 in all.
**PROGRAMS OF STUDY. Degrees:** B.A., B.S., B.S.Nurs., B.Soc.Work.
**Majors:** Accounting, American Studies, Art, Art Education, Art Therapy, Arts Management, Biology, Business/Management, Chemistry, Commercial Art, Communication Disorders, Early Childhood Education, Elementary Education, English, French, History, International Studies, Marketing, Mathematical Science, Medical Technology, Modern Language, Natural Science, Nursing, Paralegal, Psychology, Religious Studies, Secondary Education, Social Work, Sociology, Spanish.
**Distribution of degrees:** The majors with the highest enrollment are nursing, education, and business/management; languages, life sciences, and mathematical science have the lowest.
**Requirements:** General education requirement.
**Academic regulations:** Minimum 1.9 GPA must be maintained.
**Special:** Minors offered in all majors and in computer science, media communications, music, and philosophy. Associate's degrees offered. Self-designed majors. Double majors. Independent study. Internships. Graduate school at which undergraduates may take graduate-level courses. Preprofessional programs in law, medicine, veterinary science, dentistry, optometry, and podiatry. Member of Cooperating Colleges of Greater Springfield. Member of National Sisters of St. Joseph Consortium. Washington Semester. New England Regional Semester. Exchange programs with Coll of Saint Rose, St. Mary's Coll, and Trinity Coll. Teacher certification in early childhood, elementary, secondary, and bilingual/bicultural education. Certification in specific subject areas. Exchange porgram abroad in Ireland (St. Patrick's U). Study abroad also in England, Germany, Latin American countries, Spain, and Sweden. ROTC and AFROTC at Western New England Coll.
**Honors:** Phi Beta Kappa. Honors program. Honor societies.
**Academic Assistance:** Remedial reading, writing, math, and study skills. Nonremedial tutoring.
**ADMISSIONS. Academic basis for candidate selection** (in order of priority): Secondary school record, class rank, standardized test scores, essay, school's recommendation.
**Nonacademic basis for candidate selection:** Extracurricular participation is emphasized. Character and personality and alumni/ae relationship are important. Geographical distribution is considered.
**Requirements:** Graduation from secondary school is recommended; GED is accepted. No specific distribution of secondary school units required. Rank in top half of secondary

school class and minimum 2.5 GPA required; minimum SAT scores of 450 in both verbal and math recommended. ACH (chemistry and biology) required of nursing and medical technology program applicants. Academic assistance program for applicants not normally admissible. SAT is required. Campus visit and interview recommended. Off-campus interviews available with admissions and alumni representatives.
**Procedure:** Take SAT by November of 12th year. Visit college for interview by January of 12th year. Suggest filing application by January. Notification of admission on rolling basis. Reply is required by May 1. $200 tuition deposit for resident students; $150 deposit for commuters. Freshmen accepted for terms other than fall.
**Special programs:** Admission may be deferred one year. Placement may be granted through CEEB Advanced Placement exams for scores of 3 or higher. Credit and placement may be granted through life experience. Early decision program. Deadline for applying for early decision is December 15. Early entrance/early admission program.
**Transfer students:** Transfer students accepted for terms other than fall. In fall 1992, 20% of all new students were transfers into all classes. 125 transfer applications were received, 115 were accepted. Application deadline is rolling for fall; rolling for spring. Minimum 2.3 GPA required. Lowest course grade accepted is "C." Maximum number of transferable credits is 75 semester hours. At least 55 semester hours must be completed at the college to receive degree.
**Admissions contact:** Coleen S. Nauman, Director of Admissions. 800 255-ELMS.

**FINANCIAL AID. Available aid:** Pell grants, SEOG, Federal Nursing Student Scholarships, state scholarships and grants, school scholarships and grants, private scholarships and grants, ROTC scholarships, academic merit scholarships, and aid for undergraduate foreign students. Perkins Loans (NDSL), PLUS, Stafford Loans (GSL), NSL, state loans, school loans, private loans, and SLS. AMS, deferred payment plan, and family tuition reduction.
**Financial aid statistics:** In 1992-93, 84% of all undergraduate applicants received aid; 85% of freshman applicants.
**Supporting data/closing dates:** FAFSA/FAF: Priority filing date is February 1. School's own aid application: Priority filing date is February 15. State aid form: Priority filing date is February 1. Income tax forms: Priority filing date is February 15. Notification of awards on rolling basis.
**Financial aid contact:** Marian Ruzicka, Director of Financial Aid. 413 594-2761, extension 249.

# Emerson College

**Boston, MA 02116** **617 578-8500**

**1994-95 Costs.** Tuition: $15,200. Room: $4,590. Board: $3,098. Fees, books, misc. academic expenses (school's estimate): $888.
**Enrollment.** Undergraduates: 794 men, 1,130 women (full-time). Freshman class: 1,684 applicants, 1,064 accepted, 468 enrolled. Graduate enrollment: 217 men, 472 women.
**Test score averages/ranges.** Average SAT scores: 515 verbal, 505 math. Range of SAT scores of middle 50%: 460-570 verbal, 450-570 math.
**Faculty.** 110 full-time; 110 part-time. 80% of faculty holds highest degree in specific field. Student/faculty ratio: 15 to 1.
**Selectivity rating.** Competitive.

**PROFILE.** Emerson, founded in 1880, is a private college of communication and performing arts. Its urban campus is located in Boston's historic Back Bay.

**Accreditation:** NEASC. Professionally accredited by the American Speech-Language-Hearing Association.
**Religious orientation:** Emerson College is nonsectarian; no religious requirements.
**Library:** Collections totaling over 154,013 volumes, 978 periodical subscriptions, and 16,175 microform items.
**Special facilities/museums:** TV studios, film production facilities, professional theatre, speech pathology clinics, preschool nursery for the hearing impaired.
**Athletic facilities:** Fitness center on campus; off-campus facilities include gymnasium, ice rinks, athletic fields.

**STUDENT BODY. Undergraduate profile:** 35% are state residents; 33% are transfers. 1% Asian-American, 4% Black, 3% Hispanic, 1% Native American, 87% White, 4% Other. Average age of undergraduates is 20.
**Freshman profile:** 95% of accepted applicants took SAT; 5% took ACT. 65% of freshmen come from public schools.
**Undergraduate achievement:** 88% of fall 1991 freshmen returned for fall 1992 term. 63% of entering class graduated.
**Foreign students:** 86 students are from out of the country. Countries represented include Canada, France, Japan, the Netherlands, Spain, and Venezuela; 43 in all.

**PROGRAMS OF STUDY. Degrees:** B.A., B.F.A., B.Mus., B.S., B.S.Speech
**Majors:** Acting, Advertising/Public Relations, Audio, Broadcast Journalism, Business/Organizational Communication, Communication Disorders, Communication/Politics/Law, Creative Writing, Dance, Film, Musical Theatre, Print Journalism, Speech Communication, Television, Theatre Design/Technology, Theatre Production, Writing/Publishing.
**Distribution of degrees:** The majors with the highest enrollment are television, film, and acting; dance have the lowest.
**Requirements:** General education requirement.
**Academic regulations:** Freshmen must maintain minimum 1.7 GPA; sophomores, juniors, seniors, 2.0 GPA.
**Special:** Minors offered in American studies, communication/politics/law, ethics/mass media, European studies, literature, music programming, political science, psychology of mass media, visual studies/the arts, and women's studies. Interdisciplinary majors in communication/philosophy, creative service, fine arts and the religious environment, human sciences/philosophy, mass communications/business organization communication, oral literature, and visual design in the communication arts. Hands-on learning experience through children's theatre productions, drama presentations, radio/TV studio operations, and publications. Self-designed majors. Double majors. Dual degrees. Independent study. Accelerated study. Internships. Graduate school at which undergraduates may take graduate-level courses. Preprofessional programs in law and speech/language pathology. 5-1/2-year B.S./M.S. program in communication disorders. Cross-registration with Suffolk U. Member of Professional Arts Consortium of Boston; cross-registration possible. Los Angeles Semester. Teacher certification in secondary education. Certification in specific subject areas. Study abroad in the Netherlands.
**Honors:** Honors program. Honor societies.
**Academic Assistance:** Remedial study skills. Nonremedial tutoring.

**STUDENT LIFE. Housing:** All freshmen must live on campus unless living with family. Coed dorms. 50% of students live in college housing.
**Services and counseling/handicapped student services:** Placement services. Health service. Counseling services for minority and older students. Birth control, personal, and psychological counseling. Career and academic guidance services. Religious counseling. Physically disabled student services. Learning disabled services. Notetaking services. Tape recorders. Tutors. Reader services for the blind.
**Campus organizations:** Undergraduate student government. Student newspaper (Berkeley Beacon, published once/week). Literary magazine. Yearbook. Radio and TV stations. Chorus, musical theatre, drama group, forensics, film arts society, comedy workshops, Varsity Club, political awareness organization, 53 organizations in all. Four fraternities, no chapter houses; three sororities, no chapter houses. 10% of men join a fraternity. 10% of women join a sorority.
**Religious organizations:** Hillel, Catholic Organization, Office of Religious Activities.
**Minority/foreign student organizations:** EBONI, AMIGOS, ASIA, Chinese Student Association. International Club.

**ATHLETICS. Physical education requirements:** None.
**Intercollegiate competition:** 8% of students participate. Baseball (M), basketball (M,W), golf (M), ice hockey (M), soccer (M,W), softball (W), tennis (M,W). Member of ECAC, Intercollegiate Soccer Association, NCAA Division III, New England College Hockey Association, New England Women's Basketball Association.
**Intramural and club sports:** 7% of students participate. Intramural basketball, flag football, volleyball. Women's club golf.

**ADMISSIONS. Academic basis for candidate selection** (in order of priority): Secondary school record, class rank, standardized test scores, school's recommendation, essay.
**Nonacademic basis for candidate selection:** Extracurricular participation and particular talent or ability are emphasized. Character and personality and alumni/ae relationship are considered.
**Requirements:** Graduation from secondary school is recommended; GED is accepted. No specific distribution of secondary school units required. Audition required of acting and musical theatre program applicants. Conditional admission possible for applicants not meeting standard requirements. Freshman Academic Studies Program for applicants not normally admissible. SAT is required; ACT may be substituted. PSAT is recommended. Campus visit recommended. Off-campus interviews available with an admissions representative.
**Procedure:** Take SAT or ACT by fall of 12th year. Suggest filing application by February 1; no deadline. Notification of admission by April 1. Reply is required by May 1. $200 tuition deposit, refundable until May 1. $300 room deposit, refundable until May 1. Freshmen accepted for terms other than fall.
**Special programs:** Admission may be deferred one year. Credit and/or placement may be granted through CEEB Advanced Placement exams for scores of 3 or higher. Credit and/or placement may be granted through CLEP general and subject exams. Early entrance/early admission program.
**Transfer students:** Transfer students accepted for terms other than fall. In fall 1992, 33% of all new students were transfers into all classes. 502 transfer applications were received, 360 were accepted. Application deadline is March 1 for fall; December 1 for spring. Minimum 2.5 GPA required. Lowest course grade accepted is "C." Maximum number of transferable credits is 64 semester hours. At least 32 semester hours must be completed at the college to receive degree.
**Admissions contact:** Jane B. Brown, M.S., Dean of Admission. 617 578-8600.

**FINANCIAL AID. Available aid:** Pell grants, SEOG, Federal Nursing Student Scholarships, state scholarships and grants, school scholarships and grants, private scholarships and grants, and academic merit scholarships. Perkins Loans (NDSL), PLUS, Stafford Loans (GSL), private loans, and SLS. Knight Tuition Plans and AMS.
**Financial aid statistics:** 10% of aid is not need-based. In 1992-93, 94% of all undergraduate applicants received aid; 93% of freshman applicants. Average amounts of aid awarded freshmen: Scholarships and grants, $8,100; loans, $2,800.
**Supporting data/closing dates:** FAFSA/FAF: Priority filing date is March 1. School's own aid application: Priority filing date is March 1. Income tax forms: Accepted on rolling basis. Notification of awards begins April 15.
**Financial aid contact:** Bernard Pekala, M.A., Director of Financial Aid. 617 578-8655.

**STUDENT EMPLOYMENT.** College Work/Study Program. Institutional employment. 32% of full-time undergraduates work on campus during school year. Students may expect to earn an average of $1,500 during school year. Off-campus part-time employment opportunities rated "good."

**COMPUTER FACILITIES.** 85 IBM/IBM-compatible and Macintosh/Apple microcomputers; all are networked. Students may access IBM minicomputer/mainframe systems. Computer languages and software packages include Apple and IBM software; database, spreadsheet, statistical, word processing programs; 40 in all. Computer facilities are available to all students.
**Fees:** Computer fee is included in tuition/fees.
**Hours:** 8:30 AM-9:30 PM (M-F); 10 AM-6 PM (Sa); noon-8 PM (Su).

**PROMINENT ALUMNI/AE.** Norman Lear and Richard Dysart, producers; Jay Leno and Steven Wright, comedians; Morton Dean, news anchor; Henry Winkler, actor; Elma Lewis, dean, Elma Lewis School of Fine Arts.

# Emmanuel College

**Boston, MA 02115** **617 277-9340**

**1993-94 Costs.** Tuition: $11,698. Room & board: $5,800. Fees, books, misc. academic expenses (school's estimate): $775.
**Enrollment.** Undergraduates: 43 men, 682 women (full-time). Freshman class: 368 applicants, 286 accepted, 166 enrolled. Graduate enrollment: 26 men, 166 women.
**Test score averages/ranges.** N/A.
**Faculty.** 50 full-time; 50 part-time. 80% of faculty holds highest degree in specific field. Student/faculty ratio: 12 to 1.
**Selectivity rating.** N/A.

**PROFILE.** Emmanuel, founded in 1919, is a church-affiliated, liberal arts college for women. Its 16-acre, Gothic-style campus is located in Boston's Fenway section.

**Accreditation:** NEASC. Professionally accredited by the National League for Nursing.
**Religious orientation:** Emmanuel College is affiliated with the Roman Catholic Church (Sisters of Notre Dame of Namur); two semesters of theology required.
**Library:** Collections totaling over 134,000 volumes, 600 periodical subscriptions, and 1,370 microform items.
**Special facilities/museums:** Art gallery, academic resource center, language lab, science center, computer lab.
**Athletic facilities:** Gymnasium, weight room, tennis courts.

**STUDENT BODY. Undergraduate profile:** 78% are state residents; 19% are transfers. 5% Asian-American, 11% Black, 4% Hispanic, 1% Native American, 71% White, 8% Other. Average age of undergraduates is 21.
**Freshman profile:** Majority of accepted applicants took SAT. 60% of freshmen come from public schools.
**Undergraduate achievement:** 80% of fall 1991 freshmen returned for fall 1992 term. 52% of entering class graduated.
**Foreign students:** 77 students are from out of the country. Countries represented include Haiti, India, Japan, Mexico, Sri Lanka, and Vietnam; 60 in all.

**PROGRAMS OF STUDY. Degrees:** B.A., B.F.A., B.S.
**Majors:** Accounting, Art History, Art Studio, Art Therapy, Biochemistry, Biology, Chemistry, Communication Arts, Developmental Psychology, Economics, Educational Studies, Engineering, English, Foreign Languages, Graphic Design, Health Care Administration, History, Liberal Studies, Management, Mathematics, Nursing, Painting, Physics, Political Science, Pre-Dentistry, Pre-Engineering, Pre-Law, Pre-Medicine, Pre-Veterinary, Printing, Psychology, Rehabilitation Psychology, Religious Studies, Sociology, Spanish, Studio Art, Theater, Visual Communication.
**Distribution of degrees:** The majors with the highest enrollment are psychology, biology, and management; history, chemistry, and religious studies have the lowest.
**Requirements:** General education requirement.
**Academic regulations:** Minimum 2.00 GPA must be maintained.
**Special:** Minors offered in some majors and in business management, English literature, human biology, music, philosophy, and women's studies. Courses offered in computer applications and drama. Management program. Intercultural studies. Self-designed majors. Double majors. Dual degrees. Accelerated study. Pass/fail grading option. Internships. Graduate school at which undergraduates may take graduate-level courses. Preprofessional programs in law, medicine, veterinary science, dentistry, and engineering. Dual degree in engineering with Northeastern U and Wentworth Inst of Tech. Washington Semester. Exchange program with Coll of Notre Dame and Trinity Coll. Teacher certification in elementary, secondary, and special education. Certification in specific subject areas. Exchange program abroad in Japan (Seishin U), Mexico, and other countries. ROTC at Northeastern U.
**Honors:** Honor societies.
**Academic Assistance:** Remedial reading, math, and study skills. Nonremedial tutoring.

**ADMISSIONS. Academic basis for candidate selection** (in order of priority): Secondary school record, essay, school's recommendation, class rank, standardized test scores.
**Nonacademic basis for candidate selection:** Character and personality are emphasized. Extracurricular participation is important. Particular talent or ability and alumni/ae relationship are considered.
**Requirements:** Graduation from secondary school is required; GED is accepted. 16 units and the following program of study are required: 4 units of English, 3 units of math, 2 units of lab science, 3 units of foreign language, 2 units of social studies. R.N. required of nursing applicants. Conditional admission possible for applicants not meeting standard requirements. SAT is required; ACT may be substituted. ACH recommended. Campus visit recommended. Off-campus interviews available with an admissions representative.
**Procedure:** Application deadline is September. Notification of admission on rolling basis. $100 tuition deposit, refundable until May 1. $200 nonrefundable room deposit. Freshmen accepted for terms other than fall.
**Special programs:** Admission may be deferred one year. Credit and/or placement may be granted through CEEB Advanced Placement exams for scores of 3 or higher. Credit may be granted through CLEP general and subject exams, DANTES and challenge exams, and military and life experience. Credit and placement may be granted through ACT PEP exams. Early decision program. In fall 1992, three applied for early decision and three were accepted. Deadline for applying for early decision is November 1. Early entrance/early admission program.
**Transfer students:** Transfer students accepted for terms other than fall. In fall 1992, 19% of all new students were transfers into all classes. 69 transfer applications were received, 55 were accepted. Application deadline is rolling for fall; rolling for spring. Minimum 2.0 GPA required. Lowest course grade accepted is "C." Maximum number of transferable credits is 72 semester hours. At least 64 semester hours must be completed at the college to receive degree.
**Admissions contact:** Margaret Spillane Bonilla, Director of Admissions. 617 735-9715.

**FINANCIAL AID. Available aid:** Pell grants, SEOG, state scholarships and grants, school scholarships and grants, private scholarships and grants, and academic merit scholarships. Perkins Loans (NDSL), PLUS, Stafford Loans (GSL), state loans, and SLS. Tuition Plan Inc., AMS, and deferred payment plan.
**Financial aid statistics:** 2% of aid is not need-based. In 1992-93, 71% of all undergraduate applicants received aid; 81% of freshman applicants. Average amounts of aid awarded freshmen: Scholarships and grants, $6,712; loans, $2,800.
**Supporting data/closing dates:** FAFSA/FAF/FFS: Priority filing date is March 15; accepted on rolling basis. Income tax forms: Priority filing date is March 15; accepted on rolling basis. Notification of awards on rolling basis.
**Financial aid contact:** Patricia Harden, Director of Financial Aid. 617 735-9725.

# Endicott College

**Beverly, MA 01915** **508 927-0585**

**1994-95 Costs.** Tuition: $11,345. Room & board: $6,125. Fees, books, misc. academic expenses (school's estimate): $650.
**Enrollment.** Undergraduates: 800 (full-time). Freshman class: 1,002 applicants, 859 accepted, 319 enrolled.
**Test score averages/ranges.** Average SAT scores: 367 verbal, 382 math. Average ACT scores: 18 composite.
**Faculty.** 45 full-time; 45 part-time. 10% of faculty holds highest degree in specific field. Student/faculty ratio: 14 to 1.
**Selectivity rating.** Less competitive.

**PROFILE.** Endicott is a private, liberal arts college. Founded in 1939 as a women's college, it became coeducational in 1994. Its 150-acre campus is located in Beverly, 20 miles north of Boston.

**Accreditation:** NEASC. Professionally accredited by the Foundation for Interior Design Education Research, the National League for Nursing.
**Religious orientation:** Endicott College is nonsectarian; no religious requirements.
**Library:** Collections totaling over 37,540 volumes, 125 periodical subscriptions, and 4,657 microform items.
**Special facilities/museums:** Lab school for education majors.
**Athletic facilities:** Gymnasium, weight room, field hockey, soccer, and softball fields, dance studio, tennis courts.

**STUDENT BODY. Undergraduate profile:** 50% are state residents; 19% are transfers. 7% Asian-American, 7% Black, 6% Hispanic, 74% White, 6% Other. Average age of undergraduates is 19.
**Freshman profile:** 68% of accepted applicants took SAT; 3% took ACT. 67% of freshmen come from public schools.
**Undergraduate achievement:** 82% of fall 1992 freshmen returned for fall 1993 term. 75% of entering class graduated.
**Foreign students:** 80 students are from out of the country. Countries represented include Bermuda, Ecuador, England, Germany, Japan, and Panama; 34 in all.

**PROGRAMS OF STUDY. Degrees:** B.F.A., B.S., B.S.Nurs.
**Majors:** Entrepreneurial Studies, Hotel/Restaurant/Travel Administration, Interior Design, Nursing, Psychology, Psychology/Athletic Training, Psychology/Education, Psychology/Public Relations, Retailing, Visual Communications.
**Distribution of degrees:** The majors with the highest enrollment are hotel/restaurant/travel administration, interior design, and nursing.
**Requirements:** General education requirement.
**Academic regulations:** Freshmen must maintain minimum 1.6 GPA; sophomores, 1.8 GPA; juniors, 2.0 GPA; seniors, 2.0 GPA.
**Special:** Internships required each year in all majors. Associate's degrees offered. Self-designed majors. Internships. Member of NECCUM. Teacher certification in early childhood and elementary education. Certification in specific subject areas. Exchange program abroad in Switzerland (Les Roches Sch). Study abroad also in England, France, and Japan.
**Honors:** Honors program. Honor societies.
**Academic Assistance:** Remedial reading, writing, math, and study skills. Nonremedial tutoring.

**ADMISSIONS. Academic basis for candidate selection** (in order of priority): Secondary school record, school's recommendation, essay, class rank, standardized test scores.
**Nonacademic basis for candidate selection:** Character and personality, extracurricular participation, and alumni/ae relationship are important. Particular talent or ability and geographical distribution are considered.
**Requirements:** Graduation from secondary school is required; GED is accepted. 16 units and the following program of study are required: 4 units of English, 1 unit of math, 1 unit of science, 1 unit of history, 9 units of electives. 1 unit of chemistry and SAT or ACT required of nursing and physical therapy program applicants. SAT or ACT is recommended. PSAT is recommended. Campus visit and interview recommended. Off-campus interviews available with an admissions representative.
**Procedure:** Visit college for interview by spring of 12th year. Notification of admission on rolling basis. Reply is required by May 1. $300 tuition deposit, refundable until May 1. Freshmen accepted for terms other than fall.
**Special programs:** Admission may be deferred one year. Credit and/or placement may be granted through CEEB Advanced Placement exams and CLEP general and subject exams. Placement may be granted through challenge exams. Early entrance/early admission program.
**Transfer students:** Transfer students accepted for terms other than fall. In fall 1993, 19% of all new students were transfers into all classes. Application deadline is rolling for fall; rolling for spring. Minimum 2.0 GPA recommended. Lowest course grade accepted is "C." Maximum number of transferable credits is 64 semester hours. At least 64 semester hours must be completed at the college to receive degree.
**Admissions contact:** Thomas J. Redman, M.P.A., Vice-President for Admissions and Financial Aid. 508 921-1000.

**FINANCIAL AID. Available aid:** Pell grants, SEOG, state scholarships and grants, school scholarships and grants, private scholarships and grants, academic merit scholarships, and aid for undergraduate foreign students. Perkins Loans (NDSL), PLUS, Stafford Loans (GSL), state loans, private loans, and SLS. Education Plan Inc., Knight Tuition Plans, AMS, and family tuition reduction.
**Financial aid statistics:** In 1993-94, 71% of all undergraduate applicants received aid; 71% of freshman applicants. Average amounts of aid awarded freshmen: Scholarships and grants, $4,033; loans, $2,625.
**Supporting data/closing dates:** FAFSA/FAF: Accepted on rolling basis. School's own aid application: Priority filing date is March 15; accepted on rolling basis. Income tax forms: Priority filing date is March 15. Notification of awards on rolling basis.
**Financial aid contact:** Marcia Toomey, Director of Financial Aid. 508 927-0585.

## Fitchburg State College

**Fitchburg, MA 01420** 508 345-2151

**1994-95 Costs.** Tuition: $1,408 (state residents), $5,542 (out-of-state). Room & board: $3,728. Fees, books, misc. academic expenses (school's estimate): $2,326.
**Enrollment.** Undergraduates: 1,223 men, 1,656 women (full-time). Freshman class: 2,857 applicants, 2,090 accepted, 577 enrolled. Graduate enrollment: 352 men, 808 women.
**Test score averages/ranges.** Average SAT scores: 423 verbal, 465 math. Range of SAT scores of middle 50%: 370-460 verbal, 410-510 math.
**Faculty.** 234 full-time; 50 part-time. 61% of faculty holds doctoral degree. Student/faculty ratio: 16 to 1.
**Selectivity rating.** Less competitive.

**PROFILE.** Fitchburg State, founded in 1894, is a public, comprehensive college. Its 35-acre campus is located near downtown Fitchburg, 55 miles northwest of Boston.
**Accreditation:** NEASC. Professionally accredited by the American Medical Association (CAHEA), the National League for Nursing.
**Religious orientation:** Fitchburg State College is nonsectarian; no religious requirements.
**Library:** Collections totaling over 214,149 volumes, 1,435 periodical subscriptions, and 370,891 microform items.
**Special facilities/museums:** Art gallery, graphics center, on-campus teacher education school, language lab, center for studies in human behavior, 120-acre college conservation area.
**Athletic facilities:** Gymnasium, weight room, athletic fields, track.
**STUDENT BODY. Undergraduate profile:** 93% are state residents; 35% are transfers. 1% Asian-American, 3% Black, 2% Hispanic, 92% White, 2% Other. Average age of undergraduates is 21.
**Freshman profile:** 1% of freshmen who took SAT scored 700 or over on math; 3% scored 600 or over on verbal, 8% scored 600 or over on math; 15% scored 500 or over on verbal, 32% scored 500 or over on math; 62% scored 400 or over on verbal, 83% scored 400 or over on math; 97% scored 300 or over on verbal, 99% scored 300 or over on math. 98% of accepted applicants took SAT. 64% of freshmen come from public schools.
**Undergraduate achievement:** 70% of fall 1992 freshmen returned for fall 1993 term. 38% of entering class graduated. 8% of students who completed a degree program immediately went on to graduate study.
**Foreign students:** 27 students are from out of the country. Countries represented include Barbados, Cambodia, Greece, India, Japan, and Uruguay.
**PROGRAMS OF STUDY. Degrees:** B.A., B.S., B.S.Ed.
**Majors:** Biology, Business Administration, Chemistry, Communication/Media, Computer Science, Early Childhood Education, Economics, Elementary Education, English, General Studies, Geography, History, Human Services, Industrial Arts, Industrial Technology, Mathematics, Medical Technology, Middle School Education, Nursing, Psychology, Secondary Education, Sociology, Special Education.
**Distribution of degrees:** The majors with the highest enrollment are education, nursing, and business administration; chemistry, geography, and general studies have the lowest.
**Requirements:** General education requirement.
**Academic regulations:** Freshmen must maintain minimum 1.6 GPA; sophomores, 1.8 GPA; juniors, 2.0 GPA; seniors, 2.5 GPA.
**Special:** Minors offered in 24 fields. Self-designed majors. Double majors. Dual degrees. Independent study. Pass/fail grading option. Internships. Graduate school at which undergraduates may take graduate-level courses. Preprofessional programs in law, medicine, veterinary science, pharmacy, and dentistry. Teacher certification in early childhood, elementary, secondary, special education, and vo-tech education. Certification in specific subject areas. Study abroad in Austria, France, the former Soviet Republics, and Spain. ROTC.
**Honors:** Honors program. Honor societies.
**Academic Assistance:** Remedial reading, writing, math, and study skills. Nonremedial tutoring.
**STUDENT LIFE. Housing:** Students may live on or off campus. Coed and women's dorms. 55% of students live in college housing.
**Services and counseling/handicapped student services:** Placement services. Health service. Day care. Counseling services for minority, military, veteran, and older students. Birth control, personal, and psychological counseling. Career and academic guidance services. Religious counseling. Physically disabled student services. Learning disabled services. Notetaking services. Tape recorders. Tutors. Reader services for the blind.
**Campus organizations:** Undergraduate student government. Student newspaper (Strobe, published once/week). Literary magazine. Yearbook. Radio station. Glee club, Choral Arts Association, band, brass and woodwind ensembles, jazz-rock ensemble, Fine Arts Week, Dancin' Club, outing club, debating, Players Guild, Stageright, theatre workshop, Winter Carnival, PIRG, Women in Business, human services club, Amnesty International, departmental groups, 80 organizations in all. Six fraternities, no chapter houses; six sororities, no chapter houses. 18% of men join a fraternity. 20% of women join a sorority.
**Religious organizations:** Intervarsity Christian Fellowship, Newman Center, Jewish Student Union.
**Minority/foreign student organizations:** Cultural Society for Minorities, Hispanic Student Union. International Students, International Student Union.
**ATHLETICS. Physical education requirements:** Three semester hours of physical education required.
**Intercollegiate competition:** 18% of students participate. Baseball (M), basketball (M,W), cross-country (M,W), field hockey (W), football (M), ice hockey (M), soccer (M,W), softball (W), track (indoor) (M,W), track (outdoor) (M,W), track and field (M,W), volleyball (W). Member of ECAC, MASCAC, NCAA Division III, NEAC.
**Intramural and club sports:** 40% of students participate. Intramural basketball, bowling, cross-country, floor hockey, soccer, softball, tennis, touch football, volleyball, weight lifting.
**ADMISSIONS. Academic basis for candidate selection** (in order of priority): Secondary school record, class rank, standardized test scores, school's recommendation, essay.
**Nonacademic basis for candidate selection:** Extracurricular participation and particular talent or ability are important. Character and personality, geographical distribution, and alumni/ae relationship are considered.
**Requirements:** Graduation from secondary school is required; GED is accepted. No specific distribution of secondary school units required. Minimum combined SAT score of 800 and rank in top three-fifths of secondary school class required. Access program for applicants not normally admissible. SAT is required; ACT may be substituted. Campus visit and interview recommended. No off-campus interviews.
**Procedure:** Take SAT or ACT by February of 12th year. Visit college for interview by March 1 of 12th year. Suggest filing application by March 1; no deadline. Notification of admission on rolling basis. Reply is required by May 1. $135 nonrefundable tuition deposit for resident students; $85 nonrefundable tuition deposit for commuters. $50 nonrefundable room deposit. Freshmen accepted for terms other than fall.
**Special programs:** Admission may be deferred one year. Credit and/or placement may be granted through CEEB Advanced Placement exams for scores of 3 or higher. Credit may be granted through CLEP general and subject exams, DANTES and challenge exams, and military experience.
**Transfer students:** Transfer students accepted for terms other than fall. In fall 1993, 35% of all new students were transfers into all classes. 820 transfer applications were received, 516 were accepted. Application deadline is April 1 for fall; December 1 for spring. Minimum 2.0 GPA required. Lowest course grade accepted is "C-." Maximum number of transferable credits is 64 semester hours from a two-year school and 75 semester hours from a four-year school. At least 45 semester hours must be completed at the college to receive degree.
**Admissions contact:** Marke M. Vickers, M.A., Director of Admissions. 508 345-2151, extension 3144.
**FINANCIAL AID. Available aid:** Pell grants, SEOG, Federal Nursing Student Scholarships, state scholarships and grants, school scholarships and grants, private scholarships and grants, ROTC scholarships, and academic merit scholarships. Perkins Loans (NDSL), PLUS, Stafford Loans (GSL), NSL, state loans, private loans, and SLS. MEFA. TERI. Alliance. College's payment plan.
**Financial aid statistics:** 28% of aid is not need-based. In 1993-94, 75% of all undergraduate applicants received aid; 87% of freshman applicants. Average amounts of aid awarded freshmen: Scholarships and grants, $1,000; loans, $1,000.
**Supporting data/closing dates:** FAFSA/FAF/FFS: Priority filing date is March 30. Notification of awards on rolling basis.
**Financial aid contact:** Marybeth Courtright, M.A., Director of Financial Aid. 508 345-2151, extension 3155.
**STUDENT EMPLOYMENT.** College Work/Study Program. Institutional employment. 9% of full-time undergraduates work on campus during school year. Students may expect to earn an average of $1,470 during school year. Off-campus part-time employment opportunities rated "good."
**COMPUTER FACILITIES.** 425 IBM/IBM-compatible and Macintosh/Apple microcomputers; all are networked. Students may access AT&T, CDC Cyber, Digital minicomputer/mainframe systems, BITNET, Internet. Computer languages and software packages include Ada, BASIC, C, COBOL, dBASE, FORTRAN, LISP, Pascal, RDB, SPSS, WordPerfect. Computer facilities are available to all students.
**Fees:** $15 computer fee per semester; included in tuition/fees.
**Hours:** 24 hours.
**GRADUATE CAREER DATA.** Graduate school percentages: 1% enter law school. 1% enter medical school. 2% enter graduate business programs. 7% enter graduate arts and sciences programs. Highest graduate school enrollments: Fitchburg State Coll. 20% of graduates choose careers in business and industry.
**PROMINENT ALUMNI/AE.** Dorothy Kelly, M.D., authority on Sudden Infant Death Syndrome; Leo F. McManus, educational psychologist; Robert Salvatore, game inventor, *Dungeons and Dragons*.

## Framingham State College

**Framingham, MA 01701** 508 620-1220

**1993-94 Costs.** Tuition: $1,408 (state residents), $5,542 (out-of-state). Room: $2,110. Board: $1,316. Fees, books, misc. academic expenses (school's estimate): $2,226.
**Enrollment.** Undergraduates: 1,095 men, 2,034 women (full-time). Freshman class: 2,964 applicants, 2,166 accepted, 582 enrolled. Graduate enrollment: 158 men, 319 women.
**Test score averages/ranges.** Average SAT scores: 436 verbal, 472 math. Range of SAT scores of middle 50%: 380-480 verbal, 380-500 math.
**Faculty.** 170 full-time; 50 part-time. 70% of faculty holds doctoral degree. Student/faculty ratio: 16 to 1.
**Selectivity rating.** Less competitive.

**PROFILE.** Framingham State, a public college, was founded in 1839 as the first public Normal school in the country. Its 72-acre campus is located in Framingham, 20 miles west of Boston.

**Accreditation:** NEASC. Professionally accredited by the American Dietetic Association, the American Home Economics Association.
**Religious orientation:** Framingham State College is nonsectarian; no religious requirements.
**Library:** Collections totaling over 171,000 volumes, 1,205 periodical subscriptions, and 488,400 microform items.
**Special facilities/museums:** Association with Danforth Museum, art gallery, language lab, greenhouse, planetarium, nursery school.
**Athletic facilities:** Gymnasium, track, basketball court, athletic fields, tennis courts.

**STUDENT BODY. Undergraduate profile:** 94% are state residents; 45% are transfers. 2% Asian-American, 3% Black, 3% Hispanic, 89% White, 3% Other. Average age of undergraduates is 21.
**Freshman profile:** 2% of freshmen who took SAT scored 600 or over on verbal, 5% scored 600 or over on math; 18% scored 500 or over on verbal, 36% scored 500 or over on math; 76% scored 400 or over on verbal, 87% scored 400 or over on math; 100% scored 300 or over on verbal, 100% scored 300 or over on math. 100% of accepted applicants took SAT. 80% of freshmen come from public schools.
**Undergraduate achievement:** 75% of fall 1991 freshmen returned for fall 1992 term. 50% of entering class graduated. 20% of students who completed a degree program immediately went on to graduate study.
**Foreign students:** 60 students are from out of the country. Countries represented include China, Germany, Greece, Japan, Thailand, and the United Kingdom; 40 in all.

**PROGRAMS OF STUDY. Degrees:** B.A., B.S., B.S.Ed.
**Majors:** Art History/Appreciation, Art Studio, Biology, Business Administration/Management, Chemistry, Computer/Information Sciences, Consumer/Family Studies, Early Childhood Education, Earth Science, Economics, Elementary Education, English, Food Science, Food Sciences/Human Nutrition, French, Geography, History, Mathematics, Media/Communications, Medical Technology, Nursing, Philosophy, Politics, Pre-Engineering, Psychology, Sociology, Spanish, Textiles/Clothing.
**Distribution of degrees:** The majors with the highest enrollment are business administration, education, and psychology; philosophy and earth science have the lowest.
**Requirements:** General education requirement.
**Academic regulations:** Freshmen must maintain minimum 1.7 GPA; sophomores, juniors, seniors, 2.0 GPA.
**Special:** Minors offered in American studies, food chemistry, geology, Latin American studies, law/society, music, physics, and secondary education. Double majors. Independent study. Internships. Graduate school at which undergraduates may take graduate-level courses. Preprofessional programs in law, medicine, veterinary science, and dentistry. 3-1 medical technology program. 3-2 engineering program with U of Massachusetts at Amherst, Dartmouth, and Lowell. Member of College Academic Program Sharing (CAPS); cross-registration with eight other Massachusetts state colleges. Washington Semester. Teacher certification in early childhood, elementary, and secondary education. Exchange program abroad in Canada (U of Quebec). Study abroad also in England, France, and Spain. ROTC at Worcester Polytech Inst.
**Honors:** Honors program.
**Academic Assistance:** Remedial reading, writing, math, and study skills. Nonremedial tutoring.

**STUDENT LIFE. Housing:** Students may live on or off campus. Coed and women's dorms. 50% of students live in college housing.
**Social atmosphere:** Favorite hangouts include the Commuter cafe, library, dorms, Bambino's, and Bennigan's. The Gatepost and Student Government influence student life. Popular social events include the Spring Fair, Mr. FSC, Homecoming, football games, and Senior Commencement Ball.
**Services and counseling/handicapped student services:** Placement services. Health service. Day care. Counseling services for minority and older students. Personal and psychological counseling. Academic guidance services. Religious counseling. Physically disabled student services. Reader services for the blind.
**Campus organizations:** Undergraduate student government. Student newspaper (Gatepost, published once/week). Literary magazine. Yearbook. Radio station. Music groups, Hilltop Players, political and service groups, athletic and departmental groups, special-interest groups.
**Religious organizations:** Catholic, Jewish, and Protestant Campus Ministries.
**Minority/foreign student organizations:** Minority student group. International Club, Third World Organization.

**ATHLETICS. Physical education requirements:** None.
**Intercollegiate competition:** 10% of students participate. Baseball (M), basketball (M,W), cross-country (M,W), field hockey (W), football (M), ice hockey (M), soccer (M,W), softball (W), volleyball (W). Member of ECAC, MAIAW, Massachusetts State College Athletic Conference, NCAA Division III, NEAC, NECAC, NEFC.
**Intramural and club sports:** 25% of students participate. Intramural basketball, bowling, golf, ice skating, racquetball, softball, touch football, volleyball. Men's club rugby. Women's club horsemanship, rugby.

**ADMISSIONS. Academic basis for candidate selection** (in order of priority): Secondary school record, class rank, standardized test scores, school's recommendation.
**Nonacademic basis for candidate selection:** Character and personality, extracurricular participation, particular talent or ability, geographical distribution, and alumni/ae relationship are considered.
**Requirements:** Graduation from secondary school is required; GED is accepted. 16 units and the following program of study are required: 4 units of English, 3 units of math, 2 units of lab science, 2 units of foreign language, 1 unit of social studies, 1 unit of history, 3 units of academic electives. Chemistry required of biology, chemistry, home economics, and medical technology program applicants. 3 units of science, including physics, required of pre-engineering program applicants. 4 units of math required of mathematics and computer science program applicants. 3 units of French and Spanish required of applicants to those majors. Portfolio required of art program applicants. R.N. required of nursing program applicants. Academic Enrichment program for applicants not normally admissible. SAT is required. ACH recommended. Campus visit recommended. No off-campus interviews.
**Procedure:** Take SAT by December of 12th year. Suggest filing application by March 15. Application deadline is June 15. Notification of admission on rolling basis. Reply required by May 1 or within two weeks of acceptance. $50 nonrefundable tuition deposit. $50 nonrefundable room deposit. Freshmen accepted for terms other than fall.
**Special programs:** Admission may be deferred one year. Credit and/or placement may be granted through CEEB Advanced Placement exams for scores of 3 or higher. Credit may be granted through CLEP general and subject exams, DANTES exams, and military experience. Early entrance/early admission program.
**Transfer students:** Transfer students accepted for terms other than fall. In fall 1992, 45% of all new students were transfers into all classes. 1,202 transfer applications were received, 821 were accepted. Application deadline is March 15 for fall; December 1 for spring. Minimum 2.5 GPA recommended. Lowest course grade accepted is "C-." Maximum number of transferable credits is 96 semester hours. At least 32 semester hours must be completed at the college to receive degree.
**Admissions contact:** Philip M. Dooher, Ph.D., Dean of Admissions. 508 626-4500.

**FINANCIAL AID. Available aid:** Pell grants, SEOG, state scholarships, school scholarships and grants, private scholarships and grants, and academic merit scholarships. Perkins Loans (NDSL), PLUS, Stafford Loans (GSL), school loans, private loans, and SLS. AMS.
**Financial aid statistics:** 5% of aid is not need-based. In 1992-93, 40% of all undergraduate applicants received aid; 42% of freshman applicants. Average amounts of aid awarded freshmen: Scholarships and grants, $1,300; loans, $2,000.
**Supporting data/closing dates:** FAFSA/FAF/FFS: Priority filing date is March 15; accepted on rolling basis. School's own aid application: Priority filing date is March 15; accepted on rolling basis. Income tax forms: Priority filing date is March 15; accepted on rolling basis. Notification of awards begins April 1.
**Financial aid contact:** Linda Anderson-Mercier, M.Ed., Director of Financial Aid. 508 626-4534.

**STUDENT EMPLOYMENT.** College Work/Study Program. Institutional employment. 15% of full-time undergraduates work on campus during school year. Students may expect to earn an average of $1,200 during school year. Off-campus part-time employment opportunities rated "excellent."

**COMPUTER FACILITIES.** 300 IBM/IBM-compatible and Macintosh/Apple microcomputers; 200 are networked. Students may access Digital minicomputer/mainframe systems, Internet. Computer languages and software packages include BASIC, COBOL, Pascal; 15 in all. Computer facilities are available to all students.
**Fees:** None.
**Hours:** 24 hours.

**GRADUATE CAREER DATA.** Highest graduate school enrollments: U of Massachusetts at Amherst and Boston.

**PROMINENT ALUMNI/AE.** Christa McAuliffe, teacher, Teacher in Space Program.

# Gordon College

**Wenham, MA 01984** **508 927-2300**

**1994-95 Costs.** Tuition: $12,750. Room: $2,710. Board: $1,520. Fees, books, misc. academic expenses (school's estimate): $950.
**Enrollment.** Undergraduates: 437 men, 713 women (full-time). Freshman class: 593 applicants, 512 accepted, 294 enrolled.
**Test score averages/ranges.** Average SAT scores: 488 verbal, 518 math. Range of SAT scores of middle 50%: 430-540 verbal, 450-580 math.
**Faculty.** 71 full-time; 18 part-time. 73% of faculty holds doctoral degree. Student/faculty ratio: 15 to 1.
**Selectivity rating.** Competitive.

**PROFILE.** Gordon is a college of the liberal arts and sciences with religious orientation. Founded in 1889, the present institution is the result of the 1985 merger with Barrington College. Its 730-acre campus is located on Cape Ann, 25 miles north of Boston.

**Accreditation:** NEASC. Professionally accredited by the Council on Social Work Education, the National Association of Schools of Music.
**Religious orientation:** Gordon College is a nondenominational Christian school; two semesters of religion/theology required.
**Library:** Collections totaling over 241,378 volumes, 667 periodical subscriptions, and 27,732 microform items.
**Special facilities/museums:** Human performance lab, psychology lab complex, electron microscope.
**Athletic facilities:** Gymnasium, field hockey, baseball, soccer and softball fields, tennis courts, weight room.

**STUDENT BODY. Undergraduate profile:** 37% are state residents; 22% are transfers. 6% Asian-American, 3% Black, 2% Hispanic, 1% Native American, 87% White, 1% Other. Average age of undergraduates is 20.
**Freshman profile:** 1% of freshmen who took SAT scored 700 or over on verbal, 5% scored 700 or over on math; 13% scored 600 or over on verbal, 24% scored 600 or over on math; 45% scored 500 or over on verbal, 56% scored 500 or over on math; 81% scored 400 or over on verbal, 80% scored 400 or over on math; 91% scored 300 or over on verbal, 92% scored 300 or over on math. 90% of accepted applicants took SAT; 1% took ACT. 85% of freshmen come from public schools.
**Undergraduate achievement:** 82% of fall 1991 freshmen returned for fall 1992 term. 39% of entering class graduated. 19% of students who completed a degree program went on to graduate study within one year.
**Foreign students:** 60 students are from out of the country. Countries represented include China, Ethiopia, Kenya, Korea, and Mexico; 29 in all.

**PROGRAMS OF STUDY. Degrees:** A.B., B.Mus., B.S.

**Majors:** Accounting, Biblical/Theological Studies, Biology, Business Administration, Chemistry, Computer Science, Early Childhood Education, Economics, Elementary Education, English Language/Literature, French, History, International Affairs, Mathematics, Movement Science, Music Performance, Music Theory/Composition, Philosophy, Physics, Political Studies, Psychology, Recreation/Leisure Studies, Secondary/Middle School Education, Social Work, Sociology, Spanish, Special Education, Youth Ministries.
**Distribution of degrees:** The majors with the highest enrollment are business administration, English, and sociology; recreation/leisure studies, music, and Spanish have the lowest.
**Requirements:** General education requirement.
**Academic regulations:** Minimum 2.0 GPA must be maintained.
**Special:** Minors offered in all majors and in art. Self-designed majors. Double majors. Independent study. Pass/fail grading option. Internships. Cooperative education programs. Preprofessional programs in law, medicine, and theology. 2-2 programs with Thomas Jefferson U in cytotechnology, dental hygiene, medical technology, nursing, occupational therapy, physical therapy, and radiologic technology. 3-2 engineering program with U of Massachusetts at Lowell. Member of Christian College Consortium, Christian College Coalition, and Northeast Consortium of Colleges and Universities in Massachusetts; exchange possible. American Studies Program (Washington, D.C.). AuSable Inst of Environmental Studies (Michigan). Urban Studies Semester (San Francisco). Other semester-away programs available. Teacher certification in early childhood, elementary, secondary, and special education. Certification in specific subject areas. Exchange program abroad in Kenya (Daystar U Coll). Study abroad also in Costa Rica, England, France, Israel, and other countries. AFROTC at U of Massachusetts at Lowell.
**Honors:** Phi Beta Kappa. Honors program. Honor societies.
**Academic Assistance:** Remedial reading, writing, math, and study skills. Nonremedial tutoring.

**STUDENT LIFE. Housing:** All unmarried students under age 21 must live on campus unless living near campus with relatives. Coed, women's, and men's dorms. School-owned/operated apartments. 89% of students live in college housing.
**Social atmosphere:** Students frequent Nick's Roast Beef, the Sylvan Street Grille, the Liberty Tree, North Shore malls, Cristo's Coffee Cup, Wheatberry's, The Ground Round, Denny's, and local beaches. Rollerbladers, international student groups, Bible study groups, women's groups, and athletes are influential on campus. The most popular events on campus are semi-formals, theme dances, Band Night, and International Night. "Gordon is an excellent school for a solid liberal arts education with a Christian backdrop, as well as for discovering oneself, one's uniqueness, and one's ability to excel on life's path," states the editor of the student newspaper.
**Services and counseling/handicapped student services:** Placement services. Health service. Counseling services for minority students. Personal and psychological counseling. Career and academic guidance services. Religious counseling. Physically disabled student services. Learning disabled services. Notetaking services. Tape recorders. Tutors. Reader services for the blind.
**Campus organizations:** Undergraduate student government. Student newspaper (Tartan, published once/two weeks). Literary magazine. Yearbook. Choir, women's choir, bell choir, band, orchestra, Gordon Players, theatre troupe, political, service, and special-interest groups, 50 organizations in all.
**Religious organizations:** The Vine Ministries, SOS Student Ministries Program, Summer Intern Program, Summer Teams, World Focus Outreach, Habitat for Humanity.
**Minority/foreign student organizations:** AHANA. International Student Fellowship.

**ATHLETICS. Physical education requirements:** Discovery Expeditions, Concepts of Wellness program, or La Vida wilderness expedition program required in first year, followed by two activity classes.
**Intercollegiate competition:** 40% of students participate. Baseball (M), basketball (M,W), cross-country (M,W), field hockey (W), soccer (M,W), softball (W), tennis (M,W), volleyball (W). Member of Commonwealth Coast Conference, NCAA Division III.
**Intramural and club sports:** 40% of students participate. Intramural basketball, chess, frisbee, Nordic skiing, pool, soccer, softball, table tennis, tennis, volleyball. Men's club lacrosse, ultimate frisbee, volleyball. Women's club lacrosse.

**ADMISSIONS. Academic basis for candidate selection** (in order of priority): Secondary school record, essay, class rank, standardized test scores, school's recommendation.
**Nonacademic basis for candidate selection:** Character and personality are important. Extracurricular participation, particular talent or ability, and alumni/ae relationship are considered.
**Requirements:** Graduation from secondary school is required; GED is accepted. 17 units and the following program of study are required: 4 units of English, 2 units of math, 2 units of science including 1 unit of lab, 2 units of foreign language, 2 units of social studies, 5 units of academic electives. Rank in top half of secondary school class recommended. Audition required of music program applicants. SAT is required; ACT may be substituted. PSAT is recommended. Campus visit recommended. Off-campus interviews available with admissions and alumni representatives.
**Procedure:** Take SAT or ACT by November of 12th year. Visit college for interview by March of 12th year. Suggest filing application by March 15; no deadline. Notification of admission on rolling basis. Reply is required by May 1. $150 nonrefundable tuition deposit. Freshmen accepted for terms other than fall.
**Special programs:** Admission may be deferred one year. Credit may be granted through CEEB Advanced Placement for scores of 3 or higher. Credit may be granted through CLEP general and subject exams. Placement may be granted through challenge exams. Early decision program. In fall 1992, 53 applied for early decision and 48 were accepted. Deadline for applying for early decision is December 1. Early entrance/early admission program.
**Transfer students:** Transfer students accepted for terms other than fall. In fall 1992, 22% of all new students were transfers into all classes. 144 transfer applications were received, 123 were accepted. Application deadline is rolling for fall; rolling for spring. Lowest course grade accepted is "C-." Maximum number of transferable credits is 96 semester hours. At least 32 semester hours must be completed at the college to receive degree.
**Admissions contact:** Mark R. Sylvester, M.A., Dean of Admissions and Financial Aid. 508 927-2300, 800 343-1379.

**FINANCIAL AID. Available aid:** Pell grants, SEOG, state scholarships and grants, school scholarships and grants, private scholarships and grants, ROTC scholarships, academic merit scholarships, and aid for undergraduate foreign students. Perkins Loans (NDSL), PLUS, Stafford Loans (GSL), state loans, and SLS. Deferred payment plan.
**Financial aid statistics:** 6% of aid is not need-based. In 1992-93, 83% of all undergraduate applicants received aid; 94% of freshman applicants. Average amounts of aid awarded freshmen: Scholarships and grants, $6,425; loans, $2,790.
**Supporting data/closing dates:** FAFSA/FAF/FFS: Priority filing date is March 1; accepted on rolling basis. School's own aid application: Priority filing date is January 1. Income tax forms: Accepted on rolling basis. Notification of awards on rolling basis.
**Financial aid contact:** Barbara L. Boles, Director of Financial Aid. 508 927-2300, extension 4035.

**STUDENT EMPLOYMENT.** College Work/Study Program. Institutional employment. 58% of full-time undergraduates work on campus during school year. Students may expect to earn an average of $1,500 during school year. Off-campus part-time employment opportunities rated "good."

**COMPUTER FACILITIES.** 95 IBM/IBM-compatible and Macintosh/Apple microcomputers; 25 are networked. Students may access Digital minicomputer/mainframe systems. Computer languages and software packages include Ada, BASIC, C, COBOL, dBASE, FORTRAN, Lotus 1-2-3, OPS-5, Pascal, SPSS, WordPerfect. Some computers are in restricted labs.
**Fees:** Computer fee is included in tuition/fees.
**Hours:** 8 AM-1 AM.

**GRADUATE CAREER DATA.** Graduate school percentages: 2% enter law school. 2% enter medical school. 2% enter graduate business programs. Highest graduate school enrollments: Boston U, Carnegie-Mellon U, Gordon-Conwell Theological Seminary, Salem State Coll, U of Vermont, Worcester Polytech Inst. 45% of graduates choose careers in business and industry. Companies and businesses that hire graduates: Digital Equipment Corp., Raytheon.

**PROMINENT ALUMNI/AE.** Herman Smith, judge, Massachusetts; David Homer, president, North Park Coll; Rev. Everett L. Fullam, leader, Episcopal Renewal Ministries.

# Hampshire College

**Amherst, MA 01002** **413 549-4600**

**1994-95 Costs.** Tuition: $20,655. Room: $3,475. Board: $2,000. Fees, books, misc. academic expenses (school's estimate): $1,065.
**Enrollment.** Undergraduates: 456 men, 623 women (full-time). Freshman class: 1,192 applicants, 1,001 accepted, 309 enrolled.
**Test score averages/ranges.** N/A.
**Faculty.** 92 full-time; 8 part-time. 81% of faculty holds highest degree in specific field. Student/faculty ratio: 12 to 1.
**Selectivity rating.** N/A.

**PROFILE.** Hampshire, founded in 1965, is a private, liberal arts college. Programs are offered through the Schools of Communications and Cognitive Science, Humanities and Arts, Natural Science, and Social Science. Its 800-acre campus is located in Amherst, 90 miles west of Boston.
**Accreditation:** NEASC.
**Religious orientation:** Hampshire College is nonsectarian; no religious requirements.
**Library:** Collections totaling over 111,000 volumes, 800 periodical subscriptions and 400 microform items.
**Special facilities/museums:** Performing arts center, bioshelter (integrated greenhouse/aquaculture facility), farm center, electronic music and TV production studios, extensive film and photography facilities, multimedia center.
**Athletic facilities:** Outdoor tennis courts, softball field, playing fields, gymnasium, indoor swimming pool, weight training area, sauna, table tennis area, climbing wall, basketball/volleyball court, indoor running track, indoor tennis courts.

**STUDENT BODY. Undergraduate profile:** 15% are state residents; 11% are transfers. 3% Asian-American, 3% Black, 4% Hispanic, 81% White, 9% Other. Average age of undergraduates is 20.
**Freshman profile:** Majority of accepted applicants took SAT. 67% of freshmen come from public schools.
**Undergraduate achievement:** 86% of fall 1992 freshmen returned for fall 1993 term. 35% of entering class graduated. 56% of students who completed a degree program went on to graduate study.
**Foreign students:** 34 students are from out of the country. Countries represented include Bangladesh, Canada, India, and Pakistan; 18 in all.

**PROGRAMS OF STUDY. Degrees:** B.A.
**Majors:** Agriculture, American Studies, Animal Science, Anthropology, Art, Art History, Biology, Botany, Chemistry, Child Development, Cognitive Science, Communications, Computer Graphics, Computer/Information Sciences, Cultural History, Cultural Studies, Dance, Economics, Education, Environmental Design, Environmental Science, Film, Genetics, Geology, Health, History, History/Philosophy of Science, Human Movement Physiology, International Relations, Journalism, Law, Linguistics, Literature, Marine Biology, Mathematics, Media, Microbiology, Music, Neurobiology, Peace/World Security Studies, Philosophy, Photography, Physics, Political Science/Government, Psychology, Science/Public Policy, Sociology, Statistics, Studio Arts, Theatre Arts, Third World Studies, Video, Women's Studies, Writing.
**Distribution of degrees:** The majors with the highest enrollment are theater, history, and art.
**Requirements:** General education requirement.
**Special:** Interdisciplinary concentrations possible. Five-College concentrations offered in African, black, East Asian, Latin American, and peace/world security studies and in astronomy, coastal/marine sciences, dance, and international relations. Students proceed to degree through three interdisciplinary divisions (rather than traditional freshman-

through-senior sequence): Basic Studies, the Concentration (which the student designs in consultation with faculty advisers), and Advanced Studies in that concentration, including an integrative seminar. Progress and competence are gauged by six divisional competency exams which the student helps devise. Written evaluations are given rather than grades; no credit hour requirements. Self-designed majors. Independent study. Member of Five-College Consortium; cross-registration possible. Study abroad possible. ROTC at U of Massachusetts at Amherst.
**Academic Assistance:** Nonremedial tutoring.

**STUDENT LIFE. Housing:** All students must live on campus. Coed, women's, and men's dorms. School-owned/operated apartments. Off-campus privately-owned housing. 96% of students live in college housing.
**Social atmosphere:** According to the editor of the student newspaper, "We are part of the Five-College Consortium, and although we are a small, liberal arts college we have lots of contact with students from the other schools, which makes for variety." Popular on-campus gathering spots include the Airport Lounge, the Bridge Cafe, the dining commons, and the Tavern. For entertainment off campus, students frequent Banducci's Cafe and Bart's Ice Cream. Being a nontraditional school, there are not many yearly events; however, the Halloween "Trip or Treat" Party and Spring Jam are recurring favorites. "Students who survive at Hampshire are very dedicated to their work. Without the pressure of grades or tests, we must invent our own pressure to discipline ourselves."
**Services and counseling/handicapped student services:** Health service. Women's center. Day care. Counseling services for minority and older students. Birth control, personal, and psychological counseling. Career and academic guidance services. Physically disabled student services. Notetaking services. Tutors. Reader services for the blind.
**Campus organizations:** Undergraduate student government. Student newspaper (The Phoenix, published weekly). Literary magazine. TV station. Chorale, orchestra, jazz band, musical theatre, drama and dance groups, film series, sports cooperative, food cooperative, EMT group, Responsible Ecology, community council, LGBA groups, bridge club, social service groups, 100 organizations in all.
**Religious organizations:** Jewish Women's Alliance, Christian Fellowship, Students for Progressive Judaism.
**Minority/foreign student organizations:** Raices, Native American Interest Group, SOURCE, Umoja, Asian Pacific student group. Foreign Students Association.

**ATHLETICS. Physical education requirements:** None.
**Intercollegiate competition:** 30% of students participate. Member of NIRSA.
**Intramural and club sports:** 60% of students participate. Intramural Alpine skiing, badminton, basketball, bowling, frisbee, indoor tennis, kayaking, martial arts, mountaineering, rock climbing, soccer, softball, swimming, tennis, track, volleyball, weight lifting. Men's club baseball, basketball, cycling, equestrian sports, fencing, soccer, softball, tennis, ultimate frisbee, volleyball. Women's club basketball, canoeing, cross-country, cycling, equestrian sports, fencing, soccer, softball, tennis, ultimate frisbee, volleyball.

**ADMISSIONS. Academic basis for candidate selection** (in order of priority): Secondary school record, essay, school's recommendation, class rank.
**Nonacademic basis for candidate selection:** Character and personality, extracurricular participation, and particular talent or ability are considered.
**Requirements:** Graduation from secondary school is recommended; GED is accepted. 18 secondary school units are required. James Baldwin Scholars Program for applicants not normally admissible. Campus visit and interview recommended. Off-campus interviews available with admissions and alumni representatives.
**Procedure:** Visit college for interview by fall of 12th year. Suggest filing application by February. Application deadline is February. Acceptance notification sent on or after April 1. Reply is required by May 1. $200 nonrefundable tuition deposit. $200 nonrefundable room deposit. Freshmen accepted for terms other than fall.
**Special programs:** Admission may be deferred one year. Early decision program. In fall 1993, 53 applied for early decision and 43 were accepted. Deadline for applying for early decision is November 15. Early entrance/early admission program.
**Transfer students:** Transfer students accepted for terms other than fall. In fall 1993, 11% of all new students were transfers into all classes. 134 transfer applications were received, 107 were accepted. Application deadline for fall is March 15; November 15 for spring.
**Admissions contact:** Audrey Y. Smith, Director of Admissions. 413 582-5471.

**FINANCIAL AID. Available aid:** Pell grants, SEOG, state scholarships and grants, school scholarships and grants, private scholarships and grants, academic merit scholarships, and aid for undergraduate foreign students. Perkins Loans (NDSL), PLUS, Stafford Loans (GSL), state loans, private loans, and SLS. Tuition Plan Inc., Education Plan Inc., Knight Tuition Plans, and AMS.
**Financial aid statistics:** 1% of aid is not need-based. In 1993-94, 80% of all undergraduate applicants received aid; 81% of freshman applicants. Average amounts of aid awarded freshmen: Scholarships and grants, $13,800; loans, $2,625.
**Supporting data/closing dates:** FAFSA/FAF: Priority filing date is February 15. School's own aid application: Priority filing date is February 15. Income tax forms: Accepted on rolling basis. Notification of awards begins April 1.
**Financial aid contact:** Kathleen Methot, Director of Financial Aid. 413 582-5474.

**STUDENT EMPLOYMENT.** College Work/Study Program. Institutional employment. 50% of full-time undergraduates work on campus during school year. Students may expect to earn an average of $1,500 during school year. Off-campus part-time employment opportunities rated "fair."

**COMPUTER FACILITIES.** 63 IBM/IBM-compatible, Macintosh/Apple, and RISC-/UNIX-based microcomputers. Students may access Digital, SUN minicomputer/mainframe systems, BITNET, Internet. Client/LAN operating systems include Apple/Macintosh, DOS. Computer languages and software packages include APL, BASIC, C, Cricket Graph, dBASE, Excel, Hyper Card, LISP, Lotus 1-2-3, MacDraw, MacWrite II, Microsoft Word, Microsoft Works, PageMaker, Paradox, Pascal, Quattro Pro, SPSS, SuperPaint, Word for Windows, WordPerfect, Write Now. Computer facilities are available to all students.
**Fees:** Computer fee is included in tuition/fees.

**PROMINENT ALUMNI/AE.** Ken Burns, documentary filmmaker; Marta Renzi, choreographer; Aaron Lansky, director and founder, National Yiddish Book Center.

# Harvard University

**Cambridge, MA 02138** 617 495-1000

**1994-95 Costs.** Tuition: $18,485. Room & board: $6,410. Fees, books, misc. academic expenses (school's estimate): $3,255.
**Enrollment.** Undergraduates: 3,923 men, 2,939 women (full-time). Freshman class: 13,865 applicants, 2,165 accepted, 1,606 enrolled. Graduate enrollment: 6,586 men, 4,973 women.
**Test score averages/ranges.** Range of SAT scores of middle 50%: 630-720 verbal, 680-770 math.
**Faculty.** 1,658 full-time; 385 part-time. 97% of faculty holds highest degree in specific field. Student/faculty ratio: 8 to 1.
**Selectivity rating.** Most competitive.

**PROFILE.** Harvard, founded in 1636, is a private, Ivy League university. Radcliffe was established as an "annex" for women in 1879; all classes and facilities are now coeducational. Its campus is located in Cambridge, across the Charles River from Boston. Campus architecture ranges from Bulfinch to H.H. Richardson to Le Corbusier.

**Accreditation:** NEASC.
**Religious orientation:** Harvard University is nonsectarian; no religious requirements.
**Library:** Collections totaling over 13,000,000 volumes, 100,000 periodical subscriptions, and 6,800,000 microform items.
**Special facilities/museums:** Museums, language labs, observatory.
**Athletic facilities:** Gymnasium, field house, ice rink, badminton, basketball, racquetball, squash, tennis, and volleyball courts, swimming pool, tracks, stadium, boathouses, baseball, field hockey, football, lacrosse, soccer, and softball fields, weight rooms, dance studio.

**STUDENT BODY. Undergraduate profile:** 16% are state residents; 5% are transfers. 18% Asian-American, 7% Black, 8% Hispanic, 1% Native American, 61% White, 5% Other. Average age of undergraduates is 20.
**Freshman profile:** 99% of accepted applicants took SAT; 16% took ACT. 65% of freshmen come from public schools.
**Undergraduate achievement:** 99% of fall 1992 freshmen returned for fall 1993 term. 96% of entering class graduated. 28% of students who completed a degree program immediately went on to graduate study.
**Foreign students:** 450 students are from out of the country. Countries represented include Canada, China, India, Singapore, South Korea, and the United Kingdom; 95 in all.

**PROGRAMS OF STUDY. Degrees:** A.B., B.S.
**Majors:** Afro-American Studies, Anthropology, Applied Mathematics, Astronomy/Astrophysics, Biochemical Science, Biology, Chemistry, Chemistry/Physics, Classics/Allied Fields, Comparative Study of Religion, Computer Science, Earth/Planetary Sciences, East Asian Studies, Economics, Engineering Sciences, English/American Language/Literature, Environmental Sciences/Public Policy, Fine Arts, Folklore/Mythology, Germanic Languages/Literatures, Government, History, History/Literature, History/Science, Linguistics, Literature, Mathematics, Music, Near Eastern Languages/Literatures, Philosophy, Physical Sciences, Physics, Psychology, Romance Languages/Literature, Sanskrit/Indian Studies, Slavic Languages/Literatures, Social Studies, Sociology, Statistics, Visual/Environmental Studies, Women's Studies.
**Distribution of degrees:** The majors with the highest enrollment are government, English/American Literature/Language, and economics; statistics, Sanskrit/Indian studies, and physical sciences have the lowest.
**Requirements:** General education requirement.
**Academic regulations:** Minimum "C-" grade average must be maintained.
**Special:** Special concentrations and area studies programs. Tutorial system of instruction. Upperclass students live in Houses, each of which is a small college unit with its own dining hall, library, and athletic, social, and cultural activities; each House has a Master, Senior Tutor (dean), and staff of 50 resident and nonresident tutors and faculty associates. Self-designed majors. Double majors. Dual degrees. Independent study. Accelerated study. Pass/fail grading option. Internships. Graduate school at which undergraduates may take graduate-level courses. Preprofessional programs in law and medicine. 3-2 engineering program. Teacher certification in secondary education. Certification in specific subject areas. Study abroad in numerous countries. ROTC, NROTC, and AFROTC at MIT.
**Honors:** Phi Beta Kappa. Honors program.
**Academic Assistance:** Remedial reading and study skills. Nonremedial tutoring.

**STUDENT LIFE. Housing:** All freshmen must live on campus unless living with family. Coed dorms. Off-campus privately-owned housing. Off-campus married-student housing. 99% of students live in college housing.
**Services and counseling/handicapped student services:** Placement services. Health service. Women's center. Day care. Host family program houses students not from area. Counseling services for minority, veteran, and older students. Birth control, personal, and psychological counseling. Career and academic guidance services. Religious counseling. Physically disabled student services. Learning disabled services. Notetaking services. Tape recorders. Tutors. Reader services for the blind.
**Campus organizations:** Undergraduate student government. Student newspapers (Crimson; Independent; several others). Literary magazine. Yearbook. Radio station. Choral societies, glee club, orchestra, house musical societies, drama groups, debating, magazines, ad hoc committees, political, social service, and special-interest groups, 230 organizations in all.
**Religious organizations:** Several religious groups.

**Minority/foreign student organizations:** American Indians at Harvard, Asian American Association, Black Students Association, Raza, La Organizacion Boricua de Harvard/Radcliffe. International Students Association, International Assembly.

**ATHLETICS. Physical education requirements:** None.
**Intercollegiate competition:** 7% of students participate. Alpine skiing (M,W), baseball (M), basketball (M,W), crew (M,W), cross-country (M,W), diving (M,W), fencing (M,W), field hockey (W), football (M), golf (M,W), ice hockey (M,W), lacrosse (M,W), Nordic skiing (M,W), sailing (M,W), soccer (M,W), softball (W), squash (M,W), swimming (M,W), tennis (M,W), track and field (indoor) (M,W), track and field (outdoor) (M,W), volleyball (M,W), water polo (M,W), wrestling (M). Member of ECAC, Ivy League, NCAA Division I, NCAA Division I-AA for football.
**Intramural and club sports:** 60% of students participate. Intramural aerobics, ballet, fencing, jazz dance/exercise, martial arts, Nautilus, orienteering, racquetball, rugby, sailing, scuba, sculling, skating, soccer, softball, squash, swimming, table tennis, tennis, volleyball, weight lifting, yoga. Men's club badminton, basketball, boxing, cheerleading, cricket, croquet, cycling, martial arts, orienteering, polo, rugby, shooting, table tennis, ultimate frisbee, water polo. Women's club badminton, basketball, boxing, cheerleading, cricket, croquet, cycling, martial arts, orienteering, polo, rugby, shooting, table tennis, ultimate frisbee, water polo.

**ADMISSIONS. Academic basis for candidate selection** (in order of priority): Secondary school record, school's recommendation, standardized test scores.
**Nonacademic basis for candidate selection:** Extracurricular participation is emphasized. Character and personality are important. Particular talent or ability and alumni/ae relationship are considered.
**Requirements:** Graduation from secondary school is recommended; GED is accepted. 18 units and the following program of study are recommended: 4 units of English, 4 units of math, 3 units of science, 3 units of foreign language, 3 units of history, 1 unit of electives. In secondary school, students urged to pursue the most rigorous four-year programs in English, math, foreign language, and sciences. SAT is required; ACT may be substituted. ACH required. Admissions interview required. Off-campus interviews available with an alumni representative.
**Procedure:** Take SAT/ACT and ACH by end of January of 12th year. Suggest filing application by January 1; no deadline. Notification of admission by April 1. Reply is required by May 1. Freshmen accepted in fall terms only.
**Special programs:** Admission may be deferred one year. Credit and/or placement may be granted through CEEB Advanced Placement exams for scores of 4 or higher. Early action program. In fall 1993, 2,355 applied for early action and 712 were accepted. Deadline for applying for early action is November 1.
**Transfer students:** Transfer students accepted for terms other than fall. In fall 1993, 5% of all new students were transfers into all classes. 1,100 transfer applications were received, 137 were accepted. Application deadline is February 1 for fall; February 1 for spring. Lowest course grade accepted is "C-." Maximum number of transferable credits is 8 full-year courses. At least 8 full-year courses must be completed at the university to receive degree.
**Admissions contact:** Marlyn McGrath Lewis, Ph.D., Director of Admissions. 617 495-1551.

**FINANCIAL AID. Available aid:** Pell grants, SEOG, state scholarships and grants, school scholarships, private scholarships and grants, ROTC scholarships, and aid for undergraduate foreign students. Perkins Loans (NDSL), PLUS, Stafford Loans (GSL), state loans, school loans, and SLS. Knight Tuition Plans. Monthly payment plan and tuition prepayment plan.
**Financial aid statistics:** In 1993-94, 98% of all undergraduate applicants received aid; 99% of freshman applicants. Average amounts of aid awarded freshmen: Scholarships and grants, $11,411; loans, $2,850.
**Supporting data/closing dates:** FAFSA/FAF: Priority filing date is February 1. School's own aid application: Priority filing date is February 1. Income tax forms: Priority filing date is February 1. Divorced/Separated Parents Form; Business/Farm Supplement: Priority filing date is February 1. Notification of awards begins April 1.
**Financial aid contact:** James S. Miller, Director of Financial Aid. 617 495-1581.

**STUDENT EMPLOYMENT.** College Work/Study Program. Institutional employment. 70% of full-time undergraduates work on campus during school year. Students may expect to earn an average of $2,250 during school year. Off-campus part-time employment opportunities rated "excellent."

**COMPUTER FACILITIES.** 550 IBM/IBM-compatible, Macintosh/Apple, and RISC-/UNIX-based microcomputers; all are networked. Students may access AT&T, Cray, Digital, Hewlett-Packard, IBM, SUN, UNISYS minicomputer/mainframe systems, BITNET, Internet. Residence halls may be equipped with stand-alone microcomputers, networked microcomputers, modems. Client/LAN operating systems include Apple/Macintosh, DOS, OS/2, UNIX/XENIX/AIX, Windows NT, X-windows, LocalTalk/AppleTalk, Novell. Computer facilities are available to all students.
**Fees:** Computer fee is included in tuition/fees.
**Hours:** 24 hours.

**GRADUATE CAREER DATA.** Graduate school percentages: 13% enter law school. 16% enter medical school. 10% enter graduate business programs. 13% enter graduate arts and sciences programs. 1% enter theological school/seminary.

**PROMINENT ALUMNI/AE.** John Quincy Adams; T.S. Eliot; Ralph Waldo Emerson; William James; John F. Kennedy; George Santayana; Henry David Thoreau.

# Hellenic College

**Brookline, MA 02146** **617 731-3500**

**1993-94 Costs.** Tuition: $6,720. Room & board: $4,920. Fees, books, misc. academic expenses (school's estimate): $825.
**Enrollment.** Undergraduates: 56 men, 13 women (full-time). Freshman class: 15 applicants, 15 accepted, 10 enrolled. Graduate enrollment: 90 men, 13 women.
**Test score averages/ranges.** N/A.
**Faculty.** 13 full-time; 5 part-time. 80% of faculty holds doctoral degree. Student/faculty ratio: 6 to 1.
**Selectivity rating.** N/A.

**PROFILE.** Hellenic is a private, church-affiliated, liberal arts college. Its 52-acre campus is located in Brookline, three miles from downtown Boston.

**Accreditation:** NEASC.
**Religious orientation:** Hellenic College is affiliated with the Greek Orthodox Church; no religious requirements.
**Special facilities/museums:** Greek cultural center.
**Athletic facilities:** Basketball, racquetball and tennis courts, volleyball, weight/exercise area, soccer and football fields.

**STUDENT BODY. Undergraduate profile:** 2% are state residents. 2% Asian-American, 3% Black, 2% Hispanic, 87% White, 6% Other.
**Foreign students:** Countries represented include Albania, Canada, Greece, Kenya, Mexico, and Uganda.

**PROGRAMS OF STUDY. Degrees:** B.A.
**Majors:** Classics, Elementary Education, Human Development, Religious Studies.
**Requirements:** General education requirement.
**Special:** Accelerated study. Graduate school at which undergraduates may take graduate-level courses. Preprofessional programs in theology. Study abroad in Greece.

**ADMISSIONS. Academic basis for candidate selection** (in order of priority): School's recommendation, secondary school record, class rank, standardized test scores.
**Nonacademic basis for candidate selection:** Character and personality are emphasized. Extracurricular participation, particular talent or ability, and alumni/ae relationship are considered.
**Requirements:** Graduation from secondary school is required; GED is accepted. No specific distribution of secondary school units required. SAT or ACT is required. Campus visit and interview recommended. No off-campus interviews.
**Procedure:** Suggest filing application by May 11; no deadline. Notification of admission on rolling basis. Freshmen accepted for terms other than fall.
**Special programs:** Admission may be deferred. Credit and/or placement may be granted through CLEP general exams.
**Transfer students:** Transfer students accepted for terms other than fall. Minimum 2.0 GPA required.
**Admissions contact:** Rev. Dr. Albert Demos, Ph.D., Director of Admissions. 617 731-3500, extension 260.

**FINANCIAL AID. Available aid:** Perkins Loans (NDSL) and Stafford Loans (GSL).
**Financial aid statistics:** In 1992-93, 100% of all undergraduate applicants received aid.
**Supporting data/closing dates:** FAFSA/FAF: Priority filing date is May 1. School's own aid application: Priority filing date is May 1. Income tax forms: Priority filing date is May 1. Notification of awards on rolling basis.
**Financial aid contact:** Alexis McGinnis, Director of Financial Aid. 617 731-3500, extension 259.

# Lasell College

**Newton, MA 02166** **617 243-2000**

**1994-95 Costs.** Tuition: $11,475. Room & board: $6,200. Fees, books, misc. academic expenses (school's estimate): $1,125.
**Enrollment.** 500 women (full-time). Freshman class: 618 applicants, 540 accepted, 170 enrolled.
**Test score averages/ranges.** Range of SAT scores of middle 50%: 300-399 verbal, 300-399 math.
**Faculty.** 32 full-time; 57 part-time. 35% of faculty holds highest degree in specific field. Student/faculty ratio: 9 to 1.
**Selectivity rating.** Less competitive.

**PROFILE.** Lasell, founded in 1851, is a private college. Its 60-acre campus is located in Newton, eight miles from Boston.

**Accreditation:** NEASC.
**Religious orientation:** Lasell College is nonsectarian; no religious requirements.
**Library:** Collections totaling over 50,000 volumes, 429 periodical subscriptions and 134 microform items.
**Special facilities/museums:** Child care study facilities, retail management training center, inn, travel agency, art/cultural center.
**Athletic facilities:** Field, gymnasium, weight room.

**STUDENT BODY. Undergraduate profile:** 30% are transfers. 2% Asian-American, 5% Black, 3% Hispanic, 79% White, 11% Other. Average age of undergraduates is 19.
**Undergraduate achievement:** 86% of fall 1992 freshmen returned for fall 1993 term. 68% of entering class graduated.

**Foreign students:** 52 students are from out of the country. Countries represented include Colombia, the Dominican Republic, France, Hong Kong, Japan, and Taiwan; 10 in all.

**PROGRAMS OF STUDY. Degrees:** B.A., B.S.
**Majors:** Business Administration, Education, Exercise Physiology, Fashion Design, Fashion/Retail Merchandising, Hotel/Travel/Tourism Administration, Human Services, Interdisciplinary Studies.
**Requirements:** General education requirement.
**Academic regulations:** Minimum 2.0 GPA required for graduation.
**Special:** Associate's degrees offered. Pass/fail grading option. Internships. 2-2 programs in business administration, early childhood education, fashion/retail merchandising, hotel and travel/tourism administration, human services, and liberal arts/interdisciplinary studies. 2-2 1/2 program in exercise physiology/physical therapist assistant. Teacher certification in early childhood education. Study abroad in Canada and England.
**Academic Assistance:** Remedial reading, math, and study skills.

**ADMISSIONS. Academic basis for candidate selection** (in order of priority): Secondary school record, school's recommendation, class rank, essay, standardized test scores.
**Nonacademic basis for candidate selection:** Extracurricular participation is important. Character and personality and particular talent or ability are considered.
**Requirements:** Graduation from secondary school is required; GED is accepted. No specific distribution of secondary school units required. One year of lab science required of physical therapy assistant and exercise physiology program applicants. GATE Program for applicants not normally admissible. SAT is recommended. Campus visit and interview recommended. Off-campus interviews available with an admissions representative.
**Procedure:** Notification of admission on rolling basis. $300 tuition deposit, refundable until May 1. Freshmen accepted for terms other than fall.
**Special programs:** Admission may be deferred one year. Credit and/or placement may be granted through CEEB Advanced Placement exams. Credit may be granted through CLEP general and subject exams. Placement may be granted through challenge exams.
**Transfer students:** Transfer students accepted for terms other than fall. In fall 1993, 30% of all new students were transfers into all classes. 93 transfer applications were received, 88 were accepted. Application deadline is rolling for fall; rolling for spring. Minimum 2.3 GPA required. Lowest course grade accepted is "C-." Maximum 30 credits may be transferred towards an associate's degree; maximum 80 credits may be transferred towards a bachelor's degree. Minimum 45 credits must be completed at the college to receive a bachelor's degree.
**Admissions contact:** Adrienne Asiaf, Director of Admissions. 617 243-2225.

**FINANCIAL AID. Available aid:** Pell grants, SEOG, state scholarships and grants, school scholarships and grants, private scholarships and grants, academic merit scholarships, and aid for undergraduate foreign students. Perkins Loans (NDSL), PLUS, Stafford Loans (GSL), state loans, school loans, private loans, and SLS. AMS and family tuition reduction.
**Financial aid statistics:** 1% of aid is not need-based. In 1993-94, 80% of all freshman applicants received aid. Average amounts of aid awarded freshmen: Scholarships and grants, $4,140; loans, $2,444.
**Supporting data/closing dates:** FAFSA/FAF: Accepted on rolling basis. Income tax forms: Accepted on rolling basis. Notification of awards on rolling basis.
**Financial aid contact:** Michael Mullaney, Director of Financial Aid. 617 243-2227.

## Lesley College

Cambridge, MA 02138-2790 — 617 868-9600

**1994-95 Costs.** Tuition: $12,275. Room & Board: $5,600. Fees, books, misc. academic expenses (school's estimate): $670.
**Enrollment.** 499 women (full-time). Freshman class: 299 applicants, 249 accepted, 124 enrolled. Graduate enrollment: 910 men, 4,569 women.
**Test score averages/ranges.** Average SAT scores: 827 combined.
**Faculty.** 81 full-time. 60% of faculty holds highest degree in specific field. Student/faculty ratio: 14 to 1.
**Selectivity rating.** Less competitive.

**PROFILE.** Lesley, founded in 1909 as a teacher-training school, is a private college for women; men are admitted only to its graduate and adult baccalaureate degree programs. Programs are offered through the Undergraduate School, the Graduate School, and the School of Programs in Management for Business and Industry. Its five-acre campus is located in Cambridge, adjacent to Harvard University.

**Accreditation:** NEASC.
**Religious orientation:** Lesley College is nonsectarian; no religious requirements.
**Library:** Collections totaling over 100,000 volumes, 744 periodical subscriptions, and 840,000 microform items.
**Special facilities/museums:** Audio-visual department for student teachers.
**Athletic facilities:** Gymnasium, Nautilus room.

**STUDENT BODY. Undergraduate profile:** 66% are state residents; 30% are transfers. 3% Asian-American, 7% Black, 3% Hispanic, 1% Native American, 84% White, 2% Other. Average age of undergraduates is 20.
**Freshman profile:** 4% of freshmen who took SAT scored 600 or over on verbal, 6% scored 600 or over on math; 13% scored 500 or over on verbal, 25% scored 500 or over on math; 58% scored 400 or over on verbal, 59% scored 400 or over on math; 100% scored 300 or over on verbal, 100% scored 300 or over on math. Majority of accepted applicants took SAT. 70% of freshmen come from public schools.
**Undergraduate achievement:** 75% of fall 1991 freshmen returned for fall 1992 term. 60% of entering class graduated. 8% of students who completed a degree program went on to graduate study within one year.
**Foreign students:** 19 students are from out of the country. Seven countries represented in all.

**PROGRAMS OF STUDY. Degrees:** B.A.Beh.Sci., B.S., B.S.Ed., B.S.Mgmt.
**Majors:** Education, Human Services, Liberal Studies, Management.
**Distribution of degrees:** The majors with the highest enrollment are education, human services, and management.
**Requirements:** General education requirement.
**Academic regulations:** Minimum 2.00 GPA must be maintained.
**Special:** Minors offered in art, biology, computer technology, counseling, general science, history, literature and writing, math, music, physical science, psychology, and sociology. Beginning in freshmen year, students participate not only in classroom study but also in professional field placements with schools and human service organizations. Associate's degrees offered. Independent study. Pass/fail grading option. Internships. Graduate school at which undergraduates may take graduate-level courses. Five-year master's program in counseling/psychology. Washington Semester. Teacher certification in early childhood, elementary, and special education. Exchange programs abroad in England (Bradford Coll, Hull Coll).
**Academic Assistance:** Remedial reading, writing, math, and study skills. Nonremedial tutoring.

**ADMISSIONS. Academic basis for candidate selection** (in order of priority): Secondary school record, school's recommendation, standardized test scores, class rank, essay.
**Nonacademic basis for candidate selection:** Character and personality are emphasized. Extracurricular participation and particular talent or ability are important. Geographical distribution and alumni/ae relationship are considered.
**Requirements:** Graduation from secondary school is required; GED is accepted. 15 units and the following program of study are required: 4 units of English, 2 units of math, 1 unit of lab science, 1 unit of social studies, 1 unit of history, 6 units of academic electives. SAT or ACT is required. Campus visit and interview recommended. Off-campus interviews available with an admissions representative.
**Procedure:** Take SAT or ACT by December of 12th year. Visit college for interview by March of 12th year. Suggest filing application by April 1; no deadline. Notification of admission on rolling basis. Reply is required by May 1. $100 nonrefundable tuition deposit. $100 nonrefundable room deposit. Freshmen accepted for terms other than fall.
**Special programs:** Admission may be deferred one year. Credit and/or placement may be granted through CEEB Advanced Placement exams for scores of 3 or higher. Early decision program. In fall 1992, 27 applied for early decision and 25 were accepted. Deadline for applying for early decision is December 1.
**Transfer students:** Transfer students accepted for terms other than fall. In fall 1992, 30% of all new students were transfers into all classes. 75 transfer applications were received, 71 were accepted. Application deadline is June 15 for fall; December 15 for spring. Minimum 2.0 GPA required. Lowest course grade accepted is "C-." At least 63 semester hours must be completed at the college to receive degree.
**Admissions contact:** Carol Streit, Ph.D., Interim Director of Admissions. 617 349-8800.

**FINANCIAL AID. Available aid:** Pell grants, SEOG, state scholarships and grants, school scholarships and grants, private scholarships and grants, and academic merit scholarships. Perkins Loans (NDSL), PLUS, Stafford Loans (GSL), state loans, and SLS. AMS.
**Financial aid statistics:** In 1992-93, 88% of all undergraduate applicants received aid; 94% of freshman applicants. Average amounts of aid awarded freshmen: Scholarships and grants, $1,000; loans, $2,695.
**Supporting data/closing dates:** FAFSA/FAF: Priority filing date is February 1. School's own aid application: Priority filing date is March 1. State aid form: Priority filing date is February 1. Income tax forms: Priority filing date is April 30. Notification of awards begins March 15.
**Financial aid contact:** F. Duane Quinn, M.A., Director of Financial Aid. 617 349-8710.

## Massachusetts College of Art

Boston, MA 02115 — 617 232-1555

**1993-94 Costs.** Tuition: $1,465 (state residents), $6,422 (out-of-state). Room: $3,500. Board: $1,895. Fees, books, misc. academic expenses (school's estimate): $4,080.
**Enrollment.** Undergraduates: 408 men, 585 women (full-time). Freshman class: 959 applicants, 443 accepted, 288 enrolled. Graduate enrollment: 34 men, 70 women.
**Test score averages/ranges.** Average SAT scores: 476 verbal, 487 math. Range of SAT scores of middle 50%: 411-552 verbal, 410-558 math.
**Faculty.** 62 full-time; 30 part-time. 43% of faculty holds highest degree in specific field. Student/faculty ratio: 14 to 1.
**Selectivity rating.** Competitive.

**PROFILE.** The Massachusetts College of Art, founded in 1873, is a public college. Its nine-acre campus is located in the Fenway area of Boston.

**Accreditation:** NEASC. Professionally accredited by the National Association of Schools of Art and Design.
**Religious orientation:** Massachusetts College of Art is nonsectarian; no religious requirements.
**Library:** Collections totaling over 90,250 volumes, 325 periodical subscriptions, and 65,000 microform items.
**Special facilities/museums:** Seven art galleries, foundry, glass furnaces, ceramic kiln, video and film studios, performance spaces, Polaroid 20x24 camera, individual studio spaces, design research unit.
**Athletic facilities:** Gymnasium, health fitness center, performance studio, ping-pong room, swimming pool, weight training and wrestling room.

**STUDENT BODY. Undergraduate profile:** 80% are state residents; 55% are transfers. 3% Asian-American, 3% Black, 2% Hispanic, 1% Native American, 83% White, 8% Other. Average age of undergraduates is 26.
**Freshman profile:** 2% of freshmen who took SAT scored 700 or over on verbal; 11% scored 600 or over on verbal, 10% scored 600 or over on math; 41% scored 500 or over on verbal, 46% scored 500 or over on math; 80% scored 400 or over on verbal, 78% scored 400 or over on math; 96% scored 300 or over on verbal, 96% scored 300 or over on math. 100% of accepted applicants took SAT. 85% of freshmen come from public schools.

**Undergraduate achievement:** 84% of fall 1991 freshmen returned for fall 1992 term. 17% of entering class graduated. 10% of students who completed a degree program went on to graduate study within one year.
**Foreign students:** 61 students are from out of the country. Countries represented include Hong Kong, Japan, Norway, Peru, Taiwan, and Venezuela; 32 in all.

**PROGRAMS OF STUDY. Degrees:** B.F.A.
**Majors:** Architectural Design, Art Education, Art History, Ceramics, Fashion Design, Fibers, Filmmaking, Glass, Graphic Design, Illustration, Industrial Design, Interrelated Media, Metals, Painting, Photography, Printmaking, Printmaking/Graphic Design, Sculpture.
**Distribution of degrees:** The majors with the highest enrollment are design, painting, and photography; art history, fibers, and ceramics have the lowest.
**Requirements:** General education requirement.
**Special:** Minors offered in all departments and in video. Self-designed majors. Double majors. Independent study. Pass/fail grading option. Internships. Cooperative education programs. Graduate school at which undergraduates may take graduate-level courses. Member of Association of Independent Colleges of Art and Design (AICAD), College Academic Program Sharing (CAPS), Consortium of East Coast Art Schools, and Pro Arts Consortium. Exchange possible through Consortium of East Coast Art Schools and Public College Exchange Program. Teacher certification in elementary and secondary education. Certification in specific subject areas. Exchange programs abroad in England (Central St. Martins Sch of Art and Design, Chelsea Sch of Art, and West Surrey Coll of Art and Design). Study abroad also in Costa Rica, Greece, Italy, Jamaica, Mexico, and Nepal.
**Academic Assistance:** Remedial writing. Nonremedial tutoring.

**ADMISSIONS. Academic basis for candidate selection** (in order of priority): Secondary school record, essay, class rank, standardized test scores, school's recommendation.
**Nonacademic basis for candidate selection:** Particular talent or ability is emphasized. Character and personality and extracurricular participation are important. Geographical distribution and alumni/ae relationship are considered.
**Requirements:** Graduation from secondary school is required; GED is accepted. 16 units and the following program of study are required: 4 units of English, 3 units of math, 2 units of lab science, 2 units of foreign language, 1 unit of social studies, 1 unit of history, 3 units of academic electives. Portfolio required, with a minimum of 15 pieces of work. Combined SAT scores are compared with weighted class rank to determine eligibility index. Preference is given to in-state applicants. Critical Studies Presemester Program and Freshman Studio Presemester Summer Session for applicants not normally admissible. SAT is required. Campus visit and interview recommended. No off-campus interviews.
**Procedure:** Take SAT by January of 12th year. Visit college for interview by March of 12th year. Application deadline is April 1. Notification of admission on rolling basis. Reply is required by May 1 or within one month of acceptance. $50 nonrefundable tuition deposit. $300 nonrefundable room deposit. Freshmen accepted for fall term only.
**Special programs:** Admission may be deferred one year. Credit and/or placement may be granted through CEEB Advanced Placement exams for scores of 4 or higher. Credit and/or placement may be granted through CLEP general and subject exams. Credit and placement may be granted through challenge exams and life experience. Early decision program. Deadline for applying for early decision is November 1.
**Transfer students:** Transfer students accepted for terms other than fall. In fall 1992, 55% of all new students were transfers into all classes. 561 transfer applications were received, 269 were accepted. Application deadline is April 1 for fall; November 1 for spring. Minimum 3.0 GPA recommended. Lowest course grade accepted is "C." Maximum number of transferable credits is 78 semester hours. At least 66 semester hours must be completed at the college to receive degree.
**Admissions contact:** Kay Ransdell, Associate Dean for Admissions and Retention. 617 232-1555.

**FINANCIAL AID. Available aid:** Pell grants, SEOG, state scholarships and grants, school scholarships, and private grants. Perkins Loans (NDSL), PLUS, Stafford Loans (GSL), and SLS. AMS and Tuition Management Systems.
**Financial aid statistics:** 14% of aid is not need-based. In 1992-93, 100% of all undergraduate applicants received aid. Average amounts of aid awarded freshmen: Scholarships and grants, $1,780; loans, $2,100.
**Supporting data/closing dates:** FAFSA/FAF/FFS: Priority filing date is May 1; accepted on rolling basis. State aid form: Priority filing date is May 1. Income tax forms: Accepted on rolling basis. Notification of awards on rolling basis.
**Financial aid contact:** Ken Berryhill, M.A.Ed., Director of Financial Aid. 617 232-1555, extension 300.

# Massachusetts Institute of Technology

**Cambridge, MA 02139 — 617 253-1000**

**1994-95 Costs.** Tuition: $20,100. Room & board: $5,975. Fees, books, misc. academic expenses (school's estimate): $1,325.
**Enrollment.** Undergraduates: 2,962 men, 1,519 women (full-time). Freshman class: 6,411 applicants, 2,140 accepted, 1,081 enrolled. Graduate enrollment: 4,052 men, 1,229 women.
**Test score averages/ranges.** Range of SAT scores of middle 50%: 570-690 verbal, 720-780 math. Range of ACT scores of middle 50%: 27-31 English, 31-35 math.
**Faculty.** 939 full-time; 33 part-time. 99% of faculty holds highest degree in specific field. Student/faculty ratio: 5 to 1.
**Selectivity rating.** Most competitive.

**PROFILE.** MIT, founded in 1865, is a private institution. Programs are offered through the Schools of Architecture and Planning, Engineering, Humanities and Social Science, Management, and Science. Its 125-acre campus is located in Cambridge.
**Accreditation:** NEASC. Professionally accredited by the Accreditation Board for Engineering and Technology, the American Assembly of Collegiate Schools of Business, the American Psychological Association, the National Architecture Accrediting Board.
**Religious orientation:** Massachusetts Institute of Technology is nonsectarian; no religious requirements.
**Library:** Collections totaling over 2,320,524 volumes, 21,136 periodical subscriptions, and 1,969,869 microform items.
**Special facilities/museums:** Museum, theatre, visual arts center, institute for the history of science, magnet, artificial intelligence, plasma fusion, and nuclear reactor labs, linear accelerator.
**Athletic facilities:** Athletic center with ice rink, indoor track, basketball, squash, and tennis courts, swimming pool, sailing pavilion, boathouse, gymnasiums for basketball, gymnastics, volleyball, softball diamonds, practice fields, stadium for track, field hockey, football, lacrosse, soccer, and other athletic fields, fitness center, weight room.

**STUDENT BODY. Undergraduate profile:** 8% are state residents; 3% are transfers. 27% Asian-American, 6% Black, 9% Hispanic, 1% Native American, 57% White. Average age of undergraduates is 20.
**Freshman profile:** 19% of freshmen who took SAT scored 700 or over on verbal, 83% scored 700 or over on math; 62% scored 600 or over on verbal, 97% scored 600 or over on math; 83% scored 500 or over on verbal, 98% scored 500 or over on math; 88% scored 400 or over on verbal; 89% scored 300 or over on verbal. 99% of accepted applicants took SAT; 20% took ACT. 76% of freshmen come from public schools.
**Undergraduate achievement:** 97% of fall 1992 freshmen returned for fall 1993 term. 87% of entering class graduated. 55% of students who completed a degree program went on to graduate study within one year.
**Foreign students:** 373 students are from out of the country. Countries represented include Canada, China, Hong Kong, India, Mexico, and Pakistan; 84 in all.

**PROGRAMS OF STUDY. Degrees:** S.B.
**Majors:** Aeronautics/Astronautics, Anthropology/Archaeology, Architecture/Building Technology, Art/Design, Biology/Life Sciences, Biomedical Engineering, Chemical Engineering, Chemistry, Civil/Environmental Engineering, Cognitive Science, Earth/Atmospheric/Planetary Sciences, Economics, Electrical Engineering/Computer Science, Foreign Languages/Literatures, History, Humanities, Humanities/Engineering, Humanities/Science, Latin American Studies, Literature, Management Science, Materials Science/Engineering, Mathematics, Mechanical Engineering, Music, Naval Architecture/Marine Engineering, Nuclear Engineering, Ocean Engineering, Philosophy, Physics, Planning, Political Science, Russian/Slavic Studies, Science/Technology/Society, Writing.
**Distribution of degrees:** The majors with the highest enrollment are electrical engineering/computer science and mechanical engineering; ocean engineering, philosophy, and nuclear engineering have the lowest.
**Requirements:** General education requirement.
**Special:** Minors offered in all major areas. Many interdepartmental majors available. Undergraduate Research Opportunities Program (UROP). Self-designed majors. Double majors. Dual degrees. Accelerated study. Pass/fail grading option. Internships. Cooperative education programs. Graduate school at which undergraduates may take graduate-level courses. Preprofessional programs in law and medicine. 5-year M.Eng. program in the department of electrical engineering and computer science. Cross-registration with Harvard U and Wellesley Coll. Joint programs with Harvard U and Woods Hole Oceanographic Inst. One of nine institutions operating Brookhaven National Labs. Study abroad possible. ROTC, NROTC, and AFROTC.
**Honors:** Phi Beta Kappa. Honor societies.
**Academic Assistance:** Remedial writing.

**STUDENT LIFE. Housing:** All freshmen must live on campus. Coed and women's dorms. Sorority and fraternity housing. School-owned/operated apartments. On-campus married-student housing. Language and special-interest housing, student-operated cooperative houses. 93% of students live in college housing.
**Social atmosphere:** "The heavy workload has a negative impact on social life," reports the student newspaper, "but MIT was voted the twenty-fifth top party school by *Playboy* magazine. Culturally, nothing beats Boston." Students tend less to frequent outside establishments than to "congregate in their own living groups, and that is where social life is centered. Fraternities and dormitories throw frequent parties. The Lecture Series Committee has movies every weekend that are very popular."
**Services and counseling/handicapped student services:** Placement services. Health service. Women's center. Counseling services for minority, military, and veteran students. Birth control, personal, and psychological counseling. Career and academic guidance services. Religious counseling. Physically disabled student services. Notetaking services. Reader services for the blind.
**Campus organizations:** Undergraduate student government. Student newspaper (Tech, published twice/week). Literary magazine. Yearbook. Radio station. Chamber groups, glee club, concert band, brass ensemble, orchestra, debating, drama groups, outing and flying clubs, ham radio station, engineering journal, Amnesty International, Gays and Lesbians at MIT, Association of Women Students, political, service, social action, and special-interest groups, 219 organizations in all. 30 fraternities, 29 chapter houses; five sororities, one chapter house. 46% of men join a fraternity. 30% of women join a sorority.
**Religious organizations:** Groups representing all major religious faiths.
**Minority/foreign student organizations:** Black Students Union, National Society of Black Engineers, League of United Chicanos, Society of Hispanic Professional Engineers, American Indian Science and Engineering Society, other minority student groups. International Students Association, African, Brazilian, Chinese, Czech and Slovak, Filipino, Indian, Iranian, Korean, Lebanese, Pakistani, Sri Lankan, Vietnamese, and other foreign student groups.

**ATHLETICS. Physical education requirements:** Eight credit points (four activities) of physical education required; swimming test must also be passed.
**Intercollegiate competition:** 30% of students participate. Alpine skiing (M,W), baseball (M), basketball (M,W), crew (M,W), cross-country (M,W), diving (M,W), fencing (M,W), field hockey (W), football (M), golf (M), gymnastics (M,W), lacrosse (M,W), Nordic skiing (M,W), pistol (M,W), riflery (M,W), sailing (M,W), soccer (M,W), softball (W), squash (M), swimming (M,W), tennis (M,W), track and field (indoor) (M), track and field (outdoor) (M,W), volleyball (M,W), water polo (M), wrestling (M). Member of Constitu-

tion Athletic Conference, Eastern Collegiate Football Conference, ECAC, Massachusetts Association of Intercollegiate Athletics for Women, NCAA Division III, New England Women's 8.

**Intramural and club sports:** 65% of students participate. Intramural badminton, basketball, football, frisbee, ice hockey, octathon, pentathlon, pool (billiards), soccer, softball, squash, table tennis, team tennis, volleyball, water polo. Men's club archery, bowling, boxing, cheerleading, cycling, ice hockey, martial arts, rugby, ultimate frisbee. Women's club archery, bowling, boxing, cheerleading, cycling, ice hockey, martial arts, rugby, unihoc, ultimate frisbee, water polo.

**ADMISSIONS. Academic basis for candidate selection** (in order of priority): Secondary school record, standardized test scores, class rank, school's recommendation, essay.

**Nonacademic basis for candidate selection:** Character and personality, extracurricular participation, and particular talent or ability are emphasized. Alumni/ae relationship is considered.

**Requirements:** Graduation from secondary school is recommended; GED is accepted. No specific distribution of secondary school units required. Rank in top tenth of secondary school class recommended. SAT or ACT is required. ACH required. Admissions interview required. Off-campus interviews available with an alumni representative.

**Procedure:** Take SAT or ACT by January of 12th year. Take ACH by January of 12th year. Visit college for interview by December 15 of 12th year. Application deadline is January 1. Notification of admission by April 1. Reply is required by May 1. Freshmen accepted for fall term only.

**Special programs:** Admission may be deferred one year. Credit and/or placement may be granted through CEEB Advanced Placement exams for scores of 4 or higher. Early decision program. In fall 1993, 1,200 applied for early decision and 524 were accepted. Deadline for applying for early decision is November 1.

**Transfer students:** Transfer students accepted for terms other than fall. In fall 1993, 3% of all new students were transfers into all classes. 300 transfer applications were received, 43 were accepted. Application deadline is March 15 for fall; November 15 for spring. Three ACH (science, math, and either English or history) required. Minimum 3.0 GPA recommended. Lowest course grade accepted is "B."

**Admissions contact:** Michael C. Behnke, Director of Admissions. 617 253-4791.

**FINANCIAL AID. Available aid:** Pell grants, SEOG, state scholarships and grants, school grants, private scholarships and grants, ROTC scholarships, and aid for undergraduate foreign students. Perkins Loans (NDSL), PLUS, Stafford Loans (GSL), school loans, and SLS. Installment plan.

**Financial aid statistics:** In 1993-94, 91% of all undergraduate applicants received aid; 82% of freshman applicants. Average amounts of aid awarded freshmen: Scholarships and grants, $11,670; loans, $4,452.

**Supporting data/closing dates:** FAFSA/FAF: Priority filing date is March 1. School's own aid application: Priority filing date is January 14. Income tax forms: Priority filing date is May 2; accepted on rolling basis. Notification of awards begins early April.

**Financial aid contact:** Stanley Hudson, Director of Financial Aid. 617 253-4971.

**STUDENT EMPLOYMENT.** College Work/Study Program. Institutional employment. 55% of full-time undergraduates work on campus during school year. Students may expect to earn an average of $1,650 during school year. Off-campus part-time employment opportunities rated "excellent."

**COMPUTER FACILITIES.** 900 IBM/IBM-compatible, Macintosh/Apple, and RISC-/UNIX-based microcomputers; all are networked. Students may access Cray, IBM minicomputer/mainframe systems, Internet. Residence halls may be equipped with networked microcomputers. Client/LAN operating systems include Apple/Macintosh, DOS, UNIX/XENIX/AIX, Windows NT, X-windows. Numerous computer languages, applications, communications services, and packages available; 100 in all. Computer facilities are available to all students.

**Fees:** None.

**Hours:** 24 hours.

**GRADUATE CAREER DATA.** Graduate school percentages: 5% enter law school. 10% enter medical school. Highest graduate school enrollments: Boston U, Harvard U, MIT, Stanford U, UC Berkeley. 42% of graduates choose careers in business and industry. Companies and businesses that hire graduates: Bell Labs, Ford Motor Co., General Electric, Hewlett-Packard, IBM, Jet Propulsion Lab, McKinsey & Co., Motorola, Procter & Gamble, Schlumberger.

**PROMINENT ALUMNI/AE.** I.M. Pei, architect; Kenneth Olsen, founder, Digital Equipment Corp.; Les Aspin, former U.S. secretary of defense; Sheila Widnall, secretary of the Air Force.

# Massachusetts Maritime Academy

**Buzzards Bay, MA 02532-1803** — **508 830-5000**

**1993-94 Costs.** Tuition: $1,434 (state residents), $6,174 (out-of-state). Room: $1,910. Board: $2,100. Fees, books, misc. academic expenses (school's estimate): $2,435.

**Enrollment.** Undergraduates: 690 men, 44 women (full-time). Freshman class: 600 applicants, 405 accepted, 266 enrolled.

**Test score averages/ranges.** N/A.

**Faculty.** 53 full-time; 2 part-time. 70% of faculty holds highest degree in specific field. Student/faculty ratio: 13 to 1.

**Selectivity rating.** N/A.

**PROFILE.** The Massachusetts Maritime Academy is a public academy. Founded in 1891, it adopted coeducation in 1975. Its program is designed to qualify candidates to become officers in the U.S. Merchant Marine. Its 55-acre campus is located in Buzzards Bay, 55 miles south of Boston.

**Accreditation:** NEASC.

**Religious orientation:** Massachusetts Maritime Academy is nonsectarian; no religious requirements.

**Library:** Collections totaling over 42,000 volumes, 415 periodical subscriptions and 870 microform items.

**Special facilities/museums:** Maritime museum, all-weather video navigation and radar-training simulator, slow-speed diesel-training simulator, bridge-control simulator, 548-foot training ship, spill management/cargo handling simulator.

**Athletic facilities:** Gymnasiums, swimming pool, basketball, racquetball, and volleyball courts, aerobics, boxing, free weight, Nautilus, and wrestling rooms, baseball, football, lacrosse, practice, and soccer fields, sailing center, rifle range.

**STUDENT BODY. Undergraduate profile:** 80% are state residents; 12% are transfers. 1% Asian-American, 1% Black, 2% Hispanic, 96% White. Average age of undergraduates is 20.

**Undergraduate achievement:** 85% of fall 1992 freshmen returned for fall 1993 term. 70% of entering class graduated.

**Foreign students:** 13 students are from out of the country. Countries represented include Nigeria, Panama, and Taiwan; seven in all.

**PROGRAMS OF STUDY. Degrees:** B.S.

**Majors:** Environmental Protection/Marine Safety, Facilities/Plant Engineering, Marine Engineering, Marine Transportation.

**Requirements:** General education requirement.

**Special:** Concentrations offered in business management, facilities/plant engineering, marine fisheries, and mechanical engineering. Courses offered in naval science to qualify for commissions in the Navy. Cadets receiving student incentive payments must apply for and accept (if offered) a commission in the Naval Reserve. U.S. Coast Guard license exam required for graduation. Winter sea-training cruises with visits to foreign and domestic ports. Minimum of 180 days at sea required for graduation; academic credit received fulfills Maritime Administration's six-month shipboard experience requirement. Dual degrees. Cooperative education programs. Member of Southeastern Massachusetts College Consortium and SACHEM consortium. Sea Semester.

**ADMISSIONS. Academic basis for candidate selection** (in order of priority): Secondary school record, school's recommendation, standardized test scores, class rank, essay.

**Nonacademic basis for candidate selection:** Character and personality are emphasized. Extracurricular participation is important. Particular talent or ability and alumni/ae relationship are considered.

**Requirements:** Graduation from secondary school is required; GED is accepted. 16 units and the following program of study are required: 4 units of English, 3 units of math, 2 units of lab science, 3 units of social studies, 2 units of history, 1 unit of electives. Physical exam and eligibility for original U.S. Coast Guard license required. SAT is required; ACT may be substituted. ACH recommended. Campus visit and interview recommended. Off-campus interviews available with an admissions representative.

**Procedure:** Suggest filing application by November 1. Application deadline is June 1. Notification of admission on rolling basis. Reply is required within 30 days of acceptance. $100 nonrefundable tuition deposit. Freshmen accepted for fall term only.

**Special programs:** Admission may be deferred two years. Credit and/or placement may be granted through CEEB Advanced Placement exams for scores of 3 or higher. Credit and/or placement may be granted through CLEP general and subject exams. Early decision program. In fall 1993, 45 applied for early decision and 39 were accepted. Deadline for applying for early decision is November 1.

**Transfer students:** Transfer students accepted for terms other than fall. In fall 1993, 12% of all new students were transfers into all classes. 49 transfer applications were received, 18 were accepted. Application deadline is June 1. Minimum 2.0 GPA recommended. Lowest course grade accepted is "C." At least 30 semester hours must be completed at the academy to receive degree.

**Admissions contact:** Cdr. Keith D. Rabine, M.A., Director of Admissions. 508 759-5761, extension 314.

**FINANCIAL AID. Available aid:** Pell grants, SEOG, state scholarships, school scholarships, and private scholarships. Perkins Loans (NDSL), PLUS, Stafford Loans (GSL), and SLS. AMS.

**Financial aid statistics:** Average amounts of aid awarded freshmen: Scholarships and grants, $900; loans, $1,400.

**Supporting data/closing dates:** FAFSA: Priority filing date is May 1. School's own aid application: Priority filing date is May 1. Income tax forms: Priority filing date is May 1. Notification of awards begins May 1.

**Financial aid contact:** Cdr. Mary Lou Norton, Director of Financial Aid. 508 759-5761, extension 315.

# Merrimack College

**North Andover, MA 01845** — **508 837-5000**

**1994-95 Costs.** Tuition: $12,500. Room: $3,550. Board: $2,850. Fees, books, misc. academic expenses (school's estimate): $475.

**Enrollment.** Undergraduates: 1,069 men, 931 women (full-time). Freshman class: 1,981 applicants, 1,541 accepted, 517 enrolled.

**Test score averages/ranges.** Average SAT scores: 470 verbal, 490 math. Range of SAT scores of middle 50%: 450-550 verbal, 470-580 math.

**Faculty.** 126 full-time; 52 part-time. 67% of faculty holds doctoral degree. Student/faculty ratio: 15 to 1.

**Selectivity rating.** Less competitive.

**PROFILE.** Merrimack, founded in 1947, is a private, church-affiliated, liberal arts college. Programs are offered through the Divisions of Business Administration, Continuing Education, Humanities, Science and Engineering, and Social Sciences. Its 220-acre campus is located in North Andover, 25 miles north of Boston.

**Accreditation:** NEASC. Professionally accredited by the Accreditation Board for Engineering and Technology, the National Council for Accreditation of Teacher Education.

**Religious orientation:** Merrimack College is affiliated with the Roman Catholic Church (Order of St. Augustine); two semesters of religion/theology required.
**Library:** Collections totaling over 149,700 volumes, 900 periodical subscriptions, and 7,200 microform items.
**Athletic facilities:** Gymnasium, ice rink, basketball, racquetball, squash, tennis, and volleyball courts, weight room, baseball, intramural, soccer, and softball fields.

**STUDENT BODY. Undergraduate profile:** 70% are state residents; 14% are transfers. 1% Asian-American, 1% Black, 3% Hispanic, 95% White. Average age of undergraduates is 20.
**Freshman profile:** 99% of accepted applicants took SAT; 1% took ACT. 60% of freshmen come from public schools.
**Undergraduate achievement:** 82% of fall 1992 freshmen returned for fall 1993 term. 65% of entering class graduated.
**Foreign students:** 35 students are from out of the country. Countries represented include Canada, Indonesia, Japan, the Netherlands Antilles, Russia, and Saudi Arabia; 18 in all.

**PROGRAMS OF STUDY. Degrees:** B.A., B.S.
**Majors:** Accounting, Biology, Biology Teaching, Business Economics, Chemistry, Chemistry Teaching, Civil Engineering, Computer Science, Economics, Electrical Engineering, English, English Teaching, Finance, Health Sciences, History, History Teaching, International Business, Management, Marketing, Mathematics, Mathematics Teaching, Medical Technology, Philosophy, Physics, Physics Teaching, Political Science/Government, Psychology, Psychology Teaching, Religious Studies, Sociology.
**Distribution of degrees:** The majors with the highest enrollment are marketing, psychology, and English; philosophy and religious studies have the lowest.
**Requirements:** General education requirement.
**Academic regulations:** Freshmen must maintain minimum 1.5 GPA; sophomores, 1.8 GPA; juniors, 2.0 GPA; seniors, 2.0 GPA.
**Special:** Minors offered in most majors and in fine arts and modern languages. Interdepartmental major in liberal arts. Associate's degrees offered. Self-designed majors. Double majors. Dual degrees. Independent study. Pass/fail grading option. Internships. Cooperative education programs. Preprofessional programs in law, medicine, and dentistry. 3-1 medical technology program. Member of Northeast Consortium of Colleges and Universities in Massachusetts. Washington Semester. Teacher certification in elementary and secondary education. Certification in specific subject areas. Exchange program abroad in England (Richmond Coll). Study abroad also in Austria, China, France, Germany, Italy, and Spain. AFROTC at U of Massachusetts at Lowell.
**Honors:** Honor societies.
**Academic Assistance:** Nonremedial tutoring.

**STUDENT LIFE. Housing:** Students may live on or off campus. Coed dorms. School-owned/operated apartments. Townhouses. 53% of students live in college housing.
**Social atmosphere:** The student newspaper reports, "Merrimack is generally a suitcase college; therefore, Thursday night is the active party night. The Greeks really keep social life a possibility on campus. Most of their parties are sponsored off campus with bus transportation mandatory. The Student's Program Board does sponsor events but mostly on the movie, comedy, and casino nights. Students like to gather at frat parties at local bars, and Boston is only 20 minutes away. Many students attend Patriots and Celtics games. Popular events include the Semiformal, Interlude, Senior and Junior Week, Greek Games, and any hockey game–Merrimack is a Division I team."
**Services and counseling/handicapped student services:** Placement services. Health service. Personal and psychological counseling. Career and academic guidance services. Religious counseling.
**Campus organizations:** Undergraduate student government. Student newspaper (Argus, published once/month). Literary magazine. Yearbook. TV station. Liturgical chorale, On Stagers, film series, Commuters Council, Model UN, College Democrats, College Republicans, ski club, academic groups, 43 organizations in all. Five fraternities, no chapter houses; three sororities, no chapter houses.
**Religious organizations:** Merrimaction, religious studies support group, Campus Ministry, MORE retreat program, other religious groups.
**Minority/foreign student organizations:** Society Organized Against Racism. Intercultural Club.

**ATHLETICS. Physical education requirements:** None.
**Intercollegiate competition:** 13% of students participate. Baseball (M), basketball (M,W), cross-country (M,W), field hockey (W), golf (M,W), ice hockey (M), lacrosse (M), soccer (M,W), softball (W), tennis (M,W), volleyball (W). Member of ECAC, Hockey East Association, NCAA Division I for ice hockey, NCAA Division II, Northeast 10 Conference.
**Intramural and club sports:** 50% of students participate. Intramural basketball, flag football, floor hockey, ice hockey, racquetball, soccer, softball, street hockey, squash, tennis, ultimate frisbee, volleyball, walleyball. Men's club track, volleyball. Women's club track.

**ADMISSIONS. Academic basis for candidate selection** (in order of priority): Secondary school record, class rank, standardized test scores, school's recommendation, essay.
**Nonacademic basis for candidate selection:** Extracurricular participation, geographical distribution, and alumni/ae relationship are important. Character and personality and particular talent or ability are considered.
**Requirements:** Graduation from secondary school is required; GED is accepted. 16 units and the following program of study are required: 4 units of English, 3 units of math, 1 unit of science, 2 units of social studies, 6 units of electives. Minimum combined SAT score of 800, rank in top half of secondary school class, and minimum 2.5 GPA recommended. 4 units of math and 3 units of science required of engineering and science program applicants. Physics required of engineering program applicants. SAT and 3 ACHs, or ACT required. Campus visit and interview recommended. No off-campus interviews.
**Procedure:** Take SAT or ACT by January 31 of 12th year. Visit college for interview by February of 12th year. Application deadline is March 1. Notification of admission on rolling basis beginning mid-February. Reply is required by May 1. $200 tuition deposit, refundable until May 1. $100 room deposit, refundable until May 1. Freshmen accepted for terms other than fall.
**Special programs:** Admission may be deferred one year. Credit and/or placement may be granted through CEEB Advanced Placement exams for scores of 3 or higher. Early decision program. In fall 1993, 27 applied for early decision and 16 were accepted. Deadline for applying for Early Decision I is November 15; Early Decision II, January 15. Early entrance/early admission program.
**Transfer students:** Transfer students accepted for terms other than fall. In fall 1993, 14% of all new students were transfers into all classes. 209 transfer applications were received, 149 were accepted. Application deadline is June 1 for fall; December 1 for spring. Minimum 2.0 GPA required. Lowest course grade accepted is "C." Maximum number of transferable credits is 75 semester hours. At least 45 semester hours must be completed at the college to receive degree.
**Admissions contact:** John W. Hamel, M.B.A., Acting Dean of Admissions and Financial Aid. 508 837-5100.

**FINANCIAL AID. Available aid:** Pell grants, SEOG, state scholarships and grants, school scholarships and grants, private scholarships, academic merit scholarships, and athletic scholarships. Perkins Loans (NDSL), PLUS, Stafford Loans (GSL), school loans, and SLS. MEFA. TERI. Knight Tuition Plans, family tuition reduction, and guaranteed tuition.
**Financial aid statistics:** 13% of aid is not need-based. In 1993-94, 90% of all undergraduate applicants received aid; 90% of freshman applicants. Average amounts of aid awarded freshmen: Scholarships and grants, $7,500; loans, $4,000.
**Supporting data/closing dates:** FAFSA/FAF: Priority filing date is March 1. Income tax forms: Accepted on rolling basis. Notification of awards begins March 15.
**Financial aid contact:** Christine Mordach, M.B.A., Director of Financial Aid. 508 837-5186.

**STUDENT EMPLOYMENT.** College Work/Study Program. Institutional employment. 30% of full-time undergraduates work on campus during school year. Students may expect to earn an average of $1,200 during school year. Freshmen are discouraged from working during their first term. Off-campus part-time employment opportunities rated "good."

**COMPUTER FACILITIES.** 130 IBM/IBM-compatible, Macintosh/Apple, and RISC-/UNIX-based microcomputers; 100 are networked. Students may access Digital minicomputer/mainframe systems, Internet. Residence halls may be equipped with stand-alone microcomputers. Client/LAN operating systems include Apple/Macintosh, DOS, OS/2, UNIX/XENIX/AIX, X-windows, LocalTalk/AppleTalk, Microsoft, Novell. Computer languages and software packages include Ada, APL, BASIC, C, COBOL, C++, FORTRAN, LISP, MINITAB, Modula 2, Pascal, SPSS. Computer facilities are available to all students.
**Fees:** None.
**Hours:** 7:30 AM-11 PM (M-Th); 7:30 AM-6 PM (F); 9:30 AM-4 PM (Sa); 11 AM-11 PM (Su).

**GRADUATE CAREER DATA.** 85% of graduates choose careers in business and industry. Companies and businesses that hire graduates: Raytheon, Ernst & Young, Coopers & Lybrand.

**PROMINENT ALUMNI/AE.** Carl Yastrzemski, former baseball player, Boston Red Sox; Kelly Lange, TV anchor.

# Mount Holyoke College

**South Hadley, MA 01075-1488 — 413 538-2000**

**1994-95 Costs.** Tuition: $19,300. Room & board: $5,700. Fees, books, misc. academic expenses (school's estimate): $2,235.
**Enrollment.** 1,952 women (full-time). Freshman class: 1,800 applicants, 1,314 accepted, 526 enrolled.
**Test score averages/ranges.** Average SAT scores: 549 verbal, 571 math.
**Faculty.** 194 full-time; 32 part-time. Student/faculty ratio: 10 to 1.
**Selectivity rating.** Highly competitive.

**PROFILE.** Mount Holyoke, founded in 1837, is a private, liberal arts college for women. Its 800-acre campus, including numerous 19th-century buildings, is located in South Hadley, 10 miles north of Springfield.

**Accreditation:** NEASC.
**Religious orientation:** Mount Holyoke College is nonsectarian; no religious requirements.
**Library:** Collections totaling over 576,000 volumes, 1,811 periodical subscriptions, and 15,120 microform items.
**Special facilities/museums:** Art and historical museums, bronze-casting foundry, child study center, audio-visual center, language learning center, greenhouse, Japanese meditation garden, equestrian center, observatory, linear accelerator, electron microscope, refracting telescope, nuclear magnetic resonance equipment.
**Athletic facilities:** Gymnasium, basketball, racquetball, squash, tennis, and volleyball courts, swimming pool, diving tank, tracks, field hockey, lacrosse, soccer, and softball fields, dance studios, weight room, sauna, fitness trail.

**STUDENT BODY. Undergraduate profile:** 22% are state residents. 8% Asian-American, 4% Black, 3% Hispanic, 70% White, 15% Other. Average age of undergraduates is 20.
**Freshman profile:** 12% of freshmen who took SAT scored 700 or over on verbal, 16% scored 700 or over on math; 51% scored 600 or over on verbal, 60% scored 600 or over on math; 89% scored 500 or over on verbal, 93% scored 500 or over on math; 100% scored 400 or over on verbal, 100% scored 400 or over on math. Majority of accepted applicants took SAT. 74% of freshmen come from public schools.
**Undergraduate achievement:** 96% of fall 1992 freshmen returned for fall 1993 term. 25% of students who completed a degree program went on to graduate study.
**Foreign students:** 269 students are from out of the country. Countries represented include China, India, and Pakistan; 58 in all.

**PROGRAMS OF STUDY. Degrees:** A.B.
**Majors:** African American Studies, American Studies, Anthropology, Art History, Asian Studies, Astronomy, Biochemistry, Biological Sciences, Black Studies, Chemistry, Classics, Dance, Economics, English, European Studies, French, Geography, Geology, German, Greek, History, International Relations, Italian, Jewish Studies, Latin, Latin Ameri-

can Studies, Mathematics, Mathematics/Statistics/Computation, Medieval Studies, Music, Philosophy, Physics, Politics, Psychobiology, Psychology, Psychology/Education, Religion, Romance Languages, Russian, Self-Designed Majors, Sociology, Spanish, Statistics, Studio Art, Theatre Arts, Women's Studies.
**Distribution of degrees:** The majors with the highest enrollment are English, politics, and biological sciences; African American studies, dance, and Romance languages/literature have the lowest.
**Requirements:** General education requirement.
**Academic regulations:** Minimum 2.00 GPA required for graduation.
**Special:** Several options available including self-designed, interdisciplinary minors. Self-designed majors. Double majors. Independent study. Pass/fail grading option. Internships. Graduate school at which undergraduates may take graduate-level courses. Preprofessional programs in law, medicine, veterinary science, and dentistry. 3-2 engineering program with Dartmouth Coll. Member of Five College Consortium; cross-registration possible. Washington Semester. Member of Twelve College Exchange Program. Exchange programs also with Mills Coll and Spelman Coll. Teacher certification in early childhood, elementary, secondary, and bilingual/bicultural education. Certification in specific subject areas. Study abroad in Australia, Brazil, China, Ecuador, France, Germany, India, Italy, Japan, Kenya, Spain, the United Kingdom, and other countries. ROTC and AFROTC at U of Massachusetts at Amherst.
**Honors:** Phi Beta Kappa. Honors program.
**Academic Assistance:** Nonremedial tutoring.

**STUDENT LIFE. Housing:** All unmarried students under age 21 must live on campus unless living near campus with relatives. Women's dorms. Off-campus privately-owned housing. 99% of students live in college housing.
**Social atmosphere:** Students gather at Coffee Grind (a student-run coffeehouse), the Blanchard Campus Center, the Betty Shabazz House (a cultural center), at the Village Commons, and in downtown Amherst and Northampton. Influential campus groups include The Network (a campus programming board), residence hall committees, and the Association of Pan-African Unity. Students enjoy Las Vegas Night, the BMW festival, the Festival of Diversity, a capella concerts, Head of the Charles, and Something Every Friday (free events in nearby Blanchard). The editor of the Mount Holyoke News reports, "In any given week, the events calendar offers a poetry reading for every party, a film for every concert. The five-college area and the towns of Amherst and Northampton offer such a wide array of activities that a lack of something to do is virtually never a complaint."
**Services and counseling/handicapped student services:** Placement services. Health service. Women's center. Personal and psychological counseling. Career and academic guidance services. Religious counseling. Physically disabled student services. Learning disabled services. Notetaking services. Tape recorders. Tutors. Reader services for the blind.
**Campus organizations:** Undergraduate student government. Student newspaper (Mount Holyoke News, published once/week). Literary magazine. Yearbook. Radio station. Glee club, concert choir, chamber singers, orchestra, science fiction club, outing club, debating, Blue Key Guides, Athletic and Recreation Association, Alcohol Awareness Project, Action: South Africa, Amnesty International, Cambodian Tutoring Program, Children's Companionship Program, Law Society, College Democrats, College Republicans, 60 organizations in all.
**Religious organizations:** Interfaith Alliance, Intervarsity Christian Fellowship, Jewish Student Union.
**Minority/foreign student organizations:** Asian Student Association, Association of Pan-African Unity, La Unidad. International Orientation Committee, International Club, International Newsletter, International Relations Club, Islamic Cultural Alliance, Le Club Francais.

**ATHLETICS. Physical education requirements:** Three semesters of physical education required.
**Intercollegiate competition:** 18% of students participate. Basketball (W), crew (W), cross-country (W), diving (W), field hockey (W), golf (W), horsemanship (W), lacrosse (W), soccer (W), softball (W), squash (W), swimming (W), tennis (W), track (indoor) (W), track (outdoor) (W), track and field (indoor) (W), track and field (outdoor) (W), volleyball (W). Member of ECAC, NCAA Division III, NEW 8.
**Intramural and club sports:** 15% of students participate. Intramural basketball, bowling, floor hockey, folk dancing, foul shooting, fun runs, hacky sack, inner-tube water polo, tennis, ultimate frisbee, volleyball. Women's club Alpine skiing, croquet, rugby, water polo.

**ADMISSIONS. Academic basis for candidate selection** (in order of priority): Secondary school record, class rank, essay, standardized test scores, school's recommendation.
**Nonacademic basis for candidate selection:** Character and personality, extracurricular participation, particular talent or ability, geographical distribution, and alumni/ae relationship are important.
**Requirements:** Graduation from secondary school is recommended; GED is accepted. No specific distribution of secondary school units required. Additional courses in listed subject areas are recommended. SAT, ACT, and ACH required. Campus visit and interview recommended. Off-campus interviews available with an alumni representative.
**Procedure:** Take SAT by January of 12th year. Take ACH by January of 12th year. Visit college for interview by February 1 of 12th year. Application deadline is February 1. Notification of admission by April 1. Reply is required by May 1. $200 nonrefundable tuition deposit. $100 nonrefundable room deposit. Freshmen accepted for fall term only.
**Special programs:** Admission may be deferred one year. Credit may be granted through CEEB Advanced Placement for scores of 4 or higher. Early decision program. In fall 1993, 127 applied for early decision and 100 were accepted. Deadline for applying for early decision is November 15 and January 15.
**Transfer students:** Transfer students accepted for terms other than fall. In fall 1993, less than 1% of all new students were transfers into all classes. 212 transfer applications were received, 85 were accepted. Application deadline is March 15 for fall; December 1 for spring. Minimum 3.0 GPA recommended. Lowest course grade accepted is "C." Maximum number of transferable credits is 64 credit hours. At least 64 credit hours must be completed at the college to receive degree.
**Admissions contact:** Anita Smith, Director of Admissions. 413 538-2023.

**FINANCIAL AID. Available aid:** Pell grants, SEOG, state scholarships and grants, school grants, and private scholarships and grants. Perkins Loans (NDSL), PLUS, Stafford Loans (GSL), state loans, and school loans. TERI. Knight Tuition Plans and guaranteed tuition.
**Financial aid statistics:** In 1993-94, 95% of all undergraduate applicants received aid; 91% of freshman applicants. Average amounts of aid awarded freshmen: Scholarships and grants, $14,871; loans, $2,500.
**Supporting data/closing dates:** FAFSA/FAF: Priority filing date is February 1. School's own aid application: Priority filing date is February 1. Income tax forms: Priority filing date is June 1. Notification of awards begins April 1.
**Financial aid contact:** John Skarr, Director of Financial Aid and Student Financial Services. 413 538-2291.

**STUDENT EMPLOYMENT.** College Work/Study Program. Institutional employment. 60% of full-time undergraduates work on campus during school year. Students may expect to earn an average of $925 during school year. Off-campus part-time employment opportunities rated "fair."

**COMPUTER FACILITIES.** 245 IBM/IBM-compatible and Macintosh/Apple microcomputers. Residence halls may be equipped with stand-alone microcomputers, networked microcomputers. Computer languages and software packages include Assembly, BMDP, C, dBASE, DI3000, FORTRAN, Lotus 1-2-3, Pascal, Prolog, R:BASE, SPSS-X, Statview, Stella, TSP, XyWrite. Computer facilities are available to all students.
**Fees:** None.
**Hours:** 24-hour access to dormitory computer centers.

**GRADUATE CAREER DATA.** Graduate school percentages: 7% enter law school. 7% enter medical school. 2% enter graduate business programs. 11% enter graduate arts and sciences programs. Highest graduate school enrollments: Columbia U, Cornell U, Duke U, Harvard U, Stanford U, U of Chicago, U of Michigan, U of Pennsylvania, U of Virginia. 30% of graduates choose careers in business and industry. Companies and businesses that hire graduates: Aetna Life, AT&T, Bank of America, Bank of Boston, Bankers Trust, Chubb Insurance, CIGNA, Citicorp, Digital Equipment Corp., Exxon, General Electric, IBM, McGraw-Hill, Merrill Lynch, Morgan Guaranty, National Westminster Bank, Paine Webber, PIRG, Procter & Gamble, Prudential, Rockefeller U, Salomon Bros., Xerox.

**PROMINENT ALUMNI/AE.** Ella Grasso, former governor of Connecticut and first woman governor elected in her own right; Dr. Virginia Apgar, developer of the Apgar scale for testing newborns; Frances Perkins, first woman cabinet member; Emily Dickinson, poet; Sally Nunneley, NASA physician; Wendy Wasserstein, playwright.

# Mount Ida College

**Newton Centre, MA 02159** — **617 969-7000**

**1994-95 Costs.** Tuition: $10,320. Room & board: $7,220. Fees, books, misc. academic expenses (school's estimate): $600.
**Enrollment.** Undergraduates: 734 men, 896 women (full-time). Freshman class: 4,750 applicants, 4,041 accepted, 795 enrolled.
**Test score averages/ranges.** N/A.
**Faculty.** 62 full-time; 115 part-time. 22% of faculty holds doctoral degree. Student/faculty ratio: 15 to 1.
**Selectivity rating.** N/A.

**PROFILE.** Mount Ida, founded in 1899, is a private, liberal arts college. Its 85-acre campus is located in Newton Centre, eight miles west of Boston.
**Accreditation:** NEASC, CCA-ACICS.
**Religious orientation:** Mount Ida College is nonsectarian; no religious requirements.
**Library:** Collections totaling over 75,000 volumes and 352 periodical subscriptions.
**Special facilities/museums:** TV studio.
**Athletic facilities:** Gymnasium, outdoor swimming pool, tennis courts, athletic fields, weight room, fitness center, equestrian ring.

**STUDENT BODY. Undergraduate profile:** 78% are state residents; 15% are transfers. 7% Asian-American, 15% Black, 2% Hispanic, 1% Native American, 75% White. Average age of undergraduates is 19.
**Freshman profile:** Majority of accepted applicants took SAT. 80% of freshmen come from public schools.
**Undergraduate achievement:** 75% of fall 1992 freshmen returned for fall 1993 term.
**Foreign students:** 182 students are from out of the country. Countries represented include Bermuda, England, India, Ireland, Japan, and Turkey; 44 in all.

**PROGRAMS OF STUDY. Degrees:** B.Lib.Studies, B.S.
**Majors:** Bereavement Counseling, Business Administration, Criminal Justice, Fashion Design, Fashion Merchandising/Fashion Marketing, Funeral Home Management, Graphic Design, Hotel Administration, Interior Design, Journalism/Writing, Legal Studies, Liberal Studies, Management, Media Production, Public Administration, Retail Management, Teacher Certification, Veterinary Technology.
**Distribution of degrees:** The majors with the highest enrollment are liberal studies, interior design, and fashion merchandising/fashion marketing; fashion design and public administration have the lowest.
**Requirements:** General education requirement.
**Academic regulations:** Freshmen must maintain minimum 1.75 GPA; sophomores, 1.75 GPA; juniors, 2.0 GPA; seniors, 2.0 GPA.
**Special:** Associate's degrees offered. Self-designed majors. Internships. All degree programs are 2-2 programs except 3-1 veterinary technician program. Teacher certification in early childhood and elementary education. Exchange program abroad in England (Regents Coll).
**Honors:** Honor societies.
**Academic Assistance:** Remedial reading, writing, math, and study skills. Nonremedial tutoring.

**ADMISSIONS. Academic basis for candidate selection** (in order of priority): Secondary school record, school's recommendation, essay, class rank, standardized test scores.

**Nonacademic basis for candidate selection:** Character and personality, extracurricular participation, particular talent or ability, and geographical distribution are considered.
**Requirements:** Graduation from secondary school is required; GED is accepted. No specific distribution of secondary school units required. Campus visit and interview recommended. No off-campus interviews.
**Procedure:** Notification of admission on rolling basis. No set date by which applicant's must accept offer. $200 tuition and room deposit, refundable until May 1. Freshmen accepted for terms other than fall.
**Special programs:** Admission may be deferred one year. Credit and/or placement may be granted through CLEP general and subject exams. Credit and placement may be granted through life experience.
**Transfer students:** Transfer students accepted for terms other than fall. In fall 1993, 15% of all new students were transfers into all classes. 400 transfer applications were received, 350 were accepted. Application deadline is rolling for fall; rolling for spring. Minimum 2.0 GPA recommended. Lowest course grade accepted is "C-." At least 32 semester hours must be completed at the college to receive degree.
**Admissions contact:** Judy Kaufman and Harold Duvall, Co-directors of Admission. 617 969-7000, extension 153.
**FINANCIAL AID. Available aid:** Pell grants, SEOG, state scholarships and grants, school scholarships and grants, private scholarships, academic merit scholarships, athletic scholarships, and aid for undergraduate foreign students. Perkins Loans (NDSL), PLUS, Stafford Loans (GSL), state loans, private loans, and SLS. Tuition Plan Inc., Knight Tuition Plans, and AMS. TERI.
**Financial aid statistics:** 5% of aid is not need-based. In 1993-94, 57% of all undergraduate applicants received aid; 70% of freshman applicants. Average amounts of aid awarded freshmen: Scholarships and grants, $4,000; loans, $2,625.
**Supporting data/closing dates:** FAFSA/FAF: Accepted on rolling basis. School's own aid application: Accepted on rolling basis. Income tax forms: Accepted on rolling basis. Notification of awards on rolling basis.
**Financial aid contact:** Colleen Morgan, Director of Financial Aid. 617 969-7000, extension 118.

# New England Conservatory of Music

**Boston, MA 02115** — **617 262-1120**

**1994-95 Costs.** Tuition: $14,600. Room & board: $6,990. Fees, books, misc. academic expenses (school's estimate): $1,100.
**Enrollment.** Undergraduates: 153 men, 175 women (full-time). Freshman class: 425 applicants, 229 accepted, 87 enrolled. Graduate enrollment: 150 men, 218 women.
**Test score averages/ranges.** N/A.
**Faculty.** 54 full-time; 131 part-time. 22% of faculty holds highest degree in specific field. Student/faculty ratio: 7 to 1.
**Selectivity rating.** N/A.

**PROFILE.** The New England Conservatory, founded in 1867, is the oldest private conservatory of its kind in the U.S. Concert halls and faculty offices are located in three buildings in downtown Boston.
**Accreditation:** NEASC. Professionally accredited by the National Association of Schools of Music.
**Religious orientation:** New England Conservatory of Music is nonsectarian; no religious requirements.
**Library:** Collections totaling over 65,000 volumes and 250 periodical subscriptions.
**Special facilities/museums:** Rare instrument collection of over 200 pieces, recording and electronic music studios.
**Athletic facilities:** Arena, access to YMCA.
**STUDENT BODY. Undergraduate profile:** 82% are state residents; 4% are transfers. 15% Asian-American, 3% Black, 2% Hispanic, 1% Native American, 70% White, 9% Other.
**Freshman profile:** Majority of accepted applicants took SAT.
**Undergraduate achievement:** 92% of fall 1992 freshmen returned for fall 1993 term.
**Foreign students:** Countries represented include Japan, Korea, and Taiwan; 32 in all.
**PROGRAMS OF STUDY. Degrees:** B.Mus.
**Majors:** Bassoon, Cello, Clarinet, Composition, Double Bass, Euphonium, Flute, French Horn, Guitar, Harp, Harpsichord, Historical Performance, Jazz Studies, Music Education, Music History, Oboe, Organ, Percussion, Piano, Recorder, Saxophone, Theoretical Studies, Third Stream Studies, Trombone, Trumpet, Tuba, Viola, Violin, Voice.
**Distribution of degrees:** The major with the highest enrollment is performance.
**Requirements:** General education requirement.
**Special:** Participation in one of several ensembles required. New England Conservatory Symphony Orchestra provides training for instrumentalists in the standard repertoire, as well as in the less frequently explored literature, ranging from pre-Bach to contemporary music. Diploma programs available. Courses offered in economics, English, film, French, German, history, Italian, political science, and psychology. Students must pass annual promotional audition; theory and composition students must appear before jury after sophomore and junior years. Dual degrees. Internships. Graduate school at which undergraduates may take graduate-level courses. Five-year B.A. or B.S./B.Mus. program with Tufts U.
**Honors:** Honors program.
**ADMISSIONS. Academic basis for candidate selection** (in order of priority): Audition, secondary school record, school's recommendation, standardized test scores.
**Nonacademic basis for candidate selection:** Character and personality are important. Extracurricular participation is considered.
**Requirements:** Graduation from secondary school is required; GED is accepted. No specific distribution of secondary school units required. Audition required. Applicants living more than 200 miles from Boston may submit tape recording in lieu of personal audition in all majors except Third Stream studies. SAT or ACT is required. Campus visit and interview recommended. No off-campus interviews.
**Procedure:** Take SAT or ACT by February of 12th year. Suggest filing application by January 15. Application deadline is February 15. Notification of admission by April 1. Reply is required within 30 days of acceptance. $250 nonrefundable tuition deposit. $250 nonrefundable room deposit. Freshmen accepted for terms other than fall.
**Special programs:** Admission may be deferred one year. Credit may be granted through CEEB Advanced Placement for scores of 3 or higher. Placement may be granted through challenge exams.
**Transfer students:** Transfer students accepted for terms other than fall. In fall 1993, 4% of all new students were transfers into all classes. 90 transfer applications were received, 55 were accepted. Application deadline is January 15 for fall; November 15 for spring. Lowest course grade accepted is "C." Maximum number of transferable credits is 60 semester hours. At least 60 semester hours must be completed at the college to receive degree. Applicants to degree programs in music education and composition are not admitted after sophomore year.
**Admissions contact:** Robert L. Annis, M.M., Dean of Enrollment Services. 617 262-1120, extension 430.
**FINANCIAL AID. Available aid:** Pell grants, SEOG, state scholarships and grants, school scholarships and grants, private scholarships and grants, and aid for undergraduate foreign students. Perkins Loans (NDSL), PLUS, Stafford Loans (GSL), and SLS. Tuition Management Systems.
**Financial aid statistics:** In 1993-94, 79% of all undergraduate applicants received aid; 59% of freshman applicants. Average amounts of aid awarded freshmen: Scholarships and grants, $6,850.
**Supporting data/closing dates:** FAFSA: Priority filing date is January 31. School's own aid application: Priority filing date is January 15. Income tax forms: Priority filing date is January 15. Notification of awards begins April 1.
**Financial aid contact:** Robert Winkley, M.M., Director of Financial Aid. 617 262-1120, extension 440.

# Nichols College

**Dudley, MA 01571** — **508 943-1560**

**1994-95 Costs.** Tuition: $8,940. Room: $2,580. Board: $2,580. Fees, books, misc. academic expenses (school's estimate): $2,475.
**Enrollment.** Undergraduates: 462 men, 260 women (full-time). Freshman class: 705 applicants, 634 accepted, 187 enrolled. Graduate enrollment: 237 men, 171 women.
**Test score averages/ranges.** Average SAT scores: 388 verbal, 436 math. Range of SAT scores of middle 50%: 340-440 verbal, 380-490 math.
**Faculty.** 35 full-time; 14 part-time. 65% of faculty holds highest degree in specific field. Student/faculty ratio: 24 to 1.
**Selectivity rating.** Noncompetitive.

**PROFILE.** Nichols, is a private, liberal arts college. Founded in 1815 as a college for men, it adopted coeducation in 1970. Its 210-acre campus is located in Dudley.
**Accreditation:** NEASC. Professionally accredited by the American Assembly of Collegiate Schools of Business.
**Religious orientation:** Nichols College is nonsectarian; no religious requirements.
**Library:** Collections totaling over 65,000 volumes, 460 periodical subscriptions, and 2,500 microform items.
**Athletic facilities:** Gymnasium, swimming pool, field house, tennis courts, stadium, baseball, soccer, and softball fields, weight room, sandpit volleyball court.
**STUDENT BODY. Undergraduate profile:** 68% are state residents; 20% are transfers. 1% Asian-American, 1% Black, 1% Hispanic, 95% White, 2% Other. Average age of undergraduates is 20.
**Freshman profile:** 93% of accepted applicants took SAT. 82% of freshmen come from public schools.
**Undergraduate achievement:** 75% of fall 1991 freshmen returned for fall 1992 term. 52% of entering class graduated.
**Foreign students:** 10 students are from out of the country. Seven countries represented in all.
**PROGRAMS OF STUDY. Degrees:** B.A., B.S.Bus.Admin., B.S.Pub.Admin.
**Majors:** Accounting, Economics, Finance, Finance/Real Estate, General Business, History, Industrial Psychology, Management, Management Information Systems, Marketing, Psychology, Public Administration, Social Service.
**Distribution of degrees:** The majors with the highest enrollment are management, accounting, and general business; public administration, social service, and history have the lowest.
**Requirements:** General education requirement.
**Academic regulations:** Freshmen must maintain minimum 1.55 GPA; sophomores, 1.75 GPA; juniors, 1.95 GPA; seniors, 2.0 GPA.
**Special:** Minor offered in international business. Courses offered in computer science, English, environmental science, humanities, mathematics, political science, and sociology. Associate's degrees offered. Double majors. Washington Semester. Exchange program abroad in England (Regents Coll). ROTC.
**Academic Assistance:** Nonremedial tutoring.
**ADMISSIONS. Academic basis for candidate selection** (in order of priority): Secondary school record, school's recommendation, standardized test scores, class rank, essay.
**Nonacademic basis for candidate selection:** Character and personality are important. Extracurricular participation, particular talent or ability, and alumni/ae relationship are considered.
**Requirements:** Graduation from secondary school is required; GED is accepted. 16 units and the following program of study are required: 4 units of English, 3 units of math, 2 units of lab science, 2 units of social studies, 5 units of electives. Rank at or above 50th percentile on SAT or ACT and minimum "C" average recommended. SAT or ACT is required.

Campus visit and interview recommended. Off-campus interviews available with admissions and alumni representatives.
**Procedure:** Take SAT or ACT by April 15 of 12th year. Visit college for interview by April 15 of 12th year. Suggest filing application by March 1; no deadline. Notification of admission on rolling basis. Reply is required within three weeks of acceptance. $200 tuition deposit, refundable until May 1. Freshmen accepted for terms other than fall.
**Special programs:** Admission may be deferred one year. Credit may be granted through CEEB Advanced Placement for scores of 3 or higher. Credit and/or placement may be granted through CLEP general and subject exams. Credit and placement may be granted through DANTES exams. Early decision program. Deadline for applying for early decision is November 1.
**Transfer students:** Transfer students accepted for terms other than fall. In fall 1992, 20% of all new students were transfers into all classes. 87 transfer applications were received, 73 were accepted. Application deadline is rolling for fall; rolling for spring. Minimum 2.0 GPA required. Lowest course grade accepted is "C." Maximum number of transferable credits is 62 semester hours from a two-year school and 92 semester hours from a four-year school. At least 30 semester hours must be completed at the college to receive degree.
**Admissions contact:** Charlene Lowell Nemeth, M.B.A., Director of Admissions and Financial Aid. 508 943-2055.

**FINANCIAL AID. Available aid:** Pell grants, SEOG, state scholarships and grants, school scholarships and grants, private scholarships and grants, ROTC scholarships, and academic merit scholarships. PLUS, Stafford Loans (GSL), state loans, and SLS. Tuition Plan Inc., Knight Tuition Plans, family tuition reduction, and guaranteed tuition.
**Financial aid statistics:** 25% of aid is not need-based. In 1992-93, 97% of all undergraduate applicants received aid; 95% of freshman applicants.
**Supporting data/closing dates:** FAFSA/FAF: Priority filing date is March 1; accepted on rolling basis. Income tax forms: Accepted on rolling basis. Notification of awards on rolling basis.
**Financial aid contact:** Judy Bullens, Financial Aid Officer. 508 943-1560, extension 228.

# North Adams State College

**North Adams, MA 01247** **413 664-4511**

**1994-95 Costs.** Tuition: $1,408 (state residents), $5,542 (out-of-state). Room: $1,125. Board: $1,850. Fees, books, misc. academic expenses (school's estimate): $2,550.
**Enrollment.** Undergraduates: 683 men, 697 women (full-time). Freshman class: 1,563 applicants, 1,001 accepted, 240 enrolled.
**Test score averages/ranges.** Average SAT scores: 427 verbal, 470 math. Range of SAT scores of middle 50%: 400-500 verbal, 400-525 math.
**Faculty.** 98 full-time; 38 part-time. 60% of faculty holds doctoral degree. Student/faculty ratio: 15 to 1.
**Selectivity rating.** Less competitive.

**PROFILE.** North Adams State, founded in 1894, is a public, liberal arts college. Its 75-acre campus is located in North Adams, northwest of Springfield.

**Accreditation:** NEASC. Professionally accredited by the National Council for Accreditation of Teacher Education.
**Religious orientation:** North Adams State College is nonsectarian; no religious requirements.
**Library:** Collections totaling over 167,457 volumes, 510 periodical subscriptions and 570 microform items.
**Special facilities/museums:** On-campus day care, cable TV and radio facilities.
**Athletic facilities:** Gymnasiums, swimming pool, weight rooms, racquetball, squash, and tennis courts, baseball, lacrosse, rugby, soccer, and softball fields.

**STUDENT BODY. Undergraduate profile:** 92% are state residents; 38% are transfers. 1% Asian-American, 3.5% Black, 1% Hispanic, .5% Native American, 94% White. Average age of undergraduates is 23.
**Freshman profile:** 4% of freshmen who took SAT scored 600 or over on verbal, 6% scored 600 or over on math; 26% scored 500 or over on verbal, 38% scored 500 or over on math; 66% scored 400 or over on verbal, 84% scored 400 or over on math; 98% scored 300 or over on verbal, 100% scored 300 or over on math. 100% of accepted applicants took SAT.
**Undergraduate achievement:** 82% of fall 1992 freshmen returned for fall 1993 term. 48% of entering class graduated. 10% of students who completed a degree program went on to graduate study within five years.
**Foreign students:** One student is from out of the country.

**PROGRAMS OF STUDY. Degrees:** B.A., B.S.
**Majors:** Allied Health Services, Biology, Business Administration, Chemistry, Computer Science, English/Communications, Fine/Performing Arts, History, Interdisciplinary Studies, Mathematics, Medical Laboratory Technology, Philosophy, Physics, Psychology, Sociology.
**Distribution of degrees:** The majors with the highest enrollment are business administration and English/communications; physics, chemistry, and philosophy have the lowest.
**Requirements:** General education requirement.
**Academic regulations:** Freshmen must maintain minimum 1.75 GPA; sophomores, juniors, seniors, 2.0 GPA.
**Special:** Minors offered in art, economics, geography, history of civilization, and music. Courses offered in Canadian studies, political science, Spanish, theatre, and women's studies. Self-designed majors. Double majors. Independent study. Internships. Preprofessional programs in law. College Academic Program Sharing with all Massachusetts state colleges. Exchange programs with Berkshire Comm Coll and Williams Coll. Teacher certification in early childhood, elementary, and secondary education. Certification in specific subject areas. Study abroad in 21 foreign countries.
**Honors:** Honor societies.
**Academic Assistance:** Remedial reading, writing, math, and study skills. Nonremedial tutoring.

**STUDENT LIFE. Housing:** Freshmen and sophomores must live on campus. Coed dorms. Sorority and fraternity housing. Off-campus privately-owned housing. 60% of students live in college housing.
**Social atmosphere:** The Pitcher's Mound Pub, Freight Yard Pub, and Brick Oven Bar and Grille are popular gathering spots for students. Greeks, Newman Association, Student Government Association, baseball, basketball and hockey teams influence student life. Roll-A-Keg and Spring Fling are popular social events. "Because NASC is such a small school, many students take an active role in going out to parties and bars," reports the editor of the school newspaper. Sporting events are also well attended.
**Services and counseling/handicapped student services:** Placement services. Health service. Day care. Counseling services for veteran and older students. Birth control, personal, and psychological counseling. Career and academic guidance services. Physically disabled student services. Learning disabled services. Tutors.
**Campus organizations:** Undergraduate student government. Student newspaper (Beacon, published once/week). Literary magazine. Yearbook. Radio and TV stations. Chorale, concert band, jazz band, Motets, Harlequins, Readers Theatre, modern dance group, Cultural Affairs Series, Lecture-Concert Committee, athletic, departmental, service, and special-interest groups, 47 organizations in all. Four fraternities, all with chapter houses; five sororities, all with chapter houses. 10% of men join a fraternity. 10% of women join a sorority.
**Religious organizations:** Campus Christian Fellowship, Jewish Student Organization, Newman Association, Interfaith Society.
**Minority/foreign student organizations:** Multicultural Student Society.

**ATHLETICS. Physical education requirements:** Two credits of physical education required.Two credits of physical education required.
**Intercollegiate competition:** 15% of students participate. Baseball (M), basketball (M,W), cross-country (M,W), ice hockey (M), soccer (M,W), softball (W), tennis (M,W), volleyball (W). Member of ECAC, Massachusetts State College Athletic Conference, NCAA Division III.
**Intramural and club sports:** 60% of students participate. Intramural basketball, billiards, floor hockey, soccer, softball, table tennis, volleyball. Men's club boxing, rugby. Women's club boxing.

**ADMISSIONS. Academic basis for candidate selection** (in order of priority): Secondary school record, standardized test scores, class rank, school's recommendation, essay.
**Nonacademic basis for candidate selection:** Extracurricular participation is important. Character and personality, particular talent or ability, and alumni/ae relationship are considered.
**Requirements:** Graduation from secondary school is required; GED is accepted. 17 units and the following program of study are required: 4 units of English, 3 units of math, 2 units of lab science, 2 units of foreign language, 2 units of social studies, 1 unit of history, 3 units of electives. Individual Enrichment Program for applicants not normally admissible; includes four-week summer seminar. SAT is required; ACT may be substituted. Campus visit and interview recommended. No off-campus interviews.
**Procedure:** Take SAT or ACT by December of 12th year. Suggest filing application by April 1. Application deadline is June 1. Notification of admission on rolling basis. Reply is required by May 1. $100 tuition deposit, refundable until May 1. $50 room deposit, refundable until first night at school. Freshmen accepted for terms other than fall.
**Special programs:** Admission may be deferred one year. Credit may be granted through CEEB Advanced Placement for scores of 3 or higher. Credit may be granted through CLEP general and subject exams, DANTES and challenge exams, and military and life experience. Early decision program. In fall 1993, 47 applied for early decision and 14 were accepted. Deadline for applying for early decision is December 1. Early entrance/early admission program. Concurrent enrollment program.
**Transfer students:** Transfer students accepted for terms other than fall. In fall 1993, 38% of all new students were transfers into all classes. 399 transfer applications were received, 293 were accepted. Application deadline is June 1 for fall; January 1 for spring. Minimum 2.0 GPA required. Lowest course grade accepted is "D." Maximum number of transferable credits is 75 semester hours from a two-year school and 90 semester hours from a four-year school. At least 30 semester hours must be completed at the college to receive degree.
**Admissions contact:** Denise Richardello, M.Ed., Director of Admissions. 413 664-4511, extension 410.

**FINANCIAL AID. Available aid:** Pell grants, SEOG, state grants, school grants, private scholarships, and academic merit scholarships. Perkins Loans (NDSL), PLUS, Stafford Loans (GSL), and SLS. Tuition Management Systems.
**Financial aid statistics:** In 1993-94, 55% of all undergraduate applicants received aid; 90% of freshman applicants. Average amounts of aid awarded freshmen: Scholarships and grants, $1,500; loans, $2,400.
**Supporting data/closing dates:** FAFSA: Priority filing date is April 1. School's own aid application: Priority filing date is April 1; accepted on rolling basis. Income tax forms: Priority filing date is April 1; accepted on rolling basis. Notification of awards on rolling basis.
**Financial aid contact:** Gerald E. Desmarais, M.Ed., Director of Financial Aid. 413 664-4511, extension 219.

**STUDENT EMPLOYMENT.** College Work/Study Program. Institutional employment. 40% of full-time undergraduates work on campus during school year. Students may expect to earn an average of $800 during school year. Freshmen are discouraged from working during their first term. Off-campus part-time employment opportunities rated "fair."

**COMPUTER FACILITIES.** 200 IBM/IBM-compatible microcomputers; 20 are networked. Students may access Digital minicomputer/mainframe systems. Computer languages and software packages include BASIC, COBOL, COMPASS, dBASE, FORTRAN, LISP, Lotus 1-2-3, Pascal, SNOBOL, SPSS, TSP, WordPerfect, WordStar. Computer facilities are available to all students.
**Fees:** $118 computer fee per semester; included in tuition/fees.
**Hours:** 7 AM-11 PM (M-Th); 7 AM-9 PM (F-Sa); noon-9 PM (Su).

## Northeastern University

**Boston, MA 02115 617 373-2000**

**1994-95 Costs.** Tuition: $13,380. Room: $3,870. Board: $3,435. Fees, books, misc. academic expenses (school's estimate): $906.

**Enrollment.** Undergraduates: 6,686 men, 4,605 women (full-time). Freshman class: 11,901 applicants, 8,492 accepted, 2,517 enrolled. Graduate enrollment: 2,837 men, 2,334 women.

**Test score averages/ranges.** Average SAT scores: 467 verbal, 531 math. Range of SAT scores of middle 50%: 410-520 verbal, 460-600 math. Average ACT scores: 23 composite. Range of ACT scores of middle 50%: 20-26 composite.

**Faculty.** 810 full-time. 81% of faculty holds doctoral degree. Student/faculty ratio: 11 to 1.

**Selectivity rating.** Less competitive.

**PROFILE.** Northeastern is a private, comprehensive university focusing on cooperative education. Founded in 1898, it adopted coeducation in 1943. Programs are offered through the Colleges of Arts and Sciences, Business Administration, Computer Science, Engineering, Nursing, and Pharmacy and Allied Health Professions; the Schools of Engineering Technology and Journalism; and the Boston-Bouve College of Human Development Professions. Its 55-acre campus is located in Boston, near the Fenway.

**Accreditation:** NEASC. Professionally accredited by the Accreditation Board for Engineering and Technology, the American Assembly of Collegiate Schools of Business, the American Bar Association, the American Council on Pharmaceutical Education, the American Medical Association (CAHEA), the American Physical Therapy Association, the American Speech-Language-Hearing Association, the Computing Sciences Accreditation Board, the Council on Rehabilitation Education, the National League for Nursing, the National Recreation and Park Association.
**Religious orientation:** Northeastern University is nonsectarian; no religious requirements.
**Library:** Collections totaling over 691,878 volumes, 7,946 periodical subscriptions, and 1,647,689 microform items.
**Special facilities/museums:** Marine science center, African-American institute, electron microscopy center, electromagnetic research center.
**Athletic facilities:** Gymnasiums, field house, basketball, racquetball, and tennis courts, swimming pool, track, exercise, gymnastics, martial arts, and weight rooms, ice rink, baseball and football fields.

**STUDENT BODY. Undergraduate profile:** 57% are state residents; 19% are transfers. 5.3% Asian-American, 8% Black, 3% Hispanic, .2% Native American, 75% White, 8.5% Other. Average age of undergraduates is 21.
**Freshman profile:** 1% of freshmen who took SAT scored 700 or over on verbal, 5% scored 700 or over on math; 9% scored 600 or over on verbal, 25% scored 600 or over on math; 34% scored 500 or over on verbal, 65% scored 500 or over on math; 80% scored 400 or over on verbal, 92% scored 400 or over on math; 99% scored 300 or over on verbal, 99% scored 300 or over on math. 3% of freshmen who took ACT scored 30 or over on composite; 40% scored 24 or over on composite; 89% scored 18 or over on composite; 100% scored 12 or over on composite. 95% of accepted applicants took SAT; 5% took ACT.
**Undergraduate achievement:** 71% of fall 1992 freshmen returned for fall 1993 term. 38% of entering class graduated. 11% of students who completed a degree program immediately went on to graduate study.
**Foreign students:** 1,015 students are from out of the country. Countries represented include Canada, Greece, Hong Kong, Indonesia, Japan, and Korea; 99 in all.
**PROGRAMS OF STUDY. Degrees:** B.A., B.Ed., B.S.
**Majors:** Accounting, Advertising, Aerospace Maintenance Engineering Technology, African-American Studies, American Sign Language/English Interpreting, Applied Physics, Art/Architecture, Athletic Training, Biochemistry, Biology, Cardiopulmonary Science, Chemical Engineering, Chemistry, Civil Engineering, Communication Studies, Computer Engineering, Computer Science, Computer Systems, Computer Technology, Criminology/Corrections, Database Management, Early Childhood Education, Economics, Electrical Engineering, Electrical Engineering Technology, Elementary Education, English, Entrepreneurship/Small Business Management, Environmental Geology, Exercise Physiology, Finance/Insurance, French, General Engineering Program, Geology, German, Health Information Administration, History, Human Resources Management, Human Services, Industrial Engineering, International Business, Italian, Legal Studies, Linguistics, Logistics/Transportation, Management, Management Information Systems, Marketing, Mathematics, Mechanical Engineering, Mechanical Engineering Technology, Medical Laboratory Science, Music, Newspaper/Print Media, Nursing, Pharmacy, Philosophy, Physical Therapy, Physics, Policing/Security, Political Science, Power Systems Engineering, Programming Languages, Psychology, Public Relations, Radio/Television News, Respiratory Therapy, Russian, Sociology/Anthropology, Spanish, Theatre/Dance, Toxicology.
**Distribution of degrees:** The majors with the highest enrollment are criminal justice, physical therapy, and pharmacy; environmental geology has the lowest.
**Requirements:** General education requirement.
**Academic regulations:** Freshmen must maintain minimum 1.4 GPA.
**Special:** Interdisciplinary minors offered in Asian studies, cinema studies, Latino/Latin American/Caribbean studies, linguistics, marine studies, media studies, technical communication, urban studies, and women's studies. Alternative Freshman-Year Program provides opportunity to strengthen academic skills before committing to a specific field of study. University is affiliated with Forsyth Sch for Dental Hygienists for specific academic programs. Elementary Spanish offered for criminal justice and human services majors; French offered for business and economics students. East/West Marine Biology program. Associate's degrees offered. Self-designed majors. Double majors. Dual degrees. Independent study. Accelerated study. Pass/fail grading option. Internships. Cooperative education programs. Graduate school at which undergraduates may take graduate-level courses. Preprofessional programs in law, medicine, veterinary science, and dentistry. 3-2 engineering program. B.A. or B.S./J.D. program. Member of Massachusetts Bay Marine Studies Consortium. Teacher certification in early childhood, elementary, and secondary education. Exchange programs abroad in Australia (Sch of Field Studies), England (Oxford U), Ireland (Inst of Public Administration in Dublin, Queen's U of Belfast), Kenya (Sch of Field Studies), Russia (Moscow State U), and the U.S. Virgin Islands (Sch of Field Studies). Study abroad also in Belgium. ROTC. NROTC and AFROTC at Boston U.
**Honors:** Honors program. Honor societies.
**Academic Assistance:** Remedial reading, writing, math, and study skills. Nonremedial tutoring.
**STUDENT LIFE. Housing:** Students may live on or off campus. Coed, women's, and men's dorms. Fraternity housing. School-owned/operated apartments. Suites. 65% of students live in college housing.
**Social atmosphere:** According to the student newspaper, "Because we are in the heart of Boston, the campus is not unified. Groups of students go their own way off campus." Popular gathering spots for students are the Quad, the Husky Statue, Punter's Pub, Maxwell Jump's, Our House East, and A Steak in the Neighborhood. Greeks and the Northeastern News have some influence on campus. Hockey games, concerts, and lectures are among the year's favorite events.
**Services and counseling/handicapped student services:** Placement services. Health service. Women's center. Day care. Counseling services for minority and older students. Personal and psychological counseling. Career and academic guidance services. Religious counseling. Physically disabled student services. Learning disabled program/services. Notetaking services. Tape recorders. Tutors. Reader services for the blind.
**Campus organizations:** Undergraduate student government. Student newspaper (News, published once/week; NU Times, published once/month). Literary magazine. Yearbook. Radio station. Band, choral society, orchestra, dance and theatre groups, outing club, Activities Programming Board, departmental, political, professional, social service, and special-interest groups, 190 organizations in all. 18 fraternities, six chapter houses; nine sororities, no chapter houses. 9% of men join a fraternity. 5% of women join a sorority.
**Religious organizations:** Bahai Club, Campus Crusade for Christ, Chinese Christian Fellowship, Christian Student Union, Hillel, Hindu Student Association, Islamic Society.
**Minority/foreign student organizations:** Asian-American Student Association, Black Student Association, Latin American Student Organization. International Student Forum, African, Arab, Armenian, Cambodian, Cape Verdean, Caribbean, Chinese, Greek, Haitian, Indian, Indonesian, Iranian, Japanese, Korean, Lebanese, Taiwanese, and Vietnamese groups.
**ATHLETICS. Physical education requirements:** None.
**Intercollegiate competition:** 5% of students participate. Baseball (M), basketball (M,W), crew (M,W), cross-country (M,W), diving (M,W), field hockey (W), football (M), golf (M), gymnastics (W), ice hockey (M,W), soccer (M), swimming (M,W), tennis (M), track (indoor) (M,W), track (outdoor) (M,W), track and field (indoor) (M,W), track and field (outdoor) (M,W), volleyball (W). Member of ECAC, Hockey East Association, NCAA Division I, NCAA Division I-AA for football, North Atlantic Conference.
**Intramural and club sports:** 20% of students participate. Intramural aerobics, basketball, ice hockey, racquetball, soccer, softball. Men's club lacrosse, martial arts, rugby, volleyball. Women's club martial arts, soccer.
**ADMISSIONS. Academic basis for candidate selection** (in order of priority): Secondary school record, class rank, standardized test scores, school's recommendation, essay.
**Nonacademic basis for candidate selection:** Extracurricular participation is emphasized. Particular talent or ability and alumni/ae relationship are important. Character and personality and geographical distribution are considered.
**Requirements:** Graduation from secondary school is required; GED is accepted. 17 units and the following program of study are recommended: 4 units of English, 3 units of math, 3 units of science including 2 units of lab, 2 units of foreign language, 3 units of social studies, 2 units of history. Project Ujima and Alternative Freshman Year Program for applicants not normally admissible. SAT is required; ACT may be substituted. ACH recommended. Campus visit and interview recommended. No off-campus interviews.
**Procedure:** Take SAT or ACT by February of 12th year. Visit college for interview by March 31 of 12th year. Suggest filing application by March 1; no deadline. Notification of admission on rolling basis. Reply is required by May 1. $100 nonrefundable tuition deposit. $400 nonrefundable room deposit. Freshmen accepted for terms other than fall.
**Special programs:** Admission may be deferred one year. Credit and/or placement may be granted through CEEB Advanced Placement exams for scores of 3 or higher. Credit and/or placement may be granted through CLEP subject exams. Placement may be granted through challenge exams. Early entrance/early admission program. Concurrent enrollment program.
**Transfer students:** Transfer students accepted for terms other than fall. In fall 1993, 19% of all new students were transfers into all classes. 2,306 transfer applications were received, 1,181 were accepted. Application deadline is March 1 (priority filing date) for fall; February 1 for spring. Minimum 2.3 GPA required. Lowest course grade accepted is "C." Maximum number of transferable credits is 128 quarter hours. At least 48 quarter hours must be completed at the university to receive degree.
**Admissions contact:** Kevin Kelly, Dean and Director of Admissions. 617 373-2200.
**FINANCIAL AID. Available aid:** Pell grants, SEOG, state scholarships and grants, school scholarships and grants, private scholarships and grants, ROTC scholarships, academic merit scholarships, and athletic scholarships. Perkins Loans (NDSL), PLUS, Stafford Loans (GSL), NSL, Health Professions Loans, state loans, and SLS. TERI Loans, MELA Loans. Tuition Plan Inc., Knight Tuition Plans, and deferred payment plan.
**Financial aid statistics:** 8% of aid is not need-based. In 1993-94, 95% of all undergraduate applicants received aid; 71% of freshman applicants. Average amounts of aid awarded freshmen: Scholarships and grants, $5,941; loans, $2,582.
**Supporting data/closing dates:** FAFSA/FAF: Priority filing date is March 1. School's own aid application: Priority filing date is April 15. State aid form: Priority filing date is May 1. Income tax forms. Notification of awards begins April 1.
**Financial aid contact:** Jean C. Eddy, M.S., Dean of Financial Aid. 617 373-3190.
**STUDENT EMPLOYMENT.** College Work/Study Program. Institutional employment. 83% of full-time undergraduates work on campus during school year. Students may expect to earn an average of $1,709 during school year. Off-campus part-time employment opportunities rated "good."

**COMPUTER FACILITIES.** 500 IBM/IBM-compatible and Macintosh/Apple microcomputers; 275 are networked. Students may access Digital, SUN minicomputer/mainframe systems, BITNET, Internet. Residence halls may be equipped with networked microcomputers. Client/LAN operating systems include Apple/Macintosh. Computer languages and software packages include Assembler, BASIC, C, COBOL, Excel, FORTRAN, Harvard Graphics, ImSL, Lotus 1-2-3, Microsoft Word, Microsoft Windows, Paradox, Pascal, SAS, SPSS, Super Paint; numerous other financial, spreadsheet, statistical, word processing packages. Computer facilities are available to all students.
**Fees:** None.
**Hours:** 24 hours for multi-user systems and modem access; 8 AM-midn. for microcomputer labs.

**GRADUATE CAREER DATA.** Graduate school percentages: 1% enter law school. 1% enter medical school. 1% enter graduate business programs. 6% enter graduate arts and sciences programs. Highest graduate school enrollments: Boston U, Tufts U, U of California.

**PROMINENT ALUMNI/AE.** Charles A. Cocotas, President and CEO, TCBY Systems, Inc.; Richard J. Egan, Chairman, EMC Corporation; Joseph C. Farrell, Chairman and CEO, The Pittston Company; J. Philip Johnston, President, CARE; William M. McDonough, Commentator, NBC; Dennis J. Picard, Chairman and CEO, Raytheon Company; Edward L. Wax, Chairman and CEO, Saatchi & Saatchi Advertising Worldwide.

# Pine Manor College

**Chestnut Hill, MA 02167** **617 731-7000**

**1994-95 Costs.** Tuition: $15,190. Room: $3,230. Board: $3,230. Fees, books, misc. academic expenses (school's estimate): $1,175.
**Enrollment.** 370 women (full-time). Freshman class: 354 applicants, 323 accepted, 125 enrolled.
**Test score averages/ranges.** Average SAT scores: 391 verbal, 393 math. Range of SAT scores of middle 50%: 360-430 verbal, 350-440 math.
**Faculty.** 36 full-time; 25 part-time. 70% of faculty holds highest degree in specific field. Student/faculty ratio: 13 to 1.
**Selectivity rating.** Noncompetitive.

**PROFILE.** Pine Manor, founded in 1911, is a private, liberal arts college for women. Its 80-acre campus is located in Chestnut Hill, two miles from downtown Boston.

**Accreditation:** NEASC.
**Religious orientation:** Pine Manor College is nonsectarian; no religious requirements.
**Library:** Collections totaling over 83,469 volumes, 468 periodical subscriptions, and 8,000 microform items.
**Special facilities/museums:** Art gallery, on-campus preschool, communications center.
**Athletic facilities:** Gymnasium, badminton, basketball, paddle tennis, tennis, and volleyball courts, dance studio, weight room, field hockey and lacrosse fields, cross-country trail, soccer and softball fields.

**STUDENT BODY. Undergraduate profile:** 31% are state residents; 16% are transfers. 16% Asian-American, 7% Black, 8% Hispanic, 64% White, 5% Other. Average age of undergraduates is 20.
**Freshman profile:** 1% of freshmen who took SAT scored 600 or over on verbal, 2% scored 600 or over on math; 14% scored 500 or over on verbal, 15% scored 500 or over on math; 49% scored 400 or over on verbal, 40% scored 400 or over on math; 88% scored 300 or over on verbal, 87% scored 300 or over on math. 88% of accepted applicants took SAT; 12% took ACT. 49% of freshmen come from public schools.
**Undergraduate achievement:** 72% of fall 1992 freshmen returned for fall 1993 term. 51% of entering class graduated. 5% of students who completed a degree program immediately went on to graduate study.
**Foreign students:** 90 students are from out of the country. Countries represented include Brazil, Colombia, Japan, Saudi Arabia, Switzerland, and Thailand; 18 in all.

**PROGRAMS OF STUDY. Degrees:** B.A.
**Majors:** Accounting, American Studies, Art History, Biology, Biopsychology, Communication, English, Management, Psychology, Public Relations, Sociology, Visual Arts/Interior Design.
**Distribution of degrees:** The majors with the highest enrollment are management, communication, and psychology; biopsychology and American studies have the lowest.
**Requirements:** General education requirement.
**Academic regulations:** Freshmen must maintain minimum 1.80 GPA; sophomores, juniors, seniors, 2.00 GPA.
**Special:** Minors offered in most majors and in drama, French, history, international business, Italian, marketing, music, political science, Spanish, and women's studies. Associate's degrees offered. Self-designed majors. Double majors. Independent study. Accelerated study. Pass/fail grading option. Internships. Graduate school at which undergraduates may take graduate-level courses. Preprofessional programs in law and medicine. Member of Massachusetts Bay Marine Studies Consortium. Cross-registration with Babson Coll, Boston Architectural Center, Boston Washington Semester and Sea Semester. Teacher certification in early childhood and elementary education. Certification in specific subject areas. Study abroad in Australia, Canada, England, France, Italy, and Spain.
**Honors:** Honors program. Honor societies.
**Academic Assistance:** Remedial reading, writing, math, and study skills. Nonremedial tutoring.

**ADMISSIONS. Academic basis for candidate selection** (in order of priority): Secondary school record, school's recommendation, class rank, essay, standardized test scores.
**Nonacademic basis for candidate selection:** Character and personality, extracurricular participation, particular talent or ability, geographical distribution, and alumni/ae relationship are important.
**Requirements:** Graduation from secondary school is required; GED is accepted. 16 units and the following program of study are required: 4 units of English, 2 units of math, 2 units of science, 2 units of social studies, 6 units of academic electives. SAT or ACT is required. Campus visit and interview recommended. Off-campus interviews available with an admissions representative.
**Procedure:** Suggest filing application by May 1. Application deadline is August 1. Notification of admission on rolling basis. Reply is required by May 1. $500 tuition deposit, refundable until May 1. Freshmen accepted for terms other than fall.
**Special programs:** Admission may be deferred. Credit and/or placement may be granted through CEEB Advanced Placement exams for scores of 3 or higher. Credit may be granted through CLEP general exams. Early decision program. In fall 1993, six applied for early decision and five were accepted. Deadline for applying for early decision is November 25.
**Transfer students:** Transfer students accepted for terms other than fall. In fall 1993, 16% of all new students were transfers into all classes. 40 transfer applications were received, 35 were accepted. Application deadline is rolling for fall; rolling for spring. Lowest course grade accepted is "C-." Maximum number of transferable credits is 96 semester hours. At least 32 semester hours must be completed at the college to receive degree.
**Admissions contact:** Mark Gonthier, M.S., Director of Admissions & Financial Aid. 617 731-7104.

**FINANCIAL AID. Available aid:** Pell grants, SEOG, state scholarships and grants, school scholarships and grants, private scholarships and grants, and aid for undergraduate foreign students. PLUS, Stafford Loans (GSL), private loans, and SLS. Tuition Plan Inc. and AMS. TERI loans.
**Financial aid statistics:** In 1993-94, 98% of all undergraduate applicants received aid; 98% of freshman applicants. Average amounts of aid awarded freshmen: Scholarships and grants, $10,530; loans, $2,625.
**Supporting data/closing dates:** FAFSA/FAF/FFS: Priority filing date is March 15. School's own aid application: Priority filing date is March 15. Income tax forms: Accepted on rolling basis. Notification of awards on rolling basis.
**Financial aid contact:** Kathleen Russell, Director of Financial Aid. 617 731-7129.

# Regis College

**Weston, MA 02193** **617 893-1820**

**1994-95 Costs.** Tuition: $12,700. Room & board: $5,800. Fees, books, misc. academic expenses (school's estimate): $625.
**Enrollment.** 601 women (full-time). Freshman class: 423 applicants, 385 accepted, 138 enrolled. 25 women.
**Test score averages/ranges.** Average SAT scores: 432 verbal, 453 math. Range of SAT scores of middle 50%: 380-470 verbal, 390-510 math.
**Faculty.** 51 full-time; 53 part-time. 65% of faculty holds doctoral degree. Student/faculty ratio: 10 to 1.
**Selectivity rating.** Less competitive.

**PROFILE.** Regis, founded in 1927, is a church-affiliated, liberal arts college for women. Programs are offered through the Divisions of Humanities, Natural Science, Nursing, and Social Science. Its 168-acre campus, a former estate including a neo-Georgian mansion, is located in Weston.

**Accreditation:** NEASC. Professionally accredited by the Council on Social Work Education, the National League for Nursing.
**Religious orientation:** Regis College is affiliated with the Roman Catholic Church; One course in philosophy or religious studies required.
**Library:** Collections totaling over 141,290 volumes, 762 periodical subscriptions, and 28,735 microform items.
**Special facilities/museums:** Philatelic museum.
**Athletic facilities:** Gymnasium, swimming pool, badminton, basketball, racquetball, squash, tennis, and volleyball courts, dance studio, weight room, field hockey, soccer, and softball fields.

**STUDENT BODY. Undergraduate profile:** 88% are state residents; 14% are transfers. 1% Asian-American, 2% Black, 4% Hispanic, 89% White, 4% Other. Average age of undergraduates is 19.
**Freshman profile:** 2% of freshmen who took SAT scored 600 or over on verbal, 7% scored 600 or over on math; 15% scored 500 or over on verbal, 29% scored 500 or over on math; 71% scored 400 or over on verbal, 75% scored 400 or over on math; 98% scored 300 or over on verbal, 98% scored 300 or over on math. 100% of accepted applicants took SAT. 74% of freshmen come from public schools.
**Undergraduate achievement:** 81% of fall 1991 freshmen returned for fall 1992 term. 70% of entering class graduated.
**Foreign students:** 51 students are from out of the country. Countries represented include El Salvador, India, Japan, Panama, Peru, and Saudi Arabia.

**PROGRAMS OF STUDY. Degrees:** B.A., B.S.
**Majors:** Art, Biology, Chemistry, Classical Studies, Communications, Economics, English, French, German, History, Management, Mathematics, Political Science, Psychology, Social Work, Sociology, Spanish.
**Distribution of degrees:** The majors with the highest enrollment are management, communications, and English; German, Spanish, and mathematics have the lowest.
**Requirements:** General education requirement.
**Academic regulations:** Freshmen must maintain minimum 1.75 GPA; sophomores, juniors, seniors, 2.00 GPA.
**Special:** Self-designed majors. Double majors. Independent study. Pass/fail grading option. Internships. Preprofessional programs in law, medicine, veterinary science, and dentistry. 3-2 engineering program with Worcester Polytech Inst. Member of Sisters of St. Joseph Consortium. Washington Semester. Cross-registration with Babson Coll, Bentley Coll, and Boston Coll. Teacher certification in early childhood, elementary, and secondary education. Certification in specific subject areas. Study abroad in numerous countries.
**Honors:** Honors program. Honor societies.
**Academic Assistance:** Remedial reading, writing, math, and study skills.

**ADMISSIONS. Academic basis for candidate selection** (in order of priority): Secondary school record, class rank, school's recommendation, standardized test scores, essay.
**Nonacademic basis for candidate selection:** Character and personality and extracurricular participation are emphasized. Particular talent or ability is important. Alumni/ae relationship is considered.
**Requirements:** Graduation from secondary school is required; GED is accepted. 16 units and the following program of study are required: 4 units of English, 3 units of math, 2 units of science including 1 unit of lab, 2 units of foreign language, 2 units of social studies, 3 units of academic electives. R.N. required of nursing program applicants. SAT is required; ACT may be substituted. ACH recommended. Campus visit and interview recommended. Off-campus interviews available with an admissions representative.
**Procedure:** Take SAT or ACT by December of 12th year. Visit college for interview by April of 12th year. Suggest filing application by fall. Application deadline is April 1. Notification of admission on rolling basis. Reply is required by May 1. $150 nonrefundable tuition deposit. $150 nonrefundable room deposit. Freshmen accepted for terms other than fall.
**Special programs:** Admission may be deferred one year. Credit and/or placement may be granted through CEEB Advanced Placement exams for scores of 4 or higher. Credit may be granted through CLEP subject exams. Early entrance/early admission program.
**Transfer students:** Transfer students accepted for terms other than fall. In fall 1992, 14% of all new students were transfers into all classes. 56 transfer applications were received, 55 were accepted. Application deadline is August 1 for fall; January 1 for spring. Minimum 2.0 GPA required. Lowest course grade accepted is "C." Maximum number of transferable credits is 20 courses. At least 18 courses must be completed at the college to receive degree.
**Admissions contact:** Mary E. Dunn, M.B.A., Director of Admissions. 617 893-1820, extension 2050.

**FINANCIAL AID. Available aid:** Pell grants, SEOG, state scholarships and grants, school scholarships and grants, private scholarships and grants, academic merit scholarships, and aid for undergraduate foreign students. Perkins Loans (NDSL), PLUS, Stafford Loans (GSL), private loans, and SLS. Tuition Plan Inc., Knight Tuition Plans, AMS, and guaranteed tuition.
**Financial aid statistics:** 1% of aid is not need-based. In 1992-93, 86% of all undergraduate applicants received aid; 90% of freshman applicants. Average amounts of aid awarded freshmen: Scholarships and grants, $6,400; loans, $3,349.
**Supporting data/closing dates:** FAFSA/FAF: Priority filing date is February 15. School's own aid application: Priority filing date is February 15. Income tax forms: Priority filing date is February 15. Notification of awards on rolling basis.
**Financial aid contact:** Lisa Proctor, Director of Financial Aid. 617 893-1820, extension 2004.

## Salem State College

**Salem, MA 01970** **508 741-6000**

**1994-95 Costs.** Tuition: $1,408 (state residents), $5,542 (out-of-state). Room: $1,950. Board: $1,564. Fees, books, misc. academic expenses (school's estimate): $2,240.
**Enrollment.** Undergraduates: 2,395 men, 3,227 women (full-time). Freshman class: 3,976 applicants, 3,169 accepted, 1,333 enrolled. Graduate enrollment: 280 men, 670 women.
**Test score averages/ranges.** Average SAT scores: 421 verbal, 454 math.
**Faculty.** 311 full-time; 50 part-time. 70% of faculty holds highest degree in specific field. Student/faculty ratio: 18 to 1.
**Selectivity rating.** Less competitive.

**PROFILE.** Salem State, founded in 1854, is a public, liberal arts college. Programs are offered through the Schools of Arts and Sciences, Business, Education, Nursing, and Social Work and the Division of Graduate and Continuing Education. Its 62-acre campus is located in Salem, 20 miles north of Boston.

**Accreditation:** NEASC. Professionally accredited by the Council on Social Work Education, the National Association of Schools of Art and Design, the National Council for Accreditation of Teacher Education, the National League for Nursing.
**Religious orientation:** Salem State College is nonsectarian; no religious requirements.
**Library:** Collections totaling over 240,000 volumes, 1,360 periodical subscriptions, and 316,000 microform items.
**Special facilities/museums:** On-campus elementary school, color TV studio, instructional media center.
**Athletic facilities:** Gymnasium, basketball, squash, and tennis courts, swimming pool, dance studio, gymnastics and weight rooms, ice rink, baseball, field hockey, soccer, and softball fields.

**STUDENT BODY. Undergraduate profile:** 98% are state residents. 1% Asian-American, 5% Black, 3% Hispanic, 1% Native American, 90% White. Average age of undergraduates is 24.
**Freshman profile:** 98% of accepted applicants took SAT. 70% of freshmen come from public schools.
**Foreign students:** 100 students are from out of the country. Countries represented include China, France, Iceland, Japan, Nigeria, and Sweden; 30 in all.

**PROGRAMS OF STUDY. Degrees:** B.A., B.F.A., B.S.
**Majors:** Accounting, Art, Aviation Science, Biology, Business Administration, Business Economics, Business Education, Cartography, Chemistry, Communications, Computer Science, Criminal Justice, Early Childhood Education, Economics, Elementary Education, English, Finance, Fire Science, General Studies, Geography, Geological Science, Graphic Design, History, Management, Management Information Systems, Marine Biology, Mathematics, Nuclear Medical Technology, Nursing, Office Administration, Photography/Film, Political Science, Psychology, Social Service, Sociology, Sport/Fitness/Leisure, Theatre Arts.
**Distribution of degrees:** The majors with the highest enrollment are business, criminal justice, and education; chemistry and biology have the lowest.
**Requirements:** General education requirement.
**Academic regulations:** Freshmen must maintain minimum 1.40 GPA; sophomores, 1.40 GPA; juniors, 1.75 GPA; seniors, 1.75 GPA.
**Special:** Concentrations and minors in some majors and in applied math/computer science, athletic administration, drawing/painting, English literature, environment and man, health, linguistics, marketing, physical education, printmaking, pure math, quantitative management, secretarial sciences, three-dimensional design, travel/tourism, and urban studies. Cartography program. Self-designed majors. Double majors. Pass/fail grading option. Internships. Graduate school at which undergraduates may take graduate-level courses. Preprofessional programs in law, medicine, and dentistry. Member of Northeast Consortium of Colleges and Universities in Massachusetts. Teacher certification in early childhood, elementary, and secondary education. Exchange programs abroad in England and France. Study abroad also in Italy and Spain.
**Honors:** Honors program. Honor societies.
**Academic Assistance:** Remedial reading, writing, math, and study skills.

**STUDENT LIFE. Housing:** Students may live on or off campus. Coed dorms. 20% of students live in college housing.
**Social atmosphere:** The campus center, the Commons cafe, and the library are popular gathering spots. The African-American society, student theatre ensemble, and the student government association are influential in student life. Sporting events and theatre department productions are popular events. More than half of the student body commutes so "on-campus life is a struggle. People seem reluctant to attend evening functions," reports the editor of the student newspaper.
**Services and counseling/handicapped student services:** Placement services. Health service. Women's center. Day care. Counseling services for minority and older students. Birth control, personal, and psychological counseling. Career and academic guidance services. Religious counseling. Physically disabled student services. Tape recorders. Reader services for the blind.
**Campus organizations:** Undergraduate student government. Student newspaper (Log, published once/two weeks). Yearbook. Radio and TV stations. Band, glee club, folk song society, coffeehouse, Footlighters, veterans club, Young Democrats, Young Republicans, athletic, departmental, service, and special-interest groups, 41 organizations in all.
**Religious organizations:** Campus Christian Fellowship, Catholic Student Community.
**Minority/foreign student organizations:** African-American Association, Hispanic Society. International Student Association.

**ATHLETICS. Physical education requirements:** Two semester hours of physical education required.
**Intercollegiate competition:** 8% of students participate. Baseball (M), basketball (M,W), cheerleading (M,W), cross-country (M,W), diving (M,W), field hockey (W), golf (M), ice hockey (M), sailing (M,W), soccer (M,W), softball (W), swimming (M,W), tennis (M,W), track (outdoor) (M,W), track and field (outdoor) (M,W), volleyball (W). Member of ECAC, Massachusetts State College Athletic Conference, NCAA Division III, New England Collegiate Athletic Conference.
**Intramural and club sports:** 39% of students participate. Intramural aerobics, Alpine skiing, basketball, flag football, hiking, karate, racquetball, sailing, scuba diving, soccer, softball, tennis, volleyball. Men's club karate, volleyball. Women's club cheerleading, karate.

**ADMISSIONS. Academic basis for candidate selection** (in order of priority): Secondary school record, class rank, school's recommendation, standardized test scores.
**Nonacademic basis for candidate selection:** Character and personality, extracurricular participation, and alumni/ae relationship are important. Particular talent or ability is considered.
**Requirements:** Graduation from secondary school is required; GED is accepted. 16 units and the following program of study are required: 4 units of English, 3 units of math, 2 units of lab science, 2 units of foreign language, 1 unit of social studies, 1 unit of history, 3 units of academic electives. Minimum combined SAT score of 800, rank in top half of secondary school class, and minimum 2.5 GPA required of out-of-state applicants. Biology and chemistry required of nursing program applicants. Portfolio required of art program applicants. Audition required of music program applicants. Alternatives for Individual Development program for applicants not normally admissible. SAT is required; ACT may be substituted. Campus visit and interview recommended. No off-campus interviews.
**Procedure:** Take SAT or ACT by December of 12th year. Visit college for interview by December of 12th year. Suggest filing application by December 1. Application deadline is March 1. Notification of admission on rolling basis. Reply is required within 30 days of acceptance. $100 nonrefundable tuition deposit. $50 nonrefundable room deposit. Freshmen accepted for terms other than fall.
**Special programs:** Credit and/or placement may be granted through CEEB Advanced Placement exams for scores of 3 or higher. Credit and/or placement may be granted through CLEP general and subject exams. Credit and placement may be granted through ACT PEP, DANTES, and challenge exams and life experience. Early entrance/early admission program. Concurrent enrollment program.
**Transfer students:** Transfer students accepted for terms other than fall. In fall 1993, 1,526 transfer applications were received, 1,262 were accepted. Application deadline is December 15 for fall; April 1 for spring. Minimum 2.0 GPA required. Lowest course grade accepted is "C-." Maximum number of transferable credits is 90 semester hours. At least 30 semester hours must be completed at the college to receive degree.
**Admissions contact:** David Sartwell, Ed.D., Director of Admissions. 508 741-6200.

**FINANCIAL AID. Available aid:** Pell grants, SEOG, state scholarships and grants, school scholarships, and academic merit scholarships. Perkins Loans (NDSL), PLUS, Stafford Loans (GSL), NSL, state loans, school loans, and SLS. Knight Tuition Plans.
**Financial aid statistics:** 5% of aid is not need-based. In 1993-94, 62% of all undergraduate applicants received aid; 54% of freshman applicants. Average amounts of aid awarded freshmen: Scholarships and grants, $1,606; loans, $2,084.
**Supporting data/closing dates:** FAFSA/FAF: Priority filing date is April 15. Certification Statement: Priority filing date is April 15. Notification of awards begins April 15.

**Financial aid contact:** Janet Lundstrom, M.B.A., Director of Financial Aid. 508 741-6061.

**STUDENT EMPLOYMENT.** College Work/Study Program. 16% of full-time undergraduates work on campus during school year. Students may expect to earn an average of $1,250 during school year. Off-campus part-time employment opportunities rated "poor."

**COMPUTER FACILITIES.** 217 IBM/IBM-compatible and Macintosh/Apple microcomputers. Students may access Digital minicomputer/mainframe systems. Computer languages and software packages include BASIC, COBOL, FORTRAN, Lotus 1-2-3, Pascal, WordPerfect. Computer facilities are available to all students.
**Fees:** None.
**Hours:** 7 AM-10:30 PM.

# School of the Museum of Fine Arts

**Boston, MA 02115** **617 267-6100**

**1993-94 Costs.** Tuition: $12,975. Housing: None. Fees, books, misc. academic expenses (school's estimate): $1,240.
**Enrollment.** Undergraduates: 235 men, 287 women (full-time). Freshman class: 616 applicants, 172 enrolled.
**Test score averages/ranges.** N/A.
**Faculty.** 56 full-time; 126 part-time. Student/faculty ratio: 10 to 1.
**Selectivity rating.** N/A.

**PROFILE.** The School of the Museum of Fine Arts, founded in 1876, is a private college. Its 14-acre campus is located in downtown Boston.

**Accreditation:** NEASC. Professionally accredited by the National Association of Schools of Art and Design.
**Religious orientation:** School of the Museum of Fine Arts is nonsectarian; no religious requirements.
**Library:** Collections totaling over 12,000 volumes and 100 periodical subscriptions.

**STUDENT BODY. Undergraduate profile:** 70% are state residents; 51% are transfers. 3% Asian-American, 1% Black, 2% Hispanic, 81% White, 13% Other. Average age of undergraduates is 27.
**Freshman profile:** 50% of freshmen come from public schools.
**Undergraduate achievement:** 83% of fall 1992 freshmen returned for fall 1993 term.
**Foreign students:** 51 students are from out of the country. Countries represented include Argentina, Canada, Germany, Japan, Korea, and the United Kingdom; 21 in all.

**PROGRAMS OF STUDY. Degrees:** B.A., B.F.A.
**Special:** No majors as such; courses offered in ceramics, computer graphics, drawing, film, graphic design, jewelry/metalsmithing, painting, photography, printmaking, sculpture, stained glass, and video. Students construct own course programs on elective basis, with advice from teachers and administration members. Each student's work is evaluated at end of semester by review board comprised of teachers and students. Every student must produce new body of work each semester for oral and written critical review which measures total body of work produced. Self-designed majors. Double majors. Dual degrees. Independent study. Cooperative education programs. Five-year B.F.A./B.A. or B.F.A./B.S. program with Tufts U. Member of East Coast Consortium of Art Schools and Pro Arts Consortium, and Association of Independent Colleges of Art and Design (AICAD). Teacher certification in elementary and secondary education. Study abroad in numerous countries.

**ADMISSIONS. Academic basis for candidate selection** (in order of priority): Secondary school record.
**Requirements:** Graduation from secondary school is required; GED is accepted. No specific distribution of secondary school units required. Portfolio required of art program applicants. SAT is required; ACT may be substituted. Campus visit and interview recommended. Off-campus interviews available with an admissions representative.
**Procedure:** Take SAT or ACT by August 1 of 12th year. Visit college for interview by August 1 of 12th year. Suggest filing application by March 15; no deadline. Notification of admission on rolling basis. Reply is required by May 1 or within three weeks of acceptance. $200 nonrefundable tuition deposit. Freshmen accepted for terms other than fall.
**Special programs:** Admission may be deferred one year. Credit and placement may be granted through life experience.
**Transfer students:** Transfer students accepted for terms other than fall. In fall 1993, 51% of all new students were transfers into all classes. Application deadline is rolling for fall; rolling for spring. At least 72 semester hours must be completed at the college to receive degree.
**Admissions contact:** Alan Van Reed, Dean of Admissions. 617 267-1218.

**FINANCIAL AID. Available aid:** Pell grants, SEOG, state scholarships and grants, school scholarships and grants, and aid for undergraduate foreign students. PLUS, Stafford Loans (GSL), state loans, and SLS. TERI, EXCEL, and SMART loans. Installment payment plan.
**Financial aid statistics:** In 1993-94, 100% of all undergraduate applicants received aid. Average amounts of aid awarded freshmen: Scholarships and grants, $5,707; loans, $2,625.
**Supporting data/closing dates:** FAFSA/FAF: Priority filing date is February 1; accepted on rolling basis. School's own aid application: Priority filing date is March 15; accepted on rolling basis. Notification of awards on rolling basis.
**Financial aid contact:** Kathleen Joint, Director of Financial Aid. 617 267-6100, extension 645.

**STUDENT EMPLOYMENT.** College Work/Study Program. Institutional employment. Off-campus part-time employment opportunities rated "excellent."

**COMPUTER FACILITIES.** 46 Macintosh/Apple microcomputers; 30 are networked. Students may access Internet. Client/LAN operating systems include Apple/Macintosh, UNIX/XENIX/AIX, X-windows, LocalTalk/AppleTalk. Computer languages and software packages include Assembly, BASIC, C, Hypertalk, Lingo; numerous art software, word processing programs. Computer facilities are available to all students.
**Fees:** Computer fee is included in tuition/fees.

**PROMINENT ALUMNI/AE.** Doug and Mike Starn, photographers; Jim Dine, artist; Cy Twombley, painter.

# Simmons College

**Boston, MA 02115** **617 521-2000**

**1993-94 Costs.** Tuition: $15,296. Room & board: $6,740. Fees, books, misc. academic expenses (school's estimate): $938.
**Enrollment.** 1,144 women (full-time). Freshman class: 1,003 applicants, 782 accepted, 295 enrolled. Graduate enrollment: 248 men, 1,782 women.
**Test score averages/ranges.** Range of SAT scores of middle 50%: 410-550 verbal, 410-550 math. Average ACT scores: 24 composite. Range of ACT scores of middle 50%: 22-26 composite.
**Faculty.** 116 full-time; 107 part-time. 78% of faculty holds doctoral degree. Student/faculty ratio: 10 to 1.
**Selectivity rating.** Less competitive.

**PROFILE.** Simmons, founded in 1899, is a private, multipurpose college for women. Its 12-acre campus, located in Boston, includes nine Georgian-style dormitories.
**Accreditation:** NEASC. Professionally accredited by the American Library Association, the American Physical Therapy Association, the Council on Social Work Education, the National League for Nursing.
**Religious orientation:** Simmons College is nonsectarian; no religious requirements.
**Library:** Collections totaling over 259,645 volumes, 2,010 periodical subscriptions, and 1,400 microform items.
**Special facilities/museums:** Art gallery, media center, science center with dream/sleep analysis lab, physical therapy clinic areas.
**Athletic facilities:** Gymnasium, swimming pool, badminton, racquetball, squash, and volleyball courts, weight training rooms, cardiovascular area, indoor track, rowing tank, dance studio.

**STUDENT BODY. Undergraduate profile:** 59% are state residents; 16% are transfers. 7% Asian-American, 8% Black, 4% Hispanic, 65% White, 16% Other. Average age of undergraduates is 20.
**Freshman profile:** 90% of accepted applicants took SAT. 78% of freshmen come from public schools.
**Undergraduate achievement:** 81% of fall 1992 freshmen returned for fall 1993 term. 60% of entering class graduated. 10% of students who completed a degree program immediately went on to graduate study.
**Foreign students:** 69 students are from out of the country. Countries represented include Japan, Korea, the former Soviet Republics, Taiwan, Thailand, and the United Kingdom; 33 in all.

**PROGRAMS OF STUDY. Degrees:** B.A., B.S.
**Majors:** Accounting, Advertising/Public Relations, African American Studies, Art, Arts Administration, Biochemistry, Biology, Chemistry, Chemistry/Management, Communications, Computer Science, Economics, Education, English, Environmental Science, Finance, Foreign Languages/Literatures, Graphic Design, History, Human Services, International Management, International Relations, Management, Management Information Systems, Marketing, Mathematics, Music, Nursing, Nutrition, Pharmacy, Philosophy, Physical Therapy, Political Science, Pre-Law, Pre-Medicine, Psychobiology, Psychology, Retailing, Self-Planned Program, Sociology, Special Education, Women's Studies.
**Distribution of degrees:** The majors with the highest enrollment are nursing, psychology, and communications; chemistry, computer science, and African American studies have the lowest.
**Requirements:** General education requirement.
**Academic regulations:** Minimum 1.67 GPA must be maintained.
**Special:** Interdepartmental programs include accounting, advertising, journalism, and marketing. Communications students produce award-winning alumni magazine. Freshmen Honors Program. Self-designed majors. Double majors. Dual degrees. Independent study. Pass/fail grading option. Internships. Graduate school at which undergraduates may take graduate-level courses. Preprofessional programs in law, medicine, and pharmacy. 4-1 dual-degree program in chemistry and pharmacy with Massachusetts Coll of Pharmacy. Six-year physical therapy program. Member of Fenway Colleges Consortium. Cross-registration with Emmanuel Coll, Hebrew Coll, New England Conservatory of Music, and Wheelock Coll. Washington Semester. Exchange programs with Fisk U, Mills Coll, and Spelman Coll. Teacher certification in early childhood, elementary, secondary, and special education. Certification in specific subject areas. Exchange program abroad in Thailand. Study abroad also in Spain (U de Cordoba), Australia, England, France, Israel, Italy, Japan, and other countries. ROTC at Northeastern U.
**Honors:** Honors program. Honor societies.
**Academic Assistance:** Remedial writing and study skills. Nonremedial tutoring.

**STUDENT LIFE. Housing:** Students may live on or off campus. Coed and women's dorms. 70% of students live in college housing.
**Social atmosphere:** According to the editor of the student newspaper, "The social life is what you make of it. There is a lot to do." Some popular on-campus gathering spots are Fens cafeteria, Commuter Lounge, Quadside Cafe, and Bartol Hall. Favorite off-campus spots include Who's On First, Pizzeria Uno, Copperfields, and Boston Billiards. The Student Government Association, Activities Planning Board, and the Black Student organization are influential on campus. Popular campus events include Fallfest Weekend, Head of the Charles Regatta, Lecture Series, Winter Weekend, May Day, and Senior Week.

**Services and counseling/handicapped student services:** Placement services. Health service. Women's center. Counseling services for minority and older students. Birth control, personal, and psychological counseling. Career and academic guidance services. Religious counseling. Physically disabled student services. Learning disabled services. Notetaking services. Tape recorders. Tutors. Reader services for the blind.
**Campus organizations:** Undergraduate student government. Student newspaper (Simmons News, published once/week). Literary magazine. Yearbook. Chorale, drama club, Model UN, Commuter Organization, Administrative Management Society, Activity Planning Board, Amnesty International, Society Against Racism, Feminist Union, Lesbian and Bisexual Association, 70 organizations in all.
**Religious organizations:** Catholic Student Organization, Hillel, Intervarsity Christian Fellowship.
**Minority/foreign student organizations:** Black Student Organization, Asian Student Association, Latin American group. International Student Association.

**ATHLETICS. Physical education requirements:** Four semesters of physical education required.
**Intercollegiate competition:** 10% of students participate. Basketball (W), crew (W), cross-country (W), diving (W), field hockey (W), sailing (W), soccer (W), swimming (W), tennis (W), track (outdoor) (W). Member of NCAA Division III.
**Intramural and club sports:** 5% of students participate. Intramural racquetball, soccer, squash, volleyball.

**ADMISSIONS. Academic basis for candidate selection** (in order of priority): Secondary school record, class rank, standardized test scores, school's recommendation, essay.
**Nonacademic basis for candidate selection:** Extracurricular participation and alumni/ae relationship are considered.
**Requirements:** Graduation from secondary school is required; GED is accepted. 15 units and the following program of study are recommended: 4 units of English, 3 units of math, 3 units of science, 2 units of foreign language, 3 units of social studies. SAT is required; ACT may be substituted. Campus visit and interview recommended. Off-campus interviews available with admissions and alumni representatives.
**Procedure:** Take SAT or ACT by January of 12th year. Visit college for interview by January of 12th year. Application deadline is February 1. Notification of admission by April 15. Reply is required by May 1. $200 nonrefundable tuition deposit. $250 room deposit, refundable until July 1. Freshmen accepted for terms other than fall.
**Special programs:** Admission may be deferred one year. Credit and/or placement may be granted through CEEB Advanced Placement exams for scores of 4 or higher. Credit may be granted through CLEP general and subject exams and ACT PEP exams. Credit and placement may be granted through challenge exams. Early decision program. Deadline for applying for early decision is November 15 for Plan I, January 1 for Plan II. Early entrance/early admission program. Concurrent enrollment program.
**Transfer students:** Transfer students accepted for terms other than fall. In fall 1993, 16% of all new students were transfers into all classes. 172 transfer applications were received, 107 were accepted. Application deadline is April 1 for fall; December 1 for spring. Minimum 2.7 GPA recommended. Lowest course grade accepted is "C-." Maximum number of transferable credits is 80 semester hours. At least 48 semester hours must be completed at the college to receive degree.
**Admissions contact:** Deborah Wright, M.A., M.Ed., Dean of Admission. 617 521-2051, 800 345-8468.

**FINANCIAL AID. Available aid:** Pell grants, SEOG, state scholarships, school scholarships and grants, private scholarships and grants, and academic merit scholarships. Perkins Loans (NDSL), PLUS, Stafford Loans (GSL), school loans, and SLS. Knight Tuition Plans and AMS.
**Financial aid statistics:** 5% of aid is not need-based. In 1993-94, 95% of all undergraduate applicants received aid; 82% of freshman applicants. Average amounts of aid awarded freshmen: Scholarships and grants, $12,500; loans, $2,650.
**Supporting data/closing dates:** FAFSA/FAF: Priority filing date is February 1. School's own aid application: Priority filing date is February 1. Income tax forms: Accepted on rolling basis. Notification of awards begins April 1.
**Financial aid contact:** Lisa Mayer, M. Ed., Director of Financial Aid. 617 521-2036.

**STUDENT EMPLOYMENT.** College Work/Study Program. Institutional employment. 32% of full-time undergraduates work on campus during school year. Students may expect to earn an average of $1,086 during school year. Off-campus part-time employment opportunities rated "good."

**COMPUTER FACILITIES.** 91 IBM/IBM-compatible and Macintosh/Apple microcomputers; 15 are networked. Students may access Digital minicomputer/mainframe systems, Internet. Residence halls may be equipped with networked terminals. Computer languages and software packages include BASIC, C, COBOL, FORTRAN, LISP, MINITAB, Pascal, SPSS. Computer facilities are available to all students.
**Fees:** None.
**Hours:** 24 hours.

**GRADUATE CAREER DATA.** Graduate school percentages: 1% enter law school. 1% enter medical school. 10% enter graduate business programs. 14% enter graduate arts and sciences programs. Highest graduate school enrollments: Boston Coll, Boston U, Harvard U, New York U, Northeastern U, Simmons C, Suffolk U. 31% of graduates choose careers in business and industry. Companies and businesses that hire graduates: Boston public schools, Coopers & Lybrand, IDS Financial Services, KPMG Peat Marwick, Newton public schools, Prudential, Scudder Stevens & Clark, TJ Maxx.

**PROMINENT ALUMNI/AE.** Joyce Kulhawik, art and entertainment reporter, WBZ-TV Boston; Pat Collins, entertainment editor, WWOR; Anne Bryant, president, American Association of University Women.

# Simon's Rock College of Bard

**Great Barrington, MA 01230** **413 528-0771**

**1993-94 Costs.** Tuition: $16,400. Room: $2,740. Board: $2,880. Fees, books, misc. academic expenses (school's estimate): $2,120.
**Enrollment.** Undergraduates: 151 men, 150 women (full-time). Freshman class: 317 applicants, 190 accepted, 132 enrolled.
**Test score averages/ranges.** Average SAT scores: 587 verbal, 589 math.
**Faculty.** 34 full-time; 12 part-time. 90% of faculty holds doctoral degree. Student/faculty ratio: 8 to 1.
**Selectivity rating.** More competitive.

**PROFILE.** Simon's Rock College of Bard is a private, liberal arts college for students of high school age. It was founded in 1964, adopted coeducation in 1970, and became part of Bard College in 1979. Its 275-acre campus is located in Great Barrington, 60 miles west of Springfield.

**Accreditation:** NEASC.
**Religious orientation:** Simon's Rock College of Bard is nonsectarian; no religious requirements.
**Library:** Collections totaling over 60,000 volumes, 330 periodical subscriptions, and 1,800 microform items.
**Special facilities/museums:** Arts center.
**Athletic facilities:** Gymnasium, soccer and softball fields, tennis and volleyball courts, and weight rooms.

**STUDENT BODY. Undergraduate profile:** 12% are state residents; 1% are transfers. 5% Asian-American, 5% Black, 2% Hispanic, 84% White, 4% Other. Average age of undergraduates is 16.
**Freshman profile:** 11% of freshmen who took SAT scored 700 or over on verbal, 13% scored 700 or over on math; 47% scored 600 or over on verbal, 48% scored 600 or over on math; 85% scored 500 or over on verbal, 92% scored 500 or over on math; 100% scored 400 or over on verbal, 100% scored 400 or over on math. 70% of freshmen come from public schools.
**Undergraduate achievement:** 85% of fall 1992 freshmen returned for fall 1993 term. 98% of entering class graduated.
**Foreign students:** 11 students are from out of the country.

**PROGRAMS OF STUDY. Degrees:** B.A.
**Majors:** Art/Aesthetics, Environmental Studies, Intercultural Studies, Literary Studies, Natural Science, Quantitative Studies, Social Sciences, Women's Studies.
**Distribution of degrees:** The majors with the highest enrollment are literary studies, social sciences, and environmental studies; quantitative studies, natural science, and intercultural studies have the lowest.
**Requirements:** General education requirement.
**Special:** College's purpose is to provide college academics to students of secondary school age. Students enter college after completion of the 10th or 11th year and pursue a college curriculum. Liberal arts programs lead to associate's and bachelor's degrees for qualified students with at least two completed years of secondary school. One-week language and thinking workshop for all entering freshmen. Independent study. Accelerated study. Pass/fail grading option. Internships. Preprofessional programs in medicine. Study abroad in France, Japan, Thailand, Turkey, and the United Kingdom.
**Academic Assistance:** Remedial study skills. Nonremedial tutoring.

**STUDENT LIFE. Housing:** All freshmen must live on campus. Coed, women's, and men's dorms. 95% of students live in college housing.
**Social atmosphere:** The student newspaper reports, "Most folks here are so happy not to be in high school that the overall social ambiance is one of relief and low pressure." Social life is what you make of it. Students create study groups and Pictionary tournaments, as well as doing other assorted wild things in their spare time. No particular group exerts any influence so students are more or less on their own." Popular activities are going to the South Berkshire Concert Series (classical, jazz, folk), Mayfest, plays, and movies. "Halloween is always big, as are major snowfalls." Favorite gathering spots include the dormitory lounges ("pits"), theatre, music studios, downtown pizza joints, deli, and the neighboring woods.
**Services and counseling/handicapped student services:** Placement services. Health service. Women's center. Birth control, personal, and psychological counseling. Career and academic guidance services.
**Campus organizations:** Undergraduate student government. Student newspaper (The Llama, published weekly). Literary magazine. Yearbook. Radio station. Chamber music ensemble, chorus, film society, humanities forum, outing club, social/cultural committee, theatre and dance productions, Students for Social Change, PEACE (environmental group).
**Religious organizations:** Bible study.
**Minority/foreign student organizations:** Black Students Organization.

**ATHLETICS. Physical education requirements:** Four terms of physical education required.
**Intercollegiate competition:** 12% of students participate. Basketball (M,W), fencing (M), soccer (M,W), tennis (M,W), volleyball (W). Member of Colonial States Conference, National Small College Athletic Association.
**Intramural and club sports:** 30% of students participate. Intramural Alpine skiing, bowling, canoeing, contact improvisational dance, fencing, flag football, hiking, horsemanship, martial arts, mountain biking, Nordic skiing, rock climbing, soccer, softball, swimming, tai chi, tennis, ultimate frisbee, volleyball, weight lifting. Men's club basketball, soccer, volleyball. Women's club basketball, soccer, volleyball.

**ADMISSIONS. Academic basis for candidate selection** (in order of priority): Essay, secondary school record, school's recommendation, standardized test scores.

**Nonacademic basis for candidate selection:** Character and personality are emphasized. Extracurricular participation and particular talent or ability are important.
**Requirements:** Graduation from secondary school is not required. No specific distribution of secondary school units required. SAT is required; ACT may be substituted. PSAT is recommended. Campus visit and interview required. Off-campus interviews available with an admissions representative.
**Procedure:** Notification of admission on rolling basis. Reply is required within two weeks of acceptance. $350 nonrefundable tuition deposit. Freshmen accepted for terms other than fall.
**Special programs:** Admission may be deferred one year. Early entrance/early admission program.
**Transfer students:** Transfer students accepted for terms other than fall. In fall 1993, 1% of all new students were transfers into all classes. Lowest course grade accepted is "C."
**Admissions contact:** Brian Hopewell, M.A., Director of Admission. 800 235-7186.

**FINANCIAL AID. Available aid:** Pell grants, SEOG, state scholarships and grants, school scholarships and grants, private scholarships and grants, and academic merit scholarships. Perkins Loans (NDSL), PLUS, Stafford Loans (GSL), state loans, and SLS.
**Financial aid statistics:** In 1993-94, 70% of all undergraduate applicants received aid; 70% of freshman applicants. Average amounts of aid awarded freshmen: Scholarships and grants, $9,000.
**Supporting data/closing dates:** FAFSA/FAF. Income tax forms. Notification of awards on rolling basis.
**Financial aid contact:** Eve Caimano, Director of Financial Aid. 413 528-7297.

**STUDENT EMPLOYMENT.** College Work/Study Program. Institutional employment. Off-campus part-time employment opportunities rated "fair."

**COMPUTER FACILITIES.** 15 IBM/IBM-compatible and Macintosh/Apple microcomputers. Students may access minicomputer/mainframe systems, Internet. Residence halls may be equipped with stand-alone microcomputers, networked microcomputers, modems. Computer languages and software packages include AppleWorks, BASIC, C. Computer facilities are available to all students.
**Fees:** Computer fee is included in tuition/fees.
**Hours:** 8 AM-noon.

# Smith College

**Northampton, MA 01063 — 413 584-2700**

**1994-95 Costs.** Tuition: $18,820. Room & board: $6,390. Fees, books, misc. academic expenses (school's estimate): $1,263.
**Enrollment.** 2,459 women (full-time). Freshman class: 2,925 applicants, 1,598 accepted, 632 enrolled. Graduate enrollment: 14 men, 77 women.
**Test score averages/ranges.** Range of SAT scores of middle 50%: 520-630 verbal, 550-650 math. Range of ACT scores of middle 50%: 25-30 composite.
**Faculty.** 248 full-time; 28 part-time. 86% of faculty holds doctoral degree. Student/faculty ratio: 10 to 1.
**Selectivity rating.** Highly competitive.

**PROFILE.** Smith, founded in 1871, is a private, liberal arts college for women. Its 125-acre campus is located in Northampton, 20 miles from Springfield.

**Accreditation:** NEASC. Professionally accredited by the Council on Social Work Education.
**Religious orientation:** Smith College is nonsectarian; no religious requirements.
**Library:** Collections totaling over 1,092,180 volumes, 6,167 periodical subscriptions, and 68,227 microform items.
**Special facilities/museums:** Art museum, greenhouse, language lab, campus school (early childhood and elementary education), lithographic press, two electron microscopes, several observatories with reflector, refractor, and radio telescopes.
**Athletic facilities:** Gymnasiums, weight room, swimming pool, croquet and squash courts, indoor and outdoor tennis courts, indoor and outdoor tracks, riding ring and trails, athletic fields, cross-country course, softball diamond.

**STUDENT BODY. Undergraduate profile:** 19% are state residents; 11% are transfers. 12% Asian-American, 4% Black, 4% Hispanic, 74% Unreported, 6% Non-resident aliens. Average age of undergraduates is 20.
**Freshman profile:** 8% of freshmen who took SAT scored 700 or over on verbal, 10% scored 700 or over on math; 44% scored 600 or over on verbal, 52% scored 600 or over on math; 83% scored 500 or over on verbal, 91% scored 500 or over on math; 97% scored 400 or over on verbal, 100% scored 400 or over on math; 100% scored 300 or over on verbal. 97% of accepted applicants took SAT; 3% took ACT. 71% of freshmen come from public schools.
**Undergraduate achievement:** 88% of fall 1992 freshmen returned for fall 1993 term. 83% of entering class graduated. 23% of students who completed a degree program immediately went on to graduate study.
**Foreign students:** 47 students are from out of the country. Countries represented include Bangladesh, Brazil, Bulgaria, Canada, India, and Japan; 30 in all.

**PROGRAMS OF STUDY. Degrees:** A.B.
**Majors:** Afro-American Studies, American Studies, Ancient Studies, Anthropology, Art, Astronomy, Biochemistry, Biological Sciences, Chemistry, Classical Languages/Literature, Comparative Literature, Computer Science, Dance, Economics, Education/Child Study, English Language/Literature, French Language/Literature, Geology, German Language/Literature, Government, History, Italian Language/Literature, Latin American Studies, Mathematics, Medieval Studies, Music, Philosophy, Physics, Psychology, Religion/Biblical Literature, Russian Language/Literature, Sociology, Spanish/Portuguese, Theatre, Women's Studies.
**Distribution of degrees:** The majors with the highest enrollment are government, psychology, and English; astronomy and dance have the lowest.
**Academic regulations:** Minimum 2.0 GPA must be maintained.
**Special:** Minors offered in most majors and in archaeology, architecture/urbanism, art history, classics, computer science/language, East Asian languages/literature, East Asian studies, engineering, ethics, exercise/sports studies, film studies, graphic art, Greek, history of the sciences, international relations, Jewish studies, Latin, logic, marine sciences, mathematical foundations of computer science, neuroscience, political economy, public policy, simulation and modeling, studio art, systems analysis, Third World development studies, and urban studies. Self-designed majors. Double majors. Dual degrees. Independent study. Pass/fail grading option. Internships. Graduate school at which undergraduates may take graduate-level courses. Preprofessional programs in law, health, and business. Member of Five College Consortium; cross-registration possible. Washington Semester. Williams-Mystic Seaport Semester (Connecticut). Exchange programs with Howard U, North Carolina Central U, Pomona Coll, Spelman Coll, and Tougaloo Coll. Member of Twelve College Exchange Program. Teacher certification in elementary education. Exchange program abroad in Italy (Intercollegiate Center for Classical Studies). Study abroad also in China, England, France, Germany, India, Japan, the former Soviet Republics, Spain, and Switzerland. ROTC and AFROTC at U of Massachusetts at Amherst.
**Honors:** Phi Beta Kappa. Honors program. Honor societies.
**Academic Assistance:** Remedial reading, writing, math, and study skills. Nonremedial tutoring.

**STUDENT LIFE. Housing:** All students of traditional college age must live on campus. Women's dorms. School-owned/operated apartments. Off-campus privately-owned housing. 90% of students live in college housing.
**Services and counseling/handicapped student services:** Placement services. Health service. Day care. Counseling services for minority and older students. Birth control, personal, and psychological counseling. Career and academic guidance services. Religious counseling. Physically disabled student services. Learning disabled services. Notetaking services. Tape recorders. Tutors. Reader services for the blind.
**Campus organizations:** Undergraduate student government. Student newspaper (Sophian, published once/week). Literary magazine. Yearbook. Radio station. Choir, orchestra, glee club, small singing groups, drama and dance organizations, lectures, concerts, art exhibits, tutoring programs, work with the handicapped, academic, political, and special-interest groups, 92 organizations in all.
**Religious organizations:** Bahai Association, Christian Science Association, ecumenical Christian group, Newman Association, Hillel, Episcopal Fellowship, Evangelical Christian Fellowship.
**Minority/foreign student organizations:** NAACP, Black Student Alliance, Nosotras. International Student Organization, African, Asian, Korean, and South Asian groups.

**ATHLETICS. Physical education requirements:** None.
**Intercollegiate competition:** 14% of students participate. Alpine skiing (W), basketball (W), crew (W), cross-country (W), diving (W), field hockey (W), horsemanship (W), lacrosse (W), soccer (W), softball (W), squash (W), swimming (W), tennis (W), track and field (indoor) (W), track and field (outdoor) (W), volleyball (W). Member of ECAC, Massachusetts Association for Intercollegiate Athletics for Women, NCAA Division III, New England Women's 8.
**Intramural and club sports:** 31% of students participate. Intramural Alpine skiing, badminton, basketball, crew, cross-country, floor hockey, fun runs, indoor soccer, inner tube water polo, kickball, Nordic skiing, softball, squash, team handball, tennis, track meets, triathlon, ultimate frisbee, volleyball, walleyball. Women's club basketball, croquet, cycling, fencing, golf, horsemanship, Nordic skiing, outing, rugby, sailing, soccer, softball.

**ADMISSIONS. Academic basis for candidate selection** (in order of priority): Secondary school record, class rank, standardized test scores, essay, school's recommendation.
**Nonacademic basis for candidate selection:** Extracurricular participation and particular talent or ability are important. Character and personality, geographical distribution, and alumni/ae relationship are considered.
**Requirements:** Graduation from secondary school is recommended; GED is accepted. 16 units and the following program of study are recommended: 4 units of English, 3 units of math, 2 units of science, 3 units of foreign language, 2 units of social studies, 2 units of history. SAT or ACT is required. ACH recommended. Campus visit and interview recommended. Off-campus interviews available with an alumni representative.
**Procedure:** Take SAT or ACT by February of 12th year. Take ACH by February 1 of 12th year. Visit college for interview by February 1 of 12th year. Application deadline is February 1. Notification of admission by April 2. Reply is required by May 1. $100 nonrefundable tuition deposit. $200 nonrefundable room deposit. Freshmen accepted for fall term only.
**Special programs:** Admission may be deferred one year. Credit and/or placement may be granted through CEEB Advanced Placement exams for scores of 4 or higher. Early decision program. In fall 1993, 196 applied for early decision and 121 were accepted. Deadline for applying for early decision is November 15 and January 1. Early entrance/early admission program.
**Transfer students:** Transfer students accepted for terms other than fall. In fall 1993, 11% of all new students were transfers into all classes. 301 transfer applications were received, 135 were accepted. Application deadline is May 15 for fall; November 15 for spring. Lowest course grade accepted is "C." Maximum number of transferable credits is 64 semester hours. At least 64 semester hours must be completed at the college to receive degree.
**Admissions contact:** Juliet Brigham, Director of Admission. 413 585-2500.

**FINANCIAL AID. Available aid:** Pell grants, SEOG, state scholarships and grants, school grants, private scholarships and grants, and aid for undergraduate foreign students. Perkins Loans (NDSL), PLUS, Stafford Loans (GSL), state loans, school loans, private loans, and SLS. Knight Tuition Plans. Smith College 10-month payment plan. Tuition prepayment option.
**Financial aid statistics:** In 1993-94, 95% of all undergraduate applicants received aid; 87% of freshman applicants. Average amounts of aid awarded freshmen: Scholarships and grants, $12,577; loans, $2,625.
**Supporting data/closing dates:** FAFSA/FAF/FFS: Deadline is February 1. School's own aid application: Deadline is January 15. State aid form: Accepted on rolling basis. Income tax forms: Deadline is February 1. Notification of awards begins in early April.
**Financial aid contact:** Myra Baas Smith, M.A., Director of Financial Aid. 413 585-2530.

**STUDENT EMPLOYMENT.** College Work/Study Program. Institutional employment. 63% of full-time undergraduates work on campus during school year. Students may ex-

pect to earn an average of $825 during school year. Off-campus part-time employment opportunities rated "fair."

**COMPUTER FACILITIES.** 230 IBM/IBM-compatible and Macintosh/Apple microcomputers; 225 are networked. Students may access Digital, SUN minicomputer/mainframe systems, BITNET, Internet. Residence halls may be equipped with modems. Client/LAN operating systems include Apple/Macintosh, DOS, Novell. Computer languages and software packages include APL, BASIC, BMDP, C, DCL, FORTRAN, HyperCard, LISP, Mathematica, Microsoft Word, MINITAB, Modula 2, Pascal, Prolog, Quattro Pro, RSI, SPSS-X, TEX, TSP, XyWrite, WordPerfect. Computer facilities are available to all students.
**Fees:** None.
**Hours:** 8 AM-midn.; extended hours during exams.

**GRADUATE CAREER DATA.** Graduate school percentages: 10% enter law school. 2% enter medical school. 2% enter dental school. 43% enter graduate arts and sciences programs. Highest graduate school enrollments: Columbia U, Harvard U, U of Massachusetts, U of Pennsylvania. 29% of graduates choose careers in business and industry. Companies and businesses that hire graduates: U.S. Government, John Hancock, Smith Coll, U of California.

**PROMINENT ALUMNAE.** Margaret Mitchell, author, *Gone with the Wind;* Julia Child, chef, author, and TV show personality; Barbara Bush, former First Lady of the United States; Anne Morrow Lindbergh, author and navigator; Gloria Steinem, writer and founder of *Ms.* magazine; Sylvia Plath, poet and author; Glenda Reed, president, NAACP chapter, and corporate officer, Aetna Life.

# Springfield College

**Springfield, MA 01109-3797 — 413 788-3000**

**1993-94 Costs.** Tuition: $10,268. Room & board: $4,830. Fees, books, misc. academic expenses (school's estimate): $600.
**Enrollment.** Undergraduates: 1,036 men, 1,010 women (full-time). Freshman class: 2,288 applicants, 1,394 accepted, 494 enrolled.
**Test score averages/ranges.** Average SAT scores: 420 verbal, 480 math. Range of SAT scores of middle 50%: 380-470 verbal, 420-540 math.
**Faculty.** 174 full-time; 22 part-time. 52% of faculty holds doctoral degree. Student/faculty ratio: 20 to 1.
**Selectivity rating.** Competitive.

**PROFILE.** Springfield, founded in 1885, is a private, multipurpose college. Programs are offered through the Divisions of Arts and Sciences; Health, Physical Education, and Recreation; and Graduate and Continuing Studies. Its 167-acre campus is located in Springfield, 50 miles west of Worcester.
**Accreditation:** NEASC. Professionally accredited by the American Physical Therapy Association, the National Council for Accreditation of Teacher Education.
**Religious orientation:** Springfield College is nonsectarian; no religious requirements.
**Library:** Collections totaling over 147,000 volumes, 810 periodical subscriptions, and 500,000 microform items.
**Special facilities/museums:** International center, college-operated summer day camp, language lab.
**Athletic facilities:** Gymnasium, arena, weight rooms, swimming pool, baseball, football, softball, soccer fields.

**STUDENT BODY. Undergraduate profile:** 28% are state residents; 18% are transfers. 1% Asian-American, 6% Black, 1% Hispanic, 91% White, 1% Other. Average age of undergraduates is 21.
**Freshman profile:** 96% of accepted applicants took SAT; 1% took ACT. 82% of freshmen come from public schools.
**Undergraduate achievement:** 82% of fall 1991 freshmen returned for fall 1992 term. 11% of students who completed a degree program went on to graduate study within one year.
**Foreign students:** 57 students are from out of the country. Countries represented include China, England, Ireland, Japan, Sweden, and Switzerland; 12 in all.

**PROGRAMS OF STUDY. Degrees:** B.A., B.S.
**Majors:** Art, Art Therapy, Athletic Training, Biology, Business Management, Chemistry/Biology, Commercial Recreation, Community Recreation, Computer Systems Management, Early Childhood Education, Elementary Education, English, Environmental Studies, Equestrian Arts, General Community Rehabilitation, Gerontology, Group Work/Community Organization, Health Education, Health/Fitness, Health Services Administration, History, Human Services Administration, Intergroup Relations, Laboratory Science, Management/Supervision, Mathematics, Mathematics/Computer Science, Medical Technology, Physical Education, Physical Therapy, Political Science, Psychology, Rehabilitation Services, Resource Management, Social Welfare, Sociology, Therapeutic Rehabilitation/Education, Urban Life, Youth/Agency Work.
**Distribution of degrees:** The majors with the highest enrollment are physical education, business management, and rehabilitation services; art therapy, mathematics, and history have the lowest.
**Requirements:** General education requirement.
**Academic regulations:** Freshmen must maintain minimum 1.70 GPA; sophomores, 1.85 GPA; juniors, 1.95 GPA; seniors, 2.00 GPA.
**Special:** Minors offered in several majors and in approximately 12 other fields. Self-designed majors. Double majors. Independent study. Pass/fail grading option. Internships. Cooperative education programs. Graduate school at which undergraduates may take graduate-level courses. Preprofessional programs in law, medicine, veterinary science, and dentistry. 5-1/2-year entry-level master's degree program. Member of Cooperating Colleges of Greater Springfield; cross-registration possible. Teacher certification in early childhood, elementary, and secondary education. Exchange programs abroad in England (Chelsea School of Movement, Porlock Vale Equestrian Center). ROTC and AFROTC at Western New England Coll.
**Honors:** Phi Beta Kappa.
**Academic Assistance:** Nonremedial tutoring.

**STUDENT LIFE. Housing:** All freshmen, sophomores, and juniors must live on campus. Coed, women's, and men's dorms. School-owned/operated apartments. 80% of students live in college housing.
**Services and counseling/handicapped student services:** Placement services. Health service. Day care. Counseling services for minority and older students. Personal and psychological counseling. Career and academic guidance services. Religious counseling.
**Campus organizations:** Undergraduate student government. Student newspaper (Springfield Student, published once/week). Literary magazine. Yearbook. Radio station. College Singers, mixed chorus, stage band, Attic Players, Gymnastics Exhibition Dancers, speaker bureau, departmental and special-interest groups, 40 organizations in all.
**Religious organizations:** Campus Ministry, Newman Club.
**Minority/foreign student organizations:** Afro-American Club. International Relations Club.

**ATHLETICS. Physical education requirements:** Five semester hours of physical education required.
**Intercollegiate competition:** 85% of students participate. Baseball (M), basketball (M,W), cross-country (M,W), diving (M), field hockey (W), football (M), golf (M), gymnastics (M,W), lacrosse (M,W), soccer (M,W), softball (W), swimming (M,W), tennis (M,W), track and field (indoor) (M,W), track and field (outdoor) (M,W), volleyball (M,W), wrestling (M). Member of ECAC, NCAA Division I for field hockey, NCAA Division II, Northeast 10 Conference.
**Intramural and club sports:** 50% of students participate. Intramural basketball, floor hockey, flag football, soccer, softball, volleyball, water polo. Men's club cheerleading, crew, cycling, ice hockey, rugby. Women's club cheerleading, crew, cycling, rugby.

**ADMISSIONS. Academic basis for candidate selection** (in order of priority): Secondary school record, school's recommendation, class rank, standardized test scores, essay.
**Nonacademic basis for candidate selection:** Character and personality and extracurricular participation are emphasized. Particular talent or ability and alumni/ae relationship are important. Geographical distribution is considered.
**Requirements:** Graduation from secondary school is required; GED is accepted. 16 units required and the following program of study recommended: 4 units of English, 2 units of math, 2 units of science, 2 units of foreign language, 2 units of social studies, 4 units of electives. SAT is required; ACT may be substituted. Campus visit recommended. Off-campus interviews available with an alumni representative.
**Procedure:** Take SAT or ACT by December of 12th year. Visit college for interview by February 1 of 12th year. Suggest filing application by January 1. Application deadline is April 1. Notification of admission on rolling basis. Reply is required by May 1. $200 nonrefundable tuition deposit. Freshmen accepted for terms other than fall.
**Special programs:** Admission may be deferred one year. Credit may be granted through CEEB Advanced Placement for scores of 3 or higher. Credit may be granted through CLEP general and subject exams and DANTES exams. Early decision program. In fall 1992, 89 applied for early decision and 67 were accepted. Deadline for applying for early decision is December 1. Early entrance/early admission program.
**Transfer students:** Transfer students accepted for terms other than fall. In fall 1992, 18% of all new students were transfers into all classes. 226 transfer applications were received, 183 were accepted. Application deadline is June 1 for fall; December 1 for spring. Lowest course grade accepted is "C." Maximum number of transferable credits is 82 semester hours. At least 48 semester hours must be completed at the college to receive degree.
**Admissions contact:** Frederick Bartlett, M.Ed., Dean of Admissions. 413 788-3136.

**FINANCIAL AID. Available aid:** Pell grants, SEOG, state scholarships, and school scholarships. Perkins Loans (NDSL), PLUS, Stafford Loans (GSL), and SLS. Tuition Plan Inc. and Knight Tuition Plans. Monthly payment plan.
**Financial aid statistics:** In 1992-93, 75% of all undergraduate applicants received aid; 72% of freshman applicants. Average amounts of aid awarded freshmen: Scholarships and grants, $3,400.
**Supporting data/closing dates:** FAFSA/FAF: Priority filing date is April 1. School's own aid application: Deadline is April 1. Income tax forms: Deadline is April 1. Notification of awards begins March 15.
**Financial aid contact:** Linda Dagradi, Ed.D., Director of Financial Aid. 413 788-3108.

**STUDENT EMPLOYMENT.** College Work/Study Program. Institutional employment. 30% of full-time undergraduates work on campus during school year. Students may expect to earn an average of $1,100 during school year. Off-campus part-time employment opportunities rated "fair."

**COMPUTER FACILITIES.** 92 IBM/IBM-compatible and Macintosh/Apple microcomputers; all are networked. Students may access Prime minicomputer/mainframe systems. Computer languages and software packages include BASIC, COBOL, FORTRAN, Full Screen Editor, Lotus 1-2-3, Pascal, Prime Macro, RPG, SPSS-X, Word Juggler, WordStar 2000 Plus. Computer facilities are available to all students.
**Fees:** $50 computer fee per academic year; included in tuition/fees.
**Hours:** 9 AM-midn.

**GRADUATE CAREER DATA.** Highest graduate school enrollments: Smith Coll, Springfield Coll, U of Bridgeport. 14% of graduates choose careers in business and industry.

# Stonehill College

North Easton, MA 02357 508 238-1081

**1994-95 Costs.** Tuition: $12,170. Room & board: $6,172. Fees, books, misc. academic expenses (school's estimate): $760.
**Enrollment.** Undergraduates: 885 men, 1,106 women (full-time). Freshman class: 3,646 applicants, 2,300 accepted, 585 enrolled.
**Test score averages/ranges.** Average SAT scores: 480 verbal, 530 math. Range of SAT scores of middle 50%: 440-520 verbal, 480-580 math.
**Faculty.** 117 full-time; 65 part-time. 79% of faculty holds doctoral degree. Student/faculty ratio: 13 to 1.
**Selectivity rating.** Competitive.

**PROFILE.** Stonehill is a church-affiliated, multipurpose college. Founded in 1948, it adopted coeducation in 1951. Its 375-acre campus is located in North Easton, 25 miles south of Boston.

**Accreditation:** NEASC. Professionally accredited by the National Council for Accreditation of Teacher Education.
**Religious orientation:** Stonehill College is affiliated with the Roman Catholic Church (Holy Cross Fathers); two semesters of religion required.
**Library:** Collections totaling over 150,285 volumes, 1,138 periodical subscriptions, and 49,507 microform items.
**Special facilities/museums:** Institute for law and society, observatory.
**Athletic facilities:** Gymnasium, basketball, racquetball, squash, tennis, and volleyball courts, weight room, track, baseball, football, soccer, and softball fields.

**STUDENT BODY. Undergraduate profile:** 66% are state residents; 2% are transfers. 2% Asian-American, 1% Black, 1% Hispanic, 96% White. Average age of undergraduates is 20.
**Freshman profile:** 2% of freshmen who took SAT scored 700 or over on math; 5% scored 600 or over on verbal, 21% scored 600 or over on math; 37% scored 500 or over on verbal, 70% scored 500 or over on math; 86% scored 400 or over on verbal, 94% scored 400 or over on math; 98% scored 300 or over on verbal, 98% scored 300 or over on math. Majority of accepted applicants took SAT. 68% of freshmen come from public schools.
**Undergraduate achievement:** 87% of fall 1992 freshmen returned for fall 1993 term. 75% of entering class graduated. 17% of students who completed a degree program went on to graduate study within one year.
**Foreign students:** 27 students are from out of the country. Countries represented include China, Ghana, Japan, and Russia; 13 in all.

**PROGRAMS OF STUDY. Degrees:** B.A., B.S., B.S.Bus.Admin.
**Majors:** Accounting, American Studies, Biology, Chemistry, Communication, Computer Science, Criminal Justice, Economics, English, Finance, Foreign Languages, Health Care Administration, History, International Studies, Management, Managerial Economics, Marketing, Mathematics, Mathematics/Computer Science, Multidisciplinary Studies, Philosophy, Political Science, Psychology, Public Administration, Religious Studies, Sociology.
**Distribution of degrees:** The majors with the highest enrollment are communication, accounting, and psychology; chemistry, public administration, and religious studies have the lowest.
**Requirements:** General education requirement.
**Academic regulations:** Minimum 2.00 GPA must be maintained.
**Special:** Minors offered in most majors and in art history, business administration, computer information systems, early childhood education, elementary education, French, German, human or molecular biology, Irish studies, journalism/mass communication, labor studies, Middle Eastern and Asian studies, physics, Russian studies, secondary education, Spanish, and theatre arts. Biology major includes pre-dental/pre-medical and medical technology option. Self-designed majors. Independent study. Pass/fail grading option. Internships. Preprofessional programs in law, medicine, dentistry, and theology. 3-1 and 4-1 medical technology programs. Member of Southeastern Association for Cooperation of Higher Education in Massachusetts (SACHEM) and Massachusetts Bay Marine Studies Consortium. Washington Semester. Exchange program with Wheaton Coll. Teacher certification in early childhood, elementary, and secondary education. Certification in specific subject areas. Exchange programs abroad in Ireland (U Coll), Russia (Yaroslavl State U), and Quebec, Canada. Study abroad also in numerous other countries. ROTC.
**Honors:** Honors program. Honor societies.
**Academic Assistance:** Remedial writing and study skills. Nonremedial tutoring.

**STUDENT LIFE. Housing:** Students may live on or off campus. Coed, women's, and men's dorms. 80% of students live in college housing.
**Social atmosphere:** According to the editor of the student newspaper, "Stonehill has much to offer in social activities. The Theatre Company (producing one play each semester), the Student Government Association, and the residence areas all program enjoyable weekends with concerts, mixers, comedians, dramas, novelty performers, and cultural committee events off campus with transportation provided. Boston's excitement is a short distance away." Other popular events include the Boston Park Plaza semiformal, Alumni Day football game, trip to Fenway Park for a Red Sox game, and Senior 200 and 100 Days 'til Graduation parties. On campus, students gather at the dining commons; off campus, they head for local restaurants, clubs, movies, and malls.
**Services and counseling/handicapped student services:** Placement services. Health service. Counseling services for minority students. Personal and psychological counseling. Career and academic guidance services. Religious counseling. Physically disabled student services. Learning disabled services. Notetaking services. Tape recorders. Tutors. Reader services for the blind.
**Campus organizations:** Undergraduate student government. Student newspaper (Summit, published once/week). Literary magazine. Yearbook. Radio station. Academic clubs, chorus, A.C.E.S. (peer counseling group), Ames Society (service organization), Stonehill Theatre, dance group, environmental awareness group, Amnesty International, College Democrats, College Republicans, Community Services, Students for Life, alcohol awareness group, Circle K, RFK Society, wilderness bound, cheerleading, ski club, rugby, 51 organizations in all.
**Religious organizations:** Campus Ministry, Alliance for Justice and Peace, Brockton Interfaith Community, Easton Clergy, Habitat for Humanity, Into the Streets (community outreach), Knights of Columbus, Student Retreat Board, Student Worship Committee.
**Minority/foreign student organizations:** International Club.

**ATHLETICS. Physical education requirements:** None.
**Intercollegiate competition:** 15% of students participate. Baseball (M), basketball (M,W), cheerleading (W), cross-country (M,W), football (M), ice hockey (M), sailing (M,W), soccer (M,W), softball (W), tennis (M,W), track and field (indoor) (M,W), track and field (outdoor) (M,W), volleyball (W). Member of Eastern Collegiate Football Conference, ECAC, NCAA Division II, Northeast Ten Conference.
**Intramural and club sports:** 85% of students participate. Intramural basketball, cross-country, flag football, golf, indoor soccer, racquetball, softball, street hockey, volleyball, Wiffle ball. Men's club equestrian sports, rugby. Women's club equestrian sports.

**ADMISSIONS. Academic basis for candidate selection** (in order of priority): Secondary school record, class rank, standardized test scores, school's recommendation, essay.
**Nonacademic basis for candidate selection:** Character and personality, extracurricular participation, particular talent or ability, geographical distribution, and alumni/ae relationship are considered.
**Requirements:** Graduation from secondary school is required; GED is accepted. 16 units and the following program of study are required: 4 units of English, 2 units of math, 1 unit of lab science, 2 units of foreign language, 1 unit of history, 6 units of electives including 3 units of academic electives. Combined SAT score 1000-1200 and rank in top quarter of secondary school class recommended. Additional units in science and math recommended of science program applicants. SAT is required; ACT may be substituted. Campus visit recommended. No off-campus interviews.
**Procedure:** Take SAT or ACT by December of 12th year. Campus visit recommended by December. Application deadline is February 15. Acceptance notification between March 15 and April 1 for those who apply before February 15; thereafter on a space-available basis. Reply is required by May 1. $300 nonrefundable tuition deposit. Freshmen accepted for terms other than fall.
**Special programs:** Admission may be deferred one year. Credit may be granted through CEEB Advanced Placement for scores of 3 or higher. Credit may be granted through CLEP general and subject exams and military experience. Early entrance/early admission program. Concurrent enrollment program.
**Transfer students:** Transfer students accepted for terms other than fall. In fall 1993, 2% of all new students were transfers into all classes. 200 transfer applications were received, 79 were accepted. Application deadline is May 1 for fall; November 1 for spring. Minimum 2.0 GPA required. Lowest course grade accepted is "C." Maximum number of transferable credits is 60 semester hours. At least 60 semester hours must be completed at the college to receive degree.
**Admissions contact:** Brian P. Murphy, M.Ed., Dean of Admissions and Enrollment. 508 230-1373.

**FINANCIAL AID. Available aid:** Pell grants, SEOG, state scholarships and grants, school scholarships and grants, private scholarships and grants, ROTC scholarships, academic merit scholarships, and athletic scholarships. Perkins Loans (NDSL), PLUS, state loans, private loans, and SLS. MEFA. TERI. PLATO. EXCEL. Federal Direct Student Loans (FDSL). Knight Tuition Plans, AMS, family tuition reduction, and guaranteed tuition.
**Financial aid statistics:** 11% of aid is not need-based. In 1993-94, 100% of all undergraduate applicants received aid. Average amounts of aid awarded freshmen: Scholarships and grants, $4,881; loans, $3,217.
**Supporting data/closing dates:** FAFSA/FAF: Priority filing date is February 15. Income tax forms: Accepted on rolling basis. Notification of awards begins April 1.
**Financial aid contact:** Eileen K. O'Leary, Director of Financial Aid. 508 230-1088.

**STUDENT EMPLOYMENT.** College Work/Study Program. Institutional employment. 25% of full-time undergraduates work on campus during school year. Students may expect to earn an average of $800 during school year. Off-campus part-time employment opportunities rated "good."

**COMPUTER FACILITIES.** 60 IBM/IBM-compatible and Macintosh/Apple microcomputers; all are networked. Students may access Digital minicomputer/mainframe systems, Internet. Client/LAN operating systems include Apple/Macintosh, DOS, OS/2, Windows NT, DEC, LocalTalk/AppleTalk, Microsoft. Computer languages and software packages include Ada, BASIC, C, COBOL, dBASE, FORTRAN, LISP, Lotus 1-2-3, Mass-II, MINITAB, Pascal, RDB, SPSS-X, SQL, statistics, Turbo C++, WordPerfect. Computer facilities are available to all students.
**Fees:** $100 computer fee per computer lab.
**Hours:** 8 AM-11:30 PM (M-F); 8 AM-4 PM (Sa); 1 PM-midn. (Su).

**GRADUATE CAREER DATA.** Highest graduate school enrollments: Bentley Coll, Boston Coll, Boston U, Emerson Coll, Lesley Coll, New England Sch of Law, Northeastern U, Suffolk U. Companies and businesses that hire graduates: Blue Cross/Blue Shield, Coopers & Lybrand, W.B. Mason, Reebok, State Street Bank, Tufts Associated Health Plan.

**PROMINENT ALUMNI/AE.** James "Lou" Gorman, senior vice president, Boston Red Sox; Dick Flavin, national TV political commentator; Gerard O'Neill, editor, *Boston Globe's* investigative spotlight team, 1972 Pulitzer Prize winner; Dr. Judith McDowell, associate scientist, Woods Hole Oceanographic Institution.

# Suffolk University

**Boston, MA 02108** **617 573-8000**

**1994-95 Costs.** Tuition: $10,584. Housing: None. Fees, books, misc. academic expenses (school's estimate): $560.
**Enrollment.** Undergraduates: 1,027 men, 1,175 women (full-time). Freshman class: 1,263 applicants, 993 accepted, 370 enrolled. Graduate enrollment: 752 men, 600 women.
**Test score averages/ranges.** Average SAT scores: 440 verbal, 470 math. Range of SAT scores of middle 50%: 350-460 verbal, 380-520 math.
**Faculty.** 152 full-time; 146 part-time. 93% of faculty holds doctoral degree. Student/faculty ratio: 14 to 1.
**Selectivity rating.** Less competitive.

**PROFILE.** Suffolk, founded in 1906, is a private, comprehensive university. Its urban campus is located in the Beacon Hill section of Boston.

**Accreditation:** NEASC. Professionally accredited by the American Assembly of Collegiate Schools of Business, the National Association of Schools of Public Affairs and Administration.
**Religious orientation:** Suffolk University is nonsectarian; no religious requirements.
**Library:** Collections totaling over 286,600 volumes, 5,030 periodical subscriptions, and 757,900 microform items.
**Special facilities/museums:** Marine biology field station in Maine.

**STUDENT BODY. Undergraduate profile:** 95% are state residents; 48% are transfers. 6% Asian-American, 6% Black, 4% Hispanic, 66% White, 18% Other. Average age of undergraduates is 22.
**Freshman profile:** 1% of freshmen who took SAT scored 700 or over on math; 2% scored 600 or over on verbal, 6% scored 600 or over on math; 17% scored 500 or over on verbal, 31% scored 500 or over on math; 57% scored 400 or over on verbal, 68% scored 400 or over on math; 89% scored 300 or over on verbal, 96% scored 300 or over on math. 81% of accepted applicants took SAT. 70% of freshmen come from public schools.
**Undergraduate achievement:** 80% of fall 1992 freshmen returned for fall 1993 term. 40% of entering class graduated. 10% of students who completed a degree program immediately went on to graduate study.
**Foreign students:** 264 students are from out of the country. Countries represented include China, Hong Kong, Japan, Spain, Turkey, and Venezuela; 70 in all.

**PROGRAMS OF STUDY. Degrees:** B.A., B.F.A., B.S., B.S.Bus.Admin., B.S.Gen.Studies, B.S.Journ.
**Majors:** Accounting, Biochemistry, Biology, Biotechnology, Business Education/Office Technologies, Chemistry, Communications/Speech, Computer Engineering, Computer Engineering Technology, Computer Information Systems, Computer Science, Crime/Law/Deviance, Dramatic Arts/Drama, Dramatic Arts/Theatre, Economics, Education, Electronic Engineering Technology, Engineering Technology, English, Environmental Technology, Finance, Fine Arts, French, General Studies, Government, Graphic Design, History, Humanities, Industrial/Organizational Psychology, International Business, International Economics, Journalism, Life Sciences, Management, Marine Science, Marketing, Mathematics, Mathematics/Computer Science, Medical Biophysics, Medical Technology, Paralegal Studies, Philosophy, Physical Sciences, Physics, Psychology, Public Policy/Administration, Public Relations, Radiation Biology, Social Sciences, Social Work, Sociology, Spanish, Technical Communication.
**Distribution of degrees:** The majors with the highest enrollment are sociology, management, and finance; mathematics, physics, and engineering have the lowest.
**Requirements:** General education requirement.
**Academic regulations:** Freshmen must maintain minimum 1.80 GPA; sophomores, 1.90 GPA; juniors, 2.00 GPA; seniors, 2.00 GPA.
**Special:** Minors offered in criminology/law, legal studies, social work, Spanish/sociology, studio art, urban studies, and women's studies. Joint programs with New England Sch of Art & Design and Northeast Sch of Broadcasting. Certificate programs in accounting, human resource assistant, office systems, and paralegal. Associate's degrees offered. Double majors. Independent study. Accelerated study. Pass/fail grading option. Internships. Cooperative education programs. Graduate school at which undergraduates may take graduate-level courses. Preprofessional programs in law, medicine, veterinary science, and dentistry. B.S./B.A./M.B.A., B.S./B.A./J.D., B.A./J.D., B.S./J.D., M.B.A./J.D., and M.P.A./J.D. programs. 3-2 engineering programs with Boston U, Case Western Reserve U, U of Notre Dame, and Pace U. Washington Semester. Cooperative programs with Emerson Coll, Massachusetts General Hospital, New England Sch of Art & Design, and Northeast Sch of Broadcasting. Teacher certification in elementary and secondary education. Certification in specific subject areas. Exchange programs abroad in England (Regents Coll), Spain (Center for International Studies), and Switzerland (American Coll of Switzerland). Study abroad also in China (Stillwell Sch), the Czech Republic, France, Germany, Ireland, the Netherlands, Quebec, Russia (International U in Moscow), and Slovakia.
**Honors:** Phi Beta Kappa. Honors program. Honor societies.
**Academic Assistance:** Remedial reading, writing, math, and study skills.

**STUDENT LIFE. Housing:** Leased off-campus housing at neighboring college. Coed dorms. 5% of students live in college housing.
**Social atmosphere:** Favorite hangouts include local pubs, dance clubs, and the alternative music scene. Athletes, Program Council, and Council of Presidents are very influential on student life. Holiday parties, seasonal events, leadership retreat weekends, rathskellers, and the Temple Street Fair are popular social events. The student newspaper reports that the school is a commuter campus and it is difficult to encourage school social events. Students are usually carrying a full course load while working; however, they do enjoy all that Boston has to offer.
**Services and counseling/handicapped student services:** Placement services. Health service. Women's center. Counseling services for minority, veteran, and older students. Birth control, personal, and psychological counseling. Career and academic guidance services. Religious counseling. Physically disabled student services. Learning disabled services. Tape recorders.
**Campus organizations:** Undergraduate student government. Student newspaper (Suffolk Journal, published once/week). Literary magazine. Yearbook. Radio and TV stations. Drama workshop, theatre, debating, Evening Students Association, cheering club, criminology club, departmental, service, and special-interest groups, 41 organizations in all. Three fraternities, no chapter houses; one sorority, no chapter house. 1% of men join a fraternity. 1% of women join a sorority.
**Religious organizations:** Hillel.
**Minority/foreign student organizations:** Asian-American Association, Black Student Union, Haitian-American Student Association, Hispanic Association. International Student Association.

**ATHLETICS. Physical education requirements:** None.
**Intercollegiate competition:** 2% of students participate. Baseball (M), basketball (M), cross-country (M,W), golf (M), ice hockey (M), soccer (M), softball (W), tennis (M,W). Member of ECAC, NCAA Division III.
**Intramural and club sports:** 2% of students participate. Intramural basketball, football, softball. Men's club cheerleading. Women's club cheerleading.

**ADMISSIONS. Academic basis for candidate selection** (in order of priority): Secondary school record, class rank, standardized test scores, school's recommendation, essay.
**Nonacademic basis for candidate selection:** Character and personality and particular talent or ability are important. Extracurricular participation and alumni/ae relationship are considered.
**Requirements:** Graduation from secondary school is required; GED is accepted. 14 units and the following program of study are required: 4 units of English, 3 units of math, 1 unit of lab science, 1 unit of social studies, 1 unit of history, 4 units of electives. Combined SAT score of 900 and rank in top three-fifths of secondary school class recommended. Portfolio required of art program applicants. SAT or ACT is required. ACH recommended. Campus visit and interview recommended. No off-campus interviews.
**Procedure:** Take SAT or ACT by January of 12th year. Take ACH by January of 12th year. Visit college for interview by March of 12th year. Suggest filing application by April. Application deadline is June 1. Notification of admission on rolling basis. Reply is required by May 1. $100 nonrefundable tuition deposit. Freshmen accepted for terms other than fall.
**Special programs:** Admission may be deferred one year. Credit may be granted through CEEB Advanced Placement for scores of 3 or higher. Credit may be granted through CLEP general and subject exams, ACT PEP and DANTES exams, and military experience. Early entrance/early admission program.
**Transfer students:** Transfer students accepted for terms other than fall. In fall 1993, 48% of all new students were transfers into all classes. 722 transfer applications were received, 582 were accepted. Application deadline is August 1 for fall; December 15 for spring. Minimum 2.2 GPA recommended. Lowest course grade accepted is "D." Maximum number of transferable credits is 90 semester hours. At least 30 semester hours must be completed at the university to receive degree.
**Admissions contact:** William F. Coughlin, M.Ed., Director of Admissions. 617 573-8460, 800-6-SUFFOLK.

**FINANCIAL AID. Available aid:** Pell grants, SEOG, state scholarships and grants, school scholarships and grants, private scholarships and grants, and academic merit scholarships. Perkins Loans (NDSL), PLUS, Stafford Loans (GSL), school loans, private loans, and SLS. TERI loans. AMS, deferred payment plan, and family tuition reduction. Grandfathered Tuition Plan for Meritorious Students.
**Financial aid statistics:** 9% of aid is not need-based. In 1993-94, 93% of all undergraduate applicants received aid; 92% of freshman applicants. Average amounts of aid awarded freshmen: Scholarships and grants, $3,700; loans, $2,940.
**Supporting data/closing dates:** FAFSA/FAF: Priority filing date is February 15. School's own aid application: Priority filing date is March 1. State aid form: Priority filing date is May 1. Income tax forms: Priority filing date is April 15. Notification of awards begins February 15.
**Financial aid contact:** Christine Perry, M.Ed., Director of Financial Aid. 617 573-8470.

**STUDENT EMPLOYMENT.** College Work/Study Program. Institutional employment. 17% of full-time undergraduates work on campus during school year. Students may expect to earn an average of $1,190 during school year. Off-campus part-time employment opportunities rated "excellent."

**COMPUTER FACILITIES.** 200 IBM/IBM-compatible and Macintosh/Apple microcomputers; 175 are networked. Students may access Digital, Prime minicomputer/mainframe systems, BITNET, Internet. Client/LAN operating systems include Apple/Macintosh, DOS, UNIX/XENIX/AIX, DEC, Novell. Computer languages and software packages include BASIC, C, COBOL, FORTRAN, ISP, Lotus 1-2-3, MINITAB, SAS, SPSS, TSP, WordPerfect. Computer facilities are available to all students.
**Fees:** $40 computer fee per semester; included in tuition/fees.
**Hours:** 8:30 AM-9:30 PM.

**GRADUATE CAREER DATA.** Graduate school percentages: 4% enter law school. 1% enter medical school. 2% enter graduate business programs. 2% enter graduate arts and sciences programs. Highest graduate school enrollments: Bentley Coll, Boston Coll, Boston U, Northeastern U, Suffolk U. 70% of graduates choose careers in business and industry. Companies and businesses that hire graduates: high-tech companies, major banks, financial services, government, and insurance companies.

**PROMINENT ALUMNI/AE.** Edward McDonnel, president/director, Seagrams; Robert O'Leary, president/CEO, Voluntary Hospitals of America; Richard Rosenberg, chairman/CEO, BankAmerica.

# Tufts University

**Medford, MA 02155** 617 628-5000

**1994-95 Costs.** Tuition: $19,701. Room: $3,038. Board: $2,930. Fees, books, misc. academic expenses (school's estimate): $1,103.
**Enrollment.** Undergraduates: 2,172 men, 2,424 women (full-time). Freshman class: 7,616 applicants, 3,605 accepted, 1,205 enrolled. Graduate enrollment: 1,582 men, 1,820 women.
**Test score averages/ranges.** Range of SAT scores of middle 50%: 540-630 verbal, 610-700 math. Range of ACT scores of middle 50%: 26-30 composite.
**Faculty.** 335 full-time; 226 part-time. 96% of faculty holds doctoral degree. Student/faculty ratio: 13 to 1.
**Selectivity rating.** Highly competitive.

**PROFILE.** Tufts, founded in 1852, is a private, comprehensive university. Programs are offered through the College of Arts and Sciences; the Fletcher School of Law and Diplomacy; the Schools of Dental Medicine, Medicine, Nutrition, and Veterinary Medicine; and the Sackler School of Graduate Biomedical Sciences. Its 150-acre campus is located in Medford, a suburb of Boston.

**Accreditation:** NEASC. Professionally accredited by the Accreditation Board for Engineering and Technology.
**Religious orientation:** Tufts University is nonsectarian; no religious requirements.
**Library:** Collections totaling over 783,000 volumes, 4,784 periodical subscriptions, and 920,000 microform items.
**Special facilities/museums:** Language lab, nutrition institute, research lab for physical electronics, bioelectrical and biochemical labs, computer-aided design (CAD) facility, electro-optics technology and environmental management centers.
**Athletic facilities:** Aerobics dance facilities, indoor and outdoor basketball and tennis courts, squash courts, sauna, swimming pool, tracks, weight room, fitness center, Nautilus and Universal equipment.

**STUDENT BODY. Undergraduate profile:** 27% are state residents; 9% are transfers. 11% Asian-American, 4% Black, 4% Hispanic, 73% White, 8% Other.
**Freshman profile:** 3% of freshmen who took SAT scored 700 or over on verbal, 29% scored 700 or over on math; 43% scored 600 or over on verbal, 82% scored 600 or over on math; 93% scored 500 or over on verbal, 99% scored 500 or over on math; 100% scored 400 or over on verbal, 100% scored 400 or over on math. 85% of accepted applicants took SAT; 15% took ACT. 60% of freshmen come from public schools.
**Undergraduate achievement:** 99% of fall 1992 freshmen returned for fall 1993 term. 90% of entering class graduated. 35% of students who completed a degree program immediately went on to graduate study.
**Foreign students:** 368 students are from out of the country. Countries represented include Canada, Germany, Greece, India, Japan, and the United Kingdom; 62 in all.

**PROGRAMS OF STUDY. Degrees:** B.A., B.S., B.S.Chem.Eng., B.S.Civil Eng., B.S.Comp.Eng., B.S.Ed., B.S.Elec.Eng., B.S.Eng.Sci., B.S.Mech.Eng.
**Majors:** American Studies, Anthropology, Applied Physics, Archaeology, Astronomy, Biology, Biology/Psychology, Chemical Engineering, Chemical Physics, Chemistry, Child Study, Civil Engineering, Classics, Computational Mathematics, Computer Engineering, Computer Science, Drama, Economics, Electrical Engineering, Engineering Physics, Engineering Psychology, Engineering Sciences, English, Fine Arts, French, Geology, German, Greek, Greek/Roman Studies, History, International Relations, Latin, Mathematics, Mechanical Engineering, Mental Health, Music, Philosophy, Physics, Political Science, Psychology, Religion, Russian, Social Psychology, Sociology, Spanish.
**Distribution of degrees:** The majors with the highest enrollment are English, international relations, and economics.
**Requirements:** General education requirement.
**Special:** Minors offered in some liberal arts areas and in engineering management. Programs in Afro-American studies, community health, and peace/justice studies. Experimental College offers courses not available in regular curriculum. Self-designed majors. Double majors. Dual degrees. Independent study. Accelerated study. Pass/fail grading option. Internships. Graduate school at which undergraduates may take graduate-level courses. B.A./M.A. and B.S./M.S. liberal arts and engineering programs. Combined six-year B.S. or B.A./M.A.L.D. liberal arts or engineering program with the Fletcher Sch. Cross-registration with Boston Coll, Boston U, and Brandeis U. B.A./B.F.A. program with the Sch of the Museum of Fine Arts. B.A./B.Mus. program with the New England Conservatory of Music. Washington Semester. Williams-Mystic Seaport Semester (Connecticut). Exchange program with Swarthmore Coll. Teacher certification in early childhood, elementary, secondary, and special education. Study abroad in England, France, Germany, Russia, and Spain. ROTC, NROTC, and AFROTC at MIT.
**Honors:** Phi Beta Kappa. Honors program. Honor societies.
**Academic Assistance:** Nonremedial tutoring.

**STUDENT LIFE. Housing:** All freshmen and sophomores must live on campus unless living with family; freshmen and sophomores are guaranteed housing. Coed and women's dorms. Sorority and fraternity housing. Cooperative, special-interest, and cultural housing. 80% of students live in college housing.
**Social atmosphere:** According to the editor of the student newspaper, "Though they are frequently small, many of the cultural and special-interest groups hold the best, most fun, and most memorable parties." The major social advantage of Tufts is its proximity to the numerous cultural and entertainment opportunities of the Boston area and Harvard Square in nearby Cambridge. The university itself also provides exceptional cultural facilities and programs. On campus, students gather at the Campus Center for eating and ping-pong, and at The Pub and the library. Most influential groups are the Greeks, music and theatre groups, and the Tufts Center Board, which plans student activities, concerts, and films. Popular events are Spring Fling, Homecoming, and the Fall Concert.
**Services and counseling/handicapped student services:** Placement services. Health service. Women's center. Day care. Counseling services for minority, military, veteran, and older students. Birth control, personal, and psychological counseling. Career and academic guidance services. Religious counseling. Physically disabled student services. Learning disabled services.
**Campus organizations:** Undergraduate student government. Student newspaper (Tufts Daily; Tufts Observer, published once/week). Literary magazine. Yearbook. Radio and TV stations. Concert orchestra, band, chorale, music and jazz societies, music comedy group, coffeehouse, film and lecture series, theatre, modern dance club, debating, yachting and mountain clubs, environmental and consumer clubs, Young Republicans, Young Democrats, academic, professional, and volunteer service groups, 140 organizations in all. 10 fraternities, nine chapter houses; three sororities, two chapter houses. 14% of men join a fraternity. 4% of women join a sorority.
**Religious organizations:** Bahai Club, Black Christian Workshop, Catholic Community, Christian Fellowship, Hillel.
**Minority/foreign student organizations:** African-American group, Asian-American Society, Hispanic-American Society. International Club, Canadian, Indian, Japanese, Latin American, Middle Eastern, and Portuguese groups.

**ATHLETICS. Physical education requirements:** None.
**Intercollegiate competition:** 2% of students participate. Baseball (M), basketball (M,W), crew (M,W), cross-country (M,W), diving (M,W), field hockey (W), football (M), golf (M), ice hockey (M), lacrosse (M,W), sailing (M,W), soccer (M,W), softball (W), squash (M,W), swimming (M,W), tennis (M,W), track (indoor) (M,W), track (outdoor) (M,W), track and field (M,W), track and field (indoor) (M,W), track and field (outdoor) (M,W), volleyball (W). Member of ECAC, NCAA Division III, NESCAC.
**Intramural and club sports:** 3% of students participate. Intramural basketball, football, soccer, softball, volleyball. Men's club Alpine skiing, cycling, equestrian sports, fencing, rugby, shotokan, tae kwon do, ultimate frisbee, volleyball. Women's club Alpine skiing, cycling, equestrian sports, fencing, rugby, shotokan, tae kwon do, ultimate frisbee.

**ADMISSIONS. Academic basis for candidate selection** (in order of priority): Secondary school record, class rank, school's recommendation, standardized test scores, essay.
**Nonacademic basis for candidate selection:** Character and personality, extracurricular participation, and particular talent or ability are important. Geographical distribution and alumni/ae relationship are considered.
**Requirements:** Graduation from secondary school is recommended; GED is accepted. 16 units and the following program of study are recommended: 4 units of English, 3 units of math, 1 unit of science, 3 units of foreign language, 1 unit of history. 4 units of math and 2 units of lab science recommended of engineering, mathematics, and sciences program applicants. ACT, or SAT and three ACH tests required. ACH (chemistry or physics and math level I or II) required of engineering program applicants who submit SAT scores. Campus visit and interview recommended. Off-campus interviews available with an alumni representative.
**Procedure:** Take SAT or ACT by January of 12th year. Take ACH by January of 12th year. Application deadline is January 1. Notification of admission by April 1. Reply is required by May 1. $600 tuition deposit, refundable until May 1. Freshmen accepted for fall term only.
**Special programs:** Admission may be deferred one year. Credit and/or placement may be granted through CEEB Advanced Placement exams for scores of 4 or higher. Early decision program. In fall 1993, 562 applied for early decision and 299 were accepted. Deadline for applying for early decision is November 15 (first round); January 1 (second round). Early entrance/early admission program.
**Transfer students:** Transfer students accepted for terms other than fall. In fall 1993, 9% of all new students were transfers into all classes. 526 transfer applications were received, 230 were accepted. Application deadline is March 1 for fall; November 15 for spring. Lowest course grade accepted is "C." Maximum number of transferable credits is 17 courses. At least 17 courses must be completed at the university to receive degree.
**Admissions contact:** David Cuttino, Dean of Admissions. 617 627-3170.

**FINANCIAL AID. Available aid:** Pell grants, SEOG, state scholarships and grants, school scholarships and grants, private scholarships, ROTC scholarships, and academic merit scholarships. Perkins Loans (NDSL), PLUS, Stafford Loans (GSL), state loans, school loans, and SLS. AMS. MEFA. TERI. Nellie Mae. Institutional prepayment plan.
**Financial aid statistics:** In 1993-94, 92% of all undergraduate applicants received aid; 81% of freshman applicants. Average amounts of aid awarded freshmen: Scholarships and grants, $12,233; loans, $3,200.
**Supporting data/closing dates:** FAFSA/FAF: Deadline is February 1. School's own aid application: Deadline is February 1. Income tax forms: Accepted on rolling basis. Notification of awards begins April 1.
**Financial aid contact:** William Eastwood, Director of Financial Aid. 617 627-3528.

**STUDENT EMPLOYMENT.** College Work/Study Program. Institutional employment. 48% of full-time undergraduates work on campus during school year. Students may expect to earn an average of $1,500 during school year. Off-campus part-time employment opportunities rated "good."

**COMPUTER FACILITIES.** 140 IBM/IBM-compatible, Macintosh/Apple, and RISC-/UNIX-based microcomputers; 100 are networked. Students may access Digital, IBM minicomputer/mainframe systems, Internet. Client/LAN operating systems include Apple/Macintosh, DOS, UNIX/XENIX/AIX, Banyan. 75 major computer languages and software packages available. Computer facilities are available to all students.
**Fees:** None.
**Hours:** 24 hours.

**GRADUATE CAREER DATA.** Graduate school percentages: 24% enter law school. 10% enter medical school. 1% enter dental school. 20% enter graduate business programs. 35% enter graduate arts and sciences programs.

**PROMINENT ALUMNI/AE.** Malcolm Toon, ambassador; Daniel Patrick Moynihan, U.S. senator; Tracy Chapman, singer; William Hurt, actor.

# University of Massachusetts at Amherst

Amherst, MA 01003 413 545-0111

**1994-95 Costs.** Tuition: $2,220 (state residents), $8,566 (out-of-state). Room: $2,266. Board: $1,762. Fees, books, misc. academic expenses (school's estimate): $3,854.

**Enrollment.** Undergraduates: 8,307 men, 7,691 women (full-time). Freshman class: 14,438 applicants, 12,414 accepted, 3,822 enrolled. Graduate enrollment: 2,871 men, 2,988 women.

**Test score averages/ranges.** Range of SAT scores of middle 50%: 410-520 verbal, 460-590 math.

**Faculty.** 1,165 full-time; 110 part-time. 89% of faculty holds highest degree in specific field. Student/faculty ratio: 17 to 1.

**Selectivity rating.** Less competitive.

**PROFILE.** U Massachusetts at Amherst is a public, land-grant institution. Founded as an agricultural college in 1863, it became a state university in 1947. Programs are offered through the Colleges of Arts and Sciences, Engineering, and Food and Natural Resources; the Schools of Agriculture, Education, Management, Nursing, Public Health, and Physical Education; and the Division of Continuing Education. Its 1,200-acre campus is located in Amherst, 20 miles north of Springfield and 90 miles west of Boston.

**Accreditation:** NEASC. Professionally accredited by the Accreditation Board for Engineering and Technology, the American Assembly of Collegiate Schools of Business, the American Dietetic Association, the American Society of Landscape Architects, the Foundation for Interior Design Education Research, the National Association of Schools of Music, the National Council for Accreditation of Teacher Education, the National League for Nursing, the Society of American Foresters.

**Religious orientation:** University of Massachusetts at Amherst is nonsectarian; no religious requirements.

**Library:** Collections totaling over 2,587,957 volumes, 15,546 periodical subscriptions, and 1,993,325 microform items.

**Special facilities/museums:** Fine arts center, art galleries, on-campus elementary school and child guidance center, population research institute, polymer research institute.

**Athletic facilities:** Gymnasiums, swimming pools, dance studio, weight rooms, track, baseball, field hockey, football, intramural, lacrosse, soccer, and softball fields, basketball, tennis, and volleyball courts.

**STUDENT BODY. Undergraduate profile:** 77% are state residents; 25% are transfers. 5% Asian-American, 3% Black, 3% Hispanic, .5% Native American, 82% White, 6.5% Other. Average age of undergraduates is 20.

**Freshman profile:** 4% of freshmen who took SAT scored 700 or over on math; 6% scored 600 or over on verbal, 23% scored 600 or over on math; 31% scored 500 or over on verbal, 60% scored 500 or over on math; 77% scored 400 or over on verbal, 87% scored 400 or over on math; 93% scored 300 or over on verbal, 94% scored 300 or over on math. 99% of accepted applicants took SAT; 1% took ACT. 80% of freshmen come from public schools.

**Undergraduate achievement:** 76% of fall 1992 freshmen returned for fall 1993 term. 44% of entering class graduated. 41% of students who completed a degree program immediately went on to graduate study.

**Foreign students:** 1,726 students are from out of the country. Countries represented include Hong Kong, India, Japan, Malaysia, South Korea, and the United Kingdom; 74 in all.

**PROGRAMS OF STUDY. Degrees:** B.A., B.Bus.Admin., B.F.A., B.Gen.Studies, B.Mus., B.S., B.S.Chem.Eng., B.S.Civil Eng., B.S.Comp.Sys.Eng., B.S.Elec.Eng., B.S.Indust.Eng./Op.Res., B.S.Mech.Eng.

**Majors:** Accounting, Afro-American Studies, Animal Science/Pre-Veterinary Medicine, Anthropology, Apparel Marketing, Art/Design, Art Education, Art History, Art Studio, Astronomy, Bachelor's Degree with Individual Concentration, Biochemistry/Molecular Biology, Biology, Chemical Engineering, Chemistry, Chinese Language/Literature, Civil Engineering, Classics, Classics/Philosophy, Communication, Communication Disorders, Comparative Literature, Computer Science, Computer Systems Engineering, Dance, Economics, Education, Electrical Engineering, English, Entomology, Environmental Design, Environmental Sciences, Exercise Science, Family/Consumer Science, Finance/Operations Management, Food Science, Forestry, French, General Studies, Geography, Geology, German, History, Hotel/Restaurant/Travel Administration, Human Development, Human Nutrition, Industrial Engineering/Operations Research, Integrated Pest Management, Italian, Japanese Language/Literature, Journalism, Judaic Studies, Landscape Architecture, Legal Studies, Linguistics/Anthropology, Linguistics/Chinese, Linguistics/German, Linguistics/Japanese, Linguistics/Philosophy, Linguistics/Psychology, Linguistics/Russian, Management, Marketing, Mathematics, Mechanical Engineering, Medical Technology, Microbiology, Music, Natural Resource Studies, Near Eastern Studies, Nursing, Philosophy, Physics, Plant Pathology, Plant/Soil Science, Political Science, Portuguese, Pre-Dental, Pre-Medical, Psychology, Public Health, Resource Economics, Russian, Science, Social Thought/Political Economy, Sociology, Soviet/East European Studies, Spanish, Sports Management, Theater, Wildlife/Fisheries Biology, Women's Studies, Wood Science/Technology.

**Distribution of degrees:** The majors with the highest enrollment are psychology, English, and communication.

**Requirements:** General education requirement.

**Academic regulations:** Minimum 2.0 GPA must be maintained.

**Special:** Minors offered in many majors in College of Humanities and Fine Arts, in several majors in other colleges and schools, and in athletic coaching, Latin American studies, musical performance, and Polish. Residential College program offers sections of regularly scheduled courses and one-credit student-oriented and student-taught courses. Associate's degrees offered. Self-designed majors. Double majors. Independent study. Pass/fail grading option. Internships. Cooperative education programs. Graduate school at which undergraduates may take graduate-level courses. Preprofessional programs in law, medicine, veterinary science, and dentistry. Member of Five College Consortium with Amherst, Hampshire, Mount Holyoke, and Smith Colls; cross-registration possible. Washington Semester. Member of New England Regional Student Program and National Student Exchange (NSE). Teacher certification in early childhood, elementary, secondary, special education, and vo-tech education. Certification in specific subject areas. Study abroad in Argentina, Australia, Brazil, Canada, Caribbean countries, Chile, China, Colombia, Denmark, Ecuador, Egypt, France, Germany, Hungary, India, Ireland, Israel, Italy, Japan, the Netherlands, Poland, Russia, South Africa, Spain, Sweden, Switzerland, Taiwan, and the United Kingdom. ROTC and AFROTC.

**Honors:** Phi Beta Kappa. Honors program. Honor societies.

**Academic Assistance:** Remedial reading, writing, math, and study skills. Nonremedial tutoring.

**STUDENT LIFE. Housing:** All nonveteran freshmen and sophomores must live on campus unless living with family within a 40-mile radius. Coed, women's, and men's dorms. Sorority and fraternity housing. School-owned/operated apartments. 58% of students live in college housing.

**Social atmosphere:** On campus, students gather at The Hatch for fast food, at the Bluewall for coffee and ice cream, and at the People's Market, the Graduate Lounge, and the Mullins Center skating rink. Off campus, students frequent Antonio's Pizza, The Pub, the Hampshire Mall, and various Amherst bars. Athletes, the Black Student Union, the student newspaper, and the Black Mass Communication Project influence life on campus. Popular campus events include basketball games, the Southwest Week in Spring, the Jeans & T-shirt Dance, Campus BBQ, and the Spring Concert. "From the quiet solitude of the campus pond to the raucous rowdies of the William D. Mullins center, U Mass offers the best of both worlds. Have a burrito at The Hatch or fresh bean sprouts at Earthfoods. U Mass offers nearly everything," comments the student newspaper.

**Services and counseling/handicapped student services:** Placement services. Health service. Women's center. Day care. Learning Center. Counseling services for minority, military, veteran, and older students. Birth control, personal, and psychological counseling. Career and academic guidance services. Physically disabled student services. Learning disabled program/services. Notetaking services. Tape recorders. Tutors. Reader services for the blind.

**Campus organizations:** Undergraduate student government. Student newspaper (Massachusetts Daily Collegian). Literary magazine. Yearbook. Radio station. Concert, marching, and jazz bands, chamber choir, debating, PIRG, Silent Majority, outing club, Earthfoods, theatre, Science Fiction Club, Animal Rights Coalition, Lesbian/Bisexual/Gay Alliance, Republican Club, University Democrats, martial arts groups, juggling club, 190 organizations in all. 21 fraternities, 12 chapter houses; 13 sororities, eight chapter houses. 7% of men join a fraternity. 5% of women join a sorority.

**Religious organizations:** Hillel, Chabad Students Newman Club, Intervarsity Christian Fellowship, Alliance Christian Fellowship, Campus Crusade for Christ, Bahai Club, Pagan Students Organization, Ananda Marga, The Ark, Meditation League, Muslim Student Association, Upside Down.

**Minority/foreign student organizations:** Black Student Union, AFRIK-AM, Black Mass Communication Project, National Society of Black Engineers, Asian American Student Association, Concepto Latino, American Indian Student Association, Casa Domanica. International Student Association, AHORA; African, Armenian, Cambodian, Cape Verdean, Chinese, Haitian, Hellenic, Italian, Japanese, Korean, South Asian, and Vietnamese groups.

**ATHLETICS. Physical education requirements:** None.

**Intercollegiate competition:** 4% of students participate. Alpine skiing (M,W), baseball (M), basketball (M,W), cross-country (M,W), diving (M,W), field hockey (W), football (M), gymnastics (M,W), lacrosse (M), soccer (W), softball (W), swimming (M,W), track and field (indoor) (M,W), track and field (outdoor) (M,W), water polo (M). Member of Atlantic 10, ECAC, NCAA Division I, Yankee Conference.

**Intramural and club sports:** 52% of students participate. Intramural badminton, basketball, cross-country, flag football, ice hockey, racquetball, soccer, softball, squash, swimming, tennis, track and field, volleyball, wrestling. Men's club cheerleading, crew, fencing, rugby, volleyball. Women's club cheerleading, crew, fencing.

**ADMISSIONS. Academic basis for candidate selection** (in order of priority): Secondary school record, class rank, standardized test scores, school's recommendation, essay.

**Nonacademic basis for candidate selection:** Particular talent or ability is important. Character and personality, extracurricular participation, and alumni/ae relationship are considered.

**Requirements:** Graduation from secondary school is required; GED is accepted. 21 units and the following program of study are required: 4 units of English, 3 units of math, 2 units of lab science, 2 units of foreign language, 2 units of social studies, 3 units of academic electives. Audition required of music and dance program applicants. 4 units of math required of business, computer science, engineering, and math program applicants. 1/2 unit of trigometry recommended of physical sciences and math program applicants. 1 unit of chemistry required of nursing program applicants. Portfolio required of art program applicants. Conditional admission possible for applicants not meeting standard requirements. SAT is required; ACT may be substituted. PSAT is recommended. ACH is recommended. Campus visit and interview recommended. Off-campus interviews available with an alumni representative.

**Procedure:** Take SAT or ACT by November of 12th year. Take ACH by November of 12th year. Application deadline is February 15. Notification of admission on rolling basis. Reply is required by May 1. $200 tuition deposit, partially refundable. Freshmen accepted for terms other than fall.

**Special programs:** Admission may be deferred two years. Credit and/or placement may be granted through CEEB Advanced Placement exams for scores of 3 or higher. Credit and/or placement may be granted through CLEP general and subject exams. Credit and placement may be granted through challenge exams and military and life experience. Early entrance/early admission program. Concurrent enrollment program.

**Transfer students:** Transfer students accepted for terms other than fall. In fall 1993, 25% of all new students were transfers into all classes. 3,148 transfer applications were received, 2,201 were accepted. Application deadline is April 1 for fall; October 15 for spring. Minimum 2.0 GPA recommended. Lowest course grade accepted is "C." Maximum number of transferable credits is 75 semester hours. At least 45 semester hours must be completed at the university to receive degree.

**Admissions contact:** Arlene W. Cash, M.A., Director of Admissions. 413 545-0222.

**FINANCIAL AID. Available aid:** Pell grants, SEOG, state scholarships and grants, school scholarships and grants, private scholarships, ROTC scholarships, academic merit scholarships, athletic scholarships, and aid for undergraduate foreign students. Perkins Loans (NDSL), PLUS, Stafford Loans (GSL), state loans, private loans, and SLS. Knight Tuition Plans and AMS.

**Financial aid statistics:** 10% of aid is not need-based. In 1993-94, 50% of all undergraduate applicants received aid; 50% of freshman applicants. Average amounts of aid awarded freshmen: Scholarships and grants, $2,300; loans, $2,000.

**Supporting data/closing dates:** FAFSA: Priority filing date is February 15; deadline is March 1. State aid form: Deadline is May 1. Notification of awards on rolling basis.

**Financial aid contact:** Burt F. Batty, M.A., Director of Financial Aid. 413 545-0801.

**STUDENT EMPLOYMENT.** College Work/Study Program. Institutional employment. 38% of full-time undergraduates work on campus during school year. Students may expect to earn an average of $1,600 during school year. Off-campus part-time employment opportunities rated "good."

**COMPUTER FACILITIES.** IBM/IBM-compatible and Macintosh/Apple microcomputers; 180 are networked. Students may access CDC Cyber, Digital, IBM, SUN minicomputer/mainframe systems, BITNET, Internet. Residence halls may be equipped with modems. Client/LAN operating systems include Apple/Macintosh, DOS, OS/2, UNIX/XENIX/AIX, Windows NT, X-windows, DEC, LocalTalk/AppleTalk, Microsoft, Novell. Computer languages and software packages include BASIC, BMDP, C, COBOL, CYBIL, dBASE, Excel, FORTRAN, LISP, Lotus 1-2-3, Microsoft Word, Pascal, SAS, SPSS, Systat. Computer facilities are available to all students.

**Fees:** $10 computer fee per semester.

**Hours:** Approximately 14 hours/day.

**GRADUATE CAREER DATA.** Graduate school percentages: 5% enter law school. 2% enter medical school. 7% enter graduate business programs. 4% enter graduate arts and sciences programs. 73% of graduates choose careers in business and industry.

**PROMINENT ALUMNI/AE.** Bill Cosby, entertainer, comedian; Jack Walsh, chairperson and CEO, General Electric; Madeline Kunin, former governor, Vermont; Paul Theroux, author; Julius ("Dr. J") Erving, former forward, Philadelphia 76ers; Natalie Cole, singer/entertainer; George Dickerman, president, Spaulding Sports Worldwide; Richard Goldstein, chair and CEO, Unilever U.S.; Roger Johnson, director, General Services Administration; Richard Mahoney, chair and CEO, Monsanto Company; Jack Smith, chair and CEO, General Motors.

## University of Massachusetts at Boston

Boston, MA 02125-3393 — 617 287-5000

**1993-94 Costs.** Tuition: $2,200 (state residents), $8,568 (out-of-state). Housing: None. Fees, books, misc. academic expenses (school's estimate): $2,643.

**Enrollment.** Undergraduates: 2,905 men, 3,090 women (full-time). Freshman class: 2,237 applicants, 1,496 accepted, 800 enrolled. Graduate enrollment: 847 men, 1,481 women.

**Test score averages/ranges.** Average SAT scores: 427 verbal, 468 math. Range of SAT scores of middle 50%: 370-490 verbal, 410-520 math.

**Faculty.** 473 full-time; 366 part-time. 88% of faculty holds highest degree in specific field. Student/faculty ratio: 16 to 1.

**Selectivity rating.** Less competitive.

**PROFILE.** U Massachusetts at Boston, founded in 1964, is a public institution. Undergraduate and graduate programs are offered through the Colleges of Arts and Sciences, Education, Management, Nursing, and Public and Community Service. The main campus is located on Dorchester Bay, three miles south of downtown Boston.

**Accreditation:** NEASC. Professionally accredited by the American Psychological Association, the Council on Rehabilitation Education, the National League for Nursing.

**Religious orientation:** University of Massachusetts at Boston is nonsectarian; no religious requirements.

**Library:** Collections totaling over 535,971 volumes, 3,062 periodical subscriptions, and 686,369 microform items.

**Special facilities/museums:** Art gallery, tropical greenhouse, observatory, adaptive computer lab.

**Athletic facilities:** Gymnasiums, swimming pool, ice rink, athletic fields, tracks, combative, dance, and weight rooms, racquetball, squash, and tennis courts, boathouse/dock.

**STUDENT BODY. Undergraduate profile:** 98% are state residents; 68% are transfers. 8% Asian-American, 14% Black, 5% Hispanic, 1% Native American, 71% White, 1% Foreign. Average age of undergraduates is 28.

**Freshman profile:** 1% of freshmen who took SAT scored 700 or over on math; 4% scored 600 or over on verbal, 8% scored 600 or over on math; 22% scored 500 or over on verbal, 36% scored 500 or over on math; 66% scored 400 or over on verbal, 78% scored 400 or over on math; 92% scored 300 or over on verbal, 97% scored 300 or over on math. 42% of accepted applicants took SAT. 66% of freshmen come from public schools.

**Undergraduate achievement:** 70% of fall 1992 freshmen returned for fall 1993 term. 22% of students who completed a degree program went on to graduate study within .5 years.

**Foreign students:** 171 students are from out of the country. Countries represented include China, Greece, Hong Kong, Japan, South Korea, and Taiwan; 44 in all.

**PROGRAMS OF STUDY. Degrees:** B.A., B.S.

**Majors:** Adult Training in Human Services, Alternative Career, Anthropology, Applied Mathematics, Art, Biology, Biology/Medical Technology, Black Studies, Chemistry, Classics, Combined Career, Community Energy Planning, Community Planning, Community Planning/Management, Community Service Management, Computer Science, Criminal Justice/Public Safety, Economics, Engineering Physics, English, Ethics/Social/Political Philosophy, French, Geography, German, Gerontology, Greek, History, Human Performance/Fitness, Human Services, Human Services Advocacy, Independent Major, Italian, Labor Studies, Latin, Law Work, Legal Education Services, Management, Management of Human Services, Management of Legal Institutions, Music, Nursing, Philosophy, Philosophy/Public Policy, Physics, Political Science, Psychology, Pure Mathematics, Russian, Sociology, Spanish, Theatre Arts, Women's Studies.

**Distribution of degrees:** The majors with the highest enrollment are management, nursing, and English.

**Requirements:** General education requirement.

**Academic regulations:** Freshmen must maintain minimum 1.65 GPA; sophomores, 1.90 GPA; juniors, 2.00 GPA; seniors, 2.00 GPA.

**Special:** Minors offered in most majors and in coaching, human performance/fitness, and teaching in the elementary classroom. Concentrations and special programs in some majors and in alcohol/substance abuse, American studies, biobehavioral studies, biology of human population, communication studies, creative writing, East Asian studies, geographic techniques, health care studies, international relations, Irish studies, Latin American studies, linguistics, New England historical and New England prehistoric archaeology, professional writing, religion, science technology and values, technical writing, and translation. Self-designed majors. Double majors. Independent study. Accelerated study. Pass/fail grading option. Internships. Cooperative education programs. Graduate school at which undergraduates may take graduate-level courses. Preprofessional programs in law and medicine. 2-2 engineering programs with various area institutions. Semester at Nantucket Research Center. Member of National Student Exchange (NSE), New England Regional Student Exchange Program, and Boston Five Course Exchange Program. Teacher certification in early childhood, elementary, secondary, special education, vo-tech, and bilingual/bicultural education. Certification in specific subject areas. Study abroad in China, France, Germany, Ireland, Mexico, and other countries.

**Honors:** Honors program.

**Academic Assistance:** Remedial reading, writing, math, and study skills. Nonremedial tutoring.

**STUDENT LIFE. Housing:** Commuter campus; no student housing.

**Social atmosphere:** According to the editor of the student newspaper, "U Mass is a commuter campus," and "when the administration closed The Pub (the only on-campus gathering spot), they took away the only entity that kept students on campus after their classes. Off-campus gathering areas and clubs are in the city of Boston."

**Services and counseling/handicapped student services:** Placement services. Health service. Women's center. Day care. Center for Students with Disabilities. Women's Center. Counseling services for minority, military, veteran, and older students. Birth control, personal, and psychological counseling. Career and academic guidance services. Religious counseling. Physically disabled student services. Learning disabled services. Notetaking services. Tape recorders. Tutors. Reader services for the blind.

**Campus organizations:** Undergraduate student government. Student newspaper (Mass Media, published once/week). Literary magazine. Yearbook. Radio station. Music club, ballroom dance club, Amnesty International, Student Nurses Association, Gay Student Center, Freedom School, College Democrats, College Republicans, academic, athletic, service, professional, and special-interest groups, 73 organizations in all.

**Religious organizations:** Hillel Club, Christian Student Association, Newman Club, Islamic Club.

**Minority/foreign student organizations:** Black Students Center, Asian American Society, Disabled Student Association, Women's Center, Mellenia Club. Cambodian, French, Haitian, Islamic, Italian, Japanese, Korean, and Vietnamese groups, Hellenic Student Association.

**ATHLETICS. Physical education requirements:** None.

**Intercollegiate competition:** 5% of students participate. Baseball (M), basketball (M,W), cheerleading (W), cross-country (M,W), diving (M,W), football (M), ice hockey (M), lacrosse (M), soccer (M,W), softball (W), swimming (M,W), tennis (M,W), track (indoor) (M,W), track (outdoor) (M,W), track and field (indoor) (M,W), track and field (outdoor) (M,W), volleyball (W). Member of ECAC, Little East Conference, MAIAW, NCAA Division III.

**Intramural and club sports:** 40% of students participate. Intramural aerobics, basketball, flag football, floor hockey, ice hockey, racquetball, sailing, squash, volleyball, walleyball, weight training.

**ADMISSIONS. Academic basis for candidate selection** (in order of priority): Secondary school record, standardized test scores, class rank, school's recommendation, essay.

**Nonacademic basis for candidate selection:** Character and personality, particular talent or ability, and geographical distribution are considered.

**Requirements:** Graduation from secondary school is required; GED is accepted. 16 units and the following program of study are required: 4 units of English, 3 units of math, 2 units of lab science, 2 units of foreign language, 1 unit of social studies, 1 unit of history, 3 units of academic electives. Minimum combined SAT score of 800 and rank in top half of secondary school class required. Higher SAT scores and class rank required of engineering, management and nursing program applicants. EOP for applicants not normally admissible. Directions in Student Potential Program for applicants with average academic record and low SAT scores. SAT is required; ACT may be substituted. No off-campus interviews.

**Procedure:** Take SAT or ACT by December of 12th year. Application deadline is June 15. Notification of admission on rolling basis. Reply is required prior to start of classes. Freshmen accepted for terms other than fall.

**Special programs:** Admission may be deferred one year. Credit may be granted through CEEB Advanced Placement for scores of 3 or higher. Credit may be granted through CLEP general and subject exams, ACT PEP and DANTES exams. Placement may be granted through challenge exams.
**Transfer students:** Transfer students accepted for terms other than fall. In fall 1993, 68% of all new students were transfers into all classes. 3,018 transfer applications were received, 2,741 were accepted. Application deadline is June 15 for fall; November 1 for spring. Minimum 2.25 GPA required. Lowest course grade accepted is "C-." Maximum number of transferable credits is 60 semester hours from a two-year school and 90 semester hours from a four-year school. At least 30 semester hours must be completed at the university to receive degree.
**Admissions contact:** James V. Morris, Assoc. Vice Chancellor for Enrollment Management. 617 287-6100.

**FINANCIAL AID. Available aid:** Pell grants, SEOG, state scholarships and grants, school scholarships and grants, private scholarships and grants, and academic merit scholarships. Perkins Loans (NDSL), PLUS, Stafford Loans (GSL), state loans, and SLS. AMS.
**Financial aid statistics:** 10% of aid is not need-based. In 1993-94, 52% of all undergraduate applicants received aid; 66% of freshman applicants. Average amounts of aid awarded freshmen: Scholarships and grants, $2,746; loans, $2,625.
**Supporting data/closing dates:** FAFSA: Priority filing date is March 1. Institutional Application.: Priority filing date is March 1. Notification of awards begins April 1.
**Financial aid contact:** Corine Williams Byrd, Director, Financial Aid Services. 617 287-6300.

**STUDENT EMPLOYMENT.** College Work/Study Program. Institutional employment. 14% of full-time undergraduates work on campus during school year. Students may expect to earn an average of $1,507 during school year. Off-campus part-time employment opportunities rated "fair."

**COMPUTER FACILITIES.** 250 IBM/IBM-compatible, Macintosh/Apple, and RISC-/UNIX-based microcomputers; 220 are networked. Students may access Digital minicomputer/mainframe systems, Internet. Client/LAN operating systems include Apple/Macintosh, DOS, UNIX/XENIX/AIX, Banyan, DEC, LocalTalk/AppleTalk. Computer languages and software packages include BASIC, C, COBOL, DataTrieve, DECALC, Excel, FORTRAN, Lotus 1-2-3, MINITAB, Pascal, SAS, SPSS, UNIRAS graphics, WordPerfect, others. Computer facilities are available to all students.
**Fees:** None.
**Hours:** 9 AM-10 PM (M-Th); 9 AM-5 PM (F-Sa); 1 PM-8 PM (Su).

**PROMINENT ALUMNI/AE.** Joseph P. Kennedy III, U.S. congressman; Joseph Abboud, president, J.A. Apparel Corp.; Alton Brann, president and CEO, Litton Industries; Paula Lyons, consumer reporter, *Good Morning America*; Agnes "Diddy" Gullinane, philanthropist; Thomas Menino, mayor, Boston; William Bratton, New York police commissioner; Georgette Watson, founder, Drop-A-Dime; Frank Novak, actor.

# University of Massachusetts at Dartmouth

North Dartmouth, MA 02747-2300 — 508 999-8000

**1994-95 Costs.** Tuition: $1,854 (state residents), $6,988 (out-of-state). Room: $2,588. Board: $2,026. Fees, books, misc. academic expenses (school's estimate): $2,500.
**Enrollment.** Undergraduates: 2,349 men, 2,280 women (full-time). Freshman class: 3,137 applicants, 2,349 accepted, 999 enrolled. Graduate enrollment: 198 men, 202 women.
**Test score averages/ranges.** Average SAT scores: 423 verbal, 482 math. Range of SAT scores of middle 50%: 373-481 verbal, 417-550 math.
**Faculty.** 321 full-time; 110 part-time. 90% of faculty holds highest degree in specific field. Student/faculty ratio: 15 to 1.
**Selectivity rating.** Less competitive.

**PROFILE.** U Massachusetts at Dartmouth, founded in 1895, is a public, comprehensive institution. Programs are offered through the Colleges of Arts and Sciences, Business and Industry, Engineering, Nursing, and Visual and Performing Arts and the Graduate School. The Swain School of Design, in New Bedford, was recently incorporated into UMass at Dartmouth. Its 710-acre campus is located in North Dartmouth, 60 miles south of Boston.
**Accreditation:** NEASC. Professionally accredited by the Accreditation Board for Engineering and Technology, the National Association of Schools of Art and Design, the National League for Nursing.
**Religious orientation:** University of Massachusetts at Dartmouth is nonsectarian; no religious requirements.
**Library:** Collections totaling over 390,000 volumes, 2,737 periodical subscriptions, and 55,327 microform items.
**Special facilities/museums:** Art gallery, language center, Jewish culture center, Robert F. Kennedy assassination archives, electron microscope, observatory, marine research vessels.
**Athletic facilities:** Gymnasium, basketball and tennis courts, swimming pools, sports medicine and weight rooms, baseball, field hockey, football, intramural, soccer, and softball fields, track.

**STUDENT BODY. Undergraduate profile:** 94% are state residents; 36% are transfers. 2% Asian-American, 4% Black, 1% Hispanic, 91% White, 2% Other.
**Freshman profile:** 1% of freshmen who took SAT scored 700 or over on math; 2% scored 600 or over on verbal, 11% scored 600 or over on math; 17% scored 500 or over on verbal, 44% scored 500 or over on math; 63% scored 400 or over on verbal, 81% scored 400 or over on math; 96% scored 300 or over on verbal, 99% scored 300 or over on math. 98% of accepted applicants took SAT. 85% of freshmen come from public schools.
**Undergraduate achievement:** 76% of fall 1992 freshmen returned for fall 1993 term. 50% of entering class graduated.
**Foreign students:** 28 students are from out of the country. Countries represented include Cape Verde, China, Japan, Malaysia, Portugal, and Taiwan; 20 in all.

**PROGRAMS OF STUDY. Degrees:** B.A., B.F.A., B.Mus., B.S., B.S.Nurs.
**Majors:** Accounting, Art Education, Art History, Biology, Business Information Systems, Chemistry, Civil Engineering, Computer Engineering, Computer Science, Economics, Electrical Engineering, Electrical Engineering Technology, English, Fibers/Textiles, Finance, French, History, Human Resources Management, Humanities/Social Sciences, Management, Manufacturing Management, Marketing, Mathematics, Mechanical Engineering, Mechanical Engineering Technology, Medical Laboratory Science, Multidisciplinary Studies, Music, Nursing, Painting, Philosophy, Physics, Political Science, Portuguese, Printmaking, Psychology, Sculpture, Sociology, Spanish, Textile Chemistry, Textile Design, Textile Technology, Visual Design.
**Distribution of degrees:** The majors with the highest enrollment are accounting, humanities/social sciences, and management; French and fine arts have the lowest.
**Academic regulations:** Freshmen must maintain minimum 1.45 GPA; sophomores, 1.75 GPA; juniors, 1.9 GPA; seniors, 2.0 GPA.
**Special:** Minors offered in many majors and in African and African-American studies, anthropology, German, gerontology, Judaic studies, labor studies, Russian, and women's studies. Self-designed majors. Double majors. Independent study. Pass/fail grading option. Internships. Graduate school at which undergraduates may take graduate-level courses. Preprofessional programs in law, medicine, veterinary science, pharmacy, and dentistry. Five-year B.S./M.S. chemistry program. Member of Southeastern Association for Cooperation in Higher Education in Massachusetts (SACHEM); cross-registration possible. Washington Semester and other off-campus study opportunities. Exchange program with Fashion Inst of Tech. Teacher certification in elementary and secondary education. Certification in specific subject areas. Exchange programs abroad in England (Nottingham Trent U), France (U of Grenoble, Lycee du Grestraudan at Maylan), Germany (Badem-Wurtemburg U) and Portugal (Centro de Arte e Communicacado). ROTC at Providence Coll.
**Honors:** Honors program. Honor societies.
**Academic Assistance:** Remedial reading, writing, math, and study skills. Nonremedial tutoring.

**STUDENT LIFE. Housing:** Students may live on or off campus. Coed dorms. School-owned/operated apartments. 38% of students live in college housing.
**Social atmosphere:** The student newspaper reports that students congregate on campus at the Sunset Room and Corsairs Cove. Favorite gathering spots off campus are Gilligan's on the Island, Cafe Giesta, Alhambra's, and White's on the Watuppa. Greeks, SMU Theater Company, the Student Activities Board, and the campus radio station are influential organizations on campus. Popular campus events include Midnight Madness, Cultural Diversity Week, Springfest, Senior Week, and various concerts throughout the year.
**Services and counseling/handicapped student services:** Placement services. Health service. Women's center. Day care. Counseling services for minority, veteran, and older students. Birth control, personal, and psychological counseling. Career and academic guidance services. Religious counseling. Physically disabled student services. Learning disabled services. Notetaking services. Tape recorders. Tutors. Reader services for the blind.
**Campus organizations:** Undergraduate student government. Student newspaper (Torch, published once/week). Literary magazine. Yearbook. Radio station. Choir, band, music guild, drama club/theatre, outing club, student activities board, Gay/Lesbian Alliance, academic, athletic, departmental, service, and special-interest groups, 100 organizations in all.
**Religious organizations:** Catholic Student Organization, Religious Resource Center, Christian Fellowship, Eposcopal/Protestant Ministry, Hillel Jewish Student Center.
**Minority/foreign student organizations:** United Brothers and Sisters, Multicultural Student Services. Taiwan Student Organization, Indian Student Association.

**ATHLETICS. Physical education requirements:** None.
**Intercollegiate competition:** 12% of students participate. Baseball (M), basketball (M,W), cheerleading (M,W), cross-country (M,W), diving (M,W), field hockey (W), football (M), golf (M), ice hockey (M), soccer (M,W), softball (W), swimming (M,W), tennis (M,W), track (indoor) (M,W), track (outdoor) (M,W), track and field (indoor) (M,W), track and field (outdoor) (M,W), volleyball (W). Member of ECAC, Little East Conference, NAIA, NCAA Division III, New England Football Conference.
**Intramural and club sports:** 40% of students participate. Intramural basketball, cross-country, flag football, swimming, tennis, track, volleyball. Men's club lacrosse.

**ADMISSIONS. Academic basis for candidate selection** (in order of priority): Secondary school record, class rank, standardized test scores, school's recommendation, essay.
**Nonacademic basis for candidate selection:** Particular talent or ability is emphasized. Extracurricular participation is considered.
**Requirements:** Graduation from secondary school is required; GED is accepted. 16 units and the following program of study are required: 4 units of English, 3 units of math, 2 units of lab science, 2 units of foreign language, 1 unit of social studies, 1 unit of history, 3 units of academic electives. Rank in top half of secondary school class and minimum 2.3 GPA recommended. Portfolio recommended of art program applicants. Audition required of music program applicants. College Now and START programs for applicants not normally admissible. SAT is required. ACH recommended. Campus visit recommended. No off-campus interviews.
**Procedure:** Take SAT by January of 12th year. Notification of admission on rolling basis. Reply is required by May 15. $50 tuition deposit, refundable until May 15. $100 room deposit, refundable until May 15. Freshmen accepted for terms other than fall.
**Special programs:** Admission may be deferred two semesters. Credit and/or placement may be granted through CEEB Advanced Placement exams for scores of 3 or higher. Credit and/or placement may be granted through CLEP general and subject exams. Credit and placement may be granted through challenge exams and military and life experience. Early decision program. In fall 1993, 30 applied for early decision and 26 were accepted. Deadline for applying for early decision is November 15. Early entrance/early admission program. Concurrent enrollment program.
**Transfer students:** Transfer students accepted for terms other than fall. In fall 1993, 36% of all new students were transfers into all classes. 1,075 transfer applications were received, 808 were accepted. Application deadline is rolling for fall; rolling for spring. Mini-

mum 2.5 GPA recommended. Lowest course grade accepted is "C-." Maximum number of transferable credits is 60 semester hours. At least 60 semester hours must be completed at the university to receive degree.

**Admissions contact:** Raymond M. Barrows, M.P.A., Director of Admissions. 508 999-8605.

**FINANCIAL AID. Available aid:** Pell grants, SEOG, state scholarships and grants, school scholarships and grants, private scholarships, and academic merit scholarships. Tuition and fee waivers. Perkins Loans (NDSL), PLUS, Stafford Loans (GSL), NSL, Health Professions Loans, state loans, private loans, and SLS. AMS.

**Financial aid statistics:** 25% of aid is not need-based. In 1993-94, 100% of all undergraduate applicants received aid.

**Supporting data/closing dates:** FAFSA: Priority filing date is March 1; accepted on rolling basis. Notification of awards on rolling basis.

**Financial aid contact:** Gerald S. Coutinho, M.Ed., Director of Financial Aid. 508 999-8632.

**STUDENT EMPLOYMENT.** College Work/Study Program. Institutional employment. 22% of full-time undergraduates work on campus during school year. Off-campus part-time employment opportunities rated "good."

**COMPUTER FACILITIES.** 200 IBM/IBM-compatible and Macintosh/Apple microcomputers. Students may access Digital, IBM, SUN minicomputer/mainframe systems, BITNET, Internet. Residence halls may be equipped with stand-alone microcomputers, networked microcomputers, networked terminals, modems. Client/LAN operating systems include Apple/Macintosh, DOS, UNIX/XENIX/AIX, Windows NT, X-windows, DEC, LocalTalk/AppleTalk. Computer languages and software packages include Assembly, BASIC, C, COBOL, FORTRAN, LISP, MacDraw, MacPaint, Pascal, Prolog, WordStar. Computer facilities are available to all students.

**Fees:** Computer fee is included in tuition/fees.

**Hours:** 8 AM-11 PM (M-Th); 8 AM-5 PM (F); 9:30 AM-5 PM (Sa); 2 PM-9:30 PM (Su).

**PROMINENT ALUMNI/AE.** Dietmar Winkler, visual designer; Alfonse Mattia, furniture designer; Geraldine Phipps, Soviet studies; Norman Dion, founder, DYSAN Computer Disks; Steve Donovan, vice-president, Procter & Gamble; Jimmy Tingle, professional comedian.

# University of Massachusetts at Lowell

**Lowell, MA 01854** **508 934-4000**

**1993-94 Costs.** Tuition: $1,884 (state residents), $6,894 (out-of-state). Room: $2,520. Board: $1,783. Fees, books, misc. academic expenses (school's estimate): $3,068.

**Enrollment.** Undergraduates: 3,616 men, 2,124 women (full-time). Freshman class: 3,986 applicants, 3,026 accepted, 1,093 enrolled. Graduate enrollment: 1,489 men, 1,074 women.

**Test score averages/ranges.** Average SAT scores: 447 verbal, 504 math. Range of SAT scores of middle 50%: 400-490 verbal, 440-550 math.

**Faculty.** 461 full-time; 149 part-time. 82% of faculty holds doctoral degree. Student/faculty ratio: 15 to 1.

**Selectivity rating.** Less competitive.

**PROFILE.** U Massachusetts at Lowell is a public institution. Founded as a state college in 1894, it gained university status in 1959, and joined the state system in 1991. Programs are offered through the Colleges of Arts and Sciences, Engineering, Management Science, and Music. Its two campuses of 100 acres are located in Lowell, 25 miles northwest of Boston.

**Accreditation:** NEASC. Professionally accredited by the Accreditation Board for Engineering and Technology, the American Assembly of Collegiate Schools of Business, the American Medical Association (CAHEA), the American Physical Therapy Association, the Computing Sciences Accreditation Board, the National Association of Schools of Art and Design, the National Association of Schools of Music, the National Council for Accreditation of Teacher Education, the National League for Nursing.

**Religious orientation:** University of Massachusetts at Lowell is nonsectarian; no religious requirements.

**Library:** Collections totaling over 391,058 volumes, 3,757 periodical subscriptions, and 1,042,609 microform items.

**Special facilities/museums:** Language lab, media center, audio-visual department, on-campus elementary school, freshman center for learning, center for productivity enhancement, center for field studies, center for performing and visual art, center for health promotion, research nuclear reactor.

**Athletic facilities:** Gymnasium, swimming pool, ice rink, basketball, racquetball, squash, and volleyball courts, weight lifting equipment, baseball, field hockey, football, lacrosse, soccer, and softball fields.

**STUDENT BODY. Undergraduate profile:** 93% are state residents; 40% are transfers. 4.5% Asian-American, 2.1% Black, 2.4% Hispanic, .3% Native American, 81% White, 9.7% Other.

**Freshman profile:** 2% of freshmen who took SAT scored 700 or over on math; 3% scored 600 or over on verbal, 15% scored 600 or over on math; 25% scored 500 or over on verbal, 51% scored 500 or over on math; 76% scored 400 or over on verbal, 91% scored 400 or over on math; 100% scored 300 or over on verbal, 99% scored 300 or over on math. Majority of accepted applicants took SAT.

**Undergraduate achievement:** 67% of fall 1992 freshmen returned for fall 1993 term. 20% of entering class graduated.

**Foreign students:** 137 students are from out of the country. Countries represented include Canada, China, India, Indonesia, and Taiwan; 10 in all.

**PROGRAMS OF STUDY. Degrees:** B.A., B.F.A., B.Mus., B.S., B.S.Bus.Admin., B.S.Eng., B.S.Nurs., B.S.Tech.

**Majors:** Accounting, American Studies, Art, Biological Sciences, Business Administration, Chemical Engineering, Chemistry, Civil Engineering, Clinical Laboratory Sciences, Computer Science, Criminal Justice, Economics, Electrical Engineering, English, Environmental Science, Exercise Physiology, Finance, Fine Arts, French, Geology, Health Education, History, Industrial Management, Liberal Arts, Management, Management Information Systems, Marketing, Mathematics, Mechanical Engineering, Meteorology, Modern Languages, Music Business, Music Education, Music History, Music Performance, Music Theory/Composition, Musicology, Nuclear Engineering, Nursing, Operations Management, Philosophy, Physics, Plastics Engineering, Political Science, Psychology, Radiological Health Physics, Sociology, Sound Recording Technology, Spanish.

**Distribution of degrees:** The majors with the highest enrollment are business administration, criminal justice, and psychology; French, modern languages, and Spanish have the lowest.

**Requirements:** General education requirement.

**Special:** Associate's degrees offered in continuing education program. Double majors. Dual degrees. Pass/fail grading option. Internships. Graduate school at which undergraduates may take graduate-level courses. 3-2 engineering/liberal arts program with St. Anselm Coll. Member of Northeast Consortium of Colleges and Universities in Massachusetts. Teacher certification in elementary and secondary education. ROTC and AFROTC.

**Academic Assistance:** Remedial reading, writing, math, and study skills. Nonremedial tutoring.

**STUDENT LIFE. Housing:** Students may live on or off campus. Coed, women's, and men's dorms. School-owned/operated apartments. Off-campus married-student housing for graduate students. 25% of students live in college housing.

**Social atmosphere:** McGauvran Student Union, the South Cafe, Fio's Express, the Fox Den, and Abbey Road Tavern are some of the most popular student gathering-spots. Influential groups include the Connector, the Commuter Association, and the Activities Commission. Highlights of the school year are Midnight Madness hockey games, Family Day, the Head Start Christmas Party, and Spring Carnival. "U Mass Lowell is primarily a commuter college," writes the editor of the student newspaper. "As a result, the social life pales in comparison to some larger state universities. Still, all things considered, a student here can enjoy 'college life' if he/she knows where to look."

**Services and counseling/handicapped student services:** Placement services. Health service. Counseling services for minority, veteran, and older students. Personal and psychological counseling. Career and academic guidance services. Physically disabled student services. Learning disabled services. Notetaking services.

**Campus organizations:** Undergraduate student government. Student newspaper (Connector, published once/week). Yearbook. Radio station. Art co-op, drama group, PIRG, athletic, departmental, service, and special-interest groups.

**Religious organizations:** Newman Club, Intervarsity Christian Fellowship, Hillel, Muslim Student Association.

**Minority/foreign student organizations:** Black Student Union. African, Chinese, and Indian groups.

**ATHLETICS. Physical education requirements:** None.

**Intercollegiate competition:** 7% of students participate. Baseball (M), basketball (M,W), crew (M,W), cross-country (M,W), field hockey (W), football (M), golf (M), ice hockey (M), soccer (M), softball (W), swimming (M), tennis (M,W), track (indoor) (M,W), track (outdoor) (M,W), track and field (indoor) (M,W), track and field (outdoor) (M,W), volleyball (W), wrestling (M). Member of Eastern College Ski Conference, ECAC, EIAA, Freedom Football Conference, Hockey East Association, NCAA Division I for ice hockey, NCAA Division II, NCSA, NEIAAA, New England Collegiate Conference.

**Intramural and club sports:** 45% of students participate. Intramural badminton, basketball, bowling, broomball, flag football, floor hockey, golf, horseshoes, hot-shot basketball, ice hockey, indoor soccer, miniature golf, pool, racquetball, soccer, softball, squash, table tennis, tennis, triathlon, turkey trot, volleyball, weight lifting. Men's club Alpine skiing, bowling, floor hockey, horsemanship, lacrosse, martial arts, volleyball. Women's club Alpine skiing, bowling, floor hockey, horsemanship, martial arts, soccer, swimming.

**ADMISSIONS. Academic basis for candidate selection** (in order of priority): Secondary school record, standardized test scores, class rank, school's recommendation.

**Requirements:** Graduation from secondary school is required; GED is accepted. 16 units and the following program of study are required: 4 units of English, 3 units of math, 2 units of lab science, 2 units of foreign language, 3 units of social studies, 2 units of academic electives. Audition required of music program applicants. EOP for applicants not normally admissible. Encore Program for adults to begin or continue education on part-time basis; successful completion of program allows matriculation as regular undergraduate. SAT is required; ACT may be substituted. Campus visit and interview recommended. No off-campus interviews.

**Procedure:** Take SAT or ACT by January of 12th year. Suggest filing application by April 1; no deadline. Final application filing date depends on program. Notification of admission on rolling basis. Reply is required within 20 days of acceptance. $50 tuition deposit, refundable until June 1. $100 nonrefundable room deposit. Freshmen accepted for terms other than fall.

**Special programs:** Admission may be deferred one semester. Credit may be granted through CEEB Advanced Placement for scores of 3 or higher. Credit may be granted through CLEP general and subject exams. Concurrent enrollment program.

**Transfer students:** Transfer students accepted for terms other than fall. In fall 1993, 40% of all new students were transfers into all classes. 1,500 transfer applications were received, 1,209 were accepted. Application deadline is rolling for fall; rolling for spring. Minimum 2.0 GPA required. Lowest course grade accepted is "C." At least 30 semester hours must be completed at the university to receive degree.

**Admissions contact:** Lawrence R. Martin, Jr., M.Ed., Director of Admissions. 508 934-3930.

**FINANCIAL AID. Available aid:** Pell grants, SEOG, state scholarships, school scholarships, private scholarships, and athletic scholarships. Perkins Loans (NDSL), PLUS, Stafford Loans (GSL), NSL, state loans, school loans, private loans, and SLS. AMS.

**Supporting data/closing dates:** FAFSA/FAF: Deadline is May 1. Notification of awards begins in May.

**Financial aid contact:** Walter A. Costello, Director of Financial Aid. 508 934-4220.

**STUDENT EMPLOYMENT.** College Work/Study Program. Institutional employment. Off-campus part-time employment opportunities rated "fair."

**COMPUTER FACILITIES.** 600 IBM/IBM-compatible and Macintosh/Apple microcomputers. Computer languages and software packages include Ada, Assembler, BASIC, BMDP, COBOL, FORTRAN, LISP, Pascal, PL/1, SPSS; 100 in all. Computer facilities are available to all students.

**Fees:** Computer fee is included in tuition/fees.

**Hours:** 24 hours.

# Wellesley College

**Wellesley, MA 02181** **617 235-0320**

**1993-94 Costs.** Tuition: $17,390. Room & board: $6,090. Fees, books, misc. academic expenses (school's estimate): $835.

**Enrollment.** 2,136 women (full-time). Freshman class: 2,509 applicants, 1,230 accepted, 623 enrolled.

**Test score averages/ranges.** Average SAT scores: 600 verbal, 630 math.

**Faculty.** 241 full-time; 72 part-time. 97% of faculty holds highest degree in specific field. Student/faculty ratio: 10 to 1.

**Selectivity rating.** Most competitive.

**PROFILE.** Wellesley, founded in 1870, is a private, liberal arts college for women. Its 500-acre campus and arboretum is located in Wellesley, 12 miles west of Boston. Campus buildings encompass a variety of architectural styles ranging from Gothic to contemporary.

**Accreditation:** NEASC.

**Religious orientation:** Wellesley College is nonsectarian; no religious requirements.

**Library:** Collections totaling over 669,915 volumes, 2,575 periodical subscriptions, and 61,898 microform items.

**Special facilities/museums:** Learning and teaching center, writing lab, language lab, child study center, center for research on women, art museum, greenhouses and botanical gardens, two electron microscopes, observatory with three telescopes, two NMR spectrometers, laser lab, quantum mechanics lab.

**Athletic facilities:** Field house, gymnasium, basketball, racquetball, squash, and tennis courts, swimming pool, diving well, fencing salon, volleyball arena, athletic training center, weight room, dance studio, golf course, athletic fields, boathouse.

**STUDENT BODY. Undergraduate profile:** 14% are state residents; 4% are transfers. 23% Asian-American, 7% Black, 5% Hispanic, 1% Native American, 64% White. Average age of undergraduates is 20.

**Freshman profile:** 100% of accepted applicants took SAT. 64% of freshmen come from public schools.

**Undergraduate achievement:** 97% of fall 1991 freshmen returned for fall 1992 term. 82% of entering class graduated. 34% of students who completed a degree program immediately went on to graduate study.

**Foreign students:** 306 students are from out of the country. Countries represented include Canada, China, Hong Kong, Japan, Korea, and Taiwan; 66 in all.

**PROGRAMS OF STUDY. Degrees:** B.A.

**Majors:** Africana Studies, American Studies, Anthropology, Architecture, Art History, Astronomy, Biological Chemistry, Biological Sciences, Chemistry, Chinese, Chinese Studies, Classical Civilization, Classical/Near Eastern Archaeology, Cognitive Science, Computer Science, Economics, English, French, French Studies, Geology, German, German Studies, Greek, History, International Relations, Italian, Italian Culture, Japanese Studies, Jewish Studies, Language Studies, Latin, Latin American Studies, Mathematics, Medieval/Renaissance Studies, Music, Philosophy, Physics, Political Science, Psychobiology, Psychology, Religion, Russian, Russian Area Studies, Sociology, Spanish, Studio Art, Theatre Studies, Women's Studies.

**Distribution of degrees:** The majors with the highest enrollment are economics, political science, and English; Greek, Jewish studies, and Latin have the lowest.

**Requirements:** General education requirement.

**Academic regulations:** Minimum 2.0 GPA required for graduation.

**Special:** Minors offered in most majors and in art and astrophysics. Area studies, period studies, or other interdisciplinary programs may be arranged. Technology Studies Program. Peace Studies Program. Cluster Program (interdisciplinary program for first-year students). Self-designed majors. Double majors. Dual degrees. Independent study. Accelerated study. Pass/fail grading option. Internships. Preprofessional programs in law and medicine. 3-2 double degree program with MIT. Cross-registration with MIT. Sea Semester. Member of Twelve College Exchange Program. Teacher certification in secondary education. Exchange programs abroad in France, Germany, and Spain. Study abroad also in over 100 accredited programs worldwide. ROTC and AFROTC at MIT.

**Honors:** Phi Beta Kappa. Honors program. Honor societies.

**Academic Assistance:** Remedial study skills. Nonremedial tutoring.

**STUDENT LIFE. Housing:** Students may live on or off campus. Women's dorms. 99% of students live in college housing.

**Social atmosphere:** "Wellesley College students do not socialize as much as other schools," reports a student. "Students study a lot." When they are not studying, The Wellesley News reports that students frequent the Schneider Student Center, Cafe Hoop, and Bedrock Cafe on campus. Off-campus activities center around MIT, Harvard University, and Babson College. The most popular social events of the year are the Head of the Charles Regatta, Boston Marathon, TexMex Barbecue, and the annual fall gala.

**Services and counseling/handicapped student services:** Placement services. Health service. Women's center. Counseling services for minority and older students. Birth control, personal, and psychological counseling. Career and academic guidance services. Religious counseling. Physically disabled student services. Learning disabled services. Notetaking services. Tape recorders. Tutors. Reader services for the blind.

**Campus organizations:** Undergraduate student government. Student newspaper (Wellesley News, published once/week). Literary magazine. Yearbook. Radio station. Choirs, madrigal group, Chamber Music Society, MIT orchestra, coffeehouse, Carilloneurs Guild, Experimental Theatre, dance groups, film society, debating, modern drama group, Shakespeare Society, outing club, Amnesty International, academic, political, and special-interest groups, 141 organizations in all.

**Religious organizations:** Interfaith Council, Latter-Day Saints Student Association, Black Christian Fellowship, Hillel, Asian Christian Fellowship, Ministry to Black Women, Newman Catholic Ministry, Christian Fellowship, Campus Crusade for Christ, Al Muslimat, interdenominational Bible study, Episcopalian, Lutheran, and Christian Science groups.

**Minority/foreign student organizations:** Alianza, Asian Association, Harambee House, Ethos, Mezcla. Filipino Association, Chinese, Japanese, and Middle Eastern clubs, Vietnamese Student Association, Slater International, Wellesley Association for South Asian Culture, Carribean Students Association.

**ATHLETICS. Physical education requirements:** Two semesters of physical education required.

**Intercollegiate competition:** 14% of students participate. Basketball (W), crew (W), cross-country (W), diving (W), fencing (W), field hockey (W), lacrosse (W), soccer (W), squash (W), swimming (W), tennis (W), volleyball (W). Member of ECAC, NCAA Division III, New England Women's 8, Seven Sisters Group.

**Intramural and club sports:** 20% of students participate. Intramural aerobics, crew, volleyball. Women's club Alpine skiing, ice hockey, Nordic skiing, rugby, softball.

**ADMISSIONS. Academic basis for candidate selection** (in order of priority): Secondary school record, class rank, school's recommendation, standardized test scores, essay.

**Nonacademic basis for candidate selection:** Character and personality, extracurricular participation, and particular talent or ability are important. Geographical distribution and alumnae relationship are considered.

**Requirements:** Graduation from secondary school is recommended; GED is accepted. 17 units and the following program of study are recommended: 4 units of English, 3 units of math, 3 units of science, 4 units of foreign language, 3 units of social studies. SAT is required. ACH required. Campus visit and interview recommended. Off-campus interviews available with an alumni representative.

**Procedure:** Take SAT by January of 12th year. Take ACH by January of 12th year. Visit college for interview by January 15 of 12th year. Suggest filing application by January 1. Application deadline is January 15. Notification of admission by April 1. Reply is required by May 1. $200 nonrefundable tuition deposit. $150 refundable room deposit. Freshmen accepted for fall term only.

**Special programs:** Admission may be deferred one year. Credit and/or placement may be granted through CEEB Advanced Placement exams for scores of 4 or higher. Early decision program. In fall 1992, 128 applied for early decision and 72 were accepted. Deadline for applying for early decision is November 1. Early entrance/early admission program.

**Transfer students:** Transfer students accepted for terms other than fall. In fall 1992, 4% of all new students were transfers into all classes. 115 transfer applications were received, 39 were accepted. Application deadline is February 1 for fall; November 15 for spring. Minimum 3.2 GPA recommended. Lowest course grade accepted is "C." At least 16 semester hours must be completed at the college to receive degree.

**Admissions contact:** Janet A. Lavin, M.A., Director of Admission. 617 283-2270.

**FINANCIAL AID. Available aid:** Pell grants, SEOG, state scholarships and grants, school grants, private scholarships and grants, ROTC scholarships, and aid for undergraduate foreign students. Perkins Loans (NDSL), PLUS, Stafford Loans (GSL), state loans, school loans, private loans, and SLS. Knight Tuition Plans, deferred payment plan, and guaranteed tuition. Semester Payment Plan.

**Financial aid statistics:** In 1992-93, 90% of all undergraduate applicants received aid; 79% of freshman applicants. Average amounts of aid awarded freshmen: Scholarships and grants, $12,880; loans, $2,525.

**Supporting data/closing dates:** FAFSA/FAF: Priority filing date is February 1. School's own aid application: Deadline is February 1. Income tax forms: Priority filing date is March 1. Notification of awards begins April 1.

**Financial aid contact:** Kathryn Osmond, M.A., Director of Financial Aid. 617 283-2360.

**STUDENT EMPLOYMENT.** College Work/Study Program. Institutional employment. 55% of full-time undergraduates work on campus during school year. Students may expect to earn an average of $1,600 during school year. Off-campus part-time employment opportunities rated "good."

**COMPUTER FACILITIES.** 150 IBM/IBM-compatible and Macintosh/Apple microcomputers. Students may access Digital, Prime minicomputer/mainframe systems, Internet. Residence halls may be equipped with stand-alone microcomputers, networked microcomputers. Computer languages and software packages include Assembler, BASIC, C, DataTrieve, FORTRAN, LISP, MINITAB, Pascal, Prolog, SAS, SPSS-X. Computer facilities are available to all students.

Fees: None.

Hours: 24 hours.

**GRADUATE CAREER DATA.** Graduate school percentages: 23% enter law school. 16% enter medical school. 3% enter graduate business programs. 53% enter graduate arts and sciences programs. 11% of graduates choose careers in business and industry.

**PROMINENT ALUMNAE.** Alberta Bean Arthurs, director for arts and humanities, The Rockefeller Foundation; Hillary Clinton, First Lady; Laurel Cutler, vice-president, Chrysler Motors; Nora Ephron, screenwriter, producer, and director; Amalya Kearse, judge, court of appeals; Ellen R. Marram, president, Nabisco Brands; Jeanette Winter Loeb, partner, Goldman, Sachs, and Co.; Diane Sawyer, TV reporter and anchor.

# Wentworth Institute of Technology

**Boston, MA 02115** 617 442-9010

**1994-95 Costs.** Tuition: $9,850. Room & board: $6,050. Fees, books, misc. academic expenses (school's estimate): $600.
**Enrollment.** Undergraduates: 1,889 men, 294 women (full-time). Freshman class: 1,480 applicants, 1,251 accepted, 452 enrolled.
**Test score averages/ranges.** Average SAT scores: 372 verbal, 458 math. Range of SAT scores of middle 50%: 310-430 verbal, 380-530 math.
**Faculty.** 116 full-time; 100 part-time. 90% of faculty holds highest degree in specific field. Student/faculty ratio: 19 to 1.
**Selectivity rating.** Less competitive.

**PROFILE.** Wentworth is a private institute. Founded in 1904, it adopted coeducation in 1972. Its 35-acre urban campus is located in Boston.

**Accreditation:** NEASC. Professionally accredited by the Accreditation Board for Engineering and Technology, the Foundation for Interior Design Education Research, the National Architecture Accrediting Board.
**Religious orientation:** Wentworth Institute of Technology is nonsectarian; no religious requirements.
**Library:** Collections totaling over 77,000 volumes, 500 periodical subscriptions and 90 microform items.
**Athletic facilities:** Basketball, racquetball, tennis, volleyball courts, gymnasiums, ice rink, training and weight rooms.
**STUDENT BODY. Undergraduate profile:** 74% are state residents; 31% are transfers. 10% Asian-American, 9% Black, 4% Hispanic, 74% White, 3% Other. Average age of undergraduates is 22.
**Freshman profile:** 1% of freshmen who took SAT scored 700 or over on math; 1% scored 600 or over on verbal, 10% scored 600 or over on math; 8% scored 500 or over on verbal, 38% scored 500 or over on math; 40% scored 400 or over on verbal, 71% scored 400 or over on math; 81% scored 300 or over on verbal, 93% scored 300 or over on math. 90% of accepted applicants took SAT.
**Undergraduate achievement:** 66% of fall 1992 freshmen returned for fall 1993 term. 2% of students who completed a degree program immediately went on to graduate study.
**Foreign students:** 211 students are from out of the country. Countries represented include Bermuda, Hong Kong, Japan, Kuwait, Morocco, and Taiwan; 59 in all.
**PROGRAMS OF STUDY. Degrees:** B.Arch., B.S.
**Majors:** Architectural Engineering Technology, Architecture, Building Construction Technology, Civil Engineering Technology, Computer Engineering Technology, Computer Science, Construction Management, Electromechanical Engineering, Electronic Engineering Technology, Engineering Technology, Environmental Engineering, Facilities Planning/Management, Industrial Design, Interior Design, Manufacturing Engineering Technology, Mechanical Engineering Technology, Technical Communications, Technical Management.
**Distribution of degrees:** The majors with the highest enrollment are electronic engineering technology, architectural engineering technology, and mechanical engineering technology; technical communications, facilities planning/management, and manufacturing engineering technology have the lowest.
**Academic regulations:** Core curriculum required in some cases. Minimum 2.00 GPA must be maintained.
**Special:** Associate's degrees offered. Self-designed majors. Double majors. Dual degrees. Cooperative education programs. B.Arch. program has semester abroad; location varies. ROTC at Northeastern U. AFROTC at Boston U.
**Honors:** Honor societies.
**Academic Assistance:** Remedial writing, math, and study skills. Nonremedial tutoring.
**STUDENT LIFE. Housing:** Students may live on or off campus. Coed dorms. School-owned/operated apartments. 26% of students live in college housing.
**Social atmosphere:** According too the student newspaper, "The cultural life on campus is very good. Off-campus life is excellent because we are in the city of Boston." Popular campus events include Engineering Week and International Student Day. On campus, students frequent the student center and the library. Favorite off-campus spots include theatres, bars, and social clubs.
**Services and counseling/handicapped student services:** Health service. Women's center. Career Center. Counseling services for minority, military, veteran, and older students. Birth control, personal, and psychological counseling. Career and academic guidance services. Physically disabled student services. Tape recorders.
**Campus organizations:** Undergraduate student government. Student newspaper (Spectrum, once/month). Literary magazine. Yearbook. Computer programming society, American Concrete Institute, Society of Women Engineers, ski and adventure club, academic and departmental groups, 32 organizations in all.
**Religious organizations:** Bible Club.
**Minority/foreign student organizations:** Society of Black Engineers. Intercultural Student Society, Haitian, Islamic, Hellenic, and Vietnamese groups.
**ATHLETICS. Physical education requirements:** None.
**Intercollegiate competition:** 9% of students participate. Baseball (M), basketball (M,W), cheerleading (M,W), ice hockey (M), riflery (M,W), soccer (M), softball (W), tennis (M,W), volleyball (M,W). Member of Commonwealth Coast Conference, ECAC, MAIAW, NCAA Division III, New England Collegiate Athletic Conference.
**Intramural and club sports:** 21% of students participate. Intramural badminton, basketball, flag football, indoor soccer, softball, street hockey, team handball, tennis, volleyball. Men's club golf, rugby, weight lifting. Women's club golf.
**ADMISSIONS. Academic basis for candidate selection** (in order of priority): Secondary school record, standardized test scores, class rank.
**Nonacademic basis for candidate selection:** Extracurricular participation and particular talent or ability are considered.
**Requirements:** Graduation from secondary school is required; GED is accepted. 16 units and the following program of study are recommended: 4 units of English, 4 units of math, 1 unit of lab science. Minimum "C" average generally required; specific requirements vary by program. Wentworth's associate degree in architectural engineering technology is the core curriculum for the bachelor of architecture degree program. Students petition for readmission to B.Arch. program and other design and construction programs during second semester of sophomore year. Portfolio and faculty review required of applicants to B.Arch. program and Interior and Industrial Design programs. Conditional admission possible for applicants not meeting standard requirements. Tech One preparatory program for applicants not normally admissible. SAT is required; ACT may be substituted. Campus visit and interview recommended. Off-campus interviews available with admissions and alumni representatives.
**Procedure:** Take SAT or ACT by November of 12th year. Suggest filing application by June 1. Application deadline is August 1. Notification of admission on rolling basis. Reply is required by May 1 or within 21 days of acceptance. $150 tuition deposit, refundable until May 1. $400 room deposit, refundable until July 1. Freshmen accepted for terms other than fall.
**Special programs:** Admission may be deferred one year. Credit and/or placement may be granted through CEEB Advanced Placement exams for scores of 3 or higher. Credit and/or placement may be granted through CLEP subject exams. Credit and placement may be granted through DANTES and challenge exams and military and life experience.
**Transfer students:** Transfer students accepted for terms other than fall. In fall 1993, 31% of all new students were transfers into all classes. 445 transfer applications were received, 352 were accepted. Application deadline is August 1; priority filing date June 1 for fall; December 1 for spring. Lowest course grade accepted is "C." Maximum number of transferable credits is 64 credit hours. At least half of total semester hours must be completed at the institute to receive degree; exact requirements vary by program.
**Admissions contact:** Thomas J. McGinn III, M.B.A., Director of Enrollment Management. 617 442-9010, 800 556-0610.
**FINANCIAL AID. Available aid:** Pell grants, SEOG, state scholarships and grants, school scholarships and grants, private scholarships and grants, ROTC scholarships, and academic merit scholarships. Perkins Loans (NDSL), PLUS, Stafford Loans (GSL), state loans, school loans, private loans, and SLS. Knight Tuition Plans.
**Financial aid statistics:** 1% of aid is not need-based. In 1993-94, 91% of all undergraduate applicants received aid; 96% of freshman applicants. Average amounts of aid awarded freshmen: Scholarships and grants, $3,669; loans, $4,730.
**Supporting data/closing dates:** FAFSA: Priority filing date is March 1. School's own aid application: Priority filing date is March 1. State aid form: Priority filing date is May 1; accepted on rolling basis. Income tax forms: Priority filing date is March 1; accepted on rolling basis. Notification of awards on rolling basis.
**Financial aid contact:** Carol A. Rubel, M.A., Director of Financial Aid. 617 442-9010, 800 222-9368.
**STUDENT EMPLOYMENT.** College Work/Study Program. Institutional employment. 17% of full-time undergraduates work on campus during school year. Students may expect to earn an average of $1,200 during school year. Off-campus part-time employment opportunities rated "good."
**COMPUTER FACILITIES.** 220 IBM/IBM-compatible and Macintosh/Apple microcomputers; 181 are networked. Students may access Digital, SUN minicomputer/mainframe systems, Internet. Client/LAN operating systems include Apple/Macintosh, DOS, UNIX/XENIX/AIX, LocalTalk/AppleTalk, Novell. Computer languages and software packages include Assembler, AutoCAD, BASIC, C, C++, COBOL, DataCAD, dBASE, FORTRAN, Hypercard, LISP, Microsoft Word, PageMaker, Paradox, Pascal, RDB, Quattro Pro, Windows, WordPerfect, 3D-Studio. Computer facilities are available to all students.
**Fees:** Computer fee is included in tuition/fees.
**Hours:** 7:30 AM-10 PM (M-Th); 7:30 AM-9 PM (F-Sa); 1 PM-9 PM (Su).
**GRADUATE CAREER DATA.** 100% of graduates choose careers in business and industry. Companies and businesses that hire graduates: Digital Equipment Corp.
**PROMINENT ALUMNI/AE.** John A. Volpe, former governor of Massachusetts and ambassador to Italy; John F. Smith, senior vice-president, Digital Equipment Corp.; Frederick E. Hood, co-chairperson of the board, Hood Sailmakers (USA).

# Western New England College

**Springfield, MA 01119** 413 782-3111

**1993-94 Costs.** Tuition: $8,524. Room & board: $5,400. Engineering lab fee: $430. Pharmacy lab fee: $140 Other fees, books, misc. academic expenses (school's estimate): $1,250.
**Enrollment.** Undergraduates: 1,132 men, 768 women (full-time). Freshman class: 1,620 applicants, 1,469 accepted, 447 enrolled. Graduate enrollment: 1,055 men, 787 women.
**Test score averages/ranges.** Average SAT scores: 400 verbal, 460 math. Range of SAT scores of middle 50%: 350-450 verbal, 400-500 math.
**Faculty.** 106 full-time; 153 part-time. 68% of faculty holds doctoral degree. Student/faculty ratio: 17 to 1.
**Selectivity rating.** Less competitive.

**PROFILE.** Western New England, founded in 1919, is a private, multipurpose college. Programs are offered through the Pharmacy Program and the Schools of Arts and Sciences, Business, Continuing Higher Education, Engineering, and Law. Its 131-acre campus is located in a residential section of Springfield, 90 miles west of Boston.

**Accreditation:** NEASC. Professionally accredited by the Accreditation Board for Engineering and Technology, the American Bar Association, the Council on Social Work Education.
**Religious orientation:** Western New England College is nonsectarian; no religious requirements.
**Library:** Collections totaling over 116,421 volumes, 690 periodical subscriptions, and 1,729 microform items.
**Athletic facilities:** Gymnasium, areobics, weight, and wellness rooms, racquetball, squash, and tennis courts, baseball, field hockey, football, soccer, and softball fields, indoor swimming pool.

**STUDENT BODY. Undergraduate profile:** 54% are state residents; 26% are transfers. 2% Asian-American, 2% Black, 2% Hispanic, 93% White, 1% Other. Average age of undergraduates is 22.
**Freshman profile:** 1% of freshmen who took SAT scored 700 or over on math; 1% scored 600 or over on verbal, 6% scored 600 or over on math; 8% scored 500 or over on verbal, 29% scored 500 or over on math; 51% scored 400 or over on verbal, 71% scored 400 or over on math; 94% scored 300 or over on verbal, 99% scored 300 or over on math. 99% of accepted applicants took SAT. 81% of freshmen come from public schools.
**Undergraduate achievement:** 70% of fall 1991 freshmen returned for fall 1992 term. 40% of entering class graduated. 10% of students who completed a degree program went on to graduate study within one year.
**Foreign students:** 32 students are from out of the country. Countries represented include Canada, Greece, Iran, Japan, Malaysia, and Turkey; 23 in all.

**PROGRAMS OF STUDY. Degrees:** B.A., B.S., B.S.Bus.Admin., B.S.Elec.Eng., B.S.Eng., B.S.Indust.Eng., B.S.Mech.Eng., B.Soc.Work.
**Majors:** Accounting, Bioengineering, Biology, Chemistry, Computer Information Systems, Computer Science, Criminal Justice, Economics, Electrical Engineering, Engineering Management, English, Finance, General Business, Government, History, Industrial Engineering, Integrated Liberal Studies, Law Enforcement, Management, Marketing, Mathematical Sciences, Mechanical Engineering, Pharmacy, Psychology, Quantitative Economics, Quantitative Methods, Social Work, Sociology, Technical Management.
**Distribution of degrees:** The majors with the highest enrollment are law enforcement, marketing, and accounting; chemistry, biology, and bioengineering have the lowest.
**Requirements:** General education requirement.
**Academic regulations:** Minimum 2.0 GPA must be maintained.
**Special:** Minors offered in some majors and in business, education, international affairs, international business, mathematics, and philosophy,. B.A. in liberal studies and B.S. in law enforcement offered through School of Continuing Higher Education. Schools of Business and Engineering offer identical degree programs in the evening. Exploratory program available to arts and sciences freshmen and sophomores with undeclared majors. Associate's degrees offered. Self-designed majors. Double majors. Independent study. Accelerated study. Internships. Graduate school at which undergraduates may take graduate-level courses. Preprofessional programs in law, medicine, veterinary science, and dentistry. 3-2 pharmacy program with Massachusetts Coll of Pharmacy and Allied Health Sciences. Member of Cooperating Colleges of Greater Springfield. Washington Semester. Teacher certification in secondary education. Certification in specific subject areas. Study abroad possible. ROTC and AFROTC.
**Honors:** Honor societies.
**Academic Assistance:** Nonremedial tutoring.

**STUDENT LIFE. Housing:** Students may live on or off campus. Coed, women's, and men's dorms. School-owned/operated apartments. 60% of students live in college housing.
**Social atmosphere:** The Student Senate and the Council of Peer Advisors are two of the influential groups on campus. Some of the most popular social events during the year are Parent's Weekend, First Week, and Senior Week. "We are a private, homey institution that leads a semi-quiet, family life," reports the editor of the school paper. "Most people are friendly and gather in generally informal groups on and off campus."
**Services and counseling/handicapped student services:** Placement services. Health service. Counseling services for minority, military, veteran, and older students. Birth control, personal, and psychological counseling. Career and academic guidance services. Religious counseling. Physically disabled student services. Tutors.
**Campus organizations:** Undergraduate student government. Student newspaper (Westerner, published once/month). Literary magazine. Yearbook. Radio station. Stageless Players, art and literature review, photography and outing clubs, Society of Women Engineers, Helping Hands Society, academic, athletic, professional, and special-interest groups, 37 organizations in all.
**Religious organizations:** Campus Ministry.
**Minority/foreign student organizations:** United and Mutually Equal. International Student Association.

**ATHLETICS. Physical education requirements:** Two semesters of physical education required.
**Intercollegiate competition:** 20% of students participate. Baseball (M), basketball (M), bowling (M), cross-country (W), field hockey (W), football (M), golf (M), ice hockey (M), lacrosse (M), soccer (M,W), softball (W), tennis (M), wrestling (M). Member of Constitution Athletic Conference, ECAC, NCAA Division III, Northeast Women's Athletic Conference.
**Intramural and club sports:** 25% of students participate. Intramural basketball, flag football, indoor hockey, softball, volleyball, water polo. Men's club cheerleading, martial arts. Women's club martial arts.

**ADMISSIONS. Academic basis for candidate selection** (in order of priority): Secondary school record, class rank, standardized test scores, school's recommendation, essay.
**Nonacademic basis for candidate selection:** Extracurricular participation is emphasized. Character and personality are important. Particular talent or ability and alumni/ae relationship are considered.
**Requirements:** Graduation from secondary school is required; GED is accepted. 11 units and the following program of study are required: 4 units of English, 2 units of math, 2 units of lab science, 1 unit of social studies. Minimum combined SAT score of 800, rank in top two-thirds of secondary school class, and minimum 2.0 GPA recommended. SAT is required; ACT may be substituted. Campus visit and interview recommended. Off-campus interviews available with an admissions representative.
**Procedure:** Take SAT or ACT by June 1 of 12th year. Notification of admission on rolling basis. Reply is required by May 1. $100 refundable tuition deposit. $100 nonrefundable room deposit. Freshmen accepted for terms other than fall.
**Special programs:** Admission may be deferred one year. Credit and/or placement may be granted through CEEB Advanced Placement exams for scores of 3 or higher. Credit and/or placement may be granted through CLEP general and subject exams. Credit and placement may be granted through military and life experience. Concurrent enrollment program.
**Transfer students:** Transfer students accepted for terms other than fall. In fall 1992, 26% of all new students were transfers into all classes. 292 transfer applications were received, 256 were accepted. Application deadline is rolling for fall; rolling for spring. Minimum 2.0 GPA recommended. Lowest course grade accepted is "C." Maximum number of transferable credits is 70 semester hours from a two-year school and 90 semester hours from a four-year school. At least 30 semester hours must be completed at the college to receive degree.
**Admissions contact:** Lori-Ann Paterwic, M.A., Director of Admissions. 413 782-1321.

**FINANCIAL AID. Available aid:** Pell grants, SEOG, state scholarships and grants, school scholarships and grants, private scholarships and grants, ROTC scholarships, and academic merit scholarships. Perkins Loans (NDSL), PLUS, Stafford Loans (GSL), private loans, and SLS. Institutional payment plan.
**Financial aid statistics:** In 1992-93, 85% of all undergraduate applicants received aid; 77% of freshman applicants. Average amounts of aid awarded freshmen: Scholarships and grants, $1,757; loans, $3,781.
**Supporting data/closing dates:** FAFSA/FAF/FFS: Priority filing date is April 1; accepted on rolling basis. School's own aid application: Priority filing date is April 1; accepted on rolling basis. State aid form: Priority filing date is May 1. Income tax forms: Priority filing date is April 1. Notification of awards on rolling basis.
**Financial aid contact:** Kathleen M. Chambers, Director of Financial Aid. 413 782-1258.

**STUDENT EMPLOYMENT.** College Work/Study Program. Institutional employment. 29% of full-time undergraduates work on campus during school year. Students may expect to earn an average of $1,254 during school year. Off-campus part-time employment opportunities rated "fair."

**COMPUTER FACILITIES.** 300 IBM/IBM-compatible and Macintosh/Apple microcomputers; 150 are networked. Students may access Data General minicomputer/mainframe systems. Computer languages and software packages include Ada, ANSYS, BASIC, C, C++, COBOL, DI3000, FORTRAN, LISP, Pascal, PATRAN, RPG II. Computer facilities are available to all students.
**Fees:** Computer fee is included in tuition/fees.
**Hours:** 8 AM-11 PM (M-Th); 8:30 AM-8 PM (F); noon-8 PM (Sa); noon-5 PM (Su).

**GRADUATE CAREER DATA.** Graduate school percentages: 2% enter law school. 2% enter medical school. 3% enter graduate business programs. 5% enter graduate arts and sciences programs. Highest graduate school enrollments: Boston Coll, Springfield Coll, U of Massachusetts, Western New England Coll Sch of Law. 81% of graduates choose careers in business and industry. Companies and businesses that hire graduates: CIGNA, Coopers & Lybrand, FDIC, Hamilton Standard, Massachusetts Mutual, Travelers Insurance.

# Westfield State College

**Westfield, MA 01086** **413 568-3311**

**1994-95 Costs.** Tuition: $1,408 (state residents), $5,542 (out-of-state). Room: $2,575. Board: $1,200. Fees, books, misc. academic expenses (school's estimate): $2,150.
**Enrollment.** Undergraduates: 1,588 men, 1,693 women (full-time). Freshman class: 3,100 applicants, 2,150 accepted, 825 enrolled. Graduate enrollment: 225 men, 554 women.
**Test score averages/ranges.** Average SAT scores: 420 verbal, 460 math. Range of SAT scores of middle 50%: 400-499 verbal, 400-499 math.
**Faculty.** 169 full-time; 185 part-time. 75% of faculty holds doctoral degree. Student/faculty ratio: 18 to 1.
**Selectivity rating.** Competitive.

**PROFILE.** Westfield State, founded in 1838, is a public college. Its 227-acre campus is located in Westfield, 10 miles west of Springfield.

**Accreditation:** NEASC. Professionally accredited by the National Council for Accreditation of Teacher Education.
**Religious orientation:** Westfield State College is nonsectarian; no religious requirements.
**Library:** Collections totaling over 162,500 volumes, 1,100 periodical subscriptions, and 445,000 microform items.
**Special facilities/museums:** Art gallery, language lab, electron microscope.
**Athletic facilities:** Gymnasiums, baseball, football, intramural, and softball fields, swimming pool, basketball, and tennis courts, artificial turf, all-weather track.

**STUDENT BODY. Undergraduate profile:** 95% are state residents; 28% are transfers. .7% Asian-American, 2.5% Black, 1.4% Hispanic, .2% Native American, 87% White, 8.2% Other. Average age of undergraduates is 20.
**Freshman profile:** 1% of freshmen who took SAT scored 700 or over on math; 1% scored 600 or over on verbal, 5% scored 600 or over on math; 14% scored 500 or over on verbal, 31% scored 500 or over on math; 65% scored 400 or over on verbal, 79% scored 400 or over on math; 99% scored 300 or over on verbal, 99% scored 300 or over on math. 100% of accepted applicants took SAT.
**Undergraduate achievement:** 75% of fall 1992 freshmen returned for fall 1993 term. 53% of entering class graduated.
**Foreign students:** Two students are from out of the country. Countries represented include Austria and Hungary.

**PROGRAMS OF STUDY. Degrees:** B.A., B.S., B.S.Ed.
**Majors:** Applied Chemistry, Art, Biology, Business Management, Computer Information Systems, Computer Science, Criminal Justice, Early Childhood Education, Economics, Elementary Education, English, French, General Science, History, Liberal Studies, Mass

Communication, Mathematics, Movement Science, Music, Political Science, Psychology, Regional Planning, Social Sciences, Spanish, Special Education.
**Distribution of degrees:** The majors with the highest enrollment are criminal justice, business management, and education; Spanish, French, and applied chemistry have the lowest.
**Requirements:** General education requirement.
**Special:** Minors offered in most majors and in geography, philosophy, secondary education, and sociology. Double majors. Independent study. Accelerated study. Internships. Cooperative education programs. Member of Cooperating Colleges of Greater Springfield. Washington Semester. Member of New England Regional Program. Exchange programs with universities in Alaska, Arkansas, Mississippi, Oklahoma, and South Dakota. Teacher certification in early childhood, elementary, secondary, and special education. Study abroad in England and Scotland. NROTC. ROTC and AFROTC at Western New England Coll.
**Honors:** Honors program. Honor societies.
**Academic Assistance:** Nonremedial tutoring.

**STUDENT LIFE. Housing:** Students may live on or off campus. Coed, women's, and men's dorms. School-owned/operated apartments. 90% of students live in college housing.
**Social atmosphere:** According to the student newspaper, "This is a small college and everyone seems to be comfortable here. There is a distinct feeling of friendliness around campus. Seldom do you pass another person without saying 'hi,' even if you don't know them." Resident advisors, student senators, class officers, group leaders, and judicial board members, are influential on campus. Popular events include Fridays in the Owl's Nest, Spring Weekend, Homecoming, Alumni Weekend, Winter White Stag, and the Senate Banquet. The Campus Center, Shannon's, the Keg Room, and on-campus apartments are the most popular gathering spots.
**Services and counseling/handicapped student services:** Placement services. Health service. Counseling services for minority, military, veteran, and older students. Birth control, personal, and psychological counseling. Career and academic guidance services. Religious counseling. Physically disabled student services. Learning disabled services. Notetaking services. Tape recorders. Tutors. Reader services for the blind.
**Campus organizations:** Undergraduate student government. Student newspaper (Owl, published once/week). Yearbook. Radio station. Concert choir, madrigal singers, music ensembles, musical theatre, philharmonic jazz band, film society, 52 organizations in all.
**Religious organizations:** Campus Crusade for Christ.
**Minority/foreign student organizations:** AID, Third World.

**ATHLETICS. Physical education requirements:** None.
**Intercollegiate competition:** 15% of students participate. Baseball (M), basketball (M,W), cross-country (M,W), diving (W), field hockey (W), football (M), soccer (M,W), softball (W), swimming (W), track (indoor) (M,W), track (outdoor) (M,W), track and field (indoor) (M,W), track and field (outdoor) (M,W). Member of ECAC, Massachusetts State Athletic Conference, NCAA Division III.
**Intramural and club sports:** 80% of students participate. Intramural aerobics, basketball, bowling, cross-country, flag football, racquetball, soccer, softball, street hockey, volleyball, water basketball, water polo. Men's club boxing, lacrosse, swimming, volleyball. Women's club cheerleading.

**ADMISSIONS. Academic basis for candidate selection** (in order of priority): Secondary school record, class rank, standardized test scores, essay, school's recommendation.
**Nonacademic basis for candidate selection:** Extracurricular participation and particular talent or ability are important. Character and personality are considered.
**Requirements:** Graduation from secondary school is required; GED is accepted. 16 units and the following program of study are required: 4 units of English, 3 units of math, 2 units of lab science, 2 units of foreign language, 1 unit of social studies, 1 unit of history, 3 units of academic electives. Minimum combined SAT score of 750, rank in top half of secondary school class, and minimum 2.0 GPA recommended. Portfolio required of art program applicants. Audition required of music program applicants. Alternatives for Individual Development/Urban Education program for applicants not normally admissible. SAT is required. Campus visit recommended. No off-campus interviews.
**Procedure:** Take SAT by January of 12th year. Suggest filing application by December 1. Application deadline is March 1. Notification of admission on rolling basis. Reply is required by May 1. $50 nonrefundable tuition deposit. $50 nonrefundable room deposit. Freshmen accepted for terms other than fall.
**Special programs:** Credit and/or placement may be granted through CEEB Advanced Placement exams for scores of 3 or higher. Credit and/or placement may be granted through CLEP general and subject exams. Credit may be granted through challenge exams and military experience.
**Transfer students:** Transfer students accepted for terms other than fall. In fall 1993, 28% of all new students were transfers into all classes. 860 transfer applications were received, 511 were accepted. Application deadline is April 1 for fall; November 15 for spring. Minimum 2.0 GPA required. Lowest course grade accepted is "D." Maximum number of transferable credits is 67 semester hours from a two-year school and 90 semester hours from a four-year school. At least 30 semester hours must be completed at the college to receive degree.
**Admissions contact:** John F. Marcus, M.P.A., Director of Admission and Financial Aid. 413 568-3311, extension 218.

**FINANCIAL AID. Available aid:** Pell grants, SEOG, state scholarships and grants, and school scholarships and grants. Perkins Loans (NDSL), PLUS, Stafford Loans (GSL), state loans, and SLS. Institutional Payment Plan.
**Financial aid statistics:** In 1993-94, 64% of all undergraduate applicants received aid; 72% of freshman applicants. Average amounts of aid awarded freshmen: Scholarships and grants, $1,200; loans, $3,235.
**Supporting data/closing dates:** FAFSA: Priority filing date is March 1. School's own aid application: Priority filing date is April 1. Income tax forms: Priority filing date is April 1. Notification of awards on rolling basis.
**Financial aid contact:** John F. Marcus, M.P.A., Director of Admission and Financial Aid. 413 568-3311, extension 407.

**STUDENT EMPLOYMENT.** College Work/Study Program. Institutional employment. 21% of full-time undergraduates work on campus during school year. Students may expect to earn an average of $900 during school year. Off-campus part-time employment opportunities rated "fair."

**COMPUTER FACILITIES.** 175 IBM/IBM-compatible and Macintosh/Apple microcomputers. Students may access Digital minicomputer/mainframe systems. Residence halls may be equipped with networked microcomputers, modems. Computer languages and software packages include BMDP, dBASE, Lotus 1-2-3, SAS, SPSS, WordPerfect. Computer facilities are available to all students.
**Fees:** None.

**GRADUATE CAREER DATA.** Highest graduate school enrollments: U of Connecticut, U of Massachusetts at Amherst, Western New England Coll. 25% of graduates choose careers in business and industry.

# Wheaton College

**Norton, MA 02766** **508 285-8251**

**1994-95 Costs.** Tuition: $18,460. Room & board: $5,970. Fees, books, misc. academic expenses (school's estimate): $780.
**Enrollment.** Undergraduates: 436 men, 899 women (full-time). Freshman class: 1,738 applicants, 1,373 accepted, 413 enrolled.
**Test score averages/ranges.** Average SAT scores: 530 verbal, 550 math. Range of SAT scores of middle 50%: 490-570 verbal, 500-600 math. Average ACT scores: 24 composite. Range of ACT scores of middle 50%: 22-27 composite.
**Faculty.** 91 full-time; 9 part-time. 95% of faculty holds doctoral degree. Student/faculty ratio: 13 to 1.
**Selectivity rating.** Competitive.

**PROFILE.** Wheaton is a private, liberal arts college. Founded in 1834 as a seminary for women, it adopted coeducation in 1988. Its 140-acre campus is located in Norton, in southeastern Massachusetts, 35 miles from Boston.

**Accreditation:** NEASC.
**Religious orientation:** Wheaton College is nonsectarian; no religious requirements.
**Library:** Collections totaling over 309,000 volumes, 1,300 periodical subscriptions, and 39,000 microform items.
**Special facilities/museums:** Art gallery, language lab, on-campus nursery school, media center, observatory.
**Athletic facilities:** Gymnasium, swimming pool, field house, fitness trail and center, tennis courts, batting cage, indoor track, indoor archery and golf range, dance studio, athletic fields, golf range, sauna, hot tub.

**STUDENT BODY. Undergraduate profile:** 41% are state residents; 2% are transfers. 4% Asian-American, 2% Black, 2% Hispanic, 1% Native American, 84% White, 7% Other. Average age of undergraduates is 20.
**Freshman profile:** 1% of freshmen who took SAT scored 700 or over on verbal, 5% scored 700 or over on math; 15% scored 600 or over on verbal, 26% scored 600 or over on math; 70% scored 500 or over on verbal, 76% scored 500 or over on math; 98% scored 400 or over on verbal, 99% scored 400 or over on math; 100% scored 300 or over on verbal, 100% scored 300 or over on math. 32% of accepted applicants took SAT; 2% took ACT. 59% of freshmen come from public schools.
**Undergraduate achievement:** 87% of fall 1992 freshmen returned for fall 1993 term. 70% of entering class graduated. 14% of students who completed a degree program immediately went on to graduate study.
**Foreign students:** 63 students are from out of the country. Countries represented include El Salvador, Hong Kong, Japan, Korea, Spain, and Switzerland; 28 in all.

**PROGRAMS OF STUDY. Degrees:** B.A.
**Majors:** American Studies, Anthropology, Art History, Asian Studies, Biochemistry, Biology, Chemistry, Classical Civilization, Classics, Economics, English, English Dramatic Literature/Theatre, English Writing/Literature, French, German, Hispanic Studies, History, International Relations, Italian Studies, Mathematics, Mathematics/Computer Science, Mathematics/Economics, Music, Philosophy, Physics, Physics/Astronomy, Political Science, Psychobiology, Psychology, Religion, Russian, Russian Studies, Social Psychology, Sociology, Studio Art.
**Distribution of degrees:** The majors with the highest enrollment are psychology, English literature, and political science; astronomy/physics, biochemistry, and Italian studies have the lowest.
**Requirements:** General education requirement.
**Academic regulations:** Minimum 1.67 GPA must be maintained.
**Special:** Minors offered in all majors and in African studies, developmental studies, early childhood education, elementary education, environmental studies, Latin, legal studies, management, pre-health careers, theatre, urban studies, and women's studies. Courses offered in American studies, business management, drama, education, family studies, film, Greek, Hebrew, Japanese, Latin, physical education, public policy, and secondary education. Luce Family Studies Program. Self-designed majors. Double majors. Dual degrees. Independent study. Accelerated study. Pass/fail grading option. Internships. Preprofessional programs in law, medicine, veterinary science, dentistry, theology, optometry, business, communications, and education. 3-2 religion program with Andover/Newton Theology Sch. 3-2 business program with Clark U and U of Rochester. 3-2 engineering programs with Dartmouth Coll, George Washington U, and Georgia Inst of Tech. 3-2-3 Ph.D. program in optometry with New England Sch of Optometry. 3-2 communications program with Emerson Coll. Member of Southeastern Association for Cooperation in Higher Education. Cross-registration possible. Washington Semester. Member of Twelve College Exchange Program. Teacher certification in early childhood, elementary, and secondary education. Certification in specific subject areas. Study abroad in Belgium, China, France, Germany, Greece, India, Israel, Italy, Japan, Kenya, Latin American countries, Russia, Spain, Switzerland, Thailand, and the United Kingdom.
**Honors:** Phi Beta Kappa. Honors program. Honor societies.
**Academic Assistance:** Nonremedial tutoring.

**STUDENT LIFE. Housing:** All unmarried students under age 21 must live on campus unless living near campus with relatives. Coed and women's dorms. Ten special-interest houses. One all-male floor. 96% of students live in college housing.
**Social atmosphere:** The student newspaper reports, "Many students leave Wheaton on the weekends because we are so close to Providence and Boston. But more and more things are being offered on campus. The school is so small (1,200 students) that Wheaton has, pretty much, a community-type atmosphere." Students gather at the Loft, the Balfour Hood Cafe, Brown University, and Boston clubs. Spring Weekend and Commencement/Reunion are the main events of the year.
**Services and counseling/handicapped student services:** Placement services. Health service. Women's center. Counseling services for minority and older students. Birth control, personal, and psychological counseling. Career and academic guidance services. Physically disabled student services. Learning disabled services. Notetaking services. Tutors. Reader services for the blind.
**Campus organizations:** Undergraduate student government. Student newspaper (Wheaton Wire, published once/week). Literary magazine. Yearbook. Radio station. Women's Voice, Wheatones, Whims, Gentlemen Callers, dance club, Amnesty International, Lesbian/Gay/Bisexual Alliance, academic, athletic, political, service, and special-interest groups, 57 organizations in all.
**Religious organizations:** Christian Fellowship, Jewish Student Association, Catholic Club.
**Minority/foreign student organizations:** Black Students Association, Latin American Students Organization. International Student Association, Wheaton Asian Student Association.

**ATHLETICS. Physical education requirements:** Two semesters of physical education required.
**Intercollegiate competition:** 25% of students participate. Basketball (M,W), cross-country (M,W), diving (M,W), field hockey (W), lacrosse (M,W), others (W), soccer (M,W), softball (W), swimming (M,W), tennis (M,W), track (outdoor) (M,W), volleyball (W). Member of ECAC, NCAA Division III, New England Women's 8.
**Intramural and club sports:** 65% of students participate. Intramural basketball, flag football, floor hockey, golf, soccer, tennis, volleyball. Men's club Alpine skiing, golf, horsemanship, ice hockey, sailing. Women's club Alpine skiing, golf, horsemanship, sailing.

**ADMISSIONS. Academic basis for candidate selection** (in order of priority): Secondary school record, class rank, essay, school's recommendation, standardized test scores.
**Nonacademic basis for candidate selection:** Extracurricular participation is emphasized. Character and personality and particular talent or ability are important. Geographical distribution and alumni/ae relationship are considered.
**Requirements:** Graduation from secondary school is required; GED is accepted. 19 units and the following program of study are required: 4 units of English, 3 units of math, 3 units of science including 2 units of lab, 4 units of foreign language, 3 units of social studies. No standardized tests are required for admission but may be taken for placement purposes. Campus visit and interview recommended. Off-campus interviews available with admissions and alumni representatives.
**Procedure:** Visit college for interview by February 1 of 12th year. Application deadline is February 1. Notification of admission by April 1. Reply is required by May 1. $300 nonrefundable tuition deposit. Freshmen accepted for terms other than fall.
**Special programs:** Admission may be deferred one year. Credit and/or placement may be granted through CEEB Advanced Placement exams for scores of 4 or higher. Early decision program. In fall 1993, 42 applied for early decision and 40 were accepted. Deadline for applying for early decision is November 15. Early entrance/early admission program. Deadline for applying for early action is December 15. Concurrent enrollment program.
**Transfer students:** Transfer students accepted for terms other than fall. In fall 1993, 2% of all new students were transfers into all classes. 66 transfer applications were received, 44 were accepted. Application deadline is April 1 for fall; November 15 for spring. Minimum 3.0 GPA recommended. Lowest course grade accepted is "C-." Maximum number of transferable credits is 64 semester hours. At least 128 semester hours must be completed at the college to receive degree.
**Admissions contact:** Gail Berson, Dean of Admission and Student Aid. 508 285-8251.

**FINANCIAL AID. Available aid:** Pell grants, SEOG, state scholarships and grants, school grants, and private scholarships. Perkins Loans (NDSL), PLUS, Stafford Loans (GSL), state loans, school loans, private loans, and SLS. TERI loans. Mass Plan. Family education loans. Guaranteed tuition. College 10-Month Payment Plan.
**Financial aid statistics:** In 1993-94, 95% of all undergraduate applicants received aid; 91% of freshman applicants. Average amounts of aid awarded freshmen: Scholarships and grants, $11,716; loans, $3,226.
**Supporting data/closing dates:** FAFSA/FAF: Priority filing date is January 1. School's own aid application: Priority filing date is February 15. Income tax forms: Priority filing date is February 1. Notification of awards begins March 24.
**Financial aid contact:** Gary P. Allen, Director of Student Aid and College Financing. 508 285-8232.

**STUDENT EMPLOYMENT.** College Work/Study Program. Institutional employment. 80% of full-time undergraduates work on campus during school year. Students may expect to earn an average of $550 during school year. Off-campus part-time employment opportunities rated "good."

**COMPUTER FACILITIES.** 40 Macintosh/Apple microcomputers; all are networked. Students may access Internet. Client/LAN operating systems include Apple/Macintosh, LocalTalk/AppleTalk. Computer languages and software packages include DataGraph, Excel, Hyper Card, JMP, Lotus1-2-3, Mathematics, PageMaker, Pascal, Photoshop, StatView, SPSS, SuperPaint, Word; 100 in all. Computer facilities are available to all students.
**Fees:** None.
**Hours:** 8:30 AM-2 AM (M-Th); 8:30 AM-10 PM (F); 10 AM-10 PM (Sa); 10 AM-2 AM (Su).

**GRADUATE CAREER DATA.** Graduate school percentages: 12% enter law school. 3% enter medical school. 1% enter dental school. 8% enter graduate business programs. 23% enter graduate arts and sciences programs. 1% enter theological school/seminary. Highest graduate school enrollments: American U, Boston Coll, Boston U, Harvard U, New York U Law Sch, Suffolk U Law Sch, Tulane U. 45% of graduates choose careers in business and industry. Companies and businesses that hire graduates: Bloomingdale's, Boston Company, Putnam Companies, UNUM Insurance.

**PROMINENT ALUMNI/AE.** Leslie Stahl, CBS newscaster; Patricia King, professor of law, Georgetown U, and education lobbyist; Christine Todd Whitman, governor of New Jersey.

# Wheelock College

**Boston, MA 02215-4176** **617 734-5200**

**1994-95 Costs.** Tuition: $13,472. Room & board: $5,528. Fees, books, misc. academic expenses (school's estimate): $400.
**Enrollment.** Undergraduates: 23 men, 713 women (full-time). Freshman class: 399 applicants, 335 accepted, 161 enrolled. Graduate enrollment: 21 men, 526 women.
**Test score averages/ranges.** Average SAT scores: 420 verbal, 440 math. Range of SAT scores of middle 50%: 340-460 verbal, 360-500 math.
**Faculty.** 50 full-time; 72 part-time. 74% of faculty holds doctoral degree. Student/faculty ratio: 15 to 1.
**Selectivity rating.** Less competitive.

**PROFILE.** Wheelock College, founded in 1888, is a private college. Its five-acre campus is located in the Fenway section of Boston.

**Accreditation:** NEASC. Professionally accredited by the Council on Social Work Education, the National Council for Accreditation of Teacher Education.
**Religious orientation:** Wheelock College is nonsectarian; no religious requirements.
**Library:** Collections totaling over 8,500 volumes, 675 periodical subscriptions, and 318,918 microform items.
**Special facilities/museums:** Art studio, resource center with fully equipped workshop for creating and developing original curriculum tools.
**Athletic facilities:** Gymnasium, tennis courts, neighboring fields, access to athletic complex at Simmons College.

**STUDENT BODY. Undergraduate profile:** 52% are state residents; 34% are transfers. 1% Asian-American, 7% Black, 3% Hispanic, 87% White, 2% Other. Average age of undergraduates is 20.
**Freshman profile:** 3% of freshmen who took SAT scored 600 or over on verbal, 4% scored 600 or over on math; 14% scored 500 or over on verbal, 26% scored 500 or over on math; 58% scored 400 or over on verbal, 65% scored 400 or over on math; 92% scored 300 or over on verbal, 95% scored 300 or over on math. 93% of accepted applicants took SAT. 77% of freshmen come from public schools.
**Undergraduate achievement:** 81% of fall 1992 freshmen returned for fall 1993 term. 70% of entering class graduated. 7% of students who completed a degree program immediately went on to graduate study.
**Foreign students:** 12 students are from out of the country. Countries represented include Bermuda, Greece, and Japan; eight in all.

**PROGRAMS OF STUDY. Degrees:** B.A., B.S., B.Soc.Work
**Majors:** Child Life, Early Childhood Care/Education, Elementary Education, Human Development, Social Work.
**Distribution of degrees:** The majors with the highest enrollment are elementary education, social work, and child life.
**Requirements:** General education requirement.
**Academic regulations:** Freshmen must maintain minimum 1.5 GPA; sophomores, juniors, seniors, 2.0 GPA.
**Special:** Double majors. Independent study. Pass/fail grading option. Internships. Graduate school at which undergraduates may take graduate-level courses. Preprofessional programs in social work and teaching. Teacher certification in early childhood, elementary, special education, and bilingual/bicultural education. Certification in specific subject areas. Study abroad possible.
**Honors:** Honors program. Honor societies.
**Academic Assistance:** Remedial writing, math, and study skills. Nonremedial tutoring.

**ADMISSIONS. Academic basis for candidate selection** (in order of priority): Secondary school record, essay, class rank, school's recommendation, standardized test scores.
**Nonacademic basis for candidate selection:** Character and personality, extracurricular participation, and particular talent or ability are important. Geographical distribution and alumni/ae relationship are considered.
**Requirements:** Graduation from secondary school is required; GED is accepted. 16 units and the following program of study are recommended: 4 units of English, 3 units of math, 1 unit of science, 1 unit of social studies, 1 unit of history, 5 units of electives. Experience in child care recommended. SAT or ACT is required. Campus visit recommended. No off-campus interviews.
**Procedure:** Take SAT or ACT by January of 12th year. Visit college for interview by February of 12th year. Application deadline is February 15. Notification of admission on rolling basis. Reply is required by May 1. $100 nonrefundable tuition deposit. $200 nonrefundable room deposit. Freshmen accepted for terms other than fall.
**Special programs:** Admission may be deferred one year. Credit and/or placement may be granted through CEEB Advanced Placement exams for scores of 3 or higher. Credit and/or placement may be granted through CLEP general and subject exams. Credit and placement may be granted through life experience. Early decision program. In fall 1993, 39 applied for early decision and 30 were accepted. Deadline for applying for early decision is December 1.
**Transfer students:** Transfer students accepted for terms other than fall. In fall 1993, 34% of all new students were transfers into all classes. 159 transfer applications were received, 132 were accepted. Application deadline is April 15 for fall; December 1 for spring. Minimum 2.0 GPA required. Lowest course grade accepted is "C-." Maximum number of transferable credits is 66 semester hours. At least 66 semester hours must be completed at the college to receive degree.
**Admissions contact:** Joan F. Wexler, M.Ed., V.P. Enrollment Management & Admissions. 617 734-5200, extension 206.

**FINANCIAL AID. Available aid:** Pell grants, SEOG, state scholarships and grants, school scholarships and grants, private scholarships and grants, and aid for undergraduate foreign students. Perkins Loans (NDSL), PLUS, Stafford Loans (GSL), school loans, and SLS. AMS.

**Financial aid statistics:** In 1993-94, 100% of all undergraduate applicants received aid; 87% of freshman applicants. Average amounts of aid awarded freshmen: Scholarships and grants, $6,861; loans, $3,825.

**Supporting data/closing dates:** FAFSA/FAF: Deadline is March 1. School's own aid application: Deadline is March 1. Income tax forms: Accepted on rolling basis. Notification of awards on rolling basis.

**Financial aid contact:** Cheryl Rosenthal, M.Ed., Director of Financial Aid. 617 734-5200, extension 190.

# Williams College

**Williamstown, MA 01267** **413 597-3131**

**1994-95 Costs.** Tuition: $16,629. Room: $2,855. Board: $2,935. Fees, books, misc. academic expenses (school's estimate): $641.

**Enrollment.** Undergraduates: 986 men, 981 women (full-time). Freshman class: 4,186 applicants, 1,245 accepted, 526 enrolled. Graduate enrollment: 33 men, 29 women.

**Test score averages/ranges.** Range of SAT scores of middle 50%: 600-710 verbal, 650-740 math. Average ACT scores: 30 composite. Range of ACT scores of middle 50%: 29-32 composite.

**Faculty.** 233 full-time; 29 part-time. 95% of faculty holds highest degree in specific field. Student/faculty ratio: 11 to 1.

**Selectivity rating.** Most competitive.

**PROFILE.** Williams is a private, liberal arts college. Founded in 1793 as a college for men, it adopted coeducation in 1969. Its 450-acre campus is located in Williamstown, in northwestern Massachusetts.

**Accreditation:** NEASC.

**Religious orientation:** Williams College is nonsectarian; no religious requirements.

**Library:** Collections totaling over 708,320 volumes, 2,988 periodical subscriptions, and 385,499 microform items.

**Special facilities/museums:** Fine arts museum, astronomy museum, Paul Whiteman collection, theatre, language lab, social science data archive, center for development economics, observatory and planetarium, environmental studies center, three electron microscopes, nuclear magnetic resonance imager.

**Athletic facilities:** Gymnasiums, field house, swimming pool, weight room, basketball, squash, and tennis courts, dance studios, tracks, ice rink, golf course, ski areas, boathouse, athletic fields.

**STUDENT BODY. Undergraduate profile:** 16% are state residents; 3% are transfers. 11% Asian-American, 8% Black, 6% Hispanic, 72% White, 3% Other. Average age of undergraduates is 20.

**Freshman profile:** 31% of freshmen who took SAT scored 700 or over on verbal, 52% scored 700 or over on math; 76% scored 600 or over on verbal, 87% scored 600 or over on math; 95% scored 500 or over on verbal, 97% scored 500 or over on math; 99% scored 400 or over on verbal, 99% scored 400 or over on math; 100% scored 300 or over on verbal, 100% scored 300 or over on math. 69% of freshmen who took ACT scored 30 or over on composite; 97% scored 24 or over on composite; 100% scored 18 or over on composite. 98% of accepted applicants took SAT; 15% took ACT. 57% of freshmen come from public schools.

**Undergraduate achievement:** 96% of fall 1992 freshmen returned for fall 1993 term. 93% of entering class graduated. 22% of students who completed a degree program immediately went on to graduate study.

**Foreign students:** 49 students are from out of the country. Countries represented include Canada and Japan; 33 in all.

**PROGRAMS OF STUDY. Degrees:** B.A.

**Majors:** American Studies, Anthropology, Art, Art History, Asian Studies, Astronomy, Astrophysics, Biology, Chemistry, Classics, Computer Science, Economics, English, French, Geology, German, Greek, History, Latin, Mathematics, Music, Philosophy, Physics, Political Economy, Political Science, Psychology, Religion, Russian, Sociology, Spanish, Studio Art, Theatre.

**Distribution of degrees:** The majors with the highest enrollment are history, English, and political science; classics, astrophysics, and sociology have the lowest.

**Special:** Interdepartmental/interdisciplinary programs in African/Middle Eastern, Afro-American, area (people and cultures of the non-Western world), Asian, environmental, and women's studies, and in comparative literature. Course offered in creative writing. Research programs offered in biology, chemistry, developmental economics, geology, physics, public affairs, and public opinion. Concentrations offered in biochemistry, molecular biology, and neuroscience. Self-designed majors. Double majors. Independent study. Accelerated study. Pass/fail grading option. Internships. Graduate school at which undergraduates may take graduate-level courses. Preprofessional programs in medicine. 3-2 engineering programs with Columbia U and Washington U. National Theatre Institute Semester (Connecticut). Williams-Mystic Seaport Semester (Connecticut). Member of Twelve College Exchange Program. Exchange programs also with Caltech, Dartmouth Coll (Thayer Sch of Engineering), Fisk U, Howard U, and Rensselaer Polytech Inst. Exchange program abroad in England (Oxford U). Study abroad also in Denmark, Egypt, Japan, the former Soviet Republics, Spain, Sweden, and other countries.

**Honors:** Phi Beta Kappa. Honors program. Honor societies.

**Academic Assistance:** Remedial writing, math, and study skills. Nonremedial tutoring.

**STUDENT LIFE. Housing:** All first-year, sophomores, and juniors must live on campus. Coed dorms. Off-campus privately-owned housing. 96% of students live in college housing.

**Social atmosphere:** The student newspaper reports, "There are lots of alternatives if you look for them. Always do your own thing." Students tend to gather at "the weight room, the snack bar, the mail room, the Purple Pub, and the offices of the Williams Record." Influential groups on campus include Mission Park, College Council, and Connections. Popular campus events include Homecoming, Winter Carnival, Spring Weekend, dances, and concerts.

**Services and counseling/handicapped student services:** Placement services. Health service. Women's center. Day care. Counseling services for minority and older students. Birth control, personal, and psychological counseling. Career and academic guidance services. Religious counseling. Physically disabled student services. Notetaking services. Tape recorders. Tutors. Reader services for the blind.

**Campus organizations:** Undergraduate student government. Student newspaper (Williams Record, published once/week). Literary magazine. Yearbook. Radio station. Choral society, marching band, brass ensemble, orchestra, Community Service Council, dance and film societies, drama group, coffeehouse, debating, outing club, tutoring, women's group, special-interest groups, 115 organizations in all.

**Religious organizations:** Bahai group, Christian Fellowship, Christian Science Organization, Jewish Association, Lutheran Association, Newman Association, Williams Atheists, Muslim Student Union, Episcopal Connection.

**Minority/foreign student organizations:** ASIA, Bharat, Black Student Union, Grupo Unido, Students of Mixed Heritage, VISTA. International Club, Chinese and Korean groups.

**ATHLETICS. Physical education requirements:** Four semesters of physical education required.

**Intercollegiate competition:** 50% of students participate. Alpine skiing (M,W), baseball (M), basketball (M,W), crew (M,W), cross-country (M,W), diving (M,W), field hockey (W), football (M), golf (M), ice hockey (M,W), lacrosse (M,W), Nordic skiing (M,W), soccer (M,W), softball (W), squash (M,W), swimming (M,W), tennis (M,W), track (indoor) (M,W), track (outdoor) (M,W), track and field (indoor) (M,W), track and field (outdoor) (M,W), volleyball (W), wrestling (M). Member of ECAC, Little Three Conference, NCAA Division I for Alpine and Nordic skiing, NCAA Division III, New England Small College Athletic Conference.

**Intramural and club sports:** 95% of students participate. Intramural basketball, broomball, canoe and kayak, climbing, golf, ice hockey, skiing, soccer, softball, swimming, tennis, track, inner-tube water polo, volleyball. Men's club cycling, rugby, volleyball, water polo. Women's club cycling, golf, rugby, water polo.

**ADMISSIONS. Academic basis for candidate selection** (in order of priority): Secondary school record, class rank, standardized test scores, school's recommendation, essay.

**Nonacademic basis for candidate selection:** Extracurricular participation and particular talent or ability are important. Character and personality, geographical distribution, and alumni/ae relationship are considered.

**Requirements:** Graduation from secondary school is required; GED is accepted. No specific distribution of secondary school units required. SAT is required; ACT may be substituted. ACH required. Campus visit recommended. Off-campus interviews available with admissions and alumni representatives.

**Procedure:** Take SAT or ACT by January 15 of 12th year. Take ACH by January 15 of 12th year. Visit college for interview by January 15 of 12th year. Application deadline is January 1. Notification of admission by April 9. Reply is required by May 1. $200 nonrefundable tuition deposit. Freshmen accepted for fall term only.

**Special programs:** Admission may be deferred one year. Credit and/or placement may be granted through CEEB Advanced Placement exams for scores of 3 or higher. Placement may be granted through challenge exams. Early decision program. In fall 1993, 476 applied for early decision and 184 were accepted. Deadline for applying for early decision is November 15.

**Transfer students:** Transfer students accepted for terms other than fall. In fall 1993, 3% of all new students were transfers into all classes. 166 transfer applications were received, 38 were accepted. Application deadline is March 1 for fall; December 1 for spring. Minimum 3.5 GPA required. Lowest course grade accepted is "C-." Maximum number of transferable credits is 16 semester courses plus two winter study courses. At least two years must be completed at the college to receive degree.

**Admissions contact:** Thomas H. Parker, M.A.T., Director of Admissions. 413 597-2211.

**FINANCIAL AID. Available aid:** Pell grants, SEOG, state scholarships and grants, school scholarships and grants, private scholarships and grants, academic merit scholarships, and aid for undergraduate foreign students. Perkins Loans (NDSL), Stafford Loans (GSL), state loans, school loans, private loans, and SLS. Knight Tuition Plans and AMS. 10-month installment payment plan.

**Financial aid statistics:** In 1993-94, 84% of all undergraduate applicants received aid; 85% of freshman applicants. Average amounts of aid awarded freshmen: Scholarships and grants, $12,600; loans, $2,200.

**Supporting data/closing dates:** FAFSA: Priority filing date is February 1. School's own aid application: Priority filing date is February 1. Income tax forms: Priority filing date is February 1. Notification of awards begins April 10.

**Financial aid contact:** Philip G. Wick, Director of Financial Aid. 413 597-4181.

**STUDENT EMPLOYMENT.** College Work/Study Program. Institutional employment. 50% of full-time undergraduates work on campus during school year. Students may expect to earn an average of $1,000 during school year. Off-campus part-time employment opportunities rated "fair."

**COMPUTER FACILITIES.** 150 IBM/IBM-compatible, Macintosh/Apple, and RISC-/UNIX-based microcomputers; all are networked. Students may access SUN minicomputer/mainframe systems, BITNET, Internet. Client/LAN operating systems include Apple/Macintosh, DOS, UNIX/XENIX/AIX, X-windows, LocalTalk/AppleTalk, Novell. Computer languages and software packages include Ada, APL, BASIC, C, Cricket Graph, Excel, Filemaker, FORTRAN, Hypercard, LISP, Lotus 1-2-3, MacDraw, Modula 2, Multiplan, PageMaker, Pascal, SAS, SPSS-X, WordPerfect; 100 in all. Computer facilities are available to all students.

**Fees:** None.

**Hours:** 8 AM-1 AM (M-Th); 8 AM-10 PM (Fr); 10 AM-5 PM (Sa); noon-1 AM (Su). 24-hour room also available.

**GRADUATE CAREER DATA.** Graduate school percentages: 6% enter law school. 3% enter medical school. 1% enter graduate business programs. 12% enter graduate arts and sciences programs. 1% enter theological school/seminary. Highest graduate school enrollments: Harvard U, Michigan U, Stanford U, Yale U. 25% of graduates choose careers in business and industry. Companies and businesses that hire graduates: American Management Systems, Andersen Consulting Services, Bain & Co., Chemical Bank, First Boston, Goldman, Sachs, Morgan Stanley, Price Waterhouse, UNUM.

**PROMINENT ALUMNI/AE.** Hedrick Smith, former Washington bureau chief, *New York Times;* Fay Vincent, baseball commissioner; Stephen Sondheim, musician and writer.

## Worcester Polytechnic Institute

**Worcester, MA 01609** **508 831-5000**

**1993-94 Costs.** Tuition: $15,124. Room & board: $5,060. Fees, books, misc. academic expenses (school's estimate): $856.
**Enrollment.** Undergraduates: 2,260 men, 542 women (full-time). Freshman class: 2,772 applicants, 2,315 accepted, 682 enrolled. Graduate enrollment: 846 men, 208 women.
**Test score averages/ranges.** Average ACT scores: 29 composite.
**Faculty.** 228 full-time; 117 part-time. 91% of faculty holds doctoral degree. Student/faculty ratio: 12 to 1.
**Selectivity rating.** Highly competitive.

**PROFILE.** WPI is a private, polytechnic institute. Founded as an industrial institute for men in 1865, it adopted coeducation in 1968. Its 62-acre campus is located in a residential area near the center of Worcester, 45 miles west of Boston.

**Accreditation:** NEASC. Professionally accredited by the Accreditation Board for Engineering and Technology.
**Religious orientation:** Worcester Polytechnic Institute is nonsectarian; no religious requirements.
**Library:** Collections totaling over 300,000 volumes, 1,420 periodical subscriptions, and 780,000 microform items.
**Special facilities/museums:** Seven off-campus project centers, TV studio, robotics lab, CAD-CAM lab, laser labs, electron microscopes, wind tunnel, manufacturing engineering applications center, VLSI design lab, nuclear reactor.
**Athletic facilities:** Gymnasiums, swimming pool, bowling lanes, basketball, racquetball, squash, and tennis courts, sauna, track, baseball and softball fields, weight room, fitness center.

**STUDENT BODY. Undergraduate profile:** 54% are state residents. 6% Asian-American, 1% Black, 1% Hispanic, 1% Native American, 91% White. Average age of undergraduates is 20.
**Freshman profile:** 1% of freshmen who took SAT scored 700 or over on verbal, 26% scored 700 or over on math; 18% scored 600 or over on verbal, 72% scored 600 or over on math; 59% scored 500 or over on verbal, 93% scored 500 or over on math; 84% scored 400 or over on verbal, 94% scored 400 or over on math; 99% scored 300 or over on verbal. Majority of accepted applicants took SAT. 80% of freshmen come from public schools.
**Undergraduate achievement:** 95% of fall 1991 freshmen returned for fall 1992 term. 58% of entering class graduated. 20% of students who completed a degree program immediately went on to graduate study.
**Foreign students:** 175 students are from out of the country. Countries represented include Colombia, India, Indonesia, Japan, Thailand, and Venezuela; 45 in all.

**PROGRAMS OF STUDY. Degrees:** B.S.
**Majors:** Actuarial Mathematics, Aerospace Engineering, Applied Mathematics, Biology/Biotechnology, Biomedical Engineering, Chemical Engineering, Chemistry, Civil Engineering, Computer Engineering, Computer Science, Economics, Electrical Engineering, Environmental Engineering, Environmental Science, Humanities, Interdisciplinary Studies, Management, Management/Computer Applications, Management Engineering, Manufacturing Systems Engineering, Materials Engineering, Mathematics, Mechanical Engineering, Nuclear Engineering, Operations Research, Physics, Pre-Dentistry, Pre-Law, Pre-Medicine, Pre-Veterinary Medicine, Society/Technology.
**Distribution of degrees:** The majors with the highest enrollment are electrical engineering, mechanical engineering, and civil engineering; humanities and chemistry have the lowest.
**Special:** Self-designed majors. Double majors. Independent study. Accelerated study. Internships. Cooperative education programs. Graduate school at which undergraduates may take graduate-level courses. Preprofessional programs in law, medicine, and veterinary science. 3-2 dual degree programs with Anna Maria Coll, Assumption Coll, Emmanuel Coll, Regis Coll, St. Lawrence U, and Worcester State Coll. Member of Worcester Consortium of Higher Education. Member of International Student Exchange Program (ISEP). Exchange programs abroad in England (London Project Center), Germany (Fachhochschule Munchen), Ireland (The National Inst of Higher Education), Scotland (U of Stirling), Sweden (Royal Inst of Tech), and Switzerland (Federal Tech Inst). ROTC and AFROTC. NROTC at Coll of the Holy Cross.
**Academic Assistance:** Nonremedial tutoring.

**STUDENT LIFE. Housing:** Students may live on or off campus. Coed and men's dorms. School-owned/operated apartments. Special-interest housing. 50% of students live in college housing.
**Social atmosphere:** Gompei's Pizza Place, local bars/clubs, and fraternity houses are popular gathering places for students. Greeks are influential in student social life. Quad Fest, homecoming, sports events, Traditions Day, and pub shows are popular social events. The student newspaper reports that there is certain amount of apathy concerning student life; however, there are nine colleges in the area, so there is almost always something happening.
**Services and counseling/handicapped student services:** Health service. Personal and psychological counseling. Career and academic guidance services. Physically disabled student services. Learning disabled services.
**Campus organizations:** Undergraduate student government. Student newspaper (Newspeak, published once/week). Musical groups, camera club, flying club, theatre group, art club, Lens & Lights, social committee, professional groups, women's group, 99 organizations in all. 10 fraternities, all with chapter houses; three sororities, no chapter houses. 38% of men join a fraternity. 40% of women join a sorority.
**Religious organizations:** Christian Bible Fellowship, Hillel, Newman Club, Muslim Student Association.
**Minority/foreign student organizations:** African-American Cultural Society. Armenian, Asian, Hispanic, Indian, Korean, Malaysian, and Vietnamese groups.

**ATHLETICS. Physical education requirements:** Two semesters of physical education required.
**Intercollegiate competition:** 41% of students participate. Baseball (M), basketball (M,W), cross-country (M,W), diving (M,W), field hockey (W), football (M), golf (M,W), soccer (M), softball (W), swimming (M,W), tennis (M,W), track and field (indoor) (M,W), track and field (outdoor) (M,W), volleyball (W), wrestling (M). Member of Constitution Athletic Conference, ECAC, Freedom Football Conference, NCAA Division III, NECAC, New England Women's 8 Conference.
**Intramural and club sports:** 51% of students participate. Intramural basketball, cross-country, floor hockey, ice hockey, soccer, softball, swimming, table tennis, touch football, track, volleyball, water polo. Men's club Alpine skiing, crew, cycling, fencing, ice hockey, lacrosse, Nordic skiing, rugby, sailing, ultimate frisbee, volleyball, water polo. Women's club Alpine skiing, cheerleading, crew, cycling, fencing, lacrosse, Nordic skiing, rugby, sailing, soccer, ultimate frisbee, water polo.

**ADMISSIONS. Academic basis for candidate selection** (in order of priority): Secondary school record, class rank, standardized test scores, school's recommendation, essay.
**Nonacademic basis for candidate selection:** Extracurricular participation is important. Character and personality, particular talent or ability, geographical distribution, and alumni/ae relationship are considered.
**Requirements:** Graduation from secondary school is required; GED is not accepted. 10 units and the following program of study are recommended: 4 units of English, 4 units of math, 2 units of science. Early entrance encouraged if above requirements are completed. Conditional admission possible for applicants not meeting standard requirements. SAT or ACT is required. ACH required. Campus visit and interview recommended. Off-campus interviews available with an alumni representative.
**Procedure:** Take SAT or ACT by January of 12th year. Take ACH by January of 12th year. Visit college for interview by March of 12th year. Application deadline is February 15. Notification of admission by April 1. Reply is required by May 1. $250 nonrefundable tuition deposit. $100 nonrefundable room deposit. Freshmen accepted for terms other than fall.
**Special programs:** Admission may be deferred one year. Credit may be granted through CEEB Advanced Placement for scores of 4 or higher. Early decision program. In fall 1993, 177 applied for early decision and 145 were accepted. Deadline for applying for early decision is December 1. Early entrance/early admission program. Concurrent enrollment program.
**Transfer students:** Transfer students accepted for terms other than fall. Application deadline is April 15 for fall; November 15 for spring. Lowest course grade accepted is "C." Maximum number of transferable credits is 60 quarter hours. At least 60 credit hours or two years of course work must be completed at WPI to receive degree.
**Admissions contact:** Kay Dietrich, Director of Admissions. 508 831-5286.

**FINANCIAL AID. Available aid:** Pell grants, SEOG, state scholarships and grants, school scholarships and grants, private scholarships and grants, ROTC scholarships, and aid for undergraduate foreign students. Perkins Loans (NDSL), PLUS, Stafford Loans (GSL), state loans, school loans, private loans, and SLS. Tuition Plan Inc., Knight Tuition Plans, AMS, and deferred payment plan.
**Financial aid statistics:** In 1993-94, 90% of all undergraduate applicants received aid; 90% of freshman applicants. Average amounts of aid awarded freshmen: Scholarships and grants, $7,089; loans, $4,020.
**Supporting data/closing dates:** FAFSA/FAF: Priority filing date is February 1; deadline is March 1. Income tax forms: Priority filing date is March 1; deadline is May 1. Notification of awards begins April 1.
**Financial aid contact:** Michael J. Curley, M.S., Director of Freshman Financial Aid. 508 831-5469.

**STUDENT EMPLOYMENT.** College Work/Study Program. Institutional employment. 32% of full-time undergraduates work on campus during school year. Students may expect to earn an average of $1,000 during school year. Off-campus part-time employment opportunities rated "good."

**COMPUTER FACILITIES.** 620 IBM/IBM-compatible microcomputers; 400 are networked. Students may access Digital, IBM, NCR, Prime, Pyramid, SUN minicomputer/mainframe systems. Computer languages and software packages include ALGOL, BASIC, BMDP, C, C LISP, COBOL, E LISP, ExpressCalc, FORTRAN, GW Basic, Lotus 1-2-3, MINITAB, Pascal, PC Write, Prolog, SNOBOL, SPSS, STP, Turbo Pascal. Computer facilities are available to all students.
**Fees:** None.
**Hours:** 24 hours.

**GRADUATE CAREER DATA.** Graduate school percentages: 5% enter law school. 5% enter medical school. 25% enter graduate business programs. 65% enter graduate arts and sciences programs. Highest graduate school enrollments: Rensselaer Polytech Inst, U of Connecticut, U of New Hampshire, Worcester Polytech Inst. 90% of graduates choose careers in business and industry. Companies and businesses that hire graduates: General Electric, ABB Combustion Engines, United Technologies.

**PROMINENT ALUMNI/AE.** Robert Goddard, founder of modern rocketry; Paul Allaire, CEO, Xerox.

# Michigan

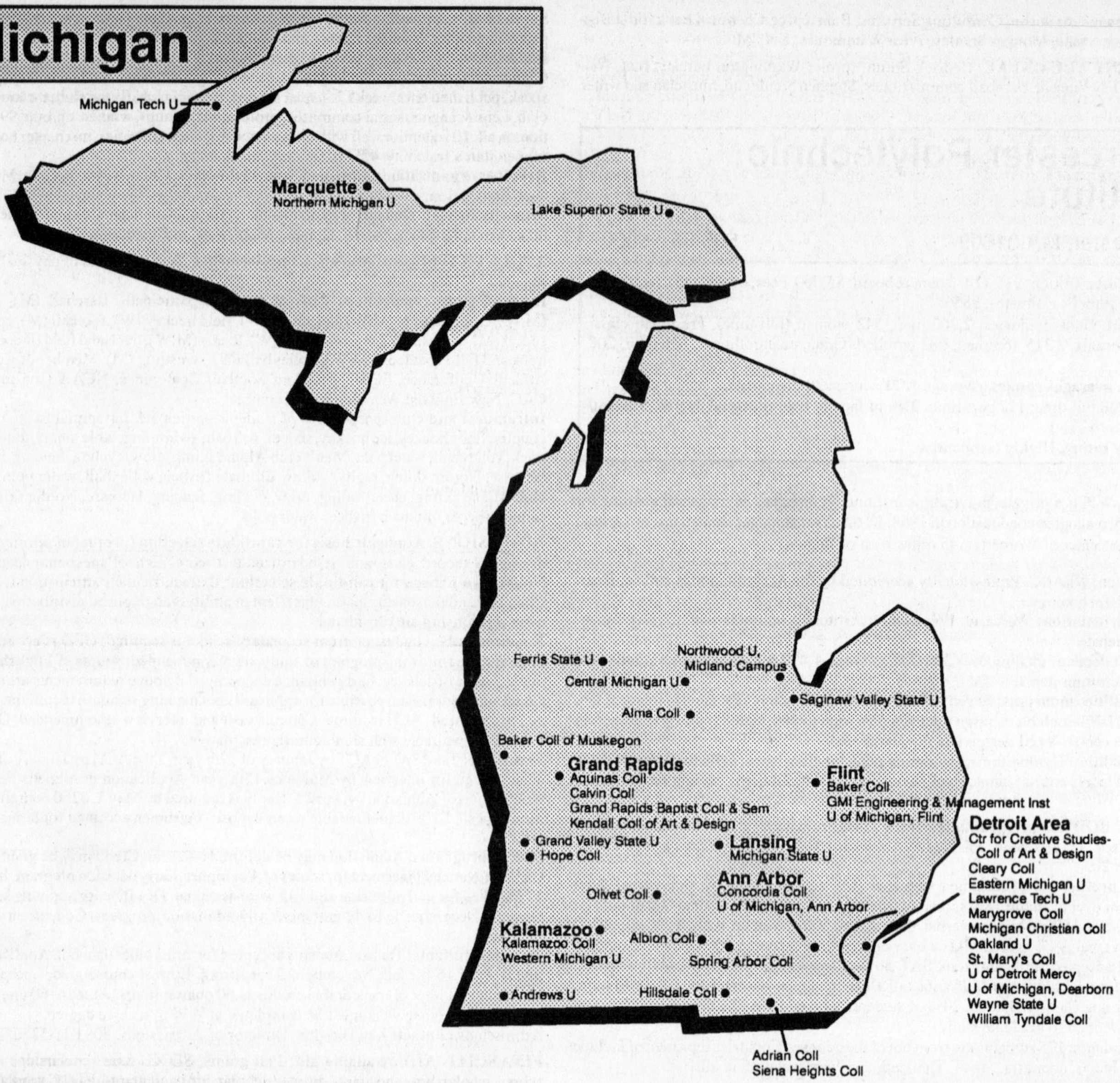


## Adrian College

**Adrian, MI 49221** **517 265-5161**

**1994-95 Costs.** Tuition: $11,250. Room: $1,590. Board: $2,160. Fees, books, misc. academic expenses (school's estimate): $500.

**Enrollment.** Undergraduates: 509 men, 527 women (full-time). Freshman class: 1,428 applicants, 1,097 accepted, 336 enrolled.

**Test score averages/ranges.** Average SAT scores: 960 combined. Average ACT scores: 23 composite. Range of ACT scores of middle 50%: 18-26 composite.

**Faculty.** 66 full-time; 30 part-time. 73% of faculty holds highest degree in specific field. Student/faculty ratio: 15 to 1.

**Selectivity rating.** Less competitive.

**PROFILE.** Adrian, founded in 1859, is a church-affiliated, liberal arts college. Its 100-acre campus and 48-acre arboretum are located in a residential area of Adrian, 35 miles northwest of Toledo. Most of the campus buildings were constructed in the last 20 years.

**Accreditation:** NCACS. Professionally accredited by the National Council for Accreditation of Teacher Education.

**Religious orientation:** Adrian College is affiliated with the United Methodist Church; one semester of religion/theology required.

**Library:** Collections totaling over 137,822 volumes, 788 periodical subscriptions, and 51,263 microform items.

**Special facilities/museums:** Art gallery, studio theatre, arboretum, education resource center, language lab, observatory, planetarium, solar greenhouse, nuclear magnetic resonance spectrometer, differential scanning calorimeter.

**Athletic facilities:** Gymnasium, badminton, basketball, handball, racquetball, tennis, and volleyball courts, aerobics studio, natatorium, tracks, athletic fields, stadium, weight room, fitness center, batting cage, human performance laboratory.

**STUDENT BODY. Undergraduate profile:** 80% are state residents; 9% are transfers. 1.2% Asian-American, 6.3% Black, 1.5% Hispanic, .4% Native American, 88% White, 2.6% Other. Average age of undergraduates is 19.

**Freshman profile:** 2% of freshmen who took SAT scored 600 or over on verbal, 18% scored 600 or over on math; 21% scored 500 or over on verbal, 60% scored 500 or over on math; 84% scored 400 or over on verbal, 87% scored 400 or over on math; 100% scored 300 or over on verbal, 100% scored 300 or over on math. 3% of freshmen who took ACT scored 30 or over on composite; 27% scored 24 or over on composite; 92% scored 18 or over on composite; 100% scored 12 or over on composite. 14% of accepted applicants took SAT; 96% took ACT. 75% of freshmen come from public schools.

**Undergraduate achievement:** 72% of fall 1992 freshmen returned for fall 1993 term. 58% of entering class graduated. 15% of students who completed a degree program went on to graduate study within one year.

**Foreign students:** 20 students are from out of the country. Countries represented include Canada, India, Japan, Singapore, South Korea, and Taiwan; nine in all.

**PROGRAMS OF STUDY. Degrees:** B.A., B.Bus.Admin., B.F.A., B.Mus., B.Mus.Ed., B.S.

**Majors:** Accounting, Art, Biology, Business Administration, Chemistry, Communication Arts/Sciences, Computer Science, Criminal Justice, Earth Science, Economics, English, Environmental Science/Studies, Exercise Science, Family Life Management, Fashion Merchandising, French, German, History, Human Services, Interior Design, International Business, International Studies, Mathematics, Music, Philosophy/Religion, Physical Education/Recreation, Physics, Political Science, Psychology, Religion, Sociology, Spanish, Teacher Education.

**Distribution of degrees:** The majors with the highest enrollment are business and biology; earth science and music have the lowest.

**Requirements:** General education requirement.

**Academic regulations:** Freshmen must maintain minimum 1.4 GPA; sophomores, 1.6 GPA; juniors, 2.0 GPA; seniors, 2.0 GPA.

**Special:** Minors offered in all majors. Bilingual/multicultural program in Spanish. Several concentrations in family arts and sciences. Associate's degrees offered. Self-designed majors. Double majors. Independent study. Internships. Preprofessional programs in law, medicine, veterinary science, pharmacy, dentistry, theology, and optometry. 3-1 medical

technology programs with affiliated hospitals. 3-1 B.F.A. program with Center for Design Studies. 3-2 pre-engineering programs with Washington U and U of Detroit. Appalachian Semester (Kentucky). Urban Life Center (Chicago). Washington Center Program. Other off-campus study opportunities. Exchange programs with Central Coll and U of Evansville. Teacher certification in elementary, secondary, and bilingual/bicultural education. Study abroad in Austria, England, France, Germany, Hong Kong, Mexico, the Netherlands, Russia, and Wales. ROTC at U of Michigan.
**Honors:** Honors program. Honor societies.
**Academic Assistance:** Remedial reading, writing, math, and study skills. Nonremedial tutoring.

**STUDENT LIFE. Housing:** All unmarried students under age 21 must live on campus unless living near campus with relatives. Coed, women's, and men's dorms. Sorority and fraternity housing. Off-campus privately-owned housing. 77% of students live in college housing.
**Social atmosphere:** "Adrian College has a really laid-back atmosphere," Reports the editor of the student newspaper. "The students and the faculty are friendly with each other, which I don't think you'd find as much at larger universities. Fall Homecoming is a big event at AC. Most of the social and professional groups have receptions with alumni. There are week-long games, competitions for the Greeks and Independent Halls, and the Walk for the Hungry usually follows on the Sunday afterwards. Adrian is a small town, but it does have a nice mall, bowling alleys, a roller rink, dance places for the over-21 crowd, and a lot of restaurants. Toledo, Ohio, and Ann Arbor are also popular off-campus hot spots."
**Services and counseling/handicapped student services:** Placement services. Health service. Counseling services for minority and older students. Personal counseling. Career and academic guidance services. Religious counseling. Physically disabled student services. Learning disabled services. Notetaking services. Tape recorders. Tutors. Reader services for the blind.
**Campus organizations:** Undergraduate student government. Student newspaper (College World, published once/week). Literary magazine. Yearbook. Radio and TV stations. Symphonic band, orchestra, singers, choir, jazz group, theatre, drama fraternity, Shakespeare Club, film society, Student Activities Committee, Nontraditional Students Group, Circle K, debate group, special-events weekends, Differently-Abled Student Group, cheerleaders, College Republicans, special-interest groups, 60 organizations in all. Five fraternities, four chapter houses; three sororities, no chapter houses. 31% of men join a fraternity. 23% of women join a sorority.
**Religious organizations:** Jewish Student Concerns, Intervarsity Christian Fellowship, Newman Center, Religious Life Council, Wesley Fellowship, Mime Troupe, Campus Crusade for Christ, Altar Guild.
**Minority/foreign student organizations:** AHORA, Ebony Connection, African-American Leadership Promoting Higher Achievement. International Club.

**ATHLETICS. Physical education requirements:** One semester of physical education required.
**Intercollegiate competition:** 40% of students participate. Baseball (M), basketball (M,W), cross-country (M,W), diving (M,W), football (M), golf (M,W), soccer (M,W), softball (W), swimming (M,W), tennis (M,W), track (outdoor) (M,W), track and field (outdoor) (M,W), volleyball (W). Member of Michigan Intercollegiate Athletic Association, NCAA Division III.
**Intramural and club sports:** 75% of students participate. Intramural basketball, flag football, over the line, racquetball, soccer, softball, tennis, volleyball, walleyball. Men's club cheerleading, volleyball. Women's club cheerleading.

**ADMISSIONS. Academic basis for candidate selection** (in order of priority): Secondary school record, standardized test scores, class rank, school's recommendation, essay.
**Nonacademic basis for candidate selection:** Character and personality, extracurricular participation, and particular talent or ability are important. Alumni/ae relationship is considered.
**Requirements:** Graduation from secondary school is required; GED is accepted. 15 units and the following program of study are recommended: 4 units of English, 2 units of math, 2 units of science, 2 units of foreign language, 2 units of social studies, 2 units of history, 1 unit of electives. Minimum composite ACT score of 20, rank in top half of secondary school class, and minimum 2.5 GPA recommended. Conditional admission possible for applicants not meeting standard requirements. SAT or ACT is required. Campus visit and interview recommended. Off-campus interviews available with an admissions representative.
**Procedure:** Take SAT or ACT by May of 12th year. Visit college for interview by May of 12th year. Suggest filing application by November 15. Application deadline is August 15. Notification of admission on rolling basis. Reply is required by May 1. $150 tuition deposit, refundable until May 1. Freshmen accepted for terms other than fall.
**Special programs:** Admission may be deferred one year. Credit and/or placement may be granted through CEEB Advanced Placement exams for scores of 4 or higher. Credit and/or placement may be granted through CLEP general and subject exams. Placement may be granted through Regents College exams. Credit and placement may be granted through ACT PEP exams. Early entrance/early admission program. Concurrent enrollment program.
**Transfer students:** Transfer students accepted for terms other than fall. In fall 1993, 9% of all new students were transfers into all classes. 90 transfer applications were received, 66 were accepted. Application deadline is August 15 for fall; December 15 for spring. Lowest course grade accepted is "C." Maximum number of transferable credits is 90 semester hours. At least 124 semester hours must be completed at the college to receive degree.
**Admissions contact:** George Wolf, Director of Admissions/Assistant VP for Enrollment Management. 800 877-2246.

**FINANCIAL AID. Available aid:** Pell grants, SEOG, state scholarships and grants, school scholarships and grants, private scholarships and grants, academic merit scholarships, and aid for undergraduate foreign students. Perkins Loans (NDSL), PLUS, Stafford Loans (GSL), state loans, private loans, and SLS. AMS and deferred payment plan.
**Financial aid statistics:** In 1993-94, 97% of all undergraduate applicants received aid; 95% of freshman applicants. Average amounts of aid awarded freshmen: Scholarships and grants, $5,013; loans, $2,600.
**Supporting data/closing dates:** FAFSA/FAF/FFS: Priority filing date is February 15; accepted on rolling basis. Notification of awards on rolling basis.
**Financial aid contact:** Christina Shell, M.S., Director of Financial Aid. 517 265-5161, extension 4306.

**STUDENT EMPLOYMENT.** College Work/Study Program. Institutional employment. 47% of full-time undergraduates work on campus during school year. Students may expect to earn an average of $750 during school year. Off-campus part-time employment opportunities rated "good."

**COMPUTER FACILITIES.** 40 IBM/IBM-compatible and Macintosh/Apple microcomputers; 25 are networked. Students may access Digital minicomputer/mainframe systems. Residence halls may be equipped with stand-alone microcomputers. Client/LAN operating systems include DOS, DEC. Computer languages and software packages include BASIC, C, COBOL, FORTRAN, Logo, Pascal; shareware library; database, spreadsheet, statistical, word processing packages. Computer facilities are available to all students.
**Fees:** None.
**Hours:** 8 AM-11 PM (M-Sa); 2 PM-11 PM (Su).

**GRADUATE CAREER DATA.** Graduate school percentages: 1% enter law school. 1% enter medical school. 1% enter dental school. 3% enter graduate business programs. 5% enter graduate arts and sciences programs. 1% enter theological school/seminary. Highest graduate school enrollments: Eastern Michigan U, Michigan State U, U of Michigan, U of Toledo. 66% of graduates choose careers in business and industry. Companies and businesses that hire graduates: Big Six accounting firms, automotive-related corporations.

**PROMINENT ALUMNI/AE.** Amos Anderson, industrialist, Anderson Development; Loran Lewis, federal judge; S. Gary Spicer, attorney; Steve N. Andrews, judge, Sixth Judicial Circuit Court, Oakland; Sanford Linden, president, Linden Medical Supply Co.; David G. Dickinson, professor emeritus of pediatrics, U of Michigan Medical School; Robert C. Dawson, president, Lawyers Title Insurance.

# Albion College

**Albion, MI 49224** **517 629-1000**

**1994-95 Costs.** Tuition: $14,770. Room: $2,400. Board: $2,426. Fees, books, misc. academic expenses (school's estimate): $640.
**Enrollment.** Undergraduates: 845 men, 829 women (full-time). Freshman class: 1,899 applicants, 1,720 accepted, 489 enrolled.
**Test score averages/ranges.** Average SAT scores: 530 verbal, 580 math. Average ACT scores: 25 composite. Range of ACT scores of middle 50%: 23-27 composite.
**Faculty.** 109 full-time; 18 part-time. 98% of faculty holds highest degree in specific field. Student/faculty ratio: 14 to 1.
**Selectivity rating.** Competitive.

**PROFILE.** Albion, founded in 1835, is a church-affiliated, liberal arts college. Its 215-acre campus is located in southcentral Michigan, 65 miles from Detroit. Campus architecture includes both mid-ninteenth century and modern buildings.

**Accreditation:** NCACS. Professionally accredited by the National Association of Schools of Music.
**Religious orientation:** Albion College is affiliated with the Methodist Church; no religious requirements.
**Library:** Collections totaling over 390,000 volumes, and 1,000 periodical subscriptions.
**Special facilities/museums:** Visual arts museum, nature center, electron microscope.
**Athletic facilities:** Gymnasium, field house, tracks, basketball, racquetball, and tennis courts, baseball, football, soccer, and softball fields, dance studio, training and weight rooms, batting cage, canoe livery.

**STUDENT BODY. Undergraduate profile:** 85% are state residents. 3.3% Asian-American, 3.9% Black, 1% Hispanic, 91.3% White, .5% Other. Average age of undergraduates is 20.
**Freshman profile:** 30% of accepted applicants took SAT; 95% took ACT. 88% of freshmen come from public schools.
**Undergraduate achievement:** 82% of fall 1992 freshmen returned for fall 1993 term. 58% of entering class graduated. 33% of students who completed a degree program immediately went on to graduate study.
**Foreign students:** 31 students are from out of the country. Countries represented include England, France, Germany, Japan, Malaysia, and Spain; 19 in all.

**PROGRAMS OF STUDY. Degrees:** B.A., B.F.A.
**Majors:** American Studies, Anthropology/Sociology, Biology, Chemistry, Computational Mathematics, Economics/Management, English, French, Geological Sciences, German, History, International Studies, Mathematics, Mathematics/Economics, Mathematics/Physics, Music, Philosophy, Physical Education, Physics, Political Science, Psychology, Religious Studies, Spanish, Speech Communication/Theatre, Visual Arts.
**Distribution of degrees:** The majors with the highest enrollment are economics/management and English; geological sciences, physics, and religious studies have the lowest.
**Requirements:** General education requirement.
**Academic regulations:** Minimum 2.0 GPA must be maintained.
**Special:** Concentrations in computer science, human services, mass communications, and women's studies. Program in professional management. Self-designed majors. Double majors. Independent study. Pass/fail grading option. Internships. Preprofessional programs in law, medicine, veterinary science, dentistry, and engineering. 3-2 program in public policy. 3-2 engineering programs with Case Western Reserve U, Columbia U, Michigan Tech U, and U of Michigan. Member of Great Lakes Colleges Association. Washington Semester. Arts Program in New York. Newberry Library Program in the Humanities (Illinois). Oak Ridge Science Semester (Tennessee). Philadelphia Urban Semester. Teacher certification in elementary and secondary education. Certification in specific subject areas. Study abroad in African countries, China, Costa Rica, the Czech Republic/Slovakia, the Dominican Republic, England, France, Germany, Greece, Hong Kong, India, Israel, Japan, Mexico, Russia, Scotland, and Spain.

**Honors:** Phi Beta Kappa. Honors program. Honor societies.
**Academic Assistance:** Nonremedial tutoring.

**STUDENT LIFE. Housing:** All unmarried students must live on campus unless living with family. Coed dorms. Fraternity housing. On-campus married-student housing. 98% of students live in college housing.
**Social atmosphere:** "Albion may look dead, but there are several events which occur each night," reports the student newspaper. "Once a student reaches his or her junior year, he or she realizes that there is much to do on this campus." Greeks, the Union Board, and the student newspaper have a great deal of influence over the student body. On campus, students frequent the Keller and the library; Cascarelli's Tavern, Charlie's Tavern, and 115 Truck Stop are popular off-campus spots. Favorite social events include stand-up comedian performances, Friday and Saturday Union Board films, Saturday football games, Homecoming, Parents' Day, Earth Day, and concerts.
**Services and counseling/handicapped student services:** Placement services. Health service. Women's center. Developing Skills Center. Birth control, personal, and psychological counseling. Career and academic guidance services.
**Campus organizations:** Undergraduate student government. Student newspaper (Pleiad, published once/week). Literary magazine. Yearbook. Radio station. Choir, music ensembles, chamber orchestra, marching and symphonic bands, drama workshop, Community Theatre, College Players, Tutorial Association, Student Volunteer Bureau, departmental and service groups. Six fraternities, all with chapter houses; six sororities, all with chapter houses. 60% of men join a fraternity. 40% of women join a sorority.
**Religious organizations:** Campus Crusade for Christ, Campus Religious Council, Canterbury Club, Catholic Campus Ministry, Fellowship of Christian Athletes, Interfaith Fellowship, Intervarsity Christian Fellowship, Orthodox Christian Fellowship, Jewish, Lutheran, and United Methodist Fellowships.
**Minority/foreign student organizations:** Black Student Alliance.

**ATHLETICS. Physical education requirements:** None.
**Intercollegiate competition:** 30% of students participate. Baseball (M), basketball (M,W), cross-country (M,W), diving (M,W), football (M), golf (M,W), soccer (M,W), softball (W), swimming (M,W), tennis (M,W), track (outdoor) (M,W), track and field (outdoor) (M,W), volleyball (W). Member of Michigan Intercollegiate Athletic Conference, NCAA Division III.
**Intramural and club sports:** 30% of students participate. Intramural badminton, basketball, biathlon, canoeing, football, golf, racquetball, soccer, softball, table tennis, tennis, turkey trot, ultimate frisbee, volleyball, walleyball. Men's club fencing, ice hockey, lacrosse, volleyball. Women's club cheerleading, fencing.

**ADMISSIONS. Academic basis for candidate selection** (in order of priority): Secondary school record, class rank, standardized test scores, school's recommendation, essay.
**Nonacademic basis for candidate selection:** Particular talent or ability is important. Extracurricular participation and alumni/ae relationship are considered.
**Requirements:** Graduation from secondary school is recommended; GED is accepted. No specific distribution of secondary school units required. 15 secondary school units are expected; no specific distribution required, but strong background in English, math, lab, and social sciences recommended. Minimum composite ACT score of 19 (combined SAT score of 900), rank in top third of secondary school class, and minimum 2.75 GPA recommended. ACT is required; SAT may be substituted. Campus visit and interview recommended.
**Procedure:** Take SAT or ACT by November of 12th year. Suggest filing application by March 1; no deadline. Notification of admission on rolling basis. Reply is required by May 1. $250 refundable tuition deposit. $150 nonrefundable general deposit. Freshmen accepted for terms other than fall.
**Special programs:** Credit and/or placement may be granted through CEEB Advanced Placement exams for scores of 3 or higher. Credit and/or placement may be granted through CLEP general and subject exams.
**Transfer students:** Transfer students accepted for terms other than fall. In fall 1993, less than 1% of all new students were transfers into all classes. 114 transfer applications were received, 56 were accepted. Minimum 2.0 GPA required. Lowest course grade accepted is "C." Maximum number of transferable credits is 64 semester hours. At least 48 semester hours must be completed at the college to receive degree.
**Admissions contact:** Frank Bonta, Ed.S., LL.D., Dean of Admissions. 517 629-0321.

**FINANCIAL AID. Available aid:** Pell grants, SEOG, state scholarships and grants, school scholarships and grants, academic merit scholarships, and aid for undergraduate foreign students. Perkins Loans (NDSL), PLUS, Stafford Loans (GSL), state loans, and SLS. Knight Tuition Plans, AMS, and deferred payment plan.
**Financial aid statistics:** 17% of aid is not need-based. In 1993-94, 95% of all undergraduate applicants received aid; 93% of freshman applicants. Average amounts of aid awarded freshmen: Scholarships and grants, $9,584; loans, $3,539.
**Supporting data/closing dates:** FAFSA/FAF: Priority filing date is February 15. Notification of awards on rolling basis.
**Financial aid contact:** Phyllis Cramer, M.S., Director of Financial Aid. 517 629-0440.

**STUDENT EMPLOYMENT.** College Work/Study Program. Institutional employment. 50% of full-time undergraduates work on campus during school year. Students may expect to earn an average of $800 during school year. Off-campus part-time employment opportunities rated "fair."

**COMPUTER FACILITIES.** 75 IBM/IBM-compatible and Macintosh/Apple microcomputers; all are networked. Students may access Digital minicomputer/mainframe systems, BITNET. Residence halls may be equipped with networked terminals. Client/LAN operating systems include Apple/Macintosh, DOS, X-windows, Novell. Computer languages and software packages include AppleWorks, BASIC, C, COBOL, FORTRAN, LISP, Lotus 1-2-3, Microsoft Word, MINITAB, Paradox, Pascal, Prolog, Quattro, WordPerfect. Computer facilities are available to all students.
**Fees:** None.
**Hours:** 8 AM-midn.

**GRADUATE CAREER DATA.** Graduate school percentages: 6% enter law school. 5% enter medical school. 2% enter graduate business programs. 11% enter graduate arts and sciences programs. Highest graduate school enrollments: Detroit Coll of Law, Michigan State U, U of Michigan, Wayne State U. 63% of graduates choose careers in business and industry. Companies and businesses that hire graduates: Arthur Andersen, Coopers & Lybrand, Andersen Consulting, Deloitte & Touche.

**PROMINENT ALUMNI/AE.** Cedric Dempsey, executive director, NCAA; William C. Ferguson, chairman/CEO, NYNEX Corp.; Richard Smith, editor-in-chief, Newsweek.

# Alma College

**Alma, MI 48801-1599** **517 463-7111**

**1993-94 Costs.** Tuition: $11,926. Room & board: $4,334. Fees, books, misc. academic expenses (school's estimate): $490.
**Enrollment.** Undergraduates: 564 men, 742 women (full-time). Freshman class: 1,267 applicants, 1,080 accepted, 385 enrolled.
**Test score averages/ranges.** Average ACT scores: 25 English, 25 math, 26 composite. Range of ACT scores of middle 50%: 22-28 English, 22-28 math.
**Faculty.** 80 full-time; 29 part-time. 84% of faculty holds highest degree in specific field. Student/faculty ratio: 15 to 1.
**Selectivity rating.** Highly competitive.

**PROFILE.** Alma, founded in 1886, is a church-affiliated, liberal arts college. Its 80-acre campus is within walking distance of downtown Alma, 40 miles from Saginaw.

**Accreditation:** NCACS. Professionally accredited by the National Association of Schools of Music.
**Religious orientation:** Alma College is affiliated with the Presbyterian Church USA; no religious requirements.
**Library:** Collections totaling over 197,700 volumes, 1,100 periodical subscriptions, and 29,800 microform items.
**Special facilities/museums:** Music and arts centers, science lab, planetarium, nuclear magnetic reactor.
**Athletic facilities:** Gymnasium, swimming pool, weight room, dance studio, handball, racquetball, and tennis courts, stadium, track, baseball, soccer, and softball fields.

**STUDENT BODY. Undergraduate profile:** 94% are state residents; 6% are transfers. 1% Asian-American, 2% Black, 1% Hispanic, 1% Native American, 94% White, 1% Other. Average age of undergraduates is 20.
**Freshman profile:** 11% of freshmen who took ACT scored 30 or over on English, 9% scored 30 or over on math, 15% scored 30 or over on composite; 64% scored 24 or over on English, 61% scored 24 or over on math, 72% scored 24 or over on composite; 100% scored 18 or over on English, 100% scored 18 or over on math, 100% scored 18 or over on composite. 91% of accepted applicants took ACT. 94% of freshmen come from public schools.
**Undergraduate achievement:** 88% of fall 1992 freshmen returned for fall 1993 term. 57% of entering class graduated. 27% of students who completed a degree program immediately went on to graduate study.
**Foreign students:** 16 students are from out of the country. Countries represented include Canada, Croatia, Japan, Korea, and Senegal; 13 in all.

**PROGRAMS OF STUDY. Degrees:** B.A., B.F.A., B.M., B.S.
**Majors:** Accounting, Art/Design, Biochemistry, Biology, Business Administration, Chemistry, Communication, Computer/Information Systems Management, Computer Science, Economics, Education, English, Exercise/Health Sciences, Finance, French, German, History, International Business, Mathematics, Music, Philosophy, Physics, Political Science, Psychology, Religious Studies, Sociology, Spanish, Theatre/Dance.
**Distribution of degrees:** The majors with the highest enrollment are business administration, biology, and education; theatre/dance, German, and speech have the lowest.
**Requirements:** General education requirement.
**Academic regulations:** Minimum 2.0 GPA must be maintained.
**Special:** Minors offered in most majors and in Christian education, cognitive science, electronics, foreign service, graphic design, Japanese, management, marketing, mathematical sciences, medical illustration, peacemaking/conflict resolution, public affairs, and women's issues. Self-designed majors. Double majors. Dual degrees. Independent study. Accelerated study. Pass/fail grading option. Internships. Graduate school at which undergraduates may take graduate-level courses. Preprofessional programs in law, medicine, dentistry, theology, engineering, occupational therapy, and physical therapy. 3-2 engineering programs with U of Michigan, Michigan Tech U, and Washington U. 3-2 occupational therapy programs with Boston U and Washington U. 3-2 forestry, fisheries, wildlife management, and natural resources programs with Duke U and U of Michigan. Member of Midwest Consortium for Study Abroad and Spring Term College Consortium. Washington Semester. Exchange program with Stillman Coll. Teacher certification in elementary, secondary, and bilingual/bicultural education. Certification in specific subject areas. Exchange programs abroad in Korea (Kyonggi U) and Puerto Rico (Inter-American U). Study abroad also in Australia, Austria, France, Germany, Japan, Mexico, Scotland, and Spain. ROTC at Central Michigan U.
**Honors:** Phi Beta Kappa. Honors program. Honor societies.
**Academic Assistance:** Remedial study skills. Nonremedial tutoring.

**STUDENT LIFE. Housing:** All unmarried students under age 21 must live on campus unless living near campus with relatives. Coed, women's, and men's dorms. Sorority and fraternity housing. School-owned/operated apartments. Off-campus college-related housing. 87% of students live in college housing. 4% of students live in off–campus college–related housing.
**Social atmosphere:** Greeks, Fellowship of Christian Athletes, Student Congress, and the Union Board influence student social activities. Students gather at the Highlandaur Lanes Bowling Alley, on-campus fraternity houses, Joe's Place, Nick's Wagon Wheel, and the Pine Knot Bar. Popular school-year events include Greek formals and weekend parties, the Irish Pub, common hour, and football and basketball games.
**Services and counseling/handicapped student services:** Placement services. Health service. Women's center. Counseling services for minority students. Birth control, personal, and psychological counseling. Career and academic guidance services. Religious coun-

seling. Physically disabled student services. Learning disabled services. Notetaking services. Tutors. Reader services for the blind.
**Campus organizations:** Undergraduate student government. Student newspaper (Almanian, published once/week). Literary magazine. Yearbook. Radio station. Choir, glee clubs, orchestras, marching band, Kiltie Dancers, gay/lesbian/bisexual social support group, Amnesty International, 89 organizations in all. Five fraternities, all with chapter houses; four sororities, all with chapter houses. 40% of men join a fraternity. 40% of women join a sorority.
**Religious organizations:** Chapel Affairs Committee, Fellowship of Christian Athletes.
**Minority/foreign student organizations:** Minority support group, United Coalition of Students. Intercultural Understanding Group.

**ATHLETICS. Physical education requirements:** None.
**Intercollegiate competition:** 46% of students participate. Baseball (M), basketball (M,W), cross-country (M,W), diving (M,W), football (M), golf (M,W), soccer (M,W), softball (W), swimming (M,W), tennis (M,W), track and field (outdoor) (M,W), volleyball (W). Member of Michigan Intercollegiate Athletic Conference, NCAA Division III.
**Intramural and club sports:** 85% of students participate. Intramural basketball, flag football, softball, volleyball, water polo. Men's club volleyball. Women's club cheerleading/pom pom.

**ADMISSIONS. Academic basis for candidate selection** (in order of priority): Secondary school record, standardized test scores, class rank, school's recommendation, essay.
**Nonacademic basis for candidate selection:** Character and personality, extracurricular participation, particular talent or ability, geographical distribution, and alumni/ae relationship are considered.
**Requirements:** Graduation from secondary school is required; GED is not accepted. 16 units and the following program of study are required: 3 units of English, 2 units of math, 2 units of science, 2 units of social studies. Minimum composite ACT score of 22 (combined SAT score of 1000) and rank in top half of secondary school class required; minimum 3.0 GPA recommended. ACT is required; SAT may be substituted. Campus visit and interview recommended. No off-campus interviews.
**Procedure:** Take SAT or ACT by October of 12th year. Visit college for interview by May of 12th year. Suggest filing application by March 1. Application deadline is August 20. Notification of admission on rolling basis. Reply is required by May 1. $200 nonrefundable tuition deposit. $100 room deposit, refundable at the end of first year. Freshmen accepted for terms other than fall.
**Special programs:** Admission may be deferred one year. Credit and/or placement may be granted through CEEB Advanced Placement exams for scores of 3 or higher. Credit and/or placement may be granted through CLEP general and subject exams. Credit and placement may be granted through challenge exams. Early decision program. In fall 1993, 214 applied for early decision and 197 were accepted. Deadline for applying for early decision is November 1. Early entrance/early admission program. Concurrent enrollment program.
**Transfer students:** Transfer students accepted for terms other than fall. In fall 1993, 6% of all new students were transfers into all classes. 79 transfer applications were received, 62 were accepted. Application deadline is August 20 for fall; December 1 for spring. Minimum 3.0 GPA required. Lowest course grade accepted is "C." Maximum number of transferable credits is 68 semester hours. At least 34 semester hours must be completed at the college to receive degree.
**Admissions contact:** John W. Seveland, M.S., Vice President for Enrollment and Student Affairs. 800 321-ALMA.

**FINANCIAL AID. Available aid:** Pell grants, SEOG, state scholarships and grants, school scholarships and grants, private scholarships, ROTC scholarships, and academic merit scholarships. Perkins Loans (NDSL), PLUS, Stafford Loans (GSL), school loans, private loans, and SLS. Tuition Plan Inc., Knight Tuition Plans, AMS, Tuition Management Systems, deferred payment plan, and guaranteed tuition. Prepayment Plan.
**Financial aid statistics:** 26% of aid is not need-based. In 1993-94, 95% of all undergraduate applicants received aid; 96% of freshman applicants. Average amounts of aid awarded freshmen: Scholarships and grants, $5,600; loans, $3,300.
**Supporting data/closing dates:** FAFSA: Priority filing date is February 15. Income tax forms: Priority filing date is February 15. Notification of awards on rolling basis.
**Financial aid contact:** Tom Freeland, Director of Financial Aid. 517 463-7347.

**STUDENT EMPLOYMENT.** College Work/Study Program. Institutional employment. 40% of full-time undergraduates work on campus during school year. Students may expect to earn an average of $800–1,000 during school year. Off-campus part-time employment opportunities rated "fair."

**COMPUTER FACILITIES.** 126 IBM/IBM-compatible and Macintosh/Apple microcomputers; 112 are networked. Students may access Digital minicomputer/mainframe systems, Internet. Residence halls may be equipped with stand-alone microcomputers, networked microcomputers, networked terminals. Client/LAN operating systems include Apple/Macintosh, DOS, DEC. Computer languages and software packages include Ada, BASIC, C, Cricket Graph, Excel, FORTRAN, LISP, Lotus 1-2-3, Pascal, SPSS-X, Super Paint, WordPerfect. Computer facilities are available to all students.
**Fees:** None.
**Hours:** 24 hours/day in residence halls; 94 hours/week in labs.

**GRADUATE CAREER DATA.** Graduate school percentages: 12% enter law school. 4% enter medical school. 1% enter dental school. 6% enter graduate business programs. 7% enter graduate arts and sciences programs. 1% enter theological school/seminary. Highest graduate school enrollments: Central Michigan U, Michigan State U, U of Detroit, U of Kentucky, U of Michigan, U of Notre Dame, Wake Forest U, Wayne State U, Western Michigan U. 26% of graduates choose careers in business and industry. Companies and businesses that hire graduates: Dow Corning, EDS, Ernst & Young, General Motors, J.C. Penney, K mart, National Bank of Detroit, Old Kent Bank, PepsiCo.

**PROMINENT ALUMNI/AE.** Jane Aldrich-Bohne, WLNS-TV (Lansing) news anchor; Bob Devaney, athletic director, U of Nebraska; Jim Northrup, commentator for Detroit Tigers.

# Andrews University

**Berrien Springs, MI 49104** **616 471-7771**

**1994-95 Costs.** Tuition: $9,996. Room: $1,815. Board: $2,175. Fees, books, misc. academic expenses (school's estimate): $1,185.
**Enrollment.** Undergraduates: 769 men, 873 women (full-time). Freshman class: 1,113 applicants, 904 accepted, 426 enrolled. Graduate enrollment: 279 men, 308 women.
**Test score averages/ranges.** Average ACT scores: 19 English, 17 math, 19 composite.
**Faculty.** 198 full-time; 72 part-time. 59% of faculty holds doctoral degree. Student/faculty ratio: 11 to 1.
**Selectivity rating.** Less competitive.

**PROFILE.** Andrews, founded in 1874, is a church-affiliated university. Programs are offered through the Colleges of Arts and Sciences and Technology, the Schools of Business and Education, and the Seventh-day Adventist Theological Seminary. Its 1,600-acre campus is located in Berrien Springs, 25 miles north of South Bend, Ind.

**Accreditation:** NCACS.
**Religious orientation:** Andrews University is affiliated with the Seventh-day Adventist Church; 18 hours of religion required.
**Library:** Collections totaling over 550,856 volumes, 2,962 periodical subscriptions, and 567,113 microform items.
**Special facilities/museums:** Audio-visual center, lab school, natural history and archaeological museums, observatory, physical therapy facilities.
**Athletic facilities:** Tennis courts, track, swimming pool, football/soccer and softball fields, badminton/volleyball and racquetball/handball courts, basketball courts, gymnastic and weight training facilities, equipment and facilities for aerobics, camping, canoeing, cross-country skiing, floor hockey, and golf.

**STUDENT BODY. Undergraduate profile:** 44% are state residents; 15% are transfers. 11% Asian-American, 21% Black, 6% Hispanic, 1% Native American, 61% White. Average age of undergraduates is 22.
**Freshman profile:** 75% of accepted applicants took ACT. 22% of freshmen come from public schools.
**Undergraduate achievement:** 69% of fall 1992 freshmen returned for fall 1993 term.
**Foreign students:** 522 students are from out of the country. Countries represented include Canada, Germany, Jamaica, Japan, and South Korea; 119 in all.

**PROGRAMS OF STUDY. Degrees:** B.A., B.Arch., B.Bus.Admin., B.F.A., B.Mus., B.S., B.S.Art Ed., B.S.Diet., B.S.Elem.Ed., B.S.Eng.Tech., B.S.Human Sci., B.S.I.T., B.S.Interiors, B.S.Med.Tech., B.S.Radiol.Tech., B.Tech.
**Majors:** Accounting, Agriculture, Aircraft Engineering Technology, Anatomy/Physiology, Apparel, Architectural Studies, Art, Art/Crafts, Automotive Technology, Aviation Technology, Behavioral Science, Biochemistry, Biology, Biology/Biomedical Option, Biophysics, Botany, Broadcasting, Building Construction Technology, Business Economics, Business Education, Chemistry, Communications, Computer-Aided Manufacturing/Robotics Technology, Computer Science, Computer Technology, Construction Engineering Technology, Economics, Education, Electronics Engineering Technology, Electronics Technology, Elementary Education, Elementary Music Education, Engineering Technology, English, Family Studies, French, General Science, German, Graphic Arts Technology, Graphics Management, Health Psychology, Health Science, History, Home Economics, Interior Design, Journalism, Language Arts, Management, Management Information Systems, Manufacturing Technology, Marketing, Mathematics, Mechanical Engineering Technology, Media Technology, Medical Technology, Molecular Biology, Music, Nursing, Nutrition, Office Administration, Operations Engineering, Physical Education, Physics, Plant Operation, Psychology, Public Relations, Radiologic Technology, Religion, Social Studies, Sociology, Spanish, Speech/Language Pathology/Audiology, Teaching English as a Second Language, Technical Plant Services, Technology Education, Theology, Zoology.
**Distribution of degrees:** The majors with the highest enrollment are business, nursing, and architecture; elementary education, mathematics, and physics have the lowest.
**Requirements:** General education requirement.
**Special:** Minors offered in many majors and in anthropology, biblical languages, bilingual education (French, German, Spanish), business administration, clothing/textiles, computerized composition, drafting, engineering, food and nutrition, geography, library science, metals technology, multi-image technology, political science, screen printing, and wood technology. Certificate programs. Associate's degrees offered. Double majors. Independent study. Pass/fail grading option. Graduate school at which undergraduates may take graduate-level courses. Preprofessional programs in law, medicine, veterinary science, pharmacy, dentistry, optometry, chiropractic, cytotechnology, dental assistant, dental hygiene, occupational therapy, physical therapy, public history, and respiratory therapy. 2-2 engineering program with Walla Walla Coll. Cooperative programs in dental assisting, dental hygiene, medical record administration, occupational therapy, physical therapy, and respiratory therapy with LaSierra U. Teacher certification in elementary and secondary education. Study abroad in Austria, France, and Spain.
**Honors:** Honors program.
**Academic Assistance:** Nonremedial tutoring.

**STUDENT LIFE. Housing:** All undergraduate students under age 22 must live on campus unless living with family. Coed, women's, and men's dorms. School-owned/operated apartments. Off-campus married-student housing. Attendance at some worship services required of undergraduates living in dorms. 68% of students live in college housing.
**Services and counseling/handicapped student services:** Placement services. Health service. Day care. Personal and psychological counseling. Career and academic guidance services. Religious counseling.
**Campus organizations:** Undergraduate student government. Student newspaper (Student Movement, published once/week). Yearbook. Radio station. Orchestra, wind sym-

phony, University Singers, Singing Men, Ladies Chorus, chamber singers, bicycling club, underwater divers club, physical education club, gymnastics group, departmental, service, and special-interest groups.
**Religious organizations:** Contemporary Christian Musicians, Ministerial Seminar, Seminary Student Forum, World Missions, BRANCH (Bringing Andrews to Christ).
**Minority/foreign student organizations:** Black Student Christian Forum, Black Student Association. Japanese, Korean, Far Eastern, Southern Asian, South Pacific, Africa-Indian Ocean, Pan-African, South African, Eastern African, Euro-African, Middle Eastern, Canadian, Franco-Haitian, Caribbean, Inter-American/Spanish, and South American Division groups.
**ATHLETICS. Physical education requirements:** Four hours of physical education required.
**Intercollegiate competition:** 1% of students participate.
**Intramural and club sports:** 30% of students participate. Intramural basketball, flagball, floor hockey, racquetball, soccer, softball, tennis, volleyball. Men's club basketball.
**ADMISSIONS. Academic basis for candidate selection** (in order of priority): Secondary school record, school's recommendation, standardized test scores.
**Nonacademic basis for candidate selection:** Character and personality are important.
**Requirements:** Graduation from secondary school is required; GED is accepted. No specific distribution of secondary school units required. Minimum 2.0 GPA recommended. Provisional admission possible for applicants not meeting standard requirements. ACT is required. Off-campus interviews available with an admissions representative.
**Procedure:** Take ACT by spring of 12th year. Suggest filing application by January; no deadline. Notification of admission on rolling basis. Reply is required by date of registration. $50 room deposit, refundable until September 1. Freshmen accepted for terms other than fall.
**Special programs:** Admission may be deferred one year. Credit may be granted through CEEB Advanced Placement for scores of 3 or higher. Credit may be granted through CLEP general and subject exams, DANTES and challenge exams. Concurrent enrollment program.
**Transfer students:** Transfer students accepted for terms other than fall. In fall 1993, 15% of all new students were transfers into all classes. 218 transfer applications were received, 218 were accepted. Application deadline is rolling for fall; rolling for spring. Minimum 2.0 GPA required. Lowest course grade accepted is "C." Maximum number of transferable semester hours is 70. At least 15-20 quarter hours must be completed at the university to receive degree.
**Admissions contact:** John F. Mentges, Director of Admissions. 616 471-3303.
**FINANCIAL AID. Available aid:** Pell grants, SEOG, state scholarships and grants, school scholarships and grants, private scholarships and grants, academic merit scholarships, and aid for undergraduate foreign students. Perkins Loans (NDSL), PLUS, Stafford Loans (GSL), and SLS. Tuition Plan Inc. and AMS.
**Financial aid statistics:** Average amounts of aid awarded freshmen: Loans, $2,300.
**Supporting data/closing dates:** FAFSA/FAF/FFS: Priority filing date is March 31; deadline is July 1. School's own aid application: Priority filing date is March 31; deadline is July 1. Income tax forms: Priority filing date is March 31; deadline is July 1. Notification of awards on rolling basis.
**Financial aid contact:** David A. Borton, M.B.A., Financial Aid Officer. 616 471-3334.
**STUDENT EMPLOYMENT.** College Work/Study Program. Institutional employment. 75% of full-time undergraduates work on campus during school year. Students may expect to earn an average of $1,200 during school year. Off-campus part-time employment opportunities rated "good."
**COMPUTER FACILITIES.** 56 IBM/IBM-compatible microcomputers; 16 are networked. Students may access Internet. Computer languages and software packages include BASIC, C, COBOL, dBASE III+, FORTRAN, LISP, Paradox, Prolog, SuperCalc 5, WordPerfect, WordStar; all other major languages and software programs. Computer facilities are available to all students.
**Fees:** None.
**Hours:** 7:30 AM-11 PM.
**GRADUATE CAREER DATA.** 65% of graduates choose careers in business and industry.
**PROMINENT ALUMNI/AE.** John David Waihee III, governor, Hawaii; Clifton Davis, actor; Glenn F. Engen, senior research meteorologist; George Vandeman, TV evangelist; Paul Cho, president, Taiwan Adventist College.

# Aquinas College

**Grand Rapids, MI 49506-1799 616 459-8281**

**1993-94 Costs.** Tuition: $10,402. Room & board: $4,124. Fees, books, misc. academic expenses (school's estimate): $500.
**Enrollment.** Undergraduates: 434 men, 817 women (full-time). Freshman class: 619 applicants, 516 accepted, 220 enrolled. Graduate enrollment: 222 men, 236 women.
**Test score averages/ranges.** Average ACT scores: 22 English, 21 math, 22 composite. Range of ACT scores of middle 50%: 19-26 English, 18-24 math.
**Faculty.** 91 full-time; 104 part-time. 62% of faculty holds highest degree in specific field. Student/faculty ratio: 14 to 1.
**Selectivity rating.** Less competitive.

**PROFILE.** Aquinas, founded in 1922, is a church-affiliated college of liberal arts and professional study. Its 90-acre campus is located in a residential area of Grand Rapids.
**Accreditation:** NCACS.
**Religious orientation:** Aquinas College is affiliated with the Roman Catholic Church (Dominican Sisters); no religious requirements.
**Library:** Collections totaling over 100,921 volumes, 944 periodical subscriptions, and 93,462 microform items.
**Athletic facilities:** Gymnasium, field house, basketball, handball, paddleball, tennis, and volleyball courts, weight room, track, golf range, baseball, soccer, and softball fields, sauna.
**STUDENT BODY. Undergraduate profile:** 97% are state residents; 29% are transfers. 1.2% Asian-American, 7% Black, 1.4% Hispanic, .4% Native American, 88.1% White, 1.9% Other. Average age of undergraduates is 23.
**Freshman profile:** 4% of freshmen who took ACT scored 30 or over on English, 3% scored 30 or over on math, 3% scored 30 or over on composite; 38% scored 24 or over on English, 29% scored 24 or over on math, 39% scored 24 or over on composite; 75% scored 18 or over on English, 76% scored 18 or over on math, 87% scored 18 or over on composite; 90% scored 12 or over on English, 94% scored 12 or over on math, 95% scored 12 or over on composite; 96% scored 6 or over on composite. 1% of accepted applicants took SAT; 99% took ACT. 76% of freshmen come from public schools.
**Undergraduate achievement:** 75% of fall 1992 freshmen returned for fall 1993 term. 33% of entering class graduated. 21% of students who completed a degree program went on to graduate study within one year.
**Foreign students:** 14 students are from out of the country. Countries represented include China, Germany, India, Japan, Russia, and Sri Lanka; eight in all.
**PROGRAMS OF STUDY. Degrees:** B.A., B.A.Gen.Ed., B.F.A., B.Mus., B.Mus.Ed., B.S., B.S.Bus.Admin.
**Majors:** Accounting/Business, Art History, Biology, Business Administration, Chemistry, Communication Arts, Computer Information Systems, Drawing, Economics, English, Environmental Studies, French, Geography, German, History, International Studies, Mathematics, Mathematics/Science, Medical Technology, Music, Music Education, Music History, Music Performance, Painting, Philosophy, Physical Education/Community Recreation, Political Science, Printmaking, Psychology, Reading Education, Religious Studies, Sculpture, Social Science, Sociology, Spanish, Urban Studies.
**Distribution of degrees:** The majors with the highest enrollment are business administration, accounting, and communication arts; philosophy, voice, and art history have the lowest.
**Requirements:** General education requirement.
**Academic regulations:** Freshmen must maintain minimum 1.7 GPA; sophomores, 1.9 GPA; juniors, 2.0 GPA; seniors, 2.0 GPA.
**Special:** Minors offered in most majors. Courses offered in education and physics. B.A. in general education requires no major. B.F.A. in advertising design, environmental design, furniture design, illustration, and interior design in association with Kendall Coll of Art and Design. Associate's degrees offered. Self-designed majors. Double majors. Independent study. Accelerated study. Pass/fail grading option. Internships. Preprofessional programs in law, medicine, dentistry, physical therapy, forestry, engineering, and social work. 3-1 program in nuclear medical technology with St. Louis U Medical Center, Mo. Member of Dominican College Consortium, the Tuition Exchange, and Catholic College Cooperative Tuition Exchange. Teacher certification in early childhood, elementary, and secondary education. Certification in specific subject areas. Study abroad in Austria, France, Germany, Ireland, Mexico, and Spain.
**Honors:** Honors program. Honor societies.
**Academic Assistance:** Remedial reading, writing, math, and study skills. Nonremedial tutoring.
**STUDENT LIFE. Housing:** All unmarried freshmen and sophomores must live on campus unless living with family. Coed, women's, and men's dorms. 45% of students live in college housing.
**Services and counseling/handicapped student services:** Placement services. Health service. Women's center. Day care. Counseling services for minority, veteran, and older students. Personal counseling. Career and academic guidance services. Religious counseling. Physically disabled student services. Learning disabled program/services. Tape recorders. Reader services for the blind.
**Campus organizations:** Undergraduate student government. Student newspaper (Aquinas Times, published four times/semester). Yearbook. Aquinas Players Theatre Club, chemical society, French club, geography association, prelaw association, Joint Council of Residence Halls, ice hockey club, fitness club, pep squad, 41 organizations in all.
**Religious organizations:** Christian Fellowship, Pastoral Center Choir, Campus Ministry.
**Minority/foreign student organizations:** Minority Student Union, JAMMIN (multicultural group). International Student Union, International Association of Business Communicators.
**ATHLETICS. Physical education requirements:** None.
**Intercollegiate competition:** 21% of students participate. Baseball (M), basketball (M,W), cheerleading (W), cross-country (M,W), golf (M), soccer (M,W), softball (W), tennis (M,W), track (indoor) (M,W), track (outdoor) (M,W), track and field (indoor) (M,W), track and field (outdoor) (M,W), volleyball (W). Member of NAIA, Wolverine-Hoosier Conference.
**Intramural and club sports:** 45% of students participate. Intramural basketball, flag football, golf, tennis, volleyball, weight training. Men's club ice hockey.
**ADMISSIONS. Academic basis for candidate selection** (in order of priority): Secondary school record, standardized test scores, school's recommendation, class rank, essay.
**Nonacademic basis for candidate selection:** Character and personality and extracurricular participation are emphasized. Particular talent or ability is important. Geographical distribution is considered.
**Requirements:** Graduation from secondary school is required; GED is not accepted. 15 units and the following program of study are required: 4 units of English, 3 units of math, 3 units of science, 4 units of social studies. Rank in top half of secondary school class and minimum 2.5 GPA required. 7th semester admissions ACT is required; SAT may be substituted. Campus visit and interview recommended. No off-campus interviews.
**Procedure:** Take SAT or ACT by May 1 of 12th year. Visit college for interview by May 1 of 12th year. Application deadline is June 1. Notification of admission on rolling basis. $200 tuition deposit, refundable until June 1. Freshmen accepted for terms other than fall.
**Special programs:** Admission may be deferred. Credit and/or placement may be granted through CEEB Advanced Placement exams for scores of 3 or higher. Credit and/or placement may be granted through CLEP general and subject exams. Credit and placement may be granted through Regents College, ACT PEP, DANTES, and challenge exams and military and life experience. Concurrent enrollment program.
**Transfer students:** Transfer students accepted for terms other than fall. In fall 1993, 29% of all new students were transfers into all classes. 188 transfer applications were received, 155 were accepted. Application deadline is rolling for fall; rolling for spring. Minimum 2.0 GPA required. Lowest course grade accepted is "D." At least 30 credits must be completed at the college to receive degree.

**Admissions contact:** Thomas Mikowski, Director of Admissions. 616 732-4460.

**FINANCIAL AID. Available aid:** Pell grants, SEOG, state scholarships and grants, school scholarships and grants, private scholarships, academic merit scholarships, athletic scholarships, and aid for undergraduate foreign students. Perkins Loans (NDSL), PLUS, Stafford Loans (GSL), state loans, and SLS. AMS and deferred payment plan.

**Financial aid statistics:** 9% of aid is not need-based. In 1993-94, 89% of all undergraduate applicants received aid; 99% of freshman applicants. Average amounts of aid awarded freshmen: Scholarships and grants, $4,300; loans, $1,894.

**Supporting data/closing dates:** FAFSA: Priority filing date is February 15; accepted on rolling basis. Notification of awards begins March 15.

**Financial aid contact:** David J. Steffee, Director of Financial Aid. 616 459-8281, extension 5129.

**STUDENT EMPLOYMENT.** College Work/Study Program. Institutional employment. 39% of full-time undergraduates work on campus during school year. Students may expect to earn an average of $1,400 during school year. Off-campus part-time employment opportunities rated "excellent."

**COMPUTER FACILITIES.** 115 IBM/IBM-compatible and Macintosh/Apple microcomputers; 62 are networked. Students may access Digital minicomputer/mainframe systems. Residence halls may be equipped with stand-alone microcomputers. Client/LAN operating systems include Apple/Macintosh, DOS, Novell. Computer languages and software packages include BAL, BASIC, COBOL, dBASE III, FORTRAN, Lotus 1-2-3, Pascal, WordPerfect; 67 in all. Computer facilities are available to all students.

**Fees:** None.

**Hours:** 8 AM-11 PM.

**GRADUATE CAREER DATA.** Graduate school percentages: 5% enter graduate business programs. 6% enter graduate arts and sciences programs. 2% enter theological school/seminary. Highest graduate school enrollments: Grand Valley State U, Western Michigan U.

**PROMINENT ALUMNI/AE.** Paul A. Assenmacher, pitcher, Chicago Cubs; James A. Brunson, assistant U.S. attorney, U.S. Dept. of Justice; Kenneth D. Neyer, owner and president, Neyer Oil Company; Adm. Albert E. Rieder, Dir. of Naval Reserve Administration; Vito J. Stellino, sports writer, *Baltimore Sun*; Dr. Patricia E. Stewart, vice president of research and development, McNeil Consumer Products.

## Baker College

**Flint, MI 48507** — **810 767-7600**

**1994-95 Costs.** Tuition: $5,760. Room: $1,100.

**Enrollment.** Undergraduates: 700 men, 2,105 women (full-time). Freshman class: 1,754 applicants, 1,754 accepted, 1,432 enrolled.

**Test score averages/ranges.** N/A.

**Faculty.** 36 full-time; 127 part-time. Student/faculty ratio: 39 to 1.

**Selectivity rating.** N/A.

**PROFILE.** Baker, founded in 1911, is a private, multipurpose college. Its 30-acre campus is located in Flint, 60 miles from Detroit.

**Accreditation:** NCACS. Professionally accredited by the Committee on Allied Health Education and Accreditation.

**Religious orientation:** Baker College is nonsectarian; no religious requirements.

**Library:** Collections totaling over 52,000 volumes, 165 periodical subscriptions, and 1,057 microform items.

**STUDENT BODY. Undergraduate profile:** 98% are state residents; 29% are transfers. 1% Asian-American, 13% Black, 1% Hispanic, 1% Native American, 84% White. Average age of undergraduates is 26.

**Undergraduate achievement:** 23% of students who completed a degree program immediately went on to graduate study.

**PROGRAMS OF STUDY. Degrees:** B.Avia.Mgmt., B.Bus.Admin., B.Graph.Comm., B.Hlth.Info.Mgmt., B.Indust.Mgmt., B.Inter.Design, B.S.Occup.Ther.

**Majors:** Accounting, Aviation Technology, Computer Information Systems, Drafting/Design Technology, Electronic Engineering Technology, Graphic Communications, Health Information Management, Industrial Technology, Interior Design, Management, Marketing, Occupational Therapy, Office Administration, SPC/Quality Improvement.

**Distribution of degrees:** The majors with the highest enrollment are management/marketing, accounting, and office administration; interior design, electronic engineering technology, and drafting/design technology have the lowest.

**Requirements:** General education requirement.

**Academic regulations:** Minimum 2.0 GPA must be maintained.

**Special:** Minors offered in some majors and in business, liberal arts, health science, medical record technology, medical science, psychology, technical flex-studies, and word processing. Associate's degrees offered. Double majors. Dual degrees. Independent study. Pass/fail grading option. Internships. Cooperative education programs.

**Academic Assistance:** Remedial reading, writing, math, and study skills. Nonremedial tutoring.

**STUDENT LIFE. Housing:** Coed dorms. 2% of students live in college housing.

**Services and counseling/handicapped student services:** Placement services. Day care. Learning center. Counseling services for minority, military, veteran, and older students. Personal and psychological counseling. Career and academic guidance services. Physically disabled student services. Notetaking services. Tape recorders. Tutors. Reader services for the blind.

**Campus organizations:** Literary magazine. Fashion Association, Health Information Management Association, Student Life Association, aviation club, travel club.

**Religious organizations:** Students with a Testimony (S.W.A.T.).

**ATHLETICS. Physical education requirements:** None.

**ADMISSIONS. Requirements:** Graduation from secondary school is required; GED is not accepted. No specific distribution of secondary school units required. Medical exam required of applicants to aviation program and some allied health programs. Campus visit and interview recommended.

**Procedure:** Application deadline is September 26. Notification of admission on rolling basis. Room deposit is refundable if notice of cancellation is given in writing prior to the start of school quarter. Freshmen accepted for terms other than fall.

**Special programs:** Credit and/or placement may be granted through CEEB Advanced Placement exams. Credit and/or placement may be granted through CLEP general exams. Credit may be granted through life experience.

**Transfer students:** Transfer students accepted for terms other than fall. In fall 1993, 29% of all new students were transfers into all classes. 591 transfer applications were received, 591 were accepted. Application deadline is September 26 for fall; April 1 for spring. Lowest course grade accepted is "C." Maximum number of transferable credits is 48 quarter hours.

**Admissions contact:** Mark Heaton, Director of Admissions. 810 766-4000.

**FINANCIAL AID. Available aid:** Pell grants, SEOG, state scholarships and grants, and private scholarships. PLUS, Stafford Loans (GSL), and SLS.

**Supporting data/closing dates:** FAFSA. School's own aid application. Income tax forms.

**Financial aid contact:** Ellis P. Salim, Director of Financial Aid. 810 766-4206.

**STUDENT EMPLOYMENT.** College Work/Study Program. Institutional employment. Off-campus part-time employment opportunities rated "good."

**COMPUTER FACILITIES.** 220 IBM/IBM-compatible and Macintosh/Apple microcomputers; all are networked. Students may access IBM minicomputer/mainframe systems, Internet. Client/LAN operating systems include Apple/Macintosh, DOS, Novell. Computer languages and software packages include COBOL, RPG; word processing, database, spreadsheet packages. Computer facilities are available to all students.

**Fees:** None.

**GRADUATE CAREER DATA.** Graduate school percentages: 13% enter graduate business programs. Companies and businesses that hire graduates: General Motors, Hurley Medical Center, Citizens Bank.

## Baker College of Muskegon

**Muskegon, MI 49442** — **800 937-0337**

**1994-95 Costs.** Tuition: $5,520. Room: $1,575. No meal plan; cafeteria service available. Fees, books, misc. academic expenses (school's estimate): $750.

**Enrollment.** Undergraduates: 464 men, 1,195 women (full-time). Freshman class: 830 applicants, 593 accepted, 593 enrolled.

**Test score averages/ranges.** N/A.

**Faculty.** Student/faculty ratio: 25 to 1.

**Selectivity rating.** N/A.

**PROFILE.** Baker College of Muskegon, founded in 1993, is a private university. Its 25-acre campus is located in Muskegon.

**Accreditation:** NCACS. Professionally accredited by the American Medical Association (CAHEA).

**Religious orientation:** Baker College of Muskegon is nonsectarian; no religious requirements.

**STUDENT BODY. Undergraduate profile:** 99% are state residents. 1% Asian-American, 10% Black, 2% Hispanic, 1% Native American, 86% White. Average age of undergraduates is 28.

**PROGRAMS OF STUDY. Degrees:** B.Avia.Mgmt., B.Bus.Admin., B.Bus.Leadership, B.Indust.Mgmt.

**Majors:** Accounting, Aviation, Business Administration, Computer Information Systems, Industrial Management, Management, Marketing, Office Administration.

**Distribution of degrees:** The majors with the highest enrollment are accounting, computer information systems, and management.

**Requirements:** General education requirement.

**Academic regulations:** Minimum 2.0 GPA must be maintained.

**Special:** Minors offered in some majors and in drafting, electronics, and word processing. Associate's degrees offered. Double majors. Pass/fail grading option. Internships. Cooperative education programs.

**Academic Assistance:** Remedial reading, writing, math, and study skills. Nonremedial tutoring.

**STUDENT LIFE. Housing:** All unmarried students under age 21 must live on campus unless living near campus with relatives. Coed dorms. 12% of students live in college housing.

**Services and counseling/handicapped student services:** Placement services. Day care. Personal counseling. Career and academic guidance services.

**ATHLETICS. Physical education requirements:** None.

**ADMISSIONS. Academic basis for candidate selection** (in order of priority): Secondary school record.

**Nonacademic basis for candidate selection:** Character and personality are important.

**Requirements:** Graduation from secondary school is required; GED is accepted. No specific distribution of secondary school units required. Campus visit and interview recommended. No off-campus interviews.

**Procedure:** Application deadline is September. Notification of admission on rolling basis. $50 room deposit, refundable until August 15. Freshmen accepted for terms other than fall.

**Special programs:** Credit and/or placement may be granted through CLEP general exams. Credit may be granted through CLEP subject exams, challenge exams, and military and life experience. Concurrent enrollment program.

**Transfer students:** Transfer students accepted for terms other than fall. Application deadline is September for fall; March for spring. Lowest course grade accepted is "C-." Maximum number of transferable credits is 98 quarter hours.
**Admissions contact:** Kathy Jacobson, Director of Admissions. 800 937-0337.

**FINANCIAL AID. Available aid:** Pell grants, SEOG, state scholarships and grants, school scholarships and grants, and private scholarships. Perkins Loans (NDSL), PLUS, Stafford Loans (GSL), and SLS.
**Financial aid statistics:** In 1993-94, 83% of all undergraduate applicants received aid.
**Supporting data/closing dates:** FAFSA/FAF/FFS: Priority filing date is February 15. School's own aid application: Priority filing date is February 15. Income tax forms: Accepted on rolling basis. Notification of awards on rolling basis.
**Financial aid contact:** Thomas Jewell, Director of Financial Aid. 800 937-0337.

**STUDENT EMPLOYMENT.** College Work/Study Program. Off-campus part-time employment opportunities rated "good."

**COMPUTER FACILITIES.** 85 IBM/IBM-compatible microcomputers. Computer languages and software packages include COBOL, RPG, WordPerfect.
**Fees:** None.

# Calvin College

**Grand Rapids, MI 49546** **616 957-6000**

**1994-95 Costs.** Tuition: $10,230. Room & board: $37170. Fees, books, misc. academic expenses (school's estimate): $400.
**Enrollment.** Undergraduates: 1,539 men, 1,862 women (full-time). Freshman class: 1,784 applicants, 1,512 accepted, 913 enrolled. Graduate enrollment: 93 men, 100 women.
**Test score averages/ranges.** Average SAT scores: 505 verbal, 567 math. Range of SAT scores of middle 50%: 440-580 verbal, 490-650 math. Average ACT scores: 24 English, 23 math, 24 composite. Range of ACT scores of middle 50%: 22-27 English, 20-26 math.
**Faculty.** 220 full-time; 57 part-time. 83% of faculty holds doctoral degree. Student/faculty ratio: 16 to 1.
**Selectivity rating.** Competitive.

**PROFILE.** Calvin, founded in 1876, is a church-affiliated, liberal arts college. Its 370-acre campus is located in a suburban area of Grand Rapids.

**Accreditation:** NCACS. Professionally accredited by the Accreditation Board for Engineering and Technology, the Council on Social Work Education, the National Association of Schools of Music, the National Council for Accreditation of Teacher Education, the National League for Nursing.
**Religious orientation:** Calvin College is affiliated with the Christian Reformed Church; two semesters of religion/theology required.
**Library:** Collections totaling over 635,000 volumes, 2,700 periodical subscriptions, and 476,090 microform items.
**Special facilities/museums:** Art gallery, observatory, ecosystem preserve, electron microscope, seismograph lab.
**Athletic facilities:** Field house, gymnasiums, swimming pool, track, baseball, soccer, and softball fields, racquetball and tennis courts.

**STUDENT BODY. Undergraduate profile:** 59% are state residents; 12% are transfers. 3% Asian-American, 1% Black, 1% Hispanic, .4% Native American, 94% White, .6% Other. Average age of undergraduates is 20.
**Freshman profile:** 3% of freshmen who took SAT scored 700 or over on verbal, 15% scored 700 or over on math; 20% scored 600 or over on verbal, 41% scored 600 or over on math; 55% scored 500 or over on verbal, 73% scored 500 or over on math; 87% scored 400 or over on verbal, 94% scored 400 or over on math; 100% scored 300 or over on verbal, 100% scored 300 or over on math. 11% of freshmen who took ACT scored 30 or over on English, 9% scored 30 or over on math, 10% scored 30 or over on composite; 58% scored 24 or over on English, 49% scored 24 or over on math, 59% scored 24 or over on composite; 94% scored 18 or over on English, 92% scored 18 or over on math, 98% scored 18 or over on composite; 100% scored 12 or over on English, 100% scored 12 or over on math, 100% scored 12 or over on composite. 28% of accepted applicants took SAT; 99% took ACT. 39% of freshmen come from public schools.
**Undergraduate achievement:** 83% of fall 1992 freshmen returned for fall 1993 term. 45% of entering class graduated. 22% of students who completed a degree program immediately went on to graduate study.
**Foreign students:** 327 students are from out of the country. Countries represented include Canada, China, India, Indonesia, Korea, and Nigeria; 31 in all.

**PROGRAMS OF STUDY. Degrees:** B.A., B.F.A., B.S., B.S.Acct., B.S.Eng., B.S.Nurs., B.S.Recr., B.Soc.Work.
**Majors:** Accounting, Art, Art History, Biochemistry, Biology, Business, Chemistry, Classical Civilization, Classical Languages, Communication Arts/Sciences, Communication Disorders, Computer Science, Criminal Justice, Dutch, Economics, Economics/Mathematics, Education, Engineering, English, French, Geography, Geology, German, Greek, History, Interdisciplinary Studies, Latin, Mathematics, Medical Technology, Music, Natural Resources, Nursing, Occupational Therapy, Philosophy, Physical Education, Physics, Political Science, Psychology, Recreation, Religion/Theology, Social Science, Social Work, Sociology, Spanish, Special Education, Visual Arts.
**Distribution of degrees:** The majors with the highest enrollment are business, English, and psychology; classical civilization, geography, and art history have the lowest.
**Requirements:** General education requirement.
**Academic regulations:** Freshmen must maintain minimum 1.65 GPA; sophomores, 1.85 GPA; juniors, 2.0 GPA; seniors, 2.0 GPA.
**Special:** Minors offered in all majors and in bilingual education, Chinese, church music, environmental studies, German studies, humanities, journalism, linguistics, missions, and Netherlandic studies. Completion of three interim courses required for graduation. Double majors. Independent study. Internships. Cooperative education programs. Graduate school at which undergraduates may take graduate-level courses. Preprofessional programs in law, medicine, pharmacy, dentistry, theology, architecture, and physical therapy. Combined-degree programs in communication disorders with Michigan State U; in medical technology with Butterworth Hospital; in occupational therapy with Washington U. Member of Christian College Coalition; exchange possible. American Studies Program (Washington, D.C.). AuSable Inst of Environmental Studies Program (Michigan). Chicago Metropolitan Program. Oregon Extension Program. Los Angeles Film Studies Center Program. Teacher certification in elementary, secondary, and special education education. Certification in specific subject areas. Study abroad in Austria, Costa Rica, France, Germany, Latin American countries, the Netherlands, Nigeria, Spain, and the United Kingdom. Interim programs in Central American countries and South Africa.
**Honors:** Honors program.
**Academic Assistance:** Remedial writing, math, and study skills. Nonremedial tutoring.

**STUDENT LIFE. Housing:** All freshmen and sophomores must live on campus unless living with family. Women's and men's dorms. School-owned/operated apartments. 60% of students live in college housing.
**Social atmosphere:** According to the student newspaper, "Calvin is a relatively small Christian liberal arts college that is private and closely affiliated with the Christian Reformed Church. Athletics are important, and there is a wonderful academic atmosphere here. Christianity tends to be a very central aspect of the Calvin community." Students tend to gather at The Cave and Easttown. Influential groups on campus include Student Senate, Chimes, and the Fellowship of Christian Athletes. A favorite event during the school year is the basketball game against their rival, Hope College.
**Services and counseling/handicapped student services:** Placement services. Health service. Counseling services for minority and older students. Personal counseling. Career and academic guidance services. Physically disabled student services. Learning disabled services. Notetaking services. Tape recorders. Tutors. Reader services for the blind.
**Campus organizations:** Undergraduate student government. Student newspaper (Chimes, published once/week). Literary magazine. Yearbook. Radio station. Musical groups, drama and literary groups, Fine Arts Guild, Student Volunteer Service, Adventure Club, Student Volunteer Services, political awareness and hunger awareness groups, Young Democrats Club, Republican Club, Associated Women Students, 70 organizations in all.
**Religious organizations:** Fellowship of Christian Athletes, Intervarsity Christian Fellowship, Christian Worldview Awareness, Bible study groups.
**Minority/foreign student organizations:** COLORS. International Student Organization.

**ATHLETICS. Physical education requirements:** Four semesters of physical education required.
**Intercollegiate competition:** 20% of students participate. Basketball (M,W), cross-country (M,W), golf (M,W), soccer (M,W), softball (W), swimming (M,W), tennis (M,W), track (outdoor) (M,W), track and field (outdoor) (M,W), volleyball (W). Member of Michigan Intercollegiate Athletic Association, NCAA Division III.
**Intramural and club sports:** 75% of students participate. Intramural badminton, basketball, fast-pitch softball, field hockey, flag football, floor hockey, golf, hocksock, ice hockey, pickleball, racquetball, soccer, softball, tennis, ultimate frisbee, volleyball, walleyball. Men's club ice hockey, lacrosse, volleyball.

**ADMISSIONS. Academic basis for candidate selection** (in order of priority): Secondary school record, class rank, standardized test scores, school's recommendation, essay.
**Nonacademic basis for candidate selection:** Character and personality are emphasized. Extracurricular participation, particular talent or ability, and alumni/ae relationship are considered.
**Requirements:** Graduation from secondary school is required; GED is not accepted. 16 units and the following program of study are required: 3 units of English, 2 units of math, 2 units of science including 1 unit of lab, 2 units of foreign language, 3 units of social studies, 3 units of electives. Required social studies units should include units of history. Required math units must include algebra and geometry. Minimum composite ACT score of 20 (combined SAT score of 810) and minimum 2.5 GPA required. Academic Support Program for applicants not normally admissible. ACT is required; SAT may be substituted. Campus visit and interview recommended. Off-campus interviews available with admissions and alumni representatives.
**Procedure:** Take SAT or ACT by January of 12th year. Visit college for interview by April of 12th year. Suggest filing application by March 1. Application deadline is August 1. Notification of admission on rolling basis. Reply is required by June 1. $200 tuition deposit, refundable until June 1. $50 room deposit, refundable until July 15. Freshmen accepted for terms other than fall.
**Special programs:** Admission may be deferred. Credit may be granted through CEEB Advanced Placement for scores of 3 or higher. Credit may be granted through CLEP subject exams and military experience. Credit and placement may be granted through challenge exams. Early entrance/early admission program. Concurrent enrollment program.
**Transfer students:** Transfer students accepted for terms other than fall. In fall 1993, 12% of all new students were transfers into all classes. 241 transfer applications were received, 223 were accepted. Application deadline is August 1 for fall; January 1 for spring. Minimum 2.5 GPA required of transfers from two year colleges; 2.0 GPA required from four year colleges. Lowest course grade accepted is "C-." Maximum number of transferable credits is 70 semester hours from a two-year school and 96 semester hours from a four-year school. At least 32 semester hours must be completed at the college to receive degree.
**Admissions contact:** Thomas E. McWhertor, M.Div., Director of Admissions. 616 957-6106, 800 688-0122.

**FINANCIAL AID. Available aid:** Pell grants, SEOG, state scholarships and grants, school scholarships and grants, private scholarships and grants, academic merit scholarships, and aid for undergraduate foreign students. PLUS, Stafford Loans (GSL), state loans, school loans, private loans, and SLS. Deferred payment plan and guaranteed tuition.
**Financial aid statistics:** 20% of aid is not need-based. In 1993-94, 95% of all undergraduate applicants received aid; 95% of freshman applicants. Average amounts of aid awarded freshmen: Scholarships and grants, $3,400; loans, $3,100.

**Supporting data/closing dates:** FAFSA/FAF/FFS: Priority filing date is February 15; accepted on rolling basis. School's own aid application: Priority filing date is February 15. Notification of awards begins March 15.
**Financial aid contact:** Wayne Hubers, M.A., Director of Financial Aid. 616 957-6134.

**STUDENT EMPLOYMENT.** College Work/Study Program. Institutional employment. 32% of full-time undergraduates work on campus during school year. Students may expect to earn an average of $1,200 during school year. Off-campus part-time employment opportunities rated "excellent."

**COMPUTER FACILITIES.** 237 IBM/IBM-compatible, Macintosh/Apple, and RISC-/UNIX-based microcomputers; all are networked. Students may access Prime, SUN minicomputer/mainframe systems, BITNET, Internet. Residence halls may be equipped with stand-alone microcomputers, networked microcomputers, networked terminals. Client/LAN operating systems include Apple/Macintosh, DOS, UNIX/XENIX/AIX, Artisoft, LocalTalk/AppleTalk, Novell. Computer languages and software packages include BASIC, C++, COBOL, FORTRAN, HyperCell, Lotus 1-2-3, PageMaker, Paradox, Pascal, Quattro Pro, Telnet, Windows, WordPerfect; 120 in all. Computer facilities are available to all students.
**Fees:** None.
**Hours:** 8 AM-midn. (some 24 hours).

**GRADUATE CAREER DATA.** Graduate school percentages: 1% enter law school. 4% enter medical school. 1% enter dental school. 4% enter graduate business programs. 8% enter graduate arts and sciences programs. 3% enter theological school/seminary. Highest graduate school enrollments: Michigan State U, Purdue U, U of Michigan, U of Notre Dame, Wayne State U, Western Michigan U. 30% of graduates choose careers in business and industry. Companies and businesses that hire graduates: Donnelly Corp., Grand Rapids area schools, Prince Corp.

**PROMINENT ALUMNI/AE.** Richard De Vos, president, Amway; Jay Van Andel, chairman, Amway; James Bere, chairman and CEO, Borg-Warner; James Wyngaarden, former director, National Institutes of Health.

## Center for Creative Studies–College of Art and Design

**Detroit, MI 48202-4034** **313 872-3118**

**1994-95 Costs.** Tuition: $11,760. Room & board: $4,100. Fees, books, misc. academic expenses (school's estimate): $2,540.
**Enrollment.** Undergraduates: 332 men, 193 women (full-time). Freshman class: 419 applicants, 396 accepted, 203 enrolled.
**Test score averages/ranges.** Average SAT scores: 450 verbal, 590 math. Range of SAT scores of middle 50%: 440-450 verbal, 480-490 math. Average ACT scores: 21 composite. Range of ACT scores of middle 50%: 20-21 composite.
**Faculty.** 46 full-time; 116 part-time. 7% of faculty holds doctoral degree. Student/faculty ratio: 11 to 1.
**Selectivity rating.** Less competitive.

**PROFILE.** The Center for Creative Studies, founded in 1926, is a private institution. Its seven-acre campus is located in downtown Detroit near the Institute of Arts.

**Accreditation:** NCACS. Professionally accredited by the National Association of Schools of Art and Design.
**Religious orientation:** Center for Creative Studies-College of Art and Design is nonsectarian; no religious requirements.
**Library:** Collections totaling over 22,000 volumes, 75 periodical subscriptions, and 60,000 microform items.
**Special facilities/museums:** Art gallery.

**STUDENT BODY. Undergraduate profile:** 87% are state residents; 63% are transfers. 5% Asian-American, 9% Black, 2% Hispanic, 1% Native American, 80% White, 3% Other. Average age of undergraduates is 23.
**Freshman profile:** 5% of freshmen who took SAT scored 700 or over on verbal, 5% scored 700 or over on math; 10% scored 600 or over on verbal, 10% scored 600 or over on math; 36% scored 500 or over on verbal, 31% scored 500 or over on math; 67% scored 400 or over on verbal, 57% scored 400 or over on math; 83% scored 300 or over on verbal, 79% scored 300 or over on math. 2% of freshmen who took ACT scored 30 or over on composite; 24% scored 24 or over on composite; 58% scored 18 or over on composite; 92% scored 12 or over on composite; 96% scored 6 or over on composite. 25% of accepted applicants took SAT; 67% took ACT. 78% of freshmen come from public schools.
**Undergraduate achievement:** 86% of fall 1992 freshmen returned for fall 1993 term. 45% of entering class graduated.
**Foreign students:** 16 students are from out of the country. Countries represented include Canada, Japan, Korea, Malaysia, and the Philippines; 15 in all.

**PROGRAMS OF STUDY. Degrees:** B.F.A.
**Majors:** Applied Photography, Art Direction, Ceramics, Fabric Design, Fine Arts Photography, Furniture Design, Glass, Graphic Design, Illustration, Interior/Environmental Design, Medical Photography, Metals/Jewelry, Painting, Printmaking, Product Design, Sculpture, Transportation Design.
**Distribution of degrees:** The majors with the highest enrollment are art direction, graphic design, and illustration.
**Requirements:** General education requirement.
**Academic regulations:** Minimum 2.0 GPA must be maintained.
**Special:** Minors offered in art history and art therapy. Self-designed majors. Double majors. Independent study. Internships. Member of Alliance of Independent Colleges of Art and Design (AICAD); exchange possible with over 25 schools. New York Studio Program. Study abroad in France, Italy, Japan, and other countries.
**Academic Assistance:** Remedial reading, writing, and study skills.

**ADMISSIONS. Academic basis for candidate selection** (in order of priority): Secondary school record, standardized test scores, essay, school's recommendation, class rank.
**Nonacademic basis for candidate selection:** Particular talent or ability is emphasized. Character and personality are important. Extracurricular participation is considered.
**Requirements:** Graduation from secondary school is required; GED is accepted. 16 units and the following program of study are recommended: 4 units of English, 2 units of math, 2 units of science, 1 unit of foreign language, 2 units of social studies, 2 units of history. Minimum SAT scores of 440 verbal and 470 math (composite ACT score of 19) and 2.5 GPA required. Portfolio required of art program applicants. Conditional admission possible for applicants not meeting standard requirements. SAT or ACT is required. Campus visit and interview required. Off-campus interview may be arranged with an admissions representative in the Detroit area.
**Procedure:** Take SAT or ACT by June 30 of 12th year. Notification of admission on rolling basis. Reply is required by July 31. $200 tuition deposit, refundable until May 1. $200 room deposit, refundable until July 1. Freshmen accepted for terms other than fall.
**Special programs:** Admission may be deferred two years. ACT required for placement and counseling. Credit and/or placement may be granted through CEEB Advanced Placement exams for scores of 4 or higher. Credit and/or placement may be granted through CLEP subject exams. Credit and placement may be granted through ACT PEP and challenge exams. Concurrent enrollment program.
**Transfer students:** Transfer students accepted for terms other than fall. In fall 1993, 63% of all new students were transfers into all classes. 309 transfer applications were received, 222 were accepted. Application deadline is July 1 for fall; December 1 for spring. Minimum 2.0 GPA required. Lowest course grade accepted is "C." Maximum number of transferable credits is 72 semester hours. At least 72 semester hours must be completed at the college to receive degree.
**Admissions contact:** Eddie Kent Tallent, Assistant Dean for Enrollment Services. 313 872-3118, extension 204.

**FINANCIAL AID. Available aid:** Pell grants, SEOG, state scholarships and grants, school scholarships and grants, private scholarships and grants, and academic merit scholarships. PLUS, Stafford Loans (GSL), state loans, and SLS. AMS and deferred payment plan. Michigan Education Trust.
**Financial aid statistics:** In 1993-94, 85% of all undergraduate applicants received aid; 80% of freshman applicants. Average amounts of aid awarded freshmen: Scholarships and grants, $3,400; loans, $2,625.
**Supporting data/closing dates:** FAFSA/FAF/FFS: Priority filing date is February 15. State aid form: Priority filing date is February 15. Income tax forms: Accepted on rolling basis. Notification of awards begins April 21.
**Financial aid contact:** Eddie Kent Tallent, B.A., Assistant Dean for Enrollment Services. 313 872-3118, extension 273.

## Central Michigan University

**Mount Pleasant, MI 48859** **517 774-4000**

**1994-95 Costs.** Tuition: $2,725 (state residents), $6,660 (out-of-state). Room & board: $3,836. Fees, books, misc. academic expenses (school's estimate): $760.
**Enrollment.** Undergraduates: 5,866 men, 7,362 women (full-time). Freshman class: 7,304 applicants, 6,263 accepted, 2,539 enrolled. Graduate enrollment: 709 men, 1,125 women.
**Test score averages/ranges.** Average ACT scores: 21 English, 20 math, 21 composite. Range of ACT scores of middle 50%: 18-23 English, 18-23 math.
**Faculty.** 662 full-time; 146 part-time. 70% of faculty holds highest degree in specific field. Student/faculty ratio: 20 to 1.
**Selectivity rating.** Less competitive.

**PROFILE.** Central Michigan, founded in 1892, is a public university. Programs are offered through the College of Arts and Sciences and the Schools of Business Administration; Education, Health, and Human Services; Extended Learning; and Graduate Studies. Its 854-acre campus is located in Mount Pleasant, 60 miles from Saginaw.

**Accreditation:** NCACS. Professionally accredited by the American Assembly of Collegiate Schools of Business, the American Speech-Language-Hearing Association, the National Association of Schools of Music, the National Council for Accreditation of Teacher Education, the National Recreation and Park Association.
**Religious orientation:** Central Michigan University is nonsectarian; no religious requirements.
**Library:** Collections totaling over 843,656 volumes, 4,940 periodical subscriptions, and 1,061,435 microform items.
**Special facilities/museums:** Cultural and natural history center, language lab.
**Athletic facilities:** Basketball, racquetball, and volleyball courts, swimming pool, recreation facility, gymnastics, power lifting, weight, and wrestling rooms, spa, sauna, bowling center, gymnasium, football, soccer, and softball fields.

**STUDENT BODY. Undergraduate profile:** 98% are state residents; 31% are transfers. 1% Asian-American, 3% Black, 1% Hispanic, 1% Native American, 93% White, 1% Other. Average age of undergraduates is 21.
**Freshman profile:** 1% of freshmen who took ACT scored 30 or over on English, 1% scored 30 or over on math, 1% scored 30 or over on composite; 24% scored 24 or over on English, 19% scored 24 or over on math, 22% scored 24 or over on composite; 78% scored 18 or over on English, 73% scored 18 or over on math, 87% scored 18 or over on composite; 99% scored 12 or over on English, 100% scored 12 or over on math, 100% scored 12 or over on composite; 100% scored 6 or over on English. 95% of accepted applicants took ACT.
**Undergraduate achievement:** 73% of fall 1992 freshmen returned for fall 1993 term. 16% of entering class graduated.
**Foreign students:** 154 students are from out of the country. Countries represented include Canada, China, India, Japan, Taiwan, and Thailand; 47 in all.

**PROGRAMS OF STUDY. Degrees:** B.A., B.Appl.Arts, B.F.A., B.Indiv.Studies, B.Mus., B.Mus.Ed., B.S., B.S.Bus.Admin., B.S.Ed.
**Majors:** Accounting, Actuarial Sciences, Administrative Systems, Allied Health Education/Administration, Anthropology, Applied Health Education/Administration, Art, Biology, Broadcast/Cinematic Arts, Business Administration/Management, Business Education, Chemistry, Child Development, Communication Disorders, Computer/Information Sciences, Court/Conference Reporting, Dietetics, Earth Science, Economics, Education, Electronics Engineering Technology, Elementary Education, English, Family Economics/Management, Finance, Food Service Administration, French, Geography, Geology, German, Health Fitness/Health Promotion, History, Home Economics, Hospitality Services Administration, Human Resources Management, Individual/Family Studies, Industrial Education, Industrial Supervision/Management, Industrial Technology, Interior Design, Interpersonal/Public Communication, Journalism, Language Arts, Linguistics, Management, Management Information Systems, Management Science, Manufacturing Technology, Marketing Management/Research, Mathematics, Mechanical Engineering Technology, Music, Philosophy, Physical Education, Physical Sciences, Physics, Political Science/Government, Production/Operations Management, Psychology, Public Health Education, Recreation, Religion, Retailing Management, School Health Education, Science, Secondary Education, Social Sciences, Sociology, Spanish, Speech/Debate/Forensics, Sports Medicine, Sports Studies, Statistics, Textiles/Clothing, Theatre/Interpretation.
**Distribution of degrees:** The majors with the highest enrollment are business, education, and psychology; religion and philosophy have the lowest.
**Requirements:** General education requirement.
**Academic regulations:** Freshmen must maintain minimum 1.0 GPA; sophomores, 1.7 GPA; juniors, 1.8 GPA; seniors, 1.95 GPA.
**Special:** Minors offered in most majors. Double majors. Dual degrees. Independent study. Pass/fail grading option. Internships. Cooperative education programs. Graduate school at which undergraduates may take graduate-level courses. Preprofessional programs in law, medicine, veterinary science, pharmacy, dentistry, optometry, architecture, conservation, engineering, forestry, nursing, occupational therapy, osteopathic, physical therapy. 2-2 inter-university engineering program with Michigan Tech U. Member of consortium with Michigan Molecular Inst and Michigan Tech U. Teacher certification in early childhood, elementary, secondary, special education, and bilingual/bicultural education. Study abroad in Australia, Austria, Canada, England, France, Germany, Japan, Mexico, and Spain. ROTC.
**Honors:** Honors program. Honor societies.
**Academic Assistance:** Remedial reading and study skills. Nonremedial tutoring.

**STUDENT LIFE. Housing:** All freshmen and sophomores under age 21 must live on campus unless living with family. Coed, women's, and men's dorms. School-owned/operated apartments. On-campus married-student housing. 39% of students live in college housing.
**Social atmosphere:** The student newspaper reports, "CMU students like to enjoy themselves and there is a wide diversity in the sort of things they like to do." Greek organizations are influential groups at the university. On-campus student hangouts include the Bovee University Center and Park Library; the Bird Bar and Grill, Wayside Central, and Nick's Saloon are some of the favorite off-campus destinations. Well attended events include Mayfest, Western Weekend, the Indian Powwow, and football games.
**Services and counseling/handicapped student services:** Placement services. Health service. Women's center. Day care. Legal aid office. Counseling services for minority students. Personal and psychological counseling. Career and academic guidance services. Physically disabled student services. Learning disabled services. Notetaking services. Tape recorders. Reader services for the blind.
**Campus organizations:** Undergraduate student government. Student newspaper (Central Michigan Life, published three times/week). Literary magazine. Yearbook. Radio and TV stations. Chorus, band, orchestra, drama group, debating, volunteer program, tenants union, departmental, political, professional, and service groups, 209 organizations in all. 17 fraternities, 14 chapter houses; 14 sororities, 12 chapter houses. 12% of men join a fraternity. 10% of women join a sorority.
**Religious organizations:** Several religious groups.
**Minority/foreign student organizations:** Several minority student groups.

**ATHLETICS. Physical education requirements:** Four one-hour activity courses required in some curricula.
**Intercollegiate competition:** 3% of students participate. Baseball (M), basketball (M,W), cheerleading (M,W), cross-country (M,W), field hockey (W), football (M), gymnastics (W), soccer (M), softball (W), track (indoor) (M,W), track (outdoor) (M,W), track and field (indoor) (M,W), track and field (outdoor) (M,W), volleyball (W), wrestling (M). Member of Mid-American Conference, NCAA Division I, NCAA Division I-A for football.
**Intramural and club sports:** 75% of students participate. Intramural basketball, billiards, bowling, cross-country, flag football, floor hockey, golf, indoor soccer, power lifting, racquetball, soccer, softball, swimming, table tennis, tennis, volleyball, walleyball, weight training, wrestling. Men's club fencing, ice hockey, martial arts, racquetball, rugby, skiing, swimming, weight lifting. Women's club fencing, gymnastics, martial arts, racquetball, skiing, soccer, swimming, weight lifting.

**ADMISSIONS. Academic basis for candidate selection** (in order of priority): Secondary school record, standardized test scores, class rank, school's recommendation, essay.
**Nonacademic basis for candidate selection:** Character and personality and extracurricular participation are considered.
**Requirements:** Graduation from secondary school is required; GED is not accepted. 13 units and the following program of study are required: 4 units of English, 3 units of math, 3 units of science, 3 units of social studies. Audition required of music program applicants. Freshman Advancement Program for applicants not normally admissible. ACT is required. Campus visit recommended.
**Procedure:** Take ACT by October of 12th year. Suggest filing application by fall; no deadline. Notification of admission on rolling basis. $80 tuition deposit required, $55 of which is refundable until June 1. $400 room deposit, refundable until June 20. Freshmen accepted for terms other than fall.
**Special programs:** Admission may be deferred one year. Credit and/or placement may be granted through CEEB Advanced Placement exams for scores of 3 or higher. Credit may be granted through CLEP general and subject exams. Credit and placement may be granted through military experience. Early entrance/early admission program. Concurrent enrollment program.
**Transfer students:** Transfer students accepted for terms other than fall. In fall 1993, 31% of all new students were transfers into all classes. 2,075 transfer applications were received, 1,583 were accepted. Minimum 2.5 GPA. Lowest course grade accepted is "C-." Maximum number of transferable credits is 94 semester hours. At least 30 semester hours must be completed at the university to receive degree.
**Admissions contact:** Michael A. Owens, M.A., Director of Admissions. 517 774-3076.

**FINANCIAL AID. Available aid:** Pell grants, SEOG, state scholarships and grants, school scholarships and grants, private scholarships and grants, ROTC scholarships, academic merit scholarships, and athletic scholarships. Perkins Loans (NDSL), PLUS, Stafford Loans (GSL), state loans, school loans, private loans, and SLS. AMS. Installment payment plan for housing.
**Financial aid statistics:** 35% of aid is not need-based. In 1993-94, 93% of all undergraduate applicants received aid; 80% of freshman applicants. Average amounts of aid awarded freshmen: Scholarships and grants, $1,730; loans, $2,050.
**Supporting data/closing dates:** FAFSA/FAF/FFS: Priority filing date is February 15. Notification of awards on rolling basis.
**Financial aid contact:** Sheryl T. Spivey, M.A., Director of Scholarships and Financial Aid. 517 774-3674.

**STUDENT EMPLOYMENT.** College Work/Study Program. Institutional employment. 30% of full-time undergraduates work on campus during school year. Students may expect to earn an average of $1,000 during school year. Off-campus part-time employment opportunities rated "fair."

**COMPUTER FACILITIES.** 600 IBM/IBM-compatible, Macintosh/Apple, and RISC-/UNIX-based microcomputers. Students may access IBM minicomputer/mainframe systems. Residence halls may be equipped with stand-alone microcomputers, networked terminals, modems. Client/LAN operating systems include Apple/Macintosh, DOS. Computer languages and software packages include APL, BASIC, COBOL, FORTRAN, ImSL, Pascal, PL/1, SAS, SPSS-X; 21 in all. Computer facilities are available to all students.
**Fees:** None.

**PROMINENT ALUMNI/AE.** Robert Griffin, Michigan supreme court justice; Dick Enberg, NBC sportscaster; Lem Tucker, CBS newscaster; Dan Majerle, professional basketball player, Phoenix Suns.

# Cleary College

**Ypsilanti, MI 48197** **313 483-4400**

**1994-95 Costs.** Tuition: $6,300. Housing: None. Fees, books, misc. academic expenses (school's estimate): $565.
**Enrollment.** Undergraduates: 75 men, 125 women (full-time). Freshman class: 35 applicants, 35 accepted, 35 enrolled.
**Test score averages/ranges.** N/A.
**Faculty.** 15 full-time; 40 part-time. 5% of faculty holds doctoral degree. Student/faculty ratio: 15 to 1.
**Selectivity rating.** N/A.

**PROFILE.** Cleary is a private college of business administration. It was founded as a school of penmanship in 1883, became a Cleary Business College in 1891, and assumed its present name in 1933. Its 22-acre campus is located in Ypsilanti, 30 miles from Detroit.

**Accreditation:** NCACS.
**Religious orientation:** Cleary College is nonsectarian; no religious requirements.
**Library:** Collections totaling over 7,000 volumes, 257 periodical subscriptions, and 1,800 microform items.
**Special facilities/museums:** Word processing lab, tax research center.
**Athletic facilities:** Gymnasium.

**STUDENT BODY. Undergraduate profile:** 92% are state residents; 40% are transfers. 3% Asian-American, 25% Black, 2% Hispanic, 70% White. Average age of undergraduates is 29.
**Freshman profile:** Majority of accepted applicants took SAT. 90% of freshmen come from public schools.
**Undergraduate achievement:** 65% of fall 1992 freshmen returned for fall 1993 term. 50% of entering class graduated.
**Foreign students:** 18 students are from out of the country. Countries represented include Canada, China, India, Japan, Mexico, and Pakistan; 11 in all.

**PROGRAMS OF STUDY. Degrees:** B.Bus.Admin.
**Majors:** Accounting, Business Computer Systems, Management, Marketing.
**Distribution of degrees:** The majors with the highest enrollment are management, accounting, and marketing.
**Requirements:** General education requirement.
**Academic regulations:** Minimum 2.0 GPA must be maintained.
**Special:** Associate's degrees offered. Double majors. Independent study. Accelerated study. Internships. Cooperative education programs. ROTC and AFROTC at U of Michigan.
**Academic Assistance:** Remedial math. Nonremedial tutoring.

**ADMISSIONS. Academic basis for candidate selection** (in order of priority): Secondary school record, essay, school's recommendation, class rank, standardized test scores.
**Nonacademic basis for candidate selection:** Extracurricular participation is important.
**Requirements:** Graduation from secondary school is required; GED is accepted. 16 units and the following program of study are recommended: 6 units of English, 4 units of math, 2 units of science, 4 units of social studies. ACT is recommended; SAT may be substituted. Campus visit and interview recommended.
**Procedure:** Take SAT or ACT by January of 12th year. Visit college for interview by spring of 12th year. Notification of admission on rolling basis. Freshmen accepted for terms other than fall.

**Special programs:** Admission may be deferred one year. Credit and/or placement may be granted through CEEB Advanced Placement exams for scores of 4 or higher. Placement may be granted through CLEP general and subject exams. Credit may be granted through challenge exams and military and life experience. Concurrent enrollment program.
**Transfer students:** Transfer students accepted for terms other than fall. In fall 1993, 40% of all new students were transfers into all classes. 70 transfer applications were received, 70 were accepted. Application deadline is rolling for fall; rolling for spring. Minimum 2.0 GPA recommended. Lowest course grade accepted is "C." Maximum number of transferable credits is 90 quarter hours. At least 45 quarter hours must be completed at the college to receive degree.
**Admissions contact:** Donna Franklin, M.A., Dean of Admissions. 313 483-4400.

**FINANCIAL AID. Available aid:** Pell grants, SEOG, state grants, school scholarships, and private scholarships. Perkins Loans (NDSL), PLUS, Stafford Loans (GSL), state loans, and private loans. Deferred payment plan.
**Financial aid statistics:** In 1993-94, 60% of all freshman applicants received aid. Average amounts of aid awarded freshmen: Scholarships and grants, $1,500; loans, $2,298.
**Supporting data/closing dates:** FAFSA. School's own aid application: Accepted on rolling basis. Notification of awards on rolling basis.
**Financial aid contact:** Rose M. Smith, Director of Financial Aid. 313 483 -4400.

## Concordia College

**Ann Arbor, MI 48105 313 995-7300**

**1993-94 Costs.** Tuition: $10,238. Room & board: $4,180. Fees, books, misc. academic expenses (school's estimate): $300.
**Enrollment.** Undergraduates: 218 men, 344 women (full-time). Freshman class: 180 applicants, 171 accepted, 74 enrolled.
**Test score averages/ranges.** Average SAT scores: 485 verbal, 500 math. Range of SAT scores of middle 50%: 430-510 verbal, 460-540 math. Average ACT scores: 19 English, 22 math, 20 composite. Range of ACT scores of middle 50%: 18-24 English, 18-24 math.
**Faculty.** 42 full-time; 17 part-time. 55% of faculty holds doctoral degree. Student/faculty ratio: 14 to 1.
**Selectivity rating.** Less competitive.

**PROFILE.** Concordia, founded in 1962, is a church-affiliated, liberal arts college. Its 234-acre campus is located in a residential area of Ann Arbor.

**Accreditation:** NCACS.
**Religious orientation:** Concordia College is affiliated with the Lutheran Church - Missouri Synod; six semesters of religion required.
**Library:** Collections totaling over 100,000 volumes, 1,600 periodical subscriptions, and 12,000 microform items.
**Athletic facilities:** Gymnasium, weight room, track, fitness trail, basketball, sand volleyball, tennis, and volleyball courts, baseball, soccer, and softball fields.

**STUDENT BODY. Undergraduate profile:** 87% are state residents; 35% are transfers. 10% Black, 90% White. Average age of undergraduates is 23.
**Freshman profile:** 3% of freshmen who took SAT scored 600 or over on verbal, 32% scored 600 or over on math; 44% scored 500 or over on verbal, 57% scored 500 or over on math; 84% scored 400 or over on verbal, 81% scored 400 or over on math; 100% scored 300 or over on verbal, 97% scored 300 or over on math. 3% of freshmen who took ACT scored 30 or over on English, 3% scored 30 or over on composite; 30% scored 24 or over on English, 23% scored 24 or over on math, 31% scored 24 or over on composite; 72% scored 18 or over on English, 73% scored 18 or over on math, 80% scored 18 or over on composite; 100% scored 12 or over on English, 99% scored 12 or over on math, 100% scored 12 or over on composite; 100% scored 6 or over on math. 1% of accepted applicants took SAT; 99% took ACT. 81% of freshmen come from public schools.
**Undergraduate achievement:** 70% of fall 1992 freshmen returned for fall 1993 term. 54% of entering class graduated.
**Foreign students:** One student is from out of the country.

**PROGRAMS OF STUDY. Degrees:** B.A.
**Majors:** Art, Biblical Languages, Biology, Business Administration/Management, Communication, English, General Science, History/Political Science, Human Resource Management, Humanities, Mathematics, Music, Philosophy, Physical Education, Psychology, Religious Studies, Sociology, Sports Management.
**Distribution of degrees:** The majors with the highest enrollment are human resource management and business administration/management.
**Requirements:** General education requirement.
**Academic regulations:** Minimum 2.0 GPA must be maintained.
**Special:** Minors offered in most majors and in classics, earth science, German, and history. Associate's degrees offered. Double majors. Independent study. Pass/fail grading option. Internships. Graduate school at which undergraduates may take graduate-level courses. Preprofessional programs in law, medicine, and dentistry. Teacher certification in early childhood, elementary, and secondary education. Certification in specific subject areas. Study abroad in Austria (U of Vienna) and England (Oak Hill Coll). ROTC and AFROTC at U of Michigan.
**Academic Assistance:** Remedial reading, writing, math, and study skills. Nonremedial tutoring.

**ADMISSIONS. Academic basis for candidate selection** (in order of priority): Secondary school record, standardized test scores, class rank, school's recommendation, essay.
**Nonacademic basis for candidate selection:** Character and personality are emphasized. Extracurricular participation and particular talent or ability are important.
**Requirements:** Graduation from secondary school is required; GED is accepted. 15 units and the following program of study are required: 3 units of English, 1 unit of math, 1 unit of science, 1 unit of social studies, 9 units of electives. Minimum combined ACT score of 18, minimum GPA 2.25 required. Academic Development Program for applicants not normally admissible. ACT is required; SAT may be substituted. Campus visit and interview recommended. Off-campus interviews available with an admissions representative.
**Procedure:** Take SAT or ACT by October of 12th year. Visit college for interview by February of 12th year. Application deadline is September 1. Notification of admission on rolling basis. rolling. $125 tuition deposit, refundable until May 1. $100 room deposit, refundable until September 1. Freshmen accepted for terms other than fall.
**Special programs:** Admission may be deferred one year. Credit and/or placement may be granted through CEEB Advanced Placement exams for scores of 4 or higher. Credit and/or placement may be granted through CLEP general and subject exams. Credit and placement may be granted through ACT PEP and challenge exams and military and life experience. Concurrent enrollment program.
**Transfer students:** Transfer students accepted for terms other than fall. In fall 1993, 35% of all new students were transfers into all classes. 66 transfer applications were received, 54 were accepted. Application deadline is September 1 of year student will attend. Minimum 2.0 GPA recommended. Lowest course grade accepted is "C." Maximum number of transferable credits is 78 semester hours from a two-year school and 98 semester hours from a four-year school. At least 30 semester hours must be completed at the college to receive degree.
**Admissions contact:** Fred A. Schebor, M.A., Director of Admissions. 313 995-7322.

**FINANCIAL AID. Available aid:** Pell grants, SEOG, state scholarships and grants, school scholarships and grants, private scholarships and grants, ROTC scholarships, academic merit scholarships, and athletic scholarships. Perkins Loans (NDSL), PLUS, Stafford Loans (GSL), state loans, school loans, private loans, and SLS. Deferred payment plan.
**Financial aid statistics:** 10% of aid is not need-based. In 1993-94, 98% of all undergraduate applicants received aid; 91% of freshman applicants. Average amounts of aid awarded freshmen: Scholarships and grants, $3,060; loans, $2,541.
**Supporting data/closing dates:** FAFSA: Priority filing date is February 15. FAF: Priority filing date is April 15. School's own aid application: Priority filing date is May 30. Income tax forms: Priority filing date is June 1; accepted on rolling basis. Notification of awards on rolling basis.
**Financial aid contact:** Brian Heinemann, M.Ed., Financial Aid Director. 313 995-7408.

## Eastern Michigan University

**Ypsilanti, MI 48197 313 487-1849**

**1994-95 Costs.** Tuition: $2,483 (state residents), $6,360 (out-of-state). Room & board: $4,031. Fees, books, misc. academic expenses (school's estimate): $835.
**Enrollment.** Undergraduates: 5,524 men, 7,445 women (full-time). Freshman class: 6,693 applicants, 5,423 accepted, 2,329 enrolled. Graduate enrollment: 1,975 men, 3,671 women.
**Test score averages/ranges.** Average SAT scores: 435 verbal, 475 math. Average ACT scores: 21 composite.
**Faculty.** 687 full-time; 359 part-time. 90% of faculty holds doctoral degree. Student/faculty ratio: 24 to 1.
**Selectivity rating.** Less competitive.

**PROFILE.** Eastern Michigan, founded in 1849, is a public, multipurpose university. Programs are offered through the Colleges of Arts and Sciences, Business, Education, Human Services, and Technology. Its 460-acre campus is located in Ypsilanti, seven miles from Ann Arbor.

**Accreditation:** NCACS. Professionally accredited by the American Assembly of Collegiate Schools of Business, the American Dietetic Association, the American Home Economics Association, the American Medical Association (CAHEA), the American Speech-Language-Hearing Association, the Council on Social Work Education, the National Association of Schools of Music, the National Council for Accreditation of Teacher Education, the National League for Nursing.
**Religious orientation:** Eastern Michigan University is nonsectarian; no religious requirements.
**Library:** Collections totaling over 800,935 volumes, 4,096 periodical subscriptions, and 692,593 microform items.
**Special facilities/museums:** Intermedia art gallery, paint research center.
**Athletic facilities:** Gymnasium, basketball, racquetball, tennis, and volleyball courts, swimming pools, weight room, tracks, sauna, bowling lanes, athletic fields, stadium, field house.

**STUDENT BODY. Undergraduate profile:** 90% are state residents; 45% are transfers. 2% Asian-American, 9% Black, 2% Hispanic, 1% Native American, 84% White, 2% Other. Average age of undergraduates is 22.
**Freshman profile:** 1% of freshmen who took SAT scored 700 or over on verbal, 1% scored 700 or over on math; 6% scored 600 or over on verbal, 7% scored 600 or over on math; 31% scored 500 or over on verbal, 45% scored 500 or over on math; 79% scored 400 or over on verbal, 85% scored 400 or over on math; 97% scored 300 or over on verbal, 96% scored 300 or over on math. 23% of accepted applicants took SAT; 91% took ACT. 92% of freshmen come from public schools.
**Undergraduate achievement:** 70% of fall 1992 freshmen returned for fall 1993 term. 41% of entering class graduated. 17% of students who completed a degree program went on to graduate study within one year.
**Foreign students:** 556 students are from out of the country. Countries represented include China, India, Japan, Malaysia, Taiwan, and Thailand; 70 in all.

**PROGRAMS OF STUDY. Degrees:** B.A., B.A.Ed., B.Art, B.Bus.Admin., B.Bus.Ed., B.F.A., B.Mus., B.Mus.Ed., B.Mus.Ther., B.S., B.S.Nurs.
**Majors:** Accounting, Africa Area Studies, Anthropology, Applied Science, Art, Arts Management, Asian/Far East Area Studies, Aviation Management Technology, Biochemistry, Biology, Business Computer Systems, Business Economics, Business French, Business German, Business Spanish, Chemistry, Communications Technology, Comparative Economic Systems, Computer-Aided Design, Computer-Aided Manufacturing, Computer Science, Construction Technology, Consumer Affairs, Consumer Services in Home

Economics, Criminal Justice/Criminology, Dietetics, Distributive Education, Dramatic Arts, Early Childhood Education, Early Elementary Education, Earth Science, Economics, Ecosystems Biology, Education of Physically/Otherwise Health Impaired, Education of the Emotionally Impaired, Education of the Hearing Impaired, Education of the Mentally Impaired, Education of the Speech/Language Impaired, Education of the Visually Impaired, Energy Management Technology, English, English/American Language/Literature, Executive Assistant, Facilities Management, Family Life, Fashion Merchandising, Finance, Food in Business, French, French Language/Literature, General Business, General Business Entrepreneurship, General Home Economics, General Science, Geography, Geology, German, German Language/Literature, Governmental Economics, Graphic Communication, Health Administration, History, Home Economics Education, Hospitality Management, Human Resources Administration/Management, Human Resources Management, Industrial Arts Education, Industrial Technology, Industrial Vocational Education, Instrumental Music Education, Intergovernmental Relations/Public Development, Interior Design/Housing, Japanese Language/Culture, Journalism, Labor Economics, Labor Studies, Land Use Analysis, Language/International Trade, Language/World Business, Later Elementary Education, Latin America Area Studies, Legal Assistant, Linguistics, Literature, Literature/Library Science/Drama for the Young, Management, Manufacturing Technology, Marketing, Mathematics, Medical Technology, Metallurgical Chemistry, Microbiology, Middle East/North Africa Area Studies, Music, Music/Liberal Arts, Music Therapy, Nursing, Occupational Therapy, Office Administrator, Office Education, Performance, Philosophy, Physical Science, Physics, Physiology, Plastics Technology, Political Science, Polymers/Coating Technology, Production Systems Analysis, Psychology, Public Administration, Public Law/Government, Public Relations, Public Sector Management, Radio/Television/Film, Secondary Education, Social Science, Social Work, Sociology, Soviet Union Area Studies, Spanish, Spanish Language/Literature, Special Education, Speech, Speech/Dramatic Arts, Strategy/Control, Supervisory Management, Theoretical/Quantitative Economics, Urban Affairs/Community Development, Urban/Regional Planning, Vocal/Keyboard Education, Word Processing Administration, Written Communications.

**Distribution of degrees:** The majors with the highest enrollment are education, marketing, and psychology.

**Requirements:** General education requirement.

**Academic regulations:** Minimum 2.0 GPA must be maintained.

**Special:** Minors offered in most majors. Self-designed majors. Double majors. Dual degrees. Independent study. Pass/fail grading option. Internships. Cooperative education programs. Graduate school at which undergraduates may take graduate-level courses. Preprofessional programs in law, medicine, veterinary science, pharmacy, dentistry, optometry, mortuary science, and podiatry. Washington Semester. Teacher certification in early childhood, elementary, secondary, special education, vo-tech, and bilingual/bicultural education. Certification in specific subject areas. Study abroad in France, Mexico, Middle Eastern countries, Spain, and other countries. ROTC. NROTC and AFROTC at U of Michigan.

**Honors:** Phi Beta Kappa. Honors program. Honor societies.

**Academic Assistance:** Nonremedial tutoring.

**STUDENT LIFE. Housing:** All freshmen and sophomores must live on campus unless living with family. Coed and women's dorms. Sorority and fraternity housing. School-owned/operated apartments. Off-campus privately-owned housing. Both on-campus and off-campus married-student housing. 16% of students live in college housing.

**Social atmosphere:** On campus, students frequent McKenny Union and Eastern Eateries. Students gather off campus at Theo's, the Tower Inn, and Abe's Coney Island. Groups with widespread influence on campus include Greeks, athletes, and the multicultural center. One of the most popular campus events is Homecoming. According to the student newspaper, "Very few students feel the need to hang around campus for fun; instead, they go to Ann Arbor or Detroit. The cultural life at EMU is diverse, more so than any other university in Michigan, but most campus events are attended poorly."

**Services and counseling/handicapped student services:** Placement services. Health service. Women's center. Day care. Counseling services for minority, military, veteran, and older students. Birth control, personal, and psychological counseling. Career and academic guidance services. Religious counseling. Physically disabled student services. Learning disabled services. Notetaking services. Tape recorders. Tutors. Reader services for the blind.

**Campus organizations:** Undergraduate student government. Student newspaper (Eastern Echo, published three times/week). Yearbook. Radio station. Debating, sailing and scuba clubs, yoga club, Campus Republicans, Young Democrats, academic/professional clubs, athletic/recreational groups, cultural/entertainment groups, 150 organizations in all. 27 fraternities, six chapter houses; 16 sororities, three chapter houses. 6% of men join a fraternity. 6% of women join a sorority.

**Religious organizations:** Bahai, Gospel Choir, Holy Trinity Peer Ministers, Intervarsity Christian Fellowship, Muslim Student Association, United Ministries in Higher Education, Hillel, BASIC, Campus Crusade for Christ, Christians in Action.

**Minority/foreign student organizations:** Black Greek Council, Hispanic Student Association, Native American Association, NAACP. International Student Association, Chinese, Hellenic, Indian, Japanese, Korean, Malaysian, Nigerian, Pakistani, Thai, and Turkish student groups.

**ATHLETICS. Physical education requirements:** Two semesters of physical education required.

**Intercollegiate competition:** 2% of students participate. Baseball (M), basketball (M,W), cross-country (M,W), diving (M,W), football (M,W), golf (M), gymnastics (W), soccer (M), softball (W), swimming (M,W), tennis (M,W), track (indoor) (M,W), track (outdoor) (M,W), track and field (indoor) (M,W), track and field (outdoor) (M,W), volleyball (W), wrestling (M). Member of Mid-America Conference, NCAA Division I, NCAA Division I-A for football.

**Intramural and club sports:** Men's club cheerleading, ice hockey, rifle. Women's club cheerleading.

**ADMISSIONS. Academic basis for candidate selection** (in order of priority): Secondary school record, standardized test scores, school's recommendation, essay, class rank.

**Nonacademic basis for candidate selection:** Extracurricular participation and particular talent or ability are considered.

**Requirements:** Graduation from secondary school is required; GED is accepted. 15 units and the following program of study are recommended: 4 units of English, 3 units of math, 3 units of science, 2 units of foreign language, 2 units of social studies, 1 unit of history. Portfolio required of art program applicants. Audition required of music program applicants. Summer Incentives Program, and Promote Academic Survival and Success program for applicants not normally admissible. SAT or ACT is required. Campus visit recommended. Off-campus interviews available with an admissions representative.

**Procedure:** Take SAT or ACT by April of 12th year. Visit college for interview by January of 12th year. Application deadline is July. Notification of admission on rolling basis. Reply is required by September. $100 room deposit, refundable until May. Freshmen accepted for terms other than fall.

**Special programs:** Admission may be deferred. Credit and/or placement may be granted through CEEB Advanced Placement exams for scores of 3 or higher. Credit and/or placement may be granted through CLEP general and subject exams. Credit may be granted through military experience. Placement may be granted through ACT PEP exams. Credit and placement may be granted through challenge exams. Concurrent enrollment program.

**Transfer students:** Transfer students accepted for terms other than fall. In fall 1993, 45% of all new students were transfers into all classes. 3,383 transfer applications were received, 2,688 were accepted. Application deadline is July 1 for fall; April 11 for spring. Minimum 2.0 GPA required. Lowest course grade accepted is "C." Maximum number of transferable credits is 75 semester hours. At least 30 semester hours must be completed at the university to receive degree.

**Admissions contact:** M. Dolan Evanovich, M.A., Director of Admissions. 313 487-3060.

**FINANCIAL AID. Available aid:** Pell grants, SEOG, state scholarships and grants, school scholarships and grants, private scholarships and grants, ROTC scholarships, academic merit scholarships, athletic scholarships, and aid for undergraduate foreign students. Disadvantaged Nursing Scholarships. Perkins Loans (NDSL), PLUS, Stafford Loans (GSL), Health Professions Loans, state loans, school loans, private loans, and SLS. Education Plan Inc. and deferred payment plan.

**Financial aid statistics:** In 1993-94, 75% of all undergraduate applicants received aid; 75% of freshman applicants. Average amounts of aid awarded freshmen: Scholarships and grants, $2,500; loans, $2,000.

**Supporting data/closing dates:** FAFSA: Priority filing date is January 31; accepted on rolling basis. Income tax forms: Accepted on rolling basis. Notification of awards begins in April.

**Financial aid contact:** Judy Benfield-Tatum, M.A., Director of Financial Aid. 313 487-0455.

**STUDENT EMPLOYMENT.** College Work/Study Program. Institutional employment. 44% of full-time undergraduates work on campus during school year. Students may expect to earn an average of $1,800 during school year. Off-campus part-time employment opportunities rated "excellent."

**COMPUTER FACILITIES.** 500 IBM/IBM-compatible, Macintosh/Apple, and RISC-/UNIX-based microcomputers; 150 are networked. Students may access Digital, IBM minicomputer/mainframe systems, BITNET, Internet, CompuServe. Residence halls may be equipped with stand-alone microcomputers. Client/LAN operating systems include Apple/Macintosh, DOS, OS/2, UNIX/XENIX/AIX, Windows NT, X-windows, Banyan, DEC, Novell. Computer languages and software packages include Ada, Assembler, BASIC, C, COBOL, dBASE, FORTRAN, Foxpro, Lotus 1-2-3, LISP, MINITAB, Paradox, Pascal, SAS, SPSS, WordPerfect; 25 in all. Computer facilities are available to all students.

**Fees:** None.

**Hours:** 24 hours.

**GRADUATE CAREER DATA.** Highest graduate school enrollments: Eastern Michigan U, U of Michigan, Michigan State U, Wayne State U. Companies and businesses that hire graduates: EDS, Ford, Northwest Air.

**PROMINENT ALUMNI/AE.** Bob Welch, pitcher for Oakland A's; Timothy McBride, Assistant Secretary of Commerce; Sharyl James, Pulitzer Prize winner; Emil Weddige, artist; Timothy Adams, president of Automobili Lamborghini.

# Ferris State University

**Big Rapids, MI 49307-2251** **616 592-2000**

**1993-94 Costs.** Tuition: $3,222 (state residents), $6,526 (out-of-state). Room & board: $3,923. Fees, books, misc. academic expenses (school's estimate): $590.

**Enrollment.** Undergraduates: 5,457 men, 3,539 women (full-time). Freshman class: 5,381 applicants, 5,177 accepted, 3,949 enrolled. Graduate enrollment: 142 men, 120 women.

**Test score averages/ranges.** Average ACT scores: 18 composite.

**Faculty.** 500 full-time; 218 part-time. 32% of faculty holds doctoral degree. Student/faculty ratio: 17 to 1.

**Selectivity rating.** Noncompetitive.

**PROFILE.** Ferris State, founded in 1884, is a public university of career-oriented education. Programs are offered through the College of Optometry; the Gerholz Institute for Lifelong Learning; and the Schools of Allied Health, Arts and Sciences, Business, Education, Pharmacy, and Technology. Its 600-acre campus is located in Big Rapids, 50 miles from Grand Rapids.

**Accreditation:** NCACS. Professionally accredited by the Accrediting Bureau of Health Education Schools, the American Council on Pharmaceutical Education, the American Dental Association, the American Optometric Association.

**Religious orientation:** Ferris State University is nonsectarian; no religious requirements.

**Library:** Collections totaling over 299,550 volumes, 3,500 periodical subscriptions, and 825,500 microform items.

**Special facilities/museums:** Art gallery.

**Athletic facilities:** Gymnasium, field house, golf course, basketball, racquetball, sand volleyball, tennis, and volleyball courts, swimming pool, tracks, aerobics, combatives, Nautilus, weight, and wrestling rooms, ice rink, athletic and football fields, par course.

**STUDENT BODY. Undergraduate profile:** 97% are state residents. 1% Asian-American, 9% Black, 1% Hispanic, 1% Native American, 85% White, 3% Other. Average age of undergraduates is 22.
**Freshman profile:** 98% of accepted applicants took ACT.
**Undergraduate achievement:** 63% of fall 1992 freshmen returned for fall 1993 term.
**Foreign students:** 251 students are from out of the country. Countries represented include Botswana, Canada, Columbia, Honduras, Japan, and Korea; 45 in all.

**PROGRAMS OF STUDY. Degrees:** B.S., B.S.Nurs., B.Soc.Work.
**Majors:** Accounting, Actuarial Science, Advertising, Advertising/Public Relations, Allied Health Education, Applied Biology, Applied Mathematics, Automotive/Heavy Equipment Management, Biotechnology, Business Administration, Business Economics, Business Education, Computer Information Systems, Construction Management, Criminal Justice, Electrical/Electronics Engineering Technology, Facilities Management, Finance, Health Services Management, Hospitality Management, Hungarian Studies, Industrial/Environmental Health Management, Insurance, Insurance/Real Estate, International Business, Management, Manufacturing Engineering Technology, Manufacturing Technology, Marketing, Marketing Retail, Marketing Sales, Mathematics Education, Medical Records Administration, Medical Technology, Nuclear Medicine Technology, Office Administration, Optometry, Personnel Management/Industrial Relations, Pharmacy, Plastics Engineering Technology, Printing Management, Production Design Engineering, Production Management, Professional Golf Management, Professional Nursing, Professional Tennis Management, Quantitative Business, Recreation Leadership/Management, Science Education, Science Education/Biology, Science Education/Chemistry, Small Business Management, Social Work, Surveying, Technical Education, Television Production, Visual Communication, Visual Science, Welding Engineering Technology.
**Distribution of degrees:** The majors with the highest enrollment are business administration/management, industrial management, and computer science.
**Requirements:** General education requirement.
**Academic regulations:** Minimum 2.0 GPA must be maintained.
**Special:** Minors offered in applied statistics, computer science, insurance, mathematics, and speech communication. "Laddering" enables student to advance career by alternating degree studies and vocational training with employment and practical experience. One-year certificate programs. Occupational education program. Career-oriented curriculum is combined with general education requirements. Associate's degrees offered. Self-designed majors. Double majors. Dual degrees. Independent study. Accelerated study. Pass/fail grading option. Internships. Cooperative education programs. Graduate school at which undergraduates may take graduate-level courses. Preprofessional programs in law, medicine, veterinary science, pharmacy, dentistry, optometry, engineering, mortuary science, physical therapy, science, and teaching. Teacher certification in secondary education. ROTC.
**Honors:** Phi Beta Kappa. Honor societies.
**Academic Assistance:** Remedial reading, writing, and study skills. Nonremedial tutoring.

**STUDENT LIFE. Housing:** All freshmen and sophomores must live on campus. Coed, women's, and men's dorms. Fraternity housing. School-owned/operated apartments. On-campus married-student housing. 46% of students live in college housing.
**Social atmosphere:** According to the student newspaper, "FSU has the reputation of being a 'suitcase college,' but the institution has devoted considerable resources to changing this image. The city of Big Rapids is a small rural community, and offers little in terms of culture or entertainment. There are no groups which exercise a particularly strong influence over the general student population. Rather, there are a large number of diverse groups which enjoy the support of students in general. Hockey is the most popular sport." Favorite off-campus gathering spots include the Alibi, the Creek, Casey McNabb's, the Sawmill, and Easttown Bar.
**Services and counseling/handicapped student services:** Placement services. Health service. Day care. Dental and optometry clinics. Counseling services for minority, military, veteran, and older students. Birth control, personal, and psychological counseling. Career and academic guidance services. Religious counseling. Physically disabled student services. Learning disabled services. Notetaking services. Reader services for the blind.
**Campus organizations:** Undergraduate student government. Student newspaper (Torch, published twice/week). Radio and TV stations. Chamber orchestra, choral union, concert band, glee clubs, gospel choir, festival chorus, jazz ensemble, marching band, symphonic band, winter arts festival, drama group, intercollegiate debating, Association of Gays and Lesbians, SADD, interfraternity council, entertainment council, academic and professional groups, service groups. 12 fraternities, seven chapter houses; seven sororities, no chapter houses. 5% of men join a fraternity. 6% of women join a sorority.
**Religious organizations:** Brothers and Sisters in Christ, Campus Crusade for Christ, Christians in Action, Fellowship Campus Ministry, His House Christian Fellowship, Intervarsity Christian Fellowship, Lutheran Campus Ministry, Wesley Foundation, Youth Ambassadors for Christ.
**Minority/foreign student organizations:** NAACP, minority student professional group.

**ATHLETICS. Physical education requirements:** None.
**Intercollegiate competition:** 1% of students participate. Basketball (M,W), cheerleading (M,W), cross-country (W), football (M), golf (M,W), ice hockey (M), softball (W), tennis (M,W), track (indoor) (W), track (outdoor) (W), track and field (indoor) (W), track and field (outdoor) (W), volleyball (W). Member of Central Collegiate Hockey Association, Great Lakes Intercollegiate Athletic Conference, Midwest Intercollegiate Football Conference, NCAA Division I for ice hockey, NCAA Division II.
**Intramural and club sports:** 78% of students participate. Intramural badminton, basketball, billiards, bowling, broom hockey, golf, field hockey, free throw, ice hockey, indoor soccer, indoor volleyball, innertube water polo, mini-golf, pickleball, racquetball, roller hockey, running, sand volleyball, skiing, snoball, softball, swimming, table tennis, tennis, touch football, track, ultimate frisbee, volleyball, walleyball. Men's club Alpine skiing, bowling, hockey, karate/martial arts, racquetball, rugby, soccer, volleyball, weight training, wrestling. Women's club Alpine skiing, bowling, karate/martial arts, racquetball, soccer, weight training.

**ADMISSIONS. Requirements:** Graduation from secondary school is required; GED is accepted. No specific distribution of secondary school units required. Portfolio required of visual communications program applicants. Collegiate Skills Program for applicants not normally admissible. ACT is required. Campus visit and interview recommended. No off-campus interviews.
**Procedure:** Notification of admission on rolling basis. Reply is required within two weeks of notification. $75 refundable tuition deposit. $75 tuition deposit, partially refundable until August 1. $90 nonrefundable room deposit. Freshmen accepted for terms other than fall.
**Special programs:** Admission may be deferred one year. Credit and/or placement may be granted through CEEB Advanced Placement exams for scores of 3 or higher. Credit and/or placement may be granted through CLEP general and subject exams. Credit may be granted through military and life experience. Credit and placement may be granted through challenge exams.
**Transfer students:** Transfer students accepted for terms other than fall. Application deadline is rolling for fall; rolling for spring. Minimum 2.0 GPA required. Lowest course grade accepted is "D." Maximum number of transferable quarter hours varies by program. At least one year of full-time course work must be completed at the university to receive degree.
**Admissions contact:** Duncan M. Sargent, Ph.D., Director of Admissions. 616 592-2100.

**FINANCIAL AID. Available aid:** Pell grants, SEOG, state scholarships, school scholarships and grants, private scholarships, ROTC scholarships, academic merit scholarships, and athletic scholarships. Perkins Loans (NDSL), PLUS, Stafford Loans (GSL), NSL, Health Professions Loans, state loans, school loans, private loans, and SLS. AMS and deferred payment plan.
**Financial aid statistics:** 10% of aid is not need-based. In 1993-94, 93% of all undergraduate applicants received aid; 94% of freshman applicants. Average amounts of aid awarded freshmen: Scholarships and grants, $2,750; loans, $1,950.
**Supporting data/closing dates:** FAFSA/FAF/FFS: Priority filing date is April 1. School's own aid application: Priority filing date is April 1. Income tax forms: Priority filing date is April 1. Notification of awards on rolling basis.
**Financial aid contact:** Robert Bopp, M.A., Director of Financial Aid. 616 592-2110.

**STUDENT EMPLOYMENT.** College Work/Study Program. Institutional employment. 23% of full-time undergraduates work on campus during school year. Students may expect to earn an average of $1,556 during school year. Off-campus part-time employment opportunities rated "good."

**COMPUTER FACILITIES.** 500 IBM/IBM-compatible, Macintosh/Apple, and RISC-/UNIX-based microcomputers; 350 are networked. Students may access IBM, UNISYS minicomputer/mainframe systems, BITNET. Computer languages and software packages include Assembler, BASIC, CICS, COBOL, dBASE, FORTRAN, MUSIC, Pascal, PL/1, RPG, SPSS; 20 in all. Computer availability varies with academic program.
**Fees:** None.
**Hours:** 8 AM-10 PM in most facilities.

**GRADUATE CAREER DATA.** 70% of graduates choose careers in business and industry. Companies and businesses that hire graduates: General Motors/EDS, Meijer, Upjohn.

## GMI Engineering & Management Institute

**Flint, MI 48504-4898** **313 955-4464**

**1994-95 Costs.** Tuition: $11,640. Room & board: $3,462. Fees, books, misc. academic expenses (school's estimate): $698.

**Enrollment.** Undergraduates: 1,874 men, 493 women (full-time). Freshman class: 1,749 applicants, 1,261 accepted, 514 enrolled. Graduate enrollment: 634 men, 140 women.

**Test score averages/ranges.** Range of SAT scores of middle 50%: 460-570 verbal, 580-690 math. Range of ACT scores of middle 50%: 22-28 English, 25-30 math.

**Faculty.** 144 full-time. 65% of faculty holds doctoral degree. Student/faculty ratio: 12 to 1.

**Selectivity rating.** Highly competitive.

**PROFILE.** GMI Engineering and Management Institute, founded in 1919, is a private, five-year institute. The school became a subsidiary of General Motors Corporation in 1926. In 1982, GMI became an independent institution, although ties with GM remain strong. Its 45-acre campus is located in Flint, 66 miles from Detroit.

**Accreditation:** NCACS. Professionally accredited by the Accreditation Board for Engineering and Technology.
**Religious orientation:** GMI Engineering & Management Institute is nonsectarian; no religious requirements.
**Library:** Collections totaling over 62,000 volumes, 877 periodical subscriptions, and 27,000 microform items.
**Special facilities/museums:** Art museum, industrial history museum, teaching labs, electron microscope.
**Athletic facilities:** Gymnasium, fitness center and track, softball, football and soccer fields.

**STUDENT BODY. Undergraduate profile:** 50% are state residents; 10% are transfers. 7% Asian-American, 5% Black, 2% Hispanic, 1% Native American, 80% White, 5% Other. Average age of undergraduates is 20.
**Freshman profile:** 1% of freshmen who took SAT scored 700 or over on verbal, 16% scored 700 or over on math; 14% scored 600 or over on verbal, 68% scored 600 or over on math; 57% scored 500 or over on verbal, 97% scored 500 or over on math; 94% scored 400 or over on verbal, 100% scored 400 or over on math; 100% scored 300 or over on verbal. 9% of freshmen who took ACT scored 30 or over on English, 22% scored 30 or over on math, 15% scored 30 or over on composite; 65% scored 24 or over on English, 92% scored 24 or over on math, 80% scored 24 or over on composite; 97% scored 18 or over on Eng-

lish, 100% scored 18 or over on math, 100% scored 18 or over on composite; 100% scored 12 or over on English. 85% of freshmen come from public schools.
**Undergraduate achievement:** 88% of fall 1992 freshmen returned for fall 1993 term. 63% of entering class graduated. 6% of students who completed a degree program immediately went on to graduate study.
**Foreign students:** 147 students are from out of the country. Countries represented include Brazil, Canada, China, Germany, Japan, and Spain; 15 in all.

**PROGRAMS OF STUDY. Degrees:** B.S.
**Majors:** Accounting/Finance, Applied Mathematics, Computer Engineering, Electrical Engineering, Industrial Engineering, Information Systems Management, Management, Manufacturing Systems Engineering, Marketing, Mechanical Engineering.
**Distribution of degrees:** The majors with the highest enrollment are mechanical engineering and electrical engineering; industrial engineering has the lowest.
**Requirements:** General education requirement. Minimum grade average of 77 must be maintained.
**Special:** All programs are cooperative; students are employees of a sponsoring company while earning degree and alternate 12-week work and study periods. All degree programs take five years to complete. Academic year continues through summer. Written reports emphasized. Thesis required. Minors offered in applied chemistry, applied mathematics, applied optics, computer science, liberal arts, and management; other cognates or concentrations can be tailored to meet student/sponsor needs. Courses also offered in chemistry/physics/materials, communication/organizational behavior, engineering mechanics, humanities/social science, math, and process engineering. Double majors. Dual degrees. Cooperative education programs. Graduate school at which undergraduates may take graduate-level courses. Student Alumni Travelships awarded to outstanding undergraduates; provide six-week work period at overseas unit. Some students perform co-op work experience terms in international locations of their corporate employer.
**Academic Assistance:** Remedial study skills.

**STUDENT LIFE. Housing:** All unmarried, first-year students must live on campus. Coed dorms. Sorority and fraternity housing. Off-campus privately-owned housing. 40% of students live in college housing.
**Social atmosphere:** The student newspaper reports, "We average about five social functions a week with year-round intramural sports. Clubs include all interests from current issues to communication, from hockey to skin diving, from student council to various honor societies. Greeks represent 50% of the student body. They have a big influence on student social life." Popular gathering spots include "all Greek houses." Favorite events include senior bar night, Greek-organized events, and GMTE council events (including the "Big Event").
**Services and counseling/handicapped student services:** Placement services. Health service. Counseling services for minority, military, veteran, and older students. Birth control, personal, and psychological counseling. Career and academic guidance services. Religious counseling. Physically disabled student services.
**Campus organizations:** Undergraduate student government. Student newspaper (Technician, published twice/month). Literary magazine. Yearbook. Radio station. Chorale, Gumpty Players, Firebirds, radio and computer clubs, Society of Women Engineers, SADD, Leadership Training, 40 organizations in all. 14 fraternities, 11 chapter houses; six sororities, two chapter houses. 60% of men join a fraternity. 60% of women join a sorority.
**Religious organizations:** Christians in Action, Intervarsity Christian Fellowship.
**Minority/foreign student organizations:** Black Unity Congress, Society of Black Engineers, Society of Hispanic Engineers. International club.

**ATHLETICS. Physical education requirements:** None.
**Intercollegiate competition:** 10% of students participate.
**Intramural and club sports:** 90% of students participate. Intramural basketball, billiards, bowling, soccer, softball, flag football, swimming, volleyball. Men's club Alpine skiing, basketball, ice hockey, martial arts, sailing, soccer, volleyball, weight lifting. Women's club Alpine skiing, martial arts, sailing, soccer, volleyball, weight lifting.

**ADMISSIONS. Academic basis for candidate selection** (in order of priority): Secondary school record, standardized test scores, class rank, essay, school's recommendation.
**Nonacademic basis for candidate selection:** Character and personality, extracurricular participation, and particular talent or ability are emphasized. Geographical distribution is important.
**Requirements:** Graduation from secondary school is required; GED is not accepted. 16.5 units and the following program of study are required: 3 units of English, 3.5 units of math, 2 units of lab science (including chemistry or physics), 8 units of academic electives. College-preparatory electives such as economics, government, history, mechanical drawing, and psychology recommended. Conditional admission possible for applicants not meeting standard requirements. SAT or ACT is required. ACH recommended. Campus visit and interview recommended. Off-campus interviews available with an admissions representative.
**Procedure:** Take SAT or ACT by December of 12th year. Take ACH by January of 12th year. Suggest filing application by November 30. Notification of admission on rolling basis. Reply is requested within 15 days of acceptance. $200 tuition deposit, refundable until May 1. Freshmen accepted for terms other than fall.
**Special programs:** Admission may be deferred one year. Credit and/or placement may be granted through CEEB Advanced Placement exams for scores of 3 or higher. Credit and/or placement may be granted through CLEP subject exams. Credit and placement may be granted through Regents College, ACT PEP, DANTES, and challenge exams.
**Transfer students:** Transfer students accepted for terms other than fall. In fall 1993, 10% of all new students were transfers into all classes. 151 transfer applications were received, 113 were accepted. Application deadline is rolling for fall; rolling for spring. Minimum 3.0 GPA recommended. Lowest course grade accepted is "C." Maximum number of transferable credits is 80 quarter hours. At least 100 quarter hours must be completed at the institute to receive degree.
**Admissions contact:** Phillip D. Lavender, M.A., Director of Admissions. 313 762-7865, 800 955-4464.

**FINANCIAL AID. Available aid:** Pell grants, SEOG, state scholarships and grants, school scholarships and grants, private scholarships and grants, and academic merit scholarships. PLUS, Stafford Loans (GSL), state loans, school loans, private loans, and SLS. Deferred payment plan.
**Financial aid statistics:** 5% of aid is not need-based. In 1993-94, 95% of all undergraduate applicants received aid; 95% of freshman applicants. Average amounts of aid awarded freshmen: Scholarships and grants, $2,659; loans, $2,500.
**Supporting data/closing dates:** FAFSA/FAF/FFS: Priority filing date is May 1. School's own aid application: Priority filing date is May 1. State aid form: Priority filing date is September 1. Notification of awards on rolling basis.
**Financial aid contact:** Mark Delorey, M.A., Director of Financial Aid. 313 762-7859.

**STUDENT EMPLOYMENT.** College Work/Study Program. Institutional employment. 21% of full-time undergraduates work on campus during school year. Students may expect to earn an average of $500 during school year. Off-campus part-time employment opportunities rated "excellent."

**COMPUTER FACILITIES.** 200 IBM/IBM-compatible, Macintosh/Apple, and RISC-/UNIX-based microcomputers; 175 are networked. Students may access SUN minicomputer/mainframe systems, Internet. Residence halls may be equipped with modems. Client/LAN operating systems include DOS, UNIX/XENIX/AIX, Novell. Computer languages and software packages include Autocad, BASIC, C, COBOL, FORTRAN, MINITAB, Pascal, PL/1, Scientific GPSS, SIMON, SLAM, SPSS-X, Unigraphics; 45 in all. Computer facilities are available to all students.
**Fees:** None.
**Hours:** 24 hours.

**GRADUATE CAREER DATA.** Highest graduate school enrollments: GMI Engineering & Management Inst, Harvard U, MIT, Purdue U, Stanford U, U of Michigan. 95% of graduates choose careers in business and industry. Companies and businesses that hire graduates: Ford, General Motors, Rockwell.

**PROMINENT ALUMNI/AE.** F. James McDonald, former president, General Motors; Robert E. Reiss, president and CEO, Interventional Tech.; Dr. Dane Miller, president and CEO, Biomet.

# Grand Rapids Baptist College and Seminary

**Grand Rapids, MI 49505** 616 458-9185

**1994-95 Costs.** Tuition: $6,480. Room: $1,800. Board: $2,088. Fees, books, misc. academic expenses (school's estimate): $932.
**Enrollment.** Undergraduates: 311 men, 371 women (full-time). Freshman class: 269 applicants, 259 accepted, 171 enrolled. Graduate enrollment: 137 men, 14 women.
**Test score averages/ranges.** Average ACT scores: 22 English, 20 math, 22 composite.
**Faculty.** 37 full-time; 33 part-time. 38% of faculty holds doctoral degree. Student/faculty ratio: 17 to 1.
**Selectivity rating.** Less competitive.

**PROFILE.** Grand Rapids, founded in 1941, is church-affiliated, liberal arts college. Its 132-acre campus is located in Grand Rapids.

**Accreditation:** NCACS.
**Religious orientation:** Grand Rapids Baptist College and Seminary is affiliated with the General Association of Regular Baptist Churches; six semesters of religion required.
**Library:** Collections totaling over 93,111 volumes, 650 periodical subscriptions and 29 microform items.
**Athletic facilities:** Gymnasium, weight room, athletic fields.

**STUDENT BODY. Undergraduate profile:** 79% are state residents; 28% are transfers. 2% Black, 96% White, 2% Other. Average age of undergraduates is 21.
**Freshman profile:** 96% of accepted applicants took ACT. 64% of freshmen come from public schools.
**Undergraduate achievement:** 67% of fall 1991 freshmen returned for fall 1992 term. 22% of entering class graduated. 14% of students who completed a degree program went on to graduate study within one year.
**Foreign students:** Six students are from out of the country. Countries represented include Brazil, Canada, and the United Kingdom; four in all.

**PROGRAMS OF STUDY. Degrees:** B.A., B.Mus., B.Relig.Ed.
**Majors:** Ancient Languages, Bible, Bible/Christian Education, Bible/Church/Parachurch Business Management, Bible/Greek, Bible/Missionary Aviation, Bible/Missions, Bible/Music/Youth Director, Bible/Pastoral Studies, Bible/Recreation/Camping, Biology, Business/Accounting, Business Administration, Business/Computer Information Systems, Business/Marketing, Business/Office Management, Church Music, Elementary/Secondary Education, English, History, Interdisciplinary Studies, Music Performance, Music Theory/Composition, Physical Education, Pre-Law, Psychology, Religion, Social Work, Sociology, Speech Communication.
**Distribution of degrees:** The majors with the highest enrollment are business, Bible, and psychology; ancient languages, social work, and history have the lowest.
**Requirements:** General education requirement.
**Academic regulations:** Freshmen must maintain minimum 1.5 GPA; sophomores, 1.7 GPA; juniors, 2.0 GPA; seniors, 2.0 GPA.
**Special:** Minors offered in many majors and in accounting, biology, drama, general science, Greek, mass communications, math, military science, philosophy, and secretarial studies. Additional minors available in teacher education program. One-year diploma program in Bible. Associate's degrees offered. Double majors. Preprofessional programs in law. Member of Christian College Coalition. Washington Semester. Teacher certification in elementary and secondary education. Exchange program abroad in England (Oxford U). Study abroad also in Costa Rica. ROTC at Western Michigan U.
**Academic Assistance:** Remedial reading, writing, math, and study skills. Nonremedial tutoring.

**ADMISSIONS. Academic basis for candidate selection** (in order of priority): Secondary school record, standardized test scores, class rank, essay, school's recommendation.

**Nonacademic basis for candidate selection:** Character and personality are emphasized. Extracurricular participation and particular talent or ability are considered. Pastor's recommendation and evidence of Christian faith are considered.
**Requirements:** Graduation from secondary school is required; GED is accepted. 17 units and the following program of study are recommended: 4 units of English, 3 units of math, 2 units of science, 1 unit of foreign language, 1 unit of social studies, 2 units of history, 4 units of electives. Electives should be chosen from history, government, language, psychology, social science, speech, and music theory. Minimum composite ACT score of 18, minimum 2.0 GPA, and rank in top half of secondary school class required; minimum 2.25 GPA recommended. Preprofessional skills test, special reference, and separate application required of education program applicants. Audition required of music program applicants. Conditional admission possible for applicants not meeting standard requirements. ACT is recommended. Campus visit and interview recommended. Off-campus interviews available with an admissions representative.
**Procedure:** Take SAT or ACT by June of 12th year. Visit college for interview by July of 12th year. Application deadline is August 1. Notification of admission on rolling basis. $200 nonrefundable tuition deposit. $100 room deposit, refundable until July 15. Freshmen accepted for terms other than fall.
**Special programs:** Admission may be deferred one year. Credit and/or placement may be granted through CEEB Advanced Placement exams for scores of 4 or higher. Credit and/or placement may be granted through CLEP subject exams. Credit may be granted through military experience. Early entrance/early admission program. Concurrent enrollment program.
**Transfer students:** Transfer students accepted for terms other than fall. In fall 1992, 28% of all new students were transfers into all classes. 119 transfer applications were received, 117 were accepted. Application deadline is August 1 for fall; December 15 for spring. Minimum 2.0 GPA required. Lowest course grade accepted is "C-." At least 32 semester hours must be completed at the college to receive degree.
**Admissions contact:** Kay Landrum, M.S., Director of Admissions. 800 968-4722, 800 354-0272.

**FINANCIAL AID. Available aid:** Pell grants, SEOG, state scholarships and grants, school scholarships and grants, private scholarships and grants, academic merit scholarships, and athletic scholarships. Perkins Loans (NDSL), PLUS, Stafford Loans (GSL), state loans, and SLS. Payment plan.
**Financial aid statistics:** Average amounts of aid awarded freshmen: Scholarships and grants, $3,177; loans, $2,350.
**Supporting data/closing dates:** FAFSA/FAF/FFS: Priority filing date is March 1. State aid form: Deadline is September 1. Notification of awards on rolling basis.
**Financial aid contact:** Open, Director of Financial Aid. 616 968-4722.

## Grand Valley State University

**Allendale, MI 49401 — 616 895-6611**

**1994-95 Costs.** Tuition: $2,622 (state residents), $6,108 (out-of-state). Room & board: $4,060. Fees, books, misc. academic expenses (school's estimate): $770.
**Enrollment.** Undergraduates: 3,454 men, 4,780 women (full-time). Freshman class: 5,165 applicants, 3,887 accepted, 1,561 enrolled. Graduate enrollment: 863 men, 1,668 women.
**Test score averages/ranges.** Average ACT scores: 23 composite. Range of ACT scores of middle 50%: 20-25 composite.
**Faculty.** 371 full-time; 228 part-time. 78% of faculty holds highest degree in specific field. Student/faculty ratio: 23 to 1.
**Selectivity rating.** Less competitive.

**PROFILE.** Grand Valley State, founded in 1960, is a public, comprehensive university. Its 900-acre campus is located in Allendale, 12 miles west of Grand Rapids and 12 miles east of Lake Michigan.

**Accreditation:** NCACS. Professionally accredited by the Accreditation Board for Engineering and Technology, the American Physical Therapy Association, the Council on Social Work Education, the National Association of Schools of Art and Design, the National Association of Schools of Music, the National Council for Accreditation of Teacher Education, the National League for Nursing.
**Religious orientation:** Grand Valley State University is nonsectarian; no religious requirements.
**Library:** Collections totaling over 430,000 volumes, 2,477 periodical subscriptions, and 577,780 microform items.
**Special facilities/museums:** Urban studies institute, 51-foot research vessel, audio-visual center, performance/recital hall, physical therapy/human performance lab.
**Athletic facilities:** Softball fields, tracks, strength/conditioning rooms, basketball, tennis, volleyball, and badminton courts.

**STUDENT BODY. Undergraduate profile:** 98% are state residents; 48% are transfers. 2% Asian-American, 5% Black, 2% Hispanic, 90% White, 1% Other. Average age of undergraduates is 23.
**Freshman profile:** 3% of freshmen who took ACT scored 30 or over on English, 3% scored 30 or over on math, 2% scored 30 or over on composite; 37% scored 24 or over on English, 33% scored 24 or over on math, 37% scored 24 or over on composite; 91% scored 18 or over on English, 89% scored 18 or over on math, 97% scored 18 or over on composite; 100% scored 12 or over on English, 100% scored 12 or over on math, 100% scored 12 or over on composite. 95% of accepted applicants took ACT. 90% of freshmen come from public schools.
**Undergraduate achievement:** 80% of fall 1992 freshmen returned for fall 1993 term.
**Foreign students:** 26 students are from out of the country. Countries represented include Canada, England, Japan, Poland, Sweden, and the former Yugoslav Republics; 12 in all.

**PROGRAMS OF STUDY. Degrees:** B.A., B.Bus.Admin., B.F.A., B.Mus., B.Mus.Ed., B.S., B.S.Eng., B.S.Nurs., B.Soc.Work.
**Majors:** Accounting, Advertising/Public Relations, Anthropology, Art/Design, Behavioral Science, Biological Computing, Biology, Biomedical Sciences, Biopsychology, Broadcasting, Business Administration/Management, Chemistry, Communications, Computer/Information Sciences, Criminal Justice, Earth Science, Economics, Education, Engineering, English Language/Literature, Facilities Management, Film/Video, Finance, French, General Business, Geology, German, Health Sciences, History, Hospitality/Tourism Management, International Relations, Journalism, Language Arts, Liberal Studies, Management, Marketing, Mathematics, Medical Technology, Music, Nursing, Occupational Safety/Health Technology, Philosophy, Photography, Physical Education, Physics, Planning/Resource Management, Political Science/Government, Pre-Dentistry, Pre-Law, Pre-Medicine, Psychology, Public Administration, Russian Studies, Science, Social Sciences, Social Studies, Social Work, Sociology, Spanish, Special Education/Psychology, Theatre, Therapeutic Recreation.
**Distribution of degrees:** The majors with the highest enrollment are business administration/management, criminal justice, and health sciences; economics and philosophy have the lowest.
**Requirements:** General education requirement.
**Academic regulations:** Minimum 2.0 GPA must be maintained.
**Special:** Minors offered in most majors. Self-designed majors. Double majors. Dual degrees. Independent study. Accelerated study. Pass/fail grading option. Internships. Cooperative education programs. Graduate school at which undergraduates may take graduate-level courses. Preprofessional programs in law, medicine, and dentistry. 2-2 and 3-2 engineering programs. Member of Consortium for Engineering Education. Teacher certification in elementary, secondary, and special education education. Exchange programs abroad in England and Japan (Christian U). Study abroad also in France, Mexico, Poland, Russia, Spain, and the former Yugoslav Republics.
**Honors:** Honors program.
**Academic Assistance:** Remedial reading, writing, math, and study skills. Nonremedial tutoring.

**STUDENT LIFE. Housing:** Some athletes must live on campus. Coed dorms. School-owned/operated apartments. Off-campus privately-owned housing. Off-campus married-student housing. 20% of students live in college housing.
**Social atmosphere:** Students are "interested in just having a good time in whatever they do," according to the student newspaper. Many small Greek organizations, sports clubs, and the Programming Board influence student social activities. Popular school-year events include Homecoming, Airband (lipsync contest), Knowledge Bowl, and Martin Luther King Day. Students meet at the student center on campus and gather at local apartment complexes, Brann's, Lincoln Lanes, and Grand Haven and Holland beaches off campus.
**Services and counseling/handicapped student services:** Placement services. Health service. Day care. Counseling services for minority, veteran, and older students. Birth control, personal, and psychological counseling. Career and academic guidance services. Religious counseling. Physically disabled student services. Learning disabled services. Tutors. Reader services for the blind.
**Campus organizations:** Undergraduate student government. Student newspaper (Lanthorn, published once/week). Literary magazine. Yearbook. Radio and TV stations. Choral groups, concert orchestra, small musical groups, community theatre, One-to-One Tutoring, Women's Information Bureau, departmental groups, special-interest groups, 138 organizations in all. Five fraternities, no chapter houses; five sororities, no chapter houses. 2% of men join a fraternity. 2% of women join a sorority.
**Religious organizations:** Interdenominational Campus Ministry, Abundant Life Fellowship, Chi Alpha Christian Fellowship, Intervarsity Christian Fellowship, His House Christian Fellowship, New Life Christian Students.
**Minority/foreign student organizations:** Minority frateries/sororities, Anishnawbe Club, Black Student Union, cross-cultural club, Latino Student Union, La Tertulia. International Club, El Renacimiento, Vietnamese group.

**ATHLETICS. Physical education requirements:** None.
**Intercollegiate competition:** 6% of students participate. Baseball (M), basketball (M,W), cheerleading (M,W), cross-country (M,W), diving (M,W), football (M), golf (M,W), softball (W), swimming (M,W), tennis (M,W), track (M,W), track and field (M,W), volleyball (W). Member of Great Lakes Intercollegiate Athletic Conference, Midwest Intercollegiate Football Conference, NCAA Division II.
**Intramural and club sports:** 27% of students participate. Intramural badminton, basketball, bowling, football, golf, tennis, volleyball, wrestling. Men's club bowling, crew, ice hockey, skiing, soccer, volleyball. Women's club bowling, crew, skiing, soccer, volleyball.

**ADMISSIONS. Academic basis for candidate selection** (in order of priority): Secondary school record, standardized test scores, school's recommendation.
**Nonacademic basis for candidate selection:** Extracurricular participation is important. Particular talent or ability is considered.
**Requirements:** Graduation from secondary school is required; GED is accepted. 20 units and the following program of study are required: 4 units of English, 3 units of math, 3 units of science including 2 units of lab, 3 units of social studies, 7 units of academic electives. Minimum composite ACT score of 19 and minimum 2.7 GPA required. Portfolio required of art program applicants. Audition required of music program applicants. ACT is required; SAT may be substituted. Campus visit and interview recommended. Off-campus interviews available with an admissions representative.
**Procedure:** Take SAT or ACT by October of 12th year. Visit college for interview by October of 12th year. Suggest filing application by February 1. Application deadline is July 31. Notification of admission on rolling basis. Applicant must accept offer of admission by final registration. $150 room deposit, refundable until June 1. Freshmen accepted for terms other than fall.
**Special programs:** Admission may be deferred one semester. Credit and/or placement may be granted through CEEB Advanced Placement exams for scores of 3 or higher. Credit and/or placement may be granted through CLEP subject exams. Credit and placement may be granted through challenge exams. Early decision program. Deadline for applying for early decision is February 1. Early entrance/early admission program. Concurrent enrollment program.
**Transfer students:** Transfer students accepted for terms other than fall. In fall 1993, 48% of all new students were transfers into all classes. 2,814 transfer applications were received, 2,368 were accepted. Application deadline is July 31 for fall; November 30 for

spring. Minimum 2.0 GPA required. Lowest course grade accepted is "C-." Maximum number of transferable credits is 62 semester hours from a two-year school and 90 semester hours from a four-year school. At least 30 semester hours must be completed at the university to receive degree.
**Admissions contact:** Jo Ann Foerster, M.A., Director of Admissions. 616 895-2025.
**FINANCIAL AID. Available aid:** Pell grants, SEOG, Federal Nursing Student Scholarships, state scholarships and grants, school scholarships and grants, private scholarships and grants, academic merit scholarships, and athletic scholarships. Perkins Loans (NDSL), PLUS, Stafford Loans (GSL), NSL, state loans, school loans, and SLS. AMS and deferred payment plan.
**Financial aid statistics:** 12% of aid is not need-based. In 1993-94, 78% of all undergraduate applicants received aid; 72% of freshman applicants. Average amounts of aid awarded freshmen: Scholarships and grants, $1,300; loans, $2,600.
**Supporting data/closing dates:** FAFSA: Priority filing date is February 15. Notification of awards begins April 15.
**Financial aid contact:** Kenneth Fridsma, M.A., Director of Financial Aid. 616 895-3234.
**STUDENT EMPLOYMENT.** College Work/Study Program. Institutional employment. 20% of full-time undergraduates work on campus during school year. Students may expect to earn an average of $1,500 during school year. Off-campus part-time employment opportunities rated "good."
**COMPUTER FACILITIES.** 1,500 IBM/IBM-compatible, Macintosh/Apple, and RISC-/UNIX-based microcomputers; 1,000 are networked. Students may access AT&T, IBM, SUN minicomputer/mainframe systems, BITNET, Internet. Residence halls may be equipped with stand-alone microcomputers, modems. Client/LAN operating systems include Apple/Macintosh, DOS, UNIX/XENIX/AIX, LocalTalk/AppleTalk, Novell. Computer languages and software packages include ALGOR, BASIC, CICS, COBOL, Falcon, FORTRAN, IDMS, Lotus 1-2-3, Microsoft Works, Modula 2, Pascal, SAS, SPSS, Windows, WordPerfect. Computer facilities are available to all students.
**Fees:** Computer fee is included in tuition/fees.
**Hours:** 18 hours/day.
**GRADUATE CAREER DATA.** Highest graduate school enrollments: Grand Valley State U, U of Michigan, Michigan State U.
**PROMINENT ALUMNI/AE.** Dr. Lawrence Paul, oncologist; Dr. David Vanderwal, plastic surgeon; Patricia Videtich, senior research geologist, CONOCO.

8 · 23

# Hillsdale College

**Hillsdale, MI 49242** **517 437-7341**

**1994-95 Costs.** Tuition: $11,090. Room: $2,100. Board: $2,600. Fees, books, misc. academic expenses (school's estimate): $1,710.
**Enrollment.** Undergraduates: 529 men, 562 women (full-time). Freshman class: 935 applicants, 738 accepted, 347 enrolled. Graduate enrollment: 542 men, 591 women.
**Test score averages/ranges.** Average SAT scores: 520 verbal, 550 math. Average ACT scores: 23 English, 23 math, 24 composite. Range of ACT scores of middle 50%: 21-26 English, 22-27 math.
**Faculty.** 80 full-time; 32 part-time. 78% of faculty holds doctoral degree. Student/faculty ratio: 12 to 1.
**Selectivity rating.** More competitive.

**PROFILE.** Hillsdale, founded in 1844, is a private, liberal arts college. Its 150-acre campus is located in the northern part of Hillsdale, 75 miles from Ann Arbor.

**Accreditation:** NCACS.
**Religious orientation:** Hillsdale College is nonsectarian; no religious requirements.
**Library:** Collections totaling over 175,000 volumes, 18,000 periodical subscriptions, and 22,000 microform items.
**Special facilities/museums:** Early childhood education lab, media center, K-8 private academy.
**Athletic facilities:** Sports complex includes indoor track, basketball arena, swimming pool, racquetball courts, tennis courts, whirlpool, saunas, weight room, training room; football stadium.
**STUDENT BODY. Undergraduate profile:** 58% are state residents; 13% are transfers. Average age of undergraduates is 20.
**Freshman profile:** 3% of freshmen who took SAT scored 700 or over on verbal, 6% scored 700 or over on math; 18% scored 600 or over on verbal, 24% scored 600 or over on math; 58% scored 500 or over on verbal, 73% scored 500 or over on math; 95% scored 400 or over on verbal, 96% scored 400 or over on math; 100% scored 300 or over on verbal, 100% scored 300 or over on math. 8% of freshmen who took ACT scored 30 or over on composite; 55% scored 24 or over on composite; 98% scored 18 or over on composite; 100% scored 12 or over on composite. 25% of accepted applicants took SAT; 75% took ACT. 71% of freshmen come from public schools.
**Undergraduate achievement:** 90% of fall 1992 freshmen returned for fall 1993 term. 80% of entering class graduated. 5% of students who completed a degree program immediately went on to graduate study.
**Foreign students:** 22 students are from out of the country. Countries represented include Canada, China, India, Japan, Kenya, and Spain; 12 in all.
**PROGRAMS OF STUDY. Degrees:** B.A., B.S.
**Majors:** Accounting, American Studies, Art, Biology, Business Administration, Chemistry, Christian Studies, Classical Studies, Communication Arts, Comparative Literature, Early Childhood Education, Economics, Elementary Education, English, Environmental Sciences, European Studies, Finance, French, German, History, International Business, Marketing, Mathematics, Music, Philosophy, Physical Education/Health, Physics, Political Economy, Political Science, Psychology, Religion, Secondary Education, Social Work, Sociology, Spanish, Speech/Theatre Arts.
**Distribution of degrees:** The majors with the highest enrollment are business, English, and history; physical education, philosophy, and religion have the lowest.
**Requirements:** General education requirement.
**Academic regulations:** Freshmen must maintain minimum 1.75 GPA; sophomores, 1.9 GPA; juniors, 2.0 GPA; seniors, 2.0 GPA.
**Special:** Minors offered. Center for Constructive Alternatives offers two one-week seminars on current issues each semester. Double majors. Internships. Preprofessional programs in law, medicine, veterinary science, pharmacy, dentistry, theology, optometry, engineering, medical technology, nursing, and social work. 2-2 engineering program with Tri-State U. 3-2 engineering program with Northwestern U. Washington Semester. Teacher certification in early childhood, elementary, and secondary education. Certification in specific subject areas. Exchange programs abroad in England (Oxford U) and Spain (U of Seville). Study abroad also in France and Germany. ROTC, NROTC, and AFROTC at U of Michigan and Michigan State U.
**Honors:** Honors program. Honor societies.
**Academic Assistance:** Nonremedial tutoring.
**STUDENT LIFE. Housing:** All freshmen must live on campus unless living with family. Women's and men's dorms. Sorority and fraternity housing. School-owned/-operated apartments. Off-campus privately-owned housing. 80% of students live in college housing.
**Social atmosphere:** According to the Collegian, fraternities, the activities board, and the football team influence student social activities. Students gather at the student union and fraternity houses on campus while frequenting Club Lido and Mike's Depot off campus. The President's Ball, Greek Week, jazz band concerts, and football games highlight the school year.
**Services and counseling/handicapped student services:** Placement services. Health service. Personal and psychological counseling. Career and academic guidance services.
**Campus organizations:** Undergraduate student government. Student newspaper (Collegian, published once/week). Literary magazine. Yearbook. Choir, jazz band, orchestra, pep band, Equestrian Club, Enterprising Leaders, Leadership Workshop, Men's and Women's Council, Praxis, Young Republicans, Young Democrats, 25 organizations in all. Five fraternities, all with chapter houses; four sororities, all with chapter houses. 50% of men join a fraternity. 50% of women join a sorority.
**Religious organizations:** Catholic Student Council, Fellowship of Christian Athletes, Intervarsity Christian Fellowship.
**Minority/foreign student organizations:** International Relations Club.
**ATHLETICS. Physical education requirements:** Two semesters of physical education required.
**Intercollegiate competition:** 40% of students participate. Baseball (M), basketball (M,W), cross-country (M,W), football (M), golf (M), softball (W), tennis (M,W), track and field (M,W), volleyball (W). Member of Great Lakes Intercollegiate Athletic Conference, MIFC, NAIA, NCAA Division II.
**Intramural and club sports:** 50% of students participate. Intramural basketball, football, volleyball. Men's club lacrosse, soccer.
**ADMISSIONS. Academic basis for candidate selection** (in order of priority): Secondary school record, standardized test scores, class rank, essay, school's recommendation.
**Nonacademic basis for candidate selection:** Character and personality and extracurricular participation are emphasized. Particular talent or ability, geographical distribution, and alumni/ae relationship are considered.
**Requirements:** Graduation from secondary school is required; GED is accepted. No specific distribution of secondary school units required. Minimum composite ACT score of 21 (combined SAT score of 1010), rank in top third of secondary school class, and minimum 3.2 GPA recommended. Audition required of music program applicants. Conditional admission possible for applicants not meeting standard requirements. SAT or ACT is required. PSAT is recommended. ACH recommended. Campus visit and interview recommended. No off-campus interviews.
**Procedure:** Take SAT or ACT by December of 12th year. Take ACH by December of 12th year. Visit college for interview by December of 12th year. Suggest filing application by January 1. Application deadline is July 15. Notification of admission on rolling basis. $200 nonrefundable tuition deposit. Freshmen accepted for terms other than fall.
**Special programs:** Admission may be deferred one year. Credit and/or placement may be granted through CEEB Advanced Placement exams for scores of 3 or higher. Credit and/or placement may be granted through CLEP general and subject exams. Early entrance/early admission program. Concurrent enrollment program.
**Transfer students:** Transfer students accepted for terms other than fall. In fall 1993, 13% of all new students were transfers into all classes. 58 transfer applications were received, 48 were accepted. Application deadline is July 15 for fall; December 15 for spring. Minimum 3.0 GPA recommended. Lowest course grade accepted is "C." Maximum number of transferable credits is 100 semester hours. At least 24 semester hours must be completed at the college to receive degree.
**Admissions contact:** Jeffrey S. Lantis, Director of Admissions. 517 437-7341, extension 2327.
**FINANCIAL AID. Available aid:** State scholarships and grants, school scholarships and grants, private scholarships and grants, academic merit scholarships, athletic scholarships, and aid for undergraduate foreign students. PLUS, Stafford Loans (GSL), school loans, private loans, and SLS. Knight Tuition Plans and AMS.
**Financial aid statistics:** 40% of aid is not need-based. In 1993-94, 95% of all undergraduate applicants received aid; 95% of freshman applicants. Average amounts of aid awarded freshmen: Scholarships and grants, $5,500; loans, $3,200.
**Supporting data/closing dates:** FAFSA/FAF/FFS: Priority filing date is April 15. School's own aid application: Priority filing date is April 15. Notification of awards on rolling basis.
**Financial aid contact:** Connie Bricker, Director of Financial Aid. 517 437-7341, extension 2350.
**STUDENT EMPLOYMENT.** Institutional employment. 40% of full-time undergraduates work on campus during school year. Students may expect to earn an average of $1,500 during school year. Off-campus part-time employment opportunities rated "good."
**COMPUTER FACILITIES.** 150 IBM/IBM-compatible and Macintosh/Apple microcomputers; 50 are networked. Students may access Digital, IBM minicomputer/mainframe systems, Internet, CompuServe. Residence halls may be equipped with stand-alone microcomputers. Client/LAN operating systems include Apple/Macintosh, DOS, UNIX/XENIX/AIX, Windows NT, LocalTalk/AppleTalk. Computer languages and software packages include Assembler, C, COBOL, LISP, Modula 2, Pascal; database, graphics,

spreadsheet, word processing software packages. Computer facilities are available to all students.
**Fees:** Computer fee is included in tuition/fees.

**GRADUATE CAREER DATA.** Graduate school percentages: 7% enter law school. 6% enter medical school. 1% enter dental school. 11% enter graduate business programs. 3% enter graduate arts and sciences programs. 1% enter theological school/seminary. Highest graduate school enrollments: Indiana U, Michigan State U, Ohio State U, U of Michigan, Wake Forest U, Wayne State U. 50% of graduates choose careers in business and industry. Companies and businesses that hire graduates: Arthur Andersen, Coopers & Lybrand, Dana Corp., Federal Mogul, Neiman Marcus, Saturn, Universal Forest Products, Comerica Bank, Ernst & Young.

**PROMINENT ALUMNI/AE.** Dr. James Seward, director of cardiovascular disease, Mayo Clinic; Dr. Ellsworth H. Brown, executive director, Chicago Historical Society; Hon. Phillip Crane, U.S. congressman, Illinois.

# Hope College

**Holland, MI 49422-9000** **616 392-5111**

**1994-95 Costs.** Tuition: $12,275. Room: $1,980. Board: $2,361. Fees, books, misc. academic expenses (school's estimate): $549.
**Enrollment.** Undergraduates: 1,082 men, 1,423 women (full-time). Freshman class: 1,712 applicants, 1,483 accepted, 626 enrolled.
**Test score averages/ranges.** Range of SAT scores of middle 50%: 940-1180 combined. Range of ACT scores of middle 50%: 21-27 composite.
**Faculty.** 182 full-time; 63 part-time. 83% of faculty holds highest degree in specific field. Student/faculty ratio: 13 to 1.
**Selectivity rating.** Competitive.

**PROFILE.** Hope College, founded in 1851, is a church-affiliated, liberal arts institution. Its 45-acre campus is located in a residential area of Holland, 30 miles southwest of Grand Rapids. Campus architecture includes 19th century structures and modern buildings.

**Accreditation:** NCACS. Professionally accredited by the National Association of Schools of Art and Design, the National Association of Schools of Dance, the National Association of Schools of Music, the National Association of Schools of Theatre, the National Council for Accreditation of Teacher Education, the National League for Nursing.
**Religious orientation:** Hope College is affiliated with the Reformed Church in America; two semesters of religion required.
**Library:** Collections totaling over 290,000 volumes, 1,494 periodical subscriptions, and 153,504 microform items.
**Special facilities/museums:** Particle accelerator, computational chemistry lab, electron microscopes, spectrometers, ultracentrifuge.
**Athletic facilities:** Gymnasium, swimming pool, track, weight rooms, badminton, basketball, handball, racquetball, and tennis courts, dance studio, baseball, field hockey, football, soccer, and softball fields, aerobic running track, indoor tennis building.

**STUDENT BODY. Undergraduate profile:** 78% are state residents; 14% are transfers. 2% Asian-American, 1% Black, 1% Hispanic, 92% White, 4% Other. Average age of undergraduates is 20.
**Freshman profile:** 2% of freshmen who took SAT scored 700 or over on verbal, 7% scored 700 or over on math; 14% scored 600 or over on verbal, 37% scored 600 or over on math; 44% scored 500 or over on verbal, 70% scored 500 or over on math; 86% scored 400 or over on verbal, 93% scored 400 or over on math; 100% scored 300 or over on verbal, 99% scored 300 or over on math. 7% of freshmen who took ACT scored 30 or over on composite; 52% scored 24 or over on composite; 96% scored 18 or over on composite; 100% scored 12 or over on composite. 37% of accepted applicants took SAT; 87% took ACT. 90% of freshmen come from public schools.
**Undergraduate achievement:** 87% of fall 1992 freshmen returned for fall 1993 term. 54% of entering class graduated. 30% of students who completed a degree program immediately went on to graduate study.
**Foreign students:** 96 students are from out of the country. Countries represented include Germany, Japan, South Africa, the former Soviet Republics, and the United Kingdom; 37 in all.

**PROGRAMS OF STUDY. Degrees:** B.A., B.Mus., B.S., B.S.Nurs.
**Majors:** Accounting, Ancient Civilization, Art, Art History, Biochemistry, Biology, Business Administration, Chemistry, Classical Languages, Communication, Computer Science, Dance, Economics, Engineering Physics, English, Environmental Geology, French, Geochemistry, Geology, Geophysics, German, History, Humanities, Instrumental Music Education, International Studies, Language Arts, Latin, Mathematics, Mathematics/Science, Music, Music Literature/History, Music Performance, Music Theory, Nursing, Philosophy, Physical Education, Physics, Political Science, Psychology, Religion, Social Studies, Social Work, Sociology, Spanish, Special Education, Theatre, Vocal Music Education.
**Distribution of degrees:** The majors with the highest enrollment are business, biology, and English; ancient civilization, music, and music performance have the lowest.
**Requirements:** General education requirement.
**Academic regulations:** Freshmen must maintain minimum 1.6 GPA; sophomores, 1.8 GPA; juniors, 1.95 GPA; seniors, 2.0 GPA.
**Special:** Minors offered in most majors and in English writing, Greek, Japanese, Russian, and women's studies. Courses offered in linguistics and dance therapy. Self-designed majors. Double majors. Independent study. Pass/fail grading option. Internships. Graduate school at which undergraduates may take graduate-level courses. Preprofessional programs in law, medicine, veterinary science, dentistry, theology, optometry, and physical therapy. 3-1 medical technology program with accredited schools of medical technology and nearby hospitals. 3-2 and 4-2 engineering programs with Case Western Reserve U, Columbia U, Rensselaer Polytech Inst, U of Michigan at Ann Arbor and Dearborn, and Washington U. Member of Great Lakes College Association and Associated Colleges of the Midwest. Washington Semester. Fine Arts Semester (New York). Oak Ridge Semester (Tennessee). Princeton Critical Languages Program (New Jersey). Urban Studies Semesters (Chicago and Philadelphia). Other semester-away programs. Teacher certification in elementary, secondary, and special education education. Certification in specific subject areas. Study abroad in over 52 countries.
**Honors:** Phi Beta Kappa.
**Academic Assistance:** Nonremedial tutoring.

**STUDENT LIFE. Housing:** All students must live on campus through junior year. Coed, women's, and men's dorms. Sorority and fraternity housing. School-owned/operated apartments. "Cottages" and language houses. 83% of students live in college housing.
**Social atmosphere:** The student newspaper reports, "This is not a 'suitcase' college. Although much of the social life is predictable, you still feel like you've missed something if you go home for the weekend. There are usually two or three parties each weekend sponsored by the Greeks. The Arcadians, the Cosmopolitans, and the Fraters throw the best off-campus bashes. All the Greek organizations are local." Popular campus events include "Homecoming in the fall, Winter Fantasia (a formal dance), and May Day in the spring. Also, traditional events such as the Pull, a tug-of-war between the sophomore and freshman men, and Nykerk, a song/drama/oration competition between the sophomore and freshman women, are popular, too."
**Services and counseling/handicapped student services:** Placement services. Health service. Academic Skills Center. Counseling services for minority and older students. Birth control, personal, and psychological counseling. Career and academic guidance services. Religious counseling. Physically disabled student services. Learning disabled services. Notetaking services. Tape recorders. Reader services for the blind.
**Campus organizations:** Undergraduate student government. Student newspaper (Anchor, published once/week). Literary magazine. Yearbook. Radio and TV stations. Choral and orchestral groups, departmental clubs, drama group, intercollegiate debating, 67 organizations in all. Six fraternities, all with chapter houses; six sororities, all with chapter houses. 9% of men join a fraternity. 10% of women join a sorority.
**Religious organizations:** Fellowship of Christian Students, Intervarsity Christian Fellowship, Ministry of Christ's People, Special Education Ministries, Students for Christ, Union of Celebrating Catholics.
**Minority/foreign student organizations:** Black Coalition, Hispanic Students Organization. International Relations Club.

**ATHLETICS. Physical education requirements:** Two semesters of physical education required.
**Intercollegiate competition:** 20% of students participate. Baseball (M,W), basketball (M,W), cheerleading (M,W), cross-country (M,W), diving (M,W), football (M), golf (M,W), soccer (M,W), softball (W), swimming (M,W), tennis (M,W), track (indoor) (M,W), track (outdoor) (M,W), track and field (outdoor) (M,W), volleyball (W). Member of Michigan Intercollegiate Athletic Association, NCAA Division III.
**Intramural and club sports:** 45% of students participate. Intramural basketball, football, soccer, softball, swimming, tennis, track. Men's club bowling, lacrosse, sailing, ultimate frisbee, volleyball, water polo, weight lifting. Women's club bowling, sailing.

**ADMISSIONS. Academic basis for candidate selection** (in order of priority): Secondary school record, class rank, standardized test scores, school's recommendation, essay.
**Nonacademic basis for candidate selection:** Character and personality and extracurricular participation are important. Alumni/ae relationship is considered.
**Requirements:** Graduation from secondary school is required; GED is accepted. 16 units and the following program of study are recommended: 4 units of English, 3 units of math, 3 units of science, 2 units of foreign language, 2 units of social studies, 1 unit of history, 5 units of electives. Special application required of applicants to nursing and sports medicine programs. ACT is required; SAT may be substituted. Campus visit and interview recommended. No off-campus interviews.
**Procedure:** Take SAT or ACT by December of 12th year. Notification of admission on rolling basis. Reply is required by May 1. $300 tuition deposit, refundable until May 1. Freshmen accepted for terms other than fall.
**Special programs:** Admission may be deferred one year. Credit and/or placement may be granted through CEEB Advanced Placement exams for scores of 4 or higher. Credit and/or placement may be granted through CLEP general exams. Credit may be granted through CLEP subject exams. Credit and placement may be granted through challenge exams. Concurrent enrollment program.
**Transfer students:** Transfer students accepted for terms other than fall. In fall 1993, 14% of all new students were transfers into all classes. 209 transfer applications were received, 174 were accepted. Minimum 2.0 GPA required. Lowest course grade accepted is "C." Maximum number of transferable credits is 65 semester hours. At least 30 semester hours must be completed at the college to receive degree.
**Admissions contact:** Gary Camp, Director of Admissions. 616 394-7850, 800 968-7850, Fax: 616 394-7130.

**FINANCIAL AID. Available aid:** Pell grants, SEOG, state scholarships and grants, school scholarships and grants, private scholarships and grants, academic merit scholarships, and aid for undergraduate foreign students. Perkins Loans (NDSL), PLUS, Stafford Loans (GSL), state loans, school loans, and SLS. MI-Loan (Michigan Loan program) Budget Payment Plan
**Financial aid statistics:** 18% of aid is not need-based. In 1993-94, 85% of all undergraduate applicants received aid; 80% of freshman applicants. Average amounts of aid awarded freshmen: Scholarships and grants, $8,145; loans, $3,141.
**Supporting data/closing dates:** FAFSA: Priority filing date is May 1. Notification of awards begins March 15.
**Financial aid contact:** Phyllis Hooyman, Director of Financial Aid. 616 394-7765.

**STUDENT EMPLOYMENT.** College Work/Study Program. Institutional employment. 47% of full-time undergraduates work on campus during school year. Students may expect to earn an average of $1,200 during school year. Off-campus part-time employment opportunities rated "excellent."

**COMPUTER FACILITIES.** 220 IBM/IBM-compatible, Macintosh/Apple, and RISC-/UNIX-based microcomputers; 100 are networked. Students may access Digital, SUN minicomputer/mainframe systems, BITNET, Internet. Residence halls may be equipped with stand-alone microcomputers, networked microcomputers, networked terminals. Client/LAN operating systems include Apple/Macintosh, DOS, UNIX/XENIX/

AIX, X-windows, LocalTalk/AppleTalk, Novell. 40 major computer languages and software packages available. Computer facilities are available to all students.
**Fees:** None.
**Hours:** 24 hours.

**GRADUATE CAREER DATA.** Graduate school percentages: 3% enter law school. 4% enter medical school. 1% enter dental school. 2% enter graduate business programs. 16% enter graduate arts and sciences programs. 2% enter theological school/seminary. Highest graduate school enrollments: Michigan State U, U of Michigan, Wayne State U. 72% of graduates choose careers in business and industry. Companies and businesses that hire graduates: Andersen Consulting, Deloitte & Touche, Ernst & Young, Universal Forestry Products.

**PROMINENT ALUMNI/AE.** Robert Schuller, minister, Crystal Cathedral; Richard Kruizenga, vice-president, Exxon; Guy Vander Jagt, former U.S. Congressman; George Zusdema, vice-provost, Medical Affairs, U of Michigan; Clifford Paine, chief designer, Golden Gate Bridge.

# Kalamazoo College

**Kalamazoo, MI 49006-3295 616 337-7000**

**1994-95 Costs.** Tuition: $16,179. Room: $2,427. Board: $2,667. Fees, books, misc. academic expenses (school's estimate): $580.
**Enrollment.** Undergraduates: 543 men, 675 women (full-time). Freshman class: 1,230 applicants, 1,109 accepted, 338 enrolled.
**Test score averages/ranges.** Range of SAT scores of middle 50%: 510-610 verbal, 550-660 math. Range of ACT scores of middle 50%: 23-28 English, 22-27 math.
**Faculty.** 92 full-time; 18 part-time. 85% of faculty holds highest degree in specific field. Student/faculty ratio: 12 to 1.
**Selectivity rating.** Highly competitive.

**PROFILE.** Kalamazoo, founded in 1833, is a private, liberal arts college. Its 60-acre campus is located in a residential area of Kalamazoo. Campus architecture includes Georgian-style buildings.

**Accreditation:** NCACS.
**Religious orientation:** Kalamazoo College is nonsectarian; two courses in religion or philosophy required.
**Library:** Collections totaling over 301,751 volumes, 1,350 periodical subscriptions, and 18,049 microform items.
**Special facilities/museums:** Science center.
**Athletic facilities:** Gymnasium, field house, swimming pool, stadium, basketball, racquetball, tennis, and volleyball courts, baseball, football, intramural, soccer, and softball fields.

**STUDENT BODY. Undergraduate profile:** 70% are state residents; 4% are transfers. 7% Asian-American, 2% Black, 1% Hispanic, 1% Native American, 85% White, 4% Other. Average age of undergraduates is 20.
**Freshman profile:** 5% of freshmen who took SAT scored 700 or over on verbal, 23% scored 700 or over on math; 44% scored 600 or over on verbal, 69% scored 600 or over on math; 85% scored 500 or over on verbal, 93% scored 500 or over on math; 99% scored 400 or over on verbal, 100% scored 400 or over on math; 100% scored 300 or over on verbal. 75% of accepted applicants took SAT; 84% took ACT. 87% of freshmen come from public schools.
**Undergraduate achievement:** 83% of fall 1992 freshmen returned for fall 1993 term. 65% of entering class graduated. 30% of students who completed a degree program went on to graduate study within one year.
**Foreign students:** 37 students are from out of the country. Countries represented include France, Germany, India, Japan, Spain, and the United Kingdom.

**PROGRAMS OF STUDY. Degrees:** B.A.
**Majors:** Anthropology, Art, Art History, Biology, Chemistry, Computer Science, Economics/Business Administration, English, French, German, Health Sciences, History, Human Development/Social Relations, International/Area Studies, Mathematics, Music, Philosophy, Physics, Political Science, Psychology, Religion, Sociology, Sociology/Anthropology, Spanish, Theatre/Communication Arts.
**Distribution of degrees:** The majors with the highest enrollment are economics, biology, and psychology; philosophy, art/art history, and religion have the lowest.
**Requirements:** General education requirement.
**Academic regulations:** Minimum 2.0 GPA must be maintained.
**Special:** Concentrations offered in all majors and in numerous other fields. Year is divided into four 11-week quarters of three subjects each. 10 quarters are spent in residence; the remaining quarters may be used for sophomore career-internship experience or foreign study (elected by 90% of students); seniors devote one quarter to individualized study in major. Special programs in African studies, American studies, business administration, computer science, international commerce, management studies, physical education, public policy studies, and teaching. Neglected-language program in Japanese, Mandarin Chinese, Portuguese, and Swahili for students of proven language aptitude. Environmental studies offers study in the Amazon rain forest and on the Galapagos Islands. Double majors. Independent study. Pass/fail grading option. Internships. Preprofessional programs in law, medicine, veterinary science, and dentistry. 3-2 engineering programs with U of Michigan and Washington U. Member of Great Lakes College Association and Kalamazoo Consortium of Higher Education. Arts Program (New York). Newberry Library Program in the Humanities (Illinois). Oak Ridge Science Semester (Tennessee). Philadelphia Urban Program. Teacher certification in secondary education. Certification in specific subject areas. Study abroad in China, Ecuador, France, Germany, Kenya, Mexico, Senegal, Sierra Leone, Spain, and Swaziland. ROTC at Western Michigan U.
**Honors:** Phi Beta Kappa. Honor societies.
**Academic Assistance:** Remedial study skills. Nonremedial tutoring.

**STUDENT LIFE. Housing:** All unmarried students under age 21 must live on campus unless living near campus with relatives. Coed dorms. 98% of students live in college housing.
**Services and counseling/handicapped student services:** Placement services. Health service. Women's center. Writing center. Collaborative learning center. Counseling services for minority students. Birth control, personal, and psychological counseling. Career and academic guidance services. Religious counseling. Physically disabled student services. Learning disabled services. Tape recorders. Tutors.
**Campus organizations:** Undergraduate student government. Student newspaper (Index, published once/week). Literary magazine. Yearbook. Radio station. Bands, orchestra, chamber choir, Guild of Change Ringers, art exhibits, film society, Habitat for Humanity, Amnesty International, Gay and Lesbian Support Group, environmental group, Women's Equity Coalition, Student Commission, 36 organizations in all.
**Religious organizations:** Chaverim, Intervarsity Christian Fellowship, Wesley/United Campus Ministries, Jewish Student Organization.
**Minority/foreign student organizations:** Black Student Organization, Asian Student Organization, Coalition on Race and Diversity. International Student Organization, Asian American Student Organization.

**ATHLETICS. Physical education requirements:** Six non-graded activity classes required.
**Intercollegiate competition:** 28% of students participate. Baseball (M), basketball (M,W), cross-country (M,W), diving (M,W), football (M), golf (M,W), soccer (M,W), softball (W), swimming (M,W), tennis (M,W), volleyball (M). Member of Michigan Intercollegiate Athletic Association, NCAA Division III.
**Intramural and club sports:** 35% of students participate. Intramural badminton, basketball, frisbee golf, racquetball, softball, swimming, tennis, triathlon, ultimate frisbee, volleyball. Men's club soccer, track, ultimate frisbee. Women's club cheerleading, track, ultimate frisbee.

**ADMISSIONS. Academic basis for candidate selection** (in order of priority): Secondary school record, class rank, standardized test scores, essay, school's recommendation.
**Nonacademic basis for candidate selection:** Extracurricular participation, particular talent or ability, and geographical distribution are important. Character and personality and alumni/ae relationship are considered.
**Requirements:** Graduation from secondary school is recommended; GED is accepted. 16 units and the following program of study are recommended: 4 units of English, 4 units of math, 3 units of science, 2 units of foreign language, 1 unit of social studies, 2 units of history. Minimum rank in top two-fifths of secondary school class and minimum 3.0 GPA recommended. Conditional admission possible for applicants not meeting standard requirements. SAT or ACT is required. PSAT is recommended. ACH recommended. Campus visit and interview recommended. Off-campus interviews available with an admissions representative.
**Procedure:** Take SAT or ACT by fall of 12th year. Take ACH by fall of 12th year. Visit college for interview by fall of 12th year. Suggest filing application by February 15. Notification of admission on rolling basis. Reply is required by May 1. $200 nonrefundable tuition deposit. Freshmen accepted for terms other than fall.
**Special programs:** Admission may be deferred one year. Credit and/or placement may be granted through CEEB Advanced Placement exams for scores of 3 or higher. Early entrance/early admission program. Concurrent enrollment program.
**Transfer students:** Transfer students accepted for terms other than fall. In fall 1993, 4% of all new students were transfers into all classes. 52 transfer applications were received, 39 were accepted. Application deadline is rolling for fall; rolling for spring. Minimum 2.8 GPA required. Lowest course grade accepted is "C." Maximum number of transferable credits is 135 quarter hours. At least 45 quarter hours must be completed at the college to receive degree.
**Admissions contact:** Teresa M. Lahti, Dean of Admissions. 616 337-7166, 800 253-3602.

**FINANCIAL AID. Available aid:** Pell grants, SEOG, state scholarships and grants, school scholarships and grants, private scholarships and grants, academic merit scholarships, and aid for undergraduate foreign students. Perkins Loans (NDSL), PLUS, Stafford Loans (GSL), state loans, and SLS. Tuition Plan Inc., Knight Tuition Plans, and deferred payment plan. Loans by special arrangement with Business Office.
**Financial aid statistics:** 44% of aid is not need-based. In 1993-94, 98% of all undergraduate applicants received aid; 98% of freshman applicants. Average amounts of aid awarded freshmen: Scholarships and grants, $6,744; loans, $3,575.
**Supporting data/closing dates:** FAFSA/FAF: Priority filing date is February 15. Income tax forms: Priority filing date is May 1; accepted on rolling basis. Notification of awards on rolling basis.
**Financial aid contact:** Joellen Silberman, M.B.A., Director of Financial Aid. 616 337-7192.

**STUDENT EMPLOYMENT.** College Work/Study Program. Institutional employment. 34% of full-time undergraduates work on campus during school year. Students may expect to earn an average of $875 during school year. Off-campus part-time employment opportunities rated "good."

**COMPUTER FACILITIES.** 70 IBM/IBM-compatible and Macintosh/Apple microcomputers; all are networked. Students may access Digital minicomputer/mainframe systems, Internet. Client/LAN operating systems include Apple/Macintosh, DOS, UNIX/XENIX/AIX, LocalTalk/AppleTalk. Computer languages and software packages include BASIC, C, COBOL, Cricket Graphics, Excel, FORTRAN, Harvard Graphics, LISP, Microsoft Word, PageMaker, Pascal, Superpaint, Windows, WordPerfect. Computer facilities are available to all students.
**Fees:** None.

**GRADUATE CAREER DATA.** Graduate school percentages: 4% enter law school. 6% enter medical school. 1% enter dental school. 1% enter graduate business programs. 18% enter graduate arts and sciences programs. Highest graduate school enrollments: U of Chicago, U of Michigan, Michigan State U, U of North Carolina, Northwestern U, U of Notre Dame. 30% of graduates choose careers in business and industry. Companies and businesses that hire graduates: Arthur Andersen, First of America Bank, IBM, Upjohn, Valassis Inserts, Warner-Lambert/Parke-Davis.

**PROMINENT ALUMNI/AE.** Vic Braden, tennis professional; Ralph McKee, scientist and discoverer of Vitamin K.

# Kendall College of Art and Design

**Grand Rapids, MI 49503-3194** **616 451-2787**

**1994-95 Costs.** Tuition: $9,990. Housing: None. Fees, books, misc. academic expenses (school's estimate): $1,610.
**Enrollment.** Undergraduates: 211 men, 203 women (full-time). Freshman class: 197 applicants, 119 accepted, 93 enrolled.
**Test score averages/ranges.** Average SAT scores: 430 verbal, 410 math. Average ACT scores: 19 English, 17 math, 19 composite.
**Faculty.** 33 full-time; 28 part-time. 5% of faculty holds doctoral degree. Student/faculty ratio: 12 to 1.
**Selectivity rating.** N/A.

**PROFILE.** Kendall College of Art and Design, founded in 1928, is a private college. Its main campus is located in a residential area of Grand Rapids.

**Accreditation:** NCACS. Professionally accredited by the Foundation for Interior Design Education Research, the National Association of Schools of Art and Design.
**Religious orientation:** Kendall College of Art and Design is nonsectarian; no religious requirements.
**Library:** Collections totaling over 16,100 volumes, 110 periodical subscriptions and 200 microform items.
**STUDENT BODY. Undergraduate profile:** 93% are state residents; 32% are transfers. 2% Asian-American, 4% Black, 3% Hispanic, 1% Native American, 86% White, 4% Other. Average age of undergraduates is 26.
**Freshman profile:** 2% of freshmen who took SAT scored 500 or over on verbal, 2% scored 500 or over on math; 5% scored 400 or over on verbal, 3% scored 400 or over on math; 10% scored 300 or over on verbal, 10% scored 300 or over on math. 1% of freshmen who took ACT scored 30 or over on English; 14% scored 24 or over on English, 4% scored 24 or over on math, 12% scored 24 or over on composite; 44% scored 18 or over on English, 33% scored 18 or over on math, 50% scored 18 or over on composite; 71% scored 12 or over on English, 70% scored 12 or over on math, 74% scored 12 or over on composite; 75% scored 6 or over on English, 74% scored 6 or over on math, 75% scored 6 or over on composite. 11% of accepted applicants took SAT; 76% took ACT. 91% of freshmen come from public schools.
**Undergraduate achievement:** 69% of fall 1992 freshmen returned for fall 1993 term. 16% of entering class graduated. 4% of students who completed a degree program went on to graduate study.
**Foreign students:** 20 students are from out of the country. Countries represented include Japan, Korea, and Vietnam; 15 in all.
**PROGRAMS OF STUDY. Degrees:** B.F.A.
**Majors:** Fine Arts, Furniture Design, Illustration, Industrial Design, Interior Design, Visual Communications.
**Distribution of degrees:** The majors with the highest enrollment are visual communication, interior design, and illustration; furniture design have the lowest.
**Requirements:** General education requirement.
**Academic regulations:** Freshmen must maintain minimum 1.0 GPA; sophomores, 1.62 GPA; juniors, 1.81 GPA; seniors, 1.9 GPA.
**Special:** Minors offered in most majors. Independent study. Internships. Cooperative education programs. Graduate school at which undergraduates may take graduate-level courses. Member of Association of Independent Colleges of Art and Design (AICAD); exchange possible. Study abroad in England, France, Italy, and Mexico.
**Academic Assistance:** Remedial reading, writing, and study skills. Nonremedial tutoring.
**ADMISSIONS. Academic basis for candidate selection** (in order of priority): Secondary school record, portfolio, standardized test scores, essay, class rank.
**Nonacademic basis for candidate selection:** Particular talent or ability is emphasized. Character and personality and alumni/ae relationship are important. Extracurricular participation and geographical distribution are considered.
**Requirements:** Graduation from secondary school is required; GED is accepted. 5.5 units and the following program of study are recommended: 2.5 units of English, 1 unit of math, 1 unit of social studies, 1 unit of history. Minimum 2.25 GPA required; minimum composite ACT score of 19 and rank in top half of secondary school class recommended. Portfolio required of art program applicants. ACT is required; SAT may be substituted. Campus visit and interview recommended. Off-campus interviews available with an admissions representative.
**Procedure:** Take SAT or ACT by spring of 12th year. Visit college for interview by spring of 12th year. Suggest filing application by April 15; no deadline. Notification of admission on rolling basis. No set date by which applicants must accept offer. $150 nonrefundable tuition deposit. Freshmen accepted for terms other than fall.
**Special programs:** Admission may be deferred two semesters. Credit and/or placement may be granted through CEEB Advanced Placement exams for scores of 3 or higher. Credit may be granted through CLEP general and subject exams, military and life experience. Early entrance/early admission program. Concurrent enrollment program.
**Transfer students:** Transfer students accepted for terms other than fall. In fall 1993, 32% of all new students were transfers into all classes. 117 transfer applications were received, 85 were accepted. Application deadline is rolling for fall; rolling for spring. Minimum 2.5 GPA required. Lowest course grade accepted is "C." Portfolio required of studio program applicants. Maximum number of transferable credits is 68 semester hours. At least 52 semester hours must be completed at the college to receive degree.
**Admissions contact:** Geoff Kehoe, B.F.A., Director of Enrollment Management. 616 451-2787, extension 42.
**FINANCIAL AID. Available aid:** Pell grants, SEOG, state scholarships and grants, school scholarships, private scholarships, and academic merit scholarships. Perkins Loans (NDSL), PLUS, Stafford Loans (GSL), and SLS. Deferred payment plan and guaranteed tuition.
**Financial aid statistics:** 20% of aid is not need-based. In 1993-94, 93% of all undergraduate applicants received aid; 83% of freshman applicants. Average amounts of aid awarded freshmen: Scholarships and grants, $2,000; loans, $2,625.
**Supporting data/closing dates:** FAFSA: Priority filing date is February 15. Notification of awards on rolling basis.
**Financial aid contact:** Sandra Preuss, M.B.A., Director of Financial Aid. 616 451-2787, extensions 24, 39.

# Lake Superior State University

**Sault Sainte Marie, MI 49783** **800 682-4800 (in-state)**

**1994-95 Costs.** Tuition: $3,312 (state residents), $6,450 (out-of-state). Room & board: $4,230. Fees, books, misc. academic expenses (school's estimate): $500.
**Enrollment.** Undergraduates: 1,558 men, 1,466 women (full-time). Freshman class: 1,406 applicants, 1,169 accepted, 522 enrolled. Graduate enrollment: 220.
**Test score averages/ranges.** Average ACT scores: 20 English, 20 math, 21 composite.
**Faculty.** 112 full-time. 30% of faculty holds doctoral degree. Student/faculty ratio: 20 to 1.
**Selectivity rating.** Less competitive.

**PROFILE.** Lake Superior State, founded in 1946, is a public university. Its 121-acre campus is located in Sault Sainte Marie, across the St. Mary's River from Sault Sainte Marie, Ontario, Canada.

**Accreditation:** NCACS. Professionally accredited by the Accreditation Board for Engineering and Technology, the National League for Nursing.
**Religious orientation:** Lake Superior State University is nonsectarian; no religious requirements.
**Library:** Collections totaling over 131,000 volumes, 775 periodical subscriptions, and 164,000 microform items.
**Special facilities/museums:** Natural science, Michigan history, and Great Lakes shipping museums, planetarium, industrial robots, atomic absorption/flame emission spectrophotometer.
**Athletic facilities:** Gymnasium, ice rink, basketball, racquetball, and tennis courts, swimming pool, diving well, rifle range, dance studio, track, combatives, weight, wrestling rooms.
**STUDENT BODY. Undergraduate profile:** 98% are state residents. 1% Asian-American, 1% Black, 5% Native American, 69% White, 24% Other. Average age of undergraduates is 24.
**Freshman profile:** Majority of accepted applicants took ACT.
**Undergraduate achievement:** 70% of fall 1991 freshmen returned for fall 1992 term.
**Foreign students:** 737 students are from out of the country. Countries represented include Canada.
**PROGRAMS OF STUDY. Degrees:** B.A., B.S.
**Majors:** Accounting, Biological Science, Biology, Business Administration, Computer Engineering Technology, Computer Information Systems Management, Computer/Mathematical Sciences, Corrections, Criminal Justice, Criminalistics, Economics/Finance, Electrical Engineering Technology, English Language/Literature, Environmental Science, Exercise Science, Fire Science, Fishery/Wildlife Management, Geology, History, Hotel/Restaurant Management, Human Services, Individualized Studies, Law Enforcement, Legal Assistance Studies, Loss Control, Management, Marketing, Mathematics, Mechanical Engineering Technology, Medical Technology, Nursing, Office Administration, Political Science, Pre-Dentistry, Pre-Law, Pre-Medicine, Pre-Veterinary, Psychology, Public Safety, Recreation Management, Robotics Engineering Technology, Social Sciences, Sociology, Therapeutic Recreation.
**Distribution of degrees:** The majors with the highest enrollment are business, criminal justice, and human services; fire science, social sciences, and medical technology have the lowest.
**Requirements:** General education requirement.
**Special:** Minors offered. Associate's degrees offered. Double majors. Dual degrees. Independent study. Pass/fail grading option. Internships. Graduate school at which undergraduates may take graduate-level courses. Preprofessional programs in law, medicine, veterinary science, pharmacy, dentistry, and optometry. 2-2 engineering program with Michigan Tech Inst. Study abroad in Canada; other programs arranged on individual basis.
**Honors:** Phi Beta Kappa. Honors program.
**Academic Assistance:** Remedial reading, writing, math, and study skills. Nonremedial tutoring.
**STUDENT LIFE. Housing:** Unmarried, nonveteran students within 27 months of secondary school graduation must live on campus. Coed, women's, and men's dorms. Sorority and fraternity housing. On-campus married-student housing. 32% of students live in college housing.
**Social atmosphere:** Students gather at The Galley on campus, and at The Alpha off campus. Greeks and the Christian Fellowship are influential groups on campus. Popular events include hockey games, Spring Fling, beach and Halloween parties, and Christian retreats. "Lake Superior State provides an awesome opportunity to meet people from all over. We're located on the Canadian border and near a Chippewa reservation, so we're exposed to Canadian and Native American perspectives," reports the student newspaper.
**Services and counseling/handicapped student services:** Placement services. Health service. Day care. Personal and psychological counseling. Career and academic guidance services. Physically disabled student services. Learning disabled services.
**Campus organizations:** Undergraduate student government. Student newspaper (Compass, published once/two weeks). Yearbook. Radio station. Orchestra, concert band, jazz and pep bands, forensics team, 44 organizations in all. Five fraternities, no chapter houses;

four sororities, no chapter houses. 10% of men join a fraternity. 10% of women join a sorority.
**Religious organizations:** Anchor House Christian Fellowship, His House Christian Fellowship, Newman Center, Campus Crusade for Christ.
**Minority/foreign student organizations:** Native American Student Council.

**ATHLETICS. Physical education requirements:** Two semesters of physical education required.
**Intercollegiate competition:** 10% of students participate. Basketball (M,W), cheerleading (M,W), cross-country (M,W), ice hockey (M), softball (W), tennis (M,W), volleyball (W), wrestling (M). Member of Central Collegiate Hockey Association, Great Lakes Intercollegiate Athletic Conference, NCAA Division I for hockey, NCAA Division II.
**Intramural and club sports:** 50% of students participate. Intramural badminton, basketball, broomball, cross-country, deer hunting, flag football, floor hockey, free throw shoot, golf, handball, ice hockey, ice skating, marathon running, racquetball, softball, tennis, three-on-three basketball, ultimate frisbee, volleyball, walleyball, water basketball, water polo, Wiffle ball, wrestling.

**ADMISSIONS. Academic basis for candidate selection** (in order of priority): Secondary school record, school's recommendation, class rank.
**Nonacademic basis for candidate selection:** Geographical distribution is important. Character and personality, extracurricular participation, particular talent or ability, and alumni/ae relationship are considered.
**Requirements:** Graduation from secondary school is required; GED is accepted. No specific distribution of secondary school units required. Minimum 2.0 GPA required. Conditional admission possible for applicants not meeting standard requirements. ACT is required. Campus visit and interview recommended. No off-campus interviews.
**Procedure:** Take ACT by June of 12th year. Visit college for interview by August of 12th year. Application deadline is August 12. Notification of admission on rolling basis. $100 room deposit, refundable until July 1. Freshmen accepted for terms other than fall.
**Special programs:** Admission may be deferred one year. Credit may be granted through CEEB Advanced Placement for scores of 3 or higher. Credit may be granted through CLEP general and subject exams, DANTES exams and military experience. Credit and placement may be granted through challenge exams. Concurrent enrollment program.
**Transfer students:** Transfer students accepted for terms other than fall. In fall 1993, 765 transfer applications were received, 564 were accepted. Application deadline is July 26 for fall; December for spring. Minimum 2.0 GPA required. Lowest course grade accepted is "D." At least 32 semester hours must be completed at the university to receive degree.
**Admissions contact:** Bruce R. Johnson, M.S., Director of Admissions. 906 635-2231.

**FINANCIAL AID. Available aid:** Pell grants, SEOG, Federal Nursing Student Scholarships, state scholarships and grants, school scholarships and grants, private scholarships, academic merit scholarships, athletic scholarships, and aid for undergraduate foreign students. PLUS, NSL, school loans, private loans, and SLS. AMS.
**Financial aid statistics:** 30% of aid is not need-based. In 1993-94, 80% of all undergraduate applicants received aid; 80% of freshman applicants. Average amounts of aid awarded freshmen: Scholarships and grants, $1,910; loans, $3,100.
**Supporting data/closing dates:** FAFSA/FAF/FFS: Priority filing date is March 1; deadline is April 1. School's own aid application: Priority filing date is March 1; deadline is April 1. Notification of awards on rolling basis.
**Financial aid contact:** William Munsell, Director of Financial Aid. 906 635-2678.

**STUDENT EMPLOYMENT.** College Work/Study Program. Institutional employment. 25% of full-time undergraduates work on campus during school year. Students may expect to earn an average of $1,400 during school year. Off-campus part-time employment opportunities rated "fair."

**COMPUTER FACILITIES.** 210 IBM/IBM-compatible and Macintosh/Apple microcomputers. Students may access Digital minicomputer/mainframe systems. Computer languages and software packages include APL, Assembler, BASIC, C, COBOL, Pascal, RPG II; database, spreadsheet, word processing packages; 45 in all. Computer facilities are available to all students.
**Fees:** $35 computer fee per semester.
**Hours:** 7:30 AM-10:30 PM (M-Th); 7:30 AM-9 PM (F); 10 AM-9 PM (Sa); 11 AM-10:30 PM (Su).

**GRADUATE CAREER DATA.** Companies and businesses that hire graduates: Emerson Electric, Ernst & Young, General Electric, General Motors, Honeywell, McDonnell Douglas.

**PROMINENT ALUMNI/AE.** Mitch Irwin, state senator; Tony Hoholik, director of marketing, Moore Business Forms; Gary Benjamin, senior vice-president, Champion, Inc.; Larry Constantineau, vice-president of marketing research, Pillsbury.

## Lawrence Technological University

**Southfield, MI 48075** **313 356-0200**

**1993-94 Costs.** Tuition: $6,795. Room: $2,500. No meal plan. Fees, books, misc. academic expenses (school's estimate): $1,320.
**Enrollment.** Undergraduates: 1,809 men, 536 women (full-time). Freshman class: 1,689 applicants, 1,443 accepted. Graduate enrollment: 195 men, 93 women.
**Test score averages/ranges.** Average ACT scores: 22 composite.
**Faculty.** 112 full-time; 195 part-time. 36% of faculty holds doctoral degree. Student/faculty ratio: 20 to 1.
**Selectivity rating.** Less competitive.

**PROFILE.** Lawrence Technological University, founded in 1932, is a private institution. Programs are offered through the Colleges of Architecture and Design, Arts and Science, Engineering, and Management. Its 100-acre campus is located in Southfield, 20 miles from the center of Detroit.
**Accreditation:** NCACS. Professionally accredited by the Accreditation Board for Engineering and Technology, the National Architecture Accrediting Board.
**Religious orientation:** Lawrence Technological University is nonsectarian; no religious requirements.
**Library:** Collections totaling over 70,000 volumes, 1,000 periodical subscriptions, and 95,000 microform items.
**Athletic facilities:** Gymnasium, field house, indoor track, weight room, racquetball courts, athletic fields.

**STUDENT BODY. Undergraduate profile:** 3% Asian-American, 9% Black, 1% Hispanic, 1% Native American, 86% White. Average age of undergraduates is 25.
**Freshman profile:** Majority of accepted applicants took ACT.
**Undergraduate achievement:** 60% of fall 1992 freshmen returned for fall 1993 term.
**Foreign students:** 124 students are from out of the country. Countries represented include Canada, Jordan, and Lebanon; 40 in all.

**PROGRAMS OF STUDY. Degrees:** B.Arch., B.S.
**Majors:** Architecture, Business Administration, Chemical Technology, Chemistry, Civil Engineering, Computer Systems, Electrical Engineering, Humanities, Industrial Management, Information Systems, Interior Architecture, Mathematics/Computer Science, Mechanical Engineering, Physics, Technology.
**Distribution of degrees:** The majors with the highest enrollment are engineering, management, and architecture.
**Requirements:** General education requirement.
**Academic regulations:** Minimum 2.0 GPA must be maintained.
**Special:** Associate's degrees offered. Self-designed majors. Double majors. Dual degrees. Independent study. Cooperative education programs. Graduate school at which undergraduates may take graduate-level courses. Study abroad in European countries.
**Academic Assistance:** Nonremedial tutoring.

**STUDENT LIFE. Housing:** Students may live on or off campus. Fraternity housing. School-owned/operated apartments. On-campus married-student housing. 7% of students live in college housing.
**Social atmosphere:** The Atrium in the Buell Management Building is a favorite on-campus gathering place for students; others include Campus Activities and Affairs Center West and the Don Ridler Field House. There are numerous groups on campus with a considerable influence on the social atmosphere, including the Greek community, the amateur radio club, the Jewish Student Association, Lawrence Christian Fellowship, student government, and the eighteen professional organizations. The university's Open House Weekend is always a big event with displays of senior projects all over campus. There are also the Greek Rush Weeks in the fall, winter, and spring, and engineering students look forward to the competition of student-built vehicles in May and June. "At Lawrence Technological University, education can be more than hours, credits, courses, and examinations," notes the student newspaper. "It can be a total experience of living and learning, encompassing recreation, entertainment, student government, athletics, culture, religion, and professional growth."
**Services and counseling/handicapped student services:** Placement services. Counseling services for minority students. Personal counseling. Career and academic guidance services.
**Campus organizations:** Undergraduate student government. Student newspaper (Tech News, published twice/month). Radio and TV stations. Society of Women Engineers. Five fraternities, one chapter house; three sororities, no chapter houses. 1% of men join a fraternity. 1% of women join a sorority.
**Minority/foreign student organizations:** Society of Black Engineers.

**ATHLETICS. Physical education requirements:** None.
**Intercollegiate competition:** 2% of students participate.
**Intramural and club sports:** 30% of students participate. Intramural basketball, bowling, touch football, golf, indoor soccer, racquetball, softball, volleyball, walleyball. Men's club golf, ice hockey, soccer.

**ADMISSIONS. Academic basis for candidate selection** (in order of priority): Secondary school record, class rank, school's recommendation, standardized test scores.
**Nonacademic basis for candidate selection:** Particular talent or ability is considered.
**Requirements:** Graduation from secondary school is required; GED is accepted. 20 units and the following program of study are recommended: 4 units of science, 4.5 units of electives. Minimum 2.0 GPA required. Minimum 2.75 GPA and portfolio required of architecture program applicants. Conditional admission possible for applicants not meeting standard requirements. ACT is required; SAT may be substituted. Campus visit and interview recommended. No off-campus interviews.
**Procedure:** Take SAT or ACT by June of 12th year. Visit college for interview by June of 12th year. Application deadline is August 1. Notification of admission on rolling basis. No set date by which applicants must accept offer. $50 refundable room deposit. Freshmen accepted for terms other than fall.
**Special programs:** Admission may be deferred one year. Credit and/or placement may be granted through CEEB Advanced Placement exams for scores of 3 or higher. Credit and/or placement may be granted through CLEP general and subject exams. Credit and placement may be granted through ACT PEP exams and military experience. Early decision program. Early entrance/early admission program. Concurrent enrollment program.
**Transfer students:** Transfer students accepted for terms other than fall. In fall 1993, 822 transfer applications were received, 748 were accepted. Application deadline is August 1 for fall; one month before beginning of term for spring. Minimum 2.0 GPA required. Lowest course grade accepted is "C." At least 45 quarter hours must be completed at the university to receive degree.
**Admissions contact:** Kevin Pollock, M.S., Director of Admissions. 313 356-0200, extension 3160.

**FINANCIAL AID. Available aid:** Pell grants, SEOG, state scholarships and grants, school scholarships and grants, private scholarships and grants, and academic merit scholarships. Perkins Loans (NDSL), PLUS, Stafford Loans (GSL), state loans, school loans, private loans, and SLS. AMS and deferred payment plan.
**Financial aid statistics:** 10% of aid is not need-based. In 1993-94, 90% of all undergraduate applicants received aid; 90% of freshman applicants. Average amounts of aid awarded freshmen: Scholarships and grants, $2,500; loans, $2,625.

**Supporting data/closing dates:** FAFSA: Priority filing date is March 1; accepted on rolling basis. FAF/FFS: Accepted on rolling basis. Income tax forms: Priority filing date is March 1; accepted on rolling basis. Notification of awards on rolling basis.
**Financial aid contact:** Paul F. Kinder, M.S., Director of Financial Aid. 313 356-0200, extension 2120.

**STUDENT EMPLOYMENT.** College Work/Study Program. Institutional employment. 60% of full-time undergraduates work on campus during school year. Students may expect to earn an average of $1,250 during school year. Off-campus part-time employment opportunities rated "excellent."

**COMPUTER FACILITIES.** 408 IBM/IBM-compatible and Macintosh/Apple microcomputers; 320 are networked. Students may access Digital minicomputer/mainframe systems, BITNET. Residence halls may be equipped with networked terminals. Numerous computer languages and software programs. Computer facilities are available to all students.
**Fees:** None.
**Hours:** 8 AM-11 PM (M-F).

**GRADUATE CAREER DATA.** Companies and businesses that hire graduates: Ford Motor Co., General Motors.

**PROMINENT ALUMNI/AE.** Edward Donley, chairperson, Air Products and Chemicals.

# Marygrove College

**Detroit, MI 48221-2599 313 862-8000**

**1994-95 Costs.** Tuition: $7,554. Room & board: $3,840. Fees, books, misc. academic expenses (school's estimate): $50.
**Enrollment.** Undergraduates: 90 men, 510 women (full-time). Freshman class: 282 applicants, 111 accepted, 138 enrolled. Graduate enrollment: 43 men, 101 women.
**Test score averages/ranges.** N/A.
**Faculty.** 52 full-time; 14 part-time. 35% of faculty holds doctoral degree. Student/faculty ratio: 17 to 1.
**Selectivity rating.** N/A.

**PROFILE.** Marygrove, founded in 1910, is a church-affiliated college. Programs are offered through the Divisions of Education, Letters, Natural Science and Mathematics, Professional Studies, Social Science, and Visual and Performing Arts. Its 68-acre campus is located in Detroit. Campus architecture includes Tudor-Gothic style buildings.

**Accreditation:** NCACS. Professionally accredited by the American Medical Association (CAHEA), the Council on Social Work Education, the National Council for Accreditation of Teacher Education.
**Religious orientation:** Marygrove College is affiliated with the Roman Catholic Church (Servants of the Immaculate Heart of Mary); one semester of religion, theology, or philosophy required.
**Library:** Collections totaling over 185,000 volumes, 800 periodical subscriptions, and 16,500 microform items.
**Special facilities/museums:** Media center, production center.
**Athletic facilities:** Gymnasium and weight room.

**STUDENT BODY. Undergraduate profile:** 99% are state residents; 46% are transfers. 80% Black, 1% Hispanic, 1% Native American, 7% White, 11% Other. Average age of undergraduates is 31.
**Freshman profile:** Majority of accepted applicants took ACT. 75% of freshmen come from public schools.
**Undergraduate achievement:** 70% of fall 1992 freshmen returned for fall 1993 term. 40% of entering class graduated.

**PROGRAMS OF STUDY. Degrees:** B.A., B.Bus.Admin., B.F.A., B.Mus., B.S., B.Soc.Work.
**Majors:** Accounting, Allied Health Science, Applied Music, Art, Art History/Appreciation, Art Therapy, Biology, Business, Business Administration, Business Education, Ceramics, Chemistry, Child Development, Clothing, Communication Studies, Computer Science, Dance, Dance Therapy, Design, Drawing, Economics, Education, English, Family/Consumer Studies, Food Sciences/Human Nutrition, French, General Human Ecology, German, Graphic Design, History, Home Economics Education, Human Ecology/Home Economics, Humanities, Journalism, Language Arts, Management, Mathematics, Music, Natural Science, Organ, Painting, Philosophy, Piano, Political Science/Government, Printmaking, Psychology, Religious Studies, Sacred Music, Social Sciences, Social Studies, Social Work, Sociology, Spanish, Special Education, Theatre, Theory, Translation, Voice.
**Distribution of degrees:** The majors with the highest enrollment are business, computer science, and psychology.
**Requirements:** General education requirement.
**Academic regulations:** Minimum 2.0 GPA must be maintained.
**Special:** Minors offered in most majors. Associate's degrees offered. Self-designed majors. Double majors. Pass/fail grading option. Internships. Cooperative education programs. Graduate school at which undergraduates may take graduate-level courses. Preprofessional programs in law, medicine, dentistry, chiropractice, and podiatry. Member of Detroit Area Catholic Higher Education Consortium; cross-registration possible. Teacher certification in early childhood, elementary, secondary, and special education education.
**Academic Assistance:** Remedial reading, writing, math, and study skills. Nonremedial tutoring.

**ADMISSIONS. Academic basis for candidate selection** (in order of priority): Secondary school record, school's recommendation, standardized test scores, class rank.
**Nonacademic basis for candidate selection:** Particular talent or ability is emphasized. Character and personality and alumni/ae relationship are important. Extracurricular participation is considered.
**Requirements:** Graduation from secondary school is required; GED is accepted. 25 units and the following program of study are recommended: 8 units of English, 4 units of math, 1 unit of science, 1 unit of foreign language, 4 units of social studies, 5 units of history. Minimum 2.7 GPA required. Separate requirements for allied health program applicants. Portfolio required of art program applicants. Audition required of music program applicants. Developmental Studies Program for applicants not normally admissible. ACT is required; SAT may be substituted. PSAT is recommended. Campus visit and interview recommended. No off-campus interviews.
**Procedure:** Take SAT or ACT by June of 12th year. Visit college for interview by March 15 of 12th year. Notification of admission on rolling basis. No set date by which applicants must accept offer. $50 nonrefundable room deposit. Freshmen accepted for terms other than fall.
**Special programs:** Admission may be deferred one year. Credit and/or placement may be granted through CEEB Advanced Placement exams for scores of 3 or higher. Credit and/or placement may be granted through CLEP general and subject exams. Credit may be granted through military experience. Credit and placement may be granted through ACT PEP, DANTES, and challenge exams and life experience. Early entrance/early admission program.
**Transfer students:** Transfer students accepted for terms other than fall. In fall 1993, 46% of all new students were transfers into all classes. 458 transfer applications were received, 236 were accepted. Minimum 2.0 GPA required. Lowest course grade accepted is "C." Maximum number of transferable credits is 98 semester hours. At least 30 credits must be completed at the college to receive degree.
**Admissions contact:** Karin Harabedian-Jahn, Director of Admissions. 313 862-5200.

**FINANCIAL AID. Available aid:** Pell grants, SEOG, state scholarships and grants, school scholarships and grants, private scholarships and grants, academic merit scholarships, and aid for undergraduate foreign students. Perkins Loans (NDSL), PLUS, Stafford Loans (GSL), state loans, private loans, and SLS. Tuition Plan Inc., Education Plan Inc., deferred payment plan, and family tuition reduction.
**Financial aid statistics:** Average amounts of aid awarded freshmen: Scholarships and grants, $1,600; loans, $1,300.
**Supporting data/closing dates:** FAFSA/FAF/FFS: Priority filing date is February 1; accepted on rolling basis. School's own aid application: Priority filing date is February 1. State aid form: Priority filing date is April 15; deadline is August 30. Income tax forms: Accepted on rolling basis. Notification of awards begins May 1.
**Financial aid contact:** Donald Hurt, Director of Financial Aid. 313 862-8000.

# Michigan Christian College

**Rochester Hills, MI 48307 800 521-6010**

**1994-95 Costs.** Tuition: $5,340. Room & board: $3,300. Fees, books, misc. academic expenses (school's estimate): $580.
**Enrollment.** Undergraduates: 97 men, 113 women (full-time). Freshman class: 250 applicants, 200 accepted, 158 enrolled.
**Test score averages/ranges.** Average ACT scores: 22 composite.
**Faculty.** 25 full-time; 7 part-time. 25% of faculty holds doctoral degree. Student/faculty ratio: 15 to 1.
**Selectivity rating.** Less competitive.

**PROFILE.** Michigan Christian, founded in 1959, is a private, church-affiliated, liberal arts college. Its 83-acre campus is located in Rochester Hills, 20 miles north of Detroit.

**Accreditation:** NCACS.
**Religious orientation:** Michigan Christian College is affiliated with the Churches of Christ; eight semesters of religion required.
**Library:** Collections totaling over 33,912 volumes, 355 periodical subscriptions, and 14,685 microform items.
**Athletic facilities:** Gymnasium; basketball, tennis, volleyball courts; athletic fields.

**STUDENT BODY. Undergraduate profile:** 73% are state residents; 12% are transfers. 1% Asian-American, 12% Black, 1% Hispanic, 83% White, 3% Other. Average age of undergraduates is 20.
**Freshman profile:** 90% of accepted applicants took ACT. 95% of freshmen come from public schools.
**Foreign students:** Nine students are from out of the country. Countries represented include Botswana, Canada, Indonesia, Japan, Korea, and Nigeria; seven in all.

**PROGRAMS OF STUDY. Degrees:** B.Bus.Admin., B.Relig.Ed.
**Majors:** Bible Studies, Biblical Studies Composite, Business Administration/Management, Child Care Management, Christian Ministry, Counseling, Criminal Justice Management, Human Resource Management, Marketing, Psychology, Social Work, Sociology.
**Distribution of degrees:** The majors with the highest enrollment are business administration, counseling, and ministry.
**Requirements:** General education requirement.
**Academic regulations:** Freshmen must maintain minimum 1.50 GPA; sophomores, juniors, seniors, 2.00 GPA.
**Special:** Minors offered in counseling, Greek, history, and specialized individualized management concentrations. Associate's degrees offered. Double majors. Independent study. Accelerated study. Internships. Graduate school at which undergraduates may take graduate-level courses. 2-2 transfer programs in several fields with numerous universities.
**Honors:** Honors program. Honor societies.
**Academic Assistance:** Remedial reading, writing, math, and study skills.

**ADMISSIONS. Academic basis for candidate selection** (in order of priority): Standardized test scores, secondary school record, class rank, essay, school's recommendation.

**Nonacademic basis for candidate selection:** Character and personality are emphasized. Extracurricular participation is important. Particular talent or ability is considered.
**Requirements:** Graduation from secondary school is required; GED is accepted. 8 units and the following program of study are recommended: 4 units of English, 2 units of math, 2 units of science. Minimum composite ACT score of 18 and minimum 2.25 GPA required. Interview required for admittance into TAP (Transitional Academic Preparation) program for under-prepared high school graduates. ACT is required. Campus visit and interview recommended. Off-campus interviews available with an admissions representative.
**Procedure:** Take ACT by fall of 12th year. Suggest filing application by April 1. Application deadline is August 1. Notification of admission on rolling basis. $25 room deposit, refundable up to 30 days prior to beginning of semester. Freshmen accepted for terms other than fall.
**Special programs:** Admission may be deferred two years. Credit and/or placement may be granted through CEEB Advanced Placement exams for scores of 3 or higher. Placement may be granted through CLEP general exams. Credit and/or placement may be granted through CLEP subject exams. Credit and placement may be granted through challenge exams and military and life experience. Early decision program. In fall 1993, 4 applied for early decision and 3 were accepted. Deadline for applying for early decision is June 1. Early entrance/early admission program. Concurrent enrollment program.
**Transfer students:** Transfer students accepted for terms other than fall. In fall 1993, 12% of all new students were transfers into all classes. 35 transfer applications were received, 30 were accepted. Application deadline is August 15 for fall; December 15 for spring. Minimum 2.0 GPA recommended. Lowest course grade accepted is "C." At least 24 semester hours must be completed at the college to receive degree.
**Admissions contact:** Toby Osburn, Dean of Enrollment Services. 313 650-6017.

**FINANCIAL AID. Available aid:** Pell grants, SEOG, state scholarships and grants, school scholarships and grants, academic merit scholarships, and athletic scholarships. Perkins Loans (NDSL), PLUS, Stafford Loans (GSL), state loans, school loans, and SLS. Deferred payment plan and family tuition reduction.
**Financial aid statistics:** 25% of aid is not need-based. In 1993-94, 91% of all undergraduate applicants received aid; 95% of freshman applicants. Average amounts of aid awarded freshmen: Scholarships and grants, $1,600.
**Supporting data/closing dates:** FAFSA: Priority filing date is June 1; deadline is August 1. School's own aid application: Priority filing date is June 1; deadline is August 1. Income tax forms: Priority filing date is June 1; deadline is August 1. Notification of awards on rolling basis.
**Financial aid contact:** Debra Rutledge, B.R.E., Director of Financial Aid. 313 650-6018.

# Michigan State University

**East Lansing, MI 48824-1046 517 355-1855**

**1994-95 Costs.** Tuition: $3,960 (state residents), $10,294 (out-of-state). Room & board: $3,672. Fees, books, misc. academic expenses (school's estimate): $1,010.
**Enrollment.** Undergraduates: 26,935 (full-time). Freshman class: 18,114 applicants, 15,096 accepted, 6,180 enrolled. Graduate enrollment: 4,426 men, 4,373 women.
**Test score averages/ranges.** Average SAT scores: 458 verbal, 524 math. Range of SAT scores of middle 50%: 400-520 verbal, 450-590 math. Average ACT scores: 23 English, 22 math, 23 composite. Range of ACT scores of middle 50%: 20-25 English, 19-25 math.
**Faculty.** 4,000 full-time; 550 part-time. 95% of faculty holds doctoral degree.
**Selectivity rating.** Less competitive.

**PROFILE.** Michigan State, founded in 1855, is a comprehensive, land-grant, public university. Programs are offered through the Colleges of Agriculture and Natural Resources, Arts and Letters, Business, Communication Arts and Sciences, Education, Engineering, Human Ecology, Human Medicine, Natural Science, Nursing, Osteopathic Medicine, Social Science, and Veterinary Medicine; the Graduate School of Business Administration; and the Honors College. Its 2,100-acre campus is located in East Lansing, 80 miles northwest of Detroit.

**Accreditation:** NCACS. Professionally accredited by the Accreditation Board for Engineering and Technology, the Accrediting Council on Education in Journalism and Mass Communication, the American Assembly of Collegiate Schools of Business, the American Dietetic Association, the American Medical Association (CAHEA), the American Society of Landscape Architects, the American Veterinary Medical Association, the Council on Social Work Education, the Foundation for Interior Design Education Research, the National Association of Schools of Music, the National Association of Schools of Theatre, the National Council for Accreditation of Teacher Education, the National League for Nursing, the Society of American Foresters.
**Religious orientation:** Michigan State University is nonsectarian; no religious requirements.
**Library:** Collections totaling over 3,800,000 volumes, 28,000 periodical subscriptions, and 4,800,000 microform items.
**Special facilities/museums:** Museums of natural history, Michigan history, art, anthropology, art center, on-campus preschool and elementary school, biological station, experimental farms, botanical garden, planetarium, two superconducting cyclotrons, observatory.
**Athletic facilities:** Gymnasiums, indoor/outdoor track, swimming pools, diving tower, badminton, basketball, racquetball, squash, tennis, and volleyball courts, rollerskating rink, dance studios, baseball, football, intramural, rugby, softball, indoor and outdoor soccer fields, saunas, exercise/fitness and weight rooms, golf course, fitness trails, arena.

**STUDENT BODY. Undergraduate profile:** 6% are transfers. 3.5% Asian-American, 8% Black, 2% Hispanic, .5% Native American, 86% White. Average age of undergraduates is 21.
**Freshman profile:** 1% of freshmen who took SAT scored 700 or over on verbal, 5% scored 700 or over on math; 9% scored 600 or over on verbal, 24% scored 600 or over on math; 33% scored 500 or over on verbal, 60% scored 500 or over on math; 76% scored 400 or over on verbal, 88% scored 400 or over on math; 96% scored 300 or over on verbal, 99% scored 300 or over on math. 38% of accepted applicants took SAT; 87% took ACT.
**Undergraduate achievement:** 84% of fall 1992 freshmen returned for fall 1993 term. 33% of entering class graduated. 21% of students who completed a degree program immediately went on to graduate study.
**Foreign students:** 564 students are from out of the country. Countries represented include Canada, China, India, Japan, South Korea, and Taiwan; 110 in all.

**PROGRAMS OF STUDY. Degrees:** B.A., B.F.A., B.Land.Arch., B.Mus., B.S.
**Majors:** Accounting, Advertising, Agricultural Engineering, Agriculture/Natural Resources Communications, Agriscience, American Studies, Ancient Studies, Animal Science, Anthropology, Apparel Design, Applied Music, Art Education, Astrophysics, Audiology/Speech Sciences, Biochemistry, Biochemistry/Biotechnology, Biological Science, Botany/Plant Pathology, Building Construction Management, Chemical Engineering, Chemistry, Child Development, Civil Engineering, Clinical Lab Sciences, Communication, Composition/Theory, Computational Mathematics, Computer Engineering, Computer Science, Criminal Justice, Crop/Soil Sciences, Dietetics, Earth Science, East Asian Languages/Culture, Economics, Education, Electrical Engineering, Elementary Education, Engineering Arts, English, Entomology, Environmental/Natural Resource Policy Studies, Family Community Services, Family/Consumer Resources, Finance, Fisheries/Wildlife, Food Engineering, Food Industry Management, Food Science, Food Systems Economics/Management, Foods/Technology/Management, Forensic Science, Forestry, French, General Business Administration, General Business Administration/Pre-Law, Geography, Geological Sciences, German, History, History of Art, Home Economics, Horticulture, Hotel/Restaurant Management, Human Resource Management, Humanities/Pre-Law, Instrumental Music Education, Interdisciplinary Humanities, Interdisciplinary Studies/Social Science, Interior Design, International Relations, Journalism, Landscape Architecture, Latin, Linguistics, Marketing, Materials/Logistics Management/Logistics, Materials/Logistics Management/Operations/Purchasing Management, Materials Science/Engineering, Mathematics, Mechanical Engineering, Mechanics, Medical Technology, Merchandising Management, Microbiology, Music, Music Performance, Music Therapy, Nursing, Nutritional Sciences, Packaging, Park/Recreation Resources, Philosophy, Physical Education/Exercise Science, Physical Science, Physics, Physiology, Political Economy, Political Science, Political Science/Pre-Law, Political Theory/Constitutional Democracy, Pre-Veterinary, Professional Accounting, Professional Education, Psychology, Public Administration, Public Resource Management, Religious Studies, Russian, Secondary Education, Social Relations, Social Work, Sociology, Spanish, Statistics, Stringed Instrument Music Education, Studio Art, Telecommunication, Theatre, Theory/Composition, Urban/Regional Planning, Vocal/General Music Education, Women's Studies, Zoology.
**Distribution of degrees:** The majors with the highest enrollment are accounting, elementary education, and advertising.
**Requirements:** General education requirement.
**Academic regulations:** Minimum 2.0 GPA must be maintained.
**Special:** Double majors. Dual degrees. Independent study. Pass/fail grading option. Internships. Cooperative education programs. Graduate school at which undergraduates may take graduate-level courses. Preprofessional programs in law, medicine, veterinary science, pharmacy, dentistry, optometry, physical therapy, osteopathy, nursing, and podiatry. M.D./Ph.D. and D.O./Ph.D. programs. Member of Consortium for Institutional Cooperation. Sea Semester. Teacher certification in early childhood, elementary, secondary, special education, and bilingual/bicultural education. Certification in specific subject areas. Exchange programs abroad in England (Roehampton Inst, U of Surrey), and Zimbabwe (U Zimbabwe). Study abroad also in 28 countries. ROTC and AFROTC.
**Honors:** Phi Beta Kappa. Honors program. Honor societies.
**Academic Assistance:** Remedial reading, writing, math, and study skills. Nonremedial tutoring.

**STUDENT LIFE. Housing:** All unmarried students under age 21 must live on campus unless living near campus with relatives. Coed and women's dorms. Sorority and fraternity housing. School-owned/operated apartments. On-campus married-student housing. 46% of students live in college housing.
**Social atmosphere:** According to the student newspaper, "Social life is thriving." Most popular events include Michigan State U versus U of Michigan football, the annual spring concert, and Greek Week. Students gather at the student union and library on campus. Off campus, they frequent Rick's American Cafe, Dooley's, America's Cup, and various other spots along Grand River Avenue bordering the campus.
**Services and counseling/handicapped student services:** Placement services. Health service. Day care. Counseling services for minority, military, veteran, and older students. Birth control, personal, and psychological counseling. Career and academic guidance services. Physically disabled student services. Learning disabled program/services. Notetaking services. Tape recorders. Tutors. Reader services for the blind.
**Campus organizations:** Undergraduate student government. Student newspaper (State News, published once/day). Yearbook. Radio and TV stations. Bands, glee club, professional fraternities and sororities, Amnesty International, Cool Action (community service group), volleyball club, Graduate Theatre Showcase, dance/cheerleading group, Alpha Phi Omega, many career-related groups, 400 organizations in all. 31 fraternities, 30 chapter houses; 21 sororities, 17 chapter houses. 10% of men join a fraternity. 10% of women join a sorority.
**Religious organizations:** Spartans for Christ, Campus Crusade for Christ, Hillel, Lutheran Student Movement, Muslim Student Association, Bahai Club, Baptist Student Union, and many others.
**Minority/foreign student organizations:** Asian Pacific American Student Organization, CRU (Chicano/Latino student organization), North American Indian Student Organization, Ebony Productions, MWENDO (Black theatre group), several black fraternities and sororities, Asian and black caucuses, and minority career-related groups. Caribbean Student Organization, Singapore Student Association, Korean Student organization, African Student Union, Turkish Student Association, Venezuelan/South American cultural organization, AIESEC (international cultural exchange organization).

ATHLETICS. **Physical education requirements:** None.

**Intercollegiate competition:** 3% of students participate. Baseball (M), basketball (M,W), cheerleading (M,W), cross-country (M,W), diving (M,W), fencing (M), field hockey (W), football (M), golf (M,W), gymnastics (M,W), ice hockey (M), lacrosse (M), soccer (M,W), softball (W), swimming (M,W), tennis (M,W), track (indoor) (M,W), track (outdoor) (M,W), track and field (indoor) (M,W), track and field (outdoor) (M,W), volleyball (W), wrestling (M). Member of Big 10 Conference, Central Collegiate Hockey Association, Midwest Lacrosse Association, NCAA Division I.

**Intramural and club sports:** 75% of students participate. Intramural aerobics, badminton, basketball, exercise fitness, floor hockey, free throw, golf, handball, hockey, paddleball, racquetball, roller skating, skiing, soccer, softball, squash, swimming, table tennis, tennis, touch football, track, ultimate frisbee, volleyball, water polo, weight lifting, wrestling. Men's club Alpine skiing, archery, bowling, crew, cycling, horsemanship, martial arts, Nordic skiing, racquetball, rodeo, rugby, sailing, ultimate frisbee, volleyball, water polo, water skiing, weight lifting, wrestling. Women's club Alpine skiing, archery, bowling, crew, cycling, horsemanship, martial arts, Nordic skiing, racquetball, rodeo, rugby, pom pom, sailing, synchronized swimming, ultimate frisbee, water skiing, weight lifting.

ADMISSIONS. **Academic basis for candidate selection** (in order of priority): Secondary school record, standardized test scores, class rank, school's recommendation.

**Nonacademic basis for candidate selection:** Extracurricular participation, particular talent or ability, and alumni/ae relationship are considered.

**Requirements:** Graduation from secondary school is required; GED is accepted. No specific distribution of secondary school units required. Minimum composite ACT score of 21 and minimum "B-" average recommended. Audition required of music program applicants. College Achievement Admissions Program (CAAP) for applicants not normally admissible. SAT or ACT is required. Campus visit recommended. No off-campus interviews.

**Procedure:** Take SAT or ACT by December of 12th year. Application deadline is July 30. Notification of admission on rolling basis. Reply is required within four weeks of notification. $100 orientation deposit, refundable until May 1. $25 room deposit, refundable until May 1. Freshmen accepted for terms other than fall.

**Special programs:** Admission may be deferred one year. Credit and/or placement may be granted through CEEB Advanced Placement exams for scores of 3 or higher. Credit and/or placement may be granted through CLEP general and subject exams. Credit may be granted through military experience. Concurrent enrollment program.

**Transfer students:** Transfer students accepted for terms other than fall. In fall 1993, 6% of all new students were transfers into all classes. 5,012 transfer applications were received, 2,832 were accepted. Application deadline is 30 days prior to registration for fall; 30 days prior to registration for spring. Minimum 2.0 GPA required. Lowest course grade accepted is "D." Maximum number of transferable credits is 60 semester hours from a two-year school and 90 semester hours from a four-year school. At least 30 semester hours must be completed at the university to receive degree.

**Admissions contact:** William H. Turner, Ph.D., Director of Admissions. 517 355-8332.

FINANCIAL AID. **Available aid:** Pell grants, SEOG, state scholarships and grants, school scholarships and grants, private scholarships and grants, ROTC scholarships, academic merit scholarships, and athletic scholarships. Perkins Loans (NDSL), PLUS, Stafford Loans (GSL), Health Professions Loans, state loans, school loans, private loans, and SLS. Deferred payment plan.

**Financial aid statistics:** In 1993-94, 50% of all undergraduate applicants received aid; 50% of freshman applicants. Average amounts of aid awarded freshmen: Scholarships and grants, $1,850; loans, $600.

**Supporting data/closing dates:** FAFSA/FAF/FFS: Accepted on rolling basis. Notification of awards on rolling basis.

**Financial aid contact:** Thomas A. Scarlett, Ph.D., Director of Financial Aid. 517 353-5940.

STUDENT EMPLOYMENT. College Work/Study Program. Institutional employment. 29% of full-time undergraduates work on campus during school year. Students may expect to earn an average of $2,400 during school year. Off-campus part-time employment opportunities rated "excellent."

COMPUTER FACILITIES. 5,000 IBM/IBM-compatible, Macintosh/Apple, and RISC-/UNIX-based microcomputers; all are networked. Students may access Digital, IBM, SUN minicomputer/mainframe systems, BITNET, Internet. Residence halls may be equipped with stand-alone microcomputers, networked microcomputers, modems. Client/LAN operating systems include Apple/Macintosh, DOS, UNIX/XENIX/AIX, Windows NT, X-windows, Banyan, LocalTalk/AppleTalk, Novell. Computer languages and software packages include APL, BASIC, CICS, COBOL, DYL 280, e-mail, FORTRAN, MBSA, OS, PSO, SAS, SPSS; database, graphics, spreadsheet, statistical, and word-processing programs. Computer facilities are available to all students.

**Fees:** None.

**Hours:** 8 AM-midn.

GRADUATE CAREER DATA. Graduate school percentages: 2% enter law school. 3% enter medical school. 1% enter dental school. 2% enter graduate business programs. Highest graduate school enrollments: Michigan St U, Wayne St U. Companies and businesses that hire graduates: Amway, Dow Chemical, Ford Motor Co., General Electric, General Motors, IBM, Upjohn.

PROMINENT ALUMNI/AE. John Engler, governor of Michigan; Molly Brennan, Rhodes scholar and manager, General Motors; Jim Cash, author, *Top Gun* and *Legal Eagles;* Steve Garvey, baseball player, San Diego Padres; Alfred Hersey, Nobel Prize-winning author, *Psychology of Medicine;* Jene Jankowski, president, CBS; Earvin "Magic" Johnson, basketball player/coach.

# Michigan Technological University

**Houghton, MI 49931** — **906 487-1885**

**1993-94 Costs.** Tuition: $3,269 (state residents), $7,550 (out-of-state). Room & board: $3,784. Fees, books, misc. academic expenses (school's estimate): $735.

**Enrollment.** Undergraduates: 4,157 men, 1,367 women (full-time). Freshman class: 2,622 applicants, 2,217 accepted, 1,051 enrolled. Graduate enrollment: 498 men, 167 women.

**Test score averages/ranges.** Average SAT scores: 513 verbal, 622 math. Range of SAT scores of middle 50%: 450-570 verbal, 560-690 math. Average ACT scores: 24 English, 26 math, 26 composite. Range of ACT scores of middle 50%: 22-27 English, 24-29 math.

**Faculty.** 358 full-time; 35 part-time. 78% of faculty holds doctoral degree. Student/faculty ratio: 15 to 1.

**Selectivity rating.** Highly competitive.

PROFILE. Michigan Tech, founded in 1855, is a public university. Its 240-acre campus is located in Houghton, on Michigan's Upper Peninsula.

**Accreditation:** NCACS. Professionally accredited by the Accreditation Board for Engineering and Technology, the Society of American Foresters.

**Religious orientation:** Michigan Technological University is nonsectarian; no religious requirements.

**Library:** Collections totaling over 781,219 volumes, 4,000 periodical subscriptions, and 367,237 microform items.

**Special facilities/museums:** Mineralogical museum, on-campus nursery school, 4,110-acre forestry center, electron microscope, scanning electron microscope, PUMA robots.

**Athletic facilities:** Gymnasiums, field house, basketball, racquetball, squash, tennis, and volleyball courts, ice rink, track, aerobics, gymnastics, and weight rooms, rifle range, swimming and diving pools, dance studio, football, intramural, soccer, and softball fields.

STUDENT BODY. **Undergraduate profile:** 81% are state residents; 22% are transfers. 1% Asian-American, 2% Black, 1% Hispanic, 1% Native American, 91% White, 4% Other. Average age of undergraduates is 20.

**Freshman profile:** 2% of freshmen who took SAT scored 700 or over on verbal, 20% scored 700 or over on math; 22% scored 600 or over on verbal, 63% scored 600 or over on math; 59% scored 500 or over on verbal, 92% scored 500 or over on math; 90% scored 400 or over on verbal, 99% scored 400 or over on math; 99% scored 300 or over on verbal, 100% scored 300 or over on math. 25% of accepted applicants took SAT; 95% took ACT.

**Undergraduate achievement:** 85% of fall 1992 freshmen returned for fall 1993 term. 15% of students who completed a degree program immediately went on to graduate study.

**Foreign students:** 251 students are from out of the country. Countries represented include Canada, China, Finland, India, Indonesia, and Malaysia; 56 in all.

PROGRAMS OF STUDY. **Degrees:** B.A., B.S.

**Majors:** Applied Geophysics, Applied Physics, Biological Sciences, Business Administration, Chemical Engineering, Chemistry, Civil Engineering, Computer Science, Economics, Electrical Engineering, Engineering Management, Environmental Engineering, Forestry, Geological Engineering, Geology, Liberal Arts, Mathematics, Mechanical Engineering, Medical Technology, Metallurgical Engineering, Mining Engineering, Physics, Scientific/Technical Communication, Social Sciences, Surveying, Wood Science.

**Distribution of degrees:** The majors with the highest enrollment are mechanical engineering, electrical engineering, and civil engineering; applied geophysics, economics, and liberal arts have the lowest.

**Requirements:** General education requirement.

**Academic regulations:** Minimum 2.0 GPA must be maintained.

**Special:** Minors offered in most majors and in foreign language, humanities, international technology and society, and teacher education. Core courses offered in accounting, behavioral science, economics, education, environmental studies, foreign languages, geography, music, philosophy, physical education, and political science. Associate's degrees offered. Self-designed majors. Double majors. Dual degrees. Independent study. Pass/fail grading option. Internships. Cooperative education programs. Graduate school at which undergraduates may take graduate-level courses. Preprofessional programs in law, medicine, veterinary science, pharmacy, dentistry, optometry, and physical therapy. 2-2 engineering programs with Central Michigan U, Delta Coll, Northwestern Michigan Coll, and Oakland Comm Coll. 3-2 engineering programs with Adrian Coll, Albion Coll, Augsburg Coll, and Coll of St. Scholastica. 3-2 engineering and forestry programs with Mt. Senario Coll, Northland Coll, and U of Wisconsin at Superior. Member of Upper Peninsula College Consortium, Graduate Studies Consortium, and Continuing Higher Education Coordinating Council. Teacher certification in secondary education. Certification in specific subject areas. Exchange programs abroad in China (U of Science and Tech), Finland (Helsinki U of Tech, Lappeenranta U of Tech, U of Oulu, Tampere U of Tech), Germany (U of Hanover, U of Stuttgart), Switzerland (Swiss Federal Inst of Tech), the former Soviet Republics (Leningrad State Polytech U, Mendeleev Inst of Chemical Tech), and the United Kingdom (U of Southhampton). ROTC and AFROTC.

**Honors:** Honor societies.

**Academic Assistance:** Remedial reading, writing, math, and study skills.

STUDENT LIFE. **Housing:** Freshmen must live on campus unless living with family. Coed dorms. Sorority and fraternity housing. On-campus married-student housing. 36% of students live in college housing.

**Social atmosphere:** According to the student newspaper, MTU is a "high-pressured, academically excellent university set in a remote area which has approximately 300 inches of snow every year." Greeks constitute 15-20% of the student population; hockey games and Greek parties occur on a weekly basis. Other popular school-year events include Winter Carnival Week with "the country's best ice sculptures" and K-Day. Students frequent Douglass House, the student union, Turn of the Century Bar & Grill, and other bars.

**Services and counseling/handicapped student services:** Placement services. Health service. Counseling services for minority, veteran, and older students. Birth control and personal counseling. Career and academic guidance services. Physically disabled student services. Notetaking services. Tape recorders.

**Campus organizations:** Undergraduate student government. Student newspaper (Lode, published once/week). Radio station. Amateur radio and chess clubs, flying club, martial arts club, Right Brain People (art club), Science Fiction and Fantasy Society, Society for Creative Anachronism, Wildlife Society, College Republicans, Young Democrats, Model UN, Circle K, departmental, professional, and service groups, 150 organizations in all. 16 fraternities, 15 chapter houses; eight sororities, all with chapter houses. 13% of men join a fraternity. 16% of women join a sorority.

**Religious organizations:** Baptist Student Union, Campus Crusade for Christ, Canterbury Club, Chi Alpha, Latter Day Saints Student Association, Lutheran Collegians, Muslim Student Association, Saint Albert the Great Catholic parish, Wesley House Organization.

**Minority/foreign student organizations:** Native American, black, Turkish-American, and Hispanic student groups. International Club, Chinese, Indian, Korean, Pakistani, Spanish, and Vietnamese groups.

**ATHLETICS. Physical education requirements:** Four terms of physical education required.

**Intercollegiate competition:** 5% of students participate. Basketball (M,W), cheerleading (M,W), cross-country (M,W), football (M), ice hockey (M), Nordic skiing (M,W), tennis (M,W), track and field (outdoor) (M,W), volleyball (M,W). Member of Great Lakes Intercollegiate Athletic Conference, Midwest Intercollegiate Football Conference, Western Collegiate Hockey Association.

**Intramural and club sports:** 50% of students participate. Intramural archery, badminton, basketball, free throw, golf, homerun contest, horseshoes, ice hockey, inner-tube water polo, paddleball, pickleball, racquetball, riflery, soccer, softball, squash, swimming, table tennis, tennis, touch football, turkey trot, volleyball, walleyball, water polo, weight lifting, wrestling. Men's club fencing, frisbee, soccer, swimming, tae kwon do, volleyball. Women's club fencing, frisbee, soccer, swimming, tae kwon do, volleyball.

**ADMISSIONS. Academic basis for candidate selection** (in order of priority): Secondary school record, class rank, standardized test scores, school's recommendation.

**Nonacademic basis for candidate selection:** Character and personality, extracurricular participation, particular talent or ability, and alumni/ae relationship are considered.

**Requirements:** Graduation from secondary school is required; GED is accepted. 7 units and the following program of study are required: 3 units of English, 3 units of math, 1 unit of lab science. Recommended test scores and class rank vary with curriculum. ACT is recommended; SAT may be substituted. Campus visit and interview recommended. Off-campus interviews available with an admissions representative.

**Procedure:** Take ACT or SAT by registration date; early in 12th year recommended. Suggest filing application by September 1 of 12th year. Application deadline is August 1. Notification of admission on rolling basis. Reply is required by May 1. $50 nonrefundable tuition deposit. $50 refundable enrollment deposit. $100 room deposit, refundable in full until June 1; $55 refundable after June 1. Freshmen accepted for terms other than fall.

**Special programs:** Admission may be deferred two years. Credit and/or placement may be granted through CEEB Advanced Placement exams for scores of 3 or higher. Credit and/or placement may be granted through CLEP subject exams. Credit and placement may be granted through challenge exams. Concurrent enrollment program.

**Transfer students:** Transfer students accepted for terms other than fall. In fall 1993, 22% of all new students were transfers into all classes. 603 transfer applications were received, 455 were accepted. Application deadline is 30 days prior to start of quarter for fall; 30 days prior to start of quarter for spring. Minimum 2.5 GPA recommended. Lowest course grade accepted is "C." Maximum number of transferable quarter hours varies. At least 36 quarter hours must be completed at the university to receive degree.

**Admissions contact:** Joseph Galetto, M.A., Director of Enrollment Management. 906 487-2335.

**FINANCIAL AID. Available aid:** Pell grants, SEOG, state scholarships and grants, school scholarships and grants, private scholarships, ROTC scholarships, academic merit scholarships, and athletic scholarships. Perkins Loans (NDSL), PLUS, Stafford Loans (GSL), school loans, and SLS. AMS. MET Plan.

**Financial aid statistics:** 50% of aid is not need-based. In 1993-94, 71% of all undergraduate applicants received aid; 71% of freshman applicants. Average amounts of aid awarded freshmen: Scholarships and grants, $2,610; loans, $2,172.

**Supporting data/closing dates:** FAFSA: Priority filing date is January 1; deadline is February 15. Income tax forms. Notification of awards begins March 30.

**Financial aid contact:** Timothy T. Malette, Director of Financial Aid. 906 487-2622.

**STUDENT EMPLOYMENT.** College Work/Study Program. Institutional employment. 38% of full-time undergraduates work on campus during school year. Students may expect to earn an average of $1,242 during school year. Off-campus part-time employment opportunities rated "fair."

**COMPUTER FACILITIES.** 500 IBM/IBM-compatible, Macintosh/Apple, and RISC-/UNIX-based microcomputers; 250 are networked. Students may access IBM, Sequent, SUN minicomputer/mainframe systems, BITNET, Internet. Residence halls may be equipped with networked microcomputers, networked terminals. Client/LAN operating systems include Apple/Macintosh. Computer languages and software packages include C, FORTRAN, Lotus 1-2-3, MINITAB, Paradox, Pascal, Quattro, SPSS, WordPerfect; 100 in all. Computer facilities are available to all students.

Fees: None.

**GRADUATE CAREER DATA.** Highest graduate school enrollments: Michigan Tech, U of Michigan. 80% of graduates choose careers in business and industry. Companies and businesses that hire graduates: Chevron, Dow Chemical, Ford, General Electric, General Motors, IBM, Westinghouse, 3M.

**PROMINENT ALUMNI/AE.** Melvin Calvin, Nobel Laureate, chemistry; Jack Real, retired president, Hughes Aircraft, former vice-president, McDonnell-Douglas; John Opie, senior vice-president, General Electric.

## Northern Michigan University

**Marquette, MI 49855** — **906 227-1000**

**1994-95 Costs.** Tuition: $2,900 (state residents), $5,530 (out-of-state). Room: $1,705. Board: $2,203. Fees, books, misc. academic expenses (school's estimate): $535.

**Enrollment.** Undergraduates: 3,051 men, 3,210 women (full-time). Freshman class: 4,519 applicants, 3,844 accepted, 1,432 enrolled. Graduate enrollment: 356 men, 646 women.

**Test score averages/ranges.** Average ACT scores: 19 English, 19 math, 20 composite. Range of ACT scores of middle 50%: 17-24 English, 17-22 math.

**Faculty.** 327 full-time; 39 part-time. 63% of faculty holds highest degree in specific field. Student/faculty ratio: 20 to 1.

**Selectivity rating.** Less competitive.

**PROFILE.** Northern Michigan, founded in 1899, is a public, comprehensive university. Its 320-acre campus is located on the shores of Lake Superior in Marquette.

**Accreditation:** NCACS. Professionally accredited by the American Dietetic Association, the American Medical Association (CAHEA), the American Speech-Language-Hearing Association, the Council on Social Work Education, the National Association of Schools of Music, the National Council for Accreditation of Teacher Education, the National League for Nursing.

**Religious orientation:** Northern Michigan University is nonsectarian; no religious requirements.

**Library:** Collections totaling over 486,951 volumes, 1,967 periodical subscriptions, and 570,357 microform items.

**Special facilities/museums:** Art museum, education learning resource center, observatory, electron microscope.

**Athletic facilities:** Gymnasiums, field house, ice rink, swimming pool, diving well, weight rooms, athletic fields, basketball, racquetball, tennis, and volleyball courts, bowling lanes, track, stadium.

**STUDENT BODY. Undergraduate profile:** 92% are state residents; 32% are transfers. 1% Asian-American, 1% Black, 1% Hispanic, 3% Native American, 92% White, 2% Other. Average age of undergraduates is 25.

**Freshman profile:** 1% of freshmen who took ACT scored 30 or over on English, 1% scored 30 or over on math, 1% scored 30 or over on composite; 14% scored 24 or over on English, 12% scored 24 or over on math, 14% scored 24 or over on composite; 58% scored 18 or over on English, 56% scored 18 or over on math, 69% scored 18 or over on composite; 98% scored 12 or over on English, 99% scored 12 or over on math, 99% scored 12 or over on composite; 100% scored 6 or over on English, 100% scored 6 or over on math, 100% scored 6 or over on composite. 78% of accepted applicants took ACT.

**Undergraduate achievement:** 68% of fall 1991 freshmen returned for fall 1992 term. 18% of entering class graduated. 13% of students who completed a degree program immediately went on to graduate study.

**Foreign students:** 71 students are from out of the country. Countries represented include Canada, China, India, Japan, Malaysia, and South Korea.

**PROGRAMS OF STUDY. Degrees:** B.A., B.F.A., B.Mus.Ed., B.S., B.S.Nurs., B.Soc.Work.

**Majors:** Accounting, Art/Design, Biochemistry, Biology, Botany, Broadcasting, Business Administration, Business Education, Ceramics, Chemistry, Clinical Science, Communication Disorders, Computer Information Systems, Computer Science, Computer Systems, Conservation, Construction Technology, Corrections, Cytotechnology, Data Processing, Dietetics, Drawing, Earth Science, Ecology, Economics, Electronic Imaging, Electronics Engineering Technology, Electronics Technology, Elementary Education, English, Environmental Design, Environmental/Occupational Hygiene, Fashion Merchandising, Filmmaking, Finance, French, Furniture Design, General Science, Geography, German, Graphic Design, Health Education, History, Home Economics, Illustration, Industrial Education, Industrial Technology, Institutional/Restaurant Management, International Studies, Justice Studies, Land-Use Planning/Management, Law Enforcement, Management, Management of Health/Fitness, Manufacturing Technology, Marketing, Mass Communications, Mathematics, Mathematics/Computer Science, Medical Technology, Mentally Impaired, Metal Crafts, Microbiology, Music, Music Education, Nursing, Office Systems, Outdoor Recreation, Package Design, Painting, Philosophy, Photography, Physical Education, Physics, Physiology, Political Science, Printmaking, Psychology, Public Administration, Public Relations, Recreation, Recreational Resource Systems, Sculpture, Secondary Education, Ski Area Management, Social Studies, Social Work, Sociology, Spanish, Speech, Sports Science, Technology, Textiles, Theatre, Water Science, Weaving, Woodworking, Zoology.

**Distribution of degrees:** The majors with the highest enrollment are nursing, management, and English; clinical science and water science have the lowest.

**Requirements:** General education requirement.

**Academic regulations:** Minimum 2.0 GPA must be maintained. Minimum GPA required for graduation varies between 2.0 and 3.0, depending on major.

**Special:** Minors offered in over 100 fields. Certificate programs offered. Courses offered in allied health and anthropology. Associate's degrees offered. Self-designed majors. Double majors. Internships. Graduate school at which undergraduates may take graduate-level courses. Preprofessional programs in law, medicine, veterinary science, pharmacy, dentistry, optometry, architecture, occupational therapy, physical therapy, and social service. 2-2 program in ski area management with Gogebic Comm Coll. Teacher certification in elementary, secondary, and special education education. Study abroad possible. ROTC.

**Academic Assistance:** Remedial reading, writing, math, and study skills. Nonremedial tutoring.

**STUDENT LIFE. Housing:** All freshmen must live on campus unless living with family. Coed and women's dorms. Off-campus privately-owned housing. On-campus married-student housing. 23% of students live in college housing.
**Social atmosphere:** According to the editor of the student newspaper, "NMU could use more high-class cultural events than local acts and a good, big facility in which to watch them. City police have cracked down on house parties, so they don't get too big for very long, but they're still available and well-attended." Influencing the social life on campus are the athletes and the Greeks. Otherwise, students enjoy attending hockey games, plays, the Seafood Fest, and holiday and special event parties.
**Services and counseling/handicapped student services:** Placement services. Health service. Counseling services for minority, military, veteran, and older students. Birth control, personal, and psychological counseling. Career and academic guidance services. Physically disabled student services. Learning disabled services. Notetaking services. Tape recorders. Tutors. Reader services for the blind.
**Campus organizations:** Undergraduate student government. Student newspaper (North-wind, published once/week). Literary magazine. Radio and TV stations. Marching and symphonic bands, orchestra, arts chorale, choir, ensembles and quartets, ski club, departmental, service, and special-interest groups, 160 organizations in all. Six fraternities, no chapter houses; two sororities, no chapter houses. 1% of men join a fraternity. 1% of women join a sorority.
**Religious organizations:** Baptist Student Fellowship, Campus Crusade for Christ, Catholic Campus Ministry, Intervarsity Christian Fellowship, Lutheran Campus Ministry, Wesley Fellowship.
**Minority/foreign student organizations:** Black Student Union, Harambee Gospel Choir.

**ATHLETICS. Physical education requirements:** Two semesters of physical education required.
**Intercollegiate competition:** 3% of students participate. Basketball (M,W), cross-country (M,W), diving (W), football (M), golf (M), ice hockey (M), Nordic skiing (M,W), swimming (W), tennis (W), volleyball (W). Member of Great Lakes Intercollegiate Athletic Conference, Midwest Intercollegiate Football Conference, NCAA Division I for ice hockey, NCAA Division II, Western Collegiate Hockey Association.
**Intramural and club sports:** Intramural badminton, basketball, bowling, flag football, floor hockey, free throw, ice hockey, inner-tube water polo, racquetball, soccer, softball, table tennis, tennis, volleyball, walleyball, wrestling. Men's club Alpine skiing. Women's club Alpine skiing.

**ADMISSIONS. Academic basis for candidate selection** (in order of priority): Secondary school record, standardized test scores, school's recommendation, class rank, essay.
**Nonacademic basis for candidate selection:** Character and personality, extracurricular participation, particular talent or ability, and alumni/ae relationship are considered.
**Requirements:** Graduation from secondary school is required; GED is accepted. 12 units required and the following program of study recommended: 4 units of English, 4 units of math, 3 units of science, 2 units of foreign language, 3 units of social studies. Minimum composite ACT score of 19 (combined SAT score of 800) and minimum 2.25 GPA in college-preparatory subjects required. Minimum 2.25 GPA required of business and justice studies program applicants; 2.5 GPA of social work program applicants; 2.6 GPA of nursing program applicants; 2.7 GPA of School of Education applicants. Freshmen Studies Program for applicants not normally admissible. ACT is required; SAT may be substituted. Campus visit and interview recommended. Off-campus interviews available with an admissions representative.
**Procedure:** Take SAT or ACT by February of 12th year. Visit college for interview by February of 12th year. Suggest filing application by February 1. Application deadline is August 1. Notification of admission on rolling basis. $60 refundable tuition deposit. $125 room deposit, partially refundable. Freshmen accepted for terms other than fall.
**Special programs:** Admission may be deferred one year. Credit and/or placement may be granted through CEEB Advanced Placement exams for scores of 3 or higher. Credit and/or placement may be granted through CLEP general and subject exams. Credit and placement may be granted through DANTES and challenge exams. Concurrent enrollment program.
**Transfer students:** Transfer students accepted for terms other than fall. In fall 1992, 32% of all new students were transfers into all classes. 1,355 transfer applications were received, 1,215 were accepted. Application deadline is August 1 for fall; December 1 for spring. Minimum 2.0 GPA required. Lowest course grade accepted is "D." At least 32 semester hours must be completed at the university to receive degree.
**Admissions contact:** Nancy Rehling, M.S.Ed., Director of Admissions. 906 227-2650.

**FINANCIAL AID. Available aid:** Pell grants, SEOG, Federal Nursing Student Scholarships, state scholarships and grants, school scholarships and grants, ROTC scholarships, academic merit scholarships, and athletic scholarships. Perkins Loans (NDSL), PLUS, Stafford Loans (GSL), state loans, private loans, and SLS. AMS.
**Financial aid statistics:** 10% of aid is not need-based. In 1992-93, 71% of all undergraduate applicants received aid; 71% of freshman applicants. Average amounts of aid awarded freshmen: Scholarships and grants, $1,775; loans, $1,568.
**Supporting data/closing dates:** FAFSA: Priority filing date is February 1; accepted on rolling basis. FAF/FFS: Priority filing date is February 1. Notification of awards begins May 1.
**Financial aid contact:** Robert Pecotte, M.S., Director of Financial Aid. 906 227-2327.

**STUDENT EMPLOYMENT.** College Work/Study Program. Institutional employment. 31% of full-time undergraduates work on campus during school year. Students may expect to earn an average of $1,310 during school year. Off-campus part-time employment opportunities rated "good."

**COMPUTER FACILITIES.** 435 IBM/IBM-compatible and Macintosh/Apple microcomputers; 170 are networked. Students may access IBM minicomputer/mainframe systems. Residence halls may be equipped with stand-alone microcomputers, networked terminals, modems. Client/LAN operating systems include Apple/Macintosh. Computer languages and software packages include Assembly, C, COBOL, FORTRAN, Pascal, PL/1; over 100 in all. Computer facilities are available to all students.
**Fees:** Computer fee is included in tuition/fees.
**Hours:** 8 AM-10 PM.

**GRADUATE CAREER DATA.** Graduate school percentages: 2% enter law school. 1% enter medical school. 1% enter dental school. 1% enter graduate business programs. 7% enter graduate arts and sciences programs. Highest graduate school enrollments: Michigan State U, U of Michigan. Companies and businesses that hire graduates: Ford, General Motors, Texas Instruments.

**PROMINENT ALUMNI/AE.** John Lautner, architect; Sharon Dillworth, writer; Robert Traver, writer; William Nault, publisher; Edward Havilik, real estate developer; Jerry Glanville, coach, Atlanta Falcons.

# Northwood University–Midland Campus

**Midland, MI 48640** **517 837-4200**

**1994-95 Costs.** Tuition: $9,450. Room: $1,785. Board: $2,600. Fees, books, misc. academic expenses (school's estimate): $865.
**Enrollment.** Undergraduates: 791 men, 488 women (full-time). Freshman class: 1,093 applicants, 998 accepted, 285 enrolled. Graduate enrollment: 55 men, 25 women.
**Test score averages/ranges.** N/A.
**Faculty.** 33 full-time; 22 part-time. 13% of faculty holds doctoral degree. Student/faculty ratio: 24 to 1.
**Selectivity rating.** N/A.

**PROFILE.** Northwood University, founded in 1959, is a private, multipurpose university including business- and industry-oriented curricula. Its 268-acre campus is located in Midland, 55 miles north of Flint.
**Accreditation:** NCACS.
**Religious orientation:** Northwood University–Midland Campus is nonsectarian; no religious requirements.
**Library:** Collections totaling over 43,000 volumes, 520 periodical subscriptions, and 1,500 microform items.
**Special facilities/museums:** Art gallery, automotive hall of fame.
**Athletic facilities:** Gymnasium, basketball, tennis, and volleyball courts, swimming pool, track, weight room, athletic fields.

**STUDENT BODY. Undergraduate profile:** 66% are state residents; 40% are transfers. 1% Asian-American, 12% Black, 2% Hispanic, 85% White. Average age of undergraduates is 20.
**Freshman profile:** Majority of accepted applicants took ACT. 85% of freshmen come from public schools.
**Undergraduate achievement:** 87% of fall 1992 freshmen returned for fall 1993 term. 20% of entering class graduated.
**Foreign students:** 100 students are from out of the country. Countries represented include Canada, Germany, India, Japan, Malawi, and the Netherlands; 21 in all.

**PROGRAMS OF STUDY. Degrees:** B.Bus.Admin.
**Majors:** Accounting, Automotive Marketing Management, Computer Information Management, Computer Science/Management, Economics, Management, Marketing.
**Distribution of degrees:** The majors with the highest enrollment are marketing, management, and accounting.
**Requirements:** General education requirement.
**Academic regulations:** Minimum 2.0 GPA must be maintained.
**Special:** Minors offered in most majors and in international business, language arts, and math. Executive M.B.A. program. Associate's degrees offered. Double majors. Dual degrees. Independent study. Accelerated study. Pass/fail grading option. Internships. Member of Associated Independent Colleges of Michigan. Study abroad in Europe; program based in Paris with extensive travel.
**Honors:** Honors program.
**Academic Assistance:** Remedial writing and math.

**STUDENT LIFE. Housing:** All unmarried freshmen under age 19 must live on campus. 65% of students live in college housing.
**Services and counseling/handicapped student services:** Placement services. Health service. Personal and psychological counseling. Academic guidance services.
**Campus organizations:** Undergraduate student government. Student newspaper (Entrepreneur, published biweekly). Yearbook. Radio station. Drama and music groups, departmental, political, service, and special-interest groups. Nine fraternities, no chapter houses; three sororities, no chapter houses. 25% of men join a fraternity. 30% of women join a sorority.
**Religious organizations:** Christian Fellowship Club, Newman Club.
**Minority/foreign student organizations:** Black Leaders Awareness Coalition. International Student Organization.

**ATHLETICS. Physical education requirements:** Two terms of physical education required.
**Intercollegiate competition:** Baseball (M), basketball (M,W), cheerleading (M,W), cross-country (M,W), football (M), golf (M), lacrosse (M), soccer (W), tennis (M,W), track and field (indoor) (M,W), track and field (outdoor) (M,W), volleyball (W). Member of Great Lakes Intercollegiate Athletic Conference, Midwest Intercollegiate Football Conference, NCAA Division II.
**Intramural and club sports:** Intramural basketball, softball, tennis, touch football, volleyball. Men's club ice hockey, soccer, track and field.

**ADMISSIONS. Academic basis for candidate selection** (in order of priority): Secondary school record, standardized test scores, class rank, school's recommendation, essay.
**Nonacademic basis for candidate selection:** Character and personality, extracurricular participation, and particular talent or ability are considered.
**Requirements:** Graduation from secondary school is recommended; GED is accepted. 8 units and the following program of study are recommended: 3 units of English, 2 units of math, 1 unit of foreign language, 2 units of social studies. Probationary admission possible for applicants not meeting standard requirements. SAT or ACT is required. Campus visit and interview recommended. Off-campus interviews available with admissions and alumni representatives.

**Procedure:** Take SAT or ACT by June of 12th year. Take ACH by June of 12th year. Visit college for interview by spring of 12th year. Suggest filing application by December 1. Notification of admission on rolling basis. No set date by which applicants must accept offer. $150 tuition deposit, refundable until May 1. $100 room deposit, refundable until May 1. Freshmen accepted for terms other than fall.
**Special programs:** Admission may be deferred. Placement may be granted through CEEB Advanced Placement exams for scores of 4 or higher. Placement may be granted through CLEP subject exams. Early entrance/early admission program. Concurrent enrollment program.
**Transfer students:** Transfer students accepted for terms other than fall. In fall 1993, 40% of all new students were transfers into all classes. 294 transfer applications were received, 289 were accepted. Application deadline is September 1 for fall; March 1 for spring. Minimum 2.0 GPA recommended. Lowest course grade accepted is "C." At least 45 quarter hours must be completed at the university to receive degree.
**Admissions contact:** David Long, D.M.D., Dean of Admissions. 515 837-4273.

**FINANCIAL AID. Available aid:** Pell grants, SEOG, state grants, school grants, private scholarships, academic merit scholarships, and athletic scholarships. PLUS and Stafford Loans (GSL). AMS and family tuition reduction.
**Financial aid statistics:** 19% of aid is not need-based. In 1993-94, 90% of all undergraduate applicants received aid; 95% of freshman applicants. Average amounts of aid awarded freshmen: Scholarships and grants, $4,900; loans, $4,100.
**Supporting data/closing dates:** FAFSA: Accepted on rolling basis. Income tax forms. Student Aid Report. Notification of awards on rolling basis.
**Financial aid contact:** Diane Todd Sprague, M.S., Director of Financial Aid. 515 837-4230.

**STUDENT EMPLOYMENT.** College Work/Study Program. Institutional employment. Students may expect to earn an average of $1,000 during school year. Freshmen are discouraged from working during their first term. Off-campus part-time employment opportunities rated "good."

**COMPUTER FACILITIES.** 85 microcomputers. Computer languages and software packages include COBOL, Image, Query. Computer facilities are available to all students. Fees: $30 computer fee per academic year.

**GRADUATE CAREER DATA.** 100% of graduates choose careers in business and industry.

# Oakland University

**Rochester, MI 48309** **313 370-2100**

**1994-95 Costs.** Tuition: $3,250 (state residents), $9,200 (out-of-state). Room & board: $4,030. Fees, books, misc. academic expenses (school's estimate): $612.
**Enrollment.** Undergraduates: 2,360 men, 4,081 women (full-time). Freshman class: 3,036 applicants, 2,576 accepted, 1,170 enrolled. Graduate enrollment: 890 men, 1,582 women.
**Test score averages/ranges.** Average ACT scores: 23 composite.
**Faculty.** 360 full-time; 258 part-time. 87% of faculty holds doctoral degree. Student/faculty ratio: 19 to 1.
**Selectivity rating.** Less competitive.

**PROFILE.** Oakland, founded in 1957, is a public, comprehensive university. Programs are offered through the College of Arts and Sciences; the Schools of Business Administration, Engineering and Computer Science, and Health Sciences; and the Division of General Studies. Its 1,500-acre campus is located in Rochester, 10 miles north of downtown Detroit.
**Accreditation:** NCACS. Professionally accredited by the Accreditation Board for Engineering and Technology, the American Assembly of Collegiate Schools of Business, the American Physical Therapy Association, the National Association of Schools of Public Affairs and Administration, the National Council for Accreditation of Teacher Education, the National League for Nursing.
**Religious orientation:** Oakland University is nonsectarian; no religious requirements.
**Library:** Collections totaling over 572,445 volumes, 2,100 periodical subscriptions, and 1,000,000 microform items.
**Special facilities/museums:** Art gallery, robotics lab, eye research institute, exercise science institute.
**Athletic facilities:** Gymnasium, sports center, swimming pool, weight room, racquetball and tennis courts, athletic fields, golf course.

**STUDENT BODY. Undergraduate profile:** 99% are state residents; 46% are transfers. 2.7% Asian-American, 6.3% Black, 1.4% Hispanic, .5% Native American, 85% White, 4.1% Other. Average age of undergraduates is 25.
**Freshman profile:** 10% of accepted applicants took SAT; 90% took ACT. 84% of freshmen come from public schools.
**Undergraduate achievement:** 67% of fall 1992 freshmen returned for fall 1993 term. 65% of entering class graduated. 25% of students who completed a degree program went on to graduate study within five years.
**Foreign students:** 48 students are from out of the country. Countries represented include Canada, China, India, Japan, and the United Kingdom; 23 in all.

**PROGRAMS OF STUDY. Degrees:** B.A., B.Gen.Studies, B.Mus., B.S., B.S.E., B.S.Nurs.
**Majors:** Accounting, Anthropology, Applied Statistics, Art History, Biochemistry, Biology, Chemistry, Chinese Language/Civilization, Communication, Computer Engineering, Computer Science, Economics, Electrical Engineering, Elementary Education, Engineering Chemistry, Engineering Physics, English, Environmental Health, Finance, French, General Management, General Studies, German, Health Sciences, History, Human Resource Development, Human Resources Management, Industrial Health/Safety, International Studies, Journalism, Latin American Language/Civilization, Linguistics, Management Information Systems, Marketing, Mathematics, Mechanical Engineering, Medical Laboratory Sciences, Medical Physics, Music, Nursing, Occupational Health/Safety, Performing Arts, Philosophy, Physics, Political Science, Psychology, Public Administration, Russian Language/Literature, Sociology, Spanish, Systems Engineering, Youth/Adult Services.
**Distribution of degrees:** The majors with the highest enrollment are nursing, psychology, and communication; German/German studies and engineering physics have the lowest.
**Requirements:** General education requirement.
**Academic regulations:** Minimum 2.0 GPA must be maintained.
**Special:** Minors offered in most majors and in African studies, Afro-American studies, American studies, applied mathematics, archaeology, comparative literature, dance, East Asian studies, energy studies, environmental studies, exercise science, film aesthetics/history, folklore/popular culture, gerontology, health/medical behavioral science, human/industrial relations, international management, Latin American studies, Michigan studies, physical education. Preprofessional studies in medicine, dentistry, and optometry, production/operations management, public relations, quantitative methods, religious studies, Slavic studies, social justice/corrections, social services, South Asian studies, speech, studio art, theatre arts, urban studies, and women's studies. Associate's degrees offered. Double majors. Dual degrees. Internships. Cooperative education programs. Graduate school at which undergraduates may take graduate-level courses. Preprofessional programs in law, medicine, veterinary science, pharmacy, dentistry, and optometry. Member of Japan Center for Michigan universities and American Heritage Association. Teacher certification in elementary and secondary education. Certification in specific subject areas. Exchange programs abroad in Austria (U of Vienna), France (U d'Orleans) and Japan (Nanzan U). Study abroad also in African, European, and South and Central American countries.
**Honors:** Honors program. Honor societies.
**Academic Assistance:** Remedial math and study skills. Nonremedial tutoring.

**STUDENT LIFE. Housing:** All unmarried students under age 21 must live on campus unless living near campus with relatives. Coed dorms. Fraternity housing. On-campus married-student housing. 11% of students live in college housing.
**Social atmosphere:** "On campus, all social and cultural life is virtually non-existent because Oakland is primarily a commuter school," reports the student newspaper. "Off-campus life is difficult to judge because it is so varied; people live in so many different areas." Popular gathering spots on campus include the Oakland Center and the Beer Lake Yacht Club. Off campus, students hang out at Dillinger's, the four Green Fields, and Griff's Grill. Greeks, the Association of Black Students, and the Student Program Board are influential groups on campus. The Greek Olympics and the Winter Festival are among the year's favorite events.
**Services and counseling/handicapped student services:** Placement services. Health service. Day care. Counseling services for minority, veteran, and older students. Birth control, personal, and psychological counseling. Career and academic guidance services. Religious counseling. Physically disabled student services. Learning disabled services. Notetaking services. Tape recorders. Tutors. Reader services for the blind.
**Campus organizations:** Undergraduate student government. Student newspaper (Oakland Post, published once/week). Radio station. Political clubs, drama groups, several vocal and instrumental music ensembles, special-interest groups, professional organizations, 82 organizations in all. Seven fraternities, one chapter house; eight sororities, no chapter houses. 3% of men join a fraternity. 4% of women join a sorority.
**Religious organizations:** Bahai Organization, Baptist Student Union, Campus Crusade for Christ, Deeper Life, Intervarsity Christian Fellowship, Lutheran Student Fellowship, St. John Student Involvement, United Students for Christ.
**Minority/foreign student organizations:** Association of Black Students, Association of Minority Engineers, Black Awareness Committee. International Student Organization, Chinese Friendship Association, Indian and Vietnamese groups.

**ATHLETICS. Physical education requirements:** None.
**Intercollegiate competition:** 2% of students participate. Baseball (M), basketball (M,W), cross-country (M), diving (M,W), golf (M), soccer (M), swimming (M,W), tennis (M,W), volleyball (W). Member of Great Lakes Intercollegiate Athletic Conference, NCAA Division II.
**Intramural and club sports:** 10% of students participate. Intramural basketball, floor hockey, football, racquetball, softball, volleyball. Men's club fencing, skiing. Women's club fencing, skiing, soccer.

**ADMISSIONS. Academic basis for candidate selection** (in order of priority): Secondary school record, standardized test scores, class rank, school's recommendation, essay.
**Nonacademic basis for candidate selection:** Character and personality, extracurricular participation, and particular talent or ability are considered.
**Requirements:** Graduation from secondary school is required; GED is not accepted. 14 units and the following program of study are required: 4 units of English, 3 units of math, 3 units of science including 1 unit of lab, 2 units of social studies, 2 units of history. Minimum 2.5 GPA required; minimum composite ACT score of 20 and minimum 2.8 GPA recommended. 3 units of math (algebra, geometry, trigonometry) required of engineering, management, math, and science program applicants. Minimum 3.0 GPA required of business, elementary education, engineering, nursing, and physical therapy program applicants. Audition required of music program applicants. Academic Opportunity Program for applicants not normally admissible. ACT is required; SAT may be substituted. Campus visit recommended. No off-campus interviews.
**Procedure:** Take SAT or ACT by February of 12th year. Suggest filing application by January. Application deadline is April. Notification of admission on rolling basis. Reply is required by May 1. $50 nonrefundable tuition deposit. Freshmen accepted for terms other than fall.
**Special programs:** Admission may be deferred two semesters. Credit and/or placement may be granted through CEEB Advanced Placement exams for scores of 3 or higher. Credit and/or placement may be granted through CLEP general and subject exams. Placement may be granted through challenge exams. Concurrent enrollment program.
**Transfer students:** Transfer students accepted for terms other than fall. In fall 1993, 46% of all new students were transfers into all classes. 2,090 transfer applications were received, 1,695 were accepted. Application deadline is July 15 for fall; December 1 for spring. Minimum 2.5 GPA required. Lowest course grade accepted is "C." Maximum number of transferable credits is 92 semester hours. At least 32 semester hours must be completed at the university to receive degree.

**Admissions contact:** Anne M. Sandoval, M.A., Acting Director of Admissions. 313 370-3360.

**FINANCIAL AID. Available aid:** Pell grants, SEOG, state scholarships and grants, school scholarships and grants, private scholarships and grants, academic merit scholarships, and athletic scholarships. Perkins Loans (NDSL), PLUS, Stafford Loans (GSL), state loans, and SLS.
**Financial aid statistics:** 36% of aid is not need-based. In 1993-94, 85% of all undergraduate applicants received aid; 94% of freshman applicants. Average amounts of aid awarded freshmen: Scholarships and grants, $1,900; loans, $1,630.
**Supporting data/closing dates:** FAFSA/FAF/FFS: Priority filing date is March 1; accepted on rolling basis. School's own aid application: Priority filing date is March 1; accepted on rolling basis. Income tax forms: Priority filing date is March 1; accepted on rolling basis. Notification of awards begins April 1.
**Financial aid contact:** Lee D. Anderson, M.A., Director of Financial Aid. 313 370-3370.

**STUDENT EMPLOYMENT.** College Work/Study Program. Institutional employment. 17% of full-time undergraduates work on campus during school year. Students may expect to earn an average of $1,200 during school year. Off-campus part-time employment opportunities rated "excellent."

**COMPUTER FACILITIES.** IBM/IBM-compatible, Macintosh/Apple, and RISC-/UNIX-based microcomputers; 350 are networked. Students may access Digital minicomputer/mainframe systems, BITNET, Internet. Residence halls may be equipped with stand-alone microcomputers, networked microcomputers, modems. Client/LAN operating systems include Apple/Macintosh, DOS, UNIX/XENIX/AIX, X-windows, DEC, LocalTalk/AppleTalk. Computer languages and software packages include BASIC, C, COBOL, Fortran, Pascal, PL/1, S, SAS; 150 in all. Computer facilities are available to all students.
**Fees:** $80 computer fee per semester; included in tuition/fees.
**Hours:** 24 hours.

**GRADUATE CAREER DATA.** Highest graduate school enrollments: Oakland U, U of Michigan, Wayne State U. 50% of graduates choose careers in business and industry. Companies and businesses that hire graduates: Chrysler, Ford, General Motors, Michigan Bell.

**PROMINENT ALUMNI/AE.** Dennis Pawley, vice-president, Mazda Corp; Barbara Dale, owner, Dale Greeting Cards; Ronna Romney, former chairperson, National Republican Party.

# Olivet College

**Olivet, MI 49076** **616 749-7000**

**1994-95 Costs.** Tuition: $11,030. Room: $2,000. Board: $1,680. Fees, books, misc. academic expenses (school's estimate): $500.
**Enrollment.** Undergraduates: 404 men, 362 women (full-time). Freshman class: 520 applicants, 465 accepted, 175 enrolled.
**Test score averages/ranges.** Average ACT scores: 18 composite.
**Faculty.** 36 full-time; 35 part-time. 48% of faculty holds doctoral degree. Student/faculty ratio: 15 to 1.
**Selectivity rating.** Less competitive.

**PROFILE.** Olivet, founded in 1844, is a church-affiliated, multipurpose college. Programs are offered in the Divisions of Education and Physical Education, Fine Arts, Science and Mathematics, and Social Sciences. Its 45-acre campus is located in Olivet, 125 miles west of Detroit.

**Accreditation:** NCACS.
**Religious orientation:** Olivet College is affiliated with the United Church of Christ (Congregational); no religious requirements.
**Library:** Collections totaling over 84,294 volumes, 850 periodical subscriptions and 604 microform items.
**Special facilities/museums:** Language lab, observatory, planetarium.
**Athletic facilities:** Indoor pool, weight room, paddleball/racquetball/handball courts, intramural building, intramural athletic fields.

**STUDENT BODY. Undergraduate profile:** 96% are state residents. 1% Asian-American, 9% Black, 1% Hispanic, 89% White.
**Freshman profile:** 92% of accepted applicants took ACT. 98% of freshmen come from public schools.
**Undergraduate achievement:** 82% of fall 1992 freshmen returned for fall 1993 term. 42% of entering class graduated. 8% of students who completed a degree program went on to graduate study within five years.
**Foreign students:** Four students are from out of the country. Countries represented include Canada, Germany, Japan, and Pakistan.

**PROGRAMS OF STUDY. Degrees:** B.A., B.Mus., B.Mus.Ed.
**Majors:** American Studies, Art, Biochemistry, Biological Anthropology, Biology, Business Administration, Chemistry, Communication, Computer Science, Economics, English, French, History, Journalism, Mathematics, Music, Physical Education, Psychology, Recreation Management, Religion, Social Studies, Sociology/Anthropology, Spanish, Theatre/Speech.
**Distribution of degrees:** The majors with the highest enrollment are business administration, education, and social sciences; chemistry and French have the lowest.
**Requirements:** General education requirement.
**Special:** Minors offered in most majors and in interpersonal communications and political science. Courses offered in astronomy. Self-designed majors. Double majors. Dual degrees. Independent study. Internships. Cooperative education programs. Graduate school at which undergraduates may take graduate-level courses. Preprofessional programs in law, medicine, and dentistry. Signatory of MACRAO Articulation Agreement. Teacher certification in elementary and secondary education. Study abroad possible.
**Honors:** Honors program.
**Academic Assistance:** Nonremedial tutoring.

**ADMISSIONS. Academic basis for candidate selection** (in order of priority): Secondary school record, class rank, standardized test scores, school's recommendation.
**Nonacademic basis for candidate selection:** Character and personality, extracurricular participation, particular talent or ability, geographical distribution, and alumni/ae relationship are considered.
**Requirements:** Graduation from secondary school is required; GED is accepted. 16 units and the following program of study are required: Minimum 2.6 GPA required. Summer session of pre-admission classwork for applicants not normally admissible. ACT is required; SAT may be substituted. Campus visit and interview recommended. Off-campus interviews available with an admissions representative.
**Procedure:** Take SAT or ACT by October of 12th year. Visit college for interview by April of 12th year. Application deadline is July. Notification of admission on rolling basis. $100 nonrefundable tuition and room deposit. Freshmen accepted for terms other than fall.
**Special programs:** Credit and/or placement may be granted through CEEB Advanced Placement exams for scores of 3 or higher. Credit and/or placement may be granted through CLEP general and subject exams. Credit and placement may be granted through military and life experience. Early decision program. In fall 1993, 10 applied for early decision and 10 were accepted. Deadline for applying for early decision is July of 11th year. Early entrance/early admission program. Concurrent enrollment program.
**Transfer students:** Transfer students accepted for terms other than fall. Application deadline is rolling for fall; rolling for spring. Minimum 2.0 GPA required. Lowest course grade accepted is "C." Maximum number of transferable credits is 78 semester hours. At least 30 semester hours must be completed at the college to receive degree.
**Admissions contact:** Durk L. Dunham, Director of Admissions. 616 749-7635.

**FINANCIAL AID. Available aid:** Pell grants, SEOG, state scholarships and grants, school grants, private scholarships and grants, and academic merit scholarships. Perkins Loans (NDSL), PLUS, Stafford Loans (GSL), state loans, and SLS. Deferred payment plan. Institutional monthly payment plan.
**Supporting data/closing dates:** FAFSA/FAF/FFS: Priority filing date is February 15; deadline is July 31. Notification of awards on rolling basis.
**Financial aid contact:** Ronald E. Thatcher, Director of Financial Aid. 616 749-7645.

# Saginaw Valley State University

**University Center, MI 48710** **517 790-4000**

**1993-94 Costs.** Tuition: $2,674 (state residents), $5,673 (out-of-state). Room & board: $3,650. Fees, books, misc. academic expenses (school's estimate): $767.
**Enrollment.** Undergraduates: 1,534 men, 2,000 women (full-time). Freshman class: 1,509 applicants, 1,334 accepted, 721 enrolled. Graduate enrollment: 721.
**Test score averages/ranges.** Average ACT scores: 18 English, 17 math, 18 composite.
**Faculty.** 170 full-time; 216 part-time. 80% of faculty holds highest degree in specific field. Student/faculty ratio: 24 to 1.
**Selectivity rating.** Less competitive.

**PROFILE.** Saginaw Valley State, founded in 1963, is a public, comprehensive university. Programs are offered through the Schools of Arts and Behavioral Sciences; Business and Management; Education; Nursing and Allied Health Sciences; and Science, Engineering, and Technology. Its 782-acre campus is located in University Center, 35 miles north of Flint.

**Accreditation:** NCACS. Professionally accredited by the Accreditation Board for Engineering and Technology, the American Medical Association (CAHEA), the Council on Social Work Education, the National Council for Accreditation of Teacher Education, the National League for Nursing.
**Religious orientation:** Saginaw Valley State University is nonsectarian; no religious requirements.
**Library:** Collections totaling over 409,760 volumes, 6,127 periodical subscriptions, and 1,469 microform items.
**Special facilities/museums:** Sculpture gallery, fine arts center, center for health and physical education, independent testing lab, center for economic and business research, applied technology research center.
**Athletic facilities:** Gymnasium, field house, basketball, racquetball, tennis, and volleyball courts, swimming pool, tracks, archery range, baseball, football, intramural, and softball fields, stadiums, arena.

**STUDENT BODY. Undergraduate profile:** 99% are state residents; 33% are transfers. 1% Asian-American, 6% Black, 3% Hispanic, 1% Native American, 87% White, 2% Other.
**Freshman profile:** 2% of accepted applicants took SAT; 98% took ACT. 98% of freshmen come from public schools.
**Undergraduate achievement:** 60% of fall 1991 freshmen returned for fall 1992 term.
**Foreign students:** 16 students are from out of the country. Countries represented include Japan and Thailand; 14 in all.

**PROGRAMS OF STUDY. Degrees:** B.A., B.Bus.Admin., B.S., B.S.Elec.Eng., B.S.Mech.Eng., B.S.Nurs., B.Soc.Work.
**Majors:** Accounting, Art, Art Education, Biochemistry, Biology, Biology Education, Business/Chemistry, Chemical Physics, Chemistry, Chemistry Education, Communication, Communication Education, Computer Information Systems, Computer Mathematics, Computer Physics, Computer Science, Criminal Justice, Design, Economics, Electrical Engineering, Elementary Education, English, English Education, Finance, French, French Education, General Business, History, History Education, Industrial Management, Industrial Technology/Supervision, Management, Marketing, Mathematics, Mathematics/Economics, Mathematics Education, Mechanical Engineering, Medical Technology, Music, Music Education, Natural Science Education, Nursing, Occupational Therapy, Optical Physics, Physical Education, Physics, Physics Education, Political Science, Pre-

Dentistry, Pre-Law, Pre-Medicine, Psychology, Public Administration, Social Work, Sociology, Spanish, Spanish Education, Special Education, Theatre, Theatre Education.
**Distribution of degrees:** The majors with the highest enrollment are business, education, and criminal justice.
**Requirements:** General education requirement. Major and minor, two majors, or approved interdisciplinary major required.
**Special:** Minors offered in many majors and in coaching, German, gerontology, legal studies, philosophy, Polish, and youth services. Courses offered in ethnic studies. Double majors. Independent study. Pass/fail grading option. Cooperative education programs. Preprofessional programs in law, medicine, dentistry, theology, engineering, forestry, occupational therapy, and physical therapy. Teacher certification in elementary, secondary, special education, and bilingual/bicultural education. Study abroad in Austria, China, France, Japan, Korea, Mexico, and Poland. ROTC at Central Michigan U.
**Honors:** Honors program.
**Academic Assistance:** Remedial reading, writing, math, and study skills. Nonremedial tutoring.

**STUDENT LIFE. Housing:** Students may live on or off campus. Coed dorms. School-owned/operated apartments. 10% of students live in college housing.
**Services and counseling/handicapped student services:** Placement services. Day care. Counseling services for minority and older students. Birth control and personal counseling. Career and academic guidance services. Physically disabled student services. Learning disabled services. Notetaking services. Tape recorders. Tutors.
**Campus organizations:** Undergraduate student government. Student newspaper (Valley Vanguard). Literary magazine. Choir, orchestra, jazz ensemble, Collegium Musicum, marching, jazz, and concert bands, drama group, theatre, cultural events, academic and social clubs, volunteer program, special-interest groups.
**Religious organizations:** Campus Ministry.
**Minority/foreign student organizations:** Progressive Student Association, Hispanic Student Association. International Student Club.

**ATHLETICS. Physical education requirements:** None.
**Intercollegiate competition:** 20% of students participate. Baseball (M), basketball (M,W), bowling (M), cheerleading (M,W), cross-country (M,W), football (M), golf (M), softball (W), tennis (W), track (indoor) (M,W), track (outdoor) (M,W), track and field (indoor) (M,W), track and field (outdoor) (M,W), volleyball (W). Member of Great Lakes Intercollegiate Athletic Conference, Midwest Intercollegiate Football Conference, NCAA Division II.
**Intramural and club sports:** 20% of students participate. Intramural basketball, floor hockey, football, soccer, softball, swimming, volleyball, walleyball. Men's club soccer. Women's club soccer.

**ADMISSIONS. Academic basis for candidate selection** (in order of priority): Secondary school record, standardized test scores, class rank, school's recommendation, essay.
**Nonacademic basis for candidate selection:** Character and personality, extracurricular participation, particular talent or ability, geographical distribution, and alumni/ae relationship are considered.
**Requirements:** Graduation from secondary school is required; GED is accepted. 18 units and the following program of study are recommended: 4 units of English, 4 units of math, 3 units of science, 2 units of foreign language, 3 units of social studies. 2 units of fine arts also recommended. Applicants offering minimum 2.5 GPA in college-preparatory courses are generally admitted; limited number of applicants with 2.0-2.49 GPA are admitted. Minimum GPA, exam, and/or interview may be required for specific majors. Special admission policy for approximately 25 applicants not normally admissible. ACT is required; SAT may be substituted. Campus visit and interview recommended. No off-campus interviews.
**Procedure:** Take SAT or ACT by December of 12th year. Notification of admission on rolling basis. Applicants must pay $25 nonrefundable matriculation fee and $200 room deposit, refundable from June 15 until August 1. Freshmen accepted for terms other than fall.
**Special programs:** Credit and/or placement may be granted through CEEB Advanced Placement exams for scores of 3 or higher. Credit and/or placement may be granted through CLEP general and subject exams. Credit and placement may be granted through challenge exams. Early entrance/early admission program. Concurrent enrollment program.
**Transfer students:** Transfer students accepted for terms other than fall. In fall 1992, 33% of all new students were transfers into all classes. 1,141 transfer applications were received, 1,040 were accepted. Application deadline is April 1 for fall; March 1 for spring. Minimum 2.0 GPA required. Lowest course grade accepted is "C." Maximum number of transferable credits is 62 semester hours from a two-year school and 93 semester hours from a four-year school. At least 31 semester hours must be completed at the university to receive degree.
**Admissions contact:** James Dwyer, Director of Admissions. 517 790-4200.

**FINANCIAL AID. Available aid:** Pell grants, SEOG, state scholarships, school scholarships and grants, private scholarships and grants, academic merit scholarships, and athletic scholarships. Perkins Loans (NDSL), PLUS, Stafford Loans (GSL), private loans, and SLS. AMS.
**Supporting data/closing dates:** FAFSA: Priority filing date is April 11. Notification of awards on rolling basis.
**Financial aid contact:** William Healy, Director of Financial Aid. 517 790-4103.

**STUDENT EMPLOYMENT.** College Work/Study Program. Institutional employment. 8% of full-time undergraduates work on campus during school year. Off-campus part-time employment opportunities rated "good."

**COMPUTER FACILITIES.** 120 IBM/IBM-compatible and Macintosh/Apple microcomputers. Students may access Digital, IBM minicomputer/mainframe systems. Computer languages and software packages include Ada, Assembler, BASIC, C, CICS, COBOL, dBASE, FORTRAN, LISP, Lotus 1-2-3, Pascal, PL/1, SAS, SPSS, SQL, WordPerfect; 30 in all. Computer facilities are available to all students.
**Fees:** None.
**Hours:** 8 AM-11 PM (M-Th); 8 AM-5 PM (F); 9 AM-5 PM (Sa); 2 PM-10 PM (Su).

**GRADUATE CAREER DATA.** Companies and businesses that hire graduates: Dow Chemical, Dow Corning, General Motors.

# Saint Mary's College

**Orchard Lake, MI 48324** — **810 682-1885**

**1994-95 Costs.** Tuition: $5,250. Room & board: $3,200. Fees, books, misc. academic expenses (school's estimate): $525.
**Enrollment.** Undergraduates: 83 men, 98 women (full-time). Freshman class: 194 applicants, 181 accepted, 166 enrolled.
**Test score averages/ranges.** Average ACT scores: 18 English, 16 math, 19 composite.
**Faculty.** 17 full-time; 28 part-time. 90% of faculty holds doctoral degree. Student/faculty ratio: 12 to 1.
**Selectivity rating.** Noncompetitive.

**PROFILE.** Saint Mary's, founded in 1885, is a private, church-affiliated, liberal arts college. Its 120-acre campus is located in Orchard Lake, 27 miles northwest of Detroit.

**Accreditation:** NCACS.
**Religious orientation:** Saint Mary's College is affiliated with the Roman Catholic Church; two semesters of theology required.
**Library:** Collections totaling over 68,000 volumes, 400 periodical subscriptions, and 5,500 microform items.
**Special facilities/museums:** Polish art museum, Polish-American museum, papal museum.
**Athletic facilities:** Field house, track, lake, gymnasium, athletic fields, beach volleyball pit.

**STUDENT BODY. Undergraduate profile:** 89% are state residents; 30% are transfers. 1% Asian-American, 12% Black, 1% Hispanic, 86% White. Average age of undergraduates is 22.
**Freshman profile:** 94% of accepted applicants took ACT. 75% of freshmen come from public schools.
**Undergraduate achievement:** 60% of fall 1991 freshmen returned for fall 1992 term. 40% of entering class graduated. 60% of students who completed a degree program went on to graduate study within five years.
**Foreign students:** 30 students are from out of the country. Countries represented include Ethiopia, Ghana, Korea, Lebanon, Pakistan, and Poland.

**PROGRAMS OF STUDY. Degrees:** B.A., B.Gen.Studies, B.Human., B.S.
**Majors:** Biology, Business Administration, Chemistry, Communication Arts, Computer Information Science, English, General Studies, Human Services, Philosophy, Polish Studies, Psychology, Radiologic Technology, Religious Studies, Social Sciences, Sociology, Theology.
**Distribution of degrees:** The majors with the highest enrollment are business administration, psychology, and communication arts; sociology and computer information science have the lowest.
**Requirements:** General education requirement.
**Special:** Minors offered in most majors and in history, Latin, natural science, physics, and religious education. Program offered in Priestly Formation is conducted with SS. Cyril and Methodius Seminary, offering those considering the priesthood an opportunity to experience community living. Double majors. Independent study. Accelerated study. Cooperative education programs. Preprofessional programs in law, medicine, veterinary science, and dentistry. Member of Detroit Area Catholic Higher Education Consortium. Study abroad in Poland.
**Academic Assistance:** Remedial reading, writing, math, and study skills.

**ADMISSIONS. Academic basis for candidate selection** (in order of priority): Secondary school record, standardized test scores, school's recommendation, class rank, essay.
**Nonacademic basis for candidate selection:** Character and personality are emphasized. Particular talent or ability is important. Extracurricular participation and alumni/ae relationship are considered.
**Requirements:** Graduation from secondary school is required; GED is accepted. 16 units and the following program of study are required: 4 units of English, 3 units of math, 3 units of science, 2 units of foreign language, 4 units of social studies. Minimum composite ACT score of 19 and minimum 2.5 GPA required. Conditional admission possible for applicants not meeting standard requirements. ACT is required; SAT may be substituted. Campus visit recommended. Off-campus interviews available with an admissions representative.
**Procedure:** Take SAT or ACT by October of 12th year. Visit college for interview by February of 12th year. Suggest filing application by April 30. Application deadline is August 15. Notification of admission on rolling basis. Reply is required by May 1. $50 nonrefundable tuition deposit. $210 refundable room deposit. Freshmen accepted for terms other than fall.
**Special programs:** Admission may be deferred one year. Credit and/or placement may be granted through CEEB Advanced Placement exams for scores of 3 or higher. Credit and/or placement may be granted through CLEP general and subject exams. Early decision program. In fall 1992, 30 applied for early decision and 27 were accepted. Early entrance/early admission program. Concurrent enrollment program.
**Transfer students:** Transfer students accepted for terms other than fall. In fall 1992, 30% of all new students were transfers into all classes. 45 transfer applications were received, 40 were accepted. Application deadline is August 15 for fall; December 15 for spring. Minimum 2.0 GPA required. Lowest course grade accepted is "C." Maximum number of transferable credits is 90 semester hours. At least 30 semester hours must be completed at the college to receive degree.
**Admissions contact:** Darrell Brockway, M.A., Dean of Enrollment Services. 810 683-0508.

**FINANCIAL AID. Available aid:** Pell grants, SEOG, state scholarships and grants, school scholarships and grants, and private scholarships. PLUS, Stafford Loans (GSL), state loans, and SLS. Deferred payment plan.

**Financial aid statistics:** In 1992-93, 90% of all undergraduate applicants received aid. Average amounts of aid awarded freshmen: Loans, $2,600.
**Supporting data/closing dates:** FAFSA/FAF/FFS: Priority filing date is January 1; deadline is March 30. School's own aid application: Priority filing date is July 1; deadline is August 30. Income tax forms: Accepted on rolling basis. Notification of awards on rolling basis.
**Financial aid contact:** Darrell Brockway, M.A., Dean of Enrollment Services. 810 683-0508.

# Siena Heights College

**Adrian, MI 49221** **517 263-0731**

**1993-94 Costs.** Tuition: $8,820. Room & board: $3,700. Fees, books, misc. academic expenses (school's estimate): $475.
**Enrollment.** Undergraduates: 287 men, 474 women (full-time). Freshman class: 480 applicants, 436 accepted, 201 enrolled. Graduate enrollment: 22 men, 101 women.
**Test score averages/ranges.** Average ACT scores: 19 English, 19 math, 20 composite.
**Faculty.** 75 full-time; 55 part-time. 42% of faculty holds doctoral degree. Student/faculty ratio: 15 to 1.
**Selectivity rating.** Noncompetitive.

**PROFILE.** Siena Heights is a private, church-affiliated, liberal arts college. Founded as a teachers college for women is 1919, it adopted coeducation in 1969. Its 140-acre campus is located in Adrian, 35 miles from Toledo.

**Accreditation:** NCACS. Professionally accredited by the National Association of Schools of Art and Design.
**Religious orientation:** Siena Heights College is affiliated with the Roman Catholic Church (Dominican Order); no religious requirements.
**Library:** Collections totaling over 115,029 volumes, 454 periodical subscriptions, and 24,459 microform items.
**Special facilities/museums:** Art gallery, Montessori school, language lab.
**Athletic facilities:** Gymnasium, track, basketball, tennis, and volleyball courts, baseball and soccer fields.

**STUDENT BODY. Undergraduate profile:** 85% are state residents. 1% Asian-American, 6% Black, 3% Hispanic, 89% White, 1% Other. Average age of undergraduates is 18.
**Freshman profile:** 2% of accepted applicants took SAT; 98% took ACT. 87% of freshmen come from public schools.
**Undergraduate achievement:** 70% of fall 1991 freshmen returned for fall 1992 term. 15% of students who completed a degree program immediately went on to graduate study.
**Foreign students:** 26 students are from out of the country. Countries represented include Africa, Canada, England, France, Japan, and South Korea.

**PROGRAMS OF STUDY. Degrees:** B.A., B.Appl.Sci., B.F.A., B.S.
**Majors:** Accounting, American Studies, Art, Biology, Business Administration, Business Education, Chemistry, Computer/Information Systems, Contracted Major, Criminal Justice, English, Fashion Merchandising, General Studies, History, Hotel/Restaurant/Institutional Management, Human Services, Humanities, Mathematics, Medical Technology, Music, Natural Science, Philosophy, Psychology, Public Administration, Religious Studies, Social Sciences, Social Work, Spanish, Theatre/Speech Communication.
**Distribution of degrees:** The majors with the highest enrollment are human services, business administration, and English; history, philosophy, and music have the lowest.
**Requirements:** General education requirement.
**Academic regulations:** Minimum 2.0 GPA must be maintained.
**Special:** Minors offered in most majors and in French, language arts, secretarial science, sociology, Spanish, and speech/drama. Minors required for those seeking teacher certification. Associate's degrees offered. Self-designed majors. Double majors. Independent study. Pass/fail grading option. Internships. Cooperative education programs. Graduate school at which undergraduates may take graduate-level courses. Preprofessional programs in law, medicine, veterinary science, pharmacy, and dentistry. 2-2 pre-engineering programs with U of Detroit and U of Michigan. Teacher certification in elementary, secondary, and vo-tech education. Study abroad in Italy.
**Honors:** Honors program.
**Academic Assistance:** Remedial study skills. Nonremedial tutoring.

**ADMISSIONS. Academic basis for candidate selection** (in order of priority): Secondary school record, standardized test scores, essay, school's recommendation, class rank.
**Nonacademic basis for candidate selection:** Character and personality are important. Extracurricular participation, particular talent or ability, and alumni/ae relationship are considered.
**Requirements:** Graduation from secondary school is required; GED is accepted. No specific distribution of secondary school units required. Minimum composite ACT score of 17 and minimum 2.3 GPA required. Conditional admission possible for applicants not meeting standard requirements. ACT is required; SAT may be substituted. Campus visit and interview recommended. No off-campus interviews.
**Procedure:** Application deadline is August 15. Notification of admission on rolling basis. $100 tuition deposit, refundable until May 1. $50 room deposit, refundable until June 1. Freshmen accepted for terms other than fall.
**Special programs:** Admission may be deferred one year. Credit and/or placement may be granted through CEEB Advanced Placement exams for scores of 3 or higher. Credit and/or placement may be granted through CLEP general and subject exams. Credit may be granted through military and life experience. Early entrance/early admission program. Concurrent enrollment program.
**Transfer students:** Transfer students accepted for terms other than fall. In fall 1992, 90 transfer applications were received, 70 were accepted. Application deadline is August 15 for fall; December 30 for spring. Minimum 2.0 GPA required. Lowest course grade accepted is "C." At least 30 semester hours must be completed at the college to receive degree.
**Admissions contact:** Norman A. Bukwaz, M.A., Dean of Admissions. 517 263-0731, extension 214.

**FINANCIAL AID. Available aid:** Pell grants, SEOG, state scholarships and grants, school scholarships and grants, private scholarships and grants, academic merit scholarships, and athletic scholarships. PLUS, Stafford Loans (GSL), and SLS. AMS, deferred payment plan, and family tuition reduction.
**Financial aid statistics:** 13% of aid is not need-based. In 1992-93, 93% of all undergraduate applicants received aid; 98% of freshman applicants. Average amounts of aid awarded freshmen: Scholarships and grants, $1,700; loans, $1,700.
**Supporting data/closing dates:** FAFSA/FAF/FFS: Priority filing date is February 15; accepted on rolling basis. Notification of awards begins March 1.
**Financial aid contact:** Joanne Iler, Director of Financial Aid. 517 263-0731, extension 211.

**STUDENT EMPLOYMENT.** College Work/Study Program. Institutional employment. 20% of full-time undergraduates work on campus during school year. Students may expect to earn an average of $1,000 during school year. Off-campus part-time employment opportunities rated "fair."

**COMPUTER FACILITIES.** 40 IBM/IBM-compatible and Macintosh/Apple microcomputers. Students may access Digital minicomputer/mainframe systems. Computer languages and software packages include Lotus 1-2-3, Paradox, Quattro, WordPerfect; 30 in all. Computer facilities are available to all students.
**Fees:** $6 computer fee per semester.
**Hours:** 8:30 AM-11 PM.

**GRADUATE CAREER DATA.** Graduate school percentages: 2% enter medical school. 3% enter graduate business programs. 5% enter graduate arts and sciences programs. Highest graduate school enrollments: U of Michigan, U of Toledo. 65% of graduates choose careers in business and industry. Companies and businesses that hire graduates: Ford Motor Co., Tecumseh Products, Toledo Trust National Bank.

**PROMINENT ALUMNI/AE.** Connie Binsfield, lieutenant governor, Michigan; Barbara Doumouchelle, Michigan State Board of Education; Leonard Weinlander, president, Weinlander Kitchen and Bath Equipment.

# Spring Arbor College

**Spring Arbor, MI 49283** **517 750-1200**

**1993-94 Costs.** Tuition: $8,600. Room & board: $3,550. Fees, books, misc. academic expenses (school's estimate): $656.
**Enrollment.** Undergraduates: 309 men, 425 women (full-time). Freshman class: 401 applicants, 361 accepted, 181 enrolled.
**Test score averages/ranges.** Average ACT scores: 21 English, 20 math, 21 composite. Range of ACT scores of middle 50%: 18-24 composite.
**Faculty.** 65 full-time; 30 part-time. 42% of faculty holds doctoral degree. Student/faculty ratio: 17 to 1.
**Selectivity rating.** Less competitive.

**PROFILE.** Spring Arbor, founded in 1873, is a church-affiliated, liberal arts college. Its 70-acre campus is located in Spring Arbor, eight miles west of Jackson.

**Accreditation:** NCACS. Professionally accredited by the Council on Social Work Education, the National Council for Accreditation of Teacher Education.
**Religious orientation:** Spring Arbor College is affiliated with the Free Methodist Church; one semester of religion required.
**Library:** Collections totaling over 84,597 volumes, 1,252 periodical subscriptions, and 280 microform items.
**Special facilities/museums:** Radio and TV studios, commercial writing/computer graphics lab, science center.
**Athletic facilities:** Field house, tracks, swimming pool, baseball, softball, and soccer fields, badminton, basketball, tennis, and volleyball courts, fitness testing lab, batting cage.

**STUDENT BODY. Undergraduate profile:** 94% are state residents; 27% are transfers. 4% Black, 93% White, 3% Other.
**Freshman profile:** 5% of freshmen who took ACT scored 30 or over on composite; 26% scored 24 or over on composite; 83% scored 18 or over on composite; 99% scored 12 or over on composite. 13% of accepted applicants took SAT; 92% took ACT. 83% of freshmen come from public schools.
**Undergraduate achievement:** 77% of fall 1992 freshmen returned for fall 1993 term. 28% of entering class graduated. 9% of students who completed a degree program immediately went on to graduate study.
**Foreign students:** 34 students are from out of the country. Countries represented include Brazil, Canada, Haiti, Hong Kong, Japan, and Kenya; nine in all.

**PROGRAMS OF STUDY. Degrees:** B.A.
**Majors:** Accounting, Art, Biochemistry, Biology, Business Administration, Chemistry, Christian Ministries, Communication, Computer Science, Contemporary Music Ministries, Economics/Business, English, English/Speech, Exercise/Sport Science, French, History, Mathematics, Music, Philosophy, Philosophy/Religion, Physics/Mathematics, Psychology, Social Science, Social Work, Sociology, Spanish, Teacher Education.
**Distribution of degrees:** The majors with the highest enrollment are business administration, elementary education, and psychology; French, Spanish, and physics/mathematics have the lowest.
**Requirements:** General education requirement.
**Academic regulations:** Minimum 2.0 GPA required for graduation.
**Special:** Minors offered in many majors and in economics, geography, physics, political science, and speech; minors in language arts and science also offered for elementary education majors. Cross-cultural studies required for all students; program involves total immersion in a different culture with options available in urban centers in the U.S. as well as abroad. Christian perspective curriculum is an interdisciplinary general education program. Programs in Christian lay ministries and supporting church ministries. Associate's

degrees offered. Self-designed majors. Double majors. Independent study. Accelerated study. Pass/fail grading option. Internships. Preprofessional programs in law, medicine, and dentistry. Member of Christian College Coalition and Wesleyan Urban Coalition. Washington Semester. AuSable Inst of Environmental Studies Program (Michigan). Teacher certification in early childhood, elementary, and secondary education. Certification in specific subject areas. Study abroad possible.
**Honors:** Honors program. Honor societies.
**Academic Assistance:** Remedial reading, writing, math, and study skills. Nonremedial tutoring.

**ADMISSIONS. Academic basis for candidate selection** (in order of priority): Secondary school record, standardized test scores, school's recommendation, class rank, essay.
**Nonacademic basis for candidate selection:** Character and personality and alumni/ae relationship are important. Extracurricular participation and particular talent or ability are considered.
**Requirements:** Graduation from secondary school is required; GED is accepted. No specific distribution of secondary school units required. Minimum composite ACT score of 20 and minimum 2.6 GPA recommended. Special admissions program for applicants not normally admissible. ACT is required; SAT may be substituted. Campus visit and interview recommended. Off-campus interviews available with an admissions representative.
**Procedure:** Take SAT or ACT by fall of 12th year. Application deadline is August 1. Notification of admission on rolling basis. $50 tuition deposit, refundable until June 1. $50 room deposit, refundable until June 1. Freshmen accepted for terms other than fall.
**Special programs:** Admission may be deferred indefinitely. Credit may be granted through CEEB Advanced Placement for scores of 3 or higher. Credit may be granted through CLEP general and subject exams, DANTES exams, and military experience. Credit and placement may be granted through life experience. Early entrance/early admission program. Concurrent enrollment program.
**Transfer students:** Transfer students accepted for terms other than fall. In fall 1993, 27% of all new students were transfers into all classes. 156 transfer applications were received, 123 were accepted. Application deadline is August 1. Minimum 2.0 GPA recommended. Lowest course grade accepted is "C." Maximum number of transferable credits is 68 semester hours from a two-year school and 94 semester hours from a four-year school. At least 30 semester hours must be completed at the college to receive degree.
**Admissions contact:** Steve Schippers, Director of Admissions. 800 968-0011.

**FINANCIAL AID. Available aid:** Pell grants, SEOG, state scholarships and grants, school scholarships and grants, private scholarships, academic merit scholarships, athletic scholarships, and aid for undergraduate foreign students. Perkins Loans (NDSL), PLUS, Stafford Loans (GSL), and SLS. Tuition Plan Inc., AMS, and deferred payment plan.
**Supporting data/closing dates:** FAFSA: Accepted on rolling basis. School's own aid application: Deadline is February 28. Notification of awards on rolling basis.
**Financial aid contact:** Lois M. Hardy, Director of Financial Aid. 517 750-1200, 800 968-0011.

# University of Detroit Mercy

**Detroit, MI 48221** **313 993-1000**

**1993-94 Costs.** Tuition: $10,800. Room & board: $3,500. Fees, books, misc. academic expenses (school's estimate): $600.
**Enrollment.** Undergraduates: 1,017 men, 1,253 women (full-time). Freshman class: 1,330 applicants, 915 accepted, 366 enrolled. Graduate enrollment: 1,681 men, 1,465 women.
**Test score averages/ranges.** Average SAT scores: 1040 combined. Average ACT scores: 23 composite.
**Faculty.** 330 full-time; 120 part-time. 85% of faculty holds doctoral degree. Student/faculty ratio: 15 to 1.
**Selectivity rating.** Less competitive.

**PROFILE.** The University of Detroit Mercy is a church-affiliated institution. It is the result of the 1991 merger of the University of Detroit (founded in 1877) and Mercy College of Detroit (founded in 1941). Programs are offered through the Colleges of Business and Administration, Engineering and Science, Health Sciences, and Liberal Arts; the Evening College of Business and Administration; and the Schools of Architecture, Dentistry, Education and Human Services, and Law. Its two campuses of 70 acres and 55 acres are located in Detroit.

**Accreditation:** NCACS. Professionally accredited by the Accreditation Board for Engineering and Technology, the American Assembly of Collegiate Schools of Business, the American Bar Association, the American Dental Association, the American Psychological Association, the Association of American Law Schools, the Council on Social Work Education, the National Architecture Accrediting Board, the National League for Nursing.
**Religious orientation:** University of Detroit Mercy is affiliated with the Roman Catholic Church (Society of Jesus and Sisters of Mercy); no religious requirements.
**Library:** Collections totaling over 784,696 volumes, 5,355 periodical subscriptions, and 735,630 microform items.
**Athletic facilities:** Gymnasiums, racquetball and tennis courts, indoor track, fitness center.

**STUDENT BODY. Undergraduate profile:** 91% are state residents; 66% are transfers. 2% Asian-American, 39% Black, 1% Hispanic, 49% White, 9% Other. Average age of undergraduates is 24.
**Freshman profile:** 2% of freshmen who took SAT scored 700 or over on math; 8% scored 600 or over on verbal, 32% scored 600 or over on math; 39% scored 500 or over on verbal, 67% scored 500 or over on math; 87% scored 400 or over on verbal, 94% scored 400 or over on math; 98% scored 300 or over on verbal, 100% scored 300 or over on math. 20% of accepted applicants took SAT; 80% took ACT. 60% of freshmen come from public schools.
**Undergraduate achievement:** 76% of fall 1991 freshmen returned for fall 1992 term. 25% of students who completed a degree program went on to graduate study within two years.
**Foreign students:** 113 students are from out of the country. Countries represented include Canada, China, India, Pakistan, Saudi Arabia, and Taiwan; 50 in all.

**PROGRAMS OF STUDY. Degrees:** A.B., A.B.Classical, B.Arch., B.Bus.Admin., B.Chem.Eng., B.Civil Eng., B.Elec.Eng., B.Eng., B.F.A., B.Mech.Eng., B.Plast.Manuf.Tech., B.S., B.S.Bus.Admin., B.S.Ed., B.Soc.Work, B.Theatre Arts.
**Majors:** Accounting, Addiction Studies, Architecture/Environmental Design, Biochemistry, Biology, Chemical Engineering, Chemistry, Chemistry/Business, Child Development, Civil Engineering, Classical Studies, Communications Studies, Computer/Information Sciences, Criminal Justice, Dental Hygiene, Economics, Educational Studies, Elementary Education, Engineering/Electrical, Engineering/Undesignated, English, Finance, Health/Physical Education, Health Services, Health Services Administration, History, Hospitality Management, Human Resource Development, Human Resources Management, Industrial Management, International Business, Legal Administration, Management Information Systems, Marketing, Mathematics, Mechanical Engineering, Medical Records Administration, Nursing, Organizational Management/Leadership, Philosophy, Plastics Manufacturing Technology, Political Science, Polymer/Plastics Engineering, Pre-Dentistry, Pre-Law, Pre-Medicine, Psychology, Public Administration, Religious Studies, Secondary Education, Social Work, Sociology, Software Production/Management, Special Education, Sports Medicine, Theatre.
**Distribution of degrees:** The majors with the highest enrollment are nursing, mechanical engineering, and architecture.
**Requirements:** General education requirement.
**Academic regulations:** Minimum 2.0 GPA must be maintained.
**Special:** Dartmouth method for intensive language study. Academic Exploration Program. Associate's degrees offered. Double majors. Dual degrees. Independent study. Pass/fail grading option. Internships. Cooperative education programs. Graduate school at which undergraduates may take graduate-level courses. Preprofessional programs in law, medicine, and dentistry. 2-2 programs in engineering and health services with 40 colleges and universities. B.A./J.D. and B.S./D.D.S. programs. Five-year architecture program. Member of Detroit Area Consortium of Catholic Colleges. Washington Semester. Teacher certification in early childhood, elementary, secondary, and special education education. Certification in specific subject areas. Study abroad in England (business, law, liberal arts), Greece (theatre), and Italy (architecture). ROTC at Eastern Michigan U.
**Honors:** Honors program.
**Academic Assistance:** Remedial reading, writing, math, and study skills. Nonremedial tutoring.

**STUDENT LIFE. Housing:** Students may live on or off campus. Coed dorms. Fraternity housing. On-campus married-student housing. Freshmen dorm. 11% of students live in college housing.
**Social atmosphere:** Detroit Mercy students gather at the Grounds Coffeehaus, the Fountain Lounge, and the Gaelic League. Greeks and the volunteer center are influential in campus social life. Popular events during the year include Homecoming, Engineering Week, and rush period for Greeks. "This is primarily a commuter school," reports the student newspaper, "therefore little in the way of organized social life exists on campus."
**Services and counseling/handicapped student services:** Placement services. Health service. Day care. Counseling services for minority and older students. Psychological counseling. Career and academic guidance services. Physically disabled student services. Notetaking services.
**Campus organizations:** Undergraduate student government. Student newspaper (Varsity News, published once/week). Yearbook. Radio station. Chorus, drama society, forensic society, debating, monthly engineering newspaper, Student Court, Broadcasting Guild, 70 organizations in all. Seven fraternities, three chapter houses; three sororities, no chapter houses. 12% of men join a fraternity. 12% of women join a sorority.
**Religious organizations:** Campus Crusade for Christ, Campus Ministry, Christian Life Community. Muslim Prayer Room.
**Minority/foreign student organizations:** Numerous minority groups. International Student Association, African, Arab, Pakistani, and Iraqi groups.

**ATHLETICS. Physical education requirements:** None.
**Intercollegiate competition:** 10% of students participate. Baseball (M), basketball (M,W), cheerleading (M), cross-country (M,W), fencing (M,W), golf (M), soccer (M,W), softball (W), tennis (M,W), track (indoor) (M,W), track (outdoor) (M,W), track and field (indoor) (M,W), track and field (outdoor) (M,W). Member of Midwestern Collegiate Conference, NCAA Division I.
**Intramural and club sports:** 1% of students participate. Intramural basketball, golf, racquetball, soccer, softball, tennis, touch football, volleyball.

**ADMISSIONS. Academic basis for candidate selection** (in order of priority): Secondary school record, class rank, school's recommendation, standardized test scores.
**Nonacademic basis for candidate selection:** Character and personality and extracurricular participation are important. Particular talent or ability and geographical distribution are considered.
**Requirements:** Graduation from secondary school is required; GED is accepted. No specific distribution of secondary school units required. College-preparatory program including English, laboratory science, math, foreign language, and social science is strongly recommended. Challenge Program for applicants not normally admissible. SAT or ACT is required. Campus visit and interview recommended. Off-campus interviews available with admissions and alumni representatives.
**Procedure:** Take SAT or ACT by December of 12th year. Application deadline is August 1. Notification of admission on rolling basis. Reply is required by May 1, or two weeks after acceptance if notified after May 1. $100 nonrefundable tuition deposit. $100 room deposit, refundable until May 15. Freshmen accepted for terms other than fall.
**Special programs:** Admission may be deferred. Credit and/or placement may be granted through CEEB Advanced Placement exams for scores of 3 or higher. Credit may be granted through CLEP general and subject exams and military and life experience.
**Transfer students:** Transfer students accepted for terms other than fall. In fall 1992, 66% of all new students were transfers into all classes. 1,643 transfer applications were received, 1,223 were accepted. Application deadline is August 1 for fall; December 1 for

spring. Minimum 2.0 GPA required. Lowest course grade accepted is "C." Maximum number of transferable credits is 64 semester hours from a two-year school and 96 semester hours from a four-year school. At least 30 semester hours must be completed at the university to receive degree.

**Admissions contact:** Dr. Robert Johnson, Dean, Enrollment Management. 313 993-1245.

**FINANCIAL AID. Available aid:** Pell grants, SEOG, Federal Nursing Student Scholarships, state scholarships and grants, school scholarships and grants, private scholarships and grants, ROTC scholarships, academic merit scholarships, athletic scholarships, and United Negro College Fund. Perkins Loans (NDSL), PLUS, Stafford Loans (GSL), NSL, school loans, and SLS. Tuition Plan Inc., AMS, and deferred payment plan.

**Financial aid statistics:** 30% of aid is not need-based. In 1992-93, 70% of all undergraduate applicants received aid; 90% of freshman applicants. Average amounts of aid awarded freshmen: Scholarships and grants, $7,800; loans, $2,625.

**Supporting data/closing dates:** FAFSA/FAF/FFS: Deadline is April 1. School's own aid application: Priority filing date is April 1. State aid form: Priority filing date is April 1; deadline is September 1. Notification of awards begins March 1.

**Financial aid contact:** Anne Watson, Director of Financial Aid and Scholarships. 313 993-1350.

**STUDENT EMPLOYMENT.** College Work/Study Program. Institutional employment. 35% of full-time undergraduates work on campus during school year. Students may expect to earn an average of $2,000 during school year. Off-campus part-time employment opportunities rated "good."

**COMPUTER FACILITIES.** 179 IBM/IBM-compatible, Macintosh/Apple, and RISC-/UNIX-based microcomputers; 73 are networked. Students may access UNISYS minicomputer/mainframe systems. Client/LAN operating systems include Apple/Macintosh. Computer languages and software packages include BASIC, C, COBOL, FORTRAN, Lotus 1-2-3, Paradox, Pascal, Quattro Pro, SPSS-X, WordPerfect. Some systems restricted to classroom or lab use.

**Fees:** None.

**Hours:** 8 AM-10 PM (M-Th); 8 AM-5 PM (F); 8 AM-8 PM (Sa); noon-5 PM (Su).

**GRADUATE CAREER DATA.** Graduate school percentages: 2% enter law school. 2% enter medical school. 3% enter dental school. 8% enter graduate business programs. 3% enter graduate arts and sciences programs. 1% enter theological school/seminary. Highest graduate school enrollments: U of Detroit Mercy, U of Michigan, Wayne State U. Companies and businesses that hire graduates: Chrysler Corp., Ford Motor Co., General Motors, local hospitals.

**PROMINENT ALUMNI/AE.** Marc Stepp, vice-president, United Auto Workers; Joseph Kutz, M.D., pioneer in reconstructive hand surgery; David Culhane, correspondent, CBS News; John P. Hayes, chairperson of the board, National Gypsum; Thomas Russell, chairperson and CEO, Federal-Mogul; M. Jane Kay, vice-president, Detroit Edison; Elmore "Dutch" Leonard, author.

## University of Michigan–Ann Arbor

**Ann Arbor, MI 48104-2210    313 764-1817**

**1993-94 Costs.** Tuition: $4,255 (state residents), $13,892 (out-of-state). Room & board: $4,855. Fees, books, misc. academic expenses (school's estimate): $635.

**Enrollment.** Undergraduates: 11,637 men, 10,408 women (full-time). Freshman class: 19,152 applicants, 12,940 accepted, 4,893 enrolled. Graduate enrollment: 7,887 men, 5,574 women.

**Test score averages/ranges.** Range of SAT scores of middle 50%: 490-600 verbal, 580-700 math. Range of ACT scores of middle 50%: 24-29 English, 25-30 math.

**Faculty.** 2,713 full-time; 621 part-time. 90% of faculty holds doctoral degree. Student/faculty ratio: 11 to 1.

**Selectivity rating.** Highly competitive.

**PROFILE.** U Michigan–Ann Arbor, founded in 1817, is a comprehensive, public institution. Programs are offered through the Colleges of Engineering; Literature, Science and the Arts; and Pharmacy and the Schools of Art, Business Administration, Education, Music, Natural Resources, and Nursing. Its 2,665-acre campus in located in Ann Arbor, 35 miles west of Detroit.

**Accreditation:** NCACS. Professionally accredited by the Accreditation Board for Engineering and Technology, the American Assembly of Collegiate Schools of Business, the American Dental Association, the National Association of Schools of Music, the National Council for Accreditation of Teacher Education, the National League for Nursing, the Society of American Foresters. Numerous professional accreditations.

**Religious orientation:** University of Michigan–Ann Arbor is nonsectarian; no religious requirements.

**Library:** Collections totaling over 6,527,636 volumes, 70,693 periodical subscriptions, and 4,905,227 microform items.

**Special facilities/museums:** Museums of anthropology, archaeology, art, natural science, paleontology, zoology, audio-visual center, planetarium, electron microscope, biology station, geology camp, athletic campus, medical center, nuclear lab, botanical garden, herbarium, and arboretum.

**Athletic facilities:** Comprehensive athletic facilities.

**STUDENT BODY. Undergraduate profile:** 70% are state residents; 15% are transfers. 10% Asian-American, 8% Black, 5% Hispanic, 1% Native American, 73% White, 3% Other. Average age of undergraduates is 20.

**Freshman profile:** 84% of accepted applicants took SAT; 59% took ACT. 80% of freshmen come from public schools.

**Undergraduate achievement:** 95% of fall 1992 freshmen returned for fall 1993 term. 61% of entering class graduated.

**Foreign students:** 619 students are from out of the country. Countries represented include Canada, China, Hong Kong, India, South Korea, and Taiwan; 71 in all.

**PROGRAMS OF STUDY. Degrees:** A.B., B.A.Ed., B.Bus.Admin., B.F.A., B.Gen.Studies, B.Mus., B.Musical Arts, B.S., B.S.Chem., B.S.Dent.Hyg., B.S.Ed., B.S.Eng., B.S.Med.Chem., B.S.Nat.Res., B.S.Nurs., B.S.Pharm.

**Majors:** Accounting, Aerospace Engineering, Afro-American/African Studies, American Culture, Ancient/Biblical Studies, Anthropology, Anthropology/Zoology, Applied Mathematics, Arabic Studies, Art Education, Arts/Ideas, Asian Studies, Astronomy, Atmospheric/Oceanic Science, Atmospheric/Oceanic/Space Sciences, Bassoon, Biological Sciences, Biology, Biomedical Sciences, Biophysics, Botany, Business Administration, Carillon, Cello, Cellular/Molecular Biology, Ceramics, Chemical Engineering, Chemistry, Chinese, Civil/Environmental Engineering, Clarinet, Classical Archaeology, Classical Studies, Communication, Comparative Literature, Composition, Computer Engineering, Computer Graphics, Computer Science, Creative Writing, Dance, Dental Hygiene, Design, Double Bass, Drama, Drawing, Economics, Electrical Engineering, Elementary Education, Engineering, Engineering Physics, Engineering Science, English, Environmental Advocacy, Environmental Communications, Environmental Instruction, Environmental Policy/Behavior, Environmental Science, Euphonium, Field Biology, Film/Video Studies, Finance, Flute, Forestry, French, French Horn, General Biology, General Studies, Geological Science, , German, Graphic Design, Greek, Harp, Harpsichord, Hebrew, History, History of Art, Human Resources, Humanities, Individualized Concentration, Industrial Design, Industrial/Operations Engineering, Interior Design, International Studies, Iranian, Islamic Studies, Italian, Japanese, Jazz Studies, Journalism, Judaic Studies, Kinesiology, Landscape Design/Planning, Latin, Latin American/Caribbean Studies, Latino/Hispanic-American Studies, Linguistics, Literature, Marketing, Materials/Metallurgical Engineering, Materials Science/Engineering, Mathematics, Mechanical Engineering, Medieval/Renaissance Collegium, Metal Work/Jewelry Design, Meteorology, Microbiology, Middle East/North Africa Area Studies, Movement Science, Music, Music Education, Music History, Music Technology, Music Theory, Musical Theater, Natural Resources, Natural Resources/Biometry, Natural Resources/Biophysics, Natural Resources/Sociobehavioral Science, Naval Architecture/Marine Engineering, Near Eastern/North African Studies, Near Eastern Studies, Nuclear Engineering, Nursing, Oboe, Oceanography, Organ, Outdoor Recreation, Painting, Percussion, Performance, Philosophy, Photography, Physics, Piano, Political Science, Printmaking, Psychology, Psychology/Science, Religion, Resource Ecology/Management, Romance Linguistics, Russian, Russian/East European Studies, Saxophone, Scandinavian Studies, Sculpture, Secondary Education, Slavic Languages/Literatures, Social Anthropology, Social Science, Sociology, Spanish, Special Education, Speech, Sports Management/Communication, Statistics, String Instruments, Teacher Education, Theater, Theatre/Drama, Trombone, Trumpet, Tuba, Turkish, Viola, Violin, Voice, Weaving/Textile Design, Western European Studies, Wildlife, Wind Instruments, Women's Studies, Zoology.

**Distribution of degrees:** The majors with the highest enrollment are psychology, engineering, and biology.

**Requirements:** General education requirement.

**Academic regulations:** Minimum 2.0 GPA must be maintained.

**Special:** Students in Coll of Literature, Science, and the Arts may elect courses in other undergraduate colleges. 10% of freshmen invited to participate in four-year Honors Program. Unified Sciences Honors Program for freshmen and sophomores includes departmental honors programs and courses. Cooperative program in natural resources. Journalism certificate. Residential College (subdivision of Coll of Literature, Science, and the Arts) offers special four-year curriculum in residential quarters with small classes and emphasis on independent study and an innovative environment. Self-designed majors. Double majors. Dual degrees. Independent study. Accelerated study. Pass/fail grading option. Internships. Cooperative education programs. Graduate school at which undergraduates may take graduate-level courses. Preprofessional programs in law, medicine, pharmacy, dentistry, architecture, and business administration. 2-2 program with Sch of Business Administration. 3-2 engineering and natural resources programs. Inter-university programs in architecture, engineering, forestry, health sciences, and natural resources. Combined bachelor's/graduate degree programs include D.D.S., M.A.Journ., M.Arch., M.D., and M.Pub.Pol. Member of Committee on Institutional Cooperation. Washington Semester. Exchange programs with Big 10 institutions and U of Chicago. Teacher certification in early childhood, elementary, and secondary education. Certification in specific subject areas. Exchange programs abroad in Germany (U of Tubingen), Great Britain (Cambridge U), and Sweden (U of Uppsala). Study abroad also in Armenia, Australia, Canada, Chile, China, France, India, Italy, Ireland, Jamaica, Japan, Mexico, Scotland, Southeast Asia, the former Soviet Republics, Spain, and West African countries. ROTC, NROTC, and AFROTC.

**Honors:** Phi Beta Kappa. Honors program. Honor societies.

**Academic Assistance:** Remedial study skills. Nonremedial tutoring.

**STUDENT LIFE. Housing:** Students may live on or off campus. Coed, women's, and men's dorms. Sorority and fraternity housing. Off-campus privately-owned housing. On-campus married-student housing. Cooperatives, special housing for handicapped students. 31% of students live in college housing.

**Social atmosphere:** The social and cultural life at Ann Arbor is "very group oriented," reports the student newspaper. The most socially influential groups on campus are the Greeks, the Michigan Student Assembly, the College Democrats and Republicans, minority student organizations, and The Michigan Daily. The most popular events of the year are the football game versus Ohio State and various music festivals. On campus, students gather at the Fishbowl, the Michigan Union Grill, and the U-Club. Favorite off-campus spots include O'Sullivan's, Rick's, and Charlie's.

**Services and counseling/handicapped student services:** Placement services. Health service. Women's center. Day care. Counseling services for minority, military, veteran, and older students. Birth control, personal, and psychological counseling. Career and academic guidance services. Religious counseling. Physically disabled student services. Learning disabled services. Notetaking services. Tape recorders. Reader services for the blind.

**Campus organizations:** Undergraduate student government. Student newspaper (Michigan Daily, published five times/week). Literary magazine. Yearbook. Radio and TV stations. Musical, drama, and literary groups, 522 organizations in all. 43 fraternities, 36

chapter houses; 24 sororities, 18 chapter houses. 25% of men join a fraternity. 25% of women join a sorority.
**Religious organizations:** Numerous religious groups.
**Minority/foreign student organizations:** Several minority groups. Numerous foreign student groups.

**ATHLETICS. Physical education requirements:** None.
**Intercollegiate competition:** 2% of students participate. Baseball (M), basketball (M,W), cross-country (M,W), diving (M,W), field hockey (W), football (M), golf (M,W), gymnastics (M,W), ice hockey (M), softball (W), swimming (M,W), tennis (M,W), track and field (indoor) (M,W), track and field (outdoor) (M,W), volleyball (W), wrestling (M). Member of Big 10 Conference, Central Collegiate Hockey Association, Midwest Field Hockey Conference, NCAA Division I, NCAA Division I-A for football.
**Intramural and club sports:** 90% of students participate. Intramural basketball, cross-country, diving, flag football, free-throw shooting, golf, ice hockey, indoor soccer, racquetball, relays, soccer, softball, swimming, table tennis, tennis, track, volleyball, water polo, wrestling. Men's club aikido, Alpine skiing, archery, bowling, boxing, cricket, cycling, equestrian sports, fencing, floor hockey, frisbee, handball, kayak, lacrosse, martial arts, Nordic skiing, paddleball, racquetball, rowing, rugby, sailing, soccer, squash, synchronized swimming, table tennis, tennis, volleyball, water polo. Women's club aikido, Alpine skiing, archery, bowling, boxing, cricket, cycling, equestrian sports, fencing, floor hockey, frisbee, handball, kayak, lacrosse, martial arts, Nordic skiing, paddleball, racquetball, rowing, rugby, sailing, soccer, squash, synchronized swimming, table tennis, tennis, volleyball, water polo.

**ADMISSIONS. Academic basis for candidate selection** (in order of priority): Secondary school record, standardized test scores, school's recommendation, class rank, essay.
**Nonacademic basis for candidate selection:** Particular talent or ability is emphasized. Extracurricular participation, geographical distribution, and alumni/ae relationship are considered.
**Requirements:** Graduation from secondary school is required; GED is accepted. 20 units and the following program of study are recommended: 4 units of English, 4 units of math, 3 units of science, 4 units of foreign language, 3 units of social studies, 1 unit of history. English units should include at least two rigorous writing courses. Some qualified applicants from in-state schools admitted before receipt of test scores. In-state applicants from unaccredited schools may be asked to take additional exam before being considered. Higher GPA and test scores required of out-of-state applicants. 3-4 units of math and 2 units of laboratory science including chemistry required of nursing program applicants. 4 units of math and at least 1 unit each of chemistry and physics required of engineering program applicants; 4 units recommended. 4 units of foreign language recommended of literature, science, and arts program applicants. Portfolio required of art program applicants. Audition required of music program applicants. Comprehensive Studies Program and Summer Bridge Program for applicants not normally admissible. SAT or ACT is required. Campus visit recommended. No off-campus interviews.
**Procedure:** Take SAT or ACT by February 1 of 12th year. Application deadline is February 1. Notification of admission on rolling basis. Reply is required by May 1. $200 nonrefundable tuition deposit. Freshmen accepted for terms other than fall.
**Special programs:** Admission may be deferred one year. Credit and/or placement may be granted through CEEB Advanced Placement exams for scores of 3 or higher. Credit and/or placement may be granted through CLEP subject exams. Credit and placement may be granted through ACT PEP and challenge exams. Early entrance/early admission program.
**Transfer students:** Transfer students accepted for terms other than fall. In fall 1993, 15% of all new students were transfers into all classes. 2,224 transfer applications were received, 1,140 were accepted. Application deadline is February 1 for fall; November 1 for spring. Minimum 2.5 GPA required. Lowest course grade accepted is "C." Maximum number of transferable credits is 60 semester hours. At least 60 semester hours must be completed at the university to receive degree.
**Admissions contact:** Theodore Spencer, M.S., Director of Admissions. 313 764-7433.

**FINANCIAL AID. Available aid:** Pell grants, SEOG, state scholarships and grants, school scholarships and grants, private scholarships and grants, ROTC scholarships, academic merit scholarships, and athletic scholarships. Perkins Loans (NDSL), PLUS, Stafford Loans (GSL), NSL, Health Professions Loans, state loans, school loans, private loans, and SLS. Installment plan.
**Financial aid statistics:** 10% of aid is not need-based. In 1993-94, 60% of all undergraduate applicants received aid; 43% of freshman applicants. Average amounts of aid awarded freshmen: Scholarships and grants, $4,600; loans, $2,000.
**Supporting data/closing dates:** FAFSA: Priority filing date is March 15; deadline is September 30. Income tax forms: Priority filing date is April 15; accepted on rolling basis; deadline is September 30. Notification of awards begins March 15.
**Financial aid contact:** Harvey Grotrian, M.A., Director of Financial Aid. 313 763-6600.

**STUDENT EMPLOYMENT.** College Work/Study Program. Institutional employment. 40% of full-time undergraduates work on campus during school year. Students may expect to earn an average of $1,200 during school year. Off-campus part-time employment opportunities rated "excellent."

**COMPUTER FACILITIES.** 3,500 IBM/IBM-compatible, Macintosh/Apple, and RISC-/UNIX-based microcomputers; all are networked. Students may access Digital, Hewlett-Packard, IBM, SUN, UNISYS minicomputer/mainframe systems, BITNET, Internet. Residence halls may be equipped with networked microcomputers. Client/LAN operating systems include Apple/Macintosh, DOS, OS/2, UNIX/XENIX/AIX, Windows NT, X-windows, Banyan, LocalTalk/AppleTalk, Novell. Numerous computer languages and software packages available. Computer facilities are available to all students.
**Fees:** None.
**Hours:** 24 hours.

**PROMINENT ALUMNI/AE.** Gerald Ford, former President of the U.S.; James Earl Jones, actor; Arthur Miller, author.

# University of Michigan–Dearborn

**Dearborn, MI 48128-1491** **313 593-5000**

**1993-94 Costs.** Tuition: $3,160 (state residents), $10,080 (out-of-state). Housing: None. Fees, books, misc. academic expenses (school's estimate): $470.
**Enrollment.** Undergraduates: 1,635 men, 1,824 women (full-time). Freshman class: 1,909 applicants, 1,306 accepted, 762 enrolled. Graduate enrollment: 771 men, 503 women.
**Test score averages/ranges.** Average SAT scores: 460 verbal, 540 math. Range of SAT scores of middle 50%: 410-510 verbal, 480-610 math. Average ACT scores: 22 English, 23 math, 23 composite. Range of ACT scores of middle 50%: 20-25 English, 20-25 math.
**Faculty.** 203 full-time; 182 part-time. 87% of faculty holds doctoral degree. Student/faculty ratio: 17 to 1.
**Selectivity rating.** Less competitive.

**PROFILE.** U Michigan–Dearborn, founded in 1959, is a comprehensive, public institution. Programs are offered through the College of Arts, Sciences, and Letters; the Divisions of Education and Interdisciplinary Studies; and the Schools of Engineering and Management. Its 202-acre campus is located in Dearborn, south of downtown Detroit.

**Accreditation:** NCACS. Professionally accredited by the Accreditation Board for Engineering and Technology, the National Council for Accreditation of Teacher Education.
**Religious orientation:** University of Michigan–Dearborn is nonsectarian; no religious requirements.
**Library:** Collections totaling over 293,284 volumes, 1,574 periodical subscriptions, and 399,641 microform items.
**Special facilities/museums:** Museum at Henry Ford estate, child development center, CAD/CAM robotics lab, environmental study area.
**Athletic facilities:** Field house, ice rink, playfield, sand volleyball courts, track, football field, tennis courts, weight room.

**STUDENT BODY. Undergraduate profile:** 99% are state residents; 48% are transfers. 4% Asian-American, 7% Black, 2% Hispanic, 1% Native American, 85% White, 1% Other. Average age of undergraduates is 22.
**Freshman profile:** 3% of freshmen who took SAT scored 700 or over on math; 6% scored 600 or over on verbal, 29% scored 600 or over on math; 34% scored 500 or over on verbal, 71% scored 500 or over on math; 79% scored 400 or over on verbal, 92% scored 400 or over on math; 97% scored 300 or over on verbal, 100% scored 300 or over on math. 13% of accepted applicants took SAT; 87% took ACT. 76% of freshmen come from public schools.
**Undergraduate achievement:** 82% of fall 1991 freshmen returned for fall 1992 term.
**Foreign students:** 43 students are from out of the country. Countries represented include Canada, Hong Kong, India, Korea, Lebanon, and Pakistan; 50 in all.

**PROGRAMS OF STUDY. Degrees:** B.A., B.Bus.Admin., B.Gen.Studies, B.S., B.S.Admin., B.S.Eng.
**Majors:** Administration, American Studies, Anthropology, Art History, Behavioral Science, Biochemistry, Biological Sciences, Biology, Business Administration, Chemistry, Computer/Information Science, Early Childhood Education, Economics, Electrical Engineering, Engineering Mathematics, English, Environmental Science, Environmental Studies, French, French Studies, General Science, Health Policy Studies, Hispanic Studies, History, Humanities, Industrial/Manufacturing Systems Engineering, International Studies, Language Arts, Liberal Studies, Manufacturing Systems Engineering, Mathematics, Mathematics Studies, Mechanical Engineering, Microbiology, Music History, Natural Science, Philosophy, Physical Science, Physics, Political Science, Psychology, Public Administration, Science Studies, Social Science, Sociology, Spanish.
**Distribution of degrees:** The majors with the highest enrollment are psychology, mechanical engineering, and electrical engineering; general science and American studies have the lowest.
**Requirements:** General education requirement.
**Academic regulations:** Minimum 2.0 GPA must be maintained.
**Special:** Minors offered in most majors and in approximately 50 other fields. Double majors. Dual degrees. Independent study. Pass/fail grading option. Internships. Cooperative education programs. Graduate school at which undergraduates may take graduate-level courses. Preprofessional programs in law, medicine, dentistry, architecture, engineering, nursing, and social work. 2-2 programs in vocational fields and education with local community colleges. 3-2 public health program with U of Michigan Sch of Public Health. Member of Community College Consortium. Washington Semester. HBC Program. Teacher certification in early childhood, elementary, and secondary education. Certification in specific subject areas. Study abroad in Canada and Japan. ROTC, NROTC, and AFROTC at U of Michigan at Ann Arbor.
**Honors:** Phi Beta Kappa. Honors program. Honor societies.
**Academic Assistance:** Remedial reading, writing, and math. Nonremedial tutoring.

**STUDENT LIFE. Housing:** No student housing.
**Social atmosphere:** Students gather on campus at the student union and on the university mall. Greeks have the greatest influence on campus life.
**Services and counseling/handicapped student services:** Placement services. Health service. Women's center. Day care. Counseling services for minority, military, veteran, and older students. Birth control, personal, and psychological counseling. Career and academic guidance services. Religious counseling. Physically disabled student services. Learning disabled services. Notetaking services. Tape recorders. Tutors. Reader services for the blind.
**Campus organizations:** Undergraduate student government. Student newspaper (Michigan Journal, published once/week). Literary magazine. Radio station. Euchre club, science fact, fiction and fantasy club, Student Activities Board, Vegetarian Society, Wolf

Pack Auto Club, stage band, choir, music club, 89 organizations in all. Three fraternities, one chapter house; three sororities, no chapter houses. 3% of men join a fraternity. 3% of women join a sorority.
**Religious organizations:** Newman Club, Campus Crusade for Christ, Intervarsity Christian Fellowship, Muslim Student Association.
**Minority/foreign student organizations:** Hispanic Student Alliance, AMIGOS, Association for Black Students, Native American Student Association. International Club, Organization for Asian-American Students, Le Cercle Francais, Society of Students of Eastern Europe.

**ATHLETICS. Physical education requirements:** None.
**Intercollegiate competition:** 2% of students participate. Basketball (M,W), volleyball (W). Member of NAIA.
**Intramural and club sports:** 5% of students participate. Intramural basketball, flag football, golf, ice hockey, scuba, special events, swimming, table tennis, tennis, volleyball, walking, walleyball. Men's club cross-country, fencing, ice hockey, soccer. Women's club cross-country, fencing.

**ADMISSIONS. Academic basis for candidate selection** (in order of priority): Secondary school record, standardized test scores, class rank, school's recommendation.
**Nonacademic basis for candidate selection:** Extracurricular participation is considered.
**Requirements:** Graduation from secondary school is recommended; GED is accepted. 45 units and the following program of study are required: 8 units of English, 6 units of math, 4 units of science, 6 units of social studies, 6 units of history, 15 units of electives. Minimum composite ACT score of 22 (combined SAT score of 1050), minimum 3.0 GPA, and rank in top fifth of secondary school class recommended. PAS (Program for Academic Support) for applicants not normally admissible. Test scores waived for adults out of school five years or more. ACT is required; SAT may be substituted. Campus visit and interview recommended. Off-campus interviews available with an admissions representative.
**Procedure:** Take SAT or ACT by fall of 12th year. Suggest filing application by March 1. Application deadline is May 1. Notification of admission on rolling basis. Reply is required by May 1 or within five days of acceptance. $50 tuition deposit, refundable until May 1. Freshmen accepted for terms other than fall.
**Special programs:** Credit and/or placement may be granted through CEEB Advanced Placement exams for scores of 3 or higher. Placement may be granted through challenge exams. Early entrance/early admission program. Concurrent enrollment program.
**Transfer students:** Transfer students accepted for terms other than fall. In fall 1992, 48% of all new students were transfers into all classes. 1,640 transfer applications were received, 1,137 were accepted. Application deadline is August 15 for fall; rolling for spring. Minimum 2.5 GPA recommended. Lowest course grade accepted is "C." Maximum number of transferable credits is 62 semester hours from a two-year school and 75 semester hours from a four-year school. At least 30 semester hours must be completed at the university to receive degree.
**Admissions contact:** Carol Mack, Director of Admissions. 313 593-5100.

**FINANCIAL AID. Available aid:** Pell grants, SEOG, state scholarships and grants, school scholarships and grants, private scholarships, ROTC scholarships, academic merit scholarships, and athletic scholarships. Perkins Loans (NDSL), PLUS, Stafford Loans (GSL), state loans, school loans, and SLS. AMS and Tuition Management Systems.
**Financial aid statistics:** In 1992-93, 55% of all undergraduate applicants received aid.
**Supporting data/closing dates:** FAFSA/FAF/FFS: Priority filing date is March 1. FAT for transfer students: Priority filing date is March 1. Notification of awards on rolling basis.
**Financial aid contact:** John A. Mason, Director of Financial Aid. 313 593-5300.

**STUDENT EMPLOYMENT.** College Work/Study Program. Institutional employment. 7% of full-time undergraduates work on campus during school year. Off-campus part-time employment opportunities rated "good."

**COMPUTER FACILITIES.** 350 IBM/IBM-compatible, Macintosh/Apple, and RISC-/UNIX-based microcomputers; all are networked. Students may access Hewlett-Packard, IBM, SUN minicomputer/mainframe systems, BITNET, Internet. Client/LAN operating systems include Apple/Macintosh. Computer languages and software packages include Assembler, BASIC, C, dBASE, Harvard Graphics, Lotus 1-2-3, Paradox, PL/1, Quattro Pro, Turbo Pascal, WordPerfect; 50 in all. Computer facilities are available to all students.
**Fees:** $20 computer fee per course; included in tuition/fees.
**Hours:** 8 AM-midn. (M-Th); 8 AM-9 PM (F); 9 AM-5 PM (Sa); 10 AM-8 PM (Su).

**GRADUATE CAREER DATA.** Companies and businesses that hire graduates: Chrysler, Ford Motor Co., Ernst & Young.

**PROMINENT ALUMNI/AE.** Bill Freehan, major league baseball player/sports commentator; Joseph G. Horonzy, executive vice-president, Commercial Bank of Detroit; Susan Heintz, director of governor's office, Southeast Michigan U.

## University of Michigan–Flint

**Flint, MI 48502** **313 762-3000**

**1994-95 Costs.** Tuition: $2,960 (state residents), $9,927 (out-of-state). Housing: None. Fees, books, misc. academic expenses (school's estimate): $710.
**Enrollment.** Undergraduates: 1,399 men, 1,711 women (full-time). Freshman class: 970 applicants, 877 accepted, 551 enrolled. Graduate enrollment: 325.
**Test score averages/ranges.** Average ACT scores: 21 English, 21 math, 22 composite. Range of ACT scores of middle 50%: 19-23 English, 18-22 math.
**Faculty.** 157 full-time; 99 part-time. 86% of faculty holds doctoral degree. Student/faculty ratio: 27 to 1.
**Selectivity rating.** Less competitive.

**PROFILE.** U Michigan–Flint, founded in 1956, is a public, comprehensive institution. Programs are offered through the College of Arts and Sciences and the Schools of Health Sciences and Management. Its 42-acre campus is located in Flint, 55 miles north of Detroit.
**Accreditation:** NCACS. Professionally accredited by the American Assembly of Collegiate Schools of Business, the National Association of Schools of Music, the National Council for Accreditation of Teacher Education, the National League for Nursing.
**Religious orientation:** University of Michigan-Flint is nonsectarian; no religious requirements.
**Library:** Collections totaling over 150,000 volumes, 1,030 periodical subscriptions, and 277,163 microform items.
**Athletic facilities:** Recreation building, basketball, racquetball, tennis, and volleyball courts, track, weight lifting and aerobics facilities, swimming pool, performance center, golf range.

**STUDENT BODY. Undergraduate profile:** 99% are state residents; 41% are transfers. 1.3% Asian-American, 10.2% Black, 2% Hispanic, 1% Native American, 73.8% White, 11.7% Other. Average age of undergraduates is 23.
**Freshman profile:** 5% of accepted applicants took SAT; 95% took ACT. 80% of freshmen come from public schools.
**Undergraduate achievement:** 75% of fall 1992 freshmen returned for fall 1993 term. 49% of entering class graduated.
**Foreign students:** Seven students are from out of the country. Seven countries represented in all.

**PROGRAMS OF STUDY. Degrees:** B.A., B.Appl.Sci., B.Bus.Admin., B.F.A., B.Gen.Studies, B.Mus.Ed., B.S., B.S.Nurs.
**Majors:** Accounting, African/Afro-American Studies, Anthropology, Applied Mathematics, Applied Science, Biology, Business Administration, Chemistry, Communications, Computer Science, Economics, Elementary Education, Engineering Sciences, English, Finance, French, General Science, General Studies, German, Health Care, History, Marketing, Mathematics, Music, Music Education, Nursing, Philosophy, Physical Geography, Physical Science, Physical Therapy, Physics, Political Science, Psychology, Public Administration, Resource/Community Sciences, Social Sciences, Social Work, Sociology, Spanish, Special Concentration, Theatre.
**Distribution of degrees:** The majors with the highest enrollment are business and education.
**Requirements:** General education requirement.
**Academic regulations:** Minimum 2.0 GPA must be maintained.
**Special:** Programs in corrections, planning/community development, substance abuse treatment/prevention, and urban administration. Joint program in liberal arts/medicine. Courses in art, comparative literature, and speech. Special courses in communication skills, environmental science; special projects in black American experience. Faculty members and 12 or more students may develop one-semester experimental courses. Self-designed majors. Double majors. Dual degrees. Independent study. Pass/fail grading option. Internships. Cooperative education programs. Preprofessional programs in law, medicine, veterinary science, pharmacy, and dentistry. Teacher certification in early childhood, elementary, and secondary education. Study abroad in any country as part of honors program.
**Honors:** Honors program. Honor societies.
**Academic Assistance:** Remedial reading, writing, math, and study skills. Nonremedial tutoring.

**STUDENT LIFE. Housing:** Commuter campus; no student housing.
**Social atmosphere:** Popular gathering spots at the school are Churchill's, Rocky's, 44 Thirsty, and the Ontario Room. Greeks, Student Government, and enviornmental groups are influential organizations on campus. The Spring Finale, Blockbuster Movies, the Student Feud, and intramural sports are among the year's favorite events.
**Services and counseling/handicapped student services:** Placement services. Health service. Women's center. Day care. Counseling services for minority and older students. Personal counseling. Career and academic guidance services. Physically disabled student services. Notetaking services. Tape recorders. Tutors. Reader services for the blind.
**Campus organizations:** Undergraduate student government. Student newspaper (Michigan Times, published twice/month). Literary magazine. Radio and TV stations. Chorale, chamber singers, wind and percussion ensembles, Organization for Women Students, athletic, departmental, service, and special-interest groups. Two fraternities, no chapter houses; four sororities, no chapter houses.
**Religious organizations:** Several religious groups.
**Minority/foreign student organizations:** MEChA, Native American group, Students for Black Achievement.

**ATHLETICS. Physical education requirements:** None.
**Intercollegiate competition:** 1% of students participate.
**Intramural and club sports:** 75% of students participate. Intramural badminton, basketball, golf, racquetball, soccer, softball, tennis, volleyball, Wiffle ball.

**ADMISSIONS. Academic basis for candidate selection** (in order of priority): Secondary school record, standardized test scores, school's recommendation, class rank, essay.
**Nonacademic basis for candidate selection:** Extracurricular participation is considered.
**Requirements:** Graduation from secondary school is required; GED is accepted. 12 units and the following program of study are required: 4 units of English, 3 units of math, 2 units of science, 3 units of social studies. 4 additional units of math required of science and behavioral science program applicants. Minimum "B" average required of business program applicants. Particular GPA requirements for nursing, physical therapy, and education program applicants. Audition required of music program applicants. Challenge Scholar Program offers supportive services for applicants not normally admissible. ACT is required; SAT may be substituted. Campus visit and interview recommended.
**Procedure:** Take SAT or ACT by December of 12th year. Suggest filing application by April 1. Application deadline is August 20. Notification of admission on rolling basis. Reply is required by May 1. $50 tuition deposit, refundable until May 1. Freshmen accepted for terms other than fall.
**Special programs:** Admission may be deferred one semester. Credit and/or placement may be granted through CEEB Advanced Placement exams for scores of 3 or higher. Credit and/or placement may be granted through CLEP subject exams. Placement may be granted through challenge exams. Early entrance/early admission program. Concurrent enrollment program.
**Transfer students:** Transfer students accepted for terms other than fall. In fall 1993, 41% of all new students were transfers into all classes. 1,553 transfer applications were received, 1,140 were accepted. Application deadline is August 20 for fall; December 1 for spring. Minimum 2.0 GPA required. Lowest course grade accepted is "C." Maximum

number of transferable credits is 62 semester hours from a two-year school and 75 semester hours from a four-year school. At least 45 semester hours must be completed at the university to receive degree.
**Admissions contact:** David L. James, M.A., Director of Admissions. 313 762-3300.

**FINANCIAL AID. Available aid:** Pell grants, SEOG, state scholarships and grants, school scholarships and grants, private scholarships, and academic merit scholarships. Perkins Loans (NDSL), PLUS, Stafford Loans (GSL), state loans, school loans, and private loans. Deferred payment plan.
**Financial aid statistics:** 10% of aid is not need-based. In 1993-94, 45% of all undergraduate applicants received aid. Average amounts of aid awarded freshmen: Scholarships and grants, $800; loans, $800.
**Supporting data/closing dates:** FAFSA/FAF/FFS: Accepted on rolling basis. School's own aid application: Accepted on rolling basis. Income tax forms: Accepted on rolling basis. Notification of awards begins mid-April.
**Financial aid contact:** Reta Pikowsky, M.A., Director of Financial Aid. 313 762-3444.

**STUDENT EMPLOYMENT.** College Work/Study Program. 10% of full-time undergraduates work on campus during school year. Students may expect to earn an average of $1,125 during school year. Off-campus part-time employment opportunities rated "excellent."

**COMPUTER FACILITIES.** 75 IBM/IBM-compatible and Macintosh/Apple microcomputers. Computer facilities are available to all students.
**Fees:** None.

# Wayne State University

**Detroit, MI 48202** **313 577-2424**

**1994-95 Costs.** Tuition: $3,234 (state residents), $7,301 (out-of-state). Housing: None. Fees, books, misc. academic expenses (school's estimate): $370.
**Enrollment.** Undergraduates: 4,184 men, 5,594 women (full-time). Freshman class: 4,219 applicants, 3,098 accepted, 1,543 enrolled. Graduate enrollment: 8,518 men, 11,715 women.
**Test score averages/ranges.** Average ACT scores: 20 English, 20 math, 21 composite. Range of ACT scores of middle 50%: 16-24 English, 16-23 math.
**Faculty.** 1,588 full-time; 1,061 part-time. 85% of faculty holds highest degree in specific field. Student/faculty ratio: 9 to 1.
**Selectivity rating.** Less competitive.

**PROFILE.** Wayne State, founded in 1933, is a public, comprehensive university. Programs are offered through the Colleges of Education; Engineering; Liberal Arts; Lifelong Learning; Nursing; Pharmacy and Allied Health Professions; and Urban, Labor, and Metropolitan Affairs; the Division of Health and Physical Education; the Graduate School; the Law School; and the Schools of Business Administration, Fine and Performing Arts, Medicine, and Social Work. Its 186-acre main campus is located in central Detroit.

**Accreditation:** NASC.
**Religious orientation:** Wayne State University is nonsectarian; no religious requirements.
**Library:** Collections totaling over 2,600,000 volumes, 24,592 periodical subscriptions, and 3,200,000 microform items.
**Athletic facilities:** Gymnasiums, football, soccer, and softball fields, basketball, racquetball, and tennis courts, weight rooms, dance studios.

**STUDENT BODY. Undergraduate profile:** 98% are state residents; 62% are transfers. 3.8% Asian-American, 21.7% Black, 1.9% Hispanic, .4% Native American, 61.6% White, 10.6% Other. Average age of undergraduates is 28.
**Freshman profile:** 2% of freshmen who took ACT scored 30 or over on English, 3% scored 30 or over on math, 2% scored 30 or over on composite; 27% scored 24 or over on English, 24% scored 24 or over on math, 26% scored 24 or over on composite; 68% scored 18 or over on English, 67% scored 18 or over on math, 72% scored 18 or over on composite; 96% scored 12 or over on English, 98% scored 12 or over on math, 99% scored 12 or over on composite; 100% scored 6 or over on English, 100% scored 6 or over on math, 100% scored 6 or over on composite. 1% of accepted applicants took SAT; 90% took ACT.
**Undergraduate achievement:** 74% of fall 1992 freshmen returned for fall 1993 term. 37% of entering class graduated.
**Foreign students:** 186 students are from out of the country. Countries represented include Canada, China, India, Korea, and Pakistan.

**PROGRAMS OF STUDY. Degrees:** B.A., B.F.A., B.Mus., B.S., B.S.Eng.Tech., B.S.Mort.Sci., B.S.Nurs., B.S.Pub.Aff., B.Soc.Work, B.Tech./Gen.Studies.
**Majors:** Accounting, American Studies, Anthropology, Anthropology/Sociology, Art, Art Education, Art History, Bilingual/Bicultural Education, Biology, Black Studies, Business Education, Chemical Engineering, Chemistry, Chicano-Boricua Studies, Church Music, Civil Engineering, Classical Civilization, Classics, Computer Science, Counseling/Guidance, Criminal Justice, Dance, Design/Merchandising, Distributive Education, Economics, Electrical/Electronic Engineering Technology, Electrical Engineering, Electromechanical Engineering Technology, Elementary Education, English, English Education, Family Life Education, Film Studies, Finance/Business Economics, Fine Arts, Foreign Language Education, French, General Studies, Geography, Geology, German, Greek, Health Occupations Education, Hebrew, History, Human Development, Humanities, Industrial Education, Information Sciences, International Studies, Italian, Journalism, Labor Studies, Latin, Linguistics, Management Information Systems, Management/Organization Sciences, Manufacturing/Industrial Engineering Technology, Marketing, Mathematics, Mathematics Education, Mechanical Engineering Sciences, Mechanical Engineering Technology, Medical Dietetics, Medical Technology, Metallurgical Engineering, Mortuary Science, Music, Music Composition, Music Education, Music Industry Management, Music/Jazz/Contemporary Media, Music Performance, Music Theory, Music Therapy, Near Eastern Languages, Near Eastern Studies, Nursery School Education, Nursing, Nutrition/Food Science, Occupational Therapy, Peace/Conflict Studies, Pharmacy, Philosophy, Physical Education, Physical Therapy, Physics, Polish, Political Science, Psychology, Public Affairs, Public Relations, Quality Control, Radiation Therapy, Radio/Television, Recreation/Park Services, Rehabilitation Services, Russian, Science, Science Education, Secondary Education, Slavic Studies, Social Studies, Social Studies Education, Social Work, Sociology, Spanish, Special Education, Speech, Speech/Dramatic Arts Education, Theatre, Urban Studies, Women's Studies.
**Distribution of degrees:** The majors with the highest enrollment are premedicine, engineering, and business administration.
**Requirements:** General education requirement.
**Academic regulations:** Minimum 2.0 GPA must be maintained.
**Special:** Minors offered in most majors; minor must be within same college as major. University centers and institutes concerning black studies, cognitive process, engineering services, gerontology, health research, labor/industrial relations, teaching about peace/war, and urban studies. Double majors. Pass/fail grading option. Internships. Cooperative education programs. Graduate school at which undergraduates may take graduate-level courses. Preprofessional programs in law, medicine, and pharmacy. Combined bachelor's/master's degrees in anthropology, biology, computer science, English, geography/urban planning, mathematics, political science, and sociology. Teacher certification in early childhood, elementary, secondary, special education, and bilingual/bicultural education. Certification in specific subject areas. Exchange program abroad in Poland (Jagellion U). Study abroad also in England and Germany. ROTC at U of Detroit. AFROTC at U of Michigan.
**Honors:** Honors program.
**Academic Assistance:** Remedial reading, writing, math, and study skills. Nonremedial tutoring.

**STUDENT LIFE. Housing:** Commuter campus; no student housing.
**Social atmosphere:** According to the student newspaper, "WSU students come from extremely diverse social and economic backgrounds. Students are residents of Detroit and also of well-to-do suburbs." This is primarily a commuter school, but one with school spirit "on the rise" and steadily increasing enrollment figures. About 80 percent of students work; 48 percent are involved in community and social organizations. On-campus, students meet at the Student Center, Circa 1890, and Prentis Building Fishbowl; Majestic Theatre, Clubland, Joe Louis Arena, and the Palace of Auburn Hills are the most common off-campus destinations. The student council, Pi Kappa Alpha, Delta Zeta, and Theta Tau are the most influential student groups. Hilberry Theatre, Tartarfest, and Greek Week are favorite social events.
**Services and counseling/handicapped student services:** Placement services. Health service. Women's center. Day care. Counseling services for minority, veteran, and older students. Personal counseling. Academic guidance services. Religious counseling. Physically disabled student services. Notetaking services. Tutors. Reader services for the blind.
**Campus organizations:** Undergraduate student government. Student newspaper (South End, published once/day). Yearbook. Radio station. Music groups, various publications, athletic, departmental, service, and special-interest groups. 16 fraternities, two chapter houses; 11 sororities, no chapter houses.
**Religious organizations:** Campus Crusade for Christ, Intervarsity Christian Fellowship.
**Minority/foreign student organizations:** Minority groups in applied sciences, engineering, and premedicine. Chinese Student Association, French Club, German Cultural Club.

**ATHLETICS. Physical education requirements:** None.
**Intercollegiate competition:** Basketball (M,W), cheerleading (M,W), cross-country (M), diving (M), fencing (M), football (M), golf (M), softball (W), swimming (M,W), tennis (M,W), volleyball (W). Member of GLIAC, Midwest Intercollegiate Football Conference, NCAA Division II.
**Intramural and club sports:** Intramural badminton, basketball, racquetball, soccer, softball, tennis, touch football, volleyball, walleyball.

**ADMISSIONS. Academic basis for candidate selection** (in order of priority): Secondary school record, standardized test scores, class rank.
**Requirements:** Graduation from secondary school is recommended; GED is accepted. 18 units and the following program of study are recommended: 4 units of English, 4 units of math, 3 units of science, 2 units of foreign language, 3 units of social studies, 2 units of electives. Unit requirements vary by college. Minimum composite ACT score of 21 (SAT scores of 450 verbal and 400 math) and minimum 2.75 GPA required. Portfolio required of art program applicants. Audition required of music program applicants. R.N. required of nursing program applicants. Conditional admission possible for applicants not meeting standard requirements. Project 350, Chicano-Boricua program, and Upward Bound for applicants not normally admissible. ACT is recommended; SAT may be substituted. Campus visit recommended. No off-campus interviews.
**Procedure:** Take SAT or ACT by August 1 of 12th year. Visit college for interview by August 1 of 12th year. Application deadline is August 1. Notification of admission on rolling basis. $70 nonrefundable tuition deposit. Freshmen accepted for terms other than fall.
**Special programs:** Credit and/or placement may be granted through CEEB Advanced Placement exams for scores of 4 or higher. Credit and/or placement may be granted through CLEP general and subject exams. Credit and placement may be granted through DANTES and challenge exams.
**Transfer students:** Transfer students accepted for terms other than fall. In fall 1993, 62% of all new students were transfers into all classes. 5,224 transfer applications were received, 3,788 were accepted. Application deadline is August 1 for fall; April 1 for spring. Minimum 2.0 GPA required. Lowest course grade accepted is "D." At least 30 semester hours must be completed at the university to receive degree.
**Admissions contact:** Ronald C. Hughes, M.A., Director of Admissions. 313 577-3577.

**FINANCIAL AID. Available aid:** Pell grants, SEOG, Federal Nursing Student Scholarships, state scholarships and grants, school scholarships and grants, private scholarships and grants, academic merit scholarships, and athletic scholarships. Perkins Loans (NDSL), PLUS, Stafford Loans (GSL), NSL, Health Professions Loans, state loans, school loans, private loans, and SLS. AMS.
**Financial aid statistics:** 30% of aid is not need-based. In 1993-94, 50% of all undergraduate applicants received aid. Average amounts of aid awarded freshmen: Scholarships and grants, $1,500.
**Supporting data/closing dates:** FAFSA: Priority filing date is May 1. Notification of awards begins April 15.

**Financial aid contact:** Judith Florian, M.B.A., Director of Financial Aid. 313 577-3378.
**STUDENT EMPLOYMENT.** College Work/Study Program. Institutional employment. Students may expect to earn an average of $2,000 during school year. Freshmen are discouraged from working during their first term. Off-campus part-time employment opportunities rated "good."
**COMPUTER FACILITIES.** 600 IBM/IBM-compatible and Macintosh/Apple microcomputers; 200 are networked. Students may access IBM minicomputer/mainframe systems. Computer languages and software packages include COBOL, FORTRAN, LISP, Pascal, SNOBOL. Computer facilities are available to all students.
**Fees:** None.
**Hours:** 8 AM-11 PM on most days.
**GRADUATE CAREER DATA.** 69% of graduates choose careers in business and industry. Companies and businesses that hire graduates: Chrysler, Ford, General Motors.
**PROMINENT ALUMNI/AE.** Lily Tomlin, actress and comedienne; Casey Kasem, "Top 40" radio musical host; John Conyers, U.S. congressman; Mary Comstock Riley, judge, Detroit; Bill Davidson, owner, Detroit Pistons; Chad Everett, actor.

# Western Michigan University

**Kalamazoo, MI 49008** **616 387-1000**

**1993-94 Costs.** Tuition: $2,430 (state residents), $6,260 (out-of-state). Room & board: $3,940. Fees, books, misc. academic expenses (school's estimate): $950.
**Enrollment.** Undergraduates: 7,578 men, 8,161 women (full-time). Freshman class: 8,565 applicants, 7,191 accepted, 2,797 enrolled. Graduate enrollment: 2,725 men, 3,813 women.
**Test score averages/ranges.** Average ACT scores: 22 English, 22 math, 23 composite. Range of ACT scores of middle 50%: 19-25 English, 19-25 math.
**Faculty.** 729 full-time; 330 part-time. 79% of faculty holds highest degree in specific field. Student/faculty ratio: 18 to 1.
**Selectivity rating.** Less competitive.

**PROFILE.** Western Michigan, founded in 1903, is a public, comprehensive university. Programs are offered through the Colleges of Arts and Sciences, Business Administration, Education, Engineering and Applied Sciences, Fine Arts, General Studies, and Health and Human Services; the Division of Continuing Education; and the Graduate College. Its 397-acre campus is located in Kalamazoo, 145 miles from Detroit.
**Accreditation:** NCACS. Professionally accredited by the Accreditation Board for Engineering and Technology, the American Assembly of Collegiate Schools of Business, the American Medical Association (CAHEA), the American Speech-Language-Hearing Association, the Council on Social Work Education, the National Association of Schools of Art and Design, the National Association of Schools of Music, the National Council for Accreditation of Teacher Education. Numerous professional accreditations.
**Religious orientation:** Western Michigan University is nonsectarian; no religious requirements.
**Library:** Collections totaling over 1,609,629 volumes, 5,403 periodical subscriptions, and 1,441,183 microform items.
**Special facilities/museums:** Pilot plant for manufacturing and printing of paper and for fiber recovery, behavior research and development center, nuclear accelerator, center for electron microscopy, particle accelerator lab.
**Athletic facilities:** Gymnasiums, field house, swimming pool, weight rooms, handball, racquetball, and tennis courts, tracks, athletic fields, ice rink.
**STUDENT BODY. Undergraduate profile:** 96% are state residents; 43% are transfers. 1% Asian-American, 6% Black, 1% Hispanic, 1% Native American, 86% White, 5% Other. Average age of undergraduates is 21.
**Freshman profile:** 4% of freshmen who took ACT scored 30 or over on English, 4% scored 30 or over on math, 4% scored 30 or over on composite; 38% scored 24 or over on English, 34% scored 24 or over on math, 39% scored 24 or over on composite; 89% scored 18 or over on English, 86% scored 18 or over on math, 95% scored 18 or over on composite; 100% scored 12 or over on English, 100% scored 12 or over on math, 100% scored 12 or over on composite. 99% of accepted applicants took ACT. 90% of freshmen come from public schools.
**Undergraduate achievement:** 79% of fall 1992 freshmen returned for fall 1993 term. 18% of entering class graduated.
**Foreign students:** 220 students are from out of the country. Countries represented include Canada, Japan, Malaysia, Singapore, South Korea, and Spain; 72 in all.
**PROGRAMS OF STUDY. Degrees:** B.A., B.Bus.Admin., B.F.A., B.Mus., B.S., B.S.Eng., B.S.Med., B.Soc.Work.
**Majors:** Accountancy, Administrative Systems, Advertising/Production, Aeronautical Engineering, Aircraft Maintenance Engineering Technology, American Studies, Anthropology, Applied Material Science, Art, Art Teaching, Automotive Engineering Technology, Aviation Technology/Operations, Biology, Biomedical Science, Broadcast/Cable Production, Business Communication, Business-Oriented Chemistry, Chemistry, Communication Studies, Composition, Computer Information Systems, Computer Science, Computer Systems Engineering, Construction Science/Management, Criminal Justice, Dance, Dietetics, Earth Science, Economics, Electrical Engineering, Elementary Education, Elementary Music, Employee Assistance Program, Engineering Graphics, English, Environmental Studies, Family Studies, Fashion Merchandising, Field Hydrogeology, Finance, Food Marketing, Food Services Administration, French, General Business, Geography, Geology, Geophysics, German, Health Chemistry, Health Education Teaching, History, Home Economics Education, Hydrogeology, Industrial Design, Industrial Education, Industrial Engineering, Industrial Marketing, Insurance, Integrated Supply Management, Interior Design, Interpersonal Communication, Jazz Studies, Latin, Latvian, Management, Manufacturing Administration, Manufacturing Engineering Technology, Marketing, Mathematics, Mechanical Engineering, Media Studies, Middle/Junior High School Education, Music, Music Education, Music History, Music Performance, Music Theatre Performer, Music Theory, Music Therapy, Occupational Therapy, Organizational Communication, Paper Engineering, Paper Science, Philosophy, Physical Education, Physical Education/Exercise Science, Physical Education/Teaching/Coaching, Physician Assistant, Physics, Political Science, Printing, Psychology, Public Administration, Public Relations, Real Estate, Recreation, Religion, Retailing, Secondary Education, Secondary Education/Business, Secondary Education/Marketing, Social Science, Social Work, Sociology, Spanish, Special Education, Speech Pathology/Audiology, Statistics, Telecommunications Management, Textile/Apparel Technology, Theatre, Theatre Education, Tourism/Travel, Visually Impaired, Vocational Education Teaching, Vocational-Technical Education, Women's Studies.
**Distribution of degrees:** The majors with the highest enrollment are finance, accountancy, and marketing.
**Requirements:** General education requirement.
**Academic regulations:** Minimum 2.0 GPA must be maintained.
**Special:** Most programs require minors. Minors offered in art history, athletic training, black American studies, botany, coaching, critical language, early childhood, family life education, gerontology, integrated creative arts, international business, Japanese, journalism, language arts, law, medieval studies, military science, plastics, practical writing, professional and applied ethics, Russian, translation study, world literature, zoology, and other fields. Courses offered in African, Chinese, Greek, and Latin American studies. Self-designed majors. Double majors. Independent study. Accelerated study. Pass/fail grading option. Cooperative education programs. Graduate school at which undergraduates may take graduate-level courses. Preprofessional programs in law, medicine, and dentistry. 3-2 occupational therapy programs with affiliated hospitals. Member of Kalamazoo Consortium. Sea Semester. Teacher certification in elementary, secondary, and votech education. Certification in specific subject areas. Exchange programs abroad in England (U of Leicester), Finland (Sibelius Academy), Germany (Free U of Berlin, U of Paderborn, U of Passau, U of Tubingen), Israel (U of Tel Aviv), Japan (Keio U), Malaysia (Sunway U), and Taiwan (National Kaohsiung Normal U). Study abroad also in other countries. ROTC.
**Honors:** Honors program. Honor societies.
**Academic Assistance:** Remedial reading, writing, math, and study skills. Nonremedial tutoring.
**STUDENT LIFE. Housing:** Students may live on or off campus. Coed, women's, and men's dorms. Sorority and fraternity housing. On-campus married-student housing. 30% of students live in college housing.
**Social atmosphere:** Favorite gathering spots for students include Bernhard Student Center, Waldo Library, Waldo's Campus Tavern, Knollwood Tavern, Gary Sports Center, and Miller Auditorium Fountain Plaza. The Panhellenic Council, the Interfraternity Council, and the Campus Activities Board are groups with a widespread influence on campus social life. Among the most popular social events of the school year are the Bronco Bash, the Barking Tuna Fest, the Kalapalooza Kalamazoo Art Fair, the Medieval Festival, and the WMU-CMU football game. The editor of the student newspaper comments, "We have a diverse community with many of the assets of a large city in a small-town setting. There is a diversity of cultural events, from dance to music to the visual arts. There is also a thriving local music scene."
**Services and counseling/handicapped student services:** Placement services. Health service. Women's center. Day care. Counseling services for minority, military, veteran, and older students. Birth control, personal, and psychological counseling. Career and academic guidance services. Religious counseling. Physically disabled student services. Learning disabled services. Notetaking services. Tape recorders. Reader services for the blind.
**Campus organizations:** Undergraduate student government. Student newspaper (Western Herald, published once/day). Radio station. Gospel choir, dance society, chess and science fiction clubs, Amnesty International, Circle of Friends, Habitat for Humanity, Pre-Law Society, Society of Women Engineers, veterans' association, departmental and political groups, 275 organizations in all. 21 fraternities, 16 chapter houses; 11 sororities, nine chapter houses. 9% of men join a fraternity. 14% of women join a sorority.
**Religious organizations:** B'nai B'rith, Hillel, Buddhadharma Society, Campus Bible Fellowship, Campus Crusade for Christ, Christians in Action, Christian Science Organization, Comparative Religions, Episcopal/Lutheran Campus Ministry, Exousia, His House, Intervaristy Christian Fellowship, Lutheran Campus Ministries, Navigators, St. Thomas More Student Parish, Tabernacle Outreach Ministry, United Campus Ministries, Wesley Foundation, Muslim group.
**Minority/foreign student organizations:** Society for Ebony Concerns, NAACP, black engineering and psychology student associations, PULL, Young Black Females/Males Support, Native American and Hispanic groups. African, Chinese, Indian, Indonesian, Japanese, Korean, Latvian, Malaysian, Nigerian, Pakistani, Russian, Thai, and other foreign groups.
**ATHLETICS. Physical education requirements:** Two semesters of physical education required.
**Intercollegiate competition:** 5% of students participate. Baseball (M), basketball (M,W), cheerleading (M,W), cross-country (M,W), football (M), gymnastics (M,W), ice hockey (M), soccer (M), softball (W), tennis (M,W), track and field (indoor) (M,W), track and field (outdoor) (M,W), volleyball (W). Member of Central Collegiate Hockey Association, Mid-American Conference, NCAA Division I.
**Intramural and club sports:** 12% of students participate. Intramural aerobics, badminton, basketball, cross-country, flag football, floor hockey, free throw, hockey, indoor soccer, Nordic skiing, racquetball, soccer, softball, swimming, table tennis, tennis, track, volleyball. Men's club Alpine skiing, badminton, cricket, goalball, judo, lacrosse, martial arts, rifle, rock climbing, rugby, sailing, swimming, volleyball, water skiing, wrestling. Women's club Alpine skiing, badminton, cricket, goalball, judo, martial arts, rifle, rock climbing, sailing, soccer, swimming, volleyball, water skiing.
**ADMISSIONS. Academic basis for candidate selection** (in order of priority): Secondary school record, standardized test scores, class rank, school's recommendation.
**Nonacademic basis for candidate selection:** Extracurricular participation and particular talent or ability are considered.
**Requirements:** Graduation from secondary school is required; GED is accepted. 12 units and the following program of study are required: 4 units of English, 3 units of math, 2 units of science, 1 unit of social studies, 2 units of history. 3 units of foreign language, 2 units of fine/performing arts, 1 unit of computer literacy, and additional units of science and math

recommended. Audition required of music and theatre program applicants. Martin Luther King Program and Alpha Student Development Program for applicants not normally admissible. ACT is required. Campus visit and interview recommended. Off-campus interviews available with an admissions representative.

**Procedure:** Take ACT by October of 12th year. Suggest filing application by March 1. Application deadline is August 15. Notification of admission on rolling basis. $50 tuition deposit, refundable until May 1. $175 room deposit, refundable until May 1. Freshmen accepted for terms other than fall.

**Special programs:** Credit and/or placement may be granted through CEEB Advanced Placement exams for scores of 3 or higher. Credit may be granted through CLEP general exams. Credit and/or placement may be granted through CLEP subject exams. Credit and placement may be granted through challenge exams and military experience. Concurrent enrollment program.

**Transfer students:** Transfer students accepted for terms other than fall. In fall 1993, 43% of all new students were transfers into all classes. 4,032 transfer applications were received, 3,396 were accepted. Application deadline is before March 1 for fall; before October 1 for spring. Minimum 2.25 GPA recommended. Lowest course grade accepted is "D." At least 30 semester hours must be completed at the university to receive degree.

**Admissions contact:** Stanley E. Henderson, M.A., Director of Admissions. 616 387-2000.

**FINANCIAL AID. Available aid:** Pell grants, SEOG, state scholarships and grants, school scholarships and grants, private scholarships and grants, ROTC scholarships, academic merit scholarships, athletic scholarships, and aid for undergraduate foreign students. Perkins Loans (NDSL), PLUS, Stafford Loans (GSL), state loans, school loans, private loans, and SLS. AMS.

**Financial aid statistics:** 45% of aid is not need-based. In 1993-94, 66% of all undergraduate applicants received aid; 65% of freshman applicants. Average amounts of aid awarded freshmen: Scholarships and grants, $2,100; loans, $2,400.

**Supporting data/closing dates:** FAFSA: Priority filing date is March 1. Notification of awards begins April 1.

**Financial aid contact:** John A. Kundel, M.A., Director of Financial Aid. 616 387-6000.

**STUDENT EMPLOYMENT.** College Work/Study Program. Institutional employment. 29% of full-time undergraduates work on campus during school year. Students may expect to earn an average of $2,050 during school year. Off-campus part-time employment opportunities rated "excellent."

**COMPUTER FACILITIES.** 900 IBM/IBM-compatible, Macintosh/Apple, and RISC-/UNIX-based microcomputers; 620 are networked. Students may access Digital, IBM, SUN minicomputer/mainframe systems, Internet. Residence halls may be equipped with stand-alone microcomputers, networked microcomputers, networked terminals, modems. Client/LAN operating systems include Apple/Macintosh, DOS, UNIX/XENIX/AIX, X-windows, DEC, LocalTalk/AppleTalk, Novell. Computer languages and software packages include Ada, BASIC, C, COBOL, dBASE, FORTRAN, LISP, Lotus 1-2-3, Microsoft Word, Microsoft Works, Pascal, RDB, SAS, SPSS, WordPerfect; 70 in all. Computer facilities are available to all students.

**Fees:** $50 computer fee per semester.

**Hours:** 24 hours.

**GRADUATE CAREER DATA.** Highest graduate school enrollments: Michigan State U, U of Michigan, Western Michigan U. 53% of graduates choose careers in business and industry. Companies and businesses that hire graduates: Big Six accounting firms, General Motors.

**PROMINENT ALUMNI/AE.** Dennis W. Archer, mayor of Detroit, former state Supreme Court justice; Mary Jackson, actress; Dr. Bill Pickard, chairman/CEO, Regal Plastics; Roy Roberts, VP/general manager, GMC Truck Division; Tim Allen, comedian, actor; Linda Kravitz, VP/national marketing, McDonald's Corp.; Jan Thompson, VP/sales operations, Mazda; Gwynn Frostic, artist and owner, Press Craft Papers.

# William Tyndale College

**Farmington Hills, MI 48331** **313 553-7200**

**1993-94 Costs.** Tuition: $5,190. Room: $1,790-$2,400. No meal plan. Fees, books, misc. academic expenses (school's estimate): $485.

**Enrollment.** Undergraduates: 127 men, 108 women (full-time). Freshman class: 259 applicants, 183 enrolled.

**Test score averages/ranges.** Average SAT scores: 360 verbal, 300 math. Average ACT scores: 21 English, 18 math, 20 composite.

**Faculty.** 11 full-time; 31 part-time. 31% of faculty holds doctoral degree.

**Selectivity rating.** Competitive.

**PROFILE.** William Tyndale, founded in 1945, is a college with religious orientation. Its 28-acre campus is located in Farmington Hills, 15 miles from Detroit.

**Accreditation:** AABC, NCACS.

**Religious orientation:** William Tyndale College is an interdenominational Christian school; two semesters of theology required.

**Library:** Collections totaling over 54,692 volumes, 230 periodical subscriptions, and 2,125 microform items.

**STUDENT BODY. Undergraduate profile:** 99% are state residents. 1% Asian-American, 31% Black, 1% Native American, 65% White, 2% Other. Average age of undergraduates is 28.

**Freshman profile:** 15% of accepted applicants took ACT. 99% of freshmen come from public schools.

**Undergraduate achievement:** 68% of students who completed a degree program went on to graduate study.

**Foreign students:** Two students are from out of the country. Countries represented include Canada and Romania.

**PROGRAMS OF STUDY. Degrees:** B.A., B.Relig.Ed., Theol.B.

**Majors:** Bible, Biblical Literature, Business Administration, Counseling, Cross-Cultural Studies/Missions, Humanities, Interdisciplinary, Music, Organ, Pastoral Studies, Psychology, Theology, Youth Studies.

**Requirements:** General education requirement.

**Academic regulations:** Freshmen must maintain minimum 1.6 GPA; sophomores, 1.9 GPA; juniors, 2.0 GPA; seniors, 2.0 GPA.

**Special:** Minors offered in some majors and in business, childhood care, education, English/speech, foreign languages, Greek language, history, philosophy, social science, and urban ministries. Associate's degrees offered. Double majors. Dual degrees. Independent study. Pass/fail grading option. Internships. Graduate school at which undergraduates may take graduate-level courses. Preprofessional programs in theology. 2-2 Bible/general studies program for students with associate's degrees. 2-3 Bachelor of Theology program. Study abroad in Israel/Jordan.

**ADMISSIONS. Academic basis for candidate selection** (in order of priority): Secondary school record, standardized test scores, school's recommendation, class rank.

**Nonacademic basis for candidate selection:** Alumni/ae relationship is emphasized. Character and personality are important. Particular talent or ability is considered.

**Requirements:** Graduation from secondary school is required; GED is accepted. No specific distribution of secondary school units required. Minimum composite ACT score of 15 and minimum 2.0 GPA recommended. Audition required of music program applicants. Conditional admission possible for applicants not meeting standard requirements. ACT is required; SAT may be substituted. Campus visit and interview recommended. Off-campus interviews available with an admissions representative.

**Procedure:** Take SAT or ACT by April of 12th year. Visit college for interview by spring of 12th year. Suggest filing application by May. Application deadline is July. Notification of admission on rolling basis. $50 refundable room deposit. Freshmen accepted for terms other than fall.

**Special programs:** Admission may be deferred one year. Credit may be granted through CEEB Advanced Placement for scores of 3 or higher. Credit may be granted through CLEP subject exams, military and life experience. Early entrance/early admission program. Concurrent enrollment program.

**Transfer students:** Transfer students accepted for terms other than fall. Application deadline is July 27. Minimum 2.0 GPA required. Lowest course grade accepted is "C." Maximum number of transferable credits is 75 semester hours. At least 45 semester hours must be completed at the college to receive degree.

**Admissions contact:** Nicole Caughell, Enrollment Coordinator. 313 553-7200.

**FINANCIAL AID. Available aid:** Pell grants, SEOG, state scholarships and grants, school scholarships and grants, private scholarships, and academic merit scholarships. PLUS, Stafford Loans (GSL), and SLS.

**Financial aid statistics:** Average amounts of aid awarded freshmen: Loans, $2,366.

**Supporting data/closing dates:** FAFSA/FAF: Priority filing date is February 15; accepted on rolling basis. School's own aid application: Priority filing date is June 15. State aid form: Priority filing date is February 15. Income tax forms: Accepted on rolling basis. Notification of awards on rolling basis.

**Financial aid contact:** Jan Jehn, Director of Financial Aid. 313 553-7200.

# Minnesota

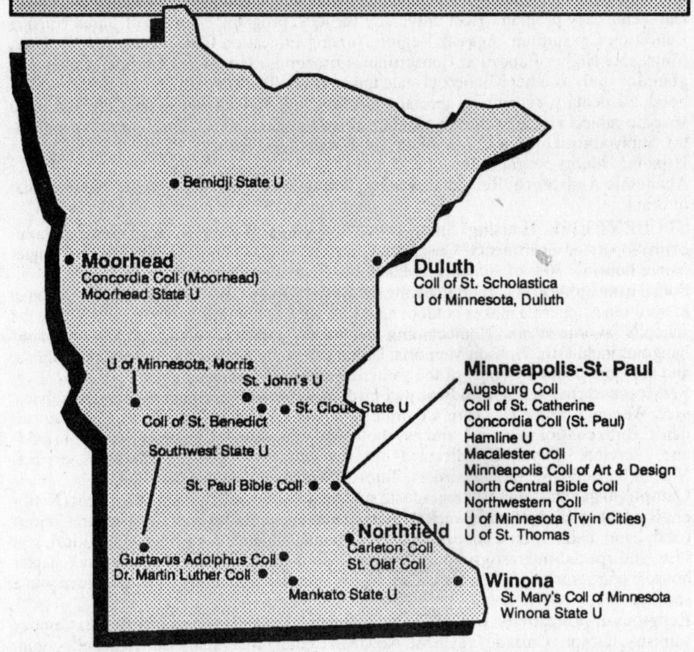


## Augsburg College

**Minneapolis, MN 55454** 612 330-1000

**1993-94 Costs.** Tuition: $11,292. Room & board: $4,204. Fees, books, misc. academic expenses (school's estimate): $1,362.
**Enrollment.** Undergraduates: 681 men, 781 women (full-time). Freshman class: 662 applicants, 513 accepted, 257 enrolled. Graduate enrollment: 37 men, 107 women.
**Test score averages/ranges.** Average SAT scores: 460 verbal, 580 math. Range of SAT scores of middle 50%: 420-470 verbal, 510-540 math. Average ACT scores: 21 composite. Range of ACT scores of middle 50%: 18-25 composite.
**Faculty.** 128 full-time; 160 part-time. 68% of faculty holds highest degree in specific field. Student/faculty ratio: 14 to 1.
**Selectivity rating.** Less competitive.

**PROFILE.** Augsburg, founded in 1869, is a church-affiliated, liberal arts college. Its 25-acre campus is located one mile from downtown Minneapolis.

**Accreditation:** NCACS. Professionally accredited by the National Council for Accreditation of Teacher Education, the National League for Nursing.
**Religious orientation:** Augsburg College is affiliated with the Evangelical Lutheran Church in America; three semesters of religion required.
**Library:** Collections totaling over 175,000 volumes, 981 periodical subscriptions, and 15,500 microform items.
**Special facilities/museums:** Electron microscope, center for atmospheric science research, theatre, pipe organ.
**Athletic facilities:** Gymnasium, basketball, handball, and racquetball court, weight and wrestling rooms, ice rinks, football, soccer, and softball fields.

**STUDENT BODY. Undergraduate profile:** 78% are state residents; 43% are transfers. 12% Asian-American, 5% Black, 1% Hispanic, 2% Native American, 78% White, 2% Other. Average age of undergraduates is 22.
**Freshman profile:** 2% of freshmen who took SAT scored 700 or over on verbal, 5% scored 700 or over on math; 10% scored 600 or over on verbal, 34% scored 600 or over on math; 37% scored 500 or over on verbal, 58% scored 500 or over on math; 72% scored 400 or over on verbal, 82% scored 400 or over on math; 90% scored 300 or over on verbal, 95% scored 300 or over on math. 5% of freshmen who took ACT scored 30 or over on composite; 33% scored 24 or over on composite; 81% scored 18 or over on composite; 91% scored 12 or over on composite. 14% of accepted applicants took SAT; 84% took ACT. 89% of freshmen come from public schools.
**Undergraduate achievement:** 75% of fall 1992 freshmen returned for fall 1993 term. 29% of entering class graduated. 11% of students who completed a degree program immediately went on to graduate study.
**Foreign students:** 57 students are from out of the country. Countries represented include Denmark, Ethiopia, Hong Kong, Japan, Norway, and Sweden; 27 in all.

**PROGRAMS OF STUDY. Degrees:** B.A., B.Mus., B.S.
**Majors:** Art History, Biology, Business Administration, Chemistry, Communications, Computer Science, East Asian Studies, Economics, Economics/Business Administration, Elementary Education, Engineering, English, French, German, Health Education, History, Humanities, International Relations, Management Information Systems, Mathematics, Metro-Urban Studies, Music, Music Education, Music Performance, Music Therapy, Natural Science, Norwegian, Nursing, Philosophy, Physical Education, Physics, Political Science, Psychology, Religion, Russian Area Studies, Scandinavian Area Studies, Secondary Education, Social Sciences, Social Work, Sociology, Space Physics, Spanish, Speech, Studio Art, Theatre Arts, Transdisciplinary.
**Distribution of degrees:** The majors with the highest enrollment are business administration, education, and communications; Scandinavian studies, East Asian studies, and foreign languages have the lowest.
**Requirements:** General education requirement.
**Academic regulations:** Freshmen must maintain minimum 1.6 GPA; sophomores, 1.7 GPA; juniors, 1.9 GPA; seniors, 2.0 GPA.
**Special:** Minors offered in most majors. Self-designed majors. Double majors. Dual degrees. Independent study. Accelerated study. Pass/fail grading option. Internships. Cooperative education programs. Preprofessional programs in law, medicine, veterinary science, pharmacy, dentistry, theology, and optometry. 3-2 engineering programs with Michigan Tech U, U of Minnesota, and Washington U. 3-2 occupational therapy program with Washington U. Member of Associated Colleges of the Twin Cities. Washington Semester, UN Semester, and Sea Semester. Interim exchange programs possible. Teacher certification in elementary, secondary, and special education. Certification in specific subject areas. Study abroad in Central American countries, England, France, Germany, Hong Kong, Mexico, Norway, and other countries. ROTC and NROTC at U of Minnesota. AFROTC at U of St. Thomas.
**Honors:** Phi Beta Kappa. Honors program. Honor societies.
**Academic Assistance:** Remedial writing, math, and study skills. Nonremedial tutoring.

**STUDENT LIFE. Housing:** Students may live on or off campus. Coed dorms. School-owned/operated apartments. Off-campus privately-owned housing. On-campus married-student housing. 48% of students live in college housing.
**Social atmosphere:** According to the editor of the student newspaper, much social activity takes place off campus as Minneapolis is a large metropolitan area, very rich in social and cultural activities. However, major on-campus events are well attended. Popular social events include Homecoming Week, Casino Night, January interim events, Spring Affair (dance), Days in May, Advent Vespers services, hockey games, and theatre events. Most influential groups on campus are the Augsburg Student Activities Council, Campus Ministry, choir, and the Echo. Students like to gather at student houses on campus, and off campus at Murphy's, the Quad, Blondie's, Tracy's Saloon, and other areas in the Cedar-Riverside community.
**Services and counseling/handicapped student services:** Placement services. Health service. Women's center. Counseling services for minority and older students. Personal and psychological counseling. Career and academic guidance services. Religious counseling. Physically disabled student services. Learning disabled program/services. Notetaking services. Tape recorders. Tutors. Reader services for the blind.
**Campus organizations:** Undergraduate student government. Student newspaper (Augsburg Echo, published once/week). Literary magazine. Yearbook. Radio station. Choir, concert band, orchestra, chapel choir, drama group, jazz band, 36 organizations in all.
**Religious organizations:** Campus Ministry, Fellowship of Christian Athletes, Intervarsity Christian Fellowship, Outreach teams, Religious Life Commission, Vocatio.
**Minority/foreign student organizations:** Black Student Union, Intertribal Student Union. Cross-cultural club.

**ATHLETICS. Physical education requirements:** Two half-semesters of physical education required.
**Intercollegiate competition:** 30% of students participate. Baseball (M), basketball (M,W), cross-country (M,W), football (M), golf (M,W), ice hockey (M), soccer (M,W), softball (W), tennis (M,W), track and field (indoor) (M,W), track and field (outdoor) (M,W), volleyball (W), wrestling (M). Member of Minnesota Intercollegiate Athletic Conference, NCAA Division III.
**Intramural and club sports:** 50% of students participate. Intramural badminton, basketball, broomball, floor hockey, softball, tennis, volleyball.

**ADMISSIONS. Academic basis for candidate selection** (in order of priority): Secondary school record, standardized test scores, class rank, school's recommendation, essay.
**Nonacademic basis for candidate selection:** Character and personality, extracurricular participation, and particular talent or ability are important. Alumni/ae relationship is considered.
**Requirements:** Graduation from secondary school is required; GED is accepted. 18 units and the following program of study are recommended: 4 units of English, 3 units of math, 3 units of science, 2 units of foreign language, 4 units of social studies, 2 units of history. Minimum composite ACT score of 18, rank in top half of secondary school class, and minimum 2.5 GPA recommended. Conditional admission possible for applicants not meeting standard requirements. ACT is required; SAT may be substituted. Campus visit and interview recommended. No off-campus interviews.
**Procedure:** Take SAT or ACT by December 15 of 12th year. Suggest filing application by April 1. Application deadline is August 15. Notification of admission on rolling basis. Reply is required by August 15. $100 tuition deposit, refundable until May 1. $100 room deposit, refundable until July 1. Freshmen accepted in terms other than fall.
**Special programs:** Admission may be deferred one year. Credit and/or placement may be granted through CEEB Advanced Placement exams for scores of 3 or higher. Credit and/or placement may be granted through CLEP general and subject exams. Credit and placement may be granted through challenge exams and military and life experience. Concurrent enrollment program.
**Transfer students:** Transfer students accepted for terms other than fall. In fall 1993, 43% of all new students were transfers into all classes. 391 transfer applications were received, 338 were accepted. Application deadline is August 15 for fall; December 31 for spring. Minimum 2.0 GPA required. Lowest course grade accepted is "C." Maximum number of transferable credits is 96 quarter hours from a two-year school and 150 quarter hours from a four-year school. At least 42 quarter hours must be completed at the college to receive degree.
**Admissions contact:** Sally Daniels, Director of Admissions. 612 330-1001, 800 788-5678.

**FINANCIAL AID. Available aid:** Pell grants, SEOG, state scholarships and grants, school scholarships and grants, private scholarships and grants, ROTC scholarships, academic merit scholarships, and aid for undergraduate foreign students. Perkins Loans (NDSL), PLUS, Stafford Loans (GSL), NSL, and SLS. Installment Plan.

**Financial aid statistics:** 5% of aid is not need-based. In 1993-94, 95% of all undergraduate applicants received aid; 95% of freshman applicants. Average amounts of aid awarded freshmen: Scholarships and grants, $7,010; loans, $2,516.
**Supporting data/closing dates:** FAFSA: Priority filing date is April 1. School's own aid application: Priority filing date is April 1. Notification of awards on rolling basis.
**Financial aid contact:** Herald A. Johnson, Assistant Vice President for Student Financial Services. 612 330-1046.

**STUDENT EMPLOYMENT.** College Work/Study Program. Institutional employment. 40% of full-time undergraduates work on campus during school year. Students may expect to earn an average of $1,300 during school year. Off-campus part-time employment opportunities rated "excellent."

**COMPUTER FACILITIES.** 105 IBM/IBM-compatible and Macintosh/Apple microcomputers; all are networked. Students may access Digital, IBM, SUN minicomputer/mainframe systems, BITNET, Internet. Residence halls may be equipped with networked microcomputers. Client/LAN operating systems include Apple/Macintosh, DOS, UNIX/XENIX/AIX, LocalTalk/AppleTalk, Novell. Computer languages and software packages include C, COBOL, FORTRAN, Pascal, UNIX; 100 in all. Computer facilities are available to all students.
**Fees:** Computer fee is included in tuition/fees.
**Hours:** 8 AM-midn.; 24 hours in residence halls.

**GRADUATE CAREER DATA.** Highest graduate school enrollments: U of Minnesota. 46% of graduates choose careers in business and industry. Companies and businesses that hire graduates: Control Data, IBM, Lutheran Brotherhood, Norwest Banks, West Publishing, 3M, area public schools.

**PROMINENT ALUMNI/AE.** Martin O. Sabo, U.S. congressman, Minnesota; Dr. Ron Fergeson, head of transplant surgery, Ohio State U; R. Luther Olson, head basketball coach, U of Arizona; James Thomas, 1983 Minority Entrepreneur of the Year; Pamela Alexander, municipal court judge, Hennipen County, Minn.; Carl Blegen, Greek archaeologist, discoverer of city of Troy; La June Lange, county court judge, Hennipen County, Minn.

## Bemidji State University

**Bemidji, MN 56601** 218 755-2040

**1993-94 Costs.** Tuition: $2,156 (state residents), $4,808 (out-of-state). Room & board: $2,672. Fees, books, misc. academic expenses (school's estimate): $660.
**Enrollment.** Undergraduates: 1,847 men, 1,947 women (full-time). Freshman class: 1,208 applicants, 877 accepted, 561 enrolled. Graduate enrollment: 113 men, 262 women.
**Test score averages/ranges.** Average ACT scores: 20 English, 20 math, 21 composite. Range of ACT scores of middle 50%: 18-23 English, 18-22 math.
**Faculty.** 217 full-time; 19 part-time. 56% of faculty holds doctoral degree. Student/faculty ratio: 20 to 1.
**Selectivity rating.** Less competitive.

**PROFILE.** Bemidji State, founded in 1919, is a public, multipurpose university. Its 89-acre campus is located along the shore of Lake Bemidji, in a residential area of Bemidji.

**Accreditation:** NCACS. Professionally accredited by the Council on Social Work Education, the National Council for Accreditation of Teacher Education.
**Religious orientation:** Bemidji State University is nonsectarian; no religious requirements.
**Library:** Collections totaling over 183,727 volumes, 886 periodical subscriptions, and 688,000 microform items.
**Special facilities/museums:** Aquatics lab.
**Athletic facilities:** Ice rink, swimming pool, gymnasium, baseball, intramural, and softball fields, football stadium, basketball, handball, tennis, and volleyball courts, dance studio, weight training room, tracks.

**STUDENT BODY. Undergraduate profile:** 94% are state residents; 50% are transfers. .6% Asian-American, .7% Black, .7% Hispanic, 4% Native American, 89% White, 5% Other. Average age of undergraduates is 23.
**Freshman profile:** 85% of accepted applicants took ACT. 96% of freshmen come from public schools.
**Undergraduate achievement:** 69% of fall 1992 freshmen returned for fall 1993 term. 11% of entering class graduated.
**Foreign students:** 253 students are from out of the country. Countries represented include Canada, China, Hong Kong, Japan, and Malaysia; 30 in all.

**PROGRAMS OF STUDY. Degrees:** B.A., B.F.A., B.S.
**Majors:** Accounting, Applied Psychology, Aquatic Biology, Art, Biology, Business Administration, Chemistry, Computer Information Systems, Computer Science, Criminal Justice, Earth Science, Economics, Elementary Education, English, Environmental Studies, French, Geography, Geology, German, Health, History, Humanities, Indian Studies, Industrial Arts, Industrial Technology, Life Science, Mass Communication, Mathematics, Medical Technology, Music, Nursing, Philosophy, Physical Education, Physical Sciences, Physics, Political Science, Psychology, Science Education, Social Studies, Social Work, Sociology, Spanish, Speech/Theatre, Sports Studies/Management, Technical Illustration/Graphic Design, Vocational Education.
**Distribution of degrees:** The majors with the highest enrollment are business administration and elementary education; philosophy, humanities, and Indian studies have the lowest.
**Requirements:** General education requirement.
**Academic regulations:** Minimum 2.0 GPA must be maintained.
**Special:** Minors offered in most majors and in anthropology, art history, chemical dependency/counseling, data processing, developmental/adapted physical education, military science, Ojibwe, recreation, religious studies, space studies, theatre production, and women's studies. Vocational licensure programs for vocational education, vocational/special needs, and athletic coaching. Associate's degrees offered. Double majors. Independent study. Accelerated study. Pass/fail grading option. Internships. Graduate school at which undergraduates may take graduate-level courses. Preprofessional programs in law, medicine, veterinary science, pharmacy, dentistry, theology, and optometry. 3-1 medical technology program. Host university for R.N. program. Member of Itasca Nursing Education Consortium, Agassiz Region Nursing Education Consortium, and Northeast Minnesota Higher Education Consortium. Eurospring Semester. Common Market Program for study at other Minnesota state universities. Teacher certification in early childhood, elementary, secondary, special education, and vo-tech education. Certification in specific subject areas. Exchange program abroad in England (Oxford U) and Japan (Akita). Study abroad also in China, Malaysia, Mexico, and Russia.
**Honors:** Honors program. Honor societies.
**Academic Assistance:** Remedial reading, writing, math, and study skills. Nonremedial tutoring.

**STUDENT LIFE. Housing:** Students may live on or off campus. Coed dorms. School-owned/operated apartments. On-campus married-student housing. On-campus single-parent housing. 30% of students live in college housing.
**Social atmosphere:** As reported by the student newspaper, Bemidji's isolated location in in northern Minnesota makes outdoor activities such as hunting, camping, and fishing the school's favorite events; Homecoming and hockey games are also popular. On-campus hangouts include the Hobson Memorial Union and Wally's cafeteria; Bottom's Up, Slim's, and the Corner Bar are some of the gathering spots off campus.
**Services and counseling/handicapped student services:** Placement services. Health service. Women's center. Day care. Counseling services for minority, veteran, and older students. Birth control, personal, and psychological counseling. Career and academic guidance services. Physically disabled student services. Learning disabled services. Notetaking services. Tape recorders. Tutors. Reader services for the blind.
**Campus organizations:** Undergraduate student government. Student newspaper (Northern Student, published once/week). Literary magazine. Radio and TV stations. Concert band, band, choir, mixed chorus, women's chorus, athletic, departmental, political, service, and special-interest groups, 80 organizations in all. Three fraternities, no chapter houses; one sorority, no chapter house. 1% of men join a fraternity. 1% of women join a sorority.
**Religious organizations:** United Campus Ministry, Bahai Campus Club, Baptist Campus Ministry, Campus Crusade for Christ, Newman Center, Intervarsity Christian Fellowship, Christian Science Organization, Latter-Day Saints Student Association, Lutheran group.
**Minority/foreign student organizations:** Council of Indian Students, Black Student Coalition. International Student Organization.

**ATHLETICS. Physical education requirements:** Two terms of physical education required.
**Intercollegiate competition:** 7% of students participate. Baseball (M), basketball (M,W), cheerleading (W), football (M), golf (M), ice hockey (M), softball (W), tennis (W), track (indoor) (M,W), track (outdoor) (M,W), track and field (indoor) (M,W), track and field (outdoor) (M,W), volleyball (W). Member of NCAA Division II, Northern Collegiate Hockey Association, Northern Sun Intercollegiate Conference.
**Intramural and club sports:** 80% of students participate. Intramural badminton, basketball, broomball, bowling, flag football, floor hockey, golf, ice hockey, indoor soccer, racquetball, soccer, softball, tennis, volleyball. Men's club cross-country, Nordic skiing, soccer, tae kwon do, volleyball. Women's club cross-country, Nordic skiing, soccer, tae kwon do, volleyball.

**ADMISSIONS. Academic basis for candidate selection** (in order of priority): Class rank, standardized test scores, secondary school record, essay, school's recommendation.
**Nonacademic basis for candidate selection:** Geographical distribution is important. Character and personality, extracurricular participation, particular talent or ability, and alumni/ae relationship are considered.
**Requirements:** Graduation from secondary school is required; GED is accepted. No specific distribution of secondary school units required. Minimum composite ACT score of 21 and rank in top half of secondary school class required. R.N. required of nursing program applicants. Conditional admission possible for applicants not meeting standard requirements. ACT is required. Campus visit and interview recommended. Off-campus interviews available with an admissions representative.
**Procedure:** Take ACT by February of 12th year. Application deadline is August 15. Notification of admission on rolling basis. No set date by which applicants must accept offer. $100 room deposit, refundable until July 15. Freshmen accepted in terms other than fall.
**Special programs:** Admission may be deferred one year. Credit and/or placement may be granted through CEEB Advanced Placement exams for scores of 4 or higher. Credit and/or placement may be granted through CLEP general and subject exams. Credit may be granted through military and life experience. Credit and placement may be granted through DANTES and challenge exams. Early entrance/early admission program. Concurrent enrollment program.
**Transfer students:** Transfer students accepted for terms other than fall. In fall 1993, 50% of all new students were transfers into all classes. 915 transfer applications were received, 738 were accepted. Application deadline is August 15 for fall; February 15 for spring. Minimum 2.0 GPA required. Lowest course grade accepted is "C." At least 45 quarter hours must be completed at the university to receive degree.
**Admissions contact:** Paul Muller, M.S., Director of Admissions. 218 755-2040.

**FINANCIAL AID. Available aid:** Pell grants, SEOG, state scholarships and grants, school scholarships and grants, private scholarships, academic merit scholarships, athletic scholarships, and aid for undergraduate foreign students. State nursing grants. State and tribal American Indian grants. Perkins Loans (NDSL), PLUS, Stafford Loans (GSL), and state loans.
**Financial aid statistics:** 28% of aid is not need-based. In 1993-94, 95% of all undergraduate applicants received aid; 91% of freshman applicants. Average amounts of aid awarded freshmen: Scholarships and grants, $1,010; loans, $1,759.
**Supporting data/closing dates:** FAFSA: Accepted on rolling basis. School's own aid application: Accepted on rolling basis. Income tax forms: Accepted on rolling basis. Notification of awards on rolling basis.
**Financial aid contact:** John Schullo, M.S., Director of Financial Aid. 218 755-2034.

**STUDENT EMPLOYMENT.** College Work/Study Program. Institutional employment. 39% of full-time undergraduates work on campus during school year. Students may

expect to earn an average of $1,500 during school year. Off-campus part-time employment opportunities rated "good."

**COMPUTER FACILITIES.** 190 IBM/IBM-compatible and Macintosh/Apple microcomputers; 140 are networked. Students may access Digital minicomputer/mainframe systems, Internet. Residence halls may be equipped with stand-alone microcomputers, networked terminals. Client/LAN operating systems include Apple/Macintosh, DOS, DEC, LocalTalk/AppleTalk, Novell. Numerous computer languages and programs available. Computer facilities are available to all students.

**Fees:** $1 computer fee per quarter hour.

## Carleton College

**Northfield, MN 55057** **507 663-4000**

**1994-95 Costs.** Tuition: $19,292. Room: $1,623. Board: $2,334. Fees, books, misc. academic expenses (school's estimate): $676.

**Enrollment.** Undergraduates: 833 men, 845 women (full-time). Freshman class: 2,693 applicants, 1,579 accepted, 489 enrolled.

**Test score averages/ranges.** Range of SAT scores of middle 50%: 560-670 verbal, 610-710 math. Range of ACT scores of middle 50%: 27-31 composite.

**Faculty.** 150 full-time; 14 part-time. 82% of faculty holds doctoral degree. Student/faculty ratio: 11 to 1.

**Selectivity rating.** Highly competitive.

**PROFILE.** Carleton, founded in 1865, is a private, liberal arts college. Its 900-acre campus, including a 450-acre arboretum, is located 35 miles south of Minneapolis-St. Paul. Campus architecture includes buildings constructed during the first two decades of the 20th century.

**Accreditation:** NCACS.

**Religious orientation:** Carleton College is nonsectarian; no religious requirements.

**Library:** Collections totaling over 488,410 volumes, 1,514 periodical subscriptions, and 17,983 microform items.

**Special facilities/museums:** Arboretum, greenhouse, observatory, scanning and transmission electron microscopes, refractor and reflector telescopes, nuclear magnetic resonance spectrometer.

**Athletic facilities:** Gymnasiums, swimming pools, indoor track, all-weather outdoor track, wrestling room, tennis courts, football stadium, weight training room, dance studio, numerous baseball and athletic fields.

**STUDENT BODY. Undergraduate profile:** 24% are state residents; 6% are transfers. 10% Asian-American, 3% Black, 4% Hispanic, 1% Native American, 81% White, 1% Other. Average age of undergraduates is 20.

**Freshman profile:** 12% of freshmen who took SAT scored 700 or over on verbal, 30% scored 700 or over on math; 56% scored 600 or over on verbal, 71% scored 600 or over on math; 83% scored 500 or over on verbal, 86% scored 500 or over on math; 88% scored 400 or over on verbal, 89% scored 400 or over on math; 89% scored 300 or over on verbal. 25% of freshmen who took ACT scored 30 or over on composite; 47% scored 24 or over on composite; 50% scored 18 or over on composite. 61% of accepted applicants took SAT; 55% took ACT. 80% of freshmen come from public schools.

**Undergraduate achievement:** 95% of fall 1992 freshmen returned for fall 1993 term. 85% of entering class graduated. 75% of students who completed a degree program went on to graduate study within five years.

**Foreign students:** 20 students are from out of the country. Countries represented include Canada, Japan, and Russia; 11 in all.

**PROGRAMS OF STUDY. Degrees:** B.A.

**Majors:** American Studies, Art History, Asian Studies, Biology, Chemistry, Classics, Computer Science, Economics, English, French, Geology, German, Greek, History, Latin, Latin American Studies, Mathematics, Music, Philosophy, Physics/Astronomy, Political Science, Psychology, Religion, Russian, Sociology/Anthropology, Spanish, Studio Art.

**Distribution of degrees:** The majors with the highest enrollment are English, history, and political science; German, music, and French have the lowest.

**Requirements:** General education requirement.

**Academic regulations:** Freshmen must maintain minimum 1.6 GPA; sophomores, 1.8 GPA; juniors, 1.9 GPA; seniors, 2.0 GPA.

**Special:** Concentrations offered in African/African American studies, archaeology, cognitive studies, East Asian studies, educational studies, French studies, Latin American studies, media studies, medieval studies, natural history, political economy, Russian studies, social thought, South Asian studies, technology/policy studies, and women's studies. Self-designed majors. Double majors. Dual degrees. Independent study. Pass/fail grading option. Internships. Preprofessional programs in medicine, veterinary science, and dentistry. 3-2 engineering programs with Columbia U and Washington U. 3-2 nursing program with Rush U. Member of Associated Colleges of the Midwest. Cooperative programs with Saint Olaf Coll. Washington Semester. Chicago Urban Studies Program, Newberry Library Program in the Humanities (Illinois), Oak Ridge Science Semester (Tennessee), and other off-campus study opportunities. Teacher certification in secondary education. Certification in specific subject areas. Study abroad in Australia, Austria, China, Costa Rica, England, France, Germany, India, Italy, Japan, Mexico, Russia, Sri Lanka, and other countries.

**Honors:** Phi Beta Kappa. Honor societies.

**Academic Assistance:** Nonremedial tutoring.

**STUDENT LIFE. Housing:** All students must live on campus for at least two years, including freshman year. Coed dorms. Off-campus privately-owned housing. Off-campus college-owned housing. 92% of students live in college housing.

**Social atmosphere:** According to the student newspaper, "Carleton's fairly intense academic pace is broken by some fairly intense recreation almost entirely on weekends. Smaller private parties have become more widespread. Interpersonal relations are generally laid-back and friendly." Favorite on-campus hangouts are the Sayles-Hill Campus Center and The Cave. Popular gathering spots off campus include the Reub, Grundy's, and Hattie's. Among the year's favorite events are Homecoming, Mid-Winter Ball, and Spring Concert.

**Services and counseling/handicapped student services:** Placement services. Health service. Women's center. Counseling services for minority students. Birth control, personal, and psychological counseling. Career and academic guidance services. Religious counseling. Learning disabled services.

**Campus organizations:** Undergraduate student government. Student newspaper (Carletonian, published once/week). Literary magazine. Yearbook. Radio station. Choir, orchestra, band, other instrumental and vocal groups, folk dance groups, theatre, Amnesty International, community service programs, Veggie Program, coffeehouse, departmental, political, and special-interest groups, 110 organizations in all.

**Religious organizations:** Christian Fellowship, Christian Science Organization, Council for Religious Understanding.

**Minority/foreign student organizations:** African American, Native American, Asian American, and Hispanic student groups.

**ATHLETICS. Physical education requirements:** Four terms of physical education required.

**Intercollegiate competition:** 30% of students participate. Alpine skiing (M,W), baseball (M), basketball (M,W), cross-country (M,W), diving (M,W), football (M), golf (M,W), Nordic skiing (M,W), soccer (M,W), swimming (M,W), tennis (M,W), track and field (indoor) (M,W), track and field (outdoor) (M,W), volleyball (W), wrestling (M). Member of Minnesota Intercollegiate Athletic Conference, NCAA Division III, NCSA.

**Intramural and club sports:** 90% of students participate. Intramural badminton, basketball, broomball, floor hockey, frisbee, racquetball, soccer, softball, squash, tennis. Men's club cycling, fencing, field hockey, horsemanship, ice hockey, lacrosse, martial arts, rugby, ultimate frisbee, volleyball, water polo. Women's club cycling, fencing, field hockey, horsemanship, lacrosse, martial arts, rugby, softball, ultimate frisbee, water polo.

**ADMISSIONS. Academic basis for candidate selection** (in order of priority): Secondary school record, school's recommendation, class rank, standardized test scores, essay.

**Nonacademic basis for candidate selection:** Character and personality, extracurricular participation, and particular talent or ability are important. Geographical distribution and alumni/ae relationship are considered.

**Requirements:** Graduation from secondary school is recommended; GED is accepted. No specific distribution of secondary school units required. SAT or ACT is required. ACH recommended. Campus visit and interview recommended. Off-campus interviews available with admissions and alumni representatives.

**Procedure:** Take SAT or ACT by February 15 of 12th year. Visit college for interview by March 1 of 12th year. Suggest filing application by February 1; no deadline. Notification of admission by April 15. Reply is required by May 1. $200 nonrefundable tuition deposit. Freshmen accepted for fall term only.

**Special programs:** Admission may be deferred one year. Credit and/or placement may be granted through CEEB Advanced Placement exams for scores of 4 or higher. Credit and placement may be granted through challenge exams. Early decision program. In fall 1993, 288 applied for early decision and 209 were accepted. Deadline for applying for early decision is are November 15 and January 15.. Early entrance/early admission program.

**Transfer students:** Transfer students accepted for terms other than fall. In fall 1993, 6% of all new students were transfers into all classes. 145 transfer applications were received, 57 were accepted. Application deadline is March 31; November 15 for winter. Minimum 3.0 GPA recommended. Lowest course grade accepted is "C." Maximum number of transferable credits is 102 credits. At least 108 credits must be completed at the college to receive degree.

**Admissions contact:** Paul Thiboutot, A.M., Dean of Admissions. 507 663-4190, 800 995-2275.

**FINANCIAL AID. Available aid:** Pell grants, SEOG, state scholarships and grants, school scholarships and grants, academic merit scholarships, and aid for undergraduate foreign students. Perkins Loans (NDSL), PLUS, Stafford Loans (GSL), state loans, and school loans. Knight Tuition Plans and AMS.

**Financial aid statistics:** 10% of aid is not need-based. In 1993-94, 98% of all undergraduate applicants received aid; 75% of freshman applicants. Average amounts of aid awarded freshmen: Scholarships and grants, $8,402; loans, $2,618.

**Supporting data/closing dates:** FAFSA/FAF: Priority filing date is March 1. State aid form: Priority filing date is March 1. Income tax forms: Priority filing date is March 1. Notification of awards on rolling basis.

**Financial aid contact:** Leonard M. Wenc, M.S., Director of Student Financial Services. 507 663-4190.

**STUDENT EMPLOYMENT.** College Work/Study Program. Institutional employment. 85% of full-time undergraduates work on campus during school year. Students may expect to earn an average of $1,750 during school year. Off-campus part-time employment opportunities rated "fair."

**COMPUTER FACILITIES.** 210 IBM/IBM-compatible and Macintosh/Apple microcomputers; 170 are networked. Students may access Digital minicomputer/mainframe systems, CompuServe. Client/LAN operating systems include Apple/Macintosh, DOS, UNIX/XENIX/AIX, X-windows, LocalTalk/AppleTalk, Novell. Computer languages and software packages include Ada, BASIC, C, Edison, FORTH, FORTRAN 77, LISP, LOGO, Modula 2, Pascal, SimScript, SNOBOL; over 40 languages and software packages. Computer facilities are available to all students.

**Fees:** None.

**Hours:** 24 hours.

**GRADUATE CAREER DATA.** Graduate school percentages: 8% enter law school. 5% enter medical school. 1% enter dental school. 4% enter graduate business programs. 50% enter graduate arts and sciences programs. 1% enter theological school/seminary. Highest graduate school enrollments: U of Chicago, U of Minnesota, U of Wisconsin, Washington U. 20% of graduates choose careers in business and industry. Companies and businesses that hire graduates: Deloitte & Touche, Ernst & Young, General Mills, Norwest Corp., Salomon Brothers.

**PROMINENT ALUMNI/AE.** Michael H. Armacost, former U.S. ambassador to Japan; Donald S. Hunt, president, Harris Bankcorp; Garrick Utley, chief foreign correspondent, ABC News.

# College of Saint Benedict

St. Joseph, MN 56374-2099 612 363-5308

**1993-94 Costs.** Tuition: $11,340. Room & board: $4,030. Fees, books, misc. academic expenses (school's estimate): $588.

**Enrollment.** 1,698 women (full-time). Freshman class: 796 applicants, 742 accepted, 443 enrolled.

**Test score averages/ranges.** Average SAT scores: 475 verbal, 510 math. Range of SAT scores of middle 50%: 390-560 verbal, 430-580 math. Average ACT scores: 23 English, 22 math, 23 composite. Range of ACT scores of middle 50%: 20-26 English, 19-25 math.

**Faculty.** 132 full-time; 27 part-time. 80% of faculty holds highest degree in specific field. Student/faculty ratio: 13 to 1.

**Selectivity rating.** Less competitive.

**PROFILE.** The College of Saint Benedict is a church-affiliated, liberal arts institution for women. Founded in 1887, it is a coordinate with Saint John's University. Its 700-acre campus is located in St. Joseph, 70 miles from Minneapolis.

**Accreditation:** NCACS. Professionally accredited by the Council on Social Work Education, the National Council for Accreditation of Teacher Education, the National League for Nursing.

**Religious orientation:** College of Saint Benedict is affiliated with the Roman Catholic Church (Sisters of the Order of St. Benedict); two semesters of religion/theology required.

**Library:** Collections totaling over 488,000 volumes, 3,200 periodical subscriptions, and 118,500 microform items.

**Special facilities/museums:** Art gallery, biology museum, nature preserve, electron microscope, neutron generator.

**Athletic facilities:** Gymnasiums, swimming pool, weight room, basketball and tennis courts.

**STUDENT BODY. Undergraduate profile:** 85% are state residents; 20% are transfers. 2% Asian-American, 1% Black, 1% Hispanic, 1% Native American, 93% White, 2% Foreign. Average age of undergraduates is 20.

**Freshman profile:** 3% of freshmen who took SAT scored 700 or over on verbal, 3% scored 700 or over on math; 8% scored 600 or over on verbal, 14% scored 600 or over on math; 42% scored 500 or over on verbal, 61% scored 500 or over on math; 73% scored 400 or over on verbal, 87% scored 400 or over on math; 99% scored 300 or over on verbal, 100% scored 300 or over on math. 9% of freshmen who took ACT scored 30 or over on English, 3% scored 30 or over on math, 5% scored 30 or over on composite; 43% scored 24 or over on English, 34% scored 24 or over on math, 39% scored 24 or over on composite; 88% scored 18 or over on English, 84% scored 18 or over on math, 93% scored 18 or over on composite; 100% scored 12 or over on English, 100% scored 12 or over on math, 100% scored 12 or over on composite. 14% of accepted applicants took SAT; 98% took ACT. 80% of freshmen come from public schools.

**Undergraduate achievement:** 84% of fall 1991 freshmen returned for fall 1992 term. 60% of entering class graduated. 25% of students who completed a degree program immediately went on to graduate study.

**Foreign students:** 33 students are from out of the country. Countries represented include the Bahamas, Hong Kong, and Japan; 11 in all.

**PROGRAMS OF STUDY. Degrees:** B.A., B.Mus., B.S.

**Majors:** Accounting, Art, Art History/Appreciation, Biology, Business Management, Chemistry, Classics, Communications, Dietetics, Economics, Elementary Education, English, French, German, Government, History, Humanities, Liberal Studies, Liturgical Music, Mathematics, Mathematics/Computer Science, Medical Technology, Medieval Studies, Music, Natural Science, Nursing, Nutritional Sciences, Pastoral Ministry, Philosophy, Physics, Physics/Computer Science, Psychology, Religious Education, Social Sciences, Social Work, Sociology, Spanish, Theatre, Theology.

**Distribution of degrees:** The majors with the highest enrollment are elementary education, management, and liberal studies; classics, medieval studies, and physics have the lowest.

**Requirements:** General education requirement.

**Academic regulations:** Freshmen must maintain minimum 1.8 GPA; sophomores, juniors, seniors 2.0 GPA.

**Special:** Minors offered in most majors and in computer science, Greek, Latin, physical education, religious studies, and secondary education. Self-designed majors. Double majors. Dual degrees. Independent study. Accelerated study. Pass/fail grading option. Internships. Preprofessional programs in law, medicine, veterinary science, pharmacy, dentistry, theology, engineering, forestry, occupational therapy, and physical therapy. 3-1 dentistry program. 3-2 engineering programs with U of Minnesota at Minneapolis and Washington U. 3-2 occupational therapy program with Washington U. Member of Higher Education Consortium for Urban Affairs. Exchange program with St. Cloud State U and St. John's U. Teacher certification in early childhood, elementary, and secondary education. Exchange program abroad in Japan (Sophia U). Study abroad also in Austria, China, England, France, Greece, Ireland, Italy, and Spain. ROTC at St. John's U.

**Honors:** Honors program. Honor societies.

**Academic Assistance:** Nonremedial tutoring.

**STUDENT LIFE. Housing:** Students may live on or off campus. Women's dorms. School-owned/-operated apartments. Off-campus privately-owned housing. 80% of students live in college housing.

**Social atmosphere:** On campus, students gather at Willy's Pub, Sexton Commons, the Loft, Mary Commons, and Claire Lynch. Off campus, students head for Sal's Bar and Grill, the LaPlayette, Loso's, The Midi, and Bo Diddley's. The Student Administrative Board, student senate, Joint Events Council, Volunteers in Service to Others, and BACCHUS are influential campus groups. The most popular events of the year are the Watab Mixer, Pinestock, the Variety Show, the Vienna Waltz, the winter and spring formals, and Homecoming. "Hot topics on campus this year are cultural awareness (racial issues), sexual discrimination, and alcohol abuse. Our college and St. John's University are close-knit schools; everyone tries to help everyone else," reports the student newspaper.

**Services and counseling/handicapped student services:** Placement services. Health service. Counseling services for minority students. Personal and psychological counseling. Career and academic guidance services. Religious counseling. Physically disabled student services. Learning disabled services. Notetaking services. Tape recorders. Tutors. Reader services for the blind.

**Campus organizations:** Undergraduate student government. Student newspaper (Independent, published twice/month). Literary magazine. Yearbook. Radio station. Vocal and instrumental groups, social justice groups, commuter student group, debating, College Republicans, Young Democrats, academic, athletic, and service groups, 110 organizations in all.

**Religious organizations:** Campus Ministry, Christian Clowns, Pax Christi, Fellowship of Christian Athletes.

**Minority/foreign student organizations:** Minority Student Organization, Coalition for Black Cultural Awareness. International Student Club, international student newspaper.

**ATHLETICS. Physical education requirements:** Two semesters of physical education required.

**Intercollegiate competition:** 10% of students participate. Basketball (W), cross-country (W), diving (W), golf (W), soccer (W), softball (W), swimming (W), tennis (W), track (indoor) (W), track (outdoor) (W), track and field (indoor) (W), track and field (outdoor) (W), volleyball (W). Member of Minnesota Intercollegiate Athletic Association, NCAA Division III.

**Intramural and club sports:** 70% of students participate. Intramural badminton, basketball, broomball, soccer, softball, tennis, volleyball, water polo. Women's club Alpine skiing, crew, cycling, lacrosse, martial arts, Nordic skiing, rugby.

**ADMISSIONS. Academic basis for candidate selection** (in order of priority): Secondary school record, class rank, standardized test scores, essay, school's recommendation.

**Nonacademic basis for candidate selection:** Extracurricular participation is important. Character and personality and particular talent or ability are considered.

**Requirements:** Graduation from secondary school is required; GED is accepted. 17 units and the following program of study are recommended: 4 units of English, 3 units of math, 2 units of lab science, 2 units of foreign language, 2 units of social studies, 4 units of electives. Minimum composite ACT score of 19 (combined SAT score of 910), rank in top half of secondary school class, and minimum 2.8 GPA in college-preparatory courses recommended. Portfolio required of art program applicants. Audition required of music program applicants. Conditional admission possible for applicants not meeting standard requirements. SAT or ACT is required; PSAT may be substituted for SAT. Campus visit and interview recommended. Off-campus interviews available with an admissions representative.

**Procedure:** Take SAT or ACT by December of 12th year. Visit college for interview by January of 12th year. Suggest filing application by May 1; no deadline. Notification of admission on rolling basis. Reply is required prior to registration. $200 nonrefundable room deposit. Freshmen accepted in terms other than fall.

**Special programs:** Admission may be deferred indefinitely. Credit and/or placement may be granted through CEEB Advanced Placement exams for scores of 3 or higher. Credit and/or placement may be granted through CLEP subject exams. Credit and placement may be granted through challenge exams. Early entrance/early admission program. Concurrent enrollment program.

**Transfer students:** Transfer students accepted for terms other than fall. In fall 1992, 20% of all new students were transfers into all classes. 178 transfer applications were received, 166 were accepted. Application deadline is rolling for fall; rolling for spring. Minimum 2.5 GPA required. Lowest course grade accepted is "C." Maximum number of transferable credits is 79 semester hours. At least 45 semester hours must be completed at the college to receive degree.

**Admissions contact:** Mary Milbert, Director of Admissions. 612 363-5308, 800 544-1489.

**FINANCIAL AID. Available aid:** Pell grants, SEOG, state grants, school scholarships and grants, private scholarships, ROTC scholarships, academic merit scholarships, and aid for undergraduate foreign students. Perkins Loans (NDSL), PLUS, Stafford Loans (GSL), state loans, and SLS. Deferred payment plan.

**Financial aid statistics:** 26% of aid is not need-based. In 1992-93, 88% of all undergraduate applicants received aid; 88% of freshman applicants. Average amounts of aid awarded freshmen: Scholarships and grants, $6,268; loans, $3,695.

**Supporting data/closing dates:** FAFSA: Accepted on rolling basis. School's own aid application: Priority filing date is August 15; accepted on rolling basis. Income tax forms: Priority filing date is August 16. Notification of awards on rolling basis.

**Financial aid contact:** Jane Haugen, Director of Financial Aid. 612 363-5388.

**STUDENT EMPLOYMENT.** College Work/Study Program. Institutional employment. 45% of full-time undergraduates work on campus during school year. Students may expect to earn an average of $1,300 during school year. Off-campus part-time employment opportunities rated "fair."

**COMPUTER FACILITIES.** 300 IBM/IBM-compatible and Macintosh/Apple microcomputers; 200 are networked. Students may access Digital minicomputer/mainframe systems, BITNET, Internet. Residence halls may be equipped with stand-alone microcomputers, networked microcomputers, modems. Computer languages and software packages include BASIC, BMDP, C, COBOL, FORTRAN, LINDO, MINITAB, Pascal, SPSS; graphics, spreadsheet, word processing packages. Computer facilities are available to all students.

**Fees:** None.

**Hours:** 8 AM-midn.

**GRADUATE CAREER DATA.** Graduate school percentages: 5% enter law school. 5% enter medical school. 5% enter graduate business programs. 10% enter graduate arts and sciences programs. Highest graduate school enrollments: U of Minnesota at St. Paul. 50% of graduates choose careers in business and industry. Companies and businesses that hire graduates: Andersen Consulting, Deluxe, EDS, West Publishing.

**PROMINENT ALUMNI/AE.** Beth Dinndorf, vice-president, First Bank of Minneapolis; Patricia Schmitt-Mische, author and cofounder of Global Education Associates; Dr. Marion Cooney, professor of pathobiology.

# The College of St. Catherine

**St. Paul, MN 55105** **612 690-6000**

**1994-95 Costs.** Tuition: $12,224. Room & board: $4,440. Fees, books, misc. academic expenses (school's estimate): $700.

**Enrollment.** Undergraduates: 5 men, 1,742 women (full-time). Freshman class: 506 applicants, 477 accepted, 235 enrolled. Graduate enrollment: 52 men, 234 women.

**Test score averages/ranges.** Average SAT scores: 482 verbal, 489 math. Range of SAT scores of middle 50%: 340-540 verbal, 430-570 math. Average ACT scores: 22 English, 20 math, 22 composite. Range of ACT scores of middle 50%: 19-25 English, 18-24 math.

**Faculty.** 131 full-time; 100 part-time. 53% of faculty holds doctoral degree. Student/faculty ratio: 14 to 1.

**Selectivity rating.** Less competitive.

**PROFILE.** The College of St. Catherine, founded in 1905, is a church-affiliated, liberal arts institution. Its 110-acre campus is located in central St. Paul.

**Accreditation:** NCACS. Professionally accredited by the American Dietetic Association, the American Medical Association (CAHEA), the Council on Social Work Education, the National Association of Schools of Music, the National Council for Accreditation of Teacher Education, the National League for Nursing.
**Religious orientation:** The College of St. Catherine is affiliated with the Roman Catholic Church (Sisters of St. Joseph of Carondelet); four semesters of religion/theology required.
**Library:** Collections totaling over 225,000 volumes, 1,200 periodical subscriptions, and 15,000 microform items.
**Special facilities/museums:** Art gallery, theatre, recital hall, experimental psychology lab, language lab, observatory.
**Athletic facilities:** Gymnasium, swimming pool, weight room, softball field, tennis courts.

**STUDENT BODY. Undergraduate profile:** 80% are state residents; 40% are transfers. 2% Asian-American, 1% Black, 1% Hispanic, 1% Native American, 85% White, 10% Unknown. Average age of undergraduates is 25.
**Freshman profile:** 2% of freshmen who took SAT scored 700 or over on verbal, 4% scored 700 or over on math; 19% scored 600 or over on verbal, 17% scored 600 or over on math; 49% scored 500 or over on verbal, 40% scored 500 or over on math; 77% scored 400 or over on verbal, 79% scored 400 or over on math; 100% scored 300 or over on verbal, 100% scored 300 or over on math. 6% of freshmen who took ACT scored 30 or over on English, 2% scored 30 or over on math, 1% scored 30 or over on composite; 38% scored 24 or over on English, 26% scored 24 or over on math, 36% scored 24 or over on composite; 81% scored 18 or over on English, 79% scored 18 or over on math, 86% scored 18 or over on composite; 96% scored 12 or over on English, 100% scored 12 or over on math, 100% scored 12 or over on composite; 97% scored 6 or over on English. 22% of accepted applicants took SAT; 92% took ACT.
**Undergraduate achievement:** 68% of fall 1991 freshmen returned for fall 1992 term. 34% of entering class graduated. 35% of students who completed a degree program went on to graduate study within 10 years.
**Foreign students:** 46 students are from out of the country. Countries represented include Japan, Kenya, Malaysia, Singapore, Tanzania, and Uganda; 25 in all.

**PROGRAMS OF STUDY. Degrees:** B.A.
**Majors:** Art, Biological Science, Business Administration, Chemistry, Communications/Theatre, Economics, Elementary Education, English, Exercise Science/Nutrition, Family Consumer/Nutritional Sciences, French, General Science, History, Information Management, International Business/Economics, International Relations, Mathematics, Medical Technology, Music, Nursing, Occupational Therapy, Philosophy, Physical Education, Physical Education/Nutrition, Physical Education/Social Work, Physics, Political Science, Psychology, Secondary Education, Social Studies, Social Work, Sociology, Soviet/East European Studies, Spanish, Theology.
**Distribution of degrees:** The majors with the highest enrollment are nursing, elementary education, and business administration.
**Requirements:** General education requirement.
**Academic regulations:** Freshmen must maintain minimum 1.5 GPA; sophomores, 1.9 GPA; juniors, 2.0 GPA; seniors, 2.0 GPA.
**Special:** Minors offered in computer science, orthodox studies, physics, social welfare, and women's studies. Self-designed majors. Double majors. Dual degrees. Independent study. Internships. Cooperative education programs. Graduate school at which undergraduates may take graduate-level courses. Preprofessional programs in law, medicine, veterinary science, pharmacy, dentistry, optometry, engineering, and health fields. 3-2 engineering programs with U of Minnesota and Washington U. 3-2 forestry and environmental studies program with Duke U. Member of Associated Colleges of the Twin Cities Consortium. Exchange programs with Avila Coll, Coll of Saint Rose, Fontbonne Coll, and Mt. St. Mary's Coll. Teacher certification in early childhood, elementary, and secondary education. Certification in specific subject areas. Study abroad in Asian, European, and Latin American countries, and the former Soviet Republics. ROTC at Coll of St. Thomas.
**Honors:** Phi Beta Kappa. Honors program. Honor societies.
**Academic Assistance:** Remedial reading, writing, math, and study skills. Nonremedial tutoring.

**STUDENT LIFE. Housing:** Students may live on or off campus. Women's dorms. School-owned/operated apartments. 39% of students live in college housing.
**Services and counseling/handicapped student services:** Placement services. Health service. Women's center. Day care. Intercultural Student Coordinator. Counseling services for minority and older students. Personal and psychological counseling. Career and academic guidance services. Religious counseling. Physically disabled student services. Learning disabled services. Notetaking services. Tape recorders. Tutors. Reader services for the blind.
**Campus organizations:** Undergraduate student government. Student newspaper (Catherine Wheel, published twice/month). Literary magazine. Yearbook. Choral groups, band, drama group, Thomas Club, Young Democrats, College Republicans, volunteer groups, athletic, departmental, and special-interest groups, 25 organizations in all.
**Religious organizations:** Campus Ministry.
**Minority/foreign student organizations:** Minority student group. International Student Association, Friendship Families, Intercultural Student Organization, International Friends Program.

**ATHLETICS. Physical education requirements:** Two semesters of physical education required.
**Intercollegiate competition:** 6% of students participate. Cross-country (W), diving (W), golf (W), softball (W), swimming (W), tennis (W), track (indoor) (W), track (outdoor) (W), track and field (indoor) (W), track and field (outdoor) (W), volleyball (W). Member of MIAC, NCAA Division III.
**Intramural and club sports:** 12% of students participate. Intramural aerobics, golf, softball, tennis, volleyball.

**ADMISSIONS. Academic basis for candidate selection** (in order of priority): Secondary school record, standardized test scores, class rank, school's recommendation.
**Nonacademic basis for candidate selection:** Character and personality and extracurricular participation are considered.
**Requirements:** Graduation from secondary school is required; GED is accepted. No specific distribution of secondary school units required. SAT or ACT is required. PSAT is recommended. Campus visit and interview recommended. Off-campus interviews available with an alumni representative.
**Procedure:** Take SAT or ACT by fall of 12th year. Notification of admission on rolling basis. Reply is required by May 1. $100 tuition deposit, refundable until May 1. $100 room deposit, refundable until May 1. Freshmen accepted in terms other than fall.
**Special programs:** Admission may be deferred one year. Credit and/or placement may be granted through CEEB Advanced Placement exams for scores of 3 or higher. Credit and/or placement may be granted through CLEP general and subject exams. Concurrent enrollment program.
**Transfer students:** Transfer students accepted for terms other than fall. In fall 1992, 40% of all new students were transfers into all classes. 600 transfer applications were received, 580 were accepted. Application deadline is rolling for fall; rolling for spring. Minimum 2.0 GPA required. Lowest course grade accepted is "C-." At least 48 semester hours must be completed at the college to receive degree.
**Admissions contact:** Mary Docken, M.A., Director of Admissions. 612 690-6505.

**FINANCIAL AID. Available aid:** Pell grants, SEOG, state scholarships and grants, school scholarships and grants, private scholarships and grants, ROTC scholarships, academic merit scholarships, and aid for undergraduate foreign students. Perkins Loans (NDSL), PLUS, Stafford Loans (GSL), NSL, state loans, and SLS. Deferred payment plan.
**Financial aid statistics:** In 1992-93, 68% of all undergraduate applicants received aid; 96% of freshman applicants. Average amounts of aid awarded freshmen: Scholarships and grants, $7,453; loans, $2,325.
**Supporting data/closing dates:** FAFSA/FAF/FFS: Priority filing date is April 1. School's own aid application: Priority filing date is April 1. Notification of awards begins March 1.
**Financial aid contact:** Susan Brady, M.A., Director of Financial Aid. 612 690-6540.

**STUDENT EMPLOYMENT.** College Work/Study Program. Institutional employment. 39% of full-time undergraduates work on campus during school year. Students may expect to earn an average of $1,375 during school year. Off-campus part-time employment opportunities rated "good."

**COMPUTER FACILITIES.** 65 IBM/IBM-compatible and Macintosh/Apple microcomputers. Students may access Digital minicomputer/mainframe systems. Residence halls may be equipped with networked terminals. Computer languages and software packages include BASIC, COBOL, FORTRAN, Pascal, Prolog; 11 in all. Computer facilities are available to all students.
**Fees:** None.
**Hours:** 24 hours.

**GRADUATE CAREER DATA.** Highest graduate school enrollments: U of Minnesota. Companies and businesses that hire graduates: 3M, Honeywell, Northern States Power.

**PROMINENT ALUMNI/AE.** Abigail Quigley McCarthy, author/activist/teacher, *One Woman Lost*; Rosemary Rader, author/theologian/professor, Arizona State U; Mary Palcich Sinclair, activist, named "Woman of the Year" 1984 by *Ms.* magazine; Mary Madonna Ashton, state commissioner of health, Minnesota; Adhiambo Odaga, first Rhodes Scholar from Kenya.

# College of St. Scholastica

**Duluth, MN 55811** **218 723-6000**

**1994-95 Costs.** Tuition: $11,844. Room & board: $3,696. Fees, books, misc. academic expenses (school's estimate): $525.

**Enrollment.** Undergraduates: 380 men, 970 women (full-time). Freshman class: 647 applicants, 596 accepted, 278 enrolled. Graduate enrollment: 82 men, 131 women.

**Test score averages/ranges.** Average SAT scores: 443 verbal, 487 math. Range of SAT scores of middle 50%: 400-540 verbal, 440-540 math. Average ACT scores: 23 English, 22 math, 23 composite. Range of ACT scores of middle 50%: 20-24 composite.

**Faculty.** 121 full-time; 53 part-time. 54% of faculty holds doctoral degree. Student/faculty ratio: 12 to 1.

**Selectivity rating.** Less competitive.

**PROFILE.** The College of St. Scholastica, founded in 1912, is a private, church-affiliated college. Programs are offered through the Divisions of Behavioral Arts and Sciences, Health Sciences, Humanities, and Natural Sciences. Its 160-acre campus is located in a residential area of Duluth.

**Accreditation:** NCACS. Professionally accredited by the American Medical Association (CAHEA), the American Physical Therapy Association, the Council on Social Work Education, the National League for Nursing.
**Religious orientation:** College of St. Scholastica is affiliated with the Roman Catholic Church (Benedictine Sisters); one quarter of religion required.
**Library:** Collections totaling over 133,342 volumes and 779 periodical subscriptions.
**Athletic facilities:** Gymnasium, basketball, racquetball, tennis, and volleyball courts, sauna, baseball, soccer, and softball fields, ice rink, weight room.

**STUDENT BODY. Undergraduate profile:** 87% are state residents; 29% are transfers. 1% Asian-American, 1% Black, 1% Hispanic, 1% Native American, 94% White, 2% Other. Average age of undergraduates is 20.
**Freshman profile:** 5% of accepted applicants took SAT; 90% took ACT.
**Undergraduate achievement:** 76% of fall 1992 freshmen returned for fall 1993 term. 20% of students who completed a degree program immediately went on to graduate study.
**Foreign students:** 11 students are from out of the country. Countries represented include Canada, Germany, and Japan.

**PROGRAMS OF STUDY. Degrees:** B.A.
**Majors:** Accounting, Biology, Chemistry, Clinical Laboratory Science, Communication, Computer Science Information Systems, Dietetics, Elementary Education, English, Exercise Science, Health Information Administration, Health Science, History, Home Economics, Humanities, International Management, Management, Mathematics, Music, Natural Sciences, Nursing, Occupational Therapy, Pastoral Ministry, Physical Therapy, Psychology, Religious Studies, Social Work, Sociology, Youth Ministry.
**Distribution of degrees:** The majors with the highest enrollment are nursing, management, and health information administration; chemistry, home economics, and sociology have the lowest.
**Requirements:** General education requirement.
**Academic regulations:** Minimum 2.0 GPA must be maintained.
**Special:** Minors offered in some majors and in American Indian studies, foreign language, peace and justice, philosophy, speech, theatre, and women's studies. Courses offered in physics. Gerontology program. Alternative Education Program grants credit for college-level learning. Professional certificate programs in health information administration, medical technology, nursing, physical therapy, and social work. Self-designed majors. Double majors. Independent study. Pass/fail grading option. Internships. Graduate school at which undergraduates may take graduate-level courses. Preprofessional programs in law, medicine, veterinary science, pharmacy, and dentistry. Other semester-away programs available. Exchange programs with U of Minnesota-Duluth and U of Wisconsin-Superior. Teacher certification in early childhood, elementary, secondary, and bilingual/bicultural education. Certification in specific subject areas. Exchange programs abroad in Costa Rica and Ireland. AFROTC at U of Minnesota at Duluth.
**Honors:** Honor societies.
**Academic Assistance:** Remedial writing, math, and study skills. Nonremedial tutoring.

**STUDENT LIFE. Housing:** Students may live on or off campus. School-owned/operated apartments. Single-parent housing. 31% of students live in college housing.
**Social atmosphere:** According to the editor of the student newspaper, "The atmosphere of the campus is almost family-like. It's a small together student body and faculty." The F.U.B.A.R. organization is the most influential on campus. The group attends athletic events and promotes school patriotism. Favorite gathering spots include Boomer's Bar, Grandma's Saloon and Deli, Fitger's on the Lake, Miller Hill Mall, Brass Phoenix, the Subway, the union games room, and the Sweat Box.
**Services and counseling/handicapped student services:** Placement services. Health service. Women's center. Day care. Counseling services for minority, veteran, and older students. Birth control, personal, and psychological counseling. Career and academic guidance services. Religious counseling. Physically disabled student services. Learning disabled services. Notetaking services. Tape recorders. Tutors. Reader services for the blind.
**Campus organizations:** Undergraduate student government. Student newspaper (Cable, published once/week). Yearbook. Abbey Minstrels, concert choir, Mod Minstrels, theatre, Danceline, 41 organizations in all.
**Religious organizations:** Peer Ministry, Campus Ministry, Youth Ministry Club.
**Minority/foreign student organizations:** American Indian Studies Association. International Club.

**ATHLETICS. Physical education requirements:** None.
**Intercollegiate competition:** 10% of students participate. Baseball (M), basketball (M,W), cheerleading (W), cross-country (M,W), golf (M,W), ice hockey (M), soccer (M,W), softball (W), tennis (M,W), volleyball (W). Member of MWAC, NAIA, NCAA Division III.
**Intramural and club sports:** 65% of students participate. Intramural basketball, flag football, floor hockey, soccer, racquetball, volleyball, Wiffle ball. Men's club Nordic skiing. Women's club Nordic skiing, rugby.

**ADMISSIONS. Academic basis for candidate selection** (in order of priority): Class rank, standardized test scores, secondary school record, school's recommendation.
**Nonacademic basis for candidate selection:** Character and personality, extracurricular participation, particular talent or ability, geographical distribution, and alumni/ae relationship are considered.
**Requirements:** Graduation from secondary school is required; GED is accepted. No specific distribution of secondary school units required. Audition required of music program applicants. Conditional admission possible for applicants not meeting standard requirements. ACT is required; SAT may be substituted. PSAT is recommended. Campus visit and interview recommended. Off-campus interviews available with an admissions representative.
**Procedure:** Take SAT or ACT by January of 12th year. Suggest filing application by November 1; no deadline. Notification of admission on rolling basis. Reply is required within 30 days of acceptance or when college offers the applicant financial aid. $100 nonrefundable tuition deposit. $75 room deposit, refundable until May 1. Freshmen accepted in terms other than fall.
**Special programs:** Admission may be deferred one year. Credit and/or placement may be granted through CEEB Advanced Placement exams for scores of 3 or higher. Credit and/or placement may be granted through CLEP general and subject exams. Credit and placement may be granted through challenge exams and military and life experience. Early entrance/early admission program. Concurrent enrollment program.
**Transfer students:** Transfer students accepted for terms other than fall. In fall 1993, 29% of all new students were transfers into all classes. 171 transfer applications were received, 164 were accepted. Application deadline is rolling for fall; rolling for spring. Minimum 2.0 GPA required. Lowest course grade accepted is "C." Maximum number of transferable credits is 144 quarter hours. At least 48 quarter hours must be completed at the college to receive degree.
**Admissions contact:** Becky Urbanski-Junkert, M.A., Vice President of Admissions and Student Financial Planning. 218 723-6046.

**FINANCIAL AID. Available aid:** Pell grants, SEOG, Federal Nursing Student Scholarships, state scholarships and grants, school scholarships and grants, private scholarships and grants, ROTC scholarships, and academic merit scholarships. Perkins Loans (NDSL), PLUS, Stafford Loans (GSL), NSL, state loans, school loans, and SLS. Family tuition reduction.
**Financial aid statistics:** 11% of aid is not need-based. In 1993-94, 93% of all undergraduate applicants received aid; 90% of freshman applicants. Average amounts of aid awarded freshmen: Scholarships and grants, $4,647; loans, $2,750.
**Supporting data/closing dates:** FAFSA/FAF: Priority filing date is March 1. FFS: Priority filing date is June 1. School's own aid application: Priority filing date is March 1. Notification of awards begins March 1.
**Financial aid contact:** Tim Rutka, Associate Dean for Student Financial Planning. 218 723-6047.

**STUDENT EMPLOYMENT.** College Work/Study Program. Institutional employment. 27% of full-time undergraduates work on campus during school year. Students may expect to earn an average of $1,275 during school year. Off-campus part-time employment opportunities rated "good."

**COMPUTER FACILITIES.** 85 IBM/IBM-compatible and Macintosh/Apple microcomputers; 82 are networked. Students may access IBM minicomputer/mainframe systems, BITNET, Internet. Residence halls may be equipped with stand-alone microcomputers. Client/LAN operating systems include Apple/Macintosh, DOS, UNIX/XENIX/AIX, Microsoft, Novell. Computer languages and software packages include AppleWorks, BASIC, C, COBOL, dBASE, Paradox, Pascal, Quattro, RPG, Turbo C, WordPerfect; 35 in all. Computer facilities are available to all students.
**Fees:** None.
**Hours:** 8 AM-midn. (M-Th); 8 AM-5 PM (F); 9 AM-5 PM (Sa); 2 PM-10 PM (Su).

**GRADUATE CAREER DATA.** Graduate school percentages: 1% enter law school. 2% enter medical school. 1% enter graduate business programs. 1% enter graduate arts and sciences programs. 11% of graduates choose careers in business and industry.

**PROMINENT ALUMNI/AE.** Katherine (Kye) Middleton Anderson, CEO, Medical Graphics Corp.; John Olund, soloist, Waverly Consort, New York City; Dr. Susan Kramer, head of research, Genentech Corp.; Mary Jean Burich LeTendre, director of Title IX, U.S. Department of Education; Dr. Marilyn Koering, professor of anatomy, George Washington U.

# Concordia College (Moorhead)

**Moorhead, MN 56562** **218 299-4000**

**1994-95 Costs.** Tuition: $10,110. Room & board: $3,165. Fees, books, misc. academic expenses (school's estimate): $500.
**Enrollment.** Undergraduates: 1,151 men, 1,766 women (full-time). Freshman class: 2,007 applicants, 1,806 accepted, 849 enrolled.
**Test score averages/ranges.** Average SAT scores: 490 verbal, 541 math. Range of SAT scores of middle 50%: 430-570 verbal, 465-610 math. Average ACT scores: 24 composite. Range of ACT scores of middle 50%: 21-27 composite.
**Faculty.** 186 full-time; 70 part-time. 63% of faculty holds doctoral degree. Student/faculty ratio: 15 to 1.
**Selectivity rating.** Competitive.

**PROFILE.** Concordia, founded in 1891, is a church-affiliated, liberal arts college. Its 120-acre campus is located in a residential area of Moorhead.

**Accreditation:** NCACS. Professionally accredited by the American Dietetic Association, the Council on Social Work Education, the National Association of Schools of Music, the National Council for Accreditation of Teacher Education, the National League for Nursing.
**Religious orientation:** Concordia College (Moorhead) is affiliated with the Evangelical Lutheran Church in America; two semesters of religion required.
**Library:** Collections totaling over 280,000 volumes, and 1,500 periodical subscriptions.
**Special facilities/museums:** Art gallery, language lab, linear accelerator, proton accelerator, microparticle accelerator.
**Athletic facilities:** Swimming pool, track, basketball and tennis courts, baseball, football, intramural, soccer, and softball fields, gymnasium, indoor track, indoor tennis courts, wrestling room.

**STUDENT BODY. Undergraduate profile:** 63% are state residents; 11% are transfers. 2% Asian-American, .5% Black, .5% Hispanic, 1% Native American, 96% White. Average age of undergraduates is 20.
**Freshman profile:** 3% of freshmen who took SAT scored 700 or over on verbal, 7% scored 700 or over on math; 13% scored 600 or over on verbal, 30% scored 600 or over on math; 47% scored 500 or over on verbal, 63% scored 500 or over on math; 81% scored 400 or over on verbal, 84% scored 400 or over on math; 94% scored 300 or over on verbal, 94% scored 300 or over on math. 19% of accepted applicants took SAT; 89% took ACT. 95% of freshmen come from public schools.

**Undergraduate achievement:** 83% of fall 1992 freshmen returned for fall 1993 term. 59% of entering class graduated. 20% of students who completed a degree program immediately went on to graduate study.
**Foreign students:** 111 students are from out of the country. Countries represented include Canada, China, Hong Kong, Norway, Sri Lanka, and the former Yugoslav Republics; 29 in all.

**PROGRAMS OF STUDY. Degrees:** B.A., B.M.
**Majors:** Accounting, Advertising/Public Relations, Art, Art History, Biology, Broadcasting/Print Journalism, Business Administration, Business Education, Chemistry, Classics, Communications, Computer Science, Economics, Education, English, English Writing, Environmental Studies, Food Sciences/Human Nutrition, French, German, Health Care Management, History, History/Political Science, Home Economics, Humanities, International Business Management, International Relations, Latin, Mathematics, Media Production/Management, Medical Technology, Music, Music Education, Music Theory, Nursing, Organizational Communications, Philosophy, Physical Education/Health/Recreation, Physics, Political Science, Psychology, Religion, Russian Studies, Social Work, Sociology, Spanish, Speech Communication/Theatre Art.
**Distribution of degrees:** The majors with the highest enrollment are business administration, communications, and psychology; business education and medical technology have the lowest.
**Requirements:** General education requirement.
**Academic regulations:** Freshmen must maintain minimum 1.70 GPA; sophomores, 1.80 GPA; juniors, 1.90 GPA; seniors, 2.00 GPA.
**Special:** Minors offered in most majors and in child development/family living, clothing/textiles, earth science, Greek, library science, and women's studies. Interdisciplinary studies. Double majors. Independent study. Pass/fail grading option. Internships. Cooperative education programs. Graduate school at which undergraduates may take graduate-level courses. Preprofessional programs in law, medicine, veterinary science, dentistry, theology, optometry, architecture, occupational therapy, and sports medicine. 3-1 program with St. Luke's Hospital Sch of Medical Tech. 3-2 architecture and engineering programs with North Dakota State U and Washington U. Member of Tri-College University Consortium. Washington Semester. Urban Studies Program (Chicago). Teacher certification in elementary and secondary education. Certification in specific subject areas. Study abroad in African, Asian, and European countries and in Mexico. ROTC and AFROTC.
**Honors:** Honors program. Honor societies.
**Academic Assistance:** Remedial reading, writing, math, and study skills. Nonremedial tutoring.

**STUDENT LIFE. Housing:** All freshmen and sophomores must live on campus unless living with family. Coed, women's, and men's dorms. School-owned/operated apartments. 59% of students live in college housing.
**Services and counseling/handicapped student services:** Placement services. Health service. Women's center. Day care. Counseling services for minority and older students. Birth control, personal, and psychological counseling. Career and academic guidance services. Religious counseling. Physically disabled student services. Learning disabled services. Notetaking services. Tutors. Reader services for the blind.
**Campus organizations:** Undergraduate student government. Student newspaper (Concordian, published once/week). Literary magazine. Yearbook. Radio and TV stations. Concert choir and band, orchestra, symphonic and other bands, freshman and chapel choirs, annual music festival, homecoming, and family weekend committee, intercollegiate debating, forensics, theatre company, political groups, volunteer service organization, departmental and special-interest groups, 150 organizations in all.
**Religious organizations:** Bread and Cheese Study Group, Fellowship of Christian Athletes, Koinonia, Mathetai, Spirit Song Promotions, Sunday Night Discipleship, Clown Troupe, outreach teams, Church Youth Day Committee, Christian Scholar Day Committee, White Earth Ministries.
**Minority/foreign student organizations:** Harambee Weuse, Indian Awareness. International Student Organization, Scandinavian club.

**ATHLETICS. Physical education requirements:** One semester of physical education required.
**Intercollegiate competition:** 15% of students participate. Baseball (M), basketball (M,W), cheerleading (M,W), cross-country (M,W), football (M), golf (M,W), ice hockey (M), soccer (M,W), softball (W), tennis (M,W), track and field (indoor) (M,W), track and field (outdoor) (M,W), volleyball (W), wrestling (M). Member of Minnesota Intercollegiate Athletic Conference, NCAA Division III.
**Intramural and club sports:** 45% of students participate. Intramural badminton, baseball, basketball, flag football, golf, racquetball, softball, swimming, table tennis, tennis, volleyball, walleyball, water basketball. Men's club martial arts, Nordic skiing, rugby, volleyball. Women's club martial arts, Nordic skiing.

**ADMISSIONS. Academic basis for candidate selection** (in order of priority): Secondary school record, class rank, standardized test scores, school's recommendation.
**Nonacademic basis for candidate selection:** Character and personality are emphasized. Extracurricular participation and alumni/ae relationship are important. Particular talent or ability and geographical distribution are considered.
**Requirements:** Graduation from secondary school is required; GED is accepted. 14 units and the following program of study are recommended: 4 units of English, 3 units of math, 3 units of science, 2 units of foreign language, 2 units of social studies. Conditional admission possible for applicants not meeting standard requirements. ACT is required; SAT may be substituted. PSAT is recommended. Campus visit and interview recommended. Off-campus interviews available with an admissions representative.
**Procedure:** Take SAT or ACT by November of 12th year. Suggest filing application by February; no deadline. Notification of admission on rolling basis. No set date by which applicant must accept offer. $100 nonrefundable tuition deposit. $100 nonrefundable room deposit. Freshmen accepted in terms other than fall.
**Special programs:** Admission may be deferred one year. Credit and/or placement may be granted through CEEB Advanced Placement exams for scores of 3 or higher. Credit may be granted through CLEP subject exams. Placement may be granted through life experience. Credit and placement may be granted through challenge exams and military experience. Concurrent enrollment program.
**Transfer students:** Transfer students accepted for terms other than fall. In fall 1993, 11% of all new students were transfers into all classes. 217 transfer applications were received, 161 were accepted. Application deadline is rolling for fall; rolling for spring. Minimum 2.0 GPA required. Lowest course grade accepted is "C." At least 32 semester hours must be completed at the college to receive degree.
**Admissions contact:** Lee E. Johnson, Director of Admissions. 218 299-3004.

**FINANCIAL AID. Available aid:** Pell grants, SEOG, state scholarships and grants, school scholarships and grants, private scholarships and grants, ROTC scholarships, academic merit scholarships, and aid for undergraduate foreign students. Perkins Loans (NDSL), PLUS, Stafford Loans (GSL), state loans, school loans, private loans, and SLS. AMS and Tuition Management Systems.
**Financial aid statistics:** 7% of aid is not need-based. In 1993-94, 83% of all undergraduate applicants received aid; 82% of freshman applicants. Average amounts of aid awarded freshmen: Scholarships and grants, $5,011; loans, $3,586.
**Supporting data/closing dates:** FAFSA: Priority filing date is April 1; accepted on rolling basis. School's own aid application: Accepted on rolling basis. Notification of awards on rolling basis.
**Financial aid contact:** Dale Thornton, Director of Financial Aid. 218 299-3010.

**STUDENT EMPLOYMENT.** College Work/Study Program. Institutional employment. 58% of full-time undergraduates work on campus during school year. Students may expect to earn an average of $600 during school year. Off-campus part-time employment opportunities rated "good."

**COMPUTER FACILITIES.** 100 IBM/IBM-compatible and Macintosh/Apple microcomputers; 75 are networked. Students may access Digital minicomputer/mainframe systems, BITNET, Internet. Client/LAN operating systems include Apple/Macintosh, DOS, UNIX/XENIX/AIX, LocalTalk/AppleTalk, Novell. Computer languages and software packages include BASIC, C, COBOL, FORTRAN, LISP, Pascal; wide variety of database, spreadsheet, statistical, utility, and word processing packages; 10 in all. Computer facilities are available to all students.
**Fees:** Computer fee is included in tuition/fees.
**Hours:** 6 AM-2 AM.

**GRADUATE CAREER DATA.** Graduate school percentages: 2% enter law school. 3% enter medical school. 1% enter dental school. 1% enter graduate business programs. 10% enter graduate arts and sciences programs. 1% enter theological school/seminary. Highest graduate school enrollments: Luther Northwestern Seminary, U of Minnesota, U of North Dakota. 40% of graduates choose careers in business and industry. Companies and businesses that hire graduates: Cargill, Deluxe Check Printers, Ernst & Young, Fargo Electronics, Minnesota Mutual, St. Paul Co.

**PROMINENT ALUMNI/AE.** Lowell Almen, editor, *The Lutheran Standard;* Dr. Charles Halgrimson, pioneer kidney transplant surgeon; Guy Doud, 1986 National Teacher of the Year; Dr. Gabriel Hauge, chairperson of the board, Manufacturers and Hanover Trust Company; Norman Lorentzsen, retired CEO, Burlington Northern.

# Concordia College (St. Paul)

**St. Paul, MN 55104-5494 — 612 641-8278**

**1994-95 Costs.** Tuition: $10,500. Room & board: $3,750. Fees, books, misc. academic expenses (school's estimate): $450.
**Enrollment.** Undergraduates: 476 men, 573 women (full-time). Freshman class: 281 applicants, 266 accepted, 139 enrolled. 4 women.
**Test score averages/ranges.** Average ACT scores: 19 English, 20 math, 20 composite. Range of ACT scores of middle 50%: 16-23 English, 17-23 math.
**Faculty.** 59 full-time; 74 part-time. 75% of faculty holds doctoral degree. Student/faculty ratio: 15 to 1.
**Selectivity rating.** Less competitive.

**PROFILE.** Concordia, founded in 1893, is a church-affiliated, liberal arts college. Its campus is located in the Midway district of St. Paul.

**Accreditation:** NCACS. Professionally accredited by the National Council for Accreditation of Teacher Education.
**Religious orientation:** Concordia College (St. Paul) is affiliated with the Lutheran Church-Missouri Synod; three terms of religion required.
**Library:** Collections totaling over 112,852 volumes, 911 periodical subscriptions, and 10,793 microform items.
**Special facilities/museums:** Museum.
**Athletic facilities:** Gymnasium, baseball, soccer, and softball fields, weight room, badminton, basketball, indoor tennis, racquetball, and volleyball courts, climbing wall.

**STUDENT BODY. Undergraduate profile:** 85% are state residents; 64% are transfers. 5% Asian-American, 5% Black, 1% Hispanic, 1% Native American, 88% White. Average age of undergraduates is 24.
**Freshman profile:** 99% of accepted applicants took ACT. 81% of freshmen come from public schools.
**Undergraduate achievement:** 63% of fall 1992 freshmen returned for fall 1993 term. 27% of entering class graduated. 3% of students who completed a degree program immediately went on to graduate study.
**Foreign students:** Four students are from out of the country. Four countries represented in all.

**PROGRAMS OF STUDY. Degrees:** B.A.
**Majors:** Accounting, Art, Bible, Biology, Communications, Director of Christian Education, Director of Evangelism, Director of Parish Music, English, Environmental Science, Family Studies, Finance, History, Literature, Management, Music, Natural Science, Organizational Management/Communication, Psychology, Public Policy, Social Science, Teacher Education.
**Distribution of degrees:** The majors with the highest enrollment are organization management, education, and psychology.

**Requirements:** General education requirement.
**Academic regulations:** Minimum 2.0 GPA must be maintained.
**Special:** Students may take two minors in place of major. Associate's degrees offered. Self-designed majors. Independent study. Pass/fail grading option. Internships. Graduate school at which undergraduates may take graduate-level courses. Preprofessional programs in law, medicine, veterinary science, pharmacy, dentistry, theology, and optometry. Member of Higher Education Consortium for Urban Affairs; cross-registration possible. Teacher certification in early childhood, elementary, and secondary education. Certification in specific subject areas. Study abroad in England, Mexico, and Scandinavian countries. ROTC and NROTC at U of Minnesota. AFROTC at U of St. Thomas.
**Academic Assistance:** Remedial reading, writing, math, and study skills. Nonremedial tutoring.

**STUDENT LIFE. Housing:** All unmarried students under age 21 must live on campus unless living near campus with relatives. 54% of students live in college housing.
**Social atmosphere:** Ganglehoff, student union, Chi Chi's, O'Garo's, Herges, Motor Oil Coffee Shop, and Tracy 1-Stop are popular hang-outs. Student senate, CREW, Amnesty International, and the student union are influential on student life. Homecoming, CIT basketball tournament, coffeehouse bands, blood drives, and movie nights are favorite social events. The social and cultural life on and off campus is growing, according to the editor of the student newspaper. "The area around our campus provides a host of activities for the students."
**Services and counseling/handicapped student services:** Placement services. Health service. Day care. Counseling services for minority, veteran, and older students. Personal and psychological counseling. Career and academic guidance services. Religious counseling. Physically disabled student services. Learning disabled services. Notetaking services. Tape recorders. Tutors. Reader services for the blind.
**Campus organizations:** Undergraduate student government. Student newspaper (Sword, published five times/quarter). Yearbook. Choir, band, orchestra, drama club.
**Minority/foreign student organizations:** UMOJA black student organization. Southeast Asian student group, international student group.

**ATHLETICS. Physical education requirements:** Four terms of physical education required.
**Intercollegiate competition:** 19% of students participate. Baseball (M), basketball (M,W), cheerleading (W), cross-country (M,W), football (M), soccer (M,W), softball (W), tennis (M), volleyball (W). Member of NAIA, Upper Midwest Athletic Conference.
**Intramural and club sports:** 23% of students participate. Intramural basketball, bowling, flag football, golf, softball, volleyball. Women's club cheerleading, soccer.

**ADMISSIONS. Academic basis for candidate selection** (in order of priority): Secondary school record, class rank, standardized test scores, school's recommendation, essay.
**Nonacademic basis for candidate selection:** Character and personality are emphasized. Particular talent or ability is important. Extracurricular participation and alumni/ae relationship are considered.
**Requirements:** Graduation from secondary school is required; GED is accepted. No specific distribution of secondary school units required. Electives should include 1 unit of fine arts and 1 unit of health/physical education. Minimum 2.0 GPA required. Academic Development Program for applicants not normally admissible. ACT is required; SAT may be substituted. Campus visit and interview recommended. Off-campus interviews available with admissions and alumni representatives.
**Procedure:** Suggest filing application by August 15; no deadline. Notification of admission on rolling basis. $100 tuition deposit, refundable until May 1. $75 room deposit, refundable until August 1. Freshmen accepted in terms other than fall.
**Special programs:** Admission may be deferred. Credit and/or placement may be granted through CEEB Advanced Placement exams for scores of 3 or higher. Credit and/or placement may be granted through CLEP general and subject exams. Credit and placement may be granted through Regents College, ACT PEP, DANTES, and challenge exams and military and life experience. Early entrance/early admission program. Concurrent enrollment program.
**Transfer students:** Transfer students accepted for terms other than fall. In fall 1993, 64% of all new students were transfers into all classes. 417 transfer applications were received, 325 were accepted. Application deadline is two weeks prior to beginning of term for fall; two weeks prior to beginning of term for spring. Minimum 2.0 GPA required. Lowest course grade accepted is "D." Maximum number of transferable credits is 108 quarter hours from a two-year school and 144 quarter hours from a four-year school. At least 48 quarter hours must be completed at the college to receive degree.
**Admissions contact:** Tim Utter, Director of Admissions. 612 641-8231.

**FINANCIAL AID. Available aid:** Pell grants, SEOG, state scholarships and grants, school scholarships and grants, private scholarships and grants, and academic merit scholarships. Perkins Loans (NDSL), PLUS, Stafford Loans (GSL), state loans, private loans, and SLS. AMS and Tuition Management Systems.
**Financial aid statistics:** In 1993-94, 89% of all undergraduate applicants received aid; 95% of freshman applicants. Average amounts of aid awarded freshmen: Scholarships and grants, $6,811; loans, $3,067.
**Supporting data/closing dates:** FAFSA: Priority filing date is March 15. School's own aid application: Priority filing date is April 15. Income tax forms: Priority filing date is May 1. Notification of awards on rolling basis.
**Financial aid contact:** Diane Borchardt, Director of Financial Aid. 612 641-8209.

**STUDENT EMPLOYMENT.** College Work/Study Program. Institutional employment. 30% of full-time undergraduates work on campus during school year. Students may expect to earn an average of $2,000 during school year. Freshmen are discouraged from working during their first term. Off-campus part-time employment opportunities rated "good."

**COMPUTER FACILITIES.** 38 IBM/IBM-compatible and Macintosh/Apple microcomputers; 30 are networked. Students may access Digital minicomputer/mainframe systems. Client/LAN operating systems include Apple/Macintosh, DOS, DEC, LocalTalk/AppleTalk. Computer languages and software packages include BASIC, Pascal; 12 in all. Computer facilities are available to all students.
**Fees:** Computer fee is included in tuition/fees.
**Hours:** 8 AM-11 PM.

**GRADUATE CAREER DATA.** Graduate school percentages: 2% enter medical school. 3% enter theological school/seminary. Highest graduate school enrollments: Concordia Seminary-Fort Wayne, Concordia Seminary-St. Louis, U of Minnesota.

# Crown College

**St. Bonifacius, MN 55375-9001 612 446-4100**

**1994-95 Costs.** Tuition: $7,650. Room: $1,850. Board: $1,850. Fees, books, misc. academic expenses (school's estimate): $925.
**Enrollment.** Undergraduates: 209 men, 207 women (full-time). Freshman class: 183 applicants, 180 accepted, 86 enrolled.
**Test score averages/ranges.** Average ACT scores: 20 composite. Range of ACT scores of middle 50%: 17-23 composite.
**Faculty.** 22 full-time; 37 part-time. 32% of faculty holds highest degree in specific field. Student/faculty ratio: 13 to 1.
**Selectivity rating.** Less competitive.

**PROFILE.** Crown College, founded in 1916, is a private, bible college and in 1992 changed its name from Saint Paul Bible College. Its 196-acre campus is located in St. Bonifacius, 20 miles west of Minneapolis.

**Accreditation:** AABC, NCACS.
**Religious orientation:** Crown College is affiliated with the Christian and Missionary Alliance; 30 credits of Bible and theology required.
**Library:** Collections totaling over 99,000 volumes, 320 periodical subscriptions, and 70,000 microform items.
**Special facilities/museums:** Language lab.
**Athletic facilities:** Gymnasium, weight room, baseball, softball, football fields, cross-country course, tennis courts.

**STUDENT BODY. Undergraduate profile:** 59% are state residents; 28% are transfers. 6% Asian-American, 1% Black, 1% Hispanic, 1% Native American, 91% White.
**Freshman profile:** 20% of freshmen who took ACT scored 24 or over on composite; 71% scored 18 or over on composite; 100% scored 12 or over on composite. 6% of accepted applicants took SAT; 94% took ACT.
**Foreign students:** 11 students are from out of the country. Countries represented include Brazil, Canada, Japan, Korea, Liberia, and Mexico.

**PROGRAMS OF STUDY. Degrees:** B.A., B.Mus.Ed., B.S., B.S.Church Mus., B.S.Miss.
**Majors:** Biblical/Theological Studies, Business Administration, Business Administration/Sports and Fitness Management, Christian Education, Church Music, Church Music/Ministries, Elementary Education, English, English Education, Family/Child Development, History, History/Pre-Counseling, History/Pre-Seminary, History/Secondary Education, Linguistics, Music Education, Pastoral Ministries, Physical Education/Coaching, Psychology, Psychology/Early Childhood Education, Psychology Education, Secondary Education/Social Science, World Mission, Youth.
**Distribution of degrees:** The majors with the highest enrollment are elementary education, world mission, and family/child development; history/preseminary and history/precounseling have the lowest.
**Requirements:** General education requirement.
**Academic regulations:** Freshmen must maintain minimum 1.5 GPA; sophomores, 1.8 GPA; juniors, 2.0 GPA; seniors, 2.0 GPA.
**Special:** Minors offered in some majors and in evangelism/church growth, music, and social science. All degree programs include a second major in Christian studies. Associate's degrees offered. Double majors. Internships. Preprofessional programs in theology. 2-2 cooperative programs with approved nonaccredited Bible colleges. Teacher certification in early childhood, elementary, and secondary education. Certification in specific subject areas.
**Academic Assistance:** Remedial writing. Nonremedial tutoring.

**ADMISSIONS.**
**Nonacademic basis for candidate selection:** Character and personality are important. Extracurricular participation and particular talent or ability are considered.
**Requirements:** Graduation from secondary school is recommended; GED is accepted. No specific distribution of secondary school units required. Conditional admission possible for applicants not meeting standard requirements. ACT is required; SAT may be substituted. Campus visit recommended. No off-campus interviews.
**Procedure:** Take SAT or ACT by June of 12th year. Suggest filing application by March 1. Application deadline is August 15. Notification of admission on rolling basis. $50 tuition deposit, refundable until June 1. $50 room deposit, refundable until June 1. Freshmen accepted in terms other than fall.
**Special programs:** Credit and/or placement may be granted through CEEB Advanced Placement exams for scores of 3 or higher. Credit may be granted through CLEP subject exams. Credit and placement may be granted through DANTES and challenge exams.
**Transfer students:** Transfer students accepted for terms other than fall. In fall 1993, 28% of all new students were transfers into all classes. 74 transfer applications were received, 73 were accepted. Application deadline is rolling for fall; rolling for spring. Lowest course grade accepted is "C." Maximum number of transferable credits is 95 credits. At least 30 credits must be completed at the college to receive degree.
**Admissions contact:** James D. Rightler, Vice President of Enrollment Services. 612 446-4142.

**FINANCIAL AID. Available aid:** Pell grants, SEOG, state grants, school scholarships and grants, and private scholarships. Perkins Loans (NDSL), PLUS, Stafford Loans (GSL), and SLS. AMS.
**Financial aid statistics:** In 1993-94, 93% of all undergraduate applicants received aid; 90% of freshman applicants. Average amounts of aid awarded freshmen: Loans, $2,185.
**Supporting data/closing dates:** FAFSA. School's own aid application: Accepted on rolling basis. Income tax forms. Notification of awards on rolling basis.
**Financial aid contact:** Janice M. Lanpher, Director of Financial Aid. 612 446-4177.

# Dr. Martin Luther College

**New Ulm, MN 56073-3300 507 354-8221**

**1994-95 Costs.** Tuition: $3,370. Room & board: $1,880. Fees, books, misc. academic expenses (school's estimate): $960.
**Enrollment.** Undergraduates: 188 men, 371 women (full-time). Freshman class: 211 applicants, 210 accepted.
**Test score averages/ranges.** Average ACT scores: 22 English, 21 math, 22 composite. Range of ACT scores of middle 50%: 19-25 English, 19-26 math.
**Faculty.** 60 full-time; 4 part-time. 17% of faculty holds doctoral degree. Student/faculty ratio: 9 to 1.
**Selectivity rating.** Less competitive.

**PROFILE.** Dr. Martin Luther College, founded in 1884, is a church-affiliated institution specializing in the training of educators for the teaching ministry. Its 50-acre campus is located in New Ulm, 90 miles southwest of the Twin Cities.

**Accreditation:** NCACS.
**Religious orientation:** Dr. Martin Luther College is affiliated with the Evangelical Lutheran Synod, Lutheran-Wisconsin; six semesters of religion required.
**Library:** Collections totaling over 115,264 volumes, 316 periodical subscriptions, and 19,424 microform items.
**Special facilities/museums:** Organ facilities for music students.
**Athletic facilities:** Gymnasium, baseball, intramural, soccer, and softball fields, tennis courts, weight lifting room.

**STUDENT BODY. Undergraduate profile:** 15% are state residents; 14% are transfers. 1% Asian-American, 1% Black, 1% Hispanic, 1% Native American, 96% White. Average age of undergraduates is 20.
**Freshman profile:** 99% of accepted applicants took ACT. 17% of freshmen come from public schools.
**Undergraduate achievement:** 76% of fall 1992 freshmen returned for fall 1993 term. 55% of entering class graduated. 2% of students who completed a degree program immediately went on to graduate study.
**Foreign students:** Six students are from out of the country. Countries represented include Antigua, Japan, and St. Lucia.

**PROGRAMS OF STUDY. Degrees:** B.S.Ed.
**Majors:** Elementary Education, Secondary Education.
**Distribution of degrees:** The major with the highest enrollment is elementary education.
**Requirements:** General education requirement.
**Academic regulations:** Freshmen must maintain minimum 1.7 GPA; sophomores, 1.9 GPA; juniors, 2.0 GPA; seniors, 2.0 GPA.
**Special:** Minors offered in English, history, music, religion, and science. The college prepares educators for teaching ministry in elementary schools affiliated with Wisconsin Evangelical Lutheran Synod. Elementary education program includes courses in general education, professional education, and one subject area of concentration. Secondary education program includes general education, professional education, and subject-matter major in English, science, or social studies. Graduates are ready for assignment to Christian ministry upon recommendation of faculty. Double majors. Independent study. Accelerated study. Graduate school at which undergraduates may take graduate-level courses. Teacher certification in elementary and secondary education. Certification in specific subject areas.
**Academic Assistance:** Remedial reading, writing, math, and study skills. Nonremedial tutoring.

**ADMISSIONS. Academic basis for candidate selection** (in order of priority): Secondary school record, standardized test scores, class rank, school's recommendation.
**Nonacademic basis for candidate selection:** Character and personality are emphasized. Particular talent or ability is important.
**Requirements:** Graduation from secondary school is required; GED is accepted. 12 units and the following program of study are required: 4 units of English, 2 units of math, 2 units of lab science, 2 units of social studies, 2 units of academic electives. Minimum 2.0 GPA required. ACT is required. Campus visit recommended. Off-campus interviews available with an admissions representative.
**Procedure:** Take ACT in 11th or 12th year, or upon matriculation. Application deadline is July 20. Notification of admission on rolling basis. No set date by which candicate must accept offer; no deposit required. Freshmen accepted in terms other than fall.
**Special programs:** Admission may be deferred one year. for scores of 3 or higher.
**Transfer students:** Transfer students accepted for terms other than fall. In fall 1993, 14% of all new students were transfers into all classes. 37 transfer applications were received, 34 were accepted. Application deadline is July 20 for fall; November 20 for spring. Lowest course grade accepted is "D." Maximum number of transferable credits is 108 semester hours. At least 30 semester hours must be completed at the college to receive degree.
**Admissions contact:** John A. Sebald, Director of Admissions and Recruitment Director. 507 354-8221, extension 280.

**FINANCIAL AID. Available aid:** Pell grants, SEOG, state scholarships and grants, school scholarships and grants, private scholarships and grants, academic merit scholarships, and aid for undergraduate foreign students. Perkins Loans (NDSL), PLUS, Stafford Loans (GSL), state loans, school loans, private loans, and SLS. Deferred payment plan.
**Financial aid statistics:** 19% of aid is not need-based. In 1993-94, 89% of all undergraduate applicants received aid; 94% of freshman applicants. Average amounts of aid awarded freshmen: Scholarships and grants, $1,875; loans, $1,775.
**Supporting data/closing dates:** FAFSA: Priority filing date is May 15; accepted on rolling basis. School's own aid application: Priority filing date is May 15; accepted on rolling basis. Notification of awards on rolling basis.
**Financial aid contact:** Robert Krueger, M.Div., Financial Aid Officer. 507 354-8221, extension 225.

# Gustavus Adolphus College

**St. Peter, MN 56082-9989 507 933-8000**

**1993-94 Costs.** Tuition (1993-94): $14,806-$16,900 per year. Room & board: $2,960-$3,500. Fees, books, misc. academic expenses (school's estimate): $435.
**Enrollment.** Undergraduates: 1,028 men, 1,253 women (full-time). Freshman class: 1,709 applicants, 1,385 accepted, 634 enrolled.
**Test score averages/ranges.** Average SAT scores: 515 verbal, 595 math. Range of SAT scores of middle 50%: 440-600 verbal, 510-670 math. Average ACT scores: 24 English, 25 math, 25 composite. Range of ACT scores of middle 50%: 22-27 English, 22-28 math.
**Faculty.** 160 full-time; 57 part-time. 83% of faculty holds highest degree in specific field. Student/faculty ratio: 13 to 1.
**Selectivity rating.** More competitive.

**PROFILE.** Gustavus Adolphus, founded in 1862, is a church-affiliated, liberal arts college. Its 246-acre campus is located in St. Peter, 65 miles southwest of Minneapolis-St. Paul.

**Accreditation:** NCACS. Professionally accredited by the National Association of Schools of Music, the National Council for Accreditation of Teacher Education, the National League for Nursing.
**Religious orientation:** Gustavus Adolphus College is affiliated with the Evangelical Lutheran Church in America; one course of religion/theology required.
**Library:** Collections totaling over 232,000 volumes, 1,300 periodical subscriptions, and 30,000 microform items.
**Special facilities/museums:** Art gallery, mineral museum, electron microscope.
**Athletic facilities:** Gymnasium, ice rink, tracks, badminton, basketball, handball, racquetball, tennis, and volleyball courts, weight room, swimming pool, baseball, football, soccer, and softball fields, archery range, aerobics and gymnastics studios, exercise stations, putting green.

**STUDENT BODY. Undergraduate profile:** 75% are state residents; 6% are transfers. 2% Asian-American, 2% Black, 94% White, 2% Other. Average age of undergraduates is 20.
**Freshman profile:** 3% of freshmen who took SAT scored 700 or over on verbal, 15% scored 700 or over on math; 28% scored 600 or over on verbal, 48% scored 600 or over on math; 58% scored 500 or over on verbal, 79% scored 500 or over on math; 94% scored 400 or over on verbal, 100% scored 400 or over on math; 100% scored 300 or over on verbal. 10% of freshmen who took ACT scored 30 or over on English, 12% scored 30 or over on math, 14% scored 30 or over on composite; 57% scored 24 or over on English, 59% scored 24 or over on math, 65% scored 24 or over on composite; 96% scored 18 or over on English, 98% scored 18 or over on math, 100% scored 18 or over on composite; 100% scored 12 or over on English, 100% scored 12 or over on math. 32% of accepted applicants took SAT; 95% took ACT. 92% of freshmen come from public schools.
**Undergraduate achievement:** 76% of fall 1992 freshmen returned for fall 1993 term. 75% of entering class graduated. 25% of students who completed a degree program immediately went on to graduate study.
**Foreign students:** 40 students are from out of the country. Countries represented include India, Japan, Namibia, the Netherlands, Russia, and Sweden; 21 in all.

**PROGRAMS OF STUDY. Degrees:** B.A.
**Majors:** Accounting, Art, Art History, Athletic Training, Biochemistry, Biology, Chemistry, Church Music, Classics, Communication Studies, Computer Science, Criminal Justice, Economics, Education, Elementary Education, English, French, General Science, Geography, Geology, German, Health Fitness, History, International Management, Japanese Studies, Management, Mathematics, Music, Nursing, Philosophy, Physical Education/Health, Physical Science, Physics, Political Science, Psychology, Religion, Russian Studies, Scandinavian Studies, Secondary Education, Sociology/Anthropology, Spanish, Speech, Theatre.
**Distribution of degrees:** The majors with the highest enrollment are psychology, political science, and biology; theatre, Japanese studies, and Russian studies have the lowest.
**Requirements:** General education requirement.
**Academic regulations:** Freshmen must maintain minimum 1.75 GPA; sophomores, 1.90 GPA; juniors, 2.00 GPA; seniors, 2.00 GPA.
**Special:** Minors offered in most majors. Interdisciplinary programs in communications, criminal justice, sciences, and social studies and in American, Japanese, Latin American, Russian, and Scandinavian area studies. Curriculum II, a four-year core program, may be taken by 10% of student body. Self-designed majors. Double majors. Dual degrees. Independent study. Internships. Preprofessional programs in law, medicine, veterinary science, dentistry, and theology. 3-2 engineering programs with U of Minnesota and Washington U. Member of Minnesota Intercollegiate Nursing Consortium. Washington Semester. Exchange possible with other 4-1-4 colleges. Teacher certification in elementary and secondary education. Certification in specific subject areas. Exchange programs abroad in Australia (Murdoch U), India (Kishinchand Chellaram Coll), Japan (Kansai Gaidai U), and Sweden (Karlstad U, Uppsala U). Study abroad also in England, France, Germany, Italy, Mexico, and Spain. ROTC at Mankato State U.
**Honors:** Phi Beta Kappa. Honors program. Honor societies.
**Academic Assistance:** Nonremedial tutoring.

**STUDENT LIFE. Housing:** All unmarried students under age 21 must live on campus unless living near campus with relatives. Coed dorms. School-owned/operated apartments. 90% of students live in college housing.
**Social atmosphere:** The favorite on-campus gathering spot is The Dive, a non-alcoholic dance club. Off campus, students frequent local bars and house parties. Greeks and athletes have a widespread influence on campus life. Sporting events, Greek banquets, the President's Ball, and Greenstock, a multi-concert event, are the most popular happenings on campus. The Nobel Conference, an annual scientific gathering, attracts thousands of scientists and reporters. According to the student newspaper, "Campus organizations try to make up for Gustavus's small-town atmosphere, and their success is apparent in how

few students leave for the weekend–very few. Greek events and successful varsity sports offer many reasons to stick around."

**Services and counseling/handicapped student services:** Placement services. Health service. Women's center. Counseling services for minority students. Personal and psychological counseling. Career and academic guidance services. Religious counseling. Learning disabled services.

**Campus organizations:** Undergraduate student government. Student newspaper (Gustavus Weekly, published once/week). Literary magazine. Yearbook. Radio station. Band, orchestra, ensembles, Gustavus Singers, concert and chapel choirs, stage bands, theatre, coffeehouse, Outdoor Enthusiasts, Big Partners, GREENS, departmental and special-interest groups, 85 organizations in all. Three fraternities, no chapter houses; five sororities, no chapter houses. 20% of men join a fraternity. 20% of women join a sorority.

**Religious organizations:** Youth Organization, Christian Community, Lutheran Student Movement, Catholic Organization.

**Minority/foreign student organizations:** Asian-American Club, Black Student Organization. International Student Organization.

**ATHLETICS. Physical education requirements:** One course of physical education required.

**Intercollegiate competition:** 30% of students participate. Baseball (M), basketball (M,W), cross-country (M,W), diving (M,W), football (M), golf (M,W), gymnastics (W), ice hockey (M), soccer (M,W), softball (W), swimming (M,W), tennis (M,W), track (indoor) (M,W), track (outdoor) (M,W), track and field (indoor) (M,W), track and field (outdoor) (M,W), volleyball (W). Member of Minnesota Intercollegiate Athletic Conference, NCAA Division III.

**Intramural and club sports:** 72% of students participate. Intramural basketball, broomball, canoe/kayak, climbing, cycling, flag football, floor hockey, Jazzercise, martial arts, Nordic skiing, rappelling, scuba, soccer, softball, volleyball. Men's club cycling, lacrosse, rugby. Women's club cycling, lacrosse, rugby.

**ADMISSIONS. Academic basis for candidate selection** (in order of priority): Secondary school record, essay, standardized test scores, class rank, school's recommendation.

**Nonacademic basis for candidate selection:** Character and personality are emphasized. Particular talent or ability is important. Extracurricular participation, geographical distribution, and alumni/ae relationship are considered.

**Requirements:** Graduation from secondary school is required; GED is accepted. 17 units and the following program of study are required: 4 units of English, 3 units of math, 2 units of lab science, 2 units of foreign language, 2 units of social studies, 2 units of history. 4 units of mathematics and 3 units of science recommended. Rank in top third of secondary school class recommended. SAT or ACT is required. PSAT is recommended. Campus visit and interview recommended. Off-campus interviews available with an admissions representative.

**Procedure:** Take SAT or ACT by December of 12th year. Visit college for interview by February of 12th year. Suggest filing application by February 15. Application deadline is April 15. Notification of admission on rolling basis. Reply is required by May 1. $200 nonrefundable tuition deposit. $200 nonrefundable room deposit. Freshmen accepted in terms other than fall.

**Special programs:** Admission may be deferred one year. Credit and/or placement may be granted through CEEB Advanced Placement exams for scores of 4 or higher. Placement may be granted through challenge exams. Early decision program. In fall 1993, 145 applied for early decision and 121 were accepted. Deadline for applying for early decision is December 1. Early entrance/early admission program. Concurrent enrollment program.

**Transfer students:** Transfer students accepted for terms other than fall. In fall 1993, 6% of all new students were transfers into all classes. 101 transfer applications were received, 72 were accepted. Application deadline is May 1 for fall; December 15 for spring. Minimum 2.4 GPA required. Lowest course grade accepted is "C." Maximum number of transferable credits is 60 semester hours. At least 18 courses must be completed at the college to receive degree.

**Admissions contact:** Mark H. Anderson, M.A., Director of Admissions. 507 933-7676.

**FINANCIAL AID. Available aid:** Pell grants, SEOG, Federal Nursing Student Scholarships, state scholarships and grants, school scholarships, private scholarships and grants, ROTC scholarships, academic merit scholarships, and aid for undergraduate foreign students. Perkins Loans (NDSL), PLUS, Stafford Loans (GSL), NSL, state loans, school loans, and SLS. Knight Tuition Plans, AMS, EFI Fund Management, and guaranteed tuition.

**Financial aid statistics:** 4% of aid is not need-based. In 1993-94, 100% of all undergraduate applicants received aid. Average amounts of aid awarded freshmen: Scholarships and grants, $7,815; loans, $2,900.

**Supporting data/closing dates:** FAFSA: Priority filing date is March 31; deadline is May 1. School's own aid application: Priority filing date is March 31; deadline is May 1. Notification of awards on rolling basis.

**Financial aid contact:** Paul Aasen, M.A., Director of Financial Aid. 507 933-7527.

**STUDENT EMPLOYMENT.** College Work/Study Program. Institutional employment. 60% of full-time undergraduates work on campus during school year. Students may expect to earn an average of $1,400 during school year. Off-campus part-time employment opportunities rated "fair."

**COMPUTER FACILITIES.** 200 IBM/IBM-compatible, Macintosh/Apple, and RISC-/UNIX-based microcomputers; all are networked. Students may access Digital minicomputer/mainframe systems, BITNET, Internet. Residence halls may be equipped with modems. Client/LAN operating systems include Apple/Macintosh. Computer languages and software packages include Claris products, Microsoft Word, Paradox, Quattro Pro, SAS, SPSS-X, WordPerfect; 20 in all. Computer facilities are available to all students.

**Fees:** None.

**Hours:** 8 AM-midn.

**GRADUATE CAREER DATA.** Graduate school percentages: 5% enter law school. 3% enter medical school. 2% enter dental school. 8% enter graduate business programs. 15% enter graduate arts and sciences programs. 2% enter theological school/seminary. 50% of graduates choose careers in business and industry.

# Hamline University

**St. Paul, MN 55101** **612 641-2800**

**1993-94 Costs.** Tuition: $12,866. Room & board: $4,100. Fees, books, misc. academic expenses (school's estimate): $555.

**Enrollment.** Undergraduates: 642 men, 822 women (full-time). Freshman class: 1,006 applicants, 825 accepted, 328 enrolled. Graduate enrollment: 495 men, 603 women.

**Test score averages/ranges.** Average SAT scores: 530 verbal, 570 math. Range of SAT scores of middle 50%: 460-610 verbal, 520-620 math. Average ACT scores: 25 composite. Range of ACT scores of middle 50%: 22-28 composite.

**Faculty.** 93 full-time; 39 part-time. 93% of faculty holds doctoral degree. Student/faculty ratio: 12 to 1.

**Selectivity rating.** Competitive.

**PROFILE.** Hamline, founded in 1854, is a church-affiliated university. Programs are offered through the College of Liberal Arts and the School of Law. Its 44-acre campus is located in the Midway section of St. Paul.

**Accreditation:** NCACS. Professionally accredited by the National Association of Schools of Music, the National Council for Accreditation of Teacher Education.

**Religious orientation:** Hamline University is affiliated with the United Methodist Church; no religious requirements.

**Library:** Collections totaling over 305,600 volumes, 3,650 periodical subscriptions, and 157,700 microform items.

**Special facilities/museums:** Language lab, theatre, music hall, science center.

**Athletic facilities:** Gymnasium, field house, basketball, racquetball, tennis, and volleyball courts, track, athletic and soccer fields, stadium, swimming pool, gymnastics, mat, and strength training rooms.

**STUDENT BODY. Undergraduate profile:** 68% are state residents; 29% are transfers. 4% Asian-American, 3% Black, 2% Hispanic, 1% Native American, 87% White, 3% Other. Average age of undergraduates is 20.

**Freshman profile:** 8% of freshmen who took SAT scored 700 or over on verbal, 8% scored 700 or over on math; 28% scored 600 or over on verbal, 40% scored 600 or over on math; 64% scored 500 or over on verbal, 87% scored 500 or over on math; 91% scored 400 or over on verbal, 100% scored 400 or over on math; 100% scored 300 or over on verbal. 21% of accepted applicants took SAT; 86% took ACT. 76% of freshmen come from public schools.

**Undergraduate achievement:** 80% of fall 1992 freshmen returned for fall 1993 term. 64% of entering class graduated. 27% of students who completed a degree program went on to graduate study within one year.

**Foreign students:** 56 students are from out of the country. Countries represented include France, Greece, Japan, Korea, Nigeria, and Spain; 29 in all.

**PROGRAMS OF STUDY. Degrees:** B.A.

**Majors:** American Studies, Anthropology, Art, Art History, Biology, Chemistry, Communication Arts, East Asian Studies, Economics, Education, English, Environmental Studies, European Studies, French, German, History, International Management, International Relations, Latin American Studies, Legal Assistant, Legal Studies, Management, Mathematics, Music, Philosophy, Physical Education, Physics, Political Science, Psychology, Religion, Russian Area Studies, Science Education, Social Studies, Sociology, Spanish, Theatre, Urban Studies, Women's Studies.

**Distribution of degrees:** The majors with the highest enrollment are psychology, English, and management.

**Requirements:** General education requirement.

**Academic regulations:** Minimum 2.0 GPA required for graduation.

**Special:** Minors offered in most majors. Curriculum composed of personal program comprising core requirements, interdisciplinary program, major, and minor. Flexible curriculum option. Interdepartmental courses. Student project for Amity Among Nations. Self-designed majors. Double majors. Dual degrees. Independent study. Pass/fail grading option. Internships. Cooperative education programs. Graduate school at which undergraduates may take graduate-level courses. Preprofessional programs in law, medicine, veterinary science, dentistry, and engineering. 3-1 medical technology program with St. Paul Ramsey Medical Center. 3-2 engineering programs with U of Minnesota. 4-2 engineering programs with U of Minnesota. 3-3 B.A./J.D. program with Hamline Law School. Occupational therapy program with Washington U. Member of Associated Colleges of the Twin Cities. Washington Semester and UN Semester. Arts Program in New York. Exchange program with Huston-Tillotson Coll. Teacher certification in elementary, secondary, and bilingual/bicultural education. Certification in specific subject areas. Study abroad in numerous countries. AFROTC at U of St. Thomas

**Honors:** Phi Beta Kappa. Honors program. Honor societies.

**Academic Assistance:** Nonremedial tutoring.

**STUDENT LIFE. Housing:** Students encouraged to live on campus. Coed dorms. Sorority and fraternity housing. Off-campus privately-owned housing. 53% of students live in college housing.

**Services and counseling/handicapped student services:** Placement services. Health service. Women's center. Project Advance. Counseling services for minority, veteran, and older students. Birth control, personal, and psychological counseling. Career and academic guidance services. Religious counseling. Physically disabled student services. Learning disabled services. Notetaking services. Tape recorders. Reader services for the blind.

**Campus organizations:** Undergraduate student government. Student newspaper (Oracle, published once/week). Literary magazine. Yearbook. A cappella choir, mixed chorus, concert band, jazz band, orchestra, Oratorio Society, intercollegiate debating, MPIRG, National Collegiate Players, Student Congress, departmental, service, and special-interest groups, 80 organizations in all. Two fraternities, all with chapter houses; two sororities, all with chapter houses. 9% of men join a fraternity. 7% of women join a sorority.

**Religious organizations:** Campus Crusade for Christ, Chaplain's Council, Intervarsity Christian Fellowship.
**Minority/foreign student organizations:** PRIDE. International Student Association, International Relations Club.
**ATHLETICS. Physical education requirements:** None.
**Intercollegiate competition:** 33% of students participate. Baseball (M), basketball (M,W), cross-country (M,W), diving (M,W), football (M), gymnastics (W), ice hockey (M), soccer (M,W), softball (W), swimming (M,W), tennis (M,W), track and field (indoor) (M,W), track and field (outdoor) (M,W), volleyball (W). Member of Minnesota Intercollegiate Athletic Conference, NCAA Division III.
**Intramural and club sports:** 60% of students participate. Intramural aerobics, basketball, bowling, football, racquetball, skiing, softball, swimming, tennis, volleyball, water polo, weight lifting. Men's club judo. Women's club cheerleading, judo, karate, skiing.
**ADMISSIONS. Academic basis for candidate selection** (in order of priority): Secondary school record, class rank, essay, school's recommendation, standardized test scores.
**Nonacademic basis for candidate selection:** Character and personality are emphasized. Extracurricular participation and particular talent or ability are important. Geographical distribution and alumni/ae relationship are considered.
**Requirements:** Graduation from secondary school is required; GED is accepted. 16 units and the following program of study are recommended: 4 units of English, 3 units of math, 3 units of science including 2 units of lab, 2 units of foreign language, 2 units of social studies, 2 units of history, 4 units of electives. SAT or ACT is required. Campus visit and interview recommended. Off-campus interviews available with an admissions representative.
**Procedure:** Take SAT or ACT by February of 12th year. Visit college for interview by March of 12th year. Suggest filing application by December 1; no deadline. Notification of admission on rolling basis. Reply is required by May 1. $100 tuition deposit, refundable until May 1. $50 room deposit, refundable until July 1. Freshmen accepted for fall term only.
**Special programs:** Admission may be deferred one year. Credit may be granted through CEEB Advanced Placement for scores of 3 or higher. Credit and/or placement may be granted through CLEP general and subject exams. Early entrance/early admission program. Early action admission program.
**Transfer students:** Transfer students accepted for terms other than fall. In fall 1993, 29% of all new students were transfers into all classes. 309 transfer applications were received, 244 were accepted. Application deadline is August 1 for fall; December 1 for spring. Minimum 2.0 GPA required. Lowest course grade accepted is "C." At least 56 semester hours must be completed at the university to receive degree.
**Admissions contact:** W. Scott Friedhoff, Ph.D., Dean of Undergraduate Admissions. 612 641-2207.
**FINANCIAL AID. Available aid:** Pell grants, SEOG, state scholarships and grants, school scholarships and grants, private scholarships and grants, academic merit scholarships, and aid for undergraduate foreign students. Perkins Loans (NDSL), PLUS, Stafford Loans (GSL), state loans, private loans, and SLS. Knight Tuition Plans. Institutional payment plan.
**Financial aid statistics:** In 1993-94, 92% of all undergraduate applicants received aid; 89% of freshman applicants. Average amounts of aid awarded freshmen: Scholarships and grants, $7,800; loans, $2,362.
**Supporting data/closing dates:** FAFSA: Deadline is March 15. Notification of awards begins March 15.
**Financial aid contact:** Richard Manderfeld, M.A., Director of Financial Aid. 612 641-2280.
**STUDENT EMPLOYMENT.** College Work/Study Program. Institutional employment. 45% of full-time undergraduates work on campus during school year. Students may expect to earn an average of $1,500 during school year. Off-campus part-time employment opportunities rated "excellent."
**COMPUTER FACILITIES.** 200 IBM/IBM-compatible and Macintosh/Apple microcomputers; 100 are networked. Students may access Digital, Sequent, SUN minicomputer/mainframe systems, Internet. Residence halls may be equipped with networked microcomputers, modems. Client/LAN operating systems include Apple/Macintosh, DOS, UNIX/XENIX/AIX, Windows NT. Computer languages and software packages include BASIC, C, COBOL, FORTRAN, Lotus 1-2-3, Paradox, Pascal, Quattro, WordPerfect. Computer facilities are available to all students.
**Fees:** $350 computer fee per year.
**GRADUATE CAREER DATA.** Graduate school percentages: 6% enter law school. 2% enter medical school. 1% enter dental school. 2% enter graduate business programs. 14% enter graduate arts and sciences programs. 1% enter theological school/seminary. Highest graduate school enrollments: U of California, U of Minnesota. 63% of graduates choose careers in business and industry. Companies and businesses that hire graduates: 3M, IDS, General Mills, state government, Control Data, Minneapolis/St. Paul school districts.
**PROMINENT ALUMNI/AE.** Rozanne Ridgeway, president, Atlantic Council of the United States; Dr. Victor Gilbertsen, chief investigator for cancer control, U of Minnesota; Thomas Jensen, music director, Colorado Ballet; Robert Mikulak, chief scientist and negotiator, U.S. Arms Control and Disarmament Agency.

# Macalester College

**St. Paul, MN 55105 612 696-6000**

**1994-95 Costs.** Tuition: $15,909. Room: $2,480. Board: $2,292. Fees, books, misc. academic expenses (school's estimate): $601.
**Enrollment.** Undergraduates: 760 men, 963 women (full-time). Freshman class: 2,939 applicants, 1,496 accepted, 452 enrolled.
**Test score averages/ranges.** Range of SAT scores of middle 50%: 560-660 verbal, 580-690 math. Range of ACT scores of middle 50%: 27-31 composite.
**Faculty.** 121 full-time; 70 part-time. 89% of faculty holds doctoral degree. Student/faculty ratio: 12 to 1.
**Selectivity rating.** Highly competitive.

**PROFILE.** Macalester, founded in 1874, is a church-affiliated, liberal arts college. Its 50-acre campus is located in a residential area of St. Paul.

**Accreditation:** NCACS. Professionally accredited by the National Council for Accreditation of Teacher Education.
**Religious orientation:** Macalester College is affiliated with the Presbyterian Church; no religious requirements.
**Library:** Collections totaling over 344,071 volumes, 1,420 periodical subscriptions, and 56,377 microform items.
**Special facilities/museums:** Humanities learning center, on-campus nursery school-kindergarten, econometrics lab, cartography lab, 250-acre nature preserve, observatory and planetarium, two electron microscopes, nuclear accelerator, nuclear magnetic resonance spectrometer, laser spectroscopy lab, X-ray diffractometer.
**Athletic facilities:** Gymnasium, field house, basketball, handball, racquetball, tennis, and volleyball courts, aerobics and weight rooms, swimming pool, athletic and softball fields, stadium, track.

**STUDENT BODY. Undergraduate profile:** 24% are state residents; 9% are transfers. 5% Asian-American, 5% Black, 5% Hispanic, 1% Native American, 71% White, 13% Other. Average age of undergraduates is 20.
**Freshman profile:** 9% of freshmen who took SAT scored 700 or over on verbal, 23% scored 700 or over on math; 58% scored 600 or over on verbal, 66% scored 600 or over on math; 91% scored 500 or over on verbal, 95% scored 500 or over on math; 98% scored 400 or over on verbal, 100% scored 400 or over on math; 100% scored 300 or over on verbal. 41% of freshmen who took ACT scored 30 or over on composite; 94% scored 24 or over on composite; 100% scored 18 or over on composite. 83% of accepted applicants took SAT; 39% took ACT. 68% of freshmen come from public schools.
**Undergraduate achievement:** 91% of fall 1992 freshmen returned for fall 1993 term. 65% of entering class graduated. 30% of students who completed a degree program immediately went on to graduate study.
**Foreign students:** 230 students are from out of the country. Countries represented include Greece, Japan, Mexico, Sweden, Turkey, and the United Kingdom; 83 in all.
**PROGRAMS OF STUDY. Degrees:** B.A.
**Majors:** Anthropology, Art, Art History, Biology, Chemistry, Classics, Communication Studies, Computer Science, Dramatic Arts, East Asian Studies, Economics, English, Environmental Studies, French, Geography, Geology, Germanic Languages/Literatures, Greek, History, International Studies, Japan Studies, Latin, Latin American Studies, Linguistics, Mathematics, Music, Philosophy, Physics/Astronomy, Political Science, Psychology, Religious Studies, Russian, Slavic Languages/Literatures, Social Science, Sociology, Spanish, Urban Studies.
**Distribution of degrees:** The majors with the highest enrollment are political science, English, and history; East Asian studies, Latin American studies, and Russian area studies have the lowest.
**Academic regulations:** Freshmen must maintain minimum 1.70 GPA; sophomores, 1.85 GPA; juniors, 2.00 GPA; seniors, 2.00 GPA. General education course is required in the first semester; two courses on diversity are required for graduation.
**Special:** Minors offered in some majors and in dance. Courses offered in physical education. Distribution requirements. Senior projects required for graduation. Self-designed majors. Double majors. Independent study. Pass/fail grading option. Internships. Preprofessional programs in law and medicine. 3-2 engineering programs with U of Minnesota and Washington U. 3-2 nursing program with Rush-Presbyterian-St. Luke's (Chicago). 3-3 architecture program. Member of Associated Colleges of the Midwest and Associated Colleges of the Twin Cities. Newberry Library Program in the Humanities (Illinois). Oak Ridge Science Semester (Tennessee). Wilderness Field Station. Other off-campus programs. Teacher certification in early childhood, elementary, and secondary education. Certification in specific subject areas. Study abroad in England, France, Germany, Japan, and other countries; over 40 in all. NROTC at U of Minnesota. AFROTC at U of St. Thomas.
**Honors:** Phi Beta Kappa. Honors program. Honor societies.
**Academic Assistance:** Remedial study skills. Nonremedial tutoring.
**STUDENT LIFE. Housing:** Students may live on or off campus. Coed dorms. 64% of students live in college housing.
**Social atmosphere:** Students gather at The Grille in the student union on campus. Off campus, students head for Dunn Bros. Coffee Shop, Cuppa Joes, and O'Gara's Bar. MACTION (a community service group), QU (a gay/lesbian/bisexual student group), and other specialized student groups have a widespread influence on campus life. Popular events include African drumming concerts, the annual campus snowball fight, QU dances, the Springfest music festival, the Scottish Country Fair, basement parties, and MacCinema weekly movies. "Off-campus students throw parties on weekends, and student organizations sponsor parties in the basements of dormitories. These parties usually feature campus bands and are central to student social life. Student performance groups (dancers, a cappella singers, theatre groups) perform regularly. The campus is located on several bus lines that allow students to travel easily to Minneapolis/St. Paul to visit theatres, museums, and clubs," reports the student newspaper.
**Services and counseling/handicapped student services:** Placement services. Health service. Counseling services for minority students. Birth control, personal, and psychological counseling. Career and academic guidance services. Physically disabled student services. Learning disabled services. Notetaking services. Tape recorders. Tutors. Reader services for the blind.
**Campus organizations:** Undergraduate student government. Student newspaper (Mac Weekly). Literary magazine. Yearbook. Radio station. Scottish Pipe Band and Dancers, African music ensemble dance ensemble, Amnesty International, Art Alliance, Poetry Circle, Environmental Action Committee, Model UN, PIRG, Gay, Lesbian, Bisexual Union, MAC Conservative Club, sky diving and outing clubs, 90 organizations in all.
**Religious organizations:** Catholic Student Organization, Christian Fellowship, Council on Religious Understanding, Jewish Organization, Muslim Student Organization, Unitarian Universalist group.
**Minority/foreign student organizations:** Adelante, BLAC, PIPE, Shades of Color, Asian student group, Native American group, Women Students of Color, Bridges. International Student Organization.

**ATHLETICS. Physical education requirements:** None.

**Intercollegiate competition:** 17% of students participate. Baseball (M), basketball (M,W), cross-country (M,W), diving (M,W), football (M), golf (M,W), soccer (M,W), softball (W), swimming (M,W), tennis (M,W), track (indoor) (M,W), track (outdoor) (M,W), track and field (indoor) (M,W), track and field (outdoor) (M,W), volleyball (W). Member of Minnesota Intercollegiate Athletic Conference, NCAA Division III.

**Intramural and club sports:** 50% of students participate. Intramural badminton, basketball, disc golf, football, floor hockey, golf, indoor soccer, inner-tube water polo, racquetball, softball, tennis, ultimate frisbee, volleyball. Men's club crew, fencing, rugby, ultimate frisbee, volleyball, water polo. Women's club crew, fencing, rugby, ultimate frisbee, water polo.

**ADMISSIONS.**

**Nonacademic basis for candidate selection:** Character and personality and extracurricular participation are emphasized. Particular talent or ability and alumni/ae relationship are considered.

**Requirements:** Graduation from secondary school is required; GED is accepted. 19 units and the following program of study are recommended: 4 units of English, 3 units of math, 3 units of science, 3 units of foreign language, 3 units of social studies, 3 units of history. Honors or advanced placement courses expected of applicants if available. SAT or ACT is required. ACH recommended. Campus visit and interview recommended. Off-campus interviews available with admissions and alumni representatives.

**Procedure:** Take SAT or ACT by January of 12th year. Take ACH by January of 12th year. Visit college for interview by January 15 of 12th year. Application deadline is January 15. Notification of admission by March 29. Reply is required by May 1. $150 nonrefundable tuition deposit. $75 room deposit, refundable until June 1. Freshmen accepted for fall term only.

**Special programs:** Admission may be deferred one year. Credit and/or placement may be granted through CEEB Advanced Placement exams. Early decision program. In fall 1993, 259 applied for early decision and 154 were accepted. Deadline for applying for early decision is November 15 and January 1. Early entrance/early admission program. Concurrent enrollment program.

**Transfer students:** Transfer students accepted for terms other than fall. In fall 1993, 9% of all new students were transfers into all classes. 269 transfer applications were received, 75 were accepted. Application deadline is April 1. Minimum 3.2 GPA recommended. Lowest course grade accepted is "C-." Maximum number of transferable credits is 68 semester hours. At least 68 semester hours must be completed at the college to receive degree.

**Admissions contact:** William M. Shain, J.D., Dean of Admissions. 612 696-6724.

**FINANCIAL AID. Available aid:** Pell grants, SEOG, state grants, school scholarships and grants, private scholarships and grants, academic merit scholarships, and aid for undergraduate foreign students. Perkins Loans (NDSL), PLUS, Stafford Loans (GSL), state loans, school loans, private loans, and SLS. Tuition Plan Inc., Knight Tuition Plans, and deferred payment plan.

**Financial aid statistics:** 2% of aid is not need-based. In 1993-94, 97% of all undergraduate applicants received aid; 92% of freshman applicants. Average amounts of aid awarded freshmen: Scholarships and grants, $9,760; loans, $2,236.

**Supporting data/closing dates:** FAFSA/FAF: Priority filing date is February 8; deadline is March 1. School's own aid application: Priority filing date is February 8; deadline is March 1. Income tax forms: Deadline is March 1. W-2 form from parents: Deadline is March 1. Notification of awards begins March 29.

**Financial aid contact:** David E. Busse, M.A., Director of Financial Aid. 612 696-6214.

**STUDENT EMPLOYMENT.** College Work/Study Program. Institutional employment. 64% of full-time undergraduates work on campus during school year. Students may expect to earn an average of $1,425 during school year. Off-campus part-time employment opportunities rated "excellent."

**COMPUTER FACILITIES.** 350 IBM/IBM-compatible, Macintosh/Apple, and RISC-/UNIX-based microcomputers; 225 are networked. Students may access Digital minicomputer/mainframe systems, BITNET, Internet. Residence halls may be equipped with stand-alone microcomputers. Client/LAN operating systems include Apple/Macintosh, DOS, UNIX/XENIX/AIX, LocalTalk/AppleTalk, Novell. Computer languages and software packages include BASIC, C, COBOL, CDD/Plus, DataTrieve, FORTRAN, MINITAB, Pascal, SAS. Computer facilities are available to all students.

**Fees:** None.

**Hours:** 8 AM-midn.

**GRADUATE CAREER DATA.** Graduate school percentages: 5% enter law school. 5% enter medical school. 1% enter graduate business programs. 20% enter graduate arts and sciences programs. 1% enter theological school/seminary. Highest graduate school enrollments: Columbia U, Cornell U, Harvard U, Northwestern U, U of Chicago, U of Minnesota. 35% of graduates choose careers in business and industry. Companies and businesses that hire graduates: Andersen Consulting, Cray Research, Honeywell, Merrill Lynch, public schools, government agencies.

**PROMINENT ALUMNI/AE.** Kofi Annan, United Nations undersecretary general; Walter Mondale, U.S. ambassador to Japan; Tim O'Brien, author.

## Mankato State University

**Mankato, MN 56002** **507 389-6767**

**1993-94 Costs.** Tuition: $2,375 (state residents), $4,675 (out-of-state). Room & board: $2,643. Fees, books, misc. academic expenses (school's estimate): $750.

**Enrollment.** Undergraduates: 4,766 men, 4,883 women (full-time). Freshman class: 3,551 applicants, 3,150 accepted, 1,547 enrolled. Graduate enrollment: 616 men, 946 women.

**Test score averages/ranges.** Average ACT scores: 21 composite. Range of ACT scores of middle 50%: 19-23 composite.

**Faculty.** 522 full-time; 180 part-time. 60% of faculty holds doctoral degree. Student/faculty ratio: 20 to 1.

**Selectivity rating.** Less competitive.

**PROFILE.** Mankato State is a public, comprehensive university. It was founded in 1867, joined the state system in 1957, and gained university status in 1975. Programs are offered through the Colleges of Arts and Humanities; Business; Education; Health and Physical Education; Natural Sciences, Mathematics, and Home Economics; Nursing; Physics, Engineering, and Technology; Social and Behavioral Sciences; and Graduate Studies. Its 400-acre campus is located in Mankato, 85 miles south of Minneapolis-St. Paul.

**Accreditation:** NCACS. Professionally accredited by the Accreditation Board for Engineering and Technology, the American Dental Association, the American Speech-Language-Hearing Association, the Council on Social Work Education, the National Association of Schools of Art and Design, the National Association of Schools of Music, the National Athletic Trainers Association, the National Council for Accreditation of Teacher Education, the National League for Nursing, the National Recreation and Park Association. Numerous professional accreditations.

**Religious orientation:** Mankato State University is nonsectarian; no religious requirements.

**Library:** Collections totaling over 1,000,000 volumes, 3,200 periodical subscriptions, and 700,000 microform items.

**Special facilities/museums:** Art gallery, day care facilities.

**Athletic facilities:** Arenas, field house, racquetball and tennis courts, baseball, soccer, and softball fields.

**STUDENT BODY. Undergraduate profile:** 85% are state residents; 37% are transfers. 2% Asian-American, 1% Black, 1% Hispanic, 1% Native American, 93% White, 2% Other. Average age of undergraduates is 22.

**Freshman profile:** 99% of accepted applicants took ACT.

**Undergraduate achievement:** 70% of fall 1992 freshmen returned for fall 1993 term. 14% of entering class graduated. 15% of students who completed a degree program immediately went on to graduate study.

**Foreign students:** 52 students are from out of the country. Countries represented include Bangladesh, Japan, and Pakistan; 40 in all.

**PROGRAMS OF STUDY. Degrees:** B.A., B.F.A., B.Mus., B.S., B.S.Elec.Eng., B.S.Mech.Eng.

**Majors:** Accounting, American Studies, Anthropology, Art, Astronomy, Athletic Training, Automotive Engineering Technology, Aviation Management, Biochemistry, Biology, Biotechnology, Business Administration, Business Education, Chemistry, Communication Disorders, Computer Science, Construction Management, Corrections, Economics, Electrical Engineering, Electronic Engineering Technology, Elementary Education, English, Environmental Studies, Finance, French, Geography, German, Health Science, History, Home Economics, Home Economics Education, Humanities, Industrial Management, Industrial Relations, International Business, International Relations, Law Enforcement, Management, Manufacturing Engineering Technology, Marketing, Mass Communications, Mathematics, Mechanical Engineering, Medical Technology, Minority/Ethnic Studies, Music, Music Education, Music Management, Nursing, Open/Liberal Studies, Philosophy, Physical Education, Physics, Political Science, Psychology, Real Estate/Insurance, Recreation/Parks/Leisure Services, Russian, Scandinavian Studies, Science Education, Secondary Education, Secretarial, Social Studies, Social Work, Sociology, Spanish, Speech Communication, Speech/Theatre Arts, Studies in Educational Alternatives, Technology Education, Theatre Arts, Toxicology, Urban/Regional Studies, Women's Studies.

**Distribution of degrees:** The majors with the highest enrollment are business administration, elementary education, and nursing; theatre arts, philosophy, and women's studies have the lowest.

**Requirements:** General education requirement.

**Special:** Minors offered in Afro-American studies, American Indian studies, corporate/community fitness, dance education, early childhood education, geology, gerontology, library media education, linguistics, middle school, military science, religious studies, social welfare, special education (EMR-TMR), and statistics. Associate's degrees offered. Self-designed majors. Double majors. Dual degrees. Independent study. Accelerated study. Pass/fail grading option. Internships. Graduate school at which undergraduates may take graduate-level courses. Preprofessional programs in law, medicine, veterinary science, pharmacy, dentistry, theology, optometry, agriculture, chiropractic, engineering, forestry, mortuary science, occupational therapy, osteopathy, physical therapy, and podiatry. Exchange programs with Gustavus Adolphus Coll and other state schools. Teacher certification in early childhood, elementary, secondary, and special education education. Study abroad in France, Germany, Japan, Mexico, and Spain. Credit possible for organized educational tours within the U.S. and abroad. ROTC.

**Honors:** Honors program.

**Academic Assistance:** Nonremedial tutoring.

**STUDENT LIFE. Housing:** Students may live on or off campus. Coed dorms. Fraternity housing. 25% of students live in college housing.

**Social atmosphere:** Students gather at the Student Union Rec Center on campus. Off campus, students head for the Albatross, Caledonia Lounge, T.J. Finnegan's, the Stockade, the What's Up Lounge, and the Square Deal. Greeks and the International Student Organization have a widespread influence on campus life. Popular campus events include Homecoming, the International Festival, Greek Week, the People's Fair, and football and basketball games.

**Services and counseling/handicapped student services:** Placement services. Health service. Women's center. Day care. Counseling services for minority, military, veteran, and older students. Birth control, personal, and psychological counseling. Career and academic guidance services. Religious counseling.

**Campus organizations:** Undergraduate student government. Student newspaper (Reporter, published twice/week). Literary magazine. Radio station. Chamber singers, opera workshop, concert choir, chorus, ensembles, orchestra, bands, Ellis Street Singers, Drama Guild, speaking groups, professional groups, academic, social, service, and special-interest groups, 125 organizations in all. Nine fraternities, five chapter houses; five sororities, no chapter houses. 2% of men join a fraternity. 1% of women join a sorority.

**Religious organizations:** 25 religious groups.

**Minority/foreign student organizations:** 15 minority and foreign student groups.

**ATHLETICS. Physical education requirements:** Seven quarter credits of physical education required.Four quarter hours of physical education required.

**Intercollegiate competition:** 1% of students participate. Baseball (M), basketball (M,W), cross-country (M,W), football (M), golf (M,W), ice hockey (M), softball (W), swimming (M,W), tennis (M,W), track (indoor) (M,W), track (outdoor) (M,W), track and field (indoor) (M,W), track and field (outdoor) (M,W), volleyball (W), wrestling (M). Member of NCAA Division II, North Central Conference.
**Intramural and club sports:** 18% of students participate. Intramural archery, badminton, basketball, billiards, bowling, field hockey, golf, handball, ice hockey, softball, swimming, table tennis, touch football, volleyball. Men's club rugby, soccer. Women's club rugby, soccer.

**ADMISSIONS. Academic basis for candidate selection** (in order of priority): Class rank, standardized test scores, secondary school record, school's recommendation, essay.
**Nonacademic basis for candidate selection:** Geographical distribution is important. Character and personality, extracurricular participation, particular talent or ability, and alumni/ae relationship are considered.
**Requirements:** Graduation from secondary school is required; GED is accepted. 16 units and the following program of study are required: 4 units of English, 3 units of math, 3 units of lab science, 2 units of foreign language, 3 units of social studies, 1 unit of electives. Minimum composite ACT score of 21 or rank in top half of secondary school class required. Applicants who do not meet standard requirements may be admitted based on ACT score, secondary class rank, and available space. ACT is required. Campus visit and interview recommended. Off-campus interviews available with an admissions representative.
**Procedure:** Take ACT by April of 12th year. Notification of admission on rolling basis. No set date by which applicants must accept offer. $100 room deposit, refundable until June 10. Freshmen accepted in terms other than fall.
**Special programs:** Admission may be deferred one year. Credit may be granted through CEEB Advanced Placement for scores of 3 or higher. Credit may be granted through CLEP general and subject exams, DANTES exams, and military experience. Early entrance/early admission program. Concurrent enrollment program.
**Transfer students:** Transfer students accepted for terms other than fall. In fall 1993, 37% of all new students were transfers into all classes. 1,748 transfer applications were received, 1,478 were accepted. Application deadline is August 15 for fall; 45 days prior to beginning of quarter for spring. Minimum 2.0 GPA required. Lowest course grade accepted is "D." At least 48 quarter hours must be completed at the university to receive degree.
**Admissions contact:** John Parkins, M.A., Director of Admissions. 507 389-1822.

**FINANCIAL AID. Available aid:** Pell grants, SEOG, state scholarships and grants, school scholarships and grants, private scholarships and grants, ROTC scholarships, academic merit scholarships, and athletic scholarships. Perkins Loans (NDSL), PLUS, Stafford Loans (GSL), state loans, school loans, and SLS. AMS.
**Financial aid statistics:** 30% of aid is not need-based. In 1993-94, 70% of all undergraduate applicants received aid; 90% of freshman applicants. Average amounts of aid awarded freshmen: Scholarships and grants, $600; loans, $1,950.
**Supporting data/closing dates:** FAFSA: Priority filing date is July 1. School's own aid application. Income tax forms. Notification of awards on rolling basis.
**Financial aid contact:** Sandra Loerts, M.A., Director of Financial Aid. 507 389-1185.

**STUDENT EMPLOYMENT.** College Work/Study Program. Institutional employment. 35% of full-time undergraduates work on campus during school year. Students may expect to earn an average of $980 during school year. Off-campus part-time employment opportunities rated "excellent."

**COMPUTER FACILITIES.** 525 IBM/IBM-compatible and Macintosh/Apple microcomputers; 380 are networked. Students may access Digital, IBM, UNISYS minicomputer/mainframe systems, BITNET, Internet. Residence halls may be equipped with standalone microcomputers, networked terminals. Client/LAN operating systems include Apple/Macintosh, LocalTalk/AppleTalk. Computer facilities are available to all students.
**Fees:** Computer fee is included in tuition/fees.
**Hours:** 7 AM-1 AM.

## Minneapolis College of Art and Design

**Minneapolis, MN 55404** 612 874-3700

**1994-95 Costs.** Tuition: $12,880. Room & board: $3,600. Fees, books, misc. academic expenses (school's estimate): $1,564.
**Enrollment.** Undergraduates: 263 men, 245 women (full-time). Freshman class: 206 applicants, 167 accepted, 79 enrolled.
**Test score averages/ranges.** N/A.
**Faculty.** 42 full-time; 3 part-time. 80% of faculty holds highest degree in specific field. Student/faculty ratio: 12 to 1.
**Selectivity rating.** Less competitive.

**PROFILE.** Minneapolis College of Art and Design, founded in 1886, is a private college. Its seven-acre campus is located in Minneapolis.

**Accreditation:** NCACS. Professionally accredited by the National Association of Schools of Art and Design.
**Religious orientation:** Minneapolis College of Art and Design is nonsectarian; no religious requirements.
**Library:** Collections totaling over 50,000 volumes, 170 periodical subscriptions and 10 microform items.
**Special facilities/museums:** Art gallery.

**STUDENT BODY. Undergraduate profile:** 78% are state residents; 50% are transfers. 5% Asian-American, 1% Black, 2% Hispanic, 1% Native American, 91% White. Average age of undergraduates is 22.
**Freshman profile:** 7% of freshmen who took SAT scored 600 or over on verbal, 29% scored 600 or over on math; 36% scored 500 or over on verbal, 44% scored 500 or over on math; 72% scored 400 or over on verbal, 65% scored 400 or over on math; 93% scored 300 or over on verbal, 93% scored 300 or over on math. 1% of freshmen who took ACT scored 30 or over on composite; 20% scored 24 or over on composite; 76% scored 18 or over on composite; 100% scored 12 or over on composite. 18% of accepted applicants took SAT; 72% took ACT.
**Undergraduate achievement:** 82% of fall 1991 freshmen returned for fall 1992 term. 26% of entering class graduated.
**Foreign students:** 19 students are from out of the country. Countries represented include Japan, Norway, Sweden, and Taiwan; nine in all.

**PROGRAMS OF STUDY. Degrees:** B.F.A.
**Majors:** Design, Fine Arts, Media Arts.
**Distribution of degrees:** The majors with the highest enrollment are design and fine arts; media arts has the lowest.
**Requirements:** General education requirement.
**Academic regulations:** Minimum 2.0 GPA must be maintained.
**Special:** Courses offered in behavioral and natural sciences, history, literature, and philosophy. Active Visiting Art Program. Commencement exhibition of student art. Self-designed majors. Pass/fail grading option. Internships. Cooperative education programs. Graduate school at which undergraduates may take graduate-level courses. Member of Association of Independent Colleges of Art and Design. Arts Program in New York. Exchange programs with Center for Creative Studies-Coll of Art and Design; Cleveland Inst of Art; Corcoran Sch of Art; Maryland Inst, Coll of Art; Memphis Coll of Art; Milwaukee Inst of Art and Design; and San Francisco Art Inst. Study abroad in Canada, Italy, and Japan.
**Honors:** Honors program.
**Academic Assistance:** Remedial reading and writing. Nonremedial tutoring.

**ADMISSIONS. Academic basis for candidate selection** (in order of priority): Secondary school record, essay, school's recommendation, standardized test scores.
**Nonacademic basis for candidate selection:** Particular talent or ability is emphasized. Extracurricular participation is important.
**Requirements:** Graduation from secondary school is required; GED is accepted. No specific distribution of secondary school units required. Minimum 2.0 GPA and portfolio required. SAT or ACT is required. Campus visit and interview recommended. Off-campus interviews available with an admissions representative.
**Procedure:** Suggest filing application by March 1; no deadline. Notification of admission on rolling basis. Reply is required by May 1. $150 tuition deposit, refundable until May 1. $100 refundable room deposit. Freshmen accepted in terms other than fall.
**Special programs:** Admission may be deferred three years. Concurrent enrollment program.
**Transfer students:** Transfer students accepted for terms other than fall. In fall 1992, 50% of all new students were transfers into all classes. 188 transfer applications were received, 149 were accepted. Application deadline is March 1 for fall; October 1 for spring. Minimum 2.0 GPA required. Lowest course grade accepted is "C." At least 30 semester hours must be completed at the college to receive degree.
**Admissions contact:** Rebecca Haas, M.F.A., Director of Admissions. 612 874-3760.

**FINANCIAL AID. Available aid:** Pell grants, SEOG, state grants, school scholarships and grants, and academic merit scholarships. Perkins Loans (NDSL), PLUS, Stafford Loans (GSL), state loans, and SLS. Tuition Plan Inc. and AMS.
**Financial aid statistics:** In 1992-93, 72% of all undergraduate applicants received aid; 85% of freshman applicants. Average amounts of aid awarded freshmen: Scholarships and grants, $3,500; loans, $2,500.
**Supporting data/closing dates:** FAFSA: Priority filing date is April 1; accepted on rolling basis. Income tax forms: Priority filing date is March 1. Notification of awards begins April 1.
**Financial aid contact:** LeAnn Winkelaar, Director of Financial Aid. 612 874-3782.

8-28

## Moorhead State University

**Moorhead, MN 56563** 218 236-2161

**1994-95 Costs.** Tuition: $2,133 (state residents), $4,459 (out-of-state). Room & board: $2,664. Fees, books, misc. academic expenses (school's estimate): $729.
**Enrollment.** Undergraduates: 2,440 men, 3,812 women (full-time). Freshman class: 2,442 applicants, 2,164 accepted. Graduate enrollment: 46 men, 78 women.
**Test score averages/ranges.** Average ACT scores: 22 composite. Range of ACT scores of middle 50%: 18-23 composite.
**Faculty.** 388 full-time; 86 part-time. 66% of faculty holds doctoral degree. Student/faculty ratio: 20 to 1.
**Selectivity rating.** Less competitive.

**PROFILE.** Moorhead State, founded in 1885, is a public, comprehensive university. Its 104-acre campus is located in Moorhead, one mile east of Fargo, N.D.

**Accreditation:** NCACS. Professionally accredited by the American Speech-Language-Hearing Association, the Council on Social Work Education, the National Association of Schools of Art and Design, the National Association of Schools of Music, the National Council for Accreditation of Teacher Education, the National League for Nursing.
**Religious orientation:** Moorhead State University is nonsectarian; no religious requirements.
**Library:** Collections totaling over 350,117 volumes, 1,482 periodical subscriptions, and 582,345 microform items.
**Special facilities/museums:** Art museum, on-campus preschool, planetarium, regional science center.
**Athletic facilities:** Racquetball and tennis courts, swimming pool, tracks, gymnasiums, football stadium, baseball diamond, intramural fields, dance, weight, and wrestling rooms, field house.

**STUDENT BODY. Undergraduate profile:** 62% are state residents; 29% are transfers. 1% Asian-American, 1% Black, 1% Hispanic, 1% Native American, 96% White. Average age of undergraduates is 23.
**Freshman profile:** 3% of freshmen who took ACT scored 30 or over on composite; 31% scored 24 or over on composite; 92% scored 18 or over on composite; 100% scored 12 or over on composite. 73% of accepted applicants took ACT. 98% of freshmen come from public schools.
**Undergraduate achievement:** 71% of fall 1992 freshmen returned for fall 1993 term. 23% of entering class graduated. 8% of students who completed a degree program went on to graduate study within one year.
**Foreign students:** 153 students are from out of the country. Countries represented include Canada, China, Hong Kong, India, and the United Kingdom; 40 in all.

**PROGRAMS OF STUDY. Degrees:** B.A., B.F.A., B.M., B.S., B.S.Nurs., B.S.Soc.Work.
**Majors:** Accounting, American Studies, Anthropology, Art, Art Education, Biology, Biology/Life Science, Business Administration, Chemistry, Communication, Computer Information Systems, Criminal Justice, Cytotechnology, Early Childhood Education, Economics, Education, Elementary Education, Energy Management, English, Exceptional Education, Film, Finance, French, German, Graphics Communications, Health Education, History, Hotel/Motel/Restaurant Management, Individualized Major, Industrial Chemistry, Industrial Education, Industrial Technology, International Business, Keyboard, Language/Hearing Science, Languages, Legal Assistant, Management, Marketing, Mass Communications, Mathematics, Medical Technology, Music, Music Industry, Music Theory, Nursing, Office Administration, Philosophy, Physical Education, Physics, Political Science, Psychology, Secondary Education, Social Work, Sociology, Spanish, Special Education, Speech, Speech Pathology/Audiology, Strings, Theatre Arts, Vocal Music, Vocational Rehabilitation Therapy, Wind Instruments.
**Distribution of degrees:** The majors with the highest enrollment are accounting, business administration, and elementary education; French and chemistry have the lowest.
**Requirements:** General education requirement.
**Special:** Minors offered in 60 fields. Self-designed majors. Double majors. Dual degrees. Independent study. Accelerated study. Pass/fail grading option. Internships. Preprofessional programs in law, medicine, veterinary science, dentistry, and optometry. 3-2 engineering program with North Dakota State U. 2-3 engineering program with U of Minnesota. 2-3 pre-pharmacy program with North Dakota State U. Member of Tri-College Consortium. Member of National Student Exchange (NSE). Teacher certification in early childhood, elementary, secondary, and special education education. Certification in specific subject areas. Exchange programs abroad in China (Nankai U), England (Portsmouth Polytech), Norway (U of Oslo), Scotland (Glasgow Sch of Art), and the Ukraine (U of Kiev). Study abroad also available in numerous other countries. ROTC and AFROTC at North Dakota State U.
**Honors:** Phi Beta Kappa. Honors program. Honor societies.
**Academic Assistance:** Remedial reading, writing, math, and study skills. Nonremedial tutoring.

**STUDENT LIFE. Housing:** Students may live on or off campus. Coed, women's, and men's dorms. Sorority and fraternity housing. 34% of students live in college housing.
**Services and counseling/handicapped student services:** Placement services. Health service. Women's center. Day care. Counseling services for minority and veteran students. Birth control, personal, and psychological counseling. Career and academic guidance services. Physically disabled student services. Learning disabled services. Notetaking services. Tape recorders. Tutors. Reader services for the blind.
**Campus organizations:** Undergraduate student government. Student newspaper (Advocate, published once/week). Literary magazine. Radio and TV stations. Feminist Collective, departmental, professional, service, and special-interest groups, 120 organizations in all. Two fraternities, all with chapter houses; three sororities, two chapter houses. 1% of men join a fraternity. 2% of women join a sorority.
**Religious organizations:** Campus Crusade for Christ, Fellowship of Christian Athletes, Intervarsity Christian Fellowship, Lutheran Student Movement.
**Minority/foreign student organizations:** Bay Students United, Chinese Student Club, Hispanic Student Organization, Unicorn. International Student Club, Hispanic Cultural Organization, Japanese and Pakistani groups.

**ATHLETICS. Physical education requirements:** None.
**Intercollegiate competition:** 10% of students participate. Basketball (M,W), cheerleading (M,W), cross-country (M,W), football (M), golf (M,W), softball (W), tennis (M,W), track (indoor) (M,W), track (outdoor) (M,W), track and field (indoor) (M,W), track and field (outdoor) (M,W), volleyball (W), wrestling (M). Member of NAIA Division I, NCAA Division II, Northern Sun Intercollegiate Conference.
**Intramural and club sports:** 40% of students participate. Intramural basketball, bowling, golf, racquetball, softball, tennis, track and field, touch football, wrestling. Men's club soccer.

**ADMISSIONS. Academic basis for candidate selection** (in order of priority): Class rank, standardized test scores.
**Requirements:** Graduation from secondary school is required; GED is accepted. No specific distribution of secondary school units required. Elective units can be chosen from world languages, world culture, and the arts. Applicants must take at least 3 years of at least 2 of these areas. Minimum composite ACT score of 21 (combined PSAT score of 90 or combined SAT score of 900) and rank in top half of secondary school class required. R.N. required of nursing program applicants. Center for Multidisciplinary Studies for applicants not normally admissible. ACT is required; SAT may be substituted. Campus visit recommended. No off-campus interviews.
**Procedure:** Take SAT or ACT by March of 12th year. Suggest filing application by January 15. Application deadline is August 15. Notification of admission on rolling basis. No set date by which applicants must accept offer. $50 room deposit, refundable until July 1. Freshmen accepted in terms other than fall.
**Special programs:** Admission may be deferred one year. Credit and/or placement may be granted through CEEB Advanced Placement exams for scores of 3 or higher. Credit and/or placement may be granted through CLEP subject exams. Credit and placement may be granted through challenge exams and military and life experience. Early entrance/early admission program. Concurrent enrollment program.
**Transfer students:** Transfer students accepted for terms other than fall. In fall 1993, 29% of all new students were transfers into all classes. 1,072 transfer applications were received, 978 were accepted. Application deadline is August 15 for fall; February 15 for spring. Minimum 2.0 GPA required. Lowest course grade accepted is "C." At least 45 quarter hours must be completed at the university to receive degree.
**Admissions contact:** Jean Lange, M.S., Director of Admissions. 218 236-2161.

**FINANCIAL AID. Available aid:** Pell grants, SEOG, state grants, school scholarships, private scholarships and grants, academic merit scholarships, and athletic scholarships. Perkins Loans (NDSL), PLUS, Stafford Loans (GSL), state loans, private loans, and SLS.
**Financial aid statistics:** 19% of aid is not need-based. In 1993-94, 73% of all undergraduate applicants received aid; 58% of freshman applicants. Average amounts of aid awarded freshmen: Scholarships and grants, $3,499; loans, $2,015.
**Supporting data/closing dates:** FAFSA/FAF/FFS: Accepted on rolling basis. School's own aid application: Accepted on rolling basis. Income tax forms: Accepted on rolling basis. Notification of awards on rolling basis.
**Financial aid contact:** David Anderson, Director of Financial Aid. 218 236-2251.

**STUDENT EMPLOYMENT.** College Work/Study Program. Institutional employment. 28% of full-time undergraduates work on campus during school year. Students may expect to earn an average of $1,520 during school year. Off-campus part-time employment opportunities rated "good."

**COMPUTER FACILITIES.** 250 IBM/IBM-compatible and Macintosh/Apple microcomputers. Students may access AT&T, Data General, Digital, SUN minicomputer/mainframe systems. Residence halls may be equipped with stand-alone microcomputers, modems. Computer languages and software packages include BASIC, C, COBOL, FORTRAN, Pascal. Computer facilities are available to all students.
**Fees:** None.
**Hours:** 24 hours.

**GRADUATE CAREER DATA.** Graduate school percentages: 2% enter law school. 5% enter graduate arts and sciences programs. Highest graduate school enrollments: Moorhead State U, North Dakota State U, U of Minnesota. 42% of graduates choose careers in business and industry. Companies and businesses that hire graduates: Arthur Andersen, Cargill, Daytons, EDS, Hendrickson & Pullen, Hormel, McGladrey, NCR.

**PROMINENT ALUMNI/AE.** Jerry VerDorn, actor; Jules Herman, musician; Judy Nygaard Broekemeier, art teacher, 1986 National Art Educator of the Year; Kristen Harris, professor, Harvard Medical School; Katie Class, Olympic speedskater.

# North Central Bible College

**Minneapolis, MN 55404** 612 332-3491

**1994-95 Costs.** Tuition: $5,280. Room: $1,680. Board: $1,640. Fees, books, misc. academic expenses (school's estimate): $1,070.
**Enrollment.** Undergraduates: 420 men, 391 women (full-time). Freshman class: 442 enrolled.
**Test score averages/ranges.** Average ACT scores: 21 composite.
**Faculty.** 37 full-time; 27 part-time. 16% of faculty holds doctoral degree. Student/faculty ratio: 18 to 1.
**Selectivity rating.** Noncompetitive.

**PROFILE.** North Central is private, church-affiliated college. Founded in 1930 to offer Bible training, it began offering baccalaureate degree-granting programs in 1955. Its six-acre campus is located in downtown Minneapolis.

**Accreditation:** NCACS.
**Religious orientation:** North Central Bible College is affiliated with the Assemblies of God; eight semesters of religion required.
**Library:** Collections totaling over 62,934 volumes, 436 periodical subscriptions, and 3,219 microform items.
**Athletic facilities:** Gymnasium with weight room, locker facilities.

**STUDENT BODY. Undergraduate profile:** 34% are state residents; 34% are transfers. 1% Asian-American, 4% Black, 2% Hispanic, 1% Native American, 92% White.
**Freshman profile:** 100% of accepted applicants took ACT.
**Foreign students:** 29 students are from out of the country. Countries represented include Australia, Canada, Denmark, Finland, Norway, and Zambia; nine in all.

**PROGRAMS OF STUDY. Degrees:** B.A., B.S.
**Majors:** Behavioral Sciences, Biblical Languages, Broadcasting, Campus Ministries, Children's Ministries, Christian Education, Christian Studies, Church Business Administration, Church Planting, Cross-Cultural Ministries, Deaf Culture Ministries, Drama, Elementary Education, Journalism, Mass Communication, Music, Pastoral Studies, Urban Studies, Youth Ministries.
**Distribution of degrees:** The majors with the highest enrollment are pastoral studies, youth ministries, and elementary education; biblical languages, children's ministries, and church planting have the lowest.
**Requirements:** General education requirement.
**Academic regulations:** Freshmen must maintain minimum 1.5 GPA; sophomores, 1.7 GPA; juniors, 1.9 GPA; seniors, 2.0 GPA.
**Special:** Minors offered in all majors and in business, early childhood education, evangelism, Greek, Hebrew, and pastoral care. Double majors. Dual degrees. Independent study. Internships. Cooperative education programs. Teacher certification in early childhood and elementary education. Study abroad in Belgium and Portugal.
**Honors:** Honor societies.
**Academic Assistance:** Remedial writing, math, and study skills. Nonremedial tutoring.

**ADMISSIONS. Academic basis for candidate selection** (in order of priority): Secondary school record, essay, school's recommendation, class rank.
**Nonacademic basis for candidate selection:** Character and personality are emphasized. Extracurricular participation and particular talent or ability are important.

**Requirements:** Graduation from secondary school is required; GED is accepted. No specific distribution of secondary school units required. ACT is required; SAT may be substituted. Campus visit and interview recommended. Off-campus interviews available with an admissions representative.
**Procedure:** Take SAT or ACT by September of 12th year. Application deadline is September 1. Notification of admission on rolling basis. $80 room deposit, refundable until August 15. Freshmen accepted in terms other than fall.
**Special programs:** Admission may be deferred one year. Credit may be granted through CEEB Advanced Placement for scores of 3 or higher. Credit may be granted through CLEP general and subject exams and military experience. Placement may be granted through ACT PEP exams. Credit and placement may be granted through DANTES and challenge exams and life experience.
**Transfer students:** Transfer students accepted for terms other than fall. In fall 1993, 34% of all new students were transfers into all classes. 171 transfer applications were received, 171 were accepted. Application deadline is rolling for fall; rolling for spring. Minimum 2.0 GPA recommended. Lowest course grade accepted is "C." Maximum number of transferable credits is 100 semester hours. At least 27 semester hours must be completed at the college to receive degree.
**Admissions contact:** Dan Neary, Director of Admissions. 800 289-6222.

**FINANCIAL AID. Available aid:** Pell grants, SEOG, state grants, school scholarships, and academic merit scholarships. Perkins Loans (NDSL), PLUS, Stafford Loans (GSL), state loans, and SLS. Tuition Management Systems.
**Financial aid statistics:** In 1993-94, 80% of all undergraduate applicants received aid.
**Supporting data/closing dates:** FAFSA: Priority filing date is May 1. School's own aid application: Priority filing date is August 1. Notification of awards on rolling basis.
**Financial aid contact:** Evie Meyer, Director of Financial Aid. 800 289-6222.

## Northwestern College

**St. Paul, MN 55113 — 612 631-5100**

**1994-95 Costs.** Tuition: $11,328. Room: $1,908. Board: $1,095. Fees, books, misc. academic expenses (school's estimate): $400.
**Enrollment.** Undergraduates: 509 men, 731 women (full-time). Freshman class: 600 applicants, 585 accepted, 352 enrolled.
**Test score averages/ranges.** Average ACT scores: 21 English, 20 math, 21 composite. Range of ACT scores of middle 50%: 19-25 composite.
**Faculty.** 59 full-time; 52 part-time. 54% of faculty holds doctoral degree. Student/faculty ratio: 17 to 1.
**Selectivity rating.** Competitive.

**PROFILE.** Northwestern, founded in 1902, is a private, liberal arts college with religious affiliation. Its 95-acre campus is located in St. Paul.

**Accreditation:** CCA-ACICS, NCACS. Professionally accredited by the National Association of Schools of Music.
**Religious orientation:** Northwestern College is a nondenominational Christian school; 12 terms of religion/theology required.
**Library:** Collections totaling over 80,000 volumes, 570 periodical subscriptions, and 35,100 microform items.
**Athletic facilities:** Gymnasium, swimming pool, baseball, football, soccer, and softball fields, weight room, basketball and volleyball courts.

**STUDENT BODY. Undergraduate profile:** 66% are state residents; 25% are transfers. 3% Asian-American, 2% Black, 1% Hispanic, 1% Native American, 93% White. Average age of undergraduates is 20.
**Freshman profile:** 15% of accepted applicants took SAT; 97% took ACT. 82% of freshmen come from public schools.
**Undergraduate achievement:** 78% of fall 1992 freshmen returned for fall 1993 term.
**Foreign students:** 19 students are from out of the country. Countries represented include Canada, China, Japan, Mexico, Norway, and Russia; 14 in all.

**PROGRAMS OF STUDY. Degrees:** B.A., B.S.
**Majors:** Accounting, Art, Art Education, Biblical Studies, Broadcasting, Children's Ministry, Christian Education, Communication, Cross-Cultural Ministries, Elementary Education, English, English Education, Finance, General Business Administration, Graphic Design, Human Resources, International Business, Management, Marketing, Mathematics, Mathematics Education, Ministries, Music, Music Education, Office Administration, Organizational Administration, Pastoral Studies, Physical Education, Psychology, Social Science, Social Studies Education, Sports Studies, Youth Ministries.
**Distribution of degrees:** The majors with the highest enrollment are elementary education, psychology, and general business; biblical studies and art have the lowest.
**Requirements:** General education requirement.
**Academic regulations:** Minimum 2.0 GPA must be maintained.
**Special:** Minors offered in most majors. Associate's degrees offered. Double majors. Independent study. Internships. Cooperative education programs. Graduate school at which undergraduates may take graduate-level courses. 3-2 engineering program and pre-nursing program with U of Minnesota. Member of Christian College Coalition and Council of Independent Colleges. Exchange program with Bethel Coll. Teacher certification in elementary and secondary education. Study abroad in England, Greece, Israel, and Japan. AFROTC at Coll of St. Thomas.
**Academic Assistance:** Remedial reading and math. Nonremedial tutoring.

**STUDENT LIFE. Housing:** All unmarried students under age 21 must live on campus unless living near campus with relatives. Women's and men's dorms. 60% of students live in college housing.
**Services and counseling/handicapped student services:** Placement services. Personal and psychological counseling. Career and academic guidance services. Religious counseling. Physically disabled student services. Learning disabled services. Notetaking services. Reader services for the blind.
**Campus organizations:** Undergraduate student government. Student newspaper (Cadence, published once/month). Literary magazine. Yearbook. Concert band, men's and women's choirs, mixed choir, chamber orchestra, instrumental and vocal ensembles, drama productions, speech team, Student Missions Fellowship.
**Religious organizations:** Campus Crusade for Christ, Fellowship of Christian Athletes, Navigators, Student Missionary Fellowship; several other religious groups.

**ATHLETICS. Physical education requirements:** Three terms of physical education required.
**Intercollegiate competition:** 15% of students participate. Baseball (M), basketball (M,W), cross-country (M,W), football (M), golf (M), soccer (M), softball (W), tennis (M), track (outdoor) (M,W), track and field (outdoor) (M,W), volleyball (W). Member of NCCAA, Upper Midwest Athletic Conference.
**Intramural and club sports:** 16% of students participate. Intramural basketball, broomball, softball, tennis, volleyball. Men's club hockey.

**ADMISSIONS. Academic basis for candidate selection** (in order of priority): Essay, secondary school record, standardized test scores, class rank, school's recommendation.
**Nonacademic basis for candidate selection:** Character and personality are emphasized. Extracurricular participation, particular talent or ability, and alumni/ae relationship are considered.
**Requirements:** Graduation from secondary school is required; GED is accepted. 16 units and the following program of study are recommended: 4 units of English, 3 units of math, 3 units of science including 1 unit of lab, 2 units of foreign language, 3 units of social studies. Minimum composite ACT score of 18, rank in top half of secondary school class, and minimum 2.0 GPA recommended. Audition required of music program applicants. Conditional admission possible for applicants not meeting standard requirements. ACT is required; SAT may be substituted. Campus visit and interview recommended. Off-campus interviews available with an admissions representative.
**Procedure:** Suggest filing application by March 1. Application deadline is August 1. Notification of admission on rolling basis. $100 refundable tuition deposit. $100 tuition deposit partially refundable until beginning of classes. $80 room deposit, refundable less damages. Freshmen accepted in terms other than fall.
**Special programs:** Admission may be deferred one year. Credit and/or placement may be granted through CEEB Advanced Placement exams for scores of 3 or higher. Credit and/or placement may be granted through CLEP general and subject exams. Credit and placement may be granted through Regents College and challenge exams. Early entrance/early admission program.
**Transfer students:** Transfer students accepted for terms other than fall. In fall 1993, 25% of all new students were transfers into all classes. 135 transfer applications were received, 130 were accepted. Application deadline is August 1 for fall; first day of classes for spring. Minimum 2.0 GPA recommended. Lowest course grade accepted is "C." At least 45 quarter hours must be completed at the college to receive degree.
**Admissions contact:** Ralph D. Anderson, M.A., Dean of Admissions. 800 827-6827, 612 631-5111.

**FINANCIAL AID. Available aid:** Pell grants, SEOG, state grants, school scholarships and grants, private scholarships and grants, ROTC scholarships, and academic merit scholarships. Perkins Loans (NDSL), PLUS, Stafford Loans (GSL), state loans, and SLS. H.E.S.
**Financial aid statistics:** In 1993-94, 85% of all undergraduate applicants received aid; 85% of freshman applicants. Average amounts of aid awarded freshmen: Scholarships and grants, $5,500; loans, $2,300.
**Supporting data/closing dates:** FAFSA: Priority filing date is March 1. FAF/FFS: Accepted on rolling basis. Income tax forms: Accepted on rolling basis. Notification of awards on rolling basis.
**Financial aid contact:** Richard L. Blatchley, Director of Financial Aid. 612 631-5211.

**STUDENT EMPLOYMENT.** College Work/Study Program. Institutional employment. 35% of full-time undergraduates work on campus during school year. Students may expect to earn an average of $1,500 during school year. Off-campus part-time employment opportunities rated "excellent."

**COMPUTER FACILITIES.** 58 IBM/IBM-compatible and Macintosh/Apple microcomputers. Client/LAN operating systems include Apple/Macintosh, DOS. Computer languages and software packages include BASIC, COBOL, dBASE, FORTRAN, Harvard Graphics, Lotus 1-2-3, Paradox, Pascal, SQL, WordPerfect, WordStar; 48 in all. Computer facilities are available to all students.
**Fees:** None.
**Hours:** 8 AM-midn. (M-Th); 8 AM-6 PM (F); 10 AM-6 PM (Sa); 1 PM-5 PM (Su).

**PROMINENT ALUMNI/AE.** Dr. Kenneth Barker, editor, academic dean of Capital Bible Seminary; George Wilson, executive vice-president of Billy Graham Association; Harold Miller, dean of continuing education and extension, U of Minnesota; Bill Maclear, assistant zone manager, Philadelphia General Motors.

9-7

## St. Cloud State University

**St. Cloud, MN 56301 — 612 255-2244**

**1994-95 Costs.** Tuition: $2,500 (state residents), $4,900 (out-of-state). Room & board: $2,625. Fees, books, misc. academic expenses (school's estimate): $706.
**Enrollment.** Undergraduates: 5,808 men, 5,732 women (full-time). Freshman class: 3,971 applicants, 3,306 accepted, 1,948 enrolled. Graduate enrollment: 383 men, 735 women.
**Test score averages/ranges.** N/A.
**Faculty.** 627 full-time; 134 part-time. 70% of faculty holds doctoral degree. Student/faculty ratio: 22 to 1.
**Selectivity rating.** Less competitive.

**PROFILE.** St. Cloud State, founded in 1869, is a public, comprehensive university. Programs are offered through the Colleges of Business, Education, Fine Arts and Humanities,

Science and Technology, and Social Sciences; All University; and the School of Graduate Studies. Its 92-acre campus is located in St. Cloud, 60 miles from the Twin Cities.

**Accreditation:** NCACS. Professionally accredited by the Accreditation Board for Engineering and Technology, the Accrediting Council on Education in Journalism and Mass Communication, the American Assembly of Collegiate Schools of Business, the Council on Rehabilitation Education, the Council on Social Work Education, the National Association of Schools of Art and Design, the National Association of Schools of Music, the National Council for Accreditation of Teacher Education.
**Religious orientation:** St. Cloud State University is nonsectarian; no religious requirements.
**Library:** Collections totaling over 2,209,971 volumes, 3,846 periodical subscriptions, and 1,347,029 microform items.
**Special facilities/museums:** Art history museum, electron microscope, planetarium.
**Athletic facilities:** Gymnasium, field house, basketball, racquetball, tennis, and volleyball courts, ice rink, track, swimming pool, baseball, football, and softball fields.

**STUDENT BODY. Undergraduate profile:** 91% are state residents; 41% are transfers. 1% Asian-American, 1% Black, 1% Hispanic, 96% White, 1% Other. Average age of undergraduates is 22.
**Freshman profile:** 95% of accepted applicants took ACT.
**Undergraduate achievement:** 76% of fall 1991 freshmen returned for fall 1992 term.
**Foreign students:** 297 students are from out of the country. Countries represented include Canada, China, Japan, Malaysia, and Pakistan; 46 in all.

**PROGRAMS OF STUDY. Degrees:** B.A., B.Elect.Studies, B.F.A., B.Mus., B.S.
**Majors:** Accounting, American Studies, Anthropology, Art, Aviation, Biological Sciences, Biology, Biotechnology, Chemistry, Communicative Disorders, Computer Science, Criminal Justice Sciences, Earth Sciences, Economics, Elective Studies, Electrical Engineering, Elementary Education, Engineering Technology, English, Environmental Studies, Finance, French, General Business, General Science, Geography, German, Health Education, History, Industrial Engineering, Industrial Studies, Information Systems, Insurance/Real Estate, International Business, International Studies, Latin American Studies, Local/Urban Affairs, Management, Manufacturing Engineering, Marketing, Mass Communications, Mathematics, Medical Technology, Meteorology, Music, Nuclear Medical Technology, Philosophy, Photographic Engineering Technology, Photographic Science/Instrumentation, Physical Education, Physical Sciences, Physics, Political Science/Government, Psychology, Public Administration, Quantitative Methods, Reading Education, Recreation, Secondary Education, Social Sciences, Social Studies, Social Work, Sociology, Spanish, Special Education, Speech Communications, Statistics, Theatre, Vocational/Technical Education.
**Distribution of degrees:** The majors with the highest enrollment are business, mass communication, and education.
**Requirements:** General education requirement.
**Academic regulations:** Minimum 2.0 GPA must be maintained.
**Special:** Programs in international, minority, and women's studies. Associate's degrees offered. Self-designed majors. Double majors. Independent study. Pass/fail grading option. Internships. Graduate school at which undergraduates may take graduate-level courses. Preprofessional programs in law, medicine, veterinary science, pharmacy, dentistry, and optometry. 2-2 occupational therapy program and 3-1 physical therapy program with Mayo Clinic (Rochester). 2-2 physical therapy program with U of Minnesota. 3-1 law enforcement program with U of Minnesota. 3-2 premedicine, prelaw, and predentistry programs with U of Minnesota. Cross-registration with Coll of St. Benedict and St. John's U. Exchange programs with state universities. Teacher certification in early childhood, elementary, secondary, special education, and vo-tech education. Certification in specific subject areas. Study abroad in China, Costa Rica, France, Germany, Japan, and Spain. ROTC.
**Honors:** Phi Beta Kappa. Honors program. Honor societies.
**Academic Assistance:** Remedial reading, writing, math, and study skills. Nonremedial tutoring.

**STUDENT LIFE. Housing:** Students may live on or off campus. Coed dorms. 19% of students live in college housing.
**Social atmosphere:** "The campus provides much of the cultural life in St. Cloud," reports the student newspaper. "Off-campus entertainment is basically a choice of music at different eating and drinking establishments." Favorite nightspots include the Red Carpet, McRudy's, the Beach Club, Charlie's, and D.B. Searle's. Influential groups on campus include the Student Senate, Greeks, and the sports teams. The most popular events of the year include plays, concerts, hockey and football games, and art exhibitions.
**Services and counseling/handicapped student services:** Placement services. Health service. Women's center. Day care. Legal assistance center. Speech/hearing clinic. Counseling services for minority, military, veteran, and older students. Birth control, personal, and psychological counseling. Career and academic guidance services. Physically disabled student services. Learning disabled services. Notetaking services. Reader services for the blind.
**Campus organizations:** Undergraduate student government. Student newspaper (Chronicle, published twice/week). Literary magazine. Radio and TV stations. Brass and jazz ensembles, concert choir, opera workshop, Aero Club, Art Student Union, creative writing club, bicycling and bowling clubs, College Republicans, gerontology club, international dance club, Lesbian/Gay/Bisexual Resource Center, Society of Women Engineers, Amnesty International, special-interest and departmental clubs. Six fraternities, five chapter houses; five sororities, four chapter houses. 1% of men join a fraternity. 1% of women join a sorority.
**Religious organizations:** Baptist Student Union, Campus Crusade for Christ, Christians in Action, Intervarsity Christian Fellowship, Latter-Day Saints Student Association, Lutheran Campus Ministry, Lutheran Student Fellowship, Newman Center, Open Forum, United Ministries in Higher Education, Moslem group.
**Minority/foreign student organizations:** American Indian Club, Council of African-American Students, Mexican-American Student Association. International Student Association, Chinese, Hmong, Korean, Pakistani, and Vietnamese groups.

**ATHLETICS. Physical education requirements:** Two quarter hours of physical education required.
**Intercollegiate competition:** 10% of students participate. Baseball (M), basketball (M,W), cheerleading (M,W), cross-country (M,W), diving (M,W), football (M), golf (M,W), ice hockey (M), softball (W), swimming (M,W), tennis (M,W), track (indoor) (M,W), track (outdoor) (M,W), track and field (indoor) (M,W), track and field (outdoor) (M,W), volleyball (W), wrestling (M). Member of NCAA Division I for men's ice hockey, NCAA Division II, North Central Conference, Western Collegiate Hockey Association.
**Intramural and club sports:** 50% of students participate. Men's club bowling, canoe/kayak, crew, fencing, martial arts, racquetball, rugby, soccer, volleyball, weight lifting. Women's club bowling, canoe/kayak, crew, fencing, martial arts, racquetball, rugby, soccer, weight lifting.

**ADMISSIONS. Academic basis for candidate selection** (in order of priority): Class rank, standardized test scores, secondary school record, school's recommendation, essay.
**Nonacademic basis for candidate selection:** Geographical distribution and alumni/ae relationship are emphasized. Character and personality, extracurricular participation, and particular talent or ability are considered.
**Requirements:** Graduation from secondary school is required; GED is accepted. 14 units and the following program of study are required: 4 units of English, 3 units of math, 3 units of science including 1 unit of lab, 3 units of social studies. Rank in top half of secondary school class required; minimum composite ACT score of 25 recommended. ACT is required; SAT may be substituted. ACH recommended. Campus visit and interview recommended. Off-campus interviews available with an alumni representative.
**Procedure:** Take ACT by summer before entering college. Suggest filing application by fall. Application deadline is August 15. Notification of admission on rolling basis. Freshmen accepted in terms other than fall.
**Special programs:** Admission may be deferred one year. Credit may be granted through CEEB Advanced Placement for scores of 3 or higher. Credit may be granted through CLEP general and subject exams. Early decision program. Concurrent enrollment program.
**Transfer students:** Transfer students accepted for terms other than fall. In fall 1993, 41% of all new students were transfers into all classes. 2,020 transfer applications were received, 1,948 were accepted. Application deadline is August 15 for fall; February 15 for spring. Lowest course grade accepted is "D-." Maximum number of transferable credits is 96 quarter hours. At least 45 quarter hours must be completed at the university to receive degree.
**Admissions contact:** Sherwood Reid, M.S., Director of Admissions. 612 255-2244.

**FINANCIAL AID. Available aid:** Pell grants, SEOG, state grants, school scholarships, private scholarships, ROTC scholarships, academic merit scholarships, and athletic scholarships. Perkins Loans (NDSL), PLUS, Stafford Loans (GSL), state loans, school loans, private loans, and SLS. AMS.
**Financial aid statistics:** 29% of aid is not need-based. In 1993-94, 80% of all undergraduate applicants received aid; 59% of freshman applicants. Average amounts of aid awarded freshmen: Scholarships and grants, $2,056; loans, $2,441.
**Supporting data/closing dates:** FAFSA: Accepted on rolling basis. School's own aid application: Accepted on rolling basis. Income tax forms: Accepted on rolling basis. Notification of awards begins June 15.
**Financial aid contact:** Frank Loncorich, Director of Financial Aid. 612 255-2047.

**STUDENT EMPLOYMENT.** College Work/Study Program. Institutional employment. 23% of full-time undergraduates work on campus during school year. Students may expect to earn an average of $1,500 during school year. Off-campus part-time employment opportunities rated "excellent."

**COMPUTER FACILITIES.** 1,275 IBM/IBM-compatible and Macintosh/Apple microcomputers; 539 are networked. Students may access Digital, IBM, SUN, UNISYS minicomputer/mainframe systems, BITNET, Internet. Residence halls may be equipped with stand-alone microcomputers. Client/LAN operating systems include Apple/Macintosh, DOS, OS/2, UNIX/XENIX/AIX, X-windows, DEC, LocalTalk/AppleTalk, Novell. Computer languages and software packages include BASIC, BMDP, C, C+, COBOL, Excel, FORTRAN, Microsoft Word, MINITAB, Modula 2, Pascal, PC-Write, SAS, SPSS, WordPerfect; database software; 133 in all. Certain lab restrictions.
**Fees:** $6 computer fee per quarter; included in tuition/fees.

**GRADUATE CAREER DATA.** Highest graduate school enrollments: U of Minnesota, North Dakota State U, U of North Dakota. 60% of graduates choose careers in business and industry. Companies and businesses that hire graduates: Daytons, Fingerhut, Control Data, Target, 3M, Honeywell, Carsons.

# Saint John's University

**Collegeville, MN 56321** **612 363-2011**

**1994-95 Costs.** Tuition: $12,247. Room: $1,921. Board: $2,160. Fees, books, misc. academic expenses (school's estimate): $588.
**Enrollment.** 1,746 men (full-time). Freshman class: 845 applicants, 745 accepted, 435 enrolled. Graduate enrollment: 55 men, 35 women.
**Test score averages/ranges.** Average SAT scores: 460 verbal, 520 math. Range of SAT scores of middle 50%: 410-510 verbal, 440-600 math. Average ACT scores: 22 English, 23 math, 23 composite. Range of ACT scores of middle 50%: 19-25 English, 20-26 math.
**Faculty.** 139 full-time; 16 part-time. 90% of faculty holds highest degree in specific field. Student/faculty ratio: 13 to 1.
**Selectivity rating.** Less competitive.

**PROFILE.** Saint John's is a church-affiliated, liberal arts university. Founded in 1857, it is a coordinate with College of Saint Benedict, for women. Programs are offered through the College of Arts and Sciences and the School of Theology. Its 2,400-acre campus is located in Collegeville, 80 miles north of Minneapolis.

**Accreditation:** NCACS. Professionally accredited by the Council on Social Work Education, the National Council for Accreditation of Teacher Education, the National League for Nursing.

**Religious orientation:** Saint John's University is affiliated with the Roman Catholic Church (Order of St. Benedict); two semesters of religion/theology required.
**Library:** Collections totaling over 488,000 volumes, 3,200 periodical subscriptions, and 118,500 microform items.
**Special facilities/museums:** Monastic Manuscript Library (largest medieval library in the world).
**Athletic facilities:** Gymnasiums, basketball, handball, racquetball, tennis, and volleyball courts, diving and swimming pools, baseball, football, intramural, and softball fields, lakes, hiking and Nordic skiing trails, ice rink, tracks, weight rooms, stadium.

**STUDENT BODY. Undergraduate profile:** 22% are state residents; 17% are transfers. 2% Asian-American, 1% Black, 1% Hispanic, 1% Native American, 93% White, 2% Foreign. Average age of undergraduates is 20.
**Freshman profile:** 5% of freshmen who took SAT scored 700 or over on math; 6% scored 600 or over on verbal, 27% scored 600 or over on math; 30% scored 500 or over on verbal, 58% scored 500 or over on math; 81% scored 400 or over on verbal, 84% scored 400 or over on math; 96% scored 300 or over on verbal, 99% scored 300 or over on math. 2% of freshmen who took ACT scored 30 or over on English, 5% scored 30 or over on math, 3% scored 30 or over on composite; 36% scored 24 or over on English, 43% scored 24 or over on math, 43% scored 24 or over on composite; 84% scored 18 or over on English, 91% scored 18 or over on math, 94% scored 18 or over on composite; 99% scored 12 or over on English, 100% scored 12 or over on math, 100% scored 12 or over on composite; 100% scored 6 or over on English. 24% of accepted applicants took SAT; 96% took ACT. 70% of freshmen come from public schools.
**Undergraduate achievement:** 83% of fall 1991 freshmen returned for fall 1992 term. 60% of entering class graduated. 25% of students who completed a degree program immediately went on to graduate study.
**Foreign students:** 42 students are from out of the country. Countries represented include the Bahamas, Hong Kong, Japan; 18 in all.

**PROGRAMS OF STUDY. Degrees:** B.A.
**Majors:** Accounting, Art, Art History, Biology, Business Management, Chemistry, Classics, Communications, Dietetics, Economics, Elementary Education, English, French, German, Government, History, Humanities, Liturgical Music, Mathematics, Mathematics/Computer Science, Medical Technology, Medieval Studies, Music, Natural Science, Nursing, Nutritional Sciences, Pastoral Ministry, Peace Studies, Philosophy, Physics, Physics/Computer Science, Psychology, Religious Education, Social Sciences, Social Work, Sociology, Spanish, Theatre, Theology.
**Distribution of degrees:** The majors with the highest enrollment are management, government, English, and accounting; medieval studies, dietetics, and classics have the lowest.
**Requirements:** General education requirement.
**Academic regulations:** Freshmen must maintain minimum 1.8 GPA; sophomores, juniors, seniors 2.0 GPA.
**Special:** Minors offered in most majors and in computer science, Greek, Latin, physical education, religious studies, and secondary education. St. John's and Coll of St. Benedict coordinate programs, combine faculties, share physical facilities, and in some cases unite academic departments with students pursuing course of study offered at other college. Courses offered in astronomy, geography, geology, journalism, and speech. Self-designed majors. Double majors. Dual degrees. Independent study. Accelerated study. Pass/fail grading option. Internships. Graduate school at which undergraduates may take graduate-level courses. Preprofessional programs in law, medicine, veterinary science, pharmacy, dentistry, theology, engineering, forestry, occupational therapy, and physical therapy. 3-1 dentistry program. 3-2 engineering programs with U of Minnesota and Washington U. 3-2 occupational therapy with Washington U. Member of Higher Education Consortium for Urban Affairs. Exchange programs with Coll of St. Benedict and St. Cloud State U. Teacher certification in early childhood, elementary, and secondary education. Exchange program abroad in Japan (Sophia U). Study abroad also in Austria, China, England, France, Greece, Ireland, Italy, and Spain. ROTC.
**Honors:** Honors program. Honor societies.
**Academic Assistance:** Nonremedial tutoring.

**STUDENT LIFE. Housing:** All freshmen must live on campus. Men's dorms. School-owned/operated apartments. Off-campus privately-owned housing. 80% of students live in college housing.
**Social atmosphere:** According to the editor of the student newspaper, there is a wide variety of social and cultural life on campus, including sports opportunities and guest speakers. Students enjoy going to football and soccer games, plays, student productions, concerts, films, and dances. Influential groups on campus include the Joint Events Council, AKS, and St. John's Senate. Favorite spots to gather are the libraries, Science Hall, and the Quad. Other favorites are the Butcher Shop, the Abbey, the MAB, and the BAC.
**Services and counseling/handicapped student services:** Placement services. Health service. Counseling services for minority students. Personal and psychological counseling. Career and academic guidance services. Religious counseling. Physically disabled student services. Learning disabled services. Notetaking services. Tape recorders. Tutors. Reader services for the blind.
**Campus organizations:** Undergraduate student government. Student newspaper (Record, published twice/month). Literary magazine. Yearbook. Radio station. Vocal and instrumental groups, debating, peer resource program, social justice groups, International Affairs Club, Young Democrats, College Republicans, academic and special-interest groups.
**Religious organizations:** Campus Ministry, Knights of Columbus, Fellowship of Christian Athletes, Christian Clowns.
**Minority/foreign student organizations:** Coalition for Black Cultural Awareness. International Student Club, international student newspaper.

**ATHLETICS. Physical education requirements:** One semester of physical education required.
**Intercollegiate competition:** 25% of students participate. Baseball (M), basketball (M), cross-country (M), diving (M), football (M), golf (M), ice hockey (M), martial arts (M), soccer (M), swimming (M), tennis (M), track (indoor) (M), track (outdoor) (M), track and field (indoor) (M), track and field (outdoor) (M), wrestling (M). Member of Minnesota Intercollegiate Athletic Conference, NCAA Division III.
**Intramural and club sports:** 85% of students participate. Intramural baseball, basketball, bowling, racquetball, soccer, softball, touch football, volleyball. Men's club crew, karate, racquetball, rugby, tae kwon do, volleyball.

**ADMISSIONS. Academic basis for candidate selection** (in order of priority): Secondary school record, class rank, standardized test scores, essay, school's recommendation.
**Nonacademic basis for candidate selection:** Extracurricular participation is important. Character and personality and particular talent or ability are considered.
**Requirements:** Graduation from secondary school is required; GED is accepted. 17 units and the following program of study are recommended: 4 units of English, 3 units of math, 2 units of lab science, 2 units of foreign language, 2 units of social studies, 4 units of electives. Minimum composite ACT score of 19 (combined SAT score of 910) and minimum 2.8 GPA required. Portfolio recommended of art program applicants. Audition recommended of music program applicants. Conditional admission possible for applicants not meeting standard requirements. SAT or ACT required; PSAT may be substituted for SAT. Campus visit and interview recommended. Off-campus interviews available with admissions and alumni representatives.
**Procedure:** Take SAT or ACT by December of 12th year. Suggest filing application by May 1; no deadline. Notification of admission on rolling basis. Reply is required prior to registration. $200 nonrefundable room deposit. Freshmen accepted in terms other than fall.
**Special programs:** Admission may be deferred. Credit and/or placement may be granted through CEEB Advanced Placement exams for scores of 3 or higher. Credit and placement may be granted through challenge exams. Early entrance/early admission program. Concurrent enrollment program.
**Transfer students:** Transfer students accepted for terms other than fall. In fall 1992, 17% of all new students were transfers into all classes. 136 transfer applications were received, 122 were accepted. Application deadline is rolling for fall; rolling for spring. Minimum 2.5 GPA required. Lowest course grade accepted is "C." Maximum number of transferable credits is 79 semester hours. At least 45 semester hours must be completed at the university to receive degree.
**Admissions contact:** Mary Milbert, Director of Admissions. 612 363-2196, 800 245-6467.

**FINANCIAL AID. Available aid:** Pell grants, SEOG, state grants, school scholarships and grants, private scholarships and grants, ROTC scholarships, academic merit scholarships, and aid for undergraduate foreign students. Perkins Loans (NDSL), PLUS, Stafford Loans (GSL), state loans, and SLS. AMS. Institutional tuition stabilization and monthly payment plans.
**Financial aid statistics:** 6% of aid is not need-based. In 1992-93, 92% of all undergraduate applicants received aid; 87% of freshman applicants. Average amounts of aid awarded freshmen: Scholarships and grants, $5,400; loans, $2,450.
**Supporting data/closing dates:** FAFSA: Priority filing date is March 1; accepted on rolling basis. School's own aid application: Priority filing date is March 1; accepted on rolling basis. State aid form: Priority filing date is March 1; accepted on rolling basis. Notification of awards on rolling basis.
**Financial aid contact:** Mike White, Director of Financial Aid. 612 363-3664.

**STUDENT EMPLOYMENT.** College Work/Study Program. Institutional employment. 45% of full-time undergraduates work on campus during school year. Students may expect to earn an average of $1,600 during school year. Off-campus part-time employment opportunities rated "good."

**COMPUTER FACILITIES.** 300 IBM/IBM-compatible and Macintosh/Apple microcomputers; 200 are networked. Students may access Digital minicomputer/mainframe systems, BITNET, Internet. Computer languages and software packages include Assembler, BASIC, BMDP, C, COBOL, FORTRAN, IML, LINDO, SPSS, MINITAB, Pascal; database, spreadsheet, statistical, word processing packages. Computer facilities are available to all students.
**Fees:** None.
**Hours:** 8 AM-midn. (M-Th); 8 AM-9 PM (F); 10 AM-9 PM (Sa); 10 AM-midn. (Su).

**GRADUATE CAREER DATA.** Graduate school percentages: 5% enter law school. 5% enter medical school. 5% enter graduate business programs. 10% enter graduate arts and sciences programs. Highest graduate school enrollments: U of Minnesota Sch of Law. 50% of graduates choose careers in business and industry. Companies and businesses that hire graduates: Big Six accounting firms, Chubb, Deluxe, Minnesota Mutual, 3M.

**PROMINENT ALUMNI/AE.** Eugene McCarthy, former U.S. senator and presidential candidate; Roger Birk, finance chairperson emeritus, Merrill Lynch; Edward Devitt, federal judge; Paul Schurke, co-navigator, Steger polar expedition; Bill Kling, communications president, Minnesota Public Radio.

# Saint Mary's College of Minnesota

**Winona, MN 55987-1399** **507 452-4430**

**1994-95 Costs.** Tuition: $10,800. Room & board: $3,680. Fees, books, misc. academic expenses (school's estimate): $480.
**Enrollment.** Undergraduates: 662 men, 581 women (full-time). Freshman class: 870 applicants, 802 accepted, 367 enrolled. Graduate enrollment: 1,599 men, 4,167 women.
**Test score averages/ranges.** Average SAT scores: 445 verbal, 475 math. Range of SAT scores of middle 50%: 400-499 verbal, 400-499 math. Average ACT scores: 21 English, 21 math, 21 composite. Range of ACT scores of middle 50%: 16-20 composite.
**Faculty.** 87 full-time; 40 part-time. 61% of faculty holds highest degree in specific field. Student/faculty ratio: 14 to 1.
**Selectivity rating.** Less competitive.

**PROFILE.** Saint Mary's is a private, church-affiliated, liberal arts college. Founded as a men's college in 1912, it adopted coeducation in 1969. Its 350-acre campus is located in Winona, southeast of the Twin Cities.

**Accreditation:** NCACS. Professionally accredited by the American Medical Association (CAHEA).
**Religious orientation:** Saint Mary's College of Minnesota is affiliated with the Roman Catholic Church (Brothers of Christian Schools); two semesters of religion/theology required.
**Library:** Collections totaling over 152,000 volumes, 717 periodical subscriptions, and 3,000 microform items.
**Special facilities/museums:** Art gallery, language lab, psychology lab.
**Athletic facilities:** Field house, ice rink, baseball, intramural, soccer, and softball fields, racquetball and tennis courts, batting cage, aerobics, training, and weight rooms, Nordic ski trails, gymnasium.

**STUDENT BODY. Undergraduate profile:** 46% are state residents; 5% are transfers. 3% Asian-American, 1% Black, 6% Hispanic, 1% Native American, 89% White. Average age of undergraduates is 20.
**Freshman profile:** 1% of freshmen who took SAT scored 700 or over on verbal, 1% scored 700 or over on math; 2% scored 600 or over on verbal, 2% scored 600 or over on math; 6% scored 500 or over on verbal, 7% scored 500 or over on math; 12% scored 400 or over on verbal, 12% scored 400 or over on math; 17% scored 300 or over on verbal, 16% scored 300 or over on math. 15% of accepted applicants took SAT; 91% took ACT. 62% of freshmen come from public schools.
**Undergraduate achievement:** 71% of fall 1992 freshmen returned for fall 1993 term. 41% of entering class graduated. 18% of students who completed a degree program immediately went on to graduate study.
**Foreign students:** 63 students are from out of the country. Countries represented include Canada, Colombia, Japan, Mexico, Saudi Arabia, and Spain; 12 in all.

**PROGRAMS OF STUDY. Degrees:** B.A., B.S.
**Majors:** Accounting, Art, Band/Classroom Music, Biology, Business Administration, Chemistry, Computer Information Systems, Computer Science, Criminal Justice, Cytotechnology, Early Childhood Education, Education, Electronic Publishing, English, English Education, English Literature, English/Writing, Environmental Biology, French, Graphic Design, Guitar/Instrumental, History, Human Services, Interdisciplinary Studies, International Business, Law Enforcement, Management, Marketing, Mathematics, Media Communications, Medical Technology, Music, Music Merchandising, Natural Science, Nuclear Medical Technology, Organ/Piano, Philosophy, Physics, Political Science, Psychology, Public Administration, Public Relations, Religious Education, Social Science, Social Science Education, Sociology, Spanish, Statistics, Studio Arts, Telecommunications, Theatre, Theatre Education, Theatre/Speech Education, Theology, Vocal/Classroom Education, Youth Ministry.
**Distribution of degrees:** The majors with the highest enrollment are marketing, management, and education; studio arts, theatre arts, and Spanish have the lowest.
**Requirements:** General education requirement.
**Academic regulations:** Freshmen must maintain minimum 1.5 GPA first semester, 1.6 second semester; sophomores must maintain minimum 1.8 GPA third semester, 2.0 fourth semester; juniors, seniors must maintain 2.0 GPA.
**Special:** Minors offered in most majors. Self-designed majors. Double majors. Independent study. Accelerated study. Pass/fail grading option. Internships. Cooperative education programs. Graduate school at which undergraduates may take graduate-level courses. Preprofessional programs in law, medicine, veterinary science, dentistry, theology, and physical therapy. 3-1 medical technology programs with United Hospitals and St. Anthony Hospital. 3-1 nuclear medical technology programs with Evanston Hospital, Hines Veterans Hospital, Mayo Foundation, and Veterans Administration Hospital. 3-1 cytotechnology program with Mayo Sch of Health Related Sciences. 3-2 engineering programs with Illinois Inst of Tech and U of Minnesota. Washington Semester. Teacher certification in early childhood, elementary, and secondary education. Certification in specific subject areas. Exchange program abroad in England. Study abroad also in Costa Rica, Ireland, Mexico, and Spain.
**Honors:** Honors program. Honor societies.
**Academic Assistance:** Remedial study skills. Nonremedial tutoring.

**STUDENT LIFE. Housing:** All freshmen and sophomores must live on campus unless living with family. Coed, women's, and men's dorms. School-owned/operated apartments. 86% of students live in college housing.
**Social atmosphere:** According to the student newspaper, "Saint Mary's is a very diverse campus where all interests are encouraged." Greek organizations, Students for a More Responsible Society, and Socratic Circle are influential on campus. The Cardinal Club is a popular meeting place on campus. Among the year's most favorite events are the Blue Angel and Gaslight talent shows, hockey games, art shows, and jazz concerts.
**Services and counseling/handicapped student services:** Counseling services for minority, veteran, and older students. Personal counseling. Career and academic guidance services. Religious counseling. Physically disabled student services. Learning disabled services. Notetaking services. Tape recorders. Tutors. Reader services for the blind.
**Campus organizations:** Undergraduate student government. Student newspapers (Cardinal, published twice/month; Troll, published daily). Literary magazine. Radio station. Chamber Singers, chorale, jazz combo and ensemble, Burbage Players, Big Brothers/Big Sisters, nursing home visiting group, youth group for retarded citizens, Campus Life Support, departmental and special-interest groups, 71 organizations in all. Two fraternities, no chapter houses; three sororities, no chapter houses. 4% of men join a fraternity. 4% of women join a sorority.
**Religious organizations:** Campus Ministry, Fellowship of Christian Athletes.
**Minority/foreign student organizations:** International Association, Intercambio.

**ATHLETICS. Physical education requirements:** Two semesters of physical education required.
**Intercollegiate competition:** 25% of students participate. Baseball (M), basketball (M,W), cross-country (M,W), golf (M), ice hockey (M), Nordic skiing (M,W), soccer (M,W), softball (W), tennis (M,W), track (outdoor) (M), volleyball (W). Member of Minnesota Intercollegiate Athletic Conference, NCAA Division III.
**Intramural and club sports:** 40% of students participate. Intramural basketball, broomball, flag football, floor hockey, fun runs, ice hockey, softball, volleyball. Women's club golf.

**ADMISSIONS. Academic basis for candidate selection** (in order of priority): Secondary school record, standardized test scores, class rank, essay, school's recommendation. **Nonacademic basis for candidate selection:** Character and personality, extracurricular participation, and particular talent or ability are important. Geographical distribution and alumni/ae relationship are considered.
**Requirements:** Graduation from secondary school is required; GED is accepted. 18 units and the following program of study are recommended: 4 units of English, 3 units of math, 2 units of science, 2 units of social studies, 7 units of electives. Minimum composite ACT score of 18 and minimum "C+" average required; rank in top half of secondary school class recommended. College Bound summer study skills program for applicants not normally admissible. ACT is required; SAT may be substituted. Campus visit and interview recommended. Off-campus interviews available with an admissions representative.
**Procedure:** Take ACT or SAT in spring of the 11th or fall of the 12th year. Visit college for interview by winter of 12th year. Notification of admission on rolling basis. No set date by which applicants must accept offer. $200 nonrefundable tuition deposit. $200 nonrefundable room deposit. Freshmen accepted in terms other than fall.
**Special programs:** Admission may be deferred one year. Credit and/or placement may be granted through CEEB Advanced Placement exams for scores of 3 or higher. Credit and/or placement may be granted through CLEP subject exams. Credit and placement may be granted through ACT PEP, DANTES, and challenge exams and military and life experience. Early entrance/early admission program. Concurrent enrollment program.
**Transfer students:** Transfer students accepted for terms other than fall. In fall 1993, 5% of all new students were transfers into all classes. Application deadline is rolling for fall; rolling for spring. Minimum 2.0 GPA required. Lowest course grade accepted is "C." Maximum number of transferable credits is 62 semester hours. At least 60 semester hours must be completed at the college to receive degree.
**Admissions contact:** Anthony M. Piscitiello, M.A., Vice President for Admissions. 800 635-5987.

**FINANCIAL AID. Available aid:** Pell grants, SEOG, state scholarships and grants, school scholarships and grants, private scholarships and grants, and academic merit scholarships. Perkins Loans (NDSL), PLUS, Stafford Loans (GSL), state loans, and SLS. Tuition Plan Inc., Knight Tuition Plans, AMS, and guaranteed tuition.
**Financial aid statistics:** 9% of aid is not need-based. In 1993-94, 84% of all undergraduate applicants received aid; 94% of freshman applicants. Average amounts of aid awarded freshmen: Scholarships and grants, $2,348; loans, $2,300.
**Supporting data/closing dates:** FAFSA/FAF/FFS: Accepted on rolling basis. School's own aid application: Accepted on rolling basis. Notification of awards on rolling basis.
**Financial aid contact:** Jayne Wobig, Director of Financial Aid. 507 457-1437.

**STUDENT EMPLOYMENT.** College Work/Study Program. Institutional employment. 53% of full-time undergraduates work on campus during school year. Students may expect to earn an average of $1,036 during school year. Off-campus part-time employment opportunities rated "fair."

**COMPUTER FACILITIES.** 160 IBM/IBM-compatible and Macintosh/Apple microcomputers; 140 are networked. Students may access Digital minicomputer/mainframe systems, Internet. Computer languages and software packages include BASIC, COBOL, FORTRAN, Lotus 1-2-3, MINITAB, Microcase, Pascal, WordPerfect. Computer facilities are available to all students.
**Fees:** Computer fee is included in tuition/fees.
**Hours:** 7:30 AM-midn. (M-Th); 10 AM-4 PM (Sa); noon-midn. (Su).

**GRADUATE CAREER DATA.** Graduate school percentages: 1% enter law school. 1% enter medical school. 3% enter graduate business programs. 12% enter graduate arts and sciences programs. 1% enter theological school/seminary. Highest graduate school enrollments: Iowa State U, Loyola U at Chicago, Mayo Medical Sch, U of Minnesota, Saint Mary's Coll. 41% of graduates choose careers in business and industry. Companies and businesses that hire graduates: Evanston Hospital, Harris Bank, Osco Drug, Peace Corps, Saint Mary's Coll of Minnesota, U.S. Fish and Wildlife Service.

**PROMINENT ALUMNI/AE.** Michael Bilandic, formery mayor of Chicago, Chief Justice of Illinois Supreme Court; LCDR Laura Folk, USN, operations officer, Defense Intelligence Agency; Jack Sharkey, playwright.

# Saint Olaf College

**Northfield, MN 55057-1098** **507 646-2222**

**1994-95 Costs.** Tuition: $14,350. Room & board: $3,750. Fees, books, misc. academic expenses (school's estimate): $500.
**Enrollment.** Undergraduates: 1,299 men, 1,589 women (full-time). Freshman class: 2,248 applicants, 1,673 accepted, 745 enrolled.
**Test score averages/ranges.** Average SAT scores: 530 verbal, 580 math. Range of SAT scores of middle 50%: 460-590 verbal, 520-650 math. Average ACT scores: 26 English, 25 math, 26 composite. Range of ACT scores of middle 50%: 23-28 composite.
**Faculty.** 267 full-time; 112 part-time. 85% of faculty holds highest degree in specific field. Student/faculty ratio: 12 to 1.
**Selectivity rating.** More competitive.

**PROFILE.** St. Olaf, founded in 1874, is a private, church-affiliated, liberal arts college. Its 350-acre campus, including several buildings from the 19th and early 20th centuries, is located in Northfield, 40 miles south of Minneapolis-St. Paul.

**Accreditation:** NCACS. Professionally accredited by the Council on Social Work Education, the National Association of Schools of Music, the National Council for Accreditation of Teacher Education, the National League for Nursing.
**Religious orientation:** Saint Olaf College is affiliated with the Evangelical Lutheran Church in America; three semesters of religion required.

**Library:** Collections totaling over 428,059 volumes, 1,968 periodical subscriptions, and 46,053 microform items.
**Special facilities/museums:** Norwegian-American history museum, language lab.
**Athletic facilities:** Field house, swimming pool, basketball, racquetball, tennis, and volleyball courts, tracks, training, weight, and wrestling rooms, baseball, football, intramural, soccer, and softball fields, aerobics studio.

**STUDENT BODY. Undergraduate profile:** 57% are state residents. 4% Asian-American, 2% Black, 1% Hispanic, 91% White, 2% Other. Average age of undergraduates is 21.
**Freshman profile:** 2% of freshmen who took SAT scored 700 or over on verbal, 14% scored 700 or over on math; 23% scored 600 or over on verbal, 43% scored 600 or over on math; 63% scored 500 or over on verbal, 82% scored 500 or over on math; 94% scored 400 or over on verbal, 98% scored 400 or over on math; 100% scored 300 or over on verbal, 100% scored 300 or over on math. 14% of freshmen who took ACT scored 30 or over on English, 11% scored 30 or over on math, 14% scored 30 or over on composite; 67% scored 24 or over on English, 63% scored 24 or over on math, 69% scored 24 or over on composite; 97% scored 18 or over on English, 97% scored 18 or over on math, 98% scored 18 or over on composite; 100% scored 12 or over on English, 100% scored 12 or over on math, 100% scored 12 or over on composite. 47% of accepted applicants took SAT; 88% took ACT. 80% of freshmen come from public schools.
**Undergraduate achievement:** 90% of fall 1992 freshmen returned for fall 1993 term. 76% of entering class graduated. 25% of students who completed a degree program went on to graduate study within one year.
**Foreign students:** 58 students are from out of the country. Countries represented include Canada, China, Germany, Japan, Norway, and Thailand; 20 in all.

**PROGRAMS OF STUDY. Degrees:** B.A., B.A.Nurs., B.Mus.
**Majors:** American Racial/Multicultural Studies, American Studies, Ancient Studies, Applied Music, Art, Art History, Asian Studies, Biology, Chemistry, Church Music, Classics, Dance, Economics, English, Family Resources, Fine Arts, French, German, Greek, Hispanic Studies, History, Latin, Literature, Mathematics, Medieval Studies, Music, Music Education, Music Theory/Composition, Norwegian, Nursing, Philosophy, Physical Education, Physics, Political Science, Psychology, Religion, Russian, Russian/Soviet Studies, Social Studies Education, Social Work, Sociology, Spanish, Speech/Theatre, Sports Science, Urban Studies, Women's Studies.
**Distribution of degrees:** The majors with the highest enrollment are economics, English, and biology; women's studies, urban studies, and American racial/multicultural studies have the lowest.
**Requirements:** General education requirement.
**Academic regulations:** Minimum 2.0 GPA must be maintained.
**Special:** Concentrations (approved interdisciplinary programs) offered in some majors and in computer science, environmental studies, historical perspectives, intercultural studies, and statistics. Paracollege offers alternative education program in which students design their own "strategies for learning," including interdisciplinary seminars, tutorials, workshops, general college classes, and a teaching project. Great Conversation program explores Western civilization from antiquity through mid-20th century. Participation in U of Minnesota SPAN program. Foreign Languages Across the Curriculum program. Self-designed majors. Double majors. Independent study. Pass/fail grading option. Internships. Graduate school at which undergraduates may take graduate-level courses. Preprofessional programs in law, medicine, veterinary science, pharmacy, dentistry, theology, optometry, and pre-physical theraphy. 3-2 engineering program with Washington U. 3-2 elementary education/fine arts program with Augsburg Coll. Member of Higher Education Consortium for Urban Affairs, Associated Colleges of the Midwest, and Minnesota Intercollegiate Nursing Consortium. Washington Semester. Newberry Library Program in the Humanities (Illinois). Other off-campus study opportunities. Exchange program with Fisk U. Cross-registration with Carleton Coll. Art courses through Union of Independent Colleges of Art and with Drew U. Teacher certification in secondary education. Certification in specific subject areas. Study abroad in African countries, Australia, the Czech Republic, China, Columbia, Costa Rica, Denmark, Ecuador, France, Germany, Greece, Hong Kong, Hungary, India, Indonesia, Italy, Korea, Japan, Liberia, New Guinea, Scandinavian countries, the former Soviet Republics, Spain, and the United Kingdom..
**Honors:** Phi Beta Kappa. Honor societies.
**Academic Assistance:** Nonremedial tutoring.

**STUDENT LIFE. Housing:** All unmarried students under age 21 must live on campus unless living near campus with relatives. Coed dorms. Off-campus privately-owned housing. 90% of students live in college housing.
**Social atmosphere:** The student newspaper reports, "A lot of people see on-campus movies and attend lectures and music performances. Northfield at times can get dull, but Minneapolis-St. Paul is only 40 minutes away." Favorite student meeting spots include the Reub-n-Stein, the Cage, the Lion's Pause, the library, and the International Coffeehouse. Popular events include Arbstock (a springfest conducted jointly with Carleton College) and the Christmas Concert.
**Services and counseling/handicapped student services:** Placement services. Health service. Women's center. Counseling services for minority and older students. Birth control, personal, and psychological counseling. Career and academic guidance services. Religious counseling. Physically disabled student services. Learning disabled services. Tutors. Reader services for the blind.
**Campus organizations:** Undergraduate student government. Student newspaper (Manitou Messenger, published once/week). Literary magazine. Yearbook. Radio station. Musical groups, chapter of National College Players, drama studio, dance company, juggling club, Amnesty International, language clubs, Feminist Awareness Caucus, political groups, 80 organizations in all.
**Religious organizations:** Bread for the World, Fellowship of Christian Athletes, informal Bible study groups, Intervarsity Christian Fellowship, Christian Outreach Teams, Student Congregation, Newman Club.
**Minority/foreign student organizations:** Harambe, Students Against Racism, Zebra Patch, Cultural Union for Black Expression. Asian Concerns, South African Concerns, World Issues Dialogue, foreign student counselors, international dance club, international dormitory group.

**ATHLETICS. Physical education requirements:** Two semesters of physical education required.
**Intercollegiate competition:** 25% of students participate. Alpine skiing (M,W), baseball (M), basketball (M,W), cross-country (M,W), diving (M,W), football (M), golf (M,W), ice hockey (M), Nordic skiing (M,W), soccer (M,W), softball (W), swimming (M,W), tennis (M,W), track and field (indoor) (M,W), track and field (outdoor) (M,W), volleyball (W), wrestling (M). Member of MIAC, NCAA Division III.
**Intramural and club sports:** 75% of students participate. Intramural badminton, basketball, broomball, hockey, indoor soccer, powderpuff football, racquetball, soccer, softball, team handball, tennis, touch football, ultimate frisbee, volleyball. Men's club cycling, ultimate frisbee, volleyball, waterpolo. Women's club cycling, ultimate frisbee, waterpolo.

**ADMISSIONS. Academic basis for candidate selection** (in order of priority): Secondary school record, standardized test scores, essay, school's recommendation, class rank.
**Nonacademic basis for candidate selection:** Character and personality, extracurricular participation, particular talent or ability, geographical distribution, and alumni/ae relationship are considered.
**Requirements:** Graduation from secondary school is required; GED is accepted. 14 units and the following program of study are recommended: 4 units of English, 3 units of math, 2 units of science, including 1 unit of lab science, 2 units of foreign language, 3 units of social studies. Minimum 3.0 GPA in academic courses recommended. Audition required of B.Mus. program applicants. SAT or ACT is required. PSAT is recommended. Campus visit and interview recommended. No off-campus interviews.
**Procedure:** Take SAT or ACT by December of 12th year. Visit college for interview any time during 12th year. Suggest filing application by February 1; no deadline. Notification of admission on rolling basis. Reply is required after applicant has received admission reply and financial aid determination from all colleges applied to. $200 nonrefundable tuition deposit. Freshmen accepted in terms other than fall.
**Special programs:** Admission may be deferred one year. Credit and/or placement may be granted through CEEB Advanced Placement exams for scores of 3 or higher. Placement may be granted through challenge exams. Early decision program. In fall 1993, 201 applied for early decision and 173 were accepted. Deadline for applying for early decision is November 15. Early entrance/early admission program.
**Transfer students:** Transfer students accepted for terms other than fall. In fall 1993, 172 transfer applications were received, 120 were accepted. Application deadline is March 1 (priority) for fall; December 1 for spring. Minimum 3.0 GPA recommended. Lowest course grade accepted is "C." Maximum number of transferable credits is 18 units of course work. At least 17 units of course work must be completed at the college to receive degree.
**Admissions contact:** Bruce Moe, Vice President, Dean of Admissions and Financial Aid. 507 646-3025.

**FINANCIAL AID. Available aid:** Pell grants, SEOG, Federal Nursing Student Scholarships, state scholarships and grants, and school scholarships and grants. Perkins Loans (NDSL), PLUS, Stafford Loans (GSL), NSL, state loans, school loans, and SLS. Knight Tuition Plans.
**Financial aid statistics:** 2% of aid is not need-based. In 1993-94, 80% of all undergraduate applicants received aid; 85% of freshman applicants. Average amounts of aid awarded freshmen: Scholarships and grants, $7,860; loans, $3,000.
**Supporting data/closing dates:** FAFSA: Priority filing date is March 1. School's own aid application: Priority filing date is March 1. Notification of awards on rolling basis.
**Financial aid contact:** Mark Gelle, M.B.A., Director of Financial Aid. 507 646-3015.

**STUDENT EMPLOYMENT.** College Work/Study Program. Institutional employment. 60% of full-time undergraduates work on campus during school year. Students may expect to earn an average of $1,000 during school year. Off-campus part-time employment opportunities rated "fair."

**COMPUTER FACILITIES.** 325 IBM/IBM-compatible and Macintosh/Apple microcomputers; 310 are networked. Students may access Digital, SUN minicomputer/mainframe systems, Internet. Residence halls may be equipped with networked microcomputers. Computer languages and software packages include BASIC, C, FORTRAN, ICON, LISP, Pascal, Prolog; 41 in all. Computer facilities are available to all students.
**Fees:** $1 computer fee per start-up disk; included in tuition/fees.
**Hours:** 24 hours.

**GRADUATE CAREER DATA.** Highest graduate school enrollments: Iowa State U, Northwestern U, U of Minnesota. 65% of graduates choose careers in business and industry. Companies and businesses that hire graduates: Arthur Andersen, Cargill, Dayton Hudson, General Motors, IBM, 3M.

**PROMINENT ALUMNI/AE.** Al Quie, former Minnesota congressman and governor; Marguerite Johnson, associate editor, *Time* magazine; L. Bruce Laingen, foreign service; Arlen Erdahl, department director, Peace Corps; Dr. Tom Savaroid, director of research, 3M; Judith Ryan, executive director, American Nurses Association.

9-11

# Southwest State University

**Marshall, MN 56258** **507 537-7021**

**1994-95 Costs.** Tuition: $2,285 (state residents), $4,785 (out-of-state). Room & board: $2,900. Fees, books, misc. academic expenses (school's estimate): $1,015.
**Enrollment.** Undergraduates: 993 men, 1,098 women (full-time). Freshman class: 1,047 applicants, 938 accepted, 511 enrolled.
**Test score averages/ranges.** N/A.
**Faculty.** 135 full-time; 1 part-time. 77% of faculty holds highest degree in specific field. Student/faculty ratio: 19 to 1.
**Selectivity rating.** N/A.

**PROFILE.** Southwest State, founded in 1963, is a public university. Programs are offered through the Schools of Business, Education, Humanities, Science, Social Science, and Technology. Its 216-acre campus, in contemporary style, is located in Marshall, 90 miles from Sioux Falls.

**Accreditation:** NCACS. Professionally accredited by the National Association of Schools of Music.

**Religious orientation:** Southwest State University is nonsectarian; no religious requirements.
**Library:** Collections totaling over 165,000 volumes, 800 periodical subscriptions, and 37,000 microform items.
**Special facilities/museums:** Art gallery, natural history museum, science museum, planetarium, greenhouse, wildlife area.
**Athletic facilities:** Gymnasium, field house, basketball, racquetball, tennis, and volleyball courts, track, stadium, weight rooms, swimming pool, diving tank, football and softball fields.

**STUDENT BODY. Undergraduate profile:** 73% are state residents; 26% are transfers. 1% Asian-American, 3% Black, 1% Hispanic, 1% Native American, 91% White, 3% Other.
**Undergraduate achievement:** 85% of fall 1992 freshmen returned for fall 1993 term. 28% of entering class graduated.
**Foreign students:** 79 students are from out of the country. Countries represented include Bangladesh, Cameroon, China, India, and Pakistan; 23 in all.

**PROGRAMS OF STUDY. Degrees:** B.A., B.Eng.Tech., B.S.
**Majors:** Accounting, Agribusiness, Art, Art Education, Biology, Biology Education, Business Administration/Management, Business Education, Chemistry, Chemistry Education, Computer Information Systems, Computer Science, Computer Science/Mathematics, Earth Science Education, Electrical Engineering Technology, Elementary Education, Health Education, History, Hotel/Restaurant Administration, Individualized Interdisciplinary, Literature, Literature/Creative Writing, Literature/Language Arts Education, Marketing, Mathematics, Mathematics Education, Mechanical Engineering Technology, Medical Technology, Music, Music Education, Office Administration, Physical Education, Physical Education Teaching, Physical Science Education, Physics, Physics Education, Political Science, Psychology, Social Work, Sociology, Speech Communication, Speech Communication/Radio/Television, Speech Communication/Secondary Education, Speech Communication/Theatre Arts, Speech Communication/Theatre Arts/Secondary Education, Theatre Arts.
**Distribution of degrees:** The majors with the highest enrollment are business administration, education, and accounting.
**Requirements:** General education requirement.
**Academic regulations:** Minimum 2.0 GPA must be maintained.
**Special:** Minors offered in many majors and in anthropology, earth/space science, English/language arts, foreign language education (French, German, and Spanish), French, German, philosophy, rural studies, and Spanish. Associate's degrees offered. Self-designed majors. Double majors. Dual degrees. Independent study. Accelerated study. Pass/fail grading option. Internships. Preprofessional programs in law, medicine, veterinary science, pharmacy, dentistry, agriculture, business, chiropractic, engineering, fishery and wildlife management, forestry, geoscience, ministry, mortuary science, nursing, and physical therapy. 2-2 nursing program with Metropolitan U. Member of Southwest and West Central Consortium and Common Market Consortium. Teacher certification in early childhood, elementary, and secondary education. Exchange program abroad in Japan. Study abroad also in Chile and China.
**Honors:** Honors program. Honor societies.
**Academic Assistance:** Remedial reading, writing, math, and study skills. Nonremedial tutoring.

**STUDENT LIFE. Housing:** Students may live on or off campus. Coed, women's, and men's dorms. 47% of students live in college housing.
**Social atmosphere:** According to the student newspaper, the Student Activities Committee, the Intervarsity Christian Fellowship, and the Nontraditional Student Union are the dominant groups on campus. A special campus event is Homecoming. Students like to gather at Lynwood Ballroom, the student center, the Wooden Nickel, and the Gambler.
**Services and counseling/handicapped student services:** Placement services. Health service. Women's center. Day care. Counseling services for minority, military, veteran, and older students. Birth control, personal, and psychological counseling. Career and academic guidance services. Religious counseling. Physically disabled student services. Learning disabled program/services. Notetaking services. Tape recorders. Tutors. Reader services for the blind.
**Campus organizations:** Undergraduate student government. Student newspaper (Impact, published twice/month). Literary magazine. 62 registered organizations.
**Religious organizations:** Fellowship of Christian Athletes, Intervarsity Christian Fellowship, Lutheran Student Commission, Newman Club.
**Minority/foreign student organizations:** Black Student Union. International Student Organization.

**ATHLETICS. Physical education requirements:** Four quarter hours of health and physical education required.
**Intercollegiate competition:** 27% of students participate. Baseball (M), basketball (M,W), football (M), softball (W), tennis (W), track (indoor) (M,W), track (outdoor) (M,W), track and field (indoor) (M,W), track and field (outdoor) (M,W), volleyball (W), wheelchair basketball (M,W), wrestling (M). Member of Central States Intercollegiate Wheelchair Conference, MAIAW, NAIA, NCAA Division II, Northern Sun Intercollegiate Conference.
**Intramural and club sports:** 40% of students participate. Intramural aerobics, basketball, cross-country, flag football, golf, softball, swimming, tennis, volleyball, weight lifting, wrestling. Men's club bowling, cheerleading. Women's club bowling, cheerleading.

**ADMISSIONS. Academic basis for candidate selection** (in order of priority): Class rank, standardized test scores, secondary school record, school's recommendation.
**Nonacademic basis for candidate selection:** Particular talent or ability is important. Character and personality are considered.
**Requirements:** Graduation from secondary school is required; GED is accepted. 16 units and the following program of study are recommended: 4 units of English, 3 units of math, 3 units of science, 2 units of foreign language, 3 units of social studies, 1 unit of history. Minimum composite ACT score of 21 or rank in top half of secondary school class required. SAT or ACT is required. Campus visit recommended. Off-campus interviews available with admissions and alumni representatives.
**Procedure:** Take SAT or ACT by August 15 of 12th year. Application deadline is August 15. Notification of admission on rolling basis. $50 room deposit, refundable until July 1. Freshmen accepted in terms other than fall.
**Special programs:** Admission may be deferred three years. Credit may be granted through CEEB Advanced Placement for scores of 3 or higher. Credit may be granted through CLEP general and subject exams, challenge exams, and military and life experience. Early entrance/early admission program. Concurrent enrollment program.
**Transfer students:** Transfer students accepted for terms other than fall. In fall 1993, 26% of all new students were transfers into all classes. 298 transfer applications were received, 247 were accepted. Minimum 2.0 GPA required. Lowest course grade accepted is "C." At least 48 quarter hours must be completed at the university to receive degree.
**Admissions contact:** Richard Shearer, M.S., Director of Admissions. 507 537-6286.

**FINANCIAL AID. Available aid:** Pell grants, SEOG, state scholarships and grants, school scholarships and grants, private scholarships and grants, academic merit scholarships, athletic scholarships, and aid for undergraduate foreign students. Perkins Loans (NDSL), PLUS, Stafford Loans (GSL), state loans, school loans, private loans, and SLS. Tuition Plan Inc. and deferred payment plan.
**Financial aid statistics:** 10% of aid is not need-based. In 1993-94, 84% of all undergraduate applicants received aid; 82% of freshman applicants. Average amounts of aid awarded freshmen: Scholarships and grants, $1,800; loans, $1,400.
**Supporting data/closing dates:** FAFSA/FFS: Priority filing date is April 15; accepted on rolling basis. School's own aid application: Priority filing date is April 15; accepted on rolling basis. Notification of awards on rolling basis.
**Financial aid contact:** Charles Johnson, Director of Financial Aid. 507 537-6281.

**STUDENT EMPLOYMENT.** College Work/Study Program. Institutional employment. 35% of full-time undergraduates work on campus during school year. Students may expect to earn an average of $1,200 during school year. Off-campus part-time employment opportunities rated "excellent."

**COMPUTER FACILITIES.** 460 IBM/IBM-compatible and Macintosh/Apple microcomputers; 350 are networked. Students may access Digital minicomputer/mainframe systems, BITNET. Residence halls may be equipped with stand-alone microcomputers. Numerous computer languages and software programs available. Computer facilities are available to all students.
**Fees:** $1 computer fee per credit hour.

9-5

# University of Minnesota–Duluth

**Duluth, MN 55812** **218 726-7500**

**1994-95 Costs.** Tuition: $3,048 (state residents), $8,993 (out-of-state). Room & board: $3,492. Fees, books, misc. academic expenses (school's estimate): $1,044.
**Enrollment.** Undergraduates: 3,120 men, 2,767 women (full-time). Freshman class: 4,192 applicants, 3,127 accepted, 1,656 enrolled. Graduate enrollment: 152 men, 204 women.
**Test score averages/ranges.** Average ACT scores: 21 English, 22 math, 22 composite. Range of ACT scores of middle 50%: 20-24 English, 20-24 math.
**Faculty.** 325 full-time; 111 part-time. 90% of faculty holds highest degree in specific field. Student/faculty ratio: 17 to 1.
**Selectivity rating.** Less competitive.

**PROFILE.** U Minnesota at Duluth, founded in 1851, is a public, liberal arts institution. Its 250-acre campus is located in Duluth, north of Minneapolis.

**Accreditation:** NCACS. Professionally accredited by the Accreditation Board for Engineering and Technology, the American Medical Association (CAHEA), the American Speech-Language-Hearing Association, the Computing Sciences Accreditation Board, the Council on Social Work Education, the National Association of Schools of Music, the National Council for Accreditation of Teacher Education.
**Religious orientation:** University of Minnesota-Duluth is nonsectarian; no religious requirements.
**Library:** Collections totaling over 422,000 volumes, 3,500 periodical subscriptions, and 231,000 microform items.
**Special facilities/museums:** Art museum, planetarium.
**Athletic facilities:** Swimming pool, gymnasium, field house, broomball and hockey rinks, intramural playing fields.

**STUDENT BODY. Undergraduate profile:** 89% are state residents; 21% are transfers. 1.8% Asian-American, .7% Black, .5% Hispanic, 1.5% Native American, 93.8% White, 1.7% International. Average age of undergraduates is 21.
**Freshman profile:** 99% of accepted applicants took ACT.
**Foreign students:** 140 students are from out of the country. Countries represented include Canada, China, and Japan; 25 in all.

**PROGRAMS OF STUDY. Degrees:** B.A., B.Acct., B.Appl.Arts, B.Appl.Sci., B.Bus.Admin., B.Chem.Eng., B.Comp.Eng., B.F.A., B.Indust.Eng., B.Mus., B.S.
**Majors:** Accounting, American Studies, Anthropology, Art, Art Education, Biochemistry, Biology, Business Administration, Chemical Engineering, Chemistry, Communication, Communication Disorders, Computer Engineering, Computer Science, Criminology, Early Childhood Studies, Economics, Elementary Education, English, Family Life Education, French, Geography, Geology, German, Graphic Design/Commercial Art, Health Education, History, Industrial Engineering, Interdisciplinary Studies, International Studies, Jazz Studies, Kindergarten/Elementary Education, Mathematics, Molecular Biology, Music, Music Education, Music Performance, Music Theory/Composition, Philosophy, Physical Education, Physics, Political Science, Psychology, Secondary Education, Sociology, Spanish, Theatre, Urban/Regional Studies, Women's Studies.

**Distribution of degrees:** The majors with the highest enrollment are business administration, communication, and accounting; American studies, music performance, and earth science have the lowest.
**Requirements:** General education requirement.
**Academic regulations:** Freshmen must maintain minimum 1.80 GPA; sophomores, juniors, seniors 2.00 GPA in most programs; 2.5 in B.F.A. and B.Mus. programs.
**Special:** Minors offered in some majors and in aerospace studies, American Indian studies, art history, dance, humanities, journalism, linguistics, military science, and recreation. Coaching certification. Self-designed majors. Double majors. Dual degrees. Independent study. Pass/fail grading option. Internships. Cooperative education programs. Graduate school at which undergraduates may take graduate-level courses. Preprofessional programs in law, medicine, veterinary science, pharmacy, dentistry, optometry, pre-engineering, pre-nursing, pre-agriculture and agricultural education, pre-forestry, pre-journalism, pre-fishery and wildlife management, and and pre-medical technology. Cross-registration with Coll of St. Scholastica and U of Wisconsin at Superior. Intercollege program allows students to pursue cross-college curriculum. Teacher certification in early childhood, elementary, secondary, special education, and vo-tech education. Certification in specific subject areas. Exchange programs abroad in England (U of Birmingham), France (U of Pau), and Sweden (U of Vaxjo). ROTC and AFROTC.
**Honors:** Honors program. Honor societies.
**Academic Assistance:** Remedial writing, math, and study skills. Nonremedial tutoring.

**STUDENT LIFE. Housing:** Coed, women's, and men's dorms. School-owned/operated apartments. Off-campus privately-owned housing. 37% of students live in college housing.
**Social atmosphere:** Kirk Cafe/Deli, Grandma's, student center, and games and outing center are favorite gathering spots. Influential student groups include recreational sports teams, program board, and the Greeks. Popular social events include hockey games, off-campus parties, intramurals, and Rockfest. "Grandma's dry night is the biggest freshman entertainment night," reports the editor of the student newspaper. "Our Greek organizations tend to be mainly social organizations. The rec sports facilities serves a majority of the students on campus. Intramurals are very important."
**Services and counseling/handicapped student services:** Placement services. Health service. Women's center. Counseling services for minority and veteran students. Birth control, personal, and psychological counseling. Career and academic guidance services. Religious counseling. Physically disabled student services. Learning disabled program/services. Notetaking services. Tape recorders. Tutors. Reader services for the blind.
**Campus organizations:** Undergraduate student government. Student newspaper (Statesman, published once/week). Radio station. Jazz ensembles, jazz choir, concert band, wind ensemble, chamber music groups, orchestra, chorus, departmental, service, and special-interest groups, 130 organizations in all. One fraternity, no chapter house; two sororities, no chapter houses.
**Religious organizations:** Council of Religious Advisers, Baptist Campus Ministry, Intervarsity Christian Fellowship, Newman Catholic Ministries, Lutheran Campus Ministry, United Campus Ministry.
**Minority/foreign student organizations:** Black Student Association, Anishinabe Club, Hispanic Organization. International Student Club, International Alumni Association, Chinese Student Organization, Southeast Asian Association.

**ATHLETICS. Physical education requirements:** None.
**Intercollegiate competition:** 30% of students participate. Baseball (M), basketball (M,W), cross-country (M,W), football (M), ice hockey (M), softball (W), tennis (M,W), track and field (indoor) (M,W), track and field (outdoor) (M,W), volleyball (W), wrestling (M). Member of NAIA, NCAA Division I for men's ice hockey, NCAA Division II, Northern Intercollegiate Conference (men), Northern Sun Conference (women).
**Intramural and club sports:** 60% of students participate. Intramural badminton, basketball, broomball, floor hockey, football, ice hockey, soccer, softball, volleyball.

**ADMISSIONS. Academic basis for candidate selection** (in order of priority): Class rank, standardized test scores, secondary school record, school's recommendation.
**Nonacademic basis for candidate selection:** Extracurricular participation and particular talent or ability are considered.
**Requirements:** Graduation from secondary school is required; GED is accepted. 14 units and the following program of study are required: 4 units of English, 3 units of math, 3 units of science, 2 units of foreign language, 2 units of social studies. Automatic admission to in-state and out-of-state applicants ranking in top third of secondary school class. Selective admission to applicants in 40th to 64th percentile of secondary school class with minimum composite ACT score of 19. ACT is required. Campus visit recommended. No off-campus interviews.
**Procedure:** Take ACT by December of 12th year. Suggest filing application by February 1. Application deadline is July 1. Notification of admission on rolling basis. $200 room deposit, $150 of which is refundable until May 2. Freshmen accepted in terms other than fall.
**Special programs:** Credit and/or placement may be granted through CEEB Advanced Placement exams for scores of 3 or higher. Credit may be granted through CLEP general and subject exams and DANTES exams. Concurrent enrollment program.
**Transfer students:** Transfer students accepted for terms other than fall. In fall 1993, 21% of all new students were transfers into all classes. 891 transfer applications were received, 727 were accepted. Application deadline is July 1 for fall; November 1 for winter; February 1 for spring. Minimum 2.0 GPA required. Lowest course grade accepted is "D." At least 45 quarter units must be completed at the university to receive degree.
**Admissions contact:** Gerald R. Allen, M.A., Director of Student Support Services. 218 726-7171.

**FINANCIAL AID. Available aid:** Pell grants, SEOG, state grants, school scholarships, ROTC scholarships, academic merit scholarships, and athletic scholarships. Perkins Loans (NDSL), PLUS, Stafford Loans (GSL), state loans, school loans, and SLS.
**Financial aid statistics:** In 1993-94, 91% of all undergraduate applicants received aid; 87% of freshman applicants. Average amounts of aid awarded freshmen: Scholarships and grants, $1,205; loans, $2,311.
**Supporting data/closing dates:** FAFSA: Priority filing date is March 31. Notification of awards begins May 1.
**Financial aid contact:** Nicholas F. Whelihan, Director of Financial Aid. 218 726-8786.

**STUDENT EMPLOYMENT.** College Work/Study Program. Institutional employment. 25% of full-time undergraduates work on campus during school year. Students may expect to earn an average of $1,500 during school year. Off-campus part-time employment opportunities rated "good."

**COMPUTER FACILITIES.** 201 IBM/IBM-compatible, Macintosh/Apple, and RISC-/UNIX-based microcomputers; all are networked. Network connections in dorms. Students may access Digital, SUN minicomputer/mainframe systems, Internet. Client/LAN operating systems include Apple/Macintosh, UNIX/XENIX/AIX, Novell. Computer languages and software packages include Ada, BASIC, C, FORTRAN, Pascal, Smalltalk; 100 in all. Computer facilities are available to all students.
**Fees:** $60 computer fee per quarter.
**Hours:** Approximately 80 hours/week in six labs.

## University of Minnesota–Morris

**Morris, MN 56267** **612 589-2211**

**1994-95 Costs.** Tuition: $3,330 (state residents), $9,843 (out-of-state). Room & board: $3,180. Fees, books, misc. academic expenses (school's estimate): $915.
**Enrollment.** Undergraduates: 857 men, 1,076 women (full-time). Freshman class: 1,458 applicants, 860 accepted, 588 enrolled.
**Test score averages/ranges.** Average SAT scores: 550 verbal, 650 math. Average ACT scores: 26 English, 25 math, 26 composite.
**Faculty.** 128 full-time; 14 part-time. 83% of faculty holds doctoral degree. Student/faculty ratio: 16 to 1.
**Selectivity rating.** Highly competitive.

**PROFILE.** U Minnesota at Morris, founded in 1959, is a public, liberal arts institution. Its 130-acre campus is located in Morris, east of Minneapolis.

**Accreditation:** NCACS. Professionally accredited by the National Council for Accreditation of Teacher Education.
**Religious orientation:** University of Minnesota-Morris is nonsectarian; no religious requirements.
**Library:** Collections totaling over 152,500 volumes, 842 periodical subscriptions, and 19,400 microform items.
**Special facilities/museums:** Art gallery.
**Athletic facilities:** Gymnasiums, weight room, swimming pool, basketball, racquetball, tennis, and volleyball courts, baseball, football, soccer, and softball fields, track, stadiums.

**STUDENT BODY. Undergraduate profile:** 80% are state residents; 5% are transfers. 4% Asian-American, 4% Black, 1% Hispanic, 3% Native American, 88% White. Average age of undergraduates is 20.
**Freshman profile:** 5% of freshmen who took SAT scored 700 or over on verbal, 18% scored 700 or over on math; 27% scored 600 or over on verbal, 50% scored 600 or over on math; 65% scored 500 or over on verbal, 81% scored 500 or over on math; 93% scored 400 or over on verbal, 95% scored 400 or over on math; 100% scored 300 or over on verbal, 100% scored 300 or over on math. 13% of freshmen who took ACT scored 30 or over on English, 10% scored 30 or over on math, 11% scored 30 or over on composite; 71% scored 24 or over on English, 68% scored 24 or over on math, 74% scored 24 or over on composite; 97% scored 18 or over on English, 96% scored 18 or over on math, 98% scored 18 or over on composite; 100% scored 12 or over on English, 100% scored 12 or over on math, 100% scored 12 or over on composite. 19% of accepted applicants took SAT; 97% took ACT. 94% of freshmen come from public schools.
**Undergraduate achievement:** 90% of fall 1992 freshmen returned for fall 1993 term. 46% of entering class graduated.
**Foreign students:** 15 students are from out of the country. 10 countries represented in all.

**PROGRAMS OF STUDY. Degrees:** B.A.
**Majors:** Art History, Biology, Business Economics, Chemistry, Computer Science, Economics, Elementary Education, English, European Studies, French, Geology, German, Health Education, History, Latin American Area Studies, Liberal Arts for the Human Services, Mathematics, Music, Philosophy, Physics, Political Science, Psychology, Social Sciences, Sociology, Spanish, Speech Communication, Studio Art, Theatre Arts.
**Distribution of degrees:** The majors with the highest enrollment are business economics, education, and liberal arts for the human services; art history, Latin American area studies, and European studies have the lowest.
**Requirements:** General education requirement.
**Special:** Minors offered in all majors and in anthropology, humanities, and women's studies. Intercollege program; cross-college curriculum leading to B.A. or B.S. Courses offered in geography, physical science, and secondary education. Undergraduate Research Opportunities Program (UROP). Self-designed majors. Double majors. Independent study. Accelerated study. Pass/fail grading option. Internships. Preprofessional programs in law, medicine, veterinary science, pharmacy, dentistry, and optometry. 2-3 engineering program with U of Minnesota at Twin Cities. Member of West Minnesota Consortium. Term-away programs. Teacher certification in elementary and secondary education. Certification in specific subject areas. Study abroad in Germany, Mexico, and other countries.
**Honors:** Honors program.

**STUDENT LIFE. Housing:** Students may live on or off campus. Coed dorms. School-owned/-operated apartments. 52% of students live in college housing.
**Social atmosphere:** According to the editor of the student newspaper, "Morris is quite small, so entertainment is highly restricted." Somewhat influential groups on campus are Christian groups and intramural sports athletes. Favorite events are Homecoming, the sorority formal dance, and Jazzfest, while Flatlands offers a venue for bands and other activities. Students enjoy gathering off campus at Frederick's (a dance club), at various homes for parties, and at Don's (a restaurant).

**Services and counseling/handicapped student services:** Placement services. Health service. Counseling services for minority and older students. Birth control, personal, and psychological counseling. Career and academic guidance services. Physically disabled student services. Learning disabled services. Tutors.
**Campus organizations:** Undergraduate student government. Student newspaper (University Register, published once/week). Literary magazine. Radio station. Stage bands, concert choir, debating, drama group, Horseman's Club, outdoor sports club, service and special-interest groups, 72 organizations in all. Two fraternities, no chapter houses; one sorority, no chapter house. 1% of men join a fraternity. 1% of women join a sorority.
**Religious organizations:** Fellowship of Christian Athletes, Intervarsity Christian Fellowship, Lutheran Campus Ministry, Shiloh Fellowship, Catholic Campus Ministries, Campus Crusade for Christ.
**Minority/foreign student organizations:** Black Student Union, Native American Student Association, United Latinos, Women of Color, Asian Student Association. International Student Association, Latin American Culture Association.

**ATHLETICS. Physical education requirements:** None.
**Intercollegiate competition:** 15% of students participate. Baseball (M), basketball (M,W), cheerleading (M,W), football (M), golf (M,W), softball (W), tennis (M,W), track (indoor) (M,W), track (outdoor) (M,W), track and field (indoor) (M,W), track and field (outdoor) (M,W), volleyball (W), wrestling (M). Member of NAIA, NCAA Division II, Northern Sun Intercollegiate Conference.
**Intramural and club sports:** 69% of students participate. Intramural basketball, flag football, racquetball, softball, swimming, tennis, volleyball. Men's club soccer.

**ADMISSIONS. Academic basis for candidate selection** (in order of priority): Class rank, standardized test scores, secondary school record, school's recommendation, essay.
**Nonacademic basis for candidate selection:** Particular talent or ability is emphasized. Extracurricular participation and alumni/ae relationship are important. Character and personality are considered.
**Requirements:** Graduation from secondary school is required; GED is accepted. 14 units and the following program of study are required: 4 units of English, 3 units of math, 3 units of science, 2 units of foreign language, 2 units of social studies. Average composite ACT score of 26 recommended. Audition required of music program applicants. ACT is required. Campus visit recommended. Off-campus interviews available with an admissions representative.
**Procedure:** Take ACT by December of 12th year. Visit college for interview by February 1 of 12th year. Suggest filing application by December 1. Application deadline is March 15. Notification of admission by April 1. Reply is required within 30 days of acceptance. $140 nonrefundable tuition deposit. $60 nonrefundable room deposit. Freshmen accepted in terms other than fall.
**Special programs:** Admission may be deferred one year. Credit and/or placement may be granted through CEEB Advanced Placement exams for scores of 3 or higher. Credit and/or placement may be granted through CLEP general and subject exams. Placement may be granted through Regents College, ACT PEP, DANTES, and challenge exams. Credit and placement may be granted through military and life experience. Early decision program. In fall 1993, 531 applied for early decision and 319 were accepted. Deadline for applying for early decision is December 1. Concurrent enrollment program.
**Transfer students:** Transfer students accepted for terms other than fall. In fall 1993, 5% of all new students were transfers into all classes. 175 transfer applications were received, 121 were accepted. Application deadline is April 15; November 1 for winter. Minimum 2.5 GPA required. Lowest course grade accepted is "D." Maximum number of transferable credits is 135 quarter hours. At least 45 quarter hours must be completed at the university to receive degree.
**Admissions contact:** Robert J. Vikander, M.S., Director of Admissions and Financial Aid. 612 589-6035.

**FINANCIAL AID. Available aid:** Pell grants, SEOG, state scholarships and grants, school scholarships and grants, private scholarships and grants, academic merit scholarships, and aid for undergraduate foreign students. Perkins Loans (NDSL), PLUS, Stafford Loans (GSL), state loans, school loans, private loans, and SLS. Tuition Plan Inc..
**Financial aid statistics:** In 1993-94, 88% of all undergraduate applicants received aid; 65% of freshman applicants. Average amounts of aid awarded freshmen: Scholarships and grants, $3,480; loans, $2,045.
**Supporting data/closing dates:** FAFSA: Priority filing date is April 1; deadline is May 2. Notification of awards on rolling basis.
**Financial aid contact:** Robert J. Vikander, M.S., Director of Admissions and Financial Aid. 612 589-6035.

**STUDENT EMPLOYMENT.** College Work/Study Program. Institutional employment. 52% of full-time undergraduates work on campus during school year. Students may expect to earn an average of $715 during school year. Off-campus part-time employment opportunities rated "fair."

**COMPUTER FACILITIES.** 130 IBM/IBM-compatible and Macintosh/Apple microcomputers. Students may access Digital minicomputer/mainframe systems. Residence halls may be equipped with networked microcomputers, modems. Computer languages and software packages include BASIC, dBASE, FORTRAN, Lotus 1-2-3, MINITAB, Pascal, SAS. Computer facilities are available to all students.
**Fees:** None.
**Hours:** 24 hours.

**GRADUATE CAREER DATA.** Highest graduate school enrollments: U of Minnesota at Twin Cities, U of North Dakota, U of Wisconsin at Madison. 12% of graduates choose careers in business and industry. Companies and businesses that hire graduates: Cargill, First Bank of Colorado, IBM, West Publishing.

**PROMINENT ALUMNI/AE.** Dennis Koslowski, 1992 Olympic silver medal-winning Greco-Roman wrestler.

# University of Minnesota, Twin Cities

**Minneapolis, MN 55455-0213 612 625-5000**

**1994-95 Costs.** Tuition: $3,585 (state residents), $9,363 (out-of-state). Room & board: $3,744. Fees, books, misc. academic expenses (school's estimate): $714.
**Enrollment.** Undergraduates: 12,250 men, 11,629 women (full-time). Freshman class: 11,054 applicants, 6,397 accepted, 3,524 enrolled. Graduate enrollment: 6,308 men, 5,625 women.
**Test score averages/ranges.** Average SAT scores: 484 verbal, 568 math. Range of SAT scores of middle 50%: 420-550 verbal, 500-650 math. Average ACT scores: 22 English, 23 math, 23 composite. Range of ACT scores of middle 50%: 19-26 English, 19-27 math.
**Faculty.** 2,663 full-time; 290 part-time. 76% of faculty holds doctoral degree. Student/faculty ratio: 15 to 1.
**Selectivity rating.** Competitive.

**PROFILE.** U Minnesota, Twin Cities, founded in 1851, is a public institution. Programs are offered through the Carlson School of Management; Colleges of Agriculture, Biological Sciences, Education, Home Economics, Liberal Arts, Natural Resources, and Pharmacy; Department of Mortuary Science; Institute of Technology; Preprofessional Programs; and the School of Nursing. Its 2,000-acre campus is located in Minneapolis.

**Accreditation:** NCACS. Professionally accredited by the American Assembly of Collegiate Schools of Business, the American Association for Counseling and Development, the American Dental Association, the American Physical Therapy Association, the National Association of Schools of Music, the National Council for Accreditation of Teacher Education, the National League for Nursing.
**Religious orientation:** University of Minnesota, Twin Cities is nonsectarian; no religious requirements.
**Library:** Collections totaling over 5,008,637 volumes, 52,018 periodical subscriptions, and 4,356,552 microform items.
**Special facilities/museums:** Art museum, art galleries, natural history museum, supercomputer institute.
**Athletic facilities:** Gymnasium, field house, track, basketball, handball, racquetball and tennis courts, football, soccer, and softball fields, aquatic center, recreation center, fitness center.

**STUDENT BODY. Undergraduate profile:** 77% are state residents. 8% Asian-American, 3% Black, 2% Hispanic, 1% Native American, 85% White, 1% Other. Average age of undergraduates is 22.
**Freshman profile:** 1% of freshmen who took SAT scored 700 or over on verbal, 13% scored 700 or over on math; 13% scored 600 or over on verbal, 45% scored 600 or over on math; 45% scored 500 or over on verbal, 76% scored 500 or over on math; 81% scored 400 or over on verbal, 94% scored 400 or over on math; 96% scored 300 or over on verbal, 100% scored 300 or over on math. 23% of accepted applicants took SAT; 93% took ACT.
**Undergraduate achievement:** 81% of fall 1992 freshmen returned for fall 1993 term. 13% of entering class graduated.
**Foreign students:** 733 students are from out of the country. Countries represented include Canada, China, India, Japan, Korea, and Taiwan; 85 in all.

**PROGRAMS OF STUDY. Degrees:** B.A., B.A.Bus.Admin., B.Aero.Eng., B.Agri.Eng., B.Arch., B.Chem., B.Chem.Eng., B.Civil Eng., B.Comp.Sci., B.Dent.Hyg.Ed., B.Ed., B.Elec. Eng., B.F.A., B.Geo-Eng., B.Internat.Studies, B.Land.Arch., B.Mat.Sci./Eng., B.Math., B.Mech.Eng., B.Mus., B.Nurs.Anes., B.Physics, B.S., B.S.Dent., B.S.Ed., B.S.Nurs., B.Stat.
**Majors:** Aerospace Engineering, Afro-American/African Studies, Agricultural Business Management, Agricultural Education, Agricultural Engineering, Agricultural Industries/Marketing, American Indian Studies, American Studies, Ancient Near Eastern Studies, Animal/Plant Systems, Anthropology, Apparel Science/Design, Applied Economics, Architecture, Art, Art History, Astronomy, Astrophysics, Biochemistry, Biology, Biostatistics, Business Education, Cell Biology, Chemical Engineering, Chemistry, Chicano Studies, Child Psychology, Chinese, Civil Engineering, Classical Civilization, Communication, Computer Science, Cultural Studies/Comparative Literature, Dance, Dental Hygiene, Dentistry, Design Communication, Design/Visual Communication, Early Childhood Education, East Asian Studies, Ecology, Economics, Education, Electrical Engineering, Elementary Education, English, Environmental Design, Evolution/Biology, Film Studies, Finnish, Fisheries/Wildlife, Food Science, Food Science/Nutrition, Forest Products, Forest Resources, French, French Area Studies, French/Italian, General Management, Genetics/Cell Biology, Geoengineering, Geography, Geology/Geophysics, German, Greek, Hebrew, History, Home Economics Education, Housing, Human Relationships/Family/Youth/Community Services, Individually-Designed Programs, Industrial Education, Interdepartmental Majors, Interior Design, International Relations, Italian, Japanese, Jewish Studies, Journalism, Journalism/Mass Communications, Kinesiology, Landscape Architecture, Latin, Latin American Studies, Law, Linguistics, Management, Marketing Education, Mass Communication, Materials Science/Engineering, Mathematics, Mechanical Engineering, Medical Technology, Medicine, Microbiology, Middle Eastern/South Asian Studies, Mortuary Sciences, Music, Music Education, Music Therapy, Natural Resources, Natural Resources/Environmental Studies, Nursing, Nutrition, Occupational Therapy, Pharmacy, Philosophy, Physical Therapy, Physics, Physiology, Plant Biology, Political Science, Psychology, Recreation/Parks/Leisure Studies, Recreation Resource Management, Religious Studies, Russian, Russian Area Studies, Science/Agriculture, Science Education, Scientific/Technical Communication, Sociology, South Asian/Middle Eastern Languages/Culture, South Asian/Middle Eastern Studies, Spanish, Spanish/Portuguese,

Speech Communication, Speech/Hearing Sciences, Statistics, Theatre Arts, Urban Forestry, Urban Studies, Veterinary Medicine, Women's Studies.
**Distribution of degrees:** The majors with the highest enrollment are business administration, psychology, and English.
**Requirements:** General education requirement.
**Academic regulations:** Minimum 2.0 GPA must be maintained.
**Special:** Minors offered in most majors. Students may register in University College and take courses in any division for B.A. or B.S. degrees. Students may transfer to College of Pharmacy or School of Nursing after one year; to Colleges of Biological Sciences, Business Administration, Dentistry, Education, Medical Technology, and Occupational or Physical Therapy after two years; to School of Medicine after three years. Programs in foreign service and pre-social work. Self-designed majors. Double majors. Dual degrees. Independent study. Accelerated study. Pass/fail grading option. Internships. Graduate school at which undergraduates may take graduate-level courses. Preprofessional programs in law, medicine, veterinary science, pharmacy, dentistry, architecture, biology, education, journalism, landscape architecture, management, medical technology, mortuary science, nursing, and occupational/physical therapy. Exchange programs with several public colleges and universities across the U.S. Teacher certification in early childhood, elementary, secondary, special education, vo-tech, and bilingual/bicultural education. Certification in specific subject areas. Study abroad in numerous countries. ROTC, NROTC, and AFROTC.
**Honors:** Phi Beta Kappa. Honors program. Honor societies.
**Academic Assistance:** Remedial reading, writing, math, and study skills. Nonremedial tutoring.

**STUDENT LIFE. Housing:** Students may live on or off campus. Coed dorms. Sorority and fraternity housing. On-campus married-student housing. 12% of students live in college housing.
**Social atmosphere:** The student newspaper reports, "Since we're located in Minneapolis, off-campus activities are as popular as on." There are "few organized campus activities, except Homecoming, which no one cares about, and Carni, put on by the Greeks in spring." Popular events on campus include Brother Jed, and the pro- and anti-CIA rallies. Minnesota students frequent First Avenue, Gluck's, Graffiti's, William's pub and nightclub, the Uptown Bar, and Lindsay's pub.
**Services and counseling/handicapped student services:** Placement services. Health service. Women's center. Day care. Counseling services for minority, military, veteran, and older students. Birth control, personal, and psychological counseling. Career and academic guidance services. Religious counseling. Physically disabled student services. Learning disabled services. Notetaking services. Tape recorders. Tutors. Reader services for the blind.
**Campus organizations:** Undergraduate student government. Student newspaper (Minnesota Daily). Literary magazine. Radio and TV stations. Student Advocate Service, Panhellenic Council, American Marketing Association, Angel Flight, National Lawyers Guild, Wildlife Rehabilitation Clinic, Women in Communication, Coalition for Peace Studies, United Student Leaders, 350 organizations in all. 27 fraternities, 23 chapter houses; 15 sororities, 13 chapter houses. 6% of men join a fraternity. 5% of women join a sorority.
**Religious organizations:** Baptist Student Fellowship, Episcopal Center, Hillel House, Newman Center, Lutheran Campus Ministry, Children of the Night, Christian Outreach, Pagan Community, Navigators, Latter-Day Saints Student Association, Eastern Orthodox Fellowship.
**Minority/foreign student organizations:** Afro-American, Asian/Pacific-American, Chicano/Latino, and Native American centers, other minority groups. International Association, International Center, Third World Caucus, Brazilian, Cambodian, Chinese, Filipino, French, German, Hellenic, Japanese, Kenyan, Korean, Laotian, Malaysian, Pakistani, Polish, Singaporean, Taiwanese, Tunisian, Turkish, Ukrainian, and Vietnamese student groups.

**ATHLETICS. Physical education requirements:** None.
**Intercollegiate competition:** 2% of students participate. Baseball (M), basketball (M,W), cross-country (M,W), diving (M,W), football (M), golf (M,W), gymnastics (M,W), ice hockey (M), soccer (W), softball (W), swimming (M,W), tennis (M,W), track (indoor) (M,W), track (outdoor) (M,W), track and field (indoor) (M,W), track and field (outdoor) (M,W), volleyball (W), wrestling (M). Member of Big 10 Conference, NCAA Division I, WCHA.
**Intramural and club sports:** 65% of students participate. Intramural badminton, baseball, basketball, bowling, broomball, flag football, floor hockey, ice hockey, racquetball, sand volleyball, soccer, softball, tennis, touch football, volleyball, water basketball, water polo. Men's club Alpine skiing, badminton, ballroom dancing, bowling, canoe/kayak, crew, cycling, fencing, handball, ice hockey, juggling, lacrosse, martial arts, Nordic skiing, racquetball, rock climbing, rugby, sailing, scuba, soccer, sport parachuting, squash, swimming, synchronized swimming, tennis, ultimate frisbee, volleyball, water polo, water skiing. Women's club Alpine skiing, badminton, ballroom dancing, bowling, canoe/kayak, crew, cycling, fencing, gymnastics, handball, ice hockey, juggling, lacrosse, martial arts, Nordic skiing, racquetball, rock climbing, rugby, sailing, scuba, soccer, softball, squash, swimming, synchronized swimming, tennis, ultimate frisbee, volleyball, water polo, water skiing.

**ADMISSIONS. Academic basis for candidate selection** (in order of priority): Secondary school record, class rank, standardized test scores, school's recommendation, essay.
**Nonacademic basis for candidate selection:** Geographical distribution is important. Extracurricular participation and particular talent or ability are considered.
**Requirements:** Graduation from secondary school is required; GED is accepted. 16 units and the following program of study are required: 4 units of English, 3 units of math, 3 units of science, 2 units of foreign language, 2 units of social studies. Portfolio required of art program applicants. Audition required of music program applicants. Conditional admission possible for applicants not meeting standard requirements. ACT is required; SAT may be substituted except by in-state applicants. Campus visit recommended. No off-campus interviews.
**Procedure:** Take SAT or ACT by December 31 of 12th year. Suggest filing application by December 15. Application deadline is June 1. Notification of admission within four weeks of receipt of application. Reply is required by May 1. $75 nonrefundable tuition deposit. $100 room deposit, refundable if not selected in lottery process. Freshmen accepted in terms other than fall.
**Special programs:** Admission may be deferred one year. Credit and/or placement may be granted through CEEB Advanced Placement exams for scores of 4 or higher. Credit may be granted through CLEP general and subject exams, DANTES exams, and military experience. Credit and placement may be granted through challenge exams. Early entrance/early admission program. Concurrent enrollment program.
**Transfer students:** Transfer students accepted for terms other than fall. In fall 1993, 7,287 transfer applications were received, 3,400 were accepted. Application deadline is April 1 for fall; June 1 for spring. Minimum 2.0 GPA required. Lowest course grade accepted is "D." Maximum number of transferable credits is 135 quarter hours. At least 45 quarter hours must be completed at the university to receive degree.
**Admissions contact:** Wayne Sigler, Ph.D., Director of Admissions. 612 625-2008.

**FINANCIAL AID. Available aid:** Pell grants, SEOG, Federal Nursing Student Scholarships, state scholarships and grants, school scholarships and grants, private scholarships and grants, ROTC scholarships, academic merit scholarships, athletic scholarships, and aid for undergraduate foreign students. Perkins Loans (NDSL), PLUS, Stafford Loans (GSL), NSL, Health Professions Loans, state loans, school loans, private loans, and SLS. Deferred payment plan.
**Supporting data/closing dates:** FAFSA. Notification of awards on rolling basis.
**Financial aid contact:** Al Miller, Director of Financial Aid. 612 624-1665.

**STUDENT EMPLOYMENT.** College Work/Study Program. Institutional employment. 27% of full-time undergraduates work on campus during school year. Students may expect to earn an average of $2,850 during school year. Freshmen are discouraged from working during their first term. Off-campus part-time employment opportunities rated "excellent."

**COMPUTER FACILITIES.** 20,000 IBM/IBM-compatible and Macintosh/Apple microcomputers. Students may access CDC Cyber, Cray, Digital, IBM, SUN minicomputer/mainframe systems, BITNET, Internet. Residence halls may be equipped with stand-alone microcomputers, networked microcomputers, networked terminals, modems. Client/LAN operating systems include Apple/Macintosh, DOS, OS/2, UNIX/XENIX/AIX, X-windows, LocalTalk/AppleTalk, Novell. Computer languages and software packages include Ada, APL, BASIC, C, C++, COBOL, FORTH, FORTRAN 77, GPSS, ICon, LISP, Modula 2, OPS, Pascal, Prolog, RPG II, SimScript, Smalltalk, SNOBOL 4; 350 in all. Computer facilities are available to all students.
**Fees:** None.

**PROMINENT ALUMNI/AE.** Hubert Humphrey and Walter Mondale, former Vice-Presidents of the U.S.; Harry Reasoner, reporter and TV anchorman; Warren Burger, former Supreme Court Chief Justice; Georgia O'Keefe, artist.

# University of St. Thomas

St. Paul, MN 55105 612 962-5000

**1993-94 Costs.** Tuition: $11,712. Room: $2,321. Board: $1,716. Fees, books, misc. academic expenses (school's estimate): $300.
**Enrollment.** Undergraduates: 2,085 men, 2,147 women (full-time). Freshman class: 1,947 applicants, 1,786 accepted, 800 enrolled. Graduate enrollment: 2,727 men, 2,508 women.
**Test score averages/ranges.** Average SAT scores: 495 verbal, 545 math. Range of SAT scores of middle 50%: 430-550 verbal, 480-610 math. Average ACT scores: 23 English, 23 math, 23 composite. Range of ACT scores of middle 50%: 20-26 English, 20-26 math.
**Faculty.** 247 full-time; 137 part-time. 61% of faculty holds doctoral degree. Student/faculty ratio: 17 to 1.
**Selectivity rating.** Less competitive.

**PROFILE.** The University of St. Thomas is a private, church-affiliated, liberal arts institution. It was founded in 1885, adopted coeducation in 1976, and gained university status in 1990. Its 78-acre campus is located in a residential section of St. Paul.

**Accreditation:** NCACS. Professionally accredited by the Council on Social Work Education, the National Council for Accreditation of Teacher Education.
**Religious orientation:** University of St. Thomas is affiliated with the Roman Catholic Church; three semesters of theology required.
**Library:** Collections totaling over 383,421 volumes, 1,810 periodical subscriptions, and 453,370 microform items.
**Athletic facilities:** Gymnasiums, field house, weight and wrestling rooms, baseball, football, soccer, and softball fields, swimming pool, badminton, basketball, handball, racquetball, squash, tennis, and volleyball courts, tracks, stadium.

**STUDENT BODY. Undergraduate profile:** 84% are state residents; 35% are transfers. 3% Asian-American, 2% Black, 1% Hispanic, 94% White. Average age of undergraduates is 21.
**Freshman profile:** 6% of freshmen who took SAT scored 700 or over on verbal, 6% scored 700 or over on math; 15% scored 600 or over on verbal, 34% scored 600 or over on math; 42% scored 500 or over on verbal, 69% scored 500 or over on math; 87% scored 400 or over on verbal, 95% scored 400 or over on math; 99% scored 300 or over on verbal, 99% scored 300 or over on math. 6% of freshmen who took ACT scored 30 or over on English, 7% scored 30 or over on math, 5% scored 30 or over on composite; 46% scored 24 or over on English, 45% scored 24 or over on math, 48% scored 24 or over on composite; 90% scored 18 or over on English, 91% scored 18 or over on math, 95% scored 18 or over on composite; 99% scored 12 or over on English, 100% scored 12 or over on math, 100% scored 12 or over on composite; 100% scored 6 or over on English. 21% of accepted applicants took SAT; 67% took ACT.
**Undergraduate achievement:** 82% of fall 1991 freshmen returned for fall 1992 term. 50% of entering class graduated. 21% of students who completed a degree program went on to graduate study within one year.

**Foreign students:** 25 students are from out of the country. Countries represented include China, Colombia, Germany, Japan, Spain, and Western Samoa; 47 in all.

**PROGRAMS OF STUDY. Degrees:** B.A.

**Majors:** Accounting, Advertising, American Studies, Anthropology, Art, Art History, Biology, Broadcast Journalism, Chemistry, Classical Languages, Corporate Fitness, Criminal Justice, East Asian Studies, Economics, Elementary Education, English, Entrepreneurship, Environmental Studies, Financial Management, French, General Business Administration, General Communication/Theater, Geography, Geology, German, Health Education, History, Home Economics, Human Resources Management, International Business, International Journalism, International Relations, International Studies, Latin American Studies, Linguistics, Literary Studies, Liturgical Music, Marketing Management, Mathematics, Music, Music/Business, Music Education, Music Performance/Studio Teaching, Music Therapy, Nursing, Nutrition, Occupational Therapy, Operations Management, Peace/Justice Studies, Philosophy, Physical Education, Physics, Political Science, Print Journalism, Psychology, Public Administration, Public Relations, Quantitative Methods/Computer Science, Russian, Social Studies, Social Work, Sociology, Soviet/East European Studies, Spanish, Speech Communication, Studio Art, Telecommunications, Textiles, Theatre, Theology, Urban Studies, Women's Studies.

**Distribution of degrees:** The majors with the highest enrollment are business, sociology, and journalism; Latin, geology, and art history have the lowest.

**Requirements:** General education requirement.

**Academic regulations:** Minimum 2.00 GPA must be maintained.

**Special:** Minors offered in over 40 areas. Self-designed majors. Double majors. Independent study. Pass/fail grading option. Internships. Preprofessional programs in law, medicine, veterinary science, pharmacy, dentistry, theology, optometry, and engineering. 3-2 engineering programs with U of Minnesota, U of Notre Dame, and Washington U. 3-3 physical therapy program with Coll of St. Catherine. Member of Associated Colleges of the Twin Cities; cross-registration possible. Washington Semester. Teacher certification in elementary and secondary education. Certification in specific subject areas. Study abroad in Austria, Colombia, Denmark, Ecuador, Egypt, England, France, Germany, Ireland, Italy, Japan, the Netherlands, Norway, Singapore, Spain, and Wales. AFROTC. NROTC at U of Minnesota.

**Honors:** Honors program.

**Academic Assistance:** Remedial reading, writing, math, and study skills. Nonremedial tutoring.

**STUDENT LIFE. Housing:** Students may live on or off campus. Women's and men's dorms. School-owned/-operated apartments. 29% of students live in college housing.

**Social atmosphere:** Popular social gathering spots off campus include O'Gara's Garage and Tiffany's Bar and Lounge ("Tiff's"). On campus, students meet at Scooter's Nightclub, a nonalcoholic bar and dance club. Popular events on campus include Fall Fest, Homecoming, Junior-Senior Nite, and the St. Thomas/St. John's football game, known as the "Tommy-Johnny" game. "There are not really any influential groups on campus, but business majors are everywhere," reports the student newspaper.

**Services and counseling/handicapped student services:** Placement services. Health service. Women's center. Counseling services for minority students. Personal and psychological counseling. Career and academic guidance services. Religious counseling. Physically disabled student services. Learning disabled program/services. Notetaking services. Reader services for the blind.

**Campus organizations:** Undergraduate student government. Student newspaper (Aquin, published bimonthly). Literary magazine. Yearbook. TV station. Women's chorus, men's glee club, orchestra, ensemble, chapel choir, concert and stage bands, opera workshop, Collegium Musicum, free film series, drama group, debating, forensics, professional, service, and volunteer groups, 72 organizations in all. One fraternity, no chapter house; one sorority, no chapter house.

**Religious organizations:** Campus Ministry, Liturgical Ministers, Peace and Justice Program, Volunteers in Action, Peer Ministry.

**Minority/foreign student organizations:** International Student Association.

**ATHLETICS. Physical education requirements:** One semester of physical education required.

**Intercollegiate competition:** 20% of students participate. Baseball (M), basketball (M,W), cheerleading (M,W), cross-country (M,W), diving (M,W), football (M), golf (M,W), ice hockey (M), soccer (M,W), softball (W), swimming (M,W), tennis (M,W), track (indoor) (M,W), track (outdoor) (M,W), track and field (indoor) (M,W), track and field (outdoor) (M,W), volleyball (W), wrestling (M). Member of Minnesota Intercollegiate Athletic Conference, NCAA Division III.

**Intramural and club sports:** 10% of students participate. Intramural badminton, basketball, floor hockey, lacrosse, martial arts, pickleball, racquetball, rowing, soccer, softball, squash, tennis, touch football, volleyball, wrestling. Men's club crew, lacrosse, rugby, volleyball. Women's club crew.

**ADMISSIONS. Academic basis for candidate selection** (in order of priority): Class rank, standardized test scores, secondary school record, school's recommendation, essay.

**Nonacademic basis for candidate selection:** Character and personality, extracurricular participation, particular talent or ability, and alumni/ae relationship are considered.

**Requirements:** Graduation from secondary school is required; GED is accepted. 16 units and the following program of study are recommended: 4 units of English, 4 units of math, 2 units of science, 4 units of foreign language, 1 unit of social studies, 1 unit of history. Minimum composite ACT score of 20 and rank in top two-fifths of secondary school class required. Conditional admission possible for applicants not meeting standard requirements. ACT is required. PSAT is recommended. Campus visit and interview recommended. No off-campus interviews.

**Procedure:** Take ACT by December 1 of 12th year. Visit college for interview by December 1 of 12th year. Suggest filing application by March 1; no deadline. Notification of admission on rolling basis. $100 tuition deposit, refundable until May 1. $100 room deposit, refundable until June 15. Freshmen accepted in terms other than fall.

**Special programs:** Admission may be deferred one year. Credit and/or placement may be granted through CEEB Advanced Placement exams for scores of 3 or higher. Credit and/or placement may be granted through CLEP general and subject exams. Placement may be granted through challenge exams. Credit and placement may be granted through military and life experience. Concurrent enrollment program.

**Transfer students:** Transfer students accepted for terms other than fall. In fall 1992, 35% of all new students were transfers into all classes. 637 transfer applications were received, 578 were accepted. Application deadline is June 1 for fall; January 1 for spring. Minimum 2.3 GPA required. Lowest course grade accepted is "D." At least 32 semester hours must be completed at the university to receive degree.

**Admissions contact:** Marla Friederichs, M.A., Director of Admissions. 612 962-6150.

**FINANCIAL AID. Available aid:** Pell grants, SEOG, state scholarships and grants, school scholarships and grants, private scholarships and grants, ROTC scholarships, academic merit scholarships, and aid for undergraduate foreign students. Perkins Loans (NDSL), PLUS, Stafford Loans (GSL), state loans, school loans, and SLS. Deferred payment plan.

**Financial aid statistics:** 15% of aid is not need-based. In 1992-93, 92% of all undergraduate applicants received aid; 94% of freshman applicants. Average amounts of aid awarded freshmen: Scholarships and grants, $5,524; loans, $3,320.

**Supporting data/closing dates:** FAFSA: Priority filing date is April 1. Notification of awards on rolling basis.

**Financial aid contact:** Richard D. Battig, Director of Financial Aid. 612 962-6550.

**STUDENT EMPLOYMENT.** College Work/Study Program. Institutional employment. 33% of full-time undergraduates work on campus during school year. Students may expect to earn an average of $1,360 during school year. Off-campus part-time employment opportunities rated "excellent."

**COMPUTER FACILITIES.** 316 IBM/IBM-compatible, Macintosh/Apple, and RISC-/UNIX-based microcomputers; 267 are networked. Students may access Digital minicomputer/mainframe systems, Internet. Residence halls may be equipped with stand-alone microcomputers, networked terminals, modems. Client/LAN operating systems include Apple/Macintosh. Computer languages and software packages include C, COBOL, dBASE, FOCUS, FORTRAN, Lotus 1-2-3, Pascal, SPSS-X, Word, WordPerfect. Computer facilities are available to all students.

**Fees:** Computer fee is included in tuition/fees.

**Hours:** 7 AM-midn.

**GRADUATE CAREER DATA.** Highest graduate school enrollments: U of Minnesota, U of St.Thomas, William Mitchell Coll of Law. Companies and businesses that hire graduates: Andersen Consulting, Arthur Andersen, Cargill, Dayton Hudson Corp., Deloitte & Touche, Ernst & Young, Grant Thornton, Honeywell, KPMG Peat Marwick, Price Waterhouse, Rosemount Inc.

**PROMINENT ALUMNI/AE.** Will Steger, Antarctic explorer; Bernard Brennan, CEO, Montgomery Ward; James Oberstar, U.S. Congressman.

9-5

## Winona State University

**Winona, MN 55987** — **507 457-5000**

**1994-95 Costs.** Tuition: $2,400 (state residents), $4,900 (out-of-state). Room & board: $2,800. Fees, books, misc. academic expenses (school's estimate): $700.

**Enrollment.** Undergraduates: 2,600 men, 3,400 women (full-time). Freshman class: 3,325 applicants, 2,050 accepted, 1,300 enrolled. Graduate enrollment: 200 men, 400 women.

**Test score averages/ranges.** Average SAT scores: 460 verbal, 490 math. Average ACT scores: 21 English, 23 math, 22 composite. Range of ACT scores of middle 50%: 21-25 composite.

**Faculty.** 325 full-time; 25 part-time. 65% of faculty holds highest degree in specific field. Student/faculty ratio: 20 to 1.

**Selectivity rating.** Competitive.

**PROFILE.** Winona State, founded in 1860, is a public, multipurpose university. Programs are offered through the Colleges of Business, Education, Liberal Arts, Nursing and Health Sciences, and Science and Engineering. Its 40-acre campus is located in Winona, southeast of Minneapolis-St. Paul.

**Accreditation:** NCACS. Professionally accredited by the Accreditation Board for Engineering and Technology, the American Bar Association, the Council on Social Work Education, the National Association of Schools of Music, the National Council for Accreditation of Teacher Education, the National League for Nursing.

**Religious orientation:** Winona State University is nonsectarian; no religious requirements.

**Library:** Collections totaling over 215,000 volumes, 1,400 periodical subscriptions, and 703,000 microform items.

**Athletic facilities:** Gymnasiums, athletic fields, handball, racquetball, and tennis courts, weight rooms, swimming pool, bowling lanes.

**STUDENT BODY. Undergraduate profile:** 65% are state residents; 30% are transfers. 2% Asian-American, 2% Black, 1% Hispanic, 1% Native American, 94% White. Average age of undergraduates is 23.

**Freshman profile:** 15% of accepted applicants took SAT; 95% took ACT. 85% of freshmen come from public schools.

**Undergraduate achievement:** 75% of fall 1992 freshmen returned for fall 1993 term. 39% of entering class graduated. 5% of students who completed a degree program immediately went on to graduate study.

**Foreign students:** 300 students are from out of the country. Countries represented include Bangladesh, China, Hong Kong, Malaysia, and Pakistan; 45 in all.

**PROGRAMS OF STUDY. Degrees:** B.A., B.S., B.S.Eng., B.S.Nurs.

**Majors:** Accounting, Advertising, Art, Biology, Broadcasting, Business Administration, Business Education, Chemistry, Communication, Composite Materials Engineering, Computer Science, Criminal Justice, Cytotechnology, Early Childhood Education, Earth Science, Economics, Education, Elementary Education, English, Exercise Science, Finance, General Studies, Geology, German, Health Care Administration, Individualized Majors, Journalism, Life Sciences, Mass Communication, Mathematics, Medical Technology, Music, Nursing, Office Administration, Paralegal, Photojournalism, Physi-

cal Education, Physical Sciences, Physics, Political Science, Production/Operations Management, Psychology, Public Administration, Public Relations, Recreational/Leisure Studies, School/Community Health Education, Social Sciences, Social Work, Sociology, Special Education, Theatre Arts.
**Distribution of degrees:** The majors with the highest enrollment are business administration, education, and nursing.
**Requirements:** General education requirement.
**Academic regulations:** Minimum 2.0 GPA must be maintained.
**Special:** Minors offered in some majors and in aviation, business law, cross-cultural communication, gerontology, history, philosophy, speech, and statistics. Certificate programs offered in coaching, learning disabilities, and teaching the mentally retarded. Associate's degrees offered. Self-designed majors. Double majors. Dual degrees. Independent study. Accelerated study. Pass/fail grading option. Internships. Graduate school at which undergraduates may take graduate-level courses. Preprofessional programs in law, medicine, veterinary science, pharmacy, dentistry, optometry, agriculture, chiropractic, engineering, fishery/wildlife management, forestry, mortuary science, physical therapy, and podiatry. Exchange programs with St. Mary's Coll and with other Minnesota state universities. Teacher certification in early childhood, elementary, secondary, special education, and bilingual/bicultural education. Certification in specific subject areas. Study abroad in China, Denmark, England, Japan, Norway, and other countries.
**Honors:** Honors program. Honor societies.
**Academic Assistance:** Remedial reading, writing, math, and study skills. Nonremedial tutoring.

**STUDENT LIFE. Housing:** Students may live on or off campus. Coed, women's, and men's dorms. Off-campus privately-owned housing. 35% of students live in college housing.
**Social atmosphere:** Smaug, the Lower Hyphen, and the Student Union are popular gathering spots. Influential groups include the BCA (Black Cultural Awareness), Pi Lams fraternity, the Klingonz, and the CIA (Christians in Action). Springfest, Homecoming, and Halloween are highlights of the school year. "This is generally a white, Christian, Protestant community that prides itself on its conservative history," reports the school newspaper. "But the demographics are slowly changing, partially due to the town's two universities, to show a more diverse city."
**Services and counseling/handicapped student services:** Placement services. Health service. Women's center. Day care. Counseling services for minority, military, veteran, and older students. Birth control, personal, and psychological counseling. Career and academic guidance services. Religious counseling. Learning disabled services.
**Campus organizations:** Undergraduate student government. Student newspaper (Winonan, published once/week). Literary magazine. Radio and TV stations. Concert, varsity, and jazz bands, orchestra, choir, Madrigal Chamber Choir, Change of Pace Singers, dance and drama groups, forensics, cultural activities committee, 60 organizations in all. Three fraternities, no chapter houses; three sororities, no chapter houses. 3% of men join a fraternity. 3% of women join a sorority.
**Religious organizations:** Baptist Student Union, Campus Crusade for Christ, Intervarsity Christian Fellowship, Lutheran Campus Ministry, Muslim Student Association, Newman Center, United Campus Ministry, Fellowship of Christian Athletes, Christians in Action.
**Minority/foreign student organizations:** Black Culture Awareness Association, Hispanic Club, American Indian Club. International Student Club, Malaysian chapter of Tai Chi Club, Hmong Club.

**ATHLETICS. Physical education requirements:** Two terms of physical education required.
**Intercollegiate competition:** 50% of students participate. Baseball (M), basketball (M,W), cross-country (M,W), football (M), golf (M,W), gymnastics (W), softball (W), tennis (M,W), track and field (indoor) (M,W), track and field (outdoor) (M,W), volleyball (W). Member of NAIA, NCAA Division II, Northern Intercollegiate Conference, Northern Sun Conference.
**Intramural and club sports:** 70% of students participate. Intramural aerobics, basketball, flag football, floor hockey, ice hockey, racquetball, softball, volleyball, walleyball, water aerobics.

**ADMISSIONS. Academic basis for candidate selection** (in order of priority): Class rank, standardized test scores, secondary school record, school's recommendation, essay.
**Nonacademic basis for candidate selection:** Character and personality, extracurricular participation, particular talent or ability, and geographical distribution are considered.
**Requirements:** Graduation from secondary school is required; GED is accepted. 18 units and the following program of study are required: 4 units of English, 3 units of math, 3 units of science including 1 unit of lab, 2 units of foreign language, 2 units of social studies, 1 unit of history, 2 units of academic electives. Minimum composite ACT score of 21 (combined SAT score of 900) and rank in top half of secondary school class required for regular admission. Admission by petition possible for applicants not normally admissible. ACT is required; SAT may be substituted. Campus visit and interview recommended. No off-campus interviews.
**Procedure:** Take SAT or ACT by October of 12th year. Visit college for interview by December of 12th year. Suggest filing application by February 15; no deadline. Notification of admission on rolling basis. $20 nonrefundable room deposit. Freshmen accepted in terms other than fall.
**Special programs:** Admission may be deferred one year. Credit and/or placement may be granted through CEEB Advanced Placement exams for scores of 3 or higher. Credit and/or placement may be granted through CLEP general and subject exams. Credit and placement may be granted through DANTES and challenge exams and military and life experience. Early entrance/early admission program. Concurrent enrollment program.
**Transfer students:** Transfer students accepted for terms other than fall. In fall 1993, 30% of all new students were transfers into all classes. 1,100 transfer applications were received, 875 were accepted. Application deadline is one month prior to start of trimester for fall; one month prior to start of trimester for spring. Minimum 2.4 GPA required. Lowest course grade accepted is "C." Maximum number of transferable credits is 96 trimester hours from a two-year school and 144 trimester hours from a four-year school. At least 45 trimester hours must be completed at the university to receive degree.
**Admissions contact:** J.A. Mootz, Ed.D., Director of Admissions. 507 457-5100.

**FINANCIAL AID. Available aid:** Pell grants, SEOG, Federal Nursing Student Scholarships, state scholarships and grants, school scholarships and grants, private scholarships and grants, academic merit scholarships, athletic scholarships, and aid for undergraduate foreign students. Perkins Loans (NDSL), PLUS, Stafford Loans (GSL), NSL, Health Professions Loans, state loans, school loans, private loans, and SLS.
**Financial aid statistics:** 23% of aid is not need-based. In 1993-94, 100% of all undergraduate applicants received aid. Average amounts of aid awarded freshmen: Scholarships and grants, $1,200; loans, $1,500.
**Supporting data/closing dates:** FAFSA: Priority filing date is April 1; accepted on rolling basis. Notification of awards begins May 1.
**Financial aid contact:** Robert Leitzau, M.S., Director of Financial Aid. 507 457-5090.

**STUDENT EMPLOYMENT.** College Work/Study Program. Institutional employment. 25% of full-time undergraduates work on campus during school year. Students may expect to earn an average of $1,500 during school year. Freshmen are discouraged from working during their first term. Off-campus part-time employment opportunities rated "good."

**COMPUTER FACILITIES.** 300 IBM/IBM-compatible, Macintosh/Apple, and RISC-/UNIX-based microcomputers; all are networked. Students may access AT&T, CDC Cyber, Cray, Data General, Digital, IBM, UNISYS minicomputer/mainframe systems, BITNET, Internet, CompuServe. Residence halls may be equipped with stand-alone microcomputers, modems. Client/LAN operating systems include Apple/Macintosh, DOS, OS/2, UNIX/XENIX/AIX, Windows NT, X-windows, Microsoft, Novell. Computer facilities are available to all students.
**Fees:** Computer fee is included in tuition/fees.
**Hours:** 8 AM-11 PM.

**GRADUATE CAREER DATA.** Highest graduate school enrollments: U of Minnesota, Winona State U. 25% of graduates choose careers in business and industry. Companies and businesses that hire graduates: Control Data, IBM, Mayo Clinic, 3M.

# Mississippi

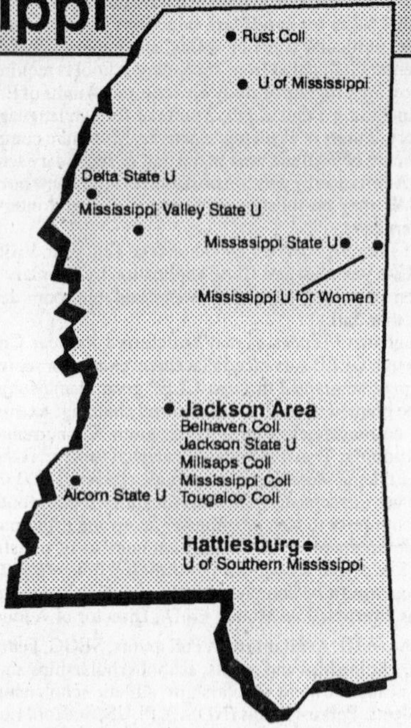


## Alcorn State University

**Lorman, MS 39096** **601 877-6147**

**1993-94 Costs.** Tuition: $2,376 (state residents), $4,518 (out-of-state). Room & board: $2,098. Fees, books, misc. academic expenses (school's estimate): $320.
**Enrollment.** Undergraduates: 1,207 men, 1,636 women (full-time). Freshman class: 3,000 applicants, 1,300 accepted, 600 enrolled. Graduate enrollment: 40 men, 163 women.
**Test score averages/ranges.** Average SAT scores: 380 verbal, 350 math. Average ACT scores: 18 English, 17 math, 19 composite.
**Faculty.** 178 full-time; 11 part-time. 50% of faculty holds doctoral degree. Student/faculty ratio: 20 to 1.
**Selectivity rating.** Less competitive.

**PROFILE.** Alcorn State, founded in 1871, is the oldest historically black, land-grant university in the country. Programs are offered through the Divisions of Agriculture and Applied Science, Arts and Sciences, Business, Education and Psychology, Graduate Studies, and Nursing. Its 1,700-acre campus is located in Lorman, 90 miles southwest of Jackson.

**Accreditation:** SACS. Professionally accredited by the National Association of Schools of Music, the National Council for Accreditation of Teacher Education, the National League for Nursing.
**Religious orientation:** Alcorn State University is nonsectarian; no religious requirements.
**Library:** Collections totaling over 161,232 volumes, 764 periodical subscriptions, and 35,904 microform items.
**Athletic facilities:** Gymnasium, basketball courts, swimming pool, handball court, dance studio, wrestling and gymnastics rooms.

**STUDENT BODY. Undergraduate profile:** 90% are state residents; 5% are transfers. 1% Asian-American, 96% Black, 3% White. Average age of undergraduates is 20.
**Freshman profile:** 5% of accepted applicants took SAT; 95% took ACT. 99% of freshmen come from public schools.
**Undergraduate achievement:** 65% of fall 1991 freshmen returned for fall 1992 term. 35% of entering class graduated. 36% of students who completed a degree program went on to graduate study within three years.
**Foreign students:** Four students are from out of the country.

**PROGRAMS OF STUDY. Degrees:** B.A., B.Mus., B.S.
**Majors:** Accounting, Agribusiness Communications, Agricultural Economics, Agricultural Education, Agronomy, Animal Science, Biology, Business Administration, Business Education, Chemistry, Computer Science/Chartered Accountancy, Criminal Justice, Early Childhood Education, Economics, Educational Psychology, Elementary Education, English, Fashion Merchandising, Food Sciences/Human Nutrition, French, General Agriculture, Health/Physical Education, Health Sciences, History, Home Economics Education, Industrial Arts Education, Industrial Technology, Institutional Management, Mathematics, Mathematics Education, Media Technology, Medical Records Administration, Music, Music Education, Music/Instrumental, Music/Piano, Music/Voice, Nursing, Office Administration, Physical Therapy, Political Science, Recreation, Social Science Education, Social Welfare, Sociology/Social Work, Special Education, Technology Education, Textile Chemistry.
**Distribution of degrees:** The majors with the highest enrollment are business, agriculture, and nursing; home economics, general education, and fashion merchandise/design have the lowest.
**Requirements:** General education requirement.
**Academic regulations:** Freshmen must maintain minimum 1.6 GPA; sophomores, 1.8 GPA; juniors, 2.0 GPA; seniors, 2.0 GPA.
**Special:** Associate's degrees offered. Double majors. Independent study. Internships. Cooperative education programs. Graduate school at which undergraduates may take graduate-level courses. Preprofessional programs in law, medicine, veterinary science, pharmacy, dentistry, and optometry. Cooperative physics program with Howard U. 2-2 preengineering program. Teacher certification in elementary education. ROTC.
**Honors:** Honors program. Honor societies.
**Academic Assistance:** Remedial reading, math, and study skills. Nonremedial tutoring.

**STUDENT LIFE. Housing:** All students receiving on-campus aid must live on campus. Women's and men's dorms. 95% of students live in college housing.
**Services and counseling/handicapped student services:** Placement services. Health service. Day care. Counseling services for military students. Personal counseling. Career and academic guidance services.
**Campus organizations:** Undergraduate student government. Student newspaper (Alcorn Herald). Yearbook. Radio station. Alcorn Players, concert and marching bands, glee club, jazz and wind ensembles, gospel choir, interfaith choir, Student Council, departmental and special-interest groups, 46 organizations in all. Four fraternities, no chapter houses; four sororities, no chapter houses. 15% of men join a fraternity. 20% of women join a sorority.
**Religious organizations:** Baptist Student Union, Newman Center, Sunday School, Church of God in Christ, United Methodist Campus Ministry.

**ATHLETICS. Physical education requirements:** Four semesters of physical education required.
**Intercollegiate competition:** 1% of students participate. Baseball (M), basketball (M,W), cross-country (M,W), football (M), golf (M), tennis (M,W), track (indoor) (M,W), track and field (M,W), volleyball (W). Member of NCAA Division 1-A for basketball, NCAA Division 1-AA, Southwestern Athletic Conference.
**Intramural and club sports:** Intramural basketball, bowling, flag football, softball, volleyball.

**ADMISSIONS. Academic basis for candidate selection** (in order of priority): Standardized test scores, class rank, secondary school record, school's recommendation, essay.
**Nonacademic basis for candidate selection:** Character and personality are important. Particular talent or ability and alumni/ae relationship are considered.
**Requirements:** Graduation from secondary school is required; GED is accepted. 13.5 units and the following program of study are required: 4 units of English, 3 units of math, 3 units of science, 1 unit of foreign language, 2.5 units of social studies. Minimum composite ACT score of 15 and minimum 2.0 GPA required of in-state applicants; minimum composite ACT score of 18 and minimum 2.0 GPA required of out-of-state applicants. Audition required of music program applicants. SAT or ACT is required. Campus visit recommended. Off-campus interviews available with an admissions representative.
**Procedure:** Application deadline is July 15. Notification of admission on rolling basis. $75 room deposit, refundable upon graduation or withdrawal. Freshmen accepted in terms other than fall.
**Special programs:** Admission may be deferred two years. Credit and/or placement may be granted through CEEB Advanced Placement exams. Credit and/or placement may be granted through CLEP general and subject exams. Early decision program. In fall 1992, 10 applied for early decision and 4 were accepted. Early entrance/early admission program. Concurrent enrollment program.
**Transfer students:** Transfer students accepted for terms other than fall. In fall 1992, 5% of all new students were transfers into all classes. 232 transfer applications were received, 95 were accepted. Application deadline is July for fall; October for spring. Minimum 2.0 GPA required. Lowest course grade accepted is "C." Maximum number of transferable credits is 64 semester hours. At least 132 semester hours must be completed at the university to receive degree.
**Admissions contact:** Albert Z. Johnson, M.S., Director of Admissions. 601 877-6147.

**FINANCIAL AID. Available aid:** Pell grants, SEOG, school scholarships, private scholarships, ROTC scholarships, academic merit scholarships, and athletic scholarships. PLUS, Stafford Loans (GSL), and SLS.
**Financial aid statistics:** 15% of aid is not need-based. In 1992-93, 95% of all undergraduate applicants received aid; 95% of freshman applicants. Average amounts of aid awarded freshmen: Loans, $1,000.
**Supporting data/closing dates:** FAFSA: Priority filing date is February 1; deadline is April 1. School's own aid application: Priority filing date is February 1; deadline is April 1. Income tax forms: Deadline is April 1. Notification of awards on rolling basis.
**Financial aid contact:** Laura Shelvy, Acting Director of Financial Aid. 601 877-6190.

**STUDENT EMPLOYMENT.** College Work/Study Program. Institutional employment. 30% of full-time undergraduates work on campus during school year. Students may expect to earn an average of $500 during school year. Freshmen are discouraged from working during their first term. Off-campus part-time employment opportunities rated "poor."

**COMPUTER FACILITIES.** IBM/IBM-compatible microcomputers. Computer languages and software packages include CICS/ICCF, COBOL, FORTRAN, PL/1, RPG. Computer facilities are available to all students.
**Fees:** None.
**Hours:** 8 AM-6 PM.

**GRADUATE CAREER DATA.** Graduate school percentages: 2% enter law school. 5% enter medical school. 1% enter dental school. 5% enter graduate business programs. 10% enter graduate arts and sciences programs. 1% enter theological school/seminary. Highest graduate school enrollments: Iowa State U, Meharry Medical Sch, Mississippi State U, U of Mississippi. 65% of graduates choose careers in business and industry. Companies and businesses that hire graduates: Allstate, Dow Chemical, federal government, IBM, State Farm Insurance.

**PROMINENT ALUMNI/AE.** Alex Haley, author, *Roots*; Medgar Evers, civil rights leader.

# Belhaven College

## Jackson, MS 39202

**1994-95 Costs.** Tuition: $7,490. Room & board: $2,900. Fees, books, misc. academic expenses (school's estimate): $430.
**Enrollment.** Undergraduates: 313 men, 423 women (full-time). Freshman class: 248 applicants, 197 accepted, 121 enrolled.
**Test score averages/ranges.** Average SAT scores: 467 verbal, 455 math. Average ACT scores: 23 composite.
**Faculty.** 35 full-time; 45 part-time. 80% of faculty holds highest degree in specific field. Student/faculty ratio: 17 to 1.
**Selectivity rating.** Less competitive.

**PROFILE.** Belhaven is a church-affiliated, liberal arts college. Founded as a women's college in 1883, it adopted coeducation in 1954. Its 42-acre campus is located in a residential area near the center of Jackson.

**Accreditation:** SACS. Professionally accredited by the National Association of Schools of Art and Design, the National Association of Schools of Music.
**Religious orientation:** Belhaven College is affiliated with the Presbyterian Church; three semesters of religion/theology required.
**Library:** Collections totaling over 83,106 volumes, 459 periodical subscriptions, and 4,276 microform items.
**Athletic facilities:** Gymnasium, swimming pool, weight room, baseball and soccer fields, basketball, tennis, and volleyball courts.
**STUDENT BODY. Undergraduate profile:** 88% are state residents; 60% are transfers. 1% Asian-American, 5% Black, 2% Hispanic, 90% White, 2% Other.
**Freshman profile:** 1% of freshmen who took SAT scored 700 or over on verbal; 1% scored 600 or over on math; 3% scored 500 or over on verbal, 3% scored 500 or over on math; 5% scored 400 or over on verbal, 5% scored 400 or over on math; 7% scored 300 or over on verbal, 7% scored 300 or over on math. 7% of freshmen who took ACT scored 30 or over on composite; 38% scored 24 or over on composite; 83% scored 18 or over on composite; 90% scored 12 or over on composite. 8% of accepted applicants took SAT; 90% took ACT.
**Undergraduate achievement:** 18% of students who completed a degree program immediately went on to graduate study.
**Foreign students:** 30 students are from out of the country. Countries represented include Brazil, Jamaica, South Africa, the United Kingdom, and Trinidad; 19 in all.
**PROGRAMS OF STUDY. Degrees:** B.A., B.A.Art, B.Mus., B.S.
**Majors:** Accounting, Art, Biblical Studies, Biology, Business Administration, Chemistry, Church Music, Computer Science, Elementary Education, English, General Sciences, History, Humanities, Mathematics, Organ, Philosophy, Piano, Psychology, Voice.
**Distribution of degrees:** The majors with the highest enrollment are business administration, accounting, and elementary education; music, art, and biblical studies have the lowest.
**Requirements:** General education requirement.
**Academic regulations:** Minimum 2.0 GPA must be maintained.
**Special:** Minors offered in most majors and in education, health/physical education, management, marketing, political science, Spanish, and sports management. Double majors. Independent study. Pass/fail grading option. Internships. Cooperative education programs. Preprofessional programs in law, medicine, veterinary science, pharmacy, dentistry, theology, optometry, health records, medical technology, nursing, occupational therapy, and physical therapy. 2-2 nursing and medical technology programs with U Medical Center. 3-2 and 2-3 preengineering programs with Mississippi State U. Teacher certification in elementary and secondary education. Certification in specific subject areas. ROTC at Jackson State U.
**Honors:** Phi Beta Kappa. Honors program. Honor societies.
**Academic Assistance:** Remedial writing, math, and study skills. Nonremedial tutoring.
**ADMISSIONS. Academic basis for candidate selection** (in order of priority): Secondary school record, standardized test scores, school's recommendation, class rank.
**Nonacademic basis for candidate selection:** Character and personality are emphasized. Extracurricular participation is important. Particular talent or ability and alumni/ae relationship are considered.
**Requirements:** Graduation from secondary school is required; GED is accepted. 16 units and the following program of study are required: 4 units of English, 2 units of math, 1 unit of science, 2 units of foreign language, 1 unit of social studies, 1 unit of history. Minimum composite ACT score of 19 (or SAT equivalent) required. Portfolio required of art program scholarship applicants. Audition required of music program scholarship applicants. Conditional admission possible for applicants not meeting standard requirements. ACT is required; SAT may be substituted. Campus visit and interview recommended. Off-campus interviews available with an admissions representative.
**Procedure:** Take SAT or ACT by April of 12th year. Visit college for interview by May 15 of 12th year. Notification of admission on rolling basis. $50 refundable tuition deposit. $100 refundable room deposit. Freshmen accepted in terms other than fall.
**Special programs:** Admission may be deferred two semesters. Credit and/or placement may be granted through CEEB Advanced Placement exams for scores of 4 or higher. Credit may be granted through CLEP general and subject exams, DANTES exams, and military experience. Credit and placement may be granted through life experience. Early entrance/early admission program.
**Transfer students:** Transfer students accepted for terms other than fall. In fall 1993, 60% of all new students were transfers into all classes. 288 transfer applications were received, 227 were accepted. Minimum 2.0 GPA required. Lowest course grade accepted is "C." Maximum number of transferable credits is 64 semester hours. At least 30 semester hours must be completed at the college to receive degree.
**Admissions contact:** Karen Walling, Director of Admissions. 601 968-5940.
**FINANCIAL AID. Available aid:** Pell grants, SEOG, state scholarships and grants, school scholarships and grants, private scholarships, academic merit scholarships, and athletic scholarships. Perkins Loans (NDSL), PLUS, Stafford Loans (GSL), school loans, private loans, and SLS. Tuition Plan Inc. and AMS.
**Financial aid statistics:** 15% of aid is not need-based. In 1993-94, 98% of all undergraduate applicants received aid; 98% of freshman applicants. Average amounts of aid awarded freshmen: Scholarships and grants, $3,000; loans, $2,000.
**Supporting data/closing dates:** FAFSA: Priority filing date is April 1. School's own aid application: Priority filing date is April 1; accepted on rolling basis. Notification of awards begins April 1.
**Financial aid contact:** Linda Phillips, M.B.A., Director of Financial Aid. 601 968-5933.

# Delta State University

## Cleveland, MS 38733 — 601 846-3000

**1994-95 Costs.** Tuition: $2,194 (state residents), $4,428 (out-of-state). Room & board: $1,880. Fees, books, misc. academic expenses (school's estimate): $350.
**Enrollment.** Undergraduates: 1,216 men, 1,612 women (full-time). Freshman class: 967 applicants, 472 accepted, 459 enrolled. Graduate enrollment: 241 men, 268 women.
**Test score averages/ranges.** Average ACT scores: 21 English, 19 math, 20 composite. Range of ACT scores of middle 50%: 18-23 English, 17-21 math.
**Faculty.** 205 full-time; 38 part-time. 56% of faculty holds doctoral degree. Student/faculty ratio: 17 to 1.
**Selectivity rating.** Less competitive.

**PROFILE.** Delta State, founded as a teachers college in 1924, is a public university. Programs are now offered through the Schools of Arts and Sciences, Business, Education, and Nursing. Its 274-acre campus is located in Cleveland, in the Mississippi Delta.

**Accreditation:** SACS. Professionally accredited by the American Home Economics Association, the Council on Social Work Education, the National Association of Schools of Art and Design, the National Association of Schools of Music, the National Council for Accreditation of Teacher Education, the National League for Nursing.
**Religious orientation:** Delta State University is nonsectarian; no religious requirements.
**Library:** Collections totaling over 263,891 volumes, 1,455 periodical subscriptions, and 718,580 microform items.
**Special facilities/museums:** Art museum, natural history museum, language lab, airport facility with 12 airplanes, flight simulator, planetarium.
**Athletic facilities:** Gymnasiums, coliseum, baseball, football, soccer, and softball fields, racquetball and tennis courts, cross-country and golf courses, swimming pool, weight room.
**STUDENT BODY. Undergraduate profile:** 92% are state residents; 55% are transfers. .6% Asian-American, 23.2% Black, .1% Hispanic, .3% Native American, 75.8% White. Average age of undergraduates is 18.
**Freshman profile:** 1% of accepted applicants took SAT; 99% took ACT. 62% of freshmen come from public schools.
**Undergraduate achievement:** 68% of fall 1992 freshmen returned for fall 1993 term. 27% of entering class graduated. 10% of students who completed a degree program immediately went on to graduate study.
**Foreign students:** 21 students are from out of the country. Countries represented include Canada, China, France, South Africa, and Sweden.
**PROGRAMS OF STUDY. Degrees:** B.A., B.Bus.Admin., B.Commercial Avia., B.F.A., B.Mus., B.Mus.Ed., B.S., B.S.Crim.Just., B.S.Ed., B.S.Gen.Studies, B.S.Nurs., B.Soc.Work.
**Majors:** Accounting, Art, Audiology/Speech Pathology, Aviation Management, Biology, Biology Education, Business Education, Chemistry, Chemistry Education, Computer Information Systems, Criminal Justice, Elementary Education, English, English Education, Environmental Science, Fashion Merchandising, Finance, Flight Operations, General Business, German Education, Health/Physical Education/Recreation, History, Home Economics, Home Economics Education, Insurance/Real Estate, Management, Marketing, Mathematics, Mathematics Education, Medical Technology, Music, Music Education, Nursing, Office Administration, Political Science, Pre-Dentistry, Pre-Engineering, Pre-Medicine, Psychology, Social Science Education, Social Sciences, Social Work, Spanish, Spanish Education, Special Education.
**Distribution of degrees:** The majors with the highest enrollment are accounting, elementary education, and management; business education, home economics education, and political science have the lowest.
**Requirements:** General education requirement.
**Academic regulations:** Minimum 2.0 GPA must be maintained.
**Special:** Minors offered in all majors. Several concentrations available in commercial aviation. Double major and internship in accounting and computer information systems. Double majors. Dual degrees. Internships. Graduate school at which undergraduates may take graduate-level courses. Preprofessional programs in medicine, veterinary science, pharmacy, dentistry, and optometry. Exchange program with Westfield State Coll. Teacher certification in elementary, secondary, and special education. Certification in specific subject areas. ROTC and AFROTC.
**Honors:** Honors program. Honor societies.
**Academic Assistance:** Remedial reading, writing, math, and study skills.
**STUDENT LIFE. Housing:** Students may live on or off campus. Women's and men's dorms. On-campus married-student housing. 43% of students live in college housing.
**Services and counseling/handicapped student services:** Placement services. Health service. Day care. Counseling services for minority, military, veteran, and older students. Personal and psychological counseling. Career and academic guidance services. Learning disabled services.
**Campus organizations:** Student newspaper (Delta Statement, published once/week). Literary magazine. Yearbook. Brass and woodwind ensembles, chorale, band, jazz band, Delta Singers, opera workshop, Delta Playhouse, traveling performers troupe, Readers Theatre, Young Republicans, departmental, professional, and special-interest groups, 35 organizations in all. Eight fraternities, no chapter houses; seven sororities, no chapter houses. 24% of men join a fraternity. 25% of women join a sorority.

**Religious organizations:** Baptist Student Union, Canterbury Club, Christian Student Center, Reform University Fellowship, Fellowship of Christian Athletes.
**Minority/foreign student organizations:** Black Student Organization.

**ATHLETICS. Physical education requirements:** Two semesters of physical education required.
**Intercollegiate competition:** 6% of students participate. Baseball (M), basketball (M,W), cheerleading (M,W), cross-country (W), diving (M,W), football (M), golf (M), softball (W), swimming (M,W), tennis (M,W). Member of Gulf South Conference, NCAA Division II, New South Conference.
**Intramural and club sports:** 10% of students participate. Intramural basketball, football, softball, walleyball.

**ADMISSIONS. Academic basis for candidate selection** (in order of priority): Standardized test scores.
**Nonacademic basis for candidate selection:** Character and personality and extracurricular participation are emphasized. Alumni/ae relationship is important. Particular talent or ability is considered.
**Requirements:** Graduation from secondary school is required; GED is accepted. 13.5 units and the following program of study are required: 4 units of English, 3 units of math, 3 units of science including 1 unit of lab, 1 unit of foreign language, 2.5 units of social studies. Minimum composite ACT score of 18 required of in-state applicants; minimum SAT score of 700 required of out-of-state applicants. ACT is required; SAT may be substituted. Campus visit recommended. Off-campus interviews available with an admissions representative.
**Procedure:** Take SAT or ACT by August of 12th year. Application deadline is August 4. Notification of admission on rolling basis. No set date by which applicants must accept offer. $50 room deposit, refundable until three weeks prior to start of term. Freshmen accepted in terms other than fall.
**Special programs:** Admission may be deferred. Credit and/or placement may be granted through CEEB Advanced Placement exams for scores of 3 or higher. Credit and/or placement may be granted through CLEP general and subject exams. Credit and placement may be granted through ACT PEP exams. Concurrent enrollment program.
**Transfer students:** Transfer students accepted for terms other than fall. In fall 1993, 55% of all new students were transfers into all classes. 793 transfer applications were received, 566 were accepted. Application deadline is August 4 for fall; December 7 for spring. Minimum 2.0 GPA required. Lowest course grade accepted is "D." Maximum number of transferable credits is 64 semester hours from a two-year school and 96 semester hours from a four-year school. At least 30 semester hours must be completed at the university to receive degree.
**Admissions contact:** Frances Short, Coordinator of Admissions. 601 846-4018.

**FINANCIAL AID. Available aid:** Pell grants, SEOG, state grants, school scholarships, ROTC scholarships, academic merit scholarships, and athletic scholarships. Perkins Loans (NDSL), PLUS, Stafford Loans (GSL), private loans, and SLS.
**Financial aid statistics:** 20% of aid is not need-based. In 1993-94, 100% of all undergraduate applicants received aid. Average amounts of aid awarded freshmen: Scholarships and grants, $1,500.
**Supporting data/closing dates:** FAFSA/FAF/FFS: Priority filing date is April 1. School's own aid application: Priority filing date is April 1. State aid form: Priority filing date is April 1. Income tax forms: Priority filing date is April 1. Notification of awards begins April 1.
**Financial aid contact:** Peggy Sledge, Director of Financial Aid. 601 846-4670.

**STUDENT EMPLOYMENT.** College Work/Study Program. Institutional employment. 12% of full-time undergraduates work on campus during school year. Students may expect to earn an average of $1,200 during school year. Off-campus part-time employment opportunities rated "fair."

**COMPUTER FACILITIES.** 270 IBM/IBM-compatible and Macintosh/Apple microcomputers; 20 are networked. Students may access NCR minicomputer/mainframe systems. Computer languages and software packages include BASIC, C, COBOL, dBASE, Lotus 1-2-3, Pascal, FORTRAN, RPG, WordPerfect; 40 in all. Computer facilities are available to all students.
**Fees:** None.
**Hours:** 8 AM-11 PM (M-Th); reduced hours on weekends.

**GRADUATE CAREER DATA.** Graduate school percentages: 2% enter law school. 4% enter medical school. 3% enter dental school. 10% enter graduate business programs. 7% enter graduate arts and sciences programs. 1% enter theological school/seminary. Highest graduate school enrollments: Delta State U, Mississippi State U, U of Mississippi, U of Southern Mississippi. 70% of graduates choose careers in business and industry.

**PROMINENT ALUMNI/AE.** Margaret Wade, National Basketball Hall of Fame Inductee and former head women's basketball coach, Delta State U; Bill LaForge, senior vice-president and general counsel, Paul Werth Associates, Inc.; Robert L. Elliott, M.D., breast cancer specialist.

# Jackson State University

**Jackson, MS 39217 — 601 968-2121**

**1993-94 Costs.** Tuition: $2,230 (state residents), $2,234 (out-of-state). Room: $1,226-$1,546. Board: $1,060-$1,220. Fees, books, misc. academic expenses (school's estimate): $500.
**Enrollment.** Undergraduates: 2,109 men, 2,744 women (full-time). Freshman class: 5,725 applicants, 3,836 accepted, 1,658 enrolled. Graduate enrollment: 261 men, 486 women.
**Test score averages/ranges.** Average ACT scores: 17 composite. Range of ACT scores of middle 50%: 15-19 composite.
**Faculty.** 315 full-time; 67 part-time. 65% of faculty holds doctoral degree. Student/faculty ratio: 17 to 1.
**Selectivity rating.** Less competitive.

**PROFILE.** Jackson State, founded in 1877, is a public university. Programs are offered through the Schools of Business, Education, Industrial and Technical Studies, and Liberal Studies. Its 128-acre campus is located in Jackson.

**Accreditation:** SACS. Professionally accredited by the Accrediting Council on Education in Journalism and Mass Communication, the Council on Social Work Education, the National Association of Schools of Music, the National Council for Accreditation of Teacher Education.
**Religious orientation:** Jackson State University is nonsectarian; no religious requirements.
**Library:** Collections totaling over 360,957 volumes and 2,715 periodical subscriptions.
**Special facilities/museums:** Research center.
**Athletic facilities:** Swimming pools, track and field, bowling lanes, baseball, football, practice, and soccer fields, martial arts and weight rooms, basketball and tennis courts, ballet, dance studios.

**STUDENT BODY. Undergraduate profile:** 67% are state residents; 3% are transfers. 1% Asian-American, 96% Black, 2% White, 1% Other. Average age of undergraduates is 20.
**Freshman profile:** 3% of freshmen who took ACT scored 24 or over on composite; 38% scored 18 or over on composite; 100% scored 12 or over on composite. Majority of accepted applicants took ACT. 85% of freshmen come from public schools.
**Undergraduate achievement:** 76% of fall 1991 freshmen returned for fall 1992 term. 38% of entering class graduated. 48% of students who completed a degree program went on to graduate study within five years.
**Foreign students:** 217 students are from out of the country. Countries represented include China, India, Iran, Kuwait, Nigeria, and Trinidad; 29 in all.

**PROGRAMS OF STUDY. Degrees:** B.A., B.Bus.Admin., B.Mus., B.Mus.Ed., B.S., B.S.Ed., B.Soc.Work.
**Majors:** Accounting, Art, Biology, Business Administration, Business Education, Chemistry, Computer Science, Criminal Justice/Correctional Services, Economics, Elementary Education, English, English Literature, Finance, Health/Physical Education/Recreation, History, Industrial Arts Education, Industrial Technology, Management, Marketing, Mass Communications, Mathematics, Mathematics Education, Meteorology, Music Education, Music/Piano Performance, Office Administration, Physics, Political Science, Psychology, Secondary Education, Social Science Education, Social Work, Sociology, Spanish, Special Education, Speech, Urban Studies.
**Distribution of degrees:** The majors with the highest enrollment are business administration, accounting, and elementary education; economics, physics, and Spanish have the lowest.
**Requirements:** General education requirement.
**Academic regulations:** Minimum 2.0 GPA must be maintained.
**Special:** Minors offered. Courses offered in early childhood education, environmental studies, historical preservation, library science, marine science, and reading. Double majors. Independent study. Internships. Cooperative education programs. Graduate school at which undergraduates may take graduate-level courses. Preprofessional programs in law, medicine, veterinary science, and dentistry. Combined-degree programs in math and chemistry with Caltech, Georgia Tech, and Mississippi State U. Medical technology/medical record administration concentration with U of Mississippi Medical Center. Research semester at Lawrence Berkeley Lab. Member of National Student Exchange (NSE). Teacher certification in elementary, secondary, and special education. Certification in specific subject areas. ROTC.
**Honors:** Phi Beta Kappa. Honors program. Honor societies.
**Academic Assistance:** Remedial reading, writing, math, and study skills.

**STUDENT LIFE. Housing:** All student athletes must live on campus. Women's and men's dorms. School-owned/operated apartments. Athletic dorm (men's). 45% of students live in college housing.
**Social atmosphere:** Favorite gathering spots include the Campus Union, JSU Gibbs/Green Memorial Plaza, the cafeteria, and off campus, the Jackson Metrocenter Mall. The Student Government Association, Pan Hellenic Council, NAACP chapter, the Baptist Student Union, Campus Crusade for Christ, and Student Advisory Councils are influential groups on campus. Students enjoy the African-American Harvest Bazaar, African-American history festivals and celebrations, Homecoming activities, the campus-wide Mardi Gras, the Soul Bowl (JSU vs. Alcorn State football game), and Greek Week. "JSU's social and cultural life is enriched by over 125 student organizations. All of the organizations facilitate the growth and community service projects JSU performs as part of its urban mission," reports the student newspaper.
**Services and counseling/handicapped student services:** Placement services. Health service. Day care. Counseling services for minority, military, veteran, and older students. Birth control, personal, and psychological counseling. Career and academic guidance services. Physically disabled student services. Notetaking services. Tape recorders. Tutors.
**Campus organizations:** Undergraduate student government. Student newspaper (Blue and White Flash, published once/week). Yearbook. Radio station. Band, orchestra, choirs, Dramatic Guild, 60 organizations in all. Four fraternities, no chapter houses; four sororities, no chapter houses.
**Religious organizations:** Bahai Club, Baptist Student Union, Campus Crusade for Christ, COGIC Collegiate, Emmanuel Club, Newman Club, Wesley Foundation.
**Minority/foreign student organizations:** Foreign Student Association, International Student Association.

**ATHLETICS. Physical education requirements:** Two semesters of physical education required.
**Intercollegiate competition:** 5% of students participate. Baseball (M), basketball (M,W), cheerleading (M,W), cross-country (M,W), football (M), golf (M), tennis (M,W), track (indoor) (M,W), track (outdoor) (M,W), track and field (indoor) (M,W), track and field (outdoor) (M,W), volleyball (W). Member of NCAA Division I, NCAA Division I-AA for football, Southwestern Athletic Conference.
**Intramural and club sports:** 62% of students participate. Intramural aerobics, basketball, karate, softball, swimming, tennis. Men's club bowling, gymnastics, martial arts, rifle, softball, swimming, weight lifting. Women's club bowling, gymnastics, martial arts, rifle, softball, swimming, weight lifting.

**ADMISSIONS. Academic basis for candidate selection** (in order of priority): Standardized test scores, secondary school record, school's recommendation, class rank.

**Nonacademic basis for candidate selection:** Character and personality, extracurricular participation, and particular talent or ability are important. Alumni/ae relationship is considered.
**Requirements:** Graduation from secondary school is recommended; GED is accepted. 13.5 units and the following program of study are required: 4 units of English, 3 units of math, 3 units of lab science, 2.5 units of social studies, 1 unit of academic electives. Minimum composite ACT score of 15 required of in-state applicants; minimum composite ACT score of 16 required of out-of-state applicants. ACT is required; SAT may be substituted. Off-campus interviews available with admissions and alumni representatives.
**Procedure:** Take SAT or ACT by December of 12th year. Application deadline is August 15. Notification of admission on rolling basis. No set date by which applicants must accept offer. $25 nonrefundable room deposit. Freshmen accepted in terms other than fall.
**Special programs:** Admission may be deferred one year. Credit may be granted through CLEP general and subject exams. Early decision program. Early entrance/early admission program. Concurrent enrollment program.
**Transfer students:** Transfer students accepted for terms other than fall. In fall 1992, 3% of all new students were transfers into all classes. Application deadline is August 15 for fall; December 15 for spring. Minimum 2.0 GPA required. Lowest course grade accepted is "C." Maximum number of transferable credits is 64 semester hours from a two-year school and 98 semester hours from a four-year school. At least 30 semester hours must be completed at the university to receive degree.
**Admissions contact:** Barbara Luckett, M.B.Ed., Director of Admissions. 601 968-2100.

**FINANCIAL AID. Available aid:** Pell grants, SEOG, state scholarships and grants, school scholarships and grants, private scholarships and grants, ROTC scholarships, academic merit scholarships, and athletic scholarships. Perkins Loans (NDSL), PLUS, Stafford Loans (GSL), school loans, private loans, and SLS.
**Financial aid statistics:** In 1992-93, 94% of all undergraduate applicants received aid.
**Supporting data/closing dates:** School's own aid application: Deadline is April 1. Notification of awards on rolling basis.
**Financial aid contact:** Stephanie Chatman, Acting Director of Financial Aid. 601 968-2227.

**STUDENT EMPLOYMENT.** College Work/Study Program. Institutional employment. 23% of full-time undergraduates work on campus during school year. Students may expect to earn an average of $2,000 during school year. Freshmen are discouraged from working during their first term. Off-campus part-time employment opportunities rated "good."

**COMPUTER FACILITIES.** 300 IBM/IBM-compatible and Macintosh/Apple microcomputers; 150 are networked. Students may access AT&T, Data General, Digital, IBM, NCR, SUN minicomputer/mainframe systems, BITNET, Internet. Computer languages and software packages include Ada, ARC-INFO, BASIC, C, C++, COBOL, Erdas, FORTRAN, Harvard Graphics, INFORMIX, SAS, SPSSX, WordPerfect. Computer facilities are available to all students.
**Fees:** None.
**Hours:** 8 AM-11 PM.

**GRADUATE CAREER DATA.** Graduate school percentages: 10% enter medical school. 9% enter graduate business programs. 16% enter graduate arts and sciences programs. Highest graduate school enrollments: U Medical Center, Jackson; U of Southern Mississippi. Companies and businesses that hire graduates: AT&T, IBM.

**PROMINENT ALUMNI/AE.** Joseph Jackson, president, National Baptist Convention; Robert Clark, state legislator; John Peoples, former president, Jackson State U; Charles Moore, contractor/entrepreneur; Walter Payton, professional athlete.

# Millsaps College

**Jackson, MS 39210** **601 974-1000**

**1993-94 Costs.** Tuition: $10,686. Room: $2,316. Board: $1,934. Fees, books, misc. academic expenses (school's estimate): $1,050.
**Enrollment.** Undergraduates: 523 men, 517 women (full-time). Freshman class: 820 applicants, 716 accepted, 263 enrolled. Graduate enrollment: 82 men, 35 women.
**Test score averages/ranges.** Average SAT scores: 520 verbal, 550 math. Average ACT scores: 26 composite. Range of ACT scores of middle 50%: 23-29 composite.
**Faculty.** 85 full-time; 21 part-time. 82% of faculty holds doctoral degree. Student/faculty ratio: 14 to 1.
**Selectivity rating.** More competitive.

**PROFILE.** Millsaps, founded in 1890, is a private, church-affiliated, liberal arts college for men. Its 100-acre campus is located in Jackson, 90 miles west of Meridian.

**Accreditation:** SACS. Professionally accredited by the American Assembly of Collegiate Schools of Business, the National Council for Accreditation of Teacher Education.
**Religious orientation:** Millsaps College is affiliated with the Methodist Church; Six credits in religion and/or philosophy required.
**Library:** Collections totaling over 265,000 volumes and 700 periodical subscriptions.
**Athletic facilities:** Physical activities center, baseball, soccer, and football fields golf course, tennis courts.

**STUDENT BODY. Undergraduate profile:** 50% are state residents. 3% Asian-American, 5% Black, 1% Hispanic, 90% White, 1% International.
**Freshman profile:** 2% of freshmen who took SAT scored 700 or over on verbal, 6% scored 700 or over on math; 18% scored 600 or over on verbal, 37% scored 600 or over on math; 56% scored 500 or over on verbal, 75% scored 500 or over on math; 94% scored 400 or over on verbal, 95% scored 400 or over on math; 100% scored 300 or over on verbal, 100% scored 300 or over on math. 48% of accepted applicants took SAT; 85% took ACT. 60% of freshmen come from public schools.
**Undergraduate achievement:** 81% of fall 1991 freshmen returned for fall 1992 term. 58% of entering class graduated.
**Foreign students:** Seven students are from out of the country. Countries represented include Japan.

**PROGRAMS OF STUDY. Degrees:** B.A., B.Bus.Admin., B.Lib.Studies, B.S.
**Majors:** Accounting, Administration, Art, Biology, Chemistry, Classical Studies, Computer Science, Economics, Elementary Education, English, European Studies, French, Geology, History, Mathematics, Music, Philosophy, Physics, Political Science, Psychology, Religion, Sociology/Anthropology, Spanish, Theatre.
**Distribution of degrees:** The majors with the highest enrollment are administration, biology, and English; religion, piano, and theatre have the lowest.
**Requirements:** General education requirement.
**Academic regulations:** Freshmen must maintain minimum 2.0 GPA; sophomores, juniors, seniors 1.5 GPA.
**Special:** Honors program includes honors paper and independent study. Writing portfolio and comprehensive exam in major field required for graduation. Interdisciplinary core curriculum. Double majors. Independent study. Internships. 3-1 medical technology program. 3-2 cooperative engineering programs with Auburn U, Columbia U, Vanderbilt U, Washington U, and Georgia Tech leading to B.S. from Millsaps and professional degree from second institution. Member of Associated Colleges of the South. Washington Semester. Teacher certification in elementary, secondary, and special education. Study abroad in Australia, England, France, Germany, Hungary, Poland, and Spain. ROTC at Jackson State U.
**Honors:** Phi Beta Kappa. Honors program. Honor societies.

**STUDENT LIFE. Housing:** All freshmen must live on campus unless living with family. All dormitories are air-conditioned. Coed, women's, and men's dorms. Fraternity housing. 72% of students live in college housing.
**Services and counseling/handicapped student services:** Placement services. Health service. Testing program. Office of Student Personnel. Chaplain. Psychological counseling. Career and academic guidance services. Learning disabled services.
**Campus organizations:** Undergraduate student government. Student newspaper. Literary magazine. Yearbook. Concert and chapel choirs, Millsaps Players, Circle K, debating, departmental and special-interest groups, 14 organizations in all. Five fraternities, all with chapter houses; four sororities, no chapter houses. 42% of men join a fraternity. 40% of women join a sorority.
**Religious organizations:** Campus Ministry Team.
**Minority/foreign student organizations:** Black Students Association. Cross Cultural Connection.

**ATHLETICS. Physical education requirements:** One semester hour of physical education required.
**Intercollegiate competition:** 16% of students participate. Baseball (M), basketball (M,W), cheerleading (M,W), cross-country (M,W), football (M), golf (M), soccer (M,W), tennis (M,W), volleyball (W). Member of NCAA Division III, Southern Collegiate Athletic Conference.
**Intramural and club sports:** 3% of students participate. Intramural basketball, soccer, softball, swimming, tennis, touch football, volleyball.

**ADMISSIONS. Academic basis for candidate selection** (in order of priority): Secondary school record, standardized test scores, essay, school's recommendation, class rank.
**Nonacademic basis for candidate selection:** Character and personality are emphasized. Extracurricular participation and alumni/ae relationship are considered.
**Requirements:** Graduation from secondary school is required; GED is accepted. 16 units required, including 4 units of English and a minimum 8 additional units in academic subjects. Conditional admission possible for applicants not meeting standard requirements. SAT or ACT is required. Admissions interview recommended. No off-campus interviews.
**Procedure:** Take SAT or ACT by December 15 of 12th year. Suggest filing application by October 15; no deadline. Notification of admission by April 1. $100 tuition deposit, refundable until May 1. $100 room deposit, refundable until May 1. Freshmen accepted in terms other than fall.
**Special programs:** Credit may be granted through CEEB Advanced Placement for scores of 4 or higher. Credit may be granted through CLEP general and subject exams. Early entrance/early admission program.
**Transfer students:** Transfer students accepted for terms other than fall. In fall 1992, 121 transfer applications were received, 94 were accepted. Minimum 2.0 GPA required. Lowest course grade accepted is "C." Maximum number of transferable credits is 16 course units. At least eight of final 10 course units must be completed at the college to receive degree.
**Admissions contact:** Gary Fretwell, M.A., Vice President for Enrollment and Student Affairs. 601 974-1050.

**FINANCIAL AID. Available aid:** Pell grants, SEOG, school scholarships, academic merit scholarships, and aid for undergraduate foreign students. Aid for United Methodist ministerial students and children of ministers of the United Methodist Church. Perkins Loans (NDSL), PLUS, Stafford Loans (GSL), school loans, private loans, and SLS. Tuition Plan Inc., Education Plan Inc., and Knight Tuition Plans. Insured Tuition Payment Plan.
**Financial aid statistics:** 36% of aid is not need-based. In 1992-93, 90% of all undergraduate applicants received aid; 91% of freshman applicants. Average amounts of aid awarded freshmen: Scholarships and grants, $6,560; loans, $3,839.
**Supporting data/closing dates:** FAFSA/FAF/FFS: Priority filing date is March 1. Notification of awards begins April 1.
**Financial aid contact:** Jack L. Woodward, B.D., Dean of Student Aid Financial Planning. 601 974-1220.

**STUDENT EMPLOYMENT.** College Work/Study Program. 51% of full-time undergraduates work on campus during school year. Students may expect to earn an average of $2,000 during school year. Off-campus part-time employment opportunities rated "good."

**COMPUTER FACILITIES.** 35 IBM/IBM-compatible microcomputers; 30 are networked. Students may access Digital minicomputer/mainframe systems, Internet. Computer languages and software packages include Lotus 1-2-3, MINITAB, WordPerfect. Computer facilities are available to all students.
**Fees:** Computer fee is included in tuition/fees.

**GRADUATE CAREER DATA.** Graduate school percentages: 9% enter law school. 6% enter medical school. 1% enter dental school. 7% enter graduate business programs. 18% enter graduate arts and sciences programs. 1% enter theological school/seminary. 54% of graduates choose careers in business and industry.

# Mississippi College

**Clinton, MS 39058 601 925-3000**

**1994-95 Costs.** Tuition: $5,580. Room: $1,210. Board: $1,600. Fees, books, misc. academic expenses (school's estimate): $900.
**Enrollment.** Undergraduates: 704 men, 998 women (full-time). Freshman class: 594 applicants, 385 accepted, 321 enrolled. Graduate enrollment: 586 men, 743 women.
**Test score averages/ranges.** Average ACT scores: 22 composite.
**Faculty.** 114 full-time; 56 part-time. 61% of faculty holds highest degree in specific field. Student/faculty ratio: 18 to 1.
**Selectivity rating.** Less competitive.

**PROFILE.** Mississippi College, founded in 1826, is a private, church-affiliated, liberal arts institution. Its 320-acre campus is located in Clinton, northeast of Jackson.

**Accreditation:** SACS. Professionally accredited by the American Bar Association, the National Association of Schools of Music, the National Council for Accreditation of Teacher Education, the National League for Nursing.
**Religious orientation:** Mississippi College is affiliated with the Southern Baptist Church; six semester hours of religion required.
**Library:** Collections totaling over 232,972 volumes, 759 periodical subscriptions, and 25,763 microform items.
**Athletic facilities:** Gymnasium, weight room.

**STUDENT BODY. Undergraduate profile:** 85% are state residents; 80% are transfers. 13% Black, 85% White, 2% Other. Average age of undergraduates is 27.
**Freshman profile:** 30% of accepted applicants took SAT; 70% took ACT. 80% of freshmen come from public schools.
**Undergraduate achievement:** 81% of fall 1992 freshmen returned for fall 1993 term. 83% of entering class graduated.
**Foreign students:** 14 students are from out of the country. Countries represented include China, Germany, India, Korea, the former Soviet Republics, and Thailand; 12 in all.

**PROGRAMS OF STUDY. Degrees:** B.A., B.Mus., B.Mus.Ed., B.S., B.S.Bus.Admin., B.S.Ed., B.S.Nurs.
**Majors:** Accounting, Administration of Justice, Art, Biological Sciences, Business Administration, Business Education, Chemistry, Church Music, Communication, Computer Science, Elementary Education, English, History, Home Economics, Interior Design, Journalism, Law, Marketing, Mathematics, Medical Technology, Modern Languages, Music, Music Education, Music Theory/Composition, Nursing, Office Administration, Paralegal Studies, Physical Education, Physics, Political Science, Psychology, Public Administration, Religion, Religious Education, Secondary Education, Social Studies, Social Work, Sociology.
**Distribution of degrees:** The majors with the highest enrollment are accounting, elementary education, and nursing; social studies, communication, and chemistry have the lowest.
**Requirements:** General education requirement.
**Special:** Minors offered in all majors except nursing. Double majors. Dual degrees. Internships. Graduate school at which undergraduates may take graduate-level courses. Preprofessional programs in law, medicine, veterinary science, pharmacy, dentistry, and theology. 3-2 engineering programs with Auburn U and U of Mississippi. Teacher certification in elementary and secondary education. Certification in specific subject areas. Exchange programs abroad in Germany (Johannes Gutenberg U) and Kazakhstan (U of Kazakhstan). Study abroad also in England. ROTC at Jackson State U.
**Honors:** Honors program.
**Academic Assistance:** Remedial study skills.

**STUDENT LIFE. Housing:** All unmarried students under age 21 must live on campus unless living near campus with relatives. Women's and men's dorms. 24% of students live in college housing.
**Social atmosphere:** On campus, students tend to gather in dorm lobbies, the cafeteria, and the student center. The Baptist Student Union, Student Government Association, women's social tribes, and men's service clubs are among the most influential groups in campus life. Football games, occasional concerts and dances, club swaps and formals are popular events, as well as student plays, concerts, and operas, and departmental speakers. "At least half of the students are commuters with no interest in the college's social and cultural life," reports the editor of the student newspaper. "Opportunities are limited on campus, but available to those who want to take advantage of what's going on. The state's largest city is ten minutes away; ballet, opera, plays, museums, and other activities abound in Jackson."
**Services and counseling/handicapped student services:** Placement services. Health service. Counseling services for minority, military, veteran, and older students. Personal and psychological counseling. Career and academic guidance services. Physically disabled student services. Notetaking services. Tutors. Reader services for the blind.
**Campus organizations:** Undergraduate student government. Student newspaper (Collegian, published once/two weeks). Literary magazine. Yearbook. Radio station. Debating, speech teams, departmental and special-interest groups, service clubs, 50 organizations in all.
**Religious organizations:** Baptist Student Union.
**Minority/foreign student organizations:** Black Student Association.

**ATHLETICS. Physical education requirements:** Three semester hours of physical education required.
**Intercollegiate competition:** 12% of students participate. Baseball (M), basketball (M,W), cross-country (M,W), football (M), golf (M), softball (W), tennis (M,W), track (indoor) (M,W), track (outdoor) (M,W), track and field (indoor) (M,W), track and field (outdoor) (M,W), volleyball (W). Member of Gulf South Conference, NCAA Division II.
**Intramural and club sports:** 10% of students participate. Intramural basketball, football, softball. Men's club soccer.

**ADMISSIONS. Academic basis for candidate selection** (in order of priority): Standardized test scores, secondary school record, class rank, school's recommendation, essay.
**Nonacademic basis for candidate selection:** Character and personality are emphasized. Extracurricular participation is important. Particular talent or ability is considered.
**Requirements:** Graduation from secondary school is required; GED is accepted. No specific distribution of secondary school units required. SAT or ACT is required. Campus visit and interview recommended. Off-campus interviews available with an admissions representative.
**Procedure:** Take SAT or ACT by August 15 of 12th year. Suggest filing application by May 1. Application deadline is August 1. Notification of admission on rolling basis. $50 room deposit, refundable until July 15. Freshmen accepted in terms other than fall.
**Special programs:** Admission may be deferred one year. Credit may be granted through CEEB Advanced Placement for scores of 3 or higher. Credit may be granted through CLEP general exams and military experience. Credit and/or placement may be granted through CLEP subject exams. Credit and placement may be granted through challenge exams. Early entrance/early admission program. Concurrent enrollment program.
**Transfer students:** Transfer students accepted for terms other than fall. In fall 1993, 80% of all new students were transfers into all classes. 624 transfer applications were received, 439 were accepted. Minimum 2.0 GPA required. Lowest course grade accepted is "D." Maximum number of transferable credits is 65 semester hours. At least 30 semester hours must be completed at the college to receive degree.
**Admissions contact:** Jennifer Trussell, M.C.C., Director of Admissions. 601 925-3240, 800 738-1236.

**FINANCIAL AID. Available aid:** Pell grants, SEOG, Federal Nursing Student Scholarships, state scholarships and grants, school scholarships and grants, private scholarships and grants, academic merit scholarships, and athletic scholarships. Ministerial grants. Perkins Loans (NDSL), PLUS, Stafford Loans (GSL), NSL, Health Professions Loans, state loans, school loans, private loans, and SLS. Deferred payment plan. Monthly payment plan.
**Supporting data/closing dates:** FAFSA: Priority filing date is April 1; accepted on rolling basis. FAF: Priority filing date is April 1. School's own aid application: Priority filing date is April 1. Notification of awards on rolling basis.
**Financial aid contact:** Thomas E. Prather, Ph.D., Director of Financial Aid. 601 925-3212, 800 738-1346.

**STUDENT EMPLOYMENT.** College Work/Study Program. Institutional employment. 16% of full-time undergraduates work on campus during school year. Students may expect to earn an average of $1,600 during school year. Off-campus part-time employment opportunities rated "good."

**COMPUTER FACILITIES.** 77 IBM/IBM-compatible and Macintosh/Apple microcomputers. Residence halls may be equipped with modems. Computer languages and software packages include BASIC, COBOL, FORTRAN, Pascal, RPG II. Computer facilities are available to all students.
Fees: None.
Hours: 8 AM-midn. (M-Th); 8 AM-11 PM (F); 8 AM-6 PM (Sa); 1 PM-11 PM (Su).

**GRADUATE CAREER DATA.** Highest graduate school enrollments: U of Mississippi, New Orleans Baptist Theological Seminary.

**PROMINENT ALUMNI/AE.** Larry Myricks, Olympic medalist; Dr. William Causey, leader in hospital infectious research; Dr. James L. Sullivan, former president, Southern Baptist Convention and Sunday School Board; Bernie Ebbeps, founder and president, LDDS long-distance carrier; Susan Morse Brown, 1987 Broadcaster of the Year.

# Mississippi State University

**Mississippi State, MS 39762 601 325-2323**

**1994-95 Costs.** Tuition: $2,494 (state residents), $4,933 (out-of-state). Room & board: $3,130. Fees, books, misc. academic expenses (school's estimate): $957.
**Enrollment.** Undergraduates: 5,904 men, 3,995 women (full-time). Freshman class: 4,255 applicants, 3,277 accepted, 1,609 enrolled. Graduate enrollment: 1,393 men, 996 women.
**Test score averages/ranges.** Average ACT scores: 23 English, 22 math, 23 composite. Range of ACT scores of middle 50%: 18-25 English, 16-23 math.
**Faculty.** 730 full-time; 100 part-time. 68% of faculty holds doctoral degree. Student/faculty ratio: 26 to 1.
**Selectivity rating.** Less competitive.

**PROFILE.** Mississippi State, founded in 1878, is a comprehensive, public university. Programs are offered through the Colleges of Agriculture and Home Economics, Architecture, Arts and Sciences, Business and Industry, Education, Engineering, Forest Resources, and Interdisciplinary Studies and the Graduate School. Its 4,200-acre campus is located in Starkville, 15 miles west of Columbus.

**Accreditation:** SACS. Professionally accredited by the Accreditation Board for Engineering and Technology, the American Assembly of Collegiate Schools of Business, the American Home Economics Association, the American Society of Landscape Architects, the American Veterinary Medical Association, the National Architecture Accrediting Board, the National Association of Schools of Art and Design, the National Association of Schools of Music, the National Association of Schools of Public Affairs and Administration, the National Council for Accreditation of Teacher Education, the Society of American Foresters.
**Religious orientation:** Mississippi State University is nonsectarian; no religious requirements.
**Library:** Collections totaling over 865,135 volumes, 7,189 periodical subscriptions, and 2,113,669 microform items.
**Special facilities/museums:** Art gallery, earth science museum, music museum, 78,000-acre experimental forest, institute of archaeology, flight research lab, planetarium.
**Athletic facilities:** Football stadium, coliseum, sports complex, swimming pool, racquetball and tennis courts, track, gymnasium, baseball, football, and intramural fields, gymnasium, golf course, field houses.

**STUDENT BODY. Undergraduate profile:** 84% are state residents; 36% are transfers. 1.1% Asian-American, 13.5% Black, .5% Hispanic, .3% Native American, 78.7% White, 5.9% Other. Average age of undergraduates is 23.
**Freshman profile:** 9% of freshmen who took ACT scored 30 or over on English, 7% scored 30 or over on math, 8% scored 30 or over on composite; 44% scored 24 or over on

English, 35% scored 24 or over on math, 37% scored 24 or over on composite; 85% scored 18 or over on English, 83% scored 18 or over on math, 90% scored 18 or over on composite; 99% scored 12 or over on English, 99% scored 12 or over on math, 100% scored 12 or over on composite; 100% scored 6 or over on English, 100% scored 6 or over on math. 4% of accepted applicants took SAT; 96% took ACT.
**Undergraduate achievement:** 77% of fall 1992 freshmen returned for fall 1993 term. 21% of entering class graduated.
**Foreign students:** 220 students are from out of the country. Countries represented include China, India, Indonesia, Malaysia, Pakistan, and Taiwan; 79 in all.

**PROGRAMS OF STUDY. Degrees:** B.A., B.Arch., B.Bus.Admin., B.F.A., B.Gen.Studies, B.Land.Arch., B.Mus.Ed., B.Prof.Acct., B.S., B.Soc.Work.
**Majors:** Accounting, Aerospace Engineering, Agribusiness, Agricommunication, Agricultural Economics, Agricultural Engineering, Agricultural Engineering Technology/Business, Agricultural/Extension Education, Agricultural Pest Management, Agriculture, Agronomy, Animal Science, Anthropology, Architecture, Art, Banking/Finance, Biochemistry, Biological Engineering, Biological Sciences, Business Administration, Business Information Systems/Quantitative Analysis, Chemical Engineering, Chemistry, Civil Engineering, Communication, Computer Engineering, Computer Science, Dairy Science, Distributive Education, Economics, Educational Psychology, Electrical Engineering, Elementary Education, Engineering/Business, English, Entomology, Fisheries Management, Food Science/Technology, Foreign Languages, Forest Products, Forestry, General Agriculture, General Liberal Arts, General Science, General Studies, Geology, History, Home Economics, Horticulture, Industrial Engineering, Industrial Technology, Insurance, Landscape Architecture, Landscape Contracting, Management, Marketing, Mathematics, Mechanical Engineering, Medical Technology, Microbiology, Music Education, Nuclear Engineering, Office Administration, Petroleum Engineering, Philosophy, Physical Education, Physics, Political Science, Poultry Science, Psychology, Real Estate/Mortgage Financing, Secondary Education, Social Work, Sociology, Special Education, Technical/Trade Studies, Technology Teacher Education, Transportation.
**Distribution of degrees:** The majors with the highest enrollment are accounting, elementary education, and marketing.
**Requirements:** General education requirement.
**Academic regulations:** Minimum 2.0 GPA must be maintained.
**Special:** Double majors. Independent study. Accelerated study. Internships. Cooperative education programs. Graduate school at which undergraduates may take graduate-level courses. Preprofessional programs in law, veterinary science, pharmacy, dentistry, theology, optometry, medical records, nursing, and physical therapy. 2-2 and 3-2 programs between Coll of Agriculture or Coll of Engineering and either Coll of Business and Industry or Coll of Liberal Arts and Sciences. 3-1 medical technology programs with approved hospitals. Member of Mississippi/Alabama Sea Grant Consortium. Washington Semester. Teacher certification in elementary, secondary, special education, and vo-tech education. Certification in specific subject areas. Study abroad in Canada, Costa Rica, Israel, Italy (honors program), Mexico. ROTC and AFROTC.
**Honors:** Honors program.
**Academic Assistance:** Remedial reading and math. Nonremedial tutoring.

**STUDENT LIFE. Housing:** Students may live on or off campus. Coed, women's, and men's dorms. Sorority and fraternity housing. On-campus married-student housing. Special-interest groupings in dorms, graduate student dorms. One coed dorm for honor students. 45% of students live in college housing.
**Social atmosphere:** According to the student newspaper, "Social and cultural life both on campus and off provide a wide array of activities for students. MSU is dedicated to providing a strong educational background as well as emotional support to all of its students. MSU goes beyond caring." Influential groups include the Student Association, Greeks, MSU Roadrunners, Panhellenic Council, the Baptist Student Union, and the Intrafraternity Council. Popular campus events include Homecoming, the Annual Egg Bowl, the Miss MSU Pageant, the Madrigal Christmas Dinner, football games, and the entire baseball season. Popular student gathering spots include the cafeteria, the drill field, and Fire Points.
**Services and counseling/handicapped student services:** Placement services. Health service. Day care. Counseling services for minority, military, veteran, and older students. Birth control, personal, and psychological counseling. Career and academic guidance services. Religious counseling. Physically disabled student services. Learning disabled services. Notetaking services. Tutors. Reader services for the blind.
**Campus organizations:** Undergraduate student government. Student newspaper (Reflector, published twice/week). Literary magazine. Yearbook. Radio and TV stations. Band, chorus, vocal and instrumental ensembles, community theatre, departmental, service, and special-interest groups, 300 organizations in all. 18 fraternities, 12 chapter houses; 11 sororities, seven chapter houses. 17% of men join a fraternity. 20% of women join a sorority.
**Religious organizations:** Campus Crusade for Christ, Chi Alpha, Fellowship of Christian Athletes, Islamic Association, Navigators, Student Christian Action, University Christian Student Center, University Common Ministries, Wesley Foundation, numerous denominational groups.
**Minority/foreign student organizations:** Afro-American Plus, African-Americans in Public Administration, Council of Black Organizations, Council on Minority Affairs, Graduate Minority Council, NAACP, Society of Black Engineers. International Partners Program, World Neighbor Association, African, Chinese, Egyptian, French, Indian, Japanese, Korean, Malaysian, Pakistani, Spanish, Thai, and Vietnamese groups.

**ATHLETICS. Physical education requirements:** None.
**Intercollegiate competition:** 3% of students participate. Baseball (M), basketball (M,W), cross-country (M,W), football (M), golf (M,W), track and field (indoor) (M,W), track and field (outdoor) (M,W), volleyball (W). Member of NCAA Division I, Southeastern Conference.
**Intramural and club sports:** 84% of students participate. Intramural basketball, bowling, football, racquetball, soccer, softball, weight lifting. Men's club soccer.

**ADMISSIONS.**
**Requirements:** Graduation from secondary school is required; GED is accepted. 16 units and the following program of study are required: 4 units of English, 3 units of math, 3 units of science including 1 unit of lab, 2.5 units of social studies, 2.5 units of electives. One elective must be from foreign languages or approved math or science. Minimum composite ACT score of 18 required; minimum combined SAT score of 710 required of out-of-state applicants submitting SAT. 2 units of biology, chemistry, or physics and 4 units of math, including algebra, geometry, or trigonometry required of engineering, forestry, math, and science program applicants. 2 units of biology, chemistry, or physics and 3 units of algebra or geometry required of architecture program applicants. 2 units of algebra, trigonometry, or geometry and 2 units of biology, chemistry, or physics required of agriculture program applicants. 2 units of math required of business program applicants. 3 units of social studies required of architecture and engineering program applicants. Conditional admission possible for applicants not meeting standard requirements. Developmental Studies Program for applicants not normally admissible. ACT is required; SAT may be substituted. Campus visit recommended. Off-campus interviews available with an alumni representative.
**Procedure:** Suggest filing application by August 1; no deadline. Notification of admission on rolling basis. Reply is required by registration. $50 room deposit, refundable until July 15. Freshmen accepted in terms other than fall.
**Special programs:** Credit may be granted through CEEB Advanced Placement for scores of 3 or higher. Credit may be granted through CLEP subject exams. Credit and placement may be granted through challenge exams. Early entrance/early admission program. Concurrent enrollment program.
**Transfer students:** Transfer students accepted for terms other than fall. In fall 1993, 36% of all new students were transfers into all classes. 1,439 transfer applications were received, 1,439 were accepted. Application deadline is 20 days prior to registration for fall; 20 days prior to registration for spring. Minimum 2.0 GPA required. Lowest course grade accepted is "C." Half the total credits required for graduation in a given curriculum may be transferred. At least 32 semester hours must be completed at the university to receive degree.
**Admissions contact:** Jerry B. Inmon, M.Ed., Director of Admissions. 601 325-2224.

**FINANCIAL AID. Available aid:** Pell grants, SEOG, state scholarships and grants, private scholarships and grants, ROTC scholarships, and athletic scholarships.
**Financial aid statistics:** 37% of aid is not need-based.
**Supporting data/closing dates:** School's own aid application: Priority filing date is August 1. Notification of awards on rolling basis.
**Financial aid contact:** Audrey S. Lambert, M.Ed., Director of Student Financial Aid. 601 325-2450.

**STUDENT EMPLOYMENT.** College Work/Study Program. Institutional employment.

**COMPUTER FACILITIES.** 3,000 IBM/IBM-compatible microcomputers; 1,000 are networked. Students may access Digital, IBM, SUN, UNISYS minicomputer/mainframe systems, BITNET, Internet. Residence halls may be equipped with stand-alone microcomputers, networked microcomputers. Client/LAN operating systems include DOS, LocalTalk/AppleTalk, Novell. Computer languages and software packages include C, COBOL, dBASE, FORTRAN, Lotus 1-2-3, MINITAB, Oracle, Pascal, SAS, SPSS, WordPerfect; specialized packages. Computer facilities are available to all students.
**Fees:** None.
**Hours:** 8 AM-midn.

**PROMINENT ALUMNI/AE.** John Stennis, former U.S. senator; Will Clark, baseball player; Richard Truly, NASA; Raphael Callejas, president, Honduras.

# Mississippi University for Women

**Columbus, MS 39701** **601 329-4750**

**1994-95 Costs.** Tuition: $2,239 (state residents), $4,381 (out-of-state). Room & board: $2,217. Fees, books, misc. academic expenses (school's estimate): $520.
**Enrollment.** Undergraduates: 275 men, 1,104 women (full-time). Freshman class: 1,128 applicants, 989 accepted, 501 enrolled. Graduate enrollment: 22 men, 155 women.
**Test score averages/ranges.** Average ACT scores: 21 English, 19 math, 21 composite. Range of ACT scores of middle 50%: 19-23 English, 17-23 math.
**Faculty.** 103 full-time; 52 part-time. 53% of faculty holds highest degree in specific field. Student/faculty ratio: 17 to 1.
**Selectivity rating.** Less competitive.

**PROFILE.** Mississippi University for Women, founded in 1884, is a public, liberal arts institution for women. Its 110-acre campus is located in Columbus, 85 miles north of Meridian.

**Accreditation:** SACS. Professionally accredited by the American Bar Association, the American Home Economics Association, the American Speech-Language-Hearing Association, the National Association of Schools of Art and Design, the National Association of Schools of Music, the National Council for Accreditation of Teacher Education, the National League for Nursing.
**Religious orientation:** Mississippi University for Women is nonsectarian; no religious requirements.
**Library:** Collections totaling over 232,598 volumes, 1,614 periodical subscriptions, and 454 microform items.
**Special facilities/museums:** Museum/gallery, university archives, language lab, TV studio, residential high school for gifted students, elementary school, center for special children, speech and hearing center.
**Athletic facilities:** Gymnasiums, swimming pool, basketball, racquetball, and tennis courts, dance studio, vita course, 3-hole pitch and putt, softball fields, gymnastics, training and weight rooms.

**STUDENT BODY. Undergraduate profile:** 92% are state residents; 29% are transfers. 20% Black, 79% White, 1% Other. Average age of undergraduates is 23.
**Freshman profile:** 3% of freshmen who took ACT scored 30 or over on English, 2% scored 30 or over on math, 3% scored 30 or over on composite; 28% scored 24 or over on English, 14% scored 24 or over on math, 22% scored 24 or over on composite; 73% scored 18 or over on English, 62% scored 18 or over on math, 77% scored 18 or over on composite; 100% scored 12 or over on English, 100% scored 12 or over on math, 100% scored 12 or over on composite. 6% of accepted applicants took SAT; 94% took ACT.

**Undergraduate achievement:** 57% of fall 1992 freshmen returned for fall 1993 term. 38% of entering class graduated.
**Foreign students:** Four students are from out of the country. Countries represented include Belize, Cameroon, China, and Japan.

**PROGRAMS OF STUDY. Degrees:** B.A., B.F.A., B.Mus., B.S., B.S.Nurs.
**Majors:** Accounting, Art, Biology, Broadcasting, Business Administration, Chemistry, Clothing/Textiles/Merchandising, Elementary Education, English, Family/Human Development, Fine Arts, History, Home Economics, Home Economics Education, Journalism, Mathematics, Microbiology, Music, Music Education, Nursing, Paralegal Studies, Physical Education, Physical Sciences, Social Sciences, Special Education, Speech Pathology, Theatre.
**Distribution of degrees:** The majors with the highest enrollment are business administration, nursing, and elementary education; home economics education has the lowest.
**Requirements:** General education requirement.
**Special:** Minors offered in all majors except nursing and educational areas. Associate's degrees offered. Double majors. Dual degrees. Pass/fail grading option. Internships. Cooperative education programs. Graduate school at which undergraduates may take graduate-level courses. Preprofessional programs in law, medicine, veterinary science, pharmacy, dentistry, engineering, and physical therapy. 3-2 engineering programs with Auburn U and Mississippi State U. Member of Academic Common Market and Hispanic Education Satellite System. Teacher certification in early childhood, elementary, secondary, and special education. Certification in specific subject areas. Study abroad in Japan, Korea, and the United Kingdom. ROTC and AFROTC at Mississippi State U.
**Honors:** Honors program. Honor societies.
**Academic Assistance:** Remedial writing and math. Nonremedial tutoring.

**STUDENT LIFE. Housing:** Students may live on or off campus. Women's and men's dorms. School-owned/operated apartments. 23% of students live in college housing.
**Social atmosphere:** The student newspaper reports,"MUW works with Columbus in providing many cultural activities for our students. Students often are busily involved with their own class work, social clubs, and other extracurricular activities. Our students enjoy social functions with students at nearby Mississippi State University and Columbus Air Force Base." Social clubs similar to sororities and student government influence student social life. On campus, students frequent the Goose, the dorms, and the Union. Favorite off-campus spots include The Club, Bonnie & Clyde's, and the local malls.
**Services and counseling/handicapped student services:** Placement services. Health service. Day care. Counseling services for minority, veteran, and older students. Personal counseling. Career and academic guidance services. Physically disabled student services. Tutors. Reader services for the blind.
**Campus organizations:** Undergraduate student government. Student newspaper (Spectator, published once/week). Literary magazine. Yearbook. Radio station. Concert choir, vocal and instrumental ensembles, special-interest groups, 90 organizations in all. One fraternity, no chapter house; three sororities, no chapter houses. 25% of men join a fraternity. 24% of women join a sorority.
**Religious organizations:** Baptist Student Union, Wesley and Newman associations, Fellowship of Christian Athletes, Ecumenical Ministry, Latter-Day Saints Student Association, United Ministries Council.
**Minority/foreign student organizations:** Black Student Council, Corettas.

**ATHLETICS. Physical education requirements:** Two semesters of physical education required.
**Intercollegiate competition:** 2% of students participate. Basketball (W), softball (W), tennis (W), volleyball (W). Member of NCAA Division II.
**Intramural and club sports:** 18% of students participate. Intramural aerobics, badminton, ballet, basketball, billiards, fencing, flag football, golf, gymnastics, racquetball, scuba, softball, swimming, table tennis, tennis, volleyball, weight lifting.

**ADMISSIONS. Academic basis for candidate selection** (in order of priority): Standardized test scores, secondary school record.
**Requirements:** Graduation from secondary school is recommended; GED is accepted. 15 units and the following program of study are required: 4 units of English, 3 units of math, 3 units of science including 2 units of lab, 2.5 units of social studies, 2 units of academic electives. At least 1 unit of foreign language recommended. Minimum composite ACT score of 18 required. Conditional admission possible for applicants not meeting standard requirements. ACT is required; SAT may be substituted. Campus visit and interview recommended. Off-campus interviews available with admissions and alumni representatives.
**Procedure:** Take SAT or ACT by spring of 12th year. Visit college for interview by spring of 12th year. Notification of admission on rolling basis. $25 room deposit, refundable until August 1. Freshmen accepted in terms other than fall.
**Special programs:** Admission may be deferred one semester. Credit may be granted through CEEB Advanced Placement for scores of 3 or higher. Credit may be granted through CLEP general and subject exams, DANTES and challenge exams, and military experience. Early entrance/early admission program. Concurrent enrollment program.
**Transfer students:** Transfer students accepted for terms other than fall. In fall 1993, 29% of all new students were transfers into all classes. 430 transfer applications were received, 430 were accepted. Minimum 2.0 GPA recommended. Lowest course grade accepted is "C." At least 30 semester hours must be completed at the university to receive degree.
**Admissions contact:** Teresa Thompson, Exec. Dir. of Enrollment/External Affairs. 601 329-7106.

**FINANCIAL AID. Available aid:** Pell grants, SEOG, state grants, school scholarships, private scholarships, ROTC scholarships, academic merit scholarships, and athletic scholarships. Perkins Loans (NDSL), PLUS, Stafford Loans (GSL), and SLS. Deferred payment plan.
**Financial aid statistics:** In 1993-94, 89% of all undergraduate applicants received aid; 91% of freshman applicants. Average amounts of aid awarded freshmen: Scholarships and grants, $1,027; loans, $2,589.
**Supporting data/closing dates:** FAFSA: Priority filing date is June 1; accepted on rolling basis. Notification of awards begins April 15.
**Financial aid contact:** Teresa Thompson, Exec. Dir. of Enrollment/External Affairs. 601 329-7114.

**STUDENT EMPLOYMENT.** College Work/Study Program. Institutional employment. 26% of full-time undergraduates work on campus during school year. Students may expect to earn an average of $1,475 during school year. Off-campus part-time employment opportunities rated "good."

**COMPUTER FACILITIES.** 132 IBM/IBM-compatible and Macintosh/Apple microcomputers; 117 are networked. Students may access IBM minicomputer/mainframe systems, Internet. Residence halls may be equipped with stand-alone microcomputers. Client/LAN operating systems include Apple/Macintosh. Computer languages and software packages include BASIC, C, COBOL, dBASE, Enable, FORTRAN, Harvard Graphics, Lotus 1-2-3, PageMaker, Pascal, PFS:First Choice, Windows, WordPerfect. Computer facilities are available to all students.
**Fees:** None.
**Hours:** 8 AM-9 PM (M-F); 8 AM-2 PM (Sa); 1 PM-7 PM (Su).

# Mississippi Valley State University

Itta Bena, MS 38941 — 601 254-9041

**1994-95 Costs.** Tuition: $2,164 (state residents), $4,306 (out-of-state). Room & board: $2,024. Fees, books, misc. academic expenses (school's estimate): $512.
**Enrollment.** Undergraduates: 951 men, 1,176 women (full-time). Freshman class: 3,537 applicants, 1,030 accepted, 528 enrolled. Graduate enrollment: 3 men, 9 women.
**Test score averages/ranges.** Average ACT scores: 17 composite. Range of ACT scores of middle 50%: 13-18 English, 14-17 math.
**Faculty.** 106 full-time; 30 part-time. 43% of faculty holds doctoral degree. Student/faculty ratio: 20 to 1.
**Selectivity rating.** Less competitive.

**PROFILE.** Mississippi Valley State, founded in 1946, is a public university. Programs are offered through the Divisions of Arts and Sciences, Business, and Education. Its 450-acre campus is located in Itta Bena, 35 miles east of Greenwood.

**Accreditation:** SACS. Professionally accredited by the Council on Social Work Education, the National Association of Schools of Art and Design, the National Association of Schools of Music, the National Council for Accreditation of Teacher Education.
**Religious orientation:** Mississippi Valley State University is nonsectarian; no religious requirements.
**Library:** Collections totaling over 106,673 volumes, 677 periodical subscriptions, and 261,574 microform items.
**Special facilities/museums:** On-campus elementary school.

**STUDENT BODY. Undergraduate profile:** 85% are state residents; 5% are transfers. 98% Black, 1% White, 1% Other. Average age of undergraduates is 20.
**Freshman profile:** 3% of freshmen who took ACT scored 24 or over on composite; 29% scored 18 or over on composite; 100% scored 12 or over on composite. 98% of accepted applicants took ACT. 98% of freshmen come from public schools.
**Undergraduate achievement:** 63% of fall 1992 freshmen returned for fall 1993 term. 37% of entering class graduated. 25% of students who completed a degree program immediately went on to graduate study.

**PROGRAMS OF STUDY. Degrees:** B.A., B.Mus.Ed., B.S., B.Soc.Work.
**Majors:** Art, Biology, Biology Education, Business Administration, Communications, Computer Science, Criminal Justice, Elementary Education, English, English Education, Environmental Health, Health/Physical Education, Industrial Technology, Mathematics, Mathematics Education, Music Education, Office Administration, Political Science, Secondary Education, Social Science Education, Social Work, Sociology, Speech.
**Distribution of degrees:** The majors with the highest enrollment are criminal justice, business administration, and education; music education, communications, and environmental health have the lowest.
**Requirements:** General education requirement.
**Academic regulations:** Freshmen must maintain minimum 1.5 GPA; sophomores, 1.7 GPA; juniors, 1.9 GPA; seniors, 2.0 GPA.
**Special:** Minors offered in accounting, biology, business administration, computer science, English, mathematics, physical education, recreation, and speech. Music major includes instrument maintenance/repair and jazz (commercial jazz, performance, theory, composition) options. Industrial/vocational education includes architectural, automotive, building construction, graphic, or machine tool technology concentrations. Special education courses offered. Freshmen may enroll in basic philosophy/humanities program before declaring major. Junior-year proficiency test in English required for directed teaching and graduation. Senior recital, exhibit, project, or comprehensive exam required for graduation. Double majors. Internships. Cooperative education programs. Graduate school at which undergraduates may take graduate-level courses. Preprofessional programs in law, medicine, and dentistry. Member of Consortium/Alliance for Minority Participation, and Writing/Thinking Consortium. Teacher certification in early childhood, elementary, secondary, and special education. Certification in specific subject areas. ROTC and AFROTC.
**Honors:** Honors program. Honor societies.
**Academic Assistance:** Remedial reading, writing, math, and study skills. Nonremedial tutoring.

**STUDENT LIFE. Housing:** Students may live on or off campus. Women's and men's dorms. Both on-campus and off-campus married-student housing. 65% of students live in college housing.
**Social atmosphere:** According to the student newspaper, social life at MVSU centers around the Student Union and the Red Room. Christian groups exert a strong influence, as does the SGA. Some of the most popular events on campus are the Miss MSU pageant, the Miss Cover Girl Pageant, Homecoming, and Valley Theatre performances.
**Services and counseling/handicapped student services:** Placement services. Health service. Counseling services for minority and older students. Birth control and personal counseling. Career and academic guidance services. Religious counseling. Physically disabled student services. Tutors.

**Campus organizations:** Undergraduate student government. Student newspaper (Delta Devils Gazette, published once/quarter). Yearbook. Radio station. Band, choirs, jazz ensembles, drama group, Trade and Industries Club, community and volunteer service, 34 organizations in all. Four fraternities, no chapter houses; four sororities, no chapter houses. 5% of men join a fraternity. 4% of women join a sorority.
**Religious organizations:** Baptist Student Union, Chapel Committee, Methodist group, Newman Club, Seventh-day Adventist group.

**ATHLETICS. Physical education requirements:** Two semesters of physical education required.
**Intercollegiate competition:** Football (M), track (M,W). Member of NCAA Division I, NCAA Division I-AA for football.
**Intramural and club sports:** Intramural basketball, gymnastics, handball, paddleball, skating, squash, swimming, volleyball, weight training.

**ADMISSIONS. Academic basis for candidate selection** (in order of priority): Standardized test scores, secondary school record, class rank, school's recommendation, essay.
**Nonacademic basis for candidate selection:** Character and personality and geographical distribution are emphasized. Extracurricular participation is important. Particular talent or ability and alumni/ae relationship are considered.
**Requirements:** Graduation from secondary school is recommended; GED is accepted. No specific distribution of secondary school units required. Minimum composite ACT score of 13 and minimum 1.8 GPA required of in-state applicants; minimum composite ACT score of 16 and minimum 1.8 GPA required of out-of-state applicants. Conditional admission possible for applicants not meeting standard requirements. ACT is required; SAT may be substituted. Campus visit and interview recommended. Off-campus interviews available with admissions and alumni representatives.
**Procedure:** Take SAT or ACT by April 30 of 12th year. Visit college for interview by April 30 of 12th year. Suggest filing application by April 30. Application deadline is August 1. Notification of admission on rolling basis. $25 refundable room deposit. Freshmen accepted in terms other than fall.
**Special programs:** Admission may be deferred one year. Credit may be granted through CLEP general and subject exams. Early entrance/early admission program.
**Transfer students:** Transfer students accepted for terms other than fall. In fall 1993, 5% of all new students were transfers into all classes. 265 transfer applications were received, 275 were accepted. Application deadline is August 1 for fall; December 1 for spring. Minimum 2.0 GPA required. Lowest course grade accepted is "C."
**Admissions contact:** Maxcine Rush, M.B.A., Director of Admissions. 601 254-9041, extension 6393.

**FINANCIAL AID. Available aid:** Pell grants, SEOG, state grants, private scholarships, ROTC scholarships, and athletic scholarships. Perkins Loans (NDSL), PLUS, Stafford Loans (GSL), and SLS. Deferred payment plan.
**Financial aid statistics:** 7% of aid is not need-based. In 1993-94, 95% of all undergraduate applicants received aid; 95% of freshman applicants. Average amounts of aid awarded freshmen: Scholarships and grants, $2,103; loans, $1,300.
**Supporting data/closing dates:** FAFSA/FAF/FFS: Priority filing date is April 1. School's own aid application: Priority filing date is April 1. Income tax forms: Priority filing date is April 1. Notification of awards on rolling basis.
**Financial aid contact:** Darrell Boyd, M.B.A., Director of Financial Aid. 601 254-9041, extension 6540.

**STUDENT EMPLOYMENT.** College Work/Study Program. Institutional employment. 8% of full-time undergraduates work on campus during school year. Students may expect to earn an average of $1,200 during school year. Off-campus part-time employment opportunities rated "poor."

**COMPUTER FACILITIES.** 125 IBM/IBM-compatible and Macintosh/Apple microcomputers. Students may access IBM minicomputer/mainframe systems. Computer languages and software packages include ABC Write, Ada, Assembler, BASIC, C, COBOL, dBASE, FORTRAN, Pascal, PC-Write, PL/1, SuperCalc, WordStar; 150 in all. Computer facilities are available to all students.
**Fees:** None.
**Hours:** 8 AM-10 PM (M-Th); 8 AM- 4 PM (F); 6 PM-10 PM (Su).

**GRADUATE CAREER DATA.** Graduate school percentages: 2% enter law school. 3% enter medical school. 3% enter dental school. 5% enter graduate business programs. 40% enter graduate arts and sciences programs. 1% enter theological school/seminary. Highest graduate school enrollments: Delta State U, Indiana U, Jackson State U, U of Southern Illinois. 12% of graduates choose careers in business and industry. Companies and businesses that hire graduates: AT&T, IBM, Standard Oil, State Corrections Department.

**PROMINENT ALUMNI/AE.** Dr. Samuel McGee and Dr. Carolyn Smith, educators; Jerry Rice, professional football player.

# Rust College

**Holly Springs, MS 38635** **601 252-8000**

**1993-94 Costs.** Tuition: $4,100. Room: $948. Board: $1,100. Fees, books, misc. academic expenses (school's estimate): $552.
**Enrollment.** Undergraduates: 373 men, 636 women (full-time). Freshman class: 1,113 applicants, 559 accepted, 288 enrolled.
**Test score averages/ranges.** Average ACT scores: 16 English, 15 math, 16 composite.
**Faculty.** 55 full-time; 6 part-time. 60% of faculty holds doctoral degree. Student/faculty ratio: 18 to 1.
**Selectivity rating.** Less competitive.

**PROFILE.** Rust, founded in 1866, is a private, church-affiliated college. Its 11-acre campus is located in Holly Springs, 35 miles from Memphis.

**Accreditation:** SACS.
**Religious orientation:** Rust College is affiliated with the United Methodist Church; one semester of religion required.
**Library:** Collections totaling over 110,002 volumes, 339 periodical subscriptions, and 6,409 microform items.
**Special facilities/museums:** Art collection, child care center.
**Athletic facilities:** Tennis court, swimming pool, exercise room, gymnasium, track, baseball and softball fields.

**STUDENT BODY. Undergraduate profile:** 67% are state residents; 4% are transfers. 94% Black, 2% White, 4% Other. Average age of undergraduates is 19.
**Freshman profile:** 72% of accepted applicants took ACT.
**Undergraduate achievement:** 73% of fall 1991 freshmen returned for fall 1992 term. 20% of entering class graduated. 30% of students who completed a degree program went on to graduate study within one year.
**Foreign students:** 41 students are from out of the country. Countries represented include Ethiopia, Gambia, Kenya, Mexico, Nigeria, and Pakistan.

**PROGRAMS OF STUDY. Degrees:** B.A., B.S.
**Majors:** Biology, Business Administration, Business Education, Chemistry, Computer Science, Economics, Elementary Education, English, English Education, Health/Physical Education/Recreation, Mass Communication/Journalism/Broadcasting Journalism, Mathematics, Mathematics Education, Medical Technology, Music, Music Education, Nursing, Political Science, Pre-Engineering, Science Education, Social Work, Sociology.
**Distribution of degrees:** The majors with the highest enrollment are business administration, social work, and political science; music and mathematics have the lowest.
**Requirements:** General education requirement.
**Academic regulations:** Freshmen must maintain minimum 1.5 GPA; sophomores, 1.85 GPA; juniors, 2.0 GPA; seniors, 2.0 GPA.
**Special:** Minors offered in most majors. Business administration major has various concentrations. Associate's degrees offered. Dual degrees. Independent study. Accelerated study. Internships. Cooperative education programs. Preprofessional programs in medicine, veterinary science, pharmacy, dentistry, and engineering. 3-2 chemistry and engineering programs, math and engineering programs, interdisciplinary science and engineering programs, and nursing and biology programs with Alcorn State U, Auburn U, Georgia Tech, Memphis State U, Mississippi State U, Tuskegee U, and U of Mississippi. Teacher certification in elementary and secondary education. Certification in specific subject areas.
**Honors:** Honors program. Honor societies.
**Academic Assistance:** Remedial reading, writing, and math.

**ADMISSIONS. Academic basis for candidate selection** (in order of priority): Secondary school record, class rank, school's recommendation, standardized test scores, essay.
**Nonacademic basis for candidate selection:** Character and personality, particular talent or ability, geographical distribution, and alumni/ae relationship are important. Extracurricular participation is considered.
**Requirements:** Graduation from secondary school is required; GED is accepted. No specific distribution of secondary school units required. Minimum 2.0 GPA required. Audition required of music program applicants. Special Services Program for students not normally admissible. ACT is required; SAT may be substituted. Campus visit and interview recommended. Off-campus interviews available with admissions and alumni representatives.
**Procedure:** Take SAT or ACT by January of 12th year. Suggest filing application by May 1. Application deadline is July 15. Notification of admission on rolling basis. Reply is required within 10 days of acceptance. $25 room deposit, refundable after graduation or withdrawal. Freshmen accepted in terms other than fall.
**Special programs:** Admission may be deferred for varying periods. Credit may be granted through CLEP general and subject exams. Placement may be granted through challenge exams. Early decision program. Deadline for applying for early decision is July 15. Early entrance/early admission program.
**Transfer students:** Transfer students accepted for terms other than fall. In fall 1992, 4% of all new students were transfers into all classes. 86 transfer applications were received, 58 were accepted. Application deadline is July 15 for fall; December 15 for spring. Minimum 2.0 GPA required. Secondary school transcript required of transfer applicants who choose not to use any credits previously earned. Lowest course grade accepted is "C." At least 124 credits must be completed at the college to receive degree.
**Admissions contact:** Jo Ann Scott, Director of Admissions. 601 252-8000, extension 4068.

**FINANCIAL AID. Available aid:** Pell grants, SEOG, state grants, school scholarships and grants, private scholarships, academic merit scholarships, aid for undergraduate foreign students, and United Negro College Fund. Perkins Loans (NDSL), PLUS, Stafford Loans (GSL), and school loans. Family tuition reduction. Installment payment plan.
**Financial aid statistics:** 20% of aid is not need-based. In 1992-93, 98% of all undergraduate applicants received aid; 95% of freshman applicants. Average amounts of aid awarded freshmen: Loans, $1,000.
**Supporting data/closing dates:** FAFSA/FFS: Priority filing date is May 1; deadline is June 15. School's own aid application: Priority filing date is May 1; deadline is June 15. Income tax forms: Priority filing date is May 1; deadline is June 15. Notification of awards begins May 1.
**Financial aid contact:** Helen Street, Director of Financial Aid. 601 252-8000, extension 4061.

# Tougaloo College

**Tougaloo, MS 39174** **601 977-7700**

**1994-95 Costs.** Tuition: $4,795. Room: $1,235. Board: $950. Fees, books, misc. academic expenses (school's estimate): $1,000.
**Enrollment.** Undergraduates: 352 men, 709 women (full-time). Freshman class: 3,784 applicants, 541 accepted, 325 enrolled.
**Test score averages/ranges.** Average SAT scores: 920 combined. Average ACT scores: 18 composite.
**Faculty.** 67 full-time; 7 part-time. 54% of faculty holds doctoral degree. Student/faculty ratio: 15 to 1.
**Selectivity rating.** Less competitive.

**PROFILE.** Tougaloo, founded in 1869, is a church-affiliated, historically black college. Its 1,265-acre campus is located in Tougaloo, just outside of Jackson.

**Accreditation:** SACS.
**Religious orientation:** Tougaloo College is affiliated with the United Church of Christ; no religious requirements.
**Library:** Collections totaling over 91,251 volumes, 450 periodical subscriptions, and 4,799 microform items.
**Special facilities/museums:** Art collection.

**STUDENT BODY. Undergraduate profile:** 88% are state residents; 11% are transfers. 99% Black, 1% Other. Average age of undergraduates is 18.
**Freshman profile:** 3% of accepted applicants took SAT; 97% took ACT. 98% of freshmen come from public schools.
**Undergraduate achievement:** 69% of fall 1991 freshmen returned for fall 1992 term. 20% of entering class graduated. 45% of students who completed a degree program immediately went on to graduate study.
**Foreign students:** Two students are from out of the country. Countries represented include Nigeria and Trinidad.

**PROGRAMS OF STUDY. Degrees:** B.A., B.S.
**Majors:** Accounting/Economics, Afro-American Studies, Art, Biology, Chemistry, Early Childhood Education, Economics, Elementary Education, English, English/Journalism, Health/Physical Education, History, Humanities, Mathematics, Mathematics/Computer Science, Music, Physics, Political Science, Psychology, Psychology/Mental Health, Sociology.
**Distribution of degrees:** The majors with the highest enrollment are economics, biology, and political science; art and physics have the lowest.
**Requirements:** General education requirement.
**Academic regulations:** Minimum 2.0 GPA must be maintained.
**Special:** Courses offered in business administration, French, geography, geology, library science, philosophy, religion, special education, and speech and drama. Social Science Advancement Institute conducts intercollegiate seminars, discussion groups, preparatory seminars for graduate study, and tutorials. Associate's degrees offered. Double majors. Dual degrees. Independent study. Accelerated study. Pass/fail grading option. Internships. Cooperative education programs. Graduate school at which undergraduates may take graduate-level courses. Preprofessional programs in law, medicine, veterinary science, dentistry, theology, engineering, nursing, lab technology, and social work. 3-1 medical technology programs with Meharry Medical Coll and St. Dominic-Jackson Hospital. 3-2 engineering programs with Brown U, Georgia Tech, Howard U, Tuskegee U, U of Mississippi, and U of Wisconsin at Madison. Cross-registration with Millsaps Coll. Washington Semester. Exchange programs with Bowdoin Coll, Brown U, and Meharry Medical Coll. Teacher certification in early childhood, elementary, and secondary education. Study abroad in African countries and France. ROTC at Jackson State U.
**Honors:** Honors program.
**Academic Assistance:** Remedial reading, writing, and math. Nonremedial tutoring.

**STUDENT LIFE. Housing:** Students must live on campus or in approved housing unless living with family. Women's and men's dorms. 80% of students live in college housing.
**Services and counseling/handicapped student services:** Placement services. Health service. Personal and psychological counseling. Career and academic guidance services. Religious counseling. Learning disabled services.
**Campus organizations:** Undergraduate student government. Student newspaper (Harambee, published once/month). Yearbook. Radio station. Heroines of Jericho, Operation Somebody Cares, Order of Eastern Stars, Panhellenic Council, prealumni, PEPS, education clubs, departmental groups, dance ensemble, cheerleaders. Four fraternities, no chapter houses; four sororities, no chapter houses.
**Religious organizations:** Baptist Student Union, Crusaders for Christ, United Church of Christ.
**Minority/foreign student organizations:** Black Expo, Black Unity Coordinating Committee, NAACP. Foreign Student Club, French Club.

**ATHLETICS. Physical education requirements:** Two semesters of physical education required.
**Intercollegiate competition:** 1% of students participate. Basketball (M,W), track (M). Member of Gulf Coast Conference, NAIA.
**Intramural and club sports:** Intramural basketball, tennis, track.

**ADMISSIONS. Academic basis for candidate selection** (in order of priority): Secondary school record, school's recommendation, standardized test scores.
**Nonacademic basis for candidate selection:** Character and personality, extracurricular participation, particular talent or ability, and alumni/ae relationship are considered.
**Requirements:** Graduation from secondary school is recommended; GED is accepted. 16 units and the following program of study are required: 3 units of English, 2 units of math, 2 units of science, 2 units of foreign language, 2 units of social studies, 1 unit of history, 4 units of academic electives. Minimum 2.0 GPA required. Algebra and geometry recommended. Foreign language recommended. Portfolio required of art program applicants. Audition required of music program applicants. Upward Bound and special services programs for applicants not normally admissible. SAT or ACT is required. Admissions interview recommended. Off-campus interviews available with admissions and alumni representatives.
**Procedure:** Take SAT or ACT by August of 12th year. Notification of admission on rolling basis. No set date by which applicants must accept offer. $50 room deposit, refundable until two weeks prior to registration. Freshmen accepted in terms other than fall.
**Special programs:** Admission may be deferred one year. Credit and/or placement may be granted through CEEB Advanced Placement exams for scores of 4 or higher. Credit and/or placement may be granted through CLEP general and subject exams. Placement may be granted through challenge exams. Early entrance/early admission program.
**Transfer students:** Transfer students accepted for terms other than fall. In fall 1992, 11% of all new students were transfers into all classes. 332 transfer applications were received, 77 were accepted. Minimum 2.0 GPA required. Lowest course grade accepted is "C." Maximum number of transferable credits is 62 semester hours.
**Admissions contact:** Washington Cole IV, Director of Admissions. 601 977-7770.

**FINANCIAL AID. Available aid:** Pell grants, SEOG, state scholarships and grants, school scholarships and grants, private scholarships, academic merit scholarships, athletic scholarships, aid for undergraduate foreign students, and United Negro College Fund. Perkins Loans (NDSL), PLUS, Stafford Loans (GSL), and SLS. Deferred payment plan.
**Financial aid statistics:** 41% of aid is not need-based. Average amounts of aid awarded freshmen: Scholarships and grants, $3,301; loans, $1,800.
**Supporting data/closing dates:** FAFSA/FAF/FFS: Priority filing date is April 15. School's own aid application: Priority filing date is April 15. Notification of awards on rolling basis.
**Financial aid contact:** Janis H. Evans, Director of Financial Aid. 601 977-7769.

**STUDENT EMPLOYMENT.** College Work/Study Program. Institutional employment. 10% of full-time undergraduates work on campus during school year. Students may expect to earn an average of $1,050 during school year. Freshmen are discouraged from working during their first term. Off-campus part-time employment opportunities rated "fair."

**COMPUTER FACILITIES.** IBM/IBM-compatible and Macintosh/Apple microcomputers. Computer facilities are available to all students.
**Fees:** Computer fee is included in tuition/fees.
**Hours:** 8 AM-midn.

# University of Mississippi

**University, MS 38677** 601 232-7111

**1994-95 Costs.** Tuition: $2,456 (state residents), $4,916 (out-of-state). Room: $1,500. Board: $1,300. Fees, books, misc. academic expenses (school's estimate): $450.
**Enrollment.** Undergraduates: 3,792 men, 3,736 women (full-time). Freshman class: 3,844 applicants, 3,383 accepted, 1,669 enrolled. Graduate enrollment: 1,243 men, 969 women.
**Test score averages/ranges.** Range of ACT scores of middle 50%: 21-26 composite.
**Faculty.** 383 full-time; 75 part-time. 79% of faculty holds doctoral degree. Student/faculty ratio: 16 to 1.
**Selectivity rating.** Less competitive.

**PROFILE.** The University of Mississippi, founded in 1844, is a comprehensive, public institution. Programs are offered through the College of Liberal Arts and the Schools of Accountancy, Business Administration, Education, Engineering, Health Related Professions, and Pharmacy. Its 2,000-acre campus is located in University, 75 miles southeast of Memphis, Tenn.

**Accreditation:** SACS. Professionally accredited by the Accreditation Board for Engineering and Technology, the Accrediting Council on Education in Journalism and Mass Communication, the American Assembly of Collegiate Schools of Business, the American Bar Association, the American Council on Pharmaceutical Education, the American Dietetic Association, the American Home Economics Association, the American Speech-Language-Hearing Association, the Association of American Law Schools, the Council on Social Work Education, the Foundation for Interior Design Education Research, the National Association of Schools of Art and Design, the National Association of Schools of Music, the National Council for Accreditation of Teacher Education.
**Religious orientation:** University of Mississippi is nonsectarian; no religious requirements.
**Library:** Collections totaling over 896,949 volumes, 9,131 periodical subscriptions, and 2,612,599 microform items.
**Special facilities/museums:** Art and archaeology museums, women's studies center, center for study of Southern culture, William Faulkner home, marine minerals research institute, center for computational hydroscience, engineering experiment station, physical acoustics center, natural products development center.
**Athletic facilities:** Gymnasium, swimming pool, tracks, basketball, racquetball, squash, and tennis courts, gymnastics and weight rooms, dance studio, athletic fields, golf course, baseball and football stadiums.

**STUDENT BODY. Undergraduate profile:** 61% are state residents; 25% are transfers. 1% Asian-American, 9% Black, 89% White, 1% Other. Average age of undergraduates is 21.
**Freshman profile:** Majority of accepted applicants took ACT. 70% of freshmen come from public schools.
**Undergraduate achievement:** 80% of fall 1992 freshmen returned for fall 1993 term. 33% of entering class graduated.
**Foreign students:** 198 students are from out of the country. Countries represented include Bangladesh, China, India, Japan, Malaysia, and the United Kingdom; 59 in all.

**PROGRAMS OF STUDY. Degrees:** B.A., B.A.Ed., B.Acct., B.Bus.Admin., B.Eng., B.F.A., B.Mus., B.Pub.Admin., B.S., B.S.Chem.Eng., B.S.Civil Eng., B.S.Comp.Sci., B.S.Elec.Eng., B.S.Geol., B.S.Geol.Eng., B.S.Home Econ., B.S.Journ., B.S.Mech.Eng., B.S.Pharm., B.Soc.Work.
**Majors:** Accountancy, Anthropology, Art, Art History, Banking/Finance, Biological Sciences, Biomedical Science, Chemical Engineering, Chemistry, Civil Engineering, Classical Civilization, Communicative Disorders, Computer Science, Court Reporting, Economics, Electrical Engineering, Elementary Education, Engineering, English, Exercise Science, Forensic Science, French, General Business, Geological Engineering, Geology, German, History, Home Economics, Insurance/Risk Management/Financial Services, Interior Design, Journalism, Journalism/Advertising, Legal Systems Administration, Leisure Management, Liberal Arts, Linguistics, Management, Management Information Systems, Managerial Finance, Marketing, Mathematics, Mechanical Engineering, Medical Technology, Music, Pharmacy, Philosophy, Physics, Political Science, Psychology, Public Administration, Radio/Television, Real Estate, Social Work, Sociology, Southern Studies, Spanish, Special Education, Telecommunications, Theatre.
**Distribution of degrees:** The majors with the highest enrollment are business management/accountancy and education; classical civilization and anthropology have the lowest.
**Requirements:** General education requirement.
**Academic regulations:** Freshmen must maintain minimum 1.5 GPA; sophomores, juniors, seniors, 2.0 GPA.

**Special:** Minors offered in majors in College of Liberal Arts and in Afro-American studies, Air Force ROTC/aerospace studies, business, education, Latin American studies, military science, naval science, religion, and telecommunications. Double majors. Independent study. Pass/fail grading option. Internships. Graduate school at which undergraduates may take graduate-level courses. Preprofessional programs in law, medicine, veterinary science, pharmacy, dentistry, and optometry. Member of Mississippi/Alabama Sea Grant Consortium, Mississippi Research Consortium, Oak Ridge Associated Universities, and Southern Association for High Energy Physics. Teacher certification in early childhood, elementary, and special education. Certification in specific subject areas. Member of International Student Exchange Program (ISEP). Exchange programs abroad in England (Liverpool Inst, U of Reading), Japan (Kansai Gaidai U), and Russia (Moscow State U). Study abroad also in European and South American countries during summer. ROTC, NROTC, and AFROTC.
**Honors:** Honors program. Honor societies.
**Academic Assistance:** Remedial reading, writing, math, and study skills. Nonremedial tutoring.

**STUDENT LIFE. Housing:** All freshmen must live on campus unless living with family. Women's and men's dorms. Sorority and fraternity housing. School-owned/operated apartments. On-campus married-student housing. 44% of students live in college housing.
**Social atmosphere:** "Greeks by far are the most influential group on campus," reports the student newspaper. "Student rock 'n' roll bands are also fairly influential." Homecoming, Dixie Week, Red/Blue Weekend, Parade of Beauties, and Miss University Pageant are the most popular events of the year. Students meet at the Hoka Theatre, the Gin, Forrester's, Syd & Harry's, Kiamie's, Four Corners, the Grove, and Fraternity Row.
**Services and counseling/handicapped student services:** Placement services. Health service. Women's center. Counseling services for minority, military, veteran, and older students. Birth control, personal, and psychological counseling. Career and academic guidance services. Religious counseling. Physically disabled student services. Learning disabled services. Notetaking services. Tape recorders. Tutors. Reader services for the blind.
**Campus organizations:** Undergraduate student government. Student newspaper (Daily Mississippian, published five times/week). Literary magazine. Yearbook. Radio and TV stations. Orchestra, marching and concert bands, chorus, debating, University Players, Students for Environmental Awareness, Young Democrats, College Republicans, 250 organizations in all. 19 fraternities, 16 chapter houses; 14 sororities, 12 chapter houses. 35% of men join a fraternity. 40% of women join a sorority.
**Religious organizations:** Baptist Student Union, Black Ministry, Campus Crusade for Christ, Catholic Student Activities, Episcopal Association, Fellowship of Christian Athletes, Hillel Foundation, Latter-Day Saints Student Organization, Islamic group, Wesley Foundation, Westminster Fellowship, other religious groups.
**Minority/foreign student organizations:** Black Student Union. Chinese, Indian, Japanese, Korean, Malaysian, Pakistani, and Singaporean groups.

**ATHLETICS. Physical education requirements:** None.
**Intercollegiate competition:** 3% of students participate. Baseball (M), basketball (M,W), cheerleading (M,W), cross-country (M,W), football (M), golf (M,W), tennis (M,W), track (indoor) (M,W), track (outdoor) (M,W), track and field (indoor) (M,W), track and field (outdoor) (M,W), volleyball (W). Member of NCAA Division I-A, Southeastern Conference.
**Intramural and club sports:** Intramural badminton, basketball, bowling, darts, flag football, floor hockey, golf, horseshoes, pickleball, racquetball, softball, swimming, tennis, track/field, ultimate frisbee, volleyball, water polo. Men's club basketball, bowling, canoeing, diving, gymnastics, handball, horsemanship, kayaking, martial arts, racquetball, rugby, soccer, softball, swimming, water polo, water skiing, weight lifting. Women's club bowling, canoeing, diving, gymnastics, horsemanship, kayaking, martial arts, racquetball, softball, swimming, water skiing.

**ADMISSIONS. Academic basis for candidate selection** (in order of priority): Secondary school record, standardized test scores.
**Nonacademic basis for candidate selection:** Particular talent or ability and alumni/ae relationship are considered.
**Requirements:** Graduation from secondary school is required; GED is not accepted. 13.5 units and the following program of study are required: 4 units of English, 3 units of math, 3 units of science including 2 units of lab, 1.5 units of social studies, 1 unit of history, 1 unit of academic electives. Minimum composite ACT score of 18 (combined SAT score of 720) and minimum 2.0 GPA required. Audition required of music and theatre program applicants. Portfolio required of art program applicants. HEOP for applicants not normally admissible. Conditional admission possible for applicants not meeting standard requirements. Special admission program for adult students. SAT or ACT is required. Campus visit and interview recommended. No off-campus interviews.
**Procedure:** Take SAT or ACT by February of 12th year. Visit college for interview by May 1 of 12th year. Suggest filing application by April 1. Application deadline is August 1. Notification of admission on rolling basis. No set date by which applicants must accept offer. $50 room deposit, refundable until July 15. Freshmen accepted in terms other than fall.
**Special programs:** Admission may be deferred one year. Credit may be granted through CEEB Advanced Placement for scores of 3 or higher. Credit may be granted through CLEP general and subject exams and military experience. Placement may be granted through challenge exams. Early entrance/early admission program.
**Transfer students:** Transfer students accepted for terms other than fall. In fall 1993, 25% of all new students were transfers into all classes. Application deadline is August 1 for fall; December 1 for spring. Minimum 2.0 GPA required. Lowest course grade accepted is "D." Maximum number of transferable credits is 63 semester hours from a two-year school and 90 semester hours from a four-year school. At least 30 semester hours must be completed at the university to receive degree.
**Admissions contact:** Beckett Howorth, M.Ed., Director of Admissions and Records. 601 232-7226.

**FINANCIAL AID. Available aid:** Pell grants, SEOG, state scholarships and grants, school scholarships, private scholarships and grants, ROTC scholarships, academic merit scholarships, athletic scholarships, and aid for undergraduate foreign students. Perkins Loans (NDSL), PLUS, Stafford Loans (GSL), Health Professions Loans, state loans, school loans, private loans, and SLS. Tuition Plan Inc. and deferred payment plan.
**Financial aid statistics:** Average amounts of aid awarded freshmen: Scholarships and grants, $1,949; loans, $2,000.
**Supporting data/closing dates:** FAFSA/FAF: Priority filing date is April 1. School's own aid application: Priority filing date is April 1. Notification of awards begins in November.
**Financial aid contact:** Thomas G. Hood, M.P.A., Director of Student Financial Aid. 601 232-7175.

**STUDENT EMPLOYMENT.** College Work/Study Program. Institutional employment. 13% of full-time undergraduates work on campus during school year. Students may expect to earn an average of $1,734 during school year. Off-campus part-time employment opportunities rated "good."

**COMPUTER FACILITIES.** 4,000 IBM/IBM-compatible, Macintosh/Apple, and RISC-/UNIX-based microcomputers; 1,500 are networked. Students may access AT&T, Cray, Digital, IBM, SUN minicomputer/mainframe systems, BITNET, Internet. Residence halls may be equipped with stand-alone microcomputers, networked terminals. Client/LAN operating systems include Apple/Macintosh, DOS, UNIX/XENIX/AIX, X-windows, Artisoft, LocalTalk/AppleTalk, Novell. Computer languages and software packages include BASIC, BMDP, C, COBOL/VS, FORTRAN 77, ImSL, Lotus 1-2-3, MOPAC, Pascal/VS, Quattro Pro, SAS, Waterloo Pascal, Windows, WordPerfect; 150 in all. Computer facilities are available to all students.
**Fees:** None.
**Hours:** 24 hours in some locations.

**GRADUATE CAREER DATA.** Companies and businesses that hire graduates: Andersen Consulting, Ernst & Young, KPMG Peat Marwick, Price Waterhouse, Federal Express, National Bank of Commerce, Sharp Manufacturing.

**PROMINENT ALUMNI/AE.** William Dunlap, printer and artist; Thad Cochran and Trent Lott, U.S. senators; Jamie Whitten, U.S. congressman; Jim Autry, president, Meredith Publishing; Thomas McGraw, Pulitzer Prize-winning historian; Charles Beall, chairperson of the board, Texas Commerce Bank; Cynthia Geary, actress; John Grisham, novelist.

# University of Southern Mississippi

**Hattiesburg, MS 39406 — 601 266-4111**

**1993-94 Costs.** Tuition: $2,392 (state residents), $4,852 (out-of-state). Room: $1,300. Board: $1,120. Fees, books, misc. academic expenses (school's estimate): $624.
**Enrollment.** Undergraduates: 3,744 men, 4,675 women (full-time). Freshman class: 2,850 applicants, 2,044 accepted, 1,046 enrolled. Graduate enrollment: 778 men, 1,104 women.
**Test score averages/ranges.** Average ACT scores: 22 English, 20 math, 21 composite.
**Faculty.** 78% of faculty holds doctoral degree. Student/faculty ratio: 17 to 1.
**Selectivity rating.** Less competitive.

**PROFILE.** The University of Southern Mississippi, founded in 1910, is a public, comprehensive institution. Programs are offered through the Colleges of the Arts, Business Administration, Education and Psychology, Health and Human Sciences, Liberal Arts, and Science and Technology; the Honors College; and the Division of Lifelong Learning. Its 840-acre campus is located in Hattiesburg, 90 miles south of Jackson.

**Accreditation:** SACS. Professionally accredited by the Accreditation Board for Engineering and Technology, the Accrediting Council on Education in Journalism and Mass Communication, the American Assembly of Collegiate Schools of Business, the American Dietetic Association, the American Home Economics Association, the American Medical Association (CAHEA), the American Speech-Language-Hearing Association, the Foundation for Interior Design Education Research, the National Association of Schools of Art and Design, the National Association of Schools of Music, the National Council for Accreditation of Teacher Education, the National League for Nursing, the National Recreation and Park Association.
**Religious orientation:** University of Southern Mississippi is nonsectarian; no religious requirements.
**Library:** Collections totaling over 858,997 volumes, 4,529 periodical subscriptions, and 3,066,777 microform items.
**Special facilities/museums:** English language institute, human performance and recreation facility, language lab, research institute, institute of microbiology, polymer science facility.
**Athletic facilities:** Swimming pool, sports arena, football and softball fields, equestrian center, recreational and fitness centers.

**STUDENT BODY. Undergraduate profile:** 80% are state residents; 53% are transfers. 3% Asian-American, 16% Black, 1% Hispanic, 80% White. Average age of undergraduates is 21.
**Freshman profile:** 5% of freshmen who took ACT scored 30 or over on English, 2% scored 30 or over on math, 4% scored 30 or over on composite; 36% scored 24 or over on English, 19% scored 24 or over on math, 28% scored 24 or over on composite; 83% scored 18 or over on English, 71% scored 18 or over on math, 77% scored 18 or over on composite; 100% scored 12 or over on English, 100% scored 12 or over on math, 100% scored 12 or over on composite. Majority of accepted applicants took ACT.
**Undergraduate achievement:** 71% of fall 1992 freshmen returned for fall 1993 term. 20% of entering class graduated.
**Foreign students:** 335 students are from out of the country. Countries represented include China, India, Japan, Sweden, Taiwan, and the United Kingdom; 49 in all.

**PROGRAMS OF STUDY. Degrees:** B.A., B.F.A., B.Mus., B.Mus.Ed., B.S., B.S.Bus. Admin., B.S.Nurs., B.Soc.Work.
**Majors:** Accounting, Advertising, American Studies, Anthropology, Architectural Engineering Technology, Art, Banking/Finance, Biological Sciences, Business Administration, Business Education, Chemistry, Child/Family Studies, Coaching/Sports Administration, Communication, Community/Regional Planning, Computer Engineering Technology, Computer Science, Construction Engineering Technology, Dance, Economics, Education of the Deaf, Electronics Engineering Technology, Elementary Education, English, Fashion Merchandising/Apparel Studies, Foreign Languages, Geography, Geology,

Health Education, History, Home Economics, Hotel/Restaurant/Tourism Management, Human Performance, Industrial Engineering Technology, Interior Design, International Studies, Journalism, Library Science, Management, Management Information Sys- tems, Marketing, Mathematics, Mechanical Engineering Technology, Medical Technology, Music, Music Education, Nursing, Nutrition/Dietetics, Office Administration, Paralegal Studies, Philosophy, Physics, Political Science, Polymer Science, Psychology, Radio/Television/Film, Recreation, Social/Rehabilitation Services, Social Work, Special Education, Speech Communication, Speech/Language Pathology/Audiology, Technical/Occupational Education, Theatre.

**Distribution of degrees:** The majors with the highest enrollment are elementary education, business administration, and psychology; philosophy, library science, and foreign language have the lowest.

**Requirements:** General education requirement.

**Academic regulations:** Freshmen must maintain minimum 1.5 GPA; sophomores, 1.75 GPA; juniors, 2.0 GPA; seniors, 2.0 GPA.

**Special:** Minors offered in many majors. Double majors. Independent study. Pass/fail grading option. Internships. Cooperative education programs. Graduate school at which undergraduates may take graduate-level courses. Preprofessional programs in law, medicine, veterinary science, pharmacy, dentistry, and engineering. Combined programs in premedicine and predentistry; B.S. granted after fourth year at professional school. Member of Mississippi Research Consortium. Teacher certification in early childhood, elementary, secondary, and special education. Certification in specific subject areas. Study abroad in Austria, Australia, Canada, Caribbean countries, France, Germany, Israel, Italy, Japan, Mexico, Switzerland, and the United Kingdom. ROTC and AFROTC.

**Honors:** Honors program. Honor societies.

**Academic Assistance:** Remedial reading, writing, and math. Nonremedial tutoring.

**STUDENT LIFE. Housing:** Freshmen under age 21 must live on campus. Women's and men's dorms. Sorority and fraternity housing. School-owned/operated apartments. On-campus married-student housing. 35% of students live in college housing.

**Social Atmosphere:** "Social energies are spent mostly on campus," states the editor of the student newspaper. Popular events include weekly movies and concerts, Homecoming, Greek Week, intramurals, and basketball games. The various Greek organizations are influential on campus. Students gather at The Hub, The End Zone, on Frat Row, and on the commons.

**Services and counseling/handicapped student services:** Placement services. Health service. Women's center. Day care. Personal and psychological counseling. Career and academic guidance services. Religious counseling. Physically disabled student services. Notetaking services. Tape recorders. Tutors. Reader services for the blind.

**Campus organizations:** Undergraduate student government. Student newspaper (Student Printz, published twice/week). Yearbook. Radio station. Concert choir, several singing groups, Covenant and Carillon, symphony orchestra, several bands, departmental groups, service organizations, support groups, games and athletic clubs, special-interest and other student groups. 13 fraternities, 11 chapter houses; 12 sororities, no chapter houses. 16% of men join a fraternity. 15% of women join a sorority.

**Religious organizations:** Baptist Student Union, Campus Crusade for Christ, Catholic Student Association, Grace Temple Campus Ministries, Fellowship of Christian Athletes, Wesley Foundation; Anglican, Latter Day Saints, Lutheran, Muslim, and other religious groups.

**Minority/foreign student organizations:** Afro-American Student Organization, Minority Engineers Society. Chinese student group.

**ATHLETICS. Physical education requirements:** One semester of physical education required.

**Intercollegiate competition:** 3% of students participate. Baseball (M), basketball (M,W), cross-country (M,W), football (M), golf (M,W), tennis (M,W), track and field (indoor) (M,W), track and field (outdoor) (M,W), volleyball (W). Member of Metropolitan Collegiate Athletic Conference, NCAA Division I-A.

**Intramural and club sports:** 46% of students participate. Intramural badminton, basketball, bowling, cross-country, floor hockey, football, golf, putt-putt golf, racquetball, soccer, softball, swimming, tennis, track, ultimate frisbee, volleyball, weight lifting, Wiffle ball. Men's club fencing, martial arts, rugby, scuba, soccer, ultimate frisbee, volleyball. Women's club fencing, martial arts, scuba, soccer, ultimate frisbee.

**ADMISSIONS.**

**Requirements:** Graduation from secondary school is required; GED is accepted. 16 units and the following program of study are required: 4 units of English, 3 units of math, 3 units of science including 1 unit of lab, 2.5 units of social studies, 2.5 units of history, 1 unit of academic electives. Minimum composite ACT score of 18 required of in-state residents; minimum combined SAT score of 690 may be submitted by out-of-state applicants. High-risk program for applicants not normally admissible. ACT is required; SAT may be substituted. No off-campus interviews.

**Procedure:** Notification of admission on rolling basis. Freshmen accepted in terms other than fall.

**Special programs:** Admission may be deferred one year. Credit and/or placement may be granted through CEEB Advanced Placement exams for scores of 3 or higher. Credit and/or placement may be granted through CLEP general and subject exams. Credit may be granted through military and life experience. Credit and placement may be granted through DANTES and challenge exams. Early entrance/early admission program. Concurrent enrollment program.

**Transfer students:** Transfer students accepted for terms other than fall. In fall 1993, 53% of all new students were transfers into all classes. 2,294 transfer applications were received, 1,834 were accepted. Minimum 2.0 GPA recommended. Lowest course grade accepted is "D." At least 32 semester hours must be completed at the university to receive degree.

**Admissions contact:** Danny Montgomery, M.E.D., Director of Admissions. 601 266-4062.

**FINANCIAL AID. Available aid:** Pell grants, SEOG, state scholarships and grants, private scholarships, ROTC scholarships, academic merit scholarships, and athletic scholarships. Perkins Loans (NDSL), PLUS, Stafford Loans (GSL), private loans, and SLS. Tuition Plan Inc., AMS, and deferred payment plan.

**Financial aid statistics:** In 1993-94, 88% of all undergraduate applicants received aid; 87% of freshman applicants.

**Supporting data/closing dates:** FAFSA/FAF/FFS: Priority filing date is March 15; accepted on rolling basis. School's own aid application: Priority filing date is March 15; accepted on rolling basis. Notification of awards begins June 1.

**Financial aid contact:** Vernetta Fairley, M.S., Director of Financial Aid. 601 266-4774.

**STUDENT EMPLOYMENT.** College Work/Study Program. Institutional employment. 10% of full-time undergraduates work on campus during school year. Students may expect to earn an average of $3,500 during school year. Off-campus part-time employment opportunities rated "good."

**COMPUTER FACILITIES.** 110 IBM/IBM-compatible and Macintosh/Apple microcomputers. Students may access Bull minicomputer/mainframe systems, BITNET, Internet. Residence halls may be equipped with networked terminals. Computer languages and software packages include BASIC, COBOL, FORTRAN, Pascal, SPSS-X. Computer facilities are available to all students.

**Fees:** None.

**Hours:** 8 AM-11 PM.

**PROMINENT ALUMNI/AE.** Robert Stewart, astronaut; Jimmy Buffet, author, singer, and entertainer; Charles Scarborough, WNBC news anchor; Gloria Norris, author/editor.

# Missouri

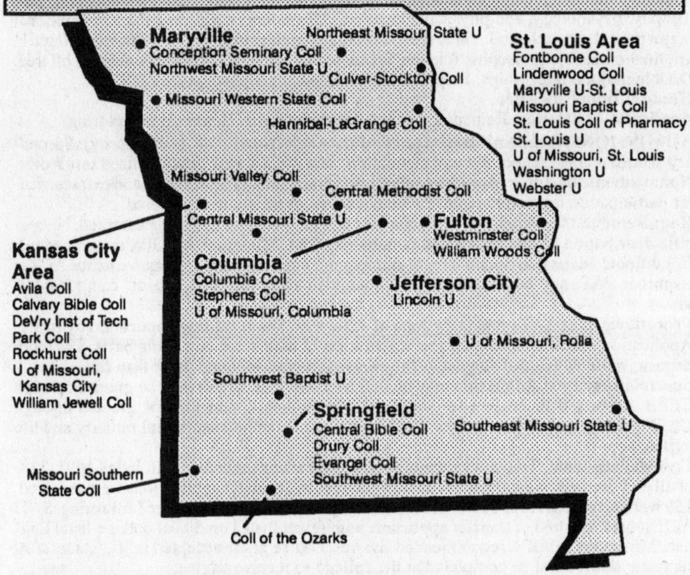


## Avila College

**Kansas City, MO 64145** 816 942-8400

**1994-95 Costs.** Tuition: $8,950. Room & board: $3,800. Fees, books, misc. academic expenses (school's estimate): $680.
**Enrollment.** Undergraduates: 179 men, 472 women (full-time). Freshman class: 368 applicants, 292 accepted, 88 enrolled. Graduate enrollment: 104 men, 144 women.
**Test score averages/ranges.** Average SAT scores: 448 verbal, 452 math. Range of SAT scores of middle 50%: 420-450 verbal, 420-480 math. Average ACT scores: 21 English, 21 math, 21 composite. Range of ACT scores of middle 50%: 18-24 English, 18-23 math.
**Faculty.** 54 full-time; 96 part-time. 69% of faculty holds highest degree in specific field. Student/faculty ratio: 14 to 1.
**Selectivity rating.** Competitive.

**PROFILE.** Avila is a church-affiliated college. It was founded in 1916, moved to its present location in 1963, and adopted coeducation in 1969. Its 48-acre campus is located 10 miles from downtown Kansas City.

**Accreditation:** NCACS. Professionally accredited by the American Bar Association, the American Medical Association (CAHEA), the Council on Social Work Education, the National League for Nursing.
**Religious orientation:** Avila College is affiliated with the Roman Catholic Church (Sisters of St. Joseph of Carondelet); nine hours of philosophy and theology required.
**Library:** Collections totaling over 80,000 volumes, 444 periodical subscriptions, and 373,413 microform items.
**Special facilities/museums:** Art gallery, Montessori preschool, reptile collection, theatre, interactive video lab, video production lab.
**Athletic facilities:** Field house, weight training area, baseball, softball, and soccer fields, outdoor basketball and tennis courts.
**STUDENT BODY. Undergraduate profile:** 68% are state residents; 62% are transfers. 1% Asian-American, 9% Black, 2% Hispanic, 1% Native American, 83% White, 4% Other. Average age of undergraduates is 24.
**Freshman profile:** 20% of accepted applicants took SAT; 92% took ACT. 75% of freshmen come from public schools.
**Undergraduate achievement:** 62% of fall 1992 freshmen returned for fall 1993 term. 34% of entering class graduated. 18% of students who completed a degree program immediately went on to graduate study.
**Foreign students:** 44 students are from out of the country. Countries represented include China, India, Japan, Taiwan, and Thailand; 13 in all.
**PROGRAMS OF STUDY. Degrees:** B.A., B.F.A., B.S., B.S.Bus.Admin., B.S.Med. Tech., B.S.Nurs., B.S.Radiol.Tech., B.Soc.Work.
**Majors:** Accounting, Art, Biology, Chemistry, Communication, Computer Science/ Mathematics, Elementary Education, English, Finance, General Management, General Studies, History, Human Resources, Information Science, International Business Management, Legal Assistant, Marketing, Mathematics, Medical Technology, Music, Natural Science, Nursing, Political Science, Pre-Medicine, Psychology, Radiologic Technology, Respiratory Therapy, Social Work, Sociology, Special Education, Theater, Theology.
**Distribution of degrees:** The majors with the highest enrollment are general management, information science, and elementary education; chemistry, international business, and general studies have the lowest.
**Requirements:** General education requirement.
**Academic regulations:** Minimum 2.0 GPA must be maintained.
**Special:** Minors offered in most majors and in anthropology, economics, secondary education, gerontology, philosophy, and women's studies. Study tours may be arranged. Associate's degrees offered. Double majors. Dual degrees. Independent study. Pass/fail grading option. Internships. Cooperative education programs. Preprofessional programs in law, medicine, veterinary science, pharmacy, dentistry, and optometry. Member of Sisters of St. Joseph College Consortium and Kansas City Regional Council for Higher Education. Washington Semester. Teacher certification in elementary, secondary, and special education. Certification in specific subject areas. ROTC at U of Missouri at Kansas City.
**Honors:** Honor societies.
**Academic Assistance:** Remedial reading, writing, math, and study skills. Nonremedial tutoring.
**ADMISSIONS. Academic basis for candidate selection** (in order of priority): Secondary school record, standardized test scores, school's recommendation, class rank, essay.
**Requirements:** Graduation from secondary school is required; GED is accepted. 16 units and the following program of study are recommended: 4 units of English, 3 units of math, 2 units of science, 2 units of foreign language, 2 units of social studies, 1 unit of electives. Minimum combined ACT score of 20 and minimum 2.5 GPA recommended. Audition and/or interview required of theatre program applicants. Portfolio required of art program applicants. Audition required of music program applicants. Conditional admission possible for applicants not meeting standard requirements. ACT is required; SAT may be substituted. Campus visit and interview recommended. Off-campus interviews available with an admissions representative.
**Procedure:** Take SAT or ACT by June of 12th year. Visit college for interview by March 30 of 12th year. Suggest filing application by May 1; no deadline. Notification of admission on rolling basis. $100 tuition deposit, refundable until May 1. $50 room deposit, refundable until May 1. Freshmen accepted in terms other than fall.
**Special programs:** Credit may be granted through CEEB Advanced Placement for scores of 3 or higher. Credit may be granted through CLEP general and subject exams, challenge exams, and military and life experience. Concurrent enrollment program.
**Transfer students:** Transfer students accepted for terms other than fall. In fall 1993, 62% of all new students were transfers into all classes. 388 transfer applications were received, 366 were accepted. Application deadline is rolling for fall; rolling for spring. Minimum 2.0 GPA recommended. Lowest course grade accepted is "D." Maximum number of transferable credits is 64 semester hours from a two-year school and 98 semester hours from a four-year school. At least 30 semester hours must be completed at the college to receive degree.
**Admissions contact:** James E. Millard, M.B.A., Director of Admissions. 816 942-8400, extension 203.
**FINANCIAL AID. Available aid:** Pell grants, SEOG, state scholarships and grants, school scholarships and grants, private scholarships and grants, academic merit scholarships, and athletic scholarships. Performing arts and family grants. Grants for Catholic secondary school graduates. Perkins Loans (NDSL), PLUS, Stafford Loans (GSL), and SLS. Deferred payment plan, family tuition reduction, and guaranteed tuition.
**Financial aid statistics:** 30% of aid is not need-based. In 1993-94, 98% of all undergraduate applicants received aid; 100% of freshman applicants. Average amounts of aid awarded freshmen: Scholarships and grants, $3,950; loans, $3,500.
**Supporting data/closing dates:** FAFSA: Priority filing date is July 1; accepted on rolling basis. School's own aid application: Accepted on rolling basis. Income tax forms: Accepted on rolling basis. Institutional Verification: Priority filing date is July 1; accepted on rolling basis. Notification of awards on rolling basis.
**Financial aid contact:** Cynthia A. Butler, Director of Financial Aid. 816 942-8400, extension 215.

## Calvary Bible College

**Kansas City, MO 64147-1341** 816 322-0110

**1994-95 Costs.** Tuition: $3,460. Room: $1,130. Board: $1,600. Fees, books, misc. academic expenses (school's estimate): $640.
**Enrollment.** Undergraduates: 108 men, 97 women (full-time). Freshman class: 98 applicants, 96 accepted, 60 enrolled. Graduate enrollment: 12.
**Test score averages/ranges.** N/A.
**Faculty.** 11 full-time; 15 part-time. 22% of faculty holds doctoral degree. Student/faculty ratio: 12 to 1.
**Selectivity rating.** Noncompetitive.

**PROFILE.** Calvary Bible, founded in 1932, is a college with religious orientation. Its 55-acre campus is located 20 miles south of downtown Kansas City.

**Accreditation:** AABC.
**Religious orientation:** Calvary Bible College is a nondenominational Christian school; eight semesters of religion/theology required.
**Library:** Collections totaling over 57,000 volumes, 307 periodical subscriptions, and 2,657 microform items.
**Athletic facilities:** Gymnasium, basketball, racquetball, and tennis courts, soccer and softball fields, track.
**STUDENT BODY. Undergraduate profile:** 42% are state residents; 23% are transfers. 1% Asian-American, 3% Black, 1% Hispanic, 2% Native American, 93% White. Average age of undergraduates is 22.
**Freshman profile:** 50% of freshmen who took SAT scored 500 or over on verbal; 100% scored 400 or over on verbal, 100% scored 400 or over on math. 55% of freshmen come from public schools.
**Undergraduate achievement:** 59% of fall 1992 freshmen returned for fall 1993 term. 28% of entering class graduated.
**Foreign students:** Six students are from out of the country. Countries represented include Bermuda, Brazil, India, Korea, Liberia, and Malaysia.
**PROGRAMS OF STUDY. Degrees:** B.A., B.Mus., B.S.
**Majors:** Biblical Counseling, Biblical Studies, Christian Broadcasting, Christian Camping, Christian Education, Christian Elementary Education, Christian Ministry, Christian Secondary Education, Church Music, Missions, Music Education, Music Performance, Pastoral Studies, Pregraduate Studies, Youth Ministry.

**Distribution of degrees:** The majors with the highest enrollment are pastoral studies, elementary education, and secondary education; Christian camping has the lowest.
**Requirements:** General education requirement.
**Special:** Double majors. Independent study. Pass/fail grading option. Internships. Graduate school at which undergraduates may take graduate-level courses. Teacher certification in elementary and secondary education.
**ADMISSIONS. Academic basis for candidate selection** (in order of priority): Secondary school record, standardized test scores, school's recommendation, class rank.
**Nonacademic basis for candidate selection:** Character and personality are emphasized.
**Requirements:** Graduation from secondary school is required; GED is accepted. No specific distribution of secondary school units required. Open admissions policy, but rank in top half of secondary school class and minimum "C" average recommended. Pastor's reference and personal statement of faith required. Audition required of music program applicants. Provisional admission possible for applicants not meeting standard requirements. ACT is required; SAT may be substituted. Campus visit and interview recommended. No off-campus interviews.
**Procedure:** Take ACT or SAT by end of 12th year. Suggest filing application by August 1. Notification of admission on rolling basis. $50 refundable room deposit. Freshmen accepted in terms other than fall.
**Special programs:** Admission may be deferred one year. Credit may be granted through CEEB Advanced Placement for scores of 3 or higher. Credit may be granted through CLEP general and subject exams and military experience. Early entrance/early admission program. Concurrent enrollment program.
**Transfer students:** Transfer students accepted for terms other than fall. In fall 1993, 23% of all new students were transfers into all classes. 84 transfer applications were received, 84 were accepted. Application deadline is rolling for fall; rolling for spring. Minimum 2.0 GPA required. Lowest course grade accepted is "C." At least 32 semester hours must be completed at the college to receive degree.
**Admissions contact:** Craig Wells, Director of Admissions. 800 326-3960.
**FINANCIAL AID. Available aid:** Pell grants, private scholarships, and aid for undergraduate foreign students. PLUS and Stafford Loans (GSL). AMS and family tuition reduction.
**Supporting data/closing dates:** FAFSA/FAF/FFS: Priority filing date is August 1. School's own aid application: Priority filing date is August 1. Notification of awards on rolling basis.
**Financial aid contact:** Tina Bridgewater, Director of Financial Aid. 816 322-0110, extension 314.

# Central Bible College

**Springfield, MO 65803 417 833-2551**

**1994-95 Costs.** Tuition: $3,720. Room & board: $2,900. Fees, books, misc. academic expenses (school's estimate): $890.
**Enrollment.** Undergraduates: 523 men, 337 women (full-time). Freshman class: 267 applicants, 267 accepted, 212 enrolled.
**Test score averages/ranges.** Average SAT scores: 409 verbal, 425 math. Range of SAT scores of middle 50%: 350-450 verbal, 340-500 math. Average ACT scores: 20 English, 18 math, 20 composite. Range of ACT scores of middle 50%: 17-23 English, 16-20 math.
**Faculty.** 35 full-time; 32 part-time. 45% of faculty holds doctoral degree. Student/faculty ratio: 25 to 1.
**Selectivity rating.** Less competitive.

**PROFILE.** Central Bible, founded in 1922, is a church-affiliated college. Its 102-acre campus is located in Springfield, near the summit of the Ozark Mountain plateau.

**Accreditation:** AABC.
**Religious orientation:** Central Bible College is affiliated with the Assemblies of God; 30 credit hours of religion/theology required.
**Library:** Collections totaling over 102,111 volumes, 493 periodical subscriptions, and 2,173 microform items.
**Athletic facilities:** Gymnasium, racquetball and tennis courts, athletic field, activities building.
**STUDENT BODY. Undergraduate profile:** 18% are state residents; 32% are transfers. 2% Asian-American, 1% Black, 2% Hispanic, 1% Native American, 94% White. Average age of undergraduates is 23.
**Freshman profile:** 3% of freshmen who took SAT scored 600 or over on math; 18% scored 500 or over on verbal, 21% scored 500 or over on math; 51% scored 400 or over on verbal, 58% scored 400 or over on math; 97% scored 300 or over on verbal, 73% scored 300 or over on math. 2% of freshmen who took ACT scored 30 or over on English, 2% scored 30 or over on math, 2% scored 30 or over on composite; 20% scored 24 or over on English, 9% scored 24 or over on math, 17% scored 24 or over on composite; 59% scored 18 or over on English, 41% scored 18 or over on math, 61% scored 18 or over on composite; 84% scored 12 or over on English, 85% scored 12 or over on math, 86% scored 12 or over on composite; 87% scored 6 or over on English, 87% scored 6 or over on math, 87% scored 6 or over on composite. 15% of accepted applicants took SAT; 80% took ACT. 86% of freshmen come from public schools.
**Undergraduate achievement:** 65% of fall 1992 freshmen returned for fall 1993 term. 21% of entering class graduated.
**Foreign students:** 11 students are from out of the country. Countries represented include Canada and Korea; six in all.
**PROGRAMS OF STUDY. Degrees:** B.A.
**Majors:** Administration of Christian Education, Bible, Biblical Languages, Children's Ministries, Christian Day School Teaching, Deaf Ministries, Missions, Music, Pastoral Ministries, Pre-Seminary, Preaching/Evangelism, Youth Ministries.
**Distribution of degrees:** The majors with the highest enrollment are biblical studies, missions, and pastoral ministry; biblical languages and pre-seminary have the lowest.
**Requirements:** General education requirement.
**Academic regulations:** Freshmen must maintain minimum 1.7 GPA; sophomores, 1.9 GPA; juniors, 2.0 GPA; seniors, 2.0 GPA.
**Special:** Minors offered in several majors and in English, history, pastoral counseling, philosophy, psychology, and physical education. All students major in Bible; an additional major may also be selected. Three-year diploma programs in all majors. Courses offered in art, mathematics, philosophy, science, Spanish, and speech. Associate's degrees offered. Double majors. Internships. Preprofessional programs in theology.
**Honors:** Honor societies.
**Academic Assistance:** Remedial writing and study skills. Nonremedial tutoring.
**ADMISSIONS. Academic basis for candidate selection** (in order of priority): Secondary school record, school's recommendation, essay, class rank, standardized test scores.
**Nonacademic basis for candidate selection:** Character and personality and extracurricular participation are emphasized. Particular talent or ability is considered.
**Requirements:** Graduation from secondary school is required; GED is accepted. No specific distribution of secondary school units required. Minimum 2.0 GPA recommended. Conditional admission possible for applicants not meeting standard requirements. ACT is required; SAT may be substituted. Campus visit recommended. No off-campus interviews.
**Procedure:** Take SAT or ACT by June of 12th year. Suggest filing application by July 1. Application deadline is August 15. Notification of admission on rolling basis. $50 room deposit, refundable until August 1. Freshmen accepted in terms other than fall.
**Special programs:** Admission may be deferred one year. Credit may be granted through CEEB Advanced Placement for scores of 3 or higher. Credit may be granted through CLEP general and subject exams, DANTES and challenge exams, and military and life experience.
**Transfer students:** Transfer students accepted for terms other than fall. In fall 1993, 32% of all new students were transfers into all classes. 162 transfer applications were received, 159 were accepted. Application deadline is August 1 for fall; December 1 for spring. SAT/ACT scores required of transfer applicants with fewer than 3 credits of college-level English. Minimum 2.0 GPA recommended. Lowest course grade accepted is "C." At least 30 semester hours must be completed at the college to receive degree.
**Admissions contact:** Eunice A. Bruegman, Director of Admissions and Records. 417 833-2551, extension 1184.
**FINANCIAL AID. Available aid:** Pell grants, SEOG, school scholarships, private scholarships, and academic merit scholarships. Perkins Loans (NDSL), PLUS, Stafford Loans (GSL), school loans, and SLS. AMS and family tuition reduction.
**Financial aid statistics:** 11% of aid is not need-based. In 1993-94, 67% of all undergraduate applicants received aid; 99% of freshman applicants. Average amounts of aid awarded freshmen: Scholarships and grants, $1,727; loans, $2,582.
**Supporting data/closing dates:** FAFSA: Priority filing date is May 1. Notification of awards begins May 1.
**Financial aid contact:** Donna See, Director of Financial Aid. 417 833-2551, extension 1205.

# Central Methodist College

**Fayette, MO 65248 816 248-3391**

**1994-95 Costs.** Tuition: $8,560. Room: $1,550. Board: $1,820. Fees, books, misc. academic expenses (school's estimate): $770.
**Enrollment.** Undergraduates: 440 men, 480 women (full-time). Freshman class: 677 applicants, 549 accepted, 240 enrolled.
**Test score averages/ranges.** Average ACT scores: 21 composite.
**Faculty.** 58 full-time; 12 part-time. 42% of faculty holds doctoral degree. Student/faculty ratio: 14 to 1.
**Selectivity rating.** Less competitive.

**PROFILE.** Central Methodist, founded in 1855, is a church-affiliated college of liberal arts and vocational education. Its 52-acre campus, designated a National Historic District, is located in the small town of Fayette, midway between St. Louis and Kansas City.

**Accreditation:** NCACS. Professionally accredited by the National Association of Schools of Music, the National Council for Accreditation of Teacher Education.
**Religious orientation:** Central Methodist College is affiliated with the Methodist Church; two semesters of religion required. Regular church attendance encouraged.
**Library:** Collections totaling over 167,398 volumes, 350 periodical subscriptions, and 81,731 microform items.
**Special facilities/museums:** Language lab, theatre, natural history museum, observatory, science lab.
**Athletic facilities:** Swimming pool, basketball, racquetball, and tennis courts, baseball, football, soccer, and softball fields, stadium, field house, recreation center.
**STUDENT BODY. Undergraduate profile:** 75% are state residents; 14% are transfers. 1% Asian-American, 7% Black, 1% Hispanic, 1% Native American, 87% White, 3% Other. Average age of undergraduates is 20.
**Freshman profile:** 5% of accepted applicants took SAT; 95% took ACT. 95% of freshmen come from public schools.
**Undergraduate achievement:** 68% of fall 1992 freshmen returned for fall 1993 term. 43% of entering class graduated. 16% of students who completed a degree program immediately went on to graduate study.
**Foreign students:** 27 students are from out of the country. Countries represented include Japan, Korea, Mexico, and Zimbabwe.
**PROGRAMS OF STUDY. Degrees:** B.A., B.Mus., B.Mus.Ed., B.S., B.S.Ed., B.S.Nurs.
**Majors:** Accounting, Biology, Business Administration/Management, Business Education, Chemistry, Communication/Theatre Arts, Computer/Information Sciences, Economics, Elementary Education, English, History, History/Political Science, Instrumental Music, Mathematics, Modern Languages/Literature, Music Education, Music History/Theory, Nursing, Philosophy, Physical Education, Physics, Political Science/Government, Psychology, Religion, Science Education, Social Science Education, Theatre Arts, Vocal Music.

**Distribution of degrees:** The majors with the highest enrollment are business administration, elementary education, and biology; music performance, English, and philosophy have the lowest.
**Requirements:** General education requirement.
**Academic regulations:** Freshmen must maintain minimum 1.8 GPA; sophomores, 1.8 GPA; juniors, 1.9 GPA; seniors, 2.0 GPA.
**Special:** Minors offered in over 30 fields. College-paid interim program grants two hours of academic credit. Associate's degrees offered. Self-designed majors. Double majors. Dual degrees. Accelerated study. Pass/fail grading option. Internships. Preprofessional programs in law, medicine, veterinary science, pharmacy, dentistry, and theology. 2-2 engineering program with U of Missouri at Rolla. Host college for business, education, and nursing programs. 3-1 medical technology programs with DePaul Sch of Medical Tech and Jewish Hospital Sch of Medical Tech. 3-3 law program with U of Missouri at Columbia. 3-2 engineering programs with Columbia U, Stanford U, and U of Missouri at Rolla. Member of Council of Independent Colleges; exchange possible. Teacher certification in early childhood, elementary, and secondary education. Study abroad in France, Germany, and Spain. ROTC.
**Honors:** Honors program. Honor societies.
**Academic Assistance:** Remedial reading, writing, math, and study skills. Nonremedial tutoring.

**ADMISSIONS. Academic basis for candidate selection** (in order of priority): Secondary school record, class rank, standardized test scores, school's recommendation, essay.
**Nonacademic basis for candidate selection:** Character and personality are important. Extracurricular participation, particular talent or ability, geographical distribution, and alumni/ae relationship are considered.
**Requirements:** Graduation from secondary school is required; GED is accepted. 16 units and the following program of study are recommended: 4 units of English, 3 units of math, 2 units of science, 4 units of social studies. Minimum 2.0 GPA required; minimum composite ACT score of 18 and rank in top two-thirds of secondary school class recommended. Departmental interviews required of nursing program applicants. Audition required of music program applicants. ACT and ACH recommended. Campus visit and interview recommended. Off-campus interviews available with an admissions representative.
**Procedure:** Take SAT or ACT by December of 12th year. Visit college for interview by December of 12th year. Suggest filing application by January 31. Application deadline is August 15. Notification of admission on rolling basis. Reply is required within 30 days of notification. $100 tuition deposit, refundable until May 1. $75 refundable room deposit. Freshmen accepted in terms other than fall.
**Special programs:** Admission may be deferred one year. Credit and/or placement may be granted through CEEB Advanced Placement exams for scores of 3 or higher. Credit may be granted through CLEP subject exams. Credit and placement may be granted through challenge exams. Early decision program. Deadline for applying for early decision is December 31. Early entrance/early admission program. Concurrent enrollment program.
**Transfer students:** Transfer students accepted for terms other than fall. In fall 1993, 14% of all new students were transfers into all classes. 140 transfer applications were received, 111 were accepted. Application deadline is rolling for fall; rolling for spring. Minimum 2.0 GPA required. Lowest course grade accepted is "C." Maximum number of transferable credits is 64 semester hours. At least 62 semester hours must be completed at the college to receive degree.
**Admissions contact:** Anthony J. Boes, M.Ed., Vice President for Student Affairs. 816 248-3391, extension 251.

**FINANCIAL AID. Available aid:** Pell grants, SEOG, state scholarships and grants, school scholarships and grants, private scholarships and grants, ROTC scholarships, academic merit scholarships, athletic scholarships, and aid for undergraduate foreign students. Methodist scholarships. Perkins Loans (NDSL), PLUS, Stafford Loans (GSL), NSL, school loans, private loans, and SLS. AMS. Payment plan.
**Financial aid statistics:** 10% of aid is not need-based. In 1993-94, 96% of all undergraduate applicants received aid; 90% of freshman applicants. Average amounts of aid awarded freshmen: Scholarships and grants, $4,875; loans, $2,400.
**Supporting data/closing dates:** FAFSA: Priority filing date is April 1. Notification of awards on rolling basis.
**Financial aid contact:** Roberta Knipp, Director of Financial Aid. 816 248-3391, extension 244.

## Central Missouri State University

**Warrensburg, MO 64093** **816 543-4111**

**1993-94 Costs.** Tuition: $2,160 (state residents), $4,320 (out-of-state). Room: $1,878. Board: $1,100. Fees, books, misc. academic expenses (school's estimate): $2,550.
**Enrollment.** Undergraduates: 3,925 men, 4,169 women (full-time). Freshman class: 4,681 applicants, 4,101 accepted, 1,613 enrolled. Graduate enrollment: 649 men, 943 women.
**Test score averages/ranges.** Average ACT scores: 21 composite. Range of ACT scores of middle 50%: 17-22 composite.
**Faculty.** 454 full-time; 37 part-time. 70% of faculty holds doctoral degree. Student/faculty ratio: 18 to 1.
**Selectivity rating.** Less competitive.

**PROFILE.** Central Missouri State, founded in 1871, is a public, multipurpose university. Programs are offered through the Colleges of Applied Sciences and Technology, Arts and Sciences, Business and Economics, and Education and Human Services. Its 1,038-acre campus is located in Warrensburg, 50 miles from Kansas City.

**Accreditation:** NCACS. Professionally accredited by the American Council for Construction Education, the American Home Economics Association, the American Speech-Language-Hearing Association, the Council on Social Work Education, the National Association of Schools of Art and Design, the National Association of Schools of Music, the National Council for Accreditation of Teacher Education, the National League for Nursing.
**Religious orientation:** Central Missouri State University is nonsectarian; no religious requirements.
**Library:** Collections totaling over 1,938,735 volumes, 2,870 periodical subscriptions, and 1,115,161 microform items.
**Special facilities/museums:** Natural history museum, language lab, speech and hearing lab, 200-acre farm, traffic management institute, driving/safety range, center for technology and business research, national police institute, international safety and health hall of fame, airport for aviation program.
**Athletic facilities:** Gymnasiums, basketball, racquetball, tennis, and volleyball courts, weight and wrestling rooms, tracks, swimming pools, aerobics studio, baseball, football, and softball fields, golf course.

**STUDENT BODY. Undergraduate profile:** 93% are state residents; 38% are transfers. .7% Asian-American, 7.6% Black, 1% Hispanic, .4% Native American, 88% White, 2.3% Other. Average age of undergraduates is 23.
**Freshman profile:** 2% of freshmen who took ACT scored 30 or over on composite; 19% scored 24 or over on composite; 71% scored 18 or over on composite; 92% scored 12 or over on composite. 92% of accepted applicants took ACT. 94% of freshmen come from public schools.
**Undergraduate achievement:** 40% of fall 1992 freshmen returned for fall 1993 term. 40% of entering class graduated. 6% of students who completed a degree program immediately went on to graduate study.
**Foreign students:** 232 students are from out of the country. Countries represented include China, India, Kenya, Malaysia, Pakistan, and Taiwan; 59 in all.

**PROGRAMS OF STUDY. Degrees:** B.A., B.F.A., B.Mus., B.Mus.Ed., B.S., B.S.Bus.Admin., B.S.Ed.
**Majors:** Accounting, Actuarial Sciences/Mathematics, Agricultural Business, Agricultural Economics, Agricultural Education, Agricultural Technology, Art Education, Aviation Technology, Biology, Broadcasting/Film, Business Education, Chemistry, Commercial Art, Computer Information Systems, Computer Science/Mathematics, Conservation Enforcement, Construction Engineering Technology, Cooperative Engineering, Corrections, Criminal Justice Administration, Dietetics, Distributive Education, Drafting Technology, Early Childhood Education, Earth Science, Economics, Education, Electricity/Electronics Technology, Elementary Education, English, Fashion/Textiles/Clothing in Business, Finance, Fire Science, French, General Recreation, Geography, Geology, German, Graphic Arts Technology/Management, History, Home Economics, Home Economics Education, Hotel/Motel/Restaurant Administration, Human Resource Management, Industrial Arts Education, Industrial Arts/Technology, Industrial Engineering Technology/Management, Industrial Hygiene, Industrial Safety, Industrial Safety Technology, Industrial Science, Industrial Technology, Instrumental Music, Interior Design, Journalism, Law Enforcement, Management, Management Technology, Marketing, Mass Communication, Mathematics, Mechanical Technology, Medical Technology, Middle School/Junior High Education, Music, Music Education, Music Theory/Composition, Nursing, Office Administration, Organizational Communication, Personnel Management, Physical Education, Physics, Political Science/Government, Power Technology, Psychology, Psychology Rehabitation, Public Relations, Safety, Safety Management, Science Education, Secondary Education, Security, Social Studies Education, Social Work, Sociology, Spanish, Special Education, Speech Communication, Speech/Dramatic Arts Education, Speech Pathology, Studio Art, Theatre, Trade/Technical/Health Occupations, Voice.
**Distribution of degrees:** The majors with the highest enrollment are elementary education, management, and criminal justice; German and science education have the lowest.
**Requirements:** General education requirement.
**Academic regulations:** Minimum 2.0 GPA must be maintained.
**Special:** Minors offered in all majors and in anthropology, health education, military science, philosophy, and photography. Associate's degrees offered. Self-designed majors. Double majors. Dual degrees. Accelerated study. Pass/fail grading option. Internships. Cooperative education programs. Graduate school at which undergraduates may take graduate-level courses. Preprofessional programs in law, medicine, veterinary science, pharmacy, dentistry, and optometry. 3-2 engineering programs with U of Kansas and U of Missouri at Columbia. Member of Kansis City Regional Council for Higher Education and Missouri London Program. Teacher certification in early childhood, elementary, secondary, special education, and vo-tech education. Certification in specific subject areas. Exchange programs abroad in Denmark (U of Denmark) and Sweden (Vaxjo U). Study abroad also in England. ROTC.
**Honors:** Honors program. Honor societies.
**Academic Assistance:** Remedial reading, writing, math, and study skills. Nonremedial tutoring.

**STUDENT LIFE. Housing:** All freshmen must live on campus. Coed, women's, and men's dorms. Sorority and fraternity housing. School-owned/operated apartments. Off-campus privately-owned housing. Both on-campus and off-campus married-student housing. 30% of students live in college housing.
**Services and counseling/handicapped student services:** Placement services. Health service. Women's center. Day care. Counseling services for minority, military, veteran, and older students. Birth control, personal, and psychological counseling. Career and academic guidance services. Physically disabled student services. Learning disabled services. Notetaking services. Tape recorders. Tutors. Reader services for the blind.
**Campus organizations:** Undergraduate student government. Student newspaper (Muleskinner, published once/week). Yearbook. Radio and TV stations. Alternative Lifestyles, Champions of Reasons, Council for Handicapped Students, Nontraditional Student Association, departmental, service, and special-interest groups, 161 organizations in all. 15 fraternities, 11 chapter houses; 10 sororities, eight chapter houses. 12% of men join a fraternity. 11% of women join a sorority.
**Religious organizations:** Baptist Student Union, Chi Alpha, Christian Campus House, Fellowship of Christian Athletes, Liahona Fellowship, Lutheran Student Assembly, Muslim Students Association, Navigators, Newman Center, United Campus Ministry, Wesley Foundation, Christian Student Fellowship.

**Minority/foreign student organizations:** Association of Black Collegiates, Black Greek Council. International Student Organization, African, Chinese, Hong Kong, Kenyan, Malaysian, Nigerian, Pakistani, and Thai groups.

**ATHLETICS. Physical education requirements:** Two semesters of physical education required.

**Intercollegiate competition:** 3% of students participate. Baseball (M), basketball (M,W), cheerleading (M,W), cross-country (M,W), football (M), golf (M), softball (W), track (indoor) (M,W), track (outdoor) (M,W), track and field (indoor) (M,W), track and field (outdoor) (M,W), volleyball (W), wrestling (M). Member of Mid-American Intercollegiate Athletic Association, NCAA Division II.

**Intramural and club sports:** 9% of students participate. Intramural basketball, football, soccer, softball.

**ADMISSIONS. Academic basis for candidate selection** (in order of priority): Class rank, standardized test scores, secondary school record, school's recommendation.

**Nonacademic basis for candidate selection:** Character and personality are important. Extracurricular participation and alumni/ae relationship are considered.

**Requirements:** Graduation from secondary school is required; GED is accepted. 12 units and the following program of study are recommended: 3 units of English, 2 units of math, 3 units of science, 1 unit of foreign language, 3 units of social studies. Rank in top two-thirds of secondary school class required. ACT is required; SAT may be substituted. Campus visit and interview recommended. Off-campus interviews available with an admissions representative.

**Procedure:** Take SAT or ACT by December of 12th year. Visit college for interview by March of 12th year. Notification of admission on rolling basis. $100 tuition deposit, refundable until August 18. $100 room deposit, refundable until August 18. Freshmen accepted in terms other than fall.

**Special programs:** Admission may be deferred one year. Credit may be granted through CEEB Advanced Placement for scores of 4 or higher. Credit may be granted through CLEP general and subject exams and DANTES exams and military experience. Credit and placement may be granted through ACT PEP and challenge exams. Early entrance/early admission program. Concurrent enrollment program.

**Transfer students:** Transfer students accepted for terms other than fall. In fall 1993, 38% of all new students were transfers into all classes. 1,724 transfer applications were received, 1,120 were accepted. Application deadline is August 15 for fall; December 15 for spring. Minimum 2.0 GPA required. Lowest course grade accepted is "D." At least 30 semester hours must be completed at the university to receive degree.

**Admissions contact:** Delores Hudson, M.S., Director of Admissions. 816 543-4290.

**FINANCIAL AID. Available aid:** Pell grants, SEOG, state scholarships and grants, school scholarships, private scholarships and grants, ROTC scholarships, academic merit scholarships, athletic scholarships, and aid for undergraduate foreign students. Perkins Loans (NDSL), PLUS, Stafford Loans (GSL), and SLS. Installment plan.

**Financial aid statistics:** In 1993-94, 70% of all undergraduate applicants received aid; 60% of freshman applicants.

**Supporting data/closing dates:** SFS: Priority filing date is March 1. Notification of awards on rolling basis.

**Financial aid contact:** Phil Shreves, M.S., Director of Financial Aid. 816 543-4040.

**STUDENT EMPLOYMENT.** College Work/Study Program. Institutional employment. 9% of full-time undergraduates work on campus during school year. Students may expect to earn an average of $1,200 during school year. Off-campus part-time employment opportunities rated "good."

**COMPUTER FACILITIES.** 871 IBM/IBM-compatible and Macintosh/Apple microcomputers; 200 are networked. Students may access IBM minicomputer/mainframe systems, BITNET, Internet. Residence halls may be equipped with stand-alone microcomputers, networked microcomputers, modems. Client/LAN operating systems include Apple/Macintosh, DOS, LocalTalk/AppleTalk, Microsoft. Computer languages and software packages include dBASE, Lotus 1-2-3, Microsoft Windows, Microsoft Works, Paradox, SMART, WordPerfect; 1,700 in all. Computer facilities are available to all students.

**Fees:** None.

**Hours:** 24 hours.

**GRADUATE CAREER DATA.** Highest graduate school enrollments: Central Missouri State U. 65% of graduates choose careers in business and industry. Companies and businesses that hire graduates: McDonnell Douglas, Missouri Public Service, PARS, Missouri Public Service.

**PROMINENT ALUMNI/AE.** Jeff Wright, NFL football player, Buffalo Bills; Dale Cornegie, pioneer of self-development and author; James W. Evans, physicist.

## College of the Ozarks

**Point Lookout, MO 65726** 417 334-6411

**1994-95 Costs.** Tuition: Paid by participation in work program and by Pell and college grants. Room & board: $1,900. Fees, books, misc. academic expenses (school's estimate): $900.

**Enrollment.** Undergraduates: 590 men, 687 women (full-time). Freshman class: 3,258 applicants, 338 accepted, 326 enrolled.

**Test score averages/ranges.** Average ACT scores: 21 composite.

**Faculty.** 86 full-time; 22 part-time. 53% of faculty holds doctoral degree. Student/faculty ratio: 15 to 1.

**Selectivity rating.** Competitive.

**PROFILE.** The College of the Ozarks, founded in 1906, is a church-affiliated, liberal arts institution. Its 930-acre campus is located in Point Lookout, 40 miles south of Springfield.

**Accreditation:** NCACS. Professionally accredited by the National Council for Accreditation of Teacher Education.

**Religious orientation:** College of the Ozarks is affiliated with the Presbyterian Church USA; two semesters of religion required.

**Library:** Collections totaling over 100,000 volumes, 797 periodical subscriptions, and 15,345 microform items.

**Special facilities/museums:** Museum containing art, natural history, music, and Ozarkiana collections, print shop, greenhouses, kitchens, farms.

**Athletic facilities:** Gymnasium, basketball, racquetball, sand volleyball, tennis, and volleyball courts, weight room, track, baseball, flag football, intramural, soccer, and softball fields, swimming pool, dance studio, saunas, jogging trails, fishing area, field house.

**STUDENT BODY. Undergraduate profile:** 67% are state residents; 5% are transfers. 1% Black, 1% Hispanic, 1% Native American, 95% White, 2% Other. Average age of undergraduates is 21.

**Freshman profile:** 1% of accepted applicants took SAT; 99% took ACT. 97% of freshmen come from public schools.

**Undergraduate achievement:** 80% of fall 1992 freshmen returned for fall 1993 term. 63% of entering class graduated. 12% of students who completed a degree program went on to graduate study within one year.

**Foreign students:** 26 students are from out of the country. Countries represented include Canada, Indonesia, Kenya, Mexico, the Netherlands, and Pakistan; 22 in all.

**PROGRAMS OF STUDY. Degrees:** B.A., B.S.

**Majors:** Accounting, Agriculture, Art, Aviation Science, Biology, Business, Chemistry, Computer Science, Criminal Justice Administration, Dietetics, Education, English, Graphic Arts, History, Home Economics, Hotel/Restaurant Management, Mass Media, Mathematics, Modern Foreign Languages, Music, Philosophy/Religion, Physical Education, Physics, Political Science, Pre-Medical, Psychology, Sociology, Speech Communications/Theatre Arts, Technology.

**Distribution of degrees:** The majors with the highest enrollment are business, elementary education, and psychology; music, dietetics, and foreign language have the lowest.

**Requirements:** General education requirement.

**Academic regulations:** Freshmen must maintain minimum 1.75 GPA; sophomores, 1.85 GPA; juniors, 2.0 GPA; seniors, 2.0 GPA.

**Special:** Minors offered in most majors and in agribusiness, animal science, French, German, and Spanish. Interdisciplinary programs. Additional programs in science. Self-designed majors. Double majors. Independent study. Internships. Cooperative education programs. Preprofessional programs in law, medicine, veterinary science, pharmacy, dentistry, theology, pre-engineering, and pre-medical technology. 3-2 engineering program. Teacher certification in early childhood, elementary, secondary, vo-tech, and bilingual/bicultural education. Certification in specific subject areas. Study abroad in France and the Netherlands. ROTC.

**Honors:** Honors program. Honor societies.

**Academic Assistance:** Remedial writing, math, and study skills. Nonremedial tutoring.

**STUDENT LIFE. Housing:** All unmarried students under age 21 must live on campus unless living near campus with relatives. Women's and men's dorms. 70% of students live in college housing.

**Services and counseling/handicapped student services:** Placement services. Health service. Day care. Counseling services for minority, military, veteran, and older students. Birth control, personal, and psychological counseling. Career and academic guidance services. Religious counseling.

**Campus organizations:** Undergraduate student government. Student newspaper (Outlook, published once/week). Literary magazine. Yearbook. Radio station. Chapel choir, chorale, jazz and wind ensembles, musicals and operas, drama productions, Circle K, volunteer fire department, service and special-interest groups, 44 organizations in all.

**Religious organizations:** Baptist Student Union, Intervarsity Christian Fellowship, Newman Club.

**Minority/foreign student organizations:** Afro-American Society. International Relations Club, French International Exchange.

**ATHLETICS. Physical education requirements:** Two semesters of physical education required.

**Intercollegiate competition:** 6% of students participate. Baseball (M), basketball (M,W), cheerleading (M,W), volleyball (W). Member of NAIA.

**Intramural and club sports:** 50% of students participate. Intramural basketball, cross-country, flag football, racquetball, softball, tennis, volleyball, water polo.

**ADMISSIONS. Academic basis for candidate selection** (in order of priority): Secondary school record, standardized test scores, school's recommendation, class rank.

**Nonacademic basis for candidate selection:** Character and personality and geographical distribution are emphasized. Extracurricular participation, particular talent or ability, and alumni/ae relationship are important.

**Requirements:** Graduation from secondary school is recommended; GED is accepted. 20 units and the following program of study are recommended: 4 units of English, 3 units of math, 2 units of science, 2 units of social studies, 2 units of history, 7 units of electives. Minimum 3.0 GPA and minimum composite ACT score of 21 recommended. Audition required of music program applicants. ACT is required; SAT may be substituted. Campus visit and interview recommended. No off-campus interviews.

**Procedure:** Take SAT or ACT by December 1 of 12th year. Suggest filing application by January 15; no deadline. Notification of admission on rolling basis. Reply is required within two weeks of acceptance. $50 room deposit, refundable until first day of term. Freshmen accepted in terms other than fall.

**Special programs:** Credit and/or placement may be granted through CEEB Advanced Placement exams for scores of 3 or higher. Placement may be granted through CLEP general exams. Credit and/or placement may be granted through CLEP subject exams. Credit may be granted through challenge exams. Early decision program. In fall 1993, 3,258 applied for early decision and 430 were accepted. Deadline for applying for early decision is January 15. Early entrance/early admission program. Concurrent enrollment program.

**Transfer students:** Transfer students accepted for terms other than fall. In fall 1993, 5% of all new students were transfers into all classes. Application deadline is August 1 for fall; December 1 for spring. Minimum 2.0 GPA required. Lowest course grade accepted is "D." At least 45 semester hours must be completed at the college to receive degree.

**Admissions contact:** Glen Cameron, Ed.D., Director of Admissions. 800 222-0525.

**FINANCIAL AID. Available aid:** Pell grants, SEOG, state scholarships and grants, school scholarships, private scholarships and grants, ROTC scholarships, academic merit scholarships, and athletic scholarships. Perkins Loans (NDSL), PLUS, Stafford Loans (GSL), and school loans.

**Financial aid statistics:** 10% of aid is not need-based. In 1993-94, 100% of all undergraduate applicants received aid. Average amounts of aid awarded freshmen: Scholarships and grants, $4,120; loans, $1,900.

**Supporting data/closing dates:** FAFSA: Priority filing date is March 1; deadline is April 1. Income tax forms: Priority filing date is March 1; deadline is April 1. Notification of awards begins February 1.
**Financial aid contact:** Helen Youngblood, Director of Financial Aid. 800 222-0525, extension 4290.

**STUDENT EMPLOYMENT.** College Work/Study Program. Institutional employment. 100% of full-time undergraduates work on campus during school year. Students may expect to earn an average of $2,380 during school year. Freshmen are discouraged from working during their first term. Off-campus part-time employment opportunities rated "excellent."

**COMPUTER FACILITIES.** 100 IBM/IBM-compatible and Macintosh/Apple microcomputers; 25 are networked. Students may access IBM minicomputer/mainframe systems. Client/LAN operating systems include Apple/Macintosh, DOS, Microsoft. Computer languages and software packages include Assembler, BASIC, C, COBOL, dBASE, EasyTrieve, FORTRAN, Lotus 1-2-3, MINITAB, Pascal, RPG, SPSS; 50 in all. Computer facilities are available to all students.
**Fees:** None.
**Hours:** 10 AM-10 PM.

**GRADUATE CAREER DATA.** Graduate school percentages: 1% enter law school. 16% enter medical school. 8% enter graduate business programs. 50% enter graduate arts and sciences programs. Highest graduate school enrollments: U of Arkansas, Central Missouri State U, U of Mississippi, U of Missouri, Washington U. 86% of graduates choose careers in business and industry. Companies and businesses that hire graduates: American Airlines, IBM, K mart, Sam's Wholesale Clubs, Silver Dollar City, Tyson, Wal-Mart.

**PROMINENT ALUMNI/AE.** Erin Hayes, ABC; Doyle Childers, Missouri state reprentative; Walter Green, judge.

# Columbia College

**Columbia, MO 65216** **800 231-2391**

**1994-95 Costs.** Tuition: $8,294. Room: $2,328. Board: $1,372. Fees, books, misc. academic expenses (school's estimate): $400.
**Enrollment.** Undergraduates: 274 men, 290 women (full-time). Freshman class: 370 applicants, 325 accepted, 182 enrolled.
**Test score averages/ranges.** Average ACT scores: 20 composite.
**Faculty.** 46 full-time; 14 part-time. 59% of faculty holds doctoral degree. Student/faculty ratio: 12 to 1.
**Selectivity rating.** Less competitive.

**PROFILE.** Columbia is a church-affiliated, liberal arts college. Founded in 1851 as a women's college, it adopted coeducation in 1969. Its 23-acre campus is located in Columbia.

**Accreditation:** NCACS.
**Religious orientation:** Columbia College is an interdenominational Christian school; no religious requirements.
**Library:** Collections totaling over 60,000 volumes, 400 periodical subscriptions and 200 microform items.
**Athletic facilities:** Gymnasium, basketball and volleyball courts, softball field.

**STUDENT BODY. Undergraduate profile:** 76% are state residents; 20% are transfers. 1% Asian-American, 14% Black, 3% Hispanic, 1% Native American, 76% White, 5% Other. Average age of undergraduates is 22.
**Freshman profile:** 4% of freshmen who took ACT scored 30 or over on composite; 14% scored 24 or over on composite; 63% scored 18 or over on composite; 98% scored 12 or over on composite; 100% scored 6 or over on composite. 88% of accepted applicants took ACT. 90% of freshmen come from public schools.
**Foreign students:** 200 students are from out of the country. Countries represented include China, Japan, Kenya, Korea, Taiwan, and Thailand; 11 in all.

**PROGRAMS OF STUDY. Degrees:** B.A., B.F.A., B.S., B.Soc.Work.
**Majors:** Art, Business Administration, Computer Information Systems, Criminal Justice Administration, Education, English, Fashion Design, Fashion Merchandising, History/Government, Meeting/Convention Planning, Psychology, Social Work, Travel Administration.
**Distribution of degrees:** The majors with the highest enrollment are business administration, criminal justice, and education; social work, psychology, and English have the lowest.
**Requirements:** General education requirement.
**Academic regulations:** Freshmen must maintain minimum 1.50 GPA; sophomores, 1.75 GPA; juniors, 2.0 GPA; seniors, 2.0 GPA.
**Special:** Optional minors. Courses offered in biology, chemistry, geography, journalism, math, philosophy, physics, sociology, Spanish, and speech. Associate's degrees offered. Self-designed majors. Double majors. Dual degrees. Independent study. Pass/fail grading option. Internships. Preprofessional programs in law, medicine, veterinary science, pharmacy, and dentistry. Member of Mid-Missouri Associated Colleges and Universities; cross-registration possible. Teacher certification in elementary and secondary education. Certification in specific subject areas. Exchange programs abroad in England (Bradford U) and Japan (Kanagawa U). ROTC, NROTC, and AFROTC at U of Missouri at Columbia.
**Honors:** Honors program. Honor societies.
**Academic Assistance:** Remedial reading, writing, math, and study skills. Nonremedial tutoring.

**STUDENT LIFE. Housing:** All unmarried students under age 21 must live on campus unless living near campus with relatives. Coed and women's dorms. 20% of students live in college housing.
**Services and counseling/handicapped student services:** Placement services. Health service. Personal counseling. Career and academic guidance services.
**Campus organizations:** Undergraduate student government. Student newspaper (Columbian, published once/month). Jane Froman Singers, arts club, Fashion Unlimited, ski club, Marketing Association, Criminal Justice Association, psychology club, Spanish club, 28 organizations in all.
**Religious organizations:** Chi Alpha, Christian Student Union.
**Minority/foreign student organizations:** Black Student Association. World Student Union.

**ATHLETICS. Physical education requirements:** None.
**Intercollegiate competition:** 20% of students participate. Basketball (M), golf (M), soccer (M), softball (W), volleyball (W). Member of NAIA, Show-Me Collegiate Conference.
**Intramural and club sports:** 40% of students participate. Intramural aerobics, basketball, billiards, flag football, horsemanship, swimming, table tennis, volleyball. Men's club cheerleading. Women's club cheerleading.

**ADMISSIONS. Academic basis for candidate selection** (in order of priority): Class rank, secondary school record, standardized test scores, essay, school's recommendation.
**Nonacademic basis for candidate selection:** Character and personality, extracurricular participation, particular talent or ability, geographical distribution, and alumni/ae relationship are important.
**Requirements:** Graduation from secondary school is required; GED is accepted. 16 units and the following program of study are required: 3 units of English, 1 unit of math, 1 unit of science, 2 units of social studies, 2 units of history, 7 units of academic electives. Rank in top half of secondary school class and minimum 2.0 GPA required. Portfolio required of art program applicants. Audition required of music program applicants. Provisional admission possible for applicants not normally admissible. ACT is required; SAT may be substituted. Campus visit and interview recommended. Off-campus interviews available with an admissions representative.
**Procedure:** Take SAT or ACT by September 7 of 12th year. Notification of admission on rolling basis. $100 nonrefundable tuition deposit. Freshmen accepted in terms other than fall.
**Special programs:** Admission may be deferred two years. Credit may be granted through CLEP general and subject exams, ACT PEP, DANTES, and challenge exams, and military and life experience. Early decision program. Early entrance/early admission program. Concurrent enrollment program.
**Transfer students:** Transfer students accepted for terms other than fall. Application deadline is rolling for fall; rolling for spring. Minimum 2.0 GPA recommended. Lowest course grade accepted is "D." Maximum number of transferable credits is 80 semester hours. At least 30 semester hours must be completed at the college to receive degree.
**Admissions contact:** R. Nelson Richter, M.A., Director of Admissions. 800 231-2391, extension 7352.

**FINANCIAL AID. Available aid:** Pell grants, SEOG, state scholarships and grants, school scholarships and grants, private scholarships and grants, ROTC scholarships, academic merit scholarships, and athletic scholarships. Perkins Loans (NDSL), PLUS, Stafford Loans (GSL), and SLS. Deferred payment plan.
**Financial aid statistics:** 42% of aid is not need-based.
**Supporting data/closing dates:** FAFSA/FAF/FFS: Accepted on rolling basis. School's own aid application: Priority filing date is March 15; accepted on rolling basis. State aid form: Priority filing date is March 15. Income tax forms: Accepted on rolling basis. SINGLEFILE: Accepted on rolling basis. Notification of awards on rolling basis.
**Financial aid contact:** Mary Lou Eldridge, Director of Financial Aid. 800 231-2391, extension 7361.

**STUDENT EMPLOYMENT.** College Work/Study Program. Institutional employment. 25% of full-time undergraduates work on campus during school year. Students may expect to earn an average of $1,200 during school year. Off-campus part-time employment opportunities rated "excellent."

**COMPUTER FACILITIES.** 30 IBM/IBM-compatible microcomputers; 20 are networked. Students may access Digital minicomputer/mainframe systems. Computer languages and software packages include AutoCAD, BASIC, COBOL, Harvard Graphics, Lotus 1-2-3, Microsoft Window, Pascal, WordPerfect; airline terminal simulation, database, financial, mathematical, spreadsheet, 3-D art, tutorial, word processing packages; 150 in all. Computer facilities are available to all students.
**Fees:** None.
**Hours:** 8 AM-10 PM.

**PROMINENT ALUMNI/AE.** Larry Young, sculptor; Jane Froman, entertainer; Kaye Herrman Steinmetz, Missouri state legislator; Richard S. Pryor, president, Bank of Jacoma, Mo.; Dr. Nancy S. Seale, pediatric dentist.

# Conception Seminary College

**Conception, MO 64433-0502** **816 944-2218**

**1993-94 Costs.** Tuition: $5,412. Room: $1,016. Board: $1,958. Fees, books, misc. academic expenses (school's estimate): $415.
**Enrollment.** 72 men (full-time). Freshman class: 28 applicants, 25 accepted, 24 enrolled.
**Test score averages/ranges.** N/A.
**Faculty.** 21 full-time; 7 part-time. 92% of faculty holds doctoral degree. Student/faculty ratio: 3 to 1.
**Selectivity rating.** Less competitive.

**PROFILE.** Conception Seminary, founded in 1886, is a private college for candidates for the Roman Catholic priesthood. Its 30-acre campus is located in Maryville, 85 miles from Kansas City.

**Accreditation:** NCACS.
**Religious orientation:** Conception Seminary College is affiliated with the Roman Catholic Church; one religion course required each semester.
**Library:** Collections totaling over 125,000 volumes, 315 periodical subscriptions and 540 microform items.

**STUDENT BODY. Undergraduate profile:** 41% are state residents. 3% Asian-American, 1% Black, 5% Hispanic, 91% White. Average age of undergraduates is 27.

**Freshman profile:** 10% of freshmen who took ACT scored 30 or over on composite; 22% scored 24 or over on composite; 96% scored 18 or over on composite; 100% scored 12 or over on composite. 14% of freshmen come from public schools.
**Undergraduate achievement:** 75% of fall 1991 freshmen returned for fall 1992 term. 45% of entering class graduated. 97% of students who completed a degree program went on to graduate study within five years.
**PROGRAMS OF STUDY. Degrees:** B.A.
**Majors:** Philosophy, Psychology, Religion.
**Requirements:** General education requirement.
**Special:** Double majors. Independent study. Preprofessional programs in theology, art and design, and engineering.
**ADMISSIONS. Academic basis for candidate selection** (in order of priority): Secondary school record, standardized test scores, school's recommendation, class rank.
**Nonacademic basis for candidate selection:** Character and personality and particular talent or ability are important. Extracurricular participation is considered.
**Requirements:** Graduation from secondary school is recommended; GED is accepted. 16 units and the following program of study are recommended: 4 units of English, 4 units of math, 4 units of science, 4 units of social studies. Psychological test is required. ACT is required. Campus visit and interview recommended. Off-campus interviews available with admissions and alumni representatives.
**Procedure:** Take ACT by spring of 12th year. Notification of admission on rolling basis. Freshmen accepted in terms other than fall.
**Special programs:** Admission may be deferred. Credit and/or placement may be granted through CEEB Advanced Placement exams. Early decision program.
**Transfer students:** Transfer students accepted for terms other than fall. Minimum 2.0 GPA recommended. Lowest course grade accepted is "C." Maximum number of transferable credits is 94 semester hours. At least 32 semester hours must be completed at the college to receive degree.
**Admissions contact:** Rev. Paul White, O.S.B., M.A., Director of Admissions. 816 944-2814.
**FINANCIAL AID. Available aid:** Pell grants, SEOG, private scholarships and grants, and academic merit scholarships. Stafford Loans (GSL).
**Supporting data/closing dates:** FAFSA/FFS: Accepted on rolling basis. Notification of awards on rolling basis.
**Financial aid contact:** Br. Justin Hernandez, O.S.B., M.A., Director of Financial Aid. 816 944-2218, extension 787.

## Culver-Stockton College

**Canton, MO 63435-1299 — 314 288-5221**

**1994-95 Costs.** Tuition: $8,000. Room & board: $3,700. Fees, books, misc. academic expenses (school's estimate): $400.
**Enrollment.** Undergraduates: 360 men, 632 women (full-time). Freshman class: 1,576 applicants, 1,110 accepted, 275 enrolled.
**Test score averages/ranges.** Average ACT scores: 22 English, 21 math, 22 composite. Range of ACT scores of middle 50%: 18-23 English, 18-23 math.
**Faculty.** 55 full-time; 20 part-time. 60% of faculty holds doctoral degree. Student/faculty ratio: 17 to 1.
**Selectivity rating.** Less competitive.

**PROFILE.** Culver-Stockton, founded in 1853, is a church-affiliated, liberal arts college. Programs are offered through the Divisions of Applied Arts and Sciences, Fine Arts, Natural and Behavioral Sciences, and Humanities. Its 143-acre campus, located in Canton, overlooks the Mississippi River.

**Accreditation:** NCACS.
**Religious orientation:** Culver-Stockton College is affiliated with the Christian Church (Disciples of Christ); one semester of religion required.
**Library:** Collections totaling over 132,260 volumes, 867 periodical subscriptions, 4,719 microform items, and 3,800 records/tapes.
**Special facilities/museums:** Art gallery, performing arts center.
**Athletic facilities:** Gymnasium, field house, basketball, racquetball, tennis, and volleyball courts, weight room, baseball, football, intramural, soccer, and softball fields, track, batting and golf cages.
**STUDENT BODY. Undergraduate profile:** 47% are state residents; 19% are transfers. 4% Black, 96% White. Average age of undergraduates is 21.
**Freshman profile:** 5% of freshmen who took ACT scored 30 or over on English, 3% scored 30 or over on math, 2% scored 30 or over on composite; 38% scored 24 or over on English, 33% scored 24 or over on math, 39% scored 24 or over on composite; 87% scored 18 or over on English, 93% scored 18 or over on math, 92% scored 18 or over on composite; 100% scored 12 or over on English, 100% scored 12 or over on math, 100% scored 12 or over on composite. 99% of accepted applicants took ACT. 93% of freshmen come from public schools.
**Undergraduate achievement:** 66% of fall 1992 freshmen returned for fall 1993 term. 40% of entering class graduated. 7% of students who completed a degree program immediately went on to graduate study.
**Foreign students:** 10 students are from out of the country. Countries represented include Brazil, China, India, Japan, Laos, and Spain.
**PROGRAMS OF STUDY. Degrees:** B.A., B.F.A., B.Mus., B.Mus.Ed., B.S., B.S.Nurs.
**Majors:** Accounting, Art, Art Education, Arts Management, Biology, Business Administration, Chemistry, Communication Arts, Criminal Justice, Elementary Education, English, History/Political Science, Individualized Major, Mathematics, Medical Technology, Music, Music Education, Nursing, Occupational Therapy, Physical Education, Psychology, Recreation Management, Religion, Secondary Education, Sociology, Speech/Theatre Arts Education.
**Distribution of degrees:** The majors with the highest enrollment are business administration, education, and nursing; chemistry, sociology, and arts management have the lowest.
**Requirements:** General education requirement.
**Academic regulations:** Freshmen must maintain minimum 1.75 GPA; sophomores, 1.9 GPA; juniors, 2.0 GPA; seniors, 2.0 GPA.
**Special:** Minors offered in some majors and in approximately 21 other fields. Freedom Studies Program (American heritage course). Self-designed majors. Double majors. Dual degrees. Independent study. Pass/fail grading option. Internships. Cooperative education programs. Preprofessional programs in law, medicine, veterinary science, pharmacy, dentistry, theology, and optometry. 2-2 engineering program with U of Missouri at Rolla. 2-2 medical technology program with St. John's Hospital Sch of Medical Tech. 3-2 business administration, engineering, and occupational therapy programs with Washington U. Teacher certification in elementary, secondary, and special education. Certification in specific subject areas. Study abroad possible.
**Honors:** Honors program. Honor societies.
**Academic Assistance:** Remedial writing. Nonremedial tutoring.
**ADMISSIONS. Academic basis for candidate selection** (in order of priority): Secondary school record, class rank, standardized test scores, school's recommendation, essay.
**Nonacademic basis for candidate selection:** Extracurricular participation, particular talent or ability, and alumni/ae relationship are important. Character and personality are considered.
**Requirements:** Graduation from secondary school is required; GED is accepted. 15 units and the following program of study are required: 4 units of English, 2 units of math, 2 units of science including 1 unit of lab, 3 units of social studies, 4 units of electives. Minimum composite ACT score of 18, rank in top half of secondary school class, and minimum 2.0 GPA required. Portfolio required of art program applicants. Audition required of music program applicants. ACT is required; SAT may be substituted. PSAT is recommended. Campus visit and interview recommended. Off-campus interviews available with an admissions representative.
**Procedure:** Take SAT or ACT by February of 12th year. Visit college for interview by May of 12th year. Suggest filing application by January. Application deadline is May. Notification of admission on rolling basis. Reply is required by May 1. $100 room deposit, refundable until May 1. Freshmen accepted in terms other than fall.
**Special programs:** Admission may be deferred one year. Credit and/or placement may be granted through CEEB Advanced Placement exams for scores of 3 or higher. Credit and/or placement may be granted through CLEP general and subject exams. Credit may be granted through military experience. Credit and placement may be granted through ACT PEP and challenge exams and life experience. Concurrent enrollment program.
**Transfer students:** Transfer students accepted for terms other than fall. In fall 1993, 19% of all new students were transfers into all classes. 158 transfer applications were received, 148 were accepted. Application deadline is June 1 for fall; December 1 for spring. Minimum 2.0 GPA required. Lowest course grade accepted is "C." Maximum number of transferable credits is 64 semester hours. At least 30 semester hours must be completed at the college to receive degree.
**Admissions contact:** Betty A. Smith, M.A., Dean of Admissions. 314 288-5221, extensions 301-303, 331-333, 800 537-1883.
**FINANCIAL AID. Available aid:** Pell grants, SEOG, state scholarships and grants, school scholarships and grants, private scholarships, academic merit scholarships, athletic scholarships, and aid for undergraduate foreign students. Perkins Loans (NDSL), PLUS, Stafford Loans (GSL), school loans, and SLS. AMS.
**Financial aid statistics:** 30% of aid is not need-based. In 1993-94, 98% of all undergraduate applicants received aid; 98% of freshman applicants. Average amounts of aid awarded freshmen: Scholarships and grants, $7,500; loans, $2,625.
**Supporting data/closing dates:** FAFSA: Priority filing date is March 15; accepted on rolling basis. Notification of awards on rolling basis.
**Financial aid contact:** Diane Bozarth, M.B.A., Director of Financial Aid. 314 288-5221, extension 306.

## DeVry Institute of Technology

**Kansas City, MO 64131 — 816 941-0430**

**1994-95 Costs.** Tuition: $5,962. Housing: None. Fees, books, misc. academic expenses (school's estimate): $580.
**Enrollment.** Undergraduates: 1,206 men, 25 women (full-time). Freshman class: 991 applicants, 912 accepted, 483 enrolled.
**Test score averages/ranges.** N/A.
**Faculty.** 61 full-time; 8 part-time. Student/faculty ratio: 26 to 1.
**Selectivity rating.** N/A.

**PROFILE.** DeVry/Kansas City, founded in 1931, is a private institution specializing in electronic technology and computer information systems. It is a member of a network of technical institutes with eight campuses in the U.S. and two in Canada. Its 10-acre campus is located in Kansas City.

**Accreditation:** NCACS. Professionally accredited by the Accreditation Board for Engineering and Technology.
**Religious orientation:** DeVry Institute of Technology is nonsectarian; no religious requirements.
**Library:** Collections totaling over 8,437 volumes, 134 periodical subscriptions, and 36,742 microform items.
**Athletic facilities:** YMCA, recreation room, golf course, skiing facilities, bowling alley, soccer and softball fields, volleyball court, karate gymnasium.
**STUDENT BODY. Undergraduate profile:** 48% are state residents; 48% are transfers. 2% Asian-American, 14% Black, 3% Hispanic, 81% White. Average age of undergraduates is 25.
**Undergraduate achievement:** 47% of fall 1992 freshmen returned for fall 1993 term. 34% of entering class graduated.
**Foreign students:** Nine students are from out of the country. Countries represented include the Bahamas, Belgium, Japan, Jordan, the Philippines, and Taiwan.
**PROGRAMS OF STUDY. Degrees:** B.S.Acct., B.S.Bus.Oper., B.S.Comp.Info.Sys., B.S.Elec.Eng.Tech., B.S.Telecomm.Mgmt.

**Majors:** Accounting, Business Operations, Computer Information Systems, Electronic Engineering Technology, Telecommunications Management.
**Distribution of degrees:** The majors with the highest enrollment are electronic engineering technology, computer information systems, and telecommunications management.
**Requirements:** General education requirement.
**Academic regulations:** Minimum 2.0 GPA must be maintained.
**Special:** Electronics technician diploma program. Associate's degrees offered. Accelerated study. Cooperative education programs.
**Honors:** Honor societies.
**Academic Assistance:** Nonremedial tutoring.

**STUDENT LIFE. Housing:** Commuter campus; no student housing.
**Social atmosphere:** Wiskers, Commons, the Volleyball Beach, and STUCO activities are popular gathering spots. Favorite on–campus events include the Chiefs football party, dinner theater night, and "Try" Athalon. "Life off campus varies greatly due to the diversity in age of the students," reports the editor of the student newspaper. "Many of the older students spend their time with family while the younger group does much of the same partying as the average college student."
**Services and counseling/handicapped student services:** Placement services. Career and academic guidance services. Physically disabled student services. Notetaking services. Reader services for the blind.
**Campus organizations:** Undergraduate student government. Student newspaper (Turning Point, published once/week). Data Processing Management Association, accounting and business operations clubs, computer club, photography club, bowling and soccer clubs, volleyball club, camping club, IEEE, 17 organizations in all.
**Minority/foreign student organizations:** DCABS. International Club.

**ATHLETICS. Physical education requirements:** None.
**Intramural and club sports:** Intramural basketball, bowling, karate, soccer, softball, volleyball.

**ADMISSIONS. Academic basis for candidate selection** (in order of priority): Standardized test scores.
**Requirements:** Graduation from secondary school is required; GED is accepted. No specific distribution of secondary school units required. All applicants must be at least 17 years of age on first day of classes. ACT or SAT is recommended. Minimum math ACT score of 16-18 (math SAT score of 400-480) required. Applicants not submitting SAT or ACT must pass DeVry entrance exam. Campus visit recommended. Off-campus interviews available with an admissions representative.
**Procedure:** Take SAT, ACT, or DeVry entrance exam. Notification of admission on rolling basis. Reply is required by registration. $75 tuition deposit, refundable until beginning of classes. Freshmen accepted in terms other than fall.
**Special programs:** Admission may be deferred one year. Credit may be granted through CLEP subject exams and DANTES and challenge exams.
**Transfer students:** Transfer students accepted for terms other than fall. In fall 1993, 48% of all new students were transfers into all classes. Application deadline is rolling for fall; rolling for spring. Minimum 2.0 GPA required. Lowest course grade accepted is "C." Maximum number of transferable semester hours is 65% of total required for degree. At least 35% of total semester hours must be completed at the institute to receive degree.
**Admissions contact:** Gayle Dykes-Grimmett, Director of Admissions. 816 941-2810.

**FINANCIAL AID. Available aid:** Pell grants, SEOG, state scholarships and grants, school scholarships, and academic merit scholarships. Perkins Loans (NDSL), PLUS, Stafford Loans (GSL), state loans, and SLS. EDUCARD Plan.
**Financial aid statistics:** In 1993-94, 83% of all undergraduate applicants received aid; 81% of freshman applicants.
**Supporting data/closing dates:** FAFSA: Accepted on rolling basis. Notification of awards on rolling basis.
**Financial aid contact:** Jim Wyant, Director of Financial Aid. 816 941-0430.

**STUDENT EMPLOYMENT.** College Work/Study Program. Institutional employment. 6% of full-time undergraduates work on campus during school year. Students may expect to earn an average of $5,200 during school year. Freshmen are discouraged from working during their first term. Off-campus part-time employment opportunities rated "excellent."

**COMPUTER FACILITIES.** 108 IBM/IBM-compatible microcomputers; all are networked. Students may access IBM minicomputer/mainframe systems, Internet, CompuServe. Client/LAN operating systems include DOS, UNIX/XENIX/AIX, Novell. 70 major computer languages and software packages available. Computer facilities are available to all students.
**Fees:** Computer fee is included in tuition/fees.

**GRADUATE CAREER DATA.** 82% of graduates choose careers in business and industry. Companies and businesses that hire graduates: Western Geophysical, KLA, Sony Service Co., Applied Materials.

## Drury College

**Springfield, MO 65802** 417 873-7800

**1994-95 Costs.** Tuition: $8,730. Room: $1,699. Board: $1,824. Fees, books, misc. academic expenses (school's estimate): $782.
**Enrollment.** Undergraduates: 490 men, 575 women (full-time). Freshman class: 710 applicants, 650 accepted, 314 enrolled. Graduate enrollment: 98 men, 220 women.
**Test score averages/ranges.** Average SAT scores: 471 verbal, 557 math. Average ACT scores: 25 composite.
**Faculty.** 86 full-time; 18 part-time. 77% of faculty holds doctoral degree. Student/faculty ratio: 14 to 1.
**Selectivity rating.** Competitive.

**PROFILE.** Drury, founded in 1873, is a liberal arts college with religious orientation. Its 37-acre campus is located in downtown Springfield.

**Accreditation:** NCACS. Professionally accredited by the National Architecture Accrediting Board, the National Council for Accreditation of Teacher Education.
**Religious orientation:** Drury College is a nondenominational Christian school; no religious requirements.
**Library:** Collections totaling over 170,000 volumes, and 1,000 periodical subscriptions.
**Special facilities/museums:** Art museum, geological field station, language lab, laser lab.
**Athletic facilities:** Gymnasium, swimming pool, fitness center, basketball and racquetball courts, soccer stadium.

**STUDENT BODY. Undergraduate profile:** 83% are state residents; 4% are transfers. 1% Asian-American, 1% Black, 1% Hispanic, 1% Native American, 96% White. Average age of undergraduates is 20.
**Freshman profile:** 10% of accepted applicants took SAT; 93% took ACT. 86% of freshmen come from public schools.
**Undergraduate achievement:** 81% of fall 1992 freshmen returned for fall 1993 term. 40% of entering class graduated. 27% of students who completed a degree program immediately went on to graduate study.
**Foreign students:** 53 students are from out of the country. Countries represented include Canada, Greece, Japan, Liberia, Nepal, and Sweden; 18 in all.

**PROGRAMS OF STUDY. Degrees:** B.A., B.Arch., B.Mus., B.Mus.Ed., B.S.Nurs.
**Majors:** Accounting, Architecture, Art History/Appreciation, Biology, Business Administration/Management, Chemistry, Communication, Criminology, Economics, Education, Elementary Education, English, Environmental Studies, French, German, History, Mathematics, Music, Philosophy, Photography, Physical Education, Physics, Political Science/Government, Psychology, Religion, Secondary Education, Sociology, Spanish, Sport/Exercise Science, Studio Arts, Theatre.
**Distribution of degrees:** The majors with the highest enrollment are business administration, architecture, and communication; philosophy, religion, and physics have the lowest.
**Requirements:** General education requirement.
**Academic regulations:** Freshmen must maintain minimum 1.6 GPA; sophomores, 2.8 GPA; juniors, 2.0 GPA; seniors, 2.0 GPA.
**Special:** Minors offered in most majors. Freshmen Studies Program. Programs offered in environmental studies and public relations. Courses offered in creative writing, geography, humanities, Latin, and library science. Double majors. Dual degrees. Independent study. Accelerated study. Pass/fail grading option. Internships. Cooperative education programs. Graduate school at which undergraduates may take graduate-level courses. Preprofessional programs in law, medicine, veterinary science, pharmacy, dentistry, theology, medical technology, and engineering. 3-1 medical technology with Lester E. Cox Medical Center, St. John's Hospital Sch of Medical Tech, St. John's Medical Center, and the Jewish Hospital of St. Louis. 4-1/2 year bachelor's and master's degrees programs with American Graduate Sch of International Management (Arizona). 3-2 engineering program with Washington U. Washington Semester. Teacher certification in elementary, secondary, and special education. Exchange program abroad in England (Regents Coll). Study abroad also in India, Italy, and Scotland.
**Honors:** Honors program. Honor societies.
**Academic Assistance:** Remedial writing and study skills. Nonremedial tutoring.

**STUDENT LIFE. Housing:** All students under age 21 must live on campus unless living with family. Coed, women's, and men's dorms. Fraternity housing. 56% of students live in college housing.
**Services and counseling/handicapped student services:** Placement services. Health service. writing center. Counseling services for minority, veteran, and older students. Personal counseling. Career and academic guidance services. Religious counseling. Physically disabled student services. Learning disabled services. Notetaking services. Tape recorders. Tutors. Reader services for the blind.
**Campus organizations:** Undergraduate student government. Student newspaper (Drury Mirror, published once/week). Literary magazine. Yearbook. Radio and TV stations. Choir, vocal ensemble, instrumental ensembles, concert band, orchestras, Drury Lane Troupers, community action group, environmental action group, House Councils, Independent Student Association, National Collegiate Players, Young Democrats, Young Republicans, Model UN, 48 organizations in all. Four fraternities, all with chapter houses; four sororities, no chapter houses. 40% of men join a fraternity. 40% of women join a sorority.
**Religious organizations:** Logos, prayer groups.
**Minority/foreign student organizations:** Black Student Organization. International Student Organization.

**ATHLETICS. Physical education requirements:** Two semesters of physical education required.
**Intercollegiate competition:** 15% of students participate. Basketball (M), cheerleading (M,W), diving (M,W), golf (M), soccer (M,W), swimming (M,W), tennis (M,W), volleyball (W). Member of NAIA, NCAA Division II.
**Intramural and club sports:** 40% of students participate. Intramural basketball, racquetball, soccer, softball, swimming, tennis, volleyball.

**ADMISSIONS. Academic basis for candidate selection** (in order of priority): Secondary school record, standardized test scores, school's recommendation, essay, class rank.
**Nonacademic basis for candidate selection:** Extracurricular participation is important. Character and personality and particular talent or ability are considered.
**Requirements:** Graduation from secondary school is required; GED is accepted. No specific distribution of secondary school units required. Minimum composite ACT score of 20 and minimum 2.5 GPA required. SAT or ACT is required. Campus visit and interview recommended. Off-campus interviews available with an admissions representative.
**Procedure:** Take SAT or ACT by fall of 12th year. Visit college for interview by February of 12th year. Suggest filing application by April 1. Application deadline is August 1. Notification of admission on rolling basis. Reply is required by May 1. $100 tuition deposit, refundable until May 1. $100 room deposit, refundable until May 1. Freshmen accepted in terms other than fall.
**Special programs:** Credit and/or placement may be granted through CEEB Advanced Placement exams for scores of 3 or higher. Credit and/or placement may be granted through CLEP general exams. Credit and placement may be granted through challenge exams. Early entrance/early admission program. Concurrent enrollment program.
**Transfer students:** Transfer students accepted for terms other than fall. In fall 1993, 4% of all new students were transfers. 120 transfer applications were received. Application deadline is August 1 for fall; December 1 for spring. Minimum 2.0 GPA required. Lowest course grade accepted is "C." Maximum number of transferable credits is 94 semester hours. At least 30 semester hours must be completed at the college to re-

ceive degree; 60 semester hours for B.Arch. program. Portfolio required of architecture program transfer applicants.
**Admissions contact:** Michael G. Thomas, M.Ed., Director of Admission. 417 873-7205.

**FINANCIAL AID. Available aid:** Pell grants, SEOG, state scholarships and grants, school scholarships and grants, private scholarships and grants, academic merit scholarships, athletic scholarships, and aid for undergraduate foreign students. Perkins Loans (NDSL), PLUS, Stafford Loans (GSL), and SLS. Federal Subsidized Student Loan Program. AMS, deferred payment plan, and guaranteed tuition.
**Financial aid statistics:** 20% of aid is not need-based. In 1993-94, 80% of all undergraduate applicants received aid; 85% of freshman applicants. Average amounts of aid awarded freshmen: Scholarships and grants, $3,700; loans, $2,200.
**Supporting data/closing dates:** FAFSA: Priority filing date is March 15; accepted on rolling basis; deadline is April 30. School's own aid application: Priority filing date is March 15; accepted on rolling basis. Notification of awards on rolling basis.
**Financial aid contact:** Annette Avery, Director of Financial Aid. 417 873-7319.

**STUDENT EMPLOYMENT.** College Work/Study Program. Institutional employment. 29% of full-time undergraduates work on campus during school year. Students may expect to earn an average of $1,500 during school year. Off-campus part-time employment opportunities rated "excellent."

**COMPUTER FACILITIES.** 21 IBM/IBM-compatible and Macintosh/Apple microcomputers. Residence halls may be equipped with stand-alone microcomputers. Computer languages and software packages include BASIC, COBOL, FORTRAN, Lotus 1-2-3, SuperCalc, WordStar. Computer facilities are available to all students.
**Fees:** None.

**GRADUATE CAREER DATA.** Graduate school percentages: 3% enter law school. 6% enter medical school. 2% enter dental school. 3% enter graduate business programs. 8% enter graduate arts and sciences programs. 2% enter theological school/seminary. Highest graduate school enrollments: U of Kansas, U of Missouri, Washington U. 46% of graduates choose careers in business and industry. Companies and businesses that hire graduates: Baird, Kurtz & Dobson, Twentieth Century, Edward D. Jones & Co., Southwestern Bell, Merck.

**PROMINENT ALUMNI/AE.** Dr. John Hammon, heart surgeon; John Morris, owner Bass Pro; Frank Clippinges, physician.

# Evangel College

**Springfield, MO 65802 — 417 865-2811**

**1993-94 Costs.** Tuition: $6,590. Room & board: $3,090. Fees, books, misc. academic expenses (school's estimate): $640.
**Enrollment.** Undergraduates: 638 men, 781 women (full-time). Freshman class: 445 applicants, 426 accepted, 388 enrolled.
**Test score averages/ranges.** Average SAT scores: 937 combined. Average ACT scores: 21 composite.
**Faculty.** 84 full-time; 31 part-time. 50% of faculty holds doctoral degree. Student/faculty ratio: 18 to 1.
**Selectivity rating.** Noncompetitive.

**PROFILE.** Evangel, founded in 1955, is a church-affiliated, liberal arts college. Its 80-acre campus is located in Springfield.

**Accreditation:** NCACS. Professionally accredited by the National Association of Schools of Music, the National Council for Accreditation of Teacher Education.
**Religious orientation:** Evangel College is affiliated with the Assembly of God; 16 semester hours of biblical studies required.
**Library:** Collections totaling over 112,000 volumes, 610 periodical subscriptions, and 23,000 microform items.
**Athletic facilities:** Gymnasium, basketball, tennis, and volleyball courts, track, baseball, practice, and softball fields.

**STUDENT BODY. Undergraduate profile:** 32% are state residents; 10% are transfers. 1% Asian-American, 3% Black, 1% Hispanic, 1% Native American, 93% White, 1% Other. Average age of undergraduates is 21.
**Freshman profile:** 19% of accepted applicants took SAT; 84% took ACT. 76% of freshmen come from public schools.
**Undergraduate achievement:** 74% of fall 1992 freshmen returned for fall 1993 term. 49% of entering class graduated.
**Foreign students:** 33 students are from out of the country. Countries represented include Canada, Ghana, India, and Spain; 13 in all.

**PROGRAMS OF STUDY. Degrees:** B.A., B.Bus.Admin., B.F.A., B.Mus., B.S.
**Majors:** Accounting, Art, Biblical Studies, Biology, Broadcasting, Business Education, Chemistry, Communications, Computer Science, Criminal Justice, Drama, Early Childhood Education, Elementary Education, English, Government, Health/Physical Education/Recreation, History, Interdisciplinary, Journalism, Management, Mathematics, Medical Technology, Music Education, Nursing, Office Administration, Psychology, Public Administration, Recreation, Science Education, Social Science, Social Work, Sociology, Spanish, Special Education, Speech.
**Distribution of degrees:** The majors with the highest enrollment are management, education, and communications; recreation, chemistry, and office administration have the lowest.
**Requirements:** General education requirement.
**Academic regulations:** Freshmen must maintain minimum 1.5 GPA; sophomores, 1.7 GPA; juniors, 1.9 GPA; seniors, 2.0 GPA.
**Special:** Minors offered in most majors and in 14 other fields. Interdisciplinary majors allow students to present two concentrations in related disciplines or one concentration with two related minors. Associate's degrees offered. Preprofessional programs in law, medicine, and theology. Two-year transfer program in engineering. 3-2 engineering program with Washington U. Member of Christian College Coalition. Washington Semester. Teacher certification in early childhood, elementary, secondary, and special education. ROTC.
**Academic Assistance:** Remedial reading, writing, math, and study skills. Nonremedial tutoring.

**STUDENT LIFE. Housing:** All students must live on campus unless living with family. Coed, women's, and men's dorms. Married-student housing. 90% of students live in college housing.
**Social atmosphere:** The Activities Board, Missions of Evangel College Students, and the Resident Hall Association influence life on campus. Popular events include Spring Fling, Harvest Fest, Fifties, Sixties, and Seventies nights, Blues Cafe, the Artist Series, and football and basketball games. "The Activities Board provides two events each month that are inexpensive and open to all students. Many students are also involved with churches and community outreach programs," reports the student newspaper.
**Services and counseling/handicapped student services:** Placement services. Health service. Counseling services for minority, veteran, and older students. Personal and psychological counseling. Career and academic guidance services. Religious counseling.
**Campus organizations:** Undergraduate student government. Student newspaper (Lance, published once/week). Yearbook. Radio station. Band, concert band, brass choir, choral union, chorale, concert choir, orchestra, Phi Mu Alpha Sinfonia, drama fraternity, Circle K, tutorial group, intercollegiate speech club, Young Democrats, Young Republicans, academic and service groups, special-interest groups.
**Religious organizations:** Student Ministries.

**ATHLETICS. Physical education requirements:** Two semester hours of physical education required.
**Intercollegiate competition:** 20% of students participate. Baseball (M), basketball (M,W), cheerleading (M,W), football (M), softball (W), track (indoor) (M,W), track (outdoor) (M,W), track and field (indoor) (M,W), track and field (outdoor) (M,W), volleyball (W). Member of Heart of America Athletic Conference, NAIA.
**Intramural and club sports:** 65% of students participate. Intramural flag football, soccer, softball, tennis, volleyball. Men's club soccer, volleyball. Women's club soccer.

**ADMISSIONS. Academic basis for candidate selection** (in order of priority): Secondary school record, standardized test scores, school's recommendation, class rank.
**Nonacademic basis for candidate selection:** Character and personality are emphasized.
**Requirements:** Graduation from secondary school is recommended; GED is accepted. 15 units required and the following program of study recommended: 3 units of English, 2 units of math, 1 unit of science, 2 units of social studies. Rank in top half of secondary school class and minimum 2.0 GPA required. ACT is required; SAT may be substituted. Campus visit recommended. No off-campus interviews.
**Procedure:** Take SAT or ACT by January of 12th year. Suggest filing application by October 1. Application deadline is August 15. Notification of admission on rolling basis. $75 refundable room deposit. Freshmen accepted in terms other than fall.
**Special programs:** Admission may be deferred one semester. Credit may be granted through CEEB Advanced Placement for scores of 3 or higher. Credit may be granted through CLEP general and subject exams. Concurrent enrollment program.
**Transfer students:** Transfer students accepted for terms other than fall. In fall 1993, 10% of all new students were transfers into all classes. 214 transfer applications were received, 189 were accepted. Application deadline is August 1 for fall; December 30 for spring. Minimum 2.0 GPA required. Lowest course grade accepted is "D." Maximum number of transferable credits is 64 semester hours. At least 30 semester hours must be completed at the college to receive degree.
**Admissions contact:** David Schoolfield, Executive Director of Enrollment. 417 865-2811.

**FINANCIAL AID. Available aid:** Pell grants, SEOG, school scholarships and grants, private scholarships and grants, ROTC scholarships, academic merit scholarships, and athletic scholarships. Perkins Loans (NDSL), PLUS, Stafford Loans (GSL), school loans, and SLS.
**Financial aid statistics:** In 1993-94, 90% of all undergraduate applicants received aid; 90% of freshman applicants. Average amounts of aid awarded freshmen: Scholarships and grants, $1,549; loans, $2,770.
**Supporting data/closing dates:** FAFSA: Priority filing date is April 1; accepted on rolling basis. School's own aid application: Priority filing date is April 1; accepted on rolling basis. Notification of awards on rolling basis.
**Financial aid contact:** Samuel Ketcher, Director of Financial Aid. 417 865-2811.

**STUDENT EMPLOYMENT.** College Work/Study Program. Institutional employment. 38% of full-time undergraduates work on campus during school year. Students may expect to earn an average of $1,700 during school year. Off-campus part-time employment opportunities rated "excellent."

**COMPUTER FACILITIES.** 93 IBM/IBM-compatible microcomputers; 36 are networked. Client/LAN operating systems include DOS. Computer facilities are available to all students.
**Fees:** Computer fee is included in tuition/fees.

# Fontbonne College

**St. Louis, MO 63105 — 314 862-3456**

**1993-94 Costs.** Tuition: $7,990. Room & board: $4,000. Fees, books, misc. academic expenses (school's estimate): $500.
**Enrollment.** Undergraduates: 253 men, 638 women (full-time). Freshman class: 291 applicants, 245 accepted, 126 enrolled. Graduate enrollment: 233 men, 316 women.
**Test score averages/ranges.** Average SAT scores: 21 combined. Average ACT scores: 22 composite.
**Faculty.** 55 full-time; 76 part-time. 55% of faculty holds highest degree in specific field. Student/faculty ratio: 14 to 1.
**Selectivity rating.** Less competitive.

PROFILE. Fontbonne, founded in 1923, is a church-affiliated, liberal arts college. Its 13-acre campus is located in a residential area of St. Louis. Campus architecture includes buildings of Red Missouri granite, trimmed with Bedford stone.

**Accreditation:** NCACS. Professionally accredited by the American Home Economics Association, the National Association of Schools of Music, the National Council for Accreditation of Teacher Education.

**Religious orientation:** Fontbonne College is affiliated with the Roman Catholic Church; three semesters of religion required.

**Library:** Collections totaling over 95,000 volumes and 510 periodical subscriptions.

**Special facilities/museums:** Art museum.

**Athletic facilities:** Gymnasium, weight room, indoor swimming pool, indoor track.

**STUDENT BODY. Undergraduate profile:** 88% are state residents; 43% are transfers. 1% Asian-American, 11% Black, 1% Hispanic, 86% White, 1% Other. Average age of undergraduates is 20.

**Freshman profile:** 98% of accepted applicants took ACT. 57% of freshmen come from public schools.

**Undergraduate achievement:** 69% of fall 1992 freshmen returned for fall 1993 term. 55% of entering class graduated. 15% of students who completed a degree program went on to graduate study within five years.

**Foreign students:** 25 students are from out of the country. Countries represented include China, Japan, Nigeria, Oman, and Taiwan; 10 in all.

**PROGRAMS OF STUDY. Degrees:** B.A., B.F.A., B.Mus., B.S.

**Majors:** Accounting, Applied Performance, Art, Behavioral Disorders, Biology, Broadcasting, Business Administration, Communication Disorders, Communications Arts, Computer Science, Deaf Education, Dietetics, Drama/Speech Education, Early Childhood, Early Childhood Music, Education/Special Education, Elementary Music Education, English, Environmental Studies, Fashion Merchandising, Finance, General Studies, Health Sciences, Health Services Administration, History, Home Economics, Human Services, Information Systems, International Business, Learning Disabilities, Management, Marketing, Mathematics, Mathematics Education, Medical Technology, Mental Retardation, Mental Retardation/Educable, Mental Retardation/Severely Handicapped, Music Business, Natural Science, Nutrition, Performance, Public Relations, Retailing, Science Education, Social Science Education, Social Sciences, Technical Theatre, Theatre.

**Distribution of degrees:** The majors with the highest enrollment are business, education, and communication arts; art, music, and social science have the lowest.

**Requirements:** General education requirement.

**Academic regulations:** Minimum 2.0 GPA must be maintained.

**Special:** Self-designed majors. Pass/fail grading option. Internships. Cooperative education programs. Graduate school at which undergraduates may take graduate-level courses. Preprofessional programs in law and medicine. 3-2 program in social work with Washington U. Member of Sisters of St. Joseph College Consortium. Exchange program with St. Louis U. Teacher certification in early childhood, elementary, secondary, special education, and vo-tech education. Certification in specific subject areas. Study abroad in Latin America countries and in Spain. ROTC at Washington U.

**Honors:** Honors program. Honor societies.

**Academic Assistance:** Remedial reading, writing, math, and study skills.

**ADMISSIONS. Academic basis for candidate selection** (in order of priority): Secondary school record, standardized test scores, class rank, school's recommendation, essay.

**Nonacademic basis for candidate selection:** Character and personality, extracurricular participation, and particular talent or ability are important. Alumni/ae relationship is considered.

**Requirements:** Graduation from secondary school is recommended; GED is accepted. 20 units and the following program of study are recommended: 4 units of English, 3 units of math, 2 units of science, 2 units of foreign language, 3 units of social studies, 3 units of history, 3 units of electives. Minimum composite ACT score of 20, rank in top half of secondary school class, and minimum 2.5 GPA recommended. Audition required of theatre program applicants. Portfolio required of art program applicants. Mentor program for applicants not meeting standard requirements. ACT is required; SAT may be substituted. Campus visit and interview recommended. Off-campus interviews available with an admissions representative.

**Procedure:** Take SAT or ACT by December of 12th year. Application deadline is August 1. Notification of admission on rolling basis. Reply is required by May 1. $100 tuition deposit, refundable until May 1. $75 room deposit, refundable until May 1. Freshmen accepted in terms other than fall.

**Special programs:** Admission may be deferred one year. Credit and/or placement may be granted through CEEB Advanced Placement exams for scores of 3 or higher. Credit may be granted through CLEP general and subject exams. Credit and placement may be granted through military and life experience. Early entrance/early admission program. Concurrent enrollment program.

**Transfer students:** Transfer students accepted for terms other than fall. In fall 1993, 43% of all new students were transfers into all classes. 238 transfer applications were received, 183 were accepted. Application deadline is August 1 for fall; December 12 for spring. Minimum 2.0 GPA recommended. Lowest course grade accepted is "C." Maximum number of transferable semester hours is 72 from two-year schools; unlimited from four-year schools. At least 32 semester hours must be completed at the college to receive degree.

**Admissions contact:** Peggy Musen, Dean of Admissions. 314 889-1400.

**FINANCIAL AID. Available aid:** Pell grants, SEOG, state scholarships and grants, school scholarships and grants, private scholarships and grants, and academic merit scholarships. Perkins Loans (NDSL), PLUS, Stafford Loans (GSL), state loans, school loans, private loans, and SLS. AMS and deferred payment plan.

**Financial aid statistics:** 20% of aid is not need-based. In 1993-94, 80% of all undergraduate applicants received aid; 84% of freshman applicants. Average amounts of aid awarded freshmen: Scholarships and grants, $2,600; loans, $2,625.

**Supporting data/closing dates:** FAFSA: Priority filing date is April 15; accepted on rolling basis. School's own aid application: Priority filing date is April 15; accepted on rolling basis. Notification of awards on rolling basis.

**Financial aid contact:** Richard W. Klemm, M.S., Director of Financial Aid. 314 889-1414.

# Hannibal-LaGrange College

**Hannibal, MO 63401** **314 221-3675**

**1994-95 Costs.** Tuition: $6,050. Room & board: $2,510. Fees, books, misc. academic expenses (school's estimate): $660.

**Enrollment.** Undergraduates: 189 men, 304 women (full-time). Freshman class: 157 enrolled.

**Test score averages/ranges.** Average ACT scores: 21 composite.

**Faculty.** 38 full-time; 19 part-time. 37% of faculty holds doctoral degree. Student/faculty ratio: 16 to 1.

**Selectivity rating.** Noncompetitive.

**PROFILE.** Hannibal-LaGrange, formed through the 1928 merger of Hannibal and La-Grange Colleges, is a church-affiliated, liberal arts college. Its 110-acre campus is located near the Mississippi River in Hannibal, 100 miles from St. Louis.

**Accreditation:** NCACS.

**Religious orientation:** Hannibal-LaGrange College is affiliated with the Southern Baptist Church; two semesters of religion required.

**Library:** Collections totaling over 74,835 volumes, 398 periodical subscriptions, and 2,742 microform items.

**Athletic facilities:** Gymnasium, basketball, racquetball, tennis, and volleyball courts, weight room, track.

**STUDENT BODY. Undergraduate profile:** 93% are state residents. 1% Asian-American, 1% Black, 1% Hispanic, 97% White. Average age of undergraduates is 22.

**Freshman profile:** 2% of accepted applicants took SAT; 98% took ACT. 93% of freshmen come from public schools.

**Undergraduate achievement:** 67% of fall 1991 freshmen returned for fall 1992 term. 13% of entering class graduated.

**Foreign students:** One student is from out of the country.

**PROGRAMS OF STUDY. Degrees:** B.Church Mus., B.Relig.Ed., B.S., B.S.Ed., B.S.Nurs., B.Theol.

**Majors:** Accounting, Business Administration, Church Music, Computer Data Processing/Information Systems, Early Childhood Education, Elementary Education, Nursing, Religious Education, Secondary Education, Theology.

**Distribution of degrees:** The majors with the highest enrollment are business administration, elementary education, and computer data processing/information systems.

**Requirements:** General education requirement.

**Special:** Program in nursing prepares students for state R.N. license exam or for transfer to bachelor's program at other colleges. Certificate programs. Associate's degrees offered. Independent study. Pass/fail grading option. Internships. Graduate school at which undergraduates may take graduate-level courses. Preprofessional programs in law, medicine, veterinary science, pharmacy, dentistry, engineering, medical technology, dental hygiene, and mathematics. Cooperative Services International Education Consortium. Teacher certification in early childhood, elementary, and secondary education. Study abroad possible in England (Harlaxton Coll).

**Honors:** Honors program. Honor societies.

**Academic Assistance:** Nonremedial tutoring.

**ADMISSIONS. Academic basis for candidate selection** (in order of priority): Standardized test scores, secondary school record, class rank, school's recommendation.

**Nonacademic basis for candidate selection:** Character and personality are emphasized.

**Requirements:** Graduation from secondary school is required; GED is accepted. No specific distribution of secondary school units required. ACT is required; SAT may be substituted. Campus visit and interview recommended.

**Procedure:** Suggest filing application by January 31; no deadline. Notification of admission on rolling basis. $100 refundable room deposit. Freshmen accepted in terms other than fall.

**Special programs:** Admission may be deferred. Credit and/or placement may be granted through CLEP general and subject exams. Credit and placement may be granted through challenge exams. Early entrance/early admission program. Concurrent enrollment program.

**Transfer students:** Transfer students accepted for terms other than fall. Lowest course grade accepted is "D."

**Admissions contact:** Bill C. Creech, Director of Admissions. 314 221-3113.

**FINANCIAL AID. Available aid:** Pell grants, SEOG, state scholarships and grants, school scholarships, athletic scholarships, and aid for undergraduate foreign students. Perkins Loans (NDSL), PLUS, Stafford Loans (GSL), state loans, and private loans. Deferred payment plan.

**Financial aid statistics:** 42% of aid is not need-based.

**Supporting data/closing dates:** FAFSA/FAF/FFS: Priority filing date is July 1; accepted on rolling basis. School's own aid application: Priority filing date is July 1. Income tax forms: Priority filing date is July 1. Notification of awards on rolling basis.

**Financial aid contact:** Dean Schoonover, Director of Financial Aid. 314 221-3675, extension 279.

# Lincoln University

**Jefferson City, MO 65102-0029 314 681-5000**

**1993-94 Costs.** Tuition: $1,800 (state residents), $3,600 (out-of-state). Room & board: $2,728. Fees, books, misc. academic expenses (school's estimate): $862.
**Enrollment.** Undergraduates: 913 men, 1,106 women (full-time). Freshman class: 1,400 applicants, 1,396 accepted, 686 enrolled. Graduate enrollment: 100 men, 223 women.
**Test score averages/ranges.** Average ACT scores: 19 composite. Range of ACT scores of middle 50%: 16-20 composite.
**Faculty.** 157 full-time; 94 part-time. 53% of faculty holds doctoral degree. Student/faculty ratio: 14 to 1.
**Selectivity rating.** Noncompetitive.

**PROFILE.** Lincoln, founded in 1866, is a public university. Programs are offered through the Colleges of Arts and Sciences and Professional Studies. Its 137-acre campus is located in Jefferson City, midway between St. Louis and Kansas City.

**Accreditation:** NCACS. Professionally accredited by the American Assembly of Collegiate Schools of Business, the National Association of Schools of Music, the National Council for Accreditation of Teacher Education, the National League for Nursing.
**Religious orientation:** Lincoln University is nonsectarian; no religious requirements.
**Library:** Collections totaling over 141,640 volumes, 748 periodical subscriptions, and 27,109 microform items.
**Athletic facilities:** Football stadium, track, baseball and soccer fields, gymnasium.

**STUDENT BODY. Undergraduate profile:** 85% are state residents; 19% are transfers. .5% Asian-American, 29% Black, .5% Hispanic, 1% Native American, 67% White, 2% Other. Average age of undergraduates is 26.
**Freshman profile:** 72% of accepted applicants took ACT.
**Undergraduate achievement:** 49% of fall 1992 freshmen returned for fall 1993 term.
**Foreign students:** 37 students are from out of the country. Countries represented include Ethiopia, Iran, Nigeria, Sierra Leone, Somalia, and Tanzania; 20 in all.

**PROGRAMS OF STUDY. Degrees:** B.A., B.Mus.Ed., B.S., B.S.Ed.
**Majors:** Accounting, Agriculture, Art, Biology, Building Engineering, Business Administration, Business Education, Chemistry, Computer Information Systems, Criminal Justice, Economics, Elementary Education, English, Fashion Merchandising, French, Health/Physical Education, History, Journalism, Marketing, Mathematics, Mechanical Technology, Medical Technology, Music, Philosophy, Physics, Political Science, Psychology, Public Administration, Radio/TV Broadcasting, Secretarial Science, Social Sciences Education, Sociology, Special Education.
**Distribution of degrees:** The majors with the highest enrollment are business administration, elementary education, and accounting; philosophy, English, and music education have the lowest.
**Requirements:** General education requirement.
**Academic regulations:** Minimum 2.0 GPA must be maintained.
**Special:** Minors offered in most majors and in Afro-American studies, anthropology, clothing/textiles, computer science, German, military science, social work, Spanish, and speech/theatre. Courses offered in geography and urban planning. Interrrelated programs in agribusiness, animal science, natural resource management, and plant/soil sciences. Associate's degrees offered. Double majors. Cooperative education programs. Graduate school at which undergraduates may take graduate-level courses. Preprofessional programs in medicine, veterinary science, pharmacy, dentistry, optometry, podiatry, and engineering. Teacher certification in elementary, secondary, and special education. ROTC.
**Honors:** Honors program.
**Academic Assistance:** Remedial reading, writing, math, and study skills. Nonremedial tutoring.

**STUDENT LIFE. Housing:** All unmarried, nonveteran students under age 21 with fewer than 60 semester hours must live on campus unless living with family. Women's and men's dorms. 13% of students live in college housing.
**Social atmosphere:** According to the editor of the student newspaper, "LU is a traditional black college [although] today more than 60% of the students are white." Most white students, however, "are commuters who tend not to be involved with campus social activities." Another student adds that the president "is attempting to address the issue of a traditional black school with a changing student population. Many people are trying to encourage student participation in LU functions. The work is great and progress is slow, but the direction is established." Greeks and the Baptist Student Association are the dominant groups on campus. Students frequent the Blue Room and Scruggs Student Union and enjoy such campus events as Homecoming and the Unity Awards in Media.
**Services and counseling/handicapped student services:** Placement services. Health service. Career and academic guidance services. Religious counseling. Physically disabled student services. Learning disabled program/services. Notetaking services. Tape recorders. Tutors. Reader services for the blind.
**Campus organizations:** Undergraduate student government. Student newspaper (Clarion). Yearbook. Radio and TV stations. Band, choir, jazz ensemble, orchestra, dance troupes, Stagecrafters, commuter students organization, academic and special-interest groups. Four fraternities, no chapter houses; four sororities, no chapter houses. 1% of women join a sorority.
**Religious organizations:** Baptist and Catholic groups.
**Minority/foreign student organizations:** International Student Association.

**ATHLETICS. Physical education requirements:** Four semesters of physical education required.
**Intercollegiate competition:** 1% of students participate. Baseball (M), basketball (M,W), golf (M), soccer (M), softball (W), tennis (W), track (indoor) (M,W), track (outdoor) (M,W), track and field (indoor) (M,W), track and field (outdoor) (M,W). Member of Mid-America Intercollegiate Athletics Association, NCAA Division II.
**Intramural and club sports:** 7% of students participate. Intramural basketball, football, softball.

**ADMISSIONS. Requirements:** Graduation from secondary school is required; GED is accepted. 16 units and the following program of study are recommended: 4 units of English, 3 units of math, 2 units of science, 3 units of social studies, 4 units of electives including 3 units of academic electives. Open admissions policy for in-state residents; minimum 2.0 GPA required of out-of-state applicants. Admissions test required of nursing program applicants. SAT or ACT is required. No off-campus interviews.
**Procedure:** Suggest filing application by April 1; no deadline. Notification of admission on rolling basis. No set date by which applicants must accept offer. $125 room deposit, refundable at the end of the semester. Freshmen accepted in terms other than fall.
**Special programs:** Admission may be deferred one year. Credit may be granted through CLEP general and subject exams. Credit and placement may be granted through challenge exams. Early decision program. Early entrance/early admission program. Concurrent enrollment program.
**Transfer students:** Transfer students accepted for terms other than fall. In fall 1993, 19% of all new students were transfers into all classes. 393 transfer applications were received, 390 were accepted. Application deadline is July 15 for fall; December 15 for spring. Minimum 2.0 GPA required. Lowest course grade accepted is "C." Maximum number of transferable credits is 64 semester hours from a two-year school and 90 semester hours from a four-year school. At least 30 semester hours must be completed at the university to receive degree.
**Admissions contact:** Stanford Baddley, M.Ed., Executive Director - Enrollment Services. 314 681-5599.

**FINANCIAL AID. Available aid:** Pell grants, SEOG, state scholarships and grants, school scholarships, private scholarships, ROTC scholarships, academic merit scholarships, and athletic scholarships. Perkins Loans (NDSL), PLUS, Stafford Loans (GSL), and SLS. Deferred payment plan.
**Financial aid statistics:** 34% of aid is not need-based. In 1993-94, 70% of all undergraduate applicants received aid. Average amounts of aid awarded freshmen: Scholarships and grants, $2,300; loans, $2,625.
**Supporting data/closing dates:** FAFSA/FAF/FFS: Priority filing date is March 1. School's own aid application: Priority filing date is March 1. State aid form: Priority filing date is March 1. Income tax forms: Accepted on rolling basis. Notification of awards on rolling basis.
**Financial aid contact:** Stanford Baddley, M.Ed., Executive Director - Enrollment Services. 314 681-6156.

**STUDENT EMPLOYMENT.** College Work/Study Program. Institutional employment. 18% of full-time undergraduates work on campus during school year. Students may expect to earn an average of $1,000 during school year. Freshmen are discouraged from working during their first term. Off-campus part-time employment opportunities rated "excellent."

**COMPUTER FACILITIES.** 250 IBM/IBM-compatible and Macintosh/Apple microcomputers; 100 are networked. Students may access IBM, SUN, UNISYS minicomputer/mainframe systems, BITNET, Internet. Client/LAN operating systems include DOS, UNIX/XENIX/AIX, X-windows, Banyan, Microsoft, Novell. Computer languages and software packages include Apple spreadsheets and word processing packages, ALGOL, BASIC, COBOL, dBASE IV, FORTRAN, Lotus 1-2-3, PL/I, SAS, WordPerfect; 20 in all. Computer facilities are available to all students.
**Fees:** None.
**Hours:** 9 AM-9 PM (M-Th); 9 AM-5PM (F).

# Lindenwood College

**St. Charles, MO 63301 314 949-2000**

**1994-95 Costs.** Tuition: $9,200. Room: $2,400. Board: $2,400. Fees, books, misc. academic expenses (school's estimate): $700.
**Enrollment.** Undergraduates: 907 men, 1,248 women (full-time). Freshman class: 797 applicants, 476 accepted, 338 enrolled. Graduate enrollment: 329 men, 453 women.
**Test score averages/ranges.** Average SAT scores: 435 verbal, 435 math. Range of SAT scores of middle 50%: 420-490 verbal, 420-490 math. Average ACT scores: 22 English, 22 math, 22 composite. Range of ACT scores of middle 50%: 19-23 English, 19-23 math.
**Faculty.** 80 full-time; 82 part-time. 66% of faculty holds doctoral degree. Student/faculty ratio: 14 to 1.
**Selectivity rating.** Competitive.

**PROFILE.** Lindenwood is a church-affiliated college. Founded as a liberal arts college for women in 1827, it adopted coeducation in 1969. Undergraduate programs are offered through the Divisions of Humanities, Natural Sciences and Mathematics, and Social Science; the Institute for Intergenerational Studies; and the International Valuation Sciences Institute. Graduate programs are also offered. Its 40-acre campus is located in a residential area of St. Louis. Campus architecture includes Tudor Gothic-style buildings.

**Accreditation:** NCACS.
**Religious orientation:** Lindenwood College is affiliated with the Presbyterian Church; one class of religion required.
**Library:** Collections totaling over 132,131 volumes, 447 periodical subscriptions, and 32,300 microform items.
**Special facilities/museums:** Archival museum.
**Athletic facilities:** Gymnasium, baseball, football, soccer, and softball fields, swimming pools, dance/aerobics, fitness, and weight rooms, stadium, track, sand volleyball courts, indoor jogging track.

**STUDENT BODY. Undergraduate profile:** 89% are state residents; 38% are transfers. 1% Asian-American, 8% Black, 1% Hispanic, 1% Native American, 85% White, 4% Other. Average age of undergraduates is 21.

**Freshman profile:** 37% of freshmen who took SAT scored 500 or over on verbal, 37% scored 500 or over on math; 87% scored 400 or over on verbal, 87% scored 400 or over on math; 100% scored 300 or over on verbal, 100% scored 300 or over on math. 4% of accepted applicants took SAT; 89% took ACT. 40% of freshmen come from public schools.
**Undergraduate achievement:** 75% of fall 1992 freshmen returned for fall 1993 term. 60% of entering class graduated. 14% of students who completed a degree program immediately went on to graduate study.
**Foreign students:** 40 students are from out of the country. Countries represented include China, Japan, Norway, Taiwan, and Thailand; 17 in all.

**PROGRAMS OF STUDY. Degrees:** B.A., B.F.A.
**Majors:** Art, Art History, Biology, Business Administration, Chemistry, Communications, Computer Science, Corporate/Industrial Communications, Criminal Justice, Early Childhood Education, Economics, Education, Elementary Education, English, European/Asian History, Fashion Marketing, French, Gerontology, Health Management, History, Human Resource Management, Management Information Systems, Mass Communications, Mathematics, Medical Technology, Music, Performing Arts, Physical Education, Political Science, Psychology, Public Administration, Sociology, Spanish, Special Education, Studio Art, Theatre, Valuation Sciences.
**Distribution of degrees:** The majors with the highest enrollment are business administration, communications, and education; French, art history, and management information systems have the lowest.
**Requirements:** General education requirement.
**Academic regulations:** Freshmen must maintain minimum 1.6 GPA; sophomores, 1.8 GPA; juniors, 1.9 GPA; seniors, 2.0 GPA.
**Special:** Minors offered. Self-designed majors. Double majors. Dual degrees. Independent study. Accelerated study. Pass/fail grading option. Internships. Cooperative education programs. Graduate school at which undergraduates may take graduate-level courses. Preprofessional programs in law, medicine, veterinary science, pharmacy, and dentistry. 3-2 engineering program with Washington U. Member of Consortium of Greater St. Louis Colleges; cross-registration possible. Teacher certification in early childhood, elementary, secondary, and special education. Certification in specific subject areas. ROTC at U of Missouri at St. Louis.
**Honors:** Honor societies.
**Academic Assistance:** Remedial reading, writing, math, and study skills. Nonremedial tutoring.

**STUDENT LIFE. Housing:** Women's and men's dorms. Fraternity housing. School-owned/-operated apartments. On-campus married-student housing. 60% of students live in college housing.
**Social atmosphere:** Students gather at the Student Center, the Fitness Center, Jekyl Theatre, the fine arts gallery, and in dorm lounges. Greeks, the Student Government, the American Humanics Student Association, and the Fellowship of Christian Athletes influence campus life. Favorite campus events include the Cotillion, Homecoming, Alumni Weekend, Spring Fling, Christmas Walk, Midnight Breakfast, Rush, and the Spring Luau. Students also enjoy the Cultural Arts Series, intramural sports, and football game barbecues. Many artists and guest speakers from nearby St. Louis give presentations on campus.
**Services and counseling/handicapped student services:** Placement services. Career and academic guidance services. Religious counseling. Physically disabled student services. Learning disabled services. Tutors. Reader services for the blind.
**Campus organizations:** Undergraduate student government. Student newspaper (LindenWorld, published once/month). Literary magazine. Yearbook. Radio station. Choir, vocal chamber music ensemble, madrigal singers, theatre, dance squad, cheerleading, Circle K, departmental and special-interest groups, 24 organizations in all. Three fraternities, two chapter houses; three sororities, one chapter house. 13% of men join a fraternity. 11% of women join a sorority.
**Religious organizations:** Religious Life Council, Christian Student Union.
**Minority/foreign student organizations:** NEXUS. International Student Club.

**ATHLETICS. Physical education requirements:** None.
**Intercollegiate competition:** 30% of students participate. Baseball (M), basketball (M,W), cheerleading (M,W), cross-country (M,W), football (M), golf (M,W), soccer (M,W), softball (W), tennis (W), track (indoor) (M,W), track (outdoor) (M,W), track and field (indoor) (M,W), track and field (outdoor) (M,W), volleyball (W), wrestling (M). Member of American Midwest Conference, Mid-States Football Association, NAIA.
**Intramural and club sports:** Intramural aerobics, basketball, bowling, flag football, free-throw contests, pocket billiards, softball, table tennis, tennis, volleyball, Wiffle ball.

**ADMISSIONS. Academic basis for candidate selection** (in order of priority): Standardized test scores, secondary school record, class rank, essay, school's recommendation.
**Nonacademic basis for candidate selection:** Character and personality are emphasized. Particular talent or ability is important. Extracurricular participation is considered.
**Requirements:** Graduation from secondary school is required; GED is accepted. No specific distribution of secondary school units required. Minimum composite ACT score of 18, rank in top half of secondary school class, and minimum 2.0 GPA required. SAT or ACT is required. Campus visit and interview recommended. Off-campus interviews available with an admissions representative.
**Procedure:** Take SAT or ACT by December 30 of 12th year. Visit college for interview by June 30 of 12th year. Suggest filing application by April 15; no deadline. Notification of admission on rolling basis. $150 nonrefundable room deposit. Freshmen accepted in terms other than fall.
**Special programs:** Admission may be deferred one year. Credit and/or placement may be granted through CEEB Advanced Placement exams for scores of 3 or higher. Credit may be granted through CLEP general and subject exams, military and life experience. Placement may be granted through challenge exams. Concurrent enrollment program.
**Transfer students:** Transfer students accepted for terms other than fall. In fall 1993, 38% of all new students were transfers into all classes. 500 transfer applications were received, 317 were accepted. Application deadline is August for fall; December for spring. Minimum 2.0 GPA required. Lowest course grade accepted is "D." Maximum number of transferable credits is 60 semester hours from a two-year school and 90 semester hours from a four-year school. At least 30 semester hours must be completed at the college to receive degree.
**Admissions contact:** John Guffey, M.A., Director of Admissions. 314 949-4949.

**FINANCIAL AID. Available aid:** Pell grants, SEOG, state scholarships and grants, school scholarships and grants, private scholarships and grants, ROTC scholarships, academic merit scholarships, athletic scholarships, and United Negro College Fund. Perkins Loans (NDSL), PLUS, Stafford Loans (GSL), state loans, private loans, and SLS. Deferred payment plan.
**Financial aid statistics:** 50% of aid is not need-based. In 1993-94, 90% of all undergraduate applicants received aid; 90% of freshman applicants. Average amounts of aid awarded freshmen: Scholarships and grants, $3,000; loans, $2,400.
**Supporting data/closing dates:** FAFSA: Priority filing date is April 1. Notification of awards on rolling basis.
**Financial aid contact:** Pamela Jones-Williams, M.B.A., Director of Financial Aid. 314 949-4923.

**STUDENT EMPLOYMENT.** College Work/Study Program. Institutional employment. 95% of full-time undergraduates work on campus during school year. Students may expect to earn an average of $1,500 during school year. Off-campus part-time employment opportunities rated "good."

**COMPUTER FACILITIES.** 65 IBM/IBM-compatible and Macintosh/Apple microcomputers; 10 are networked. Students may access Digital minicomputer/mainframe systems. Computer languages and software packages include COBOL, FORTRAN, UNIX; over 100 in all. Computer facilities are available to all students.
**Fees:** Computer fee is included in tuition/fees.
**Hours:** 8 AM-10 PM.

**GRADUATE CAREER DATA.** Graduate school percentages: 3% enter law school. 2% enter medical school. 18% enter graduate business programs. 20% enter graduate arts and sciences programs. Highest graduate school enrollments: Lindenwood Coll. Companies and businesses that hire graduates: McDonnell Douglas, Monsanto, Southwestern Bell, Contel, General Motors.

**PROMINENT ALUMNI/AE.** Frank Accarino, vice-president, NBC News; Robin Smith, news anchor.

## Maryville University of St. Louis

St. Louis, MO 63141-7299 — 314 576-9300

**1994-95 Costs.** Tuition: $9,250. Room & board: $4,550. Fees, books, misc. academic expenses (school's estimate): $425.
**Enrollment.** Undergraduates: 460 men, 893 women (full-time). Freshman class: 557 applicants, 375 accepted, 163 enrolled. Graduate enrollment: 206 men, 464 women.
**Test score averages/ranges.** Average ACT scores: 24 composite. Range of ACT scores of middle 50%: 21-27 composite.
**Faculty.** 83 full-time; 238 part-time. 76% of faculty holds highest degree in specific field. Student/faculty ratio: 15 to 1.
**Selectivity rating.** Competitive.

**PROFILE.** Maryville University of St. Louis, founded in 1872 as an academy for women, is a private institution. It became a four-year college in 1923, adopted coeducation in 1969, and gained university status in 1991. Its 290-acre campus is located 20 miles from downtown St. Louis.

**Accreditation:** NCACS. Professionally accredited by the American Physical Therapy Association, the Foundation for Interior Design Education Research, the National Association of Schools of Art and Design, the National Council for Accreditation of Teacher Education, the National League for Nursing.
**Religious orientation:** Maryville University of St. Louis is nonsectarian; no religious requirements.
**Library:** Collections totaling over 237,825 volumes, 748 periodical subscriptions, and 113,000 microform items.
**Special facilities/museums:** Art gallery, observatory.
**Athletic facilities:** Recreational center, baseball, soccer, and softball fields, sand volleyball and tennis courts.

**STUDENT BODY. Undergraduate profile:** 86% are state residents. 1% Asian-American, 4.1% Black, .8% Hispanic, 85.6% White, 8.5% Other. Average age of undergraduates is 26.
**Freshman profile:** 9% of freshmen who took ACT scored 30 or over on composite; 50% scored 24 or over on composite; 98% scored 18 or over on composite; 100% scored 12 or over on composite. 1% of accepted applicants took SAT; 99% took ACT. 74% of freshmen come from public schools.
**Undergraduate achievement:** 72% of fall 1992 freshmen returned for fall 1993 term.
**Foreign students:** 80 students are from out of the country. Countries represented include Japan, Thailand, Turkey, United Arab Emirates, and Venezuela; 15 in all.

**PROGRAMS OF STUDY. Degrees:** B.A., B.F.A., B.S., B.S.Nurs., B.S.Phys.Ther.
**Majors:** Accounting, Actuarial Science, Art Education, Biology, Chemistry, Communications, Drawing, Early Childhood Education, Elementary Education, English, Health Care Management, History, Humanities, Interior Design, Liberal Studies, Management, Management Information Systems, Marketing, Mathematics, Medical Technology, Middle Level Education, Music, Music History, Music Therapy, Nursing, Philosophy, Physical Therapy, Political Science, Pre-Engineering, Pre-Occupational Therapy, Psychology, Religious Studies, Science, Secondary Education, Sociology, Studio Art.
**Distribution of degrees:** The majors with the highest enrollment are management and health professions; education and math and sciences have the lowest.
**Requirements:** General education requirement.
**Academic regulations:** Minimum 2.0 GPA must be maintained.
**Special:** Minors offered in most majors and in art, computer science, economics, finance, human resources, international business, legal administration, physics, and writing. Double majors. Independent study. Pass/fail grading option. Internships. Cooperative education programs. Graduate school at which undergraduates may take graduate-level courses. Preprofessional programs in law, medicine, and dentistry. 3-2 engineering and occupational therapy programs with Washington U. Five-year M.B.A. program. Psychology/Sociology MSW program with St. Louis U. Member of consortium with Fontbonne

Coll, Lindenwood Coll, Missouri Baptist Coll, and Webster U. Washington Semester. Teacher certification in early childhood, elementary, and secondary education. Certification in specific subject areas. Study abroad in England and Japan. ROTC at Washington U.
**Honors:** Honors program. Honor societies.
**Academic Assistance:** Remedial writing and math. Nonremedial tutoring.

**ADMISSIONS. Academic basis for candidate selection** (in order of priority): Standardized test scores, secondary school record, class rank, school's recommendation, essay.
**Nonacademic basis for candidate selection:** Extracurricular participation and alumni/ae relationship are considered.
**Requirements:** Graduation from secondary school is required; GED is accepted. 22 units and the following program of study are required: 4 units of English, 3 units of math, 2 units of science including 1 unit of lab, 2 units of social studies, 3 units of history, 3 units of academic electives. Minimum 2.6 GPA and minimum composite ACT score of 20 (combined SAT score of 840) required. Portfolio required of art program applicants. Audition required of music program applicants. ACT is required; SAT may be substituted. Campus visit and interview recommended. Off-campus interviews available with an admissions representative.
**Procedure:** Take SAT or ACT by April of 12th year. Suggest filing application by January 1; no deadline. Notification of admission on rolling basis. Reply is required by May 1 or within 30 days of acceptance. $100 tuition deposit, refundable until May 1. $150 room deposit, refundable until August 1. Freshmen accepted in terms other than fall.
**Special programs:** Admission may be deferred one year. Credit may be granted through CEEB Advanced Placement for scores of 3 or higher. Credit may be granted through CLEP general and subject exams, Regents College, ACT PEP, and DANTES exams, and military and life experience. Credit and placement may be granted through challenge exams. Early entrance/early admission program. Concurrent enrollment program.
**Transfer students:** Transfer students accepted for terms other than fall. In fall 1993, 634 transfer applications were received, 425 were accepted. Application deadline is rolling for fall; rolling for spring. Minimum 2.0 GPA required. Lowest course grade accepted is "C." Maximum number of transferable credits is 68 semester hours from a two-year school and 98 semester hours from a four-year school. At least 30 semester hours must be completed at the university to receive degree.
**Admissions contact:** Martha Wade, Ph.D., Dean of Admissions and Enrollment Management. 314 576-9350, 800 627-9855.

**FINANCIAL AID. Available aid:** Pell grants, SEOG, state scholarships and grants, school scholarships and grants, private scholarships and grants, and academic merit scholarships. Perkins Loans (NDSL), PLUS, Stafford Loans (GSL), Health Professions Loans, and SLS. Deferred payment plan and family tuition reduction.
**Financial aid statistics:** 41% of aid is not need-based. In 1993-94, 84% of all undergraduate applicants received aid; 85% of freshman applicants. Average amounts of aid awarded freshmen: Scholarships and grants, $6,659; loans, $3,520.
**Supporting data/closing dates:** FAFSA/FFS: Priority filing date is March 1. School's own aid application: Priority filing date is February 1. Income tax forms: Priority filing date is March 1. Notification of awards on rolling basis.
**Financial aid contact:** Martha Harbaugh, M.B.A., Director of Financial Aid. 314 576-9360.

# Missouri Baptist College

**St. Louis, MO 63141 314 434-1115**

**1993-94 Costs.** Tuition: $6,440. Room & board: $2,940. Fees, books, misc. academic expenses (school's estimate): $690.
**Enrollment.** Undergraduates: 242 men, 262 women (full-time). Freshman class: 180 applicants, 160 accepted, 110 enrolled.
**Test score averages/ranges.** Average ACT scores: 21 composite.
**Faculty.** 31 full-time; 62 part-time. 55% of faculty holds doctoral degree. Student/faculty ratio: 18 to 1.
**Selectivity rating.** Less competitive.

**PROFILE.** Missouri Baptist, founded in 1968, is a private, church-affiliated, liberal arts college. Its 50-acre campus is located 15 miles from downtown St. Louis.

**Accreditation:** NCACS.
**Religious orientation:** Missouri Baptist College is affiliated with the Southern Baptist Church; two semesters of religion required.
**Library:** Collections totaling over 110,000 volumes and 150 periodical subscriptions.
**Athletic facilities:** Gymnasium, basketball and volleyball courts, baseball, soccer, and softball fields.

**STUDENT BODY. Undergraduate profile:** 98% are state residents. 2% Asian-American, 14% Black, 1% Hispanic, 80% White, 3% Other. Average age of undergraduates is 23.
**Freshman profile:** 10% of accepted applicants took SAT; 68% took ACT. 75% of freshmen come from public schools.
**Undergraduate achievement:** 79% of fall 1992 freshmen returned for fall 1993 term. 45% of entering class graduated.
**Foreign students:** 42 students are from out of the country. Countries represented include China, Kenya, Mexico, Nigeria, Saudi Arabia, and United Arab Emirates; 17 in all.

**PROGRAMS OF STUDY. Degrees:** B.A., B.S., B.S.Ed., B.S.Nurs.
**Majors:** Accounting, Behavioral Science, Biology, Business Administration, Chemistry, Child Development, Church Music, Communications, Computer/Information Systems, Computer Science, Early Childhood, Elementary Education, English, Health Education, History, Mathematics, Music, Music Education, Nursing, Philosophy, Physical Education, Psychology, Religion, Religious Education, Secondary Education, Social Sciences, Sociology.
**Distribution of degrees:** The majors with the highest enrollment are education, business administration, and religion; history, philosophy, and mathematics have the lowest.
**Requirements:** General education requirement.
**Academic regulations:** Minimum 2.0 GPA must be maintained.
**Special:** Minors offered in most majors and in marketing and management. Associate's degrees offered. Double majors. Dual degrees. Independent study. Internships. Preprofessional programs in medicine, veterinary science, pharmacy, dentistry, theology, chiropractic, nursing, and physical therapy. 3-2 engineering program with U of Missouri at Columbia and U of Missouri at Rolla. Member of consortium with Fontbonne Coll, Lindenwood Coll, Maryville U, and Webster U. Teacher certification in early childhood, elementary, and secondary education. Certification in specific subject areas. Study abroad in England. ROTC at Washington U.
**Honors:** Honors program. Honor societies.

**ADMISSIONS. Academic basis for candidate selection** (in order of priority): Secondary school record, class rank, standardized test scores, school's recommendation, essay.
**Nonacademic basis for candidate selection:** Character and personality, particular talent or ability, and alumni/ae relationship are emphasized. Extracurricular participation and geographical distribution are important.
**Requirements:** Graduation from secondary school is required; GED is accepted. 16 units and the following program of study are required: 4 units of English, 2 units of math, 2 units of science including 1 unit of lab, 2 units of social studies, 2 units of history, 4 units of electives. Minimum composite ACT score of 18, rank in top half of secondary school class, and minimum 2.0 GPA recommended. Audition required of music program applicants. R.N. required of nursing program applicants. ACT is recommended; SAT may be substituted. Campus visit and interview recommended. Off-campus interviews available with an admissions representative.
**Procedure:** Take SAT or ACT by June of 12th year. Visit college for interview by June of 12th year. Notification of admission on rolling basis. No set date by which applicants must accept offer. $125 room deposit, refundable until July 1. Freshmen accepted in terms other than fall.
**Special programs:** Credit may be granted through CLEP general and subject exams, challenge exams, and military experience. Early entrance/early admission program. Concurrent enrollment program.
**Transfer students:** Transfer students accepted for terms other than fall. Application deadline is rolling for fall; rolling for spring. Minimum 2.0 GPA recommended. Lowest course grade accepted is "D." Maximum number of transferable credits is 98 semester hours. At least 30 semester hours must be completed at the college to receive degree.
**Admissions contact:** Gloria Vertrees, Director of Admissions. 314 434-1115, extension 232.

**FINANCIAL AID. Available aid:** Pell grants, SEOG, state grants, school scholarships, academic merit scholarships, and athletic scholarships. Perkins Loans (NDSL), PLUS, Stafford Loans (GSL), and SLS. AMS and deferred payment plan.
**Supporting data/closing dates:** School's own aid application: Priority filing date is April 1. Notification of awards begins April 15.
**Financial aid contact:** Rene Bain, Director of Financial Aid. 314 434-1115, extension 228.

# Missouri Southern State College

**Joplin, MO 64801 417 625-9300**

**1994-95 Costs.** Tuition: $1,754 (state residents), $3,508 (out-of-state). Room & board: $2,700. Fees, books, misc. academic expenses (school's estimate): $1,300.
**Enrollment.** Undergraduates: 1,638 men, 2,012 women (full-time). Freshman class: 1,386 applicants, 1,375 accepted, 781 enrolled.
**Test score averages/ranges.** Average ACT scores: 21 English, 19 math, 21 composite. Range of ACT scores of middle 50%: 19-27 English, 19-27 math.
**Faculty.** 215 full-time; 85 part-time. 46% of faculty holds doctoral degree. Student/faculty ratio: 27 to 1.
**Selectivity rating.** Competitive.

**PROFILE.** Missouri Southern State, founded in 1937, is a public, liberal arts college. Its 238-acre campus is located in Joplin, 68 miles west of Springfield.

**Accreditation:** NCACS. Professionally accredited by the American Dental Association, the American Medical Association (CAHEA), the National Council for Accreditation of Teacher Education.
**Religious orientation:** Missouri Southern State College is nonsectarian; no religious requirements.
**Library:** Collections totaling over 369,587 volumes, 1,312 periodical subscriptions, and 387,575 microform items.
**Special facilities/museums:** Art museum.
**Athletic facilities:** Racquetball and tennis courts, swimming pool, softball, football, and soccer fields.

**STUDENT BODY. Undergraduate profile:** 91% are state residents; 10% are transfers. 1% Asian-American, 10% Black, 3% Hispanic, 2% Native American, 84% White. Average age of undergraduates is 24.
**Freshman profile:** 5% of accepted applicants took SAT; 95% took ACT. 96% of freshmen come from public schools.
**Undergraduate achievement:** 60% of fall 1992 freshmen returned for fall 1993 term. 53% of entering class graduated. 15% of students who completed a degree program immediately went on to graduate study.
**Foreign students:** 23 students are from out of the country. Countries represented include China, Hong Kong, India, Japan, Puerto Rico, and Vietnam; 13 in all.

**PROGRAMS OF STUDY. Degrees:** B.A., B.Gen.Studies, B.S., B.S.Bus.Admin., B.S.Ed.
**Majors:** Accounting, Art, Art Education, Biology, Biology Education, Business, Business Education, Chemistry, Chemistry Education, Communications, Computer Information Science, Criminal Justice Administration, Economics/Finance, Elementary Education, English, English Education, Environmental Health Technology, History, History Education, Management Technology, Marketing/Management, Mathematics, Mathematics

Education, Medical Technology, Music, Music Education, Nursing, Physical Education, Physics, Physics Education, Political Science, Psychology, Psychology/Special Education, Secondary Education, Social Studies Education, Sociology, Spanish, Spanish Education, Theatre, Theatre/Speech Education.
**Distribution of degrees:** The majors with the highest enrollment are business administration, criminal justice administration, and sociology; theatre, mathematics, and chemistry have the lowest.
**Requirements:** General education requirement.
**Academic regulations:** Freshmen must maintain minimum 1.6 GPA; sophomores, 1.7 GPA; juniors, 1.9 GPA; seniors, 2.0 GPA.
**Special:** Minors offered in most majors and in athletic training, education, geography, paralegal studies, social sciences, and social studies. Courses offered in astronomy, French, German, geology, health facilities administration, and philosophy. Associate's degrees offered. Self-designed majors. Double majors. Dual degrees. Independent study. Accelerated study. Internships. Preprofessional programs in law, medicine, veterinary science, pharmacy, dentistry, and optometry. 3-2 engineering program with U of Missouri at Rolla. Teacher certification in elementary, secondary, and special education. Certification in specific subject areas. Study abroad in England and Spain. ROTC.
**Honors:** Honors program. Honor societies.
**Academic Assistance:** Remedial reading, writing, math, and study skills. Nonremedial tutoring.

**STUDENT LIFE. Housing:** All freshmen and sophomores must live on campus. Women's and men's dorms. 10% of students live in college housing.
**Social atmosphere:** The student newspaper reports, "Joplin is a small conservative town so night life is limited; however, there are several larger towns nearby (Kansas City, Tulsa, Springfield) that provide a better nighttime atmosphere for those inclined to those sorts of activities." Students frequent the student union and Billingsly Student Center on campus and Legends, Park Place One, Raphaels, The Kitchen Pass, and O.K. Billiards off campus. Homecoming, Spring Fling, and movies and dances highlight the school year.
**Services and counseling/handicapped student services:** Placement services. Health service. Day care. Counseling services for minority, military, veteran, and older students. Personal and psychological counseling. Career and academic guidance services. Religious counseling. Physically disabled student services. Notetaking services. Tape recorders. Tutors. Reader services for the blind.
**Campus organizations:** Undergraduate student government. Student newspaper (Chart, published once/week). Literary magazine. Yearbook. Radio and TV stations. Concert and jazz bands, lab and marching bands, community orchestra, concert chorale, choir, College Players, debating, Residence Hall Association, Campus Activities Board, departmental and service groups, political groups, 60 organizations in all. Two fraternities, no chapter houses; two sororities, no chapter houses. 1% of men join a fraternity. 1% of women join a sorority.
**Religious organizations:** Baptist Student Union, Campus Crusade for Christ, Chi Alpha, Fellowship of Christian Athletes, Koinonia, Latter-Day Saints Student Association, Wesley Foundation, Ecumenical Campus Ministries, Newman Club.
**Minority/foreign student organizations:** Black Collegiates. International Club.

**ATHLETICS. Physical education requirements:** Two semesters of physical education required.
**Intercollegiate competition:** 5% of students participate. Baseball (M), basketball (M,W), cheerleading (M,W), cross-country (M,W), football (M), golf (M), soccer (M), tennis (W), track and field (indoor) (M,W), track and field (outdoor) (M,W), volleyball (W). Member of Mid-America Intercollegiate Athletic Association Conference, NCAA Division II.
**Intramural and club sports:** 10% of students participate. Intramural basketball, bowling, football, golf, racquetball, softball, swimming, tennis, triathlon, volleyball, walleyball.

**ADMISSIONS. Academic basis for candidate selection** (in order of priority): Class rank, standardized test scores, secondary school record, school's recommendation, essay.
**Nonacademic basis for candidate selection:** Particular talent or ability and alumni/ae relationship are considered.
**Requirements:** Graduation from secondary school is required; GED is accepted. 15 units and the following program of study are recommended: 4 units of English, 3 units of math, 3 units of science, 2 units of social studies, 3 units of electives. Minimum composite ACT score of 17 required; rank in top half of secondary school class required. Pre-entrance exams and other special requirements for honors program and nursing program applicants. Admission Appeal Process for applicants not normally admissible. ACT is required; SAT may be substituted. Campus visit recommended. No off-campus interviews.
**Procedure:** Take SAT or ACT by August 16 of 12th year. Application deadline is August 16. Notification of admission on rolling basis. Reply is required by August 16. $75 room deposit, refundable until August 16. Freshmen accepted in terms other than fall.
**Special programs:** Admission may be deferred one semester. Credit may be granted through CEEB Advanced Placement for scores of 3 or higher. Credit may be granted through CLEP general and subject exams and challenge exams. Concurrent enrollment program.
**Transfer students:** Transfer students accepted for terms other than fall. In fall 1993, 10% of all new students were transfers into all classes. 630 transfer applications were received, 620 were accepted. Application deadline is August 16 for fall; January 6 for spring. Minimum 2.0 GPA recommended. Lowest course grade accepted is "D." Maximum number of transferable credits is 64 semester hours from a two-year school and 92 semester hours from a four-year school. At least 36 semester hours must be completed at the college to receive degree.
**Admissions contact:** Richard D. Humphrey, M.S., Director of Admissions. 417 625-9300.

**FINANCIAL AID. Available aid:** Pell grants, SEOG, state scholarships and grants, school scholarships, private scholarships, ROTC scholarships, academic merit scholarships, and athletic scholarships. Perkins Loans (NDSL), PLUS, Stafford Loans (GSL), private loans, and SLS. AMS.
**Financial aid statistics:** 15% of aid is not need-based. In 1993-94, 78% of all undergraduate applicants received aid; 73% of freshman applicants. Average amounts of aid awarded freshmen: Scholarships and grants, $650; loans, $2,200.
**Supporting data/closing dates:** FAFSA/FAF/FFS: Priority filing date is February 15. School's own aid application: Priority filing date is February 15. Income tax forms: Priority filing date is February 15. IVF and FAT: Priority filing date is February 15. Notification of awards on rolling basis.
**Financial aid contact:** Jim Gilbert, M.S., Director of Financial Aid. 417 625-9300.

**STUDENT EMPLOYMENT.** College Work/Study Program. Institutional employment. 8% of full-time undergraduates work on campus during school year. Students may expect to earn an average of $1,850 during school year. Off-campus part-time employment opportunities rated "excellent."

**COMPUTER FACILITIES.** 350 IBM/IBM-compatible and Macintosh/Apple microcomputers; 8 are networked. Students may access IBM minicomputer/mainframe systems. Residence halls may be equipped with stand-alone microcomputers. Client/LAN operating systems include Novell. Computer languages and software packages include BASIC, COBOL, dBASE, FORTRAN, Lotus 1-2-3, Pascal, RPG II, VisiCalc; 35 in all. Computer facilities are available to all students.
**Fees:** $20 computer fee per semester.
**Hours:** 7 AM-11 PM (M-F); 9 AM-11 PM (Sa); 3 PM-10 PM (Su).

**GRADUATE CAREER DATA.** Graduate school percentages: 1% enter law school. 1% enter medical school. 1% enter dental school. 7% enter graduate business programs. 3% enter graduate arts and sciences programs. Highest graduate school enrollments: Pittsburg State U, Southwest Missouri State U, U of Missouri. 72% of graduates choose careers in business and industry. Companies and businesses that hire graduates: Wal-Mart, Leggett & Platt, St. John's Regional Medical Center.

**PROMINENT ALUMNI/AE.** Dennis Weaver, actor; Mike Storm, director of sales operations, American Motors, Inc., Canada.

# Missouri Valley College

**Marshall, MO 65340** **816 886-6924**

**1994-95 Costs.** Tuition: $9,000. Room & board: $4,950. Fees, books, misc. academic expenses (school's estimate): $600.
**Enrollment.** Undergraduates: 647 men, 411 women (full-time). Freshman class: 1,310 applicants, 983 accepted, 316 enrolled.
**Test score averages/ranges.** Average SAT scores: 770 combined. Average ACT scores: 18 composite.
**Faculty.** 51 full-time; 9 part-time. 40% of faculty holds doctoral degree.
**Selectivity rating.** Less competitive.

**PROFILE.** Missouri Valley, founded in 1888, is a private, church-affiliated, liberal arts college. Its 40-acre campus is located in Marshall, 85 miles east of Kansas City.

**Accreditation:** NCACS.
**Religious orientation:** Missouri Valley College is a nondenominational Christian school; one semester of religion required.
**Library:** Collections totaling over 70,000 volumes, 381 periodical subscriptions and 120 microform items.
**Athletic facilities:** Gymnasium, weight rooms, baseball, football, golf course, intramural, soccer, and softball fields, tennis courts, track, fitness trail, basketball and volleyball courts.

**STUDENT BODY. Undergraduate profile:** 65% are state residents; 36% are transfers. 4% Asian-American, 15% Black, 4% Hispanic, 2% Native American, 74% White, 1% Other. Average age of undergraduates is 20.
**Freshman profile:** 6% of freshmen who took SAT scored 500 or over on verbal, 6% scored 500 or over on math; 44% scored 400 or over on verbal, 44% scored 400 or over on math; 100% scored 300 or over on verbal, 100% scored 300 or over on math. 9% of freshmen who took ACT scored 24 or over on composite; 90% scored 18 or over on composite; 98% scored 12 or over on composite. 14% of accepted applicants took SAT; 86% took ACT. 85% of freshmen come from public schools.
**Undergraduate achievement:** 70% of fall 1992 freshmen returned for fall 1993 term. 20% of entering class graduated. 25% of students who completed a degree program went on to graduate study within five years.
**Foreign students:** 29 students are from out of the country. Countries represented include Bulgaria, Canada, Japan, Korea, Russia, and Spain; 15 in all.

**PROGRAMS OF STUDY. Degrees:** B.A., B.S.
**Majors:** Accounting, Actuarial Science, Agribusiness, Alcohol/Drug Studies, Art, Biology, Business Administration, Computer Science, Criminal Justice, Economics, Elementary Education, English, Finance, History, Human Services/Youth Agency Management, Management, Marketing, Mass Communications, Mathematics, Music, Physical Education, Political Science, Psychology, Public Administration, Recreation Administration, Religion/Philosophy, Secondary Education, Sociology, Special Education, Speech Communication/Theatre.
**Distribution of degrees:** The majors with the highest enrollment are business administration, elementary education, and mass communications.
**Requirements:** General education requirement.
**Special:** Minors offered in all majors. Associate's degrees offered. Double majors. Independent study. Pass/fail grading option. Internships. Preprofessional programs in law, medicine, veterinary science, pharmacy, dentistry, theology, optometry, engineering, and nursing. Member of Kansas City Regional Council on Higher Education. Teacher certification in elementary, secondary, and special education. Certification in specific subject areas. Exchange program abroad in Korea (Jinju Tech Schools).
**Honors:** Honor societies.
**Academic Assistance:** Remedial reading, writing, and math.

**ADMISSIONS. Academic basis for candidate selection** (in order of priority): School's recommendation, secondary school record, class rank, standardized test scores, essay.
**Nonacademic basis for candidate selection:** Character and personality are emphasized. Extracurricular participation is important. Particular talent or ability and alumni/ae relationship are considered.
**Requirements:** Graduation from secondary school is recommended; GED is accepted. 16 units and the following program of study are required: 4 units of English, 3 units of math, 2 units of science including 1 unit of lab, 2 units of social studies, 5 units of electives including 3 units of academic electives. Minimum composite ACT score of 18 (combined SAT score of 700) and rank in top half of secondary school class recommended. General

studies program for applicants not normally admissible. ACT is required; SAT may be substituted. Campus visit and interview recommended. Off-campus interviews available with admissions and alumni representatives.
**Procedure:** Take SAT or ACT by June of 12th year. Visit college for interview by May of 12th year. Suggest filing application by May. Application deadline is September. Notification of admission on rolling basis. Reply is required within 30 days of acceptance. $100 nonrefundable tuition deposit. $50 refundable room deposit. Freshmen accepted in terms other than fall.
**Special programs:** Admission may be deferred. Credit and/or placement may be granted through CLEP general and subject exams. Concurrent enrollment program.
**Transfer students:** Transfer students accepted for terms other than fall. In fall 1993, 36% of all new students were transfers into all classes. 250 transfer applications were received, 200 were accepted. Application deadline is September for fall; February for spring. Minimum 2.0 GPA recommended. Lowest course grade accepted is "C." Maximum number of transferable credits is 60 semester hours from a two-year school and 98 semester hours from a four-year school. At least 30 semester hours must be completed at the college to receive degree.
**Admissions contact:** Chadwick B. Freeman, Vice President for Admissions and Financial Aid. 816 886-6924, extension 114.

**FINANCIAL AID. Available aid:** Pell grants, SEOG, state scholarships and grants, school scholarships, private scholarships and grants, and academic merit scholarships. Perkins Loans (NDSL), PLUS, Stafford Loans (GSL), school loans, private loans, and SLS. Family tuition reduction.
**Financial aid statistics:** 31% of aid is not need-based. In 1993-94, 69% of all undergraduate applicants received aid; 69% of freshman applicants. Average amounts of aid awarded freshmen: Loans, $2,200.
**Supporting data/closing dates:** FAFSA/FAF/FFS: Accepted on rolling basis. School's own aid application: Priority filing date is April 15; accepted on rolling basis. State aid form: Priority filing date is April 15; accepted on rolling basis. Income tax forms: Accepted on rolling basis. Notification of awards on rolling basis.
**Financial aid contact:** Chadwick B. Freeman, Vice President for Admissions and Financial Aid. 816 886-6924, extension 171.

# Missouri Western State College

**St. Joseph, MO 64507-2294 816 271-4200**

**1993-94 Costs.** Tuition: $1,930 (state residents), $3,765 (out-of-state). Room & board: $2,454. Fees, books, misc. academic expenses (school's estimate): $588.
**Enrollment.** Undergraduates: 1,488 men, 2,127 women (full-time). Freshman class: 1,887 applicants, 1,870 accepted, 926 enrolled.
**Test score averages/ranges.** Average ACT scores: 19 English, 18 math, 19 composite. Range of ACT scores of middle 50%: 16-22 English, 15-19 math.
**Faculty.** 161 full-time; 10 part-time. 63% of faculty holds highest degree in specific field. Student/faculty ratio: 19 to 1.
**Selectivity rating.** Noncompetitive.

**PROFILE.** Missouri Western State, founded in 1915, is a public, multipurpose college. Programs are offered through the Divisions of Liberal Arts and Sciences and Professional Studies. Its 740-acre campus is located in St. Joseph, 40 miles north of Kansas City.

**Accreditation:** NCACS. Professionally accredited by the Accreditation Board for Engineering and Technology, the American Bar Association, the Council on Social Work Education, the National Association of Schools of Music, the National Council for Accreditation of Teacher Education, the National League for Nursing.
**Religious orientation:** Missouri Western State College is nonsectarian; no religious requirements.
**Library:** Collections totaling over 173,718 volumes, 1,390 periodical subscriptions, and 98,932 microform items.
**Special facilities/museums:** Planetarium, wilderness study area.
**Athletic facilities:** Gymnasiums, swimming pool, basketball, racquetball, tennis, and volleyball courts, baseball, football, and softball fields.

**STUDENT BODY. Undergraduate profile:** 89% are state residents; 28% are transfers. 1% Asian-American, 6% Black, 1% Hispanic, 1% Native American, 90% White, 1% Other. Average age of undergraduates is 26.
**Freshman profile:** 1% of freshmen who took ACT scored 30 or over on English, 1% scored 30 or over on math, 1% scored 30 or over on composite; 15% scored 24 or over on English, 10% scored 24 or over on math, 12% scored 24 or over on composite; 58% scored 18 or over on English, 45% scored 18 or over on math, 64% scored 18 or over on composite; 97% scored 12 or over on English, 100% scored 12 or over on math, 100% scored 12 or over on composite; 100% scored 6 or over on English. 100% of accepted applicants took ACT. 90% of freshmen come from public schools.
**Undergraduate achievement:** 55% of fall 1992 freshmen returned for fall 1993 term. 14% of entering class graduated. 5% of students who completed a degree program immediately went on to graduate study.
**Foreign students:** 15 students are from out of the country. Countries represented include Canada; 10 in all.

**PROGRAMS OF STUDY. Degrees:** B.A., B.S., B.S.Bus.Admin., B.S.Ed., B.S.Nurs., B.S.Tech., B.Soc.Work.
**Majors:** Accounting, Art, Art Education, Biology, Business, Chemistry, Commercial Art, Computer Information Systems, Computer Science, Construction Engineering Technology, Criminal Justice, Economics, Electronics Engineering Technology, Elementary Education, English, English Education, English/Literature, English/Technical Communications, English/Writing, French, French Education, History, Instrumental Music, Leisure Management, Management, Marketing, Mathematics, Medical Technology, Music, Music Education, Natural Science/Biology, Natural Science/Chemistry, Nursing, Physical Education, Political Science, Psychology, Social Work, Spanish, Spanish Education, Speech Communication, Speech/Theatre, Vocal Music.
**Distribution of degrees:** The majors with the highest enrollment are management, elementary education, and nursing; art, music, and speech/theatre education have the lowest.
**Requirements:** General education requirement.
**Academic regulations:** Minimum 2.0 GPA must be maintained.
**Special:** Minors offered in some majors and in general business, German, geography, humanities, journalism, military science, physics, and sociology. Courses offered in women's studies. Associate's degrees offered. Double majors. Dual degrees. Independent study. Pass/fail grading option. Internships. Preprofessional programs in law, medicine, veterinary science, dentistry, and optometry. 2-2 engineering programs with U of Missouri at Columbia and Rolla. Combined programs in architecture with Kansas State U and in French and Spanish with Northwest Missouri State U. Teacher certification in early childhood, elementary, secondary, and special education. Certification in specific subject areas. ROTC.
**Honors:** Honors program. Honor societies.
**Academic Assistance:** Remedial reading, writing, math, and study skills. Nonremedial tutoring.

**STUDENT LIFE. Housing:** Students may live on or off campus. Coed dorms. School-owned/-operated apartments. 17% of students live in college housing.
**Social atmosphere:** According to the editor of the student newspaper, "Most of the student body members are commuters and non-traditional students." Influential groups on campus are the Student Government Association, Dorm Council, and Campus Activities Board which sponsors assorted singers/musical groups, movies, and comedians. Students congregate on campus at the Student Union; some favorite off-campus gathering spots are Sparky's and Manhattan's Bar. Popular campus events include Homecoming, Spring Fest, Family Day, and basketball games.
**Services and counseling/handicapped student services:** Placement services. Health service. Day care. Non-traditional student center. Counseling services for minority, military, veteran, and older students. Birth control, personal, and psychological counseling. Career and academic guidance services. Learning disabled services.
**Campus organizations:** Undergraduate student government. Student newspaper (Griffon News, published once/week). Literary magazine. Yearbook. Chorale, community chorus, Renaissance Singers, bands, orchestra, ensembles, drama productions, forensics team, dance company, Circle K, Peers Reaching Others, Republican Club, departmental groups, 50 organizations in all. Three fraternities, two chapter houses; two sororities, no chapter houses. 6% of men join a fraternity. 4% of women join a sorority.
**Religious organizations:** Baptist Student Union, Campus Christian House, Fellowship of Christian Athletes, Lutheran Club, Newman Club, Wesley Foundation.
**Minority/foreign student organizations:** Ebony Collegians. International Student Organization.

**ATHLETICS. Physical education requirements:** Four credit hours of physical education required.
**Intercollegiate competition:** 10% of students participate. Baseball (M), basketball (M,W), cheerleading (M,W), football (M), golf (M), softball (W), tennis (W), volleyball (W). Member of Missouri Intercollegiate Athletic Association, NCAA Division II.
**Intramural and club sports:** 10% of students participate. Intramural basketball, flag football, indoor soccer, soccer, softball, volleyball. Men's club soccer.

**ADMISSIONS.**
**Requirements:** Graduation from secondary school is required; GED is accepted. 20 units and the following program of study are recommended: 4 units of English, 3 units of math, 2 units of science, 2 units of foreign language, 3 units of social studies. ACT is required. Minimum composite ACT score of 20 required of education and nursing program applicants. Campus visit and interview recommended. Off-campus interviews available with an admissions representative.
**Procedure:** Take ACT by February of 12th year. Application deadline is July 30. Notification of admission on rolling basis. Reply is required by semester registration date. $75 room deposit, refundable until August 1. Freshmen accepted in terms other than fall.
**Special programs:** Credit may be granted through CEEB Advanced Placement. Credit may be granted through CLEP general and subject exams, military and life experience. Early entrance/early admission program. Concurrent enrollment program.
**Transfer students:** Transfer students accepted for terms other than fall. In fall 1993, 28% of all new students were transfers into all classes. 622 transfer applications were received, 590 were accepted. Application deadline is July 30 for fall; December 20 for spring. Minimum 2.0 GPA recommended. Maximum number of transferable credits is 64 semester hours. At least 30 semester hours must be completed at the college to receive degree.
**Admissions contact:** Howard J. McCauley, M.S., Director of Admissions. 816 271-4263.

**FINANCIAL AID. Available aid:** Pell grants, SEOG, state scholarships and grants, school scholarships and grants, private scholarships, ROTC scholarships, academic merit scholarships, and athletic scholarships. Perkins Loans (NDSL), PLUS, Stafford Loans (GSL), school loans, and SLS. Deferred payment plan. Credit card payment.
**Supporting data/closing dates:** FAFSA/FFS: Deadline is April 1. School's own aid application: Accepted on rolling basis. State aid form: Priority filing date is April 1. Income tax forms. Notification of awards on rolling basis.
**Financial aid contact:** Robert Berger, M.A., Director of Financial Aid. 816 271-4361.

**STUDENT EMPLOYMENT.** College Work/Study Program. Institutional employment. 25% of full-time undergraduates work on campus during school year. Students may expect to earn an average of $1,200 during school year. Off-campus part-time employment opportunities rated "fair."

**COMPUTER FACILITIES.** 200 IBM/IBM-compatible and Macintosh/Apple microcomputers. Students may access Hewlett-Packard, IBM minicomputer/mainframe systems, Internet. Residence halls may be equipped with stand-alone microcomputers. Client/LAN operating systems include Apple/Macintosh, DOS, UNIX/XENIX/AIX, Windows NT, Novell. Computer languages and software packages include BASIC, COBOL, FORTRAN, Pascal, RPG II. Computer facilities are available to all students.
**Fees:** $2 computer fee per semester hour; included in tuition/fees.
**Hours:** 8 AM-11 PM.

**GRADUATE CAREER DATA.** Graduate school percentages: 4% enter medical school. 1% enter dental school. 5% enter graduate business programs. 27% enter graduate arts and sciences programs. 1% enter theological school/seminary. Companies and businesses that hire graduates: AT&T, Hallmark Cards, United Missouri Banks, U.S. government.

**PROMINENT ALUMNI/AE.** Robert W. Keener, president, Northwest Oil Co.; Blaine J. Yarrington, retired president, Standard Oil; Crystal Marquardt, president, Kansas Bar Association; Dr. Harry J. Sauer, Jr., dean of graduate studies, U of Missouri at Rolla.

# Northeast Missouri State University

**Kirksville, MO 63501** **816 785-4000**

**1994-95 Costs.** Tuition: $2,704 (state residents), $4,856 (out-of-state). Room & board: $3,416. Fees, books, misc. academic expenses (school's estimate): $418.

**Enrollment.** Undergraduates: 2,485 men, 3,155 women (full-time). Freshman class: 6,040 applicants, 4,577 accepted, 1,610 enrolled. Graduate enrollment: 71 men, 176 women.

**Test score averages/ranges.** Average ACT scores: 26 composite. Range of ACT scores of middle 50%: 23-28 composite.

**Faculty.** 328 full-time; 129 part-time. 72% of faculty holds highest degree in specific field. Student/faculty ratio: 16 to 1.

**Selectivity rating.** Highly competitive.

**PROFILE.** Northeast Missouri State, founded in 1867, is a public, liberal arts university. Programs are offered through the Divisions of Business and Accountancy, Communication Disorders, Education, Family Sciences, Fine Arts, Health and Exercise Science, Industrial Science, Language and Literature, Libraries and Museums, and Mathematics and Computer Science. Its 140-acre campus, with its Georgian and contemporary buildings, is located in downtown Kirksville.

**Accreditation:** NCACS. Professionally accredited by the American Home Economics Association, the American Speech-Language-Hearing Association, the National Association of Schools of Music, the National Council for Accreditation of Teacher Education, the National League for Nursing.
**Religious orientation:** Northeast Missouri State University is nonsectarian; no religious requirements.
**Library:** Collections totaling over 396,848 volumes, 1,949 periodical subscriptions, and 1,230,842 microform items.
**Special facilities/museums:** Art gallery, local history and artifacts museum, human performance lab, greenhouse, observatory, IR and NMR instrumentation.
**Athletic facilities:** Gymnasium, swimming pool, basketball, racquetball, tennis, and volleyball courts, tracks, weight rooms, baseball, football, soccer, and softball fields.

**STUDENT BODY. Undergraduate profile:** 70% are state residents; 11% are transfers. 2% Asian-American, 3% Black, 1% Hispanic, 1% Native American, 90% White, 3% Other. Average age of undergraduates is 20.
**Freshman profile:** 1% of accepted applicants took SAT; 98% took ACT. 80% of freshmen come from public schools.
**Undergraduate achievement:** 83% of fall 1992 freshmen returned for fall 1993 term. 51% of entering class graduated. 40% of students who completed a degree program immediately went on to graduate study.
**Foreign students:** 233 students are from out of the country. Countries represented include Bulgaria, China, Japan, Spain, Sri Lanka, and Taiwan; 51 in all.

**PROGRAMS OF STUDY. Degrees:** B.A., B.F.A., B.M., B.S., B.S.Nurs.
**Majors:** Accounting, Agricultural Sciences, Art, Art History, Biology, Business Administration, Chemistry, Communication, Communication Disorders, Computer Science, Economics, English, Equine Science, Exercise Science, Finance, French, German, Health, History, Journalism, Justice Systems, Management, Marketing, Mathematics, Music, Music Performance, Nursing, Philosophy/Religion, Physics, Political Science, Psychology, Russian, Sociology/Anthropology, Spanish, Speech, Theatre, Visual Communications.
**Distribution of degrees:** The majors with the highest enrollment are business administration, English, and psychology; German, theatre, and health have the lowest.
**Requirements:** General education requirement.
**Academic regulations:** Minimum 2.0 GPA must be maintained.
**Special:** Minors offered in some majors and in approximately 40 other fields. Double majors. Pass/fail grading option. Internships. Graduate school at which undergraduates may take graduate-level courses. Preprofessional programs in law, medicine, veterinary science, pharmacy, dentistry, and education. 2-2 engineering programs with U of Missouri at Columbia and U of Missouri at Rolla. Member of College Consortium for International Studies. Teacher certification in elementary, secondary, and special education. Certification in specific subject areas. Study abroad in Belgium, Bulgaria, Canada, China, Colombia, Costa Rica, Cyprus, Ecuador, England, France, Germany, Greece, Ireland, Israel, Italy, Jamaica, Japan, Korea, Mexico, Portugal, the former Soviet Republics, Spain, Switzerland, and Taiwan. ROTC.
**Honors:** Honors program. Honor societies.
**Academic Assistance:** Nonremedial tutoring.

**STUDENT LIFE. Housing:** All unmarried freshmen under age 21 must live on campus unless living with family. Coed, women's, and men's dorms. Sorority and fraternity housing. School-owned/operated apartments. On-campus married-student housing. 48% of students live in college housing.
**Social atmosphere:** According to the editor of the student newspaper, "Kirksville is a small town, and the university is the central attraction. Most social and cultural life is on campus and seems to be quite average. Homecoming Week, Dog Days, football and basketball games (if we're winning), Lyceum events (such as the Missouri Ballet, St. Louis Symphony Orchestra, and theatre groups), and graduation are the most popular social events of the year." The Student Activities Board, the Greeks, and athletes are the most dominant groups on campus. Students gather at the Student Union on campus. Off-campus spots are the frat houses, other house parties, bars, and Thousand Island State Park in warm weather.
**Services and counseling/handicapped student services:** Placement services. Health service. Women's center. Day care. Counseling services for minority and veteran students. Personal and psychological counseling. Career and academic guidance services. Physically disabled student services. Notetaking services. Reader services for the blind.
**Campus organizations:** Undergraduate student government. Student newspaper (Index, published once/week). Literary magazine. Yearbook. Radio station. High Street Dancers, Franklin Street Singers, Unique Ensemble, Amnesty International, BACCHUS, Purple Packers, World Peace Group, Young Democrats, College Republicans, 161 organizations in all. 16 fraternities, 13 chapter houses; seven sororities, no chapter houses. 30% of men join a fraternity. 19% of women join a sorority.
**Religious organizations:** Baptist Student Union, Campus Christian Fellowship, Campus Crusade for Christ, Latter-Day Saints Student Association, Lutheran Students Movement, Newman Center, Wesley House, many more religious groups.
**Minority/foreign student organizations:** Association of Black Collegians, Black Law Student Association, Black Association of Science Majors, Social Active Latino Service Association (SALSA). Bridges to International Friendship, International Club, Chinese Student Organization, Japanese Club.

**ATHLETICS. Physical education requirements:** One semester of physical education required.
**Intercollegiate competition:** 9% of students participate. Baseball (M), basketball (M,W), cheerleading (M,W), cross-country (M,W), football (M), golf (M,W), riflery (M,W), soccer (M,W), softball (W), swimming (M,W), tennis (M,W), track (indoor) (M,W), track (outdoor) (M,W), track and field (indoor) (M,W), track and field (outdoor) (M,W), volleyball (W), wrestling (M). Member of Mid-America Intercollegiate Athletic Association, NCAA Division II.
**Intramural and club sports:** 50% of students participate. Intramural badminton, basketball, horseshoes, pickleball, racquetball, soccer, softball, swimming, tennis, track and field, volleyball, weight lifting, wrestling. Men's club rugby. Women's club cheerleading, rugby.

**ADMISSIONS. Academic basis for candidate selection** (in order of priority): Secondary school record, standardized test scores, class rank, essay, school's recommendation.
**Nonacademic basis for candidate selection:** Extracurricular participation is emphasized. Character and personality and particular talent or ability are important. Geographical distribution and alumni/ae relationship are considered.
**Requirements:** Graduation from secondary school is required; GED is accepted. No specific distribution of secondary school units required. Test scores in top 40th percentile, rank in top two-fifths of secondary school class, and minimum 2.5 GPA required of in-state applicants. Test scores in top 25th percentile, rank in top two-fifths of secondary school class, and minimum 3.0 GPA required of out-of-state applicants. Separate application required of nursing program applicants. Scholastic Enhancement Experience designed to enhance the potential for success of talented students of color. ACT is required; SAT may be substituted. PSAT is recommended. Campus visit and interview recommended. Off-campus interviews available with an admissions representative.
**Procedure:** Take SAT or ACT by January of 12th year. Visit college for interview by March 15 of 12th year. Application deadline is March 1. Notification by January 1 if application is received by November 15; on rolling basis thereafter. Reply is required by May 1. $60 tuition deposit, refundable until classes begin. $50 room deposit, refundable partially until May 1. Freshmen accepted in terms other than fall.
**Special programs:** Admission may be deferred one year. Credit and/or placement may be granted through CEEB Advanced Placement exams for scores of 3 or higher. Credit and/or placement may be granted through CLEP general and subject exams. Credit may be granted through DANTES exams and military experience. Placement may be granted through challenge exams. Early entrance/early admission program. Concurrent enrollment program.
**Transfer students:** Transfer students accepted for terms other than fall. In fall 1993, 11% of all new students were transfers into all classes. 511 transfer applications were received, 296 were accepted. Application deadline is May 1 for fall; November 15 for spring. Minimum 2.5 GPA recommended. Lowest course grade accepted is "D." Maximum number of transferable credits is 64 semester hours. At least 45 semester hours must be completed at the university to receive degree.
**Admissions contact:** Kathy Rieck, M.A., Dean of Admission and Records. 816 785-4114.

**FINANCIAL AID. Available aid:** Pell grants, SEOG, state scholarships and grants, school scholarships, private scholarships and grants, ROTC scholarships, academic merit scholarships, and athletic scholarships. Perkins Loans (NDSL), PLUS, Stafford Loans (GSL), NSL, state loans, school loans, private loans, and SLS. AMS. University installment plan.
**Financial aid statistics:** Average amounts of aid awarded freshmen: Scholarships and grants, $2,348; loans, $2,800.
**Supporting data/closing dates:** FAFSA/FAF/FFS: Priority filing date is April 1. Notification of awards on rolling basis.
**Financial aid contact:** Melinda Wood, Director of Financial Aid. 816 785-4130.

**STUDENT EMPLOYMENT.** College Work/Study Program. Institutional employment. 35% of full-time undergraduates work on campus during school year. Students may expect to earn an average of $886 during school year. Off-campus part-time employment opportunities rated "good."

**COMPUTER FACILITIES.** 900 IBM/IBM-compatible and Macintosh/Apple microcomputers; 310 are networked. Students may access IBM minicomputer/mainframe systems, BITNET, Internet. Residence halls may be equipped with stand-alone microcomputers, networked microcomputers, networked terminals. Computer languages and software packages include Assembler, BASIC, C, COBOL, FORTRAN, Pascal, SAS, SPSS; 35 in all. Computer facilities are available to all students.
**Fees:** None.
**Hours:** 8 AM-2 AM (M-Th); 8 AM-10 PM (F); 10 AM-10 PM (Sa); noon-2 AM. (Su); 24 hours in residence halls.

**GRADUATE CAREER DATA.** Graduate school percentages: 3% enter law school. 5% enter medical school. 1% enter dental school. 5% enter graduate business programs. 22% enter graduate arts and sciences programs. 1% enter theological school/seminary. Highest graduate school enrollments: Indiana U, Kirksville Coll, St. Louis U, U of Illinois at Urbana-Champaign, U of Iowa, U of Missouri at Columbia, U of Missouri at St. Louis, Southern Illinois U, Washington U. 25% of graduates choose careers in business and industry. Companies and businesses that hire graduates: Big Six accounting firms, Edward D. Jones, Principle Financial Group, Lerner Corporation, United Cellular.

**PROMINENT ALUMNI/AE.** Robert Libby, Pringles inventor; Ray Armstead, Olympic gold medalist; Dr. Phyllis Mullenix, Forsyth Research Institute; Ray Bentelli, former CEO, Mallinkrodt Corp.; Bud Hunter, president, Amedco Corp.

# Northwest Missouri State University

**Maryville, MO 64468** **816 562-1212**

**1994-95 Costs.** Tuition: $2,130 (state residents), $3,735 (out-of-state). Room & board: $3,136.
**Enrollment.** Undergraduates: 2,159 men, 2,582 women (full-time). Freshman class: 2,730 applicants, 2,589 accepted, 1,252 enrolled. Graduate enrollment: 199 men, 466 women.
**Test score averages/ranges.** Average ACT scores: 21 English, 20 math, 21 composite.
**Faculty.** 244 full-time; 30 part-time. 75% of faculty holds highest degree in specific field. Student/faculty ratio: 22 to 1.
**Selectivity rating.** Less competitive.

**PROFILE.** Northwest Missouri State, founded in 1905, is a public university. Programs are offered through the Colleges of Agriculture Science and Technology; Arts and Humanities; Business, Government, and Computer Science; and Education. Its 240-acre campus is located in Maryville, 95 miles north of Kansas City.

**Accreditation:** NCACS. Professionally accredited by the American Dietetic Association, the American Home Economics Association, the National Association of Schools of Music, the National Council for Accreditation of Teacher Education.
**Religious orientation:** Northwest Missouri State University is nonsectarian; no religious requirements.
**Library:** Collections totaling over 296,324 volumes, 3,281 periodical subscriptions, and 498,660 microform items.
**Special facilities/museums:** State history and art collections, earth/science museum, broadcasting museum, on-campus elementary lab school, biomass energy plant.
**Athletic facilities:** Gymnasiums, stadium, track, aquatic center, tennis courts, baseball, intramural, and softball fields.
**STUDENT BODY. Undergraduate profile:** 60% are state residents; 19% are transfers. 1% Asian-American, 2% Black, 1% Hispanic, 96% White. Average age of undergraduates is 21.
**Freshman profile:** 3% of accepted applicants took SAT; 97% took ACT. 90% of freshmen come from public schools.
**Undergraduate achievement:** 70% of fall 1991 freshmen returned for fall 1992 term. 45% of entering class graduated.
**Foreign students:** 150 students are from out of the country. Countries represented include Hong Kong, Japan, and Taiwan; 30 in all.
**PROGRAMS OF STUDY. Degrees:** B.A., B.F.A., B.S., B.S.Elem.Ed., B.S.Med.Tech., B.S.Sec.Ed., B.Tech.
**Majors:** Accounting, Agribusiness, Agricultural Business, Agricultural Economics, Agriculture/Computer Science, Agronomy, Animal Science, Art, Art Education, Biology, Botany, Broadcasting, Business Economics, Business/Industrial Technology, Business Management, Chemistry, Computer Science, Early Childhood/Elementary Education, Earth Science Teaching, Economics, English, Family/Environmental Resources, Finance, Foods/Nutrition, French, General Agriculture, Geography, Geology, Government, History, Horticulture, Humanities/Philosophy, Instrumental Music Education, Journalism, Learning Disabilities, Marketing, Mathematics, Mathematics Education, Medical Technology, Merchandising of Textiles/Apparel/Furnishings, Middle/Junior High School Education, Music, Office Information Systems, Personnel Management, Philosophy, Physics, Psychology, Psychology/Biology, Psychology/Sociology, Public Administration, Public Relations, Recreation, Secondary Biology Education, Secondary Chemistry Education, Secondary Education, Secondary Physical Education, Social Sciences, Sociology, Spanish, Speech, Speech Communication, Speech/Theatre, Statistics, Theatre, Theatre Education, Theatre/Speech, Vocal Music Education, Vocational Agricultural Education, Vocational Home Economics Education, Wildlife Ecology, Zoology.
**Distribution of degrees:** The majors with the highest enrollment are elementary education, business management, and accounting; humanities/philosophy, mathematics, and French have the lowest.
**Requirements:** General education requirement.
**Special:** Minors offered in most majors and many specialized areas. Double majors. Cooperative education programs. Graduate school at which undergraduates may take graduate-level courses. Preprofessional programs in law, medicine, veterinary science, pharmacy, dentistry, theology, and optometry. 2-2 engineering program with U of Missouri at Rolla. 3-1 medical technology programs with approved hospitals. Washington Semester. Teacher certification in early childhood, elementary, secondary, and special education. Study abroad in England. ROTC.
**Academic Assistance:** Remedial reading, writing, math, and study skills.
**STUDENT LIFE. Housing:** All freshmen must live on campus. Coed, women's, and men's dorms. Sorority housing. 51% of students live in college housing.
**Social atmosphere:** "Many students make road trips to St. Joseph, Missouri. There are concerts there as well as in Kansas City," reports the student newspaper. Popular gathering spots on and off campus are the Bearcat Den, the Pub, and The Palms. Greeks and Amnesty International are influential groups on campus. Homecoming, Fall Freeze, and the Madrigal Feaste Celebration are among the year's favorite events.
**Services and counseling/handicapped student services:** Placement services. Health service. Counseling services for minority and veteran students. Personal counseling. Career and academic guidance services. Learning disabled services.
**Campus organizations:** Undergraduate student government. Student newspaper (Northwest Missourian, published once/week). Yearbook. Radio and TV stations. Marching band, Celebration (show choir), 100 organizations in all. Eight fraternities, all with chapter houses; four sororities, no chapter houses. 25% of men join a fraternity. 20% of women join a sorority.
**Religious organizations:** Baptist Student Union, Christ Way Inn, Fellowship of Christian Athletes, Newman Council, Religious Life Council, Lutheran Campus Center, Wesley Center.
**Minority/foreign student organizations:** Harambee, Alliance of Black Collegians. International Student Organization, Chinese Student Organization.
**ATHLETICS. Physical education requirements:** Two semesters of physical education required.
**Intercollegiate competition:** 8% of students participate. Baseball (M), basketball (M,W), cheerleading (M,W), cross-country (M,W), football (M), softball (W), tennis (M,W), track (indoor) (M,W), track (outdoor) (M,W), track and field (indoor) (M,W), track and field (outdoor) (M,W), volleyball (W). Member of Mid-America Intercollegiate Athletic Association, NCAA Division II.
**Intramural and club sports:** 75% of students participate. Intramural basketball, bench press, cross-country, flag football, free throw contest, golf, homerun contest, hot-shot basketball, pickleball, punt-pass-kick, racquetball, sand volleyball, softball, swimming, tennis, towerball, track, tug-of-war, volleyball, walleyball, water basketball, water volleyball, Wiffle ball. Men's club rodeo, soccer. Women's club rodeo, soccer.
**ADMISSIONS. Academic basis for candidate selection** (in order of priority): Secondary school record, standardized test scores, class rank.
**Nonacademic basis for candidate selection:** Extracurricular participation and particular talent or ability are considered.
**Requirements:** Graduation from secondary school is required; GED is accepted. No specific distribution of secondary school units required. Minimum 2.0 GPA required of all applicants; minimum composite ACT score of 20 or rank in top three-quarters of secondary school class recommended of in-state applicants; minimum composite ACT score of 21 or rank in top half of secondary school class recommended of out-of-state applicants. ACT is required; SAT may be substituted. Campus visit recommended. Off-campus interviews available with an admissions representative.
**Procedure:** Take SAT or ACT by spring of 12th year. Application deadline is August 1. Notification of admission on rolling basis. No set date by which applicants must accept offer. $75 room deposit, refundable until July 1. Freshmen accepted in terms other than fall.
**Special programs:** Credit may be granted through CLEP general and subject exams, challenge exams, and military experience. Early entrance/early admission program. Concurrent enrollment program.
**Transfer students:** Transfer students accepted for terms other than fall. In fall 1993, 19% of all new students were transfers into all classes. 680 transfer applications were received, 586 were accepted. Application deadline is August 1 for fall; January 1 for spring. Minimum 2.0 GPA required. Lowest course grade accepted is "D." Maximum number of transferable credits is 64 semester hours. At least 30 semester hours must be completed at the university to receive degree.
**Admissions contact:** Michael D. Walsh, M.A., Director of Admissions. 800 633-1175.
**FINANCIAL AID. Available aid:** Pell grants, SEOG, state scholarships and grants, school scholarships, private scholarships, ROTC scholarships, academic merit scholarships, and athletic scholarships. Perkins Loans (NDSL), PLUS, Stafford Loans (GSL), and SLS. Tuition Plan Inc.
**Financial aid statistics:** 30% of aid is not need-based. In 1993-94, 70% of all undergraduate applicants received aid. Average amounts of aid awarded freshmen: Scholarships and grants, $1,500; loans, $2,500.
**Supporting data/closing dates:** FAFSA/FAF/FFS: Priority filing date is April 1. Notification of awards on rolling basis.
**STUDENT EMPLOYMENT.** College Work/Study Program. Institutional employment. 15% of full-time undergraduates work on campus during school year. Students may expect to earn an average of $1,500 during school year. Off-campus part-time employment opportunities rated "fair."
**COMPUTER FACILITIES.** 100 IBM/IBM-compatible and Macintosh/Apple microcomputers; 60 are networked. Students may access Digital minicomputer/mainframe systems. Residence halls may be equipped with networked terminals. 15 major computer languages and software packages available. Computer facilities are available to all students.
**Fees:** None.
**Hours:** 24 hours.
**GRADUATE CAREER DATA.** 80% of graduates choose careers in business and industry. Companies and businesses that hire graduates: CDS, Federal Reserve, Growmark, IBP, McGoadrey & Pullen, Metropolitan Life, Mutual of Omaha, State Farm Insurance.
**PROMINENT ALUMNI/AE.** Laurie Engle, assistant to Missouri senator John Danforth; Terri McPheters, composer; Gary Gaetti, third baseman, Minnesota Twins; John McCuen, partner, McGoadrey & Pullen.

# Park College

**Parkville, MO 64152** **816 741-2000**

**1994-95 Costs.** Tuition: $3,750. Room & board: $3,900. Fees, books, misc. academic expenses (school's estimate): $600.
**Enrollment.** Undergraduates: 350 men, 350 women (full-time). Freshman class: 350 applicants, 295 accepted, 123 enrolled. Graduate enrollment: 60 men, 25 women.
**Test score averages/ranges.** Average SAT scores: 440 verbal, 400 math. Range of SAT scores of middle 50%: 400-480 verbal, 380-420 math. Average ACT scores: 21 English, 20 math, 20 composite. Range of ACT scores of middle 50%: 18-23 English, 17-22 math.
**Faculty.** 52 full-time; 23 part-time. 65% of faculty holds doctoral degree. Student/faculty ratio: 12 to 1.
**Selectivity rating.** Less competitive.

**PROFILE.** Park, founded in 1875, is a church-affiliated, liberal arts college. Its 800-acre campus is located in Parkville, 12 miles from Kansas City.

**Accreditation:** NCACS.
**Religious orientation:** Park College is affiliated with the Reorganized Church of Jesus Christ of Latter-Day Saints; no religious requirements.
**Library:** Collections totaling over 120,000 volumes, 580 periodical subscriptions, and 4,200 microform items.
**Special facilities/museums:** Campus history museum, sports medicine clinic.
**Athletic facilities:** Gymnasium, swimming pool, sand volleyball and tennis courts, soccer fields, track.

**STUDENT BODY. Undergraduate profile:** 60% are state residents; 60% are transfers. 1% Asian-American, 30% Black, 10% Hispanic, 55% White, 4% Other. Average age of undergraduates is 23.
**Freshman profile:** 2% of freshmen who took SAT scored 600 or over on verbal, 17% scored 600 or over on math; 19% scored 500 or over on verbal, 34% scored 500 or over on math; 92% scored 400 or over on verbal, 90% scored 400 or over on math; 100% scored 300 or over on verbal, 100% scored 300 or over on math. 10% of accepted applicants took SAT; 90% took ACT. 70% of freshmen come from public schools.
**Undergraduate achievement:** 66% of fall 1992 freshmen returned for fall 1993 term. 36% of entering class graduated. 20% of students who completed a degree program immediately went on to graduate study.
**Foreign students:** 70 students are from out of the country. Countries represented include Bulgaria, Ecuador, Jamaica, Korea, Micronesia, and Nigeria; 28 in all.

**PROGRAMS OF STUDY. Degrees:** B.A.
**Majors:** Accounting, Art, Athletic Training, Biology, Business Administration, Chemistry, Communication Arts, Computer-Based Information Systems, Computer Science, Criminal Justice, Economics, Education, Elementary Education, English, History, Human Services, Interior Design, International Business, Legal Studies/Pre-Law, Liberal Studies, Mathematics, Political Science/Public Administration, Psychology, Secondary Education, Social Sciences, Sociology.
**Distribution of degrees:** The majors with the highest enrollment are business administration, criminal justice, and education; sociology, human services, and chemistry have the lowest.
**Requirements:** General education requirement.
**Academic regulations:** Freshmen must maintain minimum 1.8 GPA; sophomores, 1.9 GPA; juniors, 2.0 GPA; seniors, 2.0 GPA.
**Special:** Minors offered in most majors and in music, peace studies, philosophy, religion, and theatre. Associate's degrees offered. Self-designed majors. Double majors. Dual degrees. Independent study. Internships. Graduate school at which undergraduates may take graduate-level courses. Preprofessional programs in law, medicine, veterinary science, pharmacy, dentistry, and optometry. Member of Kansas City Regional Commission on Higher Education. Washington Semester and UN Semester. Teacher certification in early childhood, elementary, and secondary education. Certification in specific subject areas. ROTC.
**Honors:** Honors program. Honor societies.
**Academic Assistance:** Remedial reading, writing, math, and study skills. Nonremedial tutoring.

**ADMISSIONS. Academic basis for candidate selection** (in order of priority): Secondary school record, class rank, standardized test scores, essay, school's recommendation.
**Nonacademic basis for candidate selection:** Character and personality, extracurricular participation, and particular talent or ability are important. Alumni/ae relationship is considered.
**Requirements:** Graduation from secondary school is recommended; GED is accepted. 18 units and the following program of study are recommended: 3 units of English, 2 units of math, 2 units of science, 2 units of foreign language, 3 units of social studies, 6 units of electives. Two of the following are required: minimum composite ACT score of 20, rank in top half of secondary school class, or minimum 2.0 GPA. L.P.N. required of nursing program applicants. ACT is required; SAT may be substituted. Campus visit and interview recommended. Off-campus interviews available with an admissions representative.
**Procedure:** Take SAT or ACT by December of 12th year. Visit college for interview by February of 12th year. Suggest filing application by February 1. Application deadline is August 1. Notification of admission on rolling basis. Reply is recommended 30 days after notification. $150 room deposit, refundable until June 1. Freshmen accepted in terms other than fall.
**Special programs:** Admission may be deferred no limit. Credit and/or placement may be granted through CEEB Advanced Placement exams for scores of 3 or higher. Credit and/or placement may be granted through CLEP general and subject exams. Credit and placement may be granted through DANTES and challenge exams and military and life experience. Early entrance/early admission program.
**Transfer students:** Transfer students accepted for terms other than fall. In fall 1993, 60% of all new students were transfers into all classes. 350 transfer applications were received, 310 were accepted. Application deadline is August 1 for fall; first day of classes for spring. Minimum 2.0 GPA required. Lowest course grade accepted is "C." Maximum number of transferable credits is 75 semester hours. Unlimited number of semester hours transferable from four-year schools. At least 24 semester hours must be completed at the college to receive degree.
**Admissions contact:** Randy Condit, M.P.A., Director of Admissions. 800 745-7275.

**FINANCIAL AID. Available aid:** Pell grants, SEOG, Federal Nursing Student Scholarships, state scholarships and grants, school scholarships and grants, private scholarships and grants, ROTC scholarships, academic merit scholarships, athletic scholarships, and aid for undergraduate foreign students. Perkins Loans (NDSL), PLUS, Stafford Loans (GSL), and SLS. AMS and Tuition Management Systems.
**Financial aid statistics:** 30% of aid is not need-based. In 1993-94, 90% of all undergraduate applicants received aid; 95% of freshman applicants. Average amounts of aid awarded freshmen: Scholarships and grants, $1,000; loans, $2,500.
**Supporting data/closing dates:** FAFSA/FAF/FFS: Priority filing date is April 1; accepted on rolling basis. School's own aid application: Priority filing date is April 1; accepted on rolling basis. Notification of awards on rolling basis.
**Financial aid contact:** Pat Hollenbeck, Director of Financial Aid. 816 741-2000.

# Rockhurst College

**Kansas City, MO 64110-2508 816 926-4000**

**1994-95 Costs.** Tuition: $9,490. Room & board: $4,100. Fees, books, misc. academic expenses (school's estimate): $800.
**Enrollment.** Undergraduates: 470 men, 711 women (full-time). Freshman class: 830 applicants, 716 accepted, 202 enrolled. Graduate enrollment: 384 men, 274 women.
**Test score averages/ranges.** Range of SAT scores of middle 50%: 400-500 verbal, 400-500 math. Range of ACT scores of middle 50%: 22-26 composite.
**Faculty.** 128 full-time; 72 part-time. 79% of faculty holds highest degree in specific field. Student/faculty ratio: 14 to 1.
**Selectivity rating.** Competitive.

**PROFILE.** Rockhurst, founded in 1910, is a private, church-affiliated, liberal arts college. Its 25-acre campus is located in Kansas City.

**Accreditation:** NCACS. Professionally accredited by the American Physical Therapy Association, the National League for Nursing.
**Religious orientation:** Rockhurst College is affiliated with the Roman Catholic Church (Society of Jesus); three semesters of theology required.
**Library:** Collections totaling over 101,235 volumes, 728 periodical subscriptions, and 77,691 microform items.
**Special facilities/museums:** Gallery.
**Athletic facilities:** Field house, weight room, handball, racquetball, tennis, and volleyball courts, soccer and softball fields.

**STUDENT BODY. Undergraduate profile:** 70% are state residents; 63% are transfers. 1% Asian-American, 6% Black, 4% Hispanic, 1% Native American, 87% White, 1% Other. Average age of undergraduates is 25.
**Freshman profile:** 4% of freshmen who took SAT scored 700 or over on math; 8% scored 600 or over on verbal, 26% scored 600 or over on math; 34% scored 500 or over on verbal, 60% scored 500 or over on math; 70% scored 400 or over on verbal, 88% scored 400 or over on math; 96% scored 300 or over on verbal, 98% scored 300 or over on math. 25% of accepted applicants took SAT; 95% took ACT. 45% of freshmen come from public schools.
**Undergraduate achievement:** 82% of fall 1991 freshmen returned for fall 1992 term. 51% of entering class graduated. 21% of students who completed a degree program immediately went on to graduate study.
**Foreign students:** 18 students are from out of the country. Countries represented include Argentina, Belize, Canada, Germany, Mexico, and the Philippines; 12 in all.

**PROGRAMS OF STUDY. Degrees:** B.A., B.S., B.S.Bus.Admin., B.S.Nurs.
**Majors:** Accounting, Biology, Business Economics, Chemistry, Communication, Computer Science, Cytotechnology, Education, English, Finance, Finance/Economics, French, Global Studies, History, Industrial Relations, Management, Marketing, Mathematics, Medical Technology, Nursing, Occupational Therapy, Personnel/Human Resources, Philosophy, Physical Therapy, Physics, Political Science, Psychology, Purchasing/Materials Management, Sociology, Spanish, Theology.
**Distribution of degrees:** The majors with the highest enrollment are accounting, nursing, and physical therapy; Spanish, communication, and business economics have the lowest.
**Requirements:** General education requirement.
**Academic regulations:** Minimum 2.0 GPA must be maintained.
**Special:** Double majors. Dual degrees. Internships. Cooperative education programs. Graduate school at which undergraduates may take graduate-level courses. Preprofessional programs in law, medicine, veterinary science, pharmacy, dentistry, and optometry. 2-2 engineering programs with U of Detroit, Marquette U, and U of Missouri at Rolla. Six-year bachelor's/master's programs in physical therapy and occupational therapy. Member of Kansas City Regional Council for Higher Education; exchange possible. Washington Semester. Teacher certification in elementary and secondary education. Certification in specific subject areas. Exchange programs abroad in England (Richmond Coll), France (Inst for American Universities), and Mexico (U of Veracruz). Study abroad also in Hong Kong, Italy, Japan, Spain, Switzerland, and Thailand. ROTC at U of Missouri at Kansas City.
**Honors:** Honors program. Honor societies.
**Academic Assistance:** Remedial writing and study skills.

**STUDENT LIFE. Housing:** All unmarried students under age 23 with fewer than 92 semester hours must live on campus unless living with family. Coed, women's, and men's dorms. Fraternity housing. School-owned/operated apartments. Townhouse Village. 43% of students live in college housing.
**Services and counseling/handicapped student services:** Placement services. Health service. Counseling services for minority students. Personal and psychological counseling. Career and academic guidance services. Religious counseling. Physically disabled student services. Learning disabled services. Tutors.
**Campus organizations:** Undergraduate student government. Student newspaper (Hawk, published biweekly). Literary magazine. Yearbook. Radio station. Choral groups, pep band, Rockhurst Players, Organization of Collegiate Women, American Humanics group, Junior Executive Association, Social Activities Board, pom-pom squad, departmental groups, 40 organizations in all. Three fraternities, all with chapter houses. 30% of men join a fraternity.
**Religious organizations:** Campus Ministry.
**Minority/foreign student organizations:** Black Student Union, Student Organization of Latinos. Multicultural Student Affairs.

**ATHLETICS. Physical education requirements:** None.
**Intercollegiate competition:** 15% of students participate. Baseball (M), basketball (M,W), soccer (M,W), tennis (M,W), volleyball (W). Member of Independent, NAIA.

**Intramural and club sports:** 50% of students participate. Intramural billiards, handball, floor hockey, golf, soccer, softball, tennis, touch football, volleyball. Men's club golf. Women's club golf.

**ADMISSIONS. Academic basis for candidate selection** (in order of priority): Secondary school record, standardized test scores, class rank, school's recommendation, essay.
**Nonacademic basis for candidate selection:** Character and personality, extracurricular participation, and particular talent or ability are important. Alumni/ae relationship is considered.
**Requirements:** Graduation from secondary school is required; GED is accepted. 15 units and the following program of study are recommended: 4 units of English, 3 units of math, 3 units of science, 2 units of foreign language, 2 units of social studies, 1 unit of history. Minimum composite ACT score of 20 (combined SAT score of 800) and rank in top two-fifths of secondary school class required. Freshman Incentive Program for applicants not normally admissible. ACT is required; SAT may be substituted. Campus visit and interview recommended. Off-campus interviews available with an admissions representative.
**Procedure:** Take SAT or ACT by April of 12th year. Visit college for interview by June of 12th year. Suggest filing application by February 1. Application deadline is June 30. Notification of admission on rolling basis. Reply is required by July 31. $100 nonrefundable tuition deposit. $100 room deposit, refundable until July 31. Freshmen accepted in terms other than fall.
**Special programs:** Admission may be deferred one year. Placement may be granted through CEEB Advanced Placement exams for scores of 3 or higher. Credit and/or placement may be granted through CLEP subject exams. Concurrent enrollment program.
**Transfer students:** Transfer students accepted for terms other than fall. In fall 1992, 63% of all new students were transfers into all classes. 642 transfer applications were received, 474 were accepted. Application deadline is June 30 for fall; December 15 for spring. Minimum 2.25 GPA required. Lowest course grade accepted is "C." Maximum number of transferable credits is 64 semester hours from a two-year school and 90 semester hours from a four-year school. At least 30 semester hours must be completed at the college to receive degree.
**Admissions contact:** Barbara O'Connell, Director of Enrollment Services. 816 926-4100, 800 842-6776.

**FINANCIAL AID. Available aid:** Pell grants, SEOG, state grants, school scholarships and grants, private scholarships and grants, academic merit scholarships, and athletic scholarships. Perkins Loans (NDSL), PLUS, Stafford Loans (GSL), and SLS. AMS, deferred payment plan, family tuition reduction, and guaranteed tuition.
**Financial aid statistics:** 25% of aid is not need-based. In 1992-93, 75% of all undergraduate applicants received aid; 75% of freshman applicants. Average amounts of aid awarded freshmen: Scholarships and grants, $5,658; loans, $3,205.
**Supporting data/closing dates:** FAFSA/FAF/FFS: Priority filing date is April 1; accepted on rolling basis. Notification of awards begins February 15.
**Financial aid contact:** Gene Buck, M.A., Director of Financial Aid. 816 926-4100.

**STUDENT EMPLOYMENT.** College Work/Study Program. Institutional employment. 30% of full-time undergraduates work on campus during school year. Students may expect to earn an average of $1,250 during school year. Off-campus part-time employment opportunities rated "good."

**COMPUTER FACILITIES.** 115 IBM/IBM-compatible, Macintosh/Apple, and RISC-/UNIX-based microcomputers; 95 are networked. Students may access Digital minicomputer/mainframe systems, BITNET. Residence halls may be equipped with stand-alone microcomputers. Client/LAN operating systems include Apple/Macintosh. Computer languages and software packages include Assembler, COBOL, FORTRAN, Lotus 1-2-3, MINITAB, Modula 2, Pascal, RDB, SAS, SPSS, WordPerfect. Computer facilities are available to all students.
**Fees:** None.
**Hours:** 8 AM-midn. (M-F); 8 AM-4:30 PM (Sa); noon-midn. (Su).

**GRADUATE CAREER DATA.** Graduate school percentages: 3% enter law school. 3% enter medical school. 1% enter dental school. 4% enter graduate business programs. 10% enter graduate arts and sciences programs. Highest graduate school enrollments: Georgetown U, St. Louis U, U of Illinois, U of Kansas, Loyola U at Chicago, U of Missouri. 47% of graduates choose careers in business and industry. Companies and businesses that hire graduates: Big Six accounting firms, Black & Veatch Engineering, Hallmark Cards, Federal Reserve Bank.

**PROMINENT ALUMNI/AE.** John Hayes, Jr., president, KPL Gas Service; John J. Sullivan, Jr., chairperson, Mid-American Bank Trust; Joseph Flaherty, vice president, CBS.

# Saint Louis College of Pharmacy

**St. Louis, MO 63110** — **314 367-8700**

**1993-94 Costs.** Tuition: $7,250. Room & board: $4,700. Fees, books, misc. academic expenses (school's estimate): $680.
**Enrollment.** Undergraduates: 302 men, 453 women (full-time). Freshman class: 298 applicants, 206 accepted, 140 enrolled. Graduate enrollment: 10 men, 6 women.
**Test score averages/ranges.** Average ACT scores: 25 composite.
**Faculty.** 52 full-time; 30 part-time. 83% of faculty holds doctoral degree. Student/faculty ratio: 13 to 1.
**Selectivity rating.** Competitive.

**PROFILE.** The St. Louis College of Pharmacy, founded in 1864, is a private college of pharmacy. Its eight-acre campus is located in St. Louis.

**Accreditation:** NCACS. Professionally accredited by the American Council on Pharmaceutical Education.
**Religious orientation:** Saint Louis College of Pharmacy is nonsectarian; no religious requirements.
**Library:** Collections totaling over 38,900 volumes and 460 periodical subscriptions.
**Athletic facilities:** Student center, fitness center, free weights, stairmaster machines, stationary bikes, cross country ski machine.

**STUDENT BODY. Undergraduate profile:** 38% are state residents; 20% are transfers. 5% Asian-American, 6% Black, 1% Hispanic, 86% White, 2% Foreign. Average age of undergraduates is 21.
**Freshman profile:** 2% of accepted applicants took SAT; 98% took ACT. 92% of freshmen come from public schools.
**Undergraduate achievement:** 86% of fall 1991 freshmen returned for fall 1992 term. 87% of entering class graduated. 12% of students who completed a degree program immediately went on to graduate study.
**Foreign students:** 15 students are from out of the country. Countries represented include Asian countries; nine in all.

**PROGRAMS OF STUDY. Degrees:** B.S.Pharm.
**Majors:** Pharmacy.
**Requirements:** General education requirement.
**Special:** Five-year B.S.Pharm. program consists of one year of preprofessional and four years of professional studies. Six-year Pharm.S. program involves one year of preprofessional study, four years of professional study, and one year of clinical residency. Pass/fail grading option. Graduate school at which undergraduates may take graduate-level courses.
**Honors:** Honor societies.
**Academic Assistance:** Remedial math and study skills. Nonremedial tutoring.

**ADMISSIONS. Academic basis for candidate selection** (in order of priority): Standardized test scores, secondary school record, class rank.
**Nonacademic basis for candidate selection:** Character and personality, extracurricular participation, and alumni/ae relationship are considered.
**Requirements:** Graduation from secondary school is required; GED is accepted. No specific distribution of secondary school units required. Minimum composite ACT score of 21, rank in top half of secondary school class, and minimum 2.5 GPA required. EOP and HEOP for applicants not normally admissible. Conditional admission possible for applicants not meeting standard requirements. ACT is required; SAT may be substituted. Campus visit and interview recommended. Off-campus interviews available with admissions and alumni representatives.
**Procedure:** Take SAT or ACT by April of 12th year. Visit college for interview by January of 12th year. Suggest filing application by December 1. Application deadline is August 1. Notification of admission on rolling basis. Reply is required by May 1. $300 tuition deposit, refundable until June 1. $50 refundable room deposit. Freshmen accepted in terms other than fall.
**Special programs:** Credit may be granted through CEEB Advanced Placement for scores of 3 or higher. Credit may be granted through CLEP general and subject exams. Early decision program. Deadline for applying for early decision is December 1.
**Transfer students:** Transfer students accepted for terms other than fall. In fall 1992, 20% of all new students were transfers into all classes. 382 transfer applications were received, 50 were accepted. Application deadline is March 1 for fall; October 1 for spring. Minimum 2.5 GPA required. Lowest course grade accepted is "C." Maximum number of transferable credits is 50 semester hours. At least 108 semester hours must be completed at the college to receive degree.
**Admissions contact:** Becky Rupp, Director of Admissions. 314 367-8700, extension 264.

**FINANCIAL AID. Available aid:** Pell grants, SEOG, state scholarships and grants, school scholarships, private scholarships, and academic merit scholarships. Perkins Loans (NDSL), PLUS, Stafford Loans (GSL), Health Professions Loans, state loans, school loans, private loans, and SLS. Deferred payment plan.
**Financial aid statistics:** In 1992-93, 85% of all undergraduate applicants received aid; 84% of freshman applicants. Average amounts of aid awarded freshmen: Scholarships and grants, $1,500; loans, $2,600.
**Supporting data/closing dates:** FAFSA/FAF: Priority filing date is March 1; deadline is May 1. School's own aid application: Priority filing date is March 1; deadline is May 1. Notification of awards on rolling basis.
**Financial aid contact:** DeDe Berkey, Director of Financial Aid. 314 367-8700, extension 269.

# Saint Louis University

**St. Louis, MO 63103** — **314 658-2222**

**1994-95 Costs.** Tuition: $11,690. Room: $2,300. Board: $2,430. Fees, books, misc. academic expenses (school's estimate): $880.
**Enrollment.** Undergraduates: 2,008 men, 2,568 women (full-time). Freshman class: 3,294 applicants, 2,853 accepted, 956 enrolled. Graduate enrollment: 2,109 men, 2,243 women.
**Test score averages/ranges.** Average SAT scores: 1030 combined. Range of SAT scores of middle 50%: 940-1170 combined. Average ACT scores: 25 composite. Range of ACT scores of middle 50%: 22-28 composite.
**Faculty.** 1,274 full-time; 80 part-time. 93% of faculty holds doctoral degree. Student/faculty ratio: 15 to 1.
**Selectivity rating.** Competitive.

**PROFILE.** Saint Louis, founded in 1818, is a private, church-affiliated university. Programs are offered through the Colleges of Arts and Sciences and Philosophy and Letters; the Schools of Allied Health Professions, Business and Administration, Nursing, Social Service, Law, and Medicine; Parks College; and the Metropolitan College. Its 225-acre campus is located two miles from downtown St. Louis.

**Accreditation:** NCACS. Professionally accredited by the Accreditation Board for Engineering and Technology, the American Assembly of Collegiate Schools of Business, the American Physical Therapy Association, the Council on Social Work Education, the Liaison Committee on Medical Education, the National Council for Accreditation of Teacher Education, the National League for Nursing.

**Religious orientation:** Saint Louis University is affiliated with the Roman Catholic Church (Society of Jesus); 15 semester hours of religion/theology required. Students are required to take two semesters each of philosophy and theology and a fifth semester of either philosophy or theology.
**Library:** Collections totaling over 2,200,000 volumes, and 11,412 periodical subscriptions.
**Special facilities/museums:** Art gallery, museum, language lab, urban affairs center.
**Athletic facilities:** Recreation center, athletic field.

**STUDENT BODY. Undergraduate profile:** 70% are state residents; 40% are transfers. 4% Asian-American, 8% Black, 2% Hispanic, 1% Native American, 72% White, 13% Other. Average age of undergraduates is 22.
**Freshman profile:** 50% of accepted applicants took SAT; 90% took ACT.
**Undergraduate achievement:** 80% of fall 1991 freshmen returned for fall 1992 term. 50% of entering class graduated. 22% of students who completed a degree program immediately went on to graduate study.
**Foreign students:** 729 students are from out of the country. Countries represented include China, Indonesia, Korea, Spain, Taiwan, and Thailand; 74 in all.

**PROGRAMS OF STUDY. Degrees:** A.B., B.S., B.S.Bus.Admin., B.S.Med.Rec.Admin., B.S.Med.Tech., B.S.Nurs., B.S.Phys.Ther., B.Soc.Work, Classical A.B.
**Majors:** Accounting, Aeronautical Administration, Aerospace Engineering, Aircraft Maintenance, Aircraft Maintenance Engineering, Aircraft Maintenance Management, Airway Science, American Studies, Art History, Arts/Sciences, Aviation Flight, Aviation Management, Aviation Science/Professional Pilot, Avionics Engineering Technology, Biology, Business Administration, Cardiovascular Perfusion Technology, Chemical Engineering, Chemistry, Classical Humanities, Communication, Communication Disorders, Computer Science, Criminal Justice/Corrections, Early Childhood Education, Economics, Education, Electrical Engineering, Elementary Education, English, Ethics/Socio-Legal Order, Finance, Fine/Performing Arts, French, Geology, Geophysics, German, Greek, Health Information Management, History, Ibero-American Studies, International Business, Jesuit Program, Latin, Logistics, Management Decisions, Management Information Systems, Marketing, Mathematics, Mathematics/Computer Science, Medical Records Administration, Medical Technology, Meteorology, Middle Education, Music, Music Education, Music History/Literature, Music Performance, Music Theory/Composition, Nuclear Medical Technology, Nursing, Occupational Therapy, Personnel/Industrial Relations, Philosophy, Physical Therapy, Physician Assistant, Physics, Physics/Engineering, Political Science, Psychology, Public Relations, Radio/Television, Russian, Secondary Education, Social Work, Spanish, Special Education, Speech/Language Disorders, Theological Studies, Transportation/Travel/Tourism, Urban Affairs.
**Distribution of degrees:** The majors with the highest enrollment are finance, nursing, and marketing; nuclear medical technology, Russian, and physics have the lowest.
**Requirements:** General education requirement.
**Special:** Minors offered in many majors, in African American, Russian, and women's studies, and in clinical chemistry, creative/professional writing, hematology, language proficiency, microbiology, political journalism, science/technology/society, and scientific translation. Business certificate program for arts & sciences students. Flight programs. Airframe/powerplant technician program. Associate's degrees offered. Self-designed majors. Double majors. Dual degrees. Independent study. Accelerated study. Pass/fail grading option. Internships. Graduate school at which undergraduates may take graduate-level courses. Preprofessional programs in law, medicine, veterinary science, dentistry, and theology. 3-2 engineering program with Washington U. Cross-registration with Washington U and other area schools. Teacher certification in early childhood, elementary, secondary, and special education. Certification in specific subject areas. Exchange program in Spain (St. Louis U, Madrid). Study abroad also possible in France and Germany. AFROTC. ROTC at Washington U.
**Honors:** Phi Beta Kappa. Honors program. Honor societies.
**Academic Assistance:** Remedial reading, writing, math, and study skills. Nonremedial tutoring.

**STUDENT LIFE. Housing:** Students may live on or off campus. Coed, women's, and men's dorms. 40% of students live in college housing.
**Social atmosphere:** Popular gathering spots for students include Humphrey's, Billiker Beach Club, and McGurk's. Black Student Alliance and International Student Federation are very active in campus life. Fall Fest and Spring Fever are two of the most anticipated events on campus.
**Services and counseling/handicapped student services:** Placement services. Health service. Counseling services for minority, military, veteran, and older students. Personal and psychological counseling. Career and academic guidance services. Religious counseling. Physically disabled student services. Learning disabled services. Notetaking services. Tape recorders. Tutors. Reader services for the blind.
**Campus organizations:** Undergraduate student government. Student newspaper (University News, published once/week). Yearbook. Radio station. Chorus, jazz band, gospel and madrigal singers, theatre, experimental theatre workshops, outdoor and sports clubs, service organizations, speakers bureau, programming boards, residence hall councils, academic and special-interest groups, 82 organizations in all. Eight fraternities, two chapter houses; four sororities, no chapter houses. 11% of men join a fraternity. 6% of women join a sorority.
**Religious organizations:** Campus Ministry, Muslim Student Association.
**Minority/foreign student organizations:** Black Student Alliance, Black business and science groups, Puerto Rican Student Association. International Student Association.

**ATHLETICS. Physical education requirements:** None.
**Intercollegiate competition:** 3% of students participate. Baseball (M), basketball (M,W), cheerleading (M,W), diving (M,W), field hockey (W), golf (M), soccer (M), softball (W), swimming (M,W), tennis (M,W), volleyball (W). Member of Midwestern Collegiate Conference, NCAA Division I.
**Intramural and club sports:** 64% of students participate. Intramural basketball, flag football, floor hockey, fun runs, golf, racquetball, soccer, softball, tennis, volleyball, water polo. Men's club martial arts, rugby, ultimate frisbee.

**ADMISSIONS. Academic basis for candidate selection** (in order of priority): Secondary school record, class rank, standardized test scores, school's recommendation, essay.
**Nonacademic basis for candidate selection:** Character and personality, extracurricular participation, particular talent or ability, and alumni/ae relationship are considered.
**Requirements:** Graduation from secondary school is required; GED is accepted. 16 units and the following program of study are recommended: 4 units of English, 3 units of math, 2 units of science, 2 units of foreign language, 2 units of social studies, 3 units of academic electives. Personal statement required for physical and occupational therapy program applicants. Portfolio required of art program applicants. Audition required of music program applicants. Conditional admission possible for applicants not meeting standard requirements. ACT is required; SAT may be substituted. Campus visit and interview recommended. Off-campus interviews available with an admissions representative.
**Procedure:** Take SAT or ACT by January of 12th year. Visit college for interview by December of 12th year. Suggest filing application by December 15. Application deadline is August 1. Application deadline for physical therapy program is December 15. Notification of admission on rolling basis. Reply is required by May 1. $200 refundable room deposit. Freshmen accepted in terms other than fall.
**Special programs:** Admission may be deferred one year. Credit and/or placement may be granted through CEEB Advanced Placement exams for scores of 3 or higher. Credit and/or placement may be granted through CLEP subject exams. Credit and placement may be granted through challenge exams and military and life experience. Early entrance/early admission program. Concurrent enrollment program.
**Transfer students:** Transfer students accepted for terms other than fall. In fall 1993, 40% of all new students were transfers into all classes. 1,962 transfer applications were received, 1,180 were accepted. Application deadline is August 1 for fall; January 1 for spring. Minimum 2.0 GPA required. Lowest course grade accepted is "C." At least 30 semester hours must be completed at the university to receive degree.
**Admissions contact:** Kent R. Hopkins, M.S., Director of Undergraduate Admissions. 314 658-2500.

**FINANCIAL AID. Available aid:** Pell grants, SEOG, state scholarships and grants, school scholarships and grants, private scholarships and grants, ROTC scholarships, academic merit scholarships, athletic scholarships, and aid for undergraduate foreign students. Family award. Perkins Loans (NDSL), PLUS, Stafford Loans (GSL), NSL, Health Professions Loans, state loans, school loans, private loans, and SLS. Deferred payment plan and family tuition reduction.
**Financial aid statistics:** 50% of aid is not need-based. In 1992-93, 80% of all undergraduate applicants received aid; 80% of freshman applicants. Average amounts of aid awarded freshmen: Scholarships and grants, $5,000; loans, $2,500.
**Supporting data/closing dates:** FAFSA/FAF/FFS: Priority filing date is January 1. School's own aid application: Priority filing date is January 1. Income tax forms: Priority filing date is May 1. Notification of awards on rolling basis.
**Financial aid contact:** Harold A. Deuser, M.B.A., Director of Financial Aid. 314 658-2350.

**STUDENT EMPLOYMENT.** College Work/Study Program. Institutional employment. 40% of full-time undergraduates work on campus during school year. Students may expect to earn an average of $2,300 during school year. Off-campus part-time employment opportunities rated "excellent."

**COMPUTER FACILITIES.** IBM/IBM-compatible, Macintosh/Apple, and RISC-/UNIX-based microcomputers. Students may access Digital, SUN minicomputer/mainframe systems, BITNET, Internet. Residence halls may be equipped with networked terminals. Computer languages and software packages include CADKEY, FOCUS, Harvard Graphics, Lotus, Microsoft Word, SAS, SPSS/X, Word Perfect; 60 in all. Computer facilities are available to all students.
**Fees:** None.
**Hours:** 8 AM-midn.; extended hours during final exams.

**GRADUATE CAREER DATA.** Graduate school percentages: 4% enter law school. 4% enter medical school. 30% enter graduate business programs. 46% enter graduate arts and sciences programs. 1% enter theological school/seminary. Highest graduate school enrollments: Saint Louis U, Washington U. 69% of graduates choose careers in business and industry. Companies and businesses that hire graduates: Ernst & Young, McDonnell Aircraft, Monsanto Chemical Company, Southwestern Bell.

# Southeast Missouri State University

**Cape Girardeau, MO 63701** **314 651-2000**

**1993-94 Costs.** Tuition: $2,052 (state residents), $3,708 (out-of-state). Room & board: $3,320. Fees, books, misc. academic expenses (school's estimate): $160.
**Enrollment.** Undergraduates: 2,692 men, 3,459 women (full-time). Freshman class: 2,874 applicants, 1,590 accepted, 1,280 enrolled. Graduate enrollment: 199 men, 555 women.
**Test score averages/ranges.** Average ACT scores: 22 English, 21 math, 23 composite.
**Faculty.** 390 full-time; 75 part-time. 90% of faculty holds doctoral degree. Student/faculty ratio: 18 to 1.
**Selectivity rating.** Competitive.

**PROFILE.** Southeast Missouri State, founded in 1873, is a public, comprehensive university. Its 200-acre campus is located in Cape Girardeau, south of St. Louis.

**Accreditation:** NCACS. Professionally accredited by the American Dietetic Association, the American Speech-Language-Hearing Association, the National Association of Schools of Music, the National Council for Accreditation of Teacher Education, the National League for Nursing.
**Religious orientation:** Southeast Missouri State University is nonsectarian; no religious requirements.
**Library:** Collections totaling over 380,271 volumes, 2,684 periodical subscriptions, and 805,200 microform items.
**Special facilities/museums:** Art museum, environmental studies institute, center for teaching and learning, writing center, clinical education lab, farm.
**Athletic facilities:** Gymnasiums, field house, basketball, racquetball, tennis, and volleyball courts, track, baseball, football, intramural, soccer, and softball fields, recreation center, swimming pool.

**STUDENT BODY. Undergraduate profile:** 88% are state residents; 30% are transfers. 6% Black, 1% Hispanic, 89% White, 4% Other. Average age of undergraduates is 22.
**Freshman profile:** 95% of accepted applicants took ACT.
**Undergraduate achievement:** 67% of fall 1992 freshmen returned for fall 1993 term. 12% of entering class graduated.
**Foreign students:** 316 students are from out of the country. Countries represented include China, Japan, Malaysia, the Netherlands, Pakistan, and Turkey; 50 in all.

**PROGRAMS OF STUDY. Degrees:** B.A., B.Gen.Studies, B.Mus., B.Mus.Ed., B.S., B.S.Bus.Admin., B.S.Ed., B.S.Interdis.Studies, B.S.Nurs., B.S.Voc.Home Econ.
**Majors:** Accounting, Agricultural Business, Agriculture, American Studies, Anthropology, Art, Biology, Chemistry, Child Development/Family Relations, Clothing/Textiles, Communication, Computer Science, Corrections, Criminal Justice, Dietetics, Early Childhood Education, Earth Sciences, Economics, Elementary Education, Engineering, Engineering Physics, Engineering Physics/Applied Physics, English, Exceptional Child Education, Fashion Merchandising, Finance, French, General Studies, Geography, Geology, High School Teaching, Historic Preservation, History, Home Economics, Housing/Interior Design, Industrial Technology, Law Enforcement, Management, Marketing, Mass Communication, Mass Communication/Journalism, Mass Communications Studies, Mathematics, Medical Technology, Middle/Junior High School Teaching, Music, Music Education, Music Theory/Composition, Nursing, Office Administration, Organ Performance, Philosophy, Physics, Piano Performance, Political Science, Psychology, Recreation, Social Work, Sociology, Spanish, Speech Communications, String Performance, Theatre, Vocal Performance, Vocational Home Economics, Wind/Percussion Performance.
**Distribution of degrees:** The majors with the highest enrollment are elementary education, criminal justice, and biology; anthropology, philosophy, and sociology have the lowest.
**Requirements:** General education requirement.
**Academic regulations:** Minimum 2.0 GPA must be maintained.
**Special:** Minors offered in most majors and in several other fields. Associate's degrees offered. Self-designed majors. Double majors. Dual degrees. Independent study. Accelerated study. Pass/fail grading option. Internships. Cooperative education programs. Graduate school at which undergraduates may take graduate-level courses. Preprofessional programs in law, medicine, veterinary science, pharmacy, dentistry, optometry, architecture, nuclear medicine, physical therapy, and podiatry. Four-year programs in agriculture and engineering and 3-2 law program with U of Missouri. 3-1 law and medical technology programs with various universities. Member of Bootheel Educational Consortium. Washington Semester. Teacher certification in early childhood, elementary, secondary, and special education. Certification in specific subject areas. Study abroad in England, Germany, Mexico, the Netherlands, and Wales. ROTC and AFROTC.
**Honors:** Honors program. Honor societies.
**Academic Assistance:** Remedial reading, writing, and math. Nonremedial tutoring.

**STUDENT LIFE. Housing:** All unmarried students under age 21 must live on campus unless living near campus with relatives. Coed, women's, and men's dorms. Sorority and fraternity housing. School-owned/operated apartments. Off-campus privately-owned housing. Off-campus married-student housing. 21% of students live in college housing.
**Services and counseling/handicapped student services:** Placement services. Health service. Counseling services for minority, military, veteran, and older students. Birth control, personal, and psychological counseling. Career and academic guidance services. Religious counseling. Learning disabled services.
**Campus organizations:** Undergraduate student government. Student newspaper (Capaha Arrow, published once/week). Radio station. Gospel choir, Historic Preservation Association, Grotto Club, Student Activities Council, Non-Traditional Student Association, departmental and special-interest groups, 125 organizations in all. 13 fraternities, nine chapter houses; eight sororities, five chapter houses. 10% of men join a fraternity. 12% of women join a sorority.
**Religious organizations:** Baptist Student Union, Black Student Fellowship, Catholic Campus Ministries, Chi Alpha, Fellowship Christian Faculty and Students, Intervarsity Christian Fellowship, Wesley Foundation.
**Minority/foreign student organizations:** Association of Black Collegians, NAACP, Pan-hellenic Council, minority fraternities/sororities. International Organization, Chinese, Indian subcontinent, and Malaysian groups.

**ATHLETICS. Physical education requirements:** None.
**Intercollegiate competition:** 4% of students participate. Baseball (M), basketball (M,W), cross-country (M,W), football (M), golf (M), gymnastics (W), softball (W), tennis (W), track and field (indoor) (M,W), track and field (outdoor) (M,W), volleyball (W). Member of NCAA Division I, NCAA Division I-AA for football, Ohio Valley Conference.
**Intramural and club sports:** 45% of students participate. Intramural basketball, bowling, climbing wall, flag football, golf, golf scramble, indoor soccer, inner-tube water polo, racquetball, sand volleyball, soccer, softball, tennis, triathlon, volleyball, walleyball, water volleyball, wrestling.

**ADMISSIONS. Academic basis for candidate selection** (in order of priority): Standardized test scores, secondary school record.
**Requirements:** Graduation from secondary school is required; GED is accepted. 15 units and the following program of study are required: 4 units of English, 2 units of math, 2 units of science, 3 units of social studies, 4 units of academic electives. Minimum composite ACT score of 18 and minimum 2.0 GPA required. Minimum composite ACT score of 20 required of education program applicants. Audition required of music program applicants. ACT is required. Campus visit recommended. No off-campus interviews.
**Procedure:** Take ACT by April of 12th year. Suggest filing application by January 15. Application deadline is June 1. Notification of admission on rolling basis. $150 room deposit, partially refundable until beginning of classes. Freshmen accepted in terms other than fall.
**Special programs:** Admission may be deferred one year. Credit may be granted through CEEB Advanced Placement for scores of 3 or higher. Credit may be granted through CLEP subject exams. Credit and placement may be granted through challenge exams and military experience. Early entrance/early admission program. Concurrent enrollment program.
**Transfer students:** Transfer students accepted for terms other than fall. In fall 1993, 30% of all new students were transfers into all classes. 1,107 transfer applications were received, 983 were accepted. Application deadline is June 15 for fall; December 15 for spring. Minimum 2.0 GPA required. Lowest course grade accepted is "F." At least 30 semester hours must be completed at the university to receive degree.
**Admissions contact:** Juan Crites, M.A., Director of Admissions. 314 651-2590.

**FINANCIAL AID. Available aid:** Pell grants, SEOG, Federal Nursing Student Scholarships, state scholarships and grants, school scholarships and grants, private scholarships and grants, ROTC scholarships, academic merit scholarships, athletic scholarships, and aid for undergraduate foreign students. Perkins Loans (NDSL), PLUS, Stafford Loans (GSL), Health Professions Loans, and SLS. Deferred payment plan.
**Financial aid statistics:** 38% of aid is not need-based. In 1993-94, 59% of all undergraduate applicants received aid.
**Supporting data/closing dates:** FAFSA: Priority filing date is April 15. State aid form: Priority filing date is April 15; deadline is April 30. Notification of awards begins March 31.
**Financial aid contact:** Karen Walker, M.A., Director of Financial Aid. 314 651-2840.

**STUDENT EMPLOYMENT.** College Work/Study Program. Institutional employment. 15% of full-time undergraduates work on campus during school year. Students may expect to earn an average of $1,500 during school year. Off-campus part-time employment opportunities rated "fair."

**COMPUTER FACILITIES.** 1,100 IBM/IBM-compatible and Macintosh/Apple microcomputers; 69 are networked. Students may access IBM minicomputer/mainframe systems, BITNET. Residence halls may be equipped with stand-alone microcomputers, networked terminals, modems. Client/LAN operating systems include Apple/Macintosh, DOS, UNIX/XENIX/AIX, Novell. Computer languages and software packages include Assembler, BASIC, COBOL, FORTRAN, Pascal, PL/1, RPG; database, spreadsheet, word processing packages. Computer facilities are available to all students.
**Fees:** None.
**Hours:** 7 AM-midn.

**GRADUATE CAREER DATA.** 91% of graduates choose careers in business and industry. Companies and businesses that hire graduates: Blue Cross/Blue Shield, Footlocker, John Hancock, McDonnell Douglas, Procter & Gamble, Southwestern Bell, Union Pacific.

**PROMINENT ALUMNI/AE.** Jerry McNeely, television producer; William G. Moll, WKRC television; Dr. Dale W. Margerum, vice-president, Purdue U; Dr. J. David Margerum, Hughs Research Lab.

# Southwest Baptist University

**Bolivar, MO 65613-2496 — 417 326-5281**

**1994-95 Costs.** Tuition: $7,070. Room & board: $2,500. Fees, books, misc. academic expenses (school's estimate): $976.
**Enrollment.** Undergraduates: 803 men, 988 women (full-time). Freshman class: 1,708 applicants, 630 accepted, 604 enrolled. Graduate enrollment: 21 men, 105 women.
**Test score averages/ranges.** Average SAT scores: 993 combined. Average ACT scores: 23 composite.
**Faculty.** 92 full-time; 110 part-time. 52% of faculty holds doctoral degree. Student/faculty ratio: 23 to 1.
**Selectivity rating.** Less competitive.

**PROFILE.** Southwest Baptist, founded in 1878, is a church-affiliated, comprehensive university. Programs are offered through the Schools of Arts and Sciences, Business, Education and Human Studies, and Fine Arts and the University College. Its 140-acre campus is located in Bolivar, 28 miles north of Springfield.

**Accreditation:** NCACS. Professionally accredited by the American Dietetic Association, the Association of Collegiate Business Schools and Programs, the National Association of Schools of Music, the National League for Nursing.
**Religious orientation:** Southwest Baptist University is affiliated with the Missouri Baptist Convention; four semesters of religion required.
**Library:** Collections totaling over 117,408 volumes, 1,227 periodical subscriptions, and 40,099 microform items.
**Athletic facilities:** Field house, gymnasium, tennis courts, tracks, swimming pool, weight rooms, soccer and softball fields, fitness trail.

**STUDENT BODY. Undergraduate profile:** 60% are state residents; 69% are transfers. 1% Asian-American, 1% Black, 96% White, 2% Other. Average age of undergraduates is 21.
**Freshman profile:** 6% of accepted applicants took SAT; 86% took ACT. 98% of freshmen come from public schools.
**Undergraduate achievement:** 66% of fall 1992 freshmen returned for fall 1993 term.
**Foreign students:** 31 students are from out of the country. Countries represented include Australia, Colombia, India, Korea, Nigeria, and the United Kingdom; 14 in all.

**PROGRAMS OF STUDY. Degrees:** B.A., B.Appl.Sci., B.Mus., B.S., B.S.Nurs.
**Majors:** Accounting, Art, Bible, Biology, Bivocational Christian Ministry, Business Administration, Business Education, Chemistry, Church Music, Commercial Art, Communication, Computer Science, Economics, Elementary Education, English, History, Human Services, Mathematics, Medical Technology, Music, Music Education, Nursing, Occupational Technology, Office Administration, Physical Education, Physical Therapy, Political Science, Psychology, Recreation, Religious Education, Religious Studies, Social Science Education, Sociology, Spanish, Speech Communication/Theatre, Sports Management, Telecommunications, Theatre, Theatre/Communication, Theatre/Telecommunications, Theological Studies.
**Distribution of degrees:** The majors with the highest enrollment are psychology, sociology, and elementary education.
**Requirements:** General education requirement.
**Special:** Minors offered in many majors and in approximately 10 other fields. Courses offered in geography, interdisciplinary studies, library science, and physical science. Certificate programs in pastoral or youth ministry, secretarial science, and theology. Associate's degrees offered. Double majors. Dual degrees. Independent study. Pass/fail grading option. Internships. Graduate school at which undergraduates may take graduate-level

courses. Preprofessional programs in law, medicine, veterinary science, pharmacy, dentistry, theology, optometry, engineering, journalism, and mortuary science. 2-2 medical engineering program with U of Missouri at Rolla. 2-2 nursing program with St. John's Sch of Nursing. 3-2 engineering programs with U of Missouri at Rolla and Washington U. Teacher certification in early childhood, elementary, and secondary education. Certification in specific subject areas. Study abroad in England. ROTC.
**Honors:** Honors program.
**Academic Assistance:** Remedial reading, writing, math, and study skills. Nonremedial tutoring.
**STUDENT LIFE. Housing:** All unmarried students under age 21 must live on campus unless living near campus with relatives. Women's and men's dorms. School-owned/operated apartments. Off-campus privately-owned housing. 50% of students live in college housing.
**Social atmosphere:** On-campus haunts include the Woody-Gotz lobby and the student union; off-campus, students gather at Mazzio's and Dunnegan Park. Small group ministries and Christian service organizations are influential groups on campus. Popular events of the school year include On-Display (talent show), basketball games, and movie nights. According to the editor of the school newspaper, "Most social life centers around Christian activities offered on campus."
**Services and counseling/handicapped student services:** Placement services. Health service. Counseling services for veteran students. Personal and psychological counseling. Career and academic guidance services. Religious counseling.
**Campus organizations:** Undergraduate student government. Student newspaper (Omnibus, published once/week). Yearbook. Ensembles, chorale, choir, Chamber Singers, Campus Singers, College Players, Contempos, nursing club, English club, behavioral science club, intercollegiate debating, forensics, Student State Teachers Association, Young Democrats, Young Republicans, 19 organizations in all.
**Religious organizations:** Church Music Conference, Fellowship of Christian Athletes, Fellowship of Christian Recreators, Ministers After Youth, revival teams.
**ATHLETICS. Physical education requirements:** Two semesters of physical education required.
**Intercollegiate competition:** 20% of students participate. Baseball (M), basketball (M,W), cheerleading (M,W), cross-country (M,W), football (M), golf (M), soccer (M,W), softball (W), tennis (M,W), track (indoor) (M,W), track (outdoor) (M,W), track and field (indoor) (M,W), track and field (outdoor) (M,W), volleyball (W). Member of Mid-America Intercollegiate Athletics Association, Missouri Intercollegiate Athletic Association, NCAA Division II.
**Intramural and club sports:** 50% of students participate. Intramural basketball, flag football, soccer, softball, table tennis, tennis, volleyball.
**ADMISSIONS. Academic basis for candidate selection** (in order of priority): Secondary school record, standardized test scores, school's recommendation, class rank.
**Requirements:** Graduation from secondary school is required; GED is accepted. 13 units and the following program of study are recommended: 4 units of English, 3 units of math, 2 units of science, 2 units of social studies, 2 units of electives. Minimum composite ACT score of 18 and minimum 2.0 GPA required. Portfolio required of art program applicants. Audition required of music program applicants. R.N. required of nursing program applicants. ACT is required; SAT may be substituted. Campus visit and interview recommended. Off-campus interviews available with an admissions representative.
**Procedure:** Take SAT or ACT by September of 12th year. Visit college for interview by September of 12th year. Application deadline is September 12. Notification of admission on rolling basis. $75 nonrefundable tuition deposit. $75 room deposit, refundable until July 1. Freshmen accepted in terms other than fall.
**Special programs:** Admission may be deferred. Credit and/or placement may be granted through CEEB Advanced Placement exams. Credit and/or placement may be granted through CLEP general and subject exams. Credit and placement may be granted through challenge exams and military and life experience. Early decision program. In fall 1993, 2,185 applied for early decision and 674 were accepted. Deadline for applying for early decision is January 31. Early entrance/early admission program. Concurrent enrollment program.
**Transfer students:** Transfer students accepted for terms other than fall. In fall 1993, 69% of all new students were transfers into all classes. 188 transfer applications were received, 188 were accepted. Application deadline is September 12 for fall; February 11 for spring. Minimum 2.0 GPA required. Lowest course grade accepted is "C." Maximum number of transferable credits is 60 semester hours from a two-year school and 90 semester hours from a four-year school. At least 32 semester hours must be completed at the university to receive degree.
**Admissions contact:** Ben Sells, Ph.D., Director of Admissions. 417 326-1810.
**FINANCIAL AID. Available aid:** Pell grants, SEOG, state scholarships and grants, school scholarships and grants, private scholarships and grants, ROTC scholarships, academic merit scholarships, athletic scholarships, and aid for undergraduate foreign students. Perkins Loans (NDSL), Stafford Loans (GSL), school loans, private loans, and SLS. Tuition Plan Inc., Education Plan Inc., and deferred payment plan.
**Supporting data/closing dates:** FAFSA/FAF/FFS: Deadline is March 30. School's own aid application: Deadline is March 30. Income tax forms: Deadline is March 30. Notification of awards on rolling basis.
**Financial aid contact:** Ronn Ramey, Director of Scholarships and Financial Assistance. 417 326-1820.
**STUDENT EMPLOYMENT.** College Work/Study Program. Institutional employment. 42% of full-time undergraduates work on campus during school year. Students may expect to earn an average of $800 during school year. Off-campus part-time employment opportunities rated "fair."
**COMPUTER FACILITIES.** 40 IBM/IBM-compatible and Macintosh/Apple microcomputers; all are networked. Students may access Digital, Hewlett-Packard minicomputer/mainframe systems. Client/LAN operating systems include Apple/Macintosh, DOS, Windows NT. Computer languages and software packages include Ada, BASIC, C, COBOL, FORTRAN, Pascal. Computer facilities are available to all students.
**Fees:** $10 computer fee per semester.
**Hours:** 7:30 AM-9 PM (M-Th), 7:30-5 PM (F), 9 AM-5 PM (Sa), 1 PM-6 PM (Su).
**GRADUATE CAREER DATA.** Graduate school percentages: 5% enter law school. 3% enter medical school. 10% enter graduate business programs. 5% enter theological school/seminary. 30% of graduates choose careers in business and industry.
**PROMINENT ALUMNI/AE.** Roy Blunt, secretary of state, Missouri.

# Southwest Missouri State University

**Springfield, MO 65804** **417 836-5000**

**1994-95 Costs.** Tuition: $2,370 (state residents), $4,740 (out-of-state). Room & board: $2,702-$3,104. Fees, books, misc. academic expenses (school's estimate): $776.
**Enrollment.** Undergraduates: 6,192 men, 6,939 women (full-time). Freshman class: 6,112 applicants, 5,254 accepted, 3,204 enrolled. Graduate enrollment: 540 men, 1,115 women.
**Test score averages/ranges.** Average ACT scores: 22 composite. Range of ACT scores of middle 50%: 19-24 composite.
**Faculty.** 685 full-time; 174 part-time. 74% of faculty holds highest degree in specific field. Student/faculty ratio: 23 to 1.
**Selectivity rating.** Less competitive.

**PROFILE.** Southwest Missouri State, founded in 1905, is a public, comprehensive university. Programs are offered through the Colleges of Arts and Letters, Business Administration, Education and Psychology, Health and Applied Sciences, Humanities and Social Sciences, and Science and Mathematics. Its 190-acre campus is located in Springfield, in southwestern Missouri.
**Accreditation:** NCACS. Professionally accredited by the American Assembly of Collegiate Schools of Business, the American Dietetic Association, the American Home Economics Association, the American Speech-Language-Hearing Association, the Computing Sciences Accreditation Board, the Council on Social Work Education, the National Association of Schools of Music, the National Association of Schools of Public Affairs and Administration, the National Athletic Trainers Association, the National Council for Accreditation of Teacher Education, the National League for Nursing, the National Recreation and Park Association.
**Religious orientation:** Southwest Missouri State University is nonsectarian; no religious requirements.
**Library:** Collections totaling over 534,000 volumes, 4,632 periodical subscriptions, and 800,000 microform items.
**Special facilities/museums:** On-campus laboratory school (K-12), 125-acre experimental farm, electron microscope, observatory.
**Athletic facilities:** Indoor and outdoor swimming pools, bowling facility, weight machines, indoor and outdoor tracks, basketball, racquetball, and tennis courts, athletic fields.
**STUDENT BODY. Undergraduate profile:** 94% are state residents; 25% are transfers. 1.2% Asian-American, 2.7% Black, .8% Hispanic, .4% Native American, 93.4% White, 1.5% Other. Average age of undergraduates is 23.
**Freshman profile:** 5% of freshmen who took ACT scored 30 or over on composite; 27% scored 24 or over on composite; 91% scored 18 or over on composite; 99% scored 12 or over on composite; 100% scored 6 or over on composite. 100% of accepted applicants took ACT. 93% of freshmen come from public schools.
**Undergraduate achievement:** 69% of fall 1992 freshmen returned for fall 1993 term.
**Foreign students:** 320 students are from out of the country. Countries represented include China, India, Indonesia, Malaysia, Taiwan, and Thailand; 52 in all.
**PROGRAMS OF STUDY. Degrees:** B.A., B.F.A., B.Mus., B.S., B.S.Ed., B.S.Nurs., B.Soc.Work.
**Majors:** Accounting, Administrative Office Administration, Agricultural Business, Agronomy, Animal Science, Antiquities, Art, Biology, Cartography/Map Technology, Cell/Molecular Biology, Chemistry, Child/Family Development, Clothing/Textiles/Merchandising, Communication Disorders, Communications, Community/Regional Planning, Computer Information Systems, Computer Science, Construction Management Technology, Dance, Design, Dietetics, Drafting/Design Technology, Earth Science, Economics, Electricity/Electronics Technology, Electronic Media, Elementary Education, Engineering Physics, English, Finance, Foods/Nutrition, French, General Agriculture, General Business, Geography, Geology, German, Gerontology, History, Horticulture, Hospitality/Restaurant Administration, Housing/Interior Design, Industrial Education, Industrial Management, Insurance/Risk Management, Latin, Latin American Studies/Spanish, Management, Manufacturing Technology, Marketing, Mathematics, Mechanical Design, Medical Technology, Music, Nursing, Philosophy, Physical Education, Physics, Political Science, Power/Transportation, Printing, Psychology, Public Administration, Radiography, Recreation/Leisure Studies, Religious Studies, Respiratory Therapy, Science, Social Work, Sociology, Spanish, Speech/Theatre, Technical Physics, Theatre, Vocational Agriculture, Vocational Home Economics, Wildlife Conservation/Management, Writing.
**Distribution of degrees:** The majors with the highest enrollment are elementary education, communications, and marketing; philosophy and religious studies have the lowest.
**Requirements:** General education requirement.
**Academic regulations:** Freshmen must maintain minimum 1.75 GPA; sophomores, juniors, seniors, 2.0 GPA.
**Special:** Minors offered in most majors and in anthropology, astronomy, biomedical sciences, coaching, criminal justice studies, decision analysis, drafting design, exercise science, gender studies, global studies, Greek, health care management, insurance, international management, international marketing, journalism, legal studies in business, library science, metals, military science, molecular biology, paralegal studies, plastics, public law, real estate, religious studies, retailing/merchandising, special education, and woods. Associate's degrees offered. Self-designed majors. Double majors. Dual degrees. Independent study. Pass/fail grading option. Internships. Cooperative education programs. Graduate school at which undergraduates may take graduate-level courses. Preprofessional programs in law, medicine, veterinary science, pharmacy, dentistry, and optometry. 2-2 engineering programs with U of Missouri at Columbia and at Rolla. Member of Midwest Student Exchange Program and Missouri Consortium for International Programs and Studies. Member of National Student Exchange (NSE). Teacher certification in early childhood, elementary, secondary, and special education. Certification in specific

subject areas. Member of International Student Exchange Program (ISEP). Study abroad in Australia, China, Costa Rica, England, France, Germany, and Mexico. ROTC.
**Honors:** Honors program. Honor societies.
**Academic Assistance:** Remedial reading, writing, math, and study skills. Nonremedial tutoring.

**STUDENT LIFE. Housing:** All unmarried freshmen and sophomores under age 21 must live on campus unless living with family. Coed, women's, and men's dorms. Sorority and fraternity housing. School-owned/operated apartments. 21% of students live in college housing.
**Social Atmosphere:** The student newspaper reports, "Campus social life seems to be very party-oriented. Greeks are very influential in campus social life, and basketball games attract the most spirited students. There are a number of Christian social gatherings throughout the year. Off campus, students socialize at frat houses and at local bars and nightclubs."
**Services and counseling/handicapped student services:** Placement services. Health service. Women's center. Day care. Escort service on campus. Counseling services for minority, military, veteran, and older students. Personal and psychological counseling. Career and academic guidance services. Religious counseling. Physically disabled student services. Learning disabled program/services. Notetaking services. Tape recorders. Reader services for the blind.
**Campus organizations:** Undergraduate student government. Student newspaper (The Southwest Standard, published once/week). Literary magazine. Radio station. Chamber Singers, chorus, concert chorale, gospel choir, concert, jazz, and marching bands, orchestra, Student Activities Council, University Ambassadors, Residence Hall Association, Resident Life Programming Boards, Association of Student Leaders, 267 organizations in all. 18 fraternities, 16 chapter houses; nine sororities, six chapter houses. 13% of men join a fraternity. 9% of women join a sorority.
**Religious organizations:** Abundant Life and You, Alpha Omega, Bahai Club, Campus Crusade for Christ, Campus Ministries International, Chi Alpha Christian Fellowship, Christian Campus House, Christian Student Center, Fellowship of Christian Athletes, ICTHUS Christian Fellowship, Lambda Delta Sigma, Midnight, Muslim Student Association, Sigma Gamma Chi, Student Gospel Fellowship, United Ministries in Higher Education, University Christian Fellowship, Wesley Foundation, and several denominational groups.
**Minority/foreign student organizations:** Association of Black Collegians, Black Data Processing Association, Hispanic Association, Native American Association, Organization for Adult Students in School, Alpha Kappa Alpha, Delta Sigma Theta, Sigma Gamma Rho, Alpha Phi Alpha, Kappa Alpha Psi, Phi Beta Sigma, Black National Pan-Hellenic Council. American-Arab Anti-Discrimination Committee, Association of International Students, Association for Chinese Students and Scholars, Malaysian Student Society, Taiwanese Student Association.

**ATHLETICS. Physical education requirements:** Four credit hours of physical education required.
**Intercollegiate competition:** 4% of students participate. Baseball (M), basketball (M,W), cross-country (M,W), field hockey (W), football (M), golf (M,W), riflery (M), soccer (M), softball (W), swimming (M), tennis (M,W), track (indoor) (M,W), track (outdoor) (M,W), track and field (indoor) (M,W), track and field (outdoor) (M,W), volleyball (W), wrestling (M). Member of Missouri Valley Conference, NCAA Division I, NCAA Division I-AA for football.
**Intramural and club sports:** Men's club bowling, handball, racquetball, rodeo, rugby. Women's club bowling.

**ADMISSIONS. Academic basis for candidate selection** (in order of priority): Class rank, standardized test scores, secondary school record, school's recommendation, essay.
**Nonacademic basis for candidate selection:** Character and personality, extracurricular participation, particular talent or ability, and geographical distribution are considered.
**Requirements:** Graduation from secondary school is required; GED is accepted. No specific distribution of secondary school units required. Minimum composite ACT score of 17 required of applicants from southwest Missouri. Minimum composite ACT score of 17 and rank in top two-thirds of secondary school class required of applicants from all other areas of Missouri. Minimum composite ACT score of 17 and rank in top half of secondary school class or composite ACT score of 19 required of out-of-state applicants. Completion of specific courses and minimum GPA required of applicants to some programs. R.N. required of nursing program applicants. ACT is required. Campus visit recommended. No off-campus interviews.
**Procedure:** Take ACT by October of 12th year. Suggest filing application by February 1. Application deadline is August 1. Notification of admission on rolling basis. $75 room deposit, refundable until June 15. Freshmen accepted in terms other than fall.
**Special programs:** Credit and/or placement may be granted through CEEB Advanced Placement exams for scores of 4 or higher. Credit may be granted through CLEP subject exams, DANTES exams, and military experience. Credit and placement may be granted through challenge exams. Concurrent enrollment program.
**Transfer students:** Transfer students accepted for terms other than fall. In fall 1993, 25% of all new students were transfers into all classes. 1,787 transfer applications were received, 1,326 were accepted. Application deadline is August 1 for fall; December 1 for spring. Minimum 2.0 GPA required. Lowest course grade accepted is "D." Maximum number of transferable credits is 64 semester hours. At least 30 semester hours must be completed at the university to receive degree.
**Admissions contact:** Donald E. Simpson, M.S., Director of Admissions and Records. 417 836-5517.

**FINANCIAL AID. Available aid:** Pell grants, SEOG, state scholarships and grants, school scholarships and grants, private scholarships and grants, ROTC scholarships, academic merit scholarships, athletic scholarships, and aid for undergraduate foreign students. Perkins Loans (NDSL), PLUS, Stafford Loans (GSL), school loans, and SLS.
**Financial aid statistics:** 28% of aid is not need-based. In 1993-94, 73% of all undergraduate applicants received aid. Average amounts of aid awarded freshmen: Scholarships and grants, $2,137; loans, $2,625.
**Supporting data/closing dates:** FAFSA: Priority filing date is March 31. Notification of awards begins June 15.
**Financial aid contact:** R. Todd Morriss, M.S., Financial Aid Director. 417 836-5262.

**STUDENT EMPLOYMENT.** College Work/Study Program. Institutional employment. 12% of full-time undergraduates work on campus during school year. Students may expect to earn an average of $800 during school year. Off-campus part-time employment opportunities rated "excellent."

**COMPUTER FACILITIES.** 4,000 IBM/IBM-compatible, Macintosh/Apple, and RISC-/UNIX-based microcomputers. Students may access AT&T, Digital, Hewlett-Packard, IBM, Prime minicomputer/mainframe systems, BITNET, Internet. Residence halls may be equipped with stand-alone microcomputers, networked microcomputers. Client/LAN operating systems include Apple/Macintosh, DOS, UNIX/XENIX/AIX, Novell. Computer languages and software packages include Assembler, BASIC, C Compiler, COBOL, FORTRAN; several other languages and software packages. Computer facilities are available to all students.
**Fees:** Computer fee is included in tuition/fees.
**Hours:** 7:30 AM-midn.

**GRADUATE CAREER DATA.** Graduate school percentages: 5% enter law school. 5% enter medical school. 1% enter dental school. 10% enter graduate business programs. 15% enter graduate arts and sciences programs. 1% enter theological school/seminary. Highest graduate school enrollments: Southwest Missouri State U. 75% of graduates choose careers in business and industry. Companies and businesses that hire graduates: McDonnell Douglas, Monsanto, Baird, Kurtz & Dobson, Koch Industries, Southwestern Bell, Hallmark, Inc., Wal-Mart, State Farm, KMPG Peat Marwick, Deloitte Touche.

**PROMINENT ALUMNI/AE.** Kathleen Turner and Tess Harper, actresses; John Goodman, actor; David Glass, CEO, Wal-Mart; John Q. Hammons, international developer; Winston Garland, NBA player.

# Stephens College

**Columbia, MO 65215** — **314 442-2211**

**1994-95 Costs.** Tuition: $13,900. Room & board: $5,200. Fees, books, misc. academic expenses (school's estimate): $600.
**Enrollment.** Undergraduates: 17 men, 590 women (full-time). Freshman class: 449 applicants, 417 accepted, 196 enrolled.
**Test score averages/ranges.** Average SAT scores: 426 verbal, 444 math. Range of SAT scores of middle 50%: 380-550 verbal, 380-540 math. Average ACT scores: 21 English, 19 math, 21 composite. Range of ACT scores of middle 50%: 18-25 English, 16-22 math.
**Faculty.** 60 full-time; 28 part-time. 85% of faculty holds highest degree in specific field. Student/faculty ratio: 11 to 1.
**Selectivity rating.** Less competitive.

**PROFILE.** Stephens, founded in 1833, is a private, liberal arts college for women; qualified men admitted to specified programs. Its 224-acre campus is located in Columbia, west of St. Louis.

**Accreditation:** NCACS.
**Religious orientation:** Stephens College is nonsectarian; no religious requirements.
**Library:** Collections totaling over 127,500 volumes, 442 periodical subscriptions, and 9,305 microform items.
**Special facilities/museums:** Museum with art and historical costume collections, on-campus preschool, kindergarten, and elementary schools, language lab.
**Athletic facilities:** Gymnasium, 9-hole golf course, tennis courts, indoor swimming pool, weight/exercise room, 11-acre lake, riding arena and stables.

**STUDENT BODY. Undergraduate profile:** 32% are state residents; 9% are transfers. 2% Asian-American, 6% Black, 2% Hispanic, 90% White. Average age of undergraduates is 21.
**Freshman profile:** 1% of freshmen who took SAT scored 700 or over on math; 3% scored 600 or over on verbal, 9% scored 600 or over on math; 22% scored 500 or over on verbal, 31% scored 500 or over on math; 64% scored 400 or over on verbal, 67% scored 400 or over on math; 93% scored 300 or over on verbal, 92% scored 300 or over on math. 7% of freshmen who took ACT scored 30 or over on English, 3% scored 30 or over on math, 6% scored 30 or over on composite; 40% scored 24 or over on English, 22% scored 24 or over on math, 31% scored 24 or over on composite; 87% scored 18 or over on English, 77% scored 18 or over on math, 90% scored 18 or over on composite; 100% scored 12 or over on English, 100% scored 12 or over on math, 100% scored 12 or over on composite. 51% of accepted applicants took SAT; 77% took ACT.
**Undergraduate achievement:** 75% of fall 1992 freshmen returned for fall 1993 term. 45% of entering class graduated.
**Foreign students:** Countries represented include Canada, Japan, and Taiwan.

**PROGRAMS OF STUDY. Degrees:** B.A., B.F.A., B.S.
**Majors:** Biology, Business Administration, Childhood Education/Early Childhood, Dance, Elementary Education, English, Equestrian Business Management, Equestrian Science, Fashion Design, Fashion Merchandising, Mass Communication/Broadcast Media, Mass Communication/Public Relations, Philosophy/Law/Rhetoric, Psychology, Social Sciences/History, Social Sciences/Political Science, Student-Initiated Major, Theatre Arts, Visual Arts.
**Distribution of degrees:** The majors with the highest enrollment are theatre, business administration, and mass communication; English and philosophy/law/rhetoric have the lowest.
**Requirements:** General education requirement.
**Special:** Minors offered in several majors and in art history, East Asian studies, environmental science, French, history, humanities, information systems, mathematics, philosophy/religion, political science, sociology, Spanish, and women's studies. Associate's degrees offered. Self-designed majors. Double majors. Dual degrees. Independent study. Accelerated study. Internships. Preprofessional programs in law, medicine, veterinary science, dentistry, and theology. Dual-degree animal science program with U of Missouri at Columbia. Dual-degree occupational therapy program with Washington U. Member of Mid-Missouri Association of Colleges and Universities. Washington Semester. Teacher certification in early childhood and elementary education. Exchange program abroad in Japan (Fukuoka Women's Coll). Study abroad also in Canada, China, England, Mexico,

African and European countries. ROTC, NROTC, and AFROTC at U of Missouri at Columbia.
**Honors:** Honors program.
**Academic Assistance:** Remedial reading, writing, and math.

**ADMISSIONS. Academic basis for candidate selection** (in order of priority): Secondary school record, essay, class rank, school's recommendation, standardized test scores.
**Nonacademic basis for candidate selection:** Character and personality and extracurricular participation are important. Particular talent or ability and alumni/ae relationship are considered.
**Requirements:** Graduation from secondary school is required; GED is accepted. 12 units and the following program of study are recommended: 4 units of English, 2 units of math, 2 units of science, 2 units of foreign language, 2 units of social studies. Minimum combined SAT score of 750 (composite ACT score of 19) and minimum 2.25 GPA required. SAT or ACT is required. Campus visit and interview recommended. Off-campus interviews available with an admissions representative.
**Procedure:** Take SAT or ACT by April of 12th year. Suggest filing application by May 31. Application deadline is August. Notification of admission on rolling basis. No set date by which applicants must accept offer. $275 tuition deposit, refundable until May 1. Freshmen accepted in terms other than fall.
**Special programs:** Admission may be deferred three years. Credit and/or placement may be granted through CEEB Advanced Placement exams for scores of 3 or higher. Credit and/or placement may be granted through CLEP general and subject exams. Early decision program. Concurrent enrollment program.
**Transfer students:** Transfer students accepted for terms other than fall. In fall 1993, 9% of all new students were transfers into all classes. 62 transfer applications were received, 45 were accepted. Application deadline is July 31 for fall; December 31 for spring. SAT/ACT scores, secondary school, and college transcripts required of transfer applicants with less than one year of college. Minimum 2.25 GPA required. Lowest course grade accepted is "D." At least 36 semester hours must be completed at the college to receive degree.
**Admissions contact:** Michael S. Brophy, Dean of Enrollment Management. 314 876-7207.

**FINANCIAL AID. Available aid:** Pell grants, SEOG, state scholarships and grants, school scholarships and grants, private scholarships and grants, and academic merit scholarships. Perkins Loans (NDSL), PLUS, Stafford Loans (GSL), school loans, and SLS. Knight Tuition Plans, deferred payment plan, and family tuition reduction.
**Financial aid statistics:** 25% of aid is not need-based. In 1993-94, 100% of all undergraduate applicants received aid. Average amounts of aid awarded freshmen: Scholarships and grants, $7,500; loans, $2,200.
**Supporting data/closing dates:** FAFSA: Priority filing date is March 15. Notification of awards begins in March.
**Financial aid contact:** Gloria Wright, Director of Financial Aid. 314 876-7106.

# University of Missouri–Columbia

**Columbia, MO 65211** **314 882-2121**

**1994-95 Costs.** Tuition: $3,232 (state residents), $8,857 (out-of-state). Room & board: $3,485. Fees, books, misc. academic expenses (school's estimate): $500.
**Enrollment.** Undergraduates: 7,375 men, 7,407 women (full-time). Freshman class: 6,574 applicants, 4,668 accepted, 2,940 enrolled. Graduate enrollment: 2,384 men, 2,289 women.
**Test score averages/ranges.** Average SAT scores: 502 verbal, 564 math. Average ACT scores: 24 English, 24 math, 25 composite. Range of ACT scores of middle 50%: 23-27 English, 21-26 math.
**Faculty.** 1,552 full-time; 40 part-time. 87% of faculty holds doctoral degree. Student/faculty ratio: 15 to 1.
**Selectivity rating.** More competitive.

**PROFILE.** U Missouri–Columbia, founded in 1839, is a comprehensive, public institution. Programs are offered through the Colleges of Agriculture, Food, and Natural Resources; Arts and Science; Business and Public Administration; Education; Health-Related Professions; and Human Environmental Sciences and the Schools of Journalism and Nursing. Its 692-acre campus is located in Columbia, 33 miles north of Jefferson City.

**Accreditation:** NCACS. Numerous professional accreditations.
**Religious orientation:** University of Missouri-Columbia is nonsectarian; no religious requirements.
**Library:** Collections totaling over 2,579,253 volumes, 22,973 periodical subscriptions, and 5,012,692 microform items.
**Special facilities/museums:** Art, archaeology, anthropology, entomology, geology, and natural history museums, NBC-TV affiliate, freedom of information center, herbarium, agricultural research farm, equine center, nuclear reactor, observatory, child development lab, engineering experiment station.
**Athletic facilities:** Field house, multipurpose center.

**STUDENT BODY. Undergraduate profile:** 88% are state residents; 31% are transfers. 2% Asian-American, 4% Black, 1% Hispanic, 1% Native American, 86% White, 6% Other. Average age of undergraduates is 21.
**Freshman profile:** 12% of freshmen who took ACT scored 30 or over on English, 9% scored 30 or over on math, 15% scored 30 or over on composite; 60% scored 24 or over on English, 46% scored 24 or over on math, 59% scored 24 or over on composite; 95% scored 18 or over on English, 93% scored 18 or over on math, 100% scored 18 or over on composite; 100% scored 12 or over on English, 100% scored 12 or over on math, 101% scored 12 or over on composite. 20% of accepted applicants took SAT; 96% took ACT.
**Undergraduate achievement:** 82% of fall 1992 freshmen returned for fall 1993 term. 30% of entering class graduated.
**Foreign students:** 493 students are from out of the country. Countries represented include China, India, Japan, Korea, Malaysia, and Taiwan; 118 in all.

**PROGRAMS OF STUDY. Degrees:** B.A., B.Ed.Studies, B.F.A., B.Hlth.Sci., B.Journ., B.S., B.S.Acct., B.S.Agri., B.S.Bus.Admin., B.S.Chem.Eng., B.S.Civil Eng., B.S.Comp. Eng., B.S.Ed., B.S.Elec.Eng., B.S.Eng., B.S.Fish.Wldlf., B.S.HumanSci., B.S.Mech.Eng., B.S.Nurs., B.Soc.Work.
**Majors:** Accountancy, Administrative Management, Advertising, Agricultural Economics, Agricultural Education, Agricultural Engineering, Agricultural Journalism, Agricultural Mechanization, Agronomy, Animal Science, Anthropology, Art, Art Education, Art History/Archaeology, Atmospheric Science, Biochemistry, Biological Sciences, Broadcast News, Business Administration, Business Logistics, Chemical Engineering, Chemistry, Civil Engineering, Classics, Clinical Laboratory Sciences, Communication/Speech, Communications/Radio/Television, Communicative Disorders, Computer Engineering, Computer Science, Consumer/Family Economics, Cytotechnology, Early Childhood Education, Economics, Educational/Counseling Psychology, Educational Studies, Electrical Engineering, Elementary Education, English, Environmental Design, Finance/Banking, Fisheries/Wildlife, Food Science/Nutrition, French, General Agriculture, General Studies, Geography, Geology, German, Health Physics, History, Horticulture, Hotel/Restaurant Management, Human Development/Family Studies, Human Environmental Sciences Journalism, Human Nutrition/Foods, Human Resource Management, Industrial Engineering, Journalism, Labor Studies, Latin American Studies, Linguistics, Magazine, Marketing, Mathematics, Mechanical Engineering, Medical Dietetics, Medical Technology, Microbiology, Music, Music Education, News/Editorial, Newspaper Publishing, Nuclear Medicine, Nursing, Occupational Therapy, Operations Management, Orthopedically Handicapped, Parks/Recreation/Tourism, Philosophy, Photojournalism, Physical Education, Physical Therapy, Physics, Political Science, Practical Arts/Vocational-Technical Education, Psychology, Radiation Therapy Technology, Radiologic Sciences, Real Estate, Religious Studies, Respiratory Therapy, Risk/Insurance, Rural Sociology, Russian, Russian Area Studies, Secondary Education, Social Work, Sociology, South Asian Studies, Spanish, Special Education, Speech Clinician, Statistics, Textile/Apparel Management, Theatre.
**Distribution of degrees:** The majors with the highest enrollment are business administration, biological sciences, and psychology.
**Requirements:** General education requirement.
**Academic regulations:** Minimum 2.0 GPA must be maintained.
**Special:** Minors offered in some majors. Black studies program. Self-designed majors. Double majors. Dual degrees. Independent study. Accelerated study. Pass/fail grading option. Internships. Cooperative education programs. Graduate school at which undergraduates may take graduate-level courses. Preprofessional programs in law, medicine, and veterinary science. 2-3 masters in architecture program with Washington U. 5-year bachelor's/master's accounting program. Member of Mid-Missouri Association of Colleges and Universities. Numerous semester-away programs. Exchange programs with Kansas State U, Kansas U, and U of Nebraska. Member of National Student Exchange (NSE). Pre-architecture program with Kansas U. Teacher certification in early childhood, elementary, secondary, special education, and vo-tech education. Certification in specific subject areas. Member of International Student Exchange Program (ISEP). Study abroad in Australia, China, Denmark, England, France, Germany, Italy, Japan, Mexico, Middle Eastern countries, the former Soviet Republics, Spain, and Taiwan. ROTC, NROTC, and AFROTC.
**Honors:** Phi Beta Kappa. Honors program. Honor societies.
**Academic Assistance:** Remedial study skills. Nonremedial tutoring.

**STUDENT LIFE. Housing:** Freshmen are required to live on campus. Coed, women's, and men's dorms. Sorority and fraternity housing. School-owned/operated apartments. Off-campus privately-owned housing. On-campus married-student housing. 32% of students live in college housing.
**Social atmosphere:** According to the student newspaper, the university has "a great social atmosphere. Greeks dominate the social scene." Favorite off-campus nightspots include the Heidelberg, the Blue Note, and Harpo's.
**Services and counseling/handicapped student services:** Placement services. Health service. Women's center. Day care. Counseling services for minority and older students. Birth control, personal, and psychological counseling. Career and academic guidance services. Physically disabled student services. Learning disabled program/services. Notetaking services. Tape recorders. Tutors. Reader services for the blind.
**Campus organizations:** Undergraduate student government. Student newspaper (Maneater, published twice/week). Yearbook. Radio and TV stations. Corner Playhouse Association, Legion of Black Collegians Gospel Choir, Amnesty For Animals, Campus for Choice, College Democrats, College Republicans, Medieval Re-enactment Society, Feminist Alliance, Pan-Hellenic Council, Gay/Lesbian Alliance, political, departmental, and service groups, 380 organizations in all. 34 fraternities, 28 chapter houses; 21 sororities, 17 chapter houses. 25% of men join a fraternity. 25% of women join a sorority.
**Religious organizations:** African Christian Students Fellowship, Baptist Student Union, Campus Crusade for Christ, Campus Outreach, Catholic Student Association, Chi Alpha, Christian Campus House, Christian Fellowship of Mizzou, Intervarsity Christian Fellowship, Jewish Student Association, Latter-Day Saints Student Association, Liahana Student Fellowship, Maranatha, Moslem Students Organization, Pagan Students Association, Religious Studies Club, University Bible Studies, Wesley Foundation Campus Ministry.
**Minority/foreign student organizations:** Association of Black Graduate and Professional Students, Barrier Free, Black Business Students, Blacks in Pursuit of Medicine, Hispano-American Leadership Organization (HALO), Hispanic Law Students Association, Legion of Black Collegians, Minority Achievement Program, Minorities Involved in Negotiating Decisions, Multicultural Journalism Association, NAACP, Society of Black Engineers. European Students Association, Cultural Association of India, Club Singapore, Bangladesh Students Association, African, Brazilian, Chinese, French, Hong Kong, Indonesian, Japanese, Korean, Latin American, Malaysian, Nigerian, Pakistani, Palestinian, Saudi, Sudanese, Taiwanese, Thai, Tunisian, and Turkish groups.

**ATHLETICS. Physical education requirements:** None.
**Intercollegiate competition:** 5% of students participate. Baseball (M), basketball (M,W), cross-country (M,W), diving (M,W), football (M), golf (M,W), gymnastics (W), softball (W), swimming (M,W), tennis (M,W), track (indoor) (M,W), track (outdoor) (M,W), track and field (indoor) (M,W), track and field (outdoor) (M,W), volleyball (W), wrestling (M). Member of Big Eight Conference, NCAA Division I-A.

**ADMISSIONS. Academic basis for candidate selection** (in order of priority): Secondary school record, class rank, standardized test scores.

**Requirements:** Graduation from secondary school is required; GED is accepted. 15 units and the following program of study are required: 4 units of English, 3 units of math, 2 units of science including 1 unit of lab, 2 units of social studies, 3 units of academic electives. 2 units of foreign language recommended. Applicants must meet standards of scale based on ACT or SAT scores and secondary school class rank. Applicants to physical therapy program must be in-state residents. Conditional admission possible for in-state applicants not meeting standard requirements. ACT is required; SAT may be substituted. Campus visit recommended. No off-campus interviews.
**Procedure:** Take SAT or ACT by October of 12th year. Application deadline is May 15. Notification of admission on rolling basis. $375 room deposit, refundable until July 1. Freshmen accepted in terms other than fall.
**Special programs:** Admission may be deferred one year. Credit may be granted through CEEB Advanced Placement for scores of 3 or higher. Credit may be granted through CLEP subject exams. Credit and placement may be granted through challenge exams. Concurrent enrollment program.
**Transfer students:** Transfer students accepted for terms other than fall. In fall 1993, 31% of all new students were transfers into all classes. 2,599 transfer applications were received, 1,852 were accepted. Application deadline is rolling for fall; rolling for spring. Minimum 2.0 GPA required. Lowest course grade accepted is "C." At least 30 semester hours must be completed at the university to receive degree.
**Admissions contact:** Georgeanne Porter, M.A., Director of Admissions. 314 882-7786, 800 225-6075.

**FINANCIAL AID. Available aid:** Pell grants, SEOG, Federal Nursing Student Scholarships, state scholarships and grants, school scholarships and grants, private scholarships and grants, ROTC scholarships, academic merit scholarships, and athletic scholarships. Perkins Loans (NDSL), PLUS, Stafford Loans (GSL), NSL, state loans, school loans, private loans, and SLS. Deferred payment plan.
**Financial aid statistics:** In 1993-94, 85% of all undergraduate applicants received aid; 85% of freshman applicants. Average amounts of aid awarded freshmen: Scholarships and grants, $2,700; loans, $2,300.
**Supporting data/closing dates:** FAFSA: Priority filing date is March 1. FAF/FFS: Priority filing date is March 1. Notification of awards begins April 15.
**Financial aid contact:** Joe Camille, M.A., Director of Financial Aid. 314 882-7506, 800 225-6075.

**STUDENT EMPLOYMENT.** College Work/Study Program. Institutional employment. 23% of full-time undergraduates work on campus during school year. Students may expect to earn an average of $800 during school year. Off-campus part-time employment opportunities rated "good."

**COMPUTER FACILITIES.** 700 IBM/IBM-compatible and Macintosh/Apple microcomputers. Students may access IBM minicomputer/mainframe systems, BITNET, Internet. Residence halls may be equipped with stand-alone microcomputers, networked microcomputers. Computer languages and software packages include Ada, APL, Assembler, COBOL, FORTRAN, Pascal, PL/1, SAS. Computer facilities are available to all students.
**Fees:** $4 computer fee per semester hour; included in tuition/fees.
**Hours:** 24 hours.

**PROMINENT ALUMNI/AE.** Sam Walton, chairman, Wal-Mart; Dick Richards, astronaut; Maj. Gen. Burton R. Moore, U.S. Army.

# University of Missouri–Kansas City

**Kansas City, MO 64110** **816 235-1000**

**1993-94 Costs.** Tuition: $2,186 (state residents), $6,538 (out-of-state). Room & board: $4,540. Fees, books, misc. academic expenses (school's estimate): $899.
**Enrollment.** Undergraduates: 1,688 men, 2,038 women (full-time). Freshman class: 1,351 applicants, 954 accepted, 542 enrolled. Graduate enrollment: 1,332 men, 2,094 women.
**Test score averages/ranges.** Average ACT scores: 24 English, 23 math, 24 composite. Range of ACT scores of middle 50%: 21-27 English, 20-26 math.
**Faculty.** 358 full-time; 186 part-time. 59% of faculty holds doctoral degree. Student/faculty ratio: 12 to 1.
**Selectivity rating.** Competitive.

**PROFILE.** U Missouri–Kansas City, founded in 1929, is a public, comprehensive institution. Programs are offered through the College of Arts and Sciences; the Schools of Basic Life Sciences, Dentistry, Education, Law, Medicine, Nursing, and Pharmacy; the Bloch School of Business and Public Administration; and the Conservatory of Music. Its 120-acre campus is located in Kansas City, 61 miles east of Topeka.

**Accreditation:** NCACS. Professionally accredited by the Accreditation Board for Engineering and Technology, the American Assembly of Collegiate Schools of Business, the American Council on Pharmaceutical Education, the American Dental Association, the National Association of Schools of Music, the National Council for Accreditation of Teacher Education, the National League for Nursing.
**Religious orientation:** University of Missouri-Kansas City is nonsectarian; no religious requirements.
**Library:** Collections totaling over 905,510 volumes, 8,569 periodical subscriptions, and 1,699,045 microform items.
**Special facilities/museums:** Art gallery, professional theater, geosciences museums, language lab.
**Athletic facilities:** Gymnasium, swimming pool, weight room, basketball, handball, tennis, and volleyball courts, tracks, baseball, football, and soccer fields.

**STUDENT BODY. Undergraduate profile:** 78% are state residents; 70% are transfers. 5% Asian-American, 8% Black, 2% Hispanic, 1% Native American, 73% White, 11% Other. Average age of undergraduates is 23.
**Freshman profile:** 92% of accepted applicants took ACT.
**Undergraduate achievement:** 74% of fall 1991 freshmen returned for fall 1992 term. 11% of entering class graduated.
**Foreign students:** 275 students are from out of the country. Countries represented include China, India, Korea, Malaysia, and Taiwan; 81 in all.

**PROGRAMS OF STUDY. Degrees:** B.A., B.Bus.Admin., B.F.A., B.Lib.Arts, B.Mus., B.Mus.Ed., B.S., B.S.Civil Eng., B.S.Dent.Hyg., B.S.Elec.Eng., B.S.Mech.Eng., B.S.Nurs., B.S.Pharm.
**Majors:** Accounting, Administration of Justice, American Culture, Art, Art History, Biology, Business Administration, Chemistry, Civil Engineering, Communications Studies, Computer Science, Dance, Dental Hygiene, Earth Sciences, Economics, Electrical Engineering, Elementary Education, English, French, Geography, Geology, German, History, Interdisciplinary Studies, Judaic Studies, Liberal Arts, Mathematics, Mechanical Engineering, Medical Technology, Music, Music Composition, Music Education, Music Performance, Music Theory, Nursing, Pharmacy, Philosophy, Physical Education, Political Science, Psychology, Secondary Education, Sociology, Spanish, Speech/Hearing Sciences, Studio Art, Theatre, Urban Affairs.
**Distribution of degrees:** The majors with the highest enrollment are business administration, biology, and elementary education; music theory, art history, and Judaic studies have the lowest.
**Requirements:** General education requirement.
**Academic regulations:** Minimum 2.0 GPA must be maintained.
**Special:** Minors offered in most majors and in classical and ancient studies, humanities, language and literature, women's studies, and writing. Area and interdepartmental majors possible. Six-year integrated arts and sciences/dental and medical programs. Self-designed majors. Double majors. Dual degrees. Independent study. Pass/fail grading option. Internships. Cooperative education programs. Graduate school at which undergraduates may take graduate-level courses. Preprofessional programs in law, medicine, veterinary science, dentistry, optometry, and osteopathy. B.A./B.S., B.A./J.D., B.A./M.D., B.A./D.D.S., and B.B.A./M.B.A. programs. Member of Kansas City Regional Council for Higher Education with 19 other schools; cross-registration possible. Teacher certification in elementary, secondary, and special education. Certification in specific subject areas. Study abroad in China, England, Germany, Korea, Mexico, South Africa, the former Soviet Republics, and Spain. ROTC.
**Honors:** Honors program. Honor societies.
**Academic Assistance:** Nonremedial tutoring.

**STUDENT LIFE. Housing:** Coed dorms. Off-campus privately-owned housing. 3% of students live in college housing.
**Social Atmosphere:** "A large percentage of our students are married, and the majority of the students commute from their respective neighborhoods," reports the student newspaper, "therefore their social lives are more work-oriented." Favorite hangouts include Mike's, Desert Heart's Club, and the Hurricane. Popular events during the year are the Roo Fair, the Community Psychic Fair, and the Holistic Health Fair.
**Services and counseling/handicapped student services:** Placement services. Women's center. Day care. Personal and psychological counseling. Career guidance services. Physically disabled student services. Learning disabled services. Notetaking services. Tutors. Reader services for the blind.
**Campus organizations:** Undergraduate student government. Student newspaper (University News, published once/week). Literary magazine. All-Student Association, debate team, departmental groups, service and social groups, 125 organizations in all. Six fraternities, three chapter houses; seven sororities, two chapter houses. 5% of men join a fraternity. 4% of women join a sorority.
**Religious organizations:** Several religious groups.
**Minority/foreign student organizations:** African-American Student Union, minority professional students organizations, minority fraternities/sororities. International Student Club, other foreign student groups.

**ATHLETICS. Physical education requirements:** Two semesters of physical education required in some programs.
**Intercollegiate competition:** 1% of students participate. Basketball (M,W), cheerleading (M,W), cross-country (M,W), golf (M,W), riflery (M,W), soccer (M), softball (W), tennis (M,W), track and field (outdoor) (M,W), volleyball (W). Member of Mid-Continent Conference, NCAA Division I.
**Intramural and club sports:** 4% of students participate. Intramural basketball, flag football, golf, racquetball, volleyball.

**ADMISSIONS. Academic basis for candidate selection** (in order of priority): Standardized test scores, class rank, secondary school record.
**Requirements:** Graduation from secondary school is recommended; GED is accepted. 15 units and the following program of study are required: 4 units of English, 3 units of math, 2 units of science including 1 unit of lab, 2 units of social studies, 4 units of electives including 3 units of academic electives. Applicants must meet standards of scale based on ACT or SAT scores and secondary school class rank. Interviews required of applicants to pharmacy program and to six-year M.D. and D.D.S. programs. Audition required of music program applicants. R.N. required of nursing program applicants. Conditional admission possible for applicants not meeting standard requirements. ACT is required; SAT may be substituted. Campus visit recommended. No off-campus interviews.
**Procedure:** Take SAT or ACT by December of 12th year. Suggest filing application by May 1; no deadline. Notification of admission on rolling basis. Freshmen accepted in terms other than fall.
**Special programs:** Admission may be deferred one semester. Credit may be granted through CEEB Advanced Placement for scores of 3 or higher. Credit may be granted through CLEP subject exams, ACT PEP and challenge exams. Early entrance/early admission program. Concurrent enrollment program.
**Transfer students:** Transfer students accepted for terms other than fall. In fall 1992, 70% of all new students were transfers into all classes. 2,020 transfer applications were received, 1,883 were accepted. Application deadline is July 1 for fall; December 1 for spring. Minimum 2.0 GPA required. Lowest course grade accepted is "D." Maximum number of transferable credits is 60 semester hours from a two-year school and 90 semester hours from a four-year school. At least 30 semester hours must be completed at the university to receive degree.
**Admissions contact:** Nancy Mead, Interim Director of Admissions. 816 235-1111.

**FINANCIAL AID. Available aid:** Pell grants, SEOG, state scholarships and grants, school scholarships and grants, private scholarships and grants, ROTC scholarships, academic merit scholarships, and athletic scholarships. Perkins Loans (NDSL), PLUS, Stafford Loans (GSL), Health Professions Loans, state loans, school loans, private loans, and SLS.
**Financial aid statistics:** 8% of aid is not need-based. In 1992-93, 47% of all undergraduate applicants received aid; 45% of freshman applicants. Average amounts of aid awarded freshmen: Scholarships and grants, $2,021; loans, $1,725.
**Supporting data/closing dates:** FAFSA: Priority filing date is March 1. School's own aid application: Priority filing date is March 15. Notification of awards on rolling basis.
**Financial aid contact:** Buford Baber, Ph.D., Director of Financial Aid. 816 235-1154.

**STUDENT EMPLOYMENT.** College Work/Study Program. Institutional employment. Students may expect to earn an average of $2,550 during school year. Off-campus part-time employment opportunities rated "excellent."

**COMPUTER FACILITIES.** 230 IBM/IBM-compatible and Macintosh/Apple microcomputers; 90 are networked. Students may access Digital minicomputer/mainframe systems, Internet. Residence halls may be equipped with stand-alone microcomputers, networked terminals. Computer languages and software packages include BMDP, C, COBOL, FORTRAN, Lotus 1-2-3, Maple, SAS, SPSS-X, WordPerfect. Computer facilities are available to all students.
**Fees:** $4 computer fee per semester hour; included in tuition/fees.
**Hours:** 8 AM-5 PM in some locations; 24 hours in others.

# University of Missouri–Rolla

**Rolla, MO 65401** **314 341-4111**

**1993-94 Costs.** Tuition: $2,733 (state residents), $8,172 (out-of-state). Room & board: $3,497. Fees, books, misc. academic expenses (school's estimate): $580.
**Enrollment.** Undergraduates: 3,036 men, 890 women (full-time). Freshman class: 1,868 applicants, 1,753 accepted, 823 enrolled. Graduate enrollment: 995 men, 199 women.
**Test score averages/ranges.** Average SAT scores: 547 verbal, 655 math. Range of SAT scores of middle 50%: 480-600 verbal, 590-700 math. Average ACT scores: 25 English, 27 math, 27 composite. Range of ACT scores of middle 50%: 24-28 English, 26-30 math.
**Faculty.** 289 full-time; 56 part-time. 92% of faculty holds doctoral degree. Student/faculty ratio: 15 to 1.
**Selectivity rating.** Highly competitive.

**PROFILE.** U Missouri–Rolla, founded in 1870, is a public, liberal arts institution. Its 105-acre campus is located in Rolla, 95 miles southwest of St. Louis.

**Accreditation:** NCACS. Professionally accredited by the Accreditation Board for Engineering and Technology.
**Religious orientation:** University of Missouri-Rolla is nonsectarian; no religious requirements.
**Library:** Collections totaling over 447,229 volumes, 1,394 periodical subscriptions, and 400,204 microform items.
**Special facilities/museums:** Museum of rocks, minerals, and gemstones, centers for environmental research, water resources, industrial research, and rock mechanics research, geophysical observatory, nuclear reactor, computerized manufacturing system, experimental mine.
**Athletic facilities:** Swimming pool, baseball, football, intramural, rugby, soccer, and softball fields, handball and tennis courts, gymnasium, golf course.

**STUDENT BODY. Undergraduate profile:** 79% are state residents; 28% are transfers. 3% Asian-American, 4% Black, 1% Hispanic, 85% White, 7% Other. Average age of undergraduates is 22.
**Freshman profile:** 2% of freshmen who took SAT scored 700 or over on verbal, 27% scored 700 or over on math; 23% scored 600 or over on verbal, 70% scored 600 or over on math; 66% scored 500 or over on verbal, 93% scored 500 or over on math; 94% scored 400 or over on verbal, 100% scored 400 or over on math; 100% scored 300 or over on verbal. 14% of freshmen who took ACT scored 30 or over on English, 32% scored 30 or over on math, 31% scored 30 or over on composite; 69% scored 24 or over on English, 83% scored 24 or over on math, 82% scored 24 or over on composite; 96% scored 18 or over on English, 99% scored 18 or over on math, 99% scored 18 or over on composite; 100% scored 12 or over on English, 100% scored 12 or over on math, 100% scored 12 or over on composite. 36% of accepted applicants took SAT; 94% took ACT. 85% of freshmen come from public schools.
**Undergraduate achievement:** 74% of fall 1992 freshmen returned for fall 1993 term. 8% of entering class graduated. 19% of students who completed a degree program immediately went on to graduate study.
**Foreign students:** 213 students are from out of the country. Countries represented include China, India, Malaysia, Taiwan, Thailand, and Turkey; 66 in all.

**PROGRAMS OF STUDY. Degrees:** B.A., B.S., B.S.Elec.Eng., B.S.Mech.Eng., B.S.Nurs.
**Majors:** Aerospace Engineering, Applied Mathematics, Ceramic Engineering, Chemical Engineering, Chemistry, Civil Engineering, Computer Science, Economics, Electrical Engineering, Engineering Management, English, Geological Engineering, Geology/Geophysics, History, Life Sciences, Management Systems, Mechanical Engineering, Metallurgical Engineering, Mining Engineering, Nuclear Engineering, Nursing, Petroleum Engineering, Philosophy, Physics, Psychology.
**Distribution of degrees:** The majors with the highest enrollment are mechanical engineering, electrical engineering, and civil engineering; English and economics have the lowest.
**Requirements:** General education requirement.
**Academic regulations:** Freshmen must maintain minimum 2.0 GPA; sophomores, 2.1 GPA; juniors, 2.2 GPA; seniors, 2.2 GPA.
**Special:** Minors offered. Double majors. Dual degrees. Pass/fail grading option. Internships. Cooperative education programs. Graduate school at which undergraduates may take graduate-level courses. Preprofessional programs in law and medicine. Exchange programs with Kansas State U, U of Kansas, and Wichita State U. Teacher certification in secondary education. Certification in specific subject areas. Study abroad in England. ROTC and AFROTC.
**Honors:** Honors program. Honor societies.

**STUDENT LIFE. Housing:** All freshmen and sophomores must live on campus. Coed dorms. Sorority and fraternity housing. School-owned/operated apartments. 68% of students live in college housing.
**Social Atmosphere:** As reported by the student newspaper, "Social life and cultural life are mainly limited to on-campus events. Fraternities, Student Union Board, Interfraternity Council, and Saint Patrick's Board organize most events." Popular on-campus gathering spots include the Library, the Courtyard, University Center East, and the Multipurpose Building. Favorite off-campus hangouts are Brewsters and Lion's Club Park. Homecoming, Greek Week, Septemberfest, and the St. Patrick's Festival are among the year's favorite events.
**Services and counseling/handicapped student services:** Placement services. Health service. Counseling services for minority students. Psychological counseling. Career and academic guidance services. Physically disabled student services. Learning disabled services. Notetaking services. Tape recorders. Tutors. Reader services for the blind.
**Campus organizations:** Undergraduate student government. Student newspaper (Missouri Miner, published once/week). Radio station. Glee club, madrigal group, concert and jazz bands, pep bands, performing arts groups, Artist Series, Young Democrats, Young Republicans, athletic, departmental, service, and special-interest groups, 165 organizations in all. 22 fraternities, 19 chapter houses; five sororities, three chapter houses. 28% of men join a fraternity. 20% of women join a sorority.
**Religious organizations:** Baptist Student Union, Campus Crusade for Christ, Chi Alpha, Christian Campus Fellowship, Christian Science Organization, Intervarsity Christian Fellowship, Koinonia, Latter-Day Saints Student Association, Lutheran student Center, Muslim Student Association, Newman Student Center, Wesley Foundation, Voices of Inspiration.
**Minority/foreign student organizations:** National Society of Black Engineers, Society of Hispanic Engineers, Association for Black Students, Society of Women Engineers. International Student Club, Chinese, Indian, Korean, Malaysian, Pakistani, Thai, and Turkish student groups.

**ATHLETICS. Physical education requirements:** None.
**Intercollegiate competition:** 7% of students participate. Baseball (M), basketball (M,W), cross-country (M,W), diving (M), football (M), golf (M), riflery (M), soccer (M,W), softball (W), swimming (M), tennis (M), track (indoor) (M,W), track (outdoor) (M,W), track and field (indoor) (M,W), track and field (outdoor) (M,W). Member of MIAA, NCAA Division II.
**Intramural and club sports:** 50% of students participate. Intramural badminton, basketball, billiards, bowling, cross-country, cycling, flag football, horseshoes, racquetball, soccer, softball, swimming, table tennis, tennis, track and field, volleyball, weight lifting, wrestling. Men's club rugby, skeet/trapshooting, volleyball, water polo.

**ADMISSIONS. Academic basis for candidate selection** (in order of priority): Class rank, standardized test scores, secondary school record, school's recommendation.
**Nonacademic basis for candidate selection:** Character and personality, extracurricular participation, particular talent or ability, and alumni/ae relationship are considered.
**Requirements:** Graduation from secondary school is required; GED is accepted. 19 units and the following program of study are required: 4 units of English, 3 units of math, 2 units of science including 1 unit of lab, 2 units of social studies, 4 units of electives (1 unit of fine arts and 3 additional units selected from foreign language, English, mathematics, science, or social studies). ACT is required; SAT may be substituted. Campus visit recommended. Off-campus interviews available with admissions and alumni representatives.
**Procedure:** Take SAT or ACT by October of 12th year. Visit college for interview by December of 12th year. Suggest filing application by November 1. Application deadline is July 1. Notification of admission on rolling basis. Reply is required by July 15. $50 nonrefundable room deposit. Freshmen accepted in terms other than fall.
**Special programs:** Credit and/or placement may be granted through CEEB Advanced Placement exams for scores of 3 or higher. Credit and/or placement may be granted through CLEP subject exams. Credit may be granted through military experience. Credit and placement may be granted through challenge exams. Concurrent enrollment program.
**Transfer students:** Transfer students accepted for terms other than fall. In fall 1993, 28% of all new students were transfers into all classes. 557 transfer applications were received, 470 were accepted. Application deadline is August for fall; January for spring. Minimum 2.5 GPA recommended. At least 60 semester hours must be completed at the university to receive degree.
**Admissions contact:** Dave Allen, M.A., Director of Admissions and Student Financial Aid. 314 341-4164.

**FINANCIAL AID. Available aid:** Pell grants, SEOG, state scholarships and grants, school scholarships and grants, private scholarships and grants, ROTC scholarships, academic merit scholarships, and athletic scholarships. Perkins Loans (NDSL), PLUS, Stafford Loans (GSL), school loans, private loans, and SLS. Deferred payment plan. VISA/Master Card/Discover.
**Financial aid statistics:** In 1993-94, 93% of all undergraduate applicants received aid; 68% of freshman applicants. Average amounts of aid awarded freshmen: Scholarships and grants, $2,000; loans, $2,000.
**Supporting data/closing dates:** FAFSA: Priority filing date is March 31. Notification of awards begins April 1.
**Financial aid contact:** Robert W. Whites, Associate Director of Admissions and Student Financial Aid. 314 341-4282.

**STUDENT EMPLOYMENT.** College Work/Study Program. Institutional employment. 27% of full-time undergraduates work on campus during school year. Students may expect to earn an average of $1,600 during school year. Off-campus part-time employment opportunities rated "fair."

**COMPUTER FACILITIES.** 400 IBM/IBM-compatible and Macintosh/Apple microcomputers; all are networked. Students may access Hewlett-Packard, IBM minicomputer/mainframe systems, BITNET, Internet. Residence halls may be equipped with networked

microcomputers. Client/LAN operating systems include Apple/Macintosh, DOS, UNIX/XENIX/AIX, X-windows, Novell. Computer languages and software packages include ADINA, Avaquas, BASIC, C, CATIA, dBASE, Fluent, FORTRAN, Ideas, Lotus 1-2-3, Mable, Mathematica, Molecular Modeling, NASTRAN, Pascal, PL/1, Quattro Pro, SAS, Systat, WordPerfect; 100 in all. Computer facilities are available to all students.
**Fees:** $5 computer fee per credit hour; included in tuition/fees.
**Hours:** 24 hours.

**GRADUATE CAREER DATA.** Highest graduate school enrollments: Auburn U, U of Missouri-Columbia, U of Missouri-Rolla, Pennsylvania State U, Stanford U, U of Texas, and Yale U. Companies and businesses that hire graduates: Black & Beatch, Ford Motors, McDonnell Douglas, Missouri Highway Transportation.

**PROMINENT ALUMNI/AE.** Vachel H. McNutt, discoverer of first commercial deposit of potash in Western Hemisphere; Harry H. Kessler, chairperson and CEO, Meehanite Metal; Enoch R. Needles, designer of world-famous bridges and highways; Lt. Col. Tom Akers, astronaut, U.S. Air Force.

# University of Missouri–St. Louis

**St. Louis, MO 63121** **314 553-5000**

**1994-95 Costs.** Tuition: $3,030 (state residents), $9,000 (out-of-state). Room & board: $3,878. Fees, books, misc. academic expenses (school's estimate): $936.
**Enrollment.** Undergraduates: 2,238 men, 2,555 women (full-time). Freshman class: 1,610 applicants, 1,051 accepted, 569 enrolled. Graduate enrollment: 853 men, 1,513 women.
**Test score averages/ranges.** Average ACT scores: 22 composite.
**Faculty.** 390 full-time; 245 part-time. 80% of faculty holds doctoral degree. Student/faculty ratio: 14 to 1.
**Selectivity rating.** Less competitive.

**PROFILE.** U Missouri–St. Louis, founded in 1963, is a public, comprehensive institution. Programs are offered through the Colleges of Arts and Sciences, Business Administration, Education, Optometry, and Nursing and the Evening College. Its 178-acre campus is located in St. Louis.

**Accreditation:** NCACS. Professionally accredited by the American Assembly of Collegiate Schools of Business, the American Optometric Association, the American Psychological Association, the Council on Social Work Education, the National Association of Schools of Music, the National Association of Schools of Public Affairs and Administration, the National Council for Accreditation of Teacher Education, the National League for Nursing.
**Religious orientation:** University of Missouri-St. Louis is nonsectarian; no religious requirements.
**Library:** Collections totaling over 571,263 volumes, 2,900 periodical subscriptions, and 1,741,337 microform items.
**Special facilities/museums:** Art gallery, language, writing labs.
**Athletic facilities:** Gymnasium, swimming pool, aerobics/exercise and weight rooms, baseball, intramural, soccer, and softball fields, badminton, basketball, handball, racquetball, tennis, and volleyball courts, track, fitness center.

**STUDENT BODY. Undergraduate profile:** 97% are state residents; 18% are transfers. 2.8% Asian-American, 13.2% Black, 1.1% Hispanic, 82.7% White, .2% Other. Average age of undergraduates is 24.
**Freshman profile:** 14% of accepted applicants took SAT; 86% took ACT. 75% of freshmen come from public schools.
**Undergraduate achievement:** 62% of fall 1992 freshmen returned for fall 1993 term. 9% of entering class graduated.
**Foreign students:** 229 students are from out of the country. Countries represented include China, India, Malaysia, Pakistan, and Taiwan; 45 in all.

**PROGRAMS OF STUDY. Degrees:** B.A., B.Gen.Studies, B.Mus., B.S., B.S.Bus.Admin., B.S.Crim./Crim.Just., B.S.Ed., B.S.Elec.Eng., B.S.Mech.Eng., B.S.Nurs., B.S.Pub.Admin., B.Soc.Work.
**Majors:** Accounting, Anthropology, Art History, Biology, Business Administration, Business Education, Chemistry, Computer Science, Criminology/Criminal Justice, Early Childhood Education, Economics, Electrical Engineering, Elementary Education, English, Finance, French, General Studies, German, History, Management Information Systems, Management/Organizational Behavior, Management Science, Marketing, Mathematics, Mechanical Engineering, Music, Music Education, Nursing, Philosophy, Physical Education, Physics, Political Science, Psychology, Public Administration, Social Work, Sociology, Spanish, Special Education, Speech Communication.
**Distribution of degrees:** The majors with the highest enrollment are business administration, education, and psychology; philosophy have the lowest.
**Requirements:** General education requirement.
**Academic regulations:** Minimum 2.0 GPA must be maintained.
**Special:** Minors offered in most majors. Extension and certificate programs offered. Urban Journalism Center in conjunction with U of Missouri at Columbia. Self-designed majors. Double majors. Dual degrees. Independent study. Accelerated study. Pass/fail grading option. Internships. Cooperative education programs. Graduate school at which undergraduates may take graduate-level courses. Preprofessional programs in law, medicine, veterinary science, pharmacy, dentistry, optometry, and engineering. Member of Higher Education Council. Exchange programs with Kansas State U, U of Kansas, U of Nebraska, St. Louis U, and Washington U. Teacher certification in early childhood, elementary, secondary, and special education. Certification in specific subject areas. Study abroad in England, France, and Germany. ROTC. AFROTC at Parks Coll.
**Honors:** Honors program. Honor societies.
**Academic Assistance:** Remedial writing, math, and study skills. Nonremedial tutoring.

**STUDENT LIFE. Housing:** Students may live on or off campus. Coed dorms. 1% of students live in college housing.
**Social Atmosphere:** The student newspaper reports, "UM-Saint Louis is an unusual campus in that it is a commuter campus and the average age is 27, therefore most students have part-time or full-time jobs." Popular on-campus spots are the Mark Twain Building, Bugg Lake, and the Quad. Whalens and the Break Away Cafe are favorite off-campus hangouts. Greeks, the swim team, and the Student Government are influential groups on campus. Popular social and cultural events are Mirthday, Hispanic-Latino Week, Greek Week, and Handicap Awareness Week.
**Services and counseling/handicapped student services:** Placement services. Health service. Women's center. Day care. Counseling services for minority, veteran, and older students. Personal and psychological counseling. Academic guidance services. Physically disabled student services. Learning disabled services. Notetaking services. Tape recorders. Tutors.
**Campus organizations:** Undergraduate student government. Student newspaper (Current, published once/week). Radio station. Disabled Student Union, film-lecture-theatre series, departmental and athletic groups, special-interest groups, 90 organizations in all. Four fraternities, all with chapter houses; five sororities, all with chapter houses.
**Religious organizations:** Baptist Student Union, Bible Study, Christian Ministry Group, Intervarsity Christian Fellowship, Jewish Student Union, Newman House, Wesley Foundation.
**Minority/foreign student organizations:** Associated Black Collegians, Minority Student Service Coalition. International Student Organization.

**ATHLETICS. Physical education requirements:** None.
**Intercollegiate competition:** 3% of students participate. Baseball (M), basketball (M,W), cheerleading (M,W), golf (M), soccer (M,W), softball (W), swimming (M,W), tennis (M,W), volleyball (W). Member of Mid-American Intercollegiate Athletic Association, NCAA Division II.
**Intramural and club sports:** 22% of students participate. Intramural basketball, bowling, flag football, golf, pickleball, racquetball, running, soccer, softball, swimming, table tennis, tennis, walleyball. Men's club ice hockey. Women's club bowling.

**ADMISSIONS. Academic basis for candidate selection** (in order of priority): Secondary school record, standardized test scores, class rank, school's recommendation.
**Nonacademic basis for candidate selection:** Extracurricular participation and particular talent or ability are considered.
**Requirements:** Graduation from secondary school is required; GED is accepted. 15 units and the following program of study are required: 4 units of English, 3 units of math, 2 units of science including 1 unit of lab, 2 units of social studies, 3 units of academic electives. 2 units of foreign language recommended. Rank in top two-thirds of secondary school class required. Associate's degree in nursing or R.N. required of B.S.N. program applicants. Conditional admission possible for applicants not meeting standard requirements. ACT is required; SAT may be substituted. Campus visit recommended. Off-campus interviews available with an admissions representative.
**Procedure:** Take SAT or ACT by July 1 of 12th year. Suggest filing application by July 1; no deadline. Notification of admission on rolling basis. Freshmen accepted in terms other than fall.
**Special programs:** Credit and/or placement may be granted through CEEB Advanced Placement exams for scores of 3 or higher. Credit may be granted through CLEP general and subject exams, ACT PEP, DANTES, and challenge exams, and military and life experience. Concurrent enrollment program.
**Transfer students:** Transfer students accepted for terms other than fall. In fall 1993, 18% of all new students were transfers into all classes. 3,397 transfer applications were received, 2,773 were accepted. Application deadline is July 1 for fall; December 1 for spring. Minimum 2.0 GPA required. Lowest course grade accepted is "D." Maximum number of transferable credits is 90 semester hours. At least 30 semester hours must be completed at the university to receive degree.
**Admissions contact:** Mimi LaMarca, M.Ed., Director of Admissions and Registrar. 314 553-5451.

**FINANCIAL AID. Available aid:** Pell grants, SEOG, state scholarships and grants, school scholarships, private scholarships, ROTC scholarships, academic merit scholarships, and athletic scholarships. Perkins Loans (NDSL), PLUS, Stafford Loans (GSL), Health Professions Loans, school loans, and SLS. Deferred payment plan.
**Financial aid statistics:** In 1993-94, 84% of all undergraduate applicants received aid; 84% of freshman applicants. Average amounts of aid awarded freshmen: Scholarships and grants, $1,066; loans, $1,563.
**Supporting data/closing dates:** FAFSA: Priority filing date is April 1; deadline is October 31. FAF/FFS: Priority filing date is April 1. Notification of awards on rolling basis.
**Financial aid contact:** Pamela Fowler, Director of Financial Aid. 314 553-5526.

**STUDENT EMPLOYMENT.** College Work/Study Program. Institutional employment. 12% of full-time undergraduates work on campus during school year. Students may expect to earn an average of $1,500 during school year. Off-campus part-time employment opportunities rated "good."

**COMPUTER FACILITIES.** 300 IBM/IBM-compatible, Macintosh/Apple, and RISC-/UNIX-based microcomputers; 200 are networked. Students may access AT&T, Data General, Digital, Hewlett-Packard, IBM, SUN minicomputer/mainframe systems, Internet. Residence halls may be equipped with stand-alone microcomputers. Client/LAN operating systems include Apple/Macintosh. Computer languages and software packages include BASIC, COBOL, FORTRAN, Pascal, PL/1, SAS; 39 in all. Computer facilities are available to all students.
**Fees:** $4 computer fee per semester hour.
**Hours:** 8 AM-10 PM.

**GRADUATE CAREER DATA.** Companies and businesses that hire graduates: Arthur Andersen, Big Six Public accounting firms, government agencies, McDonnell Douglas, Southwestern Bell.

**PROMINENT ALUMNI/AE.** Vince Schomehl, mayor of St. Louis; Marty Hendin, baseball player, St. Louis Cardinals.

# Washington University

St. Louis, MO 63130 314 935-5000

**1994-95 Costs.** Tuition: $18,350. Room & board: $5,731. Fees, books, misc. academic expenses (school's estimate): $184.
**Enrollment.** Undergraduates: 2,592 men, 2,248 women (full-time). Freshman class: 6,894 applicants, 5,239 accepted, 1,254 enrolled. Graduate enrollment: 2,911 men, 2,208 women.
**Test score averages/ranges.** Range of SAT scores of middle 50%: 510-620 verbal, 600-710 math. Range of ACT scores of middle 50%: 26-30 English, 26-31 math.
**Faculty.** 610 full-time; 364 part-time. 99% of faculty holds highest degree in specific field. Student/faculty ratio: 6 to 1.
**Selectivity rating.** Highly competitive.

**PROFILE.** Washington University, founded in 1853, is a private, comprehensive institution. Programs are offered through the College of Arts and Sciences and the Schools of Architecture, Business, Engineering and Applied Science, Fine Arts, and Medicine. Its 169-acre main campus is located in St. Louis.

**Accreditation:** NCACS. Professionally accredited by the Accreditation Board for Engineering and Technology, the American Assembly of Collegiate Schools of Business, the National Architecture Accrediting Board, the National Association of Schools of Art and Design.
**Religious orientation:** Washington University is nonsectarian; no religious requirements.
**Library:** Collections totaling over 2,979,934 volumes, 14,906 periodical subscriptions, and 2,419,941 microform items.
**Special facilities/museums:** Art gallery, business/economics experimental lab, botanical garden, NASA planetary imaging facility, TAP reactor system, triple monochromator.
**Athletic facilities:** Gymnasiums, stadium, field house, tracks, basketball, handball, racquetball, squash, tennis, and volleyball courts, saunas, baseball, football, intramural, practice, soccer, and softball fields, swimming pool, weight room.

**STUDENT BODY. Undergraduate profile:** 12% are state residents; 14% are transfers. 13% Asian-American, 6% Black, 2% Hispanic, .5% Native American, 73% White, 5.5% Other. Average age of undergraduates is 19.
**Freshman profile:** 5% of freshmen who took SAT scored 700 or over on verbal, 31% scored 700 or over on math; 35% scored 600 or over on verbal, 77% scored 600 or over on math; 79% scored 500 or over on verbal, 96% scored 500 or over on math; 95% scored 400 or over on verbal, 100% scored 400 or over on math; 98% scored 300 or over on verbal. 92% of accepted applicants took SAT; 49% took ACT. 69% of freshmen come from public schools.
**Undergraduate achievement:** 94% of fall 1992 freshmen returned for fall 1993 term. 76% of entering class graduated. 35% of students who completed a degree program immediately went on to graduate study.
**Foreign students:** 246 students are from out of the country. Countries represented include Hong Kong, India, Korea, Malayasia, Pakistan, and Taiwan; 70 in all.

**PROGRAMS OF STUDY. Degrees:** B.A., B.F.A., B.Mus., B.S., B.S.Bus.Admin., B.S.Chem., B.S.Chem.Eng., B.S.Comp.Sci., B.S.Elec.Eng., B.S.Mech.Eng., B.S.Occup. Ther., B.Tech.
**Majors:** Accounting, African/Afro-American Studies, Anthropology, Arabic, Archaeology, Architecture, Art, Art History, Asian Studies, Biochemistry, Biology, Business, Ceramics, Chemical Engineering, Chemistry, Chinese, Civil Engineering, Classics, Comparative Literature, Computer Engineering, Computer Science, Drama, Earth/Planetary Sciences, Economics, Economics/Law, Education, Electrical Engineering, Engineering/Public Policy, English, Environmental Resources, Fashion Design, Finance, French, German, Germanic Studies, Glass, Graphic Communications, Graphic Design, Graphic Illustration, Greek, Hebrew, History, History/Literature, International Business, International Studies, Italian, Japanese, Jewish/Near Eastern Studies, Latin, Latin American Studies, Linguistic Studies, Management, Marketing, Mathematics, Mechanical Engineering, Medieval/Renaissance Studies, Multimedia, Music, Painting, Philosophy, Photography, Physics, Political Science, Printmaking, Process Control Systems, Psychology, Religious Studies, Russian, Sculpture, Spanish, Systems Science/Mathematics, Western European Studies, Women's Studies.
**Distribution of degrees:** The majors with the highest enrollment are business, psychology, and English; philosophy has the lowest.
**Requirements:** General education requirement.
**Academic regulations:** Minimum 2.0 GPA must be maintained.
**Special:** Minors offered in most majors. Interdisciplinary FOCUS Program allows freshmen to concentrate on specific topics. Independent Studies Program during last two years. Courses offered in Asian studies, Islamic society/civilization, political economy, and text/traditions. Self-designed majors. Double majors. Dual degrees. Independent study. Accelerated study. Pass/fail grading option. Internships. Cooperative education programs. Graduate school at which undergraduates may take graduate-level courses. Preprofessional programs in law, medicine, veterinary science, and dentistry. Host university for 3-2 business, engineering, physical therapy, and social work programs, 3-4 architecture and engineering/architecture programs, and other dual-degree programs. Member of COFHE consortium; exchange possible. Washington Semester. Teacher certification in elementary and secondary education. Exchange programs abroad in England (Sussex U), France (U of Caen), Germany (U of Tubingen), Israel (Rothberg Sch), Japan (Waseda U), and Spain (U of Salamanca). ROTC. AFROTC at Parks Coll of St. Louis U.
**Honors:** Phi Beta Kappa. Honor societies.
**Academic Assistance:** Remedial study skills. Nonremedial tutoring.

**STUDENT LIFE. Housing:** All freshmen must live on campus. Coed dorms. Fraternity housing. School-owned/-operated apartments. 60% of students live in college housing.
**Social Atmosphere:** According to the student newspaper, "Lots of on-campus social life, especially in the Greek system. Most underclassmen stay on campus." Favorite student gathering spots include the Rat, fraternity row, and Blueberry Hill. Popular campus events include Homecoming, airband contests, and "Walk-in-Lay-Down," a semi-annual outdoor music festival.
**Services and counseling/handicapped student services:** Placement services. Health service. Women's center. Counseling services for older students. Birth control, personal, and psychological counseling. Career and academic guidance services. Religious counseling. Physically disabled student services. Learning disabled services. Notetaking services. Tape recorders. Tutors. Reader services for the blind.
**Campus organizations:** Undergraduate student government. Student newspaper (Student Life, published twice/week). Literary magazine. Yearbook. Radio station. Chamber music ensemble, orchestra, bands, choir, madrigal singers, dance theatre, drama groups, crafts fair, Campus Y social service group, departmental groups, 170 organizations in all. 12 fraternities, 11 chapter houses; seven sororities, no chapter houses. 30% of men join a fraternity. 33% of women join a sorority.
**Religious organizations:** Christian Science Organization, Hillel House, Intervarsity Christian Fellowship, Islamic Society, Lutheran Student Movement, Newman Center, Project 5, UMOJA, Wesley Foundation, other religious groups.
**Minority/foreign student organizations:** Association of Black Students, Business Minority Council, Black Law Student Association, Black Panhellenic Council, Black Pre-Med Association, National Society of Black Engineers, Hispanic Student Organization, minority fraternities/sororities. Cosmopolitan Club, International Students, Asian Student Association, Middle East Society.

**ATHLETICS. Physical education requirements:** None.
**Intercollegiate competition:** 15% of students participate. Baseball (M), basketball (M,W), cheerleading (M,W), cross-country (M,W), diving (M,W), football (M), soccer (M,W), swimming (M,W), tennis (M,W), track (indoor) (M,W), track (outdoor) (M,W), track and field (indoor) (M,W), track and field (outdoor) (M,W), volleyball (W). Member of NCAA Division III, University Athletic Association.
**Intramural and club sports:** 75% of students participate. Intramural arm wrestling, badminton, basketball, billiards, bowling, cross-country, field goal kick, flag football, free throw, golf, inner-tube water polo, mini-soccer, racquetball, soccer, softball, squash, swimming, table tennis, tennis, track/field, ultimate frisbee, volleyball, walleyball. Men's club crew, cricket, fencing, ice hockey, lacrosse, martial arts, racquetball, rugby, squash, ultimate frisbee, volleyball. Women's club crew, fencing, martial arts, racquetball, ultimate frisbee, volleyball.

**ADMISSIONS. Academic basis for candidate selection** (in order of priority): Secondary school record, class rank, school's recommendation, standardized test scores, essay.
**Nonacademic basis for candidate selection:** Character and personality, extracurricular participation, particular talent or ability, and alumni/ae relationship are important. Geographical distribution is considered.
**Requirements:** Graduation from secondary school is recommended; GED is accepted. 18 units and the following program of study are recommended: 4 units of English, 3 units of math, 3 units of science, 2 units of foreign language, 1 unit of social studies, 2 units of history. Portfolio recommended of School of Fine Arts applicants. SAT or ACT is required. ACH recommended. Campus visit recommended. Off-campus interviews available with an alumni representative.
**Procedure:** Take SAT or ACT by December of 12th year. Application deadline is January 15. Notification of admission by April 1. Reply is required by May 1. $200 nonrefundable tuition deposit. $250 nonrefundable room deposit. Freshmen accepted in terms other than fall.
**Special programs:** Admission may be deferred one year. Credit and/or placement may be granted through CEEB Advanced Placement exams for scores of 4 or higher. Credit and placement may be granted through challenge exams. Early decision program. In fall 1994, 130 applied for early decision and 117 were accepted. Deadline for applying for early decision is January 1. Early entrance/early admission program. Concurrent enrollment program.
**Transfer students:** Transfer students accepted for terms other than fall. In fall 1993, 14% of all new students were transfers into all classes. 514 transfer applications were received, 360 were accepted. Application deadline is June 1 for fall; November 15 for spring. Minimum 3.0 GPA recommended. Lowest course grade accepted is "C-." Maximum number of transferable credits is 84 semester hours. At least 36 semester hours must be completed at the university to receive degree.
**Admissions contact:** Harold Wingood, Dean of Admission. 314 935-6000, 800 638-0700.

**FINANCIAL AID. Available aid:** Pell grants, SEOG, state scholarships and grants, school scholarships and grants, private scholarships and grants, ROTC scholarships, academic merit scholarships, and aid for undergraduate foreign students. Perkins Loans (NDSL), PLUS, Stafford Loans (GSL), school loans, private loans, and SLS. Institutional cost stabilization and monthly payment plans.
**Financial aid statistics:** 11% of aid is not need-based. In 1993-94, 94% of all undergraduate applicants received aid; 85% of freshman applicants. Average amounts of aid awarded freshmen: Scholarships and grants, $12,000; loans, $3,300.
**Supporting data/closing dates:** FAFSA/FAF: Deadline is February 15. School's own aid application: Deadline is February 15. Income tax forms: Deadline is June 1. Divorced/Separated Parent statement: Deadline is February 15. Notification of awards begins April 1.
**Financial aid contact:** Dennis J. Martin, M.A., Director of Financial Aid. 314 935-5900.

**STUDENT EMPLOYMENT.** College Work/Study Program. Institutional employment. 26% of full-time undergraduates work on campus during school year. Students may expect to earn an average of $1,500 during school year. Off-campus part-time employment opportunities rated "excellent."

**COMPUTER FACILITIES.** 1,500 IBM/IBM-compatible, Macintosh/Apple, and RISC-/UNIX-based microcomputers; 4,000 are networked. Students may access AT&T, Digital, IBM, SUN minicomputer/mainframe systems, BITNET, Internet. Residence halls may be equipped with stand-alone microcomputers, networked microcomputers, modems. Client/LAN operating systems include Apple/Macintosh, DOS, UNIX/XENIX/AIX, X-windows. Computer languages and software packages include Ada, BASIC, C, C++, COBOL, FORTRAN, GPSS, LISP, Osiris, Pascal, PL/1, Prolog, SAS, SimScript; 100 in all. Computer facilities are available to all students.
**Fees:** Computer fee is included in tuition/fees.
**Hours:** 24 hours.

**GRADUATE CAREER DATA.** Graduate school percentages: 11% enter law school. 12% enter medical school. 37% enter graduate business programs. 11% enter graduate arts and sciences programs. Highest graduate school enrollments: Harvard U, Stanford U, U of Chicago, Washington U. 35% of graduates choose careers in business and industry. Companies and businesses that hire graduates: Arthur Andersen, Exxon, IBM, Procter & Gamble.

**PROMINENT ALUMNI/AE.** Mike Peters, Pulitzer Prize-winning editorial cartoonist; Daniel Nathans, Nobel laureate, medicine; Harold Ramis, movie writer/director, *Animal House, Ghostbusters, Groundhog Day.*

# Webster University

**St. Louis, MO 63119-3194 — 314 961-2660**

**1994-95 Costs.** Tuition: $9,160. Theatre program: $10,700. Room & board: $2,170. Fees, books, misc. academic expenses (school's estimate): $800.
**Enrollment.** Undergraduates: 633 men, 1,106 women (full-time). Freshman class: 562 applicants, 462 accepted, 226 enrolled. Graduate enrollment: 3,543 men, 2,962 women.
**Test score averages/ranges.** Average SAT scores: 511 verbal, 494 math. Average ACT scores: 23 composite. Range of ACT scores of middle 50%: 21-25 composite.
**Faculty.** 116 full-time; 407 part-time. 68% of faculty holds highest degree in specific field. Student/faculty ratio: 13 to 1.
**Selectivity rating.** Less competitive.

**PROFILE.** Webster is a private university. It was founded as a college for women in 1915, adopted coeducation in 1967, and gained university status in 1983. Its 47-acre main campus is located in suburban Webster Groves, 12 miles from downtown St. Louis.

**Accreditation:** NCACS. Professionally accredited by the American Bar Association, the National Association of Schools of Music, the National League for Nursing.
**Religious orientation:** Webster University is nonsectarian; no religious requirements.
**Library:** Collections totaling over 222,300 volumes, 1,233 periodical subscriptions, and 98,358 microform items.
**Special facilities/museums:** Art gallery, Repertory Theatre of St. Louis, Opera Theatre of St. Louis, multimedia center, experimental elementary school, language lab.
**Athletic facilities:** Gymnasium, swimming pool, fitness center, tennis and sand volleyball courts.

**STUDENT BODY. Undergraduate profile:** 81% are state residents; 66% are transfers. 1% Asian-American, 11% Black, 2% Hispanic, 1% Native American, 85% White. Average age of undergraduates is 24.
**Freshman profile:** 32% of accepted applicants took SAT; 82% took ACT. 70% of freshmen come from public schools.
**Undergraduate achievement:** 77% of fall 1992 freshmen returned for fall 1993 term. 38% of entering class graduated. 25% of students who completed a degree program went on to graduate study.
**Foreign students:** 47 students are from out of the country. Countries represented include China, Germany, Hong Kong, Japan, the Netherlands, and Thailand; 35 in all.

**PROGRAMS OF STUDY. Degrees:** B.A., B.F.A., B.Mus., B.Mus.Ed., B.S., B.S.Nurs.
**Majors:** Anthropology, Art, Biology, Computer Science, Dance, Education, Foreign Languages, General Science, History/Political Science, Individualized Concentration, International Studies, Jazz Studies, Literature/Language, Management, Mathematics, Media Communications, Music, Music Education, Music Theatre, Musical Composition, Musical Performance, Nursing, Philosophy, Pre-Directing, Psychology, Religion, Social Science, Sociology, Theatre Arts.
**Distribution of degrees:** The majors with the highest enrollment are management, nursing, and media communications; anthropology, philosophy, and religion have the lowest.
**Academic regulations:** Minimum 2.0 GPA must be maintained.
**Special:** Minors offered in most majors and in chemistry, fine arts, liberal arts, women's studies, and writing as a profession. Self-designed majors. Double majors. Independent study. Accelerated study. Pass/fail grading option. Internships. Cooperative education programs. Graduate school at which undergraduates may take graduate-level courses. Preprofessional programs in law, medicine, veterinary science, and dentistry. 3-2 engineering and social work programs and 3-4 architectural program with U of Missouri and Washington U. Cross-registration with Eden Seminary, Fontbonne Coll, Lindenwood Coll, Maryville Coll, and Missouri Baptist Coll. Teacher certification in early childhood, elementary, secondary, and special education. Certification in specific subject areas. Exchange program abroad with Webster U with campuses in Austria, England, the Netherlands, and Switzerland.
**Honors:** Honors program.
**Academic Assistance:** Remedial reading, writing, math, and study skills. Nonremedial tutoring.

**STUDENT LIFE. Housing:** All out-of-town freshmen must live on campus. Coed, women's, and men's dorms. School-owned/operated apartments. Honors housing. Special interest housing. 20% of students live in college housing.
**Social Atmosphere:** On campus, students gather at the University Center, the cafeteria, and the HL Course Lounge. Off campus, students head for Cicero's, Weber's Front Row Bar and Grill, Calico's, and TNG's. Art, dance, drama, and music majors have a considerable influence on campus life, as does the Student Government Association. Popular school-year events include Fall Fest, Spring Fest, The Valentine Vendue, Kwanzaa, and the art department party. According to the editor of the student newspaper, "Social life at Webster U. is divided between the graduate/business student minority and the liberal art undergraduate majority."
**Services and counseling/handicapped student services:** Placement services. Health service. Women's center. Counseling services for minority, veteran, and older students. Birth control, personal, and psychological counseling. Career and academic guidance services. Religious counseling. Physically disabled student services. Learning disabled services. Notetaking services. Tape recorders. Tutors. Reader services for the blind.
**Campus organizations:** Undergraduate student government. Student newspaper (Journal, published once/week). Literary magazine. Radio station. Choral and dance groups, Alpha Kappa Psi, Art Council, cheerleaders, College Republicans, media and education associations, philosophy club, Association for Women Students, Helping Hand Organization, Students for Life, Students for Social Action, 32 organizations in all.
**Religious organizations:** Several religious groups.
**Minority/foreign student organizations:** Association of African American Collegians. International Student Association, Thai Student Group.

**ATHLETICS. Physical education requirements:** None.
**Intercollegiate competition:** 4% of students participate. Baseball (M), basketball (M,W), cross-country (W), soccer (M), tennis (M,W), track (M,W), volleyball (W). Member of NCAA Division III, St. Louis Intercollegiate Athletic Conference.
**Intramural and club sports:** Intramural aerobics, basketball, softball, tennis, volleyball, walking, water aerobics, yoga. Men's club cheerleading, cross-county, golf, swimming, volleyball. Women's club cheerleading, golf, soccer, softball, swimming.

**ADMISSIONS. Academic basis for candidate selection** (in order of priority): Secondary school record, standardized test scores, class rank, essay, school's recommendation.
**Nonacademic basis for candidate selection:** Particular talent or ability is emphasized. Extracurricular participation and geographical distribution are considered.
**Requirements:** Graduation from secondary school is required; GED is accepted. 16 units and the following program of study are recommended: 4 units of English, 3 units of math, 2 units of science, 2 units of foreign language, 3 units of social studies, 2 units of electives. Minimum combined SAT score of 900 (composite ACT score of 20), rank in top half of secondary school class, and minimum 2.5 GPA required. Audition required of dance, music, and theatre program applicants. Portfolio required of art program applicants. SAT or ACT is required. PSAT is recommended. Campus visit and interview recommended. Off-campus interviews available with an admissions representative.
**Procedure:** Take SAT or ACT by December of 12th year. Suggest filing application by April 1. Application deadline is August 1. Notification of admission on rolling basis. Reply is required by May 1. $100 tuition deposit, refundable until May 1. $100 room deposit, refundable until May 1. Freshmen accepted in terms other than fall.
**Special programs:** Admission may be deferred one year. Credit may be granted through CEEB Advanced Placement for scores of 3 or higher. Credit may be granted through CLEP general and subject exams, Regents College, ACT PEP, DANTES, and challenge exams, and military and life experience. Early entrance/early admission program. Concurrent enrollment program.
**Transfer students:** Transfer students accepted for terms other than fall. In fall 1993, 66% of all new students were transfers into all classes. 729 transfer applications were received, 579 were accepted. Application deadline is April 1 for fall; December 1 for spring. Minimum 2.5 GPA required. Lowest course grade accepted is "C." Maximum number of transferable credits is 64 semester hours from a two-year school and 98 semester hours from a four-year school. At least 30 semester hours must be completed at the university to receive degree.
**Admissions contact:** Charles E. Beech, Director of University Admissions. 314 968-7000.

**FINANCIAL AID. Available aid:** Pell grants, SEOG, state scholarships and grants, school scholarships and grants, private scholarships and grants, and academic merit scholarships. Perkins Loans (NDSL), PLUS, Stafford Loans (GSL), private loans, and SLS. Tuition Plan Inc., AMS, EFI Fund Management, and deferred payment plan.
**Financial aid statistics:** 10% of aid is not need-based. In 1993-94, 52% of all undergraduate applicants received aid; 89% of freshman applicants. Average amounts of aid awarded freshmen: Scholarships and grants, $5,158; loans, $2,581.
**Supporting data/closing dates:** FAFSA: Priority filing date is March 1. FAF/FFS: Priority filing date is April 1. School's own aid application: Priority filing date is April 1. State aid form: Priority filing date is March 1; deadline is April 30. Notification of awards on rolling basis.
**Financial aid contact:** Sharen Lowney, Director of Financial Aid. 314 968-6977.

**STUDENT EMPLOYMENT.** College Work/Study Program. Institutional employment. 28% of full-time undergraduates work on campus during school year. Students may expect to earn an average of $2,160 during school year. Off-campus part-time employment opportunities rated "excellent."

**COMPUTER FACILITIES.** 150 IBM/IBM-compatible and Macintosh/Apple microcomputers; 100 are networked. Client/LAN operating systems include Apple/Macintosh, DOS, LocalTalk/AppleTalk, Novell. Computer languages and software packages include Adobe Illustrator, BASIC, C++, COBOL, Lotus, MacWrite, Microsoft Word, Paradox, Pascal, WordPerfect; 300 in all. Computer facilities are available to all students.
**Fees:** None.
**Hours:** 8:30 AM-10 PM (M-Th); 8:30 AM-4:30 PM (F); 9 AM-3 PM (Sa); noon-5 PM (Su).

# Westminster College

**Fulton, MO 65251 — 314 642-3361**

**1994-95 Costs.** Tuition: $10,720. Room: $1,870. Board: $2,180. Fees, books, misc. academic expenses (school's estimate): $830.
**Enrollment.** Undergraduates: 418 men, 284 women (full-time). Freshman class: 662 applicants, 553 accepted, 184 enrolled.
**Test score averages/ranges.** Average SAT scores: 480 verbal, 520 math. Range of SAT scores of middle 50%: 840-1260 combined. Average ACT scores: 24 composite. Range of ACT scores of middle 50%: 21-26 composite.
**Faculty.** 50 full-time; 10 part-time. 66% of faculty holds highest degree in specific field. Student/faculty ratio: 14 to 1.
**Selectivity rating.** Competitive.

**PROFILE.** Westminster is a church-affiliated, liberal arts college. Founded in 1851 as a college for men, it adopted coeducation in 1979. Its 250-acre campus is located in Fulton, in central Missouri, 25 miles east of Columbia.

**Accreditation:** NCACS.
**Religious orientation:** Westminster College is affiliated with the Presbyterian Church; no religious requirements.
**Library:** Collections totaling over 78,000 volumes, 390 periodical subscriptions, and 11,400 microform items.
**Special facilities/museums:** Winston Churchill Memorial Museum, language lab, NMR spectrometer, laser equipment.
**Athletic facilities:** Gymnasium, track, baseball, intramural, soccer, and softball fields, swimming pool, basketball, sand volleyball, and tennis courts, weight room.

**STUDENT BODY. Undergraduate profile:** 56% are state residents; 22% are transfers. 3% Asian/Pacific Island, 1% Black/Non-Hispanic, 1% Hispanic, 1% Native American/Alaskan, 93% White, 1% Foreign National. Average age of undergraduates is 20.
**Freshman profile:** 2% of freshmen who took SAT scored 700 or over on verbal, 4% scored 700 or over on math; 13% scored 600 or over on verbal, 29% scored 600 or over on math; 40% scored 500 or over on verbal, 62% scored 500 or over on math; 83% scored 400 or over on verbal, 84% scored 400 or over on math; 99% scored 300 or over on verbal, 97% scored 300 or over on math. 16% of accepted applicants took SAT; 84% took ACT. 70% of freshmen come from public schools.
**Undergraduate achievement:** 64% of fall 1992 freshmen returned for fall 1993 term. 64% of entering class graduated. 45% of students who completed a degree program went on to graduate study within five years.
**Foreign students:** Countries represented include Korea; 11 in all.

**PROGRAMS OF STUDY. Degrees:** B.A., B.F.A.
**Majors:** Accounting, Art, Biology, Business Administration, Chemistry, Economics, Education, English Language/Literature, French, History, International Studies, Mathematics, Philosophy, Physical Education, Physics, Political Science, Psychology, Religion, Sociology/Anthropology, Spanish.
**Distribution of degrees:** The majors with the highest enrollment are business, political science, and English; religion and philosophy have the lowest.
**Requirements:** General education requirement.
**Academic regulations:** Freshmen must maintain minimum 1.65 GPA; sophomores, 1.85 GPA; juniors, 1.95 GPA; seniors, 2.0 GPA.
**Special:** Self-designed majors. Double majors. Dual degrees. Independent study. Pass/fail grading option. Internships. Graduate school at which undergraduates may take graduate-level courses. Preprofessional programs in law, medicine, veterinary science, dentistry, engineering, government service, and osteopathy. 3-2 engineering program with Washington U. Washington Semester and UN Semester. Urban Studies Program (Chicago). Other off-campus study opportunities. Teacher certification in elementary, secondary, and special education. Certification in specific subject areas. Study abroad in Austria, England, France, Germany, Italy, Japan, Korea, and Spain. Lachish-Israel archaeological project. ROTC and AFROTC at U of Missouri at Columbia.
**Honors:** Honors program. Honor societies.
**Academic Assistance:** Remedial reading and writing.

**ADMISSIONS. Academic basis for candidate selection** (in order of priority): Secondary school record, class rank, standardized test scores, school's recommendation, essay.
**Nonacademic basis for candidate selection:** Character and personality and extracurricular participation are emphasized. Particular talent or ability, geographical distribution, and alumni/ae relationship are considered.
**Requirements:** Graduation from secondary school is required; GED is accepted. 13 units and the following program of study are required: 4 units of English, 3 units of math, 2 units of lab science, 2 units of social studies, 2 units of academic electives. ACT is required; SAT may be substituted. Campus visit and interview recommended. Off-campus interviews available with admissions and alumni representatives.
**Procedure:** Take SAT or ACT by January of 12th year. Visit college for interview by March 31 of 12th year. Notification of admission on rolling basis. Reply is required by May 1. $200 tuition deposit, refundable until May 1. Freshmen accepted in terms other than fall.
**Special programs:** Admission may be deferred one year. Credit and/or placement may be granted through CEEB Advanced Placement exams for scores of 3 or higher. Credit and/or placement may be granted through CLEP subject exams. Credit and placement may be granted through ACT PEP and challenge exams and military experience. Early entrance/early admission program. Concurrent enrollment program.
**Transfer students:** Transfer students accepted for terms other than fall. In fall 1993, 22% of all new students were transfers into all classes. 103 transfer applications were received, 81 were accepted. Application deadline is rolling for fall; rolling for spring. Minimum 2.0 GPA required. Lowest course grade accepted is "C." Maximum number of transferable credits is 61 semester hours from a two-year school and 90 semester hours from a four-year school. At least 30 semester hours must be completed at the college to receive degree.
**Admissions contact:** E. Norman Jones, M.Ed., Dean of Enrollment Management. 314 642-3365.

**FINANCIAL AID. Available aid:** Pell grants, SEOG, state scholarships and grants, school scholarships and grants, private scholarships and grants, ROTC scholarships, and academic merit scholarships. Perkins Loans (NDSL), PLUS, Stafford Loans (GSL), and SLS. Tuition Plan Inc. and AMS.
**Financial aid statistics:** 35% of aid is not need-based. In 1993-94, 75% of all undergraduate applicants received aid; 100% of freshman applicants. Average amounts of aid awarded freshmen: Scholarships and grants, $2,601; loans, $2,300.
**Supporting data/closing dates:** FAFSA/FAF/FFS: Priority filing date is March 25; accepted on rolling basis. Notification of awards on rolling basis.
**Financial aid contact:** David Humphrey, M.A., Dean of Admissions and Financial Aid. 314 642-3361.

# William Jewell College

**Liberty, MO 64068** **816 781-7700**

**1994-95 Costs.** Tuition: $10,060. Room: $1,190. Board: $1,780. Fees, books, misc. academic expenses (school's estimate): $500.
**Enrollment.** Undergraduates: 550 men, 729 women (full-time). Freshman class: 663 applicants, 547 accepted, 315 enrolled.
**Test score averages/ranges.** Average SAT scores: 500 verbal, 540 math. Range of SAT scores of middle 50%: 440-570 verbal, 490-600 math. Average ACT scores: 24 composite. Range of ACT scores of middle 50%: 20-27 composite.
**Faculty.** 100 full-time; 53 part-time. 64% of faculty holds doctoral degree. Student/faculty ratio: 14 to 1.
**Selectivity rating.** More competitive.

**PROFILE.** William Jewell, founded in 1849, is a church-affiliated, liberal arts college. Its 106-acre campus is located in Liberty, 15 miles from downtown Kansas City.
**Accreditation:** NCACS. Professionally accredited by the National Association of Schools of Music, the National League for Nursing.
**Religious orientation:** William Jewell College is affiliated with the Baptist Church; one semester of religion required.
**Library:** Collections totaling over 210,630 volumes, 833 periodical subscriptions, and 131,285 microform items.
**Special facilities/museums:** Language labs.
**Athletic facilities:** Gymnasium, stadium, field house, track, athletic fields, intramural fields, outside recreational area.
**STUDENT BODY. Undergraduate profile:** 75% are state residents; 21% are transfers. 1% Asian-American, 2% Black, 1% Hispanic, 1% Native American, 93% White, 2% Other. Average age of undergraduates is 22.
**Freshman profile:** 1% of freshmen who took SAT scored 700 or over on verbal, 7% scored 700 or over on math; 13% scored 600 or over on verbal, 30% scored 600 or over on math; 57% scored 500 or over on verbal, 75% scored 500 or over on math; 90% scored 400 or over on verbal, 95% scored 400 or over on math; 99% scored 300 or over on verbal, 99% scored 300 or over on math. 25% of accepted applicants took SAT; 95% took ACT. 90% of freshmen come from public schools.
**Undergraduate achievement:** 79% of fall 1992 freshmen returned for fall 1993 term. 50% of entering class graduated. 29% of students who completed a degree program immediately went on to graduate study.
**PROGRAMS OF STUDY. Degrees:** B.A., B.S.
**Majors:** Accounting, Art, Biology, Business Administration, Chemistry, Church Music, Communication, Computer Science, Economics, Elementary Education, English, French, German Area Studies, History, International Business/Language, International Relations, Japanese Area Studies, Management, Mathematics, Medical Technology, Music, Nursing, Philosophy, Physics, Political Science, Psychology, Public Relations, Religion, Sociology, Spanish, Systems/Data Processing.
**Distribution of degrees:** The majors with the highest enrollment are business administration, psychology, and education; international business/language, French, and physics have the lowest.
**Requirements:** General education requirement.
**Academic regulations:** Minimum 2.0 GPA must be maintained.
**Special:** Courses offered in astronomy, drama, engineering drawing, film, geography, geology, graphics, Greek, Japanese, Latin, and nutrition. Cooperative social welfare action program offers resident semester in Kansas City. Foundations general education program focuses on studies in public and private decision making. Self-designed majors. Double majors. Dual degrees. Independent study. Pass/fail grading option. Internships. Preprofessional programs in law, medicine, dentistry, theology, and journalism. 3-2 engineering programs with Columbia U, U of Kansas, and Washington U. 3-2 forestry and environmental studies program with Duke U. Washington Semester and UN Semester. Teacher certification in elementary and secondary education. Certification in specific subject areas. Member of International Student Exchange Program (ISEP). Study abroad in England, France, Japan, and Spain.
**Honors:** Honors program.
**Academic Assistance:** Remedial study skills. Nonremedial tutoring.
**STUDENT LIFE. Housing:** All students must live on campus unless living with family. Women's and men's dorms. Sorority and fraternity housing. School-owned/operated apartments. On-campus married-student housing.
**Social Atmosphere:** According to the editor of the student newspaper, cultural life "is usually intellectually fulfulling, but actual social events are somewhat constricting. Overall, students are happy here." Greeks are most influential. College Union activities are very popular with guests like Arthur Miller, rock groups (The Rainmakers, The Call), and many other entertaining shows. Students also like the Fine Arts Series for plays, classical music, and dance performances. Basketball is popular and the school's Jazz Band packs them in. Favorite gathering spot on campus is The Cage (restaurant). Off campus, students flock to Westport in Kansas City (a street filled with dance places and restaurants), Winstead's for hamburgers, and Metro North theatres.
**Services and counseling/handicapped student services:** Placement services. Health service. Counseling services for veteran students. Personal and psychological counseling. Career and academic guidance services. Physically disabled student services. Notetaking services. Tape recorders. Tutors. Reader services for the blind.
**Campus organizations:** Undergraduate student government. Student newspaper (Hilltop Monitor). Yearbook. Radio station. A cappella choir, pep band, jazz and brass ensembles, opera, orchestra, debating, William Jewell Players, Young Democrats, Young Republicans, departmental, service, and special-interest groups, 33 organizations in all. Four fraternities, all with chapter houses; four sororities, no chapter houses. 40% of men join a fraternity. 40% of women join a sorority.
**Religious organizations:** Christian Student Ministries.
**Minority/foreign student organizations:** Black Student Association, Committee on Campus Cultural Unity. Japanese-American group.

**ATHLETICS. Physical education requirements:** Two semesters of physical education required.
**Intercollegiate competition:** 20% of students participate. Baseball (M), basketball (M,W), cheerleading (M,W), cross-country (M,W), football (M), golf (M), soccer (M,W), softball (W), tennis (M,W), track (indoor) (M,W), track and field (indoor) (M,W), track and field (outdoor) (M,W), volleyball (W), wrestling (M). Member of Heart of America Conference, NAIA.
**Intramural and club sports:** 60% of students participate. Intramural badminton, baseball, cross-country, flag football, golf, racquetball, softball, swimming, tennis, track, volleyball, walleyball, wrestling. Men's club diving, swimming, wrestling. Women's club diving, golf, swimming.
**ADMISSIONS. Academic basis for candidate selection** (in order of priority): Class rank, secondary school record, standardized test scores, school's recommendation, essay.
**Nonacademic basis for candidate selection:** Character and personality are emphasized. Extracurricular participation is important. Particular talent or ability is considered.
**Requirements:** Graduation from secondary school is required; GED is accepted. 20 units and the following program of study are recommended: 4 units of English, 4 units of math, 3 units of science, 2 units of foreign language, 3 units of social studies, 3 units of electives. Rank in top half of secondary school class required. Portfolio required of art program applicants. Audition required of music program applicants. SAT or ACT is required. Campus visit and interview recommended. Off-campus interviews available with an admissions representative.
**Procedure:** Take SAT or ACT by April of 12th year. Notification of admission by April 1. $50 refundable tuition deposit. $100 room deposit, refundable until May 1 or if no residence hall space is available. Freshmen accepted in terms other than fall.
**Special programs:** Admission may be deferred. Credit and/or placement may be granted through CEEB Advanced Placement exams for scores of 4 or higher. Credit may be granted through CLEP general exams, ACT PEP and DANTES exams, and military experience. Credit and/or placement may be granted through CLEP subject exams. Credit and placement may be granted through challenge exams. Early entrance/early admission program. Concurrent enrollment program.
**Transfer students:** Transfer students accepted for terms other than fall. In fall 1993, 21% of all new students were transfers into all classes. 175 transfer applications were received, 132 were accepted. Minimum 2.0 GPA required. Lowest course grade accepted is "C." Maximum number of transferable credits is 64 semester hours from a two-year school and 94 semester hours from a four-year school. At least 30 semester hours must be completed at the college to receive degree.
**Admissions contact:** T. Edwin Norris, Director of Admission. 800 753-7009.
**FINANCIAL AID. Available aid:** Pell grants, SEOG, state scholarships and grants, school scholarships and grants, private grants, academic merit scholarships, and athletic scholarships. Perkins Loans (NDSL), PLUS, Stafford Loans (GSL), NSL, and SLS. Tuition Plan Inc., AMS, deferred payment plan, and guaranteed tuition.
**Financial aid statistics:** 48% of aid is not need-based. In 1993-94, 95% of all undergraduate applicants received aid; 98% of freshman applicants. Average amounts of aid awarded freshmen: Scholarships and grants, $5,350; loans, $4,100.
**Supporting data/closing dates:** FAFSA: Priority filing date is March 15. School's own aid application: Priority filing date is March 15. Income tax forms: Priority filing date is March 15. Notification of awards begins March 1.
**Financial aid contact:** Susan J. Armstrong, M.B.A., Director of Financial Aid. 816 781-7700, extension 5143.
**STUDENT EMPLOYMENT.** College Work/Study Program. Institutional employment. 42% of full-time undergraduates work on campus during school year. Students may expect to earn an average of $1,200 during school year. Off-campus part-time employment opportunities rated "good."
**COMPUTER FACILITIES.** 78 IBM/IBM-compatible and Macintosh/Apple microcomputers; 25 are networked. Computer languages and software packages include Ada, Assembler, BASIC, C, LISP, Lotus 1-2-3, Pagemaker, Pascal, Prolog, Windows, Word, WordPerfect. Computer facilities are available to all students.
**GRADUATE CAREER DATA.** Graduate school percentages: 4% enter law school. 1% enter medical school. 3% enter dental school. 5% enter graduate business programs. 16% enter graduate arts and sciences programs. 2% enter theological school/seminary. Highest graduate school enrollments: American U, Baylor U, Boston U, Cornell U, Johns Hopkins U, Oxford U, UCLA, U of Illinois, U of Southern California. 45% of graduates choose careers in business and industry. Companies and businesses that hire graduates: Big Six accounting firms, Citicorp, Ford, General Foods, Hallmark Cards, Metropolitan Life, Peace Corps, Ritz Carlton Hotels.
**PROMINENT ALUMNI/AE.** William E. Dreyer, president, Southwest Bell of Texas; William S. Spencer, president and CEO, SEMATECH; Stephen Turner, senior vice-president and general counsel, Texaco.

# William Woods University

**Fulton, MO 65251-1098** **314 642-2251**

**1994-95 Costs.** Tuition: $10,535. Room: $2,250. Board: $2,115. Fees, books, misc. academic expenses (school's estimate): $690.
**Enrollment.** 736 women (full-time). Freshman class: 512 applicants, 474 accepted, 235 enrolled.
**Test score averages/ranges.** Average SAT scores: 442 verbal, 457 math. Range of SAT scores of middle 50%: 370-510 verbal, 400-500 math. Average ACT scores: 21 composite. Range of ACT scores of middle 50%: 18-24 composite.
**Faculty.** 46 full-time; 27 part-time. 37% of faculty holds doctoral degree. Student/faculty ratio: 13 to 1.
**Selectivity rating.** Less competitive.

**PROFILE.** William Woods, founded in 1870, is a church-affiliated university for women. Its 160-acre campus is located in Fulton, 20 miles east of Columbia and 100 miles west of St. Louis.
**Accreditation:** NCACS. Professionally accredited by the American Bar Association, the Council on Social Work Education, the National Council for Accreditation of Teacher Education.
**Religious orientation:** William Woods University is affiliated with the Christian Church (Disciples of Christ); no religious requirements.
**Library:** Collections totaling over 77,853 volumes, 422 periodical subscriptions, and 6,760 microform items.
**Special facilities/museums:** Art gallery, theaters, on-campus preschool, computer, language, photography, sewing labs, radio and television studio, equestrian center, observatory.
**Athletic facilities:** Sports complex with gymnasium, indoor swimming pool, whirpool, sauna, training room, weight and fitness center; soccer field, tennis courts.
**STUDENT BODY. Undergraduate profile:** 53% are state residents; 14% are transfers. 1% Asian-American, 1% Black, 1% Hispanic, 97% White. Average age of undergraduates is 20.
**Freshman profile:** 2% of freshmen who took SAT scored 700 or over on verbal; 6% scored 600 or over on verbal, 6% scored 600 or over on math; 29% scored 500 or over on verbal, 29% scored 500 or over on math; 61% scored 400 or over on verbal, 74% scored 400 or over on math; 97% scored 300 or over on verbal, 97% scored 300 or over on math. 1% of freshmen who took ACT scored 30 or over on composite; 31% scored 24 or over on composite; 85% scored 18 or over on composite; 100% scored 12 or over on composite. 23% of accepted applicants took SAT; 81% took ACT. 78% of freshmen come from public schools.
**Undergraduate achievement:** 66% of fall 1992 freshmen returned for fall 1993 term. 65% of entering class graduated. 13% of students who completed a degree program immediately went on to graduate study.
**PROGRAMS OF STUDY. Degrees:** B.A., B.F.A., B.Soc.Work.
**Majors:** Administration, Art, Biology, Broadcast Communications, Business/Accounting, Business Administration, Business/Economics, Chemistry, Child Care Administration, Communications, Computer Information Systems, Early Childhood Education, Elementary Education, English, English/Communications, Equestrian Science, Fashion Merchandising, French, German, Graphic Art, History, Illustration, Interior Design, International Studies, Legal Studies, Marketing Management, Mathematics, Philosophy, Physical Education, Physics, Political Science, Pre-Law, Pre-Medicine, Psychology, Radio/Television, Secondary Education, Sign Language Communications, Social Studies Education, Social Work, Sociology, Spanish, Special Education, Studio Art, Theater.
**Distribution of degrees:** The majors with the highest enrollment are business administration, equestrian science, and education; history, broadcast communications, and political science have the lowest.
**Requirements:** General education requirement.
**Academic regulations:** Minimum 2.0 GPA must be maintained.
**Special:** Minors offered in many majors and in art history, geography, and speech. Courses offered in classical languages, journalism, and science. Associate's degrees offered. Self-designed majors. Double majors. Dual degrees. Independent study. Accelerated study. Pass/fail grading option. Internships. Preprofessional programs in law and medicine. Member of Mid-Missouri Association of Colleges and Universities. Washington Semester, UN Semester, and Sea Semester. Other off-campus study opportunities. Teacher certification in early childhood, elementary, secondary, and special education. Certification in specific subject areas. Study abroad in Ecuador, England, France, Italy, the former Soviet Republics, and Spain.
**Honors:** Honor societies.
**Academic Assistance:** Remedial study skills. Nonremedial tutoring.
**ADMISSIONS. Academic basis for candidate selection** (in order of priority): Secondary school record, standardized test scores, school's recommendation, essay, class rank.
**Nonacademic basis for candidate selection:** Character and personality and extracurricular participation are emphasized. Particular talent or ability and alumni/ae relationship are considered.
**Requirements:** Graduation from secondary school is required; GED is accepted. 16 units required and the following program of study recommended: 4 units of English, 2 units of math, 2 units of lab science, 1/2 unit of foreign language, 2 1/2 units of social studies, 1 unit of history, 8 units of electives. Portfolio required of art program applicants. Audition required of music program applicants. Conditional admission possible for applicants not meeting standard requirements. SAT or ACT is required. Campus visit and interview recommended. Off-campus interviews available with an admissions representative.
**Procedure:** Take SAT or ACT by December of 12th year. Visit college for interview by April of 12th year. Notification of admission on rolling basis. Reply is required within 30 days of acceptance. $250 tuition deposit, refundable until May 1. Freshmen accepted in terms other than fall.
**Special programs:** Admission may be deferred one year. Credit and/or placement may be granted through CEEB Advanced Placement exams for scores of 3 or higher. Credit and/or placement may be granted through CLEP general and subject exams. Placement may be granted through challenge exams. Credit and placement may be granted through life experience. Early entrance/early admission program.
**Transfer students:** Transfer students accepted for terms other than fall. In fall 1993, 14% of all new students were transfers into all classes. 61 transfer applications were received, 57 were accepted. Application deadline is rolling for fall; rolling for spring. Minimum 2.75 GPA required. Lowest course grade accepted is "C." Maximum number of transferable credits is 60 semester hours from a two-year school and 90 semester hours from a four-year school. At least 30 semester hours must be completed at the university to receive degree.
**Admissions contact:** Leslie K. Krieger, Director of Admissions. 800 995-3159.
**FINANCIAL AID. Available aid:** Pell grants, SEOG, state scholarships and grants, school scholarships and grants, private scholarships and grants, ROTC scholarships, academic merit scholarships, athletic scholarships, and aid for undergraduate foreign students. Perkins Loans (NDSL), PLUS, Stafford Loans (GSL), state loans, school loans, private loans, and SLS. Tuition Plan Inc. and family tuition reduction.
**Financial aid statistics:** 43% of aid is not need-based. In 1993-94, 73% of all undergraduate applicants received aid; 92% of freshman applicants. Average amounts of aid awarded freshmen: Scholarships and grants, $8,989; loans, $2,625.
**Supporting data/closing dates:** FAFSA: Priority filing date is April 30; deadline is June 1. School's own aid application: Priority filing date is April 30; deadline is June 1. Income tax forms: Accepted on rolling basis. Notification of awards on rolling basis.
**Financial aid contact:** Laura L. Archuleta, Director of Financial Aid. 314 592-4232.

# Montana

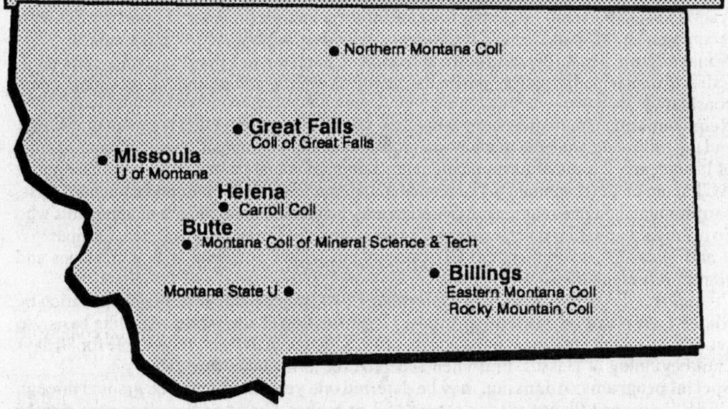


## Carroll College

**Helena, MT 59625** **406 447-4384**

**1994-95 Costs.** Tuition: $8,650. Room & board: $3,810. Fees, books, misc. academic expenses (school's estimate): $680.
**Enrollment.** Undergraduates: 426 men, 667 women (full-time). Freshman class: 819 applicants, 748 accepted, 439 enrolled.
**Test score averages/ranges.** Average ACT scores: 23 composite. Range of ACT scores of middle 50%: 22-27 composite.
**Faculty.** 74 full-time; 29 part-time. 50% of faculty holds doctoral degree. Student/faculty ratio: 14 to 1.
**Selectivity rating.** Less competitive.

**PROFILE.** Carroll, founded in 1909, is a church-affiliated, liberal arts college. Its 63-acre campus is located in central Helena, on the eastern slope of the Rocky Mountains.

**Accreditation:** NASC. Professionally accredited by the American Medical Association (CAHEA), the Council on Social Work Education, the National League for Nursing.
**Religious orientation:** Carroll College is affiliated with the Roman Catholic Church; two semesters of theology required.
**Library:** Collections totaling over 101,000 volumes, 430 periodical subscriptions, and 23,000 microform items.
**Special facilities/museums:** Arts lab, observatory, seismograph station.
**Athletic facilities:** Swimming pool, basketball and racquetball court.

**STUDENT BODY. Undergraduate profile:** 70% are state residents; 6% are transfers. 1% Asian-American, 1% Black, 1% Hispanic, 2% Native American, 92% White, 3% Other. Average age of undergraduates is 28.
**Freshman profile:** 5% of freshmen who took ACT scored 30 or over on composite; 49% scored 24 or over on composite; 92% scored 18 or over on composite; 100% scored 12 or over on composite. 30% of accepted applicants took SAT; 70% took ACT. 35% of freshmen come from public schools.
**Undergraduate achievement:** 74% of fall 1992 freshmen returned for fall 1993 term. 60% of entering class graduated. 47% of students who completed a degree program immediately went on to graduate study.
**Foreign students:** 86 students are from out of the country. Countries represented include Canada, China, India, Japan, South Korea, and Taiwan; 20 in all.

**PROGRAMS OF STUDY. Degrees:** B.A.
**Majors:** Accounting, Biology, Business Administration, Classical Languages, Combined Sciences, Communication Arts, Computer Science, Computer Science/Data Processing, Computer Software Engineering, Economics, Elementary Education, Engineering, English, English/Writing, French, Health Information Management, History, International Relations, Mathematics, Medical Technology, Nursing, Occupational Therapy, Philosophy, Physical Education, Political Science, Psychology, Public Administration, Public Relations, Social Science, Social Work, Sociology, Spanish, Speech/Communication Studies, Teaching English to Speakers of Other Languages, Theatre Arts, Theology.
**Distribution of degrees:** The majors with the highest enrollment are business administration, biology, and nursing; Spanish, medical technology, and social science have the lowest.
**Requirements:** General education requirement.
**Academic regulations:** Freshmen must maintain minimum 1.7 GPA; sophomores, 1.9 GPA; juniors, 2.0 GPA; seniors, 2.0 GPA.
**Special:** Minors offered in most majors and in art, chemistry, physics, and secondary education. Native American programs. Practicums offered in many subjects. Associate's degrees offered. Self-designed majors. Double majors. Dual degrees. Independent study. Pass/fail grading option. Internships. Cooperative education programs. Preprofessional programs in law, medicine, veterinary science, pharmacy, dentistry, theology, and optometry. 3-2 occupational therapy programs with Boston U and Washington U. 3-2 engineering programs with Columbia U, Montana State U, U of Notre Dame, and U of Southern California. 3-2 computer science program with Montana State U. Member of Independent Colleges of the Northwest. Teacher certification in elementary, secondary, and special education. Study abroad in Denmark, France, Japan, Mexico, Scotland, and Spain.
**Honors:** Honors program. Honor societies.
**Academic Assistance:** Nonremedial tutoring.

**ADMISSIONS. Academic basis for candidate selection** (in order of priority): Secondary school record, standardized test scores, school's recommendation, class rank, essay.
**Nonacademic basis for candidate selection:** Character and personality, extracurricular participation, particular talent or ability, and alumni/ae relationship are important.
**Requirements:** Graduation from secondary school is recommended; GED is accepted. No specific distribution of secondary school units required. Minimum composite ACT score of 21 (combined SAT score of 800) or minimum 2.5 GPA recommended. Conditional admission possible for applicants not meeting standard requirements. ACT is required; SAT may be substituted. Campus visit and interview recommended. Off-campus interviews available with admissions and alumni representatives.
**Procedure:** Take SAT or ACT by June 10 of 12th year. Visit college for interview by May of 12th year. Suggest filing application by February 1. Application deadline is July 1. Notification of admission on rolling basis. Reply is required by May 1. $100 nonrefundable tuition deposit. $100 nonrefundable room deposit. Freshmen accepted for terms other than fall.
**Special programs:** Admission may be deferred one year. Credit and/or placement may be granted through CEEB Advanced Placement exams for scores of 3 or higher. Credit and/or placement may be granted through CLEP general and subject exams. Placement may be granted through military experience. Credit and placement may be granted through challenge exams. Concurrent enrollment program.
**Transfer students:** Transfer students accepted for terms other than fall. In fall 1993, 6% of all new students were transfers into all classes. 106 transfer applications were received, 97 were accepted. Application deadline is July 1 for fall; December 1 for spring. Minimum 2.5 GPA required. Lowest course grade accepted is "C." Maximum number of transferable credits is 60 semester hours. At least 30 semester hours must be completed at the college to receive degree.
**Admissions contact:** Candace A. Cain, Director of Admission. 406 447-4384.

**FINANCIAL AID. Available aid:** Pell grants, SEOG, state grants, school scholarships and grants, private scholarships and grants, academic merit scholarships, athletic scholarships, and aid for undergraduate foreign students. Perkins Loans (NDSL), PLUS, Stafford Loans (GSL), and SLS. Family tuition reduction.
**Financial aid statistics:** 35% of aid is not need-based. Average amounts of aid awarded freshmen: Scholarships and grants, $3,812; loans, $4,065.
**Supporting data/closing dates:** FAFSA/FAF/FFS: Priority filing date is March 1; accepted on rolling basis. Notification of awards on rolling basis.
**Financial aid contact:** Richard Franz, Director of Financial Aid. 406 447-5425.

## College of Great Falls

**Great Falls, MT 59405** **406 761–8210**

**1994-95 Costs.** Tuition: $5,700. Room: $990. Fees, books, misc. academic expenses (school's estimate): $650.
**Enrollment.** Undergraduates: 225 men, 397 women (full-time). Freshman class: 700 applicants, 700 accepted, 478 enrolled. Graduate enrollment: 24 men, 70 women.
**Test score averages/ranges.** N/A.
**Faculty.** 42 full-time; 97 part-time. 48% of faculty holds doctoral degree. Student/faculty ratio: 16 to 1.
**Selectivity rating.** N/A.

**PROFILE.** Great Falls, founded in 1932, is a church-affiliated, liberal arts college. Its 44-acre campus is located in Great Falls, near the falls of the Missouri River.

**Accreditation:** NASC.
**Religious orientation:** College of Great Falls is affiliated with the Roman Catholic Church; one semester of religion required.
**Library:** Collections totaling over 75,457 volumes, 446 periodical subscriptions, and 21,167 microform items.
**Special facilities/museums:** Art museum.
**Athletic facilities:** Athletic center, athletic field.

**STUDENT BODY. Undergraduate profile:** 62% are state residents; 46% are transfers. 1% Black, 1% Hispanic, 6% Native American, 85% White, 7% Other. Average age of undergraduates is 29.
**Freshman profile:** 38% of freshmen come from public schools.
**Foreign students:** 92 students are from out of the country. Countries represented include Canada, England, Japan, and Korea; six in all.

**PROGRAMS OF STUDY. Degrees:** B.A., B.S.
**Majors:** Accounting, Art, Biology, Business Administration, Chemistry, Communications, Computer Science, Counseling Psychology, Criminal Justice, Elementary Education, English, General Science, Health Care Administration, History, History/Political Science, Human Services, Liberal Arts, Marketing, Mathematics, Microcomputer Management, Paralegal Studies, Physical Education, Recreation, Religious Studies, Social Sciences, Sociology.
**Requirements:** General education requirement.
**Academic regulations:** Minimum 2.0 GPA must be maintained.
**Special:** Minors offered in several majors and in early childhood education, music, Native American studies, philosophy, political science, professional writing, psychology, Spanish, special education, speech communication, and teaching music. Associate's degrees offered. Double majors. Independent study. Pass/fail grading option. Internships. Cooperative education programs. Graduate school at which undergraduates may take graduate-level courses. Preprofessional programs in law, medicine, veterinary science, pharmacy, dentistry, optometry, nursing, physical therapy, and podiatry. Member of Independent Colleges of Montana. Teacher certification in early childhood, elementary, secondary, and special education. Certification in specific subject areas.
**Academic Assistance:** Remedial reading, writing, math, and study skills. Nonremedial tutoring.

**ADMISSIONS. Academic basis for candidate selection** (in order of priority): Secondary school record, standardized test scores, class rank, school's recommendation.

**Nonacademic basis for candidate selection:** Character and personality are important. Extracurricular participation and particular talent or ability are considered.
**Requirements:** Graduation from secondary school is required; GED is accepted. 19 units and the following program of study are recommended: 4 units of English, 3 units of math, 2 units of science, 1 unit of social studies, 1 unit of history, 8 units of electives. Summer Bridge Program for limited number of applicants not normally admissible. SAT or ACT is recommended. ACH required. Campus visit and interview recommended. Off-campus interviews available with an admissions representative.
**Procedure:** Take SAT or ACT by May of 12th year. Suggest filing application by March 1; no deadline. Notification of admission on rolling basis. Freshmen accepted for terms other than fall.
**Special programs:** Admission may be deferred. Credit and/or placement may be granted through CEEB Advanced Placement exams. Credit and/or placement may be granted through CLEP general and subject exams. Credit and placement may be granted through challenge exams and military experience. Early entrance/early admission program. Concurrent enrollment program.
**Transfer students:** Transfer students accepted for terms other than fall. In fall 1992, 46% of all new students were transfers into all classes. 211 transfer applications were received, 204 were accepted. Application deadline is September 1 for fall; January 10 for spring. Minimum 2.0 GPA recommended. Lowest course grade accepted is "C." At least 30 semester hours must be completed at the college to receive degree.
**Admissions contact:** Audrey Thompson, M.Ed., Director of Admissions and Records. 406 761-8210, extension 260.

**FINANCIAL AID. Available aid:** Pell grants, SEOG, state grants, school scholarships, private scholarships, and academic merit scholarships. Perkins Loans (NDSL), PLUS, Stafford Loans (GSL), school loans, and SLS. Deferred payment plan and family tuition reduction.
**Financial aid statistics:** 5% of aid is not need-based. In 1992-93, 95% of all undergraduate applicants received aid; 95% of freshman applicants. Average amounts of aid awarded freshmen: Scholarships and grants, $1,500.
**Supporting data/closing dates:** FAFSA/FAF/FFS: Priority filing date is March 1; accepted on rolling basis. School's own aid application: Priority filing date is March 1; accepted on rolling basis. Notification of awards begins April 15.
**Financial aid contact:** Mandi Strelow Burch, M.B.A., Director of Financial Aid. 406 761-8210, extension 256.

# Montana College of Mineral Science and Technology

**Butte, MT 59701-8997** **406 496-4178**

**1993-94 Costs.** Tuition: $1,767 (state residents), $5,743 (out-of-state). Room & board: $3,210. Fees, books, misc. academic expenses (school's estimate): $500.
**Enrollment.** Undergraduates: 953 men, 517 women (full-time). Freshman class: 572 applicants, 544 accepted, 320 enrolled. Graduate enrollment: 83 men, 23 women.
**Test score averages/ranges.** Average SAT scores: 456 verbal, 554 math. Average ACT scores: 21 English, 22 math, 22 composite.
**Faculty.** 85 full-time; 54 part-time. 69% of faculty holds highest degree in specific field. Student/faculty ratio: 16 to 1.
**Selectivity rating.** Less competitive.

**PROFILE.** Montana Tech, founded in 1896, is a public, multipurpose college. Its 56-acre campus is located in Butte, south of Great Falls.

**Accreditation:** NASC. Professionally accredited by the Accreditation Board for Engineering and Technology.
**Religious orientation:** Montana College of Mineral Science and Technology is nonsectarian; no religious requirements.
**Library:** Collections totaling over 49,687 volumes, 450 periodical subscriptions, and 300,441 microform items.
**Special facilities/museums:** Mineral museum, state bureau of mines and geology, earthquake studies office, electron microscope.
**Athletic facilities:** Gymnasium, basketball, racquetball, and tennis courts, stadium, saunas, weight and wrestling rooms, swimming pool, athletic fields, human performance lab.

**STUDENT BODY. Undergraduate profile:** 84% are state residents; 3% are transfers. 1% Asian-American, 1% Black, 1% Hispanic, 1% Native American, 95% White, 1% Other. Average age of undergraduates is 25.
**Freshman profile:** 10% of accepted applicants took SAT; 90% took ACT. 98% of freshmen come from public schools.
**Undergraduate achievement:** 66% of fall 1992 freshmen returned for fall 1993 term. 50% of entering class graduated.
**Foreign students:** 68 students are from out of the country. Countries represented include Brazil, Canada, China, India, Indonesia, and Malaysia; 18 in all.

**PROGRAMS OF STUDY. Degrees:** B.S.
**Majors:** Chemistry, Computer Science, Engineering Science, Environmental Engineering, Geological Engineering, Geophysical Engineering, Mathematics, Metallurgical Engineering, Mining Engineering, Occupational Safety/Health, Petroleum Engineering, Society/Technology, Technology/Business Development.
**Distribution of degrees:** The majors with the highest enrollment are environmental engineering, engineering science, and computer science; geophysical engineering, chemistry, and geological engineering have the lowest.
**Requirements:** General education requirement.
**Academic regulations:** Minimum 2.0 GPA must be maintained.
**Special:** Minor offered in business. Credit granted for participation in band, chorus, radio programming, school newspaper, and yearbook. Associate's degrees offered. Double majors. Dual degrees. Independent study. Internships. Cooperative education programs. Graduate school at which undergraduates may take graduate-level courses. Preprofessional programs in medicine. 3-2 engineering program with Carroll Coll.
**Honors:** Honor societies.
**Academic Assistance:** Remedial math and study skills. Nonremedial tutoring.

**ADMISSIONS. Academic basis for candidate selection** (in order of priority): School's recommendation, standardized test scores, secondary school record, class rank.
**Nonacademic basis for candidate selection:** Character and personality are important. Extracurricular participation, particular talent or ability, and alumni/ae relationship are considered.
**Requirements:** Graduation from secondary school is required; GED is accepted. 14 units and the following program of study are required: 4 units of English, 3 units of math, 2 units of lab science, 2 units of foreign language, 3 units of social studies. Minimum composite ACT score of 22 (combined SAT score of 920), rank in top half of secondary school class, or minimum 2.5 GPA required. Admission may be offered to up to 15% of applicants who do not meet standard requirements. ACT is required; SAT may be substituted. Campus visit and interview recommended. Off-campus interviews available with admissions and alumni representatives.
**Procedure:** Take SAT or ACT by December 1 of 12th year. Suggest filing application by March 1. Application deadline is August 1. Notification of admission on rolling basis. No set date by which applicants must accept offer. $100 room deposit, refundable for 30 days until beginning of classes. Freshmen accepted for terms other than fall.
**Special programs:** Admission may be deferred one year. Credit may be granted through CEEB Advanced Placement for scores of 3 or higher. Credit and/or placement may be granted through CLEP general and subject exams. Credit and placement may be granted through DANTES and challenge exams and military experience. Early entrance/early admission program. Concurrent enrollment program.
**Transfer students:** Transfer students accepted for terms other than fall. In fall 1993, 3% of all new students were transfers into all classes. 235 transfer applications were received, 196 were accepted. Application deadline is August 1 for fall; December 1 for spring. Minimum 2.0 GPA required. Maximum number of transferable credits is 63 semester hours from a two-year school and 108 semester hours from a four-year school. At least 20 semester hours must be completed at the college to receive degree.
**Admissions contact:** Ed Johnson, Director of Admissions. 406 496-4178.

**FINANCIAL AID. Available aid:** Pell grants, SEOG, state scholarships, school scholarships, private scholarships, academic merit scholarships, and athletic scholarships. Perkins Loans (NDSL), PLUS, Stafford Loans (GSL), and SLS. Deferred payment plan.
**Financial aid statistics:** In 1993-94, 87% of all undergraduate applicants received aid; 65% of freshman applicants. Average amounts of aid awarded freshmen: Scholarships and grants, $1,480; loans, $2,539.
**Supporting data/closing dates:** FAFSA: Priority filing date is April 1. Income tax forms: Accepted on rolling basis. Notification of awards begins June 1.
**Financial aid contact:** Frank Kondelis, Director of Financial Aid. 406 496-4213.

# Montana State University

**Bozeman, MT 59717** **406 994-0211**

**1993-94 Costs.** Tuition: $1,933 (state residents), $5,909 (out-of-state). Room & board: $3,532. Fees, books, misc. academic expenses (school's estimate): $550.
**Enrollment.** Undergraduates: 4,896 men, 3,864 women (full-time). Freshman class: 3,500 applicants, 2,836 accepted, 1,779 enrolled. Graduate enrollment: 536 men, 348 women.
**Test score averages/ranges.** Average SAT scores: 440 verbal, 520 math. Range of SAT scores of middle 50%: 390-510 verbal, 450-600 math. Average ACT scores: 23 English, 22 math, 23 composite. Range of ACT scores of middle 50%: 19-25 English, 19-26 math.
**Faculty.** 524 full-time; 136 part-time. 65% of faculty holds doctoral degree. Student/faculty ratio: 17 to 1.
**Selectivity rating.** Less competitive.

**PROFILE.** Montana State, founded in 1893, is a public, comprehensive university. Programs are offered through the Colleges of Agriculture; Arts and Architecture; Business; Education, Health, and Human Development; Engineering; Letters and Science; Nursing; and Graduate Studies. Its 1,170-acre campus is located in Bozeman, 80 miles southeast of Butte.

**Accreditation:** NASC. Professionally accredited by the Accreditation Board for Engineering and Technology, the American Assembly of Collegiate Schools of Business, the American Dietetic Association, the National Architecture Accrediting Board, the National Association of Schools of Art and Design, the National Association of Schools of Music, the National Council for Accreditation of Teacher Education, the National League for Nursing.
**Religious orientation:** Montana State University is nonsectarian; no religious requirements.
**Library:** Collections totaling over 515,214 volumes, 5,078 periodical subscriptions, and 1,308,920 microform items.
**Special facilities/museums:** Paleontology and history museum, water resources and agricultural research centers, plant and animal nature area, planetarium, wind tunnel, electron microscopes.
**Athletic facilities:** Gymnasiums, field house, weight room, swimming pools, basketball, handball, racquetball, and tennis courts, football stadium, tracks, athletic fields.

**STUDENT BODY. Undergraduate profile:** 64% are state residents; 36% are transfers. .8% Asian-American, .4% Black, 1% Hispanic, 2.3% Native American, 92.2% White, 3.3% Foreign national. Average age of undergraduates is 23.
**Freshman profile:** 1% of freshmen who took SAT scored 700 or over on verbal, 4% scored 700 or over on math; 6% scored 600 or over on verbal, 25% scored 600 or over on math; 32% scored 500 or over on verbal, 59% scored 500 or over on math; 73% scored 400 or over on verbal, 89% scored 400 or over on math; 98% scored 300 or over on verbal, 99% scored 300 or over on math. 2% of freshmen who took ACT scored 30 or over on English,

6% scored 30 or over on math, 5% scored 30 or over on composite; 36% scored 24 or over on English, 37% scored 24 or over on math, 42% scored 24 or over on composite; 84% scored 18 or over on English, 85% scored 18 or over on math, 92% scored 18 or over on composite; 99% scored 12 or over on English, 99% scored 12 or over on math, 99% scored 12 or over on composite; 100% scored 6 or over on English, 100% scored 6 or over on math, 100% scored 6 or over on composite. 38% of accepted applicants took SAT; 70% took ACT.

**Undergraduate achievement:** 67% of fall 1992 freshmen returned for fall 1993 term. 9% of students who completed a degree program immediately went on to graduate study.

**Foreign students:** 154 students are from out of the country. Countries represented include Canada, China, Indonesia, Japan, Sweden, and Turkey; 39 in all.

**PROGRAMS OF STUDY. Degrees:** B.A., B.Arch., B.Mus.Ed., B.S.

**Majors:** Abused Land Management, Agricultural Business, Agricultural Economics, Agricultural Education, Agricultural Operations Technology, Agronomy, Animal Science, Architecture, Art, Biological Sciences, Business, Chemical Engineering, Chemistry, Civil Engineering, Computer Science, Construction Engineering Technology, Earth Science, Economics, Electrical/Electronic Engineering Technology, Electrical Engineering, Elementary Education, English, History, Home Economics, Horticulture, Industrial/Management Engineering, Interior Design, Mathematics, Mechanical Engineering, Mechanical Engineering Technology, Media/Theatre Arts, Microbiology, Modern Languages/Literature, Music Education, Nursing, Philosophy, Physical Education, Physics, Political Science, Psychology, Range Science, Secondary Education, Sociology, Soils, Speech Communication, Technology Education, Watershed Management.

**Distribution of degrees:** The majors with the highest enrollment are business, nursing, and education; agricultural economics, technology education, and soil science have the lowest.

**Requirements:** General education requirement.

**Academic regulations:** Minimum 2.0 GPA must be maintained.

**Special:** Minors offered in many majors and in apparel design, art history, biochemistry, dance, fashion merchandising, food service systems management, geography, geology, health science, human development, music, Native American studies, nutrition, public administration, religious studies, spatial analysis/GIS, statistics, and women's studies. Program in Native American studies may supplement major in College of Letters and Science. Self-designed majors. Double majors. Dual degrees. Independent study. Pass/fail grading option. Internships. Graduate school at which undergraduates may take graduate-level courses. Preprofessional programs in medicine, veterinary science, pharmacy, dentistry, optometry, occupational therapy, and physical therapy. Member of National Student Exchange (NSE). Teacher certification in early childhood, elementary, and secondary education. Certification in specific subject areas. Member of International Student Exchange Program (ISEP). Exchange programs abroad also in Australia, Germany, Japan, the Netherlands, and South Korea. ROTC and AFROTC.

**Honors:** Honors program.

**Academic Assistance:** Remedial reading, writing, and math. Nonremedial tutoring.

**STUDENT LIFE. Housing:** All students with fewer than 30 credits must live on campus. Coed, women's, and men's dorms. Sorority and fraternity housing. Off-campus privately-owned housing. On-campus married-student housing. 40% of students live in college housing.

**Social atmosphere:** Students gather at the Strand Union, the Campus Square Cinemas, Little John's Pub, and Cat's Paw. Athletes and Greeks are influential on campus. Popular events include the annual "Roskie Run" and other athletic events. According to the student newspaper, campus life is uneventful. "We're pretty isolated, although the band Poison played here once."

**Services and counseling/handicapped student services:** Placement services. Health service. Women's center. Day care. Counseling services for minority, military, veteran, and older students. Birth control, personal, and psychological counseling. Career and academic guidance services. Religious counseling. Physically disabled student services. Learning disabled services. Tape recorders. Tutors. Reader services for the blind.

**Campus organizations:** Undergraduate student government. Student newspaper (Exponent, published twice/week). Literary magazine. Radio and TV stations. Associated Women Students, bands, symphonette and symphony, vocal and instrumental ensembles, chorus, madrigal singers, drama club, sporting goods rental store, professional magazines, Residence Hall Governing Board, athletic, professional, and service groups, 82 organizations in all. 10 fraternities, all with chapter houses; five sororities, all with chapter houses. 8% of men join a fraternity. 5% of women join a sorority.

**Religious organizations:** Campus Christian Organization, Campus Crusade for Christ, Campus Ministry, other religious groups.

**Minority/foreign student organizations:** American Indian Club, Black Student Union. Chinese Student and Scholar Association, International Coordinating Council.

**ATHLETICS. Physical education requirements:** None.

**Intercollegiate competition:** Alpine skiing (W), basketball (M,W), cheerleading (M,W), cross-country (M,W), football (M), golf (W), rodeo (M,W), tennis (M,W), track (indoor) (M,W), track (outdoor) (M,W), track and field (indoor) (M,W), track and field (outdoor) (M,W), volleyball (W). Member of Big Sky Conference, National Intercollegiate Rodeo Association, NCAA Division I, NCAA Division I-AA for football.

**Intramural and club sports:** Intramural aerobics, archery, basketball, flag football, handball, racquetball, soccer, softball, squash, swimming, tennis, track and field, volleyball.

**ADMISSIONS. Academic basis for candidate selection** (in order of priority): Secondary school record, standardized test scores, class rank.

**Requirements:** Graduation from secondary school is required; GED is accepted. 14 units and the following program of study are required: 4 units of English, 3 units of math, 2 units of lab science, 3 units of social studies, 2 units of electives. Minimum combined SAT score of 920 (composite ACT score of 22), rank in top half of secondary school class, or minimum 2.5 GPA required. SAT or ACT is required. Campus visit recommended. No off-campus interviews.

**Procedure:** Application deadline is July 1. Notification of admission on rolling basis. $100 room deposit, refundable until July 15. Freshmen accepted for terms other than fall.

**Special programs:** Admission may be deferred one year. Credit and/or placement may be granted through CEEB Advanced Placement exams for scores of 3 or higher. Credit and/or placement may be granted through CLEP subject exams. Credit and placement may be granted through challenge exams. Early entrance/early admission program. Concurrent enrollment program.

**Transfer students:** Transfer students accepted for terms other than fall. In fall 1993, 36% of all new students were transfers into all classes. 1,547 transfer applications were received, 1,264 were accepted. Application deadline is July 1 for fall; December 1 for spring. Minimum 2.0 GPA required. Lowest course grade accepted is "D." No limit on number of credits that may be transferred. At least 30 semester hours must be completed at the university to receive degree.

**Admissions contact:** Charles A. Nelson, M.Ed., Director of Admissions/Registrar. 406 994-2452.

**FINANCIAL AID. Available aid:** Pell grants, SEOG, Federal Nursing Student Scholarships, state scholarships and grants, school scholarships, private scholarships, ROTC scholarships, academic merit scholarships, and athletic scholarships. Perkins Loans (NDSL), PLUS, Stafford Loans (GSL), NSL, school loans, and SLS. Deferred payment plan.

**Financial aid statistics:** In 1993-94, 89% of all undergraduate applicants received aid; 89% of freshman applicants. Average amounts of aid awarded freshmen: Scholarships and grants, $1,550; loans, $2,020.

**Supporting data/closing dates:** FAFSA: Priority filing date is March 1; deadline is March 31. School's own aid application: Priority filing date is March 1; deadline is March 31. Notification of awards on rolling basis.

**Financial aid contact:** James R. Craig, M.Ed., Director of Financial Aid. 406 994-2845.

**STUDENT EMPLOYMENT.** College Work/Study Program. Institutional employment. 18% of full-time undergraduates work on campus during school year. Students may expect to earn an average of $1,100 during school year. Off-campus part-time employment opportunities rated "good."

**COMPUTER FACILITIES.** 400 IBM/IBM-compatible and Macintosh/Apple microcomputers; 300 are networked. Students may access Digital minicomputer/mainframe systems, BITNET, Internet. Residence halls may be equipped with networked microcomputers, networked terminals. Client/LAN operating systems include Apple/Macintosh, DOS, UNIX/XENIX/AIX, X-windows, DEC. Computer languages and software packages include BASIC, C, COBOL, FORTRAN, Pascal; database, graphics, spreadsheet, statistical, and word processing packages; 50 in all. Computer facilities are available to all students.

**Fees:** Computer fee is included in tuition/fees.

**GRADUATE CAREER DATA.** Highest graduate school enrollments: Montana State U, U of Montana, U of Washington. Companies and businesses that hire graduates: Boeing, Extended Systems, Ernst & Young, Hewlett-Packard, Microsoft, Texas Instruments.

**PROMINENT ALUMNI/AE.** Dr. Loren Acton, senior scientist, space science lab for shuttle and astronauts; Paul Schmechel, president, Montana Power.

# Montana State University–Billings

**Billings, MT 59101** 406 657-2158

**1994-95 Costs.** Tuition: $2,142 (state residents), $5,866 (out-of-state). Room: $1,900. Board: $1,000. Fees, books, misc. academic expenses (school's estimate): $500.

**Enrollment.** Undergraduates: 902 men, 1,578 women (full-time). Freshman class: 931 applicants, 912 accepted, 596 enrolled. Graduate enrollment: 107 men, 277 women.

**Test score averages/ranges.** Average SAT scores: 421 verbal, 464 math. Average ACT scores: 19 English, 19 math, 20 composite.

**Faculty.** 143 full-time; 50 part-time. 70% of faculty holds doctoral degree. Student/faculty ratio: 20 to 1.

**Selectivity rating.** Less competitive.

**PROFILE.** Eastern Montana, founded in 1927, is a public college. Academic divisions include the Schools of Arts and Sciences, Business and Economics, and Education; the Human Services Program; and Special Programs. Its 90-acre campus is located in Billings.

**Accreditation:** NASC. Professionally accredited by the Council on Rehabilitation Education, the National Association of Schools of Art and Design, the National Association of Schools of Music, the National Council for Accreditation of Teacher Education.

**Religious orientation:** Eastern Montana College is nonsectarian; no religious requirements.

**Library:** Collections totaling over 140,000 volumes, 1,200 periodical subscriptions, and 660,000 microform items.

**Athletic facilities:** Gymnasiums, swimming pool, handball and racquetball courts, exercise, steam, and weight rooms, indoor track, intramural fields.

**STUDENT BODY. Undergraduate profile:** 95% are state residents; 40% are transfers. .5% Asian-American, .4% Black, 2% Hispanic, 5.4% Native American, 84% White, 7.7% Other. Average age of undergraduates is 26.

**Freshman profile:** 1% of freshmen who took SAT scored 700 or over on math; 5% scored 600 or over on verbal, 9% scored 600 or over on math; 18% scored 500 or over on verbal, 37% scored 500 or over on math; 60% scored 400 or over on verbal, 75% scored 400 or over on math; 93% scored 300 or over on verbal, 96% scored 300 or over on math. 11% of accepted applicants took SAT; 89% took ACT. 94% of freshmen come from public schools.

**Undergraduate achievement:** 51% of fall 1992 freshmen returned for fall 1993 term. 14% of entering class graduated. 7% of students who completed a degree program went on to graduate study within one year.

**Foreign students:** 10 students are from out of the country.

**PROGRAMS OF STUDY. Degrees:** B.A., B.A.Bus.Admin., B.S., B.S.Bus.Admin.

**Majors:** Accounting, Art, Biology, Business Administration, Business Economics, Chemistry, Communication Arts, Economics, Elementary Education, English, Finance, General Business Administration, General Science, German, Health/Physical Education/

Recreation, History, Human Services, Information Systems, Management, Marketing, Mass Communications, Mathematics, Music, Music Therapy, Organizational Communication, Psychology, Rehabilitation/Related Services, Secondary Education, Social Science Education, Sociology, Spanish, Special Education, Theatre Communication.
**Distribution of degrees:** The majors with the highest enrollment are elementary education, general business administration, and accounting.
**Requirements:** General education requirement.
**Academic regulations:** Minimum 2.0 GPA must be maintained.
**Special:** Minors offered include computer science, early childhood education, earth science, French, Native American studies, philosophy, physics, political science, statistics, and therapeutic recreation. Teaching minors also available. Associate's degrees offered. Double majors. Independent study. Accelerated study. Pass/fail grading option. Internships. Preprofessional programs in law, medicine, architecture, art, biology, engineering, medical science, and nursing. Teacher certification in early childhood, elementary, secondary, and special education. ROTC.
**Honors:** Honor societies.
**Academic Assistance:** Remedial writing, math, and study skills. Nonremedial tutoring.
**STUDENT LIFE. Housing:** All unmarried students under age 21 must live on campus unless living near campus with relatives. Coed dorms. 12% of students live in college housing.
**Social atmosphere:** Dudley's, Desperado's, and the L.A. Coffeeshop are favorite student haunts. The Yellowjackets basketball team, the Campus Pagan Ministry, United Christian Ministry, and Campus Christian Ministry are some of the influential groups on campus. Varsity basketball games and Homecoming are highlights of the school year.
**Services and counseling/handicapped student services:** Placement services. Health service. Women's center. Day care. Counseling services for minority, veteran, and older students. Personal and psychological counseling. Career and academic guidance services. Physically disabled student services. Learning disabled program/services. Notetaking services. Tape recorders. Tutors. Reader services for the blind.
**Campus organizations:** Undergraduate student government. Student newspaper (Retort, published once/week). Radio station. Band, jazz band, chorus, art and music clubs, rodeo club, Students with a Purpose, 46 organizations in all. One fraternity, no chapter house; one sorority, no chapter house.
**Religious organizations:** Numerous religious groups.
**Minority/foreign student organizations:** Intertribal Indian Club, American Indian Sciences and Engineering Society.
**ATHLETICS. Physical education requirements:** None.
**Intercollegiate competition:** 2% of students participate. Basketball (M,W), cross-country (M,W), tennis (M,W), volleyball (M,W). Member of NCAA Division II, Pacific West Conference.
**Intramural and club sports:** 8% of students participate. Intramural basketball, cycling, football, free-throw, golf, skiing, softball, tennis.
**ADMISSIONS. Academic basis for candidate selection** (in order of priority): Standardized test scores, secondary school record, class rank.
**Requirements:** Graduation from secondary school is required; GED is accepted. 14 units and the following program of study are required: 4 units of English, 3 units of math, 2 units of lab science, 3 units of social studies, 2 units of electives. Minimum composite ACT score of 20, rank in top half of secondary school class, or minimum 2.5 GPA required. ACT is required; SAT may be substituted. Campus visit recommended. No off-campus interviews.
**Procedure:** Notification of admission on rolling basis. Reply is required by registration. $50 room deposit, refundable until end of term. Freshmen accepted for terms other than fall.
**Special programs:** Credit and/or placement may be granted through CEEB Advanced Placement exams for scores of 3 or higher. Credit and/or placement may be granted through CLEP general and subject exams. Credit may be granted through military experience. Credit and placement may be granted through challenge exams. Early decision program. In fall 1993, 1 applied for early decision and 1 were accepted. Early entrance/early admission program. Concurrent enrollment program.
**Transfer students:** Transfer students accepted for terms other than fall. In fall 1993, 40% of all new students were transfers into all classes. Application deadline is rolling for fall; rolling for spring. Minimum 2.0 GPA required. Lowest course grade accepted is "D." At least 20 semester hours must be completed at the college to receive degree.
**Admissions contact:** Karen Everett, M.A., Director of Admissions. 406 657-2158.
**FINANCIAL AID. Available aid:** Pell grants, SEOG, state scholarships and grants, school scholarships and grants, private scholarships and grants, ROTC scholarships, academic merit scholarships, athletic scholarships, and aid for undergraduate foreign students. BIA grants. Perkins Loans (NDSL), PLUS, Stafford Loans (GSL), and SLS. Deferred payment plan.
**Financial aid statistics:** 10% of aid is not need-based. In 1993-94, 90% of all undergraduate applicants received aid; 90% of freshman applicants. Average amounts of aid awarded freshmen: Scholarships and grants, $400.
**Supporting data/closing dates:** FAFSA: Priority filing date is March 1. School's own aid application: Priority filing date is May 1. Income tax forms: Priority filing date is May 1. Notification of awards begins by May.
**Financial aid contact:** Melina Hawkins, Director of Financial Aid. 406 657-2188.
**STUDENT EMPLOYMENT.** College Work/Study Program. Institutional employment. 10% of full-time undergraduates work on campus during school year. Students may expect to earn an average of $2,000 during school year. Off-campus part-time employment opportunities rated "good."
**COMPUTER FACILITIES.** 166 IBM/IBM-compatible and Macintosh/Apple microcomputers; 80 are networked. Students may access Digital minicomputer/mainframe systems, BITNET. Computer languages and software packages include BASIC, C, COBOL, FORTRAN, Pascal, RPG; large software library. Computer facilities are available to all students.
**Fees:** $18 computer fee per 12 credits.
**Hours:** 8 AM-10 PM (M-Th); 8 AM-6 PM (F); 8 AM-1 PM (Sa); noon-5 PM (Su).
**GRADUATE CAREER DATA.** Graduate school percentages: 1% enter law school. 1% enter graduate business programs. 2% enter graduate arts and sciences programs. Highest graduate school enrollments: Eastern Montana Coll, Montana State U, U of Montana. 47% of graduates choose careers in business and industry. Companies and businesses that hire graduates: Billings School District, First Interstate Bank, State of Montana, Yellowstone Treatment Center.
**PROMINENT ALUMNI/AE.** Nancy Keenan, superintendent of public instruction, State of Montana; Ann Regan, Montana state legislator; James F. Battin, chief judge, U.S. District Court.

# Northern Montana College

**Havre, MT 59501** **406 265-3700**

**1992-93 Costs.** Tuition: $1,770 (state residents), $5,021 (out-of-state). Room & board: $3,290-$3,650. Fees, books, misc. academic expenses (school's estimate): $500.
**Enrollment.** Undergraduates: 507 men, 541 women (full-time). Freshman class: 768 applicants, 433 accepted, 308 enrolled. Graduate enrollment: 110 men, 184 women.
**Test score averages/ranges.** Average ACT scores: 19 composite.
**Faculty.** 25% of faculty holds doctoral degree. Student/faculty ratio: 17 to 1.
**Selectivity rating.** Less competitive.

**PROFILE.** Northern Montana, founded in 1929, is a public, liberal arts college. Its 170-acre campus is located in Havre, northeast of Great Falls and 50 miles from the Canadian border.

**Accreditation:** NASC. Professionally accredited by the National League for Nursing.
**Religious orientation:** Northern Montana College is nonsectarian; no religious requirements.
**Library:** Collections totaling over 110,000 volumes, 800 periodical subscriptions, and 380,000 microform items.
**Athletic facilities:** Gymnasium, pool, softball field, basketball, tennis, and volleyball courts, weight room.
**STUDENT BODY. Undergraduate profile:** 96% are state residents; 33% are transfers. 1% Black, 1% Hispanic, 9% Native American, 89% White. Average age of undergraduates is 27.
**Freshman profile:** 1% of freshmen who took ACT scored 30 or over on English, 1% scored 30 or over on math, 1% scored 30 or over on composite; 8% scored 24 or over on English, 10% scored 24 or over on math, 10% scored 24 or over on composite; 50% scored 18 or over on English, 36% scored 18 or over on math, 49% scored 18 or over on composite; 84% scored 12 or over on English, 62% scored 12 or over on math, 83% scored 12 or over on composite; 99% scored 6 or over on English, 93% scored 6 or over on math, 99% scored 6 or over on composite. 10% of accepted applicants took SAT; 90% took ACT. 98% of freshmen come from public schools.
**Undergraduate achievement:** 50% of fall 1991 freshmen returned for fall 1992 term. 30% of entering class graduated.
**Foreign students:** 21 students are from out of the country. Countries represented include Canada; seven in all.
**PROGRAMS OF STUDY. Degrees:** B.A., B.S., B.S.Ed., B.S.Nurs.
**Majors:** Automotive Technology, Business, Construction, Diesel Technology, Drafting, Electronics Technology, Elementary Education, Farm Mechanics, Interdisciplinary Studies, Mechanical Technology, Secondary Education, Trade/Technical Technology.
**Requirements:** General education requirement.
**Academic regulations:** Minimum 2.0 GPA must be maintained.
**Special:** Minors offered in most majors. Associate's degrees offered. Double majors. Dual degrees. Accelerated study. Pass/fail grading option. Internships. Cooperative education programs. Graduate school at which undergraduates may take graduate-level courses. Teacher certification in elementary and secondary education. Certification in specific subject areas.
**Academic Assistance:** Remedial reading, writing, math, and study skills. Nonremedial tutoring.
**STUDENT LIFE. Housing:** All freshmen must live on campus unless living with family. Coed, women's, and men's dorms. On-campus married-student housing. 18% of students live in college housing.
**Social atmosphere:** The student newspaper reports, "This campus is 40 percent 'nontraditional.' Students of all ages mix. Outdoor recreation activities such as ski trips and winter campus draw both traditional and nontraditional students. Each quarter, a play is put on. This draws heavily from community and campus alike. Dances and special lectures, such as on UFOs and spies, draw good crowds. No one group seems to influence the campus." Favorite off-campus spots are The Gallery, Joe's, and Gandolph's.
**Services and counseling/handicapped student services:** Placement services. Health service. Women's center. Day care. Counseling services for minority, veteran, and older students. Personal counseling. Career and academic guidance services. Physically disabled student services. Learning disabled program/services. Notetaking services. Tape recorders. Tutors. Reader services for the blind.
**Campus organizations:** Undergraduate student government. Student newspaper (Nomoco, published once/week). Literary magazine. Yearbook. Radio station. Sweetgrass Society, tutoring groups, Muscular Dystrophy Association, athletic, departmental, service, and special-interest groups, 32 organizations in all.
**ATHLETICS. Physical education requirements:** None.
**Intercollegiate competition:** 5% of students participate. Basketball (M,W), volleyball (W), wrestling (M). Member of Frontier Conference, NAIA.
**Intramural and club sports:** 35% of students participate. Intramural basketball, football, golf, softball, tennis, volleyball. Men's club climbing, swimming. Women's club climbing, swimming.
**ADMISSIONS. Academic basis for candidate selection** (in order of priority): Secondary school record, class rank, standardized test scores, school's recommendation.
**Requirements:** Graduation from secondary school is required; GED is accepted. 14 units and the following program of study are required: 4 units of English, 3 units of math, 2 units of lab science, 3 units of social studies, 2 units of academic electives. Minimum composite

ACT score of 20, rank in top half of secondary school class, or minimum 2.5 GPA required. ACT is required; SAT may be substituted. Campus visit recommended. No off-campus interviews.
**Procedure:** Take SAT or ACT by June 30 of 12th year. Notification of admission on rolling basis. No set date by which applicants must accept offer. $75 room deposit, refundable until August 15. Freshmen accepted for terms other than fall.
**Special programs:** Admission may be deferred one year. Credit and/or placement may be granted through CEEB Advanced Placement exams for scores of 3 or higher. Credit may be granted through CLEP general and subject exams and challenge exams. Early entrance/early admission program. Concurrent enrollment program.
**Transfer students:** Transfer students accepted for terms other than fall. In fall 1992, 33% of all new students were transfers into all classes. Application deadline is rolling for fall; rolling for spring. SAT/ACT required of transfers who graduated from secondary school within three years of applying. Minimum 2.0 GPA required. Lowest course grade accepted is "C." At least 36 semester hours must be completed at the college to receive degree.
**Admissions contact:** Kelly Palmer, Director of Admissions. 406 265-3704.
**FINANCIAL AID. Available aid:** Pell grants, SEOG, Federal Nursing Student Scholarships, state scholarships and grants, school scholarships, private scholarships, academic merit scholarships, athletic scholarships, and aid for undergraduate foreign students. Fee waivers for Native Americans who are state residents and for other in-state and out-of-state students. Perkins Loans (NDSL), PLUS, Stafford Loans (GSL), NSL, school loans, and SLS. Deferred payment plan.
**Financial aid statistics:** Average amounts of aid awarded freshmen: Loans, $2,400.
**Supporting data/closing dates:** FAFSA: Accepted on rolling basis. Notification of awards on rolling basis.
**Financial aid contact:** Steve Jamruszka, Director of Financial Aid. 406 265-3787.
**STUDENT EMPLOYMENT.** College Work/Study Program. Institutional employment. 35% of full-time undergraduates work on campus during school year. Students may expect to earn an average of $1,500 during school year. Off-campus part-time employment opportunities rated "fair."
**COMPUTER FACILITIES.** 140 IBM/IBM-compatible and Macintosh/Apple microcomputers. Students may access Digital minicomputer/mainframe systems. Computer languages and software packages include BASIC, CAD/CAM, COBOL, dBASE, FORTRAN, Lotus 1-2-3, Pascal, WordPerfect. Computer facilities are available to all students.
**Fees:** Computer fee is included in tuition/fees.
**Hours:** 8 AM-10 PM (M-F), weekend hours vary.

## Rocky Mountain College

**Billings, MT 59102-1796 — 406 657-1000**

**1994-95 Costs.** Tuition: $8,734. Room & board: $3,362. Fees, books, misc. academic expenses (school's estimate): $385.
**Enrollment.** Undergraduates: 304 men, 313 women (full-time). Freshman class: 658 applicants, 501 accepted, 250 enrolled.
**Test score averages/ranges.** Average SAT scores: 413 verbal, 460 math. Average ACT scores: 21 composite.
**Faculty.** 39 full-time; 23 part-time. 46% of faculty holds doctoral degree. Student/faculty ratio: 16 to 1.
**Selectivity rating.** Less competitive.

**PROFILE.** Rocky Mountain, founded in 1878, is a private, church-affiliated, liberal arts college. Its 65-acre campus is located in Billings.

**Accreditation:** NASC.
**Religious orientation:** Rocky Mountain College is an interdenominational Christian school; one semester of religion/theology required.
**Library:** Collections totaling over 65,000 volumes, 325 periodical subscriptions and 350 microform items.
**Special facilities/museums:** Elementary school, city theater, museum, studio, flight simulator.
**Athletic facilities:** Gymnasiums, aerobics, dance, and weight rooms, swimming pool, basketball and racquetball courts, tracks.
**STUDENT BODY. Undergraduate profile:** 70% are state residents; 14% are transfers. 1% Asian-American, 1% Black, 1% Hispanic, 4% Native American, 86% White, 7% Other. Average age of undergraduates is 23.
**Freshman profile:** 1% of freshmen who took SAT scored 700 or over on math; 3% scored 600 or over on verbal, 7% scored 600 or over on math; 21% scored 500 or over on verbal, 32% scored 500 or over on math; 62% scored 400 or over on verbal, 70% scored 400 or over on math; 100% scored 300 or over on verbal, 100% scored 300 or over on math. 70% of accepted applicants took SAT; 30% took ACT. 98% of freshmen come from public schools.
**Undergraduate achievement:** 70% of fall 1992 freshmen returned for fall 1993 term. 15% of students who completed a degree program immediately went on to graduate study.
**Foreign students:** 30 students are from out of the country. Countries represented include Brazil, Canada, Germany, Japan, and Pakistan.
**PROGRAMS OF STUDY. Degrees:** B.A., B.S.
**Majors:** Art, Aviation Studies, Biology, Chemistry, Christian Thought, Economics/Business Administration, Elementary Education, English/Drama, Equestrian Studies, Geology, History, History of Ideas, History/Political Science, International Studies, Mathematics, Mathematics/Computer Science, Music, Music Education, Natural Science/Mathematics, Philosophy, Physical Education, Psychology, Sociology/Anthropology, Theatre Arts.
**Distribution of degrees:** The majors with the highest enrollment are business, education, and psychology; Christian thought, geology, and philosophy have the lowest.
**Requirements:** General education requirement.
**Academic regulations:** Minimum 2.0 GPA required for graduation.
**Special:** Minors offered in all majors and in aviation, environmental, equestrian, and peace studies. Self-designed majors. Double majors. Independent study. Pass/fail grading option. Internships. Cooperative education programs. Preprofessional programs in law, medicine, veterinary science, dentistry, nursing, and occupational therapy. 3-2 programs in engineering and occupational therapy with Boston U, Montana State U, and Washington U. Exchange program with New York U. Teacher certification in elementary and secondary education. Exchange programs abroad in Egypt, Greece, and Ireland. ROTC at Eastern Montana Coll.
**Honors:** Honors program.
**Academic Assistance:** Remedial reading, writing, math, and study skills.
**ADMISSIONS. Academic basis for candidate selection** (in order of priority): Secondary school record, school's recommendation, standardized test scores, class rank, essay.
**Nonacademic basis for candidate selection:** Character and personality, extracurricular participation, and particular talent or ability are emphasized. Alumni/ae relationship is considered.
**Requirements:** Graduation from secondary school is required; GED is accepted. No specific distribution of secondary school units required. SAT or ACT is required. Campus visit recommended. Off-campus interviews available with an admissions representative.
**Procedure:** Notification of admission on rolling basis. Reply is required by May 1. $200 nonrefundable room deposit. Freshmen accepted for terms other than fall.
**Special programs:** Admission may be deferred one year. Credit and/or placement may be granted through CEEB Advanced Placement exams for scores of 3 or higher. Credit and/or placement may be granted through CLEP general and subject exams. Credit and placement may be granted through challenge exams and military and life experience. Early entrance/early admission program.
**Transfer students:** Transfer students accepted for terms other than fall. In fall 1993, 14% of all new students were transfers into all classes. 127 transfer applications were received, 93 were accepted. Minimum 2.0 GPA recommended. Lowest course grade accepted is "D." Maximum number of transferable credits is 64 semester hours from a two-year school and 94 semester hours from a four-year school. At least 30 semester hours must be completed at the college to receive degree.
**Admissions contact:** David Heringer, Director of Admissions. 406 657-1026.
**FINANCIAL AID. Available aid:** Pell grants, SEOG, school scholarships and grants, academic merit scholarships, and athletic scholarships. Perkins Loans (NDSL), PLUS, Stafford Loans (GSL), and SLS. Institutional Payment plan.
**Financial aid statistics:** In 1993-94, 93% of all undergraduate applicants received aid; 90% of freshman applicants. Average amounts of aid awarded freshmen: Scholarships and grants, $2,338; loans, $3,463.
**Supporting data/closing dates:** FAFSA/FAF/FFS: Priority filing date is April 1; accepted on rolling basis. School's own aid application: Priority filing date is April 1; accepted on rolling basis. Income tax forms: Priority filing date is April 1; accepted on rolling basis. Notification of awards on rolling basis.
**Financial aid contact:** Judy Chapman, Director of Financial Aid. 406 657-1031.

## University of Montana

**Missoula, MT 59812 — 406 243-0211**

**1993-94 Costs.** Tuition: $2,033 (state residents), $6,009 (out-of-state). Room & board: $3,661. Fees, books, misc. academic expenses (school's estimate): $550.
**Enrollment.** Undergraduates: 3,697 men, 3,857 women (full-time). Freshman class: 3,314 applicants, 1,906 accepted, 1,564 enrolled. Graduate enrollment: 742 men, 592 women.
**Test score averages/ranges.** Average SAT scores: 459 verbal, 500 math. Average ACT scores: 22 English, 21 math, 23 composite.
**Faculty.** 482 full-time; 186 part-time. 80% of faculty holds doctoral degree. Student/faculty ratio: 19 to 1.
**Selectivity rating.** Competitive.

**PROFILE.** The University of Montana, founded in 1893, is a comprehensive public institution. Programs are offered through the College of Arts and Sciences and the Schools of Business Administration, Forestry, Journalism, and Pharmacy and Allied Health Sciences. Its 220-acre campus is located in Missoula, west of Great Falls.
**Accreditation:** NASC. Professionally accredited by the Accrediting Council on Education in Journalism and Mass Communication, the American Assembly of Collegiate Schools of Business, the American Bar Association, the American Council on Pharmaceutical Education, the American Physical Therapy Association, the Association of American Law Schools, the Council on Social Work Education, the National Association of Schools of Art and Design, the National Association of Schools of Music, the National Association of Schools of Theatre, the National Athletic Trainers Association, the National Council for Accreditation of Teacher Education.
**Religious orientation:** University of Montana is nonsectarian; no religious requirements.
**Library:** Collections totaling over 750,000 volumes, 4,958 periodical subscriptions, and 280,263 microform items.
**Special facilities/museums:** Bureau of business and economic research, clinical psychology center, environmental studies lab, geology field camp, biological research center, biomedical research center.
**Athletic facilities:** Recreation center, field house, swimming pool, gymnasium, golf course, racquetball and tennis courts, athletic fields, arena, stadium, track.
**STUDENT BODY. Undergraduate profile:** 59% are state residents; 49% are transfers. 1% Asian-American, 1% Black, 1% Hispanic, 3% Native American, 94% White. Average age of undergraduates is 24.
**Freshman profile:** 1% of freshmen who took SAT scored 700 or over on verbal, 1% scored 700 or over on math; 6% scored 600 or over on verbal, 17% scored 600 or over on math; 33% scored 500 or over on verbal, 53% scored 500 or over on math; 77% scored 400 or over on verbal, 86% scored 400 or over on math; 98% scored 300 or over on verbal, 98% scored 300 or over on math. 4% of freshmen who took ACT scored 30 or over on English, 2% scored 30 or over on math, 3% scored 30 or over on composite; 35% scored 24 or over

on English, 25% scored 24 or over on math, 38% scored 24 or over on composite; 77% scored 18 or over on English, 75% scored 18 or over on math, 91% scored 18 or over on composite; 92% scored 12 or over on English, 93% scored 12 or over on math, 100% scored 12 or over on composite. 10% of accepted applicants took SAT; 85% took ACT.
**Undergraduate achievement:** 23% of students who completed a degree program immediately went on to graduate study.
**Foreign students:** 345 students are from out of the country. Countries represented include Canada, China, Germany, Japan, and Malaysia; 60 in all.

**PROGRAMS OF STUDY. Degrees:** B.A., B.A.Ed., B.F.A., B.Mus., B.Mus.Ed., B.S., B.S.Bus.Admin.
**Majors:** Anthropology, Art, Biology, Business Administration, Chemistry, Chinese, Classics, Communication Studies, Computer Science, Computer Science/Physics, Dance, Drama, Economics, Education, English, Forestry, French, Geography, Geology, German, Health/Human Performance, History, History/Political Science, Japanese, Journalism, Latin, Liberal Studies, Mathematics, Music, Music Composition, Music Performance, Music Theory, Pharmacy, Philosophy, Physical Therapy, Physics, Physics/Astronomy, Physics/Computer Science, Political Science, Political Science/History, Psychology, Radio/Television, Recreation Management, Resource Conservation, Russian, Social Work, Sociology, Spanish, Wildlife Biology.
**Requirements:** General education requirement.
**Academic regulations:** Freshmen must maintain minimum 1.75 GPA; sophomores, 1.9 GPA; juniors, 2.0 GPA; seniors, 2.0 GPA.
**Special:** Minors offered in many majors and in Asian studies, environmental studies, human development, Native American studies, prenursing, and women's studies. Wilderness Studies Program. Associate's degrees offered. Double majors. Independent study. Pass/fail grading option. Internships. Cooperative education programs. Graduate school at which undergraduates may take graduate-level courses. Preprofessional programs in law, medicine, veterinary science, pharmacy, dentistry, and optometry. Member of National Student Exchange (NSE). Teacher certification in elementary, secondary, and special education. Certification in specific subject areas. Member of International Student Exchange Program (ISEP). Study abroad in China, France, Germany, Japan, and Spain. ROTC.
**Honors:** Honors program. Honor societies.
**Academic Assistance:** Remedial reading, writing, math, and study skills. Nonremedial tutoring.

**STUDENT LIFE. Housing:** All freshmen with fewer than 30 credits must live on campus. Coed, women's, and men's dorms. Sorority and fraternity housing. Off-campus privately-owned housing. On-campus married-student housing. 30% of students live in college housing.
**Social atmosphere:** "For the person concerned about living in a beautiful setting and gaining the type of education that promotes creative thought, especially in the arts and sciences, UM is an ideal school to attend," reports the student newspaper. "The annual Foresters' Ball is probably the largest social event at UM. It's a two-day party that has drawn attention from *Playboy* magazine. The men's basketball team is a definite crowd pleaser. The student section at home games is extremely popular, and appropriately called 'The Zoo.' Culturally, UM's liberal arts background stands out. There is a strong arts, drama, and literary emphasis here. UM is a place of diverse interests and lifestyles where everyone is accepted."
**Services and counseling/handicapped student services:** Placement services. Health service. Women's center. Day care. Counseling services for minority, veteran, and older students. Birth control, personal, and psychological counseling. Career and academic guidance services. Religious counseling. Physically disabled student services. Learning disabled services. Notetaking services. Tape recorders. Tutors. Reader services for the blind.
**Campus organizations:** Undergraduate student government. Student newspaper (Montana Kaimin, published four times/week). Literary magazine. Radio station. Music organizations, theatre, professional, service, and special-interest groups, 126 organizations in all. 10 fraternities, nine chapter houses; four sororities, all with chapter houses. 9% of men join a fraternity. 7% of women join a sorority.
**Religious organizations:** Methodist Campus Crusade, Intervarsity Christian Fellowship, Baptist Fellowship, Latter-Day Saints, Catholic, and Episcopal groups.
**Minority/foreign student organizations:** Black Student Union, Native American Club, ADSUM (students with disabilities). International Student Club, Japanese and Malaysian groups.

**ATHLETICS. Physical education requirements:** None.
**Intercollegiate competition:** 2% of students participate. Basketball (M,W), cross-country (M,W), football (M), golf (W), soccer (W), tennis (M,W), track and field (indoor) (M,W), track and field (outdoor) (M,W), volleyball (W). Member of Big Sky Conference, NCAA Division I, NCAA Division I-AA for football.
**Intramural and club sports:** 45% of students participate. Intramural badminton, basketball, billiards, flag football, golf, indoor soccer, handball, racquetball, running, soccer, softball, swimming, table tennis, tennis, triathlon, volleyball, walleyball, wrestling.

**ADMISSIONS. Academic basis for candidate selection** (in order of priority): Secondary school record, class rank, standardized test scores, school's recommendation.
**Requirements:** Graduation from secondary school is required; GED is accepted. 14 units and the following program of study are required: 4 units of English, 3 units of math, 2 units of lab science, 1 unit of social studies, 2 units of history, 2 units of academic electives. Minimum composite ACT score of 22 (combined SAT score of 920), rank in top half of secondary school class, and minimum 2.5 GPA required. Portfolio required of art program applicants. Audition required of music program applicants. Conditional admission possible for applicants not meeting standard requirements. ACT is required; SAT may be substituted. Campus visit recommended. No off-campus interviews.
**Procedure:** Take SAT or ACT by December of 12th year. Suggest filing application by March 1. Application deadline is July 1. Notification of admission on rolling basis. No set date by which applicants must accept offer. $100 room deposit, refundable until July 15. Freshmen accepted for terms other than fall.
**Special programs:** Credit and/or placement may be granted through CEEB Advanced Placement exams for scores of 3 or higher. Credit and/or placement may be granted through CLEP general and subject exams. Credit may be granted through DANTES exams and military experience. Credit and placement may be granted through challenge exams. Concurrent enrollment program.
**Transfer students:** Transfer students accepted for terms other than fall. In fall 1993, 49% of all new students were transfers into all classes. 2,304 transfer applications were received, 1,195 were accepted. Application deadline is July 1 (March 1 priority) for fall; November 15 for spring. Minimum 2.0 GPA required. Lowest course grade accepted is "D." Maximum number of transferable credits is 100 semester hours. At least 30 semester hours must be completed at the university to receive degree.
**Admissions contact:** Michael L. Akin, M.S., Director of Admissions. 406 243-4277.

**FINANCIAL AID. Available aid:** Pell grants, SEOG, state scholarships and grants, school scholarships, private scholarships and grants, ROTC scholarships, academic merit scholarships, and athletic scholarships. Perkins Loans (NDSL), PLUS, Stafford Loans (GSL), and SLS. Deferred payment plan. Credit card payment plan.
**Financial aid statistics:** 25% of aid is not need-based. In 1993-94, 75% of all undergraduate applicants received aid; 74% of freshman applicants. Average amounts of aid awarded freshmen: Loans, $2,000.
**Supporting data/closing dates:** FAFSA: Priority filing date is March 1. Notification of awards begins June 15.
**Financial aid contact:** Myron Hanson, M.B.A., Director of Financial Aid. 406 243-5373.

**STUDENT EMPLOYMENT.** College Work/Study Program. Institutional employment. 27% of full-time undergraduates work on campus during school year. Students may expect to earn an average of $1,500 during school year. Off-campus part-time employment opportunities rated "excellent."

**COMPUTER FACILITIES.** 265 IBM/IBM-compatible and Macintosh/Apple microcomputers; 110 are networked. Students may access Digital minicomputer/mainframe systems, Internet. Residence halls may be equipped with stand-alone microcomputers, networked microcomputers, networked terminals. Client/LAN operating systems include Apple/Macintosh, DOS, UNIX/XENIX/AIX. Computer languages and software packages include Ada, BMDP, C, COBOL, dBASE; many other languages and software packages. Computer facilities are available to all students.
**Fees:** Computer fee is included in tuition/fees.
**Hours:** 8 AM-5 PM in some locations; 24 hours in dorms.

**GRADUATE CAREER DATA.** 32% of graduates choose careers in business and industry.

**PROMINENT ALUMNI/AE.** Don Oliver, national correspondent, NBC; Dorothy M. Johnson, author, *The Hanging Tree*; Harold Urey, Nobel Prize-winning chemist; Mike Mansfield, former U.S. senator and ambassador to Japan; Aline Mosby, correspondent, UPI; Carroll O'Connor, actor.

# Nebraska

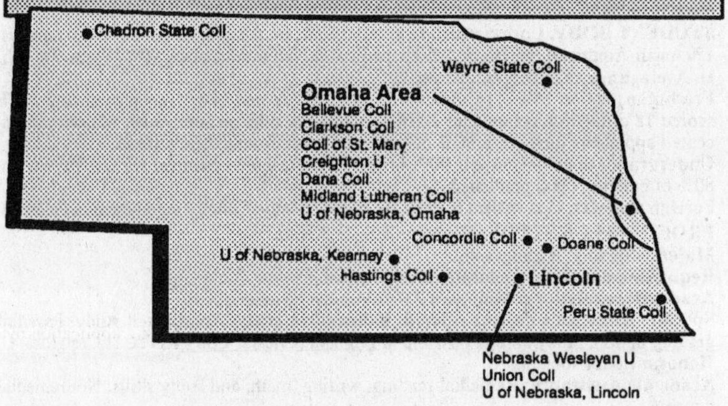


## Bellevue College

**Bellevue, NE 68005 402 291-8100**

**1993-94 Costs.** Tuition: $2,970. Housing: None. Fees, books, misc. academic expenses (school's estimate): $550.
**Enrollment.** Undergraduates: 498 men, 496 women (full-time). Freshman class: 114 enrolled. Graduate enrollment: 53 men, 39 women.
**Test score averages/ranges.** Average ACT scores: 18 composite.
**Faculty.** 40 full-time; 43 part-time. 60% of faculty holds highest degree in specific field. Student/faculty ratio: 27 to 1.
**Selectivity rating.** Noncompetitive.

**PROFILE.** Bellevue, founded in 1966, is a private college. Programs are offered through the Divisions of Behavioral and Social Sciences, Business, Humanities, and Natural Sciences and Mathematics. Its campus is located in Bellevue, in the Omaha metropolitan area.

**Accreditation:** NCACS.
**Religious orientation:** Bellevue College is nonsectarian; no religious requirements.
**Library:** Collections totaling over 103,719 volumes, 450 periodical subscriptions, and 30,000 microform items.
**Athletic facilities:** Physical health center, gymnasium, racquetball courts.

**STUDENT BODY. Undergraduate profile:** 1% Asian-American, 6% Black, 2% Hispanic, 1% Native American, 84% White, 6% Other. Average age of undergraduates is 31.
**Freshman profile:** Majority of accepted applicants took ACT. 90% of freshmen come from public schools.
**Foreign students:** 100 students are from out of the country. Countries represented include Japan, Korea, Nepal, Saudi Arabia, Thailand, and United Arab Emirates; 23 in all.

**PROGRAMS OF STUDY. Degrees:** B.A., B.F.A., B.Prof.Studies, B.S., B.Tech.Studies.
**Majors:** Accounting, Art, Art Management, Business Administration, Chemical Dependency, Communicative Arts, Computer Information Systems, Criminal Justice, English, Geography, History, Management of Human Resources, Mathematics, Philosophy, Physical Education, Political Science, Psychology, Sales/Marketing, Social Sciences, Sociology, Spanish, Sports Management, Urban Studies.
**Distribution of degrees:** The majors with the highest enrollment are business administration and accounting; geography, urban studies, and mathematics have the lowest.
**Requirements:** General education requirement.
**Academic regulations:** Freshmen must maintain minimum 1.4 GPA; sophomores, 1.8 GPA; juniors, 2.0 GPA; seniors, 2.0 GPA.
**Special:** Minors offered in most majors and in economics, information management, and women's studies. Double majors. Dual degrees. Independent study. Accelerated study. Internships. 3-1 teacher certification program with Buena Vista Coll. B.S.N. possible in conjunction with Clarkson Coll. ROTC at Creighton U. AFROTC at U of Nebraska at Omaha.
**Academic Assistance:** Remedial reading, writing, and math. Nonremedial tutoring.

**ADMISSIONS. Academic basis for candidate selection** (in order of priority): Standardized test scores, class rank, secondary school record, school's recommendation.
**Requirements:** Graduation from secondary school is required; GED is accepted. No specific distribution of secondary school units required. Provisional admission possible for applicants not meeting standard requirements. ACT is required; SAT may be substituted. Campus visit and interview recommended. Off-campus interviews available with an admissions representative.
**Procedure:** Take SAT or ACT by October 31 of 12th year. Visit college for interview by December 31 of 12th year. Acceptance notification by beginning of term. Reply is required by beginning of term. Deposit of one-third of tuition required, refundable until the fourth week of classes. Freshmen accepted in terms other than fall.
**Special programs:** Admission may be deferred one year. Credit and/or placement may be granted through CLEP general and subject exams. Credit and placement may be granted through DANTES and challenge exams and military and life experience. Early decision program. Early entrance/early admission program. Concurrent enrollment program.
**Transfer students:** Transfer students accepted for terms other than fall. Application deadline is beginning of term for fall; beginning of term for spring. Lowest course grade accepted is "C." Maximum number of transferable credits is 72 semester hours. At least 30 semester hours must be completed at the college to receive degree.
**Admissions contact:** Christel Van Meter, Director of Marketing and Enrollment. 402 293-3766.

**FINANCIAL AID. Available aid:** Pell grants, SEOG, state scholarships and grants, school scholarships, private scholarships, academic merit scholarships, athletic scholarships, and aid for undergraduate foreign students. Perkins Loans (NDSL), PLUS, Stafford Loans (GSL), and SLS. Deferred payment plan.
**Financial aid statistics:** 35% of aid is not need-based. In 1992-93, 78% of all undergraduate applicants received aid; 91% of freshman applicants. Average amounts of aid awarded freshmen: Scholarships and grants, $1,937; loans, $1,769.
**Supporting data/closing dates:** FAFSA/FAF/FFS: Priority filing date is April 15.
**Financial aid contact:** Jon Dotterer, Director of Financial Aid. 402 293-3764.

## Chadron State College

**Chadron, NE 69337-2690 308 432-6000**

**1993-94 Costs.** Tuition: $1,433 (state residents), $2,583 (out-of-state). Room & board: $2,591. Fees, books, misc. academic expenses (school's estimate): $847.
**Enrollment.** Undergraduates: 813 men, 962 women (full-time). Freshman class: 825 applicants, 825 accepted, 473 enrolled. Graduate enrollment: 340 men, 982 women.
**Test score averages/ranges.** Average ACT scores: 20 composite.
**Faculty.** 92 full-time. 67% of faculty holds doctoral degree. Student/faculty ratio: 21 to 1.
**Selectivity rating.** Less competitive.

**PROFILE.** Chadron State, founded as a Normal school in 1911, is a public college. Programs are offered through the Schools of Business and Applied Sciences, Education and Physical Education, and Humanities and Social Sciences. Its 213-acre campus is located in Chadron, 100 miles from Rapid City.

**Accreditation:** NCACS. Professionally accredited by the National Council for Accreditation of Teacher Education.
**Religious orientation:** Chadron State College is nonsectarian; no religious requirements.
**Library:** Collections totaling over 182,000 volumes, 870 periodical subscriptions, and 220,000 microform items.
**Special facilities/museums:** Planetarium, herbarium, vivarium.
**Athletic facilities:** Gymnasium, swimming pool, racquetball and tennis courts, weight rooms, track, field house.

**STUDENT BODY. Undergraduate profile:** 80% are state residents; 23% are transfers. 1.1% Asian-American, .6% Black, 1.7% Hispanic, 1.6% Native American, 95% White. Average age of undergraduates is 25.
**Freshman profile:** Majority of accepted applicants took ACT. 83% of freshmen come from public schools.
**Undergraduate achievement:** 78% of fall 1992 freshmen returned for fall 1993 term.
**Foreign students:** 17 students are from out of the country. Countries represented include Bangladesh, Canada, Ethiopia, and the Philippines; six in all.

**PROGRAMS OF STUDY. Degrees:** B.A., B.S.
**Majors:** Accounting, Administative Processes, Agri-Business, Art, Aviation, Biology, Business, Business Data Processing, Business Education, Chemistry, Child Development, Commercial Music, Computer Information Systems, Computer Systems, Criminal Justice, Early Childhood Education, Earth Science, Economics, Economics Education, Education, Elementary Education, English, English/Mass Media, Fashion Merchandising, Finance, General Office Education, General Psychology, Guidance Associate, Health Education, Health Sciences, History, Home Economics, Home Economics Education, Home Economics/Interior Design, Human Services, Industrial Agriculture, Industrial Management, Industrial Technology, Industrial Technology Education, Justice Studies/Criminal Justice, Justice Studies/Legal Study, Library Media, Management, Marketing, Mathematics, Medical Technology, Middle School Education, Mild/Moderate Handicapped Education, Music Performance, Music Theatre, Office Management, Physical Education, Physics, Political Science, Range Management, Real Estate, Recreation, School Nursing, Secondary Education, Secretarial Office Education, Social Psychology, Social Work, Sociology, Speech Communication, Speech/Theatre, Substance Abuse Psychology, Theatre, Trade/Industrial Education, Vocational Education.
**Distribution of degrees:** The majors with the highest enrollment are education, business, and criminal justice; music, art, and physical education have the lowest.
**Requirements:** General education requirement.
**Academic regulations:** Minimum 2.0 GPA must be maintained.
**Special:** Minor is required of elementary education majors and most B.A. candidates. Minors offered in several majors and in general agriculture, geography, humanities, and multicultural studies. Associate's degrees offered. Double majors. Independent study. Internships. Graduate school at which undergraduates may take graduate-level courses. Preprofessional programs in law, medicine, veterinary science, pharmacy, dentistry, optometry, architecture, chiropractic, dental hygiene, dietetics, engineering, journalism, mortuary, nursing, occupational therapy, osteopathy, physical therapy, physician assistant, podiatry, radiology, range management, and wildlife management. Teacher certification in early childhood, elementary, secondary, and special education.
**Honors:** Honors program. Honor societies.
**Academic Assistance:** Remedial reading, writing, math, and study skills. Nonremedial tutoring.

**STUDENT LIFE. Housing:** All unmarried freshmen must live on campus except for single parents or those living with family. Coed, women's, and men's dorms. On-campus married-student housing. 34% of students live in college housing.
**Social atmosphere:** Some of the popular spots for students to gather are the student center, the library, theatres, and Donald's restaurant. Some of the groups with widespread influence are Phi Alpha Theta, campus activity board, athletes, TASC Force, and the Eagle. Popular events include football games, movies, dances, theatre, historical forums, and live entertainment, such as comedians and musical groups. According to the editor of the student newspaper, "Social life revolves around small group activities, including outdoor recreation in a unique pine ridge setting, dances, concerts, and community events."

**Services and counseling/handicapped student services:** Placement services. Health service. Day care. Counseling services for minority and older students. Personal counseling. Career and academic guidance services. Physically disabled student services. Learning disabled services. Notetaking services.
**Campus organizations:** Undergraduate student government. Student newspaper (Eagle, published once/week). Choir, chorus, jazz band, symphonic band, Eagleaires, Chadron State Players, agriculture club, home economics club, Circle K, debating, photography club, rodeo and ski clubs, Young Democrats, Young Republicans.
**Religious organizations:** Unified Campus Ministries.
**Minority/foreign student organizations:** Multicultural Club. International Students.

**ATHLETICS. Physical education requirements:** Two semesters of physical education required.
**Intercollegiate competition:** 8% of students participate. Basketball (M,W), football (M), golf (W), track (indoor) (M,W), track (outdoor) (M,W), track and field (indoor) (M,W), track and field (outdoor) (M,W), volleyball (W), wrestling (M). Member of National Rodeo Association, NCAA Division II, Rocky Mountain Athletic Conference.
**Intramural and club sports:** 40% of students participate. Intramural archery, badminton, basketball, billiards, bowling, cycling, dance, golf, handball, karate, paddleball, skiing, soccer, softball, swimming, table tennis, tennis, touch football, track and field, volleyball, weight lifting. Men's club cheerleading, rodeo. Women's club cheerleading, rodeo.

**ADMISSIONS. Academic basis for candidate selection** (in order of priority): Class rank, secondary school record, standardized test scores.
**Nonacademic basis for candidate selection:** Extracurricular participation and alumni/ae relationship are emphasized.
**Requirements:** Graduation from secondary school is recommended; GED is accepted. 10 units and the following program of study are required: 4 units of English, 2 units of math, 2 units of science, 2 units of social studies. Open admission to graduates of accredited in-state secondary schools; minimum 2.0 GPA recommended. SAT or ACT is required. Campus visit and interview recommended. Off-campus interviews available with admissions and alumni representatives.
**Procedure:** Take SAT or ACT by October of 12th year. Visit college for interview by spring of 12th year. Suggest filing application by August 1; no deadline. Notification of admission on rolling basis. $100 refundable room deposit. Freshmen accepted in terms other than fall.
**Special programs:** Credit and/or placement may be granted through CEEB Advanced Placement exams. Credit and/or placement may be granted through CLEP general and subject exams. Early entrance/early admission program. Concurrent enrollment program.
**Transfer students:** Transfer students accepted for terms other than fall. In fall 1993, 23% of all new students were transfers into all classes. 259 transfer applications were received, 259 were accepted. Application deadline is August 1 (preferred) for fall; December 15 (preferred) for spring. Minimum 2.0 GPA recommended. Lowest course grade accepted is "D." Maximum number of transferable credits is 66 semester hours. At least 30 semester hours must be completed at the college to receive degree.
**Admissions contact:** Dale Williamson, M.A., Director of Admission and Records. 308 432-6464.

**FINANCIAL AID. Available aid:** Pell grants, SEOG, state grants, school scholarships, academic merit scholarships, and athletic scholarships. Perkins Loans (NDSL), PLUS, Stafford Loans (GSL), and SLS. Tuition Plan Inc. and deferred payment plan.
**Financial aid statistics:** 22% of aid is not need-based. In 1993-94, 90% of all freshman applicants received aid. Average amounts of aid awarded freshmen: Scholarships and grants, $1,904; loans, $1,200.
**Supporting data/closing dates:** FAFSA: Accepted on rolling basis. Notification of awards on rolling basis.
**Financial aid contact:** Delbert Hussey, M.S., Director of Financial Aid. 308 432-6230.

**STUDENT EMPLOYMENT.** College Work/Study Program. Institutional employment. 40% of full-time undergraduates work on campus during school year. Students may expect to earn an average of $1,100 during school year. Off-campus part-time employment opportunities rated "good."

**COMPUTER FACILITIES.** 85 IBM/IBM-compatible and Macintosh/Apple microcomputers; 15 are networked. Students may access Digital minicomputer/mainframe systems, Internet. Residence halls may be equipped with networked microcomputers. Client/LAN operating systems include Apple/Macintosh, DOS, DEC, LocalTalk/AppleTalk, Novell. Computer languages and software packages include Assembler, BASIC, COBOL, FORTRAN, Pascal, SPSS-X. Computer facilities are available to all students.
**Fees:** None.

**GRADUATE CAREER DATA.** Highest graduate school enrollments: U of Nebraska at Lincoln. 6% of graduates choose careers in business and industry.

## Clarkson College

**Omaha, NE 68131-2739** **402 552-3100**

**1993-94 Costs.** Tuition: $5,280. Room: $1,670. Fees, books, misc. academic expenses (school's estimate): $710.
**Enrollment.** Undergraduates: 21 men, 146 women (full-time). Freshman class: 451 applicants, 288 accepted, 192 enrolled. Graduate enrollment: 9 men, 52 women.
**Test score averages/ranges.** Average ACT scores: 20 composite. Range of ACT scores of middle 50%: 19-22 composite.
**Faculty.** 43 full-time; 14 part-time. 36% of faculty holds doctoral degree. Student/faculty ratio: 6 to 1.
**Selectivity rating.** Competitive.

**PROFILE.** Clarkson, founded in 1888, is a private college. Its campus is located in Omaha, in a medical area environment shared by Bishop Clarkson Memorial Hospital, the University of Nebraska Medical Center, and several other medical institutions.

**Accreditation:** NCACS. Professionally accredited by the National League for Nursing.
**Religious orientation:** Clarkson College is affiliated with the Episcopal Church; no religious requirements.
**Library:** Collections totaling over 7,512 volumes, 253 periodical subscriptions and 115 microform items.

**STUDENT BODY. Undergraduate profile:** 87% are state residents; 80% are transfers. 1% Asian-American, 3% Black, 2% Hispanic, 1% Native American, 90% White, 3% Other. Average age of undergraduates is 29.
**Freshman profile:** 14% of freshmen who took ACT scored 24 or over on composite; 82% scored 18 or over on composite; 100% scored 12 or over on composite. Majority of accepted applicants took ACT. 90% of freshmen come from public schools.
**Undergraduate achievement:** 90% of fall 1992 freshmen returned for fall 1993 term. 80% of entering class graduated.
**Foreign students:** One student is from out of the country. Country represented is Palestine.

**PROGRAMS OF STUDY. Degrees:** B.S., B.S.Nurs.
**Majors:** Nursing, Radiography.
**Requirements:** General education requirement.
**Academic regulations:** Minimum 2.0 GPA must be maintained.
**Special:** Associate's degrees offered. Independent study. Accelerated study. Pass/fail grading option. Study abroad possible in England (Chester Coll). ROTC at Creighton U.
**Honors:** Honor societies.
**Academic Assistance:** Remedial reading, writing, math, and study skills. Nonremedial tutoring.

**ADMISSIONS. Academic basis for candidate selection** (in order of priority): Secondary school record, class rank, standardized test scores, essay.
**Nonacademic basis for candidate selection:** Extracurricular participation and particular talent or ability are considered.
**Requirements:** Graduation from secondary school is required; GED is accepted. No specific distribution of secondary school units required. Miniumum composite ACT score of 20 (combined SAT score of 850), rank in top half of secondary school class, and minimum 2.0 GPA required. Conditional admission possible for applicants not meeting standard requirements. ACT is required; SAT may be substituted. Campus visit recommended.
**Procedure:** Take SAT or ACT by December of 12th year. Visit college for interview by May of 12th year. Suggest filing application by March 1; no deadline. Notification of admission on rolling basis. Reply is required within 30 days of acceptance. $100 nonrefundable tuition deposit. $100 refundable room deposit. Freshmen accepted in terms other than fall.
**Special programs:** Admission may be deferred one year. Credit and/or placement may be granted through CEEB Advanced Placement exams. Credit and/or placement may be granted through CLEP general and subject exams. Placement may be granted through military experience. Credit and placement may be granted through ACT PEP, DANTES, and challenge exams. Early entrance/early admission program. Concurrent enrollment program.
**Transfer students:** Transfer students accepted for terms other than fall. In fall 1993, 80% of all new students were transfers into all classes. 169 transfer applications were received, 85 were accepted. Application deadline is March 1 for fall; October 1 for spring. Minimum 2.5 GPA required. Lowest course grade accepted is "C." Maximum number of transferable credits is 30 semester hours from a two-year school and 36 semester hours from a four-year school. At least 40 semester hours must be completed at the college to receive degree.
**Admissions contact:** D. Lynn Taylor, Ph.D., Director of Enrollment Management. 402 552-3041, 800 647-5500.

**FINANCIAL AID. Available aid:** Pell grants, SEOG, Federal Nursing Student Scholarships, state scholarships and grants, school scholarships and grants, private scholarships and grants, ROTC scholarships, and academic merit scholarships. Perkins Loans (NDSL), PLUS, Stafford Loans (GSL), NSL, Health Professions Loans, school loans, private loans, and SLS. Deferred payment plan. Employee reimbursement plan.
**Financial aid statistics:** 14% of aid is not need-based. In 1993-94, 90% of all undergraduate applicants received aid; 94% of freshman applicants. Average amounts of aid awarded freshmen: Scholarships and grants, $565; loans, $3,419.
**Supporting data/closing dates:** FAFSA: Priority filing date is March 1; accepted on rolling basis. FAF/FFS: Accepted on rolling basis. School's own aid application: Priority filing date is March 1; accepted on rolling basis. Notification of awards on rolling basis.
**Financial aid contact:** Deb Conrad, M.S., Director of Financial Aid. 402 552-2015.

## College of Saint Mary

**Omaha, NE 68124** **402 399-2400**

**1994-95 Costs.** Tuition: $9,650. Room & board: $3,700. Fees, books, misc. academic expenses (school's estimate): $900.
**Enrollment.** Undergraduates: 13 men, 485 women (full-time). Freshman class: 370 applicants, 302 accepted, 121 enrolled.
**Test score averages/ranges.** Average ACT scores: 20 English, 19 math, 21 composite. Range of ACT scores of middle 50%: 15-24 English, 15-25 math.
**Faculty.** 62 full-time; 73 part-time. 25% of faculty holds highest degree in specific field. Student/faculty ratio: 12 to 1.
**Selectivity rating.** Competitive.

**PROFILE.** The College of Saint Mary, founded in 1923, is a private, church-affiliated college for women; qualified men admitted to evening and weekend programs. Its 45-acre campus is located in a suburban section of Omaha.

**Accreditation:** NCACS. Professionally accredited by the American Medical Association (CAHEA), the National League for Nursing.
**Religious orientation:** College of Saint Mary is affiliated with the Roman Catholic Church; three semesters of theology required.
**Library:** Collections totaling over 71,000 volumes, 490 periodical subscriptions, and 250 microform items.
**Special facilities/museums:** Art gallery.
**Athletic facilities:** Gymnasium, tennis courts, softball field, weight room.

**STUDENT BODY. Undergraduate profile:** 82% are state residents. 1% Asian-American, 3% Black, 1% Hispanic, 1% Native American, 94% White. Average age of undergraduates is 23.
**Freshman profile:** Majority of accepted applicants took ACT. 83% of freshmen come from public schools.
**Undergraduate achievement:** 70% of fall 1992 freshmen returned for fall 1993 term. 40% of entering class graduated.

**PROGRAMS OF STUDY. Degrees:** B.A., B.S., B.S.Nurs.
**Majors:** Accounting, Art, Biology, Business Administration, Chemistry, Communication, Computer Graphics, Computer Information Management, Early Childhood Education, Elementary Education, English, General Studies, Health Information Management, History, Human Resources Management, Human Services, Humanities, Language Arts, Mathematics, Medical Records Administration, Medical Technology, Music, Nursing, Occupational Therapy, Paralegal Studies, Social Sciences, Special Education.
**Distribution of degrees:** The majors with the highest enrollment are computer information management, business administration, and paralegal studies; human resources management and social sciences have the lowest.
**Requirements:** General education requirement.
**Academic regulations:** Minimum 2.0 GPA must be maintained.
**Special:** Minors offered in most majors and in child life, general science, philosophy, physical education, psychology, secondary education, sociology, telecommunications systems management, theology, and women's studies. Associate's degrees offered. Double majors. Dual degrees. Independent study. Pass/fail grading option. Internships. Preprofessional programs in law, medicine, veterinary science, pharmacy, and dentistry. Teacher certification in early childhood, elementary, secondary, and special education. ROTC at Creighton U and U of Nebraska at Omaha. AFROTC at U of Nebraska at Omaha.
**Academic Assistance:** Remedial reading, writing, math, and study skills.

**STUDENT LIFE. Housing:** All unmarried women under age 23 and not living in the Omaha metropolitan area must live on campus. Women's dorms. 14% of students live in college housing.
**Social atmosphere:** According to the student newspaper, "Students participate in typical campus activities including student government, sports, special-interest clubs, and performance groups. Being located in the heart of a major metropolitan area, they also take advantage of symphonies, ballet, theatre, an amusement park, an internationally acclaimed zoo, and many other cultural activities." Popular events include the Fall Frolics, Fine Arts Festival, Spring Fling, and Queen of Hearts Ball.
**Services and counseling/handicapped student services:** Placement services. Health service. Career and academic guidance services. Physically disabled student services. Learning disabled services. Notetaking services. Tutors.
**Campus organizations:** Undergraduate student government. Yearbook. Business, humanities, and science clubs, Professional Recreation Association, Student Ambassador Corps, 12 organizations in all.
**Religious organizations:** Campus Ministry.

**ATHLETICS. Physical education requirements:** Three semesters of physical education required.
**Intercollegiate competition:** 2% of students participate. Softball (W), tennis (W), volleyball (W). Member of NAIA.
**Intramural and club sports:** 15% of students participate. Intramural basketball, volleyball.

**ADMISSIONS. Academic basis for candidate selection** (in order of priority): Secondary school record, class rank, standardized test scores.
**Nonacademic basis for candidate selection:** Extracurricular participation is emphasized. Character and personality and particular talent or ability are important. Alumni/ae relationship is considered.
**Requirements:** Graduation from secondary school is required; GED is accepted. 16 units and the following program of study are required: 4 units of English, 2 units of math, 2 units of science, 2 units of social studies. Applicant must meet two out of three of the following criteria: minimum composite ACT score of 19, rank in top half of secondary school class, and minimum 2.0 GPA required. Chemistry and biology required of nursing program applicants; recommended of medical technology and medical records administration program applicants. Skills Development Program for applicants not meeting standard requirements. ACT is required; SAT may be substituted. ACH required. Campus visit and interview recommended. Off-campus interviews available with an admissions representative.
**Procedure:** Take ACT or SAT during 11th or 12th year. Notification of admission on rolling basis. Reply is required within 21 days. $100 tuition deposit, refundable until April 1. Freshmen accepted in terms other than fall.
**Special programs:** Admission may be deferred one semester. Credit and/or placement may be granted through CEEB Advanced Placement exams for scores of 3 or higher. Placement may be granted through CLEP general exams. Credit and/or placement may be granted through CLEP subject exams. Credit may be granted through challenge exams and military and life experience. Credit and placement may be granted through DANTES exams. Concurrent enrollment program.
**Transfer students:** Transfer students accepted for terms other than fall. In fall 1993, 288 transfer applications were received, 216 were accepted. Application deadline is August 15 for fall; January 15 for spring. Minimum 2.0 GPA required. Lowest course grade accepted is "C."
**Admissions contact:** Sheila K. Haggas, M.S., Vice President for Enrollment Services. 402 399-2405.

**FINANCIAL AID. Available aid:** Pell grants, SEOG, state grants, school scholarships and grants, private scholarships and grants, ROTC scholarships, academic merit scholarships, and athletic scholarships. Perkins Loans (NDSL), PLUS, Stafford Loans (GSL), NSL, school loans, and SLS. AMS, deferred payment plan, and family tuition reduction.
**Financial aid statistics:** Average amounts of aid awarded freshmen: Scholarships and grants, $5,432; loans, $3,714.
**Supporting data/closing dates:** School's own aid application: Priority filing date is April 15. Income tax forms: Priority filing date is April 15. Notification of awards on rolling basis.
**Financial aid contact:** Stacey Molgaard, Director of Financial Aid. 402 399-2415.

**STUDENT EMPLOYMENT.** College Work/Study Program. Institutional employment. 26% of full-time undergraduates work on campus during school year. Students may expect to earn an average of $1,100 during school year. Off-campus part-time employment opportunities rated "good."

**COMPUTER FACILITIES.** 50 IBM/IBM-compatible and Macintosh/Apple microcomputers. Students may access IBM minicomputer/mainframe systems. Computer facilities are available to all students.
**Fees:** None.
**Hours:** 8 AM-10 PM (Su-Th); 8 AM-5 PM (F-Sa).

**GRADUATE CAREER DATA.** Highest graduate school enrollments: Creighton U, U of Nebraska Medical Center. 25% of graduates choose careers in business and industry.

## Concordia College

**Seward, NE 68434** — **402 643-3651**

**1994-95 Costs.** Tuition: $9,200. Room & board: $3,370. Fees, books, misc. academic expenses (school's estimate): $450.
**Enrollment.** Undergraduates: 324 men, 459 women (full-time). Freshman class: 624 applicants, 574 accepted, 226 enrolled. Graduate enrollment: 53.
**Test score averages/ranges.** Mean ACT scores: 23 composite.
**Faculty.** 65 full-time; 19 part-time. 60% of faculty holds doctoral degree. Student/faculty ratio: 14 to 1.
**Selectivity rating.** Less competitive.

**PROFILE.** Concordia, founded in 1894, is a church-affiliated college. Its 120-acre campus is located in Seward, 30 minutes from Lincoln.

**Accreditation:** NCACS. Professionally accredited by the National Council for Accreditation of Teacher Education.
**Religious orientation:** Concordia College is affiliated with the Lutheran Church-Missouri Synod; 11-12 semester hours of religion required.
**Library:** Collections totaling over 156,135 volumes, 600 periodical subscriptions, and 4,000 microform items.
**Special facilities/museums:** Art gallery, museum of natural history, audio-visual equipment, observatory.
**Athletic facilities:** Gymnasium, track, tennis courts, football, soccer, and softball fields, swimming pool, golf course, bowling alley, weight room.

**STUDENT BODY. Undergraduate profile:** 36% are state residents; 30% are transfers. 2% Asian-American, 2% Black, 1% Hispanic, 1% Native American, 94% White. Average age of undergraduates is 18.
**Freshman profile:** Majority of accepted applicants took ACT.
**Undergraduate achievement:** 85% of fall 1992 freshmen returned for fall 1993 term.
**Foreign students:** 10 students are from out of the country. Countries represented include Barbados, China, India, Japan, Kenya, and Vietnam.

**PROGRAMS OF STUDY. Degrees:** B.A., B.F.A., B.Mus., B.S.Ed., B.S.Med.Tech.
**Majors:** Accounting, Art, Art Education, Biology, Broadcasting, Business Administration, Business Education, Chemistry, Commercial Art, Communication, Computer Science, Director of Christian Education, Dramatic Arts, Early Childhood Education, Elementary Education, English, Exercise Science, General Science, History, Home Economics, Humanities, Individualized Major, Industrial Arts Education, Journalism, Liberal Arts, Literature, Management, Mathematics, Medical Technology, Music, Music Education, Natural Science, Physical Education, Physical Science Education, Physical Sciences, Physics, Pre-Seminary Studies, Psychology, Secondary Education, Social Science Education, Social Sciences, Sociology, Spanish, Special Education, Speech/Drama, Sports Communications, Theology.
**Distribution of degrees:** The majors with the highest enrollment are education, business administration, and social sciences.
**Requirements:** General education requirement.
**Academic regulations:** Minimum 2.0 GPA required for graduation.
**Special:** Minors offered in many majors and in biblical languages, language arts, and religious education; some may be self-designed. Internships available for education, business, and director of Christian education programs. Self-designed majors. Double majors. Dual degrees. Independent study. Pass/fail grading option. Internships. Graduate school at which undergraduates may take graduate-level courses. Preprofessional programs in law, medicine, veterinary science, pharmacy, dentistry, optometry, business management, chemistry, nursing, and physical therapy. Member of consortium with U of Nebraska at Lincoln; exchange possible. Teacher certification in early childhood, elementary, secondary, and special education. Certification in specific subject areas. Exchange program abroad in England (Oak Hill Coll). ROTC. NROTC and AFROTC at U of Nebraska at Lincoln.
**Honors:** Honors program.
**Academic Assistance:** Remedial reading, writing, math, and study skills. Nonremedial tutoring.

**ADMISSIONS. Academic basis for candidate selection** (in order of priority): Secondary school record, standardized test scores, class rank, essay, school's recommendation.
**Nonacademic basis for candidate selection:** Character and personality are important. Extracurricular participation and particular talent or ability are considered.
**Requirements:** Graduation from secondary school is required; GED is accepted. 22 units and the following program of study are recommended: 4 units of English, 3 units of math, 2 units of science, 2 units of foreign language, 3 units of social studies, 2 units of history, 6 units of electives. Minimum composite ACT score of 18 and minimum 2.5 GPA required for unconditional admission. Interview required of education program applicants seeking dual certification. PPST exam required of teacher-education program applicants. Conditional admission possible for applicants not meeting standard requirements. ACT is required; SAT may be substituted. Campus visit and interview recommended. Off-campus interviews available with an admissions representative.

**Procedure:** Take SAT or ACT by June of 12th year. Suggest filing application by March 1. Application deadline is August 1. Notification of admission on rolling basis. Reply is required by August 8. $50 nonrefundable tuition deposit. $100 nonrefundable room deposit. Freshmen accepted in terms other than fall.
**Special programs:** Admission may be deferred one year. Credit and/or placement may be granted through CLEP subject exams. Credit and placement may be granted through DANTES and challenge exams and military experience. Concurrent enrollment program.
**Transfer students:** Transfer students accepted for terms other than fall. In fall 1993, 30% of all new students were transfers into all classes. Application deadline is August 1 for fall; January 5 for spring. Minimum 2.0 GPA required. Lowest course grade accepted is "C." At least 30 semester hours must be completed at the college to receive degree.
**Admissions contact:** Don Vos, Director of Admission. 800 535-5494.

**FINANCIAL AID. Available aid:** Pell grants, SEOG, state grants, school scholarships and grants, private scholarships and grants, ROTC scholarships, academic merit scholarships, athletic scholarships, and aid for undergraduate foreign students. Perkins Loans (NDSL), PLUS, Stafford Loans (GSL), and SLS. Budget payment plan.
**Financial aid statistics:** In 1993-94, 98% of all undergraduate applicants received aid; 98% of freshman applicants. Average amounts of aid awarded freshmen: Loans, $1,900.
**Supporting data/closing dates:** FAFSA: Priority filing date is May 1; accepted on rolling basis. School's own aid application: Accepted on rolling basis. Income tax forms: Accepted on rolling basis. Notification of awards on rolling basis.
**Financial aid contact:** Eveline Zwick, Director of Financial Aid. 402 643-7270.

# Creighton University

**Omaha, NE 68178** — **402 280-2700**

**1994-95 Costs.** Tuition: $10,628. Room: $2,416. Board: $1,956. Fees, books, misc. academic expenses (school's estimate): $936.
**Enrollment.** Undergraduates: 1,429 men, 2,021 women (full-time). Freshman class: 2,967 applicants, 2,836 accepted, 876 enrolled. Graduate enrollment: 1,364 men, 883 women.
**Test score averages/ranges.** Average ACT scores: 25 composite. Range of ACT scores of middle 50%: 22-27 composite.
**Faculty.** 640 full-time; 540 part-time. 88% of faculty holds highest degree in specific field. Student/faculty ratio: 14 to 1.
**Selectivity rating.** Competitive.

**PROFILE.** Creighton, founded in 1878, is a church-affiliated university. Programs are offered through the Colleges of Arts and Sciences and Business Administration; the Division of Allied Health Professions; University College; and the Schools of Dentistry, Law, Medicine, Nursing, and Pharmacy. Its campus is located on the northwest edge of downtown Omaha.

**Accreditation:** NCACS. Professionally accredited by the American Assembly of Collegiate Schools of Business, the American Dental Association, the Council on Social Work Education, the National Council for Accreditation of Teacher Education, the National League for Nursing.
**Religious orientation:** Creighton University is affiliated with the Roman Catholic Church (Society of Jesus); three semesters of theology required.
**Library:** Collections totaling over 713,250 volumes, 9,859 periodical subscriptions, and 287,561 microform items.
**Special facilities/museums:** Art gallery, health science and research complex, hospital, satellite station, observatory.
**Athletic facilities:** Gymnasium, basketball and tennis courts, track, swimming pool, baseball, intramural, soccer, and softball fields.

**STUDENT BODY. Undergraduate profile:** 47% are state residents; 12% are transfers. 5% Asian-American, 3% Black, 3% Hispanic, 1% Native American, 85% White, 3% Foreign national. Average age of undergraduates is 20.
**Freshman profile:** Majority of accepted applicants took ACT. 63% of freshmen come from public schools.
**Undergraduate achievement:** 84% of fall 1992 freshmen returned for fall 1993 term. 54% of entering class graduated. 41% of students who completed a degree program immediately went on to graduate study.
**Foreign students:** 238 students are from out of the country. Countries represented include Canada, China, India, Japan, Korea, and Malaysia; 49 in all.

**PROGRAMS OF STUDY. Degrees:** B.A., B.F.A., B.S., B.S.Arts, B.S.Bus.Admin., B.S.Chem., B.S.Nurs., B.Soc.Work.
**Majors:** Accounting, Advertising, American Studies, Art, Art History, Atmospheric Science, Biology, Broadcasting, Chemistry, Classical Civilization, Comparative Literature, Computer Science, Creative Writing, Dance, Economics, Education, Elementary Education, English, Environmental Science, Exercise Science, Finance, French, German, Greek, History, International Business, International Relations, Journalism, Latin, Management, Management Information Systems, Marketing, Mathematics, Mathematics/Computer Science, Ministry, News, Nursing, Occupational Therapy, Organizational Communication, Philosophy, Physics, Political Science, Pre-Physical Therapy, Psychology, Public Policy, Public Relations, Secondary Education, Social Work, Sociology, Spanish, Special Education, Speech, Statistics, Studio Art, Theatre, Theology.
**Distribution of degrees:** The majors with the highest enrollment are nursing, finance, and psychology; American studies, statistics, and classical civilization have the lowest.
**Requirements:** General education requirement.
**Academic regulations:** Minimum 2.0 GPA must be maintained.
**Special:** Minors are not required for graduation, but support courses are required in addition to the major in the College of Arts and Sciences. Courses offered in anatomy, Arabic, biological chemistry, black studies, cultural studies, dance, microbiology, military science, music, natural science, pharmacology, and physiology. Associate's degrees offered. Double majors. Independent study. Accelerated study. Internships. Graduate school at which undergraduates may take graduate-level courses. Preprofessional programs in law, medicine, pharmacy, dentistry, physical therapy, and occupational therapy. 3-2 engineering program with U of Detroit Mercy and Washington U. 3-3 business/law program. Member of Jesuit Universities of the Midlands. Washington Semester. Teacher certification in elementary, secondary, and special education. Certification in specific subject areas. Study abroad in England, Ireland, Italy, Japan, and Korea. ROTC. AFROTC at U of Nebraska at Omaha.
**Honors:** Honors program. Honor societies.
**Academic Assistance:** Remedial reading, writing, math, and study skills. Nonremedial tutoring.

**STUDENT LIFE. Housing:** All unmarried freshmen and sophomores must live on campus unless living with family. Coed and women's dorms. School-owned/operated apartments. On-campus married-student housing. 40% of students live in college housing.
**Social atmosphere:** On campus, students congregate at the student center; off-campus, the Bluejay Bar, Barry-O's, and Billy Frogg's are popular hangouts. Student groups with a great deal of influence on campus social life include the Greeks, the Christian Life Community, resident advisors, and the Student Board of Governor's. Soccer games are big events on-campus, especially since the Creighton team became the number one college team in the nation. Homecoming is also a popular event.
**Services and counseling/handicapped student services:** Placement services. Health service. Day care. Counseling services for minority, military, veteran, and older students. Personal and psychological counseling. Career and academic guidance services. Religious counseling. Physically disabled student services. Learning disabled services. Notetaking services.
**Campus organizations:** Undergraduate student government. Student newspaper (Creightonian, published once/week). Literary magazine. Yearbook. TV station. Music and literary clubs, drama group, communications clubs, Student Board of Governors, community service group, residence hall association, 113 organizations in all. Seven fraternities, one chapter house; six sororities, one chapter house. 33% of men join a fraternity. 30% of women join a sorority.
**Religious organizations:** Christian Medical/Dental Society, Creighton Students United for Life, Lutheran Student Fellowship.
**Minority/foreign student organizations:** Afro-American Student Association, Black Law Student Association, Latino Student Association, Women Law Students Association. International Student Association, Japanese-Nebraska Friendship Association.

**ATHLETICS. Physical education requirements:** None.
**Intercollegiate competition:** 8% of students participate. Baseball (M), basketball (M,W), cheerleading (M,W), cross-country (M,W), golf (M,W), soccer (M,W), softball (W), tennis (M,W). Member of Missouri Valley Conference, NCAA Division I.
**Intramural and club sports:** 50% of students participate. Intramural basketball, crew, flag football, soccer, softball, swimming, tennis, track. Men's club crew, rugby. Women's club crew.

**ADMISSIONS. Academic basis for candidate selection** (in order of priority): Secondary school record, class rank, standardized test scores, school's recommendation.
**Nonacademic basis for candidate selection:** Character and personality and extracurricular participation are important. Particular talent or ability is considered.
**Requirements:** Graduation from secondary school is required; GED is accepted. 16 units and the following program of study are required: 4 units of English, 3 units of math, 2 units of lab science, 2 units of foreign language, 2 units of social studies, 3 units of academic electives. Minimum composite ACT score of 18, rank in top half of secondary school class, and minimum 2.0 GPA required. EOP for applicants not normally admissible. Conditional admission possible for applicants not meeting standard requirements. ACT is required; SAT may be substituted. Campus visit and interview recommended. Off-campus interviews available with an admissions representative.
**Procedure:** Application deadline is August 1. Notification of admission on rolling basis. Reply is required by May 1. $50 tuition deposit, refundable until May 1. $50 room deposit, refundable until May 1. Freshmen accepted in terms other than fall.
**Special programs:** Admission may be deferred one year. Credit and/or placement may be granted through CEEB Advanced Placement exams for scores of 3 or higher. Credit may be granted through CLEP subject exams and military and life experience.
**Transfer students:** Transfer students accepted for terms other than fall. In fall 1993, 12% of all new students were transfers into all classes. 207 transfer applications were received, 191 were accepted. Application deadline is rolling for fall; rolling for spring. Minimum 2.0 GPA required. Lowest course grade accepted is "C." Maximum number of transferable credits is 80 semester hours. At least 48 semester hours must be completed at the university to receive degree.
**Admissions contact:** Howard J. Bachman, M.S., Director of Admissions. 402 280-2703.

**FINANCIAL AID. Available aid:** Pell grants, SEOG, Federal Nursing Student Scholarships, state scholarships and grants, school scholarships and grants, private scholarships and grants, ROTC scholarships, academic merit scholarships, and athletic scholarships. Perkins Loans (NDSL), PLUS, Stafford Loans (GSL), NSL, Health Professions Loans, private loans, and SLS. Family tuition reduction. 10-month payment plan.
**Financial aid statistics:** 47% of aid is not need-based. In 1993-94, 100% of all undergraduate applicants received aid. Average amounts of aid awarded freshmen: Scholarships and grants, $3,633; loans, $4,600.
**Supporting data/closing dates:** FAFSA/FAF/FFS: Priority filing date is April 1; accepted on rolling basis. School's own aid application: Accepted on rolling basis. Income tax forms: Accepted on rolling basis. Notification of awards begins March 1.
**Financial aid contact:** Robert D. Walker, M.S., Director of Financial Aid. 402 280-2731.

**STUDENT EMPLOYMENT.** College Work/Study Program. Institutional employment. 50% of full-time undergraduates work on campus during school year. Students may expect to earn an average of $1,500 during school year. Off-campus part-time employment opportunities rated "excellent."

**COMPUTER FACILITIES.** 250 IBM/IBM-compatible and Macintosh/Apple microcomputers. Students may access Digital, UNISYS minicomputer/mainframe systems, Internet. Residence halls may be equipped with networked terminals. Computer languages and software packages include BASIC, C+, COBOL, dBASE, FORTRAN, Lotus 1-2-3, Pascal, PL/1, Prolog, SMART, SPSS-X, WordPerfect. Most computers open to all; business and journalism students have their own facilities not open to all students.

**Fees:** None.
**Hours:** 8 AM-mid. (Su-Th); 8 AM-10 PM (F-Sa).

**GRADUATE CAREER DATA.** Graduate school percentages: 10% enter law school. 10% enter medical school. 3% enter dental school. 3% enter graduate business programs. 7% enter graduate arts and sciences programs. 3% enter theological school/seminary. Companies and businesses that hire graduates: Union Pacific Railroad, Sears, Arthur Andersen, M&M Mars.

**PROMINENT ALUMNI/AE.** Mary Alice Williams, NBC-TV broadcaster; Don Keogh, president and CEO, Coca-Cola; V.J. Skutt, CEO, Mutual of Omaha.

## Dana College

**Blair, NE 68008-1099** **402 426-9000**

**1994-95 Costs.** Tuition: $9,130. Room: $1,372. Board: $1,950. Fees, books, misc. academic expenses (school's estimate): $900.
**Enrollment.** Undergraduates: 252 men, 298 women (full-time). Freshman class: 504 applicants, 482 accepted, 185 enrolled.
**Test score averages/ranges.** Average ACT scores: 22 composite. Range of ACT scores of middle 50%: 18-24 composite.
**Faculty.** 37 full-time; 24 part-time. 45% of faculty holds doctoral degree. Student/faculty ratio: 11 to 1.
**Selectivity rating.** Less competitive.

**PROFILE.** Dana, founded in 1884, is a church-affiliated, liberal arts college. Its 150-acre campus is located in Blair, 30 miles from Omaha.

**Accreditation:** NCACS. Professionally accredited by the Council on Social Work Education, the National Council for Accreditation of Teacher Education.
**Religious orientation:** Dana College is affiliated with the Evangelical Lutheran Church in America; three semester hours of religion required.
**Library:** Collections totaling over 146,000 volumes, 569 periodical subscriptions and 369 microform items.
**Special facilities/museums:** Parnassus cultural center, performing arts center, fine arts building, Danish archives.
**Athletic facilities:** Gymnasium, racquetball, tennis, and volleyball courts, outdoor track, baseball, football, soccer, and softball fields, swimming pool, weight and wrestling rooms, batting cage.

**STUDENT BODY. Undergraduate profile:** 50% are state residents; 19% are transfers. 2.1% Asian-American, 5.1% Black, 1.1% Hispanic, 1.6% Native American, 89.1% White, 1% Other. Average age of undergraduates is 21.
**Freshman profile:** 2% of freshmen who took ACT scored 30 or over on composite; 30% scored 24 or over on composite; 85% scored 18 or over on composite; 100% scored 12 or over on composite. 6% of accepted applicants took SAT; 94% took ACT.
**Undergraduate achievement:** 64% of fall 1992 freshmen returned for fall 1993 term. 32% of entering class graduated. 10% of students who completed a degree program immediately went on to graduate study.
**Foreign students:** 27 students are from out of the country. Countries represented include Bangladesh, Canada, China, Japan, Namibia, and Nepal; 12 in all.

**PROGRAMS OF STUDY. Degrees:** B.A.
**Majors:** Accounting, Art, Biology, Business Education, Chemistry, Communication, Communication/Broadcast Media, Communication/Print Media, Economics, Education, Elementary Education, English, Environmental Studies, Finance, General Science, General Studies, German, Graphic Art, History, Humanities, Information Management, International Communication, Language Arts, Management/Organizational Behavior, Marketing, Mathematics, Mathematics/Computer Science, Medical Arts, Music, Music Education, Organizational Communication, Physical Education, Psychology, Religion, Secondary Education, Social Sciences, Social Work, Sociology, Spanish, Special Education, Speech/Theatre, Theatre/English.
**Distribution of degrees:** The majors with the highest enrollment are marketing, management, and communication; German, economics, and humanities have the lowest.
**Requirements:** General education requirement.
**Academic regulations:** Freshmen must maintain minimum 1.75 GPA; sophomores, 1.85 GPA; juniors, 2.0 GPA; seniors, 2.0 GPA.
**Special:** Minors offered in some majors and in business, coaching, computer science, Danish, philosophy, and theatre arts. Double majors. Independent study. Internships. Preprofessional programs in law, medicine, veterinary science, pharmacy, dentistry, theology, optometry, engineering, medical technology, occupational therapy, physical therapy, physician's assistant, radiologic technology, seminary, and sports medicine. Member of Nebraska Interim Colleges; cross-registration with Consortium of Eastern Nebraska Colleges. Member of Council of Independent Colleges, Association of American Colleges, Association of Independent Colleges and Universities of Nebraska, Lutheran Educational Conference of North America, Nebraska Association of Colleges and Universities, and Nebraska Educational Television Council for Higher Education. Teacher certification in elementary, secondary, and special education. Certification in specific subject areas. Exchange programs abroad in Denmark and Germany. ROTC.
**Honors:** Honor societies.
**Academic Assistance:** Remedial reading, writing, math, and study skills. Nonremedial tutoring.

**ADMISSIONS. Academic basis for candidate selection** (in order of priority): Secondary school record, standardized test scores, class rank, school's recommendation, essay.
**Nonacademic basis for candidate selection:** Character and personality, extracurricular participation, and particular talent or ability are considered.
**Requirements:** Graduation from secondary school is required; GED is accepted. 14 units and the following program of study are recommended: 4 units of English, 3 units of math, 3 units of science, 2 units of foreign language, 2 units of social studies. Minimum composite ACT score of 19 (combined SAT score of 790), rank in top half of secondary school class, and minimum 2.0 GPA recommended. Interview, testing, recommendations, and minimum 2.5 GPA required of applicants to Teacher Education program. Conditional admission possible for applicants not meeting standard requirements. ACT is required; SAT may be substituted. Campus visit and interview recommended. Off-campus interviews available with an admissions representative.
**Procedure:** Take SAT or ACT by June of 12th year. Visit college for interview by June 1 of 12th year. Suggest filing application by April 1. Application deadline is August. Notification of admission on rolling basis. Applicant must accept offer of admission by first day of classes. $100 tuition deposit, refundable until May 1. Freshmen accepted in terms other than fall.
**Special programs:** Admission may be deferred two years. Credit and/or placement may be granted through CEEB Advanced Placement exams for scores of 3 or higher. Credit and/or placement may be granted through CLEP general and subject exams. Credit and placement may be granted through Regents College, ACT PEP, DANTES, and challenge exams and military and life experience. Early entrance/early admission program. Concurrent enrollment program.
**Transfer students:** Transfer students accepted for terms other than fall. In fall 1993, 19% of all new students were transfers into all classes. 82 transfer applications were received, 81 were accepted. Application deadline is August for fall; January for spring. Minimum 2.0 GPA recommended. Lowest course grade accepted is "C." Maximum number of transferable credits is 68 semester hours from a two-year school and 96 semester hours from a four-year school. At least 32 semester hours must be completed at the college to receive degree.
**Admissions contact:** John Schueth, Director of Admissions. 800 444-3262.

**FINANCIAL AID. Available aid:** Pell grants, SEOG, state grants, school scholarships and grants, private scholarships and grants, ROTC scholarships, academic merit scholarships, athletic scholarships, and aid for undergraduate foreign students. Perkins Loans (NDSL), PLUS, Stafford Loans (GSL), school loans, and SLS. AMS, deferred payment plan, and family tuition reduction.
**Financial aid statistics:** 35% of aid is not need-based. In 1993-94, 100% of all undergraduate applicants received aid; 100% of freshman applicants. Average amounts of aid awarded freshmen: Scholarships and grants, $4,625; loans, $3,300.
**Supporting data/closing dates:** FAFSA: Priority filing date is April 1. School's own aid application: Priority filing date is April 1; accepted on rolling basis. Notification of awards begins March 1.
**Financial aid contact:** Mark Anderson, Director of Financial Aid. 402 426-7226.

## Doane College

**Crete, NE 68333** **402 826-2161**

**1994-95 Costs.** Tuition: $9,570. Room: $1,020. Board: $1,980. Fees, books, misc. academic expenses (school's estimate): $1,650.
**Enrollment.** Undergraduates: 1,088 (full-time). Freshman class: 793 applicants, 709 accepted, 244 enrolled. Graduate enrollment: 247.
**Test score averages/ranges.** Average ACT scores: 23 English, 22 math, 23 composite. Range of ACT scores of middle 50%: 20-26 English, 19-25 math.
**Faculty.** 57 full-time; 39 part-time. 64% of faculty holds doctoral degree. Student/faculty ratio: 13 to 1.
**Selectivity rating.** Less competitive.

**PROFILE.** Doane, founded in 1872, is a church-affiliated, liberal arts college. Its 360-acre campus is located in Crete, 25 miles southwest of Lincoln.

**Accreditation:** NCACS. Professionally accredited by the National Council for Accreditation of Teacher Education.
**Religious orientation:** Doane College is affiliated with the United Church of Christ; one semester of religion/theology required.
**Library:** Collections totaling over 197,521 volumes, 456 periodical subscriptions, and 9,799 microform items.
**Special facilities/museums:** Language lab, communication studies facilities, electron microscope, observatory.
**Athletic facilities:** Tracks, field house, practice fields, football stadium.

**STUDENT BODY. Undergraduate profile:** 80% are state residents; 9% are transfers. 1% Asian-American, 1% Black, 1% Hispanic, 94% White, 3% Other. Average age of undergraduates is 20.
**Freshman profile:** 7% of freshmen who took ACT scored 30 or over on English, 4% scored 30 or over on math, 4% scored 30 or over on composite; 41% scored 24 or over on English, 29% scored 24 or over on math, 45% scored 24 or over on composite; 82% scored 18 or over on English, 85% scored 18 or over on math, 92% scored 18 or over on composite; 96% scored 12 or over on English, 97% scored 12 or over on math, 98% scored 12 or over on composite; 97% scored 6 or over on English. 98% of accepted applicants took ACT. 80% of freshmen come from public schools.
**Undergraduate achievement:** 80% of fall 1992 freshmen returned for fall 1993 term. 43% of entering class graduated. 34% of students who completed a degree program immediately went on to graduate study.
**Foreign students:** 23 students are from out of the country. Countries represented include Japan, Malaysia, South Korea, Syria, Taiwan, and Vietnam.

**PROGRAMS OF STUDY. Degrees:** B.A., B.S.
**Majors:** Accounting, Allied Health/Industrial Management, Art, Biology, Business Administration, Chemistry, Computer Science, Corporate Communication, Economics, Elementary Education, English, English as a Second Language, English/Language Arts, Environmental Studies, German, History, Honors Biology, Human Services, Humanities, International Studies, Mass Communication, Mathematics, Music, Natural Science Teaching, Philosophy/Religion, Physical Education, Physical Science, Physics/Mathematics, Political Science, Psychology, Public Administration, Secondary Education, Social Science, Sociology, Spanish, Special Education, Theatre/Drama.

**Distribution of degrees:** The majors with the highest enrollment are education, business administration, and communication; German, philosophy/religion, and environmental studies have the lowest.
**Requirements:** General education requirement.
**Academic regulations:** Minimum 2.0 GPA required for graduation.
**Special:** Minors offered in most majors and in computer studies, East European studies, and speech communication. Courses offered in music therapy, French, geography, geology, and interdiscplinary studies. Credit for extracurricular activities. Self-designed majors. Double majors. Independent study. Accelerated study. Pass/fail grading option. Internships. Cooperative education programs. Graduate school at which undergraduates may take graduate-level courses. Preprofessional programs in law, medicine, veterinary science, dentistry, theology, and optometry. 3-2 engineering and occupational therapy programs with Washington U. 3-2 forestry programs with Duke U. Five-year dual degree engineering program with Columbia U. Member of consortium with Central Coll of Iowa and several international institutions. Washington Semester. Teacher certification in early childhood, elementary, secondary, and special education. Certification in specific subject areas. Member of International Student Exchange Program (ISEP). Exchange program abroad in Denmark (U of Copenhagen). Study abroad also in Africa, Asia, Australia, Austria, the Dominican Republic, England, France, Germany, Japan, Mexico, New Zealand, Russia, Spain, and Wales. ROTC and AFROTC at U of Nebraska.
**Honors:** Honors program. Honor societies.
**Academic Assistance:** Remedial reading, writing, math, and study skills. Nonremedial tutoring.

**ADMISSIONS. Academic basis for candidate selection** (in order of priority): Secondary school record, class rank, standardized test scores, school's recommendation.
**Nonacademic basis for candidate selection:** Character and personality and extracurricular participation are important. Alumni/ae relationship is considered.
**Requirements:** Graduation from secondary school is required; GED is accepted. No specific distribution of secondary school units required. Minimum composite ACT score of 21 and rank in top half of secondary school class recommended. Portfolio required of art program applicants. Audition required of music program applicants. Conditional admission possible for applicants not meeting standard requirements. ACT is required; SAT may be substituted. Campus visit and interview recommended. Off-campus interviews available with an admissions representative.
**Procedure:** Take SAT or ACT by December of 12th year. Suggest filing application by May 1; no deadline. Notification of admission on rolling basis. Reply is required by May 1. $100 tuition deposit, refundable until May 1. $50 room deposit, refundable until end of academic year. Freshmen accepted in terms other than fall.
**Special programs:** Admission may be deferred one year. Credit and/or placement may be granted through CEEB Advanced Placement exams for scores of 3 or higher. Credit and/or placement may be granted through CLEP subject exams. Credit may be granted through ACT PEP exams. Credit and placement may be granted through DANTES and challenge exams and military and life experience. Early entrance/early admission program. Concurrent enrollment program.
**Transfer students:** Transfer students accepted for terms other than fall. In fall 1993, 9% of all new students were transfers into all classes. 60 transfer applications were received, 46 were accepted. Application deadline is August 1 for fall; January 1 for spring. Minimum 2.0 GPA recommended. Lowest course grade accepted is "C-." Maximum number of transferable credits is 66 semester hours from a two-year school and 99 semester hours from a four-year school. At least 30 semester hours must be completed at the college to receive degree.
**Admissions contact:** Daniel P. Kunzman, Dean of Admissions. 402 826-8222.

**FINANCIAL AID. Available aid:** Pell grants, SEOG, state scholarships, school scholarships, academic merit scholarships, and athletic scholarships. SSIG/SSAP. Perkins Loans (NDSL), PLUS, Stafford Loans (GSL), and SLS. Tuition Plan Inc. and deferred payment plan. Advance payment plan.
**Financial aid statistics:** 18% of aid is not need-based. In 1993-94, 99% of all undergraduate applicants received aid; 99% of freshman applicants. Average amounts of aid awarded freshmen: Scholarships and grants, $4,928; loans, $3,531.
**Supporting data/closing dates:** FAFSA: Priority filing date is March 15. Notification of awards on rolling basis.
**Financial aid contact:** Karen Morris, Director of Financial Aid. 402 826-8260.

## Hastings College

**Hastings, NE 68902-0269 402 463-2402**

**1994-95 Costs.** Tuition: $9,376. Room: $1,338. Board: $1,934. Fees, books, misc. academic expenses (school's estimate): $896.
**Enrollment.** Undergraduates: 462 men, 473 women (full-time). Freshman class: 814 applicants, 708 accepted, 262 enrolled. Graduate enrollment: 15 men, 23 women.
**Test score averages/ranges.** Average ACT scores: 23 composite. Range of ACT scores of middle 50%: 20-27 composite.
**Faculty.** 67 full-time; 22 part-time. 63% of faculty holds doctoral degree. Student/faculty ratio: 13 to 1.
**Selectivity rating.** Less competitive.

**PROFILE.** Hastings, founded in 1882, is a church-affiliated, liberal arts college. Its 80-acre campus is located in a residential area of Hastings, 100 miles from Lincoln.

**Accreditation:** NCACS. Professionally accredited by the National Association of Schools of Music, the National Council for Accreditation of Teacher Education.
**Religious orientation:** Hastings College is an interdenominational Christian school; one semester of religion required.
**Library:** Collections totaling over 115,000 volumes, 450 periodical subscriptions, and 63,000 microform items.
**Special facilities/museums:** Language lab, center for communication arts, glass-blowing studio, foundry, observatory.
**Athletic facilities:** Gymnasium, football stadium, swimming pool, track, weight room, basketball, tennis, and volleyball courts, dance studio, athletic fields.

**STUDENT BODY. Undergraduate profile:** 76% are state residents; 14% are transfers. 1% Asian-American, 3% Black, 2% Hispanic, 1% Native American, 93% White. Average age of undergraduates is 22.
**Freshman profile:** 7% of freshmen who took ACT scored 30 or over on composite; 48% scored 24 or over on composite; 90% scored 18 or over on composite; 100% scored 12 or over on composite. 1% of accepted applicants took SAT; 99% took ACT. 90% of freshmen come from public schools.
**Undergraduate achievement:** 73% of fall 1992 freshmen returned for fall 1993 term. 45% of entering class graduated. 24% of students who completed a degree program immediately went on to graduate study.
**Foreign students:** Nine students are from out of the country. Countries represented include Bahamas and Pakistan; five in all.

**PROGRAMS OF STUDY. Degrees:** B.A., B.Mus.
**Majors:** Art, Biology, Business Administration, Chemistry, Communication Arts, Computer Science, Economics, Education, English, German, Health Promotion/Management, History, Human Resources Management, Human Services Administration, Mathematics, Music, Philosophy, Physical Education, Physics, Political Science, Psychology, Religion, Sociology, Spanish, Speech, Theatre Arts.
**Distribution of degrees:** The majors with the highest enrollment are business administration, education, and psychology; religion, philosophy, and foreign languages have the lowest.
**Requirements:** General education requirement.
**Academic regulations:** Freshmen must maintain minimum 1.65 GPA; sophomores, 1.8 GPA; juniors, 2.0 GPA; seniors, 2.0 GPA.
**Special:** Minors offered in many majors and in art history and studio art. Courses offerd in astronomy, French, geography, and geology. Students enroll in one course or conduct independent project during four-week January interim. Self-designed majors. Double majors. Dual degrees. Independent study. Pass/fail grading option. Internships. Graduate school at which undergraduates may take graduate-level courses. Preprofessional programs in law, medicine, veterinary science, pharmacy, dentistry, theology, optometry, engineering, library science, occupational therapy, and and physical therapy. Combined-degree programs in engineering with Columbia U, Georgia Inst of Tech, and Washington U. Combined occupational therapy degree with Boston U and Washington U. Member of Nebraska Independent College Foundation. Washington Semester. January term exchange with other colleges on 4-1-4 system. Teacher certification in elementary, secondary, and special education. Certification in specific subject areas.
**Honors:** Honor societies.
**Academic Assistance:** Remedial reading, writing, math, and study skills. Nonremedial tutoring.

**ADMISSIONS. Academic basis for candidate selection** (in order of priority): Secondary school record, class rank, standardized test scores, school's recommendation, essay.
**Nonacademic basis for candidate selection:** Character and personality, extracurricular participation, particular talent or ability, and alumni/ae relationship are considered.
**Requirements:** Graduation from secondary school is required; GED is accepted. 13 units and the following program of study are recommended: 4 units of English, 2 units of math, 2 units of science, 2 units of foreign language, 3 units of social studies. Minimum composite ACT score of 20, rank in top half of secondary school class, and minimum 2.0 GPA recommended. Portfolio required of art program applicants. Audition required of music program applicants. ATLAS program for applicants not normally admissible. ACT is required; SAT may be substituted. Campus visit and interview recommended. Off-campus interviews available with admissions and alumni representatives.
**Procedure:** Take SAT or ACT by December of 12th year. Visit college for interview by March of 12th year. Suggest filing application by January 1. Application deadline is July 15. Notification of admission on rolling basis. $200 nonrefundable tuition deposit. Freshmen accepted in terms other than fall.
**Special programs:** Admission may be deferred one year. Credit and/or placement may be granted through CEEB Advanced Placement exams for scores of 3 or higher. Credit and/or placement may be granted through CLEP general exams. Credit and placement may be granted through challenge exams and military experience. Concurrent enrollment program.
**Transfer students:** Transfer students accepted for terms other than fall. In fall 1993, 14% of all new students were transfers into all classes. 60 transfer applications were received, 45 were accepted. Application deadline is July 15 for fall; January 1 for spring. Minimum 2.0 GPA required. Lowest course grade accepted is "C." Maximum number of transferable credits is 90 semester hours. At least 30 semester hours must be completed at the college to receive degree.
**Admissions contact:** Sam Rennick, Director of Admissions. 402 463-2402.

**FINANCIAL AID. Available aid:** Pell grants, SEOG, state grants, school scholarships and grants, private scholarships and grants, academic merit scholarships, athletic scholarships, and aid for undergraduate foreign students. Perkins Loans (NDSL), PLUS, Stafford Loans (GSL), school loans, private loans, and SLS. Deferred payment plan and family tuition reduction.
**Financial aid statistics:** 25% of aid is not need-based. In 1993-94, 99% of all undergraduate applicants received aid; 100% of freshman applicants. Average amounts of aid awarded freshmen: Scholarships and grants, $4,530; loans, $3,971.
**Supporting data/closing dates:** FAFSA/FAF/FFS: Priority filing date is May 1. School's own aid application: Priority filing date is May 1. State aid form: Accepted on rolling basis. Income tax forms: Accepted on rolling basis. Notification of awards on rolling basis.
**Financial aid contact:** Ian Roberts, M.S., Director of Financial Aid. 402 463-2402.

## Midland Lutheran College

**Fremont, NE 68025** **402 721-5480**

**1994-95 Costs.** Tuition: $10,300. Room & board: $2,970. Fees, books, misc. academic expenses (school's estimate): $400.
**Enrollment.** Undergraduates: 393 men, 514 women (full-time). Freshman class: 624 applicants, 589 accepted, 272 enrolled.
**Test score averages/ranges.** Average ACT scores: 22 composite.
**Faculty.** 55 full-time; 14 part-time. 40% of faculty holds doctoral degree. Student/faculty ratio: 15 to 1.
**Selectivity rating.** Less competitive.

**PROFILE.** Midland Lutheran, founded in 1883, is a church-affiliated, liberal arts college. Its 27-acre campus is located in Fremont, 35 miles northwest of Omaha.

**Accreditation:** NCACS. Professionally accredited by the National League for Nursing.
**Religious orientation:** Midland Lutheran College is affiliated with the Evangelical Lutheran Church in America; two semesters of religion required.
**Library:** Collections totaling over 108,000 volumes and 900 periodical subscriptions.
**Special facilities/museums:** Planetarium, observatory.
**Athletic facilities:** Swimming pool, weight room, handball courts, indoor track.

**STUDENT BODY. Undergraduate profile:** 80% are state residents; 26% are transfers. 1% Asian-American, 3% Black, 1% Hispanic, 1% Native American, 94% White. Average age of undergraduates is 20.
**Freshman profile:** 98% of accepted applicants took ACT. 98% of freshmen come from public schools.
**Undergraduate achievement:** 76% of fall 1992 freshmen returned for fall 1993 term. 48% of entering class graduated. 16% of students who completed a degree program immediately went on to graduate study.
**Foreign students:** 19 students are from out of the country. Countries represented include China, Japan, Kenya, Korea, Nigeria, and Tanzania.

**PROGRAMS OF STUDY. Degrees:** B.A., B.S., B.S.Bus.Admin., B.S.Nurs.
**Majors:** Art, Biology, Business, Chemistry, Computer Science, Economics, Education, English, History, Human Services, Journalism, Mathematics, Music, Natural Science, Nursing, Physical Education, Psychology, Religion, Respiratory Therapy, Sociology.
**Distribution of degrees:** The majors with the highest enrollment are business, education, and nursing; religion, music, and history have the lowest.
**Requirements:** General education requirement.
**Academic regulations:** Freshmen must maintain minimum 1.5 GPA; sophomores, 1.75 GPA; juniors, 2.0 GPA; seniors, 2.0 GPA.
**Special:** Minors offered in all majors and in astronomy, earth science, German, physics, and Spanish. Courses offered in geography, geology, and Greek. All freshmen and any transfers who have not completed college-level course in English composition must take two-semester, interdisciplinary course, "Odyssey in the Human Spirit." Associate's degrees offered. Self-designed majors. Double majors. Independent study. Accelerated study. Pass/fail grading option. Internships. Preprofessional programs in law, medicine, veterinary science, pharmacy, dentistry, theology, optometry, and physical therapy. 3-1 respiratory therapy program. Cooperative interterm program with 300 other schools through 4-1-4 Conference. Teacher certification in early childhood, elementary, and secondary education. Certification in specific subject areas. Study abroad possible.
**Honors:** Honor societies.
**Academic Assistance:** Remedial reading, writing, math, and study skills. Nonremedial tutoring.

**ADMISSIONS. Academic basis for candidate selection** (in order of priority): Class rank, standardized test scores.
**Nonacademic basis for candidate selection:** Character and personality are important. Extracurricular participation and particular talent or ability are considered.
**Requirements:** Graduation from secondary school is required; GED is accepted. 15 units and the following program of study are required: 3 units of English, 2 units of math, 2 units of science. Rank in top half of secondary school class required. ACT is required. Campus visit and interview recommended. Off-campus interviews available with an admissions representative.
**Procedure:** Take ACT by April of 12th year. Visit college for interview by spring of 12th year. Application deadline is September 1. Notification of admission on rolling basis. No set date by which applicants must accept offer. $50 refundable room deposit. Freshmen accepted in terms other than fall.
**Special programs:** Credit may be granted through CEEB Advanced Placement for scores of 3 or higher. Credit may be granted through CLEP general exams. Credit and/or placement may be granted through CLEP subject exams. Credit and placement may be granted through ACT PEP exams.
**Transfer students:** Transfer students accepted for terms other than fall. In fall 1993, 26% of all new students were transfers into all classes. 123 transfer applications were received, 118 were accepted. Application deadline is rolling for fall; rolling for spring. Minimum 2.0 GPA recommended. Lowest course grade accepted is "C." Maximum number of transferable credits is 96 semester hours. At least 32 semester hours must be completed at the college to receive degree.
**Admissions contact:** Roland R. Kahnk, M.S., Vice President for Enrollment Services. 402 721-5480, extension 6500.

**FINANCIAL AID. Available aid:** Pell grants, SEOG, state scholarships and grants, school scholarships and grants, private scholarships and grants, academic merit scholarships, and athletic scholarships. Perkins Loans (NDSL), PLUS, Stafford Loans (GSL), school loans, and SLS. Deferred payment plan.
**Financial aid statistics:** In 1993-94, 93% of all undergraduate applicants received aid; 100% of freshman applicants. Average amounts of aid awarded freshmen: Scholarships and grants, $3,265; loans, $4,200.
**Supporting data/closing dates:** FAFSA/FAF/FFS: Priority filing date is May 1; accepted on rolling basis. School's own aid application: Priority filing date is May 1. Notification of awards begins March 10.
**Financial aid contact:** Douglas Watson, M.S., Director of Financial Aid. 402 721-5480, extension 6521.

## Nebraska Wesleyan University

**Lincoln, NE 68504** **402 466-2371**

**1994-95 Costs.** Tuition: $9,540. Room & board: $3,320. Fees, books, misc. academic expenses (school's estimate): $762.
**Enrollment.** Undergraduates: 653 men, 789 women (full-time). Freshman class: 969 applicants, 762 accepted, 382 enrolled.
**Test score averages/ranges.** Average ACT scores: 23 composite.
**Faculty.** 88 full-time; 65 part-time. 83% of faculty holds highest degree in specific field. Student/faculty ratio: 14 to 1.
**Selectivity rating.** Less competitive.

**PROFILE.** Nebraska Wesleyan, founded in 1887, is a private, church-affiliated, liberal arts university. The oldest building on campus dates back to 1888 and is listed with the National Register of Historic Landmarks. Its 44-acre campus is located five miles northeast of downtown Lincoln.

**Accreditation:** NCACS. Professionally accredited by the Council on Social Work Education, the National Association of Schools of Music, the National Council for Accreditation of Teacher Education, the National League for Nursing.
**Religious orientation:** Nebraska Wesleyan University is affiliated with the Methodist Church; no religious requirements.
**Library:** Collections totaling over 171,973 volumes, 751 periodical subscriptions, and 3,646 microform items.
**Special facilities/museums:** Art galleries, psychology/sleep lab, observatory and planetarium, carbon dating lab.
**Athletic facilities:** Gymnasium, sand volleyball and tennis courts, swimming pool, weight rooms, track, fitness center, stadium, batting cages, frisbee golf course, baseball and other athletic fields, field house.
**STUDENT BODY. Undergraduate profile:** 93% are state residents; 14% are transfers. 1% Asian-American, 2% Black, 2% Hispanic, 1% Native American, 94% White. Average age of undergraduates is 20.
**Freshman profile:** 98% of accepted applicants took ACT.
**Undergraduate achievement:** 82% of fall 1992 freshmen returned for fall 1993 term. 50% of entering class graduated.
**Foreign students:** 14 students are from out of the country. Countries represented include England, France, Germany, India, Japan, and Sweden; 14 in all.
**PROGRAMS OF STUDY. Degrees:** B.A., B.F.A., B.Mus., B.S., B.S.Nurs.
**Majors:** Applied Music, Art, Biology, Biophysics, Biopsychology, Business Administration, Business/Psychology, Business/Sociology, Chemistry, Communication, Communication Studies, Communication/Theatre Arts, Computer Science, Economics, Elementary Education, English, French, German, Global Studies, Health/Physical Education, History, Information Systems, Mathematics, Middle School Education, Music, Music Education, Nursing, Paralegal Studies, Philosophy, Physics, Political Communication, Political Science, Psychology, Religion, Social Science Education, Social Work, Sociology/Anthropology, Spanish, Special Education, Sport Management, Theatre Arts.
**Distribution of degrees:** The majors with the highest enrollment are business administration, psychology, and biology.
**Requirements:** General education requirement.
**Academic regulations:** Freshmen must maintain minimum 1.6 GPA; sophomores, 1.8 GPA; juniors, 1.9 GPA; seniors, 2.0 GPA.
**Special:** Minors offered in many majors and in accounting, American minority studies, athletic training, computer applications, criminal justice, European history, finance, graphic communication, international trade, Japanese, journalism, management/human resources, massage therapy, paralegal studies, public relations, Russian, U.S. history, and women's studies. Double majors. Dual degrees. Independent study. Pass/fail grading option. Internships. Preprofessional programs in medicine, veterinary science, pharmacy, dentistry, theology, and optometry. 3-2 engineering programs with Columbia U and Washington U. 3-2 occupational therapy program with Washington U. Washington Semester and UN Semester. Cooperative Urban Teacher Education (Kansas City). Teacher certification in elementary, secondary, and special education. Certification in specific subject areas. Member of International Student Exchange Program (ISEP). Exchange program abroad in Japan (Kwansei Gaukin). ROTC and AFROTC at U of Nebraska at Lincoln.
**Honors:** Honor societies.
**STUDENT LIFE. Housing:** All freshmen and sophomores under age 20 must live on campus unless living with family. Coed, women's, and men's dorms. Sorority and fraternity housing. 40% of students live in college housing.
**Social atmosphere:** Groups with a considerable influence on campus social life include Future Christian Athletes, Union Programs, the Rainbow club (multicultural club), New Student Orientation Ambassadors, and the Greek houses. Among popular campus events are Homecoming, LEAD retreat, and various awareness weeks, such as multicultural and alchohol awareness weeks. According to the editor of the student newspaper, "Nebraska Wesleyan is a very close-knit campus."
**Services and counseling/handicapped student services:** Health service. Counseling services for minority and older students. Birth control, personal, and psychological counseling. Career and academic guidance services. Religious counseling. Physically disabled student services.
**Campus organizations:** Undergraduate student government. Student newspaper (Cornerstone, published once/week). Literary magazine. Yearbook. Concert choir, women's glee club, dance band, orchestra, madrigal singers, experimental theatre, drama groups,

debating, drill team, Circle K, Nebraskans for Peace, College Republicans, Young Democrats, academic clubs, special-interest groups, 80 organizations in all. Four fraternities, all with chapter houses; three sororities, all with chapter houses. 38% of men join a fraternity. 32% of women join a sorority.
**Religious organizations:** Fellowship of Christian Athletes.
**Minority/foreign student organizations:** Rainbow Club. International Student Organization.
**ATHLETICS. Physical education requirements:** One semester of health required.
**Intercollegiate competition:** 20% of students participate. Baseball (M), basketball (M,W), cheerleading (W), cross-country (M,W), football (M), golf (M,W), soccer (M,W), softball (W), tennis (M,W), track (indoor) (M,W), track (outdoor) (M,W), track and field (indoor) (M,W), track and field (outdoor) (M,W), volleyball (W). Member of NAIA, NCAA Division III, Nebraska-Iowa Athletic Conference.
**Intramural and club sports:** 60% of students participate. Intramural basketball, flag football, floor hockey, frisbee golf, pool, sand volleyball, softball, table tennis, team handball, volleyball. Men's club bowling, softball, volleyball. Women's club bowling.
**ADMISSIONS. Academic basis for candidate selection** (in order of priority): Class rank, standardized test scores, secondary school record, school's recommendation, essay.
**Nonacademic basis for candidate selection:** Character and personality, extracurricular participation, particular talent or ability, geographical distribution, and alumni/ae relationship are considered.
**Requirements:** Graduation from secondary school is required; GED is accepted. No specific distribution of secondary school units required, but at least half of units should be selected from English, math, natural science, foreign language, social studies, and history. Minimum composite ACT score of 20 (combined SAT score of 800) and rank in top half of secondary school class required. Audition required of music program applicants. R.N. required of nursing program applicants. Conditional admission possible for applicants not meeting standard requirements. ACT is recommended; SAT may be substituted. Campus visit and interview recommended. Off-campus interviews available with admissions and alumni representatives.
**Procedure:** Take SAT or ACT by October of 12th year. Suggest filing application by November 15. Application deadline is May 1. Notification of admission is sent by December 15 for early decision or after March 15 for regular decision. Reply is required by January 15 for early decision or May 1 for regular decision. $50 nonrefundable tuition deposit. $50 nonrefundable room deposit. Freshmen accepted in terms other than fall.
**Special programs:** Admission may be deferred. Credit may be granted through CEEB Advanced Placement for scores of 3 or higher. Credit may be granted through CLEP general and subject exams and ACT PEP exams. Credit and placement may be granted through challenge exams. Early decision program. Deadline for applying for early decision is November 1. Concurrent enrollment program.
**Transfer students:** Transfer students accepted for terms other than fall. In fall 1993, 14% of all new students were transfers into all classes. 113 transfer applications were received, 90 were accepted. Application deadline is August 15 for fall; January 1 for spring. Minimum 2.0 GPA required. Lowest course grade accepted is "C-." Maximum number of transferable credits is 64 semester hours. At least 30 semester hours must be completed at the university to receive degree.
**Admissions contact:** Kendal E. Sieg, Director of Admissions. 402 465-2218.
**FINANCIAL AID. Available aid:** Pell grants, SEOG, state grants, school scholarships and grants, private scholarships and grants, and academic merit scholarships. Perkins Loans (NDSL), PLUS, Stafford Loans (GSL), and SLS. AMS and deferred payment plan.
**Financial aid statistics:** 20% of aid is not need-based. In 1993-94, 65% of all undergraduate applicants received aid; 74% of freshman applicants. Average amounts of aid awarded freshmen: Scholarships and grants, $3,367; loans, $3,364.
**Supporting data/closing dates:** FAFSA. Notification of awards begins December 15.
**Financial aid contact:** Claire Fredstrom, M.Ed., Director of Financial Aid. 402 465-2212.
**STUDENT EMPLOYMENT.** College Work/Study Program. Institutional employment. 25% of full-time undergraduates work on campus during school year. Students may expect to earn an average of $900 during school year. Off-campus part-time employment opportunities rated "excellent."
**COMPUTER FACILITIES.** 170 IBM/IBM-compatible and Macintosh/Apple microcomputers; 100 are networked. Students may access SUN minicomputer/mainframe systems. Residence halls may be equipped with stand-alone microcomputers. Client/LAN operating systems include Apple/Macintosh, DOS, UNIX/XENIX/AIX, LocalTalk/AppleTalk, Novell. Computer languages and software packages include Adobe PhotoShop, BASIC, C, Derive, Excel, FORTRAN, FreeHand, Hypercard, ISETL, Lisp, Modula 2, PageMaker, Paradox, Pascal, Prolog, SPSS, WordPerfect, Word; 20 in all. Computer facilities are available to all students.
**Fees:** Computer fee is included in tuition/fees.
**Hours:** 8 AM-midn.

# Peru State College

**Peru, NE 68421** **402 872-3815**

**1994-95 Costs.** Tuition: $1,500 (state residents), $2,700 (out-of-state). Room: $1,346. Board: $1,388. Fees, books, misc. academic expenses (school's estimate): $654.
**Enrollment.** Undergraduates: 954 (full-time). Freshman class: 711 applicants, 524 accepted, 482 enrolled. Graduate enrollment: 360.
**Test score averages/ranges.** N/A.
**Faculty.** 48 full-time; 100 part-time. 65% of faculty holds doctoral degree. Student/faculty ratio: 28 to 1.
**Selectivity rating.** N/A.

**PROFILE.** Peru State is a public, multipurpose college. Founded in 1867, it is the oldest college in Nebraska. Its 118-acre campus is located in Peru, 60 miles south of Omaha.

**Accreditation:** NCACS. Professionally accredited by the National Council for Accreditation of Teacher Education.
**Religious orientation:** Peru State College is nonsectarian; no religious requirements.
**Library:** Collections totaling over 100,000 volumes, 800 periodical subscriptions, and 200,000 microform items.
**Special facilities/museums:** TV studio.
**Athletic facilities:** Activity center, gymnasium, city softball field, football stadium, intramural fields, indoor pool.
**STUDENT BODY. Undergraduate profile:** 86% are state residents; 30% are transfers. 8% Black, 2% Native American, 90% White. Average age of undergraduates is 24.
**Freshman profile:** 85% of freshmen come from public schools.
**Undergraduate achievement:** 58% of fall 1992 freshmen returned for fall 1993 term. 10% of students who completed a degree program went on to graduate study.
**Foreign students:** Seven students are from out of the country.
**PROGRAMS OF STUDY. Degrees:** B.A., B.A.Ed., B.F.A.Ed., B.S., B.S.Ed., B.Tech.
**Majors:** Accounting, Art, Biological Sciences, Biology, Coaching Interscholastic Sports, Computer Science, Driver Education, Early Childhood Education, Elementary Education, English, General Science, Geography, History, Industrial Education, Industrial Technology, Language Arts, Manual Arts Education, Mathematics, Medical Technology, Music, Physical Education, Psychology/Sociology Teaching Endorsement, Robotics, Social Sciences, Special Education, Speech/Drama.
**Distribution of degrees:** The majors with the highest enrollment are education and computer science.
**Requirements:** General education requirement.
**Special:** Associate's degrees offered. Double majors. Internships. Cooperative education programs. Preprofessional programs in law, medicine, veterinary science, pharmacy, dentistry, engineering, home economics, and physical therapy. 2-2 B.Tech. program for students with associate's degree. 2-2 natural resources program with U of Nebraska at Lincoln. 3-1 programs in medical technology with approved schools of medical technology. Teacher certification in early childhood, elementary, secondary, and special education. ROTC at Creighton U.
**Honors:** Honors program. Honor societies.
**Academic Assistance:** Remedial reading, writing, math, and study skills. Nonremedial tutoring.
**ADMISSIONS. Requirements:** Graduation from secondary school is required; GED is accepted. 16 units and the following program of study are recommended: 3 units of English, 2 units of math, 2 units of science, 1 unit of foreign language, 3 units of social studies, 3 units of history, 2 units of electives. Open door policy. Guaranteed admission for in-state applicants; minimum composite ACT score of 14 required of out-of-state applicants. ACT is required; SAT may be substituted. Campus visit recommended. Off-campus interviews available with admissions and alumni representatives.
**Procedure:** Take SAT or ACT by May of 12th year. Visit college for interview by April of 12th year. Notification of admission on rolling basis. No set date by which applicants must accept offer. $20 tuition deposit, refundable until August 13. $75 room deposit, refundable until August 25. Freshmen accepted in terms other than fall.
**Special programs:** Admission may be deferred one year. Credit and/or placement may be granted through CEEB Advanced Placement exams for scores of 3 or higher. Credit and/or placement may be granted through CLEP general and subject exams. Placement may be granted through challenge exams. Credit and placement may be granted through military experience. Early decision program. Early entrance/early admission program.
**Transfer students:** Transfer students accepted for terms other than fall. In fall 1992, 30% of all new students were transfers into all classes. Minimum 2.0 GPA required. Lowest course grade accepted is "C." At least 30 semester hours must be completed at the college to receive degree.
**Admissions contact:** Curt E. Luttrell, M.A.T., Director of Admissions and School Relations. 402 872-2221.
**FINANCIAL AID. Available aid:** Pell grants, SEOG, state scholarships and grants, school scholarships and grants, academic merit scholarships, and athletic scholarships. Perkins Loans (NDSL), PLUS, Stafford Loans (GSL), school loans, and SLS.
**Financial aid statistics:** In 1993-94, 85% of all freshman applicants received aid. Average amounts of aid awarded freshmen: Loans, $1,700.
**Supporting data/closing dates:** FAFSA: Priority filing date is March 1. Notification of awards on rolling basis.
**Financial aid contact:** Dwight Garman, M.A., Director of Financial Aid. 402 872-2228.

# Union College

**Lincoln, NE 68506** **402 488-2331**

**1993-94 Costs.** Tuition: $8,460. Room: $1,600. Board: $1,100. Fees, books, misc. academic expenses (school's estimate): $550.
**Enrollment.** Undergraduates: 196 men, 251 women (full-time). Freshman class: 359 applicants, 204 accepted, 146 enrolled.
**Test score averages/ranges.** N/A.
**Faculty.** 41 full-time; 7 part-time. 35% of faculty holds doctoral degree. Student/faculty ratio: 12 to 1.
**Selectivity rating.** N/A.

**PROFILE.** Union, founded in 1891, is a church-affiliated, multipurpose college. Its 50-acre campus is located in Lincoln.

**Accreditation:** NCACS. Professionally accredited by the Council on Social Work Education, the National Council for Accreditation of Teacher Education, the National League for Nursing.
**Religious orientation:** Union College is affiliated with the Seventh-day Adventist Church; four semesters of religion/theology required.
**Library:** Collections totaling over 128,548 volumes, 750 periodical subscriptions, and 1,026 microform items.
**Athletic facilities:** Swimming pool, fitness center, gymnasium, weight room, sand volleyball and tennis courts, football, soccer, and softball fields.

**STUDENT BODY. Undergraduate profile:** 25% are state residents. 1% Asian-American, 2% Black, 2% Hispanic, 1% Native American, 85% White, 9% Other. Average age of undergraduates is 21.
**Freshman profile:** Majority of accepted applicants took ACT. 31% of freshmen come from public schools.
**Undergraduate achievement:** 71% of fall 1991 freshmen returned for fall 1992 term. 15% of entering class graduated.
**Foreign students:** 52 students are from out of the country. Countries represented include Hong Kong, Japan, Korea, and Malaysia; 21 in all.
**PROGRAMS OF STUDY. Degrees:** B.A., B.A.Theol., B.Mus., B.S., B.S.Nurs., B.Soc.Work.
**Majors:** Accounting, Art Education, Biology, Business Administration, Business Education, Chemistry, Commercial Art, Computer Information Systems, Elementary Education, English, Health/Physical Education, History, Home Economics, Institutional Development, Journalism, Language Arts, Management, Mathematics, Medical Technology, Music Education, Music Performance, Nursing, Office Administration, Physical Education, Physics, Psychology, Religion, Secondary Education, Social Sciences, Social Work, Studio Art, Theology.
**Distribution of degrees:** The majors with the highest enrollment are nursing, education, and business administration; mathematics and religion have the lowest.
**Requirements:** General education requirement.
**Academic regulations:** Freshmen must maintain minimum 1.60 GPA; sophomores, 1.75 GPA; juniors, 2.00 GPA; seniors, 2.00 GPA.
**Special:** Associate's degrees offered. Self-designed majors. Double majors. Dual degrees. Independent study. Pass/fail grading option. Internships. Preprofessional programs in law, medicine, veterinary science, pharmacy, dentistry, and optometry. 2-2 engineering program with Walla Walla Coll. 3-1 medical technology program with Hinsdale Hospital and Florida Hospital. Cross-registration with Nebraska Wesleyan U and U of Nebraska at Lincoln. Teacher certification in early childhood, elementary, secondary, and special education. Exchange programs abroad in Austria, France, and Spain. Adventist Colleges Abroad.
**Academic Assistance:** Remedial reading, writing, and math. Nonremedial tutoring.
**ADMISSIONS. Academic basis for candidate selection** (in order of priority): Secondary school record, standardized test scores, school's recommendation, class rank, essay.
**Nonacademic basis for candidate selection:** Character and personality are important.
**Requirements:** Graduation from secondary school is required; GED is accepted. 18 units and the following program of study are required: 3 units of English, 2 units of math, 2 units of science including 1 unit of lab, 1 unit of social studies, 1 unit of history, 3 units of electives including 2 units of academic electives. Minimum 2.0 GPA required. Freshman Development program for applicants not normally admissible. ACT is required; SAT may be substituted. Campus visit and interview recommended. Off-campus interviews available with an admissions representative.
**Procedure:** Suggest filing application by July 15. Application deadline is August 1. Notification of admission on rolling basis. $100 tuition deposit, refundable until classes start. $50 room deposit, refundable until classes start. Freshmen accepted in terms other than fall.
**Special programs:** Admission may be deferred one year. Credit may be granted through CEEB Advanced Placement for scores of 3 or higher. Credit may be granted through CLEP general and subject exams, Regents College exams, and military experience. Credit and placement may be granted through challenge exams. Early entrance/early admission program. Concurrent enrollment program.
**Transfer students:** Transfer students accepted for terms other than fall. In fall 1992, 66 transfer applications were received. Application deadline is July 15 for fall; November 15 for spring. Minimum 2.0 GPA recommended. Lowest course grade accepted is "C-." Maximum number of transferable credits is 64 semester hours from a two-year school and 98 semester hours from a four-year school. Minimum 30 semester hours must be completed at the college to receive degree.
**Admissions contact:** Leona Murray, Vice President for Enrollment Services. 402 486-2504, 800 228-4600.
**FINANCIAL AID. Available aid:** Pell grants, SEOG, Federal Nursing Student Scholarships, state grants, school scholarships and grants, private scholarships, academic merit scholarships, and aid for undergraduate foreign students. Perkins Loans (NDSL), PLUS, Stafford Loans (GSL), NSL, school loans, and SLS. Tuition Plan Inc. and family tuition reduction.
**Financial aid statistics:** In 1992-93, 87% of all undergraduate applicants received aid; 94% of freshman applicants. Average amounts of aid awarded freshmen: Scholarships and grants, $2,370; loans, $2,377.
**Supporting data/closing dates:** FAFSA/FAF/FFS: Priority filing date is June 15; accepted on rolling basis. Income tax forms: Accepted on rolling basis. Notification of awards on rolling basis.
**Financial aid contact:** Daniel M. Duff, Student Financial Aid Officer. 402 486-2505, 800 228-4600.

# University of Nebraska at Kearney

**Kearney, NE 68849-0661 — 308 236-8441**

**1993-94 Costs.** Tuition: $1,568 (state residents), $2,850 (out-of-state). Room & board: $2,500. Fees, books, misc. academic expenses (school's estimate): $740.
**Enrollment.** Undergraduates: 2,722 men, 3,042 women (full-time). Freshman class: 2,837 applicants, 2,697 accepted, 1,417 enrolled. Graduate enrollment: 360 men, 745 women.
**Test score averages/ranges.** Average ACT scores: 20 English, 20 math, 21 composite.
**Faculty.** 309 full-time; 114 part-time. 64% of faculty holds doctoral degree. Student/faculty ratio: 21 to 1.
**Selectivity rating.** Competitive.

**PROFILE.** U Nebraska at Kearney is a public institution. Founded as a state college in 1903, it gained university status in 1991. Programs are offered through the Schools of Business and Technology, Education, Fine Arts and Humanities, and Natural and Social Sciences. Its 235-acre campus is located in Kearney, west of Lincoln.

**Accreditation:** NCACS. Professionally accredited by the American Dietetic Association, the American Speech-Language-Hearing Association, the Council on Social Work Education, the National Association of Schools of Music, the National Council for Accreditation of Teacher Education.
**Religious orientation:** University of Nebraska at Kearney is nonsectarian; no religious requirements.
**Library:** Collections totaling over 249,955 volumes, 1,930 periodical subscriptions, and 845,997 microform items.
**Special facilities/museums:** Art gallery, language lab, museum of Nebraska art.
**Athletic facilities:** Gymnasium, basketball, racquetball, tennis, and volleyball courts, running tracks, swimming pool, stadium, football, intramural, and softball fields, exercise, weight, and wrestling rooms.

**STUDENT BODY. Undergraduate profile:** 97% are state residents; 25% are transfers. 1% Black, 2% Hispanic, 94% White, 3% Other. Average age of undergraduates is 21.
**Freshman profile:** 2% of freshmen who took ACT scored 30 or over on composite; 25% scored 24 or over on composite; 81% scored 18 or over on composite; 100% scored 12 or over on composite. 100% of accepted applicants took ACT. 90% of freshmen come from public schools.
**Undergraduate achievement:** 67% of fall 1992 freshmen returned for fall 1993 term.
**Foreign students:** 220 students are from out of the country. Countries represented include the Bahamas, Colombia, Japan, Nepal, Pakistan, and Panama; 48 in all.

**PROGRAMS OF STUDY. Degrees:** B.A., B.A.Ed., B.F.A., B.Gen.Studies, B.S., B.S.Ed.
**Majors:** Airway Computer Science, Airway Science Management, Art, Art History, Biology, Broadcasting, Business Administration, Chemistry, Communication Disorders, Computer Science, Criminal Justice, Dietetics, Economics, English, Family/Consumer Science, Fitness/Leisure Management, French, Geography, German, History, Human Development/Relationships, Human Factors, Industrial Technology, Information Systems, International Studies, Journalism, Management/Technology, Mathematics, Medical Technology, Music, Music Merchandising, Nursing, Occupational Education, Office Administration, Organizational Communication, Physical Education, Physical Science, Physics, Political Science, Professional Chemistry, Psychobiology, Psychology, Public Administration, Radiography, Recreation Leadership, Respiration Therapy Technology, Respiratory Therapy Technology, Social Science, Social Work, Sociology, Spanish, Speech Communication, Statistics, Telecommunications Management, Theatre, Translation/Interpretation, Travel/Tourism.
**Distribution of degrees:** The majors with the highest enrollment are business and physical education; economics, geography, and foreign languages have the lowest.
**Requirements:** General education requirement.
**Academic regulations:** Freshmen must maintain minimum 1.5 GPA; sophomores, 1.8 GPA; juniors, 2.0 GPA; seniors, 2.0 GPA.
**Special:** Minors offered in all majors and in arts/crafts, dance, gerontology, philosophy, regional economics, safety education, science, and sports communication. Continuing and professional education program. Independent study. Pass/fail grading option. Internships. Graduate school at which undergraduates may take graduate-level courses. Preprofessional programs in law, medicine, veterinary science, pharmacy, dentistry, optometry, architecture, engineering, meteorology, oceanography, agriculture, forestry, chemical engineering, music therapy, chiropractic, dental hygiene, medical education, mortuary science, nuclear medicine technology, occupational therapy, physical therapy, physician's assistant, podiatry, and radiologic technology. 3-1 medical technology program. Member of consortium with 54 state-supported colleges and universities. Students may attend another institution for a semester or year. Member of National Student Exchange (NSE). Teacher certification in early childhood, elementary, secondary, and special education. Certification in specific subject areas. Member of International Student Exchange Program (ISEP). ROTC.
**Honors:** Honors program.
**Academic Assistance:** Remedial study skills. Nonremedial tutoring.

**STUDENT LIFE. Housing:** All unmarried freshmen under age 20 must live on campus unless living with family. Coed, women's, and men's dorms. Sorority and fraternity housing. School-owned/operated apartments. Off-campus married-student housing. 27% of students live in college housing.
**Social atmosphere:** Students gather at the library, the student union, and at local coffee houses and bars. Athletes and Greeks are influential groups on campus. Students enjoy sporting events, movies, and the annual Homecoming activities.
**Services and counseling/handicapped student services:** Placement services. Health service. Counseling services for minority students. Personal counseling. Career and academic guidance services. Religious counseling. Physically disabled student services. Learning disabled services. Notetaking services. Tape recorders. Tutors. Reader services for the blind.
**Campus organizations:** Undergraduate student government. Student newspaper (Antelope, published once/week). Yearbook. Radio and TV stations. Choral groups, orchestra, bands, vocal and instrumental ensembles, musical theatre, dance program, debate and forensics, academic and special-interest groups, 140 organizations in all. Eight fraternities, six chapter houses; five sororities, four chapter houses.
**Religious organizations:** Campus Crusade for Christ, Christian Student Fellowship, Fellowship of Christian Athletes, Christian Fellowship, Latter-Day Saints Association, Roger Williams Fellowship.
**Minority/foreign student organizations:** International Student Association.

**ATHLETICS. Physical education requirements:** None.
**Intercollegiate competition:** 4% of students participate. Baseball (M), basketball (M,W), cheerleading (M,W), cross-country (M,W), diving (W), football (M), golf (M), softball (W), swimming (W), tennis (M,W), track and field (indoor) (M,W), track and field (outdoor) (M,W), volleyball (W), wrestling (M). Member of Independent, NCAA Division II.
**Intramural and club sports:** 15% of students participate. Intramural basketball, bowling, flag football, inner-tube water polo, punt-pass-kick, putt-putt golf, racquetball, sand vol-

leyball, soccer, softball, tennis, tug-of-war, turkey trot, volleyball, walleyball. Men's club soccer, bowling. Women's club bowling.

**ADMISSIONS. Academic basis for candidate selection** (in order of priority): Secondary school record, class rank, standardized test scores, school's recommendation.

**Nonacademic basis for candidate selection:** Extracurricular participation and particular talent or ability are considered.

**Requirements:** Graduation from secondary school is required; GED is accepted. 15 units and the following program of study are required: 4 units of English, 2 units of math, 2 units of science including 1 unit of lab, 2 units of social studies. Minimum combined SAT score of 850 (composite ACT score of 20), rank in top half of secondary school class, and completion of 10 core subjects required. SAT or ACT is required. Campus visit recommended. No off-campus interviews.

**Procedure:** Take SAT or ACT by December of 12th year. Visit college for interview by February of 12th year. Application deadline is August 1. Notification of admission on rolling basis. Reply is required by August 1. $45 room deposit, refundable until July 1. Freshmen accepted in terms other than fall.

**Special programs:** Admission may be deferred one year. Credit and/or placement may be granted through CEEB Advanced Placement exams for scores of 3 or higher. Credit may be granted through CLEP general and subject exams. Early entrance/early admission program. Concurrent enrollment program.

**Transfer students:** Transfer students accepted for terms other than fall. In fall 1993, 25% of all new students were transfers into all classes. 776 transfer applications were received, 757 were accepted. Application deadline is August 1 for fall; December 1 for spring. Minimum 2.0 GPA required. Lowest course grade accepted is "C." Maximum number of transferable credits is 66 semester hours. At least 60 semester hours must be completed at the university to receive degree.

**Admissions contact:** Wayne Samuelson, Ed.D., Director of Admissions/Associate Vice-Chancellor for Student Affairs. 308 234-8526.

**FINANCIAL AID. Available aid:** Pell grants, SEOG, state grants, school scholarships and grants, private scholarships, ROTC scholarships, academic merit scholarships, athletic scholarships, and aid for undergraduate foreign students. Perkins Loans (NDSL), PLUS, Stafford Loans (GSL), private loans, and SLS. Deferred payment plan.

**Financial aid statistics:** 44% of aid is not need-based. In 1993-94, 76% of all undergraduate applicants received aid; 84% of freshman applicants. Average amounts of aid awarded freshmen: Scholarships and grants, $1,275; loans, $1,700.

**Supporting data/closing dates:** FAFSA/FAF/FFS: Priority filing date is March 1. Notification of awards on rolling basis.

**Financial aid contact:** Patrick McTee, M.B.A., Director of Financial Aid. 308 234-8520.

**STUDENT EMPLOYMENT.** College Work/Study Program. Institutional employment. Students may expect to earn an average of $971 during school year. Off-campus part-time employment opportunities rated "excellent."

**COMPUTER FACILITIES.** 300 IBM/IBM-compatible and Macintosh/Apple microcomputers; 35 are networked. Students may access AT&T, Digital, IBM minicomputer/mainframe systems, Internet. Residence halls may be equipped with stand-alone microcomputers. Client/LAN operating systems include Apple/Macintosh, DOS. Computer languages and software packages include BASIC, C, COBOL, FORTRAN, Pascal. Computer facilities are available to all students.

**Fees:** Computer fee is included in tuition/fees.

**GRADUATE CAREER DATA.** Companies and businesses that hire graduates: EDS, Mutual of Omaha, State Farm, Union Pacific, WalMart.

**PROMINENT ALUMNI/AE.** Peter Petersen, secretary of commerce, New York Banking; Wayne Smithey, vice-president, Ford Motor Co.; Allen Smith, dean, College of Law, U of Michigan; Mary Elaine House, first female president, National Opera Association; Burnel Saum, president, Ohio National Life Insurance Co.

# University of Nebraska, Lincoln

**Lincoln, NE 68588** **402 472-7211**

**1993-94 Costs.** Tuition: $1,935 (state residents), $5,280 (out-of-state). Room & board: $2,995. Fees, books, misc. academic expenses (school's estimate): $848.

**Enrollment.** Undergraduates: 9,019 men, 7,611 women (full-time). Freshman class: 6,277 applicants, 6,003 accepted, 3,398 enrolled. Graduate enrollment: 2,656 men, 2,210 women.

**Test score averages/ranges.** Average SAT scores: 447 verbal, 513 math. Average ACT scores: 22 English, 22 math, 22 composite.

**Faculty.** 1,282 full-time; 256 part-time. 69% of faculty holds doctoral degree. Student/faculty ratio: 16 to 1.

**Selectivity rating.** Less competitive.

**PROFILE.** U Nebraska at Lincoln, founded in 1869, is a public institution. Programs are offered through the Colleges of Agriculture, Architecture, Arts and Sciences, Business Administration, Engineering and Technology, Home Economics, and Journalism; the Teachers College; and the Division of General Studies. Its 570-acre campus is located in Lincoln, 55 miles southwest of Omaha.

**Accreditation:** NCACS. Professionally accredited by the Accreditation Board for Engineering and Technology, the Accrediting Council on Education in Journalism and Mass Communication, the American Assembly of Collegiate Schools of Business, the American Bar Association, the American Council for Construction Education, the American Dietetic Association, the American Home Economics Association, the American Psychological Association, the American Speech-Language-Hearing Association, the Foundation for Interior Design Education Research, the National Architecture Accrediting Board, the National Association of Schools of Art and Design, the National Association of Schools of Music, the National Council for Accreditation of Teacher Education.

**Religious orientation:** University of Nebraska, Lincoln is nonsectarian; no religious requirements.

**Library:** Collections totaling over 2,164,254 volumes, 21,671 periodical subscriptions, and 3,723,785 microform items.

**Special facilities/museums:** Art gallery, performing arts center, food industries complex, planetarium, center for mass spectrometry, natural science museum, animal science complex, veterinary animal research/diagnosis center.

**Athletic facilities:** Stadium, tracks, sports center, recreation center, baseball, football, intramural, and softball fields, boat house, basketball, tennis, and volleyball courts, swimming pool, wrestling room, fitness trails.

**STUDENT BODY. Undergraduate profile:** 93% are state residents; 8% are transfers. 4% Asian-American, 2% Black, 2% Hispanic, 92% White. Average age of undergraduates is 21.

**Freshman profile:** 3% of freshmen who took SAT scored 700 or over on verbal, 8% scored 700 or over on math; 10% scored 600 or over on verbal, 27% scored 600 or over on math; 36% scored 500 or over on verbal, 60% scored 500 or over on math; 72% scored 400 or over on verbal, 85% scored 400 or over on math; 98% scored 300 or over on verbal, 95% scored 300 or over on math. 6% of freshmen who took ACT scored 30 or over on composite; 38% scored 24 or over on composite; 90% scored 18 or over on composite; 100% scored 12 or over on composite. 19% of accepted applicants took SAT; 98% took ACT. 88% of freshmen come from public schools.

**Undergraduate achievement:** 77% of fall 1992 freshmen returned for fall 1993 term. 16% of entering class graduated.

**Foreign students:** 712 students are from out of the country. Countries represented include China, India, Korea, Malaysia, and Pakistan; 104 in all.

**PROGRAMS OF STUDY. Degrees:** B.A., B.A.Ed., B.F.A., B.Journ., B.Mus., B.Mus.Ed., B.S., B.S.Agri., B.S.Arch., B.S.Bus.Admin., B.S.Chem.Eng., B.S.Civil Eng., B.S.Comp.Sci., B.S.Constr.Mgmt., B.S.Ed., B.S.Elec.Eng., B.S.Eng.Tech., B.S.Home Econ., B.S.Indust.Eng., B.S.Indust.Tech., B.S.Mech.Eng., B.S.Nat.Res.

**Majors:** Accounting, Actuarial Science, Administrative Resource Management, Advertising, Agribusiness, Agricultural Economics, Agricultural Education, Agricultural Engineering, Agricultural Journalism, Agronomy, Animal Science, Anthropology, Architecture, Art, Art History, Astronomy, Athletic Training, Biochemistry, Biological Sciences, Biological Systems Engineering, Biology, Broadcasting, Business Administration, Business Education, Chemical Engineering, Chemistry, Civil Engineering, Classics, Community Health Education, Computer Science, Construction Engineering Technology, Construction Management, Consumer Science/Education, Criminal Justice, Crop Protection, Dance, Drafting/Design Engineering Technology, Earth Science Education, Economics, Electrical Engineering, Electronics Engineering Technology, Elementary Education, Elementary Education/Early Childhood, English, Environmental Studies, Finance, Fisheries/Wildlife, Food Science/Technology, French, General Agriculture, General Studies, Geography, Geology, German, Great Plains Studies, Greek, Health Education, Health Education/Human Development, Health Occupations, Health/Physical Education/Recreation, Hearing Impaired Education, History, Horticulture, Human Development/Family, Industrial Education, Industrial Engineering, Industrial Technology, Integrated Studies, Interdisciplinary, International Affairs, International Business, Journalism, Language Arts, Latin, Latin American Studies, Latin Education, Management, Manufacturing Engineering Technology, Marketing, Marketing/Distributive Education, Mathematics, Mechanical Engineering, Mechanized Agriculture, Meteorology/Climatology, Middle School Education, Music, Music/Instrumental, Music Theatre, Music/Vocal, Natural Science, News/Editorial, Nutritional Sciences/Hospitality Management, Philosophy, Physical Education, Physical Science, Physics, Political Science, Pre-Nuclear Medical Technology, Pre-Physicians Assistant, Pre-Radiologic Technology, Pre-Architecture, Pre-Dental Hygiene, Pre-Dentistry, Pre-Forestry, Pre-Law, Pre-Medical Technology, Pre-Medicine, Pre-Nursing, Pre-Pharmacy, Pre-Physical Therapy, Pre-Veterinary Medicine, Pre-Social Work, Psychology, Range Science, Reading Education, Recreation, Russian, Russian Education, Social Science, Sociology, Soil Science, Spanish, Special Education, Special Education/Elementary, Special Education/Secondary, Speech Communication, Speech/Language Pathology/Audiology, Speech Pathology/Audiology, Speech/Theatre Arts, Textiles/Clothing/Design, Theatre Arts, University Studies, Veterinary Science, Vocational Technical Education, Water Science, Western European Studies, Women's Studies.

**Distribution of degrees:** The majors with the highest enrollment are psychology, business administration, and finance; actuarial science and Latin have the lowest.

**Academic regulations:** Minimum 2.0 GPA must be maintained.

**Special:** Minors offered in most majors. Associate's degrees offered. Self-designed majors. Double majors. Dual degrees. Independent study. Pass/fail grading option. Internships. Cooperative education programs. Graduate school at which undergraduates may take graduate-level courses. Preprofessional programs in law, medicine, veterinary science, pharmacy, and dentistry. 3-2 agriculture/law program. 3-2 veterinary science program with Kansas State U. Member of Mid-American State Universities Association. Sea Semester. Exchange programs with U of Missouri and Kansas State U. Teacher certification in elementary, secondary, special education, and vo-tech education. Certification in specific subject areas. Member of International Student Exchange Program (ISEP). Exchange programs abroad also in Australia (U of New England at Northern Rivers, U of Wollongong), France (Esc Dijon), Hungary (U of Economics Sciences), and the Netherlands (U of Amsterdam). Study tours abroad also offered during winter and spring breaks and during summer. ROTC, NROTC, and AFROTC.

**Honors:** Phi Beta Kappa. Honors program. Honor societies.

**Academic Assistance:** Remedial reading, writing, math, and study skills. Nonremedial tutoring.

**STUDENT LIFE. Housing:** All unmarried freshmen and sophomores under age 19 must live on campus unless living with family. Coed, women's, and men's dorms. Sorority and fraternity housing. School-owned/operated apartments. On-campus married-student housing. 20% of students live in college housing.

**Social atmosphere:** "On Saturdays during the fall, the social life revolves around the football games," reports the student newspaper. "Culturally, UNL will improve with the addition of the multimillion dollar Leid Center for Performing Arts. We have several 'cliques,' but none have a widespread influence on student social life. The Program Council plans

events for the entire campus, including music, speakers, and spring and winter break trips." One of the most popular events is the Walpurgisnacht all-night party in January. Favorite nightspots: Sandy's, O'Rourke's, The Zoo, Drumstick.
**Services and counseling/handicapped student services:** Placement services. Health service. Women's center. Day care. Counseling services for minority, military, veteran, and older students. Birth control, personal, and psychological counseling. Career and academic guidance services. Physically disabled student services. Learning disabled services. Notetaking services. Tutors. Reader services for the blind.
**Campus organizations:** Undergraduate student government. Student newspaper (Daily Nebraskan). Radio station. Musical groups, chess club, Cornhusker flying club, folk dancers, Society of Women Engineers, Amnesty International, departmental clubs and special-interest groups, 300 organizations in all. 28 fraternities, 26 chapter houses; 17 sororities, 14 chapter houses. 15% of men join a fraternity. 15% of women join a sorority.
**Religious organizations:** Christian Fellowship, Lutheran Collegians, other religious groups.
**Minority/foreign student organizations:** African-American, Mexican-American, Native American, and other minority student groups. African, Chinese, Egyptian, India, Indonesian, Korean, Malaysian, Nigerian, Palestine, Pakistani, Vietnamese, and other foreign student groups.

**ATHLETICS. Physical education requirements:** None.
**Intercollegiate competition:** 4% of students participate. Baseball (M), basketball (M,W), cheerleading (M,W), cross-country (M,W), diving (M,W), football (M), golf (M,W), gymnastics (M,W), soccer (W), softball (W), swimming (M,W), tennis (M,W), track (indoor) (M,W), track (outdoor) (M,W), track and field (indoor) (M,W), track and field (outdoor) (M,W), volleyball (W), wrestling (M). Member of Big Eight Conference, NCAA Division I, NCAA Division I-A for football.
**Intramural and club sports:** 40% of students participate. Intramural basketball, flag football, handball, martial arts, racquetball, rugby, soccer, softball, tennis, weight lifting. Men's club bowling, crew, rodeo, rugby, volleyball. Women's club bowling, crew.

**ADMISSIONS.**
**Requirements:** Graduation from secondary school is recommended; GED is accepted. 10 units and the following program of study are required: 4 units of English, 2 units of math, 2 units of science, 2 units of social studies. Minimum composite ACT score of 20 (combined SAT score of 850) or rank in top half of secondary school class required. Most undergraduate colleges have additional, specific admissions requirements. Conditional admission possible for applicants not meeting standard requirements. ACT is required; SAT may be substituted. Campus visit recommended. Off-campus interviews available with admissions and alumni representatives.
**Procedure:** Take SAT or ACT by December of 12th year. Application deadline is July 15. Notification of admission on rolling basis. Reply is required by July 15. $25 tuition deposit, refundable until August 13. $175 room deposit, refundable until three weeks prior to beginning of classes. Freshmen accepted in terms other than fall.
**Special programs:** Admission may be deferred one semester. Credit and/or placement may be granted through CEEB Advanced Placement exams for scores of 3 or higher. Credit and/or placement may be granted through CLEP general and subject exams. Credit may be granted through ACT PEP and DANTES exams and military and life experience. Credit and placement may be granted through challenge exams. Concurrent enrollment program.
**Transfer students:** Transfer students accepted for terms other than fall. In fall 1933, 8% of all new students were transfers into all classes. 1,455 transfer applications were received, 1,158 were accepted. Application deadline is July 15 for fall; December 15 for spring. Minimum 2.0 GPA required. Lowest course grade accepted is "D." Maximum number of transferable credits is 66 semester hours. At least 30 of final 36 semester hours must be completed at Lincoln to receive degree.
**Admissions contact:** John E. Beacon, M.S., Director of Admissions. 402 472-3620.

**FINANCIAL AID. Available aid:** Pell grants, SEOG, state scholarships and grants, school scholarships and grants, private scholarships, ROTC scholarships, academic merit scholarships, athletic scholarships, and aid for undergraduate foreign students. Perkins Loans (NDSL), PLUS, and Stafford Loans (GSL). Unsubsidized Stafford Loans. Deferred payment plan.
**Financial aid statistics:** In 1993-94, 64% of all undergraduate applicants received aid; 56% of freshman applicants. Average amounts of aid awarded freshmen: Scholarships and grants, $1,260; loans, $2,675.
**Supporting data/closing dates:** FAFSA: Accepted on rolling basis. Notification of awards on rolling basis.
**Financial aid contact:** John E. Beacon, M.S., Director of Scholarships/Financial Aid. 402 472-2030.

**STUDENT EMPLOYMENT.** College Work/Study Program. Institutional employment. Students may expect to earn an average of $1,600 during school year. Off-campus part-time employment opportunities rated "good."

**COMPUTER FACILITIES.** 500 IBM/IBM-compatible and Macintosh/Apple microcomputers; 300 are networked. Students may access CDC Cyber, Digital, Hewlett-Packard, IBM, SUN minicomputer/mainframe systems, Internet. Residence halls may be equipped with stand-alone microcomputers, networked microcomputers, networked terminals. Client/LAN operating systems include Apple/Macintosh. Computer languages and software packages include BMDP, C, FORTRAN, COBOL, Pascal, Macsyma, Microsoft Word, SPSS-X, SAS, WordPerfect; 43 in all. Computer facilities are available to all students.
**Fees:** None.
**Hours:** 6 AM-11 PM for some facilities; 24 hours for others.

**GRADUATE CAREER DATA.** Companies and businesses that hire graduates: Cargill, ConAgra, General Motors, Union Pacific, US West.

**PROMINENT ALUMNI/AE.** Clayton Yuetter, former U.S. Secretary of Agriculture; George W. Beadle, Nobel Prize-winning agricultural scientist; Willa Cather, Pulitzer Prize-winning novelist; Johnny Carson, entertainer.

# University of Nebraska, Omaha

**Omaha, NE 68182-0005** **402 554-2800**

**1994-95 Costs.** Tuition: $1,770 (state residents), $4,785 (out-of-state). Housing: None. Fees, books, misc. academic expenses (school's estimate): $719.
**Enrollment.** Undergraduates: 3,914 men, 4,046 women (full-time). Freshman class: 2,825 applicants, 2,584 accepted, 1,621 enrolled. Graduate enrollment: 944 men, 1,644 women.
**Test score averages/ranges.** Average ACT scores: 21 English, 21 math, 21 composite.
**Faculty.** 410 full-time; 280 part-time. 79% of faculty holds doctoral degree. Student/faculty ratio: 30 to 1.
**Selectivity rating.** Less competitive.

**PROFILE.** U Nebraska at Omaha, founded in 1908, is a comprehensive, public institution. Programs are offered through the Colleges of Arts and Sciences, Business Administration, Continuing Education, Education, Engineering and Technology, Fine Arts, Home Economics, and Public Affairs and Community Service. Its 90-acre campus is located in a residential area of Omaha.

**Accreditation:** NCACS. Professionally accredited by the Accreditation Board for Engineering and Technology, the American Assembly of Collegiate Schools of Business, the American Home Economics Association, the Council on Social Work Education, the National Council for Accreditation of Teacher Education.
**Religious orientation:** University of Nebraska, Omaha is nonsectarian; no religious requirements.
**Library:** Collections totaling over 641,000 volumes, 4,317 periodical subscriptions, and 1,300,000 microform items.
**Special facilities/museums:** Center for Afghanistan studies, language lab, physical education facility, planetarium, observatory.
**Athletic facilities:** Field house, football stadium, health, physical education and recreation center.

**STUDENT BODY. Undergraduate profile:** 95% are state residents; 67% are transfers. 2% Asian-American, 5% Black, 2% Hispanic, 1% Native American, 81% White, 9% Other. Average age of undergraduates is 27.
**Freshman profile:** Majority of accepted applicants took ACT. 70% of freshmen come from public schools.
**Foreign students:** 279 students are from out of the country. Countries represented include China, Hong Kong, India, Japan, Korea, and Pakistan; 70 in all.

**PROGRAMS OF STUDY. Degrees:** B.A., B.F.A., B.Gen.Studies, B.Mus., B.S.
**Majors:** Accounting, Administrative Secretary, Advertising Management, Applied Mathematics, Art History, Banking/Finance, Biology, Black Studies, Broadcasting, Chemistry, Civil Engineering, Community Health Education, Community Services, Computer Science, Construction Engineering Technology, Criminal Justice, Decision Sciences, Drafting Design Engineering Technology, Dramatic Arts, Economics, Education/Family Resources, Electronic Engineering Technology, Elementary Education, English, Exercise Science, Family/the Individual in Later Years, Fashion Merchandising, Fire Protection Technology, Food Service Management, French, General Science, Geography, Geology, German, Gerontology, History, Home Economics/Communication, Human Development/Family Studies, Human Nutrition, Individualized Majors, Individually Designed Specialization, Industrial Marketing, Industrial Technology, Insurance, Interdisciplinary Studies, International Studies, Journalism, Latin American Studies, Liberal Studies, Library Science, Management Information Systems, Management/Organizational Behavior, Manufacturing Engineering Technology, Marketing Management, Marketing Research, Mathematics, Music Education/Instrumental, Music Education/Vocal, Music Merchandising, Music Performance, Philosophy, Physics, Political Science, Psychology, Public Administration, Public Relations, Real Estate, Recreation/Leisure Studies, Religion, Restaurant/Institution Management, Retailing Management, Sales/Sales Management, Secondary Education, Social Work, Sociology, Spanish, Special Education, Speech, Speech Pathology, Studio Art, Textiles/Clothing/Design, Urban Studies, Writer's Workshop.
**Distribution of degrees:** The majors with the highest enrollment are criminal justice, elementary education, and accounting.
**Requirements:** General education requirement.
**Special:** Minors offered. Courses offered in Hebrew, Italian, and Russian. Associate's degrees offered. Double majors. Independent study. Cooperative education programs. Graduate school at which undergraduates may take graduate-level courses. Preprofessional programs in law, medicine, veterinary science, pharmacy, dentistry, and optometry. Six-year B.A. or B.S/J.D. program. 3-1 medical technology program with U of Nebraska Coll of Medicine. Several intercampus options with Coll of Home Economics at U of Nebraska at Lincoln. Teacher certification in elementary, secondary, and special education. Certification in specific subject areas. Study abroad in England. AFROTC. ROTC at Creighton U.
**Honors:** Phi Beta Kappa. Honors program.
**Academic Assistance:** Nonremedial tutoring.

**STUDENT LIFE. Housing:** Commuter campus; no student housing.
**Social atmosphere:** According to the editor of the student newspaper, "UNO is a commuter campus of about 16,000. The average student age is 27. UNO boasts Nebraska's largest and most prestigious business college. UNO is not a party school, but a good party can always be found." On campus, students frequent the Nebraska Room, the Maverick Room, the library, and the science center. Off campus, students can be found at the Dundee Dell, RJ's Pub, and the Old Market. The most influential campus groups are the Greeks, student government, cheerleaders, KBLZ radio, the Student Programming Organization, and athletic teams.

**Services and counseling/handicapped student services:** Placement services. Health service. Counseling services for minority, military, veteran, and older students. Personal counseling. Career and academic guidance services. Physically disabled student services. Learning disabled services. Tape recorders. Tutors.

**Campus organizations:** Undergraduate student government. Student newspaper (Gateway, published twice/week). Literary magazine. Radio and TV stations. Jazz, modern, and square dance clubs, judo and karate clubs, athletic and departmental clubs, service and special-interest groups, 110 organizations in all. Eight fraternities, one chapter house; seven sororities, no chapter houses. 3% of men join a fraternity. 3% of women join a sorority.

**Religious organizations:** Baptist Student Union, Catholic Campus Ministries, Chapter Summary Bible Study, Intervarsity Christian Fellowship, United Christian Ministries, Lutherans in Fellowship, Latter-Day Saints Student Association, Muslim group.

**Minority/foreign student organizations:** Black Liberation-Action on Campus, Hispanic and Native American groups, United Minority Students. International Student Services, International Studies Association, Afghanistan and Chinese groups.

**ATHLETICS. Physical education requirements:** None.

**Intercollegiate competition:** 1% of students participate. Baseball (M), basketball (M,W), cross-country (W), football (M), softball (W), volleyball (W), wrestling (M). Member of NCAA Division II, North Central Athletic Conference.

**Intramural and club sports:** 20% of students participate. Intramural basketball, flag football, golf, indoor soccer, judo, racquetball, softball, squash, tennis, volleyball, walleyball, wheelchair basketball, wrestling. Men's club bowling, cycling, soccer, martial arts, tennis, lacrosse, golf, badminton. Women's club bowling, soccer.

**ADMISSIONS. Academic basis for candidate selection** (in order of priority): Class rank, standardized test scores, secondary school record.

**Requirements:** Graduation from secondary school is required; GED is accepted. 10 units and the following program of study are required: 4 units of English, 2 units of math, 2 units of lab science, 2 units of social studies. Minimum composite ACT score of 20 or rank in top half of secondary school class required. 2 units of algebra required of Coll of Business Administration program applicants. 3 units of English, 2 units of algebra, 1/2 unit of trigonometry, 1 unit each of geometry, physics, and chemistry, and minimum composite ACT score of 23 required of engineering program applicants. 3 units of English and 1 unit each of algebra, geometry, and science (physics or chemistry) required of technology program applicants entering Coll of Engineering and Tech. 3 units of English, 1 unit of math, 12 units of electives including 3 units of academic electives required of Coll of Home Economics program applicants. Conditional admission possible for applicants not meeting standard requirements. SAT or ACT is required. Campus visit recommended. No off-campus interviews.

**Procedure:** Take SAT or ACT by August 1 of 12th year. Visit college for interview by August 1 of 12th year. Suggest filing application by December 1; no deadline. Notification of admission on rolling basis. $368 tuition deposit, refundable until first week of classes. Freshmen accepted in terms other than fall.

**Special programs:** Admission may be deferred one year. Credit may be granted through CEEB Advanced Placement for scores of 3 or higher. Credit may be granted through CLEP general exams, DANTES exams and military experience. Credit and/or placement may be granted through CLEP subject exams. Placement may be granted through challenge exams. Early decision program. Deadline for applying for early decision is August 1. Early entrance/early admission program. Concurrent enrollment program.

**Transfer students:** Transfer students accepted for terms other than fall. In fall 1993, 67% of all new students were transfers into all classes. 2,088 transfer applications were received, 1,874 were accepted. Application deadline is August 8 for fall; December 1 for spring. Minimum 2.0 GPA required. Lowest course grade accepted is "C." Maximum number of transferable credits is 64.

**Admissions contact:** John Flemming, M.S., Director of Admissions. 402 554-2393.

**FINANCIAL AID. Available aid:** Pell grants, SEOG, state grants, school scholarships and grants, private scholarships and grants, ROTC scholarships, academic merit scholarships, and athletic scholarships. Perkins Loans (NDSL), PLUS, Stafford Loans (GSL), school loans, private loans, and SLS. Deferred payment plan.

**Financial aid statistics:** In 1993-94, 76% of all undergraduate applicants received aid; 76% of freshman applicants. Average amounts of aid awarded freshmen: Scholarships and grants, $1,300; loans, $2,000.

**Supporting data/closing dates:** FAFSA: Priority filing date is March 1; accepted on rolling basis. School's own aid application: Priority filing date is December 1. Notification of awards on rolling basis.

**Financial aid contact:** Randy Sell, Director of Financial Aid. 402 554-2327.

**STUDENT EMPLOYMENT.** College Work/Study Program. Institutional employment. 6% of full-time undergraduates work on campus during school year. Students may expect to earn an average of $2,600 during school year. Off-campus part-time employment opportunities rated "good."

**COMPUTER FACILITIES.** 160 IBM/IBM-compatible and Macintosh/Apple microcomputers; all are networked. Students may access IBM, UNISYS minicomputer/mainframe systems, Internet. Client/LAN operating systems include Apple/Macintosh. Computer languages and software packages include Ada, BASIC, C, COBOL, DataTrieve, FORTRAN, IFPS, LISP, Mass-11, MINITAB, Oracle, Pascal, PL/1, SAS, SPSS-X. Computer facilities are available to all students.

**Fees:** None.

**Hours:** 24 hours.

**PROMINENT ALUMNI/AE.** Charles W. Schmid, executive vice-president, 7-Up; Lt. Gen. Kenneth L. Peek, Jr., vice-commander in chief, Strategic Air Command; Samuel G. Leftwich, chairperson of the board, K mart.

# Wayne State College

**Wayne, NE 68787 — 402 375-7000**

**1994-95 Costs.** Tuition: $1,500 (state residents), $2,700 (out-of-state). Room: $1,230. Board: $1,430. Fees, books, misc. academic expenses (school's estimate): $664.

**Enrollment.** Undergraduates: 1,232 men, 1,503 women (full-time). Freshman class: 1,373 applicants, 1,373 accepted, 724 enrolled. Graduate enrollment: 159 men, 426 women.

**Test score averages/ranges.** Average ACT scores: 20 English, 19 math, 20 composite. Range of ACT scores of middle 50%: 17-22 English, 16-22 math.

**Faculty.** 130 full-time; 85 part-time. 66% of faculty holds highest degree in specific field. Student/faculty ratio: 21 to 1.

**Selectivity rating.** Less competitive.

**PROFILE.** Wayne State, founded in 1910, is a public college. Programs are offered through the Divisions of Applied Science; Business; Education; Fine Arts; Humanities; Mathematics and Science; Health, Physical Education, Recreation, and Athletics; and Social Sciences. Its 128-acre campus is located in Wayne, in northeastern Nebraska, 100 miles from Omaha.

**Accreditation:** NCACS. Professionally accredited by the National Council for Accreditation of Teacher Education.

**Religious orientation:** Wayne State College is nonsectarian; no religious requirements.

**Library:** Collections totaling over 170,000 volumes, 1,000 periodical subscriptions, and 545,000 microform items.

**Special facilities/museums:** Art gallery, fine arts center, planetarium, recreation center, telecommunications network.

**Athletic facilities:** Recreation center, baseball, football, intramural, soccer, and softball fields, stadium, swimming pool.

**STUDENT BODY. Undergraduate profile:** 79% are state residents; 29% are transfers. 1% Asian-American, 2% Black, 1% Hispanic, 1% Native American, 95% White. Average age of undergraduates is 21.

**Freshman profile:** 1% of freshmen who took ACT scored 30 or over on English, 1% scored 30 or over on math, 1% scored 30 or over on composite; 22% scored 24 or over on English, 17% scored 24 or over on math, 21% scored 24 or over on composite; 68% scored 18 or over on English, 66% scored 18 or over on math, 78% scored 18 or over on composite; 98% scored 12 or over on English, 100% scored 12 or over on math, 100% scored 12 or over on composite; 100% scored 6 or over on English. Majority of accepted applicants took ACT. 90% of freshmen come from public schools.

**Undergraduate achievement:** 64% of fall 1992 freshmen returned for fall 1993 term. 15% of students who completed a degree program went on to graduate study within five years.

**Foreign students:** Eight students are from out of the country. Countries represented include the Bahamas, China, Finland, Japan, Nigeria, and Turkey; eight in all.

**PROGRAMS OF STUDY. Degrees:** B.A., B.S.

**Majors:** Accounting, Art, Biology, Broadcasting, Business Administration, Chemistry, Communication Arts, Computer Information Systems, Computer Science, Corporate/Community Relations, Criminal Justice, Early Childhood, Economics, Education, Educational Administration, Elementary Education, English, Fashion Merchandising, Finance, Food Service Management, French, Geo-Studies, German, Graphic Design, Health, Health/Physical Education, History, Home Economics, Homemaking, Human Service Counseling, Industrial Education, Industrial Management, Interdisciplinary Studies, Interior Design, International Business, International Studies, Journalism, Marketing, Mathematics, Medical Technology, Mortuary Science, Music, Music Merchandising, Office Administration, Physical Education, Political Science, Pre-Law, Psychology, Public Administration, Recreation, Secondary Education, Sociology, Spanish, Special Education, Speech Communication, Sports Management, Technology, Theatre, Wellness.

**Distribution of degrees:** The majors with the highest enrollment are business administration and counseling.

**Requirements:** General education requirement.

**Special:** Minors offered in many majors and in athletic training, earth science, geography, philosophy, and physics. B.A. and B.S. degrees require major and minor, two majors, or 50-hour major. Self-designed majors. Double majors. Independent study. Pass/fail grading option. Internships. Cooperative education programs. Graduate school at which undergraduates may take graduate-level courses. Preprofessional programs in law, medicine, veterinary science, pharmacy, dentistry, optometry, agriculture, architecture, biosystems engineering, chiropractic, diagnostic medicine, engineering, forestry, nuclear medical technology, nursing, oceanography, osteopathy, occupational therapy, physical therapy, physician's assistant, podiatry, radiation therapy technology, and radiology. 2-2 business program with Northeast Tech Commun Coll. Medical technology programs with St. Luke's and Marian Hospitals (Sioux City, Iowa). Medicine, nursing, pharmacy, dentistry, and dental hygiene programs with U of Nebraska Medical Center. Mortuary science program with colleges in Indiana and Missouri. Teacher certification in elementary, secondary, and special education. Certification in specific subject areas. Study abroad in Denmark.

**Honors:** Honors program.

**Academic Assistance:** Nonremedial tutoring.

**STUDENT LIFE. Housing:** All unmarried freshmen under age 20 must live on campus unless living with family. Coed and women's dorms. Off-campus privately-owned housing. 48% of students live in college housing.

**Social atmosphere:** According to the student newspaper, "Wayne is a small community that offers few opportunities for a variety of entertainment. With a limited budget, several campus organizations do offer students speakers, movies, and other activities." Popular activities include Homecoming, Fall Blast, Spring Happenings Week, the alumni football game, and the fall concert. Students frequent the Fourth Jug Tavern, Gay Movie Theater, Alice's Country Tavern, the student center, and the dorm lobbies. Influential groups include social fraternities and sororities and the Newman Club.

**Services and counseling/handicapped student services:** Placement services. Health service. Counseling services for minority, military, veteran, and older students. Birth control, personal, and psychological counseling. Career and academic guidance services. Physically disabled student services. Learning disabled services. Notetaking services. Tape recorders. Tutors. Reader services for the blind.

**Campus organizations:** Undergraduate student government. Student newspaper (Wayne Stater, published once/week). Literary magazine. Radio and TV stations. A cappella choir, ensembles, concert and marching bands, concert orchestra, Activities Board, drama productions, intercollegiate forensics club, Young Democrats, Young Republicans, intramural activities, departmental and special-interest groups, 80 organizations in all. Two fraternities, one chapter house; two sororities, no chapter houses. 5% of men join a fraternity. 3% of women join a sorority.

**Religious organizations:** Fellowship of Christian Athletes, Campus Crusade for Christ, Lutheran Campus Ministry, United Ministry for Higher Education.

**Minority/foreign student organizations:** Minority Student Association. International Club.

**ATHLETICS. Physical education requirements:** Two semesters of physical education required.

**Intercollegiate competition:** 10% of students participate. Baseball (M), basketball (M,W), cheerleading (M,W), cross-country (M,W), football (M), golf (M,W), softball (W), track (indoor) (M,W), track (outdoor) (M,W), track and field (indoor) (M,W), track and field (outdoor) (M,W), volleyball (W). Member of NCAA Division II.

**Intramural and club sports:** 90% of students participate. Intramural basketball, bowling, football, pitch, racquetball, softball, swimming, track, volleyball. Men's club soccer, weight lifting. Women's club soccer, weight lifting.

**ADMISSIONS. Academic basis for candidate selection** (in order of priority): Secondary school record, standardized test scores, class rank.

**Nonacademic basis for candidate selection:** Character and personality are considered.

**Requirements:** Graduation from secondary school is required; GED is accepted. 16 units and the following program of study are required: 3 units of English, 2 units of math, 2 units of science including 1 unit of lab, 1 unit of social studies, 1 unit of history. No minimum requirements for in-state applicants; minimum composite ACT score of 18 (combined SAT score of 700) and minimum 2.0 GPA required of out-of-state applicants. Minimum 2.5 GPA required of teacher education program applicants. ACT is required; SAT may be substituted. Campus visit and interview recommended. Off-campus interviews available with an admissions representative.

**Procedure:** Take SAT or ACT by December of 12th year. Visit college for interview by March 1 of 12th year. Suggest filing application by August 1. Application deadline is August 30. Notification of admission on rolling basis. $30 tuition deposit, refundable until August 1. $75 room deposit, refundable until August 1. Freshmen accepted in terms other than fall.

**Special programs:** Admission may be deferred one year. Credit may be granted through CEEB Advanced Placement for scores of 3 or higher. Credit may be granted through CLEP general and subject exams, challenge exams, and military experience. Early entrance/early admission program. Concurrent enrollment program.

**Transfer students:** Transfer students accepted for terms other than fall. In fall 1993, 29% of all new students were transfers into all classes. 347 transfer applications were received, 347 were accepted. Application deadline is August 1 for fall; January 2 for spring. SAT/ACT scores required of transfer applicants with fewer than 12 credits and have been out of high school less than three years. Minimum 2.0 GPA required. Lowest course grade accepted is "C-." Maximum number of transferable credits is 66 semester credits from a two-year school and 101 semester credits from a four-year school. At least 125 semester credits must be completed at the college to receive degree.

**Admissions contact:** Robert Zetocha, M.A., Director of Admissions. 402 375-7234.

**FINANCIAL AID. Available aid:** Pell grants, SEOG, state scholarships and grants, school scholarships, private scholarships, academic merit scholarships, athletic scholarships, and aid for undergraduate foreign students. SSIG. Perkins Loans (NDSL), PLUS, Stafford Loans (GSL), and SLS. Deferred payment plan. Installment plan for room and board.

**Financial aid statistics:** 33% of aid is not need-based. In 1993-94, 70% of all undergraduate applicants received aid; 73% of freshman applicants. Average amounts of aid awarded freshmen: Scholarships and grants, $1,945; loans, $2,895.

**Supporting data/closing dates:** FAFSA: Priority filing date is May 1. Notification of awards begins June 1.

**Financial aid contact:** Joan Zanders, Director of Financial Aid. 402 375-7230.

**STUDENT EMPLOYMENT.** College Work/Study Program. 15% of full-time undergraduates work on campus during school year. Students may expect to earn an average of $1,000 during school year. Off-campus part-time employment opportunities rated "good."

**COMPUTER FACILITIES.** 140 IBM/IBM-compatible and Macintosh/Apple microcomputers; all are networked. Students may access Digital, IBM minicomputer/mainframe systems. Client/LAN operating systems include DOS, Windows NT, Novell. Computer languages and software packages include BASIC, C, COBOL, dBASE, Excel, FORTRAN, Graph, Harvard Graphics, Lotus 1-2-3, Microsoft Windows, Microsoft Word, Paradox, Pascal, PFS, PFS File, FileWrite, RPG, WordPerfect. Computer facilities are available to all students.

Fees: None.

**GRADUATE CAREER DATA.** Highest graduate school enrollments: U Nebraska-Lincoln.

**PROMINENT ALUMNI/AE.** John Kyle, U.S. Department of the Interior (retired); Val Peterson, former governor of Nebraska and ambassador to Denmark; Drs. F.B. Decker and Anne Campbell, former commissioners of education for Nebraska; Gayle McGee, former U.S. senator.

# Nevada

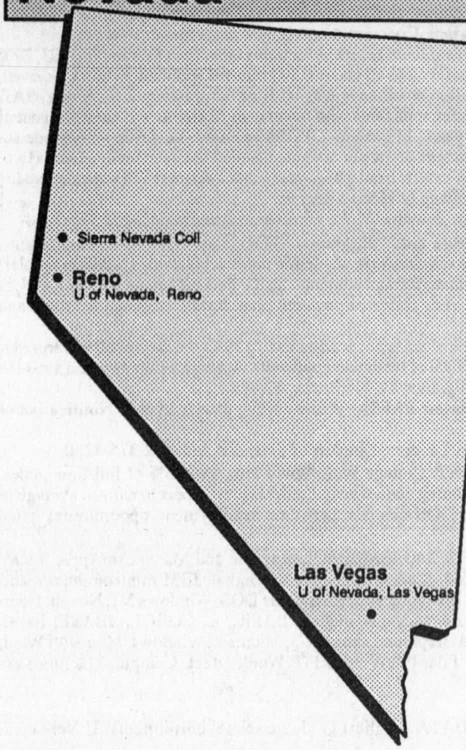


## Sierra Nevada College

**Incline Village, NV 89450** **702 831-1314**

**1994-95 Costs.** Tuition: $9,000. Room: $2,600. Fees, books, misc. academic expenses (school's estimate): $500.
**Enrollment.** Undergraduates: 135 men, 120 women (full-time). Freshman class: 90 applicants, 90 accepted, 75 enrolled. Graduate enrollment: 10 men, 27 women.
**Test score averages/ranges.** N/A.
**Faculty.** 12 full-time; 70 part-time. 5% of faculty holds doctoral degree. Student/faculty ratio: 12 to 1.
**Selectivity rating.** N/A.

**PROFILE.** Sierra Nevada, founded in 1969, is a private, liberal arts college. Its 20-acre campus is located in Incline Village, 30 miles from Reno.

**Accreditation:** NASC.
**Religious orientation:** Sierra Nevada College is nonsectarian; no religious requirements.
**Library:** Collections totaling over 20,000 volumes, 100 periodical subscriptions, and 10,000 microform items.
**Special facilities/museums:** Music studios, individual practice rooms, ceramics lab/studio, recyling center, observatory, telescope.
**Athletic facilities:** Ski hill, local facilities for aerobics, basketball, volleyball, and weight training.
**STUDENT BODY. Undergraduate profile:** 15% are state residents. 2% Asian-American, 1% Black, 1% Hispanic, 1% Native American, 95% White. Average age of undergraduates is 23.
**Freshman profile:** Majority of accepted applicants took SAT. 65% of freshmen come from public schools.
**Undergraduate achievement:** 85% of fall 1992 freshmen returned for fall 1993 term. 25% of students who completed a degree program went on to graduate study within five years.
**Foreign students:** 35 students are from out of the country. Countries represented include Canada, England, Japan, Russia, and Slovakia; 13 in all.
**PROGRAMS OF STUDY. Degrees:** B.A., B.F.A., B.S.
**Majors:** Business Administration, Environmental Science, Fine Arts, Hotel/Restaurant Management, Humanities, Music, Science, Ski Business Management, Teaching Credential Program.
**Distribution of degrees:** The majors with the highest enrollment are business administration, humanities, and teaching credential program; music and fine arts have the lowest.
**Requirements:** General education requirement.
**Academic regulations:** Minimum 2.0 GPA must be maintained.
**Special:** Artist-in-Residence and visiting artist programs. Field studies in ecology. Self-designed majors. Independent study. Pass/fail grading option. Internships. Preprofessional programs in medicine, veterinary science, and dentistry. Teacher certification in elementary and secondary education. ROTC at U of Nevada at Reno.
**Honors:** Honor societies.
**Academic Assistance:** Nonremedial tutoring.
**ADMISSIONS. Academic basis for candidate selection** (in order of priority): Secondary school record, school's recommendation, essay, standardized test scores, class rank.
**Nonacademic basis for candidate selection:** Character and personality, extracurricular participation, and particular talent or ability are considered.
**Requirements:** Graduation from secondary school is required; GED is accepted. No specific distribution of secondary school units required. Minimum 2.0 GPA required. Conditional admission possible for applicants not meeting standard requirements. SAT is recommended; ACT may be substituted. Campus visit and interview recommended. Off-campus interviews available with an admissions representative.
**Procedure:** Notification of admission on rolling basis. $100 nonrefundable tuition deposit. $250 nonrefundable room deposit. Freshmen accepted for terms other than fall.
**Special programs:** Admission may be deferred one year. Credit may be granted through CEEB Advanced Placement for scores of 3 or higher. Credit may be granted through CLEP subject exams, military and life experience. Credit and placement may be granted through challenge exams.
**Transfer students:** Transfer students accepted for terms other than fall. In fall 1993, 114 transfer applications were received, 113 were accepted. Application deadline is rolling for fall; rolling for spring. Minimum 2.0 GPA required. Lowest course grade accepted is "C." At least 24 semester hours must be completed at the college to receive degree.
**Admissions contact:** Ms. Lane Murray, Director of Admissions/Retention. 800 332-8666.
**FINANCIAL AID. Available aid:** Pell grants, SEOG, state grants, school scholarships, private scholarships, ROTC scholarships, and athletic scholarships. PLUS, Stafford Loans (GSL), and SLS. Guaranteed tuition.
**Financial aid statistics:** Average amounts of aid awarded freshmen: Scholarships and grants, $500.
**Supporting data/closing dates:** FAFSA: Accepted on rolling basis. School's own aid application: Accepted on rolling basis. Notification of awards on rolling basis.
**Financial aid contact:** Laura Whitelaw, Director of Financial Aid. 702 831-1314, extension 27.

## University of Nevada, Las Vegas

**Las Vegas, NV 89154** **702 739-3011**

**1994-95 Costs.** Tuition: $1,740 (state residents), $6,490 (out-of-state). Room & board: $5,000. Fees, books, misc. academic expenses (school's estimate): $540.
**Enrollment.** Undergraduates: 4,345 men, 4,707 women (full-time). Freshman class: 6,580 applicants, 5,481 accepted. Graduate enrollment: 1,236 men, 1,706 women.
**Test score averages/ranges.** Average ACT scores: 20 English, 19 math, 20 composite.
**Faculty.** 610 full-time; 400 part-time. 81% of faculty holds doctoral degree. Student/faculty ratio: 25 to 1.
**Selectivity rating.** Less competitive.

**PROFILE.** U Nevada at Las Vegas, founded in 1957, is a comprehensive, public institution. Its 335-acre campus is located in Las Vegas.

**Accreditation:** NASC. Professionally accredited by the American Assembly of Collegiate Schools of Business, the Council on Rehabilitation Education, the Council on Social Work Education, the National Association of Schools of Music, the National Council for Accreditation of Teacher Education, the National League for Nursing.
**Religious orientation:** University of Nevada, Las Vegas is nonsectarian; no religious requirements.
**Library:** Collections totaling over 600,000 volumes, 7,600 periodical subscriptions, and 995,000 microform items.
**Special facilities/museums:** Art galleries, on-campus preschool, athletic hall of fame, natural history museum, desert research institute, resources studies unit (National Park Service), solar observatory, EPA monitoring and support lab.
**Athletic facilities:** Gymnasiums, swimming pool, track, athletic and soccer fields, racquetball and tennis courts, weight rooms.
**STUDENT BODY. Undergraduate profile:** 83% are state residents; 30% are transfers. 5% Asian-American, 6% Black, 5% Hispanic, 1% Native American, 82% White, 1% Other. Average age of undergraduates is 23.
**Freshman profile:** 2% of freshmen who took SAT scored 700 or over on verbal, 2% scored 700 or over on math; 5% scored 600 or over on verbal, 15% scored 600 or over on math; 25% scored 500 or over on verbal, 40% scored 500 or over on math; 70% scored 400 or over on verbal, 75% scored 400 or over on math; 94% scored 300 or over on verbal, 98% scored 300 or over on math. Majority of accepted applicants took ACT.
**Foreign students:** 230 students are from out of the country. Countries represented include Canada, China, Hong Kong, India, Japan, and Taiwan; 51 in all.
**PROGRAMS OF STUDY. Degrees:** B.A., B.Ed., B.F.A., B.Lib.Studies, B.Mus., B.S., B.S.Bus.Admin., B.S.Ed., B.S.Eng., B.S.Hotel Admin.
**Majors:** Accounting, Advertising, Anthropology, Applied Physics, Art, Asian Studies, Athletic Trainer, Biology, Chemistry, Civil Engineering, Communications Studies, Comparative Literature, Computer Science, Computer Science Engineering, Criminal Justice, Dance, Earth Science, Economics, Electrical Engineering, Elementary Education, English, Environmental Studies, Film Studies, Finance, Financial Administration, French, Geology, German, Health Education, History, Hotel Administration, Industrial Accounting, Industrial Relations/Personnel, Information Sciences/Systems, Insurance, Interdisciplinary Studies, Investments, Latin American Studies, Liberal/General Studies, Linguistic Studies, Management, Management Information Systems, Marketing, Mathematical Sciences, Mechanical Engineering, Music, Nursing, Philosophy, Physical Education, Physics, Political Science, Pre-Health Sciences, Pre-Law, Psychology, Public Accounting, Quantitative Management, Radiological Sciences, Real Estate, Recreation, Romance Languages, Sales/Marketing, Secondary Education, Social Science Studies, Social

Sciences, Social Work, Sociology, Spanish, Special Education, Theatre Arts, Vocational Education, Women's Studies.
**Distribution of degrees:** The majors with the highest enrollment are hotel administration, management, and accounting.
**Requirements:** General education requirement.
**Academic regulations:** Minimum 2.0 GPA must be maintained.
**Special:** Minors offered in chemistry, engineering, ethnic studies, geology, math, physics, and sociology. Interdisciplinary programs in math, physics, sociology, and Asian, film, Latin American, and women's studies. Courses offered in astronomy, Chinese, Hebrew, Latin, library science, linguistics, and Russian. Graduate school at which undergraduates may take graduate-level courses. Preprofessional programs in law, medicine, veterinary science, and dentistry. Member of the Oak Ridge Association of Engineering. Semester-away programs. Member of National Student Exchange (NSE). Teacher certification in elementary, secondary, and special education. Study abroad in England, France, Italy, Mexico, and Spain.
**Honors:** Honors program. Honor societies.
**Academic Assistance:** Remedial study skills.

**STUDENT LIFE. Housing:** Students may live on or off campus. Coed dorms. Fraternity housing. 10% of students live in college housing.
**Social atmosphere:** Greek life is not the dominant social force as it is elsewhere. Instead, a lot of socializing surrounds basketball games and off-campus bars. Students often frequent Wet and Wild, a local water amusement park, Scandia, a giant miniature golf amusement park, Lake Mead for water skiing and boating, and Mt. Charleston for skiing and hiking. The biggest social events of the year include Homecoming, Octoberfest, and the first basketball game of the season.
**Services and counseling/handicapped student services:** Placement services. Health service. Day care. Counseling services for minority students. Career and academic guidance services. Physically disabled student services. Learning disabled program/services. Note-taking services. Tape recorders. Tutors.
**Campus organizations:** Undergraduate student government. Student newspaper (Yellin' Rebel, published twice/week). Literary magazine. Yearbook. Radio and TV stations. Marching band, chamber music groups, orchestra, jazz ensemble, choral groups, dance team, flag corps, theatre arts, film series, debating club, Young Democrats, Young Republicans, special-interest groups. 14 fraternities, five chapter houses; seven sororities, no chapter houses. 15% of men join a fraternity. 11% of women join a sorority.
**Religious organizations:** Bahai Club, Baptist Student Union, Intervarsity Christian Fellowship, Hillel, Latter-Day Saints Association, Center for Religion and Life.
**Minority/foreign student organizations:** Hispanic Association, Black Student Union, Ethnic Student Association, Filipino-American group, Native American group. International Student Organization, Korean group.

**ATHLETICS. Physical education requirements:** None.
**Intercollegiate competition:** 2% of students participate. Baseball (M), basketball (M,W), cheerleading (M,W), cross-country (W), football (M), golf (M), soccer (M), softball (W), swimming (M,W), tennis (M,W), track (W), track and field (indoor) (W), track and field (outdoor) (W). Member of Big West, NCAA Division I, NCAA Division I-A for football.
**Intramural and club sports:** Intramural archery, basketball, football, racquetball, softball, tennis.

**ADMISSIONS. Academic basis for candidate selection** (in order of priority): Secondary school record, standardized test scores.
**Requirements:** Graduation from secondary school is recommended; GED is accepted. 13.5 units and the following program of study are required: 4 units of English, 3 units of math, 3 units of science, 3 units of social studies, 1/2 unit of academic electives. Minimum 2.3 GPA required. Probationary admission for in-state applicants not meeting standard requirements; Admission by Alternative Criteria Plan. ACT is recommended; SAT may be substituted. Campus visit recommended. No off-campus interviews.
**Procedure:** Suggest filing application by July 15. Application deadline is August 15. Notification of admission on rolling basis. $250 refundable room deposit. Freshmen accepted for terms other than fall.
**Special programs:** Admission may be deferred two years. Credit and/or placement may be granted through CEEB Advanced Placement exams for scores of 3 or higher. Credit and/or placement may be granted through CLEP general and subject exams. Credit and placement may be granted through challenge exams and military experience. Early decision program. Early entrance/early admission program. Concurrent enrollment program.
**Transfer students:** Transfer students accepted for terms other than fall. In fall 1991, 30% of all new students were transfers into all classes. 2,000 transfer applications were received, 1,300 were accepted. Application deadline is August 15 for fall; January 6 for spring. Minimum 2.0 GPA required. Lowest course grade accepted is "D." At least 30 semester hours must be completed at the university to receive degree.
**Admissions contact:** Larry P. Mason, M.Ed., Director of Admissions. 702 739-3443.

**FINANCIAL AID. Available aid:** Pell grants, SEOG, school grants, private scholarships and grants, academic merit scholarships, and athletic scholarships. Perkins Loans (NDSL), PLUS, Stafford Loans (GSL), school loans, and SLS. Deferred payment plan.
**Financial aid statistics:** 43% of aid is not need-based.
**Supporting data/closing dates:** FAFSA/FAF/FFS: Priority filing date is April 1. SINGLEFILE: Priority filing date is April 1. Notification of awards on rolling basis.
**Financial aid contact:** Judy Balenger, M.Ed., Director of Financial Aid. 702 739-3424.

**STUDENT EMPLOYMENT.** College Work/Study Program. Institutional employment. Students may expect to earn an average of $3,000 during school year.

**COMPUTER FACILITIES.** IBM/IBM-compatible and Macintosh/Apple microcomputers. Computer languages and software packages include BASIC, COBOL, FORTRAN, LISP, Pascal, RPG, SNOBOL. Computer facilities are available to all students.
**Fees:** None.
**Hours:** 9 AM-midn.

**PROMINENT ALUMNI/AE.** Larry Johnson, Charlotte Hornets; Greg Anthony, New York Knicks.

# University of Nevada–Reno

Reno, NV 89557-0002 702 784-1110

**1994-95 Costs.** Tuition: $1,740 (state residents), $6,490 (out-of-state). Room & board: $4,070. Fees, books, misc. academic expenses (school's estimate): $550.
**Enrollment.** Undergraduates: 3,085 men, 3,040 women (full-time). Freshman class: 2,279 applicants, 1,924 accepted, 1,255 enrolled. Graduate enrollment: 1,338 men, 1,666 women.
**Test score averages/ranges.** Average SAT scores: 448 verbal, 492 math. Average ACT scores: 18 English, 20 math, 20 composite.
**Faculty.** 541 full-time; 50 part-time. 77% of faculty holds highest degree in specific field. Student/faculty ratio: 19 to 1.
**Selectivity rating.** Less competitive.

**PROFILE.** U Nevada–Reno is a public institution. Founded in 1864, it adopted coeducation in 1874. Programs are offered through the Colleges of Agriculture, Arts and Science, Business Administration, Education, and Human and Community Sciences; the Schools of Journalism, Medicine, Mines, and Nursing; and the Graduate School. Its 200-acre campus is located in Reno, just east of the Sierra Nevada Mountains.

**Accreditation:** NASC. Professionally accredited by the Accreditation Board for Engineering and Technology, the Accrediting Council on Education in Journalism and Mass Communication, the American Assembly of Collegiate Schools of Business, the American Home Economics Association, the American Psychological Association, the Council on Social Work Education, the Liaison Committee on Medical Education, the National Association of Schools of Music, the National Council for Accreditation of Teacher Education, the National League for Nursing.
**Religious orientation:** University of Nevada-Reno is nonsectarian; no religious requirements.
**Library:** Collections totaling over 794,878 volumes, 5,082 periodical subscriptions, and 3,430,734 microform items.
**Special facilities/museums:** Audio-visual center, theatres, state historical society, atmospherium/planetarium, seismological lab, research institutes, agricultural experimentation station.
**Athletic facilities:** Gymnasium, swimming pool, weight room, football, soccer, softball fields, racquetball, tennis, and basketball courts.

**STUDENT BODY. Undergraduate profile:** 83% are state residents; 22% are transfers. 4% Asian-American, 2% Black, 4% Hispanic, 1% Native American, 81% White, 8% Other. Average age of undergraduates is 25.
**Freshman profile:** 1% of freshmen who took SAT scored 700 or over on verbal, 4% scored 700 or over on math; 9% scored 600 or over on verbal, 24% scored 600 or over on math; 35% scored 500 or over on verbal, 62% scored 500 or over on math; 76% scored 400 or over on verbal, 88% scored 400 or over on math; 97% scored 300 or over on verbal, 99% scored 300 or over on math. 3% of freshmen who took ACT scored 30 or over on composite; 6% scored 24 or over on English, 7% scored 24 or over on math, 20% scored 24 or over on composite; 43% scored 18 or over on English, 41% scored 18 or over on math, 54% scored 18 or over on composite; 86% scored 12 or over on English, 86% scored 12 or over on math, 89% scored 12 or over on composite; 99% scored 6 or over on English, 100% scored 6 or over on math, 100% scored 6 or over on composite. Majority of accepted applicants took ACT.
**Undergraduate achievement:** 70% of fall 1992 freshmen returned for fall 1993 term.
**Foreign students:** 209 students are from out of the country. Countries represented include Canada, China, India, Japan, Pakistan, and Singapore; 54 in all.

**PROGRAMS OF STUDY. Degrees:** B.A., B.F.A., B.Gen.Studies, B.Mus., B.S.
**Majors:** Accounting, Agribusiness, Agricultural Economics, Agricultural Education, Animal Science, Anthropology, Art, Biochemistry, Biology, Chemical Engineering, Chemistry, Civil Engineering, Clinical Laboratory Science, Computer Information Systems, Computer Science, Criminal Justice, Economics, Electrical Engineering, Elementary Education, Engineering Physics, English, Finance, French, General Studies, Geography, Geological Engineering, Geology, Geophysics, German, Health Education, History, Human Development/Family Studies, Human Ecology, International Affairs, Logistics Management, Management, Marketing, Materials Science/Engineering, Mathematics, Mechanical Engineering, Medical Sciences, Metallurgical Engineering, Mining Engineering, Music, Music/Applied, Music Education, Nutrition, Philosophy, Physical Education, Physics, Political Science, Pre-Dentistry, Pre-Journalism, Pre-Medicine, Pre-Nursing, Pre-Physical Therapy, Psychology, Recreation, Resource Management, Secondary Education, Social Psychology, Social Work, Spanish, Special Education, Speech Communication, Speech Pathology, Theatre, Veterinary Science, Zoology.
**Distribution of degrees:** The majors with the highest enrollment are elementary education and general studies; zoology and geophysics have the lowest.
**Requirements:** General education requirement.
**Academic regulations:** Minimum 2.0 GPA must be maintained.
**Special:** Minors offered vary by college, school, or department. Special concentrations, interdisciplinary programs, and special programs offered. Self-designed majors. Double majors. Dual degrees. Independent study. Accelerated study. Pass/fail grading option. Internships. Cooperative education programs. Graduate school at which undergraduates may take graduate-level courses. Preprofessional programs in law, medicine, veterinary science, dentistry, and physical therapy. 3-2 veterinary medicine program through Western Interstate Commission for Higher Education (WICHE). Congressional internships in Washington, D.C. Member of National Student Exchange (NSE). Teacher certification in early childhood, elementary, secondary, special education, and bilingual/bicultural education. Basque Studies program in Spain. Study abroad also in Austria, England, France, Germany, and Mexico. ROTC.
**Honors:** Phi Beta Kappa. Honors program. Honor societies.
**Academic Assistance:** Remedial reading, writing, math, and study skills.

**Academic Assistance:** Remedial reading, writing, math, and study skills.

**STUDENT LIFE. Housing:** Students may live on or off campus. Coed, women's, and men's dorms. Sorority and fraternity housing. School-owned/operated apartments. Both on-campus and off-campus married-student housing. 12% of students live in college housing.

**Services and counseling/handicapped student services:** Placement services. Health service. Women's center. Day care. Counseling services for minority, military, veteran, and older students. Birth control, personal, and psychological counseling. Career and academic guidance services. Physically disabled student services. Learning disabled services. Notetaking services. Tutors. Reader services for the blind.

**Campus organizations:** Undergraduate student government. Student newspaper (Sagebrush, published twice/week). Literary magazine. Yearbook. Radio station. Numerous student organizations, 128 organizations in all. 11 fraternities, all with chapter houses; five sororities, all with chapter houses. 8% of men join a fraternity. 4% of women join a sorority.

**Religious organizations:** Al-Islam, Baptist Student Union, Campus Ministries International, Intervarsity Christian Fellowship, Jewish Student Union, Newman Center.

**Minority/foreign student organizations:** Black and Native American groups. International Student Organization, Asian and Chinese groups.

**ATHLETICS. Physical education requirements:** None.

**Intercollegiate competition:** 1% of students participate. Baseball (M), basketball (M,W), cross-country (W), football (M), golf (M), soccer (M), softball (W), swimming (W), tennis (M,W), track and field (indoor) (W), track and field (outdoor) (W). Member of Big West, NCAA Division I.

**Intramural and club sports:** Intramural basketball, flag football, football, raquetball, soccer, tennis, track, volleyball. Men's club cheerleading, rodeo. Women's club cheerleading, rodeo.

**ADMISSIONS. Academic basis for candidate selection** (in order of priority): Secondary school record, standardized test scores, class rank.

**Nonacademic basis for candidate selection:** Extracurricular participation, particular talent or ability, and geographical distribution are important.

**Requirements:** Graduation from secondary school is required; GED is not accepted. 1/2 unit of computer literacy required. 2 units of foreign language recommended. Minimum 2.5 GPA or minimum composite ACT score of 21 (combined SAT score of 925) required. Audition recommended of music program applicants. Portfolio recommended of art program applicants. Special Admissions for applicants not normally admissible. ACT is required; SAT may be substituted. Campus visit recommended. No off-campus interviews.

**Procedure:** Take SAT or ACT by April 3 of 12th year. Suggest filing application by February 1. Application deadline is July 1. Notification of admission on rolling basis. No set date by which applicants must accept offer. $100 refundable room deposit. Freshmen accepted for terms other than fall.

**Special programs:** Admission may be deferred one semester. Credit and/or placement may be granted through CEEB Advanced Placement exams for scores of 3 or higher. Credit may be granted through CLEP general and subject exams, ACT PEP and challenge exams. Early decision program. In fall 1993, 1,334 applied for early decision and 1,160 were accepted. Deadline for applying for early decision is January 1. Early entrance/early admission program. Concurrent enrollment program.

**Transfer students:** Transfer students accepted for terms other than fall. In fall 1993, 22% of all new students were transfers into all classes. 1,808 transfer applications were received, 1,382 were accepted. Application deadline is July 1 for fall; November 1 for spring. Minimum 2.0 GPA required. Lowest course grade accepted is "D." Maximum number of transferable credits is 64 semester hours from a two-year school and 96 semester hours from a four-year school. At least 32 semester hours must be completed at the university to receive degree.

**Admissions contact:** Melisa N. Choroszy, Ph.D., Director of Admissions. 702 784-6865.

**FINANCIAL AID. Available aid:** Pell grants, SEOG, Federal Nursing Student Scholarships, state scholarships and grants, school scholarships and grants, ROTC scholarships, academic merit scholarships, and athletic scholarships. Indian Affairs Nursing scholarship/grant. Perkins Loans (NDSL), PLUS, Stafford Loans (GSL), NSL, school loans, private loans, and SLS. Deferred payment plan.

**Financial aid statistics:** In 1993-94, 50% of all undergraduate applicants received aid; 50% of freshman applicants. Average amounts of aid awarded freshmen: Scholarships and grants, $950; loans, $1,500.

**Supporting data/closing dates:** FAFSA: Priority filing date is April 15; accepted on rolling basis. FAF/FFS: Priority filing date is April 15. Notification of awards begins May 30.

**Financial aid contact:** Melissa Choroszy, Ph.D., Director of Student Financial Services. 702 784-4666.

**STUDENT EMPLOYMENT.** College Work/Study Program. Institutional employment. 18% of full-time undergraduates work on campus during school year. Off-campus part-time employment opportunities rated "excellent."

**COMPUTER FACILITIES.** 425 IBM/IBM-compatible and Macintosh/Apple microcomputers; 125 are networked. Students may access Cray, Hewlett-Packard, SUN minicomputer/mainframe systems, BITNET, Internet. Numerous computer languages and software packages available. Computer facilities are available to all students.

**Fees:** None.

**GRADUATE CAREER DATA.** Highest graduate school enrollments: Stanford U, UC Berkeley, UC Davis, U of Nevada, Willamette U. 26% of graduates choose careers in business and industry.

**PROMINENT ALUMNI/AE.** Susan Forrest, Pulitzer prize-winning author; Sinclair Melnor, former deputy chairman of NATO; Anne Henrietta Martin, first woman candidate for U.S. Senate.

# New Hampshire

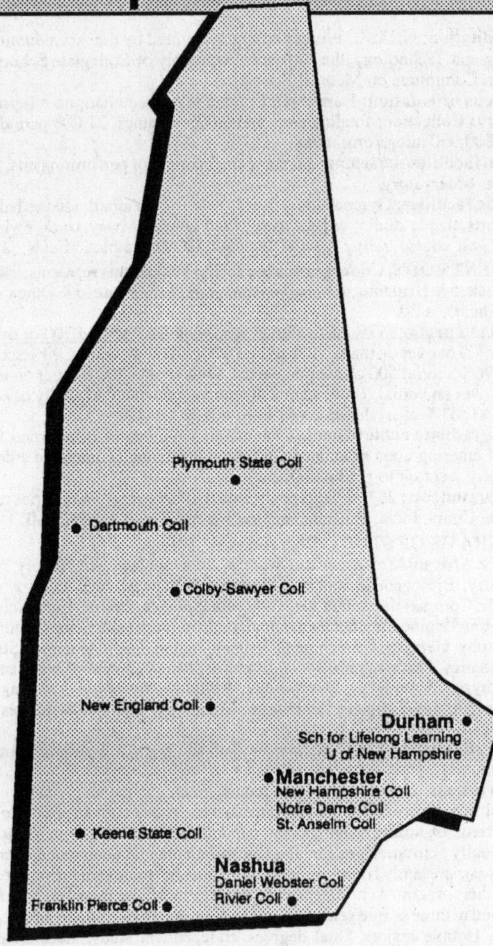


## Colby-Sawyer College

**New London, NH 03257** **603 526-2010**

**1994-95 Costs.** Tuition: $14,090. Room & board: $5,395. Fees, books, misc. academic expenses (school's estimate): $400.
**Enrollment.** Undergraduates: 210 men, 430 women (full-time). Freshman class: 910 applicants, 776 accepted, 208 enrolled.
**Test score averages/ranges.** Average SAT scores: 440 verbal, 443 math. Range of SAT scores of middle 50%: 385-485 verbal, 390-500 math. Average ACT scores: 20 composite. Range of ACT scores of middle 50%: 18-20 composite.
**Faculty.** 36 full-time; 33 part-time. 70% of faculty holds highest degree in specific field. Student/faculty ratio: 13 to 1.
**Selectivity rating.** Less competitive.

**PROFILE.** Colby-Sawyer is a private, liberal arts college. It was founded as an academy in 1837, became a junior college for women in 1928, began granting bachelor's degrees in 1943, and adopted coeducation in the fall of 1990. Its 80-acre campus is located in New London, 100 miles from Boston.

**Accreditation:** NEASC. Professionally accredited by the National League for Nursing.
**Religious orientation:** Colby-Sawyer College is nonsectarian; no religious requirements.
**Library:** Collections totaling over 70,000 volumes, 580 periodical subscriptions, and 97,500 microform items.
**Special facilities/museums:** Fine arts center, on-campus school (preschool-3).
**Athletic facilities:** Gymnasiums, field house, racquetball, squash, and tennis courts, swimming pool, athletic fields, fitness center.

**STUDENT BODY. Undergraduate profile:** 33% are state residents; 12% are transfers. 2% Asian-American, 1% Black, 1% Hispanic, 96% White. Average age of undergraduates is 20.
**Freshman profile:** 2% of freshmen who took SAT scored 600 or over on verbal, 3% scored 600 or over on math; 10% scored 500 or over on verbal, 28% scored 500 or over on math; 58% scored 400 or over on verbal, 70% scored 400 or over on math; 95% scored 300 or over on verbal, 99% scored 300 or over on math. 13% of freshmen who took ACT scored 24 or over on composite; 73% scored 18 or over on composite; 100% scored 12 or over on composite. 92% of accepted applicants took SAT; 8% took ACT.

**Undergraduate achievement:** 86% of fall 1992 freshmen returned for fall 1993 term. 55% of entering class graduated. 7% of students who completed a degree program immediately went on to graduate study.
**Foreign students:** 10 students are from out of the country. Countries represented include Canada, Japan, the former Soviet Republics, and Spain.

**PROGRAMS OF STUDY. Degrees:** B.A., B.F.A., B.S.
**Majors:** Art, Biology, Business Administration, Child Study, Communications, Early Childhood Education, English, Graphic Design, Nursing, Psychology, Secondary Education, Sports Science, Student-Designed Major.
**Distribution of degrees:** The majors with the highest enrollment are business administration, child study, and sports science; biology and art have the lowest.
**Requirements:** General education requirement.
**Academic regulations:** Minimum 2.0 GPA must be maintained.
**Special:** Minors offered in some majors and in American studies, history, philosophy and religion, and women's studies. Associate's degrees offered. Self-designed majors. Independent study. Pass/fail grading option. Internships. Preprofessional programs in law, medicine, and veterinary science. Member of New Hampshire College and University Council; cross-registration possible. Washington Semester. Exchange program with American U (Washington D.C.). Teacher certification in early childhood and secondary education. Certification in specific subject areas. Study abroad in Australia, England, France, Greece, Spain, and Switzerland. ROTC and AFROTC at U of New Hampshire.
**Honors:** Honor societies.
**Academic Assistance:** Nonremedial tutoring.

**ADMISSIONS. Academic basis for candidate selection** (in order of priority): Secondary school record, essay, school's recommendation, standardized test scores, class rank.
**Nonacademic basis for candidate selection:** Character and personality are emphasized. Extracurricular participation and particular talent or ability are important. Alumni/ae relationship is considered.
**Requirements:** Graduation from secondary school is required; GED is accepted. 15 units and the following program of study are recommended: 4 units of English, 3 units of math, 2 units of science including 1 unit of lab, 2 units of foreign language, 2 units of social studies, 2 units of electives. SAT or ACT is required. Campus visit and interview recommended. No off-campus interviews.
**Procedure:** Take SAT or ACT by December of 12th year. Notification of admission on rolling basis. Reply is required by May 1. $400 tuition deposit, refundable until May 1. Freshmen accepted for terms other than fall.
**Special programs:** Admission may be deferred one year. Credit and/or placement may be granted through CEEB Advanced Placement exams for scores of 3 or higher. Credit and/or placement may be granted through CLEP general and subject exams. Credit and placement may be granted through ACT PEP and DANTES exams and military and life experience.
**Transfer students:** Transfer students accepted for terms other than fall. In fall 1993, 12% of all new students were transfers into all classes. 59 transfer applications were received, 47 were accepted. Application deadline is August 15 for fall; December 15 for spring. Minimum 2.0 GPA recommended. Lowest course grade accepted is "C-." Maximum number of transferable credits is 90 semester hours. At least 30 semester hours must be completed at the college to receive degree.
**Admissions contact:** Joanna Henderson, Ed.D., Director of Admissions. 603 526-3700.

**FINANCIAL AID. Available aid:** Pell grants, SEOG, state scholarships and grants, school scholarships and grants, private scholarships and grants, ROTC scholarships, and academic merit scholarships. Perkins Loans (NDSL), PLUS, Stafford Loans (GSL), state loans, school loans, private loans, and SLS. AMS and Tuition Management Systems.
**Financial aid statistics:** 10% of aid is not need-based. In 1993-94, 100% of all undergraduate applicants received aid. Average amounts of aid awarded freshmen: Scholarships and grants, $9,105; loans, $2,655.
**Supporting data/closing dates:** FAFSA/FAF: Priority filing date is February 15. School's own aid application: Priority filing date is February 15. Income tax forms: Priority filing date is February 15. Notification of awards begins February.
**Financial aid contact:** Judith P. Condict, Director of Financial Aid. 603 526-3717.

## Daniel Webster College

**Nashua, NH 03063-1300** **603 883-3556**

**1993-94 Costs.** Tuition: $11,708. Room: $2,236. Board: $2,420. Fees, books, misc. academic expenses (school's estimate): $620.
**Enrollment.** Undergraduates: 368 men, 82 women (full-time). Freshman class: 585 applicants, 505 accepted, 153 enrolled.
**Test score averages/ranges.** Average SAT scores: 438 verbal, 490 math. Range of SAT scores of middle 50%: 830-1000 combined.
**Faculty.** 23 full-time; 19 part-time. 34% of faculty holds doctoral degree. Student/faculty ratio: 17 to 1.
**Selectivity rating.** Less competitive.

**PROFILE.** Daniel Webster is a private college. Founded as an aeronautical institute in 1965, it added business and engineering programs in 1969. Its 50-acre campus is located adjacent to Nashua's municipal airport.

**Accreditation:** NEASC.
**Religious orientation:** Daniel Webster College is nonsectarian; no religious requirements.
**Library:** Collections totaling over 35,000 volumes, 600 periodical subscriptions and 410 microform items.
**Special facilities/museums:** Campus is adjacent to municipal airport; 25 aircraft are available for flight training. Three flight simulators, aerospace center.
**Athletic facilities:** Gymnasium, weight facility, soccer and softball field, tennis courts.

**STUDENT BODY. Undergraduate profile:** 18% are state residents; 18% are transfers. 2% Asian-American, 2% Black, 2% Hispanic, 1% Native American, 2% White, 1% Other. Average age of undergraduates is 20.
**Freshman profile:** 1% of freshmen who took SAT scored 700 or over on verbal, 2% scored 700 or over on math; 2% scored 600 or over on verbal, 12% scored 600 or over on math; 16% scored 500 or over on verbal, 45% scored 500 or over on math; 64% scored 400 or over on verbal, 84% scored 400 or over on math; 96% scored 300 or over on verbal, 99% scored 300 or over on math. 98% of accepted applicants took SAT; 2% took ACT. 84% of freshmen come from public schools.
**Undergraduate achievement:** 69% of fall 1992 freshmen returned for fall 1993 term. 47% of entering class graduated. 10% of students who completed a degree program went on to graduate study within one year.
**Foreign students:** Six students are from out of the country. Countries represented include the Bahamas, Canada, Ethiopia, Germany, and Indonesia; six in all.

**PROGRAMS OF STUDY. Degrees:** B.S.
**Majors:** Air Traffic Control Management, Aviation Management, Aviation Management/Flight Training, Business Management, Computer Science, Computer Systems.
**Distribution of degrees:** The majors with the highest enrollment are aviation management/flight training, aviation management, and business management.
**Requirements:** General education requirement.
**Academic regulations:** Minimum 2.0 GPA must be maintained.
**Special:** Minors offered in most majors. Courses offered in behavioral and social sciences, humanities and fine arts, and natural sciences and math. Associate's degrees offered. Double majors. Pass/fail grading option. Internships. Cooperative education programs. 2-2 programs in aeronautical engineering and engineering science with U of Massachusetts at Lowell and U of New Hampshire. Member of New Hampshire College and University Council. AFROTC. ROTC at U of New Hampshire. NROTC at U of Massachusetts at Lowell.
**Honors:** Honor societies.
**Academic Assistance:** Nonremedial tutoring.

**ADMISSIONS. Academic basis for candidate selection** (in order of priority): Secondary school record, school's recommendation, class rank, standardized test scores.
**Nonacademic basis for candidate selection:** Character and personality are emphasized. Extracurricular participation, geographical distribution, and alumni/ae relationship are important. Particular talent or ability is considered.
**Requirements:** Graduation from secondary school is required; GED is accepted. 20 units and the following program of study are required: 4 units of English, 3 units of math, 2 units of lab science, 4 units of social studies, 2 units of history. Rank in top half of secondary school class recommended. SAT is required; ACT may be substituted. ACH recommended. Campus visit and interview recommended. Off-campus interviews available with an admissions representative.
**Procedure:** Take SAT or ACT by January of 12th year. Visit college for interview by March of 12th year. Suggest filing application by February 1. Application deadline is June 1. Notification of admission on rolling basis. Reply is required by May 1. $200 refundable tuition deposit. $100 nonrefundable room deposit. Freshmen accepted for terms other than fall.
**Special programs:** Admission may be deferred one year. Credit and/or placement may be granted through CEEB Advanced Placement exams for scores of 3 or higher. Credit and/or placement may be granted through CLEP general and subject exams. Credit and placement may be granted through challenge exams and military and life experience. Early entrance/early admission program. Concurrent enrollment program.
**Transfer students:** Transfer students accepted for terms other than fall. In fall 1993, 18% of all new students were transfers into all classes. Application deadline is June 1 for fall; December 1 for spring. Minimum 2.0 GPA required. Lowest course grade accepted is "C." Maximum number of transferable credits is 90 semester hours. At least 30 semester hours must be completed at the college to receive degree.
**Admissions contact:** Terry E. Whittum, Director of Admissions. 603 883-3556, extension 224.

**FINANCIAL AID. Available aid:** Pell grants, SEOG, state scholarships and grants, school scholarships and grants, private scholarships, and ROTC scholarships. Perkins Loans (NDSL), PLUS, Stafford Loans (GSL), private loans, and SLS. Tuition Plan Inc., AMS, and Tuition Management Systems.
**Financial aid statistics:** In 1993-94, 87% of all undergraduate applicants received aid; 93% of freshman applicants. Average amounts of aid awarded freshmen: Scholarships and grants, $6,434; loans, $2,940.
**Supporting data/closing dates:** FAFSA: Priority filing date is March 15. School's own aid application: Priority filing date is March 15; accepted on rolling basis. Income tax forms: Priority filing date is April 16; accepted on rolling basis. Notification of awards on rolling basis.
**Financial aid contact:** Barbara Webber, Director of Financial Aid. 603 883-3556, extension 217.

# Dartmouth College

**Hanover, NH 03755** **603 646-1110**

**1994-95 Costs.** Tuition: $19,545. Room: $3,255. Board: $2,610. Fees, books, misc. academic expenses (school's estimate): $605.
**Enrollment.** Undergraduates: 2,278 men, 1,932 women (full-time). Freshman class: 8,587 applicants, 2,273 accepted, 1,087 enrolled. Graduate enrollment: 754 men, 471 women.
**Test score averages/ranges.** Range of SAT scores of middle 50%: 590-690 verbal, 660-740 math.
**Faculty.** 316 full-time. 94% of faculty holds highest degree in specific field. Student/faculty ratio: 12 to 1.
**Selectivity rating.** Most competitive.

**PROFILE.** Dartmouth, founded in 1769, is a private, Ivy League college. Programs are offered through the Amos Tuck School of Business Administration, the Thayer School of Engineering, and the Medical and Graduate School. Its 265-acre campus is located in Hanover, northwest of Boston.

**Accreditation:** NEASC. Professionally accredited by the Accreditation Board for Engineering and Technology, the American Assembly of Collegiate Schools of Business, the Liaison Committee on Medical Education.
**Religious orientation:** Dartmouth College is nonsectarian; no religious requirements.
**Library:** Collections totaling over 1,900,000 volumes, 21,000 periodical subscriptions, and 1,800,000 microform items.
**Special facilities/museums:** Art museum, centers for performing arts, social science, and science, observatory.
**Athletic facilities:** Gymnasiums, fitness center, basketball, racquetball, squash, and tennis courts, dance studio, weight room, field house, skiway, track, swimming pools, boat house, golf course, riding farm, rifle range, ice rink, athletic fields, sailing facilities.
**STUDENT BODY. Undergraduate profile:** 9% are state residents. 9% Asian-American, 7% Black, 5% Hispanic, 4% Native American, 70% White, 5% Other. Average age of undergraduates is 20.
**Freshman profile:** 17% of freshmen who took SAT scored 700 or over on verbal, 56% scored 700 or over on math; 72% scored 600 or over on verbal, 90% scored 600 or over on math; 96% scored 500 or over on verbal, 99% scored 500 or over on math; 100% scored 400 or over on verbal, 100% scored 400 or over on math. Majority of accepted applicants took SAT. 63% of freshmen come from public schools.
**Undergraduate achievement:** 97% of fall 1992 freshmen returned for fall 1993 term. 94% of entering class graduated. 26% of students who completed a degree program immediately went on to graduate study.
**Foreign students:** 253 students are from out of the country. Countries represented include Canada, China, India, Pakistan, and the United Kingdom; 54 in all.

**PROGRAMS OF STUDY. Degrees:** A.B., B.Eng.
**Majors:** African/Afro-American Studies, Anthropology, Art History, Asian Studies, Biochemistry, Biological Sciences, Chemistry, Classical Archaeology, Classical Studies, Classics, Comparative Literature, Computer Science, Drama, Earth Sciences, Economics, Education, Engineering Sciences, English, Environmental Science, Film Studies, French, Geography, German, Government, History, Italian, Latin American Studies, Linguistics, Mathematics, Mathematics/Social Sciences, Music, Native American Studies, Philosophy, Physics/Astronomy, Psychology, Religion, Romance Languages, Russian Area Studies, Russian Language/Literature, Sociology, Spanish/Portuguese, Visual Studies, Women's Studies.
**Distribution of degrees:** The majors with the highest enrollment are government and history.
**Requirements:** General education requirement.
**Special:** All majors offer honors groups in which juniors and seniors are treated on an individual basis regarding requirements, capabilities, and instruction. Teaching is conducted individually or in small groups. The Dartmouth plan for year-round operation is four equal terms/year; presently freshmen and seniors follow traditional fall/winter/spring sequence, and sophomores must enroll for the summer term. Under this plan, bachelor's degrees may be earned in three or five years rather than four. Associate's degrees offered. Self-designed majors. Double majors. Dual degrees. Independent study. Accelerated study. Pass/fail grading option. Internships. Graduate school at which undergraduates may take graduate-level courses. Preprofessional programs in medicine. 3-2 A.B./M.B.A. program and 3-2 A.B. or B.E./M.E. program. Member of New Hampshire College and University Council. Washington Semester. Member of Twelve College Exchange Program. Exchange program also with UC San Diego. Teacher certification in elementary and secondary education. Certification in specific subject areas. Exchange programs abroad in Canada (McGill U), China (Beijing Normal U), Hungary (Karl Marx U), and Japan (Keio U). Study abroad also in Bulgaria, Costa Rica, France, Germany, Greece, Italy, Kenya, Mexico, New Zealand, Scotland, the former Soviet Republics, and Spain. ROTC at Norwich U.
**Honors:** Phi Beta Kappa. Honors program.
**Academic Assistance:** Remedial writing and study skills. Nonremedial tutoring.

**STUDENT LIFE. Housing:** All freshmen must live on campus. Coed dorms. Sorority and fraternity housing. Off-campus privately-owned housing. Off-campus married-student housing. 92% of students live in college housing.
**Social atmosphere:** According to the student newspaper, Greeks and athletes have the greatest influence on social life. Popular school events include Winter Carnival, Green Key, Summer Carnival, Homecoming, and Harvard Weekend. Bentley's and Five Old Nugget Alley are favorite student places.
**Services and counseling/handicapped student services:** Placement services. Health service. Women's center. Day care. Counseling services for minority, military, veteran, and older students. Birth control, personal, and psychological counseling. Career and academic guidance services. Religious counseling. Physically disabled student services. Learning disabled services. Tape recorders. Tutors. Reader services for the blind.
**Campus organizations:** Undergraduate student government. Student newspaper (Dartmouth, published once/day). Literary magazine. Yearbook. Radio and TV stations. Jazz and chamber music groups, band, orchestra, chorus, glee club, experimental theatre, World Affairs Council, Dartmouth Players, film society, forensic union, 70 organizations in all. 17 fraternities, all with chapter houses; seven sororities, six chapter houses. 55% of men join a fraternity. 40% of women join a sorority.
**Religious organizations:** Baptist Student Union, CSO, Campus Crusade for Christ, Bahai, Catholic, Episcopal, Hillel, and other religious groups.
**Minority/foreign student organizations:** Afro-American Society, Asian Association, La Alianza Latina, Interracial Concerns Committee, Native Americans at Dartmouth, Society of Black Engineers, Black Underground Theatre and Arts, African-American Drumming Ensemble, Ujima Dance Group, AFRICASO, Korean Student Association, Hispanic-American Forum. International Student Association.

**ATHLETICS. Physical education requirements:** Three terms of physical education required.
**Intercollegiate competition:** 40% of students participate. Alpine skiing (M,W), baseball (M), basketball (M,W), crew (M,W), cross-country (M,W), diving (M,W), field hockey (W), football (M), golf (M,W), gymnastics (M), ice hockey (M,W), lacrosse (M,W), Nor-

dic skiing (M,W), sailing (M,W), soccer (M,W), squash (M,W), swimming (M,W), tennis (M,W), track and field (indoor) (M,W), track and field (outdoor) (M,W), volleyball (M,W). Member of ECAC, Ivy League, NCAA Division I.

**Intramural and club sports:** 85% of students participate. Intramural Alpine skiing, baseball, basketball, bowling, cycling, diving, golf, handball, ice hockey, inner-tube water polo, lacrosse, Nordic skiing, racquetball, rifle, soccer, softball, squash, swimming, table tennis, tennis, touch football, ultimate frisbee, volleyball, walleyball, weight lifting, wrestling. Men's club Alpine skiing, canoe, fencing, horsemanship, martial arts, Nordic skiing, rugby, shotokean, tae kwon do, ultimate frisbee, water polo, water skiing, wrestling. Women's club Alpine skiing, canoe, fencing, horsemanship, martial arts, Nordic skiing, rugby, shotokean, softball, tae kwon do, ultimate frisbee, water polo, water skiing, wrestling.

**ADMISSIONS. Academic basis for candidate selection** (in order of priority): Secondary school record, class rank, school's recommendation, standardized test scores, essay.

**Nonacademic basis for candidate selection:** Character and personality, extracurricular participation, and particular talent or ability are important. Geographical distribution and alumni/ae relationship are considered.

**Requirements:** Graduation from secondary school is recommended; GED is accepted. 17 units and the following program of study are recommended: 4 units of English, 4 units of math, 3 units of science including 2 units of lab, 3 units of foreign language, 3 units of social studies. SAT is required; ACT may be substituted. ACH required. Campus visit and interview recommended. Off-campus interviews available with an alumni representative.

**Procedure:** Take SAT or ACT by January of 12th year. Take ACH by January of 12th year. Visit college for interview by January of 12th year. Application deadline is January. Notification of admission by April 15. Reply is required by May 1. Freshmen accepted for fall term only.

**Special programs:** Admission may be deferred one year. Credit and/or placement may be granted through CEEB Advanced Placement exams for scores of 4 or higher. Credit and placement may be granted through challenge exams. Early decision program. In fall 1993, 1,033 applied for early decision and 296 were accepted. Deadline for applying for early decision is November 10.

**Transfer students:** Transfer students accepted for fall term. In fall 1993, less than 1% of all new students were transfers into all classes. 264 transfer applications were received, 70 were accepted. Application deadline is April 15. Lowest course grade accepted is "C."

**Admissions contact:** Karl M. Furstenberg, M.B.A., Dean of Admissions and Financial Aid. 603 646-2875.

**FINANCIAL AID. Available aid:** Pell grants, SEOG, state scholarships and grants, school scholarships and grants, ROTC scholarships, and aid for undergraduate foreign students. Perkins Loans (NDSL), PLUS, Stafford Loans (GSL), state loans, and school loans. Knight Tuition Plans. Tuition prepayment plan.

**Financial aid statistics:** In 1993-94, 83% of all undergraduate applicants received aid; 86% of freshman applicants. Average amounts of aid awarded freshmen: Scholarships and grants, $12,614; loans, $3,100.

**Supporting data/closing dates:** FAFSA: Priority filing date is February 10. FAF: Deadline is February 10. School's own aid application: Deadline is February 1. Income tax forms: Deadline is February 1. Notification of awards begins in April.

**Financial aid contact:** Virginia S. Hazen, M.B.A., Director of Financial Aid. 603 646-2451.

**STUDENT EMPLOYMENT.** College Work/Study Program. Institutional employment. 55% of full-time undergraduates work on campus during school year. Students may expect to earn an average of $1,500 during school year. Off-campus part-time employment opportunities rated "good."

**COMPUTER FACILITIES.** 7,000 IBM/IBM-compatible and Macintosh/Apple microcomputers; all are networked. Students may access BITNET, Internet. Residence halls may be equipped with networked microcomputers. Computer facilities are available to all students.

**Fees:** Computer fee is included in tuition/fees.

**Hours:** 24 hours.

**GRADUATE CAREER DATA.** Companies and businesses that hire graduates: over 150 companies and corporations recruit each year on campus.

**PROMINENT ALUMNI/AE.** Daniel Webster, 19th century statesman; Nelson Rockefeller, former governor of New York and former Vice President of the U.S.; Theodore Geisel (Dr. Seuss), author of children's books; C. Everett Koop, former U.S. surgeon general.

## Franklin Pierce College

**Rindge, NH 03461-0060 — 603 899-4000**

**1994-95 Costs.** Tuition: $13,320. Room: $2,500. Board: $2,130. Fees, books, misc. academic expenses (school's estimate): $660.

**Enrollment.** Undergraduates: 614 men, 574 women (full-time). Freshman class: 5,787 applicants, 4,471 accepted, 445 enrolled.

**Test score averages/ranges.** Average SAT scores: 402 verbal, 423 math. Range of SAT scores of middle 50%: 352-458 verbal, 363-494 math.

**Faculty.** 76 full-time; 30 part-time. 62% of faculty holds highest degree in specific field. Student/faculty ratio: 14 to 1.

**Selectivity rating.** Less competitive.

**PROFILE.** Franklin Pierce, founded in 1962, is a private college. Its 1,000-acre campus is located at the base of Mount Monadnock, 20 miles from Keene, 65 miles from Boston.

**Accreditation:** NEASC.

**Religious orientation:** Franklin Pierce College is nonsectarian; no religious requirements.

**Library:** Collections totaling over 69,587 volumes, 523 periodical subscriptions, and 25,600 microform items.

**Athletic facilities:** Soccer field, baseball field, sailboats, lake, canoes, basketball gym, exercise facility, ski slopes, cross country trails.

**STUDENT BODY. Undergraduate profile:** 13% are state residents; 7% are transfers. 1% Asian-American, 5% Black, 1% Hispanic, 93% White. Average age of undergraduates is 20.

**Freshman profile:** 1% of freshmen who took SAT scored 700 or over on math; 1% scored 600 or over on verbal, 5% scored 600 or over on math; 14% scored 500 or over on verbal, 23% scored 500 or over on math; 52% scored 400 or over on verbal, 57% scored 400 or over on math; 92% scored 300 or over on verbal, 93% scored 300 or over on math. 75% of accepted applicants took SAT. 86% of freshmen come from public schools.

**Undergraduate achievement:** 68% of fall 1992 freshmen returned for fall 1993 term. 35% of entering class graduated.

**Foreign students:** Countries represented include Bermuda, England, Japan, Morocco, and the former Yugoslav Republics; 16 in all.

**PROGRAMS OF STUDY. Degrees:** B.A., B.S.

**Majors:** Accounting, Advertising, Anthropology, Archaeology, Biology, Business Management, Computer Mathematics, Computer Science/Management, Economic Theory, Education, English, Environmental Science, Financial Management, Fine Arts, French, Graphic Arts, History, International Business, Marketing, Mass Communication, Mathematics, Music, Political Science, Pre-Law, Pre-Medicine, Psychology, Radio/Television, Recreation Management, Self-Designed Majors, Social Work/Counseling, Sociology, Spanish, Theatre Arts.

**Distribution of degrees:** The majors with the highest enrollment are mass communication, education, and management; French, mathematics, and Spanish have the lowest.

**Requirements:** General education requirement.

**Academic regulations:** Minimum 2.0 GPA must be maintained.

**Special:** Minors offered in several majors and in art history, business administration, chemistry, dance, field biology, graphic communication, philosophy, professional writing, and social theory. Self-designed majors. Double majors. Dual degrees. Independent study. Accelerated study. Internships. Preprofessional programs in law, medicine, veterinary science, dentistry, and optometry. Member of New Hampshire College and University Council; cross-registration possible. Teacher certification in elementary and secondary education. Certification in specific subject areas. Exchange program abroad in England (Richmond Coll). AFROTC at U of New Hampshire.

**Honors:** Honors program. Honor societies.

**Academic Assistance:** Remedial reading, writing, math, and study skills. Nonremedial tutoring.

**STUDENT LIFE. Housing:** All unmarried students under age 21 must live on campus unless living near campus with relatives. Coed, women's, and men's dorms. School-owned/operated apartments. Off-campus privately-owned housing. Lakeside cottages. 85% of students live in college housing.

**Social atmosphere:** Students gather at the Pub, the Greenhouse, and fraternity houses. Athletes and resident advisors have the most influence on campus life. Students enjoy soccer and basketball games, Fall Weekend, Spring Weekend, Midnight Madness, the Valakis Series, and the Crimson and Gray Series. The student newspaper reports, "Franklin Pierce College offers religious services once a week, and vendors visit campus often. This is good for students who don't have cars and can't get off campus."

**Services and counseling/handicapped student services:** Placement services. Health service. Counseling services for veteran students. Personal and psychological counseling. Career and academic guidance services. Physically disabled student services. Learning disabled services. Notetaking services. Tape recorders. Reader services for the blind.

**Campus organizations:** Undergraduate student government. Student newspaper (Pierce Arrow, published once/two weeks). Literary magazine. Yearbook. Radio and TV stations. Choir, chamber chorus, instrumental ensemble, performing arts series, Amnesty International, environmental awareness club, outing club, cheerleaders; academic, athletic, departmental, and special-interest groups, 34 organizations in all.

**Religious organizations:** Catholic student group.

**Minority/foreign student organizations:** Minority student group.

**ATHLETICS. Physical education requirements:** None.

**Intercollegiate competition:** 6% of students participate. Baseball (M), basketball (M,W), cross-country (M), golf (M), skiing (M,W), soccer (M,W), softball (W), tennis (M,W), volleyball (W). Member of Eastern College Athletic Association, NCAA Division II, New England Collegiate Conference.

**Intramural and club sports:** 2% of students participate. Intramural baseball, basketball, cross-country, golf, ice hockey, skiing, soccer, softball, tennis, volleyball.

**ADMISSIONS. Academic basis for candidate selection** (in order of priority): Secondary school record, school's recommendation, standardized test scores, class rank.

**Nonacademic basis for candidate selection:** Extracurricular participation is emphasized. Character and personality and particular talent or ability are important. Alumni/ae relationship is considered.

**Requirements:** Graduation from secondary school is recommended; GED is accepted. 16 units and the following program of study are required: 4 units of English, 2 units of math, 2 units of science including 1 unit of lab, 1 unit of social studies, 1 unit of history, 6 units of electives. Minimum combined SAT score of 700 and minimum 2.0 GPA recommended. Conditional admission possible for applicants not meeting standard requirements. ADVANCE program for applicants not normally admissible. SAT is required; ACT may be substituted. Campus visit and interview recommended. No off-campus interviews.

**Procedure:** Take SAT or ACT by November of 12th year. Visit college for interview by February of 12th year. Notification of admission on rolling basis. Reply is required by May 1 or within 30 days of acceptance. $100 tuition deposit, refundable until May 1. Freshmen accepted for terms other than fall.

**Special programs:** Admission may be deferred one year. Credit and/or placement may be granted through CEEB Advanced Placement exams for scores of 3 or higher. Credit and/or placement may be granted through CLEP general and subject exams. Credit and placement may be granted through Regents College, ACT PEP, and DANTES exams and military and life experience. Early entrance/early admission program. Concurrent enrollment program.

**Transfer students:** Transfer students accepted for terms other than fall. In fall 1993, 7% of all new students were transfers into all classes. 218 transfer applications were received, 132 were accepted. Application deadline is rolling for fall; rolling for spring. Minimum

2.0 GPA recommended. Lowest course grade accepted is "C-." Maximum number of transferable credits is 60 semester hours from a two-year school and 90 semester hours from a four-year school. At least 38 semester hours must be completed at the college to receive degree.

**Admissions contact:** Thomas E. Desrosiers, M.A., Director of Admissions. 800 437-0048, 603 899-4050.

**FINANCIAL AID. Available aid:** Pell grants, SEOG, state scholarships and grants, school scholarships and grants, private scholarships and grants, academic merit scholarships, athletic scholarships, and aid for undergraduate foreign students. Perkins Loans (NDSL), PLUS, Stafford Loans (GSL), state loans, and SLS. Deferred payment plan and family tuition reduction. Institutional payment plans.

**Financial aid statistics:** 28% of aid is not need-based. In 1993-94, 95% of all undergraduate applicants received aid; 95% of freshman applicants. Average amounts of aid awarded freshmen: Scholarships and grants, $3,955; loans, $4,000.

**Supporting data/closing dates:** FAFSA: Priority filing date is March 15. School's own aid application: Deadline is December 31. Income tax forms: Accepted on rolling basis. Notification of awards on rolling basis.

**Financial aid contact:** Susan Howard, M.Ed., Director of Financial Aid. 800 437-0048, 603 899-4185.

**STUDENT EMPLOYMENT.** College Work/Study Program. Institutional employment. 36% of full-time undergraduates work on campus during school year. Students may expect to earn an average of $1,000 during school year. Off-campus part-time employment opportunities rated "fair."

**COMPUTER FACILITIES.** 110 IBM/IBM-compatible and Macintosh/Apple microcomputers; 85 are networked. Students may access Digital minicomputer/mainframe systems. Client/LAN operating systems include Apple/Macintosh, DOS, Windows NT, Novell. Computer languages and software packages include BASIC, C, COBOL, FORTRAN, LISP, LOGO, Modula 2, Pascal, SPSS; database, spreadsheet, statistical, word processing packages. Computer facilities are available to all students.

**Fees:** None.

**Hours:** 9 AM-1 AM (M-Th); 9 AM-5 PM (F); noon-5 PM (Sa); 1 PM-1 AM (Su).

**PROMINENT ALUMNI/AE.** John Burke, supervisor of special agents, FBI; Robert Dole, president of Bed & Bath division, Fieldcrest-Cannon, Inc.; Peter McGrath, environmental trial attorney, U.S. Dept. of Justice; Temple Grandin, owner, Grandin Livestock Systems.

# Keene State College

**Keene, NH 03431** **603 352-1909**

**1993-94 Costs.** Tuition: $2,520 (state residents), $7,350 (out-of-state). Room: $2,572. Board: $1,388. Fees, books, misc. academic expenses (school's estimate): $1,095.

**Enrollment.** Undergraduates: 1,523 men, 1,960 women (full-time). Freshman class: 3,150 applicants, 2,443 accepted, 762 enrolled. Graduate enrollment: 139 men, 246 women.

**Test score averages/ranges.** Average SAT scores: 431 verbal, 462 math.

**Faculty.** 179 full-time; 171 part-time. 71% of faculty holds doctoral degree. Student/faculty ratio: 19 to 1.

**Selectivity rating.** Less competitive.

**PROFILE.** Keene State, founded in 1909, is a public college. Its 160-acre campus is located in Keene, in the southwestern corner of New Hampshire.

**Accreditation:** NEASC. Professionally accredited by the National Association of Schools of Music, the National Council for Accreditation of Teacher Education.

**Religious orientation:** Keene State College is nonsectarian; no religious requirements.

**Library:** Collections totaling over 187,831 volumes, 994 periodical subscriptions, and 567,530 microform items.

**Special facilities/museums:** Art gallery, theatre arts and film production facilities, Holocaust resource center, learning resource center, safety center, elementary school, early childhood development center, 400-acre nature preserve.

**Athletic facilities:** Gymnasium, athletic fields, racquetball and squash courts, swimming pool, weight rooms, fitness center.

**STUDENT BODY. Undergraduate profile:** 60% are state residents; 28% are transfers. 1% Asian-American, 1% Hispanic, 84% White, 14% Other. Average age of undergraduates is 22.

**Freshman profile:** 2% of freshmen who took SAT scored 600 or over on verbal, 6% scored 600 or over on math; 18% scored 500 or over on verbal, 33% scored 500 or over on math; 67% scored 400 or over on verbal, 79% scored 400 or over on math; 98% scored 300 or over on verbal, 99% scored 300 or over on math. 97% of accepted applicants took SAT.

**Undergraduate achievement:** 74% of fall 1991 freshmen returned for fall 1992 term. 37% of entering class graduated. 15% of students who completed a degree program immediately went on to graduate study.

**Foreign students:** 45 students are from out of the country. Countries represented include England, France, Ireland, Japan, Spain, and Taiwan; 24 in all.

**PROGRAMS OF STUDY. Degrees:** B.A., B.Mus., B.S.

**Majors:** American Studies, Applied Computer Science, Art, Biology, Chemistry, Chemistry/Biology, Chemistry/Physics, Computer Mathematics, Drafting/Design Technology, Early Childhood Development, Economics, Education, Electronics Technology, Elementary Education, English, Environmental Studies, Film Studies, French, General Studies, Geography, Geology, Graphic Arts, Graphic Design, Health Teacher Education, History, History Education, Home Economics, Home Economics Education, Individualized Majors, Industrial Arts Education, Industrial Chemistry, Industrial Management, Industrial Technology, Journalism, Journalism/Graphic Arts, Management, Manufacturing Technology, Mathematics, Mathematics/Physics, Middle School/Junior High Mathematics, Music, Music Education, Performance, Physical Education, Political Science, Psychology, Safety Studies, Secondary Education, Social Science, Social Science Education, Sociology, Spanish, Special Education, Theatre Arts/Speech, Theatre Studies, Vocational Teacher Education.

**Distribution of degrees:** The majors with the highest enrollment are management, elementary education, and psychology.

**Requirements:** General education requirement.

**Academic regulations:** Freshmen must maintain minimum 1.8 GPA; sophomores, 1.9 GPA; juniors, 2.0 GPA; seniors, 2.0 GPA.

**Special:** Minors offered in many majors and in chemical dependency, dance, driver safety, German, nutrition, philosophy, physics, speech communication, statistics, technology, and women's studies. Freshman Year Experience Program. Associate's degrees offered. Self-designed majors. Double majors. Dual degrees. Independent study. Internships. Cooperative education programs. Graduate school at which undergraduates may take graduate-level courses. 2-2 engineering program with U of New Hampshire. 3-2 engineering program with Clarkson U. Member of New Hampshire College and University Council; cross-registration or exchange possible. Teacher certification in early childhood, elementary, secondary, special education, and vo-tech education. Certification in specific subject areas. Exchange programs abroad in Ecuador (Catholic U), England, Ireland (U of Limerick), Japan (Kansai Gaidai U), and Russia. Study abroad also in Australia, France, and other countries. ROTC and AFROTC at U of New Hampshire.

**Honors:** Honors program. Honor societies.

**Academic Assistance:** Remedial reading, writing, and math. Nonremedial tutoring.

**STUDENT LIFE. Housing:** Students may live on or off campus. Coed and women's dorms. Sorority and fraternity housing. School-owned/operated apartments. Off-campus privately-owned housing. On-campus married-student housing. 52% of students live in college housing.

**Services and counseling/handicapped student services:** Placement services. Health service. Women's center. Day care. Counseling services for veteran and older students. Birth control, personal, and psychological counseling. Career and academic guidance services. Religious counseling. Physically disabled student services. Learning disabled services. Notetaking services. Tape recorders. Tutors. Reader services for the blind.

**Campus organizations:** Undergraduate student government. Student newspaper (Equinox, published once/week). Literary magazine. Yearbook. Radio and TV stations. Choir, chamber singers, band, orchestra, ensembles, theatre group, film society, community service opportunities, council for women, recycling committee, Public Affairs Forum, Concerned Student Coalition, Social Activities Council, athletic, departmental, and special-interest groups, 75 organizations in all. Six fraternities, no chapter houses; six sororities, no chapter houses. 21% of men join a fraternity. 14% of women join a sorority.

**Religious organizations:** Campus Ministry, Newman Center, Jewish Student Organization.

**Minority/foreign student organizations:** African Alliance.

**ATHLETICS. Physical education requirements:** None.

**Intercollegiate competition:** 10% of students participate. Baseball (M), basketball (M,W), cross-country (M,W), diving (M,W), field hockey (W), soccer (M,W), softball (W), swimming (M,W), track (indoor) (M,W), track (outdoor) (M,W), volleyball (W). Member of ECAC, NCAA Division II, NECC.

**Intramural and club sports:** 50% of students participate. Intramural basketball, flag football, ice hockey, lacrosse, racquetball, rugby, soccer, ultimate frisbee, volleyball. Men's club ice hockey, judo, kocondo, lacrosse, martial arts, rugby, skiing, ultimate frisbee, volleyball. Women's club judo, kocondo, martial arts, rugby.

**ADMISSIONS. Academic basis for candidate selection** (in order of priority): Secondary school record, class rank, standardized test scores, school's recommendation, essay.

**Nonacademic basis for candidate selection:** Character and personality and particular talent or ability are emphasized. Extracurricular participation is important. Alumni/ae relationship is considered.

**Requirements:** Graduation from secondary school is required; GED is accepted. 12 units and the following program of study are required: 4 units of English, 3 units of math, 2 units of science including 1 unit of lab, 2 units of social studies. Minimum combined SAT score of 750 and rank in top three-fifths of secondary school class required of in-state applicants; minimum combined SAT score of 800 and rank in top half of secondary school class required of out-of-state applicants. Portfolio required of art program applicants. Audition required of music program applicants. TRIO program for applicants not normally admissible. SAT is required. Campus visit and interview recommended. No off-campus interviews.

**Procedure:** Take SAT by January of 12th year. Application deadline is April 1. Notification of admission on rolling basis. Reply is required by May 1. $100 nonrefundable tuition deposit. $100 nonrefundable room deposit. Freshmen accepted for terms other than fall.

**Special programs:** Admission may be deferred one year. Credit and/or placement may be granted through CEEB Advanced Placement exams for scores of 3 or higher. Credit and/or placement may be granted through CLEP general and subject exams. Credit may be granted through military and life experience. Early entrance/early admission program.

**Transfer students:** Transfer students accepted for terms other than fall. In fall 1992, 28% of all new students were transfers into all classes. 614 transfer applications were received, 527 were accepted. Application deadline is June 1 for fall; December 1 for spring. Minimum 2.0 GPA required. Lowest course grade accepted is "C." At least 30 semester hours must be completed at the college to receive degree.

**Admissions contact:** Kathryn Dodge, M.A., Interim Director of Admissions. 603 358-2276.

**FINANCIAL AID. Available aid:** Pell grants, SEOG, school scholarships, and athletic scholarships. Perkins Loans (NDSL), PLUS, Stafford Loans (GSL), school loans, and SLS. Tuition Plan Inc., Knight Tuition Plans, and AMS.

**Financial aid statistics:** 18% of aid is not need-based. In 1992-93, 84% of all undergraduate applicants received aid; 76% of freshman applicants. Average amounts of aid awarded freshmen: Scholarships and grants, $702; loans, $2,564.

**Supporting data/closing dates:** FAFSA/FAF: Priority filing date is March 1. State aid form: Priority filing date is March 1; deadline is May 1. Income tax forms: Priority filing date is April 15; accepted on rolling basis. Notification of awards on rolling basis.

**Financial aid contact:** Patricia Blodgett, Interim Director of Financial Aid. 603 358-2280.

**STUDENT EMPLOYMENT.** College Work/Study Program. Institutional employment. 22% of full-time undergraduates work on campus during school year. Students may

expect to earn an average of $1,150 during school year. Off-campus part-time employment opportunities rated "good."

**COMPUTER FACILITIES.** 75 IBM/IBM-compatible and Macintosh/Apple microcomputers; 19 are networked. Students may access Digital minicomputer/mainframe systems. Residence halls may be equipped with stand-alone microcomputers. Client/LAN operating systems include DEC. Computer languages and software packages include BASIC, C, COBOL, Excel, FORTRAN, HyperCard, Lotus 1-2-3, Microsoft Word, Microsoft Works, Pascal; 100 in all. Computer facilities are available to all students.
**Fees:** Computer fee is included in tuition/fees.
**Hours:** 8 AM-midn. (M-Th); 8 AM-8 PM (F); noon-6 PM (Sa); 1 PM-10 PM (Su).

**GRADUATE CAREER DATA.** Graduate school percentages: 14% enter graduate arts and sciences programs. Highest graduate school enrollments: Indiana U of Pennsylvania, Keene State Coll, U of Connecticut, U of New Hampshire, U of Notre Dame. Companies and businesses that hire graduates: Beech Hill Hospital, Cheshire Medical Center, IBM, Internal Revenue Service, Kingsbury Corp., Markem Corp., Peace Corps.

**PROMINENT ALUMNI/AE.** Frank H. Blackington, president, U of Pittsburgh at Johnstown; Richard Hopwood, retired member, U.S. Foreign Service; Joel Maiola, chief of staff for New Hampshire governor; Ernest Hebert, author; Wallace Tripp, originator of PawPrints Cards.

## New England College

**Henniker, NH 03242 — 603 428-2232**

**1994-95 Costs.** Tuition: $13,165. Room: $2,770. Board: $2,565. Fees, books, misc. academic expenses (school's estimate): $560.
**Enrollment.** Undergraduates: 480 men, 320 women (full-time). Freshman class: 1,268 applicants, 1,042 accepted, 263 enrolled.
**Test score averages/ranges.** Average SAT scores: 420 verbal, 420 math.
**Faculty.** 68 full-time; 25 part-time. 65% of faculty holds highest degree in specific field. Student/faculty ratio: 14 to 1.
**Selectivity rating.** Less competitive.

**PROFILE.** New England College, founded in 1946, is a private, liberal arts institution. Its 210-acre campus is located in Henniker, 17 miles from Concord.

**Accreditation:** NEASC. Professionally accredited by the Accreditation Board for Engineering and Technology.
**Religious orientation:** New England College is nonsectarian; no religious requirements.
**Library:** Collections totaling over 100,000 volumes, 650 periodical subscriptions, and 35,000 microform items.
**Special facilities/museums:** Art gallery, research island on Maine coast, electron microscope.
**Athletic facilities:** Gymnasium, field house, basketball and tennis courts, weight room, ice rink, baseball, field hockey, intramural, lacrosse, soccer, and softball fields, cross-country ski trails.

**STUDENT BODY. Undergraduate profile:** 12% are state residents; 20% are transfers. 1% Asian-American, 2% Black, 93% White, 4% Other. Average age of undergraduates is 19.
**Freshman profile:** 85% of accepted applicants took SAT; 10% took ACT. 62% of freshmen come from public schools.
**Foreign students:** 80 students are from out of the country. Countries represented include Canada, Japan, Kuwait, and Turkey; 32 in all.

**PROGRAMS OF STUDY. Degrees:** B.A., B.S.
**Majors:** Accounting, Art, Biology, Business, Communication, Education, English, International Administration, Physical Education/Sports Studies, Political Science, Psychology, Social/Economic Development, Theatre.
**Distribution of degrees:** The majors with the highest enrollment are business, communication, and education.
**Requirements:** General education requirement.
**Academic regulations:** Minimum 2.0 GPA must be maintained.
**Special:** Minors offered in many majors. Courses offered in chemistry, ecology, folk music, folklore, French, German, music, physics, and religion. Internships for semester or full year in business, communications, human services, environmental studies, and government. Self-designed majors. Double majors. Independent study. Pass/fail grading option. Internships. Member of New Hampshire College and University Council; exchange possible. Teacher certification in elementary and secondary education. Certification in specific subject areas. Exchange programs abroad in Canada, Japan, Lithuania, and other countries. Study abroad also at college's overseas campus in England. ROTC at U of New Hampshire. AFROTC at Daniel Webster Coll.
**Honors:** Honors program. Honor societies.
**Academic Assistance:** Nonremedial tutoring.

**ADMISSIONS. Academic basis for candidate selection** (in order of priority): Secondary school record, essay, school's recommendation, class rank, standardized test scores.
**Nonacademic basis for candidate selection:** Character and personality are emphasized. Extracurricular participation, particular talent or ability, and alumni/ae relationship are important.
**Requirements:** Graduation from secondary school is required; GED is accepted. 13 units and the following program of study are required: 4 units of English, 2 units of math, 2 units of science including 1 unit of lab, 3 units of social studies, 1 unit of history. Minimum 2.0 GPA recommended. Conditional admission possible for applicants not meeting standard requirements. Campus visit and interview recommended. Off-campus interviews available with an admissions representative.
**Procedure:** Take SAT or ACT by December of 12th year. Visit college for interview by March 31 of 12th year. Notification of admission on rolling basis. Reply is required by May 1. $300 tuition deposit, refundable until May 1. Freshmen accepted for terms other than fall.
**Special programs:** Admission may be deferred two years. Credit and/or placement may be granted through CEEB Advanced Placement exams for scores of 3 or higher. Credit may be granted through CLEP general and subject exams and life experience. Concurrent enrollment program.
**Transfer students:** Transfer students accepted for terms other than fall. In fall 1992, 20% of all new students were transfers into all classes. 125 transfer applications were received, 82 were accepted. Application deadline is rolling for fall; rolling for spring. Minimum 2.0 GPA recommended. Lowest course grade accepted is "C-." Maximum number of transferable credits is 60 semester hours. At least 60 semester hours must be completed at the college to receive degree.
**Admissions contact:** Donald N. Parker, Director of Admissions. 603 428-2223, 800 521-7642.

**FINANCIAL AID. Available aid:** Pell grants, SEOG, state scholarships and grants, school scholarships and grants, private scholarships and grants, academic merit scholarships, and aid for undergraduate foreign students. Perkins Loans (NDSL), PLUS, Stafford Loans (GSL), state loans, and SLS. Tuition Plan Inc., Knight Tuition Plans, and family tuition reduction.
**Financial aid statistics:** In 1992-93, 50% of all undergraduate applicants received aid; 92% of freshman applicants. Average amounts of aid awarded freshmen: Scholarships and grants, $4,500; loans, $3,000.
**Supporting data/closing dates:** FAFSA/FAF/FFS: Priority filing date is March 1. School's own aid application: Priority filing date is March 1. Income tax forms: Priority filing date is March 1. Notification of awards begins March 1.
**Financial aid contact:** Grace Krebs, Director of Financial Aid. 603 428-2284, 800 521-7642.

## New Hampshire College

**Manchester, NH 03106-1045 — 603 668-2211**

**1994-95 Costs.** Tuition: $10,608. Room & board: $4,740. Fees, books, misc. academic expenses (school's estimate): $880.
**Enrollment.** Undergraduates: 622 men, 409 women (full-time). Freshman class: 1,926 applicants, 1,430 accepted, 364 enrolled. Graduate enrollment: 1,000 men, 700 women.
**Test score averages/ranges.** Average SAT scores: 383 verbal, 433 math.
**Faculty.** 57 full-time; 39 part-time. 40% of faculty holds doctoral degree. Student/faculty ratio: 18 to 1.
**Selectivity rating.** Less competitive.

**PROFILE.** New Hampshire, founded in 1932, is a private, liberal arts college. Programs are offered in the School of Business, the Culinary Institute, and the Graduate School. Its 700-acre campus is located in Manchester, 50 miles north of Boston.

**Accreditation:** NEASC.
**Religious orientation:** New Hampshire College is nonsectarian; no religious requirements.
**Library:** Collections totaling over 80,000 volumes, 846 periodical subscriptions, and 250,185 microform items.
**Special facilities/museums:** Art gallery, TV studio.
**Athletic facilities:** Racquetball courts, aerobics room, swimming pool, gymnasiums, Nautilus room, lighted tennis courts, refrigerated outdoor ice rink, playing fields.

**STUDENT BODY. Undergraduate profile:** 30% are state residents; 10% are transfers. 3% Asian-American, 2% Black, 1% Hispanic, 79% White, 15% Other. Average age of undergraduates is 19.
**Freshman profile:** 2% of freshmen who took SAT scored 600 or over on math; 6% scored 500 or over on verbal, 21% scored 500 or over on math; 39% scored 400 or over on verbal, 63% scored 400 or over on math; 89% scored 300 or over on verbal, 93% scored 300 or over on math. 94% of accepted applicants took SAT. 80% of freshmen come from public schools.
**Undergraduate achievement:** 64% of fall 1992 freshmen returned for fall 1993 term. 32% of entering class graduated.
**Foreign students:** 191 students are from out of the country. Countries represented include Colombia, India, Japan, Korea, Pakistan, and Taiwan; 40 in all.

**PROGRAMS OF STUDY. Degrees:** B.S.
**Majors:** Accounting, Business Administration, Business Communication, Business/Distributive Teacher Education, Business Studies, Communication, Computer Information Systems, Economics/Finance, English Language/Literature, English Teacher Education, Hotel Management, Humanities, International Business, Management Advisory Systems, Marketing, Marketing Teacher Education, Mathematics Teacher Education, Office Administration, Restaurant Management, Retailing, Social Science, Sport Management, Technical Management, Travel/Tourism.
**Distribution of degrees:** The majors with the highest enrollment are business studies, business administration, and marketing; teacher education and management advisory services have the lowest.
**Requirements:** General education requirement.
**Academic regulations:** Minimum 2.0 GPA must be maintained.
**Special:** Minors offered in some majors. Technical management program designed for students with associate's degree in area other than business; leads to B.S. in business. Certificate programs in accounting, computer programming, education and the family, human resource management, micro-computer production/inventory control retailing. Associate's degrees offered. Double majors. Dual degrees. Independent study. Accelerated study. Internships. Cooperative education programs. Preprofessional programs in business. Member of New Hampshire College and University Council. Teacher certification in secondary education. Certification in specific subject areas. Study abroad in England. ROTC and AFROTC at U of New Hampshire.
**Honors:** Honors program.
**Academic Assistance:** Remedial reading, writing, math, and study skills. Nonremedial tutoring.

**ADMISSIONS. Academic basis for candidate selection** (in order of priority): Secondary school record, school's recommendation, essay, standardized test scores, class rank.
**Nonacademic basis for candidate selection:** Character and personality are emphasized. Extracurricular participation is important. Particular talent or ability and alumni/ae relationship are considered.
**Requirements:** Graduation from secondary school is required; GED is accepted. 16 units and the following program of study are required: 4 units of English, 2 units of math. Minimum 2.5 GPA and rank in top half of secondary school class recommended. SAT is required; ACT may be substituted. Campus visit and interview recommended. Off-campus interviews available with admissions and alumni representatives.
**Procedure:** Take SAT or ACT by December of 12th year. Visit college for interview by May of 12th year. Suggest filing application by January. Notification of admission on rolling basis. Reply is required by May 1. $100 tuition deposit, refundable until May 1. $100 room deposit, refundable until May 1. Freshmen accepted for terms other than fall.
**Special programs:** Admission may be deferred one year. Credit may be granted through CEEB Advanced Placement for scores of 3 or higher. Credit may be granted through CLEP general and subject exams, ACT PEP and DANTES exams, and military experience. Placement may be granted through challenge exams. Credit and placement may be granted through life experience. Early entrance/early admission program.
**Transfer students:** Transfer students accepted for terms other than fall. In fall 1993, 10% of all new students were transfers into all classes. Application deadline is rolling for fall; rolling for spring. Minimum 2.0 GPA required. Lowest course grade accepted is "C." Maximum number of transferable credits is 90 semester hours. At least 30 semester hours must be completed at the college to receive degree.
**Admissions contact:** Brad Poznanski, Director of Admission. 603 645-9611, 800 NHC-4-YOU.

**FINANCIAL AID. Available aid:** Pell grants, SEOG, state scholarships and grants, school scholarships and grants, private scholarships and grants, ROTC scholarships, academic merit scholarships, and athletic scholarships. Perkins Loans (NDSL), PLUS, Stafford Loans (GSL), and SLS. Tuition Plan Inc.
**Financial aid statistics:** 54% of aid is not need-based. In 1993-94, 80% of all undergraduate applicants received aid; 80% of freshman applicants. Average amounts of aid awarded freshmen: Scholarships and grants, $2,000; loans, $1,500.
**Supporting data/closing dates:** FAFSA/FAF: Priority filing date is March 15. Notification of awards on rolling basis.
**Financial aid contact:** Clint Hanson, M.Ed., Director of Financial Aid. 603 645-9645.

## Plymouth State College

**Plymouth, NH 03264** **603 535-5000**

**1994-95 Costs.** Tuition: $2,650 (state residents), $7,870 (out-of-state). Room & board: $4,038. Fees, books, misc. academic expenses (school's estimate): $1,300.
**Enrollment.** Undergraduates: 1,750 men, 1,750 women (full-time). Freshman class: 3,514 applicants, 2,404 accepted, 716 enrolled. Graduate enrollment: 150 men, 50 women.
**Test score averages/ranges.** Average SAT scores: 420 verbal, 460 math.
**Faculty.** 171 full-time. 85% of faculty holds highest degree in specific field. Student/faculty ratio: 20 to 1.
**Selectivity rating.** Less competitive.

**PROFILE.** Plymouth State, founded in 1871, is a public, multipurpose college. Its 150-acre campus is located in Plymouth, 40 miles north of Concord.

**Accreditation:** NEASC. Professionally accredited by the National Council for Accreditation of Teacher Education.
**Religious orientation:** Plymouth State College is nonsectarian; no religious requirements.
**Library:** Collections totaling over 750,000 volumes, 1,200 periodical subscriptions, and 500,000 microform items.
**Special facilities/museums:** Art gallery, cultural arts center, environmental studies center, institute for New Hampshire studies, interactive TV with Keene State U and U of New Hampshire, planetarium.
**Athletic facilities:** Gymnasium, field house, swimming pool, basketball, racquetball, tennis, and volleyball courts, dance studio, aerobics, dance, fitness, training, and wrestling rooms, baseball, field hockey, football, intramural, lacrosse, soccer, and softball fields.

**STUDENT BODY. Undergraduate profile:** 60% are state residents; 25% are transfers. 98% White, 2% Other. Average age of undergraduates is 20.
**Freshman profile:** Majority of accepted applicants took SAT. 95% of freshmen come from public schools.
**Undergraduate achievement:** 85% of fall 1992 freshmen returned for fall 1993 term.
**Foreign students:** 40 students are from out of the country. Countries represented include Canada, France, Greece, and Japan; 10 in all.

**PROGRAMS OF STUDY. Degrees:** B.A., B.F.A., B.S.
**Majors:** Accounting, Actuarial Sciences, Anthropology, Applied Computer Science, Applied Economics, Applied Mathematics, Art, Athletic Training, Bilingual Languages, Biological Sciences, Biology, Chemistry, Computer Information Systems, Computer Mathematics, Data Processing, Elementary Education, English, Environmental Biology, Finance, French, Geography, Graphic Design, Health/Physical Education, History, Interdisciplinary Studies, Local/Regional Planning, Management, Mathematics, Medieval Studies, Meteorology, Music, Philosophy, Physical Education, Physical Sciences, Political Science, Psychology, Public Management, Secretarial, Social Sciences, Social Work, Sociology, Spanish, Studio Art, Theatre.
**Distribution of degrees:** The majors with the highest enrollment are business and education; Spanish, medieval studies, and philosophy have the lowest.
**Requirements:** General education requirement.
**Academic regulations:** Freshmen must maintain minimum 1.5 GPA; sophomores, 1.7 GPA; juniors, 1.85 GPA; seniors, 2.0 GPA.
**Special:** Minors offered in 50 fields. Courses offered in Canadian studies, economics, German, and New Hampshire/Northern New England studies. Introduction to the Academic Community program. Associate's degrees offered. Self-designed majors. Double majors. Dual degrees. Independent study. Pass/fail grading option. Internships. Graduate school at which undergraduates may take graduate-level courses. Preprofessional programs in law. Member of New Hampshire College and University Council; cross-registration possible. Member of New England Regional Student Program. Semester-away programs may be individually arranged. Teacher certification in early childhood, elementary, and secondary education. Certification in specific subject areas. Study abroad in Canada, England, France, Mexico, and Spain. ROTC at U of New Hampshire.
**Honors:** Phi Beta Kappa. Honors program. Honor societies.
**Academic Assistance:** Nonremedial tutoring.

**STUDENT LIFE. Housing:** All first-year students must live on campus. Coed, women's, and men's dorms. Sorority and fraternity housing. School-owned/operated apartments. 70% of students live in college housing.
**Social atmosphere:** The College Union Building and Biederman's Deli are two popular hangouts for Plymouth State students. Campus organizations include Greeks and athletic teams. Homecoming, Canada Conference, Evening of Swing, and the Battle of the Bands are some of the most popular annual campus events.
**Services and counseling/handicapped student services:** Placement services. Health service. Women's center. Day care. Counseling services for veteran and older students. Birth control, personal, and psychological counseling. Career and academic guidance services. Religious counseling. Physically disabled student services. Learning disabled services. Notetaking services. Tape recorders. Tutors.
**Campus organizations:** Undergraduate student government. Student newspaper (Clock, published once/week). Literary magazine. Yearbook. Radio and TV stations. Chorale, women's glee club, concert and brass choirs, chamber orchestra, jazz band, pep band, woodwind ensemble, Plymouth Players, debating, outing club, athletic, departmental, and special-interest groups, 50 organizations in all. Seven fraternities, no chapter houses; five sororities, no chapter houses. 10% of men join a fraternity. 10% of women join a sorority.
**Religious organizations:** Campus Ministry, Chi Alpha.
**Minority/foreign student organizations:** International Student Organization.

**ATHLETICS. Physical education requirements:** Two semesters of physical education required.
**Intercollegiate competition:** 25% of students participate. Alpine skiing (M,W), baseball (M), basketball (M,W), diving (W), field hockey (W), football (M), ice hockey (M), lacrosse (M,W), soccer (M,W), softball (W), swimming (W), tennis (M,W), wrestling (M). Member of Cox Conference, ECAC, Freedom Football Conference, Little East Conference, NCAA Division III, NEFC.
**Intramural and club sports:** 65% of students participate. Intramural badminton, basketball, flag football, floor hockey, frisbee, racquetball, rugby, soccer, softball, tennis, volleyball. Men's club cheerleading, crew, cross-country, cycling, hang gliding, indoor track/field, martial arts, outdoor track/field, rugby, sailing, skateboarding, ski diving, snowboarding, volleyball. Women's club cheerleading, crew, cross-country, cycling, hang gliding, indoor track/field, martial arts, outdoor track/field, rugby, sailing, skateboarding, ski diving, snowboarding, volleyball.

**ADMISSIONS. Academic basis for candidate selection** (in order of priority): Secondary school record, class rank, school's recommendation, essay, standardized test scores.
**Nonacademic basis for candidate selection:** Character and personality are emphasized. Extracurricular participation and particular talent or ability are important. Geographical distribution is considered.
**Requirements:** Graduation from secondary school is required; GED is accepted. No specific distribution of secondary school units required. Minimum combined SAT score of 800, rank in top half of secondary school class, and minimum "C+" average recommended. Audition required of music program applicants. SAT is required; ACT may be substituted. Campus visit recommended.
**Procedure:** Take SAT or ACT by January of 12th year. Suggest filing application by April 1; no deadline. Notification of admission on rolling basis. Reply is required by May 1. $100 nonrefundable tuition deposit. $100 nonrefundable room deposit. Freshmen accepted for terms other than fall.
**Special programs:** Credit and/or placement may be granted through CEEB Advanced Placement exams for scores of 3 or higher. Credit and/or placement may be granted through CLEP general and subject exams. Credit and placement may be granted through DANTES and challenge exams and military experience.
**Transfer students:** Transfer students accepted for terms other than fall. In fall 1993, 25% of all new students were transfers into all classes. 600 transfer applications were received, 403 were accepted. Application deadline is April 1 for fall; January 1 for spring. Minimum 2.0 GPA required. Lowest course grade accepted is "C." Maximum number of transferable credits is 90 semester hours. At least 30 semester hours must be completed at the college to receive degree.
**Admissions contact:** Eugene Fahey, M.Ed., Director of Admissions. 603 535-2237.

**FINANCIAL AID. Available aid:** Pell grants, SEOG, state scholarships and grants, school scholarships, private scholarships and grants, ROTC scholarships, academic merit scholarships, and aid for undergraduate foreign students. Perkins Loans (NDSL), PLUS, Stafford Loans (GSL), private loans, and SLS. Knight Tuition Plans and AMS.
**Financial aid statistics:** 36% of aid is not need-based. In 1993-94, 73% of all undergraduate applicants received aid; 73% of freshman applicants. Average amounts of aid awarded freshmen: Scholarships and grants, $2,371; loans, $2,100.
**Supporting data/closing dates:** FAFSA: Priority filing date is March 1. Notification of awards on rolling basis.
**Financial aid contact:** Robert Tuveson, Director of Financial Aid. 603 535-2238.

**STUDENT EMPLOYMENT.** College Work/Study Program. Institutional employment. 31% of full-time undergraduates work on campus during school year. Students may expect to earn an average of $820 during school year. Off-campus part-time employment opportunities rated "good."

**COMPUTER FACILITIES.** 200 IBM/IBM-compatible and Macintosh/Apple microcomputers; all are networked. Students may access Digital minicomputer/mainframe

systems. Residence halls may be equipped with networked microcomputers. Computer languages and software packages include BASIC, COBOL, FORTRAN, LISP, Pascal, WordPerfect; 6 in all. Computer facilities are available to all students.
**Fees:** Computer fee is included in tuition/fees.
**Hours:** 24 hours.

# Rivier College

**Nashua, NH 03060-5086** **603 888-1311**

**1994-95 Costs.** Tuition: $10,170. Room & board: $5,000. Fees, books, misc. academic expenses (school's estimate): $2,525.
**Enrollment.** Undergraduates: 71 men, 527 women (full-time). Freshman class: 456 applicants, 350 accepted, 202 enrolled. Graduate enrollment: 353 men, 662 women.
**Test score averages/ranges.** Average SAT scores: 417 verbal, 460 math. Range of SAT scores of middle 50%: 360-470 verbal, 380-520 math.
**Faculty.** 64 full-time; 138 part-time. 41% of faculty holds highest degree in specific field. Student/faculty ratio: 17 to 1.
**Selectivity rating.** Less competitive.

**PROFILE.** Rivier is a private, church-affiliated college. Programs are offered through the Undergraduate School for Women, the Rivier College/St. Joseph Hospital School of Nursing, and the Schools of Continuing Education and Graduate Studies. Its 50-acre campus is one mile from downtown Nashua.

**Accreditation:** NEASC. Professionally accredited by the American Bar Association, the National League for Nursing.
**Religious orientation:** Rivier College is affiliated with the Roman Catholic Church; three semesters of religion required.
**Library:** Collections totaling over 120,440 volumes, 60 periodical subscriptions, and 26,350 microform items.
**Special facilities/museums:** Art gallery, on-campus education centers, language lab, TV microscope, video/laser disk system, photospectrometer, high-performance liquid chromatograph.
**Athletic facilities:** Gymnasium, weight room, basketball and tennis courts, athletic fields.

**STUDENT BODY. Undergraduate profile:** 58% are state residents; 36% are transfers: 1% Asian-American, 1% Black, 2% Hispanic, 78% White, 18% Other. Average age of undergraduates is 19.
**Freshman profile:** 2% of freshmen who took SAT scored 600 or over on verbal, 6% scored 600 or over on math; 18% scored 500 or over on verbal, 28% scored 500 or over on math; 57% scored 400 or over on verbal, 67% scored 400 or over on math; 94% scored 300 or over on verbal, 99% scored 300 or over on math. 93% of accepted applicants took SAT. 76% of freshmen come from public schools.
**Undergraduate achievement:** 66% of fall 1992 freshmen returned for fall 1993 term. 22% of students who completed a degree program went on to graduate study within five years.
**Foreign students:** Two students are from out of the country. Countries represented include Japan.

**PROGRAMS OF STUDY. Degrees:** B.A., B.F.A., B.S.
**Majors:** Accounting, Art, Art Education, Biology, Biology Education, Business, Business Education, Chemistry, Chemistry Education, Communications, Computer Science, Design, Early Childhood Education, Elementary Education, English, English Education, French, History/Political Science, Human Development, Information Management, Liberal/General Studies, Management, Marketing, Mathematics, Mathematics/Computer Science Education, Modern Language Education, Nursing, Paralegal Studies, Pre-Dentistry, Pre-Education, Pre-Law, Pre-Medicine, Pre-Veterinary, Psychology, Secondary Education, Social Sciences, Sociology, Spanish, Studio Art.
**Distribution of degrees:** The majors with the highest enrollment are business, education, and behavioral sciences.
**Requirements:** General education requirement.
**Academic regulations:** Minimum 2.0 GPA must be maintained.
**Special:** Minors offered in most majors and in philosophy, public relations, religion, and social work. Associate's degrees offered. Dual degrees. Internships. Graduate school at which undergraduates may take graduate-level courses. Preprofessional programs in law, medicine, veterinary science, dentistry, and education. Member of New Hampshire College and University Council; cross-registration or exchange possible. Teacher certification in early childhood, elementary, secondary, and special education. Certification in specific subject areas. AFROTC at Daniel Webster Coll.
**Academic Assistance:** Nonremedial tutoring.

**ADMISSIONS. Academic basis for candidate selection** (in order of priority): Secondary school record, standardized test scores, school's recommendation, essay, class rank.
**Nonacademic basis for candidate selection:** Character and personality and extracurricular participation are important. Particular talent or ability and alumni/ae relationship are considered.
**Requirements:** Graduation from secondary school is required; GED is accepted. 16 units and the following program of study are required: 4 units of English, 2 units of math, 1 unit of lab science, 2 units of foreign language, 2 units of social studies, 5 units of academic electives. Algebra and chemistry required of nursing program applicants. R.N. required of applicants to B.S.N. program. Portfolio required of art program applicants. SAT is required; ACT may be substituted. Campus visit and interview recommended. Off-campus interviews available with an admissions representative.
**Procedure:** Take SAT or ACT by January of 12th year. Visit college for interview by March of 12th year. Suggest filing application by March; no deadline. Notification of admission on rolling basis. Reply is required by May 1. $50 tuition deposit, refundable until May 1. $100 room deposit, refundable until May 1. Freshmen accepted for terms other than fall.
**Special programs:** Admission may be deferred one year. Credit and/or placement may be granted through CEEB Advanced Placement exams for scores of 3 or higher. Credit and/or placement may be granted through CLEP general and subject exams. Credit may be granted through life experience. Credit and placement may be granted through ACT PEP and challenge exams and military experience. Early entrance/early admission program.
**Transfer students:** Transfer students accepted for terms other than fall. In fall 1993, 36% of all new students were transfers into all classes. 274 transfer applications were received, 199 were accepted. Application deadline is March for fall; December for spring. Minimum 2.0 GPA required. Lowest course grade accepted is "D." Maximum number of transferable credits is 45 semester hours from a two-year school and 90 semester hours from a four-year school. At least 30 semester hours must be completed at the college to receive degree.
**Admissions contact:** Jolene Greene-Mitchell, Director of Admissions. 603 888-1311, extension 8507, 800 44-RIVIER.

**FINANCIAL AID. Available aid:** Pell grants, SEOG, state scholarships and grants, school scholarships and grants, private scholarships and grants, academic merit scholarships, and aid for undergraduate foreign students. Perkins Loans (NDSL), PLUS, Stafford Loans (GSL), state loans, school loans, private loans, and SLS. Deferred payment plan.
**Financial aid statistics:** 5% of aid is not need-based. In 1993-94, 85% of all undergraduate applicants received aid; 90% of freshman applicants. Average amounts of aid awarded freshmen: Scholarships and grants, $2,200; loans, $2,250.
**Supporting data/closing dates:** FAFSA/FAF: Priority filing date is March 16. School's own aid application: Priority filing date is March 16. Income tax forms: Priority filing date is March 16. Verification statement: Priority filing date is March 16. Notification of awards on rolling basis.
**Financial aid contact:** Jolene Greene-Mitchell, Director of Financial Aid. 603 888-1311, extension 8510.

# Saint Anselm College

**Manchester, NH 03102** **603 641-7000**

**1994-95 Costs.** Tuition: $12,950. Room & board: $5,400. Fees, books, misc. academic expenses (school's estimate): $750.
**Enrollment.** Undergraduates: 823 men, 1,050 women (full-time). Freshman class: 2,095 applicants, 1,553 accepted, 514 enrolled.
**Test score averages/ranges.** Average SAT scores: 481 verbal, 512 math. Range of SAT scores of middle 50%: 430-530 verbal, 440-560 math.
**Faculty.** 116 full-time; 39 part-time. 70% of faculty holds doctoral degree. Student/faculty ratio: 16 to 1.
**Selectivity rating.** Less competitive.

**PROFILE.** Saint Anselm, founded in 1889, is a church-affiliated, liberal arts college. Its 420-acre campus is located in Manchester, 50 miles north of Boston.

**Accreditation:** NEASC. Professionally accredited by the National League for Nursing.
**Religious orientation:** Saint Anselm College is affiliated with the Roman Catholic Church (Order of Saint Benedict); three courses of theology required.
**Library:** Collections totaling over 192,000 volumes, 1,350 periodical subscriptions, and 16,000 microform items.
**Special facilities/museums:** Arts center, observatory.
**Athletic facilities:** Gymnasium, recreation center, swimming pools, soccer, baseball, softball, football, lacrosse, and rugby fields, indoor and outdoor tennis courts.

**STUDENT BODY. Undergraduate profile:** 20% are state residents; 7% are transfers. 97% White, 3% Other. Average age of undergraduates is 20.
**Freshman profile:** 4% of freshmen who took SAT scored 600 or over on verbal, 12% scored 600 or over on math; 38% scored 500 or over on verbal, 55% scored 500 or over on math; 91% scored 400 or over on verbal, 94% scored 400 or over on math; 100% scored 300 or over on verbal, 100% scored 300 or over on math. 99% of accepted applicants took SAT; 1% took ACT. 65% of freshmen come from public schools.
**Undergraduate achievement:** 87% of fall 1992 freshmen returned for fall 1993 term. 75% of entering class graduated. 22% of students who completed a degree program immediately went on to graduate study.
**Foreign students:** Three students are from out of the country.

**PROGRAMS OF STUDY. Degrees:** B.A., B.S.Nurs.
**Majors:** Accounting, Biochemistry, Biology, Business, Chemistry, Classical Languages, Computer Science, Computer Science/Business, Computer Science/Mathematics, Criminal Justice, Economics, English, Financial Economics, Fine Arts, French, History, Liberal Studies, Mathematics, Mathematics/Economics, Natural Science, Nursing, Philosophy, Politics, Psychology, Sociology, Spanish, Theology.
**Distribution of degrees:** The majors with the highest enrollment are nursing, history, and business; theology, philosophy, and classical languages have the lowest.
**Requirements:** General education requirement.
**Academic regulations:** Minimum 2.0 GPA must be maintained.
**Special:** Certificates offered in Russian area studies. Special studies certificates offered for advanced study in French, German, Greek, Latin, and Spanish for students not majoring in these areas. Courses offered in art, astronomy, education, geography/urban studies, human work behavior, international relations, music, physics, and Russian. Associate's degrees offered. Independent study. Internships. Preprofessional programs in law, medicine, pharmacy, dentistry, theology, and optometry. 3-2 engineering programs with Catholic U, Manhattan Coll, U of Massachusetts at Lowell, and U of Notre Dame. Member of New Hampshire College and University Council; cross-registration possible. Washington Semester. Teacher certification in secondary education. Certification in specific subject areas. Study abroad in England, France, Ireland, Italy, Scotland, and Spain. ROTC and AFROTC at various schools.
**Honors:** Honor societies.
**Academic Assistance:** Nonremedial tutoring.

**STUDENT LIFE. Housing:** All freshmen must live on campus unless living with family. Women's and men's dorms. School-owned/operated apartments. 65% of students live in college housing.

**Social atmosphere:** On campus, students gather at the Coffee Shop and Pub. Off campus, students frequent the Rack-Em-Up Lounge, the Red Arrow Diner, and Shirley D's Diner. The Center for Volunteers and the Student Programming Board influence life on campus. Saint Anselm students enjoy the annual Cabaret, the lip-sync contest, and class formals. According to the student newspaper, the campus social scene is not very diverse. "Social life on campus centers around drinking. There isn't much off campus to attract students, either, so many students go home frequently."
**Services and counseling/handicapped student services:** Placement services. Health service. Counseling services for minority, veteran, and older students. Personal counseling. Career and academic guidance services. Religious counseling. Physically disabled student services. Learning disabled services. Notetaking services. Tape recorders. Tutors. Reader services for the blind.
**Campus organizations:** Undergraduate student government. Student newspaper (Saint Anselm Crier, published once/two weeks). Literary magazine. Yearbook. Choir, jazz band, debating, Anselmian Abbey Players, Anselmian Music Society, Center for Volunteers, Political Union, Alpine Club, Commission on the Arts, Knights of Columbus, departmental groups, special-interest groups, 53 organizations in all. Three fraternities, no chapter houses; one sorority, no chapter house. 12% of men join a fraternity. 4% of women join a sorority.
**Religious organizations:** Campus Ministry, Oblates of St. Benedict, Pax Christi, Chi Sigma.

**ATHLETICS. Physical education requirements:** None.
**Intercollegiate competition:** 25% of students participate. Alpine skiing (M,W), baseball (M), basketball (M,W), cross-country (M,W), golf (M), ice hockey (M), lacrosse (M), skiing (M,W), soccer (M,W), softball (W), tennis (M,W), volleyball (W). Member of ECAC, NCAA Division II, Northeast Ten.
**Intramural and club sports:** 65% of students participate. Intramural aerobics, basketball, dance, golf, gymnastics, hockey, racquetball, soccer, softball, swimming, tennis, touch football, volleyball, weight lifting. Men's club Alpine skiing, crew, karate, rugby, volleyball. Women's club Alpine skiing, cheerleading, crew, karate, ruby.

**ADMISSIONS. Academic basis for candidate selection** (in order of priority): Secondary school record, class rank, standardized test scores, essay, school's recommendation.
**Nonacademic basis for candidate selection:** Character and personality are emphasized. Extracurricular participation and particular talent or ability are important. Geographical distribution and alumni/ae relationship are considered.
**Requirements:** Graduation from secondary school is recommended; GED is accepted. 16 units and the following program of study are required: 4 units of English, 3 units of math, 3 units of lab science, 2 units of foreign language, 1 unit of social studies, 1 unit of history, 2 units of academic electives. SAT is required; ACT may be substituted. Campus visit and interview recommended. Off-campus interviews available with admissions and alumni representatives.
**Procedure:** Take SAT or ACT by December of 12th year. Visit college for interview by February of 12th year. Suggest filing application by February 15; no deadline. Notification of admission on rolling basis. Reply is required by May 1. $200 nonrefundable tuition deposit. Freshmen accepted for terms other than fall.
**Special programs:** Admission may be deferred one year. Credit and/or placement may be granted through CEEB Advanced Placement exams for scores of 3 or higher. Credit may be granted through CLEP general exams. Credit and/or placement may be granted through CLEP subject exams. Early decision program. In fall 1993, 61 applied for early decision and 51 were accepted. Deadline for applying for early decision is December 1. Early entrance/early admission program.
**Transfer students:** Transfer students accepted for terms other than fall. In fall 1993, 7% of all new students were transfers into all classes. 138 transfer applications were received, 81 were accepted. Application deadline is June 1 for fall; December 1 for spring. Minimum 2.5 GPA recommended. Lowest course grade accepted is "C." Maximum number of transferable credits is the equivalent of two years of course work (20 courses). At least two years of course work (20 courses) must be completed at the college to receive degree.
**Admissions contact:** Donald E. Healy, Director of Admissions. 603 641-7500.

**FINANCIAL AID. Available aid:** Pell grants, SEOG, state scholarships, school scholarships and grants, private scholarships, ROTC scholarships, and athletic scholarships. Perkins Loans (NDSL), PLUS, Stafford Loans (GSL), NSL, private loans, and SLS. Tuition Plan Inc., AMS, and family tuition reduction.
**Financial aid statistics:** 11% of aid is not need-based. In 1993-94, 82% of all undergraduate applicants received aid; 84% of freshman applicants. Average amounts of aid awarded freshmen: Scholarships and grants, $5,708; loans, $2,366.
**Supporting data/closing dates:** FAFSA/FAF/FFS: Priority filing date is April 15. Income tax forms: Accepted on rolling basis. Notification of awards begins March 15.
**Financial aid contact:** Francis X. Fraitzl, Director of Financial Aid. 603 641-7110.

**STUDENT EMPLOYMENT.** College Work/Study Program. Institutional employment. 42% of full-time undergraduates work on campus during school year. Students may expect to earn an average of $665 during school year. Off-campus part-time employment opportunities rated "good."

**COMPUTER FACILITIES.** 160 IBM/IBM-compatible and Macintosh/Apple microcomputers; 105 are networked. Students may access Digital minicomputer/mainframe systems, Internet. Residence halls may be equipped with modems. Client/LAN operating systems include Apple/Macintosh, DOS, UNIX/XENIX/AIX, DEC, Novell. Computer languages and software packages include BASIC, C, COBOL, FORTRAN, LISP, MacWrite, Pascal, Prolog, SPSS, 20/20, UNIX, WordPerfect; several hundred languages and software packages available. Computer facilities are available to all students.
**Fees:** $30 computer fee per semester.
**Hours:** 8 AM-midn.

**GRADUATE CAREER DATA.** Graduate school percentages: 4% enter law school. 2% enter medical school. 2% enter dental school. 7% enter graduate business programs. 5% enter graduate arts and sciences programs. 1% enter theological school/seminary. Highest graduate school enrollments: Boston Coll, Boston U, Catholic U, Georgetown U, Tufts U, U of Connecticut, U of Massachusetts, U of New Hampshire, U of Notre Dame. 60% of graduates choose careers in business and industry. Companies and businesses that hire graduates: American Express, Digital Equipment Corp., Kidder Peabody, New England Telephone, IBM, Sanders, Xerox.

**PROMINENT ALUMNI/AE.** John King, former New Hampshire governor and supreme court chief justice; Robert Weiler, president and COO, Cullinet; Joyce Clifford, director of nursing, Beth Israel Hospital; Dr. Armand Brodeur, pediatric radiologist and former dean, St. Louis U Sch of Medicine.

## School for Lifelong Learning

**Durham, NH 03824-3545** **603 862-1692**

**1993-94 Costs.** Tuition: $2,574 (state residents), $2,814 (out-of-state). Housing: None. Fees, books, misc. academic expenses (school's estimate): $30.
**Enrollment.** Undergraduates: 70 men, 160 women (full-time).
**Test score averages/ranges.** N/A.
**Faculty.** 216 part-time. Student/faculty ratio: 15 to 1.
**Selectivity rating.** N/A.

**PROFILE.** The School for Lifelong Learning, founded in 1972, is a public, liberal arts school for continuing-education adults. The school has no central campus; it is based in over 70 citites in New Hampshire with nine regional offices.

**Accreditation:** NEASC.
**Religious orientation:** School for Lifelong Learning is nonsectarian; no religious requirements.
**STUDENT BODY. Undergraduate profile:** 80% are state residents. Average age of undergraduates is 36.
**Foreign students:** One student is from out of the country.
**PROGRAMS OF STUDY. Degrees:** B.Gen.Studies, B.Prof.Studies.
**Majors:** Behavioral Science, Management, Self-Designed Majors.
**Distribution of degrees:** The majors with the highest enrollment are behavioral science and management.
**Requirements:** General education requirement.
**Academic regulations:** Minimum 2.0 GPA required for graduation.
**Special:** The School is for adults, most of whom attend part-time while maintaining home, work, and community commitments. Five certificate programs offered. Associate's degrees offered. Self-designed majors. Double majors. Independent study. Accelerated study. Pass/fail grading option. Member of New Hampshire College and University Council.
**ADMISSIONS. Academic basis for candidate selection** (in order of priority): Essay.
**Requirements:** No specific distribution of secondary school units required. Campus visit and interview required.
**Procedure:** Freshmen accepted for fall term only.
**Special programs:** Credit may be granted through CEEB Advanced Placement for scores of 3 or higher. Credit may be granted through CLEP general and subject exams, ACT PEP and DANTES exams, and military and life experience. Placement may be granted through challenge exams.
**Transfer students:** Transfer students accepted for terms other than fall. Lowest course grade accepted is "C." Maximum number of transferable credits is 94 semester hours. At least 30 semester hours must be completed at the school to receive degree.
**Admissions contact:** Tessa McDonnell, Assistant Dean. 603 862-1692.
**FINANCIAL AID. Available aid:** Pell grants, state scholarships and grants, and school grants. PLUS, Stafford Loans (GSL), and state loans. (Graduation from secondary school is required for financial aid.) Average amount of scholarships and grants awarded (1992-93): $2,400.
**Supporting data/closing dates:** FAFSA/FAF/FFS: Accepted on rolling basis. Income tax forms: Accepted on rolling basis. Notification of awards on rolling basis.

## University of New Hampshire

**Durham, NH 03824** **603 862-1234**

**1993-94 Costs.** Tuition: $3,844 (state residents), $11,467 (out-of-state). Room & board: $3,862. Fees, books, misc. academic expenses (school's estimate): $1,049.
**Enrollment.** Undergraduates: 4,578 men, 5,644 women (full-time). Freshman class: 9,750 applicants, 7,640 accepted, 2,529 enrolled. Graduate enrollment: 750 men, 816 women.
**Test score averages/ranges.** Average SAT scores: 476 verbal, 536 math. Range of SAT scores of middle 50%: 430-530 verbal, 480-600 math.
**Faculty.** 649 full-time; 216 part-time. 85% of faculty holds doctoral degree. Student/faculty ratio: 17 to 1.
**Selectivity rating.** Competitive.

**PROFILE.** University of New Hampshire, founded in 1866, is a comprehensive, public institution. Programs are offered through the Colleges of Engineering and Physical Sciences, Health Studies, Liberal Arts, and Life Sciences and Agriculture and the Whittemore School of Business and Economics. Its 200-acre campus is located in Durham, north of Portsmouth.

**Accreditation:** NEASC. Professionally accredited by the Accreditation Board for Engineering and Technology, the American Dietetic Association, the American Medical Association (CAHEA), the Computing Sciences Accreditation Board, the Council on Social Work Education, the National Association of Schools of Music, the National Athletic Trainers Association, the National Council for Accreditation of Teacher Education, the National League for Nursing, the Society of American Foresters.
**Religious orientation:** University of New Hampshire is nonsectarian; no religious requirements.
**Library:** Collections totaling over 1,023,000 volumes, 6,500 periodical subscriptions, and 714,199 microform items.

**Special facilities/museums:** Art galleries, language lab, marine science labs, observatory, electron microscope, hyperbaric chamber.
**Athletic facilities:** Gymnasium, field house, athletic fields, basketball, handball, racquetball, squash, and tennis courts, ice rink, weight rooms, swimming pool, tracks, arena.

**STUDENT BODY. Undergraduate profile:** 60% are state residents; 18% are transfers. 1.3% Asian-American, .6% Black, .9% Hispanic, .1% Native American, 91.5% White, 5.6% Other. Average age of undergraduates is 20.
**Freshman profile:** 3% of freshmen who took SAT scored 700 or over on math; 6% scored 600 or over on verbal, 25% scored 600 or over on math; 39% scored 500 or over on verbal, 68% scored 500 or over on math; 86% scored 400 or over on verbal, 95% scored 400 or over on math; 99% scored 300 or over on verbal, 100% scored 300 or over on math. 100% of accepted applicants took SAT.
**Undergraduate achievement:** 84% of fall 1992 freshmen returned for fall 1993 term. 51% of entering class graduated.
**Foreign students:** 70 students are from out of the country. Countries represented include China, India, Japan, Korea, Thailand, and Turkey; 30 in all.

**PROGRAMS OF STUDY. Degrees:** B.A., B.F.A., B.Mus., B.S., B.S.Forestry.
**Majors:** Adult/Occupational Education, Animal Sciences, Anthropology, Art History, Biochemistry, Biology, Business Administration, Chemical Engineering, Chemistry, Chemistry/Physics Teaching, Civil Engineering, Classics, Communication, Communication Disorders, Community Development, Computer Sciences, Dairy Management, Earth Science Teaching, Earth Sciences, Economics, Electrical Engineering, Electrical Engineering Technology, English, English Teaching, Entomology, Environmental Conservation, Family/Consumer Studies, Fine Arts, Forestry, French, Geography, Geology, German, Greek, Health Management/Policy, History, Horticulture/Agronomy, Hotel Administration, Humanities, Hydrology, Journalism, Latin, Leisure Management, Linguistics, Mathematics, Mathematics Education, Mechanical Engineering, Mechanical Engineering Technology, Medical Laboratory Science, Microbiology, Music Education, Music History, Music Theory, Nursing, Nutritional Sciences, Occupational Therapy, Performance Study, Philosophy, Physical Education, Physics, Plant Biology, Political Science, Psychology, Resource Economics, Russian, Social Work, Sociology, Soil Science, Spanish, Studio Art, Theater, Tourism, Water Resources Management, Wildlife Management, Women's Studies, Zoology.
**Distribution of degrees:** The majors with the highest enrollment are business administration, English, and political science; Greek, Latin, and hydrology have the lowest.
**Requirements:** General education requirement.
**Academic regulations:** Minimum 2.00 GPA must be maintained.
**Special:** Interdisciplinary minors offered in over 15 areas. Undergraduate Research Program supports undergraduate research in numerous fields of study. Combined undergraduate/graduate program in education. Interdisciplinary dual major in international affairs possible in combination with any of the university's other majors. Associate's degrees offered. Self-designed majors. Double majors. Dual degrees. Independent study. Accelerated study. Pass/fail grading option. Internships. Graduate school at which undergraduates may take graduate-level courses. Preprofessional programs in law, medicine, veterinary science, and theology. Four-year combined program with Mary Hitchcock Memorial Hospital Sch of Medical Tech (Hanover) leads to B.S. and M.T. certificate. New England Regional Student Program. Member of consortium with other New Hampshire four-year schools. Washington Semester and Sea Semester. Member of National Student Exchange (NSE). Teacher certification in elementary, secondary, special education, and bilingual/bicultural education. Study abroad in numerous countries. ROTC and AFROTC.
**Honors:** Phi Beta Kappa. Honors program.
**Academic Assistance:** Remedial study skills. Nonremedial tutoring.

**STUDENT LIFE. Housing:** Students may live on or off campus. Coed, women's, and men's dorms. Sorority and fraternity housing. School-owned/operated apartments. On-campus married-student housing. Special-interest minidorms. Independent-living residence halls. 51% of students live in college housing.
**Social atmosphere:** "Slightly homogenous campus, but enjoyable," reports the student newspaper. "Approximately 20 percent of the student body is Greek, influencing Homecoming, Winter Carnival, and weekend parties." In addition to Homecoming and Winter Carnival, popular events include Parents Weekend, hockey and football games, concerts, and Springfest. On campus, UNH students meet at the Memorial Union Building Pub. Off campus, they frequent Benjamin's, Nick's, "Portsmouth bars, and even Boston bars."
**Services and counseling/handicapped student services:** Placement services. Health service. Women's center. Day care. Testing service. Counseling services for minority, military, veteran, and older students. Birth control, personal, and psychological counseling. Career and academic guidance services. Physically disabled student services. Learning disabled services. Notetaking services. Tape recorders. Reader services for the blind.
**Campus organizations:** Undergraduate student government. Student newspaper (New Hampshire, published biweekly). Literary magazine. Yearbook. Radio and TV stations. Amnesty International, departmental groups, musical and drama groups, outing, ski, and chess clubs, student environmental action coalition, collegiate 4-H club, 94 organizations in all. Nine fraternities, all with chapter houses; six sororities, all with chapter houses. 10% of men join a fraternity. 10% of women join a sorority.
**Religious organizations:** Hillel, Catholic Student Organization, Christian Impact, Christian Science Student Organization, Intervarsity Christian Fellowship, New Testament Fellowship, United Campus Ministry.
**Minority/foreign student organizations:** Minority Awareness Committee, Black Student Union, Asociacion de Estudiantes Latino Americanos, Chinese Students Friendship Association, Diversity Support Coalition, Native American Cultural Association. International Festival, International Forum, French Club, German Club, Japanese Society.

**ATHLETICS. Physical education requirements:** None.
**Intercollegiate competition:** 16% of students participate. Alpine skiing (M,W), baseball (M), basketball (M,W), cross-country (M,W), field hockey (W), football (M), golf (M,W), gymnastics (W), ice hockey (M,W), lacrosse (M,W), Nordic skiing (M,W), soccer (M,W), softball (W), swimming (M,W), tennis (M), track (indoor) (M,W), track (outdoor) (M,W), track and field (indoor) (M), track and field (outdoor) (M), volleyball (W). Member of ECAC, Hockey East, NCAA Division I, NCAA Division I-AA for football, North Atlantic Conference, Yankee Conference for football.
**Intramural and club sports:** 60% of students participate. Intramural basketball, bowling, broomball, floor hockey, football, ice hockey, squash, soccer, softball, volleyball, water polo. Men's club badminton, crew, cycling, fencing, judo, rugby, sailing, shotokan, volleyball, woodsmen. Women's club badminton, crew, cycling, horsemanship, judo, rugby, sailing, shotokan.

**ADMISSIONS. Academic basis for candidate selection** (in order of priority): Secondary school record, class rank, school's recommendation, standardized test scores, essay.
**Nonacademic basis for candidate selection:** Character and personality and alumni/ae relationship are important. Extracurricular participation, particular talent or ability, and geographical distribution are considered.
**Requirements:** Graduation from secondary school is required; GED is accepted. No specific distribution of secondary school units required. Higher SAT scores and class rank and stronger secondary school programs of study required of out-of-state applicants. Portfolio required of art program applicants. Audition required of music program applicants. SAT or ACT is required. Campus visit and interview recommended. No off-campus interviews.
**Procedure:** Take SAT by January of 12th year. Visit college for interview by February 25 of 12th year. Suggest filing application by fall. Application deadline is February 1. Notification of admission by April 15. Reply is required by May 1. $300 refundable tuition deposit. $200 refundable room deposit. Freshmen accepted for terms other than fall.
**Special programs:** Admission may be deferred one year. Credit and/or placement may be granted through CEEB Advanced Placement exams for scores of 3 or higher. Credit and/or placement may be granted through CLEP general and subject exams. Credit may be granted through military and life experience. Credit and placement may be granted through ACT PEP exams. Early decision program. In fall 1993, 1,541 applied for early decision and 923 were accepted. Deadline for applying for early decision is December 1.
**Transfer students:** Transfer students accepted for terms other than fall. In fall 1993, 18% of all new students were transfers into all classes. 1,473 transfer applications were received, 852 were accepted. Application deadline is March 1 for fall; November 1 for spring. Minimum 2.8 GPA required. Lowest course grade accepted is "C." Maximum number of transferable credits is 96 semester hours. At least 32 semester hours must be completed at the university to receive degree.
**Admissions contact:** David Kraus, M.S., Director of Admissions. 603 862-1360.

**FINANCIAL AID. Available aid:** SEOG, state scholarships and grants, school scholarships and grants, private scholarships and grants, ROTC scholarships, academic merit scholarships, athletic scholarships, and aid for undergraduate foreign students. Perkins Loans (NDSL), PLUS, Stafford Loans (GSL), school loans, private loans, and SLS. Tuition Plan of New England.
**Financial aid statistics:** 11% of aid is not need-based. In 1993-94, 87% of all undergraduate applicants received aid; 82% of freshman applicants. Average amounts of aid awarded freshmen: Scholarships and grants, $3,752; loans, $3,519.
**Supporting data/closing dates:** FAFSA: Priority filing date is January 1; deadline is March 1. Notification of awards on rolling basis.
**Financial aid contact:** Richard Craig, M.Ed., Director of Financial Aid. 603 862-3600.

**STUDENT EMPLOYMENT.** College Work/Study Program. Institutional employment. 30% of full-time undergraduates work on campus during school year. Students may expect to earn an average of $1,750 during school year. Off-campus part-time employment opportunities rated "excellent."

**COMPUTER FACILITIES.** 300 IBM/IBM-compatible, Macintosh/Apple, and RISC-/UNIX-based microcomputers. Students may access AT&T, Digital, IBM, Prime, SUN minicomputer/mainframe systems, Internet. Residence halls may be equipped with networked microcomputers, networked terminals. Client/LAN operating systems include Apple/Macintosh, DOS, UNIX/XENIX/AIX, Windows NT, DEC, LocalTalk/AppleTalk, Novell. Computer languages and software packages include BASIC, C, COBOL, dBASE, Excel, FORTRAN, LISP, Lotus 1-2-3, MacDraw, MacWrite, MINITAB, Pascal, PL/1, Prolog, PSX, S1032, SAS, WordPerfect. Computer facilities are available to all students.
**Fees:** None.
**Hours:** 8 AM-midn. (other hours available).

**PROMINENT ALUMNI/AE.** John Irving, novelist; Maryann Plunkett, Tony Award-winning actress; Natalie Jacobson, broadcast journalist; Marcia Carsey, executive producer, *The Cosby Show;* Susan Mercandetti, producer, ABC's *Nightline;* Barbara Walsh, Pulitzer Prize-winning journalist; James Nassikas, owner of San Francisco's Stanford Court; Ron Noble, assistant secretary, U.S. Treasury.

# New Jersey

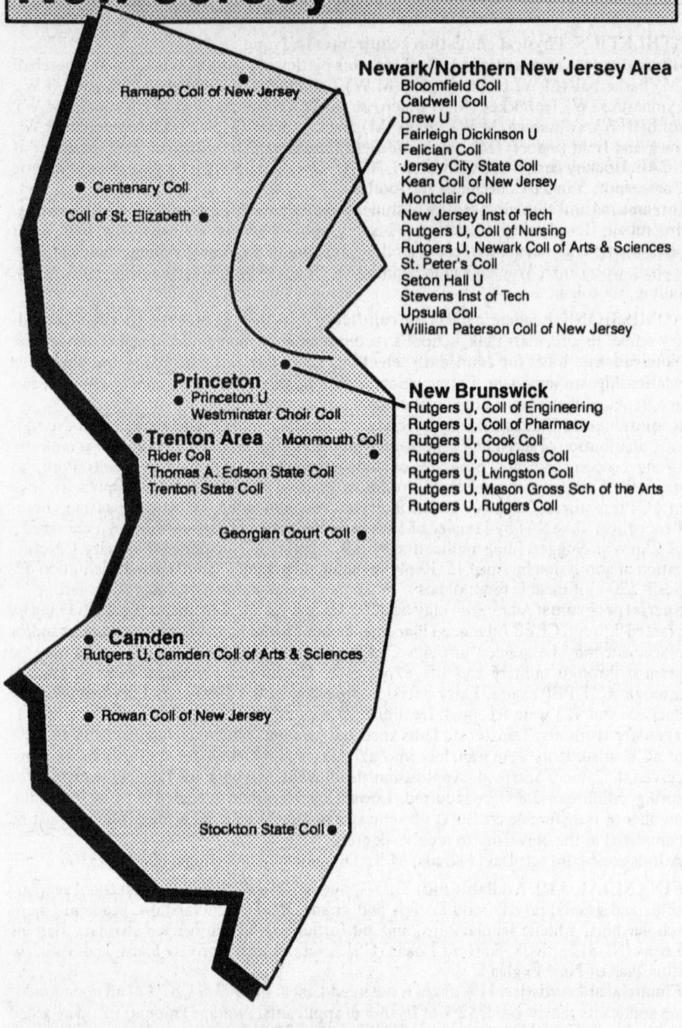


## Caldwell College

**Caldwell, NJ 07006** **201 228-4424**

**1994-95 Costs.** Tuition: $8,700. Room & board: $4,400. Fees, books, misc. academic expenses (school's estimate): $1,385.
**Enrollment.** Undergraduates: 240 men, 453 women (full-time). Freshman class: 1,011 applicants, 604 accepted, 213 enrolled. Graduate enrollment: 3 men, 20 women.
**Test score averages/ranges.** Average SAT scores: 441 verbal, 461 math. Range of SAT scores of middle 50%: 400-490 verbal, 440-500 math.
**Faculty.** 59 full-time; 43 part-time. 36% of faculty holds doctoral degree. Student/faculty ratio: 12 to 1.
**Selectivity rating.** Less competitive.

**PROFILE.** Caldwell is a church-affiliated, liberal arts college. Founded as a college for women in 1939, it adopted coeducation in 1986. Its 100-acre campus is located in Caldwell, 20 miles from New York City.

**Accreditation:** MSACS.
**Religious orientation:** Caldwell College is affiliated with the Roman Catholic Church (Dominican Order); three semesters of religion required.
**Library:** Collections totaling over 102,958 volumes, 390 periodical subscriptions, and 2,510 microform items.
**Special facilities/museums:** Art gallery, theatre, library with media center, TV studio.
**Athletic facilities:** Gymnasium, tennis courts, swimming pool, weight rooms, soccer and softball fields.

**STUDENT BODY. Undergraduate profile:** 79% are state residents; 42% are transfers. 2% Asian-American, 10% Black, 6% Hispanic, 64% White, 17% Other. Average age of undergraduates is 20.
**Freshman profile:** 2% of freshmen who took SAT scored 700 or over on math; 5% scored 600 or over on verbal, 10% scored 600 or over on math; 19% scored 500 or over on verbal, 35% scored 500 or over on math; 71% scored 400 or over on verbal, 81% scored 400 or over on math; 98% scored 300 or over on verbal, 100% scored 300 or over on math. 100% of accepted applicants took SAT. 70% of freshmen come from public schools.
**Undergraduate achievement:** 73% of fall 1992 freshmen returned for fall 1993 term. 38% of entering class graduated. 6% of students who completed a degree program immediately went on to graduate study.
**Foreign students:** 119 students are from out of the country. Countries represented include Japan, Korea, and Spain; 21 in all.

**PROGRAMS OF STUDY. Degrees:** B.A., B.F.A., B.S.
**Majors:** Art, Biology, Business Administration, Chemistry, Computer Information Systems, Computer Science, Elementary Education, English, Fine Arts, French, History, Mathematics, Medical Technology, Music, Psychology, Religious Studies, Social Studies, Sociology, Spanish.
**Distribution of degrees:** The majors with the highest enrollment are business administration, psychology, and education; religious studies, French, and chemistry have the lowest.
**Requirements:** General education requirement.
**Academic regulations:** Minimum 2.0 GPA must be maintained.
**Special:** Minors offered in all majors and in criminal justice, physical sciences, and political science. Numerous professional and area studies certification programs. Special programs in English as a Second Language and American English language studies. Medical technology program includes 12-month training in approved hospital, qualifying students for Registry of Medical Technologists exam. Double majors. Independent study. Pass/fail grading option. Internships. Cooperative education programs. Teacher certification in early childhood, elementary, and secondary education. Certification in specific subject areas. Study abroad in England, France, and Spain. ROTC at Seton Hall U.
**Honors:** Honors program. Honor societies.
**Academic Assistance:** Remedial reading, writing, math, and study skills. Nonremedial tutoring.

**ADMISSIONS. Academic basis for candidate selection** (in order of priority): Class rank, standardized test scores, secondary school record, school's recommendation.
**Nonacademic basis for candidate selection:** Character and personality, extracurricular participation, particular talent or ability, and alumni/ae relationship are considered.
**Requirements:** Graduation from secondary school is required; GED is accepted. 16 units and the following program of study are required: 4 units of English, 2 units of math, 2 units of science including 1 unit of lab, 2 units of foreign language, 1 unit of history, 5 units of electives. Minimum combined SAT score of 900 and rank in top half of secondary school class recommended. Portfolio required of art program applicants. Audition required of music program applicants. R.N. required of nursing program applicants. EOP for applicants not normally admissible. Conditional admission possible for applicants not meeting standard requirements. SAT is required; ACT may be substituted. Campus visit and interview recommended. Off-campus interviews available with an admissions representative.
**Procedure:** Take SAT or ACT by January 22 of 12th year. Notification of admission on rolling basis. No set date by which applicants must accept offer. $150 tuition deposit, refundable until May 1. $150 room deposit, refundable until May 1. Freshmen accepted in terms other than fall.
**Special programs:** Admission may be deferred one year. Credit may be granted through CLEP general and subject exams, ACT PEP and DANTES exams and life experience. Early entrance/early admission program. Concurrent enrollment program.
**Transfer students:** Transfer students accepted for terms other than fall. In fall 1993, 42% of all new students were transfers into all classes. 568 transfer applications were received, 461 were accepted. Application deadline is September 1 for fall; January 1 for spring. Minimum 2.0 GPA required. Lowest course grade accepted is "C." Maximum number of transferable credits is 60 semester hours from a two-year school and 75 semester hours from a four-year school. At least 45 semester hours must be completed at the college to receive degree.
**Admissions contact:** J. Raymond Sheenan, M.A., Director of Admissions. 201 228-4424, extension 220.

**FINANCIAL AID. Available aid:** Pell grants, SEOG, state scholarships and grants, school scholarships and grants, private scholarships and grants, ROTC scholarships, academic merit scholarships, athletic scholarships, and aid for undergraduate foreign students. Veteran's Benefits. Perkins Loans (NDSL), PLUS, Stafford Loans (GSL), and SLS. Tuition Plan Inc., AMS, deferred payment plan, and family tuition reduction.
**Financial aid statistics:** 50% of aid is not need-based. In 1993-94, 62% of all undergraduate applicants received aid; 59% of freshman applicants. Average amounts of aid awarded freshmen: Scholarships and grants, $5,338; loans, $2,424.
**Supporting data/closing dates:** FAFSA/FAF/FFS: Accepted on rolling basis. State aid form: Accepted on rolling basis. Income tax forms: Accepted on rolling basis. Notification of awards on rolling basis.
**Financial aid contact:** Margaret T. Murnane, Director of Financial Aid. 201 228-4424, extension 221.

## Centenary College

**Hackettstown, NJ 07840** **908 852-1400**

**1992-93 Costs.** Tuition: $10,815. Room & board: $5,130. Fees, books, misc. academic expenses (school's estimate): $490.
**Enrollment.** Undergraduates: 115 men, 310 women (full-time). Freshman class: 417 applicants, 253 accepted, 118 enrolled.
**Test score averages/ranges.** Range of SAT scores of middle 50%: 350-390 verbal, 350-390 math. Average ACT scores: 14 English, 16 math, 16 composite. Range of ACT scores of middle 50%: 13-18 English, 13-19 math.
**Faculty.** 32 full-time; 66 part-time. 65% of faculty holds doctoral degree. Student/faculty ratio: 12 to 1.
**Selectivity rating.** Less competitive.

**PROFILE.** Centenary College is a church-affiliated, liberal arts institution. It was founded in 1867 and operated as a women's college throughout much of its history before adopting coeducation in 1988. Its 42-acre campus is located in Hackettstown, approximately 50 miles west of New York City.

**Accreditation:** MSACS. Professionally accredited by the National Council for Accreditation of Teacher Education.
**Religious orientation:** Centenary College is affiliated with the United Methodist Church; no religious requirements.
**Library:** Collections totaling over 50,000 volumes, 375 periodical subscriptions, and 12,400 microform items.
**Special facilities/museums:** Art gallery, on-campus preschool.
**Athletic facilities:** Swimming pool, tennis courts, playing fields, basketball and volleyball courts, dance studio, fitness center, game room, equestrian center.

**STUDENT BODY. Undergraduate profile:** 80% are state residents; 31% are transfers. 5% Asian-American, 12% Black, 5% Hispanic, 69% White, 9% Other. Average age of undergraduates is 19.
**Freshman profile:** 2% of freshmen who took SAT scored 600 or over on verbal, 2% scored 600 or over on math; 6% scored 500 or over on verbal, 16% scored 500 or over on math; 34% scored 400 or over on verbal, 46% scored 400 or over on math; 84% scored 300 or over on verbal, 85% scored 300 or over on math. 25% of freshmen who took ACT scored 18 or over on English, 50% scored 18 or over on math, 50% scored 18 or over on composite; 100% scored 12 or over on English, 100% scored 12 or over on math, 100% scored 12 or over on composite. 98% of accepted applicants took SAT; 2% took ACT. 87% of freshmen come from public schools.
**Undergraduate achievement:** 85% of fall 1991 freshmen returned for fall 1992 term. 45% of entering class graduated. 5% of students who completed a degree program went on to graduate study within one year.
**Foreign students:** 38 students are from out of the country. Countries represented include Japan, Korea, Taiwan, and Thailand; eight in all.

**PROGRAMS OF STUDY. Degrees:** B.A., B.F.A., B.S.
**Majors:** Accounting, Art/Design, Business Administration, Communications, Education, English, Equine Studies, Fashion, History, Individualized Studies, Interior Design, International Studies, Mathematics, Psychology.
**Distribution of degrees:** The majors with the highest enrollment are business administration, equine studies, and psychology; individualized studies, communications, and mathematics have the lowest.
**Requirements:** General education requirement.
**Academic regulations:** Freshmen must maintain minimum 1.6 GPA; sophomores, 1.8 GPA; juniors, 2.0 GPA; seniors, 2.0 GPA.
**Special:** Minors offered in most major areas. Courses offered in biology, chemistry, economics, foreign languages, philosophy, physical science, religion, sociology, and speech. Associate's degrees offered. Self-designed majors. Independent study. Pass/fail grading option. Internships. Teacher certification in early childhood, elementary, secondary, and special education. Certification in specific subject areas. Semester abroad in England for equine studies.
**Honors:** Honor societies.
**Academic Assistance:** Remedial reading, writing, math, and study skills. Nonremedial tutoring.

**ADMISSIONS. Academic basis for candidate selection** (in order of priority): Secondary school record, school's recommendation, standardized test scores, essay, class rank.
**Nonacademic basis for candidate selection:** Extracurricular participation is emphasized. Particular talent or ability is important. Character and personality and alumni/ae relationship are considered.
**Requirements:** Graduation from secondary school is required; GED is accepted. 12 units and the following program of study are required: 4 units of English, 3 units of math, 3 units of science, 2 units of social studies. Minimum combined SAT score of 850, rank in top third of secondary school class, and minimum 2.3 GPA recommended. Portfolio required of art/design and interior design program applicants. Educational Opportunity Fund (EOF) for in-state applicants not normally admissible. Conditional admission possible for applicants not meeting standard requirements. SAT is required; ACT may be substituted. Campus visit and interview recommended. Off-campus interviews available with admissions and alumni representatives.
**Procedure:** Take SAT or ACT by November 15 of 12th year. Take ACH by November 15 of 12th year. Visit college for interview by April 15 of 12th year. Notification of admission on rolling basis. Reply is required within 30 days of acceptance. $150 tuition deposit, refundable until May 15. $150 room deposit, refundable until May 15. Freshmen accepted in terms other than fall.
**Special programs:** Admission may be deferred two years. Credit and/or placement may be granted through CEEB Advanced Placement exams for scores of 3 or higher. Credit and/or placement may be granted through CLEP general and subject exams. Credit may be granted through life experience.
**Transfer students:** Transfer students accepted for terms other than fall. In fall 1992, 31% of all new students were transfers into all classes. 120 transfer applications were received, 114 were accepted. Application deadline is rolling for fall; rolling for spring. Minimum 2.0 GPA required. Lowest course grade accepted is "C-." Maximum number of transferable credits is 72 semester hours. At least 32 semester hours must be completed at the college to receive degree.
**Admissions contact:** Michael McGraw, M.A., Vice President for Enrollment Management. 908 852-1400, extension 273.

**FINANCIAL AID. Available aid:** Pell grants, SEOG, state scholarships and grants, school scholarships, private scholarships and grants, and academic merit scholarships. Perkins Loans (NDSL), PLUS, Stafford Loans (GSL), and SLS. Tuition Plan Inc., AMS, EFI Fund Management, and family tuition reduction.
**Financial aid statistics:** 30% of aid is not need-based. In 1992-93, 75% of all undergraduate applicants received aid; 40% of freshman applicants. Average amounts of aid awarded freshmen: Scholarships and grants, $2,000; loans, $2,000.
**Supporting data/closing dates:** FAFSA/FAF: Priority filing date is March 1; accepted on rolling basis. School's own aid application: Priority filing date is March 1; accepted on rolling basis. Income tax forms: Priority filing date is March 1; accepted on rolling basis. Notification of awards on rolling basis.
**Financial aid contact:** Kim Adamson, M.A., Director of Financial Aid. 908 852-1400, extension 350.

## College of Saint Elizabeth

**Morristown, NJ 07960** 201 292-6300

**1994-95 Costs.** Tuition: $10,900. Room & board: $5,250. Fees, books, misc. academic expenses (school's estimate): $880.
**Enrollment.** Undergraduates: 5 men, 468 women (full-time). Freshman class: 413 applicants, 330 accepted, 119 enrolled. Graduate enrollment: 3 men, 14 women.
**Test score averages/ranges.** Average SAT scores: 439 verbal, 476 math. Range of SAT scores of middle 50%: 380-490 verbal, 400-510 math.
**Faculty.** 46 full-time; 81 part-time. 69% of faculty holds highest degree in specific field. Student/faculty ratio: 10 to 1.
**Selectivity rating.** Less competitive.

**PROFILE.** The College of Saint Elizabeth, founded in 1899, is a church-affiliated, liberal arts college for women; some men are enrolled part-time. Its 200-acre campus, including prominent buildings in the Gothic Revival style, is located in Convent Station, in northern New Jersey.

**Accreditation:** MSACS. Professionally accredited by the National League for Nursing.
**Religious orientation:** College of Saint Elizabeth is affiliated with the Roman Catholic Church (Sisters of Charity); one semester of religion required.
**Library:** Collections totaling over 187,078 volumes, 802 periodical subscriptions, and 25,173 microform items.
**Special facilities/museums:** On-campus nursery and secondary schools, volunteer services center, Shakespeare garden, Greek theatre, TV studio.
**Athletic facilities:** Swimming pool, gymnasium, weight room, tennis courts, bike path, dance studio, archery range, all-purpose field.

**STUDENT BODY. Undergraduate profile:** 97% are state residents; 25% are transfers. 3% Asian-American, 6% Black, 10% Hispanic, 1% Native American, 75% White, 5% Other. Average age of undergraduates is 21.
**Freshman profile:** 3% of freshmen who took SAT scored 700 or over on math; 7% scored 600 or over on verbal, 12% scored 600 or over on math; 18% scored 500 or over on verbal, 34% scored 500 or over on math; 61% scored 400 or over on verbal, 76% scored 400 or over on math; 89% scored 300 or over on verbal, 93% scored 300 or over on math. 95% of accepted applicants took SAT. 61% of freshmen come from public schools.
**Undergraduate achievement:** 72% of fall 1991 freshmen returned for fall 1992 term. 50% of entering class graduated. 17% of students who completed a degree program immediately went on to graduate study.
**Foreign students:** 30 students are from out of the country. Countries represented include Japan, Malaysia, the Philippines, Sri Lanka, and Taiwan; 12 in all.

**PROGRAMS OF STUDY. Degrees:** B.A., B.S., B.S.Nurs.
**Majors:** Accounting, Art, Biochemistry, Biology, Business, Business Administration, Chemistry, Computer Information Systems, Computer Science, Early Childhood Education, Economics, Education, Elementary Education, English, Fashion/Design, Food/Nutrition, French, History, Home Economics, Home Economics Education, Management, Mathematics, Medical Technology, Music, Nursing, Philosophy, Psychology, Sociology, Spanish, Special Education, Toxicology.
**Distribution of degrees:** The majors with the highest enrollment are business, psychology, and education; philosophy, Spanish, and economics have the lowest.
**Requirements:** General education requirement.
**Academic regulations:** Freshmen must maintain minimum 1.8 GPA; sophomores, juniors, seniors, 2.0 GPA.
**Special:** Minors offered. Courses offered in German, religious studies, and speech. Programs in communication, gerontology, and secondary education. Double majors. Independent study. Pass/fail grading option. Internships. Preprofessional programs in law, medicine, and dentistry. 3-1 medical technology and cytotechnology programs with U of Medicine and Dentistry of New Jersey. Cross-registration with Drew U and Fairleigh Dickinson U. Washington Semester and UN Semester. Exchange programs with Coll of Mt. St. Joseph, Coll of Mt. St. Vincent-on-Hudson, Elizabeth Seton Coll, and Seton Hill Coll. Teacher certification in early childhood, elementary, secondary, and special education. Certification in specific subject areas. Exchange program abroad in Canada (Mt. St. Vincent U).
**Honors:** Honors program. Honor societies.
**Academic Assistance:** Remedial reading and math. Nonremedial tutoring.

**ADMISSIONS. Academic basis for candidate selection** (in order of priority): Secondary school record, standardized test scores, class rank, school's recommendation, essay.
**Nonacademic basis for candidate selection:** Character and personality, extracurricular participation, and alumni/ae relationship are important. Particular talent or ability and geographical distribution are considered.
**Requirements:** Graduation from secondary school is required; GED is accepted. 16 units and the following program of study are required: 3 units of English, 3 units of math and science, 2 units of foreign language, 1 unit of history, 7 units of academic electives. Minimum combined SAT score of 800, rank in top half of secondary school class, and minimum 2.5 GPA recommended. R.N. required of nursing program applicants. Educational Opportunity Fund program for in-state applicants not normally admissible. SAT is required; ACT may be substituted. ACH recommended. Campus visit and interview recommended. Off-campus interviews available with admissions and alumni representatives.
**Procedure:** Take SAT or ACT by January of 12th year. Suggest filing application by February 1. Application deadline is August 15. Notification of admission on rolling basis. Reply is required by May 1. $150 tuition deposit, refundable until May 1. $150 room deposit, refundable until May 1. Freshmen accepted in terms other than fall.
**Special programs:** Admission may be deferred one year. Credit and/or placement may be granted through CEEB Advanced Placement exams for scores of 3 or higher. Credit and/or placement may be granted through CLEP subject exams. Credit and placement may be granted through Regents College and ACT PEP exams and military experience. Early decision program. In fall 1992, 14 applied for early decision and six were accepted. Dead-

line for applying for early decision is November 15. Early entrance/early admission program.
**Transfer students:** Transfer students accepted for terms other than fall. In fall 1992, 25% of all new students were transfers into all classes. 142 transfer applications were received, 79 were accepted. Application deadline is August 15 for fall; January 15 for spring. Minimum 2.0 GPA recommended. Lowest course grade accepted is "C." Maximum number of transferable credits is 64 semester hours. At least 64 semester hours must be completed at the college to receive degree.
**Admissions contact:** George P. Lynes II, Dean of Admission and Financial Aid. 201 292-6351.

**FINANCIAL AID. Available aid:** Pell grants, SEOG, state scholarships and grants, school scholarships and grants, private scholarships and grants, academic merit scholarships, and aid for undergraduate foreign students. Perkins Loans (NDSL), PLUS, Stafford Loans (GSL), state loans, and SLS. Tuition Plan Inc., AMS, and family tuition reduction.
**Financial aid statistics:** 20% of aid is not need-based. In 1992-93, 93% of all undergraduate applicants received aid; 90% of freshman applicants. Average amounts of aid awarded freshmen: Scholarships and grants, $4,300; loans, $2,625.
**Supporting data/closing dates:** FAFSA/FAF: Accepted on rolling basis. Income tax forms: Accepted on rolling basis. Notification of awards on rolling basis.
**Financial aid contact:** Camille Green-Thomas, Director of Financial Aid. 201 292-6344.

# Drew University

**Madison, NJ 07940** **201 408-3000**

**1993-94 Costs.** Tuition: $17,568. Room & board: $5,348. Fees, books, misc. academic expenses (school's estimate): $1,010.
**Enrollment.** Undergraduates: 483 men, 685 women (full-time). Freshman class: 2,150 applicants, 1,580 accepted, 323 enrolled. Graduate enrollment: 454 men, 307 women.
**Test score averages/ranges.** Average SAT scores: 574 verbal, 614 math. Range of SAT scores of middle 50%: 510-630 verbal, 550-680 math. Average ACT scores: 27 composite.
**Faculty.** 100 full-time; 79 part-time. 93% of faculty holds highest degree in specific field. Student/faculty ratio: 11 to 1.
**Selectivity rating.** Highly competitive.

**PROFILE.** Drew, founded in 1867, is a private university. Programs are offered through the College of Liberal Arts, the Graduate School, and the Theological School. Its 186-acre campus is located in Madison, 27 miles from New York City. Many of its buildings date from the 19th and early 20th centuries.

**Accreditation:** MSACS.
**Religious orientation:** Drew University is affiliated with the Methodist Church (historically); no religious requirements.
**Library:** Collections totaling over 429,636 volumes, 2,049 periodical subscriptions, and 296,414 microform items.
**Special facilities/museums:** Art gallery, photography gallery, language lab, child development center, research greenhouse, arboretum, observatory, laser holography lab, nuclear magnetic resonator, electron microscope, optical and radio telescopes.
**Athletic facilities:** Basketball, racquetball, squash, tennis, and volleyball courts, indoor track, stadium, athletic fields, swimming pool, weight room.

**STUDENT BODY. Undergraduate profile:** 55% are state residents; 9% are transfers. 6% Asian-American, 4% Black, 5% Hispanic, 73% White, 12% Other. Average age of undergraduates is 20.
**Freshman profile:** 8% of freshmen who took SAT scored 700 or over on verbal, 20% scored 700 or over on math; 43% scored 600 or over on verbal, 59% scored 600 or over on math; 81% scored 500 or over on verbal, 88% scored 500 or over on math; 97% scored 400 or over on verbal, 98% scored 400 or over on math; 99% scored 300 or over on verbal, 99% scored 300 or over on math. 98% of accepted applicants took SAT; 2% took ACT. 70% of freshmen come from public schools.
**Undergraduate achievement:** 90% of fall 1992 freshmen returned for fall 1993 term. 74% of entering class graduated. 21% of students who completed a degree program immediately went on to graduate study.
**Foreign students:** Countries represented include Canada, Indonesia, Japan, Korea, Portugal, and Switzerland; 22 in all.

**PROGRAMS OF STUDY. Degrees:** B.A.
**Majors:** American Studies, Anthropology, Art, Behavioral Science, Biology, Chemistry, Classics, Computer Science, Economics, English, French, German, History, Mathematics, Music, Philosophy, Physics, Political Science, Psychobiology, Psychology, Religion, Russian, Sociology, Spanish, Theatre Arts.
**Distribution of degrees:** The majors with the highest enrollment are political science, psychology, and English; religion, classics, and German have the lowest.
**Requirements:** General education requirement.
**Academic regulations:** Minimum 2.0 GPA must be maintained.
**Special:** Minors offered in all majors and in archaeology, arts/administration/museology, business management, Jewish studies, linguistics, women's studies, and writing. African-American, Asian, Latin American, Middle Eastern, and Russian area studies programs. Self-designed majors. Double majors. Dual degrees. Independent study. Pass/fail grading option. Internships. Cooperative education programs. Graduate school at which undergraduates may take graduate-level courses. Preprofessional programs in law, medicine, veterinary science, dentistry, theology, engineering, physical therapy, and podiatry. 3-2 forestry and environmental studies program with Duke U. 3-2 engineering programs with Stevens Inst of Tech and Washington U. 3-4 medical program with U of Medicine and Dentistry of New Jersey. Washington Semester and UN Semester. Contemporary Arts Program in New York. Teacher certification in early childhood, elementary, secondary, and special education. Exchange programs abroad in England (Sheffield U), Japan (Obirin U), and Korea (Yonsei U). Study abroad also in Belgium, Chile, the Ivory Coast, and Mali.
**Honors:** Phi Beta Kappa. Honors program. Honor societies.
**Academic Assistance:** Nonremedial tutoring.

**STUDENT LIFE. Housing:** All unmarried students must live on campus unless living with family. Coed, women's, and men's dorms. Off-campus privately-owned housing. On-campus married-student housing. Coed theme and language houses. 90% of students live in college housing.
**Social atmosphere:** Drew students frequent The Other End Coffee House and The Pub. The University Programming Board, Women's Concerns, and Kuumba are major influences on student life. Jamnesty, November Fest, and The Block Party are highlights of the school year. "The town of Madison is not a great college town, so we do it all ourselves," reports the editor of the school newspaper. "When we need to get off campus, we usually go to New York City, only forty minutes away. Drew's cultural life is great; there are always special lectures, symposiums, art openings, etc."
**Services and counseling/handicapped student services:** Placement services. Health service. Day care. Counseling services for minority students. Birth control, personal, and psychological counseling. Career and academic guidance services. Religious counseling. Physically disabled student services. Learning disabled services. Tape recorders. Tutors.
**Campus organizations:** Undergraduate student government. Student newspaper (Acorn, published once/week). Literary magazine. Yearbook. Radio station. Orchestra, chorale, dance and drama groups, photography club, Amnesty International, Peacemakers, environmental group, center for social outreach, College Democrats, College Republicans, Women's Concerns, academic, political, and special-interest groups.
**Religious organizations:** Intervarsity Christian Fellowship, Order of St. Luke, Black Ministerial Caucus, Drew People Concerned, Baptist, Episcopal, Catholic, Orthodox Christian, Jewish, and ecumenical groups.
**Minority/foreign student organizations:** KUUMBA, Ariel, Hyera, Asian Students in America. International Student Organization, Korean Caucus, Kelly Club, Russian Studies Club.

**ATHLETICS. Physical education requirements:** None.
**Intercollegiate competition:** 40% of students participate. Baseball (M), basketball (M,W), cross-country (M,W), fencing (M,W), field hockey (W), horsemanship (M,W), lacrosse (M,W), martial arts (M,W), soccer (M,W), softball (W), tennis (M,W). Member of ECAC, Middle Atlantic Collegiate Fencing Association, Middle Atlantic Conference, NCAA Division III.
**Intramural and club sports:** 70% of students participate. Intramural basketball, flag football, indoor soccer, racquetball, softball, squash, swimming, tennis, volleyball. Men's club rugby, ultimate frisbee. Women's club rugby, ultimate frisbee.

**ADMISSIONS. Academic basis for candidate selection** (in order of priority): Secondary school record, class rank, standardized test scores, school's recommendation, essay.
**Nonacademic basis for candidate selection:** Particular talent or ability is emphasized. Character and personality and extracurricular participation are important.
**Requirements:** Graduation from secondary school is required; GED is accepted. 16 units and the following program of study are recommended: 4 units of English, 3 units of math, 2 units of science, 2 units of foreign language, 2 units of social studies, 3 units of electives. EOP for applicants not normally admissible. SAT is required; ACT may be substituted. ACH recommended. Campus visit and interview recommended. Off-campus interviews available with admissions and alumni representatives.
**Procedure:** Take SAT or ACT by January of 12th year. Take ACH by January of 12th year. Visit college for interview by February 15 of 12th year. Application deadline is February 15. Priority filing date is January 1 for Drew Scholar program and 3-4 B.A./M.D. program. Notification of admission by March 15. Reply is required by May 1. $300 nonrefundable tuition deposit. $200 room deposit, refundable upon graduation or withdrawal from the university. Room deposit included in tuition deposit. Freshmen accepted in terms other than fall.
**Special programs:** Admission may be deferred one year. Credit and/or placement may be granted through CEEB Advanced Placement exams for scores of 4 or higher. Credit and/or placement may be granted through CLEP general and subject exams. Credit and placement may be granted through challenge exams. Early decision program. In fall 1993, 90 applied for early decision and 78 were accepted. Deadline for applying for early decision is December 1 and January 15. Early entrance/early admission program.
**Transfer students:** Transfer students accepted for terms other than fall. In fall 1993, 9% of all new students were transfers into all classes. 105 transfer applications were received, 62 were accepted. Application deadline is July 1 for fall; December 1 for spring. Minimum 3.0 GPA recommended. Lowest course grade accepted is "C." Maximum number of transferable credits is 60 semester hours. At least 60 semester hours must be completed at the university to receive degree.
**Admissions contact:** Roberto Noya, M.Ed., Director of Admissions. 201 408-DREW.

**FINANCIAL AID. Available aid:** Pell grants, SEOG, state scholarships and grants, school scholarships and grants, ROTC scholarships, and academic merit scholarships. Perkins Loans (NDSL), PLUS, Stafford Loans (GSL), state loans, private loans, and SLS. Knight Tuition Plans and AMS. Summit Trust loans.
**Financial aid statistics:** 40% of aid is not need-based. In 1993-94, 67% of all undergraduate applicants received aid; 84% of freshman applicants. Average amounts of aid awarded freshmen: Scholarships and grants, $9,751; loans, $2,301.
**Supporting data/closing dates:** FAFSA: Priority filing date is March 1. Notification of awards on rolling basis.
**Financial aid contact:** Francine Andrea, Director of Financial Aid. 201 408-3112.

**STUDENT EMPLOYMENT.** College Work/Study Program. Institutional employment. 62% of full-time undergraduates work on campus during school year. Students may expect to earn an average of $825 during school year. Off-campus part-time employment opportunities rated "good."

**COMPUTER FACILITIES.** 2,500 IBM/IBM-compatible microcomputers; all are networked. Students may access Digital minicomputer/mainframe systems, BITNET, Internet. Computer languages and software packages include Quattro Pro, SPSS, WordPerfect; various programming languages; 315 in all. Computer facilities are available to all students.
**Fees:** None.

**GRADUATE CAREER DATA.** Graduate school percentages: 5% enter law school. 3% enter medical school. 13% enter graduate arts and sciences programs. 1% enter theological school/seminary. Highest graduate school enrollments: Rutgers U, State U of New York, U of Medicine and Dentistry of New Jersey, U of Pennsylvania. 20% of graduates choose careers in business and industry. Companies and businesses that hire graduates: Chubb & Son, U.S. government, Prudential.

**PROMINENT ALUMNI/AE.** J. Rand Castile, director, Asian Art Museum of San Francisco; Patricia L. Gauch, editor-in-chief, Philomel Books; the Honorable William Gray, president and CEO, United Negro College Fund; Richard Walker, U.S. ambassador to Korea; Theodore Greenberg, senior litigator for assistant attorney general; Dr. Richard Krammerer, drug tester, 1984 Olympics.

# Fairleigh Dickinson University

**Madison, NJ 07940** **201 593-8500**

**1993-94 Costs.** Tuition: $10,410. Room & board: $5,336. Fees, books, misc. academic expenses (school's estimate): $1,304.
**Enrollment.** Undergraduates: 1,484 men, 1,429 women (full-time). Freshman class: 2,912 applicants, 1,648 accepted, 481 enrolled. Graduate enrollment: 2,181 men, 2,165 women.
**Test score averages/ranges.** Average SAT scores: 438 verbal, 490 math. Range of SAT scores of middle 50%: 380-490 verbal, 430-540 math.
**Faculty.** 277 full-time; 329 part-time. 92% of faculty holds highest degree in specific field. Student/faculty ratio: 17 to 1.
**Selectivity rating.** Competitive.

**PROFILE.** Fairleigh Dickinson, founded in 1942 is a private university. It operates three campuses in the northern New Jersey suburbs (Rutherford, Florham-Madison, and Teaneck-Hackensack) and campuses in England and the U.S. Virgin Islands.

**Accreditation:** MSACS. Professionally accredited by the Accreditation Board for Engineering and Technology, the American Dental Association, the American Medical Association (CAHEA), the American Physical Therapy Association, the American Psychological Association, the National Association of Schools of Public Affairs and Administration, the National League for Nursing.
**Religious orientation:** Fairleigh Dickinson University is nonsectarian; no religious requirements.
**Library:** Collections totaling over 553,801 volumes, 3,225 periodical subscriptions, and 496,655 microform items.
**Athletic facilities:** Gymnasiums, basketball and tennis courts, weight rooms, baseball, intramural, and soccer fields.

**STUDENT BODY. Undergraduate profile:** 79% are state residents; 22% are transfers. 4% Asian-American, 12% Black, 5% Hispanic, 65% White, 14% Other. Average age of undergraduates is 21.
**Freshman profile:** 1% of freshmen who took SAT scored 700 or over on math; 3% scored 600 or over on verbal, 13% scored 600 or over on math; 23% scored 500 or over on verbal, 46% scored 500 or over on math; 69% scored 400 or over on verbal, 87% scored 400 or over on math; 96% scored 300 or over on verbal, 99% scored 300 or over on math. 82% of accepted applicants took SAT.
**Undergraduate achievement:** 70% of fall 1991 freshmen returned for fall 1992 term. 27% of entering class graduated.
**Foreign students:** 246 students are from out of the country. Countries represented include India, Japan, Korea, Saudi Arabia, Taiwan, and Thailand; 33 in all.

**PROGRAMS OF STUDY. Degrees:** B.A., B.S., B.S.Elec.Eng.
**Majors:** Accounting, Art, Biochemistry, Biological Sciences, Biology, Business Management, Chemistry, Civil Engineering Technology, Clinical Laboratory Science, Communication, Computer Science, Construction Engineering Technology, Economics, Economics/Finance, Electrical Engineering, Electrical Engineering Technology, English Education, English Language/Literature, Environmental Science, Fine Arts, French Language/Literature, History, Hotel/Restaurant Management, Humanities, International Studies, Marine Biology, Marketing, Mathematics, Mathematics Education, Mechanical Engineering Technology, Medical Technology, Nursing, Philosophy, Physics, Political Science, Psychology, Radiologic Technology, Science, Sociology, Spanish Language/Literature.
**Distribution of degrees:** The majors with the highest enrollment are business management, marketing, and psychology; philosophy, French language/literature, and Spanish language/literature have the lowest.
**Requirements:** General education requirement.
**Academic regulations:** Minimum 2.0 GPA must be maintained.
**Special:** Minors offered in approximately 32 fields. Associate's degrees offered. Double majors. Independent study. Accelerated study. Pass/fail grading option. Internships. Cooperative education programs. Graduate school at which undergraduates may take graduate-level courses. Preprofessional programs in law, medicine, veterinary science, pharmacy, and dentistry. 2-3 pre-pharmacy program with Long Island U. Six-year B.S./D.M.D. program with U of Medicine and Dentistry of New Jersey. Five-year B.A./M.A. program in psychology. Five-year B.A. or B.S./M.B.A. program. Five-year B.A. or B.S./M.A.T. program. Five-year B.A./M.P.A. program. Teacher certification in elementary, secondary, special education, and bilingual/bicultural education. Exchange program abroad in England (Wroxton Coll). ROTC at Seton Hall U. AFROTC at New Jersey Inst of Tech.
**Honors:** Honors program. Honor societies.
**Academic Assistance:** Remedial reading, writing, math, and study skills. Nonremedial tutoring.

**STUDENT LIFE. Housing:** Students may live on or off campus. Coed dorms. 37% of students live in college housing.
**Services and counseling/handicapped student services:** Placement services. Health service. Counseling services for minority and older students. Birth control, personal, and psychological counseling. Career and academic guidance services. Religious counseling. Physically disabled student services. Learning disabled program/services. Notetaking services. Tape recorders. Tutors. Reader services for the blind.
**Campus organizations:** Undergraduate student government. Student newspaper (Spectator, published biweekly). Literary magazine. Yearbook. Radio and TV stations. Choir, debating, drama group, 31 organizations in all. 10 fraternities, all with chapter houses; eight sororities, five chapter houses. 30% of men join a fraternity. 35% of women join a sorority.
**Minority/foreign student organizations:** Association of Black Scholars, Circulo Latino, 100 Black Men, Association of Blacks and Hispanics. International Student Organization, Afro Carribe Organization, Korean Student Association.

**ATHLETICS. Physical education requirements:** One credit of physical education required.
**Intercollegiate competition:** 25% of students participate. Baseball (M,W), basketball (M,W), cross-country (M,W), fencing (W), field hockey (W), football (M), golf (M,W), horsemanship (M,W), lacrosse (M), soccer (M), softball (W), tennis (M,W), track (indoor) (M,W), track (outdoor) (M,W), track and field (indoor) (M,W), track and field (outdoor) (M,W), volleyball (W). Member of ECAC, MAC Freedom, NCAA Division III.
**Intramural and club sports:** 40% of students participate. Intramural basketball, bowling, flag football, golf, softball, swimming, tennis, volleyball, weight lifting. Men's club rugby.

**ADMISSIONS. Academic basis for candidate selection** (in order of priority): Secondary school record, standardized test scores, class rank, school's recommendation, essay.
**Nonacademic basis for candidate selection:** Character and personality and particular talent or ability are important. Extracurricular participation and alumni/ae relationship are considered.
**Requirements:** Graduation from secondary school is required; GED is accepted. 19 units and the following program of study are required: 4 units of English, 2 units of math, 2 units of science including 1 unit of lab, 2 units of foreign language, 2 units of social studies, 2 units of history, 2 units of academic electives. Minimum combined SAT score of 930, or minimum combined SAT score of 850 and either rank in top two-fifths of secondary school class or a "C+" average. 3 units of math and 2 units of lab science required of engineering and science program applicants. 1 unit of chemistry, 1 unit of biology, 2-1/2 years of math, and 1 unit of physics required of health sciences program applicants. EOP for applicants not normally admissible. Freshman Intensive Studies program for applicants not normally admissible at Madison campus. SAT is required; ACT may be substituted. Campus visit and interview recommended. Off-campus interviews available with an admissions representative.
**Procedure:** Take SAT or ACT by fall of 12th year. Suggest filing application by November 15; no deadline. Notification of admission on rolling basis. Reply is required by May 1 or within two weeks of acceptance. $100 nonrefundable tuition deposit. $100 nonrefundable room deposit. Freshmen accepted in terms other than fall.
**Special programs:** Admission may be deferred one year. Credit may be granted through CEEB Advanced Placement for scores of 3 or higher. Credit may be granted through CLEP general and subject exams, military and life experience. Credit and placement may be granted through challenge exams. Early decision program. In fall 1992, six applied for early decision and two were accepted. Deadline for applying for early decision is November 15. Early entrance/early admission program. Concurrent enrollment program.
**Transfer students:** Transfer students accepted for terms other than fall. In fall 1992, 22% of all new students were transfers into all classes. 1,257 transfer applications were received, 878 were accepted. Application deadline is rolling for fall; rolling for spring. Minimum 2.0 GPA required. Lowest course grade accepted is "C." Maximum number of transferable credits is 64 semester hours from a two-year school and 96 semester hours from a four-year school. At least 32 semester hours must be completed at the university to receive degree.
**Admissions contact:** Dale Herold, University Director of Admissions and Financial Aid. 201 460-5294.

**FINANCIAL AID. Available aid:** Pell grants, SEOG, Federal Nursing Student Scholarships, state scholarships and grants, school scholarships and grants, private scholarships and grants, academic merit scholarships, and athletic scholarships. Perkins Loans (NDSL), PLUS, Stafford Loans (GSL), NSL, Health Professions Loans, school loans, private loans, and SLS. AMS, deferred payment plan, and family tuition reduction. Monthly payment plan.
**Financial aid statistics:** In 1992-93, 60% of all freshman applicants received aid.
**Supporting data/closing dates:** FAFSA/FAF: Priority filing date is March 15. Notification of awards on rolling basis.
**Financial aid contact:** Dale Herold, University Director of Admissions and Financial Aid. 201 460-5294.

**STUDENT EMPLOYMENT.** College Work/Study Program. Institutional employment. 14% of full-time undergraduates work on campus during school year. Students may expect to earn an average of $1,150 during school year. Off-campus part-time employment opportunities rated "fair."

**COMPUTER FACILITIES.** 250 IBM/IBM-compatible and Macintosh/Apple microcomputers; 150 are networked. Students may access Digital minicomputer/mainframe systems, BITNET, Internet. Client/LAN operating systems include Apple/Macintosh, LocalTalk/AppleTalk. Computer languages and software packages include Assembly, C, dBASE, Lotus 1-2-3, Pascal, WordPerfect. Computer facilities are available to all students.
**Fees:** Computer fee is included in tuition/fees.
**Hours:** 24 hours.

**GRADUATE CAREER DATA.** Companies and businesses that hire graduates: AT&T, Big Six accounting firms, The Prudential, Dunn & Bradstreet, MACY's Northeast, United Parcel Service, Metropolitan Life, United Jersey Bank, John Hancock Mutual Life, Kellogg's Sales, Enterprise Rent-A-Car, Beneficial Management.

**PROMINENT ALUMNI/AE.** Edwary L. Hennessey, Jr., former chairman and CEO, Allied Signal; Peggy Noonan, author and former Presidential speech writer; Michael G. King, president and CEO, King World Productions.

# Felician College

**Lodi, NJ 07644** **201 778-1190**

**1994-95 Costs.** Tuition: $8,100. Housing: None. Fees, books, misc. academic expenses (school's estimate): $750.
**Enrollment.** Undergraduates: 70 men, 435 women (full-time). Freshman class: 420 applicants, 280 accepted, 155 enrolled.
**Test score averages/ranges.** Average SAT scores: 450 verbal, 450 math. Range of SAT scores of middle 50%: 440-490 verbal, 420-460 math.
**Faculty.** 50 full-time; 49 part-time. 60% of faculty holds highest degree in specific field. Student/faculty ratio: 11 to 1.
**Selectivity rating.** Less competitive.

**PROFILE.** Felician is a church-affiliated, liberal arts college. Founded as a women's college in 1923, it adopted coeducation in 1986. Its 27-acre campus is located in Lodi, 15 miles from New York City.

**Accreditation:** MSACS. Professionally accredited by the American Medical Association (CAHEA), the National League for Nursing.
**Religious orientation:** Felician College is affiliated with the Roman Catholic Church; one semester of religion required.
**Library:** Collections totaling over 111,585 volumes, 570 periodical subscriptions, and 11,000 microform items.
**Special facilities/museums:** On-campus elementary school for exceptional children.

**STUDENT BODY. Undergraduate profile:** 99% are state residents; 50% are transfers. 8% Asian-American, 5% Black, 11% Hispanic, 1% Native American, 74% White, 1% Other. Average age of undergraduates is 24.
**Freshman profile:** 6% of freshmen who took SAT scored 600 or over on verbal, 1% scored 600 or over on math; 12% scored 500 or over on verbal, 7% scored 500 or over on math; 65% scored 400 or over on verbal, 77% scored 400 or over on math; 94% scored 300 or over on verbal, 94% scored 300 or over on math. 73% of accepted applicants took SAT. 70% of freshmen come from public schools.
**Undergraduate achievement:** 70% of fall 1992 freshmen returned for fall 1993 term.
**Foreign students:** 17 students are from out of the country. Countries represented include India, Japan, the Philippines, and Trinidad; 11 in all.

**PROGRAMS OF STUDY. Degrees:** B.A., B.S., B.S.Nurs.
**Majors:** Art, Biology, Business, Clinical Laboratory Sciences, Computer Science, Elementary Education, English, History, Humanities, Liberal Arts, Mathematics, Natural Science, Nursing, Psychology, Religious Studies, Social/Behavioral Sciences, Special Education.
**Distribution of degrees:** The majors with the highest enrollment are nursing and elementary education.
**Requirements:** General education requirement.
**Academic regulations:** Freshmen must maintain minimum 1.8 GPA; sophomores, juniors, seniors, 2.0 GPA.
**Special:** Minors offered in accounting, communication, and sociology. Associate's degrees offered. Self-designed majors. Double majors. Independent study. Internships. Preprofessional programs in law, medicine, veterinary science, and dentistry. 3-2 clinical lab science program with U of Medicine and Dentistry of New Jersey. Teacher certification in elementary and special education. Certification in specific subject areas.
**Honors:** Honors program.
**Academic Assistance:** Remedial reading, writing, math, and study skills. Nonremedial tutoring.

**ADMISSIONS. Academic basis for candidate selection** (in order of priority): Secondary school record, standardized test scores, class rank, school's recommendation.
**Nonacademic basis for candidate selection:** Character and personality, extracurricular participation, and alumni/ae relationship are considered.
**Requirements:** Graduation from secondary school is required; GED is accepted. 16 units and the following program of study are recommended: 4 units of English, 3 units of math, 2 units of science, 2 units of foreign language, 2 units of social studies. Chemistry and biology with lab required of nursing program applicants. Educational Opportunity Fund for in-state applicants not normally admissible. SAT is required; ACT may be substituted. Campus visit and interview required. No off-campus interviews.
**Procedure:** Take SAT or ACT by August of 12th year. Visit college for interview by August of 12th year. Notification of admission on rolling basis. Reply is required within 30 days of acceptance. $100 nonrefundable tuition deposit. Freshmen accepted in terms other than fall.
**Special programs:** Admission may be deferred one year. Credit and/or placement may be granted through CEEB Advanced Placement exams for scores of 4 or higher. Credit and/or placement may be granted through CLEP subject exams. Credit may be granted through ACT PEP and DANTES exams. Placement may be granted through challenge exams. Early entrance/early admission program. Concurrent enrollment program.
**Transfer students:** Transfer students accepted for terms other than fall. In fall 1993, 50% of all new students were transfers into all classes. 337 transfer applications were received, 257 were accepted. Application deadline is rolling for fall; rolling for spring. Lowest course grade accepted is "C." Maximum number of transferable credits is 75 semester hours from a two-year school and 90 semester hours from a four-year school. At least 30 semester hours must be completed at the college to receive degree.
**Admissions contact:** Sr. Mary Austin Blank, O.S.B., M.S., Director of Admissions. 201 778-1029.

**FINANCIAL AID. Available aid:** Pell grants, SEOG, state scholarships and grants, school scholarships and grants, private scholarships and grants, and academic merit scholarships. PLUS, Stafford Loans (GSL), state loans, and SLS. Deferred payment plan and family tuition reduction.
**Financial aid statistics:** In 1993-94, 75% of all undergraduate applicants received aid; 75% of freshman applicants. Average amounts of aid awarded freshmen: Loans, $2,000.
**Supporting data/closing dates:** FAFSA/FAF: Accepted on rolling basis. School's own aid application: Accepted on rolling basis. State aid form: Accepted on rolling basis. Notification of awards on rolling basis.
**Financial aid contact:** Sr. Dorothy Marie Krzewinska, M.S., Director of Financial Aid.

# Georgian Court College

**Lakewood, NJ 08701-2697** **908 364-2200**

**1994-95 Costs.** Tuition: $9,150. Room & board: $3,950. Fees, books, misc. academic expenses (school's estimate): $930.
**Enrollment.** Undergraduates: 49 men, 985 women (full-time). Freshman class: 330 applicants, 281 accepted, 143 enrolled. Graduate enrollment: 87 men, 583 women.
**Test score averages/ranges.** Average SAT scores: 418 verbal, 455 math. Range of SAT scores of middle 50%: 360-450 verbal, 370-480 math.
**Faculty.** 85 full-time; 97 part-time. 50% of faculty holds highest degree in specific field. Student/faculty ratio: 10 to 1.
**Selectivity rating.** Competitive.

**PROFILE.** Georgian Court, founded in 1908, is a church-affiliated, liberal arts college. Traditionally a women's college, the institution added a coeducational undergraduate evening division in 1979. Its 152-acre campus, a designated National Historic Site, is located 60 miles from Philadelphia and New York City.

**Accreditation:** MSACS.
**Religious orientation:** Georgian Court College is affiliated with the Roman Catholic Church (Sisters of Mercy); one semester of religion required.
**Library:** Collections totaling over 102,074 volumes, 906 periodical subscriptions, and 415,761 microform items.
**Special facilities/museums:** Art gallery, arboretum.
**Athletic facilities:** Gymnasium, swimming pool, basketball, tennis, and volleyball courts, weight room, fitness center.

**STUDENT BODY. Undergraduate profile:** 99% are state residents; 66% are transfers. 1% Asian-American, 4% Black, 1% Hispanic, 2% Native American, 88% White, 4% Other. Average age of undergraduates is 23.
**Freshman profile:** 1% of freshmen who took SAT scored 600 or over on verbal, 2% scored 600 or over on math; 12% scored 500 or over on verbal, 16% scored 500 or over on math; 54% scored 400 or over on verbal, 61% scored 400 or over on math; 76% scored 300 or over on verbal, 77% scored 300 or over on math. Majority of accepted applicants took SAT.
**Undergraduate achievement:** 84% of fall 1991 freshmen returned for fall 1992 term. 46% of entering class graduated. 25% of students who completed a degree program went on to graduate study within five years.
**Foreign students:** Six students are from out of the country. Five countries represented in all.

**PROGRAMS OF STUDY. Degrees:** B.A., B.S., B.Soc.Work.
**Majors:** Accounting, Art, Art History, Biochemistry, Biology, Business Administration, Chemistry, English, French, History, Humanities, Mathematics, Music, Physics, Psychology, Religious Studies, Social Work, Sociology, Spanish, Special Education.
**Distribution of degrees:** The majors with the highest enrollment are business administration, psychology, and humanities.
**Requirements:** General education requirement.
**Special:** Minors offered in most majors and in classical studies, computer science, economics, German, gerontology, interdisciplinary areas, Italian, marketing, modern/classical languages, philosophy, political science, and sociology/anthropology. Double majors. Pass/fail grading option. Cooperative education programs. Preprofessional programs in law, medicine, and dentistry. 3-2 engineering program with George Washington U. Teacher certification in early childhood, elementary, secondary, special education, and bilingual/bicultural education. Certification in specific subject areas. Study abroad in England, France, Germany, and Spain.
**Honors:** Honors program. Honor societies.
**Academic Assistance:** Remedial reading, writing, math, and study skills.

**ADMISSIONS. Academic basis for candidate selection** (in order of priority): Secondary school record, class rank, standardized test scores, essay, school's recommendation.
**Nonacademic basis for candidate selection:** Character and personality and particular talent or ability are emphasized. Extracurricular participation is important. Alumni/ae relationship is considered.
**Requirements:** Graduation from secondary school is required; GED is accepted. 16 units and the following program of study are required: 4 units of English, 2 units of math, 1 unit of lab science, 2 units of foreign language, 1 unit of history, 6 units of academic electives. Minimum combined SAT score of 750, rank in top half of secondary school class, and minimum 2.75 GPA required. Audition required of music program applicants. SEP for applicants not normally admissible. Educational Opportunity Fund (EOF) for in-state applicants not normally admissible. SAT is required. Campus visit and interview recommended. No off-campus interviews.
**Procedure:** Take SAT by January of 12th year. Suggest filing application by November 15. Application deadline is July 1. Notification of admission on rolling basis. Reply is required by May 1. $50 nonrefundable tuition deposit. $100 nonrefundable room deposit. Freshmen accepted in terms other than fall.
**Special programs:** Credit and/or placement may be granted through CEEB Advanced Placement exams for scores of 3 or higher. Credit may be granted through CLEP general and subject exams, DANTES exams, and military experience. Placement may be granted through life experience. Early decision program. Deadline for applying for early decision is November 15. Early entrance/early admission program. Concurrent enrollment program.
**Transfer students:** Transfer students accepted for terms other than fall. In fall 1992, 66% of all new students were transfers into all classes. 451 transfer applications were received, 433 were accepted. Application deadline is July 1 for fall; December 1 for spring. Minimum 2.0 GPA required. Lowest course grade accepted is "D." Maximum number of trans-

ferable credits is 82 semester hours. At least 50 semester hours must be completed at the college to receive degree.
**Admissions contact:** John P. Burke, M.Ed., Director of Admissions. 908 367-4440.

**FINANCIAL AID. Available aid:** Pell grants, SEOG, state scholarships and grants, school scholarships and grants, private scholarships and grants, academic merit scholarships, and athletic scholarships. Perkins Loans (NDSL), PLUS, Stafford Loans (GSL), state loans, and SLS. AMS and family tuition reduction. Chemical Bank Tuition Plan.
**Financial aid statistics:** 10% of aid is not need-based. In 1992-93, 94% of all undergraduate applicants received aid; 90% of freshman applicants. Average amounts of aid awarded freshmen: Scholarships and grants, $1,705; loans, $2,185.
**Supporting data/closing dates:** FAFSA/FAF: Priority filing date is August 1; accepted on rolling basis. School's own aid application: Priority filing date is August 1. State aid form: Priority filing date is June 1. Income tax forms: Accepted on rolling basis. Notification of awards on rolling basis.
**Financial aid contact:** Sr. Francesca Holly, R.S.M., M.Ed., Director of Financial Aid. 908 364-2200, extension 258.

# Jersey City State College

**Jersey City, NJ 07305 — 201 200-2000**

**1993-94 Costs.** Tuition: $2,152 (state residents), $3,300 (out-of-state). Room & board: $5,000. Fees, books, misc. academic expenses (school's estimate): $1,045.
**Enrollment.** Undergraduates: 1,765 men, 2,052 women (full-time). Freshman class: 2,957 applicants, 1,423 accepted, 691 enrolled. Graduate enrollment: 294 men, 940 women.
**Test score averages/ranges.** Average SAT scores: 400 verbal, 440 math.
**Faculty.** 241 full-time; 193 part-time. 63% of faculty holds highest degree in specific field. Student/faculty ratio: 16 to 1.
**Selectivity rating.** Competitive.

**PROFILE.** Jersey City State, founded in 1927, is a public college. Programs are offered through the Schools of Arts and Sciences and Professional Studies and Education. Its 17-acre campus is located in Jersey City, 15 miles from New York City.

**Accreditation:** MSACS. Professionally accredited by the National Association of Schools of Art and Design, the National Association of Schools of Music, the National Council for Accreditation of Teacher Education, the National League for Nursing.
**Religious orientation:** Jersey City State College is nonsectarian; no religious requirements.
**Library:** Collections totaling over 244,949 volumes, 1,445 periodical subscriptions, and 641,488 microform items.
**Special facilities/museums:** Art galleries, catalyst teaching center, lab school for special education, center for media and technology, criminal justice institute, electron microscope.
**Athletic facilities:** Gymnasiums, basketball, racquetball, and tennis courts, swimming pool, weight rooms, baseball, football, soccer, and softball fields, dance and exercise studios, indoor track.

**STUDENT BODY. Undergraduate profile:** 99% are state residents; 35% are transfers. 8% Asian-American, 18% Black, 17% Hispanic, 45% White, 12% Other. Average age of undergraduates is 24.
**Freshman profile:** 1% of freshmen who took SAT scored 600 or over on verbal, 3% scored 600 or over on math; 8% scored 500 or over on verbal, 21% scored 500 or over on math; 42% scored 400 or over on verbal, 66% scored 400 or over on math; 82% scored 300 or over on verbal, 92% scored 300 or over on math. 95% of accepted applicants took SAT. 60% of freshmen come from public schools.
**Undergraduate achievement:** 70% of fall 1992 freshmen returned for fall 1993 term. 25% of students who completed a degree program went on to graduate study within three years.
**Foreign students:** 268 students are from out of the country. Countries represented include China, India, Kenya, Nigeria, the Philippines, and Poland; 52 in all.

**PROGRAMS OF STUDY. Degrees:** B.A., B.F.A., B.S., B.S.Nurs.
**Majors:** Art, Biology, Business Administration, Chemistry, Computer Science, Criminal Justice/Fire Safety/Security Administration, Early Childhood Education, Economics, Elementary Education, English, Geoscience, Health Sciences, History, Mathematics, Media Arts, Music, Nursing, Philosophy, Political Science, Psychology, Sociology, Spanish, Special Education, Sports Management.
**Distribution of degrees:** The majors with the highest enrollment are business administration, criminal justice, and computer science; Spanish, geoscience, and chemistry have the lowest.
**Requirements:** General education requirement.
**Academic regulations:** Freshmen must maintain minimum 1.6 GPA; sophomores, 1.75 GPA; juniors, 1.85 GPA; seniors, 2.0 GPA.
**Special:** Minors offered in most majors. Double majors. Independent study. Accelerated study. Pass/fail grading option. Internships. Cooperative education programs. Graduate school at which undergraduates may take graduate-level courses. Preprofessional programs in law, medicine, veterinary science, pharmacy, dentistry, and optometry. Member of New Jersey State Colleges Consortium. Washington Semester. Teacher certification in early childhood, elementary, secondary, and special education. Certification in specific subject areas. Study abroad in China, Colombia, Cyprus, Denmark, Ecuador, England, France, Germany, Greece, Israel, Italy, Jamaica, Mexico, Portugal, Scotland, Spain, and Sweden.
**Honors:** Honors program. Honor societies.
**Academic Assistance:** Remedial reading, writing, math, and study skills.

**STUDENT LIFE. Housing:** Students may live on or off campus. Coed dorms. 3% of students live in college housing.
**Social atmosphere:** Bently's, Park Tavern, the game room, Shooter's, and New York City are hot spots for students. Influential student groups include Gothic Players, TKE, Phi Beta Sigma, Student Government, Black Freedom Society, and radio station WGKR. Homecoming, football and basketball games, musical plays, Unity banquet, and formal dances are popular social events. The editor of the student newspaper describes the college as a "diverse campus, average age 23, co-op college in an urban setting near NYC."
**Services and counseling/handicapped student services:** Placement services. Health service. Women's center. Day care. Counseling services for veteran students. Personal and psychological counseling. Career and academic guidance services. Physically disabled student services. Learning disabled program/services. Tape recorders. Tutors. Reader services for the blind.
**Campus organizations:** Undergraduate student government. Student newspaper (Knight Examiner, published once/two weeks). Literary magazine. Yearbook. Radio station. Concert and jazz bands, ensembles, choral and dance groups, orchestra, gospel choir, departmental and special-interest groups, 32 organizations in all. Seven fraternities, no chapter houses; five sororities, no chapter houses. 1% of men join a fraternity. 1% of women join a sorority.
**Religious organizations:** Campus Christian Fellowship.
**Minority/foreign student organizations:** Black Freedom Society, Latin Power Association, Africana Journal. International Student Association, Middle Eastern and Polish groups.

**ATHLETICS. Physical education requirements:** None.
**Intercollegiate competition:** 6% of students participate. Baseball (M), basketball (M,W), cheerleading (M,W), cross-country (W), football (M), soccer (M,W), softball (W), tennis (M), volleyball (M,W). Member of ECAC, NCAA Division III, NJAC.
**Intramural and club sports:** 30% of students participate. Intramural basketball, billiards, bowling, cross-country, flag football, floor football, floor hockey, foul shooting, karate, racquetball, swimming, softball, table tennis, tennis, volleyball, walleyball, Wiffle ball.

**ADMISSIONS. Academic basis for candidate selection** (in order of priority): Secondary school record, class rank, standardized test scores, essay, school's recommendation.
**Nonacademic basis for candidate selection:** Character and personality, extracurricular participation, and particular talent or ability are important. Alumni/ae relationship is considered.
**Requirements:** Graduation from secondary school is required; GED is accepted. 16 units and the following program of study are required: 4 units of English, 3 units of math, 2 units of lab science, 2 units of social studies, 5 units of academic electives. Mimimum combined SAT score of 800, rank in top half of secondary school class, and minimum 2.5 GPA required. Audition required of music program applicants. R.N. required of nursing program applicants. EOP for applicants not normally admissible. SAT is required; ACT may be substituted. Campus visit recommended. No off-campus interviews.
**Procedure:** Take SAT or ACT by January of 12th year. Suggest filing application by April 1. Application deadline is May 1. Notification of admission on rolling basis. Reply is required by May 1. $50 nonrefundable tuition deposit. $150 nonrefundable room deposit. Freshmen accepted in terms other than fall.
**Special programs:** Admission may be deferred one year. Credit and/or placement may be granted through CEEB Advanced Placement exams for scores of 3 or higher. Credit and/or placement may be granted through CLEP general and subject exams. Credit may be granted through DANTES exams and military experience. Placement may be granted through challenge exams. Credit and placement may be granted through ACT PEP exams. Early entrance/early admission program. Concurrent enrollment program.
**Transfer students:** Transfer students accepted for terms other than fall. In fall 1993, 35% of all new students were transfers into all classes. 1,436 transfer applications were received, 976 were accepted. Application deadline is July 1 for fall; November 1 for spring. Minimum 2.0 GPA required. Lowest course grade accepted is "C." Maximum number of transferable credits is 64 semester hours from a two-year school and 96 semester hours from a four-year school. At least 36 semester hours must be completed at the college to receive degree.
**Admissions contact:** Samuel T. McGhee, M.A., Director of Admissions. 201 200-3234, 800 441-5272.

**FINANCIAL AID. Available aid:** Pell grants, SEOG, state scholarships and grants, school scholarships, private scholarships and grants, ROTC scholarships, academic merit scholarships, and United Negro College Fund. Perkins Loans (NDSL), PLUS, Stafford Loans (GSL), state loans, private loans, and SLS.
**Financial aid statistics:** 2% of aid is not need-based. In 1993-94, 69% of all undergraduate applicants received aid; 65% of freshman applicants. Average amounts of aid awarded freshmen: Scholarships and grants, $3,479; loans, $2,582.
**Supporting data/closing dates:** FAFSA: Priority filing date is April 15. FAF/FFS: Accepted on rolling basis. State aid form: Deadline is October 1. Notification of awards on rolling basis.
**Financial aid contact:** Robert J. McBride, M.S., Director of Financial Aid. 201 200-3173.

**STUDENT EMPLOYMENT.** College Work/Study Program. Institutional employment. 6% of full-time undergraduates work on campus during school year. Students may expect to earn an average of $2,212 during school year. Off-campus part-time employment opportunities rated "good."

**COMPUTER FACILITIES.** 1,400 IBM/IBM-compatible and Macintosh/Apple microcomputers; 65 are networked. Students may access Digital, SUN minicomputer/mainframe systems, Internet. Client/LAN operating systems include Apple/Macintosh, LocalTalk/AppleTalk. Computer languages and software packages include Ada, BASIC, COBOL, FORTRAN, Pascal, RPG, SPSS; 200 in all. Computer facilities are available to all students.
**Fees:** None.
**Hours:** 8 AM-10 PM.

**GRADUATE CAREER DATA.** Graduate school percentages: 1% enter law school. 1% enter medical school. 15% enter graduate business programs. 15% enter graduate arts and sciences programs. 60% of graduates choose careers in business and industry. Companies and businesses that hire graduates: Paine Webber Group, Bank of Tokyo, K mart, Prudential-Bache, UPS.

**PROMINENT ALUMNI/AE.** Pam Fiore, vice president/editor-in-chief, American Express Publishing Co.; Dr. Deborah Cannon Wolfe, educator; Robert Janiszewski, county executive, Hudson County, N.J.

# Kean College of New Jersey

**Union, NJ 07083 908 527-2000**

**1993-94 Costs.** Tuition: $2,555 (state residents), $3,485 (out-of-state). Room & board: $3,840. Fees, books, misc. academic expenses (school's estimate): $675.
**Enrollment.** Undergraduates: 2,793 men, 4,011 women (full-time). Freshman class: 3,344 applicants, 2,320 accepted, 1,223 enrolled. Graduate enrollment: 392 men, 1,372 women.
**Test score averages/ranges.** Average SAT scores: 417 verbal, 463 math. Range of SAT scores of middle 50%: 400-449 verbal, 450-499 math.
**Faculty.** 329 full-time; 484 part-time. 76% of faculty holds doctoral degree. Student/faculty ratio: 13 to 1.
**Selectivity rating.** Less competitive.

**PROFILE.** Kean, founded in 1855, is a public college. Programs are offered through the Schools of Business, Government, and Technology; Education; Liberal Arts; and Natural Sciences, Nursing, and Mathematics. Its 128-acre campus is located in Union, 12 miles from New York City.

**Accreditation:** MSACS. Professionally accredited by the American Physical Therapy Association, the Council on Social Work Education, the National Association of Schools of Music, the National Council for Accreditation of Teacher Education.
**Religious orientation:** Kean College of New Jersey is nonsectarian; no religious requirements.
**Library:** Collections totaling over 265,000 volumes, 1,350 periodical subscriptions, and 300,000 microform items.
**Athletic facilities:** Gymnasiums, swimming pool, dance, fitness, and weight rooms, tennis courts, athletic fields.

**STUDENT BODY. Undergraduate profile:** 97% are state residents; 36% are transfers. 4% Asian-American, 14% Black, 14% Hispanic, 66% White, 2% Other. Average age of undergraduates is 20.
**Freshman profile:** 2% of freshmen who took SAT scored 600 or over on verbal, 3% scored 600 or over on math; 11% scored 500 or over on verbal, 32% scored 500 or over on math; 63% scored 400 or over on verbal, 82% scored 400 or over on math; 97% scored 300 or over on verbal, 99% scored 300 or over on math.
**Undergraduate achievement:** 79% of fall 1991 freshmen returned for fall 1992 term. 49% of entering class graduated.
**Foreign students:** 233 students are from out of the country. 67 countries represented in all.

**PROGRAMS OF STUDY. Degrees:** B.A., B.F.A., B.S., B.S.Nurs., B.Soc.Work.
**Majors:** Accounting, Art History, Biology, Chemistry, Chemistry/Physics, Computer Science, Early Childhood Education, Earth Sciences, Economics, Elementary Education, English, Fine Arts, French, History, Industrial Education, Industrial Technology, Library/Media Specialist, Management Science, Mathematics, Medical Record Administration, Medical Technology, Music, Music Education, Nursing, Occupational Therapy, Philosophy/Religion, Physical Education, Physical Therapy, Political Science, Psychology, Public Administration, Social Work, Sociology, Spanish, Speech/Hearing, Teacher of the Handicapped, Urban/Outdoor Education.
**Distribution of degrees:** The majors with the highest enrollment are management science, accounting, and elementary education; industrial education, chemistry/physics, and music education have the lowest.
**Requirements:** General education requirement.
**Academic regulations:** Minimum 2.0 GPA required for graduation.
**Special:** Spanish Speaking Program offers selection of general education courses in Spanish each semester. Double majors. Independent study. Pass/fail grading option. Graduate school at which undergraduates may take graduate-level courses. Member of Consortium of East New Jersey. Teacher certification in early childhood and special education. Study abroad in many countries through New Jersey State College Consortium for International Education. ROTC at Seton Hall U. AFROTC at New Jersey Inst of Tech.
**Honors:** Honor societies.
**Academic Assistance:** Remedial reading, writing, and math.

**STUDENT LIFE. Housing:** Students may live on or off campus. Coed dorms. School-owned/operated apartments. Off-campus privately-owned housing. Freshman housing. 12% of students live in college housing.
**Social atmosphere:** The student newspaper reports, "The college is about half commuters and half residents. The residents throw parties every Thursday night and often other times. Many commuters join in and bring residents to off-campus hot spots." Fraternities, sororities, cultural groups, and the National Student Affairs office have the greatest influence on campus social life. The most popular campus events include Homecoming, Springfest, Hell Week, and Campus Awareness Festival. Off campus, students gather at Makadoos, the Sports Place, and McDougal Street.
**Services and counseling/handicapped student services:** Placement services. Health service. Day care. Counseling services for minority, military, veteran, and older students. Birth control, personal, and psychological counseling. Career and academic guidance services.
**Campus organizations:** Undergraduate student government. Student newspaper (Independent, published once/week). Literary magazine. Yearbook. Radio and TV stations. Chorus, orchestra, gospel choir, drama groups, poetry group, Kean Komix, Commuter Club, BACCHUS, SADD, Circle K, photography and chess clubs, First Aid Squad, Peace Center, Young Democrats, College Republicans, academic and special-interest groups, 117 organizations in all. 14 fraternities, no chapter houses; 16 sororities, no chapter houses. 3% of men join a fraternity. 3% of women join a sorority.
**Religious organizations:** Campus Advance, Catholic Student Organization, Intervarsity Christian Fellowship.
**Minority/foreign student organizations:** Brothers in the Struggle. International Student Association; African, Chinese, Cuban, Filipino, Haitian, Indian, Latin American, Pakistani, Portuguese, and Vietnamese groups.

**ATHLETICS. Physical education requirements:** None.
**Intercollegiate competition:** 10% of students participate. Baseball (M), basketball (M,W), cheerleading (W), field hockey (W), football (M), lacrosse (M), soccer (M,W), softball (W), swimming (W), volleyball (W), wrestling (M). Member of ECAC, NCAA Division III, New Jersey State Athletic Conference.
**Intramural and club sports:** 25% of students participate. Intramural basketball, flag football, soccer, softball, volleyball. Men's club ice hockey.

**ADMISSIONS. Academic basis for candidate selection** (in order of priority): Class rank, standardized test scores, secondary school record, school's recommendation.
**Nonacademic basis for candidate selection:** Character and personality, extracurricular participation, and particular talent or ability are considered.
**Requirements:** Graduation from secondary school is required; GED is accepted. 16 units and the following program of study are required: 4 units of English, 3 units of math, 2 units of lab science, 2 units of social studies, 3 units of electives. R.N. required of nursing program applicants. Exceptional Educational Opportunities Program and Passport Program for applicants not normally admissible. SAT is required; ACT may be substituted. Campus visit recommended. No off-campus interviews.
**Procedure:** Take SAT or ACT by December of 12th year. Suggest filing application by February 15. Application deadline is June 15. Notification of admission on rolling basis. Reply is required by May 1 or within 10 days if accepted after May 1. $50 nonrefundable tuition deposit. $75 nonrefundable room deposit. Freshmen accepted in terms other than fall.
**Special programs:** Credit and/or placement may be granted through CEEB Advanced Placement exams for scores of 3 or higher. Credit and/or placement may be granted through CLEP general and subject exams. Credit and placement may be granted through ACT PEP and challenge exams and military and life experience.
**Transfer students:** Transfer students accepted for terms other than fall. In fall 1992, 36% of all new students were transfers into all classes. 1,972 transfer applications were received, 1,850 were accepted. Application deadline is June 15 for fall; November 15 for spring. Minimum 2.0 GPA required. Lowest course grade accepted is "C." Maximum number of transferable credits is 90 semester hours. At least 32 semester hours must be completed at the college to receive degree.
**Admissions contact:** Audley Bridges, Acting Director of Admissions. 908 527-2195.

**FINANCIAL AID. Available aid:** Pell grants, SEOG, state scholarships, and aid for undergraduate foreign students. Perkins Loans (NDSL), PLUS, and Stafford Loans (GSL).
**Financial aid statistics:** 50% of aid is not need-based. In 1992-93, 57% of all undergraduate applicants received aid; 77% of freshman applicants. Average amounts of aid awarded freshmen: Scholarships and grants, $900; loans, $1,500.
**Supporting data/closing dates:** FAFSA/FAF/FFS: Accepted on rolling basis.
**Financial aid contact:** Patricia D. Early, M.A., Director of Financial Aid. 908 527-2855.

**STUDENT EMPLOYMENT.** College Work/Study Program. Institutional employment. 13% of full-time undergraduates work on campus during school year. Students may expect to earn an average of $1,000 during school year. Off-campus part-time employment opportunities rated "excellent."

**COMPUTER FACILITIES.** 680 IBM/IBM-compatible, Macintosh/Apple, and RISC-/UNIX-based microcomputers; 250 are networked. Students may access IBM, Prime, SUN minicomputer/mainframe systems, Internet. Computer languages and software packages include Lotus 1-2-3, Turbo Pascal, WordPerfect. Computer facilities are available to all students.
**Fees:** None.

# Monmouth College

**West Long Branch, NJ 07764-1898 908 571-3400**

**1994-95 Costs.** Tuition: $12,480. Room & board: $5,290. Fees, books, misc. academic expenses (school's estimate): $490.
**Enrollment.** Undergraduates: 830 men, 965 women (full-time). Freshman class: 2,223 applicants, 1,816 accepted, 436 enrolled. Graduate enrollment: 763 men, 681 women.
**Test score averages/ranges.** Average SAT scores: 437 verbal, 489 math.
**Faculty.** 156 full-time; 130 part-time. 70% of faculty holds doctoral degree. Student/faculty ratio: 15 to 1.
**Selectivity rating.** Less competitive.

**PROFILE.** Monmouth, founded in 1933, is a private, liberal arts college. Its 125-acre campus is located in West Long Branch, 50 miles south of New York City.

**Accreditation:** MSACS. Professionally accredited by the Accreditation Board for Engineering and Technology, the Council on Social Work Education, the National League for Nursing.
**Religious orientation:** Monmouth College is nonsectarian; no religious requirements.
**Library:** Collections totaling over 240,677 volumes, 1,490 periodical subscriptions, and 275,485 microform items.
**Special facilities/museums:** Art museum, instructional media center, on-campus lab school.
**Athletic facilities:** Gymnasium, athletic fields, tennis courts, swimming pool, track, weight room.

**STUDENT BODY. Undergraduate profile:** 93% are state residents; 50% are transfers. 3% Asian-American, 5% Black, 5% Hispanic, 84% White, 3% Other. Average age of undergraduates is 22.
**Freshman profile:** 2% of freshmen who took SAT scored 700 or over on math; 3% scored 600 or over on verbal, 14% scored 600 or over on math; 22% scored 500 or over on verbal, 45% scored 500 or over on math; 69% scored 400 or over on verbal, 85% scored 400 or over on math; 99% scored 300 or over on verbal, 99% scored 300 or over on math. Majority of accepted applicants took SAT.

**Undergraduate achievement:** 15% of students who completed a degree program immediately went on to graduate study.
**Foreign students:** 38 students are from out of the country. Countries represented include China, Greece, India, Kuwait, Taiwan, and the United Kingdom.

**PROGRAMS OF STUDY. Degrees:** B.A., B.S., B.S.Nurs., B.Soc.Work.
**Majors:** Anthropology, Art, Biology, Business Administration, Chemistry, Communications/Speech, Computer Science, Criminal Justice, Education, Electronics Engineering, English, Finance, Foreign Languages/Multiple Emphasis, History, History/Political Science, Mathematics, Medical Technology, Music, Music Education, Nursing, Philosophy, Physics, Physics/Computer Science, Political Science/Government, Psychology, Social Work, Sociology, Special Education.
**Distribution of degrees:** The majors with the highest enrollment are business administration, education, and communications; anthropology, art, and music have the lowest.
**Requirements:** General education requirement.
**Academic regulations:** Freshmen must maintain minimum 1.6 GPA; sophomores, 1.8 GPA; juniors, 2.0 GPA; seniors, 2.0 GPA.
**Special:** Minors offered in most majors and in theatre and women's studies. Courses offered in German, Hebrew, Italian, Latin, physical education, religious studies, and Russian. Certificate programs offered in African American studies and computer science. Program offered in development of leadership and social responsibility. Associate's degrees offered. Self-designed majors. Double majors. Dual degrees. Independent study. Accelerated study. Internships. Cooperative education programs. Graduate school at which undergraduates may take graduate-level courses. Preprofessional programs in law, medicine, and veterinary science. 3-1 medical technology program. Five-year B.S./M.B.A. program. Member of New Jersey Marine Science Consortium. Washington Semester. Teacher certification in early childhood, elementary, secondary, and special education. Study abroad in England, France, Peru, and Spain. ROTC at Rutgers U.
**Honors:** Honors program. Honor societies.
**Academic Assistance:** Remedial reading, writing, math, and study skills. Nonremedial tutoring.

**STUDENT LIFE. Housing:** Students may live on or off campus. Coed, women's, and men's dorms. School-owned/operated apartments. 50% of students live in college housing.
**Social atmosphere:** According to the student newspaper, those who gather on campus congregate at the student center and dining hall. Popular events include a formal ball and concerts featuring big-name musicians. Greeks and the radio station are influential on campus.
**Services and counseling/handicapped student services:** Placement services. Health service. Women's center. Day care. Counseling services for minority and older students. Birth control, personal, and psychological counseling. Career and academic guidance services. Physically disabled student services. Learning disabled program/services. Notetaking services. Tape recorders. Tutors. Reader services for the blind.
**Campus organizations:** Undergraduate student government. Student newspaper (Outlook, published once/week). Literary magazine. Yearbook. Radio station. Music, dance, and theatre groups, Council for Exceptional Children, Democratic Club, karate club, Oral Interpretation Society, Rotaract, Resident Hall Association, student activities club, athletic, departmental, and service groups, 72 organizations in all. Six fraternities, no chapter houses; five sororities, no chapter houses. 8% of men join a fraternity. 13% of women join a sorority.
**Religious organizations:** Christian Ambassadors.
**Minority/foreign student organizations:** African-American Student Union, Hispanic-American Club. International Student Club.

**ATHLETICS. Physical education requirements:** Two semesters of physical education required.
**Intercollegiate competition:** 20% of students participate. Baseball (M), cheerleading (M,W), cross-country (M,W), football (M), golf (M), soccer (M,W), softball (W), tennis (M,W), track (indoor) (M,W), track (outdoor) (M,W), track and field (indoor) (M,W), track and field (outdoor) (M,W). Member of ECAC, NCAA Division I, NCAA Division I-AA for football, Northeast Conference.
**Intramural and club sports:** 25% of students participate. Intramural basketball, flag football, floor hockey, softball, volleyball.

**ADMISSIONS. Academic basis for candidate selection** (in order of priority): Standardized test scores, secondary school record, class rank, school's recommendation, essay.
**Nonacademic basis for candidate selection:** Particular talent or ability is important. Character and personality, extracurricular participation, and alumni/ae relationship are considered.
**Requirements:** Graduation from secondary school is required; GED is accepted. 16 units and the following program of study are required: 4 units of English, 2 units of math, 2 units of science including 1 unit of lab, 2 units of history, 6 units of academic electives. Minimum combined SAT score of 900, rank in top three-fifths of secondary school class, and minimum 2.0 GPA required. R.N. required of nursing program applicants. Educational Opportunity Fund and Edward G. Schlaefer programs for applicants not normally admissible. SAT is required. ACH recommended. Campus visit and interview recommended. Off-campus interviews available with an admissions representative.
**Procedure:** Take SAT by January of 12th year. Visit college for interview by March of 12th year. Suggest filing application by January 1. Application deadline is March 1. Notification of admission on rolling basis. Reply is required by May 1. $160 nonrefundable tuition deposit. $160 nonrefundable room deposit. Freshmen accepted in terms other than fall.
**Special programs:** Admission may be deferred one year. Credit may be granted through CEEB Advanced Placement for scores of 3 or higher. Credit may be granted through CLEP general and subject exams, military and life experience. Credit and placement may be granted through challenge exams. Early decision program. Deadline for applying for early decision is January 1. Concurrent enrollment program.
**Transfer students:** Transfer students accepted for terms other than fall. In fall 1992, 50% of all new students were transfers into all classes. 746 transfer applications were received, 561 were accepted. Application deadline is rolling for fall; rolling for spring. Minimum 2.0 GPA required. Lowest course grade accepted is "C." Maximum number of transferable credits is 72 semester hours from a two-year school and 96 semester hours from a four-year school. At least 56 semester hours must be completed at the college to receive degree.
**Admissions contact:** Barry Ward, M.B.A., Director of Admissions. 908 571-3456, 800 543-9671.

**FINANCIAL AID. Available aid:** Pell grants, SEOG, state scholarships and grants, school scholarships and grants, academic merit scholarships, and athletic scholarships. Perkins Loans (NDSL), PLUS, Stafford Loans (GSL), state loans, school loans, and SLS. Knight Tuition Plans, EFI Fund Management, family tuition reduction, and guaranteed tuition.
**Financial aid statistics:** 25% of aid is not need-based. In 1992-93, 63% of all undergraduate applicants received aid; 75% of freshman applicants.
**Supporting data/closing dates:** FAFSA/FAF/FFS: Priority filing date is March 1. School's own aid application: Priority filing date is March 1. Income tax forms: Priority filing date is March 1. Notification of awards begins March 10.
**Financial aid contact:** Hank Mackiewicz, M.A., Director of Financial Aid. 908 571-3463.

**STUDENT EMPLOYMENT.** College Work/Study Program. Institutional employment. 8% of full-time undergraduates work on campus during school year. Off-campus part-time employment opportunities rated "good."

**COMPUTER FACILITIES.** 100 IBM/IBM-compatible microcomputers; 50 are networked. Students may access AT&T, Digital, SUN minicomputer/mainframe systems. Computer languages and software packages include Ada, BASIC, COBOL, Crystal Writer, dBASE, FORTRAN, Lotus 1-2-3, Pascal, SPSS, WordPerfect, numerous other spreadsheet, statistical, and word processing programs. Computer facilities are available to all students.
**Fees:** Computer fee is included in tuition/fees.
**Hours:** 8 AM-midn.

**GRADUATE CAREER DATA.** Highest graduate school enrollments: Monmouth Coll, New Jersey Inst of Tech, Rutgers U. 75% of graduates choose careers in business and industry. Companies and businesses that hire graduates: AT&T, Coopers & Lybrand, Internal Revenue Service.

**PROMINENT ALUMNI/AE.** Bartholomew P. Donohue, product management engineering vice-president, AT&T Information Management Services; Stanley S. Bey, business owner; Dr. Yvonne Thornton, consultant in prenatal obstetrics, Morristown Memorial Hospital.

# Montclair State College

**Upper Montclair, NJ 07043-1624 — 201 893-4000**

**1993-94 Costs.** Tuition: $2,285 (state residents), $3,456 (out-of-state). Room & board: $4,700. Fees, books, misc. academic expenses (school's estimate): $1,184.
**Enrollment.** Undergraduates: 2,697 men, 3,966 women (full-time). Freshman class: 5,681 applicants, 2,268 accepted, 916 enrolled. Graduate enrollment: 1,108 men, 2,484 women.
**Test score averages/ranges.** Range of SAT scores of middle 50%: 431-513 verbal, 480-566 math.
**Faculty.** 420 full-time; 396 part-time. 85% of faculty holds highest degree in specific field. Student/faculty ratio: 15 to 1.
**Selectivity rating.** Competitive.

**PROFILE.** Montclair State, founded in 1908, is a public, liberal arts college. Programs are offered through the Colleges of Business Administration, Fine and Performing Arts, Humanities and Social Sciences, Mathematical and Natural Sciences, and Professional Studies. Its 200-acre campus is located in Upper Montclair, 30 miles northwest of Newark.

**Accreditation:** MSACS. Professionally accredited by the American Dietetic Association, the American Home Economics Association, the American Speech-Language-Hearing Association, the National Association of Schools of Art and Design, the National Association of Schools of Music, the National Council for Accreditation of Teacher Education, the National Recreation and Park Association.
**Religious orientation:** Montclair State College is nonsectarian; no religious requirements.
**Library:** Collections totaling over 388,527 volumes, 3,397 periodical subscriptions, and 1,030,039 microform items.
**Athletic facilities:** Gymnasium, field house, basketball, tennis, and volleyball courts, swimming pool, track, athletic fields, weight rooms.

**STUDENT BODY. Undergraduate profile:** 99% are state residents; 43% are transfers. 3% Asian-American, 8% Black, 11% Hispanic, 64% White, 14% Other. Average age of undergraduates is 19.
**Freshman profile:** 1% of freshmen who took SAT scored 700 or over on math; 5% scored 600 or over on verbal, 17% scored 600 or over on math; 33% scored 500 or over on verbal, 71% scored 500 or over on math; 88% scored 400 or over on verbal, 99% scored 400 or over on math; 99% scored 300 or over on verbal, 100% scored 300 or over on math. 100% of accepted applicants took SAT. 85% of freshmen come from public schools.
**Undergraduate achievement:** 84% of fall 1991 freshmen returned for fall 1992 term. 30% of entering class graduated.
**Foreign students:** 217 students are from out of the country. Countries represented include China, Cyprus, India, Japan, Kenya, and Peru; 98 in all.

**PROGRAMS OF STUDY. Degrees:** B.A., B.F.A., B.Mus., B.S.
**Majors:** Allied Health Services, Anthropology, Biochemistry, Biology, Business Administration, Business Education, Chemistry, Classics, Computer Science, Dance, Economics, English, Fine Arts, French, Geography, Geoscience, German, Health Education, History, Home Economics, Humanities, Industrial Technology/Education, Italian, Latin, Linguistics, Mathematics, Molecular Biology, Music, Music Therapy, Philosophy, Physical Education, Physics, Political Science, Psychology, Recreation Professions, Religious Studies, Sociology, Spanish, Speech/Theatre, Theatre.

**Distribution of degrees:** The majors with the highest enrollment are business administration, psychology, and English; linguistics, geoscience, and Latin have the lowest.
**Requirements:** General education requirement.
**Academic regulations:** Freshmen must maintain minimum 1.6 GPA; sophomores, 1.8 GPA; juniors, 2.0 GPA; seniors, 2.0 GPA.
**Special:** Minors offered in many majors and in over 20 other fields. Double majors. Pass/fail grading option. Internships. Cooperative education programs. Graduate school at which undergraduates may take graduate-level courses. Preprofessional programs in law, medicine, pharmacy, and dentistry. Five-year bachelor's/master's practical anthropology program. Member of New Jersey Marine Sciences Consortium. Washington Semester. Teacher certification in early childhood, elementary, secondary, special education, vo-tech, and bilingual/bicultural education. Certification in specific subject areas. Member of International Student Exchange Program (ISEP). Exchange programs abroad in Denmark (U of Copenhagen), England, Ireland (U of Limerick), Israel U (Hebrew U of Jerusalem, U of Tel Aviv), Mexico (U of Guadalajara), and Scotland (Duncan of Jordanstone Coll of Art in Dundee). Study abroad also in China, Colombia, Cyprus, Ecuador, Germany, Greece, Italy, Jamaica, Portugal, Spain, Sweden, and Switzerland. ROTC at Seton Hall U. AFROTC at New Jersey Inst of Tech.
**Honors:** Honors program.
**Academic Assistance:** Remedial reading, writing, math, and study skills.

**STUDENT LIFE. Housing:** Students may live on or off campus. Coed, women's, and men's dorms. School-owned/operated apartments. Off-campus privately-owned housing. 20% of students live in college housing.
**Social atmosphere:** As reported by the student newspaper, campus social life suffers from an abundance of commuting students. However, fraternities, sororities, the school newspaper and yearbook, and the Student Government Association have some influence on campus. Popular campus events include Homecoming, Carnival, Spring Day, various concerts, drama productions, lip sync contests, and Latin Month.
**Services and counseling/handicapped student services:** Placement services. Health service. Women's center. Day care. Counseling services for minority, veteran, and older students. Birth control, personal, and psychological counseling. Career and academic guidance services.
**Campus organizations:** Undergraduate student government. Student newspaper (Montclarion, published once/week). Literary magazine. Yearbook. Radio station. Class One Concerts, drama group, human relations organization, conservation club, 86 organizations in all.
**Religious organizations:** Jewish Student Union, Newman Community, Chi Alpha, Protestant Foundation, Intervarsity Christian Fellowship.
**Minority/foreign student organizations:** Organization of Students for African Unity, Latin American Student Organization. International Student Organization.

**ATHLETICS. Physical education requirements:** One semester hour of physical education required.
**Intercollegiate competition:** 43% of students participate. Baseball (M), basketball (M,W), cheerleading (M,W), cross-country (M,W), diving (M,W), field hockey (W), football (M), golf (M), lacrosse (M), soccer (M,W), softball (W), swimming (M,W), tennis (M,W), track and field (indoor) (M,W), track and field (outdoor) (M,W), volleyball (W), wrestling (M). Member of ECAC, Metropolitan Collegiate Athletic Conference, NCAA Division III, New Jersey Athletic Conference.
**Intramural and club sports:** 78% of students participate. Intramural basketball, flag football, softball, volleyball, water polo. Men's club bowling, Nordic skiing.

**ADMISSIONS. Academic basis for candidate selection** (in order of priority): Secondary school record, class rank, standardized test scores, school's recommendation, essay.
**Nonacademic basis for candidate selection:** Extracurricular participation and particular talent or ability are important.
**Requirements:** Graduation from secondary school is required; GED is accepted. 16 units and the following program of study are required: 4 units of English, 3 units of math, 2 units of lab science, 2 units of foreign language, 2 units of social studies, 3 units of academic electives. Minimum combined SAT score of 1000 and rank in top quarter of secondary school class recommended. Algebra II required of business administration program applicants. 4 units of mathematics, including trigonometry, required of computer science program applicants. Portfolio, audition, and/or interview required of broadcasting, dance, fine arts, music, speech communication, and theatre program applicants. Educational Opportunity Fund (EOF), Program for Academic Student Support (PASS), and Special Talent Admission for applicants not normally admissible. SAT is required. Campus visit and interview recommended. Off-campus interviews available with an admissions representative.
**Procedure:** Take SAT by January of 12th year. Application deadline is March 1. Notification of admission on rolling basis. Reply is required by May 1. $50 nonrefundable tuition deposit. $60 room deposit, refundable if applicant decides not to attend Montclair. Freshmen accepted in terms other than fall.
**Special programs:** Admission may be deferred one year. Credit and/or placement may be granted through CEEB Advanced Placement exams for scores of 3 or higher. Credit may be granted through CLEP general and subject exams. Credit may be granted through Regents College, DANTES, and challenge exams and military and life experience.
**Transfer students:** Transfer students accepted for terms other than fall. In fall 1992, 43% of all new students were transfers into all classes. 1,969 transfer applications were received, 983 were accepted. Application deadline is May 1 for fall; October 15 for spring. Minimum 2.5 GPA required. Lowest course grade accepted is "C." Maximum number of transferable credits is 96 semester hours. At least 32 semester hours must be completed at the college to receive degree.
**Admissions contact:** Alan Buechler, Ed.D., Director of Admissions. 800 331-9205.

**FINANCIAL AID. Available aid:** Pell grants, SEOG, state scholarships and grants, school scholarships, and academic merit scholarships. Perkins Loans (NDSL), PLUS, Stafford Loans (GSL), state loans, and SLS.
**Financial aid statistics:** In 1992-93, 55% of all undergraduate applicants received aid; 55% of freshman applicants. Average amounts of aid awarded freshmen: Scholarships and grants, $500; loans, $2,500.
**Supporting data/closing dates:** FAFSA/FAF: Priority filing date is March 1. Notification of awards begins April 1.
**Financial aid contact:** Randall W. Richards, Ed.D., Director of Financial Aid. 201 893-4461.

**STUDENT EMPLOYMENT.** College Work/Study Program. Institutional employment. 8% of full-time undergraduates work on campus during school year. Students may expect to earn an average of $900 during school year. Off-campus part-time employment opportunities rated "good."

**COMPUTER FACILITIES.** 450 IBM/IBM-compatible and Macintosh/Apple microcomputers; 300 are networked. Students may access Digital, SUN minicomputer/mainframe systems, Internet. Client/LAN operating systems include Apple/Macintosh, LocalTalk/AppleTalk. Computer languages and software packages include C, FORTRAN, INGRES, LISP, Maple, Pascal, SAS, SPSS; 50 in all. Computer facilities are available to all students.
**Fees:** None.
**Hours:** 8 AM-midn (on-site use); 24 hours (modem use).

**PROMINENT ALUMNI/AE.** Marge Roukema, U.S. congresswoman; Jeff Torborg, manager, New York Mets; Eugene T. Maleska, editor, *New York Times* crossword puzzle.

# New Jersey Institute of Technology

**Newark, NJ 07102-1982** **201 596-3000**

**1993-94 Costs.** Tuition: $4,198 (state residents), $8,759 (out-of-state). Room & board: $5,175. Fees, books, misc. academic expenses (school's estimate): $1,492.
**Enrollment.** Undergraduates: 2,784 men, 527 women (full-time). Freshman class: 1,879 applicants, 1,216 accepted, 483 enrolled. Graduate enrollment: 1,917 men, 677 women.
**Test score averages/ranges.** Average SAT scores: 466 verbal, 600 math. Range of SAT scores of middle 50%: 410-530 verbal, 550-650 math.
**Faculty.** 327 full-time; 140 part-time. 98% of faculty holds highest degree in specific field. Student/faculty ratio: 13 to 1.
**Selectivity rating.** Competitive.

**PROFILE.** New Jersey Institute of Technology, founded in 1881, is a public, technical institution. The campus is located in downtown Newark.

**Accreditation:** MSACS. Professionally accredited by the Accreditation Board for Engineering and Technology, the National Architecture Accrediting Board.
**Religious orientation:** New Jersey Institute of Technology is nonsectarian; no religious requirements.
**Library:** Collections totaling over 134,500 volumes, 1,233 periodical subscriptions, and 3,723 microform items.
**Special facilities/museums:** Hazardous waste management research center.
**Athletic facilities:** Gymnasiums, fitness center, swimming pool, fencing, free weight, martial arts, and wrestling rooms, bowling lanes, basketball, racquetball, and tennis courts, athletic fields, soccer stadium, track, aerobics/dance studio, sauna.

**STUDENT BODY. Undergraduate profile:** 97% are state residents; 48% are transfers. 17% Asian-American, 13% Black, 13% Hispanic, .5% Native American, 53% White, 3.5% Other. Average age of undergraduates is 22.
**Freshman profile:** 10% of freshmen who took SAT scored 700 or over on math; 7% scored 600 or over on verbal, 49% scored 600 or over on math; 35% scored 500 or over on verbal, 96% scored 500 or over on math; 81% scored 400 or over on verbal, 100% scored 400 or over on math; 96% scored 300 or over on verbal. 100% of accepted applicants took SAT. 80% of freshmen come from public schools.
**Undergraduate achievement:** 80% of fall 1992 freshmen returned for fall 1993 term. 42% of entering class graduated. 10% of students who completed a degree program immediately went on to graduate study.
**Foreign students:** 222 students are from out of the country. Countries represented include China, India, Pakistan, and Taiwan; 45 in all.

**PROGRAMS OF STUDY. Degrees:** B.A., B.Arch., B.S.
**Majors:** Applied Chemistry, Applied Mathematics, Applied Physics, Architecture, Chemical Engineering, Civil Engineering, Computer Engineering, Computer Science, Electrical Engineering, Engineering Science, Engineering Technology, Industrial Engineering, Information Processing Systems, Management, Manufacturing Engineering, Materials Science/Engineering, Mechanical Engineering, Science/Technology/Society, Statistics/Actuarial Science.
**Distribution of degrees:** The majors with the highest enrollment are electrical engineering, engineering technology, and mechanical engineering; applied chemistry, applied mathematics, and applied physics have the lowest.
**Requirements:** General education requirement.
**Academic regulations:** Minimum 2.0 GPA must be maintained.
**Special:** Courses offered in art, economics, English, environmental engineering, history, humanities, management engineering, materials science, nuclear engineering, organizational science, and philosophy. Corrective Writing Program required of some students. Self-designed majors. Double majors. Dual degrees. Independent study. Internships. Cooperative education programs. Preprofessional programs in medicine and dentistry. 2-2 engineering, engineering technology, and management programs. 3-2 engineering/liberal arts programs with Lincoln U, Seton Hall U, and Upsala Coll. Cross-registration with Essex County Coll, Rutgers U, and U of Medicine and Dentistry of New Jersey. Exchange programs abraod in France (Inst National Des Sciences Appliquees) and Germany (Fachhochschule). AFROTC.
**Honors:** Honors program. Honor societies.
**Academic Assistance:** Remedial reading, writing, math, and study skills. Nonremedial tutoring.

**STUDENT LIFE. Housing:** Students may live on or off campus. Coed dorms. 25% of students live in college housing.

**Social atmosphere:** Popular spots include the Pub, Jasmine's, McGovern's, and fraternity houses. Greeks and the National Society of Black Engineers influence student social life. Eagerly anticipated social events include Greek parties, World Week, and Spring Week. "The student body is a mix of many diverse cultures and races," reports the editor of the student newspaper. Many students go home for the weekend.
**Services and counseling/handicapped student services:** Placement services. Health service. Counseling services for minority, military, veteran, and older students. Personal and psychological counseling. Career and academic guidance services. Physically disabled student services. Learning disabled services.
**Campus organizations:** Undergraduate student government. Student newspaper (Vector, published once/week). Yearbook. Radio station. Drama group, Society of Women Engineers, band, chess and outing clubs, athletic and professional groups, 45 organizations in all. 18 fraternities, 14 chapter houses; seven sororities, no chapter houses. 18% of men join a fraternity. 19% of women join a sorority.
**Religious organizations:** Christian Fellowship.
**Minority/foreign student organizations:** Hispanic Organization of Students in Technology, Black Association of Student Engineers. International Student Association, Chinese and Indian groups.

**ATHLETICS. Physical education requirements:** Two semesters of physical education required.
**Intercollegiate competition:** 7% of students participate. Baseball (M), basketball (M,W), bowling (M,W), cross-country (M,W), fencing (M,W), golf (M), soccer (M), softball (W), tennis (M,W), volleyball (M,W). Member of Eastern Intercollegiate Volleyball Association, ECAC, IAC, Jersey Nine Association, NCAA Division III, Skyline Conference, WIAC.
**Intramural and club sports:** 50% of students participate. Intramural archery, badminton, basketball, bowling, flag football, floor hockey, free-throw, indoor soccer, pentathlon, racquetball, soccer, softball, swimming, tennis, track and field, turkey trot, volleyball, weight lifting. Men's club Alpine skiing, cheerleading, ice hockey, martial arts, swimming, track & field. Women's club Alpine skiing, cheerleading, martial arts, soccer, swimming, track & field.

**ADMISSIONS. Academic basis for candidate selection** (in order of priority): Secondary school record, standardized test scores, school's recommendation, class rank, essay.
**Nonacademic basis for candidate selection:** Character and personality, extracurricular participation, and particular talent or ability are considered.
**Requirements:** Graduation from secondary school is required; GED is accepted. 16 units and the following program of study are required: 4 units of English, 4 units of math, 2 units of lab science, 4 units of electives. Portfolio required of architecture program applicants. A.A.S. (or equivalent) required of engineering technology program applicants. EOP for applicants not normally admissible. Conditional admission possible for applicants not meeting standard requirements. SAT is required; ACT may be substituted. ACH required. Campus visit and interview recommended. No off-campus interviews.
**Procedure:** Take SAT or ACT by November of 12th year. Take ACH by November of 12th year. Visit college for interview by February of 12th year. Suggest filing application by March 1. Application deadline is April 1. Notification of admission on rolling basis. Reply is required by May 1. $100 nonrefundable tuition deposit. $80 nonrefundable room deposit. Freshmen accepted in terms other than fall.
**Special programs:** Credit may be granted through CEEB Advanced Placement for scores of 3 or higher. Credit may be granted through CLEP subject exams and challenge exams. Placement may be granted through DANTES exams. Credit and placement may be granted through ACT PEP exams. Early decision program. In fall 1993, 108 applied for early decision and 30 were accepted. Deadline for applying for early decision is December 1. Early entrance/early admission program.
**Transfer students:** Transfer students accepted for terms other than fall. In fall 1993, 48% of all new students were transfers into all classes. 1,039 transfer applications were received, 639 were accepted. Application deadline is May 1 (architecture), June 1 (others) for fall; November 1 (architecture), December 1 (others) for spring. Minimum 2.5 GPA recommended. Lowest course grade accepted is "C." Maximum number of transferable credits varies according to program. At least 33 semester hours must be completed at the university to receive degree.
**Admissions contact:** Kathryn Kelly, M.A., Director of Admissions. 201 596-3300.

**FINANCIAL AID. Available aid:** Pell grants, SEOG, state scholarships and grants, school scholarships and grants, private scholarships and grants, ROTC scholarships, and academic merit scholarships. Perkins Loans (NDSL), PLUS, Stafford Loans (GSL), school loans, and SLS. Deferred payment plan.
**Financial aid statistics:** 8% of aid is not need-based. In 1993-94, 86% of all undergraduate applicants received aid; 73% of freshman applicants. Average amounts of aid awarded freshmen: Scholarships and grants, $4,541; loans, $2,593.
**Supporting data/closing dates:** FAFSA/FAF: Priority filing date is March 15. School's own aid application: Priority filing date is March 15. State aid form: Priority filing date is March 15. Income tax forms: Priority filing date is March 15. Notification of awards on rolling basis.
**Financial aid contact:** Kaveh Kamiar, M.B.A., Acting Director of Financial Aid. 201 596-3480.

**STUDENT EMPLOYMENT.** College Work/Study Program. Institutional employment. 20% of full-time undergraduates work on campus during school year. Students may expect to earn an average of $2,333 during school year. Freshmen are discouraged from working during their first term. Off-campus part-time employment opportunities rated "good."

**COMPUTER FACILITIES.** 3,000 IBM/IBM-compatible, Macintosh/Apple, and RISC-/UNIX-based microcomputers; 400 are networked. Students may access AT&T, Cray, Digital, Hewlett-Packard, IBM, SUN minicomputer/mainframe systems, Internet. Residence halls may be equipped with stand-alone microcomputers, networked microcomputers, networked terminals, modems. Client/LAN operating systems include Apple/Macintosh, DOS, OS/2, UNIX/XENIX/AIX, X-windows, DEC, LocalTalk/AppleTalk, Novell. 100 major computer languages and software packages available. Computer facilities are available to all students.
**Fees:** $70 computer fee per semester.

**GRADUATE CAREER DATA.** Graduate school percentages: 2% enter law school. 1% enter medical school. 1% enter dental school. 2% enter graduate business programs. 4% enter graduate arts and sciences programs. 90% of graduates choose careers in business and industry. Companies and businesses that hire graduates: AT&T, Allied Signal, General Electric, IBM, PSE & G.

# Princeton University

**Princeton, NJ 08544 — 609 258-3000**

**1994-95 Costs.** Tuition: $19,900. Room: $2,696. Board: $3,214. Fees, books, misc. academic expenses (school's estimate): $2,165.
**Enrollment.** Undergraduates: 2,549 men, 1,976 women (full-time). Freshman class: 12,857 applicants, 2,041 accepted, 1,140 enrolled. Graduate enrollment: 1,259 men, 654 women.
**Test score averages/ranges.** Range of SAT scores of middle 50%: 600-700 verbal, 660-750 math.
**Faculty.** 774 full-time; 161 part-time. 99% of faculty holds highest degree in specific field. Student/faculty ratio: 6 to 1.
**Selectivity rating.** Most competitive.

**PROFILE.** Princeton, founded in 1746, is a private, Ivy League, comprehensive university. Its 1,000-acre campus is located in a residential section of Princeton, 50 miles southwest of New York City. The main campus includes Georgian and Gothic architectural styles and contemporary structures by I.M. Pei and Robert Venturi.
**Accreditation:** MSACS. Professionally accredited by the Accreditation Board for Engineering and Technology, the National Architecture Accrediting Board.
**Religious orientation:** Princeton University is nonsectarian; no religious requirements.
**Library:** Collections totaling over 4,713,716 volumes, 34,287 periodical subscriptions, and 2,400,000 microform items.
**Special facilities/museums:** Art and natural history museums, supercomputer at John von Neumann Center, energy and environmental studies center, plasma physics lab.
**Athletic facilities:** Gymnasiums, field house, ice rink, swimming pools, aerobics, fencing, Nautilus, and weight rooms, athletic fields, stadium, basketball, squash, tennis, and volleyball courts, rowing course, boathouse, golf course, track.

**STUDENT BODY. Undergraduate profile:** 14% are state residents. 9% Asian-American, 6% Black, 6% Hispanic, 72% White, 7% Other. Average age of undergraduates is 20.
**Freshman profile:** 29% of freshmen who took SAT scored 700 or over on verbal, 59% scored 700 or over on math; 78% scored 600 or over on verbal, 93% scored 600 or over on math; 98% scored 500 or over on verbal, 100% scored 500 or over on math; 100% scored 400 or over on verbal. Majority of accepted applicants took SAT. 56% of freshmen come from public schools.
**Undergraduate achievement:** 98% of fall 1991 freshmen returned for fall 1992 term. 95% of entering class graduated.
**Foreign students:** 265 students are from out of the country. 60 countries represented in all.

**PROGRAMS OF STUDY. Degrees:** A.B., B.S.Eng.
**Majors:** Anthropology, Architecture, Art/Archaeology, Astrophysics, Biology, Chemical Engineering, Chemistry, Civil Engineering, Classics, Comparative Literature, Computer Science, East Asian Studies, Economics, Electrical Engineering, English, Geological/Geophysical Sciences, German Language/Literature, History, Mathematics, Mechanical/Aerospace Engineering, Molecular Biology, Music, Near Eastern Studies, Philosophy, Physics, Politics, Psychology, Public/International Affairs, Religion, Romance Languages/Literature, Slavic Languages/Literatures, Sociology.
**Distribution of degrees:** The majors with the highest enrollment are history, politics, and English; Slavic languages/literatures, Near Eastern studies, and astrophysics have the lowest.
**Requirements:** General education requirement.
**Special:** Self-designed majors. Independent study. Pass/fail grading option. Graduate school at which undergraduates may take graduate-level courses. Preprofessional programs in law and medicine. Member of Consortium for Scientific Computing. Exchange programs with Princeton Theological Seminary, Rutgers U, and Westminster Choir Coll. Study abroad in over 30 countries. ROTC. AFROTC at Rutgers U.
**Honors:** Phi Beta Kappa. Honors program.
**Academic Assistance:** Nonremedial tutoring.

**STUDENT LIFE. Housing:** All freshmen and sophomores must live on campus. Coed, women's, and men's dorms. School-owned/operated apartments. Off-campus married-student housing. 98% of students live in college housing.
**Services and counseling/handicapped student services:** Placement services. Health service. Women's center. Counseling services for minority students. Birth control, personal, and psychological counseling. Career and academic guidance services. Religious counseling.
**Campus organizations:** Undergraduate student government. Student newspaper (Daily Princetonian). Literary magazine. Yearbook. Radio station. Orchestra, band, chamber chorus, chapel choir, glee club, informal music groups, debating, public speaking, Community House, student volunteers council, 200 organizations in all.
**Religious organizations:** Bahai Club, Christian Science Organization, Hillel, Yavneh, Latter-Day Saints.
**Minority/foreign student organizations:** Black, Chicano, Puerto Rican, Asian, and Native American groups. International Student Association.

**ATHLETICS. Physical education requirements:** Physical education required of freshmen.
**Intercollegiate competition:** 43% of students participate. Baseball (M), basketball (M,W), crew (M,W), cross-country (M,W), diving (M,W), fencing (M,W), field hockey (W), football (M), golf (M,W), ice hockey (M,W), lacrosse (M,W), lightweight football (M), soccer (M,W), softball (W), squash (M,W), swimming (M,W), tennis (M,W), track (indoor) (M,W), track (outdoor) (M,W), track and field (indoor) (M,W), track and field

(outdoor) (M,W), volleyball (W), wrestling (M). Member of ECAC, Ivy League, NCAA Division I.

**Intramural and club sports:** 70% of students participate. Intramural badminton, basketball, billiards, bowling, broomball, cross-country, flag football, golf, ice hockey, indoor soccer, inner-tube water polo, mini-marathon, pool, soccer, softball, squash, swimming, table tennis, tennis, track and field, volleyball. Men's club Alpine skiing, badminton, cheerleading, cycling, dance, gymnastics, horsemanship, lacrosse, martial arts, rifle, rugby, sailing, soccer, table tennis, ultimate frisbee, volleyball, water polo. Women's club Alpine skiing, badminton, cheerleading, cycling, dance, gymnastics, horsemanship, lacrosse, martial arts, rifle, rugby, sailing, soccer, table tennis, ultimate frisbee, volleyball, water polo.

**ADMISSIONS. Academic basis for candidate selection** (in order of priority): Secondary school record, class rank, school's recommendation, standardized test scores, essay.
**Nonacademic basis for candidate selection:** Character and personality, extracurricular participation, and particular talent or ability are important. Alumni/ae relationship is considered.
**Requirements:** Graduation from secondary school is required; GED is accepted. 20 units and the following program of study are recommended: 4 units of English, 4 units of math, 2 units of science, 4 units of foreign language, 2 units of history. Additional units should be chosen from social studies, science, language, art, and music. SAT is required; ACT may be substituted. ACH recommended. Campus visit and interview recommended. Off-campus interviews available with an alumni representative.
**Procedure:** Take SAT or ACT by January of 12th year. Take ACH by January of 12th year. Visit college for interview by December 31 of 12th year. Application deadline is January 2. Notification of acceptance by early April. Reply is required by May 1. Freshmen accepted in fall terms only.
**Special programs:** Admission may be deferred one year. Credit and/or placement may be granted through CEEB Advanced Placement exams for scores of 4 or higher. Placement may be granted through challenge exams. Early entrance/early admission program.
**Transfer students:** Transfer students accepted for fall term. Application deadline is April 1. Minimum 3.0 GPA recommended. Lowest course grade accepted is "C." Maximum number of transferable credits is the equivalent of two years of course work.
**Admissions contact:** Fred Hargadon, Dean of Admissions. 609 258-3060.

**FINANCIAL AID. Available aid:** Pell grants, SEOG, state scholarships and grants, school scholarships, private scholarships and grants, ROTC scholarships, and aid for undergraduate foreign students. Perkins Loans (NDSL), PLUS, Stafford Loans (GSL), school loans, and SLS. Monthly payment plan. Princeton Parent Loan Program.
**Financial aid statistics:** Average amounts of aid awarded freshmen: Scholarships and grants, $12,290; loans, $2,725.
**Supporting data/closing dates:** FAFSA/FAF: Deadline is February 1. School's own aid application: Deadline is February 1. Income tax forms: Deadline is June 1. Notification of awards begins early April.
**Financial aid contact:** Don Betterton, Director of Financial Aid. 609 258-3330.

**STUDENT EMPLOYMENT.** College Work/Study Program. Institutional employment. 60% of full-time undergraduates work on campus during school year. Students may expect to earn an average of $1,000 during school year. Off-campus part-time employment opportunities rated "excellent."

**COMPUTER FACILITIES.** 438 IBM/IBM-compatible, Macintosh/Apple, and RISC-/UNIX-based microcomputers. Students may access IBM, SUN minicomputer/mainframe systems. Residence halls may be equipped with networked microcomputers, networked terminals, modems. Computer languages and software packages include C, FORTRAN, PL/1; numerous database, spreadsheet, statistical, word processing packages. Computer facilities are available to all students.
**Fees:** None.
**Hours:** 24 hours.

**PROMINENT ALUMNI/AE.** Bill Bradley, U.S. senator; James Baker, former U.S. secretary of state; Jimmy Stewart, actor; Lewis Thomas, physician and author; Lee Iacocca, president, Chrysler Corp.

# Ramapo College of New Jersey

**Mahwah, NJ 07430** **201 529-7500**

**1994-95 Costs.** Tuition: $2,456 (state residents), $3,800 (out-of-state). Room: $3,400. Board: $1,400. Fees, books, misc. academic expenses (school's estimate): $1,400.
**Enrollment.** Undergraduates: 1,461 men, 1,314 women (full-time). Freshman class: 2,300 applicants, 1,007 accepted, 457 enrolled.
**Test score averages/ranges.** Average SAT scores: 450 verbal, 490 math. Range of SAT scores of middle 50%: 420-500 verbal, 440-540 math.
**Faculty.** 136 full-time. 95% of faculty holds highest degree in specific field. Student/faculty ratio: 19 to 1.
**Selectivity rating.** Competitive.

**PROFILE.** Ramapo, founded in 1969, is a public, liberal arts college. Programs are offered through the Schools of Administration/Business, American/International Studies, Contemporary Arts, Environmental Studies, Social Science/Human Services, and Theoretical/Applied Science and the Division of Basic Studies. Its 300-acre campus is located in Mahwah, north of Newark.

**Accreditation:** MSACS. Professionally accredited by the Council on Social Work Education.
**Religious orientation:** Ramapo College of New Jersey is nonsectarian; no religious requirements.
**Library:** Collections totaling over 150,000 volumes, 1,300 periodical subscriptions, and 3,000 microform items.
**Special facilities/museums:** Art museum, media center, international telecommunications center, electron microscope.
**Athletic facilities:** Gymnasium, swimming pool, basketball and tennis courts, weight room, baseball, intramural, soccer, and softball fields, track.

**STUDENT BODY. Undergraduate profile:** 81% are state residents; 59% are transfers. 4% Asian-American, 10% Black, 4% Hispanic, 82% White. Average age of undergraduates is 21.
**Freshman profile:** 2% of freshmen who took SAT scored 700 or over on math; 4% scored 600 or over on verbal, 8% scored 600 or over on math; 22% scored 500 or over on verbal, 45% scored 500 or over on math; 80% scored 400 or over on verbal, 92% scored 400 or over on math; 100% scored 300 or over on verbal, 100% scored 300 or over on math. 98% of accepted applicants took SAT. 92% of freshmen come from public schools.
**Undergraduate achievement:** 71% of fall 1991 freshmen returned for fall 1992 term. 30% of entering class graduated. 5% of students who completed a degree program immediately went on to graduate study.
**Foreign students:** 170 students are from out of the country. Countries represented include China, India, Kenya, Namibia, Pakistan, and Sweden; 41 in all.

**PROGRAMS OF STUDY. Degrees:** B.A., B.S., B.S.Nurs., B.Soc.Work.
**Majors:** Accounting, American Studies, Biology, Business Administration, Chemistry, Communication Arts, Computer Science, Contemporary Arts, Economics, Environmental Science, Environmental Studies, Finance, Fine Arts, History, Information Systems, International Business, International Studies, Law/Society, Literature, Management, Marketing, Mathematics, Metropolitan Studies, Nursing, Philosophy, Physics, Political Science/Government, Psychology, Social Work, Sociology.
**Distribution of degrees:** The majors with the highest enrollment are business administration, communication arts, and psychology; chemistry, physics, and contemporary arts have the lowest.
**Requirements:** General education requirement.
**Academic regulations:** Minimum 2.0 GPA must be maintained.
**Special:** Minors offered in African American studies, anthropology, foreign languages, gerontology, Judaic studies, Latin American studies, public policy, substance abuse, and women's studies. Courses offered by Division of Physical Education/Athletics and Learning Skills. Self-designed majors. Double majors. Dual degrees. Independent study. Accelerated study. Pass/fail grading option. Internships. Cooperative education programs. Preprofessional programs in law, medicine, veterinary science, and dentistry. Combined degree programs in biology and chemistry with Rutgers U. Teacher certification in secondary education. Certification in specific subject areas. Exchange program abroad in England. Study abroad also in China, France, Ireland, Italy, Kenya, and the former Soviet Republics.
**Honors:** Honors program. Honor societies.
**Academic Assistance:** Remedial reading, writing, and math. Nonremedial tutoring.

**STUDENT LIFE. Housing:** Students may live on or off campus. Coed, women's, and men's dorms. School-owned/operated apartments. 45% of students live in college housing.
**Social atmosphere:** The student newspaper reports, "Basically, any good entertainment gets overlooked. Like any other college, apathy runs wild here, and yet there is quite a bit of interest in clubs, something for everyone. Earth Week in March is extremely popular. Springfest is also hot, as are the WRPR meetings. Comedy Night is also popular." Influential student groups include the Office of American Unity, WRPR, the Ramapo News, and the New Arts Alliance. Favorite gathering spots include WRPR and the Suffern Hotel.
**Services and counseling/handicapped student services:** Placement services. Health service. Women's center. Day care. Counseling services for minority, veteran, and older students. Birth control, personal, and psychological counseling. Career and academic guidance services. Physically disabled student services. Learning disabled services. Notetaking services. Tape recorders. Tutors. Reader services for the blind.
**Campus organizations:** Undergraduate student government. Student newspaper (Ramapo News, published once/week). Literary magazine. Yearbook. Radio station. Jazz band, choral group, drama group, horseback riding club, departmental groups, special-interest groups, 51 organizations in all. Eight fraternities, no chapter houses; four sororities, no chapter houses. 4% of men join a fraternity. 4% of women join a sorority.
**Religious organizations:** Intervarsity Christian Fellowship, Jewish Student Association, Newman Club.
**Minority/foreign student organizations:** Black and Latino groups. International Student Organization.

**ATHLETICS. Physical education requirements:** None.
**Intercollegiate competition:** 10% of students participate. Baseball (M), basketball (M,W), cheerleading (M,W), cross-country (M,W), football (M), golf (M), soccer (M,W), softball (W), tennis (M,W), track (outdoor) (M,W), track and field (outdoor) (M,W), volleyball (M,W). Member of ECAC, NCAA Division III, New Jersey State College Athletic Conference, WIAC.
**Intramural and club sports:** 65% of students participate. Intramural basketball, flag football, fun runs, hockey, prediction walks, softball, volleyball, water polo.

**ADMISSIONS. Academic basis for candidate selection** (in order of priority): Secondary school record, class rank, standardized test scores, school's recommendation, essay.
**Nonacademic basis for candidate selection:** Character and personality, extracurricular participation, and particular talent or ability are important.
**Requirements:** Graduation from secondary school is recommended; GED is accepted. 18 units and the following program of study are required: 4 units of English, 3 units of math, 2 units of lab science, 2 units of foreign language, 2 units of history, 5 units of academic electives. R.N. required of nursing program applicants. EOP for applicants not normally admissible. SAT is required; ACT may be substituted. ACH recommended. Campus visit and interview recommended. No off-campus interviews.
**Procedure:** Take SAT or ACT by January of 12th year. Take ACH by January of 12th year. Visit college for interview by February of 12th year. Application deadline is March 15. Notification of admission on rolling basis. Reply is required by May 1. $100 nonrefundable tuition deposit. $100 room deposit, refundable until August 1. Freshmen accepted in terms other than fall.
**Special programs:** Admission may be deferred one year. Credit and/or placement may be granted through CEEB Advanced Placement exams for scores of 3 or higher. Credit and/or placement may be granted through CLEP general and subject exams. Placement may be

granted through challenge exams. Credit and placement may be granted through Regents College, ACT PEP, and DANTES exams, and military and life experience. Early entrance/early admission program. Concurrent enrollment program.
**Transfer students:** Transfer students accepted for terms other than fall. In fall 1992, 59% of all new students were transfers into all classes. 1,189 transfer applications were received, 975 were accepted. Application deadline is May 1 for fall; November 15 for spring. Minimum 2.0 GPA required. Lowest course grade accepted is "C." Maximum number of transferable credits is 75 semester hours from a two-year school and 83 semester hours from a four-year school. At least 45 semester hours must be completed at the college to receive degree.
**Admissions contact:** Nancy E. Jaeger, Director of Admissions. 201 529-7600.

**FINANCIAL AID. Available aid:** Pell grants, SEOG, state scholarships and grants, school scholarships and grants, private scholarships, and academic merit scholarships. Perkins Loans (NDSL), PLUS, Stafford Loans (GSL), and SLS. AMS.
**Supporting data/closing dates:** FAFSA/FAF: Accepted on rolling basis. Income tax forms: Accepted on rolling basis. Notification of awards begins May 1.
**Financial aid contact:** Mark Singer, Director of Financial Aid. 201 529-7550.

**STUDENT EMPLOYMENT.** College Work/Study Program. Institutional employment. 11% of full-time undergraduates work on campus during school year. Students may expect to earn an average of $1,000 during school year. Off-campus part-time employment opportunities rated "excellent."

**COMPUTER FACILITIES.** 200 IBM/IBM-compatible and Macintosh/Apple microcomputers; 150 are networked. Students may access Digital minicomputer/mainframe systems, BITNET, Internet. Residence halls may be equipped with networked terminals. Computer languages and software packages include COBOL, dBASE, FORTRAN, Lotus 1-2-3, Microsoft Windows, Pascal, WordPerfect, others. Computer facilities are available to all students.
**Fees:** None.
**Hours:** 8 AM-10 PM.

**GRADUATE CAREER DATA.** Graduate school percentages: 2% enter law school. 1% enter medical school. 3% enter graduate business programs. 1% enter graduate arts and sciences programs. Highest graduate school enrollments: Columbia U, Fairleigh Dickinson U, Fordham U, New York U, Rutgers U. Companies and businesses that hire graduates: IBM, Sony, Union Camp, United Parcel Service.

# Rider College

**Lawrenceville, NJ 08648-3099 — 609 896-5000**

**1994-95 Costs.** Tuition: $13,250. Room: $2,840. Board: $2,580. Fees, books, misc. academic expenses (school's estimate): $600.
**Enrollment.** Undergraduates: 1,254 men, 1,522 women (full-time). Freshman class: 3,586 applicants, 2,424 accepted, 668 enrolled.
**Test score averages/ranges.** Average SAT scores: 439 verbal, 501 math. Range of SAT scores of middle 50%: 425-475 verbal, 450-525 math.
**Faculty.** 226 full-time; 187 part-time. 92% of faculty holds highest degree in specific field. Student/faculty ratio: 16 to 1.
**Selectivity rating.** Less competitive.

**PROFILE.** Rider, founded in 1865, is a private, multipurpose college. Programs are offered through the Schools of Business Administration, Continuing Studies, Education, and Liberal Arts and Science. Its 340-acre campus in Lawrenceville, two miles north of Trenton.

**Accreditation:** MSACS. Professionally accredited by the National Council for Accreditation of Teacher Education.
**Religious orientation:** Rider College is nonsectarian; no religious requirements.
**Library:** Collections totaling over 350,000 volumes, 2,000 periodical subscriptions, and 450,000 microform items.
**Special facilities/museums:** Art gallery, language lab, multicultural center, holocaust/genocide center, electron scanning microscope.
**Athletic facilities:** Gymnasiums, tennis and volleyball courts, track, fitness center, football, soccer, and softball fields, swimming pool, aerobics room.

**STUDENT BODY. Undergraduate profile:** 78% are state residents; 25% are transfers. 3% Asian-American, 7% Black, 4% Hispanic, 1% Native American, 79% White, 6% Other. Average age of undergraduates is 21.
**Freshman profile:** 1% of freshmen who took SAT scored 700 or over on verbal, 2% scored 700 or over on math; 4% scored 600 or over on verbal, 14% scored 600 or over on math; 19% scored 500 or over on verbal, 46% scored 500 or over on math; 69% scored 400 or over on verbal, 91% scored 400 or over on math; 98% scored 300 or over on verbal, 100% scored 300 or over on math. 99% of accepted applicants took SAT; 1% took ACT.
**Undergraduate achievement:** 72% of fall 1992 freshmen returned for fall 1993 term. 47% of entering class graduated. 10% of students who completed a degree program immediately went on to graduate study.
**Foreign students:** 31 students are from out of the country. Countries represented include Bangladesh, China, the Dominican Republic, India, Pakistan, and Turkey; 25 in all.

**PROGRAMS OF STUDY. Degrees:** B.A., B.S., B.S.Bus.Admin.
**Majors:** Accounting, Actuarial Sciences, Advertising, American Studies, Art, Biochemistry, Biology, Business Administration, Business Economics, Business Education, Chemistry, Computer Information Systems, Early Childhood Education, Economics, Elementary Education, English Literature, English Writing, Finance, Fine Arts, French, Geology, German, History, Human Resource Management, Journalism, Management/Organizational Behavior, Management Sciences, Marine Sciences, Marketing, Mathematics, Music, Philosophy, Physics, Political Science, Psychology, Russian, Secondary Education, Sociology, Spanish, Speech/Communication Arts, Theatre.
**Distribution of degrees:** The majors with the highest enrollment are accounting, finance, and marketing; Russian, German, and American studies have the lowest.
**Requirements:** General education requirement.
**Academic regulations:** Freshmen must maintain minimum 1.67 GPA; sophomores, 1.80 GPA; juniors, 1.90 GPA; seniors, 2.00 GPA.
**Special:** Minors offered in many majors and in communications, environmental studies, ethics, geochemistry, geosciences, international studies, Russian/Soviet studies, social work, and women's studies. Intercultural studies program is an interdisciplinary program taken in conjunction with major. Double majors. Dual degrees. Pass/fail grading option. Internships. Cooperative education programs. Graduate school at which undergraduates may take graduate-level courses. Preprofessional programs in law, medicine, veterinary science, and dentistry. Member of New Jersey Marine Science Consortium. Teacher certification in early childhood, elementary, secondary, and bilingual/bicultural education. Study abroad in Austria, England, France, Israel, Japan, Puerto Rico, and Spain. ROTC. AFROTC at Rutgers U.
**Honors:** Honors program. Honor societies.
**Academic Assistance:** Remedial reading, math, and study skills. Nonremedial tutoring.

**STUDENT LIFE. Housing:** Students may live on or off campus. Coed, women's, and men's dorms. Sorority and fraternity housing. School-owned/operated apartments. 75% of students live in college housing.
**Services and counseling/handicapped student services:** Placement services. Health service. Women's center. Birth control, personal, and psychological counseling. Career and academic guidance services. Religious counseling. Physically disabled student services. Learning disabled services. Tutors. Reader services for the blind.
**Campus organizations:** Undergraduate student government. Student newspaper (Rider News, published once/week). Yearbook. Radio station. Chorus, jazz ensemble, pep band, inspirational choir, debating, tutoring program, athletic, departmental, and special-interest groups, 60 organizations in all. Four fraternities, three chapter houses; four sororities, three chapter houses. 8% of men join a fraternity. 7% of women join a sorority.
**Religious organizations:** Protestant Campus Ministry, Catholic Campus Ministry, Christian Fellowship, Hillel.
**Minority/foreign student organizations:** Black Student Union, Asian Students at Rider, Latin American Student Organization, Rider Organization of Caribbean-Affiliated Students. International Students Club.

**ATHLETICS. Physical education requirements:** None.
**Intercollegiate competition:** 15% of students participate. Baseball (M), basketball (M,W), cheerleading (M,W), cross-country (M,W), diving (M,W), field hockey (W), golf (M), soccer (M), softball (W), swimming (M,W), tennis (M,W), track (indoor) (M,W), track (outdoor) (M,W), track and field (indoor) (M,W), track and field (outdoor) (M,W), volleyball (W), wrestling (M). Member of East Coast Wrestling Association, ECAC, ECC, Metropolitan Collegiate Swimming Conference, NCAA Division I, NJAIAW, Northeast Conference.
**Intramural and club sports:** 53% of students participate. Intramural basketball, billiards, bowling, cage soccer, flag football, floor hockey, golf, handball, inner-tube water polo, soccer, softball, street hockey, tennis, track, volleyball, weight lifting, Wiffle ball, wrestling. Men's club lacrosse, volleyball, ice hockey.

**ADMISSIONS. Academic basis for candidate selection** (in order of priority): Secondary school record, standardized test scores, class rank, school's recommendation, essay.
**Nonacademic basis for candidate selection:** Extracurricular participation is important. Character and personality and particular talent or ability are considered.
**Requirements:** Graduation from secondary school is required; GED is accepted. 16 units (including 4 units of English) required. Algebra I and II and geometry required of business, mathematics, and science program applicants. Minimum combined SAT score of 800, rank in top half of secondary school class, and minimum "B-" average recommended. EOP for applicants not normally admissible. Conditional admission possible for applicants not meeting standard requirements. Summer Trial Program for applicants not normally admissible. SAT is required; ACT may be substituted. PSAT is recommended. Campus visit and interview recommended. No off-campus interviews.
**Procedure:** Take SAT or ACT by December of 12th year. Notification of admission on rolling basis. Reply is required by May 1. $200 nonrefundable tuition deposit. $200 nonrefundable room deposit. Freshmen accepted in terms other than fall.
**Special programs:** Admission may be deferred one year. Credit and/or placement may be granted through CEEB Advanced Placement exams for scores of 3 or higher. Credit may be granted through CLEP general and subject exams. Credit and placement may be granted through challenge exams. Early entrance/early admission program. Concurrent enrollment program.
**Transfer students:** Transfer students accepted for terms other than fall. In fall 1993, 25% of all new students were transfers into all classes. 443 transfer applications were received, 389 were accepted. Application deadline is rolling for fall; rolling for spring. Minimum 2.5 GPA recommended. Lowest course grade accepted is "C-." Maximum number of transferable credits is 60 semester hours from a two-year school and 90 semester hours from a four-year school. At least 30 semester hours must be completed at the college to receive degree.
**Admissions contact:** Susan C. Christian, Director of Admissions. 609 896-5042, 800 257-9026.

**FINANCIAL AID. Available aid:** Pell grants, SEOG, state scholarships and grants, school scholarships and grants, private scholarships and grants, ROTC scholarships, academic merit scholarships, and athletic scholarships. Perkins Loans (NDSL), PLUS, Stafford Loans (GSL), state loans, school loans, and SLS. Knight Tuition Plans and AMS.
**Financial aid statistics:** In 1993-94, 81% of all undergraduate applicants received aid; 75% of freshman applicants. Average amounts of aid awarded freshmen: Scholarships and grants, $8,500; loans, $2,625.
**Supporting data/closing dates:** FAFSA: Priority filing date is March 1; accepted on rolling basis. Income tax forms: Priority filing date is March 1; accepted on rolling basis. Notification of awards begins in March.
**Financial aid contact:** John Brugle, Ph.D., Director of Financial Aid. 609 896-5042.

**STUDENT EMPLOYMENT.** College Work/Study Program. Institutional employment. 22% of full-time undergraduates work on campus during school year. Students may expect to earn an average of $1,000 during school year. Off-campus part-time employment opportunities rated "good."

**COMPUTER FACILITIES.** 200 IBM/IBM-compatible and Macintosh/Apple microcomputers. Students may access Digital minicomputer/mainframe systems, BITNET, In-

ternet. Client/LAN operating systems include Apple/Macintosh, DOS, DEC, LocalTalk/AppleTalk, Novell. Computer languages and software packages include BASIC, C, COBOL, dBASE, DISSPLA, Excel, FORTRAN, IMSL, LINDO, Lotus 1-2-3, MAPLE, Oracle, Pascal, Professional Write, SAS, SPSS-X, Tell-a-graf, TEX, Windows, Word for Windows, VAX Notes. Computer facilities are available to all students.
**Fees:** None.
**Hours:** 24 hours.

**GRADUATE CAREER DATA.** Graduate school percentages: 1% enter law school. 1% enter medical school. 2% enter graduate business programs. 6% enter graduate arts and sciences programs. Highest graduate school enrollments: Drexel U, Rider Coll, Rutgers U. 55% of graduates choose careers in business and industry. Companies and businesses that hire graduates: AT&T, Johnson & Johnson, Squibb, Prudential, Big Six accounting firms.

**PROMINENT ALUMNI/AE.** Susan Polis Schutz, greeting card designer and poet; Digger Phelps, former basketball coach, U of Notre Dame; Harry Gamble, general manager, Philadelphia Eagles; William Mastrosimone, playwright.

# Rowan College of New Jersey

Glassboro, NJ 08028 — 609 863-5000

**1993-94 Costs.** Tuition: $2,733 (state residents), $3,783 (out-of-state). Room & board: $4,800. Fees, books, misc. academic expenses (school's estimate): $800.
**Enrollment.** Undergraduates: 2,239 men, 3,231 women (full-time). Freshman class: 4,027 applicants, 1,601 accepted, 896 enrolled. Graduate enrollment: 388 men, 1,101 women.
**Test score averages/ranges.** Average SAT scores: 470 verbal, 510 math.
**Faculty.** 291 full-time; 118 part-time. 52% of faculty holds highest degree in specific field. Student/faculty ratio: 17 to 1.
**Selectivity rating.** Competitive.

**PROFILE.** Rowan College, founded in 1923, is a public, comprehensive college. Programs are offered through the Schools of Business Administration, Education and Related Professional Studies, Fine and Performing Arts, and Liberal Arts and Sciences. Its 180-acre campus is located in Glassboro, 20 miles from Philadelphia.

**Accreditation:** MSACS. Professionally accredited by the National Association of Schools of Music, the National Council for Accreditation of Teacher Education.
**Religious orientation:** Rowan College of New Jersey is nonsectarian; no religious requirements.
**Library:** Collections totaling over 4,000,000 volumes, 1,700 periodical subscriptions, and 100,000 microform items.
**Special facilities/museums:** Glass collection, on-campus elementary school and early childhood demonstration center, animal penthouse, greenhouse for biological studies, observatory.
**Athletic facilities:** Gymnasium, athletic fields, weight rooms, basketball and tennis courts, fitness trail, swimming pool, recreation center.

**STUDENT BODY. Undergraduate profile:** 97% are state residents; 50% are transfers. 2% Asian-American, 10% Black, 4% Hispanic, 83% White, 1% Other. Average age of undergraduates is 21.
**Freshman profile:** 1% of freshmen who took SAT scored 700 or over on math; 3% scored 600 or over on verbal, 12% scored 600 or over on math; 30% scored 500 or over on verbal, 57% scored 500 or over on math; 88% scored 400 or over on verbal, 100% scored 400 or over on math; 99% scored 300 or over on verbal. 99% of accepted applicants took SAT; 1% took ACT.
**Undergraduate achievement:** 77% of fall 1991 freshmen returned for fall 1992 term. 25% of entering class graduated. 31% of students who completed a degree program went on to graduate study within one year.
**Foreign students:** 70 students are from out of the country. Countries represented include China, Japan, Nigeria, and Somalia; 30 in all.

**PROGRAMS OF STUDY. Degrees:** B.A., B.Mus., B.S.
**Majors:** Art, Biological Science, Business Administration, Chemistry, Communications, Computer Science, Economics, Elementary/Early Childhood Education, English, Geography, Health/Physical Education, History, Law/Justice, Mathematics, Music, Physical Science, Political Science, Psychology, Sociology, Spanish, Speech/Theater/Dance, Teacher of the Handicapped.
**Distribution of degrees:** The majors with the highest enrollment are business administration, elementary education, and communications; health/physical education and music have the lowest.
**Requirements:** General education requirement.
**Academic regulations:** Freshmen must maintain minimum 1.6 GPA; sophomores, 1.8 GPA; juniors, 2.0 GPA; seniors, 2.0 GPA.
**Special:** Minors offered in some majors and in French and technology. Interdisciplinary concentrations in American studies, anthropology, applied math, aviation/aerospace, behavioral science, creative writing, drug information/education, German, international studies, philosophy/religion, puppetry, and women's studies. Senior Scholar Program. Double majors. Independent study. Accelerated study. Internships. Cooperative education programs. Graduate school at which undergraduates may take graduate-level courses. Preprofessional programs in medicine, pharmacy, dentistry, optometry, and physical therapy. 3-2 engineering programs with Drexel U, Rutgers U, and Temple U. 3-2 optometry program with Pennsylvania Coll of Optometry. 3-2 pharmacy program with Philadelphia Coll of Pharmacy. 3-3 podiatry program with Pennsylvania Coll of Podiatric Medicine. Teacher certification in early childhood, elementary, secondary, special education, vo-tech, and bilingual/bicultural education. Certification in specific subject areas. Study abroad in Australia, Denmark, France, Germany, Great Britain, and Spain. ROTC.
**Honors:** Phi Beta Kappa. Honors program. Honor societies.
**Academic Assistance:** Remedial reading, writing, math, and study skills. Nonremedial tutoring.

**STUDENT LIFE. Housing:** All freshmen and sophomores must live on campus unless living with family. Coed and women's dorms. School-owned/operated apartments. 34% of students live in college housing.
**Services and counseling/handicapped student services:** Placement services. Health service. Day care. Counseling services for minority and older students. Personal and psychological counseling. Career and academic guidance services. Religious counseling. Physically disabled student services. Learning disabled services. Notetaking services. Tape recorders. Tutors.
**Campus organizations:** Undergraduate student government. Student newspaper (Whit, published once/week). Literary magazine. Yearbook. Radio station. Contemporary music ensemble, wind ensemble, Campus Players, American Marketing Association, American Society for Personnel Administration, Cinema Workshop, Printmakers Guild, Public Relations Student Society of America, 150 organizations in all. 10 fraternities, one chapter house; 11 sororities, no chapter houses.
**Religious organizations:** Christians on the Move for Christ, Hillel, Newman Club, Intervarsity Christian Fellowship.
**Minority/foreign student organizations:** Black Culture League, Puerto Rican Students in Action.

**ATHLETICS. Physical education requirements:** One semester of physical education required.
**Intercollegiate competition:** 8% of students participate. Baseball (M), basketball (M,W), cheerleading (M,W), cross-country (M,W), diving (M,W), field hockey (W), football (M), lacrosse (W), soccer (M), softball (W), swimming (M,W), tennis (M,W), track and field (outdoor) (M,W). Member of ECAC, NCAA Division III, New Jersey Athletic Conference.
**Intramural and club sports:** 55% of students participate. Intramural badminton, basketball, flag football, floor hockey, racquetball, soccer, softball, tennis, volleyball.

**ADMISSIONS. Academic basis for candidate selection** (in order of priority): Secondary school record, class rank, standardized test scores, school's recommendation, essay.
**Nonacademic basis for candidate selection:** Particular talent or ability is important. Character and personality and extracurricular participation are considered.
**Requirements:** Graduation from secondary school is required; GED is accepted. 16 units and the following program of study are required: 4 units of English, 3 units of math, 2 units of science, 2 units of foreign language, 2 units of social studies, 2 units of history, 1 unit of electives. Minimum combined SAT score of 900, rank in top two-fifths of secondary school class, and minimum 3.0 GPA recommended. Audition required of music program applicants. Educational Opportunity Fund for in-state applicants not normally admissible. SAT is required; ACT may be substituted. Campus visit recommended. No off-campus interviews.
**Procedure:** Take SAT or ACT by January 25 of 12th year. Application deadline is March 15. Notification of admission on rolling basis. Reply is required by May 1. $50 nonrefundable tuition deposit. $150 room deposit, refundable until June 1. Freshmen accepted in terms other than fall.
**Special programs:** Admission may be deferred one year. Credit and/or placement may be granted through CEEB Advanced Placement exams for scores of 3 or higher. Credit may be granted through CLEP general and subject exams. Credit and placement may be granted through DANTES and challenge exams and military experience.
**Transfer students:** Transfer students accepted for terms other than fall. In fall 1992, 50% of all new students were transfers into all classes. 2,164 transfer applications were received, 1,366 were accepted. Application deadline is April 15 for fall; November 15 for spring. Minimum 2.5 GPA recommended. Lowest course grade accepted is "C." Maximum number of transferable credits is 90 semester hours. At least 30 semester hours must be completed at the college to receive degree.
**Admissions contact:** Marvin Sills, Director of Admissions. 609 863-5346.

**FINANCIAL AID. Available aid:** Pell grants, SEOG, state scholarships and grants, school scholarships and grants, private scholarships and grants, ROTC scholarships, and academic merit scholarships. Perkins Loans (NDSL), PLUS, Stafford Loans (GSL), and SLS. Deferred payment plan.
**Financial aid statistics:** 5% of aid is not need-based. In 1992-93, 83% of all undergraduate applicants received aid; 80% of freshman applicants. Average amounts of aid awarded freshmen: Scholarships and grants, $1,000; loans, $2,300.
**Supporting data/closing dates:** FAFSA/FAF: Priority filing date is April 15. School's own aid application: Priority filing date is April 15. SINGLEFILE: Priority filing date is April 15. Notification of awards begins June 25.
**Financial aid contact:** William Murphy, M.A., Director of Financial Aid. 609 863-6141.

**STUDENT EMPLOYMENT.** College Work/Study Program. Institutional employment. 12% of full-time undergraduates work on campus during school year. Students may expect to earn an average of $1,200 during school year. Off-campus part-time employment opportunities rated "excellent."

**COMPUTER FACILITIES.** 600 IBM/IBM-compatible and Macintosh/Apple microcomputers; 300 are networked. Students may access Digital, IBM minicomputer/mainframe systems, BITNET, Internet. Client/LAN operating systems include Novell. Computer languages and software packages include Lotus 1-2-3, MacWrite, Microsoft Word, PageMaker. Computer facilities are available to all students.
**Fees:** Computer fee is included in tuition/fees.

**GRADUATE CAREER DATA.** Highest graduate school enrollments: Drexel U, Rowan Coll of New Jersey, Rutgers U, Temple U. Companies and businesses that hire graduates: CIGNA, Prudential, school districts.

**PROMINENT ALUMNI/AE.** Betty Bowe Castor, Florida commissioner of education; Robert Heydges, actor; Kenneth Wooden, author and ABC News reporter/producer.

## Rutgers University–Camden College of Arts and Sciences

**Camden, NJ 08101** **609 225-1766**

**1993-94 Costs.** Tuition: $3,417 (state residents), $6,955 (out-of-state). Room: $2,598. Board: $1,856. Fees, books, misc. academic expenses (school's estimate): $1,415.
**Enrollment.** Undergraduates: 885 men, 1,128 women (full-time). Freshman class: 3,366 applicants, 1,752 accepted, 232 enrolled.
**Test score averages/ranges.** Average SAT scores: 489 verbal, 545 math. Range of SAT scores of middle 50%: 450-530 verbal, 510-590 math.
**Faculty.** 136 full-time. 95% of faculty holds highest degree in specific field. Student/faculty ratio: 16 to 1.
**Selectivity rating.** More competitive.

**PROFILE.** Rutgers U–Camden College of Arts and Sciences is a public, comprehensive university. Founded in 1927, it became part of the state system in 1950. Its 25-acre campus is located in Camden.

**Accreditation:** MSACS. Professionally accredited by the American Medical Association (CAHEA), the Council on Social Work Education, the National Association of Schools of Music, the National Council for Accreditation of Teacher Education, the National League for Nursing.
**Religious orientation:** Rutgers University-Camden College of Arts and Sciences is nonsectarian; no religious requirements.
**Library:** Collections totaling over 357,701 volumes, 2,106 periodical subscriptions, and 214,499 microform items.
**Special facilities/museums:** Art gallery, poetry center, music synthesizer, electron microscope.
**Athletic facilities:** Gymnasium, swimming pool, weight room, tennis, handball, racquetball, and squash courts, athletic fields.

**STUDENT BODY. Undergraduate profile:** 97% are state residents; 67% are transfers. 4% Asian-American, 13% Black, 6% Hispanic, 71% White, 6% Other. Average age of undergraduates is 23.
**Freshman profile:** 2% of freshmen who took SAT scored 700 or over on math; 8% scored 600 or over on verbal, 23% scored 600 or over on math; 45% scored 500 or over on verbal, 81% scored 500 or over on math; 95% scored 400 or over on verbal, 98% scored 400 or over on math; 98% scored 300 or over on verbal, 99% scored 300 or over on math. 99% of accepted applicants took SAT; 1% took ACT.
**Undergraduate achievement:** 79% of fall 1991 freshmen returned for fall 1992 term. 25% of entering class graduated. 27% of students completing a degree program immediately went on to graduate study.
**Foreign students:** 15 students are from out of the country. Countries represented include India, Japan, Korea, Pakistan, the Philippines, and Russia.

**PROGRAMS OF STUDY. Degrees:** B.A., B.S.
**Majors:** Afro-American Studies, Art, Biological Sciences/Biology, Chemistry, Computer Science, Economics, English, French, General Science, German, History, Independent/Individualized Major, Mathematics, Medical Technology, Music, Nursing, Philosophy, Physics, Political Science, Psychology, Social Work, Sociology, Spanish, Student-Proposed Major, Theatre Arts, Urban Studies.
**Distribution of degrees:** The majors with the highest enrollment are psychology, English, and nursing.
**Requirements:** General education requirement.
**Academic regulations:** Minimum 2.0 GPA must be maintained.
**Special:** Minors offered in most majors. Self-designed majors. Double majors. Dual degrees. Independent study. Accelerated study. Pass/fail grading option. Graduate school at which undergraduates may take graduate-level courses. Preprofessional programs in law, medicine, veterinary science, pharmacy, and dentistry. 2-2 and 3-2 engineering programs with Rutgers Coll of Engineering. 1-3 agriculture program with Cook Coll (Rutgers). Eight-year B.A./M.D. program with U of Medicine and Dentistry of New Jersey. 2-3 pharmacy program with Rutgers Coll of Pharmacy. Teacher certification in early childhood, elementary, and secondary education. Certification in specific subject areas. Study abroad in England, France, Germany, Ireland, Israel, Italy, Mexico, Portugal, and Spain. ROTC. AFROTC at St. Joseph's U.
**Honors:** Honors program. Honor societies.
**Academic Assistance:** Remedial reading, writing, math, and study skills. Nonremedial tutoring.

**STUDENT LIFE. Housing:** Students may live on or off campus. Coed dorms. School-owned/operated apartments. 7% of students live in college housing.
**Social atmosphere:** Gathering spots for students include the student center, McDonald's, Hank's, and the Bull's Head. Influential groups include campus activities board, student congress, Women's Students Organization, and the Latin American Student Organization. Popular social/cultural events are Fall Day, Spring Day, Cafe Teatro, Comedy Night, Black History Month, Women's History, and Latin-American Heritage Month. Since it is a commuter campus, events are not always well attended, according to the school newspaper. However, some events, such as the ones listed, have managed to attract a following and consistently go well. On Mondays and Wednesdays, the campus is erupting with activity.
**Services and counseling/handicapped student services:** Placement services. Health service. Learning Resources Center. Counseling services for minority, military, veteran, and older students. Birth control, personal, and psychological counseling. Career and academic guidance services. Religious counseling. Physically disabled student services. Learning disabled services. Notetaking services. Tape recorders. Tutors. Reader services for the blind.
**Campus organizations:** Undergraduate student government. Student newspaper (Gleaner, published once/week). Literary magazine. Yearbook. Theatre group, activities board, Organization for Career Success, academic and departmental groups, All Students Coalition, Democrat and Republican clubs, martial arts group, 45 organizations in all. Four fraternities, two chapter houses; seven sororities, no chapter houses. 6% of men join a fraternity. 6% of women join a sorority.
**Religious organizations:** Intervarsity Christian Fellowship.
**Minority/foreign student organizations:** Black Student Union. International Society, Latin American Student Organization.

**ATHLETICS. Physical education requirements:** None.
**Intercollegiate competition:** 12% of students participate. Baseball (M), basketball (M,W), cheerleading (M,W), cross-country (M,W), golf (M), soccer (M), softball (W), swimming (M,W), tennis (M,W), track (outdoor) (M,W), track and field (outdoor) (M,W), wrestling (M). Member of ECAC, NCAA Division III, NJAC, NJAIAW.
**Intramural and club sports:** 48% of students participate. Intramural badminton, basketball, flag football, handball, racquetball, soccer, softball, squash, volleyball, weight lifting. Men's club martial arts. Women's club martial arts.

**ADMISSIONS. Academic basis for candidate selection** (in order of priority): Secondary school record, class rank, standardized test scores, school's recommendation.
**Nonacademic basis for candidate selection:** Particular talent or ability is important. Extracurricular participation and geographical distribution are considered.
**Requirements:** Graduation from secondary school is required; GED is accepted. 16 units and the following program of study are required: 4 units of English, 3 units of math, 2 units of science, 2 units of foreign language, 5 units of academic electives. Educational Opportunity Fund (EOF) program for in-state applicants not normally admissible. SAT or ACT is required. Campus visit recommended.
**Procedure:** Take SAT or ACT by December of 12th year. Application deadline is May 1. Notification of admission on rolling basis. Reply is required by May 1 or within two weeks of acceptance. $125 nonrefundable tuition deposit. $200 nonrefundable room deposit. Freshmen accepted in terms other than fall.
**Special programs:** Admission may be deferred one semester. Credit and/or placement may be granted through CEEB Advanced Placement exams for scores of 4 or higher. Credit and/or placement may be granted through CLEP subject exams. Credit and placement may be granted through ACT PEP and challenge exams. Early entrance/early admission program. Concurrent enrollment program.
**Transfer students:** Transfer students accepted for terms other than fall. In fall 1993, 67% of all new students were transfers into all classes. 1,663 transfer applications were received, 945 were accepted. Application deadline is May 1 for fall; November 30 for spring. Lowest course grade accepted is "C." Maximum number of transferable credits is 64 semester hours. At least 30 of final 40 semester hours must be completed at Camden to receive degree.
**Admissions contact:** Elizabeth Mitchell, Ph.D., Assistant Vice President for University Undergraduate Admissions. 609 225-6104.

**FINANCIAL AID. Available aid:** Pell grants, SEOG, state scholarships and grants, school scholarships and grants, ROTC scholarships, and academic merit scholarships. Perkins Loans (NDSL), PLUS, Stafford Loans (GSL), state loans, school loans, and SLS. AMS and deferred payment plan.
**Financial aid statistics:** 9% of aid is not need-based. In 1993-94, 83% of all undergraduate applicants received aid; 79% of freshman applicants. Average amounts of aid awarded freshmen: Scholarships and grants, $4,114; loans, $1,973.
**Supporting data/closing dates:** FAFSA: Priority filing date is March 1. Income tax forms: Accepted on rolling basis. Notification of awards on rolling basis.
**Financial aid contact:** Richard Woodland, Director of Financial Aid. 609 225-6039.

**STUDENT EMPLOYMENT.** College Work/Study Program. Institutional employment. 11% of full-time undergraduates work on campus during school year. Students may expect to earn an average of $591 during school year. Off-campus part-time employment opportunities rated "fair."

**COMPUTER FACILITIES.** 93 IBM/IBM-compatible, Macintosh/Apple, and RISC-/UNIX-based microcomputers; 77 are networked. Students may access Digital, IBM, SUN minicomputer/mainframe systems, BITNET, Internet. Residence halls may be equipped with stand-alone microcomputers, modems. Client/LAN operating systems include Apple/Macintosh, DOS, UNIX/XENIX/AIX, X-windows, LocalTalk/AppleTalk, Novell. Computer languages and software packages include BASIC, C, dBASE, Lotus, Pascal, SAS, SPSS. Word, WordPerfect; 50 in all. Computer facilities are available to all students.
**Fees:** $50/semester.
**Hours:** 8:30 AM-11 PM (M-F); shorter hours on weekends

**GRADUATE CAREER DATA.** Graduate school percentages: 12% enter law school. 4% enter medical school. 7% enter graduate business programs. 62% enter graduate arts and sciences programs. Highest graduate school enrollments: Georgetown U, U of Medicine and Denistry of New Jersey, U of Pennsylvania, Rutgers U, Temple U, Villanova U. Companies and businesses that hire graduates: KPMG Peat Marwick, CIGNA, Federal Reserve Bank, Computer Sciences Corp.

## Rutgers University–College of Engineering

**New Brunswick, NJ 08903** **908 932-1766**

**1993-94 Costs.** Tuition: $3,792 (state residents), $7,716 (out-of-state). Room: $2,598. Board: $1,856. Fees, books, misc. academic expenses (school's estimate): $890.
**Enrollment.** Undergraduates: 1,936 men, 412 women (full-time). Freshman class: 3,593 applicants, 2,499 accepted, 582 enrolled.
**Test score averages/ranges.** Average SAT scores: 504 verbal, 663 math. Range of SAT scores of middle 50%: 440-570 verbal, 620-720 math.
**Faculty.** 126 full-time. 95% of faculty holds highest degree in specific field. Student/faculty ratio: 12 to 1.
**Selectivity rating.** Highly competitive.

**PROFILE.** Rutgers U–College of Engineering, founded in 1864, is a public, engineering university. Programs are offered through the Departments of Ceramics, Chemical and Biochemical Engineering, Civil and Environmental Engineering, Electrical Engineering, Industrial Engineering, Mechanical and Aerospace Engineering, and Mechanics and Materials Science. Its campus is located in New Brunswick, 40 miles from New York City.

**Accreditation:** MSACS. Professionally accredited by the Accreditation Board for Engineering and Technology.
**Religious orientation:** Rutgers University-College of Engineering is nonsectarian; no religious requirements.
**Library:** Collections totaling over 4,387,960 volumes, 19,822 periodical subscriptions, and 2,630,211 microform items.
**Special facilities/museums:** Agricultural, art, and geology museums, center for fiber optics materials research, center for ceramics research, center for advanced biotechnology and medicine, center for computer aids to industrial productivity, draw tower lab.
**Athletic facilities:** Gymnasiums, athletic fields, indoor practice bubble, golf course, tennis courts, swimming pools, recreation centers, stadium.

**STUDENT BODY. Undergraduate profile:** 87% are state residents; 14% are transfers. 22% Asian-American, 7% Black, 6% Hispanic, 57% White, 8% Other. Average age of undergraduates is 20.
**Freshman profile:** 1% of freshmen who took SAT scored 700 or over on verbal, 33% scored 700 or over on math; 18% scored 600 or over on verbal, 86% scored 600 or over on math; 57% scored 500 or over on verbal, 99% scored 500 or over on math; 89% scored 400 or over on verbal, 100% scored 400 or over on math; 97% scored 300 or over on verbal. 100% of accepted applicants took SAT; 1% took ACT.
**Undergraduate achievement:** 89% of fall 1991 freshmen returned for fall 1992 term. 30% of entering class graduated. 34% of students who completed a degree program immediately went on to graduate study.
**Foreign students:** 141 students are from out of the country. Countries represented include Bangladesh, Hong Kong, India, Korea, Pakistan, and Turkey; 38 in all.

**PROGRAMS OF STUDY. Degrees:** B.S.
**Majors:** Applied Sciences in Engineering, Bioresource Engineering, Ceramic Engineering, Chemical Engineering, Civil Engineering, Electrical Engineering, Industrial Engineering, Mechanical Engineering.
**Distribution of degrees:** The majors with the highest enrollment are electrical engineering, mechanical engineering, and civil engineering.
**Requirements:** General education requirement.
**Academic regulations:** Freshmen must maintain minimum 1.8 GPA; sophomores, juniors, seniors, 2.0 GPA.
**Special:** Programs also offered in aerospace engineering, biochemical engineering, bioenvironmental engineering, computer engineering, food engineering, and horticultural engineering. Self-designed majors. Double majors. Dual degrees. Independent study. Pass/fail grading option. Internships. Graduate school at which undergraduates may take graduate-level courses. Five-year B.S./M.B.A. program with Rutgers Graduate Sch of Management. Exchange program abroad in England (City U). Study abroad also in France, Germany, Ireland, Israel, Italy, Mexico, Portugal, and Spain. ROTC and AFROTC.
**Honors:** Honors program. Honor societies.
**Academic Assistance:** Remedial reading, writing, math, and study skills. Nonremedial tutoring.

**STUDENT LIFE. Housing:** Students may live on or off campus. Coed dorms. School-owned/operated apartments. Off-campus privately-owned housing. 66% of students live in college housing.
**Social atmosphere:** According to the student newspaper, Rutgers "is a very large university. If you are looking for something to do you can usually find something." On campus, students gather at the Student Center, while some popular off-campus spots include Stuff Yer Face, Thomas Sweets, and the Old Queens Tavern. The campus sponsors concerts with nationally known bands, such as the Hooters and Squeeze. Athletic events, especially basketball games and the Homecoming football game, are well attended.
**Services and counseling/handicapped student services:** Placement services. Health service. Women's center. Day care. Learning Resources Center. Counseling services for minority, military, veteran, and older students. Birth control, personal, and psychological counseling. Career and academic guidance services. Religious counseling. Physically disabled student services. Learning disabled services. Notetaking services. Reader services for the blind.
**Campus organizations:** Undergraduate student government. Student newspaper (Daily Targum; THE MOMENT). Literary magazine. Yearbook. Radio and TV stations. Orchestra, bands, many engineering groups, numerous cultural, professional, recreational, service, and special-interest groups, 300 organizations in all. 32 fraternities, 19 chapter houses; 15 sororities, no chapter houses. 7% of men join a fraternity. 3% of women join a sorority.
**Religious organizations:** Bahai Club, B'nai B'rith Hillel, Campus Crusade for Christ, Chinese Christian Fellowship, Intervarsity Christian Fellowship, Islamic Society and Friends, Jewish University Students Together, Korean Christian Fellowship, Meditation Club, New Hope Church, University Christian Outreach.
**Minority/foreign student organizations:** Blacks United to Save Themselves, Black Voice/Carta Boricua, Black Women's Association, El Circulo Hispanica, Minority Affairs Committee, Minority Mentor Club, Minority Engineering Task Force, NAACP, Native American Organization, Paul Robeson Club, Society of Hispanic Engineers. International Student Association, African, Arab, Armenian, Asian, Chinese, Filipino, French, Haitian, Indian, Iranian, Japanese, Korean, Latin American, Pakistani, Polish, Portuguese/Brazilian, Puerto Rican, Turkish, Ukrainian, Vietnamese, and West Indian groups.

**ATHLETICS. Physical education requirements:** None.
**Intercollegiate competition:** 3% of students participate. Baseball (M), basketball (M,W), cheerleading (M,W), crew (M,W), cross-country (M,W), diving (M,W), fencing (M,W), field hockey (W), football (M), golf (M,W), gymnastics (W), lacrosse (M,W), soccer (M,W), softball (W), swimming (M,W), tennis (M,W), track and field (indoor) (M,W), track and field (outdoor) (M,W), volleyball (W), wrestling (M). Member of Atlantic 10 Conference, Big East Football Conference, ECAC, NCAA Division I.
**Intramural and club sports:** Intramural aerobics, basketball, body building, bowling, floor hockey, flag football, golf, racquetball, soccer, table tennis, tennis, touch football, triathlon, ultimate frisbee, volleyball, walleyball, wrestling. Men's club aerobics, badminton, equestrian sports, field hockey, football, gymnastics, ice hockey, lacrosse, martial arts, modern dance, mountain bike, outdoors, racquetball, rangers, rugby, sailing, scuba, skiing, squash, synchronized swimming, table tennis, volleyball, water polo. Women's club aerobics, badminton, equestrian sports, field hockey, football, gymnastics, lacrosse, martial arts, modern dance, mountain bike, outdoors, racquetball, rangers, rugby, sailing, scuba, skiing, squash, synchronized swimming, table tennis, volleyball, water polo.

**ADMISSIONS. Academic basis for candidate selection** (in order of priority): Secondary school record, class rank, standardized test scores, school's recommendation.
**Nonacademic basis for candidate selection:** Extracurricular participation, particular talent or ability, and geographical distribution are considered.
**Requirements:** Graduation from secondary school is required; GED is accepted. 16 units and the following program of study are required: 4 units of English, 4 units of math, 2 units of lab science, 6 units of academic electives. Educational Opportunity Fund (EOF) program for in-state applicants not normally admissible. SAT or ACT is required. Campus visit recommended.
**Procedure:** Take SAT or ACT by December of 12th year. Application deadline is January 15. Notification of admission by April 15. Reply is required by May 1 or within two weeks of acceptance. $125 nonrefundable tuition deposit. $100 room deposit, refundable until June 30. Freshmen accepted in fall terms only.
**Special programs:** Admission may be deferred one year. Credit may be granted through CEEB Advanced Placement for scores of 4 or higher. Placement may be granted through life experience. Credit and placement may be granted through ACT PEP and challenge exams and military experience. Early entrance/early admission program. Concurrent enrollment program.
**Transfer students:** Transfer students accepted for terms other than fall. In fall 1993, 14% of all new students were transfers into all classes. 507 transfer applications were received, 170 were accepted. Application deadline is March 15 for fall; November 1 for spring. Lowest course grade accepted is "C." Maximum number of transferable credits is 60 semester hours. At least 30 of final 42 credits must be completed at Coll of Engineering to receive degree.
**Admissions contact:** Elizabeth Mitchell, Ph.D., Assistant Vice President for University Undergraduate Admissions. 908 932-3770.

**FINANCIAL AID. Available aid:** Pell grants, SEOG, state scholarships and grants, school scholarships and grants, ROTC scholarships, academic merit scholarships, and athletic scholarships. Perkins Loans (NDSL), PLUS, Stafford Loans (GSL), state loans, and school loans. AMS and deferred payment plan.
**Financial aid statistics:** 19% of aid is not need-based. In 1993-94, 88% of all undergraduate applicants received aid; 85% of freshman applicants. Average amounts of aid awarded freshmen: Scholarships and grants, $5,342; loans, $2,120.
**Supporting data/closing dates:** FAFSA: Priority filing date is March 1. Income tax forms: Accepted on rolling basis. Notification of awards on rolling basis.
**Financial aid contact:** Steve Rouff, M.A., Acting Director of Financial Aid. 908 932-8811 (A-Led), 908 932-7057 (Lee-Z).

**STUDENT EMPLOYMENT.** College Work/Study Program. Institutional employment. 8% of full-time undergraduates work on campus during school year. Students may expect to earn an average of $639 during school year. Off-campus part-time employment opportunities rated "fair."

**COMPUTER FACILITIES.** 688 IBM/IBM-compatible, Macintosh/Apple, and RISC-/UNIX-based microcomputers; 599 are networked. Students may access Digital, Hewlett-Packard, IBM, Pyramid, SUN minicomputer/mainframe systems, BITNET, Internet, CompuServe. Residence halls may be equipped with stand-alone microcomputers, networked microcomputers. Client/LAN operating systems include Apple/Macintosh, DOS, OS/2, UNIX/XENIX/AIX, Windows NT, X-windows, LocalTalk/AppleTalk, Novell. Computer languages and software packages include Ansys, AutoCAD, BASIC, C, CAD/CAM, CAEDS, FORTRAN, GPSS, Lindo, Lotus 1-2-3, MacWrite, Maple, Mathematica, MARC, PageMaker, Pascal, SAS, SPSS-X, Word, WordPerfect. Computer facilities are available to all students.
**Fees:** $50 computer fee per semesters.
**Hours:** 24 hours in some locations.

**GRADUATE CAREER DATA.** Highest graduate school enrollments: Rutgers U, Stevens Inst of Tech, U of Pennsylvania. Companies and businesses that hire graduates: Bellcore, Exxon, Ingersoll and Rand, Merck, Procter and Gamble.

# Rutgers University–College of Nursing

Newark, NJ 07102 201 648-1766

**1993-94 Costs.** Tuition: $3,417 (state residents), $6,955 (out-of-state). Room: $2,598. Board: $1,856. Fees, books, misc. academic expenses (school's estimate): $1,401.
**Enrollment.** Undergraduates: 41 men, 347 women (full-time). Freshman class: 933 applicants, 162 accepted, 43 enrolled.
**Test score averages/ranges.** Average SAT scores: 499 verbal, 559 math. Range of SAT scores of middle 50%: 470-540 verbal, 520-610 math.
**Faculty.** 37 full-time. 95% of faculty holds highest degree in specific field. Student/faculty ratio: 9 to 1.
**Selectivity rating.** More competitive.

**PROFILE.** Rutgers U–College of Nursing, founded in 1956, is a private university of nursing. Its 23-acre campus is located in Newark, 15 miles from New York City.

**Accreditation:** MSACS. Professionally accredited by the National League for Nursing.
**Religious orientation:** Rutgers University-College of Nursing is nonsectarian; no religious requirements.

**Library:** Collections totaling over 591,536 volumes, 3,748 periodical subscriptions, and 675,962 microform items.
**Athletic facilities:** Gymnasiums, swimming pool, soccer, softball, and baseball fields, Nautilus and free-weight equipment, racquetball and tennis courts, recreation facility, dance room, saunas.

**STUDENT BODY. Undergraduate profile:** 98% are state residents; 67% are transfers. 18% Asian-American, 20% Black, 10% Hispanic, 47% White, 5% Other. Average age of undergraduates is 21.
**Freshman profile:** 4% of freshmen who took SAT scored 700 or over on math; 4% scored 600 or over on verbal, 30% scored 600 or over on math; 56% scored 500 or over on verbal, 82% scored 500 or over on math; 100% scored 400 or over on verbal, 100% scored 400 or over on math. 100% of accepted applicants took SAT; 1% took ACT.
**Undergraduate achievement:** 86% of fall 1991 freshmen returned for fall 1992 term. 47% of entering class graduated. 5% of students who completed a degree program immediately went on to graduate study.
**Foreign students:** Four students are from out of the country. Countries represented include South Africa, the Philippines, and Taiwan.

**PROGRAMS OF STUDY. Degrees:** B.S.Nurs.
**Majors:** Nursing.
**Requirements:** General education requirement.
**Academic regulations:** Freshmen must maintain minimum 1.4 GPA; sophomores, 1.75 GPA; juniors, 2.0 GPA; seniors, 2.0 GPA.
**Special:** Minors offered through Newark Coll of Arts and Sciences. Independent study. Accelerated study. Pass/fail grading option. Graduate school at which undergraduates may take graduate-level courses. M.S. in nursing and a post-master's concentration in nurse psychotherapy are offered in conjunction with Rutgers Graduate Sch in Newark. ROTC at New Jersey Inst of Tech. AFROTC at Rutgers U, New Brunswick.
**Honors:** Honors program. Honor societies.
**Academic Assistance:** Remedial reading, writing, math, and study skills. Nonremedial tutoring.

**ADMISSIONS. Academic basis for candidate selection** (in order of priority): Secondary school record, class rank, standardized test scores, school's recommendation.
**Nonacademic basis for candidate selection:** Character and personality, extracurricular participation, particular talent or ability, and geographical distribution are considered.
**Requirements:** Graduation from secondary school is required; GED is accepted. 16 units and the following program of study are required: 4 units of English, 3 units of math, 2 units of lab science, 7 units of academic electives. Educational Opportunity Fund (EOF) program for in-state applicants not normally admissible. SAT or ACT is required. Campus visit recommended.
**Procedure:** Take SAT or ACT by December of 12th year. Application deadline is January 15. Notification of admission on rolling basis. Reply is required by May 1 or within two weeks of acceptance. $100 room deposit, refundable until July 1. Freshmen accepted in fall terms only.
**Special programs:** Admission may be deferred one semester. Credit may be granted through CEEB Advanced Placement for scores of 4 or higher. Credit may be granted through CLEP general exams. Credit and placement may be granted through Regents College, ACT PEP, and challenge exams. Early entrance/early admission program. Concurrent enrollment program.
**Transfer students:** Transfer students accepted for fall term. In fall 1993, 67% of all new students were transfers into all classes. 567 transfer applications were received, 138 were accepted. Application deadline is March 15. Lowest course grade accepted is "C." Maximum number of transferable credits is 94 semester hours. At least 30 of final 42 semester hours must be completed at Coll of Nursing to receive degree.
**Admissions contact:** Elizabeth Mitchell, Ph.D., Assistant Vice President for University Undergraduate Admissions. 201 648-5205.

**FINANCIAL AID. Available aid:** Pell grants, SEOG, state scholarships and grants, school scholarships and grants, ROTC scholarships, academic merit scholarships, and athletic scholarships. Perkins Loans (NDSL), PLUS, Stafford Loans (GSL), state loans, school loans, and SLS. AMS and deferred payment plan.
**Financial aid statistics:** 8% of aid is not need-based. In 1993-94, 85% of all undergraduate applicants received aid; 60% of freshman applicants. Average amounts of aid awarded freshmen: Scholarships and grants, $4,868; loans, $1,624.
**Supporting data/closing dates:** FAFSA: Priority filing date is March 1. Income tax forms: Accepted on rolling basis. Notification of awards on rolling basis.
**Financial aid contact:** Paul Gilroy, Director of Financial Aid. 201 648-5357.

## Rutgers University–College of Pharmacy

**New Brunswick, NJ 08903** **908 932-1766**

**1993-94 Costs.** Tuition: $3,792 (state residents), $7,716 (out-of-state). Room: $2,598. Board: $1,856. Fees, books, misc. academic expenses (school's estimate): $890.

**Enrollment.** Undergraduates: 310 men, 556 women (full-time). Freshman class: 1,591 applicants, 552 accepted, 194 enrolled. Graduate enrollment: 9 men, 27 women.

**Test score averages/ranges.** Average SAT scores: 527 verbal, 654 math. Range of SAT scores of middle 50%: 470-580 verbal, 610-700 math.

**Faculty.** 52 full-time. 95% of faculty holds highest degree in specific field. Student/faculty ratio: 12 to 1.

**Selectivity rating.** Highly competitive.

**PROFILE.** Rutgers U–College of Pharmacy is a public, pharmaceutical university. Founded in 1892, it became part of the state system in 1927. Its campus is located in New Brunswick, 40 miles from New York City.

**Accreditation:** MSACS. Professionally accredited by the American Council on Pharmaceutical Education.
**Religious orientation:** Rutgers University-College of Pharmacy is nonsectarian; no religious requirements.
**Library:** Collections totaling over 4,387,960 volumes, 19,822 periodical subscriptions, and 2,630,211 microform items.
**Special facilities/museums:** Agricultural, art, and geology museums, controlled drug delivery research center, pharmaceutical manufacturing lab.
**Athletic facilities:** Gymnasiums, athletic fields, indoor practice bubble, golf course, tennis courts, swimming pools, recreation centers, stadium.

**STUDENT BODY. Undergraduate profile:** 87% are state residents; 14% are transfers. 36% Asian-American, 4% Black, 8% Hispanic, 48% White, 4% Other. Average age of undergraduates is 20.
**Freshman profile:** 28% of freshmen who took SAT scored 700 or over on math; 19% scored 600 or over on verbal, 83% scored 600 or over on math; 66% scored 500 or over on verbal, 99% scored 500 or over on math; 98% scored 400 or over on verbal, 100% scored 400 or over on math; 100% scored 300 or over on verbal. 100% of accepted applicants took SAT; 1% took ACT.
**Undergraduate achievement:** 88% of fall 1992 freshmen returned for fall 1993 term. 26% of students who completed a degree program immediately went on to graduate study.
**Foreign students:** 17 students are from out of the country. Countries represented include China, Hong Kong, Korea, Nigeria, Taiwan, and the United Kingdom; 11 in all.

**PROGRAMS OF STUDY. Degrees:** B.S.
**Majors:** Pharmacy.
**Requirements:** General education requirement.
**Academic regulations:** Minimum 2.0 GPA must be maintained.
**Special:** Internships. Graduate school at which undergraduates may take graduate-level courses. Study abroad in England, France, Germany, Ireland, Israel, Italy, Mexico, Portugal, and Spain. ROTC and AFROTC.
**Honors:** Honors program. Honor societies.
**Academic Assistance:** Remedial reading, writing, math, and study skills. Nonremedial tutoring.

**ADMISSIONS. Academic basis for candidate selection** (in order of priority): Secondary school record, class rank, standardized test scores, school's recommendation.
**Nonacademic basis for candidate selection:** Extracurricular participation, particular talent or ability, and geographical distribution are considered.
**Requirements:** Graduation from secondary school is required; GED is accepted. 16 units and the following program of study are required: 4 units of English, 3 units of math, 2 units of lab science, 2 units of foreign language, 5 units of academic electives. Educational Opportunity Fund (EOF) program for in-state applicants not normally admissible. Either SAT or ACT is required. Campus visit recommended.
**Procedure:** Take SAT or ACT by December of 12th year. Application deadline is January 15. Notification of admission by April 15. Reply is required by May 1 or within two weeks of acceptance. $125 nonrefundable tuition deposit. $100 room deposit, refundable until June 30. Freshmen accepted in fall terms only.
**Special programs:** Admission may be deferred one year. Credit and/or placement may be granted through CEEB Advanced Placement exams for scores of 4 or higher. Credit may be granted through CLEP subject exams and Regents College exams. Early entrance/early admission program. Concurrent enrollment program.
**Transfer students:** Transfer students accepted for fall term. In fall 1993, 14% of all new students were transfers into all classes. 639 transfer applications were received, 54 were accepted. Application deadline is March 15. Lowest course grade accepted is "C." Maximum number of transferable credits is 70 semester hours. At least the final year must be completed at the Coll of Pharmacy to receive degree.
**Admissions contact:** Elizabeth Mitchell, Ph.D., Assistant Vice President for University Undergraduate Admissions. 908 932-3770.

**FINANCIAL AID. Available aid:** Pell grants, SEOG, state scholarships and grants, school scholarships and grants, ROTC scholarships, academic merit scholarships, and athletic scholarships. Perkins Loans (NDSL), PLUS, Stafford Loans (GSL), state loans, school loans, and SLS. AMS and deferred payment plan.
**Financial aid statistics:** 20% of aid is not need-based. In 1993-94, 90% of all undergraduate applicants received aid; 92% of freshman applicants. Average amounts of aid awarded freshmen: Scholarships and grants, $4,058; loans, $2,949.
**Supporting data/closing dates:** FAFSA: Priority filing date is March 1. Income tax forms: Accepted on rolling basis. Notification of awards on rolling basis.
**Financial aid contact:** Steve Rouff, M.A., Acting Director of Financial Aid. 908 932-8811 (A-Led), 908 932-7057 (Lee-Z).

## Rutgers University–Cook College

**New Brunswick, NJ 08903** **908 932-1766**

**1993-94 Costs.** Tuition: $3,792 (state residents), $7,716 (out-of-state). Room: $2,598. Board: $1,856. Fees, books, misc. academic expenses (school's estimate): $1,583.

**Enrollment.** Undergraduates: 1,391 men, 1,183 women (full-time). Freshman class: 7,097 applicants, 4,006 accepted, 545 enrolled.

**Test score averages/ranges.** Average SAT scores: 510 verbal, 584 math. Range of SAT scores of middle 50%: 460-560 verbal, 530-640 math.

**Faculty.** 97 full-time. 95% of faculty holds highest degree in specific field. Student/faculty ratio: 16 to 1.

**Selectivity rating.** More competitive.

**PROFILE.** Rutgers U–Cook College, founded in 1921, is a public, comprehensive university focusing on applied sciences. Its campus is located in New Brunswick, 40 miles from New York City.

**Accreditation:** MSACS. Professionally accredited by the American Society of Landscape Architects.
**Religious orientation:** Rutgers University-Cook College is nonsectarian; no religious requirements.
**Library:** Collections totaling over 4,387,960 volumes, 19,822 periodical subscriptions, and 2,630,211 microform items.
**Special facilities/museums:** Agricultural, art, and geology museums, center for advanced food technology, center for agricultural molecular biology, marine and coastal sciences institute, center for coastal and environmental studies.
**Athletic facilities:** Gymnasiums, athletic fields, indoor practice bubble, golf course, tennis courts, swimming pool, recreation centers, stadium.

**STUDENT BODY. Undergraduate profile:** 90% are state residents; 24% are transfers. 10% Asian-American, 5% Black, 6% Hispanic, 77% White, 2% Other. Average age of undergraduates is 21.
**Freshman profile:** 1% of freshmen who took SAT scored 700 or over on verbal, 8% scored 700 or over on math; 11% scored 600 or over on verbal, 45% scored 600 or over on math; 58% scored 500 or over on verbal, 89% scored 500 or over on math; 95% scored 400 or over on verbal, 99% scored 400 or over on math; 99% scored 300 or over on verbal. 99% of accepted applicants took SAT; 1% took ACT.
**Undergraduate achievement:** 93% of fall 1991 freshmen returned for fall 1992 term. 37% of entering class graduated. 38% of students who completed a degree program immediately went on to graduate study.
**Foreign students:** 20 students are from out of the country. Countries represented include Germany, Hong Kong, Japan, St. Vincent/Grenadines, Uruguay, and Venezuela; 15 in all.

**PROGRAMS OF STUDY. Degrees:** B.A., B.S.
**Majors:** Agricultural Science, Animal Science, Atmospheric Sciences, Biochemistry, Biological Sciences, Bioresource Engineering, Biotechnology, Chemistry, Chemistry/Foods/Nutrition, Communication, Computer Science, Environmental/Business Economics, Environmental Planning/Design, Environmental Sciences, Exercise Science/Sports Studies, Food Science, Geography, Geological Sciences, Human Ecology, Independent Major, International Environmental Studies, Journalism/Mass Media, Natural Resource Management, Nutritional Sciences, Plant Science, Professional/Occupational Education, Public Health.
**Distribution of degrees:** The majors with the highest enrollment are environmental sciences, biological sciences, and environmental/business economics.
**Requirements:** General education requirement.
**Academic regulations:** Freshmen must maintain minimum 1.75 GPA; sophomores, 1.7 GPA; juniors, 1.8 GPA; seniors, 2.0 GPA.
**Special:** Minors offered in several majors and in agricultural engineering technology, agrioecology, entomology, equine science, health care, marine science, meteorology and physical oceanography, professional youth work, and science and agriculture teacher education. Most majors include several options. Certificate programs offered in environmental planning, environmental resource monitoring, international agriculture/environment, social strategies for environmental protection, and teacher education. Self-designed majors. Double majors. Dual degrees. Independent study. Accelerated study. Pass/fail grading option. Internships. Cooperative education programs. Graduate school at which undergraduates may take graduate-level courses. Preprofessional programs in law, medicine, veterinary science, and dentistry. Eight-year B.A./M.D. program with U of Medicine and Dentistry of New Jersey. Five-year bioresource engineering program. B.S./M.B.A. program. Exchange program with Tuskegee U. Teacher certification in secondary education. Certification in specific subject areas. Exchange programs abroad in England (U of Reading) and Israel (Technion-Israel Inst of Tech). Study abroad also in France, Germany, Ireland, Italy, Mexico, Portugal, and Spain. ROTC and AFROTC.
**Honors:** Honors program. Honor societies.
**Academic Assistance:** Remedial reading, writing, math, and study skills. Nonremedial tutoring.

**STUDENT LIFE. Housing:** Students may live on or off campus. Coed and men's dorms. School-owned/operated apartments. Substance-free housing. 62% of students live in college housing.
**Social atmosphere:** The student newspaper reports, "Most social events take place on campus. The university sponsors lectures, forums, dances, etc." The most popular events on campus include Homecoming, the SBT Dance Marathon, and Halloweek, sponsored by Sigma Phi Epsilon. "Greeks control the social life at Rutgers. They sponsor parties, mixers, and holiday events." Students frequent Thomas Sweet Ice Creamery, Skinny Vinnie's Pizzeria, and the fraternity houses.
**Services and counseling/handicapped student services:** Placement services. Health service. Women's center. Day care. Learning Resource Center. Counseling services for minority, military, veteran, and older students. Birth control, personal, and psychological counseling. Career and academic guidance services. Religious counseling. Physically disabled student services. Learning disabled services. Notetaking services. Reader services for the blind.
**Campus organizations:** Undergraduate student government. Student newspaper (Daily Targum; Green Print, published once/week). Literary magazine. Yearbook. Radio and TV stations. Orchestra, bands, film committee, program/activities council, Enlightenment Club, ethnic programs, committee, student advisory board, commuter club, academic and departmental groups, baseball and soccer clubs, recreation association, 300 organizations in all. 32 fraternities, 19 chapter houses; 15 sororities, no chapter houses. 7% of men join a fraternity. 3% of women join a sorority.
**Religious organizations:** Bahai Club, B'nai B'rith Hillel, Campus Crusade for Christ, Chinese Christian Fellowship, Intervarsity Christian Fellowship, Islamic Society and Friends, Jewish University Students Together, Korean Christian Fellowship, Meditation Club, New Hope Church, University Christian Outreach.
**Minority/foreign student organizations:** Blacks United to Save Themselves, Black Voice/Carta Boricua, El Circulo Hispanica, Latino Pre-Law group, Minority Affairs Committee, Minority Mentor Club, minority engineering and science groups, NAACP, Native American Organization, Paul Robeson Club. International Student Association, African, Arab, Armenian, Asian, Chinese, Filipino, French, Haitian, Indian, Iranian, Japanese, Korean, Latin American, Pakistani, Polish, Portuguese/Brazilian, Puerto Rican, Turkish, Ukrainian, Vietnamese, and West Indian groups.

**ATHLETICS. Physical education requirements:** None.
**Intercollegiate competition:** 7% of students participate. Baseball (M), basketball (M,W), cheerleading (M,W), crew (M,W), cross-country (M,W), diving (M,W), fencing (M,W), field hockey (W), football (M), golf (M,W), gymnastics (W), lacrosse (M,W), soccer (M,W), softball (W), swimming (M,W), tennis (M,W), track and field (indoor) (M,W), track and field (outdoor) (M,W), volleyball (W), wrestling (M). Member of Atlantic 10 Conference, Big East Football Conference, ECAC, NCAA Division I.
**Intramural and club sports:** Intramural aerobics, basketball, body building, bowling, floor hockey, flag football, golf, racquetball, soccer, table tennis, tennis, touch football, triathlon, ultimate frisbee, volleyball, walleyball, wrestling. Men's club aerobics, badminton, equestrian sports, field hockey, football, gymnastics, ice hockey, lacrosse, martial arts, modern dance, mountain bike, outdoors, racquetball, rangers, rugby, sailing, scuba, skiing, squash, synchronized swimming, table tennis, volleyball, water polo. Women's club aerobics, badminton, equestrian sports, field hockey, football, gymnastics, lacrosse, martial arts, modern dance, mountain bike, outdoors, racquetball, rangers, rugby, sailing, scuba, skiing, squash, synchronized swimming, table tennis, volleyball, water polo.

**ADMISSIONS. Academic basis for candidate selection** (in order of priority): Secondary school record, class rank, standardized test scores, school's recommendation.
**Nonacademic basis for candidate selection:** Particular talent or ability is important. Extracurricular participation and geographical distribution are considered.
**Requirements:** Graduation from secondary school is required; GED is accepted. 16 units and the following program of study are required: 4 units of English, 3 units of math, 9 units of academic electives. Educational Opportunity Fund (EOF) for in-state applicants not normally admissible. SAT or ACT is required. Campus visit recommended.
**Procedure:** Take SAT or ACT by December of 12th year. Application deadline is January 15. Notification of admission by April 15. Reply is required by May 1 or within two weeks of acceptance. $125 nonrefundable tuition deposit. $100 room deposit, refundable until June 30. Freshmen accepted in fall terms only.
**Special programs:** Admission may be deferred one year. Credit and/or placement may be granted through CEEB Advanced Placement exams for scores of 4 or higher. Credit and placement may be granted through challenge exams. Early entrance/early admission program. Concurrent enrollment program.
**Transfer students:** Transfer students accepted for terms other than fall. In fall 1993, 24% of all new students were transfers into all classes. 1,669 transfer applications were received, 595 were accepted. Application deadline is March 15 for fall; November 1 for spring. Lowest course grade accepted is "C." At least 30 of final 42 semester hours must be completed at the college to receive degree.
**Admissions contact:** Elizabeth Mitchell, Ph.D., Assistant Vice President for University Undergraduate Admissions. 908 932-3770.

**FINANCIAL AID. Available aid:** Pell grants, SEOG, state scholarships and grants, school scholarships and grants, ROTC scholarships, academic merit scholarships, and athletic scholarships. Perkins Loans (NDSL), PLUS, Stafford Loans (GSL), state loans, school loans, and SLS. AMS and deferred payment plan.
**Financial aid statistics:** 19% of aid is not need-based. In 1993-94, 82% of all undergraduate applicants received aid; 73% of freshman applicants. Average amounts of aid awarded freshmen: Scholarships and grants, $4,137; loans, $2,582.
**Supporting data/closing dates:** FAFSA: Priority filing date is March 1. Income tax forms: Accepted on rolling basis. Notification of awards on rolling basis.
**Financial aid contact:** Steve Rouff, M.A., Acting Director of Financial Aid. 908 932-8811 (A-Led), 908 932-7057 (Lee-Z).

**STUDENT EMPLOYMENT.** College Work/Study Program. Institutional employment. 11% of full-time undergraduates work on campus during school year. Students may expect to earn an average of $488 during school year. Off-campus part-time employment opportunities rated "fair."

**COMPUTER FACILITIES.** 482 IBM/IBM-compatible and Macintosh/Apple microcomputers; 452 are networked. Students may access Digital, IBM, SUN minicomputer/mainframe systems, BITNET, Internet. Client/LAN operating systems include Apple/Macintosh, DOS, UNIX/XENIX/AIX, X-windows, LocalTalk/AppleTalk, Novell. Computer languages and software packages include ClarisWorks, FORTRAN, Lotus 1-2-3, MacWrite, SAS, SPSS-X, WordPerfect; 50 in all. Microcomputers available to all students; mainframes restricted to classroom instructional use.
**Fees:** $50/semester.
**Hours:** Vary; 24 hours/day in some locations.

**GRADUATE CAREER DATA.** Highest graduate school enrollments: New York U, Rutgers U, U of Medicine & Dentistry of New Jersey. Companies and businesses that hire graduates: Deloitte and Touche, Merck, Wal-Mart, KPMG Peat Marwick, Procter and Gamble.

# Rutgers University–Douglass College

**New Brunswick, NJ 08903** **908 932-1766**

**1993-94 Costs.** Tuition: $3,417 (state residents), $6,955 (out-of-state). Room: $2,598. Board: $1,856. Fees, books, misc. academic expenses (school's estimate): $1,558.
**Enrollment.** 2,830 women (full-time). Freshman class: 5,887 applicants, 3,963 accepted, 659 enrolled.
**Test score averages/ranges.** Average SAT scores: 500 verbal, 545 math. Range of SAT scores of middle 50%: 450-550 verbal, 500-590 math.
**Faculty.** 761 full-time. 95% of faculty holds highest degree in specific field. Student/faculty ratio: 17 to 1.
**Selectivity rating.** Competitive.

**PROFILE.** Rutgers U–Douglass College is a public, comprehensive university for women. Founded in 1918, it is the largest women's college in the U.S. Its campus is located in New Brunswick, 40 miles from New York City.

**Accreditation:** MSACS. Professionally accredited by the American Assembly of Collegiate Schools of Business, the American Medical Association (CAHEA), the National Association of Schools of Music, the National Council for Accreditation of Teacher Education.

**Religious orientation:** Rutgers University-Douglass College is nonsectarian; no religious requirements.

**Library:** Collections totaling over 4,387,960 volumes, 19,822 periodical subscriptions, and 2,630,211 microform items.

**Special facilities/museums:** Agricultural, art, and geology museums, theatres, concert halls, center for global issues and women's leadership, center for the American woman and politics, center for women and work.

**Athletic facilities:** Gymnasiums, athletic fields, indoor practice bubble, golf course, tennis courts, swimming pools, recreation centers, stadium.

**STUDENT BODY. Undergraduate profile:** 93% are state residents; 20% are transfers. 13% Asian-American, 10% Black, 6% Hispanic, 67% White, 4% Other. Average age of undergraduates is 20.

**Freshman profile:** 1% of freshmen who took SAT scored 700 or over on verbal, 2% scored 700 or over on math; 12% scored 600 or over on verbal, 23% scored 600 or over on math; 49% scored 500 or over on verbal, 76% scored 500 or over on math; 94% scored 400 or over on verbal, 97% scored 400 or over on math; 100% scored 300 or over on verbal, 100% scored 300 or over on math. 100% of accepted applicants took SAT; 1% took ACT.

**Undergraduate achievement:** 91% of fall 1991 freshmen returned for fall 1992 term. 65% of entering class graduated. 36% of students who completed a degree program immediately went on to graduate study.

**Foreign students:** 39 students are from out of the country. Countries represented include Austria, Hong Kong, India, Japan, Taiwan, and the United Kingdom; 19 in all.

**PROGRAMS OF STUDY. Degrees:** B.A., B.S.

**Majors:** Accounting, Africana Studies, American Studies, Anthropology, Art History, Atmospheric Sciences, Biochemistry, Biological Sciences/Biology, Biomathematics, Biotechnology, Chemistry, Chemistry/Foods/Nutrition, Chinese, Classical Humanities, Communication, Comparative Literature, Computer Science, Dance, East Asian Language/Area Studies, Economics, English, Exercise Science/Sport Studies, Finance, Food Science, French, Geography, Geology, German, Greek, Greek/Latin, Hebraic Studies, History, History/Political Science, Human Ecology, Individualized Major, Italian, Journalism/Mass Media, Labor Studies, Latin, Latin American Studies, Linguistics, Management, Marketing, Mathematics, Medical Technology, Middle Eastern Studies, Music, Nutritional Sciences, Philosophy, Physics, Political Science, Portuguese, Psychology, Public Health, Puerto Rican/Hispanic Caribbean Studies, Religion, Russian, Slavic/East European Studies, Sociology, Spanish, Statistics, Statistics/Mathematics, Theatre Arts, Urban Studies, Visual Arts, Women's Studies.

**Distribution of degrees:** The majors with the highest enrollment are psychology, English, and communications.

**Requirements:** General education requirement.

**Academic regulations:** Freshmen must maintain minimum 1.71 GPA; sophomores, 1.94 GPA; juniors, 1.96 GPA; seniors, 1.96 GPA.

**Special:** Minors offered in many majors and in approximately 20 other fields. Certificate programs in many areas including cartography, coaching, criminology, environmental planning, enviromental resource monitoring, foreign language, international studies, science management, and translation proficiency. Self-designed majors. Double majors. Dual degrees. Independent study. Accelerated study. Pass/fail grading option. Internships. Graduate school at which undergraduates may take graduate-level courses. Preprofessional programs in law, medicine, and dentistry. 2-3 engineering with Rutgers Coll of Enginering. 3-2 B.A./M.B.A. program with Rutgers Graduate Sch of Management. Five-year B.A./M.Ed. program with Rutgers Graduate Sch of Education. Eight-year B.A./M.D. program with U of Medicine and Dentistry of New Jersey. Science management certificate. Washington Semester. Member of National Student Exchange. Exchange program with Howard U. Teacher certification in early childhood, elementary, secondary, and special education. Certification in specific subject areas. Study abroad in France, Germany, Great Britain, Ireland, Israel, Italy, Mexico, Portugal, and Spain. ROTC and AFROTC.

**Honors:** Phi Beta Kappa. Honors program. Honor societies.

**Academic Assistance:** Remedial reading, writing, math, and study skills. Nonremedial tutoring.

**STUDENT LIFE. Housing:** Students may live on or off campus. Women's dorms. School-owned/operated apartments. Language and cultural houses. Math-science house. Substance-free housing. 61% of students live in college housing.

**Social atmosphere:** According to the student newspaper, "Many students go home for weekends. Thursday and Friday nights are party nights." Fraternities hold parties and fundraising events, dorms and ethnic/cultural groups organize dances and other activities, and the College Center Board offers movies, speakers, parties, and other events. Popular on-campus spots are the College Center, the Cafe, the Passion Puddle, and the campus lake, where students picnic, have barbecues, and relax. Off campus, students frequent Stuff Yer Face restaurant, Shelly's, Thomas Sweets, Old Queens, Roxy, and the Knight Club. Homecoming, Mom's Day, Dad's Day, Ag Field Day, the Annual Women's Conference, and athletic events are popular.

**Services and counseling/handicapped student services:** Placement services. Health service. Women's center. Day care. Learning Resources Center. Counseling services for minority, military, veteran, and older students. Birth control, personal, and psychological counseling. Career and academic guidance services. Religious counseling. Physically disabled student services. Learning disabled services. Notetaking services. Reader services for the blind.

**Campus organizations:** Undergraduate student government. Student newspaper (Daily Targum; Caellian). Literary magazine. Yearbook. Radio and TV stations. Orchestra, bands, activities board, Feminist Collective, numerous academic, cultural, professional, recreational, service, and special-interest groups, 300 organizations in all. 15 sororities, no chapter houses. 3% of women join a sorority.

**Religious organizations:** Bahai Club, B'nai B'rith Hillel, Campus Crusade for Christ, Chinese Christian Fellowship, Intervarsity Christian Fellowship, Islamic Society and Friends, Jewish University Students Together, Korean Christian Fellowship, Meditation Club, New Hope Church, University Christian Outreach.

**Minority/foreign student organizations:** Blacks United to Save Themselves, Black Voice/Carta Boricua, Black Women's Association, Douglass Black Student Congress, El Circulo Hispanica, Minority Affairs Committee, Minority Mentor Club, minority engineering and science groups, NAACP, Native American Organization, Paul Robeson Club. International Student Association, African, Armenian, Asian, Chinese, Filipino, French, Greek, Haitian, Indian, Iranian, Italian, Japanese, Korean, Latin American, Pakistani, Polish, Portuguese/Brazilian, Puerto Rican, Turkish, Ukrainian, Vietnamese, and West Indian groups.

**ATHLETICS. Physical education requirements:** None.

**Intercollegiate competition:** 3% of students participate. Basketball (W), cheerleading (W), crew (W), cross-country (W), diving (W), fencing (W), field hockey (W), golf (W), gymnastics (W), lacrosse (W), soccer (W), softball (W), swimming (W), tennis (W), track and field (indoor) (W), track and field (outdoor) (W), volleyball (W). Member of Atlantic 10 Conference, ECAC, NCAA Division I.

**Intramural and club sports:** Intramural aerobics, basketball, body building, bowling, floor hockey, golf, racquetball, soccer, table tennis, tennis, triathlon, ultimate frisbee, volleyball, walleyball. Women's club aerobics, badminton, equestrian sports, field hockey, football, gymnastics, lacrosse, martial arts, modern dance, mountain bike, outdoors, racquetball, rangers, rugby, sailing, scuba, skiing, squash, synchronized swimming, table tennis, volleyball, water polo.

**ADMISSIONS. Academic basis for candidate selection** (in order of priority): Secondary school record, class rank, standardized test scores, school's recommendation.

**Nonacademic basis for candidate selection:** Particular talent or ability is important. Extracurricular participation and geographical distribution are considered.

**Requirements:** Graduation from secondary school is required; GED is accepted. 16 units and the following program of study are required: 4 units of English, 3 units of math, 2 units of science, 2 units of foreign language, 5 units of academic electives. Educational Opportunity Fund (EOF) program for in-state applicants not normally admissible. SAT or ACT is required. Campus visit recommended.

**Procedure:** Take SAT or ACT by December of 12th year. Application deadline is January 15. Notification of admission by April 15. Reply is required by May 1 or within two weeks of acceptance. $125 nonrefundable tuition deposit. $100 room deposit, refundable until June 30. Freshmen accepted in fall terms only.

**Special programs:** Admission may be deferred one year. Credit and/or placement may be granted through CEEB Advanced Placement exams for scores of 4 or higher. Credit may be granted through CLEP subject exams and challenge exams. Early entrance/early admission program. Concurrent enrollment program.

**Transfer students:** Transfer students accepted for terms other than fall. In fall 1993, 20% of all new students were transfers into all classes. 1,521 transfer applications were received, 643 were accepted. Application deadline is March 15 for fall; November 1 for spring. Lowest course grade accepted is "C." Maximum number of transferable credits is 60 semester hours. At least 30 of final 42 semester hours must be completed at the college to receive degree.

**Admissions contact:** Elizabeth Mitchell, Ph.D., Assistant Vice President for University Undergraduate Admissions. 908 932-3770.

**FINANCIAL AID. Available aid:** Pell grants, SEOG, state scholarships and grants, school scholarships and grants, ROTC scholarships, academic merit scholarships, and athletic scholarships. Perkins Loans (NDSL), PLUS, Stafford Loans (GSL), state loans, school loans, and SLS. AMS and deferred payment plan.

**Financial aid statistics:** 18% of aid is not need-based. In 1993-94, 86% of all undergraduate applicants received aid; 77% of freshman applicants. Average amounts of aid awarded freshmen: Scholarships and grants, $4,076; loans, $2,261.

**Supporting data/closing dates:** FAFSA: Priority filing date is March 1. Income tax forms: Accepted on rolling basis. Notification of awards on rolling basis.

**Financial aid contact:** Steve Rouff, M.A., Acting Director of Financial Aid. 908 932-8811 (A-Led), 908 932-7057 (Lee-Z).

**STUDENT EMPLOYMENT.** College Work/Study Program. Institutional employment. 21% of full-time undergraduates work on campus during school year. Students may expect to earn an average of $504 during school year. Off-campus part-time employment opportunities rated "fair."

**COMPUTER FACILITIES.** 482 IBM/IBM-compatible and Macintosh/Apple microcomputers; 452 are networked. Students may access Digital, IBM, SUN minicomputer/mainframe systems, BITNET, Internet. Residence halls may be equipped with stand-alone microcomputers. Client/LAN operating systems include Apple/Macintosh, DOS, UNIX/XENIX/AIX, X-windows, LocalTalk/AppleTalk, Novell. Computer languages and software packages include ClarisWorks, FORTRAN, Lotus 1-2-3, MacWrite, SAS, SPSS-X, WordPerfect; 50 in all. Microcomputers available to all students; mainframes restricted to classroom instructional use.

**Fees:** $50 computer fee per semester.

**Hours:** Vary; 24 hours in some locations.

**GRADUATE CAREER DATA.** Highest graduate school enrollments: Georgetown U, New York U, Rutgers U, U of Medicine & Dentistry of New Jersey. Companies and businesses that hire graduates: Deloitte & Touche, Prudential, Merck, KPMG Peat Marwick, Bloomingdale's.

**PROMINENT ALUMNI/AE.** Cheryl Washington, news anchor; Judith Viorst, writer.

# Rutgers University–Livingston College

**New Brunswick, NJ 08903 908 932-1766**

**1993-94 Costs.** Tuition: $3,417 (state residents), $6,955 (out-of-state). Room: $2,598. Board: $1,856. Fees, books, misc. academic expenses (school's estimate): $1,640.
**Enrollment.** Undergraduates: 2,073 men, 1,360 women (full-time). Freshman class: 11,996 applicants, 7,212 accepted, 661 enrolled.
**Test score averages/ranges.** Average SAT scores: 481 verbal, 551 math. Range of SAT scores of middle 50%: 430-530 verbal, 500-600 math.
**Faculty.** 761 full-time. 95% of faculty holds highest degree in specific field. Student/faculty ratio: 17 to 1.
**Selectivity rating.** Competitive.

**PROFILE.** Rutgers U–Livingston College, founded in 1969, is a public, liberal arts university. Its campus is located in New Brunswick, 40 miles from New York City.
**Accreditation:** MSACS. Professionally accredited by the American Assembly of Collegiate Schools of Business, the American Medical Association (CAHEA), the Council on Education for Public Health, the Council on Social Work Education, the National Association of Schools of Music, the National Council for Accreditation of Teacher Education.
**Religious orientation:** Rutgers University-Livingston College is nonsectarian; no religious requirements.
**Library:** Collections totaling over 4,387,960 volumes, 19,822 periodical subscriptions, and 2,630,211 microform items.
**Special facilities/museums:** Agricultural, art, and geology museums, black-box theatre, forest ecological preserve, Van de Graaff tandem accelerator.
**Athletic facilities:** Gymnasiums, athletic fields, indoor practice bubble, golf course, tennis courts, swimming pools, recreation centers, stadium.
**STUDENT BODY. Undergraduate profile:** 89% are state residents; 36% are transfers. 12% Asian-American, 14% Black, 7% Hispanic, 62% White, 5% Other. Average age of undergraduates is 21.
**Freshman profile:** 1% of freshmen who took SAT scored 700 or over on verbal, 3% scored 700 or over on math; 6% scored 600 or over on verbal, 29% scored 600 or over on math; 44% scored 500 or over on verbal, 78% scored 500 or over on math; 89% scored 400 or over on verbal, 99% scored 400 or over on math; 99% scored 300 or over on verbal, 100% scored 300 or over on math. 100% of accepted applicants took SAT.
**Undergraduate achievement:** 87% of fall 1992 freshmen returned for fall 1993 term. 36% of entering class graduated. 34% of students who completed a degree program immediately went on to graduate study.
**Foreign students:** 81 students are from out of the country. Countries represented include India, Japan, Korea, Taiwan, Trinidad/Tobago, and the United Kingdom; 34 in all.
**PROGRAMS OF STUDY. Degrees:** B.A., B.S.
**Majors:** Accounting, Administration of Justice, Africana Studies, American Studies, Anthropology, Art History, Biochemistry, Biological Sciences/Biology, Biomathematics, Chemistry, Chemistry/Foods/Nutrition, Chinese, Classical Humanities, Communication, Comparative Literature, Computer Science, Dance, East Asian Language/Area Studies, Economics, English, Exercise Science/Sports Studies, Finance, French, Geography, Geology, German, Greek, Greek/Latin, Hebraic Studies, History, History/Political Science, Individualized Major, Italian, Journalism/Mass Media, Labor Studies, Latin, Latin American Studies, Linguistics, Management, Marketing, Mathematics, Medical Technology, Middle Eastern Studies, Music, Philosophy, Physician Assistant, Physics, Political Science, Portuguese, Psychology, Public Health, Puerto Rican/Hispanic Caribbean Studies, Religion, Russian, Slavic/East European Studies, Social Work, Sociology, Spanish, Statistics, Statistics/Mathematics, Theatre Arts, Urban Studies, Visual Arts, Women's Studies.
**Distribution of degrees:** The majors with the highest enrollment are economics, psychology, and administration of justice.
**Requirements:** General education requirement.
**Academic regulations:** Freshmen must maintain minimum 1.6 GPA; sophomores, 1.6 GPA; juniors, 1.7 GPA; seniors, 1.8 GPA.
**Special:** Minors offered in many majors and in approximately 25 other fields. Eagleton Institute associate's certificate for senior political science majors. Certificate programs in many areas including cartography, coaching, criminology, environmental planning, environmental resource monitoring, foreign language proficiency, international studies, science management, translation proficiency, and urban planning. Self-designed majors. Double majors. Dual degrees. Independent study. Accelerated study. Pass/fail grading option. Internships. Graduate school at which undergraduates may take graduate-level courses. Preprofessional programs in law, medicine, and dentistry. 2-3 engineering program with Rutgers Coll of Engineering. 3-2 B.A./M.B.A. program with Rutgers Graduate Sch of Management. Five-year B.A./M.Ed. program with Rutgers Graduate Sch of Education. Eight-year B.A./M.D. program with U of Medicine and Dentistry of New Jersey. Washington Semester. Teacher certification in early childhood, elementary, secondary, and special education. Certification in specific subject areas. Study abroad in France, Germany, Ireland, Israel, Italy, Mexico, Portugal, Spain, and the United Kingdom. ROTC and AFROTC.
**Honors:** Phi Beta Kappa. Honors program. Honor societies.
**Academic Assistance:** Remedial reading, writing, math, and study skills. Nonremedial tutoring.
**STUDENT LIFE. Housing:** Students may live on or off campus. Coed dorms. Fraternity housing. School-owned/operated apartments. Off-campus privately-owned housing. 43% of students live in college housing.
**Social atmosphere:** The student newspaper reports, "Livingston students are no longer always going home on the weekends. Weekend programming and a changing student body are making Livingston a more cohesive unit all week long." Popular events include Homecoming and Spring Weekend, "when the whole campus becomes a party." Fraternities have some influence on student social life; however, "it's mainly a diffuse collection of individuals, a small college within a large university." A common student gathering spot is the new student center, while "the popular hangouts are still across the river at Rutgers College."
**Services and counseling/handicapped student services:** Placement services. Health service. Women's center. Day care. Learning Resources Center. Counseling services for minority, military, veteran, and older students. Birth control, personal, and psychological counseling. Career and academic guidance services. Religious counseling. Physically disabled student services. Learning disabled services. Notetaking services. Reader services for the blind.
**Campus organizations:** Undergraduate student government. Student newspaper (Daily Targum; Livingston Medium). Literary magazine. Yearbook. Radio and TV stations. Livingston's Own Concert Organization, orchestra, bands, entertainment committee, program board, numerous academic, cultural, professional, recreational, service, and special-interest groups, 300 organizations in all. 32 fraternities, 19 chapter houses; 15 sororities, no chapter houses. 7% of men join a fraternity. 3% of women join a sorority.
**Religious organizations:** Bahai Club, B'nai B'rith Hillel, Campus Crusade for Christ, Chinese Christian Fellowship, Intervarsity Christian Fellowship, Islamic Society and Friends, Jewish University Students Together, Korean Christian Fellowship, Meditation Club, New Hope Church, University Christian Outreach.
**Minority/foreign student organizations:** Blacks United to Save Themselves, Black Voice/Carta Boricua, Black Women's Association, El Circulo Hispanica, Minority Affairs Committee, Minority Mentor Club, minority engineering and science groups, NAACP, Native American Organization, Paul Robeson Club. International Student Association, African, Arab, Armenian, Asian, Chinese, Filipino, French, Haitian, Indian, Iranian, Japanese, Korean, Latin American, Pakistani, Polish, Portuguese/Brazilian, Puerto Rican, Turkish, Ukrainian, Vietnamese, and West Indian groups.
**ATHLETICS. Physical education requirements:** None.
**Intercollegiate competition:** 7% of students participate. Baseball (M), basketball (M,W), cheerleading (M,W), crew (M,W), cross-country (M,W), diving (M,W), fencing (M,W), field hockey (W), football (M), golf (M,W), gymnastics (W), lacrosse (M,W), soccer (M,W), softball (W), swimming (M,W), tennis (M,W), track and field (indoor) (M,W), track and field (outdoor) (M,W), volleyball (W), wrestling (M). Member of Atlantic 10 Conference, Big East Football Conference, ECAC, NCAA Division I.
**Intramural and club sports:** Intramural aerobics, basketball, body building, bowling, floor hockey, flag football, golf, racquetball, soccer, table tennis, tennis, touch football, triathlon, ultimate frisbee, volleyball, walleyball, wrestling. Men's club aerobics, badminton, equestrian sports, field hockey, football, gymnastics, ice hockey, lacrosse, martial arts, modern dance, mountain bike, outdoors, racquetball, rangers, rugby, sailing, scuba, skiing, squash, synchronized swimming, table tennis, volleyball, water polo. Women's club aerobics, badminton, equestrian sports, field hockey, football, gymnastics, lacrosse, martial arts, modern dance, mountain bike, outdoors, racquetball, rangers, rugby, sailing, scuba, skiing, squash, synchronized swimming, table tennis, volleyball, water polo.
**ADMISSIONS. Academic basis for candidate selection** (in order of priority): Secondary school record, class rank, standardized test scores, school's recommendation.
**Nonacademic basis for candidate selection:** Particular talent or ability is important. Extracurricular participation and geographical distribution are considered.
**Requirements:** Graduation from secondary school is required; GED is accepted. 16 units and the following program of study are required: 4 units of English, 3 units of math, 2 units of science, 2 units of foreign language, 5 units of academic electives. Educational Opportunity Fund (EOF) program for in-state applicants not normally admissible. SAT or ACT is required. Campus visit recommended.
**Procedure:** Take SAT or ACT by December of 12th year. Application deadline is January 15. Notification of admission by April 15. Reply is required by May 1 or within two weeks of acceptance. $125 nonrefundable tuition deposit. $100 room deposit, refundable until June 30. Freshmen accepted in fall terms only.
**Special programs:** Admission may be deferred one year. Credit and/or placement may be granted through CEEB Advanced Placement exams for scores of 4 or higher. Credit and/or placement may be granted through CLEP general and subject exams. Credit and placement may be granted through life experience. Early entrance/early admission program. Concurrent enrollment program.
**Transfer students:** Transfer students accepted for terms other than fall. In fall 1993, 36% of all new students were transfers into all classes. 3,844 transfer applications were received, 1,679 were accepted. Application deadline is March 15 for fall; November 1 for spring. Lowest course grade accepted is "C." Maximum number of transferable credits is 60 semester hours. At least 30 of final 42 semester hours must be completed at Livingston to receive degree.
**Admissions contact:** Elizabeth Mitchell, Ph.D., Assistant Vice President for University Undergraduate Admissions. 908 932-3770.
**FINANCIAL AID. Available aid:** Pell grants, SEOG, state scholarships and grants, school scholarships and grants, ROTC scholarships, academic merit scholarships, and athletic scholarships. Perkins Loans (NDSL), PLUS, Stafford Loans (GSL), state loans, school loans, and SLS. AMS and deferred payment plan.
**Financial aid statistics:** 16% of aid is not need-based. In 1993-94, 83% of all undergraduate applicants received aid; 76% of freshman applicants. Average amounts of aid awarded freshmen: Scholarships and grants, $4,948; loans, $2,006.
**Supporting data/closing dates:** FAFSA: Priority filing date is March 1. Income tax forms: Accepted on rolling basis. Notification of awards on rolling basis.
**Financial aid contact:** Steve Rouff, M.A., Acting Director of Financial Aid. 908 932-8811 (A-Led), 908 932-7057 (Lee-Z).
**STUDENT EMPLOYMENT.** College Work/Study Program. Institutional employment. 18% of full-time undergraduates work on campus during school year. Students may expect to earn an average of $500 during school year. Off-campus part-time employment opportunities rated "fair."
**COMPUTER FACILITIES.** 482 IBM/IBM-compatible and Macintosh/Apple microcomputers; 452 are networked. Students may access Digital, IBM, SUN minicomputer/mainframe systems, BITNET, Internet. Client/LAN operating systems include Apple/Macintosh, DOS, UNIX/XENIX/AIX, X-windows, LocalTalk/AppleTalk, Novell. Computer languages and software packages include ClarisWorks, FORTRAN, Lotus

1-2-3, MacWrite, SAS, SPSS-X, WordPerfect; 50 in all. Microcomputers available to all students; mainframes restricted to instructional classroom use.
**Fees:** $50/semester.
**Hours:** Vary; 24 hours in some locations.

**GRADUATE CAREER DATA.** Companies and businesses that hire graduates: Deloitte & Touche, Johnson & Johnson, Merck, Kettering Cancer Center, KPMG Peat Marwick.

## Rutgers University–Mason Gross School of the Arts

**New Brunswick, NJ 08903** **908 932-1766**

**1993-94 Costs.** Tuition: $3,417 (state residents), $6,955 (out-of-state). Room: $2,598. Board: $1,856. Fees, books, misc. academic expenses (school's estimate): $890.
**Enrollment.** Undergraduates: 184 men, 214 women (full-time). Freshman class: 1,087 applicants, 270 accepted, 119 enrolled. Graduate enrollment: 104 men, 120 women.
**Test score averages/ranges.** Average SAT scores: 485 verbal, 526 math. Range of SAT scores of middle 50%: 430-540 verbal, 470-580 math.
**Faculty.** 78 full-time. 95% of faculty holds highest degree in specific field. Student/faculty ratio: 11 to 1.
**Selectivity rating.** More competitive.

**PROFILE.** Rutgers U–The Mason Gross School of the Arts, founded in 1976, is a public university for the arts. Its campus is located in New Brunswick, 40 miles from New York City.

**Accreditation:** MSACS. Professionally accredited by the National Association of Schools of Art and Design, the National Association of Schools of Music, the National Council for Accreditation of Teacher Education.
**Religious orientation:** Rutgers University-Mason Gross School of the Arts is nonsectarian; no religious requirements.
**Library:** Collections totaling over 4,387,960 volumes, 19,822 periodical subscriptions, and 2,630,211 microform items.
**Special facilities/museums:** Agricultural, art, and geology museums, dance, music, and art studios, concert and recital halls, theatres, institute of jazz studies.
**Athletic facilities:** Gymnasiums, athletic fields, indoor practice bubble, golf course, tennis courts, swimming pools, recreation centers, stadium.

**STUDENT BODY. Undergraduate profile:** 86% are state residents; 18% are transfers. 7% Asian-American, 6% Black, 7% Hispanic, 76% White, 4% Other. Average age of undergraduates is 21.
**Freshman profile:** 3% of freshmen who took SAT scored 700 or over on math; 9% scored 600 or over on verbal, 21% scored 600 or over on math; 48% scored 500 or over on verbal, 65% scored 500 or over on math; 88% scored 400 or over on verbal, 92% scored 400 or over on math; 98% scored 300 or over on verbal, 99% scored 300 or over on math. 99% of accepted applicants took SAT; 1% took ACT.
**Undergraduate achievement:** 76% of fall 1991 freshmen returned for fall 1992 term. 41% of entering class graduated. 22% of students who completed a degree program immediately went on to graduate study.
**Foreign students:** 10 students are from out of the country. Countries represented include Austria, Canada, Indonesia, Korea, Taiwan, and the United Kingdom; nine in all.

**PROGRAMS OF STUDY. Degrees:** B.F.A., B.Mus.
**Majors:** Dance, Music, Theatre Arts, Visual Arts.
**Distribution of degrees:** The majors with the highest enrollment are visual arts, music, and theatre arts.
**Requirements:** General education requirement.
**Academic regulations:** Minimum 1.8 GPA must be maintained.
**Special:** Concentrations in acting, design, design/technical theatre, drawing, film/video, jazz, music education, music performance, painting, photography, printmaking, production/management in theatre arts, sculpture/ceramics. Internships. Graduate school at which undergraduates may take graduate-level courses. Teacher certification in elementary and secondary education. Certification in specific subject areas. Study abroad in England, France, Germany, Ireland, Israel, Italy, Mexico, Portugal, and Spain. ROTC and AFROTC.
**Academic Assistance:** Remedial reading, writing, math, and study skills. Nonremedial tutoring.

**ADMISSIONS. Academic basis for candidate selection** (in order of priority): Secondary school record, class rank, standardized test scores, school's recommendation.
**Nonacademic basis for candidate selection:** Particular talent or ability is emphasized.
**Requirements:** Graduation from secondary school is required; GED is accepted. 16 units and the following program of study are required: 4 units of English, 3 units of math, 9 units of academic electives. Audition required of dance, music program, and theatre arts applicants. Portfolio required of art program applicants. Education Opportunity Fund (EOF) program for in-state applicants not normally admissible. SAT or ACT is required. Campus visit recommended. Off-campus interviews available with an admissions representative.
**Procedure:** Take SAT or ACT by December of 12th year. Application deadline is January 15 for visual arts program; March 15 for music, dance, and theatre arts programs. Notification of admission by April 15. Reply is required by May 1 or within two weeks of acceptance. $125 nonrefundable tuition deposit. $100 room deposit, refundable until June 30. Freshmen accepted in fall terms only.
**Special programs:** Admission may be deferred one year. Credit and/or placement may be granted through CEEB Advanced Placement exams for scores of 4 or higher. Credit and/or placement may be granted through CLEP subject exams. Early entrance/early admission program. Concurrent enrollment program.
**Transfer students:** Transfer students accepted for terms other than fall. In fall 1993, 18% of all new students were transfers into all classes. 263 transfer applications were received, 44 were accepted. Application deadline is March 15 for fall; November 1 for spring. Lowest course grade accepted is "C." Two or three years of course work must be completed at the college to receive degree; varies by major.
**Admissions contact:** Elizabeth Mitchell, Ph.D., Assistant Vice President for University Undergraduate Admissions. 908 932-3770.

**FINANCIAL AID. Available aid:** Pell grants, SEOG, state scholarships and grants, school scholarships and grants, ROTC scholarships, academic merit scholarships, and athletic scholarships. Perkins Loans (NDSL), PLUS, Stafford Loans (GSL), state loans, school loans, and SLS. AMS and deferred payment plan.
**Financial aid statistics:** 15% of aid is not need-based. In 1993-94, 84% of all undergraduate applicants received aid; 78% of freshman applicants. Average amounts of aid awarded freshmen: Scholarships and grants, $3,367; loans, $2,713.
**Supporting data/closing dates:** FAFSA: Priority filing date is March 1. Income tax forms: Accepted on rolling basis. Notification of awards on rolling basis.
**Financial aid contact:** Steve Rouff, M.A., Acting Director of Financial Aid. 908 932-8811 (A-Led), 908 932-7057 (Lee-Z).

## Rutgers University–Newark College of Arts and Sciences

**Newark, NJ 07102** **201 648-1766**

**1993-94 Costs.** Tuition: $3,417 (state residents), $6,955 (out-of-state). Room: $2,598. Board: $1,856. Fees, books, misc. academic expenses (school's estimate): $1,408.
**Enrollment.** Undergraduates: 1,484 men, 1,638 women (full-time). Freshman class: 4,852 applicants, 2,528 accepted, 456 enrolled.
**Test score averages/ranges.** Average SAT scores: 456 verbal, 527 math. Range of SAT scores of middle 50%: 400-500 verbal, 470-580 math.
**Faculty.** 184 full-time. 95% of faculty holds highest degree in specific field. Student/faculty ratio: 15 to 1.
**Selectivity rating.** Competitive.

**PROFILE.** Rutgers U–Newark College of Arts and Sciences, founded in 1930, is a public, liberal arts university. Its 23-acre campus is located in Newark, 15 miles from New York City.

**Accreditation:** MSACS. Professionally accredited by the American Assembly of Collegiate Schools of Business, the American Medical Association (CAHEA), the Council on Social Work Education, the National Association of Schools of Music.
**Religious orientation:** Rutgers University-Newark College of Arts and Sciences is nonsectarian; no religious requirements.
**Library:** Collections totaling over 591,536 volumes, 3,708 periodical subscriptions, and 675,962 microform items.
**Special facilities/museums:** Institute of jazz studies, TV/radio media center, animal behavior institute, molecular and behavioral neuroscience, electron microscope.
**Athletic facilities:** Gymnasiums, swimming pool, soccer, softball, and baseball fields, Nautilus and free-weight equipment, tennis and racquetball courts, recreation facility, dance room, saunas.

**STUDENT BODY. Undergraduate profile:** 94% are state residents; 48% are transfers. 14% Asian-American, 18% Black, 16% Hispanic, 1% Native American, 39% White, 12% Other. Average age of undergraduates is 22.
**Freshman profile:** 2% of freshmen who took SAT scored 700 or over on math; 5% scored 600 or over on verbal, 19% scored 600 or over on math; 25% scored 500 or over on verbal, 66% scored 500 or over on math; 75% scored 400 or over on verbal, 96% scored 400 or over on math; 98% scored 300 or over on verbal, 98% scored 300 or over on math. 98% of accepted applicants took SAT; 1% took ACT.
**Undergraduate achievement:** 83% of fall 1991 freshmen returned for fall 1992 term. 23% of entering class graduated. 39% of students who completed a degree program immediately went on to graduate study.
**Foreign students:** 144 students are from out of the country. Countries represented include Cyprus, India, Indonesia, Japan, the Philippines, and Taiwan; 44 in all.

**PROGRAMS OF STUDY. Degrees:** B.A., B.F.A., B.S.
**Majors:** Accounting, Afro-American/African Studies, American Studies, Anthropology, Applied Mathematics, Applied Physics, Art, Biology, Botany, Chemistry, Classical Civilization, Clinical Lab Sciences, Computer Science, Criminal Justice, Economics, English, Finance, French, Geology, German, Graphic Design, Hebraic Studies, History, Information Processing Systems, Interdisciplinary Major, Italian, Journalism, Management, Marketing, Mathematics, Medical Technology, Music, Philosophy, Physics, Political Science, Psychology, Puerto Rican Studies, Science/Technology/Society, Slavic, Social Work, Sociology, Spanish, Theatre Arts/Speech, Women's Studies, Zoology/Physiology.
**Distribution of degrees:** The majors with the highest enrollment are accounting, management, and biology.
**Requirements:** General education requirement.
**Academic regulations:** Minimum 2.0 GPA must be maintained.
**Special:** Minors offered in most majors and in archaeology, criminal justice, international affairs, legal studies, religion, and television. Self-designed majors. Double majors. Dual degrees. Independent study. Accelerated study. Pass/fail grading option. Internships. Graduate school at which undergraduates may take graduate-level courses. Preprofessional programs in law, medicine, veterinary science, pharmacy, and dentistry. 2-2 and 2-3 engineering programs with Rutgers Coll of Engineering. 2-3 pharmacy program with Rutgers Coll of Pharmacy. 3-2 B.A./M.B.A. program with Rutgers Graduate Sch of Management. B.A. or B.S./M.A. criminal justice program with Rutgers Sch of Criminal Justice. Eight-year B.A./M.D. program with U of Medicine and Dentistry of New Jersey. Member of consortium with Essex County Coll, New Jersey Inst of Tech, and U of Medicine and Dentistry of New Jersey. Teacher certification in early childhood, elementary, and secondary education. Certification in specific subject areas. Study abroad in England, France, Germany, Ireland, Israel, Italy, Mexico, Portugal, and Spain. ROTC at New Jersey Inst of Tech. AFROTC at Rutgers New Brunswick.

**Honors:** Phi Beta Kappa. Honors program. Honor societies.
**Academic Assistance:** Remedial reading, writing, math, and study skills. Nonremedial tutoring.

**STUDENT LIFE. Housing:** Students may live on or off campus. Coed dorms. School-owned/operated apartments. 6% of students live in college housing.
**Social atmosphere:** According to the editor of the student newspaper, Newark College of Arts and Sciences is "a culturally diverse campus with easy access to some of the largest museums and libraries in the country. It has a friendly and welcoming atmosphere with plenty for the active student to do." Influential groups around campus are athletes, the Student Governing Association, and the program board. Popular events include the Golden Dome Volleyball Classic, the Fright Night Halloween Party, fraternity parties, and guest speakers. Among spots students enjoy are the On Campus Pub, the Student Center, the campus cafeteria, the library, and McGovern's Bar and Grill.
**Services and counseling/handicapped student services:** Placement services. Health service. Day care. Counseling services for minority, military, veteran, and older students. Birth control, personal, and psychological counseling. Career and academic guidance services. Religious counseling. Physically disabled student services. Learning disabled services. Notetaking services. Tape recorders. Tutors. Reader services for the blind.
**Campus organizations:** Undergraduate student government. Student newspaper (Observer, published once/week). Literary magazine. Yearbook. Radio station. Chorus, art organization, theatre arts group, photography, debate, program board, martial arts groups, outdoor and ski clubs, academic, professional, service, and special-interest groups, 85 organizations in all. Five fraternities, one chapter house; seven sororities, two chapter houses.
**Religious organizations:** Islamic Student Organization, Jewish Student Union, Newman Club.
**Minority/foreign student organizations:** Black Organization of Students, Haitian American Student Association, Hispanic Club, Italian American Club, Minority Science Club, Nelson Mandela Club, Progresso Hispano Organization, Robeson Network. International Student Organization, People from Around the World, African, Arab, Chinese, Cuban, Egyptian, Filipino, Korean, Puerto Rican, Ukrainian, and West Indian groups.

**ATHLETICS. Physical education requirements:** None.
**Intercollegiate competition:** 8% of students participate. Baseball (M), basketball (M,W), soccer (M), softball (W), tennis (M,W), volleyball (M,W). Member of Eastern Intercollegiate Volleyball Association, ECAC, NCAA Division I for men's volleyball, NCAA Division III, NJAC.
**Intramural and club sports:** 10% of students participate. Intramural aerobics, basketball, flag football, floor hockey, martial arts, Nautilus, racquetball, soccer, table tennis, tennis, volleyball, weight training. Men's club fencing, table tennis. Women's club fencing.

**ADMISSIONS. Academic basis for candidate selection** (in order of priority): Secondary school record, class rank, standardized test scores, school's recommendation.
**Nonacademic basis for candidate selection:** Particular talent or ability is important. Extracurricular participation and geographical distribution are considered.
**Requirements:** Graduation from secondary school is required; GED is accepted. 16 units and the following program of study are required: 4 units of English, 3 units of math, 2 units of science, 2 units of foreign language, 5 units of academic electives. Educational Opportunity Fund (EOF) program for in-state applicants not normally admissible. SAT or ACT is required. Campus visit recommended.
**Procedure:** Take SAT or ACT by December of 12th year. Application deadline is May 1. Notification of admission on rolling basis. Reply is required by May 1 or within two weeks of acceptance. $100 room deposit, refundable until July 1. Freshmen accepted in terms other than fall.
**Special programs:** Admission may be deferred one semester. Credit and/or placement may be granted through CEEB Advanced Placement exams for scores of 4 or higher. Credit may be granted through CLEP general and subject exams. Early entrance/early admission program. Concurrent enrollment program.
**Transfer students:** Transfer students accepted for terms other than fall. In fall 1993, 48% of all new students were transfers into all classes. 2,013 transfer applications were received, 972 were accepted. Application deadline is May 1 for fall; November 30 for spring. Lowest course grade accepted is "C." Maximum number of transferable credits is 94 semester hours. At least 30 of final 42 semester hours must be completed at Newark to receive degree.
**Admissions contact:** Elizabeth Mitchell, Ph.D., Assistant Vice President for University Undergraduate Admissions. 201 648-5205.

**FINANCIAL AID. Available aid:** Pell grants, SEOG, state scholarships and grants, school scholarships and grants, ROTC scholarships, academic merit scholarships, and athletic scholarships. Perkins Loans (NDSL), PLUS, Stafford Loans (GSL), state loans, school loans, and SLS. AMS and deferred payment plan.
**Financial aid statistics:** 7% of aid is not need-based. In 1993-94, 84% of all undergraduate applicants received aid; 81% of freshman applicants. Average amounts of aid awarded freshmen: Scholarships and grants, $4,564; loans, $1,594.
**Supporting data/closing dates:** FAFSA: Priority filing date is March 1. Income tax forms: Accepted on rolling basis. Notification of awards on rolling basis.
**Financial aid contact:** Paul Gilroy, Director of Financial Aid. 201 648-5357.

**STUDENT EMPLOYMENT.** College Work/Study Program. Institutional employment. 8% of full-time undergraduates work on campus during school year. Students may expect to earn an average of $639 during school year. Off-campus part-time employment opportunities rated "good."

**COMPUTER FACILITIES.** 400 IBM/IBM-compatible and Macintosh/Apple microcomputers; all are networked. Students may access Digital, Hewlett-Packard, IBM, Pyramid, SUN minicomputer/mainframe systems, BITNET, Internet. Residence halls may be equipped with stand-alone microcomputers. Client/LAN operating systems include Apple/Macintosh, Novell. Computer languages and software packages include C, FORTRAN, Lindo, Pascal, SAS, SPSS-X. Computer facilities are available to all students.
**Fees:** $100 computer fee per year.
**Hours:** 9 AM-10 PM.

**GRADUATE CAREER DATA.** Companies and businesses that hire graduates: Deloitte and Touche, Price Waterhouse, Wal-Mart, Merck, Federal Reserve Bank.

# Rutgers University–Rutgers College

**New Brunswick, NJ 08903** **908 932-1766**

**1993-94 Costs.** Tuition: $3,417 (state residents), $6,955 (out-of-state). Room: $2,598. Board: $1,856. Fees, books, misc. academic expenses (school's estimate): $1,604.
**Enrollment.** Undergraduates: 4,068 men, 4,162 women (full-time). Freshman class: 16,843 applicants, 7,808 accepted, 1,760 enrolled.
**Test score averages/ranges.** Average SAT scores: 534 verbal, 608 math. Range of SAT scores of middle 50%: 470-600 verbal, 550-670 math.
**Faculty.** 761 full-time. 95% of faculty holds highest degree in specific field. Student/faculty ratio: 17 to 1.
**Selectivity rating.** Highly competitive.

**PROFILE.** Rutgers U–Rutgers College, founded in 1766, is a public, liberal arts university. Founded in 1766, it adopted coeducation in 1972. Its campus is located in New Brunswick, 40 miles from New York City.

**Accreditation:** MSACS. Professionally accredited by the American Assembly of Collegiate Schools of Business, the National Association of Schools of Music, the National Council for Accreditation of Teacher Education.
**Religious orientation:** Rutgers University-Rutgers College is nonsectarian; no religious requirements.
**Library:** Collections totaling over 4,387,960 volumes, 19,822 periodical subscriptions, and 2,630,211 microform items.
**Special facilities/museums:** Art and geology museums, language lab, TV studio, research institutes.
**Athletic facilities:** Gymnasiums, athletic fields, indoor practice bubble, golf course, tennis courts, swimming pools, recreation centers, stadium.

**STUDENT BODY. Undergraduate profile:** 89% are state residents; 21% are transfers. 15% Asian-American, 8% Black, 12% Hispanic, 62% White, 3% Other. Average age of undergraduates is 20.
**Freshman profile:** 2% of freshmen who took SAT scored 700 or over on verbal, 16% scored 700 or over on math; 25% scored 600 or over on verbal, 58% scored 600 or over on math; 68% scored 500 or over on verbal, 91% scored 500 or over on math; 96% scored 400 or over on verbal, 99% scored 400 or over on math; 99% scored 300 or over on verbal. 100% of accepted applicants took SAT; 1% took ACT.
**Undergraduate achievement:** 91% of fall 1991 freshmen returned for fall 1992 term. 61% of entering class graduated. 37% of students who completed a degree program immediately went on to graduate study.
**Foreign students:** 180 students are from out of the country. Countries represented include Cyprus, Hong Kong, India, Japan, Korea, and Pakistan; 44 in all.

**PROGRAMS OF STUDY. Degrees:** B.A., B.S.
**Majors:** Accounting, Administration of Justice, Africana Studies, American Studies, Anthropology, Art History, Biochemistry, Biological Sciences/Biology, Biomathematics, Chemistry, Chemistry/Foods/Nutrition, Chinese, Classical Humanities, Communication, Comparative Literature, Computer Science, Dance, East Asian Language/Area Studies, Economics, English, Exercise Science/Sport Studies, Finance, French, Geography, Geology, German, Greek, Greek/Latin, Hebraic Studies, History, History/Political Science, Individualized Major, Italian, Journalism/Mass Media, Labor Studies, Latin, Latin American Studies, Linguistics, Management, Marketing, Mathematics, Middle Eastern Studies, Music, Philosophy, Physics, Political Science, Portuguese, Psychology, Public Health, Puerto Rican/Hispanic Caribbean Studies, Religion, Russian, Slavic/Eastern European Studies, Sociology, Spanish, Statistics, Statistics/Mathematics, Theatre Arts, Urban Studies, Visual Arts, Women's Studies.
**Distribution of degrees:** The majors with the highest enrollment are psychology, English, and economics.
**Requirements:** General education requirement.
**Academic regulations:** Minimum 2.0 GPA must be maintained.
**Special:** Minors offered in many majors. Certificate programs in many areas including cartography, coaching, criminology, environmental planning, foreign language proficiency, international studies, translation proficiency, and urban planning. Self-designed majors. Double majors. Dual degrees. Independent study. Accelerated study. Pass/fail grading option. Internships. Graduate school at which undergraduates may take graduate-level courses. Preprofessional programs in law, medicine, and dentistry. 2-3 engineering program with Rutgers Coll of Engineering. 3-2 B.A./M.B.A. program with Rutgers Graduate Sch of Management. B.A./M.Ed. and B.S/M.Ed. programs with Rutgers Graduate Sch of Education. Eight-year B.A./M.D. program with U of Medicine and Dentistry of New Jersey. Washington Semester. Member of National Student Exchange (NSE). Teacher certification in early childhood, elementary, secondary, and special education. Certification in specific subject areas. Study abroad in France, Germany, Ireland, Israel, Italy, Mexico, Portugal, Spain, and the United Kingdom. ROTC and AFROTC.
**Honors:** Phi Beta Kappa. Honors program. Honor societies.
**Academic Assistance:** Remedial reading, writing, math, and study skills. Nonremedial tutoring.

**STUDENT LIFE. Housing:** Students may live on or off campus. Coed dorms. Fraternity housing. School-owned/operated apartments. Off-campus privately-owned housing. New residential facility, to be completed in spring of 1994, will include parking and health club. 57% of students live in college housing.
**Services and counseling/handicapped student services:** Placement services. Health service. Women's center. Day care. Learning Resources Center. Counseling services for minority, military, veteran, and older students. Birth control, personal, and psychological counseling. Career and academic guidance services. Religious counseling. Physically disabled student services. Learning disabled services. Notetaking services. Reader services for the blind.

**Campus organizations:** Undergraduate student government. Student newspapers (Daily Targum; Rutgers Review). Literary magazine. Yearbook. Radio and TV stations. Orchestra, bands, performing dance club, talent showcase, many other cultural groups, geography and political science clubs, many other academic groups, community outreach, environmental group, Republican and Democrat groups, cycling and outdoor clubs, sailing and scuba clubs, other special-interest and recreational groups, 300 organizations in all. 32 fraternities, 19 chapter houses; 15 sororities, no chapter houses. 7% of men join a fraternity. 3% of women join a sorority.
**Religious organizations:** Bahai Club, B'nai B'rith Hillel, Campus Crusade for Christ, Chinese Christian Fellowship, Intervarsity Christian Fellowship, Islamic Society and Friends, Jewish Perspectives, Jewish University Students Together, Korean Christian Fellowship, Meditation Club, New Hope Church, University Christian Outreach, other religious groups.
**Minority/foreign student organizations:** Blacks United to Save Themselves, Black Voice/Carta Boricua, El Circulo Hispanico, Latino Pre-Law group, Minority Affairs Committee, Minority Mentor Club, NAACP, Native American Organization, minority engineering and science groups, Paul Robeson Club. International Student Association, African, Arab, Armenian, Asian, Chinese, Filipino, French, Haitian, Indian, Iranian, Japanese, Korean, Latin American, Pakistani, Polish, Portuguese/Brazilian, Puerto Rican, Turkish, Ukrainian, Vietnamese, and West Indian groups.

**ATHLETICS. Physical education requirements:** None.
**Intercollegiate competition:** 8% of students participate. Baseball (M), basketball (M,W), cheerleading (M,W), crew (M,W), cross-country (M,W), diving (M,W), fencing (M,W), field hockey (W), football (M), golf (M,W), gymnastics (W), lacrosse (M,W), soccer (M,W), softball (W), swimming (M,W), tennis (M,W), track and field (outdoor) (M,W), volleyball (W), wrestling (M). Member of Atlantic 10 Conference, Big East Football Conference, ECAC, NCAA Division I.
**Intramural and club sports:** Intramural aerobics, basketball, body building, bowling, floor hockey, flag football, golf, racquetball, soccer, table tennis, tennis, touch football, triathlon, ultimate frisbee, volleyball, walleyball, wrestling. Men's club aerobics, badminton, equestrian sports, field hockey, football, gymnastics, ice hockey, lacrosse, martial arts, modern dance, mountain bike, outdoors, racquetball, rangers, rugby, sailing, scuba, skiing, squash, sychronized swimming, table tennis, volleyball, water polo. Women's club aerobics, badminton, equestrian sports, field hockey, football, gymnastics, lacrosse, martial arts, modern dance, mountain bike, outdoors, racquetball, rangers, rugby, sailing, scuba, skiing, squash, sychronized swimming, table tennis, volleyball, water polo.

**ADMISSIONS. Academic basis for candidate selection** (in order of priority): Secondary school record, class rank, standardized test scores, school's recommendation.
**Nonacademic basis for candidate selection:** Particular talent or ability is important. Extracurricular participation and geographical distribution are considered.
**Requirements:** Graduation from secondary school is required; GED is accepted. 16 units and the following program of study are required: 4 units of English, 3 units of math, 2 units of science, 2 units of foreign language, 5 units of academic electives. Educational Opportunity Fund (EOF) program for in-state applicants not normally admissible. SAT or ACT is required. Campus visit recommended.
**Procedure:** Take SAT or ACT by December of 12th year. Application deadline is January 15. Notification of admission by April 15. Reply is required by May 1 or within two weeks of acceptance. $125 nonrefundable tuition deposit. $100 room deposit, refundable until June 30. Freshmen accepted in fall terms only.
**Special programs:** Admission may be deferred one year. Credit may be granted through CEEB Advanced Placement for scores of 4 or higher. Credit and placement may be granted through challenge exams. Early entrance/early admission program. Concurrent enrollment program.
**Transfer students:** Transfer students accepted for terms other than fall. In fall 1993, 21% of all new students were transfers into all classes. 4,080 transfer applications were received, 1,032 were accepted. Application deadline is March 15 for fall; November 1 for spring. Lowest course grade accepted is "C." Maximum number of transferable credits is 60 semester hours. At least 30 of final 42 semester hours must be completed at Rutgers to receive degree.
**Admissions contact:** Elizabeth Mitchell, Ph.D., Assistant Vice President for University Undergraduate Admissions. 908 932-3770.

**FINANCIAL AID. Available aid:** Pell grants, SEOG, state scholarships and grants, school scholarships and grants, ROTC scholarships, academic merit scholarships, and athletic scholarships. Perkins Loans (NDSL), PLUS, Stafford Loans (GSL), state loans, school loans, and SLS. AMS and deferred payment plan.
**Financial aid statistics:** 20% of aid is not need-based. In 1993-94, 88% of all undergraduate applicants received aid; 81% of freshman applicants. Average amounts of aid awarded freshmen: Scholarships and grants, $4,447; loans, $2,251.
**Supporting data/closing dates:** FAFSA: Priority filing date is March 1. Income tax forms: Accepted on rolling basis. Notification of awards on rolling basis.
**Financial aid contact:** Steve Rouff, M.A., Acting Director of Financial Aid. 908 932-8811 (A-Led), 908 932-7057 (Lee-Z).

**STUDENT EMPLOYMENT.** College Work/Study Program. Institutional employment. 16% of full-time undergraduates work on campus during school year. Students may expect to earn an average of $510 during school year. Off-campus part-time employment opportunities rated "fair."

**COMPUTER FACILITIES.** 482 IBM/IBM-compatible and Macintosh/Apple microcomputers; 452 are networked. Students may access Digital, IBM, SUN minicomputer/mainframe systems, BITNET, Internet. Residence halls may be equipped with stand-alone microcomputers. Client/LAN operating systems include Apple/Macintosh, DOS, UNIX/XENIX/AIX, X-windows, LocalTalk/AppleTalk, Novell. Computer languages and software packages include ClarisWorks, FORTRAN, Lotus 1-2-3, MacWrite, SAS, SPSS-X, WordPerfect; 50 in all. Microcomputers available to all students; mainframes restricted to instructional classroom use.
**Fees:** $50/semester.
**Hours:** 24 hours in some locations.

**GRADUATE CAREER DATA.** Highest graduate school enrollments: Columbia U, New York U, Rutgers U, U of Medicine & Dentistry of New Jersey. Companies and businesses that hire graduates: Merck, Prudential, IBM, Deloitte & Touche, KPMG Peat Marwick, Wal-Mart, Morgan Stanley.

# Saint Peter's College

**Jersey City, NJ 07306** **201 915-9000**

**1993-94 Costs.** Tuition: $9,150. Room: $2,680. Board: $2,200-$2,600. Fees, books, misc. academic expenses (school's estimate): $795.
**Enrollment.** Undergraduates: 925 men, 1,056 women (full-time). Freshman class: 1,607 applicants, 1,413 accepted, 616 enrolled. Graduate enrollment: 205 men, 173 women.
**Test score averages/ranges.** Average SAT scores: 429 verbal, 476 math.
**Faculty.** 117 full-time. 87% of faculty holds highest degree in specific field. Student/faculty ratio: 17 to 1.
**Selectivity rating.** Less competitive.

**PROFILE.** Saint Peter's is a private, church-affiliated, multipurpose college. Founded in 1872, it adopted coeducation in 1966. Its 10-acre campus is located in Jersey City, three miles from New York City.
**Accreditation:** MSACS. Professionally accredited by the National League for Nursing.
**Religious orientation:** Saint Peter's College is affiliated with the Roman Catholic Church (Society of Jesus); two semesters of theology required.
**Library:** Collections totaling over 318,684 volumes, 1,487 periodical subscriptions, and 5,809 microform items.
**Special facilities/museums:** TV production facilities.
**Athletic facilities:** Gymnasium, basketball, racquetball, squash, and tennis courts, swimming pool, baseball, football, soccer, and softball fields, track, weight room, fitness/conditioning room.

**STUDENT BODY. Undergraduate profile:** 85% are state residents. 8% Asian-American, 10% Black, 17% Hispanic, 53% White, 12% Other. Average age of undergraduates is 20.
**Freshman profile:** 3% of freshmen who took SAT scored 600 or over on verbal, 9% scored 600 or over on math; 17% scored 500 or over on verbal, 37% scored 500 or over on math; 54% scored 400 or over on verbal, 68% scored 400 or over on math; 80% scored 300 or over on verbal, 82% scored 300 or over on math. Majority of accepted applicants took SAT. 54% of freshmen come from public schools.
**Undergraduate achievement:** 75% of fall 1992 freshmen returned for fall 1993 term.
**Foreign students:** Countries represented include China, Cuba, Egypt, Japan, Korea, and Pakistan; 12 in all.

**PROGRAMS OF STUDY. Degrees:** B.A., B.S., B.S.Nurs.
**Majors:** Accounting, American Studies, Art History, Biological Chemistry, Biology, Business Management, Chemistry, Classical Civilization, Classical Languages, Computer Science, Cytotechnology, Economics, Elementary Education, English Literature, French, Health Care Management, History, Humanities, Marketing Management, Mathematical Economics, Mathematics, Medical Technology, Natural Science, Nursing, Philosophy, Physics, Political Science, Psychology, Social Sciences, Sociology, Spanish, Theology, Toxicology, Urban Studies.
**Distribution of degrees:** The majors with the highest enrollment are business management, accounting, and marketing management; classical languages, philosophy, and theology have the lowest.
**Requirements:** General education requirement.
**Academic regulations:** Freshmen must maintain minimum 1.8 GPA; sophomores, juniors, seniors, 2.0 GPA.
**Special:** Minors offered in many majors and in criminal justice, data processing, education, electronics, finance, fine arts, journalism, international studies, and music. Associate's degrees offered. Self-designed majors. Double majors. Independent study. Accelerated study. Pass/fail grading option. Internships. Cooperative education programs. Preprofessional programs in law, medicine, veterinary science, and dentistry. Seven-year B.S./D.D.S. program with New York U. 3-2 clinical lab sciences program with U of Medicine and Dentistry of New Jersey. Member of Institute for the Advancement of Urban Education. Washington Semester. Teacher certification in early childhood, elementary, secondary, and special education. Certification in specific subject areas. Member of International Student Exchange Program (ISEP). ROTC at Seton Hall U.
**Honors:** Honors program. Honor societies.
**Academic Assistance:** Remedial reading, writing, math, and study skills. Nonremedial tutoring.

**STUDENT LIFE. Housing:** Students may live on or off campus. School-owned/operated apartments. 13% of students live in college housing.
**Social atmosphere:** According to the student newspaper, "The social and cultural life at SPC is rather quiet. Lectures and events of cultural significance are provided by the college." Students hang out at the cafeteria, the Quadrangle, and the McIntyre Lounge. The Student Senate is an influential group on campus. The Halloween Dance, Homecoming Week, and basketball games are among the year's favorite events.
**Services and counseling/handicapped student services:** Placement services. Health service. Counseling services for minority, military, veteran, and older students. Birth control, personal, and psychological counseling. Career and academic guidance services. Religious counseling. Physically disabled student services. Learning disabled services. Notetaking services. Tutors. Reader services for the blind.
**Campus organizations:** Undergraduate student government. Student newspaper (Pauw Wow, published once/month). Literary magazine. Yearbook. Radio station. Glee club, pep band, drama group, Circle K, debating, peace and justice group, Knights of Columbus, martial arts group, academic groups, 52 organizations in all. One fraternity, no chapter house. 2% of men join a fraternity.
**Religious organizations:** Campus Ministry.
**Minority/foreign student organizations:** Black Action Committee, Asian-American, Hispanic, and Native American groups. International Club.

**ATHLETICS. Physical education requirements:** None.
**Intercollegiate competition:** 25% of students participate. Baseball (M), basketball (M,W), bowling (M), cheerleading (M,W), cross-country (M,W), diving (M,W), football (M), golf (M), soccer (M,W), softball (W), swimming (M,W), tennis (M,W), track (indoor) (M,W), track (outdoor) (M,W), track and field (indoor) (M,W), track and field (outdoor) (M,W), volleyball (W). Member of ECAC, Metro Atlantic Athletic Conference, NCAA Division I.
**Intramural and club sports:** 30% of students participate. Intramural basketball, cross-country, floor hockey, football, golf, softball, swimming, table tennis, tennis, ultimate frisbee, volleyball.

**ADMISSIONS. Academic basis for candidate selection** (in order of priority): Secondary school record, class rank, standardized test scores, essay, school's recommendation.
**Nonacademic basis for candidate selection:** Character and personality and particular talent or ability are emphasized. Extracurricular participation is important. Alumni/ae relationship is considered.
**Requirements:** Graduation from secondary school is recommended; GED is accepted. 16 units and the following program of study are required: 4 units of English, 3 units of math, 2 units of science including 1 unit of lab, 2 units of foreign language, 2 units of history, 3 units of academic electives. Minimum SAT score of 400 in both verbal and math, rank in top two-fifths of secondary school class, and minimum 2.0 GPA recommended. R.N. required of nursing program applicants. Educational Opportunity Fund (EOF) program and Educational Student Support Program for applicants not normally admissible. SAT is required; ACT may be substituted. Campus visit and interview recommended. Off-campus interviews available with admissions and alumni representatives.
**Procedure:** Suggest filing application by May 1; no deadline. Notification of admission on rolling basis. Reply is required by May 1. $100 tuition deposit, refundable until May 1. $200 room deposit, refundable until May 1. Freshmen accepted in terms other than fall.
**Special programs:** Admission may be deferred one year. Credit and/or placement may be granted through CEEB Advanced Placement exams for scores of 4 or higher. Credit and/or placement may be granted through CLEP general and subject exams. Credit and placement may be granted through Regents College, ACT PEP, DANTES, and challenge exams and military and life experience. Early decision program. Deadline for applying for early decision is December 1. Early entrance/early admission program. Concurrent enrollment program.
**Transfer students:** Transfer students accepted for terms other than fall. In fall 1992, 69 transfer applications were received, 47 were accepted. Application deadline is rolling for fall; rolling for spring. Minimum 2.0 GPA required. Lowest course grade accepted is "C." Maximum number of transferable credits is 69 semester hours. At least 69 semester hours must be completed at the college to receive degree.
**Admissions contact:** Mary Beth Carey, M.A., Director of Admissions. 201 915-9213.

**FINANCIAL AID. Available aid:** Pell grants, SEOG, state scholarships and grants, school scholarships and grants, private scholarships and grants, ROTC scholarships, academic merit scholarships, athletic scholarships, and aid for undergraduate foreign students. Perkins Loans (NDSL), PLUS, Stafford Loans (GSL), state loans, and SLS. Deferred payment plan. Institutional installment plan.
**Financial aid statistics:** 34% of aid is not need-based. In 1993-94, 75% of all undergraduate applicants received aid; 75% of freshman applicants. Average amounts of aid awarded freshmen: Scholarships and grants, $7,600; loans, $2,100.
**Supporting data/closing dates:** FAFSA: Priority filing date is February 15. FAF: Priority filing date is February 15; accepted on rolling basis. State aid form: Priority filing date is February 15; accepted on rolling basis. Notification of awards on rolling basis.
**Financial aid contact:** Thomas C. Scott, M.A., Director of Financial Aid. 201 915-9308.

**STUDENT EMPLOYMENT.** College Work/Study Program. Institutional employment. 13% of full-time undergraduates work on campus during school year. Students may expect to earn an average of $1,000 during school year. Off-campus part-time employment opportunities rated "excellent."

**COMPUTER FACILITIES.** 125 IBM/IBM-compatible and Macintosh/Apple microcomputers; 100 are networked. Students may access Digital minicomputer/mainframe systems, BITNET, Internet. Residence halls may be equipped with modems. Computer languages and software packages include Assembly, BASIC, C, COBOL, FORTRAN, Harvard Graphics, Management Scientist, Paradox, Pascal, PL/1, RPG, SPSS, WordPerfect; 30 in all. Computer facilities are available to all students.
**Fees:** $10 computer fee per credit.
**Hours:** 8 AM-10 PM (M-Th); 8 AM-5 PM (F); 9 AM-2 PM (Sa).

**PROMINENT ALUMNI/AE.** Dennis James, TV personality; Anthony Terracciano, president, First Fidelity Bank; Thomas D. Carver, president, Atlantic City Casino Association.

# Seton Hall University

**South Orange, NJ 07079-2689 — 201 761-9000**

**1994-95 Costs.** Tuition: $12,000. Room & board: $6,484. Fees, books, misc. academic expenses (school's estimate): $1,200.
**Enrollment.** Undergraduates: 2,174 men, 2,224 women (full-time). Freshman class: 4,697 applicants, 3,566 accepted, 1,003 enrolled. Graduate enrollment: 2,062 men, 2,558 women.
**Test score averages/ranges.** Average SAT scores: 442 verbal, 496 math. Range of SAT scores of middle 50%: 400-490 verbal, 440-550 math.
**Faculty.** 299 full-time; 90 part-time. 66% of faculty holds highest degree in specific field. Student/faculty ratio: 17 to 1.
**Selectivity rating.** Less competitive.

**PROFILE.** Seton Hall, founded in 1856, is a private, church-affiliated, comprehensive university. Programs are offered through the Colleges of Arts and Sciences and Nursing; the Schools of Business, Education, and Law; and the University College. Its 58-acre campus is located in South Orange, 14 miles from New York City.
**Accreditation:** MSACS. Professionally accredited by the American Assembly of Collegiate Schools of Business, the National League for Nursing.
**Religious orientation:** Seton Hall University is affiliated with the Roman Catholic Church (Archdiocese of Newark); one semester of religion required.
**Library:** Collections totaling over 403,350 volumes, 2,163 periodical subscriptions, and 24,250 microform items.
**Special facilities/museums:** Art, natural history, and Native American museums, theatre-in-the-round, archaeological research center, TV studio.
**Athletic facilities:** Gymnasium, baseball, intramural, soccer, and softball fields, weight room, dance studio, track, basketball, racquetball, tennis, and volleyball courts.

**STUDENT BODY. Undergraduate profile:** 83% are state residents; 20% are transfers. 4% Asian-American, 10% Black, 7% Hispanic, 78% White, 1% Other. Average age of undergraduates is 20.
**Freshman profile:** 99% of accepted applicants took SAT; 1% took ACT. 60% of freshmen come from public schools.
**Undergraduate achievement:** 86% of fall 1992 freshmen returned for fall 1993 term. 19% of students who completed a degree program immediately went on to graduate study.
**Foreign students:** 56 students are from out of the country. Countries represented include China, Ireland, Italy, Japan, Korea, and Taiwan; 31 in all.

**PROGRAMS OF STUDY. Degrees:** B.A., B.S., B.S.Ed., B.S.Nurs.
**Majors:** Accounting, African-American Studies, Anthropology, Art/Music, Asian Studies, Biology, Chemistry, Classical Studies, Communication, Computer/Information Sciences, Computer Science, Criminal Justice, Economics, Elementary Education, English, Finance, French, Health/Physical Education, History, Italian, Liberal Studies, Management, Marketing, Mathematics, Modern Languages, Nursing, Philosophy, Physics, Political Science, Psychology, Religious Studies, Secondary Education, Social/Behavioral Science, Social Work, Sociology, Spanish.
**Distribution of degrees:** The majors with the highest enrollment are accounting, communication, and finance; philosophy, religious studies, and foreign languages have the lowest.
**Requirements:** General education requirement.
**Academic regulations:** Freshmen must maintain minimum 1.75 GPA; sophomores, 1.90 GPA; juniors, 2.00 GPA; seniors, 2.00 GPA.
**Special:** Minors offered in most majors and in archaeology, art history, business administration, and German. Humanistic studies programs. Certificate program offered in gerontology. Courses offered in Chinese, geography, German, Hebrew, Italian, Japanese, music, and Russian. ESL courses available. Double majors. Dual degrees. Independent study. Accelerated study. Pass/fail grading option. Internships. Cooperative education programs. Graduate school at which undergraduates may take graduate-level courses. Preprofessional programs in law, medicine, dentistry, and optometry. 3-2 engineering program with New Jersey Inst of Tech and Stevens Inst of Tech. Five-year B.A./M.B.A. program. Washington Semester. Teacher certification in elementary, secondary, special education, and bilingual/bicultural education. Study abroad in China, France, Japan, Poland, and numerous other countries. ROTC. AFROTC at New Jersey Inst of Tech.
**Honors:** Honors program. Honor societies.
**Academic Assistance:** Remedial reading, writing, math, and study skills. Nonremedial tutoring.

**STUDENT LIFE. Housing:** Students may live on or off campus. Coed and women's dorms. School-owned/operated apartments. 50% of students live in college housing.
**Social atmosphere:** On campus, students gather at the Greek Room and the cafeteria; off campus, students head for The Hall, Pauley's, and Toro Loco. Greeks, the Student Activities Board, and the student newspaper are influential on campus life. Popular campus events include basketball games and tournaments, concerts, movies, and guest lectures. The student newspaper reports, "Greeks are many. Sports are the biggest highlight, but if you look closely there is a moderate amount of stuff to do for everyone. We're close to New York City, so that helps, and Seton Hall is small enough to get involved and meet lots of people."
**Services and counseling/handicapped student services:** Placement services. Health service. Women's center. Counseling services for minority, military, and veteran students. Personal and psychological counseling. Career and academic guidance services. Religious counseling. Physically disabled student services. Learning disabled services. Notetaking services. Tape recorders. Tutors. Reader services for the blind.
**Campus organizations:** Undergraduate student government. Student newspaper (Setonian, published once/week). Literary magazine. Yearbook. Radio station. Glee club, debating, drama and film societies, Young Democrats, Young Republicans, PIRG, academic, professional, and special-interest groups, 100 organizations in all. 12 fraternities, no chapter houses; 10 sororities, no chapter houses. 25% of men join a fraternity. 25% of women join a sorority.
**Religious organizations:** Campus Ministry.
**Minority/foreign student organizations:** Black Student Union, Caribe, Adelante, Association of Black Accountants. International Student Association, African, Chinese, Filipino, and Korean groups.

**ATHLETICS. Physical education requirements:** None.
**Intercollegiate competition:** 5% of students participate. Baseball (M), basketball (M,W), cheerleading (M,W), cross-country (M,W), diving (M,W), golf (M), soccer (M,W), softball (W), swimming (M,W), tennis (M,W), track (indoor) (M,W), track (outdoor) (M,W), track and field (indoor) (M,W), track and field (outdoor) (M,W), volleyball (W), wrestling (M). Member of Big East Conference, ECAC, NCAA Division I.
**Intramural and club sports:** Intramural basketball, golf, racquetball, soccer, softball, tennis, volleyball, walleyball, wrestling, weight lifting. Men's club bowling, cheerleading, ice hockey, lacrosse, martial arts, rugby, volleyball. Women's club bowling, cheerleading, martial arts, soccer.

**ADMISSIONS. Academic basis for candidate selection** (in order of priority): Secondary school record, class rank, standardized test scores, essay, school's recommendation.
**Nonacademic basis for candidate selection:** Alumni/ae relationship is important. Character and personality, extracurricular participation, particular talent or ability, and geographical distribution are considered.

**Requirements:** Graduation from secondary school is required; GED is accepted. 16 units and the following program of study are required: 4 units of English, 3 units of math, 1 unit of lab science, 2 units of foreign language, 2 units of social studies, 4 units of academic electives. Minimum combined SAT score of 900, rank in top two-fifths of secondary school class, and minimum 2.5 GPA recommended. 2 units of lab science required of nursing program applicants. EOP for applicants not normally admissible. Either SAT or ACT is required. Campus visit and interview recommended. No off-campus interviews.
**Procedure:** Take SAT or ACT by March 30 of 12th year. Suggest filing application by March 1; no deadline. Acceptance notification begins on a rolling basis starting January 1. Reply is required by May 1. $150 nonrefundable tuition deposit. $250 room deposit, refundable until May 1. Freshmen accepted in terms other than fall.
**Special programs:** Admission may be deferred one year. Credit and/or placement may be granted through CEEB Advanced Placement exams for scores of 3 or higher. Credit and/or placement may be granted through CLEP general and subject exams. Placement may be granted through challenge exams.
**Transfer students:** Transfer students accepted for terms other than fall. In fall 1993, 20% of all new students were transfers into all classes. 885 transfer applications were received, 579 were accepted. Application deadline is June 1 for fall; December 1 for spring. Minimum 2.75 GPA required. Lowest course grade accepted is "C." Maximum number of transferable credits is 70 semester hours from a two-year school and 90 semester hours from a four-year school. At least 30 semester hours must be completed at the university to receive degree.
**Admissions contact:** Patricia Burgh, M.A., Dean of Enrollment Services, Admissions, and Financial Aid. 201 761-9332.

**FINANCIAL AID. Available aid:** Pell grants, SEOG, Federal Nursing Student Scholarships, state scholarships and grants, school scholarships and grants, private scholarships and grants, ROTC scholarships, academic merit scholarships, and athletic scholarships. Perkins Loans (NDSL), PLUS, Stafford Loans (GSL), NSL, state loans, school loans, private loans, and SLS. Tuition Plan Inc., AMS, deferred payment plan, and family tuition reduction.
**Financial aid statistics:** 30% of aid is not need-based. In 1993-94, 74% of all undergraduate applicants received aid; 74% of freshman applicants. Average amounts of aid awarded freshmen: Scholarships and grants, $1,200; loans, $2,500.
**Supporting data/closing dates:** FAFSA: Accepted on rolling basis. Notification of awards on rolling basis.
**Financial aid contact:** Michael Menendez, M.A., Director of Financial Aid. 201 761-9350.

**STUDENT EMPLOYMENT.** College Work/Study Program. Institutional employment. 25% of full-time undergraduates work on campus during school year. Students may expect to earn an average of $1,000 during school year. Off-campus part-time employment opportunities rated "excellent."

**COMPUTER FACILITIES.** 350 IBM/IBM-compatible and Macintosh/Apple microcomputers; 290 are networked. Students may access IBM minicomputer/mainframe systems, BITNET, Internet. Residence halls may be equipped with stand-alone microcomputers. Client/LAN operating systems include Apple/Macintosh, DOS. Computer languages and software packages include BASIC, C, C++, COBOL, dBASE, FORTRAN, Harvard Graphics, Illustrator, Lotus 1-2-3, Lunena, MINITAB, PageMaker, Pascal, Persuasion, Quark Xpress, SAS, SPSS-X, WordPerfect; 100 in all. Computer facilities are available to all students.
**Fees:** Computer fee is included in tuition/fees.
**Hours:** 8 AM-2 AM.

**GRADUATE CAREER DATA.** Highest graduate school enrollments: George Mason U, Harvard U, New York U, Rutgers U, SUNY-Stony Brook, Seton Hall U, Tufts U. 85% of graduates choose careers in business and industry. Companies and businesses that hire graduates: AT&T, Ciba Geigy, Cooper & Lybrand, Scherung Plough, Prudential.

**PROMINENT ALUMNI/AE.** Robert Brennan, chairperson, First Securities; Ellen O'Kane Lee, stock analyst; Robert Wussler, president and CEO, Comset Video; Rick Cerone, baseball player; Lucile Joel, president, American Nurses Association; W. Cary Edwards, New Jersey attorney general.

# Stevens Institute of Technology

**Hoboken, NJ 07030** **201 216-5000**

**1994-95 Costs.** Tuition: $16,900. Room & board: $5,520. Fees, books, misc. academic expenses (school's estimate): $550.
**Enrollment.** Undergraduates: 1,025 men, 238 women (full-time). Freshman class: 1,768 applicants, 1,249 accepted, 380 enrolled. Graduate enrollment: 1,254 men, 348 women.
**Test score averages/ranges.** Average SAT scores: 521 verbal, 652 math.
**Faculty.** 157 full-time; 90 part-time. 90% of faculty holds doctoral degree. Student/faculty ratio: 10 to 1.
**Selectivity rating.** Highly competitive.

**PROFILE.** Stevens Institute is a private institute of technology. Founded in 1870, it adopted coeducation in 1972. Its 55-acre campus is located in Hoboken, overlooking the Hudson River.

**Accreditation:** MSACS. Professionally accredited by the Accreditation Board for Engineering and Technology.
**Religious orientation:** Stevens Institute of Technology is nonsectarian; no religious requirements.
**Library:** Collections totaling over 150,000 volumes, 1,000 periodical subscriptions, and 20 microform items.
**Special facilities/museums:** Art museum, electron microscope, ocean engineering lab, HDTV research facility.
**Athletic facilities:** Gymnasium, recreation center, basketball, platform tennis, racquetball, squash, and tennis courts, swimming pool, weight room, athletic fields.

**STUDENT BODY. Undergraduate profile:** 62% are state residents. 26% Asian-American, 5% Black, 9% Hispanic, 57% White, 3% Other. Average age of undergraduates is 19.
**Freshman profile:** 3% of freshmen who took SAT scored 700 or over on verbal, 32% scored 700 or over on math; 27% scored 600 or over on verbal, 77% scored 600 or over on math; 65% scored 500 or over on verbal, 100% scored 500 or over on math; 91% scored 400 or over on verbal; 97% scored 300 or over on verbal. 98% of accepted applicants took SAT; 5% took ACT.
**Undergraduate achievement:** 83% of fall 1992 freshmen returned for fall 1993 term. 75% of entering class graduated. 70% of students who completed a degree program went on to graduate study within five years.
**Foreign students:** 44 students are from out of the country. Countries represented include China, Germany, Greece, the Philippines, and the United Kingdom; 26 in all.

**PROGRAMS OF STUDY. Degrees:** B.A., B.Eng., B.S.
**Majors:** Biology, Chemical Biology, Chemical Engineering, Chemistry, Civil Engineering, Computer Science, Computer Systems, Electrical Engineering, Engineering, Engineering Management, Engineering Physics, Humanities, Management/Business Administration, Management Information Systems, Management Sciences, Materials/Metallurgical Engineering, Materials Science, Mathematics, Mechanical Engineering, Ocean Engineering, Physics, Technology Management.
**Distribution of degrees:** The majors with the highest enrollment are engineering, science, and computer science.
**Requirements:** General education requirement.
**Academic regulations:** Minimum 2.0 GPA must be maintained.
**Special:** Minors offered in all majors. Engineering majors take elective courses in junior and senior years; program teaches fundamentals of engineering which apply to all fields. Systems planning and management majors take core courses in science and mathematics and in economic, political, and social analysis; program designed to educate for both professional technology and social science; options for concentrations in applied psychology, computer systems, management, management science, and technological systems. Undergraduate technology and medicine projects. Self-designed majors. Double majors. Dual degrees. Independent study. Accelerated study. Pass/fail grading option. Internships. Cooperative education programs. Graduate school at which undergraduates may take graduate-level courses. Preprofessional programs in law, medicine, and dentistry. 3-2 engineering program with New York U. Study abroad in Germany and Scotland. ROTC and AFROTC.
**Honors:** Honors program.
**Academic Assistance:** Nonremedial tutoring.

**STUDENT LIFE. Housing:** Coed and men's dorms. Sorority and fraternity housing. Both on-campus and off-campus married-student housing. 80% of students live in college housing.
**Social atmosphere:** According to the editor of the student newspaper, "Social life is somewhat inhibited by an unbalanced male-female student ratio. Cultural life is very diverse due to many different active cultural groups. Stevens is very close to New York City." Students tend to gather at the Student Center and the Student Union Gymnasium. Popular groups on campus include the Student Council, Greeks, and ethnic organizations. Some of the favorite events during the school year are the Techfest in the fall and the Boken party week in the spring.
**Services and counseling/handicapped student services:** Placement services. Health service. Women's center. Day care. Counseling services for minority students. Birth control, personal, and psychological counseling. Career and academic guidance services. Religious counseling. Physically disabled student services. Tape recorders. Tutors.
**Campus organizations:** Undergraduate student government. Student newspaper (Stute, published once/week). Literary magazine. Yearbook. Radio and TV stations. Jazz and stage bands, interdormitory council, commuter council, athletic association, skydiving and yachting clubs, karate team, 50 organizations in all. 10 fraternities, all with chapter houses; three sororities, all with chapter houses. 40% of men join a fraternity. 40% of women join a sorority.
**Religious organizations:** Christian Fellowship, Hillel, Newman Association, Chinese Christian Fellowship.
**Minority/foreign student organizations:** Black Student Union, Latin American Association, Society of Black Engineers. Chinese, Hellenic, Indian, and Korean groups.

**ATHLETICS. Physical education requirements:** Six semesters of physical education required.
**Intercollegiate competition:** 35% of students participate. Baseball (M), basketball (M), cross-country (M,W), fencing (W), lacrosse (M), soccer (M,W), squash (M), tennis (M,W), volleyball (M). Member of East Coast Collegiate Squash League, Eastern Intercollegiate Volleyball Association, ECAC, Hudson Valley Lacrosse League, IAC, NCAA Division III, Women's Intercollegiate Athletic Conference.
**Intramural and club sports:** 40% of students participate. Intramural archery, badminton, basketball, box lacrosse, floor hockey, racquetball, softball, squash, table tennis, tennis, touch football, volleyball. Men's club Alpine skiing, archery, bowling, golf, ice hockey. Women's club archery, basketball, cross-country, golf.

**ADMISSIONS. Academic basis for candidate selection** (in order of priority): Secondary school record, school's recommendation, class rank, standardized test scores, essay.
**Nonacademic basis for candidate selection:** Character and personality, extracurricular participation, and particular talent or ability are emphasized. Alumni/ae relationship is considered.
**Requirements:** Graduation from secondary school is required; GED is accepted. No specific distribution of secondary school units required. SAT is required; ACT may be substituted. ACH required. Campus visit and interview required. Off-campus interviews available with an admissions representative.
**Procedure:** Take SAT or ACT by March of 12th year. Take ACH by March of 12th year. Visit college for interview by March of 12th year. Application deadline is March 1. Notification of admission on rolling basis. Reply is required by May 1. $200 nonrefundable tuition deposit. $150 nonrefundable room deposit. Freshmen accepted in fall terms only.

**Special programs:** Admission may be deferred one year. Credit and/or placement may be granted through CEEB Advanced Placement exams for scores of 4 or higher. Credit and placement may be granted through challenge exams. Early decision program. In fall 1993, 36 applied for early decision and 23 were accepted. Deadline for applying for early decision is November 1. Early entrance/early admission program.
**Transfer students:** Transfer students accepted for terms other than fall. In fall 1993, 150 transfer applications were received, 103 were accepted. Application deadline is March 1 for fall; November 1 for spring. Lowest course grade accepted is "C." At least half of semester hours must be completed at the institute to receive degree.
**Admissions contact:** Maureen Weatherall, M.A., Dean of Admissions. 201 216-5194.

**FINANCIAL AID. Available aid:** Pell grants, SEOG, state scholarships and grants, school scholarships and grants, private scholarships and grants, ROTC scholarships, and academic merit scholarships. Perkins Loans (NDSL), PLUS, Stafford Loans (GSL), school loans, and SLS. EFI Fund Management.
**Financial aid statistics:** 20% of aid is not need-based. In 1993-94, 92% of all undergraduate applicants received aid; 90% of freshman applicants. Average amounts of aid awarded freshmen: Scholarships and grants, $5,400; loans, $17,850.
**Supporting data/closing dates:** FAFSA/FAF: Priority filing date is March 1. Income tax forms: Priority filing date is March 1. Notification of awards on rolling basis.
**Financial aid contact:** Carol Zeblocki, M.A., Director of Financial Aid. 201 216-5201.

**STUDENT EMPLOYMENT.** College Work/Study Program. Institutional employment. 50% of full-time undergraduates work on campus during school year. Students may expect to earn an average of $1,000 during school year. Off-campus part-time employment opportunities rated "excellent."

**COMPUTER FACILITIES.** 820 IBM/IBM-compatible and Macintosh/Apple microcomputers; 800 are networked. Students may access AT&T, Digital, Hewlett-Packard, IBM, NCR, SUN minicomputer/mainframe systems, BITNET, Internet. Residence halls may be equipped with networked microcomputers, modems. Client/LAN operating systems include Apple/Macintosh, DOS, UNIX/XENIX/AIX, Windows NT, X-windows, DEC, LocalTalk/AppleTalk, Microsoft, Novell. 150 major computer languages and software packages available. Computer facilities are available to all students.
**Fees:** None.
**Hours:** 24 hours.

**GRADUATE CAREER DATA.** Graduate school percentages: 1% enter law school. 1% enter medical school. 1% enter dental school. 6% enter graduate business programs. 1% enter graduate arts and sciences programs. Highest graduate school enrollments: Stevens Institute of Technology. 90% of graduates choose careers in business and industry. Companies and businesses that hire graduates: AT&T, IBM, Prudential, Westinghouse.

**PROMINENT ALUMNI/AE.** Charles Mott, co-founder and past director, General Motors; Eugene McDermott, member of Board of Directors, Texas Instruments; Wesley J. Howe, chairperson and CEO, Becton Dickinson; Leon Febres Cordero, former president of Ecuador; Caleb Hurt, CEO, Martin Marietta; Alexander Calder, artist/sculptor; Richard Reeves, national columnist.

# Stockton College of New Jersey

**Pomona, NJ 08240** **609 652-1776**

**1994-95 Costs.** Tuition: $2,176 (state residents), $2,880 (out-of-state). Room: $2,700. Board: $1,544. Fees, books, misc. academic expenses (school's estimate): $1,415.
**Enrollment.** Undergraduates: 2,118 men, 2,247 women (full-time). Freshman class: 4,019 applicants, 1,579 accepted, 716 enrolled.
**Test score averages/ranges.** Average SAT scores: 490 verbal, 552 math. Range of SAT scores of middle 50%: 450-530 verbal, 550-600 math.
**Faculty.** 193 full-time; 114 part-time. 92% of faculty holds highest degree in specific field. Student/faculty ratio: 17 to 1.
**Selectivity rating.** More competitive.

**PROFILE.** Stockton College, founded in 1969 as Stockton State College, is a public, multipurpose college. Its 1,600-acre campus is located in Pomona, west of Atlantic City.

**Accreditation:** MSACS. Professionally accredited by the American Physical Therapy Association, the Council on Social Work Education, the National League for Nursing.
**Religious orientation:** Stockton State College is nonsectarian; no religious requirements.
**Library:** Collections totaling over 224,972 volumes, 1,558 periodical subscriptions, and 298,388 microform items.
**Special facilities/museums:** Art gallery, performing arts center, Holocaust resource center, community justice institute, environmental research center, observatory, marine lab and field station.
**Athletic facilities:** Gymnasium, swimming pool, track, baseball, football, lacrosse, soccer, and softball fields, basketball, racquetball, sand volleyball, street hockey, and tennis courts, weight rooms, sauna.

**STUDENT BODY. Undergraduate profile:** 97% are state residents; 48% are transfers. 3% Asian-American, 8% Black, 4% Hispanic, 85% White. Average age of undergraduates is 22.
**Freshman profile:** 1% of freshmen who took SAT scored 700 or over on verbal, 4% scored 700 or over on math; 7% scored 600 or over on verbal, 27% scored 600 or over on math; 44% scored 500 or over on verbal, 79% scored 500 or over on math; 95% scored 400 or over on verbal, 100% scored 400 or over on math; 100% scored 300 or over on verbal. 99% of accepted applicants took SAT; 1% took ACT. 65% of freshmen come from public schools.
**Undergraduate achievement:** 83% of fall 1992 freshmen returned for fall 1993 term. 34% of entering class graduated. 39% of students who completed a degree program went on to graduate study within five years.
**Foreign students:** Countries represented include African countries, Greece, Japan, Malaysia, the Netherlands, and Pakistan; 30 in all.

**PROGRAMS OF STUDY. Degrees:** B.A., B.S., B.S.Nurs., B.Soc.Work.
**Majors:** Applied Physics, Biology, Business Studies, Chemistry, Criminal Justice, Economics, Environmental Studies, Geology, Historical Studies, Information/Systems Sciences, Liberal Studies, Literature/Language, Marine Science, Mathematics, Nursing, Philosophy/Religion, Physical Therapy, Political Science, Psychology, Public Health, Social Work, Sociology/Anthropology, Speech Pathology/Audiology, Studies in the Arts.
**Distribution of degrees:** The majors with the highest enrollment are business, environmental studies, and psychology; geology, philosophy, and physics have the lowest.
**Requirements:** General education requirement.
**Academic regulations:** Minimum 2.0 GPA must be maintained.
**Special:** Programs in basic studies, gerontology, topical concentrations, and writing. Certificate programs. Self-designed majors. Independent study. Accelerated study. Pass/fail grading option. Internships. Cooperative education programs. Graduate school at which undergraduates may take graduate-level courses. Preprofessional programs in law, medicine, veterinary science, dentistry, audiology, political science, and speech pathology. 3-2 engineering programs with New Jersey Inst of Tech and Rutgers U. 3-4 medical and dental programs with U of Medicine and Dentistry of New Jersey. Washington Semester. Teacher certification in secondary education. Certification in specific subject areas. Study abroad in Australia, China, Denmark, Greece, Israel, Japan, Mexico, Spain, Sweden, and the United Kingdom.
**Honors:** Honor societies.
**Academic Assistance:** Remedial reading, writing, and math. Nonremedial tutoring.

**STUDENT LIFE. Housing:** Students may live on or off campus. Coed dorms. School-owned/operated apartments. Housing for the physically handicapped. 41% of students live in college housing.
**Social atmosphere:** According to the editor of the student newspaper, "Social life on campus is a bit weak, but what there is of it is diverse. The weekends tend to be quiet. The college is only 20 minutes from Atlantic City, 45 minutes from Philadelphia, and 20 minutes from the beach, yet it is set away in the pine barrens like a hideaway." Students like to congregate on campus at the Lakeside Center, the Student Center, and the Rathskellar. Off-campus activities center around the Arrowhead Inn, Atlantic City, Margate Clubs, and the Hangin' Horse Saloon. Most influential groups are the Board of Activities, Tenants Association, some Greeks, and the Student Senate. Favorite events are Spring Challenge, Earthweek, and basketball season.
**Services and counseling/handicapped student services:** Placement services. Health service. Women's center. Day care. Counseling services for minority and older students. Birth control, personal, and psychological counseling. Career and academic guidance services. Religious counseling. Physically disabled student services. Learning disabled services. Notetaking services. Tape recorders.
**Campus organizations:** Undergraduate student government. Student newspaper (Argo). Literary magazine. Yearbook. Radio and TV stations. Jazz/music workshop, Gospel Troubadours, art collegium, drama group, outing club, programming committee, Women's Union, athletic, departmental, service, and special-interest groups, 76 organizations in all. 11 fraternities, no chapter houses; seven sororities, no chapter houses. 19% of men join a fraternity. 10% of women join a sorority.
**Religious organizations:** Hillel, Jewish Student Union, New Life Christian Fellowship.
**Minority/foreign student organizations:** Los Latinos Unidos, Unified Black Student Society, minorities committee. International Student Organization.

**ATHLETICS. Physical education requirements:** None.
**Intercollegiate competition:** 60% of students participate. Baseball (M), basketball (M,W), crew (M), cross-country (M,W), soccer (M), softball (W), track and field (M,W), volleyball (W). Member of ECAC, NCAA Division III, NJAC.
**Intramural and club sports:** 1% of students participate. Intramural basketball, flag football, softball, street hockey, volleyball. Men's club aikido, Alpine skiing, baseball, crew, fencing, karate, lacrosse, sailing, scuba, swimming, tennis. Women's club aikido, Alpine skiing, baseball, crew, fencing, field hockey, frisbee, karate, lacrosse, sailing, scuba, swimming, tennis.

**ADMISSIONS. Academic basis for candidate selection** (in order of priority): Secondary school record, class rank, standardized test scores, essay, school's recommendation.
**Nonacademic basis for candidate selection:** Character and personality, extracurricular participation, and particular talent or ability are considered.
**Requirements:** Graduation from secondary school is required; GED is accepted. 16 units and the following program of study are recommended: 4 units of English, 3 units of math, 2 units of science, 2 units of social studies, 5 units of electives. CEEB Achievement Tests (English, math level I or II, and chemistry or physics) required of accelerated medical school applicants only. Selective admissions for physical therapy program applicants. R.N. required of nursing program applicants. EOF program for applicants not normally admissible. SAT or ACT is required. Campus visit and interview recommended. No off-campus interviews.
**Procedure:** Take SAT or ACT by April of 12th year. Visit college for interview by May of 12th year. Application deadline is May 1. Notification of admission on rolling basis. Reply is required by May 1. $100 nonrefundable tuition deposit. $50 room deposit, refundable until June 1. Freshmen accepted in terms other than fall.
**Special programs:** Credit may be granted through CEEB Advanced Placement for scores of 3 or higher. Credit may be granted through CLEP subject exams, military and life experience. Placement may be granted through DANTES and challenge exams. Early decision program. In fall 1993, 187 applied for early decision and 82 were accepted. Deadline for applying for early decision is January 15. Early entrance/early admission program. Concurrent enrollment program.
**Transfer students:** Transfer students accepted for terms other than fall. In fall 1993, 48% of all new students were transfers into all classes. 2,107 transfer applications were received, 1,038 were accepted. Application deadline is June 1 for fall; December 1 for spring. Minimum 2.5 GPA recommended. Lowest course grade accepted is "C." Maximum number of transferable credits is 64 semester hours from a two-year school and 96 semester hours from a four-year school. At least 32 semester hours must be completed at the college to receive degree.
**Admissions contact:** Sal Catalfamo, M.A., Dean of Enrollment Management. 609 652-4261.

**FINANCIAL AID. Available aid:** Pell grants, SEOG, state scholarships and grants, school scholarships and grants, private scholarships and grants, and academic merit scholarships.

Perkins Loans (NDSL), PLUS, Stafford Loans (GSL), state loans, and SLS. Deferred payment plan.
**Financial aid statistics:** 17% of aid is not need-based. In 1993-94, 65% of all undergraduate applicants received aid; 77% of freshman applicants. Average amounts of aid awarded freshmen: Scholarships and grants, $1,159; loans, $2,578.
**Supporting data/closing dates:** FAFSA/FAF/FFS: Priority filing date is March 1; accepted on rolling basis. Income tax forms: Accepted on rolling basis. Notification of awards on rolling basis.
**Financial aid contact:** Jeanne Lewis, M.A., Director of Financial Aid. 609 652-4201.

**STUDENT EMPLOYMENT.** College Work/Study Program. Institutional employment. 13% of full-time undergraduates work on campus during school year. Students may expect to earn an average of $1,000 during school year. Off-campus part-time employment opportunities rated "excellent."

**COMPUTER FACILITIES.** 385 IBM/IBM-compatible, Macintosh/Apple, and RISC-/UNIX-based microcomputers; 210 are networked. Students may access AT&T, Digital, IBM minicomputer/mainframe systems, Internet. Residence halls may be equipped with stand-alone microcomputers, networked microcomputers, modems. Client/LAN operating systems include Apple/Macintosh, DOS, OS/2, UNIX/XENIX/AIX, Windows NT, X-windows, DEC, LocalTalk/AppleTalk, Novell. Computer languages and software packages include Ada, C, COBOL, FOCUS, FORTRAN, Modula 2, PL/1, Pascal, RDB, SAS, SPSS-X. Computer facilities are available to all students.
**Fees:** None.
**Hours:** 8 AM-midn.

**GRADUATE CAREER DATA.** Graduate school percentages: 7% enter law school. 8% enter medical school. 2% enter dental school. 13% enter graduate business programs. 6% enter graduate arts and sciences programs. 4% enter theological school/seminary.

# Thomas A. Edison State College

**Trenton, NJ 08608-1176 — 609 984-1150**

**1993-94 Costs.** Tuition: $400 (state residents), $710 (out-of-state). Housing: None.
**Enrollment.** Freshman class: 4,720 applicants, 4,720 accepted, 2,840 enrolled.
**Test score averages/ranges.** N/A.
**Faculty.** N/A.
**Selectivity rating.** N/A.

**PROFILE.** Thomas Edison State, founded in 1972, is a public college serving adult, continuing-education students. Students earn credit through achievement testing, guided study, telecourses, and life and work experience. Its two-acre campus is in downtown Trenton, 35 miles northeast of Philadelphia.

**Accreditation:** MSACS. Professionally accredited by the National League for Nursing.
**Religious orientation:** Thomas A. Edison State College is nonsectarian; no religious requirements.

**STUDENT BODY. Undergraduate achievement:** 29% of students completing a degree program went on to graduate study within one year.
**Foreign students:** Countries represented include Canada, Germany, Mexico, the Philippines, and the United Kingdom; 65 in all.

**PROGRAMS OF STUDY. Degrees:** B.A., B.S., B.S./B.A., B.S.Nurs.
**Majors:** Accounting, Administrative Office Management, Advertising Management, African-American Studies, Agricultural Mechanics, Air Traffic Control, American Studies, Anthropology, Archaeology, Architectural Design, Art, Art Therapy, Asian Studies, Aviation, Banking, Biological Laboratory Science, Biology, Biomedical Electronics, Chemical Laboratory Science, Chemistry, Child Development Services, Civil Engineering Technology, Communications, Community Education Services, Community Legal Services, Community Services, Computer Science, Computer Science/Technology, Construction, Counseling Services, Criminal Justice, Dance, Data Processing, Dental Hygiene, Economics, Electrical Technology, Electronics Engineering Technology, Emergency Disaster Management, Engineering Graphics, Environmental Science/Technology, Environmental Studies, Finance, Fire Protection Science, Food Technology, Foreign Language, Forestry, General Management, Geography, Geology, Gerontology, Health/Nutrition, Health Services, Health Services Administration, Health Services Education, History, Horticulture, Hospital Health Care Administration, Hotel/Motel/Restaurant Management, Humanities, Industrial Engineering Technology, Insurance, International Business, Journalism, Labor Studies, Laboratory Animal Science, Liberal Arts/General Studies, Literature, Logistics, Management of Human Resources, Management of Information Systems, Marine Engineering Technology, Marketing, Materials Science, Mathematics, Mechanical Engineering Technology, Medical Laboratory Science, Mental Health Services, Mental Retardation Services, Music, Natural Science/Mathematics, Nondestructive Evaluation, Nuclear Engineering Technology, Nuclear Medicine, Nursing, Operations Management, Perfusion Technology, Philosophy, Photography, Physics, Political Science, Procurement, Psychology, Public Administration, Public Safety Services, Purchasing/Material Management, Radiation Protection, Radiation Therapy, Radiologic Science, Radiologic Technology, Real Estate, Recreation Services, Rehabilitation Services, Religion, Respiratory Therapy, Retailing Management, School Business Administration, Services for the Deaf, Social Science/History, Social Services, Social Services Administration, Sociology, Surveying, Technical Services in Audiology, Theatre Arts, Transportation Management, Urban Studies, Water Resources Management, Women's Studies.
**Distribution of degrees:** The majors with the highest enrollment are social science/history, general management, and applied science/technology/aviation.
**Requirements:** General education requirement.
**Academic regulations:** Minimum 2.0 GPA required for graduation.
**Special:** Associate's degrees offered. Self-designed majors. Double majors. Dual degrees. Independent study. Member of New Jersey Statewide Testing and Assessment Center.

**ADMISSIONS. Requirements:** Graduation from secondary school is required; GED is accepted. No specific distribution of secondary school units required. Certification required for applicants to some health profession fields. R.N. required of nursing program applicants. No off-campus interviews.
**Procedure:** Notification of admission on rolling basis. Reply is required within one year of acceptance. Freshmen accepted in fall terms only.
**Special programs:** Credit may be granted through CEEB Advanced Placement for scores of 3 or higher. Credit may be granted through CLEP general and subject exams, Regents College, ACT PEP, DANTES, and challenge exams, and military and life experience.
**Transfer students:** Transfer students accepted for terms other than fall. Lowest course grade accepted is "D."
**Admissions contact:** Janice Toliver, M.A., Director of Admissions. 609 984-1150.

**FINANCIAL AID. Available aid:** Pell grants, state grants, and private grants. College-administered funds. Stafford Loans (GSL). AMS.
**Supporting data/closing dates:** FAFSA: Deadline is July 1. School's own aid application: Deadline is July 1. State aid form: Priority filing date is July 1. Notification of awards begins July 1.
**Financial aid contact:** Jules Kann, M.S., Director of Financial Aid. 609 756-2430.

# Trenton State College

**Trenton, NJ 08650-4700 — 609 771-1855**

**1993-94 Costs.** Tuition: $3,110 (state residents), $4,790 (out-of-state). Room & board: $5,400. Fees, books, misc. academic expenses (school's estimate): $1,000.
**Enrollment.** Undergraduates: 2,010 men, 3,155 women (full-time). Freshman class: 5,044 applicants, 2,312 accepted, 943 enrolled. Graduate enrollment: 182 men, 761 women.
**Test score averages/ranges.** Average SAT scores: 519 verbal, 592 math. Range of SAT scores of middle 50%: 470-570 verbal, 540-650 math.
**Faculty.** 316 full-time; 240 part-time. 79% of faculty holds doctoral degree. Student/faculty ratio: 15 to 1.
**Selectivity rating.** Highly competitive.

**PROFILE.** Trenton State, founded in 1855, is a public college. Programs are offered through the Schools of Arts and Sciences, Business, Education, Industrial Education and Engineering Technology, and Nursing and the Divisions of Continuing and Adult Education and Graduate Studies. Its 210-acre campus is located four miles from downtown Trenton.

**Accreditation:** MSACS. Professionally accredited by the American Speech-Language-Hearing Association, the Foundation for Interior Design Education Research, the National Association of Schools of Music, the National Council for Accreditation of Teacher Education, the National League for Nursing.
**Religious orientation:** Trenton State College is nonsectarian; no religious requirements.
**Library:** Collections totaling over 505,000 volumes, 1,566 periodical subscriptions, and 558,000 microform items.
**Special facilities/museums:** Art gallery, observatory, scanning and transmission electron microscopes.
**Athletic facilities:** Recreation center with tennis, basketball, volleyball and racquetball courts, gymnasium, weight room, indoor track, combatives room, stadium with artificial turf, basketball arena, gymnastics room, dance studio, baseball and softball stadiums, aquatics center, outdoor track, tennis courts, athletic fields.

**STUDENT BODY. Undergraduate profile:** 91% are state residents; 33% are transfers. 3% Asian-American, 7% Black, 4% Hispanic, 85% White, 1% Other. Average age of undergraduates is 22.
**Freshman profile:** 1% of freshmen who took SAT scored 700 or over on verbal, 11% scored 700 or over on math; 14% scored 600 or over on verbal, 49% scored 600 or over on math; 62% scored 500 or over on verbal, 90% scored 500 or over on math; 100% scored 400 or over on verbal, 100% scored 400 or over on math. 100% of accepted applicants took SAT. 68% of freshmen come from public schools.
**Undergraduate achievement:** 95% of fall 1992 freshmen returned for fall 1993 term.
**Foreign students:** 33 students are from out of the country. Countries represented include China, Cyprus, India, and Japan; 16 in all.

**PROGRAMS OF STUDY. Degrees:** B.A., B.F.A., B.Mus., B.S., B.S.Nurs.
**Majors:** Art, Art Therapy, Biology, Business Administration, Chemistry, Communication, Computer Science, Early Childhood Education, Economics, Education of the Hearing Impaired, Elementary Education, Engineering Science, English, Finance, Fine Art, Graphic Design, Health/Physical Education, History, Interior Design, Journalism, Law/Justice, Management, Marketing, Mathematics, Music, Nursing, Philosophy, Physics, Political Science, Professional Writing, Psychology, Sociology, Special Education for the Developmentally Handicapped, Speech Pathology/Audiology, Statistics, Technology Education.
**Distribution of degrees:** The majors with the highest enrollment are elementary education, English, and business administration; health education and philosophy have the lowest.
**Requirements:** General education requirement.
**Academic regulations:** Minimum 2.0 GPA must be maintained.
**Special:** Minors offered in many majors and in African-American studies, classical studies, deaf studies, French, German, international/area studies, media/communication, Italian, religion, Spanish, and women's studies. Double majors. Independent study. Pass/fail grading option. Internships. Graduate school at which undergraduates may take graduate-level courses. Preprofessional programs in law, medicine, and dentistry. Seven-year B.S./M.D. program with U of Medicine and Dentistry of New Jersey. Seven-year B.S./O.D. degree with SUNY Coll of Optometry. Member of New Jersey Marine Biology Consortium. Member of National Student Exchange (NSE). Teacher certification in early childhood, elementary, secondary, and special education. Certification in specific subject areas.

Member of International Student Exchange Program (ISEP). ROTC at Rider Coll. AFROTC at Rutgers U.
**Honors:** Honors program. Honor societies.
**Academic Assistance:** Remedial reading, writing, and math. Nonremedial tutoring.

**STUDENT LIFE. Housing:** Students may live on or off campus. Coed and women's dorms. 53% of students live in college housing.
**Social atmosphere:** To relax, students head for the Rat, a campus bar, or to the City Gardens, an off-campus dance club. The Student Center All-Nighter, an all-night party, is a favorite event on campus. The student newspaper comments, "Our campus is only 15% Greek, so fraternities and sororities do not rule social life, but fraternity parties, which are usually off campus, are fairly popular. For the most part, it's a do-it-yourself social life."
**Services and counseling/handicapped student services:** Placement services. Health service. Women's center. Day care. Counseling services for minority and military students. Birth control, personal, and psychological counseling. Career and academic guidance services. Religious counseling. Physically disabled student services. Learning disabled services. Notetaking services. Tape recorders. Tutors. Reader services for the blind.
**Campus organizations:** Undergraduate student government. Student newspaper (Signal, published once/week). Literary magazine. Yearbook. Radio station. Band, brass choir, theatre, Amnesty International, Circle K, aikido club, Students Acting for the Environment, Students Against Drunk Driving, academic, athletic, professional, and special-interest groups, 140 organizations in all. 14 fraternities, no chapter houses; 13 sororities, no chapter houses. 11% of men join a fraternity. 13% of women join a sorority.
**Religious organizations:** Catholic Campus Ministry, Chi Alpha, Episcopal Church, Hillel, Intervarsity Christian Fellowship, Islamic Society, Newman Club, Protestant Fellowship, Unitarian Universalist Association.
**Minority/foreign student organizations:** Asian American Association, Gay Union, Union Latina, Minority Programming, Black Student Union, Caribbean Student Association, minority fraternities/sororities, Minority Student Coalition, NAACP, National Society of Black Engineers, Utimme Umana/La Voz Oculta. International Relations Council, International Student Association, Student Exchange Organization.

**ATHLETICS. Physical education requirements:** None.
**Intercollegiate competition:** 15% of students participate. Baseball (M), basketball (M,W), cheerleading (M,W), cross-country (M,W), diving (M,W), field hockey (W), football (M), golf (M), lacrosse (W), soccer (M,W), softball (W), swimming (M,W), tennis (M,W), track (indoor) (M,W), track (outdoor) (M,W), track and field (indoor) (M,W), track and field (outdoor) (M,W), wrestling (M). Member of Collegiate Track Conference, ECAC, Metropolitan, NCAA Division III, NJAC.
**Intramural and club sports:** 70% of students participate. Intramural basketball, bowling, flag football, floor hockey, ice hockey, inner-tube water polo, racquetball, soccer, softball, super trot, volleyball. Men's club cycling, fencing, ice hockey, lacrosse, martial arts, rugby, volleyball, weight lifting. Women's club cycling, fencing, martial arts, volleyball, weight lifting.

**ADMISSIONS. Academic basis for candidate selection** (in order of priority): Secondary school record, class rank, standardized test scores, essay, school's recommendation.
**Nonacademic basis for candidate selection:** Extracurricular participation and particular talent or ability are emphasized.
**Requirements:** Graduation from secondary school is required; GED is accepted. 16 units and the following program of study are required: 4 units of English, 3 units of math, 2 units of lab science, 2 units of social studies, 5 units of electives including 6 units of academic electives. Minimum combined SAT score of 800 and rank in top half of secondary school class required. Interview and portfolio required of some applicants to communication studies program. Portfolio required of art program applicants. Audition required of music program applicants. CEEB Achievement Test (Math level I or II) required of electronics engineering technology program applicants. EOP for applicants not normally admissible. SAT is required; ACT may be substituted. Campus visit recommended. No off-campus interviews.
**Procedure:** Take SAT or ACT by December of 12th year. Application deadline is March 1. Notification of admission by April 1. Reply is required by May 1. $100 nonrefundable tuition deposit. $100 nonrefundable room deposit. Freshmen accepted in terms other than fall.
**Special programs:** Credit may be granted through CEEB Advanced Placement for scores of 4 or higher. Credit may be granted through CLEP general and subject exams, ACT PEP and DANTES exams. Early decision program. In fall 1993, 420 applied for early decision and 176 were accepted. Deadline for applying for early decision is November 15. Early entrance/early admission program. Concurrent enrollment program.
**Transfer students:** Transfer students accepted for terms other than fall. In fall 1993, 33% of all new students were transfers into all classes. 1,200 transfer applications were received, 520 were accepted. Application deadline is March 1 for fall; November 1 for spring. Minimum 2.75 GPA required. Lowest course grade accepted is "C." Maximum number of transferable credits is 64 semester hours from a two-year school and 83 semester hours from a four-year school. At least 45 semester hours must be completed at the college to receive degree.
**Admissions contact:** John Iacovelli, M.Ed., Director of Admissions and Financial Aid. 609 771-2131.

**FINANCIAL AID. Available aid:** Pell grants, SEOG, state scholarships and grants, school scholarships, private scholarships, ROTC scholarships, and academic merit scholarships. Perkins Loans (NDSL), PLUS, Stafford Loans (GSL), NSL, state loans, and SLS. Tuition Plan Inc., AMS, and deferred payment plan.
**Financial aid statistics:** 60% of aid is not need-based. In 1993-94, 48% of all undergraduate applicants received aid; 55% of freshman applicants. Average amounts of aid awarded freshmen: Scholarships and grants, $2,600; loans, $3,250.
**Supporting data/closing dates:** FAFSA: Priority filing date is April 1. School's own aid application: Priority filing date is April 1. Notification of awards begins April 1.
**Financial aid contact:** John Iacovelli, M.Ed., Director of Admissions and Financial Aid. 609 771-2211.

**STUDENT EMPLOYMENT.** College Work/Study Program. Institutional employment. 15% of full-time undergraduates work on campus during school year. Students may expect to earn an average of $900 during school year. Off-campus part-time employment opportunities rated "good."

**COMPUTER FACILITIES.** 470 IBM/IBM-compatible and Macintosh/Apple microcomputers; all are networked. Students may access IBM minicomputer/mainframe systems, BITNET, Internet. Residence halls may be equipped with networked microcomputers. Client/LAN operating systems include Apple/Macintosh, DOS, UNIX/XENIX/AIX, Novell. Computer languages and software packages include BASIC, C, COBOL, dBASE, FORTRAN, LISP, LOGO, Lotus 1-2-3, Pascal, PL/1, Professional Write, Prolog, Quattro Pro, SAS, Turbo Pascal, WordPerfect; 15 in all. Computer facilities are available to all students.
**Fees:** None.
**Hours:** 9 AM-11 PM.

**GRADUATE CAREER DATA.** Graduate school percentages: 3% enter law school. 2% enter medical school. 8% enter graduate business programs. 17% enter graduate arts and sciences programs. Highest graduate school enrollments: Columbia U, Pennsylvania State U, Rutgers U, Seton Hall U, Temple U, Trenton State Coll, U of Dayton, U of Maryland, U of Medicine and Dentistry of New Jersey, U of Pennsylvania. 73% of graduates choose careers in business and industry. Companies and businesses that hire graduates: Big Six accounting firms, Johnson & Johnson, Merrill Lynch, Pillsbury, Prudential, State of New Jersey, Eli Lilly, Carter-Wallace.

**PROMINENT ALUMNI/AE.** James Florio, governor, New Jersey; Christopher Smith, U.S. congressman.

# Upsala College

**East Orange, NJ 07019** **201 266-7000**

**1993-94 Costs.** Tuition: $12,500. Room: $2,300. Board: $2,440. Fees, books, misc. academic expenses (school's estimate): $850.
**Enrollment.** Undergraduates: 480 men, 405 women (full-time). Freshman class: 1,420 applicants, 1,142 accepted, 360 enrolled. Graduate enrollment: 17 men, 31 women.
**Test score averages/ranges.** Average SAT scores: 420 verbal, 470 math.
**Faculty.** 58 full-time; 54 part-time. 80% of faculty holds doctoral degree. Student/faculty ratio: 16 to 1.
**Selectivity rating.** Less competitive.

**PROFILE.** Upsala, founded in 1893, is a private, church-affiliated, liberal arts college. Its 45-acre main campus is located in East Orange, 15 miles from New York City.

**Accreditation:** MSACS. Professionally accredited by the Council on Social Work Education.
**Religious orientation:** Upsala College is affiliated with the Evangelical Lutheran Church in America; no religious requirements.
**Library:** Collections totaling over 162,500 volumes, 720 periodical subscriptions, and 1,500 microform items.
**Special facilities/museums:** Center for Adult Degrees.
**Athletic facilities:** Gymnasium, basketball, tennis, and volleyball courts, dance studio, weight and wrestling rooms, baseball, football, soccer, and softball fields.

**STUDENT BODY. Undergraduate profile:** 79% are state residents; 20% are transfers. 12% Asian-American, 45% Black, 12% Hispanic, 1% Native American, 30% White. Average age of undergraduates is 20.
**Freshman profile:** 2% of freshmen who took SAT scored 600 or over on verbal, 2% scored 600 or over on math; 12% scored 500 or over on verbal, 17% scored 500 or over on math; 62% scored 400 or over on verbal, 73% scored 400 or over on math; 96% scored 300 or over on verbal, 100% scored 300 or over on math. 70% of accepted applicants took SAT. 67% of freshmen come from public schools.
**Undergraduate achievement:** 75% of fall 1991 freshmen returned for fall 1992 term. 20% of entering class graduated. 32% of students who completed a degree program went on to graduate study within five years.
**Foreign students:** 92 students are from out of the country. Countries represented include Japan, Korea, Namibia, and Sweden; 24 in all.

**PROGRAMS OF STUDY. Degrees:** B.A., B.S., B.Soc.Work.
**Majors:** Accounting, Anthropology, Biochemistry, Biology, Business Administration, Chemistry, Communication, Computer Information Systems, Creative/Performing Arts, Economics, English, History, Human Resources Management, Mathematics, Multinational Corporate Studies, Philosophy, Political Science, Psychology, Religion, Social Work, Sociology, Spanish, Theatre.
**Distribution of degrees:** The majors with the highest enrollment are business administration, human resources management, and psychology.
**Requirements:** General education requirement.
**Academic regulations:** Freshmen must maintain minimum 1.75 GPA; sophomores, 1.80 GPA; juniors, 1.90 GPA; seniors, 2.00 GPA.
**Special:** Minors offered in all majors. Concentrations offered in American Studies, ancient Near East studies, art history, black studies, cytotechnology, environmental studies, Judaic studies, and urban studies. ESL program. Self-designed majors. Double majors. Independent study. Accelerated study. Pass/fail grading option. Internships. Cooperative education programs. Graduate school at which undergraduates may take graduate-level courses. Preprofessional programs in law, medicine, veterinary science, and dentistry. 3-2 engineering programs with New Jersey Inst of Tech and Washington U. 3-2 forestry and environmental studies program with Duke U. 3-2 cytotechnology program with U of Medicine and Dentistry of New Jersey. Seven-year optometry program with Pennsylvania Coll of Optometry. Washington Semester. Study abroad in France and Sweden.
**Honors:** Honors program.
**Academic Assistance:** Remedial reading, writing, math, and study skills. Nonremedial tutoring.

**ADMISSIONS. Academic basis for candidate selection** (in order of priority): Secondary school record, class rank, standardized test scores, essay, school's recommendation.
**Nonacademic basis for candidate selection:** Particular talent or ability and geographical distribution are important. Character and personality, extracurricular participation, and alumni/ae relationship are considered.

**Requirements:** Graduation from secondary school is required; GED is accepted. 16 units and the following program of study are required: 4 units of English, 3 units of math, 2 units of lab science, 2 units of foreign language, 2 units of social studies. Minimum 2.0 GPA required. EOP for applicants not normally admissible. Challenge program for applicants not normally admissible. SAT is required; ACT may be substituted. Campus visit and interview recommended. Off-campus interviews available with an admissions representative.
**Procedure:** Take SAT or ACT by December of 12th year. Suggest filing application by November 1; no deadline. Notification of admission on rolling basis. Reply is required within two weeks of acceptance. $300 nonrefundable tuition deposit. $200 nonrefundable room deposit. Freshmen accepted in terms other than fall.
**Special programs:** Admission may be deferred one year. Credit and/or placement may be granted through CEEB Advanced Placement exams for scores of 3 or higher. Credit and/or placement may be granted through CLEP general and subject exams. Credit and placement may be granted through Regents College, ACT PEP, DANTES, and challenge exams, military and life experience. Early decision program. Deadline for applying for early decision is November 1. Early entrance/early admission program. Concurrent enrollment program.
**Transfer students:** Transfer students accepted for terms other than fall. In fall 1992, 20% of all new students were transfers into all classes. 120 transfer applications were received, 73 were accepted. Application deadline is rolling for fall; rolling for spring. Minimum 2.0 GPA required. Lowest course grade accepted is "C." Maximum number of transferable credits is 96 semester hours. At least 32 semester hours must be completed at the college to receive degree.
**Admissions contact:** Susan M. Chalfin, M.S.Ed., Dean of Admissions. 201 266-7191.

**FINANCIAL AID. Available aid:** Pell grants, SEOG, state scholarships and grants, school scholarships and grants, private scholarships and grants, academic merit scholarships, and aid for undergraduate foreign students. Lutheran Church scholarships. Perkins Loans (NDSL), PLUS, Stafford Loans (GSL), state loans, and SLS. Family tuition reduction.
**Financial aid statistics:** In 1992-93, 98% of all undergraduate applicants received aid; 88% of freshman applicants. Average amounts of aid awarded freshmen: Scholarships and grants, $4,000; loans, $2,000.
**Supporting data/closing dates:** FAFSA/FAF/FFS: Priority filing date is April 1; accepted on rolling basis. State aid form: Accepted on rolling basis. Income tax forms: Priority filing date is April 1; accepted on rolling basis. IEADC, SSI: Priority filing date is April 1; accepted on rolling basis. Notification of awards on rolling basis.
**Financial aid contact:** Pamela Pappas, Director of Financial Aid. 201 266-7191.

## Westminster Choir College, The School of Music of Rider College

**Princeton, NJ 08540** **609 921-7100**

**1993-94 Costs.** Tuition: $12,750. Room & board: $5,515. Fees, books, misc. academic expenses (school's estimate): $1,020.
**Enrollment.** Undergraduates: 79 men, 142 women (full-time). Freshman class: 146 applicants, 135 accepted, 73 enrolled. Graduate enrollment: 43 men, 61 women.
**Test score averages/ranges.** Average SAT scores: 490 verbal, 510 math. Range of SAT scores of middle 50%: 450-520 verbal, 460-540 math. Average ACT scores: 22 composite. Range of ACT scores of middle 50%: 20-25 composite.
**Faculty.** 40 full-time; 29 part-time. 60% of faculty holds doctoral degree. Student/faculty ratio: 6 to 1.
**Selectivity rating.** Competitive.

**PROFILE.** Westminster Choir College is a private college of music. Founded in 1926 in Ohio, it moved to New Jersey in 1932. Its 23-acre campus is located in Princeton, 50 miles from both New York City and Philadelphia.

**Accreditation:** MSACS. Professionally accredited by the National Association of Schools of Music.
**Religious orientation:** Westminster Choir College, The School of Music of Rider College is nonsectarian; one semester of religion/theology required.
**Library:** Collections totaling over 56,260 volumes, 175 periodical subscriptions and 414 microform items.
**Special facilities/museums:** Archives of organ historical society, more than 20 pipe organs, 120 pianos, music computing center, performance collection center, music education resource center, voice resource center.
**Athletic facilities:** Swimming pool at local YMCA.

**STUDENT BODY. Undergraduate profile:** 37% are state residents; 30% are transfers. 3% Asian-American, 7% Black, 2% Hispanic, 75% White, 13% Other. Average age of undergraduates is 21.
**Freshman profile:** 14% of freshmen who took ACT scored 30 or over on composite; 43% scored 24 or over on composite; 72% scored 18 or over on composite; 100% scored 12 or over on composite. 88% of accepted applicants took SAT; 12% took ACT.
**Undergraduate achievement:** 82% of fall 1992 freshmen returned for fall 1993 term. 50% of entering class graduated. 29% of students completing a degree program immediately went on to graduate study.

**PROGRAMS OF STUDY. Degrees:** B.A.Mus., B.Mus.
**Majors:** Church Music, Music Education, Organ Performance, Piano Pedagogy, Piano Performance, Theory/Composition, Voice Performance.
**Distribution of degrees:** The majors with the highest enrollment are music education, voice performance, and church music; theory/composition, piano performance, and organ performance have the lowest.
**Requirements:** General education requirement.
**Academic regulations:** Minimum 2.0 GPA must be maintained.
**Special:** All students sing with the Symphonic Choir, performing regularly with the New York Philharmonic and the Philadelphia Orchestras. The Westminster Choir is the choir-in-residence for the Spoleto Festival of Three Worlds. Computer-based theory instruction. All students learn word processing. Minors offered in organ, piano, and voice. Double majors. Independent study. Pass/fail grading option. Internships. Graduate school at which undergraduates may take graduate-level courses. Teacher certification in elementary and secondary education. Certification in specific subject areas. ROTC at Rider Coll. AFROTC at Rutgers U.
**Academic Assistance:** Remedial reading, writing, math, and study skills. Nonremedial tutoring.

**ADMISSIONS. Academic basis for candidate selection** (in order of priority): Secondary school record, standardized test scores, class rank, school's recommendation, essay.
**Nonacademic basis for candidate selection:** Particular talent or ability is emphasized. Extracurricular participation is important. Character and personality are considered.
**Requirements:** Graduation from secondary school is required; GED is accepted. 7 units and the following program of study are required: 4 units of English, 1 unit of math, 2 units of history. Three units of science, two units of foreign language, and two units of electives are recommended. Minimum combined SAT score of 700 (SAT score of 350 in math). Audition required of all applicants. EOP for applicants not normally admissible. SAT or ACT is required. Campus visit and interview recommended. Off-campus interviews available with admissions and alumni representatives.
**Procedure:** Take SAT or ACT by August 1 of 12th year. Take ACH by August 1 of 12th year. Notification of admission on rolling basis. Reply is required by May 1. $200 nonrefundable tuition deposit. $200 nonrefundable room deposit. Freshmen accepted in terms other than fall.
**Special programs:** Admission may be deferred one year. Credit may be granted through CEEB Advanced Placement for scores of 3 or higher. Early decision program. Deadline for applying for early decision is November 1. Early entrance/early admission program.
**Transfer students:** Transfer students accepted for terms other than fall. In fall 1993, 30% of all new students were transfers into all classes. 43 transfer applications were received, 34 were accepted. Application deadline is rolling for fall; rolling for spring. Minimum 2.0 GPA required. Lowest course grade accepted is "C." Maximum number of transferable credits is 60 semester hours. At least 60 semester hours must be completed at the college to receive degree.
**Admissions contact:** Deborah J. Erie, M.Ed., Director of Admissions. 609 921-7144.

**FINANCIAL AID. Available aid:** Pell grants, SEOG, state scholarships and grants, school scholarships and grants, ROTC scholarships, and academic merit scholarships. Perkins Loans (NDSL), PLUS, Stafford Loans (GSL), state loans, school loans, and SLS. AMS.
**Financial aid statistics:** In 1993-94, 80% of all undergraduate applicants received aid; 80% of freshman applicants. Average amounts of aid awarded freshmen: Scholarships and grants, $4,677; loans, $2,049.
**Supporting data/closing dates:** FAFSA: Priority filing date is March 1; accepted on rolling basis. Stafford Loan: Priority filing date is March 1; accepted on rolling basis. Notification of awards begins February 1.
**Financial aid contact:** Audrey MacKellar, Associate Director of Financial Aid. 609 896-5360.

## William Paterson College of New Jersey

**Wayne, NJ 07470** **201 595-2000**

**1993-94 Costs.** Tuition: $2,832 (state residents), $3,728 (out-of-state). Room & board: $4,510. Fees, books, misc. academic expenses (school's estimate): $300.
**Enrollment.** Undergraduates: 2,478 men, 3,183 women (full-time). Freshman class: 5,232 applicants, 2,607 accepted, 1,044 enrolled. Graduate enrollment: 198 men, 734 women.
**Test score averages/ranges.** Average SAT scores: 436 verbal, 482 math.
**Faculty.** 307 full-time; 13 part-time. 78% of faculty holds doctoral degree. Student/faculty ratio: 14 to 1.
**Selectivity rating.** Competitive.

**PROFILE.** William Paterson, founded in 1855, is a public, multipurpose college. Programs are offered through the Colleges of Arts and Communication, Education and Community Service, Health Professions and Nursing, Humanities, Management, Science and Mathematics, and Social Science. Its 250-acre campus is located in Wayne, 20 miles west of New York City.

**Accreditation:** MSACS. Professionally accredited by the American Speech-Language-Hearing Association, the National Association of Schools of Music, the National Council for Accreditation of Teacher Education, the National League for Nursing.
**Religious orientation:** William Paterson College of New Jersey is nonsectarian; no religious requirements.
**Library:** Collections totaling over 307,000 volumes, 1,400 periodical subscriptions, and 861,000 microform items.
**Special facilities/museums:** Art gallery, audio-visual center, film library, computer graphics lab, collection of William Paterson's private papers, nonprofit communications center, electron microscopes.
**Athletic facilities:** Gymnasium, swimming pool, basketball, racquetball, and tennis courts, weight rooms, sauna, dance studio, track, baseball, field hockey, football, soccer, and softball fields.

**STUDENT BODY. Undergraduate profile:** 98% are state residents; 38% are transfers. 3% Asian-American, 7% Black, 8% Hispanic, 1% Native American, 80% White, 1% Other. Average age of undergraduates is 21.
**Freshman profile:** 98% of accepted applicants took SAT; 5% took ACT.

**Undergraduate achievement:** 78% of fall 1991 freshmen returned for fall 1992 term. 15% of entering class graduated. 16% of students who completed a degree program immediately went on to graduate study.
**Foreign students:** 72 students are from out of the country. Countries represented include China, England, Japan, Kenya, and Nigeria; 32 in all.

**PROGRAMS OF STUDY. Degrees:** B.A., B.F.A., B.Mus., B.S.
**Majors:** Accounting, African/African-American/Caribbean Studies, Art History, Biology, Biotechnology, Business Administration, Chemistry, Community Health/School Health Education, Computer Science, Dramatic Arts, Economics, Elementary Education, English, Environmental Science, Fine Arts, Geography, History, Jazz Studies, Liberal Studies, Mathematics, Music Management, Music Performance, Musical Studies, Nursing, Philosophy, Physical Education, Political Science, Psychology, Sociology/Anthropology, Spanish, Special Education, Speech Pathology, Studio Art.
**Distribution of degrees:** The majors with the highest enrollment are business administration and elementary education; African/African-American/Caribbean studies has the lowest.
**Requirements:** General education requirement.
**Academic regulations:** Minimum 2.0 GPA must be maintained.
**Special:** Honors programs in biopsychology, humanities, jazz studies, and international business. Double majors. Independent study. Accelerated study. Pass/fail grading option. Internships. Preprofessional programs in law, medicine, veterinary science, and pharmacy. Member of National Student Exchange (NSE). Teacher certification in elementary, secondary, and special education. Certification in specific subject areas. Member of New Jersey Consortium for International Education Exchange. Study abroad in Australia, Denmark, Greece, Israel, Spain, the United Kingdom, and other countries. ROTC at New Jersey Inst of Tech and Seton Hall U.
**Honors:** Honors program.
**Academic Assistance:** Remedial reading, writing, math, and study skills. Nonremedial tutoring.

**STUDENT LIFE. Housing:** Students may live on or off campus. Coed dorms. School-owned/operated apartments. 16% of students live in college housing.
**Social atmosphere:** According to the student newspaper, William Paterson College offers many worthwhile social diversions. Springfest, concerts, the Distinguished Lecturer Series, and Homecoming are just some of the popular social events. Off campus, students frequent the Sandwich Pub and J&E's; on campus, they prefer to hang out at Billy Pat's Club, the Student Center, and the Rec Center. Of the numerous groups on campus, those with the most social influence are Greeks, the Christian Fellowship, the Catholic Campus Ministry Club, and the Student Activities Planning Board (SAPB).
**Services and counseling/handicapped student services:** Placement services. Health service. Day care. Counseling services for minority, veteran, and older students. Birth control, personal, and psychological counseling. Career and academic guidance services. Religious counseling. Physically disabled student services. Learning disabled services. Tape recorders. Tutors. Reader services for the blind.
**Campus organizations:** Undergraduate student government. Student newspaper (Beacon, published once/week). Literary magazine. Yearbook. Radio and TV stations. Choir, chorus, gospel choir, bands, ensembles, college-community sinfonetta, coffeehouse, outdoor club, Society for Creative Anachronism, dance ensemble, BACCHUS, academic, political, and special-interest groups, 53 organizations in all. 11 fraternities, no chapter houses; 10 sororities, no chapter houses. 10% of men join a fraternity. 12% of women join a sorority.
**Religious organizations:** Catholic Campus Ministry, Christian Fellowship, Jewish Student Association.
**Minority/foreign student organizations:** Black Student Association, Sisters for Awareness, Black Leadership, and Equality (SABLE). International Student Organization, Caribbean, Chinese, Latin American, and Palestinian groups.

**ATHLETICS. Physical education requirements:** One semester of physical education required.
**Intercollegiate competition:** 10% of students participate. Baseball (M), basketball (M,W), cheerleading (W), cross-country (M,W), diving (M,W), field hockey (W), football (M), soccer (M), softball (W), swimming (M,W), track (indoor) (M,W), track (outdoor) (M,W), track and field (indoor) (M,W), track and field (outdoor) (M,W), volleyball (W). Member of Collegiate Track Conference, ECAC, Metropolitan Swimming Conference, NCAA Division III, New Jersey Athletic Conference, New Jersey Intercollegiate Athletic Association for Women.
**Intramural and club sports:** 40% of students participate. Intramural aerobics, basketball, bowling, flag football, floor hockey, racquetball, running, softball, swimming, table tennis, tennis, track, volleyball, walleyball, water polo, weight lifting. Men's club bowling, cycling, horsemanship, ice hockey. Women's club bowling, cycling, horsemanship, soccer.

**ADMISSIONS. Academic basis for candidate selection** (in order of priority): Secondary school record, class rank, standardized test scores, school's recommendation, essay.
**Nonacademic basis for candidate selection:** Character and personality, extracurricular participation, particular talent or ability, geographical distribution, and alumni/ae relationship are considered.
**Requirements:** Graduation from secondary school is required; GED is accepted. 16 units and the following program of study are required: 4 units of English, 3 units of math, 2 units of lab science, 2 units of social studies, 3 units of academic electives. Portfolio required of art program applicants. Audition required of music program applicants. EOP and Sponsored Admissions Program for applicants not normally admissible. SAT is required; ACT may be substituted. Campus visit recommended. Off-campus interviews available with admissions and alumni representatives.
**Procedure:** Take SAT or ACT by February of 12th year. Visit college for interview by November of 12th year. Suggest filing application by April 15. Application deadline is June 30. Notification of admission on rolling basis. Reply is required by May 1. $50 nonrefundable tuition deposit. $75 nonrefundable room deposit. Freshmen accepted in terms other than fall.
**Special programs:** Admission may be deferred one year. Credit and/or placement may be granted through CEEB Advanced Placement exams for scores of 3 or higher. Credit and/or placement may be granted through CLEP general and subject exams. Credit and placement may be granted through ACT PEP and challenge exams. Early decision program. Early entrance/early admission program. Concurrent enrollment program.
**Transfer students:** Transfer students accepted for terms other than fall. In fall 1992, 38% of all new students were transfers into all classes. 1,782 transfer applications were received, 1,406 were accepted. Application deadline is June 30 for fall; November 1 for spring. Minimum 2.0 GPA required. Lowest course grade accepted is "C." Maximum number of transferable credits is 90 semester hours. At least 30 semester hours must be completed at the college to receive degree.
**Admissions contact:** Leo J. DeBartolo, M.Ed., Director of Admissions. 201 595-2125.

**FINANCIAL AID. Available aid:** Pell grants and state scholarships and grants. Perkins Loans (NDSL), PLUS, Stafford Loans (GSL), state loans, and SLS. Deferred payment plan.
**Financial aid statistics:** 69% of aid is not need-based.
**Supporting data/closing dates:** FAFSA/FAF: Priority filing date is April 15. Income tax forms: Priority filing date is April 15. Notification of awards on rolling basis.
**Financial aid contact:** Georgia Daniel, Director of Financial Aid. 201 595-2202.

**STUDENT EMPLOYMENT.** College Work/Study Program. Institutional employment. 4% of full-time undergraduates work on campus during school year. Students may expect to earn an average of $1,500 during school year. Off-campus part-time employment opportunities rated "good."

**COMPUTER FACILITIES.** IBM/IBM-compatible and Macintosh/Apple microcomputers. Students may access AT&T, IBM minicomputer/mainframe systems, Internet. Computer languages and software packages include dBASE, Lotus 1-2-3, SAS, SPSS, word processing packages. Computer facilities are available to all students.
Fees: None.
**Hours:** 8 AM-10 PM (M-Th); 8 AM-8 PM (F); 8 AM-4 PM (Sa).

**GRADUATE CAREER DATA.** Graduate school percentages: 2% enter law school. 1% enter medical school. 2% enter graduate business programs. 10% enter graduate arts and sciences programs. Highest graduate school enrollments: William Paterson Coll. 52% of graduates choose careers in business and industry.

**PROMINENT ALUMNI/AE.** Dr. Douglas Arella, pediatric orthopedics specialist; Michael Burns, president, Rymer Co.; John Byrne, managing editor, *Business Week* magazine; Cora-Ann Mahalik, anchor/reporter *A Current Affair;* Judi Buckalew, vice-president and managing director for government relations, International Association for Financial Planning.

# New Mexico

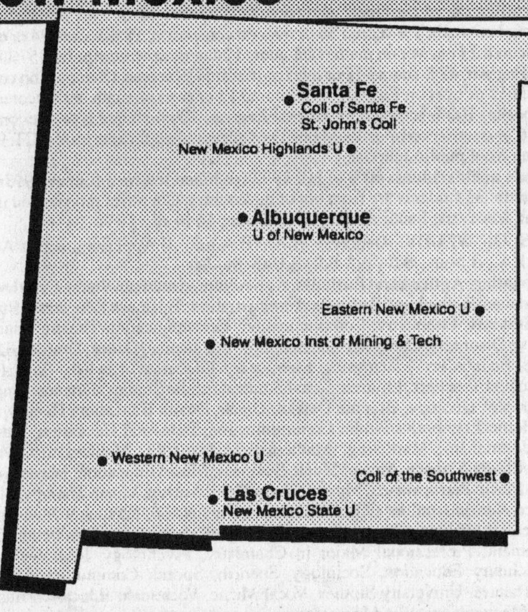


## College of Santa Fe

**Santa Fe, NM 87501** **505 473-6011**

**1994-95 Costs.** Tuition: $11,138. Room & board: $4,210. Fees, books, misc. academic expenses (school's estimate): $840.
**Enrollment.** Undergraduates: 404 men, 469 women (full-time). Freshman class: 546 applicants, 453 accepted, 189 enrolled. Graduate enrollment: 37 men, 108 women.
**Test score averages/ranges.** Average SAT scores: 480 verbal, 490 math. Average ACT scores: 21 composite.
**Faculty.** 54 full-time; 91 part-time. 75% of faculty holds doctoral degree. Student/faculty ratio: 14 to 1.
**Selectivity rating.** Less competitive.

**PROFILE.** The College of Santa Fe is a private, liberal arts college. Founded in 1874, it adopted coeducation in 1966. Its 98-acre campus is located in Santa Fe, 60 miles from Albuquerque.

**Accreditation:** NCACS.
**Religious orientation:** College of Santa Fe is affiliated with the Roman Catholic Church (Christian Brothers); six semesters of religion/theology required.
**Library:** Collections totaling over 165,000 volumes and 321 periodical subscriptions.
**Special facilities/museums:** Art gallery, film/TV studio.
**Athletic facilities:** Tennis center, basketball, racquetball, squash, and volleyball courts, flag football and soccer fields, gymnasiums, Universal equipment, aerobics/cardiovascular and wrestling rooms.
**STUDENT BODY. Undergraduate profile:** 28% are transfers. 2.7% Asian-American, 2.6% Black, 14.6% Hispanic, 1.9% Native American, 75.8% White, 2.4% Other. Average age of undergraduates is 27.
**Freshman profile:** 39% of accepted applicants took SAT; 41% took ACT. 73% of freshmen come from public schools.
**Undergraduate achievement:** 62% of fall 1992 freshmen returned for fall 1993 term. 55% of entering class graduated. 80% of students who completed a degree program went on to graduate study within one year.
**Foreign students:** 15 students are from out of the country. Countries represented include Canada, Germany, Japan, Japan, Mexico, and Spain; 10 in all.
**PROGRAMS OF STUDY. Degrees:** B.A., B.F.A., B.S.
**Majors:** Accounting Applications, Acting, Applied Mathematics/Computer Science, Applied Psychology, Art History, Art Therapy, Arts/Entertainment Management, Biology, Chemistry, Computer Applications Design, Computer Science, Contemporary Music, Corporate Communications, Creative Writing, Design Technology, English, English Education, Environmental Management, Environmental Science, General Psychology, Humanities, Managerial Psychology, Mathematics, Mathematics Education, Moving Image Arts, Music Theatre, Organizational Management, Pastoral Studies, Religion Studies, Science Education, Social Science, Southwest American Studies, Studio Arts, Technical Communication, Theatre Management.
**Distribution of degrees:** The majors with the highest enrollment are education, performing arts, and moving image arts; religion studies, environmental science, and biology have the lowest.
**Requirements:** General education requirement.
**Academic regulations:** Minimum 2.0 GPA must be maintained.
**Special:** Minors offered in some majors and in contemporary music, dance, history, philosophy, physical education, political science, Spanish, and theatre, Associate's degrees offered. Self-designed majors. Double majors. Dual degrees. Pass/fail grading option. Graduate school at which undergraduates may take graduate-level courses. Preprofessional programs in law, medicine, veterinary science, and dentistry. Teacher certification in elementary, secondary, and bilingual/bicultural education. Certification in specific subject areas.
**Academic Assistance:** Remedial reading, writing, math, and study skills. Nonremedial tutoring.
**ADMISSIONS. Academic basis for candidate selection** (in order of priority): Secondary school record, standardized test scores, essay, school's recommendation, class rank. **Nonacademic basis for candidate selection:** Particular talent or ability is important. Character and personality and extracurricular participation are considered.
**Requirements:** Graduation from secondary school is required; GED is accepted. 21 units and the following program of study are required: 3 units of English, 2 units of math, 2 units of lab science, 2 units of social studies, 10 units of electives. Minimum composite ACT score of 19 (combined SAT score of 960) and minimum 2.3 GPA required. Audition required of performing arts, moving image arts, and music program applicants. SAT or ACT is required. Campus visit and interview recommended. Off-campus interviews available with admissions and alumni representatives.
**Procedure:** Suggest filing application by March 1. Application deadline is July 30. Notification of admission on rolling basis. Reply is required by first week of classes. $100 nonrefundable tuition deposit. $200 refundable room deposit. Freshmen accepted for terms other than fall.
**Special programs:** Admission may be deferred two years. Credit and/or placement may be granted through CEEB Advanced Placement exams for scores of 3 or higher. Credit and/or placement may be granted through CLEP general and subject exams. Credit and placement may be granted through challenge exams and military and life experience. Concurrent enrollment program.
**Transfer students:** Transfer students accepted for terms other than fall. In fall 1993, 28% of all new students were transfers into all classes. 272 transfer applications were received, 191 were accepted. Application deadline is July 30 for fall; January 3 for spring. Minimum 2.5 GPA required. Lowest course grade accepted is "C." At least 30 semester hours must be completed at the college to receive degree.
**Admissions contact:** Monica Martinez, Director of Admissions. 505 473-6131, 800 473-6131.
**FINANCIAL AID. Available aid:** Pell grants, SEOG, state grants, school scholarships, private scholarships, and academic merit scholarships. Perkins Loans (NDSL), PLUS, Stafford Loans (GSL), and SLS. Tuition Management Systems.
**Financial aid statistics:** 22% of aid is not need-based. In 1993-94, 75% of all undergraduate applicants received aid; 85% of freshman applicants. Average amounts of aid awarded freshmen: Scholarships and grants, $1,000; loans, $2,625.
**Supporting data/closing dates:** FAFSA: Priority filing date is March 1; accepted on rolling basis. School's own aid application. State aid form: Accepted on rolling basis. Income tax forms: Accepted on rolling basis. Notification of awards on rolling basis.
**Financial aid contact:** Cy Martinez, Associate Director of Financial Aid. 505 473-6127.

## College of the Southwest

**Hobbs, NM 88240** **505 392-6561**

**1993-94 Costs.** Tuition: $3,120. Room & board: $2,410. Fees, books, misc. academic expenses (school's estimate): $550.
**Enrollment.** Undergraduates: 95 men, 120 women (full-time). Freshman class: 77 applicants, 61 accepted, 47 enrolled.
**Test score averages/ranges.** Average SAT scores: 395 verbal, 365 math. Average ACT scores: 17 English, 18 math, 18 composite.
**Faculty.** 12 full-time; 27 part-time. 34% of faculty holds doctoral degree. Student/faculty ratio: 8 to 1.
**Selectivity rating.** Less competitive.

**PROFILE.** The College of the Southwest, founded in 1962, is a private college of arts and sciences with religious affiliation. Its 162-acre campus is located in Hobbs, southwest of Lubbock, Tex.

**Accreditation:** NCACS.
**Religious orientation:** College of the Southwest is nonsectarian; two semesters of religion required.
**Library:** Collections totaling over 87,440 volumes, 240 periodical subscriptions, and 12,628 microform items.
**Athletic facilities:** Gymnasium, racquetball and volleyball courts, weight room, baseball and soccer fields, fitness center.
**STUDENT BODY. Undergraduate profile:** 82% are state residents; 23% are transfers. 2% Black, 13% Hispanic, 1% Native American, 84% White. Average age of undergraduates is 28.
**Freshman profile:** 25% of freshmen who took SAT scored 500 or over on verbal; 50% scored 400 or over on verbal, 50% scored 400 or over on math; 75% scored 300 or over on verbal, 75% scored 300 or over on math. 4% of freshmen who took ACT scored 24 or over on English, 15% scored 24 or over on math, 15% scored 24 or over on composite; 46% scored 18 or over on English, 50% scored 18 or over on math, 50% scored 18 or over on composite; 92% scored 12 or over on English, 100% scored 12 or over on math, 100% scored 12 or over on composite; 100% scored 6 or over on English. 13% of accepted applicants took SAT; 87% took ACT. 93% of freshmen come from public schools.
**Undergraduate achievement:** 20% of fall 1992 freshmen returned for fall 1993 term. 4% of entering class graduated. 30% of students who completed a degree program went on to graduate study.
**Foreign students:** Nine students are from out of the country. Countries represented include the Bahamas, Canada, and the Netherlands; seven in all.
**PROGRAMS OF STUDY. Degrees:** B.A.Lib.Studies, B.A.Sci., B.Bus.Admin., B.S.
**Majors:** Accounting, Biology, Chemistry, Elementary Education, English, Geology, History, Management, Marketing, Mathematics, Psychology, Secondary Education, Special Education, The Arts.

**Distribution of degrees:** The majors with the highest enrollment are elementary education, psychology, and management; secondary education, accounting, and marketing have the lowest.
**Requirements:** General education requirement.
**Academic regulations:** Freshmen must maintain minimum 1.75 GPA; sophomores, 1.75 GPA; juniors, 2.00 GPA; seniors, 2.00 GPA.
**Special:** Self-designed majors. Internships. Graduate school at which undergraduates may take graduate-level courses. Preprofessional programs in law and medicine. Teacher certification in elementary, secondary, special education, and bilingual/bicultural education. Certification in specific subject areas.
**Honors:** Honor societies.

**ADMISSIONS. Academic basis for candidate selection** (in order of priority): Secondary school record, class rank, standardized test scores.
**Nonacademic basis for candidate selection:** Character and personality, extracurricular participation, particular talent or ability, geographical distribution, and alumni/ae relationship are emphasized.
**Requirements:** Graduation from secondary school is recommended; GED is accepted. No specific distribution of secondary school units required. Minimum composite ACT score of 18 (combined SAT score of 740) and rank in top half of secondary school class or minimum 2.0 GPA required. Interview and written exam required of education program applicants. Conditional admission possible for applicants not meeting standard requirements. ACT is required; SAT may be substituted. Campus visit and interview recommended. Off-campus interviews available with an admissions representative.
**Procedure:** Take SAT or ACT by June of 12th year. Suggest filing application by July 1; no deadline. Notification of admission on rolling basis. Reply is required by August 15. $150 room deposit, refundable until the start of classes. Freshmen accepted for terms other than fall.
**Special programs:** Admission may be deferred up to 30 days after registration. Credit may be granted through CEEB Advanced Placement for scores of 2 or higher. Credit may be granted through CLEP general and subject exams, ACT PEP, DANTES, and challenge exams, and military and life experience. Early entrance/early admission program. Concurrent enrollment program.
**Transfer students:** Transfer students accepted for terms other than fall. In fall 1993, 23% of all new students were transfers into all classes. 102 transfer applications were received, 102 were accepted. Application deadline is August 1 for fall; December 1 for spring. Minimum 2.0 GPA required. Lowest course grade accepted is "D." Maximum number of transferable credits is 66 semester hours from a two-year school and 98 semester hours from a four-year school. At least 30 semester hours must be completed at the college to receive degree.
**Admissions contact:** Rhonda Tyler, Director of Student Services. 505 392-6561, extension 320.

**FINANCIAL AID. Available aid:** Pell grants, SEOG, state scholarships and grants, school scholarships, private scholarships, academic merit scholarships, and athletic scholarships. PLUS, Stafford Loans (GSL), and SLS. Deferred payment plan.
**Financial aid statistics:** 43% of aid is not need-based. In 1993-94, 95% of all undergraduate applicants received aid; 100% of freshman applicants. Average amounts of aid awarded freshmen: Scholarships and grants, $1,338; loans, $2,625.
**Supporting data/closing dates:** FAFSA/FAF/FFS: Priority filing date is April 1; deadline is June 1. School's own aid application: Priority filing date is April 1; deadline is June 1. Income tax forms: Priority filing date is June 1; deadline is August 1. Notification of awards begins July 1.
**Financial aid contact:** Glenna M. Ohaver, M.A., Director of Financial Aid. 505 392-6561, extension 208.

# Eastern New Mexico University

**Portales, NM 88130** **505 562-1011**

**1994-95 Costs.** Tuition: $1,443 (state residents), $5,283 (out-of-state). Room: $1,160. Board: $1,350. Fees, books, misc. academic expenses (school's estimate): $600.
**Enrollment.** Undergraduates: 1,250 men, 1,543 women (full-time). Freshman class: 1,297 applicants. Graduate enrollment: 229 men, 393 women.
**Test score averages/ranges.** Average SAT scores: 510 verbal, 455 math. Range of SAT scores of middle 50%: 850-1080 combined. Average ACT scores: 24 English, 19 math, 21 composite. Range of ACT scores of middle 50%: 18-29 English, 14-25 math.
**Faculty.** 156 full-time; 91 part-time. 49% of faculty holds doctoral degree. Student/faculty ratio: 22 to 1.
**Selectivity rating.** Noncompetitive.

**PROFILE.** Eastern New Mexico, founded in 1934, is a public, comprehensive university. Programs are offered through the Colleges of Business, Education and Technology, Fine Arts, and Liberal Arts and Sciences and the Graduate School. Its 400-acre campus is located in Portales, in east-central New Mexico.

**Accreditation:** NCACS. Professionally accredited by the National Association of Schools of Music, the National Council for Accreditation of Teacher Education.
**Religious orientation:** Eastern New Mexico University is nonsectarian; no religious requirements.
**Library:** Collections totaling over 350,000 volumes, 4,150 periodical subscriptions, and 1,944 microform items.
**Special facilities/museums:** Natural history and historical museums, theatre, child development center, audio-visual center, electron microscopes, laser.
**Athletic facilities:** Basketball, tennis, volleyball, and racquetball courts, natatorium, weight room, conditioning/cardiovascular room, track.

**STUDENT BODY. Undergraduate profile:** 72% are state residents. 1% Asian-American, 5% Black, 20% Hispanic, 2% Native American, 70% White, 2% Other. Average age of undergraduates is 21.
**Freshman profile:** 2% of freshmen who took ACT scored 30 or over on English, 1% scored 30 or over on math, 1% scored 30 or over on composite; 18% scored 24 or over on English, 8% scored 24 or over on math, 12% scored 24 or over on composite; 57% scored 18 or over on English, 42% scored 18 or over on math, 57% scored 18 or over on composite; 95% scored 12 or over on English, 99% scored 12 or over on math, 99% scored 12 or over on composite; 100% scored 6 or over on English, 100% scored 6 or over on math, 100% scored 6 or over on composite. Majority of accepted applicants took ACT. 96% of freshmen come from public schools.
**Undergraduate achievement:** 60% of fall 1992 freshmen returned for fall 1993 term.
**Foreign students:** 31 students are from out of the country. Countries represented include China, Kuwait, Malaysia, Saudi Arabia, and Taiwan; 16 in all.

**PROGRAMS OF STUDY. Degrees:** B.A., B.A.Ed., B.Appl.Sci., B.Bus.Admin., B.Bus.Ed., B.F.A., B.Mus., B.S., B.S.Ed., B.Univ.Studies.
**Majors:** Accounting, Agricultural Business, Agriculture, American Studies, Anthropology, Art, Art Education, Biology, Business Administration, Business Education, Business Information Systems, Chemistry, Communication, Communication/Theatre Education, Communicative Disorders, Computer Science, Criminal Justice, Dance, Drafting/Design, Earth Science, Economics, Electronics, Elementary Education, English, English Language for Bilingual Teachers, Environmental Studies, Ethnic Studies, Finance, Fine Arts, French, Geography, Geology, Graphic Design, Greek, Health Education, History, Home Economics, Home Economics/Public Communication, Industrial Education, Industrial Technology, Journalism, Marketing, Mathematical Statistics, Mathematics, Medical Technology, Military Science, Music, Music Business, Music Education, Music History/Appreciation, Music Performance, Music Theory/Composition, Music Therapy, Musical Theatre, Office Administration, Office Education, Percussion, Personnel Management, Physical Education, Physics, Piano, Political Science/Government, Production/Operations Management, Professional Major in Chemistry, Psychology, Radio/Television, Religion, Secondary Education, Sociology, Spanish, Speech Communication, String Instruments, Theatre, University Studies, Vocal Music, Vocational Education/Business, Wildlife/Fish Management, Wind Instruments.
**Distribution of degrees:** The majors with the highest enrollment are elementary education, communication, and psychology; chemistry, marketing, and art education have the lowest.
**Requirements:** General education requirement.
**Academic regulations:** Minimum 2.0 GPA must be maintained.
**Special:** Minors offered in some majors and in biophysics and library science. Associate's degrees offered. Self-designed majors. Double majors. Independent study. Internships. Cooperative education programs. Graduate school at which undergraduates may take graduate-level courses. Preprofessional programs in medicine, veterinary science, pharmacy, and dentistry. Member of National Student Exchange (NSE). Teacher certification in early childhood, elementary, secondary, special education, vo-tech, and bilingual/bicultural education. Certification in specific subject areas. Member of International Student Exchange Program (ISEP). ROTC.
**Honors:** Honors program. Honor societies.
**Academic Assistance:** Remedial reading, writing, math, and study skills. Nonremedial tutoring.

**STUDENT LIFE. Housing:** Students may live on or off campus. Coed, women's, and men's dorms. School-owned/operated apartments. On-campus married-student housing. 80% of students live in college housing.
**Services and counseling/handicapped student services:** Placement services. Health service. Counseling services for minority, military, veteran, and older students. Birth control, personal, and psychological counseling. Career and academic guidance services. Religious counseling. Physically disabled student services. Learning disabled services. Notetaking services. Tape recorders. Reader services for the blind.
**Campus organizations:** Undergraduate student government. Student newspaper (Chase, published once/week). Literary magazine. Yearbook. Radio and TV stations. 100 registered organizations. Five fraternities, all with chapter houses; two sororities, all with chapter houses. 16% of men join a fraternity. 8% of women join a sorority.
**Religious organizations:** Baptist Union Center, Campus Christian House, Church of Christ, Newman Center, Wesley Foundation.
**Minority/foreign student organizations:** Several minority student groups. International Student Club, European Society.

**ATHLETICS. Physical education requirements:** Two semesters of physical education required.
**Intercollegiate competition:** 8% of students participate. Baseball (M), basketball (M,W), football (M), riflery (M,W), tennis (W), volleyball (W). Member of Lone Star Conference, NCAA Division II.
**Intramural and club sports:** 12% of students participate. Intramural badminton, basketball, football, golf, horseshoes, soccer, tennis.

**ADMISSIONS. Academic basis for candidate selection** (in order of priority): Secondary school record, standardized test scores, school's recommendation, class rank, essay.
**Nonacademic basis for candidate selection:** Particular talent or ability is considered.
**Requirements:** Graduation from secondary school is required; GED is accepted. 13 units and the following program of study are recommended: 4 units of English, 3 units of math, 2 units of science, 1 unit of foreign language, 2 units of social studies, 1 unit of history. Minimum composite ACT score of 21 (combined SAT score of 860) or minimum 2.5 GPA required. R.N. required of nursing program applicants. Project Forward program for applicants not normally admissible. ACT is required; SAT may be substituted. Campus visit and interview recommended. Off-campus interviews available with admissions and alumni representatives.
**Procedure:** Take SAT or ACT by August 1 of 12th year. Suggest filing application by August 1. Application deadline is August 15. Notification of admission on rolling basis. No set date by which applicants must accept offer. $75 nonrefundable room deposit. Freshmen accepted for terms other than fall.
**Special programs:** Credit and/or placement may be granted through CEEB Advanced Placement exams for scores of 3 or higher. Credit may be granted through CLEP general and subject exams, DANTES exams, and military experience. Placement may be granted

through challenge exams. Credit and placement may be granted through ACT PEP exams. Early entrance/early admission program. Concurrent enrollment program.
**Transfer students:** Transfer students accepted for terms other than fall. In fall 1993, 621 transfer applications were received, 602 were accepted. Application deadline is rolling for fall; rolling for spring. Minimum 2.0 GPA recommended. Lowest course grade accepted is "D." At least 32 semester hours must be completed at the university to receive degree.
**Admissions contact:** Larry N. Fuqua, M.A., Director of Admissions. 505 562-2178, 800 367-3668.

**FINANCIAL AID. Available aid:** Pell grants, SEOG, state scholarships and grants, school scholarships, private scholarships, ROTC scholarships, academic merit scholarships, and athletic scholarships. Perkins Loans (NDSL), PLUS, Stafford Loans (GSL), school loans, and SLS. AMS and deferred payment plan.
**Financial aid statistics:** 15% of aid is not need-based. In 1993-94, 92% of all undergraduate applicants received aid; 90% of freshman applicants. Average amounts of aid awarded freshmen: Scholarships and grants, $1,312; loans, $1,200.
**Supporting data/closing dates:** FAFSA/FAF/FFS: Priority filing date is March 1. Notification of awards on rolling basis.
**Financial aid contact:** Carol Holden, M.A., Director of Financial Aid. 505 562-2194.

**STUDENT EMPLOYMENT.** College Work/Study Program. Institutional employment. 58% of full-time undergraduates work on campus during school year. Students may expect to earn an average of $987 during school year. Off-campus part-time employment opportunities rated "fair."

**COMPUTER FACILITIES.** 75 IBM/IBM-compatible and Macintosh/Apple microcomputers. Students may access Digital minicomputer/mainframe systems. Residence halls may be equipped with stand-alone microcomputers. Computer languages and software packages include BASIC, COBOL, dBASE, Lotus 1-2-3, Paradox, Pascal, WordPerfect. Computer facilities are available to all students.
**Fees:** Computer fee is included in tuition/fees.
**Hours:** 7 AM-8 PM.

# New Mexico Highlands University

**Las Vegas, NM 87701** **505 425-7511**

**1994-95 Costs.** Tuition: $1,464 (state residents), $5,663 (out-of-state). Room: $1,000. Board: $1,300. Fees, books, misc. academic expenses (school's estimate): $280.
**Enrollment.** Undergraduates: 742 men, 850 women (full-time). Freshman class: 782 applicants, 645 accepted, 461 enrolled. Graduate enrollment: 296 men, 458 women.
**Test score averages/ranges.** Average ACT scores: 17 English, 17 math, 18 composite.
**Faculty.** 65% of faculty holds doctoral degree. Student/faculty ratio: 23 to 1.
**Selectivity rating.** Less competitive.

**PROFILE.** New Mexico Highlands is a public university. Founded in 1898, it gained university status in 1941. Programs are offered through the Schools of Liberal and Fine Arts, Science and Technology, and Professional Studies. Its 150-acre campus is located in the center of Las Vegas, 70 miles east of Santa Fe.

**Accreditation:** NCACS. Professionally accredited by the Council on Social Work Education.
**Religious orientation:** New Mexico Highlands University is nonsectarian; no religious requirements.
**Library:** Collections totaling over 450,000 volumes, 2,394 periodical subscriptions, and 107,000 microform items.
**Athletic facilities:** Baseball, football, soccer, and softball fields, badminton, basketball, racquetball, tennis, and volleyball courts, tracks, swimming pool, golf course, gymnasium, aerobics and weight rooms.

**STUDENT BODY. Undergraduate profile:** 92% are state residents. 2% Black, 68% Hispanic, 4% Native American, 25% White, 1% Other. Average age of undergraduates is 22.
**Freshman profile:** 6% of accepted applicants took SAT; 94% took ACT. 94% of freshmen come from public schools.
**Undergraduate achievement:** 55% of fall 1992 freshmen returned for fall 1993 term. 23% of entering class graduated.
**Foreign students:** 15 students are from out of the country. Countries represented include Argentina, China, and India; eight in all.

**PROGRAMS OF STUDY. Degrees:** B.A., B.Bus.Admin., B.F.A., B.S., B.S.Elec.Eng., B.S.Eng., B.Soc.Work.
**Majors:** Art, Biology, Business Administration, Chemistry, Computer Science, Electrical Engineering, Electronic Engineering, Elementary Education, Engineering Technology, English, Environmental Science, Fine Arts, Graphic Design, History, Human Performance, Leisure Services, Mass Communications, Mathematics, Music, Music Education, Political Science, Psychology, Social Work, Sociology/Anthropology, Spanish, Special Education, Technology Education.
**Distribution of degrees:** The majors with the highest enrollment are business administration, education, and social work.
**Requirements:** General education requirement.
**Academic regulations:** Freshmen must maintain minimum 1.75 GPA; sophomores, juniors, seniors, 2.0 GPA.
**Special:** Minors offered in some majors and in bilingual education, coaching, cognitive science, combined science, early childhood education, French, German, secondary education, and speech. Associate's degrees offered. Double majors. Independent study. Internships. Cooperative education programs. Graduate school at which undergraduates may take graduate-level courses. Preprofessional programs in law, medicine, veterinary science, pharmacy, dentistry, optometry, and physical therapy. Teacher certification in early childhood, elementary, secondary, special education, vo-tech, and bilingual/bicultural education. Certification in specific subject areas.
**Honors:** Honors program.
**Academic Assistance:** Remedial reading, writing, math, and study skills. Nonremedial tutoring.

**STUDENT LIFE. Housing:** Coed, women's, and men's dorms. School-owned/operated apartments. On-campus married-student housing. 45% of students live in college housing.
**Services and counseling/handicapped student services:** Placement services. Health service. Women's center. Day care. Counseling services for minority, military, veteran, and older students. Birth control, personal, and psychological counseling. Career and academic guidance services. Religious counseling. Physically disabled student services. Learning disabled services. Notetaking services. Tape recorders. Tutors. Reader services for the blind.
**Campus organizations:** Undergraduate student government. Student newspaper (La Mecha, published once/week). Radio and TV stations. Challengers, Circle K, Esquire Club, Servisios Especiales, Veterans of America, professional and special-interest groups.
**Religious organizations:** Baptist Student Union, Fellowship of Christian Athletes.
**Minority/foreign student organizations:** Black Student Union, Native American Club. Chinese Student Association.

**ATHLETICS. Physical education requirements:** Two semesters of physical education required.
**Intercollegiate competition:** 13% of students participate. Baseball (M), basketball (M,W), cross-country (M,W), football (M), softball (W), volleyball (W). Member of NCAA Division II, Rocky Mountain Athletic Conference.
**Intramural and club sports:** 23% of students participate. Intramural badminton, basketball, bowling, flag football, floor hockey, frisbee golf, golf, racquetball, softball, swimming, tennis, volleyball, walleyball.

**ADMISSIONS. Academic basis for candidate selection** (in order of priority): Secondary school record, standardized test scores, class rank, school's recommendation.
**Nonacademic basis for candidate selection:** Character and personality, extracurricular participation, particular talent or ability, and geographical distribution are important. Alumni/ae relationship is considered.
**Requirements:** Graduation from secondary school is required; GED is accepted. No specific distribution of secondary school units required. Minimum 2.0 GPA required. Conditional admission possible for applicants not meeting standard requirements. ACT is required; SAT may be substituted. Campus visit recommended. Off-campus interviews available with an admissions representative.
**Procedure:** Take SAT or ACT by June 1 of 12th year. Suggest filing application by January 1; no deadline. Notification of admission on rolling basis. Reply is required by registration. $50 refundable tuition deposit. $75 nonrefundable room deposit. Freshmen accepted for terms other than fall.
**Special programs:** Admission may be deferred one year. Credit and/or placement may be granted through CEEB Advanced Placement exams for scores of 4 or higher. Credit and/or placement may be granted through CLEP general and subject exams. Credit and placement may be granted through ACT PEP, DANTES, and challenge exams and military experience. Early decision program. Deadline for applying for early decision is August 1. Early entrance/early admission program. Concurrent enrollment program.
**Transfer students:** Transfer students accepted for terms other than fall. In fall 1993, 253 transfer applications were received, 221 were accepted. Application deadline is August 1 for fall; December 1 for spring. Minimum 2.0 GPA required. Lowest course grade accepted is "C." Maximum number of transferable credits is 88 semester hours from a two-year school and 96 semester hours from a four-year school. At least 32 semester hours must be completed at the university to receive degree.
**Admissions contact:** John Coca, Director of Admissions. 505 454-3439.

**FINANCIAL AID. Available aid:** Pell grants, SEOG, state scholarships and grants, school scholarships, private scholarships and grants, academic merit scholarships, athletic scholarships, and aid for undergraduate foreign students. Perkins Loans (NDSL), PLUS, Stafford Loans (GSL), state loans, and SLS. Deferred payment plan.
**Financial aid statistics:** In 1993-94, 71% of all undergraduate applicants received aid; 70% of freshman applicants. Average amounts of aid awarded freshmen: Scholarships and grants, $3,000; loans, $1,500.
**Supporting data/closing dates:** FAFSA/FAF/FFS: Priority filing date is March 1; accepted on rolling basis. Notification of awards on rolling basis.
**Financial aid contact:** Darlene Ortiz, M.B.A., Director of Financial Aid. 505 454-3317.

**STUDENT EMPLOYMENT.** College Work/Study Program. Institutional employment. 45% of full-time undergraduates work on campus during school year. Students may expect to earn an average of $1,460 during school year. Off-campus part-time employment opportunities rated "fair."

**COMPUTER FACILITIES.** 300 IBM/IBM-compatible and Macintosh/Apple microcomputers. Students may access Digital minicomputer/mainframe systems, Internet. Residence halls may be equipped with stand-alone microcomputers, modems. Client/LAN operating systems include Apple/Macintosh, DOS, UNIX/XENIX/AIX, Windows NT, X-windows, DEC, LocalTalk/AppleTalk, Microsoft. Computer languages and software packages include Aldridge, APL, BASIC, C, COBOL, FORTRAN, IsML, PL/1, Prolog, SAS. Computer facilities are available to all students.
**Fees:** None.
**Hours:** 8 AM-10 PM.

# New Mexico Institute of Mining and Technology

**Socorro, NM 87801** **505 835-5011**

**1994-95 Costs.** Tuition: $1,302 (state residents), $5,376 (out-of-state). Room: $1,346. Board: $2,080. Fees, books, misc. academic expenses (school's estimate): $1,156.
**Enrollment.** Undergraduates: 690 men, 327 women (full-time). Freshman class: 787 applicants, 601 accepted, 233 enrolled. Graduate enrollment: 222 men, 69 women.
**Test score averages/ranges.** Average SAT scores: 506 verbal, 594 math. Average ACT scores: 26 composite. Range of ACT scores of middle 50%: 23-26 English, 24-27 math.
**Faculty.** 99 full-time; 4 part-time. 96% of faculty holds doctoral degree. Student/faculty ratio: 14 to 1.
**Selectivity rating.** Highly competitive.

**PROFILE.** New Mexico Tech, founded in 1889, is a public, technical institution. Programs are offered int the Bureau of Mines and Mineral Resources, the Division of Research and Development, and the New Mexico Petroleum Recovery Research Center. Its 320-acre campus is located in Socorro, 75 miles south of Albuquerque.

**Accreditation:** NCACS. Professionally accredited by the Accreditation Board for Engineering and Technology.
**Religious orientation:** New Mexico Institute of Mining and Technology is nonsectarian; no religious requirements.
**Library:** Collections totaling over 155,000 volumes, 1,030 periodical subscriptions, and 36,000 microform items.
**Special facilities/museums:** Mineral museum, electron microscopes, observatory, radio telescope.
**Athletic facilities:** Athletic fields, gymnasiums, racquetball, squash, and tennis courts, weight room, swimming center, golf course.

**STUDENT BODY. Undergraduate profile:** 60% are state residents. 3% Asian-American, 1% Black, 17% Hispanic, 3% Native American, 69% White, 7% Other. Average age of undergraduates is 24.
**Freshman profile:** 3% of freshmen who took SAT scored 700 or over on verbal, 19% scored 700 or over on math; 22% scored 600 or over on verbal, 54% scored 600 or over on math; 55% scored 500 or over on verbal, 81% scored 500 or over on math; 83% scored 400 or over on verbal, 94% scored 400 or over on math; 96% scored 300 or over on verbal, 98% scored 300 or over on math. Majority of accepted applicants took ACT. 70% of freshmen come from public schools.
**Undergraduate achievement:** 69% of fall 1992 freshmen returned for fall 1993 term.
**Foreign students:** 174 students are from out of the country. Countries represented include Canada, China, India, Malaysia, and Taiwan; 43 in all.

**PROGRAMS OF STUDY. Degrees:** B.Eng., B.Gen.Studies, B.S., B.S.Bus.Admin.
**Majors:** Basic Sciences, Biology, Business Administration, Chemical Processing, Chemistry, Computer Science, Electrical Engineering, Engineering Mechanics, Environmental Engineering, Environmental Sciences, General Studies, Geological Engineering, Geology, Geophysics, Materials Engineering, Mathematics, Medical Technology, Metallurgical Engineering, Mineral Engineering, Petroleum Engineering, Physics, Psychology, Technical Communication.
**Distribution of degrees:** The majors with the highest enrollment are environmental engineering, physics, and biology.
**Requirements:** General education requirement.
**Academic regulations:** Freshmen must maintain minimum 1.6 GPA; sophomores, 1.8 GPA; juniors, 2.0 GPA; seniors, 2.0 GPA.
**Special:** Courses offered in economics, education, English, fine arts, languages, music, philosophy, physical recreation, and political science. Numerous research facilities and opportunities for undergraduates in atmospheric research, mines/minerals research, petroleum recovery/research, explosives technology, cometary studies, seismic research, and groundwater tracer studies. Associate's degrees offered. Self-designed majors. Double majors. Dual degrees. Independent study. Accelerated study. Pass/fail grading option. Internships. Cooperative education programs. Graduate school at which undergraduates may take graduate-level courses. Preprofessional programs in medicine, veterinary science, and dentistry. 3-2 engineering/hydrology program. 3-2 geoscience program. Member of Western Interstate Commission for Higher Education (WICHE) and Waste Energy Research Consortium. Exchange programs through Western Undergraduate Exchange program and with St. John's Coll (New Mexico). Teacher certification in secondary education. Certification in specific subject areas. Exchange program abroad in Italy.
**Honors:** Honor societies.
**Academic Assistance:** Remedial reading, writing, math, and study skills. Nonremedial tutoring.

**ADMISSIONS. Academic basis for candidate selection** (in order of priority): Secondary school record, standardized test scores, class rank, school's recommendation.
**Nonacademic basis for candidate selection:** Extracurricular participation, particular talent or ability, geographical distribution, and alumni/ae relationship are considered.
**Requirements:** Graduation from secondary school is required; GED is accepted. 15 units and the following program of study are required: 4 units of English, 3 units of math, 2 units of science including 1 unit of lab, 3 units of social studies, 2 units of academic electives. Minimum composite ACT score of 21 and minimum 2.0 GPA required. Conditional admission possible for applicants not meeting standard requirements. ACT is required; SAT may be substituted. Campus visit recommended. No off-campus interviews.
**Procedure:** Take SAT or ACT by February 28 of 12th year. Visit college for interview by April of 12th year. Suggest filing application by March 1. Application deadline is August 15. Notification of admission on rolling basis. Reply is required by August 15. $50 tuition deposit, refundable until May 1. $100 room deposit, refundable on pro rata basis. Freshmen accepted for terms other than fall.
**Special programs:** Admission may be deferred one year. Credit and/or placement may be granted through CEEB Advanced Placement exams for scores of 3 or higher. Credit and placement may be granted through challenge exams. Early entrance/early admission program. Concurrent enrollment program.
**Transfer students:** Transfer students accepted for terms other than fall. In fall 1993, 190 transfer applications were received, 153 were accepted. Application deadline is August 1 for fall; December 15 for spring. Minimum 2.0 GPA required. Lowest course grade accepted is "C." At least 30 semester hours must be completed at the institute to receive degree.
**Admissions contact:** Louise E. Chamberlin, M.S.T., Director of Admissions. 505 835-5424, 800 428-TECH.

**FINANCIAL AID. Available aid:** Pell grants, SEOG, state scholarships and grants, school scholarships, private scholarships, and academic merit scholarships. Perkins Loans (NDSL), PLUS, Stafford Loans (GSL), school loans, and SLS. Deferred payment plan. Payment by credit card.
**Financial aid statistics:** 40% of aid is not need-based. In 1993-94, 96% of all undergraduate applicants received aid; 93% of freshman applicants. Average amounts of aid awarded freshmen: Scholarships and grants, $1,975; loans, $1,910.
**Supporting data/closing dates:** FAFSA: Priority filing date is March 1. School's own aid application: Priority filing date is March 1. Notification of awards on rolling basis.
**Financial aid contact:** Ann Hansen, Director of Financial Aid. 505 835-5333.

# New Mexico State University

**Las Cruces, NM 88003** **505 646-0111**

**1994-95 Costs.** Tuition: $1,980 (state residents), $6,432 (out-of-state). Room: $1,588. Board: $1,560. Fees, books, misc. academic expenses (school's estimate): $500.
**Enrollment.** Undergraduates: 4,926 men, 4,557 women (full-time). Freshman class: 3,763 applicants, 2,990 accepted, 1,092 enrolled. Graduate enrollment: 1,398 men, 1,145 women.
**Test score averages/ranges.** Average ACT scores: 21 composite.
**Faculty.** 650 full-time; 144 part-time. 79% of faculty holds doctoral degree. Student/faculty ratio: 19 to 1.
**Selectivity rating.** Noncompetitive.

**PROFILE.** New Mexico State, founded in 1888, is a public, multipurpose university. Programs are offered through the Colleges of Agriculture and Home Economics, Arts and Sciences, Business Administration and Economics, Education, Engineering, and Human and Community Services. Its 5,800-acre campus is located in Las Cruces, 42 miles north of El Paso, Texas.

**Accreditation:** NCACS. Professionally accredited by the Accreditation Board for Engineering and Technology, the American Assembly of Collegiate Schools of Business, the American Home Economics Association, the American Speech-Language-Hearing Association, the Council on Social Work Education, the National Association of Schools of Music, the National Council for Accreditation of Teacher Education, the National League for Nursing.
**Religious orientation:** New Mexico State University is nonsectarian; no religious requirements.
**Library:** Collections totaling over 850,000 volumes, 6,600 periodical subscriptions, and 400,000 microform items.
**Special facilities/museums:** University and art department museums, theatre, horse farm, sports medicine training clinic, observatory, electron microscope.
**Athletic facilities:** Basketball, racquetball, and tennis courts, swimming pool, weight room, track, athletic fields.

**STUDENT BODY. Undergraduate profile:** 91% are state residents; 35% are transfers. 1% Asian-American, 2% Black, 29% Hispanic, 3% Native American, 65% White. Average age of undergraduates is 25.
**Freshman profile:** Majority of accepted applicants took ACT.
**Undergraduate achievement:** 73% of fall 1991 freshmen returned for fall 1992 term.
**Foreign students:** 164 students are from out of the country. Countries represented include China, India, Malaysia, Mexico, and Taiwan; 80 in all.

**PROGRAMS OF STUDY. Degrees:** B.A., B.Acct., B.Bus.Admin., B.F.A., B.Mus., B.Mus.Ed., B.S., B.S.Ed., B.S.M.T., B.S.Nurs., B.Soc.Work.
**Majors:** Accounting, Agricultural Biology, Agricultural Business Management, Agricultural Engineering, Agricultural/Extension Education, Agriculture, Animal Science, Anthropology, Art, Art Education, Athletic Training, Biochemistry, Biology, Biology Education, Business Computer Systems, Business Education, Chemical Engineering, Chemistry, Chemistry Education, City/Regional Planning, Civil Engineering, Communication Disorders, Communication Studies, Community Health, Computer Engineering, Computer Science, Criminal Justice, Crop Science, Drama, Earth Science Education, Economics, Electrical Engineering, Elementary Education, Engineering Technology, English, English Education, Environmental/Resource Economics, Family/Consumer Studies, Farm/Ranch Management, Finance, Fine Arts, Fishery Science, Foods/Nutrition Services, Foreign Language Education, Foreign Languages, General Agronomy, General Business, General Science Education, Geography, Geological Engineering, Geology, Government, Health Science, Health Science Education, History, History Education, Home Economics, Home Economics Business, Home Economics Education, Horticulture, Industrial Engineering, International Business, Journalism/Mass Communications, Journalism/Mass Communications Education, Management, Marketing, Mathematics, Mathematics Education, Mechanical Engineering, Medical Technology, Microbiology, Music, Music Education, Nursing, Pest Management, Philosophy, Physical Education, Physics, Physics Education, Professional Golf Management, Psychology, Range Science, Real Estate, Recreation Areas Management, Secondary Education, Social Studies Education, Social Work, Sociology, Soil Science, Speech Communication Education, Surveying, Technical Education, Theatre Arts Education, Wildlife Science.

**Distribution of degrees:** The majors with the highest enrollment are elementary education, accounting, and electrical engineering.
**Requirements:** General education requirement.
**Academic regulations:** Minimum 2.0 GPA must be maintained.
**Special:** Minors offered in most majors. Associate's degrees offered. Self-designed majors. Double majors. Independent study. Pass/fail grading option. Internships. Cooperative education programs. Graduate school at which undergraduates may take graduate-level courses. Preprofessional programs in law, medicine, veterinary science, pharmacy, dentistry, chiropractic, forestry, physical therapy, and public health. Member of WICHE consortium. Member of National Student Exchange (NSE). Teacher certification in elementary, secondary, special education, and bilingual/bicultural education. Certification in specific subject areas. Study abroad possible. ROTC and AFROTC.
**Honors:** Honors program.
**Academic Assistance:** Remedial reading, writing, math, and study skills. Nonremedial tutoring.

**STUDENT LIFE. Housing:** Students may live on or off campus. Coed and women's dorms. Sorority and fraternity housing. School-owned/operated apartments. On-campus married-student housing. Handicapped-student housing. Honors housing. 22% of students live in college housing.
**Social atmosphere:** Popular gathering spots for students are the Village Inn, the Corbett Center, and the Activity Center. Influential organizations on campus include Associated Students of NMSU, Greeks, and Campus Crusade for Christ. The Cruces Rally and Scavenger Hunt, Greek Week, Homecoming, basketball games, and the Whole Enchilada Fiesta are among the year's favorite events.
**Services and counseling/handicapped student services:** Placement services. Health service. Women's center. Diagnostic testing service. Counseling services for minority, military, veteran, and older students. Personal and psychological counseling. Career and academic guidance services. Physically disabled student services. Learning disabled program/services. Notetaking services. Tape recorders. Tutors. Reader services for the blind.
**Campus organizations:** Undergraduate student government. Student newspaper (Round Up, published three times/week). Literary magazine. Yearbook. Radio and TV stations. Choirs, chamber music group, orchestra, symphonic wind and percussion ensembles, marching and concert bands, Playmakers, tutoring groups, athletic and political groups, departmental and special-interest groups, 218 organizations in all. 10 fraternities, all with chapter houses; six sororities, five chapter houses. 6% of men join a fraternity. 5% of women join a sorority.
**Religious organizations:** Aggies for Christ, Baptist Student Union, BASHA Gospel Ensemble of NMSU, Campus Crusade for Christ, Christian Science Organization, Intervarsity Christian Fellowship, Muslim Student Association.
**Minority/foreign student organizations:** Black Allied Student Association, Los Chicanos de NMSU, Organization of African Students, United Native American Organization. Chinese, Iraqi, and Mexican student groups.

**ATHLETICS. Physical education requirements:** None.
**Intercollegiate competition:** 3% of students participate. Baseball (M), basketball (M,W), cheerleading (M,W), cross-country (M,W), diving (M,W), football (M), golf (M,W), rodeo (M,W), swimming (M,W), tennis (M,W), track (outdoor) (M,W), track and field (outdoor) (M,W), volleyball (W). Member of Big West Conference for men, Big West Conference for women, NCAA Division I.
**Intramural and club sports:** 8% of students participate. Men's club rugby, soccer.

**ADMISSIONS. Academic basis for candidate selection** (in order of priority): Secondary school record, standardized test scores, class rank.
**Requirements:** Graduation from secondary school is required; GED is accepted. 12 units and the following program of study are required: 4 units of English, 3 units of math, 2 units of lab science, 1 unit of foreign language. Minimum composite ACT score of 19 (combined SAT score of 740) and minimum 2.25 GPA required. ACT is required; SAT may be substituted. Campus visit recommended. No off-campus interviews.
**Procedure:** Notification of admission on rolling basis. Tuition deposit equal to 20% of tuition, refundable until February 21. $100 room deposit, refundable until July 1. Freshmen accepted for terms other than fall.
**Special programs:** Admission may be deferred one year. Credit may be granted through CEEB Advanced Placement for scores of 3 or higher. Credit may be granted through CLEP general and subject exams, DANTES exams, and military experience. Early entrance/early admission program. Concurrent enrollment program.
**Transfer students:** Transfer students accepted for terms other than fall. In fall 1992, 35% of all new students were transfers into all classes. 1,259 transfer applications were received, 1,200 were accepted. Application deadline is six weeks prior to date of registration for fall; January 1 for spring. Minimum 2.0 GPA recommended. Lowest course grade accepted is "C." At least 30 semester hours must be completed at the university to receive degree.
**Admissions contact:** Bill J. Bruner, M.S., Director of Admissions and Records. 505 646-3121.

**FINANCIAL AID. Available aid:** Pell grants, SEOG, state scholarships and grants, school scholarships, private scholarships, ROTC scholarships, academic merit scholarships, and athletic scholarships. Perkins Loans (NDSL), PLUS, Stafford Loans (GSL), Health Professions Loans, school loans, and SLS.
**Financial aid statistics:** 16% of aid is not need-based. In 1992-93, 65% of all undergraduate applicants received aid; 60% of freshman applicants. Average amounts of aid awarded freshmen: Scholarships and grants, $1,756.
**Supporting data/closing dates:** FAFSA: Priority filing date is March 1. School's own aid application: Priority filing date is March 1. Income tax forms: Priority filing date is March 1. Notification of awards on rolling basis.
**Financial aid contact:** Greeley W. Myers, M.Ed., Director of Financial Aid. 505 646-4105.

**STUDENT EMPLOYMENT.** College Work/Study Program. Institutional employment. 27% of full-time undergraduates work on campus during school year. Students may expect to earn an average of $2,144 during school year. Off-campus part-time employment opportunities rated "good."

**COMPUTER FACILITIES.** 3,683 IBM/IBM-compatible and Macintosh/Apple microcomputers; 600 are networked. Students may access Digital minicomputer/mainframe systems. Residence halls may be equipped with stand-alone microcomputers, networked microcomputers. Computer languages and software packages include BASIC, COBOL, FORTRAN, Lotus 1-2-3, Microsoft, Pascal, SAS, Script, WordPerfect, WordStar. Computer facilities are available to all students.
**Fees:** None.

# St. John's College

**Santa Fe, NM 87501** **505 984-6060**

**1994-95 Costs.** Tuition: $17,430. Room & board: $5,720. Fees, books, misc. academic expenses (school's estimate): $700.
**Enrollment.** Undergraduates: 231 men, 180 women (full-time). Freshman class: 285 applicants, 243 accepted, 126 enrolled. Graduate enrollment: 40 men, 44 women.
**Test score averages/ranges.** Range of SAT scores of middle 50%: 550-650 verbal, 520-650 math. Average ACT scores: 29 English, 26 math, 27 composite.
**Faculty.** 45 full-time; 9 part-time. 60% of faculty holds doctoral degree. Student/faculty ratio: 8 to 1.
**Selectivity rating.** More competitive.

**PROFILE.** St. John's is a private, liberal arts college. Founded in Annapolis, Maryland, in 1696, the Santa Fe campus opened in 1964. At the core of St. John's curriculum is a list of "great books." Its 300-acre campus is located in Sante Fe, 60 miles from Albuquerque.

**Accreditation:** NCACS.
**Religious orientation:** St. John's College is nonsectarian; no religious requirements.
**Library:** Collections totaling over 60,000 volumes and 160 periodical subscriptions.
**Special facilities/museums:** Art gallery.
**Athletic facilities:** Tennis courts, soccer field, track, dance room, weight room; off-campus gymnasium and swimming pool.

**STUDENT BODY. Undergraduate profile:** 9% are state residents; 20% are transfers. 3% Asian-American, 1% Black, 6% Hispanic, 1% Native American, 89% White. Average age of undergraduates is 20.
**Freshman profile:** 6% of freshmen who took SAT scored 700 or over on verbal, 8% scored 700 or over on math; 52% scored 600 or over on verbal, 46% scored 600 or over on math; 94% scored 500 or over on verbal, 89% scored 500 or over on math; 100% scored 400 or over on verbal, 100% scored 400 or over on math. 61% of accepted applicants took SAT; 20% took ACT. 68% of freshmen come from public schools.
**Undergraduate achievement:** 85% of fall 1992 freshmen returned for fall 1993 term. 53% of entering class graduated. 20% of students who completed a degree program immediately went on to graduate study.
**Foreign students:** Eight students are from out of the country. Countries represented include Canada, France, Germany, and Mexico; five in all.

**PROGRAMS OF STUDY. Degrees:** B.A.Lib.Arts
**Requirements:** General education requirement.
**Special:** All students take the same required program based on a four-year study of great books, focusing on literature, mathematics, philosophy, theology, sciences, political theory, music, history, and economics. Students and faculty work together in small discussion classes without lecture courses, written finals, or emphasis on grades. Preprofessional programs in law. One year may be spent at college's Maryland campus.
**Academic Assistance:** Remedial writing and math. Nonremedial tutoring.

**STUDENT LIFE. Housing:** All freshmen, sophomores, and juniors must live on campus. Coed, women's, and men's dorms. 80% of students live in college housing.
**Services and counseling/handicapped student services:** Placement services. Health service. Individual tutoring. Birth control, personal, and psychological counseling. Career and academic guidance services.
**Campus organizations:** Undergraduate student government. Student newspaper (Moon, published once/week). Literary magazine. Chorus, chamber groups, film club, drawing, painting and poetry groups, karate club, yoga and dance groups.

**ATHLETICS. Physical education requirements:** None.
**Intercollegiate competition:** 7% of students participate.
**Intramural and club sports:** 2% of students participate. Intramural Alpine skiing, fencing, martial arts, Nordic skiing, soccer, softball, volleyball, yoga. Men's club Alpine skiing, baseball, basketball, fencing, martial arts, soccer, softball, swimming, tennis, volleyball, weight lifting.

**ADMISSIONS. Academic basis for candidate selection** (in order of priority): Essay, secondary school record, school's recommendation, class rank, standardized test scores.
**Nonacademic basis for candidate selection:** Character and personality are emphasized. Particular talent or ability is important. Extracurricular participation and alumni/ae relationship are considered.
**Requirements:** Graduation from secondary school is recommended; GED is accepted. No specific distribution of secondary school units required. College-preparatory courses required. No minimum GPA or standardized test scores required. SAT or ACT is recommended. Campus visit and interview recommended. Off-campus interviews available with admissions and alumni representatives.
**Procedure:** Take SAT or ACT by fall of 12th year. Visit college for interview by April of 12th year. Suggest filing application by March 1. Notification of admission on rolling basis. Reply is required by May 1. $250 nonrefundable tuition deposit. $150 nonrefundable room deposit. Freshmen accepted for terms other than fall.
**Special programs:** Admission may be deferred one year. Early entrance/early admission program.
**Transfer students:** Transfer students accepted for terms other than fall. In fall 1993, 20% of all new students were transfers into all classes. 35 transfer applications were received, 30 were accepted. Application deadline is March 1 for fall; December 15 for spring. At least 132 semester hours must be completed at the college to receive degree.

**Admissions contact:** Larry Clendenin, M.A., Director of Admissions. 800 332-5232.

**FINANCIAL AID. Available aid:** Pell grants, SEOG, state scholarships and grants, school grants, private scholarships, and aid for undergraduate foreign students. Perkins Loans (NDSL), PLUS, Stafford Loans (GSL), and SLS. Tuition Plan Inc., AMS, and guaranteed tuition.

**Financial aid statistics:** In 1993-94, 95% of all undergraduate applicants received aid; 95% of freshman applicants. Average amounts of aid awarded freshmen: Scholarships and grants, $9,598; loans, $2,400.

**Supporting data/closing dates:** FAFSA/FAF/FFS: Priority filing date is February 15. School's own aid application: Priority filing date is February 15. State aid form: Priority filing date is February 15. Income tax forms: Priority filing date is February 15. Notification of awards on rolling basis.

**Financial aid contact:** Michael Rodriguez, Director of Financial Aid. 505 984-6058.

**STUDENT EMPLOYMENT.** College Work/Study Program. Institutional employment. 35% of full-time undergraduates work on campus during school year. Students may expect to earn an average of $1,700 during school year. Off-campus part-time employment opportunities rated "excellent."

**COMPUTER FACILITIES.** 11 IBM/IBM-compatible, Macintosh/Apple, and RISC-/UNIX-based microcomputers; five are networked. Residence halls may be equipped with modems. Client/LAN operating systems include Apple/Macintosh, DOS, Microsoft. Computer languages and software packages include BASIC, MacWrite, WordPerfect, Excel, math programs, physics programs; 12 in all. Computer facilities are available to all students.

**Fees:** None.

**Hours:** 8 AM-midn.

**GRADUATE CAREER DATA.** Graduate school percentages: 7% enter law school. 6% enter medical school. 3% enter graduate business programs. 42% enter graduate arts and sciences programs. 1% enter theological school/seminary. Highest graduate school enrollments: U of Chicago, Harvard U, Johns Hopkins U, U of New Mexico, U of Pennsylvania, U of Texas, U of Washington. 20% of graduates choose careers in business and industry. Companies and businesses that hire graduates: Los Alamos National Lab, New Mexico elementary and secondary schools, Naval Research Lab.

**PROMINENT ALUMNI/AE.** Ray Cave, managing editor, Time-Life; Robert A. Goldwin, scholar, American Enterprise Institute, and former White House adviser on education; Ahmet Ertegun, CEO and founder, Atlantic Records; Mark Krinock, neurosurgeon, Baylor Medical School; Seth Cropsey, Deputy Assistant to the Secretary of Defense.

# University of New Mexico

**Albuquerque, NM 87131** **505 277-0111**

**1994-95 Costs.** Tuition: $1,884 (state residents), $7,115 (out-of-state). Room & board: $3,021-$3,279. Fees, books, misc. academic expenses (school's estimate): $584.

**Enrollment.** Undergraduates: 5,847 men, 6,570 women (full-time). Freshman class: 3,653 applicants, 3,066 accepted, 1,722 enrolled. Graduate enrollment: 2,494 men, 2,704 women.

**Test score averages/ranges.** Average ACT scores: 22 composite. Range of ACT scores of middle 50%: 19-24 composite.

**Faculty.** 1,315 full-time; 465 part-time. 88% of faculty holds highest degree in specific field. Student/faculty ratio: 15 to 1.

**Selectivity rating.** Less competitive.

**PROFILE.** The University of New Mexico, founded in 1889, is a public, comprehensive institution. Programs are offered through the Colleges of Architecture, Arts and Sciences, Dental Programs, Education, Engineering, Fine Arts, Nursing, Pharmacy, and University Studies and the Schools of Management and Medicine. Its 625-acre campus is located in Albuquerque.

**Accreditation:** NCACS. Professionally accredited by the American Assembly of Collegiate Schools of Business, the American Bar Association, the American Council on Pharmaceutical Education, the American Medical Association (CAHEA), the Association of American Law Schools, the National Architecture Accrediting Board, the National Association of Schools of Music, the National Council for Accreditation of Teacher Education, the National League for Nursing.

**Religious orientation:** University of New Mexico is nonsectarian; no religious requirements.

**Library:** Collections totaling over 1,815,957 volumes, 21,933 periodical subscriptions, and 5,111,453 microform items.

**Special facilities/museums:** Museums of art, anthropology, geology, and Southwestern biology, lithography institute, meteoritics institute, electron and electron scanning microscopes, nuclear reactor.

**Athletic facilities:** Gymnasiums, swimming pools, basketball, racquetball, and tennis courts, stadium, arena, gymnastics facility, track, baseball, practice, soccer, and softball fields, golf courses, ski slopes.

**STUDENT BODY. Undergraduate profile:** 90% are state residents; 50% are transfers. 2% Asian-American, 2% Black, 27% Hispanic, 4% Native American, 64% White, 1% Other. Average age of undergraduates is 25.

**Freshman profile:** Majority of accepted applicants took ACT.

**Undergraduate achievement:** 72% of fall 1991 freshmen returned for fall 1992 term.

**Foreign students:** 122 students are from out of the country. Countries represented include Canada, China, Germany, India, Israel, and the United Kingdom; 87 in all.

**PROGRAMS OF STUDY. Degrees:** B.A., B.A.Ed., B.Bus.Admin., B.Mus., B.Mus.Ed., B.S., B.Univ.Studies.

**Majors:** Accounting, American Studies, Anthropology, Architecture, Art, Art Education, Art Studio, Asian Studies, Astrophysics, Athletic Training, Bilingual Education, Biochemistry, Biology, Business Computer Systems, Business Education, Chemical Engineering, Chemistry, Child Development/Family Relations, Civil Engineering, Classical Studies, Classics, Communication, Communication Arts Education, Communicative Disorders, Comparative Literature, Computer Engineering, Computer Science, Construction Engineering, Construction Management, Creative Writing, Criminal Justice, Dance, Dental Hygiene, Earth Science Education, Economics, Economics/Philosophy, Electrical Engineering, Elementary Education, Elementary Physical Education, Emergency Medical Technology, English, English/Philosophy, Entrepreneurial Studies, Environmental Design, Exercise Technology, Family Studies, Family Studies Education, Financial Management, French, General Management, Geography, Geology, German, Health Education, History, Human Resources Management, Industrial Education, Interdisciplinary, International Management, Journalism, Languages, Latin American Studies, Life Science Education, Linguistics, Management Sciences, Marketing/Management, Mathematics, Mathematics Education, Mechanical Engineering, Medical Technology, Music, Music Education, Nuclear Engineering, Nuclear Medicine Technology, Nursing, Nutrition/Dietetics, Pharmacy, Philosophy, Philosophy/Pre-Law, Physical Education, Physical Science Education, Physical Therapy, Physics, Political Science, Portuguese, Production/Operations Management, Professional Writing, Psychology, Radiation Therapy Technology, Radiography, Recreation, Religious Studies, Respiratory Therapy, Russian Studies, Sign Language Interpretation, Social Studies Education, Sociology, Sonography, Spanish, Special Education, Teaching English as a Second Language, Technology and Training, Theatre Arts, Travel/Tourism, University Studies.

**Distribution of degrees:** The majors with the highest enrollment are university studies, psychology, and elementary education; American studies, art, and classics have the lowest.

**Academic regulations:** Freshmen must maintain minimum 1.7 GPA; sophomores, juniors, seniors, 2.0 GPA.

**Special:** Minors offered in over 80 fields. All freshmen enroll in University College and enter other colleges in sophomore year; at beginning of junior year, students declare major and minor, or two majors, or a special curriculum. Electives for degree credit may be chosen from various colleges. Certificate programs. Special summer programs in German and French. Associate's degrees offered. Double majors. Dual degrees. Internships. Cooperative education programs. Graduate school at which undergraduates may take graduate-level courses. Preprofessional programs in law, medicine, veterinary science, dentistry, and forestry. 3-2 civil engineering/M.B.A. program. 3-2 Latin American studies/M.B.A. program. Member of Western Interstate Commission for Higher Education (WICHE). Member of National Student Exchange (NSE). Teacher certification in early childhood, elementary, secondary, special education, and bilingual/bicultural education. Certification in specific subject areas. Member of International Student Exchange Program (ISEP). Study abroad in Canada, France, Germany, Japan, Mexico, Spain, and the United Kingdom. ROTC and AFROTC.

**Honors:** Phi Beta Kappa. Honors program. Honor societies.

**Academic Assistance:** Remedial study skills. Nonremedial tutoring.

**STUDENT LIFE. Housing:** Students may live on or off campus. Coed, women's, and men's dorms. Sorority and fraternity housing. School-owned/operated apartments. Off-campus married-student housing. 8% of students live in college housing.

**Social atmosphere:** The student newspaper characterizes the university as "a beautiful adobe campus with a siesta-like atmosphere in the summer. Very mixed culturally: Native Americans, Hispanics, whites, but few blacks. It is a bilingual campus." Influential groups on campus include the College Republicans, lesbian groups, and Hispanic groups. The most popular event of the year is the Welcome Back Daze, with week-long festivities, free food, and music. The Frontier Restaurant across from the university is a favorite gathering spot for students.

**Services and counseling/handicapped student services:** Placement services. Health service. Women's center. Day care. Counseling services for minority, military, and veteran students. Personal and psychological counseling. Career and academic guidance services. Religious counseling. Physically disabled student services. Learning disabled services. Notetaking services. Tape recorders. Tutors. Reader services for the blind.

**Campus organizations:** Undergraduate student government. Student newspaper (Lobo, published once/day). Radio and TV stations. Chorus, civic orchestra, opera workshop, wind ensemble, theatre, military and political groups, sports and recreation groups, professional groups, departmental and service groups, special-interest groups, 250 organizations in all. 12 fraternities, 10 chapter houses; five sororities, four chapter houses. 2% of men join a fraternity. 1% of women join a sorority.

**Religious organizations:** Aquinas Newman Center, Bahai Association, Baptist Student Union, Campus Crusade for Christ, Canterbury Campus Ministry, Christian Fellowship, Christian Science Organization, Great Commission Students, Hillel Jewish Student Union, Latter-Day Saints Student Association, Life Student Union, Lutheran Student Movement, Navigators, United Campus Ministry.

**Minority/foreign student organizations:** Association for People of African Descent, Black Student Union, MEChA, NAACP, Southwest Indian Student Coalition, United Mexican-American Students. International Center, Chinese, Indian, Korean, and Vietnamese groups.

**ATHLETICS. Physical education requirements:** None.

**Intercollegiate competition:** 4% of students participate. Alpine skiing (M,W), baseball (M), basketball (M,W), cheerleading (M,W), cross-country (M,W), diving (M,W), football (M), golf (M,W), gymnastics (M), Nordic skiing (M,W), soccer (M,W), softball (W), swimming (M,W), tennis (M,W), track (indoor) (M,W), track (outdoor) (M,W), track and field (indoor) (M,W), track and field (outdoor) (M,W), volleyball (W), wrestling (M). Member of NCAA Division I, NCAA Division I-A for football, Western Athletic Conference.

**Intramural and club sports:** 40% of students participate. Intramural basketball, flag football, golf, racquetball, soccer, softball, tennis, volleyball. Men's club bowling, cycling, rugby. Women's club bowling, cycling.

**ADMISSIONS. Academic basis for candidate selection** (in order of priority): Secondary school record, standardized test scores, class rank, essay, school's recommendation.

**Nonacademic basis for candidate selection:** Extracurricular participation and particular talent or ability are considered.

**Requirements:** Graduation from secondary school is required; GED is accepted. 14 units and the following program of study are required: 4 units of English, 3 units of math, 2 units of science including 1 unit of lab, 2 units of foreign language, 2 units of social studies, 1

unit of history. Minimum 2.0 GPA required. Portfolio required of art program applicants. Special admissions and College Enrichment Program for applicants not meeting standard requirements. ACT is required; SAT may be substituted. Campus visit recommended. No off-campus interviews.
**Procedure:** Take SAT or ACT by August of 12th year. Application deadline is one month prior to beginning of semester. Notification of admission on rolling basis. Reply is required by beginning of term. $50 room deposit, refundable until July 1. Freshmen accepted for terms other than fall.
**Special programs:** Admission may be deferred three semesters. Credit may be granted through CEEB Advanced Placement for scores of 3 or higher. Credit may be granted through CLEP general and subject exams, DANTES and challenge exams, and military experience. Early entrance/early admission program. Concurrent enrollment program.
**Transfer students:** Transfer students accepted for terms other than fall. In fall 1992, 50% of all new students were transfers into all classes. Application deadline is one month prior to beginning of semester for fall; one month prior to beginning of semester for spring. Minimum 2.0 GPA required. Lowest course grade accepted is "C." At least 30 semester hours must be completed at the university to receive degree.
**Admissions contact:** Cynthia Stuart, M.A.P.A., Director of Admissions. 505 277-2446.

**FINANCIAL AID. Available aid:** Pell grants, SEOG, Federal Nursing Student Scholarships, state scholarships and grants, school scholarships and grants, private scholarships, ROTC scholarships, academic merit scholarships, and athletic scholarships. Perkins Loans (NDSL), PLUS, Stafford Loans (GSL), NSL, Health Professions Loans, school loans, private loans, and SLS. Deferred payment plan.
**Financial aid statistics:** 24% of aid is not need-based. In 1992-93, 88% of all undergraduate applicants received aid; 92% of freshman applicants. Average amounts of aid awarded freshmen: Scholarships and grants, $2,381; loans, $1,524.
**Supporting data/closing dates:** FAFSA: Priority filing date is March 1. Notification of awards begins May 1.
**Financial aid contact:** John Whiteside, M.A., Director of Financial Aid. 505 277-2041.

**STUDENT EMPLOYMENT.** College Work/Study Program. Institutional employment. 27% of full-time undergraduates work on campus during school year. Students may expect to earn an average of $2,500 during school year. Off-campus part-time employment opportunities rated "excellent."

**COMPUTER FACILITIES.** 216 IBM/IBM-compatible and Macintosh/Apple microcomputers; all are networked. Students may access Digital, IBM minicomputer/mainframe systems, BITNET, Internet. Residence halls may be equipped with stand-alone microcomputers. Client/LAN operating systems include Novell. 123 major computer languages and software packages available. Computer facilities are available to all students.
**Fees:** Computer fee is included in tuition/fees.

**PROMINENT ALUMNI/AE.** Henry Trewhitt, managing editor, *U.S. News and World Report*; Harold Enarson, past president, Ohio State U; John Hernandez, deputy administrator, Environmental Protection Agency; Shirley Hufstedler, former U.S. secretary of education; Pete Domenici, U.S. senator and chairperson of Senate Budget Committee.

# Western New Mexico University

**Silver City, NM 88062** **505 538-6011**

**1993-94 Costs.** Tuition: $1,294 (state residents), $4,652 (out-of-state). Room: $920. Board: $1,260. Fees, books, misc. academic expenses (school's estimate): $600.
**Enrollment.** Undergraduates: 630 men, 728 women (full-time). Freshman class: 1,263 applicants, 1,262 accepted, 589 enrolled. Graduate enrollment: 76 men, 138 women.
**Test score averages/ranges.** Average SAT scores: 661 combined. Average ACT scores: 16 composite.
**Faculty.** 70 full-time; 33 part-time. 48% of faculty holds doctoral degree. Student/faculty ratio: 18 to 1.
**Selectivity rating.** Noncompetitive.

**PROFILE.** Western New Mexico, founded in 1893, is a public, multipurpose university. Its 80-acre campus is located in Silver City, in southwestern New Mexico, 100 miles from El Paso.

**Accreditation:** NCACS.
**Religious orientation:** Western New Mexico University is nonsectarian; no religious requirements.
**Library:** Collections totaling over 140,000 volumes, 1,000 periodical subscriptions, and 370,000 microform items.
**Special facilities/museums:** Museum.
**Athletic facilities:** Swimming pool, weight room, racquetball and tennis courts, intramural gymnasium.

**STUDENT BODY. Undergraduate profile:** 7% are transfers. 1% Asian-American, 2% Black, 42% Hispanic, 2% Native American, 52% White, 1% Other. Average age of undergraduates is 20.
**Freshman profile:** 5% of freshmen who took ACT scored 24 or over on composite; 33% scored 18 or over on composite; 92% scored 12 or over on composite; 98% scored 6 or over on composite. 6% of accepted applicants took SAT; 56% took ACT.
**Foreign students:** 18 students are from out of the country. Countries represented include Japan, Mexico, Nigeria, Palau, and the United Kingdom.

**PROGRAMS OF STUDY. Degrees:** B.A., B.Acad.Studies, B.S., B.Tech.
**Majors:** Administration of Justice, Art, Biology, Business Education, Chemistry, Computer Science, Elementary Education, English, Hispanic Studies, History, Humanities, Mathematics, Medical Technology, Music, Physical Education, Psychology, Public Administration, Secondary Education, Social Science, Sociology, Special Education.
**Distribution of degrees:** The majors with the highest enrollment are education, business, and sociology; fine arts, math, and natural science have the lowest.
**Requirements:** General education requirement.
**Special:** Minors offered in most majors and in approximately 25 other fields. Police Training Academy program leads to certification as law enforcement officer; other certificate programs. Courses offered in anthropology and journalism. Associate's degrees offered. Self-designed majors. Double majors. Dual degrees. Independent study. Pass/fail grading option. Internships. Cooperative education programs. Graduate school at which undergraduates may take graduate-level courses. Preprofessional programs in law, medicine, veterinary science, pharmacy, dentistry, and forestry. 2-3 engineering program with New Mexico State U. Teacher certification in early childhood, elementary, secondary, special education, vo-tech, and bilingual/bicultural education. Certification in specific subject areas.
**Honors:** Phi Beta Kappa.
**Academic Assistance:** Remedial reading, writing, math, and study skills.

**STUDENT LIFE. Housing:** All freshmen under age 21 must live on campus unless living with family. Coed, women's, and men's dorms. On-campus married-student housing. 25% of students live in college housing.
**Services and counseling/handicapped student services:** Placement services. Women's center. Day care. Counseling services for veteran students. Personal counseling. Religious counseling. Learning disabled services.
**Campus organizations:** Undergraduate student government. Student newspaper (Mustang, published twice/month). Yearbook. Athletes in Motion, biology, criminal justice, home economics, and social science groups, martial arts group, skiing and outdoor groups, nontraditional student group, SAM club, WMNU Ambassadors, Sho' Band.
**Religious organizations:** Baptist Student Union, St. Francis Newman Club, United Campus Ministry.
**Minority/foreign student organizations:** MEChA, Native American Club. International Club.

**ATHLETICS. Physical education requirements:** None.
**Intercollegiate competition:** 10% of students participate. Basketball (M,W), cross-country (M,W), football (M), golf (M), rodeo (M,W), track (outdoor) (W), track and field (M,W), volleyball (W). Member of NAIA.
**Intramural and club sports:** 1% of students participate. Intramural badminton, flag football, golf, racquetball, soccer, softball, swimming, tennis, track, volleyball, wrestling.

**ADMISSIONS. Academic basis for candidate selection** (in order of priority): Secondary school record, standardized test scores, class rank.
**Nonacademic basis for candidate selection:** Particular talent or ability and alumni/ae relationship are considered.
**Requirements:** Graduation from secondary school is required; GED is accepted. 16 units and the following program of study are recommended: 3 units of English, 2 units of math, 2 units of science, 2 units of social studies. Minimum 2.0 GPA required. 1 unit of intermediate algebra and 1 unit of plane geometry recommended of business administration, dentistry, engineering, pharmacy, and science program applicants. Admission possible for applicants not meeting standard requirements; special appeal required. ACT is required; SAT may be substituted. Campus visit recommended. No off-campus interviews.
**Procedure:** Take SAT or ACT by December of 12th year. Suggest filing application by April. Application deadline is August. Notification of admission on rolling basis. $75 room deposit, refundable partially. Freshmen accepted for terms other than fall.
**Special programs:** Admission may be deferred one year. Credit may be granted through CEEB Advanced Placement. Credit and/or placement may be granted through CLEP general and subject exams. Early entrance/early admission program. Concurrent enrollment program.
**Transfer students:** Transfer students accepted for terms other than fall. In fall 1992, 7% of all new students were transfers into all classes. 347 transfer applications were received, 347 were accepted. Application deadline is August for fall; January for spring. Minimum 2.0 GPA recommended. Lowest course grade accepted is "C-."
**Admissions contact:** Michael Alecksen, M.B.A., Director of Admissions. 505 538-6106.

**FINANCIAL AID. Available aid:** Pell grants, SEOG, state scholarships and grants, school scholarships, private scholarships, academic merit scholarships, and athletic scholarships. Perkins Loans (NDSL), PLUS, Stafford Loans (GSL), NSL, and SLS. Deferred payment plan, family tuition reduction, and guaranteed tuition.
**Financial aid statistics:** Average amounts of aid awarded freshmen: Loans, $2,625.
**Supporting data/closing dates:** FAFSA/FAF/FFS: Accepted on rolling basis. School's own aid application: Priority filing date is April 1. Income tax forms: Accepted on rolling basis. Verification forms: Accepted on rolling basis. Notification of awards on rolling basis.
**Financial aid contact:** Charles Kelly, M.A., Director of Financial Aid. 505 538-6173.

**STUDENT EMPLOYMENT.** College Work/Study Program. Institutional employment. 32% of full-time undergraduates work on campus during school year. Students may expect to earn an average of $2,075 during school year. Off-campus part-time employment opportunities rated "fair."

**COMPUTER FACILITIES.** IBM/IBM-compatible and Macintosh/Apple microcomputers. Computer languages and software packages include AppleWorks, Assembly, BASIC, Chart, COBOL, dBASE, FORTRAN, Lotus 1-2-3, MacPaint, MacWrite, Microsoft Word, WordStar. Computer facilities are available to all students.
**Fees:** $10 computer fee per semester.
**Hours:** 8 AM-9 PM.

# New York

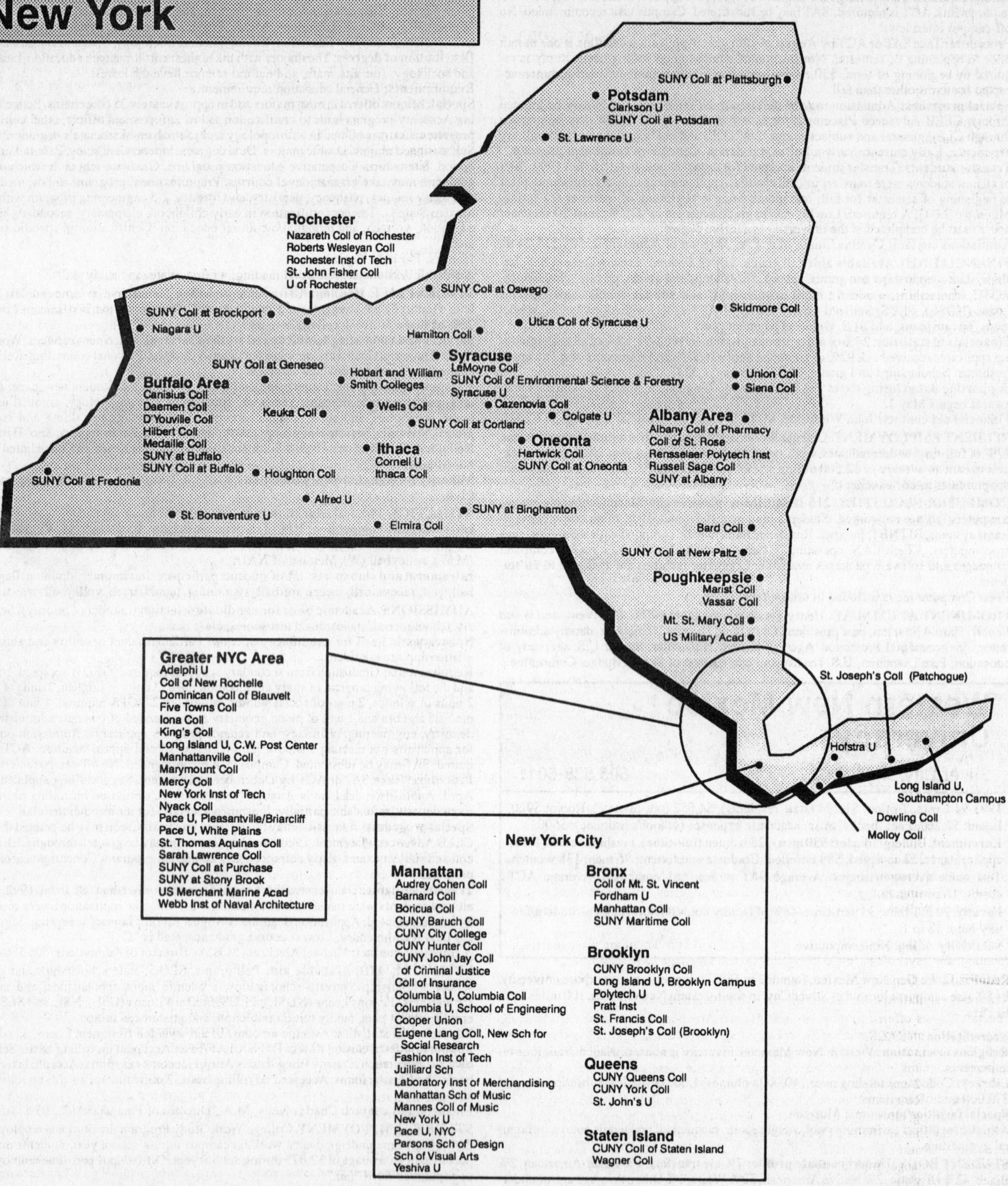
SUNY Coll at Plattsburgh
Potsdam
Clarkson U
SUNY Coll at Potsdam
St. Lawrence U
Rochester
Nazareth Coll of Rochester
Roberts Wesleyan Coll
Rochester Inst of Tech
St. John Fisher Coll
U of Rochester
SUNY Coll at Oswego
SUNY Coll at Brockport
Niagara U
Skidmore Coll
Utica Coll of Syracuse U
Hamilton Coll
Syracuse
LeMoyne Coll
SUNY Coll of Environmental Science & Forestry
Syracuse U
SUNY Coll at Geneseo
Hobart and William
Smith Colleges
Buffalo Area
Canisius Coll
Daemen Coll
D'Youville Coll
Hilbert Coll
Medaille Coll
SUNY at Buffalo
SUNY Coll at Buffalo
Union Coll
Siena Coll
Keuka Coll
Wells Coll
Cazenovia Coll
Colgate U
SUNY Coll at Cortland
Albany Area
Albany Coll of Pharmacy
Coll of St. Rose
Rensselaer Polytech Inst
Russell Sage Coll
SUNY at Albany
Oneonta
Hartwick Coll
SUNY Coll at Oneonta
Ithaca
Cornell U
Ithaca Coll
SUNY Coll at Fredonia
Houghton Coll
Alfred U
St. Bonaventure U
SUNY at Binghamton
Elmira Coll
Bard Coll
SUNY Coll at New Paltz
Poughkeepsie
Marist Coll
Vassar Coll
Mt. St. Mary Coll
US Military Acad
St. Joseph's Coll (Patchogue)
Hofstra U
Long Island U,
Southampton Campus
Dowling Coll
Molloy Coll
Greater NYC Area
Adelphi U
Coll of New Rochelle
Dominican Coll of Blauvelt
Five Towns Coll
Iona Coll
King's Coll
Long Island U, C.W. Post Center
Manhattanville Coll
Marymount Coll
Mercy Coll
New York Inst of Tech
Nyack Coll
Pace U, Pleasantville/Briarcliff
Pace U, White Plains
St. Thomas Aquinas Coll
Sarah Lawrence Coll
SUNY Coll at Purchase
SUNY at Stony Brook
US Merchant Marine Acad
Webb Inst of Naval Architecture
New York City
Manhattan
Audrey Cohen Coll
Barnard Coll
Boricua Coll
CUNY Baruch Coll
CUNY City College
CUNY Hunter Coll
CUNY John Jay Coll
of Criminal Justice
Coll of Insurance
Columbia U, Columbia Coll
Columbia U, School of Engineering
Cooper Union
Eugene Lang Coll, New Sch for
Social Research
Fashion Inst of Tech
Juilliard Sch
Laboratory Inst of Merchandising
Manhattan Sch of Music
Mannes Coll of Music
New York U
Pace U, NYC
Parsons Sch of Design
Sch of Visual Arts
Yeshiva U
Bronx
Coll of Mt. St. Vincent
Fordham U
Manhattan Coll
SUNY Maritime Coll
Brooklyn
CUNY Brooklyn Coll
Long Island U, Brooklyn Campus
Polytech U
Pratt Inst
St. Francis Coll
St. Joseph's Coll (Brooklyn)
Queens
CUNY Queens Coll
CUNY York Coll
St. John's U
Staten Island
CUNY Coll of Staten Island
Wagner Coll

# Adelphi University

Garden City, NY 11530 516 877-3000

**1993-94 Costs.** Tuition: $14,000. Room & board: $5,500. Fees, books, misc. academic expenses (school's estimate): $750.

**Enrollment.** Undergraduates: 1,054 men, 1,840 women (full-time). Freshman class: 2,831 applicants, 2,463 accepted, 1,162 enrolled. Graduate enrollment: 1,095 men, 3,013 women.

**Test score averages/ranges.** Average SAT scores: 453 verbal, 494 math. Range of SAT scores of middle 50%: 400-500 verbal, 430-560 math.

**Faculty.** 269 full-time; 396 part-time. 73% of faculty holds doctoral degree. Student/faculty ratio: 13 to 1.

**Selectivity rating.** Less competitive.

**PROFILE.** Adelphi is a private, multipurpose university. Founded as a boys' preparatory school, it became a college in 1896, and gained university status in 1963. Programs are offered through the College of Arts and Sciences; the Schools of Business, Nursing, and Social Work; the University College; and the Institute for Teaching and Education Studies. Its 75-acre campus is located in western Long Island, 20 miles from New York City.

**Accreditation:** MSACS. Professionally accredited by the American Psychological Association, the American Speech-Language-Hearing Association, the Council on Social Work Education, the National League for Nursing.

**Religious orientation:** Adelphi University is nonsectarian; no religious requirements.

**Library:** Collections totaling over 461,673 volumes, 4,490 periodical subscriptions, and 650,063 microform items.

**Special facilities/museums:** Art gallery, sculpture and ceramics studios, bronze-casting foundry, theatre, language labs.

**Athletic facilities:** Gymnasium, swimming pool, tracks, weight room, dance studio, racquetball, squash, and tennis courts, baseball, soccer, and softball fields.

**STUDENT BODY. Undergraduate profile:** 91% are state residents; 48% are transfers. 3% Asian-American, 10% Black, 5% Hispanic, 1% Native American, 62% White, 19% Other. Average age of undergraduates is 26.

**Freshman profile:** 1% of freshmen who took SAT scored 700 or over on verbal, 1% scored 700 or over on math; 7% scored 600 or over on verbal, 14% scored 600 or over on math; 28% scored 500 or over on verbal, 47% scored 500 or over on math; 81% scored 400 or over on verbal, 88% scored 400 or over on math; 98% scored 300 or over on verbal, 99% scored 300 or over on math. 87% of accepted applicants took SAT. 80% of freshmen come from public schools.

**Undergraduate achievement:** 62% of fall 1991 freshmen returned for fall 1992 term. 26% of entering class graduated.

**Foreign students:** 168 students are from out of the country. Countries represented include China, Cyprus, Greece, Japan, and Korea; 41 in all.

**PROGRAMS OF STUDY. Degrees:** B.A., B.Bus.Admin., B.F.A., B.S., B.S.Ed., B.Soc.Work.

**Majors:** Accounting, Anthropology, Art, Art Education, Banking/Money Management, Biochemistry, Biology, Business Management, Chemistry, Communications, Computer Science, Dance, Earth Science, Economics, Elementary Education, English, Foreign Language Studies, French, History, Latin American Studies, Mathematics, Music, Music Education, Nursing, Philosophy, Physical Education, Physics, Political Studies, Psychology, Social Welfare, Sociology, Spanish, Speech Arts/Communicative Disorders, Theatre.

**Distribution of degrees:** The majors with the highest enrollment are management, accounting, and psychology; philosophy, music, and language have the lowest.

**Requirements:** General education requirement.

**Academic regulations:** Minimum 2.0 GPA must be maintained.

**Special:** Minors offered in most majors. African-American and women's studies programs. Double majors. Dual degrees. Independent study. Pass/fail grading option. Internships. Graduate school at which undergraduates may take graduate-level courses. Preprofessional programs in law, medicine, veterinary science, dentistry, optometry, business, and podiatry. 3-2 engineering programs with Columbia U, Newark Coll of Engineering, Polytechnic U, Rensselaer Polytech Inst, and Stevens Inst of Tech. Five-year programs in business, nursing, physics, and social work. Seven-year joint programs with Tufts U Sch of Dental Medicine and SUNY Coll of Optometry. Teacher certification in elementary and secondary education. Certification in specific subject areas. Member of Council on International Exchange. Study abroad in over 30 countries. ROTC at Hofstra U. AFROTC at New York Inst of Tech.

**Honors:** Honors program.

**Academic Assistance:** Remedial reading, writing, math, and study skills. Nonremedial tutoring.

**STUDENT LIFE. Housing:** Students may live on or off campus. Coed and women's dorms. School-owned/operated apartments. 12% of students live in college housing.

**Social atmosphere:** Sharros, the Rathskellar, university center dining room, fire-side lounge, New York City, and Roosevelt Field Mall are popular on- and off- campus gathering spots. Influential groups include Greeks, Circle K, Environmental Action Coalition, Christian Fellowship, APO, UMOJA, athletes, Caliber, and La Union Latino. Popular social events include Homecoming, comedy nights, dances, Spring-In, Kwanza, African-American Solidarity Day, and Starlight Showdown. "Adelphi is what you make it," reports the student newspaper. "If you want to meet people, there are plenty of opportunities."

**Services and counseling/handicapped student services:** Placement services. Health service. Day care. Counseling services for minority, veteran, and older students. Birth control, personal, and psychological counseling. Career and academic guidance services. Religious counseling. Physically disabled student services. Learning disabled program/services. Notetaking services. Tape recorders. Tutors. Reader services for the blind.

**Campus organizations:** Undergraduate student government. Student newspaper (Delphian, published once/week). Literary magazine. Yearbook. Radio station. Choral ensemble, dance group, SADD, WE CARE, Circle K, communications club, marketing and advertising clubs, physical education/fitness club, President's Circle, Student Activities Board, 80 organizations in all. Eight fraternities, no chapter houses; seven sororities, no chapter houses. 7% of men join a fraternity. 5% of women join a sorority.

**Religious organizations:** Catholic Campus Community, Hillel, Christian Fellowship.

**Minority/foreign student organizations:** International Student Society, African Peoples Organization, La Union Latina, Asian Student Association, Third World Pre-Med Association.

**ATHLETICS. Physical education requirements:** None.

**Intercollegiate competition:** 5% of students participate. Baseball (M), basketball (M,W), cheerleading (M,W), cross-country (M,W), golf (M), handball (M,W), lacrosse (M), soccer (M,W), softball (W), swimming (M,W), tennis (M,W), volleyball (W). Member of ECAC, NCAA Division I for men's soccer, NCAA Division II, New York Collegiate Athletic Conference.

**Intramural and club sports:** 20% of students participate. Intramural basketball, flag football, floor hockey, soccer, softball, swimming, tennis, volleyball. Men's club team handball. Women's club cheerleading, equestrian sports, team handball.

**ADMISSIONS. Academic basis for candidate selection** (in order of priority): Secondary school record, class rank, standardized test scores, essay, school's recommendation.

**Nonacademic basis for candidate selection:** Character and personality, extracurricular participation, particular talent or ability, geographical distribution, and alumni/ae relationship are considered.

**Requirements:** Graduation from secondary school is required; GED is accepted. 16 units and the following program of study are recommended: 4 units of English, 3 units of math, 3 units of science, 2 units of foreign language, 4 units of electives. Minimum combined SAT score of 950, rank in top third of secondary school class, and minimum 3.0 GPA recommended. Audition required of performing arts and music program applicants. Portfolio required of technical theatre and art program applicants. HEOP for applicants not normally admissible. General studies program for applicants not normally admissible. SAT or ACT is required. Campus visit and interview recommended. No off-campus interviews.

**Procedure:** Take SAT or ACT by January of 12th year. Visit college for interview by April 15 of 12th year. Suggest filing application by March 1; no deadline. Notification of admission on rolling basis. Reply is required by May 1; April 1 for learning disabled applicants. $250 nonrefundable tuition deposit. $100 nonrefundable room deposit. Freshmen accepted for terms other than fall.

**Special programs:** Admission may be deferred one year. Credit and/or placement may be granted through CEEB Advanced Placement exams for scores of 3 or higher. Credit and/or placement may be granted through CLEP general and subject exams. Credit may be granted through life experience. Early entrance/early admission program. Concurrent enrollment program.

**Transfer students:** Transfer students accepted for terms other than fall. In fall 1992, 48% of all new students were transfers into all classes. 1,080 transfer applications were received, 948 were accepted. Application deadline is rolling for fall; rolling for spring. Minimum 2.5 GPA recommended. Lowest course grade accepted is "C-." Maximum number of transferable credits is 64 semester hours from a two-year school and 90 semester hours from a four-year school. At least 30 semester hours must be completed at the university to receive degree.

**Admissions contact:** Scott Healy, M.S., Vice President of Enrollment Planning and Management. 516 877-3050.

**FINANCIAL AID. Available aid:** Pell grants, SEOG, Federal Nursing Student Scholarships, state scholarships and grants, school scholarships and grants, private scholarships and grants, ROTC scholarships, academic merit scholarships, and athletic scholarships. Perkins Loans (NDSL), PLUS, Stafford Loans (GSL), NSL, Health Professions Loans, and SLS. Tuition Plan Inc., AMS, and deferred payment plan.

**Financial aid statistics:** 48% of aid is not need-based. In 1992-93, 66% of all undergraduate applicants received aid; 74% of freshman applicants. Average amounts of aid awarded freshmen: Scholarships and grants, $3,127; loans, $2,436.

**Supporting data/closing dates:** FAFSA/FAF: Priority filing date is May 1. School's own aid application: Accepted on rolling basis. Notification of awards begins February 15.

**Financial aid contact:** Timothy Burton, Director of Financial Aid. 516 877-3080.

**STUDENT EMPLOYMENT.** College Work/Study Program. Institutional employment. 27% of full-time undergraduates work on campus during school year. Students may expect to earn an average of $1,500 during school year. Off-campus part-time employment opportunities rated "good."

**COMPUTER FACILITIES.** 450 IBM/IBM-compatible and Macintosh/Apple microcomputers; all are networked. Students may access Digital minicomputer/mainframe systems. Computer languages and software packages include BASIC, BMDP, C, COBOL, dBASE II, FORTRAN, LISP, Lotus 1-2-3, MINITAB, Pascal, SAS, SPSS-X, Unix, WordPerfect; 50 in all. Computer facilities are available to all students.

**Fees:** None.

**Hours:** 8 AM-11 PM (M-Th); 8 AM-10 PM (F); 9 AM-2 PM (Sa); 11 AM-4 PM (Su).

**PROMINENT ALUMNI/AE.** John J. Phelan, Jr., chairperson and chief executive, New York Stock Exchange; Frederick Salerno, president and CEO, New York Telephone Co.; Edolphos Towns, U.S. congressman.

# Albany College of Pharmacy

**Albany, NY 12208** **518 445-7200**

**1994-95 Costs.** Tuition: $9,000. Room: $2,800. Board: $1,900. Fees, books, misc. academic expenses (school's estimate): $820.
**Enrollment.** Undergraduates: 244 men, 396 women (full-time). Freshman class: 363 applicants, 265 accepted, 140 enrolled. Graduate enrollment: 2 men, 13 women.
**Test score averages/ranges.** Average SAT scores: 453 verbal, 541 math.
**Faculty.** 35 full-time; 26 part-time. 46% of faculty holds doctoral degree. Student/faculty ratio: 17 to 1.
**Selectivity rating.** Less competitive.

**PROFILE.** Albany College of Pharmacy was founded in 1881. A private institution, it is a functionally autonomous branch of Union University. The one-acre campus is located in Albany.

**Accreditation:** MSACS. Professionally accredited by the American Council on Pharmaceutical Education.
**Religious orientation:** Albany College of Pharmacy is nonsectarian; no religious requirements.
**Library:** Collections totaling over 8,000 volumes, 155 periodical subscriptions and 100 microform items.
**Special facilities/museums:** Pharmaceutical museum.
**Athletic facilities:** Gymnasium, soccer fields.

**STUDENT BODY. Undergraduate profile:** 92% are state residents; 23% are transfers. 8% Asian-American, 1% Black, 2% Hispanic, 1% Native American, 88% White. Average age of undergraduates is 21.
**Freshman profile:** 2% of freshmen who took SAT scored 700 or over on math; 2% scored 600 or over on verbal, 23% scored 600 or over on math; 25% scored 500 or over on verbal, 72% scored 500 or over on math; 84% scored 400 or over on verbal, 99% scored 400 or over on math; 94% scored 300 or over on verbal. 96% of accepted applicants took SAT. 91% of freshmen come from public schools.
**Undergraduate achievement:** 88% of fall 1992 freshmen returned for fall 1993 term. 78% of entering class graduated. 13% of students who completed a degree program went on to graduate study.
**Foreign students:** 10 students are from out of the country. Countries represented include Canada and Hong Kong; five in all.

**PROGRAMS OF STUDY. Degrees:** B.S.Pharm.
**Majors:** Pharmacy.
**Requirements:** General education requirement.
**Academic regulations:** Minimum 2.0 GPA must be maintained.
**Special:** B.S.Pharm. curriculum is a five-year program. Courses offered in liberal arts. Dual degrees. Independent study. Five-year B.S.Pharm./M.S. Health Systems Management program with Union Coll. B.S.Pharm./D.Pharm. program. Member of Hudson-Mohawk Association of Colleges and Universities; cross-registration possible.
**Honors:** Honor societies.
**Academic Assistance:** Remedial writing. Nonremedial tutoring.

**ADMISSIONS. Academic basis for candidate selection** (in order of priority): Secondary school record, class rank, standardized test scores, school's recommendation, essay.
**Nonacademic basis for candidate selection:** Character and personality, extracurricular participation, particular talent or ability, geographical distribution, and alumni/ae relationship are considered.
**Requirements:** Graduation from secondary school is required; GED is accepted. 17 units and the following program of study are required: 4 units of English, 4 units of math, 3 units of science including 2 units of lab, 6 units of academic electives. Minimum combined SAT score of 1000, rank in top half of secondary school class, and minimum 85 average recommended. SAT is required; ACT may be substituted. Campus visit recommended. No off-campus interviews.
**Procedure:** Take SAT or ACT by December 1 of 12th year. Visit college for interview by December 1 of 12th year. Suggest filing application by December 1; no deadline. Notification of admission on rolling basis. Reply is required by date specified in letter of acceptance. $100 nonrefundable tuition deposit. $100 room deposit, refundable until May 1. Freshmen accepted for fall terms only.
**Special programs:** Credit may be granted through CEEB Advanced Placement for scores of 4 or higher. Credit may be granted through CLEP general and subject exams and Regents College exams. Deadline for applying for early decision is December 1. Early entrance/early admission program.
**Transfer students:** Transfer students accepted for fall term only. In fall 1993, 23% of all new students were transfers into all classes. 255 transfer applications were received, 61 were accepted. Application deadline is March 1. Minimum 3.0 GPA recommended. Lowest course grade accepted is "C." Maximum number of transferable credits is 66 semester hours from a two-year school and 80 semester hours from a four-year school. At least 85 semester hours must be completed at the college to receive degree.
**Admissions contact:** Janis L. Fisher, Director of Admissions/Registrar. 518 445-7221.

**FINANCIAL AID. Available aid:** Pell grants, SEOG, state scholarships and grants, school scholarships and grants, and private scholarships and grants. Perkins Loans (NDSL), PLUS, Stafford Loans (GSL), Health Professions Loans, state loans, and SLS. AMS.
**Financial aid statistics:** 25% of aid is not need-based. In 1993-94, 85% of all undergraduate applicants received aid; 85% of freshman applicants. Average amounts of aid awarded freshmen: Scholarships and grants, $800; loans, $1,200.
**Supporting data/closing dates:** FAFSA: Priority filing date is March 15. Notification of awards begins April 1.
**Financial aid contact:** Thomas Dalton, Director of Financial Aid. 518 445-7258.

# Alfred University

**Alfred, NY 14802** **607 871-2111**

**1993-94 Costs.** Tuition: $16,048. (Tuition for the New York State College of Ceramics: $6,320.) Room & board: $5,006. Fees, books, misc. academic expenses (school's estimate): $1,000.
**Enrollment.** Undergraduates: 1,029 men, 801 women (full-time). Freshman class: 1,732 applicants, 1,425 accepted, 479 enrolled. Graduate enrollment: 187 men, 199 women.
**Test score averages/ranges.** Average SAT scores: 510 verbal, 580 math. Range of SAT scores of middle 50%: 480-580 verbal, 540-660 math. Range of ACT scores of middle 50%: 23-28 composite.
**Faculty.** 169 full-time; 60 part-time. 83% of faculty holds doctoral degree. Student/faculty ratio: 12 to 1.
**Selectivity rating.** Competitive.

**PROFILE.** Alfred University was founded in 1836. Programs are offered through the privately endowed Colleges of Business and Administration, Liberal Arts and Sciences, and Nursing; the Division of Industrial Engineering; and the Graduate School, as well as the publicly funded New York State College of Ceramics. Its 232-acre campus is located in Alfred, in southwestern New York.

**Accreditation:** MSACS. Professionally accredited by the Accreditation Board for Engineering and Technology, the American Assembly of Collegiate Schools of Business, the National Association of Schools of Art and Design.
**Religious orientation:** Alfred University is nonsectarian; no religious requirements.
**Library:** Collections totaling over 285,260 volumes, 1,895 periodical subscriptions, and 37,000 microform items.
**Special facilities/museums:** Art museums, carillon, language labs, electron microscope, observatory, extensive engineering equipment.
**Athletic facilities:** Basketball, volleyball, racquetball, and tennis courts, football, soccer, lacrosse, and softball fields, track, swimming pool, weight room.

**STUDENT BODY. Undergraduate profile:** 70% are state residents; 19% are transfers. 2% Asian-American, 5% Black, 3% Hispanic, 1% Native American, 88% White, 1% Other. Average age of undergraduates is 20.
**Freshman profile:** 5% of freshmen who took SAT scored 700 or over on verbal, 14% scored 700 or over on math; 20% scored 600 or over on verbal, 49% scored 600 or over on math; 57% scored 500 or over on verbal, 89% scored 500 or over on math; 96% scored 400 or over on verbal, 99% scored 400 or over on math; 100% scored 300 or over on verbal, 100% scored 300 or over on math. 11% of freshmen who took ACT scored 30 or over on composite; 60% scored 24 or over on composite; 99% scored 18 or over on composite; 100% scored 12 or over on composite. 75% of accepted applicants took SAT; 25% took ACT. 83% of freshmen come from public schools.
**Undergraduate achievement:** 82% of fall 1992 freshmen returned for fall 1993 term. 68% of entering class graduated. 28% of students who completed a degree program immediately went on to graduate study.
**Foreign students:** 14 students are from out of the country. Countries represented include Canada, China, Germany, Japan, Korea, and Taiwan.

**PROGRAMS OF STUDY. Degrees:** B.A., B.F.A., B.S.
**Majors:** Accounting, Art Education, Biology, Business Administration, Ceramic Art, Ceramic Engineering, Ceramic Engineering Science, Chemistry, Communication Studies, Computer Science, Criminal Justice Studies, Economics, Electrical Engineering, Elementary Education, English, Environmental Studies, Fine Arts, French, General Science, General Studies, Geology, German, Gerontology, Glass Art, Glass Engineering Science, Graphic Design, History, History of Art, Mathematics, Mechanical Engineering, Painting, Performing Arts, Philosophy, Photography, Physics, Political Science, Pre-Art Therapy, Printmaking, Psychology, Public Administration, Sculpture, Secondary Education, Sociology, Spanish, Video/Computer Graphics/Electronic Imaging, Wood Design.
**Distribution of degrees:** The majors with the highest enrollment are ceramic engineering science, business administration, and psychology.
**Requirements:** General education requirement.
**Academic regulations:** Freshmen must maintain minimum 1.75 GPA; sophomores, juniors, seniors, 2.0 GPA.
**Special:** Minors offered in most majors and in American cultural studies, anthropology, astronomy, coaching, computer instrumentation, dance, equestrian studies, industrial engineering, literature, music, public law, religious studies, social science research, speech, sports medicine, women's studies, and writing. Students may specialize in illustration. Students enrolled in College of Liberal Arts may elect any course in the university provided prerequisites are met. World Campus Afloat Program. Self-designed majors. Double majors. Dual degrees. Independent study. Accelerated study. Pass/fail grading option. Internships. Cooperative education programs. Graduate school at which undergraduates may take graduate-level courses. Preprofessional programs in law, medicine, veterinary science, and dentistry. 3-2 engineering program with Columbia U. 3-2 forestry studies program with Duke U. 3-2 liberal arts/M.B.A. program with Clarkson U. Member of Rochester Area Colleges Consortium and College Center of the Finger Lakes. Washington Semester, UN Semester, and Sea Semester. Albany Semester. Teacher certification in elementary and secondary education. Certification in specific subject areas. Exchange programs abroad in England (Brighton Polytech, Camberwell Sch of Art, Manchester Polytech, U of Leeds, U of Sheffield), Germany (Technical U, U of Erlangen-Nuremburg), and Switzerland (Federal Polytech Inst of Lausanne). ROTC.
**Honors:** Honors program.
**Academic Assistance:** Remedial reading, writing, math, and study skills. Nonremedial tutoring.

**STUDENT LIFE. Housing:** All freshmen and sophomores must live on campus unless living with family. Coed dorms. Sorority and fraternity housing. School-owned/operated apartments. Suites. 87% of students live in college housing.

**Social atmosphere:** According to the editor of the student newspaper, "Students always say, 'There is nothing to do in Alfred,' but they are completely wrong. They just need to get more involved with student organizations and their events. There is always something to do in Alfred." Special events include Hot Dog Day (a fundraiser in April) and sport and theatre events. "The Student Senate sponsors a great number of social events through organizations funded by the Senate. The Greek system sponsors a lot of social events also." Favorite gathering spots include Rogers Campus Center, the Saxon Inne, Gentleman Jim's, Alex's College Spot, and the fraternities.
**Services and counseling/handicapped student services:** Placement services. Health service. Counseling services for minority students. Personal counseling. Career and academic guidance services. Physically disabled student services. Learning disabled services. Tape recorders.
**Campus organizations:** Undergraduate student government. Student newspaper (Fiat Lux, published once/week). Literary magazine. Yearbook. Radio station. Major drama productions, karate club, career women's association chapter, 70 organizations in all. Seven fraternities, six chapter houses; five sororities, three chapter houses. 27% of men join a fraternity. 13% of women join a sorority.
**Religious organizations:** Hillel, Brothers and Sisters in Christ, Emmanuel Ministries.
**Minority/foreign student organizations:** Ibero American Student Union (IASU), Concerned Brothers, Shades of Ebony, UMOJA. World Friends, International Student Organization.

**ATHLETICS. Physical education requirements:** Two semesters of physical education required.
**Intercollegiate competition:** 20% of students participate. Alpine skiing (M,W), basketball (M,W), cross-country (M,W), diving (M,W), football (M), golf (M), horsemanship (M,W), lacrosse (M,W), soccer (M,W), softball (W), swimming (M,W), tennis (M,W), track (M), track and field (indoor) (M), track and field (outdoor) (M), volleyball (W). Member of EAA, ECAC, IHSA, NCAA Division III, NCSA, New York State Women's College Athletic Association.
**Intramural and club sports:** 70% of students participate. Intramural aerobics, basketball, flag football, karate, racquetball, soccer, softball, volleyball. Men's club karate, rugby. Women's club rugby.

**ADMISSIONS. Academic basis for candidate selection** (in order of priority): Secondary school record, class rank, school's recommendation, standardized test scores, essay.
**Nonacademic basis for candidate selection:** Extracurricular participation is emphasized. Particular talent or ability, geographical distribution, and alumni/ae relationship are important. Character and personality are considered.
**Requirements:** Graduation from secondary school is required; GED is accepted. 16 units and the following program of study are recommended: 4 units of English, 3 units of math, 3 units of science, 2 units of foreign language, 4 units of social studies. Portfolio required of art program applicants. EOP and HEOP for applicants not normally admissible. SAT or ACT is required. Campus visit and interview recommended. Off-campus interviews available with an admissions representative.
**Procedure:** Take SAT or ACT by January of 12th year. Suggest filing application by February 15; no deadline. Notification of admission by March. Reply is required by May 1. $200 nonrefundable tuition deposit. $100 nonrefundable room deposit. Freshmen accepted for terms other than fall.
**Special programs:** Admission may be deferred two years. Credit and/or placement may be granted through CEEB Advanced Placement exams for scores of 4 or higher. Credit and/or placement may be granted through CLEP general exams. Early decision program. In fall 1993, 70 applied for early decision and 48 were accepted. Deadline for applying for early decision is December 1. Early entrance/early admission program. Concurrent enrollment program.
**Transfer students:** Transfer students accepted for terms other than fall. In fall 1993, 19% of all new students were transfers into all classes. 201 transfer applications were received, 155 were accepted. Application deadline is August 1 for fall; December 1 for spring. Minimum 2.5 GPA required. Lowest course grade accepted is "C." Maximum number of transferable credits is 72 quarter hours. At least 30 quarter hours must be completed at the university to receive degree.
**Admissions contact:** Laurie Richer, Acting Director of Admissions. 607 871-2115, 800 541-9229.

**FINANCIAL AID. Available aid:** Pell grants, SEOG, state scholarships and grants, school scholarships and grants, private scholarships and grants, ROTC scholarships, academic merit scholarships, and aid for undergraduate foreign students. Perkins Loans (NDSL), PLUS, Stafford Loans (GSL), school loans, and SLS. AMS and guaranteed tuition.
**Financial aid statistics:** 20% of aid is not need-based. In 1993-94, 95% of all undergraduate aid recipients received aid; 95% of freshman applicants. Average amounts of aid awarded freshmen: Scholarships and grants, $10,000; loans, $3,000.
**Supporting data/closing dates:** FAFSA: Accepted on rolling basis. School's own aid application: Accepted on rolling basis. State aid form: Accepted on rolling basis. Income tax forms: Accepted on rolling basis. Notification of awards on rolling basis.
**Financial aid contact:** Earl Pierce, M.A., Director of Financial Aid. 607 871-2159.

**STUDENT EMPLOYMENT.** College Work/Study Program. Institutional employment. 65% of full-time undergraduates work on campus during school year. Students may expect to earn an average of $800 during school year. Off-campus part-time employment opportunities rated "fair."

**COMPUTER FACILITIES.** 400 IBM/IBM-compatible, Macintosh/Apple, and RISC-/UNIX-based microcomputers; 350 are networked. Students may access Digital minicomputer/mainframe systems, BITNET, Internet. Residence halls may be equipped with stand-alone microcomputers, networked microcomputers, networked terminals, modems. Client/LAN operating systems include Apple/Macintosh, DOS, UNIX/XENIX/AIX, X-windows, DEC, LocalTalk/AppleTalk, Novell. Computer languages and software packages include BASIC, C, COBOL, FORTRAN, Lotus 1-2-3, MINITAB, Pascal, Graphics, SPSS-X, WordPerfect. Computer facilities are available to all students.
**Fees:** None.
**Hours:** 24 hours.

**GRADUATE CAREER DATA.** Highest graduate school enrollments: Alfred U, Pennsylvania State U, Syracuse U, U of Buffalo, U of Rochester. 63% of graduates choose careers in business and industry. Companies and businesses that hire graduates: Price Waterhouse, General Electric, Corning Glass Works, KPMG Peat Marwick, Norton Company.
**PROMINENT ALUMNI/AE.** Robert Klein, comedian; Leah Napolin, playwright; Peter Jenkins and Robert Littell, authors; Val Cushing, artist.

# Audrey Cohen College

**New York, NY 10014 — 212 989-2002**

**1994-95 Costs.** Tuition: $7,840. Housing: None. Fees, books, misc. academic expenses (school's estimate): $300.
**Enrollment.** Undergraduates: 266 men, 677 women (full-time). Freshman class: 631 applicants, 531 accepted, 265 enrolled. Graduate enrollment: 20 men, 37 women.
**Test score averages/ranges.** N/A.
**Faculty.** 17 full-time; 56 part-time. 40% of faculty holds doctoral degree. Student/faculty ratio: 20 to 1.
**Selectivity rating.** N/A.

**PROFILE.** Audrey Cohen, founded in 1964, is a private college offering business and professional service programs. Its one-acre campus is located in Manhattan.
**Accreditation:** MSACS.
**Religious orientation:** Audrey Cohen College is nonsectarian; no religious requirements.
**Library:** Collections totaling over 20,170 volumes, 201 periodical subscriptions and 310 microform items.

**STUDENT BODY. Undergraduate profile:** 95% are state residents; 51% are transfers. 2% Asian-American, 58% Black, 19% Hispanic, 5% Native American, 16% White. Average age of undergraduates is 30.
**Undergraduate achievement:** 75% of fall 1992 freshmen returned for fall 1993 term. 40% of entering class graduated. 50% of students who completed a degree program went on to graduate study within one year.

**PROGRAMS OF STUDY. Degrees:** B.Prof.Studies
**Majors:** Business, Service Professions.
**Requirements:** General education requirement.
**Academic regulations:** Minimum 2.0 GPA must be maintained.
**Special:** College requires class work integrated with field work; class learning is applied, tested, documented, and assessed in the field. Internships. Preprofessional programs in law.
**Academic Assistance:** Remedial reading, writing, math, and study skills. Nonremedial tutoring.

**ADMISSIONS. Academic basis for candidate selection** (in order of priority): Standardized test scores, essay, school's recommendation, secondary school record, class rank.
**Nonacademic basis for candidate selection:** Character and personality, extracurricular participation, and particular talent or ability are important.
**Requirements:** Graduation from secondary school is recommended; GED is accepted. 16 units and the following program of study are required: 4 units of English, 2 units of math, 1 unit of science, 4 units of social studies, 2 units of history, 3 units of electives. Stanford Task Test required. Campus visit and interview required.
**Procedure:** Suggest filing application by May 1; no deadline. Notification of admission on rolling basis. Freshmen accepted for terms other than fall.
**Special programs:** Admission may be deferred one year. Credit and/or placement may be granted through CLEP subject exams. Credit and placement may be granted through life experience.
**Transfer students:** Transfer students accepted for terms other than fall. In fall 1993, 51% of all new students were transfers into all classes. Application deadline is August 15 for fall; December 15 for spring. Lowest course grade accepted is "C." Maximum number of transferable credits is 64 semester hours. At least 128 semester hours must be completed at the college to receive degree.
**Admissions contact:** Steven K. Lenhart, Director of Admissions. 212 989-2002, extension 501.

**FINANCIAL AID. Available aid:** Pell grants, state scholarships and grants, school scholarships and grants, private scholarships and grants, and academic merit scholarships. Stafford Loans (GSL). Monthly payment plans.
**Supporting data/closing dates:** State aid form. Income tax forms. Notification of awards on rolling basis.
**Financial aid contact:** Rosibel Gomez, Director of Financial Aid. 212 989-2002, extension 504.

# Bard College

**Annandale-on-Hudson, NY 12504-5000 — 914 758-6822**

**1994-95 Costs.** Tuition: $19,264. Room & Board: $6,206. Fees, books, misc. academic expenses (school's estimate): $1,500.
**Enrollment.** Undergraduates: 501 men, 522 women (full-time). Freshman class: 1,857 applicants, 910 accepted, 313 enrolled. Graduate enrollment: 60 men, 50 women.
**Test score averages/ranges.** Range of SAT scores of middle 50%: 550-670 verbal, 550-690 math.
**Faculty.** 92 full-time; 43 part-time. 95% of faculty holds doctoral degree. Student/faculty ratio: 10 to 1.
**Selectivity rating.** Highly competitive.

**PROFILE.** Bard, founded in 1860, is a private, liberal arts college. Programs are offered through the Divisions of Arts, Language and Literature, Natural Sciences and Mathematics, and Social Studies. Its 600-acre campus is located in Annandale-on-Hudson, 90 miles north of New York City.

**Accreditation:** MSACS.
**Religious orientation:** Bard College is nonsectarian; no religious requirements.
**Library:** Collections totaling over 260,000 volumes, 730 periodical subscriptions, and 5,670 microform items.
**Special facilities/museums:** Performing arts center, gallery, art museum, collection of late twentieth century art, center for curatorial studies, language lab, nursery school, ecology field station.
**Athletic facilities:** Indoor swimming/diving pool, weight rooms, outdoor tennis courts, squash, racquetball, and basketball courts, gymnasium.

**STUDENT BODY. Undergraduate profile:** 25% are state residents; 12% are transfers. 5% Asian-American, 8% Black, 5% Hispanic, 1% Native American, 65% White, 16% Other. Average age of undergraduates is 20.
**Freshman profile:** 74% of accepted applicants took SAT. 70% of freshmen come from public schools.
**Undergraduate achievement:** 89% of fall 1992 freshmen returned for fall 1993 term. 77% of entering class graduated. 60% of students who completed a degree program went on to graduate study within five years.
**Foreign students:** 127 students are from out of the country. Countries represented include Czechoslovakia, France, Greece, Peru, Russia, and Sweden; 48 in all.

**PROGRAMS OF STUDY. Degrees:** B.A.
**Majors:** American Studies, Anthropology, Area Studies, Art History, Asian Studies, Biology, Chemistry, Classics, Community/Regional Environmental Studies, Creative Writing, Drama/Dance, Ecology, Economics, English, Film, Fine Arts, French, Gender Studies, German, History, History of Ideas, Intensive Language Immersion Program/German, Literature, Mathematics, Multicultural/Ethnic Studies, Music, Natural Science, Philosophy, Photography, Physics, Political Science, Psychology, Religion, Russian/Soviet Studies, Sociology, Spanish.
**Distribution of degrees:** The majors with the highest enrollment are fine arts and literature; natural science and mathematics have the lowest.
**Requirements:** General education requirement.
**Academic regulations:** Minimum 2.0 GPA must be maintained.
**Special:** Self-designed majors. Double majors. Dual degrees. Independent study. Accelerated study. Pass/fail grading option. Internships. Preprofessional programs in law, medicine, veterinary science, pharmacy, dentistry, theology, and optometry. Accelerated law program with Cardozo Law Sch. 3-2 engineering program with Columbia U. 3-2 business program with U of Rochester. 3-2 forestry and environmental studies program with Duke U. 3-2 M.P.A. program with Syracuse U. 3-2 M.S.W. program with Hunter Coll and U of Pennsylvania. 3-2 public health program with Yale U. 3-2 city and regional planning program and 2-3 architecture program with Pratt Inst. Washington Semester. Exchange programs with numerous schools. Exchange programs abroad in Greece (American Sch of Classical Studies) and Russia (Leningrad Herzen U). Study abroad also in several other countries.
**Academic Assistance:** Nonremedial tutoring.

**STUDENT LIFE. Housing:** All freshmen must live on campus. Coed and women's dorms. 85% of students live in college housing.
**Social atmosphere:** As reported by the student newspaper, "The small student body at Bard provides both opportunities and limits to students. An individual, with determination and charisma, can change the campus atmosphere." Influential groups on campus include the Coalition for Choice and the International Students Organization. International student parties, Autumn Fest, Spring Fling, and the Tent Party are among the year's favorite events.
**Services and counseling/handicapped student services:** Placement services. Health service. Women's center. Counseling services for minority and older students. Birth control, personal, and psychological counseling. Career and academic guidance services. Religious counseling. Physically disabled student services. Notetaking services. Tape recorders. Tutors. Reader services for the blind.
**Campus organizations:** Student newspaper (Observer, published once/week). Literary magazine. Yearbook. Radio station. Chorus, drama productions, psychology journal, departmental, language, and political groups, 60 organizations in all.
**Religious organizations:** Several religious groups.
**Minority/foreign student organizations:** Black Student Organization, Latin American Student Organization, Asian Student Organization, Multicultural Club. International Student Organization.

**ATHLETICS. Physical education requirements:** None.
**Intercollegiate competition:** 5% of students participate. Basketball (M,W), cross-country (M,W), soccer (M), softball (W), tennis (M,W), volleyball (M,W). Member of NAIA.
**Intramural and club sports:** 2% of students participate. Intramural basketball, road running, soccer, softball, squash, tennis, volleyball.

**ADMISSIONS. Academic basis for candidate selection** (in order of priority): Secondary school record, essay, school's recommendation, class rank.
**Nonacademic basis for candidate selection:** Extracurricular participation and particular talent or ability are emphasized. Character and personality are important.
**Requirements:** Graduation from secondary school is required; GED is accepted. No specific distribution of secondary school units required. Rank in top two-fifths of secondary school class recommended. HEOP for in-state applicants not normally admissible. SP/ARC (Superior Potential/Admission Risk Candidate) program for talented underachievers. Campus visit and interview recommended. No off-campus interviews.
**Procedure:** Visit college for interview by February 15 of 12th year. Application deadline is February 15. Acceptance notification by the first week of April. Reply is required by May 1. $350 nonrefundable tuition deposit. Freshmen accepted for terms other than fall.
**Special programs:** Admission may be deferred one year. Credit may be granted through CEEB Advanced Placement for scores of 4 or higher. Early decision program. In fall 1993, 20 applied for early decision and 16 were accepted. Deadline for applying for early decision is December 1. Early entrance/early admission program.
**Transfer students:** Transfer students accepted for terms other than fall. In fall 1993, 12% of all new students were transfers into all classes. 150 transfer applications were received, 95 were accepted. Application deadline is June 1 for fall; December 1 for spring. Minimum 3.0 GPA recommended. Lowest course grade accepted is "C." Maximum number of transferable credits is 60 semester hours. At least 64 semester hours must be completed at the college to receive degree.
**Admissions contact:** Mary I. Backlund, M.S., Director of Admissions. 914 758-7472.

**FINANCIAL AID. Available aid:** Pell grants, SEOG, state scholarships and grants, school scholarships and grants, academic merit scholarships, and aid for undergraduate foreign students. Perkins Loans (NDSL), PLUS, Stafford Loans (GSL), and SLS. Knight Tuition Plans. 10-Month Budgeted Payment Plan.
**Financial aid statistics:** 10% of aid is not need-based. In 1993-94, 97% of all undergraduate applicants received aid; 97% of freshman applicants. Average amounts of aid awarded freshmen: Scholarships and grants, $12,820; loans, $2,800.
**Supporting data/closing dates:** FAFSA/FAF/FFS: Priority filing date is March 15. School's own aid application: Priority filing date is March 15. Income tax forms: Accepted on rolling basis. Divorced/Separated Parents Statement: Accepted on rolling basis. Notification of awards begins April 1.
**Financial aid contact:** Gerald Kelly, J.C.D., Director of Financial Aid. 914 758-7526.

**STUDENT EMPLOYMENT.** College Work/Study Program. Institutional employment. 50% of full-time undergraduates work on campus during school year. Students may expect to earn an average of $1,000 during school year. Off-campus part-time employment opportunities rated "fair."

**COMPUTER FACILITIES.** 90 IBM/IBM-compatible and Macintosh/Apple microcomputers; 70 are networked. Students may access IBM minicomputer/mainframe systems, BITNET, Internet, CompuServe. Client/LAN operating systems include Apple/Macintosh, DOS, OS/2, UNIX/XENIX/AIX. Computer languages and software packages include BASIC, C, FORTRAN, Pascal, Turbo Pascal; numerous database, word processing, spreadsheet, graphics packages. Computer facilities are available to all students.
**Fees:** None.
**Hours:** 9 AM-2 AM.

**PROMINENT ALUMNI/AE.** Asher Edelman, financier; Donald Fagen, musician; Blythe Danner, actress; Ran Blake, musician; Anthony Hecht, poet; Larry Hagman and Chevy Chase, actors; Carl Davis, composer; William Sherman, Pulitzer Prize-winning journalist; Peter Stone, writer; Richard Pousette-Dart, painter; Jin Kinoshita, bio-chemist; Howard Koch and Richard Rovere, writers.

# Barnard College

**New York, NY 10027-6598** **212 854-5262**

**1993-94 Costs.** Tuition: $17,088. Room & board: $7,736. Fees, books, misc. academic expenses (school's estimate): $520.
**Enrollment.** 2,190 women (full-time). Freshman class: 2,496 applicants, 1,212 accepted, 531 enrolled.
**Test score averages/ranges.** Range of SAT scores of middle 50%: 550-640 verbal, 570-660 math. Range of ACT scores of middle 50%: 26-29 composite.
**Faculty.** 160 full-time; 104 part-time. 98% of faculty holds doctoral degree. Student/faculty ratio: 11 to 1.
**Selectivity rating.** Highly competitive.

**PROFILE.** Barnard, founded in 1889, is a private, liberal arts college for women affiliated with Columbia University. Its four-acre campus is located in midtown Manhattan.

**Accreditation:** MSACS.
**Religious orientation:** Barnard College is nonsectarian; no religious requirements.
**Library:** Collections totaling over 166,213 volumes, 724 periodical subscriptions, and 14,018 microform items.
**Special facilities/museums:** Professional theatre, infant-toddler center, greenhouse, academic computer center.
**Athletic facilities:** Aquatic center, track, cycling and weight rooms, saunas, racquet sports and tennis courts, gymnasiums.

**STUDENT BODY. Undergraduate profile:** 42% are state residents; 15% are transfers. 25% Asian-American, 4% Black, 6% Hispanic, 1% Native American, 60% White, 4% Other. Average age of undergraduates is 19.
**Freshman profile:** 6% of freshmen who took SAT scored 700 or over on verbal, 13% scored 700 or over on math; 50% scored 600 or over on verbal, 66% scored 600 or over on math; 94% scored 500 or over on verbal, 98% scored 500 or over on math; 100% scored 400 or over on verbal, 100% scored 400 or over on math. 98% of accepted applicants took SAT; 2% took ACT. 57% of freshmen come from public schools.
**Undergraduate achievement:** 95% of fall 1992 freshmen returned for fall 1993 term. 73% of entering class graduated. 36% of students who completed a degree program immediately went on to graduate study.
**Foreign students:** 80 students are from out of the country. Countries represented include Canada, England, France, Hong Kong, Israel, and Japan; 36 in all.

**PROGRAMS OF STUDY. Degrees:** B.A.
**Majors:** American Studies, Ancient Studies, Anthropology, Applied Mathematics, Architecture, Art History, Asian Studies, Astronomy, Biochemistry, Biological Sciences, Biopsychology, Chemistry, Classics, Computer Science, Dance, East Asian Studies, Economics, English, Environmental Science, European Studies, Foreign Area Studies, French, French Language/Literature, German, Greek, Greek/Latin, History, Italian, Latin, Latin America Area Studies, Mathematical Statistics, Mathematics, Medieval Studies, Middle Eastern Studies, Music, Pan-African Studies, Philosophy, Physics, Political Science, Psychology, Pure Mathematics, Religion, Russian, Russian Area Studies, Sociology, Spanish, Theatre, Urban Affairs, Western European Studies, Women's Studies.
**Distribution of degrees:** The majors with the highest enrollment are English, political science, and psychology; Italian and Russian have the lowest.
**Requirements:** General education requirement.
**Academic regulations:** Minimum 2.0 GPA must be maintained.
**Special:** Minors offered in all majors. Senior Scholar and Centennial Scholar Programs. Self-designed majors. Double majors. Dual degrees. Independent study. Accelerated

study. Pass/fail grading option. Internships. Graduate school at which undergraduates may take graduate-level courses. Preprofessional programs in law, medicine, veterinary science, and dentistry. 3-2 B.A./M.A. and B.A./M.Public Admin. programs with Columbia U School of International Affairs. 3-2 engineering program and 3-3 law program with Columbia U. 3-2 B.A./M.A. music program with Juilliard Sch. Double degree program in Judaic studies with Jewish Theological Seminary. Member of Consortium for Excellence in Teacher Education (CETE). Exchange program with Manhattan Sch of Music. Teacher certification in elementary and secondary education. Certification in specific subject areas. Exchange programs abroad in England (Cambridge U, London Sch of Economics, Oxford U), France (the Sorbonne), Italy (Intercollegiate Center for Classical Studies, Rome), and Japan (Kyoto U). Study abroad also in other countries.
**Honors:** Phi Beta Kappa. Honors program. Honor societies.
**Academic Assistance:** Nonremedial tutoring.

**STUDENT LIFE. Housing:** Students may live on or off campus. Coed and women's dorms. Wheelchair-accessible housing. 90% of students live in college housing.
**Social atmosphere:** As reported by the student newspaper, "Because we are in Manhattan, we have endless opportunities for social and cultural activities. Students generally take advantage of the city's abundance. There are no specific groups which have any overpowering influence. There is a well-kept balance of influence between groups." Students meet on the Columbia steps and in the McIntosh Student Center. Off campus, students frequent the Village, downtown clubs, and local restaurants and bars.
**Services and counseling/handicapped student services:** Placement services. Health service. Women's center. Office for disability services. Counseling services for minority students. Personal and psychological counseling. Career and academic guidance services. Physically disabled student services. Learning disabled services. Notetaking services. Tape recorders. Tutors. Reader services for the blind.
**Campus organizations:** Undergraduate student government. Student newspaper (Barnard Bulletin, published once/week). Literary magazine. Yearbook. Radio station. Chorus, cultural, literary, orchestra, Gilbert and Sullivan Society, dance and drama groups, debating, community service groups, academic, departmental, political, and professional groups, 80 organizations in all.
**Religious organizations:** Numerous religious groups.
**Minority/foreign student organizations:** Numerous minority organizations. Foreign student groups.

**ATHLETICS. Physical education requirements:** Two semesters of physical education required.
**Intercollegiate competition:** 30% of students participate. Archery (W), basketball (W), crew (W), cross-country (W), diving (W), fencing (W), soccer (W), swimming (W), tennis (W), track and field (indoor) (W), track and field (outdoor) (W), volleyball (W). Member of NCAA Division I.
**Intramural and club sports:** 50% of students participate. Women's club cheerleading, cycling, lacrosse, martial arts, rugby, sailing, softball, ultimate frisbee.

**ADMISSIONS. Academic basis for candidate selection** (in order of priority): Secondary school record, standardized test scores, school's recommendation, essay, class rank.
**Nonacademic basis for candidate selection:** Extracurricular participation is important. Character and personality, particular talent or ability, geographical distribution, and alumni/ae relationship are considered.
**Requirements:** Graduation from secondary school is recommended; GED is accepted. 16 units and the following program of study are recommended: 4 units of English, 3 units of math, 3 units of science, 2 units of foreign language, 1 unit of social studies, 1 unit of history, 1 unit of electives. Rank in top tenth of secondary school class or minimum 3.5 GPA recommended. Audition required of applicants to exchange program with the Juilliard Sch or Manhattan Sch of Music. HEOP for applicants not normally admissible. SAT or ACT is required. ACH required. Campus visit and interview recommended. Off-campus interviews available with admissions and alumni representatives.
**Procedure:** Take SAT or ACT by January of 12th year. Take ACH by January of 12th year. Visit college for interview by January of 12th year. Application deadline is January 15. Notification of admission by April 1. Reply is required by May 1. $200 nonrefundable tuition deposit. $200 nonrefundable room deposit. Freshmen accepted for terms other than fall.
**Special programs:** Admission may be deferred one year. Credit and/or placement may be granted through CEEB Advanced Placement exams for scores of 4 or higher. Placement may be granted through challenge exams. Early decision program. In fall 1993, 144 applied for early decision and 85 were accepted. Deadline for applying for early decision is November 15 (Plan I) and January 2 (Plan II). Early entrance/early admission program.
**Transfer students:** Transfer students accepted for terms other than fall. In fall 1993, 15% of all new students were transfers into all classes. 289 transfer applications were received, 150 were accepted. Application deadline is March 1, April 1, May 1 for fall; December 15 for spring. Minimum 3.5 GPA recommended. Lowest course grade accepted is "C." Maximum number of transferable credits is 60 semester hours. At least 60 semester hours must be completed at the college to receive degree.
**Admissions contact:** Doris Davis, M.A., Director of Admissions. 212 854-2014, FAX: 212 854-6220.

**FINANCIAL AID. Available aid:** Pell grants, SEOG, state scholarships and grants, school scholarships and grants, and private scholarships and grants. Perkins Loans (NDSL), PLUS, Stafford Loans (GSL), state loans, school loans, and private loans. Tuition Plan Inc., Education Plan Inc., Knight Tuition Plans, AMS, Tuition Management Systems, and deferred payment plan.
**Financial aid statistics:** In 1993-94, 60% of all undergraduate applicants received aid; 60% of freshman applicants. Average amounts of aid awarded freshmen: Scholarships and grants, $14,802; loans, $2,600.
**Supporting data/closing dates:** FAFSA/FAF: Deadline is February 1. School's own aid application: Deadline is February 1. Income tax forms: Deadline is February 1. Notification of awards begins April 4.
**Financial aid contact:** Suzanne Clair Guard, Director of Financial Aid. 212 854-2154.

**STUDENT EMPLOYMENT.** College Work/Study Program. Institutional employment. 25% of full-time undergraduates work on campus during school year. Students may expect to earn an average of $1,200 during school year. Off-campus part-time employment opportunities rated "excellent."

**COMPUTER FACILITIES.** 120 IBM/IBM-compatible and Macintosh/Apple microcomputers; all are networked. Students may access Digital, IBM minicomputer/mainframe systems, BITNET, Internet. Residence halls may be equipped with stand-alone microcomputers, networked microcomputers. Client/LAN operating systems include Apple/Macintosh, DOS, OS/2, UNIX/XENIX/AIX, LocalTalk/AppleTalk, Novell. Computer languages and software packages include dBASE IV, Lotus 1-2-3, MacWrite, SPSS, Turbo Pascal, Word, WordPerfect; 15 in all. Computer facilities are available to all students.
**Fees:** None.
**Hours:** 24 hours.

**GRADUATE CAREER DATA.** Graduate school percentages: 7% enter law school. 6% enter medical school. 1% enter dental school. 1% enter graduate business programs. 6% enter graduate arts and sciences programs. Highest graduate school enrollments: Columbia U, Harvard U, Yale U. 25% of graduates choose careers in business and industry.

**PROMINENT ALUMNI/AE.** Erica Jong, author; Twyla Tharp, dancer, choreographer; Margaret Mead, anthropologist; Jeane Kirkpatrick, former U.N. ambassador; Anna Quindlen, author and columnist, *New York Times*.

# Boricua College

**New York, NY 10032 — 212 694-1000**

**1993-94 Costs.** Tuition: $5,700. Housing: None. Fees, books, misc. academic expenses (school's estimate): $1,000.
**Enrollment.** Undergraduates: 246 men, 896 women (full-time). Freshman class: 389 applicants, 345 accepted, 260 enrolled.
**Test score averages/ranges.** N/A.
**Faculty.** 48 full-time; 46 part-time. 31% of faculty holds doctoral degree. Student/faculty ratio: 20 to 1.
**Selectivity rating.** N/A.

**PROFILE.** Boricua, founded in 1974, is a private, liberal arts college with an English/Spanish bilingual and bicultural curriculum. Its campus is located in Manhattan.

**Accreditation:** MSACS.
**Religious orientation:** Boricua College is nonsectarian; no religious requirements.
**Library:** Collections totaling over 128,727 volumes and 227 periodical subscriptions.

**STUDENT BODY. Undergraduate profile:** 1% Asian-American, 5% Black, 93% Hispanic, 1% White. Average age of undergraduates is 28.

**PROGRAMS OF STUDY. Degrees:** B.A., B.S.
**Majors:** Business Administration, Business Law, Business Planning, Curriculum Planning, Elementary Education, Human Services, Management, Organizational Development, Teaching Language Skills.
**Requirements:** General education requirement.
**Special:** College offers fully bilingual program and serves educational needs of Puerto Rican and other Spanish-speaking people. Curriculum is process-oriented and student-centered; comprises three applied studies courses (individualized instruction, colloquium, experiential), one theoretical course, and one cultural course per semester. Hispanic Caseworker Training Program. Associate's degrees offered. Internships. Graduate school at which undergraduates may take graduate-level courses. Teacher certification in elementary education.

**STUDENT LIFE. Housing:** Commuter campus; no student housing.
**Services and counseling/handicapped student services:** Academic guidance services. Learning disabled services.
**Campus organizations:** Undergraduate student government. Chorus.

**ADMISSIONS. Academic basis for candidate selection** (in order of priority): Essay, secondary school record, school's recommendation.
**Nonacademic basis for candidate selection:** Character and personality are important. Extracurricular participation, particular talent or ability, and alumni/ae relationship are considered.
**Requirements:** Graduation from secondary school is required; GED is accepted. No specific distribution of secondary school units required. HEOP for applicants not normally admissible. College Prep Program for applicants not normally admissible. Campus visit recommended. No off-campus interviews.
**Procedure:** Notification of admission by September 7. Freshmen accepted for terms other than fall.
**Special programs:** Admission may be deferred one year.
**Transfer students:** Transfer students accepted for terms other than fall. In fall 1992, 75 transfer applications were received, 60 were accepted. Application deadline is September 6 for fall; January 7 for spring. Lowest course grade accepted is "C."
**Admissions contact:** Miriam Santiago Pagan, M.S.Ed., Director of Admissions. 212 694-1000, extensions 530-532.

**FINANCIAL AID. Available aid:** Pell grants, SEOG, state grants, and private grants. PLUS, Stafford Loans (GSL), and SLS. Deferred payment plan.
**Financial aid statistics:** In 1992-93, 90% of all undergraduate applicants received aid; 90% of freshman applicants. Average amounts of aid awarded freshmen: Loans, $2,300.
**Supporting data/closing dates:** FAFSA/FAF/FFS: Priority filing date is May 4; deadline is June 30. Income tax forms: Priority filing date is April 15; deadline is June 30. Notification of awards on rolling basis.
**Financial aid contact:** Abraham Cruz, Director of Financial Aid. 212 694-1000, extensions 213-216.

**STUDENT EMPLOYMENT.** College Work/Study Program. Freshmen are discouraged from working during their first term.

# Canisius College

**Buffalo, NY 14208** **716 883-7000**

**1993-94 Costs.** Tuition: $9,950. Room & board: $5,240. Fees, books, misc. academic expenses (school's estimate): $720.
**Enrollment.** Undergraduates: 1,685 men, 1,363 women (full-time). Freshman class: 2,853 applicants, 1,634 accepted, 515 enrolled. Graduate enrollment: 575 men, 751 women.
**Test score averages/ranges.** Average SAT scores: 479 verbal, 536 math. Range of SAT scores of middle 50%: 420-530 verbal, 480-580 math. Average ACT scores: 24 composite. Range of ACT scores of middle 50%: 20-24 composite.
**Faculty.** 198 full-time; 141 part-time. 91% of faculty holds doctoral degree. Student/faculty ratio: 17 to 1.
**Selectivity rating.** More competitive.

**PROFILE.** Canisius, founded in 1870, is a church-affiliated, liberal arts college. Programs are offered through the College of Arts and Sciences, the Continuing Studies and Graduate Divisions, and the School of Business Administration. Its 25-acre campus is located in downtown Buffalo.

**Accreditation:** MSACS. Professionally accredited by the American Assembly of Collegiate Schools of Business, the National Council for Accreditation of Teacher Education.
**Religious orientation:** Canisius College is affiliated with the Roman Catholic Church (Society of Jesus); three semesters of religion/theology required.
**Library:** Collections totaling over 272,570 volumes, 1,161 periodical subscriptions, and 489,887 microform items.
**Special facilities/museums:** TV studio, language lab, electron microscope, seismograph, molecular biology and physics labs.
**Athletic facilities:** Athletic center.

**STUDENT BODY. Undergraduate profile:** 92% are state residents; 18% are transfers. 1% Asian-American, 5% Black, 2% Hispanic, 90% White, 2% Other. Average age of undergraduates is 21.
**Freshman profile:** 5% of freshmen who took SAT scored 700 or over on verbal, 3% scored 700 or over on math; 13% scored 600 or over on verbal, 20% scored 600 or over on math; 41% scored 500 or over on verbal, 69% scored 500 or over on math; 94% scored 400 or over on verbal, 98% scored 400 or over on math; 100% scored 300 or over on math. 97% of accepted applicants took SAT; 31% took ACT. 70% of freshmen come from public schools.
**Undergraduate achievement:** 94% of fall 1991 freshmen returned for fall 1992 term. 47% of entering class graduated. 31% of students who completed a degree program went on to graduate study within one year.
**Foreign students:** 46 students are from out of the country. Countries represented include Canada, China, France, India, Jordan, and Taiwan; 33 in all.

**PROGRAMS OF STUDY. Degrees:** B.A., B.S.
**Majors:** Accounting, Art History, Biochemistry, Biology, Business Education, Chemistry, Communications, Computer Science, Economics, Education, Elementary/Early/Secondary Education, English, Finance, French, German, History, International Relations, Management, Management Information, Marketing, Mathematics, Medical Technology, Philosophy, Physical Education, Physics, Political Science, Psychology, Religious Studies, Sociology/Anthropology, Spanish, Urban Studies.
**Distribution of degrees:** The majors with the highest enrollment are management, English, and communications; medical technology, philosophy, and religious studies have the lowest.
**Requirements:** General education requirement.
**Academic regulations:** Freshmen must maintain minimum 1.75 GPA; sophomores, juniors, seniors, 2.0 GPA.
**Special:** Students enrolled in the College of Arts and Sciences may take courses in School of Business. Minors offered in some majors and in gerontology and music. Courses offered in Greek, Latin, and Russian. Certificate programs offered in athletic training, international business, and women's studies. Associate's degrees offered. Double majors. Dual degrees. Independent study. Pass/fail grading option. Internships. Graduate school at which undergraduates may take graduate-level courses. Preprofessional programs in law, medicine, veterinary science, pharmacy, dentistry, and optometry. Bachelor's/M.B.A., bachelor's/M.B.A. in Prof.Acct., and M.Public Admin. programs. Environmental science and forestry program with SUNY Coll of Environmental Science and Forestry. Member of Western New York Consortium of Higher Education. Washington Semester. Exchange program with Fashion Institute of Technology. Teacher certification in elementary and secondary education. Certification in specific subject areas. Exchange programs abroad in Italy (Loyola U of Chicago in Rome) and Spain (U do Oviedo). ROTC.
**Honors:** Honors program. Honor societies.
**Academic Assistance:** Remedial writing, math, and study skills. Nonremedial tutoring.

**STUDENT LIFE. Housing:** All students must live on campus unless living within a 40-mile radius. Coed dorms. School-owned/operated apartments. 32% of students live in college housing.
**Social atmosphere:** The student newspaper reports, "Except for a few popular events, on-campus activities are not very well attended. Because its a city campus, most students meet off campus in pubs and bars." Students like to hang out on campus at the Rathskellar and head off campus to the Locker Room, the Brick Bar, and Mister Goodbar's. An influential group is the Campus Programming Board which sponsors speakers, mixers, parties, and bands. The Spring Quad party, the 100 Daze party, and Oktoberfest are among the year's favorite events.
**Services and counseling/handicapped student services:** Placement services. Health service. Counseling services for minority, veteran, and older students. Personal and psychological counseling. Career and academic guidance services. Religious counseling. Physically disabled student services. Notetaking services. Tutors. Reader services for the blind.
**Campus organizations:** Undergraduate student government. Student newspaper (Griffin, published once/week). Literary magazine. Yearbook. Radio station. Chorale, glee club, jazz ensemble, orchestra, Little Theatre, ski club, television studio, special-interest groups, 90 organizations in all. Two fraternities, all with chapter houses; two sororities, no chapter houses. 4% of men join a fraternity. 4% of women join a sorority.
**Religious organizations:** Reverence for Life, Pax Christi.
**Minority/foreign student organizations:** Afro-American Society. Global Horizons, International Affairs Society, Asian, French, German, Italian, Polish, and Spanish clubs.

**ATHLETICS. Physical education requirements:** Four units of physical education required.
**Intercollegiate competition:** 15% of students participate. Baseball (M), basketball (M,W), crew (M,W), cross-country (M,W), football (M), golf (M), ice hockey (M), lacrosse (M), riflery (M,W), soccer (M,W), softball (W), swimming (M,W), tennis (M,W), track (indoor) (M,W), track (outdoor) (M,W), track and field (indoor) (M,W), track and field (outdoor) (M,W), volleyball (W). Member of ECAC, Metro Atlantic Athletic Conference, NCAA Division I.
**Intramural and club sports:** 10% of students participate. Intramural basketball, floor hockey, football, softball, tennis, volleyball. Men's club cheerleading, rugby. Women's club cheerleading, lacrosse.

**ADMISSIONS. Academic basis for candidate selection** (in order of priority): Secondary school record, standardized test scores, class rank, school's recommendation, essay.
**Nonacademic basis for candidate selection:** Extracurricular participation, particular talent or ability, and alumni/ae relationship are considered.
**Requirements:** Graduation from secondary school is required; GED is accepted. 16 units and the following program of study are required: 4 units of English, 3 units of math, 1 unit of science, 2 units of foreign language, 2 units of social studies, 4 units of academic electives. Minimum combined SAT score of 900, rank in top half of secondary school class, and minimum 80 average recommended. HEOP for applicants not normally admissible. SAT is required; ACT may be substituted. Campus visit and interview recommended. Off-campus interviews available with admissions and alumni representatives.
**Procedure:** Take SAT or ACT by June of 12th year. Suggest filing application by fall; no deadline. Notification of admission on rolling basis. Reply is required by May 1. $100 tuition deposit, refundable until May 1. $100 room deposit, refundable until June 15. Freshmen accepted for terms other than fall.
**Special programs:** Admission may be deferred one year. Credit and/or placement may be granted through CEEB Advanced Placement exams for scores of 4 or higher. Credit and/or placement may be granted through CLEP subject exams. Credit and placement may be granted through Regents College, ACT PEP, DANTES, and challenge exams and military and life experience. Early entrance/early admission program.
**Transfer students:** Transfer students accepted for terms other than fall. In fall 1992, 18% of all new students were transfers into all classes. 375 transfer applications were received, 264 were accepted. Application deadline is rolling for fall; rolling for spring. Minimum 2.0 GPA required. Lowest course grade accepted is "C." Maximum number of transferable credits is 60 semester hours from a two-year school and 90 semester hours from a four-year school. At least 30 semester hours must be completed at the college to receive degree.
**Admissions contact:** Penelope Lips, M.Ed., Director of Admissions. 716 888-2200, 800 843-1517.

**FINANCIAL AID. Available aid:** Pell grants, SEOG, state scholarships and grants, school scholarships and grants, private scholarships and grants, ROTC scholarships, academic merit scholarships, and athletic scholarships. Perkins Loans (NDSL), PLUS, Stafford Loans (GSL), school loans, private loans, and SLS. Tuition Plan Inc., deferred payment plan, and guaranteed tuition. Monthly payment plan.
**Financial aid statistics:** 17% of aid is not need-based. In 1992-93, 83% of all undergraduate applicants received aid; 92% of freshman applicants. Average amounts of aid awarded freshmen: Scholarships and grants, $6,128; loans, $2,796.
**Supporting data/closing dates:** FAFSA/FAF/FFS: Priority filing date is February 1. State aid form: Priority filing date is May 1. Income tax forms: Priority filing date is April 15. Notification of awards begins April.
**Financial aid contact:** Curtis Gaume, M.Ed., Director of Financial Aid. 716 888-2300, 800 541-6348.

**STUDENT EMPLOYMENT.** College Work/Study Program. Institutional employment. 26% of full-time undergraduates work on campus during school year. Students may expect to earn an average of $1,459 during school year. Off-campus part-time employment opportunities rated "good."

**COMPUTER FACILITIES.** 129 IBM/IBM-compatible and Macintosh/Apple microcomputers; all are networked. Students may access Digital minicomputer/mainframe systems, BITNET, Internet. Client/LAN operating systems include Apple/Macintosh. Computer languages and software packages include COBOL, Excel, FORTRAN, IFPS, ImSL, INGRES, Lotus 1-2-3, Microsoft Word, Modula 2, PageMaker, Pascal, SAS, SPSS-X. Computer facilities are available to all students.
**Fees:** $40 computer fee per course.
**Hours:** 8 AM-11:30 PM in library lab.

**GRADUATE CAREER DATA.** Graduate school percentages: 4% enter law school. 3% enter medical school. 1% enter dental school. 6% enter graduate business programs. 6% enter graduate arts and sciences programs. 1% enter theological school/seminary. Highest graduate school enrollments: Canisius Coll, Marquette U, Syracuse U, SUNY Albany, SUNY Buffalo, SUNY Coll at Buffalo, U of Pittsburgh, U of Rochester. 65% of graduates choose careers in business and industry. Companies and businesses that hire graduates: Price Waterhouse, M & T Bank, Rich Products, Deloitte & Touche, Marine Midland, Ernst & Young.

**PROMINENT ALUMNI/AE.** Elaine Sciolino, chief diplomatic correspondent, *New York Times;* William D. Hassett, Jr., chairperson and CEO, Boston Garden; Dr. Donald Pinkel, chief of pediatric leukemia, Anderson Hospital and Tumor Institute; Henry J. Nowak, John J. LaFalce, and L. William Paxon, U.S. congressmen, New York.

# Cazenovia College

**Cazenovia, NY 13035** 315 655-9446

**1994-95 Costs.** Tuition: $9,160. Room & board: $4,932. Fees, books, misc. academic expenses (school's estimate): $887.
**Enrollment.** Undergraduates: 324 men, 668 women (full-time). Freshman class: 3,847 applicants, 3,433 accepted, 527 enrolled.
**Test score averages/ranges.** Average SAT scores: 379 verbal, 402 math. Average ACT scores: 18 composite.
**Faculty.** 45 full-time; 72 part-time. 29% of faculty holds doctoral degree. Student/faculty ratio: 16 to 1.
**Selectivity rating.** Less competitive.

**PROFILE.** Cazenovia is a private, multipurpose college. Founded in 1824, it adopted coeducation in 1983. Its 25-acre campus is located in Cazenovia, 20 miles from Syracuse.

**Accreditation:** MSACS.
**Religious orientation:** Cazenovia College is nonsectarian; no religious requirements.
**Library:** Collections totaling over 63,536 volumes, 400 periodical subscriptions, and 7,986 microform items.
**Special facilities/museums:** Equine center.
**Athletic facilities:** Gymnasiums, Olympic-sized swimming pool, weight and training rooms, racquetball and tennis courts.

**STUDENT BODY. Undergraduate profile:** 81% are state residents. 1% Asian-American, 14% Black, 5% Hispanic, 1% Native American, 79% White. Average age of undergraduates is 20.
**Freshman profile:** 82% of accepted applicants took SAT; 18% took ACT. 91% of freshmen come from public schools.
**Undergraduate achievement:** 67% of fall 1992 freshmen returned for fall 1993 term. 10% of entering class graduated. 73% of students who completed a degree program immediately went on to graduate study.
**Foreign students:** Eight students are from out of the country. Countries represented include Canada, Japan, and Panama; five in all.

**PROGRAMS OF STUDY. Degrees:** B.F.A., B.Prof.Studies, B.S.
**Majors:** Advertising/Graphic Design, Business Management, Commercial Illustration, Fine Arts, Interior Design, Literature/Humanities, Retail Management, Science/Technology, Social Institutions.
**Academic regulations:** Freshmen must maintain minimum 1.8 GPA; sophomores, juniors, seniors, 2.0 GPA.
**Special:** Associate's degrees offered. Self-designed majors. Internships. Study abroad in England, Puerto Rico, and Switzerland.
**Honors:** Honors program. Honor societies.
**Academic Assistance:** Remedial reading, writing, math, and study skills. Nonremedial tutoring.

**ADMISSIONS. Academic basis for candidate selection** (in order of priority): Secondary school record, class rank, school's recommendation, standardized test scores.
**Requirements:** Graduation from secondary school is required; GED is accepted. No specific distribution of secondary school units required. Portfolio required of art program applicants. HEOP for applicants not normally admissible. Conditional admission possible for applicants not meeting standard requirements. SAT or ACT is recommended. Campus visit and interview recommended. No off-campus interviews.
**Procedure:** Take SAT or ACT by June 30 of 12th year. Notification of admission on rolling basis. No set date by which applicants must accept offer. $285 tuition deposit, refundable partially until April 30. Freshmen accepted for terms other than fall.
**Special programs:** Admission may be deferred three years. Credit and/or placement may be granted through CEEB Advanced Placement exams for scores of 3 or higher. Credit may be granted through CLEP general exams. Credit may be granted through ACT PEP and challenge exams and military and life experience.
**Transfer students:** Transfer students accepted for terms other than fall. Application deadline is September 1 for fall; January 1 for spring. Minimum 2.0 GPA required. Lowest course grade accepted is "C." Maximum of 60 semester hours may be transferred. At least 60 semester hours must be completed at the college to receive degree.
**Admissions contact:** James T. Parker, Ph.D., Director of Admissions. 800 654-3210.

**FINANCIAL AID. Available aid:** Pell grants, SEOG, state scholarships and grants, school scholarships and grants, private scholarships and grants, academic merit scholarships, and athletic scholarships. Perkins Loans (NDSL), PLUS, Stafford Loans (GSL), school loans, and SLS. Deferred payment plan.
**Financial aid statistics:** In 1993-94, 89% of all undergraduate applicants received aid; 89% of freshman applicants. Average amounts of aid awarded freshmen: Scholarships and grants, $1,832; loans, $3,461.
**Supporting data/closing dates:** FAFSA/FAF: Accepted on rolling basis. Income tax forms: Accepted on rolling basis. Notification of awards on rolling basis.
**Financial aid contact:** Mary C. David, M.S., Director of Financial Aid. 800 654-3210.

# City University of New York, Baruch College

**New York, NY 10010** 212 447-3000

**1993-94 Costs.** Tuition: $2,450 (state residents), $5,050 (out-of-state). Housing: None. Fees, books, misc. academic expenses (school's estimate): $750.
**Enrollment.** Undergraduates: 3,482 men, 4,910 women (full-time). Freshman class: 5,209 applicants, 3,027 accepted, 1,423 enrolled. Graduate enrollment: 1,458 men, 1,158 women.
**Test score averages/ranges.** N/A.
**Faculty.** 440 full-time; 380 part-time. 87% of faculty holds doctoral degree. Student/faculty ratio: 33 to 1.
**Selectivity rating.** N/A.

**PROFILE.** Baruch, founded in 1961, is a public college. Programs are offered through the Schools of Business and Public Administration, Education and Educational Services, and Liberal Arts and Sciences. Its campus is located in the center of New York's central business district.

**Accreditation:** MSACS. Professionally accredited by the American Assembly of Collegiate Schools of Business.
**Religious orientation:** City University of New York, Baruch College is nonsectarian; no religious requirements.
**Library:** Collections totaling over 412,000 volumes, 4,000 periodical subscriptions, and 1,700,000 microform items.
**Special facilities/museums:** Art gallery.
**Athletic facilities:** Gymnasium, swimming pool, weight room, dance/karate studio.

**STUDENT BODY. Undergraduate profile:** 99% are state residents. 23% Asian/Pacific Islander, 21% Black, 12% Hispanic, 5% Puerto Rican, 21% White, 18% Other. Average age of undergraduates is 22.
**Freshman profile:** 90% of freshmen come from public schools.
**Foreign students:** 93 students are from out of the country. Countries represented include China, Hong Kong, India, Japan, Taiwan, and Trinidad; 90 in all.

**PROGRAMS OF STUDY. Degrees:** B.A., B.Bus.Admin., B.S.Ed.
**Majors:** Accounting, Actuarial Science, Advertising, Art Administration, Business Communications, Business Education, Computer Information Systems Analysis, Creative Writing, Early Childhood/Elementary Education, Economics, Education, English, Finance, Hebrew, History, Industrial Psychology, International Marketing, Journalism, Literature, Management, Management of Musical Enterprises, Marketing, Marketing/Consumer Research, Marketing Management, Mathematics, Music, Natural Sciences, Office Administration/Technology, Operations Research, Philosophy, Political Science, Psychology, Public Administration, Quantitative Methods in Marketing, Religion/Culture, Retailing/Sales, Sociology, Spanish, Special Education, Statistical Analysis, Statistics.
**Distribution of degrees:** The majors with the highest enrollment are accounting and finance; religion/culture, operations research, and statistics have the lowest.
**Requirements:** General education requirement.
**Academic regulations:** Minimum 2.0 GPA must be maintained.
**Special:** Minor or its equivalent is required for graduation. Minors offered in some majors and in art, black and Hispanic studies, computer information systems, law, modern languages/comparative literature, and speech. Self-designed majors. Independent study. Pass/fail grading option. Internships. Albany semester. Teacher certification in early childhood, elementary, and special education. Exchange programs abroad in England (Middlesex Polytech), France (U of Lyon, U of Paris), Germany (Mannheim U), Israel (Tel Aviv U), and Mexico (U Iberoamericana).
**Honors:** Honors program. Honor societies.
**Academic Assistance:** Remedial reading, writing, math, and study skills. Nonremedial tutoring.

**STUDENT LIFE. Housing:** Commuter campus; no student housing.
**Social atmosphere:** The student newspaper reports that there is "very little social and cultural life at Baruch because it is a commuter school. Most people work outside school, so they don't have time for these things." Active groups on campus include the Carribean clubs, the American Marketing Association, and the Accounting Society. Popular social events are Hispanic Week, Italian Week, Black History Week, Caribbean Week, the Street Fair, and the Club Fair. On campus, students gather at the student center, various cafeterias, and the Live Bait Club.
**Services and counseling/handicapped student services:** Placement services. Health service. Day care. Counseling services for older students. Birth control, personal, and psychological counseling. Career and academic guidance services. Physically disabled student services. Learning disabled services. Notetaking services. Tape recorders. Tutors. Reader services for the blind.
**Campus organizations:** Undergraduate student government. Student newspapers (Ticker; Reporter). Literary magazine. Yearbook. Radio station. Chorus, band, ensemble, orchestra, athletic, political, professional, and social groups, 95 organizations in all.
**Religious organizations:** Buddhist, Christian, Jewish, and Muslim student organizations.
**Minority/foreign student organizations:** International Student Organization and other foreign student groups.

**ATHLETICS. Physical education requirements:** One semester of physical education required in some majors.
**Intercollegiate competition:** 10% of students participate. Baseball (M), basketball (M,W), cheerleading (W), fencing (M,W), soccer (M), tennis (M,W), volleyball (M,W). Member of CUNY Athletic Conference, ECAC, NCAA Division III.

**Intramural and club sports:** 15% of students participate. Intramural badminton, basketball, cross-country, soccer, volleyball, weight lifting. Men's club martial arts. Women's club martial arts.

**ADMISSIONS. Academic basis for candidate selection** (in order of priority): Secondary school record, class rank, standardized test scores.

**Requirements:** Graduation from secondary school is required; GED is accepted. No specific distribution of secondary school units required. Minimum combined SAT score of 900, rank in the top two-thirds of secondary school class, and minimum 80% average required. SEEK (Search for Education, Elevation, and Knowledge) program for applicants not normally admissible. SAT is recommended; ACT may be substituted. Campus visit recommended. No off-campus interviews.

**Procedure:** Suggest filing application by January 16; no deadline. Notification of admission on rolling basis. Freshmen accepted for terms other than fall.

**Special programs:** Admission may be deferred one year. Credit and/or placement may be granted through CEEB Advanced Placement exams for scores of 3 or higher. Credit may be granted through CLEP general and subject exams, Regents College, ACT PEP, DANTES, and challenge exams and military experience.

**Transfer students:** Transfer students accepted for terms other than fall. In fall 1992, 2,930 transfer applications were received, 2,113 were accepted. Application deadline is March 15 for fall; November 1 for spring. Lowest course grade accepted is "C." Maximum number of transferable credits is 70 semester hours from a two-year school and 96 semester hours from a four-year school. At least 32 semester hours must be completed at the college to receive degree.

**Admissions contact:** Ellen Washington, Director of Admissions. 212 447-3750.

**FINANCIAL AID. Available aid:** Pell grants, SEOG, state scholarships and grants, school scholarships and grants, private scholarships and grants, academic merit scholarships, and aid for undergraduate foreign students. Perkins Loans (NDSL), PLUS, Stafford Loans (GSL), private loans, and SLS.

**Financial aid statistics:** 28% of aid is not need-based. In 1992-93, 59% of all undergraduate applicants received aid; 66% of freshman applicants. Average amounts of aid awarded freshmen: Scholarships and grants, $2,750; loans, $1,700.

**Supporting data/closing dates:** FAFSA/FAF: Priority filing date is April 15. State aid form: Accepted on rolling basis. Notification of awards on rolling basis.

**Financial aid contact:** James F. Murphy, M.A., Director of Financial Aid. 212 447-3775.

**STUDENT EMPLOYMENT.** College Work/Study Program. Institutional employment. 6% of full-time undergraduates work on campus during school year. Students may expect to earn an average of $1,600 during school year. Freshmen are discouraged from working during their first term. Off-campus part-time employment opportunities rated "fair."

**COMPUTER FACILITIES.** 265 IBM/IBM-compatible and Macintosh/Apple microcomputers; 140 are networked. Students may access IBM, SUN minicomputer/mainframe systems, BITNET, Internet. Computer languages and software packages include C++, COBOL, dBASE, FORTRAN, Lotus, Pascal, SPSS, Symphony, WordPerfect, WordStar; mathematical and statistical packages. Computer facilities are available to all students.

**Fees:** $25 computer fee per semester; included in tuition/fees.

# City University of New York, Brooklyn College

**Brooklyn, NY 11210** **718 951-5000**

**1993-94 Costs.** Tuition: $2,450 (state residents), $5,050 (out-of-state). Housing: None. Fees, books, misc. academic expenses (school's estimate): $655.

**Enrollment.** Undergraduates: 3,529 men, 4,490 women (full-time). Freshman class: 3,914 applicants, 2,505 accepted, 1,428 enrolled. Graduate enrollment: 5,597.

**Test score averages/ranges.** N/A.

**Faculty.** 594 full-time; 256 part-time. Student/faculty ratio: 16 to 1.

**Selectivity rating.** N/A.

**PROFILE.** Brooklyn College, founded in 1930, is a public, liberal arts institution. Programs are offered through the College of Liberal Arts, the School of General Studies, and the Division of Graduate Studies. Its 26-acre campus is located in Brooklyn's Flatbush section.

**Accreditation:** MSACS. Professionally accredited by the National Council for Accreditation of Teacher Education.

**Religious orientation:** City University of New York, Brooklyn College is nonsectarian; no religious requirements.

**Library:** Collections totaling over 957,130 volumes, and 3,833 periodical subscriptions.

**Special facilities/museums:** Art museum, language lab, TV studios, speech clinic, research centers and institutes, particle accelerator.

**Athletic facilities:** Gymnasiums, swimming pools, basketball, racquetball, squash, tennis, and volleyball courts, track, athletic fields, fencing, weight, and wrestling rooms.

**STUDENT BODY. Undergraduate profile:** 98% are state residents. 9% Asian-American, 23% Black, 10% Hispanic, 1% Native American, 57% White. Average age of undergraduates is 20.

**Freshman profile:** 61% of freshmen come from public schools.

**Foreign students:** 482 students are from out of the country. Countries represented include Grenada, Hong Kong, Jamaica, St. Vincent, and Trinidad; 50 in all.

**PROGRAMS OF STUDY. Degrees:** B.A., B.F.A., B.S.

**Majors:** Accounting, Africana Studies, American Studies, Anthropology, Archaeology, Area Studies, Art, Art History, Biology, Broadcast Journalism, Business/Management/Finance, Caribbean Studies, Chemistry, Classics, Comparative Literature, Computational Mathematics, Computer/Information Science/Economics, Computer/Information Sciences, Computers/Programming, Early Childhood Education, Earth Science Teacher, Economics, Education, Education of the Speech/Hearing Handicapped, Elementary Education, English, Film, French, Geology, German, Greek, Health/Nutrition Sciences, Health Sciences, Hebrew, History, Home Economics, Interdepartmental Major in Science, Italian, Journalism, Judaic Studies, Latin, Linguistics, Mathematics, Music, Music Composition, Music Performance, Philosophy, Physical Education, Physics, Political Science, Psychology, Puerto Rican Studies, Religious Studies, Russian, Social Studies Teacher, Sociology, Spanish, Special Education, Speech, Speech Pathology/Audiology, Speech Teacher, Television/Radio, Theatre, Urban Administration/Computer/Information Science, Urban Studies, Women's Studies.

**Distribution of degrees:** The majors with the highest enrollment are accounting, business/management/finance, and psychology; Puerto Rican studies, physics, and classics have the lowest.

**Requirements:** General education requirement.

**Academic regulations:** Freshmen must maintain minimum 1.5 GPA; sophomores, juniors, seniors, 2.0 GPA.

**Special:** Double majors. Dual degrees. Independent study. Accelerated study. Pass/fail grading option. Internships. Graduate school at which undergraduates may take graduate-level courses. Preprofessional programs in law, medicine, and engineering. 2-2 engineering programs with CUNY City Coll and Polytech U. 4-1/2-year B.A./M.A. urban administration/computer and information science program. 4-1/2-year B.S./M.P.S. computer and information science/economics program. Four-year B.A./M.A. biology, chemistry, physics, and psychology programs. Eight-year B.A./M.D. honors program with SUNY Health Science Center at Brooklyn. Washington Semester. Teacher certification in early childhood, elementary, secondary, special education, and bilingual/bicultural education. Study abroad in the Caribbean, England, France, Ireland, Israel, Italy, Japan, and Spain.

**Honors:** Phi Beta Kappa. Honors program.

**Academic Assistance:** Remedial reading, writing, and math. Nonremedial tutoring.

**STUDENT LIFE. Housing:** Commuter campus; no student housing.

**Social atmosphere:** According to the student newspaper, the social and cultural life can be described as vibrant and diversified. The most socially influential groups on campus are the Gay and Lesbian Alliance, the New York Public Interest Research Group, fraternities, and sports teams. Students congregate in front of Boylan Hall and in the basement of the student union building.

**Services and counseling/handicapped student services:** Placement services. Health service. Women's center. Day care. Counseling services for minority, military, veteran, and older students. Birth control, personal, and psychological counseling. Career and academic guidance services. Religious counseling. Physically disabled student services. Learning disabled services. Notetaking services. Tape recorders. Tutors. Reader services for the blind.

**Campus organizations:** Undergraduate student government. Student newspapers (Kingsman; Excelsior, both published once/week). Literary magazine. Yearbook. Radio station. Academic Club Association, forensics, accounting society, chess club, martial arts group, 109 organizations in all. Seven fraternities, no chapter houses; seven sororities, no chapter houses. 5% of men join a fraternity. 5% of women join a sorority.

**Religious organizations:** Hillel, Chinese Christian Fellowship, Newman Center.

**Minority/foreign student organizations:** Black Science Student Association, Haitian-American, Italian-American, and Russian-American groups. Caribbean, Chinese, Greek, and Indian groups.

**ATHLETICS. Physical education requirements:** None.

**Intercollegiate competition:** 5% of students participate.

**Intramural and club sports:** 6% of students participate. Intramural aerobics, basketball, flag football, racquetball, softball, squash, swimming, tennis, track, volleyball, weight training.

**ADMISSIONS. Academic basis for candidate selection** (in order of priority): Secondary school record, standardized test scores, class rank.

**Requirements:** Graduation from secondary school is required; GED is accepted. 15 units and the following program of study are recommended: 4 units of English, 3 units of math, 1 unit of science, 3 units of foreign language, 4 units of social studies. Minimum combined SAT score of 900, rank in top third of secondary school class, or minimum 80% average recommended. Audition required of music program applicants. Search for Education, Elevation, and Knowledge (SEEK) program for applicants not normally admissible. SAT is recommended. PSAT is recommended. Campus visit recommended. No off-campus interviews.

**Procedure:** Take SAT or ACT by October of 12th year. Notification of admission on rolling basis. Freshmen accepted for terms other than fall.

**Special programs:** Admission may be deferred one semester. Credit may be granted through CEEB Advanced Placement for scores of 3 or higher. Credit may be granted through CLEP subject exams, Regents College, and DANTES exams, and military experience. Placement may be granted through challenge exams. Early entrance/early admission program. Concurrent enrollment program.

**Transfer students:** Transfer students accepted for terms other than fall. In fall 1992, 1,957 transfer applications were received, 1,163 were accepted. Application deadline is rolling for fall; rolling for spring. Minimum 2.0 GPA required. Lowest course grade accepted is "C." Maximum number of transferable credits is 64 semester hours. At least 48 semester hours must be completed at the college to receive degree.

**Admissions contact:** Marianne Booufall Tynan, M.S., Associate Director of Recruitment. 718 951-5051.

**FINANCIAL AID. Available aid:** Pell grants, SEOG, state scholarships and grants, school scholarships, and athletic scholarships. Perkins Loans (NDSL), PLUS, Stafford Loans (GSL), and SLS.

**Financial aid statistics:** In 1992-93, 51% of all undergraduate applicants received aid; 50% of freshman applicants. Average amounts of aid awarded freshmen: Scholarships and grants, $500; loans, $1,800.

**Supporting data/closing dates:** School's own aid application: Priority filing date is April 1. State aid form: Priority filing date is April 1. Income tax forms: Priority filing date is April 1. Notification of awards on rolling basis.

**STUDENT EMPLOYMENT.** College Work/Study Program. Institutional employment. 3% of full-time undergraduates work on campus during school year. Students may expect to earn an average of $1,000 during school year. Off-campus part-time employment opportunities rated "good."

**COMPUTER FACILITIES.** 250 IBM/IBM-compatible, Macintosh/Apple, and RISC-/UNIX-based microcomputers; all are networked. Students may access IBM mini-

computer/mainframe systems. Client/LAN operating systems include Novell. Computer languages and software packages include Assembler, BASIC, C, COBOL, dBASE, DOS, FORTRAN, LISP, Lotus 1-2-3, Pascal, PL/1, SPITBOL, WordStar. Computer facilities are available to all students.
**Fees:** Computer fee is included in tuition/fees.
**Hours:** 8 AM-10:45 PM (M-Th); 9 AM-4:45 PM (F-Su).

**GRADUATE CAREER DATA.** Graduate school percentages: 3% enter law school. 4% enter medical school. 1% enter dental school. Highest graduate school enrollments: Brooklyn Law Sch, New York U Sch of Dentistry, SUNY Health Science Center. Companies and businesses that hire graduates: Bell Cove, Chase Manhattan Bank, Deloitte & Touche, J.P. Morgan.

**PROMINENT ALUMNI/AE.** Stanley Cohen, Nobel Prize-winning biochemist; Peter Nero, pianist; Barbara Boxer, U.S. congresswoman; Barbara Aronstein Black, dean, Columbia U School of Law; Jimmy Smits, actor; Oscar Brand, folksinger and humorist; Irwin Shaw, author; Shirley Chisholm, former U.S. congresswoman; Frank Field, meteorologist; Alan Dershowitz, professor, Harvard Law School.

# City University of New York, City College

**New York, NY 10031** **212 650-7000**

**1993-94 Costs.** Tuition: $2,450 (state residents), $5,050 (out-of-state). Housing: None. Fees, books, misc. academic expenses (school's estimate): $594.
**Enrollment.** Undergraduates: 4,472 men, 3,426 women (full-time). Freshman class: 3,396 applicants, 2,582 accepted, 1,160 enrolled. Graduate enrollment: 1,653 men, 1,589 women.
**Test score averages/ranges.** N/A.
**Faculty.** 588 full-time; 522 part-time. 85% of faculty holds doctoral degree. Student/faculty ratio: 15 to 1.
**Selectivity rating.** N/A.

**PROFILE.** City College, founded in 1847 as the Free Academy, is a public institution. Programs are offered through the College of Liberal Arts and Science and the Schools of Architecture and Environmental Studies, Education, Engineering, and Nursing. Its 35-acre campus of Gothic and modern architecture is located in New York's St. Nicholas Heights section.

**Accreditation:** MSACS. Professionally accredited by the Accreditation Board for Engineering and Technology, the National Architecture Accrediting Board, the National Council for Accreditation of Teacher Education, the National League for Nursing.
**Religious orientation:** City University of New York, City College is nonsectarian; no religious requirements.
**Library:** Collections totaling over 1,157,470 volumes, 3,470 periodical subscriptions, and 577,547 microform items.
**Special facilities/museums:** Art museum, electron microscope, spectroscopy lab, planetarium, aquarium, weather station.
**Athletic facilities:** Swimming pools, gymnasiums, athletic fields, tracks, tennis courts, weight rooms.

**STUDENT BODY. Undergraduate profile:** 46% are transfers. 16% Asian-American, 39% Black, 27% Hispanic, 12% White, 6% Other. Average age of undergraduates is 26.
**Freshman profile:** 90% of freshmen come from public schools.
**Undergraduate achievement:** 70% of fall 1991 freshmen returned for fall 1992 term.
**Foreign students:** 113 students are from out of the country. Countries represented include Bangladesh, China, Greece, India, Pakistan, and West Indies; 80 in all.

**PROGRAMS OF STUDY. Degrees:** B.A., B.Arch., B.Eng., B.F.A., B.S., B.S.Ed., B.S.Nurs., B.Tech.
**Majors:** American Studies, Anthropology, Architecture, Art, Art History, Asian Studies, Bilingual Education, Biochemistry, Biology, Black Studies, Chemical Engineering, Chemistry, Civil Engineering, Classics, Communication/Film/Video, Comparative Literature, Computer Science, Dance, Early Childhood Education, Earth Science, Economics, Electrical Engineering, Elementary Education, English, French, Geography, German, Greek, Hebrew, History, International Studies, Italian, Jewish Studies, Latin, Latin American/Hispanic Caribbean Studies, Linguistics, Mathematics, Mechanical Engineering, Meteorology, Music, Nursing, Oceanography, Philosophy, Physical Education, Physics, Political Science, Pre-Law, Pre-Veterinary, Psychology, Russian, Russian Studies, Secondary Education, Slavic Studies, Social Studies, Sociology, Spanish, Special Education, Swahili, Technology Education, Theatre, Theatre/Dance, Urban Landscape Architecture, Vocational/Occupational Education.
**Distribution of degrees:** The majors with the highest enrollment are electrical engineering, architecture, and nursing; classics and Asian studies have the lowest.
**Requirements:** General education requirement.
**Academic regulations:** Freshmen must maintain minimum 1.5 GPA; sophomores, juniors, seniors, 2.0 GPA.
**Special:** Programs in actuarial math, community health education, history of science/technology, labor studies, management/administration, medieval and Renaissance studies, physician assistant, and women's studies. Double majors. Dual degrees. Accelerated study. Cooperative education programs. Graduate school at which undergraduates may take graduate-level courses. Preprofessional programs in law, medicine, veterinary science, and dentistry. Accelerated seven-year B.S./M.D. program with CUNY Medical School. Accelerated six-year B.A./J.D. program with CUNY Center for Legal Education. Combined bachelor's/master's programs in economics, English, math, math education, psychology, sociology, and Spanish. Students may take courses at any CUNY college. Teacher certification in early childhood, elementary, secondary, and special education. Study abroad in China, the Dominican Republic, England, France, Germany, Israel, Japan, and Kenya.
**Honors:** Phi Beta Kappa. Honors program.
**Academic Assistance:** Remedial reading, writing, math, and study skills. Nonremedial tutoring.

**STUDENT LIFE. Housing:** Commuter campus; no student housing.
**Social atmosphere:** The student newspaper reports that campus social life is influenced by the Day Student Government and the Students for Educational Rights. A popular event is the CUNY Intercollegiate Sports Conference. On-campus gathering spots include Aaron Davis Hall, Marshall Gym, Cohen library, NAC ballroom, and lecture halls.
**Services and counseling/handicapped student services:** Placement services. Health service. Day care. Counseling services for veteran students. Psychological counseling. Career and academic guidance services. Physically disabled student services. Notetaking services. Tape recorders. Reader services for the blind.
**Campus organizations:** Undergraduate student government. Student newspaper (Campus Nightwatch). Literary magazine. Yearbook. Radio station. 100 registered organizations.
**Religious organizations:** Chinese Christian Fellowship, Jewish group.
**Minority/foreign student organizations:** Black and Haitian groups, Society of Black Engineers. International Student Organization.

**ATHLETICS. Physical education requirements:** Two semesters of physical education required.
**Intercollegiate competition:** 2% of students participate. Baseball (M), basketball (M,W), cheerleading (M,W), cross-country (M,W), diving (M,W), fencing (M,W), gymnastics (M), lacrosse (M), soccer (M), swimming (M,W), tennis (M,W), track (indoor) (M,W), track (outdoor) (M,W), track and field (indoor) (M,W), track and field (outdoor) (M,W), volleyball (M,W). Member of CUNY Athletic Conference, ECAC, NCAA Division III.
**Intramural and club sports:** 10% of students participate. Intramural badminton, basketball, jogging, martial arts, road racing, softball, swimming, tennis, touch football, weight training, volleyball.

**ADMISSIONS. Academic basis for candidate selection** (in order of priority): Secondary school record, class rank, standardized test scores.
**Requirements:** Graduation from secondary school is required; GED is accepted. 12 units required and the following program of study recommended: 4 units of English, 2 units of math, 2 units of science, 3 units of foreign language, 3.5 units of social studies. Minimum combined SAT score of 900 (composite ACT score of 20), rank in top third of secondary school class, and minimum grade average of 80% required. Audition required of music program applicants. Search for Elevation, Education, and Knowledge (SEEK) program for applicants not normally admissible. SAT or ACT is recommended. No off-campus interviews.
**Procedure:** Suggest filing application by January 15; no deadline. Notification of admission on rolling basis. No set date by which applicants must accept offer. Freshmen accepted for terms other than fall.
**Special programs:** Credit and/or placement may be granted through CEEB Advanced Placement exams for scores of 3 or higher. Early entrance/early admission program. Concurrent enrollment program.
**Transfer students:** Transfer students accepted for terms other than fall. In fall 1992, 46% of all new students were transfers into all classes. 2,797 transfer applications were received, 1,883 were accepted. Application deadline is March 15 for fall; November 1 for spring. Minimum 2.0 GPA required. Lowest course grade accepted is "C." At least 32 semester hours must be completed at the college to receive degree.
**Admissions contact:** Nancy P. Campbell, M.A., Director of Admissions. 212 650-6977.

**FINANCIAL AID. Available aid:** Pell grants, SEOG, Federal Nursing Student Scholarships, state scholarships and grants, school scholarships, private scholarships, and academic merit scholarships. Perkins Loans (NDSL) and Stafford Loans (GSL).
**Financial aid statistics:** Average amounts of aid awarded freshmen: Scholarships and grants, $3,600.
**Supporting data/closing dates:** School's own aid application: Priority filing date is April 1. Notification of awards begins early August.
**Financial aid contact:** Thelma Mason, M.A., Director of Financial Aid. 212 650-6645.

**STUDENT EMPLOYMENT.** College Work/Study Program. Institutional employment. 10% of full-time undergraduates work on campus during school year. Off-campus part-time employment opportunities rated "fair."

**COMPUTER FACILITIES.** 3,000 IBM/IBM-compatible and Macintosh/Apple microcomputers; 2,500 are networked. Students may access Digital, IBM, SUN minicomputer/mainframe systems, Internet. Computer languages and software packages include Assembly, COBOL, dBASE, FORTRAN, LISP, Lotus 1-2-3, Microsoft Word, Pascal, WordPerfect; 50 in all. Computer facilities are available to all students.
**Fees:** $25 computer fee per year; included in tuition/fees.
**Hours:** 9 AM-9 PM.

**GRADUATE CAREER DATA.** Graduate school percentages: 3% enter law school. 15% enter medical school. 2% enter graduate business programs. 10% enter graduate arts and sciences programs. 13% of graduates choose careers in business and industry. Companies and businesses that hire graduates: AT&T, government agencies, IBM.

**PROMINENT ALUMNI/AE.** Colin Powell, chairman, Joint Chiefs of Staff; Edward Koch, former mayor, New York City; Jonas Salk, M.D., developer of polio vaccine; A.M. Rosenthal, former editor, *New York Times*; Stanley Kaplan, founder, Stanley H. Kaplan Educational Centers; Herman Badillo, former New York City borough president.

## City University of New York, The College of Staten Island

**Staten Island, NY 10314** **718 390-7733**

**1993-94 Costs.** Tuition: $2,450 (state residents), $5,050 (out-of-state). Housing: None. Fees, books, misc. academic expenses (school's estimate): $606.
**Enrollment.** Undergraduates: 2,669 men, 3,181 women (full-time). Freshman class: 2,936 applicants, 2,936 accepted, 1,532 enrolled. Graduate enrollment: 275 men, 876 women.
**Test score averages/ranges.** N/A.
**Faculty.** 293 full-time; 441 part-time. 74% of faculty holds highest degree in specific field. Student/faculty ratio: 23 to 1.
**Selectivity rating.** Noncompetitive.

**PROFILE.** The College of Staten Island, a public institution, was created in 1976 through the merger of Staten Island Community College and Richmond College, an upper-division institution. The college offers four-year programs with majors in the traditional disciplines, but emphasizes upper-division programs for graduates of its Division of Associate Studies and for graduates of community colleges. Its 43-acre campus is located at two sites in Staten Island.

**Accreditation:** MSACS. Professionally accredited by the Accreditation Board for Engineering and Technology, the American Medical Association (CAHEA), the National League for Nursing.
**Religious orientation:** City University of New York, The College of Staten Island is nonsectarian; no religious requirements.
**Library:** Collections totaling over 190,239 volumes, 1,398 periodical subscriptions, and 455,300 microform items.
**Special facilities/museums:** Video/film studio. Laboratory science building.
**Athletic facilities:** Gymnasium, basketball and tennis courts, baseball, football, and soccer fields, outdoor track, weight room.

**STUDENT BODY. Undergraduate profile:** 96% are state residents; 20% are transfers. 8% Asian-American, 10% Black, 6% Hispanic, 76% White. Average age of undergraduates is 28.
**Undergraduate achievement:** 67% of fall 1991 freshmen returned for fall 1992 term. 12% of entering class graduated.
**Foreign students:** 511 students are from out of the country. Countries represented include China, Greece, India, Japan, Korea, and Pakistan; 60 in all.

**PROGRAMS OF STUDY. Degrees:** B.A., B.S.
**Majors:** Accounting, African-American Studies, American Studies, Applied Social Sciences, Art, Biochemistry, Biology, Business, Chemistry, Cinema Studies, Communications, Computer Science, Dramatic Arts, Economics, Education, Engineering Sciences, English, History, International Studies, Mathematics, Medical Technology, Music, Nursing, Philosophy, Physics, Political Science, Psychology, Romance Languages, Sociology/Anthropology, Spanish, Women's Studies.
**Distribution of degrees:** The majors with the highest enrollment are psychology, business, and accounting; biochemistry, music, and anthropology have the lowest.
**Academic regulations:** Minimum 2.0 GPA required for graduation.
**Special:** Minors offered in most majors. B.S. may be earned in two years by students with appropriate associate's degree. Each undergraduate must successfully complete CUNY Skills Assessment Exams in reading, writing, and math. Associate's degrees offered. Double majors. Dual degrees. Independent study. Internships. Graduate school at which undergraduates may take graduate-level courses. Preprofessional programs in law, medicine, veterinary science, and dentistry. Member of College Consortium for International Studies, Staten Island Consortium of Education, and CUNY Film Consortium. Cross-registration with CUNY colleges. Teacher certification in early childhood, elementary, secondary, and special education. Certification in specific subject areas. Study abroad in Denmark, Ecuador, England, France, Greece, Italy, and Spain.
**Honors:** Honors program. Honor societies.
**Academic Assistance:** Remedial reading, writing, math, and study skills. Nonremedial tutoring.

**STUDENT LIFE. Housing:** Commuter campus; no student housing.
**Social atmosphere:** "The social and cultural life of CSI students is always evolving," reports the student newspaper. "There are many clubs and fraternities on campus which are very active. However, as CSI is a commuter school, most students' social lives take place off-campus." Students gather at club offices, the Quadrangle, the cafeteria, and area nightclubs.
**Services and counseling/handicapped student services:** Placement services. Health service. Women's center. Day care. Counseling services for veteran and older students. Personal counseling. Career and academic guidance services. Physically disabled student services. Learning disabled services. Notetaking services. Tape recorders. Tutors. Reader services for the blind.
**Campus organizations:** Undergraduate student government. Student newspaper (College Voice, published twice/month). Literary magazine. Yearbook. Radio station. Chorus, poetry magazine, cultural, professional, and special-interest groups, 63 organizations in all.
**Religious organizations:** Christian Fellowship, Hillel, Newman Club.
**Minority/foreign student organizations:** Minority student groups. International Club.

**ATHLETICS. Physical education requirements:** Two semesters of physical education required.
**Intercollegiate competition:** 2% of students participate. Baseball (M), basketball (M,W), soccer (M), softball (W), tennis (M,W), volleyball (W). Member of CUNY Athletic Association, ECAC, NCAA Division III, NYSWAC, Skyline Conference.
**Intramural and club sports:** 10% of students participate. Intramural aerobics, basketball, bowling, frisbee golf, golf, gymnastics, racquetball, soccer, softball, table tennis, touch football, volleyball.

**ADMISSIONS.**
**Requirements:** Graduation from secondary school is recommended; GED is accepted. 11 units and the following program of study are recommended: 4 units of English, 2 units of math, 1 unit of science, 4 units of electives. Minimum 3.0 GPA and rank in top two-thirds of secondary school class required of applicants to four-year programs. Open admissions policy for New York State applicants to two-year programs. Audition required of music program applicants. No off-campus interviews.
**Procedure:** Suggest filing application by January 12. Application deadline is July 1. Notification of admission on rolling basis. No set date by which applicants must accept offer. Freshmen accepted for terms other than fall.
**Special programs:** Admission may be deferred one year. Credit may be granted through CLEP general and subject exams. Credit and placement may be granted through life experience. Concurrent enrollment program.
**Transfer students:** Transfer students accepted for terms other than fall. In fall 1992, 20% of all new students were transfers into all classes. 950 transfer applications were received, 875 were accepted. Application deadline is July 1 for fall; December 1 for spring. Minimum 2.0 GPA required. Lowest course grade accepted is "C-." Maximum number of transferable credits is 98 semester hours. At least 30 semester hours must be completed at the college to receive degree.
**Admissions contact:** Ramon Hulsey, M.Phil., M.Int'l.Affairs., Admissions. 718 390-7557.

**FINANCIAL AID. Available aid:** Pell grants, SEOG, state scholarships and grants, school scholarships, private grants, and academic merit scholarships. Perkins Loans (NDSL), PLUS, Stafford Loans (GSL), and SLS.
**Financial aid statistics:** In 1992-93, 40% of all undergraduate applicants received aid; 40% of freshman applicants. Average amounts of aid awarded freshmen: Scholarships and grants, $2,100; loans, $1,900.
**Supporting data/closing dates:** School's own aid application: Priority filing date is May 28. AFSA: Priority filing date is May 31. Notification of awards begins July 1.
**Financial aid contact:** Sherman Whipkey, M.Ed., Director of Financial Aid. 718 390-7710.

**STUDENT EMPLOYMENT.** College Work/Study Program. Institutional employment. 7% of full-time undergraduates work on campus during school year. Students may expect to earn an average of $1,700 during school year. Off-campus part-time employment opportunities rated "good."

**COMPUTER FACILITIES.** 360 IBM/IBM-compatible, Macintosh/Apple, and RISC-/UNIX-based microcomputers; 250 are networked. Students may access Digital, IBM minicomputer/mainframe systems, BITNET, Internet. Computer languages and software packages include Assembler, C, COBOL, FORTRAN, Microsoft Word, MINITAB, Pascal, PL/1, SAS, SPSS, WordPerfect; 250 in all. Computer facilities are available to all students.
**Fees:** $25 computer fee per semester.
**Hours:** 24 hours in some locations.

## City University of New York, Hunter College

**New York, NY 10021** **212 772-4000**

**1993-94 Costs.** Tuition: $2,450 (state residents), $5,050 (out-of-state). Room: $1,600. Fees, books, misc. academic expenses (school's estimate): $503.
**Enrollment.** Undergraduates: 3,116 men, 5,601 women (full-time). Freshman class: 2,380 accepted, 1,025 enrolled. Graduate enrollment: 1,065 men, 3,378 women.
**Test score averages/ranges.** N/A.
**Faculty.** 696 full-time. 85% of faculty holds highest degree in specific field. Student/faculty ratio: 17 to 1.
**Selectivity rating.** N/A.

**PROFILE.** Hunter College, founded in 1870, is a public institution. In addition to its liberal arts and education programs, degrees are offered through the Schools of Health Sciences, Nursing, and Social Work. Its three-block campus is located in New York City.

**Accreditation:** MSACS. Professionally accredited by the American Dietetic Association, the American Physical Therapy Association, the American Speech-Language-Hearing Association, the Council on Education for Public Health, the Council on Social Work Education, the National Council for Accreditation of Teacher Education, the National League for Nursing.
**Religious orientation:** City University of New York, Hunter College is nonsectarian; no religious requirements.
**Library:** Collections totaling over 617,000 volumes, and 4,100 periodical subscriptions.
**Special facilities/museums:** Art gallery, geology lab, on-campus elementary and secondary schools.
**Athletic facilities:** Aerobics room, basketball, racquetball, tennis, and volleyball courts, intramural and soccer fields, swimming pools, weight rooms.

**STUDENT BODY. Undergraduate profile:** 97% are state residents. 13% Asian-American, 24% Black, 23% Hispanic, 1% Native American, 39% White. Average age of undergraduates is 27.
**Undergraduate achievement:** 77% of fall 1991 freshmen returned for fall 1992 term.
**Foreign students:** 74 countries represented in all.

**PROGRAMS OF STUDY. Degrees:** B.A., B.F.A., B.Mus., B.S.
**Majors:** Accounting, Anthropology, Art, Biological Sciences, Black/Puerto Rican Studies, Chemistry, Chinese, Classical Archaeology, Classical Studies, Communications, Community Health Education, Comparative Literature, Computer Science, Dance, Early Childhood/Elementary Education, Economics, Energy Policy Studies, English, English

Language Arts, Fine Arts, French, Geography, Geology, German, Greek, Health Education, Hebrew, History, Human Movement, Italian, Jewish Social Studies, Latin, Latin American/Caribbean Studies, Mathematics, Medical Laboratory Sciences, Music, Nursing, Nutrition/Food Science, Philosophy, Physical Education, Physical Therapy, Physics, Political Science, Psychology, Religion, Romance Languages, Russian, Secondary Education, Sociology, Spanish, Statistics, Theatre/Film, Urban Studies, Women's Studies.
**Distribution of degrees:** The majors with the highest enrollment are psychology, English, and communications.
**Requirements:** General education requirement.
**Academic regulations:** Minimum 2.0 GPA must be maintained.
**Special:** Minors offered in all majors. Self-designed majors. Double majors. Independent study. Accelerated study. Pass/fail grading option. Internships. Graduate school at which undergraduates may take graduate-level courses. Preprofessional programs in law, medicine, veterinary science, pharmacy, and dentistry. 2-2 engineering program with CUNY City Coll. Cross-registration with Mannes Coll of Music, Marymount Manhattan Coll, and YIVO Inst of Jewish Research. Exchange program abroad in France (U of Paris).
**Honors:** Phi Beta Kappa. Honors program.
**Academic Assistance:** Remedial reading, writing, math, and study skills. Nonremedial tutoring.

**STUDENT LIFE. Housing:** Students may live on or off campus. Coed dorms. 1% of students live in college housing.
**Social atmosphere:** "Because Hunter is a commuter campus in the heart of the greatest city in the world, the on-campus activities are not where it's most happening. New York's cultural activities beat everything else cold," reports the editor of the student newspaper. Students like to hang out in the third floor walkways and the West Building lobbies and court. Off campus, they gather at places like the 68th Street subway station, the East Village, the Underground, and Wetlands. Groups with influence on campus include Rock Against Racism and the newspaper staff. Popular events of the year include Homecoming, the Rock Against Racism concert, commencement, Central American activities, and celebrity visits and lectures.
**Services and counseling/handicapped student services:** Placement services. Health service. Women's center. Day care. Counseling services for older students. Personal and psychological counseling. Career and academic guidance services. Physically disabled student services. Learning disabled services. Notetaking services. Tutors. Reader services for the blind.
**Campus organizations:** Undergraduate student government. Student newspaper (Hunter Envoy). Literary magazine. Radio station. Band, orchestra, choirs, drama club, departmental groups, special-interest groups, 130 organizations in all. Four fraternities, no chapter houses.
**Religious organizations:** Chinese Christian, Korean Christian, other Christian, Jewish, Islamic, and Buddhist groups.
**Minority/foreign student organizations:** African Descendants Organization, Black Literary Collective, Black Nation Support Committee, Filipino-American group, Hispanic group, Daughters of Afrika. Arab, Asian/Pacific, Caribbean, Haitian, Indian, Indo-Caribbean, and Lebanese groups, Third World Women/Women of Color group.

**ATHLETICS. Physical education requirements:** One semester of physical education required.
**Intercollegiate competition:** 4% of students participate. Baseball (M), basketball (M,W), cheerleading (M,W), cross-country (M,W), fencing (M,W), soccer (M), softball (W), swimming (W), tennis (M,W), track (indoor) (M,W), track (outdoor) (M,W), track and field (indoor) (M,W), track and field (outdoor) (M,W), volleyball (M,W), wrestling (M). Member of CTC, CUNY Athletic Conference, ECAC, Metropolitan, NCAA Division III, New York State Women's Collegiate Athletic Association, NIWFA, PAC, Skyline.
**Intramural and club sports:** Intramural basketball, floor hockey, football, racquetball, soccer, volleyball.

**ADMISSIONS. Academic basis for candidate selection** (in order of priority): Secondary school record, standardized test scores, class rank.
**Requirements:** Graduation from secondary school is required; GED is accepted. 10 academic secondary school units required; no specific distribution required. Minimum combined SAT score of 900, rank in top third of secondary school class, or minimum 80% average required. Audition required of dance, music, and theatre program applicants. R.N. required of applicants to R.N. pathway nursing program. Portfolio required of art program applicants. Search for Education, Elevation, and Knowledge (SEEK) program for applicants not normally admissible. SAT is recommended. No off-campus interviews.
**Procedure:** Take SAT or ACT by November of 12th year. Application deadline is January 15. Notification of admission on rolling basis. No set date by which applicants must accept offer. Freshmen accepted for terms other than fall.
**Special programs:** Admission may be deferred one year. Credit and/or placement may be granted through CEEB Advanced Placement exams for scores of 3 or higher. Credit and/or placement may be granted through CLEP subject exams.
**Transfer students:** Transfer students accepted for terms other than fall. Application deadline is March 15 for fall; November 1 for spring. Minimum 2.0 GPA required. Lowest course grade accepted is "C-." Maximum number of transferable credits is 75 semester hours from a two-year school and 95 semester hours from a four-year school. At least 30 semester hours must be completed at the college to receive degree.
**Admissions contact:** William Zlata, Director of Admissions. 212 772-4490.

**FINANCIAL AID. Available aid:** Pell grants, SEOG, state scholarships and grants, school scholarships and grants, private scholarships, academic merit scholarships, and aid for undergraduate foreign students. Perkins Loans (NDSL), PLUS, Stafford Loans (GSL), state loans, school loans, and SLS.
**Financial aid statistics:** In 1992-93, 85% of all undergraduate applicants received aid; 75% of freshman applicants.
**Supporting data/closing dates:** School's own aid application: Accepted on rolling basis; deadline is May 1. Notification of awards on rolling basis.
**Financial aid contact:** Marie Leonard, M.A., Director of Financial Aid. 212 772-4820.

**STUDENT EMPLOYMENT.** College Work/Study Program. Institutional employment. Off-campus part-time employment opportunities rated "good."

**COMPUTER FACILITIES.** 58 IBM/IBM-compatible and Macintosh/Apple microcomputers. Students may access IBM minicomputer/mainframe systems. Computer languages and software packages include Assembler, C, COBOL, FORTRAN, LISP, PL/1. Computer facilities are available to all students.
**Fees:** None.

**PROMINENT ALUMNI/AE.** Audre Lorde, poet and feminist; Ruby Dee, actress; Bella Abzug, lawyer and politician; Robert Morris, artist; Martina Arroyo, Metropolitan Opera star; Judith Crist, syndicated movie reviewer; Hortense Gabel, New York supreme court justice; Jack Newfield, columnist.

# City University of New York, John Jay College of Criminal Justice

**New York, NY 10019** **212 237-8000**

**1993-94 Costs.** Tuition: $2,450 (state residents), $5,050 (out-of-state). Housing: None. Fees, books, misc. academic expenses (school's estimate): $500.
**Enrollment.** Undergraduates: 2,449 men, 2,797 women (full-time). Freshman class: 2,518 applicants, 2,518 accepted, 1,367 enrolled. Graduate enrollment: 372 men, 307 women.
**Test score averages/ranges.** N/A.
**Faculty.** 283 full-time; 134 part-time. 75% of faculty holds doctoral degree. Student/faculty ratio: 17 to 1.
**Selectivity rating.** N/A.

**PROFILE.** John Jay College of Criminal Justice is a public institution of liberal arts and criminal justice. Founded in 1964, it grew out of a program of higher education for New York City police officers. Its campus is located in the Lincoln Center area of Manhattan.
**Accreditation:** MSACS.
**Religious orientation:** City University of New York, John Jay College of Criminal Justice is nonsectarian; no religious requirements.
**Library:** Collections totaling over 200,000 volumes, 1,325 periodical subscriptions, and 125,000 microform items.
**Special facilities/museums:** Criminal justice center, center for productive public management, center for ethics.
**Athletic facilities:** Gymnasiums, swimming pool, strength training room, cardiovascular fitness center, combatives room, tennis and basketball courts, jogging track, volleyball and racquetball courts, wrestling room, dance studio.

**STUDENT BODY. Undergraduate profile:** 95% are state residents; 32% are transfers. 4% Asian-American, 37% Black, 32% Hispanic, 25% White, 2% Other. Average age of undergraduates is 27.
**Freshman profile:** 90% of freshmen come from public schools.
**Undergraduate achievement:** 75% of fall 1991 freshmen returned for fall 1992 term.
**Foreign students:** 80 students are from out of the country. 10 countries represented in all.

**PROGRAMS OF STUDY. Degrees:** B.A., B.S.
**Majors:** Computer Information Systems, Correctional Administration, Criminal Justice, Criminal Justice Administration/Planning, Criminology, Deviant Behavior/Social Control, Fire Service Administration/Fire Science, Forensic Psychology, Forensic Science, Government/Public Administration, Legal Studies, Police Science, Security Management.
**Distribution of degrees:** The majors with the highest enrollment are criminal justice, police science, and legal studies; forensic science, forensic psychology, and fire science have the lowest.
**Requirements:** General education requirement.
**Special:** Minors offered in economics, English, language, psychology, public administration, and sociology. Thematic studies program is a four-year interdisciplinary program focusing on various criminal justice themes. Independent study. Pass/fail grading option. Internships. Graduate school at which undergraduates may take graduate-level courses. Cross-registration with other CUNY colleges. Study abroad in Denmark, England, France, Germany, Greece, Ireland, Italy, Israel, Mexico, Puerto Rico, Scotland, Spain, and Switzerland.
**Academic Assistance:** Remedial reading, writing, math, and study skills. Nonremedial tutoring.

**STUDENT LIFE. Housing:** Commuter campus; no student housing.
**Social atmosphere:** According to the editor of the student newspaper, "John Jay is not only a college which fosters academic excellence, it is an institution which helps to develop a well-rounded individual. Because of our Manhattan location, the city of New York and all it has to offer serves as our campus." The newspaper office, the cafeteria, the Rathskeller, Lincoln Center, the Hard Rock Cafe, and the Blarney Stone are favorite student gathering spots. The JJC Bloodhounds is a popular athletic group. John Jay parties and various club parties are also popular.
**Services and counseling/handicapped student services:** Placement services. Health service. Women's center. Day care. Counseling services for minority, military, veteran, and older students. Birth control, personal, and psychological counseling. Career and academic guidance services. Learning disabled services.
**Campus organizations:** Undergraduate student government. Student newspaper (Lex Review, published once/month). Literary magazine. Yearbook. Radio station. Glee club, dance club, drama groups, Kuumba Players, Women's Coalition, Federal Criminal Justice Society, Forensic Science Society, Veterans Society, departmental clubs, special-interest groups.
**Religious organizations:** Christian Seekers Fellowship Club, Jewish Club.
**Minority/foreign student organizations:** Black Student Organization, Haitian Student Society.

**ATHLETICS. Physical education requirements:** One semester of physical education required.

**Intercollegiate competition:** 5% of students participate. Baseball (M), basketball (M,W), cheerleading (W), cross-country (M), softball (W), tennis (M,W), volleyball (W), wrestling (M). Member of City University of New York Athletic Conference (CUNYAC), ECAC, Hudson Valley Women's Athletic Conference (HVWAC), Metropolitan Collegiate Tennis Conference (MCTC), NCAA Division III.
**Intramural and club sports:** 2% of students participate. Intramural basketball, body building, fitness and excercise, karate, judo, power lifting, racquetball, soccer, strength training, swimming, tennis, triathlon, volleyball. Men's club martial arts, racquetball, soccer, swimming. Women's club racquetball, soccer, swimming.

**ADMISSIONS. Academic basis for candidate selection** (in order of priority): Secondary school record, class rank, standardized test scores, school's recommendation.
**Requirements:** Graduation from secondary school is required; GED is accepted. No specific distribution of secondary school units required. Rank in top half of secondary school class and minimum grade average of 75% required. Search for Education, Elevation, and Knowledge (SEEK) program for applicants not normally admissible. Campus visit and interview recommended. No off-campus interviews.
**Procedure:** Suggest filing application by January 1; no deadline. Notification of admission on rolling basis. No set date by which applicants must accept offer. Freshmen accepted for terms other than fall.
**Special programs:** Admission may be deferred one semester. Credit may be granted through CEEB Advanced Placement for scores of 3 or higher. Credit and/or placement may be granted through CLEP general and subject exams. Credit may be granted through military and life experience. Placement may be granted through challenge exams. Early entrance/early admission program. Concurrent enrollment program.
**Transfer students:** Transfer students accepted for terms other than fall. In fall 1992, 32% of all new students were transfers into all classes. Application deadline is rolling for fall; rolling for spring. Minimum 2.0 GPA required. Lowest course grade accepted is "C." Maximum number of transferable credits is 72 semester hours from a two-year school and 96 semester hours from a four-year school. At least 32 semester hours must be completed at the college to receive degree.
**Admissions contact:** Frank W. Marousek, M.A., Director of Admissions. 212 237-8865.

**FINANCIAL AID. Available aid:** Pell grants, SEOG, state grants, school scholarships and grants, private scholarships, ROTC scholarships, and academic merit scholarships. Perkins Loans (NDSL), PLUS, and Stafford Loans (GSL).
**Financial aid statistics:** In 1992-93, 85% of all undergraduate applicants received aid.
**Supporting data/closing dates:** School's own aid application: Accepted on rolling basis. State aid form: Accepted on rolling basis. CSAF: Accepted on rolling basis. Notification of awards on rolling basis.
**Financial aid contact:** John Emmons, M.A., Director of Financial Aid. 212 237-8151.

**STUDENT EMPLOYMENT.** College Work/Study Program. Institutional employment. 5% of full-time undergraduates work on campus during school year. Students may expect to earn an average of $1,000 during school year. Off-campus part-time employment opportunities rated "fair."

**COMPUTER FACILITIES.** 120 IBM/IBM-compatible and Macintosh/Apple microcomputers. Students may access IBM minicomputer/mainframe systems. Computer facilities are available to all students.
**Fees:** None.

**GRADUATE CAREER DATA.** Highest graduate school enrollments: John Jay Coll of Criminal Justice. 15% of graduates choose careers in business and industry. Companies and businesses that hire graduates: City of New York, State of New York, federal government.

**PROMINENT ALUMNI/AE.** Richard Condon, first deputy commissioner, New York City Police Department; Terrence McCann, vice-president for security services, Citibank NA; Hubert Williams, president, Police Foundation.

# City University of New York, Queens College

**Flushing, NY 11367** **718 997-5000**

**1993-94 Costs.** Tuition: $2,450 (state residents), $5,050 (out-of-state). Housing: None. Fees, books, misc. academic expenses (school's estimate): $600.
**Enrollment.** Undergraduates: 5,855 men, 8,623 women (full-time). Freshman class: 5,500 applicants, 3,522 accepted, 1,647 enrolled. Graduate enrollment: 979 men, 2,464 women.
**Test score averages/ranges.** N/A.
**Faculty.** 628 full-time; 646 part-time. 87% of faculty holds highest degree in specific field. Student/faculty ratio: 18 to 1.
**Selectivity rating.** N/A.

**PROFILE.** Queens College, founded in 1937, is a public institution. Programs are offered through the College of Liberal Arts (including the Divisions of Arts and Humanities, Mathematics and Natural Sciences, and Social Sciences and the Schools of Education and Music), the School of General Studies (the evening division), and the Graduate Division. Its 76-acre campus is located in Flushing.

**Accreditation:** MSACS. Professionally accredited by the American Library Association, the American Speech-Language-Hearing Association.
**Religious orientation:** City University of New York, Queens College is nonsectarian; no religious requirements.
**Library:** Collections totaling over 650,000 volumes, 4,000 periodical subscriptions, and 630,000 microform items.
**Special facilities/museums:** Art museum, centers for Asian, Byzantine, modern Greek, and Jewish studies, centers for the new American work force, urban programs, and environmental education, TV and sound labs.
**Athletic facilities:** Gymnasium, swimming pool, baseball, lacrosse, soccer, and softball fields, tennis courts, weight room, track.

**STUDENT BODY. Undergraduate profile:** 95% are state residents; 28% are transfers. 16% Asian-American, 7% Black, 17% Hispanic, 53% White, 7% Other. Average age of undergraduates is 22.
**Freshman profile:** 65% of freshmen come from public schools.
**Undergraduate achievement:** 70% of fall 1991 freshmen returned for fall 1992 term.
**Foreign students:** 773 students are from out of the country.

**PROGRAMS OF STUDY. Degrees:** B.A., B.F.A., B.Mus., B.S.
**Majors:** Accounting, Anthropology, Art, Art History, Biology, Chemistry, Communication Arts/Sciences, Comparative Literature, Computer Science, Drama/Theatre/Dance, Early Childhood, Earth Sciences, Economics, Education, Elementary Education, English, Film Studies, French, Geology, German, Greek, Hebrew, History, Home Economics, Honors/Western Tradition, Interdisciplinary Studies, Italian, Jewish Studies, Labor Studies, Latin, Linguistics, Mathematics, Music, Philosophy, Physical Education, Physics, Political Science/Government, Portuguese, Psychology, Russian, Secondary Education, Sociology, Spanish, Urban Studies, Yiddish.
**Distribution of degrees:** The majors with the highest enrollment are accounting, communication arts/sciences, and elementary education.
**Requirements:** General education requirement.
**Academic regulations:** Minimum 2.0 GPA required for graduation.
**Special:** Interdisciplinary programs in Africana, American, Byzantine/modern Greek, East Asian, Irish, Italian-American, Jewish, Latin American, Puerto Rican and religious studies. Business/liberal arts and journalism/liberal arts programs. Self-designed majors. Double majors. Dual degrees. Independent study. Accelerated study. Pass/fail grading option. Internships. Cooperative education programs. Graduate school at which undergraduates may take graduate-level courses. Preprofessional programs in law, medicine, veterinary science, dentistry, optometry, and engineering. Combined B.A./M.A. programs in chemistry, music, philosophy, physics, and political science. 3-2 engineering program with Columbia U. Cross-registration with other CUNY colleges. Teacher certification in early childhood, elementary, and secondary education. Certification in specific subject areas. Study abroad in France and Italy.
**Honors:** Phi Beta Kappa. Honors program.
**Academic Assistance:** Remedial reading, writing, math, and study skills. Nonremedial tutoring.

**STUDENT LIFE. Housing:** Commuter campus; no student housing.
**Services and counseling/handicapped student services:** Placement services. Health service. Day care. Counseling services for minority and older students. Personal and psychological counseling. Career and academic guidance services. Physically disabled student services. Learning disabled services. Notetaking services. Tape recorders. Tutors. Reader services for the blind.
**Campus organizations:** Undergraduate student government. Student newspaper (Quad, published once/week). Literary magazine. Radio station. Orchestral and choral societies, brass and jazz ensembles, opera club, drama productions, academic and political groups.
**Religious organizations:** Religious groups.
**Minority/foreign student organizations:** Minority and ethnic student groups. Foreign student groups.

**ATHLETICS. Physical education requirements:** One semester of physical education required.
**Intercollegiate competition:** 3% of students participate. Baseball (M), basketball (M,W), cross-country (M,W), diving (M,W), golf (M), lacrosse (M), soccer (M), softball (W), swimming (M,W), tennis (M,W), track and field (indoor) (M,W), track and field (outdoor) (M,W), volleyball (M,W), water polo (M). Member of Eastern College Soccer Conference, ECAC, Knickerbocker Lacrosse Conference, Metropolitan Swim Conference, Metropolitan Tennis Conference, NCAA Division II, New York Collegiate Athletic Conference.
**Intramural and club sports:** 10% of students participate. Intramural basketball, cross-country, football, softball, volleyball.

**ADMISSIONS. Academic basis for candidate selection** (in order of priority): Secondary school record, class rank, standardized test scores, essay, school's recommendation.
**Nonacademic basis for candidate selection:** Extracurricular participation and particular talent or ability are considered.
**Requirements:** Graduation from secondary school is required; GED is accepted. 17 units and the following program of study are recommended: 4 units of English, 3 units of math, 3 units of science, 3 units of foreign language, 4 units of social studies. Minimum combined SAT score of 900, rank in top third of secondary school class, or minimum 3.0 GPA required. Audition required of music program applicants. Search for Education, Elevation, and Knowledge (SEEK) program for applicants not normally admissible. SAT is recommended. PSAT is recommended. Campus visit recommended. No off-campus interviews.
**Procedure:** Take SAT or ACT by November of 12th year. Suggest filing application by January 15; no deadline. Notification of admission on rolling basis. No set date by which applicants must accept offer. Freshmen accepted for terms other than fall.
**Special programs:** Credit and/or placement may be granted through CEEB Advanced Placement exams for scores of 3 or higher. Credit may be granted through CLEP subject exams and life experience. Early entrance/early admission program. Concurrent enrollment program.
**Transfer students:** Transfer students accepted for terms other than fall. In fall 1992, 28% of all new students were transfers into all classes. Application deadline is March 15 for fall; November 15 for spring. Minimum 2.0 GPA required. Lowest course grade accepted is "C." Maximum number of transferable credits is 83 semester hours. At least 45 semester hours must be completed at the college to receive degree.
**Admissions contact:** Susan Reantillo, M.A., Executive Director of Admissions. 718 997-5600.

**FINANCIAL AID. Available aid:** Pell grants, SEOG, state grants, school scholarships, private scholarships, academic merit scholarships, and athletic scholarships. Perkins Loans (NDSL), PLUS, Stafford Loans (GSL), and SLS.
**Supporting data/closing dates:** School's own aid application: Priority filing date is May 15; deadline is August 1.

**Financial aid contact:** Doug Strauss, Director of Financial Aid. 718 997-5100.

**STUDENT EMPLOYMENT.** College Work/Study Program. Institutional employment. 5% of full-time undergraduates work on campus during school year. Students may expect to earn an average of $700 during school year. Freshmen are discouraged from working during their first term. Off-campus part-time employment opportunities rated "good."

**COMPUTER FACILITIES.** 50 IBM/IBM-compatible and Macintosh/Apple microcomputers. Computer facilities are available to all students.

**Fees:** None.

## City University of New York, York College

**Jamaica, NY 11451** **718 262-2000**

**1993-94 Costs.** Tuition: $2,450 (state residents), $5,050 (out-of-state). Housing: None.

**Enrollment.** Undergraduates: 1,458 men, 2,153 women (full-time).

**Test score averages/ranges.** N/A.

**Faculty.** 150 full-time; 50 part-time. 80% of faculty holds doctoral degree. Student/faculty ratio: 17 to 1.

**Selectivity rating.** N/A.

**PROFILE.** York College, founded in 1966, is a public institution offering liberal and career education. Its 50-acre campus is located in Jamaica.

**Accreditation:** MSACS. Professionally accredited by the American Medical Association (CAHEA), the Council on Social Work Education.
**Religious orientation:** City University of New York, York College is nonsectarian; no religious requirements.
**Library:** Collections totaling over 153,000 volumes, 11,000 periodical subscriptions, and 110,000 microform items.
**Special facilities/museums:** Center for educational technology.
**Athletic facilities:** Gymnasium, swimming pool, fitness center, handball and tennis courts, soccer and softball fields.

**STUDENT BODY. Undergraduate profile:** 88% are state residents; 40% are transfers. 10% Asian-American, 61% Black, 16% Hispanic, 13% White. Average age of undergraduates is 32.
**Foreign students:** 420 students are from out of the country. Countries represented include Bangladesh, China, Cyprus, Greece, Hong Kong, and India; 27 in all.

**PROGRAMS OF STUDY. Degrees:** B.A., B.S.
**Majors:** Accounting, African-American Studies, Anthropology, Art History, Bilingual Program, Biology, Business Administration, Chemistry, Community Health Education, Early Childhood Education, Economics, Elementary Education, English, Environmental Health Science, Fine Arts, French, Geology, Gerontology, Health Education, History, Information Systems Management, Italian, Marketing, Mathematics, Medical Technology, Music, Nursing, Occupational Therapy, Philosophy, Physical Education, Physics, Political Science, Psychology, Social Work, Sociology, Spanish, Special Education, Speech, Studio Art.
**Distribution of degrees:** The majors with the highest enrollment are information systems management, business administration, and elementary education.
**Requirements:** General education requirement.
**Special:** Concentrations offered in Judaic studies, Latin American studies, and Puerto Rican studies. Courses offered in behavioral science, communications, comparative literature, humanities, and managerial studies. Self-designed majors. Independent study. Pass/fail grading option. Internships. Cooperative education programs. Preprofessional programs in medicine, dentistry, and engineering. Teacher certification in early childhood, elementary, secondary, and special education. Study abroad in France.
**Honors:** Honors program.
**Academic Assistance:** Nonremedial tutoring.

**STUDENT LIFE. Housing:** Commuter campus; no student housing.
**Services and counseling/handicapped student services:** Placement services. Health service. Counseling services for minority, veteran, and older students. Personal counseling. Career and academic guidance services. Learning disabled services.
**Campus organizations:** Undergraduate student government. Academic, athletic, cultural, musical, and political groups.

**ATHLETICS. Physical education requirements:** Two credits of physical education required.
**Intercollegiate competition:** 2% of students participate. Basketball (M,W), cheerleading (W), cross-country (M,W), soccer (M), tennis (M), track (indoor) (M,W), track (outdoor) (M,W), track and field (indoor) (M,W), track and field (outdoor) (M,W), volleyball (M,W). Member of CUNYAC, ECAC, Hudson Valley Women's Athletic Conference, MCTC, NCAA Division III, NYSWAA.
**Intramural and club sports:** 14% of students participate. Intramural badminton, basketball, flag football, table tennis.

**ADMISSIONS. Academic basis for candidate selection** (in order of priority): Secondary school record, class rank.
**Requirements:** Graduation from secondary school is required; GED is accepted. No specific distribution of secondary school units required. Admissions criteria determined by number of openings available and by action of CUNY Board of Trustees (subject to change each semester). Special admissions requirements for health profession, social work, and cooperative education programs. Search for Education, Elevation, and Knowledge (SEEK) program for applicants not normally admissible. Flexible admissions requirements for veterans and adult (over age 25) applicants. Campus visit recommended. No off-campus interviews.
**Procedure:** Suggest filing application by February 1; no deadline. Notification of admission on rolling basis. No set date by which applicants must accept offer. Freshmen accepted for terms other than fall.
**Special programs:** Admission may be deferred one semester. Credit and/or placement may be granted through CEEB Advanced Placement exams for scores of 3 or higher. Credit and/or placement may be granted through CLEP subject exams. Credit and placement may be granted through challenge exams and military and life experience. Early entrance/early admission program. Concurrent enrollment program.
**Transfer students:** Transfer students accepted for terms other than fall. In fall 1992, 40% of all new students were transfers into all classes. Minimum 2.0 GPA required. Lowest course grade accepted is "C." Maximum number of transferable credits is 64 semester hours from a two-year school and 98 semester hours from a four-year school. At least 30 semester hours must be completed at the college to receive degree.
**Admissions contact:** Sally Nelson, M.A., Director of Admissions. 718 262-2165.

**FINANCIAL AID. Available aid:** Pell grants, SEOG, and state scholarships. Perkins Loans (NDSL), PLUS, and Stafford Loans (GSL).
**Supporting data/closing dates:** School's own aid application: Accepted on rolling basis.
**Financial aid contact:** Adolphus C. Frazier, M.A., Director of Financial Aid. 718 262-2230.

**STUDENT EMPLOYMENT.** College Work/Study Program. 70% of full-time undergraduates work on campus during school year.

**COMPUTER FACILITIES.** IBM/IBM-compatible microcomputers. Students may access IBM minicomputer/mainframe systems.

**Fees:** None.

## Clarkson University

**Potsdam, NY 13699** **315 268-6400**

**1993-94 Costs.** Tuition: $15,060. Room: $2,498. Board: $2,828. Fees, books, misc. academic expenses (school's estimate): $1,020.

**Enrollment.** Undergraduates: 1,812 men, 520 women (full-time). Freshman class: 2,100 applicants, 560 enrolled. Graduate enrollment: 275 men, 84 women.

**Test score averages/ranges.** N/A.

**Faculty.** 184 full-time; 19 part-time. 90% of faculty holds doctoral degree. Student/faculty ratio: 15 to 1.

**Selectivity rating.** Highly competitive.

**PROFILE.** Clarkson, founded in 1896, is a private university. Programs are offered through the Faculty of Liberal Studies and the Schools of Engineering, Management, and Science. Its 600-acre campus is located in Potsdam, in northern New York.

**Accreditation:** MSACS. Professionally accredited by the Accreditation Board for Engineering and Technology, the American Assembly of Collegiate Schools of Business.
**Religious orientation:** Clarkson University is nonsectarian; no religious requirements.
**Library:** Collections totaling over 207,453 volumes, 1,954 periodical subscriptions, and 253,834 microform items.
**Special facilities/museums:** Nuclear reactor, electron microscope.
**Athletic facilities:** Gymnasium, arena, ice rink, athletic fields, recreation building, swimming pool.

**STUDENT BODY. Undergraduate profile:** 77% are state residents; 23% are transfers. 2% Asian-American, 2% Black, 2% Hispanic, 1% Native American, 89% White, 4% Other. Average age of undergraduates is 20.
**Freshman profile:** 3% of freshmen who took SAT scored 700 or over on verbal, 10% scored 700 or over on math; 18% scored 600 or over on verbal, 58% scored 600 or over on math; 58% scored 500 or over on verbal, 95% scored 500 or over on math; 99% scored 400 or over on verbal, 100% scored 400 or over on math; 100% scored 300 or over on verbal. Majority of accepted applicants took SAT. 75% of freshmen come from public schools.
**Undergraduate achievement:** 85% of fall 1992 freshmen returned for fall 1993 term. 64% of entering class graduated. 15% of students who completed a degree program immediately went on to graduate study.
**Foreign students:** 100 students are from out of the country. Countries represented include Canada, India, Japan, Malaysia, Spain, and Venezuela; 29 in all.

**PROGRAMS OF STUDY. Degrees:** B.S.
**Majors:** Accounting, Aeronautical Engineering, Biology, Chemical Engineering, Chemistry, Civil/Environmental Engineering, Computer Engineering, Computer Science, Economics, Electrical Engineering, Finance, History, Humanities, Industrial Hygiene/Environmental Toxicology, Industrial Management, Interdisciplinary Engineering/Management, Liberal Studies/Business, Management, Management Information Systems, Marketing, Mathematics, Mechanical Engineering, Physics, Political Science, Psychology, Social Sciences, Sociology, Technical Communication.
**Distribution of degrees:** The majors with the highest enrollment are engineering, accounting, and mathematics.
**Requirements:** General education requirement.
**Special:** School of Management offers 16 career concentration areas. Double majors. Dual degrees. Independent study. Cooperative education programs. Graduate school at which undergraduates may take graduate-level courses. Preprofessional programs in law, medicine, veterinary science, and dentistry. 2-2 engineering program through State U of New York. 3-2 B.A./B.S.E. program with several SUNY liberal arts colleges. 4-1 B.A. or B.S./M.B.A. program. Member of Associated Colleges of the St. Lawrence Valley. Cross-registration with St. Lawrence U, SUNY Agricultural and Tech Coll at Canton, SUNY Coll at Potsdam. Exchange program abroad in Canada (U of Ottawa and Queen's U), England (City U), and Sweden (Lulea U). ROTC and AFROTC.
**Honors:** Honor societies.
**Academic Assistance:** Remedial study skills.

**STUDENT LIFE. Housing:** All unmarried students under age 21 must live on campus unless living near campus with relatives. Coed, women's, and men's dorms. Sorority and

fraternity housing. School-owned/operated apartments. 86% of students live in college housing.
**Social atmosphere:** According to the editor of the student newspaper, "Campus life is somewhat dull. Schoolwork takes up a significant amount of students' time." However, the Greeks and the hockey team do provide some fun and strongly influence social life. Without a student union or central gathering place on campus, local bars are the most popular places to meet other students. Lewis House is another popular gathering spot. A highlight for entertainment in winter is the annual Ice Carnival.
**Services and counseling/handicapped student services:** Placement services. Health service. Women's center. Counseling services for minority, military, and veteran students. Personal and psychological counseling. Career and academic guidance services. Physically disabled student services. Learning disabled services. Tutors. Reader services for the blind.
**Campus organizations:** Undergraduate student government. Student newspaper (Integrater, published once/week). Yearbook. Radio and TV stations. Glee club, jazz band, concert and pep bands, theatre, humor magazine, athletic, professional, and special-interest groups, 70 organizations in all. 13 fraternities, no chapter houses; three sororities, no chapter houses. 25% of men join a fraternity. 25% of women join a sorority.
**Religious organizations:** Intervarsity Christian Fellowship.
**Minority/foreign student organizations:** American Indian Science and Engineering Society, SPECTRUMM, National Society of Black Engineers, Society of Hispanic Professional Engineers. International Students Club.

**ATHLETICS. Physical education requirements:** Two semesters of physical education required.
**Intercollegiate competition:** 20% of students participate. Alpine skiing (M,W), baseball (M), basketball (M,W), cross-country (M), diving (M,W), golf (M), ice hockey (M), lacrosse (M,W), Nordic skiing (M,W), soccer (M,W), swimming (M,W), tennis (M,W), volleyball (W). Member of ECAC, Empire Athletic Association, NCAA Division I for ice hockey, NCAA Division III, USCSA.
**Intramural and club sports:** 45% of students participate. Intramural basketball, box lacrosse, broomball, floor hockey, ice hockey, soccer, softball, touch football, volleyball, water polo. Men's club rugby.

**ADMISSIONS. Academic basis for candidate selection** (in order of priority): Secondary school record, class rank, standardized test scores, school's recommendation, essay.
**Nonacademic basis for candidate selection:** Character and personality are important. Extracurricular participation, particular talent or ability, geographical distribution, and alumni/ae relationship are considered.
**Requirements:** Graduation from secondary school is required; GED is accepted. 16 units and the following program of study are required: 4 units of English, 3 units of math, 2 units of science. Rank in top quarter of secondary school class and minimum "B" average recommended. Conditional admission possible for applicants not meeting standard requirements. SAT or ACT is required. ACH recommended. Campus visit and interview recommended. Off-campus interviews available with admissions and alumni representatives.
**Procedure:** Take SAT or ACT by November of 12th year. Suggest filing application by February; no deadline. Notification of admission on rolling basis beginning February 1. Reply is required by May 1. $300 nonrefundable tuition deposit. Freshmen accepted for terms other than fall.
**Special programs:** Admission may be deferred one year. Credit and/or placement may be granted through CEEB Advanced Placement exams for scores of 3 or higher. Credit and/or placement may be granted through CLEP subject exams. Early decision program. Deadline for applying for early decision is December 1. Early entrance/early admission program.
**Transfer students:** Transfer students accepted for terms other than fall. In fall 1993, 23% of all new students were transfers into all classes. 500 transfer applications were received. Application deadline is rolling for fall; rolling for spring. Minimum 2.75 GPA. Lowest course grade accepted is "C." Maximum number of transferable credits is 72 semester hours from a two-year school and 90 semester hours from a four-year school. At least 30 semester hours must be completed at the university to receive degree.
**Admissions contact:** Robert A. Croot, Executive Director of Undergraduate Admission. 315 268-6479, 315 268-6480.

**FINANCIAL AID. Available aid:** Pell grants, SEOG, state scholarships and grants, school scholarships and grants, private scholarships and grants, ROTC scholarships, academic merit scholarships, and athletic scholarships. Perkins Loans (NDSL), PLUS, and Stafford Loans (GSL).
**Financial aid statistics:** 5% of aid is not need-based. In 1993-94, 85% of all undergraduate applicants received aid; 90% of freshman applicants. Average amounts of aid awarded freshmen: Scholarships and grants, $4,000; loans, $4,000.
**Supporting data/closing dates:** FAFSA/FAF/FFS: Priority filing date is February 15. Notification of awards begins April 1.
**Financial aid contact:** G. Brown, Executive of Financial Assistance. 315 268-6471.

**STUDENT EMPLOYMENT.** College Work/Study Program. Institutional employment. 40% of full-time undergraduates work on campus during school year. Students may expect to earn an average of $700 during school year. Freshmen are discouraged from working during their first term. Off-campus part-time employment opportunities rated "good."

**COMPUTER FACILITIES.** 2,805 IBM/IBM-compatible microcomputers; 200 are networked. Students may access IBM, SUN minicomputer/mainframe systems. Residence halls may be equipped with stand-alone microcomputers, networked microcomputers, modems. Numerous computer languages and software packages available. Computer facilities are available to all students.
**Fees:** None.
**Hours:** 24 hours.

**GRADUATE CAREER DATA.** 20% of graduates choose careers in business and industry. Companies and businesses that hire graduates: IBM, General Electric, Eastman Kodak, Xerox, Procter & Gamble, Big Six accounting firms, Texas Instruments.

# Colgate University

**Hamilton, NY 13346** **315 824-1000**

**1994-95 Costs.** Tuition: $19,510. Room: $2,690. Board: $2,875. Fees, books, misc. academic expenses (school's estimate): $695.
**Enrollment.** Undergraduates: 1,299 men, 1,353 women (full-time). Freshman class: 4,856 applicants, 2,541 accepted, 729 enrolled. Graduate enrollment: 8 men, 5 women.
**Test score averages/ranges.** Range of SAT scores of middle 50%: 546-638 verbal, 603-700 math. Range of ACT scores of middle 50%: 25-29 composite.
**Faculty.** 198 full-time; 56 part-time. 98% of faculty holds highest degree in specific field. Student/faculty ratio: 11 to 1.
**Selectivity rating.** Highly competitive.

**PROFILE.** Colgate, founded in 1819, is a private, liberal arts university. Its 1,100-acre campus is located in Hamilton, 38 miles southeast of Syracuse. Campus architecture includes 19th- and early 20th-century buildings as well as contemporary structures.

**Accreditation:** MSACS.
**Religious orientation:** Colgate University is nonsectarian; no religious requirements.
**Library:** Collections totaling over 530,000 volumes, and 2,540 periodical subscriptions.
**Special facilities/museums:** Art gallery, anthropology museum, language lab, closed-circuit TV system, life sciences complex, geology/fossil collection, observatory, electron microscopes, laser lab.
**Athletic facilities:** Gymnasiums, golf course, weight rooms, ice rink, swimming pools, tracks, batting cage, varsity and practice fields, basketball, racquetball, squash, and tennis courts, bowling alleys, boat house, field house, sauna, trap range.

**STUDENT BODY. Undergraduate profile:** 34% are state residents. 5% Asian-American, 5% Black, 3% Hispanic, 1% Native American, 85% White, 1% Other. Average age of undergraduates is 20.
**Freshman profile:** 3% of freshmen who took SAT scored 700 or over on verbal, 18% scored 700 or over on math; 37% scored 600 or over on verbal, 67% scored 600 or over on math; 83% scored 500 or over on verbal, 94% scored 500 or over on math; 97% scored 400 or over on verbal, 99% scored 400 or over on math; 100% scored 300 or over on verbal, 100% scored 300 or over on math. 80% of accepted applicants took SAT; 20% took ACT. 69% of freshmen come from public schools.
**Undergraduate achievement:** 94% of fall 1992 freshmen returned for fall 1993 term. 85% of entering class graduated. 26% of students who completed a degree program immediately went on to graduate study.
**Foreign students:** 67 students are from out of the country. Countries represented include Canada, France, India, Japan, Korea, and the United Kingdom; 21 in all.

**PROGRAMS OF STUDY. Degrees:** B.A.
**Majors:** Africana Studies, Art/Art History, Asian Studies, Astrogeophysics, Astronomy/Physics, Biochemistry, Biology, Chemistry, Classical Studies, Computer Science, Economics, Educational Studies, English, French, Geography, Geology, German, Greek, History, Humanities, International Relations, Latin, Latin American Studies, Mathematical Economics, Mathematics, Molecular Biology, Music, Native American Studies, Natural Science, Neurosciences, Peace Studies, Philosophy, Philosophy/Religion, Physical Sciences, Physics, Political Science, Psychology, Religion, Russian Studies, Social Sciences, Sociology/Anthropology, Spanish, Women's Studies.
**Distribution of degrees:** The majors with the highest enrollment are English, economics, and history; Latin, German, and computer science/mathematics have the lowest.
**Requirements:** General education requirement.
**Academic regulations:** Freshmen must maintain minimum 1.6 GPA; sophomores, 1.8-2.0 GPA; juniors, 2.0 GPA; seniors, 2.0 GPA.
**Special:** Minors offered in all majors and in African-American studies, Chinese, cognitive science, creative writing, environmental studies, Japanese, and theatre arts. Self-designed majors. Double majors. Independent study. Pass/fail grading option. Graduate school at which undergraduates may take graduate-level courses. Preprofessional programs in law, medicine, veterinary science, dentistry, and theology. 3-2 engineering programs with Columbia U, Cornell U, Dartmouth Coll, and Rensselaer Polytech Inst. 3-2 architecture program with Washington U. Four-year B.A./M.A. program may be entered in junior year. Washington Semester and Sea Semester. Other semester-away programs available. Member of New York State Visiting Student Program. Teacher certification in elementary and secondary education. Certification in specific subject areas. Exchange program abroad in Sweden (Stockholm U). Study abroad also in China, England, France, Germany, India, Italy, Japan, Mexico, Nigeria, Poland, the former Soviet Republics, Spain, Switzerland, and Wales.
**Honors:** Phi Beta Kappa. Honors program.
**Academic Assistance:** Remedial writing and study skills. Nonremedial tutoring.

**STUDENT LIFE. Housing:** All first- and second-year students must live on campus. Coed and women's dorms. Sorority and fraternity housing. School-owned/operated apartments. Special-interest (peace, ecology) houses. 64% of students live in college housing.
**Social atmosphere:** As reported by the student newspaper, the Jug, the Coop, and Donovan's Pub are some of the most popular gathering places on and around campus. Greek-letter organizations and athletics have always been important elements in the social life around Colgate. A very popular event is the annual Spring Party Weekend.
**Services and counseling/handicapped student services:** Placement services. Health service. Women's center. Counseling services for minority students. Birth control, personal, and psychological counseling. Career and academic guidance services. Religious counseling. Physically disabled student services. Learning disabled services. Notetaking services. Tape recorders. Tutors. Reader services for the blind.

**Campus organizations:** Undergraduate student government. Student newspaper (Maroon/News, published weekly). Literary magazine. Yearbook. Radio and TV stations. Chamber singers, band, chorus, concert and dance orchestras, debating, theatre, environmental awareness group, used bookstore, student travel agency, Amnesty International, outing club, Amnesty International, College Democrats/Republicans, Women's Coalition, Gay/Lesbian Student Alliance, departmental and community service groups, 90 organizations in all. Nine fraternities, all with chapter houses; four sororities, three chapter houses. 45% of men join a fraternity. 25% of women join a sorority.

**Religious organizations:** University Church, Jewish Student Union, Newman Community, Christian Fellowship, Orthodox Student Fellowship.

**Minority/foreign student organizations:** Black Student Union, African-American Student Alliance, Unidad. Japan Club, Asian, Caribbean, Korean, and West Indian groups.

**ATHLETICS. Physical education requirements:** Four semesters of physical education required.

**Intercollegiate competition:** 30% of students participate. Baseball (M), basketball (M,W), cheerleading (M,W), cross-country (M,W), diving (M,W), field hockey (W), football (M), golf (M), ice hockey (M), lacrosse (M,W), soccer (M,W), softball (W), swimming (M,W), tennis (M,W), track and field (indoor) (M,W), track and field (outdoor) (M,W), volleyball (W). Member of ECAC, NCAA Division I, Patriot League.

**Intramural and club sports:** 75% of students participate. Intramural backpacking, basketball, billiards, bocci, bowling, canoeing, camping, cross-country, cycling, fishing, flag football, foosball, golf, hiking, horseback riding, ice hockey, jogging, kayaking, lacrosse, Nordic skiing, racquetball, skating, skiing, soccer, softball, squash, swimming, table tennis, tennis, track and field, trap shooting, ultimate frisbee, volleyball, weight training, white water rafting. Men's club Alpine skiing, crew, ice hockey, indoor soccer, Nordic skiing, rugby, sailing, squash, ultimate frisbee, volleyball, water polo. Women's club Alpine skiing, crew, ice hockey, lacrosse, Nordic skiing, rugby, sailing, squash, ultimate frisbee.

**ADMISSIONS. Academic basis for candidate selection** (in order of priority): Secondary school record, school's recommendation, class rank, standardized test scores, essay.

**Nonacademic basis for candidate selection:** Extracurricular participation and particular talent or ability are important. Character and personality, geographical distribution, and alumni/ae relationship are considered.

**Requirements:** Graduation from secondary school is recommended; GED is accepted. 16 units and the following program of study are recommended: 4 units of English, 4 units of math, 3 units of science, 3 units of foreign language, 2 units of social studies. HEOP for applicants not normally admissible. University Scholars program for applicants not normally admissible. SAT or ACT is required. ACH required. Campus visit and interview recommended. Off-campus interviews available with an alumni representative.

**Procedure:** Take SAT or ACT by December of 12th year. Take ACH by December of 12th year. Application deadline is January 15. Notification of admission by April 1. Reply is required by May 1. $500 nonrefundable tuition deposit. Freshmen accepted for terms other than fall.

**Special programs:** Admission may be deferred two years. Credit and/or placement may be granted through CEEB Advanced Placement exams for scores of 4 or higher. Credit and/or placement may be granted through CLEP general and subject exams. Placement may be granted through challenge exams. Early decision program. In fall 1993, 320 applied for early decision and 170 were accepted. Deadline for applying for early decision is January 15. Early entrance/early admission program. Concurrent enrollment program.

**Transfer students:** Transfer students accepted for terms other than fall. In fall 1993, less than 1% of all new students were transfers into all classes. 115 transfer applications were received, 47 were accepted. Application deadline is March 15 for fall; November 15 for spring. Minimum 3.0 GPA required. Lowest course grade accepted is "C." Maximum number of transferable credits is 16 courses. At least 16 courses must be completed at the college to receive degree.

**Admissions contact:** Gary L. Ross, M.S., Director of Admission. 315 824-7401.

**FINANCIAL AID. Available aid:** Pell grants, SEOG, state scholarships and grants, school scholarships and grants, and private scholarships and grants. Perkins Loans (NDSL), PLUS, Stafford Loans (GSL), state loans, school loans, private loans, and SLS. Institutional payment plan.

**Financial aid statistics:** In 1993-94, 97% of all undergraduate applicants received aid; 91% of freshman applicants. Average amounts of aid awarded freshmen: Scholarships and grants, $15,000; loans, $2,200.

**Supporting data/closing dates:** FAFSA/FAF: Priority filing date is February 1. School's own aid application: Priority filing date is January 1. Income tax forms: Priority filing date is May 1. Notification of awards begins April 1.

**Financial aid contact:** Marcelle Tyburski, Director of Student Aid. 315 824-7431.

**STUDENT EMPLOYMENT.** College Work/Study Program. Institutional employment. 53% of full-time undergraduates work on campus during school year. Students may expect to earn an average of $1,000 during school year. Off-campus part-time employment opportunities rated "poor."

**COMPUTER FACILITIES.** 260 IBM/IBM-compatible, Macintosh/Apple, and RISC-/UNIX-based microcomputers; 200 are networked. Students may access Digital, SUN minicomputer/mainframe systems, BITNET, Internet. Client/LAN operating systems include Apple/Macintosh, DOS, UNIX/XENIX/AIX, DEC, LocalTalk/AppleTalk. Computer languages and software packages include Assembler, BASIC, C, DCL, FORTRAN, HyperCard, Lotus 1-2-3, Microsoft Word, Pascal, WordPerfect; 50 in all. Approximately 50 computers are priority-use for science students.

**Fees:** None.

**Hours:** 8 AM-1 AM; 24 hours on Sundays and at end of term.

**GRADUATE CAREER DATA.** Graduate school percentages: 9% enter law school. 5% enter medical/dental school. 2% enter graduate business programs. 10% enter graduate arts and sciences programs. Highest graduate school enrollments: Boston U, Columbia U, New York U, U of Michigan, U of Pennsylvania. 33% of graduates choose careers in business and industry. Companies and businesses that hire graduates: Arthur Andersen, Chase Manhattan Bank, IBM, Merrill Lynch, Prudential-Bache.

**PROMINENT ALUMNI/AE.** Gloria Borger, news editor/commentator; J. Richard Munro, retired chair, Time/Warner; Andy Rooney, broadcaster.

# The College of Insurance

**New York, NY 10007** **212 962-4111**

**1994-95 Costs.** Tuition: $11,480. Room & board: $7,400. Fees, books, misc. academic expenses (school's estimate): $660.

**Enrollment.** Undergraduates: 80 men, 54 women (full-time). Freshman class: 180 applicants, 105 accepted, 74 enrolled. Graduate enrollment: 124 men, 67 women.

**Test score averages/ranges.** N/A.

**Faculty.** 22 full-time; 65 part-time. 25% of faculty holds doctoral degree. Student/faculty ratio: 15 to 1.

**Selectivity rating.** More competitive.

**PROFILE.** The College of Insurance, founded in 1962, is a private institution of insurance and related areas. Its 10-story building is located in lower Manhattan.

**Accreditation:** MSACS.

**Religious orientation:** The College of Insurance is nonsectarian; no religious requirements.

**Library:** Collections totaling over 103,517 volumes, 481 periodical subscriptions, and 2,753 microform items.

**Athletic facilities:** Gymnasium with Nautilus equipment, weight room.

**STUDENT BODY. Undergraduate profile:** 7% Asian-American, 17% Black, 10% Hispanic, 62% White, 4% Other. Average age of undergraduates is 20.

**Freshman profile:** 7% of freshmen who took SAT scored 700 or over on math; 53% scored 600 or over on math; 47% scored 500 or over on verbal, 93% scored 500 or over on math; 90% scored 400 or over on verbal, 100% scored 400 or over on math; 100% scored 300 or over on verbal. 95% of accepted applicants took SAT; 5% took ACT.

**Undergraduate achievement:** 97% of fall 1992 freshmen returned for fall 1993 term.

**Foreign students:** 18 countries represented in all.

**PROGRAMS OF STUDY. Degrees:** B.Bus.Admin., B.S.

**Majors:** Actuarial Science, Business, Finance, Insurance.

**Requirements:** General education requirement.

**Special:** Visiting Minority Honors Intern Program. Associate's degrees offered. Dual degrees. Accelerated study. Internships. Cooperative education programs. Five-year B.B.A./M.B.A. and B.S./M.B.A. programs. Study abroad in China and England.

**Honors:** Honors program.

**ADMISSIONS. Academic basis for candidate selection** (in order of priority): Secondary school record, class rank, standardized test scores, school's recommendation, essay.

**Nonacademic basis for candidate selection:** Character and personality and extracurricular participation are important. Particular talent or ability and alumni/ae relationship are considered.

**Requirements:** Graduation from secondary school is required; GED is accepted. No specific distribution of secondary school units required. Minimum combined SAT score of 900-1200 required (varies for B.Bus.Admin. and B.S. degree applicants); minimum 2.5 GPA recommended. Conditional admission possible for applicants not meeting standard requirements. SAT is required; ACT may be substituted. Campus visit recommended. Off-campus interviews available with admissions and alumni representatives.

**Procedure:** Take SAT or ACT by December of 12th year. Visit college for interview by December of 12th year. Suggest filing application by December. Application deadline is May. Notification of admission on rolling basis. Reply is required by May 1. $120 nonrefundable tuition deposit. $100 nonrefundable room deposit. Freshmen accepted for terms other than fall.

**Special programs:** Admission may be deferred one year. Credit may be granted through CEEB Advanced Placement for scores of 4 or higher. Credit may be granted through CLEP subject exams. Credit and placement may be granted through challenge exams. Early decision program. Deadline for applying for early decision is December.

**Transfer students:** Transfer students accepted for terms other than fall. In fall 1993, 45 transfer applications were received, 35 were accepted. Application deadline is July 1 for fall; December 1 for spring. Minimum 2.5 GPA required. Lowest course grade accepted is "C." Maximum number of transferable credits is 60 semester hours from a two-year school and 75 semester hours from a four-year school. At least 45 semester hours must be completed at the college to receive degree.

**Admissions contact:** Theresa C. Marro, M.B.A., Director of Admissions. 212 815-9232.

**FINANCIAL AID. Available aid:** Pell grants, SEOG, state scholarships and grants, and school scholarships and grants. Perkins Loans (NDSL), PLUS, Stafford Loans (GSL), and SLS. Installment payment plan.

**Financial aid statistics:** 10% of aid is not need-based. In 1993-94, 95% of all freshman applicants received aid. Average amounts of aid awarded freshmen: Scholarships and grants, $8,700.

**Supporting data/closing dates:** FAFSA/FAF: Accepted on rolling basis. Notification of awards on rolling basis.

**Financial aid contact:** Marjorie Melikian, Director of Financial Aid. 212 815-9222.

# College of Mount St. Vincent

**Riverdale, NY 10471** **718 405-3200**

**1993-94 Costs.** Tuition: $11,130. Room & board: $5,600. Fees, books, misc. academic expenses (school's estimate): $520.

**Enrollment.** Undergraduates: 126 men, 573 women (full-time). Freshman class: 751 applicants, 536 accepted, 177 enrolled. Graduate enrollment: 35 women.

**Test score averages/ranges.** Average SAT scores: 414 verbal, 426 math. Range of SAT scores of middle 50%: 360-460 verbal, 390-500 math.

**Faculty.** 59 full-time; 38 part-time. 78% of faculty holds highest degree in specific field. Student/faculty ratio: 12 to 1.

**Selectivity rating.** Less competitive.

**PROFILE.** The College of Mount St. Vincent, founded in 1847, is a private, church-affiliated, liberal arts college. Its 70-acre campus is located in Riverdale along the Hudson River.

**Accreditation:** MSACS. Professionally accredited by the National League for Nursing.
**Religious orientation:** College of Mount St. Vincent is affiliated with the Roman Catholic Church (Sisters of Charity of St. Vincent de Paul); one semester of religion/theology required.
**Library:** Collections totaling over 148,094 volumes, 521 periodical subscriptions, and 11,000 microform items.
**Special facilities/museums:** Language lab, TV studio, electron microscope.
**Athletic facilities:** Gymnasium, swimming pool, weight room, dance studio, racquetball and outdoor tennis courts.

**STUDENT BODY. Undergraduate profile:** 90% are state residents. 8% Asian-American, 10% Black, 19% Hispanic, 59% White, 4% Other. Average age of undergraduates is 20.
**Freshman profile:** 1% of freshmen who took SAT scored 700 or over on verbal, 1% scored 700 or over on math; 3% scored 600 or over on verbal, 7% scored 600 or over on math; 18% scored 500 or over on verbal, 32% scored 500 or over on math; 65% scored 400 or over on verbal, 66% scored 400 or over on math; 94% scored 300 or over on verbal, 99% scored 300 or over on math. 38% of freshmen come from public schools.
**Undergraduate achievement:** 91% of fall 1991 freshmen returned for fall 1992 term. 55% of entering class graduated. 20% of students who completed a degree program immediately went on to graduate study.
**Foreign students:** Countries represented include the Bahamas, China, India, Japan, the Philippines, and Russia.

**PROGRAMS OF STUDY. Degrees:** B.A., B.S.
**Majors:** Biochemistry, Biology, Business, Chemistry, Communication, Computer Science, Economics, English, French, Health Education, History, International Studies, Liberal Arts, Mathematics, Modern Foreign Languages, Nursing, Peace Studies, Philosophy, Physical Education, Physics, Psychology, Religious Studies, Sociology, Spanish, Special Education, Urban Affairs.
**Distribution of degrees:** The majors with the highest enrollment are psychology, business, and communication.
**Requirements:** General education requirement.
**Academic regulations:** Freshmen must maintain minimum 1.7 GPA; sophomores, 1.9 GPA; juniors, 2.0 GPA; seniors, 2.0 GPA.
**Special:** Minors offered in all majors except nursing. Cooperative program arrangement with Manhattan Coll. Program in international business. Associate's degrees offered. Self-designed majors. Double majors. Dual degrees. Accelerated study. Internships. Preprofessional programs in law, medicine, and dentistry. 3-2 engineering program with Manhattan Coll. Exchange programs with Coll of Mount St. Joseph, Coll of St. Elizabeth, Elizabeth Seton Coll, Mount St. Vincent U, and Seton Hill Coll. Teacher certification in early childhood, elementary, secondary, and special education. Study abroad possible. AFROTC at Manhattan Coll.
**Honors:** Honors program. Honor societies.
**Academic Assistance:** Remedial reading, writing, and math. Nonremedial tutoring.

**ADMISSIONS. Academic basis for candidate selection** (in order of priority): Secondary school record, standardized test scores, class rank, school's recommendation, essay.
**Nonacademic basis for candidate selection:** Character and personality, extracurricular participation, and particular talent or ability are important. Geographical distribution and alumni/ae relationship are considered.
**Requirements:** Graduation from secondary school is required; GED is accepted. 16 units and the following program of study are recommended: 4 units of English, 2 units of math, 1 unit of science, 2 units of foreign language, 1 unit of social studies, 2 units of history, 4 units of electives. Minimum SAT scores of 400 in both verbal and math, rank in top half of secondary school class, and minimum 2.5 GPA recommended. Chemistry required of nursing program applicants. HEOP and Bridge Program for applicants not normally admissible. SAT is required; ACT may be substituted. Campus visit and interview recommended. Off-campus interviews available with admissions and alumni representatives.
**Procedure:** Take SAT or ACT by January of 12th year. Visit college for interview by March 30 of 12th year. Suggest filing application by fall; no deadline. Notification of admission on rolling basis. $200 nonrefundable tuition deposit. $200 nonrefundable room deposit. Freshmen accepted for terms other than fall.
**Special programs:** Admission may be deferred one year. Credit and/or placement may be granted through CEEB Advanced Placement exams for scores of 3 or higher. Credit and/or placement may be granted through CLEP general and subject exams. Early decision program. Deadline for applying for early decision is November 15. Early entrance/early admission program. Concurrent enrollment program.
**Transfer students:** Transfer students accepted for terms other than fall. In fall 1992, 119 transfer applications were received, 65 were accepted. Application deadline is rolling for fall; rolling for spring. Minimum 2.5 GPA required. Lowest course grade accepted is "C." Maximum number of transferable credits is 65 semester hours from a two-year school and 75 semester hours from a four-year school. At least 45 semester hours must be completed at the college to receive degree.
**Admissions contact:** Lenore Mott, Dean of Admissions and Financial Aid. 718 405-3267.

**FINANCIAL AID. Available aid:** Pell grants, SEOG, state scholarships and grants, school scholarships and grants, private scholarships and grants, ROTC scholarships, academic merit scholarships, and aid for undergraduate foreign students. Perkins Loans (NDSL), PLUS, Stafford Loans (GSL), NSL, state loans, and SLS. Tuition Plan Inc., Knight Tuition Plans, AMS, deferred payment plan, and family tuition reduction.
**Financial aid statistics:** 24% of aid is not need-based. In 1992-93, 99% of all undergraduate applicants received aid; 90% of freshman applicants. Average amounts of aid awarded freshmen: Scholarships and grants, $5,400; loans, $2,000.
**Supporting data/closing dates:** FAFSA/FAF: Priority filing date is March 15. School's own aid application: Priority filing date is March 15. Notification of awards begins March 26.
**Financial aid contact:** Margo McDonagh, M.A., Director of Financial Aid. 718 405-3290.

# College of New Rochelle

**New Rochelle, NY 10805** **914 632-5300**

**1994-95 Costs.** Tuition: $11,400. Room & board: $5,000. Fees, books, misc. academic expenses (school's estimate): $550.

**Enrollment.** Undergraduates: 12 men, 639 women (full-time). Freshman class: 600 applicants, 376 accepted, 136 enrolled. Graduate enrollment: 208 men, 1,315 women.

**Test score averages/ranges.** Average SAT scores: 416 verbal, 424 math. Range of SAT scores of middle 50%: 370-470 verbal, 360-490 math.

**Faculty.** 53 full-time; 43 part-time. 66% of faculty holds doctoral degree. Student/faculty ratio: 10 to 1.

**Selectivity rating.** Competitive.

**PROFILE.** The College of New Rochelle is a private college. Founded in 1904 as a women's college, the School of Arts and Sciences continues the tradition of enrolling women only, while the other three schools admit both men and women. Programs also offered through the Schools of Nursing, the School of New Resources, and the Graduate School. Its 16-acre campus, with its Gothic-style architecture, is located near Long Island Sound in New Rochelle.

**Accreditation:** MSACS. Professionally accredited by the Council on Social Work Education, the National League for Nursing.
**Religious orientation:** College of New Rochelle is nonsectarian; no religious requirements.
**Library:** Collections totaling over 183,133 volumes, 1,409 periodical subscriptions, and 276 microform items.
**Special facilities/museums:** Art gallery, multimedia theatre/teleconference center, language lab, centers for media, computer studies, TV studio.
**Athletic facilities:** Gymnasium, swimming pool, Nautilus room, tennis courts, dance studio.

**STUDENT BODY. Undergraduate profile:** 92% are state residents; 31% are transfers. 4% Asian-American, 24% Black, 16% Hispanic, 55% White, 1% Other. Average age of undergraduates is 22.
**Freshman profile:** 1% of freshmen who took SAT scored 700 or over on verbal, 1% scored 700 or over on math; 2% scored 600 or over on verbal, 4% scored 600 or over on math; 13% scored 500 or over on verbal, 23% scored 500 or over on math; 64% scored 400 or over on verbal, 63% scored 400 or over on math; 96% scored 300 or over on verbal, 96% scored 300 or over on math. 99% of accepted applicants took SAT; 1% took ACT. 70% of freshmen come from public schools.
**Undergraduate achievement:** 81% of fall 1992 freshmen returned for fall 1993 term. 31% of entering class graduated. 9% of students who completed a degree program immediately went on to graduate study.
**Foreign students:** 26 students are from out of the country. Countries represented include China, Japan, Kenya, the Philippines, Thailand, and the West Indies; nine in all.

**PROGRAMS OF STUDY. Degrees:** B.A., B.F.A., B.S.
**Majors:** Advertising, American Studies, Art Education, Art History, Art Therapy, Biology, Broadcasting, Business, Chemistry, Classical Humanities, Classics, Communication Arts, Economics, English, French, History, Interdisciplinary Studies, International Studies, Italian, Journalism, Latin/Greek, Mathematics, Nursing, Philosophy, Physics, Political Science/Government, Psychology, Public Relations, Religious Studies, Social Work, Sociology, Spanish, Studio Art, Women's Studies.
**Distribution of degrees:** The majors with the highest enrollment are communication arts, psychology, and studio art; classics, religious studies, and philosophy have the lowest.
**Requirements:** General education requirement.
**Academic regulations:** Minimum 2.0 GPA must be maintained.
**Special:** Senior seminar may be taken on an interdisciplinary basis. Community action/education program includes field work in community. Externships in chemistry and premedicine. Self-designed majors. Double majors. Independent study. Accelerated study. Pass/fail grading option. Internships. Cooperative education programs. Graduate school at which undergraduates may take graduate-level courses. Preprofessional programs in law, medicine, veterinary science, and dentistry. Five-year bachelor's/master's degree programs in community/school psychology and therapeutic education. Washington Semester and UN Semester. Exchange programs with Concordia Coll, Iona Coll, and Marymount Coll. Teacher certification in early childhood, elementary, secondary, and special education. Certification in specific subject areas. Study abroad in England, France, Germany, Ireland, Mexico, Scotland, and Spain.
**Honors:** Honors program. Honor societies.
**Academic Assistance:** Remedial reading, writing, math, and study skills. Nonremedial tutoring.

**ADMISSIONS. Academic basis for candidate selection** (in order of priority): Secondary school record, class rank, standardized test scores, school's recommendation, essay.
**Nonacademic basis for candidate selection:** Character and personality, extracurricular participation, particular talent or ability, and alumni/ae relationship are considered.
**Requirements:** Graduation from secondary school is required; GED is accepted. 15 units and the following program of study are required: 4 units of English, 3 units of math, 3 units of science, 2 units of foreign language, 3 units of social studies. Minimum combined SAT score of 800, rank in top half of secondary school class, and minimum 2.0 GPA recommended. Minimum SAT scores of 400 in both verbal and math required of nursing program applicants. Portfolio required of art program applicants. HEOP for applicants not normally admissible. Conditional admission possible for applicants not meeting standard requirements. SAT is required; ACT may be substituted. PSAT is recommended. Campus visit and interview recommended. Off-campus interviews available with admissions and alumni representatives.
**Procedure:** Take SAT or ACT by spring of 12th year. Visit college for interview by July 30 of 12th year. Application deadline is August 15. Notification of admission on rolling basis. $300 nonrefundable tuition deposit. $50 nonrefundable room deposit. Freshmen accepted for terms other than fall.
**Special programs:** Admission may be deferred three years. Credit and/or placement may be granted through CEEB Advanced Placement exams for scores of 5 or higher. Credit may be granted through CLEP general and subject exams and Regents College exams. Placement may be granted through challenge exams. Early decision program. Deadline for applying for early decision is November 1. Early entrance/early admission program. Concurrent enrollment program.
**Transfer students:** Transfer students accepted for terms other than fall. In fall 1993, 31% of all new students were transfers into all classes. 317 transfer applications were received, 105 were accepted. Application deadline is rolling for fall; rolling for spring. Minimum 2.0 GPA required. Lowest course grade accepted is "C." Maximum number of transferable semester hours is 75 for School of Arts and Sciences; 90 for School of Nursing. At least 30 semester hours must be completed at the college to receive degree.
**Admissions contact:** John P. Hine, Jr., Director of Admission. 914 654-5452.

**FINANCIAL AID. Available aid:** Pell grants, SEOG, Federal Nursing Student Scholarships, state scholarships and grants, school scholarships and grants, private scholarships and grants, academic merit scholarships, aid for undergraduate foreign students, and United Negro College Fund. Perkins Loans (NDSL), PLUS, Stafford Loans (GSL), NSL, state loans, private loans, and SLS. Tuition Plan Inc., AMS, deferred payment plan, and family tuition reduction. CNR Installment Plan.
**Financial aid statistics:** 19% of aid is not need-based. In 1993-94, 98% of all undergraduate applicants received aid; 80% of freshman applicants. Average amounts of aid awarded freshmen: Scholarships and grants, $7,082; loans, $3,758.
**Supporting data/closing dates:** FAFSA: Accepted on rolling basis. School's own aid application: Accepted on rolling basis. State aid form: Accepted on rolling basis. Income tax forms: Accepted on rolling basis. Notification of awards on rolling basis.
**Financial aid contact:** Ronald Pollack, Ph.D., Director of Financial Aid. 914 654-5224.

# The College of Saint Rose

**Albany, NY 12203 518 454-5111**

**1993-94 Costs.** Tuition: $9,422. Room & board: $5,288. Fees, books, misc. academic expenses (school's estimate): $1,570.
**Enrollment.** Undergraduates: 468 men, 1,114 women (full-time). Freshman class: 740 applicants, 537 accepted, 246 enrolled. Graduate enrollment: 700 men, 1,641 women.
**Test score averages/ranges.** Average SAT scores: 460 verbal, 500 math.
**Faculty.** 123 full-time; 97 part-time. 75% of faculty holds doctoral degree. Student/faculty ratio: 17 to 1.
**Selectivity rating.** Less competitive.

**PROFILE.** The College of Saint Rose is a private, liberal arts institution. Founded in 1920, it adopted coeducation in 1970. Its 22-acre campus is located in a residential section of Albany.

**Accreditation:** MSACS. Professionally accredited by the American Speech-Language-Hearing Association, the National Association of Schools of Art and Design.
**Religious orientation:** The College of Saint Rose is a nondenominational Christian school; no religious requirements.
**Library:** Collections totaling over 161,890 volumes, 1,002 periodical subscriptions, and 88,000 microform items.
**Special facilities/museums:** Art gallery, TV production studio, radio lab, music recording studio, screen print facility, observatory.
**Athletic facilities:** Gymnasium, indoor swimming pool, weight room, multipurpose room.

**STUDENT BODY. Undergraduate profile:** 97% are state residents; 60% are transfers. 2% Asian-American, 3% Black, 1% Hispanic, .2% Native American, 93% White, .8% Other. Average age of undergraduates is 25.
**Freshman profile:** 1% of freshmen who took SAT scored 700 or over on verbal, 2% scored 700 or over on math; 5% scored 600 or over on verbal, 11% scored 600 or over on math; 29% scored 500 or over on verbal, 49% scored 500 or over on math; 77% scored 400 or over on verbal, 92% scored 400 or over on math; 99% scored 300 or over on verbal, 99% scored 300 or over on math. 100% of accepted applicants took SAT; 25% took ACT. 70% of freshmen come from public schools.
**Undergraduate achievement:** 62% of fall 1992 freshmen returned for fall 1993 term. 55% of entering class graduated. 42% of students who completed a degree program went on to graduate study within one year.
**Foreign students:** 40 students are from out of the country. Countries represented include China, Japan, and Turkey; 29 in all.

**PROGRAMS OF STUDY. Degrees:** B.A., B.S.
**Majors:** Accounting, American Studies, Art Education, Biology, Biology/Cytotechnology, Biology/Electron Microscopy, Biology/Secondary Education, Business Administration, Chemistry, Chemistry/Secondary Education, Communication Disorders, Computer Information Systems, Elementary Education, English, English/Secondary Education, Graphic Design, History, History/Political Science, History/Political Science/Secondary Education, Interdepartmental Studies, Mathematics, Mathematics/Secondary Education, Medical Technology, Music, Music Education, Public Communication, Religious Studies, Sociology, Spanish, Spanish/Secondary Education, Special Education, Studio Art.
**Distribution of degrees:** The majors with the highest enrollment are education, business, and communication disorders; chemistry, mathematics, and foreign language have the lowest.
**Requirements:** General education requirement.
**Academic regulations:** Minimum 2.0 GPA must be maintained.
**Special:** Minors offered in most majors and in art, drama, philosophy, and writing. Double majors. Dual degrees. Pass/fail grading option. Internships. Graduate school at which undergraduates may take graduate-level courses. Preprofessional programs in law, medicine, veterinary science, and dentistry. 3-2 engineering program. Member of Hudson-Mohawk Association of Colleges and Universities and Sisters of Saint Joseph College Consortium; cross-registration possible. Exchange programs with 13 Carondelet colleges and eight other colleges. Member of New York State Visiting Student Program. Teacher certification in elementary, secondary, and special education. Certification in specific subject areas. Study abroad in Greece and Britain. NROTC at Siena Coll and Rensselaer Polytech Inst.
**Honors:** Honor societies.
**Academic Assistance:** Remedial writing, math, and study skills. Nonremedial tutoring.

**STUDENT LIFE. Housing:** Students may live on or off campus. Coed, women's, and men's dorms. 50% of students live in college housing.
**Social atmosphere:** As reported by a school official, "Participation in Saint Rose co-curricular activities provides students the opportunity to develop important leadership and interpersonal skills while having fun in the process." On campus, students like to congregate at the Camelot Room, the Campus Center Main Lounge, and the Activities Center. Off campus, students frequently go to the Knickerbocker Arena, Crossgates Mall, Saratoga Performing Arts Center, and Madison Avenue Theater. Popular groups on campus include the Student Events Board, the Student Association, and athletic teams. Some favorite campus events are Senior Week, Silver Bay Leadership Experience, semiformal balls, Coffee House Series, and gallery openings.
**Services and counseling/handicapped student services:** Placement services. Health service. Counseling services for minority and older students. Personal and psychological counseling. Career and academic guidance services. Religious counseling. Physically disabled student services. Learning disabled services. Notetaking services. Tape recorders. Tutors. Reader services for the blind.
**Campus organizations:** Undergraduate student government. Student newspaper (Chronicle, published twice/month). Literary magazine. Yearbook. Chamber Singers, Masterworks Chorale, jazz and wind ensembles, drama groups, coffeehouse, film series, Oktoberfest, student art shows, 25 organizations in all.
**Religious organizations:** Campus Ministry, Canticleers (folk mass singers).
**Minority/foreign student organizations:** Spectrum. International Student Organization.

**ATHLETICS. Physical education requirements:** Two semesters of physical education required.
**Intercollegiate competition:** 10% of students participate. Baseball (M), basketball (M,W), cheerleading (M,W), cross-country (M,W), diving (M,W), soccer (M,W), softball (W), swimming (M,W), tennis (M,W), track (indoor) (M,W), track (outdoor) (M,W), track and field (indoor) (M,W), track and field (outdoor) (M,W), volleyball (W). Member of ECAC, NCAA Division II, New York Collegiate Athletic Conference.
**Intramural and club sports:** 4% of students participate. Intramural basketball, flag football, swimming, volleyball. Men's club canoe/kayak. Women's club canoe/kayak.

**ADMISSIONS. Academic basis for candidate selection** (in order of priority): Secondary school record, standardized test scores, class rank, school's recommendation, essay.
**Nonacademic basis for candidate selection:** Character and personality, extracurricular participation, particular talent or ability, and alumni/ae relationship are considered.
**Requirements:** Graduation from secondary school is required; GED is accepted. 16 units and the following program of study are required: 4 units of English, 3 units of math, 2 units of science including 1 unit of lab, 4 units of history. Minimum combined SAT score of 800 and rank in top half of secondary school class required. Portfolio required of art program applicants. Audition required of music program applicants. HEOP for applicants not normally admissible. ACCESS program for applicants not normally admissible. SAT is required; ACT may be substituted. Campus visit and interview recommended. No off-campus interviews.
**Procedure:** Take SAT or ACT by November of 12th year. Visit college for interview by spring of 12th year. Suggest filing application by March 1; no deadline. Notification of admission on rolling basis. No set date by which applicants must accept offer. $100 tuition deposit, refundable until May 1. $100 room deposit, refundable until May 1. Freshmen accepted for terms other than fall.
**Special programs:** Admission may be deferred one semester. Credit may be granted through CEEB Advanced Placement for scores of 3 or higher. Credit may be granted through CLEP general and subject exams and DANTES exams. Credit and placement may be granted through military and life experience. Concurrent enrollment program.
**Transfer students:** Transfer students accepted for terms other than fall. In fall 1993, 60% of all new students were transfers into all classes. 798 transfer applications were received. Application deadline is rolling for fall; rolling for spring. Minimum 2.5 GPA required. Lowest course grade accepted is "C-." Maximum number of transferable credits is 62 credit hours. At least 60 credit hours must be completed at the college to receive degree.
**Admissions contact:** Mary M. O'Donnell, M.A., Director of Admissions. 518 454-5150.

**FINANCIAL AID. Available aid:** Pell grants, SEOG, state grants, academic merit scholarships, and athletic scholarships. Talent, art, music, English, and Spanish scholarships. Perkins Loans (NDSL) and Stafford Loans (GSL). AMS.
**Supporting data/closing dates:** FAFSA/FAF/FFS: Priority filing date is February 1; accepted on rolling basis. School's own aid application: Priority filing date is February 1; accepted on rolling basis. Income tax forms: Priority filing date is February 1; accepted on rolling basis. W-2. Notification of awards on rolling basis.

**Financial aid contact:** Jean E. Cossey, Director of Financial Aid. 518 454-5168.

**STUDENT EMPLOYMENT.** College Work/Study Program. Institutional employment. 18% of full-time undergraduates work on campus during school year. Students may expect to earn an average of $750 during school year. Off-campus part-time employment opportunities rated "excellent."

**COMPUTER FACILITIES.** 200 IBM/IBM-compatible and Macintosh/Apple microcomputers; 100 are networked. Students may access UNISYS minicomputer/mainframe systems. Residence halls may be equipped with stand-alone microcomputers, networked microcomputers, modems. Client/LAN operating systems include Apple/Macintosh. Computer languages and software packages include BASIC, COBOL, FORTRAN, Pascal, RPG. Computer facilities are available to all students.
**Fees:** None.
**Hours:** 24 hours for mainframe; 114 hours/week in labs.

**GRADUATE CAREER DATA.** Highest graduate school enrollments: New York State U at Albany. 20% of graduates choose careers in business and industry.

# Columbia University–Columbia College

**New York, NY 10027** **212 854-1754**

**1994-95 Costs.** Tuition: $18,550. Room & board: $7,000. Fees, books, misc. academic expenses (school's estimate): $1,014.
**Enrollment.** Undergraduates: 1,783 men, 1,664 women (full-time). Freshman class: 6,756 applicants, 2,053 accepted, 871 enrolled.
**Test score averages/ranges.** Range of SAT scores of middle 50%: 600-700 verbal, 650-750 math.
**Faculty.** 481 full-time. Student/faculty ratio: 7 to 1.
**Selectivity rating.** Most competitive.

**PROFILE.** Columbia University–Columbia College, founded in 1754, is a private, Ivy League, comprehensive university. Its 27-acre campus is located in the residential Morningside Heights section of Manhattan.

**Accreditation:** MSACS. Professionally accredited by the Accreditation Board for Engineering and Technology, the American Assembly of Collegiate Schools of Business, the National Architecture Accrediting Board.
**Religious orientation:** Columbia University–Columbia College is nonsectarian; no religious requirements.
**Library:** Collections totaling over 6,000,000 volumes, 59,000 periodical subscriptions, and 4,000,000 microform items.
**Special facilities/museums:** Art and architecture galleries, theatres.
**Athletic facilities:** Gymnasium, swimming pool, weight rooms, tracks, basketball, racquetball, and tennis courts, aerobic, fencing, and martial arts rooms, athletic fields, football and soccer stadiums, boathouse.

**STUDENT BODY. Undergraduate profile:** 19.9% Asian-American, 9% Black, 8.8% Hispanic, .1% Native American, 62.2% White.
**Freshman profile:** Majority of accepted applicants took SAT. 60% of freshmen come from public schools.
**Undergraduate achievement:** 96% of fall 1992 freshmen returned for fall 1993 term. 80% of entering class graduated. 90% of students who completed a degree program went on to graduate study.
**Foreign students:** Countries represented include Canada, France, Hong Kong, India, Japan, and the United Kingdom; 77 in all.

**PROGRAMS OF STUDY. Degrees:** A.B.
**Majors:** African-American Studies, Ancient Studies, Anthropology, Archaeology, Architecture, Art History, Astronomy, Astrophysics, Biochemistry, Biology, Biology/Psychology, Biophysics, Chemical Physics, Chemistry, Classics, Comparative Literature, Computer Science, Dance, East Asian Studies, Economics, Economics/Mathematics, Economics/Philosophy, Economics/Statistics, English, Environmental Science, Film Studies, French, Geochemistry, Geological Science, Geophysics, German Language/Literature, German Studies, Greek, History, History/Sociology, Italian, Latin, Mathematics, Middle East Studies, Music, Philosophy, Physics, Political Science, Psychology, Regional Studies, Religion, Russian Language/Literature, Russian Regional Studies, Sociology, Spanish Language/Literature, Terrestrial Geology, Theatre Arts/Drama, Urban Studies, Visual Arts, Women's Studies.
**Distribution of degrees:** The majors with the highest enrollment are English, history, and political science.
**Requirements:** General education requirement.
**Academic regulations:** Minimum 2.0 GPA must be maintained.
**Special:** Concentrations offered in many majors. Regional studies major offers concentrations in African, East Central European, and Latin American studies. Special programs in chemistry. Great Books colloquium. Seminar Institute allows selected juniors and seniors to take one intensive course/semester. Self-designed majors. Double majors. Dual degrees. Independent study. Pass/fail grading option. Internships. Graduate school at which undergraduates may take graduate-level courses. 3-2 engineering program. Five-year B.A./M.I.A. (international affairs) and B.A./M.F.A. programs. Five-year B.A./M.Mus. program with Juilliard Sch. Six-year B.A./J.D. program. Exchange programs abroad in England (Cambridge U, Oxford U), France, and Japan (Kyoto Center for Japanese Studies). ROTC at Fordham U and CUNY John Jay Coll. AFROTC at Manhattan Coll.
**Honors:** Phi Beta Kappa.
**Academic Assistance:** Nonremedial tutoring.

**STUDENT LIFE. Housing:** All freshmen must live on campus unless living with family. Coed dorms. Fraternity housing. 90% of students live in college housing.
**Social atmosphere:** According to the editor of the student newspaper, "Columbia students spend much of their social and cultural life around New York City. It is a very fun school but not centered around campus or typically collegiate events." Columbiafest weekends, Furnald Folkfest, and Realityfest parties are some of the most popular social events of the year. There is a small but active Greek life on campus. On-campus gathering spots include the Ferris-Booth Hall Cafe and dorm lounges. Favorite nightspots among Columbia students include Drew's, Blue Star, The Marlin, and Cannon's.
**Services and counseling/handicapped student services:** Placement services. Health service. Women's center. Counseling services for minority students. Birth control, personal, and psychological counseling. Career and academic guidance services. Religious counseling. Physically disabled student services. Learning disabled services. Reader services for the blind.
**Campus organizations:** Undergraduate student government. Student newspaper (Columbia Daily Spectator, published once/day). Literary magazine. Yearbook. Radio and TV stations. Glee club, gospel choir, Kingsmen, jazz band, marching band, Orchesis, Gilbert and Sullivan Society, Columbia Players, Musical Theatre Society, debating, Big Brothers/Big Sisters, Amnesty International, Community Clothes Closet, Lesbian, Bisexual and Gay Coalition, athletic, departmental, service, and special-interest groups. 12 fraternities, no chapter houses; seven sororities, no chapter houses; six coed fraternities. 18% of men join a fraternity. 8% of women join a sorority.
**Religious organizations:** Baptist, Catholic, Episcopal, Lutheran, Methodist, and Presbyterian Campus Ministries, Orthodox Christian Fellowship, Jewish Student Union, Muslim Student Association.
**Minority/foreign student organizations:** Black Students Organization, National Society of Black Engineers, Accion Boricua, Chicano Caucus, United Minorities Board, Society of Hispanic Professional Engineers, Alianza Latinoamericana, Arab Association, Asian Student Union, Asian Women's Coalition, Italian Cultural Club, Chinese, Indian, Italian, and Korean groups.

**ATHLETICS. Physical education requirements:** Two semesters of physical education required.
**Intercollegiate competition:** 40% of students participate. Archery (W), baseball (M), basketball (M,W), crew (M,W), cross-country (M,W), diving (M,W), fencing (M,W), football (M), golf (M), soccer (M,W), swimming (M,W), tennis (M,W), track (indoor) (M,W), track (outdoor) (M,W), track and field (indoor) (M,W), track and field (outdoor) (M,W), volleyball (W), wrestling (M). Member of ECAC, Ivy League, NCAA Division I, NCAA Division I-AA in football.
**Intramural and club sports:** 60% of students participate. Intramural basketball, flag football, paddleball, racquetball, soccer, softball, squash, swimming, tennis, volleyball. Men's club Alpine skiing, archery, badminton, cricket, cycling, equestrian sports, floor hockey, handball, hiking, ice hockey, kayak, lacrosse, martial arts, raquetball, road running, rifle, rugby, SCUBA, sailing, squash, skiing, table tennis, triathlon, ultimate frisbee, volleyball, water polo, weight lifting. Women's club Alpine skiing, badmiton, cheerleading, cricket, cycling, equestrian sports, field hockey, floor hockey, hiking, ice hockey, lacrosse, kayak, martial arts, racquetball, road running, rifle, rugby, sailing, SCUBA, skiing, softball, table tennis, triathlon, ultimate frisbee, water polo, weight lifting.

**ADMISSIONS. Academic basis for candidate selection** (in order of priority): Secondary school record, class rank, school's recommendation, standardized test scores, essay.
**Nonacademic basis for candidate selection:** Character and personality and extracurricular participation are emphasized. Particular talent or ability is important. Geographical distribution and alumni/ae relationship are considered.
**Requirements:** Graduation from secondary school is required; GED is accepted. 16 units and the following program of study are recommended: 4 units of English, 3 units of math, 3 units of science including 1 unit of lab, 3 units of foreign language, 3 units of social studies. EOP and HEOP for applicants not normally admissible. SAT or ACT is required. ACH required. Campus visit and interview recommended. Off-campus interviews available with an alumni representative.
**Procedure:** Take SAT or ACT by January of 12th year. Visit college for interview by December of 12th year. Application deadline is January 1. Notification of admission by April 15. Reply is required by May 1. $250 nonrefundable tuition deposit. Freshmen accepted for fall terms only.
**Special programs:** Admission may be deferred one year. Credit and/or placement may be granted through CEEB Advanced Placement exams for scores of 4 or higher. Placement may be granted through challenge exams. Early decision program. In fall 1993, 387 applied for early decision and 190 were accepted. Deadline for applying for early decision is November 1. Early entrance/early admission program.
**Transfer students:** Transfer students accepted for terms other than fall. In fall 1993, 710 transfer applications were received, 108 were accepted. Application deadline is May 1 for fall; November 1 for spring. Minimum 3.0 GPA required. Lowest course grade accepted is "C." Maximum number of transferable credits is 64 semester hours. At least 60 semester hours must be completed at the university to receive degree.
**Admissions contact:** Drusilla Blackman, M.B.A., Dean of Undergraduate Admissions and Financial Aid. 212 854-2521.

**FINANCIAL AID. Available aid:** Pell grants, SEOG, state scholarships, school scholarships, ROTC scholarships, and aid for undergraduate foreign students. Perkins Loans (NDSL), PLUS, Stafford Loans (GSL), and school loans. AMS, deferred payment plan, and guaranteed tuition.
**Financial aid statistics:** In 1993-94, 85% of all freshman applicants received aid. Average amounts of aid awarded freshmen: Scholarships and grants, $10,000.
**Supporting data/closing dates:** FAFSA/FAF: Deadline is February 1. School's own aid application: Deadline is January 1. Income tax forms: Deadline is February 1. Notification of awards begins April 15.

**STUDENT EMPLOYMENT.** College Work/Study Program. Institutional employment. 60% of full-time undergraduates work on campus during school year. Students may expect to earn an average of $1,500 during school year. Off-campus part-time employment opportunities rated "good."

**COMPUTER FACILITIES.** 100 IBM/IBM-compatible and Macintosh/Apple microcomputers; all are networked. Students may access SUN minicomputer/mainframe systems, BITNET, Internet. Residence halls may be equipped with networked terminals. Computer languages and software packages include ALGOL, BASIC, C, FORTRAN, LISP, Pascal, Prolog, SAS, SPSS. Computer facilities are available to all students.
**Fees:** $45 computer fee per semester; included in tuition/fees.
**Hours:** 24 hours in dormitories.

**GRADUATE CAREER DATA.** Graduate school percentages: 25% enter law school. 15% enter medical school. Highest graduate school enrollments: Columbia U, Harvard U, New York U. 30% of graduates choose careers in business and industry. Companies and businesses that hire graduates: Associated Press, IBM, Merrill Lynch, *New York Times*, Salomon Bros., Shearson Lehman Bros.

**PROMINENT ALUMNI/AE.** Armand Hammer, industrialist and philanthropist; Herman Wouk and Allen Ginsburg, writers; Lou Gehrig and Sid Luckman, athletes; Richard Rodgers and Oscar Hammerstein, writers of Broadway musicals; Emmanuel Ax, pianist; Art Garfunkel, singer and actor; James Cagney, actor; Brian De Palma, filmmaker.

# Columbia University–School of Engineering and Applied Science

**New York, NY 10027** **212 854-1754**

**1994-95 Costs.** Tuition: $18,550. Room & board: $7,000. Fees, books, misc. academic expenses (school's estimate): $1,150.

**Enrollment.** Undergraduates: 806 men, 202 women (full-time). Freshman class: 1,213 applicants, 618 accepted, 242 enrolled.

**Test score averages/ranges.** Range of SAT scores of middle 50%: 550-700 verbal, 700-800 math.

**Faculty.** 100 full-time; 36 part-time. 100% of faculty holds doctoral degree. Student/faculty ratio: 10 to 1.

**Selectivity rating.** Most competitive.

**PROFILE.** Columbia University–School of Engineering and Applied Science, founded in 1864, is a private, Ivy League, comprehensive university. Its campus is located in the residential Morningside Heights section of Manhattan.

**Accreditation:** MSACS. Professionally accredited by the Accreditation Board for Engineering and Technology.

**Religious orientation:** Columbia University–School of Engineering and Applied Science is nonsectarian; no religious requirements.

**Library:** Collections totaling over 170,000 volumes, 1,300 periodical subscriptions, and 1,000,000 microform items.

**Special facilities/museums:** Center for advanced research in computer and information technologies, high-tech and telecommunications research centers, observatory, reactor, fusion research equipment, microcomponent clean room, electron microscope, robotics lab, materials testing and strength of materials labs.

**Athletic facilities:** Gymnasium, aerobic, fencing, weight, and martial arts rooms, swimming pool, tracks, athletic fields, football and soccer stadiums, basketball, racquetball, and tennis courts, boathouse.

**STUDENT BODY. Undergraduate profile:** 45% are state residents. 48.2% Asian-American, 4.3% Black, 4.5% Hispanic, 40% White, 3% Other. Average age of undergraduates is 20.

**Undergraduate achievement:** 89% of fall 1992 freshmen returned for fall 1993 term. 74% of entering class graduated. 41% of students who completed a degree program immediately went on to graduate study.

**Foreign students:** Countries represented include Canada, China, India, Malaysia, Singapore, and South Korea; 48 in all.

**PROGRAMS OF STUDY. Degrees:** B.S.

**Majors:** Applied Mathematics, Applied Physics, Bioengineering Studies, Biomechanics, Chemical Engineering, Civil Engineering, Computer Science, Electrical Engineering, Environmental Engineering, Industrial Engineering, Materials Science, Mechanical Engineering, Metallurgy, Mineral Sciences, Mining, Nuclear Engineering, Operations Research.

**Distribution of degrees:** The majors with the highest enrollment are computer science, electrical engineering, and mechanical engineering; chemical engineering and applied physics have the lowest.

**Requirements:** General education requirement.

**Academic regulations:** Minimum 2.2 GPA must be maintained.

**Special:** Dual degrees. Internships. Graduate school at which undergraduates may take graduate-level courses. Preprofessional programs in law, medicine, and dentistry. Host institution for 3-2 engineering program with participation by over 80 colleges and universities. Joint degree program with Columbia College. Five-year program with the Sch of International and Public Affairs culminating in a B.S./M.Internat.Aff. Six-year B.S/J.D. program with the Sch of Law.

**Honors:** Honors program.

**Academic Assistance:** Nonremedial tutoring.

**STUDENT LIFE. Housing:** Freshmen are required to live on campus unless commuting from home. Coed dorms. Fraternity housing. School-owned/operated apartments. Both on-campus and off-campus married-student housing. 90% of students live in college housing.

**Services and counseling/handicapped student services:** Placement services. Health service. Women's center. Counseling services for minority students. Birth control, personal, and psychological counseling. Career and academic guidance services. Religious counseling.

**Campus organizations:** Undergraduate student government. Student newspaper (Columbia Daily Spectator, published once/day). Literary magazine. Yearbook. Radio and TV stations. SEAS Student Council, Amnesty International, Big Brothers/Big Sisters, Black Theatre and Performing Arts Society, Clef Hangers, Filmmakers, Gilbert and Sullivan Society, glee club, gospel choir, jazz band, marching band, musical theatre society, orchestra, Players, numerous arts, service, and pre-professional organizations, 80 organizations in all. 12 fraternities, seven sororities. 18% of men join a fraternity. 8% of women join a sorority.

**Religious organizations:** Numerous religious groups.

**Minority/foreign student organizations:** Accion Boricua, Alianza Latinoamericana, Asian Women's Coalition, Black Students Organization, Chicano Caucus, Italian Cultural Club, National Society of Black Engineers, Society of Hispanic Professional Engineers, United Minorities Board. Arab Association, Asian Student Union, Chinese Students club, Club Zamana (for Indian Students), Korean Students Association.

**ATHLETICS. Physical education requirements:** Two semesters of physical education required.

**Intercollegiate competition:** 40% of students participate. Archery (W), baseball (M), basketball (M,W), crew (M,W), cross-country (M,W), diving (M,W), fencing (M,W), football (M), golf (M), soccer (M,W), swimming (M,W), tennis (M,W), track (indoor) (M,W), track (outdoor) (M,W), track and field (indoor) (M,W), track and field (outdoor) (M,W), volleyball (W), wrestling (M). Member of ECAC, EISL, EIWA, Ivy League, NCAA Division I.

**Intramural and club sports:** 60% of students participate. Intramural basketball, flag football, paddleball, racquetball, soccer, softball, squash, swimming, tennis, volleyball. Men's club Alpine skiing, archery, badmiton, cricket, cycling, equestrian sports, floor hockey, handball, hiking, ice hockey, kayak, lacrosse, martial arts, raquetball, rifle, road running, rugby, sailing, SCUBA, squash, table tennis, triathlon, ultimate frisbee, volleyball, water polo, weight lifting. Women's club Alpine skiing, badminton, cricket, cycling, equestrian sports, handball, hiking, floor hockey, field hockey, ice hockey, kayak, lacrosse, martial arts, rifle, racquetball, road running, rugby, sailing, SCUBA, softball, table tennis, triathlon, ultimate frisbee, water polo, weight lifting.

**ADMISSIONS. Academic basis for candidate selection** (in order of priority): Secondary school record, school's recommendation, essay, class rank, standardized test scores.

**Nonacademic basis for candidate selection:** Character and personality and extracurricular participation are important. Particular talent or ability, geographical distribution, and alumni/ae relationship are considered.

**Requirements:** Graduation from secondary school is required; GED is not accepted. The following program of study is required: 4 units of English, 4 units of mathematics, 4 units of science including three units of lab. Math units should include calculus; science units should include chemistry and physics. Two or three units of foreign language and three or four units of history and social studies recommended. HEOP for applicants not normally admissible. SAT is required; ACT may be substituted. ACH required. Campus visit and interview recommended. Off-campus interviews available with an alumni representative.

**Procedure:** Take SAT or ACT by January of 12th year. Take ACH by January of 12th year. Visit college for interview by January of 12th year. Suggest filing application by January 1; no deadline. Notification of admission by April 15. Reply is required by May 1. $250 nonrefundable tuition deposit. Freshmen accepted for fall terms only.

**Special programs:** Admission may be deferred one year. Credit and/or placement may be granted through CEEB Advanced Placement exams for scores of 4 or higher. Early decision program. In fall 1993, 28 applied for early decision and 18 were accepted. Deadline for applying for early decision is November 1.

**Transfer students:** Transfer students accepted for fall term only. In fall 1993, 101 transfer applications were received, 22 were accepted. Application deadline is April 1. Minimum 3.5 GPA required. Lowest course grade accepted is "C."

**Admissions contact:** Drusilla Blackman, M.B.A., Dean of Undergraduate Admissions and Financial Aid. 212 854-2521.

**FINANCIAL AID. Available aid:** Pell grants, SEOG, state scholarships and grants, school scholarships and grants, and private scholarships and grants. Perkins Loans (NDSL), PLUS, Stafford Loans (GSL), state loans, school loans, private loans, and SLS. AMS and guaranteed tuition.

**Financial aid statistics:** In 1993-94, 85% of all undergraduate applicants received aid; 93% of freshman applicants. Average amounts of aid awarded freshmen: Scholarships and grants, $12,000; loans, $2,400.

**Supporting data/closing dates:** FAFSA/FAF: Priority filing date is February 1. School's own aid application: Priority filing date is February 1. Income tax forms: Priority filing date is April 15. Notification of awards begins April 15.

**STUDENT EMPLOYMENT.** College Work/Study Program. Institutional employment. 48% of full-time undergraduates work on campus during school year. Students may expect to earn an average of $1,850 during school year. Off-campus part-time employment opportunities rated "good."

**COMPUTER FACILITIES.** IBM/IBM-compatible and Macintosh/Apple microcomputers. Students may access Digital, IBM minicomputer/mainframe systems. Computer languages and software packages include ALGOL, APL, BASIC, COBOL, FORTRAN, LISP, Pascal, PL/1, SNOBOL; variety of specialized engineering computational and graphics packages, general software for word processing and work in social sciences. Fees: None.

**GRADUATE CAREER DATA.** Graduate school percentages: 4% enter law school. 5% enter medical school. 1% enter graduate business programs. 22% enter graduate arts and sciences programs. Highest graduate school enrollments: Columbia U.

# The Cooper Union

**New York, NY 10003** **212 353-4100**

**1993-94 Costs.** Tuition: None. Room: $4,545. Fees, books, misc. academic expenses (school's estimate): $4,300.

**Enrollment.** Undergraduates: 637 men, 322 women (full-time). Freshman class: 2,339 applicants, 307 accepted, 197 enrolled. Graduate enrollment: 79 men, 10 women.

**Test score averages/ranges.** Average SAT scores: 600 verbal, 740 math. Range of SAT scores of middle 50%: 540-660 verbal, 690-760 math.

**Faculty.** 60 full-time; 175 part-time. 60% of faculty holds doctoral degree. Student/faculty ratio: 7 to 1.

**Selectivity rating.** Most competitive.

**PROFILE.** The Cooper Union, founded in 1859, is a private, multipurpose institution offering tuition-free education. Programs are offered through the Schools of Architecture, Art, and Engineering. Its five-building campus, located in lower Manhattan, includes the Foundation Building, a Registered Historic Landmark.

**Accreditation:** MSACS. Professionally accredited by the Accreditation Board for Engineering and Technology, the National Architecture Accrediting Board, the National Association of Schools of Art and Design.
**Religious orientation:** The Cooper Union is nonsectarian; no religious requirements.
**Library:** Collections totaling over 98,000 volumes, 370 periodical subscriptions, and 100,000 microform items.
**Special facilities/museums:** Art gallery, air pollution control center, computer graphics and robotics lab, infrastructure institute.
**Athletic facilities:** Rented facilities nearby.

**STUDENT BODY. Undergraduate profile:** 60% are state residents; 20% are transfers. 27% Asian-American, 8% Black, 9% Hispanic, 1% Native American, 50% White, 5% Other. Average age of undergraduates is 20.
**Freshman profile:** 9% of freshmen who took SAT scored 700 or over on verbal, 75% scored 700 or over on math; 50% scored 600 or over on verbal, 100% scored 600 or over on math; 88% scored 500 or over on verbal; 100% scored 400 or over on verbal. 99% of accepted applicants took SAT; 1% took ACT. 70% of freshmen come from public schools.
**Undergraduate achievement:** 87% of fall 1992 freshmen returned for fall 1993 term. 60% of entering class graduated. 55% of students who completed a degree program went on to graduate study within five years.
**Foreign students:** 81 students are from out of the country. Countries represented include Canada, China, Germany, India, Korea, and Romania; 33 in all.

**PROGRAMS OF STUDY. Degrees:** B.Arch., B.Eng., B.F.A., B.S.
**Majors:** Architecture, Chemical Engineering, Civil Engineering, Electrical Engineering, Engineering, Fine Art, Graphic Design, Mechanical Engineering.
**Distribution of degrees:** The majors with the highest enrollment are fine arts, electrical engineering, and architecture; engineering, chemical engineering, and mechanical engineering have the lowest.
**Requirements:** General education requirement.
**Academic regulations:** Minimum 2.5 GPA must be maintained.
**Special:** Independent study. Accelerated study. Internships. Graduate school at which undergraduates may take graduate-level courses. Member of East Coast National Association of Schools of Art and Design. Exchange program with Otis Sch of Art and Design. Study abroad in England, Germany, Israel, Japan, Kenya, the Netherlands, and Switzerland.
**Honors:** Honors program. Honor societies.
**Academic Assistance:** Nonremedial tutoring.

**STUDENT LIFE. Housing:** School-owned/operated apartments. No meal plan. 19% of students live in college housing.
**Social atmosphere:** Favorite off-campus gathering spots include Billy's, Carty's, Veniero's, Central Park, McSorley's, Angelika Film Center and many, many other local cafes and bars. Popular campus activities include Hewitt parties, comedy night, ProMusic concerts, the Turkey Trot (Thanksgiving jog around Central Park), and the many lectures, conferences, and performances sponsored by the ethnic societies. "There's not really much of a campus at Cooper," observes the editor of the student newspaper. "But then as we're fond of saying: 'Manhattan is our campus'."
**Services and counseling/handicapped student services:** Placement services. Health service. Personal and psychological counseling. Career and academic guidance services. Physically disabled student services. Learning disabled services. Tape recorders. Tutors.
**Campus organizations:** Undergraduate student government. Student newspaper (Pioneer, published once/month). Literary magazine. Yearbook. Cooper Greens, Habitat for Humanity, Pro Musica, theatre and drama groups, film society, graphics publication, speech and debate clubs, 25 organizations in all. Two fraternities, no chapter houses; two sororities, no chapter houses. 20% of men join a fraternity. 10% of women join a sorority.
**Religious organizations:** Campus Crusade for Christ, Christian Fellowship, The Meditation Place, Kesher organization.
**Minority/foreign student organizations:** ONYX (black student group), AMIGOS (Hispanic student group), Chinese and Korean groups.

**ATHLETICS. Physical education requirements:** None.
**Intercollegiate competition:** 5% of students participate. Bowling (M,W), tennis (M,W).
**Intramural and club sports:** Intramural basketball, bowling, softball, table tennis, volleyball.

**ADMISSIONS. Academic basis for candidate selection** (in order of priority): Secondary school record, standardized test scores, school's recommendation, class rank.
**Nonacademic basis for candidate selection:** Particular talent or ability is emphasized. Character and personality are important. Extracurricular participation is considered.
**Requirements:** Graduation from secondary school is required; GED is accepted. 16 units and the following program of study are required: 4 units of English, 6 units of electives. 1 unit of math, 1 unit of science, 2 units of history/social studies, and 8 units of electives required of art program applicants. 3 units of math (including trigonometry), 1 unit of science, and 2 units of history/social studies required of architecture program applicants. 3.5 units of math (including pre-calculus), 2 units of science (including physics and chemistry) and 2 units of history/social studies required of engineering program applicants. Home projects demonstrating design aptitude and related abilities required of art and architecture program applicants. Portfolio required of art program applicants. SAT is required; ACT may be substituted. ACH required. CEEBs in math, chemistry, or physics required for engineering programs applicants. No off-campus interviews.
**Procedure:** Take SAT or ACT by January of 12th year. Take ACH by January of 12th year. Priority filing dates are January 1 for architecture program applicants, January 10 for art program applicants, and February 1 for engineering program applicants. Notification of admission by April 1. Reply is required by May 1. $450 nonrefundable room deposit. Freshmen accepted for fall terms only.
**Special programs:** Admission may be deferred one year. Credit may be granted through CEEB Advanced Placement for scores of 4 or higher. Credit may be granted through CLEP subject exams. Early decision program. In fall 1993, 66 applied for early decision and 33 were accepted. Deadline for applying for early decision is December 1. Early entrance/early admission program.
**Transfer students:** Transfer students accepted for fall term only. In fall 1993, 20% of all new students were transfers into all classes. 777 transfer applications were received, 35 were accepted. Application deadline is Jan. 10 (art), Feb. 15 (arch.), April 15 (eng.). Lowest course grade accepted is "B." Maximum number of transferable credits is 60 semester hours.
**Admissions contact:** Richard Bory, M.Div., M.S., Dean of Admissions. 212 353-4120.

**FINANCIAL AID. Available aid:** Pell grants, SEOG, state scholarships, school scholarships and grants, and private grants. All students enrolled on a tuition-free basis. Perkins Loans (NDSL), Stafford Loans (GSL), state loans, school loans, and private loans.
**Financial aid statistics:** In 1993-94, 72% of all undergraduate applicants received aid; 70% of freshman applicants.
**Supporting data/closing dates:** FAFSA/FAF: Priority filing date is in February; accepted on rolling basis; deadline is in May. Notification of awards on rolling basis.
**Financial aid contact:** Ann-Marie Weimer-Sumner, Ph.D., Director of Financial Aid. 212 353-4112.

**STUDENT EMPLOYMENT.** College Work/Study Program. Institutional employment. 35% of full-time undergraduates work on campus during school year. Students may expect to earn an average of $3,000 during school year. Freshmen are discouraged from working during their first term. Off-campus part-time employment opportunities rated "excellent."

**COMPUTER FACILITIES.** 130 IBM/IBM-compatible, Macintosh/Apple, and RISC-/UNIX-based microcomputers; 95 are networked. Students may access AT&T, Digital, Hewlett-Packard, SUN minicomputer/mainframe systems, Internet. Residence halls may be equipped with stand-alone microcomputers. Client/LAN operating systems include Apple/Macintosh, DOS, UNIX/XENIX/AIX, X-windows, LocalTalk/AppleTalk. Computer languages and software packages include BASIC, C, FORTRAN, Pascal; 100 in all. Computer facilities are available to all students.
**Fees:** None.
**Hours:** 9 AM-midn. (M-F); 9 AM-midn. (Sa-Su).

**GRADUATE CAREER DATA.** Graduate school percentages: 3% enter law school. 3% enter medical school. 10% enter graduate business programs. 34% enter graduate arts and sciences programs. Highest graduate school enrollments: UC Berkeley, Columbia U, MIT, Princeton. 40% of graduates choose careers in business and industry. Companies and businesses that hire graduates: Bell Labs, AT&T, major art/design, engineering, and architectural companies/firms.

**PROMINENT ALUMNI/AE.** Thomas Edison, inventor; Felix Frankfurter, former chief justice of U.S. Supreme Court; William Pfann, developer of first transistor prototype; Israel Taback, senior engineer, NASA spacecraft; Tom Wesselmann, painter; Rulse, 1993 Nobel Prize winner, physics.

# Cornell University

**Ithaca, NY 14853** | **607 255-2000**

**1994-95 Costs.** Tuition: $19,000. State Division: $7,740 (in-state); $14,900 (out-of-state). Room & board: $6,148. Fees, books, misc. academic expenses (school's estimate): $666.

**Enrollment.** Undergraduates: 6,878 men, 5,935 women (full-time). Freshman class: 20,324 applicants, 7,171 accepted, 3,286 enrolled. Graduate enrollment: 3,485 men, 2,151 women.

**Test score averages/ranges.** Range of SAT scores of middle 50%: 540-640 verbal, 640-740 math.

**Faculty.** 1,542 full-time; 52 part-time. 94% of faculty holds highest degree in specific field. Student/faculty ratio: 8 to 1.

**Selectivity rating.** Most competitive.

**PROFILE.** Cornell, founded in 1865, is a land-grant institution. Programs are offered through the Colleges of Agriculture and Life Sciences; Architecture, Art, and Planning; Arts and Sciences; Engineering; and Human Ecology; the Schools of Hotel Administration and Industrial and Labor Relations; the Graduate School; the Graduate School of Management; and the Law School. Its 745-acre campus is located in Ithaca, 45 miles from Syracuse.

**Accreditation:** MSACS. Professionally accredited by the American Society of Landscape Architects, the Council on Social Work Education.
**Religious orientation:** Cornell University is nonsectarian; no religious requirements.
**Library:** Collections totaling over 5,579,629 volumes, 61,068 periodical subscriptions, and 6,129,806 microform items.
**Special facilities/museums:** Art museum, Africana studies and research center, theory center.
**Athletic facilities:** Gymnasium, baseball, field hockey, football, lacrosse, rugby, soccer, and softball fields, basketball, racquetball, squash, and tennis courts, crew facilities, swimming pools, dance studio, golf course, ice rink, equitation center, fencing and weight rooms, track, field houses, stadium, bowling alley.

**STUDENT BODY. Undergraduate profile:** 49% are state residents; 14% are transfers. 15% Asian-American, 5% Black, 6% Hispanic, 69% White, 5% Other. Average age of undergraduates is 20.
**Freshman profile:** 99% of accepted applicants took SAT.
**Undergraduate achievement:** 96% of fall 1992 freshmen returned for fall 1993 term. 79% of entering class graduated. 32% of students who completed a degree program went on to graduate study within one year.
**Foreign students:** 626 students are from out of the country. 116 countries represented in all.

**PROGRAMS OF STUDY. Degrees:** B.A., B.Arch., B.F.A., B.S.
**Majors:** Africana Studies, Agricultural Business Management/Marketing, Agricultural Economics, Agricultural Education, Agricultural Engineering, American Studies, Animal Physiology/Anatomy, Animal Science, Anthropology, Aquatic Science, Archaeology,

Architecture, Asian Studies, Astronomy, Atmospheric Science, Behavioral/Social Sciences, Biochemistry, Biological Sciences, Biology/Society, Botany, Cell Biology, Chemical Engineering, Chemistry, City/Regional Planning, Civil/Environmental Engineering, Classics, College Scholar Major, Communication Arts, Comparative Literature, Computer Science, Consumer Economics/Housing, Dance, Design/Environmental Analysis, Ecology/Evolution, Economics, Electrical Engineering, Engineering Physics, English, Entomology, Environmental Horticulture, Environmental Technology, Farm Finance/Farm Management, Field Crops, Fine Arts, Floriculture/Ornamental Horticulture, Food Industry Management, Food Science, French, General Studies, Genetics/Development Neurology/Behavior, Geological Sciences, German, German Area Studies, Government, History, History of Architecture/Urban Development, History of Art, Hotel/Restaurant Administration, Human Development/Family Studies, Human Services Studies, Independent Major, Individual Curriculum, Industrial/Labor Relations, Interdisciplinary, International Agriculture, Italian, Landscape Architecture, Linguistics, Materials Science/Engineering, Mathematics, Mechanical Engineering, Microbiology, Music, Natural Resources, Near Eastern Studies, Nutritional Sciences, Operations Research/Industrial Engineering, Philosophy, Physics, Plant Biology, Plant Breeding, Plant Pathology, Plant Protection, Plant Sciences, Policy Analysis, Pomology, Psychology, Religious Studies, Resource Economics, Rural Sociology, Russian, Russian/Soviet Studies, Social Relations, Sociology, Soils Science, Spanish, Statistics/Biometry, Textiles/Apparel, Theatre Arts, Urban/Regional Studies, Vegetable Crops.
**Distribution of degrees:** The majors with the highest enrollment are biological sciences and government; pomology, social relations, and astronomy have the lowest.
**Special:** Interdisciplinary programs. Women's studies program. Instruction in approximately 40 languages. Dual registration possible for seniors accepted by one of university's professional schools. Self-designed majors. Double majors. Dual degrees. Independent study. Accelerated study. Pass/fail grading option. Internships. Cooperative education programs. Graduate school at which undergraduates may take graduate-level courses. Preprofessional programs in law, medicine, and veterinary science. Five-year B.A./M.A. program in business administration. Six-year B.S./M.B.A./M.E. program. B.A./B.S. and B.A./B.F.A. programs. Member of Consortium on Financing Higher Education. Washington Semester, UN Semester, and Sea Semester. Teacher certification in secondary education. Certification in specific subject areas. Study abroad in numerous countries. Archaeological investigations during summer in Cyprus, Greece, and Israel. ROTC, NROTC, and AFROTC.
**Honors:** Phi Beta Kappa. Honors program. Honor societies.
**Academic Assistance:** Remedial reading. Nonremedial tutoring.

**STUDENT LIFE. Housing:** Students may live on or off campus. Coed, women's, and men's dorms. Sorority and fraternity housing. School-owned/operated apartments. Special-interest houses. Cooperative dormitories and dining plans. 76% of students live in college housing.
**Social atmosphere:** Students gather at Ruloff's, The Palms, Willard Straight Hall, the Robert Purcell Community Center, and Collegetown. Greeks have a widespread influence on campus life. Popular events include Slope Day and hockey games.
**Services and counseling/handicapped student services:** Placement services. Health service. Women's center. Counseling services for minority and veteran students. Birth control, personal, and psychological counseling. Career and academic guidance services. Religious counseling. Physically disabled student services. Learning disabled services. Notetaking services. Tape recorders. Tutors. Reader services for the blind.
**Campus organizations:** Undergraduate student government. Student newspaper (Cornell Daily Sun). Literary magazine. Yearbook. Radio station. Choral groups, concert and jazz bands, marching and pep bands, music ensembles, orchestra, dance and drama groups, debating, public speaking, volunteer community service groups, departmental groups, special-interest groups, 500 organizations in all. 47 fraternities, 46 chapter houses; 18 sororities, 16 chapter houses. 32% of men join a fraternity. 28% of women join a sorority.
**Religious organizations:** Hillel, CARP, Chinese Bible Study, Campus Crusade for Christ, Africana American Worship Service, Intervarsity Christian Fellowship, Hong Kong Christian Fellowship, Bahai Club, Catholic Community, Jewish Student Appeal, Lutheran Student Fellowship, Navigators, Latter-Day Saints Student Association, Protestant Cooperative Ministry, Episcopal and Unitarian Universalist chaplaincies.
**Minority/foreign student organizations:** Africana Student Association, Black Students United, La Asociacion Latina, Native American group, Minority Veterinary Association, National Society of Black Engineers, Society of Minority Hoteliers, Association of Students of Color. Asian, Baltic, Canadian, Caribbean, Chilean, Chinese, Colombian, Egyptian, Filipino, Indian, Japanese, Korean, Mexican, Pakistani, Persian, Sri Lankan, Taiwanese, Vietnamese, and other foreign student groups.

**ATHLETICS. Physical education requirements:** Two semesters of physical education required.
**Intercollegiate competition:** 15% of students participate. Baseball (M), basketball (M,W), crew (M,W), cross-country (M,W), diving (M,W), field hockey (W), football (M), golf (M), ice hockey (M,W), lacrosse (M,W), lightweight football (M), polo (M,W), soccer (M,W), softball (W), squash (M), swimming (M,W), tennis (M,W), track (indoor) (M,W), track (outdoor) (M,W), track and field (indoor) (M,W), track and field (outdoor) (M,W), volleyball (W), wrestling (M). Member of ECAC, Ivy League, NCAA Division I, NCAA Division I-AA for football.
**Intramural and club sports:** 70% of students participate. Intramural Alpine skiing, badminton, basketball, bowling, box lacrosse, broomstick polo, cross-country, fencing, floor hockey, golf, homerun contest, horseshoes, ice hockey, inner-tube water polo, Nordic skiing, soccer, softball, squash, swimming, table tennis, tennis, touch football, track, volleyball, wrestling. Men's club Alpine skiing, archery, cheerleading, cycling, handball, horsemanship, martial arts, Nordic skiing, racquetball, rifle, rugby, sailing, ultimate frisbee, water polo, water skiing, weight lifting. Women's club cheerleading, cycling, handball, horsemanship, martial arts, Nordic skiing, racquetball, rifle, rugby, sailing, squash, ultimate frisbee, water skiing, weight lifting.

**ADMISSIONS. Academic basis for candidate selection** (in order of priority): Secondary school record, class rank, school's recommendation, standardized test scores, essay.
**Nonacademic basis for candidate selection:** Extracurricular participation and particular talent or ability are emphasized. Character and personality are important. Geographical distribution and alumni/ae relationship are considered.
**Requirements:** Graduation from secondary school is recommended; GED is accepted. 16 units and the following program of study are required: 4 units of English, 3 units of math. Other requirements vary significantly depending upon program. Applicants must have satisfactory knowledge of subjects required by individual colleges for admission to those colleges. Interview and portfolio required of applicants to College of Architecture, Art, and Planning. Interview required of applicants to School of Hotel Administration and School of Industrial and Labor Relations. EOP and HEOP for applicants not normally admissible. SAT or ACT is required. Campus visit recommended. Off-campus interviews available with admissions and alumni representatives.
**Procedure:** Take SAT or ACT by December of 12th year. Application deadline is January 1. Notification of admissions by mid-April. Reply is required by May 1. $200 tuition deposit, refundable until July 1. Freshmen accepted for terms other than fall.
**Special programs:** Admission may be deferred one year. Credit and/or placement may be granted through CEEB Advanced Placement exams. Early decision program. In fall 1993, 1,808 applied for early decision and 691 were accepted. Deadline for applying for early decision is November 10. Early entrance/early admission program.
**Transfer students:** Transfer students accepted for terms other than fall. In fall 1993, 14% of all new students were transfers into all classes. 1,672 transfer applications were received, 677 were accepted. Application deadline is March 1 for fall; October 15 for spring. At least 60 credits must be completed at the university to receive degree.
**Admissions contact:** Nancy Meislahn, Director of Admissions. 607 255-5241.

**FINANCIAL AID. Available aid:** Pell grants, SEOG, state scholarships and grants, school scholarships and grants, private scholarships and grants, ROTC scholarships, and aid for undergraduate foreign students. Perkins Loans (NDSL), PLUS, Stafford Loans (GSL), school loans, and SLS. Installment plan. Multiple-year tuition payment plan.
**Financial aid statistics:** In 1993-94, 95% of all undergraduate applicants received aid; 89% of freshman applicants. Average amounts of aid awarded freshmen: Scholarships and grants, $11,750; loans, $3,850.
**Supporting data/closing dates:** FAFSA/FAF: Priority filing date is February 15. School's own aid application: Priority filing date is February 15. Income tax forms: Accepted on rolling basis. Notification of awards begins April 2.
**Financial aid contact:** Donald A. Saleh, M.A., Director of Financial Aid. 607 255-5145.

**STUDENT EMPLOYMENT.** College Work/Study Program. Institutional employment. 44% of full-time undergraduates work on campus during school year. Students may expect to earn an average of $1,499 during school year. Off-campus part-time employment opportunities rated "good."

**COMPUTER FACILITIES.** IBM/IBM-compatible and Macintosh/Apple microcomputers. Students may access Digital, IBM minicomputer/mainframe systems, BITNET, Internet. Residence halls may be equipped with modems. Client/LAN operating systems include Apple/Macintosh, DOS, OS/2, UNIX/XENIX/AIX, Windows NT, X-windows, LocalTalk/AppleTalk. Computer languages and software packages include C, Excel, LISP, Lotus 1-2-3, Mathematica, SAS, Word, Write Now. Computer facilities are available to all students.
**Fees:** Computer fee is included in tuition/fees.
**Hours:** 8 AM-2 AM.

**GRADUATE CAREER DATA.** Graduate school percentages: 6% enter law school. 7% enter medical school. 1% enter graduate business programs. 11% enter graduate arts and sciences programs. Highest graduate school enrollments: Cornell U, U of Pennsylvania, Stanford U. Companies and businesses that hire graduates: Andersen Consulting, Procter & Gamble, Chase Manhattan.

**PROMINENT ALUMNI/AE.** Ruth Bader Ginsberg, U.S. Supreme Court justice; Toni Morrison, author; Janet Reno, U.S. attorney general; E.B. White, author.

# Daemen College

**Amherst, NY 14226** **716 839-3600**

**1994-95 Costs.** Tuition: $8,800. Room & board: $4,600. Fees, books, misc. academic expenses (school's estimate): $320.
**Enrollment.** Undergraduates: 433 men, 824 women (full-time). Freshman class: 406 enrolled. Graduate enrollment: 4 men, 8 women.
**Test score averages/ranges.** N/A.
**Faculty.** 70 full-time; 66 part-time. 78% of faculty holds highest degree in specific field. Student/faculty ratio: 15 to 1.
**Selectivity rating.** N/A.

**PROFILE.** Daemen, founded in 1947, is a private, career-oriented, liberal arts college. Programs are offered through the Divisions of Business and Commerce, Fine and Performing Arts, Humanities and Social Sciences, and Natural and Health Sciences. Its 37-acre campus is located in a suburb of Buffalo.

**Accreditation:** MSACS. Professionally accredited by the American Physical Therapy Association, the Council on Social Work Education, the National League for Nursing.
**Religious orientation:** Daemen College is nonsectarian; no religious requirements.
**Library:** Collections totaling over 130,000 volumes, 850 periodical subscriptions, and 1,200 microform items.
**Special facilities/museums:** Teaching resource center, academic resource center, language lab.
**Athletic facilities:** Basketball courts, weight rooms, trainer's and exercise rooms, tennis courts; free access to YMCA swimming pool across from campus.

**STUDENT BODY. Undergraduate profile:** 89% are state residents. 1% Asian-American, 7% Black, 2% Hispanic, 87% White, 3% Other. Average age of undergraduates is 20.

**Freshman profile:** Majority of accepted applicants took SAT.
**Foreign students:** 60 students are from out of the country. Countries represented include African and Asian countries; 17 in all.

**PROGRAMS OF STUDY. Degrees:** B.A., B.F.A., B.S.
**Majors:** Accounting, Applied Design, Art, Biology, Business Administration, Elementary Education, English, French, Graphic Design, History/Government, Humanities, Mathematics, Medical Technology, Natural Science, Nursing, Physical Therapy, Psychology, Religious Studies, Social Work, Spanish, Special Education, Transportation/Travel Management.
**Requirements:** General education requirement.
**Special:** Certificate programs offered in accounting, government/urban problems, medical technology, and transportation studies. Self-designed majors. Double majors. Dual degrees. Independent study. Pass/fail grading option. Internships. Cooperative education programs. Preprofessional programs in law, medicine, veterinary science, and dentistry. Member of Western New York Consortium of Higher Education. Washington Semester. Teacher certification in elementary, secondary, and special education. Certification in specific subject areas. Exchange program abroad in Poland (Catholic U of Lublin). Study abroad also in England, France, Mexico, and Spain. ROTC at Canisius Coll.
**Honors:** Honor societies.
**Academic Assistance:** Remedial reading, writing, math, and study skills. Nonremedial tutoring.

**STUDENT LIFE. Housing:** Students may live on or off campus. Women's and men's dorms. 28% of students live in college housing.
**Services and counseling/handicapped student services:** Placement services. Personal and psychological counseling. Career and academic guidance services. Religious counseling. Physically disabled student services. Learning disabled services. Tutors.
**Campus organizations:** Undergraduate student government. Student newspaper (Ascent, published once/month). Literary magazine. Yearbook. Glee club, drama club, ski club, Community Action Corps, departmental groups, special-interest groups, 22 organizations in all. Two fraternities, no chapter houses; four sororities, no chapter houses. 14% of men join a fraternity. 15% of women join a sorority.
**Religious organizations:** Campus Ministry.
**Minority/foreign student organizations:** Unity Among Us. International Student Club.

**ATHLETICS. Physical education requirements:** None.
**Intercollegiate competition:** 3% of students participate. Baseball (M), basketball (M,W), soccer (M,W), softball (W), track (M,W). Member of National Small Colleges Athletic Association.
**Intramural and club sports:** Intramural basketball, skiing, tennis, touch football, volleyball.

**ADMISSIONS. Academic basis for candidate selection** (in order of priority): Secondary school record, standardized test scores, class rank, school's recommendation.
**Nonacademic basis for candidate selection:** Character and personality, extracurricular participation, particular talent or ability, geographical distribution, and alumni/ae relationship are considered.
**Requirements:** Graduation from secondary school is required; GED is accepted. No specific distribution of secondary school units required. Portfolio required of art program applicants. R.N. required of nursing program applicants. HEOP for applicants not normally admissible. Conditional admission possible for applicants not meeting standard requirements. SAT or ACT is required. Campus visit and interview recommended. Off-campus interviews available with an admissions representative.
**Procedure:** Take SAT or ACT by December of 12th year. Visit college for interview by April of 12th year. Suggest filing application by December; no deadline. Notification of admission on rolling basis. Reply is required by May 1. $100 nonrefundable tuition deposit. $100 room deposit, refundable until May 1. Freshmen accepted for terms other than fall.
**Special programs:** Credit and/or placement may be granted through CEEB Advanced Placement exams for scores of 3 or higher. Credit and/or placement may be granted through CLEP subject exams. Credit and placement may be granted through Regents College, DANTES, and challenge exams, and life experience. Early decision program. Deadline for applying for early decision is August 1. Early entrance/early admission program. Concurrent enrollment program.
**Transfer students:** Transfer students accepted for terms other than fall. Application deadline is rolling for fall; rolling for spring. Minimum 2.0 GPA required. Lowest course grade accepted is "C." At least 30 semester hours must be completed at the college to receive degree.
**Admissions contact:** Maria Dillard, M.A., Director of Enrollment Management. 716 839-8225.

**FINANCIAL AID. Available aid:** Pell grants, SEOG, state scholarships and grants, school scholarships and grants, private scholarships and grants, ROTC scholarships, academic merit scholarships, and athletic scholarships. Perkins Loans (NDSL), PLUS, Stafford Loans (GSL), school loans, and SLS. AMS, deferred payment plan, and family tuition reduction.
**Financial aid statistics:** In 1993-94, 94% of all undergraduate applicants received aid; 96% of freshman applicants. Average amounts of aid awarded freshmen: Scholarships and grants, $3,500; loans, $2,300.
**Supporting data/closing dates:** FAFSA/FAF/FFS: Accepted on rolling basis. School's own aid application: Accepted on rolling basis. State aid form: Accepted on rolling basis. Income tax forms. Notification of awards on rolling basis.
**Financial aid contact:** Helen Lukasik, M.A., Director of Financial Aid. 716 839-3600.

**STUDENT EMPLOYMENT.** College Work/Study Program. Institutional employment. 2% of full-time undergraduates work on campus during school year. Students may expect to earn an average of $1,200 during school year. Off-campus part-time employment opportunities rated "excellent."

**COMPUTER FACILITIES.** 80 IBM/IBM-compatible and Macintosh/Apple microcomputers. Students may access Digital minicomputer/mainframe systems. Computer languages and software packages include Assembler, BASIC, C, COBOL, Dual System, FORTRAN, LISP, Pascal. Computer facilities are available to all students.
**Hours:** 8 AM-midn. (M-F); noon-midn. (Sa-Su).

# Dominican College of Blauvelt

**Orangeburg, NY 10962** **914 359-7800**

**1992-93 Costs.** Tuition: $7,140. Room & board: $5,300. Fees, books, misc. academic expenses (school's estimate): $975.
**Enrollment.** Undergraduates: 217 men, 421 women (full-time). Freshman class: 360 applicants, 329 accepted, 108 enrolled.
**Test score averages/ranges.** N/A.
**Faculty.** 40 full-time; 86 part-time. 45% of faculty holds doctoral degree. Student/faculty ratio: 12 to 1.
**Selectivity rating.** N/A.

**PROFILE.** Dominican, founded in 1952, is a private, liberal arts college. Its 14-acre campus is located in Rockland County, 17 miles north of New York City.

**Accreditation:** MSACS. Professionally accredited by the American Library Association, the Council on Social Work Education, the National League for Nursing.
**Religious orientation:** Dominican College of Blauvelt is nonsectarian; no religious requirements.
**Library:** Collections totaling over 98,586 volumes, 637 periodical subscriptions, and 11,318 microform items.
**Athletic facilities:** Gymnasiums, softball field.

**STUDENT BODY. Undergraduate profile:** 70% are state residents; 47% are transfers. 3% Asian-American, 7% Black, 85% White, 5% Other. Average age of undergraduates is 28.
**Freshman profile:** 95% of accepted applicants took SAT. 79% of freshmen come from public schools.
**Undergraduate achievement:** 67% of fall 1992 freshmen returned for fall 1993 term. 33% of entering class graduated.
**Foreign students:** 20 students are from out of the country. Countries represented include Ireland, Japan, Namibia, St. Lucia, Taiwan, and Turkey.

**PROGRAMS OF STUDY. Degrees:** B.A., B.S., B.S.Ed., B.S.Nurs.
**Majors:** Accounting, American Social Sciences, Business Administration, Computer Information Systems, Economics, Elementary Education, English, Health Services Administration, History, Humanities, Management, Mathematics, Natural Science, Nursing, Occupational Therapy, Psychology, Rehabilitation Teaching, Social Sciences, Social Work, Spanish, Special Education.
**Distribution of degrees:** The majors with the highest enrollment are management, nursing, and occupational therapy; history, Spanish, and special education have the lowest.
**Requirements:** General education requirement.
**Academic regulations:** Freshmen must maintain minimum 1.8 GPA; sophomores, juniors, seniors, 2.0 GPA.
**Special:** Courses offered in art, biological sciences, chemistry, dance, earth science, music, philosophy, physics, political science, religious studies, and speech. Course clusters (interdisciplinary courses designed by students and faculty) vary from year to year and include areas such as American social sciences, business computer systems, and communications. Certificate programs offered in community residence personnel, computer information systems, and computer programming. Associate's degrees offered. Double majors. Independent study. Accelerated study. Internships. Cooperative education programs. Preprofessional programs in law. 3-2 engineering program with Manhattan Coll. Teacher certification in elementary, secondary, and special education. ROTC at St. Peter's Coll.
**Honors:** Honors program. Honor societies.
**Academic Assistance:** Remedial reading, writing, math, and study skills. Nonremedial tutoring.

**ADMISSIONS. Academic basis for candidate selection** (in order of priority): Secondary school record, class rank, school's recommendation, standardized test scores.
**Nonacademic basis for candidate selection:** Character and personality and particular talent or ability are important. Extracurricular participation and alumni/ae relationship are considered.
**Requirements:** Graduation from secondary school is required; GED is accepted. 16 units and the following program of study are recommended: 4 units of English, 1 unit of math, 1 unit of science, 2 units of foreign language, 3 units of social studies, 5 units of electives. Minimum combined SAT score of 800 and minimum 2.0 GPA recommended. SAT is required; ACT may be substituted. Campus visit and interview recommended. Off-campus interviews available with admissions and alumni representatives.
**Procedure:** Take SAT or ACT by November of 12th year. Visit college for interview by January of 12th year. Suggest filing application by spring; no deadline. Notification of admission on rolling basis. Reply is required by May 1. $100 tuition deposit, refundable until May 1. $100 room deposit, refundable until May 1. Freshmen accepted for terms other than fall.
**Special programs:** Admission may be deferred one year. Credit and/or placement may be granted through CEEB Advanced Placement exams for scores of 2 or higher. Credit may be granted through CLEP general and subject exams. Early decision program. Early entrance/early admission program.
**Transfer students:** Transfer students accepted for terms other than fall. In fall 1993, 47% of all new students were transfers into all classes. 225 transfer applications were received, 200 were accepted. Application deadline is rolling for fall; rolling for spring. Minimum 2.0 GPA required. Lowest course grade accepted is "C." Maximum number of transferable credits is 70 semester hours. At least 30 semester hours must be completed at the college to receive degree.
**Admissions contact:** Louis Kern, Director of Admissions. 914 359-7800, extension 208.

**FINANCIAL AID. Available aid:** Pell grants, SEOG, Federal Nursing Student Scholarships, state scholarships and grants, school scholarships and grants, private scholarships and grants, ROTC scholarships, academic merit scholarships, and athletic scholarships.

Perkins Loans (NDSL), PLUS, Stafford Loans (GSL), NSL, state loans, school loans, and private loans. Tuition Plan Inc. and AMS.
**Financial aid statistics:** 5% of aid is not need-based. In 1993-94, 76% of all undergraduate applicants received aid; 75% of freshman applicants. Average amounts of aid awarded freshmen: Scholarships and grants, $2,000; loans, $1,900.
**Supporting data/closing dates:** FAFSA/FAF: Priority filing date is March 15. State aid form: Priority filing date is March 15. Notification of awards on rolling basis.
**Financial aid contact:** Eileen Felske, Director of Financial Aid. 914 359-7800, extension 225.

**STUDENT EMPLOYMENT.** College Work/Study Program. Institutional employment. 8% of full-time undergraduates work on campus during school year. Students may expect to earn an average of $900 during school year. Freshmen are discouraged from working during their first term. Off-campus part-time employment opportunities rated "excellent."

**COMPUTER FACILITIES.** 86 IBM/IBM-compatible and Macintosh/Apple microcomputers; 10 are networked. Students may access Digital minicomputer/mainframe systems. Residence halls may be equipped with stand-alone microcomputers. Computer languages and software packages include Assembly, BASIC, C, COBOL, dBASE, FORTRAN, Lotus 1-2-3, PageMaker, Pascal, SPSS, WordPerfect, WordStar. Computer facilities are available to all students.
**Fees:** Computer fee is included in tuition/fees.
**Hours:** 8:30 AM-10 PM.

# Dowling College

**Oakdale, NY 11769** **516 244-3000**

**1993-94 Costs.** Tuition: $8,160. Room: $2,915. Fees, books, misc. academic expenses (school's estimate): $1,040.
**Enrollment.** Undergraduates: 472 men, 582 women (full-time). Freshman class: 1,011 applicants, 829 accepted, 410 enrolled. Graduate enrollment: 694 men, 1,154 women.
**Test score averages/ranges.** Average SAT scores: 376 verbal, 433 math. Average ACT scores: 18 composite.
**Faculty.** 93 full-time; 286 part-time. 75% of faculty holds highest degree in specific field. Student/faculty ratio: 19 to 1.
**Selectivity rating.** Less competitive.

**PROFILE.** Dowling, founded in 1959, is a private college. Its 36-acre campus is located in Oakdale, on the south shore of Long Island. The campus focal point was built at the turn of the century by William K. Vanderbilt.

**Accreditation:** MSACS. Professionally accredited by the American Library Association.
**Religious orientation:** Dowling College is nonsectarian; no religious requirements.
**Library:** Collections totaling over 135,000 volumes, 872 periodical subscriptions, and 462,000 microform items.
**Special facilities/museums:** Art gallery, cultural study center, media center, human factors lab, meteorology lab.
**Athletic facilities:** Weight and exercise equipment.

**STUDENT BODY. Undergraduate profile:** 99% are state residents; 61% are transfers. 1% Asian-American, 2% Black, 5% Hispanic, 92% White. Average age of undergraduates is 25.
**Freshman profile:** 1% of freshmen who took SAT scored 600 or over on verbal, 7% scored 600 or over on math; 8% scored 500 or over on verbal, 28% scored 500 or over on math; 40% scored 400 or over on verbal, 61% scored 400 or over on math; 82% scored 300 or over on verbal, 93% scored 300 or over on math. 10% of freshmen who took ACT scored 24 or over on composite; 46% scored 18 or over on composite; 95% scored 12 or over on composite; 100% scored 6 or over on composite. 81% of accepted applicants took SAT; 19% took ACT.
**Undergraduate achievement:** 71% of fall 1992 freshmen returned for fall 1993 term. 37% of entering class graduated. 25% of students who completed a degree program went on to graduate study within five years.
**Foreign students:** Four students are from out of the country. Four countries represented in all.

**PROGRAMS OF STUDY. Degrees:** B.A., B.Bus.Admin., B.S.
**Majors:** Accounting, Aeronautics, Aeronautics/Applied Mathematics, Aeronautics/Management, Aircraft System Management, Airway Computer Sciences, Airway Science Management, Biology, Computer Information Systems, Computer Science, Economics, Education, English, Finance, History, Humanities, Management, Marine Studies, Marketing, Mathematics, Music, Music Education, Natural Science/Mathematics, Professional/Liberal Studies, Psychology, Romance Languages, Social Sciences, Sociology/Anthropology, Special Education, Speech/Dramatic Art, The Arts, Visual Arts.
**Distribution of degrees:** The majors with the highest enrollment are business, aeronautics, and education; marine studies, speech/dramatic art, and music have the lowest.
**Requirements:** General education requirement.
**Academic regulations:** Minimum 2.0 GPA must be maintained.
**Special:** Minors offered. Professional and liberal studies major for students with associate's degree or similar preparation and a professional orientation. Certificate programs in coaching, foreign language proficiency, and writing. Post master's diplomas in total quality management and aviation management. Professional diplomas in educational administration and computers in education. Independent study. Pass/fail grading option. Internships. Cooperative education programs. Graduate school at which undergraduates may take graduate-level courses. Preprofessional programs in law, medicine, veterinary science, and dentistry. Member of Long Island Region Advisory Council for Higher Education. Teacher certification in elementary, secondary, and special education. AFROTC. ROTC at New York Inst of Tech.
**Honors:** Honor societies.
**Academic Assistance:** Remedial reading, writing, math, and study skills. Nonremedial tutoring.

**STUDENT LIFE. Housing:** Students may live on or off campus. Men's dorms. Apartment-style residence complex for men and women. 10% of students live in college housing.
**Social atmosphere:** The Lion's Den is a favorite hang-out. The Spanish club, Pan club, and Alpha Ehto Rho are influential groups. Sporting events, the Fall Regatta, and the Comedy Zone are popular social events.
**Services and counseling/handicapped student services:** Placement services. Health service. Computer assisted instruction. Counseling services for minority students. Career and academic guidance services. Physically disabled student services. Learning disabled program/services. Notetaking services. Tape recorders. Tutors. Reader services for the blind.
**Campus organizations:** Undergraduate student government. Student newspaper (Lion's Voice, published biweekly). Literary magazine. Yearbook. Radio station. Chorus, orchestra, jazz, dance ensemble, Improvisational Players, aeronautics club, flying team, Presidential Scholars, 27 organizations in all.
**Religious organizations:** Bible Enrichment Club.
**Minority/foreign student organizations:** Pan Club, Spanish Club.

**ATHLETICS. Physical education requirements:** None.
**Intercollegiate competition:** 5% of students participate. Baseball (M), basketball (M,W), golf (M), lacrosse (M), soccer (M), softball (W), tennis (M,W), volleyball (W). Member of ECAC, NCAA Division II, New York Collegiate Athletic Conference.
**Intramural and club sports:** 10% of students participate. Intramural basketball, floor hockey, karate, soccer, touch football, volleyball, weight lifting. Men's club cheerleading, crew/rowing. Women's club cheerleading, crew/rowing, kickline.

**ADMISSIONS. Academic basis for candidate selection** (in order of priority): Secondary school record, class rank, school's recommendation, standardized test scores.
**Nonacademic basis for candidate selection:** Character and personality, extracurricular participation, particular talent or ability, geographical distribution, and alumni/ae relationship are considered.
**Requirements:** Graduation from secondary school is required; GED is accepted. 16 units and the following program of study are recommended: 4 units of English, 2 units of math, 2 units of science, 2 units of foreign language, 3 units of social studies. HEOP for applicants not normally admissible. College-preparatory work program for in-state applicants not normally admissible. SAT or ACT is required. Campus visit and interview recommended.
**Procedure:** Take SAT or ACT by January of 12th year. Suggest filing application as early as possible in 12th year. Notification of admission on rolling basis. $200 refundable tuition deposit. $200 refundable room deposit. Freshmen accepted for terms other than fall.
**Special programs:** Admission may be deferred. Credit and/or placement may be granted through CEEB Advanced Placement exams for scores of 3 or higher. Credit may be granted through CLEP general and subject exams. Credit and placement may be granted through DANTES and challenge exams. Early entrance/early admission program. Concurrent enrollment program.
**Transfer students:** Transfer students accepted for terms other than fall. In fall 1993, 61% of all new students were transfers into all classes. 960 transfer applications were received, 922 were accepted. Application deadline is rolling for fall; rolling for spring. Lowest course grade accepted is "C." Maximum number of transferable credits is 60 semester hours from a two-year school and 90 semester hours from a four-year school. At least 30 semester hours must be completed at the college to receive degree.
**Admissions contact:** Kate Rowe, M.A., Director of Admissions. 516 244-3030.

**FINANCIAL AID. Available aid:** Pell grants, SEOG, state scholarships and grants, school scholarships and grants, private scholarships and grants, ROTC scholarships, academic merit scholarships, athletic scholarships, and aid for undergraduate foreign students. Perkins Loans (NDSL), PLUS, Stafford Loans (GSL), and SLS. Consern Loans. Focus Loans. Tuition Plan Inc., Education Plan Inc., AMS, deferred payment plan, and guaranteed tuition. College Funding, Inc.
**Supporting data/closing dates:** FAFSA/FAF/FFS: Priority filing date is May 1. School's own aid application: Priority filing date is May 1. State aid form: Priority filing date is May 1. Notification of awards on rolling basis.
**Financial aid contact:** Kristina Smith, M.B.A., Director of Financial Aid. 516 244-3110.

**STUDENT EMPLOYMENT.** College Work/Study Program. Institutional employment. Off-campus part-time employment opportunities rated "excellent."

**COMPUTER FACILITIES.** 315 IBM/IBM-compatible and Macintosh/Apple microcomputers; 285 are networked. Client/LAN operating systems include Apple/Macintosh, DOS. Numerous computer languages and software packages available. Computer facilities are available to all students.
**Fees:** Computer fee is included in tuition/fees.
**Hours:** 7 AM-11 PM (M-Th); 8 AM-4 PM (F); 8 AM-5 PM (Sa-Su).

# D'Youville College

**Buffalo, NY 14201** **716 881-3200**

**1994-95 Costs.** Tuition: $8,920. Room: $2,155. Board: $2,155. Fees, books, misc. academic expenses (school's estimate): $860.
**Enrollment.** Undergraduates: 290 men, 782 women (full-time). Freshman class: 887 applicants, 630 accepted, 163 enrolled. Graduate enrollment: 44 men, 344 women.
**Test score averages/ranges.** Average SAT scores: 435 verbal, 497 math. Range of SAT scores of middle 50%: 420-470 verbal, 480-540 math. Average ACT scores: 22 composite.
**Faculty.** 84 full-time; 55 part-time. 60% of faculty holds doctoral degree. Student/faculty ratio: 14 to 1.
**Selectivity rating.** Less competitive.

**PROFILE.** D'Youville is a private college. Founded as a women's college in 1908, it adopted coeducation in 1971. Its one-acre campus is less than a mile from the center of downtown Buffalo.

**Accreditation:** MSACS. Professionally accredited by the American Dietetic Association, the American Medical Association (CAHEA), the American Physical Therapy Association, the Council on Social Work Education, the National League for Nursing.
**Religious orientation:** D'Youville College is nonsectarian; no religious requirements.
**Library:** Collections totaling over 154,010 volumes, 719 periodical subscriptions, and 339 microform items.
**Special facilities/museums:** On-campus elementary and secondary schools, language lab, closed-circuit TV studio.
**Athletic facilities:** Gymnasium, swimming pool, weight room.

**STUDENT BODY. Undergraduate profile:** 90% are state residents; 53% are transfers. 1% Asian-American, 8% Black, 3% Hispanic, 1% Native American, 72% White, 15% Other. Average age of undergraduates is 19.
**Freshman profile:** 1% of freshmen who took SAT scored 600 or over on verbal, 10% scored 600 or over on math; 20% scored 500 or over on verbal, 55% scored 500 or over on math; 71% scored 400 or over on verbal, 88% scored 400 or over on math; 100% scored 300 or over on verbal, 100% scored 300 or over on math. 75% of accepted applicants took SAT; 25% took ACT. 70% of freshmen come from public schools.
**Undergraduate achievement:** 64% of fall 1991 freshmen returned for fall 1992 term. 45% of entering class graduated. 15% of students who completed a degree program went on to graduate study within five years.
**Foreign students:** 217 students are from out of the country. Countries represented include Canada, Jamaica, Japan, Puerto Rico, and Venezuela.

**PROGRAMS OF STUDY. Degrees:** B.A., B.S., B.S.Nurs.
**Majors:** Accounting, Biology, Business, Business Management, Dietetics, Education, Education/Bilingual, Education of Blind/Visually Impaired, Elementary Education, English, History, Management, Nursing, Occupational Therapy, Philosophy, Physical Therapy, Physician Assistant, Secondary Education, Social Work, Sociology, Special Education.
**Distribution of degrees:** The majors with the highest enrollment are physical therapy, nursing, and business; philosophy, history, and sociology have the lowest.
**Requirements:** General education requirement.
**Academic regulations:** Freshmen must maintain minimum 1.8 GPA; sophomores, juniors, seniors, 2.0 GPA.
**Special:** Minors offered in accounting, general business, English, gerontology, health care management, management, mathematics/computer science, philosophy, psychology, Spanish, and written communications. Courses offered in dance, religious studies, Spanish, and other areas. Double majors. Dual degrees. Independent study. Pass/fail grading option. Internships. Graduate school at which undergraduates may take graduate-level courses. Preprofessional programs in law, medicine, veterinary science, and dentistry. Five-year B.S./M.S. programs in physical therapy, occupational therapy, and dietetics. B.S.N./M.S. program. Member of Colleges of Western New York Consortium; cross-registration possible. Teacher certification in early childhood, elementary, secondary, special education, and bilingual/bicultural education. ROTC at Canisius Coll.
**Honors:** Honors program. Honor societies.
**Academic Assistance:** Remedial reading, writing, math, and study skills.

**ADMISSIONS. Academic basis for candidate selection** (in order of priority): Secondary school record, standardized test scores, class rank, school's recommendation, essay.
**Nonacademic basis for candidate selection:** Character and personality and extracurricular participation are important. Particular talent or ability and alumni/ae relationship are considered.
**Requirements:** Graduation from secondary school is required; GED is accepted. 18 units and the following program of study are recommended: 4 units of English, 3 units of math, 3 units of science, 3 units of foreign language, 4 units of social studies. Minimum combined SAT score of 800, rank in top half of secondary school class, and minimum grade average of 80 required. Biology, chemistry, minimum combined SAT score of 900, and minimum grade average of 85 required of dietetics, nursing, occupational therapy, and physical therapy program applicants. Minimum combined SAT score of 1000 required of physician's assistant program applicants. HEOP for applicants not normally admissible. Conditional admission possible for applicants not meeting standard requirements. SAT or ACT is required. PSAT is recommended. Campus visit and interview recommended. Off-campus interviews available with an admissions representative.
**Procedure:** Take SAT or ACT by fall of 12th year. Notification of admission on rolling basis. No set date by which applicants must accept offer. \$100-\$150 tuition deposit. \$100 room deposit, refundable prior to June 1. Freshmen accepted for terms other than fall.
**Special programs:** Admission may be deferred one year. Credit may be granted through CEEB Advanced Placement for scores of 3 or higher. Credit may be granted through CLEP general and subject exams, DANTES and challenge exams, and military experience.
**Transfer students:** Transfer students accepted for terms other than fall. In fall 1993, 53% of all new students were transfers into all classes. 787 transfer applications were received, 387 were accepted. Application deadline is August for fall; January for spring. Minimum 2.0 GPA required. Lowest course grade accepted is "C." Maximum number of transferable credits is 64 semester hours from a two-year school and 90 semester hours from a four-year school. At least 30 semester hours must be completed at the college to receive degree.
**Admissions contact:** Ronald H. Dannecker, Director of Admissions and Financial Aid. 800 777-3921, 716 881-7600.

**FINANCIAL AID. Available aid:** Pell grants, SEOG, Federal Nursing Student Scholarships, state scholarships and grants, school scholarships and grants, private scholarships and grants, ROTC scholarships, academic merit scholarships, athletic scholarships, and aid for undergraduate foreign students. Perkins Loans (NDSL), PLUS, Stafford Loans (GSL), NSL, Health Professions Loans, state loans, school loans, private loans, and SLS. Tuition Plan Inc., deferred payment plan, family tuition reduction, and guaranteed tuition.
**Financial aid statistics:** 19% of aid is not need-based. In 1993-94, 93% of all undergraduate applicants received aid; 93% of freshman applicants. Average amounts of aid awarded freshmen: Scholarships and grants, \$1,000; loans, \$2,500.
**Supporting data/closing dates:** FAFSA: Accepted on rolling basis. State aid form: Accepted on rolling basis. Notification of awards begins April.
**Financial aid contact:** Ronald H. Dannecker, Director of Admissions and Financial Aid. 800 777-3921, 716 881-7691.

# Elmira College

**Elmira, NY 14901** **607 735-1800**

**1994-95 Costs.** Tuition: \$14,990. Room & board: \$4,980. Fees, books, misc. academic expenses (school's estimate): \$750.
**Enrollment.** Undergraduates: 440 men, 659 women (full-time). Freshman class: 1,457 applicants, 1,045 accepted, 345 enrolled.
**Test score averages/ranges.** Average SAT scores: 462 verbal, 497 math. Range of SAT scores of middle 50%: 410-520 verbal, 430-550 math. Average ACT scores: 22 English, 24 math, 23 composite. Range of ACT scores of middle 50%: 20-24 English, 22-26 math.
**Faculty.** 66 full-time; 10 part-time. 98% of faculty holds highest degree in specific field. Student/faculty ratio: 16 to 1.
**Selectivity rating.** Less competitive.

**PROFILE.** Elmira is a private, liberal arts college. Founded as a women's college in 1855, it adopted coeducation in 1969. Its 40-acre campus is located in a residential area of Elmira.

**Accreditation:** MSACS. Professionally accredited by the National League for Nursing.
**Religious orientation:** Elmira College is nonsectarian; no religious requirements.
**Library:** Collections totaling over 349,279 volumes, 844 periodical subscriptions, and 360,290 microform items.
**Special facilities/museums:** Center for Mark Twain studies, American studies center.
**Athletic facilities:** Athletic center, gymnasiums, ice rink, swimming pool, racquetball and tennis courts, dance studio, weight room, golf course, athletic fields.

**STUDENT BODY. Undergraduate profile:** 53% are state residents; 25% are transfers. 3% Asian-American, 2% Black, 3% Hispanic, 1% Native American, 83% White, 8% Foreign. Average age of undergraduates is 21.
**Freshman profile:** 1% of freshmen who took SAT scored 700 or over on verbal, 2% scored 700 or over on math; 7% scored 600 or over on verbal, 18% scored 600 or over on math; 27% scored 500 or over on verbal, 48% scored 500 or over on math; 75% scored 400 or over on verbal, 87% scored 400 or over on math; 100% scored 300 or over on verbal, 100% scored 300 or over on math. 4% of freshmen who took ACT scored 30 or over on English, 9% scored 30 or over on math, 8% scored 30 or over on composite; 27% scored 24 or over on English, 48% scored 24 or over on math, 38% scored 24 or over on composite; 87% scored 18 or over on English, 91% scored 18 or over on math, 89% scored 18 or over on composite; 100% scored 12 or over on English, 100% scored 12 or over on math, 100% scored 12 or over on composite. 90% of accepted applicants took SAT; 28% took ACT. 72% of freshmen come from public schools.
**Undergraduate achievement:** 89% of fall 1992 freshmen returned for fall 1993 term. 65% of entering class graduated. 50% of students who completed a degree program went on to graduate study within one year.
**Foreign students:** 86 students are from out of the country. Countries represented include Bahamas, Canada, Japan, Korea, Spain, and Thailand; 23 in all.

**PROGRAMS OF STUDY. Degrees:** B.A., B.S.
**Majors:** Accounting, American Studies, Art, Biology, Biology/Chemistry, Business Administration, Chemistry, Classical Studies, Computer Information Systems, Criminal Justice, Economics, Elementary Education, English Literature, Environmental Studies, Foreign Languages, History, Human Services, Individualized Studies, International Business, International Studies, Management, Marketing, Mathematics, Medical Technology, Music, Nursing, Philosophy/Religion, Political Science, Psychology, Public Affairs, Social Studies, Sociology/Anthropology, Speech/Hearing, Theatre.
**Distribution of degrees:** The majors with the highest enrollment are elementary education, marketing, and psychology; chemistry, classical studies, and philosophy/religion have the lowest.
**Requirements:** General education requirement.
**Academic regulations:** Minimum 2.0 GPA must be maintained.
**Special:** Minors offered in some majors and in anthropology, botany, computer science, French, German, information systems, Latin, physics, Spanish, women's studies, and zoology. Required six-week April-May period for independent study or field experience with faculty-student projects or foreign travel groups. Self-designed majors. Double majors. Dual degrees. Independent study. Accelerated study. Pass/fail grading option. Internships. Graduate school at which undergraduates may take graduate-level courses. Preprofessional programs in law, medicine, veterinary science, dentistry, and optometry. Member of College Consortium of the Finger Lakes. Spring Term Consortium provides third-term exchanges with Alma Coll, Hanover Coll, Indiana Central U, Northland Coll, and Westminster Coll. Washington Semester and UN Semester. Teacher certification in elementary and secondary education. Certification in specific subject areas. Exchange programs abroad in the Bahamas, Germany, Japan, and Taiwan. Study abroad also in Australia, England, France, Germany, India, Italy, Japan, the Philippines, Spain, and Thailand. ROTC. AFROTC at Cornell U.
**Honors:** Phi Beta Kappa. Honor societies.
**Academic Assistance:** Nonremedial tutoring.

**STUDENT LIFE. Housing:** All unmarried students under age 21 must live on campus unless living near campus with relatives. Coed and women's dorms. School-owned/operated apartments. 85% of students live in college housing.
**Social atmosphere:** Mackenzies, the Branch, Kingsbury's, Sheehans, the Arnot Mall, and Harris Hill are favorite hang-outs. Student Association, Residence Life, the Octagon, Student Activities Board, Big Event Committee, and the Guys & Girls House have widespread influence on campus life. Popular social/cultural events include concerts, ice hockey games, other sports, comedians, poets, and speakers. "The entertainment-based organizations do an excellent job of bringing fun and educational acts to campus," reports the editor of the student newspaper. There is something going on around campus every

weekend. "If you are looking for a college where everyone knows your name, this is the one you are looking for!"
**Services and counseling/handicapped student services:** Placement services. Health service. Counseling services for minority, veteran, and older students. Personal and psychological counseling. Career and academic guidance services. Religious counseling. Learning disabled services.
**Campus organizations:** Undergraduate student government. Student newspaper (Octagon, published once/week). Literary magazine. Yearbook. Radio station. Student Activities Board, classical concert group, choruses, concert ensemble, drama group, modern dance group, outing and ski clubs, Student Fellowship, departmental and political groups, 44 organizations in all.
**Religious organizations:** Campus Ministry.
**Minority/foreign student organizations:** Minority Student Union. International Club.

**ATHLETICS. Physical education requirements:** Two semesters of physical education required.
**Intercollegiate competition:** 13% of students participate. Basketball (M,W), cheerleading (M,W), golf (M), ice hockey (M), lacrosse (M), soccer (M,W), softball (W), tennis (M,W), volleyball (W). Member of ECAC, Empire Lacrosse League, NCAA Division III, NYSWCAA.
**Intramural and club sports:** 50% of students participate. Intramural aerobics, badminton, basketball, billiards, bowling, flag football, ice hockey, indoor soccer, martial arts, pickleball, racquetball, softball, table tennis, tennis, volleyball, walleyball, water aerobics. Men's club rugby. Women's club field hockey.

**ADMISSIONS. Academic basis for candidate selection** (in order of priority): Secondary school record, school's recommendation, class rank, essay, standardized test scores.
**Nonacademic basis for candidate selection:** Character and personality and extracurricular participation are emphasized. Particular talent or ability and geographical distribution are important. Alumni/ae relationship is considered.
**Requirements:** Graduation from secondary school is required; GED is accepted. 16 units and the following program of study are required: 4 units of English, 2 units of math, 2 units of lab science, 3 units of social studies, 1 unit of history, 2 units of electives. SAT or ACT is required. Campus visit and interview recommended. Off-campus interviews available with admissions and alumni representatives.
**Procedure:** Take SAT or ACT by February of 12th year. Visit college for interview by February of 12th year. Suggest filing application by March 15; no deadline. Notification of admission on rolling basis. Reply is required by May 1. $200 nonrefundable tuition deposit. Freshmen accepted for terms other than fall.
**Special programs:** Admission may be deferred one year. Credit and/or placement may be granted through CEEB Advanced Placement exams for scores of 3 or higher. Credit and/or placement may be granted through CLEP general and subject exams. Credit and placement may be granted through Regents College, ACT PEP, DANTES, and challenge exams and military experience. Early decision program. Deadline for applying for early decision is January 15. Early entrance/early admission program. Concurrent enrollment program.
**Transfer students:** Transfer students accepted for terms other than fall. In fall 1993, 25% of all new students were transfers into all classes. 210 transfer applications were received, 186 were accepted. Application deadline is July 15 for fall; November 15 for spring. Minimum 2.0 GPA required. Lowest course grade accepted is "C-." Maximum number of transferable credits is 60 semester hours from a two-year school and 90 semester hours from a four-year school. At least 30 semester hours must be completed at the college to receive degree.
**Admissions contact:** William S. Neal, M.S., Dean of Admissions. 607 735-1724.

**FINANCIAL AID. Available aid:** Pell grants, SEOG, state scholarships and grants, school scholarships and grants, private scholarships and grants, ROTC scholarships, academic merit scholarships, and aid for undergraduate foreign students. Perkins Loans (NDSL), PLUS, Stafford Loans (GSL), state loans, school loans, private loans, and SLS. Tuition Plan Inc., Knight Tuition Plans, and AMS.
**Financial aid statistics:** 35% of aid is not need-based. In 1993-94, 100% of all undergraduate applicants received aid; 100% of freshman applicants. Average amounts of aid awarded freshmen: Scholarships and grants, $8,200; loans, $3,300.
**Supporting data/closing dates:** FAFSA: Priority filing date is March 1. FAF: Priority filing date is March 1; accepted on rolling basis. State aid form: Priority filing date is March 1; deadline is May 1. Income tax forms: Priority filing date is April 15. Notification of awards begins March 15.
**Financial aid contact:** Kathleen L. Cohen, Dean of Financial Aid. 607 735-1728.

**STUDENT EMPLOYMENT.** College Work/Study Program. Institutional employment. 50% of full-time undergraduates work on campus during school year. Students may expect to earn an average of $1,100 during school year. Off-campus part-time employment opportunities rated "good."

**COMPUTER FACILITIES.** 70 IBM/IBM-compatible and Macintosh/Apple microcomputers; 30 are networked. Students may access Digital minicomputer/mainframe systems. Client/LAN operating systems include Apple/Macintosh, DOS, DEC, LocalTalk/AppleTalk. Computer languages and software packages include Excel, Filemaker PRC, Hypercard, Maple, MINITAB, Pascal, SoftLab for Windows, SuperPaint, Systemed, Word. Computer facilities are available to all students.
**Fees:** None.
**Hours:** 6 AM-midn. (weekdays).

**GRADUATE CAREER DATA.** Graduate school percentages: 5% enter law school. 1% enter medical school. 1% enter dental school. 12% enter graduate business programs. 30% enter graduate arts and sciences programs. Highest graduate school enrollments: Cornell U, Elmira Coll, Syracuse U. 53% of graduates choose careers in business and industry. Companies and businesses that hire graduates: Corning Inc., IBM, State of New York.

**PROMINENT ALUMNI/AE.** Alair Townsend, former deputy mayor for finance and economic development, New York City; Gail Shaffer, secretary of state, New York; Fay Kanin, author; Wilhelmina Cole Holladay, founder, National Museum of Women in the Arts, Washington, D.C.

# Eugene Lang College of the New School for Social Research

**New York, NY 10011** **212 229-5600**

**1993-94 Costs.** Tuition: $13,760. Room & board: $7,310. Fees, books, misc. academic expenses (school's estimate): $950.
**Enrollment.** Undergraduates: 355 (full-time). Freshman class: 255 applicants, 198 accepted, 77 enrolled.
**Test score averages/ranges.** Average SAT scores: 540 verbal, 520 math. Average ACT scores: 28 composite.
**Faculty.** 13 full-time; 46 part-time. 95% of faculty holds doctoral degree. Student/faculty ratio: 9 to 1.
**Selectivity rating.** Competitive.

**PROFILE.** The New School for Social Research, founded in 1919, is a private university. Programs are offered through the Eugene Lang College, founded in 1976; the Graduate Faculty of Political and Social Science; and the Graduate School of Management and Urban Professions. Its urban campus, consisting of six buildings, is located in Greenwich Village, New York City.

**Accreditation:** MSACS. Professionally accredited by the National Association of Schools of Art and Design.
**Religious orientation:** Eugene Lang College of the New School for Social Research is nonsectarian; no religious requirements.
**Library:** Collections totaling over 3,100,000 volumes, and 24,660 periodical subscriptions.
**Special facilities/museums:** Art gallery, photography museum, extensive collections of contemporary art, TV studio.

**STUDENT BODY. Undergraduate profile:** 25% are state residents; 50% are transfers. 6% Asian-American, 5% Black, 6% Hispanic, 1% Native American, 82% White. Average age of undergraduates is 20.
**Freshman profile:** 93% of accepted applicants took SAT; 10% took ACT. 55% of freshmen come from public schools.
**Undergraduate achievement:** 85% of fall 1992 freshmen returned for fall 1993 term. 55% of entering class graduated. 55% of students who completed a degree program went on to graduate study within one year.
**Foreign students:** 30 students are from out of the country. Countries represented include Bulgaria, China, Germany, Japan, the Netherlands, and the United Kingdom.

**PROGRAMS OF STUDY. Degrees:** B.A., B.A./B.F.A.
**Concentrations of Study:** Art/Culture/Society, Drama, Economics/Politics, Gender/Knowledge, History, Individually-Designed Programs, Music/Language, Philosophy, Psychology, Science/Technology/Power, Urban Studies, Writing/Literature.
**Distribution of degrees:** The majors with the highest enrollment are writing/literature, art/culture/society, and urban studies.
**Academic regulations:** Minimum 2.0 GPA must be maintained.
**Special:** All students design their own academic program in consultation with faculty advisers. Students select seminars at Eugene Lang Coll or combine seminars with courses offered by the New School's Adult Division, Graduate Faculty of Political and Social Science, Graduate Sch of Management and Urban Professions, Mannes Coll of Music, and Parsons Sch of Design. Freshmen are required to participate in at least three seminars per semester, including a freshman writing seminar. Self-designed majors. Double majors. Dual degrees. Independent study. Internships. Graduate school at which undergraduates may take graduate-level courses. Preprofessional programs in law. B.A./M.A. programs in anthropology, economics, media studies, psychology, and public policy analysis. B.A./B.F.A. or a professional certificate in eight areas of art specialization offered through affiliation with Parsons Sch of Design. 3-2 early childhood, elementary, and museum education programs with Bank Street Coll of Education. Exchange programs with Polytech U and The Cooper Union. Teacher certification in elementary and secondary education. Exchange programs abroad in France (Dijon U) and the Netherlands (U of Amsterdam).
**Academic Assistance:** Remedial writing. Nonremedial tutoring.

**ADMISSIONS. Academic basis for candidate selection** (in order of priority): Secondary school record, school's recommendation, standardized test scores, essay, class rank.
**Nonacademic basis for candidate selection:** Character and personality, extracurricular participation, and particular talent or ability are considered.
**Requirements:** Graduation from secondary school is recommended; GED is accepted. 16 units required and the following program of study recommended: 4 units of English, 3 units of math, 2 units of science, 2 units of foreign language, 1 unit of social studies, 1 unit of history. Portfolio and home exam required of B.A./B.F.A. program applicants. Audition required of music program applicants. LEAP (Lang Educational Achievement Program, division of HEOP) for applicants not normally admissible. SAT or ACT is required. Campus visit recommended.
**Procedure:** Take SAT or ACT by January of 12th year. Visit college for interview by February of 12th year. Suggest filing application by February 1; no deadline. Notification of admission by April 1. Reply is required by May 1. $200 nonrefundable tuition deposit. $220 nonrefundable room deposit. Freshmen accepted for terms other than fall.
**Special programs:** Admission may be deferred one year. Credit may be granted through CEEB Advanced Placement for scores of 4 or higher. Early decision program. Deadline for applying for early decision is November 15. Early entrance/early admission program. Concurrent enrollment program.
**Transfer students:** Transfer students accepted for terms other than fall. In fall 1993, 50% of all new students were transfers into all classes. 85 transfer applications were received,

76 were accepted. Application deadline is July 1 for fall; November 15 for spring. Minimum 2.5 GPA recommended. Lowest course grade accepted is "C." Maximum number of transferable credits is 60 semester hours. At least 60 semester hours must be completed at the college to receive degree.
**Admissions contact:** Jennifer Gill Fondiller, M.A., Director of Admissions. 212 229-5665.

**FINANCIAL AID. Available aid:** Pell grants, SEOG, state scholarships and grants, school scholarships and grants, private scholarships and grants, and aid for undergraduate foreign students. Perkins Loans (NDSL), PLUS, Stafford Loans (GSL), state loans, school loans, and SLS. AMS.
**Financial aid statistics:** Average amounts of aid awarded freshmen: Scholarships and grants, $6,324; loans, $4,000.
**Supporting data/closing dates:** FAFSA/FAF: Priority filing date is March 1. School's own aid application: Priority filing date is March 1. State aid form: Priority filing date is June 1. Income tax forms: Priority filing date is June 1. Notification of awards begins April 1.
**Financial aid contact:** Nancy Brewer, Director of Financial Aid. 212 229-8930.

# Fashion Institute of Technology

**New York, NY 10001-5992 — 212 760-7675**

**1994-95 Costs.** Tuition: $2,100 (state residents), $5,100 (out-of-state). Room & board: $5,000. Fees, books, misc. academic expenses (school's estimate): $1,440.
**Enrollment.** Undergraduates: 789 men, 3,464 women (full-time). Freshman class: 4,831 applicants, 1,841 accepted, 1,614 enrolled. Graduate enrollment: 18 men, 46 women.
**Test score averages/ranges.** Average SAT scores: 420 verbal, 400 math.
**Faculty.** 225 full-time; 595 part-time. Student/faculty ratio: 15 to 1.
**Selectivity rating.** Competitive.

**PROFILE.** The Fashion Institute of Technology, founded in 1944, is a college of art and design and business and technology. It is a public institution, receiving its principal financial support from the State and City of New York. Its campus is located in midtown Manhattan, near the center of New York's fashion industry.

**Accreditation:** MSACS. Professionally accredited by the Foundation for Interior Design Education Research, the National Association of Schools of Art and Design.
**Religious orientation:** Fashion Institute of Technology is nonsectarian; no religious requirements.
**Library:** Collections totaling over 105,027 volumes, 588 periodical subscriptions, and 3,564 microform items.
**Special facilities/museums:** Technical classrooms, production labs, studios, TV studio, lighting, design, knitting, and technology demonstration labs, fashion/arts galleries, clothing and fabric collections.
**Athletic facilities:** Gymnasiums, weight room with Nautilus and Universal machines, dance studio, game room.
**STUDENT BODY. Undergraduate profile:** 60% are state residents; 45% are transfers. 12% Asian-American, 6% Black, 7% Hispanic, 1% Native American, 51% White, 23% Other. Average age of undergraduates is 20.
**Freshman profile:** 85% of accepted applicants took SAT; 15% took ACT.
**Undergraduate achievement:** 65% of fall 1992 freshmen returned for fall 1993 term.
**PROGRAMS OF STUDY. Degrees:** B.F.A., B.S.
**Majors:** Advertising Design, Fabric Styling, Fashion Design, Fashion Merchandising, Graphic Arts, Illustration, Interior Design, Jewelry Design, Marketing/Fashion/Related Industries, Packaging Design, Photography, Production Management/Apparel, Production Management/Textiles, Restoration, Textile Marketing, Textile/Surface Design, Toy Design, Visual Merchandising/Display.
**Distribution of degrees:** The majors with the highest enrollment are marketing/fashion/related industries, advertising design, and illustration; restoration, toy design, and packaging design have the lowest.
**Requirements:** General education requirement.
**Academic regulations:** Minimum 2.0 GPA must be maintained.
**Special:** Courses offered in educational skills, English, humanities, mathematics, physical education, and social sciences. Associate's degrees offered. All students must earn associate's degree before being accepted into bachelor's degree program. Internships. Cooperative education programs. Member of College Consortium for International Study. Study abroad in England, France, and Italy.
**Academic Assistance:** Remedial reading, writing, math, and study skills. Nonremedial tutoring.
**STUDENT LIFE. Housing:** Students may live on or off campus. Coed and women's dorms. 30% of students live in college housing.
**Social atmosphere:** As reported by the student newspaper, "There is no real social life on campus, but all of New York City is our campus." Since the school is located in the middle of the city, there are so many activities and choices that there is really no favorite spot. Students like to gather on campus at the gym or in the basements of the dorms. Some enjoyable activities on campus are the Monday night movies and nightly aerobics classes.
**Services and counseling/handicapped student services:** Placement services. Health service. Personal counseling. Academic guidance services. Physically disabled student services. Learning disabled services. Tape recorders. Reader services for the blind.
**Campus organizations:** Undergraduate student government. Student newspaper (West 27, published once/month). Literary magazine. Yearbook. Radio station. Student-Faculty Corps, Programming Board, 70 organizations in all.
**Minority/foreign student organizations:** International Student Organization, Siddhartha, Asian, Chinese, French, Greek, Italian, Japanese, and Korean groups.
**ATHLETICS. Physical education requirements:** Two semesters of physical education required.
**Intercollegiate competition:** 27% of students participate. Basketball (M), bowling (M,W), cheerleading (M), tennis (M,W), volleyball (W). Member of Metropolitan Community College Athletic Conference, National Junior College Athletic Association.
**Intramural and club sports:** 10% of students participate. Intramural aerobics, basketball, pool, table tennis, tennis, volleyball.
**ADMISSIONS. Academic basis for candidate selection** (in order of priority): Secondary school record, essay, class rank, school's recommendation.
**Nonacademic basis for candidate selection:** Particular talent or ability is emphasized. Character and personality and extracurricular participation are considered.
**Requirements:** Graduation from secondary school is required; GED is accepted. No specific distribution of secondary school units required. Minimum 2.0 GPA required. Portfolio required of art program applicants. EOP for applicants not normally admissible. SAT or ACT is recommended. Campus visit recommended. No off-campus interviews.
**Procedure:** Application deadline is March 15. Notification of admission on rolling basis. Reply is required by May 1 or within 15 days of acceptance. $50 tuition deposit, refundable until July 1. $50 room deposit, refundable until August 15. Freshmen accepted for terms other than fall.
**Special programs:** Credit and/or placement may be granted through CEEB Advanced Placement exams for scores of 3 or higher. Credit and/or placement may be granted through CLEP subject exams. Credit and placement may be granted through challenge exams.
**Transfer students:** Transfer students accepted for terms other than fall. In fall 1992, 45% of all new students were transfers into all classes. Application deadline is March 1 for fall; October 15 for spring. Minimum 2.0 GPA required. Lowest course grade accepted is "C."
**Admissions contact:** James C. Pidgeon, Director of Admissions. 212 760-7675.
**FINANCIAL AID. Available aid:** Pell grants, SEOG, state scholarships and grants, school scholarships and grants, and private scholarships and grants. Perkins Loans (NDSL), PLUS, Stafford Loans (GSL), and SLS. AMS. Manufacturers Hanover Plan.
**Financial aid statistics:** In 1993-94, 75% of all undergraduate applicants received aid; 77% of freshman applicants. Average amounts of aid awarded freshmen: Scholarships and grants, $1,852; loans, $1,780.
**Supporting data/closing dates:** FAFSA/FAF: Priority filing date is March 15. School's own aid application: Accepted on rolling basis. Income tax forms: Accepted on rolling basis. Notification of awards on rolling basis.
**Financial aid contact:** Lucille Higgins, Director of Financial Aid. 212 760-7684.
**STUDENT EMPLOYMENT.** College Work/Study Program. Institutional employment. 10% of full-time undergraduates work on campus during school year. Students may expect to earn an average of $1,400 during school year. Off-campus part-time employment opportunities rated "excellent."
**COMPUTER FACILITIES.** 240 IBM/IBM-compatible and Macintosh/Apple microcomputers; 75 are networked. Client/LAN operating systems include Apple/Macintosh, LocalTalk/AppleTalk. Computer languages and software packages include BASIC, COBOL, FORTRAN, INGRES, Quel, SQL, WordPerfect; programs for advertising, fashion, interior, and textile design; 25 in all. Computer use restricted to students in applicable courses.
**Fees:** Computer fee is included in tuition/fees.
**Hours:** 9 AM-9 PM in most locations.
**PROMINENT ALUMNI/AE.** Calvin Klein, fashion designer; Antonio, illustrator; Linda Beauchamp, vice-president, Saks Fifth Avenue; Norma Kamali, fashion designer; Allyn St. George, men's fashion designer; Alfred Fornay, Jr., executive editor, *Ebony Man.*

# Five Towns College

**Dix Hills, NY 11746-6055 — 516 424-7000**

**1994-95 Costs.** Tuition: $7,400. Room: $3,500. Board: $1,200. Fees, books, misc. academic expenses (school's estimate): $1,600.
**Enrollment.** Undergraduates: 499 men, 189 women (full-time). Freshman class: 475 applicants, 426 accepted, 309 enrolled.
**Test score averages/ranges.** Average SAT scores: 440 verbal, 450 math.
**Faculty.** 29 full-time; 36 part-time. 38% of faculty holds doctoral degree. Student/faculty ratio: 12 to 1.
**Selectivity rating.** Less competitive.

**PROFILE.** Five Towns, founded in 1972, is a private college offering programs in music and music education. Its 34-acre campus is located in the town of Dix Hills, 18 miles from New York City.

**Accreditation:** MSACS.
**Religious orientation:** Five Towns College is nonsectarian; no religious requirements.
**Library:** Collections totaling over 22,410 volumes, 360 periodical subscriptions and 45 microform items.
**Special facilities/museums:** 48- and 24-track recording studios, MIDI studio, video studio.
**Athletic facilities:** Basketball courts, gym/field house, indoor volleyball courts, softball fields.
**STUDENT BODY. Undergraduate profile:** 94% are state residents; 37% are transfers. 1% Asian-American, 18% Black, 8% Hispanic, 72% White, 1% Other. Average age of undergraduates is 20.
**Freshman profile:** 5% of freshmen who took SAT scored 600 or over on verbal, 6% scored 600 or over on math; 25% scored 500 or over on verbal, 25% scored 500 or over on math; 85% scored 400 or over on verbal, 87% scored 400 or over on math; 97% scored 300 or over on verbal, 97% scored 300 or over on math. Majority of accepted applicants took SAT. 88% of freshmen come from public schools.
**Undergraduate achievement:** 63% of fall 1992 freshmen returned for fall 1993 term.
**Foreign students:** Nine students are from out of the country. Countries represented include Japan, Korea, and Russia.

**PROGRAMS OF STUDY. Degrees:** B.Prof.Studies, Mus.B.
**Majors:** Business Management, Jazz/Commercial Music, Music Education.
**Requirements:** General education requirement.
**Academic regulations:** Minimum 2.0 GPA must be maintained.
**Special:** Concentrations offered in audio recording technology, broadcasting, composition/songwriting, music business, musical theatre, performance, and video music. Associate's degrees offered. Double majors. Dual degrees. Independent study. Accelerated study. Internships. Cooperative education programs. Teacher certification in elementary and secondary education. Certification in specific subject areas.
**Honors:** Honor societies.
**Academic Assistance:** Remedial reading, writing, math, and study skills. Nonremedial tutoring.

**ADMISSIONS. Academic basis for candidate selection** (in order of priority): Secondary school record, school's recommendation, class rank, standardized test scores, essay.
**Nonacademic basis for candidate selection:** Particular talent or ability is emphasized. Character and personality are important. Extracurricular participation and alumni/ae relationship are considered.
**Requirements:** Graduation from secondary school is recommended; GED is accepted. 21 units and the following program of study are recommended: 4 units of English, 3 units of math, 3 units of science, 2 units of foreign language, 3 units of social studies, 2 units of history, 4 units of electives. Minimum combined SAT score of 850 and minimum 2.75 GPA required. Audition required of music program applicants. HEOP for applicants not normally admissible. SAT is recommended. Campus visit recommended. No off-campus interviews.
**Procedure:** Take SAT or ACT by April of 12th year. Notification of admission on rolling basis. No set date by which applicants must accept offer. $350 nonrefundable tuition deposit. $100 nonrefundable room deposit. Freshmen accepted for terms other than fall.
**Special programs:** Admission may be deferred one year. Placement may be granted through life experience. Credit and placement may be granted through challenge exams. Early entrance/early admission program. Concurrent enrollment program.
**Transfer students:** Transfer students accepted for terms other than fall. In fall 1993, 37% of all new students were transfers into all classes. 179 transfer applications were received, 168 were accepted. Application deadline is rolling for fall; rolling for spring. Minimum 2.5 GPA recommended. Lowest course grade accepted is "C." Maximum number of transferable credits is 83 semester hours. At least 45 semester hours must be completed at the college to receive degree.
**Admissions contact:** Robert Goldschlager, M.A., Director of Admissions. 516 424-7000, extension 110.

**FINANCIAL AID. Available aid:** Pell grants, SEOG, state grants, school scholarships, and academic merit scholarships. Music scholarships. PLUS, Stafford Loans (GSL), and SLS. AMS.
**Financial aid statistics:** 10% of aid is not need-based. In 1993-94, 80% of all undergraduate applicants received aid; 70% of freshman applicants. Average amounts of aid awarded freshmen: Scholarships and grants, $2,400; loans, $2,625.
**Supporting data/closing dates:** FAFSA: Priority filing date is May 1; accepted on rolling basis. School's own aid application: Priority filing date is May 1; accepted on rolling basis. State aid form: Priority filing date is May 1; accepted on rolling basis. Income tax forms: Priority filing date is May 1; accepted on rolling basis. Notification of awards on rolling basis.
**Financial aid contact:** Ellen Murray, Director of Financial Aid. 516 424-7000, extension 114.

## Fordham University

**Bronx, NY 10458** **718 817-1000**

**1993-94 Costs.** Tuition: $13,200. Room & board: $6,700-$7,715. Fees, books, misc. academic expenses (school's estimate): $750.
**Enrollment.** Undergraduates: 2,322 men, 2,418 women (full-time). Freshman class: 4,200 applicants, 2,874 accepted, 942 enrolled. Graduate enrollment: 3,126 men, 5,099 women.
**Test score averages/ranges.** Average SAT scores: 506 verbal, 535 math.
**Faculty.** 351 full-time. 97% of faculty holds doctoral degree. Student/faculty ratio: 17 to 1.
**Selectivity rating.** Competitive.

**PROFILE.** Fordham, founded in 1841, is a church-affiliated university. In addition to the liberal arts and sciences offered through Fordham College, undergraduate programs are offered through the College of Business Administration and the College at Lincoln Center. Graduate programs are offered through the Schools of Arts and Sciences, Business Administration, Education, Law, Religion and Religious Education, and Social Service. Its 86-acre Rose Hill campus is located in the Bronx, adjacent to the Botanical Gardens and Bronx Zoo; its seven-acre Lincoln Center campus is located in Manhattan.

**Accreditation:** MSACS. Professionally accredited by the American Assembly of Collegiate Schools of Business, the National Council for Accreditation of Teacher Education.
**Religious orientation:** Fordham University is affiliated with the Roman Catholic Church (Society of Jesus); one to two units of religion may be required; varies by major.
**Library:** Collections totaling over 1,553,549 volumes, 9,968 periodical subscriptions, and 1,850,575 microform items.
**Athletic facilities:** Gymnasium, athletic center, athletic fields, tennis courts, parade grounds.

**STUDENT BODY. Undergraduate profile:** 69% are state residents; 15% are transfers. 5% Asian-American, 6% Black, 15% Hispanic, 71% White, 3% Other. Average age of undergraduates is 19.
**Freshman profile:** 1% of freshmen who took SAT scored 700 or over on verbal, 6% scored 700 or over on math; 16% scored 600 or over on verbal, 27% scored 600 or over on math; 58% scored 500 or over on verbal, 73% scored 500 or over on math; 97% scored 400 or over on verbal, 97% scored 400 or over on math; 100% scored 300 or over on verbal, 100% scored 300 or over on math. 97% of accepted applicants took SAT; 3% took ACT. 36% of freshmen come from public schools.
**Undergraduate achievement:** 92% of fall 1992 freshmen returned for fall 1993 term. 84% of entering class graduated. 24% of students who completed a degree program immediately went on to graduate study.
**Foreign students:** 188 students are from out of the country. Countries represented include Brazil, Italy, Japan, the Philippines, Spain, and the United Kingdom; 48 in all.

**PROGRAMS OF STUDY. Degrees:** B.A., B.S., B.S.Bus.Admin.
**Majors:** Accounting, African-American/African Studies, American Studies, Anthropology, Art, Art History, Art/Music, Bilingual/Bicultural Studies, Biology, Broadcasting, Business Economics, Business/Pre-Professional Program, Chemistry, Classical Civilization, Classical Languages, Communications, Comparative Literature, Computer Science, Creative Writing, Criminal Justice, Economics, Economics/Mathematics, Engineering, English, Film Study, Finance, Fine Arts, French, French Language/Literature, General Science, German, Greek, Greek/Latin, History, Information/Communication Systems, Information Sciences, International Business, International/Intercultural Studies, Italian, Italian Language/Literature, Journalism, Latin, Management Systems, Managerial Accounting, Marketing, Mathematics, Mathematics/Economics, Media Studies, Medieval Studies, Middle East Studies, Modern Languages, Natural Science, Peace/Justice Studies, Pharmacy, Philosophy, Photography/Graphic Arts, Physics, Political Science, Pre-Architecture, Pre-Dental Studies, Pre-Health Studies, Pre-Law Studies, Pre-Medical Studies, Pre-Veterinary Medicine Studies, Psychology, Public Accounting, Public Administration, Puerto Rican/Latin American Studies, Radio/Television, Religious Studies, Russian, Social Science, Sociology, Soviet Studies, Spanish, Spanish Language/Literature, Studio Art, Theatre/Drama, Theology, Urban Studies, Women's Studies.
**Distribution of degrees:** The majors with the highest enrollment are business administration, communications/media studies, and English/comparative literature; African-American/African Studies, urban studies, and anthropology have the lowest.
**Requirements:** General education requirement.
**Academic regulations:** Freshmen must maintain minimum 1.6 GPA; sophomores, 1.8 GPA; juniors, 2.0 GPA; seniors, 2.0 GPA.
**Special:** Self-designed majors. Double majors. Independent study. Accelerated study. Internships. Graduate school at which undergraduates may take graduate-level courses. Preprofessional programs in law, medicine, veterinary science, and dentistry. 3-2 engineering program (chemical, civil, electrical, industrial, metallurgical, mining, nuclear) with Case Western Reserve U and Columbia U. Five-year bachelor's/master's degree program in political science/economics. 3-3 law program. 3-3 pharmacy program with Long Island U. Exchange programs with Talladega Coll and U of San Francisco. Teacher certification in elementary and secondary education. Study abroad in numerous countries. ROTC. NROTC at SUNY Maritime. AFROTC at Manhattan Coll.
**Honors:** Phi Beta Kappa. Honors program. Honor societies.
**Academic Assistance:** Remedial study skills. Nonremedial tutoring.

**STUDENT LIFE. Housing:** Students may live on or off campus. Coed dorms. 70% of students live in college housing.
**Social atmosphere:** According to the editor of the student newspaper, "Fordham has a mediocre social life. Most of it is done off campus and at private parties. Kegs are not allowed on campus. School mixers are not very popular." Among the influential groups on campus is Catharsis, a group of writers associated with the student newspaper. The Homecoming football game, Spring Weekend, and Senior Week are the biggest social events of the year. Off-campus night spots popular with Fordham students include Clarke's Bar, The Lantern Bar, and Bronx River Yacht Club.
**Services and counseling/handicapped student services:** Placement services. Health service. Reading and speech improvement programs. Counseling services for minority students. Personal and psychological counseling. Career and academic guidance services. Religious counseling. Physically disabled student services. Learning disabled services. Notetaking services. Tutors. Reader services for the blind.
**Campus organizations:** Undergraduate student government. Student newspaper (The Ram and the Observer, published once/week). Literary magazine. Yearbook. Radio station. Band, theatre and film study groups, public speaking groups, debating, service fraternities, Global Outreach, community service programs, Weekend Activities Committee, academic clubs, 130 organizations in all.
**Religious organizations:** Campus Ministry.
**Minority/foreign student organizations:** IBSU, El Greto, Philippine-American Society, Dante Society. International Club.

**ATHLETICS. Physical education requirements:** None.
**Intercollegiate competition:** Baseball (M), basketball (M,W), cheerleading (M,W), cross-country (M,W), diving (M,W), football (M), golf (M), soccer (M), softball (W), squash (M), swimming (M,W), tennis (M,W), track (M,W), water polo (M). Member of ECAC, EISL, ICAAAA, MAAC, NCAA Division I, NCAA Division I-AA for football.
**Intramural and club sports:** 1% of students participate. Intramural basketball, flag football, softball. Men's club crew, horsemanship, ice hockey, lacrosse, martial arts, modern dance, rifle, rugby, volleyball, wrestling. Women's club crew, field hockey, horsemanship, martial arts, modern dance, rifle, soccer.

**ADMISSIONS. Academic basis for candidate selection** (in order of priority): Secondary school record, class rank, standardized test scores, school's recommendation, essay.
**Nonacademic basis for candidate selection:** Extracurricular participation and alumni/ae relationship are important. Character and personality, particular talent or ability, and geographical distribution are considered.
**Requirements:** Graduation from secondary school is required; GED is accepted. 18 units and the following program of study are required: 4 units of English, 3 units of math, 1 unit of science, 2 units of foreign language, 2 units of social studies, 6 units of electives. 4 units of math and 1 unit each of chemistry and physics required of science program applicants. Stronger math background required of applicants to College of Business. HEOP for in-state applicants not normally admissible. SAT or ACT is required. ACH recommended. Campus visit and interview recommended. Off-campus interviews available with an alumni representative.

**Procedure:** Take SAT or ACT by January of 12th year. Take ACH by February of 12th year. Visit college for interview by February of 12th year. Suggest filing application by February 1. Application deadline is April 1. Notification of admission by March 1. Reply is required by May 1. $100 nonrefundable tuition deposit. $200 room deposit, refundable until June 1. Freshmen accepted for terms other than fall.
**Special programs:** Admission may be deferred one year. Credit and/or placement may be granted through CEEB Advanced Placement exams for scores of 3 or higher. Credit and/or placement may be granted through CLEP general and subject exams. Credit and placement may be granted through challenge exams. Early decision program. In fall 1993, 45 applied for early decision and 31 were accepted. Deadline for applying for early decision is November 1. Early entrance/early admission program.
**Transfer students:** Transfer students accepted for terms other than fall. In fall 1993, 15% of all new students were transfers into all classes. 432 transfer applications were received, 273 were accepted. Application deadline is July 1 for fall; December 1 for spring. Minimum 2.5 GPA. Lowest course grade accepted is "C." Maximum number of transferable semester hours is 60 for the College of Business; 64 for Fordham College; and 80 for the Coll at Lincoln Center. At least 60 semester hours must be completed at the university to receive degree.
**Admissions contact:** John Buckley, M.S.Ed., Director of Admissions. 718 817-4000.

**FINANCIAL AID. Available aid:** Pell grants, SEOG, state scholarships and grants, school scholarships and grants, private scholarships and grants, ROTC scholarships, academic merit scholarships, and athletic scholarships. Perkins Loans (NDSL), PLUS, Stafford Loans (GSL), state loans, school loans, private loans, and SLS. Tuition Plan Inc., Education Plan Inc., and Knight Tuition Plans. Major credit cards.
**Financial aid statistics:** 10% of aid is not need-based. In 1993-94, 90% of all undergraduate applicants received aid; 84% of freshman applicants. Average amounts of aid awarded freshmen: Scholarships and grants, $6,600; loans, $2,200.
**Supporting data/closing dates:** FAFSA/FAF: Priority filing date is February 1. School's own aid application: Priority filing date is February 1. Notification of awards begins April 1.
**Financial aid contact:** Angela Van Dekker, Director of Financial Aid. 718 817-3800.

**STUDENT EMPLOYMENT.** College Work/Study Program. 40% of full-time undergraduates work on campus during school year. Students may expect to earn an average of $1,600 during school year. Off-campus part-time employment opportunities rated "excellent."

**COMPUTER FACILITIES.** 221 IBM/IBM-compatible and Macintosh/Apple microcomputers; all are networked. Students may access Digital minicomputer/mainframe systems, Internet. Residence halls may be equipped with modems. Computer languages and software packages include APL, BMDP, C, COBOL, FOCUS, FORTRAN, Pascal, SPSS-X; 20 in all. Computer facilities are available to all students.
**Fees:** $25 computer fee per year.
**Hours:** 8:30 AM-11 PM (weekdays); 9 AM-11 PM (weekends).

**GRADUATE CAREER DATA.** Graduate school percentages: 10% enter law school. 1% enter medical school. 5% enter graduate business programs. 8% enter graduate arts and sciences programs. Highest graduate school enrollments: Albany Medical School, Columbia U, Duke U, Georgetown U, Harvard U, SUNY at Buffalo, U of Pennsylvania. 58% of graduates choose careers in business and industry. Companies and businesses that hire graduates: Price Waterhouse, Morgan Guarantee, Xerox, Aetna.

**PROMINENT ALUMNI/AE.** Denzel Washington and Alan Alda, actors; Mary Higgins Clark, author.

# Hamilton College

**Clinton, NY 13323** — **315 859-4011**

**1993-94 Costs.** Tuition: $18,650. Room: $2,450. Board: $2,400. Fees, books, misc. academic expenses (school's estimate): $400.
**Enrollment.** Undergraduates: 904 men, 742 women (full-time). Freshman class: 3,140 applicants, 1,783 accepted, 454 enrolled.
**Test score averages/ranges.** Range of SAT scores of middle 50%: 500-590 verbal, 550-650 math.
**Faculty.** 168 full-time; 27 part-time. 96% of faculty holds highest degree in specific field. Student/faculty ratio: 10 to 1.
**Selectivity rating.** Highly competitive.

**PROFILE.** Hamilton is a private, liberal arts college. Founded in 1812, it adopted coeducation in 1978. Its 1,200-acre campus is located in Clinton, nine miles from Utica.

**Accreditation:** MSACS.
**Religious orientation:** Hamilton College is nonsectarian; no religious requirements.
**Library:** Collections totaling over 484,634 volumes, 2,784 periodical subscriptions, and 881 microform items.
**Special facilities/museums:** Art gallery, language lab, fitness center, observatory, two electron microscopes.
**Athletic facilities:** Gymnasiums, fitness center, field house, swimming pool, nine-hole golf course, artificial turf field, all-weather track, football stadium, intramural fields, outdoor paddle tennis, racquetball, squash, and tennis courts.

**STUDENT BODY. Undergraduate profile:** 41% are state residents; 3% are transfers. 4% Asian-American, 3% Black, 3% Hispanic, 85% White, 5% Foreign. Average age of undergraduates is 20.
**Freshman profile:** 1% of freshmen who took SAT scored 700 or over on verbal, 10% scored 700 or over on math; 20% scored 600 or over on verbal, 49% scored 600 or over on math; 70% scored 500 or over on verbal, 92% scored 500 or over on math; 95% scored 400 or over on verbal, 98% scored 400 or over on math; 100% scored 300 or over on verbal, 100% scored 300 or over on math. 99% of accepted applicants took SAT; 3% took ACT. 56% of freshmen come from public schools.
**Undergraduate achievement:** 98% of fall 1992 freshmen returned for fall 1993 term. 90% of entering class graduated. 19% of students who completed a degree program immediately went on to graduate study.
**Foreign students:** 94 students are from out of the country. Countries represented include Canada, China, India, Japan, Pakistan, and Turkey; 33 in all.

**PROGRAMS OF STUDY. Degrees:** B.A.
**Majors:** American Studies, Ancient Mediterranean Civilization, Anthropology, Art History, Asian Studies, Biology, Chemistry, Classics, Comparative Literature, Computer Sciences, Dance, Economics, English, Foreign Languages/Multiple Emphasis, French, Geology, German, Government, History, Linguistics, Mathematics, Molecular Biology/Biochemistry, Music, Philosophy, Physics, Psychobiology, Psychology, Public Policy, Religion, Russian Studies, Sociology, Spanish, Studio Art, Theatre, Women's Studies, World Politics, Writing.
**Distribution of degrees:** The majors with the highest enrollment are government, history, and economics; ancient Mediterranean civilization, linguistics, and American studies have the lowest.
**Requirements:** General education requirement.
**Special:** Minors offered in all majors and in Africana studies, astronomy, Latin American studies, and medieval/Renaissance studies. Courses offered in eight additional languages and in speech. Senior comprehensive exam or senior project required in major field. Self-designed majors. Double majors. Independent study. Accelerated study. Pass/fail grading option. Internships. Preprofessional programs in law, medicine, and dentistry. Cooperative Public Policy A.B./M.S. program with U of Rochester. Early Assurance Program in medicine with several institutions. 3-2 engineering programs with Columbia U, Rensselaer Polytech Inst, and Washington U. 3-3 law program with Columbia U. M.A.T. program with Union Coll. Washington Semester. Williams-Mystic Seaport Semester (Connecticut). Exchange programs with Colgate U and Utica Coll of Syracuse U. Study abroad in France, Greece, Italy, the former Soviet Republics, Spain, Sweden, and other countries. ROTC at Utica Coll of Syracuse U.
**Honors:** Phi Beta Kappa. Honors program. Honor societies.
**Academic Assistance:** Nonremedial tutoring.

**STUDENT LIFE. Housing:** All first-year students must live on campus; permission required for upperclass students to live off campus. Coed dorms. Fraternity housing. School-owned/operated apartments. Off-campus privately-owned housing. 97% of students live in college housing.
**Social atmosphere:** The student newspaper reports, "Generally, there is not a central location and students socialize somewhat chaotically. The size of the campus, however, makes this fact unimportant. The Greek system is strong but not dominating." Spring Weekend Festival is one of the popular social events of the year; movies, football and hockey games, and bands are also popular.
**Services and counseling/handicapped student services:** Placement services. Health service. Women's center. Day care. Reading and writing center. Study skills center. Quantitative literacy center. Counseling services for minority and older students. Birth control, personal, and psychological counseling. Career and academic guidance services. Religious counseling.
**Campus organizations:** Undergraduate student government. Student newspaper (Spectator, published once/week). Literary magazine. Yearbook. Radio station. Chamber orchestra, choir, glee club, woodwind ensemble, brass choir, jazz band, theatre, dance group, debating, film society, outing club, Model UN, Gay/Lesbian/Bisexual Alliance, volunteer organizations, departmental groups, 64 organizations in all. Seven fraternities, all with chapter houses; two sororities, no chapter houses. 41% of men join a fraternity. 16% of women join a sorority.
**Religious organizations:** Christian Fellowship, Hillel, Newman Association, Muslim Student Association.
**Minority/foreign student organizations:** Asian Cultural Society, Black and Latin Student Union, La Vanguardia. International Student Association, Middle Eastern student group.

**ATHLETICS. Physical education requirements:** One to three semesters of physical education required. Students must pass swimming test and several proficiency tests.
**Intercollegiate competition:** 40% of students participate. Baseball (M), basketball (M,W), cross-country (M,W), field hockey (W), football (M), golf (M), ice hockey (M), lacrosse (M,W), soccer (M,W), softball (W), squash (M,W), swimming (M,W), tennis (M,W), track (M,W), volleyball (W). Member of ECAC, NCAA Division III, NESCAC.
**Intramural and club sports:** 65% of students participate. Intramural basketball, cross-country, golf, flag football, hockey, soccer, softball, swimming, track and field. Men's club bicycling, crew, cricket, fencing, judo, platform tennis, rugby, sailing, skiing, ultimate frisbee, water polo. Women's club bicycling, crew, fencing, ice hockey, judo, platform tennis, rugby, sailing, skiing, ultimate frisbee.

**ADMISSIONS. Academic basis for candidate selection** (in order of priority): Secondary school record, class rank, school's recommendation, standardized test scores, essay.
**Nonacademic basis for candidate selection:** Character and personality and alumni/ae relationship are emphasized. Extracurricular participation and particular talent or ability are important. Geographical distribution is considered.
**Requirements:** Graduation from secondary school is recommended; GED is accepted. 16 units and the following program of study are recommended: 4 units of English, 3 units of math, 2 units of science, 3 units of foreign language, 3 units of social studies. Only academic subjects may be counted. HEOP for applicants not normally admissible. SAT or ACT is required. ACH recommended. Campus visit and interview recommended. Off-campus interviews available with admissions and alumni representatives.
**Procedure:** Take SAT or ACT by January 31 of 12th year. Take ACH by January 31 of 12th year. Visit college for interview by February 15 of 12th year. Application deadline is January 15. Notification of admission by April 15. Reply is required by May 1. $200 nonrefundable tuition deposit. Freshmen accepted for fall terms only.
**Special programs:** Admission may be deferred one year. Credit and/or placement may be granted through CEEB Advanced Placement exams for scores of 4 or higher. Placement may be granted through challenge exams. Early decision program. In fall 1993, 239 applied for early decision and 132 were accepted. Deadline for applying for early decision is November 15 (Plan I) and January 15 (Plan II). Early entrance/early admission program. Concurrent enrollment program.

**Transfer students:** Transfer students accepted for terms other than fall. In fall 1993, 3% of all new students were transfers into all classes. 125 transfer applications were received, 24 were accepted. Application deadline is March 15 for fall; December 15 for spring. Minimum 3.0 GPA recommended. Lowest course grade accepted is "C." Maximum number of transferable credits is the equivalent of two years of course work. At least 64 credit hours must be completed at the college to receive degree. At least two years of course work must be completed at the college to receive degree.

**FINANCIAL AID. Available aid:** Pell grants, SEOG, state scholarships and grants, school scholarships and grants, and aid for undergraduate foreign students. Perkins Loans (NDSL), PLUS, Stafford Loans (GSL), school loans, private loans, and SLS. Tuition Plan Inc., Knight Tuition Plans, AMS, and Tuition Management Systems.
**Financial aid statistics:** In 1993-94, 97% of all undergraduate applicants received aid; 94% of freshman applicants. Average amounts of aid awarded freshmen: Scholarships and grants, $11,100; loans, $2,500.
**Supporting data/closing dates:** School's own aid application: Deadline is February 1. Income tax forms: Priority filing date is February 1; deadline is March 1. Notification of awards begins April 1.
**Financial aid contact:** Ken Kogut, M.Ed., Director of Financial Aid. 315 859-4434.

**STUDENT EMPLOYMENT.** College Work/Study Program. Institutional employment. 46% of full-time undergraduates work on campus during school year. Students may expect to earn an average of $1,400 during school year. Off-campus part-time employment opportunities rated "fair."

**COMPUTER FACILITIES.** 327 IBM/IBM-compatible and Macintosh/Apple microcomputers; 125 are networked. Students may access Digital, Hewlett-Packard, IBM minicomputer/mainframe systems, Internet. Client/LAN operating systems include Apple/Macintosh, LocalTalk/AppleTalk. Computer languages and software packages include Excel, Hyper Card, Lotus 1-2-3, MacWrite, MAPLE, Multimate, Pascal, Super Paint, statistics packages, scanning software, several word processing programs. Computer facilities are available to all students.
**Fees:** Computer fee is included in tuition/fees.
**Hours:** 8:30 AM-11:45 PM.

**GRADUATE CAREER DATA.** Graduate school percentages: 6% enter law school. 5% enter medical school. 1% enter graduate business programs. 8% enter graduate arts and sciences programs. Highest graduate school enrollments: Boston U, Columbia U, Cornell U, Harvard U, New York U, Syracuse U.

**PROMINENT ALUMNI/AE.** B.F. Skinner, behavioral psychologist; Ezra Pound, poet; William Masters, sex researcher; Alexander Woollcott, writer and literary critic; Elihu Root, diplomat.

# Hartwick College

**Oneonta, NY 13820-4020 607 431-4200**

**1994-95 Costs.** Tuition: $17,480. Room: $2,250. Board: $2,530. Fees, books, misc. academic expenses (school's estimate): $800.
**Enrollment.** Undergraduates: 673 men, 783 women (full-time). Freshman class: 2,112 applicants, 1,725 accepted, 430 enrolled.
**Test score averages/ranges.** Average SAT scores: 478 verbal, 524 math. Range of SAT scores of middle 50%: 420-520 verbal, 470-570 math. Average ACT scores: 23 composite. Range of ACT scores of middle 50%: 21-26 composite.
**Faculty.** 105 full-time; 22 part-time. 87% of faculty holds highest degree in specific field. Student/faculty ratio: 13 to 1.
**Selectivity rating.** Competitive.

**PROFILE.** Hartwick, founded in 1797, is a private college. Its 375-acre campus is located in Oneonta, 75 miles from Albany.
**Accreditation:** MSACS. Professionally accredited by the National Association of Schools of Art and Design, the National Association of Schools of Music, the National League for Nursing.
**Religious orientation:** Hartwick College is nonsectarian; no religious requirements.
**Library:** Collections totaling over 238,618 volumes, 1,188 periodical subscriptions, and 47,535 microform items.
**Special facilities/museums:** Art and history museums, Indian artifact collection, environmental center, observatory, electron microscope, tissue culture lab, spectrophotometers.
**Athletic facilities:** Gymnasiums, swimming pool, practice and game soccer fields, track, basketball, racquetball, squash, and tennis courts, weight room, fitness center, saunas, dance room, all-purpose Astroturf field with lights.

**STUDENT BODY. Undergraduate profile:** 63% are state residents; 11% are transfers. 2% Asian-American, 3% Black, 2% Hispanic, 93% White. Average age of undergraduates is 20.
**Freshman profile:** 1% of freshmen who took SAT scored 700 or over on verbal, 2% scored 700 or over on math; 8% scored 600 or over on verbal, 17% scored 600 or over on math; 37% scored 500 or over on verbal, 65% scored 500 or over on math; 88% scored 400 or over on verbal, 94% scored 400 or over on math; 100% scored 300 or over on verbal, 100% scored 300 or over on math. 6% of freshmen who took ACT scored 30 or over on composite; 42% scored 24 or over on composite; 94% scored 18 or over on composite; 100% scored 12 or over on composite. 95% of accepted applicants took SAT; 27% took ACT. 75% of freshmen come from public schools.
**Undergraduate achievement:** 82% of fall 1992 freshmen returned for fall 1993 term. 57% of entering class graduated. 20% of students who completed a degree program immediately went on to graduate study.
**Foreign students:** 27 students are from out of the country. Countries represented include China, England, Italy, Japan, Russia, and Spain; 15 in all.

**PROGRAMS OF STUDY. Degrees:** B.A., B.S.
**Majors:** Accounting, Anthropology, Art, Art History, Biochemistry, Biology, Chemistry, Computer Science, Economics, English, French, Geology, German, History, Individual Studies, Information Science, Management, Mathematics, Medical Technology, Music, Music Education, Nursing, Philosophy, Philosophy/Religion, Physics, Political Science, Psychology, Religion, Sociology, Spanish, Theatre Arts.
**Distribution of degrees:** The majors with the highest enrollment are political science, psychology, and management; medical technology, religion, and German have the lowest.
**Requirements:** General education requirement.
**Academic regulations:** Minimum 2.0 GPA must be maintained.
**Special:** Minors offered in comparative literature, education (secondary), museum studies, and myth and folklore. Environmental science and policy program. Self-designed majors. Double majors. Dual degrees. Independent study. Internships. Preprofessional programs in law, medicine, veterinary science, dentistry, optometry, and engineering. 3-1 and 4-1 medical technology programs may be arranged. 3-2 engineering programs with Clarkson U and Columbia U. 3-3 law program with Albany Law Sch. Member of College Consortium of the Finger Lakes; cross-registration possible. Member of Hudson Mohawk Association and New York State Independent College Consortium. Washington Semester. Exchange program with SUNY at Oneonta. Teacher certification in elementary and secondary education. Certification in specific subject areas. Study abroad in Austria, the Bahamas, Brazil, China, Costa Rica, England, France, Germany, Greece, India, Ireland, Japan, Mexico, Russia, Scotland, Spain, and Thailand.
**Honors:** Honors program. Honor societies.
**Academic Assistance:** Remedial study skills. Nonremedial tutoring.

**STUDENT LIFE. Housing:** All freshmen and sophomores must live on campus unless living with family. Coed dorms. Sorority and fraternity housing. School-owned/operated apartments. 81% of students live in college housing.
**Services and counseling/handicapped student services:** Placement services. Health service. Women's center. Counseling services for minority and older students. Birth control, personal, and psychological counseling. Career and academic guidance services. Religious counseling. Learning disabled services.
**Campus organizations:** Undergraduate student government. Student newspaper (Hilltops, published once/week). Literary magazine. Yearbook. Radio station. Band, concert choir, dance club, alternative film society, Amnesty International, wilderness experience program, The Women's Center, SADD, Cardboard Alley Players, art club, karate club, ice hockey club, philosophy forum, writing and math clubs, ski club, academic, athletic, and special-interest groups, 46 organizations in all. Four fraternities, all with chapter houses; four sororities, three chapter houses. 23% of men join a fraternity. 26% of women join a sorority.
**Religious organizations:** Campus Ambassadors, Campus Student Ministry, Jewish Student Association.
**Minority/foreign student organizations:** Ethnic Coalition.

**ATHLETICS. Physical education requirements:** Four half units of physical education required.
**Intercollegiate competition:** 30% of students participate. Baseball (M), basketball (M,W), cheerleading (W), cross-country (M,W), diving (M,W), field hockey (W), football (M), golf (M), lacrosse (M,W), soccer (M,W), softball (W), swimming (M,W), tennis (M,W), track (indoor) (M,W), track (outdoor) (M,W), track and field (indoor) (M,W), track and field (outdoor) (M,W), volleyball (W). Member of ECAC, Empire Athletic Association, NCAA Division I for men's soccer, NCAA Division III.
**Intramural and club sports:** 60% of students participate. Intramural archery, badminton, basketball, cross-country, flag football, floor hockey, soccer, softball, tennis, volleyball, walleyball, water polo. Men's club Alpine skiing, ice hockey, rugby, water polo. Women's club Alpine skiing, water polo.

**ADMISSIONS. Academic basis for candidate selection** (in order of priority): Secondary school record, class rank, standardized test scores, school's recommendation, essay.
**Nonacademic basis for candidate selection:** Character and personality and extracurricular participation are emphasized. Particular talent or ability is important. Alumni/ae relationship is considered.
**Requirements:** Graduation from secondary school is required; GED is accepted. 18 units and the following program of study are required: 4 units of English, 3 units of math, 3 units of lab science, 2 units of foreign language, 3 units of social studies. Portfolio recommended of art program applicants. Audition required of music program applicants. Conditional admission possible for applicants not meeting standard requirements. SAT or ACT is required. ACH recommended. Campus visit and interview recommended. Off-campus interviews available with admissions and alumni representatives.
**Procedure:** Take SAT or ACT by December of 12th year. Take ACH by December of 12th year. Visit college for interview by February 15 of 12th year. Application deadline is February 15. Notification of admission is sent by mid-March. Reply is required by May 1. $300 tuition deposit, refundable until May 1. $200 refundable room deposit. Freshmen accepted for terms other than fall.
**Special programs:** Admission may be deferred one year. Credit and/or placement may be granted through CEEB Advanced Placement exams for scores of 3 or higher. Credit may be granted through CLEP general and subject exams, Regents College, ACT PEP, and DANTES exams and military experience. Credit and placement may be granted through challenge exams and life experience. Early decision program. In fall 1993, 47 applied for early decision and 41 were accepted. Deadline for applying for early decision is January 1.
**Transfer students:** Transfer students accepted for terms other than fall. In fall 1993, 11% of all new students were transfers into all classes. 132 transfer applications were received, 97 were accepted. Application deadline is August 1 for fall; January 1 for spring. Minimum 2.5 GPA required. Lowest course grade accepted is "C." Maximum number of transferable credits is the equivalent of two years of course work. At least 18 course units must be completed at the college to receive degree.
**Admissions contact:** Karyl B. Clemens, Dean of Admissions. 607 431-4150, 800 828-2200.

**FINANCIAL AID. Available aid:** Pell grants, SEOG, Federal Nursing Student Scholarships, state scholarships and grants, school scholarships and grants, private scholarships, academic merit scholarships, athletic scholarships, and aid for undergraduate foreign students. Perkins Loans (NDSL), PLUS, Stafford Loans (GSL), NSL, school loans, and SLS. Knight Tuition Plans and family tuition reduction.
**Financial aid statistics:** 32% of aid is not need-based. In 1993-94, 95% of all undergraduate applicants received aid; 95% of freshman applicants. Average amounts of aid awarded freshmen: Scholarships and grants, $6,915; loans, $5,600.

**Supporting data/closing dates:** FAFSA/FAF: Deadline is February 15. School's own aid application: Deadline is February 15. Income tax forms: Deadline is February 15. Notification of awards begins mid-March.
**Financial aid contact:** Ellen P. Miller, M.A., Director of Financial Aid. 607 431-4130, 800 828-2200.

**STUDENT EMPLOYMENT.** College Work/Study Program. Institutional employment. 57% of full-time undergraduates work on campus during school year. Students may expect to earn an average of $1,300 during school year. Off-campus part-time employment opportunities rated "fair."

**COMPUTER FACILITIES.** 500 IBM/IBM-compatible and Macintosh/Apple microcomputers; all are networked. Students may access Digital minicomputer/mainframe systems, BITNET, Internet. Client/LAN operating systems include Apple/Macintosh, DOS, DEC, LocalTalk/AppleTalk. Computer languages and software packages include Assembly, C, COBOL, dBASE, FORTRAN, Hypercard, LISP, PageMaker, Paradox, Pascal, Prolog, Quattro Pro, SAS, SPSS, Wing 2, WordPerfect. Computer facilities are available to all students. Each enrolled freshman receives his or her own notebook-sized computer and printer.
**Fees:** Computer fee is included in tuition/fees.
**Hours:** 8 AM-1 AM (labs); networked services 24 hrs.

**GRADUATE CAREER DATA.** Graduate school percentages: 2% enter law school. 2% enter medical school. 1% enter dental school. 6% enter graduate business programs. 3% enter graduate arts and sciences programs. Highest graduate school enrollments: American U, Cornell U, SUNY Albany, Syracuse U, U of Rochester. 33% of graduates choose careers in business and industry. Companies and businesses that hire graduates: Coopers & Lybrand, IBM, Digital Equipment Corp., KPMG Peat Marwick.

**PROMINENT ALUMNI/AE.** John Johnstone, CEO, Olin Corp.; Charles Cook, former New York senator; Scott Adams, syndicated cartoonist, "Dilbert".

## Hilbert College

**Hamburg, NY 14075-1597** **716 649-7900**

**1994-95 Costs.** Tuition: $7,000. Room & board: $4,500. Fees, books, misc. academic expenses (school's estimate): $925.
**Enrollment.** Undergraduates: 191 men, 311 women (full-time). Freshman class: 385 applicants, 252 accepted, 119 enrolled.
**Test score averages/ranges.** Average SAT scores: 370 verbal, 385 math. Average ACT scores: 18 composite.
**Faculty.** 30 full-time; 30 part-time. 45% of faculty holds doctoral degree. Student/faculty ratio: 20 to 1.
**Selectivity rating.** Less competitive.

**PROFILE.** Hilbert is a private, church-affiliated college. Founded in 1957, it adopted coeducation in 1969. Its 40-acre campus is located in the town of Hamburg, 10 miles from Buffalo.

**Accreditation:** MSACS. Professionally accredited by the American Bar Association.
**Religious orientation:** Hilbert College is an interdenominational Christian school; no religious requirements.
**Library:** Collections totaling over 43,000 volumes.
**Athletic facilities:** Recreation complex, fields, weight room.

**STUDENT BODY. Undergraduate profile:** 99% are state residents; 40% are transfers. 3% Black, 1% Hispanic, 1% Native American, 94% White, 1% Other. Average age of undergraduates is 20.
**Freshman profile:** 1% of freshmen who took SAT scored 700 or over on math; 2% scored 600 or over on verbal; 10% scored 500 or over on verbal, 9% scored 500 or over on math; 23% scored 400 or over on verbal, 36% scored 400 or over on math; 90% scored 300 or over on verbal, 92% scored 300 or over on math. 3% of freshmen who took ACT scored 30 or over on composite; 17% scored 24 or over on composite; 48% scored 18 or over on composite; 100% scored 12 or over on composite. 32% of accepted applicants took SAT; 6% took ACT. 93% of freshmen come from public schools.
**Undergraduate achievement:** 67% of fall 1992 freshmen returned for fall 1993 term. 60% of students who completed a degree program immediately went on to graduate study.
**Foreign students:** Three students are from out of the country. Countries represented include Japan and the former Soviet Republics; three in all.

**PROGRAMS OF STUDY. Degrees:** B.A., B.S.
**Majors:** Business Administration, Criminal Justice, English, Human Services, Legal Assistant.
**Requirements:** General education requirement.
**Academic regulations:** Freshmen must maintain minimum 1.74 GPA; sophomores, 1.94 GPA; juniors, 2.0 GPA; seniors, 2.0 GPA.
**Special:** Associate's degrees offered. Independent study. Pass/fail grading option. Internships. Member of Western New York Consortium.
**Honors:** Honor societies.
**Academic Assistance:** Remedial writing, math, and study skills. Nonremedial tutoring.

**ADMISSIONS. Academic basis for candidate selection** (in order of priority): Secondary school record, class rank, school's recommendation, essay, standardized test scores.
**Nonacademic basis for candidate selection:** Character and personality are important. Extracurricular participation and particular talent or ability are considered.
**Requirements:** Graduation from secondary school is recommended; GED is accepted. 16 units and the following program of study are required: 4 units of English, 1 unit of math, 1 unit of science, 2 units of social studies, 2 units of history, 6 units of electives. Minimum 2.0 GPA required. Conditional admission possible for applicants not meeting standard requirements. SAT is recommended; ACT may be substituted. Campus visit and interview recommended. Off-campus interviews available with an admissions representative.
**Procedure:** Suggest filing application by June 30. Application deadline is September 1. Notification of admission on rolling basis. Reply is required by September 1. $50 nonrefundable tuition deposit. $100 nonrefundable room deposit. Freshmen accepted for terms other than fall.
**Special programs:** Credit and/or placement may be granted through CEEB Advanced Placement exams for scores of 2 or higher. Credit and/or placement may be granted through CLEP general and subject exams. Placement may be granted through life experience. Credit and placement may be granted through Regents College, ACT PEP, and DANTES exams and military experience. Early entrance/early admission program. Concurrent enrollment program.
**Transfer students:** Transfer students accepted for terms other than fall. In fall 1993, 40% of all new students were transfers into all classes. 199 transfer applications were received, 188 were accepted. Application deadline is August 1 for fall; December 1 for spring. Minimum 2.0 GPA required. Lowest course grade accepted is "D." Maximum number of transferable credits is 60 semester hours. At least 60 semester hours must be completed at the college to receive degree.
**Admissions contact:** Beatrice Slick, M.S.W., Director of Admissions.

**FINANCIAL AID. Available aid:** Pell grants, SEOG, state grants, school scholarships and grants, private scholarships, and academic merit scholarships. Perkins Loans (NDSL), PLUS, Stafford Loans (GSL), and SLS. Deferred payment plan.
**Financial aid statistics:** 20% of aid is not need-based. In 1993-94, 82% of all undergraduate applicants received aid; 98% of freshman applicants. Average amounts of aid awarded freshmen: Scholarships and grants, $3,248; loans, $2,625.
**Supporting data/closing dates:** FAFSA/FAF/FFS: Priority filing date is February 28. State aid form: Priority filing date is May 1. Income tax forms: Priority filing date is April 15. Notification of awards begins April.
**Financial aid contact:** Libby Miller, Director of Financial Aid.

## Hobart and William Smith Colleges

**Geneva, NY 14456** **315 789-5500**

**1994-95 Costs.** Tuition: $19,029. Room: $2,969. Board: $2,877. Fees, books, misc. academic expenses (school's estimate): $1,031.
**Enrollment.** Undergraduates: 953 men, 839 women (full-time). Freshman class: 2,688 applicants, 2,081 accepted, 500 enrolled.
**Test score averages/ranges.** Range of SAT scores of middle 50%: 490-540 verbal, 550-600 math. Range of ACT scores of middle 50%: 24-27 composite.
**Faculty.** 145 full-time; 28 part-time. 97% of faculty holds doctoral degree. Student/faculty ratio: 13 to 1.
**Selectivity rating.** Competitive.

**PROFILE.** Hobart College, founded in 1822, is a private, liberal arts college for men. Coordinate college, William Smith, founded in 1908, is a private liberal arts college for women. Its 280-acre combined campus is located in Geneva.

**Accreditation:** MSACS.
**Religious orientation:** Hobart and William Smith Colleges are nonsectarian; no religious requirements.
**Library:** Collections totaling over 306,000 volumes, 1,872 periodical subscriptions, and 42,000 microform items.
**Special facilities/museums:** Art gallery, language lab, 100-acre nature preserve, research vessel.
**Athletic facilities:** Gymnasiums, swimming pool, field house, basketball, racquetball, squash, and tennis courts, weight rooms, aerobics and dance studios, athletic fields, recreation center.

**STUDENT BODY. Undergraduate profile:** 40% are state residents; 5% are transfers. 2% Asian-American, 5% Black, 4% Hispanic, 89% White. Average age of undergraduates is 20.
**Freshman profile:** 4% of freshmen who took SAT scored 700 or over on math; 8% scored 600 or over on verbal, 28% scored 600 or over on math; 47% scored 500 or over on verbal, 75% scored 500 or over on math; 90% scored 400 or over on verbal, 97% scored 400 or over on math; 99% scored 300 or over on verbal, 100% scored 300 or over on math. 95% of accepted applicants took SAT; 5% took ACT. 58% of freshmen come from public schools.
**Undergraduate achievement:** 93% of fall 1992 freshmen returned for fall 1993 term. 80% of entering class graduated. 24% of students who completed a degree program immediately went on to graduate study.
**Foreign students:** 59 students are from out of the country. Countries represented include China, India, Japan, Pakistan, and Sri Lanka; 24 in all.

**PROGRAMS OF STUDY. Degrees:** B.A., B.S.
**Majors:** American Studies, Anthropology/Sociology, Art History/Studio, Asian Studies, Biology, Chemistry, Chinese, Classics, Comparative Literature, Computer/Information Sciences, Economics, English, Environmental Studies, French, Geoscience, German, Greek, History, Latin, Mathematics, Music, Philosophy, Physics, Political Science/Government, Psychology, Religious Studies, Russian, Spanish, Third World Studies, Urban Studies, Women's Studies.
**Distribution of degrees:** The majors with the highest enrollment are English, individual majors, and history; anthropology, physics, and music have the lowest.
**Requirements:** General education requirement.
**Academic regulations:** Minimum 2.0 GPA must be maintained.
**Special:** Minors offered in all majors. Classes are coeducational, but each college directs its own undergraduate life and has its own dean, student government, and athletic administration. Self-designed majors. Double majors. Dual degrees. Independent study. Accelerated study. Pass/fail grading option. Internships. Preprofessional programs in law, medicine, veterinary science, and dentistry. 3-2 engineering programs with Columbia U, Dartmouth Coll, Rensselaer Polytech Inst, and U of Rochester. Five-year M.B.A. program with Clarkson U. Seven-year architecture program with Washington U. Member of Rochester Area Colleges consortium; cross-registration possible. Washington Semester, UN

Semester, and Sea Semester. New York City fine and performing arts program. Los Angeles term. Teacher certification in elementary, secondary, and special education. Certification in specific subject areas. Study abroad in Australia, the Bahamas, China, the Dominican Republic, Ecuador, England, Egypt, France, India, Italy, Japan, Korea, Mexico, Scotland, Spain, Sri Lanka, and Switzerland.
**Honors:** Phi Beta Kappa. Honors program. Honor societies.
**Academic Assistance:** Nonremedial tutoring.

**STUDENT LIFE. Housing:** All first-year students must live on campus. Coed, women's, and men's dorms. Fraternity housing. Theme houses. Cooperative houses. 80% of students live in college housing.
**Social atmosphere:** According to the editor of one student newspaper, "The social life on campus focuses on fraternity parties, sports events, guest lecturers, and other campus events. Cultural life focuses on art exhibitions, films, and plays." Students like to gather on campus at the frats, The Cafe, and the sports and recreation center. Off campus, they often go to the Smith Opera House, a concert hall. Favorite events of the year include lacrosse games, campus concerts (10,000 Maniacs and Pat Metheny, to name a few), the Greek Fest, the Lobster Bash, Winter Carnival, and the Fall Ball. Influential groups are the Greeks, the Hobart Student Association, the William Smith Congress, and the Concert Committee.
**Services and counseling/handicapped student services:** Placement services. Health service. Women's center. Counseling services for minority and older students. Birth control, personal, and psychological counseling. Career and academic guidance services. Religious counseling. Physically disabled student services. Learning disabled services. Notetaking services. Tape recorders. Tutors. Reader services for the blind.
**Campus organizations:** Undergraduate student government. Student newspapers (Herald, Waves, published weekly). Literary magazine. Yearbook. Radio station. Jazz organization/ensemble, orchestra, choral groups, musicians collective, gospel choir, drama and dance groups, film society, crafts guild, academic groups, cricket, cycling and ski clubs, farm club, environmental awareness group, Amnesty International, literacy corps, sign language club, Big Brothers/Big Sisters, service network, social affairs group, Political Education Network, Entrepreneurs Club, College Democrats/Republicans, Women's Resource Center, Men's Action Coalition, Gay/Lesbian/Bisexual/Friends Network, 60 organizations in all. Seven fraternities, all with chapter houses. 30% of men join a fraternity.
**Religious organizations:** Canterbury Club, Christian Fellowship, Hillel, Newman Community.
**Minority/foreign student organizations:** African-American Student Coalition, Latin American Organization, Pan-African Latin Organization, United magazine, Umoja House for Women of Color. International Student Club, Chinese and Japanese clubs, KI SWAHLI Club.

**ATHLETICS. Physical education requirements:** None.
**Intercollegiate competition:** 45% of students participate. Baseball (M), basketball (M,W), crew (W), cross-country (M), diving (M,W), field hockey (W), football (M), golf (M), ice hockey (M), lacrosse (M,W), soccer (M,W), squash (M), swimming (M,W), tennis (M,W). Member of ECAC, Empire Athletic Association, NCAA Division III.
**Intramural and club sports:** 85% of students participate. Intramural basketball, ice hockey, lacrosse, soccer, softball, tennis, touch football, volleyball, walleyball. Men's club Alpine skiing, canoe, crew, cycling, ice hockey, indoor track and field, martial arts, racquetball, rugby, sailing, ultimate frisbee, volleyball, weight lifting. Women's club Alpine skiing, canoe, crew, cross-country, cycling, ice hockey, indoor track and field, martial arts, outdoor track and field, racquetball, rugby, sailing, squash, ultimate frisbee, volleyball, weight lifting.

**ADMISSIONS. Academic basis for candidate selection** (in order of priority): Secondary school record, standardized test scores, school's recommendation, class rank, essay.
**Nonacademic basis for candidate selection:** Character and personality, extracurricular participation, and particular talent or ability are important. Geographical distribution and alumni/ae relationship are considered.
**Requirements:** Graduation from secondary school is required; GED is accepted. 18 units and the following program of study are required: 4 units of English, 3 units of math, 2 units of lab science, 2 units of foreign language, 2 units of history, 5 units of academic electives. HEOP for applicants not normally admissible. SAT or ACT is required. ACH recommended. Campus visit and interview recommended. Off-campus interviews available with admissions and alumni representatives.
**Procedure:** Take SAT or ACT by January of 12th year. Take ACH by January of 12th year. Visit college for interview by February 15 of 12th year. Application deadline is February 15. Notification of admission by April 1. Reply is required by May 1. $300 nonrefundable tuition deposit. Freshmen accepted for fall terms only.
**Special programs:** Admission may be deferred two years. Credit and/or placement may be granted through CEEB Advanced Placement exams for scores of 4 or higher. Credit and/or placement may be granted through CLEP general and subject exams. Early decision program. In fall 1993, 109 applied for early decision and 90 were accepted. Deadline for applying for early decision is November 15 and January 1. Early entrance/early admission program. Concurrent enrollment program.
**Transfer students:** Transfer students accepted for terms other than fall. In fall 1993, 5% of all new students were transfers into all classes. 146 transfer applications were received, 96 were accepted. Application deadline is rolling for fall; rolling for spring. Minimum 3.0 GPA recommended. Lowest course grade accepted is "C." Maximum number of transferable credits is 18 courses. At least 18 courses must be completed at the coordinate colleges to receive degree.
**Admissions contact:** Mara O'Laughlin, Director of Admissions. 800 852-2256 (Hobart), 800 245-0100 (William Smith).

**FINANCIAL AID. Available aid:** Pell grants, SEOG, state scholarships and grants, school scholarships and grants, private scholarships and grants, academic merit scholarships, and aid for undergraduate foreign students. Perkins Loans (NDSL), PLUS, Stafford Loans (GSL), and SLS. Tuition Plan Inc., AMS, and guaranteed tuition.
**Financial aid statistics:** 1% of aid is not need-based. In 1993-94, 90% of all undergraduate applicants received aid; 92% of freshman applicants. Average amounts of aid awarded freshmen: Scholarships and grants, $11,300; loans, $2,625.
**Supporting data/closing dates:** FAFSA/FAF: Priority filing date is February 15. School's own aid application: Priority filing date is February 15. State aid form: Priority filing date is June 1; accepted on rolling basis. Income tax forms: Priority filing date is May 15. Notification of awards begins April 1.
**Financial aid contact:** Robert Freeman, M.B.A., Director of Financial Aid. 315 781-3315.

**STUDENT EMPLOYMENT.** College Work/Study Program. Institutional employment. 43% of full-time undergraduates work on campus during school year. Students may expect to earn an average of $1,000 during school year. Off-campus part-time employment opportunities rated "fair."

**COMPUTER FACILITIES.** 122 IBM/IBM-compatible and Macintosh/Apple microcomputers; 98 are networked. Students may access Digital minicomputer/mainframe systems, BITNET. Client/LAN operating systems include Apple/Macintosh, DOS, DEC. Computer languages and software packages include Ada, BASIC, C, Editor, FORTRAN, LISP, Lotus 1-2-3, Macro, Modula 2, Pascal, PC-Solve, SAS, SPSS WordPerfect, Windows. Computer facilities are available to all students.
**Fees:** None.
**Hours:** 9 AM-midn., longer during exams.

**GRADUATE CAREER DATA.** Graduate school percentages: 7% enter law school. 4% enter medical school. 6% enter graduate business programs. 23% enter graduate arts and sciences programs. Highest graduate school enrollments: Bryn Mawr Coll, Columbia U, Cornell U, Dartmouth Coll, Duke U, Georgetown U, Harvard U, Johns Hopkins U, Maxwell Sch of Public Administration, Middlebury Coll, Princeton U, Stanford U, U of Rochester, Yale U. 47% of graduates choose careers in business and industry. Companies and businesses that hire graduates: Aetna, Bantam Doubleday, Chubb, Citibank, Federal Reserve Bank, IBM, J.P. Morgan, Merck, Morgan Stanley, Peace Corps, Sharpe & Dahme, Strawbridge & Clothier, Xerox.

**PROMINENT ALUMNI/AE.** Eric Lax, author; Dr. Robert Gale, cancer researcher; Beth Brophy, senior editor, *U.S. News & World Report*; Edward Regan, comptroller, State of New York; Reynold Levy, president, AT&T; Dr. Priscilla Shaffer, Dana Farber Cancer Inst; Susan Bonay, financial analyst, Harvard U.

# Hofstra University

**Hempstead, NY 11550 — 516 463-6600**

**1992-93 Costs.** Tuition: $10,490. Room & board: $5,606. Fees, books, misc. academic expenses (school's estimate): $925.
**Enrollment.** Undergraduates: 3,113 men, 3,664 women (full-time). Freshman class: 7,428 applicants, 5,860 accepted, 1,498 enrolled. Graduate enrollment: 1,596 men, 2,232 women.
**Test score averages/ranges.** Average SAT scores: 480 verbal, 545 math. Range of SAT scores of middle 50%: 450-550 verbal, 500-600 math. Average ACT scores: 24 composite.
**Faculty.** 452 full-time; 527 part-time. 90% of faculty holds doctoral degree. Student/faculty ratio: 18 to 1.
**Selectivity rating.** More competitive.

**PROFILE.** Hofstra, founded in 1935, is a private university. Programs are offered through the College of Liberal Arts and Sciences; New College; and the Schools of Business, Education, and Law. Its 238-acre campus is located in Hempstead, 25 miles east of New York City.
**Accreditation:** MSACS. Professionally accredited by the Accreditation Board for Engineering and Technology, the American Assembly of Collegiate Schools of Business, the American Speech-Language-Hearing Association, the National Council for Accreditation of Teacher Education.
**Religious orientation:** Hofstra University is nonsectarian; no religious requirements.
**Library:** Collections totaling over 1,340,650 volumes, and 5,870 periodical subscriptions.
**Special facilities/museums:** Art galleries, exhibition areas, arboretum, child care and family center, TV institute, communications facilities, electron microscopes.
**Athletic facilities:** Stadium; physical fitness center; swim center; numerous playing fields.

**STUDENT BODY. Undergraduate profile:** 60% are state residents; 35% are transfers. 3% Asian-American, 5% Black, 5% Hispanic, 87% White. Average age of undergraduates is 21.
**Freshman profile:** 1% of freshmen who took SAT scored 700 or over on verbal, 4% scored 700 or over on math; 11% scored 600 or over on verbal, 28% scored 600 or over on math; 56% scored 500 or over on verbal, 75% scored 500 or over on math; 100% scored 400 or over on verbal, 100% scored 400 or over on math. 80% of accepted applicants took SAT; 20% took ACT. 75% of freshmen come from public schools.
**Undergraduate achievement:** 86% of fall 1992 freshmen returned for fall 1993 term. 58% of entering class graduated. 64% of students who completed a degree program went on to graduate study within five years.
**Foreign students:** 320 students are from out of the country. Countries represented include India, Israel, Japan, Korea, Norway, and Pakistan; 65 in all.

**PROGRAMS OF STUDY. Degrees:** B.A., B.Bus.Admin., B.Eng., B.F.A., B.S., B.S.Ed.
**Majors:** Accounting, African Studies, American Studies, Anthropology, Applied Economics, Applied Social Science, Aqua/Mariculture, Art History, Asian Studies, Athletic Training, Banking/Finance, Biochemistry, Biology, Business Computer Information Systems, Business Education, Chemistry, Classics, Communication Arts, Communications, Computer Science, Creative Studies, Dance, Drama, Earth Resources, Economics, Electrical Engineering, Elementary Education, Engineering Science, English, Exercise Specialist, Fine Arts, Fine Arts Education, French, Geography, Geology, German, Hebrew, History, Humanities, Ibero-American Studies, Industrial Engineering, Interdisciplinary Studies, International Business, Italian, Jewish Studies, Liberal Arts, Management, Marketing, Mathematics, Mechanical Engineering, Music, Music Education, Natural Science, Philosophy, Physical Education, Physics, Political Science, Psychology, Russian, School/Community Health Education, Secretarial/Office Studies, Social Science, Sociology,

Spanish, Speech Arts, Speech/Language Pathology, Teacher of Speech/Hearing Handicapped, Theatre Arts, University Without Walls.
**Distribution of degrees:** The majors with the highest enrollment are accounting, psychology, and marketing; geology, German, and Italian have the lowest.
**Requirements:** General education requirement.
**Academic regulations:** Freshmen must maintain minimum 1.5 GPA; sophomores, 1.7 GPA; juniors, 1.9 GPA; seniors, 2.0 GPA.
**Special:** Minors offered in most majors. Associate's degrees offered. Self-designed majors. Double majors. Dual degrees. Independent study. Accelerated study. Pass/fail grading option. Internships. Graduate school at which undergraduates may take graduate-level courses. Preprofessional programs in law, medicine, veterinary science, dentistry, and optometry. 3-2 engineering program with Columbia U. Washington Semester. Teacher certification in elementary and secondary education. Certification in specific subject areas. Summer session in Jamaica. Study abroad also in China, England, France, and Spain. ROTC.
**Honors:** Phi Beta Kappa. Honors program. Honor societies.
**Academic Assistance:** Nonremedial tutoring.

**STUDENT LIFE. Housing:** Students may live on or off campus. Coed and women's dorms. School-owned/operated apartments. 59% of students live in college housing.
**Social atmosphere:** According to the editor of the student newspaper, social and cultural life is "excellent–very diverse. Programming Club sees to it there's something going on every night. If that's not enough, New York City is a train ride away!" Special campus events include The Freak Formal (Halloween party), Homecoming, concerts, frequent museum exhibitions, and the Shakespeare Festival.
**Services and counseling/handicapped student services:** Placement services. Health service. Women's center. Day care. Counseling services for minority, military, veteran, and older students. Birth control, personal, and psychological counseling. Career and academic guidance services. Religious counseling. Physically disabled student services. Learning disabled program/services. Notetaking services. Tape recorders. Tutors. Reader services for the blind.
**Campus organizations:** Undergraduate student government. Student newspaper (Chronicle, published once/week). Literary magazine. Yearbook. Radio and TV stations. Hofstra Singers, chorus, band, orchestra, drama performances, annual Shakespeare Festival, debating, The Satellite, HELP community service group, chess club, Circle K, College Conservatives, College Republicans, Green Future, SADD, 118 organizations in all. 16 fraternities, no chapter houses; 10 sororities, no chapter houses. 14% of men join a fraternity. 12% of women join a sorority.
**Religious organizations:** Christian Fellowship, Hillel, Newman Society.
**Minority/foreign student organizations:** African People's Organization, African/Latino Society, Asian- American Organization, National Society of Black Engineers, Organization of Latin Americans. International Student Organization, African Caribbean Society, Nirvana, French, Gaelic, German, Italian, Iranian, Japanese, and Spanish groups.

**ATHLETICS. Physical education requirements:** None.
**Intercollegiate competition:** 10% of students participate. Baseball (M), basketball (M,W), cheerleading (M,W), cross-country (M,W), field hockey (W), football (M), golf (M), lacrosse (M,W), soccer (M,W), softball (W), tennis (M,W), volleyball (W), wrestling (M). Member of ECAC, ECC, NCAA Division I, NCAA Division I-AA for football.
**Intramural and club sports:** 35% of students participate. Intramural basketball, floor hockey, soccer, softball, touch football, volleyball, water polo, water volleyball, Wiffle ball. Women's club crew, horsemanship, ice hockey, rugby.

**ADMISSIONS. Academic basis for candidate selection** (in order of priority): Secondary school record, class rank, standardized test scores, school's recommendation, essay.
**Nonacademic basis for candidate selection:** Character and personality, extracurricular participation, particular talent or ability, geographical distribution, and alumni/ae relationship are considered.
**Requirements:** Graduation from secondary school is required; GED is accepted. 16 units and the following program of study are required: 4 units of English, 2 units of math, 2 units of science including 1 unit of lab, 2 units of foreign language, 3 units of social studies, 3 units of academic electives. Minimum combined SAT score of 1000 and rank in top third of secondary school class recommended. NOAH (New Opportunities at Hofstra) program and Division of Special Studies for applicants not normally admissible. SAT or ACT is required. Campus visit and interview recommended. No off-campus interviews.
**Procedure:** Take SAT or ACT by December of 12th year. Suggest filing application by February 15; no deadline. Notification of admission on rolling basis. Reply is required by May 1. $100 tuition deposit, refundable until June 1. $100 room deposit, refundable until June 1. Freshmen accepted for terms other than fall.
**Special programs:** Admission may be deferred one year. Credit and/or placement may be granted through CEEB Advanced Placement exams for scores of 4 or higher. Credit and/or placement may be granted through CLEP general and subject exams. Credit and placement may be granted through challenge exams and life experience. Early decision program. Deadline for applying for early decision is December 1. Early entrance/early admission program.
**Transfer students:** Transfer students accepted for terms other than fall. In fall 1993, 35% of all new students were transfers into all classes. 1,598 transfer applications were received, 1,288 were accepted. Application deadline is August 1 for fall; rolling for spring. Minimum 2.5 GPA required. Lowest course grade accepted is "C-." Maximum number of transferable credits is 64 semester hours from a two-year school and 94 semester hours from a four-year school. At least 30 semester hours must be completed at the university to receive degree.
**Admissions contact:** Margaret A. Shields, Dean of Admissions. 516 463-6700.

**FINANCIAL AID. Available aid:** Pell grants, SEOG, state grants, school scholarships and grants, private scholarships, ROTC scholarships, academic merit scholarships, and athletic scholarships. Perkins Loans (NDSL), PLUS, Stafford Loans (GSL), and SLS. Tuition Plan Inc., Knight Tuition Plans, and AMS.
**Financial aid statistics:** 30% of aid is not need-based. In 1993-94, 80% of all undergraduate applicants received aid; 82% of freshman applicants. Average amounts of aid awarded freshmen: Scholarships and grants, $2,500; loans, $2,625.
**Supporting data/closing dates:** FAFSA/FAF: Priority filing date is March 1; accepted on rolling basis. State aid form: Priority filing date is March 1; accepted on rolling basis. Notification of awards on rolling basis.

**STUDENT EMPLOYMENT.** College Work/Study Program. Institutional employment. 40% of full-time undergraduates work on campus during school year. Students may expect to earn an average of $1,200 during school year. Off-campus part-time employment opportunities rated "excellent."

**COMPUTER FACILITIES.** 150 IBM/IBM-compatible and Macintosh/Apple microcomputers; all are networked. Students may access Digital, IBM minicomputer/mainframe systems, BITNET, Internet. Client/LAN operating systems include Apple/Macintosh. Computer languages and software packages include Ada, APL, BAL, BASIC, BMDP, C, CDD, COBOL, DataTrieve, FORTRAN, IFPS, LPS, MANOVA, MINITAB, MPS, Pascal, PL/1, REXX, SAS, SPSS, STRESS, TEX. Computer facilities are available to all students.
**Fees:** None.
**Hours:** 8 AM-midn.

**GRADUATE CAREER DATA.** Highest graduate school enrollments: Columbia U, New York U, U of Pennsylvania. Companies and businesses that hire graduates: Citibank, Grumman Aerospace, Big Six accounting firms.

**PROMINENT ALUMNI/AE.** Francis Ford Coppola, film director; Madeline Kahn, Lanie Kazan, and Susan Sullivan, actresses; Christopher Walken, actor; Norman Lent, U.S. congressman; Joseph Dionne, president, McGraw-Hill; Peter Kalikow and William Caunitz, publishers; Nelson DeMille, author; Carol Alt, model; Ellie Greenwich, singer/songwriter.

# Houghton College

**Houghton, NY 14744** **716 567-9200**

**1994-95 Costs.** Tuition: $9,990. Room & board: $3,550. Fees, books, misc. academic expenses (school's estimate): $1,510.
**Enrollment.** Undergraduates: 483 men, 727 women (full-time). Freshman class: 949 applicants, 786 accepted, 302 enrolled.
**Test score averages/ranges.** Average SAT scores: 500 verbal, 535 math. Range of SAT scores of middle 50%: 440-560 verbal, 470-600 math. Average ACT scores: 24 composite. Range of ACT scores of middle 50%: 22-27 composite.
**Faculty.** 64 full-time; 36 part-time. 71% of faculty holds highest degree in specific field. Student/faculty ratio: 14 to 1.
**Selectivity rating.** Competitive.

**PROFILE.** Houghton, founded in 1883, is a church-affiliated, liberal arts college. Its 1,300-acre campus is located in Houghton, 65 miles southeast of Buffalo.

**Accreditation:** MSACS. Professionally accredited by the National Association of Schools of Music.
**Religious orientation:** Houghton College is affiliated with the Wesleyan Church; three semesters of religion required.
**Library:** Collections totaling over 216,500 volumes, 625 periodical subscriptions, and 13,684 microform items.
**Special facilities/museums:** Electron microscope.
**Athletic facilities:** Gymnasium, basketball courts, racquetball courts, swimming pool, weight room, training room, indoor and outdoor tracks, ski slope, cross-country ski trails, tennis courts, ropes/initiatives course, athletic fields.

**STUDENT BODY. Undergraduate profile:** 63% are state residents; 13% are transfers. 1% Asian-American, 2% Black, 1% Hispanic, 1% Native American, 90% White, 5% International. Average age of undergraduates is 20.
**Freshman profile:** 3% of freshmen who took SAT scored 700 or over on verbal, 6% scored 700 or over on math; 22% scored 600 or over on verbal, 26% scored 600 or over on math; 51% scored 500 or over on verbal, 69% scored 500 or over on math; 93% scored 400 or over on verbal, 95% scored 400 or over on math; 100% scored 300 or over on verbal, 100% scored 300 or over on math. 82% of accepted applicants took SAT; 27% took ACT. 80% of freshmen come from public schools.
**Undergraduate achievement:** 87% of fall 1992 freshmen returned for fall 1993 term. 59% of entering class graduated. 21% of students who completed a degree program immediately went on to graduate study.
**Foreign students:** 18 students are from out of the country. Countries represented include Canada, Hong Kong, Japan, and Korea; 14 in all.

**PROGRAMS OF STUDY. Degrees:** B.A., B.Mus., B.S.
**Majors:** Accounting, Applied Music, Art, Bible, Biology, Brass Instrument, Business Administration/Management, Chemistry, Christian Education, Church Ministries, Church Music, Communication, Elementary Education, English, French, General Science, History, Humanities, International Studies, Mathematics, Ministerial, Music Education, Music Theory, Organ, Philosophy, Physical Education, Physics, Piano, Political Science, Psychology, Recreation, Religion, Social Sciences, Sociology, Spanish, String Instruments, Voice, Writing.
**Distribution of degrees:** The majors with the highest enrollment are psychology, business administration, and elementary education; French, church music, and humanities have the lowest.
**Requirements:** General education requirement.
**Academic regulations:** Minimum 2.0 GPA must be maintained.
**Special:** Minors offered in most majors and in earth science, economics, German, and theology. Tutorial course plan. Associate's degrees offered. Double majors. Dual degrees. Independent study. Internships. Preprofessional programs in law, medicine, veterinary science, dentistry, theology, and optometry. 3-2 engineering program and five-year B.A. or B.S./M.B.A. program with Clarkson U. Member of Christian College Consortium and Western New York Consortium; cross-registration possible. American Studies Program

(Washington, D.C.). Teacher certification in early childhood, elementary, and secondary education. Certification in specific subject areas. Study abroad in China, Costa Rica, England, France, Germany, Israel/Jordan, Portugal, and Spain. ROTC at St. Bonaventure U.
**Honors:** Honors program.
**Academic Assistance:** Remedial reading, writing, math, and study skills. Nonremedial tutoring.

**STUDENT LIFE. Housing:** All freshmen and sophomores must live on campus. Women's and men's dorms. School-owned/operated apartments. Off-campus privately-owned housing. Off-campus married-student housing. 90% of students live in college housing.
**Social atmosphere:** The student newspaper reports, "The campus is nestled in a hamlet in the southern tier of New York State, isolated from cities and towns. The rural country atmosphere enhances the community-centered feeling the student receives at this small liberal arts college." Popular events include Homecoming, Winter Weekend, the Junior/Senior Banquet, and Madrigals. Off campus, students frequent Big Al's Pizza and Snack Shop, the Dugout in nearby Fillmore, and the local minimart. Influential groups on campus include Allegheny County Outreach, Christian Student Outreach and World Missions Fellowship, and the Campus Activities Board.
**Services and counseling/handicapped student services:** Health service. Personal and psychological counseling. Career guidance services. Religious counseling. Learning disabled services.
**Campus organizations:** Undergraduate student government. Student newspaper (Houghton Star, published once/week). Literary magazine. Yearbook. Radio station. Choirs, madrigal singers, concert band, orchestra, Campus Activity Board, academic, athletic, and special-interest groups.
**Religious organizations:** Allegheny County Outreach, Christian Student Outreach, Prison Ministry, World Missions Fellowship.
**Minority/foreign student organizations:** African American Cultural Exchange. International Student Association.

**ATHLETICS. Physical education requirements:** Two semesters of physical education required.
**Intercollegiate competition:** 15% of students participate. Basketball (M,W), cheerleading (W), cross-country (M,W), field hockey (W), soccer (M,W), track (indoor) (M,W), track (outdoor) (M,W), track and field (indoor) (M,W), track and field (outdoor) (M,W), volleyball (W). Member of Keystone-Empire Athletic Conference, NAIA.
**Intramural and club sports:** 60% of students participate. Intramural floor hockey, indoor soccer, soccer, softball, volleyball, water polo. Men's club Alpine skiing, cheerleading, gymnastics, horsemanship, Nordic skiing. Women's club Alpine skiing, cheerleading, gymnastics, horsemanship, Nordic skiing.

**ADMISSIONS. Academic basis for candidate selection** (in order of priority): Secondary school record, class rank, standardized test scores, essay, school's recommendation.
**Nonacademic basis for candidate selection:** Character and personality, extracurricular participation, particular talent or ability, and alumni/ae relationship are considered.
**Requirements:** Graduation from secondary school is required; GED is accepted. 16 units and the following program of study are required: 4 units of English, 2 units of math, 2 units of science including 1 unit of lab, 2 units of foreign language, 3 units of social studies. Minimum SAT scores of 400 in both verbal and math, rank in top half of secondary school class, and minimum 2.5 GPA required. Separate application and audition required of applicants to School of Music. Achievement Program for applicants not normally admissible. SAT is required; ACT may be substituted. Campus visit and interview recommended. No off-campus interviews.
**Procedure:** Take SAT or ACT by December of 12th year. Visit college for interview by April 1 of 12th year. Suggest filing application by January 1; no deadline. Notification of admission on rolling basis. Reply is required by May 1. $100 nonrefundable tuition deposit. Freshmen accepted for terms other than fall.
**Special programs:** Admission may be deferred one year. Credit and/or placement may be granted through CEEB Advanced Placement exams for scores of 4 or higher. Credit and/or placement may be granted through CLEP subject exams. Credit may be granted through military experience. Placement may be granted through challenge exams. Credit and placement may be granted through Regents College and DANTES exams. Early entrance/early admission program. Concurrent enrollment program.
**Transfer students:** Transfer students accepted for terms other than fall. In fall 1993, 13% of all new students were transfers into all classes. 98 transfer applications were received, 95 were accepted. Application deadline is August 1 for fall; December 15 for spring. Minimum 2.5 GPA required. Lowest course grade accepted is "C-." Maximum number of transferable credits is 94 semester hours. At least 30 semester hours must be completed at the college to receive degree.
**Admissions contact:** Tim R. Fuller, M.B.A., Executive Director of Alumni and Admissions. 800 777-2556.

**FINANCIAL AID. Available aid:** Pell grants, SEOG, state scholarships and grants, school scholarships and grants, private scholarships and grants, ROTC scholarships, academic merit scholarships, athletic scholarships, and aid for undergraduate foreign students. Perkins Loans (NDSL), PLUS, Stafford Loans (GSL), and SLS. AMS and family tuition reduction.
**Financial aid statistics:** 35% of aid is not need-based. In 1993-94, 98% of all undergraduate applicants received aid; 96% of freshman applicants. Average amounts of aid awarded freshmen: Scholarships and grants, $2,446; loans, $2,750.
**Supporting data/closing dates:** FAFSA/FAF: Priority filing date is March 1. School's own aid application: Priority filing date is March 1. Notification of awards begins March 15.
**Financial aid contact:** Troy Martin, M.B.A., Director of Financial Aid. 716 567-9328.

**STUDENT EMPLOYMENT.** College Work/Study Program. Institutional employment. 65% of full-time undergraduates work on campus during school year. Students may expect to earn an average of $900 during school year. Off-campus part-time employment opportunities rated "poor."

**COMPUTER FACILITIES.** 110 IBM/IBM-compatible and Macintosh/Apple microcomputers; 64 are networked. Students may access Digital minicomputer/mainframe systems. Residence halls may be equipped with networked terminals. Computer languages and software packages include BASIC, COBOL, FORTRAN, Lotus 1-2-3, Pascal, WordPerfect, WordStar. Computer facilities are available to all students.
**Fees:** $30 computer fee per semester.
**Hours:** Six hours/day (microcomputers); 18 hours/day (terminals).

**GRADUATE CAREER DATA.** Graduate school percentages: 2% enter law school. 3% enter medical school. 1% enter dental school. 1% enter graduate business programs. 7% enter graduate arts and sciences programs. 4% enter theological school/seminary. Highest graduate school enrollments: SUNY at Buffalo, Syracuse U, U of Rochester. 28% of graduates choose careers in business and industry. Companies and businesses that hire graduates: Eastman Kodak, IBM, M&T Bank.

**PROMINENT ALUMNI/AE.** George Beverly Shea, gospel music evangelist; Dr. Richard Dominguez, sports medicine physician and author; Dr. Joseph Fortner, research physician, Sloan-Kettering Memorial Institute; Robert Mackenzie, Nashville music producer; Dr. M. Dudley Phillips, nominee, AAFP Physician of the Year.

# Iona College

**New Rochelle, NY 10801 914 633-2000**

**1993-94 Costs.** Tuition: $9,990. Room & board: $5,200-$6,200. Fees, books, misc. academic expenses (school's estimate): $720.
**Enrollment.** Undergraduates: 1,862 men, 2,044 women (full-time). Freshman class: 4,892 applicants, 3,530 accepted, 913 enrolled. Graduate enrollment: 715 men, 929 women.
**Test score averages/ranges.** Average SAT scores: 410 verbal, 457 math. Range of SAT scores of middle 50%: 350-460 verbal, 400-510 math.
**Faculty.** 192 full-time; 215 part-time. 53% of faculty holds doctoral degree. Student/faculty ratio: 18 to 1.
**Selectivity rating.** Less competitive.

**PROFILE.** Iona, founded in 1940, is a church-affiliated, liberal arts college. Programs are offered through the Schools of Arts and Sciences, Business Administration, and General Studies. Its 35-acre campus is located in New Rochelle on Long Island Sound, 16 miles from New York City.
**Accreditation:** MSACS, CCA-ACICS. Professionally accredited by the American Assembly of Collegiate Schools of Business, the National League for Nursing.
**Religious orientation:** Iona College is nonsectarian; two semesters of religion required.
**Library:** Collections totaling over 313,134 volumes, 1,247 periodical subscriptions, and 26,000 microform items.
**Special facilities/museums:** Community arts center, Irish and rare book collection, language lab, electron microscope.
**Athletic facilities:** Swimming pool, gymnasium, track, basketball, baseball, football, lacrosse, and soccer fields, weight rooms, saunas.

**STUDENT BODY. Undergraduate profile:** 91% are state residents; 3% are transfers. 2% Asian-American, 17% Black, 13% Hispanic, 68% White. Average age of undergraduates is 20.
**Freshman profile:** 1% of freshmen who took SAT scored 700 or over on math; 3% scored 600 or over on verbal, 6% scored 600 or over on math; 14% scored 500 or over on verbal, 30% scored 500 or over on math; 55% scored 400 or over on verbal, 75% scored 400 or over on math; 97% scored 300 or over on verbal, 98% scored 300 or over on math. 98% of accepted applicants took SAT. 45% of freshmen come from public schools.
**Undergraduate achievement:** 79% of fall 1992 freshmen returned for fall 1993 term. 44% of entering class graduated. 10% of students who completed a degree program immediately went on to graduate study.
**Foreign students:** 60 students are from out of the country. Countries represented include India, Ireland, Japan, Morocco, Nigeria, and United Kingdom; 42 in all.

**PROGRAMS OF STUDY. Degrees:** B.A., B.Bus.Admin., B.S.
**Majors:** Accounting, American Studies, Biochemistry, Biology, Business Economics, Chemistry, Communication Arts, Computer-Based Business Majors, Computer/Information Sciences, Criminal Justice, Ecology, Economics, Education, English, Finance, French, History, Interdisciplinary Science, Interdisciplinary Studies, International Business, International Studies, Italian, Management, Management Information Systems, Management Science, Marketing, Mathematics, Medical Technology, Philosophy, Physics, Political Science/Government, Production/Operations Management, Psychology, Religious Studies, Social Work, Sociology, Spanish, Speech/Dramatic Arts, Urban Studies.
**Distribution of degrees:** The majors with the highest enrollment are communication arts, accounting, and management; interdisciplinary science, French, and physics have the lowest.
**Requirements:** General education requirement.
**Academic regulations:** Minimum 2.0 GPA must be maintained.
**Special:** Minors offered in all majors and in classical humanities, fine arts, gerontology, peace and justice, and women's studies. Associate's degrees offered. Double majors. Dual degrees. Independent study. Accelerated study. Pass/fail grading option. Internships. Cooperative education programs. Graduate school at which undergraduates may take graduate-level courses. Preprofessional programs in law, medicine, veterinary science, and dentistry. 3-2 ecology program with Concordia Coll. 3-2 social work programs with Coll of New Rochelle, Concordia Coll, and Marymount Coll. Member of Consortium of Colleges in Westchester and Westchester Social Work Educational Consortium. Teacher certification in early childhood, elementary, secondary, and special education. Certification in specific subject areas. Study abroad in Belgium, France, Ireland, Italy, Morocco, and Spain. ROTC at Fordham U.
**Honors:** Phi Beta Kappa. Honors program. Honor societies.
**Academic Assistance:** Remedial reading, writing, math, and study skills. Nonremedial tutoring.

**STUDENT LIFE. Housing:** Students may live on or off campus. Coed and women's dorms. Off-campus privately-owned housing. 11% of students live in college housing.

**Services and counseling/handicapped student services:** Placement services. Health service. Women's center. Counseling services for minority, military, veteran, and older students. Personal and psychological counseling. Career and academic guidance services. Religious counseling. Physically disabled student services. Learning disabled program/services. Notetaking services. Reader services for the blind.
**Campus organizations:** Undergraduate student government. Student newspaper (Ionian, published once/week). Literary magazine. Yearbook. Radio and TV stations. Iona Singers, Iona Players, departmental, service, and special-interest groups, 61 organizations in all. 10 fraternities, no chapter houses; nine sororities, no chapter houses. 5% of men join a fraternity. 5% of women join a sorority.
**Religious organizations:** Campus Ministry, Religious Studies Club.
**Minority/foreign student organizations:** Black fraternity/sorority club, Council on Minority Leaders.

**ATHLETICS. Physical education requirements:** None.
**Intercollegiate competition:** 11% of students participate. Baseball (M), basketball (M,W), crew (M,W), cross-country (M,W), diving (M,W), football (M), golf (M), ice hockey (M), soccer (M,W), softball (W), swimming (M,W), tennis (M,W), track (indoor) (M), track (outdoor) (M), track and field (indoor) (M), track and field (outdoor) (M), volleyball (W), water polo (M). Member of ECAC, IC4A for track, Metro Atlantic Athletic Conference, NCAA Division I, NCAA Division IAA for football.
**Intramural and club sports:** 12% of students participate. Intramural basketball, football, hockey, soccer, softball. Men's club cheerleading, lacrosse, martial arts, rugby, weight lifting. Women's club cheerleading, kickline, rugby.

**ADMISSIONS. Academic basis for candidate selection** (in order of priority): Secondary school record, standardized test scores, school's recommendation, class rank.
**Nonacademic basis for candidate selection:** Character and personality, extracurricular participation, particular talent or ability, and alumni/ae relationship are considered.
**Requirements:** Graduation from secondary school is required; GED is accepted. 16 units and the following program of study are recommended: 4 units of English, 3 units of math, 1 unit of science, 2 units of foreign language, 1 unit of social studies, 1 unit of history, 4 units of electives. Rank in top half of secondary school class and minimum 2.5 GPA recommended. 2 units of lab science required of science program applicants. HEOP and Community Leadership Program for applicants not normally admissible. SAT is required; ACT may be substituted. ACH recommended. Campus visit and interview recommended. Off-campus interviews available with admissions and alumni representatives.
**Procedure:** Take SAT or ACT by fall of 12th year. Take ACH by fall of 12th year. Suggest filing application by March 15; no deadline. Acceptance notification on rolling basis beginning January 1. Reply is required by May 1 or within four weeks of acceptance. $100 nonrefundable tuition deposit. $200 refundable room deposit. Freshmen accepted for terms other than fall.
**Special programs:** Admission may be deferred one year. Credit and/or placement may be granted through CEEB Advanced Placement exams for scores of 3 or higher. Credit and/or placement may be granted through CLEP general and subject exams. Credit may be granted through challenge exams and life experience. Deadline for applying for early decision is November 1. Early entrance/early admission program.
**Transfer students:** Transfer students accepted for terms other than fall. In fall 1993, 3% of all new students were transfers into all classes. 641 transfer applications were received, 230 were accepted. Application deadline is August 1 for fall; December 1 for spring. Minimum 2.5 GPA required. Lowest course grade accepted is "C." Maximum number of transferable credits is 64 semester hours from a two-year school and 90 semester hours from a four-year school. At least 36 semester hours must be completed at the college to receive degree.
**Admissions contact:** Laurie Austin, M.A., Director of Admissions. 914 633-2502.

**FINANCIAL AID. Available aid:** Pell grants, SEOG, Federal Nursing Student Scholarships, state scholarships and grants, school scholarships and grants, private scholarships and grants, academic merit scholarships, athletic scholarships, and aid for undergraduate foreign students. Perkins Loans (NDSL), PLUS, Stafford Loans (GSL), state loans, private loans, and SLS. Tuition Plan Inc. and AMS.
**Financial aid statistics:** 7% of aid is not need-based. In 1993-94, 93% of all undergraduate applicants received aid; 96% of freshman applicants. Average amounts of aid awarded freshmen: Scholarships and grants, $5,803; loans, $4,846.
**Supporting data/closing dates:** FAFSA/FAF/FFS: Priority filing date is April 15; accepted on rolling basis. School's own aid application: Priority filing date is April 15; accepted on rolling basis. Income tax forms: Priority filing date is April 15; accepted on rolling basis. Notification of awards on rolling basis.
**Financial aid contact:** Norma Abrams-McNerney, Director of Financial Aid. 914 633-2497.

**STUDENT EMPLOYMENT.** College Work/Study Program. Institutional employment. 14% of full-time undergraduates work on campus during school year. Students may expect to earn an average of $1,500 during school year. Off-campus part-time employment opportunities rated "excellent."

**COMPUTER FACILITIES.** 1,000 IBM/IBM-compatible and Macintosh/Apple microcomputers; 350 are networked. Students may access IBM minicomputer/mainframe systems, BITNET, Internet. Residence halls may be equipped with stand-alone microcomputers, networked microcomputers. Client/LAN operating systems include DOS, Novell. Computer languages and software packages include BASIC, COBOL, dBASE, DBMS, FORTRAN, Paradox, Pascal, PL/1, Quattro Pro, Script, SPSS, STATPAC, WATBOL, WordPerfect. Computer facilities are available to all students.
**Fees:** $20 computer fee per semester; included in tuition/fees.
**Hours:** 24 hours.

**GRADUATE CAREER DATA.** 7% of graduates choose careers in business and industry. Companies and businesses that hire graduates: Arthur Andersen, Chase Manhattan, Coopers & Lybrand, Ernst & Young, IBM, KPMG Peat Marwick, Shearson Lehman Bros., Xerox.

**PROMINENT ALUMNI/AE.** Cathleen Ruane Kinney, executive VP, equities and audit, New York Stock Exchange; Most Rev. John Nevins, bishop of Venice, Fla.; Edward Robinson, president, Avon Corp.

# Ithaca College

**Ithaca, NY 14850** **607 274-3013**

**1994-95 Costs.** Tuition: $14,424. Room: $3,062. Board: $3,130. Fees, books, misc. academic expenses (school's estimate): $634.
**Enrollment.** Undergraduates: 2,795 men, 3,132 women (full-time). Freshman class: 7,113 applicants, 5,372 accepted, 1,588 enrolled. Graduate enrollment: 43 men, 90 women.
**Test score averages/ranges.** Range of SAT scores of middle 50%: 440-530 verbal, 490-590 math.
**Faculty.** 456 full-time; 129 part-time. 83% of faculty holds highest degree in specific field. Student/faculty ratio: 13 to 1.
**Selectivity rating.** Competitive.

**PROFILE.** Ithaca, founded in 1892, is a private college. Programs are offered through the Schools of Allied Health Professions; Business; Communications; Health, Physical Education, and Recreation; Humanities and Science; and Music. Its 600-acre campus is located in Ithaca, 50 miles south of Syracuse.

**Accreditation:** MSACS. Professionally accredited by the American Medical Association (CAHEA), the American Physical Therapy Association, the National Association of Schools of Music, the National Council for Accreditation of Teacher Education.
**Religious orientation:** Ithaca College is nonsectarian; no religious requirements.
**Library:** Collections totaling over 320,821 volumes, 2,460 periodical subscriptions, and 173,055 microform items.
**Special facilities/museums:** Speech and physical therapy clinics, specialized exercise science and sciences labs, TV/radio and cinema/photography studios, business and mathematics computer labs.
**Athletic facilities:** Gymnasium, swimming pools, playing fields, weight room.

**STUDENT BODY. Undergraduate profile:** 44% are state residents; 9% are transfers. 1% Asian-American, 2% Black, 2% Hispanic, 93% White, 2% Other. Average age of undergraduates is 20.
**Freshman profile:** 1% of freshmen who took SAT scored 700 or over on verbal, 3% scored 700 or over on math; 8% scored 600 or over on verbal, 28% scored 600 or over on math; 46% scored 500 or over on verbal, 75% scored 500 or over on math; 94% scored 400 or over on verbal, 98% scored 400 or over on math; 100% scored 300 or over on verbal, 100% scored 300 or over on math. 95% of accepted applicants took SAT; 7% took ACT. 80% of freshmen come from public schools.
**Undergraduate achievement:** 87% of fall 1991 freshmen returned for fall 1992 term. 67% of entering class graduated. 26% of students who completed a degree program immediately went on to graduate study.
**Foreign students:** 52 students are from out of the country. 28 countries represented in all.

**PROGRAMS OF STUDY. Degrees:** B.A., B.F.A., B.Mus., B.S.
**Majors:** Accounting, Acting, Administration of Health Services, Anthropology, Applied Economics, Applied Psychology, Art, Art History, Athletic Training/Exercise Science, Biochemistry, Biology, Chemistry, Cinema/Photography, Clinical Science, Community Health Education, Composition, Computer Information Science, Computer Science, Computer Science/Mathematics, Corporate Communication, Drama, Economics, Economics/Management, English, Exercise Science, Film/Photography/Visual Arts, Finance, Fitness/Cardiac Rehabilitation/Exercise Science, French, German, Health Education, History, Human Resource Management, International Business, Jazz Studies, Journalism, Management, Marketing, Mathematics, Mathematics/Economics, Mathematics/Physics, Media Studies, Medical Records Administration, Music, Music Education, Musical Theatre, Performance, Performance/Music Education, Philosophy, Philosophy of Religion, Physical Education, Physical Education Teacher, Physical Therapy, Physics, Physics/Computing, Planned Studies, Politics, Psychology, Recreation, Religious Studies, Social Studies, Sociology, Spanish, Speech Communication, Speech/Language Pathology/Audiology, Sport Management, Sport Studies, Sports Information/Communication, Teachers of Speech/Hearing Handicapped, Telecommunications Management, Television/Radio, Theatre Arts Management, Theatrical Production Arts, Theory.
**Distribution of degrees:** The majors with the highest enrollment are television/radio, management, and sociology.
**Academic regulations:** Freshmen must maintain minimum 1.8 GPA; sophomores, juniors, seniors, 2.0 GPA.
**Special:** Minors offered in many majors and in adult fitness, advertising/public relations, applied exercise science, audio production, comparative literature, computing, dance, environmental studies, gerontology, health, Italian, nutrition, organizational studies, outdoor recreation, scriptwriting, social work, still photography, and writing. Self-designed majors. Double majors. Dual degrees. Independent study. Accelerated study. Pass/fail grading option. Internships. Graduate school at which undergraduates may take graduate-level courses. Preprofessional programs in law and medicine. 3-1 optometry program with Pennsylvania Coll of Optometry. Five-year clinical science/physical therapy program. 3-2 engineering programs with Cornell U, Rensselaer Polytech Inst, and SUNY Binghamton. Teacher certification in elementary and secondary education. Certification in specific subject areas. Study abroad in England. ROTC and AFROTC at Cornell U.
**Honors:** Honors program.
**Academic Assistance:** Nonremedial tutoring.

**STUDENT LIFE. Housing:** All unmarried students under age 21 must live on campus unless living near campus with relatives. Coed and women's dorms. Sorority and fraternity housing. School-owned/operated apartments. 80% of students live in college housing.
**Social atmosphere:** The most popular on-campus gathering spots are the Pub/Coffeehouse, campus center television lounges, and the dining halls. Off campus, downtown bars, the Gorges and Falls, and The Commons are popular. The Student Activities Board, Bureau of Concerts, football, crew, and rugby teams are the most influential groups on campus life. Rocktoberfest, the Cortaca Jug Game (Ithaca vs. SUNY Cortland football

game), the all-campus semi-formal, Winterfest, and Senior Week are among the most popular events of the school year. "Culturally, we have a campus that is almost 96% white and middle class," reports the student newspaper. "The downtown scene is hopping, with plenty of bars, restaurants, and places to shop."
**Services and counseling/handicapped student services:** Placement services. Health service. Counseling services for minority, military, veteran, and older students. Birth control, personal, and psychological counseling. Career and academic guidance services. Religious counseling. Learning disabled services.
**Campus organizations:** Undergraduate student government. Student newspaper (Ithacan, published once/week). Literary magazine. Yearbook. Radio and TV stations. Amani Singers, Voices Unlimited, Trombone Troupe, Kuumba Repertory Theatre, Oracle Society, Community Service Network, Habitat for Humanity, Adventurers Guild, College Republicans, academic, athletic, political, professional, service, and special-interest groups, 133 organizations in all. Six fraternities, six chapter houses. Two sororities, no chapter houses. 2% of women join a sorority.
**Religious organizations:** Hillel, Catholic group, Lutheran Student Fellowship, other Protestant groups, United Jewish Appeal.
**Minority/foreign student organizations:** African Latino Society. International Club, Friends of Native Nations, Italian and Spanish clubs.

**ATHLETICS. Physical education requirements:** None.
**Intercollegiate competition:** 15% of students participate. Baseball (M), basketball (M,W), crew (M,W), cross-country (M,W), diving (M,W), field hockey (W), football (M), golf (M), gymnastics (W), lacrosse (M,W), soccer (M,W), softball (W), swimming (M,W), tennis (M,W), track (indoor) (M,W), track (outdoor) (M,W), track and field (indoor) (M,W), track and field (outdoor) (M,W), volleyball (W), wrestling (M). Member of ECAC, Empire Athletic Association, NCAA Division III, New York State Women's Collegiate Athletic Association.
**Intramural and club sports:** 20% of students participate. Intramural basketball, golf, soccer, softball, swimming, tennis, touch football, volleyball, wrestling. Men's club Alpine skiing, cycling, ice hockey, martial arts, sailing, volleyball, weight lifting. Women's club Alpine skiing, martial arts, weight lifting.

**ADMISSIONS. Academic basis for candidate selection** (in order of priority): Secondary school record, class rank, school's recommendation, standardized test scores, essay.
**Nonacademic basis for candidate selection:** Character and personality are emphasized. Extracurricular participation and particular talent or ability are important. Alumni/ae relationship is considered.
**Requirements:** Graduation from secondary school is required; GED is accepted. 16 units and the following program of study are recommended: 4 units of English, 2 units of math, 2 units of science, 2 units of foreign language, 2 units of social studies, 4 units of electives. 3 to 4 units of math recommended of business and social sciences program applicants. Biology, chemistry, physics, and 3 units of math recommended of physical therapy program applicaants. Audition required of music and theatre program applicants. EOP and HEOP for applicants not normally admissible. SAT is required; ACT may be substituted. PSAT is recommended. ACH recommended. Campus visit and interview recommended. No off-campus interviews.
**Procedure:** Take SAT or ACT by December of 12th year. Application deadline is March 1. Notification of admission on rolling basis. Reply is required by May 1. $250 nonrefundable tuition deposit. Freshmen accepted for terms other than fall.
**Special programs:** Admission may be deferred one year. Credit and/or placement may be granted through CEEB Advanced Placement exams for scores of 3 or higher. Credit and/or placement may be granted through CLEP general and subject exams. Early decision program. In fall 1992, 316 applied for early decision and 198 were accepted. Deadline for applying for early decision is November 1. Early entrance/early admission program.
**Transfer students:** Transfer students accepted for terms other than fall. In fall 1992, 9% of all new students were transfers into all classes. 652 transfer applications were received, 320 were accepted. Application deadline is March 1 for fall; November 1 for spring. Minimum 2.6 GPA required. Lowest course grade accepted is "C." Maximum number of transferable credits is 90 semester hours. At least 30 semester hours must be completed at the college to receive degree.
**Admissions contact:** Paula J. Mitchell, Director of Admissions. 607 274-3124.

**FINANCIAL AID. Available aid:** Pell grants, SEOG, Federal Nursing Student Scholarships, state scholarships and grants, school scholarships and grants, private scholarships and grants, ROTC scholarships, academic merit scholarships, and aid for undergraduate foreign students. Perkins Loans (NDSL), PLUS, Stafford Loans (GSL), private loans, and SLS. AMS.
**Financial aid statistics:** In 1992-93, 55% of all undergraduate applicants received aid; 55% of freshman applicants. Average amounts of aid awarded freshmen: Scholarships and grants, $9,000; loans, $2,100.
**Supporting data/closing dates:** FAFSA/FAF: Priority filing date is March 1. Income tax forms: Priority filing date is May 1. Notification of awards on rolling basis.
**Financial aid contact:** Jan Klotz, Director of Financial Aid. 607 274-3131.

**STUDENT EMPLOYMENT.** College Work/Study Program. Institutional employment. 40% of full-time undergraduates work on campus during school year. Students may expect to earn an average of $1,000 during school year. Off-campus part-time employment opportunities rated "good."

**COMPUTER FACILITIES.** 300 IBM/IBM-compatible and Macintosh/Apple microcomputers; all are networked. Students may access Digital minicomputer/mainframe systems, BITNET, Internet. Client/LAN operating systems include UNIX/XENIX/AIX. Computer languages and software packages include COBOL, FORTRAN, Lotus 1-2-3, Microsoft Works, Modula 2, PageMaker, Pascal, Quattro Pro, R:BASE, SPSS-X, Super Paint, Turbo Pascal, WordPerfect. Computer facilities are available to all students.
**Fees:** None.

**GRADUATE CAREER DATA.** Graduate school percentages: 5% enter law school. 1% enter medical school. 1% enter dental school. 3% enter graduate business programs. 20% enter graduate arts and sciences programs. Highest graduate school enrollments: Ithaca Coll, New York U, Syracuse U, U of Connecticut. 46% of graduates choose careers in business and industry.

# The Juilliard School

**New York, NY 10023-6590 212 799-5000**

**1994-95 Costs.** Tuition: $12,200. Room & board: $6,300-$7,900. Fees, books, misc. academic expenses (school's estimate): $2,400.
**Enrollment.** Undergraduates: 221 men, 284 women (full-time). Freshman class: 841 applicants, 159 accepted, 111 enrolled. Graduate enrollment: 180 men, 187 women.
**Test score averages/ranges.** N/A.
**Faculty.** Student/faculty ratio: 4 to 1.
**Selectivity rating.** N/A.

**PROFILE.** The Juilliard School, founded in 1905, is a private college of the performing arts. Programs are offered through the Divisions of Dance, Drama, and Music. Its campus is located at Lincoln Center in New York City.

**Accreditation:** MSACS, CCA-ACICS.
**Religious orientation:** The Juilliard School is nonsectarian; no religious requirements.
**Library:** Collections totaling over 65,000 volumes, 175 periodical subscriptions, and 1,300 microform items.
**Special facilities/museums:** Five major theatres, two-story studios, private teaching studios, 300 practice rooms, organ studios, concert and production spaces.

**STUDENT BODY. Undergraduate profile:** 21% are state residents; 18% are transfers. 14% Asian-American, 5% Black, 3% Hispanic, 1% Native American, 46% White, 31% Other. Average age of undergraduates is 21.
**Undergraduate achievement:** 85% of fall 1991 freshmen returned for fall 1992 term. 80% of entering class graduated.
**Foreign students:** 137 students are from out of the country. Countries represented include Canada, France, Israel, Japan, Korea, and Taiwan; 38 in all.

**PROGRAMS OF STUDY. Degrees:** B.F.A., B.Mus.
**Majors:** Brass Instruments, Classical Guitar, Composition, Conducting, Dance, Drama, Harp, Harpsichord, Music, Orchestral Instruments, Organ, Percussion, Piano, String Instruments, Voice, Woodwind Instruments.
**Distribution of degrees:** The majors with the highest enrollment are piano, dance, and violin; harpsichord and tuba have the lowest.
**Requirements:** General education requirement.
**Special:** Diploma programs offered in all major fields of study. Liberal arts courses. Master classes with world-renowned musicians, dancers, and actors. Double majors. Dual degrees. Accelerated study. Pass/fail grading option. Internships. Graduate school at which undergraduates may take graduate-level courses. 3-2 B.Mus./M.M. program with Barnard Coll and Columbia U. Affiliated with the Lincoln Center for the Performing Arts. Exchange programs abroad in England (Guildhall, Royal Academy and London Sch of Contemporary Dance), Israel (Rubin Academy), and the former Soviet Republics (St. Petersburg, Moscow, and Tbilisi Conservatories).

**STUDENT LIFE. Housing:** First-time freshmen must live on campus. Coed dorms. 48% of students live in college housing.
**Social atmosphere:** "The Juilliard School is a small community that provides a lot of entertainment to the rest of those interested in the Arts. Our students are very busy, but many do develop interests outside the school. The most popular entertainment is provided by the students themselves: dance recitals, music recitals, drama performances, etc." Favorite gathering spots in Manhattan are West Side Diner, The World (nightclub), and anywhere in the Village or Central Park.
**Services and counseling/handicapped student services:** Placement services. Health service. Counseling services for minority students. Birth control, personal, and psychological counseling. Career and academic guidance services. Learning disabled services.
**Campus organizations:** Undergraduate student government. Student newspaper (Juilliard Journal, published once/month). Yearbook. Chorus, orchestra, large and small ensembles, dance and drama groups, Celluloid Club, Residence Life Committee, lectures.
**Religious organizations:** Korean Christian Fellowship.
**Minority/foreign student organizations:** Minority Student Affairs. Foreign Student Association.

**ATHLETICS. Physical education requirements:** None.
**Intramural and club sports:** Intramural ice hockey, tennis.

**ADMISSIONS. Academic basis for candidate selection** (in order of priority): Audition, secondary school record, essay.
**Nonacademic basis for candidate selection:** Particular talent or ability is emphasized. Character and personality are important.
**Requirements:** Graduation from secondary school is required; GED is accepted. No specific distribution of secondary school units required. Preparation in proposed major required. Auditions required of dance, drama, and music program applicants. Provisional year of study possible for foreign students not normally admissible. Campus visit required for audition. No off-campus interviews.
**Procedure:** Suggest filing application by January 8. Application deadline is March 15. Acceptance notification one month after audition. Reply is required by May 1; July 1 for May applicants. $200 nonrefundable tuition deposit. $200 nonrefundable room deposit. Freshmen accepted for fall terms only.
**Special programs:** Early entrance/early admission program.
**Transfer students:** Transfer students accepted for fall term only. In fall 1992, 18% of all new students were transfers into all classes. 665 transfer applications were received, 65 were accepted. Application deadline is January 8 for fall; March 15 for spring. Lowest course grade accepted is "C." Maximum number of transferable credits is 12 semester hours.
**Admissions contact:** Carole J. Everett, M.A.T., Director of Admissions. 212 799-5000, extension 223.

**FINANCIAL AID. Available aid:** Pell grants, SEOG, state scholarships and grants, school scholarships and grants, private scholarships and grants, academic merit scholar-

ships, and aid for undergraduate foreign students. Perkins Loans (NDSL), PLUS, Stafford Loans (GSL), school loans, private loans, and SLS. Knight Tuition Plans.
**Financial aid statistics:** In 1992-93, 100% of all undergraduate applicants received aid. Average amounts of aid awarded freshmen: Scholarships and grants, $4,714; loans, $3,000.
**Supporting data/closing dates:** FAFSA/FAF: Priority filing date is March 17. School's own aid application: Priority filing date is February 17. Income tax forms: Priority filing date is April 17. Notification of awards on rolling basis.
**Financial aid contact:** Rhoda Payne, D.M.A., Director of Financial Aid. 212 799-5000, extension 211.

**STUDENT EMPLOYMENT.** College Work/Study Program. Institutional employment. 50% of full-time undergraduates work on campus during school year. Students may expect to earn an average of $1,500 during school year. Off-campus part-time employment opportunities rated "good."

**GRADUATE CAREER DATA.** Highest graduate school enrollments: The Juilliard School. Companies and businesses that hire graduates: New York Philharmonic; other major orchestras, dance companies, opera companies, films, and Broadway.

**PROMINENT ALUMNI/AE.** Leontyne Price, opera singer; Itzhak Perlman, violinist; Wynton Marsalis, trumpet player; Kevin Kline, Kelly McGillis, Robin Williams, Christopher Reeves, and Patty LuPone, actors; Paul Taylor, dancer.

# Keuka College

**Keuka Park, NY 14478 — 315 536-4411**

**1994-95 Costs.** Tuition: $9,500. Room & board: $4,550. Fees, books, misc. academic expenses (school's estimate): $840.
**Enrollment.** Undergraduates: 204 men, 523 women (full-time). Freshman class: 470 applicants, 387 accepted, 174 enrolled.
**Test score averages/ranges.** Average SAT scores: 451 verbal, 495 math. Range of SAT scores of middle 50%: 420-490 verbal, 455-530 math. Average ACT scores: 22 composite.
**Faculty.** 47 full-time; 29 part-time. 96% of faculty holds highest degree in specific field. Student/faculty ratio: 15 to 1.
**Selectivity rating.** Less competitive.

**PROFILE.** Keuka is a church-affiliated college. Founded as a women's college in 1890, it adopted coeducation in 1984. Its 176-acre campus is located in Keuka Park, 50 miles from Rochester.

**Accreditation:** MSACS. Professionally accredited by the Council on Social Work Education, the National League for Nursing.
**Religious orientation:** Keuka College is affiliated with the American Baptist Church; one semester of religion/theology required.
**Library:** Collections totaling over 100,000 volumes and 325 periodical subscriptions.
**Athletic facilities:** Gymnasium, lacrosse and soccer fields, sauna, swimming pool, weight room, fitness center.

**STUDENT BODY. Undergraduate profile:** 94% are state residents; 34% are transfers. 1% Asian-American, 5% Black, 1% Hispanic, 1% Native American, 92% White. Average age of undergraduates is 23.
**Freshman profile:** 2% of freshmen who took SAT scored 700 or over on math; 3% scored 600 or over on verbal, 11% scored 600 or over on math; 24% scored 500 or over on verbal, 51% scored 500 or over on math; 82% scored 400 or over on verbal, 95% scored 400 or over on math; 100% scored 300 or over on verbal, 100% scored 300 or over on math. 84% of accepted applicants took SAT; 28% took ACT. 91% of freshmen come from public schools.
**Undergraduate achievement:** 71% of fall 1992 freshmen returned for fall 1993 term. 56% of entering class graduated. 12% of students who completed a degree program immediately went on to graduate study.
**Foreign students:** 10 students are from out of the country. Countries represented include China, Japan, Nicaragua, Switzerland, and Zaire; six in all.

**PROGRAMS OF STUDY. Degrees:** B.A., B.S.
**Majors:** Biochemistry, Biology, Chemistry, Early Childhood Education, Elementary Education, English, Environmental Science, Food/Resort Management, Human Resource Management, Management, Marketing, Mathematics, Medical Technology, Nursing, Occupational Therapy, Political Science, Psychology, Public Administration Management, Secondary Education, Social Work, Sociology, Special Education.
**Distribution of degrees:** The majors with the highest enrollment are occupational therapy, education, and nursing; mathematics, English, and psychology have the lowest.
**Requirements:** General education requirement.
**Academic regulations:** Freshmen must maintain minimum 1.5 GPA; sophomores, 1.8 GPA; juniors, 1.95 GPA; seniors, 2.0 GPA.
**Special:** Minors offered in several majors and in computer information services, criminal justice, and gerontology. Self-designed majors. Double majors. Independent study. Internships. Cooperative education programs. Preprofessional programs in law, medicine, veterinary science, and dentistry. 3-1 medical technology program. 3-2 engineering program with Clarkson U. Member of the College Consortium of the Finger Lakes and Rochester Area Colleges Consortium. Washington Semester. Teacher certification in early childhood, elementary, secondary, and special education. Certification in specific subject areas. ROTC at Rochester Polytech Inst.
**Honors:** Honors program. Honor societies.
**Academic Assistance:** Remedial reading, writing, math, and study skills. Nonremedial tutoring.

**ADMISSIONS. Academic basis for candidate selection** (in order of priority): Secondary school record, standardized test scores, class rank, essay, school's recommendation.
**Nonacademic basis for candidate selection:** Extracurricular participation is emphasized. Character and personality and particular talent or ability are important. Alumni/ae relationship is considered.
**Requirements:** Graduation from secondary school is required; GED is accepted. 16 units and the following program of study are required: 4 units of English, 3 units of math, 3 units of science including 1 unit of lab, 2 units of foreign language, 3 units of social studies. Mininum combined SAT score of 940 and rank in the top 30% of secondary school class. HEOP for applicants not normally admissible. Conditional admission possible for applicants not meeting standard requirements. Summer Foundations program possible for applicants not meeting standard requirements. SAT or ACT is required. ACH recommended. Campus visit and interview recommended. Off-campus interviews available with an admissions representative.
**Procedure:** Take SAT or ACT by November of 12th year. Take ACH by January of 12th year. Visit college for interview by November 15 of 12th year. Suggest filing application by August 1; no deadline. Notification of admission on rolling basis. Reply is required by May 1 or within 30 days of acceptance. $150 tuition deposit, refundable until May 1. $150 room deposit, refundable until May 1. Freshmen accepted for terms other than fall.
**Special programs:** Admission may be deferred one year. Credit and/or placement may be granted through CEEB Advanced Placement exams for scores of 3 or higher. Credit and/or placement may be granted through CLEP general and subject exams. Credit and placement may be granted through challenge exams. Early decision program. In fall 1993, 20 applied for early decision and 12 were accepted. Deadline for applying for early decision is November 15. Early entrance/early admission program.
**Transfer students:** Transfer students accepted for terms other than fall. In fall 1993, 34% of all new students were transfers into all classes. 215 transfer applications were received, 168 were accepted. Application deadline is April 15 for fall; November 15 for spring. Minimum 2.5 GPA required. Lowest course grade accepted is "C-." Maximum number of transferable credits is 60 semester hours from a two-year school and 90 semester hours from a four-year school. At least 30 semester hours must be completed at the college to receive degree.
**Admissions contact:** Robert J. Iannuzzo, M.S., Dean of Admissions and Financial Aid. 315 536-5254, 800 54-KEUKA.

**FINANCIAL AID. Available aid:** Pell grants, SEOG, state scholarships and grants, school scholarships and grants, private scholarships and grants, ROTC scholarships, and academic merit scholarships. Perkins Loans (NDSL), PLUS, Stafford Loans (GSL), school loans, private loans, and SLS. Tuition Plan Inc. and AMS.
**Financial aid statistics:** 8% of aid is not need-based. In 1993-94, 95% of all undergraduate applicants received aid; 98% of freshman applicants. Average amounts of aid awarded freshmen: Scholarships and grants, $2,450; loans, $2,625.
**Supporting data/closing dates:** FAFSA/FAF: Priority filing date is March 15. School's own aid application: Priority filing date is March 15. Notification of awards on rolling basis.
**Financial aid contact:** Debra Schreiber, Director of Financial Aid. 315 536-5232.

# The King's College

**Briarcliff Manor, NY 10510 — 914 944-7200**

**1994-95 Costs.** Tuition: $8,190. Room & board: $3,920. Fees, books, misc. academic expenses (school's estimate): $750.
**Enrollment.** Undergraduates: 80 men, 191 women (full-time). Freshman class: 356 applicants, 233 accepted, 72 enrolled. Graduate enrollment: 89 men, 150 women.
**Test score averages/ranges.** Average SAT scores: 442 verbal, 465 math.
**Faculty.** 26 full-time; 23 part-time. 53% of faculty holds doctoral degree. Student/faculty ratio: 9 to 1.
**Selectivity rating.** Less competitive.

**PROFILE.** The King's College, founded in 1938, is a liberal arts institution with religious orientation. Its 80-acre campus is located in Briarcliff Manor, 30 miles from New York City. The campus contains Tudor-style architecture.
**Accreditation:** MSACS.
**Religious orientation:** The King's College is a nondenominational Christian school; 16 semesters of religion required.
**Library:** Collections totaling over 100,000 volumes, 600 periodical subscriptions, and 11,067 microform items.
**Special facilities/museums:** Computer center.
**Athletic facilities:** Gymnasium, swimming pool, track, tennis courts, baseball, intramural, soccer, and softball fields, weight room, table tennis, pool tables.

**STUDENT BODY. Undergraduate profile:** 32% are transfers. 5% Asian-American, 12% Black, 2% Hispanic, 81% White. Average age of undergraduates is 21.
**Freshman profile:** 85% of accepted applicants took SAT; 15% took ACT. 40% of freshmen come from public schools.
**Undergraduate achievement:** 85% of fall 1991 freshmen returned for fall 1992 term. 53% of entering class graduated.
**Foreign students:** 16 students are from out of the country. Countries represented include Canada, China, Ecuador, England, Hong Kong, and Korea.

**PROGRAMS OF STUDY. Degrees:** B.A., B.S.
**Majors:** Accounting, Applied Music, Biblical Studies, Biology, Business Administration/Economics, Chemistry, Computer Science, Early Childhood Education, Elementary Education, English, French, History, Mathematical Sciences, Mathematics, Medical Technology, Modern Foreign Languages, Music, Music Education, Nursing, Physical Education, Psychology, Religion, Religious Education, Sociology, Spanish, Writing.
**Distribution of degrees:** The majors with the highest enrollment are elementary education, business administration/economics, and English; chemistry and sociology have the lowest.
**Requirements:** General education requirement.
**Academic regulations:** Minimum 2.0 GPA required for graduation.

**Special:** Minors offered in most majors and in business, communications, fine arts, geology, and languages. Courses offered in anthropology, fine arts, geography, German, Greek, and linguistics. Interdepartmental courses. Associate's degrees offered. Double majors. Independent study. Internships. Graduate school at which undergraduates may take graduate-level courses. Preprofessional programs in law, medicine, and therapy. B.S./M.B.A. program in accounting and A.A./B.S.N. program with Pace U. Member of Christian College Coalition; exchange possible. American Studies Program (Washington, D.C.) and AuSable Inst of Environmental Studies Program (Michigan). Teacher certification in early childhood, elementary, and secondary education. Certification in specific subject areas. Study abroad in the Dominican Republic, England, France, Germany, Latin American countries, and Spain.
**Academic Assistance:** Remedial reading, writing, math, and study skills. Nonremedial tutoring.

**ADMISSIONS. Academic basis for candidate selection** (in order of priority): Secondary school record, standardized test scores, class rank, school's recommendation, essay.
**Nonacademic basis for candidate selection:** Character and personality, extracurricular participation, and particular talent or ability are important. Alumni/ae relationship is considered.
**Requirements:** Graduation from secondary school is required; GED is accepted. 16 units and the following program of study are required: 3 units of English, 2 units of math, 2 units of science, 2 units of foreign language, 2 units of social studies, 2 units of history, 3 units of academic electives. Minimum combined SAT score of 800 and minimum 2.5 GPA recommended. Audition required of music program applicants. Provisional admission possible for applicants not meeting standard requirements. SAT or ACT is required. Campus visit and interview recommended. Off-campus interviews available with an alumni representative.
**Procedure:** Take SAT or ACT by January of 12th year. Application deadline is August. Notification of admission on rolling basis. $100 nonrefundable tuition deposit. Freshmen accepted for terms other than fall.
**Special programs:** Admission may be deferred one year. Credit and/or placement may be granted through CEEB Advanced Placement exams for scores of 3 or higher. Credit and/or placement may be granted through CLEP general and subject exams. Early entrance/early admission program.
**Transfer students:** Transfer students accepted for terms other than fall. In fall 1993, 32% of all new students were transfers into all classes. Application deadline is August 1 for fall; December 15 for spring. Minimum 2.0 GPA recommended. Lowest course grade accepted is "C." Maximum number of transferable credits is 63 quarter hours. At least 30 quarter hours must be completed at the college to receive degree.
**Admissions contact:** Cheryl L. Burdick, M.P.S., Director of Admissions. 914 944-5650.

**FINANCIAL AID. Available aid:** Pell grants, SEOG, state scholarships, school scholarships and grants, private scholarships, academic merit scholarships, and athletic scholarships. Perkins Loans (NDSL), PLUS, and Stafford Loans (GSL). Deferred payment plan. King's College Three-Payment Plan.
**Financial aid statistics:** In 1993-94, 85% of all undergraduate applicants received aid; 89% of freshman applicants. Average amounts of aid awarded freshmen: Scholarships and grants, $9,885; loans, $2,550.
**Supporting data/closing dates:** FAFSA/FAF: Priority filing date is February 15. School's own aid application: Priority filing date is February 15. Income tax forms: Priority filing date is February 15. Notification of awards begins March 15.
**Financial aid contact:** Susan Spitzer, Acting Director of Financial Aid. 914 944-5663.

# Laboratory Institute of Merchandising

**New York, NY 10022** **212 752-1530**

**1994-95 Costs.** Tuition: $9,800. Housing: None. Fees, books, misc. academic expenses (school's estimate): $450.
**Enrollment.** Undergraduates: 9 men, 161 women (full-time). Freshman class: 193 applicants, 143 accepted, 68 enrolled.
**Test score averages/ranges.** N/A.
**Faculty.** 7 full-time; 33 part-time. 15% of faculty holds doctoral degree. Student/faculty ratio: 8 to 1.
**Selectivity rating.** N/A.

**PROFILE.** The Laboratory Institute of Merchandising, founded in 1939, is a private institute. Its facilities are located in Manhattan.

**Accreditation:** MSACS.
**Religious orientation:** Laboratory Institute of Merchandising is nonsectarian; no religious requirements.
**Library:** Collections totaling over 9,660 volumes, 122 periodical subscriptions and 337 microform items.

**STUDENT BODY. Undergraduate profile:** 15% are transfers. 2% Asian-American, 25% Black, 20% Hispanic, 53% White. Average age of undergraduates is 20.
**Freshman profile:** 98% of accepted applicants took SAT. 65% of freshmen come from public schools.
**Undergraduate achievement:** 89% of fall 1992 freshmen returned for fall 1993 term. 91% of entering class graduated.
**Foreign students:** Seven students are from out of the country. Countries represented include Canada and Japan; six in all.

**PROGRAMS OF STUDY. Degrees:** B.Prof.Studies
**Majors:** Fashion Merchandising, Visual Merchandising.
**Requirements:** General education requirement.
**Special:** Upper-division students may take liberal arts courses at Fordham U. Associate's degrees offered. Independent study. Pass/fail grading option. Internships. Cooperative education programs. Study abroad in England and France.
**Academic Assistance:** Remedial writing and math.

**ADMISSIONS. Academic basis for candidate selection** (in order of priority): Secondary school record, standardized test scores, class rank, essay, school's recommendation.
**Nonacademic basis for candidate selection:** Character and personality, extracurricular participation, and particular talent or ability are important. Alumni/ae relationship is considered.
**Requirements:** Graduation from secondary school is required; GED is accepted. No specific distribution of secondary school units required. Rank in top half of secondary school class and minimum "B/C" average recommended. SAT or ACT is required. Campus visit recommended.
**Procedure:** Suggest filing application by April 15; no deadline. Notification of admission on rolling basis. No set date by which applicants must accept offer. $350 nonrefundable tuition deposit. Freshmen accepted for terms other than fall.
**Special programs:** Admission may be deferred one year. Credit and/or placement may be granted through CEEB Advanced Placement exams. Credit may be granted through CLEP general and subject exams.
**Transfer students:** Transfer students accepted for terms other than fall. In fall 1993, 15% of all new students were transfers into all classes. 50 transfer applications were received, 39 were accepted. Application deadline is rolling for fall; rolling for spring. Minimum 2.5 GPA recommended. Lowest course grade accepted is "C." At least 46 semester hours must be completed at the institute to receive degree.
**Admissions contact:** Sandy Joseph, Acting Director of Admissions. 212 752-1530.

**FINANCIAL AID. Available aid:** Pell grants, SEOG, state scholarships and grants, private grants, and academic merit scholarships. Perkins Loans (NDSL), PLUS, Stafford Loans (GSL), and SLS.
**Financial aid statistics:** In 1993-94, 65% of all undergraduate applicants received aid.
**Supporting data/closing dates:** FAFSA: Priority filing date is April 1; accepted on rolling basis. State aid form: Accepted on rolling basis; deadline is April 1. Income tax forms: Accepted on rolling basis; deadline is April 1. Notification of awards on rolling basis.
**Financial aid contact:** Jonathan Kenler, M.B.A., Director of Financial Aid. 212 752-1530.

# LeMoyne College

**Syracuse, NY 13214** **315 445-4100**

**1994-95 Costs.** Tuition: $11,040. Room: $2,890. Board: $1,950. Fees, books, misc. academic expenses (school's estimate): $665.
**Enrollment.** Undergraduates: 823 men, 997 women (full-time). Freshman class: 1,470 applicants, 1,199 accepted, 425 enrolled. Graduate enrollment: 76 men, 58 women.
**Test score averages/ranges.** Range of SAT scores of middle 50%: 420-510 verbal, 480-590 math. Range of ACT scores of middle 50%: 22-27 English, 22-26 math.
**Faculty.** 119 full-time; 91 part-time. 93% of faculty holds doctoral degree. Student/faculty ratio: 13 to 1.
**Selectivity rating.** Competitive.,

**PROFILE.** LeMoyne, founded in 1946, is a church-affiliated, liberal arts college. Its 150-acre campus is located in a residential area, two miles from downtown Syracuse.

**Accreditation:** MSACS.
**Religious orientation:** LeMoyne College is affiliated with the Roman Catholic Church (Society of Jesus); two semesters of religion required.
**Library:** Collections totaling over 205,949 volumes, 1,734 periodical subscriptions, and 30,363 microform items.
**Special facilities/museums:** Art gallery, audio-visual center, electron microscopes.
**Athletic facilities:** Gymnasiums, basketball, racquetball, and tennis courts, weight room, baseball, football, intramural, lacrosse, soccer, and softball fields, recreation center.

**STUDENT BODY. Undergraduate profile:** 92% are state residents; 24% are transfers. 2% Asian-American, 4% Black, 3% Hispanic, 1% Native American, 88% White, 2% Other. Average age of undergraduates is 20.
**Freshman profile:** 1% of freshmen who took SAT scored 700 or over on verbal, 3% scored 700 or over on math; 6% scored 600 or over on verbal, 23% scored 600 or over on math; 35% scored 500 or over on verbal, 69% scored 500 or over on math; 89% scored 400 or over on verbal, 97% scored 400 or over on math; 100% scored 300 or over on verbal, 100% scored 300 or over on math. 10% of freshmen who took ACT scored 30 or over on English, 10% scored 30 or over on math, 14% scored 30 or over on composite; 62% scored 24 or over on English, 56% scored 24 or over on math, 62% scored 24 or over on composite; 98% scored 18 or over on English, 100% scored 18 or over on math, 100% scored 18 or over on composite; 100% scored 12 or over on English. 99% of accepted applicants took SAT; 41% took ACT. 62% of freshmen come from public schools.
**Undergraduate achievement:** 92% of fall 1992 freshmen returned for fall 1993 term. 69% of entering class graduated. 32% of students who completed a degree program went on to graduate study within one year.
**Foreign students:** 25 students are from out of the country. Countries represented include the Bahamas, Belize, Canada, Jordan, and Nigeria.

**PROGRAMS OF STUDY. Degrees:** B.A., B.S.
**Majors:** Accounting, Biology, Business Administration, Chemistry, Computer Science, Economics, English, French, History, Industrial Relations/Human Resources Management, Mathematics, Mathematics/Actuarial Science, Mathematics/Education, Mathematics/Operations Research, Mathematics/Statistics, Multiple Science, Philosophy, Physics, Political Science, Psychology, Psychology/Special Education, Religious Studies, Sociology, Sociology/Criminology/Criminal Justice, Sociology/Human Services, Sociology Research, Spanish.

**Distribution of degrees:** The majors with the highest enrollment are business administration, accounting, and English; religious studies, physics, and mathematics/management have the lowest.
**Requirements:** General education requirement.
**Academic regulations:** Freshmen must maintain minimum 1.61 GPA; sophomores, 1.81 GPA; juniors, 1.91 GPA; seniors, 2.0 GPA.
**Special:** Minors offered in most majors and in international and urban studies. Concentrations offered in business language, communications, criminology/criminal justice, drama, finance, human resources, management, management information systems, marketing, and operations management. Double majors. Independent study. Pass/fail grading option. Internships. Graduate school at which undergraduates may take graduate-level courses. Preprofessional programs in law, medicine, veterinary science, dentistry, and optometry. 2-2 environmental science and forestry program with SUNY Coll of Environmental Science and Forestry. 2-2 physical therapy program with SUNY Health Science Center at Syracuse. 3-4 dentistry program with SUNY at Buffalo. 3-4 optometry program with Pennsylvania Coll of Optometry. 3-4 podiatry program with New York Coll of Podiatric Medicine. Early Assurance Program with SUNY at Buffalo and SUNY Health Science Center at Syracuse. 3-2 engineering programs with Clarkson U, Manhattan Coll, and U of Detroit Mercy. Member of Consortium for the Cultural Foundations of Medicine. Albany Semester. Visiting Student Program. CUPGAS Program (physics) with Virginia Polytech Inst and State U. Teacher certification in elementary, secondary, special education, and bilingual/bicultural education. Certification in specific subject areas. Study abroad in Australia, Austria, Egypt, England, France, Ireland, Israel, Italy, Japan, Mexico, Spain, and other countries. ROTC and AFROTC at Syracuse U.
**Honors:** Honors program. Honor societies.
**Academic Assistance:** Remedial writing and math. Nonremedial tutoring.

**STUDENT LIFE. Housing:** All students must live on campus unless living with family. Coed, women's, and men's dorms. School-owned/operated apartments. 73% of students live in college housing.
**Social atmosphere:** As reported by the student newspaper, some of the most popular student gathering spots, on and off campus, are the Dewittshire, the Dolphin Den, Marshall Square, and the 21 Club. Influential groups include LSPB, the Values Committee, International House, POWER, and the Dolphin paper. Basketball games, the Christmas Semiformal, Spring Formal, and Dolphy Day are some of the more popular campus events.
**Services and counseling/handicapped student services:** Placement services. Health service. Counseling services for minority and older students. Personal and psychological counseling. Career and academic guidance services. Religious counseling. Physically disabled student services. Learning disabled services. Tape recorders. Tutors. Reader services for the blind.
**Campus organizations:** Undergraduate student government. Student newspaper (Dolphin, published once/week). Literary magazine. Yearbook. Radio station. Choral society, religious folk group, debating, drama group, Performing Arts Society, Young Democrats, Young Republicans, academic, service, and special-interest groups, 61 organizations in all.
**Religious organizations:** Campus Ministry, Christian Fellowship, Emmaus Retreat Program.
**Minority/foreign student organizations:** Minority Cultural Society, Pride in Our Work Ethic & Race (POWER), El Progresso. International House.

**ATHLETICS. Physical education requirements:** Two semesters of physical education required.
**Intercollegiate competition:** 30% of students participate. Baseball (M), basketball (M,W), cheerleading (M,W), cross-country (M,W), diving (M,W), golf (M), lacrosse (M,W), soccer (M,W), softball (W), swimming (M,W), tennis (M,W), volleyball (W). Member of ECAC, MAAC, NCAA Division I for baseball, NCAA Division II, New England Collegiate Conference.
**Intramural and club sports:** 75% of students participate. Intramural basketball, flag football, indoor soccer, inner-tube water polo, racquetball, soccer, softball, volleyball, walleyball. Men's club ice hockey, rugby, volleyball.

**ADMISSIONS. Academic basis for candidate selection** (in order of priority): Secondary school record, class rank, school's recommendation, standardized test scores, essay.
**Nonacademic basis for candidate selection:** Extracurricular participation is emphasized. Character and personality and particular talent or ability are important. Alumni/ae relationship is considered.
**Requirements:** Graduation from secondary school is required; GED is not accepted. 16 units and the following program of study are required: 4 units of English, 3 units of math, 3 units of science, 3 units of foreign language, 3 units of social studies. HEOP for applicants not normally admissible. SAT or ACT is required. Campus visit and interview recommended. No off-campus interviews.
**Procedure:** Take SAT or ACT by January of 12th year. Take ACH by January of 12th year. Visit college for interview by April of 12th year. Suggest filing application by February 1. Application deadline is March 15. Notification of admission on rolling basis. Reply is required by May 1. $100 nonrefundable tuition deposit. $100 nonrefundable room deposit. Freshmen accepted for terms other than fall.
**Special programs:** Admission may be deferred one year. Credit and/or placement may be granted through CEEB Advanced Placement exams for scores of 3 or higher. Credit may be granted through CLEP subject exams and Regents College exams. Early decision program. In fall 1993, 76 applied for early decision and 74 were accepted. Deadline for applying for early decision is December 1. Early entrance/early admission program.
**Transfer students:** Transfer students accepted for terms other than fall. In fall 1993, 24% of all new students were transfers into all classes. 279 transfer applications were received, 176 were accepted. Application deadline is June 1 for fall; December 1 for spring. Minimum 2.6 GPA required. Lowest course grade accepted is "C." Maximum number of transferable credits is 60 semester hours from a two-year school and 90 semester hours from a four-year school. At least 30 semester hours must be completed at the college to receive degree.
**Admissions contact:** Edwin B. Harris, Ph.D., Director of Admissions. 315 445-4300, 800 333-4733.

**FINANCIAL AID. Available aid:** Pell grants, SEOG, state scholarships and grants, school scholarships and grants, private scholarships and grants, academic merit scholarships, athletic scholarships, and aid for undergraduate foreign students. Perkins Loans (NDSL), PLUS, Stafford Loans (GSL), and SLS. AMS.
**Financial aid statistics:** 20% of aid is not need-based. In 1993-94, 100% of all undergraduate applicants received aid. Average amounts of aid awarded freshmen: Scholarships and grants, $6,500; loans, $2,625.
**Supporting data/closing dates:** FAFSA/FAF/FFS: Priority filing date is February 15; deadline is April 15. School's own aid application: Priority filing date is March 15; deadline is May 1. Income tax forms: Deadline is May 1. Notification of awards begins March 15.
**Financial aid contact:** Darryl Anderson, M.Ed., Director of Financial Aid. 315 445-4400.

**STUDENT EMPLOYMENT.** College Work/Study Program. Institutional employment. 35% of full-time undergraduates work on campus during school year. Students may expect to earn an average of $1,200 during school year. Off-campus part-time employment opportunities rated "excellent."

**COMPUTER FACILITIES.** 85 IBM/IBM-compatible and Macintosh/Apple microcomputers; 45 are networked. Students may access Digital, IBM minicomputer/mainframe systems, BITNET, Internet. Residence halls may be equipped with stand-alone microcomputers, networked terminals. Client/LAN operating systems include Apple/Macintosh, DOS. Computer languages and software packages include Ada, BASIC, BMDP, C, COBOL, dBASE, Excel, FORTRAN, LISP, Lotus 1-2-3, Microsoft Word, MINITAB, Pascal, PC-Solve, Powerpoint, Quattro, SAS, SPSS, WordPerfect. Computer facilities are available to all students.
**Fees:** $10 computer fee per semester.
**Hours:** 24 hours.

**GRADUATE CAREER DATA.** Graduate school percentages: 5% enter law school. 3% enter medical school. 1% enter dental school. 4% enter graduate business programs. 14% enter graduate arts and sciences programs. Highest graduate school enrollments: SUNY, Syracuse U. 50% of graduates choose careers in business and industry. Companies and businesses that hire graduates: Aetna, Carrier Corp., Big Six accounting firms, General Electric, Key Bank, Agway.

**PROMINENT ALUMNI/AE.** Carl J. Schramm, executive vice president, Fortis Inc.; Jack Curry, managing editor, *TV Guide;* Michael Madden, executive managing director, Kidder Peabody.

# Long Island University, Brooklyn Campus

**Brooklyn, NY 11201** 718 488-1000

**1994-95 Costs.** Tuition: $11,000. Room: $2,950. Board: $3,050. Fees, books, misc. academic expenses (school's estimate): $650.
**Enrollment.** Undergraduates: 1,544 men, 2,903 women (full-time). Freshman class: 1,952 applicants, 1,922 accepted, 987 enrolled.
**Test score averages/ranges.** N/A.
**Faculty.** 222 full-time. 53% of faculty holds doctoral degree. Student/faculty ratio: 9 to 1.
**Selectivity rating.** N/A.

**PROFILE.** Long Island University, Brooklyn Campus, founded in 1926, is a private institution. Programs are offered through the Colleges of Liberal Arts and Sciences and Pharmacy and Health Sciences and the Schools of Business, Public Administration, and Information Sciences; Communications, Visual, and Performing Arts; Education; and Health Professions. Its 23-acre campus is located in downtown Brooklyn.

**Accreditation:** MSACS.
**Religious orientation:** Long Island University, Brooklyn Campus is nonsectarian; no religious requirements.
**Library:** Collections totaling over 250,000 volumes, 1,265 periodical subscriptions, and 40,500 microform items.
**Special facilities/museums:** Language lab, instructional resources center.
**Athletic facilities:** Athletic center, tennis courts, athletic field, gymnasium.

**STUDENT BODY. Undergraduate profile:** 88% are state residents; 44% are transfers. 10.8% Asian-American, 43.3% Black, 16.5% Hispanic, .3% Native American, 29.1% White. Average age of undergraduates is 25.
**Freshman profile:** 82% of freshmen come from public schools.
**Undergraduate achievement:** 65% of fall 1992 freshmen returned for fall 1993 term.
**Foreign students:** 47 students are from out of the country. Countries represented include China, India, Korea, Nigeria, Pakistan, and Russia; 30 in all.

**PROGRAMS OF STUDY. Degrees:** B.A., B.F.A., B.S., B.S.Pharm.
**Majors:** Accounting, Banking/Finance, Biology, Business Administration, Chemistry, Communication Studies, Computer Science, Cytotechnology, Economics, Elementary Education, English, Finance, History, Humanities, Journalism, Management, Marketing, Mathematics, Media Studies, Medical Technology, Molecular Biology, Music, Nursing, Operations Management/Operations Research, Pharmacy, Philosophy, Physical Education, Physical Therapy, Physician's Assistant, Psychology, Public Administration, Respiratory Therapy, Secondary Education, Social Sciences, Sociology/Anthropology, Spanish, Speech/Theatre, Visual Arts.
**Requirements:** General education requirement.
**Special:** Certificate programs in criminal justice, international studies, and social welfare. Paralegal studies program. Courses offered in linguistics. Associate's degrees offered. Self-designed majors. Double majors. Accelerated study. Pass/fail grading option. Internships. Cooperative education programs. Graduate school at which undergraduates may take graduate-level courses. Preprofessional programs in law and medicine. Five-year B.A./M.B.A. program. Six-year B.S.Pharm./M.B.A programs. 3-1 cytotechnology and medical technology programs with approved school or hospital. UN Semester. Teacher certification in early childhood, elementary, and secondary education.
**Honors:** Phi Beta Kappa. Honors program. Honor societies.
**Academic Assistance:** Nonremedial tutoring.

**STUDENT LIFE. Housing:** Students may live on or off campus. Coed, women's, and men's dorms. 15% of students live in college housing.
**Social atmosphere:** Avena lounge, the library, and SGA office are popular gathering places. SGA, Seawanhaka, and Latinos Unidos are influential groups. Homecoming, Spring Day, and Orientation Day are popular events. According to the editor of the student newspaper, "Everyone keeps mostly to themselves here because it's a commuter college."
**Services and counseling/handicapped student services:** Placement services. Health service. Women's center. Freshman counseling. Guided studies. International student services. Counseling services for veteran students. Birth control, personal, and psychological counseling. Career and academic guidance services. Learning disabled program/services.
**Campus organizations:** Undergraduate student government. Student newspaper (Seawanhaka, published once/week). Literary magazine. Yearbook. Radio and TV stations. Theatre, Women's Movement, departmental, political, and special-interest groups, 64 organizations in all. Three fraternities, no chapter houses; three sororities, no chapter houses.
**Religious organizations:** Intervarsity Christian Fellowship, Bible study group, Muslim Society.
**Minority/foreign student organizations:** Black Active Student Association, Caribbean Student Movement. International Student Organization.
**ATHLETICS. Physical education requirements:** None.
**Intercollegiate competition:** 3% of students participate. Baseball (M), basketball (M,W), cheerleading (W), cross-country (M,W), golf (M), soccer (M), softball (W), tennis (W), track (indoor) (M,W), track (outdoor) (M,W), track and field (indoor) (M,W), track and field (outdoor) (M,W). Member of ECAC, NCAA Division I, Northeast Conference.
**Intramural and club sports:** Intramural baseball, flag football, table tennis, tennis, volleyball. Men's club indoor track, indoor track/field, outdoor track, outdoor track/field. Women's club indoor track, indoor track/field, outdoor track, outdoor track/field.
**ADMISSIONS. Academic basis for candidate selection** (in order of priority): Secondary school record, standardized test scores, class rank, school's recommendation, essay.
**Requirements:** Graduation from secondary school is required; GED is accepted. 16 units and the following program of study are required: 4 units of English, 2 units of math, 1 unit of science, 2 units of foreign language, 3 units of social studies, 4 units of electives including 1 unit of academic electives. HEOP for applicants not normally admissible. SAT is recommended. ACT is recommended. Campus visit recommended. No off-campus interviews.
**Procedure:** Notification of admission on rolling basis. $100 nonrefundable tuition deposit. $100 nonrefundable room deposit. Freshmen accepted for terms other than fall.
**Special programs:** Admission may be deferred one year. Credit and/or placement may be granted through CEEB Advanced Placement exams for scores of 3 or higher. Credit may be granted through CLEP general and subject exams and Regents College and ACT PEP exams and military and life experience. Concurrent enrollment program.
**Transfer students:** Transfer students accepted for terms other than fall. In fall 1993, 44% of all new students were transfers into all classes. 2,333 transfer applications were received. Application deadline is rolling for fall; rolling for spring. Lowest course grade accepted is "C." Maximum number of transferable credits is 96 semester hours. At least 32 semester hours must be completed at the university to receive degree.
**Admissions contact:** Alan B. Chaves, M.Div., Dean of Admissions. 718 488-1011.
**FINANCIAL AID. Available aid:** Pell grants, SEOG, Federal Nursing Student Scholarships, state scholarships and grants, school scholarships and grants, private scholarships and grants, academic merit scholarships, athletic scholarships, and aid for undergraduate foreign students. Perkins Loans (NDSL), PLUS, Stafford Loans (GSL), Health Professions Loans, state loans, and SLS. Tuition Plan Inc. and deferred payment plan.
**Financial aid statistics:** In 1993-94, 91% of all undergraduate applicants received aid; 90% of freshman applicants. Average amounts of aid awarded freshmen: Scholarships and grants, $6,000; loans, $1,500.
**Supporting data/closing dates:** FAFSA/FAF: Accepted on rolling basis. School's own aid application: Accepted on rolling basis. State aid form: Accepted on rolling basis. Income tax forms: Accepted on rolling basis. Notification of awards on rolling basis.
**Financial aid contact:** Rosa Iannicelli, Director of Financial Aid. 718 488-1037.
**STUDENT EMPLOYMENT.** College Work/Study Program. Institutional employment. 10% of full-time undergraduates work on campus during school year. Students may expect to earn an average of $1,200 during school year. Freshmen are discouraged from working during their first term. Off-campus part-time employment opportunities rated "good."
**COMPUTER FACILITIES.** 650 IBM/IBM-compatible and Macintosh/Apple microcomputers; 400 are networked. Students may access Digital, IBM, Sequent minicomputer/mainframe systems, BITNET, Internet. Residence halls may be equipped with stand-alone microcomputers, networked microcomputers, networked terminals, modems. Client/LAN operating systems include Novell. Computer languages and software packages include BASIC, C, COBOL, Lotus, MS Word, Pascal, SPSS-X, Windows, WordPerfect; 300 in all. Computer facilities are available to all students.
**Hours:** 9 AM-9 PM.

## Long Island University, C.W. Post Campus

**Brookville, NY 11548** **800 548-7526**

**1993-94 Costs.** Tuition: $10,940. Room & board: $5,280. Fees, books, misc. academic expenses (school's estimate): $1,030.
**Enrollment.** Undergraduates: 1,652 men, 2,038 women (full-time). Freshman class: 3,129 applicants, 2,665 accepted, 778 enrolled. Graduate enrollment: 1,186 men, 2,167 women.
**Test score averages/ranges.** Average SAT scores: 479 verbal, 547 math. Range of SAT scores of middle 50%: 450-550 verbal, 500-600 math.
**Faculty.** 317 full-time; 402 part-time. 87% of faculty holds highest degree in specific field. Student/faculty ratio: 12 to 1.
**Selectivity rating.** Competitive.

**PROFILE.** Long Island University, C.W. Post Center, founded in 1954, is a private institution. Programs are offered through the College of Liberal Arts and Sciences; the Schools of Arts, Business Administration, Education, Health and Public Service, and Professional Accountancy; and the Graduate Library School. Its 400-acre campus is located in Brookville, 45 minutes from Manhattan.

**Accreditation:** MSACS. Professionally accredited by the American Dietetic Association, the American Medical Association (CAHEA), the American Speech-Language-Hearing Association, the National Association of Schools of Music, the National Association of Schools of Public Affairs and Administration, the National League for Nursing.
**Religious orientation:** Long Island University, C.W. Post Campus is nonsectarian; no religious requirements.
**Library:** Collections totaling over 2,169,157 volumes, 8,042 periodical subscriptions, and 913,544 microform items.
**Special facilities/museums:** Art museum, performing arts center, concert theatre, television equipment, three electron microscopes.
**Athletic facilities:** Field house, weight rooms, athletic fields, racquetball/squash courts, swimming pool, equestrian stables, gymnasium.

**STUDENT BODY. Undergraduate profile:** 66% are state residents; 44% are transfers. 4% Asian-American, 7% Black, 5% Hispanic, 1% Native American, 76% White, 7% unknown. Average age of undergraduates is 21.
**Freshman profile:** 4% of freshmen who took SAT scored 700 or over on math; 10% scored 600 or over on verbal, 31% scored 600 or over on math; 41% scored 500 or over on verbal, 72% scored 500 or over on math; 89% scored 400 or over on verbal, 96% scored 400 or over on math; 100% scored 300 or over on verbal, 99% scored 300 or over on math. 90% of accepted applicants took SAT; 10% took ACT. 71% of freshmen come from public schools.
**Undergraduate achievement:** 69% of fall 1992 freshmen returned for fall 1993 term. 39% of entering class graduated. 62% of students who completed a degree program went on to graduate study within one year.
**Foreign students:** 299 students are from out of the country. Countries represented include Cyprus, Greece, Japan, Korea, Taiwan, and Turkey; 34 in all.
**PROGRAMS OF STUDY. Degrees:** B.A., B.F.A., B.Prof.Studies, B.S., B.S.Ed.
**Majors:** Accounting, Acting, Applied Art, Art Education, Art History, Art Therapy, Arts Management, Biology, Biology Education, Broadcasting, Business Administration/Management, Chemistry, Chemistry Education, Communication Arts, Comparative Languages, Computational Mathematics, Computer/Information Sciences, Conservation, Criminal Justice, Design, Earth Science Education, Economics, Education in Non-School Settings, Elementary Education, English, English Education, Environmental Studies, Film, Finance, Fine Arts, French, French Education, Geography, Geology, German, German Education, Health Administration, Health Education, Health/Physical Education, History, Information Systems, Interdisciplinary Studies, International Studies, Italian, Italian Education, Journalism, Latin American Studies, Management, Managerial Accounting, Marketing, Mathematics, Mathematics Education, Medical Biology, Medical Records Administration, Medical Technology, Molecular Biology, Music, Music Education, Nursing, Nutrition, Pharmacy, Philosophy, Photography, Physical Education, Physics, Physics Education, Political Science/Government, Pre-Engineering, Pre-Pharmacy, Pre-Respiratory Therapy, Psychology, Public Accounting, Public Administration, Public Relations, Radiologic Technology, Russian Area Studies, Social Studies, Social Studies Education, Sociology, Spanish, Spanish Education, Speech Education, Studio Art, Teacher of Speech/Hearing Handicapped, Theatre.
**Distribution of degrees:** The majors with the highest enrollment are business administration, education, and political science.
**Requirements:** General education requirement.
**Academic regulations:** Minimum 2.0 GPA must be maintained.
**Special:** Minors offered in approximately 70 fields. Associate's degrees offered. Self-designed majors. Double majors. Dual degrees. Independent study. Accelerated study. Pass/fail grading option. Internships. Cooperative education programs. Graduate school at which undergraduates may take graduate-level courses. Preprofessional programs in law, medicine, and pharmacy. 3-2 engineering program with Polytech U of New York. B.S./M.S. biology program. B.A./M.S. criminal justice program. B.A./M.P.A. health administration and public administration programs. B.A./M.A. political science program. B.A./M.B.A. international studies/business administration program. Member of Nassau Higher Education Consortium and LIRACHE (Long Island Regional Advisory Council on Higher Education). Washington Semester, UN Semester, and Sea Semester. Exchange programs with other Long Island universities. Teacher certification in early childhood, elementary, secondary, special education, and bilingual/bicultural education. Certification in specific subject areas. Study abroad in Egypt, England, France, Greece, Italy, Japan, Korea, the Netherlands, and Switzerland. Friends World Program locations in Costa Rica, England, Israel, Kenya, India, Japan, and Taiwan. ROTC and AFROTC at New York Inst of Tech and Hofstra U.
**Honors:** Honors program. Honor societies.
**Academic Assistance:** Remedial reading, writing, math, and study skills. Nonremedial tutoring.

**STUDENT LIFE. Housing:** Students may live on or off campus. Coed dorms. 31% of students live in college housing.
**Services and counseling/handicapped student services:** Placement services. Health service. Women's center. Day care. Counseling services for minority, military, veteran, and older students. Birth control, personal, and psychological counseling. Career and academic guidance services. Religious counseling. Physically disabled student services. Learning disabled program/services. Notetaking services. Tape recorders. Tutors. Reader services for the blind.
**Campus organizations:** Undergraduate student government. Student newspaper (Pioneer, published once/week). Literary magazine. Yearbook. Radio station. Chorus, orchestra, band, Chamber Madrigal Singers, Student Art League, drama group, debating, Broadcasters of Tomorrow, Gay/Lesbian Student Association, SADD, departmental, social, and special-interest groups, 60 organizations in all. 10 fraternities, no chapter houses; 10 sororities, no chapter houses. 6% of men join a fraternity. 4% of women join a sorority.

**Religious organizations:** Campus Crusade for Christ, Jewish Student Association, Newman Club.

**Minority/foreign student organizations:** African People's Organization, Council for Latin American Students, Caribbean/African student group. Chinese Student Association, Hellenic Society, International Student Association.

**ATHLETICS. Physical education requirements:** None.

**Intercollegiate competition:** 13% of students participate. Baseball (M), basketball (M,W), cheerleading (M,W), cross-country (M,W), field hockey (W), football (M), lacrosse (M), soccer (M), softball (W), tennis (W), track (indoor) (M,W), track (outdoor) (M,W), track and field (indoor) (M,W), track and field (outdoor) (M,W), volleyball (W). Member of ECAC, NCAA Division I for baseball, NCAA Division II, NCAA Division III for football, NYCAC.

**Intramural and club sports:** 6% of students participate. Intramural basketball, flag football, softball, volleyball. Men's club equestrian sports, ice hockey, rugby. Women's club equestrian sports.

**ADMISSIONS. Academic basis for candidate selection** (in order of priority): Secondary school record, standardized test scores, class rank, school's recommendation, essay.

**Nonacademic basis for candidate selection:** Character and personality, extracurricular participation, and particular talent or ability are important.

**Requirements:** Graduation from secondary school is required; GED is accepted. 21 units and the following program of study are required: 4 units of English, 2 units of math, 2 units of lab science, 2 units of foreign language, 3 units of social studies, 3 units of history, 3 units of electives including 2 units of academic electives. Minimum combined SAT score of 900 and minimum grade average of 75 required. Portfolio required of art program applicants. Audition required of music program applicants. R.N. required of nursing program applicants. HEOP for applicants not normally admissible. Conditional admission possible for applicants not meeting standard requirements. General Studies Program. SAT is required; ACT may be substituted. PSAT is recommended. ACH recommended. Campus visit and interview recommended. Off-campus interviews available with an admissions representative.

**Procedure:** Take SAT or ACT by November of 12th year. Visit college for interview by December of 12th year. Notification of admission on rolling basis. No set date by which applicants must accept offer; scholarship recipients must accept offer by May 1 or within two weeks of acceptance. $100 nonrefundable tuition deposit. $100 room deposit, refundable until July 1. Freshmen accepted for terms other than fall.

**Special programs:** Admission may be deferred one year. Credit may be granted through CEEB Advanced Placement for scores of 4 or higher. Credit may be granted through CLEP general and subject exams, Regents College and DANTES exam,s and life experience. Placement may be granted through ACT PEP and challenge exams. Credit and placement may be granted through military experience. Deadline for applying for early decision is rolling. Early entrance/early admission program. Concurrent enrollment program.

**Transfer students:** Transfer students accepted for terms other than fall. In fall 1993, 44% of all new students were transfers into all classes. 1,197 transfer applications were received, 1,163 were accepted. Minimum 2.0 GPA required. Lowest course grade accepted is "C." Maximum number of transferable credits is 64 semester hours. At least 32 semester hours must be completed at the university to receive degree.

**Admissions contact:** Christine C. Natali, M.S., Director of Admissions. 516 299-2413.

**FINANCIAL AID. Available aid:** Pell grants, SEOG, state scholarships and grants, school scholarships and grants, private scholarships and grants, academic merit scholarships, athletic scholarships, and aid for undergraduate foreign students. Perkins Loans (NDSL), PLUS, Stafford Loans (GSL), state loans, private loans, and SLS. Tuition Plan Inc., Knight Tuition Plans, AMS, and deferred payment plan.

**Financial aid statistics:** 45% of aid is not need-based. In 1993-94, 75% of all undergraduate applicants received aid; 77% of freshman applicants. Average amounts of aid awarded freshmen: Scholarships and grants, $3,000; loans, $2,000.

**Supporting data/closing dates:** FAFSA: Priority filing date is May 15. FAF: Priority filing date is May 15; accepted on rolling basis. State aid form: Accepted on rolling basis. Income tax forms: Accepted on rolling basis. Notification of awards on rolling basis.

**Financial aid contact:** Joanne Graziano, M.B.A., Director of Financial Aid. 516 299-2338.

**STUDENT EMPLOYMENT.** College Work/Study Program. Institutional employment. 31% of full-time undergraduates work on campus during school year. Students may expect to earn an average of $900 during school year. Off-campus part-time employment opportunities rated "good."

**COMPUTER FACILITIES.** 400 IBM/IBM-compatible and Macintosh/Apple microcomputers; all are networked. Students may access Digital, IBM, Sequent minicomputer/mainframe systems, BITNET, Internet. Residence halls may be equipped with stand-alone microcomputers, networked microcomputers, networked terminals, modems. Client/LAN operating systems include Apple/Macintosh, DOS, UNIX/XENIX/AIX, DEC, LocalTalk/AppleTalk, Novell. Computer languages and software packages include Ada, BASIC, C, COBOL, FORTRAN, GPSS, LISP, Pascal, RPG II, SimScript; 700 in all. Computer facilities are available to all students.

**Fees:** Computer fee is included in tuition/fees.

**Hours:** 8 AM-11 PM; computers within dormitories available 8 AM-4 AM.

**GRADUATE CAREER DATA.** Highest graduate school enrollments: Long Island University, C.W. Post Campus. 39% of graduates choose careers in business and industry.

**PROMINENT ALUMNI/AE.** Rita Sands, broadcaster, WCBS; Dr. Nath, noted for work with DNA and biology; Franklin Coleman, public relations director for Senator D'Amato.

# Long Island University, Southampton Campus

**Southampton, NY 11968** **516 283-4000**

**1993-94 Costs.** Tuition: $11,600. Room & board: $5,810. Fees, books, misc. academic expenses (school's estimate): $1,500.

**Enrollment.** Undergraduates: 450 men, 766 women (full-time). Freshman class: 1,123 applicants, 990 accepted, 325 enrolled. Graduate enrollment: 41 men, 70 women.

**Test score averages/ranges.** Average SAT scores: 450 verbal, 500 math.

**Faculty.** 72 full-time; 43 part-time. 91% of faculty holds highest degree in specific field. Student/faculty ratio: 17 to 1.

**Selectivity rating.** Less competitive.

**PROFILE.** Long Island University, Southampton Campus, founded in 1963, is a private institution. Programs are offered through the Divisions of Business, Fine Arts, Humanities, Natural Science, Social Science, and Teacher Education. Its 110-acre campus is located in Southampton, 100 miles east of New York City.

**Accreditation:** MSACS.

**Religious orientation:** Long Island University, Southampton Campus is nonsectarian; no religious requirements.

**Library:** Collections totaling over 144,000 volumes, 680 periodical subscriptions, and 34,000 microform items.

**Special facilities/museums:** Art galleries, on-campus nursery school, psychobiology lab, marine station and fleet of research vessels.

**Athletic facilities:** Gymnasiums, weight room, tennis and volleyball courts, swimming pool, fitness trail, sailing facilities.

**STUDENT BODY. Undergraduate profile:** 55% are state residents; 28% are transfers. 1.4% Asian-American, 8.7% Black, 5.1% Hispanic, 2.1% Native American, 82.7% White. Average age of undergraduates is 21.

**Freshman profile:** 8% of freshmen who took SAT scored 600 or over on verbal, 11% scored 600 or over on math; 30% scored 500 or over on verbal, 43% scored 500 or over on math; 76% scored 400 or over on verbal, 72% scored 400 or over on math; 100% scored 300 or over on verbal, 100% scored 300 or over on math. Majority of accepted applicants took SAT.

**Undergraduate achievement:** 89% of fall 1992 freshmen returned for fall 1993 term. 51% of entering class graduated. 28% of students who completed a degree program immediately went on to graduate study.

**Foreign students:** 24 students are from out of the country. Countries represented include England, India, Japan, Romania, the Netherlands, and Trinidad/Tobago; eight in all.

**PROGRAMS OF STUDY. Degrees:** B.A., B.F.A., B.S.

**Majors:** Accounting, Art, Art Education, Art/Graphic Design, Arts Management, Biology, Business Administration, Chemistry, Communication Arts, Elementary Education, English/Writing, Environmental Science, Environmental Studies, Geology, History/Politics, Interdisciplinary Studies, Marine Science, Pre-Law, Psychology, Psychology/Biology, Secondary Education, Social Sciences, Sociology.

**Distribution of degrees:** The majors with the highest enrollment are marine science, business administration, and art; sociology, chemistry, and geology have the lowest.

**Requirements:** General education requirement.

**Academic regulations:** Minimum 2.0 GPA must be maintained.

**Special:** Minors offered in all majors and in economics, film, music, and theatre. Courses offered in American studies, computer science, dance, economics, music, theatre, and writing. Self-designed majors. Double majors. Independent study. Pass/fail grading option. Internships. Cooperative education programs. Graduate school at which undergraduates may take graduate-level courses. Preprofessional programs in law, medicine, veterinary science, and pharmacy. 2-2 pre-pharmacy program with Long Island U at Brooklyn. UN Semester and Sea Semester. Teacher certification in elementary and secondary education. Certification in specific subject areas. Study abroad in China, Costa Rica, England, India, Israel, Japan, and Kenya. ROTC at Hofstra U.

**Honors:** Honors program. Honor societies.

**Academic Assistance:** Remedial reading, writing, math, and study skills. Nonremedial tutoring.

**STUDENT LIFE. Housing:** All unmarried students under age 21 must live on campus unless living near campus with relatives. Coed and women's dorms. 75% of students live in college housing.

**Services and counseling/handicapped student services:** Placement services. Health service. Personal and psychological counseling. Career and academic guidance services. Physically disabled student services. Learning disabled services. Notetaking services. Tutors.

**Campus organizations:** Undergraduate student government. Student newspaper (Windmill, published once/week). Literary magazine. Yearbook. Radio station. Chorus, instrumental ensemble, drama group, film committee, Readers and Writers Club, academic, athletic, service, and special-interest groups, 38 organizations in all.

**Religious organizations:** Campus Ministry.

**Minority/foreign student organizations:** Spectrum of Unity.

**ATHLETICS. Physical education requirements:** None.

**Intercollegiate competition:** 12% of students participate. Basketball (M,W), lacrosse (M), soccer (M,W), softball (W), volleyball (M,W). Member of ECAC, NCAA Division II, New York Collegiate Athletic Conference.

**Intramural and club sports:** 20% of students participate. Intramural badminton, basketball, bowling, flag football, golf, indoor soccer, softball, tennis, ultimate frisbee, volleyball. Men's club sailing, ultimate frisbee. Women's club cheerleading, sailing, ultimate frisbee.

**ADMISSIONS. Academic basis for candidate selection** (in order of priority): Secondary school record, standardized test scores, class rank, school's recommendation, essay.
**Nonacademic basis for candidate selection:** Extracurricular participation is emphasized. Character and personality are important. Particular talent or ability and alumni/ae relationship are considered.
**Requirements:** Graduation from secondary school is required; GED is accepted. 18 units and the following program of study are recommended: 4 units of English, 2 units of math, 3 units of science, 2 units of foreign language, 3 units of social studies, 4 units of electives. Minimum combined SAT score of 900 and minimum "C" average recommended. HEOP for applicants not normally admissible. SAT or ACT is required. Campus visit and interview recommended. No off-campus interviews.
**Procedure:** Take SAT or ACT by November of 12th year. Visit college for interview by June of 12th year. Notification of admission on rolling basis. No set date by which applicants must accept offer. $100 tuition deposit, refundable until May 1. $100 room deposit, refundable until May 1. Freshmen accepted for terms other than fall.
**Special programs:** Admission may be deferred one year. Credit and/or placement may be granted through CEEB Advanced Placement exams for scores of 3 or higher. Credit and/or placement may be granted through CLEP general and subject exams. Credit may be granted through military experience. Credit and placement may be granted through Regents College, DANTES, and challenge exams and life experience. Early entrance/early admission program. Concurrent enrollment program.
**Transfer students:** Transfer students accepted for terms other than fall. In fall 1993, 28% of all new students were transfers into all classes. 341 transfer applications were received, 280 were accepted. Application deadline is rolling for fall; rolling for spring. Minimum 2.0 GPA required. Lowest course grade accepted is "C." Maximum number of transferable credits is 68 semester hours from a two-year school and 96 semester hours from a four-year school. At least 30 semester hours must be completed at the university to receive degree.
**Admissions contact:** Carol G. Gilbert, Director of Admissions. 516 283-4000, extension 200.

**FINANCIAL AID. Available aid:** Pell grants, SEOG, state scholarships and grants, school scholarships and grants, private scholarships and grants, academic merit scholarships, and athletic scholarships. Perkins Loans (NDSL), PLUS, Stafford Loans (GSL), state loans, school loans, private loans, and SLS. Tuition Plan Inc., Knight Tuition Plans, AMS, and deferred payment plan. Individual payment plan.
**Financial aid statistics:** 30% of aid is not need-based. In 1993-94, 80% of all undergraduate applicants received aid; 80% of freshman applicants. Average amounts of aid awarded freshmen: Scholarships and grants, $4,600.
**Supporting data/closing dates:** FAFSA/FAF: Accepted on rolling basis. School's own aid application: Accepted on rolling basis. Income tax forms: Accepted on rolling basis. Notification of awards on rolling basis.
**Financial aid contact:** Susan Taylor, M.S., Director of Financial Aid. 516 283-4000, extension 321.

**STUDENT EMPLOYMENT.** College Work/Study Program. Institutional employment. 12% of full-time undergraduates work on campus during school year. Students may expect to earn an average of $800 during school year. Off-campus part-time employment opportunities rated "good."

**COMPUTER FACILITIES.** 130 IBM/IBM-compatible microcomputers; all are networked. Students may access Digital, IBM minicomputer/mainframe systems, BITNET. Residence halls may be equipped with networked terminals. Client/LAN operating systems include DOS, LocalTalk/AppleTalk, Microsoft, Novell. Computer languages and software packages include BASIC, C, COBOL, FORTRAN, LISP, Pascal. Computer facilities are available to all students.
**Fees:** Computer fee is included in tuition/fees.
**Hours:** 7:30 AM-midn.

**GRADUATE CAREER DATA.** Graduate school percentages: 1% enter law school. 1% enter medical school. 1% enter dental school. 3% enter graduate business programs. 21% enter graduate arts and sciences programs. Highest graduate school enrollments: SUNY Stony Brook, U of Rhode Island.

# Manhattan College

**Riverdale, NY 10471** **212 920-0100**

**1994-95 Costs.** Tuition: $12,370. Room & board: $6,800. Fees, books, misc. academic expenses (school's estimate): $1,200.
**Enrollment.** Undergraduates: 1,492 men, 1,088 women (full-time). Freshman class: 2,432 applicants, 1,678 accepted, 559 enrolled. Graduate enrollment: 402 men, 238 women.
**Test score averages/ranges.** Average SAT scores: 467 verbal, 539 math.
**Faculty.** 192 full-time; 84 part-time. 89% of faculty holds doctoral degree. Student/faculty ratio: 15 to 1.
**Selectivity rating.** Competitive.

**PROFILE.** Manhattan is a church-affiliated, liberal arts college. Founded in 1853, it adopted coeducation in 1974. Programs are offered through the Schools of Arts and Sciences, Business, Education and Human Services, Engineering, and General Studies. Its 47-acre campus is located in the Riverdale section of New York City.

**Accreditation:** MSACS. Professionally accredited by the Accreditation Board for Engineering and Technology.
**Religious orientation:** Manhattan College is affiliated with the Roman Catholic Church; three semesters of religion/theology required.
**Library:** Collections totaling over 280,000 volumes, 1,530 periodical subscriptions, and 8,000 microform items.
**Special facilities/museums:** On-campus special education program for student teaching, research and learning center, plant morphogenesis lab, nuclear reactor.
**Athletic facilities:** Indoor track, basketball, tennis, and volleyball courts, swimming pool, exercise and weight rooms, athletic fields.

**STUDENT BODY. Undergraduate profile:** 77% are state residents; 25% are transfers. 7% Asian-American, 5% Black, 12% Hispanic, 76% White. Average age of undergraduates is 20.
**Freshman profile:** 1% of freshmen who took SAT scored 700 or over on math; 1% scored 600 or over on verbal, 21% scored 600 or over on math; 25% scored 500 or over on verbal, 62% scored 500 or over on math; 83% scored 400 or over on verbal, 87% scored 400 or over on math; 98% scored 300 or over on verbal, 98% scored 300 or over on math. Majority of accepted applicants took SAT. 36% of freshmen come from public schools.
**Undergraduate achievement:** 86% of fall 1992 freshmen returned for fall 1993 term. 40% of students who completed a degree program went on to graduate study within five years.
**Foreign students:** 11 students are from out of the country. Countries represented include China, Ireland, Japan, Jordan, Lebanon, and the former Soviet Republics; nine in all.

**PROGRAMS OF STUDY. Degrees:** B.A., B.S., B.S.Eng.
**Majors:** Accounting, American Studies, Biochemistry, Bioengineering, Biology, Chemical Engineering, Chemistry, Civil Engineering, Classical Languages, Communications, Computer Engineering, Computer/Information Sciences, Computer Science, Economics, Electrical Engineering, Elementary Education, English, Environmental Engineering, Exercise Physiology, Finance, Fine Arts, French, German, Government/Politics, Health Education, History, Industrial Engineering, International Business, International Studies, Italian, Management Sciences, Marketing, Mathematics, Mechanical Engineering, Nuclear Engineering, Peace Studies, Philosophy, Physical Education, Physics, Pre-Physical Therapy, Psychology, Radiological/Health Sciences, Religious Studies, Russian/Slavic Studies, Social Studies, Sociology, Spanish, Special Education, Sports Medicine, Urban Affairs.
**Distribution of degrees:** The majors with the highest enrollment are marketing, civil engineering, and finance; Italian, philosophy, and French have the lowest.
**Requirements:** General education requirement.
**Academic regulations:** Freshmen must maintain minimum 1.8 GPA; sophomores, juniors, seniors, 2.0 GPA.
**Special:** Minors offered in some majors. Associate's degrees offered. Double majors. Independent study. Accelerated study. Pass/fail grading option. Internships. Cooperative education programs. Graduate school at which undergraduates may take graduate-level courses. Preprofessional programs in law, medicine, veterinary science, dentistry, and podiatry. Early Assurance Program with SUNY Buffalo Medical Sch. Cooperative programs with Columbia U Sch of Dental and Oral Surgery, National Academy Sch of Fine Arts, and New York Coll of Podiatric Medicine. Host college for 3-2 engineering programs with Coll of Mount St. Vincent, Coll of the Sacred Heart, Dominican Coll, LeMoyne Coll, Pace U, St. John Fisher Coll, St. Thomas Aquinas Coll, and Siena Coll. Albany Semester. Exchange program with Coll of Mount St. Vincent. Teacher certification in elementary, secondary, and special education. Certification in specific subject areas. Study abroad in Austria, France, Germany, Italy, Japan, Mexico, Singapore, Spain, and the United Kingdom. AFROTC.
**Honors:** Phi Beta Kappa. Honor societies.
**Academic Assistance:** Remedial math and study skills. Nonremedial tutoring.

**STUDENT LIFE. Housing:** Students may live on or off campus. Coed and men's dorms. 55% of students live in college housing.
**Services and counseling/handicapped student services:** Placement services. Health service. Counseling services for military and veteran students. Personal and psychological counseling. Career and academic guidance services. Religious counseling. Learning disabled program/services.
**Campus organizations:** Undergraduate student government. Student newspaper (Quadrangle, published once/week). Literary magazine. Yearbook. Radio station. College Singers, pep band, College Players, Amnesty International, Pen & Sword, Women's Awareness Coalition, Young Republicans, Gaelic Society, community groups, academic and service groups, 70 organizations in all. Four fraternities, no chapter houses; two sororities, no chapter houses. 5% of men join a fraternity. 2% of women join a sorority.
**Religious organizations:** Campus Ministry, Muslim Student Association.
**Minority/foreign student organizations:** African-American/Caribbean group, Minority Student Union. International Student Association, Arabic Club, Chinese Student Association.

**ATHLETICS. Physical education requirements:** None.
**Intercollegiate competition:** 12% of students participate. Baseball (M), basketball (M,W), cross-country (M,W), golf (M), soccer (M,W), softball (W), swimming (W), tennis (M,W), track and field (indoor) (M,W), track and field (outdoor) (M,W), volleyball (W), wrestling (M). Member of ECAC, Metro Atlantic Athletic Conference, NCAA Division I.
**Intramural and club sports:** 53% of students participate. Intramural aerobics, basketball, flag football, softball, swimming, tennis, track, volleyball, weight lifting. Men's club cheerleading, crew, lacrosse. Women's club crew.

**ADMISSIONS. Academic basis for candidate selection** (in order of priority): Secondary school record, standardized test scores, school's recommendation, class rank, essay.
**Nonacademic basis for candidate selection:** Character and personality, extracurricular participation, particular talent or ability, geographical distribution, and alumni/ae relationship are considered.
**Requirements:** Graduation from secondary school is required; GED is accepted. 16 units and the following program of study are required: 4 units of English, 3 units of math, 2 units of lab science, 2 units of foreign language, 3 units of social studies, 2 units of academic electives. Rank in top half of secondary school class and minimum grade average of 80 recommended. HEOP for applicants not normally admissible. SAT is required; ACT may be substituted. Campus visit and interview recommended. Off-campus interviews available with an alumni representative.
**Procedure:** Take SAT or ACT by December of 12th year. Suggest filing application by December 1. Application deadline is March 1. Notification of admission on rolling basis. Reply is required by May 1. $200 nonrefundable tuition deposit. $500 nonrefundable room deposit. Freshmen accepted for terms other than fall.
**Special programs:** Admission may be deferred one year. Credit and/or placement may be granted through CEEB Advanced Placement exams for scores of 3 or higher. Credit and/or

placement may be granted through CLEP subject exams. Credit and placement may be granted through Regents College exams. Early decision program. In fall 1993, 30 applied for early decision and 20 were accepted. Deadline for applying for early decision is December 1. Early entrance/early admission program. Concurrent enrollment program.
**Transfer students:** Transfer students accepted for terms other than fall. In fall 1993, 25% of all new students were transfers into all classes. 507 transfer applications were received, 374 were accepted. Application deadline is July 1 for fall; December 1 for spring. Minimum 2.5 GPA required. Lowest course grade accepted is "C." Maximum number of transferable credits is 66 semester hours. At least 66 semester hours must be completed at the college to receive degree.
**Admissions contact:** John J. Brennan, Jr., M.A., Dean of Admissions. 212 920-0200.

**FINANCIAL AID. Available aid:** Pell grants, SEOG, state scholarships and grants, school scholarships and grants, private scholarships and grants, ROTC scholarships, academic merit scholarships, and athletic scholarships. Perkins Loans (NDSL), PLUS, Stafford Loans (GSL), state loans, and SLS. Deferred payment plan.
**Financial aid statistics:** In 1993-94, 95% of all undergraduate applicants received aid; 90% of freshman applicants. Average amounts of aid awarded freshmen: Scholarships and grants, $4,500; loans, $2,625.
**Supporting data/closing dates:** FAFSA/FAF/FFS: Priority filing date is February 15. School's own aid application: Priority filing date is February 15. Income tax forms: Priority filing date is March 1. Notification of awards begins April 1.
**Financial aid contact:** Lori Farrier, Acting Director of Financial Aid. 212 920-0381.

**STUDENT EMPLOYMENT.** College Work/Study Program. Institutional employment. 11% of full-time undergraduates work on campus during school year. Students may expect to earn an average of $1,500 during school year. Off-campus part-time employment opportunities rated "good."

**COMPUTER FACILITIES.** 320 IBM/IBM-compatible and Macintosh/Apple microcomputers; 80 are networked. Students may access Digital minicomputer/mainframe systems, BITNET, Internet. Residence halls may be equipped with stand-alone microcomputers. 40 major computer languages and software packages available. Computer facilities are available to all students.
**Fees:** Computer fee is included in tuition/fees.
**Hours:** 24 hour dial-in service; 9 AM-10:30 PM (M-F); 10 AM-5:30 PM (Sa-Su).

**GRADUATE CAREER DATA.** Graduate school percentages: 2% enter law school. 2% enter medical school. 1% enter graduate business programs. 4% enter graduate arts and sciences programs. Highest graduate school enrollments: Adelphi U, Downstate New York Medical Sch, Fordham Law Sch, Manhattan Coll, New York U Law School, Notre Dame Coll, Rensselaer Polytech Inst. Companies and businesses that hire graduates: AT&T, Big Six accounting firms, IBM, Mobil Oil, NASA, New York Stock Exchange, United Nations.

**PROMINENT ALUMNI/AE.** Rudolph Giuliani, U.S. district attorney, State of New York; Robert J. Farrell, vice-president and chief market analyst, Merrill Lynch; L. Jay Oliva, president, New York U; Charles Gargano, U.S. ambassador to Trinidad and Tobago; James Patterson, CEO, J. Walter Thompson.

# Manhattan School of Music

**New York, NY 10027 — 212 749-2802**

**1994-95 Costs.** Tuition: $12,500. Room: $4,000-$4,500. Fees, books, misc. academic expenses (school's estimate): $1,180.
**Enrollment.** Undergraduates: 205 men, 214 women (full-time). Freshman class: 351 applicants, 161 accepted, 69 enrolled. Graduate enrollment: 186 men, 255 women.
**Test score averages/ranges.** N/A.
**Faculty.** 20 full-time; 230 part-time. 20% of faculty holds doctoral degree. Student/faculty ratio: 11 to 1.
**Selectivity rating.** N/A.

**PROFILE.** The Manhattan School of Music, founded in 1918, is a private conservatory. Its facilities are located in the Morningside Heights section of Manhattan.

**Accreditation:** MSACS.
**Religious orientation:** Manhattan School of Music is nonsectarian; no religious requirements.
**Library:** Collections totaling over 70,000 volumes and 119 periodical subscriptions.
**Special facilities/museums:** Collection of 20,000 recordings. Electronic music studios, electronic piano lab, recording studio, practice rooms, 1,000-seat auditorium, recital halls.

**STUDENT BODY. Undergraduate profile:** 29% are state residents; 51% are transfers. 11% Asian-American, 6% Black, 4% Hispanic, 1% Native American, 41% White, 37% Foreign. Average age of undergraduates is 22.
**Freshman profile:** 74% of freshmen come from public schools.
**Undergraduate achievement:** 85% of fall 1992 freshmen returned for fall 1993 term. 50% of entering class graduated. 50% of students who completed a degree program immediately went on to graduate study.
**Foreign students:** 161 students are from out of the country. Countries represented include Canada, Hong Kong, Israel, Japan, Korea, and Taiwan; 31 in all.

**PROGRAMS OF STUDY. Degrees:** B.Mus.
**Majors:** Brass, Composition, Guitar, Harp, Harpsichord, Jazz, Organ, Percussion, Piano, String Instruments, Voice, Woodwind.
**Distribution of degrees:** The majors with the highest enrollment are piano, voice, and jazz; bassoon, harp, and harpsicord have the lowest.
**Requirements:** General education requirement.
**Academic regulations:** Minimum 2.0 GPA must be maintained.
**Special:** Independent study. Graduate school at which undergraduates may take graduate-level courses. Cross-registration with Barnard Coll of Columbia U.

**ADMISSIONS. Academic basis for candidate selection** (in order of priority): Secondary school record, school's recommendation, class rank, standardized test scores, essay.
**Nonacademic basis for candidate selection:** Particular talent or ability is emphasized. Character and personality and extracurricular participation are important. Geographical distribution is considered.
**Requirements:** Graduation from secondary school is recommended; GED is accepted. 24 units and the following program of study are recommended: 8 units of English, 2 units of math, 2 units of science, 4 units of foreign language, 4 units of social studies, 4 units of history. Admission is by audition in major field. Audition required of performance program applicants. Written and aural exams and personal interview required of composition program applicants. Secondary piano required of all majors other than accompanying, harpsichord, piano, and organ. SAT or ACT is recommended. Campus visit and interview recommended. No off-campus interviews.
**Procedure:** Suggest filing application by January 15. Application deadline is April 15. Acceptance notification within one month after audition. Reply is required by May 1. $200 nonrefundable tuition deposit. $300 nonrefundable room deposit. Freshmen accepted for terms other than fall.
**Special programs:** Credit may be granted through CEEB Advanced Placement for scores of 4 or higher. Credit may be granted through CLEP general and subject exams. Placement may be granted through challenge exams.
**Transfer students:** Transfer students accepted for terms other than fall. In fall 1993, 51% of all new students were transfers into all classes. 306 transfer applications were received, 115 were accepted. Application deadline is April 15 for fall; December 1 for spring. Minimum 2.5 GPA required. Lowest course grade accepted is "C." Maximum number of transferable credits is 60 semester hours. At least 62 semester hours must be completed at the college to receive degree.
**Admissions contact:** James Gandre, M.M., Dean of Admission and Alumni. 212 749-3025.

**FINANCIAL AID. Available aid:** Pell grants, SEOG, state grants, and school scholarships and grants. Perkins Loans (NDSL), PLUS, Stafford Loans (GSL), and SLS. AMS.
**Financial aid statistics:** 40% of aid is not need-based. In 1993-94, 80% of all undergraduate applicants received aid; 80% of freshman applicants. Average amounts of aid awarded freshmen: Scholarships and grants, $5,000; loans, $3,000.
**Supporting data/closing dates:** FAFSA/FAF: Priority filing date is February 15; deadline is April 15. School's own aid application: Priority filing date is February 15; deadline is April 15. Income tax forms: Priority filing date is February 15; deadline is April 15. Notification of awards begins February 15.
**Financial aid contact:** Samuel Manning, M.A., Director of Financial Aid. 212 749-2802.

# Manhattanville College

**Purchase, NY 10577 — 914 694-2200**

**1994-95 Costs.** Tuition: $14,700. Room & board: $6,550. Fees, books, misc. academic expenses (school's estimate): $800.
**Enrollment.** Undergraduates: 321 men, 550 women (full-time). Freshman class: 874 applicants, 693 accepted, 214 enrolled.
**Test score averages/ranges.** Average SAT scores: 512 verbal, 519 math. Range of SAT scores of middle 50%: 400-499 verbal, 500-599 math. Average ACT scores: 24 English, 24 math, 24 composite.
**Faculty.** 76 full-time; 131 part-time. 85% of faculty holds highest degree in specific field. Student/faculty ratio: 12 to 1.
**Selectivity rating.** Competitive.

**PROFILE.** Manhattanville is a private, liberal arts college. Founded as an academy for girls in 1841, it adopted coeducation in 1971. Its 100-acre campus is located in Purchase, 25 miles from New York City.

**Accreditation:** MSACS. Professionally accredited by the National Association of Schools of Music.
**Religious orientation:** Manhattanville College is nonsectarian; no religious requirements.
**Library:** Collections totaling over 255,000 volumes, 1,600 periodical subscriptions, and 6,200 microform items.
**Special facilities/museums:** Art gallery, art and music studios, English language institute, two electron microscopes.
**Athletic facilities:** Gymnasium, swimming pool, dance studio, fitness center, training rooms, basketball and tennis courts, baseball, field hockey, lacrosse, soccer, and softball fields, batting cage.

**STUDENT BODY. Undergraduate profile:** 51% are state residents; 18% are transfers. 4% Asian-American, 8% Black, 9% Hispanic, 1% Native American, 69% White, 9% Foreign. Average age of undergraduates is 21.
**Freshman profile:** 85% of accepted applicants took SAT; 5% took ACT. 57% of freshmen come from public schools.
**Undergraduate achievement:** 90% of fall 1992 freshmen returned for fall 1993 term. 81% of entering class graduated. 35% of students who completed a degree program immediately went on to graduate study.
**Foreign students:** 49 students are from out of the country. Countries represented include Brazil, Japan, Mexico, and Switzerland; 26 in all.

**PROGRAMS OF STUDY. Degrees:** B.A., B.F.A., B.Mus.
**Majors:** Art, Art History/Appreciation, Asian Studies, Biochemistry, Biology, Business/Management, Chemistry, Classics, Computer Science, Dance/Theatre, Economics, English, French, History, International Studies, Mathematics, Music, Music Education, Music Management, Music Performance, Philosophy, Physics, Political Science/Government, Psychology, Religion, Romance Languages, Russian, Russian Area Studies, Sociology, Spanish.
**Distribution of degrees:** The majors with the highest enrollment are management, political science, and psychology; physics, classics, and chemistry have the lowest.
**Requirements:** General education requirement.
**Academic regulations:** Freshmen must maintain minimum 1.8 GPA; sophomores, juniors, seniors, 2.0 GPA.

**Special:** Minors offered in all majors and in education (with option for provisional state certification), German, Italian, and women's studies. Interdisciplinary majors in American, Asian, classical, international, medieval, Renaissance, and Russian area studies. Student must demonstrate competency in three broad fields (research, analytical writing, and use of quantitative methods to solve research problems). Special courses on educating women for leadership, analyzing relation between humanities and law, and journalism. Seminars in American culture. Self-designed majors. Double majors. Independent study. Accelerated study. Pass/fail grading option. Internships. Graduate school at which undergraduates may take graduate-level courses. Preprofessional programs in law, medicine, and dentistry. 3-2 B.A./M.B.A. program with New York U. 3-2 B.A./B.S. nursing program with New York U. 3-2 B.A./B.S. engineering program with Clarkson U. 3-4 B.A./D.D.S. program with Columbia U. Washington Semester. Exchange program with Mills Coll. New York State Visiting Students Program. Teacher certification in early childhood, elementary, secondary, and special education. Certification in specific subject areas. Exchange programs abroad in Austria (U of Vienna), England (St. Clare's Hall and St. Michael's Center for Medieval and Renaissance Studies), and Italy (Scuola Lorenzo de Medici). Study abroad also in France and Spain.
**Honors:** Honors program. Honor societies.
**Academic Assistance:** Remedial reading, writing, math, and study skills. Nonremedial tutoring.

**ADMISSIONS. Academic basis for candidate selection** (in order of priority): Secondary school record, school's recommendation, standardized test scores, essay, class rank.
**Nonacademic basis for candidate selection:** Character and personality and extracurricular participation are important. Particular talent or ability and alumni/ae relationship are considered.
**Requirements:** Graduation from secondary school is required; GED is accepted. No specific distribution of secondary school units required. Minimum 3.0 GPA recommended. Portfolio required of art program applicants. Audition required of music program applicants. HEOP for applicants not normally admissible. Conditional admission possible for applicants not meeting standard requirements. SAT is required; ACT may be substituted. ACH recommended. Campus visit and interview recommended. Off-campus interviews available with admissions and alumni representatives.
**Procedure:** Take SAT or ACT by February 1 of 12th year. Take ACH by February 1 of 12th year. Visit college for interview by March 1 of 12th year. Application deadline is March 1. Notification of admission on rolling basis. Reply is required by May 1. $200 nonrefundable tuition deposit. $100 nonrefundable room deposit. Freshmen accepted for terms other than fall.
**Special programs:** Admission may be deferred one year. Credit and/or placement may be granted through CEEB Advanced Placement exams for scores of 4 or higher. Credit and/or placement may be granted through CLEP general exams. Credit may be granted through CLEP subject exams. Placement may be granted through challenge exams. Early decision program. In fall 1993, 11 applied for early decision and 6 were accepted. Deadline for applying for early decision is December 1. Early entrance/early admission program.
**Transfer students:** Transfer students accepted for terms other than fall. In fall 1993, 18% of all new students were transfers into all classes. 141 transfer applications were received, 87 were accepted. Application deadline is June 1 for fall; December 1 for spring. Minimum 2.0 GPA required. Lowest course grade accepted is "C-." Maximum number of transferable credits is 60 semester hours. At least 60 semester hours must be completed at the college to receive degree.
**Admissions contact:** R. David Harvey, M.Ed., Director of Admissions. 914 694-2200, extension 464.

**FINANCIAL AID. Available aid:** Pell grants, SEOG, state scholarships, school scholarships and grants, private scholarships and grants, academic merit scholarships, and aid for undergraduate foreign students. Perkins Loans (NDSL), PLUS, Stafford Loans (GSL), and SLS. Tuition Plan Inc., Knight Tuition Plans, and AMS.
**Financial aid statistics:** 10% of aid is not need-based. In 1993-94, 85% of all undergraduate applicants received aid; 95% of freshman applicants. Average amounts of aid awarded freshmen: Scholarships and grants, $11,100; loans, $2,600.
**Supporting data/closing dates:** FAFSA: Priority filing date is March 1; accepted on rolling basis. FAF: Priority filing date is March 1. Income tax forms: Accepted on rolling basis. Notification of awards begins March 1.
**Financial aid contact:** Kathleen Dixon, Associate Director of Financial Planning. 914 694-2200, extension 513.

# The Mannes College of Music

**New York, NY 10024 — 212 580-0210**

**1994-95 Costs.** Tuition: $12,750. Room: $5,200. Fees, books, misc. academic expenses (school's estimate): $1,150.
**Enrollment.** Undergraduates: 51 men, 58 women (full-time). Freshman class: 137 applicants, 48 accepted, 19 enrolled. Graduate enrollment: 59 men, 87 women.
**Test score averages/ranges.** N/A.
**Faculty.** 25 full-time; 125 part-time. 90% of faculty holds highest degree in specific field. Student/faculty ratio: 5 to 1.
**Selectivity rating.** N/A.

**PROFILE.** Mannes, founded in 1916, is a private college. Its facilities are located in Manhattan.

**Accreditation:** MSACS.
**Religious orientation:** The Mannes College of Music is nonsectarian; no religious requirements.
**Library:** Collections totaling over 28,000 volumes and 50 periodical subscriptions.

**STUDENT BODY. Undergraduate profile:** 65% are state residents; 60% are transfers. 10% Asian-American, 4% Black, 5% Hispanic, 46% White, 35% international students. Average age of undergraduates is 20.
**Undergraduate achievement:** 98% of fall 1992 freshmen returned for fall 1993 term. 85% of entering class graduated. 45% of students who completed a degree program immediately went on to graduate study.
**Foreign students:** 35 students are from out of the country. Countries represented include Canada, China, Japan, Korea, and Mexico; 26 in all.

**PROGRAMS OF STUDY. Degrees:** B.Mus., B.S.
**Majors:** Choral Conducting, Composition, Instruments, Orchestral Conducting, Theory/Composition, Voice.
**Distribution of degrees:** The majors with the highest enrollment are voice, piano, and violin; conducting and theory have the lowest.
**Requirements:** General education requirement.
**Academic regulations:** Minimum "B-" grade average must be maintained.
**Special:** Performance is main emphasis. Orchestra gives four to five concerts per year. Double majors. Graduate school at which undergraduates may take graduate-level courses. Cross-registration with CUNY Hunter Coll, Marymount Manhattan Coll, and the New Sch for Social Research. Summer study abroad in France (Conservatoire at Fontainebleau).
**Academic Assistance:** Nonremedial tutoring.

**ADMISSIONS. Academic basis for candidate selection** (in order of priority): Secondary school record, school's recommendation, class rank.
**Nonacademic basis for candidate selection:** Particular talent or ability is emphasized. Character and personality are important.
**Requirements:** Graduation from secondary school is required; GED is accepted. 9 units and the following program of study are required: 4 units of English, 2 units of math, 1 unit of science, 2 units of foreign language. Audition and institutional entrance exam covering theory, training, and dictation required. Relatively strong musical background, including ear training and command of theory and major instrument recommended. Campus visit and interview recommended. No off-campus interviews.
**Procedure:** Visit college for interview by August 1 of 12th year. Application deadline is August 1. Acceptance notification two to three weeks after audition. Reply is required by date specified in letter of acceptance. $300 nonrefundable tuition deposit. $220 refundable room deposit. Freshmen accepted for terms other than fall.
**Special programs:** Admission may be deferred one year. Credit and/or placement may be granted through CEEB Advanced Placement exams. Placement may be granted through challenge exams. Early entrance/early admission program. Concurrent enrollment program.
**Transfer students:** Transfer students accepted for terms other than fall. In fall 1993, 60% of all new students were transfers into all classes. 126 transfer applications were received, 55 were accepted. Application deadline is August 1 for fall; December 1 for spring. Lowest course grade accepted is "C."
**Admissions contact:** Marilyn Groves, Director of Admissions. 212 580-0210, extensions 46, 47.

**FINANCIAL AID. Available aid:** Pell grants, SEOG, state scholarships and grants, school scholarships and grants, private scholarships, and aid for undergraduate foreign students. Perkins Loans (NDSL), PLUS, Stafford Loans (GSL), private loans, and SLS. Tuition Plan Inc. and deferred payment plan.
**Financial aid statistics:** 40% of aid is not need-based. In 1993-94, 75% of all undergraduate applicants received aid; 70% of freshman applicants. Average amounts of aid awarded freshmen: Scholarships and grants, $3,700; loans, $3,000.
**Supporting data/closing dates:** FAFSA/FAF: Accepted on rolling basis. School's own aid application: Accepted on rolling basis. Notification of awards on rolling basis.
**Financial aid contact:** Michael Lynch, Director of Financial Aid. 212 580-0210, extension 48.

# Marist College

**Poughkeepsie, NY 12601 — 914 575-3000**

**1993-94 Costs.** Tuition: $10,700. Room & board: $5,800. Fees, books, misc. academic expenses (school's estimate): $880.
**Enrollment.** Undergraduates: 1,521 men, 1,644 women (full-time). Freshman class: 4,730 applicants, 3,164 accepted, 836 enrolled. Graduate enrollment: 310 men, 288 women.
**Test score averages/ranges.** Range of SAT scores of middle 50%: 930-1080 combined. Average ACT scores: 25 composite.
**Faculty.** 151 full-time; 180 part-time. 68% of faculty holds doctoral degree. Student/faculty ratio: 17 to 1.
**Selectivity rating.** Competitive.

**PROFILE.** Marist is a private, liberal arts college. Founded as a college for men in 1929, it adopted coeducation in 1968. Its 120-acre campus is located in Poughkeepsie, 75 miles north of New York City.

**Accreditation:** MSACS, CCA-ACICS. Professionally accredited by the American Medical Association (CAHEA), the Council on Social Work Education.
**Religious orientation:** Marist College is nonsectarian; no religious requirements.
**Library:** Collections totaling over 145,000 volumes, 1,470 periodical subscriptions, and 53,154 microform items.
**Special facilities/museums:** Art gallery, language lab, estuarine and environmental studies lab, public opinion institute, audio-visual/TV center, communications center.
**Athletic facilities:** Gymnasium, baseball, football, intramural, lacrosse, rugby, soccer, and softball fields, basketball, racquetball, volleyball, and tennis courts, track, swimming pool, weight room, field house, rowing tank, dance studio.

**STUDENT BODY. Undergraduate profile:** 52% are state residents; 13% are transfers. 2% Asian-American, 5% Black, 3% Hispanic, 89% White, 1% Other. Average age of undergraduates is 20.
**Freshman profile:** 1% of freshmen who took SAT scored 700 or over on verbal, 2% scored 700 or over on math; 5% scored 600 or over on verbal, 10% scored 600 or over on math; 45% scored 500 or over on verbal, 58% scored 500 or over on math; 88% scored 400

or over on verbal, 92% scored 400 or over on math; 92% scored 300 or over on verbal. 96% of accepted applicants took SAT; 4% took ACT. 74% of freshmen come from public schools.
**Undergraduate achievement:** 94% of fall 1992 freshmen returned for fall 1993 term. 64% of entering class graduated. 15% of students who completed a degree program immediately went on to graduate study.
**Foreign students:** 28 students are from out of the country. Countries represented include India, Japan, Malaysia, Nigeria, Panama, and Taiwan; 14 in all.

**PROGRAMS OF STUDY. Degrees:** B.A., B.Prof.Studies, B.S.
**Majors:** Accounting, American Studies, Biology, Business Administration, Chemistry, Communication Arts, Computer Information Systems, Computer Mathematics, Computer Science, Criminal/Juvenile Justice, Economics, English, Environmental Science, Fashion Design, Fine Arts, French, History, Mathematics, Medical Technology, Political Science, Psychology, Russian, Social Work, Spanish.
**Distribution of degrees:** The majors with the highest enrollment are communication arts, business administration, and psychology; French, Spanish, and economics have the lowest.
**Requirements:** General education requirement.
**Academic regulations:** Minimum 2.0 GPA must be maintained.
**Special:** Minors offered in most majors and in anthropology, Franklin D. Roosevelt studies, Jewish studies, philosophy, religious studies, and Russian area studies. Concentrations offered in business, education, English, fine arts, police science, and public administration. Comprehensive exams and GRE required by some departments for graduation. Seminars. Double majors. Dual degrees. Independent study. Pass/fail grading option. Internships. Cooperative education programs. Graduate school at which undergraduates may take graduate-level courses. Preprofessional programs in law, medicine, and dentistry. Five-year B.A./M.A. program in psychology. Member of Associated Colleges of the Mid-Hudson Area and New York State Visiting Student Program. Washington Semester. Marist Abroad Program. Teacher certification in elementary, secondary, and special education. Certification in specific subject areas. Exchange program abroad in Australia, Austria, France, Germany, the Netherlands, Scandinavia, Spain, the United Kingdom, and other countries.
**Honors:** Honors program. Honor societies.
**Academic Assistance:** Remedial reading, writing, math, and study skills. Nonremedial tutoring.

**STUDENT LIFE. Housing:** Freshmen must live on campus. Coed dorms. School-owned/operated apartments. Off-campus privately-owned housing. Upperclass townhouses, freshman residences. 76% of students live in college housing.
**Social atmosphere:** The student newspaper reports that students socialize on campus at the Campus Center deli and pizza bar, while off campus they gather at local bars and student houses. Popular events include basketball games, the Christmas and spring formals, and Community Unity Barbeques.
**Services and counseling/handicapped student services:** Placement services. Health service. Internships. Counseling services for minority, military, veteran, and older students. Birth control, personal, and psychological counseling. Career and academic guidance services. Religious counseling. Physically disabled student services. Learning disabled program/services. Notetaking services. Tape recorders. Tutors. Reader services for the blind.
**Campus organizations:** Undergraduate student government. Student newspaper (Circle, published once/week). Literary magazine. Yearbook. Radio and TV stations. Glee club, Marist College Singers, drama groups, debating, Circle K, Knights of Columbus, Young Americans for Freedom, Young Democrats, Young Republicans, special-interest groups, 72 organizations in all. Four fraternities, one chapter house; two sororities, one chapter house. 6% of men join a fraternity. 9% of women join a sorority.
**Religious organizations:** Campus Ministry, Youth Ministry.
**Minority/foreign student organizations:** Black Student Union, Hispanic Club. International Student Union.

**ATHLETICS. Physical education requirements:** None.
**Intercollegiate competition:** 21% of students participate. Baseball (M), basketball (M,W), crew (M,W), cross-country (M,W), diving (M,W), football (M), lacrosse (M), soccer (M), softball (W), swimming (M,W), tennis (M,W), track (indoor) (M,W), track (outdoor) (M,W), track and field (indoor) (M,W), track and field (outdoor) (M,W), volleyball (W). Member of ECAC, MET Swimming League, NCAA Division I-AA, Northeast Conference.
**Intramural and club sports:** 50% of students participate. Intramural aerobics, basketball, bowling, flag football, running, soccer, softball, volleyball. Men's club horsemanship, ice hockey, racquetball, rugby, skiing, volleyball, wrestling. Women's club cheerleading, horsemanship, lacrosse, racquetball, skiing, soccer.

**ADMISSIONS. Academic basis for candidate selection** (in order of priority): Secondary school record, class rank, standardized test scores, school's recommendation, essay.
**Nonacademic basis for candidate selection:** Particular talent or ability is emphasized. Extracurricular participation and geographical distribution are important. Character and personality and alumni/ae relationship are considered.
**Requirements:** Graduation from secondary school is required; GED is accepted. 16 units are required and the following program of study is recommended: 4 units of English, 3 units of mathematics, 2 units of science, 2 units of foreign language, 3 units of social studies, 2 units of history. 4 units of math recommended of computer science and science program applicants. HEOP for applicants not normally admissible. SAT or ACT is required. Campus visit and interview recommended. Off-campus interviews available with an admissions representative.
**Procedure:** Take SAT or ACT by January of 12th year. Visit college for interview by March of 12th year. Suggest filing application by December 1. Application deadline is March 1. Acceptance notification beginning February 1. Reply is required by May 1. $150 tuition deposit, refundable until May 1. $200 room deposit, refundable until May 1. Freshmen accepted for terms other than fall.
**Special programs:** Admission may be deferred one year or more. Credit and/or placement may be granted through CEEB Advanced Placement exams for scores of 3 or higher. Credit and/or placement may be granted through CLEP subject exams. Credit and placement may be granted through Regents College and ACT PEP exams. Early decision program. In fall 1993, 710 applied for early decision and 544 were accepted. Deadline for applying for early decision is December 1. Early entrance/early admission program. Concurrent enrollment program.
**Transfer students:** Transfer students accepted for terms other than fall. In fall 1993, 13% of all new students were transfers into all classes. 388 transfer applications were received, 266 were accepted. Application deadline is rolling for fall; rolling for spring. Minimum 2.5 GPA recommended. Lowest course grade accepted is "C-." Maximum number of transferable credits is 60 semester hours from a two-year school and 90 semester hours from a four-year school. At least 30 semester hours must be completed at the college to receive degree.
**Admissions contact:** Harry W. Wood, M.A., Vice President, Admissions and Enrollment Planning. 914 575-3226.

**FINANCIAL AID. Available aid:** Pell grants, SEOG, state scholarships and grants, school scholarships and grants, private scholarships and grants, academic merit scholarships, and athletic scholarships. Perkins Loans (NDSL), PLUS, Stafford Loans (GSL), and SLS. Tuition Plan Inc., Education Plan Inc., Knight Tuition Plans, and AMS.
**Financial aid statistics:** 19% of aid is not need-based. In 1993-94, 80% of all undergraduate applicants received aid; 80% of freshman applicants. Average amounts of aid awarded freshmen: Scholarships and grants, $3,800; loans, $2,600.
**Supporting data/closing dates:** FAFSA: Priority filing date is March 1; accepted on rolling basis. FAF/FFS: Priority filing date is March 1. Income tax forms: Priority filing date is May 1; accepted on rolling basis. Notification of awards on rolling basis.
**Financial aid contact:** Christine M. McCormack, M.A., Director of Financial Aid. 914 575-3230.

**STUDENT EMPLOYMENT.** College Work/Study Program. Institutional employment. 20% of full-time undergraduates work on campus during school year. Students may expect to earn an average of $1,200 during school year. Off-campus part-time employment opportunities rated "good."

**COMPUTER FACILITIES.** 350 IBM/IBM-compatible microcomputers; 100 are networked. Students may access IBM minicomputer/mainframe systems, BITNET. Residence halls may be equipped with stand-alone microcomputers, networked microcomputers, networked terminals. Client/LAN operating systems include OS/2. Computer languages and software packages include APL, COBOL, dBASE, FORTRAN, Lotus 1-2-3, Pascal, PL/1, Q&A, R:BASE, REXX, WordPerfect, Writing Assistant. Computer facilities are available to all students.
**Fees:** None.
**Hours:** 16 hours (M-F); 24 hours (Sa-Su).

**GRADUATE CAREER DATA.** Graduate school percentages: 9% enter law school. 2% enter medical school. 1% enter dental school. 11% enter graduate business programs. 14% enter graduate arts and sciences programs. Highest graduate school enrollments: Albany Law and Medical Sch, Columbia U, Fairfield U, Fordham U, New York U, Notre Dame U, St. John's U, SUNY at Albany, Villanova U. 72% of graduates choose careers in business and industry. Companies and businesses that hire graduates: IBM, NBC, CBS, Westinghouse, Big Six accounting firms, Shearson-Lehman, E.F. Hutton.

**PROMINENT ALUMNI/AE.** Bill C. Davis, playwright; Brendon T. Burke, director of personnel, ABC-TV; Bill O'Reilly, ABC network reporter; Charles Milligan, senior vice-president, Paine Webber; Bill Kuffner, senior vice-president, Citibank Corp; Peter Pirner, CEO, Adidas.

# Marymount College

**Tarrytown, NY 10591** — **914 631-3200**

**1993-94 Costs.** Tuition: $11,150. Room & board: $6,200. Fees, books, misc. academic expenses (school's estimate): $915.
**Enrollment.** Undergraduates: 40 men, 691 women (full-time). Freshman class: 478 applicants, 327 accepted, 117 enrolled.
**Test score averages/ranges.** Average SAT scores: 460 verbal, 456 math. Range of SAT scores of middle 50%: 380-490 verbal, 380-500 math.
**Faculty.** 56 full-time; 70 part-time. 86% of faculty holds highest degree in specific field. Student/faculty ratio: 12 to 1.
**Selectivity rating.** Less competitive.

**PROFILE.** Marymount, founded in 1907, is a private, liberal arts college for women; qualified men admitted to weekend program. Its 25-acre campus is located in Tarrytown, 35 miles from New York City.

**Accreditation:** MSACS. Professionally accredited by the American Dietetic Association, the Council on Social Work Education.
**Religious orientation:** Marymount College is nonsectarian; one semester of religion required.
**Library:** Collections totaling over 118,000 volumes, 650 periodical subscriptions and 173 microform items.
**Special facilities/museums:** Language lab.
**Athletic facilities:** Gymnasium, swimming pool, fitness center, tennis courts, bowling alley, athletic field, dance studio.

**STUDENT BODY. Undergraduate profile:** 77% are state residents; 36% are transfers. 4% Asian-American, 16% Black, 14% Hispanic, 60% White, 6% Other. Average age of undergraduates is 22.
**Freshman profile:** 4% of freshmen who took SAT scored 600 or over on verbal, 8% scored 600 or over on math; 26% scored 500 or over on verbal, 31% scored 500 or over on math; 59% scored 400 or over on verbal, 80% scored 400 or over on math; 77% scored 300 or over on verbal, 98% scored 300 or over on math. 91% of accepted applicants took SAT; 1% took ACT. 74% of freshmen come from public schools.
**Undergraduate achievement:** 95% of fall 1992 freshmen returned for fall 1993 term. 60% of entering class graduated. 28% of students who completed a degree program immediately went on to graduate study.

**Foreign students:** 41 students are from out of the country. Countries represented include France, Japan, Kenya, Korea, and the Philippines; 15 in all.

**PROGRAMS OF STUDY. Degrees:** B.A., B.S., B.Soc.Work.

**Majors:** American Studies, Art History, Art Studio, Biology, Business, Chemistry, Economics, Education, English, Fashion Design, Fashion Merchandising, Foods/Nutrition, French, History, Home Economics, Information Systems, Interior Design, International Business, International Studies, Mathematics, Politics, Pre-Law, Pre-Medicine, Psychology, Religious Studies, Social Work, Sociology, Spanish, Speech/Drama.

**Distribution of degrees:** The majors with the highest enrollment are business, education, and psychology.

**Requirements:** General education requirement.

**Academic regulations:** Minimum 2.0 GPA must be maintained.

**Special:** Minors offered in most majors and in many specialized areas. Innovations workshop. Seminar approach is widely used. Senior seminar and project in major field required. Evaluation as well as grades in major field. Up to three courses may be taken on credit/no credit basis. Self-designed majors. Double majors. Dual degrees. Independent study. Pass/fail grading option. Internships. Preprofessional programs in law, medicine, and dentistry. 3-2 M.Ed. program with Fordham U. 3-2 speech-language pathology/audiology and occupational therapy programs with New York U. Member of Westchester Consortium for International Studies. Washington Semester. Teacher certification in elementary, secondary, and special education. Certification in specific subject areas. Study abroad in Australia, England, Japan, Scotland, and other countries.

**Honors:** Honors program. Honor societies.

**Academic Assistance:** Remedial reading, writing, math, and study skills. Nonremedial tutoring.

**ADMISSIONS. Academic basis for candidate selection** (in order of priority): Secondary school record, school's recommendation, standardized test scores, essay, class rank.

**Nonacademic basis for candidate selection:** Character and personality are emphasized. Extracurricular participation is important. Particular talent or ability, geographical distribution, and alumni/ae relationship are considered.

**Requirements:** Graduation from secondary school is recommended; GED is accepted. 16 units are required and the following program of study is recommended: 4 units of English, 3 units of mathematics, 3 units of science, 3 units of foreign language, 3 units of social studies. Minimum 2.5 GPA recommended. HEOP for applicants not normally admissible. SAT is required; ACT may be substituted. ACH recommended. Campus visit and interview recommended. Off-campus interviews available with admissions and alumni representatives.

**Procedure:** Take SAT or ACT by January of 12th year. Suggest filing application by April 15. Application deadline is August 15. Notification of admission on rolling basis. Reply is required by May 1. $100 nonrefundable tuition deposit. $150 nonrefundable room deposit. Freshmen accepted for terms other than fall.

**Special programs:** Admission may be deferred one year. Credit may be granted through CEEB Advanced Placement for scores of 3 or higher. Credit may be granted through CLEP general and subject exams and life experience. Early entrance/early admission program.

**Transfer students:** Transfer students accepted for terms other than fall. In fall 1993, 36% of all new students were transfers into all classes. 127 transfer applications were received, 108 were accepted. Application deadline is August 15 for fall; January 15 for spring. Minimum 2.5 GPA required. Lowest course grade accepted is "C." Maximum number of transferable credits is 75 semester hours. At least 45 semester hours must be completed at the college to receive degree.

**Admissions contact:** Gina R. Campbell, M.A., Director of Admissions. 914 332-8295.

**FINANCIAL AID. Available aid:** Pell grants, SEOG, state scholarships and grants, school scholarships and grants, and academic merit scholarships. Perkins Loans (NDSL), PLUS, Stafford Loans (GSL), and SLS. Knight Tuition Plans and family tuition reduction.

**Financial aid statistics:** In 1993-94, 100% of all undergraduate applicants received aid. Average amounts of aid awarded freshmen: Scholarships and grants, $3,512; loans, $3,825.

**Supporting data/closing dates:** FAFSA/FAF: Accepted on rolling basis. School's own aid application: Accepted on rolling basis. Income tax forms: Accepted on rolling basis. Notification of awards begins in February.

**Financial aid contact:** Annidia Finaro, M.S., Director of Financial Aid. 914 332-8345.

## Medaille College

**Buffalo, NY 14214** **716 884-3281**

**1994-95 Costs.** Tuition: $8,760. Room: $2,500. Board: $1,900. Fees, books, misc. academic expenses (school's estimate): $660.

**Enrollment.** Undergraduates: 399 men, 511 women (full-time). Freshman class: 384 applicants, 223 accepted, 143 enrolled.

**Test score averages/ranges.** N/A.

**Faculty.** 46 full-time; 48 part-time. 65% of faculty holds doctoral degree. Student/faculty ratio: 17 to 1.

**Selectivity rating.** N/A.

**PROFILE.** Medaille is a private, liberal arts college. Founded in 1875 as a Catholic teachers college for women, it became a coeducational, nonsectarian college in 1967. Its 13-acre campus is located in Buffalo, 75 miles southwest of Rochester.

**Accreditation:** MSACS.

**Religious orientation:** Medaille College is nonsectarian; no religious requirements.

**Library:** Collections totaling over 50,000 volumes, 387 periodical subscriptions, and 28,791 microform items.

**Athletic facilities:** Recreation center, athletic fields.

**STUDENT BODY. Undergraduate profile:** 99% are state residents; 70% are transfers. 1% Asian-American, 22% Black, 2% Hispanic, 2% Native American, 73% White. Average age of undergraduates is 27.

**Undergraduate achievement:** 11% of students who completed a degree program immediately went on to graduate study.

**Foreign students:** Countries represented include Canada.

**PROGRAMS OF STUDY. Degrees:** B.A., B.S.

**Majors:** Business Administration, Child/Youth Services, Computer/Information Sciences, Elementary Education, Financial Services, Government Service, Human Resource Development, Human Services, Humanities, Liberal/General Studies, Management of Nonprofit Organizations, Media Communications, Social Sciences, Sports Management.

**Distribution of degrees:** The majors with the highest enrollment are elementary education and business administration; arts management, humanities, and social sciences have the lowest.

**Academic regulations:** Freshmen must maintain minimum 1.3 GPA; sophomores, 1.75 GPA; juniors, 1.9 GPA; seniors, 2.0 GPA.

**Special:** Minors offered in business, computer information systems, human resource development, literature, and writing. Certificate programs offered. Master's degree program in reading with Canisius Coll. Associate's degrees offered. Double majors. Dual degrees. Independent study. Pass/fail grading option. Internships. Preprofessional programs in law. Member of Western New York Consortium of Higher Education; cross-registration possible. Teacher certification in elementary education. Certification in specific subject areas. Exchange program abroad in England (Rockland Coll). ROTC at Canisius Coll.

**Honors:** Honors program. Honor societies.

**Academic Assistance:** Remedial reading, writing, math, and study skills. Nonremedial tutoring.

**ADMISSIONS. Academic basis for candidate selection** (in order of priority): Secondary school record, class rank, standardized test scores, school's recommendation, essay.

**Nonacademic basis for candidate selection:** Character and personality are emphasized. Extracurricular participation and particular talent or ability are important. Alumni/ae relationship is considered.

**Requirements:** Graduation from secondary school is required; GED is accepted. 18 units and the following program of study are recommended: 3 units of English, 3 units of math, 3 units of science, 1 unit of foreign language, 2 units of social studies, 2 units of history. Minimum 2.5 GPA recommended. Minimum 2.5 GPA required of veterinary and elementary education program applicants. HEOP for applicants not normally admissible. SAT or ACT is recommended. Admissions interview required. Off-campus interviews available with an admissions representative.

**Procedure:** Visit college for interview by August 1 of 12th year. Suggest filing application by May 15; no deadline. Notification of admission on rolling basis. Reply is required by first day of classes. $50 nonrefundable tuition deposit. $100 nonrefundable room deposit. Freshmen accepted for terms other than fall.

**Special programs:** Admission may be deferred one semester. Credit may be granted through CEEB Advanced Placement for scores of 3 or higher. Credit may be granted through CLEP general and subject exams. Credit and placement may be granted through Regents College, ACT PEP, DANTES, and challenge exams and military and life experience.

**Transfer students:** Transfer students accepted for terms other than fall. In fall 1993, 70% of all new students were transfers into all classes. 674 transfer applications were received, 356 were accepted. Application deadline is rolling for fall; rolling for spring. Minimum 2.0 GPA recommended. Lowest course grade accepted is "D." Maximum number of transferable credits is 72 semester hours from a two-year school and 90 semester hours from a four-year school. At least 30 semester hours must be completed at the college to receive degree.

**Admissions contact:** Jacqueline S. Matheny, Director of Enrollment Management. 716 884-3281, extensions 203-206.

**FINANCIAL AID. Available aid:** Pell grants, SEOG, state scholarships and grants, school scholarships and grants, private scholarships and grants, academic merit scholarships, aid for undergraduate foreign students, and United Negro College Fund. Stafford Loans (GSL), state loans, and SLS. AMS and deferred payment plan.

**Financial aid statistics:** 1% of aid is not need-based. In 1993-94, 91% of all undergraduate applicants received aid; 70% of freshman applicants. Average amounts of aid awarded freshmen: Scholarships and grants, $3,545; loans, $2,625.

**Supporting data/closing dates:** FAFSA/FAF/FFS: Priority filing date is March 15. School's own aid application: Priority filing date is March 15. Income tax forms: Accepted on rolling basis. Notification of awards on rolling basis.

**Financial aid contact:** Carolyn Jamison, Director of Financial Aid. 716 884-3281, extensions 256-258.

## Mercy College

**Dobbs Ferry, NY 10522** **914 693-7500**

**1992-93 Costs.** Tuition: $7,200. Housing: None. Fees, books, misc. academic expenses (school's estimate): $500.

**Enrollment.** Undergraduates: 1,641 men, 2,481 women (full-time). Freshman class: 2,163 applicants, 1,957 accepted, 1,287 enrolled. Graduate enrollment: 29 men, 120 women.

**Test score averages/ranges.** N/A.

**Faculty.** 171 full-time. 60% of faculty holds doctoral degree. Student/faculty ratio: 14 to 1.

**Selectivity rating.** N/A.

**PROFILE.** Mercy, founded in 1960, is a private, multipurpose college. Its 70-acre campus is located in Dobbs Ferry in Westchester County, 30 miles north of New York City.

**Accreditation:** MSACS. Professionally accredited by the National League for Nursing.

**Religious orientation:** Mercy College is nonsectarian; no religious requirements.

**Library:** Collections totaling over 310,000 volumes and 1,200 periodical subscriptions.

**Special facilities/museums:** Lower Hudson Valley environmental center, continuing biomedical education institute.

**Athletic facilities:** Gymnasium, track, weight room, baseball, soccer, and softball fields.

**STUDENT BODY. Undergraduate profile:** 97% are state residents. 1% Asian-American, 20% Black, 19% Hispanic, 60% White.
**Freshman profile:** 75% of freshmen come from public schools.
**Undergraduate achievement:** 75% of fall 1991 freshmen returned for fall 1992 term. 45% of entering class graduated. 9% of students who completed a degree program went on to graduate study within five years.
**Foreign students:** Countries represented include African countries and Middle Eastern countries; 50 in all.

**PROGRAMS OF STUDY. Degrees:** B.A., B.S.
**Majors:** Accounting, Behavioral Science, Biology, Business Administration, Computer Information Systems, Computer Science, Criminal Justice, English, Government, History, Interdisciplinary Studies, Journalism/Media, Mathematics, Medical Technology, Music, Nursing, Paralegal Studies, Photography, Pre-Chiropractic, Psychology, Public Safety, Social Work, Sociology, Spanish, Speech, Therapeutic Recreation, Veterinary Technology.
**Distribution of degrees:** The majors with the highest enrollment are business, behavioral science, psychology, and computer science; foreign languages, sociology, and history have the lowest.
**Requirements:** General education requirement.
**Academic regulations:** Minimum 2.0 GPA required for graduation.
**Special:** Minors offered in some majors and in over 10 other areas. Certificate programs offered. Courses offered in earth science, fire science, gerontology, linguistics, occupational safety/health administration, and visual/plastic arts. Dance courses offered at Humphrey Dance Center. Studies in medieval culture at the Verrazzano Inst. Bilingual (Spanish/English) bachelor's degree programs in accounting, business administration, computer science, education, mathematics, and psychology. Associate's degrees offered. Self-designed majors. Double majors. Dual degrees. Independent study. Accelerated study. Pass/fail grading option. Internships. Cooperative education programs. Graduate school at which undergraduates may take graduate-level courses. Preprofessional programs in law, medicine, dentistry, optometry, osteopathy, and podiatry. 3-2 pharmacy and 4-1 M.B.A. programs with Long Island U. Member of Consortium of Colleges in Westchester County; cross-registration possible. Teacher certification in elementary, secondary, and special education. Study abroad in Italy. ROTC at Fordham U. AFROTC at Manhattan Coll.
**Honors:** Honors program.
**Academic Assistance:** Nonremedial tutoring.

**STUDENT LIFE. Housing:** Commuter campus; no student housing.
**Social atmosphere:** Among the year's popular events at Mercy College are the Annual Halloween/Costume Party, Reporter's Impact/Journalism Club's Annual Media Bowl, Spring Break Mixer, Christmas Tree Lighting, Media Auction, and other parties and get-togethers sponsored by the various clubs on campus. The most influential groups on campus are the Reporter's Impact staff, WMCY radio staff, and the Social Enterprise Club.
**Services and counseling/handicapped student services:** Placement services. Health service. Day care. Peer support groups. Counseling services for minority, military, veteran, and older students. Birth control, personal, and psychological counseling. Career and academic guidance services. Religious counseling. Physically disabled student services. Learning disabled program/services.
**Campus organizations:** Undergraduate student government. Student newspaper (Reporter's Impact, published bimonthly). Literary magazine. Yearbook. Radio station. Chorus, drama group, departmental and special-interest groups.
**Minority/foreign student organizations:** Minority student groups. Several foreign student groups.

**ATHLETICS. Physical education requirements:** None.
**Intercollegiate competition:** 10% of students participate. Baseball (M), basketball (M,W), cross-country (M,W), golf (M), soccer (M), softball (W), tennis (M), volleyball (W). Member of ECAC, NCAA Division II, NYCAC.
**Intramural and club sports:** 15% of students participate. Intramural badminton, basketball, table tennis, volleyball.

**ADMISSIONS. Academic basis for candidate selection** (in order of priority): Secondary school record, standardized test scores, class rank, school's recommendation.
**Nonacademic basis for candidate selection:** Character and personality and particular talent or ability are emphasized.
**Requirements:** Graduation from secondary school is required; GED is accepted. 15 units and the following program of study are recommended: 4 units of English, 3 units of math, 2 units of science, 2 units of foreign language, 4 units of social studies. Portfolio required of art program applicants. Audition required of music program applicants. R.N. required of nursing program applicants. College Opportunity Program for students not normally admissible. SAT is recommended; ACT may be substituted. Campus visit and interview recommended. Off-campus interviews available with an admissions representative.
**Procedure:** Take SAT or ACT by December of 12th year. Visit college for interview by March of 12th year. Suggest filing application by November. Notification of admission on rolling basis. Freshmen accepted for terms other than fall.
**Special programs:** Admission may be deferred one year. Credit may be granted through CEEB Advanced Placement for scores of 3 or higher. Credit may be granted through CLEP general and subject exams, DANTES exams, and military experience. Early decision program. Early entrance/early admission program. Concurrent enrollment program.
**Transfer students:** Transfer students accepted for terms other than fall. In fall 1992, 1,369 transfer applications were received. Application deadline is rolling for fall; rolling for spring. Minimum 2.0 GPA required. Lowest course grade accepted is "C." Maximum number of transferable credits is 75 semester hours from a two-year school and 90 semester hours from a four-year school. At least 30 semester hours must be completed at the college to receive degree.
**Admissions contact:** William Rothenberg, M.S., Dean of Admissions. 914 693-7600.

**FINANCIAL AID. Available aid:** Pell grants, SEOG, state scholarships, school scholarships and grants, private scholarships and grants, academic merit scholarships, athletic scholarships, and aid for undergraduate foreign students. Institutional Free Tuition Program. Perkins Loans (NDSL), Stafford Loans (GSL), NSL, state loans, and SLS. Tuition Plan Inc. and deferred payment plan.
**Financial aid statistics:** Average amounts of aid awarded freshmen: Scholarships and grants, $2,600.
**Supporting data/closing dates:** FAFSA/FAF/FFS: Accepted on rolling basis. State aid form: Deadline is February 15.
**Financial aid contact:** Marion Dale, Director of Financial Aid. 914 674-7328, extension 7327.

**STUDENT EMPLOYMENT.** College Work/Study Program. Institutional employment. 80% of full-time undergraduates work on campus during school year. Off-campus part-time employment opportunities rated "fair."

**COMPUTER FACILITIES.** 135 IBM/IBM-compatible and Macintosh/Apple microcomputers. Students may access IBM minicomputer/mainframe systems. Computer languages and software packages include Assembly, BASIC, COBOL, FORTRAN, JCL, Pascal; several software packages.
**Fees:** None.

**GRADUATE CAREER DATA.** Highest graduate school enrollments: Fordham U, Long Island U, New York U. 70% of graduates choose careers in business and industry. Companies and businesses that hire graduates: AT&T, General Foods, IBM, NYNEX.

**PROMINENT ALUMNI/AE.** Walter Anderson, editor, *Parade* magazine.

# Molloy College

**Rockville Centre, NY 11570** **516 678-5000**

**1994-95 Costs.** Tuition: $8,800. Housing: None. Fees, books, misc. academic expenses (school's estimate): $978.
**Enrollment.** Undergraduates: 741 men, 2,351 women (full-time). Freshman class: 466 applicants, 367 accepted, 181 enrolled. Graduate enrollment: 100 women.
**Test score averages/ranges.** Average SAT scores: 410 verbal, 450 math. Range of SAT scores of middle 50%: 390-490 verbal, 400-540 math.
**Faculty.** 89 full-time; 99 part-time. 25% of faculty holds doctoral degree. Student/faculty ratio: 11 to 1.
**Selectivity rating.** Less competitive.

**PROFILE.** Molloy, founded in 1955, is a private, church-affiliated, liberal arts college. Its 25-acre campus is located in Rockville Centre, 20 miles east of New York City.

**Accreditation:** MSACS. Professionally accredited by the Council on Social Work Education, the National League for Nursing.
**Religious orientation:** Molloy College is affiliated with the Roman Catholic Church (Dominican Sisters); three semesters of religion required.
**Library:** Collections totaling over 87,900 volumes, 850 periodical subscriptions, and 1,426 microform items.
**Special facilities/museums:** Professional Repertory Theatre Company in residence, dance studio, institute of cross-cultural and cross-ethnic studies, institute of gerontology, cablevision studio.
**Athletic facilities:** Gymnasium, basketball and tennis courts, baseball, soccer, and softball fields, training, weight rooms.

**STUDENT BODY. Undergraduate profile:** 71% are transfers. 2% Asian-American, 9% Black, 4% Hispanic, 1% Native American, 84% White. Average age of undergraduates is 21.
**Freshman profile:** 1% of freshmen who took SAT scored 600 or over on verbal, 8% scored 600 or over on math; 13% scored 500 or over on verbal, 32% scored 500 or over on math; 63% scored 400 or over on verbal, 72% scored 400 or over on math; 89% scored 300 or over on verbal, 97% scored 300 or over on math. 96% of accepted applicants took SAT. 55% of freshmen come from public schools.
**Undergraduate achievement:** 98% of fall 1991 freshmen returned for fall 1992 term. 75% of entering class graduated. 26% of students who completed a degree program went on to graduate study within five years.
**Foreign students:** Two students are from out of the country.

**PROGRAMS OF STUDY. Degrees:** B.A., B.S., B.S.Nurs.
**Majors:** Accounting, Art, Biology, Business Management, Cardiorespiratory Sciences, Computer Science, English, French, Gerontology, History, Interdisciplinary Studies, International Peace/Justice Studies, Mathematics, Music, Music Therapy, Nursing, Philosophy, Political Science, Psychology, Social Work, Sociology, Spanish, Speech, Theology.
**Distribution of degrees:** The majors with the highest enrollment are nursing and business management.
**Requirements:** General education requirement.
**Academic regulations:** Minimum 2.0 GPA must be maintained.
**Special:** Minors offered in many majors and in art history, chemistry/earth science, chemistry/physical science, communication, Irish studies, journalism, photography, and women's studies. Associate's degrees offered. Double majors. Dual degrees. Independent study. Accelerated study. Pass/fail grading option. Internships. Preprofessional programs in law, medicine, veterinary science, and dentistry. Member of Academic Enrichment Program of Long Island Regional Advisory Council on Higher Education; cross-registration possible. Teacher certification in early childhood, elementary, secondary, and special education. Study abroad in France and Spain. ROTC at Hofstra U and St. John's U. AFROTC at New York Inst of Tech.
**Honors:** Phi Beta Kappa. Honor societies.
**Academic Assistance:** Remedial reading, writing, math, and study skills.

**STUDENT LIFE. Housing:** Commuter campus; no student housing.
**Social atmosphere:** "There does need to be some improvement made in students getting involved at Molloy," reports the editor of the student newspaper. "The problem stems from the amount of working time needed to pay for college which ultimately leaves little free time." Popular on-campus gathering spots include Scoops and the Anselma Room, while off-campus students hang out at Dunigan's Restaurant and Cafe 20 South. The Equestrian Team, Campus Ministries, the Molloy Forum, the Psychology Club, and the Gaelic Society are influential groups on campus. Favorite events during the school year include 55

Nights for Seniors, Sophomore Tradition, and the Molloy Equestrian Home Horse Show Competition.
**Services and counseling/handicapped student services:** Placement services. Health service. Women's center. Day care. Counseling services for minority and older students. Personal counseling. Career and academic guidance services. Religious counseling. Physically disabled student services. Learning disabled program/services. Notetaking services. Tape recorders. Tutors. Reader services for the blind.
**Campus organizations:** Undergraduate student government. Student newspaper (Ivy Towers, published once/month). Literary magazine. Yearbook. TV station. Vocal ensemble, drama and music clubs, women's club, Spanish Institute, service and special-interest groups, 30 organizations in all.
**Religious organizations:** Campus Ministry.
**Minority/foreign student organizations:** Afro-American Cultural Association, Spanish club, Philipino club.

**ATHLETICS. Physical education requirements:** Two semesters of physical education required.
**Intercollegiate competition:** 5% of students participate. Baseball (M), basketball (M,W), cross-country (M,W), golf (M,W), horsemanship (M,W), soccer (W), softball (W), tennis (W), volleyball (W). Member of ECAC, NCAA Division II, NYCAC.
**Intramural and club sports:** 8% of students participate. Intramural equestrian sports, softball, touch football. Women's club cross-country, golf, soccer.

**ADMISSIONS. Academic basis for candidate selection** (in order of priority): Secondary school record, standardized test scores, school's recommendation, essay, class rank.
**Nonacademic basis for candidate selection:** Extracurricular participation and particular talent or ability are important. Character and personality and alumni/ae relationship are considered.
**Requirements:** Graduation from secondary school is required; GED is accepted. 13 units and the following program of study are required: 4 units of English, 2 units of math, 2 units of science, 2 units of foreign language, 3 units of social studies. Minimum combined SAT score of 800 and minimum grade average of 80 required. Portfolio required of art program applicants. Audition required of music program applicants. HEOP for applicants not normally admissible. Conditional admission possible for applicants not meeting standard requirements. SAT or ACT is required. Admissions interview recommended. Off-campus interviews available with an admissions representative.
**Procedure:** Suggest filing application by December 1; no deadline. Notification of admission on rolling basis. Reply is required by May 1. $200 nonrefundable tuition deposit. Freshmen accepted for terms other than fall.
**Special programs:** Admission may be deferred one year. Credit may be granted through CLEP general and subject exams. Placement may be granted through Regents College exams. Credit and placement may be granted through challenge exams and military and life experience. Early entrance/early admission program.
**Transfer students:** Transfer students accepted for terms other than fall. In fall 1992, 71% of all new students were transfers into all classes. 758 transfer applications were received, 561 were accepted. Application deadline is rolling for fall; rolling for spring. Minimum 2.0 GPA required. Lowest course grade accepted is "D." Maximum number of transferable credits is 98 semester hours. At least 32 semester hours must be completed at the college to receive degree.
**Admissions contact:** Wayne F. James, M.S., C.A.G.S., Director of Admissions. 516 678-5000, extension 240.

**FINANCIAL AID. Available aid:** Pell grants, SEOG, Federal Nursing Student Scholarships, school scholarships and grants, private scholarships and grants, and athletic scholarships. Perkins Loans (NDSL), PLUS, Stafford Loans (GSL), state loans, private loans, and SLS. Tuition Plan Inc., deferred payment plan, and family tuition reduction.
**Financial aid statistics:** Average amounts of aid awarded freshmen: Scholarships and grants, $1,000; loans, $2,750.
**Supporting data/closing dates:** FAFSA/FAF/FFS: Accepted on rolling basis. School's own aid application: Accepted on rolling basis. State aid form: Accepted on rolling basis. Income tax forms: Accepted on rolling basis. Notification of awards on rolling basis.
**Financial aid contact:** Susan Swisher, Director of Financial Aid. 516 678-5000, extension 249.

**STUDENT EMPLOYMENT.** College Work/Study Program. Institutional employment. Off-campus part-time employment opportunities rated "excellent."

**COMPUTER FACILITIES.** 68 IBM/IBM-compatible microcomputers; all are networked. Computer facilities are available to all students.
**Fees:** Computer fee is included in tuition/fees.

**GRADUATE CAREER DATA.** Graduate school percentages: 2% enter law school. 20% enter medical school. 4% enter dental school.

# Mount Saint Mary College

**Newburgh, NY 12550-3598 914 569-3248**

**1993-94 Costs.** Tuition: $7,700. Room & board: $4,850. Fees, books, misc. academic expenses (school's estimate): $640.
**Enrollment.** Undergraduates: 318 men, 737 women (full-time). Freshman class: 1,055 applicants, 800 accepted, 238 enrolled. Graduate enrollment: 38 men, 146 women.
**Test score averages/ranges.** Average SAT scores: 465 verbal, 465 math. Range of SAT scores of middle 50%: 440-480 verbal, 440-480 math. Average ACT scores: 20 composite.
**Faculty.** 68 full-time; 92 part-time. 73% of faculty holds doctoral degree. Student/faculty ratio: 13 to 1.
**Selectivity rating.** Less competitive.

**PROFILE.** Mount Saint Mary is a private, church-affiliated, liberal arts college. Founded in 1960, it adopted coeducation in 1968. Its 36-acre campus is located in Newburgh, 58 miles north of New York City.
**Accreditation:** MSACS. Professionally accredited by the American Medical Association (CAHEA), the National League for Nursing.
**Religious orientation:** Mount Saint Mary College is affiliated with the Roman Catholic Church; three semesters of religion/philosophy required.
**Library:** Collections totaling over 115,000 volumes, 650 periodical subscriptions, and 33,000 microform items.
**Special facilities/museums:** On-campus elementary school, television station and editing room.
**Athletic facilities:** Gymnasium, baseball, soccer, and softball fields, basketball and volleyball courts, free weight room, cardiovascular fitness center, natatorium.

**STUDENT BODY. Undergraduate profile:** 72% are state residents; 33% are transfers. 2% Asian-American, 7% Black, 3% Hispanic, 1% Native American, 86% White, 1% Other. Average age of undergraduates is 21.
**Freshman profile:** 4% of freshmen who took SAT scored 600 or over on verbal, 5% scored 600 or over on math; 34% scored 500 or over on verbal, 33% scored 500 or over on math; 96% scored 400 or over on verbal, 96% scored 400 or over on math; 100% scored 300 or over on verbal, 100% scored 300 or over on math. 88% of accepted applicants took SAT; 7% took ACT. 50% of freshmen come from public schools.
**Undergraduate achievement:** 87% of fall 1992 freshmen returned for fall 1993 term. 68% of entering class graduated. 38% of students who completed a degree program went on to graduate study within seven years.
**Foreign students:** 17 students are from out of the country. Countries represented include China, France, Greece, Hungary, Korea, and Poland; 11 in all.

**PROGRAMS OF STUDY. Degrees:** B.A., B.S., B.S.Ed., B.S.Nurs.
**Majors:** Accounting, Biology, Business Management/Administration, Chemistry, Communication Arts, Computer Science, Education, Elementary Education, English, Hispanic Studies, History, History/Political Science, Human Services, Interdisciplinary Studies, International Studies, Mathematics, Media Studies, Medical Technology, Nursing, Pre-Dental, Pre-Law, Pre-Medical, Pre-Veterinary, Psychology, Public Relations, Secondary Education, Social Sciences, Sociology, Special Education, Theatre Arts.
**Distribution of degrees:** The majors with the highest enrollment are education, business management/administration, and nursing; Hispanic studies, sociology, and theatre arts have the lowest.
**Requirements:** General education requirement.
**Academic regulations:** Freshmen must maintain minimum 1.7 GPA; sophomores, 1.85 GPA; juniors, 2.0 GPA; seniors, 2.0 GPA.
**Special:** Minors offered in most majors and in biblical studies, French, philosophy, religious studies, Spanish, and theatre/music. Courses offered in anthropology, art, earth science, economics, fine arts, geography, music, and speech. Self-designed majors. Double majors. Dual degrees. Independent study. Accelerated study. Pass/fail grading option. Internships. Cooperative education programs. Graduate school at which undergraduates may take graduate-level courses. Preprofessional programs in law, medicine, veterinary science, and dentistry. Member of Mid-Hudson College Consortium; cross-registration possible. Washington Semester and Sea Semester. Teacher certification in elementary, secondary, and special education. Certification in specific subject areas. Study abroad in Australia, Austria, China, England, France, Ireland, Italy, Mexico, Russia, Scotland, Spain, and other countries. ROTC at Fordham U.
**Honors:** Honors program. Honor societies.
**Academic Assistance:** Remedial reading, writing, math, and study skills. Nonremedial tutoring.

**ADMISSIONS. Academic basis for candidate selection** (in order of priority): Secondary school record, class rank, standardized test scores, school's recommendation, essay.
**Nonacademic basis for candidate selection:** Alumni/ae relationship is important. Character and personality, extracurricular participation, particular talent or ability, and geographical distribution are considered.
**Requirements:** Graduation from secondary school is recommended; GED is accepted. 24.5 units and the following program of study are recommended: 4 units of English, 3 units of math, 3 units of science, 3 units of foreign language, 4 units of social studies, 4 units of history, 3.5 units of electives. Minimum combined SAT score of 900, rank in top half of secondary school class, and minimum 80 average recommended. Biology and chemistry required of nursing program applicants. HEOP for applicants not normally admissible. Conditional admission possible for applicants not meeting standard requirements. SAT or ACT is required. Campus visit and interview recommended. Off-campus interviews available with an admissions representative.
**Procedure:** Take SAT or ACT by December of 12th year. Visit college for interview by May of 12th year. Suggest filing application by December. Application deadline is August. Notification of admission on rolling basis. No set date by which applicants must accept offer. $100 tuition deposit, refundable until May 1. $100 room deposit, refundable until May 1. Freshmen accepted for terms other than fall.
**Special programs:** Admission may be deferred two years. Credit and/or placement may be granted through CEEB Advanced Placement exams. Credit and/or placement may be granted through CLEP general and subject exams. Placement may be granted through challenge exams. Credit and placement may be granted through Regents College, ACT PEP, and DANTES exams, and military and life experience. Early decision program. In fall 1993, 8 applied for early decision and 5 were accepted. Deadline for applying for early decision is December 1. Early entrance/early admission program. Concurrent enrollment program.
**Transfer students:** Transfer students accepted for terms other than fall. In fall 1993, 33% of all new students were transfers into all classes. 262 transfer applications were received, 160 were accepted. Application deadline is September 1 for fall; January 15 for spring. Minimum 2.0 GPA required. Lowest course grade accepted is "C." Maximum number of transferable credits is 60 semester hours from a two-year school and 90 semester hours from a four-year school. At least 30 semester hours must be completed at the college to receive degree.
**Admissions contact:** J. Randall Ognibene, M.A., Director of Admissions. 914 569-3248, 800 558-0942 (in-state).

**FINANCIAL AID. Available aid:** Pell grants, SEOG, Federal Nursing Student Scholarships, state scholarships and grants, school scholarships and grants, private scholarships

and grants, ROTC scholarships, and academic merit scholarships. Perkins Loans (NDSL), PLUS, Stafford Loans (GSL), NSL, and SLS. Tuition Plan Inc. and AMS.
**Financial aid statistics:** 26% of aid is not need-based. In 1993-94, 80% of all undergraduate applicants received aid; 90% of freshman applicants. Average amounts of aid awarded freshmen: Scholarships and grants, $2,000; loans, $2,000.
**Supporting data/closing dates:** FAFSA/FAF/FFS: Priority filing date is March 15; accepted on rolling basis. State aid form: Priority filing date is March 15; accepted on rolling basis. Income tax forms: Priority filing date is March 15; accepted on rolling basis. Notification of awards begins March 1.
**Financial aid contact:** David Stacey, M.A., Director of Financial Aid. 914 569-3195, extension 3195.

# Nazareth College of Rochester

**Rochester, NY 14618** **716 586-2525**

**1994-95 Costs.** Tuition: $10,240. Room & board: $4,910. Fees, books, misc. academic expenses (school's estimate): $640.
**Enrollment.** Undergraduates: 341 men, 962 women (full-time). Freshman class: 942 applicants, 793 accepted, 275 enrolled. Graduate enrollment: 141 men, 794 women.
**Test score averages/ranges.** Average SAT scores: 494 verbal, 540 math. Range of SAT scores of middle 50%: 444-544 verbal, 490-590 math. Average ACT scores: 24 composite. Range of ACT scores of middle 50%: 23-27 composite.
**Faculty.** 111 full-time; 69 part-time. 74% of faculty holds doctoral degree. Student/faculty ratio: 14 to 1.
**Selectivity rating.** Competitive.

**PROFILE.** Nazareth College of Rochester is a private, liberal arts institution. Founded as a women's college in 1924, it adopted coeducation in 1974. Its 75-acre campus is located in Rochester.

**Accreditation:** MSACS. Professionally accredited by the Council on Social Work Education, the National Association of Schools of Music.
**Religious orientation:** Nazareth College of Rochester is nonsectarian; one semester of religion required.
**Library:** Collections totaling over 256,216 volumes, 1,620 periodical subscriptions, and 285,144 microform items.
**Special facilities/museums:** Speech, hearing, and language clinic, reading clinic, psychology center.
**Athletic facilities:** Athletic fields, gymnasium, basketball, racquetball, and tennis courts, fitness center, swimming pool, dance studio.

**STUDENT BODY. Undergraduate profile:** 95% are state residents; 44% are transfers. 1% Asian-American, 4% Black, 2% Hispanic, 1% Native American, 92% White. Average age of undergraduates is 20.
**Freshman profile:** 3% of freshmen who took SAT scored 700 or over on math; 10% scored 600 or over on verbal, 20% scored 600 or over on math; 52% scored 500 or over on verbal, 70% scored 500 or over on math; 95% scored 400 or over on verbal, 99% scored 400 or over on math; 100% scored 300 or over on verbal, 100% scored 300 or over on math. 95% of accepted applicants took SAT; 5% took ACT. 88% of freshmen come from public schools.
**Undergraduate achievement:** 85% of fall 1992 freshmen returned for fall 1993 term. 57% of entering class graduated. 30% of students who completed a degree program went on to graduate study within one year.
**Foreign students:** Three students are from out of the country.

**PROGRAMS OF STUDY. Degrees:** B.A., B.Mus., B.S.
**Majors:** Accounting, American Studies, Anthropology, Art, Art History, Biochemistry, Biology, Business Administration, Business Administration/Management, Business/Distributive Education, Chemistry, Computer/Information Science, Economics, Education, Elementary Education, English, Environmental Science, Fine Arts, French, German, History, International Studies, Italian, Literature/Language, Mathematics, Modern Foreign Language, Music, Music Therapy, Nursing, Philosophy, Political Science, Psychology, Religion, Social Science, Social Work, Sociology, Spanish, Speech Pathology, Theatre Arts.
**Distribution of degrees:** The majors with the highest enrollment are business administration, psychology, and social work; biology, chemistry, and German have the lowest.
**Requirements:** General education requirement.
**Academic regulations:** Freshmen must maintain minimum 1.8 GPA; sophomores, 1.9 GPA; juniors, 2.0 GPA; seniors, 2.0 GPA.
**Special:** Minors offered in all majors. Courses offered in anthropology, education, physics, and Russian. Seminars and research in biology, chemistry, English, foreign languages, international business, mathematics, psychology, and sports management. Double majors. Independent study. Accelerated study. Pass/fail grading option. Internships. Preprofessional programs in law, medicine, veterinary science, and dentistry. 2-2 programs in accounting, business, and liberal arts with Monroe Comm Coll. 3-2 program in chemical engineering with Clarkson U. Member of Rochester Area Colleges Consortium. Washington Semester. Albany Semester. Teacher certification in elementary, secondary, and special education. Study abroad in France, Germany, Ireland, Italy, and Spain. AFROTC at Rochester Inst of Tech.
**Honors:** Honors program.
**Academic Assistance:** Remedial reading, writing, math, and study skills.

**STUDENT LIFE. Housing:** Students may live on or off campus. Coed and women's dorms. 61% of students live in college housing.
**Social atmosphere:** The student newspaper comments, "Being a small campus, it's sometimes hard to find a single time when the 'social life' is the best. We do pretty well with what we've got." On campus, students gather at the Roost, the 21 Club, and the Cabaret. Popular destinations off campus are Thirsty's, J.W. Prepps, Prince George's, and Pattim's. Marathon Men Weekend, Springfest, Senior Week (or Spirit Week), and the 100 Days Mixer are all popular events.
**Services and counseling/handicapped student services:** Placement services. Health service. Day care. Counseling services for minority and older students. Birth control, personal, and psychological counseling. Career and academic guidance services. Religious counseling. Physically disabled student services. Learning disabled services. Notetaking services. Tape recorders. Tutors. Reader services for the blind.
**Campus organizations:** Undergraduate student government. Student newspaper (Gleaner, published once/month). Yearbook. Radio station. Wind and jazz ensembles, concert and jazz bands, concert choir, drama club, social workers association, commuter association, Circle K, Rotaract, Amnesty International, 30 organizations in all.
**Religious organizations:** Young in Spirit, Campus Ministry.
**Minority/foreign student organizations:** Black Interest Group. French, German, Italian, and Spanish clubs.

**ATHLETICS. Physical education requirements:** Two semesters of physical education required.
**Intercollegiate competition:** 14% of students participate. Basketball (M,W), cheerleading (M,W), diving (M,W), golf (M,W), lacrosse (M,W), soccer (M,W), swimming (M,W), tennis (M,W), volleyball (W). Member of ECAC, NCAA Division III, NYSAIAW.
**Intramural and club sports:** 30% of students participate. Intramural basketball, floor hockey, football, racquetball, soccer, volleyball. Men's club volleyball.

**ADMISSIONS. Academic basis for candidate selection** (in order of priority): Secondary school record, standardized test scores, class rank, school's recommendation, essay.
**Nonacademic basis for candidate selection:** Extracurricular participation, particular talent or ability, geographical distribution, and alumni/ae relationship are important. Character and personality are considered.
**Requirements:** Graduation from secondary school is required; GED is accepted. 19 units and the following program of study are recommended: 4 units of English, 3 units of math, 3 units of science including 2 units of lab, 3 units of foreign language, 4 units of social studies. Minimum combined SAT score of 850 (composite ACT score of 20), rank in top third of secondary school class, and minimum 2.5 GPA recommended. Portfolio required of art program applicants. Audition required of music program applicants. R.N. required of nursing program applicants. HEOP for applicants not normally admissible. SAT or ACT is required. Campus visit and interview recommended. Off-campus interviews available with admissions and alumni representatives.
**Procedure:** Take SAT or ACT by January of 12th year. Suggest filing application by February 15; no deadline. Notification of admission on rolling basis. Reply is required by May 1. $200 tuition deposit, refundable prior to May 1. Freshmen accepted for terms other than fall.
**Special programs:** Admission may be deferred one semester. Credit and/or placement may be granted through CEEB Advanced Placement exams for scores of 3 or higher. Credit and/or placement may be granted through CLEP general and subject exams. Credit may be granted through challenge exams and military experience. Early entrance/early admission program.
**Transfer students:** Transfer students accepted for terms other than fall. In fall 1993, 44% of all new students were transfers into all classes. 305 transfer applications were received, 235 were accepted. Application deadline is July 1 for fall; December 15 for spring. Minimum 2.5 GPA required. Lowest course grade accepted is "C." Maximum number of transferable credits is 90 semester hours. At least 30 semester hours must be completed at the college to receive degree.
**Admissions contact:** Thomas DaRin, M.S., Director of Admissions. 800 462-3944, 800 248-3939.

**FINANCIAL AID. Available aid:** Pell grants, SEOG, state scholarships and grants, school scholarships and grants, private scholarships and grants, and academic merit scholarships. Perkins Loans (NDSL), PLUS, Stafford Loans (GSL), and SLS. AMS and family tuition reduction.
**Financial aid statistics:** 21% of aid is not need-based. In 1993-94, 100% of all undergraduate applicants received aid. Average amounts of aid awarded freshmen: Scholarships and grants, $5,801; loans, $2,810.
**Supporting data/closing dates:** FAFSA/FAF: Priority filing date is March 30. Income tax forms: Accepted on rolling basis. Notification of awards on rolling basis.
**Financial aid contact:** Bruce Woolley, Ph.D., Director of Financial Aid. 716 586-2525.

**STUDENT EMPLOYMENT.** College Work/Study Program. Institutional employment. 44% of full-time undergraduates work on campus during school year. Students may expect to earn an average of $1,014 during school year. Off-campus part-time employment opportunities rated "excellent."

**COMPUTER FACILITIES.** 82 IBM/IBM-compatible and Macintosh/Apple microcomputers; all are networked. Students may access Digital, IBM, SUN minicomputer/mainframe systems, Internet. Residence halls may be equipped with networked terminals. Client/LAN operating systems include Apple/Macintosh, DOS, UNIX/XENIX/AIX, DEC, LocalTalk/AppleTalk, Novell. 850 major computer languages and software packages available. Computer facilities are available to all students.
**Fees:** None.
**Hours:** 24 hours.

**GRADUATE CAREER DATA.** Graduate school percentages: 2% enter law school. 1% enter medical school. 2% enter graduate business programs. 5% enter graduate arts and sciences programs. Highest graduate school enrollments: Nazareth Coll, Rochester Inst of Tech, SUNY Coll at Brockport, SUNY at Buffalo, SUNY Coll at Geneseo, Syracuse U, U of Rochester. 30% of graduates choose careers in business and industry. Companies and businesses that hire graduates: BOCES #1 Fairport, Eastman Kodak, Nazareth College, Paychex, U of Rochester, Xerox, Rochester city school district.

# New York Institute of Technology

**Old Westbury, NY 11568 516 686-7516**

**1994-95 Costs.** Tuition: $8,650. Room: $2,000-$3,000. Board: $1,800-$2,400. Fees, books, misc. academic expenses (school's estimate): $900.
**Enrollment.** Undergraduates: 3,377 men, 1,353 women (full-time). Freshman class: 2,541 applicants, 1,977 accepted, 1,509 enrolled. Graduate enrollment: 1,559 men, 891 women.
**Test score averages/ranges.** Average SAT scores: 389 verbal, 447 math.
**Faculty.** 228 full-time; 450 part-time. 58% of faculty holds doctoral degree. Student/faculty ratio: 20 to 1.
**Selectivity rating.** Less competitive.

**PROFILE.** New York Institute of Technology, founded in 1910, is a private institution of technology. Programs are offered in the Centers for Energy Policy and Research and Labor and Industrial Relations and the Schools of Architecture, Engineering and Technology, Hotel Administration and Culinary Arts, Management, Media and Arts, and Natural Sciences. Its 700-acre campus, including the C.V. Whitney estate, is located in Old Westbury, east of New York City.

**Accreditation:** MSACS. Professionally accredited by the Accreditation Board for Engineering and Technology, the American Osteopathic Association, the Foundation for Interior Design Education Research, the National Architecture Accrediting Board.
**Religious orientation:** New York Institute of Technology is nonsectarian; no religious requirements.
**Library:** Collections totaling over 175,875 volumes, 3,466 periodical subscriptions, and 300,000 microform items.
**Athletic facilities:** Gymnasium, basketball, handball, and tennis courts, weight room, swimming pool, athletic fields, bowling alley, aerobics room, golf course.

**STUDENT BODY. Undergraduate profile:** 74% are state residents; 33% are transfers. 8% Asian-American, 14% Black, 7% Hispanic, 57% White, 14% Other. Average age of undergraduates is 24.
**Freshman profile:** 1% of freshmen who took SAT scored 700 or over on math; 1% scored 600 or over on verbal, 2% scored 600 or over on math; 11% scored 500 or over on verbal, 17% scored 500 or over on math; 54% scored 400 or over on verbal, 57% scored 400 or over on math; 91% scored 300 or over on verbal, 92% scored 300 or over on math. 76% of freshmen come from public schools.
**Undergraduate achievement:** 52% of fall 1992 freshmen returned for fall 1993 term. 31% of entering class graduated. 25% of students who completed a degree program went on to graduate study within five years.
**Foreign students:** 1,964 students are from out of the country. Countries represented include China, India, Korea, and Taiwan; 70 in all.

**PROGRAMS OF STUDY. Degrees:** B.A., B.Arch., B.F.A., B.Prof.Studies, B.S., B.Tech.
**Majors:** Accounting, Aerospace Engineering, Architectural Technology, Architecture, Art Education, Behavioral Sciences, Behavioral Sciences/CAPP, Biology Education, Business Administration, Business Administration Education, Business/Distributive Education, Chemistry Education, Communication Arts, Computer Science, Design Graphics, Economics, Electrical Engineering Technology, Electromechanical Technology, Engineering/Electrical, Finance, Fine Arts, General Studies, Health Education, Hotel/Restaurant Administration, Industrial Engineering, Industrial Engineering Technology, Industrial Hygiene, Industrial Technology, Interior Design, Labor Management Option, Life Science/Chiropractic, Life Sciences, Life Sciences/Osteopathy, Management, Management of Information Systems, Manufacturing, Marketing, Mathematics Education, Mechanical Engineering, Mechanical Engineering Technology, Mechanical Technology, Medical Technology, Physics, Physics Education, Plant Operation, Political Science, Radiologic Specialist's Assistant, Secretarial Administration, Teacher Education, Technical Education, Technical Writing, Technological Management, Telecommunications Management, Trade Education.
**Distribution of degrees:** The majors with the highest enrollment are architecture, business, and communication arts; economics, political science, and physics have the lowest.
**Requirements:** General education requirement.
**Academic regulations:** Freshmen must maintain minimum 1.70 GPA; sophomores, 1.90 GPA; juniors, 2.0 GPA; seniors, 2.0 GPA.
**Special:** Certificate programs offered. Courses offered in English, math, social sciences, speech, and television. Associate's degrees offered. Self-designed majors. Double majors. Independent study. Accelerated study. Graduate school at which undergraduates may take graduate-level courses. Preprofessional programs in law, medicine, veterinary science, pharmacy, and dentistry. Combined B.S./D.O. with NYIT's New York Coll of Osteopathic Medicine. Architectural Technology/M.B.A. program. Teacher certification in vo-tech education. Study abroad in England, France, and Italy. AFROTC.
**Honors:** Honor societies.
**Academic Assistance:** Remedial reading, writing, math, and study skills. Nonremedial tutoring.

**STUDENT LIFE. Housing:** Students may live on or off campus. Coed dorms. 50% of students live in college housing.
**Social atmosphere:** The most popular events on campus, according to the Campus Slate newspaper, are T.M. Dealy's 48-hour poetry marathon/short story recital, the homemade film contest, baseball games, Natalie Petito's Choir group Christmas show, and Ray Lambaise's charity ball. The most influential student organizations are the Campus Slate, Heavy Metal Dave's Rock'n'Roll Show, Paumonok Fletcher's Art Revival Group, and John Bradley's Christian Group. On campus, students meet at the Pac building and the workout gym. Favorite off-campus spots include Aquilino's Ribs, Denny's Sports Cafe, and Eggy's.
**Services and counseling/handicapped student services:** Placement services. Health service. Counseling services for minority, veteran, and older students. Birth control, personal, and psychological counseling. Career and academic guidance services. Religious counseling. Physically disabled student services. Learning disabled program/services. Notetaking services. Tape recorders. Tutors. Reader services for the blind.
**Campus organizations:** Undergraduate student government. Student newspapers (Campus Slate; Campus Voice). Literary magazine. Yearbook. Radio station. American Institute of Architecture Students (AIAS), Criminal Justice Club, Financial Management Association, Political Science Club, United Artists, Cultural Diversity Council, 40 organizations in all. 10 fraternities, no chapter houses; two sororities, no chapter houses. 40% of men join a fraternity. 20% of women join a sorority.
**Religious organizations:** Christian Fellowship, Heaven on Earth, Jewish Student Union, Life Talks.
**Minority/foreign student organizations:** African Peoples Organization, National Society of Black Engineers, Society of Hispanic Professional Engineers, Hispanic Student Council. International Student Association, Greek Culture Club, Indian Culture Club, Chinese Student Association, Korean Student Association, South Asian Cultural Organization.

**ATHLETICS. Physical education requirements:** None.
**Intercollegiate competition:** 2% of students participate. Baseball (M), basketball (M), cross-country (M,W), lacrosse (M), soccer (M,W), softball (W), track (indoor) (M,W), track (outdoor) (M,W), track and field (indoor) (M,W), track and field (outdoor) (M,W), volleyball (W). Member of Diamond Baseball Conference, ECAC, NCAA Division I for baseball, NCAA Division II, NYCAC.
**Intramural and club sports:** 4% of students participate. Intramural arena football, basketball, dodge ball, flag football, football, softball, tennis, volleyball, water basketball, water polo, Wiffle ball. Women's club cheerleading.

**ADMISSIONS. Academic basis for candidate selection** (in order of priority): Secondary school record, standardized test scores, class rank, school's recommendation.
**Nonacademic basis for candidate selection:** Particular talent or ability is emphasized. Character and personality, extracurricular participation, and alumni/ae relationship are considered.
**Requirements:** Graduation from secondary school is recommended; GED is accepted. No specific distribution of secondary school units required. Minimum SAT scores of 400 verbal and 450 math recommended. Portfolio required of art program applicants. EOP and HEOP for applicants not normally admissible. Conditional admission possible for applicants not meeting standard requirements. SAT is required; ACT may be substituted. Campus visit and interview recommended. Off-campus interviews available with an admissions representative.
**Procedure:** Take SAT or ACT by spring of 12th year. Notification of admission on rolling basis. No set date by which applicants must accept offer. $300 nonrefundable tuition deposit. $100 nonrefundable room deposit. Freshmen accepted for terms other than fall.
**Special programs:** Admission may be deferred. Credit and/or placement may be granted through CEEB Advanced Placement exams for scores of 3 or higher. Credit and/or placement may be granted through CLEP general and subject exams. Credit may be granted through military experience. Credit and placement may be granted through Regents College, ACT PEP, DANTES, and challenge exams and life experience. Early entrance/early admission program. Concurrent enrollment program.
**Transfer students:** Transfer students accepted for terms other than fall. In fall 1993, 33% of all new students were transfers into all classes. 1,012 transfer applications were received, 1,000 were accepted. Minimum 1.7 GPA recommended. Lowest course grade accepted is "D." Maximum number of transferable credits is 90 semester hours from a two-year school and 108 semester hours from a four-year school. At least 30 semester hours must be completed at the institute to receive degree.
**Admissions contact:** Arthur Lambert, Executive Director of Enrollment Services. 516 686-7520.

**FINANCIAL AID. Available aid:** Pell grants, SEOG, state scholarships and grants, school scholarships and grants, private scholarships and grants, ROTC scholarships, academic merit scholarships, and athletic scholarships. Perkins Loans (NDSL), PLUS, Stafford Loans (GSL), and SLS. Deferred payment plan.
**Financial aid statistics:** 50% of aid is not need-based. In 1993-94, 80% of all undergraduate applicants received aid; 80% of freshman applicants. Average amounts of aid awarded freshmen: Scholarships and grants, $1,000; loans, $2,625.
**Supporting data/closing dates:** FAFSA/FAF: Accepted on rolling basis. School's own aid application: Accepted on rolling basis. State aid form: Accepted on rolling basis. Income tax forms: Accepted on rolling basis. Notification of awards on rolling basis.
**Financial aid contact:** Doreen Meyer, Director of Financial Aid. 516 686-7680.

**STUDENT EMPLOYMENT.** College Work/Study Program. Institutional employment. 10% of full-time undergraduates work on campus during school year. Students may expect to earn an average of $1,500 during school year. Off-campus part-time employment opportunities rated "good."

**COMPUTER FACILITIES.** 263 IBM/IBM-compatible and Macintosh/Apple microcomputers; 191 are networked. Students may access Digital minicomputer/mainframe systems. Computer languages and software packages include BASIC, COBOL, FORTRAN, Microsoft Works, PageMaker, Pascal, WordPerfect. Computer facilities are available to all students.
**Fees:** Computer fee is included in tuition/fees.
**Hours:** 8 AM-11 PM (M-F); 9 AM-7 PM (Sa-Su).

**GRADUATE CAREER DATA.** Graduate school percentages: 3% enter law school. 15% enter graduate business programs. Highest graduate school enrollments: Columbia U, Harvard U, New York U, Pratt Inst, U of Pennsylvania. 70% of graduates choose careers in business and industry. Companies and businesses that hire graduates: AT&T, Grumman Aerospace, IBM.

**PROMINENT ALUMNI/AE.** Angelo F. Corva, president, Angelo F. Corva Associates; Richard Torrenzano, director/senior vice-president for corporate affairs, Smith, Kline, Beecham; Ronald K. Breuer, vice-president, The Morgan Bank.

# New York University

**New York, NY 10011** **212 998-1212**

**1994-95 Costs.** Tuition: $18,739. Room & board: $7,262. Fees, books, misc. academic expenses (school's estimate): $450.
**Enrollment.** Undergraduates: 6,437 men, 8,788 women (full-time). Freshman class: 13,594 applicants, 7,244 accepted, 2,505 enrolled. Graduate enrollment: 6,485 men, 8,759 women.
**Test score averages/ranges.** N/A.
**Faculty.** 1,218 full-time; 2,892 part-time. 99% of faculty holds highest degree in specific field. Student/faculty ratio: 13 to 1.
**Selectivity rating.** Highly competitive.

**PROFILE.** NYU, founded in 1831, is a private, comprehensive university. Programs are offered through the Colleges of Arts and Sciences and Business and Public Administration; the Schools of the Arts; Education, Health, Nursing, and Arts Professions; and Social Work; and the Stern School of Business. Its 29-acre campus is located in Greenwich Village, New York City.

**Accreditation:** MSACS.
**Religious orientation:** New York University is nonsectarian; no religious requirements.
**Library:** Collections totaling over 3,601,904 volumes, 29,254 periodical subscriptions, and 3,074,824 microform items.
**Special facilities/museums:** Art galleries, exhibition spaces, institutes of fine arts, mathematics, and science, center for Hellenic studies, foreign language and cultural centers.
**Athletic facilities:** Sport center, racquetball and tennis courts, weight training facility, mini-gymnasium, field house, swimming pool and diving tank, fencing salle, dance studio, track, fitness/exercise facility.

**STUDENT BODY. Undergraduate profile:** 70% are state residents; 38% are transfers. 18% Asian-American, 9% Black, 8% Hispanic, 51% White, 14% Unknown.
**Freshman profile:** 4% of freshmen who took SAT scored 700 or over on verbal, 13% scored 700 or over on math; 29% scored 600 or over on verbal, 54% scored 600 or over on math; 76% scored 500 or over on verbal, 88% scored 500 or over on math; 98% scored 400 or over on verbal, 98% scored 400 or over on math; 100% scored 300 or over on verbal, 100% scored 300 or over on math. 93% of accepted applicants took SAT; 5% took ACT. 66% of freshmen come from public schools.
**Undergraduate achievement:** 87% of fall 1992 freshmen returned for fall 1993 term. 59% of entering class graduated.
**Foreign students:** 937 students are from out of the country. Countries represented include Asian and European countries; 120 in all.

**PROGRAMS OF STUDY. Degrees:** B.A., B.F.A., B.S.
**Majors:** Accounting, Actuarial Science, Anthropology, Applied Science, Archaeology, Art, Art Education, Art History, Biochemistry, Biology, Chemical Engineering, Chemistry, Cinema Studies, Civil Engineering, Classical Civilization, Classics, Classics/Anthropology, Classics/Fine Arts, Communications Studies, Comparative Literature, Computer Engineering, Computer Science, Computer Science/Mathematics, Dance, Dance Education, Drama, Dramatic Literature/Theatre/History/Cinema, Dramatic Writing, Early Childhood/Elementary Education, East Asian Studies, Economics, Educational Theatre, Electrical Engineering, Engineering Physics, English, English/American Literature, European Studies, Film Production, Finance, Fine Arts, French Language/Literature, French/Linguistics, General Business, German/Linguistics, Germanic Languages/Literatures, Graphic Communications, Greek, Hebrew Language/Literature, History, Hotel/Restaurant/Food Management, Individualized Study, Information Systems, International Business, Italian Language/Literature, Italian/Linguistics, Jewish History/Civilization, Journalism/Mass Communications, Latin, Latin American Literature, Latin American Studies, Latin/Greek, Linguistics, Luso-Brazilian Language/Literature, Management/Organizational Behavior, Management/Technology, Marketing, Mathematics, Mathematics/Computer Science, Mechanical Engineering, Medieval/Renaissance Studies, Metropolitan Studies, Music, Music/Business, Music Education, Music Performance/Composition, Music/Technology, Music Theory/Composition, Musical Theatre, Near Eastern Civilization, Near Eastern Languages/Literatures, Neural Science, Nursing, Nutrition/Dietetics, Philosophy, Photography, Physical Therapy, Physics, Politics, Portuguese Language/Literature, Psychology, Radio Production, Religious Studies, Romance Languages, Russian, Russian Area Studies, Secondary Education, Slavic Languages/Literatures, Social Work, Sociology, Spanish Language/Literature, Spanish/Linguistics, Special Education, Speech/Language Pathology/Audiology, Statistics/Operations Research, Studio Art, Television Production, Theatrical/Film Design, Urban Design, Urban Studies, Women's Studies.
**Distribution of degrees:** The majors with the highest enrollment are film/television, individualized study, and accounting.
**Requirements:** General education requirement.
**Academic regulations:** Minimum 2.0 GPA required for graduation.
**Special:** Minors offered in most majors and in African-American studies, Arabic, astronomy, Chinese, earth/environmental science, East Asian civilization, geology, literature in translation, Persian, Turkish, and writing. Associate's degrees offered. Self-designed majors. Double majors. Dual degrees. Independent study. Internships. Graduate school at which undergraduates may take graduate-level courses. Preprofessional programs in law, medicine, veterinary science, dentistry, and optometry. B.S./B.E. engineering program with Stevens Inst of Tech. B.A./D.D.S. and B.A./M.D. programs. Washington Semester. Teacher certification in early childhood, elementary, secondary, and special education. Certification in specific subject areas. Exchange programs abroad in France (Ecole Superieur de Commerce), Italy (Luigi Bocconi U), and Japan (Sanna Coll). Study abroad also in England, Germany, Greece, India, Kenya, Portugal, Spain, and Sweden. ROTC at Polytech U.
**Honors:** Phi Beta Kappa. Honors program.
**Academic Assistance:** Nonremedial tutoring.

**STUDENT LIFE. Housing:** Students may live on or off campus. Coed dorms. Sorority and fraternity housing. School-owned/operated apartments. 40% of students live in college housing.
**Social atmosphere:** As reported by the student newspaper, "The Village has a lot to offer NYU students, including clubs, bars, movies, plays, and concerts. Most popular bars include the Kettle-of-Fish, the Red Lion, and the Dugout. For a cup of herbal tea or cappuccino, there's Cafe Figaro. Many go to the Ritz, CBGB's, or the Village Update when good popular bands and NYU bands play there. Also, on a nice, warm day, Washington Square Park serves as an enjoyable place to hang out and watch and listen to the park entertainers, jugglers, musicians, acrobats. There are enough happenings going on around the city. One can never get bored, even at four A.M.; 24-hour diners and after-hour places keep the NYU students busy and happy all evening."
**Services and counseling/handicapped student services:** Placement services. Health service. Counseling services for minority and older students. Birth control, personal, and psychological counseling. Career and academic guidance services. Religious counseling. Physically disabled student services. Learning disabled program/services. Notetaking services. Tape recorders. Tutors. Reader services for the blind.
**Campus organizations:** Undergraduate student government. Student newspaper (Washington Square News; Courier; Forum). Literary magazine. Radio and TV stations. 230 registered organizations. 11 fraternities, no chapter houses; seven sororities, no chapter houses. 7% of men join a fraternity. 5% of women join a sorority.
**Religious organizations:** Protestant Campus Ministry, Jewish Cultural Foundation, Catholic Center.
**Minority/foreign student organizations:** Several minority student groups. Numerous foreign student groups.

**ATHLETICS. Physical education requirements:** None.
**Intercollegiate competition:** Basketball (M,W), cross-country (M,W), diving (M,W), fencing (M,W), golf (M), soccer (M), swimming (M,W), tennis (M,W), track (indoor) (M,W), track (outdoor) (M,W), track and field (outdoor) (M,W), volleyball (M,W), wrestling (M). Member of ECAC, ECS, ICAAAA, ISA, NAAU, NACDA, NCAA Division III, NIWFA, NWAU, Met Association, UAA.
**Intramural and club sports:** Intramural soccer, touch football. Men's club badminton, ballroom/social dancing, baseball, crew, cycling, equestrian sports, ice hockey, lacrosse, martial arts, racquetball, running, squash, triathlon, water polo. Women's club badminton, ballroom/social dancing, crew, cycling, equestrian sports, martial arts, racquetball, running, soccer, softball, squash, triathlon, water polo.

**ADMISSIONS. Academic basis for candidate selection** (in order of priority): Secondary school record, standardized test scores, school's recommendation, essay.
**Nonacademic basis for candidate selection:** Character and personality, extracurricular participation, and particular talent or ability are important. Alumni/ae relationship is considered.
**Requirements:** Graduation from secondary school is required; GED is accepted. 16 units and the following program of study are required: 4 units of English, 3 units of math, 2 units of lab science, 2 units of foreign language, 3 units of social studies. Minimum combined SAT score of 1100 and minimum 3.0 GPA recommended. Submission of creative material or audition required of performing arts, art, and music program applicants and applicants for non-performance areas in the school of the arts. Interview required of physical therapy and occupational therapy program applicants. HEOP for applicants not normally admissible. SAT or ACT is required. Campus visit recommended. No off-campus interviews.
**Procedure:** Take SAT or ACT by January of 12th year. Visit college for interview by January of 12th year. Application deadline is February 1. Notification of admission by April 1. Reply is required by May 1. $200 nonrefundable tuition deposit. $100 nonrefundable room deposit. Freshmen accepted for terms other than fall.
**Special programs:** Admission may be deferred one year. Credit and/or placement may be granted through CEEB Advanced Placement exams for scores of 3 or higher. Credit may be granted through CLEP subject exams, ACT PEP exams, and military and life experience. Early decision program. In fall 1993, 1,020 applied for early decision and 560 were accepted. Deadline for applying for early decision is December 15. Early entrance/early admission program.
**Transfer students:** Transfer students accepted for terms other than fall. In fall 1993, 38% of all new students were transfers into all classes. 4,011 transfer applications were received, 2,062 were accepted. Application deadline is December 1 for fall; March 1 for spring. Minimum 2.8 GPA required. Lowest course grade accepted is "C." Maximum number of transferable credits is 64 semester hours.
**Admissions contact:** Richard A. Avitabile, M.S., Director of Admissions/Enrollment Management. 212 998-4500.

**FINANCIAL AID. Available aid:** Pell grants, SEOG, state scholarships and grants, school scholarships and grants, and academic merit scholarships. Perkins Loans (NDSL), PLUS, Stafford Loans (GSL), NSL, private loans, and SLS. Tuition Plan Inc. Tuition stabilization and prepayment plans.
**Financial aid statistics:** 10% of aid is not need-based. In 1993-94, 96% of all undergraduate applicants received aid; 97% of freshman applicants. Average amounts of aid awarded freshmen: Scholarships and grants, $8,894; loans, $3,620.
**Supporting data/closing dates:** FAFSA: Priority filing date is February 15. State aid form. Notification of awards begins April 1.
**Financial aid contact:** Keith Jepsen, Ed.D., Director of Financial Aid. 212 998-4444.

**STUDENT EMPLOYMENT.** College Work/Study Program. Institutional employment. 23% of full-time undergraduates work on campus during school year. Students may expect to earn an average of $2,500 during school year. Off-campus part-time employment opportunities rated "excellent."

**COMPUTER FACILITIES.** 940 IBM/IBM-compatible and Macintosh/Apple microcomputers; 870 are networked. Students may access Digital, IBM minicomputer/mainframe systems, BITNET, Internet. Residence halls may be equipped with networked microcomputers. Client/LAN operating systems include Apple/Macintosh. Computer languages and software packages include Ada, APL, BASIC, C, C-Prolog, COBOL, FORTRAN, Graphic Outlook, ICON, INGRES, LISP, M77, Macro 32, MATHLAB, Modula 2, NAG, Pascal, PL/1, SAS, Shell, SPITBOL, SPSS Graphics, SPSS-X, SPSS/PC; 150 in all. Computer facilities are available to all students.
**Fees:** Computer fee is included in tuition/fees.

**GRADUATE CAREER DATA.** Graduate school percentages: 15% enter law school. 14% enter medical school. 2% enter dental school. 8% enter graduate business programs. 38% enter graduate arts and sciences programs. Highest graduate school enrollments: Columbia U, Harvard U, Yale U. 50% of graduates choose careers in business and industry.

**PROMINENT ALUMNI/AE.** Lawrence A. Tisch, CEO, CBS; Oliver Stone, director; Martin Scorsese, filmmaker; Joseph Heller, novelist; Robert Jarvik, developer of the artificial heart; Albert Sabin, developer of oral polio vaccine; George D. Wald, Nobel Prize-winning biologist; Henry Greenwald, editor-in-chief, *Time* magazine.

# Niagara University

**Niagara University, NY 14109 716 285-1212**

**1994-95 Costs.** Tuition: $9,660. Room & board: $4,638. Fees, books, misc. academic expenses (school's estimate): $760.

**Enrollment.** Undergraduates: 767 men, 1,152 women (full-time). Freshman class: 2,220 applicants, 1,796 accepted, 467 enrolled. Graduate enrollment: 224 men, 359 women.

**Test score averages/ranges.** Range of SAT scores of middle 50%: 400-500 verbal, 430-525 math. Range of ACT scores of middle 50%: 19-24 composite.

**Faculty.** 112 full-time; 125 part-time. 85% of faculty holds highest degree in specific field. Student/faculty ratio: 16 to 1.

**Selectivity rating.** Less competitive.

**PROFILE.** Niagara, founded in 1856, is a private, liberal arts university, rooted in a Catholic tradition. Programs are offered through the Colleges of Arts and Sciences, Business Administration, and Nursing; the School of Education; and the Institute of Transportation, Travel, and Tourism. Its 160-acre campus is located four miles north of Niagara Falls, in Niagara University.

**Accreditation:** MSACS. Professionally accredited by the Council on Social Work Education, the National Council for Accreditation of Teacher Education, the National League for Nursing.
**Religious orientation:** Niagara University is historically affiliated with the Roman Catholic Church (Vincentian Fathers and Brothers); three semesters of religion required.
**Library:** Collections totaling over 284,647 volumes, 1,272 periodical subscriptions, and 73,456 microform items.
**Special facilities/museums:** Art museum, fine arts center.
**Athletic facilities:** Aerobics room, weight room, gymnasium, swimming pools, baseball, and soccer fields, basketball, racquetball, tennis, and volleyball courts.

**STUDENT BODY. Undergraduate profile:** 94% are state residents; 31% are transfers. 1% Asian-American, 5% Black, 2% Hispanic, 1% Native American, 86% White, 5% Other. Average age of undergraduates is 20.
**Freshman profile:** 85% of accepted applicants took SAT; 34% took ACT. 75% of freshmen come from public schools.
**Undergraduate achievement:** 75% of fall 1992 freshmen returned for fall 1993 term. 85% of entering class graduated. 11% of students who completed a degree program immediately went on to graduate study.
**Foreign students:** 131 students are from out of the country. Countries represented include Canada, China, Germany, and Japan; 20 in all.

**PROGRAMS OF STUDY. Degrees:** B.A., B.Bus.Admin., B.F.A., B.S.
**Majors:** Accounting, Biochemistry, Biology, Biotechnology, Chemistry, Communication Studies, Computer/Information Sciences, Criminology/Criminal Justice, Economics, Elementary Education, English, French, General Business, History, Hotel/Restaurant Administration, Human Resources, International Studies, Life Sciences, Management, Marketing, Mathematics, Nursing, Philosophy, Political Science, Psychology, Religious Studies, Secondary Education, Social Sciences, Social Work, Sociology, Spanish, Theatre, Transportation, Travel/Tourism Administration.
**Distribution of degrees:** The majors with the highest enrollment are accounting, travel/tourism/hotel/restaurant, and education; languages, theatre, and computer/information systems have the lowest.
**Requirements:** General education requirement.
**Academic regulations:** Minimum 2.0 GPA must be maintained.
**Special:** Minors offered in all majors. Academic Exploration Program for undeclared majors. Minority Group Studies programs. Walt Disney World College Program for students in Institute of Travel, Hotel, and Restaurant Administration. Associate's degrees offered. Double majors. Dual degrees. Independent study. Accelerated study. Pass/fail grading option. Internships. Cooperative education programs. Graduate school at which undergraduates may take graduate-level courses. Preprofessional programs in law, medicine, and dentistry. 2-3 engineering program with U of Detroit. Member of Western New York Consortium; exchange possible. Albany Semester, New York City Semester, and Washington Semester. Visiting Student Program. Teacher certification in elementary and secondary education. Certification in specific subject areas. Study abroad in England, France, Germany, Spain, and Switzerland. ROTC.
**Honors:** Honors program. Honor societies.
**Academic Assistance:** Remedial reading, writing, math, and study skills. Nonremedial tutoring.

**STUDENT LIFE. Housing:** All first-time freshmen and sophomores must live on campus unless living with family. Coed, women's, and men's dorms. 55% of students live in college housing.
**Social atmosphere:** The Student Centre and dorms are popular gathering spots on campus. The student government and residence life staff are the most influential groups on student social life. Highlights of the school year include basketball games, comedy nights, concerts, trips to Toronto, and to Buffalo Bills football games. The school newspaper reports that Niagara has a "good atmosphere, very friendly," with a "real sense of community."
**Services and counseling/handicapped student services:** Placement services. Health service. Counseling services for minority, military, veteran, and older students. Personal and psychological counseling. Career and academic guidance services. Religious counseling. Physically disabled student services. Learning disabled services. Notetaking services. Tape recorders. Tutors. Reader services for the blind.
**Campus organizations:** Undergraduate student government. Student newspaper (Index, published once/two weeks). Literary magazine. Yearbook. Radio and TV stations. Chapel choir, Gospel Sound, University Players, films committee, orienteering and ski clubs, Knights of Columbus, aviation club, Programming Board, Interdorm Council, Muscular Dystrophy Association, academic groups, 70 organizations in all. Two fraternities, no chapter houses. 1% of men join a fraternity.
**Religious organizations:** Campus Ministry, St. Vincent de Paul Society.
**Minority/foreign student organizations:** Ethnic Awareness Association, Black Student Union, Hispanic Society. Foreign Student Council, Club International.

**ATHLETICS. Physical education requirements:** None.
**Intercollegiate competition:** 16% of students participate. Baseball (M), basketball (M,W), cheerleading (W), cross-country (M,W), golf (M), soccer (M,W), softball (W), swimming (M,W), tennis (M,W), volleyball (W). Member of ECAC, Metro Atlantic Athletic Conference, NCAA Division I.
**Intramural and club sports:** 15% of students participate. Intramural basketball, floor hockey, football, racquetball, softball. Men's club hockey, lacrosse, rugby.

**ADMISSIONS. Academic basis for candidate selection** (in order of priority): Secondary school record, class rank, standardized test scores, school's recommendation.
**Nonacademic basis for candidate selection:** Character and personality, extracurricular participation, particular talent or ability, and alumni/ae relationship are considered.
**Requirements:** Graduation from secondary school is required; GED is accepted. 16 units and the following program of study are required: 4 units of English, 2 units of math, 2 units of lab science, 2 units of foreign language, 2 units of social studies, 4 units of academic electives. Minimum SAT scores of 450 in both verbal and math (composite ACT score of 21), rank in top half of secondary school class, and minimum "B" average recommended. 3 units each of science and math required of computer/information sciences, mathematics, nursing, and science program applicants. HEOP for applicants not normally admissible. Niagara University Opportunity Program (NUOP) for applicants not meeting standard requirements. SAT or ACT is required. Campus visit and interview recommended. Off-campus interviews available with an admissions representative.
**Procedure:** Take SAT or ACT by fall of 12th year. Visit college for interview by spring of 12th year. Application deadline is August 1. Notification of admission on rolling basis. Reply is required by May 1. $50 nonrefundable tuition deposit. $50 nonrefundable room deposit. Freshmen accepted for terms other than fall.
**Special programs:** Admission may be deferred three years. Credit and/or placement may be granted through CEEB Advanced Placement exams for scores of 3 or higher. Credit and/or placement may be granted through CLEP general and subject exams. Credit may be granted through military and life experience. Credit and placement may be granted through Regents College, ACT PEP, DANTES, and challenge exams. Early decision program. Deadline for applying for early decision is August 1. Early entrance/early admission program. Concurrent enrollment program.
**Transfer students:** Transfer students accepted for terms other than fall. In fall 1993, 31% of all new students were transfers into all classes. 569 transfer applications were received, 430 were accepted. Application deadline is rolling for fall; rolling for spring. Minimum 2.0 GPA required. Lowest course grade accepted is "C." Maximum number of transferable credits is 90 semester hours. At least 30 semester hours must be completed at the university to receive degree.
**Admissions contact:** George C. Pachter, Jr., M.S.Ed., Dean of Admissions. 716 286-8700, 800 462-2111.

**FINANCIAL AID. Available aid:** Pell grants, SEOG, state scholarships and grants, school scholarships and grants, private scholarships and grants, ROTC scholarships, academic merit scholarships, and athletic scholarships. Perkins Loans (NDSL), PLUS, Stafford Loans (GSL), NSL, and SLS. Tuition Plan Inc., AMS, and deferred payment plan.
**Financial aid statistics:** 25% of aid is not need-based. In 1993-94, 95% of all undergraduate applicants received aid; 95% of freshman applicants. Average amounts of aid awarded freshmen: Scholarships and grants, $3,800; loans, $4,300.
**Supporting data/closing dates:** FAFSA: Priority filing date is February 15. Income tax forms. Notification of awards on rolling basis.
**Financial aid contact:** Maureen E. Salfi, M.S.Ed., Director of Financial Aid. 716 286-8686.

**STUDENT EMPLOYMENT.** College Work/Study Program. Institutional employment. 25% of full-time undergraduates work on campus during school year. Students may expect to earn an average of $1,600 during school year. Off-campus part-time employment opportunities rated "excellent."

**COMPUTER FACILITIES.** 150 IBM/IBM-compatible and Macintosh/Apple microcomputers; all are networked. Students may access Digital minicomputer/mainframe systems, Internet. Residence halls may be equipped with stand-alone microcomputers, networked microcomputers, modems. Client/LAN operating systems include Apple/Macintosh, DOS, UNIX/XENIX/AIX, Novell. Computer languages and software packages include BASIC, C, C++, COBOL, dBASE, FORTRAN, Framework II, Lotus 1-2-3, MINITAB, PageMaker, Pascal, SAS, SPSS, VM Compiler, WordPerfect. Computer facilities are available to all students.
**Fees:** Computer fee is included in tuition/fees.
**Hours:** 9 AM-11 PM (M-Th); 9 AM-5 PM (F); noon-5 PM (Sa); 3 PM-10 PM (Su).

**GRADUATE CAREER DATA.** Graduate school percentages: 1% enter law school. 2% enter medical school. 2% enter graduate business programs. 3% enter graduate arts and sciences programs. Highest graduate school enrollments: New York U, Niagara U, St. John's U, SUNY Buffalo, SUNY Health Center at Syracuse. Companies and businesses that hire graduates: Carborundum, Disney World, Marriot Corp., Marine Midland Bank, Price Waterhouse, Ritz-Carlton, Upjohn, Xerox.

**PROMINENT ALUMNI/AE.** Robert Dwyer, vice-president of marketing, Dean Witter Reynolds; Frank P. Layden, president and general manager, Utah Jazz basketball team; Dawn Church, actress; Calvin Murphy, Basketball Hall of Fame.

# Nyack College

**Nyack, NY 10960-3698** **914 358-1710**

**1993-94 Costs.** Tuition: $7,950. Room: $1,680. Board: $2,130. Fees, books, misc. academic expenses (school's estimate): $950.
**Enrollment.** Undergraduates: 229 men, 296 women (full-time). Graduate enrollment: 239.
**Test score averages/ranges.** Average SAT scores: 406 verbal, 444 math.
**Faculty.** 42 full-time; 32 part-time. 26% of faculty holds doctoral degree. Student/faculty ratio: 13 to 1.
**Selectivity rating.** Noncompetitive.

**PROFILE.** Nyack, founded in 1882, is a private, church-affiliated, liberal arts college. Its 63-acre campus, overlooking the Hudson River, is located in Nyack, 25 miles north of New York City.

**Accreditation:** MSACS. Professionally accredited by the National Association of Schools of Music.
**Religious orientation:** Nyack College is affiliated with the Christian and Missionary Alliance; six semesters of theology required.
**Library:** Collections totaling over 76,000 volumes and 500 periodical subscriptions.
**Athletic facilities:** Gymnasium, tennis courts, baseball, softball, and soccer fields, trainers and weight rooms.

**STUDENT BODY. Undergraduate profile:** 63% are state residents; 41% are transfers. 16% Asian-American, 10% Black, 14% Hispanic, 60% White. Average age of undergraduates is 21.
**Freshman profile:** Majority of accepted applicants took SAT.
**Undergraduate achievement:** 71% of fall 1991 freshmen returned for fall 1992 term. 49% of entering class graduated.
**Foreign students:** 11 students are from out of the country. Countries represented include the Bahamas, Canada, Colombia, Ecuador, Jordan, and Korea.

**PROGRAMS OF STUDY. Degrees:** B.A., B.Mus., B.S.
**Majors:** Bible, Business Administration, Christian Education, Church Music, Communications, Elementary Education, English, History, Interdisciplinary Studies, Keyboard/Orchestral Instruments, Missiology, Music Composition, Music Education, Organizational Management, Pastoral Ministry, Philosophy, Psychology, Religion, Secondary Education, Social Science, Voice, Youth Ministry.
**Distribution of degrees:** The majors with the highest enrollment are elementary education, psychology, and Bible; philosophy and music composition have the lowest.
**Requirements:** General education requirement.
**Academic regulations:** Freshmen must maintain minimum 1.7 GPA; sophomores, 1.8/1.9 GPA; juniors, 2.0 GPA; seniors, 2.0 GPA.
**Special:** Independent study. Pass/fail grading option. Internships. Graduate school at which undergraduates may take graduate-level courses. Preprofessional programs in theology. Member of Christian College Coalition; exchange possible. American Studies Program (Washington, D.C.). Teacher certification in early childhood, elementary, and secondary education. Study abroad in England, France, Israel, Latin American countries, and other countries.
**Academic Assistance:** Nonremedial tutoring.

**ADMISSIONS. Academic basis for candidate selection** (in order of priority): Secondary school record, standardized test scores, class rank, essay, school's recommendation.
**Nonacademic basis for candidate selection:** Character and personality are emphasized. Extracurricular participation is important. Particular talent or ability is considered.
**Requirements:** Graduation from secondary school is required; GED is accepted. 16 units are required and the following program of study is recommended: 4 units of English, 3 units of mathematics, 3 units of science, 2 units of foreign language, 3 units of social studies, 3 units of history, 4 units of electives. Minimum combined SAT score of 850 (composite ACT score of 18), rank in top two-fifths of secondary school class, and minimum 2.5 GPA recommended. Audition required of music program applicants. HEOP for qualified state residents. SAT or ACT is required. PSAT is recommended. Campus visit and interview recommended. Off-campus interviews available with an admissions representative.
**Procedure:** Take SAT or ACT by March of 12th year. Visit college for interview by January of 12th year. Notification of admission on rolling basis. Reply is required by January 31 or within one month if accepted after that date. $100 tuition deposit, refundable until May 1. $50 room deposit, refundable until September 1. Freshmen accepted for terms other than fall.
**Special programs:** Admission may be deferred two semesters. Credit may be granted through CEEB Advanced Placement for scores of 3 or higher. Credit may be granted through CLEP general and subject exams. Placement may be granted through challenge exams. Credit and placement may be granted through military and life experience.
**Transfer students:** Transfer students accepted for terms other than fall. In fall 1992, 41% of all new students were transfers into all classes. Application deadline is rolling for fall; rolling for spring. Minimum 2.0 GPA required. Lowest course grade accepted is "C." Maximum number of transferable credits is 100 semester hours. At least 30 semester hours must be completed at the college to receive degree.
**Admissions contact:** Dennis Whalen, Director of Admissions. 800 33-NYACK.

**FINANCIAL AID. Available aid:** Pell grants, SEOG, state scholarships and grants, school scholarships and grants, private scholarships, academic merit scholarships, and athletic scholarships. Perkins Loans (NDSL), PLUS, Stafford Loans (GSL), and school loans. Tuition Plan Inc., AMS, and Tuition Management Systems.
**Supporting data/closing dates:** FAFSA/FAF: Priority filing date is May 1. School's own aid application: Priority filing date is May 1. Notification of awards on rolling basis.
**Financial aid contact:** Evelyn Stolarski, M.P.S., Director of Financial Aid. 914 358-1710, extension 151.

# Pace University (New York City)

**New York, NY 10038** **212 346-1200**

**1993-94 Costs.** Tuition: $10,480. Room: $3,320. Board: $1,340. Fees, books, misc. academic expenses (school's estimate): $800.
**Enrollment.** Undergraduates: 1,257 men, 1,593 women (full-time). Graduate enrollment: 1,286 men, 921 women.
**Test score averages/ranges.** N/A.
**Faculty.** 512 full-time; 700 part-time. 70% of faculty holds doctoral degree. Student/faculty ratio: 22 to 1.
**Selectivity rating.** Less competitive.

**PROFILE.** Pace, New York City, founded in 1906, is a private, comprehensive university. Programs are offered through the Colleges of Arts and Sciences; the Schools of Computer Science and Information Systems, Business, Education, Nursing, and Law; the University College; and the Graduate Center. Its three-acre urban campus is located in downtown New York City.

**Accreditation:** MSACS. Professionally accredited by the National League for Nursing.
**Religious orientation:** Pace University (New York City) is nonsectarian; no religious requirements.
**Library:** Collections totaling over 376,740 volumes, 1,901 periodical subscriptions, and 85,641 microform items.
**Special facilities/museums:** Museum/gallery.
**Athletic facilities:** Facilities for baseball, basketball, football, tennis, soccer, cross-country, lacrosse, softball, volleyball, gymnasiums, swimming pools, weight/fitness rooms.

**STUDENT BODY. Undergraduate profile:** 88% are state residents; 29% are transfers. 9% Asian-American, 16% Black, 14% Hispanic, 1% Native American, 47% White, 13% Other.

**PROGRAMS OF STUDY. Degrees:** B.A., B.Bus.Admin., B.F.A., B.S., B.S.Nurs.
**Majors:** Accounting, Acting, Advertising, Banking, Biology, Business Education, Chemistry, Computer Science, Dramatic Arts, Early Childhood Development, Economics, English/Communications, English/Film Studies, Finance, French, General Business, General Science, History, History of Drama, Hotel Management, Human Relations, Human Resources Development, Industrial Relations, Insurance, International Management, International Marketing, Labor Management Relations, Management, Management Information Systems, Management Science, Marketing, Marketing Management, Mathematics, Mathematics/Computer Science, Mathematics/Economics, Medical Technology, Nursing, Office Automation, Office Information Systems, Operations Management, Political Science, Psychology, Real Estate, Respiratory Therapy, Retail Management, Scenic Design, Secondary Education, Social Science, Sociology/Anthropology, Spanish, Speech Communication, Speech Pathology, Theatre Technology.
**Distribution of degrees:** The majors with the highest enrollment are accounting, marketing, and management; foreign languages have the lowest.
**Requirements:** General education requirement.
**Academic regulations:** Minimum 2.0 GPA required for graduation.
**Special:** Minors offered in many majors and in applied statistics, art history, human services, and youth agency administration. Associate's degrees offered. Double majors. Independent study. Internships. Cooperative education programs. Graduate school at which undergraduates may take graduate-level courses. Preprofessional programs in medicine and dentistry. Cooperative diagnostic medical sonography and medical records administration programs with SUNY Downstate Medical Center. B.A./M.B.A., B.S./M.B.A., and B.B.A./M.B.A. programs. Cross-registration with Pleasantville/Briarcliff and White Plains campuses. Teacher certification in early childhood and secondary education. Study abroad possible. AFROTC at Manhattan Coll.
**Honors:** Honors program.
**Academic Assistance:** Nonremedial tutoring.

**STUDENT LIFE. Housing:** Students may live on or off campus. Coed dorms. 10% of students live in college housing.
**Social atmosphere:** According to the editor of the student newspaper, many students are commuters, so the social life on campus is pretty much limited to organizational activities. On campus, students migrate to the Student Union and the cafeteria. Off campus, they head for Killarney Rose. Influential groups are the Alpha Chi Epsilon fraternity and the Caribbean Student Association. Most popular annual event is Spirit Night in November.
**Services and counseling/handicapped student services:** Placement services. Health service. Counseling services for veteran students. Personal counseling. Career and academic guidance services. Physically disabled student services.
**Campus organizations:** Undergraduate student government. Student newspaper (Pace Press, published bimonthly). Literary magazine. Yearbook. Radio and TV stations. Music club, drama group, World Politics Society, service groups. Five fraternities, no chapter houses; five sororities, no chapter houses.
**Religious organizations:** Newman Club, Jewish Student Association, Christian Fellowship.
**Minority/foreign student organizations:** Black Student Organization. Asian Cultural Society, Caribbean Student Association, International Student Organization.

**ATHLETICS. Physical education requirements:** None.
**Intercollegiate competition:** 3% of students participate. Baseball (M), basketball (M,W), cross-country (M,W), football (M), lacrosse (M), softball (W), tennis (M,W), track (indoor) (M,W), track (outdoor) (M,W), track and field (indoor) (M,W), track and field (outdoor) (M,W), volleyball (W). Member of ECAC, NCAA, NYCAC.
**Intramural and club sports:** 25% of students participate. Intramural badminton, basketball, football, golf, softball, tennis, volleyball. Men's club ice hockey. Women's club cheerleading, horsemanship.

**ADMISSIONS. Academic basis for candidate selection** (in order of priority): Secondary school record, school's recommendation, standardized test scores, class rank, essay.
**Nonacademic basis for candidate selection:** Character and personality, extracurricular participation, particular talent or ability, and alumni/ae relationship are considered.
**Requirements:** Graduation from secondary school is required; GED is accepted. 16 units and the following program of study are required: 4 units of English, 2 units of math, 2 units of lab science, 2 units of foreign language, 3 units of social studies, 4 units of electives. SAT or ACT is required. ACH recommended. Campus visit and interview recommended. No off-campus interviews.
**Procedure:** Take SAT or ACT by fall of 12th year. Application deadline is August 15. Notification of admission on rolling basis. Reply is required by May 1. $100 nonrefundable tuition deposit. $250 nonrefundable room deposit. Freshmen accepted for terms other than fall.
**Special programs:** Admission may be deferred two semesters. Credit and/or placement may be granted through CEEB Advanced Placement exams for scores of 3 or higher. Credit may be granted through CLEP general and subject exams. Credit and placement may be granted through challenge exams and military and life experience. Early decision program. Deadline for applying for early decision is November 1. Early entrance/early admission program.
**Transfer students:** Transfer students accepted for terms other than fall. Application deadline is rolling for fall; rolling for spring. Minimum 2.5 GPA required. Lowest course grade accepted is "C." Maximum number of transferable credits is 68 semester hours from a two-year school and 96 semester hours from a four-year school. At least 32 semester hours must be completed at the university to receive degree.
**Admissions contact:** Mark J. Brooks, University Director of Admissions. 212 346-1323.

**FINANCIAL AID. Available aid:** Pell grants, SEOG, state scholarships and grants, school scholarships and grants, private scholarships and grants, academic merit scholarships, and athletic scholarships. Perkins Loans (NDSL), PLUS, Stafford Loans (GSL), NSL, private loans, and SLS. Tuition Plan Inc., AMS, and deferred payment plan.
**Supporting data/closing dates:** FAFSA/FAF/FFS: Priority filing date is March 15. Notification of awards on rolling basis.
**Financial aid contact:** James Hanbury, University Director of Financial Aid. 212 346-1300.

**STUDENT EMPLOYMENT.** College Work/Study Program. Institutional employment. 9% of full-time undergraduates work on campus during school year. Students may expect to earn an average of $1,500 during school year. Off-campus part-time employment opportunities rated "excellent."

**COMPUTER FACILITIES.** 150 IBM/IBM-compatible microcomputers. Computer languages and software packages include APL, Assembler, BASIC, COBOL, FORTRAN, Pascal, PL/C, Pascal; 29 in all. Computer facilities are available to all students.
**Fees:** None.

## Pace University (Pleasantville/Briarcliff)

Pleasantville, NY 10570 914 773-3300

**1993-94 Costs.** Tuition: $10,480. Room: $3,320. Board: $1,340. Fees, books, misc. academic expenses (school's estimate): $800.
**Enrollment.** Undergraduates: 1,340 men, 1,566 women (full-time).
**Test score averages/ranges.** Average SAT scores: 438 verbal, 506 math.
**Faculty.** 512 full-time; 700 part-time. 70% of faculty holds doctoral degree. Student/faculty ratio: 22 to 1.
**Selectivity rating.** Less competitive.

**PROFILE.** Pace, Pleasantville/Briarcliff, founded in 1962, is a private, comprehensive university. Programs are offered through the Colleges of Arts and Sciences; the Schools of Computer Science and Information Systems, Business, Education, Nursing, and Law; the University College; and the Graduate Center. Its 200-acre campus is located in Pleasantville, 20 miles north of New York City.

**Accreditation:** MSACS. Professionally accredited by the National League for Nursing.
**Religious orientation:** Pace University (Pleasantville/Briarcliff) is nonsectarian; no religious requirements.
**Library:** Collections totaling over 186,176 volumes, 1,301 periodical subscriptions, and 14,308 microform items.
**Special facilities/museums:** Museum/gallery.
**Athletic facilities:** Basketball, tennis, and volleyball courts, baseball, football, lacrosse, soccer, and softball fields, gymnasiums, fitness centers, swimming pool.

**STUDENT BODY. Undergraduate profile:** 71% are state residents; 37% are transfers. 2% Asian-American, 3% Black, 5% Hispanic, 1% Native American, 87% White, 2% Other.

**PROGRAMS OF STUDY. Degrees:** B.A., B.Bus.Admin., B.F.A., B.S., B.S.Nurs.
**Majors:** Accounting, Advertising, Art, Biochemistry, Biological Sciences, Biology, Business Education, Chemistry, Computer Science, Criminal Justice, Economics, Elementary Education, Entrepreneurship, Finance, French, General Business, Global Studies, History, Human Relations, Human Resources Development, Information Systems, International Management, International Marketing, Literature/Communications, Management, Management Information Systems, Marketing, Marketing Management, Mathematics, Medical Technology, Nursing, Office Automation, Operations Management, Physics, Political Science, Psychology, Retail Management, Science/Physics Concentration, Secondary Education, Social Science, Sociology/Anthropology, Spanish, Urban Studies.
**Distribution of degrees:** The majors with the highest enrollment are accounting, marketing, and management; foreign languages have the lowest.
**Special:** Minors offered in most majors and in business, equine science, music, philosophy, religious studies, and statistics. Associate's degrees offered. Double majors. Independent study. Pass/fail grading option. Internships. Graduate school at which undergraduates may take graduate-level courses. Preprofessional programs in medicine and dentistry. 3-2 electrical and chemical engineering programs with Manhattan Coll. B.A./M.B.A., B.S./M.B.A., and B.B.A./M.B.A. programs. Cross-registration with New York City and White Plains campuses. Teacher certification in secondary education. Study abroad possible. AFROTC at Manhattan Coll.
**Honors:** Honors program.
**Academic Assistance:** Nonremedial tutoring.

**STUDENT LIFE. Housing:** Students may live on or off campus. Coed dorms. 52% of students live in college housing.
**Social atmosphere:** According to the editor of the student newspaper, campus life has improved since the recent adoption of a student activities fee. On campus, students migrate to the Campus Center, and they head off campus for Foley's Club and Lock, Stock, and Barrel in Pleasantville. Favorite annual events center around Homecoming, spring and winter formals, campus concerts, the Ray Boston Party, and the campus movies.
**Services and counseling/handicapped student services:** Placement services. Health service. Counseling services for veteran students. Personal counseling. Career and academic guidance services.
**Campus organizations:** Undergraduate student government. Student newspaper (New Morning, published twice/month). Literary magazine. Yearbook. Radio station. Glee club, dance club, Parnassus Players, debating, Peer Helpers, Student Affairs Committee, Commuter Council. Four fraternities, no chapter houses; four sororities, no chapter houses.
**Religious organizations:** Hillel, Newman Apostolate, Campus Crusade for Christ, Jewish Student Association.
**Minority/foreign student organizations:** UMOJA. International Student Organization, Organizacion Latino Espanola.

**ATHLETICS. Physical education requirements:** None.
**Intercollegiate competition:** 3% of students participate. Baseball (M), basketball (M), cross-country (M,W), football (M), horsemanship (W), lacrosse (M), softball (W), tennis (M,W), track (indoor) (M,W), track (outdoor) (M,W), track and field (indoor) (M,W), track and field (outdoor) (M,W), volleyball (W). Member of ECAC, NCAA Division I for baseball, NCAA Division II, New York Collegiate Athletic Conference (NYCAC).
**Intramural and club sports:** 25% of students participate. Intramural football, soccer, softball, tennis, volleyball. Men's club ice hockey. Women's club cheerleading, equestrian sports, riding.

**ADMISSIONS. Academic basis for candidate selection** (in order of priority): Secondary school record, school's recommendation, standardized test scores, class rank, essay.
**Nonacademic basis for candidate selection:** Character and personality, extracurricular participation, particular talent or ability, and alumni/ae relationship are considered.
**Requirements:** Graduation from secondary school is required; GED is accepted. 16 units and the following program of study are required: 4 units of English, 2 units of math, 2 units of lab science, 2 units of foreign language, 3 units of social studies, 4 units of electives. Portfolio required of art program applicants. SAT or ACT is required. ACH recommended. Campus visit and interview recommended. No off-campus interviews.
**Procedure:** Take SAT or ACT by fall of 12th year. Visit college for interview by January of 12th year. Suggest filing application by August 15; no deadline. Notification of admission on rolling basis. No set date by which applicants must accept offer. $100 nonrefundable tuition deposit. $250 nonrefundable room deposit. Freshmen accepted for terms other than fall.
**Special programs:** Admission may be deferred two semesters. Credit and/or placement may be granted through CEEB Advanced Placement exams for scores of 3 or higher. Credit and/or placement may be granted through CLEP general and subject exams. Credit and placement may be granted through challenge exams and military and life experience. Early decision program. Deadline for applying for early decision is November 1. Early entrance/early admission program.
**Transfer students:** Transfer students accepted for terms other than fall. Application deadline is August 15 for fall; January 15 for spring. Minimum 2.5 GPA required. Lowest course grade accepted is "C." Maximum number of transferable credits is 68 semester hours from a two-year school and 96 semester hours from a four-year school. At least 32 semester hours must be completed at the university to receive degree.
**Admissions contact:** Mark J. Brooks, University Director of Admissions. 914 773-3746.

**FINANCIAL AID. Available aid:** Pell grants, SEOG, state scholarships and grants, school scholarships and grants, private grants, academic merit scholarships, and athletic scholarships. Perkins Loans (NDSL), PLUS, Stafford Loans (GSL), NSL, private loans, and SLS. Tuition Plan Inc., AMS, and deferred payment plan.
**Supporting data/closing dates:** FAFSA/FAF/FFS: Priority filing date is March 15. Notification of awards on rolling basis.
**Financial aid contact:** James Hanbury, University Director of Financial Aid. 914 773-3751.

**STUDENT EMPLOYMENT.** College Work/Study Program. Institutional employment. Students may expect to earn an average of $1,500 during school year. Off-campus part-time employment opportunities rated "good."

**COMPUTER FACILITIES.** 150 IBM/IBM-compatible microcomputers. Computer languages and software packages include APL, Assembler, BASIC, COBOL, FORTRAN, Pascal, PL/C; 29 in all. Computer facilities are available to all students.
**Fees:** None.

## Pace University (White Plains)

White Plains, NY 10603 914 422-4000

**1993-94 Costs.** Tuition: $10,480. Room: $3,320. Board: $1,340. Fees, books, misc. academic expenses (school's estimate): $800.
**Enrollment.** Undergraduates: 305 men, 493 women (full-time). Graduate enrollment: 855 men, 963 women.
**Test score averages/ranges.** Average SAT scores: 436 verbal, 486 math.
**Faculty.** 512 full-time; 700 part-time. 70% of faculty holds doctoral degree. Student/faculty ratio: 22 to 1.
**Selectivity rating.** Less competitive.

**PROFILE.** Pace, White Plains, founded in 1906, is a private, comprehensive university. Programs are offered through the Colleges of Arts and Sciences; the Schools of Computer Science and Information Systems, Business, Education, Nursing, and Law; the University College; and the Graduate Center. Its 15-acre campus is located in White Plains, 15 miles from New York City.

**Accreditation:** MSACS. Professionally accredited by the American Bar Association.
**Religious orientation:** Pace University (White Plains) is nonsectarian; no religious requirements.
**Library:** Collections totaling over 99,962 volumes, 918 periodical subscriptions, and 34,278 microform items.
**Athletic facilities:** Baseball, football, lacrosse, soccer, and softball fields, basketball, tennis, and volleyball courts, bowling lanes, goft course, coross–country track, fencing room.

**STUDENT BODY. Undergraduate profile:** 86% are state residents; 42% are transfers. 4% Asian-American, 8% Black, 7% Hispanic, 1% Native American, 77% White, 3% Other.

**PROGRAMS OF STUDY. Degrees:** B.A., B.Bus.Admin., B.F.A., B.S., B.S.Nurs.
**Majors:** Accounting, Advertising, Biology, Business Education, Chemistry, Computer Science, Economics, Elementary Education, English/Communications, Entrepreneurship, Finance, French, History, Human Relations, Human Resources Development, Human Services, Information Systems, International Management, International Marketing, Journalism, Management, Management Information Systems, Marketing, Marketing Management, Mathematics, Office Automation, Office Information Systems, Operations Management, Political Science, Psychology, Retail Management, Secondary Education, Sociology/Anthropology, Spanish.
**Distribution of degrees:** The majors with the highest enrollment are accounting, marketing, and management; foreign languages have the lowest.
**Requirements:** General education requirement.
**Special:** Minors offered in most majors and in art, business, criminal justice, global studies, human relations, information systems, music, philosophy, psychology, religious studies, statistics, and theatrical arts. Associate's degrees offered. Double majors. Independent study. Pass/fail grading option. Internships. Cooperative education programs. Graduate school at which undergraduates may take graduate-level courses. Preprofessional programs in law and medicine. 3-2 electrical and chemical engineering programs with Manhattan Coll. B.A./M.B.A., B.S./M.B.A., B.B.A./M.B.A., and B.A./M.P.A. programs. Cross-registration with New York City and Pleasantville campuses. Teacher certification in early childhood, elementary, and secondary education. Study abroad possible. AFROTC at Manhattan Coll.
**Honors:** Honors program.
**Academic Assistance:** Nonremedial tutoring.

**ADMISSIONS. Academic basis for candidate selection** (in order of priority): Secondary school record, school's recommendation, standardized test scores, class rank, essay.
**Nonacademic basis for candidate selection:** Character and personality are emphasized. Extracurricular participation, particular talent or ability, geographical distribution, and alumni/ae relationship are considered.
**Requirements:** Graduation from secondary school is required; GED is accepted. 16 units required and the following program of study recommended: 4 units of English, 2 units of math, 2 units of science, 2 units of foreign language, 2 units of social studies, 2 units of history, 4 units of electives. Conditional admission possible for applicants not meeting standard requirements. SAT or ACT is required. ACH recommended. Campus visit and interview recommended. No off-campus interviews.
**Procedure:** Suggest filing application by fall; no deadline. Notification of admission on rolling basis. No set date by which applicants must accept offer. $100 nonrefundable tuition deposit. $250 nonrefundable room deposit. Freshmen accepted for terms other than fall.
**Special programs:** Admission may be deferred two semesters. Credit and/or placement may be granted through CEEB Advanced Placement exams for scores of 3 or higher. Credit and/or placement may be granted through CLEP general and subject exams. Credit and placement may be granted through challenge exams and military and life experience. Early decision program. Deadline for applying for early decision is November 1. Early entrance/early admission program.
**Transfer students:** Transfer students accepted for terms other than fall. Application deadline is August 15 for fall; January 15 for spring. Minimum 2.5 GPA required. Lowest course grade accepted is "C." Maximum number of transferable credits is 68 semester hours from a two-year school and 96 semester hours from a four-year school. Maximum number of transferable credits is 68 semester hours from two-year schools; 96 from four-year schools. At least 32 semester hours must be completed at the university to receive degree.
**Admissions contact:** Mark J. Brooks, University Director of Admissions. 914 422-4070.

**FINANCIAL AID. Available aid:** Pell grants, SEOG, state scholarships and grants, school scholarships and grants, private scholarships and grants, academic merit scholarships, and athletic scholarships. Perkins Loans (NDSL), PLUS, Stafford Loans (GSL), NSL, private loans, and SLS. Tuition Plan Inc., AMS, and deferred payment plan.
**Supporting data/closing dates:** FAFSA/FAF/FFS: Priority filing date is March 15. Notification of awards on rolling basis.
**Financial aid contact:** James Hanbury, University Director of Financial Aid. 914 422-4050.

## Parsons School of Design

New York, NY 10011 212 229-8900

**1994-95 Costs.** Tuition: $15,030. Room: $6,240. Board: $4,380. Fees, books, misc. academic expenses (school's estimate): $1,750.
**Enrollment.** Undergraduates: 504 men, 1,123 women (full-time). Freshman class: 932 applicants, 694 accepted, 370 enrolled. Graduate enrollment: 45 men, 92 women.
**Test score averages/ranges.** Average SAT scores: 460 verbal, 490 math.
**Faculty.** 35 full-time; 350 part-time. Student/faculty ratio: 15 to 1.
**Selectivity rating.** N/A.

**PROFILE.** Parsons School of Design is a private college of the arts. Founded as a coeducational institution in 1896, it became affiliated with the New School for Social Research in 1970. Its two-acre campus is located in New York City.

**Accreditation:** MSACS. Professionally accredited by the National Association of Schools of Art and Design.
**Religious orientation:** Parsons School of Design is nonsectarian; no religious requirements.
**Library:** Collections totaling over 45,000 volumes, 250 periodical subscriptions, and 35,000 microform items.
**Special facilities/museums:** Fashion Education Center in New York's garment district with labs and studios for fashion design students.

**STUDENT BODY. Undergraduate profile:** 40% are state residents; 50% are transfers. 9% Asian-American, 3% Black, 4% Hispanic, 46% White, 38% Other. Average age of undergraduates is 20.
**Freshman profile:** Majority of accepted applicants took SAT.
**Undergraduate achievement:** 88% of fall 1992 freshmen returned for fall 1993 term. 75% of entering class graduated. 10% of students who completed a degree program went on to graduate study within one year.
**Foreign students:** 151 students are from out of the country. Countries represented include Canada, China, France, Hong Kong, Japan, and Korea; 60 in all.

**PROGRAMS OF STUDY. Degrees:** B.A./B.F.A., B.Bus.Admin., B.F.A.
**Majors:** Communication Design, Design Marketing, Environmental Design, Fashion Design, Fine Arts, Illustration, Interior Design, Photography, Product Design.
**Requirements:** General education requirement.
**Special:** Minors offered in art education and art history. Professional certificates offered. Courses offered in English and humanities, math, natural sciences, printmaking, and social sciences. Associate's degrees offered. Dual degrees. Graduate school at which undergraduates may take graduate-level courses. Five-year B.A./B.F.A. program with Eugene Lang Coll of New Sch for Social Research. Member of Association of Independent Colleges of Art and Design (AICAD); exchange possible. Teacher certification in elementary and secondary education. Study abroad in France, Israel, the Netherlands, Sweden, and the United Kingdom.
**Academic Assistance:** Nonremedial tutoring.

**STUDENT LIFE. Housing:** Students may live on or off campus. Coed dorms. School-owned/operated apartments. 35% of students live in college housing.
**Services and counseling/handicapped student services:** Placement services. Personal and psychological counseling. Career and academic guidance services.
**Campus organizations:** Undergraduate student government. Student newspaper (Parsons Paper). Literary magazine. Exhibition committee, annual exhibition/fashion show.
**Minority/foreign student organizations:** Black Student Association. International Student Association.

**ATHLETICS. Physical education requirements:** None.

**ADMISSIONS. Academic basis for candidate selection** (in order of priority): Portfolio, secondary school record, standardized test scores, school's recommendation, class rank.
**Nonacademic basis for candidate selection:** Particular talent or ability is emphasized. Character and personality and extracurricular participation are considered.
**Requirements:** Graduation from secondary school is required; GED is accepted. 16 units required and the following program of study recommended: 4 units of English, 4 units of social studies. Well-rounded secondary school program in academic subjects, with as much artwork as program will allow, and above-average grades recommended. Portfolio (minimum of 12 pieces) and home art test required. Conditional admission possible for applicants not meeting standard requirements. HEOP for in-state applicants not normally admissible. SAT or ACT is required. Campus visit and interview recommended. No off-campus interviews.
**Procedure:** Suggest filing application by March 1. Application deadline is July 1. Notification of admission on rolling basis. Reply is required by May 1 or within one month of acceptance. $300 nonrefundable tuition deposit. $220 nonrefundable room deposit. Freshmen accepted for terms other than fall.
**Special programs:** Credit and/or placement may be granted through CEEB Advanced Placement exams for scores of 4 or higher. Early entrance/early admission program.
**Transfer students:** Transfer students accepted for terms other than fall. In fall 1993, 50% of all new students were transfers into all classes. Application deadline is July 1 for fall; December 1 for spring. Minimum 2.0 GPA required. Lowest course grade accepted is "C." Maximum number of transferable credits is 67 semester hours. At least 67 semester hours must be completed at the college to receive degree.
**Admissions contact:** Nadine M. Bourgeois, M.A., Director of Admissions. 212 229-8910, 800 252-0852, FAX 212 229-8975.

**FINANCIAL AID. Available aid:** Pell grants, SEOG, state scholarships and grants, school scholarships and grants, private scholarships and grants, and aid for undergraduate

foreign students. Perkins Loans (NDSL), PLUS, Stafford Loans (GSL), state loans, private loans, and SLS. School-administered extended payment plan.
**Financial aid statistics:** In 1993-94, 80% of all undergraduate applicants received aid; 80% of freshman applicants. Average amounts of aid awarded freshmen: Scholarships and grants, $3,070.
**Supporting data/closing dates:** FAFSA/FAF: Priority filing date is March 1; accepted on rolling basis. School's own aid application: Priority filing date is March 1; accepted on rolling basis. Notification of awards on rolling basis.
**Financial aid contact:** Nancy Brewer, M.B.A., Director of Financial Aid. 212 229-8930.

**STUDENT EMPLOYMENT.** College Work/Study Program. Institutional employment. 22% of full-time undergraduates work on campus during school year. Students may expect to earn an average of $1,500 during school year. Freshmen are discouraged from working during their first term. Off-campus part-time employment opportunities rated "good."

**COMPUTER FACILITIES.** IBM/IBM-compatible and Macintosh/Apple microcomputers. Client/LAN operating systems include Apple/Macintosh, DOS, UNIX/XENIX/AIX, Novell. Numerous computer languages and software packages available. Computers are available only to students enrolled in computer classes; departmental permission required.
**Fees:** None.

**GRADUATE CAREER DATA.** Highest graduate school enrollments: Columbia U, Yale U.

**PROMINENT ALUMNI/AE.** Donna Karan, fashion designer; Peter De Seve, illustrator; Arthur Kugelman, graphic designer; Michael Bray, interior designer.

# Polytechnic University

**Brooklyn, NY 11201** **718 260-3600**

**1994-95 Costs.** Tuition: $16,200. Room & board: $4,700. Fees, books, misc. academic expenses (school's estimate): $797.
**Enrollment.** Undergraduates: 1,186 men, 193 women (full-time). Freshman class: 1,132 applicants, 847 accepted, 302 enrolled. Graduate enrollment: 1,749 men, 295 women.
**Test score averages/ranges.** Average SAT scores: 480 verbal, 630 math. Range of SAT scores of middle 50%: 410-560 verbal, 560-670 math.
**Faculty.** 176 full-time; 126 part-time. 90% of faculty holds doctoral degree. Student/faculty ratio: 14 to 1.
**Selectivity rating.** Highly competitive.

**PROFILE.** Polytechnic is a private university. Founded in 1854, it adopted coeducation in 1935, and merged with New York University's School of Engineering and Science in 1973. Programs are offered through the Divisions of Arts and Sciences, Engineering, and Management. Its main campus is located in Brooklyn.

**Accreditation:** MSACS. Professionally accredited by the Accreditation Board for Engineering and Technology.
**Religious orientation:** Polytechnic University is nonsectarian; no religious requirements.
**Library:** Collections totaling over 350,000 volumes, 2,000 periodical subscriptions, and 56,648 microform items.
**Special facilities/museums:** Electron microscope, supersonic windtunnel.
**Athletic facilities:** Weight room, gymnasium, racquetball courts, athletic fields.

**STUDENT BODY. Undergraduate profile:** 97% are state residents. 33% Asian-American, 11% Black, 8% Hispanic, 41% White, 7% Other. Average age of undergraduates is 21.
**Freshman profile:** 99% of accepted applicants took SAT; 1% took ACT. 77% of freshmen come from public schools.
**Undergraduate achievement:** 75% of fall 1992 freshmen returned for fall 1993 term. 28% of entering class graduated. 15% of students who completed a degree program went on to graduate study within one year.
**Foreign students:** 22 students are from out of the country. Countries represented include China, Hong Kong, India, Israel, Korea, and Pakistan; 12 in all.

**PROGRAMS OF STUDY. Degrees:** B.S.
**Majors:** Aerospace Engineering, Chemical Engineering, Chemistry, Civil Engineering, Computer Engineering, Computer Science, Electrical Engineering, Environmental Engineering, Environmental Science, Humanities, Industrial Engineering, Mathematics, Mechanical Engineering, Physics, Social Sciences, Technical Writing/Journalism.
**Distribution of degrees:** The majors with the highest enrollment are electrical engineering, mechanical engineering, and civil engineering; social science has the lowest.
**Requirements:** General education requirement.
**Academic regulations:** Minimum 2.0 GPA must be maintained.
**Special:** Independent study. Accelerated study. Cooperative education programs. Graduate school at which undergraduates may take graduate-level courses. Preprofessional programs in law and medicine. 2-2 engineering program with CUNY Brooklyn Coll. 3-2 engineering programs with Adelphi U, Long Island U-C.W. Post Campus, St. John's U, and SUNY Coll at Oneonta. ROTC. AFROTC at New York Inst of Tech.
**Honors:** Honors program. Honor societies.
**Academic Assistance:** Remedial reading, writing, math, and study skills. Nonremedial tutoring.

**STUDENT LIFE. Housing:** Students may live on or off campus. Coed dorms. Fraternity housing. Housing provided for Brooklyn campus students through Long Island U and Pratt Inst. Two coed dormitories on Long Island campus. 15% of students live in college housing.
**Social atmosphere:** Students gather on campus at the student lounge, in club offices, and at the Cafe Poly. International students, the Society of Hispanic Professional Engineers, and the National Society of Black Engineers are influential groups on campus. Popular events include Club Day, Latin American Day, comedy shows, the Chinese New Year, the spring dance, the Awards Banquet, and the Great Adventure Trip. According to the student newspaper, "Poly is primarily a commuter school, but clubs and organizations are strong and well funded. We have a lot of ethnic diversity."
**Services and counseling/handicapped student services:** Placement services. Personal counseling. Career and academic guidance services. Physically disabled student services. Learning disabled services. Notetaking services. Tape recorders. Tutors.
**Campus organizations:** Undergraduate student government. Student newspaper (Polytechnic Reporter; Bohican). Yearbook. Radio station. Musicians Guild, debating, Astronomical Society, Microcomputer Society, chess and photography clubs, freshman publications, Pershing Rifles, academic, professional, and special-interest groups, 68 organizations in all. Four fraternities, two chapter houses. 17% of men join a fraternity.
**Religious organizations:** Christian Fellowship, Jewish Student Union, Muslim Student Association.
**Minority/foreign student organizations:** Celtic Society, Latin American Association, National Society of Black Engineers, Society of Hispanic Engineers, Society of Women Engineers. International Student Organization, Chinese, Haitian, Iranian, Korean, and Indian groups.

**ATHLETICS. Physical education requirements:** None.
**Intercollegiate competition:** 18% of students participate. Baseball (M), basketball (M), cross-country (M,W), lacrosse (M), martial arts (M,W), soccer (M), softball (W), tennis (M,W), volleyball (W). Member of ECAC, Independent Athletic Conference, NCAA Division III.
**Intramural and club sports:** 12% of students participate. Intramural basketball, football, handball, racquetball, volleyball. Men's club volleyball.

**ADMISSIONS. Academic basis for candidate selection** (in order of priority): Secondary school record, standardized test scores, class rank, school's recommendation.
**Nonacademic basis for candidate selection:** Particular talent or ability is important. Character and personality, extracurricular participation, and alumni/ae relationship are considered.
**Requirements:** Graduation from secondary school is required; GED is accepted. No specific distribution of secondary school units required. Minimum SAT scores of 450 verbal and 550 math and minimum 2.75 GPA required. Additional courses in math and science recommended. HEOP for applicants not normally admissible. SAT is required; ACT may be substituted. ACH recommended. Campus visit and interview recommended. No off-campus interviews.
**Procedure:** Take SAT or ACT by December of 12th year. Suggest filing application by February 1. Notification of admission on rolling basis. Reply is required by May 1. $250 tuition deposit, refundable until May 1. $300 room deposit, refundable until first day of classes. Freshmen accepted for terms other than fall.
**Special programs:** Admission may be deferred one year. Credit may be granted through CEEB Advanced Placement for scores of 4 or higher. Early decision program. In fall 1993, 19 applied for early decision and 15 were accepted. Deadline for applying for early decision is November 1. Early entrance/early admission program. Concurrent enrollment program.
**Transfer students:** Transfer students accepted for terms other than fall. In fall 1993, 379 transfer applications were received, 291 were accepted. Application deadline is rolling for fall; rolling for spring. Minimum 2.75 GPA required. Lowest course grade accepted is "C." At least 34 semester hours must be completed at the university to receive degree.
**Admissions contact:** Peter G. Jordan, Dean of Admissions. 718 260-3100 (Brooklyn), 516 755-4200 (Farmingdale).

**FINANCIAL AID. Available aid:** Pell grants, SEOG, state scholarships and grants, school scholarships and grants, private scholarships and grants, ROTC scholarships, academic merit scholarships, and aid for undergraduate foreign students. Perkins Loans (NDSL), PLUS, Stafford Loans (GSL), state loans, school loans, and SLS. Knight Tuition Plans, EFI Fund Management, and deferred payment plan.
**Financial aid statistics:** 10% of aid is not need-based. In 1993-94, 86% of all undergraduate applicants received aid; 88% of freshman applicants. Average amounts of aid awarded freshmen: Scholarships and grants, $11,758; loans, $2,546.
**Supporting data/closing dates:** FAFSA: Priority filing date is March 1; accepted on rolling basis; deadline is May 1. FAF: Priority filing date is April 15; accepted on rolling basis; deadline is May 1. School's own aid application: Priority filing date is March 1; accepted on rolling basis; deadline is May 1. Notification of awards begins March 15.
**Financial aid contact:** Veronica Lucas, Director of Financial Aid. 718 260-3300.

**STUDENT EMPLOYMENT.** College Work/Study Program. Institutional employment. 30% of full-time undergraduates work on campus during school year. Students may expect to earn an average of $1,500 during school year. Freshmen are discouraged from working during their first term. Off-campus part-time employment opportunities rated "good."

**COMPUTER FACILITIES.** 160 IBM/IBM-compatible, Macintosh/Apple, and RISC-/UNIX-based microcomputers; all are networked. Students may access IBM, SUN minicomputer/mainframe systems, Internet. Client/LAN operating systems include DOS, UNIX/XENIX/AIX, X-windows, Novell. Computer languages and software packages include Assembler, C, COBOL, dBASE, Derive, FORTRAN, Pascal, Prolog, Quattro Pro, SimScript, WordPerfect; 11 in all. Computer facilities are available to all students.
**Fees:** Computer fee is included in tuition/fees.
**Hours:** 8 AM-11 PM (M-F); 10 AM-4 PM (Sa).

**GRADUATE CAREER DATA.** Companies and businesses that hire graduates: IBM, Bell Labs, Grumman, Raytheon, General Dynamics, LILCO, Westinghouse.

# Pratt Institute

**Brooklyn, NY 11205** **718 636-3600**

**1994-95 Costs.** Tuition: $13,975. Room: $4,360. Board: $2,380. Fees, books, misc. academic expenses (school's estimate): $1,880.
**Enrollment.** Undergraduates: 1,050 men, 606 women (full-time). Freshman class: 1,127 applicants, 879 accepted, 304 enrolled. Graduate enrollment: 461 men, 577 women.
**Test score averages/ranges.** Average SAT scores: 469 verbal, 524 math. Range of SAT scores of middle 50%: 340-490 verbal, 430-580 math.
**Faculty.** 110 full-time; 371 part-time. 83% of faculty holds highest degree in specific field. Student/faculty ratio: 12 to 1.
**Selectivity rating.** Less competitive.

**PROFILE.** Pratt Institute, founded in 1887, is a private, multipurpose institute. Programs are offered through the Schools of Architecture, Art and Design, and Engineering. Its 25-acre campus is located in Brooklyn.

**Accreditation:** MSACS. Professionally accredited by the Foundation for Interior Design Education Research, the National Architecture Accrediting Board, the National Association of Schools of Art and Design.
**Religious orientation:** Pratt Institute is nonsectarian; no religious requirements.
**Library:** Collections totaling over 208,174 volumes, 500 periodical subscriptions, and 50,000 microform items.
**Special facilities/museums:** Art gallery, fine arts center, printmaking center, computer graphics lab.
**Athletic facilities:** Athletic courts, gymnasium, indoor track, saunas, weight rooms, dance studios, soccer field.

**STUDENT BODY. Undergraduate profile:** 54% are state residents; 29% are transfers. 13% Asian-American, 10% Black, 9% Hispanic, 55% White, 13% Other. Average age of undergraduates is 23.
**Freshman profile:** 2% of freshmen who took SAT scored 700 or over on verbal, 5% scored 700 or over on math; 17% scored 600 or over on verbal, 35% scored 600 or over on math; 44% scored 500 or over on verbal, 64% scored 500 or over on math; 72% scored 400 or over on verbal, 81% scored 400 or over on math; 82% scored 300 or over on verbal, 97% scored 300 or over on math. 75% of accepted applicants took SAT; 1% took ACT. 81% of freshmen come from public schools.
**Undergraduate achievement:** 90% of fall 1992 freshmen returned for fall 1993 term. 55% of entering class graduated. 4% of students who completed a degree program went on to graduate study within one year.
**Foreign students:** 254 students are from out of the country. Countries represented include Hong Kong, Israel, Japan, Korea, Taiwan, and Thailand; 59 in all.

**PROGRAMS OF STUDY. Degrees:** B.Arch., B.F.A., B.Indust.Design, B.Prof.Studies, B.S.
**Majors:** Architecture, Art Education, Art History, Communications Design, Computer Graphics, Construction Management, Fashion Design, Film/Video, Fine Arts, Industrial Design, Interior Design, Merchandising/Fashion Management, Photography.
**Distribution of degrees:** The majors with the highest enrollment are architecture, electrical engineering, and communications design; computer science, chemical engineering, and merchandising have the lowest.
**Requirements:** General education requirement.
**Academic regulations:** Minimum 2.0 GPA must be maintained.
**Special:** Associate's degrees offered. Dual degrees. Independent study. Internships. Graduate school at which undergraduates may take graduate-level courses. Combined B.Arch./M.Arch., B.Arch./M.S., B.S./B.P.S. programs in architecture. Combined B.F.A./M.S., B.F.A./M.F.A., B.I.D./M.I.D., B.I.D./M.S., M.S./M.F.A., and M.S./M.S. programs. Combined M.S./J.D. program with Brooklyn Law Sch. Member of East Coast Consortium of Schools of Art and Design. Teacher certification in elementary, secondary, and special education. Certification in specific subject areas. Study abroad in Denmark, Italy, and Japan. ROTC at four local universities.
**Honors:** Honor societies.
**Academic Assistance:** Remedial study skills.

**STUDENT LIFE. Housing:** Students may live on or off campus. Coed dorms. School-owned/operated apartments. On-campus married-student housing. 41% of students live in college housing.
**Social atmosphere:** On campus, students gather at art openings or in art studios. Bars, music clubs, and museums are popular off-campus spots. Influential campus groups include Greeks, the Pratt House Project in Restoration and Communal Living, the Parties and Concerts Committee, and Encore, a comedy organization. Favorite campus events are the International Food Fair, Encore comedy nights, parties sponsored by the Hispanic Association, and performances by Hot Walrus, a student band. "The Pratt community consists of very creative, artistic students. Although big parties on campus are attended, most students are involved with individual interests and with the scene outside the campus," reports the student newspaper.
**Services and counseling/handicapped student services:** Placement services. Health service. Birth control, personal, and psychological counseling. Career and academic guidance services. Religious counseling. Physically disabled student services. Learning disabled services. Notetaking services. Tutors. Reader services for the blind.
**Campus organizations:** Undergraduate student government. Student newspaper (Prattler, published once/month). Literary magazine. Yearbook. Radio station. Fashion society, film society, comedy club, aerobics club, cycling club, martial arts club, ski club, Inter-Greek Council, Pratt Ambassadors, Commuting Students Organization, Environmental Resource Group, Gay/Lesbians/Bisexuals at Pratt, PIRG, Student Alumni Council, 50 organizations in all. Three fraternities, one chapter house; one sorority, no chapter house. 2% of men join a fraternity. 1% of women join a sorority.
**Religious organizations:** Christian Fellowship, Jewish Student Union, Muslim Student Association.
**Minority/foreign student organizations:** Black Architecture Coalition, The Agenda, Hispanic Student Union, Women's History Month Committee. International Student Organization, Asian Student Organization, Caribbean South American Club, Chinese Student Club, Indian Student Club, Korean Student Association, Vietnamese Student Organization.

**ATHLETICS. Physical education requirements:** None.
**Intercollegiate competition:** 10% of students participate. Basketball (M), cross-country (M,W), soccer (M), tennis (M,W), track (indoor) (M,W), track (outdoor) (M,W), track and field (indoor) (M,W), track and field (outdoor) (M,W), volleyball (W). Member of CTC, ECAC, Hudson Valley Women's Athletic Conference, MCTC, NCAA Division III, WFC.
**Intramural and club sports:** 25% of students participate. Intramural aerobics, basketball, flag football, indoor track, martial arts, running, soccer, table tennis, tennis, volleyball, weight lifting. Men's club martial arts, volleyball. Women's club martial arts.

**ADMISSIONS. Academic basis for candidate selection** (in order of priority): Secondary school record, class rank, standardized test scores, school's recommendation, essay.
**Nonacademic basis for candidate selection:** Particular talent or ability is emphasized. Character and personality are important. Extracurricular participation and alumni/ae relationship are considered.
**Requirements:** Graduation from secondary school is required; GED is accepted. 14 units and the following program of study are recommended: 4 units of English, 2 units of math, 2 units of science, 2 units of social studies, 2 units of history, 2 units of electives. Minimum combined SAT score of 900 and rank in top fifth of secondary school class or minimum 2.8 GPA recommended. Portfolio required of architecture and art program applicants. HEOP for applicants not normally admissible. Conditional admission possible for applicants not meeting standard requirements. SAT or ACT is required. ACH recommended. Campus visit and interview recommended. Off-campus interviews available with admissions and alumni representatives.
**Procedure:** Take SAT or ACT by January of 12th year. Take ACH by April of 12th year. Visit college for interview by March of 12th year. Suggest filing application by February 1. Notification of admission on rolling basis. Reply is required by May 1 or within two weeks of acceptance. $200 nonrefundable tuition deposit. $150 refundable room deposit and $150 one-time security deposit. Freshmen accepted for terms other than fall.
**Special programs:** Admission may be deferred one year. Credit and/or placement may be granted through CEEB Advanced Placement exams for scores of 3 or higher. Credit and/or placement may be granted through CLEP general and subject exams. Early decision program. Deadline for applying for early decision is December 1.
**Transfer students:** Transfer students accepted for terms other than fall. In fall 1993, 29% of all new students were transfers into all classes. 526 transfer applications were received, 422 were accepted. Application deadline is rolling for fall; rolling for spring. Minimum 2.0 GPA required. Lowest course grade accepted is "C." Maximum number of transferable credits is one quarter of total required for degree. At least 48 semester hours must be completed at the institute to receive degree.
**Admissions contact:** Judith Aaron, M.L.S., Dean of Admissions. 718 636-3669, 800 331-0834.

**FINANCIAL AID. Available aid:** Pell grants, SEOG, state scholarships and grants, school scholarships and grants, private scholarships and grants, and academic merit scholarships. Perkins Loans (NDSL), PLUS, Stafford Loans (GSL), school loans, and SLS. Knight Tuition Plans and deferred payment plan. Tuition Installment Plan. VISA/MasterCard. Universal Education Loan. Chemical Bank Educational Finance Programs.
**Financial aid statistics:** 14% of aid is not need-based. In 1993-94, 93% of all undergraduate applicants received aid; 98% of freshman applicants. Average amounts of aid awarded freshmen: Scholarships and grants, $6,385; loans, $3,375.
**Supporting data/closing dates:** FAFSA/FAF/FFS: Priority filing date is March 1. School's own aid application: Priority filing date is March 1. Income tax forms: Priority filing date is April 15. Notification of awards on rolling basis.
**Financial aid contact:** Joan Warren, Director of Financial Aid. 718 636-3599.

**STUDENT EMPLOYMENT.** College Work/Study Program. Institutional employment. 32% of full-time undergraduates work on campus during school year. Students may expect to earn an average of $2,100 during school year. Off-campus part-time employment opportunities rated "excellent."

**COMPUTER FACILITIES.** 250 IBM/IBM-compatible, Macintosh/Apple, and RISC-/UNIX-based microcomputers; 100 are networked. Students may access SUN minicomputer/mainframe systems, BITNET. Residence halls may be equipped with stand-alone microcomputers. Client/LAN operating systems include Apple/Macintosh, LocalTalk/AppleTalk. Computer languages and software packages include Autocad, Cubicorp picturemaker, Lumera paint system, Tips paint/image processing program; computer-aided mapping, 3-D modeling and animation, rendering, simulation, spreadsheet, and telecommunications packages; 100 in all. Computer facilities are available to all students.
**Fees:** None.
**Hours:** 14-24 hours daily.

**GRADUATE CAREER DATA.** Graduate school percentages: 6% enter graduate business programs. 19% enter graduate arts and sciences programs. 89% of graduates choose careers in business and industry. Companies and businesses that hire graduates: Westinghouse, Doubleday & Co., AT&T, Owings & Merril.

**PROMINENT ALUMNI/AE.** Adele Simpson and Betsey Johnson, fashion designers; Peter Max and Gertrude Schweitzer, artists; Norman Steisel, first deputy mayor, New York City; Robert Redford, film actor and director; Naomi Leff, interior designer; George Segal, sculptor; Tomie DePaola, illustrator; Robert Wilson, artist.

# Rensselaer Polytechnic Institute

Troy, NY 12180 518 276-6000

**1993-94 Costs.** Tuition: $16,800. Room & board: $5,742. Fees, books, misc. academic expenses (school's estimate): $1,050.
**Enrollment.** Undergraduates: 3,427 men, 879 women (full-time). Freshman class: 5,110 applicants, 4,088 accepted, 1,084 enrolled. Graduate enrollment: 1,760 men, 456 women.
**Test score averages/ranges.** Range of SAT scores of middle 50%: 480-590 verbal, 620-710 math. Average ACT scores: 26 composite.
**Faculty.** 99% of faculty holds highest degree in specific field. Student/faculty ratio: 11 to 1.
**Selectivity rating.** Highly competitive.

**PROFILE.** RPI, founded in 1824, is a private, technical institution. Programs are offered through the Schools of Architecture, Engineering, Humanities and Social Sciences, Management, and Science. Its 260-acre campus is located in Troy, 15 miles from Albany.

**Accreditation:** MSACS. Professionally accredited by the Accreditation Board for Engineering and Technology, the American Assembly of Collegiate Schools of Business, the National Architecture Accrediting Board.
**Religious orientation:** Rensselaer Polytechnic Institute is nonsectarian; no religious requirements.
**Library:** Collections totaling over 394,954 volumes, 3,484 periodical subscriptions, and 541,219 microform items.
**Special facilities/museums:** Gallery, iear studios, observatory, fresh water institute at Lake George, technology park, center for industrial innovation, wind tunnel, linear accelerator, incubator center.
**Athletic facilities:** Gymnasiums, field house, swimming pool, weight room, indoor track, wrestling room, ice rink, handball, squash, and tennis courts, athletic fields.

**STUDENT BODY. Undergraduate profile:** 43% are state residents; 17% are transfers. 13% Asian-American, 4% Black, 5% Hispanic, 72% White, 6% Other. Average age of undergraduates is 21.
**Freshman profile:** 95% of accepted applicants took SAT; 5% took ACT. 72% of freshmen come from public schools.
**Undergraduate achievement:** 85% of fall 1992 freshmen returned for fall 1993 term. 20% of students who completed a degree program immediately went on to graduate study.
**Foreign students:** 248 students are from out of the country. Countries represented include Canada, Hong Kong, India, Korea, Malaysia, and Taiwan; 60 in all.

**PROGRAMS OF STUDY. Degrees:** B.Arch., B.S.
**Majors:** Aeronautical Engineering, Architecture, Biochemistry/Biophysics, Bioengineering/Biomedical Engineering, Biology, Building Sciences, Chemical Engineering, Chemistry, Civil Engineering, Communication, Computer Science, Computer/Systems Engineering, Economics, Electric Power Engineering, Electrical Engineering, Engineering Physics, Engineering Science, Environmental Engineering, Geology, Industrial/Management Engineering, Interdisciplinary Science, Management, Materials Engineering, Mathematics, Mechanical Engineering, Mechanics, Nuclear Engineering, Philosophy, Physics, Psychology, Science/Technology Studies.
**Distribution of degrees:** The majors with the highest enrollment are mechanical engineering, electrical engineering, and biology.
**Requirements:** General education requirement.
**Academic regulations:** Freshmen must maintain minimum 1.6 GPA; sophomores, 1.7 GPA; juniors, 1.8 GPA; seniors, 1.8 GPA.
**Special:** Courses offered in French and German. Double majors. Dual degrees. Accelerated study. Pass/fail grading option. Internships. Cooperative education programs. Graduate school at which undergraduates may take graduate-level courses. Preprofessional programs in law, medicine, and dentistry. 2-2 engineering and/or science programs with 146 community colleges. 3-2, 3-3, and 4-2 engineering programs with over 20 liberal arts institutions. Six-year combined B.S./M.D. program in biology/medicine with Albany Medical Coll. Six-year B.S./D.M.D. program in biology/dentistry with U of Pennsylvania Sch of Dental Medicine. Six-year B.S./J.D. program in management/law with Albany Law Sch. Member of Hudson-Mohawk Association of Colleges and Universities; cross-registration possible. Exchange programs with Harvey Mudd Coll and Williams Coll. Teacher certification in secondary education. Certification in specific subject areas. Roman studies architecture program offers one or two semesters of study in Rome. Exchange programs in France (U Tech de Compiegne), Switzerland (Swiss Federal Inst of Tech in Zurich), and the United Kingdom (Imperial Coll and U Coll, U of Leeds, U of Sussex, Swansea U, and U of Wales). ROTC, NROTC, and AFROTC.
**Honors:** Honors program. Honor societies.
**Academic Assistance:** Nonremedial tutoring.

**STUDENT LIFE. Housing:** All freshmen must live on campus unless living with family. Coed and men's dorms. Sorority and fraternity housing. School-owned/operated apartments. Both on-campus and off-campus married-student housing. 54% of students live in college housing.
**Social atmosphere:** According to the student newspaper, Rensselaer has one of the largest Greek systems in the state, and they are very influential on campus. There are also over 128 union clubs to join. Special social events include all RPI hockey games, especially the Big Red Freakout Game, and concerts at the RPI field house which in the past have featured Heart, Bon Jovi, Jethro Tull, Robert Plant, Debbie Gibson, Stryper, Yes, and others.
**Services and counseling/handicapped student services:** Placement services. Health service. Women's center. Day care. International Student Office, Office of Minority Student Affairs. Counseling services for minority and military students. Birth control, personal, and psychological counseling. Career and academic guidance services. Religious counseling. Physically disabled student services. Learning disabled services. Notetaking services. Tape recorders. Tutors. Reader services for the blind.
**Campus organizations:** Undergraduate student government. Student newspaper (Polytechnic, published once/week). Literary magazine. Yearbook. Radio station. Band, glee club, orchestra, ensembles, RPI Players, activities committee, academic, professional, and special-interest groups, 120 organizations in all. 31 fraternities, 25 chapter houses; five sororities, four chapter houses. 40% of men join a fraternity. 40% of women join a sorority.
**Religious organizations:** Brothers and Sisters in Christ, Christian Association, Hillel, Islamic and Muslim Student Associations, Newman Foundation.
**Minority/foreign student organizations:** Black Student Alliance, Society of Black Engineers, Society of Hispanic Professional Engineers. Chinese, Filipino, Greek, Indian, Japanese, Latino, Korean, Pakistani, Taiwanese, Turkish, and Vietnamese groups.

**ATHLETICS. Physical education requirements:** Three semesters of physical education required.
**Intercollegiate competition:** 15% of students participate. Baseball (M), basketball (M,W), cross-country (M,W), diving (M,W), field hockey (W), football (M), golf (M), ice hockey (M), lacrosse (M,W), soccer (M,W), softball (W), swimming (M,W), tennis (M,W), track (indoor) (M,W), track (outdoor) (M,W), track and field (indoor) (M,W), track and field (outdoor) (M,W). Member of EAA, ECAC, ICAC, NCAA Division I for ice hockey, NCAA Division III.
**Intramural and club sports:** 70% of students participate. Intramural aerobics, basketball, bowling, court hockey, flag football, golf, ice hockey, indoor soccer, inner-tube water polo, pool, soccer, softball, swimming, table tennis, tennis, track, volleyball, walleyball, water aerobics, wrestling, yoga. Men's club Alpine skiing, bowling, cheerleading, crew, fencing, gymnastics, Nordic skiing, racquetball, rifle, rugby, ultimate frisbee, volleyball, water polo, weight lifting. Women's club ice hockey, racquetball, rifle, ultimate frisbee, volleyball, weight lifting.

**ADMISSIONS. Academic basis for candidate selection** (in order of priority): Secondary school record, standardized test scores, school's recommendation, class rank, essay.
**Nonacademic basis for candidate selection:** Character and personality, extracurricular participation, particular talent or ability, geographical distribution, and alumni/ae relationship are considered.
**Requirements:** Graduation from secondary school is required; GED is not accepted. 10 units and the following program of study are required: 4 units of English, 4 units of math, 2 units of science. The following courses are strongly recommended (in order of importance): calculus, Advanced Placement chemistry, and Advanced Placement physics. Portfolio required of architecture program applicants. HEOP for applicants not normally admissible. Conditional admission possible for applicants not meeting standard requirements. SAT or ACT is required. ACH recommended. Campus visit and interview recommended. Off-campus interviews available with an admissions representative.
**Procedure:** Take SAT or ACT by January of 12th year. Take ACH by January of 12th year. Visit college for interview by January of 12th year. Application deadline is January 15. Notification of admission by March 15. Reply is required by May 1. $250 nonrefundable tuition deposit. Freshmen accepted for terms other than fall.
**Special programs:** Admission may be deferred one year. Credit and/or placement may be granted through CEEB Advanced Placement exams for scores of 4 or higher. Placement may be granted through challenge exams and military and life experience. Early decision program. In fall 1992, 207 applied for early decision and 162 were accepted. Deadline for applying for early decision is January 1. Concurrent enrollment program.
**Transfer students:** Transfer students accepted for terms other than fall. In fall 1993, 17% of all new students were transfers into all classes. 578 transfer applications were received, 444 were accepted. Application deadline is August 1 for fall; November 1 for spring. Minimum 3.0 GPA recommended. Lowest course grade accepted is "C." At least 30 semester hours with two years of residency must be completed at the institute to receive degree.

**FINANCIAL AID. Available aid:** Pell grants, SEOG, state scholarships and grants, school scholarships and grants, private scholarships and grants, ROTC scholarships, academic merit scholarships, and athletic scholarships. Perkins Loans (NDSL), PLUS, Stafford Loans (GSL), state loans, school loans, private loans, and SLS. Knight Tuition Plans, AMS, and Tuition Management Systems. Monthly Installment Plan.
**Financial aid statistics:** 2% of aid is not need-based. In 1993-94, 76% of all undergraduate applicants received aid; 74% of freshman applicants. Average amounts of aid awarded freshmen: Scholarships and grants, $10,434; loans, $3,072.
**Supporting data/closing dates:** FAFSA/FAF: Priority filing date is February 15. School's own aid application: Accepted on rolling basis. Notification of awards begins early April.
**Financial aid contact:** James Stevenson, Director of Financial Aid. 518 276-6813.

**STUDENT EMPLOYMENT.** College Work/Study Program. Institutional employment. 25% of full-time undergraduates work on campus during school year. Students may expect to earn an average of $1,400 during school year. Off-campus part-time employment opportunities rated "good."

**COMPUTER FACILITIES.** 600 IBM/IBM-compatible, Macintosh/Apple, and RISC-/UNIX-based microcomputers; 580 are networked. Students may access IBM minicomputer/mainframe systems, BITNET, Internet. Residence halls may be equipped with networked microcomputers. Computer languages and software packages include ALGOL, Assembler, C, COBOL, DOS, FORTRAN, LISP, PL/1, SAS, SPSS-X. Computer facilities are available to all students.
**Fees:** None.
**Hours:** 24 hours.

**GRADUATE CAREER DATA.** Highest graduate school enrollments: U of California at Berkeley, Cornell U, Rensselaer Polytech Inst, Stanford U. 58% of graduates choose careers in business and industry. Companies and businesses that hire graduates: Anderson Consulting, General Electric, IBM, Northern Telecom, Procter and Gamble, United Technologies, Xerox.

**PROMINENT ALUMNI/AE.** J. Erik Jonsson, founder, Texas Instruments; William Mau, founder, Bugle Boy Industries; Robert Sageman, former president and CEO, AT&T; Jim Forsese, vice-president, IBM; George Strichman, former president, Colt Industries; Nancy Fitzroy, first woman president of the American Society of Mechanical Engineers; George Lowe, manager, NASA's Apollo Project/Mission; George Ferris, inventor of the ferris wheel; Washington Roebling, Brooklyn Bridge architect.

# Roberts Wesleyan College

Rochester, NY 14624-1997 716 594-6000

**1994-95 Costs.** Tuition: $10,220. Room: $2,352. Board: $1,194. Fees, books, misc. academic expenses (school's estimate): $724.
**Enrollment.** Undergraduates: 365 men, 567 women (full-time). Freshman class: 459 applicants, 422 accepted, 212 enrolled. Graduate enrollment: 17 men, 59 women.
**Test score averages/ranges.** Average SAT scores: 464 verbal, 503 math. Average ACT scores: 23 composite.
**Faculty.** 51 full-time; 56 part-time. 50% of faculty holds doctoral degree. Student/faculty ratio: 15 to 1.
**Selectivity rating.** Less competitive.

**PROFILE.** Roberts Wesleyan, founded in 1866, is a private, church-affiliated, liberal arts college. Its 75-acre campus is located eight miles from downtown Rochester.

**Accreditation:** MSACS. Professionally accredited by the Council on Social Work Education, the National Association of Schools of Art and Design, the National Association of Schools of Music, the National League for Nursing.
**Religious orientation:** Roberts Wesleyan College is affiliated with the Free Methodist Church; six semester hours of religion required.
**Library:** Collections totaling over 99,869 volumes, 678 periodical subscriptions, and 50,419 microform items.
**Special facilities/museums:** Nuclear magnetic resonator, mass spectrometer.
**Athletic facilities:** Swimming pool, sauna, indoor track, weight room, track, soccer field, life fitness center, basketball, racquetball, tennis, and volleyball courts.
**STUDENT BODY. Undergraduate profile:** 88% are state residents; 27% are transfers. .9% Asian-American, 6% Black, 2% Hispanic, .4% Native American, 85% White, 5.7% Other. Average age of undergraduates is 19.
**Undergraduate achievement:** 73% of fall 1992 freshmen returned for fall 1993 term. 46% of entering class graduated. 30% of students who completed a degree program went on to graduate study within one year.
**Foreign students:** Countries represented include Canada, Jamaica, and Japan; eight in all.
**PROGRAMS OF STUDY. Degrees:** B.A., B.S.
**Majors:** Accounting, Art, Art Education, Biochemistry, Biology, Business Administration, Chemistry, Communication, Comprehensive Science, Comprehensive Social Studies, Computer Science, Contemporary Ministries, Criminal Justice, Elementary Education, Engineering, English, Fine Arts, General Science, Gerontology, History, Humanities, Management of Human Resources, Mathematics, Medical Technology, Music, Music Education, Natural Science, Nursing, Physical Science, Physics, Psychology, Religion/Philosophy, Social Work, Sociology.
**Distribution of degrees:** The majors with the highest enrollment are management of human resources, elementary education, and nursing; gerontology, physics, and chemistry have the lowest.
**Requirements:** General education requirement.
**Academic regulations:** Freshmen must maintain minimum 1.5 GPA; sophomores, 1.75 GPA; juniors, 2.0 GPA; seniors, 2.0 GPA.
**Special:** Minors offered in many majors and in biblical studies, business, economics, foreign languages, general science, philosophy, religious studies, and social welfare. January Experience Program offers courses in transcultural and enrichment education. Associate's degrees offered. Double majors. Dual degrees. Independent study. Internships. Graduate school at which undergraduates may take graduate-level courses. Preprofessional programs in law, medicine, veterinary science, pharmacy, and dentistry. 3-2 engineering programs with Clarkson U, Rensselaer Polytech Inst, and Rochester Inst of Tech. Member of Christian College Coalition, Rochester Area Colleges Consortium, Council of Independent Colleges and Universities, and Association of Free Methodist Educational Institutions. Cross-registration with Rochester-area colleges. Washington Semester and UN Semester. American Studies program (Washington, D.C.) and AuSable Inst of Environmental Studies Program (Michigan). Teacher certification in early childhood, elementary, and secondary education. Study abroad in England. AFROTC. ROTC and AFROTC at Rochester Inst of Tech.
**Honors:** Phi Beta Kappa. Honors program.
**Academic Assistance:** Remedial reading, writing, math, and study skills.
**ADMISSIONS. Academic basis for candidate selection** (in order of priority): Secondary school record, school's recommendation, standardized test scores, essay, class rank.
**Nonacademic basis for candidate selection:** Character and personality and particular talent or ability are emphasized. Extracurricular participation and alumni/ae relationship are important. Geographical distribution is considered.
**Requirements:** Graduation from secondary school is required; GED is accepted. 15 units and the following program of study are required: 4 units of English, 2 units of math, 1 unit of lab science, 3 units of foreign language, 3 units of social studies, 2 units of history. Minimum combined SAT score of 800, rank in top three-fifths of secondary school class, and minimum 2.5 GPA recommended. Portfolio required of art program applicants. Audition required of music program applicants. Conditional admission possible for applicants not meeting standard requirements. SAT or ACT is required. PSAT is recommended. Campus visit and interview recommended. Off-campus interviews available with an admissions representative.
**Procedure:** Take SAT or ACT by March of 12th year. Visit college for interview by May of 12th year. Application deadline is August 1. Notification of admission on rolling basis. Reply is required by May 1. $100 tuition deposit, refundable until May 1. $50 room deposit, refundable until May 1. Freshmen accepted for terms other than fall.
**Special programs:** Admission may be deferred one semester. Credit and/or placement may be granted through CEEB Advanced Placement exams for scores of 3 or higher. Credit may be granted through CLEP general and subject exams, Regents College, and ACT PEP exams. Early entrance/early admission program. Concurrent enrollment program.
**Transfer students:** Transfer students accepted for terms other than fall. In fall 1993, 27% of all new students were transfers into all classes. 153 transfer applications were received, 127 were accepted. Application deadline is August 1 for fall; December 15 for spring. Minimum 2.0 GPA required. Lowest course grade accepted is "C." Maximum number of transferable credits is 92 semester hours. At least 30 semester hours must be completed at the college to receive degree.
**Admissions contact:** Linda Kurtz, Director of Admissions. 716 594-6400, 800 777-4RWC.
**FINANCIAL AID. Available aid:** Pell grants, SEOG, state scholarships and grants, school scholarships and grants, private scholarships and grants, academic merit scholarships, and athletic scholarships. Perkins Loans (NDSL), PLUS, Stafford Loans (GSL), NSL, and SLS. AMS and Tuition Management Systems.
**Financial aid statistics:** 40% of aid is not need-based. In 1993, 96% of all undergraduate applicants received aid; 99% of freshman applicants. Average amounts of aid awarded freshmen: Scholarships and grants, $6,150; loans, $3,400.
**Supporting data/closing dates:** FAFSA/FAF/FFS: Accepted on rolling basis. Notification of awards on rolling basis.
**Financial aid contact:** Karl G. Somerville, Director of Financial Aid. 716 594-6422.

# Rochester Institute of Technology

Rochester, NY 14623 716 475-2411

**1993-94 Costs.** Tuition: $13,266. Room: $2,934. Board: $2,505. Fees, books, misc. academic expenses (school's estimate): $1,649.
**Enrollment.** Undergraduates: 5,632 men, 2,437 women (full-time). Freshman class: 4,837 applicants, 3,916 accepted, 1,530 enrolled. Graduate enrollment: 1,223 men, 748 women.
**Test score averages/ranges.** Range of SAT scores of middle 50%: 430-540 verbal, 510-630 math. Range of ACT scores of middle 50%: 22-27 composite.
**Faculty.** 640 full-time; 413 part-time. 70% of faculty holds highest degree in specific field. Student/faculty ratio: 12 to 1.
**Selectivity rating.** Competitive.

**PROFILE.** RIT, founded in 1829, is a private, technological institution. Programs are offered through the Colleges of Applied Science and Technology, Business, Engineering, Fine and Applied Arts, Liberal Arts, Graphic Arts and Photography, and Science and the National Technical Institute for the Deaf. Its 1,300-acre campus is located five miles from downtown Rochester.

**Accreditation:** MSACS. Professionally accredited by the Accreditation Board for Engineering and Technology, the American Dietetic Association, the Council on Social Work Education, the National Association of Schools of Art and Design.
**Religious orientation:** Rochester Institute of Technology is nonsectarian; no religious requirements.
**Library:** Collections totaling over 324,000 volumes, 3,768 periodical subscriptions, and 203,830 microform items.
**Special facilities/museums:** Student-managed restaurant, media resource, TV, and graphic arts centers, center for imaging science, microelectronic engineering center.
**Athletic facilities:** Gymnasiums, swimming pool, weight and wrestling rooms, ice skating arena, gymnasiums, dance and martial arts studios, fitness center, tracks, basketball, racquetball, tennis, and volleyball courts, baseball, lacrosse, multi-purpose, soccer, and softball fields.
**STUDENT BODY. Undergraduate profile:** 67% are state residents; 40% are transfers. 5% Asian-American, 5% Black, 3% Hispanic, 1% Native American, 78% White, 8% Other. Average age of undergraduates is 21.
**Freshman profile:** 1% of freshmen who took SAT scored 700 or over on verbal, 7% scored 700 or over on math; 11% scored 600 or over on verbal, 40% scored 600 or over on math; 45% scored 500 or over on verbal, 79% scored 500 or over on math; 86% scored 400 or over on verbal, 96% scored 400 or over on math; 99% scored 300 or over on verbal, 100% scored 300 or over on math. 90% of accepted applicants took SAT; 30% took ACT. 85% of freshmen come from public schools.
**Undergraduate achievement:** 85% of fall 1991 freshmen returned for fall 1992 term. 55% of entering class graduated. 50% of students who completed a degree program went on to graduate study within five years.
**Foreign students:** 405 students are from out of the country. Countries represented include Canada, China, India, Japan, Korea, and Taiwan; 80 in all.
**PROGRAMS OF STUDY. Degrees:** B.F.A., B.S., B.Tech.
**Majors:** Accounting, Advertising Photography, Applied Mathematics, Applied Statistics, Biology, Biomedical Computing, Biomedical Photographic Communications, Biotechnology, Business Administration, Ceramics/Ceramic Sculpture, Chemistry, Civil Engineering Technology, Computational Mathematics, Computer Engineering, Computer Engineering Technology, Computer Science, Criminal Justice, Economics, Electrical Engineering, Electrical Engineering Technology, Environmental Management, Film/Video, Finance, Fine Arts Photography, Food Management, Food Marketing/Distribution, General Dietetics/Nutritional Care, Glass, Graphic Design, Hotel/Resort Management, Imaging/Photographic Technology, Imaging Science, Industrial Design, Industrial Engineering, Information Systems, Information Technology, Interior Design, International Business, Management, Manufacturing Engineering Technology, Marketing, Mechanical/Aerospace Engineering, Mechanical Engineering, Mechanical Engineering Technology, Medical Illustration, Medical Technology, Metalcrafts/Jewelry, Microelectronic Engineering, Newspaper Production Management, Nuclear Medical Technology, Packaging Design, Packaging Science, Painting, Painting/Illustration, Photographic Marketing Management, Photographic Processing/Finishing Management, Photojournalism, Physics, Polymer Chemistry, Pre-Dental, Pre-Medicine, Pre-Veterinary, Printing, Printing/Applied Computer Science, Printing Systems, Printmaking, Printmaking/Illustration, Professional Photographic Illustration, Professional/Technical Communication, Social Work,

Telecommunications Technology, Travel Management, Ultrasound Technology, Weaving/Textile Design, Woodworking/Furniture Design.
**Distribution of degrees:** The majors with the highest enrollment are business administration, engineering, and engineering technology; physics, economics, and social work have the lowest.
**Requirements:** General education requirement.
**Academic regulations:** Freshmen must maintain minimum 1.4 GPA; sophomores, juniors, seniors, 2.0 GPA.
**Special:** Field experience in social work and criminal justice. Upperclass students in Colleges of Business, Engineering, Science, and Applied Science and Technology participate in cooperative program for alternating quarters of study and work. Cooperative options in School of Printing, Department of Packaging, and Department of Environmental Management also offered. Associate's degrees offered. Self-designed majors. Independent study. Internships. Cooperative education programs. Graduate school at which undergraduates may take graduate-level courses. Preprofessional programs in law, medicine, veterinary science, dentistry, and optometry. Five-year B.S./M.S. engineering program. Five-year B.S./M.B.A. program. Member of Consortium of Rochester-Area Colleges. Exchange program with Spellman Coll. Teacher certification in elementary and secondary education. Certification in specific subject areas. Exchange programs abroad in Austria (U of Salzburg) and England (U of Oxford, U of Sheffield). ROTC and AFROTC. NROTC at U of Rochester.
**Honors:** Honors program. Honor societies.
**Academic Assistance:** Remedial reading, writing, math, and study skills. Nonremedial tutoring.

**STUDENT LIFE. Housing:** All freshmen must live on campus unless living with family. Coed, women's, and men's dorms. Sorority and fraternity housing. School-owned/operated apartments. On-campus married-student housing. 70% of students live in college housing.
**Social atmosphere:** The student newspaper reports that, "New alcohol policies have made Greek parties rather dull affairs. Occasionally, however, excellent speakers and live bands are featured on campus; this adds significantly to the social life." Movies, hockey games, and Friday happy hours are also well-attended social events. Students at RIT most often congregate at the Red Creek, Club Zero, Jay's Diner, and Marketplace Mall when getting together off campus. On campus, the "Ritskeller" is a popular place to hang out.
**Services and counseling/handicapped student services:** Placement services. Health service. Day care. Counseling services for minority, military, veteran, and older students. Birth control, personal, and psychological counseling. Career and academic guidance services. Religious counseling. Physically disabled student services. Learning disabled program/services. Notetaking services. Tape recorders. Tutors. Reader services for the blind.
**Campus organizations:** Undergraduate student government. Student newspaper (Reporter, published once/month). Literary magazine. Yearbook. Radio and TV stations. Society of Automotive Engineers, RIT Singers, jazz ensemble, gospel ensemble, dance company, drama group, debating, Amnesty International, professional, service, and special-interest groups, 70 organizations in all. 10 fraternities, no chapter houses; five sororities, no chapter houses. 10% of men join a fraternity. 10% of women join a sorority.
**Religious organizations:** Campus Crusade for Christ, Hillel, Intervarsity Christian Fellowship, Bible Believers Club.
**Minority/foreign student organizations:** Black Awareness Committee, Hispanic Student Association, Black Sisters group, Ebony club, Society of Black Engineers and Scientists. International Student Association, Caribbean Student Association, Chinese Student Society.

**ATHLETICS. Physical education requirements:** Six terms of physical education required.
**Intercollegiate competition:** 5% of students participate. Baseball (M), basketball (M,W), cheerleading (W), cross-country (M), diving (M,W), ice hockey (M,W), lacrosse (M), soccer (M,W), softball (W), swimming (M,W), tennis (M,W), track (indoor) (M,W), track (outdoor) (M,W), track and field (indoor) (M,W), track and field (outdoor) (M,W), volleyball (W), wrestling (M). Member of ECAC, Empire Athletic Association, NCAA Division III, NYSWCAA, United States Intercollegiate Lacrosse Association.
**Intramural and club sports:** 80% of students participate. Intramural aerobics, archery, badminton, basketball, billiards, bowling, canoeing, cheerleading, cycling, dodgeball, fencing, figure skating, fishing, flag football, floor hockey, frisbee, golf, horsemanship, hunting, ice fishing, ice hockey, inner-tube water polo, lacrosse, lifesaving, martial arts, outdoor education, racquetball, rope climbing, rugby, running, scuba diving, skeet shooting, skiing, soccer, softball, swimming, table tennis, triathlon, tennis, volleyball, water polo, weight lifting, yoga. Men's club Alpine skiing, cycling, lacrosse, rugby, soccer, ultimate frisbee. Women's club Alpine skiing, cycling, lacrosse, ultimate frisbee.

**ADMISSIONS. Academic basis for candidate selection** (in order of priority): Secondary school record, standardized test scores, class rank, essay, school's recommendation.
**Nonacademic basis for candidate selection:** Character and personality, extracurricular participation, particular talent or ability, geographical distribution, and alumni/ae relationship are considered.
**Requirements:** Graduation from secondary school is required; GED is accepted. 16 units and the following program of study are recommended: 4 units of English, 3 units of math, 3 units of science, 4 units of social studies, 2 units of electives. Portfolio required of art design and crafts program applicants. HEOP for applicants not normally admissible. Conditional admission possible for applicants not meeting standard requirements. College Anticipation Program and Institute Opportunity Program for applicants not normally admissible. SAT or ACT is required. PSAT is recommended. Campus visit and interview recommended. No off-campus interviews.
**Procedure:** Take SAT or ACT by fall of 12th year. Suggest filing application by March 1. Application deadline is August 1. Reply is required by May 1 or within two weeks of acceptance. $200 nonrefundable tuition deposit. Freshmen accepted for terms other than fall.
**Special programs:** Admission may be deferred one year. Credit and/or placement may be granted through CEEB Advanced Placement exams for scores of 3 or higher. Credit and/or placement may be granted through CLEP general and subject exams. Credit and placement may be granted through DANTES and challenge exams and life experience. Early decision program. In fall 1992, 290 applied for early decision and 258 were accepted. Deadline for applying for early decision is December 1. Early entrance/early admission program. Concurrent enrollment program.
**Transfer students:** Transfer students accepted for terms other than fall. In fall 1992, 40% of all new students were transfers into all classes. 2,013 transfer applications were received, 1,583 were accepted. Application deadline is rolling for fall; rolling for winter; rolling for spring. Minimum 2.5 GPA recommended. Lowest course grade accepted is "C-." Maximum number of transferable credits is 90 quarter hours from a two-year school and 135 quarter hours from a four-year school. At least 45 quarter hours must be completed at the university to receive degree.
**Admissions contact:** Daniel R. Shelley, M.S., Director of Admissions. 716 475-6631.

**FINANCIAL AID. Available aid:** Pell grants, SEOG, state scholarships and grants, school scholarships and grants, private scholarships and grants, ROTC scholarships, academic merit scholarships, and aid for undergraduate foreign students. Perkins Loans (NDSL), PLUS, Stafford Loans (GSL), state loans, private loans, and SLS. Knight Tuition Plans, AMS, deferred payment plan, and guaranteed tuition. RIT 12-month payment plan.
**Financial aid statistics:** 7% of aid is not need-based. In 1992-93, 85% of all undergraduate applicants received aid; 94% of freshman applicants. Average amounts of aid awarded freshmen: Scholarships and grants, $7,612; loans, $3,360.
**Supporting data/closing dates:** FAFSA/FAF/FFS: Priority filing date is March 15. Notification of awards begins March 15.
**Financial aid contact:** Verna Hazen, M.Ed., Director of Financial Aid. 716 475-2186.

**STUDENT EMPLOYMENT.** College Work/Study Program. Institutional employment. 45% of full-time undergraduates work on campus during school year. Students may expect to earn an average of $1,450 during school year. Off-campus part-time employment opportunities rated "excellent."

**COMPUTER FACILITIES.** 850 IBM/IBM-compatible, Macintosh/Apple, and RISC-/UNIX-based microcomputers. Students may access Digital, IBM, SUN minicomputer/mainframe systems. Residence halls may be equipped with stand-alone microcomputers, networked terminals. Client/LAN operating systems include Apple/Macintosh. Computer languages and software packages include Ada, Algol, Assembly, C, FORTRAN, Mesa, Modula-2, Pascal. Computer facilities are available to all students.
**Fees:** None.
**Hours:** 8 AM-11 PM.

**GRADUATE CAREER DATA.** Highest graduate school enrollments: Cornell U, Ohio State U, Pennsylvania State U, Rochester Inst of Tech, SUNY at Buffalo, Syracuse U, U of Rochester. Companies and businesses that hire graduates: Eastman Kodak, General Electric, Xerox, U.S. Government, IBM, Strong Medical Center, Marriott.

**PROMINENT ALUMNI/AE.** Fred Tucker, corporate vice-president, Motorola; William Buckingham, CEO, Manufacturers Hanover Bank; Tom Curley, president, *USA Today*; William Snyder, Pulitzer-prize winning photojournalist.

# Russell Sage College

**Troy, NY 12180** **518 270-2000**

**1994-95 Costs.** Tuition: $12,350. Room & board: $5,240. Fees, books, misc. academic expenses (school's estimate): $770.
**Enrollment.** 1,009 women (full-time). Freshman class: 550 applicants, 510 accepted, 181 enrolled.
**Test score averages/ranges.** Range of SAT scores of middle 50%: 400-499 verbal, 425-499 math. Range of ACT scores of middle 50%: 19-24 composite.
**Faculty.** 120 full-time; 50 part-time. 86% of faculty holds highest degree in specific field. Student/faculty ratio: 9 to 1.
**Selectivity rating.** Less competitive.

**PROFILE.** Russell Sage, founded in 1916, is a private college for women. Its eight-acre campus, containing several 19th-century buildings, is located in Troy.

**Accreditation:** MSACS. Professionally accredited by the American Physical Therapy Association, the National League for Nursing.
**Religious orientation:** Russell Sage College is nonsectarian; no religious requirements.
**Library:** Collections totaling over 198,000 volumes, 1,050 periodical subscriptions, and 12,000 microform items.
**Special facilities/museums:** Art gallery, theatre, child study and development center, women's education center, media center, electronic classroom.
**Athletic facilities:** Gymnasiums, weight room, swimming pool, bowling lanes, tennis courts, athletic field.

**STUDENT BODY. Undergraduate profile:** 86% are state residents; 46% are transfers. 2% Asian-American, 5% Black, 4% Hispanic, 1% Native American, 82% White, 6% Other. Average age of undergraduates is 22.
**Freshman profile:** 3% of freshmen who took SAT scored 600 or over on verbal, 8% scored 600 or over on math; 25% scored 500 or over on verbal, 48% scored 500 or over on math; 75% scored 400 or over on verbal, 84% scored 400 or over on math; 100% scored 300 or over on verbal, 100% scored 300 or over on math. 95% of accepted applicants took SAT; 20% took ACT.
**Undergraduate achievement:** 81% of fall 1992 freshmen returned for fall 1993 term. 60% of entering class graduated. 13% of students who completed a degree program immediately went on to graduate study.
**Foreign students:** Three students are from out of the country. Three countries represented in all.

**PROGRAMS OF STUDY. Degrees:** B.A., B.S.
**Majors:** Accounting, Arts Management, Athletic Training, Biochemistry, Biology, Chemistry, Communications, Computer Information Systems, Computer Science, Creative Arts in Therapy, Criminal Justice, Economics, Elementary Education, Elementary Education/Natural Sciences, English, French, History, Interdisciplinary Studies, International Studies, Marketing, Mathematics, Medical Technology, Nursing, Nutrition, Occupational Therapy, Physical Therapy, Political Science, Psychology/Human Services/Pre-Social Work, Sociology, Spanish, Special Education.

**Distribution of degrees:** The majors with the highest enrollment are physical therapy, nursing, and psychology; medical technology has the lowest.
**Requirements:** General education requirement.
**Academic regulations:** Freshmen must maintain minimum 1.8 GPA; sophomores, juniors, seniors, 2.0 GPA.
**Special:** Minors offered in most majors and in business administration, coaching, dance, German, music, retailing, theatre, visual arts, and women's studies. Courses offered in anatomy, anthropology, religion, and speech. Double majors. Independent study. Pass/fail grading option. Internships. Cooperative education programs. Graduate school at which undergraduates may take graduate-level courses. Preprofessional programs in law, medicine, veterinary science, and dentistry. Five-year bachelor's/master's programs in business administration and public administration. 3-2 engineering program with Rensselaer Polytech Inst. Six-year law program with Albany Law School. Member of Hudson-Mohawk Consortium. Washington Semester. Exchange programs with Bennett Coll, Mills Coll, and Mt Vernon Coll. Teacher certification in elementary, secondary, and special education. Certification in specific subject areas. Study abroad in England, France, Germany, Japan, and Spain. ROTC, NROTC, and AFROTC at Rensselaer Polytech Inst.
**Honors:** Honors program.
**Academic Assistance:** Remedial reading, writing, math, and study skills. Nonremedial tutoring.

**STUDENT LIFE. Housing:** All unmarried students must live on campus unless living with family. Women's dorms. 70% of students live in college housing.
**Social atmosphere:** Popular gathering spots include the Student Center, Elda's, the student union, and fraternities. Greeks exert the most influence on campus life. Popular campus events include Secret Sophomore Week, Sagefest, Rally Week, and the Slippin' into the Semester parties. "Campus social life is fairly dead; the student government tries to provide activities for students, but they have a poor turnout. Most students end up going to bars or fraternity parties," reports The Quill.
**Services and counseling/handicapped student services:** Placement services. Health service. Women's center. Day care. Counseling services for older students. Birth control, personal, and psychological counseling. Career and academic guidance services. Religious counseling. Learning disabled services.
**Campus organizations:** Undergraduate student government. Student newspaper (Quill, published once/week). Literary magazine. Yearbook. Choral, dance, ski, riding, recreation, drama, and foreign language groups, glee and outing clubs, Model UN, 40 organizations in all.
**Religious organizations:** Campus Ministry, Hillel, Christian Association.
**Minority/foreign student organizations:** Black and Latin American student groups, Intercultural Awareness Committee, multicultural center.

**ATHLETICS. Physical education requirements:** None.
**Intercollegiate competition:** 17% of students participate. Basketball (W), soccer (W), softball (W), tennis (W), volleyball (W). Member of NCAA Division III, New York State Women's Collegiate Athletic Association.
**Intramural and club sports:** 45% of students participate. Intramural aerobics, badminton, basketball, bowling, cross-country, field hockey, floor hockey, lacrosse, soccer, swimming, tennis, volleyball, weight training. Women's club cross-country, field hockey, horsemanship, indoor soccer, lacrosse.

**ADMISSIONS. Academic basis for candidate selection** (in order of priority): Secondary school record, standardized test scores, class rank, essay, school's recommendation.
**Nonacademic basis for candidate selection:** Extracurricular participation and particular talent or ability are emphasized. Character and personality and geographical distribution are important. Alumni/ae relationship is considered.
**Requirements:** Graduation from secondary school is required; GED is accepted. 17 units and the following program of study are recommended: 4 units of English, 3 units of math, 2 units of science, 2 units of foreign language, 3 units of social studies, 1 unit of electives. Minimum combined SAT score of 800, rank in top half of secondary school class, and minimum 2.5 GPA recommended. Minimum "B" average in biology, chemistry, and physics required of physical therapy and occupational therapy program applicants. HEOP for applicants not normally admissible. SAT is required; ACT may be substituted. Campus visit and interview recommended. No off-campus interviews.
**Procedure:** Take SAT or ACT by May of 12th year. Suggest filing application by March 1. Application deadline is August 1. Notification of admission on rolling basis. Reply is required by May 1. $200 nonrefundable tuition deposit. $100 room deposit, refundable until May 1. Freshmen accepted for terms other than fall.
**Special programs:** Admission may be deferred one year. Credit and/or placement may be granted through CEEB Advanced Placement exams for scores of 3 or higher. Credit and/or placement may be granted through CLEP subject exams. Placement may be granted through challenge exams. Credit and placement may be granted through military and life experience. Early decision program. In fall 1993, 35 applied for early decision and 25 were accepted. Deadline for applying for early decision is November 1. Early entrance/early admission program.
**Transfer students:** Transfer students accepted for terms other than fall. In fall 1993, 46% of all new students were transfers into all classes. 400 transfer applications were received, 360 were accepted. Application deadline is August 1 for fall; December 15 for spring. Minimum 2.0 GPA recommended. Lowest course grade accepted is "C." Maximum number of transferable credits is 60 semester hours from a two-year school and 75 semester hours from a four-year school. At least 45 semester hours must be completed at the college to receive degree.
**Admissions contact:** Patrice M. Tate, Director of Admissions. 800 999-3RSC, 518 270-2217.

**FINANCIAL AID. Available aid:** Pell grants, SEOG, state scholarships and grants, school scholarships and grants, private scholarships and grants, and academic merit scholarships. Perkins Loans (NDSL), PLUS, Stafford Loans (GSL), school loans, private loans, and SLS. Tuition Plan Inc., Knight Tuition Plans, AMS, Tuition Management Systems, and family tuition reduction.
**Financial aid statistics:** 10% of aid is not need-based. In 1993-94, 90% of all undergraduate applicants received aid; 95% of freshman applicants. Average amounts of aid awarded freshmen: Scholarships and grants, $7,400; loans, $3,800.
**Supporting data/closing dates:** FAFSA: Priority filing date is March 1. Income tax forms: Accepted on rolling basis. Verification Worksheet: Accepted on rolling basis. Notification of awards begins in March.
**Financial aid contact:** Dennis Tillman, M.A., Director of Financial Aid. 518 270-2341.

**STUDENT EMPLOYMENT.** College Work/Study Program. Institutional employment. 45% of full-time undergraduates work on campus during school year. Students may expect to earn an average of $1,200 during school year. Off-campus part-time employment opportunities rated "good."

**COMPUTER FACILITIES.** 70 IBM/IBM-compatible and Macintosh/Apple microcomputers; 17 are networked. Students may access Digital, IBM, Prime minicomputer/mainframe systems. Client/LAN operating systems include Apple/Macintosh, DOS, Windows NT, DEC, Microsoft. Computer languages and software packages include BASIC, COBOL, FORTRAN, Pascal; database management, desktop publishing, spreadsheet, word processing packages; 50 in all. Computer facilities are available to all students.
**Fees:** None.
**Hours:** 17 hours/day.

**GRADUATE CAREER DATA.** Highest graduate school enrollments: Coll of St. Rose, Russell Sage Coll, SUNY at Albany. 30% of graduates choose careers in business and industry.

**PROMINENT ALUMNI/AE.** Nancy Meuller, president, Nancy's Quiches; Linda Nee, researcher, National Institutes of Health.

# St. Bonaventure University

**St. Bonaventure, NY 14778-2284 — 716 375-2000**

**1994-95 Costs.** Tuition: $10,456. Room & board: $4,826. Fees, books, misc. academic expenses (school's estimate): $870.
**Enrollment.** Undergraduates: 877 men, 867 women (full-time). Freshman class: 1,500 applicants, 1,313 accepted, 374 enrolled. Graduate enrollment: 339 men, 364 women.
**Test score averages/ranges.** Average SAT scores: 478 verbal, 536 math. Range of SAT scores of middle 50%: 420-530 verbal, 490-590 math. Average ACT scores: 24 English, 23 math, 25 composite. Range of ACT scores of middle 50%: 22-27 English, 21-25 math.
**Faculty.** 160 full-time; 15 part-time. 98% of faculty holds doctoral degree. Student/faculty ratio: 14 to 1.
**Selectivity rating.** Competitive.

**PROFILE.** St. Bonaventure, founded in 1856, is a church-affiliated, comprehensive university. Programs are offered through the Schools of Arts and Sciences, Business, Education, and Graduate Studies. Its 600-acre campus, with a combination of traditional Florentine and modern brick buildings, is located in St. Bonaventure, 65 miles from Buffalo. The campus includes a Friary for the community's Franciscan Friars.

**Accreditation:** MSACS.
**Religious orientation:** St. Bonaventure University is affiliated with the Roman Catholic Church (Franciscan Friars); three semesters of theology required.
**Library:** Collections totaling over 241,000 volumes, 1,500 periodical subscriptions, and 97,000 microform items.
**Athletic facilities:** Fitness center, racquetball and tennis courts, Nautilus, swimming pool, gymnasiums.

**STUDENT BODY. Undergraduate profile:** 75% are state residents; 17% are transfers. .5% Asian-American, 2% Black, 1% Hispanic, .5% Native American, 96% White, 6% Other. Average age of undergraduates is 20.
**Freshman profile:** 8% of freshmen who took SAT scored 600 or over on verbal, 19% scored 600 or over on math; 31% scored 500 or over on verbal, 57% scored 500 or over on math; 69% scored 400 or over on verbal, 81% scored 400 or over on math; 80% scored 300 or over on verbal, 82% scored 300 or over on math. 2% of freshmen who took ACT scored 30 or over on English, 1% scored 30 or over on composite; 11% scored 24 or over on English, 7% scored 24 or over on math, 12% scored 24 or over on composite; 18% scored 18 or over on English, 18% scored 18 or over on math, 18% scored 18 or over on composite. 98% of accepted applicants took SAT; 37% took ACT. 61% of freshmen come from public schools.
**Undergraduate achievement:** 82% of fall 1992 freshmen returned for fall 1993 term. 70% of entering class graduated. 21% of students who completed a degree program immediately went on to graduate study.
**Foreign students:** 22 students are from out of the country. Countries represented include Canada, Poland, South Africa, Spain, Sweden, and the West Indies; 16 in all.

**PROGRAMS OF STUDY. Degrees:** B.A., B.Bus.Admin., B.S., B.S.Ed.
**Majors:** Accounting, Biology, Chemistry, Classical Languages, Computer Science, Economics, Elementary Education, English, Finance, French, German, Greek, History, Interdisciplinary Studies, Latin, Management Sciences, Marketing, Mass Communication, Mathematics, Medical Technology, Philosophy, Physical Education, Physics, Political Science, Psychology, Social Sciences, Sociology, Spanish, Theological Studies.
**Distribution of degrees:** The majors with the highest enrollment are elementary education, accounting, and marketing; classical languages, chemistry, and physics have the lowest.
**Requirements:** General education requirement.
**Academic regulations:** Minimum 2.0 GPA must be maintained.
**Special:** Minors offered in most majors and in business administration, education, geography, international business, justice/peace/conflict studies, management information systems, marketing communications, music, philosophy/applied ethics, philosophy/law, pre-engineering, quantitative methods, social work, and visual arts. Courses offered in anthropology, fine arts, and political science. Self-designed majors. Double majors. Dual degrees. Independent study. Accelerated study. Pass/fail grading option. Internships. Graduate school at which undergraduates may take graduate-level courses. Preprofessional programs in law, medicine, veterinary science, dentistry, and optometry. 2-2 engi-

neering program with Clarkson U and U of Detroit. B.A./M.A. programs in English and psychology. B.S./M.S. physics program. B.A. or B.S./M.B.A. programs in English, math, and physics. Member of Western New York Consortium of Colleges and Universities. Washington Semester. Teacher certification in elementary and secondary education. Certification in specific subject areas. Exchange programs abroad in China (Shanghai Teachers U), Cyprus (Frederick Polytech U), Ecuador (Spanish Language and Latin American Culture and Civilization Inst; Coll Americano de Guayaquil), England (Ealing Coll), France (Inst of American Universities), Germany (Coll Platinum; Schiller International U), Greece (American U), Ireland (St. Patrick U), Italy (American U; Loyola Rome Center of Liberal Arts), Japan (Sophia U), Mexico (U of the Americas), Portugal (Centro de Linguas), Scotland (Moray House Coll of Education; Napier Polytech; U of Stirling), Spain (U of Seville), and Switzerland (Franklin Coll). ROTC.

**Honors:** Honors program. Honor societies.

**Academic Assistance:** Remedial reading, writing, math, and study skills. Nonremedial tutoring.

**STUDENT LIFE. Housing:** All unmarried students under age 21 must live on campus unless living near campus with relatives. Coed dorms. School-owned/operated apartments. 75% of students live in college housing.

**Social atmosphere:** Popular on-campus gathering spots include the RC Cafe and the residence halls; off campus, students frequent local bars and the fitness center. Influential groups on campus include the student government, Campus Ministry, and the Residence Life staff. Spring weekend and Division I basketball are highlights of the school year. The school newspaper reports, "Students at St. Bonaventure develop close friendships in a welcoming setting."

**Services and counseling/handicapped student services:** Placement services. Health service. Counseling services for veteran students. Birth control, personal, and psychological counseling. Career and academic guidance services. Religious counseling. Physically disabled student services. Learning disabled services. Notetaking services. Tape recorders. Tutors.

**Campus organizations:** Undergraduate student government. Student newspaper (Bona Venture, published once/week). Literary magazine. Yearbook. Radio station. Glee club, chamber singers, orchestra, concert and stage bands, Garret Theatre Players, Big Brothers/Big Sisters, Women's Council, Knights of Columbus, Amnesty International, College Democrats, College Republicans, Non-traditional Student Association, commuter club, departmental, service, and special-interest groups, 58 organizations in all.

**Religious organizations:** Campus Ministry, The Warming House, Guidepost, Brush-Up.

**Minority/foreign student organizations:** Black Student Union. International Student Organization.

**ATHLETICS. Physical education requirements:** None.

**Intercollegiate competition:** 14% of students participate. Baseball (M), basketball (M,W), cross-country (M,W), diving (M,W), golf (M), soccer (M,W), softball (W), swimming (M,W), tennis (M,W), volleyball (W). Member of Atlantic 10, ECAC, NCAA Division I.

**Intramural and club sports:** Intramural basketball, billiards, bowling, flag football, floor hockey, soccer, softball, swimming, table tennis, tennis, volleyball, weight lifting. Men's club lacrosse, rugby. Women's club lacrosse.

**ADMISSIONS. Academic basis for candidate selection** (in order of priority): Secondary school record, standardized test scores, school's recommendation, class rank, essay.

**Nonacademic basis for candidate selection:** Character and personality, extracurricular participation, particular talent or ability, and alumni/ae relationship are considered.

**Requirements:** Graduation from secondary school is required; GED is accepted. 16 units and the following program of study are required: 4 units of English, 3 units of math, 3 units of science, 2 units of foreign language, 4 units of social studies. Minimum combined SAT score of 1000, rank in top two-fifths of secondary school class, and minimum 3.0 GPA recommended. HEOP for applicants not normally admissible. SAT or ACT is required. Campus visit and interview recommended. No off-campus interviews.

**Procedure:** Take SAT or ACT by November of 12th year. Suggest filing application by April 15; no deadline. Notification of admission on rolling basis. Reply is required by May 1 or by date specified in letter of acceptance. $200 nonrefundable tuition deposit. Freshmen accepted for terms other than fall.

**Special programs:** Admission may be deferred one year. Credit and/or placement may be granted through CEEB Advanced Placement exams for scores of 3 or higher. Credit and/or placement may be granted through CLEP subject exams. Placement may be granted through challenge exams. Early entrance/early admission program. Concurrent enrollment program.

**Transfer students:** Transfer students accepted for terms other than fall. In fall 1993, 17% of all new students were transfers into all classes. 167 transfer applications were received, 134 were accepted. Application deadline is August 1 for fall; December 1 for spring. Minimum 2.0 GPA required. Lowest course grade accepted is "D." Final 36 semester hours and half of major courses must be completed at the college to receive degree.

**Admissions contact:** June T. Solan, M.S.Ed., Director of Admissions. 716 375-2400.

**FINANCIAL AID. Available aid:** Pell grants, SEOG, state scholarships and grants, school scholarships and grants, private scholarships and grants, ROTC scholarships, academic merit scholarships, athletic scholarships, and aid for undergraduate foreign students. Perkins Loans (NDSL), PLUS, Stafford Loans (GSL), school loans, private loans, and SLS. Tuition Plan Inc., AMS, deferred payment plan, and family tuition reduction.

**Financial aid statistics:** 16% of aid is not need-based. In 1992-93, 98% of all undergraduate applicants received aid; 97% of freshman applicants. Average amounts of aid awarded freshmen: Scholarships and grants, $6,000; loans, $2,750.

**Supporting data/closing dates:** FAFSA/FAF/FFS: Priority filing date is March 1. Notification of awards begins April 1.

**Financial aid contact:** Mary Piccioli, M.B.A., Director of Financial Aid. 716 375-2528.

**STUDENT EMPLOYMENT.** College Work/Study Program. Institutional employment. 39% of full-time undergraduates work on campus during school year. Students may expect to earn an average of $800 during school year. Off-campus part-time employment opportunities rated "fair."

**COMPUTER FACILITIES.** 140 IBM/IBM-compatible and Macintosh/Apple microcomputers; all are networked. Students may access AT&T, Hewlett-Packard, IBM, SUN minicomputer/mainframe systems, BITNET, Internet. Client/LAN operating systems include Apple/Macintosh, DOS, UNIX/XENIX/AIX, Windows NT, DEC, LocalTalk/AppleTalk, Novell. Computer languages and software packages include Ada, AmiPro, BASIC, C, COBOL, dBASE, FORTRAN, LISP, Lotus 1-2-3, MINITAB, Paradox, Pascal, Systat, TurboTax, Windows, WordPerfect, WordStar; 50 in all. Computer facilities are available to all students.

**Fees:** Computer fee is included in tuition/fees.

**GRADUATE CAREER DATA.** Highest graduate school enrollments: St. Bonaventure U, SUNY Buffalo, Syracuse U, U of Buffalo. 50% of graduates choose careers in business and industry. Companies and businesses that hire graduates: Big Six accounting firms, IBM, Xerox.

**PROMINENT ALUMNI/AE.** Rick Farina, senior vice president, Shearson Lehman Hutton; Robert Dubill, Pulitzer Prize-winner, senior editor, *USA Today.*

# St. Francis College

**Brooklyn Heights, NY 11201** **718 522-2300**

**1993-94 Costs.** Tuition: $6,550. Housing: None. Fees, books, misc. academic expenses (school's estimate): $450.

**Enrollment.** Undergraduates: 661 men, 901 women (full-time). Freshman class: 1,013 applicants, 916 accepted, 401 enrolled.

**Test score averages/ranges.** N/A.

**Faculty.** 57 full-time; 94 part-time. 64% of faculty holds doctoral degree. Student/faculty ratio: 23 to 1.

**Selectivity rating.** N/A.

**PROFILE.** St. Francis is a private, liberal arts college, rooted in a Catholic tradition. Founded in 1884 with the purpose of providing higher education for students with limited economic resources, it adopted coeducation in 1969. Its urban campus is located in Brooklyn Heights.

**Accreditation:** MSACS.

**Religious orientation:** St. Francis College is historically affiliated with the Roman Catholic Church; three semester hours of religion/theology required.

**Library:** Collections totaling over 160,849 volumes, 700 periodical subscriptions, and 12,500 microform items.

**Special facilities/museums:** Institute for local historical studies, archival collection for New York City, greenhouse, electronic classroom.

**Athletic facilities:** Gymnasium, swimming pool, recreation, training, and weight rooms, athletic fields.

**STUDENT BODY. Undergraduate profile:** 99% are state residents; 28% are transfers. 2% Asian-American, 23% Black, 15% Hispanic, 1% Native American, 54% White, 5% Other. Average age of undergraduates is 21.

**Freshman profile:** 44% of freshmen come from public schools.

**Undergraduate achievement:** 74% of fall 1992 freshmen returned for fall 1993 term. 26% of entering class graduated.

**Foreign students:** 105 students are from out of the country. Countries represented include Asian countries, Cyprus, European countries, Latin American countries, and the West Indies; 37 in all.

**PROGRAMS OF STUDY. Degrees:** B.A., B.S.

**Majors:** Accounting, Accounting/Business Practice, Aviation Administration, Aviation Business Studies, Biology, Biomedical Science, Communications, Economics, English, Health Care Management, Health Services Administration, History, International Cultural Studies, Management, Mathematics, Medical Technology, Physical Education, Political Science, Psychology, Social Studies, Sociology, Special Studies.

**Distribution of degrees:** The majors with the highest enrollment are management, special studies, and accounting; biomedical science, aviation administration, and health services administration have the lowest.

**Requirements:** General education requirement.

**Academic regulations:** Freshmen must maintain minimum 1.5 GPA; sophomores, 1.75 GPA; juniors, 2.0 GPA; seniors, 2.0 GPA.

**Special:** Minors offered in some majors and in chemistry, computer systems, French, health science, religious studies, and Spanish. Courses offered in fine arts, German, physics, and speech and communications. Associate's degrees offered. Self-designed majors. Independent study. Internships. Preprofessional programs in law, medicine, and dentistry. 2-2 medical sonography, nursing, occupational therapy, and radiologic science programs with SUNY Health Science Center at Brooklyn. Podiatric medicine program with New York Coll of Podiatric Medicine. Inter-American Studies Program. New York State Legislative Program. Teacher certification in secondary education. Certification in specific subject areas. Study abroad possible. ROTC at Polytech U. AFROTC at Manhattan Coll.

**Honors:** Honors program. Honor societies.

**Academic Assistance:** Remedial reading, writing, math, and study skills. Nonremedial tutoring.

**STUDENT LIFE. Housing:** Commuter campus; no student housing.

**Social atmosphere:** On campus, the cafeteria and student lounge are the usual gathering-spots; off campus, the local bars and restaurants are popular. Student government and athletic teams have strong influence on student social life. Highlights of the school year include home athletic games, ski trips, on- and off-campus parties, and the Semi-Formal. According to the student newspaper, "Being a commuter school, most activities at St. Francis are held during the day. Many students take advantage of our close proximity to New York City for socializing and entertainment, as well as employment."

**Services and counseling/handicapped student services:** Placement services. Health service. Counseling services for older students. Personal counseling. Career and academic guidance services. Religious counseling. Physically disabled student services. Learning disabled services. Notetaking services. Tape recorders. Tutors. Reader services for the blind.

**Campus organizations:** Undergraduate student government. Student newspaper (Voice, published 12 times/year). Literary magazine. Yearbook. Music and drama groups, Gaelic Society, Model UN, St. Francis Flyers, history/political science society, billiards club, St. Thomas More Pre-Law Society, academic, athletic, and special-interest groups, 28 organizations in all. Two fraternities, no chapter houses; one sorority, no chapter house. 5% of men join a fraternity. 2% of women join a sorority.

**Religious organizations:** Christian Club, interdenominational choir.

**Minority/foreign student organizations:** Black Student Organization, Latin American Society, Association of Black Accountants. Foreign Student Association, Caribbean Student Association.

**ATHLETICS. Physical education requirements:** One semester of physical education required.

**Intercollegiate competition:** 15% of students participate. Baseball (M), basketball (M,W), cross-country (M,W), soccer (M), softball (W), swimming (M,W), tennis (M,W), track (indoor) (M,W), track (outdoor) (M,W), track and field (indoor) (M,W), track and field (outdoor) (M,W), water polo (M). Member of NCAA Division I, Northeast Conference.

**Intramural and club sports:** 30% of students participate. Intramural basketball, soccer, volleyball. Men's club bowling. Women's club bowling.

**ADMISSIONS. Academic basis for candidate selection** (in order of priority): Secondary school record, school's recommendation, class rank, standardized test scores, essay.

**Nonacademic basis for candidate selection:** Character and personality are important. Extracurricular participation, particular talent or ability, and alumni/ae relationship are considered.

**Requirements:** Graduation from secondary school is required; GED is accepted. 16 units and the following program of study are required: 4 units of English, 2 units of math, 1 unit of science, 3 units of social studies, 6 units of academic electives. Conditional admission possible for applicants not meeting standard requirements. SAT is required. Campus visit and interview recommended. Off-campus interviews available with admissions and alumni representatives.

**Procedure:** Take SAT by January of 12th year. Notification of admission on rolling basis. No set date by which applicants must accept offer. Freshmen accepted for terms other than fall.

**Special programs:** Admission may be deferred one semester. Placement may be granted through CEEB Advanced Placement exams for scores of 3 or higher. Credit and/or placement may be granted through CLEP general and subject exams. Credit may be granted through Regents College, ACT PEP, and DANTES exams and military and life experience.

**Transfer students:** Transfer students accepted for terms other than fall. In fall 1993, 28% of all new students were transfers into all classes. 278 transfer applications were received, 195 were accepted. Application deadline is rolling for fall; rolling for spring. Minimum 2.0 GPA required. Lowest course grade accepted is "C." Maximum number of transferable credits is 98 semester hours. At least 30 semester hours must be completed at the college to receive degree.

**Admissions contact:** Br. George Larkin, O.S.F., Dean of Admissions. 718 522-2300, extension 200.

**FINANCIAL AID. Available aid:** Pell grants, SEOG, state scholarships and grants, school scholarships, private scholarships, academic merit scholarships, and athletic scholarships. Perkins Loans (NDSL), PLUS, Stafford Loans (GSL), and SLS. Monthly budget plan.

**Financial aid statistics:** 15% of aid is not need-based. In 1993-94, 87% of all undergraduate applicants received aid; 83% of freshman applicants. Average amounts of aid awarded freshmen: Scholarships and grants, $4,360; loans, $2,625.

**Supporting data/closing dates:** FAFSA: Priority filing date is February 15. FAF/FFS: Priority filing date is February 15; accepted on rolling basis. School's own aid application: Priority filing date is February 15; accepted on rolling basis. State aid form: Priority filing date is February 15. Notification of awards begins March 15.

**Financial aid contact:** Br. Thomas O'Neill, O.S.F., M.S., Director of Financial Aid. 718 522-2300, extension 246.

**STUDENT EMPLOYMENT.** College Work/Study Program. Institutional employment. 9% of full-time undergraduates work on campus during school year. Students may expect to earn an average of $1,200 during school year. Off-campus part-time employment opportunities rated "good."

**COMPUTER FACILITIES.** 50 IBM/IBM-compatible and Macintosh/Apple microcomputers; all are networked. Students may access IBM minicomputer/mainframe systems. Residence halls may be equipped with stand-alone microcomputers, networked microcomputers, modems. Client/LAN operating systems include DOS, Novell. Computer languages and software packages include COBOL, dBASE, Lotus 1-2-3, Pascal, WordPerfect; 10 in all. Computer facilities are available to all students.

**Fees:** $35 computer fee per course; included in tuition/fees.

**Hours:** 8 AM-9 PM (M-Th); 8 AM-7 PM (F); 10 AM-4 PM (Sa).

**GRADUATE CAREER DATA.** Graduate school percentages: 3% enter law school. 1% enter medical school. 18% enter graduate business programs. 3% enter graduate arts and sciences programs. Companies and businesses that hire graduates: Big Six accounting firms.

**PROMINENT ALUMNI/AE.** Nicholas Trivisonno, executive vice-president, GTE; Roy L. Reardon, partner, Simpson Thacher and Bartlett law firm; Frank X. Altimari, federal judge; Francis McCormack, senior vice-president, Arco.

## St. John Fisher College

**Rochester, NY 14618** **716 385-8000**

**1994-95 Costs.** Tuition: $10,570. Room: $3,550. Board: $1,880. Fees, books, misc. academic expenses (school's estimate): $785.

**Enrollment.** Undergraduates: 744 men, 943 women (full-time). Freshman class: 1,368 applicants, 1,064 accepted, 354 enrolled. Graduate enrollment: 115 men, 165 women.

**Test score averages/ranges.** Average SAT scores: 465 verbal, 525 math. Range of SAT scores of middle 50%: 419-520 verbal, 458-587 math. Average ACT scores: 21 English, 21 math, 22 composite. Range of ACT scores of middle 50%: 22-25 English, 22-28 math.

**Faculty.** 106 full-time; 86 part-time. 84% of faculty holds doctoral degree. Student/faculty ratio: 16 to 1.

**Selectivity rating.** Less competitive.

**PROFILE.** St. John Fisher is a church-affiliated, liberal arts college. Founded in 1948 as a men's college, it adopted coeducation in 1971. Its 126-acre campus is located in a suburban section of Rochester.

**Accreditation:** MSACS. Professionally accredited by the American Assembly of Collegiate Schools of Business, the National Council for Accreditation of Teacher Education, the National League for Nursing.

**Religious orientation:** St. John Fisher College is affiliated with the Roman Catholic Church (Basilian Priests); four courses in religious studies/philosophy required.

**Library:** Collections totaling over 175,000 volumes, 1,000 periodical subscriptions, and 111,940 microform items.

**Special facilities/museums:** Greenhouse, TV studio, radio station, computer and language labs, human and animal psychology lab, marine aquarium, two electron microscopes, radiation lab, microbial fermenters, X-ray diffraction, spectrometer, microphotometer, reflecting telescopes.

**Athletic facilities:** Student life center, track, basketball, handball, racquetball, tennis, and volleyball courts, football, soccer, and softball fields, 9-hole golf course, gymnasium.

**STUDENT BODY. Undergraduate profile:** 97% are state residents; 37% are transfers. 2% Asian-American, 5% Black, 2% Hispanic, 1% Native American, 85% White, 5% Other. Average age of undergraduates is 21.

**Freshman profile:** 1% of freshmen who took SAT scored 700 or over on math; 5% scored 600 or over on verbal, 20% scored 600 or over on math; 30% scored 500 or over on verbal, 60% scored 500 or over on math; 85% scored 400 or over on verbal, 96% scored 400 or over on math; 100% scored 300 or over on verbal, 100% scored 300 or over on math. 2% of freshmen who took ACT scored 30 or over on English, 3% scored 30 or over on math, 2% scored 30 or over on composite; 29% scored 24 or over on English, 33% scored 24 or over on math, 33% scored 24 or over on composite; 83% scored 18 or over on English, 87% scored 18 or over on math, 91% scored 18 or over on composite; 100% scored 12 or over on English, 100% scored 12 or over on math, 100% scored 12 or over on composite. 73% of accepted applicants took SAT; 27% took ACT. 60% of freshmen come from public schools.

**Undergraduate achievement:** 80% of fall 1992 freshmen returned for fall 1993 term. 50% of entering class graduated. 13% of students who completed a degree program immediately went on to graduate study.

**Foreign students:** 15 students are from out of the country. Countries represented include Antigua, Colombia, Ethiopia, Germany, Ghana, and Kenya; 15 in all.

**PROGRAMS OF STUDY. Degrees:** B.A., B.Bus.Admin., B.S., B.S.Nurs.

**Majors:** Accounting, Anthropology, Biology, Business Management, Chemistry, Communication/Journalism, Computer Science, Economics, Elementary Education, English, French, German, History, Industrial/Commercial Accounting, International Studies, Italian, Liberal Studies, Management, Mathematics, Nursing, Philosophy, Physics, Political Science, Psychology, Religious Studies, Social Studies Teaching, Sociology, Spanish.

**Distribution of degrees:** The majors with the highest enrollment are business management, accounting, and psychology; religious studies, philosophy, and German have the lowest.

**Requirements:** General education requirement.

**Academic regulations:** Minimum 2.0 GPA must be maintained.

**Special:** Minors offered in biochemistry, classical languages, clinical sociology, community studies, criminology/criminal justice, English writing, finance, gerontology, human resource management, international business management, management, management information systems, marketing, and Polish studies. International simulation program in political science. Independent research courses in all sciences. Self-designed majors. Double majors. Independent study. Accelerated study. Pass/fail grading option. Internships. Graduate school at which undergraduates may take graduate-level courses. Preprofessional programs in law, medicine, veterinary science, pharmacy, dentistry, and optometry. 2-2 environmental science program with SUNY at Syracuse. 2-2 engineering program with U of Detroit. 3-4 engineering programs with Clarkson U, Manhattan Coll, and SUNY at Buffalo. 3-2 optometry program with Pennsylvania Coll of Optometry. 3-2 B.S.Mgmt./M.B.A. program. 3-2 international studies/M.B.A. program. 3-2 Bachelor's/M.A. public policy program with U of Rochester. 4-2 engineering program with Columbia U. Member of Rochester Area Colleges; cross-registration possible. Washington Semester. Teacher certification in elementary and secondary education. Certification in specific subject areas. Study abroad in Australia, Austria, the Dominican Republic, Egypt, England, France, Germany, Ireland, Italy, Poland, South Africa, the former Soviet Republics, Spain, and Wales. ROTC and AFROTC at Rochester Inst of Tech.

**Honors:** Honors program. Honor societies.

**Academic Assistance:** Remedial writing, math, and study skills. Nonremedial tutoring.

**STUDENT LIFE. Housing:** Students may live on or off campus. Coed and women's dorms. 50% of students live in college housing.

**Services and counseling/handicapped student services:** Placement services. Health service. Day care. Counseling services for veteran students. Personal and psychological counseling. Career and academic guidance services. Religious counseling. Physically disabled student services. Learning disabled services. Notetaking services. Tape recorders. Tutors. Reader services for the blind.
**Campus organizations:** Undergraduate student government. Student newspaper (Pioneer, published once/week). Literary magazine. Yearbook. Radio station. Glee club, pep band, gospel choir, Fisher Players, Circle K, Amnesty International, Women in Communications, Pope Law Association, Residence Council, Commuter Council, Student Activities Board, astronomy club, athletic, departmental, service, and special-interest groups, 52 organizations in all.
**Religious organizations:** Campus Ministry.
**Minority/foreign student organizations:** Black Student Union, Latino Student Union, United Culture Club, International Studies Association. Latino Student Union.

**ATHLETICS. Physical education requirements:** None.
**Intercollegiate competition:** 20% of students participate. Baseball (M), basketball (M,W), cheerleading (M,W), cross-country (M,W), football (M), golf (M,W), soccer (M,W), softball (W), tennis (M,W), volleyball (W). Member of ECAC, NCAA Division III.
**Intramural and club sports:** 60% of students participate. Intramural football, floor hockey, racquetball, soccer, softball. Men's club crew, lacrosse, rugby. Women's club crew.

**ADMISSIONS. Academic basis for candidate selection** (in order of priority): Secondary school record, class rank, standardized test scores, school's recommendation, essay.
**Nonacademic basis for candidate selection:** Character and personality are emphasized. Extracurricular participation is important. Particular talent or ability, geographical distribution, and alumni/ae relationship are considered.
**Requirements:** Graduation from secondary school is required; GED is accepted. 16 units and the following program of study are required: 4 units of English, 4 units of history. 3 units of mathematics, 3 units of science, and 2 units of foreign language are recommended. HEOP for applicants not normally admissible. SAT or ACT is required. Campus visit and interview recommended. No off-campus interviews.
**Procedure:** Take SAT or ACT by November of 12th year. Visit college for interview by December of 12th year. Suggest filing application by November 15; no deadline. Notification of admission on rolling basis. Reply is required by May 1. $75 nonrefundable tuition deposit. $75 nonrefundable room deposit. Freshmen accepted for terms other than fall.
**Special programs:** Admission may be deferred one year. Credit and/or placement may be granted through CEEB Advanced Placement exams for scores of 3 or higher. Credit and/or placement may be granted through CLEP subject exams. Credit and placement may be granted through Regents College, DANTES, and challenge exams and military experience. Early decision program. Deadline for applying for early decision is November 15. Early entrance/early admission program. Concurrent enrollment program.
**Transfer students:** Transfer students accepted for terms other than fall. In fall 1993, 37% of all new students were transfers into all classes. 463 transfer applications were received, 394 were accepted. Application deadline is rolling for fall; rolling for spring. Minimum 2.0 GPA required. Lowest course grade accepted is "C." Maximum number of transferable credits is 66 semester hours from a two-year school and 90 semester hours from a four-year school. At least 30 semester hours must be completed at the college to receive degree.
**Admissions contact:** Peter E. Lindsey, Dean of Admissions. 716 385-8064.

**FINANCIAL AID. Available aid:** Pell grants, SEOG, state scholarships and grants, school scholarships and grants, private scholarships and grants, ROTC scholarships, and academic merit scholarships. Perkins Loans (NDSL), PLUS, Stafford Loans (GSL), and SLS. AMS and deferred payment plan.
**Financial aid statistics:** 17% of aid is not need-based. In 1993-94, 100% of all undergraduate applicants received aid. Average amounts of aid awarded freshmen: Scholarships and grants, $5,090; loans, $2,682.
**Supporting data/closing dates:** FAFSA: Priority filing date is March 1. State aid form: Priority filing date is March 1. Notification of awards on rolling basis.
**Financial aid contact:** Anne Steger, M.S., Director of Financial Aid. 716 385-8042.

**STUDENT EMPLOYMENT.** College Work/Study Program. Institutional employment. 21% of full-time undergraduates work on campus during school year. Students may expect to earn an average of $1,200 during school year. Off-campus part-time employment opportunities rated "excellent."

**COMPUTER FACILITIES.** 98 IBM/IBM-compatible, Macintosh/Apple, and RISC-/UNIX-based microcomputers; all are networked. Students may access Digital, SUN minicomputer/mainframe systems, BITNET, Internet. Client/LAN operating systems include Apple/Macintosh, DOS, OS/2, UNIX/XENIX/AIX, X-windows, DEC, LocalTalk/AppleTalk. Computer languages and software packages include BASIC, C, COBOL, dBASE, FORTRAN, LISP, Lotus 1-2-3, Microsoft Word, MINITAB, Modula 2, Paradox, Pascal, SPSS, Windows, WordPerfect; 25 in all. Computer facilities are available to all students.
**Fees:** None.
**Hours:** 98 hours/week.

**GRADUATE CAREER DATA.** Graduate school percentages: 2% enter law school. 1% enter medical school. 1% enter dental school. 5% enter graduate business programs. 4% enter graduate arts and sciences programs. Highest graduate school enrollments: Nazareth Coll, Rochester Inst of Tech, St. John Fisher Coll, SUNY at Albany, SUNY at Buffalo, SUNY Coll at Brockport, Syracuse U, U of Rochester. Companies and businesses that hire graduates: Eastman Kodak, First Federal Bank, Paychex, Sutherland Group, Xerox, Wegmans, U of Rochester, St. John Fisher Coll.

**PROMINENT ALUMNI/AE.** Timothy Kinsella, senior investigator, National Cancer Institute; Leon Lesniak, vice-president and regional manager, IBM; Davis Larimer, federal court judge; Raphael Ndingi, bishop, Kenya; Robert Agostinelli, partner, Lazard Freres; Thomas Hogan, managing partner, Deloitte & Touche; Eugene Welch, assistant district attorney, Rochester region.

# St. John's University

**Jamaica, NY 11439 — 718 990-6161**

**1993-94 Costs.** Tuition: $8,600. Housing: None. Fees, books, misc. academic expenses (school's estimate): $380.
**Enrollment.** Undergraduates: 5,654 men, 6,131 women (full-time). Freshman class: 7,653 applicants, 2,587 accepted, 2,400 enrolled. Graduate enrollment: 2,448 men, 2,828 women.
**Test score averages/ranges.** Average SAT scores: 430 verbal, 501 math.
**Faculty.** 623 full-time; 414 part-time. 80% of faculty holds highest degree in specific field. Student/faculty ratio: 20 to 1.
**Selectivity rating.** Competitive.

**PROFILE.** St. John's, founded in 1870, is a church-affiliated university. Programs are offered through the Colleges of Business Administration, Education and Human Services, Liberal Arts and Sciences, and Pharmacy and Allied Health Professions; Institute of Asian Studies; and Evening and Weekend College. Its 95-acre campus is located in Jamaica, 16 miles from Staten Island.

**Accreditation:** MSACS. Professionally accredited by the American Assembly of Collegiate Schools of Business, the American Bar Association, the American Council on Pharmaceutical Education, the American Library Association, the American Psychological Association, the Association of American Law Schools.
**Religious orientation:** St. John's University is affiliated with the Roman Catholic Church (Vincentian Fathers); three semesters of theology required.
**Library:** Collections totaling over 1,122,412 volumes, 14,969 periodical subscriptions, and 1,778,017 microform items.
**Special facilities/museums:** Art gallery, cultural museum, Asian cultural center, TV center.
**Athletic facilities:** Gymnasiums, swimming pool, track, baseball, football, lacrosse, soccer, and softball fields, rifle range, basketball, squash, and racquetball courts, exercise, fencing, weight rooms.

**STUDENT BODY. Undergraduate profile:** 95% are state residents; 7% are transfers. 10% Asian-American, 11% Black, 12% Hispanic, 1% Native American, 66% White. Average age of undergraduates is 20.
**Freshman profile:** 95% of accepted applicants took SAT; 5% took ACT.
**Undergraduate achievement:** 75% of fall 1991 freshmen returned for fall 1992 term. 61% of entering class graduated.
**Foreign students:** 452 students are from out of the country. Countries represented include China, Hong Kong, India, Korea, Taiwan, and the United Kingdom; 82 in all.

**PROGRAMS OF STUDY. Degrees:** B.A., B.F.A., B.S., B.S.Ed., B.S.Med.Tech., B.S.Pharm.
**Majors:** Accounting, American Studies, Anthropology, Applied Statistics, Art, Art Education, Asian Studies, Athletic Administration, Biology, Biology Education, Chemistry, Chemistry Education, Chinese Education, Communication Arts, Computer Science, Creative Photography, Criminal Justice, Economics, Elementary/Bilingual Education, Elementary Education, Elementary Education/Special Education, English, English Education, Environmental Studies, Environmental Studies Education, Finance, Fine Arts, French, French Education, Funeral Service Administration, German, German Education, Government/Politics, Graphic Design, Health Care Administration, History, Human Services, Italian, Italian Education, Japanese Education, Journalism, Literature/Speech, Management, Marketing, Mathematical Physics, Mathematics, Mathematics Education, Medical Technology, Microcomputer Systems, Paralegal Studies, Pathologist's Assistant, Pharmacy, Philosophy, Philosophy/Theology, Physical Science, Physician Assistant, Physics, Physics Education, Political Science, Professional Career Photography, Psychology, Public Administration/Public Service, Quantitative Analysis, Security Administration, Social Sciences, Social Studies, Social Studies Education, Sociology, Spanish, Spanish Education, Speech, Speech Education, Speech/Hearing Handicapped Education, Speech Pathology/Audiology, Theology, Toxicology, Transportation.
**Distribution of degrees:** The majors with the highest enrollment are management, pharmacy, and accounting; security administration, philosophy/theology, and physical science have the lowest.
**Requirements:** General education requirement.
**Academic regulations:** Minimum 2.0 GPA must be maintained.
**Special:** Minors and concentrations offered in many majors. Associate's degrees offered. Double majors. Dual degrees. Independent study. Accelerated study. Pass/fail grading option. Internships. Graduate school at which undergraduates may take graduate-level courses. Preprofessional programs in law, medicine, pharmacy, dentistry, and theology. 3-2 engineering program with Polytech U. Member of International Association of Universities and International Council on Education for Teaching. Teacher certification in early childhood, elementary, secondary, special education, and bilingual/bicultural education. Certification in specific subject areas. Study abroad in Hungary and Ireland. ROTC.
**Honors:** Honors program. Honor societies.
**Academic Assistance:** Remedial reading, writing, math, and study skills. Nonremedial tutoring.

**STUDENT LIFE. Housing:** Commuter campus; no student housing.
**Social atmosphere:** As reported by the student newspaper, "On-campus activities are gaining popularity, despite the change in the drinking age." Popular events on campus include basketball games, International Night, and Comedy Nights. Influential groups on campus include the student government and Greeks. Off campus, students meet at J.P.O.D.'s and Gantry's. Favorite on-campus spots include the Quad Lounge, the Rathskeller, and the cafeterias.

**Services and counseling/handicapped student services:** Placement services. Health service. Speech and hearing clinic. Counseling services for minority and veteran students. Personal and psychological counseling. Career and academic guidance services. Religious counseling. Physically disabled student services. Learning disabled services. Tape recorders. Tutors.
**Campus organizations:** Undergraduate student government. Student newspapers (St. John's Today; Torch; Arrow). Literary magazine. Yearbook. Radio and TV stations. Glee club, mixed chorus, gospel choir, Chappell Players, Circle K, CAUSE, De Paul Social Action Group, Student Union Board, Accounting Society, 130 organizations in all. 20 fraternities, no chapter houses; 18 sororities, no chapter houses. 5% of men join a fraternity. 5% of women join a sorority.
**Religious organizations:** Campus Liturgy Group, Catholic League, Catholic Student Association, Chinese Christian Fellowship, Christian Fellowship, Jewish Student Organization, St. Vincent de Paul Society.
**Minority/foreign student organizations:** Haraya (black student group), Multi-Cultural Student Association, Organization of Latin American Students. International Student Association, African, Armenian, Asian, Caribbean, Chinese, Filipino, German, Greek, Guyanese, Haitian, Indian, Irish, Italian, Japanese, Latin American, Spanish, and Ukrainian groups.

**ATHLETICS. Physical education requirements:** None.
**Intercollegiate competition:** 4% of students participate. Baseball (M), basketball (M,W), cross-country (M,W), diving (M,W), fencing (M), football (M), golf (M), lacrosse (M), riflery (M,W), soccer (M,W), softball (W), swimming (M,W), tennis (M,W), track (indoor) (M,W), track (outdoor) (M,W), track and field (indoor) (M,W), track and field (outdoor) (M,W), volleyball (W). Member of Big East Conference, ECAC, NCAA Division I, NCAA Division I-AA for football.
**Intramural and club sports:** 10% of students participate. Intramural aerobics, basketball, crew, fencing, judo, racquetball, squash, swimming, touch football, volleyball, wrestling. Men's club bowling, cheerleading, crew, handball, horsemanship, martial arts, racquetball, squash, volleyball, weight lifting, wrestling. Women's club cheerleading, crew, martial arts, squash, volleyball, weight lifting, wrestling.

**ADMISSIONS. Academic basis for candidate selection** (in order of priority): Secondary school record, standardized test scores, school's recommendation, class rank.
**Requirements:** Graduation from secondary school is required; GED is accepted. 16 units and the following program of study are required: 4 units of English, 2 units of math, 1 unit of science, 2 units of foreign language, 1 unit of social studies, 6 units of electives including 3 units of academic electives. Minimum combined SAT score of 1000 or minimum 3.0 GPA required. Portfolio required of art program applicants. HEOP for applicants not normally admissible. Self-Pace and College Admissions Program for applicants not normally admissible. SAT is required; ACT may be substituted. No off-campus interviews.
**Procedure:** Take SAT or ACT in 11th or 12th year. Notification of admission on rolling basis. Reply is required within four weeks of acceptance. $100 nonrefundable tuition deposit. Freshmen accepted for terms other than fall.
**Special programs:** Admission may be deferred one year. Credit and/or placement may be granted through CEEB Advanced Placement exams for scores of 3 or higher. Credit and/or placement may be granted through CLEP general and subject exams. Credit may be granted through life experience. Credit and placement may be granted through Regents College and DANTES exams and military experience. Early entrance/early admission program. Concurrent enrollment program.
**Transfer students:** Transfer students accepted for terms other than fall. In fall 1992, 7% of all new students were transfers into all classes. Minimum 2.0 GPA required for most programs; higher for allied health, pharmacy, and science programs. Lowest course grade accepted is "C." 2,636 transfer applications were received, 1,143 were accepted. Application deadline is August 1 for fall; December 1 for spring. Maximum number of transferable semester hours varies from 90 to 96 for bachelor's degree programs. At least 30 semester hours must be completed at the university to receive degree.
**Admissions contact:** Vivian Liu, M.A., Director of Admissions. 718 990-6240.

**FINANCIAL AID. Available aid:** Pell grants, SEOG, state scholarships and grants, school scholarships and grants, private scholarships and grants, ROTC scholarships, academic merit scholarships, and athletic scholarships. Perkins Loans (NDSL), PLUS, Stafford Loans (GSL), and SLS. Knight Tuition Plans.
**Financial aid statistics:** 40% of aid is not need-based. In 1992-93, 73% of all undergraduate applicants received aid; 90% of freshman applicants. Average amounts of aid awarded freshmen: Scholarships and grants, $4,542; loans, $2,225.
**Supporting data/closing dates:** FAFSA/FAF: Priority filing date is April 1. Notification of awards begins May 1.
**Financial aid contact:** Joseph Sciame, Director of Financial Aid. 718 990-6403.

**STUDENT EMPLOYMENT.** College Work/Study Program. Institutional employment. 5% of full-time undergraduates work on campus during school year. Students may expect to earn an average of $5,304 during school year. Freshmen are discouraged from working during their first term. Off-campus part-time employment opportunities rated "excellent."

**COMPUTER FACILITIES.** 360 IBM/IBM-compatible and Macintosh/Apple microcomputers; all are networked. Students may access IBM minicomputer/mainframe systems, BITNET. Computer languages and software packages include APL, BASIC, COBOL, DISSPLA, FORTRAN, LISP, Lotus 1-2-3, Pascal, PL/1; graphics, statistical, word processing packages. Computer facilities are available to all students.
**Fees:** Computer fee is included in tuition/fees.
**Hours:** 8 AM-11:30 PM (M-F); 9 AM-5 PM (Sa); 11 AM-5 PM (Su).

**PROMINENT ALUMNI/AE.** George Deukmejian, former governor, California; Mario Cuomo, governor, New York; Hugh Carey, former governor, New York; Jill M. Considine, superintendent of banks, New York State Banking Commission; Daniel P. Tully, president and CEO, Merrill Lynch; Ron Brown, U.S. secretary of commerce.

# St. Joseph's College (Brooklyn)

**Brooklyn, NY 11205** — **718 636-6800**

**1994-95 Costs.** Tuition: $7,140. Housing: None. Fees, books, misc. academic expenses (school's estimate): $922.
**Enrollment.** Undergraduates: 85 men, 327 women (full-time). Freshman class: 268 applicants, 163 accepted, 73 enrolled.
**Test score averages/ranges.** Average SAT scores: 426 verbal, 460 math.
**Faculty.** 43 full-time; 67 part-time. 50% of faculty holds doctoral degree. Student/faculty ratio: 10 to 1.
**Selectivity rating.** Less competitive.

**PROFILE.** St. Joseph's, Brooklyn, is a private, liberal arts college. Founded as a women's college in 1916, it adopted coeducation in 1971. Its two-acre campus is located in a residential section of Brooklyn.

**Accreditation:** MSACS. Professionally accredited by the National League for Nursing.
**Religious orientation:** St. Joseph's College (Brooklyn) is nonsectarian; no religious requirements.
**Library:** Collections totaling over 116,505 volumes, 431 periodical subscriptions, and 3,095 microform items.
**Special facilities/museums:** Child study center, on-campus preschool.
**Athletic facilities:** Gymnasium.

**STUDENT BODY. Undergraduate profile:** 99% are state residents. 5% Asian-American, 38% Black, 8% Hispanic, 49% White. Average age of undergraduates is 20.
**Freshman profile:** 96% of accepted applicants took SAT. 23% of freshmen come from public schools.
**Undergraduate achievement:** 80% of fall 1992 freshmen returned for fall 1993 term. 65% of entering class graduated. 40% of students who completed a degree program immediately went on to graduate study.

**PROGRAMS OF STUDY. Degrees:** B.A., B.S.
**Majors:** Accounting, Biology, Business Administration, Chemistry, Child Study, Child Study/Special Education Option, Community Health, English, French, General Studies, Health Administration, History, Human Relations, Management of Human Resources, Mathematics, Nursing, Psychology, Social Sciences, Spanish, Speech Communication.
**Distribution of degrees:** The majors with the highest enrollment are health administration, child study, and community health; biology, history, and accounting have the lowest.
**Requirements:** General education requirement.
**Academic regulations:** Minimum 2.0 GPA must be maintained.
**Special:** Certificate programs in data/information processing, criminology/criminal justice, and other subjects. Independent study. Pass/fail grading option. Internships. Preprofessional programs in law, medicine, nursing, and occupational therapy. 2-4 podiatry program with New York Coll of Podiatry. 3-2 occupational therapy program with New York U. Teacher certification in early childhood, elementary, secondary, and special education. Study abroad possible.
**Honors:** Honor societies.
**Academic Assistance:** Nonremedial tutoring.

**ADMISSIONS. Academic basis for candidate selection** (in order of priority): Secondary school record, standardized test scores, school's recommendation, class rank.
**Nonacademic basis for candidate selection:** Character and personality, extracurricular participation, particular talent or ability, and alumni/ae relationship are considered.
**Requirements:** Graduation from secondary school is required; GED is accepted. 16 units and the following program of study are required: 4 units of English, 2 units of math, 1 unit of lab science, 2 units of foreign language, 1 unit of history, 6 units of electives. Special program for applicants not normally admissible. SAT is required; ACT may be substituted. Campus visit and interview recommended. No off-campus interviews.
**Procedure:** Take SAT or ACT by January of 12th year. Suggest filing application by March 15. Application deadline is August 15. Notification of admission on rolling basis. Reply is required by May 1. $200 nonrefundable tuition deposit. Freshmen accepted for terms other than fall.
**Special programs:** Admission may be deferred one year. Credit and/or placement may be granted through CEEB Advanced Placement exams for scores of 3 or higher. Credit and/or placement may be granted through CLEP subject exams. Early decision program. Early entrance/early admission program. Concurrent enrollment program.
**Transfer students:** Transfer students accepted for terms other than fall. Application deadline is August 15 for fall; December 15 for spring. Minimum 2.0 GPA required. Lowest course grade accepted is "C." Maximum number of transferable credits is 64 semester hours. At least 48 semester hours must be completed at the college to receive degree.
**Admissions contact:** Geraldine Foudy, M.P.A., Director of Admissions. 718 636-6868.

**FINANCIAL AID. Available aid:** Pell grants, SEOG, state scholarships and grants, school scholarships and grants, private scholarships and grants, and academic merit scholarships. Alumni Scholarships. Tuition Remission. Perkins Loans (NDSL), PLUS, and SLS. Tuition Plan Inc. and AMS.
**Financial aid statistics:** 50% of aid is not need-based. In 1993-94, 98% of all undergraduate applicants received aid; 98% of freshman applicants. Average amounts of aid awarded freshmen: Scholarships and grants, $3,000; loans, $2,000.
**Supporting data/closing dates:** FAFSA: Priority filing date is February 25. School's own aid application: Priority filing date is March 15. State aid form: Priority filing date is February 25. Income tax forms: Deadline is March 25. Notification of awards begins April 1.
**Financial aid contact:** Carol Sullivan, Director of Financial Aid. 718 636-6800, extension 205.

# St. Joseph's College (Patchogue)

**Patchogue, NY 11772** **516 447-3200**

**1993-94 Costs.** Tuition: $7,000. Housing: None. Fees, books, misc. academic expenses (school's estimate): $732.
**Enrollment.** Undergraduates: 324 men, 935 women (full-time). Freshman class: 446 applicants, 349 accepted, 149 enrolled.
**Test score averages/ranges.** Average SAT scores: 451 verbal, 483 math.
**Faculty.** 55 full-time; 113 part-time. 47% of faculty holds doctoral degree. Student/faculty ratio: 12 to 1.
**Selectivity rating.** Less competitive.

**PROFILE.** St. Joseph's, Patchogue, founded in 1916, is a private, liberal arts college. Its 28-acre campus, established in 1976, was redesignated the Suffolk Campus in 1979.

**Accreditation:** MSACS.
**Religious orientation:** St. Joseph's College (Patchogue) is nonsectarian; no religious requirements.
**Library:** Collections totaling over 71,898 volumes, 488 periodical subscriptions, and 3,670 microform items.
**Special facilities/museums:** Long Island history museum, theatre.
**Athletic facilities:** Gymnasium, tennis courts, baseball and soccer fields, weight room.

**STUDENT BODY. Undergraduate profile:** 61% are transfers. 1% Asian-American, 3% Black, 4% Hispanic, 92% White. Average age of undergraduates is 26.
**Freshman profile:** 2% of freshmen who took SAT scored 700 or over on math; 5% scored 600 or over on verbal, 10% scored 600 or over on math; 23% scored 500 or over on verbal, 46% scored 500 or over on math; 78% scored 400 or over on verbal, 88% scored 400 or over on math; 99% scored 300 or over on verbal, 100% scored 300 or over on math. 99% of accepted applicants took SAT; 1% took ACT. 83% of freshmen come from public schools.
**Undergraduate achievement:** 73% of fall 1992 freshmen returned for fall 1993 term. 51% of entering class graduated. 35% of students who completed a degree program immediately went on to graduate study.

**PROGRAMS OF STUDY. Degrees:** B.A., B.S.
**Majors:** Accounting, Biology, Business Administration, Child Study, Child Study/Special Education Option, English, History, Human Relations, Mathematics/Computer Science, Psychology, Recreation, Social Sciences.
**Distribution of degrees:** The majors with the highest enrollment are child study, business administration, and accounting; recreation and biology have the lowest.
**Requirements:** General education requirement.
**Academic regulations:** Minimum 2.0 GPA must be maintained.
**Special:** Pass/fail grading option. Internships. Preprofessional programs in law, medicine, veterinary science, and dentistry. 3-1 biomedical program with Columbia U Sch of Dental and Oral Surgery and New York Coll of Podiatric Medicine. 3-2 occupational therapy with New York U. Member of Long Island Regional Advisory Council for Higher Education. Teacher certification in early childhood, elementary, secondary, and special education. Certification in specific subject areas. ROTC at Hofstra U. AFROTC at New York Inst of Tech.

**STUDENT LIFE. Housing:** Commuter campus; no student housing.
**Social atmosphere:** As reported by the student newspaper, "Patchogue is a great shopping town. There are lots of things to do between classes. Student Services at SJC is constantly coming up with new events to raise student interest. Everyone knows everyone here because everyone is involved in expanding and making SJC better each year." Influential student groups include Campus Ministry and Student Government. "The student lounge on the first floor is packed every day of the week." Also popular is "common hour where activities are held in the Rathskeller, Board Room, or Music Room."
**Services and counseling/handicapped student services:** Placement services. Counseling services for veteran and older students. Personal counseling. Career and academic guidance services. Physically disabled student services. Learning disabled services. Notetaking services. Tape recorders.
**Campus organizations:** Undergraduate student government. Student newspaper (Talon). Literary magazine. Yearbook. Campus Activity Board, business and child study clubs, Circle K, cultural affairs committee, drama and folk music clubs, English and foreign language clubs, fitness club, cheerleaders kickline, 18 organizations in all.
**Religious organizations:** Campus Ministry Club, Pax Christi.

**ATHLETICS. Physical education requirements:** None.
**Intercollegiate competition:** 10% of students participate. Baseball (M), basketball (M), cheerleading (W), horsemanship (W), soccer (M), softball (W), tennis (M,W), volleyball (W). Member of Central Atlantic Collegiate Conference, NAIA.
**Intramural and club sports:** 2% of students participate. Intramural billiards, soccer, table tennis, tennis, volleyball. Men's club softball. Women's club bowling, soccer.

**ADMISSIONS. Academic basis for candidate selection** (in order of priority): Secondary school record, standardized test scores, class rank, school's recommendation, essay.
**Requirements:** Graduation from secondary school is required; GED is accepted. 16 units and the following program of study are required: 4 units of English, 2 units of math, 1 unit of lab science, 2 units of foreign language, 1 unit of history, 6 units of academic electives. Minimum combined SAT score of 850 and minimum 2.0 GPA required. R.N. required of nursing program applicants. SAT is required; ACT may be substituted. Campus visit and interview recommended. No off-campus interviews.
**Procedure:** Take SAT or ACT by November of 12th year. Application deadline is August 15. Notification of admission on rolling basis. No set date by which applicants must accept offer. $205 nonrefundable tuition deposit. Freshmen accepted for terms other than fall.
**Special programs:** Admission may be deferred two years. Credit may be granted through CEEB Advanced Placement for scores of 3 or higher. Credit may be granted through CLEP general and subject exams, Regents College and DANTES exams, and military and life experience. Early entrance/early admission program. Concurrent enrollment program.
**Transfer students:** Transfer students accepted for terms other than fall. In fall 1993, 61% of all new students were transfers into all classes. 489 transfer applications were received, 431 were accepted. Application deadline is August 15 for fall; January 1 for spring. Minimum 2.0 GPA required. Lowest course grade accepted is "C." Maximum number of transferable credits is 64 semester hours from a two-year school and 96 semester hours from a four-year school. At least 35 semester hours must be completed at the college to receive degree.
**Admissions contact:** Marion E. Salgado, M.A., Director of Admissions. 516 447-3219.

**FINANCIAL AID. Available aid:** Pell grants, SEOG, state scholarships and grants, school scholarships and grants, and private scholarships and grants. Perkins Loans (NDSL), PLUS, Stafford Loans (GSL), and SLS. Tuition Plan Inc. and AMS.
**Financial aid statistics:** 15% of aid is not need-based. In 1993-94, 66% of all undergraduate applicants received aid; 55% of freshman applicants. Average amounts of aid awarded freshmen: Scholarships and grants, $2,100; loans, $2,625.
**Supporting data/closing dates:** FAFSA/FAF: Priority filing date is February 25. School's own aid application: Priority filing date is February 25. Income tax forms. Notification of awards begins April 15.
**Financial aid contact:** Carol Sullivan, Director of Financial Aid. 516 447-3200.

**STUDENT EMPLOYMENT.** College Work/Study Program. Institutional employment. 3% of full-time undergraduates work on campus during school year. Students may expect to earn an average of $1,000 during school year. Off-campus part-time employment opportunities rated "good."

**COMPUTER FACILITIES.** 45 IBM/IBM-compatible, Macintosh/Apple, and RISC-/UNIX-based microcomputers. Students may access IBM minicomputer/mainframe systems. Client/LAN operating systems include Apple/Macintosh, DOS, UNIX/XENIX/AIX, X-windows. Computer languages and software packages include BASIC, C, COBOL, dBASE, ISETL, Lotus 1-2-3, Pascal, Professional Write, Prolog, SAS, SPS, Word Works, WordPerfect. Computer facilities are available to all students.
**Fees:** None.
**Hours:** 7:30 AM-10 PM.

**GRADUATE CAREER DATA.** Graduate school percentages: 5% enter law school. 1% enter medical school. 1% enter dental school. 10% enter graduate business programs. 25% enter graduate arts and sciences programs. 1% enter theological school/seminary. Highest graduate school enrollments: Adelphi U, Hofstra U, Long Island U-C.W. Post Campus, SUNY Coll at Stony Brook. 50% of graduates choose careers in business and industry. Companies and businesses that hire graduates: Grumman, National Westminster.

# St. Lawrence University

**Canton, NY 13617** **315 379-5011**

**1994-95 Costs.** Tuition: $18,720. Room & board: $5,730. Fees, books, misc. academic expenses (school's estimate): $320.
**Enrollment.** Undergraduates: 942 men, 987 women (full-time). Freshman class: 2,753 applicants, 1,820 accepted, 505 enrolled. Graduate enrollment: 33 men, 57 women.
**Test score averages/ranges.** Average SAT scores: 515 verbal, 573 math. Range of SAT scores of middle 50%: 470-550 verbal, 520-620 math.
**Faculty.** 152 full-time; 17 part-time. 94% of faculty holds highest degree in specific field. Student/faculty ratio: 12 to 1.
**Selectivity rating.** Competitive.

**PROFILE.** St. Lawrence, founded in 1856, is a private, liberal arts university. The campus includes a building dating from 1856 registered with the National Register of Historic Places. Its 1,000-acre campus is located in Canton, in northern New York.

**Accreditation:** MSACS.
**Religious orientation:** St. Lawrence University is nonsectarian; no religious requirements.
**Library:** Collections totaling over 404,545 volumes, 2,371 periodical subscriptions, and 360,604 microform items.
**Special facilities/museums:** Art gallery, language lab, center for international education, mobile environmental research facility, 76-acre forest preserve, two electron microscopes.
**Athletic facilities:** Gymnasium, field house, swimming pool, basketball, squash, and tennis courts, weight room, sauna, tracks, athletic fields, ice rink, riding arena, outdoor trails.

**STUDENT BODY. Undergraduate profile:** 54% are state residents; 8% are transfers. 2% Asian-American, 3% Black, 2% Hispanic, 1% Native American, 92% White. Average age of undergraduates is 20.
**Freshman profile:** Majority of accepted applicants took SAT. 62% of freshmen come from public schools.
**Undergraduate achievement:** 88% of fall 1992 freshmen returned for fall 1993 term. 72% of entering class graduated. 25% of students who completed a degree program immediately went on to graduate study.
**Foreign students:** 23 students are from out of the country. Countries represented include Bulgaria, Canada, China, India, Kenya, and Soviet Union; 20 in all.

**PROGRAMS OF STUDY. Degrees:** B.A., B.S.
**Majors:** Anthropology, Asian Studies, Biology, Biology/Physics, Canadian Studies, Chemistry, Economics, Economics/Mathematics, English, Environmental Studies, Fine Arts, French, Geology, Geology/Physics, German, Government, History, Mathematics, Mathematics/Computer Studies, Multifield Major, Multilanguage, Music, Philosophy, Physics, Psychology, Religious Studies/Classical Languages, Sociology, Spanish, Speech/Theatre, Sport/Leisure Studies.
**Distribution of degrees:** The majors with the highest enrollment are English, economics, and psychology; German, physics, and music have the lowest.
**Requirements:** General education requirement.
**Academic regulations:** Minimum 2.0 GPA must be maintained.

**Special:** Minors offered in most majors and in African, Caribbean/Latin American, and gender studies, applied statistics, English literature, and writing. Self-designed majors. Double majors. Independent study. Pass/fail grading option. Internships. Graduate school at which undergraduates may take graduate-level courses. Preprofessional programs in law, medicine, veterinary science, dentistry, and optometry. 3-2 engineering programs with Clarkson U, Columbia U, Rensselaer Polytech Inst, U of Rochester, U of Southern California, Washington U, and Worcester Polytech Inst. 3-2 nursing program with U of Rochester. 4-1 M.B.A. program with Clarkson U. Member of Associated Colleges of the St. Lawrence Valley; cross-registration possible. Washington Semester. Teacher certification in secondary education. Certification in specific subject areas. Member of International Student Exchange Program (ISEP). Study abroad in Austria, Canada, Costa Rica, Denmark, France, India, Japan, Kenya, the former Soviet Republics, Spain, and the United Kingdom. AFROTC at Clarkson U.
**Honors:** Phi Beta Kappa. Honor societies.
**Academic Assistance:** Nonremedial tutoring.

**STUDENT LIFE. Housing:** All unmarried students under age 21 must live on campus unless living near campus with relatives. Coed dorms. Sorority and fraternity housing. Off-campus privately-owned housing. Theme cottages. 98% of students live in college housing.
**Social atmosphere:** The University Center, the Pub, Tick Tock, and ODY (library) are favorite student hangouts. Groups with an influence on campus social life include Greeks, athletes, student government, and ACE, which provides a wide array of social and cultural activities from movies to plays to art openings. Peak Week is a big event at St. Lawrence, when groups hike up all 46 of the Adirondack High Peaks. Also popular are hockey games and concerts.
**Services and counseling/handicapped student services:** Health service. Women's center. Counseling services for minority students. Personal and psychological counseling. Career and academic guidance services. Physically disabled student services. Learning disabled services. Tape recorders. Tutors.
**Campus organizations:** Undergraduate student government. Student newspaper (Hill News, published once/week). Literary magazine. Yearbook. Radio station. Annual arts festival, The Laurentian Singers, drama productions, Association for Campus Entertainment (ACE), Panhellenic Council, outing and riding clubs, photography club, environmental awareness group, debating, Forensic Society, Community Development Corps, Habitat for Humanity, Big Brothers/Big Sisters, 75 organizations in all. Seven fraternities, six chapter houses; five sororities, all with chapter houses. 35% of men join a fraternity. 35% of women join a sorority.
**Religious organizations:** Intervarsity Christian Fellowship, Jewish Student Union, Newman Center.
**Minority/foreign student organizations:** AHORA (Hispanic group), Black Student Union, LAMDA, Students of Color for Action, Native American student group, ASIA (Asian-American group). International House.

**ATHLETICS. Physical education requirements:** One semester of physical education required.
**Intercollegiate competition:** 30% of students participate. Alpine skiing (M,W), baseball (M), basketball (M,W), cross-country (M,W), diving (M,W), field hockey (W), football (M), horsemanship (M,W), ice hockey (M,W), lacrosse (M,W), Nordic skiing (M,W), soccer (M,W), swimming (M,W), tennis (M,W), track (indoor) (M,W), track (outdoor) (M,W), track and field (indoor) (M,W), track and field (outdoor) (M,W), volleyball (W), wrestling (M). Member of EAA, ECAC, NCAA Division I for men's ice hockey, NCAA Division III.
**Intramural and club sports:** 70% of students participate. Intramural basketball, golf, ice hockey, lacrosse, soccer, softball, squash, tennis, touch football, volleyball.

**ADMISSIONS. Academic basis for candidate selection** (in order of priority): Secondary school record, class rank, school's recommendation, essay, standardized test scores.
**Nonacademic basis for candidate selection:** Character and personality are emphasized. Extracurricular participation and particular talent or ability are important. Alumni/ae relationship is considered.
**Requirements:** Graduation from secondary school is required; GED is accepted. No specific distribution of secondary school units required. HEOP for applicants not normally admissible. SAT or ACT is required. ACH recommended. Campus visit and interview recommended. Off-campus interviews available with admissions and alumni representatives.
**Procedure:** Take SAT or ACT by January of 12th year. Take ACH by January of 12th year. Application deadline is February 1. Acceptance notification begins March 15. Reply is required by May 1. $500 nonrefundable tuition deposit. Freshmen accepted for terms other than fall.
**Special programs:** Admission may be deferred one year. Credit and/or placement may be granted through CEEB Advanced Placement exams for scores of 4 or higher. Credit and/or placement may be granted through CLEP subject exams. Placement may be granted through challenge exams. Early decision program. In fall 1993, 134 applied for early decision and 124 were accepted. Deadline for applying for early decision is December 15.
**Transfer students:** Transfer students accepted for terms other than fall. In fall 1992, 8% of all new students were transfers into all classes. 95 transfer applications were received, 60 were accepted. Application deadline is May 1 for fall; December 1 for spring. Minimum 3.0 GPA required. Lowest course grade accepted is "C." Maximum number of transferable credits is 63 semester hours. At least 60 semester hours must be completed at the university to receive degree.
**Admissions contact:** Joel Wincowski, M.A., Dean of Admissions and Financial Aid. 315 379-5261, 800 285-1856.

**FINANCIAL AID. Available aid:** Pell grants, SEOG, state scholarships and grants, school scholarships and grants, private scholarships and grants, academic merit scholarships, and aid for undergraduate foreign students. Perkins Loans (NDSL), PLUS, Stafford Loans (GSL), and school loans. Tuition Plan Inc., Knight Tuition Plans, and AMS. School's own payment plan.
**Financial aid statistics:** 1% of aid is not need-based. In 1993-94, 95% of all undergraduate applicants received aid; 97% of freshman applicants. Average amounts of aid awarded freshmen: Scholarships and grants, $12,817; loans, $2,655.
**Supporting data/closing dates:** FAFSA/FAF: Deadline is February 15. School's own aid application: Deadline is February 15. Income tax forms: Deadline is May 31. Notification of awards begins March 15.
**Financial aid contact:** Philip M. Bisselle, M.A.T., Director of Financial Aid. 315 379-5265.

**STUDENT EMPLOYMENT.** College Work/Study Program. Institutional employment. 39% of full-time undergraduates work on campus during school year. Students may expect to earn an average of $1,330 during school year. Off-campus part-time employment opportunities rated "poor."

**COMPUTER FACILITIES.** 600 IBM/IBM-compatible and Macintosh/Apple microcomputers; all are networked. Students may access minicomputer/mainframe systems, BITNET. Residence halls may be equipped with networked microcomputers. Computer languages and software packages include BMDP, CMS, COBOL, dBASE, FORTRAN, Lotus 1-2-3, MINITAB, MUSIC, Pascal, PL/1, SAS, SPSS, Word for Windows, WordPerfect, XyWrite. Computer facilities are available to all students.
**Fees:** Computer fee is included in tuition/fees.
**Hours:** 24 hours.

**GRADUATE CAREER DATA.** Graduate school percentages: 12% enter law school. 10% enter medical school. 8% enter graduate business programs. 46% enter graduate arts and sciences programs. Highest graduate school enrollments: Boston U, U of Chicago, Clarkson U, Columbia U, Cornell U, Syracuse U. 75% of graduates choose careers in business and industry. Companies and businesses that hire graduates: Boston Company, Chase Manhattan, Chubb Insurance, General Electric, Xerox.

**PROMINENT ALUMNI/AE.** Kirk Douglas, actor; Dr. Paul Parkman, co-discoverer of the rubella vaccine; Grace Fippinger, vice president, treasurer, and secretary, NYNEX; Dave Jennings, former professional football player, New York Giants.

# St. Thomas Aquinas College

**Sparkill, NY 10976 — 914 398-4000**

**1993-94 Costs.** Tuition: $8,000. Room & board: $5,400. Fees, books, misc. academic expenses (school's estimate): $650.
**Enrollment.** Undergraduates: 476 men, 633 women (full-time). Freshman class: 861 applicants, 650 accepted, 226 enrolled. Graduate enrollment: 25 men, 80 women.
**Test score averages/ranges.** Average SAT scores: 440 verbal, 450 math.
**Faculty.** 75 full-time; 55 part-time. 92% of faculty holds doctoral degree. Student/faculty ratio: 17 to 1.
**Selectivity rating.** Less competitive.

**PROFILE.** St. Thomas Aquinas is a private, liberal arts college. Founded in 1952, it adopted coeducation in 1969. Its 46-acre campus is located in Sparkill, 15 miles from New York City.

**Accreditation:** MSACS.
**Religious orientation:** St. Thomas Aquinas College is nonsectarian; one semester of religion required.
**Library:** Collections totaling over 102,000 volumes, 935 periodical subscriptions, and 21,000 microform items.
**Special facilities/museums:** On-campus preschool, language lab.
**Athletic facilities:** Gymnasium, fitness center, basketball and tennis courts.

**STUDENT BODY. Undergraduate profile:** 65% are state residents; 45% are transfers. 3% Asian-American, 4.2% Black, 7.7% Hispanic, 83.3% White, 1.8% Other. Average age of undergraduates is 21.
**Freshman profile:** 100% of accepted applicants took SAT. 80% of freshmen come from public schools.
**Undergraduate achievement:** 80% of fall 1992 freshmen returned for fall 1993 term. 47% of entering class graduated. 38% of students who completed a degree program went on to graduate study within one year.
**Foreign students:** 23 students are from out of the country. Countries represented include Germany, India, Ireland, Japan, and the Philippines; nine in all.

**PROGRAMS OF STUDY. Degrees:** B.A., B.S., B.S.Ed.
**Majors:** Accounting, Art, Art Education, Art Therapy, Business Administration, Commercial Design, Communication Arts, Criminal Justice, Elementary Education, Engineering, English, Finance, Gerontology, History, Marketing, Mathematics, Medical Technology, Natural Science, Philosophy/Religious Studies, Psychology, Recreation/Leisure, Romance Languages, Secondary Education, Social Sciences, Spanish, Special Education.
**Distribution of degrees:** The majors with the highest enrollment are business administration, education, and communication arts; gerontology has the lowest.
**Requirements:** General education requirement.
**Academic regulations:** Freshmen must maintain minimum 1.85 GPA; sophomores, juniors, seniors, 2.0 GPA.
**Special:** Courses offered in astronomy, biology, chemistry, computer programming, economics, French, geography, geology, German, Italian, library science, music, physics, political science, and sociology. Off-campus courses for credit available at various centers in Rockland County. Associate's degrees offered. Double majors. Dual degrees. Independent study. Accelerated study. Pass/fail grading option. Internships. Cooperative education programs. Graduate school at which undergraduates may take graduate-level courses. Preprofessional programs in law, medicine, and dentistry. 3-2 engineering programs with George Washington U and Manhattan Coll. Teacher certification in elementary, secondary, special education, and bilingual/bicultural education. Certification in specific subject areas. Study abroad in England. AFROTC at Manhattan Coll.
**Honors:** Honors program. Honor societies.
**Academic Assistance:** Remedial writing, math, and study skills.

**STUDENT LIFE. Housing:** Students may live on or off campus. Coed dorms. School-owned/operated apartments. 35% of students live in college housing.
**Social atmosphere:** Popular events at St. Thomas Aquinas include dances, concerts, poetry readings, dorm events, game shows, and art expositions. According to the student

newspaper, "If there were more funds available there could be a better social and cultural life. St. Thomas Aquinas College is predominantly a commuter school; it's tough to maintain student interest." Athletes, the radio station, and dorm students have the most influence on campus.
**Services and counseling/handicapped student services:** Placement services. Counseling services for older students. Personal and psychological counseling. Career and academic guidance services. Religious counseling. Learning disabled program/services.
**Campus organizations:** Undergraduate student government. Student newspaper (Thoma, published once/two weeks). Literary magazine. Yearbook. Radio station. Chorus, Laetare Players, Cultural Affairs, ski and video clubs, Political Union, academic and special-interest groups, 20 organizations in all.
**Religious organizations:** Campus Ministry.
**Minority/foreign student organizations:** International Club.

**ATHLETICS. Physical education requirements:** None.
**Intercollegiate competition:** 16% of students participate. Baseball (M), basketball (M,W), cross-country (M), golf (M), soccer (W), softball (W), volleyball (W). Member of Central Atlantic Collegiate Conference, NAIA.
**Intramural and club sports:** 5% of students participate. Intramural basketball, fitness, floor hockey, Wiffle ball. Men's club soccer. Women's club cheerleading, cross-country.

**ADMISSIONS. Academic basis for candidate selection** (in order of priority): Secondary school record, class rank, standardized test scores, school's recommendation, essay.
**Nonacademic basis for candidate selection:** Character and personality, extracurricular participation, particular talent or ability, and alumni/ae relationship are considered.
**Requirements:** Graduation from secondary school is required; GED is accepted. 16 units and the following program of study are required: 4 units of English, 2 units of math, 2 units of science, 1 unit of foreign language, 1 unit of history, 7 units of academic electives. Minimum SAT scores of 400 in both verbal and math, rank in top half of secondary school class, and minimum "C+" average recommended. HEOP for applicants not normally admissible. SAT is required. Campus visit and interview recommended. No off-campus interviews.
**Procedure:** Take SAT by November of 12th year. Visit college for interview by December of 12th year. Suggest filing application by January; no deadline. Notification of admission on rolling basis. Reply is required by May 1. $100 tuition deposit, refundable until May 1. $250 room deposit, refundable until May 1. Freshmen accepted for terms other than fall.
**Special programs:** Admission may be deferred one year. Credit and/or placement may be granted through CEEB Advanced Placement exams for scores of 3 or higher. Credit and/or placement may be granted through CLEP general and subject exams. Credit and placement may be granted through DANTES exams and military and life experience. Early entrance/early admission program. Concurrent enrollment program.
**Transfer students:** Transfer students accepted for terms other than fall. In fall 1993, 45% of all new students were transfers into all classes. 353 transfer applications were received, 335 were accepted. Application deadline is rolling for fall; rolling for spring. Minimum 2.0 GPA required. Lowest course grade accepted is "C." Maximum number of transferable credits is 90 semester hours. At least 30 semester hours must be completed at the college to receive degree.
**Admissions contact:** Leo Flynn, M.A., Dean of Enrollment Management. 914 398-4100.

**FINANCIAL AID. Available aid:** Pell grants, SEOG, state grants, school scholarships and grants, academic merit scholarships, and athletic scholarships. Perkins Loans (NDSL), PLUS, Stafford Loans (GSL), and SLS. Tuition Plan Inc., Education Plan Inc., AMS, deferred payment plan, and family tuition reduction.
**Financial aid statistics:** In 1993-94, 65% of all undergraduate applicants received aid; 70% of freshman applicants. Average amounts of aid awarded freshmen: Scholarships and grants, $1,500; loans, $2,200.
**Supporting data/closing dates:** FAFSA/FAF: Accepted on rolling basis. School's own aid application: Accepted on rolling basis. Income tax forms: Accepted on rolling basis. Notification of awards on rolling basis.
**Financial aid contact:** Peter Brennan, M.A., Director of Financial Aid. 914 398-4100.

**STUDENT EMPLOYMENT.** College Work/Study Program. Institutional employment. Students may expect to earn an average of $2,000 during school year. Off-campus part-time employment opportunities rated "good."

**COMPUTER FACILITIES.** 50 IBM/IBM-compatible and Macintosh/Apple microcomputers; all are networked. Students may access Hewlett-Packard minicomputer/mainframe systems. Computer languages and software packages include Assembler, BASIC, COBOL, dBASE, FORTRAN, Lotus 1-2-3, Pascal, SPSS, WordPerfect, WordStar. Computer facilities are available to all students.
**Fees:** $30 computer fee per course.
**Hours:** 8 AM-9:30 PM (M-F); 9 AM-5 PM (Sa-Su).

**GRADUATE CAREER DATA.** Graduate school percentages: 3% enter law school. 1% enter medical school. 19% enter graduate business programs. Highest graduate school enrollments: Fordham U, Iona Coll, Pace U. 35% of graduates choose careers in business and industry. Companies and businesses that hire graduates: Big Six accounting firms.

## Sarah Lawrence College

**Bronxville, NY 10708** **914 337-0700**

**1994-95 Costs.** Tuition: $19,300. Room: $4,816. Board: $2,400. Fees, books, misc. academic expenses (school's estimate): $898.
**Enrollment.** Undergraduates: 233 men, 699 women (full-time). Freshman class: 1,380 applicants, 770 accepted, 256 enrolled. Graduate enrollment: 26 men, 196 women.
**Test score averages/ranges.** Average ACT scores: 27 composite. Range of ACT scores of middle 50%: 24-27 composite.
**Faculty.** 163 full-time; 63 part-time. 92% of faculty holds doctoral degree. Student/faculty ratio: 6 to 1.
**Selectivity rating.** Highly competitive.

**PROFILE.** Sarah Lawrence is a private, liberal arts college. Founded as a women's college in 1926, it adopted coeducation in 1968. Its 35-acre campus, with Tudor-style buildings, is located in Bronxville, north of New York City.

**Accreditation:** MSACS.
**Religious orientation:** Sarah Lawrence College is nonsectarian; no religious requirements.
**Library:** Collections totaling over 210,253 volumes, 1,193 periodical subscriptions, and 13,534 microform items.
**Special facilities/museums:** Performing arts center, child development institute, on-campus preschool, greenhouse, environmental theater.
**Athletic facilities:** Fitness center, racquetball and tennis courts, gymnasium, swimming pool, ice rink, dance studio, athletic field, bowling alley.

**STUDENT BODY. Undergraduate profile:** 23% are state residents; 20% are transfers. 5% Asian-American, 6% Black, 5% Hispanic, 1% Native American, 78% White, 5% Other. Average age of undergraduates is 20.
**Freshman profile:** 7% of freshmen who took SAT scored 700 or over on verbal, 4% scored 700 or over on math; 45% scored 600 or over on verbal, 31% scored 600 or over on math; 81% scored 500 or over on verbal, 72% scored 500 or over on math; 95% scored 400 or over on verbal, 92% scored 400 or over on math; 98% scored 300 or over on verbal, 98% scored 300 or over on math. Majority of accepted applicants took SAT. 60% of freshmen come from public schools.
**Undergraduate achievement:** 96% of fall 1992 freshmen returned for fall 1993 term. 80% of entering class graduated. 70% of students who completed a degree program went on to graduate study within five years.
**Foreign students:** 88 students are from out of the country. Countries represented include Canada, England, France, Japan, Spain, and Switzerland; 35 in all.

**PROGRAMS OF STUDY. Degrees:** B.A.
**Majors:** American Studies, Anthropology, Art History, Asian Studies, Biology, Chemistry, Computer Science, Creative Writing, Dance, Economics, Film, French, Geology, German, History, International Studies, Italian, Latin, Literature, Mathematics, Music, Philosophy, Physics, Political Science, Psychology, Public Policy, Religion, Russian, Science, Sociology, Spanish, Studio Art, Theatre, Women's Studies, Writing.
**Distribution of degrees:** The majors with the highest enrollment are literature, history, and psychology.
**Special:** Students are not required to major in a particular field; they may choose an area of concentration rather than completing strict major or minor requirements. Professional-level creative arts program is an integral part of academic curriculum. Self-designed majors. Double majors. Independent study. Internships. Graduate school at which undergraduates may take graduate-level courses. Preprofessional programs in law and medicine. Member of American Collegiate Consortium. Marine Biology Semester (St. Croix). Exchange programs abroad in England (London Theatre Inst, Oxford U), France, and Italy (U of Florence). Study abroad also in the former Soviet Republics.
**Academic Assistance:** Nonremedial tutoring.

**STUDENT LIFE. Housing:** Students may live on or off campus. Coed, women's, and men's dorms. School-owned/operated apartments. 90% of students live in college housing.
**Social atmosphere:** As reported by the student newspaper, the post office and Valceann House are popular on-campus areas. Off campus, students frequent Nathan's and the Spinning Wheel. Special campus events are the Bob Dylan Look-Alike Contest and the celebration of Hemingway's birthday.
**Services and counseling/handicapped student services:** Placement services. Health service. Counseling services for minority and older students. Birth control, personal, and psychological counseling. Career and academic guidance services.
**Campus organizations:** Undergraduate student government. Student newspaper (SLC Newspaper, published once/week). Literary magazine. Yearbook. Chamber music groups, chorus, orchestra, concert and guest lecture series, dance group, film series, Feminist Alliance, Amnesty International, AIDS peer counselors, Homeless Task Force, Environmental Awareness, outdoors club, museum club, 38 organizations in all.
**Religious organizations:** Jewish Student Union, Bible Study, Christian Fellowship, Newman Club, Unitarian Universalist group, Society of Friends group.
**Minority/foreign student organizations:** Harambe, Unidad, Asian Student Union, Men of Color (MOCA).

**ATHLETICS. Physical education requirements:** Two semesters of physical education required.
**Intercollegiate competition:** 10% of students participate. Crew (M,W), horsemanship (M,W), tennis (M,W), volleyball (W). Member of Hudson Valley Women's Athletic Conference, Intercollegiate Horse Show Association, Metropolitan Rowing Association, National Collegiate Cycling Association.
**Intramural and club sports:** 20% of students participate. Intramural badminton, basketball, bowling, fencing, flag football, pickleball, softball, tennis, ultimate frisbee, volleyball.

**ADMISSIONS. Academic basis for candidate selection** (in order of priority): Secondary school record, essay, school's recommendation, class rank, standardized test scores.
**Nonacademic basis for candidate selection:** Character and personality, extracurricular participation, and particular talent or ability are emphasized. Alumni/ae relationship is important. Geographical distribution is considered.
**Requirements:** Graduation from secondary school is recommended; GED is accepted. No specific distribution of secondary school units required. SAT or ACT is required. ACH required. Campus visit and interview recommended. Off-campus interviews available with admissions and alumni representatives.
**Procedure:** Take SAT or ACT by January of 12th year. Take ACH by January of 12th year. Visit college for interview by February 1 of 12th year. Application deadline is February 1. Notification of admission by April 1. Reply is required by May 1. $400 nonrefundable tuition deposit. Freshmen accepted for terms other than fall.
**Special programs:** Admission may be deferred one year. Credit may be granted through CEEB Advanced Placement for scores of 4 or higher. Early decision program. In fall 1993, 97 applied for early decision and 65 were accepted. Deadline for applying for early decision is November 15 and January 1. Early entrance/early admission program.

**Transfer students:** Transfer students accepted for terms other than fall. In fall 1993, 20% of all new students were transfers into all classes. 218 transfer applications were received, 95 were accepted. Application deadline is April 15 for fall; December 1 for spring. Minimum 3.0 GPA recommended. Lowest course grade accepted is "C." Maximum number of transferable credits is 60 semester hours. At least 60 semester hours must be completed at the college to receive degree.
**Admissions contact:** Barbara Friend, M.A., Dean of Admissions. 914 395-2510.

**FINANCIAL AID. Available aid:** Pell grants, SEOG, state grants, school grants, private scholarships and grants, and academic merit scholarships. Perkins Loans (NDSL), PLUS, Stafford Loans (GSL), and SLS. Knight Tuition Plans. NELLIE MAE, Educational Credit Corp.
**Financial aid statistics:** In 1993-94, 88% of all undergraduate applicants received aid; 83% of freshman applicants. Average amounts of aid awarded freshmen: Scholarships and grants, $12,197; loans, $2,550.
**Supporting data/closing dates:** FAFSA/FAF: Priority filing date is February 1. School's own aid application: Priority filing date is February 1. Income tax forms: Priority filing date is April 15. Notification of awards begins April 1.
**Financial aid contact:** Heather McDonnell, M.Ed., Director of Financial Aid. 914 395-2570.

**STUDENT EMPLOYMENT.** College Work/Study Program. Institutional employment. 45% of full-time undergraduates work on campus during school year. Students may expect to earn an average of $1,400 during school year. Off-campus part-time employment opportunities rated "good."

**COMPUTER FACILITIES.** 20 IBM/IBM-compatible and Macintosh/Apple microcomputers; 4 are networked. Residence halls may be equipped with networked terminals. Computer languages and software packages include C, dBASE, LISP, Lotus 1-2-3, Microsoft Word, Paint Brush, Pascal, Prolog, Windows, WordPerfect. Computer facilities are available to all students.
**Fees:** None.
**Hours:** 24 hours.

**GRADUATE CAREER DATA.** Graduate school percentages: 14% enter law school. 7% enter medical school. 1% enter dental school. 4% enter graduate business programs. 49% enter graduate arts and sciences programs. Highest graduate school enrollments: UC Berkeley, Columbia U, Middlebury Coll, New York U. 14% of graduates choose careers in business and industry.

**PROMINENT ALUMNI/AE.** Jane Alexander, actress, head of National Endowment for the Arts; Alice Walker, novelist; Barbara Walters, journalist; Jon Avnet and Brian DePalma, filmmakers; Holly Robinson, actress; Jean Baker Miller, psychiatrist and author, *Toward a New Psychology of Women*; Janice Simpson, editor, *Time* magazine; Meredith Monk, composer, choreographer, and director; Ellen James, superior court justice.

# School of Visual Arts

**New York, NY 10010-3994** **212 592-2100**

**1993-94 Costs.** Tuition: $11,000. Room: $4,500. Fees, books, misc. academic expenses (school's estimate): $980.
**Enrollment.** Graduate enrollment: 230.
**Test score averages/ranges.** Average SAT scores: 480 verbal, 460 math.
**Faculty.** Student/faculty ratio: 12 to 1.
**Selectivity rating.** Noncompetitive.

**PROFILE.** The School of Visual Arts, founded in 1947, is a private college of art. Its campus of five buildings is located in lower Manhattan.

**Accreditation:** MSACS. Professionally accredited by the National Association of Schools of Art and Design.
**Religious orientation:** School of Visual Arts is nonsectarian; no religious requirements.
**Library:** Collections totaling over 60,000 volumes and 255 periodical subscriptions.
**Special facilities/museums:** Art musuem, student galleries, animation studio, amphitheatre.

**STUDENT BODY. Undergraduate profile:** 70% are state residents; 40% are transfers. 6% Asian-American, 5% Black, 4% Hispanic, 85% White. Average age of undergraduates is 19.
**Freshman profile:** Majority of accepted applicants took SAT.
**Undergraduate achievement:** 85% of fall 1992 freshmen returned for fall 1993 term.
**Foreign students:** 200 students are from out of the country. Countries represented include China, England, Germany, India, Japan, and Korea; 32 in all.

**PROGRAMS OF STUDY. Degrees:** B.F.A.
**Majors:** Advertising, Animation, Art Education, Art Therapy, Cartooning, Computer Art, Film, Fine Arts, Graphic Design, Illustration, Interior Design, Photography, Video.
**Special:** Independent study. Pass/fail grading option. Internships. Member of National Portfolio Days Association. Exchange programs in Israel (Bezalel Acad of Arts and Design), England (Middlesex Polytech and Central/St. Martin's), France (ESAG), and the Netherlands (Amsterdam Sch of the Arts). Study abroad also in Japan (Tokyo Gakuin Designer's Coll), Italy, Ireland, Greece, and Spain.
**Academic Assistance:** Remedial reading, writing, and study skills.

**ADMISSIONS. Academic basis for candidate selection** (in order of priority): Secondary school record, standardized test scores, essay.
**Nonacademic basis for candidate selection:** Particular talent or ability is emphasized. Character and personality and extracurricular participation are important.
**Requirements:** Graduation from secondary school is required; GED is accepted. No specific distribution of secondary school units required. Portfolio required of most applicants; shooting script and essay required of film and video program applicants. Conditional admission possible for applicants not meeting standard requirements. SAT or ACT is required. Campus visit recommended. Off-campus interviews available with an admissions representative.
**Procedure:** Take SAT or ACT by February of 12th year. Visit college for interview by April of 12th year. Suggest filing application by January. Notification of admission on rolling basis. Reply is required by May 1. $100 nonrefundable tuition deposit. $200 nonrefundable room deposit. Freshmen accepted for terms other than fall.
**Special programs:** Admission may be deferred one year. Credit may be granted through CEEB Advanced Placement for scores of 3 or higher. Credit and/or placement may be granted through CLEP general and subject exams.
**Transfer students:** Transfer students accepted for terms other than fall. In fall 1993, 40% of all new students were transfers into all classes. Application deadline is rolling for fall; rolling for spring. Minimum 2.0 GPA required. Lowest course grade accepted is "C." Maximum number of transferable credits is 64 semester hours. At least 64 semester hours must be completed at the school to receive degree.
**Admissions contact:** Lawrence E. Wilson, Director of Admissions. 212 679-7350, extension 299.

**FINANCIAL AID. Available aid:** Pell grants, SEOG, state scholarships and grants, and school scholarships and grants. Perkins Loans (NDSL), PLUS, Stafford Loans (GSL), state loans, private loans, and SLS. Tuition Plan Inc.
**Supporting data/closing dates:** FAFSA/FAF: Deadline is March 1. School's own aid application: Deadline is March 1. Notification of awards on rolling basis.
**Financial aid contact:** Howard Leslie, Director of Financial Aid. 212 679-7350.

# Siena College

**Loudonville, NY 12211-1462** **518 783-2300**

**1994-95 Costs.** Tuition: $10,800. Room: $2,980. Board: $2,120. Fees, books, misc. academic expenses (school's estimate): $910.
**Enrollment.** Undergraduates: 1,247 men, 1,422 women (full-time). Freshman class: 2,961 applicants, 1,932 accepted, 628 enrolled.
**Test score averages/ranges.** Average SAT scores: 491 verbal, 560 math. Average ACT scores: 24 composite.
**Faculty.** 169 full-time; 84 part-time. 69% of faculty holds doctoral degree. Student/faculty ratio: 16 to 1.
**Selectivity rating.** More competitive.

**PROFILE.** Siena is a church-affiliated, multipurpose college. Founded in 1937, it adopted coeducation in 1969. Programs are offered through the Divisions of Arts, Business, and Science. Its 155-acre campus is located in Loudonville, 15 miles north of Albany.

**Accreditation:** MSACS. Professionally accredited by the Council on Social Work Education.
**Religious orientation:** Siena College is affiliated with the Roman Catholic Church (Franciscan Friars); two semesters of religion/theology required.
**Library:** Collections totaling over 244,564 volumes, 1,767 periodical subscriptions, and 29,613 microform items.
**Athletic facilities:** Swimming pool, aerobics, exercise machinery, weight rooms, lacrosse, baseball, and soccer fields, basketball, racquetball, squash, tennis, and volleyball courts, track.

**STUDENT BODY. Undergraduate profile:** 85% are state residents; 24% are transfers. 2% Asian-American, 2% Black, 2% Hispanic, 93% White, 1% Other. Average age of undergraduates is 20.
**Freshman profile:** 92% of accepted applicants took SAT; 30% took ACT. 73% of freshmen come from public schools.
**Undergraduate achievement:** 93% of fall 1992 freshmen returned for fall 1993 term. 74% of entering class graduated. 24% of students who completed a degree program immediately went on to graduate study.
**Foreign students:** 26 students are from out of the country. Countries represented include Canada and England; 10 in all.

**PROGRAMS OF STUDY. Degrees:** B.A., B.Bus.Admin., B.S.
**Majors:** Accounting, American Studies, Biology, Chemistry, Classical Languages, Computer Science, Economics, English, Finance, French, History, Marketing/Management, Mathematics, Philosophy, Physics, Political Science, Psychology, Religious Studies, Social Work, Sociology, Spanish.
**Distribution of degrees:** The majors with the highest enrollment are marketing/management, accounting, and finance; classical languages, religious studies, and Spanish have the lowest.
**Requirements:** General education requirement.
**Academic regulations:** Freshmen must maintain minimum 1.5 GPA; sophomores, 1.7 GPA; juniors, 1.9 GPA; seniors, 2.0 GPA.
**Special:** Courses offered in business law, fine arts, German, Greek, Latin, Russian, and statistics. International studies/foreign language/business program. Certificate programs in accounting, computer science, peace studies, and theatre arts. Concentration requirements. Dual degrees. Independent study. Accelerated study. Pass/fail grading option. Internships. Graduate school at which undergraduates may take graduate-level courses. Preprofessional programs in law, medicine, veterinary science, dentistry, and optometry. 2-2 program with SUNY Syracuse Sch of Environmental Science and Forestry. 4-1 M.B.A. program with Clarkson U. Siena-Albany Medical Coll Program in Medicine. 3-2 engineering programs with Catholic U, Clarkson U, Manhattan Coll, Rensselaer Polytech Inst, Western New England Coll, SUNY Binghamton. Member of Hudson-Mohawk Association of Colleges and Universities. Washington Semester. Exchange program with American U. Teacher certification in secondary education. Certification in specific subject areas. Member of International Student Exchange Program (ISEP). ROTC. AFROTC at Rensselaer Polytech Inst.
**Honors:** Phi Beta Kappa. Honors program. Honor societies.
**Academic Assistance:** Remedial writing and study skills.

**STUDENT LIFE. Housing:** All freshmen living beyond a 50-mile radius must live on campus. Coed dorms. College-owned townhouses for seniors. 70% of students live in college housing.

**Social atmosphere:** According to the editor of the student newspaper, "New York State's alcohol law makes a lot of places off–limits, but many off-campus spots have under-over nights. Siena is still adjusting to the change in the law in terms of on-campus programming." On campus, students gather at the Arc and the Rat. Favorite spots off campus include TGI Friday's, Madden's, O'Flaherty's, Dapper's, Poppy's, and the 21 Club. Influential groups on campus are athletes and the Black/Latin Student Union. Favorite events during the school year are basketball games, Winter Weekend, Rock for Human Concerns, and Spring Weekends.
**Services and counseling/handicapped student services:** Placement services. Health service. Women's program. Counseling services for minority, military, and older students. Personal and psychological counseling. Career and academic guidance services. Religious counseling. Physically disabled student services. Learning disabled services. Notetaking services. Tape recorders. Tutors.
**Campus organizations:** Undergraduate student government. Student newspaper (Promethean, published once/two weeks). Literary magazine. Yearbook. Radio station. Big Brothers/Big Sisters, film series, Stage III, Human Concerns Committee, 61 organizations in all.
**Religious organizations:** Campus Ministry.
**Minority/foreign student organizations:** Black and Latin Student Union, Multicultural Society. Asian Student Organization.

**ATHLETICS. Physical education requirements:** None.
**Intercollegiate competition:** 20% of students participate. Baseball (M), basketball (M,W), cross-country (M,W), field hockey (W), football (M), golf (M), lacrosse (M), soccer (M,W), softball (W), tennis (M,W), track (W), track (indoor) (M,W), track and field (indoor) (M,W), volleyball (W). Member of ECAC, Metro Atlantic Athletic Conference.
**Intramural and club sports:** 80% of students participate. Intramural basketball, football, golf, soccer, softball, volleyball, walleyball. Men's club cheerleading, fencing, ice hockey, martial arts, rugby, skiing, track. Women's club cheerleading, fencing, lacrosse, martial arts, skiing.

**ADMISSIONS. Academic basis for candidate selection** (in order of priority): Secondary school record, class rank, school's recommendation, standardized test scores, essay.
**Nonacademic basis for candidate selection:** Character and personality are emphasized. Extracurricular participation is important. Particular talent or ability, geographical distribution, and alumni/ae relationship are considered.
**Requirements:** Graduation from secondary school is required; GED is accepted. 16 units and the following program of study are required: 4 units of English, 3 units of math, 3 units of science, 2 units of foreign language, 4 units of social studies. Additional units of math and science recommended. HEOP for applicants not normally admissible. SAT or ACT is required. Campus visit and interview recommended. No off-campus interviews.
**Procedure:** Take SAT or ACT by January of 12th year. Take ACH by January of 12th year. Visit college for interview by February of 12th year. Application deadline is March 1. Notification of admission by March 15. Reply is required by May 1. $200 tuition deposit, refundable until May 1. Freshmen accepted for terms other than fall.
**Special programs:** Admission may be deferred one year. Credit and/or placement may be granted through CEEB Advanced Placement exams for scores of 4 or higher. Credit and/or placement may be granted through CLEP general and subject exams. Credit and placement may be granted through challenge exams. Early decision program. In fall 1993, 398 applied for early decision and 335 were accepted. Deadline for applying for early decision is December 1. Early entrance/early admission program.
**Transfer students:** Transfer students accepted for terms other than fall. In fall 1993, 24% of all new students were transfers into all classes. 416 transfer applications were received, 312 were accepted. Application deadline is July 1 for fall; December 1 for spring. Minimum 2.5 GPA recommended. Lowest course grade accepted is "C." Maximum number of transferable credits is 66 semester hours from a two-year school and 90 semester hours from a four-year school. At least 30 semester hours must be completed at the college to receive degree.
**Admissions contact:** Katherine M. McCarthy, M.B.A., Dean of Admissions. 518 783-2423.

**FINANCIAL AID. Available aid:** Pell grants, SEOG, state scholarships and grants, school scholarships and grants, private scholarships and grants, ROTC scholarships, academic merit scholarships, and athletic scholarships. Perkins Loans (NDSL), PLUS, Stafford Loans (GSL), private loans, and SLS. Tuition Plan Inc., Knight Tuition Plans, and AMS.
**Financial aid statistics:** 24% of aid is not need-based. In 1993-94, 100% of all undergraduate applicants received aid. Average amounts of aid awarded freshmen: Scholarships and grants, $5,295; loans, $2,480.
**Supporting data/closing dates:** FAFSA: Priority filing date is February 1. School's own aid application: Priority filing date is February 1. State aid form: Priority filing date is February 1. Income tax forms: Priority filing date is April 15. Notification of awards begins April 1.
**Financial aid contact:** Ann Donovan White, M.S.Ed., Director of Financial Aid. 518 783-2427.

**STUDENT EMPLOYMENT.** College Work/Study Program. Institutional employment. 20% of full-time undergraduates work on campus during school year. Students may expect to earn an average of $800 during school year. Off-campus part-time employment opportunities rated "good."

**COMPUTER FACILITIES.** 120 IBM/IBM-compatible and Macintosh/Apple microcomputers; 75 are networked. Students may access Digital minicomputer/mainframe systems, BITNET. Client/LAN operating systems include Apple/Macintosh, DOS, DEC. Computer languages and software packages include APL, BASIC, C, C++, COBOL, Enable, FORTRAN, Harvard Graphics, ImSL, LISP, Lotus, MacroAssembler, Mass-II, MINITAB, Pascal, PC Globe, PL/1, Prolog, RDB, Regis, SPSS, WordPerfect. Computer facilities are available to all students.
**Fees:** Computer fee is included in tuition/fees.
**Hours:** 24 hours.

**GRADUATE CAREER DATA.** Graduate school percentages: 3% enter law school. 4% enter medical school. 1% enter dental school. 2% enter graduate business programs. 9% enter graduate arts and sciences programs. Highest graduate school enrollments: Albany Law School, Albany Medical Coll, Renssaeler Polytech Inst, State U of New York. Companies and businesses that hire graduates: Albany Medical Center, Coopers & Lybrand, Fleet Bank, Geary Corp., General Electric, KPMG Peat Marwick, Key Bank, State of New York.

**PROMINENT ALUMNI/AE.** George Deukmejian, governor of California; J. Patrick Barrett, CEO, Carpat; William Kennedy, Pulitzer Prize-winning author.

# Skidmore College

**Saratoga Springs, NY 12866 518 584-5000**

**1994-95 Costs.** Tuition: $18,710. Room: $3,170. Board: $2,515. Fees, books, misc. academic expenses (school's estimate): $756.
**Enrollment.** Undergraduates: 879 men, 1,248 women (full-time). Freshman class: 4,024 applicants, 2,700 accepted, 596 enrolled.
**Test score averages/ranges.** Average SAT scores: 520 verbal, 560 math. Range of SAT scores of middle 50%: 470-570 verbal, 510-610 math.
**Faculty.** 184 full-time; 17 part-time. 92% of faculty holds highest degree in specific field. Student/faculty ratio: 11 to 1.
**Selectivity rating.** Competitive.

**PROFILE.** Skidmore is a private, liberal arts college. Founded in 1903, it adopted coeducation in 1971. Its 800-acre campus is located in Saratoga Springs, 30 miles from Albany.

**Accreditation:** MSACS. Professionally accredited by the American Assembly of Collegiate Schools of Business, the Council on Social Work Education, the National Association of Schools of Art and Design.
**Religious orientation:** Skidmore College is nonsectarian; no religious requirements.
**Library:** Collections totaling over 377,000 volumes, 1,600 periodical subscriptions, and 160,000 microform items.
**Special facilities/museums:** Art galleries, center for child study, art, music, dance, and theatre facilities, quantitative reasoning lab, electron microscope, X-ray fluorescence spectrometer.
**Athletic facilities:** Gymnasium, swimming pool, weight room, basketball, racquetball, squash, tennis, and volleyball courts, baseball, field hockey, lacrosse, soccer, softball, and touch football fields, cross-country trails, riding center, driving range.

**STUDENT BODY. Undergraduate profile:** 31% are state residents; 1% are transfers. 4% Asian-American, 3% Black, 4% Hispanic, 86% White, 3% Other. Average age of undergraduates is 20.
**Freshman profile:** 4% of freshmen who took SAT scored 700 or over on verbal; 31% scored 600 or over on verbal, 15% scored 600 or over on math; 79% scored 500 or over on verbal, 60% scored 500 or over on math; 96% scored 400 or over on verbal, 94% scored 400 or over on math; 97% scored 300 or over on verbal, 97% scored 300 or over on math. 100% of accepted applicants took SAT; 9% took ACT. 58% of freshmen come from public schools.
**Undergraduate achievement:** 91% of fall 1991 freshmen returned for fall 1992 term. 73% of entering class graduated. 25% of students who completed a degree program went on to graduate study within one year.
**Foreign students:** 16 students are from out of the country. Countries represented include Canada, England, France, Germany, Japan, and Switzerland.

**PROGRAMS OF STUDY. Degrees:** B.A., B.S.
**Majors:** American Studies, Anthropology, Art Education, Art History, Biology, Biology/Chemistry, Biology/Philosophy, Biology/Psychology, Business, Business/Economics, Business/French, Business/German, Business/Government, Business/Mathematics, Business/Physical Education, Business/Spanish, Chemistry, Classics, Computer Science, Dance, Dance/Theatre, Economics, Economics/French, Economics/German, Economics/Mathematics, Economics/Philosophy, Economics/Sociology, Economics/Spanish, Elementary Education, English, English/French, English/German, English/Philosophy, English/Spanish, French, French Area Studies, Geology, German, Government, Government/French, Government/German, Government/History, Government/Philosophy, Government/Sociology, Government/Spanish, History, History/Philosophy, Mathematics, Music, Philosophy, Physical Education, Physics, Political Economy, Psychology, Psychology/Sociology, Self-Determined Majors, Social Work, Sociology, Sociology/Anthropology, Spanish, Studio Art, Theatre, University Without Walls.
**Distribution of degrees:** The majors with the highest enrollment are English, business, and government; physical education, dance, and German have the lowest.
**Requirements:** General education requirement.
**Academic regulations:** Freshmen must maintain minimum 1.67 GPA; sophomores, juniors, seniors, 2.0 GPA.
**Special:** Minors offered in most majors and in Asian studies, early childhood education, environmental studies, Italian, law/society, religion, and women's studies. Individually designed programs, including work experience, through University Without Walls program. College Venture Program provides placement and counseling for students taking leave of absence to pursue full-time internships. Self-designed majors. Double majors. Dual degrees. Independent study. Accelerated study. Pass/fail grading option. Internships. Preprofessional programs in law, medicine, veterinary science, and dentistry. 4-1 M.B.A. program with Clarkson U. Accelerated law school entry program with Cardozo Law Sch of Yeshiva U. 3-2 engineering programs with Clarkson U and Dartmouth Coll. 3-2 M.B.A. program with Rensselaer Polytech Inst. M.A. teaching program with Union Coll. Member of Hudson-Mohawk Association of Colleges and Universities; cross-registration possible. Washington Semester. Teacher certification in elementary education. Certification in specific subject areas. Member of American Collegiate Consortium for East-West Cultural and Academic Exchange. Exchange programs abroad in China (Qufu U) and Japan (Sophia U). Study abroad also in African countries, Australia, Austria, England, France, Germany, India, Israel, Italy, Scotland, and Spain. ROTC at Rensselaer Polytech Inst. and Siena Coll. NROTC and AFROTC at Rensselaer Polytech Inst.
**Honors:** Phi Beta Kappa. Honor societies.
**Academic Assistance:** Nonremedial tutoring.

**STUDENT LIFE. Housing:** All freshmen and sophomores must live on campus. Coed dorms. School-owned/operated apartments. 81% of students live in college housing.
**Social atmosphere:** The student newspaper reports, "On-campus social life consists of approximately five all-campus parties per year or small dorm parties. Off-campus social life is in bars, local ski areas, and the Saratoga Performing Arts Center. Saratoga is known for its Victorian charm, the Saratoga race track open only in August, and the American ballet center. Socially, no one group prevails, although the art department contributes to the campus. Athletics are still fairly small and unimportant. Campus organizations such as student government are not as influential as on other campuses." Favorite gathering spots are Desperate Annie's, Tin & Lint, the Broadway, Trattoria, Margarita's, and Longfellow's.
**Services and counseling/handicapped student services:** Health service. Day care. Counseling services for minority, veteran, and older students. Birth control, personal, and psychological counseling. Career and academic guidance services. Religious counseling. Physically disabled student services. Notetaking services. Reader services for the blind.
**Campus organizations:** Undergraduate student government. Student newspaper (Skidmore News, published once/week). Literary magazine. Yearbook. Radio and TV stations. Collegium Musicum, chorus, singing groups, orchestra, jazz and wind ensembles, dance club, PRO Arts, outing club, Student Entertainment Company, College Democrats, Republican Coalition, Interclass Council, Student Speakers Bureau, art and social sciences/philosophy magazines, 80 organizations in all.
**Religious organizations:** Christian Fellowship, Episcopal Club, Jewish Student Union, Newman Foundation, Tagar.
**Minority/foreign student organizations:** Society Opposed to All Racism, Black Action Movement. International Student Association, Asian Club, Alliance, Latino Cultural Society, International Relations Club.

**ATHLETICS. Physical education requirements:** None.
**Intercollegiate competition:** 25% of students participate. Baseball (M), basketball (M,W), crew (M,W), field hockey (W), golf (M), horsemanship (M,W), ice hockey (M), lacrosse (M,W), soccer (M,W), softball (W), swimming (M,W), tennis (M,W), volleyball (W). Member of ECAC, NCAA Division III, NYSWCAA.
**Intramural and club sports:** 50% of students participate. Intramural basketball, cross country, racquetball, soccer, softball, squash, tennis, touch football, volleyball. Men's club Alpine skiing, polo, volleyball, wrestling. Women's club Alpine skiing, ice hockey, polo.

**ADMISSIONS. Academic basis for candidate selection** (in order of priority): Secondary school record, school's recommendation, standardized test scores, class rank, essay.
**Nonacademic basis for candidate selection:** Character and personality and extracurricular participation are emphasized. Particular talent or ability and geographical distribution are important. Alumni/ae relationship is considered.
**Requirements:** Graduation from secondary school is required; GED is accepted. No specific distribution of secondary school units required. HEOP for applicants not normally admissible. SAT or ACT is required. ACH recommended. Campus visit and interview recommended. Off-campus interviews available with admissions and alumni representatives.
**Procedure:** Take SAT or ACT by December of 12th year. Take ACH by December of 12th year. Visit college for interview by February of 12th year. Application deadline is February 1. Notification of admission by April 1. Reply is required by May 1. $300 nonrefundable tuition deposit. Freshmen accepted for terms other than fall.
**Special programs:** Admission may be deferred two years. Credit and/or placement may be granted through CEEB Advanced Placement exams for scores of 4 or higher. Credit and/or placement may be granted through CLEP subject exams. Early decision program. In fall 1992, 319 applied for early decision and 215 were accepted. Deadline for applying for early decision is December 1 or January 15. Early entrance/early admission program.
**Transfer students:** Transfer students accepted for terms other than fall. In fall 1992, 1% of all new students were transfers into all classes. 119 transfer applications were received, 58 were accepted. Application deadline is April 1 for fall; November 15 for spring. Minimum 2.7 GPA recommended. Lowest course grade accepted is "C." Maximum number of transferable credits is 60 semester hours. At least 60 semester hours must be completed at the college to receive degree.
**Admissions contact:** Mary Lou W. Bates, Director of Admissions. 518 587-7569.

**FINANCIAL AID. Available aid:** Pell grants, SEOG, state scholarships and grants, school grants, private scholarships and grants, and ROTC scholarships. Music scholarships. Perkins Loans (NDSL), PLUS, Stafford Loans (GSL), school loans, and SLS. Guaranteed tuition. Institutional installment plan.
**Financial aid statistics:** In 1992-93, 49% of all undergraduate applicants received aid; 33% of freshman applicants. Average amounts of aid awarded freshmen: Scholarships and grants, $10,247; loans, $2,300.
**Supporting data/closing dates:** FAFSA/FAF: Deadline is February 1. School's own aid application: Deadline is February 1. Notification of awards begins April 1.
**Financial aid contact:** Robert D. Shorb, M.S., Director of Financial Aid. 518 584-5000, extension 2144.

**STUDENT EMPLOYMENT.** College Work/Study Program. Institutional employment. 45% of full-time undergraduates work on campus during school year. Students may expect to earn an average of $800 during school year. Off-campus part-time employment opportunities rated "good."

**COMPUTER FACILITIES.** 250 IBM/IBM-compatible and Macintosh/Apple microcomputers; 80 are networked. Students may access Prime, SUN minicomputer/mainframe systems, BITNET, Internet. Residence halls may be equipped with stand-alone microcomputers, networked microcomputers, networked terminals. Client/LAN operating systems include Apple/Macintosh. Computer languages and software packages include BASIC, C, dBASE, Excel, LOGO, Lotus 1-2-3, MacWrite, Pascal, Super Paint, WordPerfect; 50 in all. Computer facilities are available to all students.
**Fees:** Computer fee is included in tuition/fees.
**Hours:** 24 hours.

**GRADUATE CAREER DATA.** Highest graduate school enrollments: Boston U, Columbia U, New York U, Rensselaer Polytech Inst; SUNY at Albany. 25% of graduates choose careers in business and industry. Companies and businesses that hire graduates: Chubb Group, Ernst & Young, General Electric, Paine Webber, Quad Graphics, Shawmut International.

# State University of New York at Albany

**Albany, NY 12222** — **518 442-3300**

**1993-94 Costs.** Tuition: $2,650 (state residents), $6,550 (out-of-state). Room: $2,798. Board: $1,338. Fees, books, misc. academic expenses (school's estimate): $873.
**Enrollment.** Undergraduates: 5,432 men, 5,103 women (full-time). Freshman class: 14,397 applicants, 9,017 accepted, 1,924 enrolled. Graduate enrollment: 2,064 men, 2,952 women.
**Test score averages/ranges.** Average SAT scores: 522 verbal, 602 math. Range of SAT scores of middle 50%: 470-550 verbal, 540-640 math.
**Faculty.** 670 full-time; 232 part-time. 96% of faculty holds highest degree in specific field. Student/faculty ratio: 18 to 1.
**Selectivity rating.** More competitive.

**PROFILE.** SUNY at Albany, founded in 1844, is a public, comprehensive university. Programs are offered through the Colleges of Humanities and Fine Arts, Science and Mathematics, and Social and Behavioral Science and the Schools of Business, Criminal Justice, Education, Public Affairs, and Public Welfare. Its 560-acre campus is located in Albany.
**Accreditation:** MSACS. Professionally accredited by the American Assembly of Collegiate Schools of Business, the Council on Social Work Education.
**Religious orientation:** State University of New York at Albany is nonsectarian; no religious requirements.
**Library:** Collections totaling over 1,300,000 volumes, 7,000 periodical subscriptions, and 2,400,000 microform items.
**Special facilities/museums:** Art gallery, performing arts center, meteorological lab, atmospheric science research center, particle accelerator for ion implantation, nuclear accelerator.
**Athletic facilities:** Gymnasiums, sports bubble with tennis courts, swimming pool, weight and wrestling rooms, dance studio, fitness center, basketball, handball/racquetball, squash, and volleyball courts, baseball, lacrosse, soccer, and softball fields, indoor and outdoor tracks.

**STUDENT BODY. Undergraduate profile:** 97% are state residents; 33% are transfers. 7% Asian-American, 9% Black, 6% Hispanic, 1% Native American, 70% White, 7% Other. Average age of undergraduates is 21.
**Freshman profile:** 1% of freshmen who took SAT scored 700 or over on verbal, 8% scored 700 or over on math; 13% scored 600 or over on verbal, 53% scored 600 or over on math; 63% scored 500 or over on verbal, 95% scored 500 or over on math; 99% scored 400 or over on verbal, 100% scored 400 or over on math; 100% scored 300 or over on verbal. 99% of accepted applicants took SAT; 1% took ACT.
**Undergraduate achievement:** 89% of fall 1991 freshmen returned for fall 1992 term. 45% of students who completed a degree program went on to graduate study within one year.
**Foreign students:** 107 students are from out of the country. Countries represented include Cyprus, Hong Kong, India, Japan, Korea, and Malaysia; 26 in all.

**PROGRAMS OF STUDY. Degrees:** B.A., B.S.
**Majors:** Accounting, African/Afro-American Studies, Anthropology, Art History, Asian Studies, Atmospheric Science, Biology, Business Administration, Chemistry, Chinese Studies, Communication, Computer Science, Computer Science/Applied Mathematics, Criminal Justice, Earth Science, East Asian Studies, Economics, Education, English, French, Geography, Geological Sciences, German, Greek, Greek/Roman Civilization, History, Inter-American Studies, Interdisciplinary Studies, Italian, Japanese Studies, Judaic Studies, Latin, Latin American/Caribbean Studies, Linguistics, Mathematics, Medical Technology, Music, Philosophy, Physics, Political Science, Pre-Professional Business Sequence, Psychology, Public Affairs, Puerto Rican Studies, Religious Studies, Russian, Russian/East European Studies, Secondary Education, Social Studies, Social Welfare, Sociology, Spanish, Studio Art, Theatre, Women's Studies.
**Distribution of degrees:** The majors with the highest enrollment are psychology, English, and business administration.
**Requirements:** General education requirement.
**Academic regulations:** Minimum 2.0 GPA must be maintained.
**Special:** Programs in journalism, legal studies, peace studies, and urban affairs. Interdisciplinary programs in biochemistry, human biology, information science, and molecular biology. Self-designed majors. Double majors. Independent study. Accelerated study. Pass/fail grading option. Internships. Graduate school at which undergraduates may take graduate-level courses. Preprofessional programs in law and medicine. 3-2 engineering program with Rensselaer Polytech Inst. 3-3 law program with Albany Law Sch. Member of Hudson-Mohawk Association of Colleges and Universities; cross-registration possible. Semester or year may be spent at any of 60 participating schools in New York State through Visiting Student Program. Teacher certification in secondary, special education, and bilingual/bicultural education. Certification in specific subject areas. Study abroad in China, Denmark, France, Germany, Israel, Japan, Singapore, the former Soviet Republics, Spain, the United Kingdom, and other countries. ROTC, NROTC, and AFROTC at Siena Coll.
**Honors:** Phi Beta Kappa. Honors program.
**Academic Assistance:** Remedial reading, writing, math, and study skills. Nonremedial tutoring.

**STUDENT LIFE. Housing:** Students may live on or off campus. Coed dorms. School-owned/operated apartments. On-campus married-student housing. 60% of students live in college housing.
**Social atmosphere:** The Rat, Washington Tavern, and Bogart's are favorite gathering places for students. Greeks influence student life. Popular social events include Fountain Day, Fallfest, and Mayfest.
**Services and counseling/handicapped student services:** Health service. Day care. Counseling services for minority students. Personal and psychological counseling. Career and academic guidance services. Religious counseling. Physically disabled student ser-

vices. Learning disabled services. Notetaking services. Tape recorders. Tutors. Reader services for the blind.

**Campus organizations:** Undergraduate student government. Student newspaper (Albany Student Press, published once/week). Yearbook. Radio station. Mixed chorus, University Singers, ensembles, orchestra, band, drama productions, departmental and special-interest groups, 100 organizations in all. 26 fraternities, no chapter houses; 13 sororities, no chapter houses. 20% of men join a fraternity. 10% of women join a sorority.

**Religious organizations:** Chapel House, several religious groups.

**Minority/foreign student organizations:** Black and Hispanic groups. Several foreign groups.

**ATHLETICS. Physical education requirements:** None.

**Intercollegiate competition:** 5% of students participate. Baseball (M), basketball (M,W), cross-country (M,W), diving (M,W), football (M), lacrosse (M,W), soccer (M,W), softball (W), swimming (M,W), tennis (M,W), track (indoor) (M,W), track (outdoor) (M,W), track and field (indoor) (M,W), track and field (outdoor) (M,W), volleyball (W), wrestling (M). Member of CTC, ECAC, NCAA Division III, NYSWCAA.

**Intramural and club sports:** 35% of students participate. Intramural badminton, basketball, flag football, floor hockey, racquetball, soccer, softball, squash, tennis, volleyball.

**ADMISSIONS. Academic basis for candidate selection** (in order of priority): Secondary school record, standardized test scores, class rank, school's recommendation.

**Nonacademic basis for candidate selection:** Character and personality, extracurricular participation, and particular talent or ability are considered.

**Requirements:** Graduation from secondary school is required; GED is accepted. 18 units and the following program of study are required: 4 units of English, 2 units of math, 2 units of lab science, 3 units of social studies, 5 units of electives. Minimum combined SAT score of 1100, rank in top fifth of secondary school class, and minimum 87.5 average recommended. Portfolio required of art program applicants. Audition required of music program applicants. EOP for applicants not normally admissible. Talented Student Admission Program and Minority Recruitment Program for applicants not normally admissible. SAT is required; ACT may be substituted. Campus visit recommended. No off-campus interviews.

**Procedure:** Take SAT or ACT by December 1 of 12th year. Suggest filing application by November 15. Application deadline is February 15. Notification of admission on rolling basis. Reply is required by May 1. $150 tuition deposit, refundable until May 1. Freshmen accepted for terms other than fall.

**Special programs:** Admission may be deferred one year. Credit and/or placement may be granted through CEEB Advanced Placement exams for scores of 3 or higher. Credit and/or placement may be granted through CLEP general and subject exams. Early decision program. Early entrance/early admission program. Concurrent enrollment program.

**Transfer students:** Transfer students accepted for terms other than fall. In fall 1992, 33% of all new students were transfers into all classes. 4,560 transfer applications were received, 2,278 were accepted. Application deadline is April 1 for fall; November 1 for spring. Lowest course grade accepted is "C." Maximum number of transferable credits is 64 semester hours. At least 30 semester hours must be completed at the university to receive degree.

**Admissions contact:** Micheileen Treadwell, Ed.D., Director of Admissions. 518 442-5435.

**FINANCIAL AID. Available aid:** Pell grants, SEOG, state scholarships and grants, private scholarships and grants, and ROTC scholarships. Perkins Loans (NDSL), Stafford Loans (GSL), and school loans.

**Financial aid statistics:** In 1992-93, 80% of all undergraduate applicants received aid; 80% of freshman applicants.

**Supporting data/closing dates:** FAFSA/FAF/FFS: Priority filing date is April 25. Notification of awards on rolling basis.

**Financial aid contact:** Richard Tastor, M.A., Interim Director of Financial Aid. 518 442-5435.

**STUDENT EMPLOYMENT.** College Work/Study Program. 8% of full-time undergraduates work on campus during school year. Students may expect to earn an average of $851 during school year. Off-campus part-time employment opportunities rated "good."

**COMPUTER FACILITIES.** 500 IBM/IBM-compatible, Macintosh/Apple, and RISC-/UNIX-based microcomputers; 400 are networked. Students may access Digital, IBM, UNISYS minicomputer/mainframe systems. Residence halls may be equipped with stand-alone microcomputers, networked microcomputers, networked terminals, modems. Client/LAN operating systems include UNIX/XENIX/AIX. Computer languages and software packages include BASIC, BMDP, COBOL, dBASE, DISSPLA, FORTRAN, ImSL, LISREL, Lotus 1-2-3, MINITAB, Pascal, PL/1, SAS, SPSS. Computer facilities are available to all students.

**Hours:** 24 hours.

**PROMINENT ALUMNI/AE.** Harold Gould, actor; Leroy Irvis, speaker, Pennsylvania House of Representatives.

## State University of New York at Binghamton

**Binghamton, NY 13902-6000** **607 777-2000**

**1994-95 Costs.** Tuition: $2,650 (state residents), $6,550 (out-of-state). Room & board: $5,080. Fees, books, misc. academic expenses (school's estimate): $1,111.

**Enrollment.** Undergraduates: 3,875 men, 4,669 women (full-time). Freshman class: 14,463 applicants, 6,166 accepted, 1,764 enrolled. Graduate enrollment: 1,473 men, 1,309 women.

**Test score averages/ranges.** Average SAT scores: 533 verbal, 615 math. Range of SAT scores of middle 50%: 1050-1260 combined.

**Faculty.** 492 full-time; 185 part-time. 95% of faculty holds highest degree in specific field. Student/faculty ratio: 19 to 1.

**Selectivity rating.** Highly competitive.

**PROFILE.** SUNY at Binghamton is a public, comprehensive university. It was founded in 1946, adopted coeducation in 1948, and joined the state system in 1950. Programs are offered through the Schools of Advanced Technology, Education, Management, and Nursing and the Clinical Campus. Its 606-acre campus is located in Binghamton.

**Accreditation:** MSACS. Professionally accredited by the Accreditation Board for Engineering and Technology, the National League for Nursing.

**Religious orientation:** State University of New York at Binghamton is nonsectarian; no religious requirements.

**Library:** Collections totaling over 1,471,424 volumes, 9,595 periodical subscriptions, and 1,321,894 microform items.

**Special facilities/museums:** Performing arts center, art and dance studios, sculpture foundry, several research centers, greenhouse, botanical teaching collection.

**Athletic facilities:** Gymnasiums, athletic fields, basketball, raquetball, squash, and tennis courts, weight rooms, dance studio, swimming pools, tracks, trails, nature preserve.

**STUDENT BODY. Undergraduate profile:** 94% are state residents; 32% are transfers. 9% Asian-American, 5% Black, 4% Hispanic, 1% Native American, 80% White, 1% Other. Average age of undergraduates is 20.

**Freshman profile:** 99% of accepted applicants took SAT.

**Undergraduate achievement:** 92% of fall 1991 freshmen returned for fall 1992 term. 45% of students who completed a degree program went on to graduate study within five years.

**Foreign students:** 154 students are from out of the country. Countries represented include Brazil, Germany, Malaysia, Panama, Taiwan, and the United Kingdom; 40 in all.

**PROGRAMS OF STUDY. Degrees:** B.A., B.F.A., B.Mus., B.S.

**Majors:** Accounting, African/Afro-American Studies, Anthropology, Applied Social Sciences, Arabic, Art, Art History, Biochemistry, Biological Sciences, Chemistry, Cinema, Classical Studies, Comparative Literature, Computer Science/Information Science, Economics, Electrical Engineering, English, English/Rhetoric, Environmental Studies, French, Geography, Geological Sciences, Geophysics, German, Greek, Hebrew, History, Interdepartmental Studies, Italian, Judaic Studies, Latin, Latin American/Caribbean Area Studies, Law/Society, Liberal Studies, Management, Mathematical Physics, Mathematical Sciences, Mechanical Engineering, Medieval Studies, Music, Nursing, Philosophy, Philosophy/Politics/Law, Physics, Political Science, Psychobiology, Psychology, Social Sciences, Sociology, Spanish, Theatre.

**Distribution of degrees:** The majors with the highest enrollment are management, English, and psychology; classics, Italian, and geology have the lowest.

**Academic regulations:** Minimum 2.0 GPA required for graduation.

**Special:** Minors offered in many majors and in classical/Near Eastern studies, geology, human services/society, Romance languages, and women's studies. Self-designed majors. Double majors. Dual degrees. Independent study. Pass/fail grading option. Internships. Graduate school at which undergraduates may take graduate-level courses. Preprofessional programs in law, medicine, veterinary science, dentistry, and optometry. 2-2 engineering programs. 3-1 and 3-4 optometry programs with SUNY Coll of Optometry. 3-2 management program. 3-2 engineering programs with Clarkson U, Columbia U, Rochester Inst of Tech, and SUNY at Buffalo. Washington Semester. Other off-campus study opportunities. Member of New York State Visiting Student Program. Study abroad in Austria, China, Denmark, England, France, Israel, Japan, Mexico, and other countries.

**Honors:** Phi Beta Kappa. Honors program. Honor societies.

**Academic Assistance:** Nonremedial tutoring.

**STUDENT LIFE. Housing:** All unmarried freshmen must live on campus unless living with family. Coed dorms. School-owned/operated apartments. Both on-campus and off-campus married-student housing. Single-sex corridors in dorms. 50% of students live in college housing.

**Social atmosphere:** As reported by the student newspaper, "Despite long and cold winters, social life has been increasing in spirit and participation. Many students are off campus during their junior year and virtually all are off by their senior year. The student body remains diverse and minorities are prominent on campus. Most of the social life is geared toward being off campus." Gathering places include Bourbon Street, the Rathskeller, Scandals, and Esprit. Popular groups on campus include Greeks, intramural teams, and minority organizations. Favorite events during the school year are Homecoming and Spring Fling.

**Services and counseling/handicapped student services:** Placement services. Health service. Women's center. Day care. Counseling services for minority, military, veteran, and older students. Birth control, personal, and psychological counseling. Career and academic guidance services. Religious counseling. Physically disabled student services. Learning disabled services. Notetaking services. Tape recorders. Tutors. Reader services for the blind.

**Campus organizations:** Undergraduate student government. Student newspaper (Pipe Dream, published twice/week). Literary magazine. Yearbook. Radio and TV stations. Chorus, chorale, University Singers, orchestra, opera and jazz workshops, ensembles, theatre, student volunteer services, Students for a Barrier-Free Campus, science and world issues journals. 21 fraternities, no chapter houses; 14 sororities, no chapter houses. 15% of men join a fraternity. 15% of women join a sorority.

**Religious organizations:** Brothers and Sisters in Christ, Campus Bible Fellowship, Chabad House, Intervarsity Christian Fellowship, Jewish Student Union, Newman Association, Protestant Campus Ministry.

**Minority/foreign student organizations:** Black Student Union, Latin American Student Union, Asian Student Union, minority management organization. International Student Association, Caribbean and Nigerian groups.

**ATHLETICS. Physical education requirements:** Two semesters of physical education required of students in Harpur Coll, School of Management, and School of Nursing.

**Intercollegiate competition:** 10% of students participate. Baseball (M), basketball (M,W), cheerleading (M,W), cross-country (M,W), diving (M,W), golf (M), soccer (M,W), softball (W), swimming (M,W), tennis (M,W), track (indoor) (M,W), track (outdoor) (M,W), track and field (indoor) (M,W), track and field (outdoor) (M,W), volleyball (W), wrestling (M). Member of ECAC, NCAA Division III, NYSWCAA, SUNYAC.

**Intramural and club sports:** 50% of students participate. Intramural badminton, basketball, bowling, floor hockey, golf, inner-tube water polo, paddleball, pickleball, racquetball, soccer, softball, squash, table tennis, tennis, flag football, turkey trot, volleyball, walleyball, wrestling. Men's club Alpine skiing, badminton, bowling, boxing, crew, cycling, deck hockey, fencing, fishing, gymnastics, horsemanship, hunting, lacrosse, martial arts, racquetball, rugby, ultimate frisbee, volleyball. Women's club Alpine skiing, badminton, bowling, crew, cycling, deck hockey, fencing, fishing, gymnastics, horsemanship, hunting, lacrosse, martial arts, racquetball, rugby, ultimate frisbee.

**ADMISSIONS. Academic basis for candidate selection** (in order of priority): Secondary school record, class rank, essay, school's recommendation, standardized test scores.
**Nonacademic basis for candidate selection:** Character and personality and extracurricular participation are emphasized. Particular talent or ability is important. Geographical distribution and alumni/ae relationship are considered.
**Requirements:** Graduation from secondary school is required; GED is accepted. 21 units and the following program of study are recommended: 4 units of math, 4 units of science, 3 units of foreign language, 2 units of social studies, 2 units of history. 3 units of one foreign language or 2 units of two languages required of Harpur Coll applicants. 1 unit of chemistry recommended of nursing program applicants. EOP for applicants not normally admissible. SAT or ACT is required. Campus visit recommended. No off-campus interviews.
**Procedure:** Take SAT or ACT by November of 12th year. Suggest filing application by January 1. Application deadline is February 15. Notification of admission between March 15 and April 15. Reply is required by May 1 or within 30 days. $50 tuition deposit, refundable until May 1. $175 room deposit, refundable until May 1. Freshmen accepted for terms other than fall.
**Special programs:** Admission may be deferred one year. Credit and/or placement may be granted through CEEB Advanced Placement exams for scores of 3 or higher. Credit and/or placement may be granted through CLEP subject exams. Credit and placement may be granted through Regents College, ACT PEP, DANTES, and challenge exams and military experience. Early decision program. In fall 1993, 350 applied for early decision and 147 were accepted. Deadline for applying for early decision is November 1. Early entrance/early admission program. Concurrent enrollment program.
**Transfer students:** Transfer students accepted for terms other than fall. In fall 1993, 32% of all new students were transfers into all classes. 3,408 transfer applications were received, 1,508 were accepted. Application deadline varies by program for fall; November 15 for spring. Lowest course grade accepted is "C-."
**Admissions contact:** Geoffrey D. Gould, Ed.D., Director of Admissions. 607 777-2171.

**FINANCIAL AID. Available aid:** Pell grants, SEOG, Federal Nursing Student Scholarships, state scholarships and grants, school scholarships and grants, private scholarships and grants, and academic merit scholarships. Perkins Loans (NDSL), PLUS, Stafford Loans (GSL), NSL, and SLS. College-based time payment plan.
**Financial aid statistics:** 5% of aid is not need-based. In 1993-94, 31% of all undergraduate applicants received aid; 61% of freshman applicants. Average amounts of aid awarded freshmen: Scholarships and grants, $3,801; loans, $1,284.
**Supporting data/closing dates:** FAFSA. State aid form: Accepted on rolling basis. EOP supplement: Priority filing date is March 1. Notification of awards begins March 25.
**Financial aid contact:** Christina Knickerbocker, M.Ed., Director of Financial Aid. 607 777-2428.

**STUDENT EMPLOYMENT.** College Work/Study Program. Institutional employment. 10% of full-time undergraduates work on campus during school year. Students may expect to earn an average of $1,000 during school year. Off-campus part-time employment opportunities rated "excellent."

**COMPUTER FACILITIES.** IBM/IBM-compatible, Macintosh/Apple, and RISC-/UNIX-based microcomputers. Students may access Internet. Computer languages and software packages include APL, C, COBOL, FORTRAN, Pascal, PL/1. Computer facilities are available to all students.
**Fees:** None.
**Hours:** 9 AM-3 AM (M-Th); 9 AM-midn. (Sa-Su).

**GRADUATE CAREER DATA.** Graduate school percentages: 11% enter law school. 8% enter medical school. 2% enter graduate business programs. 24% enter graduate arts and sciences programs. Highest graduate school enrollments: Columbia U, New York U, St. John's U, SUNY at Binghamton, SUNY at Buffalo, SUNY at Stony Brook, Syracuse U, U of Connecticut, U of Maryland.

**PROMINENT ALUMNI/AE.** Susan Clark-Jackson, president and publisher, *Reno Gazette*; Arnold Levine, head of microbiology department, Princeton U; Paul Reiser, actor, *Mad About You;* Andrew Bergman, screenwriter, *Blazing Saddles*; Nan Ross Huhn, Superior Court judge, Washington, D.C.

# State University of New York at Buffalo

**Buffalo, NY 14260** **716 645-2000**

**1993-94 Costs.** Tuition: $2,650 (state residents), $6,550 (out-of-state). Room & board: $4,822. Fees, books, misc. academic expenses (school's estimate): $874.
**Enrollment.** Undergraduates: 8,066 men, 5,897 women (full-time). Freshman class: 15,039 applicants, 9,649 accepted, 3,087 enrolled. Graduate enrollment: 4,512 men, 4,036 women.
**Test score averages/ranges.** Average SAT scores: 479 verbal, 572 math. Range of SAT scores of middle 50%: 450-550 verbal, 550-650 math.
**Faculty.** 1,236 full-time; 165 part-time. 97% of faculty holds highest degree in specific field. Student/faculty ratio: 15 to 1.
**Selectivity rating.** Competitive.

**PROFILE.** SUNY at Buffalo, founded in 1846, is a public, comprehensive university. Its main 160-acre campus is located in downtown Buffalo.

**Accreditation:** MSACS. Professionally accredited by the Accreditation Board for Engineering and Technology, the American Assembly of Collegiate Schools of Business, the American Bar Association, the American Council on Pharmaceutical Education, the American Dental Association, the American Library Association, the American Medical Association (CAHEA), the American Physical Therapy Association, the American Psychological Association, the American Speech-Language-Hearing Association, the Council on Social Work Education, the Liaison Committee on Medical Education, the National Architecture Accrediting Board, the National Association of Schools of Art and Design, the National Association of Schools of Music, the National League for Nursing.
**Religious orientation:** State University of New York at Buffalo is nonsectarian; no religious requirements.
**Library:** Collections totaling over 2,724,222 volumes, 22,643 periodical subscriptions, and 4,093,112 microform items.
**Special facilities/museums:** Anthropology museum, concert hall with pipe organ, nature preserve, health and sciences center, national earthquake center, numerous other research centers, nuclear reactor.
**Athletic facilities:** Gymnasium, swimming pools, basketball, racquetball, and tennis courts, indoor and outdoor tracks, field house, playing fields, sports arena, weight room.

**STUDENT BODY. Undergraduate profile:** 99% are state residents; 39% are transfers. 9% Asian-American, 7% Black, 4% Hispanic, 1% Native American, 78% White, 1% Nonresident alien. Average age of undergraduates is 22.
**Freshman profile:** 1% of freshmen who took SAT scored 700 or over on verbal, 8% scored 700 or over on math; 8% scored 600 or over on verbal, 39% scored 600 or over on math; 41% scored 500 or over on verbal, 83% scored 500 or over on math; 86% scored 400 or over on verbal, 99% scored 400 or over on math; 100% scored 300 or over on verbal, 100% scored 300 or over on math. 98% of accepted applicants took SAT; 22% took ACT.
**Undergraduate achievement:** 88% of fall 1991 freshmen returned for fall 1992 term. 28% of entering class graduated.
**Foreign students:** 270 students are from out of the country. Countries represented include Canada, China, Hong Kong, Japan, Malaysia, and Pakistan; 49 in all.

**PROGRAMS OF STUDY. Degrees:** B.A., B.F.A., B.Mus., B.Prof.Studies, B.S.
**Majors:** Accounting, Aerospace Engineering, African-American Studies, American Studies, Anthropology, Architecture, Art Education, Art History, Biochemical Pharmacology, Biochemistry, Biology, Biophysical Sciences, Business Administration, Chemical Engineering, Chemistry, Civil Engineering, Classics, Communication, Computer Science, Economics, Electrical Engineering, Engineering Physics, English, Environmental Design, Exercise Science, Fine Arts, French, Geography, Geological Sciences, German, History, Industrial Engineering, Interdisciplinary Social Sciences, Italian, Linguistics, Mathematical Physics, Mathematics, Mechanical Engineering, Media Study, Medical Technology, Medicinal Chemistry, Music, Music Education, Music Performance, Nuclear Medical Technology, Nursing, Occupational Therapy, Pharmaceutics, Pharmacy, Philosophy, Physical Therapy, Physics, Political Science, Psychology, Sociology, Spanish, Speech/Hearing Sciences, Statistics, Studio Art, Theatre, Women's Studies.
**Distribution of degrees:** The majors with the highest enrollment are business administration, interdisciplinary social sciences, and psychology; African-American studies, art education, and engineering physics have the lowest.
**Requirements:** General education requirement.
**Academic regulations:** Minimum 2.0 GPA must be maintained.
**Special:** Minors offered in many majors and in biotechnology, comparative politics, cartography, design, geography of international trade and world business, Polish studies, public law, and other areas. Self-designed majors. Double majors. Dual degrees. Independent study. Accelerated study. Pass/fail grading option. Internships. Graduate school at which undergraduates may take graduate-level courses. Preprofessional programs in law, medicine, veterinary science, pharmacy, dentistry, and optometry. Early assurance of admission to SUNY at Buffalo Medical Sch for students with minimum 3.5 GPA after three semesters. Joint B.A./J.D., B.A./M.S.W., and B.A./M.B.A. programs. 3-4 optometry program with SUNY State Coll of Optometry. Member of Western New York Consortium and Association of Colleges and Universities of the State of New York Consortium. Washington Semester. Teacher certification in early childhood, elementary, secondary, and bilingual/bicultural education. Certification in specific subject areas. Study abroad in China, Costa Rica, France, Germany, Japan, Latvia, Mexico, Poland, and the United Kingdom. ROTC at Canisius Coll.
**Honors:** Phi Beta Kappa. Honors program. Honor societies.
**Academic Assistance:** Remedial reading, writing, math, and study skills. Nonremedial tutoring.

**STUDENT LIFE. Housing:** Students may live on or off campus. Coed dorms. 20% of students live in college housing.
**Social atmosphere:** On campus, students frequent the Student Union and the Commons; off campus, P.J. Bottoms and Third Base are popular bars. The Student Association is an influential organization on campus. Homecoming and the Fall and Spring Fests highlight the school year. "UB does pretty well considering it has two campuses, North and South, that separate the students," writes the editor of the student newspaper. "Only recently, with the construction of a Student Union and the upgrade of our athletic programs to Division I, has the school had any school spirit."
**Services and counseling/handicapped student services:** Placement services. Health service. Women's center. Day care. Counseling services for minority, veteran, and older students. Birth control, personal, and psychological counseling. Career and academic guidance services. Religious counseling. Physically disabled student services. Learning disabled services. Notetaking services. Tape recorders. Tutors. Reader services for the blind.
**Campus organizations:** Undergraduate student government. Student newspaper (Spectrum, published three times/week). Literary magazine. Yearbook. Radio station. Cheerleaders, volunteer ambulance corps, departmental, professional, service, and special-interest groups, 415 organizations in all. 22 fraternities, no chapter houses; nine sororities, no chapter houses.
**Religious organizations:** Bahai, Baptist, Methodist, Lutheran, and Catholic groups, Chinese Christian Church, Hebrew Christian Mission, Christian Messianic Fellowship, other religious groups.
**Minority/foreign student organizations:** Black Student Union, black health professions group, Gray Panthers, the Independents, minority nursing group, Society of Black Engineers, Native American People's Alliance, PODER. African, Brazilian, Caribbean, German, Greek, Hellenic, Hungarian, Indian, Iranian, Irish, Israeli, Italian, Korean, Latin American, Lebanese, Muslim, Nigerian, Pakistani, and other foreign student groups.

**ATHLETICS. Physical education requirements:** None.

**Intercollegiate competition:** 5% of students participate. Basketball (M,W), cheerleading (M,W), cross-country (M,W), diving (M,W), football (M), soccer (M,W), swimming (M,W), tennis (M,W), track (indoor) (M,W), track (outdoor) (M,W), track and field (indoor) (M,W), track and field (outdoor) (M,W), volleyball (W), wrestling (M). Member of ECAC, NCAA Division I, NCAA Division I-AA for football.
**Intramural and club sports:** 15% of students participate. Intramural badminton, basketball, body building, flag football, floor hockey, power lifting, racquetball, soccer, softball, squash, tennis, turkey trot, volleyball. Men's club badminton, baseball, bowling, cycling, fencing, frisbee, gymnastics, ice hockey, karate, kite, lacrosse, power lifting, rowing, rugby, running, tennis, sailing, skiing, snow boarding, volleyball. Women's club badminton, bowling, cycling, fencing, frisbee, gymnastics, karate, kite, lacrosse, power lifting, rowing, rugby, running, sailing, skiing, snow boarding.

**ADMISSIONS. Academic basis for candidate selection** (in order of priority): Secondary school record, class rank, standardized test scores.
**Requirements:** Graduation from secondary school is required; GED is accepted. No specific distribution of secondary school units required. Portfolio required of art program applicants. Audition required of music program applicants. EOP for applicants not normally admissible. Minority Academic Achievement Program for applicants not normally admissible. SAT or ACT is required. Campus visit recommended. No off-campus interviews.
**Procedure:** Take SAT or ACT by November of 12th year. Suggest filing application by January 5; no deadline. Notification of admission by February 15. Reply is required by May 1. $150 tuition deposit, refundable until May 1. $175 room deposit, refundable until May 1. Freshmen accepted for terms other than fall.
**Special programs:** Credit may be granted through CEEB Advanced Placement for scores of 4 or higher. Credit may be granted through CLEP general and subject exams, Regents College, ACT PEP, DANTES, and challenge exams, and military experience. Early entrance/early admission program. Concurrent enrollment program.
**Transfer students:** Transfer students accepted for terms other than fall. In fall 1993, 39% of all new students were transfers into all classes. 5,742 transfer applications were received, 3,693 were accepted. Application deadline is early in semester preceding entrance for fall; early in semester preceding entrance for spring. Minimum 2.0 GPA required. Lowest course grade accepted is "D." At least 32 semester hours must be completed at the university to receive degree.
**Admissions contact:** Kevin Durkin, M.S., Director of Admissions.

**FINANCIAL AID. Available aid:** Pell grants, SEOG, Federal Nursing Student Scholarships, state scholarships and grants, school scholarships and grants, private scholarships and grants, academic merit scholarships, and athletic scholarships. Perkins Loans (NDSL), PLUS, Stafford Loans (GSL), NSL, Health Professions Loans, school loans, private loans, and SLS. Tuition Plan Inc. and AMS.
**Financial aid statistics:** 15% of aid is not need-based. In 1993-94, 60% of all undergraduate applicants received aid; 60% of freshman applicants. Average amounts of aid awarded freshmen: Scholarships and grants, $1,337; loans, $2,625.
**Supporting data/closing dates:** FAFSA: Deadline is April 1. Notification of awards begins April 15.
**Financial aid contact:** Michael Randall, M.B.A., Director of Financial Aid. 716 829-3724.

**STUDENT EMPLOYMENT.** College Work/Study Program. Institutional employment. 20% of full-time undergraduates work on campus during school year. Students may expect to earn an average of $1,000 during school year. Off-campus part-time employment opportunities rated "good."

**COMPUTER FACILITIES.** 450 IBM/IBM-compatible and Macintosh/Apple microcomputers; 350 are networked. Students may access Digital, IBM, SUN minicomputer/mainframe systems, BITNET, Internet. Residence halls may be equipped with stand-alone microcomputers, networked terminals. Client/LAN operating systems include Apple/Macintosh, DOS, UNIX/XENIX/AIX, X-windows, Microsoft, Novell. Computer languages and software packages include BASIC, C, COBOL, FORTRAN, FRANZ LISP, LISP, MACRO-11, MINITAB, Modula 2, Pascal, PL/1, Prolog, SAS, SPSS-X; various database, graphics, mathematical, statistical, text processing, desktop publishing software packages. Computer facilities are available to all students.
**Fees:** None.
**Hours:** 24 hours.

**GRADUATE CAREER DATA.** Companies and businesses that hire graduates: ALCOA, Corning Glass, CVS, Electronic Data Systems, General Electric, NCR, Occidental Chemical, Union Carbide, Westinghouse.

**PROMINENT ALUMNI/AE.** Ellen Shulman Baker, astronaut and NASA mission specialist; Thomas G. Toles, Pulitzer Prize-winning editorial cartoonist; Wolf I. Blitzer, CNN Pentagon correspondent; Wilson Greatbatch, inventor of pacemaker; Jerome Kassirer, editor, *New England Journal of Medicine*; Linda J. Wacher, president, WARNACO.

# State University of New York College at Brockport

**Brockport, NY 14420-2915** **716 395-2211**

**1994-95 Costs.** Tuition: $2,650 (state residents), $6,550 (out-of-state). Room & board: $4,360. Fees, books, misc. academic expenses (school's estimate): $790.
**Enrollment.** Undergraduates: 2,685 men, 3,073 women (full-time). Freshman class: 7,294 applicants, 3,561 accepted, 987 enrolled. Graduate enrollment: 654 men, 1,231 women.
**Test score averages/ranges.** Average SAT scores: 449 verbal, 504 math. Range of SAT scores of middle 50%: 400-500 verbal, 450-550 math. Average ACT scores: 22 composite. Range of ACT scores of middle 50%: 20-23 composite.
**Faculty.** 347 full-time; 227 part-time. 78% of faculty holds doctoral degree. Student/faculty ratio: 20 to 1.
**Selectivity rating.** Competitive.

**PROFILE.** SUNY College at Brockport, founded in 1835, is a public, liberal arts college. Its 600-acre campus is located in Brockport, 16 miles west of Rochester.

**Accreditation:** MSACS. Professionally accredited by the Council on Social Work Education, the National Association of Schools of Dance, the National Association of Schools of Public Affairs and Administration, the National League for Nursing, the National Recreation and Park Association.
**Religious orientation:** State University of New York College at Brockport is nonsectarian; no religious requirements.
**Library:** Collections totaling over 514,000 volumes, 2,300 periodical subscriptions, and 2,000,000 microform items.
**Special facilities/museums:** Theatre, leadership development institute, greenhouse, planetarium, electron microscope.
**Athletic facilities:** Gymnasiums, stadium for football and track, swimming pools, athletic fields, athletic, weight and wrestling rooms, bowling alleys, indoor ice hockey rink, gymnastics area, wrestling facility, handball, racquetball, squash, and tennis courts.

**STUDENT BODY. Undergraduate profile:** 99% are state residents; 55% are transfers. 1% Asian-American, 6% Black, 2% Hispanic, 91% White. Average age of undergraduates is 23.
**Freshman profile:** 1% of freshmen who took SAT scored 700 or over on math; 1% scored 600 or over on verbal, 11% scored 600 or over on math; 21% scored 500 or over on verbal, 56% scored 500 or over on math; 78% scored 400 or over on verbal, 96% scored 400 or over on math; 100% scored 300 or over on verbal, 100% scored 300 or over on math. 1% of freshmen who took ACT scored 30 or over on composite; 28% scored 24 or over on composite; 97% scored 18 or over on composite; 100% scored 12 or over on composite. 95% of accepted applicants took SAT; 31% took ACT. 94% of freshmen come from public schools.
**Undergraduate achievement:** 75% of fall 1992 freshmen returned for fall 1993 term. 28% of entering class graduated. 24% of students who completed a degree program went on to graduate study within one year.
**Foreign students:** 34 students are from out of the country. Countries represented include Germany, Hong Kong, India, Japan, and South Africa; 16 in all.

**PROGRAMS OF STUDY. Degrees:** B.A., B.F.A., B.S., B.S.Nurs.
**Majors:** Accounting, African/Afro-American Studies, American Studies, Anthropology, Art History, Arts for Children, Biological Sciences, Business Administration, Chemistry, Communication, Communication Study, Computer Science, Criminal Justice, Dance, Earth Science, Economics, English, French, Geology, Health Sciences, History, International Business/Economics, International Studies, Liberal Studies, Mathematics, Medical Technology, Meteorology, Nursing, Philosophy, Physical Education/Sport, Physics, Political Science, Psychology, Recreation/Leisure, Social Work, Sociology, Spanish, Studio Art, Theatre, Water Resources.
**Distribution of degrees:** The majors with the highest enrollment are business administration, criminal justice, and psychology; philosophy, water resources, and theatre have the lowest.
**Requirements:** General education requirement.
**Academic regulations:** Minimum 2.0 GPA must be maintained.
**Special:** Minors offered in most majors and in applied social research, Canadian studies, communications/meteorology, environmental studies, film studies, gerontology, Jewish studies, Latin American studies, modern war society, scientific writing, and women's studies. Courses offered in Chinese, counselor education, Hebrew, Italian, Latin, natural sciences, oceanography, and zoology. Three-year degree program. Contractual liberal arts program. Self-designed majors. Double majors. Independent study. Accelerated study. Internships. Graduate school at which undergraduates may take graduate-level courses. Preprofessional programs in law, medicine, veterinary science, dentistry, and optometry. 3-2 engineering programs with Case Western Reserve U, Clarkson U, SUNY at Binghamton, SUNY at Buffalo, and Syracuse U. Member of Rochester Area Colleges Consortium. Washington Semester. Albany Semester. Teacher certification in elementary, secondary, and bilingual/bicultural education. Certification in specific subject areas. Exchange programs abroad in Canada (Dalhousie U), England (Brunel U, Chelsea Coll, Middlesex Polytechnic), and Japan (Kansai Gaidai U). Study abroad also in the Bahamas, France, Ghana, Greece, Jamaica, and Mexico. ROTC. NROTC at U of Rochester. AFROTC at Rochester Inst of Tech.
**Honors:** Honors program. Honor societies.
**Academic Assistance:** Remedial reading, writing, math, and study skills. Nonremedial tutoring.

**STUDENT LIFE. Housing:** All freshmen must live on campus unless living with family. Coed dorms. Sorority and fraternity housing. Off-campus privately-owned housing. 30% of students live in college housing.
**Social atmosphere:** Football and hockey are popular at Brockport, as are the free movies, air band contests, Spring Weekend, and Homecoming. Influential groups on campus include the student government, Campus Crusade for Christ, Greeks, and the Organization of Students of African Descent. Favorite off-campus spots include Northbound Junction, the Lincoln, Canalside Sports Clubs, C & S, Barber's, and the apartment complex Lechase. "Bars are popular and crowded, and parties are always popular," reports the student newspaper.
**Services and counseling/handicapped student services:** Placement services. Health service. Women's center. Day care. Counseling services for minority, veteran, and older students. Personal and psychological counseling. Career and academic guidance services. Physically disabled student services. Learning disabled program/services. Notetaking services. Tutors. Reader services for the blind.
**Campus organizations:** Undergraduate student government. Student newspaper (Stylus, published once/week). Yearbook. Radio and TV stations. Orchestra, dance group, Harlequin Dance Club, theatre club, academic, athletic, cultural, service, and special-interest groups, 86 organizations in all. Nine fraternities, no chapter houses; seven sororities, no chapter houses. 4% of men join a fraternity. 4% of women join a sorority.
**Religious organizations:** Hillel, Newman Club, Intervarsity Christian Fellowship, Bible study group.
**Minority/foreign student organizations:** ALAS (Association of Latin American Students), OSAD (black student group), Native American Student Association, Leadership

Development Institute, NAACP, Black women and men support groups. International Student Association, Caribbean and Latin American groups.

**ATHLETICS. Physical education requirements:** None.
**Intercollegiate competition:** 28% of students participate. Baseball (M), basketball (M,W), cheerleading (M,W), cross-country (M,W), diving (M,W), field hockey (W), football (M), gymnastics (W), ice hockey (M), soccer (M,W), softball (W), swimming (M,W), tennis (W), track (indoor) (M,W), track (outdoor) (M,W), track and field (indoor) (M,W), track and field (outdoor) (M,W), volleyball (W), wrestling (M). Member of ECAC, NCAA Division III, NYSWCAA, SUNYAC.
**Intramural and club sports:** 60% of students participate. Intramural badminton, baseball, basketball, broomball, cross-country, football, golf, ice hockey, lacrosse, racquetball, soccer, softball, squash, table tennis, tennis, track, volleyball, water polo, wrestling, wrist wrestling. Men's club lacrosse, martial arts, Nordic skiing, rugby, volleyball. Women's club lacrosse, martial arts, Nordic skiing, rugby.

**ADMISSIONS. Academic basis for candidate selection** (in order of priority): Secondary school record, class rank, standardized test scores, school's recommendation.
**Nonacademic basis for candidate selection:** Character and personality, extracurricular participation, and particular talent or ability are important. Alumni/ae relationship is considered.
**Requirements:** Graduation from secondary school is recommended; GED is accepted. 17 units and the following program of study are required: 4 units of English, 2 units of math, 2 units of science including 1 unit of lab, 2 units of foreign language, 4 units of history, 4 units of electives including 1 unit of academic electives. Minimum combined SAT scores of 350 in both verbal and math and minimum "B" average required. Portfolio recommended of art program applicants. Audition recommended of dance program applicants. EOP for applicants not normally admissible. Conditional admission possible for applicants not meeting standard requirements. Exceptional Talent Program for applicants not normally admissible. SAT or ACT is required. PSAT is recommended. Campus visit and interview recommended. No off-campus interviews.
**Procedure:** Take SAT or ACT by November of 12th year. Suggest filing application by December 1; no deadline. Acceptance notification on modified rolling basis beginning January 15. Reply is required by May 1. $50 tuition deposit, refundable until May 1. $100 room deposit, refundable until June 1. Freshmen accepted for terms other than fall.
**Special programs:** Admission may be deferred one year. Credit and/or placement may be granted through CEEB Advanced Placement exams for scores of 3 or higher. Credit and/or placement may be granted through CLEP general and subject exams. Credit and placement may be granted through Regents College, ACT PEP, DANTES, and challenge exams and military and life experience. Early decision program. In fall 1993, 35 applied for early decision and 10 were accepted. Deadline for applying for early decision is November 15. Early entrance/early admission program. Concurrent enrollment program.
**Transfer students:** Transfer students accepted for terms other than fall. In fall 1993, 55% of all new students were transfers into all classes. 3,535 transfer applications were received, 2,364 were accepted. Application deadline is March 1 for fall; December 1 for spring. Minimum 2.25 GPA required. Lowest course grade accepted is "D." Maximum number of transferable credits is 96 semester hours. At least 24 semester hours must be completed at the college to receive degree.
**Admissions contact:** James R. Cook, M.S., Acting Director of Admissions. 716 395-2751.

**FINANCIAL AID. Available aid:** Pell grants, SEOG, Federal Nursing Student Scholarships, state scholarships and grants, school scholarships, private scholarships and grants, ROTC scholarships, and academic merit scholarships. Perkins Loans (NDSL), PLUS, Stafford Loans (GSL), NSL, school loans, private loans, and SLS. Time Payment Plan.
**Financial aid statistics:** 5% of aid is not need-based. In 1993-94, 85% of all undergraduate applicants received aid; 83% of freshman applicants. Average amounts of aid awarded freshmen: Scholarships and grants, $1,463; loans, $1,884.
**Supporting data/closing dates:** FAFSA. School's own aid application: Priority filing date is March 18; deadline is May 2. Notification of awards on rolling basis.
**Financial aid contact:** Scott Atkinson, M.S., Director of Financial Aid. 716 395-2501, 800 295-9150.

**STUDENT EMPLOYMENT.** College Work/Study Program. Institutional employment. 40% of full-time undergraduates work on campus during school year. Students may expect to earn an average of $592 during school year. Off-campus part-time employment opportunities rated "good."

**COMPUTER FACILITIES.** 150 IBM/IBM-compatible and Macintosh/Apple microcomputers; 28 are networked. Students may access Digital, Prime, SUN minicomputer/mainframe systems, BITNET, Internet. Residence halls may be equipped with stand-alone microcomputers. Client/LAN operating systems include Apple/Macintosh, DOS, UNIX/XENIX/AIX, LocalTalk/AppleTalk, Novell. Computer languages and software packages include Assembler, C, COBOL, FORTRAN, LISP, MINITAB, Modula 2, Pascal, SAS, SimScript, SPSS. Computer facilities are available to all students.
**Fees:** Computer fee is included in tuition/fees.
**Hours:** 8 AM-11 PM (M-Th); 8 AM-9 PM (F); 1 PM-9 PM (Sa); 1 PM-11 PM (Su).

**GRADUATE CAREER DATA.** Graduate school percentages: 1% enter law school. 1% enter medical school. 1% enter dental school. 5% enter graduate business programs. 5% enter graduate arts and sciences programs. Highest graduate school enrollments: Nazareth Coll, Rochester Inst of Tech, SUNY at Albany, SUNY at Brockport, SUNY at Buffalo. 47% of graduates choose careers in business and industry. Companies and businesses that hire graduates: Bausch & Lomb, Eastman Kodak, Hillside Children's Center, Rochester City School District, Xerox.

**PROMINENT ALUMNI/AE.** Raymond McGrath, U.S. congressman; Peter McWalters, commissioner of education, Rhode Island; Marion Schrank, vice-president for student affairs, SUNY at Brockport.

# State University of New York College at Buffalo

Buffalo, NY 14222 — 716 878-4000

**1994-95 Costs.** Tuition: $2,650 (state residents), $6,250 (out-of-state). Room: $2,680. Board: $1,360-$1,760. Fees, books, misc. academic expenses (school's estimate): $670.
**Enrollment.** Undergraduates: 3,367 men, 4,703 women (full-time). Freshman class: 5,845 applicants, 3,471 accepted, 1,080 enrolled. Graduate enrollment: 502 men, 1,403 women.
**Test score averages/ranges.** N/A.
**Faculty.** 429 full-time; 148 part-time. 90% of faculty holds doctoral degree. Student/faculty ratio: 22 to 1.
**Selectivity rating.** N/A.

**PROFILE.** SUNY College at Buffalo, founded in 1867, is a public, multipurpose college of arts and sciences. Its 115-acre, urban campus is located in Buffalo.

**Accreditation:** MSACS. Professionally accredited by the Accreditation Board for Engineering and Technology, the American Dietetic Association, the American Speech-Language-Hearing Association, the Council on Social Work Education, the National Council for Accreditation of Teacher Education.
**Religious orientation:** State University of New York College at Buffalo is nonsectarian; no religious requirements.
**Library:** Collections totaling over 575,898 volumes, 3,740 periodical subscriptions, and 755,558 microform items.
**Special facilities/museums:** Art center, performing arts center, Great Lakes Center for Environmental Research, planetarium.
**Athletic facilities:** Gymnasium, natatorium, athletic bubble with indoor track, tennis courts, ice rink, sports arena, athletic fields.

**STUDENT BODY. Undergraduate profile:** 53% are transfers. 1% Asian-American, 10% Black, 3% Hispanic, 1% Native American, 85% White. Average age of undergraduates is 22.
**Freshman profile:** Majority of accepted applicants took SAT.
**Undergraduate achievement:** 73% of fall 1991 freshmen returned for fall 1992 term. 14% of entering class graduated.
**Foreign students:** 133 students are from out of the country. Countries represented include Canada, China, Hong Kong, and Japan; 34 in all.

**PROGRAMS OF STUDY. Degrees:** B.A., B.F.A., B.S., B.S.Ed., B.Tech.
**Majors:** Anthropology, Art, Art Education, Art History, Biology, Broadcasting, Business Education, Business Studies, Chemistry, Computer Information Systems, Consumer/Family Studies, Criminal Justice, Criminalistics, Design, Dietetics, Distributive Education, Early Childhood Education, Earth Sciences, Economics, Electro/Mechanical Engineering Technology, Elementary Education, English, Exceptional Education, Food Systems Management, French, General Studies, Geography, Geology, Health/Wellness, History, Humanities, Industrial Technology, Italian, Journalism, Mass Media, Mathematics, Music, Painting, Philosophy, Photography, Physics, Political Science, Printmaking, Psychology, Public Communications, Sculpture, Secondary Education/Biology, Secondary Education/Chemistry, Secondary Education/Earth Science, Secondary Education/English, Secondary Education/French, Secondary Education/Mathematics, Secondary Education/Physics, Secondary Education/Social Studies, Secondary Education/Spanish, Social Work, Sociology, Spanish, Speech/Language/Auditory Pathology, Technology Education, The Arts, Theatre Arts, Urban Regional Analysis/Planning, Vocational-Technical Education.
**Distribution of degrees:** The majors with the highest enrollment are business studies, elementary education, and criminal justice; sculpture, secondary education/earth science, and Spanish have the lowest.
**Requirements:** General education requirement.
**Academic regulations:** Minimum 2.0 GPA must be maintained.
**Special:** Minors offered in most majors. Double majors. Dual degrees. Independent study. Pass/fail grading option. Internships. Cooperative education programs. Graduate school at which undergraduates may take graduate-level courses. Preprofessional programs in law and health professions. 3-2 engineering programs with Clarkson U and SUNY at Binghamton. Member of Western New York Consortium. Washington Semester. Member of National Student Exchange (NSE). Teacher certification in elementary, secondary, special education, and vo-tech education. Certification in specific subject areas. Member of International Student Exchange Program (ISEP). ROTC at Canisius Coll.
**Honors:** Honors program.
**Academic Assistance:** Remedial reading, writing, math, and study skills. Nonremedial tutoring.

**STUDENT LIFE. Housing:** Students may live on or off campus. Coed dorms. 17% of students live in college housing.
**Services and counseling/handicapped student services:** Placement services. Health service. Women's center. Day care. Counseling services for minority, veteran, and older students. Birth control, personal, and psychological counseling. Career and academic guidance services. Religious counseling. Physically disabled student services. Learning disabled services. Reader services for the blind.
**Campus organizations:** Undergraduate student government. Student newspaper (Record, published twice/week). Yearbook. Radio station. Chorus, concert and jazz bands, dance ensemble, PIRG, athletic, political, service, and special-interest groups, 75 organizations in all. 12 fraternities, no chapter houses; 10 sororities, no chapter houses.
**Religious organizations:** Intervarsity Christian Fellowship, Newman Center, Hosanna Christian Fellowship, Campus Crusade for Christ, Muslim Student Organization.

**Minority/foreign student organizations:** Adelantes Estudiantes Latinos, Afro-American Student Organization, Black Active Minds, Native American Student Association. International Student Organization, Caribbean Student Organization.

**ATHLETICS. Physical education requirements:** Two semester hours of physical education required.

**Intercollegiate competition:** 5% of students participate. Basketball (M,W), cross-country (M,W), diving (M,W), football (M), ice hockey (M), lacrosse (W), soccer (M,W), softball (W), swimming (M,W), tennis (M,W), track and field (indoor) (M,W), track and field (outdoor) (M,W), volleyball (W). Member of ECAC, NCAA Division III, SUNYAC.

**Intramural and club sports:** 6% of students participate. Intramural badminton, baseball, basketball, bowling, cross-country, field hockey, flag football, floor hockey, lacrosse, racquetball, softball, squash, volleyball. Men's club baseball, bowling, rugby, lacrosse. Women's club bowling, cheerleading, rugby.

**ADMISSIONS. Academic basis for candidate selection** (in order of priority): Secondary school record, class rank, school's recommendation, standardized test scores.

**Nonacademic basis for candidate selection:** Extracurricular participation and particular talent or ability are considered.

**Requirements:** Graduation from secondary school is required; GED is accepted. 16 units and the following program of study are required: 4 units of English, 2 units of math, 3 units of science, 2 units of foreign language, 4 units of social studies. Rank in top half of secondary school class and minimum "B-" average recommended. Portfolio required of fine arts program applicants. EOP for applicants not normally admissible. SAT is recommended; ACT may be substituted. Campus visit recommended. No off-campus interviews.

**Procedure:** Suggest filing application by December 15. Notification of admission on rolling basis. Reply is required within four weeks of acceptance. $50 nonrefundable tuition deposit. $100 nonrefundable room deposit. Freshmen accepted for terms other than fall.

**Special programs:** Admission may be deferred one year. Credit may be granted through CEEB Advanced Placement for scores of 3 or higher. Credit may be granted through CLEP general and subject exams, Regents College and DANTES exams, and military and life experience. Placement may be granted through challenge exams. Early decision program. Deadline for applying for early decision is November 15. Early entrance/early admission program. Concurrent enrollment program.

**Transfer students:** Transfer students accepted for terms other than fall. In fall 1992, 53% of all new students were transfers into all classes. 2,772 transfer applications were received, 2,310 were accepted. Application deadline is rolling for fall; rolling for spring. Minimum 2.0 GPA required. Lowest course grade accepted is "D." Maximum number of transferable credits is 65 semester hours from a two-year school and 91 semester hours from a four-year school. At least 32 semester hours must be completed at the college to receive degree.

**Admissions contact:** Deborah K. Renzi, M.S.W., Director of Admissions. 716 878-4017.

**FINANCIAL AID. Available aid:** Pell grants, SEOG, state scholarships and grants, private scholarships, and academic merit scholarships. Perkins Loans (NDSL), PLUS, Stafford Loans (GSL), private loans, and SLS. AMS.

**Financial aid statistics:** 5% of aid is not need-based. In 1992-93, 70% of all undergraduate applicants received aid; 70% of freshman applicants. Average amounts of aid awarded freshmen: Scholarships and grants, $1,000.

**Supporting data/closing dates:** FAFSA/FAF/FFS: Priority filing date is March 15. Income tax forms: Accepted on rolling basis. Notification of awards on rolling basis.

**Financial aid contact:** Daniel R. Hunter, Jr., Ed.M., Director of Financial Aid. 716 878-4901.

**STUDENT EMPLOYMENT.** College Work/Study Program. Institutional employment. 10% of full-time undergraduates work on campus during school year. Students may expect to earn an average of $1,275 during school year. Freshmen are discouraged from working during their first term. Off-campus part-time employment opportunities rated "good."

**COMPUTER FACILITIES.** 250 IBM/IBM-compatible and Macintosh/Apple microcomputers; 100 are networked. Students may access Digital minicomputer/mainframe systems, BITNET. Computer languages and software packages include APL, Assembler, BASIC, COBOL, dBASE, FORTRAN, Lotus 1-2-3, Oracle, Pascal, SAS, SPSS-X, WordPerfect. Computer facilities are available to all students.

**Fees:** None.

**Hours:** 24 hours.

**PROMINENT ALUMNI/AE.** Tom Fontana, Emmy award winner, *St. Elsewhere;* Harry Ausprich, president, Bloomsburg U of Pennsylvania; Eugene T. Reville, former superintendent, Buffalo public schools; Diane English, playwright and TV producer, *Murphy Brown*; James H. Young, chancellor, U of Arkansas at Little Rock.

## State University of New York College at Cortland

**Cortland, NY 13045** **607 753-2011**

**1993-94 Costs.** Tuition: $2,650 (state residents), $6,550 (out-of-state). Room: $2,400. Board: $2,000. Fees, books, misc. academic expenses (school's estimate): $976.

**Enrollment.** Undergraduates: 2,217 men, 2,799 women (full-time). Freshman class: 7,888 applicants, 3,598 accepted, 1,036 enrolled. Graduate enrollment: 384 men, 974 women.

**Test score averages/ranges.** Average SAT scores: 460 verbal, 524 math. Range of SAT scores of middle 50%: 440-493 verbal, 476-559 math. Average ACT scores: 22 English, 22 math, 23 composite. Range of ACT scores of middle 50%: 22-25 composite.

**Faculty.** 243 full-time; 216 part-time. 81% of faculty holds doctoral degree. Student/faculty ratio: 20 to 1.

**Selectivity rating.** Competitive.

**PROFILE.** SUNY College at Cortland, founded in 1868, is a public, multipurpose college of arts and sciences. Its 191-acre campus is located in Cortland, 30 miles from Syracuse.

**Accreditation:** MSACS.

**Religious orientation:** State University of New York College at Cortland is nonsectarian; no religious requirements.

**Library:** Collections totaling over 371,974 volumes, 2,419 periodical subscriptions, and 620,481 microform items.

**Special facilities/museums:** Natural history museum, fine arts center, education center in the Adirondacks, center for speech and hearing disorders, nature preserve, geological field station, greenhouse, planetarium, scanning electron microscopes.

**Athletic facilities:** Physical education center, field house, gymnasium, intramural facilities, playing fields.

**STUDENT BODY. Undergraduate profile:** 97% are state residents; 38% are transfers. 1% Asian-American, 2% Black, 2% Hispanic, .5% Native American, 94.5% White. Average age of undergraduates is 20.

**Freshman profile:** 1% of freshmen who took SAT scored 600 or over on verbal, 9% scored 600 or over on math; 19% scored 500 or over on verbal, 58% scored 500 or over on math; 78% scored 400 or over on verbal, 98% scored 400 or over on math; 100% scored 300 or over on verbal, 100% scored 300 or over on math. 1% of freshmen who took ACT scored 30 or over on composite; 51% scored 24 or over on composite; 99% scored 18 or over on composite; 100% scored 12 or over on composite. 81% of accepted applicants took SAT; 33% took ACT. 91% of freshmen come from public schools.

**Undergraduate achievement:** 76% of fall 1992 freshmen returned for fall 1993 term. 39% of entering class graduated. 18% of students who completed a degree program immediately went on to graduate study.

**Foreign students:** 16 students are from out of the country. Countries represented include China, Cyprus, Germany, Japan, Spain, and United Kingdom; 15 in all.

**PROGRAMS OF STUDY. Degrees:** B.A., B.S., B.S.Ed.

**Majors:** Anthropology, Art, Biology, Black Studies, Chemistry, Cinema Study, Communication Studies, Early/Secondary Education, Economics, Economics/Management Science, Elementary Education, English, Environmental Science, French, General Studies, Geography, Geology, Geology/Chemistry, German, Health Education, Health Sciences, History, International Studies, Mathematics, Mathematics/Physics, Music, Philosophy, Physical Education, Physics, Political Science, Psychology, Recreation, Recreation Education, Social Studies, Sociology, Spanish, Speech, Speech Pathology/Audiology, Theatre Arts.

**Distribution of degrees:** The majors with the highest enrollment are elementary education, physical education, and communication studies; cinema study and philosophy have the lowest.

**Requirements:** General education requirement.

**Academic regulations:** Minimum 2.0 GPA must be maintained.

**Special:** Programs in arts management, art for special populations, Asian studies, computer science, geophysics, journalism, management, outdoor education, psychology of exceptional children, and public administration/policy. Social gerontology and urban studies. Cooperative education programs. Graduate school at which undergraduates may take graduate-level courses. Preprofessional programs in law, medicine, veterinary science, dentistry, engineering, and physical therapy. 2-2 biology, forestry, and environmental science programs with SUNY Coll of Environmental Science and Forestry. 3-1 art education program with SUNY Coll at Buffalo. 3-2 forestry and environmental studies program with Duke U. 3-2 engineering programs with Alfred U, Case Western Reserve U, Clarkson U, SUNY at Binghamton, SUNY at Buffalo, and SUNY at Stony Brook. 3-2 B.A./B.S. programs in foreign language studies and agriculture/life sciences with Cornell U. Washington Semester. Albany Semester. Teacher certification in early childhood, elementary, and secondary education. Certification in specific subject areas. Study abroad in Belize, China, England, France, Germany, Ireland, Mexico, Spain, and Switzerland. ROTC. AFROTC at Cornell U.

**Honors:** Honors program. Honor societies.

**Academic Assistance:** Remedial writing, math, and study skills. Nonremedial tutoring.

**STUDENT LIFE. Housing:** All unmarried students under age 21 must live on campus unless living near campus with relatives. Coed dorms. Sorority and fraternity housing. School-owned/operated apartments. 60% of students live in college housing.

**Social atmosphere:** Off-campus, students frequent Friday's, the Dark Horse Tavern, and Woodman's and Murphy's Pubs; on-campus gathering-spots include Corey Union and the Tannery. Football, Greeks, the CCSA (Student Association), and off-campus parties are predominant in student life at Cortland. The most popular events of the school year are the "CORTACA JUG" (annual football game between C-State and Ithaca College), rugby games, the Spring Picnic, Clayton and Monroe Street block parties, and various on-campus seminars, speakers, and cultural events. "Cultural diversity is a major element of extra-curricular and academic life at SUNY Cortland," says the editor of the student newspaper. "Campus clubs range from the Latin Student Union to the Ballroom Dance Team."

**Services and counseling/handicapped student services:** Placement services. Health service. Counseling services for minority and older students. Personal and psychological counseling. Career and academic guidance services. Learning disabled services.

**Campus organizations:** Undergraduate student government. Student newspaper (Dragon Chronicle, published once/week). Literary magazine. Yearbook. Radio and TV stations. College Singers, glee club, symphonic wind ensemble, college/community orchestra, dance group, debating, Masquers Guild, art exhibition association, Hunger-Homelessness Coalition of New York, PIRG, SADD, outing club, 100 organizations in all. Seven fraternities, five chapter houses; four sororities, all with chapter houses. 10% of men join a fraternity. 5% of women join a sorority.

**Religious organizations:** Interfaith Center, Jewish Student Society, Newman Center, Brothers and Sisters in Christ, Campus Bible Study, Campus Christian Association.

**Minority/foreign student organizations:** Black Student Union, Latin Student Union. International Student Organization.

**ATHLETICS. Physical education requirements:** None.

**Intercollegiate competition:** 12% of students participate. Baseball (M), basketball (M,W), cross-country (M,W), field hockey (W), football (M), gymnastics (M,W), ice hockey (M), lacrosse (M,W), soccer (M,W), softball (W), swimming (M,W), track (indoor) (M,W), track (outdoor) (M,W), track and field (indoor) (M,W), track and field (outdoor) (M,W), volleyball (W), wrestling (M). Member of ECAC, NCAA Division III, SUNYAC.

**Intramural and club sports:** 20% of students participate. Intramural archery, badminton, basketball, bowling, box lacrosse, cross-country, fencing, field hockey, flag football, football, golf, handball, lacrosse, paddleball, soccer, softball, squash, swimming, table tennis, tennis, track/field, volleyball, wrestling. Men's club cheerleading, ice hockey, volleyball. Women's club cheerleading, equestrian sports.

**ADMISSIONS. Academic basis for candidate selection** (in order of priority): Secondary school record, standardized test scores, school's recommendation, class rank, essay.

**Nonacademic basis for candidate selection:** Character and personality are emphasized. Extracurricular participation, particular talent or ability, and alumni/ae relationship are important. Geographical distribution is considered.

**Requirements:** Graduation from secondary school is required; GED is accepted. 16 units and the following program of study are required: 4 units of English, 4 units of history/social studies, 2 units of math, 2 units of science including 1 unit of lab, 1 unit of academic electives. College-preparatory program required. Minimum combined SAT score of 900 (composite ACT score of 22), rank in top half of secondary school class, and minimum "B" average recommended. Audition required of music program applicants. EOP for applicants not normally admissible. SAT or ACT is required. Campus visit and interview recommended. Off-campus interviews available with admissions and alumni representatives.

**Procedure:** Take SAT or ACT by November of 12th year. Visit college for interview by February of 12th year. Suggest filing application by February 1. Application deadline is July 1. Notification of admission by March 22. Reply is required by May 1. $50 tuition deposit, refundable until May 1. $150 room deposit, refundable until May 1. Freshmen accepted for terms other than fall.

**Special programs:** Admission may be deferred one year. Credit and/or placement may be granted through CEEB Advanced Placement exams for scores of 3 or higher. Credit and/or placement may be granted through CLEP subject exams. Credit and placement may be granted through Regents College and challenge exams. Early decision program. In fall 1993, 47 early decision applicants were accepted. Deadline for applying for early decision is November 15. Early entrance/early admission program.

**Transfer students:** Transfer students accepted for terms other than fall. In fall 1993, 38% of all new students were transfers into all classes. 2,762 transfer applications were received, 1,095 were accepted. Application deadline is March 15 for fall; December 1 for spring. Minimum 2.5 GPA recommended. Lowest course grade accepted is "C-." Maximum number of transferable credits is 64 semester hours from a two-year school and 79 semester hours from a four-year school. At least 45 semester hours must be completed at the college to receive degree.

**Admissions contact:** Michael K. McKeon, M.A., Director of Admission. 607 753-4711.

**FINANCIAL AID. Available aid:** Pell grants, SEOG, state scholarships and grants, school scholarships, private scholarships and grants, ROTC scholarships, and academic merit scholarships. Perkins Loans (NDSL), PLUS, Stafford Loans (GSL), and SLS. Tuition Budget Plan, Inc.

**Supporting data/closing dates:** FAFSA/FFS: Priority filing date is May 1. School's own aid application: Priority filing date is May 1. Notification of awards begins May 1.

**Financial aid contact:** Keith Bundy, M.S., Director of Financial Aid. 607 753-4717.

**STUDENT EMPLOYMENT.** College Work/Study Program. Institutional employment. 30% of full-time undergraduates work on campus during school year. Students may expect to earn an average of $1,200 during school year. Off-campus part-time employment opportunities rated "good."

**COMPUTER FACILITIES.** 412 IBM/IBM-compatible and Macintosh/Apple microcomputers; 165 are networked. Students may access Digital, UNISYS minicomputer/mainframe systems, BITNET, Internet. Residence halls may be equipped with networked microcomputers. Client/LAN operating systems include Apple/Macintosh, DOS, OS/2, DEC, LocalTalk/AppleTalk, Novell. Computer languages and software packages include ALGOL, COBOL, FORTRAN, Lotus 1-2-3, MINITAB, Pascal, PL/1, RPG, SPSS, WordPerfect; 36 in all. Computer facilities are available to all students.

**Fees:** $25 computer fee per semester; included in tuition/fees.

**PROMINENT ALUMNI/AE.** David Truax, associate vice chancellor, State University of New York.

# State University of New York College at Fredonia

**Fredonia, NY 14063** 716 673-3111

**1992-93 Costs.** Tuition: $2,650 (state residents), $6,550 (out-of-state). Room & board: $3,980. Fees, books, misc. academic expenses (school's estimate): $896.

**Enrollment.** Undergraduates: 1,857 men, 2,267 women (full-time). Freshman class: 4,877 applicants, 2,798 accepted, 885 enrolled. Graduate enrollment: 102 men, 314 women.

**Test score averages/ranges.** Average SAT scores: 472 verbal, 525 math. Range of SAT scores of middle 50%: 430-510 verbal, 480-570 math. Average ACT scores: 23 composite. Range of ACT scores of middle 50%: 21-24 composite.

**Faculty.** 234 full-time; 51 part-time. 90% of faculty holds highest degree in specific field. Student/faculty ratio: 20 to 1.

**Selectivity rating.** Competitive.

**PROFILE.** SUNY College at Fredonia, founded in 1826, is a public, multipurpose college of arts and sciences. Its 230-acre campus, designed by architect I.M. Pei, is located in Fredonia, 45 miles southwest of Buffalo.

**Accreditation:** MSACS. Professionally accredited by the American Speech-Language-Hearing Association, the National Association of Schools of Art and Design, the National Association of Schools of Music, the National Association of Schools of Theatre.

**Religious orientation:** State University of New York College at Fredonia is nonsectarian; no religious requirements.

**Library:** Collections totaling over 381,405 volumes, 1,936 periodical subscriptions, and 932,635 microform items.

**Special facilities/museums:** Art center, education and local history museums, teacher education research center, developmental reading center, writing center.

**Athletic facilities:** Field house, swimming pool, ice rink, basketball, handball, racquetball, tennis, and volleyball courts, tracks, dance studio, gymnasiums, weight room, athletic fields.

**STUDENT BODY. Undergraduate profile:** 98% are state residents; 34% are transfers. 1% Asian-American, 3% Black, 2% Hispanic, 1% Native American, 93% White. Average age of undergraduates is 20.

**Freshman profile:** 97% of accepted applicants took SAT; 39% took ACT. 65% of freshmen come from public schools.

**Undergraduate achievement:** 86% of fall 1992 freshmen returned for fall 1993 term. 26% of students who completed a degree program went on to graduate study within one year.

**Foreign students:** Seven students are from out of the country. Countries represented include Canada, Germany, and Japan; seven in all.

**PROGRAMS OF STUDY. Degrees:** B.A., B.A.Spec.Studies, B.F.A., B.Mus., B.S., B.S.Ed., B.S.Spec.Studies.

**Majors:** Accounting, Applied Music, Art, Biology, Business Administration, Chemistry, Communication/Media, Computer Science, Cooperative Agriculture, Cooperative Engineering, Cooperative Special Education, Early Childhood Education, Economics, Elementary Education, English, French, Geology, Geophysics, Health Services Administration, History, Industrial Management, Mathematics, Mathematics/Physics, Medical Technology, Music, Music Education, Music History, Music Performance, Music Theory, Music Therapy, Musical Theatre, Philosophy, Physics, Recombinant Gene Technology, Social Studies, Sociology, Spanish, Special Studies, Speech Pathology/Audiology, Theatre, Theatre Arts.

**Distribution of degrees:** The majors with the highest enrollment are business administration, elementary education, and English.

**Requirements:** General education requirement.

**Academic regulations:** Minimum 2.0 GPA must be maintained.

**Special:** Minors offered. Self-designed majors. Double majors. Dual degrees. Independent study. Accelerated study. Pass/fail grading option. Internships. Graduate school at which undergraduates may take graduate-level courses. Preprofessional programs in law, medicine, veterinary science, pharmacy, and dentistry. 3-2 engineering programs with Alfred U, Case Western Reserve U, Clarkson U, Columbia U, Cornell U, Louisiana Tech U, Ohio State U, Rensselaer Polytech Inst, Rochester Inst of Tech, SUNY at Binghamton, SUNY at Buffalo, Syracuse U, and Tri-State U. B.S./M.B.A. programs with Clarkson U, SUNY at Binghamton, SUNY at Buffalo, and U of Pittsburgh. Member of Western New York Consortium Colleges. Washington Semester and other off-campus study opportunities. Exchange possible through SUNY system. Teacher certification in early childhood, elementary, and secondary education. Certification in specific subject areas. Study abroad possible. ROTC at Canisius Coll.

**Honors:** Honors program.

**Academic Assistance:** Nonremedial tutoring.

**STUDENT LIFE. Housing:** All freshmen and sophomores must live on campus. Coed, women's, and men's dorms. School-owned/operated apartments. 55% of students live in college housing.

**Social atmosphere:** According to the student newspaper, "Fredonia's reputation is built solely on going to classes, then going out. Sure, the 21-year-old drinking laws have hurt some, but that has not made the village of Fredonia any less quiet during the week and weekends. The most popular gathering spots are off-campus houses having weekly parties (e.g. The Blue Anchor) and bars downtown such as OMI, Rooney's, J & D's, and BJ's." On campus, students congregate at the Campus Center. Greek organizations and the campus media have some influence on student life, while popular events include Cultural Extravaganza, Homecoming, and on-campus concerts.

**Services and counseling/handicapped student services:** Placement services. Health service. Day care. Counseling services for minority and veteran students. Birth control, personal, and psychological counseling. Career and academic guidance services. Physically disabled student services. Notetaking services. Tape recorders. Tutors. Reader services for the blind.

**Campus organizations:** Undergraduate student government. Student newspaper (Leader, published once/week). Literary magazine. Radio and TV stations. Choir, chorus, chamber singers, band, orchestra, jazz workshop, instrumental ensembles, opera theatre, Campus Libertarians, Amnesty International, Circle K, drill team, Inter-Greek Council, Nontraditional Students Alliance, Project Environment, ski club, Tae Kwon Do club, TV and radio clubs, wilderness club, Writers Guild/Promethean Society, academic, athletic, service, and special-interest groups, 150 organizations in all. Three fraternities, no chapter houses; two sororities, no chapter houses. 3% of men join a fraternity. 3% of women join a sorority.

**Religious organizations:** Chi Alpha, Intervarsity Christian Fellowship, Jewish Student Union, Newman Club.

**Minority/foreign student organizations:** Black Student Union, Hispanic Society, Native American Society.

**ATHLETICS. Physical education requirements:** None.

**Intercollegiate competition:** 10% of students participate. Baseball (M), basketball (M,W), cheerleading (M,W), cross-country (M,W), ice hockey (M), soccer (M,W), tennis (M,W), track (indoor) (M,W), track (outdoor) (M,W), track and field (indoor) (M,W), track and field (outdoor) (M,W), volleyball (W). Member of ECAC, NCAA Division III, NYSWCAA, SUNYAC.

**Intramural and club sports:** 45% of students participate. Intramural basketball, beach volleyball, broomball, horseshoes, inner-tube water polo, inner-tube basketball, racquetball, soccer, softball, tennis, touch football, volleyball, walleyball, Wiffle ball. Men's club cheerleading, lacrosse, martial arts, rugby, volleyball. Women's club cheerleading, field hockey, martial arts, volleyball.

**ADMISSIONS. Academic basis for candidate selection** (in order of priority): Secondary school record, class rank, standardized test scores, school's recommendation, essay.

**Nonacademic basis for candidate selection:** Particular talent or ability is important. Extracurricular participation and alumni/ae relationship are considered.
**Requirements:** Graduation from secondary school is required; GED is accepted. 16 units and the following program of study are required: 4 units of English, 4 units of math, 3 units of science including 1 unit of lab, 3 units of foreign language, 4 units of social studies. Minimum combined SAT score of 900 (composite ACT score of 18), rank in top two-fifths of secondary school class, and minimum 2.5 GPA recommended. Portfolio required of art program applicants. Audition required of music program applicants. EOP for applicants not normally admissible. Minority/Special Talent Full Opportunity Programs for applicants not normally admissible. SAT or ACT is required. Campus visit recommended. No off-campus interviews.
**Procedure:** Take SAT or ACT by December of 12th year. Suggest filing application by January 15. Application deadline is April 1. Notification of admission on rolling basis. Reply is required by May 1. $50 tuition deposit, refundable until May 1. $50 room deposit, refundable until June 1. Freshmen accepted for terms other than fall.
**Special programs:** Admission may be deferred one year. Credit and/or placement may be granted through CEEB Advanced Placement exams for scores of 3 or higher. Credit and/or placement may be granted through CLEP general and subject exams. Credit and placement may be granted through Regents College exams. Concurrent enrollment program.
**Transfer students:** Transfer students accepted for terms other than fall. In fall 1993, 34% of all new students were transfers into all classes. 1,570 transfer applications were received, 926 were accepted. Application deadline is March 15 for fall; November 1 for spring. Minimum 2.0 GPA required. Lowest course grade accepted is "D." Maximum number of transferable credits is 75 semester hours. At least 45 semester hours must be completed at the college to receive degree.
**Admissions contact:** William S. Clark, M.S.Ed., Director of Admissions and Enrollment. 716 673-3251.

**FINANCIAL AID. Available aid:** Pell grants, SEOG, state scholarships and grants, school scholarships, private scholarships, and academic merit scholarships. Perkins Loans (NDSL), PLUS, Stafford Loans (GSL), and SLS. Tuition Plan Inc., AMS, and deferred payment plan. Institutional installment payment plan.
**Financial aid statistics:** 5% of aid is not need-based. In 1993-94, 65% of all undergraduate applicants received aid; 67% of freshman applicants. Average amounts of aid awarded freshmen: Scholarships and grants, $1,438; loans, $2,235.
**Supporting data/closing dates:** FAFSA/FAF/FFS: Priority filing date is February 28; accepted on rolling basis. State aid form: Accepted on rolling basis. Notification of awards begins March 15.
**Financial aid contact:** Karen Klose, M.S.Ed., Director of Financial Aid. 716 673-3253.

**STUDENT EMPLOYMENT.** College Work/Study Program. Institutional employment. 35% of full-time undergraduates work on campus during school year. Students may expect to earn an average of $950 during school year. Off-campus part-time employment opportunities rated "fair."

**COMPUTER FACILITIES.** 500 IBM/IBM-compatible, Macintosh/Apple, and RISC-/UNIX-based microcomputers; 100 are networked. Students may access Digital, SUN, UNISYS minicomputer/mainframe systems, BITNET, Internet. Residence halls may be equipped with stand-alone microcomputers, networked terminals. Client/LAN operating systems include Apple/Macintosh, DOS, UNIX/XENIX/AIX, Windows NT, LocalTalk/AppleTalk, Microsoft, Novell. Computer languages and software packages include Ada, ALGOL, APL, AppleDOS, BASIC, COBOL, dBASE, FORTRAN, LISP, Lotus 1-2-3, MacWrite, MINITAB, Pascal, RPG, SPSS, WordPerfect, WordStar. Computer facilities are available to all students.
**Fees:** Computer fee is included in tuition/fees.
**Hours:** 24 hours.

**PROMINENT ALUMNI/AE.** Paul Cambria, leading first-amendment lawyer; Peter Michael Goetz, actor, *The Cavanaughs, Brighton Beach Memoirs*; Barbar Kilduff, soprano; Brian Frons, vice-president for creative affairs, NBC; Neil Postman, educator and author, *Teaching as a Subversive Activity*; Diane Pennica, biologist and researcher, Genetech; Mary McDonnell, actress.

# State University of New York College at Geneseo

Geneseo, NY 14454 716 245-5211

**1994-95 Costs.** Tuition: $2,650 (state residents), $6,550 (out-of-state). Room: $2,620. Board: $1,550. Fees, books, misc. academic expenses (school's estimate): $905.
**Enrollment.** Undergraduates: 1,796 men, 3,260 women (full-time). Freshman class: 8,598 applicants, 4,562 accepted, 1,143 enrolled. Graduate enrollment: 90 men, 335 women.
**Test score averages/ranges.** Average SAT scores: 541 verbal, 608 math. Range of SAT scores of middle 50%: 490-580 verbal, 560-680 math. Average ACT scores: 26 composite.
**Faculty.** 246 full-time; 82 part-time. 82% of faculty holds doctoral degree. Student/faculty ratio: 20 to 1.
**Selectivity rating.** Highly competitive.

**PROFILE.** SUNY College at Geneseo, founded in 1867, is a public, multipurpose college of liberal arts and sciences. Its 220-acre campus is located in Geneseo, 30 miles south of Rochester.

**Accreditation:** MSACS. Professionally accredited by the American Speech-Language-Hearing Association.
**Religious orientation:** State University of New York College at Geneseo is nonsectarian; no religious requirements.
**Library:** Collections totaling over 445,187 volumes, 3,078 periodical subscriptions, and 810,893 microform items.
**Special facilities/museums:** Three theatres, electron microscopes.
**Athletic facilities:** Gymnasiums, ice rink, swimming pools, handball, racquetball, squash, and tennis courts, weight room, track, athletic fields, fitness center, dance studio, bowling alleys.

**STUDENT BODY. Undergraduate profile:** 98% are state residents; 22% are transfers. 6% Asian-American, 2% Black, 4% Hispanic, 1% Native American, 87% White. Average age of undergraduates is 20.
**Freshman profile:** 1% of freshmen who took SAT scored 700 or over on verbal, 10% scored 700 or over on math; 20% scored 600 or over on verbal, 58% scored 600 or over on math; 73% scored 500 or over on verbal, 96% scored 500 or over on math; 99% scored 400 or over on verbal, 98% scored 400 or over on math. Majority of accepted applicants took SAT. 85% of freshmen come from public schools.
**Undergraduate achievement:** 92% of fall 1992 freshmen returned for fall 1993 term. 70% of entering class graduated. 28% of students who completed a degree program immediately went on to graduate study.
**Foreign students:** Nine students are from out of the country. Countries represented include China, Finland, Japan, Sweden, and Taiwan.

**PROGRAMS OF STUDY. Degrees:** B.A., B.S., B.S.Ed.
**Majors:** Accounting, American Civilization, Anthropology, Applied Physics, Art, Art History, Biochemistry, Biology, Black Studies, Chemistry, Communication, Comparative Literature, Computer Science, Economics, Elementary Education, English, French, Geochemistry, Geography, Geological Sciences, Geophysics, History, Management Sciences, Mathematics, Medical Technology, Music, Natural Science, Philosophy, Physics, Political Science, Psychology, Sociology, Spanish, Special Education, Speech Pathology/Audiology, Studio Art, Theatre.
**Distribution of degrees:** The majors with the highest enrollment are biology, psychology, and elementary education; American civilization, black studies, and comparative literature have the lowest.
**Requirements:** General education requirement.
**Academic regulations:** Minimum 2.0 GPA required for graduation.
**Special:** Minors offered in cognitive science, computer science, criminal justice, dance, environmental studies, human development, linguistics, medieval history, museum studies, musical theatre, organizational and occupational behavior, photolithography, public relations, urban studies, information systems, legal studies, religious studies, modern European studies, and women's studies. Up to 30 hours of elective credit is given for independent study, contract study, and proficiency exams. Double majors. Independent study. Pass/fail grading option. Internships. Graduate school at which undergraduates may take graduate-level courses. Preprofessional programs in law, medicine, veterinary science, pharmacy, dentistry, theology, optometry, nursing, planning, and public service. 2-2 environmental science and forestry program with SUNY Coll of Environmental Science and Forestry. 2-2 physical therapy program with SUNY Health Science Center at Syracuse. 3-2 engineering programs with Alfred U, Case Western Reserve U, Clarkson U, Columbia U, Ohio State U, Rochester Inst of Tech, U of Rochester, SUNY at Buffalo, SUNY at Stony Brook, and Syracuse U. 3-2 M.B.A. (economics/management) program with Pace U, Rochester Inst of Tech, SUNY at Buffalo, and Syracuse U. Member of Rochester Area College Consortium; cross-registration possible. Washington Semester. Visiting Student Program with other New York institutions. Teacher certification in elementary, secondary, and special education. Certification in specific subject areas. Study abroad possible. ROTC and AFROTC at Rochester Inst of Tech.
**Honors:** Honors program. Honor societies.
**Academic Assistance:** Remedial writing and math. Nonremedial tutoring.

**STUDENT LIFE. Housing:** All freshmen must live on campus unless living with family. Coed dorms. Sorority and fraternity housing. 61% of students live in college housing.
**Social atmosphere:** As the student newspaper reports, "The small village atmosphere coupled with the location of the school set just above the gorgeous Genesee Valley provides for an enjoyable, cultured social life." Greeks, the Activities Commission, and the Inter–Residence Council have a strong influence on campus social life. The College Union, The Hub, The Gazebo, and the lower quad are all popular hang-outs on campus; off campus, students frequent The Palace Lounge, The Inn Between, The Vital Spot, Gentlemen Jim's, The Village Park, and Main Street. Social highlights of the year include Homecoming Weekend, Homecoming Concert, soccer, lacrosse, and hockey games, Spring Weekend, intramural sports, Senior Week, and graduation.
**Services and counseling/handicapped student services:** Placement services. Health service. Women's center. Counseling services for minority, military, veteran, and older students. Birth control, personal, and psychological counseling. Career and academic guidance services. Physically disabled student services. Tape recorders. Reader services for the blind.
**Campus organizations:** Undergraduate student government. Student newspaper (Lamron, published once/week). Literary magazine. Yearbook. Radio station. Band, carol choristers, chamber singers, debating, drama group, jazz ensemble, string band, 175 organizations in all. 10 fraternities, no chapter houses; 10 sororities, no chapter houses. 19% of men join a fraternity. 15% of women join a sorority.
**Religious organizations:** Agape, Baptist Student Union, Brothers and Sisters in Christ, Christian Fellowship, Hillel, Interfaith Center, Latter-Day Saints Student Association, Newman Center, Wesley Fellowship.
**Minority/foreign student organizations:** Minority Student Council, HUG (Hispanic group), Black Student Union, Caribbean Connection, Bahai Unity Club, United Students Continent of Asia. International Relations Organization, Asian Culture Exchange.

**ATHLETICS. Physical education requirements:** None.
**Intercollegiate competition:** 12% of students participate. Basketball (M,W), cheerleading (W), cross-country (M,W), diving (M,W), ice hockey (M), lacrosse (M), soccer (M,W), softball (W), swimming (M,W), track (indoor) (M,W), track (outdoor) (M,W), track and field (indoor) (M,W), track and field (outdoor) (M,W), volleyball (W). Member of ECAC, Empire Lacrosse, NCAA Division III, New York State Collegiate Track and Field, NYSWCAA, SUNYAC.
**Intramural and club sports:** 80% of students participate. Intramural basketball, broomball, flag football, handball, inner-tube water polo, soccer, softball, volleyball. Men's club crew, golf, horsemanship, martial arts, rugby, squash, tennis, volleyball, water polo. Women's club crew, field hockey, horsemanship, lacrosse, martial arts, rugby, squash, tennis.

**ADMISSIONS. Academic basis for candidate selection** (in order of priority): Secondary school record, class rank, standardized test scores, essay, school's recommendation.
**Nonacademic basis for candidate selection:** Character and personality, extracurricular participation, particular talent or ability, and alumni/ae relationship are considered.
**Requirements:** Graduation from secondary school is required; GED is accepted. 18 units and the following program of study are recommended: 4 units of English, 4 units of math, 4 units of science, 4 units of foreign language, 4 units of social studies, 2 units of electives. Audition or portfolio required of music, drama, and studio art program applicants. EOP for applicants not normally admissible. Special Talent Program for applicants not normally admissible. SAT or ACT is required. Campus visit and interview recommended. No off-campus interviews.
**Procedure:** Suggest filing application by November. Application deadline is January 15. Acceptance notification on rolling basis after February 1. Reply is required by May 1. $100 nonrefundable tuition deposit. $50 nonrefundable room deposit. Freshmen accepted for terms other than fall.
**Special programs:** Admission may be deferred two semesters. Credit may be granted through CEEB Advanced Placement for scores of 3 or higher. Credit may be granted through CLEP general and subject exams, Regents College, ACT PEP, and DANTES exams. Credit and placement may be granted through challenge exams. Early decision program. In fall 1993, 222 applied for early decision and 170 were accepted. Deadline for applying for early decision is November 15. Early entrance/early admission program.
**Transfer students:** Transfer students accepted for terms other than fall. In fall 1993, 22% of all new students were transfers into all classes. 1,789 transfer applications were received, 778 were accepted. Application deadline is February 1 for fall; September 15 for spring. Minimum 2.0 GPA. Lowest course grade accepted is "D." Maximum number of transferable credits is 60 semester hours from a two-year school and 90 semester hours from a four-year school. At least 30 semester hours must be completed at the college to receive degree.
**Admissions contact:** Jill E. Conlon, M.A., Director of Admissions. 716 245-5571.

**FINANCIAL AID. Available aid:** Pell grants, SEOG, state scholarships and grants, school scholarships, private scholarships, ROTC scholarships, and academic merit scholarships. Perkins Loans (NDSL), PLUS, Stafford Loans (GSL), private loans, and SLS. AMS.
**Financial aid statistics:** 35% of aid is not need-based. In 1993-94, 80% of all freshman applicants received aid. Average amounts of aid awarded freshmen: Scholarships and grants, $2,000; loans, $2,135.
**Supporting data/closing dates:** FAFSA: Deadline is February 15. Notification of awards begins April 1.
**Financial aid contact:** Archie L. Cureton, M.S., Director of Financial Aid. 716 245-5731.

**STUDENT EMPLOYMENT.** College Work/Study Program. Institutional employment. 28% of full-time undergraduates work on campus during school year. Students may expect to earn an average of $1,200 during school year. Off-campus part-time employment opportunities rated "good."

**COMPUTER FACILITIES.** 417 IBM/IBM-compatible and Macintosh/Apple microcomputers; 150 are networked. Students may access Digital minicomputer/mainframe systems, BITNET, Internet. Residence halls may be equipped with stand-alone microcomputers. Client/LAN operating systems include Apple/Macintosh, DOS, LocalTalk/AppleTalk. Computer languages and software packages include Assembly, BASIC, C, COBOL, FORTRAN, LISP, Pascal, PL/1, SPSS, statistical packages. Computer facilities are available to all students.
**Fees:** None.
**Hours:** 8 AM-2 AM.

**GRADUATE CAREER DATA.** Graduate school percentages: 2% enter law school. 2% enter graduate business programs. 7% enter graduate arts and sciences programs. Highest graduate school enrollments: Cornell U, Johns Hopkins U, SUNY at Buffalo, Syracuse U, U of Rochester. 30% of graduates choose careers in business and industry. Companies and businesses that hire graduates: Eastman Kodak, Bausch & Lomb, Xerox.

**PROMINENT ALUMNI/AE.** Glenn Gordon Caron, executive TV producer, *Moonlighting;* Kurt Smith, political speechwriter and author.

# State University of New York College at New Paltz

New Paltz, NY 12561-2499 914 257-2121

**1994-95 Costs.** Tuition: $2,650 (state residents), $6,550 (out-of-state). Room: $2,720. Board: $2,060. Fees, books, misc. academic expenses (school's estimate): $855.
**Enrollment.** Undergraduates: 1,985 men, 2,761 women (full-time). Freshman class: 8,399 applicants, 3,609 accepted, 798 enrolled. Graduate enrollment: 456 men, 1,310 women.
**Test score averages/ranges.** Average SAT scores: 479 verbal, 537 math. Range of SAT scores of middle 50%: 423-560 verbal, 476-590 math.
**Faculty.** 289 full-time; 275 part-time. 78% of faculty holds doctoral degree. Student/faculty ratio: 16 to 1.
**Selectivity rating.** More competitive.

**PROFILE.** SUNY College at New Paltz, founded in 1828, is a public, multipurpose college of arts and sciences. Its 216-acre campus is located in New Paltz, 75 miles from Albany.

**Accreditation:** MSACS. Professionally accredited by the Accreditation Board for Engineering and Technology, the Computing Sciences Accreditation Board, the National Association of Schools of Music, the National League for Nursing.
**Religious orientation:** State University of New York College at New Paltz is nonsectarian; no religious requirements.
**Library:** Collections totaling over 397,699 volumes, 1,385 periodical subscriptions, and 929,681 microform items.
**Special facilities/museums:** Art gallery, theatres, theatre design collection, national center for study of foreign languages, cartography lab, computerized journalism lab, greenhouse, speech and hearing center, music therapy training facility, robotics lab, planetarium, two electron microscope labs.
**Athletic facilities:** Gymnasium, swimming pool, dance studio, body mechanics and weight rooms, fitness lab, basketball, racquetball, tennis, and volleyball courts, indoor and outdoor tracks, cross-country course, baseball, soccer, and softball fields.

**STUDENT BODY. Undergraduate profile:** 94% are state residents; 54% are transfers. 4% Asian-American, 10% Black, 9% Hispanic, 1% Native American, 73% White, 3% Other. Average age of undergraduates is 23.
**Freshman profile:** 1% of freshmen who took SAT scored 700 or over on verbal, 2% scored 700 or over on math; 7% scored 600 or over on verbal, 22% scored 600 or over on math; 38% scored 500 or over on verbal, 70% scored 500 or over on math; 86% scored 400 or over on verbal, 98% scored 400 or over on math; 99% scored 300 or over on verbal, 99% scored 300 or over on math. 90% of accepted applicants took SAT; 10% took ACT. 95% of freshmen come from public schools.
**Undergraduate achievement:** 78% of fall 1992 freshmen returned for fall 1993 term. 61% of entering class graduated.
**Foreign students:** 450 students are from out of the country. Countries represented include China, Greece, Japan, Korea, Pakistan, and United Kingdom; 41 in all.

**PROGRAMS OF STUDY. Degrees:** B.A., B.F.A., B.S., B.S.Elec.Eng., B.S.Nurs.
**Majors:** Accounting, Anthropology, Art Education, Art History, Bilingual/Bicultural Education, Biology, Black Studies, Business Administration, Ceramics, Chemistry, Communication/Media, Computer Engineering, Computer Science, Economics, Electrical Engineering, Elementary/Early Secondary Education, Elementary Education, English, French, Geography, Geological Science, German, Gold/Silversmithing, Graphic Design, History, International Relations, Jazz Studies, Journalism, Mathematics, Music, Music Therapy, Nursing, Painting, Philosophy, Photography, Physics, Planning/Regional Affairs, Political Science, Printmaking, Psychology, Scenography, Sculpture, Secondary Education, Sociology, Spanish, Speech/Hearing, Studio Art, Theatre Arts, Visual Arts, Women's Studies.
**Distribution of degrees:** The majors with the highest enrollment are elementary education, business administration, and psychology; philosophy, black studies, and women's studies have the lowest.
**Requirements:** General education requirement.
**Academic regulations:** Minimum 2.0 GPA must be maintained.
**Special:** Minors offered in many majors and in approximately 20 other fields. Courses offered in Arabic, Chinese studies, Hebrew, Italian, Latin, and Swahili. Self-designed majors. Double majors. Dual degrees. Independent study. Accelerated study. Pass/fail grading option. Internships. Cooperative education programs. Graduate school at which undergraduates may take graduate-level courses. Preprofessional programs in law, medicine, veterinary science, dentistry, and optometry. 3-2/2-2 program with SUNY Coll of Environmental Science & Forestry. 2-2 physical therapy program with SUNY Coll of Health Related Professions at Syracuse. 3-2 geological engineering program with New Mexico Inst of Mining and Tech. 3-4 optometry program with SUNY Coll of Optometry. 3-4 osteopathy program with New York Coll of Osteopathic Medicine. Member of Mid-Hudson College Consortium. UN Semester. Teacher certification in early childhood, elementary, secondary, and bilingual/bicultural education. Certification in specific subject areas. Study abroad in China, England, France, Germany, Greece, Israel, Italy, Japan, the Netherlands, New Zealand, the former Soviet Republics, and Spain.
**Honors:** Honors program.
**Academic Assistance:** Remedial reading, writing, math, and study skills. Nonremedial tutoring.

**STUDENT LIFE. Housing:** All freshmen (students with fewer than 30 credits) must live on campus unless living with family within a 25-mile radius. Coed dorms. 46% of students live in college housing.
**Social atmosphere:** SUNY College at New Paltz is a school of great ethnic, academic, and social diversity. There are over 80 different student organizations on campus; the athletic and Greek communities are both influential groups. Many parties, stepdances, semi-formals, and concerts provide entertainment during the school year. According to editor of the student newspaper, "While our past reputation as a party school is somewhat unfounded, SUNY at New Paltz does offer numerous social opportunities as well as many off-campus outlets. The best is probably the nearby wilderness region, one of the most beautiful areas anywhere." On-campus, students usually gather at the Student Union or Oscars, while bars and taverns are popular for off-campus get-togethers.
**Services and counseling/handicapped student services:** Placement services. Health service. Women's center. Day care. Counseling services for older students. Birth control, personal, and psychological counseling. Career and academic guidance services. Religious counseling. Physically disabled student services. Learning disabled services. Notetaking services. Tape recorders. Tutors. Reader services for the blind.
**Campus organizations:** Undergraduate student government. Student newspaper (Oracle, published once/week). Literary magazine. Yearbook. Radio and TV stations. Voices of Unity, Collegium Musicum, concert choir, jazz ensemble, theatre society, academic, service, social, and special-interest groups, 152 organizations in all. 15 fraternities, no chapter houses; eight sororities, no chapter houses. 3% of men join a fraternity. 3% of women join a sorority.
**Religious organizations:** Campus Catholic Center, Fountain of Faith, Student Christian Center, Jewish Student Union.
**Minority/foreign student organizations:** African Women's Alliance, Asian-Pacific Student Association, Black Student Union, Hermanos Latinos. International Students Society, Asian Student Union, Latin American Student Union.

**ATHLETICS. Physical education requirements:** Two semesters of physical education required.
**Intercollegiate competition:** 4% of students participate. Baseball (M), basketball (M,W), cross-country (M,W), diving (M,W), golf (M), soccer (M,W), softball (W), swimming (M,W), tennis (M,W), volleyball (M,W). Member of ECAC, NCAA Division III, SUNY-AC-East.

**Intramural and club sports:** Intramural aerobics, badminton, basketball, cross-country, free-throw shooting, golf, handball, inner-tube water polo, racquetball, softball, table tennis, tennis, touch football, volleyball, walleyball, water relays. Men's club tennis. Women's club cheerleading.

**ADMISSIONS. Academic basis for candidate selection** (in order of priority): Secondary school record, standardized test scores, class rank, school's recommendation, essay.
**Nonacademic basis for candidate selection:** Character and personality, extracurricular participation, and particular talent or ability are considered.
**Requirements:** Graduation from secondary school is required; GED is accepted. 21 units and the following program of study are recommended: 4 units of English, 3 units of math, 3 units of science including 2 units of lab, 3 units of foreign language, 4 units of social studies, 4 units of history. Minimum combined SAT score of 950, rank in top half of secondary school class, and minimum "B" academic average recommended. Portfolio required of art program applicants. Audition required of music and theatre program applicants. R.N. required of nursing program applicants. EOP for applicants not normally admissible. SAT or ACT is required. Campus visit recommended. No off-campus interviews.
**Procedure:** Take SAT or ACT by December 1 of 12th year. Suggest filing application by January 1. Application deadline is May 1. Notification of admission on rolling basis. Reply is required by May 1 or within 30 days of acceptance. $50 refundable tuition deposit. $50 refundable room deposit. Freshmen accepted for terms other than fall.
**Special programs:** Admission may be deferred one year. Credit and/or placement may be granted through CEEB Advanced Placement exams for scores of 3 or higher. Credit may be granted through CLEP subject exams and military experience. Early decision program. Deadline for applying for early decision is November 1. Early entrance/early admission program.
**Transfer students:** Transfer students accepted for terms other than fall. In fall 1993, 54% of all new students were transfers into all classes. 3,457 transfer applications were received, 2,040 were accepted. Application deadline is May 15 for fall; October 15 for spring. Minimum 2.5 GPA required. Lowest course grade accepted is "D." Maximum number of transferable credits is 70 semester hours from a two-year school and 90 semester hours from a four-year school. At least 30 semester hours must be completed at the college to receive degree.
**Admissions contact:** Robert J. Seaman, M.A., Dean of Admissions. 914 257-3200.

**FINANCIAL AID. Available aid:** Pell grants, SEOG, state scholarships and grants, school scholarships, and private scholarships. Perkins Loans (NDSL), PLUS, Stafford Loans (GSL), and SLS. AMS.
**Financial aid statistics:** 5% of aid is not need-based. In 1993-94, 80% of all undergraduate applicants received aid; 80% of freshman applicants. Average amounts of aid awarded freshmen: Scholarships and grants, $1,000; loans, $2,000.
**Supporting data/closing dates:** FAFSA: Priority filing date is March 15. State aid form: Priority filing date is March 15. Notification of awards begins April 1.
**Financial aid contact:** Daniel Sistarenik, M.S., Director of Financial Aid. 914 257-3250.

**STUDENT EMPLOYMENT.** College Work/Study Program. Institutional employment. 25% of full-time undergraduates work on campus during school year. Students may expect to earn an average of $800 during school year. Off-campus part-time employment opportunities rated "good."

**COMPUTER FACILITIES.** 210 IBM/IBM-compatible, Macintosh/Apple, and RISC-/UNIX-based microcomputers; 180 are networked. Students may access IBM minicomputer/mainframe systems, BITNET, Internet. Residence halls may be equipped with networked terminals. Client/LAN operating systems include Apple/Macintosh, DOS, UNIX/XENIX/AIX, X-windows, LocalTalk/AppleTalk, Novell. Computer languages and software packages include Assembler, C, C++, Fortran, LISP, PASCAL, PC-Solve, Mathematica, Modula, PROLOG, Quattro Pro, Smalltalk, Spice, Statgraphics, Textra, WordPerfect; 16 in all. Computer facilities are available to all students.
**Fees:** None.
**Hours:** Mainframe/workstations: 24 hrs. Dial-in LANS: 8 AM-11 PM (M-Th), 8 AM-4:30 PM (F), 10 AM-8 PM (Sa), 10 AM-11 PM (Su).

**GRADUATE CAREER DATA.** Companies and businesses that hire graduates: Fortune 500 companies; Big Five accounting firms; federal, state, and local governments and agencies.

**PROMINENT ALUMNI/AE.** Andria Hall, broadcast journalist (FOX), *Front Page;* Maurice Hinchey, congressman; Carl Lenarsky, clinical director of Division of Research Immunology and Bone Marrow Transplantation at Childrens Hospital of Southern California Sch of Medicine; John Turturro, actor, writer, director.

## State University of New York College at Oneonta

**Oneonta, NY 13820** **607 436-3500**

**1994-95 Costs.** Tuition: $2,650 (state residents), $6,550 (out-of-state). Room: $3,068. Board: $2,450. Fees, books, misc. academic expenses (school's estimate): $875.
**Enrollment.** Undergraduates: 1,851 men, 2,776 women (full-time). Freshman class: 7,500 applicants, 4,350 accepted, 902 enrolled. Graduate enrollment: 142 men, 413 women.
**Test score averages/ranges.** Average SAT scores: 463 verbal, 509 math. Range of SAT scores of middle 50%: 410-490 verbal, 460-550 math. Average ACT scores: 22 composite. Range of ACT scores of middle 50%: 20-23 composite.
**Faculty.** 260 full-time; 64 part-time. 70% of faculty holds doctoral degree. Student/faculty ratio: 19 to 1.
**Selectivity rating.** Less competitive.

**PROFILE.** SUNY College at Oneonta, founded in 1889, is a public, multipurpose college of liberal arts and sciences. Its 200-acre campus is located in Oneonta, 75 miles southwest of Albany.

**Accreditation:** MSACS. Professionally accredited by the American Dietetic Association, the American Home Economics Association, the National Council for Accreditation of Teacher Education.
**Religious orientation:** State University of New York College at Oneonta is nonsectarian; no religious requirements.
**Library:** Collections totaling over 525,215 volumes, 2,750 periodical subscriptions, and 721,766 microform items.
**Special facilities/museums:** Science discovery museum with hands-on exhibits, biological field station on Otsego Lake, planetarium and observatory, college camp, wildlife preserve.
**Athletic facilities:** Gymnasium, swimming pool, racquetball and tennis courts, weight room, field house, track, athletic fields.

**STUDENT BODY. Undergraduate profile:** 99% are state residents; 44% are transfers. 1.3% Asian-American, 2.5% Black, 3% Hispanic, .1% Native American, 92.6% White, .5% Other. Average age of undergraduates is 20.
**Freshman profile:** 94% of accepted applicants took SAT; 6% took ACT.
**Undergraduate achievement:** 80% of fall 1992 freshmen returned for fall 1993 term.
**Foreign students:** 50 students are from out of the country. Countries represented include Canada, England, Iran, Japan, Sweden, and Taiwan.

**PROGRAMS OF STUDY. Degrees:** B.A., B.S.
**Majors:** Accounting, Adulthood/Aging Studies, Anthropology, Art History, Art Studio, Biology, Black/Hispanic Studies, Business Economics, Chemistry, Child/Family Studies, Computer Science, Dietetics, Earth Science, Economics, Elementary Education, English, Environmental Science, Food/Business, French, Geography, Geology, History, Home Economics, Home Economics Education, Interdisciplinary Studies, International Studies, Mathematics, Meteorology, Music, Philosophy, Physics, Political Science, Psychology, School Nursing, Secondary Education, Sociology, Spanish, Speech Communication, Statistics, Theatre, Water Resources.
**Distribution of degrees:** The majors with the highest enrollment are education, business economics, and psychology.
**Requirements:** General education requirement.
**Academic regulations:** Minimum 2.0 GPA must be maintained.
**Special:** Minors offered in over 60 fields. Double majors. Independent study. Pass/fail grading option. Internships. Cooperative education programs. Graduate school at which undergraduates may take graduate-level courses. Preprofessional programs in law, medicine, veterinary science, dentistry, and optometry. 2-2 physical therapy, respiratory care, medical technology, and cytotechnology programs with SUNY Health Science Center at Syracuse. 2-2 nursing programs with SUNY Health Science Center at Brooklyn and Johns Hopkins U. 2-2 environmental science and forestry program with SUNY Coll of Environmental Science and Forestry. 3-1 fashion program with Fashion Inst of Tech. 3-1 art education program with SUNY Coll at Buffalo. 3-2 engineering programs with Clarkson U, Georgia Tech, Polytech U, SUNY at Alfred, Binghamton, and Buffalo, and Syracuse U. 3-2 accounting program with SUNY at Binghamton. 3-2 management programs with SUNY at Binghamton and U of Rochester. 4-1 bachelor's/M.B.A. program with Clarkson U. 3-4 optometry program with SUNY College of Optometry. Cross-registration/exchange with Hartwick Coll. Member of New York Visiting Student Program. Washington Semester. Teacher certification in elementary and secondary education. Certification in specific subject areas. Exchange program abroad in Germany (U of Wuerzburg). Study abroad also in England, India, Ireland, Israel, Japan, and other countries.
**Honors:** Honors program.
**Academic Assistance:** Remedial reading, writing, math, and study skills.

**STUDENT LIFE. Housing:** Students may live on or off campus. Coed and women's dorms. Special-interest housing. 60% of students live in college housing.
**Social atmosphere:** The student newspaper comments, "Unfortunately, socializing at downtown bars is the main social function." In addition, students gather at the College Camp, dance clubs, and various points of interest in Albany and, on campus, meet at the Union for movies, pinball, and occasional comedians. The most influential groups on campus are Greek organizations and the soccer team. The Mayor's Cup soccer game, Parents Weekend, and Halloween and St. Patrick's Day events are all popular on campus.
**Services and counseling/handicapped student services:** Placement services. Health service. Day care. Counseling services for minority, veteran, and older students. Birth control and personal counseling. Career and academic guidance services. Physically disabled student services. Learning disabled services. Notetaking services. Tape recorders. Tutors. Reader services for the blind.
**Campus organizations:** Undergraduate student government. Student newspaper (State Times, published once/week). Yearbook. Radio station. Concert band, orchestra, concert choir, brass ensemble, chamber singers Mask and Hammer, outing club, service club, Women's Alliance, athletic and departmental groups, 50 organizations in all. 13 fraternities, no chapter houses; eight sororities, two chapter houses.
**Religious organizations:** Campus Ministry.
**Minority/foreign student organizations:** Students of Color Coalition, HOLA. International Student Organization.

**ATHLETICS. Physical education requirements:** None.
**Intercollegiate competition:** 10% of students participate. Baseball (M), basketball (M,W), cheerleading (W), cross-country (M,W), field hockey (W), lacrosse (M,W), soccer (M,W), softball (W), swimming (W), tennis (M,W), volleyball (W), wrestling (M). Member of ECAC, NCAA Division I for men's soccer, NCAA Division III, New York State Women's Collegiate Athletic Association, SUNY Athletic Conference.
**Intramural and club sports:** 40% of students participate. Intramural aerobics, volleyball, football, soccer, racquetball, floor hockey, walleyball, basketball, badminton, European handball, softball. Men's club cheerleading, frisbee, kickline, rugby, skiing, volleyball. Women's club cheerleading, frisbee, kickline, rugby, skiing.

**ADMISSIONS. Academic basis for candidate selection** (in order of priority): Secondary school record, class rank, standardized test scores, school's recommendation, essay.

**Nonacademic basis for candidate selection:** Extracurricular participation and particular talent or ability are important. Character and personality and alumni/ae relationship are considered.

**Requirements:** Graduation from secondary school is required; GED is accepted. 16 units and the following program of study are required: 4 units of English, 4 units of social studies. Units in social studies should include history. 3 units of foreign language recommended. Minimum combined SAT score of 950 (composite ACT score of 22), rank in top third of secondary school class, and mean grade average of 85 recommended. EOP for applicants not normally admissible. SAT or ACT is required. Campus visit recommended. No off-campus interviews.

**Procedure:** Take SAT or ACT by December of 12th year. Suggest filing application by January 2; no deadline. Notification of admission on rolling basis. Reply is required by May 1 or within 30 days of acceptance if after May 1. $50 tuition deposit, refundable until May 1. $100 room deposit, refundable until July 1. Freshmen accepted for terms other than fall.

**Special programs:** Admission may be deferred one year. Credit and/or placement may be granted through CEEB Advanced Placement exams for scores of 3 or higher. Credit may be granted through CLEP general exams and military experience. Credit and/or placement may be granted through CLEP subject exams. Credit and placement may be granted through Regents College, ACT PEP, DANTES, and challenge exams and life experience. Early entrance/early admission program. Concurrent enrollment program.

**Transfer students:** Transfer students accepted for terms other than fall. In fall 1993, 44% of all new students were transfers into all classes. 2,700 transfer applications were received, 1,650 were accepted. Application deadline is rolling for fall; rolling for spring. Minimum 2.5 GPA recommended. Lowest course grade accepted is "C." Maximum number of transferable credits is 66 semester hours from a two-year school and 77 semester hours from a four-year school. At least 45 semester hours must be completed at the college to receive degree.

**Admissions contact:** Richard H. Burr, M.S., Director of Admissions. 607 436-2524.

**FINANCIAL AID. Available aid:** Pell grants, SEOG, state scholarships and grants, school scholarships and grants, private scholarships, and academic merit scholarships. Perkins Loans (NDSL), PLUS, Stafford Loans (GSL), and SLS. Tuition Plan Inc. and AMS. Institutional payment plan.

**Financial aid statistics:** 1% of aid is not need-based. In 1993-94, 67% of all freshman applicants received aid. Average amounts of aid awarded freshmen: Scholarships and grants, $1,670; loans, $2,625.

**Supporting data/closing dates:** FAFSA: Accepted on rolling basis; deadline is April 15. State aid form: Accepted on rolling basis. Notification of awards begins May 1.

**Financial aid contact:** Donald Moore, M.A., Director of Financial Aid. 607 436-2532.

**STUDENT EMPLOYMENT.** College Work/Study Program. Institutional employment. 40% of full-time undergraduates work on campus during school year. Students may expect to earn an average of $1,200 during school year. Off-campus part-time employment opportunities rated "good."

**COMPUTER FACILITIES.** 200 IBM/IBM-compatible and Macintosh/Apple microcomputers. Students may access Digital minicomputer/mainframe systems, BITNET, Internet. Residence halls may be equipped with stand-alone microcomputers. Client/LAN operating systems include Apple/Macintosh, DOS, UNIX/XENIX/AIX, X-windows, DEC, LocalTalk/AppleTalk. Computer languages and software packages include BASIC, COBOL, C++, FORTRAN, LISP, LOGO, MINITAB, Pascal, SAS. Computer facilities are available to all students.

**Fees:** Computer fee is included in tuition/fees.

**Hours:** Vary by facility; most open 70 to 80 hours/week.

**GRADUATE CAREER DATA.** Companies and businesses that hire graduates: Banking and financial institutions, wholesale and retail companies, school districts.

# State University of New York College at Oswego

**Oswego, NY 13126** **315 341-2500**

**1992-93 Costs.** Tuition: $2,650 (state residents), $6,550 (out-of-state). Room & board: $4,440. Fees, books, misc. academic expenses (school's estimate): $705.

**Enrollment.** Undergraduates: 3,050 men, 3,600 women (full-time). Freshman class: 8,000 applicants, 4,500 accepted, 1,450 enrolled. Graduate enrollment: 169 men, 960 women.

**Test score averages/ranges.** Average SAT scores: 480 verbal, 550 math. Range of SAT scores of middle 50%: 450-550 verbal, 450-515 math. Average ACT scores: 24 composite. Range of ACT scores of middle 50%: 23-26 composite.

**Faculty.** 326 full-time; 65 part-time. 78% of faculty holds doctoral degree. Student/faculty ratio: 20 to 1.

**Selectivity rating.** More competitive.

**PROFILE.** SUNY College at Oswego, founded in 1861, is a public, multipurpose college of arts and sciences. Its 696-acre campus is located in Oswego, 35 miles northwest of Syracuse, on the shore of Lake Ontario.

**Accreditation:** MSACS. Professionally accredited by the National Association of Schools of Music.

**Religious orientation:** State University of New York College at Oswego is nonsectarian; no religious requirements.

**Library:** Collections totaling over 409,000 volumes, 1,726 periodical subscriptions, and 1,600,000 microform items.

**Special facilities/museums:** Art galleries, biological field station, curriculum materials center, electron microscopy lab, planetarium.

**Athletic facilities:** Field house, ice hockey arena, fitness center, wellness center, dance studio, basketball, racquetball, squash, and tennis courts, indoor swimming pools, fencing and weight rooms, outdoor track, baseball, field hockey, lacrosse, soccer, softball, and volleyball fields.

**STUDENT BODY. Undergraduate profile:** 96% are state residents; 37% are transfers. 2% Asian-American, 4% Black, 3.5% Hispanic, .5% Native American, 89% White, 1% Other. Average age of undergraduates is 21.

**Freshman profile:** 1% of freshmen who took SAT scored 700 or over on math; 5% scored 600 or over on verbal, 23% scored 600 or over on math; 35% scored 500 or over on verbal, 83% scored 500 or over on math; 95% scored 400 or over on verbal, 98% scored 400 or over on math; 100% scored 300 or over on verbal, 100% scored 300 or over on math. 88% of accepted applicants took SAT; 40% took ACT. 90% of freshmen come from public schools.

**Undergraduate achievement:** 88% of fall 1992 freshmen returned for fall 1993 term. 52% of entering class graduated. 21% of students who completed a degree program immediately went on to graduate study.

**Foreign students:** 45 students are from out of the country. Countries represented include Canada, China, Hong Kong, Japan, and Nigeria.

**PROGRAMS OF STUDY. Degrees:** B.A., B.F.A., B.S.

**Majors:** Accounting, American Studies, Anthropology, Applied Mathematical Economics, Applied Mathematics, Art, Biology, Broadcasting/Mass Communications, Business Administration, Chemistry, Communications Studies, Computer Science, Economics, Elementary Education, English, French, General Studies, Geochemistry, Geology, German, History, Industrial Arts, Industrial Training/Development, Linguistics, Management Sciences, Marketing, Mathematics, Meteorology, Music, Philosophy, Philosophy/Psychology, Physics, Political Science, Psychology, Public Justice, Russian, Secondary Education, Sociology, Spanish, Technology Education, Theatre, Vocational/Technical Education, Zoology.

**Distribution of degrees:** The majors with the highest enrollment are business administration, communications, and elementary education; geochemistry, general studies, and American studies have the lowest.

**Requirements:** General education requirement.

**Academic regulations:** Minimum 2.0 GPA must be maintained.

**Special:** Minors offered in most majors and in Afro-American studies, Asian studies, athletic coaching, creative writing, forensic science, health science, international studies, Italian, marine sciences, medieval/Renaissance studies, museum studies, Native American studies, reading education, East European studies, and women's studies. Double majors. Independent study. Pass/fail grading option. Internships. Cooperative education programs. Preprofessional programs in law, medicine, veterinary science, dentistry, and optometry. 2-2 medical technology/cytotechnology program with SUNY Health Science Center at Syracuse. 2-2 zoo technology program with Santa Fe Comm Coll. 2-2 environmental science program with SUNY Coll of Environmental Science and Forestry. 3-2 engineering programs with Case Western Reserve U, Clarkson U, and SUNY at Binghamton. 3-4 optometry program with SUNY Coll of Optometry. Washington Semester. Member of New York State Visiting Student Program. Teacher certification in early childhood, elementary, secondary, and vo-tech education. Certification in specific subject areas. Exchange program abroad in St. Etienne. Study abroad also in Australia, Austria, Belgium, China, the Dominican Republic, England, France, Germany, Greece, Jamaica, Japan, Mexico, Scotland, Spain, and Wales. ROTC.

**Honors:** Phi Beta Kappa. Honors program. Honor societies.

**Academic Assistance:** Remedial reading, writing, math, and study skills. Nonremedial tutoring.

**STUDENT LIFE. Housing:** All unmarried students under age 21 must live on campus unless living with family. Coed, women's, and men's dorms. Sorority and fraternity housing. Off-campus privately-owned housing. 67% of students live in college housing.

**Social atmosphere:** On campus, students gather at Timepieces and Hewitt Union. Off campus, students head for The Shed, The Patch, Water Street, American Foundry, The Sting, Caddyshack, and Breitbeck Park. Greeks, athletes, and the student media influence campus life. Students enjoy Springfest, the Bridge Street Run, concerts, comedy shows, plays, musicals, and art gallery events. According to the student newspaper, Oswego is an active place on weekends: "On weekend nights the downtown area is crowded with bar-hopping students. There are also several socials on campus each weekend. Lake Ontario is popular during warm weather."

**Services and counseling/handicapped student services:** Placement services. Health service. Women's center. Day care. Counseling services for minority, military, veteran, and older students. Birth control, personal, and psychological counseling. Career and academic guidance services. Religious counseling. Physically disabled student services. Learning disabled services. Reader services for the blind.

**Campus organizations:** Undergraduate student government. Student newspaper (Oswegonian, published once/week). Literary magazine. Yearbook. Radio and TV stations. Choir, festival chorus, gospel choir, Statesingers, symphonic choir, chamber singers, men's glee club, orchestra, concert band, folk dancing, dance group, drama groups, Community Services Office, Amnesty International, academic, political, and special-interest groups, 125 organizations in all. 14 fraternities, eight chapter houses; 14 sororities, seven chapter houses. 15% of men join a fraternity. 15% of women join a sorority.

**Religious organizations:** Campus Crusade for Christ, Brothers and Sisters in Christ, Newman Center, Jewish Student Center.

**Minority/foreign student organizations:** ALANA League, Black Student Union, Asian and Latin student unions. International Student Association.

**ATHLETICS. Physical education requirements:** None.

**Intercollegiate competition:** 5% of students participate. Baseball (M), basketball (M,W), cross-country (M,W), diving (M,W), field hockey (W), golf (M), ice hockey (M), lacrosse (M,W), soccer (M,W), softball (W), swimming (M,W), tennis (M,W), volleyball (W), wrestling (M). Member of ECAC, NCAA Division III, NYSWCAA, SUNY Athletic Conference.

**Intramural and club sports:** 65% of students participate. Intramural aerobics, badminton, basketball, bowling, broomball, fencing, foul shooting, golf, gymnastics, indoor soccer, inner-tube water polo, racquetball, softball, swimming, tennis, touch football, track, turkey trot, volleyball, wrestling. Men's club canoe/kayak, rugby, volleyball. Women's club cheerleading, rugby.

**ADMISSIONS. Academic basis for candidate selection** (in order of priority): Secondary school record, standardized test scores, class rank, essay, school's recommendation.

**Nonacademic basis for candidate selection:** Character and personality, extracurricular participation, and particular talent or ability are important. Alumni/ae relationship is considered.

**Requirements:** Graduation from secondary school is required; GED is accepted. 18 units and the following program of study are required: 4 units of English, 3 units of math, 3 units of science including 2 units of lab, 2 units of foreign language, 4 units of social studies, 2 units of history. EOP for applicants not normally admissible. SAT or ACT is required. Campus visit and interview recommended. No off-campus interviews.

**Procedure:** Take SAT or ACT by November of 12th year. Visit college for interview by spring of 12th year. Suggest filing application by January 15; no deadline. Acceptance notification on rolling basis beginning February 1. Reply is required by May 1. $100 tuition deposit, refundable until May 1. $100 room deposit, refundable until May 1. Freshmen accepted for terms other than fall.

**Special programs:** Admission may be deferred one year. Credit may be granted through CEEB Advanced Placement for scores of 3 or higher. Credit may be granted through CLEP general and subject exams, Regents College, ACT PEP, DANTES, and challenge exams, and military and life experience. Early entrance/early admission program.

**Transfer students:** Transfer students accepted for terms other than fall. In fall 1993, 37% of all new students were transfers into all classes. 2,500 transfer applications were received, 1,740 were accepted. Application deadline is January 15 (priority date) for fall; November 15 (priority date) for spring. Minimum 2.5 GPA recommended. Lowest course grade accepted is "C." Maximum number of transferable credits is 62 semester hours from a two-year school and 92 semester hours from a four-year school. At least 30 semester hours must be completed at the college to receive degree.

**Admissions contact:** Joseph F. Grant, Jr., Ed.D., Dean of Admissions. 315 341-2250.

**FINANCIAL AID. Available aid:** Pell grants, SEOG, state scholarships and grants, school scholarships and grants, private scholarships and grants, ROTC scholarships, and academic merit scholarships. Perkins Loans (NDSL), PLUS, Stafford Loans (GSL), state loans, and SLS. AMS.

**Financial aid statistics:** 1% of aid is not need-based. In 1993-94, 60% of all undergraduate applicants received aid; 52% of freshman applicants. Average amounts of aid awarded freshmen: Scholarships and grants, $931; loans, $2,135.

**Supporting data/closing dates:** FAFSA/FAF: Priority filing date is March 1. State aid form: Priority filing date is March 1. Notification of awards begins April 1.

**Financial aid contact:** Margaret Sternberg, M.S., Director of Financial Aid. 315 341-2248.

**STUDENT EMPLOYMENT.** College Work/Study Program. Institutional employment. 35% of full-time undergraduates work on campus during school year. Students may expect to earn an average of $1,000 during school year. Off-campus part-time employment opportunities rated "fair."

**COMPUTER FACILITIES.** 250 IBM/IBM-compatible and Macintosh/Apple microcomputers; 200 are networked. Students may access Digital, SUN minicomputer/mainframe systems, BITNET, Internet. Residence halls may be equipped with networked microcomputers, modems. Client/LAN operating systems include Apple/Macintosh. Computer languages and software packages include Assembler, BASIC, C, FORTRAN, LISP, Pascal; graphics, spreadsheet, word processing packages; 35 in all. Computer facilities are available to all students.

**Fees:** None.

**GRADUATE CAREER DATA.** Graduate school percentages: 2% enter law school. 1% enter medical school. 1% enter dental school. 8% enter graduate business programs. 6% enter graduate arts and sciences programs. 1% enter theological school/seminary. Highest graduate school enrollments: SUNY at Albany, SUNY at Buffalo, Syracuse U. 45% of graduates choose careers in business and industry. Companies and businesses that hire graduates: Aetna, Big Six accounting firms, Ford Motor Co., General Electric, IBM, Lever Brothers, Marine Midland, United Technologies, Xerox.

**PROMINENT ALUMNI/AE.** Ken Auletta, author and political columnist; Al Roker, weatherman, NBC's *Sunday Today;* Robin Curtis, actress; Alice McDermott, author, *That Night;* Richard Alexander, Broadway producer/director; Harold Morse, CEO and founder, American Management TV Corp. and American Media Foundation.

# State University of New York College at Plattsburgh

**Plattsburgh, NY 12901** — **518 564-2000**

**1994-95 Costs.** Tuition: $2,650 (state residents), $6,550 (out-of-state). Room: $2,520. Board: $1,656. Fees, books, misc. academic expenses (school's estimate): $911.

**Enrollment.** Undergraduates: 2,219 men, 2,852 women (full-time). Freshman class: 4,618 applicants, 3,583 accepted, 846 enrolled. Graduate enrollment: 190 men, 528 women.

**Test score averages/ranges.** Average SAT scores: 460 verbal, 520 math. Range of SAT scores of middle 50%: 410-500 verbal, 470-580 math. Average ACT scores: 22 composite. Range of ACT scores of middle 50%: 20-23 composite.

**Faculty.** 265 full-time; 119 part-time. 80% of faculty holds doctoral degree. Student/faculty ratio: 20 to 1.

**Selectivity rating.** Less competitive.

**PROFILE.** SUNY College at Plattsburgh, founded in 1889, is a public, multipurpose college of arts and sciences. Its 300-acre campus is located in Plattsburgh, 60 miles from Montreal, Canada.

**Accreditation:** MSACS. Professionally accredited by the American Dietetic Association, the National League for Nursing.

**Religious orientation:** State University of New York College at Plattsburgh is nonsectarian; no religious requirements.

**Library:** Collections totaling over 354,299 volumes, 1,447 periodical subscriptions, and 801,551 microform items.

**Special facilities/museums:** Art galleries, sculpture courtyard, communications/lecture hall, interactive video for telecourses, radio and TV broadcasting facilities, planetarium, on-site research center for biotechnology and environmental science, enzymology lab, electron microscope, remote sensing lab, NMR spectrophotometer, computer-operated infrared spectrophotometer, gas chromatograph, mass spectrometer, computerized liquid scintillation counter.

**Athletic facilities:** Gymnasiums, racquetball and tennis courts, bowling lanes, swimming pool, weight rooms, tracks, cross-country trails, ice arena, field house, dance studio.

**STUDENT BODY. Undergraduate profile:** 97% are state residents; 48% are transfers. 2% Asian-American, 3% Black, 3% Hispanic, 82% White, 10% Other. Average age of undergraduates is 21.

**Freshman profile:** 1% of freshmen who took SAT scored 700 or over on math; 2% scored 600 or over on verbal, 14% scored 600 or over on math; 28% scored 500 or over on verbal, 64% scored 500 or over on math; 82% scored 400 or over on verbal, 95% scored 400 or over on math; 100% scored 300 or over on verbal, 100% scored 300 or over on math. Majority of accepted applicants took SAT. 95% of freshmen come from public schools.

**Undergraduate achievement:** 78% of fall 1992 freshmen returned for fall 1993 term. 38% of entering class graduated. 35% of students who completed a degree program immediately went on to graduate study.

**Foreign students:** 90 students are from out of the country. Countries represented include Canada, Japan, and United Kingdom; 22 in all.

**PROGRAMS OF STUDY. Degrees:** B.A., B.S., B.S.Ed.

**Majors:** Accounting, Anthropology, Art, Biochemistry, Biology, Business, Business/Economics, Canadian Studies, Chemistry, Child Care Management, Child/Family Services, Communications, Computer Science, Criminal Justice, Dietetics, Economics, Education, Engineering, English, Environmental Chemistry, Environmental Geology, Environmental Science, Food/Nutrition, French, Geography, Geology, Hearing/Speech Science, History, Hotel/Restaurant Management, Human Services, In Vitro Cell Biology/Biotechnology, Individualized Studies, International Policy Studies, Latin American Studies, Mathematics, Medical Technology, Nursing, Philosophy, Physics, Political Science, Psychology, Social Work, Sociology, Spanish, Theatre.

**Distribution of degrees:** The majors with the highest enrollment are education, business, and psychology; Latin American studies and geology have the lowest.

**Requirements:** General education requirement.

**Academic regulations:** Minimum 2.0 GPA must be maintained.

**Special:** Minors offered in many majors and in approximately 25 other fields. Minority and women's studies programs. Undeclared majors. Self-designed majors. Double majors. Dual degrees. Independent study. Accelerated study. Pass/fail grading option. Internships. Cooperative education programs. Graduate school at which undergraduates may take graduate-level courses. Preprofessional programs in law, medicine, veterinary science, dentistry, and optometry. 3-2 international policy studies program with Monterey Inst of International Studies. 3-2 engineering programs with various universities. 4-1 business program with Clarkson U. 3-4 optometry program with SUNY Coll of Optometry. Off-campus study opportunities available. Exchange program with other SUNY colleges. Teacher certification in elementary, secondary, and special education. Certification in specific subject areas. Exchange programs abroad in Canada (U of Laval, U of Toronto), England (Chester Coll of Education, Leeds Coll, Liverpool Inst of Higher Education), and in Chile. Study abroad also possible in many other countries, including Australia and Asia.

**Honors:** Honors program. Honor societies.

**Academic Assistance:** Remedial reading, writing, math, and study skills. Nonremedial tutoring.

**STUDENT LIFE. Housing:** All unmarried students under age 21 must live on campus unless living near campus with relatives. Coed dorms. Fraternity housing. Off-campus privately-owned housing. 49% of students live in college housing.

**Social atmosphere:** The student newspaper reports, "Although weekends are the focus of much attention, Plattsburgh provides a mix of events from educational to social. Plattsburgh has been known for its parties and also for its hockey team." Popular campus events include Homecoming, hockey games, parents' weekend, Mainstage Productions by the Arts Department, and Student Association Movies. Influential student groups include the Activities Coordination Board, the student newspaper staff, and the NCAA Champion hockey team. Students enjoy socializing at the Point, the Blue Room Lounge, fraternity houses, and Champlain Centres.

**Services and counseling/handicapped student services:** Placement services. Health service. Day care. Counseling services for minority, military, veteran, and older students. Birth control, personal, and psychological counseling. Career and academic guidance services. Religious counseling. Physically disabled student services. Learning disabled services. Notetaking services. Tape recorders. Tutors. Reader services for the blind.

**Campus organizations:** Undergraduate student government. Student newspaper (Cardinal Points, published once/week). Literary magazine. Yearbook. Radio and TV stations. Chorale, concert and symphonic bands, theatre association, debating, forensic union, Circle K, Amnesty International, Environmental Action Committee, Adult Student Group, Adirondack Experience Club, center for women's concerns, academic, athletic, service, social action, and special-interest groups, 108 organizations in all. 10 fraternities, three chapter houses; nine sororities, no chapter houses. 13% of men join a fraternity. 12% of women join a sorority.

**Religious organizations:** Intervarsity Christian Fellowship, Hillel, Newman Association.

**Minority/foreign student organizations:** Akeba, Akwekon, El Pueblo, Asian Students Promoting Cultural Enrichment. Club International, Club Canada.

**ATHLETICS. Physical education requirements:** None.

**Intercollegiate competition:** 6% of students participate. Basketball (M,W), cross-country (M,W), diving (M,W), ice hockey (M), soccer (M,W), swimming (M,W), tennis (W), track (indoor) (M,W), track (outdoor) (M,W), track and field (indoor) (M,W), track and field (outdoor) (M,W), volleyball (W). Member of ECAC, NCAA Division III, NYST&FA, NYSWCAA, SUNYAC.

**Intramural and club sports:** 50% of students participate. Intramural basketball, bowling, broomball, floor hockey, indoor soccer, racquetball, soccer, softball, tennis, touch football, volleyball, walleyball. Men's club baseball, lacrosse, racquetball, rugby. Women's club cheerleading, racquetball, rugby.

**ADMISSIONS. Academic basis for candidate selection** (in order of priority): Secondary school record, standardized test scores, class rank, school's recommendation, essay.

**Nonacademic basis for candidate selection:** Extracurricular participation and particular talent or ability are important. Character and personality and alumni/ae relationship are considered.

**Requirements:** Graduation from secondary school is required; GED is accepted. 12 units and the following program of study are required: 4 units of English, 3 units of math, 3 units of science, 4 units of social studies. 3 units of foreign language and additional mathematics and science units recommended. Minimum combined SAT score of 900, rank in top quarter of secondary school class, and minimum grade average of 82 recommended. EOP for applicants not normally admissible. SAT or ACT is required. Campus visit and interview recommended. No off-campus interviews.

**Procedure:** Take SAT or ACT by December of 12th year. Visit college for interview by April of 12th year. Suggest filing application by November; no deadline. Notification of admission on rolling basis beginning January 15. Reply is required by May 1. $100 tuition deposit, refundable until May 1. $50 room deposit, refundable until July 1. Freshmen accepted for terms other than fall.

**Special programs:** Admission may be deferred one year. Credit and/or placement may be granted through CEEB Advanced Placement exams for scores of 3 or higher. Credit and/or placement may be granted through CLEP general and subject exams. Credit and placement may be granted through Regents College, ACT PEP, DANTES, and challenge exams and military experience. Early decision program. Early entrance/early admission program. Concurrent enrollment program.

**Transfer students:** Transfer students accepted for terms other than fall. In fall 1993, 48% of all new students were transfers into all classes. 1,981 transfer applications were received, 1,699 were accepted. Application deadline is March 1 for fall; November 1 for spring. Minimum 2.3 GPA recommended. Lowest course grade accepted is "D." Maximum number of transferable credits is 72 semester hours from a two-year school and 89 semester hours from a four-year school. At least 36 semester hours must be completed at the college to receive degree.

**Admissions contact:** Richard J. Higgins, M.S., Director of Admissions. 518 564-2040.

**FINANCIAL AID. Available aid:** Pell grants, SEOG, state scholarships and grants, school scholarships and grants, private scholarships, academic merit scholarships, and aid for undergraduate foreign students. Perkins Loans (NDSL), PLUS, Stafford Loans (GSL), NSL, private loans, and SLS. AMS.

**Financial aid statistics:** 10% of aid is not need-based. In 1993-94, 80% of all undergraduate applicants received aid; 80% of freshman applicants. Average amounts of aid awarded freshmen: Scholarships and grants, $1,160; loans, $2,165.

**Supporting data/closing dates:** FAFSA: Priority filing date is March 1. State aid form: Priority filing date is March 1. Notification of awards on rolling basis.

**Financial aid contact:** Suzanne Sokolowski, M.Ed., Director of Financial Aid. 518 564-2072.

**STUDENT EMPLOYMENT.** College Work/Study Program. Institutional employment. 20% of full-time undergraduates work on campus during school year. Students may expect to earn an average of $1,000 during school year. Off-campus part-time employment opportunities rated "good."

**COMPUTER FACILITIES.** 150 IBM/IBM-compatible and Macintosh/Apple microcomputers; 140 are networked. Students may access Digital minicomputer/mainframe systems, BITNET, Internet. Client/LAN operating systems include Apple/Macintosh, DOS, UNIX/XENIX/AIX, X-windows, DEC, LocalTalk/AppleTalk. Computer languages and software packages include C, COBOL, FORTRAN, LOGO, MINITAB, Modula 2, Oracle, Pascal, SAS, SAS/GRAPH, SPSS-X. Computer facilities are available to all students.

**Hours:** 8 AM-11 PM.

**GRADUATE CAREER DATA.** Graduate school percentages: 1% enter law school. 1% enter medical school. 3% enter graduate business programs. 23% enter graduate arts and sciences programs. Highest graduate school enrollments: Clarkson U, New York U, Pace U, SUNY at Albany, SUNY Coll at Plattsburgh, Syracuse U. 34% of graduates choose careers in business and industry. Companies and businesses that hire graduates: CVPH Medical Center, IBM, Macy's, Marriott, Wyeth-Ayerst Labs.

**PROMINENT ALUMNI/AE.** Tom Chapin, TV host, Public Television; Kathy Hopkins McGaw, vice-president, Chase Manhattan Bank; Dawn Fratangelo, TV news anchor.

# State University of New York College at Potsdam

**Potsdam, NY 13676** **315 267-2000**

**1994-95 Costs.** Tuition: $2,650 (state residents), $6,550 (out-of-state). Room: $2,750. Board: $1,820. Fees, books, misc. academic expenses (school's estimate): $755.

**Enrollment.** Undergraduates: 1,452 men, 2,162 women (full-time). Freshman class: 3,150 applicants, 2,289 accepted, 650 enrolled. Graduate enrollment: 134 men, 435 women.

**Test score averages/ranges.** Average SAT scores: 500 verbal, 540 math. Average ACT scores: 22 English, 24 math, 23 composite.

**Faculty.** 231 full-time; 110 part-time. 66% of faculty holds doctoral degree. Student/faculty ratio: 20 to 1.

**Selectivity rating.** Competitive.

**PROFILE.** SUNY College at Potsdam, founded in 1816, is a public, liberal arts college. Programs are offered through the School of Liberal Studies; the Crane School of Music; and the School of Graduate, Professional, and Lifelong Learning. Its 240-acre campus is located in Potsdam, north of Syracuse.

**Accreditation:** MSACS. Professionally accredited by the National Association of Schools of Music.

**Religious orientation:** State University of New York College at Potsdam is nonsectarian; no religious requirements.

**Library:** Collections totaling over 393,819 volumes, 1,417 periodical subscriptions, and 605,863 microform items.

**Special facilities/museums:** Art gallery, ecology museum, three performance halls, theatre, on-campus school (N-6), planetarium, electron microscope, nuclear magnetic resonator.

**Athletic facilities:** Gymnasiums, ice arena, field house, tracks, swimming pool, basketball, handball, racquetball, squash, and tennis courts, gymnastics, training/therapy, weight, and wrestling rooms, dance studio, playing fields.

**STUDENT BODY. Undergraduate profile:** 95% are state residents; 33% are transfers. 1% Asian-American, 1% Black, 1% Hispanic, 1% Native American, 81% White, 15% Unknown. Average age of undergraduates is 21.

**Freshman profile:** 2% of freshmen who took SAT scored 700 or over on verbal, 2% scored 700 or over on math; 8% scored 600 or over on verbal, 12% scored 600 or over on math; 37% scored 500 or over on verbal, 61% scored 500 or over on math; 95% scored 400 or over on verbal, 98% scored 400 or over on math; 100% scored 300 or over on verbal, 100% scored 300 or over on math. 75% of accepted applicants took SAT; 25% took ACT. 80% of freshmen come from public schools.

**Undergraduate achievement:** 84% of fall 1992 freshmen returned for fall 1993 term. 30% of entering class graduated. 26% of students who completed a degree program went on to graduate study within one year.

**Foreign students:** 44 students are from out of the country. Countries represented include Canada, China, England, Greece, Japan, and Mexico; 11 in all.

**PROGRAMS OF STUDY. Degrees:** B.A., B.A.Ed., B.A.Mus., B.Mus.

**Majors:** Anthropology, Art History, Biology, Chemistry, Computer/Information Science, Dance, Drama, Economics, Elementary Education, English, French, Geology, History, Industrial Labor Relations, Interdepartmental Natural Science, Mathematics, Music, Music Education, Music Performance, Musical Studies, Philosophy, Physics, Political Science, Psychology, Secondary Education, Sociology, Spanish, Speech Communications, Student-Initiated Interdepartmental Major, Studio Art.

**Distribution of degrees:** The majors with the highest enrollment are music and music education, psychology, and English; philosophy, dance, and drama have the lowest.

**Requirements:** General education requirement.

**Academic regulations:** Minimum 2.0 GPA must be maintained.

**Special:** Minors offered in many majors and in acting, archaeology, business economics, business of music, criminal justice, directing, European history, health science, hearing science, international studies, journalism, literature, Native American studies, personnel management, social/human services, U.S. history, U.S. legal systems, U.S. politics, urban studies, women's studies, and writing. Education majors must choose additional arts or sciences major. Career-oriented courses in many fields. Paraprofessional training in the helping professions and in personnel management, public justice, rural studies, speech/language pathology and psychology, and urban studies. Star Lake Campus for recreation and education. Learning communities. Freshman interest groups. Self-designed majors. Double majors. Dual degrees. Independent study. Accelerated study. Pass/fail grading option. Internships. Cooperative education programs. Graduate school at which undergraduates may take graduate-level courses. Preprofessional programs in law and medicine. 3-4 optometry program with SUNY Coll of Optometry. 3-2 engineering and engineering technology programs with Clarkson U and SUNY Coll of Tech at Canton. 3-2 management and accounting program with SUNY Coll of Tech at Canton. Member of Associated Colleges of the St. Lawrence Valley; cross-registration possible. Member of National Student Exchange (NSE). Teacher certification in early childhood, elementary, and secondary education. Certification in specific subject areas. Exchange programs abroad in Australia (Western Australia Conservatory of Music), England (Liverpool Inst of Higher Education), and Mexico (U de las Americas). Study abroad also in Colombia, France, Japan, Poland, and Switzerland. ROTC and AFROTC at Clarkson U.

**Honors:** Honors program. Honor societies.

**Academic Assistance:** Nonremedial tutoring.

**STUDENT LIFE. Housing:** All freshmen, sophomores, and juniors must live on campus. Coed, women's, and men's dorms. 60% of students live in college housing.

**Social atmosphere:** "Potsdam College has a very warm, friendly atmosphere and is located in northern New York in a small college-town setting," reports the student newspaper. "Some of the most popular events are the annual Ice Carnival with Clarkson University, the Crane School of Music concerts and recitals, fundraisers such as the annual Dance-A-Thon, and the Potsdam Bears basketball games. Although only 20 percent of our student body belongs to fraternities and sororities, many students attend Greek functions. Athletic events, both intercollegiate and intramural, are also very popular among our students. The most popular gathering spots off campus are fraternity and sorority houses, and several downtown establishments."

**Services and counseling/handicapped student services:** Placement services. Health service. Day care. Counseling services for minority, military, veteran, and older students. Birth control, personal, and psychological counseling. Career and academic guidance services. Physically disabled student services. Learning disabled services. Notetaking services. Tape recorders. Tutors. Reader services for the blind.

**Campus organizations:** Undergraduate student government. Student newspaper (Racquette, published once/week). Literary magazine. Yearbook. Radio station. Collegiate Singers, chamber singers, Crane chorus, jazz ensemble, orchestra, concert bands, ensembles, dance group, theatre guild, debating, ice carnival, fall festival, academic, athletic, departmental, political, service, social, and special-interest groups, 88 organizations in all. Six fraternities, two chapter houses; eight sororities, five chapter houses. 10% of men join a fraternity. 15% of women join a sorority.

**Religious organizations:** Intervarsity Christian Fellowship, Bible Club, Jewish Culture Club.

**Minority/foreign student organizations:** Black Student Association, Hispanos Unidos para Progressar, Association of Native Americans. International Student Organization.

**ATHLETICS. Physical education requirements:** Four semesters of physical education required.

**Intercollegiate competition:** 4% of students participate. Basketball (M,W), horsemanship (W), ice hockey (M), lacrosse (M), soccer (M,W), swimming (M,W), tennis (W), vol-

leyball (W). Member of ECAC, Empire Lacrosse League, NCAA Division III, NYSAIAW, State University of New York Athletic Conference.
**Intramural and club sports:** 60% of students participate. Intramural basketball, broomball, racquetball, soccer, softball, tennis, touch football, volleyball, water polo, wrestling.
**ADMISSIONS. Academic basis for candidate selection** (in order of priority): Secondary school record, standardized test scores, class rank, school's recommendation.
**Nonacademic basis for candidate selection:** Character and personality, extracurricular participation, and particular talent or ability are important. Alumni/ae relationship is considered.
**Requirements:** Graduation from secondary school is required; GED is accepted. 16 units and the following program of study are required: 4 units of English, 2 units of math, 2 units of lab science, 4 units of social studies, 1 unit of academic electives. Minimum SAT scores of 400 verbal and 400 math (composite ACT score of 20) and minimum "B-" average required. 3 units of French or Spanish required of French and Spanish program applicants. 3 units each of math and science required of math and science program applicants. Scores and tapes of original works required of music composition program applicants. Portfolio recommended of art program applicants. Audition required of music program applicants. EOP for applicants not normally admissible. Conditional admission possible for applicants not meeting standard requirements. SAT or ACT is required. Campus visit and interview recommended. Off-campus interviews available with an admissions representative.
**Procedure:** Take SAT or ACT by December of 12th year. Take ACH by December of 12th year. Visit college for interview by March 1 of 12th year. Suggest filing application by December 1. Application deadline is March 1. Notification of admission on rolling basis. Reply is required by May 1. $50 tuition deposit, refundable until May 1. $50 room deposit, refundable until May 1. Freshmen accepted for terms other than fall.
**Special programs:** Admission may be deferred one year. Credit and/or placement may be granted through CEEB Advanced Placement exams for scores of 3 or higher. Credit and/or placement may be granted through CLEP general and subject exams. Credit and placement may be granted through Regents College exams and military experience. Early entrance/early admission program. Concurrent enrollment program.
**Transfer students:** Transfer students accepted for terms other than fall. In fall 1993, 33% of all new students were transfers into all classes. 1,314 transfer applications were received, 810 were accepted. Application deadline is May 1 for fall; December 1 for spring. Minimum 2.3 GPA required. Lowest course grade accepted is "C." Maximum number of transferable credits is 60 semester hours from a two-year school and 90 semester hours from a four-year school. At least 30 semester hours must be completed at the college to receive degree.
**Admissions contact:** Mary Lou Retelle, M.Ed., Director of Enrollment Management. 315 267-2180.
**FINANCIAL AID. Available aid:** Pell grants, SEOG, state scholarships, school scholarships, and academic merit scholarships. Perkins Loans (NDSL), PLUS, Stafford Loans (GSL), and SLS. AMS. Institutional payment plan.
**Financial aid statistics:** 25% of aid is not need-based. In 1993-94, 72% of all undergraduate applicants received aid. Average amounts of aid awarded freshmen: Scholarships and grants, $1,000; loans, $2,000.
**Supporting data/closing dates:** FAFSA: Priority filing date is March 1. Notification of awards on rolling basis.
**Financial aid contact:** Karen O'Brien, M.S.Ed., Director of Financial Aid. 315 267-2162.
**STUDENT EMPLOYMENT.** College Work/Study Program. Institutional employment. 50% of full-time undergraduates work on campus during school year. Students may expect to earn an average of $900 during school year. Off-campus part-time employment opportunities rated "good."
**COMPUTER FACILITIES.** 300 IBM/IBM-compatible, Macintosh/Apple, and RISC-/UNIX-based microcomputers; 200 are networked. Students may access Digital, SUN minicomputer/mainframe systems, BITNET, Internet. Residence halls may be equipped with stand-alone microcomputers, networked microcomputers, networked terminals. Client/LAN operating systems include Apple/Macintosh, DOS, UNIX/XENIX/AIX, DEC, LocalTalk/AppleTalk, Novell. Computer languages and software packages include BioQuest, C, E-mail, EXCEL, Finale, FORTRAN, Gopher, Hypercard, LISP, Mathematica, Pascal, Word; charting, database, graphics, simulation, spreadsheet programs. Computer facilities are available to all students.
**Hours:** 24-hour access in dorms and in one lab. Other labs open 14 hrs/day.
**GRADUATE CAREER DATA.** Graduate school percentages: 1% enter law school. 1% enter medical school. 3% enter graduate business programs. 3% enter graduate arts and sciences programs. Highest graduate school enrollments: Clarkson U, St. Lawrence U, SUNY Coll at Potsdam, Syracuse U. 35% of graduates choose careers in business and industry. Companies and businesses that hire graduates: IBM, Tel-Tech, Xerox.
**PROMINENT ALUMNI/AE.** David Conner, music director, *Sesame Street;* Robert T. Washburn, composer; T. Coraghessan Boyle, author.

## State University of New York College at Purchase

Purchase, NY 10577 914 251-6000

**1994-95 Costs.** Tuition: $2,650 (state residents), $6,550 (out-of-state). Room & board: $4,294. Fees, books, misc. academic expenses (school's estimate): $1,330.
**Enrollment.** Undergraduates: 1,125 men, 1,352 women (full-time). Freshman class: 2,119 applicants, 1,264 accepted, 390 enrolled. Graduate enrollment: 29 men, 28 women.
**Test score averages/ranges.** Average SAT scores: 466 verbal, 487 math. Range of SAT scores of middle 50%: 390-540 verbal, 420-560 math.
**Faculty.** 130 full-time; 168 part-time. 90% of faculty holds doctoral degree. Student/faculty ratio: 18 to 1.
**Selectivity rating.** Competitive.

**PROFILE.** SUNY College at Purchase, founded in 1967, is a public, multipurpose college and conservatory of both liberal and fine arts. Programs are offered through the College of Letters and Science and the School of the Arts. Its 550-acre campus is located in Purchase, three miles from White Plains.
**Accreditation:** MSACS.
**Religious orientation:** State University of New York College at Purchase is nonsectarian; no religious requirements.
**Library:** Collections totaling over 243,000 volumes, 1,560 periodical subscriptions, and 224,000 microform items.
**Special facilities/museums:** Museum, four-theatre performing arts center, visual arts facility, children's center, recording studio, electron microscopes.
**Athletic facilities:** Gymnasiums, swimming pool, aerobics studio, weight rooms, racquetball, squash, and tennis courts, soccer and softball fields.
**STUDENT BODY. Undergraduate profile:** 86% are state residents; 55% are transfers. 3% Asian-American, 8% Black, 8% Hispanic, 1% Native American, 78% White, 2% Other. Average age of undergraduates is 24.
**Freshman profile:** 74% of accepted applicants took SAT.
**Undergraduate achievement:** 73% of fall 1992 freshmen returned for fall 1993 term. 21% of entering class graduated. 40% of students who completed a degree program went on to graduate study within five years.
**Foreign students:** 77 students are from out of the country. Countries represented include Canada, Japan, South Korea, Switzerland, and the United Kingdom; 21 in all.
**PROGRAMS OF STUDY. Degrees:** B.A., B.F.A., B.S.
**Majors:** Acting, Anthropology, Art History, Biology, Chemistry, Dance, Economics, Environmental Science, Film, History, Language/Culture, Library Media, Literature, Mathematics, Music, Philosophy, Physics, Political Science, Psychology, Sociology, Theatre Design/Technology, Visual Arts.
**Distribution of degrees:** The majors with the highest enrollment are visual arts, literature, and psychology; chemistry, language/culture, and physics have the lowest.
**Requirements:** General education requirement.
**Academic regulations:** Minimum 2.0 GPA must be maintained (on a 4.3 scale).
**Special:** Concentrations in art of the book, ballet, costume design, creative writing, dance composition, dance production, drama studies, furniture, graphic design, lighting design, modern dance, music composition, music performance, painting/drawing, photography, printmaking, sculpture/3-D media, set design, social sciences/arts, stage management, studio composition, technical direction, and women's studies. Self-designed majors. Double majors. Independent study. Pass/fail grading option. Internships. Preprofessional programs in law and medicine. Cross-registration with Manhattanville Coll. Exchange program abroad in the Netherlands (Amsterdam Sch of the Arts). Study abroad also in numerous other countries.
**Academic Assistance:** Remedial reading, writing, math, and study skills. Nonremedial tutoring.
**STUDENT LIFE. Housing:** Students may live on or off campus. Coed, women's, and men's dorms. School-owned/operated apartments. On-campus married-student housing. 39% of students live in college housing.
**Social atmosphere:** As reported by the student newspaper, "Purchase is very diverse socially. Port Chester is the only nearby town; however, N.Y.C. is within easy distance." Popular student groups include the Gay, Lesbian, Bisexual Union and the acting and dance departments. On-campus hangouts include the Pub, the Henry Moore, and the mailroom; the Beat, Las Brisas, and Marty's are common off-campus destinations. Popular campus events include Happy Homo Hop, American Pictures, Womyn's Week, the Visual Arts Senior Show, and the Senior Film Showing.
**Services and counseling/handicapped student services:** Placement services. Health service. Day care. Birth control, personal, and psychological counseling. Career and academic guidance services. Physically disabled student services. Learning disabled services. Tape recorders. Tutors.
**Campus organizations:** Undergraduate student government. Student newspaper (Load, published once/two weeks). Literary magazine. Radio station. Gospel choir, cabaret, video club, General Programming Committee, ultimate frisbee team, 36 organizations in all.
**Religious organizations:** Jewish Student Coalition, Newman Club.
**Minority/foreign student organizations:** Organization of African People in America, Latinos Unidos, Women of Many Backgrounds.
**ATHLETICS. Physical education requirements:** Two credits in either physical education or dance required of students in College of Letters and Science.
**Intercollegiate competition:** Fencing (M,W), soccer (M), tennis (M,W), volleyball (W). Member of Hudson Valley Women's Athletic Conference.
**Intramural and club sports:** Intramural aerobics, basketball, flag football, hockey, racquetball, soccer, softball, swimming, tennis, volleyball, weight lifting. Men's club ultimate frisbee. Women's club ultimate frisbee.
**ADMISSIONS. Academic basis for candidate selection** (in order of priority): Secondary school record, standardized test scores, class rank, essay, school's recommendation.
**Nonacademic basis for candidate selection:** Character and personality, extracurricular participation, and particular talent or ability are important. Geographical distribution and alumni/ae relationship are considered.
**Requirements:** Graduation from secondary school is recommended; GED is accepted. 16 units and the following program of study are recommended: 4 units of English, 3 units of math, 3 units of science, 2 units of foreign language, 1 unit of social studies, 3 units of history. Minimum combined SAT score of 1000, rank in top fifth of secondary school class, or minimum 80 average required. Audition required of acting, dance, and music program applicants. Interview required of theatre design/technology and film program applicants. Portfolio required of art program applicants. EOP and Multicultural Access Program (MAP) for applicants not normally admissible. SAT or ACT is required. Campus visit and interview recommended. No off-campus interviews.
**Procedure:** Take SAT or ACT by November of 12th year. Visit college for interview by March of 12th year. Suggest filing application by December 1. Application deadline is July 1. Notification of admission on rolling basis. Reply is required by May 1. $100 tuition deposit, refundable until May 1. $50 room deposit, refundable until July 1. Freshmen accepted for terms other than fall.

**Special programs:** Credit and/or placement may be granted through CEEB Advanced Placement exams for scores of 3 or higher. Credit and/or placement may be granted through CLEP general and subject exams. Credit may be granted through Regents College exams and military experience. Placement may be granted through challenge exams. Credit and placement may be granted through ACT PEP and DANTES exams. Early entrance/early admission program.
**Transfer students:** Transfer students accepted for terms other than fall. In fall 1993, 55% of all new students were transfers into all classes. 975 transfer applications were received, 720 were accepted. Application deadline is March 15 for fall; October 15 for spring. Minimum 2.0 GPA required. Lowest course grade accepted is "D." Maximum number of transferable credits is 90 semester hours. At least 30 semester hours must be completed at the college to receive degree.
**Admissions contact:** Betsy Immergut, M.S., Director of Admissions. 914 251-6300.

**FINANCIAL AID. Available aid:** Pell grants, SEOG, state scholarships and grants, school scholarships and grants, private scholarships, and academic merit scholarships. Perkins Loans (NDSL), PLUS, Stafford Loans (GSL), state loans, private loans, and SLS. Institutional installment plan.
**Financial aid statistics:** 5% of aid is not need-based. In 1993-94, 100% of all undergraduate applicants received aid. Average amounts of aid awarded freshmen: Scholarships and grants, $1,410; loans, $2,000.
**Supporting data/closing dates:** FAFSA: Priority filing date is February 15; accepted on rolling basis. School's own aid application: Priority filing date is February 1; accepted on rolling basis. State aid form: Priority filing date is February 15; accepted on rolling basis. Income tax forms: Priority filing date is February 15; accepted on rolling basis. Notification of awards begins April 15.
**Financial aid contact:** Emilie Devine, M.S., Ed.S., Director of Financial Aid. 914 251-6350.

**STUDENT EMPLOYMENT.** College Work/Study Program. Institutional employment. 30% of full-time undergraduates work on campus during school year. Students may expect to earn an average of $1,000 during school year. Off-campus part-time employment opportunities rated "excellent."

**COMPUTER FACILITIES.** 34 IBM/IBM-compatible and Macintosh/Apple microcomputers; 12 are networked. Students may access IBM minicomputer/mainframe systems. Computer languages and software packages include Assembler, BASIC, C, COBOL, FORTRAN, Pascal, SPSS-X, Windows, WordPerfect, WordStar. Computer facilities are available to all students.
**Fees:** Computer fee is included in tuition/fees.
**Hours:** 11 AM-11 PM (M-Th); 10 AM-4:30 PM (F); noon-6 PM (Sa); 1 PM-10 PM (Su).

**GRADUATE CAREER DATA.** Graduate school percentages: 2% enter law school. 2% enter medical school. 2% enter dental school. 5% enter graduate business programs. 45% enter graduate arts and sciences programs. Highest graduate school enrollments: Columbia U, Fordham U, New York U, Yale U. Companies and businesses that hire graduates: Cornell U Medical Center, Harper Collins.

**PROMINENT ALUMNI/AE.** Hal Hartley, independent film maker; Wesley Snipes, actor; Theresa Capucelli, dancer, Martha Graham Dance Company.

# State University of New York College of Environmental Science and Forestry

Syracuse, NY 13210 — 315 470-6500

**1994-95 Costs.** Tuition: $2,650 (state residents), $6,550 (out-of-state). Room: $3,250. Board: $3,280. Fees, books, misc. academic expenses (school's estimate): $887.
**Enrollment.** Undergraduates: 716 men, 297 women (full-time). Freshman class: 710 applicants, 153 accepted, 67 enrolled. Graduate enrollment: 409 men, 233 women.
**Test score averages/ranges.** Average SAT scores: 555 verbal, 590 math.
**Faculty.** 119 full-time; 12 part-time. 90% of faculty holds doctoral degree. Student/faculty ratio: 25 to 1.
**Selectivity rating.** Highly competitive.

**PROFILE.** SUNY College of Environmental Science and Forestry, founded in 1911, is a public, multipurpose college. Programs are offered through the Schools of Biology, Chemistry, and Ecology; Environmental and Resource Engineering; Forestry; and Landscape Architecture. Its 12-acre campus is located in Syracuse.

**Accreditation:** MSACS. Professionally accredited by the Accreditation Board for Engineering and Technology, the American Society of Landscape Architects, the Society of American Foresters.
**Religious orientation:** State University of New York College of Environmental Science and Forestry is nonsectarian; no religious requirements.
**Library:** Collections totaling over 94,000 volumes, 1,700 periodical subscriptions, and 91,000 microform items.
**Special facilities/museums:** Museum, art galleries, plant growth and animal environmental simulating chambers, wildlife collection, electron microscope, industrial-sized paper machine, photogrammetric and geodetic facilities.
**Athletic facilities:** Gymnasiums, fitness centers, swimming pools, tennis, racquetball, and squash courts, outdoor athletic fields (all facilities through Syracuse U).

**STUDENT BODY. Undergraduate profile:** 90% are state residents; 78% are transfers. 1% Asian-American, 2% Black, 1% Hispanic, 1% Native American, 94% White, 1% Other. Average age of undergraduates is 24.
**Freshman profile:** 98% of accepted applicants took SAT; 2% took ACT. 95% of freshmen come from public schools.
**Undergraduate achievement:** 90% of fall 1991 freshmen returned for fall 1992 term. 10% of students who completed a degree program immediately went on to graduate study.
**Foreign students:** 11 students are from out of the country. Countries represented include Austria, China, Grenada, Iran, Sri Lanka, and Thailand; eight in all.

**PROGRAMS OF STUDY. Degrees:** B.Land.Arch., B.S.
**Majors:** Biochemistry/Natural Products, Chemistry, Environmental Chemistry, Environmental/Forest Biology, Environmental Studies, Forest Engineering, Forest Resource Management, Forestry/Biology, Landscape Architecture, Natural/Synthetic Polymer Chemistry, Paper Science/Engineering, Wood Products Engineering.
**Distribution of degrees:** The majors with the highest enrollment are forest biology, landscape architecture, and environmental studies; paper science/engineering, chemistry, and wood products engineering have the lowest.
**Requirements:** General education requirement.
**Academic regulations:** Minimum 2.0 GPA must be maintained.
**Special:** Second year of A.A.S. in forest technology offered. Associate's degrees offered. Independent study. Accelerated study. Pass/fail grading option. Internships. Graduate school at which undergraduates may take graduate-level courses. Preprofessional programs in law, medicine, veterinary science, and dentistry. Off-campus semester for landscape architecture students. Teacher certification in secondary education. Certification in specific subject areas. Study abroad through Syracuse U program. ROTC and AFROTC.
**Honors:** Phi Beta Kappa. Honors program.
**Academic Assistance:** Remedial reading, writing, math, and study skills. Nonremedial tutoring.

**ADMISSIONS. Academic basis for candidate selection** (in order of priority): Secondary school record, class rank, standardized test scores, school's recommendation, essay.
**Nonacademic basis for candidate selection:** Extracurricular participation and alumni/ae relationship are considered.
**Requirements:** Graduation from secondary school is required; GED is not accepted. 18 units and the following program of study are recommended: 4 units of English, 2 units of foreign language, 3 units of social studies, 3 units of electives. College enrolls 60-80 freshmen in the following majors: chemistry, environmental/forest biology, forest engineering, forest resource management, and paper science/engineering. Applicants not admitted for freshman year may be given guarantee of admission for sophomore or junior year under Guaranteed Transfer Admissions Program. Most students spend two years at another college prior to entering SUNY-ESF; applicants are encouraged to enroll in a pre-ESF cooperative program in their freshman and sophomore years. EOP for applicants not normally admissible. SAT or ACT is required. Campus visit and interview recommended. No off-campus interviews.
**Procedure:** Suggest filing application by December 1. Application deadline is July 15. Notification of admission on rolling basis. Reply is required by May 1. $100 tuition deposit, refundable until May 1. Freshmen accepted for fall terms only.
**Special programs:** Admission may be deferred one year. Credit may be granted through CEEB Advanced Placement for scores of 3 or higher. Credit may be granted through CLEP general and subject exams, Regents College, ACT PEP, and DANTES exams, and military experience. Early decision program. In fall 1992, 36 applied for early decision and 24 were accepted. Deadline for applying for early decision is November 15.
**Transfer students:** Transfer students accepted for terms other than fall. In fall 1992, 78% of all new students were transfers into all classes. 850 transfer applications were received, 442 were accepted. Application deadline is December 1 for fall; November 1 for spring. Minimum 2.0 GPA required. Lowest course grade accepted is "C." At least 30 semester hours must be completed at the college to receive degree.
**Admissions contact:** Dennis O. Stratton, M.S., Director of Admissions. 315 470-6600, 800 777-7373.

**FINANCIAL AID. Available aid:** Pell grants, SEOG, state scholarships and grants, school scholarships and grants, private scholarships, ROTC scholarships, and academic merit scholarships. Perkins Loans (NDSL), PLUS, and Stafford Loans (GSL). AMS.
**Financial aid statistics:** In 1992-93, 85% of all undergraduate applicants received aid.
**Supporting data/closing dates:** FAFSA/FFS: Priority filing date is March 15. School's own aid application: Priority filing date is March 15. Notification of awards begins April 1.
**Financial aid contact:** John E. View, M.A., M.B.A., Director of Financial Aid. 315 470-6670.

# State University of New York Maritime College

Throggs Neck, NY 10465 — 718 409-7392

**1994-95 Costs.** Tuition: $2,650 (state residents), $6,550 (out-of-state). Room: $2,830. Board: $2,000. Fees, books, misc. academic expenses (school's estimate): $3,359.
**Enrollment.** Undergraduates: 617 men, 65 women (full-time). Freshman class: 763 applicants, 405 accepted, 217 enrolled. Graduate enrollment: 162 men, 22 women.
**Test score averages/ranges.** Average SAT scores: 452 verbal, 528 math. Range of SAT scores of middle 50%: 420-500 verbal, 460-580 math. Average ACT scores: 21 English, 23 math.
**Faculty.** 65 full-time; 14 part-time. 36% of faculty holds doctoral degree. Student/faculty ratio: 15 to 1.
**Selectivity rating.** Competitive.

**PROFILE.** SUNY Maritime College, founded in 1874, is a public, multipurpose college for the maritime and related industries. Its 55-acre campus is located in Throggs Neck.

**Accreditation:** MSACS. Professionally accredited by the Accreditation Board for Engineering and Technology.
**Religious orientation:** State University of New York Maritime College is nonsectarian; no religious requirements.
**Library:** Collections totaling over 75,643 volumes, 484 periodical subscriptions, and 25,462 microform items.

**Special facilities/museums:** Maritime industry museum, extensive engineering and science lab facilities, center for simulated marine operations, 1,700-ton training ship, tugboat, barge.
**Athletic facilities:** Gymnasium, athletic fields, swimming pool, Universal gym, dance studio, basketball, racquetball, and tennis courts, rifle range, exercise and weight rooms, sailboats, crew shells, wind surfing.

**STUDENT BODY. Undergraduate profile:** 81% are state residents; 14% are transfers. 7% Asian-American, 6% Black, 7% Hispanic, 80% White. Average age of undergraduates is 20.
**Freshman profile:** 2% of freshmen who took SAT scored 700 or over on math; 10% scored 600 or over on verbal, 22% scored 600 or over on math; 32% scored 500 or over on verbal, 68% scored 500 or over on math; 83% scored 400 or over on verbal, 100% scored 400 or over on math; 100% scored 300 or over on verbal. 72% of accepted applicants took SAT; 3% took ACT. 54% of freshmen come from public schools.
**Undergraduate achievement:** 81% of fall 1992 freshmen returned for fall 1993 term. 63% of entering class graduated. 1% of students who completed a degree program immediately went on to graduate study.
**Foreign students:** 38 students are from out of the country. Countries represented include Egypt, Greece, Hong Kong, Jamaica, Korea, and Taiwan; 21 in all.

**PROGRAMS OF STUDY. Degrees:** B.Eng., B.S.
**Majors:** Business Administration/Marine Transportation, Electrical Engineering, Facility Engineering, Humanities, Marine Engineering, Mechanical Engineering, Meteorology/Oceanography, Naval Architecture.
**Distribution of degrees:** The majors with the highest enrollment are business administration/marine transportation, marine engineering, and electrical engineering; humanities and mechanical engineering have the lowest.
**Requirements:** General education requirement.
**Academic regulations:** Minimum 2.0 GPA must be maintained.
**Special:** Minors offered in environmental science, international business, management, marine operations, and transportation management. College program includes required three summer sea terms on training vessel. Cadets passing required U.S. Coast Guard exams receive Merchant Marine License as Third Mate or Third Assistant Engineer. Cadets receiving Federal Incentive Payment must complete two courses in Naval Science, leading to eligibility for commission in Merchant Marine Reserve Program of Naval Reserve (inactive duty). They must also agree to sail on their license or work in marine industry on shore for three years after graduation. Out-of-state students in program pay in-state tuition rates; all participants receive stipend of $3,000/year. Graduate school at which undergraduates may take graduate-level courses. B.S./M.S. program in marine transportation/transportation management. Sea Semester. NROTC. AFROTC at Manhattan Coll.
**Honors:** Honor societies.
**Academic Assistance:** Remedial writing and study skills. Nonremedial tutoring.
**Campus organizations:** Undergraduate student government. Student newspaper (Porthole, published once/month). Yearbook. Radio station. Glee club, marching band, Circle K, radio club, sailing squadron, Eagle Scout fraternity, academic, athletic, political, and special-interest groups, 38 organizations in all. One fraternity, no chapter house. 4% of men join a fraternity.

**ADMISSIONS. Academic basis for candidate selection** (in order of priority): Secondary school record, standardized test scores, class rank, school's recommendation, essay.
**Nonacademic basis for candidate selection:** Character and personality, extracurricular participation, and particular talent or ability are emphasized. Alumni/ae relationship is important.
**Requirements:** Graduation from secondary school is required; GED is accepted. 16 units and the following program of study are required: 4 units of English, 3 units of math, 2 units of lab science, 2 units of foreign language, 1 unit of social studies, 3 units of history, 1 unit of academic electives. Applicants encouraged to pursue science and math beyond required minimum; 4 units of math, foreign language, and both physics and chemistry are usually presented. Minimum combined SAT score of 1050, rank in top fifth of secondary school class, and minimum 85 average recommended. Physical exam required of all applicants. EOP for applicants not normally admissible. Flex Program for applicants not normally admissible. SAT is required; ACT may be substituted. PSAT is required. ACH recommended. Campus visit and interview recommended. Off-campus interviews available with admissions and alumni representatives.
**Procedure:** Take SAT or ACT by December of 12th year. Suggest filing application by November 15; no deadline. Notification of admission on rolling basis. Reply is required by May 1. $50 tuition deposit, refundable until May 1. $50 room deposit, refundable until May. Freshmen accepted for terms other than fall.
**Special programs:** Admission may be deferred one year. Credit and/or placement may be granted through CEEB Advanced Placement exams for scores of 4 or higher. Credit and/or placement may be granted through CLEP subject exams. Credit and placement may be granted through Regents College, DANTES, and challenge exams and military experience. Early decision program. In fall 1993, 41 applied for early decision and 28 were accepted. Deadline for applying for early decision is December 1. Early entrance/early admission program.
**Transfer students:** Transfer students accepted for terms other than fall. In fall 1993, 14% of all new students were transfers into all classes. 129 transfer applications were received, 76 were accepted. Application deadline is December 15 for fall; August 1 for spring. Minimum 2.5 GPA required. Lowest course grade accepted is "C." Maximum number of transferable credits is 70 semester hours. At least 40 semester hours must be completed at the college to receive degree.
**Admissions contact:** Peter Cooney, M.S., Director of Admissions and Financial Aid. 718 409-7220.

**FINANCIAL AID. Available aid:** Pell grants, SEOG, state grants, school scholarships, and ROTC scholarships. Student Incentive Program. MARTP. Perkins Loans (NDSL), PLUS, Stafford Loans (GSL), and SLS. Parent's Association short-term loans. Tuition Plan Inc. and AMS.
**Financial aid statistics:** 25% of aid is not need-based. In 1993-94, 79% of all undergraduate applicants received aid; 81% of freshman applicants. Average amounts of aid awarded freshmen: Scholarships and grants, $950; loans, $2,625.
**Supporting data/closing dates:** FAFSA: Priority filing date is March 15. School's own aid application: Accepted on rolling basis. State aid form: Priority filing date is March 15. Income tax forms: Priority filing date is February 15; accepted on rolling basis. Admiral's Scholarship Application: Priority filing date is January 1; deadline is February 1. Notification of awards on rolling basis.
**Financial aid contact:** Peter Cooney, M.S., Director of Admissions and Financial Aid. 718 409-7268.

# State University of New York at Stony Brook

**Stony Brook, NY 11794** 516 689-6000

**1993-94 Costs.** Tuition: $2,650 (state residents), $6,550 (out-of-state). Room & board: $4,712. Fees, books, misc. academic expenses (school's estimate): $1,096.
**Enrollment.** Undergraduates: 4,875 men, 4,869 women (full-time). Freshman class: 12,512 applicants, 6,969 accepted, 1,724 enrolled. Graduate enrollment: 2,883 men, 3,227 women.
**Test score averages/ranges.** Average SAT scores: 473 verbal, 547 math.
**Faculty.** 1,284 full-time; 293 part-time. 95% of faculty holds doctoral degree. Student/faculty ratio: 17 to 1.
**Selectivity rating.** More competitive.

**PROFILE.** SUNY at Stony Brook, founded in 1957, is a public comprehensive university. Programs are offered through the College of Arts and Sciences, the W. Averell Harriman School for Management and Policy, the College of Engineering and Applied Sciences, and the Health Sciences Center. Its 1,100-acre is located in Stony Brook, 60 miles from New York City.
**Accreditation:** MSACS. Professionally accredited by the Accreditation Board for Engineering and Technology, the American Medical Association (CAHEA), the American Physical Therapy Association, the Council on Social Work Education, the National League for Nursing.
**Religious orientation:** State University of New York at Stony Brook is nonsectarian; no religious requirements.
**Library:** Collections totaling over 1,807,481 volumes, 21,517 periodical subscriptions, and 3,073,547 microform items.
**Special facilities/museums:** Fine arts center, natural sciences museum, federated learning center, curriculum development center, economic research bureau, instructional resource center, marine sciences research center, Van de Graaff accelerator.
**Athletic facilities:** Gymnasiums, swimming pool, basketball, racquetball, squash, and tennis courts, weight rooms, athletic fields, sports complex.

**STUDENT BODY. Undergraduate profile:** 98% are state residents. 16.7% Asian-American, 8.9% Black, 6.9% Hispanic, .2% Native American, 50.8% White, 16.5% Other. Average age of undergraduates is 21.
**Freshman profile:** 6% of freshmen who took SAT scored 700 or over on math; 6% scored 600 or over on verbal, 27% scored 600 or over on math; 36% scored 500 or over on verbal, 72% scored 500 or over on math; 86% scored 400 or over on verbal, 96% scored 400 or over on math; 97% scored 300 or over on verbal, 99% scored 300 or over on math. 83% of accepted applicants took SAT. 85% of freshmen come from public schools.
**Undergraduate achievement:** 83% of fall 1992 freshmen returned for fall 1993 term. 75% of students who completed a degree program went on to graduate study within five years.
**Foreign students:** 342 students are from out of the country. Countries represented include China, Hong Kong, India, Iran, and Korea.

**PROGRAMS OF STUDY. Degrees:** B.A., B.Eng., B.S.
**Majors:** Africana Studies, Anthropology, Applied Mathematics/Statistics, Art History/Criticism, Astronomy/Planetary Science, Atmospheric Sciences/Meteorology, Biochemistry, Biological Sciences, Business Management, Chemistry, Comparative Literature, Computer Science, Earth/Space Sciences, Economics, Electrical Engineering, Engineering Chemistry, Engineering Science, English, French Language/Literature, Geology, German Language/Literature, Hispanic Language/Literature, History, Humanities, Information Systems, Italian, Linguistics, Mathematics, Mechanical Engineering, Medical Technology, Multidisciplinary Studies, Music, Nursing, Philosophy, Physical Therapy, Physician Assistant, Physics, Political Science, Psychology, Religious Studies, Russian Language/Literature, Social Sciences, Social Work, Sociology, Studio Art, Theatre Arts.
**Distribution of degrees:** The majors with the highest enrollment are psychology, multidisciplinary studies, and biological sciences; German language/literature, comparative literature, and Africana studies have the lowest.
**Requirements:** General education requirement.
**Academic regulations:** Minimum 2.0 GPA required for graduation.
**Special:** Minors offered in child/family studies, health/society, journalism, Judaic studies, Korean studies, Long Island regional studies, Middle Eastern studies, women's studies, and other areas. URECA program enables students to participate in research projects with faculty. Double majors. Dual degrees. Independent study. Pass/fail grading option. Internships. Graduate school at which undergraduates may take graduate-level courses. Preprofessional programs in law, medicine, and dentistry. Five-year dual degree program in engineering/liberal arts. B.S./M.S. program in nursing. Member of Long Island Regional Advisory Council for Higher Education. Washington Semester. Albany Semester. New York State Visiting Student Program. Member of the National Student Exchange (NSE). Teacher certification in secondary education. Certification in specific subject areas. Study

abroad in Bolivia, China, France, Germany, Italy, Korea, Poland, and the United Kingdom.

**Honors:** Phi Beta Kappa. Honors program.

**Academic Assistance:** Remedial writing and math. Nonremedial tutoring.

**STUDENT LIFE. Housing:** Students may live on or off campus. Coed dorms. Single-sex floors and living/learning centers in some dormitories. 55% of students live in college housing.

**Social atmosphere:** The student newspaper reports that because of poor living conditions on campus, "most civilized people are driven to commute." Students congregate at the graduate student lounge and the End of the Bridge on campus, and at the Park Bench, Checkmate, and the Tara Inn off campus. Popular events include SAB concerts and Tokyo Joe's.

**Services and counseling/handicapped student services:** Health service. Women's center. Day care. Counseling services for minority, veteran, and older students. Birth control, personal, and psychological counseling. Career and academic guidance services. Religious counseling. Learning disabled services.

**Campus organizations:** Undergraduate student government. Student newspapers (Statesman; Stony Brook Press). Yearbook. Radio station. Chorale, band, orchestra, coffeehouse, Theatre of Movement, craft shop, Young Democrats, Young Republicans, Students for a Democratic Society, 140 organizations in all. 12 fraternities, no chapter houses; 11 sororities, no chapter houses.

**Religious organizations:** Several religious groups.

**Minority/foreign student organizations:** Black Student Union, black theatre workshop. Several foreign student groups.

**ATHLETICS. Physical education requirements:** None.

**Intercollegiate competition:** 10% of students participate. Baseball (M), basketball (M,W), cheerleading (M,W), cross-country (M,W), diving (M,W), football (M), lacrosse (M), soccer (M,W), softball (W), squash (M), swimming (M,W), tennis (M,W), track (indoor) (M,W), track (outdoor) (M,W), track and field (indoor) (M,W), track and field (outdoor) (M,W), volleyball (W). Member of ECAC, Freedom Football Conference, NCAA Division I for men's lacrosse and women's soccer, NCAA Division III, NYSWCAA, Skyline Conferences.

**Intramural and club sports:** 60% of students participate. Intramural badminton, basketball, bowling, cross-country, golf, handball, paddleball, soccer, softball, squash, swimming, tennis, volleyball. Men's club fencing, horsemanship, ice hockey, martial arts, racquetball, rugby. Women's club racquetball.

**ADMISSIONS. Academic basis for candidate selection** (in order of priority): Secondary school record, class rank, school's recommendation, standardized test scores.

**Nonacademic basis for candidate selection:** Extracurricular participation and particular talent or ability are important. Character and personality, geographical distribution, and alumni/ae relationship are considered.

**Requirements:** Graduation from secondary school is required; GED is accepted. No specific distribution of secondary school units required. Chemistry, physics, and 4 units of math recommended of sciences, engineering, and mathematics program applicants. Applicants planning to major in computer science must successfully complete one semester at Stony Brook. Additional requirements for upper-division nursing and engineering program applicants. EOP for applicants not normally admissible. Individual Merit Program for applicants not normally admissible. SAT or ACT is required. Campus visit and interview recommended. No off-campus interviews.

**Procedure:** Notification of admission on rolling basis, except for health sciences. $100 tuition deposit, refundable until May 1. $200 room deposit, refundable until June 30. Freshmen accepted for terms other than fall.

**Special programs:** Admission may be deferred one year. Credit and/or placement may be granted through CEEB Advanced Placement exams for scores of 3 or higher. Credit and/or placement may be granted through CLEP general and subject exams. Credit and placement may be granted through challenge exams. Early entrance/early admission program. Concurrent enrollment program.

**Transfer students:** Transfer students accepted for terms other than fall. In fall 1993, 4,543 transfer applications were received, 2,522 were accepted. Minimum 2.5 GPA required of all transfers except those holding associate's degrees from in-state community colleges (no minimum required). Lowest course grade accepted is "D." At least the final 36 credits must be completed at the university to receive degree.

**Admissions contact:** Gigi Lamens, Director of Admissions. 516 632-6868.

**FINANCIAL AID. Available aid:** Pell grants, SEOG, state scholarships and grants, school scholarships, private scholarships and grants, and academic merit scholarships. Perkins Loans (NDSL), PLUS, Stafford Loans (GSL), NSL, Health Professions Loans, and state loans. Tuition Plan Inc.

**Financial aid statistics:** 57% of aid is not need-based. In 1993-94, 95% of all freshman applicants received aid.

**Supporting data/closing dates:** FAFSA/FAF: Deadline is March 15. School's own aid application: Accepted on rolling basis. Notification of awards on rolling basis.

**Financial aid contact:** Anna M. Torres, Director of Financial Aid. 516 632-6840.

**STUDENT EMPLOYMENT.** College Work/Study Program. Institutional employment. 10% of full-time undergraduates work on campus during school year. Students may expect to earn an average of $1,200 during school year. Off-campus part-time employment opportunities rated "good."

**COMPUTER FACILITIES.** IBM/IBM-compatible and Macintosh/Apple microcomputers. Students may access Digital, IBM, SUN minicomputer/mainframe systems, BITNET, Internet. Client/LAN operating systems include Apple/Macintosh, DOS, OS/2, UNIX/XENIX/AIX, Novell. Computer languages and software packages include C, COBOL, DISSPLA, FORTRAN, ImSL, Pascal, SAS, SPSS-X, Tell-a-graf. Computer facilities are available to all students.

**Fees:** None.

# Syracuse University

**Syracuse, NY 13244** **315 443-1870**

**1993-94 Costs.** Tuition: $14,360. Room: $3,480. Board: $3,120. Fees, books, misc. academic expenses (school's estimate): $925.

**Enrollment.** Undergraduates: 5,027 men, 5,115 women (full-time). Freshman class: 10,477 applicants, 7,260 accepted, 2,442 enrolled. Graduate enrollment: 2,272 men, 2,212 women.

**Test score averages/ranges.** Range of SAT scores of middle 50%: 450-560 verbal, 520-640 math.

**Faculty.** 897 full-time; 768 part-time. 84% of faculty holds highest degree in specific field. Student/faculty ratio: 11 to 1.

**Selectivity rating.** Competitive.

**PROFILE.** Syracuse, founded in 1870, is a private, comprehensive university. Programs are offered through the Colleges of Arts and Sciences, Human Development, Nursing, and Visual and Performing Arts; the Schools of Architecture, Computer and Information Science, Education, Management, Social Work, and Information Studies; the L.C. Smith College of Engineering; and the Newhouse School of Public Communications. Its 600-acre campus, including 15 buildings registered with the National Register of Historic Places, is located in Syracuse.

**Accreditation:** MSACS. Professionally accredited by the Accreditation Board for Engineering and Technology, the Accrediting Council on Education in Journalism and Mass Communication, the American Assembly of Collegiate Schools of Business, the American Dietetic Association, the American Library Association, the American Medical Association (CAHEA), the American Psychological Association, the American Society of Landscape Architects, the American Speech-Language-Hearing Association, the Council on Rehabilitation Education, the Council on Social Work Education, the Foundation for Interior Design Education Research, the National Architecture Accrediting Board, the National Association of Schools of Art and Design, the National Association of Schools of Music, the National Council for Accreditation of Teacher Education, the National League for Nursing.

**Religious orientation:** Syracuse University is nonsectarian; no religious requirements.

**Library:** Collections totaling over 2,300,000 volumes, 16,559 periodical subscriptions, and 4,300,000 microform items.

**Special facilities/museums:** Art gallery, American costume collection, language labs, audio-visual center, audio archives, nursery school, on-campus day care center, center for science and technology, computer applications center, CAD studio.

**Athletic facilities:** Gymnasiums, field house, basketball, handball, racquetball, squash, and tennis courts, athletic fields, stadium, tracks, dance, fencing, and weight rooms, swimming pools, rifle range, golf course.

**STUDENT BODY. Undergraduate profile:** 39% are state residents; 14% are transfers. 6% Asian-American, 10% Black, 5% Hispanic, 1% Native American, 78% White. Average age of undergraduates is 20.

**Freshman profile:** 2% of freshmen who took SAT scored 700 or over on verbal, 7% scored 700 or over on math; 14% scored 600 or over on verbal, 36% scored 600 or over on math; 68% scored 500 or over on verbal, 87% scored 500 or over on math; 99% scored 400 or over on verbal, 99% scored 400 or over on math; 100% scored 300 or over on verbal, 100% scored 300 or over on math. 95% of accepted applicants took SAT; 5% took ACT. 75% of freshmen come from public schools.

**Undergraduate achievement:** 89% of fall 1992 freshmen returned for fall 1993 term. 20% of students who completed a degree program went on to graduate study within one year.

**Foreign students:** 336 students are from out of the country. Countries represented include Canada, Japan, Malaysia, South Korea, Taiwan, and Turkey; 62 in all.

**PROGRAMS OF STUDY. Degrees:** B.A., B.Arch., B.F.A., B.Indust.Design, B.Mus., B.S.

**Majors:** Accounting, Advertising, Advertising Design, Aerospace Engineering, African-American Studies, American Studies, Anthropology, Architecture, Art Education, Art History, Art/Photography, Art/Video, Bioengineering, Biological Sciences, Broadcast Journalism, Ceramics, Chemical Engineering, Chemistry, Child/Family Studies, Civil Engineering, Classical Civilization, Classics, Communication Design, Communication Sciences/Disorders, Comparative Literature, Computer Engineering, Computer Graphics, Computer/Information Sciences, Consumer Studies, Design/Technical Theatre, Dietetics, Drama, Economics, Electrical Engineering, Elementary Education, Engineering Physics, English, English Literature, Environmental Engineering, Environmental/Interior Design, European Literature, Experimental Studies, Family/Community Services, Fashion Design, Fashion Illustration, Fiber Structure/Interlocking, Film, Film/Art, Film/Drama, Finance, Fine Arts, Food Systems Management, Foreign Language Education, Foreign Languages/Cultures, French, General Studies, Geography, Geology, German, Health Education, History, Illustration, Industrial Design, Information Studies, Interior Design, International Relations, Italian, Latin American Studies, Linguistics, Magazine, Management Information Systems, Managerial Law/Public Policy, Managerial Statistics, Manufacturing Engineering, Marketing Management, Mathematics, Mathematics Education, Mechanical Engineering, Medieval Studies, Metalsmithing, Music, Music Composition, Music Education, Music Industry, Music Theory, Musical Theatre, Newspaper, Nonviolent Conflict/Change, Nursing, Nutritional Sciences, Operations Management, Organ, Painting, Percussion, Personnel/Industrial Relations, Philosophy, Photography, Physical Education, Physics, Piano, Policy Studies, Political Philosophy, Political Science, Printmaking, Producing for Electronic Media, Psychology, Public Relations, Publishing, Radio/Television, Rehabilitation Services, Religion, Restaurant/Food Service Management, Retailing, Russian, Russian Studies, Science Education, Science Teaching, Sculpture, Secondary Education, Selected Studies, Social Studies Education, Social Work, Sociology, Spanish, Special Education, Speech Communication, Speech Pathology, String Instru-

ments, Design/Surface/Pattern, Telecommunications Management, Textile Studies, Transportation/Distribution Management, Voice, Wind Instruments, Women's Studies.
**Distribution of degrees:** The majors with the highest enrollment are management, social sciences, and communication; mathematics, languages, and philosophy have the lowest.
**Requirements:** General education requirement.
**Academic regulations:** Minimum 2.0 GPA must be maintained.
**Special:** Minors required for graduation in some programs. Minors offered in many majors. Selected studies program provides courses meeting individual needs and interests. Self-designed majors. Double majors. Dual degrees. Independent study. Accelerated study. Pass/fail grading option. Internships. Cooperative education programs. Graduate school at which undergraduates may take graduate-level courses. Preprofessional programs in law, medicine, veterinary science, and dentistry. 3-3 law program. 3-2 engineering program. 3-2 M.B.A. program. Teacher certification in early childhood, elementary, secondary, and special education. Certification in specific subject areas. Study abroad in England, France, Germany, Israel, Italy, Spain, and Zimbabwe. ROTC and AFROTC.
**Honors:** Phi Beta Kappa. Honors program. Honor societies.
**Academic Assistance:** Remedial reading, writing, math, and study skills. Nonremedial tutoring.

**STUDENT LIFE. Housing:** All freshmen and sophomores must live on campus. Coed and women's dorms. Sorority and fraternity housing. School-owned/operated apartments. On-campus married-student housing. 75% of students live in college housing.
**Social atmosphere:** On-campus gathering spots include the Schine Student Center and the steps of the Hendricks Chapel. Favorite off-campus destinations include Marshall Street, Westcott Street, and the Carousel Mall. The Student African-American Society, the University Union, the Black Box Players, and athletes influence campus life. Students enjoy the annual Dance Marathon, Block Party, Greek Freak, the Media Cup, Homecoming, the Christmas Cabaret, and Flip Night at Faegan's. The Daily Orange reports, "The university has really pushed to provide alternatives to drinking, but drinking is still common on campus. Minority organizations are excellent at sponsoring speakers, films, and programs."
**Services and counseling/handicapped student services:** Placement services. Health service. Women's center. Day care. Counseling services for minority, military, and veteran students. Birth control, personal, and psychological counseling. Career and academic guidance services. Religious counseling. Physically disabled student services. Learning disabled services. Notetaking services. Tape recorders. Tutors. Reader services for the blind.
**Campus organizations:** Undergraduate student government. Student newspaper (Daily Orange). Literary magazine. Yearbook. Radio and TV stations. Drama and musical groups, Women's Club, literary magazines and publications, ski club, debating, political groups, special-interest groups, 250 organizations in all. 30 fraternities, 21 chapter houses; 22 sororities, 16 chapter houses. 24% of men join a fraternity. 33% of women join a sorority.
**Religious organizations:** Baptist Student Union, Campus Crusade for Christ, Chabad House, Christian Science Organization, Hillel, Hindu Samaj, Muslim Students Association, Newman Club, other religious groups.
**Minority/foreign student organizations:** Afro-American Society, La Casa Latinoamericana, Minority Architects, Minority Management Society, NAACP, Native American Indian Association, other minority organizations. International Student Association, Armenian, Caribbean, Filipino, and West Indian groups.

**ATHLETICS. Physical education requirements:** None.
**Intercollegiate competition:** 5% of students participate. Basketball (M,W), crew (M,W), cross-country (M,W), field hockey (W), football (M), gymnastics (M), lacrosse (M), soccer (M), swimming (M,W), tennis (W), track (indoor) (M,W), track (outdoor) (M,W), track and field (indoor) (M,W), track and field (outdoor) (M,W), volleyball (W), wrestling (M). Member of Big East Conference, ECAC, NCAA Division I.
**Intramural and club sports:** 20% of students participate. Intramural badminton, basketball, billiards, body building, bowling, cross-country, floor hockey, golf, handball, horseshoes, indoor soccer, racquetball, rifle, softball, squash, swimming, table tennis, tennis, track and field, volleyball, walleyball, water polo, weight lifting. Men's club Alpine skiing, baseball, cricket, cycling, dance, fencing, figure skating, golf, horsemanship, ice hockey, juggling, lacrosse, martial arts, Nordic skiing, racquetball, rugby, sailing, scuba diving, soccer, squash, tennis, ultimate frisbee, volleyball, weight lifting. Women's club Alpine skiing, cricket, cycling, dance, fencing, field hockey, figure skating, golf, gymnastics, horsemanship, juggling, lacrosse, martial arts, Nordic skiing, racquetball, sailing, scuba diving, soccer, softball, squash, tennis, ultimate frisbee, weight lifting.

**ADMISSIONS. Academic basis for candidate selection** (in order of priority): Secondary school record, class rank, standardized test scores, school's recommendation, essay.
**Nonacademic basis for candidate selection:** Character and personality are important. Extracurricular participation, particular talent or ability, and alumni/ae relationship are considered.
**Requirements:** Graduation from secondary school is required; GED is accepted. 20 units and the following program of study are required: 4 units of English, 3 units of math, 3 units of science including 2 units of lab, 2 units of foreign language, 3 units of social studies, 5 units of academic electives. Portfolio required of architecture and art program applicants. Audition required of drama and music program applicants. HEOP for applicants not normally admissible. SAT is required; ACT may be substituted. Campus visit and interview recommended. No off-campus interviews.
**Procedure:** Take SAT or ACT by December of 12th year. Visit college for interview by February of 12th year. Suggest filing application by February; no deadline. Notification of admission by March 15. Reply is required by May 1. $250 nonrefundable tuition deposit. $250 room deposit, refundable until June 1. Freshmen accepted for terms other than fall.
**Special programs:** Admission may be deferred one year. Credit and/or placement may be granted through CEEB Advanced Placement exams for scores of 3 or higher. Credit may be granted through CLEP subject exams. Early decision program. In fall 1993, 400 applied for early decision and 366 were accepted. Deadline for applying for early decision is November 15. Early entrance/early admission program. Concurrent enrollment program.
**Transfer students:** Transfer students accepted for terms other than fall. In fall 1993, 14% of all new students were transfers into all classes. 1,199 transfer applications were received, 753 were accepted. Application deadline is June 1 (priority) for fall; November 15 (priority) for spring. Minimum 2.5 GPA required. Lowest course grade accepted is "C." Maximum number of transferable credits is 90 semester hours. At least 30 semester hours must be completed at the university to receive degree.
**Admissions contact:** David C. Smith, Director of Admissions. 315 443-1513.

**FINANCIAL AID. Available aid:** Pell grants, SEOG, state scholarships and grants, school scholarships and grants, private scholarships and grants, ROTC scholarships, academic merit scholarships, and athletic scholarships. Perkins Loans (NDSL), PLUS, Stafford Loans (GSL), NSL, state loans, private loans, and SLS. Twelve-Month Payment Plan.
**Financial aid statistics:** 16% of aid is not need-based. In 1993-94, 60% of all undergraduate applicants received aid; 85% of freshman applicants. Average amounts of aid awarded freshmen: Scholarships and grants, $7,500; loans, $3,300.
**Supporting data/closing dates:** FAFSA/FAF: Deadline is March 1. Notification of awards begins March 15.
**Financial aid contact:** Christopher Walsh, Director of Financial Aid Services. 315 443-1513.

**STUDENT EMPLOYMENT.** College Work/Study Program. Institutional employment. 40% of full-time undergraduates work on campus during school year. Students may expect to earn an average of $1,900 during school year. Off-campus part-time employment opportunities rated "good."

**COMPUTER FACILITIES.** 400 IBM/IBM-compatible, Macintosh/Apple, and RISC-/UNIX-based microcomputers; all are networked. Students may access Digital, IBM, SUN minicomputer/mainframe systems, BITNET, Internet. Residence halls may be equipped with networked microcomputers, modems. Client/LAN operating systems include Apple/Macintosh, DOS, UNIX/XENIX/AIX, LocalTalk/AppleTalk, Microsoft, Novell. Computer languages and software packages include database, graphics, spreadsheet, and wordprocessing programs. Computer facilities are available to all students.
**Fees:** None.
**Hours:** 24 hours.

**GRADUATE CAREER DATA.** Graduate school percentages: 5% enter law school. 2% enter medical school. 7% enter graduate business programs. Highest graduate school enrollments: Cornell U, SUNY Albany, SUNY Buffalo, Syracuse U. 30% of graduates choose careers in business and industry. Companies and businesses that hire graduates: Bloomingdale's, Coopers & Lybrand, Estee Lauder, Gannett Newspapers, IBM, Price Waterhouse.

**PROMINENT ALUMNI/AE.** Steve Kroft, co-editor, *60 Minutes*; Betsey Johnson, fashion designer; Ted Koppel, journalist; Donna Shalala, U.S. Secretary of Health & Human Services; Joyce Carol Oates, novelist.

# Union College

**Schenectady, NY 12308** **518 388-6000**

**1994-95 Costs.** Tuition: $18,732. Room: $3,297. Board: $2,907. Fees, books, misc. academic expenses (school's estimate): $640.
**Enrollment.** Undergraduates: 1,060 men, 855 women (full-time). Freshman class: 3,495 applicants, 1,712 accepted, 529 enrolled. Graduate enrollment: 288 men, 166 women.
**Test score averages/ranges.** Average SAT scores: 540 verbal, 620 math. Average ACT scores: 28 composite. Range of ACT scores of middle 50%: 26-32 composite.
**Faculty.** 182 full-time; 20 part-time. 93% of faculty holds doctoral degree. Student/faculty ratio: 11 to 1.
**Selectivity rating.** Highly competitive.

**PROFILE.** Union is a private, multipurpose college. Founded for men in 1795, it adopted coeducation in 1970. Its 100-acre campus is located in Schenectady, 15 miles from Albany.

**Accreditation:** MSACS. Professionally accredited by the Accreditation Board for Engineering and Technology.
**Religious orientation:** Union College is nonsectarian; no religious requirements.
**Library:** Collections totaling over 489,504 volumes, 2,123 periodical subscriptions, and 554,877 microform items.
**Special facilities/museums:** Horticultural garden, superconducting nuclear magnetic resonance spectrometer, two electron microscopes, tandem pelletron positive ion accelerator.
**Athletic facilities:** Field house, fitness center, swimming pool, weight rooms, basketball, racquetball, squash, and tennis courts, ice rink, tracks, baseball, football, lacrosse, soccer, and softball fields.

**STUDENT BODY. Undergraduate profile:** 55% are state residents; 6% are transfers. 6% Asian-American, 3% Black, 3% Hispanic, 85% White, 3% Other. Average age of undergraduates is 20.
**Freshman profile:** 25% of accepted applicants took ACT. 67% of freshmen come from public schools.
**Undergraduate achievement:** 95% of fall 1992 freshmen returned for fall 1993 term. 79% of entering class graduated. 32% of students who completed a degree program went on to graduate study within one year.
**Foreign students:** 51 students are from out of the country. Countries represented include Canada, Greece, Japan, and Spain; 10 in all.

**PROGRAMS OF STUDY. Degrees:** B.A., B.S., B.S.Civil Eng., B.S.Elec.Eng., B.S.Mech.Eng.
**Majors:** American Studies, Biology, Chemistry, Civil Engineering, Classics, Computer Information Systems, Computer Science, East Asian Studies, Economics, Electrical Engineering, English, Geology, History, Humanities, Industrial Economics, Interdepartmental Program, Latin American Studies, Managerial Economics, Mathematics, Mechanical Engineering, Modern Languages, Philosophy, Physics, Political Science, Psychology, Russian/East European Studies, Science, Social Science, Sociology, The Arts, Women's Studies.

**Distribution of degrees:** The majors with the highest enrollment are political science, history, and biology; women's studies has the lowest.
**Requirements:** General education requirement.
**Academic regulations:** Minimum 2.0 GPA must be maintained.
**Special:** Minors offered in most majors and in astronomy, classical civilization, cultural anthropology, Greek, Latin, music, theatre arts, visual arts, and world music. Self-designed majors. Double majors. Dual degrees. Independent study. Accelerated study. Pass/fail grading option. Internships. Graduate school at which undergraduates may take graduate-level courses. Five-year liberal arts/engineering program. Five-year B.A./M.B.A. and B.S./M.B.A. programs. Accelerated six-year program in law and public policy with Albany Law School and seven-year program in medicine with Albany Medical Coll. Member of the Hudson-Mohawk Association of Colleges and Universities; cross-registration possible. Washington Semester. Albany Semester. Teacher certification in secondary education. Certification in specific subject areas. Exchange programs abroad in China (Nanjing Normal U), England (Coll of Ripon and York St. John), Russia, and Switzerland (Swiss Federal Inst of Tech). Study abroad also in Austria, Barbados, Bermuda, Brazil, France, Germany, Greece, Holland, Hungary, Israel, Italy, Japan, Mexico, South Korea, and Spain. ROTC at Siena Coll. NROTC and AFROTC at Rensselaer Polytech Inst.
**Honors:** Phi Beta Kappa. Honor societies.
**Academic Assistance:** Remedial writing.

**STUDENT LIFE. Housing:** All freshmen, sophomores, and juniors must live on campus unless living with family. Coed, women's, and men's dorms. Sorority and fraternity housing. 80% of students live in college housing.
**Social atmosphere:** The student newspaper reports that, "The social life of this campus depends heavily on Greek life." The most popular social events of the year are Homecoming, hockey and football games, Camp Union, Greek Week, Fitzhugh Ludlow Day, Delta Gamma Olympics, Sigma Chi Derby Days, Winterfest, and other annual Greek-sponsored parties. The favorite student hangouts are fraternities, local bars, and off-campus student residences.
**Services and counseling/handicapped student services:** Placement services. Health service. Women's center. Birth control, personal, and psychological counseling. Career and academic guidance services. Religious counseling.
**Campus organizations:** Undergraduate student government. Student newspaper (Concordiensis, published once/week). Literary magazine. Yearbook. Radio station. Choir and dance ensemble, pep, concert, and jazz bands, chamber orchestra, drama group, tutoring groups, film workshop, departmental, professional, and service groups, 88 organizations in all. 19 fraternities, 14 chapter houses; four sororities, all with chapter houses. 45% of men join a fraternity. 25% of women join a sorority.
**Religious organizations:** Campus Protestant Ministry, Protestant Student Council, United Jewish Appeal, Jewish Student Union, Newman Club, Christian Fellowship.
**Minority/foreign student organizations:** African and Latino Student Alliance, Asian Student Union. International Student Union, International House, International Relations Club.

**ATHLETICS. Physical education requirements:** None.
**Intercollegiate competition:** 35% of students participate. Baseball (M), basketball (M,W), cross-country (M,W), diving (M,W), field hockey (W), football (M), ice hockey (M), lacrosse (M,W), soccer (M,W), softball (W), swimming (M,W), tennis (M,W), track (indoor) (M,W), track (outdoor) (M,W), track and field (indoor) (M,W), track and field (outdoor) (M,W), volleyball (W). Member of ECAC, NCAA Division III, NYSWCAA.
**Intramural and club sports:** 70% of students participate. Intramural aerobics, basketball, flag football, golf, judo, karate, lacrosse, racquetball, soccer, softball, squash, swimming, tennis, volleyball, water polo. Men's club Alpine skiing, crew, fencing, handball, Nordic skiing, raquetball, rugby, squash, ultimate frisbee, water polo, weight lifting. Women's club Alpine skiing, cheerleading, crew, fencing, handball, Nordic skiing, racquetball, rugby, squash, ultimate frisbee, water polo, weight lifting.

**ADMISSIONS. Academic basis for candidate selection** (in order of priority): Secondary school record, class rank, school's recommendation, essay, standardized test scores.
**Nonacademic basis for candidate selection:** Character and personality and extracurricular participation are emphasized. Particular talent or ability is important. Geographical distribution and alumni/ae relationship are considered.
**Requirements:** Graduation from secondary school is required; GED is not accepted. 16 secondary school units required, including 4 units of English. 2.5 units of math and 2 units of foreign language required of liberal arts applicants. Intermediate algebra, plane geometry, trigonometry, chemistry, and physics required of engineering program applicants. 3.5 units of math required of B.S./M.D. program applicants (seven-year program). ACT or 3 ACH tests required. HEOP for in-state applicants who are not normally admissible; Academic Opportunity Program for applicants from any state who are not normally admissible. Campus visit and interview recommended. Off-campus interviews available with an alumni representative.
**Procedure:** Take ACT by January 1 of 12th year. Take ACH by January 1 of 12th year. Visit college for interview by February 1 of 12th year. Application deadline is February 1. Notification of admission by April 1. Reply is required by May 1. $400 nonrefundable tuition deposit. Freshmen accepted for fall terms only.
**Special programs:** Admission may be deferred. Credit and/or placement may be granted through CEEB Advanced Placement exams for scores of 4 or higher. Early decision program. In fall 1993, 254 applied for early decision and 178 were accepted. Deadline for applying for early decision is February 1. Early entrance/early admission program. Concurrent enrollment program.
**Transfer students:** Transfer students accepted for terms other than fall. In fall 1993, 6% of all new students were transfers into all classes. 84 transfer applications were received, 52 were accepted. Application deadline is June 15 for fall; November 1 for winter; February 1 for spring. ACT or 3 CEEB Achievement Tests required of all transfer applicants. Minimum 3.0 GPA recommended. Lowest course grade accepted is "C." At least 18 courses must be completed at the college to receive degree.
**Admissions contact:** Daniel Lundquist, Ed.M., Dean of Admissions and Financial Aid. 518 388-6112.

**FINANCIAL AID. Available aid:** Pell grants, SEOG, state scholarships and grants, school scholarships and grants, private scholarships and grants, ROTC scholarships, and aid for undergraduate foreign students. Perkins Loans (NDSL), PLUS, Stafford Loans (GSL), school loans, private loans, and SLS. Tuition Plan Inc., Knight Tuition Plans, and AMS.
**Financial aid statistics:** 1% of aid is not need-based. In 1993-94, 95% of all undergraduate applicants received aid; 95% of freshman applicants. Average amounts of aid awarded freshmen: Scholarships and grants, $12,000; loans, $3,000.
**Supporting data/closing dates:** FAFSA/FAF: Priority filing date is February 1. School's own aid application: Deadline is February 1. Income tax forms: Priority filing date is June 1. Notification of awards begins March 30.
**Financial aid contact:** Michael Brown, Director of Financial Aid. 518 388-6123.

**STUDENT EMPLOYMENT.** College Work/Study Program. Institutional employment. 34% of full-time undergraduates work on campus during school year. Students may expect to earn an average of $815 during school year. Off-campus part-time employment opportunities rated "good."

**COMPUTER FACILITIES.** 175 IBM/IBM-compatible, Macintosh/Apple, and RISC-/UNIX-based microcomputers; 125 are networked. Students may access Digital, SUN minicomputer/mainframe systems, Internet. Residence halls may be equipped with modems. Client/LAN operating systems include Apple/Macintosh, DOS, UNIX/XENIX/AIX, X-windows, DEC, LocalTalk/AppleTalk. Computer languages and software packages include BASIC, C, C++, Excel, engineering application programs, FLUENT, FORTRAN, LISP, Lotus 1-2-3, MATHCAD, Mathematica, Microsoft Word, Pascal, SAS, SPSS-X, WordPerfect; 50 in all. Computer facilities are available to all students.
**Fees:** None.
**Hours:** 24 hours.

**GRADUATE CAREER DATA.** Graduate school percentages: 10% enter law school. 9% enter medical school. 1% enter dental school. 1% enter graduate business programs. 16% enter graduate arts and sciences programs. Highest graduate school enrollments: Albany Medical Coll, Boston U, Columbia U, Cornell U, Harvard U, New York U, U of Chicago. 60% of graduates choose careers in business and industry. Companies and businesses that hire graduates: AT&T, Bankers Trust, Coopers & Lybrand, General Electric.

**PROMINENT ALUMNI/AE.** Baruch Blumberg, Nobel Prize-winning physiologist; R. Gordon Gould, inventor of the laser; Michael Fuchs, chairperson and CEO, Home Box Office; Phil Alden Robinson, author and film director; Victor Fazio, U.S. congressman; Robert Chartoff, film producer.

# United States Merchant Marine Academy

**Kings Point, NY 11024-1699** **516 773-5000**

**1993-94 Costs.** Four-year scholarship covers tuition, room, board, and some medical/dental expenses. Required fees: $4,000 (freshmen); $1,000 (others).
**Enrollment.** Undergraduates: 892 men, 95 women (full-time). Freshman class: 942 applicants, 365 accepted, 283 enrolled.
**Test score averages/ranges.** Average SAT scores: 542 verbal, 593 math. Range of SAT scores of middle 50%: 530-530 verbal, 590-590 math.
**Faculty.** 74 full-time; 8 part-time. 50% of faculty holds doctoral degree. Student/faculty ratio: 11 to 1.
**Selectivity rating.** Highly competitive.

**PROFILE.** The U.S. Merchant Marine Academy is a public service academy. Founded in 1943, it adopted coeducation in 1974. Its 82-acre campus is located in Kings Point, on the north shore of Long Island, 20 miles east of New York City.

**Accreditation:** MSACS. Professionally accredited by the Accreditation Board for Engineering and Technology.
**Religious orientation:** United States Merchant Marine Academy is nonsectarian; no religious requirements.
**Library:** Collections totaling over 228,806 volumes, 918 periodical subscriptions, and 109,694 microform items.
**Special facilities/museums:** American Merchant Marine museum, national maritime research center, computer-aided operations research center, more than 80 vessels and small craft, steam and diesel labs, nuclear engineering facility, tanker simulator, ship's bridge simulator, radar labs.
**Athletic facilities:** Gymnasium, indoor and outdoor swimming pools, basketball, racquetball, squash, and tennis courts, track, aerobics and weight rooms, baseball, football, lacrosse, and soccer fields, sailboats.

**STUDENT BODY. Undergraduate profile:** 14% are state residents. 4% Asian-American, 1% Black, 2% Hispanic, 1% Native American, 92% White. Average age of undergraduates is 20.
**Freshman profile:** 7% of freshmen who took SAT scored 700 or over on verbal, 7% scored 700 or over on math; 26% scored 600 or over on verbal, 44% scored 600 or over on math; 65% scored 500 or over on verbal, 100% scored 500 or over on math; 100% scored 400 or over on verbal. Majority of accepted applicants took SAT.
**Undergraduate achievement:** 80% of fall 1992 freshmen returned for fall 1993 term. 2% of students who completed a degree program immediately went on to graduate study.
**Foreign students:** 33 students are from out of the country. Countries represented include Argentina, Colombia, Greece, Panama, Russia, and the Philippines.

**PROGRAMS OF STUDY. Degrees:** B.S.
**Majors:** Dual License, Marine Engineering, Marine Engineering Systems, Marine Transportation, Ship's Officer/Deck.
**Requirements:** General education requirement.
**Academic regulations:** Minimum 2.0 GPA must be maintained.
**Special:** Four-year program leads to license as merchant marine deck or engineering officer and commission as ensign in the U.S. Naval Reserve. Graduates must serve in U.S. Naval Reserve for eight years, six years on active, two inactive duty. Concentrations offered in chemistry, computer science, law, management, marine electronics, marine machinery design, marine petroleum operations, marine thermal power systems and control,

maritime transportation, mathematics, naval architecture, nuclear engineering, marine electrical power and control, and physics. Courses offered in humanities, management, and sciences. Five months of second and third years are spent aboard U.S. flag ships. Double majors. Internships. Cooperative education programs. Preprofessional programs in admiralty law.
**Honors:** Honors program.
**Academic Assistance:** Remedial math. Nonremedial tutoring.

**STUDENT LIFE. Housing:** All students must live on campus, except during shipboard training. Coed dorms. 100% of students live in college housing.
**Social atmosphere:** As reported by the student newspaper, "Situated in posh Great Neck, midshipmen are only 20 minutes from New York City and a wide variety of entertainment. The school has a pub, open to seniors on Friday night. The local ale houses, such as C.J.'s, Fishtale's, and Chi Chi's are frequented by midshipmen. The America's Cup is of great interest, as our school sponsored the "America II."
**Services and counseling/handicapped student services:** Personal and psychological counseling. Career and academic guidance services. Religious counseling.
**Campus organizations:** Student newspaper (Hear This, published four or five times/ year). Yearbook. Chapel choir, glee club, regimental band, debating, radio, camera, and chess clubs, Knights of Columbus, international relations club, Marlenspike and Trident clubs, sailing squadron, professional groups, 45 organizations in all.
**Religious organizations:** Newman Club, Bible Study Club.
**Minority/foreign student organizations:** Ethnic Culture Club.

**ATHLETICS. Physical education requirements:** 12 terms of physical education required.
**Intercollegiate competition:** 75% of students participate. Baseball (M), basketball (M), crew (M,W), cross-country (M,W), diving (M,W), football (M), golf (M,W), lacrosse (M), pistol (M,W), riflery (M,W), rugby (M), sailing (M,W), soccer (M), softball (W), swimming (M,W), tennis (M,W), track (indoor) (M,W), track (outdoor) (M,W), track and field (indoor) (M,W), track and field (outdoor) (M,W), volleyball (M,W), water polo (M), wrestling (M). Member of ECAC, Freedom Football Conference, Metropolitan Swimming and Wrestling Conferences, NCAA Division III, Skyline Athletic Conference.
**Intramural and club sports:** 100% of students participate. Intramural basketball, bowling, flag football, racquetball, soccer, softball, volleyball, water polo. Men's club cycling, fencing, hockey, martial arts, power lifting, rugby. Women's club cycling, fencing, power lifting.

**ADMISSIONS. Academic basis for candidate selection** (in order of priority): Secondary school record, class rank, standardized test scores, school's recommendation, essay.
**Nonacademic basis for candidate selection:** Character and personality and geographical distribution are emphasized. Extracurricular participation is important. Particular talent or ability and alumni/ae relationship are considered.
**Requirements:** Graduation from secondary school is recommended; GED is accepted. 15 units and the following program of study are required: 3 units of English, 3 units of math, 1 unit of lab science. 4 units of math and 2 units of science recommended. Minimum combined SAT score of 950 with minimum scores of 400 verbal and 500 math and rank in top two-fifths of secondary school class required. Applicants must be U.S. citizens between 17 and 25 years of age and must be nominated by a member of Congress or other nominating authority (not the President or Vice President). Good physical condition and physical exam required. SAT or ACT is required. Campus visit recommended. Off-campus interviews available with an alumni representative.
**Procedure:** Take SAT or ACT by February of 12th year. Application deadline is March 1. Acceptance notification on rolling basis beginning in December. Reply is required by May 1. Freshmen accepted for fall terms only.
**Transfer students:** Transfer students accepted for fall term only. Application deadline is March 1. Minimum 3.0 GPA recommended. At least 160 semester hours must be completed at the service academy to receive degree.
**Admissions contact:** Capt. James M. Skinner, M.S., Director of Admissions. 516 773-5391.

**FINANCIAL AID. Available aid:** Private scholarships. Federal Service Academy Scholarships. PLUS, Stafford Loans (GSL), and SLS.
**Financial aid statistics:** In 1993-94, 11% of all undergraduate applicants received aid; 28% of freshman applicants. Average amounts of aid awarded freshmen: Loans, $2,500.
**Supporting data/closing dates:** FAFSA: Priority filing date is March 15. Income tax forms: Accepted on rolling basis. Notification of awards begins April 20.
**Financial aid contact:** Capt. James M. Skimner, M.S., Director of Financial Aid. 516 773-5711.

**STUDENT EMPLOYMENT.** 1% of full-time undergraduates work on campus during school year. Freshmen are discouraged from working during their first term. Off-campus part-time employment opportunities rated "good."

**COMPUTER FACILITIES.** 1,200 IBM/IBM-compatible and Macintosh/Apple microcomputers; all are networked. Residence halls may be equipped with networked microcomputers. Client/LAN operating systems include Apple/Macintosh, DOS, UNIX/XENIX/AIX, X-windows, Microsoft, Novell. Computer languages and software packages include Ada, Assembler, BASIC, C, COBOL, FORTH, FORTRAN, Pascal, PL/1. Computer facilities are available to all students.
**Fees:** None.
**Hours:** 8 AM-8 PM.

**GRADUATE CAREER DATA.** Graduate school percentages: 1% enter graduate business programs. Highest graduate school enrollments: Adelphi U, SUNY at Stony Brook, Tulane U. 74% of graduates choose careers in business and industry. Companies and businesses that hire graduates: American President Lines, Exxon, Lykes Bros. Steamship Co., Sea-Land Services, Texaco.

**PROMINENT ALUMNI/AE.** Lane Kirkland, president, AFL-CIO; Vice Adm. Albert Herberger; Charles R. Cushing, president, Charles Cushing & Co. (naval architects); Capt. Warren Leback, U.S. Maritime Administration; Nancy Wagner, pilot, San Francisco Bar Harbor Pilots Association.

# United States Military Academy

**West Point, NY 10996 — 914 938-4011**

**1994-95 Costs.** All cadets are members of the U.S. Army and receive an annual salary of more than $6,500. Tuition, room and board, and medical and dental care are provided at no cost to cadets. First-year students pay $1,500 deposit in order to purchase a computer, books, uniforms, and other incidentals.
**Enrollment.** Undergraduates: 3,742 men, 495 women (full-time). Freshman class: 10,464 applicants, 1,610 accepted, 1,212 enrolled.
**Test score averages/ranges.** Average SAT scores: 558 verbal, 653 math. Range of SAT scores of middle 50%: 500-599 verbal, 600-700 math. Average ACT scores: 27 English, 28 math, 28 composite. Range of ACT scores of middle 50%: 26-29 English, 27-30 math.
**Faculty.** 464 full-time. 26% of faculty holds doctoral degree. Student/faculty ratio: 9 to 1.
**Selectivity rating.** Highly competitive.

**PROFILE.** The U.S. Military Academy is a public service academy. Founded in 1802, it adopted coeducation in 1976. Its 16,080-acre campus is located in West Point, on the Hudson River, 50 miles north of New York City.

**Accreditation:** MSACS. Professionally accredited by the Accreditation Board for Engineering and Technology.
**Religious orientation:** United States Military Academy is nonsectarian; no religious requirements.
**Library:** Collections totaling over 414,711 volumes, 2,400 periodical subscriptions, and 718,666 microform items.
**Special facilities/museums:** Museum.
**Athletic facilities:** Gymnasiums, field house, ice rink, rifle and pistol ranges, tracks, swimming pools, boxing, gymnastics, weight, and wrestling rooms, basketball, handball, racquetball, squash, tennis, and volleyball courts, golf course, lakes, bowling alleys, ski slope, baseball, football, intramural, soccer, and softball fields, stadium, trap shooting area.

**STUDENT BODY. Undergraduate profile:** 8% are state residents. 5% Asian-American, 7% Black, 4% Hispanic, 1% Native American, 83% White. Average age of undergraduates is 20.
**Freshman profile:** 3% of freshmen who took SAT scored 700 or over on verbal, 29% scored 700 or over on math; 30% scored 600 or over on verbal, 81% scored 600 or over on math; 81% scored 500 or over on verbal, 100% scored 500 or over on math; 100% scored 400 or over on verbal. 63% of accepted applicants took SAT; 37% took ACT.
**Undergraduate achievement:** 94% of fall 1992 freshmen returned for fall 1993 term. 82% of entering class graduated.
**Foreign students:** 36 students are from out of the country. Countries represented include Columbia, Malaysia, Nigeria, Singapore, Thailand, and Turkey; 21 in all.

**PROGRAMS OF STUDY. Degrees:** B.S.
**Majors:** Aerospace Systems, American Legal System, American Studies, Applied Science/Engineering Interdisciplinary, Arabic, Automotive Systems, Basic Science Interdisciplinary, Behavioral Science, Chemical Engineering, Chemistry, Chinese, Civil Engineering, Computer Engineering, Computer Science, East Asian Studies, Economics, Electrical/Electronics Engineering, Electrical Engineering, Energy Systems, Engineering Management, Engineering Physics, Environmental Engineering, Environmental Science, Foreign Area Studies, Foreign Languages, French, Geography, German, History, Human Factors Psychology, Individual Psychology, Latin American Studies, Life Sciences, Literature, Management, Mathematical Science, Mechanical Engineering, Mechanical Systems, Middle Eastern Studies, Military History, Military Science, Modern History, Nuclear Engineering, Nuclear Reactor Technology, Operations Research, Philosophy, Physical Electronics, Physics, Political Science, Portuguese, Russian, Sociology, Spanish, Systems Engineering, Western European Studies.
**Distribution of degrees:** The majors with the highest enrollment are engineering, management, and political science; military studies and foreign area studies have the lowest.
**Requirements:** General education requirement.
**Academic regulations:** Freshmen must maintain minimum 1.7 GPA; sophomores, 1.8 GPA; juniors, 1.9 GPA; seniors, 2.0 GPA (on a 4.33 scale).
**Special:** The primary purpose of the academy is to educate and train the country's future professional military leaders. Upon graduation, every cadet is commissioned as a Second Lieutenant of the U.S. Army and must serve six years active duty in the Army. All cadets must complete four-year academic program. Freshmen enter in summer for Cadet Basic Training. The Third Class sophomore summer program includes military field training, armor training in Kentucky, and artillery, infantry, and air defense training. Second Class junior summer program emphasizes advanced training and troop leadership, mountain warfare school in Vermont, northern warfare school in Alaska, airborne school in Georgia, survival techniques in Colorado. Cadets may choose from over 150 academic opportunities during summer. Double majors. Independent study. Internships. Preprofessional programs in medicine. Exchange programs with U.S. Air Force, Coast Guard, and Naval Academies.
**Honors:** Phi Beta Kappa. Honors program. Honor societies.
**Academic Assistance:** Remedial reading and study skills. Nonremedial tutoring.

**STUDENT LIFE. Housing:** All cadets must live on campus. Coed dorms. 100% of students live in college housing.
**Social atmosphere:** According to the editor of the student newspaper, there are excellent cultural offerings on campus through theatre arts productions and concerts, as well as opportunities to engage in club activities. In addition, "New York City provides an environment

unsurpassed for social and cultural experience." On campus, students frequent Eisenhower Hall, Grant Hall, and the Post Theatre. Popular events include cadet class dances and the weekend dances held in Eisenhower Hall.

**Services and counseling/handicapped student services:** Health service. Counseling services for military students. Birth control, personal, and psychological counseling. Career and academic guidance services. Religious counseling.

**Campus organizations:** Undergraduate student government. Literary magazine. Yearbook. Radio station. Glee club, choirs, bands, Theatre Arts Guild, Cadet Fine Arts Forum, film and performing arts series, debating, Corbin Seminar (women's group), Annual Conference on U.S. Affairs, academic clubs, parachuting club, drill team, 104 organizations in all.

**Religious organizations:** Baptist Student Union, Christian Fellowship, Navigators, Fellowship of Christian Athletes, God's Gang, Episcopal Club, Knights of Columbus, Jewish Squad, Latter-Day Saints Student Association, Lutheran Cadet Club, Christian Science Club.

**Minority/foreign student organizations:** Contemporary Affairs Seminar, Korean/American Relations Seminar.

**ATHLETICS. Physical education requirements:** Eight semesters of physical education required.

**Intercollegiate competition:** 45% of students participate. Baseball (M), basketball (M,W), cross-country (M,W), diving (M,W), football (M), golf (M), gymnastics (M), ice hockey (M), lacrosse (M), lightweight football (M), pistol (M,W), riflery (M,W), soccer (M,W), softball (W), swimming (M,W), tennis (M,W), track (indoor) (M,W), track (outdoor) (M,W), track and field (indoor) (M,W), track and field (outdoor) (M,W), volleyball (W), water polo (M), wrestling (M). Member of ECAC, NCAA Division I, NCAA Division I-A for football, Patriot League.

**Intramural and club sports:** 75% of students participate. Intramural Alpine skiing, basketball, bowling, boxing, crew, cross-country, cycling, fencing, flag football, flickerball, floor hockey, handball, horsemanship, judo, karate, lacrosse, marathon, Nordic skiing, orienteering, power lifting, racquetball, rugby, sailing, skeet/trapshooting, soccer, softball, squash, swimming, team handball, triathalon, volleyball, walleyball, wrestling. Men's club Alpine skiing, bowling, crew, cycling, fencing, handball, horsemanship, martial arts, Nordic skiing, racquetball, rugby, sailing, squash, volleyball, weight lifting. Women's club Alpine skiing, bowling, crew, cycling, fencing, handball, horsemanship, martial arts, Nordic skiing, racquetball, sailing, weight lifting.

**ADMISSIONS. Academic basis for candidate selection** (in order of priority): Standardized test scores, class rank, secondary school record, school's recommendation, essay.

**Nonacademic basis for candidate selection:** Character and personality and extracurricular participation are emphasized. Particular talent or ability is considered.

**Requirements:** Graduation from secondary school is required; GED is accepted. 19 units and the following program of study are recommended: 4 units of English, 4 units of math, 2 units of lab science, 2 units of foreign language, 3 units of social studies, 1 unit of history, 3 units of academic electives. Every applicant must obtain a nomination from an approved source (Congress, President, Vice President, or Department of the Army). Entrants must be at least 17 years of age and not yet 22 on July 1 of year of entry. All applicants must be unmarried U.S. citizens in good health with no parental obligations or responsibilities and must demonstrate leadership ability. SAT or ACT is required. PSAT is recommended. ACH recommended. Campus visit and interview recommended. Off-campus interviews available with admissions and alumni representatives.

**Procedure:** Seek nomination and submit Service Academies Precandidate Questionnaire in spring of 11th year. Applicants are advised to seek nominations from as many sources as possible and to contact the Admissions Office between July 1 and January 15 of 12th year. Take SAT or ACT by fall of 12th year. Suggest filing application by December 1. Application deadline is March 21. Notification of admission on rolling basis. Reply is required by May 1. Freshmen accepted for fall terms only.

**Special programs:** Credit/placement offered for Advanced Placement scores of 4 or higher. Placement may be granted through CLEP subject exams. Credit and placement may be granted through challenge exams. Early decision program. In fall 1993, 711 applied for early decision and 594 were accepted. Deadline for applying for early decision is October 25.

**Transfer students:** All transfers enter as freshmen. Transfer students accepted for fall term only. Application deadline is March 21.

**Admissions contact:** Col. Pierce A. Rushton, Jr., M.S., Director of Admissions. 914 938-4041.

**FINANCIAL AID. Available aid:** No-interest loans of $100-$1,500 available to students who cannot pay $1,500 deposit. Every cadet receives $2,700 interest-free advance payment.

**Financial aid contact:** Major Naeditch, M.S., Treasurer. 914 938-3516.

**COMPUTER FACILITIES.** 5,500 IBM/IBM-compatible microcomputers; all are networked. Students may access AT&T, Digital, UNISYS minicomputer/mainframe systems, BITNET, Internet, CompuServe. Residence halls may be equipped with stand-alone microcomputers, networked microcomputers. Client/LAN operating systems include DOS, UNIX/XENIX/AIX, Microsoft, Novell. Computer languages and software packages include Ada, Autocad, Drafix, FORTRAN, Mathcad, Microsoft Word, Turbo Pascal, Quattro Pro, SPSS, Windows, WordPerfect. Computer facilities are available to all students.

**Fees:** None.

**Hours:** 24 hours.

**GRADUATE CAREER DATA.** Graduate school percentages: 2% enter medical school. 97% of graduates who remain on active duty for 20 years obtain an advanced degree.

**PROMINENT ALUMNI/AE.** Ulysses S. Grant and Dwight D. Eisenhower, U.S. Presidents; Douglas MacArthur, Omar Bradley, and Norman Schwarzkopf, generals, U.S. Army.

# University of Rochester

**Rochester, NY 14627** **716 275-2121**

**1994-95 Costs.** Tuition: $17,840. Room: $3,978. Board: $2,605. Fees, books, misc. academic expenses (school's estimate): $910.

**Enrollment.** Undergraduates: 2,694 men, 2,382 women (full-time). Freshman class: 8,777 applicants, 5,498 accepted, 1,243 enrolled. Graduate enrollment: 1,840 men, 1,291 women.

**Test score averages/ranges.** Range of SAT scores of middle 50%: 470-590 verbal, 550-670 math. Range of ACT scores of middle 50%: 23-29 composite.

**Faculty.** 505 full-time; 72 part-time. 99% of faculty holds highest degree in specific field. Student/faculty ratio: 12 to 1.

**Selectivity rating.** Highly competitive.

**PROFILE.** The University of Rochester, founded in 1850, is a private, comprehensive university. Programs are offered through the Colleges of Arts and Science and Engineering and Applied Science; the University College of Liberal and Applied Studies; the Eastman School of Music; the Graduate School of Education and Human Development; the William E. Simon Graduate School of Business Administration; and the Schools of Medicine and Dentistry and Nursing. Its urban campus is located in Rochester.

**Accreditation:** MSACS. Professionally accredited by the Accreditation Board for Engineering and Technology, the American Assembly of Collegiate Schools of Business, the American Medical Association (CAHEA), the American Psychological Association, the Council on Education for Public Health, the Liaison Committee on Medical Education, the National Association of Schools of Music, the National League for Nursing.

**Religious orientation:** University of Rochester is nonsectarian; no religious requirements.

**Library:** Collections totaling over 2,774,892 volumes, 13,309 periodical subscriptions, and 3,661,525 microform items.

**Special facilities/museums:** Art center and gallery, African and African-American studies institute, center for women's studies, visual science and space science centers, institute of optics, observatory, laser energetics and nuclear structure research labs, electron microscopes.

**Athletic facilities:** Sports center, stadium, field house, gymnasium, ice rink, swimming pool, diving tank, weight rooms, fitness center, basketball, racquetball, squash, tennis, and volleyball courts, track, athletic fields, jogging trails.

**STUDENT BODY. Undergraduate profile:** 43% are state residents; 14% are transfers. 6% Asian-American, 6% Black, 4% Hispanic, 1% Native American, 70% White, 13% Other.

**Freshman profile:** 2% of freshmen who took SAT scored 700 or over on verbal, 16% scored 700 or over on math; 21% scored 600 or over on verbal, 57% scored 600 or over on math; 62% scored 500 or over on verbal, 87% scored 500 or over on math; 90% scored 400 or over on verbal, 97% scored 400 or over on math; 99% scored 300 or over on verbal, 100% scored 300 or over on math. 93% of accepted applicants took SAT; 24% took ACT.

**Undergraduate achievement:** 94% of fall 1992 freshmen returned for fall 1993 term. 65% of entering class graduated. 35% of students who completed a degree program immediately went on to graduate study.

**Foreign students:** 420 students are from out of the country. Countries represented include Canada, China, India, Japan, Korea, and Taiwan; 75 in all.

**PROGRAMS OF STUDY. Degrees:** B.A., B.Mus., B.S.

**Majors:** Anthropology, Applied Mathematics, Applied Music, Art History, Biochemistry, Biological Sciences, Biology, Biology/Geology, Cell/Developmental Biology, Chemical Engineering, Chemistry, Classics, Cognitive Science, Computer Sciences/Applied Mathematics, Computer Sciences/Mathematics, Ecology/Evolutionary Biology, Economics, Electrical Engineering, Engineering/Applied Science, Engineering Science, English, Environmental Science, Environmental Studies, Film Studies, Foreign Literature, French, Geology, Geomechanics, German, Health/Society, History, Integrated Science, Interdepartmental Studies, Japanese, Linguistics, Mathematics, Mathematics/Statistics, Mechanical Engineering, Microbiology, Molecular Genetics, Music, Music Composition, Music Education, Music History, Music Theory, Neuroscience, Nursing, Optics, Philosophy, Physics, Physics/Astronomy, Political Science, Psychology, Religious Studies, Russian, Spanish, Statistics, Studio Art, Women's Studies.

**Distribution of degrees:** The majors with the highest enrollment are psychology, economics, and political science; applied mathematics, math/statistics, and classics have the lowest.

**Requirements:** General education requirement.

**Academic regulations:** Minimum 2.0 GPA must be maintained.

**Special:** Minors offered in many majors and in approximately 25 other areas. Certificate programs offered. Undergraduate research, preceptorials (small freshman seminars), residential, and student-initiated courses. Freshman curriculum offers the Traditional Approach, allowing students to select from entire range of courses open to freshmen; Freshman Ventures allows students to take half of first year's work as an integrated sequence. Special programs include project-oriented part-time "experienceships" and full-time summer placement program. "Take Five" program allows selected students to take a fifth year tuition-free. Rochester Early Medical Scholars Program. Senior Scholars Program. Self-designed majors. Double majors. Dual degrees. Independent study. Pass/fail grading option. Internships. Graduate school at which undergraduates may take graduate-level courses. Preprofessional programs in law, medicine, and dentistry. 3-2 engineering program. Numerous bachelor's/master's degree programs. Member of Rochester Area Consortium Colleges. Washington Semester. Teacher certification in secondary and special education. Certification in specific subject areas. Exchange program abroad in England. Study abroad also in Australia, Austria, Belgium, China, the Czech Republic, Egypt,

France, Germany, Hungary, Israel, Italy, Japan, Poland, Russia, Singapore, Spain, and Taiwan. NROTC. ROTC and AFROTC at Rochester Inst of Tech.
**Honors:** Phi Beta Kappa. Honor societies.
**Academic Assistance:** Nonremedial tutoring.

**STUDENT LIFE. Housing:** All freshmen must live on campus unless living with family. Coed, women's, and men's dorms. Sorority and fraternity housing. School-owned/operated apartments. Off-campus privately-owned housing. On-campus married-student housing. 82% of students live in college housing.
**Social atmosphere:** Students gather at The Pit, Creme de la Creme, Java Joe's, Wilson Commons, and Heaven. Influential campus groups include Hillel, Greeks, the Black Student Union, and the Chinese Student Association. The most popular events of the year are Dandelion Day, Winter Carnival, the International Fiesta, and the Boar's Head Dinner. According to the student newspaper, "student life is varied and active, although there isn't really a 'college town' nearby."
**Services and counseling/handicapped student services:** Placement services. Health service. Women's center. Day care. Study skills center. Counseling services for minority and older students. Birth control, personal, and psychological counseling. Career and academic guidance services. Physically disabled student services. Learning disabled services. Notetaking services. Tape recorders. Tutors. Reader services for the blind.
**Campus organizations:** Undergraduate student government. Student newspaper (Campus Times, published once/week). Literary magazine. Yearbook. Radio station. Gospel choir, jazz ensemble, chamber singers, ski and sailing groups, amateur radio group, cinema group, arts group, social activities board, women's caucus, numerous musical, drama, and dance groups, 139 organizations in all. 16 fraternities, six chapter houses; 10 sororities, no chapter houses. 24% of men join a fraternity. 19% of women join a sorority.
**Religious organizations:** Brothers and Sisters in Christ, Interdenominational Worship Group, Newman Community, Intervarsity Christian Fellowship, Protestant Community, Hillel, Hindu Association, Bahai and Muslim groups, International Christian Fellowship, Chinese Christian Fellowship.
**Minority/foreign student organizations:** African and Caribbean Culture Club, Black Student Union, Association of Black Drama and Arts, Charles Drew Pre-Med Society, Thurgood Marshall Pre-Law Society, Black and Hispanic Women's Alliance, Asian Cultural Exchange, Chinese Students Association, Chinese Students and Scholars, Spanish and Latin Association. International Student Association, Taiwanese, Hong Kong, Indian, Japanese, Korean, Pakistani, and Vietnamese groups.

**ATHLETICS. Physical education requirements:** None.
**Intercollegiate competition:** 15% of students participate. Baseball (M), basketball (M,W), cross-country (M,W), diving (M,W), field hockey (W), football (M), golf (M), soccer (M,W), squash (M), swimming (M,W), tennis (M,W), track and field (indoor) (M,W), track and field (outdoor) (M,W), volleyball (W). Member of ECAC, NCAA Division III, NYSWCAA, University Athletic Association.
**Intramural and club sports:** 60% of students participate. Intramural floor hockey, racquetball, soccer, softball, touch football, tennis, tube water polo, volleyball. Men's club Alpine skiing, canoe/kayak, crew, cycling, fencing, gymnastics, horsemanship, ice hockey, lacrosse, martial arts, Nordic skiing, rugby, sailing, ultimate frisbee, volleyball, wrestling. Women's club Alpine skiing, canoe/kayak, cheerleading, crew, cycling, fencing, gymnastics, lacrosse, martial arts, Nordic skiing, sailing, softball.

**ADMISSIONS. Academic basis for candidate selection** (in order of priority): Secondary school record, school's recommendation, class rank, standardized test scores, essay.
**Nonacademic basis for candidate selection:** Character and personality and extracurricular participation are emphasized. Particular talent or ability, geographical distribution, and alumni/ae relationship are considered.
**Requirements:** Graduation from secondary school is recommended; GED is accepted. 15 units and the following program of study are recommended: 4 units of English, 3 units of math, 2 units of science, 2 units of foreign language, 4 units of social studies. Physics required of physics and physics/astronomy program applicants; recommended of engineering program applicants. Chemistry strongly recommended of biology, chemistry, chemical engineering, and nursing program applicants. Audition required of B.Mus. program applicants; recommended of B.A. music program applicants. HEOP for applicants not normally admissible. SAT or ACT is required. ACH recommended. Campus visit and interview recommended. Off-campus interviews available with an alumni representative.
**Procedure:** Take SAT or ACT by February of 12th year. Visit college for interview by fall of 12th year. Suggest filing application by January 30; no deadline. Notification of admission by April 15. Reply is required by May 1. $400 nonrefundable tuition deposit. Freshmen accepted for terms other than fall.
**Special programs:** Admission may be deferred one year. Credit and/or placement may be granted through CEEB Advanced Placement exams for scores of 4 or higher. Placement may be granted through challenge exams. Early decision program. In fall 1993, 307 applied for early decision and 167 were accepted. Deadline for applying for early decision is November 15, but requests are considered until February 1. Early entrance/early admission program. Concurrent enrollment program.
**Transfer students:** Transfer students accepted for terms other than fall. In fall 1993, 14% of all new students were transfers into all classes. 364 transfer applications were received, 308 were accepted. Application deadline is rolling for fall; rolling for spring. Minimum 2.8 GPA recommended. Lowest course grade accepted is "C-." Maximum number of transferable credits is 96 semester hours. At least 32 semester hours must be completed at the university to receive degree.
**Admissions contact:** Wayne A. Locust, M.S., Director of Admissions, River Campus. 716 275-3221.

**FINANCIAL AID. Available aid:** Pell grants, SEOG, state scholarships and grants, school scholarships and grants, private scholarships and grants, ROTC scholarships, academic merit scholarships, and aid for undergraduate foreign students. Perkins Loans (NDSL), PLUS, Stafford Loans (GSL), NSL, school loans, private loans, and SLS. Deferred payment plan and guaranteed tuition.
**Financial aid statistics:** 11% of aid is not need-based. In 1993-94, 95% of all undergraduate applicants received aid; 91% of freshman applicants. Average amounts of aid awarded freshmen: Scholarships and grants, $13,250; loans, $3,475.
**Supporting data/closing dates:** FAFSA/FAF/FFS: Priority filing date is February 1. School's own aid application: Priority filing date is February 1. Income tax forms: Deadline is May 31. Notification of awards begins April 2.
**Financial aid contact:** Ryan C. Williams, M.S.E., Director of Financial Aid. 716 275-3226.

**STUDENT EMPLOYMENT.** College Work/Study Program. Institutional employment. 60% of full-time undergraduates work on campus during school year. Students may expect to earn an average of $2,800 during school year. Off-campus part-time employment opportunities rated "good."

**COMPUTER FACILITIES.** 180 IBM/IBM-compatible, Macintosh/Apple, and RISC-/UNIX-based microcomputers; 160 are networked. Students may access Digital, IBM minicomputer/mainframe systems, BITNET, Internet. Residence halls may be equipped with stand-alone microcomputers, networked microcomputers, networked terminals, modems. Client/LAN operating systems include Apple/Macintosh. Computer languages and software packages include BMDP, C, COBOL, DISSPLA, FORTRAN, ImSL, INGRES, Mathematica, MINITAB, NAG, Pascal, PL/1, SAS, SPSS-X; 200 in all. Computer facilities are available to all students.
**Fees:** None.
**Hours:** 24 hours, six days/week; shorter weekend hours.

**GRADUATE CAREER DATA.** Graduate school percentages: 6% enter law school. 8% enter medical school. 1% enter dental school. 1% enter graduate business programs. 16% enter graduate arts and sciences programs. Highest graduate school enrollments: SUNY system, Syracuse U, U of Rochester. 19% of graduates choose careers in business and industry. Companies and businesses that hire graduates: Aetna, Bloomberg L.P., Eastman Kodak, Strong Memorial Hospital, U of Rochester, Union Carbide, U.S. Armed Forces, Xerox.

**PROMINENT ALUMNI/AE.** David Kearns, former Xerox CEO and former U.S. Secretary of Education; Chuck Mangione, musician; Helen Baker Crouch, director, Literacy Volunteers of America; George Abbott, playwright, producer, director; Dr. Arthur Kornberg, Nobel Prize winner.

# Utica College of Syracuse University

**Utica, NY 13502** **315 782-8884**

**1993-94 Costs.** Tuition: $11,890. Room & board: $4,734. Fees, books, misc. academic expenses (school's estimate): $1,090.
**Enrollment.** Undergraduates: 655 men, 938 women (full-time). Freshman class: 1,511 applicants, 1,195 accepted, 326 enrolled.
**Test score averages/ranges.** Average SAT scores: 420 verbal, 468 math. Range of SAT scores of middle 50%: 380-480 verbal, 420-550 math. Average ACT scores: 22 English, 21 math, 22 composite.
**Faculty.** 111 full-time; 81 part-time. 87% of faculty holds highest degree in specific field. Student/faculty ratio: 15 to 1.
**Selectivity rating.** Competitive.

**PROFILE.** Utica, founded in 1946, is a private college and a division of Syracuse University. Its 130-acre campus is located in Utica, 50 miles east of Syracuse.

**Accreditation:** MSACS. Professionally accredited by the National League for Nursing.
**Religious orientation:** Utica College of Syracuse University is nonsectarian; no religious requirements.
**Library:** Collections totaling over 148,616 volumes, 1,258 periodical subscriptions, and 6,640 microform items.
**Special facilities/museums:** Art gallery, gerontology and public relations institutes, wildlife sanctuary.
**Athletic facilities:** Mini-gymnasium, basketball, racquetball, tennis, and volleyball courts, aerobics, dance, free-weight, and Nautilus rooms, swimming pool, baseball, flag football, lacrosse, soccer, and softball fields, sauna.

**STUDENT BODY. Undergraduate profile:** 41% are transfers. 2% Asian-American, 7% Black, 5% Hispanic, 82% White, 4% Other.
**Freshman profile:** 1% of freshmen who took SAT scored 700 or over on math; 3% scored 600 or over on verbal, 9% scored 600 or over on math; 19% scored 500 or over on verbal, 38% scored 500 or over on math; 60% scored 400 or over on verbal, 71% scored 400 or over on math; 91% scored 300 or over on verbal, 95% scored 300 or over on math. 88% of accepted applicants took SAT; 19% took ACT.
**Undergraduate achievement:** 66% of fall 1991 freshmen returned for fall 1992 term. 37% of entering class graduated. 17% of students who completed a degree program went on to graduate study within five years.
**Foreign students:** Countries represented include England, France, Germany, Italy, Kenya, and Norway; 16 in all.

**PROGRAMS OF STUDY. Degrees:** B.A., B.S.
**Majors:** Accounting, Actuarial Sciences, Anthropology/Sociology, Biology, Business Administration, Business/Economics, Chemistry, Child Life, Computer Science, Construction Management, Criminal Justice, Criminal Justice/Economic Crime Investigation, Economics, Electrical Engineering, English, Fine Arts, Gerontology, History, Human Studies, International Studies, Journalism Studies, Mathematics, Nursing, Occupational Therapy, Philosophy, Physics, Political Science, Psychology, Public Relations, Public Relations/Journalism, Social Studies, Sociology, Speech Communication/Dramatic Arts, Therapeutic Recreation.
**Distribution of degrees:** The majors with the highest enrollment are business administration, speech communication/dramatic arts, and occupational therapy; actuarial sciences, human studies, and social studies have the lowest.
**Requirements:** General education requirement.

**Academic regulations:** Minimum 2.0 GPA must be maintained.
**Special:** Minors offered in many majors and in education, film, French, government, literature, music, Spanish, theatre, and writing. Double majors. Pass/fail grading option. Internships. Cooperative education programs. Preprofessional programs in law, medicine, veterinary science, pharmacy, dentistry, and optometry. 2-2, 3-2, and 2-1-1 engineering programs with Syracuse U and other engineering schools. Teacher certification in secondary education. Certification in specific subject areas. Study abroad in Belgium, China, England, France, Germany, Israel, Italy, Poland, the former Soviet Republics, and Spain. ROTC. AFROTC at Syracuse U.
**Honors:** Phi Beta Kappa. Honors program.
**Academic Assistance:** Remedial reading, writing, and math. Nonremedial tutoring.

**STUDENT LIFE. Housing:** Students may live on or off campus. Coed dorms. 70% of students live in college housing.
**Social atmosphere:** According to the student newspaper, favorite student gathering spots include Lemons & Limes Lounge, Burrstone House, Spilkas, and the Bearded Dolphin. Greek-letter organizations and sports teams are among the most socially influential groups on campus. Popular campus events include Homecoming and the men's basketball game against Hamilton College.
**Services and counseling/handicapped student services:** Placement services. Health service. Counseling services for minority students. Birth control and personal counseling. Career and academic guidance services. Religious counseling. Physically disabled student services. Learning disabled services. Tape recorders. Tutors.
**Campus organizations:** Undergraduate student government. Student newspaper (Tangerine, published once/week). Literary magazine. Yearbook. Radio station. Chorus, instrumental ensemble, drama group, debating, humanities circle, Amnesty International, academic, cultural, departmental, service, and special-interest groups, 70 organizations in all. Seven fraternities, no chapter houses; six sororities, no chapter houses. 18% of men join a fraternity. 15% of women join a sorority.
**Religious organizations:** Jewish Student Union, Intervarsity Christian Fellowship, Newman Community.
**Minority/foreign student organizations:** Black Student Union. International Student Association, Latin American Student Union.

**ATHLETICS. Physical education requirements:** None.
**Intercollegiate competition:** 16% of students participate. Baseball (M), basketball (M,W), diving (M,W), golf (M,W), soccer (M,W), softball (W), swimming (M,W), tennis (M,W). Member of NCAA Division III.
**Intramural and club sports:** 65% of students participate. Intramural badminton, basketball, billiards, bowling, broomball, flag football, golf, indoor soccer, racquetball, softball, table tennis, volleyball, water polo, walleyball, Wiffle ball. Men's club cheerleading, cross-country, fencing, lacrosse, martial arts, rifle, volleyball. Women's club cheerleading, cross-country, fencing, martial arts, rifle, volleyball.

**ADMISSIONS. Academic basis for candidate selection** (in order of priority): Secondary school record, class rank, essay, school's recommendation, standardized test scores.
**Nonacademic basis for candidate selection:** Character and personality are emphasized. Extracurricular participation is important. Particular talent or ability is considered.
**Requirements:** Graduation from secondary school is required; GED is accepted. 16 units and the following program of study are recommended: 4 units of English, 3 units of math, 3 units of science, 2 units of foreign language, 3 units of social studies. Rank in top two-fifths of secondary school class and minimum 2.5 GPA recommended. HEOP for applicants not normally admissible. SAT is recommended; ACT may be substituted. PSAT is recommended. ACH recommended. Campus visit and interview recommended. Off-campus interviews available with an admissions representative.
**Procedure:** Take SAT or ACT by December of 12th year. Take ACH by December of 12th year. Visit college for interview by January of 12th year. Notification of admission on rolling basis. Reply is required by May 1. $200 nonrefundable tuition deposit. Freshmen accepted for terms other than fall.
**Special programs:** Admission may be deferred one year. Credit and/or placement may be granted through CEEB Advanced Placement exams for scores of 4 or higher. Credit and/or placement may be granted through CLEP general and subject exams. Credit and placement may be granted through military and life experience. Early decision program. Deadline for applying for early decision is December 1.
**Transfer students:** Transfer students accepted for terms other than fall. In fall 1992, 41% of all new students were transfers into all classes. 489 transfer applications were received, 425 were accepted. Application deadline is rolling for fall; rolling for spring. Minimum 2.5 GPA recommended. Lowest course grade accepted is "C." Maximum number of transferable credits is 90 semester hours. At least 30 semester hours must be completed at the college to receive degree.
**Admissions contact:** Dominic P. Passalacqua, M.A., Director of Admissions. 800 782-8884.

**FINANCIAL AID. Available aid:** Pell grants, SEOG, state scholarships and grants, school scholarships and grants, private scholarships and grants, ROTC scholarships, and academic merit scholarships. Perkins Loans (NDSL), PLUS, Stafford Loans (GSL), private loans, and SLS. AMS, Tuition Management Systems, and deferred payment plan.
**Financial aid statistics:** 3% of aid is not need-based. In 1992-93, 88% of all undergraduate applicants received aid; 78% of freshman applicants. Average amounts of aid awarded freshmen: Scholarships and grants, $3,210; loans, $2,414.
**Supporting data/closing dates:** FAFSA/FAF: Priority filing date is March 1. State aid form: Priority filing date is March 1. Income tax forms: Accepted on rolling basis. Notification of awards on rolling basis.
**Financial aid contact:** Elizabeth C. Wilson, Director of Financial Aid. 315 792-3179.

**STUDENT EMPLOYMENT.** College Work/Study Program. Institutional employment. 31% of full-time undergraduates work on campus during school year. Students may expect to earn an average of $1,182 during school year. Off-campus part-time employment opportunities rated "good."

**COMPUTER FACILITIES.** 100 IBM/IBM-compatible and Macintosh/Apple microcomputers. Students may access IBM, Prime minicomputer/mainframe systems. Computer languages and software packages include APL, Assembler, BASIC, COBOL, FORTRAN, Pascal. Computer facilities are available to all students.
**Fees:** None.
**Hours:** 8 AM-midn. (Su-Th); 8 AM-10 PM (F-Sa).

**GRADUATE CAREER DATA.** Graduate school percentages: 4% enter law school. 3% enter medical school. 3% enter dental school. 4% enter graduate business programs. 2% enter graduate arts and sciences programs. Highest graduate school enrollments: Syracuse U. 70% of graduates choose careers in business and industry. Companies and businesses that hire graduates: Big Six accounting firms, Fortune 100 companies.

**PROMINENT ALUMNI/AE.** Sherwood Boehlert, U.S. congressman.

# Vassar College

**Poughkeepsie, NY 12601** **914 437-7000**

**1994-95 Costs.** Tuition: $18,920. Room & board: $5,950. Fees, books, misc. academic expenses (school's estimate): $1,265.
**Enrollment.** Undergraduates: 841 men, 1,323 women (full-time). Freshman class: 3,550 applicants, 1,887 accepted, 651 enrolled.
**Test score averages/ranges.** Average SAT scores: 600 verbal, 630 math. Range of SAT scores of middle 50%: 560-650 verbal, 580-680 math. Average ACT scores: 28 composite. Range of ACT scores of middle 50%: 25-30 composite.
**Faculty.** 202 full-time; 21 part-time. 90% of faculty holds doctoral degree. Student/faculty ratio: 11 to 1.
**Selectivity rating.** Highly competitive.

**PROFILE.** Vassar is a private, liberal arts college. Founded for women in 1861, it adopted coeducation in 1969. Its 1,000-acre campus is located on the outskirts of Poughkeepsie, 75 miles north of New York City. It includes a range of architecture from Gothic to modernist.
**Accreditation:** MSACS.
**Religious orientation:** Vassar College is nonsectarian; no religious requirements.
**Library:** Collections totaling over 716,921 volumes, 3,900 periodical subscriptions, and 350,000 microform items.
**Special facilities/museums:** Art center, theatres, nursery school, environmental field station, geology museum, Russian TV satellite, electron microscope.
**Athletic facilities:** Field house, gymnasium, golf course, swimming pool, racquetball, squash, and tennis courts, track, baseball, field hockey, soccer fields, fitness rooms.

**STUDENT BODY. Undergraduate profile:** 32% are state residents. 9% Asian-American, 6% Black, 6% Hispanic, 76% White, 3% Non-resident alien. Average age of undergraduates is 20.
**Freshman profile:** 7% of freshmen who took SAT scored 700 or over on verbal, 15% scored 700 or over on math; 51% scored 600 or over on verbal, 63% scored 600 or over on math; 93% scored 500 or over on verbal, 94% scored 500 or over on math; 100% scored 400 or over on verbal, 99% scored 400 or over on math; 100% scored 300 or over on math. 80% of accepted applicants took SAT; 20% took ACT. 60% of freshmen come from public schools.
**Undergraduate achievement:** 94% of fall 1992 freshmen returned for fall 1993 term. 80% of entering class graduated. 24% of students who completed a degree program immediately went on to graduate study.
**Foreign students:** 93 students are from out of the country. Countries represented include England, France, Germany, and India; 45 in all.

**PROGRAMS OF STUDY. Degrees:** A.B.
**Majors:** Africana Studies, American Culture, Anthropology, Art, Asian Studies, Astronomy, Biochemistry, Biology, Biopsychology, Chemistry, Cognitive Science Studies, Computer Science, Drama, Economics, English, French, Geography, Geography/Anthropology, Geology, German, Greek, Hispanic Studies, History, International Studies, Italian, Latin, Latin American Studies, Mathematics, Medieval/Renaissance Studies, Music, Philosophy, Physics, Political Science, Psychology, Religion, Russian, Science/Technology/Society, Sociology, Urban Studies, Victorian Studies, Women's Studies.
**Distribution of degrees:** The majors with the highest enrollment are English, psychology, and political science; Victorian studies, Greek, and biochemistry have the lowest.
**Academic regulations:** Minimum 2.0 GPA must be maintained.
**Special:** Independent Program. Self-designed majors. Double majors. Dual degrees. Independent study. Pass/fail grading option. Internships. Graduate school at which undergraduates may take graduate-level courses. Preprofessional programs in law and medicine. Four-year A.B./M.A. program in chemistry. 3-2 engineering program with Dartmouth Coll. Member of Inter-University Consortium for Educational Computing. National Theatre Institute Semester (Connecticut), Washington Semester, Williams-Mystic Seaport Semester (Connecticut), and other off-campus study opportunities. Member of Twelve College Exchange Program. Teacher certification in early childhood, elementary, and secondary education. Exchange programs abroad in England, Germany, Greece, Italy, and Spain. Study abroad also in France, Ireland, and the former Soviet Republics.
**Honors:** Phi Beta Kappa.
**Academic Assistance:** Nonremedial tutoring.

**STUDENT LIFE. Housing:** All freshmen must live on campus; four-year students must spend three years in residence. Coed dorms. School-owned/operated apartments. One women's dormitory. Cooperative housing for 29 upperclass students. 98% of students live in college housing.
**Social atmosphere:** The student newspaper reports, "Social life centers on the Vassar campus. Not very many big parties, rather emphasis on small, intimate things and some all-campus events, formals in fall and spring." The most popular campus events include Winter Weekend, "a two-day festival celebrating student spirit during winter," and Founder's Day, "a celebration of the founding and founder of Vassar College, traditionally held in the spring with old-fashioned carnival spirit." Peter's Place is a favorite gathering spot.
**Services and counseling/handicapped student services:** Placement services. Health service. Counseling services for minority and older students. Birth control, personal, and psychological counseling. Career and academic guidance services. Physically disabled student services. Learning disabled services. Tutors.
**Campus organizations:** Undergraduate student government. Student newspaper (Miscellany News, published once/week). Literary magazine. Yearbook. Radio station. Choir, mixed chorus, madrigal group, informal singing groups, band, orchestra, experimental

film society, dance and drama groups, Student Entertainment Committee, community service projects, tutoring for local school children, 85 organizations in all.
**Religious organizations:** Christian Fellowship, Interfaith Council, Jewish Student Union, Catholic and Episcopal groups.
**Minority/foreign student organizations:** Black Student Union, A.S.A., Poder Latino, Black Commencement Committee, Ebony Theatre. International Student Association.

**ATHLETICS. Physical education requirements:** None.
**Intercollegiate competition:** 20% of students participate. Baseball (M), basketball (M,W), cross-country (M,W), fencing (M,W), field hockey (W), lacrosse (M,W), soccer (M,W), squash (M,W), swimming (M,W), tennis (M,W), volleyball (M,W). Member of ECAC, NCAA Division III, NYSWCAA, Seven Sisters Athletic Conference.
**Intramural and club sports:** 45% of students participate. Intramural basketball, cycling, equestrian sports, floor hockey, football, racquetball, sailing, soccer, softball, squash, ultimate frisbee, volleyball. Men's club crew, rugby. Women's club crew, rugby.

**ADMISSIONS. Academic basis for candidate selection** (in order of priority): Secondary school record, essay, standardized test scores, class rank, school's recommendation.
**Nonacademic basis for candidate selection:** Extracurricular participation and particular talent or ability are emphasized. Character and personality are important. Geographical distribution is considered.
**Requirements:** Graduation from secondary school is required; GED is accepted. No specific distribution of secondary school units required. Audio tape and portfolio recommended of music and art program applicants. SAT is required; ACT may be substituted. ACH required. Campus visit and interview recommended. Off-campus interviews available with admissions and alumni representatives.
**Procedure:** Take SAT or ACT by December of 12th year. Take ACH by December of 12th year. Visit college for interview by February 1 of 12th year. Suggest filing application by fall. Application deadline is January 15. Acceptance notification by early April. Reply is required by May 1. $500 nonrefundable tuition deposit. Freshmen accepted for fall terms only.
**Special programs:** Admission may be deferred one year. Credit may be granted through CEEB Advanced Placement for scores of 4 or higher. Credit may be granted through CLEP subject exams. Early decision program. In fall 1993, 354 applied for early decision and 177 were accepted. Deadline for applying for early decision is January 15. Early entrance/early admission program.
**Transfer students:** Transfer students accepted for terms other than fall. In fall 1993, 247 transfer applications were received, 49 were accepted. Application deadline is March 1 for fall; November 15 for spring. Minimum 3.0 GPA. Lowest course grade accepted is "C." Maximum number of transferable credits is 17 units (one unit equals 3.53 semester hours). At least 17 units must be completed at the college to receive degree.
**Admissions contact:** Thomas Matos, Director of Admissions. 914 437-7300.

**FINANCIAL AID. Available aid:** Pell grants, SEOG, state scholarships and grants, school scholarships, private scholarships and grants, and aid for undergraduate foreign students. Perkins Loans (NDSL), PLUS, Stafford Loans (GSL), school loans, and SLS. Tuition Plan Inc., Knight Tuition Plans, and AMS. EXCEL Parent Loan. Vassar Parent Loan.
**Financial aid statistics:** In 1993-94, 94% of all undergraduate applicants received aid; 83% of freshman applicants. Average amounts of aid awarded freshmen: Scholarships and grants, $14,430; loans, $2,508.
**Supporting data/closing dates:** FAFSA: Deadline is February 1. School's own aid application: Deadline is January 1. Income tax forms: Deadline is January 1. Notification of awards begins in early April.
**Financial aid contact:** Michael P. Fraher, Director of Financial Aid. 914 437-5320.

**STUDENT EMPLOYMENT.** College Work/Study Program. 58% of full-time undergraduates work on campus during school year. Students may expect to earn an average of $950 during school year. Off-campus part-time employment opportunities rated "fair."

**COMPUTER FACILITIES.** 30 IBM/IBM-compatible and Macintosh/Apple microcomputers. Students may access Digital minicomputer/mainframe systems. Residence halls may be equipped with stand-alone microcomputers, networked microcomputers. Numerous computer languages and software packages available. Computer facilities are available to all students.
**Fees:** None.
**Hours:** 24 hours.

**GRADUATE CAREER DATA.** Graduate school percentages: 9% enter law school. 5% enter medical school. 3% enter graduate business programs. 13% enter graduate arts and sciences programs. Highest graduate school enrollments: Harvard U, Johns Hopkins U, New York U, Stanford U, Yale U. 17% of graduates choose careers in business and industry. Companies and businesses that hire graduates: Prudential-Bache, Marine Midland Bank, IBM.

**PROMINENT ALUMNI/AE.** Meryl Streep, actress; Edna St. Vincent Millay, poet; Mary McCarthy and Elizabeth Bishop, authors; Dr. Mary Calderone, Planned Parenthood; Vera Cooper Rubin, astronomer.

# Wagner College

**Staten Island, NY 10301 — 718 390-3100**

**1994-95 Costs.** Tuition: $13,500. Room & board: $5,800. Fees, books, misc. academic expenses (school's estimate): $500.
**Enrollment.** Undergraduates: 582 men, 742 women (full-time). Freshman class: 1,416 applicants, 1,015 accepted, 416 enrolled. Graduate enrollment: 99 men, 203 women.
**Test score averages/ranges.** Average SAT scores: 480 verbal, 510 math. Range of SAT scores of middle 50%: 430-540 verbal, 450-560 math.
**Faculty.** 76 full-time; 101 part-time. 85% of faculty holds highest degree in specific field. Student/faculty ratio: 12 to 1.
**Selectivity rating.** Less competitive.

**PROFILE.** Wagner, founded in 1883, is a non-sectarian liberal arts college. Its 86-acre campus is located on Staten Island.
**Accreditation:** MSACS. Professionally accredited by the National League for Nursing.
**Religious orientation:** Wagner College is nonsectarian; no religious requirements.
**Library:** Collections totaling over 300,000 volumes, 1,000 periodical subscriptions, and 22,500 microform items.
**Special facilities/museums:** Art gallery, on-campus nursery school, early childhood center, nursing resource center, planetarium, two electron microscopes, solar energy project.
**Athletic facilities:** Gymnasium, weight and wrestling rooms, basketball, squash, and tennis courts, baseball and football fields, fitness center.

**STUDENT BODY. Undergraduate profile:** 65% are state residents; 18% are transfers. 1% Asian-American, 5% Black, 2% Hispanic, 87% White, 5% Other. Average age of undergraduates is 20.
**Freshman profile:** 1% of freshmen who took SAT scored 700 or over on verbal, 3% scored 700 or over on math; 10% scored 600 or over on verbal, 15% scored 600 or over on math; 47% scored 500 or over on verbal, 62% scored 500 or over on math; 81% scored 400 or over on verbal, 90% scored 400 or over on math; 99% scored 300 or over on verbal, 98% scored 300 or over on math. 96% of accepted applicants took SAT; 4% took ACT. 63% of freshmen come from public schools.
**Undergraduate achievement:** 84% of fall 1992 freshmen returned for fall 1993 term. 62% of entering class graduated. 10% of students who completed a degree program immediately went on to graduate study.
**Foreign students:** 70 students are from out of the country. Countries represented include Greece, India, Japan, Korea, Taiwan, and Thailand; 27 in all.

**PROGRAMS OF STUDY. Degrees:** B.A., B.S., B.S.Ed.
**Majors:** Accounting, Art, Arts Administration, Biology, Chemistry, Computer, Economics/Business Administration, Education, English, Gerontology, History, Mathematics, Medical Technology, Microbiology, Music, Nursing, Physician Assistant, Physics, Political Science, Psychology, Sociology/Anthropology, Theatre/Speech.
**Distribution of degrees:** The majors with the highest enrollment are economics/business administration, education, and nursing; chemistry, physics, and medical technology have the lowest.
**Requirements:** General education requirement.
**Academic regulations:** Minimum 2.0 GPA must be maintained.
**Special:** Minors offered in all majors and in criminal justice, family studies, foreign languages, global studies, philosophy, public administration, religious studies, and social work. Double majors. Independent study. Pass/fail grading option. Internships. Graduate school at which undergraduates may take graduate-level courses. Preprofessional programs in law, medicine, veterinary science, pharmacy, dentistry, optometry, chiropractic, and engineering. 3-2 occupational therapy and speech pathology programs with New York U. 3-4 dentistry program with New York U. Exchange program with California Lutheran Coll. Teacher certification in elementary, secondary, and special education. Study abroad through Institute for Asian and European Studies. ROTC at St. John's U. AFROTC at Rutgers U and Stevens Inst of Tech.
**Honors:** Honors program. Honor societies.
**Academic Assistance:** Remedial reading, writing, math, and study skills. Nonremedial tutoring.

**STUDENT LIFE. Housing:** Students may live on or off campus. Coed dorms. 65% of students live in college housing.
**Social atmosphere:** "Wagner is just a ferry ride away from Manhattan, which has an abundance of social and cultural hot spots," writes the editor of the student newspaper. "Wagner also has, on campus, many events sponsored by different student organizations that give students a wide variety of social and cultural experiences." On and around campus students gather in residence hall lounges, fraternity and sorority lounges, the Hawk's Nest and the Union Plaza. Homecoming, the Songfest, the annual Halloween Party and football games are among some favorite campus events.
**Services and counseling/handicapped student services:** Placement services. Health service. Personal and psychological counseling. Career and academic guidance services. Religious counseling. Physically disabled student services. Learning disabled services. Notetaking services. Tape recorders. Tutors. Reader services for the blind.
**Campus organizations:** Undergraduate student government. Student newspaper (Wagnerian, published once/month). Literary magazine. Yearbook. Radio station. Choir, community orchestra, concert and jazz bands, music society, theatre, Associated Women Students, academic groups, Circle K, Big Brothers, Residence Hall Council, 65 organizations in all. Eight fraternities, no chapter houses; five sororities, no chapter houses. 20% of men join a fraternity. 15% of women join a sorority.
**Religious organizations:** Lutheran Student Association, Newman Club, Christian Fellowship, Hillel.
**Minority/foreign student organizations:** Black Concern. International Student Association, Chinese and Korean groups.

**ATHLETICS. Physical education requirements:** None.
**Intercollegiate competition:** 45% of students participate. Baseball (M), basketball (M,W), cheerleading (M,W), cross-country (M,W), football (M), golf (M), soccer (W), softball (W), tennis (M,W), track (indoor) (M,W), track (outdoor) (M,W), track and field (indoor) (M,W), track and field (outdoor) (M,W), volleyball (W), wrestling (M). Member of ECAC, NCAA Division I, NCAA Division I-AA for football, New England Conference, Northeast Conference.
**Intramural and club sports:** 65% of students participate. Intramural basketball, floor hockey, soccer, softball, touch football, volleyball. Men's club hockey, lacrosse. Women's club cheerleading.

**ADMISSIONS. Academic basis for candidate selection** (in order of priority): Secondary school record, standardized test scores, class rank, school's recommendation, essay.
**Nonacademic basis for candidate selection:** Extracurricular participation and particular talent or ability are emphasized. Character and personality are important. Geographical distribution and alumni/ae relationship are considered.
**Requirements:** Graduation from secondary school is required; GED is accepted. 16 units and the following program of study are required: 4 units of English, 2 units of math, 2 units of science including 1 unit of lab, 2 units of foreign language, 2 units of social studies, 4 units of electives including 3 units of academic electives. Minimum combined SAT score of 900, rank in top half of secondary school class, and minimum "B-" average recommended. Audition required of music and theatre program applicants. Freshman Intensive

Study Program for applicants not normally admissible. SAT is required; ACT may be substituted. Campus visit and interview recommended. No off-campus interviews.
**Procedure:** Take SAT or ACT by December of 12th year. Visit college for interview by February of 12th year. Suggest filing application by February 15. Notification of admission by March 1. Reply is required by May 1. $300 tuition deposit, refundable until May 1. $300 nonrefundable room deposit. Freshmen accepted for terms other than fall.
**Special programs:** Admission may be deferred one year. Credit and/or placement may be granted through CEEB Advanced Placement exams for scores of 4 or higher. Credit and/or placement may be granted through CLEP general and subject exams. Credit may be granted through life experience. Credit and placement may be granted through Regents College, DANTES, and challenge exams and military experience. Early decision program. In fall 1993, 70 applied for early decision and 42 were accepted. Deadline for applying for early decision is December 15. Early entrance/early admission program. Concurrent enrollment program.
**Transfer students:** Transfer students accepted for terms other than fall. In fall 1993, 18% of all new students were transfers into all classes. 232 transfer applications were received, 179 were accepted. Application deadline is July 15 for fall; December 15 for spring. Minimum 2.0 GPA required. Lowest course grade accepted is "C-." Maximum number of transferable credits is 64 semester hours from a two-year school and 90 semester hours from a four-year school. At least 30 semester hours must be completed at the college to receive degree.
**Admissions contact:** Joseph Foulke, M.A., Dean of Admissions and Financial Aid. 718 390-3411.

**FINANCIAL AID. Available aid:** Pell grants, SEOG, state scholarships and grants, school scholarships and grants, private scholarships and grants, ROTC scholarships, academic merit scholarships, and athletic scholarships. Perkins Loans (NDSL), PLUS, Stafford Loans (GSL), NSL, and SLS. AMS and family tuition reduction.
**Financial aid statistics:** 30% of aid is not need-based. In 1993-94, 95% of all undergraduate applicants received aid; 95% of freshman applicants. Average amounts of aid awarded freshmen: Scholarships and grants, $4,000; loans, $2,500.
**Supporting data/closing dates:** FAFSA/FAF/FFS: Priority filing date is April 1. School's own aid application: Priority filing date is April 1. Notification of awards on rolling basis.
**Financial aid contact:** Joseph Foulke, M.A., Dean of Admissions and Financial Aid. 718 390-3183.

**STUDENT EMPLOYMENT.** College Work/Study Program. Institutional employment. 30% of full-time undergraduates work on campus during school year. Students may expect to earn an average of $1,100 during school year. Off-campus part-time employment opportunities rated "good."

**COMPUTER FACILITIES.** 75 IBM/IBM-compatible and Macintosh/Apple microcomputers; all are networked. Students may access Digital minicomputer/mainframe systems, BITNET. Client/LAN operating systems include Apple/Macintosh, DOS, Windows NT, DEC. Computer languages and software packages include Ada, ALGOL, BASIC, COBOL, dBASE, FORTRAN, LISP, Lotus 1-2-3, PL/1, SNOBOL, VAX BASIC, WordPerfect. Computer facilities are available to all students.
**Fees:** Computer fee is included in tuition/fees.
**Hours:** 9 AM-10 PM (microcomputers); 7 AM-11 PM (mainframe).

**GRADUATE CAREER DATA.** Graduate school percentages: 3% enter law school. 4% enter medical school. 3% enter dental school. 15% enter graduate business programs. Highest graduate school enrollments: New York U, St. John's U, Wagner Coll. 35% of graduates choose careers in business and industry. Companies and businesses that hire graduates: AT&T, Merrill Lynch, Price Waterhouse.

**PROMINENT ALUMNI/AE.** Richard Kotite, head coach, Philadelphia Eagles; Donald Spiro, CEO, Oppenheimer Fund; Robert Loggia, actor; Guy Molinari, former U.S. congressman and Staten Island borough president; Randy Graff, Tony Award winner, *City of Angels*.

## Webb Institute of Naval Architecture

**Glen Cove, NY 11542** **516 671-2213**

**1993-94 Costs.** Tuition: None. Room & board: $4,800. Fees, books, misc. academic expenses (school's estimate): $700.
**Enrollment.** Undergraduates: 64 men, 18 women (full-time). Freshman class: 88 applicants, 29 accepted, 23 enrolled.
**Test score averages/ranges.** Average SAT scores: 600 verbal, 710 math. Range of SAT scores of middle 50%: 570-640 verbal, 680-740 math.
**Faculty.** 9 full-time; 5 part-time. 50% of faculty holds doctoral degree. Student/faculty ratio: 5 to 1.
**Selectivity rating.** Most competitive.

**PROFILE.** Webb is a private institute of naval architecture and marine engineering. Founded in 1889, it adopted coeducation in 1974. Its 26-acre campus is located in Glen Cove, on the north shore of Long Island, 22 miles from New York City.

**Accreditation:** MSACS. Professionally accredited by the Accreditation Board for Engineering and Technology.
**Religious orientation:** Webb Institute of Naval Architecture is nonsectarian; no religious requirements.
**Library:** Collections totaling over 42,514 volumes, 196 periodical subscriptions, and 1,137 microform items.
**Special facilities/museums:** Towing tank for model testing, marine engineering lab.
**Athletic facilities:** Gymnasium, locker and weight rooms, practice, soccer, and softball fields, tennis courts, nautilus, boat house, yacht club.

**STUDENT BODY. Undergraduate profile:** 26% are state residents. 6% Asian-American, 1% Black, 2% Hispanic, 91% White. Average age of undergraduates is 20.
**Freshman profile:** 4% of freshmen who took SAT scored 700 or over on verbal, 57% scored 700 or over on math; 61% scored 600 or over on verbal, 100% scored 600 or over on math; 91% scored 500 or over on verbal; 100% scored 400 or over on verbal. 100% of accepted applicants took SAT. 83% of freshmen come from public schools.
**Undergraduate achievement:** 76% of fall 1991 freshmen returned for fall 1992 term. 67% of entering class graduated.

**PROGRAMS OF STUDY. Degrees:** B.S.
**Majors:** Naval Architecture/Marine Engineering.
**Requirements:** General education requirement.
**Academic regulations:** Minimum 2.5 GPA must be maintained.
**Special:** Double majors. Internships.

**STUDENT LIFE. Housing:** All students must live on campus. Women's and men's dorms.
**Services and counseling/handicapped student services:** Placement services. Personal counseling. Academic guidance services.
**Campus organizations:** Undergraduate student government. Yearbook.

**ATHLETICS. Physical education requirements:** None.
**Intercollegiate competition:** 80% of students participate. Basketball (M), cheerleading (W), sailing (M,W), soccer (M), tennis (M,W), ultimate frisbee (M), volleyball (M,W). Member of Independent.
**Intramural and club sports:** 90% of students participate. Intramural basketball, billiards, floor hockey, soccer, softball, table tennis, tennis, ultimate frisbee, volleyball, windsurfing.

**ADMISSIONS. Academic basis for candidate selection** (in order of priority): Secondary school record, class rank, standardized test scores, school's recommendation.
**Nonacademic basis for candidate selection:** Character and personality, extracurricular participation, and particular talent or ability are important.
**Requirements:** Graduation from secondary school is required; GED is not accepted. 16 units and the following program of study are required: 4 units of English, 4 units of math, 2 units of lab science, 1 unit of foreign language, 2 units of social studies, 3 units of electives. Rank in top tenth of secondary school class and 85 average in math, physics, and chemistry required. Mechanical drawing and computer education recommended. SAT is required. ACH required. Campus visit and interview required. No off-campus interviews.
**Procedure:** Take SAT by December 30 of 12th year. Visit college for interview by December 30 of 12th year. Suggest filing application by October 15. Application deadline is February 15. Acceptance notification from March 1 to April 30. Reply is required within 10 days of acceptance. $150 nonrefundable room deposit. Freshmen accepted for fall terms only.
**Special programs:** Early decision program. In fall 1992, 4 applied for early decision and 1 was accepted. Deadline for applying for early decision is October 15.
**Transfer students:** Transfer students accepted for fall term only. In fall 1992, 3 transfer applications were received. Application deadline is February 15. Minimum 3.2 GPA required. Lowest course grade accepted is "B." At least 140 semester hours must be completed at the institute to receive degree.
**Admissions contact:** William G. Murray, M.S., Director of Admissions and Financial Aid.

**FINANCIAL AID. Available aid:** Pell grants, state scholarships, school grants, private scholarships, and academic merit scholarships. PLUS and Stafford Loans (GSL).
**Financial aid statistics:** In 1992-93, 15% of all undergraduate applicants received aid; 9% of freshman applicants. Average amounts of aid awarded freshmen: Scholarships and grants, $1,300; loans, $3,800.
**Supporting data/closing dates:** FAFSA/FAF: Deadline is July 1. Notification of awards on rolling basis.
**Financial aid contact:** William G. Murray, M.S., Director of Admissions and Financial Aid. 516 671-2213.

**STUDENT EMPLOYMENT.** College Work/Study Program. Freshmen are discouraged from working during their first term.

**COMPUTER FACILITIES.** 18 IBM/IBM-compatible microcomputers. Residence halls may be equipped with stand-alone microcomputers. Computer languages and software packages include BASIC, C, FORTRAN, Pascal. Computer facilities are available to all students.
**Fees:** None.
**Hours:** 24 hours.

**GRADUATE CAREER DATA.** Highest graduate school enrollments: MIT, U of California at Berkeley, U of Maryland, U of Michigan. 100% of graduates choose careers in business and industry. Companies and businesses that hire graduates: Marine transportation companies, yacht designers, naval design and research firms.

## Wells College

**Aurora, NY 13026** **315 364-3278**

**1994-95 Costs.** Tuition: $14,900. Room & board: $5,550. Fees, books, misc. academic expenses (school's estimate): $960.
**Enrollment.** 396 women (full-time). Freshman class: 318 applicants, 235 accepted, 130 enrolled. Graduate enrollment: 415 women.
**Test score averages/ranges.** Average SAT scores: 540 verbal, 540 math. Range of SAT scores of middle 50%: 490-600 verbal, 490-590 math. Average ACT scores: 24 composite. Range of ACT scores of middle 50%: 22-27 composite.
**Faculty.** 48 full-time; 10 part-time. 96% of faculty holds highest degree in specific field. Student/faculty ratio: 8 to 1.
**Selectivity rating.** Competitive.

PROFILE. Wells, founded in 1868, is a private, liberal arts college for women. Its 360-acre campus is located in Aurora, in central New York's Finger Lake region, 40 miles southwest of Syracuse.

**Accreditation:** MSACS.
**Religious orientation:** Wells College is nonsectarian; no religious requirements.
**Library:** Collections totaling over 233,000 volumes and 664 periodical subscriptions.
**Athletic facilities:** Swimming pool, gymnasium, basketball, platform tennis, and tennis courts, weight room, athletic fields, golf course, boathouse.

STUDENT BODY. **Undergraduate profile:** 60% are state residents; 19% are transfers. 7% Asian-American, 5% Black, 3% Hispanic, 1% Native American, 83% White, 1% Other. Average age of undergraduates is 19.
**Freshman profile:** 1% of freshmen who took SAT scored 700 or over on verbal; 21% scored 600 or over on verbal, 13% scored 600 or over on math; 53% scored 500 or over on verbal, 58% scored 500 or over on math; 89% scored 400 or over on verbal, 91% scored 400 or over on math; 100% scored 300 or over on verbal, 100% scored 300 or over on math. 7% of freshmen who took ACT scored 30 or over on composite; 44% scored 24 or over on composite; 100% scored 18 or over on composite. 83% of accepted applicants took SAT; 35% took ACT. 86% of freshmen come from public schools.
**Undergraduate achievement:** 75% of fall 1992 freshmen returned for fall 1993 term. 64% of entering class graduated. 25% of students who completed a degree program immediately went on to graduate study.
**Foreign students:** Six students are from out of the country. Countries represented include France and Japan.

PROGRAMS OF STUDY. **Degrees:** B.A.
**Majors:** American Studies, Economics/Management, English, Environmental Policy/Science/Values, Foreign Languages/Literatures/Cultures, History, International Studies, Mathematics/Physical Science, Psychology, Public Affairs, Religious Studies/Human Values, Sociology, Visual Arts, Women's Studies.
**Distribution of degrees:** The majors with the highest enrollment are psychology and English; math/physics and religious studies/human values have the lowest.
**Requirements:** General education requirement.
**Academic regulations:** Minimum 2.0 GPA must be maintained.
**Special:** Minors offered in most majors and in several other fields. Self-designed majors. Dual degrees. Independent study. Pass/fail grading option. Internships. Preprofessional programs in law, medicine, veterinary science, and dentistry. 3-2 engineering programs with Clarkson U, Columbia U, Cornell U, Texas A&M U, and Washington U. 3-2 B.A./M.B.A. program with U of Rochester. 3-2 B.A./M.S. community health program with U of Rochester. Washington Semester. Exchange program with Cornell U. Teacher certification in elementary and secondary education. Certification in specific subject areas. Study abroad in Denmark, England, France, Germany, Italy, Mexico, Scotland, Senegal, and Spain. ROTC at Cornell U.
**Honors:** Phi Beta Kappa.
**Academic Assistance:** Remedial writing and math. Nonremedial tutoring.

ADMISSIONS. **Academic basis for candidate selection** (in order of priority): Secondary school record, class rank, school's recommendation, essay, standardized test scores.
**Nonacademic basis for candidate selection:** Character and personality and extracurricular participation are emphasized. Particular talent or ability and alumni/ae relationship are considered.
**Requirements:** Graduation from secondary school is required; GED is not accepted. 16 units and the following program of study are required: 4 units of English, 3 units of math, 3 units of science including 2 units of lab, 4 units of social studies, 4 units of electives. Minimum "C+" average in college prep curriculum and rank in top half of secondary school class required; rank in top fifth recommended. Standardized tests considered on sliding scale depending on GPA and rigor of secondary school curriculum and preparation. SAT or ACT is required. Campus visit and interview recommended. Off-campus interviews available with admissions and alumni representatives.
**Procedure:** Take SAT or ACT by December of 12th year. Visit college for interview by February 15 of 12th year. Suggest filing application by January 15. Application deadline is March 1. Notification of admission by April 1. Reply is required by May 1. $300 nonrefundable tuition deposit. Freshmen accepted for fall terms only.
**Special programs:** Admission may be deferred one year. Credit and/or placement may be granted through CEEB Advanced Placement exams for scores of 4 or higher. Credit may be granted through life experience. Placement may be granted through challenge exams. Early decision program. In fall 1993, 40 applied for early decision and 35 were accepted. Deadline for applying for early decision is December 15. Early entrance/early admission program. Concurrent enrollment program.
**Transfer students:** Transfer students accepted for terms other than fall. In fall 1993, 19% of all new students were transfers into all classes. 55 transfer applications were received, 45 were accepted. Application deadline is July 15 for fall; January 1 for spring. Minimum 2.5 GPA required. Lowest course grade accepted is "C-." Maximum number of transferable credits is 60 semester hours. At least 60 semester hours must be completed at the college to receive degree.
**Admissions contact:** Mary Ann Kalbaugh, Dean of Admissions. 315 364-3264, 800 952-9355.

FINANCIAL AID. **Available aid:** Pell grants, SEOG, state scholarships and grants, school scholarships and grants, private scholarships, academic merit scholarships, and aid for undergraduate foreign students. PLUS, Stafford-Loans (GSL), school loans, and SLS. Knight Tuition Plans, AMS, and guaranteed tuition. College Payment Plan.
**Financial aid statistics:** In 1993-94, 89% of all undergraduate applicants received aid; 92% of freshman applicants. Average amounts of aid awarded freshmen: Scholarships and grants, $9,935; loans, $2,500.
**Supporting data/closing dates:** FAFSA/FAF: Priority filing date is February 15; deadline is May 1. Notification of awards begins December 1.
**Financial aid contact:** Cathleen Bellomo, M.S., Director of Financial Aid. 315 364-3289.

# Yeshiva University

**New York, NY 10033-3201 — 212 960-5400**

**1993-94 Costs.** Tuition: $12,100. Room: $2,780. Board: $3,150. Fees, books, misc. academic expenses (school's estimate): $800.
**Enrollment.** Undergraduates: 1,029 men, 919 women (full-time). Freshman class: 1,333 applicants, 1,104 accepted, 711 enrolled. Graduate enrollment: 1,374 men, 1,625 women.
**Test score averages/ranges.** Average SAT scores: 559 verbal, 629 math.
**Faculty.** 120 full-time; 114 part-time. 67% of faculty holds highest degree in specific field. Student/faculty ratio: 8 to 1.
**Selectivity rating.** More competitive.

PROFILE. Yeshiva, founded in 1886, is a private, comprehensive university. Programs are offered through the Colleges of Hebraic Studies and Medicine; Graduate Division of Medical Sciences; Graduate Institute of Jewish Education and Administration; Graduate School; Graduate School of Psychology; Institute for Advanced Biomedical Studies; Schools of Business, General Jewish Studies, Law, and Social Work; Stern College for Women; Yeshiva College; and Yeshiva Program/School of Talmudic Studies. Its facilities are located at three centers in Manhattan and one in the Bronx.

**Accreditation:** MSACS.
**Religious orientation:** Yeshiva University is nonsectarian; no religious requirements.
**Library:** Collections totaling over 977,217 volumes, 6,471 periodical subscriptions, and 919,952 microform items.
**Special facilities/museums:** Archives and rare book collection, museum of Jewish art, architecture, history, and culture, writing center.
**Athletic facilities:** Gymnasium, swimming pool, exercise rooms, fencing and wrestling areas, track.

STUDENT BODY. **Undergraduate profile:** 57% are state residents. Average age of undergraduates is 19.
**Freshman profile:** 10% of freshmen who took SAT scored 700 or over on verbal, 25% scored 700 or over on math; 35% scored 600 or over on verbal, 65% scored 600 or over on math; 74% scored 500 or over on verbal, 94% scored 500 or over on math; 96% scored 400 or over on verbal, 100% scored 400 or over on math; 100% scored 300 or over on verbal. 96% of accepted applicants took SAT; 4% took ACT. 5% of freshmen come from public schools.
**Undergraduate achievement:** 80% of fall 1992 freshmen returned for fall 1993 term. 45% of entering class graduated. 80% of students who completed a degree program went on to graduate study within five years.
**Foreign students:** 104 students are from out of the country. Countries represented include Australia, Canada, Iran, Israel, Russia, and Syria; 31 in all.

PROGRAMS OF STUDY. **Degrees:** B.A., B.S.
**Majors:** Accounting, Biology, Chemistry, Classical Languages/Greek/Latin, Communications, Computer Science, Economics, Education, English, Finance, French, Hebrew, History, Jewish Education, Jewish Studies, Management, Management Information Systems, Marketing, Mathematics, Music, Philosophy, Physics, Political Science, Pre-Engineering, Pre-Health Sciences, Pre-Law, Psychology, Sociology, Speech/Communication Disorders, Speech/Drama.
**Distribution of degrees:** The majors with the highest enrollment are psychology, economics, and accounting; music, classical languages, and physics have the lowest.
**Requirements:** General education requirement.
**Academic regulations:** Minimum 2.0 GPA must be maintained.
**Special:** Minors offered in most majors and in art. Courses and tracks offered in American studies, Arabic, business, Japanese, library science, physical education, Russian, Spanish, statistics, and Yiddish. All students take courses in Jewish studies. Associate's degrees offered. Self-designed majors. Double majors. Dual degrees. Independent study. Pass/fail grading option. Internships. Graduate school at which undergraduates may take graduate-level courses. Preprofessional programs in law, medicine, dentistry, engineering, nursing, occupational therapy, and podiatry. 3-2 and 4-2 engineering programs with Columbia U. 3-2 nursing program with New York U. 3-2 occupational therapy programs with Columbia U and New York U. 3-4 podiatry program with New York Coll of Podiatric Medicine. Stern Coll students may take courses in advertising, photography, and design at Fashion Inst of Tech. Teacher certification in elementary education. Study abroad in Israel.
**Honors:** Honors program. Honor societies.

STUDENT LIFE. **Housing:** All students must live on campus unless living with family. Women's and men's dorms. 85% of students live in college housing.
**Social atmosphere:** Favorite student haunts include Beit Midrash, Time-Out Pizza, Deli-Kasbah, Yum Yum Shoppe, and the MSAC. The YCDS and The Commentator have a considerable influence on campus social life. Popular events of the school year include the Chanuka concert, the MACS game, and Purim Chagigas.
**Services and counseling/handicapped student services:** Placement services. Health service. Personal and psychological counseling. Career and academic guidance services.
**Campus organizations:** Undergraduate student government. Student newspaper (Commentator, published once/two weeks). Yearbook. Radio station. Community volunteer work, debating, drama group, departmental, philanthropic, political, professional, and special-interest groups.
**Minority/foreign student organizations:** Club Canada, Russian Club.

ATHLETICS. **Physical education requirements:** Two semesters of physical education required.
**Intercollegiate competition:** 20% of students participate. Basketball (M), cross-country (M), fencing (M), golf (M), tennis (M), volleyball (M), wrestling (M). Member of ECAC, Independent Athletic Conference, NCAA Division III.

**Intramural and club sports:** 50% of students participate. Intramural basketball, floor hockey, foosball, indoor track, swimming, table tennis, weight lifting, wrestling. Women's club basketball.

**ADMISSIONS. Academic basis for candidate selection** (in order of priority): Secondary school record, standardized test scores, school's recommendation, essay, class rank. **Nonacademic basis for candidate selection:** Character and personality are important. Extracurricular participation, particular talent or ability, and alumni/ae relationship are considered.

**Requirements:** Graduation from secondary school is required; GED is accepted. 16 units and the following program of study are required: 4 units of English, 2 units of math, 2 units of science, 2 units of foreign language, 2 units of history, 4 units of academic electives. Minimum SAT scores of 550 in both verbal and math and minimum 3.3 GPA required. SAT or ACT is required. ACH recommended. Campus visit recommended. Off-campus interviews available with admissions and alumni representatives.

**Procedure:** Take SAT or ACT by November of 12th year. Application deadline is February 15. Notification of admission on rolling basis. Reply is required by May 1. $150 nonrefundable tuition deposit. $20 nonrefundable room deposit. Freshmen accepted for terms other than fall.

**Special programs:** Admission may be deferred one year. Credit and/or placement may be granted through CEEB Advanced Placement exams for scores of 4 or higher. Credit and/or placement may be granted through CLEP subject exams. Credit may be granted through military experience. Early entrance/early admission program.

**Transfer students:** Transfer students accepted for terms other than fall. Application deadline is February 15 for fall; rolling for spring. Minimum 3.0 GPA required. Lowest course grade accepted is "C." Maximum number of transferable semester hours is 22 per semester or 43 per year. At least four full-time semesters must be completed at the university to receive degree.

**Admissions contact:** Michael Kranzler, Associate Director of Admissions. 212 960-5277.

**FINANCIAL AID. Available aid:** Pell grants, SEOG, state scholarships and grants, school scholarships and grants, private scholarships and grants, and academic merit scholarships. Perkins Loans (NDSL), PLUS, Stafford Loans (GSL), state loans, school loans, and SLS. America's Tuition Assistance Corporation (ATAC).

**Financial aid statistics:** 2% of aid is not need-based. In 1993-94, 75% of all undergraduate applicants received aid; 75% of freshman applicants. Average amounts of aid awarded freshmen: Scholarships and grants, $3,343; loans, $1,500.

**Supporting data/closing dates:** FAFSA: Priority filing date is April 15. School's own aid application: Priority filing date is April 15; accepted on rolling basis. State aid form: Priority filing date is April 15; accepted on rolling basis. Income tax forms: Priority filing date is April 15; accepted on rolling basis. Notification of awards on rolling basis.

**Financial aid contact:** Jack Nussbaum, M.P.A., Director of Student Finances. 212 960-5269.

**STUDENT EMPLOYMENT.** College Work/Study Program. 35% of full-time undergraduates work on campus during school year. Students may expect to earn an average of $500 during school year. Freshmen are discouraged from working during their first term. Off-campus part-time employment opportunities rated "good."

**COMPUTER FACILITIES.** 125 IBM/IBM-compatible and RISC-/UNIX-based microcomputers; 109 are networked. Students may access IBM minicomputer/mainframe systems, Internet. Client/LAN operating systems include DOS, OS/2, UNIX/XENIX/AIX, X-windows, Microsoft. Computer languages and software packages include C, C++, dBASE, FORTRAN, LISP, Lotus 1-2-3, Pascal, Prolog, SPSS, WordPerfect, WordStar; chemistry and biology modeling and tutorials; 126 in all. Computer facilities are available to all students.

**Fees:** $50 computer fee per course; no charge for general use.

**Hours:** 24 hours via modem. Other hours vary.

**GRADUATE CAREER DATA.** Graduate school percentages: 12% enter law school. 9% enter medical school. 6% enter dental school. 8% enter graduate business programs. 18% enter graduate arts and sciences programs. 4% enter theological school/seminary. Highest graduate school enrollments: Columbia U, New York U, Yeshiva U (Albert Einstein Coll of Medicine, Benjamin N. Cardozo Sch of Law). 15% of graduates choose careers in business and industry. Companies and businesses that hire graduates: Big Six accounting firms.

**PROMINENT ALUMNI/AE.** Dr. Morton R. Axelrod, chief of oncology, Bronx-Lebanon Hospital; Chaim Potok, novelist; Jerome Hornblass, New York State supreme court justice; Nathan Lewin, attorney.

# North Carolina

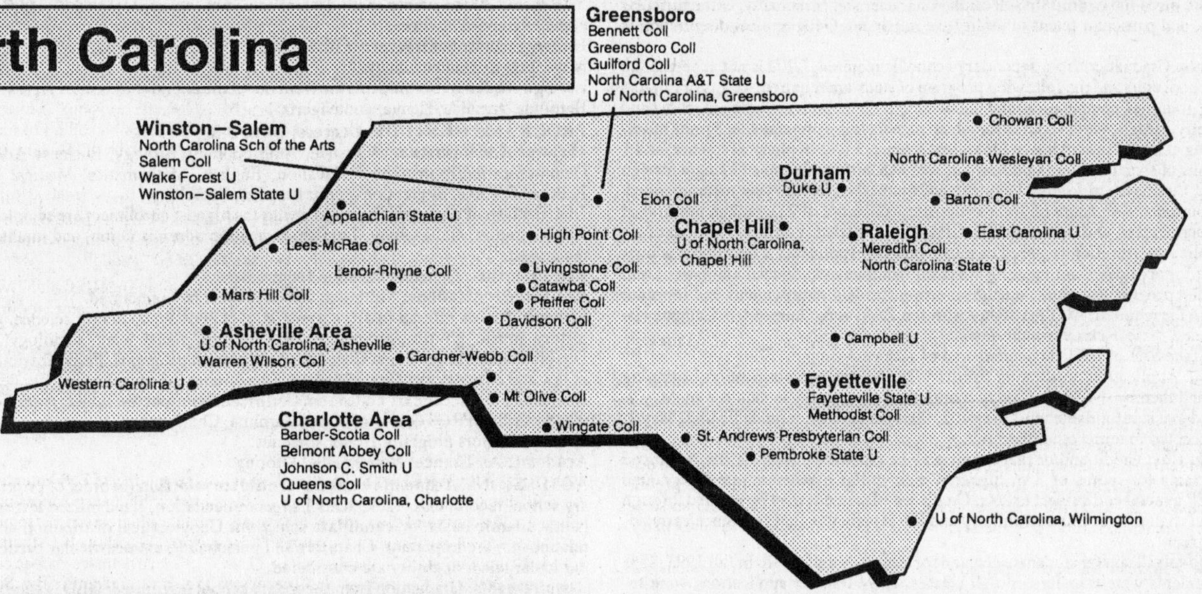


## Appalachian State University

**Boone, NC 28608** **704 262-2000**

**1994-95 Costs.** Tuition: $1,480 (state residents), $6,806 (out-of-state). Room & board: $2,630. Fees, books, misc. academic expenses (school's estimate): $1,078.
**Enrollment.** Undergraduates: 4,841 men, 5,073 women (full-time). Freshman class: 7,313 applicants, 4,664 accepted, 1,910 enrolled. Graduate enrollment: 371 men, 577 women.
**Test score averages/ranges.** Average SAT scores: 471 verbal, 519 math. Range of SAT scores of middle 50%: 420-520 verbal, 470-570 math.
**Faculty.** 535 full-time; 158 part-time. 68% of faculty holds doctoral degree. Student/faculty ratio: 16 to 1.
**Selectivity rating.** Competitive.

**PROFILE.** Appalachian State is a public university. It was founded in 1899, designated a Normal school in 1925, became a state teachers college in 1929, and gained university status in 1967. Programs are offered through the Colleges of Arts and Sciences, Business, Fine and Applied Arts, and Education. Its 75- and 185-acre campuses are located in Boone, 95 miles from Charlotte and Winston-Salem.

**Accreditation:** SACS. Professionally accredited by the American Assembly of Collegiate Schools of Business, the American Dietetic Association, the American Speech-Language-Hearing Association, the National Association of Schools of Music, the National Council for Accreditation of Teacher Education.
**Religious orientation:** Appalachian State University is nonsectarian; no religious requirements.
**Library:** Collections totaling over 629,576 volumes, 3,789 periodical subscriptions, and 1,115,245 microform items.
**Special facilities/museums:** Museum of Appalachian history, language lab, observatory, meteorological reporting station.
**Athletic facilities:** Gymnasiums, athletic center, football stadium, basketball, racquetball, and tennis courts, baseball, football, field hockey, and soccer fields, aerobics, gymnastics, and weight rooms.

**STUDENT BODY. Undergraduate profile:** 89% are state residents; 28% are transfers. 1% Asian-American, 4% Black, 1% Hispanic, 94% White. Average age of undergraduates is 21.
**Freshman profile:** 1% of freshmen who took SAT scored 700 or over on verbal, 2% scored 700 or over on math; 7% scored 600 or over on verbal, 16% scored 600 or over on math; 33% scored 500 or over on verbal, 60% scored 500 or over on math; 85% scored 400 or over on verbal, 96% scored 400 or over on math; 99% scored 300 or over on verbal, 100% scored 300 or over on math.
**Undergraduate achievement:** 86% of fall 1992 freshmen returned for fall 1993 term. 32% of entering class graduated. 20% of students who completed a degree program went on to graduate study within one year.
**Foreign students:** 45 students are from out of the country. Countries represented include England, Finland, Hong Kong, Japan, and Sweden; 25 in all.

**PROGRAMS OF STUDY. Degrees:** B.A., B.F.A., B.Mus., B.S., B.S.Bus.Admin., B.S.Crim.Just., B.Soc.Work, B.Tech.
**Majors:** Accounting, Anthropology, Applied Communication, Art, Art Education, Art Marketing/Production, Banking, Biology, Business Education, Business/Technology, Chemistry, Child Development, Clothing/Textiles, Communication Disorders, Community Health Education, Community/Regional Planning, Computer Science, Criminal Justice, Driver/Safety Education, Economics, Elementary Education, English, Finance, Foods/Nutrition, French, Geography, Geology, Graphic Design, Habilitative Sciences, Health Care Management, Health Education, Health Promotion, History, Home Economics, Hospitality Management, Housing/Interiors, Individualized Majors, Industrial Education/Technology, Industrial Technology, Information Systems, Interdisciplinary Studies, Management, Marketing, Marketing Education for Teachers, Mathematics, Medical Technology, Middle Grades Education, Music Education, Music Industry Studies, Music Performance, Office Systems Management, Philosophy/Religion, Physical Education, Physics, Political Science, Psychology, Reading Education, Real Estate/Urban Analysis, Recreation Management, Risk/Insurance, Social Sciences, Social Work, Sociology, Spanish, Special Education, Speech, Speech Teaching, Speech/Theatre, Statistics, Studio Art.
**Distribution of degrees:** The majors with the highest enrollment are management, communications, and elementary education.
**Requirements:** General education requirement.
**Academic regulations:** Freshmen must maintain minimum 1.5 GPA; sophomores, 1.9 GPA; juniors, 2.0 GPA; seniors, 2.0 GPA.
**Special:** Minors offered in many majors and in approximately 20 other fields. Self-designed majors. Double majors. Dual degrees. Independent study. Accelerated study. Pass/fail grading option. Internships. Graduate school at which undergraduates may take graduate-level courses. Preprofessional programs in law, medicine, pharmacy, dentistry, theology, engineering, forest resources, and nursing. Combined programs with professional schools. Two-year transfer programs in engineering, forestry, nursing, and pharmacy. 3-2 engineering program with Auburn U. Member of Appalachian Consortium. Teacher certification in elementary, secondary, and special education. Study abroad in Barbados, China, England, France, Germany, Honduras, Mexico, the Netherlands, Spain, Sweden, and Switzerland. ROTC.
**Honors:** Honors program. Honor societies.
**Academic Assistance:** Nonremedial tutoring.

**STUDENT LIFE. Housing:** Unmarried, nonveteran freshmen must live on campus unless living with family. Coed, women's, and men's dorms. Sorority and fraternity housing. School-owned/operated apartments. On-campus married-student housing. 38% of students live in college housing.
**Social atmosphere:** Popular activities include football games, the Yofest outdoor music festival, night skiing, and outdoor programs sponsored by ASU. Greeks, the SGA, the Christian Varsity Fellowship, and BACCHUS are among the influential groups on campus. Students enjoy spending free time at the Klondike Cafe, Sollicito's Pizza, the Pub, the Sweet Shop, the Sheraton lounge, and the cafeteria.
**Services and counseling/handicapped student services:** Placement services. Health service. Day care. Counseling services for minority, military, veteran, and older students. Birth control, personal, and psychological counseling. Career and academic guidance services. Physically disabled student services. Learning disabled program/services. Notetaking services. Tape recorders. Reader services for the blind.
**Campus organizations:** Undergraduate student government. Student newspaper (Appalachian, published twice/week). Literary magazine. Yearbook. Men's and women's glee clubs, University Singers, marching and stage bands, symphonic band, symphony orchestra, wind and jazz ensembles, majorettes, debating, Big Brothers/Big Sisters, departmental, service, and special-interest groups, 170 organizations in all. 12 fraternities, no chapter houses; nine sororities, no chapter houses. 5% of men join a fraternity. 5% of women join a sorority.
**Minority/foreign student organizations:** Black Student Association. International Student Association.

**ATHLETICS. Physical education requirements:** Two semesters of physical education required.
**Intercollegiate competition:** 5% of students participate. Baseball (M), basketball (M,W), cheerleading (M,W), cross-country (M,W), field hockey (W), football (M), golf (M,W), soccer (M), tennis (M,W), track (indoor) (M,W), track (outdoor) (M,W), track and field (indoor) (M,W), track and field (outdoor) (M,W), volleyball (W), wrestling (M). Member of NCAA Division I, NCAA Division I-AA for football, Southern Conference.
**Intramural and club sports:** 80% of students participate. Intramural arm wrestling, badminton, basketball, canoeing, field hockey, flag football, frisbee, golf, handball, racquetball, road racing, skiing, soccer, softball, swimming, team handball, tennis, track, water polo, wrestling. Men's club Alpine skiing, canoe/kayak, crew, football, frisbee, Nordic skiing, rugby, volleyball. Women's club canoe/kayak, crew, Nordic skiing, soccer, volleyball.

**ADMISSIONS. Academic basis for candidate selection** (in order of priority): Secondary school record, class rank, standardized test scores, essay, school's recommendation.

**Nonacademic basis for candidate selection:** Character and personality, extracurricular participation, and particular talent or ability are important. Geographical distribution is considered.
**Requirements:** Graduation from secondary school is required; GED is not accepted. 20 secondary school units and the following program of study are required: 4 units of English emphasizing grammar, composition, and literature; 3 units of math including algebra I and II and geometry or higher-level course for which algebra II is a prerequisite; 3 units of science including at least 1 unit in life or biological science, 1 unit of physical science, and 1 lab unit; 2 units of social studies including 1 unit of U.S. history. 2 units of a single foreign language and 1 unit each of foreign language and math taken in 12th year recommended. Minimum combined SAT score of 960 (composite ACT score of 21), rank in top fifth of secondary school class, and minimum 3.1 GPA recommended. Portfolio required of art program applicants. Audition required of music program applicants. Conditional admission possible for applicants not meeting standard requirements. Special admissions and Upward Bound program for applicants not meeting standard requirements and for older applicants. SAT is required; ACT may be substituted. PSAT is recommended. Campus visit recommended. No off-campus interviews.
**Procedure:** Take SAT or ACT by September 1 of 12th year. Suggest filing application by September 30. Application deadline is February 28. Acceptance notification beginning October 31 and then by the 30th of every month thereafter. Reply is required by May 1. $100 tuition deposit, refundable until May 1. $100 room deposit, refundable until May 1. Freshmen accepted in terms other than fall.
**Special programs:** Credit and/or placement may be granted through CEEB Advanced Placement exams for scores of 3 or higher. Credit and/or placement may be granted through CLEP general and subject exams. Credit and placement may be granted through DANTES and challenge exams and military and life experience. Early entrance/early admission program.
**Transfer students:** Transfer students accepted for terms other than fall. In fall 1993, 28% of all new students were transfers into all classes. 1,994 transfer applications were received, 1,425 were accepted. Minimum 2.0 GPA required. Lowest course grade accepted is "C." At least 30 semester hours must be completed at the university to receive degree.
**Admissions contact:** T. Joseph Watts, M.A., Director of Admissions. 704 262-2120.

**FINANCIAL AID. Available aid:** Pell grants, SEOG, state scholarships and grants, school scholarships and grants, private scholarships and grants, ROTC scholarships, academic merit scholarships, and athletic scholarships. Minority Presence grants. Perkins Loans (NDSL), PLUS, Stafford Loans (GSL), school loans, private loans, and SLS.
**Financial aid statistics:** In 1993-94, 66% of all undergraduate applicants received aid; 95% of freshman applicants. Average amounts of aid awarded freshmen: Scholarships and grants, $500; loans, $2,000.
**Supporting data/closing dates:** FAFSA/FAF: Priority filing date is March 15; accepted on rolling basis. School's own aid application: Priority filing date is March 15; accepted on rolling basis. Notification of awards begins April 15.
**Financial aid contact:** Bob Feid, M.A., Acting Director of Financial Aid. 704 262-2190.

**STUDENT EMPLOYMENT.** College Work/Study Program. Institutional employment. 28% of full-time undergraduates work on campus during school year. Students may expect to earn an average of $1,200 during school year. Off-campus part-time employment opportunities rated "good."

**COMPUTER FACILITIES.** 450 IBM/IBM-compatible and Macintosh/Apple microcomputers; 90 are networked. Students may access AT&T, Digital, IBM minicomputer/mainframe systems. Residence halls may be equipped with networked microcomputers, networked terminals. 45 major computer languages and software packages available. Computer facilities are available to all students.
**Fees:** $15 computer fee per semester.
**Hours:** 24 hours.

**GRADUATE CAREER DATA.** 75% of graduates choose careers in business and industry. Companies and businesses that hire graduates: Gallo, Nations Bank, First Union Bank, Burlington Industries.

# Barber-Scotia College

**Concord, NC 28025** **704 786-5171**

**1993-94 Costs.** Tuition: $3,969. Room: $1,300. Board: $1,440. Fees, books, misc. academic expenses (school's estimate): $690.
**Enrollment.** Undergraduates: 352 men, 352 women (full-time). Freshman class: 933 applicants, 933 accepted, 480 enrolled.
**Test score averages/ranges.** Average SAT scores: 300 verbal, 350 math. Range of SAT scores of middle 50%: 250-349 verbal, 250-349 math.
**Faculty.** 50 full-time; 5 part-time. 50% of faculty holds doctoral degree. Student/faculty ratio: 14 to 1.
**Selectivity rating.** Noncompetitive.

**PROFILE.** Barber-Scotia is a private, church-affiliated, liberal arts college. Founded in 1867, it adopted coeducation in 1954. Its 23-acre campus is located in the town of Concord, 20 miles from Charlotte.

**Accreditation:** SACS. Professionally accredited by the National Council for Accreditation of Teacher Education.
**Religious orientation:** Barber-Scotia College is affiliated with the Presbyterian Church (USA); no religious requirements.
**Library:** Collections totaling over 26,356 volumes, 193 periodical subscriptions, and 1,100 microform items.

**STUDENT BODY. Undergraduate profile:** 53% are state residents; 3% are transfers. 99% Black, 1% White.
**Freshman profile:** 2% of freshmen who took SAT scored 500 or over on math; 6% scored 400 or over on verbal, 8% scored 400 or over on math; 38% scored 300 or over on verbal, 57% scored 300 or over on math. 19% of accepted applicants took SAT. 100% of freshmen come from public schools.
**Undergraduate achievement:** 10% of students completing a degree program immediately went on to graduate study.
**Foreign students:** Six students are from out of the country. Countries represented include Bermuda, Jamaica, Kenya, and Nigeria.

**PROGRAMS OF STUDY. Degrees:** B.A., B.S.
**Majors:** Administration of Justice, Anthropology, Biology, Business Administration, Communication/Journalism, Education, English, Mathematics, Medical Technology, Political Science, Recreation Administration, Sociology.
**Distribution of degrees:** The majors with the highest enrollment are sociology, business administration, and biology; English, recreation administration, and mathematics have the lowest.
**Requirements:** General education requirement.
**Academic regulations:** Minimum 2.0 GPA must be maintained.
**Special:** Minors offered in art, chiropractic, chemistry, computer science, gerontology, history, music, physics, pre-engineering, pre-law, social work, sociology, and theatre. Double majors. Internships. Cooperative education programs. Preprofessional programs in law and chiropractic. Charlotte Area Educational Consortium. Teacher certification in elementary and secondary education. Certification in specific subject areas. ROTC at Davidson Coll. AFROTC at U of North Carolina, Charlotte.
**Honors:** Honors program. Honor societies.
**Academic Assistance:** Nonremedial tutoring.

**ADMISSIONS. Academic basis for candidate selection** (in order of priority): Secondary school record, class rank, school's recommendation, standardized test scores.
**Nonacademic basis for candidate selection:** Geographical distribution and alumni/ae relationship are important. Character and personality, extracurricular participation, and particular talent or ability are considered.
**Requirements:** Graduation from secondary school is required; GED is accepted. No specific distribution of secondary school units required. SAT or ACT is required. Campus visit recommended. Off-campus interviews available with admissions and alumni representatives.
**Procedure:** Application deadline is August 1. Notification of admission on rolling basis. $100 room deposit, refundable until August 15. Freshmen accepted in terms other than fall.
**Special programs:** Credit and/or placement may be granted through CEEB Advanced Placement exams for scores of 3 or higher. Credit and/or placement may be granted through CLEP general and subject exams. Placement may be granted through ACT PEP exams.
**Transfer students:** Transfer students accepted for terms other than fall. In fall 1992, 3% of all new students were transfers into all classes. 21 transfer applications were received, 21 were accepted. Application deadline is August 1 for fall; December 1 for spring. Minimum 2.0 GPA required. Lowest course grade accepted is "C." Maximum number of transferable credits is 65 semester hours. At least 60 semester hours must be completed at the college to receive degree.
**Admissions contact:** Abbie Butler, Director of Admissions. 704 786-5171, extension 247.

**FINANCIAL AID. Available aid:** Pell grants, SEOG, state scholarships and grants, school scholarships and grants, private scholarships and grants, ROTC scholarships, athletic scholarships, and United Negro College Fund. Perkins Loans (NDSL), PLUS, Stafford Loans (GSL), state loans, and SLS.
**Financial aid statistics:** 5% of aid is not need-based. In 1992-93, 99% of all undergraduate applicants received aid. Average amounts of aid awarded freshmen: Scholarships and grants, $5,000.
**Supporting data/closing dates:** FAFSA/FAF: Accepted on rolling basis. School's own aid application: Accepted on rolling basis. State aid form: Accepted on rolling basis. Income tax forms: Accepted on rolling basis. Notification of awards on rolling basis.
**Financial aid contact:** Patsy Nwagbaraocha. 704 786-5171, extension 247.

# Barton College

**Wilson, NC 27893** **919 399-6300**

**1994-95 Costs.** Tuition: $7,420. Room: $1,720. Board: $1,720. Fees, books, misc. academic expenses (school's estimate): $830.
**Enrollment.** Undergraduates: 376 men, 733 women (full-time). Freshman class: 709 applicants, 642 accepted, 242 enrolled.
**Test score averages/ranges.** Average SAT scores: 396 verbal, 444 math.
**Faculty.** 87 full-time; 27 part-time. 64% of faculty holds highest degree in specific field. Student/faculty ratio: 14 to 1.
**Selectivity rating.** Less competitive.

**PROFILE.** Barton is a church-affiliated college. It was founded in 1902, and in 1990 its name was changed from Atlantic Christian College. Its 62-acre campus is located in Wilson, 45 miles from Raleigh.

**Accreditation:** SACS. Professionally accredited by the American Medical Association (CAHEA), the National League for Nursing.
**Religious orientation:** Barton College is affiliated with the Disciples of Christ Church; one semester of religion required.
**Library:** Collections totaling over 160,993 volumes, 981 periodical subscriptions, and 195,343 microform items.
**Special facilities/museums:** Art gallery.
**Athletic facilities:** Gymnasium, weight room, tennis courts, athletic fields.

**STUDENT BODY. Undergraduate profile:** 76% are state residents; 40% are transfers. 1% Asian-American, 11% Black, 1% Hispanic, 1% Native American, 84% White, 2% Other. Average age of undergraduates is 20.
**Freshman profile:** 5% of freshmen who took SAT scored 600 or over on math; 9% scored 500 or over on verbal, 26% scored 500 or over on math; 51% scored 400 or over on verbal,

65% scored 400 or over on math; 90% scored 300 or over on verbal, 97% scored 300 or over on math. 96% of accepted applicants took SAT; 4% took ACT. 80% of freshmen come from public schools.

**Undergraduate achievement:** 73% of fall 1992 freshmen returned for fall 1993 term. 10% of students completing a degree program went on to graduate study within one year.

**Foreign students:** 20 students are from out of the country. Countries represented include China, India, Japan, Mexico, South Africa, and Turkey; 15 in all.

**PROGRAMS OF STUDY. Degrees:** B.A., B.F.A., B.Lib.Studies, B.S.

**Majors:** Accounting, American Studies, Art Education, Biology, Business Administration, Cell Biology, Ceramics, Chemistry, Commercial Design, Communications, Drawing, Early Childhood Education, Education of the Hearing Impaired, English, Environmental Science, French, Graphics, History, Intermediate Education, International Studies, Mathematics, Middle School Education, Music, Music Education, Music Recording Technology, Nursing, Painting, Photography, Physical Education, Political Science, Printmaking, Psychology, Psychology/Business, Religion/Philosophy, Sculpture, Social Studies, Social Work, Sociology, Spanish, Sports Administration, Sports Science, Studio Art.

**Distribution of degrees:** The majors with the highest enrollment are business, nursing, and education; music, religion, and studio art have the lowest.

**Requirements:** General education requirement.

**Academic regulations:** Freshmen must maintain minimum 1.45 GPA; sophomores, 1.60 GPA; juniors, 1.85 GPA; seniors, 2.0 GPA.

**Special:** Minors offered in all majors and in computer science, drama, economics, geography, and visual arts. Double majors. Independent study. Internships. Preprofessional programs in law, medicine, veterinary science, pharmacy, and dentistry. 2-2 medical technology programs with East Carolina U and U of North Carolina at Chapel Hill. 3-1 and 4-1 medical technology programs with various hospitals. Washington Semester. Teacher certification in early childhood, elementary, secondary, and special education. Certification in specific subject areas. Study abroad in Japan, South Korea, and Switzerland.

**Honors:** Honors program. Honor societies.

**Academic Assistance:** Nonremedial tutoring.

**STUDENT LIFE. Housing:** All unmarried students under age 21 must live on campus unless living near campus with relatives. Coed, women's, and men's dorms. 50% of students live in college housing.

**Social atmosphere:** "Sports play an important role at Barton," reports the student newspaper. "We also have a strong arts department. Plays and concerts are student favorites as well as student productions in the communications department." A couple of popular spots at Barton are Bully's and Off the Wall. Greeks, Stage and Script, the Student Union Committee, Student Government Association, and the Baptist Student Union are influential organizations on campus. Some of the favorite events of the year are the Lighting of the Luminaries, Homecoming, and concerts.

**Services and counseling/handicapped student services:** Placement services. Health service. Counseling services for minority and older students. Personal counseling. Career and academic guidance services. Religious counseling. Physically disabled student services. Notetaking services. Tape recorders. Tutors. Reader services for the blind.

**Campus organizations:** Undergraduate student government. Student newspaper (Barton Collegiate, published once/two weeks). Literary magazine. Yearbook. Accounting club, commercial design club, trivia club, Circle K, Gospel Choir, Jaycees, photography club, interdormitory association, Republican club, Young Democrats, 42 organizations in all. Four fraternities, all with chapter houses; three sororities, no chapter houses. 10% of men join a fraternity. 15% of women join a sorority.

**Religious organizations:** Disciple Student Union, Fellowship of Christian Athletes, Hands for Christ, Alpha Omega Fellowship, Baptist Student Union, Campus Christian Association, other religious groups.

**Minority/foreign student organizations:** Afro-American Awareness Society, Minority Organization Council, Black Student Union. International Club.

**ATHLETICS. Physical education requirements:** Three semesters of physical education required.

**Intercollegiate competition:** 7% of students participate. Baseball (M), basketball (M,W), cheerleading (W), golf (M), soccer (M,W), softball (W), tennis (M,W), volleyball (W). Member of Carolinas Intercollegiate Athletic Conference, NAIA, NCAA.

**Intramural and club sports:** 50% of students participate. Intramural basketball, flag football, floor hockey, golf, racquetball, soccer, softball, tennis, volleyball, walleyball.

**ADMISSIONS. Academic basis for candidate selection** (in order of priority): Secondary school record, standardized test scores, class rank, school's recommendation, essay.

**Nonacademic basis for candidate selection:** Character and personality, particular talent or ability, and geographical distribution are important. Extracurricular participation and alumni/ae relationship are considered.

**Requirements:** Graduation from secondary school is required; GED is accepted. 12 units and the following program of study are recommended: 4 units of English, 3 units of math, 3 units of science, 2 units of foreign language, 2 units of social studies, 2 units of history, 4 units of electives. Minimum combined SAT score of 800, rank in top half of secondary school class, and minimum 2.0 GPA recommended. Portfolio required of art program applicants. Audition required of music program applicants. R.N. required of nursing program applicants. SAT is required; ACT may be substituted. Campus visit and interview recommended. Off-campus interviews available with admissions and alumni representatives.

**Procedure:** Take SAT or ACT by December of 12th year. Take ACH by May of 12th year. Visit college for interview by February of 12th year. Suggest filing application by December 15. Application deadline is August 15. Notification of admission on rolling basis. Reply is required by May 1. $100 tuition deposit, refundable until May 1. Freshmen accepted in terms other than fall.

**Special programs:** Admission may be deferred one year. Credit may be granted through CLEP subject exams. Credit and placement may be granted through Regents College, ACT PEP, and challenge exams. Early entrance/early admission program. Concurrent enrollment program.

**Transfer students:** Transfer students accepted for terms other than fall. In fall 1993, 40% of all new students were transfers into all classes. 281 transfer applications were received, 224 were accepted. Application deadline is July 31 for fall; November 30 for spring. Minimum 2.0 GPA recommended. Lowest course grade accepted is "C." Maximum number of transferable credits is 64 semester hours. At least 45 semester hours must be completed at the college to receive degree.

**Admissions contact:** Anthony C. Britt, M.B.A., Director of Admissions. 800 345-4973.

**FINANCIAL AID. Available aid:** Pell grants, SEOG, state scholarships and grants, school scholarships and grants, academic merit scholarships, athletic scholarships, and aid for undergraduate foreign students. Perkins Loans (NDSL), PLUS, Stafford Loans (GSL), and SLS. AMS. School's payment plan.

**Financial aid statistics:** 46% of aid is not need-based. In 1993-94, 82% of all undergraduate applicants received aid; 85% of freshman applicants. Average amounts of aid awarded freshmen: Scholarships and grants, $1,200; loans, $2,625.

**Supporting data/closing dates:** FAFSA: Accepted on rolling basis. School's own aid application: Priority filing date is July 1; accepted on rolling basis. Income tax forms: Accepted on rolling basis. Notification of awards on rolling basis.

**Financial aid contact:** Miriam Landing, Director of Financial Aid. 800 345-4973.

**STUDENT EMPLOYMENT.** College Work/Study Program. Institutional employment. 36% of full-time undergraduates work on campus during school year. Students may expect to earn an average of $1,200 during school year. Off-campus part-time employment opportunities rated "good."

**COMPUTER FACILITIES.** 65 IBM/IBM-compatible and Macintosh/Apple microcomputers. Computer languages and software packages include Assembler, BASIC, C, COBOL, FORTRAN, Harvard Graphics, Lotus 1-2-3, Paradox, Pascal, Quattro Pro, RPG, Windows; 13 in all. Computer facilities are available to all students.

**Fees:** $15 computer fee per semester; included in tuition/fees.

**Hours:** 2 PM-9 PM (M-Th), 8 AM-3 PM (F), 2 PM-9 PM (Sa-Su).

**GRADUATE CAREER DATA.** Graduate school percentages: 2% enter law school. 2% enter medical school. 1% enter dental school. 2% enter graduate business programs. 1% enter graduate arts and sciences programs. 2% enter theological school/seminary. Highest graduate school enrollments: North Carolina State U, East Carolina U. 45% of graduates choose careers in business and industry. Companies and businesses that hire graduates: Public school systems, hospitals.

**PROMINENT ALUMNI/AE.** Dr. William E. Tucker, Chancellor, Texas Christian U; Ava Gardner, actress.

# Belmont Abbey College

**Belmont, NC 28012** **704 825-6700**

**1994-95 Costs.** Tuition: $7,850 (state residents), $9,000 (out-of-state). Room & board: $4,850. Fees, books, misc. academic expenses (school's estimate): $940.

**Enrollment.** Undergraduates: 334 men, 375 women (full-time). Freshman class: 632 applicants, 494 accepted, 129 enrolled. Graduate enrollment: 9 men, 49 women.

**Test score averages/ranges.** Average SAT scores: 427 verbal, 463 math. Range of SAT scores of middle 50%: 400-449 verbal, 449-499 math.

**Faculty.** 46 full-time; 35 part-time. 83% of faculty holds doctoral degree. Student/faculty ratio: 16 to 1.

**Selectivity rating.** Less competitive.

**PROFILE.** Belmont Abbey, founded in 1886, is a church-affiliated college. Programs are offered through the Divisions of Humanities, Mathematics and Natural Sciences, Social and Behavioral Sciences, and Professional Studies. Its 650-acre campus is located in Belmont, 10 miles from Charlotte. Campus architecture includes 19th-century buildings built by monks; the neo-Gothic Abbey Church is listed in the National Register of Historic Places.

**Accreditation:** SACS. Professionally accredited by the National Council for Accreditation of Teacher Education.

**Religious orientation:** Belmont Abbey College is affiliated with the Roman Catholic Church (Benedictine Monks); two semesters of theology required.

**Library:** Collections totaling over 110,050 volumes, 609 periodical subscriptions, and 59,000 microform items.

**Special facilities/museums:** Museum with rare book collection, language lab.

**Athletic facilities:** Swimming pool, jogging track, basketball, tennis courts, baseball and soccer fields, golf range, weight room.

**STUDENT BODY. Undergraduate profile:** 53% are state residents; 18% are transfers. 2% Asian-American, 6% Black, 1% Hispanic, 1% Native American, 87% White, 3% nonresident aliens. Average age of undergraduates is 22.

**Freshman profile:** 2% of freshmen who took SAT scored 600 or over on verbal, 6% scored 600 or over on math; 16% scored 500 or over on verbal, 30% scored 500 or over on math; 59% scored 400 or over on verbal, 75% scored 400 or over on math; 98% scored 300 or over on verbal, 100% scored 300 or over on math. 91% of accepted applicants took SAT; 9% took ACT. 50% of freshmen come from public schools.

**Undergraduate achievement:** 70% of fall 1992 freshmen returned for fall 1993 term. 40% of entering class graduated.

**Foreign students:** 32 students are from out of the country. Countries represented include the Bahamas, Bulgaria, India, Israel, Malaysia, and Norway; 15 in all.

**PROGRAMS OF STUDY. Degrees:** B.A., B.S.

**Majors:** Accounting, Biology, Business Administration, Chemistry, Computer Information Science, Early Childhood Education, Economics, Education (General), English, History, Liberal Studies, Management Accounting, Mathematics, Medical Technology, Philosophy, Political Science, Psychology, Recreational Studies, Religious Education, Secondary Education, Sociology, Special Education, Sports Management, Theology, Therapeutic Recreation.

**Distribution of degrees:** The majors with the highest enrollment are business, education, and biology; chemistry, economics, and philosophy have the lowest.

**Requirements:** General education requirement.

**Academic regulations:** Freshmen must maintain minimum 1.50 GPA; sophomores, 1.75 GPA; juniors, 1.90 GPA; seniors, 2.00 GPA.

**Special:** Minors offered in all majors. Courses offered in astronomy, Chinese, engineering, fine arts, French, geography, German, great books, Greek, Hebrew, Latin music, mythology, physical education, and Spanish. Double majors. Dual degrees. Independent study. Internships. Cooperative education programs. Preprofessional programs in law, medicine, veterinary science, pharmacy, and dentistry. 3-2 engineering programs with Clemson U, Georgia Tech, and U of Notre Dame. Member of Charlotte Area Educational Consortium. Sea Semester. Teacher certification in elementary, secondary, and special education. Certification in specific subject areas. Exchange program abroad in Japan (Kansai Gaidai U). Study abroad also possible in other countries. ROTC and AFROTC at U of North Carolina at Charlotte.
**Honors:** Honors program. Honor societies.
**Academic Assistance:** Remedial writing, math, and study skills. Nonremedial tutoring.

**ADMISSIONS. Academic basis for candidate selection** (in order of priority): Secondary school record, class rank, standardized test scores, school's recommendation, essay.
**Nonacademic basis for candidate selection:** Character and personality, extracurricular participation, particular talent or ability, and alumni/ae relationship are considered.
**Requirements:** Graduation from secondary school is required; GED is accepted. 16 units and the following program of study are required: 4 units of English, 3 units of math, 2 units of science, 2 units of foreign language, 1 unit of social studies, 1 unit of history, 3 units of academic electives. Minimum combined SAT score of 750, rank in top quarter of secondary school class, and minimum 2.3 GPA recommended. SAT is required; ACT may be substituted. Campus visit and interview recommended. Off-campus interviews available with an admissions representative.
**Procedure:** Take SAT or ACT by June of 12th year. Visit college for interview by May 1 of 12th year. Application deadline is August 1. Notification of admission on rolling basis. $100 tuition deposit, refundable until May 1. $300 room deposit, refundable until May 1. Freshmen accepted in terms other than fall.
**Special programs:** Admission may be deferred one year. Credit and/or placement may be granted through CEEB Advanced Placement exams for scores of 3 or higher. Credit and/or placement may be granted through CLEP general and subject exams. Credit and placement may be granted through challenge exams and military and life experience. Early entrance/early admission program. Concurrent enrollment program.
**Transfer students:** Transfer students accepted for terms other than fall. In fall 1993, 18% of all new students were transfers into all classes. 228 transfer applications were received, 212 were accepted. Application deadline is August 1 for fall; December 1 for spring. Minimum 2.0 GPA required. Lowest course grade accepted is "C." Maximum number of transferable credits is 65 semester hours. At least 30 semester hours must be completed at the college to receive degree.
**Admissions contact:** Laurie W. Taylor, Dean of Admissions. 800 523-2355.

**FINANCIAL AID. Available aid:** Pell grants, SEOG, state grants, school scholarships and grants, private scholarships and grants, ROTC scholarships, athletic scholarships, and aid for undergraduate foreign students. Perkins Loans (NDSL), PLUS, Stafford Loans (GSL), private loans, and SLS. Deferred payment plan and family tuition reduction.
**Financial aid statistics:** 77% of aid is not need-based. In 1993-94, 98% of all freshman applicants received aid. Average amounts of aid awarded freshmen: Scholarships and grants, $2,366; loans, $2,625.
**Supporting data/closing dates:** FAFSA/FAF: Priority filing date is March 1; accepted on rolling basis. Income tax forms: Accepted on rolling basis. Notification of awards on rolling basis.
**Financial aid contact:** Anne Stevens, Director of Financial Aid. 800 523-2355.

# Bennett College

**Greensboro, NC 27401** **919 273-4431**

**1994-95 Costs.** Tuition: $5,600. Room: $1,465. Board: $1,630. Fees, books, misc. academic expenses (school's estimate): $1,780.
**Enrollment.** Undergraduates: 650 men, 617 women (full-time). Freshman class: 774 applicants, 542 accepted, 193 enrolled.
**Test score averages/ranges.** Average SAT scores: 385 verbal, 395 math. Average ACT scores: 18 composite.
**Faculty.** 52 full-time; 6 part-time. 63% of faculty holds doctoral degree. Student/faculty ratio: 11 to 1.
**Selectivity rating.** Less competitive.

**PROFILE.** Bennett is a church-affiliated college. It was founded as a coeducational seminary in 1873, gained college status in 1889, and became a senior college for women in 1926. Its 55-acre campus is located in Greensboro.

**Accreditation:** SACS. Professionally accredited by the American Dietetic Association, the Council on Social Work Education, the National Council for Accreditation of Teacher Education.
**Religious orientation:** Bennett College is affiliated with the United Methodist Church; three semester hours of religion/theology required.
**Library:** Collections totaling over 95,293 volumes, 325 periodical subscriptions, and 1,800 microform items.
**Special facilities/museums:** Children's House, Constance Maiteena collection, college archives, telecommunications satellite dish.
**Athletic facilities:** Gymnasium, swimming pool, ball courts, fitness equipment.

**STUDENT BODY. Undergraduate profile:** 32% are state residents; 11% are transfers. 99% Black, 1% Hispanic. Average age of undergraduates is 20.
**Freshman profile:** 1% of freshmen who took SAT scored 600 or over on verbal, 2% scored 600 or over on math; 4% scored 500 or over on verbal, 7% scored 500 or over on math; 27% scored 400 or over on verbal, 33% scored 400 or over on math; 62% scored 300 or over on verbal, 60% scored 300 or over on math. 21% of freshmen who took ACT scored 24 or over on composite; 80% scored 18 or over on composite; 100% scored 12 or over on composite. 89% of accepted applicants took SAT; 11% took ACT. 91% of freshmen come from public schools.
**Undergraduate achievement:** 71% of fall 1992 freshmen returned for fall 1993 term. 26% of entering class graduated. 35% of students completing a degree program immediately went on to graduate study.
**Foreign students:** 16 students are from out of the country. Countries represented include Gambia, Ghana, Jamaica, Liberia, Zambia, and Zimbabwe; 10 in all.

**PROGRAMS OF STUDY. Degrees:** B.A., B.A./S.Interdis.Studies, B.S., B.Soc.Work.
**Majors:** Accounting, Arts Management, Biology, Business Administration, Chemistry, Clothing/Fashion Merchandising, Communications, Computer Science, Elementary Education, English, English Education, Home Economics, Interdisciplinary Studies, Mathematics, Mathematics Education, Medical Technology, Middle Grades Education, Music, Music Education, Nutrition/Dietetics, Political Science, Psychology, Science Education, Social Work, Sociology, Special Education, Visual Arts.
**Distribution of degrees:** The majors with the highest enrollment are business administration, education, and interdisciplinary studies; music, chemistry, and computer science have the lowest.
**Requirements:** General education requirement.
**Academic regulations:** Freshmen must maintain minimum 1.75 GPA; sophomores, juniors, seniors, 2.0 GPA.
**Special:** Minors offered in economics, history, and women's studies. Associate's degrees offered. Self-designed majors. Dual degrees. Independent study. Internships. Preprofessional programs in medicine, pharmacy, and dentistry. 3-1 medical technology program with the Bowman Gray Sch of Medicine at Wake Forest U. 3-2 nursing program with North Carolina A&T State U. Five-year dual degree program in electrical or mechanical engineering with North Carolina A&T State U. Special programs with five areas of concentration offered in conjunction with U of North Carolina at Greensboro and North Carolina A&T State U. Member of the Piedmont Independent College Association (PICA) and Greater Greensboro Consortium. Washington Semester. Exchange programs with Mt. Vernon Coll, New York U, Randolph-Macon Coll, and Union Coll. Teacher certification in early childhood, elementary, secondary, and special education. Certification in specific subject areas. ROTC and AFROTC at North Carolina A&T State U.
**Honors:** Honors program. Honor societies.
**Academic Assistance:** Remedial reading, writing, math, and study skills. Nonremedial tutoring.

**STUDENT LIFE. Housing:** All students must live on campus for first two years. 80% of students live in college housing.
**Social atmosphere:** The most popular on-campus gathering spot at Bennett is the student union. Four sororities have widespread influence on student life. Founder's Day and the Bennett Coronation highlight the school year. "We are a private, religious college," reports the editor of the school newspaper. Many students participate in the social activities at the local state university, only three blocks away.
**Services and counseling/handicapped student services:** Placement services. Health service. Day care. Student Support Services Program. Personal and psychological counseling. Career and academic guidance services. Religious counseling. Learning disabled services.
**Campus organizations:** Undergraduate student government. Student newspaper (Bennett Banner, published quarterly). Yearbook. Theatre group, Academic/Cultural Enrichment Series, Bennett College Choir, community service and departmental groups, 28 organizations in all. Four sororities, no chapter houses. 20% of women join a sorority.
**Religious organizations:** Belles of Harmony, Christian Fellowship.
**Minority/foreign student organizations:** International Students Organization.

**ATHLETICS. Physical education requirements:** Four semester hours of physical education required.

**ADMISSIONS. Academic basis for candidate selection** (in order of priority): Secondary school record, standardized test scores, class rank, school's recommendation, essay.
**Nonacademic basis for candidate selection:** Character and personality and extracurricular participation are emphasized. Particular talent or ability is important. Geographical distribution and alumni/ae relationship are considered.
**Requirements:** Graduation from secondary school is required; GED is accepted. 16 units and the following program of study are required: 4 units of English, 2 units of math, 1 unit of science, 2 units of foreign language, 1 unit of social studies, 6 units of electives. HEOP for applicants not normally admissible. Special student status possible for applicants not meeting standard requirements. SAT is required; ACT may be substituted. Campus visit and interview recommended. Off-campus interviews available with an alumni representative.
**Procedure:** Take SAT or ACT by spring of 12th year. Suggest filing application by February 15; no deadline. Notification of admission within two weeks of receipt of all credentials. Reply is required by June 30. $100 refundable room deposit. Freshmen accepted in terms other than fall.
**Special programs:** Admission may be deferred one semester. Credit and/or placement may be granted through CLEP general and subject exams. Early entrance/early admission program.
**Transfer students:** Transfer students accepted for terms other than fall. In fall 1993, 11% of all new students were transfers into all classes. 74 transfer applications were received, 40 were accepted. Application deadline is rolling for fall; rolling for spring. Minimum 2.0 GPA recommended. Lowest course grade accepted is "C." At least 36 semester hours must be completed at the college to receive degree.
**Admissions contact:** Yolanda Johnson, Acting Director of Admissions. 919 370-8624.

**FINANCIAL AID. Available aid:** Pell grants, SEOG, state grants, school scholarships and grants, private scholarships and grants, academic merit scholarships, and United Negro College Fund. Perkins Loans (NDSL), PLUS, Stafford Loans (GSL), and SLS. Deferred payment plan.
**Financial aid statistics:** 36% of aid is not need-based. In 1993-94, 89% of all undergraduate applicants received aid; 86% of freshman applicants. Average amounts of aid awarded freshmen: Scholarships and grants, $1,678; loans, $5,037.
**Supporting data/closing dates:** FAFSA/FAF: Accepted on rolling basis. Notification of awards on rolling basis.

**STUDENT EMPLOYMENT.** College Work/Study Program. Institutional employment. 32% of full-time undergraduates work on campus during school year. Students may expect to earn an average of $1,080 during school year. Off-campus part-time employment opportunities rated "good."

**COMPUTER FACILITIES.** 110 IBM/IBM-compatible microcomputers; 60 are networked. Students may access Digital, IBM minicomputer/mainframe systems. Client/LAN operating systems include DOS, Novell. Computer languages and software packages include BASIC, dBASE, FORTRAN, ICISS, Lotus, Pascal, WordPerfect. Computer facilities are available to all students.
**Fees:** None.
**Hours:** 8 AM-9 PM.

**GRADUATE CAREER DATA.** Graduate school percentages: 1% enter law school. 35% enter medical school. 10% enter dental school. 8% enter graduate business programs. 25% enter graduate arts and sciences programs. Highest graduate school enrollments: Howard U, Meharry Medical Coll, U of North Carolina. 30% of graduates choose careers in business and industry. Companies and businesses that hire graduates: U.S. government, public and private schools.

**PROMINENT ALUMNI/AE.** Mayde Norman, actress; Glendora Putnam, attorney; Dorothyn Brown, surgeon.

# Campbell University

**Buies Creek, NC 27506** **800 334-4111**

**1993-94 Costs.** Tuition: $7,550. Room & board: $2,825. Fees, books, misc. academic expenses (school's estimate): $500.
**Enrollment.** Undergraduates: 905 men, 1,139 women (full-time). Freshman class: 2,087 applicants, 1,339 accepted, 610 enrolled. Graduate enrollment: 523 men, 507 women.
**Test score averages/ranges.** Average SAT scores: 439 verbal, 476 math.
**Faculty.** 134 full-time; 168 part-time. 77% of faculty holds doctoral degree. Student/faculty ratio: 18 to 1.
**Selectivity rating.** Competitive.

**PROFILE.** Campbell is a church-affiliated university. It was founded as an academy in 1887, became a four-year college in 1961, and gained university status in 1979. Its 990-acre campus is located in Buies Creek, 30 miles from Raleigh and Fayetteville.

**Accreditation:** SACS. Professionally accredited by the National Council for Accreditation of Teacher Education.
**Religious orientation:** Campbell University is affiliated with the North Carolina Baptist Convention; Two semester hours of religion required.
**Library:** Collections totaling over 174,900 volumes, 995 periodical subscriptions, and 950,000 microform items.
**Special facilities/museums:** Language lab.
**Athletic facilities:** Gymnasium, stadium, baseball, intramural, soccer, and softball fields, golf course, weight, and wrestling rooms, swimming pool, basketball, tennis, and volleyball courts, fitness course.

**STUDENT BODY. Undergraduate profile:** 62% are state residents; 27% are transfers. 5% Asian-American, 8% Black, 3% Hispanic, 1% Native American, 83% White. Average age of undergraduates is 22.
**Freshman profile:** 1% of freshmen who took SAT scored 700 or over on verbal, 1% scored 700 or over on math; 5% scored 600 or over on verbal, 12% scored 600 or over on math; 25% scored 500 or over on verbal, 41% scored 500 or over on math; 60% scored 400 or over on verbal, 72% scored 400 or over on math; 86% scored 300 or over on verbal, 89% scored 300 or over on math. Majority of accepted applicants took SAT. 90% of freshmen come from public schools.
**Undergraduate achievement:** 76% of fall 1992 freshmen returned for fall 1993 term. 50% of entering class graduated.
**Foreign students:** 139 students are from out of the country. Countries represented include Bahamas, Canada, China, Japan, Malaysia, and Thailand; 41 in all.

**PROGRAMS OF STUDY. Degrees:** B.A., B.Appl.Sci., B.Bus.Admin., B.Hlth.Sci., B.S.
**Majors:** Accounting, Art, Biology, Business Administration, Chemistry, Clothing/Textile/Fashion Merchandising, Computer Information Systems, Data Processing, Dramatic Art, Economics, Elementary Education, English, Food Service Management, French, Government, History, Home Economics, Home Furnishing/Merchandising, Mass Communication, Mathematics, Medical Technology, Military Science, Music, Music Education, Physical Education, Psychology, Religion, Religion/Philosophy, Social Science, Social Services, Social Work, Spanish, Trust Management.
**Distribution of degrees:** The majors with the highest enrollment are business administration, government, and mass communication; drama and home economics have the lowest.
**Requirements:** General education requirement.
**Academic regulations:** Minimum 2.0 GPA required for graduation.
**Special:** Courses offered in geography, German, Greek, journalism, Latin, secretarial science, and speech/drama. Concentrations available in several majors. Associate's degrees offered. Double majors. Independent study. Internships. Cooperative education programs. Graduate school at which undergraduates may take graduate-level courses. Preprofessional programs in law, medicine, veterinary science, pharmacy, and dentistry. 2-3 engineering program with North Carolina State U. 3-1 medical technology and physician assistant programs with local hospitals. 3-3 accelerated law program. 3-2 business program. Member of North Carolina Consortium of Independent Colleges and Universities. American Studies Program (Washington, D.C.). Teacher certification in elementary and secondary education. Certification in specific subject areas. Exchange program abroad in Wales (Baptist Coll of Wales). Study abroad also in France and Mexico. ROTC.
**Honors:** Honor societies.
**Academic Assistance:** Nonremedial tutoring.

**STUDENT LIFE. Housing:** Undergraduates must live on campus unless living with family. Women's and men's dorms. School-owned/operated apartments. On-campus married-student housing. 80% of students live in college housing.
**Social atmosphere:** Chele's Place (a coffeehouse), the student center, and Faces are favorite gathering spots for students. The Baptist Student Union, the Student Government Association, men's and women's basketball and soccer teams, and Kappa Psi (pharmacy fraternity) influence student life. Eagerly anticipated social events include homecoming, Spring Fling, concerts, dances, Christian Focus week, and Spring Pig Out BBQ picnic. Buies Creek is a small town, still quiet and safe, according to the student newspaper. "In fact, there aren't any stop signs."
**Services and counseling/handicapped student services:** Placement services. Health service. Counseling services for military, veteran, and older students. Psychological counseling. Career and academic guidance services.
**Campus organizations:** Undergraduate student government. Student newspaper (Campbell Times, published once/week). Literary magazine. Yearbook. Radio station. Brass ensemble, collegiate and touring choirs, Morning Star, gospel choir, concert and stage bands, Campbell Players, departmental and special-interest groups, 40 organizations in all.
**Religious organizations:** Baptist Student Union, Catholic Young Adults, Clowns for Christ, Fellowship of Christian Athletes.
**Minority/foreign student organizations:** International Students Club, Omega Nu Alpha. International Student Club.

**ATHLETICS. Physical education requirements:** Two semester hours of physical education required.
**Intercollegiate competition:** 8% of students participate. Baseball (M), basketball (M,W), cheerleading (M,W), cross-country (M,W), golf (M,W), soccer (M,W), softball (W), tennis (M,W), track and field (indoor) (M,W), track and field (outdoor) (M,W), volleyball (W), wrestling (M). Member of Big South Conference, NCAA Division I.
**Intramural and club sports:** 20% of students participate. Intramural badminton, basketball, billiards, diving, flag football, golf, putt-putt golf, softball, swimming, table tennis, tennis, volleyball, water polo, weight lifting.

**ADMISSIONS. Academic basis for candidate selection** (in order of priority): Secondary school record, standardized test scores, class rank, school's recommendation, essay.
**Nonacademic basis for candidate selection:** Character and personality and extracurricular participation are important. Particular talent or ability and alumni/ae relationship are considered.
**Requirements:** Graduation from secondary school is required; GED is accepted. 18 units and the following program of study are required: 4 units of English, 3 units of math, 2 units of science, 2 units of foreign language, 2 units of social studies, 5 units of academic electives. Minimum combined SAT score of 825 and minimum GPA of 2.0 required. Conditional admission possible for applicants not meeting standard requirements. SAT or ACT is required. Campus visit and interview recommended. Off-campus interviews available with an admissions representative.
**Procedure:** Take SAT or ACT by October of 12th year. Visit college for interview by June of 12th year. Application deadline is July 31. Notification of admission on rolling basis. $100 tuition deposit, refundable until July 1. Freshmen accepted in terms other than fall.
**Special programs:** Admission may be deferred. Credit and/or placement may be granted through CEEB Advanced Placement exams for scores of 3 or higher. Credit and/or placement may be granted through CLEP general and subject exams. Credit and placement may be granted through DANTES exams and military experience. Early entrance/early admission program. Concurrent enrollment program.
**Transfer students:** Transfer students accepted for terms other than fall. In fall 1993, 27% of all new students were transfers into all classes. 583 transfer applications were received, 408 were accepted. Application deadline is August for fall; December for spring. Minimum 2.0 GPA required. Lowest course grade accepted is "F." Maximum number of transferable credits is 64 semester hours from two-year schools; no limit for four-year schools. At least 32 semester hours must be completed at the university to receive degree.
**Admissions contact:** Herbert V. Kerner, M.A., Dean of Admissions. 800 334-4111, extension 1320.

**FINANCIAL AID. Available aid:** Pell grants, SEOG, state scholarships and grants, school scholarships and grants, private scholarships and grants, ROTC scholarships, academic merit scholarships, and athletic scholarships. Perkins Loans (NDSL), PLUS, Stafford Loans (GSL), Health Professions Loans, state loans, school loans, private loans, and SLS. AMS. University payment plan.
**Financial aid statistics:** 20% of aid is not need-based. In 1993-94, 88% of all undergraduate applicants received aid; 88% of freshman applicants. Average amounts of aid awarded freshmen: Scholarships and grants, $3,641; loans, $2,625.
**Supporting data/closing dates:** FAFSA: Priority filing date is March 15. Notification of awards on rolling basis.
**Financial aid contact:** Mrs. Rue Stewart, Director of Financial Aid. 800 334-4111, extension 1313.

**STUDENT EMPLOYMENT.** College Work/Study Program. Institutional employment. 30% of full-time undergraduates work on campus during school year. Students may expect to earn an average of $523 during school year. Off-campus part-time employment opportunities rated "good."

**COMPUTER FACILITIES.** 32 IBM/IBM-compatible microcomputers; all are networked. Students may access IBM minicomputer/mainframe systems. Client/LAN operating systems include OS/2. Computer languages and software packages include BASIC, COBOL, dBASE, Lotus 1-2-3, Pascal, RPG. Computer facilities are available to all students.
**Fees:** None.
**Hours:** 8:30 AM-10 PM (M-F); 5 PM-10 PM (Su).

## Catawba College

**Salisbury, NC 28144** **704 637-4111**

**1994-95 Costs.** Tuition: $9,270. Room & board: $4,100. Fees, books, misc. academic expenses (school's estimate): $600.
**Enrollment.** Undergraduates: 482 men, 433 women (full-time). Freshman class: 1,083 applicants, 880 accepted, 290 enrolled. 7 women.
**Test score averages/ranges.** Average SAT scores: 434 verbal, 481 math. Range of SAT scores of middle 50%: 380-480 verbal, 420-530 math.
**Faculty.** 63 full-time; 13 part-time. 80% of faculty holds doctoral degree. Student/faculty ratio: 14 to 1.
**Selectivity rating.** Less competitive.

**PROFILE.** Catawba, founded in 1851, is a church-affiliated, liberal arts college. Programs are offered through the Divisions of General Education, Humanities, Mathematics and Sciences, Social and Behavioral Sciences, and Teacher Education and the Schools of Physical Education and Athletics, Performing Arts, and Business. Its 210-acre campus is located in Salisbury, within 50 miles of Charlotte, Greensboro, and Winston-Salem.

**Accreditation:** SACS. Professionally accredited by the National Council for Accreditation of Teacher Education.
**Religious orientation:** Catawba College is affiliated with the United Church of Christ; no religious requirements.
**Library:** Collections totaling over 174,108 volumes, 907 periodical subscriptions, and 492,932 microform items.
**Special facilities/museums:** Ecology preserve.
**Athletic facilities:** Gymnasium, field house, swimming pool, basketball, outdoor volleyball, racquetball, and tennis courts, weight rooms, field hockey, football, soccer, and softball fields.

**STUDENT BODY. Undergraduate profile:** 50% are state residents; 14% are transfers. 1% Asian-American, 7% Black, 1% Hispanic, 90% White, 1% Other.
**Freshman profile:** 3% of freshmen who took SAT scored 600 or over on verbal, 10% scored 600 or over on math; 22% scored 500 or over on verbal, 42% scored 500 or over on math; 69% scored 400 or over on verbal, 84% scored 400 or over on math; 98% scored 300 or over on verbal, 98% scored 300 or over on math. 98% of accepted applicants took SAT.
**Undergraduate achievement:** 66% of fall 1992 freshmen returned for fall 1993 term. 32% of entering class graduated. 11% of students completing a degree program immediately went on to graduate study.
**Foreign students:** 11 students are from out of the country. Countries represented include Canada and England; six in all.

**PROGRAMS OF STUDY. Degrees:** B.A.
**Majors:** Accounting, American Politics, Arts Administration, Biology, Business Administration, Chemistry, Chemistry Education, Church Music, Communication Arts, Computer Information Systems, Computer Science, Elementary Education, English, Forestry/Environmental Studies, French, History, International Business, International Relations, Mathematics, Medical Technology, Middle School Education, Music, Music Education, Music Industry, Musical Theatre, Physical Education, Physician Assistant, Political Science, Pre-Medical Science, Psychological Services, Psychology, Recreation, Religion/Philosophy, Sociology, Spanish, Special Education, Sports Medicine, Theatre Arts, Therapeutic Recreation.
**Distribution of degrees:** The majors with the highest enrollment are business, communication arts, and elementary education; Spanish, religion/philosophy, and chemistry have the lowest.
**Requirements:** General education requirement.
**Academic regulations:** Freshmen must maintain minimum 1.50 GPA; sophomores, 1.75 GPA; juniors, 2.00 GPA; seniors, 2.00 GPA.
**Special:** Minors offered in most majors and in art, athletic coaching, dance, economics, environmental science, German, journalism, secondary/special subjects education, and speech. Self-designed majors. Double majors. Independent study. Pass/fail grading option. Internships. Preprofessional programs in law and medicine. 3-2 forestry and environmental science program with Duke U. Medical technology and physician's assistant programs with Wake Forest U. Engineering program with North Carolina State U. Deaf education program with Appalachian State U. Washington Semester. Teacher certification in early childhood, elementary, and secondary education. Certification in specific subject areas. Study abroad in England. ROTC at Davidson Coll.
**Honors:** Honors program. Honor societies.
**Academic Assistance:** Nonremedial tutoring.

**ADMISSIONS. Academic basis for candidate selection** (in order of priority): Secondary school record, standardized test scores, class rank, school's recommendation, essay.
**Nonacademic basis for candidate selection:** Particular talent or ability is important. Character and personality, extracurricular participation, and alumni/ae relationship are considered.
**Requirements:** Graduation from secondary school is recommended; GED is accepted. 16 units and the following program of study are required: 4 units of English, 2 units of math, 2 units of lab science, 2 units of social studies, 6 units of electives including 2 units of academic electives. Minimum 2.5 GPA required of applicants to teacher education and sports medicine programs. Audition required of music program applicants. Conditional admission possible for applicants not meeting standard requirements. SAT is required; ACT may be substituted. Campus visit and interview recommended. Off-campus interviews available with admissions and alumni representatives.
**Procedure:** Notification of admission on rolling basis. Reply is required prior to registration. $100 tuition deposit, refundable until May 1. $100 room deposit, refundable until May 1. Freshmen accepted in terms other than fall.
**Special programs:** Admission may be deferred one year. Credit and/or placement may be granted through CEEB Advanced Placement exams for scores of 3 or higher. Credit may be granted through CLEP subject exams and military experience. Early entrance/early admission program.
**Transfer students:** Transfer students accepted for terms other than fall. In fall 1993, 14% of all new students were transfers into all classes. 151 transfer applications were received, 131 were accepted. Minimum 2.0 GPA recommended. Lowest course grade accepted is "C." Maximum number of transferable credits is 64 semester hours from a two-year school and 96 semester hours from a four-year school. At least 32 semester hours must be completed at the college to receive degree.
**Admissions contact:** Robert W. Bennett, M.S., Director of Admissions. 800 CATAWBA.

**FINANCIAL AID. Available aid:** Pell grants, SEOG, state scholarships and grants, school scholarships and grants, private scholarships and grants, academic merit scholarships, and athletic scholarships. Perkins Loans (NDSL), PLUS, Stafford Loans (GSL), school loans, private loans, and SLS. AMS.
**Financial aid statistics:** 62% of aid is not need-based. In 1993-94, 96% of all undergraduate applicants received aid; 79% of freshman applicants. Average amounts of aid awarded freshmen: Scholarships and grants, $1,715; loans, $2,597.
**Supporting data/closing dates:** FAFSA/FAF/FFS: Priority filing date is March 15. School's own aid application: Priority filing date is March 15. State aid form: Accepted on rolling basis. Income tax forms: Accepted on rolling basis. Notification of awards on rolling basis.
**Financial aid contact:** Rebecca Brewster, M.B.A., Director of Scholarships and Financial Assistance. 704 637-4416.

## Chowan College

**Murfreesboro, NC 27855** **919 398-4101**

**1994-95 Costs.** Tuition: $8,000. Room: $1,420. Board: $2,060. Fees, books, misc. academic expenses (school's estimate): $500.
**Enrollment.** Undergraduates: 403 men, 226 women (full-time). Freshman class: 898 applicants, 664 accepted, 232 enrolled.
**Test score averages/ranges.** Average SAT scores: 400 verbal, 300 math. Range of SAT scores of middle 50%: 300-400 verbal, 300-400 math. Average ACT scores: 18 composite. Range of ACT scores of middle 50%: 16-19 composite.
**Faculty.** 52 full-time. Student/faculty ratio: 12 to 1.
**Selectivity rating.** Less competitive.

**PROFILE.** Chowan, founded in 1848, is a private, church-affiliated, liberal arts college. Its 280-acre campus is located in Murfreesboro, 60 miles from Norfolk.

**Accreditation:** SACS.
**Religious orientation:** Chowan College is an interdenominational Christian school; two semesters of religion/theology required.
**Library:** Collections totaling over 90,000 volumes.
**Athletic facilities:** Recreation center, basketball, racquetball, and tennis courts, steam, suana, and weight rooms, swimming pool.

**STUDENT BODY. Undergraduate profile:** 47% are state residents; 57% are transfers. 1% Asian-American, 22% Black, 1% Hispanic, 1% Native American, 75% White. Average age of undergraduates is 20.
**Freshman profile:** 90% of accepted applicants took SAT; 3% took ACT.
**Foreign students:** 22 students are from out of the country. Countries represented include China, Iran, Japan, Korea, and Mexico; 16 in all.

**PROGRAMS OF STUDY.**
**Majors:** Art/Commercial Art, English, Graphic Communications, Health/Physical Education, K-12 Education, Liberal Studies, Mathematics, Religion, Science, Sports Management, Studio Art.
**Requirements:** General education requirement.
**Academic regulations:** Minimum 2.0 GPA must be maintained.
**Special:** Associate's degrees offered. Self-designed majors. Double majors. Dual degrees. Independent study. Accelerated study. Internships. Preprofessional programs in medicine, veterinary science, pharmacy, dentistry, theology, and optometry. Teacher certification in elementary and secondary education.
**Honors:** Honors program.
**Academic Assistance:** Remedial reading, writing, math, and study skills. Nonremedial tutoring.

**ADMISSIONS. Academic basis for candidate selection** (in order of priority): Secondary school record, standardized test scores, class rank, school's recommendation, essay.
**Nonacademic basis for candidate selection:** Character and personality, extracurricular participation, particular talent or ability, and alumni/ae relationship are considered.
**Requirements:** Graduation from secondary school is required; GED is accepted. 19 units and the following program of study are required: 4 units of English, 2 units of math, 2 units of science including 1 unit of lab, 2 units of social studies, 1 unit of history, 8 units of electives including 6 units of academic electives. Minimum SAT score of 700, rank in top half of secondary school class, and minimum 2.0 GPA required. Conditional admission possible for applicants not meeting standard requirements. SAT or ACT is required. Campus visit and interview recommended. Off-campus interviews available with admissions and alumni representatives.
**Procedure:** Take SAT or ACT by February of 12th year. Take ACH by February of 12th year. Suggest filing application by June 1. Application deadline is August 1. Notification of admission on rolling basis. Reply is required by August 1. $200 tuition deposit, refundable until May 1. Freshmen accepted in terms other than fall.
**Special programs:** Admission may be deferred one year. Credit and/or placement may be granted through CEEB Advanced Placement exams for scores of 3 or higher. Credit and/or placement may be granted through CLEP general exams. Credit may be granted through CLEP subject exams. Credit and placement may be granted through Regents College, ACT PEP, DANTES, and challenge exams and military and life experience. Early entrance/early admission program. Concurrent enrollment program.

**Transfer students:** Transfer students accepted for terms other than fall. In fall 1992, 57% of all new students were transfers into all classes. 119 transfer applications were received, 86 were accepted. Minimum 2.0 GPA recommended. Lowest course grade accepted is "C." Maximum number of transferable credits is 100 semester hours. At least 28 semester hours must be completed at the college to receive degree.
**Admissions contact:** Mary Jo Byrd, Director of Admissions. 800 488-4101.

**FINANCIAL AID. Available aid:** Pell grants, SEOG, state scholarships and grants, school scholarships and grants, private scholarships and grants, and academic merit scholarships. Perkins Loans (NDSL), PLUS, Stafford Loans (GSL), state loans, and SLS. Deferred payment plan and family tuition reduction.
**Financial aid statistics:** 20% of aid is not need-based. In 1992-93, 80% of all undergraduate applicants received aid; 80% of freshman applicants.
**Supporting data/closing dates:** FAFSA/FAF/FFS: Priority filing date is March 15; accepted on rolling basis; deadline is August 1.Notification of awards on rolling basis.
**Financial aid contact:** Cliff Collins, Director of Financial Aid. 919 398-4101, extension 249.

# Davidson College

**Davidson, NC 28036 — 704 892-2000**

**1994-95 Costs.** Tuition: $16,850. Room & board: $5,070. Fees, books, misc. academic expenses (school's estimate): $1,214.
**Enrollment.** Undergraduates: 819 men, 729 women (full-time). Freshman class: 2,245 applicants, 882 accepted, 414 enrolled.
**Test score averages/ranges.** Average SAT scores: 570 verbal, 630 math. Range of SAT scores of middle 50%: 520-630 verbal, 590-680 math.
**Faculty.** 127 full-time; 10 part-time. 98% of faculty holds highest degree in specific field. Student/faculty ratio: 12 to 1.
**Selectivity rating.** Most competitive.

**PROFILE.** Davidson is a church-affiliated, liberal arts college. Founded as a men's college in 1837, it adopted coeducation in 1972. Its 450-acre campus and recreational lake are located in Davidson, 20 miles north of Charlotte.

**Accreditation:** SACS.
**Religious orientation:** Davidson College is affiliated with the Presbyterian Church USA; one semester of religion required.
**Library:** Collections totaling over 385,270 volumes, 2,827 periodical subscriptions, and 324,655 microform items.
**Special facilities/museums:** Art gallery, scanning electron microscopes, UV-visible spectrometer, laser systems.
**Athletic facilities:** Baseball, football, and soccer stadiums, track, football, practice, rugby, soccer, and softball fields, golf practice course, gymnasium, basketball, racquetball, squash, tennis, and volleyball courts, dance studio, training and weight rooms, natatorium, lake, canoeing, sailing, and water skiing facilities.

**STUDENT BODY. Undergraduate profile:** 25% are state residents; 1% are transfers. 2% Asian-American, 4% Black, 1% Hispanic, 89% White, 4% Other. Average age of undergraduates is 19.
**Freshman profile:** 4% of freshmen who took SAT scored 700 or over on verbal, 19% scored 700 or over on math; 40% scored 600 or over on verbal, 70% scored 600 or over on math; 85% scored 500 or over on verbal, 96% scored 500 or over on math; 98% scored 400 or over on verbal, 98% scored 400 or over on math. 98% of accepted applicants took SAT; 7% took ACT. 60% of freshmen come from public schools.
**Undergraduate achievement:** 92% of fall 1991 freshmen returned for fall 1992 term. 81% of entering class graduated. 50% of students completing a degree program immediately went on to graduate study.
**Foreign students:** 58 students are from out of the country. Countries represented include France, Germany, India, Malaysia, Russia, and Sri Lanka; 28 in all.

**PROGRAMS OF STUDY. Degrees:** B.A., B.S.
**Majors:** Art, Biology, Chemistry, Classics, Economics, English, French, German, Greek, History, Latin, Mathematics, Music, Philosophy, Physics, Political Science, Psychology, Religion, Sociology, Spanish, Theatre.
**Distribution of degrees:** The majors with the highest enrollment are history, psychology, and political science; theatre and music have the lowest.
**Requirements:** General education requirement.
**Academic regulations:** Freshmen must maintain minimum 1.5 GPA; sophomores, 1.8 GPA; juniors, 2.0 GPA; seniors, 2.0 GPA.
**Special:** Concentrations offered in applied mathematics, gender studies, international studies, medical humanities, and neurosciences. Courses offered in education, interdisciplinary humanities, and South Asian studies. Non-Western studies program. Self-designed majors. Independent study. Accelerated study. Pass/fail grading option. Internships. Preprofessional programs in law and medicine. 3-2 engineering programs with Columbia U, Duke U, Georgia Tech, North Carolina State U, and Washington U. Member of Charlotte Area Educational Consortium and American Collegiate Consortium for East-West Cultural and Academic Exchange. Washington Semester. Philadelphia Semester, other semester-away programs available. Exchange programs with Howard U and Morehouse Coll. Teacher certification in secondary education. Certification in specific subject areas. Study abroad in England, France, Germany, Greece, India, Italy, Mexico, and Spain. ROTC.
**Honors:** Phi Beta Kappa. Honors program. Honor societies.
**Academic Assistance:** Nonremedial tutoring.

**STUDENT LIFE. Housing:** All freshmen must live on campus; upperclass students must receive permission to live off campus. Coed, women's, and men's dorms. School-owned/operated apartments. Off-campus privately-owned housing. 89% of students live in college housing.
**Social atmosphere:** Patterson Court (fraternities and eating houses), Grey Student Union, the Korner Pub, the Back Street Cafe, The Soda Shop, Davidson College Presbyterian Church, and the Library are popular student social gathering spots. Social life is widely influenced by the Greek system and other groups such as Intervarsity Christian Fellowship and Davidson Outdoors. Three big weekends highlight life at Davidson: Homecoming, Midwinters, and Spring Frolics, which involve fraternity parties and campus-wide concerts of nationally-renowned rock groups. "Above all," reports the editor of the student newspaper, "the Honor Code provides the most distinct characteristic of Davidson. Students leave their Walkmans on library desks, doors are always left unlocked, and exams are self-scheduled. I have known a student to leave 15 cents on a copy machine for several days, come back, and find it there untouched."
**Services and counseling/handicapped student services:** Placement services. Health service. Counseling services for minority students. Birth control, personal, and psychological counseling. Career and academic guidance services. Religious counseling. Physically disabled student services. Learning disabled services. Notetaking services. Tape recorders. Tutors. Reader services for the blind.
**Campus organizations:** Undergraduate student government. Student newspaper (Davidsonian, published once/week). Literary magazine. Yearbook. Radio station. 100 registered organizations. Six fraternities, all with chapter houses; three sororities, no chapter houses. 65% of men join a fraternity. 71% of women join a sorority.
**Religious organizations:** Catholic Campus Ministry, Chapel Committee, Fellowship of Christian Athletes, Intervarsity Christian Fellowship, Westminster Fellowship.
**Minority/foreign student organizations:** ACES, Black Student Coalition, SEN, La Union Hispanica, Mentor Program.

**ATHLETICS. Physical education requirements:** Participation in three individual sports and one team sport by end of sophomore year required.
**Intercollegiate competition:** 30% of students participate. Baseball (M), basketball (M,W), cheerleading (M,W), cross-country (M,W), diving (M,W), field hockey (W), football (M), golf (M), lacrosse (W), soccer (M,W), swimming (M,W), tennis (M,W), track and field (indoor) (M,W), track and field (outdoor) (M,W), volleyball (W), wrestling (M). Member of NCAA Division I, NCAA Division I-AA for football, Southern Conference.
**Intramural and club sports:** 80% of students participate. Intramural basketball, flickerball, golf, soccer, softball, street hockey, swimming, tennis, volleyball. Men's club crew, lacrosse, rugby, sailing, soccer, tennis, volleyball, water skiing. Women's club crew, sailing, soccer, tennis, water skiing.

**ADMISSIONS. Academic basis for candidate selection** (in order of priority): Secondary school record, class rank, school's recommendation, essay, standardized test scores.
**Nonacademic basis for candidate selection:** Character and personality and particular talent or ability are important. Extracurricular participation, geographical distribution, and alumni/ae relationship are considered.
**Requirements:** Graduation from secondary school is required; GED is not accepted. 16 units and the following program of study are required: 4 units of English, 3 units of math, 2 units of science, 2 units of foreign language, 1 unit of history, 4 units of academic electives. SAT or ACT is required. ACH recommended. Campus visit and interview recommended. No off-campus interviews.
**Procedure:** Take SAT or ACT by January of 12th year. Suggest filing application by January 15. Application deadline is February 1. Notification of admission by April 1. Reply is required by May 1. $300 nonrefundable tuition/room deposit. Freshmen accepted for fall term only.
**Special programs:** Admission may be deferred one year. Credit and/or placement may be granted through CEEB Advanced Placement exams for scores of 4 or higher. Early decision program. In fall 1992, 233 applied for early decision and 165 were accepted. Deadline for applying for early decision is December 1. Early entrance/early admission program.
**Transfer students:** Transfer students accepted for terms other than fall. In fall 1992, 1% of all new students were transfers into all classes. 149 transfer applications were received, 10 were accepted. Application deadline is March 15 for fall; October 15 for spring. Minimum 3.0 GPA recommended. Lowest course grade accepted is "C." Maximum number of transferable credits is 18 courses from a two-year school and 16 courses from a four-year school. At least two years of course work (16 courses) must be completed at the college to receive degree.
**Admissions contact:** Nancy Cable Wells, Ph.D., Director of Admissions. 704 892-2230.

**FINANCIAL AID. Available aid:** Pell grants, SEOG, state scholarships and grants, school scholarships and grants, private scholarships and grants, ROTC scholarships, academic merit scholarships, athletic scholarships, and aid for undergraduate foreign students. Perkins Loans (NDSL), PLUS, Stafford Loans (GSL), school loans, and SLS. Knight Tuition Plans and AMS.
**Financial aid statistics:** 23% of aid is not need-based. In 1992-93, 85% of all undergraduate applicants received aid; 85% of freshman applicants. Average amounts of aid awarded freshmen: Scholarships and grants, $7,500; loans, $2,500.
**Supporting data/closing dates:** FAFSA: Deadline is February 15. FAF: Priority filing date is February 15. School's own aid application: Deadline is February 15. Income tax forms: Deadline is March 15. Notification of awards begins April 1.
**Financial aid contact:** Gordon Peck, M.A.T., Director of Financial Aid. 704 892-2232.

**STUDENT EMPLOYMENT.** College Work/Study Program. Institutional employment. 35% of full-time undergraduates work on campus during school year. Students may expect to earn an average of $1,200 during school year. Off-campus part-time employment opportunities rated "fair."

**COMPUTER FACILITIES.** 138 IBM/IBM-compatible, Macintosh/Apple, and RISC-/UNIX-based microcomputers; all are networked. Students may access Digital minicomputer/mainframe systems, Internet. Client/LAN operating systems include Apple/Macintosh. Computer languages and software packages include BASIC, Excel, FORTRAN, LISP, MINITAB, Pascal, PL/1, Quattro, SAS, SPSS-X, VAXNOTES, WordPerfect; 125 in all. Computer facilities are available to all students.
**Fees:** None.
**Hours:** 24 hours.

**GRADUATE CAREER DATA.** Graduate school percentages: 10% enter law school. 10% enter medical school. 2% enter dental school. 15% enter graduate business programs. 23% enter graduate arts and sciences programs. 1% enter theological school/seminary.

Highest graduate school enrollments: Duke U, U of North Carolina at Chapel Hill, U of Virginia, Vanderbilt U. Companies and businesses that hire graduates: Anderson Consulting, Nations Bank, Teacher Search.

**PROMINENT ALUMNI/AE.** James Batten, chairperson of the board and CEO, Knight-Ridder; Edward E. Crutchfield, chairperson and CEO, First Union Corp.; Joseph Robinson, musician, New York Philharmonic Orchestra; Dean Rusk, former U.S. secretary of state; James G. Martin, former governor of North Carolina.

# Duke University

**Durham, NC 27708** **919 684-8111**

**1994-95 Costs.** Tuition: $18,590. $19,210 (School of Engineering). Room & Board: $5,904. Fees, books, misc. academic expenses (school's estimate): $1,104.

**Enrollment.** Undergraduates: 3,300 men, 2,767 women (full-time). Freshman class: 14,528 applicants, 3,859 accepted, 1,618 enrolled. Graduate enrollment: 3,224 men, 2,072 women.

**Test score averages/ranges.** Range of SAT scores of middle 50%: 570-670 verbal, 650-740 math. Range of ACT scores of middle 50%: 29-30 English, 28-32 math.

**Faculty.** 650 full-time; 96 part-time. 97% of faculty holds highest degree in specific field. Student/faculty ratio: 9 to 1.

**Selectivity rating.** Most competitive.

**PROFILE.** Duke is a church-affiliated university. Founded as the Union Institute in 1839, it was reorganized as a teachers college in 1851, became a liberal arts college in 1859, and was renamed Duke University in 1924. Programs are offered through the Trinity College of Arts and Sciences and the School of Engineering. Its 8,500-acre campus, including English Gothic architecture style, is located in a residential section of Durham.

**Accreditation:** SACS. Professionally accredited by the Accreditation Board for Engineering and Technology, the American Assembly of Collegiate Schools of Business, the American Bar Association, the American Medical Association (CAHEA), the American Physical Therapy Association, the Association of Theological Schools in the United States and Canada, the National League for Nursing, the Society of American Foresters.
**Religious orientation:** Duke University is affiliated with the United Methodist Church; no religious requirements.
**Library:** Collections totaling over 4,134,361 volumes, 31,107 periodical subscriptions, and 1,391,803 microform items.
**Special facilities/museums:** Art museum, language lab, university forest, primate center, phytotron, electron laser, nuclear magnetic resonance machine, nuclear lab.
**Athletic facilities:** Gymnasiums, swimming pools, basketball, racquetball, squash, tennis, and volleyball courts, tracks, golf course, athletic fields, stadium, weight room, fitness course.

**STUDENT BODY. Undergraduate profile:** 14% are state residents; 2% are transfers. 8% Asian-American, 8% Black, 4% Hispanic, 1% Native American, 79% White. Average age of undergraduates is 20.
**Freshman profile:** 99% of accepted applicants took SAT; 26% took ACT. 66% of freshmen come from public schools.
**Undergraduate achievement:** 98% of fall 1991 freshmen returned for fall 1992 term. 92% of entering class graduated. 38% of students who completed a degree program went on to graduate study within one year.
**Foreign students:** 33 students are from out of the country. Countries represented include Canada, France, Germany, Hong Kong, Japan, and the United Kingdom; 21 in all.

**PROGRAMS OF STUDY. Degrees:** A.B., B.S., B.S.Eng.
**Majors:** Afro-American Studies, Art History, Biological Anthropology/Anatomy, Biology, Biomedical Engineering Studies, Chemistry, Civil/Environmental Engineering, Classical Languages, Classical Studies, Comparative Area Studies, Computer Science, Cultural Anthropology, Design, Drama, Economics, Electrical Engineering, English, Environmental Science/Policy, French, Geology, Germanic Languages/Literatures, History, Italian Studies, Literature, Mathematics, Mechanical Engineering/Materials Science, Medieval/Renaissance Studies, Music, Philosophy, Physics, Political Science, Psychology, Public Policy Studies, Religion, Slavic Languages/Literatures, Sociology, Spanish.
**Distribution of degrees:** The majors with the highest enrollment are English, political science, and history; geology and literature have the lowest.
**Requirements:** General education requirement.
**Academic regulations:** Minimum 1.7 GPA required for graduation.
**Special:** Program II allows students to structure individual courses of study for committee approval. Certificates offered in African and Afro-American studies, institute of the arts, Asian and African languages and literature, dance, film and video, genetics, health policy, human development, interdisciplinary German studies, Judaic studies, marine biology, markets and management studies, neurosciences, science/technology/human values, women's studies, perspectives on Marxism and society, and primatology. Self-designed majors. Double majors. Independent study. Accelerated study. Pass/fail grading option. Internships. Graduate school at which undergraduates may take graduate-level courses. Pre-business, pre-law, and pre-medicine advising available. 3-2 engineering program. 3-2 and 4-1 medical technology programs. Combined bachelor's/master's degree programs in business, engineering, environmental management, forestry, law, and teaching. Member of Consortium on Financing Higher Education. New York Arts Program. Exchange program with Howard U. Cross-registration with North Carolina Central U, North Carolina State U, and U of North Carolina at Chapel Hill. Teacher certification in elementary and secondary education. Certification in specific subject areas. Exchange programs abroad in Canada (McGill U) and Japan (International Christian U). Study abroad also in Austria, Belgium, China, Egypt, England, France, Germany, Greece, India, Israel, Italy, Morocco, Poland, Scotland, the former Soviet Republics, Spain, Taiwan, and Zimbabwe. ROTC, NROTC, and AFROTC.
**Honors:** Phi Beta Kappa. Honor societies.
**Academic Assistance:** Nonremedial tutoring.

**STUDENT LIFE. Housing:** All first-semester freshmen must live on campus. Coed, women's, and men's dorms. Fraternity housing. School-owned/operated apartments. Theme dorms. Theme halls. 88% of students live in college housing.
**Social atmosphere:** The editor of the student newspaper observes, "It has been said we work hard and we play hard. Freshmen tend to be frenetic, but everything mellows as we get older. Some people move off campus, most try to live on West Campus, the happenin' place. Everybody loves Duke basketball. Most stuff happens on campus." Some of the more popular events include Duke basketball games, the Umbria Jazz Festival, Oktoberfest, Springfest, Handel's Messiah in the Chapel, Myrtle Beach, Martin Luther King Day, the Christmas tree lighting, Homecoming, the Freewater Film Series and Quad Flix, and Broadway at Duke. Students frequent Satisfaction Pizza and Ninth Street, "a street of neat sorts of bohemian shops."
**Services and counseling/handicapped student services:** Placement services. Health service. Women's center. Day care. Counseling services for minority, military, veteran, and older students. Birth control, personal, and psychological counseling. Career and academic guidance services. Religious counseling. Physically disabled student services. Learning disabled services. Notetaking services. Tape recorders. Tutors. Reader services for the blind.
**Campus organizations:** Undergraduate student government. Student newspaper (Chronicle, published once/day). Literary magazine. Yearbook. Radio and TV stations. Two Broadway previews each year, chapel choir, chorale, bands, symphony orchestra, wind symphony, other musical groups, dance and drama groups, Amnesty International, Circle K, coffeehouse, outing and photo clubs, debating, art groups, programming committees, political, service, and special-interest groups, 200 organizations in all. 23 fraternities, 18 chapter houses; 12 sororities, no chapter houses. 42% of men join a fraternity. 42% of women join a sorority.
**Religious organizations:** Bahai group, Baptist Student Union, Black Campus Ministry, Cambridge Christian Fellowship, Campus Crusade for Christ, Catholic Campus Ministry, Episcopal Center, Fellowship of Christian Athletes, Hillel, Intervarsity Christian Fellowship, Islamic Association, Lutheran Campus Ministry, Navigators, Newman Center, United Church of Christ group, Wesley Foundation.
**Minority/foreign student organizations:** Asian Student Association, Black Student Alliance, Center for Black Culture, Muslim Students Association, Spanish-American-Latin Students. International Association, Asian, Chinese, Indian, and Japanese groups.

**ATHLETICS. Physical education requirements:** None.
**Intercollegiate competition:** 10% of students participate. Baseball (M), basketball (M,W), cross-country (M,W), diving (M,W), fencing (M,W), field hockey (W), football (M), golf (M,W), lacrosse (M), soccer (M,W), swimming (M,W), tennis (M,W), track and field (indoor) (M,W), track and field (outdoor) (M,W), volleyball (W), wrestling (M). Member of Atlantic Coast Conference, NCAA Division I, NCAA Division I-A for football.
**Intramural and club sports:** 65% of students participate. Intramural baseball, basketball, crew, cycling, equestrian sports, football, golf, ice hockey, lacrosse, martial arts, racquetball, rugby, sailing, skiing, soccer, squash, swimming, tennis, track and field, water polo. Men's club badminton, baseball, crew, cycling, equestrian sports, field hockey, football, frisbee, golf, ice hockey, karate, lacrosse, racquetball, running, rugby, skiing, sky diving, soccer, softball, tae kwon do, tennis, triathlon, volleyball, water polo, sailing. Women's club badminton, crew, cycling, dancing, equestrian sports, field hockey, ice hockey, karate, lacrosse, racquetball, running, skiing, sky diving, soccer, softball, tae kwon do, tennis, triathlon, volleyball, water polo.

**ADMISSIONS. Academic basis for candidate selection** (in order of priority): Secondary school record, school's recommendation, class rank, standardized test scores, essay.
**Nonacademic basis for candidate selection:** Character and personality, extracurricular participation, and particular talent or ability are important. Geographical distribution and alumni/ae relationship are considered.
**Requirements:** Graduation from secondary school is required; GED is not accepted. 15 units and the following program of study are recommended: 4 units of English, 3 units of math, 3 units of science, 3 units of foreign language, 2 units of social studies. 4 units of math and 1 unit of physics or chemistry required of engineering program applicants. SAT or ACT is required. ACH required. Campus visit and interview recommended. Off-campus interviews available with an alumni representative.
**Procedure:** Take SAT or ACT by January of 12th year. Take ACH by January of 12th year. Visit college for interview by December 15 of 12th year. Suggest filing application by December 1. Application deadline is January 2. Notification of admission by April 15. Reply is required by May 1. $360 nonrefundable tuition deposit. $100 nonrefundable room deposit. Freshmen accepted in terms other than fall.
**Special programs:** Admission may be deferred one year. Credit and/or placement may be granted through CEEB Advanced Placement exams for scores of 4 or higher. Early decision program. In fall 1992, 976 applied for early decision and 465 were accepted. Deadline for applying for early decision is November 1. Early entrance/early admission program.
**Transfer students:** Transfer students accepted for terms other than fall. In fall 1992, 2% of all new students were transfers into all classes. 271 transfer applications were received, 69 were accepted. Application deadline is April 1 for fall; October 15 for spring. Minimum 3.0 GPA recommended. Lowest course grade accepted is "C-." Maximum number of transferable credits is 17 courses. At least 17 courses must be completed at the university to receive degree.
**Admissions contact:** Christoph Guttentag, M.A., Director of Undergraduate Admissions. 919 684-3214.

**FINANCIAL AID. Available aid:** Pell grants, SEOG, state scholarships and grants, school scholarships and grants, private scholarships and grants, ROTC scholarships, academic merit scholarships, and athletic scholarships. Perkins Loans (NDSL), PLUS, Stafford Loans (GSL), Health Professions Loans, state loans, school loans, and SLS. Knight Tuition Plans. Multiple Payment Plan.
**Financial aid statistics:** 10% of aid is not need-based. In 1992-93, 39% of all undergraduate applicants received aid; 37% of freshman applicants. Average amounts of aid awarded freshmen: Scholarships and grants, $11,162; loans, $2,800.
**Supporting data/closing dates:** FAFSA/FAF/FFS: Priority filing date is February 1. Income tax forms: Priority filing date is February 1.

**Financial aid contact:** James A. Belvin, Jr., Director of Financial Aid. 919 684-6225.

**STUDENT EMPLOYMENT.** College Work/Study Program. Institutional employment. 28% of full-time undergraduates work on campus during school year. Students may expect to earn an average of $1,400 during school year. Off-campus part-time employment opportunities rated "good."

**COMPUTER FACILITIES.** 340 IBM/IBM-compatible and Macintosh/Apple microcomputers; 300 are networked. Students may access IBM, SUN minicomputer/mainframe systems, BITNET, Internet. Residence halls may be equipped with stand-alone microcomputers, networked microcomputers. Client/LAN operating systems include Apple/Macintosh. Computer languages and software packages include Maple, Mathematica, MATHLAB, Microsoft Word, MINITAB, PC Write, SAS, SPSS, Stat Graphics, WordPerfect. Computer facilities are available to all students.
**Fees:** Computer fee is included in tuition/fees.

**GRADUATE CAREER DATA.** Graduate school percentages: 11% enter law school. 12% enter medical school. 1% enter graduate business programs. 35% of graduates choose careers in business and industry.

**PROMINENT ALUMNI/AE.** Richard Nixon, former U.S. president; Elizabeth Dole, former U.S. secretary of labor; Juanita Kreps, former U.S. secretary of commerce; William Styron, author; Reynolds Price, author; George Grune, CEO, *Reader's Digest.*

## East Carolina University

**Greenville, NC 27858-4353 — 919 757-6131**

**1993-94 Costs.** Tuition: $1,426 (state residents), $7,098 (out-of-state). Room: $1,500. Board: $1,650. Fees, books, misc. academic expenses (school's estimate): $550.
**Enrollment.** Undergraduates: 5,875 men, 7,293 women (full-time). Freshman class: 9,274 applicants, 6,362 accepted, 2,435 enrolled. Graduate enrollment: 1,104 men, 1,855 women.
**Test score averages/ranges.** Average SAT scores: 433 verbal, 483 math. Range of SAT scores of middle 50%: 390-470 verbal, 430-530 math. Average ACT scores: 18 composite. Range of ACT scores of middle 50%: 17-18 composite.
**Faculty.** 746 full-time; 14 part-time. 68% of faculty holds doctoral degree. Student/faculty ratio: 19 to 1.
**Selectivity rating.** Less competitive.

**PROFILE.** East Carolina, founded in 1907, is a public university. Programs are offered through the College of Arts and Sciences; the Graduate School; the General College; the Schools of Allied Health Sciences, Art, Business, Education, Home Economics, Industry and Technology, Medicine, Music, Nursing, and Social Work; and the Divisions of Academic Library Services, Continuing Education, and Health Sciences. Its 373-acre campus is located in Greenville.

**Accreditation:** SACS. Professionally accredited by the American Assembly of Collegiate Schools of Business, the American Dietetic Association, the American Home Economics Association, the American Medical Association (CAHEA), the American Physical Therapy Association, the American Speech-Language-Hearing Association, the Council on Social Work Education, the Liaison Committee on Medical Education, the National Association of Schools of Art and Design, the National Association of Schools of Music, the National Council for Accreditation of Teacher Education, the National League for Nursing, the National Recreation and Park Association. Numerous professional accreditations.
**Religious orientation:** East Carolina University is nonsectarian; no religious requirements.
**Library:** Collections totaling over 1,088,523 volumes, 6,858 periodical subscriptions, and 1,543,083 microform items.
**Special facilities/museums:** Art museum, coastal resources center, language lab.
**Athletic facilities:** Coliseum, field house, track, stadium, natatorium, athletic, baseball, and softball fields, tennis courts.

**STUDENT BODY. Undergraduate profile:** 83% are state residents; 36% are transfers. 1% Asian-American, 9% Black, 1% Hispanic, 1% Native American, 88% White. Average age of undergraduates is 21.
**Freshman profile:** 1% of freshmen who took SAT scored 700 or over on math; 2% scored 600 or over on verbal, 7% scored 600 or over on math; 16% scored 500 or over on verbal, 41% scored 500 or over on math; 69% scored 400 or over on verbal, 88% scored 400 or over on math; 97% scored 300 or over on verbal, 98% scored 300 or over on math. 1% of freshmen who took ACT scored 24 or over on composite; 37% scored 18 or over on composite; 52% scored 12 or over on composite. 99% of accepted applicants took SAT; 1% took ACT. 90% of freshmen come from public schools.
**Undergraduate achievement:** 77% of fall 1992 freshmen returned for fall 1993 term. 18% of entering class graduated.
**Foreign students:** 22 students are from out of the country. Countries represented include Denmark, England, Germany, Italy, Norway, and Sweden; seven in all.

**PROGRAMS OF STUDY. Degrees:** B.A., B.F.A., B.S., B.S.Bus.Admin.
**Majors:** Accounting/Management, Administrative Services, Anthropology, Applied Physics, Art, Art Education, Banking, Biochemistry, Biology, Business/Commerce/Distributive Education, Chemistry, Child Development/Family Relations, Clinical Laboratory Science, Clothing/Textiles, Communication Arts, Community Arts Management, Computer/Information Sciences, Criminal Justice, Cytotechnology, Dance, Dance Education, Decision Science, Early Childhood Education, Economics, Elementary Education, English, Environmental Health, Finance, French, General Business, Geography, Geology, German, Health Information Management, Health/Physical Education, History, Home Economics, Home Economics Education, Hospitality Management, Industrial/Technical Education, Industrial Technology, Interior Design, Leisure Systems Studies, Library Science Education, Management, Marketing, Mathematics, Middle Education, Music/Church Music, Music Education, Music Performance, Music/Piano Pedagogy, Music Theory/Composition, Music Therapy, Music/Voice Pedagogy, Nursing, Nutrition/Dietetics, Occupational Therapy, Philosophy, Physical Education, Physical Therapy, Physics, Political Science, Psychology, Public History, Real Estate, School/Community Health Education, Science Education, Secondary Education, Social Work, Sociology, Spanish, Special Education, Speech/Language/Auditory Pathology, Technical Education, Theatre Arts, Urban/Regional Planning.
**Distribution of degrees:** The majors with the highest enrollment are business/management, elementary education, and industrial arts education; community arts management, French, and philosophy have the lowest.
**Requirements:** General education requirement.
**Academic regulations:** Freshmen must maintain minimum 1.75 GPA; sophomores, juniors, seniors, 2.0 GPA.
**Special:** Minors are offered in 59 areas of study of which eight are interdisciplinary and two are aerospace/military studies. Double majors. Dual degrees. Independent study. Internships. Cooperative education programs. Graduate school at which undergraduates may take graduate-level courses. Preprofessional programs in law, medicine, veterinary science, pharmacy, dentistry, optometry, and engineering. 3-2 engineering programs with North Carolina A&T U, North Carolina State U, and U of North Carolina at Charlotte. BSA/MSA program in accounting. Transfer program in industrial technology. Member of Water Resources Research Institute, Institute for Nutrition, Oak Ridge Associated Universities, and Sea Grant College Program. UN Semester. Member of National Student Exchange (NSE). Teacher certification in early childhood, elementary, secondary, special education, and vo-tech education. Certification in specific subject areas. Member of International Student Exchange Program (ISEP). Exchange programs abroad in England (Richmond Coll), France (the Sorbonne), and Italy (U of Ferrara). Study abroad also in Costa Rica and Japan. ROTC and AFROTC.
**Honors:** Honors program. Honor societies.
**Academic Assistance:** Remedial reading, writing, math, and study skills. Nonremedial tutoring.

**STUDENT LIFE. Housing:** Students may live on or off campus. Coed, women's, and men's dorms. Sorority and fraternity housing. 33% of students live in college housing.
**Social atmosphere:** Popular spots on and off campus are the Student Union, Student Stores, Attic Nite Club, Chicos, and Bogies. The rugby and football teams influence campus life. Football games, Halloween, Barefoot on the Mall, and basketball games are popular social events. "Most social life for students is either from Greek functions or going to bars or clubs downtown," reports the student newspaper.
**Services and counseling/handicapped student services:** Placement services. Health service. Couples and group counseling. Legal counseling. Counseling services for minority, military, veteran, and older students. Birth control, personal, and psychological counseling. Career and academic guidance services. Religious counseling. Physically disabled student services. Learning disabled program/services. Notetaking services. Tape recorders. Tutors. Reader services for the blind.
**Campus organizations:** Undergraduate student government. Student newspaper (East Carolinian, published twice/week). Literary magazine. Yearbook. Radio station. Choirs, bands, music groups, Opera Theatre, coffeehouse, East Carolina Playhouse, poetry forum, crafts center, films, lectures, debating, Young Democrats, Young Republicans, People United to Support the Handicapped, peer health educators, recreational clubs, athletic, departmental, and service groups, 175 organizations in all. 20 fraternities, 13 chapter houses; 12 sororities, eight chapter houses. 15% of men join a fraternity. 15% of women join a sorority.
**Religious organizations:** Students for Christ, Buddhist Meditation/Study Group, Campus Crusade for Christ, Navigators, Hillel, King Youth, New Generation, Newman Club, Baptist Student Union.
**Minority/foreign student organizations:** Native Americans of ECU, Blacks for Leadership/Equality, Minority Arts Committee. International Student Association, Spanish, German, and Chinese clubs.

**ATHLETICS. Physical education requirements:** One semester of physical education required.
**Intercollegiate competition:** 2% of students participate. Baseball (M), basketball (M,W), cross-country (M,W), diving (M,W), football (M), golf (M), soccer (M), softball (W), swimming (M,W), tennis (M,W), track (indoor) (M,W), track (outdoor) (M,W), volleyball (W). Member of Colonial Athletic Association, NCAA Division I.
**Intramural and club sports:** 47% of students participate. Intramural badminton, basketball, bowling, cross-country, golf, horseback riding, racquetball, skiing, soccer, softball, tennis, water polo. Men's club crew, disc golf, frisbee, karate, kayak, lacrosse, rugby, tae kwon do, volleyball, weightlifting, wind surfing. Women's club soccer, frisbee, karate, tae kwon do, volleyball.

**ADMISSIONS. Academic basis for candidate selection** (in order of priority): Secondary school record, standardized test scores, class rank.
**Nonacademic basis for candidate selection:** Particular talent or ability and geographical distribution are considered.
**Requirements:** Graduation from secondary school is required; GED is not accepted. No specific distribution of secondary school units required. Minimum combined SAT score of 800 and minimum 2.0 GPA required of in-state applicants; rank in top half of secondary school class recommended. Minimum combined SAT score of 900 and minimum 2.0 GPA required of out-of-state applicants; rank in top half of secondary school class recommended. Audition required of music program applicants. SAT or ACT is required. Campus visit recommended. No off-campus interviews.
**Procedure:** Take SAT or ACT by February of 12th year. Suggest filing application by December 15. Application deadline is March 15. Notification of admission on rolling basis. Reply is required by May 1. $30 nonrefundable tuition deposit. $100 room deposit, refundable until July 1. Freshmen accepted in terms other than fall.
**Special programs:** Credit may be granted through CEEB Advanced Placement for scores of 3 or higher. Credit may be granted through CLEP general and subject exams, DANTES and challenge exams, and military experience. Early entrance/early admission program. Concurrent enrollment program.
**Transfer students:** Transfer students accepted for terms other than fall. In fall 1993, 36% of all new students were transfers into all classes. 2,493 transfer applications were received, 2,096 were accepted. Application deadline is April 15 for fall; November 1 for

spring. Minimum 2.0 GPA required. Lowest course grade accepted is "C." Maximum number of transferable credits is 60 semester hours. 30 semester hours and half of major must be completed at the university to receive degree.
**Admissions contact:** Thomas E. Powell, Ph.D., Director of Admissions. 919 757-6640.

**FINANCIAL AID. Available aid:** Pell grants, SEOG, state scholarships and grants, school scholarships and grants, private scholarships and grants, ROTC scholarships, academic merit scholarships, and athletic scholarships. Perkins Loans (NDSL), PLUS, Stafford Loans (GSL), NSL, Health Professions Loans, state loans, private loans, and SLS.
**Financial aid statistics:** 10% of aid is not need-based. In 1993-94, 52% of all undergraduate applicants received aid; 52% of freshman applicants. Average amounts of aid awarded freshmen: Scholarships and grants, $2,553.
**Supporting data/closing dates:** FAFSA: Priority filing date is April 15. SINGLEFILE: Accepted on rolling basis. Notification of awards on rolling basis.
**Financial aid contact:** Rosemary Stelma, M.S., Director of Financial Aid. 919 757-6610.

**STUDENT EMPLOYMENT.** College Work/Study Program. Institutional employment. 13% of full-time undergraduates work on campus during school year. Students may expect to earn an average of $1,600 during school year. Off-campus part-time employment opportunities rated "good."

**COMPUTER FACILITIES.** 1,200 IBM/IBM-compatible and Macintosh/Apple microcomputers; 600 are networked. Students may access AT&T, Cray, Digital, Hewlett-Packard, IBM, SUN minicomputer/mainframe systems, BITNET, Internet. Residence halls may be equipped with stand-alone microcomputers, networked microcomputers, networked terminals, modems. Client/LAN operating systems include Apple/Macintosh, DOS, UNIX/XENIX/AIX, Novell. Computer languages and software packages include Assembler, BASIC, C, COBOL, dBASE, DW4, FORTRAN, Lotus 1-2-3, MINITAB, Multiplan, Pascal, SAS, SPSS-X, SQL, Videotext, Word; 90 in all. Computer facilities are available to all students.
**Fees:** $25/semester.
**Hours:** 7 AM-12 midn.

**GRADUATE CAREER DATA.** Companies and businesses that hire graduates: Various banks and accounting firms; textile, transportation, and insurance companies; retail firms.

**PROMINENT ALUMNI/AE.** James H. Maynard, founder of Golden Corral and CEO of Investors Management; Valeria O. Lovelace, vice-president for research and circulation, "Sesame Street"; Robert B. Morgan, former U.S. senator, currently director of State Bureau of Investigation, North Carolina.

# Elon College

**Elon College, NC 27244** **910 584-9711**

**1994-95 Costs.** Tuition: $9,100. Room: $1,782. Board: $2,101. Fees, books, misc. academic expenses (school's estimate): $650.
**Enrollment.** Undergraduates: 1,295 men, 1,638 women (full-time). Freshman class: 3,624 applicants, 2,786 accepted, 857 enrolled. Graduate enrollment: 76 men, 62 women.
**Test score averages/ranges.** Average SAT scores: 439 verbal, 483 math. Range of SAT scores of middle 50%: 390-480 verbal, 430-530 math.
**Faculty.** 138 full-time; 55 part-time. 75% of faculty holds doctoral degree. Student/faculty ratio: 17 to 1.
**Selectivity rating.** Less competitive.

**PROFILE.** Elon, founded in 1889, is a church-affiliated, liberal arts college. Its 275-acre campus is located west of North Carolina's primary high-tech region, the Research Triangle.

**Accreditation:** SACS. Professionally accredited by the National Council for Accreditation of Teacher Education.
**Religious orientation:** Elon College is affiliated with the United Church of Christ; no religious requirements.
**Library:** Collections totaling over 179,222 volumes, 1,000 periodical subscriptions, and 509,427 microform items.
**Special facilities/museums:** Resource center, fine arts center with recital hall, theatre, television studio, music rooms, art gallery.
**Athletic facilities:** Gymnasiums, swimming pool, handball, racquetball, and tennis courts, field house, lacrosse, soccer, and softball fields, track.

**STUDENT BODY. Undergraduate profile:** 40% are state residents; 15% are transfers. 1% Asian-American, 7% Black, 1% Hispanic, 90% White, 1% Other. Average age of undergraduates is 20.
**Freshman profile:** 1% of freshmen who took SAT scored 700 or over on math; 3% scored 600 or over on verbal, 8% scored 600 or over on math; 20% scored 500 or over on verbal, 43% scored 500 or over on math; 74% scored 400 or over on verbal, 90% scored 400 or over on math; 99% scored 300 or over on verbal, 100% scored 300 or over on math. 98% of accepted applicants took SAT; 2% took ACT. 85% of freshmen come from public schools.
**Undergraduate achievement:** 79% of fall 1992 freshmen returned for fall 1993 term. 45% of entering class graduated. 23% of students who completed a degree program went on to graduate study within one year.
**Foreign students:** 41 students are from out of the country. Countries represented include England, Japan, Pakistan, Spain, Taiwan, and Thailand; 19 in all.

**PROGRAMS OF STUDY. Degrees:** B.A., B.S.
**Majors:** Accounting, Biology, Business Administration, Chemistry, Communications/Broadcast/Corporate, Computer Science, Economics, Education, English, French, Health Education, History, Human Services, Journalism, Leisure Sports Management, Mathematics, Medical Technology, Music, Music Education, Music Performance, Music Theatre, Philosophy, Physical Education/Health, Physics, Political Science, Psychology, Public Administration, Religious Studies, Science Education, Social Sciences, Sociology, Spanish, Sports Medicine, Theatre Arts.
**Distribution of degrees:** The majors with the highest enrollment are business administration, communications, and education; physics, French, and theatre arts have the lowest.
**Requirements:** General education requirement.
**Academic regulations:** Freshmen must maintain minimum 1.8 GPA; sophomores, 1.8 GPA; juniors, 2.0 GPA; seniors, 2.0 GPA.
**Special:** Minors offered in many majors and in anthropology, dance, geography, international studies, studio art, and women's studies. Several concentrations available in communications, including corporate broadcasting and journalism. Courses offered in Chinese, coaching, geology, German, and Greek. Teaching Fellows Program. Isabella Cannon Leadership Program. Double majors. Independent study. Accelerated study. Pass/fail grading option. Internships. Cooperative education programs. Preprofessional programs in law, medicine, veterinary science, pharmacy, dentistry, theology, optometry, podiatry, and osteopathy. 3-2 engineering programs with North Carolina A&T U, North Carolina State U, and U of North Carolina at Charlotte. Member of Piedmont Independent Colleges Association. Washington Semester. Exchanges programs with Augustana Coll, Austin Coll, Bethany Coll, Birmingham-Southern Coll, Carthage Coll, Chapman U, Coe Coll, DePauw U, Eckerd Coll, Gustavus Adolphus Coll, Hastings Coll, Pacific Lutheran U, St. Mary's Coll, St. Olaf Coll, Tabor Coll, Washington and Jefferson Coll, Westminster Coll, and Whitworth Coll. Teacher certification in early childhood, elementary, and secondary education. Certification in specific subject areas. Exchange programs abroad in Japan (Nagasaki Wesleyan Coll, Kansai U). Study abroad also in Belize, China, Costa Rica, England, Guadeloupe, Jamaica, Mexico, the Netherlands, and Spain. ROTC.
**Honors:** Honors program. Honor societies.
**Academic Assistance:** Remedial reading, writing, math, and study skills. Nonremedial tutoring.

**STUDENT LIFE. Housing:** Students may live on or off campus. Women's and men's dorms. Sorority and fraternity housing. School-owned/operated apartments. 55% of students live in college housing.
**Services and counseling/handicapped student services:** Placement services. Health service. Women's center. Counseling services for minority and older students. Personal counseling. Career and academic guidance services. Religious counseling. Physically disabled student services. Learning disabled services. Notetaking services. Tape recorders. Tutors.
**Campus organizations:** Undergraduate student government. Student newspaper (Pendulum, published once/week). Literary magazine. Yearbook. Radio and TV stations. Concert choir, chamber singers, gospel choir, Elan (vocal jazz ensemble), pep and jazz bands, Student Government Association, Habitat for Humanity, Liberal Arts Forum, Model UN, Young Democrats, Lyceum Committee, Civinettes, BACCHUS, Elon Volunteers, Student Union Board, 88 organizations in all. 10 fraternities, four chapter houses; nine sororities, four chapter houses. 23% of men join a fraternity. 29% of women join a sorority.
**Religious organizations:** Christian Student Union, Fellowship of Christian Athletes, Newman Society, Baptist Student Union, Intervarsity Christian Fellowship, Discover Fellowship.
**Minority/foreign student organizations:** Black Cultural Society. International Student Association.

**ATHLETICS. Physical education requirements:** One semester of physical education required.
**Intercollegiate competition:** 11% of students participate. Baseball (M), basketball (M,W), cheerleading (M,W), cross-country (M,W), football (M), golf (M), soccer (M,W), softball (W), tennis (M,W), track (outdoor) (M), track and field (outdoor) (M), volleyball (W). Member of NCAA Division II, South Atlantic Conference.
**Intramural and club sports:** 40% of students participate. Intramural basketball, football, racquetball, soccer, softball, tennis, volleyball, water polo. Men's club lacrosse. Women's club lacrosse.

**ADMISSIONS. Academic basis for candidate selection** (in order of priority): Secondary school record, standardized test scores, class rank, school's recommendation, essay.
**Nonacademic basis for candidate selection:** Character and personality are important. Extracurricular participation, particular talent or ability, and alumni/ae relationship are considered.
**Requirements:** Graduation from secondary school is required; GED is accepted. 14 units and the following program of study are required: 4 units of English, 3 units of math, 2 units of science including 1 unit of lab, 2 units of foreign language, 1 unit of social studies, 1 unit of history. Additional units of math, science, social studies, and history recommended. Rank in top half of secondary school class and minimum 2.5 GPA recommended. Audition required of music program applicants. SAT or ACT is required. Campus visit and interview recommended. No off-campus interviews.
**Procedure:** Take SAT or ACT by fall of 12th year. Visit college for interview by fall of 12th year. Suggest filing application by June 1; no deadline. Notification of admission on rolling basis. Reply is recommended within one month of acceptance. $50 tuition deposit, refundable until May 1. $150 room deposit, refundable until May 1. Freshmen accepted in terms other than fall.
**Special programs:** Admission may be deferred one year. Credit may be granted through CEEB Advanced Placement for scores of 3 or higher. Credit may be granted through CLEP general and subject exams, ACT PEP exams, and military experience. Credit and placement may be granted through challenge exams. Early decision program. In fall 1993, 194 applied for early decision and 149 were accepted. Deadline for applying for early decision is December 1. Concurrent enrollment program.
**Transfer students:** Transfer students accepted for terms other than fall. In fall 1993, 15% of all new students were transfers into all classes. 252 transfer applications were received, 208 were accepted. Application deadline is July 15 for fall; December 1 for spring. Minimum 2.0 GPA required. Lowest course grade accepted is "C." Maximum number of transferable credits is 65 semester hours. At least 32 semester hours must be completed at the college to receive degree.
**Admissions contact:** Nan P. Perkins, M.A., Dean of Admissions and Financial Planning. 800 334-8448, extension 1.

**FINANCIAL AID. Available aid:** Pell grants, SEOG, state scholarships and grants, school scholarships and grants, private scholarships and grants, ROTC scholarships, academic merit scholarships, and athletic scholarships. Leadership scholarships. Perkins

Loans (NDSL), PLUS, Stafford Loans (GSL), state loans, school loans, private loans, and SLS. Tuition Plan Inc., Knight Tuition Plans, and AMS.
**Financial aid statistics:** 48% of aid is not need-based. In 1993-94, 81% of all undergraduate applicants received aid; 65% of freshman applicants. Average amounts of aid awarded freshmen: Scholarships and grants, $3,539; loans, $3,310.
**Supporting data/closing dates:** FAFSA/FAF: Priority filing date is April 1. School's own aid application: Priority filing date is April 1; accepted on rolling basis. Notification of awards on rolling basis.
**Financial aid contact:** Joel Speckhard, J.D., Associate Dean of Admissions and Financial Planning. 800 334-8448, extension 2.

**STUDENT EMPLOYMENT.** College Work/Study Program. Institutional employment. 28% of full-time undergraduates work on campus during school year. Students may expect to earn an average of $1,300 during school year. Off-campus part-time employment opportunities rated "excellent."

**COMPUTER FACILITIES.** 140 IBM/IBM-compatible, Macintosh/Apple, and RISC-/UNIX-based microcomputers; 100 are networked. Students may access Digital, SUN minicomputer/mainframe systems, Internet. Client/LAN operating systems include Apple/Macintosh, DOS, UNIX/XENIX/AIX, Novell. Computer languages and software packages include Ada, APL, BASIC, C++, COBOL, dBASE, FORTRAN, Lotus, Macro, Minitab, Pascal, SAS, Smartstar, SPSS, Turbo C, Turbo Pascal, WordPerfect. Computer facilities are available to all students.
**Fees:** Computer fee is included in tuition/fees.
**Hours:** 8 AM-1 AM (M-Th); 10 AM-5 PM (F); 12 AM-6 PM (Sa); 2 PM-1 AM (Su).

**GRADUATE CAREER DATA.** Graduate school percentages: 2% enter law school. 1% enter medical school. 6% enter graduate business programs. Highest graduate school enrollments: Elon Coll, U of Maryland, U of North Carolina at Greensboro, Wake Forest U. 69% of graduates choose careers in business and industry. Companies and businesses that hire graduates: AT&T, First Wachovia Bank, Roche Biomedical Labs, Purdue Farms, Burlington Industries, Arthur Andersen, IBM, Atcom Telecommunications, Ernst and Young.

**PROMINENT ALUMNI/AE.** Dr. John R. Kernodle, former chairperson, American Medical Association; Doug Moe, former coach, San Antonio Spurs; Eugene Gordon, federal judge, U.S. District Court; Martin Ritt, film producer and director; Marjorie Hunter, former Washington correspondent, *New York Times*; C. Kenneth Utt, Oscar-winning film producer, *Silence of the Lambs*.

# Fayetteville State University

**Fayetteville, NC 28301 — 919 486-1133**

**1994-95 Costs.** Tuition: $740 (state residents), $6,806 (out-of-state). Room: $1,400. Board: $1,150. Fees, books, misc. academic expenses (school's estimate): $636.
**Enrollment.** Undergraduates: 958 men, 1,658 women (full-time). Freshman class: 1,201 applicants, 784 accepted, 353 enrolled. Graduate enrollment: 230 men, 548 women.
**Test score averages/ranges.** Average SAT scores: 396 verbal, 420 math.
**Faculty.** 185 full-time; 25 part-time. 71% of faculty holds doctoral degree. Student/faculty ratio: 15 to 1.
**Selectivity rating.** Noncompetitive.

**PROFILE.** Fayetteville State, founded in 1867, is a public university. Programs are offered through the College of Arts and Sciences and the Schools of Business and Economics and Education and Human Development. Its 136-acre campus is located in Fayetteville.

**Accreditation:** SACS. Professionally accredited by the National Council for Accreditation of Teacher Education.
**Religious orientation:** Fayetteville State University is nonsectarian; no religious requirements.
**Library:** Collections totaling over 174,778 volumes, 2,550 periodical subscriptions, and 470,285 microform items.
**Special facilities/museums:** Planetarium.
**Athletic facilities:** Gymnasiums, swimming pool, football and softball fields, tennis courts, track, stadium.

**STUDENT BODY. Undergraduate profile:** 91% are state residents; 39% are transfers. 1% Asian-American, 68% Black, 2% Hispanic, 1% Native American, 28% White. Average age of undergraduates is 20.
**Freshman profile:** 1% of freshmen who took SAT scored 600 or over on math; 8% scored 500 or over on verbal, 15% scored 500 or over on math; 36% scored 400 or over on verbal, 50% scored 400 or over on math; 90% scored 300 or over on verbal, 96% scored 300 or over on math. 100% of accepted applicants took SAT.
**Undergraduate achievement:** 76% of fall 1991 freshmen returned for fall 1992 term. 12% of entering class graduated. 10% of students who completed a degree program immediately went on to graduate study.
**Foreign students:** Countries represented include Nigeria.

**PROGRAMS OF STUDY. Degrees:** B.A., B.S., B.S.M.T., B.S.Nurs.
**Majors:** Accounting, Biology, Business Administration, Business Education, Chemistry, Computer Science, Criminal Justice, Early Childhood Education, Economics, English Language/Literature, Geography, Health Education, History, Intermediate Education, Marketing, Mathematics, Medical Technology, Middle Grade Education, Music, Music Education, Nursing, Office Administration, Physical Education, Political Science, Psychology, Secondary Education/Social Sciences, Sociology, Spanish, Speech/Theatre, Visual Arts.
**Distribution of degrees:** The majors with the highest enrollment are business administration, sociology, and education; chemistry, medical technology, and music have the lowest.
**Requirements:** General education requirement.
**Academic regulations:** Freshmen must maintain minimum 1.0 GPA; sophomores, 1.6 GPA; juniors, 1.85 GPA; seniors, 1.99 GPA.
**Special:** Minors offered in all majors and in art education and recreation. Associate's degrees offered. Double majors. Independent study. Internships. Cooperative education programs. 2-2 programs in applied math, conservation, engineering, natural resource and recreation management, physics, pulp and paper science, recreation and park administration, textile chemistry, and textiles technology with North Carolina State U. Teacher certification in early childhood, elementary, secondary, and special education. Certification in specific subject areas. AFROTC.
**Honors:** Honors program.
**Academic Assistance:** Remedial reading, writing, and math. Nonremedial tutoring.

**STUDENT LIFE. Housing:** Students may live on or off campus. Women's and men's dorms. 31% of students live in college housing.
**Social atmosphere:** Students gather at the student center, the SBE Lounge, and the Taylor Science Annex Lounge. Popular campus events include Homecoming, Martin Luther King celebrations, and the Lyceum lecture series. According to the student newspaper, "Fayetteville State is one of the most culturally diverse universities in the North Carolina system. Students and faculty reach for the best in education while trying to learn and accept each culture's qualities. This leads to large groups of students interacting in numerous activities both on and off campus."
**Services and counseling/handicapped student services:** Placement services. Health service. Day care. Counseling services for minority, military, and veteran students. Personal counseling. Career and academic guidance services.
**Campus organizations:** Undergraduate student government. Student newspaper (Broncos' Voice, published bimonthly). Yearbook. Radio and TV stations. Choir, band, pep club, marching dance group, class organizations, special-interest groups. Four fraternities, no chapter houses; four sororities, no chapter houses. 3% of men join a fraternity. 3% of women join a sorority.
**Religious organizations:** Baptist Student Union, Fellowship of Christian Students.
**Minority/foreign student organizations:** Afro-American Society.

**ATHLETICS. Physical education requirements:** One semester of physical education required.
**Intercollegiate competition:** 4% of students participate. Basketball (M,W), cheerleading (M,W), cross-country (M,W), football (M), golf (M), softball (W), volleyball (W). Member of Central Intercollegiate Athletic Association, NCAA Division II.
**Intramural and club sports:** 20% of students participate. Intramural basketball, bowling, flag football, powderpuff football, softball, tennis, track, volleyball.

**ADMISSIONS. Academic basis for candidate selection** (in order of priority): Standardized test scores, secondary school record, class rank, school's recommendation.
**Nonacademic basis for candidate selection:** Character and personality are important. Extracurricular participation, particular talent or ability, and geographical distribution are considered.
**Requirements:** Graduation from secondary school is recommended; GED is accepted. 18 units and the following program of study are required: 4 units of English, 3 units of math, 3 units of science including 1 unit of lab, 1 unit of social studies, 1 unit of history, 6 units of academic electives. SAT is required; ACT may be substituted. PSAT is recommended. No off-campus interviews.
**Procedure:** Notification of admission on rolling basis. $75 refundable room deposit. Freshmen accepted in terms other than fall.
**Special programs:** Admission may be deferred one year. Credit and/or placement may be granted through CEEB Advanced Placement exams for scores of 3 or higher. Credit may be granted through CLEP general and subject exams, DANTES exams, and military experience. Early entrance/early admission program. Concurrent enrollment program.
**Transfer students:** Transfer students accepted for terms other than fall. In fall 1992, 39% of all new students were transfers into all classes. 764 transfer applications were received, 682 were accepted. Application deadline is August 1 for fall; December 1 for spring. Minimum 2.0 GPA required. Lowest course grade accepted is "C." Maximum number of transferable credits is 60 semester hours from a two-year school and 90 semester hours from a four-year school. At least 30 semester hours must be completed at the university to receive degree.
**Admissions contact:** Charles Darlington, M.Ed., Academic Dean. 919 486-1371.

**FINANCIAL AID. Available aid:** Pell grants, SEOG, Federal Nursing Student Scholarships, state scholarships and grants, school scholarships, private scholarships and grants, ROTC scholarships, academic merit scholarships, athletic scholarships, and aid for undergraduate foreign students. American Indian Student Legislative Program. Perkins Loans (NDSL), PLUS, and Stafford Loans (GSL). Deferred payment plan.
**Supporting data/closing dates:** FAFSA/FAF/FFS: Deadline is May 1. Income tax forms: Accepted on rolling basis. Notification of awards on rolling basis.
**Financial aid contact:** Mae Graves, Director of Financial Aid. 919 486-1325.

**STUDENT EMPLOYMENT.** College Work/Study Program. Institutional employment. 36% of full-time undergraduates work on campus during school year. Students may expect to earn an average of $650 during school year. Off-campus part-time employment opportunities rated "fair."

**COMPUTER FACILITIES.** 250 IBM/IBM-compatible and Macintosh/Apple microcomputers. Students may access Digital, Sequent minicomputer/mainframe systems. Computer languages and software packages include Ada, Assembly, BASIC, C, COBOL, FORTRAN, Pascal, POISE, Systems Analysis. Computer facilities are available to all students.
**Fees:** None.
**Hours:** 24 hours.

**GRADUATE CAREER DATA.** Highest graduate school enrollments: Fayetteville State U. 12% of graduates choose careers in business and industry. Companies and businesses that hire graduates: Bell, Monsanto, IBM.

**PROMINENT ALUMNI/AE.** Dr. Jesse Williams, director, Cumberland County Health Department; Dr. Willis McCloud, superintendent, Northampton County Schools; Dr. Jessica Daniels, clinical psychologist, Baker Guidance Center, Boston, Mass.; James Ivery, assistant to deputy undersecretary, U.S. Department of Health and Human Services.

# Gardner-Webb College

**Boiling Springs, NC 28017-9980 704 434-4798**

**1993-94 Costs.** Tuition: $7,680. Room: $1,940. Board: $2,130. Fees, books, misc. academic expenses (school's estimate): $500.
**Enrollment.** Undergraduates: 740 men, 863 women (full-time). Freshman class: 1,110 applicants, 930 accepted, 338 enrolled. Graduate enrollment: 112 men, 104 women.
**Test score averages/ranges.** Average SAT scores: 400 verbal, 445 math.
**Faculty.** 83 full-time; 80 part-time. 70% of faculty holds doctoral degree. Student/faculty ratio: 17 to 1.
**Selectivity rating.** Less competitive.

**PROFILE.** Gardner-Webb, founded in 1905, is a church-affiliated college of liberal and professional studies. Its 200-acre campus is located in Boiling Springs, in the Piedmont section of North Carolina.
**Accreditation:** SACS. Professionally accredited by the National Association of Schools of Music, the National League for Nursing.
**Religious orientation:** Gardner-Webb College is an interdenominational Christian school; two semesters of religion required.
**Library:** Collections totaling over 260,000 volumes and 937 periodical subscriptions.
**Special facilities/museums:** Observatory.
**Athletic facilities:** Gymnasiums, swimming pool, basketball, racquetball, tennis, and volleyball courts, baseball, softball, and soccer fields, football stadium, weight lifting and wrestling rooms.
**STUDENT BODY. Undergraduate profile:** 76% are state residents; 42% are transfers. 1% Asian-American, 11% Black, 83% White, 5% Other. Average age of undergraduates is 20.
**Freshman profile:** 2% of freshmen who took SAT scored 600 or over on verbal, 6% scored 600 or over on math; 12% scored 500 or over on verbal, 27% scored 500 or over on math; 46% scored 400 or over on verbal, 64% scored 400 or over on math; 82% scored 300 or over on verbal, 89% scored 300 or over on math. Majority of accepted applicants took SAT. 85% of freshmen come from public schools.
**Undergraduate achievement:** 80% of fall 1992 freshmen returned for fall 1993 term. 40% of entering class graduated.
**Foreign students:** 63 students are from out of the country. Countries represented include the Bahamas, Cameroon, India, Japan, Nigeria, and Trinidad; 19 in all.
**PROGRAMS OF STUDY. Degrees:** B.A., B.S., B.S.Nurs.
**Majors:** Biology, Business Administration, Chemistry, Communications, Early Childhood Education, English, French, General Science, Health/Physical Education, History, Intermediate Education, Mathematics, Medical Technology, Music, Nursing, Psychology, Religion, Religious Education, Social Sciences, Spanish.
**Distribution of degrees:** The majors with the highest enrollment are business administration, intermediate education, and religion.
**Requirements:** General education requirement.
**Academic regulations:** Freshmen must maintain minimum 1.5 GPA; sophomores, 1.7 GPA; juniors, 1.9 GPA; seniors, 2.0 GPA.
**Special:** Minors offered in all majors. Associate's degrees offered. Double majors. Dual degrees. Independent study. Internships. Graduate school at which undergraduates may take graduate-level courses. Preprofessional programs in law, medicine, pharmacy, dentistry, and theology. Medical technology and physician's assistant programs with Bowman Gray Sch of Medicine. 3-2 engineering program with Auburn U and U of North Carolina at Charlotte. Teacher certification in early childhood, elementary, and secondary education.
**Honors:** Honors program. Honor societies.
**Academic Assistance:** Remedial reading, writing, math, and study skills.
**STUDENT LIFE. Housing:** Unmarried students must live on campus unless living with family. Women's and men's dorms. 70% of students live in college housing.
**Social atmosphere:** "We are a small, private, Southern Baptist institution in a rural area," reports the student newspaper. "Students go home on the weekend for entertainment. We also have many day students and adult learners." Popular events on campus include football and basketball games, and pop concerts. Influential groups include the Student Government Association, Big Brothers and Big Sisters, and the Baptist Student Union. Students meet at the Dover Campus Center and, off campus, at the Bulldog Quik Snak.
**Services and counseling/handicapped student services:** Placement services. Health service. Personal and psychological counseling. Career and academic guidance services. Religious counseling. Physically disabled student services. Learning disabled services. Notetaking services. Tape recorders. Tutors. Reader services for the blind.
**Campus organizations:** Undergraduate student government. Student newspaper (Pilot). Yearbook. Radio station. World Trade Resource Club, folk singers, chorus, drama group, pep band, ensemble, Student Entertainment Association, Residence Hall Association, Association of Women Students, athletic, departmental, service, and special-interest groups.
**Religious organizations:** Baptist Young Women, Baptist Student Union, Fellowship of Christian Athletes, Religious Education club, Focus Revival Teams, Ministerial Alliance, Jail and Prison Ministry, Rest Home Ministry.
**Minority/foreign student organizations:** Afro-American Society. International Student Club.
**ATHLETICS. Physical education requirements:** Two semesters of physical education required.
**Intercollegiate competition:** 40% of students participate. Baseball (M), basketball (M,W), cheerleading (M,W), cross-country (M,W), football (M), golf (M), soccer (M,W), softball (W), tennis (M,W), volleyball (W), wrestling (M). Member of NCAA Division II, South Atlantic Conference.
**Intramural and club sports:** 25% of students participate. Intramural basketball, flag football, golf, pool, racquetball, softball, table tennis, tennis, volleyball, walleyball.

**ADMISSIONS. Academic basis for candidate selection** (in order of priority): Secondary school record, class rank, standardized test scores, school's recommendation, essay.
**Nonacademic basis for candidate selection:** Character and personality, extracurricular participation, and particular talent or ability are important.
**Requirements:** Graduation from secondary school is required; GED is accepted. 15 units and the following program of study are recommended: 4 units of English, 3 units of math, 1 unit of science, 2 units of foreign language, 2 units of social studies, 3 units of electives. Rank in top half of secondary school class recommended. SAT is required; ACT may be substituted. Campus visit and interview recommended. Off-campus interviews available with admissions and alumni representatives.
**Procedure:** Take SAT or ACT by December of 12th year. Visit college for interview by March of 12th year. Notification of admission on rolling basis. Reply is required within 30 days of notification. $150 room deposit, refundable until May 1. Freshmen accepted in terms other than fall.
**Special programs:** Credit and/or placement may be granted through CLEP general and subject exams. Credit may be granted through ACT PEP, DANTES, and challenge exams and military experience. Early decision program. Early entrance/early admission program. Concurrent enrollment program.
**Transfer students:** Transfer students accepted for terms other than fall. In fall 1993, 42% of all new students were transfers into all classes. Application deadline is rolling for fall; rolling for spring. Minimum 2.0 GPA required. Lowest course grade accepted is "C." Maximum number of transferable credits is 64 semester hours from a two-year school and 98 semester hours from a four-year school. At least 30 semester hours must be completed at the college to receive degree.
**Admissions contact:** Ray M. Hardee, M.A., Director of Admissions. 800 253-6472.
**FINANCIAL AID. Available aid:** Pell grants, SEOG, state scholarships and grants, school scholarships and grants, private scholarships, academic merit scholarships, and athletic scholarships. Perkins Loans (NDSL), PLUS, Stafford Loans (GSL), NSL, Health Professions Loans, state loans, school loans, private loans, and SLS. Tuition Plan Inc. and deferred payment plan.
**Supporting data/closing dates:** FAFSA/FAF/FFS: Accepted on rolling basis.
**Financial aid statistics:** 20% of aid is not need-based. In 1993-94, 80% of all undergraduate applicants received aid. Average amounts of aid awarded freshmen: Scholarships and grants, $2,800; loans, $2,625.
**STUDENT EMPLOYMENT.** College Work/Study Program. Institutional employment. 32% of full-time undergraduates work on campus during school year. Students may expect to earn an average of $1,300 during school year. Off-campus part-time employment opportunities rated "good."
**COMPUTER FACILITIES.** 70 IBM/IBM-compatible microcomputers. Students may access IBM minicomputer/mainframe systems. Computer languages and software packages include BASIC, COBOL, dBASE, FORTRAN, Lotus 1-2-3, PL/1, RPG, WordPerfect.
**Fees:** None.
**Hours:** 7:45 AM-11 PM.
**PROMINENT ALUMNI/AE.** Dr. Sam Craver, professor of education, Virginia Commonwealth U; Dr. Roland Yow, architect; Roger King, TV producer and syndicator.

# Greensboro College

**Greensboro, NC 27401-1875 919 272-7102**

**1993-94 Costs.** Tuition: $7,646. Room: $1,640. Board: $2,040. Fees, books, misc. academic expenses (school's estimate): $720.
**Enrollment.** Undergraduates: 305 men, 507 women (full-time). Freshman class: 753 applicants, 597 accepted, 222 enrolled.
**Test score averages/ranges.** Average SAT scores: 440 verbal, 460 math.
**Faculty.** 42 full-time; 38 part-time. 86% of faculty holds highest degree in specific field. Student/faculty ratio: 18 to 1.
**Selectivity rating.** Less competitive.

**PROFILE.** Greensboro College is a church-affiliated institution. Founded as a women's college in 1938, it adopted coeducation in 1954. Programs are offered through the Divisions of Applied Arts and Social Sciences, Fine Arts, Humanities, and Natural Sciences and Mathematics. Its 27-acre campus is located near downtown Greensboro.
**Accreditation:** SACS. Professionally accredited by the National Association of Schools of Music.
**Religious orientation:** Greensboro College is affiliated with the United Methodist Church; two semesters of religion required.
**Library:** Collections totaling over 90,000 volumes, 450 periodical subscriptions, and 3,600 microform items.
**Special facilities/museums:** Art gallery, historical museum, language lab.
**Athletic facilities:** Gymnasium, swimming pool, athletic field, weight room, basketball, tennis, and volleyball courts, dance studio.
**STUDENT BODY. Undergraduate profile:** 62% are state residents; 22% are transfers. 1% Asian-American, 11% Black, 1% Hispanic, 1% Native American, 86% White. Average age of undergraduates is 20.
**Freshman profile:** 1% of freshmen who took SAT scored 700 or over on verbal, 1% scored 700 or over on math; 7% scored 600 or over on verbal, 9% scored 600 or over on math; 20% scored 500 or over on verbal, 32% scored 500 or over on math; 64% scored 400 or over on verbal, 68% scored 400 or over on math; 98% scored 300 or over on verbal, 98% scored 300 or over on math. 98% of accepted applicants took SAT; 2% took ACT. 90% of freshmen come from public schools.
**Undergraduate achievement:** 68% of fall 1991 freshmen returned for fall 1992 term. 40% of entering class graduated. 18% of students who completed a degree program went on to graduate study within five years.
**Foreign students:** 11 students are from out of the country.
**PROGRAMS OF STUDY. Degrees:** B.A., B.S.

**Majors:** Accounting, Allied Health, Art, Biology, Business Administration, Chemistry, Education, Elementary Education, English, French, History, Mathematics, Medical Technology, Middle Grades Education, Music, Physical Education, Physician's Assistant, Political Science, Psychology, Radiological Technology, Religion/Philosophy, Secondary Education, Sociology, Spanish, Special Education, Theatre.
**Distribution of degrees:** The majors with the highest enrollment are business administration, education, and biology; chemistry and mathematics have the lowest.
**Requirements:** General education requirement.
**Special:** Minors offered in all majors and in computer science and legal administration. Double majors. Independent study. Accelerated study. Pass/fail grading option. Internships. Graduate school at which undergraduates may take graduate-level courses. Preprofessional programs in law, medicine, veterinary science, dentistry, and theology. 2-2 radiologic technology program with Moses H. Cone Hospital. 3-1 medical technology program with Moses H. Cone and Baptist Hospitals. 3-2 physician assistant program with Bowman Gray Sch of Medicine. Member of Greater Greensboro Consortium and Piedmont Independent College Association. Teacher certification in elementary, secondary, and special education. ROTC and AFROTC at North Carolina A&T State U.
**Honors:** Honors program.
**Academic Assistance:** Nonremedial tutoring.

**ADMISSIONS. Academic basis for candidate selection** (in order of priority): Secondary school record, class rank, standardized test scores, essay, school's recommendation.
**Nonacademic basis for candidate selection:** Character and personality, extracurricular participation, particular talent or ability, and alumni/ae relationship are considered.
**Requirements:** Graduation from secondary school is recommended; GED is accepted. No specific distribution of secondary school units required. Academic Development Program with one-semester conditional admission for applicants not meeting standard requirements. SAT or ACT is required. ACH recommended. Campus visit and interview recommended. Off-campus interviews available with an alumni representative.
**Procedure:** Take SAT or ACT by October of 12th year. Visit college for interview by January of 12th year. Notification of admission on rolling basis. Reply is required within four weeks of acceptance. $150 nonrefundable tuition deposit. $150 nonrefundable deposit. Freshmen accepted in terms other than fall.
**Special programs:** Admission may be deferred one year. Credit and/or placement may be granted through CEEB Advanced Placement exams for scores of 3 or higher. Credit and/or placement may be granted through CLEP general and subject exams. Credit and placement may be granted through Regents College, ACT PEP, DANTES, and challenge exams and military and life experience. Early entrance/early admission program. Concurrent enrollment program.
**Transfer students:** Transfer students accepted for terms other than fall. In fall 1992, 22% of all new students were transfers into all classes. 189 transfer applications were received, 118 were accepted. Application deadline is rolling for fall; rolling for spring. Minimum 2.0 GPA recommended. Lowest course grade accepted is "C." Maximum number of transferable credits is 100 semester hours. At least 30 semester hours must be completed at the college to receive degree. At least 30 semester hours must be completed at the college to receive degree.
**Admissions contact:** Martha Bunch, Director of Admissions. 800 346-8226.

**FINANCIAL AID. Available aid:** Pell grants, SEOG, state grants, school scholarships, private scholarships and grants, and academic merit scholarships. Perkins Loans (NDSL), PLUS, Stafford Loans (GSL), school loans, and SLS. AMS and Tuition Management Systems.
**Financial aid statistics:** Average amounts of aid awarded freshmen: Scholarships and grants, $2,181; loans, $2,765.
**Supporting data/closing dates:** FAFSA/FAF/FFS: Priority filing date is March 15. Notification of awards on rolling basis.
**Financial aid contact:** Katharine Bonisolli, Director of Financial Aid. 800 346-8226.

# Guilford College

**Greensboro, NC 27410** **910 316-2000**

**1994-95 Costs.** Tuition: $13,400. Room: $2,704. Board: $2,456. Fees, books, misc. academic expenses (school's estimate): $1,410.
**Enrollment.** Undergraduates: 657 men, 753 women (full-time). Freshman class: 1,205 applicants, 1,054 accepted, 326 enrolled.
**Test score averages/ranges.** Average SAT scores: 499 verbal, 531 math. Range of SAT scores of middle 50%: 430-560 verbal, 470-590 math. Average ACT scores: 24 composite. Range of ACT scores of middle 50%: 20-27 composite.
**Faculty.** 88 full-time; 20 part-time. 74% of faculty holds doctoral degree. Student/faculty ratio: 14 to 1.
**Selectivity rating.** Competitive.

**PROFILE.** Guilford, founded in 1837, is a church-affiliated college. Its 300-acre campus is located in northwest Greensboro in the Piedmont section of North Carolina. Campus architecture reflects a Georgian Colonial influence.

**Accreditation:** SACS.
**Religious orientation:** Guilford College is affiliated with the Society of Friends; no religious requirements.
**Library:** Collections totaling over 226,000 volumes, and 1,225 periodical subscriptions.
**Special facilities/museums:** Friends Historical Collection, art gallery, language lab, research-grade observatory, telecommunications center.
**Athletic facilities:** Gymnasium, field house, baseball, football, intramural, lacrosse, and soccer fields, stadium, YMCA swimming pool, weight room.

**STUDENT BODY. Undergraduate profile:** 39% are state residents; 14% are transfers. 1% Asian-American, 7% Black, 2% Hispanic, 1% Native American, 89% White. Average age of undergraduates is 21.
**Freshman profile:** 89% of accepted applicants took SAT; 14% took ACT. 65% of freshmen come from public schools.
**Undergraduate achievement:** 74% of fall 1992 freshmen returned for fall 1993 term. 52% of entering class graduated. 20% of students who completed a degree program went on to graduate study within five years.
**Foreign students:** 18 students are from out of the country. Countries represented include Guatemala, Singapore, Thailand, Venezuela, and the former Yugoslav Republics; 14 in all.

**PROGRAMS OF STUDY. Degrees:** A.B., B.F.A., B.Mus., B.S.
**Majors:** Accounting, Art, Biology, Chemistry, Economics, Education Studies, English, French, Geology, German, German Area Studies, History, Humanistic Studies, International Studies, Justice/Policy Studies, Management, Mathematics, Music, Philosophy, Physical Education, Physics, Political Science, Psychology, Religious Studies, Sociology/Anthropology, Spanish, Sport Management, Sports Medicine, Theatre Studies.
**Distribution of degrees:** The majors with the highest enrollment are management and justice/policy studies; French and Spanish have the lowest.
**Requirements:** General education requirement.
**Academic regulations:** Minimum 2.0 GPA must be maintained.
**Special:** Concentrations offered in Afro-American studies, communications, computing, environmental studies, intercultural studies, medieval studies, peace and conflict, and women's studies. Minors offered. Geology field trips to numerous locations. Self-designed majors. Double majors. Dual degrees. Independent study. Accelerated study. Pass/fail grading option. Internships. Preprofessional programs in law, medicine, veterinary science, dentistry, and theology. 3-1 medical technology and physician's assistant programs with Bowman Gray Sch of Medicine. 3-2 forestry and environmental studies program with Duke U. 3-2 engineering programs with Georgia Tech and Washington U. Cooperative consortium programs. Member of Piedmont Independent College Association and Greater Greensboro Consortium. Cross-registration with Bennett Coll, Elon Coll, Greensboro Coll, Guilford Tech Comm Coll, High Point Coll, North Carolina A&T State U, and U of North Carolina at Greensboro. Washington Semester and UN Semester. One-week semesters in Philadelphia, the Outer Banks, and Florida. Teacher certification in elementary and secondary education. Certification in specific subject areas. Exchange programs abroad in Japan (International Christian U). Study abroad also in China, England, France, Germany, Ghana, Italy, and Mexico. ROTC and AFROTC at North Carolina A&T State U.
**Honors:** Honors program. Honor societies.
**Academic Assistance:** Remedial reading, writing, math, and study skills. Nonremedial tutoring.

**STUDENT LIFE. Housing:** All unmarried students under age 23 must live on campus unless living with family. Coed, women's, and men's dorms. School-owned/operated apartments. On-campus married-student housing. Theme housing. 78% of students live in college housing.
**Social atmosphere:** The editor of the student newspaper comments, "Since Guilford has no fraternity or sororities, parties are held on an individual basis. That means that it's harder to find something to do, but at the same time the college is less polarized by such groups." Popular gathering spots around Guilford include Jam's Deli, Jan's House, the Underground, The Edge, Dolley's, and Village Tavern. Influential groups on campus include the College Union and radical feminists. A favorite event during the school year is Serendipity, which is the spring blowout with bands, events, etc.
**Services and counseling/handicapped student services:** Placement services. Health service. Women's center. Counseling services for minority, veteran, and older students. Birth control, personal, and psychological counseling. Career and academic guidance services. Religious counseling. Physically disabled student services. Learning disabled services. Notetaking services. Tape recorders. Tutors. Reader services for the blind.
**Campus organizations:** Undergraduate student government. Student newspaper (Guilfordian, published once/week). Literary magazine. Yearbook. Radio station. Choir, Revelers (drama group), Websterian Prelaw Society, community volunteer groups, College Republicans, Young Democrats, scholarly journals, departmental, service, and special-interest groups., 38 organizations in all.
**Religious organizations:** Intervarsity Christian Fellowship, Hillel, Young Friends Quaker Concerns, Fellowship of Christian Athletes.
**Minority/foreign student organizations:** African American Cultural Society, Native American Club. International Relations Club.

**ATHLETICS. Physical education requirements:** None.
**Intercollegiate competition:** 30% of students participate. Baseball (M), basketball (M,W), cheerleading (M,W), football (M), golf (M), lacrosse (M,W), soccer (M,W), tennis (M,W), volleyball (W). Member of NCAA Division III, Old Dominion Athletic Conference.
**Intramural and club sports:** 60% of students participate. Intramural basketball, bowling, flag football, golf, soccer, softball, swimming, table tennis, tennis, ultimate frisbee, volleyball. Men's club rugby. Women's club rugby.

**ADMISSIONS. Academic basis for candidate selection** (in order of priority): Class rank, secondary school record, standardized test scores, essay, school's recommendation.
**Nonacademic basis for candidate selection:** Character and personality, extracurricular participation, particular talent or ability, and geographical distribution are emphasized. Alumni/ae relationship is considered.
**Requirements:** Graduation from secondary school is required; GED is accepted. 18 units and the following program of study are required: 4 units of English, 3 units of math, 2 units of lab science, 2 units of foreign language, 2 units of social studies, 1 unit of history, 4 units of electives including 2 units of academic electives. Conditional admission possible for applicants not meeting standard requirements. SAT or ACT is required. ACH recommended. Campus visit and interview recommended. Off-campus interviews available with admissions and alumni representatives.
**Procedure:** Take SAT or ACT by December of 12th year. Take ACH by December of 12th year. Visit college for interview by May of 12th year. Application deadline is February 1. Notification of admission by March 15. Reply is required by May 1. $300 tuition deposit, refundable until May 1. Freshmen accepted in terms other than fall.
**Special programs:** Admission may be deferred one year. Credit and/or placement may be granted through CEEB Advanced Placement exams for scores of 4 or higher. Credit and/or

placement may be granted through CLEP general and subject exams. Early decision program. In fall 1993, 26 applied for early decision and 25 were accepted. Deadline for applying for early decision is December 1. Early entrance/early admission program. Concurrent enrollment program.
**Transfer students:** Transfer students accepted for terms other than fall. In fall 1993, 14% of all new students were transfers into all classes. 160 transfer applications were received, 120 were accepted. Application deadline is June 1 for fall; December 1 for spring. Minimum 2.0 GPA required. Lowest course grade accepted is "C." Maximum number of transferable credits is 64 semester hours. At least 32 semester hours must be completed at the college to receive degree.
**Admissions contact:** Larry M. West, M.A., Director of Admissions. 800 992-7759.

**FINANCIAL AID. Available aid:** Pell grants, SEOG, state scholarships and grants, school scholarships and grants, private scholarships and grants, ROTC scholarships, and academic merit scholarships. Perkins Loans (NDSL), PLUS, Stafford Loans (GSL), state loans, school loans, private loans, and SLS. College monthly installment plan.
**Financial aid statistics:** 19% of aid is not need-based. In 1993-94, 98% of all undergraduate applicants received aid; 98% of freshman applicants. Average amounts of aid awarded freshmen: Scholarships and grants, $8,795; loans, $3,350.
**Supporting data/closing dates:** FAFSA: Priority filing date is March 1. School's own aid application: Priority filing date is March 1. Income tax forms: Accepted on rolling basis. Notification of awards on rolling basis.
**Financial aid contact:** Anthony E. Gurley, Director of Financial Aid. 910 316-2354.

**STUDENT EMPLOYMENT.** College Work/Study Program. Institutional employment. 44% of full-time undergraduates work on campus during school year. Students may expect to earn an average of $1,250 during school year. Off-campus part-time employment opportunities rated "good."

**COMPUTER FACILITIES.** 101 IBM/IBM-compatible and Macintosh/Apple microcomputers; 99 are networked. Students may access Digital minicomputer/mainframe systems, Internet. Residence halls may be equipped with direct connections to VAX (Null modem) or 10 Boset. Client/LAN operating systems include Apple/Macintosh, DOS, DEC. Computer languages and software packages include BASIC, C, FORTRAN, IDL, MINITAB, Pascal, Quattro, SPSS-X, Super Paint, WordPerfect. Computer facilities are available to all students.
**Fees:** Computer fee is included in tuition/fees.
**Hours:** 24 hours.

**GRADUATE CAREER DATA.** Graduate school percentages: 3% enter law school. 2% enter medical school. 3% enter graduate business programs. 12% enter graduate arts and sciences programs. Highest graduate school enrollments: Duke U, U of North Carolina at Chapel Hill, Penn State, U of Virginia, Wake Forest U. 15% of graduates choose careers in business and industry. Companies and businesses that hire graduates: AT&T, Arthur Andersen, Ciba Geigy, First Wachovia.

**PROMINENT ALUMNI/AE.** Dewey Trogdon, CEO, Cone Mills; M.L. Carr, professional basketball player; Warren Mitofsky, head of network election polling consortium.

## High Point University

**High Point, NC 27262-3598 — 910 841-9000**

**1994-95 Costs.** Tuition: $7,550. Room & board: $4,050. Fees, books, misc. academic expenses (school's estimate): $1,250.
**Enrollment.** Undergraduates: 831 men, 1,216 women (full-time). Freshman class: 1,412 applicants, 1,149 accepted, 341 enrolled. Graduate enrollment: 11 men, 14 women.
**Test score averages/ranges.** Average SAT scores: 423 verbal, 456 math. Range of SAT scores of middle 50%: 380-470 verbal, 390-520 math.
**Faculty.** 94 full-time; 4 part-time. 60% of faculty holds doctoral degree. Student/faculty ratio: 14 to 1.
**Selectivity rating.** Less competitive.

**PROFILE.** High Point is a church-affiliated university. Founded in 1924, it gained university status in 1991. Its 75-acre campus is located in a residential area of High Point, 17 miles from Winston-Salem and 15 miles from Greensboro.
**Accreditation:** SACS. Professionally accredited by the National Council for Accreditation of Teacher Education.
**Religious orientation:** High Point University is affiliated with the United Methodist Church; one semester of religion required.
**Library:** Collections totaling over 141,563 volumes, 1,205 periodical subscriptions, and 55,000 microform items.
**Athletic facilities:** Gymnasiums, baseball, field hockey, and intramural fields, baseball and soccer stadiums, track, tennis courts, swimming pool.

**STUDENT BODY. Undergraduate profile:** 45% are state residents; 28% are transfers. 1% Asian-American, 7% Black, 1% Hispanic, 1% Native American, 90% White. Average age of undergraduates is 21.
**Freshman profile:** 1% of freshmen who took SAT scored 700 or over on math; 2% scored 600 or over on verbal, 7% scored 600 or over on math; 15% scored 500 or over on verbal, 31% scored 500 or over on math; 56% scored 400 or over on verbal, 64% scored 400 or over on math; 84% scored 300 or over on verbal, 85% scored 300 or over on math. 98% of accepted applicants took SAT. 88% of freshmen come from public schools.
**Undergraduate achievement:** 20% of students who completed a degree program immediately went on to graduate study.
**Foreign students:** 28 students are from out of the country. Countries represented include Brazil, Canada, Jordan, Korea, Sweden, and the United Kingdom; 18 in all.

**PROGRAMS OF STUDY. Degrees:** B.A., B.S.
**Majors:** Accounting, Art, Art Education, Biology, Business Administration/Economics, Chemistry, Chemistry/Business, Computer Information Systems, Elementary Education, English/Communications, English/Literature, English/Writing, Forestry, French, History, Home Furnishings/Interior Design, Home Furnishings Marketing, Human Relations, Individualized Major, Industrial/Organizational Psychology, International Business, International Studies, Mathematics, Medical Technology, Middle Grades Education, Philosophy, Physical Education/Recreation, Political Science, Psychology, Religion, Social Studies, Special Education, Sports Medicine, Theatre Arts.
**Distribution of degrees:** The majors with the highest enrollment are business administration/economics, accounting, and psychology; chemistry, medical technology, and forestry have the lowest.
**Requirements:** General education requirement.
**Academic regulations:** Minimum 2.0 GPA must be maintained.
**Special:** Minors offered all majors and in American free enterprise, athletic coaching, computer science, music, and social work. Human relations major, offered in cooperation with American Humanics, trains students for service-oriented careers in youth services (scouting, YMCA, etc.) and with volunteer community agencies. Home furnishings marketing major receives support from furniture industry. Self-designed majors. Double majors. Independent study. Pass/fail grading option. Internships. Preprofessional programs in law, medicine, veterinary science, pharmacy, dentistry, theology, and optometry. 3-1 medical technology program. 3-2 forestry and environmental studies program with Duke U. Member of Greater Greensboro Consortium and Piedmont Independent College Association. Teacher certification in early childhood, secondary, and special education. Certification in specific subject areas. Exchange program abroad in England (Oxford U). Study abroad also in Brazil, France, Germany, and Spain. ROTC and AFROTC at North Carolina A&T U.
**Honors:** Honors program. Honor societies.
**Academic Assistance:** Remedial reading, writing, math, and study skills. Nonremedial tutoring.

**STUDENT LIFE. Housing:** All unmarried students under age 21 must live on campus unless living near campus with relatives. Coed, women's, and men's dorms. Sorority and fraternity housing. School–owned/operated apartments. 62% of students live in college housing.
**Social atmosphere:** According to the editor of the student newspaper, social life at High Point is dominated by the Greeks. Popular events include basketball games, Homecoming, Spring Formal, Christmas Lessons and Carols ritual, and Senior Send Off. On campus, students meet at the student center, the library, and the cafeteria. There are a number of nearby bars frequented by students from High Point and several neighboring colleges.
**Services and counseling/handicapped student services:** Placement services. Health service. Counseling services for veteran students. Personal and psychological counseling. Career and academic guidance services. Religious counseling.
**Campus organizations:** Undergraduate student government. Student newspaper (Hi Po, published once/month). Literary magazine. Yearbook. Radio station. University Singers, Tower Players, Student Union Board, international business club, student chemical society, Collegiate Journalist, 53 organizations in all. Four fraternities, all with chapter houses; four sororities, no chapter houses. 38% of men join a fraternity. 32% of women join a sorority.
**Religious organizations:** Baptist Student Union, Board of Stewards, Fellowship of Christian Athletes.
**Minority/foreign student organizations:** Black Cultural Awareness. International Club.

**ATHLETICS. Physical education requirements:** Two semesters of physical education required.
**Intercollegiate competition:** 28% of students participate. Baseball (M), basketball (M,W), cheerleading (W), cross-country (M,W), field hockey (W), golf (M), soccer (M,W), tennis (M,W), track (outdoor) (M), track and field (outdoor) (M), volleyball (W). Member of Carolinas Intercollegiate Athletic Conference, NAIA.
**Intramural and club sports:** 64% of students participate. Intramural badminton, frisbee, golf, soccer, softball, tag football, track, volleyball. Women's club field hockey.

**ADMISSIONS. Academic basis for candidate selection** (in order of priority): Secondary school record, standardized test scores, class rank, school's recommendation.
**Nonacademic basis for candidate selection:** Character and personality are important. Extracurricular participation and alumni/ae relationship are considered.
**Requirements:** Graduation from secondary school is required; GED is accepted. 15 units and the following program of study are required: 4 units of English, 2 units of math, 2 units of lab science, 3 units of social studies, 2 units of history. Rank in top half of secondary class and minimum "C" average recommended. SAT is required; ACT may be substituted. ACH recommended. Campus visit and interview recommended. No off-campus interviews.
**Procedure:** Take SAT or ACT by spring of 12th year. Visit college for interview by spring of 12th year. Suggest filing application by January; no deadline. Notification of admission on rolling basis. Reply is required within 30 days of acceptance. $100 tuition deposit, refundable until May 1. Freshmen accepted in terms other than fall.
**Special programs:** Admission may be deferred three terms. Credit and/or placement may be granted through CEEB Advanced Placement exams for scores of 3 or higher. Credit may be granted through CLEP general exams, DANTES exams, and life experience. Credit and/or placement may be granted through CLEP subject exams. Placement may be granted through challenge exams. Credit and placement may be granted through military experience. Early entrance/early admission program. Concurrent enrollment program.
**Transfer students:** Transfer students accepted for terms other than fall. In fall 1993, 28% of all new students were transfers into all classes. 348 transfer applications were received, 279 were accepted. Application deadline is rolling for fall; rolling for spring. Minimum 2.0 GPA required. Lowest course grade accepted is "C." Maximum number of transferable credits is 94 semester hours. At least 31 semester hours must be completed at the university to receive degree.
**Admissions contact:** Jim Schlimmer, Dean of Admissions. 910 841-9216.

**FINANCIAL AID. Available aid:** Pell grants, SEOG, state grants, school scholarships and grants, private scholarships and grants, academic merit scholarships, and athletic scholarships. Perkins Loans (NDSL), PLUS, Stafford Loans (GSL), private loans, and SLS. Tuition Plan Inc., Knight Tuition Plans, and deferred payment plan.
**Financial aid statistics:** 38% of aid is not need-based. In 1993-94, 83% of all undergraduate applicants received aid; 65% of freshman applicants. Average amounts of aid awarded freshmen: Scholarships and grants, $6,100; loans, $2,700.

**Supporting data/closing dates:** FAFSA: Priority filing date is March 1; accepted on rolling basis. School's own aid application: Priority filing date is March 1; accepted on rolling basis. Income tax forms: Accepted on rolling basis. Notification of awards on rolling basis.
**Financial aid contact:** Kay Stroud, Director of Financial Aid. 910 841-9128.

**STUDENT EMPLOYMENT.** College Work/Study Program. Institutional employment. 21% of full-time undergraduates work on campus during school year. Students may expect to earn an average of $1,025 during school year. Off-campus part-time employment opportunities rated "good."

**COMPUTER FACILITIES.** 106 IBM/IBM-compatible and Macintosh/Apple microcomputers. Students may access Data General minicomputer/mainframe systems, Internet. Client/LAN operating systems include Apple/Macintosh, DOS. Computer languages and software packages include Assembly, C, COBOL, dBASE, FORTRAN, Lotus 1-2-3, Pascal, WordPerfect. Computer facilities are available to all students.
**Fees:** None.
**Hours:** 10 AM-midn.

**GRADUATE CAREER DATA.** Graduate school percentages: 1% enter law school. 2% enter medical school. 3% enter dental school. 1% enter graduate business programs. 7% enter graduate arts and sciences programs. 1% enter theological school/seminary. Highest graduate school enrollments: U of North Carolina at Chapel Hill, U of North Carolina at Greensboro, Wake Forest U. 48% of graduates choose careers in business and industry. Companies and businesses that hire graduates: banks, furniture industry, insurance companies, retail stores.

# Johnson C. Smith University

**Charlotte, NC 28216** **704 378-1000**

**1994-95 Costs.** Tuition: $6,338. Room & board: $2,438. Fees, books, misc. academic expenses (school's estimate): $1,285.
**Enrollment.** Undergraduates: 531 men, 816 women (full-time). Freshman class: 2,138 applicants, 1,347 accepted.
**Test score averages/ranges.** Average SAT scores: 339 verbal, 362 math.
**Faculty.** 86 full-time; 19 part-time. 73% of faculty holds doctoral degree. Student/faculty ratio: 15 to 1.
**Selectivity rating.** Less competitive.

**PROFILE.** Johnson C. Smith University is a private, liberal arts institution. Programs are offered through the Divisions of Education and Psychology, Humanities, Mathematics and Sciences, and Social Sciences. Its 85-acre campus, located near downtown Charlotte, includes buildings of traditional and modern design.

**Accreditation:** SACS.
**Religious orientation:** Johnson C. Smith University is nonsectarian; three hours of philosophy or religion required.
**Library:** Collections totaling over 115,226 volumes, 800 periodical subscriptions, and 24,069 microform items.
**Special facilities/museums:** Language lab, honors college, banking and finance center.
**Athletic facilities:** Gymnasium, tennis courts, swimming pool.

**STUDENT BODY. Undergraduate profile:** 25% are state residents; 12% are transfers. 100% Black. Average age of undergraduates is 20.
**Freshman profile:** 3% of freshmen who took SAT scored 500 or over on verbal, 3% scored 500 or over on math; 17% scored 400 or over on verbal, 21% scored 400 or over on math; 60% scored 300 or over on verbal, 71% scored 300 or over on math. 92% of accepted applicants took SAT.
**Undergraduate achievement:** 67% of fall 1992 freshmen returned for fall 1993 term. 20% of entering class graduated.
**Foreign students:** One student is from out of the country.

**PROGRAMS OF STUDY. Degrees:** B.A., B.S., B.Soc.Work.
**Majors:** Accounting, Banking/Finance, Biology, Business Administration, Chemistry, Communication Arts, Computer Science, Early Childhood Education, Economics, Education, Elementary Education, English, Health Education, History, Marketing, Mathematics, Mathematics/Physics, Music, Music Business, Music Education, Physical Education, Political Science, Psychology, Secondary Education, Social Work, Sociology, Urban Studies.
**Distribution of degrees:** The majors with the highest enrollment are business administration, communication arts, and social work; health education, music business, and mathematics have the lowest.
**Requirements:** General education requirement.
**Academic regulations:** Minimum 2.5 GPA required for graduation. Convocations required for freshmen only.
**Special:** Double majors. Independent study. Accelerated study. Internships. Cooperative education programs. Preprofessional programs in law, medicine, and dentistry. 3-2 engineering and education programs with U of North Carolina at Charlotte. Member of Charlotte Area Educational Consortium. Teacher certification in early childhood, elementary, secondary, and special education. Study abroad in Canada, European countries, and Mexico. ROTC and AFROTC at U of North Carolina at Charlotte.
**Honors:** Phi Beta Kappa. Honors program.
**Academic Assistance:** Remedial reading, writing, math, and study skills. Nonremedial tutoring.

**STUDENT LIFE. Housing:** Students may live on or off campus. Women's and men's dorms. Honors College Center accommodates 15 students. 77% of students live in college housing.
**Services and counseling/handicapped student services:** Placement services. Health service. Day care. Counseling services for veteran students. Birth control and personal counseling. Career and academic guidance services. Religious counseling.
**Campus organizations:** Undergraduate student government. Student newspaper (Student News, published twice/year). Yearbook. Radio station. Band, choir, Shaki/Shaki dance club, drama club, political science club, special-interest groups. Four fraternities, no chapter houses; four sororities, no chapter houses. 20% of men join a fraternity. 25% of women join a sorority.
**Religious organizations:** Spiritual Choir, Student Christian Association.
**Minority/foreign student organizations:** NAACP.

**ATHLETICS. Physical education requirements:** Four hours of physical education required.
**Intercollegiate competition:** 3% of students participate. Baseball (M), basketball (M,W), cross-country (M,W), football (M), golf (M), softball (W), tennis (M), track and field (M,W), volleyball (W). Member of Central Intercollegiate Athletic Association, NCAA Division II.
**Intramural and club sports:** 1% of students participate. Intramural badminton, basketball, swimming, volleyball.

**ADMISSIONS. Academic basis for candidate selection** (in order of priority): Secondary school record, standardized test scores, school's recommendation, class rank.
**Nonacademic basis for candidate selection:** Character and personality are important. Extracurricular participation, particular talent or ability, and alumni/ae relationship are considered.
**Requirements:** Graduation from secondary school is required; GED is accepted. 16 units and the following program of study are required: 4 units of English, 2 units of math, 1 unit of lab science, 2 units of social studies, 7 units of academic electives. Minimum combined SAT score of 600, rank in top two-thirds of secondary school class, and minimum 2.0 GPA required. SAT is required; ACT may be substituted. Campus visit and interview recommended. Off-campus interviews available with admissions and alumni representatives.
**Procedure:** Take SAT or ACT by February of 12th year. Visit college for interview by February of 12th year. Suggest filing application by December. Application deadline is August 1. Notification of admission on rolling basis. Tuition deposit equal to 75% of total tuition, refundable until eight weeks after start of classes. $100 nonrefundable room deposit. Freshmen accepted in terms other than fall.
**Special programs:** Admission may be deferred two years. Credit and/or placement may be granted through CEEB Advanced Placement exams for scores of 3 or higher. Credit and/or placement may be granted through CLEP general and subject exams. Early decision program.
**Transfer students:** Transfer students accepted for terms other than fall. In fall 1993, 12% of all new students were transfers into all classes. 199 transfer applications were received, 101 were accepted. Application deadline is August 1 for fall; November 1 for spring. Minimum 2.0 GPA required. Lowest course grade accepted is "C." Maximum number of transferable credits is 64 semester hours. At least 32 semester hours must be completed at the university to receive degree.
**Admissions contact:** Marvin Dunlap, Director of Admissions. 800 782-7303.

**FINANCIAL AID. Available aid:** Pell grants, SEOG, state scholarships and grants, school scholarships and grants, private scholarships and grants, academic merit scholarships, athletic scholarships, and aid for undergraduate foreign students. Perkins Loans (NDSL), PLUS, Stafford Loans (GSL), state loans, and school loans. Tuition Plan Inc., Tuition Management Systems, and deferred payment plan.
**Financial aid statistics:** 15% of aid is not need-based. In 1993-94, 76% of all undergraduate applicants received aid; 95% of freshman applicants. Average amounts of aid awarded freshmen: Scholarships and grants, $2,476; loans, $2,625.
**Supporting data/closing dates:** FAFSA/FAF/FFS: Priority filing date is April 15. Notification of awards begins April 16.
**Financial aid contact:** Carolyn Smith, Director of Financial Aid. 704 378-1034.

**STUDENT EMPLOYMENT.** College Work/Study Program. Institutional employment. 30% of full-time undergraduates work on campus during school year. Students may expect to earn an average of $2,000 during school year. Off-campus part-time employment opportunities rated "fair."

**COMPUTER FACILITIES.** 100 IBM/IBM-compatible and Macintosh/Apple microcomputers. Computer languages and software packages include COBOL, RPG III; statistical, word processing programs. Computer facilities are available to all students.
**Fees:** None.

**GRADUATE CAREER DATA.** Highest graduate school enrollments: Duke U, Emory U, Georgia Tech, Howard U, North Carolina A&T State U, North Carolina Central U, U of North Carolina, Ohio State U.

**PROMINENT ALUMNI/AE.** Curley Neal and Twiggy Sanders, basketball players; Pettis Norman, former NFL player, Dallas Cowboys; Horace Davenport, judge; Eva Clayton, U.S. congresswoman.

# Lees-McRae College

**Banner Elk, NC 28604** **704 898-5241**

**1994-95 Costs.** Tuition: $8,530. Room: $1,404. Board: $1,716. Fees, books, misc. academic expenses (school's estimate): $400.
**Enrollment.** Undergraduates: 422 men, 235 women (full-time). Freshman class: 653 applicants, 586 accepted, 260 enrolled.
**Test score averages/ranges.** Average SAT scores: 340 verbal, 370 math. Range of SAT scores of middle 50%: 300-399 verbal, 300-399 math.
**Faculty.** 45 full-time; 22 part-time. Student/faculty ratio: 15 to 1.
**Selectivity rating.** Less competitive.

**PROFILE.** Lees-McRae is a private, church-affiliated, liberal arts college. Founded in 1900, it adopted coeducation in 1923. Its 40-acre campus is located in Banner Elk, 50 miles from Johnson City, Tenn.

**Accreditation:** SACS.
**Religious orientation:** Lees-McRae College is affiliated with the Presbyterian Church; one semester of religion required.

**Library:** Collections totaling over 84,300 volumes, 453 periodical subscriptions, and 164,170 microform items.
**Special facilities/museums:** Appalachian culture museum, curriculum center for teacher education.
**Athletic facilities:** Gymnasiums, swimming pool, tennis courts, athletic fields.

**STUDENT BODY.**
**Freshman profile:** 1% of freshmen who took SAT scored 600 or over on math; 4% scored 500 or over on verbal, 8% scored 500 or over on math; 34% scored 400 or over on verbal, 40% scored 400 or over on math; 71% scored 300 or over on verbal, 75% scored 300 or over on math. Majority of accepted applicants took SAT.
**Foreign students:** 15 students are from out of the country. Countries represented include China, England, and Japan; 15 in all.

**PROGRAMS OF STUDY. Degrees:** B.A., B.S.
**Majors:** Biology, Business Administration, Communications, Criminal Justice, Dance, English, History, Humanities, Interdisciplinary Studies, Mathematics, Musical Theatre, Religious Studies, Social Studies, Theatre Arts.
**Distribution of degrees:** The majors with the highest enrollment are performing arts, communications, and criminal justice; religion and mathematics have the lowest.
**Requirements:** General education requirement.
**Academic regulations:** Freshmen must maintain minimum 1.4 GPA; sophomores, 1.8 GPA; juniors, 2.0 GPA; seniors, 2.0 GPA.
**Special:** Minors offered in several majors and in accompaniment, athletic training, computer information systems, physical education, and religious studies. Self-designed majors. Internships. Preprofessional programs in law, medicine, veterinary science, dentistry, and theology. Teacher certification in secondary education. Certification in specific subject areas. Exchange program abroad in the United Kingdom (Comparative Center for Study). Study abroad also in Ireland.
**Honors:** Honors program. Honor societies.
**Academic Assistance:** Remedial reading, writing, math, and study skills. Nonremedial tutoring.

**ADMISSIONS. Academic basis for candidate selection** (in order of priority): Secondary school record, standardized test scores, school's recommendation, class rank, essay.
**Nonacademic basis for candidate selection:** Character and personality, extracurricular participation, particular talent or ability, and geographical distribution are considered.
**Requirements:** Graduation from secondary school is recommended; GED is accepted. No specific distribution of secondary school units required. Minimum combined SAT score of 700 and minimum 2.0 GPA required. Conditional admission possible for applicants not meeting standard requirements. SAT or ACT is required. Campus visit and interview recommended. Off-campus interviews available with an admissions representative.
**Procedure:** Notification of admission on rolling basis. Reply is required by May 1. $200 tuition deposit, refundable until May 1. Freshmen accepted in terms other than fall.
**Special programs:** Admission may be deferred two years. Credit and/or placement may be granted through CEEB Advanced Placement exams for scores of 3 or higher. Credit and/or placement may be granted through CLEP general and subject exams. Early entrance/early admission program.
**Transfer students:** Transfer students accepted for terms other than fall. Application deadline is rolling for fall; rolling for spring.
**Admissions contact:** Michael Andrews, Director of Admissions. 704 898-8723.

**FINANCIAL AID. Available aid:** Pell grants, SEOG, state scholarships and grants, school scholarships and grants, private scholarships, academic merit scholarships, athletic scholarships, and aid for undergraduate foreign students. Perkins Loans (NDSL), PLUS, Stafford Loans (GSL), school loans, and SLS. AMS.
**Financial aid statistics:** In 1993-94, 71% of all undergraduate applicants received aid; 90% of freshman applicants.
**Supporting data/closing dates:** FAFSA/FAF/FFS: Priority filing date is April 1. School's own aid application: Priority filing date is April 1. Notification of awards begins April 15.
**Financial aid contact:** Carter Hammett McGrury, M.A., Director of Student Financial Planning. 704 898-8793.

# Lenoir-Rhyne College

**Hickory, NC 28603** **704 328-1741**

**1994-95 Costs.** Tuition: $10,100. Room: $1,760. Board: $2,240. Fees, books, misc. academic expenses (school's estimate): $1,910.
**Enrollment.** Undergraduates: 477 men, 696 women (full-time). Freshman class: 865 applicants, 701 accepted, 254 enrolled. Graduate enrollment: 7 men, 8 women.
**Test score averages/ranges.** Average SAT scores: 451 verbal, 496 math. Range of SAT scores of middle 50%: 400-500 verbal, 450-550 math. Average ACT scores: 21 composite. Range of ACT scores of middle 50%: 21-23 composite.
**Faculty.** 96 full-time; 22 part-time. 67% of faculty holds doctoral degree. Student/faculty ratio: 12 to 1.
**Selectivity rating.** Less competitive.

**PROFILE.** Lenoir-Rhyne, founded in 1891, is a church-affiliated college of the liberal arts and sciences. Programs are offered through the Divisions of Humanities, Natural Sciences and Mathematics, Professional Programs, and Social and Behavioral Sciences. Its 100-acre campus is located in Hickory, in North Carolina's Piedmont region.

**Accreditation:** SACS. Professionally accredited by the National Council for Accreditation of Teacher Education, the National League for Nursing.
**Religious orientation:** Lenoir-Rhyne College is affiliated with the Lutheran Church; two semesters of religion required.
**Library:** Collections totaling over 130,000 volumes, 1,000 periodical subscriptions, and 250,000 microform items.
**Special facilities/museums:** Language lab.
**Athletic facilities:** Gymnasiums, swimming pool, racquetball courts, baseball, football, intramural, soccer, and softball fields, stadium.

**STUDENT BODY. Undergraduate profile:** 50% are state residents; 29% are transfers. 1% Asian-American, 5% Black, 1% Hispanic, 93% White. Average age of undergraduates is 21.
**Freshman profile:** 1% of freshmen who took SAT scored 700 or over on verbal, 2% scored 700 or over on math; 6% scored 600 or over on verbal, 14% scored 600 or over on math; 29% scored 500 or over on verbal, 49% scored 500 or over on math; 73% scored 400 or over on verbal, 86% scored 400 or over on math; 98% scored 300 or over on verbal, 99% scored 300 or over on math. 94% of accepted applicants took SAT; 1% took ACT. 83% of freshmen come from public schools.
**Undergraduate achievement:** 88% of fall 1992 freshmen returned for fall 1993 term. 46% of entering class graduated. 33% of students who completed a degree program immediately went on to graduate study.
**Foreign students:** Three students are from out of the country. Countries represented include England, Japan, and Spain.

**PROGRAMS OF STUDY. Degrees:** B.A., B.Mus.Ed., B.S.
**Majors:** Accounting, Applied Music, Art Education, Biology, Biology Education, Business Administration, Business Education, Chemistry, Classics, Communication, Computer Science, Economics, Education, Elementary Education, English, Environmental Studies, French, General Studies, German, Health/Physical Education, History, International Business, Mathematics, Music, Music Education, Nursing, Parish Education, Philosophy, Physician's Assistant, Physics, Political Science, Psychology, Religious Studies, Secondary Education, Sociology, Spanish, Special Education for the Deaf, Theatre Arts.
**Distribution of degrees:** The majors with the highest enrollment are business, education, and communication.
**Requirements:** General education requirement.
**Academic regulations:** Freshmen must maintain minimum 1.2 GPA; sophomores, 1.5 GPA; juniors, 1.9 GPA; seniors, 2.0 GPA.
**Special:** Minors offered in most majors. Self-designed majors. Double majors. Dual degrees. Independent study. Pass/fail grading option. Internships. Graduate school at which undergraduates may take graduate-level courses. Preprofessional programs in law and medicine. 3-1 medical technology program. 2-3 pharmacy program. 3-2 engineering programs with Duke U, Georgia Tech, and North Carolina State U. 3-2 forestry and environmental studies program with Duke U. Washington Semester and UN Semester. Teacher certification in early childhood, elementary, and secondary education. Certification in specific subject areas. Study abroad in England, France, Germany, Mexico, and Spain. ROTC at Davidson Coll.
**Honors:** Honors program.
**Academic Assistance:** Remedial math.

**STUDENT LIFE. Housing:** Students may live on or off campus. Coed, women's, and men's dorms. 70% of students live in college housing.
**Social atmosphere:** According to the editor of the student newspaper, Greeks are the most influential group at Lenoir-Rhyne. Popular events include rush, Spring Fling, sorority/fraternity socials, football games, Push Field Day, and the skate-a-thon. In addition, many convocations and forums are offered, the Playmakers theatre group performs several times a year, and the Program Board and Greeks plan parties and events. On campus, students gather at the Bear's Lair, Cromer Center, and the quad. Frequented spots off campus include Homer's, McGuire's, Rockola Cafe, and Fizz and Don's.
**Services and counseling/handicapped student services:** Placement services. Health service. Counseling services for minority and veteran students. Personal counseling. Career and academic guidance services. Physically disabled student services. Learning disabled services. Notetaking services.
**Campus organizations:** Undergraduate student government. Student newspaper (Lenoir-Rhynean, published once/week). Literary magazine. Yearbook. Radio and TV stations. A cappella choir, choral ensembles, concert band, drama groups, community service organizations, outdoor club, creative writing magazines, departmental, political, and special-interest groups. Four fraternities, three chapter houses; four sororities, no chapter houses. 30% of men join a fraternity. 35% of women join a sorority.
**Religious organizations:** Intervarsity Christian Fellowship, Baptist Student Union, Fools for Christ, Chapel Council, Lutheran Student Movement, Newman Club.
**Minority/foreign student organizations:** Black Student Union.

**ATHLETICS. Physical education requirements:** Two semesters of physical education required.
**Intercollegiate competition:** 20% of students participate. Baseball (M,W), basketball (M,W), cheerleading (M,W), cross-country (M,W), football (M), golf (M), soccer (M,W), softball (W), tennis (M,W), track and field (outdoor) (W), volleyball (W). Member of NCAA Division II, South Atlantic Conference.
**Intramural and club sports:** 33% of students participate. Intramural basketball, flag football, soccer, softball, swimming, volleyball.

**ADMISSIONS. Academic basis for candidate selection** (in order of priority): Secondary school record, class rank, standardized test scores, school's recommendation, essay.
**Nonacademic basis for candidate selection:** Character and personality, particular talent or ability, and alumni/ae relationship are emphasized. Extracurricular participation and geographical distribution are important.
**Requirements:** Graduation from secondary school is recommended; GED is accepted. 16 units and the following program of study are required: 4 units of English, 3 units of math, 1 unit of lab science, 1 unit of history, 5 units of academic electives. Rank in top half of secondary school class and minimum 2.5 GPA required. Audition required of music program applicants. Conditional admission possible for applicants not meeting standard requirements. SAT is required; ACT may be substituted. Campus visit and interview recommended. Off-campus interviews available with an admissions representative.
**Procedure:** Take SAT or ACT by December 15 of 12th year. Suggest filing application by January 1. Application deadline is August 1. Notification of admission on rolling basis. Reply is required by May 1. $200 tuition deposit, refundable until May 1. Freshmen accepted in terms other than fall.
**Special programs:** Admission may be deferred one year. Credit and/or placement may be granted through CEEB Advanced Placement exams for scores of 3 or higher. Credit and/or placement may be granted through CLEP general and subject exams. Credit and

placement may be granted through DANTES and challenge exams and life experience. Early entrance/early admission program. Concurrent enrollment program.
**Transfer students:** Transfer students accepted for terms other than fall. In fall 1993, 29% of all new students were transfers into all classes. 201 transfer applications were received, 155 were accepted. Application deadline is rolling for fall; rolling for spring. Minimum 2.0 GPA required. Lowest course grade accepted is "C." Maximum number of transferable credits is 64 semester hours from a two-year school and 90 semester hours from a four-year school. At least 30 semester hours must be completed at the college to receive degree.
**Admissions contact:** Timothy L. Jackson, M.S., Director of Admissions. 704 328-7300.

**FINANCIAL AID. Available aid:** Pell grants, SEOG, Federal Nursing Student Scholarships, state scholarships and grants, school scholarships and grants, private scholarships and grants, academic merit scholarships, athletic scholarships, and aid for undergraduate foreign students. Perkins Loans (NDSL), PLUS, Stafford Loans (GSL), state loans, school loans, private loans, and SLS. Knight Tuition Plans, deferred payment plan, and family tuition reduction.
**Financial aid statistics:** 40% of aid is not need-based. In 1993-94, 85% of all undergraduate applicants received aid; 85% of freshman applicants. Average amounts of aid awarded freshmen: Scholarships and grants, $2,400.
**Supporting data/closing dates:** Income tax forms: Accepted on rolling basis. Notification of awards on rolling basis.
**Financial aid contact:** Daniel Klock, M.S., Director of Financial Aid. 704 328-1741, extension 141.

**STUDENT EMPLOYMENT.** College Work/Study Program. Institutional employment. 50% of full-time undergraduates work on campus during school year. Students may expect to earn an average of $1,075 during school year. Off-campus part-time employment opportunities rated "excellent."

**COMPUTER FACILITIES.** 60 IBM/IBM-compatible and Macintosh/Apple microcomputers. Students may access IBM minicomputer/mainframe systems, Internet. Client/LAN operating systems include Apple/Macintosh, DOS. Computer languages and software packages include BASIC, COBOL, FORTRAN, LISP, Modula 2, Pascal; eight in all. Computer facilities are available to all students.
**Fees:** Computer fee is included in tuition/fees.
**Hours:** 8 AM-11 PM (M-F); noon-5 PM (Sa); 2 PM-11 PM (Su).

## Livingstone College

**Salisbury, NC 28144** — **704 638-5500**

**1994-95 Costs.** Tuition: $4,400. Room & board: $3,400. Fees, books, misc. academic expenses (school's estimate): $2,000.
**Enrollment.** Undergraduates: 354 men, 278 women (full-time). Freshman class: 882 applicants, 473 accepted, 211 enrolled. Graduate enrollment: 17 men, 9 women.
**Test score averages/ranges.** Average SAT scores: 295 verbal, 322 math.
**Faculty.** 55 full-time; 9 part-time. 34% of faculty holds doctoral degree. Student/faculty ratio: 10 to 1.
**Selectivity rating.** Less competitive.

**PROFILE.** Livingstone, founded in 1879, is a church-affiliated college. Programs are offered through the College of Arts and Sciences and Hood Theological Seminary. Its 272-acre campus is located in Salisbury, 38 miles northeast of Charlotte.

**Accreditation:** SACS. Professionally accredited by the Council on Social Work Education.
**Religious orientation:** Livingstone College is affiliated with the African Methodist Episcopal Zion Church; four semesters of religion required.
**Library:** Collections totaling over 78,000 volumes, 245 periodical subscriptions, and 40,650 microform items.
**Special facilities/museums:** Learning center, museum.
**Athletic facilities:** Gymnasium, football and softball fields, track, tennis courts, weight room.

**STUDENT BODY. Undergraduate profile:** 53% are state residents; 1% are transfers. 90% Black, 5% White, 5% Other. Average age of undergraduates is 18.
**Freshman profile:** 1% of freshmen who took SAT scored 500 or over on math; 5% scored 400 or over on verbal, 8% scored 400 or over on math; 40% scored 300 or over on verbal, 50% scored 300 or over on math. 90% of accepted applicants took SAT; 10% took ACT. 95% of freshmen come from public schools.
**Undergraduate achievement:** 85% of fall 1992 freshmen returned for fall 1993 term. 60% of entering class graduated.
**Foreign students:** 15 students are from out of the country. Countries represented include Bermuda, Liberia, Nigeria, the Virgin Islands, and the West Indies.

**PROGRAMS OF STUDY. Degrees:** B.A., B.S., B.Soc.Work.
**Majors:** Accounting, Biology, Business Administration, Chemistry, Criminal Justice, Elementary Education, English, History, Mathematics, Music, Music Education, Physical Education, Political Science, Psychology, Social Studies, Social Welfare, Sociology.
**Distribution of degrees:** The majors with the highest enrollment are business administration and psychology; music, English, and biology have the lowest.
**Requirements:** General education requirement.
**Special:** Double majors. Dual degrees. Independent study. Internships. Cooperative education programs. Preprofessional programs in law, medicine, and pharmacy. Dual degree pharmacy program with Howard U. Dual degree law program with Saint John U. Dual degree engineering program with North Carolina A&T State U. Teacher certification in early childhood, elementary, and secondary education. ROTC at Davidson Coll.
**Honors:** Honors program.
**Academic Assistance:** Remedial reading, writing, math, and study skills.

**ADMISSIONS. Academic basis for candidate selection** (in order of priority): Secondary school record, standardized test scores, class rank, school's recommendation.
**Nonacademic basis for candidate selection:** Character and personality and particular talent or ability are important. Extracurricular participation and geographical distribution are considered.
**Requirements:** Graduation from secondary school is required; GED is accepted. 20 units and the following program of study are required: 4 units of English, 2 units of math, 2 units of science including 1 unit of lab, 2 units of foreign language, 1 unit of social studies, 1 unit of history, 7 units of electives. Minimum 2.0 GPA recommended. Audition required of music program applicants. Conditional admission possible for applicants not meeting standard requirements. SAT is required; ACT may be substituted. Campus visit recommended. Off-campus interviews available with an admissions representative.
**Procedure:** Take SAT or ACT by June 1 of 12th year. Application deadline is July 15. Notification of admission on rolling basis. Reply is required by August 1. $150 room deposit, refundable until July 1. Freshmen accepted in terms other than fall.
**Special programs:** Admission may be deferred one year. Credit and/or placement may be granted through CEEB Advanced Placement exams for scores of 3 or higher. Credit and/or placement may be granted through CLEP subject exams. Placement may be granted through challenge exams and military experience.
**Transfer students:** Transfer students accepted for terms other than fall. In fall 1993, 1% of all new students were transfers into all classes. 21 transfer applications were received, 21 were accepted. Application deadline is July 1 for fall; December 1 for spring. Minimum 2.0 GPA recommended. Lowest course grade accepted is "C." Maximum number of transferable credits is 64 semester hours. At least 45 semester hours must be completed at the college to receive degree.
**Admissions contact:** Grady Deese, Jr., M.A., Coordinator of Recruiting. 704 638-5502.

**FINANCIAL AID. Available aid:** Pell grants, SEOG, state scholarships and grants, school scholarships and grants, private scholarships, academic merit scholarships, athletic scholarships, aid for undergraduate foreign students, and United Negro College Fund. PLUS, Stafford Loans (GSL), and SLS.
**Financial aid statistics:** 30% of aid is not need-based. In 1993-94, 98% of all undergraduate applicants received aid; 95% of freshman applicants. Average amounts of aid awarded freshmen: Scholarships and grants, $1,750; loans, $2,500.
**Supporting data/closing dates:** FAFSA: Priority filing date is March 31. FAF/FFS: Accepted on rolling basis. School's own aid application: Priority filing date is March 31. SINGLEFILE: Priority filing date is April 15. Notification of awards on rolling basis.
**Financial aid contact:** Wanda White, M.S., Director of Financial Aid. 704 638-5562.

## Mars Hill College

**Mars Hill, NC 28754** — **704 689-1201**

**1994-95 Costs.** Tuition: $7,500. Room & board: $3,550. Fees, books, misc. academic expenses (school's estimate): $1,050.
**Enrollment.** Undergraduates: 554 men, 577 women (full-time). Freshman class: 1,056 applicants, 873 accepted, 383 enrolled.
**Test score averages/ranges.** Average SAT scores: 407 verbal, 454 math. Average ACT scores: 19 English, 19 math, 20 composite.
**Faculty.** 78 full-time; 55 part-time. 60% of faculty holds doctoral degree. Student/faculty ratio: 13 to 1.
**Selectivity rating.** Less competitive.

**PROFILE.** Mars Hill, founded in 1856, is a church-affiliated, liberal arts college. Programs are offered through the Divisions of Business Administration and Economics; Education; Fine Arts; Health, Physical Education, Recreation, and Athletics; Humanities; Natural Sciences, Computer Science, and Mathematics; and Social and Behavioral Sciences. Its 180-acre campus is located in the mountains of western North Carolina, 18 miles north of Asheville.

**Accreditation:** SACS. Professionally accredited by the Council on Social Work Education, the National Association of Schools of Music.
**Religious orientation:** Mars Hill College is affiliated with the North Carolina Baptist Convention; no religious requirements.
**Library:** Collections totaling over 90,000 volumes, 750 periodical subscriptions, and 70,000 microform items.
**Special facilities/museums:** Language lab, Appalachian artifacts museum, rural life museum.
**Athletic facilities:** Gymnasiums, track, swimming pool, basketball, racquetball, and tennis courts, soccer and softball fields, Nautilus.

**STUDENT BODY. Undergraduate profile:** 63% are state residents; 15% are transfers. 1% Asian-American, 7% Black, 1% Native American, 87% White, 4% Other. Average age of undergraduates is 20.
**Freshman profile:** Majority of accepted applicants took SAT. 65% of freshmen come from public schools.
**Undergraduate achievement:** 73% of fall 1992 freshmen returned for fall 1993 term. 49% of entering class graduated. 40% of students who completed a degree program went on to graduate study within one year.
**Foreign students:** 23 students are from out of the country. Countries represented include Bermuda, Canada, France, Japan, Spain, and the former Yugoslav Republics; 18 in all.

**PROGRAMS OF STUDY. Degrees:** B.A., B.F.A., B.Mus., B.S., B.Soc.Work.
**Majors:** Accounting, Allied Health, Art, Art Education, Art History, Biology, Botany, Business Administration, Chemistry, Church Music, Communications/Public Relations, Computer/Information Sciences, Elementary Education, English, Fashion Merchandising, History, International Studies, Mathematics, Music, Music Education, Music Performance, Music Theatre, Political Science, Psychology, Religion/Philosophy, Social Work, Sociology, Spanish, Theatre Arts, Theatre Arts Education, Zoology.
**Distribution of degrees:** The majors with the highest enrollment are business, elementary education, and music.
**Requirements:** General education requirement.

**Academic regulations:** Freshmen must maintain minimum 1.3 GPA; sophomores, 1.5 GPA; juniors, 1.8 GPA; seniors, 2.0 GPA.
**Special:** Minors offered in coaching, gerontology, human services, regional studies, research and computer applications, social science, and sports medicine. Southern Appalachian Center focuses on regional history, culture, and community renewal. Appalachian Studies Concentration. One year internship for elementary and middle grade education. Self-designed majors. Double majors. Dual degrees. Independent study. Internships. Cooperative education programs. Preprofessional programs in law, medicine, veterinary science, pharmacy, dentistry, and theology. Cooperative program with U of North Carolina. 2-2 programs in dental hygiene, nursing, physical therapy, radiology technology, respiratory therapy. 3-1 medical technology program. B.S. in allied health awarded after certification from technical school. 3-2 physician's assistant program with Bowman Gray Sch of Medicine. Member of Appalachian Colleges Assessment Consortium. Washington Semester and other off-campus study opportunities. Teacher certification in elementary and secondary education. Certification in specific subject areas. Member of International Student Exchange Program (ISEP). Study abroad in England and in Latin American and Western European countries.
**Honors:** Honors program.
**Academic Assistance:** Nonremedial tutoring.

**STUDENT LIFE. Housing:** All unmarried, nonveteran freshmen and sophomores under 21 must live on campus unless living with family. Women's and men's dorms. School-owned/operated apartments. On-campus married-student housing. 67% of students live in college housing.
**Social atmosphere:** Students often gather off-campus at Denny's in Asheville, and at the Timberline coffee house and The Loft night club on campus. Greeks and the Christian Student Movement are influential groups on campus. Popular campus events include the Christmas formal, Homecoming, Spring Fling, and the Spring formal. According to the student newspaper, social life on campus is growing steadily.
**Services and counseling/handicapped student services:** Placement services. Health service. "Mentor groups" of faculty and freshmen provide orientation throughout first semester. Personal counseling. Career and academic guidance services. Religious counseling. Physically disabled student services. Learning disabled services. Notetaking services. Tape recorders. Tutors. Reader services for the blind.
**Campus organizations:** Undergraduate student government. Student newspaper (Hilltop, published twice/month). Literary magazine. Yearbook. Radio station. Sinfonia, chorus, band, orchestra, theatre, business club, Bailey Mountain Cloggers, New Beginning Singers, Show Stoppers, Circle K, College Union Committees, academic, departmental, and social service groups. Six fraternities, no chapter houses; five sororities, no chapter houses. 10% of men join a fraternity. 12% of women join a sorority.
**Religious organizations:** Christian Student Movement, Fellowship of Christian Athletes.
**Minority/foreign student organizations:** Black Students in Action, Kappa Alpha Psi. International Club.

**ATHLETICS. Physical education requirements:** Two semesters of physical education required.
**Intercollegiate competition:** 33% of students participate. Baseball (M), basketball (M,W), cheerleading (M,W), cross-country (M,W), football (M), golf (M), soccer (M,W), softball (W), tennis (M,W), volleyball (W). Member of NCAA Divison II, South Atlantic Conference.
**Intramural and club sports:** 45% of students participate. Intramural basketball, bowling, flag football, soccer, softball, water polo. Men's club weight lifting.

**ADMISSIONS. Academic basis for candidate selection** (in order of priority): Secondary school record, school's recommendation, standardized test scores, class rank, essay.
**Nonacademic basis for candidate selection:** Character and personality and extracurricular participation are important. Particular talent or ability and alumni/ae relationship are considered.
**Requirements:** Graduation from secondary school is required; GED is accepted. 13 units and the following program of study are required: 4 units of English, 3 units of math, 2 units of science including 1 unit of lab, 2 units of social studies, 2 units of history. Audition required of music program applicants. Academic Enrichment Program offered in summer for applicants not normally admissible. SAT is required; ACT may be substituted. Campus visit and interview recommended. No off-campus interviews.
**Procedure:** Application deadline is May 1. Notification of admission on rolling basis. $150 tuition deposit, refundable until May 1. Freshmen accepted in terms other than fall.
**Special programs:** Placement may be granted through CEEB Advanced Placement exams for scores of 3 or higher. Credit and/or placement may be granted through CLEP general and subject exams. Early entrance/early admission program. Concurrent enrollment program.
**Transfer students:** Transfer students accepted for terms other than fall. In fall 1993, 15% of all new students were transfers into all classes. 138 transfer applications were received. Application deadline is rolling for fall; rolling for spring. Minimum 2.0 GPA required. Lowest course grade accepted is "C." Maximum number of transferable credits is 68 semester hours. At least 30 semester hours (12 within major) must be completed at the college to receive degree.
**Admissions contact:** Rick Hinshaw, Dean of Admissions. 800 543-1514.

**FINANCIAL AID. Available aid:** Pell grants, SEOG, state scholarships and grants, school scholarships, private scholarships and grants, academic merit scholarships, and athletic scholarships. Perkins Loans (NDSL), PLUS, Stafford Loans (GSL), state loans, school loans, private loans, and SLS. Tuition Plan Inc., Knight Tuition Plans, AMS, and deferred payment plan.
**Financial aid statistics:** 20% of aid is not need-based. In 1993-94, 80% of all undergraduate applicants received aid; 95% of freshman applicants. Average amounts of aid awarded freshmen: Scholarships and grants, $3,000; loans, $2,000.
**Supporting data/closing dates:** FAFSA/FAF: Priority filing date is May 1; accepted on rolling basis. State aid form: Priority filing date is February 15; accepted on rolling basis. Income tax forms: Accepted on rolling basis. Notification of awards on rolling basis.
**Financial aid contact:** Ann McAnear, Director of Financial Aid. 800 543-1514.

**STUDENT EMPLOYMENT.** College Work/Study Program. Institutional employment. 45% of full-time undergraduates work on campus during school year. Students may expect to earn an average of $1,000 during school year. Off-campus part-time employment opportunities rated "good."

**COMPUTER FACILITIES.** 90 IBM/IBM-compatible and Macintosh/Apple microcomputers. Computer languages and software packages include BASIC, C, COBOL, Pascal. Computer facilities are available to all students.
**Fees:** None.
**Hours:** 8 AM-9 PM.

**PROMINENT ALUMNI/AE.** John Chandler, president, American Association of Colleges; Dean Probst, chancellor, University System of Georgia; Dr. William Brown Deal, chairperson, School of Medicine, and dean and associate vice-president, U of Florida; Woodrow Jones, judge, U.S. District court; William L. Brown, CEO and chairperson, Bank of Boston; Dr. Max Lennon, president, Clemson U.

# Meredith College

**Raleigh, NC 27607-5298** **919 829-8600**

**1993-94 Costs.** Tuition: $6,340. Room & board: $3,100. Fees, books, misc. academic expenses (school's estimate): $450.
**Enrollment.** 1,721 women (full-time). Freshman class: 899 applicants, 772 accepted, 376 enrolled. 154 women.
**Test score averages/ranges.** Range of SAT scores of middle 50%: 400-490 verbal, 430-540 math.
**Faculty.** 103 full-time; 91 part-time. 76% of faculty holds highest degree in specific field. Student/faculty ratio: 17 to 1.
**Selectivity rating.** Less competitive.

**PROFILE.** Meredith, founded in 1835, is a church-affiliated, liberal arts college for women. Its 225-acre campus is located in Raleigh.

**Accreditation:** SACS. Professionally accredited by the American Dietetic Association, the Council on Social Work Education, the National Association of Schools of Music.
**Religious orientation:** Meredith College is affiliated with the North Carolina Baptist Convention; two semesters of religion required.
**Library:** Collections totaling over 144,000 volumes, 770 periodical subscriptions, and 76,800 microform items.
**Special facilities/museums:** Art gallery, amphitheatre, child-care lab, greenhouse, writing center.
**Athletic facilities:** Gymnasium, swimming pool, putting green, badminton, basketball, tennis, and volleyball courts, weight room, softball field, archery range, golf driving area.

**STUDENT BODY. Undergraduate profile:** 82% are state residents; 20% are transfers. 1% Asian-American, 4% Black, 92% White, 3% Other. Average age of undergraduates is 21.
**Freshman profile:** 1% of freshmen who took SAT scored 700 or over on math; 3% scored 600 or over on verbal, 8% scored 600 or over on math; 22% scored 500 or over on verbal, 43% scored 500 or over on math; 77% scored 400 or over on verbal, 85% scored 400 or over on math; 98% scored 300 or over on verbal, 99% scored 300 or over on math. 99% of accepted applicants took SAT. 86% of freshmen come from public schools.
**Undergraduate achievement:** 83% of fall 1992 freshmen returned for fall 1993 term. 61% of entering class graduated. 16% of students who completed a degree program immediately went on to graduate study.
**Foreign students:** 38 students are from out of the country. Countries represented include China, England, Japan, and Korea; 18 in all.

**PROGRAMS OF STUDY. Degrees:** B.A., B.Mus., B.S.
**Majors:** American Civilization, Applied Music, Art, Biology, Business Administration, Chemistry, Clothing/Fashion Merchandising, Computer/Mathematical Sciences, Dance, Economics, English, Fashion Merchandising, Foods/Nutrition, French, Health Science, History, Home Economics, Interior Design, International Studies, Mathematics, Medical Technology, Music, Music Education, Political Studies, Psychology, Religion, Self-Designed Majors, Social Work, Sociology, Spanish, Speech Communication, Theatre.
**Distribution of degrees:** The majors with the highest enrollment are business administration, child development, and psychology; dance, chemistry, and religion have the lowest.
**Requirements:** General education requirement.
**Academic regulations:** Freshmen must maintain minimum 1.35 GPA; sophomores, 1.65 GPA; juniors, 1.85 GPA; seniors, 1.9 GPA.
**Special:** Minors offered in most majors and in accounting, chemical physics, computer systems, finance, geography, management, marketing, music theatre, philosophy, physical education/fitness, and statistics. Concentrations in criminal justice and professional communications. Individually tailored minors possible in all departments. Courses offered in women's studies. Capstone Studies Courses. Three-month postbaccalaureate legal assistance program. Certification programs in teacher education, social work, and school social work. Over 400 leadership positions on campus enable students to develop leadership skills. Self-designed majors. Double majors. Dual degrees. Independent study. Accelerated study. Pass/fail grading option. Internships. Cooperative education programs. Graduate school at which undergraduates may take graduate-level courses. Preprofessional programs in law, medicine, veterinary science, pharmacy, dentistry, theology, and optometry. Individualized program leading to a second degree in engineering may be arranged with North Carolina State U. Member of Cooperating Raleigh Colleges. Cross-registration with North Carolina State U, Peace Coll, St. Augustine's Coll, St. Mary's Coll, and Shaw U. Washington Semester and UN Semester. Exchange program offered with Marymount Manhattan Coll. Teacher certification in elementary, middle grades, secondary, and vo-tech education. Certification in specific subject areas. Exchange programs abroad in England (Humberside U, U of Hull), France (U Catholique de L'Ouest), Japan (Obirin U), and Spain (U Nebrissenis). Study abroad also in China, Italy, Switzerland, and other countries. ROTC and AFROTC at North Carolina State U.
**Honors:** Honors program. Honor societies.
**Academic Assistance:** Remedial writing, math, and study skills. Nonremedial tutoring.

**STUDENT LIFE. Housing:** All full-time unmarried undergraduates under age 23 not living with relatives must live in campus, except by permission. Women's dorms. International dorm. 68% of full-time students live in college housing.
**Services and counseling/handicapped student services:** Placement services. Health service. Academic and preprofessional advising. Counseling services for older students. Personal and psychological counseling. Career and academic guidance services. Religious counseling. Physically disabled student services. Learning disabled services.
**Campus organizations:** Undergraduate student government. Student newspaper (Meredith Herald, published once/week). Literary magazine. Yearbook. Choir, ensembles, theatre groups, entertainment association, social service societies, College Democrats, Young Republicans, Meredith Performs, synchronized swimming group, recreational and departmental groups, 71 organizations in all.
**Religious organizations:** Christian Association, Freeman Religion Club.
**Minority/foreign student organizations:** Association for Black Awareness. International Association.

**ATHLETICS. Physical education requirements:** Four semesters of physical education required.
**Intercollegiate competition:** 3% of students participate. Basketball (W), soccer (W), softball (W), tennis (W), volleyball (W). Member of NCAA Division III.
**Intramural and club sports:** 10% of students participate. Intramural basketball, flag football, soccer, swimming, volleyball. Women's club synchronized swimming.

**ADMISSIONS. Academic basis for candidate selection** (in order of priority): Secondary school record, class rank, standardized test scores, school's recommendation, essay.
**Nonacademic basis for candidate selection:** Character and personality, extracurricular participation, particular talent or ability, geographical distribution, and alumni/ae relationship are considered.
**Requirements:** Graduation from secondary school is required; GED is not accepted. 16 units and the following program of study are required: 4 units of English, 3 units of math, 1 unit of foreign language, 8 units of electives including 5 units of academic electives. Minimum GPA of 2.0 in academic subjects required; rank in top half of secondary school class recommended. Audition recommended of music program applicants. Portfolio recommended of art program applicants. SAT is required; ACT may be substituted. Campus visit and interview recommended. No off-campus interviews.
**Procedure:** Take SAT or ACT by January of 12th year. Suggest filing application by February 15; no deadline. Notification of admission on rolling basis beginning in early November. Reply is required by May 1. $100 nonrefundable room deposit. Freshmen accepted in terms other than fall.
**Special programs:** Admission may be deferred one year. Credit and/or placement may be granted through CEEB Advanced Placement exams for scores of 3 or higher. Credit and/or placement may be granted through CLEP general and subject exams. Credit and placement may be granted through challenge exams and military and life experience. Early decision program. In fall 1994, 99 applied for early decision and 84 were accepted. Deadline for applying for early decision is October 15. Early entrance/early admission program. Concurrent enrollment program.
**Transfer students:** Transfer students accepted for terms other than fall. In fall 1993, 20% of all new students were transfers into all classes. 188 transfer applications were received, 147 were accepted. Recommended application deadline is February 15 for fall; December 1 for spring. Minimum 2.0 GPA required. Lowest course grade accepted is "D." Maximum of 35 transferable semester hours from nursing schools. At least 30 semester hours must be completed at the college to receive degree.
**Admissions contact:** Sue E. Kearney, A.M., Director of Admissions. 919 829-8581.

**FINANCIAL AID. Available aid:** Pell grants, SEOG, state scholarships and grants, school scholarships, academic merit scholarships, and aid for undergraduate foreign students. Perkins Loans (NDSL), PLUS, Stafford Loans (GSL), and SLS. AMS.
**Financial aid statistics:** 23% of aid is not need-based. In 1993-94, 97% of all undergraduate applicants received aid; 96% of freshman applicants. Average amounts of aid awarded freshmen: Scholarships and grants, $3,600; loans, $2,300.
**Supporting data/closing dates:** FAFSA: Priority filing date is February 15. School's own aid application: Priority filing date is February 15; accepted on rolling basis. Notification of awards begins April 1.
**Financial aid contact:** Elizabeth McDuffie, Director of Scholarships and Financial Assistance. 919 829-8565.

**STUDENT EMPLOYMENT.** College Work/Study Program. Institutional employment. 20% of full-time undergraduates work on campus during school year. Students may expect to earn an average of $1,200 during school year. Off-campus part-time employment opportunities rated "excellent."

**COMPUTER FACILITIES.** 90 IBM/IBM-compatible and Macintosh/Apple microcomputers. Students may access minicomputer/mainframe systems. Residence halls may be equipped with stand-alone microcomputers. Client/LAN operating systems include Apple/Macintosh, DOS, Windows NT. Computer languages and software packages include Assembly, BASIC, C, COBOL, Harvard Graphics, LISP, MAPLE, MINITAB, Pascal, SPSS, WordPerfect, calculus and spreadsheet software. Computer facilities are available to all students.
**Fees:** None.
**Hours:** 24 hours in residence halls; 7 AM-1 AM in classrooms.

**GRADUATE CAREER DATA.** Graduate school percentages: 1% enter law school. 1% enter medical school. 1% enter dental school. 2% enter graduate business programs. 7% enter graduate arts and sciences programs. 1% enter theological school/seminary. Highest graduate school enrollments: Appalachian State U, Campbell U, East Carolina U, Meredith Coll, North Carolina State U, U of North Carolina at Chapel Hill, U of North Carolina at Greensboro, U of South Carolina, U of Virginia, Wake Forest U. 49% of graduates choose careers in business and industry. Companies and businesses that hire graduates: Atcom, Burroughs Wellcome, Carolina Telegraph & Telephone, CP&L, IBM, Northern Telecom, SAS Institute.

**PROMINENT ALUMNI/AE.** BetsyLane Cochrane, senate whip, N.C. General Assembly; Beth Leavel-Milne, actress; Roxie Collie Laybourne, Smithsonian Institute.

# Methodist College

**Fayetteville, NC 28311** **910 630-7000**

**1994-95 Costs.** Tuition: $9,400. Room: $1,600. Board: $2,150. Fees, books, misc. academic expenses (school's estimate): $450.
**Enrollment.** Undergraduates: 590 men, 524 women (full-time). Freshman class: 1,348 applicants, 962 accepted, 657 enrolled.
**Test score averages/ranges.** Average SAT scores: 410 verbal, 457 math. Range of SAT scores of middle 50%: 350-399 verbal, 400-449 math. Average ACT scores: 19 composite.
**Faculty.** 53 full-time; 32 part-time. 68% of faculty holds doctoral degree. Student/faculty ratio: 14 to 1.
**Selectivity rating.** Less competitive.

**PROFILE.** Methodist is a private, church-affiliated, liberal arts college. Its 600-acre campus is located in Fayetteville, 60 miles south of Raleigh.

**Accreditation:** SACS.
**Religious orientation:** Methodist College is affiliated with the United Methodist Church (North Carolina Conference); two semesters of religion required.
**Library:** Collections totaling over 82,920 volumes, 530 periodical subscriptions, and 10,100 microform items.
**Special facilities/museums:** Art gallery, Bible collection, language lab, nature trail.
**Athletic facilities:** Gymnasium, free weights, basketball, raquetball, tennis, and volleyball courts, football and soccer fields, track, golf course.

**STUDENT BODY. Undergraduate profile:** 66% are state residents; 30% are transfers. 4% Asian-American, 10% Black, 3% Hispanic, 1% Native American, 81% White, 1% Other. Average age of undergraduates is 21.
**Freshman profile:** 1% of freshmen who took SAT scored 700 or over on math; 1% scored 600 or over on verbal, 5% scored 600 or over on math; 8% scored 500 or over on verbal, 25% scored 500 or over on math; 39% scored 400 or over on verbal, 66% scored 400 or over on math; 90% scored 300 or over on verbal, 97% scored 300 or over on math. 79% of accepted applicants took SAT; 21% took ACT. 88% of freshmen come from public schools.
**Undergraduate achievement:** 60% of fall 1992 freshmen returned for fall 1993 term.
**Foreign students:** 38 students are from out of the country. Countries represented include Canada, China, England, Germany, Ireland, and Japan; 17 in all.

**PROGRAMS OF STUDY. Degrees:** B.A., B.Appl.Sci., B.Mus., B.S.
**Majors:** Accounting, Art, Art Education, Arts Management, Biology, Business Administration/Chemistry, Business Administration/Golf Management, Business Administration/Professional Tennis Management, Communication, Computer Science, Criminal Justice/Legal Studies, Early Childhood Education, Elementary Education, English, French, History, Intermediate Education, International Studies, Liberal Arts Studies, Mathematics, Music, Music Education, Music Management, Physical Education, Political Science, Psychology, Religion, Science, Social Work, Spanish, Special Education, Theatre, Theatre Arts Education, Theatre Management, Visual Arts/Management, Writing.
**Distribution of degrees:** The majors with the highest enrollment are business administration, education, and sociology; computer science, Spanish, and mathematics have the lowest.
**Requirements:** General education requirement.
**Academic regulations:** Freshmen must maintain minimum 1.40 GPA; sophomores, 1.60 GPA; juniors, 1.80 GPA; seniors, 1.90 GPA.
**Special:** Associate's degrees offered. Double majors. Independent study. Pass/fail grading option. Internships. Cooperative education programs. Graduate school at which undergraduates may take graduate-level courses. Preprofessional programs in law, medicine, veterinary science, pharmacy, dentistry, and theology. 2-2 and 2-3 engineering programs with Georgia Tech, North Carolina State U, and U of South Carolina. Washington Semester. Teacher certification in early childhood, elementary, secondary, and special education. Study abroad in Korea. ROTC. AFROTC at Fayetteville State U.
**Honors:** Honors program. Honor societies.
**Academic Assistance:** Remedial reading, writing, math, and study skills. Nonremedial tutoring.

**ADMISSIONS. Academic basis for candidate selection** (in order of priority): Secondary school record, standardized test scores, class rank, school's recommendation, essay.
**Nonacademic basis for candidate selection:** Character and personality are emphasized. Extracurricular participation is important. Alumni/ae relationship is considered.
**Requirements:** Graduation from secondary school is required; GED is accepted. 18 units and the following program of study are required: 4 units of English, 2 units of math, 2 units of science, 2 units of social studies, 2 units of history, 6 units of academic electives. 2 units of a single foreign language recommended. Minimum combined SAT score of 750, rank in top half of secondary school class, and minimum 2.0 GPA required of in-state applicants; minimum combined SAT score of 750, rank in top half of secondary school class, and minimum 2.5 GPA required of out-of-state applicants. Conditional admission possible for applicants not meeting standard requirements. SAT or ACT is required. Campus visit and interview recommended. Off-campus interviews available with an admissions representative.
**Procedure:** Take SAT or ACT by June of 12th year. Visit college for interview by June of 12th year. Application deadline is August. Notification of admission on rolling basis. $100 tuition deposit, refundable until May 1. $200 room deposit, refundable until May 1. Freshmen accepted in terms other than fall.
**Special programs:** Admission may be deferred one year. Credit may be granted through CEEB Advanced Placement for scores of 3 or higher. Credit may be granted through CLEP general and subject exams, DANTES and challenge exams, and military and life experience. Concurrent enrollment program.

**Transfer students:** Transfer students accepted for terms other than fall. In fall 1993, 30% of all new students were transfers into all classes. 201 transfer applications were received, 197 were accepted. Application deadline is August for fall; January for spring. Minimum 2.0 GPA recommended. Lowest course grade accepted is "C." Maximum number of transferable credits is 62 semester hours from a two-year school and 95 semester hours from a four-year school. At least 24 semester hours must be completed at the college to receive degree.
**Admissions contact:** J. Alan Coheley, M.Ed., Vice President for Enrollment Services. 910 630-7027.

**FINANCIAL AID. Available aid:** Pell grants, SEOG, state scholarships and grants, school scholarships and grants, private scholarships and grants, ROTC scholarships, academic merit scholarships, and aid for undergraduate foreign students. Perkins Loans (NDSL), PLUS, Stafford Loans (GSL), and SLS.
**Financial aid statistics:** 28% of aid is not need-based. Average amounts of aid awarded freshmen: Scholarships and grants, $4,000; loans, $2,625.
**Supporting data/closing dates:** FAFSA/FAF/FFS: Priority filing date is May 1. School's own aid application: Accepted on rolling basis. SINGLEFILE: Priority filing date is May 1. Notification of awards on rolling basis.
**Financial aid contact:** John R. Keso, M.Ed., Director of Financial Aid. 910 630-7189.

## Mount Olive College

**Mount Olive, NC 28365** **919 658-2502**

**1994-95 Costs.** Tuition: $7,450. Room & board: $2,800. Fees, books, misc. academic expenses (school's estimate): $600.
**Enrollment.** Undergraduates: 210 men, 218 women (full-time). Freshman class: 407 applicants, 335 accepted, 138 enrolled.
**Test score averages/ranges.** Average SAT scores: 381 verbal, 437 math. Range of SAT scores of middle 50%: 330-430 verbal, 380-490 math. Average ACT scores: 17 composite. Range of ACT scores of middle 50%: 16-18 composite.
**Faculty.** 35 full-time; 24 part-time. 40% of faculty holds doctoral degree. Student/faculty ratio: 12 to 1.
**Selectivity rating.** Less competitive.

**PROFILE.** Mount Olive, founded in 1951, is a private, church-affiliated, liberal arts college. Its 110-acre campus is located in Mount Olive, south of Charlotte.

**Accreditation:** SACS.
**Religious orientation:** Mount Olive College is affiliated with the Free Will Baptist Church; two semesters of religion required.
**Library:** Collections totaling over 55,000 volumes, 360 periodical subscriptions and 300 microform items.
**Special facilities/museums:** Art collection, Free Will Baptist archives.
**Athletic facilities:** Athletic center, baseball, soccer, and softball fields, tennis courts, gymnasium, training and weight room, basketball, racquetball, and volleyball courts, golf course.
**STUDENT BODY. Undergraduate profile:** 95% are state residents. 2% Asian-American, 19% Black, 1% Hispanic, 78% White. Average age of undergraduates is 27.
**Freshman profile:** 6% of freshmen who took SAT scored 600 or over on math; 7% scored 500 or over on verbal, 22% scored 500 or over on math; 36% scored 400 or over on verbal, 61% scored 400 or over on math; 80% scored 300 or over on verbal, 88% scored 300 or over on math. 38% of freshmen who took ACT scored 18 or over on composite; 100% scored 12 or over on composite. Majority of accepted applicants took SAT. 92% of freshmen come from public schools.
**Undergraduate achievement:** 60% of fall 1992 freshmen returned for fall 1993 term. 20% of entering class graduated. 5% of students who completed a degree program went on to graduate study within one year.
**Foreign students:** Two students are from out of the country. Two countries represented in all.
**PROGRAMS OF STUDY. Degrees:** B.A., B.Appl.Sci., B.S.
**Majors:** Accounting, Business, Church Ministries, Computer Information Systems, English, Fine Arts/Art, Fine Arts/Music, Human Resources Management, Liberal Arts, Psychology, Recreation, Religion, Science, Social Science, Visual Communications.
**Distribution of degrees:** The majors with the highest enrollment are business, recreation, and psychology; English has the lowest.
**Requirements:** General education requirement.
**Academic regulations:** Freshmen must maintain minimum 1.25 GPA; sophomores, 1.65 GPA; juniors, 1.85 GPA; seniors, 1.9 GPA.
**Special:** Minors offered in all majors. Associate's degrees offered. Double majors. Dual degrees. Independent study. Accelerated study. Internships. Cooperative education programs. Preprofessional programs in law, medicine, veterinary science, pharmacy, dentistry, theology, and nursing. Member of Eastern North Carolina Career Alliance.
**Honors:** Honors program. Honor societies.
**Academic Assistance:** Remedial writing, math, and study skills. Nonremedial tutoring.
**ADMISSIONS. Academic basis for candidate selection** (in order of priority): Secondary school record, class rank, school's recommendation, standardized test scores.
**Nonacademic basis for candidate selection:** Character and personality are emphasized. Extracurricular participation is important. Particular talent or ability and alumni/ae relationship are considered.
**Requirements:** Graduation from secondary school is required; GED is accepted. 14 units and the following program of study are recommended: 4 units of English, 3 units of math, 3 units of science, 2 units of foreign language, 2 units of history. Minimum combined SAT score of 700, rank in top half of secondary school class, and minimum 2.0 GPA recommended. Portfolio required of art program applicants. Audition required of music program applicants. Conditional admission possible for applicants not meeting standard requirements. SAT is required; ACT may be substituted. Campus visit and interview recommended. Off-campus interviews available with an admissions representative.
**Procedure:** Notification of admission on rolling basis. Reply is required within two weeks of acceptance. $50 tuition deposit, refundable until May 31. $25 room deposit, refundable until May 31. Freshmen accepted in terms other than fall.
**Special programs:** Credit and/or placement may be granted through CEEB Advanced Placement exams for scores of 3 or higher. Credit may be granted through CLEP general and subject exams, Regents College, ACT PEP, and DANTES exams, and military and life experience. Credit and placement may be granted through challenge exams. Early entrance/early admission program. Concurrent enrollment program.
**Transfer students:** Transfer students accepted for terms other than fall. In fall 1993, 122 transfer applications were received, 103 were accepted. Application deadline is rolling for fall; rolling for spring. Minimum 2.0 GPA recommended. Lowest course grade accepted is "C." Maximum number of transferable credits is 64 semester hours from a two-year school and 96 semester hours from a four-year school. At least 30 semester hours must be completed at the college to receive degree.
**Admissions contact:** Dianne B. Riley, M.A., Director of Admissions. 919 658-7164.
**FINANCIAL AID. Available aid:** Pell grants, SEOG, state scholarships and grants, school scholarships and grants, private scholarships and grants, academic merit scholarships, and athletic scholarships. Perkins Loans (NDSL), PLUS, Stafford Loans (GSL), and SLS. AMS.
**Financial aid statistics:** In 1993-94, 50% of all undergraduate applicants received aid. Average amounts of aid awarded freshmen: Loans, $2,625.
**Supporting data/closing dates:** FAFSA: Priority filing date is March 1. School's own aid application: Priority filing date is March 1. Notification of awards on rolling basis.
**Financial aid contact:** Vicky Cotton, M.A., Director of Financial Aid. 919 658-7164.

## North Carolina Agricultural and Technical State University

**Greensboro, NC 27411** **919 334-7500**

**1993–94 Costs.** Tuition: $407 (state residents), $6,806 (out-of-state). Room: $1,780. Board: $1,330. Fees, books, misc. academic expenses (school's estimate): $1,227.
**Enrollment.** Undergraduates: 2,908 men, 2,990 women (full-time). Freshman class: 5,074 applicants, 3,124 accepted, 1,495 enrolled. Graduate enrollment: 420 men, 467 women.
**Test score averages/ranges.** Average SAT scores: 385 verbal, 436 math. Range of SAT scores of middle 50%: 300-400 verbal, 300-400 math. Average ACT scores: 19 composite.
**Faculty.** 355 full-time; 69 part-time. 60% of faculty holds doctoral degree. Student/faculty ratio: 14 to 1.
**Selectivity rating.** Less competitive.

**PROFILE.** North Carolina A&T State, founded in 1891, is a public, historically black university. Programs are offered through the Schools of Agriculture, Arts and Sciences, Business, Education, Engineering, Nursing, and Technology. Its 187-acre campus is located in Greensboro, 90 miles north of Charlotte.

**Accreditation:** SACS. Professionally accredited by the Accreditation Board for Engineering and Technology, the American Assembly of Collegiate Schools of Business, the American Home Economics Association, the Council on Social Work Education, the National Association of Schools of Music, the National Council for Accreditation of Teacher Education, the National League for Nursing.
**Religious orientation:** North Carolina Agricultural and Technical State University is nonsectarian; no religious requirements.
**Library:** Collections totaling over 372,438 volumes, 1,802 periodical subscriptions, and 21,105 microform items.
**Special facilities/museums:** Art gallery, African heritage center, child development laboratory, microelectronics center of North Carolina, planetarium, herbarium.
**Athletic facilities:** Swimming pool, gymnasium, basketball, racquetball, and volleyball courts, weight lifting facility, track, football stadium.
**STUDENT BODY. Undergraduate profile:** 84% are state residents; 23% are transfers. 90% Black, 9% White, 1% Other. Average age of undergraduates is 22.
**Freshman profile:** 1% of freshmen who took SAT scored 700 or over on math; 1% scored 600 or over on verbal, 4% scored 600 or over on math; 6% scored 500 or over on verbal, 20% scored 500 or over on math; 35% scored 400 or over on verbal, 55% scored 400 or over on math; 81% scored 300 or over on verbal, 92% scored 300 or over on math. 95% of accepted applicants took SAT.
**Undergraduate achievement:** 76% of fall 1991 freshmen returned for fall 1992 term. 14% of entering class graduated.
**Foreign students:** Countries represented include the Bahamas, China, India, Indonesia, Nigeria, and Pakistan; 26 in all.
**PROGRAMS OF STUDY. Degrees:** B.A., B.F.A., B.S., B.S.Nurs., B.Soc.Work.
**Majors:** Accounting, Administrative Services, Agricultural Education, Agricultural Engineering, Agricultural Science, Agricultural Technology, Architectural Engineering, Biology, Business Education, Business Finance, Business Management, Business Marketing, Chemical Engineering, Chemistry, Child Development, Clothing/Textiles, Computer Science, Driver/Safety Education, Early Childhood Education, Economics, Education, Electrical Engineering, Electronics, Engineering Mathematics, Engineering Physics, English, Food Administration, Food/Nutrition, French, Graphics Communications, Health/Physical Education, History, Home Economics Education, Industrial Arts Education, Industrial Education, Industrial Engineering, Industrial Technology, Laboratory Animal Technology, Landscape Architecture, Manufacturing, Mathematics, Mechanical Engineering, Music, Nursing, Occupational Safety/Health, Physics, Political Science,

Professional Theatre, Psychology, Recreation Administration, Social Sciences, Social Services, Sociology, Speech, Transportation, Vocational Education, Vocational Industrial Education.
**Distribution of degrees:** The majors with the highest enrollment are business administration, electrical engineering, and accounting; French and physics have the lowest.
**Requirements:** General education requirement.
**Academic regulations:** Minimum 2.0 GPA must be maintained.
**Special:** Double majors. Internships. Cooperative education programs. Graduate school at which undergraduates may take graduate-level courses. Member of Piedmont Independent Association of North Carolina. Teacher certification in early childhood, elementary, secondary, special education, and vo-tech education. Study abroad in England, France, and Mexico. ROTC and AFROTC.
**Honors:** Honors program. Honor societies.
**Academic Assistance:** Remedial reading, writing, and math. Nonremedial tutoring.

**STUDENT LIFE. Housing:** Students may live on or off campus. Women's and men's dorms. 41% of students live in college housing.
**Services and counseling/handicapped student services:** Placement services. Health service. Personal and psychological counseling. Academic guidance services. Religious counseling. Physically disabled student services. Learning disabled services. Notetaking services. Tape recorders. Tutors. Reader services for the blind.
**Campus organizations:** Undergraduate student government. Student newspaper (A&T Register, published once/week). Richard B. Harrison Players, senior band, symphony concert band, choirs, Fellowship Gospel Choir, departmental groups. Four fraternities, no chapter houses; four sororities, no chapter houses. 1% of men join a fraternity. 1% of women join a sorority.
**Religious organizations:** Brothers in Christ, Sisters of Brothers in Christ, Newman Club, Wesley Foundation, University Usher Board.
**Minority/foreign student organizations:** Minority Student Association. International Student Association.

**ATHLETICS. Physical education requirements:** Two semesters of physical education required.
**Intercollegiate competition:** 3% of students participate. Baseball (M), basketball (M,W), cheerleading (M,W), cross-country (M,W), football (M), softball (W), tennis (M,W), track (indoor) (M,W), track (outdoor) (M,W), track and field (indoor) (M,W), track and field (outdoor) (M,W), volleyball (W). Member of Mid Eastern Athletic Conference, NCAA Division I, NCAA Division I-AA for football.
**Intramural and club sports:** 8% of students participate. Intramural aerobics, basketball, bowling, card, chess, and pool tournaments, dance, football, softball, swimming, tennis, track, volleyball.

**ADMISSIONS. Academic basis for candidate selection** (in order of priority): Secondary school record, standardized test scores, class rank, school's recommendation.
**Requirements:** Graduation from secondary school is required; GED is not accepted. 16 units and the following program of study are required: 4 units of English, 3 units of math, 3 units of science including 1 unit of lab, 2 units of social studies, 4 units of academic electives. Secondary school units must include biology and history. Minimum 2.0 GPA recommended of in-state applicants; minimum combined SAT score of 800 (composite ACT score of 21) and minimum 2.5 GPA recommended of out-of-state applicants. 2 units of algebra, 1/2 unit of plane geometry, and 1/2 unit of trigonometry required of business, economics, and science program applicants. Auditions required of fine arts program applicants. SAT or ACT is required. No off-campus interviews.
**Procedure:** Take SAT or ACT by December of 12th year. Notification of admission on rolling basis. Reply is required by May 1. $75 room deposit, refundable until July 16. Freshmen accepted in terms other than fall.
**Special programs:** Credit may be granted through CEEB Advanced Placement for scores of 3 or higher. Credit may be granted through CLEP general and subject exams, DANTES exams, and military experience. Credit and placement may be granted through challenge exams.
**Transfer students:** Transfer students accepted for terms other than fall. In fall 1992, 23% of all new students were transfers into all classes. Application deadline is June 1 for fall; December 1 for spring. Minimum 2.0 GPA required. Lowest course grade accepted is "C." Maximum number of transferable credits is 80 semester hours. At least 36 semester hours must be completed at the university to receive degree.
**Admissions contact:** John F. Smith, M.S., Director of Admissions. 919 334-7946.

**FINANCIAL AID. Available aid:** Pell grants, SEOG, Federal Nursing Student Scholarships, state scholarships and grants, school scholarships and grants, private scholarships and grants, ROTC scholarships, academic merit scholarships, and athletic scholarships. Perkins Loans (NDSL), PLUS, Stafford Loans (GSL), Health Professions Loans, state loans, private loans, and SLS. Deferred payment plan.
**Financial aid statistics:** 26% of aid is not need-based. In 1992-93, 90% of all undergraduate applicants received aid; 95% of freshman applicants. Average amounts of aid awarded freshmen: Scholarships and grants, $275; loans, $1,800.
**Supporting data/closing dates:** FAFSA: Priority filing date is March 15. Notification of awards on rolling basis.
**Financial aid contact:** Dolores S. Davis, M.S., Director of Financial Aid. 919 334-7973.

**STUDENT EMPLOYMENT.** College Work/Study Program. Institutional employment. 14% of full-time undergraduates work on campus during school year. Students may expect to earn an average of $1,600 during school year. Off-campus part-time employment opportunities rated "good."

**COMPUTER FACILITIES.** 225 IBM/IBM-compatible and Macintosh/Apple microcomputers; 28 are networked. Students may access Digital minicomputer/mainframe systems. Computer languages and software packages include Ada, BASIC, C, COBOL, DataTrieve, DBMS, FORTRAN, Pascal, SAS, SMART, SPSS-X, Smart Star. Computer facilities are available to all students.
**Fees:** None.
**Hours:** 8 AM-midn. (M-F); 8 AM-5 PM (Sa).

**PROMINENT ALUMNI/AE.** Dr. Ronald McNair, astronaut; Col. Clara Adams-Ender, chief Army nurse; Dwaine Board, lineman for San Francisco 49ers; Lou Donaldson, jazz musician and composer; Henry E. Frye, associate justice, North Carolina supreme court; Dr. Dwight Davis, coronary medicine; Hon. Adolphus Towns, congressman, New York State; Rev. Jesse Jackson.

# North Carolina School of the Arts

**Winston-Salem, NC 27117-2189 919 770-3399**

**1994-95 Costs.** Tuition: $1,194 (state residents), $8,112 (out-of-state). Room & board: $3,486. Fees, books, misc. academic expenses (school's estimate): $1,085.
**Enrollment.** Undergraduates: 223 men, 196 women (full-time). Freshman class: 315 applicants, 181 accepted, 122 enrolled. Graduate enrollment: 29 men, 25 women.
**Test score averages/ranges.** Average SAT scores: 506 verbal, 533 math.
**Faculty.** 93 full-time; 37 part-time. 15% of faculty holds doctoral degree. Student/faculty ratio: 7 to 1.
**Selectivity rating.** Competitive.

**PROFILE.** The North Carolina School of the Arts, founded in 1964, is a public school of the arts. Its modern campus is located in Winston-Salem's central section.

**Accreditation:** SACS.
**Religious orientation:** North Carolina School of the Arts is nonsectarian; no religious requirements.
**Library:** Collections totaling over 107,510 volumes, 460 periodical subscriptions, and 17,956 microform items.

**STUDENT BODY. Undergraduate profile:** 35% are state residents; 18% are transfers. 2% Asian-American, 6% Black, 2% Hispanic, 1% Native American, 84% White, 5% Other. Average age of undergraduates is 20.
**Freshman profile:** 1% of freshmen who took SAT scored 700 or over on verbal, 1% scored 700 or over on math; 9% scored 600 or over on verbal, 16% scored 600 or over on math; 32% scored 500 or over on verbal, 37% scored 500 or over on math; 55% scored 400 or over on verbal, 54% scored 400 or over on math; 61% scored 300 or over on verbal, 60% scored 300 or over on math. Majority of accepted applicants took SAT. 95% of freshmen come from public schools.
**Undergraduate achievement:** 67% of fall 1992 freshmen returned for fall 1993 term. 27% of entering class graduated.
**Foreign students:** 16 students are from out of the country. Countries represented include Canada, Germany, Hungary, Israel, Italy, and Japan; nine in all.

**PROGRAMS OF STUDY. Degrees:** B.F.A., B.Mus.
**Majors:** Dance, Filmmaking, Music, Theatre, Theatre Design/Production.
**Distribution of degrees:** The majors with the highest enrollment are design/production, music, and drama.
**Requirements:** General education requirement.
**Special:** Internships. Graduate school at which undergraduates may take graduate-level courses.
**Academic Assistance:** Remedial reading and writing.

**ADMISSIONS. Academic basis for candidate selection** (in order of priority): Secondary school record, standardized test scores, school's recommendation, class rank.
**Nonacademic basis for candidate selection:** Particular talent or ability is emphasized. Character and personality and extracurricular participation are important. Geographical distribution and alumni/ae relationship are considered.
**Requirements:** Graduation from secondary school is recommended; GED is accepted. 20 units and the following program of study are required: 4 units of English, 3 units of math, 3 units of science including 1 unit of lab, 1 unit of social studies, 1 unit of history, 4 units of academic electives. Portfolio required of design/production and filmmaking program applicants. Audition required of dance and drama program applicants. Four-year diploma program for applicants not normally admissible. SAT is required; ACT may be substituted. Campus visit recommended. Off-campus interviews available with an admissions representative.
**Procedure:** Take SAT or ACT by November of 12th year. Visit college for interview by March of 12th year. Suggest filing application by March; no deadline. Notification of admission by April 1. Reply is required by May 1. $100 tuition deposit, refundable until May 1. $50 room deposit, refundable until May 1. Freshmen accepted in terms other than fall.
**Special programs:** Credit and/or placement may be granted through CEEB Advanced Placement exams for scores of 3 or higher. Credit may be granted through CLEP general and subject exams. Concurrent enrollment program.
**Transfer students:** Transfer students accepted for terms other than fall. In fall 1993, 18% of all new students were transfers into all classes. 140 transfer applications were received, 75 were accepted. Application deadline is March 1. Lowest course grade accepted is "C."
**Admissions contact:** Carol Palm, Director of Admissions. 919 770-3290.

**FINANCIAL AID. Available aid:** Pell grants, state scholarships and grants, school scholarships and grants, and private scholarships. Perkins Loans (NDSL), PLUS, Stafford Loans (GSL), state loans, and SLS. Tuition Plan Inc. and Education Plan Inc.
**Financial aid statistics:** 25% of aid is not need-based. In 1993-94, 79% of all undergraduate applicants received aid; 75% of freshman applicants. Average amounts of aid awarded freshmen: Scholarships and grants, $875; loans, $2,000.
**Supporting data/closing dates:** FAFSA/FAF/FFS: Priority filing date is April 1; accepted on rolling basis. School's own aid application: Priority filing date is March 15; accepted on rolling basis. Notification of awards begins April 15.
**Financial aid contact:** Ginger Klock, Director of Student Financial Aid. 919 770-3297.

## North Carolina State University

Raleigh, NC 27695-7103 919 515-2011

**1994-95 Costs.** Tuition: $1,492 (state residents), $8,886 (out-of-state). Room: $1,500. Board: $1,900. Fees, books, misc. academic expenses (school's estimate): $700.

**Enrollment.** Undergraduates: 10,269 men, 6,187 women (full-time). Freshman class: 10,678 applicants, 7,059 accepted, 3,176 enrolled. Graduate enrollment: 3,272 men, 2,490 women.

**Test score averages/ranges.** Average SAT scores: 493 verbal, 578 math. Range of SAT scores of middle 50%: 420-530 verbal, 510-620 math.

**Faculty.** 1,359 full-time; 221 part-time. 85% of faculty holds doctoral degree. Student/faculty ratio: 14 to 1.

**Selectivity rating.** More competitive.

**PROFILE.** North Carolina State, founded in 1887, is a public, comprehensive university. Programs are offered through the Colleges of Agriculture and Life Sciences, Education and Psychology, Engineering, Forest Resources, Humanities and Social Science, Physical and Mathematical Science, Textiles, and Veterinary Medicine and the School of Design. Its 1600-acre campus is located in Raleigh.

**Accreditation:** SACS. Professionally accredited by the Accreditation Board for Engineering and Technology, the Council on Social Work Education, the National Architecture Accrediting Board, the National Council for Accreditation of Teacher Education, the Society of American Foresters.

**Religious orientation:** North Carolina State University is nonsectarian; no religious requirements.

**Library:** Collections totaling over 2,000,000 volumes, 18,086 periodical subscriptions, and 3,700,000 microform items.

**Special facilities/museums:** Art and arts/crafts galleries, research farms and forest, pulp/paper and wood products labs, processing equipment for fiber, fabric, and garment manufacture, electron microscopes, nuclear reactor, stable isotope lab, phytophotron with controlled atmosphere growth chambers.

**Athletic facilities:** Swimming pools, basketball, racquetball, squash, and volleyball courts, track, aerobics, fencing, gymnastics, weight, and wrestling rooms, indoor rock climbing facility, athletic fields.

**STUDENT BODY. Undergraduate profile:** 86% are state residents; 29% are transfers. 3% Asian-American, 9% Black, 1% Hispanic, 1% Native American, 82% White, 4% Other. Average age of undergraduates is 22.

**Freshman profile:** 1% of freshmen who took SAT scored 700 or over on verbal, 10% scored 700 or over on math; 11% scored 600 or over on verbal, 40% scored 600 or over on math; 45% scored 500 or over on verbal, 84% scored 500 or over on math; 92% scored 400 or over on verbal, 98% scored 400 or over on math; 100% scored 300 or over on verbal, 99% scored 300 or over on math. 99% of accepted applicants took SAT; 5% took ACT. 96% of freshmen come from public schools.

**Undergraduate achievement:** 93% of fall 1992 freshmen returned for fall 1993 term. 28% of entering class graduated. 28% of students who completed a degree program went on to graduate study within one year.

**Foreign students:** 223 students are from out of the country. Countries represented include Egypt, India, and Pacific Rim countries; 93 in all.

**PROGRAMS OF STUDY. Degrees:** B.A., B.Arch., B.Env.Design, B.S., B.Soc.Work.

**Majors:** Accounting, Aerospace Engineering, Agricultural Business/Management, Agricultural Economics, Agricultural Education, Agricultural Systems Technology, Agronomy, Animal Science, Applied Sociology, Architecture, Biochemistry, Biological/Agricultural Engineering, Biological Sciences, Botany, Business, Chemical Engineering, Chemistry, Civil Engineering, Communication, Computer Engineering, Computer Science/Information Systems, Conservation, Construction Management, Economics, Education, Electrical Engineering, English, Environmental Design, Environmental Design in Architecture, Environmental Design in Landscape Architecture, Environmental Engineering, Fisheries/Wildlife Sciences, Food Science, Forestry, French Language/Literature, Furniture Manufacturing/Management, Geology, Graphic Design, Health Occupations Education, History, Horticultural Science, Individualized Studies, Industrial Design, Industrial Engineering, Marketing Education, Materials Science/Engineering, Mathematics, Mathematics Education, Mechanical Engineering, Medical Technology, Meteorology, Microbiology, Middle Grades Education, Multidisciplinary Study, Natural Resources, Nuclear Engineering, Parks/Recreation/Tourist Management, Philosophy, Physics, Political Science/Government, Poultry Science, Pre-Dental, Pre-Medical, Pre-Optometry, Pre-Veterinary, Psychology, Pulp/Paper Science/Technology, Science Education, Social Work, Sociology, Spanish Language/Literature, Statistics, Technical Education, Technology Education, Textile/Apparel Management, Textile Chemistry, Textile Engineering, Textile Materials Science, Textile Science, Veterinary Medicine, Vocational Industrial Education, Wood Science/Technology, Zoology.

**Distribution of degrees:** The majors with the highest enrollment are electrical engineering and mechanical engineering.

**Requirements:** General education requirement.

**Academic regulations:** Freshmen must maintain minimum 1.5 GPA; sophomores, 1.7 GPA; juniors, 1.8 GPA; seniors, 2.0 GPA.

**Special:** Minors offered in many majors. Options offered in construction, criminal justice, human resource development, microbiology, teacher education, textile design, and writing/editing. Two-year Agricultural Institute. Associate's degrees offered. Self-designed majors. Double majors. Dual degrees. Independent study. Accelerated study. Pass/fail grading option. Internships. Cooperative education programs. Graduate school at which undergraduates may take graduate-level courses. Preprofessional programs in law, medicine, veterinary science, dentistry, and optometry. 3-2 engineering program with U of North Carolina at Asheville. Member of International University Consortium for Telecommunications and Cooperating Raleigh Colleges. Cross-registration with Meredith Coll, Peace Coll, St. Augustine's Coll, St. Mary's Coll, and Shaw U. Member of National Student Exchange (NSE). Teacher certification in secondary education. Certification in specific subject areas. Member of International Student Exchange Program (ISEP). Study abroad in over 90 countries including Austria, Chile, England, France, Germany, Japan, Jordan, Mexico, the Netherlands, Scotland, and Spain. ROTC, NROTC, and AFROTC.

**Honors:** Honors program. Honor societies.

**Academic Assistance:** Remedial reading, writing, math, and study skills. Nonremedial tutoring.

**STUDENT LIFE. Housing:** Students may live on or off campus. Coed, women's, and men's dorms. Sorority and fraternity housing. On-campus married-student housing. 40% of students live in college housing.

**Social atmosphere:** According to the student newspaper, the student population is very diversified: "Greeks, Campus Crusade for Christ, bohemians, freaks, design students, engineering majors, nerds." Popular events include basketball games, state fairs, design school parties, and the Wolfstock concert. Favorite off-campus destinations include Barry's bar and dancing, the various nightspots along Hillsboro Street across from the campus, the Rose Garden park, the mall, and Cheers bar.

**Services and counseling/handicapped student services:** Placement services. Health service. Women's center. Day care. Counseling services for minority, military, veteran, and older students. Birth control, personal, and psychological counseling. Career and academic guidance services. Religious counseling. Physically disabled student services. Learning disabled program/services. Notetaking services. Tape recorders. Tutors. Reader services for the blind.

**Campus organizations:** Undergraduate student government. Student newspaper (Technician, published three times/week). Literary magazine. Yearbook. Radio and TV stations. Symphonic, marching, and ROTC bands, glee club, drama group, political, professional, service, and special-interest groups, 350 organizations in all. 24 fraternities, 18 chapter houses; 10 sororities, six chapter houses. 15% of men join a fraternity. 15% of women join a sorority.

**Religious organizations:** Bahai Club, Baptist Student Union, Canterbury Club, Catholic Student Center, Christian Science Organization, Collegian Christian Fellowship, many other religious groups.

**Minority/foreign student organizations:** Society of African-American Culture, Native American Organization, Black Students Board, Peer Mentor Program, National Society of Black Engineers, Kemetic Benu Order. Chinese, Ethiopian, Hong Kong, Indian, Indonesian, Japanese, Korean, Latin American, Malaysian, Pakistan, Taiwanese, Thai, Vietnamese, and Zimbabwe groups.

**ATHLETICS. Physical education requirements:** Four semesters of physical education required.

**Intercollegiate competition:** 2% of students participate. Baseball (M), basketball (M,W), cheerleading (M,W), cross-country (M,W), diving (M,W), football (M), golf (M), gymnastics (W), riflery (M,W), soccer (M,W), swimming (M,W), tennis (M,W), track (indoor) (M,W), track (outdoor) (M,W), track and field (indoor) (M,W), track and field (outdoor) (M,W), volleyball (W), wrestling (M). Member of Atlantic Coast Conference, NCAA Division I.

**Intramural and club sports:** 40% of students participate. Intramural aerobics, archery, badminton, baseball, basketball, bowling, cycling, field hockey, frisbee, handball, ice hockey, lacrosse, martial arts, mountain cycling, racquetball, rodeo, rowing, rugby, sailing, skiing, soccer, squash, tennis, volleyball, water aerobics, water polo, water skiing, windsurfing, wrestling. Men's club Alpine skiing, archery, bowling, canoe/kayak, crew, cycling, field hockey, handball, ice hockey, lacrosse, martial arts, Nordic skiing, polo, racquetball, rugby, sailing, softball, squash, ultimate frisbee, water polo, water skiing. Women's club Alpine skiing, archery, bowling, canoe/kayak, crew, cycling, field hockey, handball, ice hockey, lacrosse, martial arts, Nordic skiing, polo, racquetball, rugby, sailing, softball, squash, ultimate frisbee, water polo, water skiing.

**ADMISSIONS. Academic basis for candidate selection** (in order of priority): Secondary school record, class rank, standardized test scores, essay, school's recommendation.

**Nonacademic basis for candidate selection:** Geographical distribution is important. Character and personality, extracurricular participation, particular talent or ability, and alumni/ae relationship are considered.

**Requirements:** Graduation from secondary school is required; GED is accepted. 20 units and the following program of study are required: 4 units of English, 3 units of math, 3 units of science including 1 unit of lab, 2 units of foreign language, 2 units of social studies, 1 unit of history, 3 units of electives including 1 unit of academic electives. Portfolio required of art program applicants. Special consideration given to applicants who have graduated from nonaccredited secondary schools or who are holders of equivalency certificates. SAT or ACT is required. PSAT is recommended. ACH required. Campus visit recommended. No off-campus interviews.

**Procedure:** Take SAT or ACT by December of 12th year. Take ACH by May of 12th year. Suggest filing application by November 1. Application deadline is February 1. Final filing date for School of Design is January 1. Notification of admission on rolling basis. Reply is required by May 1. $100 tuition deposit of which $50 is refundable until May 1. Freshmen accepted in terms other than fall.

**Special programs:** Admission may be deferred one year. Credit and/or placement may be granted through CEEB Advanced Placement exams for scores of 3 or higher. Credit and/or placement may be granted through CLEP subject exams. Credit and placement may be granted through Regents College, ACT PEP, DANTES, and challenge exams. Concurrent enrollment program.

**Transfer students:** Transfer students accepted for terms other than fall. In fall 1993, 29% of all new students were transfers into all classes. 3,498 transfer applications were received, 1,716 were accepted. Application deadline is April 1 for fall; November 1 for spring. Minimum 2.0 GPA required. Lowest course grade accepted is "C." Maximum number of transferable semester hours is between 80 and 90. 30-48 semester hours must be completed at the university to receive degree.

**Admissions contact:** George R. Dixon, M.P.A., Ed.D., Director of Admissions. 919 515-2434.

**FINANCIAL AID. Available aid:** Pell grants, SEOG, state scholarships and grants, school scholarships and grants, private scholarships and grants, ROTC scholarships,

academic merit scholarships, and athletic scholarships. Perkins Loans (NDSL), PLUS, Stafford Loans (GSL), Health Professions Loans, state loans, school loans, private loans, and SLS.
**Financial aid statistics:** In 1993-94, 60% of all undergraduate applicants received aid; 60% of freshman applicants. Average amounts of aid awarded freshmen: Scholarships and grants, $800; loans, $1,000.
**Supporting data/closing dates:** FAFSA: Deadline is March 1. FAF/FFS: Accepted on rolling basis. School's own aid application: Deadline is March 1. Income tax forms: Accepted on rolling basis. Notification of awards on rolling basis.
**Financial aid contact:** Julia E. Rice, M.A., Director of Financial Aid. 919 515-2421.

**STUDENT EMPLOYMENT.** College Work/Study Program. Institutional employment. Freshmen are discouraged from working during their first term. Off-campus part-time employment opportunities rated "excellent."

**COMPUTER FACILITIES.** 3,200 IBM/IBM-compatible and Macintosh/Apple microcomputers. Students may access Cray, Digital, IBM minicomputer/mainframe systems, Internet. Residence halls may be equipped with stand-alone microcomputers, networked microcomputers, networked terminals, modems. Client/LAN operating systems include Apple/Macintosh, DOS, UNIX/XENIX/AIX, X-windows. Computer languages and software packages include BASIC, C, C++, COBOL, FORTRAN, Pascal, SAS, SPSS. Computer facilities are available to all students.
**Fees:** $100 computer fee per semester for some majors.
**Hours:** 24 hours.

**GRADUATE CAREER DATA.** Highest graduate school enrollments: Georgia Tech, North Carolina State U, U of North Carolina at Chapel Hill. 60% of graduates choose careers in business and industry. Companies and businesses that hire graduates: IBM, Dupont, General Electric, AT&T.

**PROMINENT ALUMNI/AE.** Roy Park, CEO, Park Communications; James B. Hunt, Jr., governor, North Carolina; Dr. William Friday, president emeritus, U of North Carolina system; John Tesh, "Entertainment Tonight" co-host; Ed Woolard, CEO, DuPont; General Maxwell Thurman, U.S. Army.

# North Carolina Wesleyan College

**Rocky Mount, NC 27804** **919 985-5100**

**1994-95 Costs.** Tuition: $8,242. Room: $1,900. Board: $2,330. Fees, books, misc. academic expenses (school's estimate): $1,100.
**Enrollment.** Undergraduates: 309 men, 337 women (full-time). Freshman class: 812 applicants, 689 accepted, 195 enrolled.
**Test score averages/ranges.** Average SAT scores: 394 verbal, 432 math. Average ACT scores: 18 composite.
**Faculty.** 43 full-time; 28 part-time. 68% of faculty holds doctoral degree. Student/faculty ratio: 13 to 1.
**Selectivity rating.** Less competitive.

**PROFILE.** North Carolina Wesleyan, founded in 1956, is a private, church-affiliated, liberal arts college. Its 200-acre campus is located four miles north of Rocky Mount.

**Accreditation:** SACS.
**Religious orientation:** North Carolina Wesleyan College is affiliated with the United Methodist Church; three semester hours of religion required.
**Library:** Collections totaling over 58,000 volumes, 560 periodical subscriptions, and 12,227 microform items.
**Special facilities/museums:** Black Mountain Collection, Robert Lynch Collection of Outsider Art.
**Athletic facilities:** Gymnasium, basketball, tennis, and volleyball courts, baseball, intramural, soccer, and softball fields, weight room.

**STUDENT BODY. Undergraduate profile:** 49% are state residents; 33% are transfers. 1% Asian-American, 18% Black, 2% Hispanic, 78% White, 1% Other. Average age of undergraduates is 18.
**Freshman profile:** 2% of freshmen who took SAT scored 600 or over on verbal, 4% scored 600 or over on math; 13% scored 500 or over on verbal, 17% scored 500 or over on math; 41% scored 400 or over on verbal, 65% scored 400 or over on math; 92% scored 300 or over on verbal, 96% scored 300 or over on math. 92% of accepted applicants took SAT; 6% took ACT. 85% of freshmen come from public schools.
**Undergraduate achievement:** 71% of fall 1992 freshmen returned for fall 1993 term. 35% of entering class graduated. 30% of students who completed a degree program went on to graduate study within one year.
**Foreign students:** 10 students are from out of the country. Countries represented include Bermuda, Burma, India, Indonesia, and Venezuela; eight in all.

**PROGRAMS OF STUDY. Degrees:** B.A., B.S.
**Majors:** Accounting, Biology, Business Administration, Chemistry, Computer Information Systems, Education, Elementary Education, English, Environmental Science, Food Services/Hotel Management, History, Justice/Public Policy, Mathematics, Middle School Education, Music, Philosophy, Philosophy/Religion, Physical Education, Psychology, Religion, Sociology/Anthropology, Theatre.
**Distribution of degrees:** The majors with the highest enrollment are business administration, justice/public policy, and computer information systems; philosophy/religion, music, and middle school education have the lowest.
**Requirements:** General education requirement.
**Academic regulations:** Minimum 2.0 GPA must be maintained.
**Special:** Minors offered in most majors and in journalism, legal studies, and politics. Double majors. Dual degrees. Independent study. Pass/fail grading option. Internships. Cooperative education programs. Preprofessional programs in legal studies. Member of Eastern North Carolina Teacher Education Consortium and Teacher Education Consortium. Teacher certification in elementary and secondary education. Certification in specific subject areas.
**Honors:** Honors program. Honor societies.
**Academic Assistance:** Remedial study skills. Nonremedial tutoring.

**ADMISSIONS. Academic basis for candidate selection** (in order of priority): Secondary school record, standardized test scores, class rank, school's recommendation, essay.
**Nonacademic basis for candidate selection:** Particular talent or ability is emphasized. Character and personality and extracurricular participation are important. Geographical distribution and alumni/ae relationship are considered.
**Requirements:** Graduation from secondary school is required; GED is accepted. 16 units and the following program of study are recommended: 4 units of English, 3 units of math, 2 units of science, 2 units of foreign language, 1 unit of social studies, 2 units of history, 2 units of electives. Combined SAT score of 800, rank in top half of secondary school class, and 2.0 GPA recommended. SAT is required; ACT may be substituted. Campus visit and interview recommended. No off-campus interviews.
**Procedure:** Take SAT or ACT by April of 12th year. Application deadline is July 15. Notification of admission on rolling basis. Reply is required by August 1. $200 tuition deposit, refundable until May 1. $100 room deposit, refundable until June 1. Freshmen accepted in terms other than fall.
**Special programs:** Admission may be deferred two years. Credit may be granted through CEEB Advanced Placement for scores of 3 or higher. Credit may be granted through CLEP general and subject exams, ACT PEP, DANTES, and challenge exams, and military experience. Early entrance/early admission program. Concurrent enrollment program.
**Transfer students:** Transfer students accepted for terms other than fall. In fall 1993, 33% of all new students were transfers into all classes. 184 transfer applications were received, 145 were accepted. Application deadline is July 15 for fall; December 15 for spring. Minimum 2.0 GPA recommended. Lowest course grade accepted is "C." Maximum number of transferable credits is 64 semester hours from a two-year school and 94 semester hours from a four-year school. At least 30 semester hours must be completed at the college to receive degree.
**Admissions contact:** Brett Freshour, Director of Admissions. 919 985-5200.

**FINANCIAL AID. Available aid:** Pell grants, SEOG, state scholarships and grants, school scholarships and grants, private scholarships and grants, and academic merit scholarships. Perkins Loans (NDSL), PLUS, Stafford Loans (GSL), and SLS. Institutional tuition payment plan.
**Financial aid statistics:** 30% of aid is not need-based. In 1993-94, 78% of all undergraduate applicants received aid; 67% of freshman applicants. Average amounts of aid awarded freshmen: Scholarships and grants, $1,300; loans, $2,625.
**Supporting data/closing dates:** FAFSA/FAF: Deadline is April 1. Notification of awards on rolling basis.
**Financial aid contact:** Vickie Edwards, Director of Financial Aid. 919 985-5200.

# Pembroke State University

**Pembroke, NC 28372** **919 521-6000**

**1994-95 Costs.** Tuition: $1,078 (state residents), $6,442 (out-of-state). Room & board: $2,460. Fees, books, misc. academic expenses (school's estimate): $400.
**Enrollment.** Undergraduates: 980 men, 1,194 women (full-time). Freshman class: 946 applicants, 774 accepted, 440 enrolled. Graduate enrollment: 84 men, 258 women.
**Test score averages/ranges.** Average SAT scores: 385 verbal, 433 math.
**Faculty.** 150 full-time; 51 part-time. 77% of faculty holds doctoral degree. Student/faculty ratio: 16 to 1.
**Selectivity rating.** Less competitive.

**PROFILE.** Pembroke State is a public, arts and sciences university. Founded in 1887 to serve the Native Americans of the area, in 1954, admission was opened to all qualified applicants. Its 100-acre campus is located in Pembroke, in south-central North Carolina.

**Accreditation:** SACS. Professionally accredited by the Council on Social Work Education, the National Association of Schools of Music, the National Association of Schools of Public Affairs and Administration, the National Council for Accreditation of Teacher Education.
**Religious orientation:** Pembroke State University is nonsectarian; one semester of religion required.
**Library:** Collections totaling over 177,000 volumes, 1,439 periodical subscriptions, and 279,000 microform items.
**Special facilities/museums:** Native American resource center.
**Athletic facilities:** Gymnasium, swimming pool, sauna, basketball, tennis, and volleyball courts, track, baseball, soccer, and softball fields, weight and wrestling rooms.

**STUDENT BODY. Undergraduate profile:** 97% are state residents; 31% are transfers. 1% Asian-American, 12% Black, 1% Hispanic, 25% Native American, 61% White. Average age of undergraduates is 25.
**Freshman profile:** 1% of freshmen who took SAT scored 600 or over on verbal, 3% scored 600 or over on math; 8% scored 500 or over on verbal, 21% scored 500 or over on math; 40% scored 400 or over on verbal, 61% scored 400 or over on math; 85% scored 300 or over on verbal, 91% scored 300 or over on math. 90% of accepted applicants took SAT.
**Undergraduate achievement:** 74% of fall 1992 freshmen returned for fall 1993 term. 17% of entering class graduated. 17% of students who completed a degree program went on to graduate study within one year.
**Foreign students:** 13 students are from out of the country. Countries represented include Canada, Finland, Japan, and Korea; nine in all.

**PROGRAMS OF STUDY. Degrees:** B.A., B.Mus., B.S., B.S.Appl.Sci., B.S.Nurs., B.Soc.Work.
**Majors:** Accounting, American Indian Studies, Art, Art Education, Biology, Biology Education, Business Administration, Business/Applied Science, Business Education, Chemistry, Communicative Arts, Computer Science, Contracted Major, Criminal Justice, Dramatic Literature/Performance, Economics, Elementary Education, English Education, Health/Physical Education/Recreation, History, Learning Disabilities, Literature,

Management, Mathematics, Mathematics Education, Medical Technology, Mental Retardation, Middle Grade Education, Music, Music Education/Instrumental, Music Education/Keyboard/Instrumental, Music Education/Keyboard/Vocal, Music Education/Vocal, Music Industry, Music Performance, Nursing, Office Management, Philosophy, Physical Education, Political Science/Government, Pre-Law, Psychology, Public Administration, Recreational Management, Religion, Science Education, Social Studies Education, Social Work, Sociology, Special Education, Theatre Arts.
**Distribution of degrees:** The majors with the highest enrollment are business management/administration, elementary education, and sociology; nursing and philosophy/religion have the lowest.
**Requirements:** General education requirement.
**Academic regulations:** Freshmen must maintain minimum 1.38 GPA; sophomores, 1.63 GPA; juniors, 1.88 GPA; seniors, 2.00 GPA.
**Special:** Minors offered in many majors and in applied gerontology, athletic coaching, French, geography, geology, health education, jazz studies, journalism, language, legal studies, medical sociology, personnel/organizational leadership, public relations communication, sacred music, social welfare, speech, world studies, and writing. Double majors. Internships. Graduate school at which undergraduates may take graduate-level courses. Preprofessional programs in law and medicine. 3-4 podiatric medicine program with Pennsylvania Coll of Podiatric Medicine. Washington Semester. Teacher certification in elementary, secondary, and special education. Certification in specific subject areas. ROTC and AFROTC.
**Honors:** Honors program. Honor societies.
**Academic Assistance:** Remedial reading, writing, math, and study skills. Nonremedial tutoring.

**STUDENT LIFE. Housing:** Women's and men's dorms. 22% of students live in college housing.
**Social atmosphere:** According to the editor of the student newspaper, student apathy at PSU is quite high, but students do get involved with Homecoming and Spring Break, two of the biggest annual events. Basketball is also popular. Greeks are influential on campus. Students hang out at Bert's and the Student Center at the university. Off campus they head for The Corner.
**Services and counseling/handicapped student services:** Placement services. Health service. Counseling services for minority, veteran, and older students. Birth control, personal, and psychological counseling. Career and academic guidance services. Religious counseling. Physically disabled student services. Learning disabled services. Notetaking services. Tape recorders. Tutors. Reader services for the blind.
**Campus organizations:** Undergraduate student government. Student newspaper (Pine Needle, published twice/month). Yearbook. TV station. Gospel choir, jazz groups, concert choir, student and faculty art shows, cheerleaders, University Players, pep band, concert band, Campus Activities Board, 60 organizations in all. Eight fraternities, no chapter houses; six sororities, no chapter houses. 2% of men join a fraternity. 2% of women join a sorority.
**Religious organizations:** Baptist Student Union, Fellowship of Christian Athletes, Methodist Campus Ministry.
**Minority/foreign student organizations:** Black Student Organization, Native American Student Organization. International Student Club.

**ATHLETICS. Physical education requirements:** Two semesters of physical education required.
**Intercollegiate competition:** 10% of students participate. Baseball (M), basketball (M,W), cheerleading (M,W), cross-country (M,W), golf (M), soccer (M), softball (W), track and field (indoor) (M), track and field (outdoor) (M), volleyball (W), wrestling (M). Member of NCAA Division II, Peach Belt Athletic Conference.
**Intramural and club sports:** 5% of students participate. Intramural archery, baseball, basketball, bowling, golf, soccer, softball, tennis, volleyball, wrestling.

**ADMISSIONS. Academic basis for candidate selection** (in order of priority): Secondary school record, class rank, standardized test scores, school's recommendation, essay.
**Nonacademic basis for candidate selection:** Character and personality, extracurricular participation, and particular talent or ability are considered.
**Requirements:** Graduation from secondary school is required; GED is accepted. 13 units and the following program of study are required: 4 units of English, 3 units of math, 3 units of science including 1 unit of lab, 2 units of social studies. Minimum combined SAT score of 800, rank in top half of secondary school class, and minimum 2.0 GPA required. Conditional admission possible for applicants not meeting standard requirements. SAT or ACT is required. Campus visit and interview recommended. No off-campus interviews.
**Procedure:** Take SAT or ACT by December 31 of 12th year. Application deadline is July 15. Notification of admission on rolling basis. $75 room deposit, refundable until July 15 or within 10 days of acceptance. Freshmen accepted in terms other than fall.
**Special programs:** Credit and/or placement may be granted through CEEB Advanced Placement exams for scores of 3 or higher. Credit and/or placement may be granted through CLEP general and subject exams. Credit may be granted through military experience. Credit and placement may be granted through DANTES exams. Concurrent enrollment program.
**Transfer students:** Transfer students accepted for terms other than fall. In fall 1993, 31% of all new students were transfers into all classes. 499 transfer applications were received, 434 were accepted. Application deadline is July 15 for fall; December 1 for spring. Minimum 2.0 GPA required. Lowest course grade accepted is "C." Maximum number of transferable credits is 60 semester hours. At least 30 semester hours must be completed at the university to receive degree.
**Admissions contact:** Anthony Locklear, M.A.Ed., Director of Admissions. 919 521-6262.

**FINANCIAL AID. Available aid:** Pell grants, SEOG, state scholarships and grants, school scholarships, private scholarships, ROTC scholarships, academic merit scholarships, and athletic scholarships. Perkins Loans (NDSL), PLUS, Stafford Loans (GSL), state loans, private loans, and SLS. AMS. Credit card
**Financial aid statistics:** 24% of aid is not need-based. In 1993-94, 39% of all undergraduate applicants received aid; 87% of freshman applicants. Average amounts of aid awarded freshmen: Scholarships and grants, $1,110; loans, $975.
**Supporting data/closing dates:** FAFSA: Priority filing date is April 15; accepted on rolling basis. Notification of awards on rolling basis.
**Financial aid contact:** Sue Simms, M.S., Director of Financial Aid. 919 521-6255.

**STUDENT EMPLOYMENT.** College Work/Study Program. Institutional employment. 11% of full-time undergraduates work on campus during school year. Students may expect to earn an average of $1,275 during school year. Off-campus part-time employment opportunities rated "poor."

**COMPUTER FACILITIES.** 225 IBM/IBM-compatible and Macintosh/Apple microcomputers; 110 are networked. Students may access Data General, Digital minicomputer/mainframe systems, BITNET, Internet. Client/LAN operating systems include DOS, UNIX/XENIX/AIX, DEC, Novell. Computer languages and software packages include Ada, BASIC, C, COBOL, dBASE, Focus, FORTRAN, Gramatik 5, Harvard Graphics, Kwik Stat, Lanskool, LISP, Lotus 1-2-3, Pascal, SAS, Spin, Windows, WordPerfect. Computer facilities are available to all students.
**Fees:** None.
**Hours:** 8 AM-5 PM (M-F) for most computers. 8 AM-10 PM (M-Th); 8 AM-4:30 PM (F); 2 PM-9:45 PM (Su) in library lab.

**GRADUATE CAREER DATA.** Highest graduate school enrollments: Campbell U, East Carolina U, Pembroke State U, Fayetteville State U, North Carolina State U, U of North Carolina. 29% of graduates choose careers in business and industry.

**PROMINENT ALUMNI/AE.** Dr. Adolph Dial, state legislator, North Carolina; Kelvin Sampson, coach, Washington State U; Marion Bass, owner, Bass subsidiary; Dennis Lowery, owner, Continental Chemical.

# Pfeiffer College

**Misenheimer, NC 28109** **704 463-1360**

**1993-94 Costs.** Tuition: $8,190. Room & board: $3,180. Fees, books, misc. academic expenses (school's estimate): $400.
**Enrollment.** Undergraduates: 320 men, 334 women (full-time). Freshman class: 838 applicants, 651 accepted, 159 enrolled. Graduate enrollment: 95 men, 94 women.
**Test score averages/ranges.** Average SAT scores: 390 verbal, 441 math. Range of SAT scores of middle 50%: 330-440 verbal, 370-500 math. Average ACT scores: 19 composite.
**Faculty.** 47 full-time; 44 part-time. 57% of faculty holds doctoral degree. Student/faculty ratio: 16 to 1.
**Selectivity rating.** Less competitive.

**PROFILE.** Pfeiffer, founded in 1885, is a private, church-affiliated, liberal arts college. Its 365-acre main campus is located in Misenheimer, 40 miles north of Charlotte.

**Accreditation:** SACS. Professionally accredited by the National Association of Schools of Music.
**Religious orientation:** Pfeiffer College is affiliated with the United Methodist Church; two semesters of religion required.
**Library:** Collections totaling over 111,500 volumes, 430 periodical subscriptions, and 9,000 microform items.
**Special facilities/museums:** Art gallery, language lab.
**Athletic facilities:** Gymnasiums, swimming pool, weight room, baseball, lacrosse, soccer, and softball fields, tennis courts.

**STUDENT BODY. Undergraduate profile:** 61% are state residents; 44% are transfers. 1% Asian-American, 8% Black, 1% Hispanic, 1% Native American, 87% White, 2% Other. Average age of undergraduates is 22.
**Freshman profile:** 1% of freshmen who took SAT scored 700 or over on math; 1% scored 600 or over on verbal, 7% scored 600 or over on math; 8% scored 500 or over on verbal, 26% scored 500 or over on math; 42% scored 400 or over on verbal, 60% scored 400 or over on math; 92% scored 300 or over on verbal, 97% scored 300 or over on math. 97% of accepted applicants took SAT; 2% took ACT. 95% of freshmen come from public schools.
**Undergraduate achievement:** 59% of fall 1992 freshmen returned for fall 1993 term. 22% of entering class graduated.
**Foreign students:** 10 students are from out of the country. Countries represented include Brazil, Canada, India, Japan, and the United Kingdom; nine in all.

**PROGRAMS OF STUDY. Degrees:** A.B., B.S.
**Majors:** Accounting, Arts Administration, Biology, Business Administration, Chemistry, Christian Education, Christian Education/Music, Communications, Computer Information Systems, Criminal Justice, Economics, Elementary Education, English/Literary Studies, Health Care Management, Health/Physical Education, History, Mathematics, Music, Pre-Engineering, Pre-Medical, Psychology, Religion, Social Studies, Sociology, Special Education, Sports Management, Sports Medicine, Theatre.
**Distribution of degrees:** The majors with the highest enrollment are business administration, criminal justice, and sociology; theatre, social studies, and pre-engineering have the lowest.
**Requirements:** General education requirement.
**Academic regulations:** Freshmen must maintain minimum 1.2 GPA; sophomores, 1.6 GPA; juniors, 1.8 GPA; seniors, 2.0 GPA.
**Special:** Minors offered in many majors and in art, athletic training, coaching, physics, and political science. Major and supporting courses and cultural program activities required. Students proceed at their own pace and file application for degree one semester before anticipated graduation. Credit units determined by quality of work rather than number of specific courses. Physician's assistant program. English competency exam and GRE required for graduation. Double majors. Dual degrees. Independent study. Accelerated study. Internships. Cooperative education programs. Preprofessional programs in law, medicine, veterinary science, dentistry, theology, and engineering. 3-2 engineering programs with Auburn U and Georgia Tech. Member of Charlotte Area Consortium. Washington Semester. Teacher certification in early childhood, elementary, secondary,

and special education. Certification in specific subject areas. Exchange program abroad in Japan (Obirin U). Study abroad also in other countries.
**Honors:** Honors program. Honor societies.
**Academic Assistance:** Remedial reading and math.

**ADMISSIONS. Academic basis for candidate selection** (in order of priority): Secondary school record, standardized test scores, class rank, school's recommendation.
**Nonacademic basis for candidate selection:** Extracurricular participation is emphasized. Particular talent or ability is important. Character and personality and alumni/ae relationship are considered.
**Requirements:** Graduation from secondary school is recommended; GED is accepted. 16 units and the following program of study are recommended: 4 units of English, 3 units of math, 2 units of science, 2 units of foreign language, 3 units of social studies, 2 units of history. Audition required of music program applicants. Conditional admission possible for applicants not meeting standard requirements. SAT is required; ACT may be substituted. Campus visit and interview recommended. Off-campus interviews available with admissions and alumni representatives.
**Procedure:** Take SAT or ACT by January of 12th year. Visit college for interview by April of 12th year. Suggest filing application by March 15. Application deadline is August 1. Notification of admission on rolling basis. No set date by which applicants must accept offer. $150 tuition deposit, refundable until May 1. Freshmen accepted in terms other than fall.
**Special programs:** Admission may be deferred one semester. Credit and/or placement may be granted through CEEB Advanced Placement exams for scores of 3 or higher. Credit and/or placement may be granted through CLEP general and subject exams. Credit and placement may be granted through ACT PEP, DANTES, and challenge exams, and military and life experience. Early entrance/early admission program. Concurrent enrollment program.
**Transfer students:** Transfer students accepted for terms other than fall. In fall 1993, 44% of all new students were transfers into all classes. 258 transfer applications were received, 174 were accepted. Application deadline is August 1 for fall; January 1 for spring. Minimum 2.0 GPA recommended. Lowest course grade accepted is "D." At least 45 semester hours must be completed at the college to receive degree.
**Admissions contact:** David J. Maltby, Dean of Admission and Financial Aid. 800 338-2060.

**FINANCIAL AID. Available aid:** Pell grants, SEOG, state scholarships and grants, school scholarships and grants, private scholarships and grants, ROTC scholarships, academic merit scholarships, athletic scholarships, and aid for undergraduate foreign students. Perkins Loans (NDSL), PLUS, Stafford Loans (GSL), school loans, private loans, and SLS. Tuition Plan Inc., Education Plan Inc., Knight Tuition Plans, AMS, EFI Fund Management, Tuition Management Systems, deferred payment plan, and family tuition reduction.
**Financial aid statistics:** 49% of aid is not need-based. In 1993-94, 98% of all undergraduate applicants received aid; 97% of freshman applicants. Average amounts of aid awarded freshmen: Scholarships and grants, $4,213; loans, $3,937.
**Supporting data/closing dates:** FAFSA/FAF/FFS: Priority filing date is March 15. Income tax forms: Priority filing date is March 15. Notification of awards on rolling basis.
**Financial aid contact:** Ruby Mason, Director of Financial Aid. 800 338-2060.

# Queens College

**Charlotte, NC 28274** **704 332-7121**

**1994-95 Costs.** Tuition: $11,020. Room: $2,810. Board: $2,160. Fees, books, misc. academic expenses (school's estimate): $610.
**Enrollment.** Undergraduates: 165 men, 465 women (full-time). Freshman class: 516 applicants, 391 accepted, 154 enrolled. Graduate enrollment: 161 men, 209 women.
**Test score averages/ranges.** Average SAT scores: 491 verbal, 514 math. Range of SAT scores of middle 50%: 420-550 verbal, 460-570 math. Average ACT scores: 25 composite. Range of ACT scores of middle 50%: 23-26 composite.
**Faculty.** 65 full-time; 30 part-time. 74% of faculty holds highest degree in specific field. Student/faculty ratio: 12 to 1.
**Selectivity rating.** Competitive.

**PROFILE.** Queens, founded in 1857, is a private, church-affiliated, liberal arts college. Programs are offered through the College of Arts and Sciences and the New College. Its 25-acre campus, located in Charlotte, includes buildings constructed in a Georgian architectural style.

**Accreditation:** SACS. Professionally accredited by the Association of Collegiate Business Schools and Programs, the National Association of Schools of Music, the National Council for Accreditation of Teacher Education, the National League for Nursing.
**Religious orientation:** Queens College is affiliated with the Presbyterian Church; no religious requirements.
**Library:** Collections totaling over 115,000 volumes, 590 periodical subscriptions, and 25,000 microform items.
**Special facilities/museums:** Three art galleries, rare books museum.
**Athletic facilities:** Gymnasium, tennis courts, swimming pool, weight room, soccer and softball fields.

**STUDENT BODY. Undergraduate profile:** 46% are state residents; 55% are transfers. 1% Asian-American, 10% Black, 3% Hispanic, 1% Native American, 81% White, 4% Other. Average age of undergraduates is 20.
**Freshman profile:** 13% of freshmen who took SAT scored 600 or over on verbal, 13% scored 600 or over on math; 38% scored 500 or over on verbal, 53% scored 500 or over on math; 81% scored 400 or over on verbal, 91% scored 400 or over on math; 100% scored 300 or over on verbal, 100% scored 300 or over on math. Majority of accepted applicants took SAT. 80% of freshmen come from public schools.
**Undergraduate achievement:** 85% of fall 1992 freshmen returned for fall 1993 term. 54% of entering class graduated. 23% of students who completed a degree program immediately went on to graduate study.
**Foreign students:** 27 students are from out of the country. Countries represented include China, India, Kenya, Russia, Sweden, and Venezuela.

**PROGRAMS OF STUDY. Degrees:** B.A., B.M., B.Mus., B.S., B.S.Nurs.
**Majors:** Accounting, Applied Music, Art, Art History, Biochemistry, Biology, Business Administration, Business/Foreign Language, Communications, Early Childhood Education, English, English/Drama, European Studies, French, History, Mathematics, Music, Music/Elective Studies in Business, Music Therapy, Nursing, Philosophy, Political Science, Psychology, Sociology, Spanish.
**Distribution of degrees:** The majors with the highest enrollment are business administration, communications, and English; mathematics has the lowest.
**Requirements:** General education requirement.
**Academic regulations:** Freshmen must maintain minimum 1.8 GPA; sophomores, 1.9 GPA; juniors, 2.0 GPA; seniors, 2.0 GPA.
**Special:** Minors offered in most majors and in religion. Foundation of Liberal Learning core curriculum in freshman and sophomore years includes interdisciplinary sequence investigating the humanities, fine arts, social sciences, and natural sciences. Degree plan is composed of liberal arts core curriculum including major with internship, an international experience, and professional development. Double majors. Independent study. Pass/fail grading option. Internships. Graduate school at which undergraduates may take graduate-level courses. Preprofessional programs in law and medicine. 3-2 B.A. in liberal arts/M.A. in Christian education with Presbyterian Sch of Christian Education, Richmond, Va. Member of Charlotte Area Educational Consortium. Washington Semester. Teacher certification in early childhood, elementary, and secondary education. Certification in specific subject areas. Exchange program abroad in Korea (Hon Nam U). Study abroad also in China, England, Italy, Spain, Wales, and central European countries. ROTC at Davidson Coll. AFROTC at U of North Carolina at Charlotte.
**Honors:** Honors program. Honor societies.
**Academic Assistance:** Remedial writing, math, and study skills. Nonremedial tutoring.

**STUDENT LIFE. Housing:** All unmarried students under age 21 must live on campus unless living near campus with relatives. Unmarried students under age 21 must live on campus unless granted permission by dean of students. Coed, women's, and men's dorms. 71% of students live in college housing.
**Services and counseling/handicapped student services:** Placement services. Health service. Counseling services for minority and older students. Personal and psychological counseling. Career and academic guidance services. Religious counseling.
**Campus organizations:** Undergraduate student government. Student newspaper (Paw Print, published twice/month). Literary magazine. Yearbook. Concert choir, gospel choir, adventure club, dance club, sailing club, Amnesty International, College Republicans, College Democrats, Justinian Society (prelaw), student legislature, National Organization for Women, OASIS, Student Union, departmental groups, 39 organizations in all. Two fraternities, one chapter house; five sororities, four chapter houses. 50% of men join a fraternity. 50% of women join a sorority.
**Religious organizations:** Fellowship of Christian Athletes, Religious Life Committee, Westminster Fellowship, Baptist Student Union.
**Minority/foreign student organizations:** Students for Black Awareness, Minority Taskforce. International Club.

**ATHLETICS. Physical education requirements:** Two semesters of physical education required.
**Intercollegiate competition:** 25% of students participate. Basketball (M,W), cheerleading (M,W), golf (M), soccer (M,W), softball (W), tennis (M,W), volleyball (W). Member of NCAA Division II.
**Intramural and club sports:** 40% of students participate. Intramural aerobics, basketball, bowling, football, softball, tennis, volleyball.

**ADMISSIONS. Academic basis for candidate selection** (in order of priority): Secondary school record, standardized test scores, class rank, school's recommendation, essay.
**Nonacademic basis for candidate selection:** Character and personality, extracurricular participation, and particular talent or ability are important.
**Requirements:** Graduation from secondary school is required; GED is accepted. 16 units and the following program of study are required: 4 units of English, 3 units of math, 1 unit of lab science, 2 units of foreign language, 2 units of social studies, 4 units of electives. Minimum combined SAT score of 800, rank in top half of secondary school class, and minimum 2.5 GPA recommended. Two National Teacher Examination Core Batteries (general education and communication skills) required of education/teacher certification program applicants. Interview and additional application required of nursing program applicants. Strong background in science and math highly recommended of computer science, math, and sciences program applicants. Portfolio recommended of art program applicants. Audition required of music program applicants. Conditional admission possible for applicants not meeting standard requirements. SAT or ACT is required. ACH recommended. Campus visit and interview recommended. Off-campus interviews available with admissions and alumni representatives.
**Procedure:** Take SAT or ACT by October of 12th year. Take ACH by April of 12th year. Visit college for interview by February of 12th year. Suggest filing application by March 15. Notification of admission on rolling basis. Reply is required by May 1 or within three weeks if notified after May 1. $100 tuition deposit, refundable until May 1. $100 room deposit, refundable until May 1. Freshmen accepted in terms other than fall.
**Special programs:** Admission may be deferred one year. Credit and/or placement may be granted through CEEB Advanced Placement exams for scores of 4 or higher. Credit and/or placement may be granted through CLEP subject exams. Placement may be granted through Regents College and challenge exams. Early entrance/early admission program. Concurrent enrollment program.
**Transfer students:** Transfer students accepted for terms other than fall. In fall 1993, 55% of all new students were transfers into all classes. 323 transfer applications were received, 260 were accepted. Application deadline is rolling for fall; rolling for spring. Minimum 2.0 GPA required. Lowest course grade accepted is "C." Maximum number of transferable credits is 60 semester hours. At least 45 semester hours must be completed at the college to receive degree.

**Admissions contact:** D. Stephen Cloniger, Ph.D., Vice President for Enrollment Management. 704 337-2212, 800 849-0202.

**FINANCIAL AID. Available aid:** Pell grants, SEOG, state scholarships and grants, school scholarships and grants, private scholarships and grants, academic merit scholarships, athletic scholarships, and aid for undergraduate foreign students. Perkins Loans (NDSL), PLUS, Stafford Loans (GSL), state loans, private loans, and SLS. Tuition Plan Inc., Knight Tuition Plans, AMS, deferred payment plan, and family tuition reduction.
**Financial aid statistics:** 35% of aid is not need-based. In 1993-94, 90% of all undergraduate applicants received aid; 90% of freshman applicants. Average amounts of aid awarded freshmen: Scholarships and grants, $7,400; loans, $2,625.
**Supporting data/closing dates:** FAFSA/FAF: Priority filing date is March 1. Notification of awards on rolling basis.
**Financial aid contact:** Betty Whalen, M.A., Director of Financial Aid. 704 337-2225, 800 849-0202.

**STUDENT EMPLOYMENT.** College Work/Study Program. Institutional employment. 40% of full-time undergraduates work on campus during school year. Students may expect to earn an average of $1,500 during school year. Off-campus part-time employment opportunities rated "excellent."

**COMPUTER FACILITIES.** 70 IBM/IBM-compatible microcomputers; 20 are networked. Students may access Digital minicomputer/mainframe systems, Internet. Residence halls may be equipped with stand-alone microcomputers. Computer languages and software packages include Assembly, C, COBOL, dBASE, FORTRAN, Lisp, Lotus 1-2-3, Pascal, Turbo Pascal, Pl/1, WordPerfect. Computer facilities are available to all students.
**Fees:** Computer fee is included in tuition/fees.
**Hours:** 24 hours.

**GRADUATE CAREER DATA.** Graduate school percentages: 3% enter law school. 2% enter medical school. 5% enter graduate business programs. 10% enter graduate arts and sciences programs. Highest graduate school enrollments: Emory U, U of North Carolina at Chapel Hill, U of North Carolina at Charlotte, U of South Carolina, Wake Forest U. 60% of graduates choose careers in business and industry. Companies and businesses that hire graduates: Bix Six accounting firms, Carolinas Medical Center, Duke Power, First Union National Bank, IBM, Nations Bank, Presbyterian Hospital.

**PROMINENT ALUMNI/AE.** Myrta Pulliam, editor, *Indianapolis Star*, Pulitzer Prize winner; Julia Jones, superior court judge; Sara McMahon, corporate executive, Day's Inn; Dr. Marilyn MacQueen, transplant immunology researcher; Betsy Cromer Byars, author, Newberry Literary Award winner; Margaret Hackett Murphy, U.S. federal judge; Janice Partel, vice-president, Citicorp.

## St. Andrews Presbyterian College

**Laurinburg, NC 28352-5598** **919 277-5000**

**1994-95 Costs.** Tuition: $10,375. Room: $1,825. Board: $2,750. Fees, books, misc. academic expenses (school's estimate): $300.

**Enrollment.** Undergraduates: 286 men, 326 women (full-time). Freshman class: 843 applicants, 681 accepted.

**Test score averages/ranges.** Average SAT scores: 451 verbal, 479 math. Range of SAT scores of middle 50%: 350-500 verbal, 400-550 math.

**Faculty.** 51 full-time; 16 part-time. 70% of faculty holds doctoral degree. Student/faculty ratio: 11 to 1.

**Selectivity rating.** Less competitive.

**PROFILE.** St. Andrews Presbyterian, founded in 1958, is a church-affiliated, liberal arts college. Its 600-acre lakeside campus is located in Laurinburg, 40 miles from Fayetteville.

**Accreditation:** SACS.
**Religious orientation:** St. Andrews Presbyterian College is affiliated with the Presbyterian Church (Synod of North Carolina); no religious requirements.
**Library:** Collections totaling over 104,852 volumes, 400 periodical subscriptions, and 66,127 microform items.
**Special facilities/museums:** Art gallery, anthropology museum, 20,000-square-foot science lab, electron microscopy center with three electron microscopes, psychology lab, artronics graphics computer.
**Athletic facilities:** Racquetball and tennis courts, swimming pool, baseball, football, soccer, and softball fields, weight rooms, gymnasiums, track, golf course, equestrian facilities.

**STUDENT BODY. Undergraduate profile:** 42% are state residents; 27% are transfers. 1% Asian-American, 10% Black, 2% Hispanic, 1% Native American, 82% White, 4% Other. Average age of undergraduates is 22.
**Freshman profile:** 3% of freshmen who took SAT scored 700 or over on verbal, 2% scored 700 or over on math; 16% scored 600 or over on verbal, 11% scored 600 or over on math; 34% scored 500 or over on verbal, 33% scored 500 or over on math; 68% scored 400 or over on verbal, 77% scored 400 or over on math; 98% scored 300 or over on verbal, 100% scored 300 or over on math. 98% of accepted applicants took SAT; 2% took ACT.
**Undergraduate achievement:** 74% of fall 1992 freshmen returned for fall 1993 term. 58% of entering class graduated. 53% of students who completed a degree program immediately went on to graduate study.
**Foreign students:** Countries represented include China, Japan, Korea, Scotland, and Zimbabwe; 16 in all.

**PROGRAMS OF STUDY. Degrees:** B.A., B.S.
**Majors:** Allied Health, Art, Asian Studies, Biochemistry, Biology, Business Administration, Chemical Physics, Chemistry, Communications, Education, English, French, History, Literature, Mathematics, Mathematics/Computer Science, Modern Language, Music, Philosophy, Philosophy/Religion, Physical Education, Politics, Psychology, Religion, Theatre.
**Distribution of degrees:** The majors with the highest enrollment are business administration, biology, and politics; communications, foreign languages, and allied health have the lowest.
**Requirements:** General education requirement.
**Academic regulations:** Minimum 2.0 GPA required for graduation.
**Special:** Minors offered in many majors and in visual arts. Self-designed and individualized thematic majors offered, including art history, children's theatre, Christian education, college administration, comparative cultures, ecological studies, horticulture, international business, intercultural studies, legal anthropology, occupational therapy, personnel management, social work, and Southern culture. Self-designed majors. Double majors. Dual degrees. Independent study. Pass/fail grading option. Internships. Cooperative education programs. Preprofessional programs in law, medicine, and veterinary science. 3-2 engineering program with Georgia Tech and North Carolina St U. 3-2 accounting program with U of Georgia. Member of Central College Consortium. Washington Semester. Teacher certification in early childhood and elementary education. Exchange programs abroad in Japan (Kansai Gaidai U, Oberin Coll), Korea (Han-Nam U), Ecuador (Cuenca U), and Scotland (Sterling U). Study abroad also in China, Egypt, England, Greece, India, Italy, Mexico, Switzerland, and Venezuela.
**Honors:** Honors program.
**Academic Assistance:** Remedial writing and study skills.

**ADMISSIONS. Academic basis for candidate selection** (in order of priority): Secondary school record, standardized test scores, school's recommendation, class rank, essay.
**Nonacademic basis for candidate selection:** Extracurricular participation is emphasized. Character and personality and particular talent or ability are important. Alumni/ae relationship is considered.
**Requirements:** Graduation from secondary school is required; GED is accepted. 20 units and the following program of study are recommended: 4 units of English, 3 units of math, 3 units of science, 2 units of foreign language, 1 unit of social studies, 1 unit of history, 2 units of electives. Minimum SAT scores of 400 in both verbal and math and minimum 2.0 GPA recommended. Conditional admission possible for applicants not meeting standard requirements. SAT or ACT is required. Campus visit recommended. Off-campus interviews available with an admissions representative.
**Procedure:** Notification of admission on rolling basis. $200 tuition deposit, refundable until May 1. Freshmen accepted in terms other than fall.
**Special programs:** Admission may be deferred one year. Credit may be granted through CEEB Advanced Placement for scores of 3 or higher. Credit and/or placement may be granted through CLEP general and subject exams. Early entrance/early admission program.
**Transfer students:** Transfer students accepted for terms other than fall. In fall 1993, 27% of all new students were transfers into all classes. 115 transfer applications were received, 107 were accepted. Application deadline is rolling for fall; rolling for spring. Minimum 2.0 GPA. Lowest course grade accepted is "D." Maximum number of transferable credits is 65 semester hours. At least 32 semester hours must be completed at the college to receive degree.
**Admissions contact:** Dale Montague, Dean of Admissions and Financial Aid. 800 763-0198.

**FINANCIAL AID. Available aid:** Pell grants, SEOG, state scholarships and grants, school scholarships and grants, private scholarships and grants, academic merit scholarships, athletic scholarships, and aid for undergraduate foreign students. Perkins Loans (NDSL), PLUS, Stafford Loans (GSL), school loans, and SLS. Knight Tuition Plans and AMS.
**Financial aid statistics:** Average amounts of aid awarded freshmen: Scholarships and grants, $4,500; loans, $3,572.
**Supporting data/closing dates:** FAFSA/FAF/FFS: Priority filing date is March 1. Notification of awards begins April 1.
**Financial aid contact:** Ann Todd, Director of Financial Aid. 800 763-0198.

## Salem College

**Winston-Salem, NC 27108** **910 721-2600**

**1994-95 Costs.** Tuition: $10,475. Room: $3,025. Board: $3,275. Fees, books, misc. academic expenses (school's estimate): $735.

**Enrollment.** Undergraduates: 11 men, 533 women (full-time). Freshman class: 335 applicants, 290 accepted, 132 enrolled. Graduate enrollment: 2 men, 74 women.

**Test score averages/ranges.** Average SAT scores: 498 verbal, 511 math.

**Faculty.** 45 full-time; 22 part-time. 82% of faculty holds highest degree in specific field. Student/faculty ratio: 11 to 1.

**Selectivity rating.** Competitive.

**PROFILE.** Salem, founded in 1772, is a private, church-affiliated, liberal arts college for women; qualified men admitted only to evening college. Its 57-acre campus, situated in a historic 18th-century village, is located in Winston-Salem, 30 miles west of Greensboro.

**Accreditation:** SACS. Professionally accredited by the National Association of Schools of Music, the National Council for Accreditation of Teacher Education.
**Religious orientation:** Salem College is affiliated with the Moravian Church in America; One semester of religion or philosophy required.
**Library:** Collections totaling over 113,000 volumes, 540 periodical subscriptions, and 110,100 microform items.
**Special facilities/museums:** Art gallery, fine arts center, language lab.
**Athletic facilities:** Gymnasiums, badminton, basketball, tennis, and volleyball courts, swimming pool, field hockey, intramural, and soccer fields, dance studio, weight room.

**STUDENT BODY. Undergraduate profile:** 67% are state residents; 6% are transfers. 1% Asian-American, 5% Black, 1% Hispanic, 1% Native American, 90% White, 2% Other. Average age of undergraduates is 27.
**Freshman profile:** 3% of freshmen who took SAT scored 700 or over on verbal, 8% scored 700 or over on math; 13% scored 600 or over on verbal, 40% scored 600 or over on math; 47% scored 500 or over on verbal, 87% scored 500 or over on math; 88% scored 400 or over on verbal, 97% scored 400 or over on math; 100% scored 300 or over on verbal,

100% scored 300 or over on math. 95% of accepted applicants took SAT; 5% took ACT. 61% of freshmen come from public schools.
**Undergraduate achievement:** 87% of fall 1992 freshmen returned for fall 1993 term. 46% of entering class graduated.
**Foreign students:** 13 students are from out of the country. Countries represented include China, Gambia, India, Japan, and Sri Lanka.

**PROGRAMS OF STUDY. Degrees:** B.A., B.Mus., B.S.
**Majors:** Accounting, American Studies, Art, Arts Management, Biology, Business Administration, Chemistry, Communications, Economics, English, Foreign Language/Management, French, German, History, Interior Design, International Relations, Mathematics, Medical Technology, Music, Music Performance, Philosophy/Religion, Physician's Assistant, Psychology, Sociology, Spanish.
**Distribution of degrees:** The majors with the highest enrollment are communications, English, and business management; American studies, economics, and foreign language/management have the lowest.
**Requirements:** General education requirement.
**Academic regulations:** Sophomores must maintain minimum 1.5 GPA; juniors, 1.7 GPA; seniors, 2.0 GPA.
**Special:** Minors offered in many majors and in women's studies. Interdisciplinary courses include drama, education, Greek, physics, and political science concentrations. Self-designed majors. Double majors. Independent study. Pass/fail grading option. Internships. Preprofessional programs in law, medicine, veterinary science, and dentistry. 3-1 medical technology programs with Duke U, Wake Forest U at Bowman Gray Sch of Medicine, and Forsyth City Hospital. 3-2 engineering programs with Duke U and Vanderbilt U. 3-2 physician's assistant programs with Wake Forest U at Bowman Gray Sch of Medicine. Washington Semester and UN Semester. Teacher certification in elementary, secondary, and special education. Certification in specific subject areas. Exchange program abroad in Japan (Obiron U). Study abroad also in England, France, and Mexico. ROTC at Wake Forest U.
**Honors:** Honors program. Honor societies.
**Academic Assistance:** Remedial reading and study skills.

**ADMISSIONS. Academic basis for candidate selection** (in order of priority): Secondary school record, standardized test scores, essay, school's recommendation, class rank.
**Nonacademic basis for candidate selection:** Character and personality are emphasized. Extracurricular participation is important. Particular talent or ability is considered.
**Requirements:** Graduation from secondary school is required; GED is accepted. 15 units and the following program of study are required: 4 units of English, 3 units of math, 3 units of science including 1 unit of lab, 2 units of foreign language, 2 units of history. Minimum combined SAT score of 900 and minimum 2.5 GPA recommended. SAT or ACT is required. Campus visit and interview recommended. Off-campus interviews available with admissions and alumni representatives.
**Procedure:** Take SAT or ACT by January of 12th year. Visit college for interview by February of 12th year. Application deadline is August 1. Notification of admission on rolling basis. Reply is required by May 1. $250 nonrefundable tuition deposit. $75 room deposit, refundable upon graduation or withdrawal. Freshmen accepted in terms other than fall.
**Special programs:** Admission may be deferred one year. Credit and/or placement may be granted through CEEB Advanced Placement exams for scores of 3 or higher. Credit and/or placement may be granted through CLEP general and subject exams. Credit and placement may be granted through ACT PEP and challenge exams. Early entrance/early admission program. Concurrent enrollment program.
**Transfer students:** Transfer students accepted for terms other than fall. In fall 1993, 6% of all new students were transfers into all classes. 50 transfer applications were received, 37 were accepted. Application deadline is rolling for fall; January 15 for spring. Minimum 2.0 GPA recommended. Lowest course grade accepted is "D." At least 32 semester hours must be completed at the college to receive degree.
**Admissions contact:** Katherine Knapp, Director of Admissions. 910 721-2621.

**FINANCIAL AID. Available aid:** Pell grants, SEOG, state scholarships and grants, school scholarships and grants, private scholarships and grants, academic merit scholarships, and aid for undergraduate foreign students. Perkins Loans (NDSL), PLUS, Stafford Loans (GSL), and SLS. Knight Tuition Plans. College payment plan.
**Financial aid statistics:** 14% of aid is not need-based. In 1993-94, 60% of all undergraduate applicants received aid; 79% of freshman applicants. Average amounts of aid awarded freshmen: Scholarships and grants, $7,233; loans, $2,625.
**Supporting data/closing dates:** FAFSA/FAF/FFS: Priority filing date is April 1. School's own aid application: Priority filing date is April 1. Notification of awards begins March 1.
**Financial aid contact:** Neville Watkins, M.Ed., Director of Financial Aid. 910 721-2808.

# University of North Carolina at Asheville

**Asheville, NC 28804-3299 — 704 251-6600**

**1994-95 Costs.** Tuition: $640 (state residents), $6,272 (out-of-state). Room & board: $3,470. Fees, books, misc. academic expenses (school's estimate): $1,412.
**Enrollment.** Undergraduates: 958 men, 1,075 women (full-time). Freshman class: 1,757 applicants, 979 accepted, 397 enrolled. Graduate enrollment: 29 men, 25 women.
**Test score averages/ranges.** Average SAT scores: 504 verbal, 550 math. Range of SAT scores of middle 50%: 450-550 verbal, 500-610 math. Average ACT scores: 24 composite. Range of ACT scores of middle 50%: 22-26 composite.
**Faculty.** 147 full-time; 95 part-time. 83% of faculty holds highest degree in specific field. Student/faculty ratio: 14 to 1.
**Selectivity rating.** More competitive.

**PROFILE.** UNC at Asheville, founded in 1927, is a public, liberal arts institution. Its 265-acre campus is located in Asheville, in the Blue Ridge Mountains of western North Carolina.
**Accreditation:** SACS.
**Religious orientation:** University of North Carolina at Asheville is nonsectarian; no religious requirements.
**Library:** Collections totaling over 214,000 volumes, 2,000 periodical subscriptions, and 611,000 microform items.
**Special facilities/museums:** Research center, creative retirement center, music recording center, botanical gardens, arboretum, environmental quality institute, simulation labs, microwave communication center.
**Athletic facilities:** Swimming pool, baseball, soccer, and softball fields, weight room, basketball and tennis courts, track.

**STUDENT BODY. Undergraduate profile:** 91% are state residents; 35% are transfers. 1% Asian-American, 4% Black, 1% Hispanic, 1% Native American, 93% White. Average age of undergraduates is 19.
**Freshman profile:** 2% of freshmen who took SAT scored 700 or over on verbal, 4% scored 700 or over on math; 14% scored 600 or over on verbal, 28% scored 600 or over on math; 50% scored 500 or over on verbal, 73% scored 500 or over on math; 91% scored 400 or over on verbal, 94% scored 400 or over on math; 96% scored 300 or over on verbal, 96% scored 300 or over on math. 96% of accepted applicants took SAT; 4% took ACT. 85% of freshmen come from public schools.
**Undergraduate achievement:** 78% of fall 1992 freshmen returned for fall 1993 term. 18% of entering class graduated. 5% of students who completed a degree program went on to graduate study within one year.
**Foreign students:** 29 students are from out of the country. Countries represented include Columbia, Hong Kong, Japan, Kenya, and Peru; 18 in all.

**PROGRAMS OF STUDY. Degrees:** B.A., B.F.A., B.S.
**Majors:** Accounting, Art, Atmospheric Science, Biology, Chemistry, Computer/Information Sciences, Drama, Economics, Environmental Studies, French, German, History, Literature, Management, Mass Communication, Mathematics, Music, Philosophy, Physics, Political Science, Psychology, Social Sciences, Sociology, Spanish.
**Distribution of degrees:** The majors with the highest enrollment are management, psychology, and sociology; French and German have the lowest.
**Requirements:** General education requirement.
**Academic regulations:** Minimum 2.0 GPA must be maintained.
**Special:** Minors offered in most majors. Interdisciplinary minors offered in health promotion, humanities, international studies, and women's studies. Courses offered in arts and ideas, education, humanities, meteorology, and electronic music and recording. Self-designed majors. Double majors. Independent study. Internships. Graduate school at which undergraduates may take graduate-level courses. Preprofessional programs in law, medicine, and dentistry. 2-2 engineering and nursing programs with North Carolina State U and Western Carolina U. 3-1 dentistry, forest resources, and textile chemistry programs with North Carolina State U. Asheville Area Educational Consortium. Washington Semester. Exchange program with Duke U, Mars Hill Coll, North Carolina A&T State U, North Carolina State U, U of North Carolina at Charlotte, Warren Wilson Coll, and Winston-Salem State U. Teacher certification in early childhood, elementary, and secondary education. Certification in specific subject areas. Exchange programs abroad in China (Najing U) and Ecuador. Study abroad also in Canada, England, France, Germany, and Spain.
**Honors:** Honors program. Honor societies.
**Academic Assistance:** Remedial reading, writing, math, and study skills. Nonremedial tutoring.

**STUDENT LIFE. Housing:** Students may live on or off campus. Coed, women's, and men's dorms. 40% of students live in college housing.
**Social atmosphere:** Prominent organizations include the Student Government Association, Underground Productions, Greeks, and athletes. Popular gathering places on campus are Daunte's Grill and the Highsmith Center. Off-campus, Sonny's Bistro, 45 Cherry, and Magnolia's are among the favorite places where students hang out.
**Services and counseling/handicapped student services:** Placement services. Health service. Women's center. Counseling services for minority, veteran, and older students. Birth control, personal, and psychological counseling. Career and academic guidance services. Physically disabled student services. Learning disabled services. Notetaking services. Tutors. Reader services for the blind.
**Campus organizations:** Undergraduate student government. Student newspaper (Blue Banner, published once/week). Literary magazine. Band, jazz band, pep band, chorus, Ebony Choir, Underdog Productions, drama group, Encore, College Democrats, College Republicans, ecology club, Free Inquiry Association, Student Health Advisory Council, chess and ski clubs, athletic, departmental, service, and special-interest groups, 70 organizations in all. Two fraternities, no chapter houses; three sororities, no chapter houses. 6% of men join a fraternity. 6% of women join a sorority.
**Religious organizations:** Baptist Student Union, Intervarsity Christian Fellowship, Campus Crusade for Christ, Christian Action Fellowship, Fellowship of Christian Athletes.
**Minority/foreign student organizations:** African-American Student Association, Project WHY (We Hear You). International Student Association, French and Spanish clubs.

**ATHLETICS. Physical education requirements:** Two semesters of physical education required.
**Intercollegiate competition:** 8% of students participate. Baseball (M), basketball (M,W), cheerleading (M,W), cross-country (M,W), golf (M), soccer (M,W), tennis (M,W), track (indoor) (M,W), track and field (outdoor) (M,W), volleyball (W). Member of Big South Conference, NCAA Division I.
**Intramural and club sports:** 40% of students participate. Intramural basketball, camping, climbing, flag football, hiking, kayaking, mountain biking, soccer, softball, tennis, volleyball.

**ADMISSIONS. Academic basis for candidate selection** (in order of priority): Secondary school record, class rank, standardized test scores, school's recommendation, essay.
**Nonacademic basis for candidate selection:** Character and personality, extracurricular participation, particular talent or ability, geographical distribution, and alumni/ae relationship are considered.
**Requirements:** Graduation from secondary school is required; GED is not accepted. 15 units and the following program of study are required: 4 units of English, 3 units of math, 3 units of science including 1 unit of lab, 1 unit of social studies, 1 unit of history. SAT or ACT is required. Campus visit recommended. No off-campus interviews.

**Procedure:** Take SAT or ACT by October of 12th year. Suggest filing application by October 1. Application deadline is April. Notification of admission on rolling basis. $50 tuition deposit, refundable until June 1. $100 room deposit, refundable until June 1. Freshmen accepted in terms other than fall.
**Special programs:** Admission may be deferred one year. Credit and/or placement may be granted through CEEB Advanced Placement exams for scores of 3 or higher. Credit may be granted through CLEP general and subject exams. Credit and placement may be granted through challenge exams. Early entrance/early admission program. Concurrent enrollment program.
**Transfer students:** Transfer students accepted for terms other than fall. In fall 1993, 35% of all new students were transfers into all classes. 698 transfer applications were received, 441 were accepted. Application deadline is June 15 for fall; December 1 for spring. Minimum 2.0 GPA recommended. Lowest course grade accepted is "C." Maximum number of transferable credits is 60 semester hours. At least 30 semester hours must be completed at the university to receive degree.
**Admissions contact:** John W. White, M.Ed., Director of Admissions. 704 251-6481.

**FINANCIAL AID. Available aid:** Pell grants, SEOG, state scholarships and grants, school scholarships and grants, private scholarships and grants, academic merit scholarships, and athletic scholarships. Perkins Loans (NDSL), PLUS, Stafford Loans (GSL), state loans, school loans, private loans, and SLS. Tuition Plan Inc.
**Financial aid statistics:** 36% of aid is not need-based. In 1993-94, 99% of all undergraduate applicants received aid; 99% of freshman applicants. Average amounts of aid awarded freshmen: Scholarships and grants, $2,286; loans, $2,374.
**Supporting data/closing dates:** FAFSA/FAF: Priority filing date is March 1. School's own aid application: Priority filing date is March 1. Notification of awards on rolling basis.
**Financial aid contact:** Carolyn McElrath, Director of Financial Aid. 704 251-6535.

**STUDENT EMPLOYMENT.** College Work/Study Program. Institutional employment. 15% of full-time undergraduates work on campus during school year. Students may expect to earn an average of $975 during school year. Freshmen are discouraged from working during their first term. Off-campus part-time employment opportunities rated "good."

**COMPUTER FACILITIES.** 181 IBM/IBM-compatible and Macintosh/Apple microcomputers; all are networked. Students may access Cray, Digital, SUN minicomputer/mainframe systems, BITNET, Internet. Residence halls may be equipped with modems. Client/LAN operating systems include Apple/Macintosh. Computer languages and software packages include APL, BASIC, C, COBOL, FORTRAN, Pascal, SAS, SPSS; 100 in all. Computer facilities are available to all students.
**Fees:** None.
**Hours:** 8 AM-10 PM.

**GRADUATE CAREER DATA.** Highest graduate school enrollments: U of North Carolina at Chapel Hill, Western Carolina U. 65% of graduates choose careers in business and industry.

# University of North Carolina at Chapel Hill

**Chapel Hill, NC 27599-2200 919 962-2211**

**1994-95 Costs.** Tuition: $1,419 (state residents), $8,461 (out-of-state). Room & board: $4,050. Fees, books, misc. academic expenses (school's estimate): $500.
**Enrollment.** Undergraduates: 6,220 men, 9,454 women (full-time). Freshman class: 15,041 applicants, 5,977 accepted, 3,331 enrolled. Graduate/professional enrollment: 4,078 men, 4,547 women.
**Test score averages/ranges.** Average SAT scores: 527 verbal, 594 math.
**Faculty.** 2,249 full-time; 186 part-time. 67% of faculty holds doctoral degree. Student/faculty ratio: 10 to 1.
**Selectivity rating.** Highly competitive.

**PROFILE.** UNC Chapel Hill, founded in 1795, is a public, comprehensive institution. Programs are offered through the College of Arts and Sciences and the Schools of Allied Health Professions, Business Administration, Education, and Journalism. Its 638-acre campus is located in Chapel Hill, 15 miles northeast of Durham.
**Accreditation:** SACS.
**Religious orientation:** University of North Carolina at Chapel Hill is nonsectarian; no religious requirements.
**Library:** Collections totaling over 3,301,751 volumes, 23,000 periodical subscriptions, and 5,575,758 microform items.
**Special facilities/museums:** Art museum, folklore council, institute of folk music, communications center, institute of Latin American Studies, institute of fisheries research, institute of natural science, research laboratory of anthropology, planetarium.
**Athletic facilities:** Gymnasiums, field house, badminton, basketball, handball, racquetball, squash, tennis, and volleyball courts, fencing and weight rooms, aerobics studio, natatorium, track, athletic fields, golf course, stadium.

**STUDENT BODY. Undergraduate profile:** Average age of undergraduates is 20.
**Freshman profile:** Majority of accepted applicants took SAT. 87% of freshmen come from public schools.
**Foreign students:** 128 students are from out of the country. Countries represented include Canada, England, Hong Kong, Japan, Pakistan, and Singapore; 55 in all.

**PROGRAMS OF STUDY. Degrees:** B.A., B.S.
**Majors:** Accounting, Actuarial Sciences, Administration of Criminal Justice, Advertising, African Studies, Afro-American Studies, American Studies, Anthropology, Applied Mathematics, Applied Sciences, Archaeology, Art, Art History, Biological Sciences, Biostatistics, Broadcast Journalism, Business Administration, Chemistry, Classical Civilization, Classics, Communication Skills, Comparative Literature, Computer/Information Sciences, Dental Hygiene, Design/Technology for Theatre, Dramatic Arts, Early Childhood Education, East Asian Studies, Economics, English, Environmental Protection, French, Geography, Geology, German, Germanic Languages, Greek, Health Administration, Health/Physical Education, History, Industrial Relations, Interdisciplinary Studies, Intermediate Education, International Studies, Italian, Latin, Linguistics/Non-Western Languages, Mass Communication, Material Science, Mathematical Sciences, Mathematics, Medical Technology, Middle School Education, Music, Music Education, Natural Sciences, News/Editorial Journalism, Nursing, Nutrition, Operations Research, Peace/War/Defense, Pharmacy, Philosophy, Photojournalism, Physical Education, Physical Therapy, Physics/Astronomy, Political Science/Government, Polymer Science, Portuguese, Psychology, Public Health, Public Policy Analysis, Public Relations, Radio/Television/Motion Pictures, Radiologic Sciences, Recreation Administration, Religious Studies, Romance Languages, Russian, Russian/East European Studies, Social Sciences, Social Studies, Sociology, Spanish, Speech, Speech Communication, Statistics, Studio Art.
**Distribution of degrees:** The majors with the highest enrollment are biology, business administration, and psychology; African studies and Italian have the lowest.
**Requirements:** General education requirement.
**Academic regulations:** Freshmen must maintain minimum 1.5 GPA; sophomores, 1.75 GPA; juniors, 1.9 GPA; seniors, 2.0 GPA.
**Special:** All freshmen and sophomores enroll in General College. Courses in Arabic, Celtic, Chinese, folklore, Hebrew, information science, Norwegian, Polish, and Sanskrit. North Carolina Fellows. Self-designed majors. Double majors. Dual degrees. Independent study. Pass/fail grading option. Graduate school at which undergraduates may take graduate-level courses. Predental, prelaw, and premedical adviser available to help students choose majors appropriate to their postgraduate education. Law/M.B.A. accounting program. Teacher certification in early childhood, elementary, secondary, and special education. Exchange programs abroad in Colombia (U of Antioquia), France (U of Paris), and Germany (U of Dusseldorf, U of Goettingen). Study abroad also possible in Australia, Brazil, China, Denmark, England, Israel, Italy, Japan, Mexico, Peru, Scotland, the former Soviet Republics, and Spain. Negev archaeology seminar. ROTC, NROTC, and AFROTC.
**Honors:** Phi Beta Kappa. Honors program.
**Academic Assistance:** Remedial math.

**STUDENT LIFE. Housing:** Students may live on or off campus. Coed, women's, and men's dorms. Sorority and fraternity housing. School-owned/operated apartments. Off-campus privately-owned housing. On-campus married-student housing. 35% of students live in college housing.
**Services and counseling/handicapped student services:** Placement services. Health service. Counseling services for minority, military, veteran, and older students. Birth control, personal, and psychological counseling. Career and academic guidance services. Learning disabled services.
**Campus organizations:** Undergraduate student government. Student newspaper (Daily Tar Heel). Literary magazine. Yearbook. Radio and TV stations. Clef Hangers, musical ensemble groups, Carolina Choir, High Kicking Heels, 250 organizations in all. 15 fraternities, all with chapter houses; 12 sororities, all with chapter houses. 20% of men join a fraternity. 20% of women join a sorority.
**Religious organizations:** Many religious organizations.
**Minority/foreign student organizations:** Black Student Movement, Indian Circle. International Student Center.

**ATHLETICS. Physical education requirements:** Two semesters of physical education required.
**Intercollegiate competition:** 5% of students participate. Baseball (M), basketball (M,W), cross-country (M,W), diving (M,W), fencing (M,W), field hockey (W), football (M), golf (M,W), gymnastics (W), lacrosse (M), soccer (M,W), softball (W), swimming (M,W), tennis (M,W), track (indoor) (M,W), track (outdoor) (M,W), track and field (indoor) (M,W), track and field (outdoor) (M,W), volleyball (W), wrestling (M). Member of Atlantic Coast Conference, NCAA Division I.
**Intramural and club sports:** 50% of students participate. Intramural badminton, basketball, biathlon, bowling, fencing, floor hockey, flag football, football, frisbee golf, golf, gymnastics, inner-tube water basketball, inner-tube water polo, racquetball, soccer, softball, squash, swimming, table tennis, tennis, triathlon, track/field, ultimate frisbee, volleyball, walleyball, Wiffle ball, wrestling. Men's club Alpine skiing, badminton, baseball, bowling, crew, cricket, cycling, fencing, football, gymnastics, ice hockey, lacrosse, martial arts, outing, racquetball, rugby, sailing, scuba diving, soccer, swimming, tae kwon do, team handball, tennis, ultimate frisbee, volleyball, water polo, water skiing. Women's club Alpine skiing, badminton, bowling, crew, cycling, equestrian sports, fencing, field hockey, gymnastics, lacrosse, martial arts, modern extension, outing, racquetball, sailing, soccer, swimming, tae kwon do, team handball, tennis, ultimate frisbee, scuba diving, volleyball, water polo, water skiing.

**ADMISSIONS. Academic basis for candidate selection** (in order of priority): Secondary school record, class rank, standardized test scores, school's recommendation, essay.
**Nonacademic basis for candidate selection:** Extracurricular participation, particular talent or ability, and alumni/ae relationship are considered.
**Requirements:** Graduation from secondary school is required; GED is not accepted. 16 units and the following program of study are required: 4 units of English, 3 units of math, 3 units of science including 1 unit of lab, 2 units of foreign language, 2 units of social studies, 2 units of academic electives. Minimum combined SAT score of 800 required. Applicants are advised to take advantage of most difficult course programs offered in secondary school. Audition required of music program applicants. SAT is required; ACT may be substituted. Campus visit recommended. No off-campus interviews.
**Procedure:** Take SAT or ACT by November of 12th year. Application deadline is January 15. Notification of admission on rolling basis. Reply is required by May 1. $25 nonrefundable tuition deposit. $75 room deposit, refundable partially. Freshmen accepted for fall term only.
**Special programs:** Credit and/or placement may be granted through CEEB Advanced Placement exams for scores of 3 or higher. Credit and/or placement may be granted through CLEP general and subject exams. Credit may be granted through military and life experience. Credit and placement may be granted through DANTES and challenge exams.
**Transfer students:** Transfer students accepted for fall term. In fall 1993, 3,011 transfer applications were received, 1,329 were accepted. Application deadline is March 15

(January 15 preferred). Minimum 2.0 GPA required. Lowest course grade accepted is "C." Maximum number of transferable credits is 62 semester hours. At least 30 semester hours must be completed at the university to receive degree.

**Admissions contact:** James C. Walters, Ed.D., Associate Provost/Director of Undergraduate Admissions. 919 966-3621.

**FINANCIAL AID. Available aid:** Pell grants, SEOG, Federal Nursing Student Scholarships, state scholarships and grants, school scholarships and grants, private scholarships and grants, ROTC scholarships, academic merit scholarships, and athletic scholarships. Perkins Loans (NDSL), PLUS, Stafford Loans (GSL), NSL, Health Professions Loans, state loans, and school loans.

**Financial aid statistics:** Average amounts of aid awarded freshmen: Scholarships and grants, $2,000.

**Supporting data/closing dates:** School's own aid application: Priority filing date is January 15; deadline is March 1. Notification of awards begins April 15.

**Financial aid contact:** Eleanor Morris, Director of Student Aid. 919 962-8396.

**STUDENT EMPLOYMENT.** College Work/Study Program. Institutional employment. 30% of full-time undergraduates work on campus during school year. Students may expect to earn an average of $900 during school year. Off-campus part-time employment opportunities rated "good."

**COMPUTER FACILITIES.** 200 IBM/IBM-compatible and Macintosh/Apple microcomputers. Residence halls may be equipped with stand-alone microcomputers, networked terminals, modems. Numerous computer languages and software programs available. Computer facilities are available to all students.

**Fees:** None.

**GRADUATE CAREER DATA.** Highest graduate school enrollments: Duke U, East Carolina U, U of North Carolina at Chapel Hill, Wake Forest U. 78% of graduates choose careers in business and industry. Companies and businesses that hire graduates: IBM, NCNB, First Union, Wachovia, Procter & Gamble, Arthur Andersen, NCR, Northern Telecom.

**PROMINENT ALUMNI/AE.** Charles Kuralt, CBS News; Roger Mudd, CBS News; Jeff McNally, cartoonist; Richard Adler, playwright; Richard Jenrette, co-founder of Donaldson Lufkin Jenrette; Vermont Royster, *Wall Street Journal*; Andy Griffith, actor; Thomas Wolfe, author.

# University of North Carolina at Charlotte

Charlotte, NC 28223 704 547-2000

**1993-94 Costs.** Tuition: $1,300 (state residents), $7,580 (out-of-state). Room & board: $3,212. Fees, books, misc. academic expenses (school's estimate): $1,195.

**Enrollment.** Undergraduates: 5,100 men, 4,999 women (full-time). Freshman class: 5,803 applicants, 4,441 accepted, 1,730 enrolled. Graduate enrollment: 1,020 men, 1,409 women.

**Test score averages/ranges.** Average SAT scores: 435 verbal, 491 math. Range of SAT scores of middle 50%: 390-470 verbal, 440-540 math.

**Faculty.** 646 full-time; 244 part-time. 79% of faculty holds doctoral degree. Student/faculty ratio: 16 to 1.

**Selectivity rating.** Less competitive.

**PROFILE.** UNC Charlotte, founded in 1946, is a public, comprehensive university. Programs are offered through the Colleges of Architecture, Arts and Sciences, Business Administration, Education and Allied Health Professions, Engineering, and Nursing and the Graduate School. Its 950-acre campus is located five miles from downtown Charlotte.

**Accreditation:** SACS. Professionally accredited by the Accreditation Board for Engineering and Technology, the American Assembly of Collegiate Schools of Business, the National Architecture Accrediting Board, the National Council for Accreditation of Teacher Education, the National League for Nursing.

**Religious orientation:** University of North Carolina at Charlotte is nonsectarian; no religious requirements.

**Library:** Collections totaling over 557,729 volumes, 5,032 periodical subscriptions, and 1,155,404 microform items.

**Special facilities/museums:** Urban studies and community service institute, mock court room, applied research center, language lab, 63-acre ecological reserve, botanical and horticultural complex, tropical rainforest conservatory.

**Athletic facilities:** Basketball, handball, squash, and tennis courts, training, weight, and wrestling rooms, swimming pool, track, gymnasium, baseball and intramural, soccer fields.

**STUDENT BODY. Undergraduate profile:** 87% are state residents; 49% are transfers. 3% Asian-American, 14% Black, 1% Hispanic, 1% Native American, 79% White, 2% Other. Average age of undergraduates is 23.

**Freshman profile:** 1% of freshmen who took SAT scored 700 or over on math; 3% scored 600 or over on verbal, 11% scored 600 or over on math; 21% scored 500 or over on verbal, 49% scored 500 or over on math; 68% scored 400 or over on verbal, 84% scored 400 or over on math; 97% scored 300 or over on verbal, 98% scored 300 or over on math. 99% of accepted applicants took SAT; 1% took ACT.

**Undergraduate achievement:** 80% of fall 1992 freshmen returned for fall 1993 term. 25% of entering class graduated.

**Foreign students:** 324 students are from out of the country. Countries represented include China, India, Japan, Malaysia, Taiwan, and United Arab Emirates; 70 in all.

**PROGRAMS OF STUDY. Degrees:** B.A., B.Arch., B.Creat.Arts, B.F.A., B.Mus., B.S., B.S.Bus.Admin., B.S.Civil Eng., B.S.Elec.Eng., B.S.Eng.Tech., B.S.Mech.Eng., B.S.Nurs., B.Soc.Work.

**Majors:** Accounting, African/Afro-American Studies, Anthropology, Architecture, Art, Biology, Business Administration, Chemistry, Child/Family Development, Civil Engineering, Civil Engineering Technology, Computer Science, Criminal Justice, Earth Science, Economics, Electrical Engineering, Electrical Engineering Technology, Elementary Education, Engineering Technology, English, Finance, French, Geography, German, Health Fitness, History, Human Services, Individualized Major, Industrial/Operations Management, International Business, Management, Management Information Systems, Manufacturing Engineering Technology, Marketing, Mathematics, Mechanical Engineering, Mechanical Engineering Technology, Middle Grade Education, Nursing, Performing Arts/Dance, Performing Arts/Music, Performing Arts/Theatre, Philosophy, Physics, Political Science, Psychology, Religious Studies, Social Work, Sociology, Spanish, Special Education.

**Distribution of degrees:** The majors with the highest enrollment are psychology, elementary education, and English; physics, manufacturing engineering technology, and music have the lowest.

**Requirements:** General education requirement.

**Academic regulations:** Minimum 2.0 GPA must be maintained.

**Special:** Minors offered in many majors and in American studies, communication studies, foreign languages, gerontology, international studies, journalism, museum studies, substance abuse, and women's studies. Department of Health and Physical Education offers programs in athletic training specialty and athletic training endorsement including 24-hour concentration in prevention and treatment of athletic injuries. Venture Program wilderness experience for academic credit. Medical technology program. Double majors. Dual degrees. Independent study. Pass/fail grading option. Internships. Cooperative education programs. Graduate school at which undergraduates may take graduate-level courses. Preprofessional programs in law, medicine, veterinary science, pharmacy, dentistry, optometry, chemical engineering, forest resources, and medical technology. Member of Charlotte Area Educational Consortium. Teacher certification in elementary, secondary, and special education. Certification in specific subject areas. Exchange programs abroad in England (Kingston Polytech) and Germany (Ludwigsburg). Member of International Student Exchange Program (ISEP). Study abroad in Australia, Canada, and in African, Asian, and Latin American countries. ROTC and AFROTC.

**Honors:** Honors program. Honor societies.

**Academic Assistance:** Nonremedial tutoring.

**STUDENT LIFE. Housing:** Students may live on or off campus. Coed dorms. Fraternity housing. School-owned/operated apartments. 24% of students live in college housing.

**Social atmosphere:** The popular places on campus are Afterhours, Cone Center, and the Greek Wall. The Pterodactyl Club, the Underground, the Upperdeck, Sandwich Construction Company, and Fraternity Row are favorite off–campus spots. Greeks, Student Government Association, student media, university programming board, Black Student Union, resident student association, Association of Student Commuters, Black Greek council, Intersorority, and Interfraternity Council are influential student groups. Popular on-campus events include the AZ Most Eligible Bachelor Contest, the Greek Sing, Greek Week, the Boo Bash, the Backyard Bash, Midnight Madness, and the Annual International Festival. Students also enjoy jazz, films, and sporting events. According to the school newspaper, the campus is only active during the week since it is a commuter campus. Uptown Charlotte, which offers clubs and cultural activities, is five minutes away.

**Services and counseling/handicapped student services:** Placement services. Health service. Counseling services for minority, military, veteran, and older students. Birth control, personal, and psychological counseling. Career and academic guidance services. Religious counseling. Physically disabled student services. Learning disabled services. Notetaking services. Tape recorders. Tutors. Reader services for the blind.

**Campus organizations:** Undergraduate student government. Student newspaper (University Times, published once/week). Literary magazine. Yearbook. Radio station. Chorus, gospel choir, pep band, dance ensemble, debating, Rathskeller, Non-Traditional Students Association, sign language club, departmental, political, social, and special-interest groups, 135 organizations in all. 12 fraternities, six chapter houses; eight sororities, no chapter houses. 11% of men join a fraternity. 9% of women join a sorority.

**Religious organizations:** Bahai Club, Baptist Student Union, Campus Crusade for Christ, Canterbury Club, Chi-Rho Catholic Campus Ministry, Latter-Day Saints Association, Methodist/Presbyterian Campus Ministry, Muslim Student Association, Students for Christ.

**Minority/foreign student organizations:** Black Greek Council, Black Student Union, Children of the Sun Cultural Choir, National Society of Black Accountants, National Society of Black Engineers, other minority groups. Chinese Student Association, General Union of Palestinian Students, German Club, India Student Association, Japan Club, UNCC International Club, Vietnamese Student Association.

**ATHLETICS. Physical education requirements:** None.

**Intercollegiate competition:** 4% of students participate. Baseball (M), basketball (M,W), cheerleading (M,W), cross-country (M,W), golf (M), soccer (M,W), softball (W), tennis (M,W), track (indoor) (M,W), track (outdoor) (M,W), track and field (outdoor) (M,W), volleyball (W). Member of Metro Conference, NCAA Division I.

**Intramural and club sports:** 40% of students participate. Intramural badminton, basketball, bowling, football, golf, handball, horseshoes, racquetball, soccer, softball, swimming, table tennis, tennis, track and field, tug-of-war, volleyball, water polo. Men's club aerobics, crew, lacrosse, martial arts, rugby, volleyball, water skiing. Women's club aerobics, crew, lacrosse, martial arts, rugby, soccer, water skiing.

**ADMISSIONS. Academic basis for candidate selection** (in order of priority): Secondary school record, class rank, standardized test scores, school's recommendation.

**Nonacademic basis for candidate selection:** Particular talent or ability and geographical distribution are considered.

**Requirements:** Graduation from secondary school is recommended; GED is accepted. 16 units and the following program of study are required: 4 units of English, 3 units of math, 2 units of science including 1 unit of lab, 2 units of foreign language, 2 units of social studies. Minimum combined SAT score of 850, rank in top half of secondary school class, and minimum 2.0 GPA required. 1 additional unit of foreign language, 1 additional unit of math, 1 unit of world history, 1/2 unit of health education recommended, and/or a minimum of three academic courses in the twelfth year. Minimum SAT math score of 400 and ACT math score of 20 required of business administration and architecture program applicants; portfolio and interview also required of architecture program applicants. Solid geometry and trigonometry required of architecture and engineering program applicants. Minimum SAT math score of 500 required of engineering program applicants to be admitted directly to a lower division of a department; minimum SAT math score of 450 required of freshman engineering program applicants to the College of Engineering. SAT is required; ACT may be substituted. Campus visit recommended. No off-campus interviews.

**Procedure:** Take SAT or ACT by December of 12th year. Suggest filing application by July 1; no deadline. Acceptance notification on December 15, February 1, and March 15. $100 room deposit, refundable until June 1. Freshmen accepted in terms other than fall.

**Special programs:** Admission may be deferred one year. Credit may be granted through CEEB Advanced Placement for scores of 3 or higher. Credit may be granted through CLEP general and subject exams. Concurrent enrollment program.

**Transfer students:** Transfer students accepted for terms other than fall. In fall 1993, 49% of all new students were transfers into all classes. 2,762 transfer applications were received, 2,424 were accepted. Application deadline is July 1 for fall; November 15 for spring. Minimum 2.0 GPA required. Lowest course grade accepted is "C." Maximum number of transferable credits is 64 semester hours from a two-year school and 90 semester hours from a four-year school. At least 30 semester hours must be completed at the university to receive degree.

**Admissions contact:** Kathi M. Baucom, M.Ed., Director of Admissions. 704 547-2213.

**FINANCIAL AID. Available aid:** Pell grants, SEOG, state scholarships and grants, school scholarships and grants, private scholarships and grants, ROTC scholarships, academic merit scholarships, and athletic scholarships. Perkins Loans (NDSL), PLUS, Stafford Loans (GSL), school loans, and SLS. Room and board payment plan.

**Financial aid statistics:** 20% of aid is not need-based. In 1993-94, 92% of all undergraduate applicants received aid; 90% of freshman applicants. Average amounts of aid awarded freshmen: Scholarships and grants, $1,700; loans, $2,300.

**Supporting data/closing dates:** FAFSA: Priority filing date is April 1; accepted on rolling basis. Notification of awards on rolling basis.

**Financial aid contact:** Curtis R. Whalen, M.Ed., Financial Aid Director. 704 547-2461.

**STUDENT EMPLOYMENT.** College Work/Study Program. Institutional employment. 17% of full-time undergraduates work on campus during school year. Students may expect to earn an average of $1,200 during school year. Off-campus part-time employment opportunities rated "excellent."

**COMPUTER FACILITIES.** 650 IBM/IBM-compatible and Macintosh/Apple microcomputers; 450 are networked. Students may access Cray, Digital, IBM minicomputer/mainframe systems, BITNET, Internet. Residence halls may be equipped with stand-alone microcomputers, networked terminals. Client/LAN operating systems include Apple/Macintosh, DOS, UNIX/XENIX/AIX, LocalTalk/AppleTalk, Novell. Computer languages and software packages include ANSYS, APL, C, FORTRAN, Paradox, Pascal, Quattro Pro, SAS, SPSS, WordPerfect; 25 in all. Computer facilities are available to all students.

**Fees:** $25 computer fee per semester; included in tuition/fees.

**Hours:** 24-hour labs, 9 AM-10 PM staffed labs; 8 AM-midn.

**GRADUATE CAREER DATA.** Companies and businesses that hire graduates: Burlington Industries, Duke Power, First Union Bank, Hoechst Celanese, Microsoft, Milliken, NationsBank, Price Waterhouse, Underwriters Lab.

**PROMINENT ALUMNI/AE.** Martha Bedell Alexander and Robert J. Hensley, Jr., representatives, N.C. General Assembly; Benjamin F. Chavis, Jr., executive director, NAACP; David and Carlton Moody, Grammy award-winning musicians; Reece A. Overcash, chairman/CEO, Associates Corp. of North America.

# University of North Carolina at Greensboro

Greensboro, NC 27412 — 910 334-5000

**1993-94 Costs.** Tuition: $846 (state residents), $7,888 (out-of-state). Room: $1,715. Board: $1,760. Fees, books, misc. academic expenses (school's estimate): $1,321.

**Enrollment.** Undergraduates: 2,683 men, 4,849 women (full-time). Freshman class: 5,191 applicants, 4,134 accepted, 1,525 enrolled. Graduate enrollment: 899 men, 1,836 women.

**Test score averages/ranges.** Range of SAT scores of middle 50%: 400-500 verbal, 450-550 math.

**Faculty.** 591 full-time; 124 part-time. 72% of faculty holds highest degree in specific field. Student/faculty ratio: 14 to 1.

**Selectivity rating.** Less competitive.

**PROFILE.** UNC Greensboro is a public, comprehensive university. Founded in 1891 as a women's college, it adopted coeducation when it joined the state system in 1963. Its 141-acre campus is located one mile from downtown Greensboro.

**Accreditation:** SACS. Professionally accredited by the American Assembly of Collegiate Schools of Business, the American Dietetic Association, the American Home Economics Association, the American Library Association, the American Medical Association (CAHEA), the American Psychological Association, the American Speech-Language-Hearing Association, the Council on Social Work Education, the Foundation for Interior Design Education Research, the National Association of Schools of Music, the National Association of Schools of Public Affairs and Administration, the National Council for Accreditation of Teacher Education, the National League for Nursing, the National Recreation and Park Association.

**Religious orientation:** University of North Carolina at Greensboro is nonsectarian; no religious requirements.

**Library:** Collections totaling over 850,098 volumes, 5,525 periodical subscriptions, and 874,988 microform items.

**Special facilities/museums:** 42-acre recreational site, art gallery, language lab, observatory.

**Athletic facilities:** Gymnasium, rugby and softball fields, soccer stadium, health/human performance building, student recreation center.

**STUDENT BODY. Undergraduate profile:** 86% are state residents; 34% are transfers. 2% Asian-American, 13% Black, 1% Hispanic, 82% White, 2% Other. Average age of undergraduates is 20.

**Freshman profile:** 1% of freshmen who took SAT scored 700 or over on verbal, 2% scored 700 or over on math; 7% scored 600 or over on verbal, 11% scored 600 or over on math; 28% scored 500 or over on verbal, 49% scored 500 or over on math; 79% scored 400 or over on verbal, 93% scored 400 or over on math; 99% scored 300 or over on verbal, 100% scored 300 or over on math. 99% of accepted applicants took SAT. 95% of freshmen come from public schools.

**Undergraduate achievement:** 75% of fall 1992 freshmen returned for fall 1993 term. 29% of entering class graduated.

**Foreign students:** 161 students are from out of the country. Countries represented include Bahamas, Bermuda, China, India, Japan, and the United Kingdom; 51 in all.

**PROGRAMS OF STUDY. Degrees:** B.A., B.F.A., B.S., B.S.Home Econ., B.S.Mus., B.S.Nurs.

**Majors:** Accounting, Acting, Anthropology, Apparel Design, Apparel Marketing/Merchandising, Archaeology, Art, Art Education, Art History/Appreciation, Biology, Broadcast Journalism, Business Education, Chemistry, Child Development, Child Development/Family Relations, Clothing/Textiles, Communication Studies, Composition, Computer/Information Science, Dance, Dance Teacher Education, Dance Teaching in Alternative Settings, Design, Design/Technical Theatre Direction, Developmental Foundations in Pre-School Education, Dietetics, Drama, Economics, Education of the Deaf, Elementary Education, English, Exercise Science/Sports Studies, Financial Management, Food/Nutrition, French, General Music, General Music Education/Choral, General Speech, Geography, German, Gerontology, Greek, Greek Civilization, Health Education, History, History/Philosophy of Science, Home Economics, Human Relations, Instrumental Music Education, Interior Design, International Studies, Latin, Leisure Services/Tourist Management, Linguistics, Management, Management Information Systems, Marketing, Marketing Education, Mathematics, Media Production, Merchandising Management, Middle Grades Education, Music History, Nursing, Office Systems Administration, Operations Management, Painting, Performance, Performance/Jazz Studies, Philosophy, Physical Education Teacher Education, Physics, Political Science, Psychology, Religious Studies, Restaurant/Food Service Management, Risk Management/Insurance, Roman Civilization, Russian Studies, Sculpture, Social Work, Sociology, Spanish, Speech Communication, Speech Pathology/Audiology, Statistics, Textiles, Theatre Arts, Therapeutic Recreation.

**Distribution of degrees:** The majors with the highest enrollment are business administration, speech, and elementary education; Greek, physics, and German have the lowest.

**Requirements:** General education requirement.

**Academic regulations:** Freshmen must maintain minimum 1.30 GPA; sophomores, 1.49 GPA; juniors, 1.72 GPA; seniors, 2.00 GPA.

**Special:** Minors offered in all majors and in African, Asian, black, international, population, and women's studies. Several concentrations available in art education, health education, child development and family relations, and liberal studies. Interdepartmental studies in gerontology, history and philosophy of science, international studies, linguistics, urban studies, and world literature. Residential college and Plan II programs offered. Certificate program in school social work. Self-designed majors. Double majors. Dual degrees. Independent study. Accelerated study. Graduate school at which undergraduates may take graduate-level courses. Preprofessional programs in law, medicine, veterinary science, pharmacy, and dentistry. 2-2 engineering programs with North Carolina A&T State U, North Carolina State U, and U of North Carolina at Charlotte. Member of Greater Greensboro Consortium. Washington Semester. Teacher certification in special education. Certification in specific subject areas. Study abroad in Germany, Italy, Spain, and European Common Market countries. ROTC and AFROTC at North Carolina A&T State U.

**Honors:** Phi Beta Kappa. Honors program. Honor societies.

**Academic Assistance:** Remedial reading, writing, math, and study skills. Nonremedial tutoring.

**STUDENT LIFE. Housing:** Students may live on or off campus. Coed, women's, and men's dorms. School-owned/operated apartments. 33% of students live in college housing.

**Social atmosphere:** Off campus, students frequent the Spring Garden Bar & Grill and New York Pizza. Student media organizations have widespread influence on student social life. Popular events of the year include the Fall Kick-off, Spring Fling, and soccer and basketball games. "UNC/Greensboro has a large commuter population," reports the school newspaper, "and of the on-campus residents, over 75 percent of them leave for the weekend."

**Services and counseling/handicapped student services:** Placement services. Health service. Women's center. Counseling services for minority, veteran, and older students. Personal and psychological counseling. Career and academic guidance services. Physically disabled student services. Learning disabled services. Notetaking services. Tape recorders. Tutors. Reader services for the blind.

**Campus organizations:** Undergraduate student government. Student newspaper (Carolinian, published once/week). Literary magazine. Yearbook. Radio station. Music and drama groups, Amnesty International, Anthropological Society, Art Education Association, political and special-interest groups, 145 organizations in all. Eight fraternities, no chapter houses; eight sororities, no chapter houses. 15% of men join a fraternity. 15% of women join a sorority.

**Religious organizations:** Campus Ministries, Hillel, Bahai, all major Christian groups.

**Minority/foreign student organizations:** Neo-Black Society, Black Business Student Association, Black Greek Unity, NAACP. International Student Association.

**ATHLETICS. Physical education requirements:** None.

**Intercollegiate competition:** 2% of students participate. Baseball (M), basketball (M,W), cross-country (M,W), golf (M,W), soccer (M,W), softball (W), tennis (M,W), volleyball (W), wrestling (M). Member of Big South Conference, NCAA Division I.

**Intramural and club sports:** 9% of students participate. Intramural basketball, billiards, bowling, cheerleading, flag football, golf, soccer, racquetball, soccer, softball, table tennis, tennis, volleyball. Men's club baseball, dance, karate, lacrosse, outdoor activity, scuba, soccer. Women's club dance, karate, lacrosse, outdoor activity, scuba, soccer.

**ADMISSIONS. Academic basis for candidate selection** (in order of priority): Secondary school record, standardized test scores, class rank, school's recommendation.

**Nonacademic basis for candidate selection:** Character and personality, extracurricular participation, particular talent or ability, geographical distribution, and alumni/ae relationship are important.
**Requirements:** Graduation from secondary school is required; GED is accepted. 15 units and the following program of study are required: 4 units of English, 3 units of math, 3 units of science including 1 unit of lab, 2 units of foreign language, 2 units of social studies, 1 unit of academic electives. Science must include 1 unit in life or biological science and 1 unit in physical science. Social studies must include 1 unit in U.S. history and 1 unit in history, economics, sociology, or civics. Portfolio required of art program applicants. Audition required of music program applicants. SAT is required; ACT may be substituted. ACH recommended. Campus visit and interview recommended. No off-campus interviews.
**Procedure:** Take SAT or ACT by December of 12th year. Application deadline is August 1. Notification of admission on rolling basis. Reply is required by May 1. $150 room deposit, refundable until June 1. Freshmen accepted in terms other than fall.
**Special programs:** Admission may be deferred one year. Credit and/or placement may be granted through CEEB Advanced Placement exams for scores of 3 or higher. Credit and/or placement may be granted through CLEP general and subject exams. Early decision program. Deadline for applying for early decision is October 10. Early entrance/early admission program. Concurrent enrollment program.
**Transfer students:** Transfer students accepted for terms other than fall. In fall 1993, 34% of all new students were transfers into all classes. 1,599 transfer applications were received, 1,328 were accepted. Application deadline is August 1 for fall; December 1 for spring. Minimum 2.0 GPA required. Lowest course grade accepted is "C." Maximum number of transferable credits is 90 semester hours. At least 30 semester hours must be completed at the university to receive degree.
**Admissions contact:** Jerry Harrelson, M.A., Acting Director of Admissions. 910 334-5243.

**FINANCIAL AID. Available aid:** Pell grants, SEOG, Federal Nursing Student Scholarships, state scholarships and grants, school scholarships and grants, academic merit scholarships, and athletic scholarships. Perkins Loans (NDSL), Stafford Loans (GSL), school loans, and SLS.
**Financial aid statistics:** In 1993-94, 79% of all undergraduate applicants received aid; 79% of freshman applicants. Average amounts of aid awarded freshmen: Scholarships and grants, $3,000.
**Supporting data/closing dates:** FAFSA: Priority filing date is March 1. Notification of awards on rolling basis.

**STUDENT EMPLOYMENT.** College Work/Study Program. Institutional employment. 20% of full-time undergraduates work on campus during school year. Students may expect to earn an average of $3,000 during school year. Freshmen are discouraged from working during their first term. Off-campus part-time employment opportunities rated "good."

**COMPUTER FACILITIES.** 800 IBM/IBM-compatible and Macintosh/Apple microcomputers; all are networked. Students may access Digital minicomputer/mainframe systems. Computer languages and software packages include BMDP, BASIC, COBOL, FORTRAN, Pascal, SAS, SPSS-X; 100 in all. Computer facilities are available to all students.
**Fees:** $30 computer fee per semester.
**Hours:** Mainframe available 24 hours.

**PROMINENT ALUMNI/AE.** Bonnie Angelo, correspondent, *Time* magazine; Margaret Coit Elwell, Pulitzer Prize-winning author; Meredith M. Fernstrom, senior vice-president, office of public responsibility, American Express; Donna Oliver, 1987 National Teacher of the Year; Susan M. Sharp, former chief justice of state supreme court.

## University of North Carolina at Wilmington

**Wilmington, NC 28403-3297** **919 395-3000**

**1993-94 Costs.** Tuition: $1,344 (state residents), $7,016 (out-of-state). Room & board: $3,680. Fees, books, misc. academic expenses (school's estimate): $1,252.
**Enrollment.** Undergraduates: 2,750 men, 3,885 women (full-time). Freshman class: 6,071 applicants, 3,856 accepted, 1,449 enrolled. Graduate enrollment: 161 men, 216 women.
**Test score averages/ranges.** Average SAT scores: 441 verbal, 494 math. Average ACT scores: 22 composite.
**Faculty.** 346 full-time; 80 part-time. 69% of faculty holds doctoral degree. Student/faculty ratio: 17 to 1.
**Selectivity rating.** Competitive.

**PROFILE.** UNC at Wilmington is a public, comprehensive university. Founded in 1947 as a two-year institution, it became a four-year university in 1963 and joined the state system in 1969. Undergraduate programs are offered through the College of Arts and Sciences, the Cameron School of Business Administration, the School of Education, and the School of Nursing. Its 650-acre campus, with buildings of modified Georgian design, is located in the southeastern part of the state, 10 to 15 miles from several Atlantic coast beaches.

**Accreditation:** SACS. Professionally accredited by the National Council for Accreditation of Teacher Education, the National League for Nursing.
**Religious orientation:** University of North Carolina at Wilmington is nonsectarian; no religious requirements.
**Library:** Collections totaling over 376,273 volumes, 4,981 periodical subscriptions, and 622,383 microform items.
**Special facilities/museums:** Museum of world culture, wildflower preserve, center for marine science research.
**Athletic facilities:** Swimming and diving pools, basketball courts, baseball field, soccer field, handball and tennis courts, track and cross-country complex, fitness courses, game room, coliseum.

**STUDENT BODY. Undergraduate profile:** 87% are state residents; 11% are transfers. 1% Asian-American, 7% Black, 1% Hispanic, 91% White. Average age of undergraduates is 20.
**Freshman profile:** 3% of freshmen who took SAT scored 600 or over on verbal, 9% scored 600 or over on math; 21% scored 500 or over on verbal, 50% scored 500 or over on math; 74% scored 400 or over on verbal, 88% scored 400 or over on math; 99% scored 300 or over on verbal, 99% scored 300 or over on math. 26% of freshmen who took ACT scored 24 or over on composite; 91% scored 18 or over on composite; 100% scored 12 or over on composite. 98% of accepted applicants took SAT; 2% took ACT.
**Undergraduate achievement:** 76% of fall 1992 freshmen returned for fall 1993 term. 25% of entering class graduated. 2% of students who completed a degree program immediately went on to graduate study.
**Foreign students:** 33 students are from out of the country. Countries represented include Canada, China, Mexico, Turkey, and the United Kingdom; 29 in all.

**PROGRAMS OF STUDY. Degrees:** B.A., B.S., B.Soc.Work.
**Majors:** Accounting, Anthropology, Art, Biology, Business Administration/Management, Chemistry, Computer/Information Sciences, Drama, Early Childhood Education, Economics, Elementary Education, English, Environmental Studies, Fine Arts, French, Geography, Geology, History, Law Enforcement/Corrections, Marine Biology, Marketing, Mathematics, Medical Technology, Middle Grades Education, Music, Nursing, Parks/Recreation Management, Philosophy/Religion, Physical Education/Health, Physics, Political Science/Government, Psychology, Social Sciences, Social Work, Sociology, Spanish, Special Education, Speech Communication.
**Distribution of degrees:** The majors with the highest enrollment are psychology, English, and marine biology; social science, music, and French have the lowest.
**Requirements:** General education requirement.
**Academic regulations:** Freshmen must maintain minimum 1.2 GPA; sophomores, 1.5 GPA; juniors, 1.8 GPA; seniors, 2.0 GPA.
**Special:** Double majors. Dual degrees. Independent study. Internships. Cooperative education programs. Graduate school at which undergraduates may take graduate-level courses. Preprofessional programs in law, medicine, veterinary science, pharmacy, dentistry, optometry, agriculture, engineering, and forestry. 2-2 and 3-2 engineering programs. Teacher certification in early childhood, elementary, secondary, and special education. Study abroad in Australia, England, France, and the Netherlands.
**Honors:** Honors program.
**Academic Assistance:** Remedial reading, writing, math, and study skills. Nonremedial tutoring.

**STUDENT LIFE. Housing:** Students may live on or off campus. Coed dorms. School-owned/-operated apartments. 24% of students live in college housing.
**Social atmosphere:** Student gathering-spots include New Zoo, the Mad Monk, Stemmerman's, and The Ice House. Athletes have a widespread influence on campus life. The most popular event of the year is the NCAA basketball tournament. According to the student newspaper, "the beach is a big part of life; it's a big drawing point. The campus is quite environmentally active."
**Services and counseling/handicapped student services:** Placement services. Health service. Counseling services for minority, military, veteran, and older students. Birth control, personal, and psychological counseling. Career and academic guidance services. Physically disabled student services. Learning disabled program/services. Notetaking services. Tape recorders. Tutors. Reader services for the blind.
**Campus organizations:** Undergraduate student government. Student newspaper (Seahawk, published once/week). Literary magazine. Radio station. Chamber singers, mixed chorus, concert choir, community orchestra, wind and jazz ensembles, theatre groups, debating, SADD, Divers Association, campus entertainment association, marine science journal, departmental groups, 95 organizations in all. 13 fraternities, one chapter house; 11 sororities, no chapter houses. 14% of men join a fraternity. 9% of women join a sorority.
**Religious organizations:** Baptist Student Union, Campus Crusade for Christ, Catholic Christian Ministry, Fellowship of Christian Athletes, FOCUS.
**Minority/foreign student organizations:** Black Student Union, NAACP, Minority Mentor Program, Black History Month, minority achievement awards.

**ATHLETICS. Physical education requirements:** One semester of physical education required.
**Intercollegiate competition:** 2% of students participate. Baseball (M), basketball (M,W), cross-country (M,W), golf (M,W), soccer (M), softball (W), swimming (M,W), tennis (M,W), track and field (outdoor) (M,W), volleyball (W). Member of Colonial Athletic Association, ECAC South, NCAA Division I.
**Intramural and club sports:** Intramural archery, bowling, fishing derby, free throw, frisbee, pool, racquetball, roller skating, surfing, table tennis. Men's club crew, lacrosse, rugby, sailing, scuba, skateboarding, surfing, ultimate frisbee, volleyball, water skiing. Women's club crew, dance, equestrian sports, rifle, soccer, ultimate frisbee.

**ADMISSIONS. Academic basis for candidate selection** (in order of priority): Secondary school record, standardized test scores, class rank.
**Nonacademic basis for candidate selection:** Geographical distribution is considered.
**Requirements:** Graduation from secondary school is recommended; GED is accepted. 20 units and the following program of study are required: 4 units of English, 3 units of math, 3 units of science including 1 unit of lab, 2 units of foreign language, 2 units of social studies, 5 units of academic electives. 1 unit of history also required. Applicants may be admitted with deficiency in foreign language units but must complete foreign language requirements before graduation. Minimum combined SAT score of 800 and minimum 2.0 GPA required. SAT is required; ACT may be substituted. No off-campus interviews.
**Procedure:** Take SAT or ACT by December of 12th year. Notification of admission on rolling basis. Reply is required by May 15. $25 nonrefundable tuition deposit. $100 room deposit, refundable until May 15 under certain circumstances. Freshmen accepted in terms other than fall.
**Special programs:** Credit and/or placement may be granted through CEEB Advanced Placement exams for scores of 3 or higher. Credit and/or placement may be granted

through CLEP general and subject exams. Credit and placement may be granted through military experience. Concurrent enrollment program.
**Transfer students:** Transfer students accepted for terms other than fall. In fall 1993, 11% of all new students were transfers into all classes. 1,815 transfer applications were received, 1,235 were accepted. Application deadline is March 15 for fall; December 1 for spring. Minimum 2.0 GPA required. Lowest course grade accepted is "C." Maximum number of transferable credits is 62 semester hours from a two-year school and 94 semester hours from a four-year school. At least 30 semester hours must be completed at the university to receive degree.
**Admissions contact:** Diane M. Zeeman, M.A., Director of Admissions. 919 395-3243.

**FINANCIAL AID. Available aid:** Pell grants, SEOG, state scholarships and grants, school scholarships and grants, private scholarships and grants, academic merit scholarships, athletic scholarships, and aid for undergraduate foreign students. Perkins Loans (NDSL), PLUS, Stafford Loans (GSL), state loans, private loans, and SLS. AMS.
**Financial aid statistics:** 46% of aid is not need-based. In 1993-94, 78% of all undergraduate applicants received aid; 88% of freshman applicants. Average amounts of aid awarded freshmen: Scholarships and grants, $453; loans, $2,697.
**Supporting data/closing dates:** FAFSA: Priority filing date is March 15; accepted on rolling basis. School's own aid application: Priority filing date is March 15. Notification of awards begins April 15.
**Financial aid contact:** Joseph V. Capell, M.Div., Director of Financial Aid. 919 395-3177.

**STUDENT EMPLOYMENT.** College Work/Study Program. Institutional employment. 6% of full-time undergraduates work on campus during school year. Students may expect to earn an average of $1,094 during school year. Off-campus part-time employment opportunities rated "good."

**COMPUTER FACILITIES.** 52 IBM/IBM-compatible and Macintosh/Apple microcomputers; all are networked. Students may access Digital, Sequent minicomputer/mainframe systems, Internet. Residence halls may be equipped with networked microcomputers. Client/LAN operating systems include Apple/Macintosh, DOS, UNIX/XENIX/AIX, LocalTalk/AppleTalk, Novell. Computer languages and software packages include Assembler, BASIC, COBOL, FORTRAN, Pascal, PL/1, SAS, SPSS-X, 20/20, WordPerfect; 11 in all. Computer facilities are available to all students.
**Fees:** None.
**Hours:** 8 AM-11 PM; 24-hour access via modem.

**GRADUATE CAREER DATA.** Highest graduate school enrollments: North Carolina State U, U of North Carolina at Wilmington. 50% of graduates choose careers in business and industry. Companies and businesses that hire graduates: DuPont, General Electric.

# Wake Forest University

**Winston-Salem, NC 27109 — 910 759-5000**

**1994-95 Costs.** Tuition: $13,850. Room & board: $4,360. Fees, books, misc. academic expenses (school's estimate): $500.
**Enrollment.** Undergraduates: 1,804 men, 1,754 women (full-time). Freshman class: 5,661 applicants, 2,392 accepted, 903 enrolled. Graduate enrollment: 1,139 men, 744 women.
**Test score averages/ranges.** Range of SAT scores of middle 50%: 550-650 verbal, 600-700 math.
**Faculty.** 272 full-time; 62 part-time. 85% of faculty holds doctoral degree. Student/faculty ratio: 13 to 1.
**Selectivity rating.** Highly competitive.

**PROFILE.** Wake Forest is a church-affiliated university. Founded in 1834, it adopted coeducation in 1942. Programs are offered through the Schools of Business and Accountancy, Law, and Medicine; Wake Forest College; and the Graduate School. Its 470-acre campus is located in Winston-Salem. Most of its buildings are of modified Georgian architecture.

**Accreditation:** SACS. Professionally accredited by the American Assembly of Collegiate Schools of Business, the National Council for Accreditation of Teacher Education.
**Religious orientation:** Wake Forest University is affiliated with the North Carolina Baptist Convention; one semester of religion required.
**Library:** Collections totaling over 1,337,142 volumes, 19,252 periodical subscriptions, and 1,342,814 microform items.
**Special facilities/museums:** American art and anthropological museums, student art gallery, laser and electron microscope labs, primate research station.
**Athletic facilities:** Basketball, handball, racquetball, and tennis courts, football and soccer fields, baseball and softball diamonds, golf practice area, track, weight room.

**STUDENT BODY. Undergraduate profile:** 34% are state residents. 1% Asian-American, 8% Black, 89% White, 2% Other. Average age of undergraduates is 20.
**Freshman profile:** 99% of accepted applicants took SAT. 75% of freshmen come from public schools.
**Undergraduate achievement:** 97% of fall 1992 freshmen returned for fall 1993 term. 75% of entering class graduated. 32% of students who completed a degree program immediately went on to graduate study.
**Foreign students:** 46 students are from out of the country. Countries represented include Canada, France, Germany, India, the Netherlands, and Spain; 25 in all.

**PROGRAMS OF STUDY. Degrees:** B.A., B.S.
**Majors:** Accounting, Anthropology, Art, Biology, Business, Chemistry, Classics, Computer Science, Economics, Education, English, French, German, Greek, Health/Sports Science, History, Latin, Mathematical Economics, Mathematics, Music, Philosophy, Physics, Politics, Psychology, Religion, Russian, Sociology, Spanish, Spanish/French, Speech Communication, Theatre.
**Distribution of degrees:** The majors with the highest enrollment are English, biology, and business; classics/Greek, music, and German have the lowest.
**Requirements:** General education requirement.
**Academic regulations:** Freshmen must maintain minimum 1.45 GPA; sophomores, 1.60 GPA; juniors, 1.75 GPA; seniors, 1.90 GPA.
**Special:** Minors offered in most majors and in educational studies, French language and culture, French literature, Hispanic literature, Italian and Spanish language and culture. Courses offered in Asian studies, Chinese, Hebrew, Hindi, journalism, and natural sciences. Interdisciplinary and departmental honors program. All freshmen and sophomores enroll in School of Arts and Sciences for general distribution requirements. English composition proficiency required in all departments. Students admitted to upper divisions after successful completion of basic courses. Double majors. Dual degrees. Independent study. Pass/fail grading option. Internships. Cooperative education programs. Graduate school at which undergraduates may take graduate-level courses. Preprofessional programs in law, medicine, veterinary science, dentistry, and theology. 3-2 engineering programs with North Carolina State U. 3-2 forestry and environmental studies program with Duke U. 3-2 programs in dentistry and microbiology with approved schools. Combined degrees in law, medical sciences, medical technology, microbiology, and physician assistant with university's professional schools of business, law, and medicine. Cross-registration with Salem Coll. Summer business program for liberal arts students. Teacher certification in elementary and secondary education. Certification in specific subject areas. Exchange programs abroad in Japan (Tokai U) and Russia (Moscow State U). Study abroad also in Austria, China, England, France, Germany, Italy, and Spain. ROTC.
**Honors:** Phi Beta Kappa. Honors program. Honor societies.
**Academic Assistance:** Remedial reading, writing, math, and study skills. Nonremedial tutoring.

**STUDENT LIFE. Housing:** Unmarried freshmen must live on campus unless living with family. Coed, women's, and men's dorms. Sorority and fraternity housing. School-owned/operated apartments. Off-campus privately-owned housing. On-campus married-student housing. Theme houses. 83% of students live in college housing.
**Social atmosphere:** The student newspaper reports, "Because we have a small campus with 3,500 undergraduates, much of the social life is on campus. There is always something to do, whether it's a lecture, concert, party, or movie. Fraternity and society parties entertain many students on weekends, while off-campus spots are more popular during the week. Since over 40 percent of the student body is Greek, they have a wide influence. The Student Union Network sponsors everything from parties to concerts to 'coffeehouse' nights to movies. The Residence Student Association also sponsors social events such as cookouts. Football tailgates and ballgames are popular, as are various formals."
**Services and counseling/handicapped student services:** Placement services. Health service. Counseling services for minority, veteran, and older students. Birth control, personal, and psychological counseling. Career and academic guidance services. Religious counseling. Physically disabled student services. Learning disabled services. Notetaking services. Tutors. Reader services for the blind.
**Campus organizations:** Undergraduate student government. Student newspaper (Old Gold and Black, published once/week). Literary magazine. Yearbook. Radio station. Literary Society, Gospel choir, French, Hispanic, and Russian clubs, accounting, anthropology, politics, and sociology groups, peer educators, Resident Student Association, Habitat for Humanity, Student Alumni Council, Volunteer Service Corps, Amnesty International, College Democrats, College Republicans, Model United Nations Society, Harbinger Corps, 90 organizations in all. 15 fraternities, one chapter house; 10 sororities, no chapter houses. 42% of men join a fraternity. 51% of women join a sorority.
**Religious organizations:** Black Christian Fellowship, Baptist Student Union, Catholic Student Union, Episcopal Student Association, Fellowship of Christian Athletes, Intervarsity Christian Fellowship, Wesley Foundation, Lutheran Campus Fellowship, Presbyterian Student Fellowship.
**Minority/foreign student organizations:** Black Student Alliance, NAACP. International Club, Asian Student Union.

**ATHLETICS. Physical education requirements:** Two semesters of physical education required.
**Intercollegiate competition:** 10% of students participate. Baseball (M), basketball (M,W), cross-country (M,W), field hockey (W), football (M), golf (M,W), soccer (M), tennis (M,W), track (indoor) (M,W), track (outdoor) (M,W). Member of Atlantic Coast Conference, NCAA Division I.
**Intramural and club sports:** 1% of students participate. Intramural baseball, biathlon, cross-country, football, golf, racquetball, soccer, softball, swimming, tennis, volleyball, weight lifting, wrestling.

**ADMISSIONS. Academic basis for candidate selection** (in order of priority): Secondary school record, class rank, standardized test scores, school's recommendation, essay.
**Nonacademic basis for candidate selection:** Character and personality, extracurricular participation, and particular talent or ability are emphasized. Alumni/ae relationship is important. Geographical distribution is considered.
**Requirements:** Graduation from secondary school is recommended; GED is accepted. 16 units and the following program of study are required: 4 units of English, 3 units of math, 1 unit of science, 2 units of foreign language, 2 units of social studies, 2 units of history, 2 units of academic electives. SAT is required. ACH recommended. Campus visit recommended. No off-campus interviews.
**Procedure:** Take SAT by fall of 12th year. Take ACH by fall of 12th year. Application deadline is January 15. Notification of admission by April 1. Reply is required by May 1. $200 nonrefundable tuition deposit. Freshmen accepted in terms other than fall.
**Special programs:** Admission may be deferred one year. Credit and/or placement may be granted through CEEB Advanced Placement exams for scores of 4 or higher. Credit and/or placement may be granted through CLEP subject exams. Credit and placement may be granted through challenge exams. Early decision program. In fall 1993, 400 applied for early decision and 153 were accepted. Deadline for applying for early decision is November 15. Early entrance/early admission program. Concurrent enrollment program.
**Transfer students:** Transfer students accepted for terms other than fall. In fall 1993, less than 1% of all new students were transfers into all classes. 305 transfer applications were received, 122 were accepted. Application deadline is February 15 for fall; November 15 for spring. Minimum 2.0 GPA required. Lowest course grade accepted is "D." Maximum number of transferable credits is 64 semester hours. At least 72 credits must be completed at the university to receive degree.

**Admissions contact:** William G. Starling, Director of Admissions and Financial Aid. 910 759-5201.

**FINANCIAL AID. Available aid:** Pell grants, SEOG, state scholarships and grants, school scholarships and grants, private scholarships and grants, ROTC scholarships, academic merit scholarships, and athletic scholarships. Perkins Loans (NDSL), PLUS, Stafford Loans (GSL), state loans, school loans, private loans, and SLS. Knight Tuition Plans. Institutional payment plan.
**Financial aid statistics:** 40% of aid is not need-based. In 1993-94, 100% of all undergraduate applicants received aid. Average amounts of aid awarded freshmen: Scholarships and grants, $6,800; loans, $4,450.
**Supporting data/closing dates:** FAFSA/FAF: Priority filing date is March 1. School's own aid application: Priority filing date is March 1. Income tax forms: Priority filing date is March 1. Notification of awards begins April 15.
**Financial aid contact:** William G. Starling, Director of Admissions and Financial Aid. 910 759-5176.

**STUDENT EMPLOYMENT.** College Work/Study Program. Institutional employment. Students may expect to earn an average of $1,500 during school year. Off-campus part-time employment opportunities rated "good."

**COMPUTER FACILITIES.** 161 IBM/IBM-compatible and Macintosh/Apple microcomputers; all are networked. Students may access Hewlett-Packard, SUN minicomputer/mainframe systems, BITNET, Internet. Residence halls may be equipped with networked microcomputers. Computer languages and software packages include C, Disspla, FORTRAN, Harvard Graphics, HyperCard, MacPaint, MacWrite, Microsoft Word, NCSA Telnet Deltagraph, Pascal, SAS, SPSSX, Taste, Word for Windows, WordPerfect. Computer facilities are available to all students.
**Fees:** None.
**Hours:** 24 hours.

**GRADUATE CAREER DATA.** Graduate school percentages: 6% enter law school. 6% enter medical school. 2% enter graduate business programs. 16% enter graduate arts and sciences programs. 1% enter theological school/seminary. Highest graduate school enrollments: Duke U, U of Georgia, U of North Carolina at Chapel Hill, U of South Carolina, U of Virginia, Washington and Lee U, Coll of William and Mary. 60% of graduates choose careers in business and industry. Companies and businesses that hire graduates: Andersen Consulting, Chubb Insurance, Coopers Lybrand, First Union, General Electric, KPMG Peat Marwick, Nations Bank, Pepsico, S.D. Warren.

**PROMINENT ALUMNI/AE.** Arnold Palmer, professional golfer; C.C. Hope, director, FDIC; Wayne Calloway, chairperson of the board, PepsiCo; A.R. Ammons, poet; Albert Hunt, Washington bureau chief, *Wall Street Journal*.

## Warren Wilson College

**Swannanoa, NC 28778** **704 298-3325**

**1994-95 Costs.** Tuition: $10,000. Room & board: $3,052. Fees, books, misc. academic expenses (school's estimate): $1,015.
**Enrollment.** Undergraduates: 204 men, 264 women (full-time). Freshman class: 299 applicants, 236 accepted, 116 enrolled. Graduate enrollment: 16 men, 52 women.
**Test score averages/ranges.** Average SAT scores: 521 verbal, 522 math. Range of SAT scores of middle 50%: 440-600 verbal, 450-590 math.
**Faculty.** 44 full-time; 26 part-time. 44% of faculty holds highest degree in specific field. Student/faculty ratio: 11 to 1.
**Selectivity rating.** Competitive.

**PROFILE.** Warren Wilson is a church-affiliated, liberal arts college. Founded in 1894 as a boys' school, it became a two-year college in 1942 and a four-year college in 1965. Its 1,000-acre campus is located in Swannanoa, 10 miles from the city of Asheville.

**Accreditation:** SACS. Professionally accredited by the Council on Social Work Education.
**Religious orientation:** Warren Wilson College is affiliated with the Presbyterian Church USA; no religious requirements.
**Library:** Collections totaling over 90,000 volumes, 469 periodical subscriptions and 103 microform items.
**Special facilities/museums:** Two child development centers.
**Athletic facilities:** Gymnasium, fitness and weight rooms, swimming pool, baseball, soccer, softball, and fields, basketball and tennis courts.

**STUDENT BODY. Undergraduate profile:** 38% are state residents; 22% are transfers. 2% Asian-American, 3% Black, 1% Hispanic, 1% Native American, 83% White, 10% Other. Average age of undergraduates is 20.
**Freshman profile:** 1% of freshmen who took SAT scored 700 or over on verbal, 1% scored 700 or over on math; 12% scored 600 or over on verbal, 7% scored 600 or over on math; 31% scored 500 or over on verbal, 31% scored 500 or over on math; 62% scored 400 or over on verbal, 59% scored 400 or over on math; 68% scored 300 or over on verbal, 68% scored 300 or over on math. 91% of accepted applicants took SAT; 9% took ACT.
**Undergraduate achievement:** 72% of fall 1991 freshmen returned for fall 1992 term.
**Foreign students:** Countries represented include Ethiopia, India, Japan, Kenya, Lebanon, and Suriname; 10 in all.

**PROGRAMS OF STUDY. Degrees:** B.A.
**Majors:** Biological Sciences, Chemistry, Economics/Business Administration, Education, English, English/Theatre Arts, Environmental Studies, General Studies, History/Political Science, Humanities, Intercultural Studies, Mathematics/Computer Science, Psychology, Social Work, Sociology.
**Distribution of degrees:** The majors with the highest enrollment are economics/business administration, environmental studies, and education.
**Requirements:** General education requirement.
**Academic regulations:** Minimum 2.0 GPA required for graduation.
**Special:** Minors offered in some majors and in Appalachian studies, art, modern language, music, philosophy, physics, and religion. Interdisciplinary major offered in United States studies. All residential students work 15 hours/week in campus work program to pay most of cost of room and board; students are carpenters, gardeners, librarians, accountants, foresters, farmers raising livestock and crops on 300-acre working farm, plumbers, electricians, and office workers. Double majors. Dual degrees. Independent study. Pass/fail grading option. Internships. Preprofessional programs in medicine and veterinary science. 3-2 engineering program with Washington U. 3-2 forestry and environmental studies program with Duke U. Member of Appalachian Consortium. Exchange program with Appalachian State U. Teacher certification in elementary and secondary education. Study abroad in England and Japan.
**Academic Assistance:** Remedial study skills.

**ADMISSIONS. Academic basis for candidate selection** (in order of priority): Secondary school record, standardized test scores, school's recommendation, class rank, essay.
**Nonacademic basis for candidate selection:** Character and personality are emphasized. Extracurricular participation, particular talent or ability, geographical distribution, and alumni/ae relationship are considered.
**Requirements:** Graduation from secondary school is required; GED is accepted. 11 units and the following program of study are required: 4 units of English, 3 units of math, 2 units of lab science, 1 unit of social studies, 1 unit of history. Minimum SAT scores of 400 in both verbal and math, rank in top half of secondary school class, and minimum 2.0 GPA recommended. SAT is required; ACT may be substituted. Campus visit and interview recommended. Off-campus interviews available with an admissions representative.
**Procedure:** Take SAT or ACT by May of 12th year. Visit college for interview by December of 12th year. Application deadline is July 1. Notification of admission on rolling basis. Reply is required by May 1. $360 nonrefundable tuition deposit. $50 nonrefundable room deposit. Freshmen accepted in terms other than fall.
**Special programs:** Admission may be deferred one year. Credit and/or placement may be granted through CEEB Advanced Placement exams for scores of 3 or higher. Placement may be granted through CLEP general and subject exams. Credit may be granted through military and life experience. Early entrance/early admission program.
**Transfer students:** Transfer students accepted for terms other than fall. In fall 1992, 22% of all new students were transfers into all classes. 104 transfer applications were received, 83 were accepted. Application deadline is rolling for fall; rolling for spring. Minimum 2.0 GPA required. Lowest course grade accepted is "C."
**Admissions contact:** Thomas Weede, Director of Admissions. 704 298-3325, extension 240.

**FINANCIAL AID. Available aid:** Pell grants, state grants, school scholarships, and private scholarships. Perkins Loans (NDSL), Stafford Loans (GSL), state loans, and school loans.
**Financial aid statistics:** Average amounts of aid awarded freshmen: Scholarships and grants, $2,700; loans, $2,000.
**Supporting data/closing dates:** FAFSA: Priority filing date is May 2. FAF/FFS: Deadline is May 2. State aid form: Priority filing date is May 2. Income tax forms: Priority filing date is May 2. Notification of awards on rolling basis.
**Financial aid contact:** Kathy Pack, M.A., Director of Financial Aid. 704 298-3325, extension 249.

## Western Carolina University

**Cullowhee, NC 28723** **704 227-7211**

**1993-94 Costs.** Tuition: $740 (state residents), $6,806 (out-of-state). Room: $1,280. Board: $1,140. Fees, books, misc. academic expenses (school's estimate): $986.
**Enrollment.** Undergraduates: 2,554 men, 2,446 women (full-time). Freshman class: 3,224 applicants, 2,519 accepted, 1,057 enrolled. Graduate enrollment: 317 men, 534 women.
**Test score averages/ranges.** Average SAT scores: 410 verbal, 457 math. Range of SAT scores of middle 50%: 360-450 verbal, 400-510 math.
**Faculty.** 334 full-time; 154 part-time. 69% of faculty holds doctoral degree. Student/faculty ratio: 17 to 1.
**Selectivity rating.** Less competitive.

**PROFILE.** Western Carolina, founded in 1889, is a public, multipurpose university. Programs are offered through the Schools of Arts and Sciences, Business, Education and Psychology, Nursing and Health Sciences, and Technology and Applied Science and the Graduate School. Its 400-acre campus is located in Cullowhee, 50 miles west of Asheville.

**Accreditation:** SACS. Professionally accredited by the Accreditation Board for Engineering and Technology, the American Assembly of Collegiate Schools of Business, the American Dietetic Association, the American Home Economics Association, the American Medical Association (CAHEA), the Council on Social Work Education, the National Association of Schools of Music, the National Council for Accreditation of Teacher Education, the National League for Nursing.
**Religious orientation:** Western Carolina University is nonsectarian; no religious requirements.
**Library:** Collections totaling over 420,933 volumes, 2,119 periodical subscriptions, and 1,124,547 microform items.
**Special facilities/museums:** Two art galleries, geology and history museums, mountain heritage and life centers, reading center, rural education institute, state center for the advancement of teaching, speech and hearing center, state cardiac/rehabilitation program and wildlife commission.
**Athletic facilities:** Gymnasium, stadium, baseball, football, intramural, soccer, and softball fields, track, basketball, handball, and tennis courts, jogging course, golf driving range, putting green, swimming pools, archery, rifle, and skeet ranges, bowling alley, weight room.

**STUDENT BODY. Undergraduate profile:** 91% are state residents; 32% are transfers. .9% Asian-American, 3.9% Black, .3% Hispanic, 1.6% Native American, 93% White, .3% Other. Average age of undergraduates is 20.

**Freshman profile:** 1% of freshmen who took SAT scored 700 or over on math; 2% scored 600 or over on verbal, 5% scored 600 or over on math; 13% scored 500 or over on verbal, 29% scored 500 or over on math; 55% scored 400 or over on verbal, 78% scored 400 or over on math; 97% scored 300 or over on verbal, 99% scored 300 or over on math. 99% of accepted applicants took SAT. 95% of freshmen come from public schools.

**Undergraduate achievement:** 71% of fall 1992 freshmen returned for fall 1993 term. 19% of entering class graduated. 16% of students who completed a degree program went on to graduate study within five years.

**Foreign students:** Five students are from out of the country.

**PROGRAMS OF STUDY. Degrees:** B.A., B.F.A., B.S., B.S.Bus.Admin., B.S.Ed., B.S.Nurs.

**Majors:** Accounting, Anthropology, Art, Art Education, Biology, Biology/Secondary Education, Business Administration/Law, Business Education, Chemistry, Child Development/Family Relations, Clinical Lab Sciences, Clothing/Textiles/Merchandising, Communications, Communications Disorders Education, Computer/Information Sciences, Computer Information Systems, Criminal Justice, Dramatic Arts/Radio/TV, Early Childhood Education, Economics, Education of the Mentally Retarded, Electrical Engineering Technology, Emergency Medical Care, Engineering Technology, English, English Education, Environmental Health, Finance, Food Service Management, French, French Education, Geography, Geology, German, German Education, Health Education, Health Information Management, Health Services Management/Supervision, History, Home Economics, Home Economics Education, Industrial Arts Education, Industrial Chemistry, Industrial Distribution, Industrial Technology, Interior Design, Intermediate Education, International Business, Learning Disabilities Education, Management, Manufacturing Engineering Technology, Marketing, Mathematics, Mathematics Education, Middle Grade Education, Music, Music Education, Music Education/Instrumental, Natural Resources Management, Nursing, Nutrition/Dietetics, Office Administration, Parks/Recreation Management, Philosophy, Physical Education, Physics, Political Science/Government, Psychology, Radio/Television, Science Education, Social Science Education, Social Sciences, Social Work, Sociology, Spanish, Spanish Education, Special Education, Special Studies, Speech/Theatre Arts, Speech/Theatre Arts Education, Sports Management, Theatre, Therapeutic Recreation.

**Distribution of degrees:** The majors with the highest enrollment are marketing, criminal justice, and nursing; geology, sociology, and health services management/supervision have the lowest.

**Requirements:** General education requirement.

**Academic regulations:** Minimum 2.0 GPA must be maintained.

**Special:** Minors offered in most majors and in American studies, Cherokee studies, fashion merchandising, guidance/counseling, international studies, journalism, lifespan development, and professional writing. Dual degrees. Independent study. Accelerated study. Pass/fail grading option. Internships. Cooperative education programs. Graduate school at which undergraduates may take graduate-level courses. Preprofessional programs in law, medicine, veterinary science, pharmacy, dentistry, and optometry. Two-year transfer programs in agriculture, engineering, and forestry with North Carolina State U. Health information management and clinical lab science programs offered in cooperation with affiliated hospitals. Member of Southern Appalachian Research-Resource Management Cooperative. Interinstitutional programs with U of North Carolina at Asheville. Teacher certification in early childhood, elementary, secondary, special education, and vo-tech education. Certification in specific subject areas. Study abroad in Central American countries, Colombia, England, Mexico, and the West Indies. ROTC.

**Honors:** Honors program. Honor societies.

**Academic Assistance:** Remedial reading, writing, math, and study skills. Nonremedial tutoring.

**STUDENT LIFE. Housing:** All unmarried freshmen must live on campus unless living with family. Women's and men's dorms. School-owned/operated apartments. On-campus married-student housing. 46% of students live in college housing.

**Social atmosphere:** Students gather at University Center and at Bailey's, a local bar. Greeks, the Organization of Ebony Students, and Last Minute Productions influence campus life. Favorite campus events include Homecoming, intramural sporting events, and concerts. The editor of the student newspaper reports, "Social life could be better, considering all the organizations on campus--more concerts, maybe."

**Services and counseling/handicapped student services:** Placement services. Health service. Counseling services for minority, veteran, and older students. Birth control, personal, and psychological counseling. Career and academic guidance services. Physically disabled student services. Learning disabled services. Notetaking services. Tape recorders. Tutors. Reader services for the blind.

**Campus organizations:** Undergraduate student government. Student newspaper (Western Carolinian, published once/week). Literary magazine. Yearbook. Radio station. Band, choral ensembles, chorus, University Players, professional, service, and special-interest groups, 140 organizations in all. 14 fraternities, 11 chapter houses; eight sororities, no chapter houses. 20% of men join a fraternity. 10% of women join a sorority.

**Religious organizations:** Baptist Student Union, Canterbury House, Catholic Student Center, Chi Alpha, Church of Christ, Covenant Student Fellowship, Latter-Day Saints Organization, Lutheran Student Organization, Presbyterian Campus Ministry, Wesley Foundation.

**Minority/foreign student organizations:** Alpha Phi Alpha, Black Student Fellowship, Ebony Students, Kappa Alpha Psi, Omega Psi Phi. International Student Organization.

**ATHLETICS. Physical education requirements:** Two semesters of physical education required.

**Intercollegiate competition:** 4% of students participate. Baseball (M), basketball (M,W), cheerleading (M,W), cross-country (M,W), football (M), golf (M,W), tennis (M,W), track (indoor) (M,W), track (outdoor) (M,W), track and field (indoor) (M,W), track and field (outdoor) (M,W), volleyball (W). Member of NCAA Division I, NCAA Division I-AA for football, Southern Conference.

**Intramural and club sports:** 30% of students participate. Intramural arm wrestling, badminton, basketball, billiards, bowling, cross-country, fishing derby, flag football, football, homerun contest, horseshoes, racquetball, soccer, softball, swimming, table tennis, tennis, track and field, trapshooting, volleyball, water polo, weight lifting, wrestling. Men's club rugby.

**ADMISSIONS. Academic basis for candidate selection** (in order of priority): Secondary school record, class rank, standardized test scores, school's recommendation, essay.

**Nonacademic basis for candidate selection:** Extracurricular participation and particular talent or ability are important. Character and personality are considered.

**Requirements:** Graduation from secondary school is required; GED is accepted. 20 units and the following program of study are required: 4 units of English, 3 units of math, 3 units of science including 1 unit of lab, 2 units of social studies, 1 unit of history. Minimum SAT scores of 350 in both verbal and math, rank in top half of secondary school class, and minimum 2.0 GPA recommended. Aptitude exam and audition required of music program applicants. Conditional admission possible for applicants not meeting standard requirements. SAT is required. Campus visit recommended. Off-campus interviews available with an admissions representative.

**Procedure:** Take SAT by December of 12th year. Visit college for interview by spring of 12th year. Suggest filing application by fall. Application deadline is July. Notification of admission on rolling basis. Reply is required within 30 days of acceptance. $75 room deposit, refundable until June 1. $75 room deposit, $65 of which is refundable if applicant withdraws before June 1. Freshmen accepted in terms other than fall.

**Special programs:** Admission may be deferred two years. Credit and/or placement may be granted through CEEB Advanced Placement exams for scores of 3 or higher. Credit and/or placement may be granted through CLEP subject exams. Credit and placement may be granted through challenge exams and military and life experience. Early entrance/early admission program. Concurrent enrollment program.

**Transfer students:** Transfer students accepted for terms other than fall. In fall 1993, 32% of all new students were transfers into all classes. 983 transfer applications were received, 838 were accepted. Application deadline is July 1 for fall; December 1 for spring. Minimum 2.0 GPA required. Lowest course grade accepted is "C." At least 30 semester hours must be completed at the university to receive degree.

**Admissions contact:** Drumont Bowman, M.A., Director of Admissions. 704 227-7317.

**FINANCIAL AID. Available aid:** Pell grants, SEOG, state scholarships and grants, school scholarships and grants, private scholarships and grants, ROTC scholarships, academic merit scholarships, and athletic scholarships. Perkins Loans (NDSL), PLUS, Stafford Loans (GSL), NSL, Health Professions Loans, state loans, and SLS.

**Financial aid statistics:** 25% of aid is not need-based. In 1993-94, 87% of all undergraduate applicants received aid; 80% of freshman applicants. Average amounts of aid awarded freshmen: Scholarships and grants, $1,200; loans, $1,850.

**Supporting data/closing dates:** FAFSA: Priority filing date is March 31. Notification of awards begins May 1.

**Financial aid contact:** Thomas W. Grant, M.S., Director of Student Financial Aid. 704 227-7290.

**STUDENT EMPLOYMENT.** College Work/Study Program. Institutional employment. 35% of full-time undergraduates work on campus during school year. Students may expect to earn an average of $2,000 during school year. Off-campus part-time employment opportunities rated "fair."

**COMPUTER FACILITIES.** 400 IBM/IBM-compatible and Macintosh/Apple microcomputers; 85 are networked. Students may access Digital minicomputer/mainframe systems, Internet. Client/LAN operating systems include Apple/Macintosh, LocalTalk/AppleTalk. Computer languages and software packages include Ada, BASIC, C, COBOL, Di3000, FORTRAN, INGRES, Macro, MINITAB, OPSS, Pascal, Rally, RDB, SAS, Shazam, SOL, SPSS-X, 20/20, TDMS. Computer facilities are available to all students.

**Fees:** None.

**Hours:** 8 AM-10 PM (M-F), 24-hour dial-in access.

**GRADUATE CAREER DATA.** Graduate school percentages: 1% enter law school. 1% enter medical school. 4% enter graduate business programs. 2% enter graduate arts and sciences programs. Highest graduate school enrollments: North Carolina State U, U of North Carolina at Chapel Hill, Western Carolina U. Companies and businesses that hire graduates: Millikan, North Carolina National Bank, Wachovia Bank, Wal-Mart.

**PROMINENT ALUMNI/AE.** Charles West, retired chief news writer, CBS Evening News; Dr. Robert Failing, pathologist and renowned mountain climber; Dr. Wallace Hyde, national political fundraiser and insurance company owner; Robert Terrell, author and associate editor, *The Asheville Citizen*; Bishop Ernest Fitzgerald, resident bishop, North Georgia Conference, United Methodist Church.

# Wingate College

**Wingate, NC 28174-0157** **704 233-8000**

**1993-94 Costs.** Tuition: $7,070. Room & board: $3,200. Fees, books, misc. academic expenses (school's estimate): $740.

**Enrollment.** Undergraduates: 637 men, 599 women (full-time). Freshman class: 1,239 applicants, 1,017 accepted, 389 enrolled. Graduate enrollment: 33 men, 35 women.

**Test score averages/ranges.** Average SAT scores: 398 verbal, 444 math.

**Faculty.** 78 full-time; 21 part-time. 75% of faculty holds doctoral degree. Student/faculty ratio: 16 to 1.

**Selectivity rating.** Less competitive.

**PROFILE.** Wingate, founded in 1896, is a church-affiliated college. Undergraduate programs are offered through the Divisions of Business and Economics, Education and Social Science, Fine Arts, Humanities, and Science and Mathematics. Its 15-acre campus is located in Wingate, 25 miles southeast of Charlotte.

**Accreditation:** SACS. Professionally accredited by the National Association of Schools of Music, the National League for Nursing.

**Religious orientation:** Wingate College is affiliated with the Baptist Church; two semesters of religion required.

**Library:** Collections totaling over 110,000 volumes, 670 periodical subscriptions, and 20,000 microform items.

**Special facilities/museums:** Art gallery, electron microscope, TV studio, outdoor recreation lab.
**Athletic facilities:** Gymnasiums, weight room, baseball, football, soccer, and softball fields, field house, basketball, racquetball, and tennis courts, arena, golf driving range, swimming pool.

**STUDENT BODY. Undergraduate profile:** 60% are state residents; 19% are transfers. 1% Asian-American, 9% Black, 1% Hispanic, 1% Native American, 87% White, 1% Other. Average age of undergraduates is 20.
**Freshman profile:** 1% of freshmen who took SAT scored 700 or over on math; 2% scored 600 or over on verbal, 6% scored 600 or over on math; 9% scored 500 or over on verbal, 22% scored 500 or over on math; 37% scored 400 or over on verbal, 56% scored 400 or over on math; 82% scored 300 or over on verbal, 82% scored 300 or over on math. Majority of accepted applicants took SAT. 90% of freshmen come from public schools.
**Undergraduate achievement:** 81% of fall 1992 freshmen returned for fall 1993 term. 66% of entering class graduated. 30% of students who completed a degree program immediately went on to graduate study.
**Foreign students:** 10 students are from out of the country. Eight countries represented in all.

**PROGRAMS OF STUDY. Degrees:** B.A., B.Mus., B.Mus.Ed., B.S.
**Majors:** Accounting, Allied Health, American Studies, Art, Art Education, Biology, Business Administration, Business/Mathematics, Chemistry, Church Music, Communication Studies, Computer Information Systems, Economics, Elementary Education, English, English Education, General Business, History, Human Services, Management, Mathematics, Mathematics/Business, Mathematics Education, Middle Grades Education, Music, Music Business, Music Education, Music Performance, Parks/Recreation Administration, Pre-Engineering, Psychology, Reading Education, Religious Studies, Science Education, Secondary Education, Social Sciences Education, Sociology, Sport Management, Sports Medicine, Technology.
**Distribution of degrees:** The majors with the highest enrollment are business, communications, and education; math, art, and allied health have the lowest.
**Requirements:** General education requirement.
**Academic regulations:** Freshmen must maintain minimum 1.8 GPA; sophomores, 1.8 GPA; juniors, 1.8 GPA; seniors, 2.0 GPA.
**Special:** Optional minors offered in many majors and in coaching, family studies, finance, French, international studies, speech communication, sports medicine, and telecommunication. Great American Heritage program offers travel to major cities in the U.S. "W'International," a semester seminar culminating in 10-day trip to Europe. Associate's degrees offered. Double majors. Independent study. Accelerated study. Internships. Cooperative education programs. Preprofessional programs in law, medicine, veterinary science, pharmacy, and dentistry. 3-2 engineering programs with Clemson U, North Carolina State U, and Virginia Polytech Inst. Member of Charlotte Area Educational Consortium. Teacher certification in elementary and secondary education. Certification in specific subject areas. Study abroad in England. ROTC at Davidson Coll. AFROTC at U of North Carolina at Charlotte.
**Honors:** Honors program. Honor societies.
**Academic Assistance:** Nonremedial tutoring.

**STUDENT LIFE. Housing:** All unmarried students under age 21 not living with relatives must live on campus. Women's and men's dorms. School-owned/operated apartments. 80% of students live in college housing.
**Social atmosphere:** Popular student gathering spots are the Student Center, the Cellar, the Pterodactyl, and the Dog Pound. Greeks, the Christian Student Union, and the Fellowship of Christian Athletes are among the influential groups on campus. Fall Fest, Spring Fling, and one annual big-name concert are highlights of the school year. Wingate prides itself on the openness and diversity of its students and social life.
**Services and counseling/handicapped student services:** Placement services. Health service. Counseling services for older students. Personal and psychological counseling. Career and academic guidance services. Religious counseling. Physically disabled student services. Learning disabled services. Tape recorders. Reader services for the blind.
**Campus organizations:** Undergraduate student government. Student newspaper (Weekly Triangle). Literary magazine. Yearbook. TV station. Cheerleaders, color guard, departmental societies, ensembles, literary and outing clubs, student handbook, SGA newsletter, Young Democrats, Young Republicans, UCAN (service club), 42 organizations in all. Three fraternities, no chapter houses; two sororities, no chapter houses. 15% of men join a fraternity. 11% of women join a sorority.
**Religious organizations:** Christian Student Union, Fellowship of Christian Athletes.
**Minority/foreign student organizations:** Black Awareness Club. International Club.

**ATHLETICS. Physical education requirements:** One semester of physical education required.
**Intercollegiate competition:** 20% of students participate. Baseball (M), basketball (M,W), cheerleading (M,W), cross-country (M,W), football (M), golf (M), soccer (M,W), softball (W), tennis (M,W), volleyball (W). Member of NCAA Division II, South Atlantic Conference.
**Intramural and club sports:** 60% of students participate. Intramural basketball, bowling, football, golf, pool, racquetball, softball, swimming, table tennis, tennis, volleyball. Men's club volleyball.

**ADMISSIONS. Academic basis for candidate selection** (in order of priority): Secondary school record, class rank, standardized test scores, school's recommendation, essay.
**Nonacademic basis for candidate selection:** Character and personality and particular talent or ability are emphasized. Extracurricular participation and alumni/ae relationship are important. Geographical distribution is considered.
**Requirements:** Graduation from secondary school is required; GED is accepted. No specific distribution of secondary school units required. Minimum 2.0 GPA required. Conditional admission possible for applicants not meeting standard requirements. SAT is required; ACT may be substituted. Campus visit and interview recommended. Off-campus interviews available with an admissions representative.
**Procedure:** Take SAT or ACT by December of 12th year. Suggest filing application by January. Application deadline is August 15. Notification of admission on rolling basis. Reply is required within 10 days of acceptance. $200 tuition deposit, refundable until May 1. Freshmen accepted in terms other than fall.
**Special programs:** Admission may be deferred one year. Credit and/or placement may be granted through CEEB Advanced Placement exams for scores of 3 or higher. Credit may be granted through CLEP subject exams. Early entrance/early admission program. Concurrent enrollment program.
**Transfer students:** Transfer students accepted for terms other than fall. In fall 1993, 19% of all new students were transfers into all classes. 203 transfer applications were received, 150 were accepted. Application deadline is August 1 for fall; December 15 for spring. Minimum 2.0 GPA required. Lowest course grade accepted is "C." Maximum number of transferable credits is 64 semester hours. At least 30 semester hours must be completed at the college to receive degree.
**Admissions contact:** Christopher J. Keller, M.S., Director of Admissions. 800 755-5550.

**FINANCIAL AID. Available aid:** Pell grants, SEOG, state scholarships and grants, school scholarships and grants, private scholarships and grants, academic merit scholarships, and athletic scholarships. Music and ministerial scholarships. Yearbook, newspaper, and R.A. stipends. PLUS, Stafford Loans (GSL), private loans, and SLS. Tuition Management Systems.
**Financial aid statistics:** 48% of aid is not need-based. In 1993-94, 85% of all undergraduate applicants received aid; 80% of freshman applicants. Average amounts of aid awarded freshmen: Scholarships and grants, $2,800; loans, $2,500.
**Supporting data/closing dates:** FAFSA: Priority filing date is May 1; accepted on rolling basis. School's own aid application: Priority filing date is May 1; accepted on rolling basis. Notification of awards begins February 15.
**Financial aid contact:** Sarah Cousins, Director of Financial Planning. 800 755-5550.

**STUDENT EMPLOYMENT.** College Work/Study Program. Institutional employment. 25% of full-time undergraduates work on campus during school year. Students may expect to earn an average of $1,000 during school year. Off-campus part-time employment opportunities rated "good."

**COMPUTER FACILITIES.** 75 IBM/IBM-compatible and Macintosh/Apple microcomputers. Students may access Hewlett-Packard, IBM minicomputer/mainframe systems. Computer languages and software packages include BASIC, COBOL, Data Structures, FORTRAN, Pascal, SPSS. Computer facilities are available to all students.
**Fees:** None.
**Hours:** 8:30 AM-10 PM (M-Th); 8:30 AM-5 PM (F); 6 PM-10 PM (Su).

**GRADUATE CAREER DATA.** Graduate school percentages: 5% enter law school. 5% enter medical school. 10% enter graduate business programs. 15% enter graduate arts and sciences programs. 2% enter theological school/seminary. Highest graduate school enrollments: U of Virginia, Wake Forest U. 60% of graduates choose careers in business and industry. Companies and businesses that hire graduates: banks, retail stores, hospitals, mental health centers.

**PROMINENT ALUMNI/AE.** Jesse Helms, U.S. senator.

# Winston-Salem State University

**Winston-Salem, NC 27110** — **910 750-2000**

**1994-95 Costs.** Tuition: $1,242 (state residents), $6,606 (out-of-state). Room & board: $2,900. Fees, books, misc. academic expenses (school's estimate): $1,434.
**Enrollment.** Undergraduates: 776 men, 1,293 women (full-time). Freshman class: 1,065 applicants, 922 accepted, 385 enrolled.
**Test score averages/ranges.** Average SAT scores: 369 verbal, 405 math.
**Faculty.** 152 full-time; 26 part-time. 70% of faculty holds doctoral degree. Student/faculty ratio: 15 to 1.
**Selectivity rating.** Less competitive.

**PROFILE.** Winston-Salem State, founded in 1892, is a public, comprehensive university. Its 81-acre campus is located in Winston-Salem.
**Accreditation:** SACS. Professionally accredited by the National Council for Accreditation of Teacher Education, the National League for Nursing.
**Religious orientation:** Winston-Salem State University is nonsectarian; no religious requirements.
**Library:** Collections totaling over 162,358 volumes, 1,125 periodical subscriptions, and 98,185 microform items.
**Special facilities/museums:** Art gallery.
**Athletic facilities:** Gymnasium, swimming pool, basketball courts, tennis courts, track.

**STUDENT BODY. Undergraduate profile:** 93% are state residents; 47% are transfers. .8% Asian-American, 78% Black, .1% Hispanic, .1% Native American, 21% White. Average age of undergraduates is 25.
**Freshman profile:** 2% of freshmen who took SAT scored 500 or over on verbal, 7% scored 500 or over on math; 18% scored 400 or over on verbal, 33% scored 400 or over on math; 70% scored 300 or over on verbal, 83% scored 300 or over on math. 95% of accepted applicants took SAT.
**Undergraduate achievement:** 70% of fall 1992 freshmen returned for fall 1993 term. 11% of entering class graduated.
**Foreign students:** Countries represented include African countries, Bangladesh, China, Pakistan, and the West Indies.

**PROGRAMS OF STUDY. Degrees:** B.A., B.S.
**Majors:** Accounting, Applied Science, Art, Biology, Business Administration, Chemistry, Commercial Music, Computer/Information Sciences, Economics, Elementary Education, English, History, Information Systems Management, Mass Communication, Mathematics, Medical Technology, Middle Grades Education, Music Education, Nursing, Physical Education, Physical Therapy, Political Science/Government, Psychology, Sociology, Spanish, Special Education, Sports Management, Therapeutic Recreation, Urban Affairs.
**Distribution of degrees:** The majors with the highest enrollment are business administration, nursing, and accounting; chemistry, urban affairs, and Spanish have the lowest.

**Requirements:** General education requirement.
**Academic regulations:** Freshmen must maintain minimum 1.50 GPA; seniors, 2.00 GPA.
**Special:** Minors offered in some majors and in black studies, dramatic arts, environmental sciences, French, housing management, Romance languages, sacred music, and social welfare. Certificate program in computer programming. Courses offered in geography, mass communications, philosophy, physics, and religion. Double majors. Dual degrees. Independent study. Internships. Cooperative education programs. Fourth year B.A. or B.S. in Project Strengthen (health-related science programs) allows seniors to spend year in cooperating dental, medical, or graduate school. Member of U of North Carolina Consortium. Teacher certification in early childhood, elementary, secondary, and special education. ROTC.
**Honors:** Phi Beta Kappa. Honors program.
**Academic Assistance:** Nonremedial tutoring.

**STUDENT LIFE. Housing:** Students may live on or off campus. Coed, women's, and men's dorms. 39% of students live in college housing.
**Social atmosphere:** Favorite student gathering spots include the Hauser Student Union and Gaines Gym. Sororities, the National Broadcasting Society, and the Student Government Association influence campus life. Popular events include the Mr. Ram Pageant, the coronation of Miss Winston-Salem State, Homecoming Week, Greek Week, and football and basketball games. The student newspaper reports, "Most social events take place on campus. Winston-Salem Greeks often co-sponsor events with the Greeks at Wake Forest U. We have many diverse cultural programs throughout the year."
**Services and counseling/handicapped student services:** Placement services. Health service. Counseling services for minority, military, and older students. Career and academic guidance services. Physically disabled student services. Tutors.
**Campus organizations:** Undergraduate student government. Student newspaper (News Argus, published once/month). Yearbook. Radio station. Band, stage band, University Singers, male octet, choir, music fraternity, Drama Guild, charm club, Circle K, Ram Beautification Club, departmental groups, 70 organizations in all. Six fraternities, no chapter houses; eight sororities, no chapter houses. 30% of men join a fraternity. 25% of women join a sorority.
**Religious organizations:** Several religious groups.

**ATHLETICS. Physical education requirements:** Four semesters of physical education required.
**Intercollegiate competition:** Basketball (M,W), cross-country (M), football (M), softball (W), tennis (M,W), track and field (M,W), volleyball (W), wrestling (M). Member of CIAA, NCAA Division II.
**Intramural and club sports:** Men's club bowling. Women's club bowling.

**ADMISSIONS. Academic basis for candidate selection** (in order of priority): Secondary school record, class rank, standardized test scores, school's recommendation, essay.
**Nonacademic basis for candidate selection:** Character and personality are important. Extracurricular participation, particular talent or ability, and alumni/ae relationship are considered.
**Requirements:** Graduation from secondary school is required; GED is accepted. No specific distribution of secondary school units required. Minimum combined SAT score of 725, rank in top half of secondary school class, and minimum 1.75 GPA recommended. Algebra I and II, geometry, and 2 units of foreign language required of business, English, history, and science program applicants. Minimum SAT verbal score of 390, grade 11 reading level, completion of university core curriculum with minimum 2.6 GPA, and application by second semester of sophomore year required of nursing program applicants. Audition required of music program applicants. Supplemental Education Program for applicants not normally admissible. Those with academic deficiencies are required to take noncredit courses prior to sophomore year. SAT is required; ACT may be substituted. Campus visit recommended. No off-campus interviews.
**Procedure:** Take SAT or ACT by January of 12th year. Notification of admission on rolling basis. No set date by which applicants must accept offer. $25 room deposit, refundable until August 1. Freshmen accepted in terms other than fall.
**Special programs:** Admission may be deferred one year. Credit and/or placement may be granted through CEEB Advanced Placement exams for scores of 3 or higher. Credit and/or placement may be granted through CLEP general and subject exams. Credit and placement may be granted through challenge exams. Early entrance/early admission program. Concurrent enrollment program.
**Transfer students:** Transfer students accepted for terms other than fall. In fall 1993, 47% of all new students were transfers into all classes. 653 transfer applications were received, 622 were accepted. Application deadline is rolling for fall; rolling for spring. Minimum 2.0 GPA required. Lowest course grade accepted is "C." Maximum number of transferable credits is 64 semester hours from a two-year school and 96 semester hours from a four-year school. At least 30 semester hours must be completed at the university to receive degree.
**Admissions contact:** Van Wilson, Director of Admissions. 910 750-2070.

**FINANCIAL AID. Available aid:** Pell grants, SEOG, Federal Nursing Student Scholarships, state scholarships and grants, school scholarships and grants, private scholarships and grants, ROTC scholarships, academic merit scholarships, and athletic scholarships. Perkins Loans (NDSL), PLUS, Stafford Loans (GSL), state loans, school loans, and private loans. Tuition Plan Inc.
**Financial aid statistics:** 10% of aid is not need-based. In 1993-94, 89% of all undergraduate applicants received aid; 81% of freshman applicants. Average amounts of aid awarded freshmen: Scholarships and grants, $500.
**Supporting data/closing dates:** FAFSA/FAF/FFS: Priority filing date is April 15. School's own aid application: Priority filing date is April 15. Notification of awards begins May 15.
**Financial aid contact:** Theodore Hindsman, Director of Financial Aid. 910 750-3280.

**STUDENT EMPLOYMENT.** College Work/Study Program. Institutional employment. 29% of full-time undergraduates work on campus during school year. Students may expect to earn an average of $600 during school year. Off-campus part-time employment opportunities rated "good."

**COMPUTER FACILITIES.** 57 IBM/IBM-compatible and Macintosh/Apple microcomputers; all are networked. Students may access Digital minicomputer/mainframe systems, BITNET. Computer languages and software packages include BASIC; database, spreadsheet, word processing programs. Computer facilities are available to all students.
**Fees:** $20 computer fee per course.
**Hours:** 8 AM-11 PM (M-Th); 8 AM-5 PM (F-Sa); 1 PM-6 PM (Su).

**GRADUATE CAREER DATA.** Companies and businesses that hire graduates: Wachovia Bank, IBM.

**PROMINENT ALUMNI/AE.** Timmy Newsome, professional football player; Earl "The Pearl" Monroe, professional basketball player; Selma Burke, sculptor.

# North Dakota

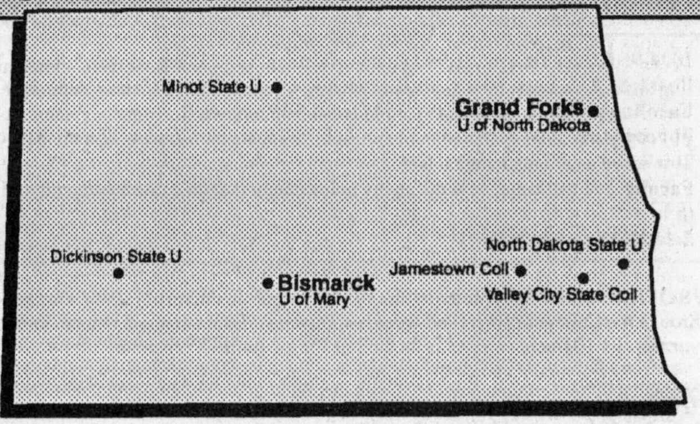


## Dickinson State University

**Dickinson, ND 58601** **800 279-4295**

**1994-95 Costs.** Tuition: $1,680 (state residents), $4,486 (out-of-state). Room & board: $2,150. Fees, books, misc. academic expenses (school's estimate): $777.
**Enrollment.** Undergraduates: 589 men, 789 women (full-time). Freshman class: 434 applicants, 412 accepted, 319 enrolled.
**Test score averages/ranges.** N/A.
**Faculty.** 76 full-time; 31 part-time. 45% of faculty holds doctoral degree. Student/faculty ratio: 18 to 1.
**Selectivity rating.** Noncompetitive.

**PROFILE.** Dickinson State, founded in 1918, is a public university. Programs are offered through the Schools of Arts and Sciences; Business and Administration; Education; Health Sciences; Physical Education and Recreation; Psychology; and Applied Science and Technology. Its 40-acre campus is located in the town of Dickinson, 100 miles from Bismarck.

**Accreditation:** NCACS. Professionally accredited by the National League for Nursing.
**Religious orientation:** Dickinson State University is nonsectarian; no religious requirements.
**Library:** Collections totaling over 80,000 volumes, 678 periodical subscriptions and 272 microform items.
**Special facilities/museums:** Art gallery, audio-visual equipment, language lab.
**Athletic facilities:** Gymnasium, sports hall with indoor track and wrestling/weight room, stadium, outdoor track, indoor rodeo arena.

**STUDENT BODY. Undergraduate profile:** 79% are state residents; 11% are transfers. 1.6% Native American, 95% White, 3.4% Other. Average age of undergraduates is 21.
**Freshman profile:** 1% of accepted applicants took SAT; 99% took ACT. 95% of freshmen come from public schools.
**Undergraduate achievement:** 70% of fall 1992 freshmen returned for fall 1993 term. 10% of students who completed a degree program went on to graduate study within five years.
**Foreign students:** 19 students are from out of the country. Countries represented include Canada, China, and Germany.

**PROGRAMS OF STUDY. Degrees:** B.A., B.S., B.S.Ed., B.S.Nurs., B.Univ.Studies.
**Majors:** Accounting, Art, Art Education, Biology, Business Administration, Business Education, Chemistry, Choral Music, Communication Arts, Communications Education, Composite Science, Computer Science, Elementary Education, English, History, Instrumental Music, Mathematics, Music, Music Education, Nursing, Physical Education, Political Science, Social/Behavioral Science, Social Work, Spanish, Speech, Theatre, University Studies.
**Distribution of degrees:** The majors with the highest enrollment are elementary education, business administration, and secondary education (with various majors); art, social work, and theatre have the lowest.
**Requirements:** General education requirement.
**Academic regulations:** Freshmen must maintain minimum 1.6 GPA; sophomores, 1.75 GPA; juniors, 1.9 GPA; seniors, 2.0 GPA. Minimum GPA required to graduate is 2.0 in major.
**Special:** Minors offered in most majors and in coaching, driver education, earth science, geography, German, journalism, psychology, recreation, science, and sociology. Associate's degrees offered. Self-designed majors. Double majors. Dual degrees. Independent study. Pass/fail grading option. Internships. Cooperative education programs. Preprofessional programs in law, medicine, veterinary science, pharmacy, dentistry, optometry, agriculture, engineering, forestry, medical technology, mortuary science, and wildlife. 2-2 social work program with U of North Dakota. Member of Northern Plains Consortium. Teacher certification in early childhood, elementary, and secondary education. Certification in specific subject areas. Exchange programs abroad in Australia, China, England (Wroxton Coll), Russia, and Saudi Arabia.
**Academic Assistance:** Remedial reading, writing, math, and study skills. Nonremedial tutoring.

**STUDENT LIFE. Housing:** All unmarried students under age 21 with fewer than 64 semester hours must live on campus unless living with family. Coed, women's, and men's dorms. On-campus married-student housing. 25% of students live in college housing.
**Social atmosphere:** The Student Center is a favorite on-campus gathering spot. Popular social and cultural events include Hilltop Holiday, Homecoming, and the production of Handel's *Messiah*.
**Services and counseling/handicapped student services:** Placement services. Health service. Counseling services for older students. Birth control, personal, and psychological counseling. Career and academic guidance services. Religious counseling. Physically disabled student services. Notetaking services. Tape recorders. Tutors. Reader services for the blind.
**Campus organizations:** Undergraduate student government. Student newspaper (Western Concept, published once/two weeks). Literary magazine. Yearbook. Chorale, pop vocal and jazz ensembles, marching and concert bands, art and drama clubs, speech team, rodeo club, business and agriculture clubs, Student Education Association, Student Nurses Association, Student Ambassadors, Young Democrats, 30 organizations in all. Two fraternities, no chapter houses; one sorority, no chapter house. 3% of men join a fraternity. 6% of women join a sorority.
**Religious organizations:** Catholic Student Association, Lutheran Campus Ministry, Navigators, United Ministries of Higher Education.
**Minority/foreign student organizations:** International Student Club.

**ATHLETICS. Physical education requirements:** Two semester hours of physical education required.
**Intercollegiate competition:** 10% of students participate. Baseball (M), basketball (M,W), cheerleading (W), cross-country (M,W), football (M), golf (M,W), tennis (M,W), track (indoor) (M,W), track (outdoor) (M,W), track and field (indoor) (M,W), track and field (outdoor) (M,W), volleyball (W), wrestling (M). Member of NAIA, National Intercollegiate Rodeo Association, North Dakota College Athletic Conference.
**Intramural and club sports:** 8% of students participate. Intramural basketball, football, softball, volleyball.

**ADMISSIONS. Academic basis for candidate selection** (in order of priority): Secondary school record, standardized test scores, class rank, school's recommendation.
**Nonacademic basis for candidate selection:** Character and personality, extracurricular participation, and particular talent or ability are considered.
**Requirements:** Graduation from secondary school is recommended; GED is accepted. 20 units and the following program of study are required: 4 units of English, 3 units of math, 3 units of lab science, 3 units of social studies. Minimum composite ACT score of 18 or minimum 2.0 GPA and secondary school algebra and chemistry required of nursing program applicants. ACT is required; SAT may be substituted. Campus visit and interview recommended. Off-campus interviews available with an admissions representative.
**Procedure:** Take SAT or ACT by January of 12th year. Notification of admission on rolling basis. Reply is required by registration date. $50 room deposit, refundable until August 1. Freshmen accepted in terms other than fall.
**Special programs:** Admission may be deferred indefinitely. Credit may be granted through CLEP general and subject exams.
**Transfer students:** Transfer students accepted for terms other than fall. In fall 1993, 11% of all new students were transfers into all classes. 183 transfer applications were received, 174 were accepted. Minimum 2.0 GPA required. Lowest course grade accepted is "D." At least 32 semester hours must be completed at the university to receive degree.
**Admissions contact:** Marshall Melbye, Director of Admissions/Registrar. 701 227-2175.

**FINANCIAL AID. Available aid:** Pell grants, SEOG, Federal Nursing Student Scholarships, state scholarships and grants, school scholarships, private scholarships, academic merit scholarships, athletic scholarships, and aid for undergraduate foreign students. Perkins Loans (NDSL), PLUS, Stafford Loans (GSL), NSL, Health Professions Loans, and SLS. Alaska state loans.
**Financial aid statistics:** 2% of aid is not need-based. In 1993-94, 95% of all undergraduate applicants received aid; 95% of freshman applicants. Average amounts of aid awarded freshmen: Scholarships and grants, $1,163.
**Supporting data/closing dates:** FAFSA: Priority filing date is April 15. Notification of awards begins in mid June.
**Financial aid contact:** Sandy Klein, Director of Financial Aid. 701 227-2371.

**STUDENT EMPLOYMENT.** College Work/Study Program. Institutional employment. 20% of full-time undergraduates work on campus during school year. Students may expect to earn an average of $900 during school year. Freshmen are discouraged from working during their first term. Off-campus part-time employment opportunities rated "good."

**COMPUTER FACILITIES.** 124 IBM/IBM-compatible and Macintosh/Apple microcomputers; 100 are networked. Students may access IBM minicomputer/mainframe systems. Residence halls may be equipped with stand-alone microcomputers, networked microcomputers. Computer languages and software packages include BASIC, C, COBOL, FORTRAN, Lotus 1-2-3, Open Access, PageMaker, Pascal, Quattro Pro, WordPerfect; 10 in all. Computer facilities are available to all students.
**Fees:** $4.50/computer credit hour.
**Hours:** 7 AM-10 PM (M-F); eight hours/day (Sa-Su).

**GRADUATE CAREER DATA.** Highest graduate school enrollments: Montana State U, North Dakota State U, Northern State U, U of Minnesota, U of North Dakota.

**PROMINENT ALUMNI/AE.** Steve Easton, U.S. Attorney General's office; Al Jaeger, secretary of state, North Dakota; Dr. Erna Yackel, mathematics professor, Purdue U.

# Jamestown College

**Jamestown, ND 58401** **701 252-3467**

**1994-95 Costs.** Tuition: $7,620. Room: $1,380. Board: $1,700. Fees, books, misc. academic expenses (school's estimate): $5.
**Enrollment.** Undergraduates: 486 men, 509 women (full-time). Freshman class: 472 applicants, 410 accepted, 262 enrolled.
**Test score averages/ranges.** Average ACT scores: 20 English, 21 math, 22 composite. Range of ACT scores of middle 50%: 20-24 composite.
**Faculty.** 53 full-time; 19 part-time. 51% of faculty holds doctoral degree. Student/faculty ratio: 18 to 1.
**Selectivity rating.** Less competitive.

PROFILE. Jamestown, founded in 1884, is a church-affiliated, liberal arts college. Its 107-acre campus is located in the city of Jamestown, 100 miles from both Bismarck and Fargo. The campus chapel is listed in the National Register of Historic Places.

**Accreditation:** NCACS. Professionally accredited by the National League for Nursing.
**Religious orientation:** Jamestown College is affiliated with the Presbyterian Church; one semester of religion required.
**Library:** Collections totaling over 86,277 volumes, 332 periodical subscriptions, and 15,830 microform items.
**Athletic facilities:** Gymnasiums, swimming pool, basketball, racquetball, and tennis courts, track, free weight, and Nautilus rooms, batting cage, athletic fields.

**STUDENT BODY. Undergraduate profile:** 64% are state residents; 16% are transfers. 1% Asian-American, 1% Black, 1% Hispanic, 2% Native American, 95% White.
**Freshman profile:** 5% of accepted applicants took SAT; 95% took ACT. 95% of freshmen come from public schools.
**Undergraduate achievement:** 71% of fall 1992 freshmen returned for fall 1993 term. 40% of entering class graduated. 7% of students who completed a degree program immediately went on to graduate study.
**Foreign students:** 79 students are from out of the country. Countries represented include Canada, Japan, and Russia; 12 in all.

**PROGRAMS OF STUDY. Degrees:** B.A.
**Majors:** Accounting, Actuarial Science, Art/Business, Biology, Business Administration, Chemistry, Computer Science, Education, English, Fine Arts, Health/Physical Education/Recreation, History/Political Science, Management Information Science, Mathematics, Music, Nursing, Psychology, Religion/Philosophy.
**Distribution of degrees:** The majors with the highest enrollment are business administration, nursing, and history/political science; chemistry, music, and religion/philosophy have the lowest.
**Requirements:** General education requirement.
**Academic regulations:** Minimum 2.0 GPA required for graduation.
**Special:** Minors offered. Double majors. Independent study. Pass/fail grading option. Internships. Cooperative education programs. Preprofessional programs in law, medicine, veterinary science, pharmacy, dentistry, theology, optometry, engineering, medical technology, and physical therapy. 2-2 engineering programs with North Dakota State U, South Dakota State U, and U of North Dakota. 3-2 engineering program with Washington U. Teacher certification in early childhood, elementary, and secondary education.
**Honors:** Honors program.
**Academic Assistance:** Remedial reading, writing, math, and study skills. Nonremedial tutoring.

**ADMISSIONS. Academic basis for candidate selection** (in order of priority): Secondary school record, standardized test scores, class rank, school's recommendation.
**Nonacademic basis for candidate selection:** Character and personality, extracurricular participation, and particular talent or ability are emphasized. Geographical distribution and alumni/ae relationship are considered.
**Requirements:** Graduation from secondary school is required; GED is accepted. 16 units and the following program of study are recommended: 4 units of English, 2 units of math, 2 units of science, 1 unit of foreign language, 1 unit of social studies. Minimum composite ACT score of 18, rank in top half of secondary school class, and minimum 2.5 GPA required. ACT is recommended; SAT may be substituted. Campus visit and interview recommended. No off-campus interviews.
**Procedure:** Notification of admission on rolling basis. $75 nonrefundable tuition deposit. Freshmen accepted in terms other than fall.
**Special programs:** Admission may be deferred. Credit and/or placement may be granted through CEEB Advanced Placement exams for scores of 3 or higher. Credit and/or placement may be granted through CLEP general and subject exams. Credit may be granted through challenge exams. Early entrance/early admission program. Concurrent enrollment program.
**Transfer students:** Transfer students accepted for terms other than fall. In fall 1993, 16% of all new students were transfers into all classes. 91 transfer applications were received, 80 were accepted. Minimum 2.5 GPA recommended. Lowest course grade accepted is "C."
**Admissions contact:** Carol Schmeichel, M.Ed., Director of Admissions. 701 252-3467.

**FINANCIAL AID. Available aid:** Pell grants, SEOG, state scholarships and grants, school scholarships and grants, private scholarships, academic merit scholarships, and aid for undergraduate foreign students. Perkins Loans (NDSL), PLUS, Stafford Loans (GSL), NSL, and SLS. AMS.
**Financial aid statistics:** In 1993-94, 100% of all undergraduate applicants received aid. Average amounts of aid awarded freshmen: Scholarships and grants, $5,000; loans, $2,500.
**Supporting data/closing dates:** FAFSA: Accepted on rolling basis. Notification of awards on rolling basis.
**Financial aid contact:** Eileen McDaniel, Director of Financial Aid. 701 252-3467.

# Minot State University

**Minot, ND 58707** **701 857-3000**

**1994-95 Costs.** Tuition: $1,960 (state residents), $4,933 (out-of-state). Room: $752. Board: $1,235. Fees, books, misc. academic expenses (school's estimate): $600.
**Enrollment.** Undergraduates: 1,354 men, 1,945 women (full-time). Freshman class: 914 applicants, 904 accepted, 652 enrolled. Graduate enrollment: 11 men, 41 women.
**Test score averages/ranges.** N/A.
**Faculty.** 171 full-time. 44% of faculty holds doctoral degree. Student/faculty ratio: 19 to 1.
**Selectivity rating.** N/A.

PROFILE. Minot State, founded in 1924, is a public university. Programs are offered through the Colleges of Arts and Sciences, Business, Education and Human Services, and Nursing. Its 104-acre campus is located in Minot, north of Bismark.

**Accreditation:** NCACS. Professionally accredited by the American Speech-Language-Hearing Association, the Council on Social Work Education, the National Association of Schools of Music, the National Council for Accreditation of Teacher Education, the National League for Nursing.
**Religious orientation:** Minot State University is nonsectarian; no religious requirements.
**Library:** Collections totaling over 226,933 volumes, 850 periodical subscriptions, and 40,676 microform items.
**Special facilities/museums:** Natural history museum.
**Athletic facilities:** Stadiums, gymnasium.

**STUDENT BODY. Undergraduate profile:** 94% are state residents. 1% Asian-American, 1% Black, 1% Hispanic, 3% Native American, 93% White, 1% Other.
**Undergraduate achievement:** 74% of fall 1992 freshmen returned for fall 1993 term.
**Foreign students:** 10 students are from out of the country. Countries represented include Canada; eight in all.

**PROGRAMS OF STUDY. Degrees:** B.A., B.S., B.S.Ed., B.S.Nurs., B.S.Soc.Work.
**Majors:** Addiction Studies, Art, Biological Science, Broadcasting, Business Administration, Business Education, Chemistry, College Studies, Communication Arts, Communication Disorders, Computer Science, Criminal Justice, Earth Science, Economics, Education of the Deaf, Elementary Education, English, Environmental Science, Foreign Language, Mathematics, Medical Technology, Mental Retardation, Music, Nursing, Physical Education, Physical Sciences, Physics, Psychology, Social Sciences, Social Work, Sociology, X-Ray Technology.
**Distribution of degrees:** The majors with the highest enrollment are business administration, education, social work, and criminal justice.
**Requirements:** General education requirement.
**Academic regulations:** Minimum 2.0 GPA required for graduation.
**Special:** Minors offered in most majors and in coaching, driver/safety education, geography, health education, home economics, Indian studies, philosophy, political science, and Spanish. Correspondence courses. Associate's degrees offered. Self-designed majors. Double majors. Dual degrees. Independent study. Accelerated study. Pass/fail grading option. Internships. Graduate school at which undergraduates may take graduate-level courses. Preprofessional programs in law, medicine, veterinary science, pharmacy, dentistry, optometry, chiropractic, dental hygiene, dietetics, engineering, occupational therapy, and physical therapy. 3-1 medical technology program. Semester-away programs available. Teacher certification in elementary, secondary, and special education. Study abroad possible.
**Honors:** Honors program.
**Academic Assistance:** Nonremedial tutoring.

**STUDENT LIFE. Housing:** Students may live on or off campus. Coed, women's, and men's dorms. School-owned/operated apartments. On-campus married-student housing. 49% of students live in college housing.
**Social atmosphere:** The most popular gathering spot on campus is the student union. Athletes and the Student Association influence campus life. Favorite campus events include Native American Awareness Week, Spring Breakout, Homecoming, Snosations, and movie nights.
**Services and counseling/handicapped student services:** Placement services. Health service. Women's center. Counseling services for minority and older students. Personal and psychological counseling. Career and academic guidance services. Physically disabled student services. Learning disabled services. Notetaking services.
**Campus organizations:** Undergraduate student government. Student newspaper (Red and Green, published once/week). Literary magazine. Yearbook. Radio station. Concert and marching bands, concert choir, choruses, jazz ensemble, madrigal singers, opera, orchestra, wind ensemble, concert and lecture series, Campus Players, departmental, athletic, and political groups, 45 organizations in all.
**Religious organizations:** Student Lutheran Movement, Intervarsity Christian Fellowship, Catholic Student Association.
**Minority/foreign student organizations:** Native American Club. Global Society.

**ATHLETICS. Physical education requirements:** None.
**Intercollegiate competition:** 20% of students participate. Basketball (M,W), cheerleading (W), cross-country (M,W), football (M), golf (M), softball (W), tennis (M,W), track (indoor) (M,W), track (outdoor) (M,W), track and field (indoor) (M,W), track and field (outdoor) (M,W), volleyball (W). Member of NAIA, North Dakota College Athletic Conference.
**Intramural and club sports:** 25% of students participate. Intramural basketball, flag football, racquetball, softball, swimming, tennis, volleyball, walleyball.

**ADMISSIONS. Academic basis for candidate selection** (in order of priority): Secondary school record, standardized test scores.
**Requirements:** Graduation from secondary school is required; GED is accepted. 23 units and the following program of study are required: 4 units of English, 3 units of math, 3 units of lab science, 3 units of social studies, 7 units of electives, of which 6 must be academic. 2

units of foreign language recommended. ACT is required; SAT may be substituted. PSAT is recommended. Campus visit recommended. No off-campus interviews.
**Procedure:** Notification of admission on rolling basis. $100 room deposit, refundable until July 1. Freshmen accepted in terms other than fall.
**Special programs:** Admission may be deferred indefinitely. Credit and/or placement may be granted through CLEP general and subject exams. Concurrent enrollment program.
**Transfer students:** Transfer students accepted for terms other than fall. Application deadline is rolling for fall; rolling for spring. Minimum 2.0 GPA required. Lowest course grade accepted is "D." At least 45 semester hours must be completed at the university to receive degree.
**Admissions contact:** Angela Kirchmeier, Admissions Adviser. 701 857-3350.
**FINANCIAL AID. Available aid:** Pell grants, SEOG, Federal Nursing Student Scholarships, state scholarships and grants, school scholarships, academic merit scholarships, and athletic scholarships. Perkins Loans (NDSL), PLUS, Stafford Loans (GSL), NSL, and SLS. Small emergency loans.
**Financial aid statistics:** In 1993-94, 72% of all undergraduate applicants received aid; 72% of freshman applicants. Average amounts of aid awarded freshmen: Scholarships and grants, $1,450.
**Supporting data/closing dates:** FAFSA: Priority filing date is April 15. Notification of awards on rolling basis.
**Financial aid contact:** Dale Gehring, Director of Financial Aid. 701 857-3375.
**STUDENT EMPLOYMENT.** College Work/Study Program. Institutional employment. 4% of full-time undergraduates work on campus during school year. Students may expect to earn an average of $975 during school year. Off-campus part-time employment opportunities rated "good."
**COMPUTER FACILITIES.** IBM/IBM-compatible and Macintosh/Apple microcomputers. Students may access BITNET, Internet. Computer facilities are available to all students.
**Fees:** None.
**Hours:** 8 AM-10 PM.

# North Dakota State University

**Fargo, ND 58105** **701 237-8011**

**1993-94 Costs.** Tuition: $1,986 (in-state), $2,482 (Minnesota residents), $5,300 (out-of-state, excluding Minnesota residents). Room & board: $2,590. Fees, books, misc. academic expenses (school's estimate): $798.
**Enrollment.** Undergraduates: 4,434 men, 2,989 women (full-time). Freshman class: 3,038 applicants, 2,285 accepted, 1,631 enrolled. Graduate enrollment: 589 men, 375 women.
**Test score averages/ranges.** Average ACT scores: 22 English, 22 math, 22 composite. Range of ACT scores of middle 50%: 18-24 English, 18-25 math.
**Faculty.** 464 full-time; 33 part-time. 87% of faculty holds doctoral degree. Student/faculty ratio: 19 to 1.
**Selectivity rating.** Less competitive.

**PROFILE.** North Dakota State, founded in 1890, is a public university. Programs are offered through the Colleges of Agriculture, Business Administration, Engineering and Architecture, Home Economics, Humanities and Social Sciences, Pharmacy, and University Studies, and the School of Education. Its 2,300-acre campus is located in Fargo.

**Accreditation:** NCACS. Professionally accredited by the Accreditation Board for Engineering and Technology, the American Council on Pharmaceutical Education, the American Dietetic Association, the American Home Economics Association, the National Architecture Accrediting Board, the National Association of Schools of Music, the National Council for Accreditation of Teacher Education, the National League for Nursing.
**Religious orientation:** North Dakota State University is nonsectarian; no religious requirements.
**Library:** Collections totaling over 455,338 volumes, 4,265 periodical subscriptions, and 220,119 microform items.
**Special facilities/museums:** Art gallery, language lab, genetics institute, regional studies institute.
**Athletic facilities:** Field house with facilities for basketball, swimming, wrestling, handball, racquetball, paddleball, indoor skiing instruction, baseball practice, physical education classes and weight training; Astroturf field.
**STUDENT BODY. Undergraduate profile:** 63% are state residents; 56% are transfers. 1% Asian-American, 1% Black, 1% Hispanic, 1% Native American, 96% White. Average age of undergraduates is 23.
**Freshman profile:** Majority of accepted applicants took ACT. 93% of freshmen come from public schools.
**Undergraduate achievement:** 75% of fall 1992 freshmen returned for fall 1993 term. 45% of entering class graduated. 14% of students who completed a degree program went on to graduate study within five years.
**Foreign students:** 73 students are from out of the country. Countries represented include Canada, China, Hong Kong, India, Korea, and Taiwan; 46 in all.
**PROGRAMS OF STUDY. Degrees:** B.A., B.Arch., B.F.A., B.S., B.S.Ed., B.S.Nurs., B.Univ.Studies.
**Majors:** Accounting, Aero Manufacturing Engineering Technology, Agricultural Economics, Agricultural Education, Agricultural Engineering, Agricultural Extension, Agricultural Mechanization, Animal/Range Sciences, Apparel/Textiles, Architecture, Art, Athletic Training, Biological Sciences, Biology, Biotechnology, Botany, Business Administration, Chemistry, Child Development/Family Science, Civil Engineering, Composite Science, Computer Science, Construction Engineering, Construction Management, Construction Technology, Corporate/Community Fitness, Crop/Weed Sciences, Earth Science, Economics, Electrical/Electronics Engineering, Elementary Education, Engineering Physics, English, Entomology, Family Economics, Food/Nutrition, Food Science/Technology, French, General Agriculture, General Home Economics, German, History, Home Economics Education, Horticulture, Hotel/Motel/Restaurant Management, Humanities, Industrial Engineering/Management, Interior Design, International Business, Landscape Architecture, Leisure Studies/Community Recreational Services, Management Information Systems, Mass Communication, Mathematics, Mechanical Engineering, Medical Technology, Microbiology, Microbiology/Bacteriology, Music, Nursing, Pharmacy, Physical Education, Physics, Plant Pathology, Political Science, Psychology, Respiratory Therapy, Secondary Education, Social Sciences, Sociology, Soil Science, Spanish, Speech Communication, Statistics, Theatre Arts, Transportation Engineering, University Studies, Veterinary Technology, Zoology.
**Distribution of degrees:** The majors with the highest enrollment are business administration, electrical/electronics engineering, and pharmacy.
**Requirements:** General education requirement.
**Academic regulations:** Freshmen must maintain minimum 1.60 GPA; sophomores, 1.75 GPA; juniors, 2.00 GPA; seniors, 2.00 GPA.
**Special:** Minors offered in most majors and in geography, gerontology, religion, and women's studies. Self-designed majors. Double majors. Dual degrees. Independent study. Accelerated study. Pass/fail grading option. Internships. Cooperative education programs. Graduate school at which undergraduates may take graduate-level courses. Preprofessional programs in law, medicine, veterinary science, dentistry, optometry, chiropractic, mortuary science, osteopathy, and physical therapy. 2-2 pre-physical therapy program. Member of Tri-College University Consortium. Teacher certification in elementary and secondary education. Certification in specific subject areas. Study abroad possible. ROTC and AFROTC.
**Honors:** Honors program. Honor societies.
**Academic Assistance:** Remedial reading, writing, math, and study skills. Nonremedial tutoring.
**STUDENT LIFE. Housing:** All unmarried freshmen under age 19 must live on campus unless living with family. Coed, women's, and men's dorms. Sorority and fraternity housing. School-owned/operated apartments. Off-campus privately-owned housing. Both on-campus and off-campus married-student housing. 39% of students live in college housing.
**Social atmosphere:** According to the student newspaper, students tend to hang out at the Memorial Union Building, the Bison Turf Pub, and Old Broadway. Greek organizations are influential on campus. Popular campus events include football games, hockey games, Spring Blast Week, and Homecoming.
**Services and counseling/handicapped student services:** Placement services. Health service. Day care. Counseling services for minority, military, veteran, and older students. Birth control, personal, and psychological counseling. Career and academic guidance services. Religious counseling. Physically disabled student services. Learning disabled program/services. Notetaking services. Tape recorders. Tutors. Reader services for the blind.
**Campus organizations:** Undergraduate student government. Student newspaper (Spectrum, published twice/week). Radio station. Concert choir, marching and concert bands, jazz ensemble, Circle K, Student Alumni Association, YMCA, College Democrats, College Republicans, Arnold Air Society, 185 organizations in all. Eight fraternities, all with chapter houses; five sororities, all with chapter houses. 9% of men join a fraternity. 7% of women join a sorority.
**Religious organizations:** Campus Crusade for Christ, First Assembly Campus Ministry, Fellowship of Christian Athletes, Intervarsity Christian Fellowship, Navigators, Newman Center, United Campus Ministry, University Lutheran Center, other religious groups.
**Minority/foreign student organizations:** Native American Student Association. International Student Association, Chinese, Hong Kong, Indian, Korean, Kurdistanian, Latin American, Malaysian, Singapore, and other foreign groups.
**ATHLETICS. Physical education requirements:** Two semesters of physical education required.
**Intercollegiate competition:** 1% of students participate. Baseball (M), basketball (M,W), cross-country (M,W), football (M), golf (M), softball (W), track (indoor) (M,W), track (outdoor) (M,W), track and field (M,W), volleyball (W), wrestling (M). Member of NCAA Division II.
**Intramural and club sports:** Men's club cheerleading. Women's club cheerleading.
**ADMISSIONS.**
**Requirements:** Graduation from secondary school is required; GED is accepted. 13 units and the following program of study are required: 4 units of English, 3 units of math, 3 units of lab science, 3 units of social studies. Minimum composite ACT score of 20 and minimum 2.5 GPA or minimum 2.5 GPA and rank in top half of secondary school class required of applicants deficient in any one of the required core units. Audition required of music program applicants. Minimum math ACT score of 23 or rank in top 30% of secondary school class with minimum math ACT score of 20 required of electrical/electronics engineering program applicants. Rank in top 30% of secondary school class required of mechanical engineering program applicants. Minimum composite ACT score of 22 recommended of architecture program applicants. Conditional admission possible for applicants not meeting standard requirements. ACT is required; SAT may be substituted. Campus visit and interview recommended. Off-campus interviews available with admissions and alumni representatives.
**Procedure:** Take SAT or ACT by April of 12th year. Acceptance notification on rolling basis, within one week of completion of file. No set date by which applicants must accept offer. $50 room deposit, refundable until July 1. Freshmen accepted in terms other than fall.
**Special programs:** Admission may be deferred one year. Credit and/or placement may be granted through CEEB Advanced Placement exams for scores of 3 or higher. Credit may be granted through CLEP general and subject exams, ACT PEP and challenge exams, and military and life experience. Early entrance/early admission program. Concurrent enrollment program.
**Transfer students:** Transfer students accepted for terms other than fall. In fall 1993, 56% of all new students were transfers into all classes. 1,368 transfer applications were received, 1,109 were accepted. Application deadline is rolling for fall; rolling for spring. Minimum 2.0 GPA required. Lowest course grade accepted is "D." At least 30 semester hours must be completed at the university to receive degree.
**Admissions contact:** Carolyn Schnell, M.A., Interim Director of Admission. 701 237-8643, 800 488-NDSU.

**FINANCIAL AID. Available aid:** Pell grants, SEOG, state scholarships and grants, school scholarships, private scholarships, ROTC scholarships, academic merit scholarships, and athletic scholarships. Perkins Loans (NDSL), PLUS, Stafford Loans (GSL), NSL, private loans, and SLS. AMS. Monthly payment plan.
**Financial aid statistics:** 47% of aid is not need-based. In 1993-94, 62% of all undergraduate applicants received aid. Average amounts of aid awarded freshmen: Scholarships and grants, $1,500; loans, $2,000.
**Supporting data/closing dates:** FAFSA: Priority filing date is April 15. Notification of awards begins June 1.
**Financial aid contact:** Wayne Tesmer, Director of Student Financial Aid. 701 237-7533, 800 726-3188.

**STUDENT EMPLOYMENT.** College Work/Study Program. Institutional employment. 17% of full-time undergraduates work on campus during school year. Students may expect to earn an average of $750 during school year. Off-campus part-time employment opportunities rated "excellent."

**COMPUTER FACILITIES.** 2,000 IBM/IBM-compatible, Macintosh/Apple, and RISC-/UNIX-based microcomputers; 1,000 are networked. Students may access Hewlett-Packard, IBM, NCR, SUN minicomputer/mainframe systems, BITNET, Internet. Residence halls may be equipped with stand-alone microcomputers, networked microcomputers. Client/LAN operating systems include Apple/Macintosh, DOS, OS/2, UNIX/XENIX/AIX, Windows NT, Banyan, LocalTalk/AppleTalk, Microsoft, Novell. Computer languages and software packages include Assembler, BASIC, BMDP, COBOL, DISSPLA, FORTRAN, LISP, Modula 2, Pascal, SAS, SimScript, SPSS; 45 in all. Computer facilities are available to all students.
**Fees:** Computer fee is included in tuition/fees.
**Hours:** 24 hours for some.

**GRADUATE CAREER DATA.** Highest graduate school enrollments: North Dakota State U, U of Minnesota, U of North Dakota. 80% of graduates choose careers in business and industry. Companies and businesses that hire graduates: 3M, Boeing, Rockwell International, Hewlett-Packard, Hughes Aircraft.

# University of Mary

**Bismarck, ND 58501-9652 — 701 255-7500**

**1994-95 Costs.** Tuition: $6,490. Room & board: $2,660. Fees, books, misc. academic expenses (school's estimate): $650.
**Enrollment.** Undergraduates: 538 men, 938 women (full-time). Freshman class: 674 applicants, 654 accepted, 350 enrolled. Graduate enrollment: 45 men, 90 women.
**Test score averages/ranges.** Average ACT scores: 20 English, 20 math, 21 composite. Range of ACT scores of middle 50%: 17-23 English, 17-23 math.
**Faculty.** 75 full-time; 43 part-time. 31% of faculty holds doctoral degree. Student/faculty ratio: 17 to 1.
**Selectivity rating.** Less competitive.

**PROFILE.** The University of Mary, founded in 1959, is a church-affiliated institution. Programs are offered through the Divisions of Business Administration, Education, Humanities, Mathematics and Natural Sciences, Nursing, Philosophy and Theology, and Social and Behavioral Sciences. Its 180-acre campus is located seven miles from downtown Bismarck. The campus, completed in 1969, contains buildings designed by Marcel Breuer.

**Accreditation:** NCACS. Professionally accredited by the Council on Social Work Education, the National League for Nursing.
**Religious orientation:** University of Mary is affiliated with the Roman Catholic Church (Benedictine Sisters); no religious requirements.
**Library:** Collections totaling over 52,000 volumes, 500 periodical subscriptions, and 2,500 microform items.
**Special facilities/museums:** Art gallery.
**Athletic facilities:** Gymnasium, swimming pool, fitness center, sauna, training, weight, and wrestling rooms, basketball, racquetball, and tennis courts, track, football and softball fields.

**STUDENT BODY. Undergraduate profile:** 79% are state residents. 1% Asian-American, 1% Black, 1% Hispanic, 3% Native American, 93% White, 1% Other. Average age of undergraduates is 23.
**Freshman profile:** 1% of freshmen who took ACT scored 30 or over on English, 3% scored 30 or over on math, 1% scored 30 or over on composite; 21% scored 24 or over on English, 20% scored 24 or over on math, 23% scored 24 or over on composite; 66% scored 18 or over on English, 65% scored 18 or over on math, 77% scored 18 or over on composite; 93% scored 12 or over on English, 92% scored 12 or over on math, 94% scored 12 or over on composite; 94% scored 6 or over on English, 93% scored 6 or over on math. 2% of accepted applicants took SAT; 93% took ACT. 90% of freshmen come from public schools.
**Undergraduate achievement:** 71% of fall 1992 freshmen returned for fall 1993 term. 35% of entering class graduated. 5% of students who completed a degree program immediately went on to graduate study.
**Foreign students:** 18 students are from out of the country. Countries represented include Canada, China, and India.

**PROGRAMS OF STUDY. Degrees:** B.A., B.S., B.Univ.Studies.
**Majors:** Accounting, Addiction Counseling, Athletic Training, Biology, Business Administration, Christian Ministry, Communications, Computer Information Systems, Early Childhood Education, Elementary Education, English, Mathematics, Mathematics/Science Composite, Medical Technology, Music, Nursing, Physical Education, Radiologic Technology, Respiratory Care, Social/Behavioral Science, Social Work, Special Education.
**Distribution of degrees:** The majors with the highest enrollment are nursing, business administration, and elementary education; communications, mathematics, and Christian ministry have the lowest.
**Requirements:** General education requirement.
**Academic regulations:** Minimum 2.0 GPA must be maintained.
**Special:** Minors offered in many majors and in business communications, coaching, French, German, health education, history, Indian studies, philosophy, philosophy/theology, psychology, public relations, religious education, secondary education, sociology, Spanish, and theology. Career-oriented areas of emphasis in broadcasting, emergency care, energy management, financial institutions management, health administration, health education, hotel/motel management, and management information systems; classes during May term, internships during summer session. Associate's degrees offered. Double majors. Independent study. Internships. Cooperative education programs. Graduate school at which undergraduates may take graduate-level courses. Preprofessional programs in law, medicine, veterinary science, pharmacy, dentistry, and optometry. 2-2 radiological technology and respiratory care programs. 3-1 medical technology program. Teacher certification in early childhood, elementary, secondary, and special education. Study abroad in England, France, Germany, and Spain. Broadcasting program in London with Catholic Radio & Television Centre.
**Honors:** Honors program. Honor societies.
**Academic Assistance:** Remedial writing, math, and study skills.

**STUDENT LIFE. Housing:** All freshmen and sophomores must live on campus unless living with family. Women's and men's dorms. School-owned/operated apartments. 40% of students live in college housing.
**Services and counseling/handicapped student services:** Placement services. Health service. Women's center. Counseling services for minority, veteran, and older students. Personal counseling. Career and academic guidance services. Religious counseling. Physically disabled student services. Learning disabled services. Tutors.
**Campus organizations:** Undergraduate student government. Student newspaper (Summit, published once/month). Yearbook. Radio and TV stations. Concert band and choir, jazz band, University Singers, various small ensembles, Circle K, forensics, ski club, academic, professional, and special-interest groups.
**Religious organizations:** Campus Ministry.
**Minority/foreign student organizations:** Sacred Hoop Club.

**ATHLETICS. Physical education requirements:** None.
**Intercollegiate competition:** 23% of students participate. Basketball (M,W), cross-country (M,W), football (M), softball (W), tennis (M,W), track (indoor) (M,W), track (outdoor) (M,W), track and field (indoor) (M,W), track and field (outdoor) (M,W), volleyball (W), wrestling (M). Member of NAIA, North Dakota Collegiate Athletic Conference.
**Intramural and club sports:** 18% of students participate. Intramural archery, basketball, billiards, bowling, flag football, frisbee, handball, Nordic skiing, racquetball, sledding, softball, table tennis, tennis, track, turkey run, volleyball, walleyball, water basketball.

**ADMISSIONS. Academic basis for candidate selection** (in order of priority): Secondary school record, standardized test scores, class rank, school's recommendation.
**Requirements:** Graduation from secondary school is required; GED is accepted. No specific distribution of secondary school units required. Minimum composite ACT score of 18, rank in top half of secondary school class, and minimum 2.5 GPA recommended. Audition required of music program applicants. Conditional admission possible for applicants not meeting standard requirements. ACT is required; SAT may be substituted. PSAT is recommended. Campus visit recommended. Off-campus interviews available with an admissions representative.
**Procedure:** Take SAT or ACT by June of 12th year. Application deadline is August 15. Notification of admission on rolling basis. No set date by which applicants must accept offer. $50 room deposit, refundable until August 1. Freshmen accepted in terms other than fall.
**Special programs:** Admission may be deferred one year. Credit may be granted through CLEP general and subject exams, ACT PEP and challenge exams, and military and life experience. Early entrance/early admission program.
**Transfer students:** Transfer students accepted for terms other than fall. In fall 1993, 346 transfer applications were received, 343 were accepted. Application deadline is August 15 for fall; December 15 for spring. Minimum 2.0 GPA recommended. Lowest course grade accepted is "D." Maximum number of transferable credits is 64 semester hours. At least 32 semester hours must be completed at the university to receive degree.
**Admissions contact:** Steph Storey, Director of Admissions. 701 255-7500, extension 329.

**FINANCIAL AID. Available aid:** Pell grants, SEOG, state scholarships and grants, school scholarships and grants, private scholarships, academic merit scholarships, athletic scholarships, and aid for undergraduate foreign students. Perkins Loans (NDSL), PLUS, Stafford Loans (GSL), NSL, and SLS. Family tuition reduction.
**Financial aid statistics:** In 1993-94, 89% of all undergraduate applicants received aid; 91% of freshman applicants. Average amounts of aid awarded freshmen: Scholarships and grants, $3,200; loans, $2,900.
**Supporting data/closing dates:** FAFSA/FAF/FFS: Accepted on rolling basis. School's own aid application: Accepted on rolling basis. Notification of awards on rolling basis.
**Financial aid contact:** Sr. Rosanne Zastoupil, Director of Financial Aid. 701 255-7500, extension 383.

**STUDENT EMPLOYMENT.** College Work/Study Program. Institutional employment. 18% of full-time undergraduates work on campus during school year. Students may expect to earn an average of $975 during school year. Off-campus part-time employment opportunities rated "good."

**COMPUTER FACILITIES.** 56 IBM/IBM-compatible and Macintosh/Apple microcomputers; 21 are networked. Students may access IBM minicomputer/mainframe systems. Client/LAN operating systems include Apple/Macintosh, DOS, UNIX/XENIX/AIX. Computer languages and software packages include COBOL, RPG, UNIX; 10 in all. Computer facilities are available to all students.
**Fees:** $20 computer fee per semester.
**Hours:** 7 AM-midn.

**GRADUATE CAREER DATA.** Graduate school percentages: 1% enter medical school. 1% enter dental school. 1% enter graduate business programs. 1% enter graduate arts and sciences programs. 1% enter theological school/seminary. Highest graduate school enrollments: Iowa, Minnesota, North Dakota, and Wisconsin public institutions. 40% of graduates choose careers in business and industry.

**PROMINENT ALUMNI/AE.** Greg Nelson, composer, arranger, and recorder of spiritual music.

# University of North Dakota

**Grand Forks, ND 58202-8172 701 777-4463**

**1994-95 Costs.** Tuition: $2,428 (state residents), $5,952 (out-of-state). Room: $1,033. Board: $1,670. Fees, books, misc. academic expenses (school's estimate): $600.

**Enrollment.** Undergraduates: 4,466 men, 3,868 women (full-time). Freshman class: 2,777 applicants, 2,249 accepted, 1,652 enrolled. Graduate enrollment: 596 men, 773 women.

**Test score averages/ranges.** Average SAT scores: 465 verbal, 535 math. Range of SAT scores of middle 50%: 390-510 verbal, 460-610 math. Average ACT scores: 22 English, 22 math, 23 composite. Range of ACT scores of middle 50%: 18-24 English, 18-25 math.

**Faculty.** 481 full-time; 93 part-time. 57% of faculty holds doctoral degree. Student/faculty ratio: 17 to 1.

**Selectivity rating.** Less competitive.

**PROFILE.** The University of North Dakota, founded in 1883, is a public university. Programs are offered through the Center for Aerospace Sciences and Teaching and Learning; the Colleges of Arts and Sciences, Business and Public Administration, Engineering and Mines, Fine Arts, Human Resources Development, and Nursing; and the School of Medicine. Its 508-acre campus is located in Grand Forks, in the center of the Red River Valley.

**Accreditation:** NCACS. Professionally accredited by the Accreditation Board for Engineering and Technology, the American Assembly of Collegiate Schools of Business, the American Dietetic Association, the American Home Economics Association, the American Medical Association (CAHEA), the American Physical Therapy Association, the American Psychological Association, the Council on Social Work Education, the National Association of Schools of Art and Design, the National Association of Schools of Music, the National Council for Accreditation of Teacher Education, the National League for Nursing.

**Religious orientation:** University of North Dakota is nonsectarian; no religious requirements.

**Library:** Collections totaling over 1,200,000 volumes, 8,673 periodical subscriptions, and 2,257,965 microform items.

**Special facilities/museums:** Art gallery, fine arts center, mining/mineral resources research institute/energy research center, remote sensing institute, aviation facilities, meteorology data center.

**Athletic facilities:** Field house, ice rink, stadium, golf course, sports center, basketball, racquetball, and tennis courts, weight rooms, athletic fields, track, swimming pool.

**STUDENT BODY. Undergraduate profile:** 63% are state residents; 34% are transfers. 1% Asian-American, 1% Black, 1% Hispanic, 3% Native American, 91% White, 3% Other. Average age of undergraduates is 23.

**Freshman profile:** 3% of freshmen who took SAT scored 700 or over on verbal, 8% scored 700 or over on math; 10% scored 600 or over on verbal, 30% scored 600 or over on math; 32% scored 500 or over on verbal, 62% scored 500 or over on math; 75% scored 400 or over on verbal, 87% scored 400 or over on math; 98% scored 300 or over on verbal, 94% scored 300 or over on math. Majority of accepted applicants took ACT.

**Undergraduate achievement:** 78% of fall 1992 freshmen returned for fall 1993 term. 43% of entering class graduated.

**Foreign students:** 394 students are from out of the country. Countries represented include Canada, China, India, Norway, Saudi Arabia, and Taiwan; 44 in all.

**PROGRAMS OF STUDY. Degrees:** B.A., B.Acct., B.Bus.Admin., B.F.A., B.Mus., B.Pub.Admin., B.S., B.S.Ed., B.S.Med.Tech., B.S.Nurs.

**Majors:** Accounting, Advertising, Aeronautical Studies, Air Traffic Control Operations, Aircraft Systems Management, Airport Administration, Airway Computer Sciences, Airway Science, Airway Science Management, American Studies, Anthropology, Athletic Training, Aviation Administration, Banking/Finance, Biology, Broadcasting, Chemical Engineering, Chemistry, Civil Engineering, Classical Languages, Communication Disorders, Community Dietetics, Computer Science, Criminal Justice Studies, Cytotechnology, Early Childhood Education, Earth Science, Economics, Electrical Engineering, Elementary Education, Engineering Management, Engineering Physics, English, English/Theatre Arts, Environmental Geology/Technology, Fishery/Wildlife Management, French, General Management, Geography, Geological Engineering, Geology, German, History, Home Economics Education, Indian Studies, Industrial Technology, Information Management, International Studies, Journalism, Languages, Latin, Marketing, Mathematics, Mechanical Engineering, Medical Technology, Meteorological Studies, Middle School/Junior High Education, Music, Music Education, Music Performance, Natural Science, Norwegian, Nursing, Occupational Therapy, Peace Studies, Philosophy, Philosophy/Religion, Physical Education, Physical Sciences, Physical Therapy, Physics, Political Science, Psychology, Public Administration, Public Relations, Recreation, Religion, Russian/Soviet Studies, Secondary Education, Social Sciences, Social Work, Sociology, Spanish, Special Education, Speech, Textiles/Clothing/Merchandising, Theatre Arts, Visual Arts.

**Distribution of degrees:** The majors with the highest enrollment are business, accounting, and aerospace sciences; American studies, religious studies, and earth science have the lowest.

**Requirements:** General education requirement.

**Academic regulations:** Minimum 2.0 GPA must be maintained.

**Special:** Minors offered in most majors and in aerospace studies, athletic coaching, ceramics, intellectual history, and professional flight. Integrated studies program. Self-designed majors. Double majors. Dual degrees. Independent study. Accelerated study. Pass/fail grading option. Internships. Cooperative education programs. Graduate school at which undergraduates may take graduate-level courses. Preprofessional programs in law, medicine, veterinary science, dentistry, optometry, and mortuary science. Member of Western Interstate Commission for Higher Education (WICHE). Teacher certification in early childhood, elementary, secondary, and special education. Member of International Student Exchange Program (ISEP). Study abroad also in Canada, Costa Rica, Norway, and 36 other countries. ROTC.

**Honors:** Honors program. Honor societies.

**Academic Assistance:** Nonremedial tutoring.

**STUDENT LIFE. Housing:** Students may live on or off campus. Coed, women's, and men's dorms. Sorority and fraternity housing. School-owned/operated apartments. Off-campus privately-owned housing. Both on-campus and off-campus married-student housing. 35% of students live in college housing.

**Services and counseling/handicapped student services:** Placement services. Health service. Women's center. Day care. Tutoring, Learning Center. Counseling services for minority, military, veteran, and older students. Birth control, personal, and psychological counseling. Career and academic guidance services. Physically disabled student services. Learning disabled program/services. Notetaking services. Tape recorders. Tutors. Reader services for the blind.

**Campus organizations:** Undergraduate student government. Student newspaper (Dakota Student, published twice/week). Radio station. Academic, political, professional, service, and special-interest groups, 196 organizations in all. 17 fraternities, 16 chapter houses; seven sororities, all with chapter houses. 12% of men join a fraternity. 8% of women join a sorority.

**Religious organizations:** Campus Crusade for Christ, Campus Ministry International, Christian Dental and Medical Society, Christian Legal Society, Conquerors in Christ, Free Church College Fellowship, Grace University Ministries, Intervarsity Christian Fellowship, Jewish Student Organization, Latter-Day Saints Student Association, Maranatha Campus Advent, Muslim Student Association, Newman Center.

**Minority/foreign student organizations:** American Native Student Association, Black Student Organization, Hispanic American Council. International Student Organization, African, Chinese, and Indian groups.

**ATHLETICS. Physical education requirements:** None.

**Intercollegiate competition:** 4% of students participate. Baseball (M), basketball (M,W), cheerleading (M,W), cross-country (M,W), diving (M,W), football (M), golf (M), ice hockey (M), softball (W), swimming (M,W), track (indoor) (M,W), track (outdoor) (M,W), track and field (indoor) (M,W), track and field (outdoor) (M,W), volleyball (W), wrestling (M). Member of NCAA Division I for ice hockey, NCAA Division II, North Central Conference, WCHA.

**Intramural and club sports:** 40% of students participate. Intramural basketball, football, rugby, soccer, softball, tennis, volleyball.

**ADMISSIONS. Academic basis for candidate selection** (in order of priority): Secondary school record, class rank, standardized test scores, school's recommendation, essay.

**Nonacademic basis for candidate selection:** Character and personality, extracurricular participation, and particular talent or ability are important.

**Requirements:** Graduation from secondary school is required; GED is accepted. 16 units and the following program of study are required: 4 units of English, 3 units of math, 3 units of science including 2 units of lab, 3 units of social studies. Minimum composite ACT score of 17 and completion of secondary school core curriculum required. Admissions appeal possible for applicants not meeting standard requirements. ACT is required; SAT may be substituted. Campus visit and interview recommended. Off-campus interviews available with an admissions representative.

**Procedure:** Take SAT or ACT by April of 12th year. Suggest filing application by March 1. Application deadline is July 1. Notification of admission on rolling basis. No set date by which applicants must accept offer. $25 nonrefundable room deposit. Freshmen accepted in terms other than fall.

**Special programs:** Admission may be deferred one year. Credit and/or placement may be granted through CEEB Advanced Placement exams for scores of 3 or higher. Credit may be granted through CLEP subject exams. Credit and placement may be granted through ACT PEP and challenge exams and military experience. Early entrance/early admission program. Concurrent enrollment program.

**Transfer students:** Transfer students accepted for terms other than fall. In fall 1993, 34% of all new students were transfers into all classes. 1,378 transfer applications were received, 1,198 were accepted. Application deadline is July 1 for fall; November 15 for spring. Minimum 2.0 GPA required. Lowest course grade accepted is "D." No limit on number of credits that may be transferred, but minimum of 60 credits must be completed at a four-year college. At least 30 semester hours must be completed at the university to receive degree.

**Admissions contact:** Alice Poehls, Ph.D., Interim Director of Admissions/Records. 701 777-3821.

**FINANCIAL AID. Available aid:** Pell grants, SEOG, Federal Nursing Student Scholarships, state scholarships and grants, school scholarships, private scholarships, ROTC scholarships, academic merit scholarships, athletic scholarships, and aid for undergraduate foreign students. Perkins Loans (NDSL), PLUS, Stafford Loans (GSL), Unsubsidized Stafford Loans, NSL, Health Professions Loans, state loans, school loans, private loans, and SLS. AMS and deferred payment plan. Payment by credit card.

**Financial aid statistics:** 22% of aid is not need-based. In 1993-94, 46% of all undergraduate applicants received aid; 60% of freshman applicants. Average amounts of aid awarded freshmen: Scholarships and grants, $1,326; loans, $1,611.

**Supporting data/closing dates:** FAFSA: Priority filing date is April 15; accepted on rolling basis. Notification of awards begins in late May.

**Financial aid contact:** Gerald Hamerlik, Ed.D., Director of Financial Aid. 701 777-3121.

**STUDENT EMPLOYMENT.** College Work/Study Program. Institutional employment. 10% of full-time undergraduates work on campus during school year. Students may expect to earn an average of $1,350 during school year. Off-campus part-time employment opportunities rated "good."

**COMPUTER FACILITIES.** 3,500 IBM/IBM-compatible and Macintosh/Apple microcomputers; 600 are networked. Students may access AT&T, Cray, Digital, IBM, UNISYS minicomputer/mainframe systems, BITNET, Internet. Residence halls may be equipped with stand-alone microcomputers, networked microcomputers, modems. Client/

LAN operating systems include Apple/Macintosh, DOS, UNIX/XENIX/AIX, LocalTalk/AppleTalk, Novell. Computer languages and software packages include Ada, Assembler, C, CICS, COBOL, FORTRAN, Modula 2, Natural, PL/1, SAS, SPSS-X; 20 in all. Computer facilities are available to all students.
**Fees:** None.
**Hours:** 24 hours in some locations.

**GRADUATE CAREER DATA.** Companies and businesses that hire graduates: Big Six accounting firms, Boeing, Cargill, Honeywell, Hutchinson Technology, IBM, Iowa Electric, Kennedy & Coe, Koch Industries, McGladrey & Pullen, Norwest Bank, Rockwell, State Farm Insurance, Target, 3M.

**PROMINENT ALUMNI/AE.** James Olson, chairperson of the board, AT&T; Gen. David Jones, former chairman, Joint Chiefs of Staff; Carl Ben Eillson, Arctic aviator; Thomas Barger, former president, Aramco Oil.

# Valley City State University

**Valley City, ND 58072-4098 — 701 845-7990**

**1994-95 Costs.** Tuition: $1,680 (state residents), $4,486 (out-of-state). Room: $790. Board: $1,870. Fees, books, misc. academic expenses (school's estimate): $809.
**Enrollment.** Undergraduates: 448 men, 555 women (full-time). Freshman class: 322 applicants, 322 accepted, 209 enrolled.
**Test score averages/ranges.** Average ACT scores: 19 English, 20 math, 20 composite. Range of ACT scores of middle 50%: 19-24 composite.
**Faculty.** 54 full-time; 14 part-time. 39% of faculty holds doctoral degree. Student/faculty ratio: 15 to 1.
**Selectivity rating.** Noncompetitive.

**PROFILE.** Valley City State, founded in 1890, is a public, comprehensive university. Programs are offered in the Divisions of Business; Communication Arts and Social Science; Education and Psychology; Fine Arts; Health and Physical Education; and Mathematics, Science, and Technology. Its 55-acre campus is located in Valley City, 58 miles west of Fargo.
**Accreditation:** NCACS. Professionally accredited by the National Council for Accreditation of Teacher Education.
**Religious orientation:** Valley City State University is nonsectarian; no religious requirements.
**Library:** Collections totaling over 85,877 volumes, 409 periodical subscriptions, and 29,159 microform items.
**Special facilities/museums:** Art gallery, planetarium.
**Athletic facilities:** Gymnasium, field house, racquetball courts, swimming pool, track, athletic field.

**STUDENT BODY. Undergraduate profile:** 87% are state residents; 27% are transfers. 1% Black, 1% Hispanic, 1% Native American, 97% White. Average age of undergraduates is 20.
**Freshman profile:** 11% of freshmen who took ACT scored 24 or over on English, 12% scored 24 or over on math, 11% scored 24 or over on composite; 36% scored 18 or over on English, 32% scored 18 or over on math, 39% scored 18 or over on composite; 52% scored 12 or over on English, 53% scored 12 or over on math, 53% scored 12 or over on composite; 54% scored 6 or over on English, 54% scored 6 or over on math, 54% scored 6 or over on composite. Majority of accepted applicants took ACT. 93% of freshmen come from public schools.
**Undergraduate achievement:** 64% of fall 1991 freshmen returned for fall 1992 term. 18% of entering class graduated. 5% of students completing a degree program immediately went on to graduate study.
**Foreign students:** 40 students are from out of the country. Countries represented include Canada and Mexico; four in all.

**PROGRAMS OF STUDY. Degrees:** B.A., B.S., B.S.Ed., B.Univ.Studies.
**Majors:** Art, Art Education, Biology, Biology Education, Business Administration, Business Education, Chemistry, Chemistry Education, Computer Information Systems, Elementary Education, English, English Education, Health Education, History, History Education, Human Resources, Industrial Technology, Mathematics, Mathematics Education, Music, Music Education, Office Administration/Management, Physical Education, Science Education, Social Science, Social Science Education, Spanish, Spanish Education, Technology Education.
**Distribution of degrees:** The majors with the highest enrollment are elementary education, business administration, and physical education; art and Spanish have the lowest.
**Requirements:** General education requirement.
**Academic regulations:** Freshmen must maintain minimum 1.6 GPA; sophomores, 1.8 GPA; juniors, 2.0 GPA; seniors, 2.0 GPA.
**Special:** Minors offered. Self-designed majors. Double majors. Independent study. Accelerated study. Internships. Preprofessional programs in law, medicine, veterinary science, pharmacy, dentistry, optometry, engineering, mortuary science, nursing, physical therapy, and social work. Teacher certification in elementary and secondary education. Certification in specific subject areas.
**Academic Assistance:** Remedial reading, writing, math, and study skills. Nonremedial tutoring.

**ADMISSIONS. Academic basis for candidate selection** (in order of priority): Secondary school record, class rank.
**Requirements:** Graduation from secondary school is required; GED is accepted. No specific distribution of secondary school units required. Conditional admission possible for applicants not meeting standard requirements. ACT is required; SAT may be substituted. Campus visit recommended.
**Procedure:** Take SAT or ACT by June 30 of 12th year. Application deadline is the last day of registration. Notification of admission on rolling basis. $50 room deposit, refundable until 30 days before registration. Freshmen accepted in terms other than fall.
**Special programs:** Credit may be granted through CLEP general and subject exams, military and life experience. Placement may be granted through challenge exams. Early entrance/early admission program. Concurrent enrollment program.
**Transfer students:** Transfer students accepted for terms other than fall. In fall 1992, 27% of all new students were transfers into all classes. 107 transfer applications were received, 104 were accepted. Application deadline is the last day of registration for fall; the last day of registration for spring. Lowest course grade accepted is "D." At least 24 semester hours must be completed at the university to receive degree.
**Admissions contact:** Monte Johnson, Director of Admission. 701 845-7101.

**FINANCIAL AID. Available aid:** Pell grants, SEOG, state scholarships and grants, school scholarships, private scholarships and grants, academic merit scholarships, athletic scholarships, and aid for undergraduate foreign students. Perkins Loans (NDSL), PLUS, Stafford Loans (GSL), school loans, and SLS.
**Financial aid statistics:** 10% of aid is not need-based. In 1992-93, 84% of all undergraduate applicants received aid; 94% of freshman applicants. Average amounts of aid awarded freshmen: Scholarships and grants, $1,695; loans, $1,578.
**Supporting data/closing dates:** FAFSA/FAF/FFS: Priority filing date is April 15; accepted on rolling basis. Notification of awards on rolling basis.
**Financial aid contact:** Betty Schumacher, Director of Student Financial Aid. 701 845-7412.

# Ohio

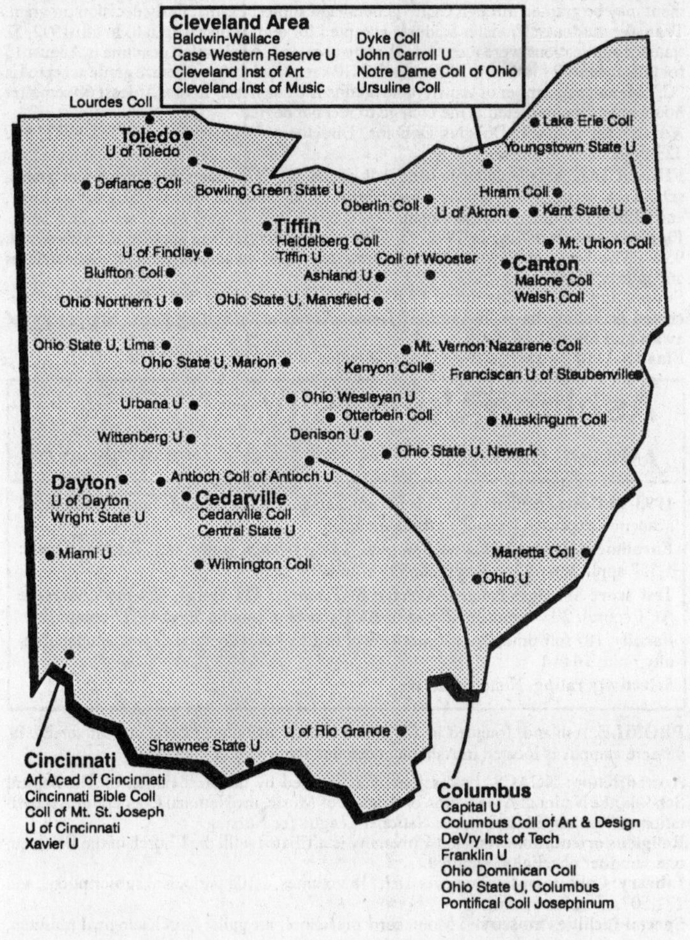


# Antioch College of Antioch University

**Yellow Springs, OH 45387** **513 767-7331**

**1993-94 Costs.** Tuition: $14,740. Room: $1,464. Board: $1,712. Fees, books, misc. academic expenses (school's estimate): $1,702.
**Enrollment.** Undergraduates: 256 men, 456 women (full-time). Freshman class: 568 applicants, 532 accepted, 185 enrolled.
**Test score averages/ranges.** Average SAT scores: 520 verbal, 500 math. Range of SAT scores of middle 50%: 460-580 verbal, 420-580 math. Average ACT scores: 24 English, 21 math, 24 composite. Range of ACT scores of middle 50%: 21-27 English, 17-24 math.
**Faculty.** 62 full-time; 30 part-time. 68% of faculty holds highest degree in specific field. Student/faculty ratio: 13 to 1.
**Selectivity rating.** Competitive.

**PROFILE.** Antioch is a private, liberal arts college. Founded in 1852, it gained university status in 1978. Its 100-acre campus is located in Yellow Springs, 18 miles east of Dayton; the college's 1,000-acre nature preserve is adjacent to the campus.

**Accreditation:** NCACS.
**Religious orientation:** Antioch College of Antioch University is nonsectarian; no religious requirements.
**Library:** Collections totaling over 273,250 volumes, 1,059 periodical subscriptions, and 45,603 microform items.
**Special facilities/museums:** 1,000-acre nature preserve.
**Athletic facilities:** Basketball, racquetball, tennis, and volleyball courts, swimming pool, weight room, outdoor fields.

**STUDENT BODY. Undergraduate profile:** 19% are state residents; 25% are transfers. 2% Asian-American, 9% Black, 4% Hispanic, 1% Native American, 82% White, 2% Other. Average age of undergraduates is 21.
**Freshman profile:** 2% of freshmen who took SAT scored 700 or over on verbal, 1% scored 700 or over on math; 21% scored 600 or over on verbal, 20% scored 600 or over on math; 60% scored 500 or over on verbal, 55% scored 500 or over on math; 89% scored 400 or over on verbal, 81% scored 400 or over on math; 99% scored 300 or over on verbal, 97% scored 300 or over on math. 10% of freshmen who took ACT scored 30 or over on English, 2% scored 30 or over on math, 7% scored 30 or over on composite; 54% scored 24 or over on English, 30% scored 24 or over on math, 48% scored 24 or over on composite; 89% scored 18 or over on English, 67% scored 18 or over on math, 94% scored 18 or over on composite; 99% scored 12 or over on English, 99% scored 12 or over on math, 99% scored 12 or over on composite; 100% scored 6 or over on English, 100% scored 6 or over on math, 100% scored 6 or over on composite. 64% of accepted applicants took SAT; 41% took ACT.
**Undergraduate achievement:** 75% of fall 1992 freshmen returned for fall 1993 term. 28% of entering class graduated.
**Foreign students:** Two students are from out of the country. Countries represented include Germany and Japan.

**PROGRAMS OF STUDY. Degrees:** B.A., B.S.
**Majors:** African/African-American Studies, Anthropology/Sociology, Biology, Chemistry, Communications/Media Arts, Economics, Education Studies, Environmental Science/Studies, History, International Languages/Cultures, International Relations/Peace Studies, Literature/Creative Writing, Management, Mathematics/Computer Science, Music, Peace Studies, Performing Arts, Philosophy, Physics, Political Science, Pre-Medicine, Psychology, Theatre, Visual Arts, Women's Studies.
**Distribution of degrees:** The majors with the highest enrollment are communication, biology, and visual arts; education and philosophy have the lowest.
**Requirements:** General education requirement.
**Special:** Off-campus education including jobs, apprenticeships, and research assistantships required of all students. Cooperative plan alternates on- and off-campus quarters on a year-round calendar; about two-thirds of students are on campus at one time. Self-designed majors. Double majors. Dual degrees. Independent study. Graduate school at which undergraduates may take graduate-level courses. Preprofessional programs in medicine. 3-2 engineering program with Washington U. Member of Great Lakes Colleges Association and Southwestern Ohio Council for Higher Education; joint education programs possible. Arts Program in New York, Newberry Library Program in the Humanities (Illinois), Oak Ridge Science Semester (Tennessee), and Philadelphia Urban Semester. Teacher certification in elementary and secondary education. Certification in specific subject areas. Study abroad in Brazil, China, Colombia, Egypt, England, Germany, Hong Kong, India, Israel, Japan, Kenya, Liberia, the Netherlands, Poland, Scotland, Sierra Leone, the former Soviet Republics, and the former Yugoslav Republics.
**Academic Assistance:** Remedial writing and math.

**STUDENT LIFE. Housing:** All first-year students must live on campus. Coed dorms. Substance-free housing. 95% of students live in college housing.
**Social atmosphere:** According to the editor of the student newspaper, the social and cultural life at Antioch can be described as "irreverent, creative, extreme, small, gossipy, worldly, informed, and very intense." Antioch's most popular events include the Quasi-Prom, the Camelot Bike Race, May Day, the Halloween party, and the Algonquin canoe trip. Influential groups on campus include the community government, Jewish groups, gay and lesbian groups, the Third World Alliance, and the Co-op. Students gather at Trails Tavern, Dayton Street Gulch, and Connor House, a student-run coffeehouse.
**Services and counseling/handicapped student services:** Placement services. Health service. Women's center. Birth control, personal, and psychological counseling. Academic guidance services. Learning disabled services.
**Campus organizations:** Undergraduate student government. Student newspaper (Antioch Record, published once/week). Literary magazine. Radio station. Instrumental and vocal groups, theatre, dance group, filmmaking and photography groups, Green Politics Group, organic garden, recycling center, student-run fire department, Peace Center, Lesbian/Gay Center, women's and men's groups, creative groups, scientific interest group, departmental, political, service, and special-interest groups, 28 organizations in all.
**Religious organizations:** Bahai group.
**Minority/foreign student organizations:** Third World Alliance, Men of African Descent, Women of Color, Unidad!.

**ATHLETICS. Physical education requirements:** Four terms of physical education required.
**Intramural and club sports:** 17% of students participate. Intramural soccer, volleyball.

**ADMISSIONS. Academic basis for candidate selection** (in order of priority): School's recommendation, essay, secondary school record, class rank, standardized test scores.
**Nonacademic basis for candidate selection:** Character and personality, extracurricular participation, and particular talent or ability are important. Alumni/ae relationship is considered.
**Requirements:** Graduation from secondary school is required; GED is accepted. No specific distribution of secondary school units required. Full college-preparatory program recommended. Special review required of applicants not normally admissible. SAT is recommended; ACT may be substituted. Campus visit and interview recommended. Off-campus interviews available with admissions and alumni representatives.
**Procedure:** Suggest filing application by February 1; no deadline. Notification of admission by April 1. Reply is required by May 1. $150 nonrefundable tuition deposit. Freshmen accepted for terms other than fall.
**Special programs:** Admission may be deferred one year. Credit and/or placement may be granted through CEEB Advanced Placement exams for scores of 4 or higher. Credit and/or placement may be granted through CLEP general and subject exams. Credit and placement may be granted through ACT PEP and DANTES exams, and military experience. Early decision program. In fall 1993, 70 applied for early decision and 69 were accepted. Deadline for applying for early decision is November 15. Early entrance/early admission program. Concurrent enrollment program.
**Transfer students:** Transfer students accepted for terms other than fall. In fall 1993, 25% of all new students were transfers into all classes. 140 transfer applications were received, 126 were accepted. Application deadline is March 1. Lowest course grade accepted is "C." Maximum number of transferable credits is 80 quarter hours. At least 80 quarter hours must be completed at the college to receive degree.
**Admissions contact:** James H. Williams, Jr., Dean of Admissions. 513 767-6400.

**FINANCIAL AID. Available aid:** Pell grants, SEOG, state grants, school scholarships and grants, academic merit scholarships, and aid for undergraduate foreign students. Per-

kins Loans (NDSL), PLUS, Stafford Loans (GSL), school loans, and SLS. Tuition Management Systems and family tuition reduction.
**Financial aid statistics:** 15% of aid is not need-based. In 1993-94, 98% of all undergraduate applicants received aid; 98% of freshman applicants. Average amounts of aid awarded freshmen: Scholarships and grants, $7,442; loans, $3,960.
**Supporting data/closing dates:** FAFSA/FAF/FFS: Priority filing date is March 1. School's own aid application: Priority filing date is March 1. Income tax forms: Priority filing date is March 1. W-2's/Divorced Parent's form: Priority filing date is March 1. Notification of awards begins April 1.
**Financial aid contact:** Sandra Tarbox, M.A., Director of Financial Aid. 513 767-6367.

**STUDENT EMPLOYMENT.** College Work/Study Program. Institutional employment. 67% of full-time undergraduates work on campus during school year. Students may expect to earn an average of $1,700 during school year. Off-campus part-time employment opportunities rated "fair."

**COMPUTER FACILITIES.** 50 IBM/IBM-compatible and Macintosh/Apple microcomputers. Students may access Digital minicomputer/mainframe systems, Internet. Residence halls may be equipped with stand-alone microcomputers. Client/LAN operating systems include Apple/Macintosh, DOS, OS/2, LocalTalk/AppleTalk, Novell. Computer languages and software packages include COBOL, FORTRAN, Pascal, SPSS-X, WPS-Plus. Computer facilities are available to all students.
**Fees:** None.
**Hours:** 8:30 AM-2 AM (weekdays); limited hours on weekends.

**PROMINENT ALUMNI/AE.** Steven Jay Gould, author and professor of zoology, Harvard U; Virginia Hamilton, prize-winning author of children's books; Coretta Scott King, civil rights leader; Rod Serling, creator of *The Twilight Zone;* Theodore Levitt, editor, *Harvard Business Review;* Dr. Leland Clark, inventor of heart-lung machine.

# Art Academy of Cincinnati

**Cincinnati, OH 45202** **513 721-5205**

**1993-94 Costs.** Tuition: $8,450. Housing: None. Fees, books, misc. academic expenses (school's estimate): $1,570.
**Enrollment.** Undergraduates: 109 men, 90 women (full-time). Freshman class: 130 applicants, 82 accepted, 33 enrolled.
**Test score averages/ranges.** Average SAT scores: 427 verbal, 399 math. Average ACT scores: 17 composite.
**Faculty.** 18 full-time; 22 part-time. Student/faculty ratio: 11 to 1.
**Selectivity rating.** Less competitive.

**PROFILE.** The Art Academy of Cincinnati, founded in 1887, is a private institution. Its 184-acre campus is located between the residential communities of Mt. Adams and Walnut Hills.

**Accreditation:** NCACS. Professionally accredited by the National Association of Schools of Art and Design.
**Religious orientation:** Art Academy of Cincinnati is nonsectarian; no religious requirements.
**Library:** Collections totaling over 50,000 volumes and 350 periodical subscriptions.
**Special facilities/museums:** Academy is physically connected to and affiliated with Cincinnati Art Museum.
**Athletic facilities:** Athletic facilities through intercollege consortium and local city facilities.

**STUDENT BODY. Undergraduate profile:** 75% are state residents. 1% Asian-American, 7% Black, 92% White. Average age of undergraduates is 25.
**Freshman profile:** 4% of freshmen who took SAT scored 600 or over on verbal; 37% scored 500 or over on verbal, 21% scored 500 or over on math; 58% scored 400 or over on verbal, 46% scored 400 or over on math; 87% scored 300 or over on verbal, 87% scored 300 or over on math. 10% of freshmen who took ACT scored 24 or over on composite; 40% scored 18 or over on composite; 80% scored 12 or over on composite; 100% scored 6 or over on composite. 40% of accepted applicants took SAT; 60% took ACT.
**Undergraduate achievement:** 75% of fall 1991 freshmen returned for fall 1992 term. 50% of entering class graduated.
**Foreign students:** Two students are from out of the country. Two countries represented in all.

**PROGRAMS OF STUDY. Degrees:** B.F.A.
**Majors:** Art History, Graphic Design, Illustration, Painting, Photography, Printmaking, Sculpture.
**Distribution of degrees:** The majors with the highest enrollment are graphic design, illustration, and painting; sculpture, photography, and printmaking have the lowest.
**Special:** Associate's degrees offered. Independent study. Cooperative education programs. Member of Greater Cincinnati Consortium of Colleges and Universities. Art College Exchange Semester. Study abroad in England and other countries. ROTC, NROTC, and AFROTC through Greater Cincinnati Consortium.
**Academic Assistance:** Nonremedial tutoring.

**ADMISSIONS. Academic basis for candidate selection** (in order of priority): Secondary school record, standardized test scores.
**Nonacademic basis for candidate selection:** Particular talent or ability is emphasized. Character and personality are important. Extracurricular participation and alumni/ae relationship are considered.
**Requirements:** Graduation from secondary school is required; GED is accepted. 16 units and the following program of study are recommended: 4 units of English, 3 units of math, 2 units of science, 2 units of foreign language, 3 units of social studies, 3 units of history, 4 units of electives. Fine art electives recommended. Minimum 2.0 GPA required. Portfolio required. Provisional admission possible for applicants not meeting standard requirements. SAT or ACT is required. Campus visit recommended. No off-campus interviews.
**Procedure:** Take SAT or ACT by March of 12th year. Visit college for interview by June of 12th year. Suggest filing application by March. Notification of admission on rolling basis. $100 nonrefundable tuition deposit. Freshmen accepted for terms other than fall.
**Special programs:** Admission may be deferred. Credit and/or placement may be granted through CEEB Advanced Placement exams for scores of 5 or higher. Credit and/or placement may be granted through CLEP general and subject exams. Early decision program.
**Transfer students:** Transfer students accepted for terms other than fall. In fall 1992, 52 transfer applications were received, 41 were accepted. Application deadline is August 15 for fall; January 2 for spring. Minimum 2.0 GPA required. Lowest course grade accepted is "C." Maximum number of transferable credits is 69 semester hours. At least 60 semester hours must be completed at the college to receive degree.
**Admissions contact:** Douglas Dobbins, Director of Admissions. 513 562-8757, 800 323-5692.

**FINANCIAL AID. Available aid:** Pell grants, SEOG, state scholarships and grants, school scholarships, and private scholarships. PLUS, Stafford Loans (GSL), school loans, and SLS. Institutional payment plan.
**Financial aid statistics:** In 1992-93, 97% of all undergraduate applicants received aid; 95% of freshman applicants. Average amounts of aid awarded freshmen: Scholarships and grants, $600.
**Supporting data/closing dates:** FAFSA: Accepted on rolling basis. State aid form: Accepted on rolling basis. Income tax forms: Accepted on rolling basis. Notification of awards on rolling basis.
**Financial aid contact:** Karen Geiger, Director of Financial Aid. 513 562-8751.

# Ashland University

**Ashland, OH 44805** **419 289-4142**

**1993-94 Costs.** Tuition: $10,733. Room: $2,382. Board: $2,138. Fees, books, misc. academic expenses (school's estimate): $705.
**Enrollment.** Undergraduates: 884 men, 1,063 women (full-time). Freshman class: 1,557 applicants, 1,388 accepted, 538 enrolled.
**Test score averages/ranges.** Average SAT scores: 417 verbal, 454 math. Average ACT scores: 20 composite. Range of ACT scores of middle 50%: 19-23 composite.
**Faculty.** 187 full-time; 8 part-time. 41% of faculty holds doctoral degree. Student/faculty ratio: 16 to 1.
**Selectivity rating.** Noncompetitive.

**PROFILE.** Ashland, founded in 1878, is a church-affiliated, liberal arts university. Its 98-acre campus is located in Ashland, 60 miles southwest of Cleveland.

**Accreditation:** NCACS. Professionally accredited by the Association of Theological Schools, the National Association of Schools of Music, the National Council for Accreditation of Teacher Education, the National League for Nursing.
**Religious orientation:** Ashland University is affiliated with the Church of the Brethren; one semester of religion required.
**Library:** Collections totaling over 187,718 volumes, 1,108 periodical subscriptions, and 171,507 microform items.
**Special facilities/museums:** Montesorri preschool, art gallery, archaeological museum, numismatic center.
**Athletic facilities:** Gymnasiums, tracks, natatorium, athletic fields.

**STUDENT BODY. Undergraduate profile:** 85% are state residents; 33% are transfers. 5% Black, 1% Hispanic, 89% White, 5% Other. Average age of undergraduates is 21.
**Freshman profile:** 3% of freshmen who took SAT scored 600 or over on verbal, 7% scored 600 or over on math; 19% scored 500 or over on verbal, 32% scored 500 or over on math; 59% scored 400 or over on verbal, 74% scored 400 or over on math; 94% scored 300 or over on verbal, 95% scored 300 or over on math. 2% of freshmen who took ACT scored 30 or over on composite; 19% scored 24 or over on composite; 79% scored 18 or over on composite; 100% scored 12 or over on composite. 10% of accepted applicants took SAT; 90% took ACT. 82% of freshmen come from public schools.
**Undergraduate achievement:** 70% of fall 1991 freshmen returned for fall 1992 term. 38% of entering class graduated. 9% of students who completed a degree program immediately went on to graduate study.
**Foreign students:** 162 students are from out of the country. Countries represented include Japan, Korea, Malaysia, and Thailand; 14 in all.

**PROGRAMS OF STUDY. Degrees:** B.A., B.S.
**Majors:** Accounting, Adaptive Physical Education, American Studies, Applied Music, Art, Art Education, Biochemistry, Biology, Broadcast Sales/Station Management, Broadcast Technology/Production, Business Administration, Business Education, Business Management, Chemistry, Child Care Services, Christian Education, Clothing Fashion Merchandising, Communications, Community/Home Services, Computer Information Systems, Creative Writing, Criminal Justice, Dramatics, Earth Science, Economics, Elementary Education, English, Family Services, Finance, Food Services, French, Geology, Health Education, Health Services Management, History, Home Economics, Home Economics/Human Development, Hotel/Restaurant Management, Human Development, International Studies, Journalism, Marketing, Mathematics, Music, Music Composition, Music Education, Music Theory, Nursing, Physical Education, Physics, Political Science, Professional Video, Psychology, Public Communication, Radio/Television, Recreation, Religion, Science, Secondary Education, Secretarial Science, Social Psychology, Social Studies, Social Work, Sociology, Spanish, Special Education, Speech, Speech Education, Sports Communications, Studio Art, Toxicology, Vocational Education.
**Distribution of degrees:** The majors with the highest enrollment are elementary education, management, and criminal justice; English and religion have the lowest.
**Requirements:** General education requirement.
**Special:** Minors offered in 40 areas. Associate's degrees offered. Double majors. Independent study. Pass/fail grading option. Internships. Graduate school at which undergraduates may take graduate-level courses. Preprofessional programs in law, medicine, veterinary science, pharmacy, dentistry, and optometry. Engineering program with U of Detroit. Art programs with Drew U, Hunter Coll, and various art institutes. Member of Northwest Ohio Consortium. Washington Semester. Exchange programs with American U, Art Inst

of Pittsburgh, Drew U. Teacher certification in early childhood, elementary, secondary, and special education. Certification in specific subject areas. Study abroad in Austria, China, Colombia, Cyprus, Denmark, Ecuador, England, France, Germany, Greece, Hong Kong, Ireland, Israel, Italy, Jamaica, and Mexico. AFROTC at U of Akron.
**Honors:** Honors program. Honor societies.
**Academic Assistance:** Remedial reading, writing, math, and study skills. Nonremedial tutoring.

**STUDENT LIFE. Housing:** All unmarried students under age 21 must live on campus unless living near campus with relatives. Coed, women's, and men's dorms. 71% of students live in college housing.
**Social atmosphere:** Popular gathering spots include the cafeteria, student center gameroom, library, and gym. Influential student groups include HOPE Fellowship, Campus Activities Board, WRDL-TV and radio, the Collegian, student senate, and Greeks. Students enjoy yearly social events such as Homecoming (activities include Good Split Hope, a quarter-of-a-mile-long banana split), Springfest, and the Christmas Dance. The Campus Activities Board provides many activities, such as entertainers, which are successful. "We're known, however, as not the most exciting social campus around because of our dry status. But, personally, I like it and so do others because it's less trouble overall," reports the editor of the student newspaper.
**Services and counseling/handicapped student services:** Placement services. Health service. Counseling services for minority, military, veteran, and older students. Personal and psychological counseling. Career guidance services. Religious counseling. Physically disabled student services. Learning disabled services. Tape recorders. Tutors. Reader services for the blind.
**Campus organizations:** Undergraduate student government. Student newspaper (Collegian, published once/week). Yearbook. Radio and TV stations. Band, orchestra, chapel choir, college choir, intercollegiate debating, Campus Activity Board, outdoor club, departmental and service groups, 75 organizations in all. Five fraternities, all with chapter houses; four sororities, no chapter houses. 10% of men join a fraternity. 30% of women join a sorority.
**Religious organizations:** Fellowship of Christian Athletes, Hope Christian Fellowship, Newman Club.
**Minority/foreign student organizations:** Black Student Union. International Club.

**ATHLETICS. Physical education requirements:** Two semesters of physical education required.
**Intercollegiate competition:** 6% of students participate. Baseball (M), basketball (M,W), cheerleading (M,W), cross-country (M,W), diving (M,W), football (M), golf (M), soccer (M), softball (W), swimming (M,W), track and field (indoor) (M,W), track and field (outdoor) (M,W), volleyball (W), wrestling (M). Member of Great Lakes Valley Conference, Midwest Intercollegiate Football Conference, NCAA Division II.
**Intramural and club sports:** 3% of students participate. Men's club volleyball.

**ADMISSIONS. Academic basis for candidate selection** (in order of priority): Secondary school record, standardized test scores, school's recommendation, essay, class rank.
**Nonacademic basis for candidate selection:** Character and personality are important. Extracurricular participation, particular talent or ability, and alumni/ae relationship are considered.
**Requirements:** Graduation from secondary school is required; GED is accepted. 17 units and the following program of study are recommended: 4 units of English, 3 units of math, 3 units of science, 2 units of foreign language, 3 units of social studies, 1 unit of history, 1 unit of electives. Minimum composite ACT score of 18 (combined SAT score of 850) and rank in top half of secondary school class recommended. R.N. required of nursing applicants. ACT is required; SAT may be substituted. Campus visit and interview recommended. No off-campus interviews.
**Procedure:** Take SAT or ACT by October of 12th year. Visit college for interview by January of 12th year. Suggest filing application by December. Application deadline is August. Notification of admission on rolling basis. No set date by which applicants must accept offer. $100 tuition deposit, refundable until May 1. Freshmen accepted for terms other than fall.
**Special programs:** Admission may be deferred one year. Credit and/or placement may be granted through CEEB Advanced Placement exams for scores of 3 or higher. Credit and/or placement may be granted through CLEP general and subject exams. Credit and placement may be granted through DANTES and challenge exams, and military experience. Concurrent enrollment program.
**Transfer students:** Transfer students accepted for terms other than fall. In fall 1992, 33% of all new students were transfers into all classes. 299 transfer applications were received, 246 were accepted. Application deadline is August for fall; December for spring. Minimum 2.0 GPA required. Lowest course grade accepted is "C." Maximum number of transferable credits is 64 semester hours. At least 32 semester hours must be completed at the university to receive degree.
**Admissions contact:** Carl Gerbasi, Jr., Executive Director of Admission and Financial Aid. 419 289-5052.

**FINANCIAL AID. Available aid:** Pell grants, SEOG, state scholarships and grants, school scholarships and grants, private scholarships and grants, academic merit scholarships, athletic scholarships, and aid for undergraduate foreign students. Perkins Loans (NDSL), PLUS, Stafford Loans (GSL), state loans, school loans, private loans, and SLS. AMS and family tuition reduction.
**Financial aid statistics:** 1% of aid is not need-based. In 1992-93, 97% of all undergraduate applicants received aid; 90% of freshman applicants. Average amounts of aid awarded freshmen: Scholarships and grants, $5,500; loans, $3,200.
**Supporting data/closing dates:** FAFSA/FAF/FFS: Accepted on rolling basis. School's own aid application: Priority filing date is March 15. State aid form: Deadline is September 25. Income tax forms: Accepted on rolling basis. Notification of awards on rolling basis.
**Financial aid contact:** Stephen Howell, M.A., Director of Financial Aid. 419 289-5001.

**STUDENT EMPLOYMENT.** College Work/Study Program. Institutional employment. 35% of full-time undergraduates work on campus during school year. Students may expect to earn an average of $800 during school year. Off-campus part-time employment opportunities rated "fair."

**COMPUTER FACILITIES.** 120 IBM/IBM-compatible and Macintosh/Apple microcomputers; 100 are networked. Students may access Digital minicomputer/mainframe systems. Computer languages and software packages include Assembler, BASIC, C, COBOL, dBASE, First Choice, Lotus 1-2-3, WordPerfect, WordStar. Computer facilities are available to all students.
**Fees:** None.
**Hours:** 8:30 AM-10 PM.

**GRADUATE CAREER DATA.** Highest graduate school enrollments: U of Akron, Ashland U, Cleveland State U. Companies and businesses that hire graduates: Electronic Data Systems, K mart, Rubbermaid.

**PROMINENT ALUMNI/AE.** Dwight Schar, president and chairperson, NV Homes; Dweier Brown, actor; Bryan Wittman, promotion division, Disney World.

9-11

# Baldwin-Wallace College

**Berea, OH 44017** **216 826-2900**

**1994-95 Costs.** Tuition: $10,995. Room & board: $4,410. Fees, books, misc. academic expenses (school's estimate): $985.
**Enrollment.** Undergraduates: 1,092 men, 1,626 women (full-time). Freshman class: 1,558 applicants, 1,359 accepted, 658 enrolled. Graduate enrollment: 289 men, 305 women.
**Test score averages/ranges.** Average SAT scores: 460 verbal, 530 math. Range of SAT scores of middle 50%: 870-1110 combined. Average ACT scores: 23 composite. Range of ACT scores of middle 50%: 20-25 composite.
**Faculty.** 149 full-time; 128 part-time. 67% of faculty holds doctoral degree. Student/faculty ratio: 18 to 1.
**Selectivity rating.** Less competitive.

**PROFILE.** Baldwin-Wallace, founded in 1845, is a church-affiliated, liberal arts college. Its 56-acre campus is located in Berea, 14 miles southeast of downtown Cleveland. Campus architecture includes ivy-covered sandstone buildings as well as colonial-style structures.

**Accreditation:** NCACS. Professionally accredited by the National Association of Schools of Music, the National Council for Accreditation of Teacher Education.
**Religious orientation:** Baldwin-Wallace College is affiliated with the United Methodist Church; no religious requirements.
**Library:** Collections totaling over 240,000 volumes and 1,003 periodical subscriptions.
**Special facilities/museums:** Art gallery, electron microscope, observatory.
**Athletic facilities:** Extensive facilities.

**STUDENT BODY. Undergraduate profile:** 90% are state residents; 30% are transfers. 1% Asian-American, 5% Black, 2% Hispanic, 91% White, 1% Other. Average age of undergraduates is 23.
**Freshman profile:** 1% of freshmen who took SAT scored 700 or over on verbal, 4% scored 700 or over on math; 6% scored 600 or over on verbal, 25% scored 600 or over on math; 39% scored 500 or over on verbal, 64% scored 500 or over on math; 100% scored 400 or over on verbal, 100% scored 400 or over on math. 4% of freshmen who took ACT scored 30 or over on composite; 41% scored 24 or over on composite; 95% scored 18 or over on composite; 100% scored 12 or over on composite. 50% of accepted applicants took SAT; 83% took ACT. 85% of freshmen come from public schools.
**Undergraduate achievement:** 82% of fall 1992 freshmen returned for fall 1993 term. 12% of students who completed a degree program immediately went on to graduate study.
**Foreign students:** 51 students are from out of the country. Countries represented include India, Indonesia, Japan, Korea, Thailand, and Turkey; 22 in all.

**PROGRAMS OF STUDY. Degrees:** B.A., B.Mus., B.Mus.Ed., B.S., B.S.Ed.
**Majors:** Accounting, Art, Art Education, Art History, Athletic Training, Biological Science, Broadcasting, Business Administration, Chemistry, Computer Information Systems, Computer Science, Criminal Justice, Economics, Elementary Education, English, French, Geology, German, Health/Physical Education, History, Home Economics, International Studies, Mathematics, Medical Technology, Music, Music Education, Music History/Literature, Music Management, Music Performance, Music Theory, Music Therapy, Musical Theatre, Philosophy, Physics, Political Science, Psychology, Religion, Secondary Education, Social Work, Sociology, Spanish, Speech/Theatre, Sports/Dance/Arts Management, Sports Medicine, Studio Art.
**Distribution of degrees:** The majors with the highest enrollment are business administration, education, and English; religion, philosophy, and geology have the lowest.
**Requirements:** General education requirement.
**Academic regulations:** Freshmen must maintain minimum 1.7 GPA; sophomores, 1.9 GPA; juniors, 2.0 GPA; seniors, 2.0 GPA.
**Special:** Minors offered in most majors and in dance and environmental studies. Courses offered in aging studies, astronomy, black studies, Greek/Middle East studies, and Russian. Intercultural Studies Program. Self-designed majors. Double majors. Dual degrees. Independent study. Accelerated study. Pass/fail grading option. Internships. Preprofessional programs in law, medicine, veterinary science, pharmacy, dentistry, theology, optometry, engineering, library science, social work, and speech pathology. 3-2 engineering programs with Case Western Reserve U, Columbia U, and Washington U. 3-2 forestry program with Duke U. Combined degree programs in social work and biology with Case Western Reserve U. Member of Cleveland Music Therapy Consortium. Washington Semester and UN Semester. Teacher certification in elementary, secondary, and special education. Certification in specific subject areas. Study abroad in Austria, Colombia, England, Egypt, France, the Galapagos Islands, Greece, Germany, India, Israel, Italy, Japan, Jordan, the Netherlands, Puerto Rico, and Turkey. ROTC at Cleveland State U. AFROTC at U of Akron.
**Honors:** Honors program. Honor societies.
**Academic Assistance:** Remedial writing, math, and study skills. Nonremedial tutoring.

**STUDENT LIFE. Housing:** All freshmen must live on campus unless living with family. Coed, women's, and men's dorms. 60% of students live in college housing.
**Social atmosphere:** Students frequent the Hive, Berea Cafe, Topps Bar & Grill, the Student Activity Center, and Eastlands. Greeks, the college radio station, campus entertainment productions, and the Student Senate are strong influences on campus life. Some of the most popular events of the year are the Greek Sing, Greek Week, Latin Carnival, World

9-5

Student Alliance Thanksgiving Dinner, and the Freshman Dance Mixer. "Berea is a small town with a few minor areas to socialize, including a first-run theater, bars, and a coffeeshop," reports the student newspaper. "We are twenty minutes from downtown Cleveland, where there is much to do."

**Services and counseling/handicapped student services:** Placement services. Health service. Day care. Counseling services for minority and older students. Birth control, personal, and psychological counseling. Career and academic guidance services. Religious counseling. Physically disabled student services. Learning disabled services. Notetaking services. Tutors.

**Campus organizations:** Undergraduate student government. Student newspaper (Exponent, published once/week). Literary magazine. Yearbook. Radio station. Music ensembles, dance club, psychology club, pre-law club, Young Democrats, Young Republicans, Teaching Together, 100 organizations in all. Five fraternities, no chapter houses; seven sororities, no chapter houses. 13% of men join a fraternity. 15% of women join a sorority.

**Religious organizations:** Campus Crusade for Christ, Fellowship of Christian Athletes, BASIC, Lutheran Student Association, Newman Student Organization, Hillel, Kappa Phi, Intervarsity Christian Fellowship.

**Minority/foreign student organizations:** Black Student Alliance, Hispanic-American Student Association. World Student Association.

**ATHLETICS. Physical education requirements:** Three quarters of physical education required.

**Intercollegiate competition:** 9% of students participate. Baseball (M), basketball (M,W), cheerleading (M,W), cross-country (M,W), football (M), golf (M), soccer (M,W), softball (W), swimming (M,W), tennis (M,W), track and field (M,W), volleyball (W), wrestling (M). Member of NCAA Division III, Ohio Athletic Conference.

**Intramural and club sports:** 6% of students participate.

**ADMISSIONS. Academic basis for candidate selection** (in order of priority): Secondary school record, class rank, standardized test scores, school's recommendation, essay.

**Nonacademic basis for candidate selection:** Extracurricular participation is important. Character and personality, particular talent or ability, geographical distribution, and alumni/ae relationship are considered.

**Requirements:** Graduation from secondary school is required; GED is accepted. 16 units and the following program of study required: 4 units of English, 3 units of math, 3 units of science, 2 units of foreign language, 1 unit of social studies, 2 units of history. Minimum combined SAT score of 950 (composite ACT score of 20), rank top third of secondary school class, and minimum 2.75 GPA recommended. Audition required of music program applicants. SAT or ACT is required. Campus visit and interview recommended. No off-campus interviews.

**Procedure:** Take SAT or ACT by February 8 of 12th year. Suggest filing application by March 1; no deadline. Notification of admission on rolling basis. Reply is required by May 1. $100 tuition deposit, refundable until May 1. $100 room deposit, refundable until May 1. Freshmen accepted for terms other than fall.

**Special programs:** Admission may be deferred. Credit and/or placement may be granted through CEEB Advanced Placement exams for scores of 3 or higher. Credit may be granted through CLEP general and subject exams, and life experience. Concurrent enrollment program.

**Transfer students:** Transfer students accepted for terms other than fall. In fall 1993, 30% of all new students were transfers into all classes. 456 transfer applications were received, 317 were accepted. Application deadline is rolling for fall; rolling for spring. Minimum 2.75 GPA recommended. Lowest course grade accepted is "C." Maximum number of transferable credits is 93 quarter hours. At least 48 quarter hours must be completed at the college to receive degree.

**Admissions contact:** Juliann K. Baker, M.Ed., Director of Undergraduate Admission. 216 826-2222.

**FINANCIAL AID. Available aid:** Pell grants, SEOG, state scholarships and grants, school scholarships and grants, private scholarships, and academic merit scholarships. Perkins Loans (NDSL), PLUS, Stafford Loans (GSL), school loans, and SLS. AMS.

**Financial aid statistics:** 26% of aid is not need-based. In 1993-94, 96% of all undergraduate applicants received aid; 96% of freshman applicants. Average amounts of aid awarded freshmen: Scholarships and grants, $6,737; loans, $2,083.

**Supporting data/closing dates:** FAFSA: Priority filing date is May 1. FAF/FFS: Priority filing date is May 1; accepted on rolling basis. School's own aid application: Priority filing date is May 1; accepted on rolling basis. State aid form: Deadline is September 24. Notification of awards begins March 1.

**Financial aid contact:** George Rolleston, Ph.D., Director of Financial Aid. 216 826-2108.

**STUDENT EMPLOYMENT.** College Work/Study Program. Institutional employment. 30% of full-time undergraduates work on campus during school year. Students may expect to earn an average of $732 during school year. Off-campus part-time employment opportunities rated "good."

**COMPUTER FACILITIES.** 490 IBM/IBM-compatible, Macintosh/Apple, and RISC-/UNIX-based microcomputers; 175 are networked. Students may access IBM minicomputer/mainframe systems, Internet. Residence halls may be equipped with stand-alone microcomputers, modems. Client/LAN operating systems include OS/2. Computer languages and software packages include Ada, AutoCAD, BASIC, COBOL, C, dBASE, FORTRAN, IFPS, Lotus 1-2-3, Pascal, SAS, SPSS. Computer facilities are available to all students.

**Fees:** Computer fee is included in tuition/fees.

**Hours:** 8 AM-11 PM (M-Su).

**GRADUATE CAREER DATA.** Graduate school percentages: 2% enter law school. 1% enter medical school. 1% enter dental school. 4% enter graduate business programs. 3% enter graduate arts and sciences programs. Highest graduate school enrollments: Bowling Green State U, Case Western Reserve U, Cleveland State U. 56% of graduates choose careers in business and industry. Companies and businesses that hire graduates: Arthur Andersen, Ernest & Young, Firestone, IBM, National City Bank, Ameritrust, BP America.

**PROMINENT ALUMNI/AE.** Jack Overmyer, astronaut; Bud Collins, TV sports analyst; Thomas Riemenschneider, associate vice-president for clinical affairs, SUNY Buffalo Medical Sch; Arlene Saunders, soprano with Metropolitan Opera; Willard Carmel, CEO, McDonald & Co. Securities; Harrison Dillard, two-time Olympic gold medalist.

# Bluffton College

**Bluffton, OH 45817** **419 358-3000**

**1994-95 Costs.** Tuition: $9,900. Room: $1,617. Board: $2,373. Fees, books, misc. academic expenses (school's estimate): $1,200.

**Enrollment.** Undergraduates: 374 men, 386 women (full-time). Freshman class: 568 applicants, 514 accepted, 209 enrolled.

**Test score averages/ranges.** Average SAT scores: 449 verbal, 523 math. Average ACT scores: 23 English, 22 math, 23 composite.

**Faculty.** 45 full-time; 36 part-time. 69% of faculty holds highest degree in specific field. Student/faculty ratio: 15 to 1.

**Selectivity rating.** Less competitive.

**PROFILE.** Bluffton, founded in 1899, is a church-affiliated, liberal arts college. Its 65-acre campus, with some buildings dating from 1900, is located in Bluffton, 15 miles from Lima.

**Accreditation:** NCACS. Professionally accredited by the American Dietetic Association, the Council on Social Work Education, the National Association of Schools of Music.

**Religious orientation:** Bluffton College is affiliated with the General Conference Mennonite Church; two courses in religious studies required.

**Library:** Collections totaling over 130,000 volumes, 600 periodical subscriptions, and 56,000 microform items.

**Special facilities/museums:** Mennonite historical library, peace arts center, nature preserve.

**Athletic facilities:** Basketball, racquetball, and tennis courts, weight room, baseball, soccer, and softball fields, football/track stadium.

**STUDENT BODY. Undergraduate profile:** 90% are state residents; 19% are transfers. 1% Asian-American, 3% Black, 1% Hispanic, 90% White, 5% Other. Average age of undergraduates is 20.

**Freshman profile:** 6% of freshmen who took SAT scored 700 or over on math; 4% scored 600 or over on verbal, 25% scored 600 or over on math; 33% scored 500 or over on verbal, 61% scored 500 or over on math; 69% scored 400 or over on verbal, 90% scored 400 or over on math; 100% scored 300 or over on verbal, 100% scored 300 or over on math. Majority of accepted applicants took ACT. 95% of freshmen come from public schools.

**Undergraduate achievement:** 72% of fall 1992 freshmen returned for fall 1993 term. 52% of entering class graduated. 3% of students who completed a degree program immediately went on to graduate study.

**Foreign students:** 42 students are from out of the country. Countries represented include African countries, China, India, and Palestine; 19 in all.

**PROGRAMS OF STUDY. Degrees:** B.A., B.S.

**Majors:** Accounting, Art, Biology, Business Administration, Chemistry, Child Development, Church Work, Clothing/Textiles/Retailing, Communication, Computer/Information Sciences, Criminal Justice, Economics, Elementary Education, English, Foods/Nutrition, Health/Physical Education/Recreation, History, Home Economics, Humanities, Mathematics, Music, Pre-Medicine, Psychology, Recreation Management, Religion, Secondary Education, Sociology, Spanish, Spanish/Economics, Special Education, Sport Management, Wellness.

**Distribution of degrees:** The majors with the highest enrollment are business administration, elementary education, and sociology; religion, home economics, and Spanish have the lowest.

**Requirements:** General education requirement.

**Academic regulations:** Freshmen must maintain minimum 1.5 GPA; sophomores, 1.7 GPA; juniors, 1.9 GPA; seniors, 2.0 GPA.

**Special:** Minors offered in home economics, music, peace/conflict studies, pre-law, and religion. Self-designed majors. Double majors. Independent study. Pass/fail grading option. Internships. Preprofessional programs in law, medicine, theology, and peace/conflict studies. Member of Christian College Coalition, Greater Cincinnati Council on World Affairs, Indiana Consortium for International Programs, and Northwest Ohio Consortium. Washington Semester. Other term-away programs available. Teacher certification in early childhood, elementary, secondary, and special education. Certification in specific subject areas. Study abroad in Costa Rica, France, Guatemala, Nicaragua, Northern Ireland, and Poland.

**Honors:** Honors program.

**Academic Assistance:** Remedial reading, writing, math, and study skills. Nonremedial tutoring.

**ADMISSIONS. Academic basis for candidate selection** (in order of priority): Secondary school record, standardized test scores, class rank, school's recommendation.

**Nonacademic basis for candidate selection:** Character and personality and extracurricular participation are emphasized. Particular talent or ability and geographical distribution are considered.

**Requirements:** Graduation from secondary school is required; GED is accepted. 16 units and the following program of study are recommended: 4 units of English, 3 units of math, 3 units of science, 3 units of foreign language, 3 units of social studies. Minimum combined SAT score of 800 (composite ACT score of 19), rank in top half of secondary school class, and minimum 2.3 GPA required. Audition required of music program applicants. Academic Resources/Study Skills Program for applicants not normally admissible. SAT or ACT is required. Campus visit and interview recommended. Off-campus interviews available with an admissions representative.

**Procedure:** Take SAT or ACT by December of 12th year. Visit college for interview by April 1 of 12th year. Application deadline is August 15. Notification of admission on rolling basis. No set date by which applicants must accept offer. $50 nonrefundable room deposit. Freshmen accepted for terms other than fall.

**Special programs:** Admission may be deferred two years. Credit and/or placement may be granted through CEEB Advanced Placement exams for scores of 4 or higher. Credit and/or placement may be granted through CLEP general and subject exams. Credit and

placement may be granted through DANTES and challenge exams and life experience. Early entrance/early admission program. Concurrent enrollment program.
**Transfer students:** Transfer students accepted for terms other than fall. In fall 1993, 19% of all new students were transfers into all classes. 67 transfer applications were received, 64 were accepted. Application deadline is two weeks prior to start of quarter for fall; two weeks prior to start of quarter for spring. Minimum 2.0 GPA required. Lowest course grade accepted is "C-." Maximum number of transferable credits is 139 quarter hours. At least 45 quarter hours must be completed at the college to receive degree.
**Admissions contact:** Michael Hieronimus, M.Ed., Dean of Admissions. 800-488-3257.

**FINANCIAL AID. Available aid:** Pell grants, SEOG, state scholarships and grants, school scholarships and grants, private scholarships and grants, academic merit scholarships, and aid for undergraduate foreign students. Art, music, and leadership awards. Church scholarships. Perkins Loans (NDSL), PLUS, Stafford Loans (GSL), state loans, private loans, and SLS. Institutional payment plans.
**Financial aid statistics:** In 1993-94, 100% of all undergraduate applicants received aid. Average amounts of aid awarded freshmen: Scholarships and grants, $3,892; loans, $2,200.
**Supporting data/closing dates:** FAFSA: Accepted on rolling basis. State aid form: Accepted on rolling basis. Notification of awards on rolling basis.
**Financial aid contact:** Lawrence Matthews, Director of Financial Aid. 419 358-3246, 800-488-3257.

5-3 8-30

# Bowling Green State University

**Bowling Green, OH 43403 419 372-2531**

**1993-94 Costs.** Tuition: $2,910 (state residents), $4,152 (out-of-state). Room: $1,840. Board: $1,308. Fees, books, misc. academic expenses (school's estimate): $924.
**Enrollment.** Undergraduates: 5,792 men, 8,160 women (full-time). Freshman class: 9,067 applicants, 6,840 accepted, 2,977 enrolled. Graduate enrollment: 1,107 men, 1,304 women.
**Test score averages/ranges.** Average SAT scores: 457 verbal, 498 math. Range of SAT scores of middle 50%: 400-510 verbal, 430-560 math. Average ACT scores: 22 English, 21 math, 22 composite. Range of ACT scores of middle 50%: 19-24 English, 19-23 math.
**Faculty.** 680 full-time; 172 part-time. 80% of faculty holds doctoral degree. Student/faculty ratio: 20 to 1.
**Selectivity rating.** Less competitive.

**PROFILE.** Bowling Green State is a public university. Founded as a teacher-training institution in 1910, it began granting bachelor's degrees in 1929. Programs are offered through the Colleges of Business Administration, Education, Health and Community Services, Liberal Arts, and Musical Arts, and the Graduate College. Its 1,250-acre campus is located in Bowling Green, 23 miles south of Toledo.

**Accreditation:** NCACS. Professionally accredited by the Accrediting Council on Education in Journalism and Mass Communication, the American Assembly of Collegiate Schools of Business, the American Dietetic Association, the American Medical Association (CAHEA), the American Physical Therapy Association, the American Psychological Association, the American Speech-Language-Hearing Association, the Council on Social Work Education, the National Association of Schools of Art and Design, the National Association of Schools of Music, the National Council for Accreditation of Teacher Education, the National League for Nursing.
**Religious orientation:** Bowling Green State University is nonsectarian; no religious requirements.
**Library:** Collections totaling over 1,758,223 volumes, 6,071 periodical subscriptions, and 1,622,423 microform items.
**Special facilities/museums:** Gulf Coast marine biology research lab, Great Lakes research institute, national drosophila stock center, center for photochemical sciences, planetarium, electron microscopes.
**Athletic facilities:** Gymnasium, golf course, basketball, handball, racquetball, tennis, and volleyball courts, track, ice rink, stadium, baseball, football, intramural, soccer, and softball fields, swimming pool, weight room, arena, fieldhouse.

**STUDENT BODY. Undergraduate profile:** 92% are state residents; 2% are transfers. 1% Asian-American, 4% Black, 1% Hispanic, 94% White. Average age of undergraduates is 19.
**Freshman profile:** 36% of accepted applicants took SAT; 80% took ACT.
**Undergraduate achievement:** 79% of fall 1991 freshmen returned for fall 1992 term. 32% of entering class graduated. 15% of students who completed a degree program went on to graduate study within one year.
**Foreign students:** 147 students are from out of the country. Countries represented include Canada, China, France, Hong Kong, India, and Japan; 60 in all.

**PROGRAMS OF STUDY. Degrees:** B.A., B.A.Comm., B.F.A., B.Lib.Studies, B.Mus., B.S., B.S.Appl.Microbio., B.S.Art Ther., B.S.Bus.Admin., B.S.Comm.Disorders, B.S.Crim.Just., B.S.Diet., B.S.Econ., B.S.Ed., B.S.Env.Hlth., B.S.Gerontol., B.S.Journ., B.S.Med.Tech., B.S.Nurs., B.S.Phys.Ther., B.S.Soc.Work, B.S.Tech.
**Majors:** Accounting, Actuarial Sciences, Administrative Management, Advanced Technical Teaching, Aerotechnology, American Cultural Studies, Apparel Design/History, Applied Microbiology, Art, Art Education, Art History, Art Therapy, Asian Studies, Biological Sciences/Microbiology, Biology, Biology/Pre-Dental, Biology/Pre-Medical, Biology/Pre-Osteopathy, Broadcast Journalism, Business Education, Business/Pre-Law, Ceramics, Chemistry, Chemistry/Biochemistry, Chemistry/Pre-Dentistry, Chemistry/Pre-Medicine, Chemistry/Pre-Osteopathy, Child/Family/Community Services, Child/Family Development, Classical Studies, Communication Disorders, Communications, Computer Art, Computer Science, Construction Technology, Consumer/Family Resource Management, Crafts, Creative Writing, Criminal Justice, Dance, Design Technology, Dietetics, Drawing, Early Childhood Education, Earth Science, Economics, Electronic Technology, Elementary Education, English, English/Pre-Law, Environmental Analysis/Policy, Environmental Design, Environmental Health, Environmental Science, Ethnic Studies, Executive Secretarial, Fashion Merchandising, Fiber/Fabric, Film Studies, Finance, Food Science/Nutrition, French, General Business, General Home Economics, General Studies/Business, Geography, Geology, Geology/Geochemistry, Geology/Geophysics, Geology/Paleobiology, German, Gerontology, Glass, Graphic Design, Health Care Administration, Health Education, Health Promotion, History, History/Pre-Law, Home Economics, Hospitality Management, Human Resource Management, Individualized Program, Industrial/Labor Relations, Industrial Technology, Interior Design, International Business, International Studies, Interpersonal/Public Communication, Jazz Studies, Jewelry/Metalsmithing, Journalism, Latin, Latin American Studies, Liberal Studies, Long-term Care Administration, Magazine Journalism, Management Information Systems, Manufacturing Technology, Marketing, Marketing Education, Mathematics, Mathematics/Computer Science, Medical Technology, Music, Music Composition, Music Education, Music Literature/History, Music Performance, News/Editorial, Nursing, Office Administration, Operations Research, Painting, Philosophy, Philosophy/Pre-Law, Photography, Photojournalism, Physical Education, Physical Education/Health/Coaching, Physical Therapy, Physics, Political Science, Political Science/Pre-Law, Popular Culture, Printmaking, Production/Operations Management, Psychology, Psychology/Sociology, Public/Institutional Administration, Public Relations, Purchasing/Materials Management, Radio/Television/Film, Recreation, Restaurant Management/Institutional Food Service, Russian, Science Comprehensive, Scientific/Technical Communication, Sculpture, Social Studies, Social Work, Sociology, Sociology/Pre-Law, Soviet Studies, Spanish, Special Education for the Developmentally Handicapped, Special Education/Hearing Handicapped, Special Education/Learning Disabilities, Special Education/Multihandicapped, Special Education/Severe Behavior Handicapped, Sport Management, Statistics, Technology Education, Theatre, Visual Communications Technology, Women's Studies.
**Distribution of degrees:** The majors with the highest enrollment are elementary education, marketing, and nursing; philosophy, art (two-dimensional studies), and business education have the lowest.
**Requirements:** General education requirement.
**Academic regulations:** Minimum 2.0 GPA must be maintained.
**Special:** Minors offered in most majors and in other areas, including aquatics, bookkeeping, broadcast meteorology, and recording technology. Time-flexible degree program. Cluster Colleges. Thematic quarters. Associate's degrees offered. Self-designed majors. Double majors. Dual degrees. Independent study. Accelerated study. Pass/fail grading option. Internships. Cooperative education programs. Graduate school at which undergraduates may take graduate-level courses. Preprofessional programs in law, medicine, veterinary science, pharmacy, dentistry, theology, optometry, and mortuary science. Washington Semester. Member of National Student Exchange (NSE). Teacher certification in early childhood, elementary, secondary, special education, and vo-tech education. Certification in specific subject areas. Study abroad in Austria, Brazil, China, France, Germany, Italy, Japan, Korea, the former Soviet Republics, Spain, and the United Kingdom. ROTC and AFROTC.
**Honors:** Phi Beta Kappa. Honors program. Honor societies.
**Academic Assistance:** Remedial reading, writing, math, and study skills. Nonremedial tutoring.

**STUDENT LIFE. Housing:** All freshmen and sophomores must live on campus unless living with family. Coed, women's, and men's dorms. Sorority and fraternity housing. 48% of students live in college housing.
**Social atmosphere:** According to the student newspaper, "Hockey games are big draws; concerts are always popular, too. But many students go home every weekend and that hurts social life. Greeks only make up about 20% of the campus." Favorite hangouts are Howard's Club H, Uptown, the Brauthaus, and three on-campus nonalcoholic nightclubs.
**Services and counseling/handicapped student services:** Placement services. Health service. Women's center. Counseling services for minority, military, veteran, and older students. Birth control, personal, and psychological counseling. Career and academic guidance services. Physically disabled student services. Learning disabled services. Tutors. Reader services for the blind.
**Campus organizations:** Undergraduate student government. Student newspaper (Bowling Green News, published once/day). Literary magazine. Yearbook. Radio and TV stations. Bands, orchestras, choirs, chorale, drama groups, speaking and debating groups, interpretive reading groups, women's group, 132 organizations in all. 23 fraternities, 19 chapter houses; 17 sororities, 14 chapter houses. 24% of men join a fraternity. 21% of women join a sorority.
**Religious organizations:** Active Christians Today, Baptist Student Union, Bible Studies, Campus Crusade for Christ, Chi Alpha Christian Fellowship, Christian Outreach Bible Ministry, Christian Student Fellowship, Intervarsity Christian Fellowship, University Lutheran Chapel.
**Minority/foreign student organizations:** Black Student Union, Latino Student Union, NAACP, Board of Black Cultural Activities, Black Greek Council, minority business student group, Young Men of Black Alliance. World Student Association.

**ATHLETICS. Physical education requirements:** Two semesters of physical education required.
**Intercollegiate competition:** 3% of students participate. Baseball (M), basketball (M,W), cross-country (M,W), diving (M,W), football (M), golf (M,W), gymnastics (W), ice hockey (M), soccer (M), softball (W), swimming (M,W), tennis (M,W), track (indoor) (M,W), track (outdoor) (M,W), track and field (indoor) (M,W), track and field (outdoor) (M,W), volleyball (W). Member of Central Collegiate Hockey Association, Mid-American Conference, NCAA Division I.
**Intramural and club sports:** Intramural basketball, bowling, cross-country, curling, flag football, floor hockey, golf, ice hockey, racquetball, soccer, softball, tennis, volleyball, walleyball, wrestling. Men's club ice hockey, ice skating, lacrosse, racquetball, riflery, rugby, sailing, ski racing, soccer, squash, volleyball, water skiing, weight lifting. Women's club ice skating, racquetball, rugby, sailing, ski racing, soccer, squash, water skiing, weight lifting.

**ADMISSIONS. Academic basis for candidate selection** (in order of priority): Secondary school record, standardized test scores, class rank.

**Nonacademic basis for candidate selection:** Character and personality, extracurricular participation, particular talent or ability, and alumni/ae relationship are considered.
**Requirements:** Graduation from secondary school is required; GED is accepted. 16 units and the following program of study are required: 4 units of English, 3 units of math, 3 units of science including 2 units of lab, 2 units of foreign language, 3 units of social studies, 1 unit of academic electives. Minimum composite ACT score of 17 (combined SAT score of 700) required. Audition required of music program applicants. Summer Freshman Program for applicants not normally admissible. ACT is required; SAT may be substituted. Campus visit and interview recommended. No off-campus interviews.
**Procedure:** Take SAT or ACT by December 15 of 12th year. Suggest filing application by February 1. Application deadline is August 1. Notification of admission on rolling basis. Reply is required by two weeks prior to beginning of semester. $100 room deposit, refundable in full until May 1. Freshmen accepted for terms other than fall.
**Special programs:** Admission may be deferred one year. Credit and/or placement may be granted through CEEB Advanced Placement exams for scores of 3 or higher. Credit may be granted through CLEP subject exams, challenge exams, and military and life experience. Concurrent enrollment program.
**Transfer students:** Transfer students accepted for terms other than fall. In fall 1992, 2% of all new students were transfers into all classes. 1,013 transfer applications were received, 839 were accepted. Application deadline is August 1 for fall; December 15 for spring. Minimum 2.0 GPA recommended. Lowest course grade accepted is "D." At least 30 semester hours must be completed at the university to receive degree.
**Admissions contact:** John W. Martin, M.Ed., Director of Admissions. 419 372-2086.

**FINANCIAL AID. Available aid:** Pell grants, SEOG, state scholarships and grants, school scholarships and grants, private scholarships and grants, ROTC scholarships, academic merit scholarships, athletic scholarships, and aid for undergraduate foreign students. Perkins Loans (NDSL), PLUS, Stafford Loans (GSL), NSL, private loans, and SLS. Deferred payment plan. Short-term loans.
**Financial aid statistics:** 38% of aid is not need-based. In 1992-93, 50% of all undergraduate applicants received aid; 55% of freshman applicants. Average amounts of aid awarded freshmen: Scholarships and grants, $1,270; loans, $1,900.
**Supporting data/closing dates:** FAFSA/FAF/FFS: Accepted on rolling basis. State aid form: Deadline is September 15. Notification of awards begins May 1.
**Financial aid contact:** Conrad McRoberts, M.S., Director of Financial Aid. 419 372-2651.

**STUDENT EMPLOYMENT.** College Work/Study Program. Institutional employment. 30% of full-time undergraduates work on campus during school year. Students may expect to earn an average of $1,100 during school year. Off-campus part-time employment opportunities rated "good."

**COMPUTER FACILITIES.** 707 IBM/IBM-compatible and Macintosh/Apple microcomputers; 290 are networked. Students may access Digital, IBM minicomputer/mainframe systems, Internet. Residence halls may be equipped with stand-alone microcomputers, networked microcomputers. Client/LAN operating systems include Apple/Macintosh. Computer languages and software packages include BMDP, C, COBOL, FORTRAN, HyperCard, LISREL, Microsoft Works, Pascal, SAS, SPSS; 200 in all. Some computer labs restricted to graduate students and faculty.
Fees: None.
**Hours:** 8 AM-midn. (M-F); weekend hours.

**GRADUATE CAREER DATA.** Companies and businesses that hire graduates: Arthur Andersen, Lazarus, Marathon Oil, Motorola, Nationwide Insurance.

**PROMINENT ALUMNI/AE.** Eva Marie Saint, actress; Ruth Otte, president, cable TV's Discovery Channel; Tim Conway, actor.

8-28

## Capital University

**Columbus, OH 43209-2394** **614 236-6801**

**1994-95 Costs.** Tuition: $13,050. Room & board: $4,000. Fees, books, misc. academic expenses (school's estimate): $435.
**Enrollment.** Undergraduates: 585 men, 960 women (full-time). Freshman class: 1,747 applicants, 1,382 accepted, 449 enrolled. Graduate enrollment: 725 men, 477 women.
**Test score averages/ranges.** Average SAT scores: 465 verbal, 510 math. Range of SAT scores of middle 50%: 410-520 verbal, 440-580 math. Average ACT scores: 23 English, 22 math, 23 composite. Range of ACT scores of middle 50%: 21-26 English, 20-25 math.
**Faculty.** 107 full-time; 56 part-time. 78% of faculty holds highest degree in specific field. Student/faculty ratio: 14 to 1.
**Selectivity rating.** Less competitive.

**PROFILE.** Capital, founded in 1830, is a church-affiliated university. Programs are offered through the Adult Degree Program, the College of Arts and Sciences, the Conservatory of Music, the Graduate School of Administration, the Law School, and the School of Nursing. Its 48-acre campus is in a suburban area three miles from downtown Columbus.

**Accreditation:** NCACS. Professionally accredited by the American Bar Association, the Council on Social Work Education, the National Association of Schools of Music, the National Council for Accreditation of Teacher Education, the National League for Nursing.
**Religious orientation:** Capital University is affiliated with the Evangelical Lutheran Church in America; two semesters of theology required.
**Library:** Collections totaling over 191,742 volumes, 880 periodical subscriptions, and 93,082 microform items.
**Special facilities/museums:** Art gallery, language lab.
**Athletic facilities:** Gymnasiums, basketball, tennis, and volleyball courts, baseball, football, soccer, and softball fields, weight and wrestling rooms, stadium, arena.

**STUDENT BODY. Undergraduate profile:** 90% are state residents; 22% are transfers. 2% Asian-American, 6% Black, 92% White. Average age of undergraduates is 20.
**Freshman profile:** 6% of freshmen who took ACT scored 30 or over on English, 4% scored 30 or over on math, 5% scored 30 or over on composite; 48% scored 24 or over on English, 35% scored 24 or over on math, 42% scored 24 or over on composite; 90% scored 18 or over on English, 88% scored 18 or over on math, 87% scored 18 or over on composite; 99% scored 12 or over on English, 99% scored 12 or over on math, 91% scored 12 or over on composite; 100% scored 6 or over on English, 100% scored 6 or over on math. 33% of accepted applicants took SAT; 91% took ACT. 93% of freshmen come from public schools.
**Undergraduate achievement:** 74% of fall 1992 freshmen returned for fall 1993 term. 65% of entering class graduated. 35% of students who completed a degree program went on to graduate study within five years.
**Foreign students:** 41 students are from out of the country. Countries represented include China, Indonesia, Japan, Korea, Russia, and Taiwan; 30 in all.

**PROGRAMS OF STUDY. Degrees:** B.A., B.F.A., B.Gen.Studies, B.Mus., B.S.Nurs., B.Soc.Work.
**Majors:** Accounting, Art, Art Therapy, Athletic Training, Biology, Business Administration, Business/French, Chemistry, Computer/Information Sciences, Criminology, Economics, Education, Elementary Education, English, Fine Arts, French, Health/Fitness Management, History, International Studies, Jazz, Keyboard Pedagogy, Management, Mathematics, Music, Music Composition, Music Education, Music Industry, Music Performance, Nursing, Philosophy, Physical Education, Political Science/Government, Psychology, Public Administration, Public Relations, Religion, Secondary Education, Social Work, Sociology, Spanish, Speech/Communication Arts, Sports Medicine.
**Distribution of degrees:** The majors with the highest enrollment are nursing, education, and accounting; religion, French, and public administration have the lowest.
**Requirements:** General education requirement.
**Academic regulations:** Minimum 2.0 GPA required for graduation.
**Special:** Minors offered in many majors and in biblical languages, coaching, finance, historic preservation, Lutheran elementary education, marketing, physics, public speaking, social welfare, and transcultural studies. Certificate programs offered. Courses offered in anthropology, ethnic studies, geography, and Greek. Management training program. Social work program includes field work. Multidisciplinary majors in many areas including economic/political science, history/government, and humanities. Self-designed majors. Double majors. Independent study. Pass/fail grading option. Internships. Cooperative education programs. Preprofessional programs in law, medicine, veterinary science, pharmacy, dentistry, theology, physical therapy, and allied health fields. 3-2 engineering programs with Case Western Reserve U and Washington U. 3-2 occupational therapy program with Washington U. Member of Higher Educational Council of Columbus; cross-registration possible. Washington Semester. Teacher certification in elementary and secondary education. Study abroad in Jamaica, Japan, Mexico, European, Middle Eastern and South American countries. ROTC. NROTC and AFROTC at Ohio State U.
**Honors:** Honors program.
**Academic Assistance:** Nonremedial tutoring.

**STUDENT LIFE. Housing:** All students under age 23 must live on campus unless living with family. Coed, women's, and men's dorms. 60% of students live in college housing.
**Social atmosphere:** Students gather at the Crusader Club, the Drexel Movie Theatre, Grater's Ice Cream Shop, and High Street bars. Influential campus groups include the University Programming Board, Greeks, the Student Environmental Action Coalition, the conservatory of music, and the women's basketball team. Homecoming, sporting events, the Martin Luther King Day of Learning, Greek parties, ice skating, and Wicked Wednesday events (comedians and bands) at the Crusader Club are favorite campus activities. "Greek parties are very popular, and University Programming does a good job providing quality events on Wednesdays and Fridays," reports the student newspaper. "There's a lot to do in Columbus–students can get cheap symphony, ballet, and opera tickets–but you need a car to get to these events."
**Services and counseling/handicapped student services:** Placement services. Health service. Counseling services for minority students. Birth control, personal, and psychological counseling. Career and academic guidance services. Religious counseling. Learning disabled services.
**Campus organizations:** Undergraduate student government. Student newspaper (Chimes, published once/week). Literary magazine. Yearbook. Chapel choir, chorale, jazz ensembles, wind symphony, theatre, forensics, Circle K, cheerleaders, professional and service groups. Four fraternities, no chapter houses; four sororities, no chapter houses. 20% of men join a fraternity. 25% of women join a sorority.
**Religious organizations:** Baptist Student Union, Bible study group, Capital Volunteers, Catholics on Campus, Fellowship of Christian Athletes, Intervarsity Christian Fellowship, university congregation.
**Minority/foreign student organizations:** Afro-American cultural group, Ebony Brothers. International Student Association.

**ATHLETICS. Physical education requirements:** None.
**Intercollegiate competition:** 35% of students participate. Baseball (M), basketball (M,W), football (M), golf (M), soccer (M,W), softball (W), tennis (M,W), volleyball (W), wrestling (M). Member of NCAA Division III, Ohio Athletic Conference.
**Intramural and club sports:** 75% of students participate. Intramural aerobics, basketball, billiards, bowling, cycling, fitness room, floor hockey, football, golf, soccer, softball, swimming, tennis, volleyball.

**ADMISSIONS. Academic basis for candidate selection** (in order of priority): Secondary school record, class rank, standardized test scores, school's recommendation.
**Nonacademic basis for candidate selection:** Character and personality are emphasized. Extracurricular participation and particular talent or ability are important. Alumni/ae relationship is considered.
**Requirements:** Graduation from secondary school is required; GED is accepted. 16 units and the following program of study are required: 4 units of English, 3 units of math, 3 units of science including 2 units of lab, 2 units of foreign language, 2 units of social studies, 1 unit of history, 1 unit of electives. Rank in top half of secondary school class and minimum 2.5 GPA recommended. Chemistry required of nursing program applicants. Audition required of music program applicants. SAT or ACT is required. Campus visit and interview recommended. No off-campus interviews.
**Procedure:** Take SAT or ACT by December of 12th year. Visit college for interview by December of 12th year. Application deadline is August 1. Notification of admission on rolling basis. Reply is required by May 1. $200 tuition deposit, refundable until May 1. $100 room deposit, refundable until May 1. Freshmen accepted for terms other than fall.

**Special programs:** Admission may be deferred one year. Credit and/or placement may be granted through CEEB Advanced Placement exams for scores of 3 or higher. Credit and/or placement may be granted through CLEP subject exams. Credit and placement may be granted through ACT PEP, DANTES, and challenge exams, and military and life experience. Early entrance/early admission program. Concurrent enrollment program.
**Transfer students:** Transfer students accepted for terms other than fall. In fall 1993, 22% of all new students were transfers into all classes. 283 transfer applications were received, 194 were accepted. Application deadline is August 1 for fall; December 1 for spring. Minimum 2.25 GPA required. Lowest course grade accepted is "C-." At least 30 semester hours must be completed at the university to receive degree.
**Admissions contact:** Dolphus E. Henry, Ph.D., Vice President for Enrollment Management. 614 236-6101, 800 289-6289.

**FINANCIAL AID. Available aid:** Pell grants, SEOG, state scholarships and grants, school scholarships and grants, private grants, ROTC scholarships, academic merit scholarships, and aid for undergraduate foreign students. Proficiency Awards for music students. Perkins Loans (NDSL), PLUS, Stafford Loans (GSL), NSL, and SLS. Tuition Management Systems.
**Financial aid statistics:** 50% of aid is not need-based. In 1993-94, 97% of all undergraduate applicants received aid; 91% of freshman applicants. Average amounts of aid awarded freshmen: Scholarships and grants, $6,500; loans, $2,200.
**Supporting data/closing dates:** FAFSA: Priority filing date is February 15. School's own aid application: Priority filing date is February 15. Notification of awards begins April 1.
**Financial aid contact:** June Schlabach, M.A., Director of Financial Aid. 614 236-6511.

**STUDENT EMPLOYMENT.** College Work/Study Program. Institutional employment. 52% of full-time undergraduates work on campus during school year. Students may expect to earn an average of $1,500 during school year. Off-campus part-time employment opportunities rated "excellent."

**COMPUTER FACILITIES.** 60 IBM/IBM-compatible and Macintosh/Apple microcomputers. Students may access Prime, SUN minicomputer/mainframe systems. Client/LAN operating systems include Apple/Macintosh, DOS. Computer languages and software packages include Assembler, BASIC, C, COBOL, dBASE, FORTRAN, Pascal, SPSS; graphics, word processing packages. Multi-user system may be used only for relevant class work.
**Fees:** None.
**Hours:** 8 AM-11 PM (M-Th); 8 AM-5 PM (F); 9 AM-5 PM (Sa); 1 PM-1 AM (Su).

**GRADUATE CAREER DATA.** Highest graduate school enrollments: Capital U Law School, Ohio State U. 78% of graduates choose careers in business and industry. Companies and businesses that hire graduates: Bank One, Children's Hospital, Deloitte & Touche, KPMG Peat Marwick, Nationwide Insurance, Ohio State U Hospitals.

**PROMINENT ALUMNI/AE.** George Dell, author; Armin Meyer, ambassador to Iran; Charles Oestreich, president, Texas Lutheran Coll; Dr. Richard Bord, former director, Martha Holden Jennings Foundation.

8-28

# Case Western Reserve University

**Cleveland, OH 44106-7055** **216 368-2000**

**1994-95 Costs.** Tuition: $15,700. Room: $2,960. Board: $2,180. Fees, books, misc. academic expenses (school's estimate): $650.
**Enrollment.** Undergraduates: 1,823 men, 1,228 women (full-time). Freshman class: 3,877 applicants, 3,156 accepted, 713 enrolled. Graduate enrollment: 3,275 men, 2,437 women.
**Test score averages/ranges.** Range of SAT scores of middle 50%: 510-640 verbal, 610-730 math. Range of ACT scores of middle 50%: 26-31 composite.
**Faculty.** 1,769 full-time undergraduate and graduate; 47 part-time undergraduate and graduate. 97% of faculty holds highest degree in specific field. Student/faculty ratio: 8 to 1.
**Selectivity rating.** Highly competitive.

**PROFILE.** Case Western Reserve is a private, comprehensive university. It is the result of the 1967 merger of Case Institute of Technology and Western Reserve University. Its 128-acre campus is located in Cleveland's University Circle, four miles from downtown Cleveland.

**Accreditation:** NCACS. Professionally accredited by the Accreditation Board for Engineering and Technology, the American Assembly of Collegiate Schools of Business, the American Medical Association (CAHEA), the National Association of Schools of Music, the National League for Nursing.
**Religious orientation:** Case Western Reserve University is nonsectarian; no religious requirements.
**Library:** Collections totaling over 1,802,042 volumes, 14,344 periodical subscriptions, and 2,089,795 microform items.
**Special facilities/museums:** Art, natural history, and auto-aviation museums, historical society, garden center, biology field stations, observatory.
**Athletic facilities:** Gymnasiums, track, basketball, racquetball, squash, tennis, and volleyball courts, swimming pools, archery and rifle ranges, baseball, football, intramural, soccer, and softball fields, fitness trail, weight and wrestling rooms.

**STUDENT BODY. Undergraduate profile:** 62% are state residents; 16% are transfers. 10% Asian-American, 7% Black, 2% Hispanic, 1% Native American, 68% White, 12% Other. Average age of undergraduates is 20.
**Freshman profile:** 42% of freshmen who took ACT scored 30 or over on composite; 93% scored 24 or over on composite; 100% scored 18 or over on composite. 87% of accepted applicants took SAT; 60% took ACT. 70% of freshmen come from public schools.
**Undergraduate achievement:** 91% of fall 1992 freshmen returned for fall 1993 term. 43% of entering class graduated. 39% of students who completed a degree program immediately went on to graduate study.
**Foreign students:** 290 students are from out of the country. Countries represented include Canada, China, India, Indonesia, Japan, and Malaysia; 49 in all.

**PROGRAMS OF STUDY. Degrees:** B.A., B.S., B.S.Nurs.
**Majors:** Accounting, Aerospace Engineering, American Studies, Anthropology, Applied Mathematics, Applied Physics, Art Education, Art History, Asian Studies, Astronomy, Biochemistry, Biology, Biomedical Engineering, Chemical Engineering, Chemistry, Civil Engineering, Classics, Communication Sciences/Disorders, Comparative Literature, Computer Engineering, Computer Science, Economics, Electrical Engineering, Engineering, English, Environmental Geology, Fluid/Thermal Sciences, French, Geological Sciences, German, German Studies, Gerontological Studies, History, History/Philosophy of Science/Technology, Industrial Engineering, International Studies, Literature, Management, Management Science, Materials Science, Mathematics, Mechanical Engineering, Medical Technology, Music, Music Education, Natural Sciences, Nursing, Nutrition, Nutritional Biochemistry/Metabolism, Operations Management/Operations Research, Philosophy, Physics, Political Science, Polymer Science/Engineering, Pre-Architecture, Psychology, Religion, Sociology, Spanish, Statistics, Systems/Control Engineering, Theatre.
**Distribution of degrees:** The majors with the highest enrollment are mechanical engineering, management, and accounting; comparative literature, applied mathematics, and pre-architecture have the lowest.
**Requirements:** General education requirement.
**Academic regulations:** Minimum 2.0 GPA required for graduation.
**Special:** Minors offered in all majors and in art studio, artificial intelligence, arts in a technological age, Chinese, dance, education, electronics, forms/roots of modern consciousness, history of technology/science, human development, Japanese, photography, physical education, Russian, and women's studies. LAMBDA Program (Liberal Arts Math Based Alternative) combines liberal arts discipline with strong quantitative background. Preprofessional Scholars Program (dentistry, law, management, medicine, nursing, social work) leads to conditional admission to related professional school of the university. Self-designed majors. Double majors. Dual degrees. Independent study. Accelerated study. Pass/fail grading option. Internships. Cooperative education programs. Graduate school at which undergraduates may take graduate-level courses. Preprofessional programs in veterinary science, dentistry, theology, and education. 3-1 medical technology programs with University Hospitals. Five-year bachelor's/M.B.A. program. Host university for 3-2 programs in astronomy, biochemistry, and engineering. Full-time students may cross-register for one course/semester at 13 Cleveland area colleges. Washington Semester. Teacher certification in elementary and secondary education. Certification in specific subject areas. Study abroad in Australia, Austria, Denmark, England, France, Germany, Israel, Italy, Japan, Korea, New Zealand, Scotland, and Spain. ROTC at John Carroll U. AFROTC at U of Akron.
**Honors:** Phi Beta Kappa. Honors program. Honor societies.
**Academic Assistance:** Nonremedial tutoring.

**STUDENT LIFE. Housing:** All unmarried students under age 21 must live on campus unless living near campus with relatives. Coed and women's dorms. Sorority and fraternity housing. 77% of students live in college housing.
**Services and counseling/handicapped student services:** Placement services. Health service. Women's center. Dental clinic. Developmental learning strategies. Counseling services for minority, veteran, and older students. Birth control, personal, and psychological counseling. Career and academic guidance services. Religious counseling. Physically disabled student services. Learning disabled services. Notetaking services. Tape recorders. Tutors. Reader services for the blind.
**Campus organizations:** Undergraduate student government. Student newspaper (Observer, published once/week). Literary magazine. Yearbook. Radio station. Musical ensembles, performing arts groups, film society, community service groups, outing club, commuter and older-student clubs, Gay/Lesbian Student Union, academic and professional groups, 100 organizations in all. 18 fraternities, 15 chapter houses; five sororities, three chapter houses. 40% of men join a fraternity. 20% of women join a sorority.
**Religious organizations:** University Christian Movement, Hillel, Campus Crusade for Christ, Korean Undergraduate Bible Study, Hallinan Center, other religious groups.
**Minority/foreign student organizations:** African American Society, Asian American Alliance, Hispanic Society, National Society of Black Engineers. International Club; Arab, Caribbean, Indian, Indonesian, Japanese, Korean, Malaysian, and Pakistani groups.

**ATHLETICS. Physical education requirements:** Two semesters of physical education required.
**Intercollegiate competition:** 16% of students participate. Baseball (M), basketball (M,W), cheerleading (M,W), cross-country (M,W), diving (M,W), fencing (M,W), football (M), golf (M), soccer (M,W), swimming (M,W), tennis (M,W), track (indoor) (M,W), track and field (indoor) (M,W), track and field (outdoor) (M,W), volleyball (W), wrestling (M). Member of NCAA Division III, North Coast Athletic Conference, University Athletic Association.
**Intramural and club sports:** 70% of students participate. Intramural badminton, basketball, bench press, bowling, cross-country, flag football, free throw, frisbee, golf, indoor soccer, inner-tube water polo, racquetball, soccer, softball, squash, table tennis, tennis, track, volleyball, walleyball, wrestling. Men's club archery, bowling, crew, ice hockey, lacrosse, martial arts, squash, volleyball, water polo. Women's club archery, bowling, softball.

**ADMISSIONS. Academic basis for candidate selection** (in order of priority): Secondary school record, class rank, standardized test scores, school's recommendation, essay.
**Nonacademic basis for candidate selection:** Particular talent or ability is emphasized. Extracurricular participation is important. Character and personality, geographical distribution, and alumni/ae relationship are considered.
**Requirements:** Graduation from secondary school is required; GED is accepted. 16 units and the following program of study are required: 4 units of English, 3 units of math, 1 unit of lab science. 4 units of math required of math, science, and engineering program applicants. 1 unit of chemistry and 1 unit of physics required of engineering program applicants. 2 units of lab science, including chemistry, required of math, science, and premedical studies program applicants. Portfolio required of art education program applicants. Audition required of music education program applicants. Portfolio required of art program applicants. Audition required of music program applicants. SAT or ACT is required. ACH recommended. Campus visit and interview recommended. Off-campus interviews available with admissions and alumni representatives.

**Procedure:** Take SAT or ACT by December of 12th year. Visit college for interview by January of 12th year. Suggest filing application by fall. Application deadline is February 15. Notification of admission by April 1. Reply is required by May 1. $200 nonrefundable tuition deposit. Freshmen accepted for terms other than fall.
**Special programs:** Admission may be deferred one year. Credit and/or placement may be granted through CEEB Advanced Placement exams for scores of 4 or higher. Credit and placement may be granted through challenge exams. Early decision program. In fall 1993, 128 applied for early decision and 111 were accepted. Deadline for applying for early decision is January 15. Early entrance/early admission program. Concurrent enrollment program.
**Transfer students:** Transfer students accepted for terms other than fall. In fall 1993, 16% of all new students were transfers into all classes. 497 transfer applications were received, 271 were accepted. Application deadline is June 30 (February 15 for nursing) for fall; November 15 for spring. Minimum 3.0 GPA recommended. Lowest course grade accepted is "C." At least 60 semester hours must be completed at the university to receive degree.
**Admissions contact:** William T. Conley, M.Ed., Director of Admissions. 216 368-4450.

**FINANCIAL AID. Available aid:** Pell grants, SEOG, state scholarships and grants, school scholarships and grants, private scholarships, ROTC scholarships, and academic merit scholarships. Perkins Loans (NDSL), PLUS, Stafford Loans (GSL), school loans, and SLS. Knight Tuition Plans, AMS, deferred payment plan, and guaranteed tuition. Tuition stabilization plan. Private financing plans.
**Financial aid statistics:** 30% of aid is not need-based. Average amounts of aid awarded freshmen: Scholarships and grants, $10,926; loans, $6,052.
**Supporting data/closing dates:** FAFSA/FAF/FFS: Priority filing date is February 1. Income tax forms: Priority filing date is March 1. Notification of awards on rolling basis.
**Financial aid contact:** Donald Chenelle, Director of Financial Aid. 216 368-4530.

**STUDENT EMPLOYMENT.** College Work/Study Program. Institutional employment. 80% of full-time undergraduates work on campus during school year. Students may expect to earn an average of $1,200 during school year. Off-campus part-time employment opportunities rated "good."

**COMPUTER FACILITIES.** 200 IBM/IBM-compatible, Macintosh/Apple, and RISC-/UNIX-based microcomputers; all are networked. Students may access IBM minicomputer/mainframe systems, BITNET, Internet, CompuServe. Residence halls may be equipped with networked microcomputers. Client/LAN operating systems include Apple/Macintosh, DOS, OS/2, UNIX/XENIX/AIX, Novell. Computer languages and software packages include BASIC, COBOL, FORTRAN, Mathematica, Turbo C, Turbo Pascal; graphics, spreadsheet, statistical, word processing programs, special software for various departments/programs. Computer facilities are available to all students.
**Fees:** Computer fee is included in tuition/fees.
**Hours:** Some facilities restrict hours for class use.

**GRADUATE CAREER DATA.** Graduate school percentages: 5% enter law school. 8% enter medical school. 1% enter dental school. 4% enter graduate business programs. 20% enter graduate arts and sciences programs. Highest graduate school enrollments: Case Western Reserve U, Cornell U, MIT, Ohio State U, Stanford U, U of Illinois. 35% of graduates choose careers in business and industry. Companies and businesses that hire graduates: Arthur Andersen, BP America, Dow Chemical, Ernest & Young, General Motors, IBM, Lincoln Electric.

**PROMINENT ALUMNI/AE.** Herbert Henry Dow, founder, Dow Chemical; William Baker, president, WNET-TV; Michael McCaskey, CEO, Chicago Bears; Dr. David Satcher, director, Federal Centers for Disease Control; Richard LeFauve, president, Saturn Corporation.

## Cedarville College

**Cedarville, OH 45314** **513 766-2211**

**1993-94 Costs.** Tuition: $6,192. Room: $1,788. Board: $1,968. Fees, books, misc. academic expenses (school's estimate): $1,402.
**Enrollment.** Undergraduates: 950 men, 1,246 women (full-time). Freshman class: 1,307 applicants, 1,090 accepted, 616 enrolled.
**Test score averages/ranges.** Average SAT scores: 486 verbal, 524 math. Range of SAT scores of middle 50%: 420-550 verbal, 450-600 math. Average ACT scores: 24 English, 22 math, 24 composite. Range of ACT scores of middle 50%: 21-27 English, 19-25 math.
**Faculty.** 130 full-time; 40 part-time. 54% of faculty holds doctoral degree. Student/faculty ratio: 17 to 1.
**Selectivity rating.** Competitive.

**PROFILE.** Cedarville, founded in 1887, is a church-affiliated, liberal arts college. Programs are offered through the Departments of Biblical Education, Business Administration, Communication Arts, Education, Health and Physical Education, Language and Literature, Music, Nursing, Psychology, Science and Mathematics, and Social Sciences and History. Its 105-acre campus is located in Cedarville, 20 miles from Dayton.

**Accreditation:** NCACS. Professionally accredited by the National League for Nursing.
**Religious orientation:** Cedarville College is affiliated with the Baptist Church; six quarters of religion required.
**Library:** Collections totaling over 122,220 volumes, 1,030 periodical subscriptions, and 20,776 microform items.
**Special facilities/museums:** Observatory.
**Athletic facilities:** Gymnasium, field house, badminton, basketball, racquetball, tennis, and volleyball courts, baseball, intramural, soccer, and softball fields, weight room, track.

**STUDENT BODY. Undergraduate profile:** 35% are state residents; 14% are transfers. 1% Asian-American, 1% Black, .5% Hispanic, .5% Native American, 96% White, 1% Other. Average age of undergraduates is 20.
**Freshman profile:** 1% of freshmen who took SAT scored 700 or over on verbal, 4% scored 700 or over on math; 13% scored 600 or over on verbal, 27% scored 600 or over on math; 43% scored 500 or over on verbal, 58% scored 500 or over on math; 85% scored 400 or over on verbal, 86% scored 400 or over on math; 100% scored 300 or over on verbal, 99% scored 300 or over on math. 51% of accepted applicants took SAT; 69% took ACT. 54% of freshmen come from public schools.
**Undergraduate achievement:** 80% of fall 1992 freshmen returned for fall 1993 term. 45% of entering class graduated. 18% of students who completed a degree program immediately went on to graduate study.
**Foreign students:** 23 students are from out of the country. Countries represented include Brazil and Canada; 11 in all.

**PROGRAMS OF STUDY. Degrees:** B.A., B.S.Elec.Eng., B.S.Mus.Ed., B.S.Nurs.
**Majors:** Accounting, American Studies, Applied Psychology, Behavioral Science, Bible Studies, Biology, Broadcasting, Business Communications Technology, Business Education, Chemistry, Church Music, Communication Arts, Computer/Information Sciences, Criminal Justice, Electrical Engineering, Elementary Education, English, Finance, Global Economics, History, History/Political Science, International Business, International Studies, Management, Marketing, Mathematics, Mechanical Engineering, Missiology, Music, Music Education, Nursing, Philosophy, Physical Education, Political Science/Government, Pre-Law, Pre-Medicine, Pre-Physical Therapy, Professional Writing, Psychology, Public Administration, Science, Social Sciences, Social Work, Sociology, Spanish.
**Distribution of degrees:** The majors with the highest enrollment are business, education, and nursing; American studies, Spanish, and music have the lowest.
**Requirements:** General education requirement.
**Academic regulations:** Freshmen must maintain minimum 1.50 GPA; sophomores, 1.65 GPA; juniors, 1.90 GPA; seniors, 2.0 GPA.
**Special:** Minor in Bible required for graduation. One-year certificate program in Bible. TESOL and special education certification. Associate's degrees offered. Double majors. Independent study. Pass/fail grading option. Internships. Preprofessional programs in law, medicine, veterinary science, pharmacy, dentistry, theology, optometry, agriculture, medical technology, and physical therapy. Off-campus study opportunities. Teacher certification in early childhood, elementary, secondary, and special education. Certification in specific subject areas. Study abroad in Costa Rica, the Dominican Republic, England, France, Germany, Peru, Scotland, and Spain. ROTC and AFROTC.
**Honors:** Honors program. Honor societies.
**Academic Assistance:** Remedial math and study skills. Nonremedial tutoring.

**STUDENT LIFE. Housing:** All unmarried students under age 25 must live on campus unless living with family. Women's and men's dorms. Off-campus privately-owned housing. Off-campus married-student housing. 79% of students live in college housing.
**Services and counseling/handicapped student services:** Placement services. Health service. Counseling services for veteran students. Personal and psychological counseling. Career and academic guidance services. Religious counseling. Physically disabled student services. Learning disabled services. Reader services for the blind.
**Campus organizations:** Undergraduate student government. Student newspaper (Cedars, published biweekly). Yearbook. Radio station. Concert chorale, debating, drama group, campus spirit organization, Republican club, forensics, Earth Stewardship Organization, Married Student Fellowship, professional and special-interest groups, 46 organizations in all.
**Religious organizations:** Advisory 7, Fellowship for World Missions, Swordbearers.
**Minority/foreign student organizations:** Iota Chi. Mu Keppe.

**ATHLETICS. Physical education requirements:** Two quarters of physical education required.
**Intercollegiate competition:** 10% of students participate. Baseball (M), basketball (M,W), cheerleading (M,W), cross-country (M,W), golf (M), soccer (M), softball (W), tennis (M,W), track and field (indoor) (M,W), track and field (outdoor) (M,W), volleyball (W). Member of Mid-Ohio Conference, NAIA, NCCAA.
**Intramural and club sports:** 60% of students participate. Intramural aerobics, bowling, flag football, floor hockey, golf, pool, racquetball, sand volleyball, soccer, softball, table tennis, team handball, tennis, volleyball, wallyball. Men's club volleyball.

**ADMISSIONS. Academic basis for candidate selection** (in order of priority): Secondary school record, standardized test scores, class rank, school's recommendation, essay.
**Nonacademic basis for candidate selection:** Character and personality are emphasized. Extracurricular participation, particular talent or ability, and alumni/ae relationship are considered.
**Requirements:** Graduation from secondary school is required; GED is accepted. 18 units and the following program of study are recommended: 4 units of English, 3 units of math, 3 units of science, 2 units of foreign language, 3 units of social studies, 3 units of history. Three units of history and social studies required. Minimum composite ACT score of 21 (combined SAT score of 900), rank in top half of secondary school class, and minimum 2.8 GPA required. Audition required of music program applicants. Conditional admission possible for applicants not meeting standard requirements. Academic Development Program possible for applicants not normally admissible. ACT is required; SAT may be substituted. Campus visit and interview recommended. Off-campus interviews available with an admissions representative.
**Procedure:** Take SAT or ACT by December of 12th year. Notification of admission on rolling basis. Reply is required by May 1 or within 30 days after receiving letter of acceptance. $250 tuition deposit, refundable partially until September 1. Freshmen accepted for terms other than fall.
**Special programs:** Admission may be deferred one year. Credit and/or placement may be granted through CEEB Advanced Placement exams for scores of 3 or higher. Credit and/or placement may be granted through CLEP general and subject exams. Credit and placement may be granted through challenge exams. Early entrance/early admission program. Concurrent enrollment program.
**Transfer students:** Transfer students accepted for terms other than fall. In fall 1993, 14% of all new students were transfers into all classes. 341 transfer applications were received, 215 were accepted. Application deadline is rolling for fall; rolling for spring. Minimum 2.5 GPA recommended. Lowest course grade accepted is "C-." At least 48 quarter hours must be completed at the college to receive degree.
**Admissions contact:** David M. Ormsbee, Director of Admissions. 800 233-2784, 800 CEDARVILLE.

**FINANCIAL AID. Available aid:** Pell grants, SEOG, state scholarships and grants, school scholarships and grants, private scholarships and grants, ROTC scholarships, academic merit scholarships, and athletic scholarships. Perkins Loans (NDSL), PLUS, Staf-

ford Loans (GSL), NSL, state loans, school loans, private loans, and SLS. Deferred payment plan. Interest-Bearing Prepayment Plan.
**Financial aid statistics:** 32% of aid is not need-based. In 1993-94, 63% of all undergraduate applicants received aid; 90% of freshman applicants. Average amounts of aid awarded freshmen: Scholarships and grants, $987; loans, $3,284.
**Supporting data/closing dates:** FAFSA: Priority filing date is March 1; accepted on rolling basis. School's own aid application: Priority filing date is March 1; accepted on rolling basis. State aid form: Priority filing date is March 1; accepted on rolling basis. Income tax forms: Priority filing date is March 1; accepted on rolling basis. Notification of awards begins April 1.
**Financial aid contact:** Fred E. Merritt, Director of Financial Aid. 800 444-2433.
**STUDENT EMPLOYMENT.** College Work/Study Program. Institutional employment. 25% of full-time undergraduates work on campus during school year. Students may expect to earn an average of $1,300 during school year. Freshmen are discouraged from working during their first term. Off-campus part-time employment opportunities rated "fair."
**COMPUTER FACILITIES.** 900 IBM/IBM-compatible microcomputers; all are networked. Students may access IBM minicomputer/mainframe systems, Internet. Residence halls may be equipped with stand-alone microcomputers, networked microcomputers. 100 major computer languages and software packages available. Computer facilities are available to all students.
**Fees:** $80 computer fee per quarter.
**Hours:** 7 AM-11 PM (M-F); 8 AM-11 PM (Sa).
**GRADUATE CAREER DATA.** Highest graduate school enrollments: Indiana U, Miami U, Ohio State U, Michigan State U, U of Michigan. 35% of graduates choose careers in business and industry. Companies and businesses that hire graduates: Arthur Anderson, Ernst & Young, Best Lock, ESKO, Mercy Medical Center.
**PROMINENT ALUMNI/AE.** Jim Englemen, plant manager, General Motors; Dave Hole, state representative; Missouri; Dr. Rex Rogers, president, Grand Rapids Baptist College; Michael Stephens, CEO, Greene Memorial Hospital; Roy Linton, former chairman, Standard Register; Frank Jeniste, foreign diplomat, International Cultural Affairs.

## Central State University

**Wilberforce, OH 45384 — 513 376-6011**

**1993-94 Costs.** Tuition: $1,515 (state residents), $4,731 (out-of-state). Room & board: $4,725. Fees, books, misc. academic expenses (school's estimate): $1,825.
**Enrollment.** Undergraduates: 1,277 men, 1,315 women (full-time). Freshman class: 3,556 applicants, 2,474 accepted, 710 enrolled. Graduate enrollment: 4 men, 14 women.
**Test score averages/ranges.** N/A.
**Faculty.** 127 full-time; 20 part-time. 46% of faculty holds doctoral degree. Student/faculty ratio: 15 to 1.
**Selectivity rating.** N/A.

**PROFILE.** Central State, founded in 1887, is a comprehensive, public university. Programs are offered through the Colleges of Arts and Sciences, Business Administration, and Education. Its 550-acre campus is located in Wilberforce, 18 miles east of Dayton.
**Accreditation:** NCACS.
**Religious orientation:** Central State University is nonsectarian; no religious requirements.
**Library:** Collections totaling over 155,643 volumes, 890 periodical subscriptions, and 555,443 microform items.
**Special facilities/museums:** Museum/gallery, TV studio, language lab.
**Athletic facilities:** Gymnasiums, nautilus and dance rooms, swimming pool, baseball and softball fields.
**STUDENT BODY. Undergraduate profile:** 65% are state residents; 3% are transfers. 90% Black, 5% White, 5% Other. Average age of undergraduates is 19.
**Freshman profile:** Majority of accepted applicants took ACT.
**Undergraduate achievement:** 20% of fall 1992 freshmen returned for fall 1993 term. 65% of students who completed a degree program went on to graduate study within five years.
**Foreign students:** Countries represented include Ethiopia, Jamaica, Jordan, Kenya, Lebanon, and Zimbabwe.
**PROGRAMS OF STUDY. Degrees:** B.A., B.Mus., B.S., B.S.Ed., B.S.Mus.Ed.
**Majors:** Accounting, Allied Health, Art Education, Biology, Business Administration/Management, Chemistry, Community Health, Community Recreation, Computer Technology, Construction, Drawing/Design/Planning, Earth Science, Economics, Electronics, Elementary Education, English, English Literature, Finance, French, Geography, Geology, Graphic Arts, Graphic/Commercial Art, Health Education, Health/Physical Education/Recreation, History, Industrial Arts Education, Industrial Technology, Journalism, Management, Management Information Systems, Manufacturing Engineering, Marketing Management/Research, Mathematics, Military Science, Music, Music Education, Music Performance, Philosophy, Physical Education, Physics, Political Science/Government, Psychology, Public Administration, Radio/Television, Secondary Education, Social Welfare, Sociology/Anthropology, Spanish, Special Education, Speech/Debate/Forensics, Studio Art, Systems Engineering, Theatre, Water Resources Management.
**Distribution of degrees:** The majors with the highest enrollment are business administration and education; water resources management and manufacturing engineering have the lowest.
**Requirements:** General education requirement.
**Academic regulations:** Minimum 2.0 GPA must be maintained.
**Special:** Minors offered in most majors. Associate's degrees offered. Double majors. Independent study. Internships. Cooperative education programs. Graduate school at which undergraduates may take graduate-level courses. Preprofessional programs in law, medicine, veterinary science, pharmacy, dentistry, and engineering. 2-2 and 3-2 engineering programs with Wright State U. Member of Southwestern Ohio Council for Higher Education (SOCHE); cross-registration possible. Teacher certification in elementary, secondary, and special education. ROTC. AFROTC at Wright St U.
**Honors:** Honors program. Honor societies.
**Academic Assistance:** Remedial reading, writing, and math. Nonremedial tutoring.
**STUDENT LIFE. Housing:** All freshmen must live on campus unless living with family. Coed, women's, and men's dorms. 50% of students live in college housing.
**Social atmosphere:** According to the student newspaper, CSU offers a quiet campus life in a rural setting, although three urban centers are located within an hour's drive. Favorite on-campus gathering spots include the Union, the Breezeway, and Central Park. Popular groups on campus include Student Government, Inter-faith Campus Ministry, and Greeks. Homecoming, May Weekend, and football and basketball games are popular events.
**Services and counseling/handicapped student services:** Placement services. Health service. Counseling services for military students. Personal and psychological counseling. Career and academic guidance services. Religious counseling. Physically disabled student services. Notetaking services.
**Campus organizations:** Undergraduate student government. Student newspaper (Gold Torch, published twice/month). Yearbook. Radio station. Concert/jazz band, choirs, marching band, drama groups, service and special-interest groups. Four fraternities, no chapter houses; three sororities, no chapter houses. 35% of men join a fraternity. 25% of women join a sorority.
**Religious organizations:** Interfaith Campus Ministry.
**ATHLETICS. Physical education requirements:** Five quarter hours of physical education required.Five hours of physical education required.
**Intercollegiate competition:** 8% of students participate. Baseball (M), basketball (M,W), cross-country (M,W), football (M), track and field (indoor) (M,W), track and field (outdoor) (M,W), volleyball (W). Member of NAIA Division I.
**Intramural and club sports:** 15% of students participate. Intramural basketball, flag football, softball, volleyball.
**ADMISSIONS. Academic basis for candidate selection** (in order of priority): Secondary school record, class rank, standardized test scores, school's recommendation, essay.
**Requirements:** Graduation from secondary school is required; GED is accepted. No specific distribution of secondary school units required. Minimum 2.0 GPA required of out-of-state applicants. University College program for applicants not normally admissible. ACT is required. Campus visit and interview recommended. No off-campus interviews.
**Procedure:** Take ACT before submission of application. Suggest filing application by June 15. Application deadline is August 1. Notification of admission on rolling basis. $60 nonrefundable room deposit. Freshmen accepted for terms other than fall.
**Special programs:** Admission may be deferred. Early entrance/early admission program. Concurrent enrollment program.
**Transfer students:** Transfer students accepted for terms other than fall. In fall 1993, 3% of all new students were transfers into all classes. 279 transfer applications were received, 198 were accepted. Application deadline is June 15 for fall; February 15 for spring. Minimum 2.0 GPA required. Lowest course grade accepted is "C." At least 45 credits must be completed at the university to receive degree.
**Admissions contact:** Robert E. Johnson, M.Ed., Director of Admissions. 513 376-6348.
**FINANCIAL AID. Available aid:** Pell grants, SEOG, state grants, school scholarships and grants, ROTC scholarships, academic merit scholarships, and athletic scholarships. Perkins Loans (NDSL), PLUS, Stafford Loans (GSL), state loans, and SLS. Tuition installment plan.
**Supporting data/closing dates:** FAFSA/FAF/FFS: Priority filing date is March 31; accepted on rolling basis. School's own aid application: Priority filing date is March 31; accepted on rolling basis. State aid form: Priority filing date is March 31; accepted on rolling basis. Notification of awards on rolling basis.
**Financial aid contact:** Sunny Terrell, Director of Financial Aid. 513 376-6579.
**STUDENT EMPLOYMENT.** College Work/Study Program. 30% of full-time undergraduates work on campus during school year. Students may expect to earn an average of $1,200 during school year. Off-campus part-time employment opportunities rated "fair."
**COMPUTER FACILITIES.** IBM/IBM-compatible and Macintosh/Apple microcomputers. Students may access IBM minicomputer/mainframe systems. Computer languages and software packages include Assembly, COBOL, Harvard Graphics, Professional Plan, WordPerfect. Computers are available to all students; use is supervised.
**Fees:** $25 computer fee per quarter.
**Hours:** 8 AM-4 PM, 6 PM-11 PM (M-F).
**GRADUATE CAREER DATA.** Companies and businesses that hire graduates: General Electric Aircrafts, MCI Telecommunications, Procter & Gamble.

8-30/9-4

## Cincinnati Bible College

**Cincinnati, OH 45204-3200 — 513 244-8100**

**1993-94 Costs.** Tuition: $3,872. Room & board: $3,124. Fees, books, misc. academic expenses (school's estimate): $500.
**Enrollment.** Undergraduates: 310 men, 209 women (full-time). Freshman class: 292 applicants, 292 accepted, 210 enrolled. Graduate enrollment: 235 men, 50 women.
**Test score averages/ranges.** N/A.
**Faculty.** 28 full-time; 25 part-time. 21% of faculty holds doctoral degree. Student/faculty ratio: 20 to 1.
**Selectivity rating.** N/A.

**PROFILE.** Cincinnati Bible, founded in 1924, is a church-affiliated college. Its 35-acre campus is located three miles from downtown Cinncinnati.
**Accreditation:** AABC, NCACS.
**Religious orientation:** Cincinnati Bible College is a nondenominational Christian school; eight semesters of religion/theology required.
**Library:** Collections totaling over 86,883 volumes, 721 periodical subscriptions, and 34,000 microform items.
**Special facilities/museums:** Museum.
**Athletic facilities:** Gymnasium.

**STUDENT BODY. Undergraduate profile:** 60% are state residents; 7% are transfers. 1% Asian-American, 3% Black, 96% White. Average age of undergraduates is 20.
**Freshman profile:** 85% of accepted applicants took ACT. 98% of freshmen come from public schools.
**Undergraduate achievement:** 66% of fall 1991 freshmen returned for fall 1992 term. 25% of entering class graduated. 25% of students who completed a degree program went on to graduate study within five years.
**Foreign students:** 12 students are from out of the country. Countries represented include Australia, Canada, Japan, and Thailand; nine in all.
**PROGRAMS OF STUDY. Degrees:** B.A., B.Mus., B.S.
**Majors:** Bible/General Studies, Christian Education, Christian Ministries, Church Music, Elementary Education, Missions, Secondary Education.
**Distribution of degrees:** The majors with the highest enrollment are Christian ministries, Christian education, and Bible/general studies.
**Requirements:** General education requirement.
**Academic regulations:** Minimum 2.0 GPA must be maintained.
**Special:** Minors offered in journalism, ministry, and psychology. Education program for deaf students. Associate's degrees offered. Double majors. Independent study. Internships. Graduate school at which undergraduates may take graduate-level courses. Numerous 2-2 programs with Fort Hays State U. Member of Greater Cincinnati Consortium of Colleges and Universities. Elementary, secondary, and music education certification offered through cooperative program with Coll of Mount St. Joseph. Teacher certification in early childhood, elementary, and secondary education.
**ADMISSIONS. Academic basis for candidate selection** (in order of priority): Secondary school record, class rank, essay, standardized test scores, school's recommendation.
**Nonacademic basis for candidate selection:** Character and personality and alumni/ae relationship are emphasized.
**Requirements:** Graduation from secondary school is required; GED is accepted. No specific distribution of secondary school units required. College-preparatory courses recommended. Conditional admission possible for applicants not meeting standard requirements. ACT is required. Campus visit and interview recommended. Off-campus interviews available with an admissions representative.
**Procedure:** Take ACT by June of 12th year. Take ACH by May 15 of 12th year. Visit college for interview by May 15 of 12th year. Suggest filing application by December 31. Application deadline is August 10. Notification of admission on rolling basis. $55 room deposit, refundable until August 28. Freshmen accepted for terms other than fall.
**Special programs:** Credit may be granted through CEEB Advanced Placement for scores of 3 or higher. Credit may be granted through CLEP general and subject exams, challenge exams, and military experience.
**Transfer students:** Transfer students accepted for terms other than fall. In fall 1992, 7% of all new students were transfers into all classes. 45 transfer applications were received, 45 were accepted. Application deadline is August 10 for fall; November 30 for spring. Minimum 2.0 GPA required. Lowest course grade accepted is "C." Maximum number of transferable credits is 100 semester hours. At least 32 semester hours must be completed at the college to receive degree.
**Admissions contact:** Philip G. Coleman, Director of Admissions. 513 244-8141.
**FINANCIAL AID. Available aid:** Pell grants, SEOG, state scholarships and grants, school scholarships, private scholarships and grants, academic merit scholarships, and aid for undergraduate foreign students. PLUS, Stafford Loans (GSL), private loans, and SLS.
**Financial aid statistics:** In 1992-93, 78% of all freshman applicants received aid. Average amounts of aid awarded freshmen: Loans, $2,200.
**Supporting data/closing dates:** FAFSA/FAF/FFS: Priority filing date is May 1. School's own aid application: Priority filing date is May 1; accepted on rolling basis. State aid form: Priority filing date is September 29. Notification of awards on rolling basis.
**Financial aid contact:** Linda Weaver, Director of Financial Aid. 513 244-8450.

## Cleveland Institute of Art

**Cleveland, OH 44106** 216 421-7400

**1994-95 Costs.** Tuition: $11,400. Room: $2,650. Board: $2,120. Fees, books, misc. academic expenses (school's estimate): $1,400.
**Enrollment.** Undergraduates: 236 men, 205 women (full-time). Freshman class: 389 applicants, 365 accepted, 119 enrolled.
**Test score averages/ranges.** Average SAT scores: 449 verbal, 469 math. Average ACT scores: 21 composite.
**Faculty.** 29 full-time; 48 part-time. 90% of faculty holds highest degree in specific field. Student/faculty ratio: 10 to 1.
**Selectivity rating.** Less competitive.

**PROFILE.** Cleveland Institute of Art, founded in 1881, is a private institution. Its 500-acre campus is located in University Circle, four miles east of downtown Cleveland.

**Accreditation:** NCACS. Professionally accredited by the National Association of Schools of Art and Design.
**Religious orientation:** Cleveland Institute of Art is nonsectarian; no religious requirements.
**Library:** Collections totaling over 40,000 volumes, 200 periodical subscriptions and 100 microform items.
**Special facilities/museums:** Art museum, auto/aviation museum, natural history museum.
**STUDENT BODY. Undergraduate profile:** 74% are state residents; 40% are transfers. 4% Asian-American, 4% Black, 4% Hispanic, 88% White. Average age of undergraduates is 24.
**Freshman profile:** 3% of freshmen who took SAT scored 700 or over on verbal; 9% scored 600 or over on verbal, 11% scored 600 or over on math; 34% scored 500 or over on verbal, 46% scored 500 or over on math; 85% scored 400 or over on verbal, 78% scored 400 or over on math; 95% scored 300 or over on verbal, 97% scored 300 or over on math. 98% of freshmen come from public schools.
**Undergraduate achievement:** 72% of fall 1992 freshmen returned for fall 1993 term. 38% of entering class graduated.
**Foreign students:** Eight students are from out of the country. Countries represented include Japan, Korea, and Romania.
**PROGRAMS OF STUDY. Degrees:** B.F.A.
**Majors:** Art Education, Ceramics, Drawing, Enameling, Fiber, Glass, Graphics, Illustration, Industrial Design, Interior Design, Medical Illustration, Metals, Painting, Photography, Printmaking, Sculpture.
**Requirements:** General education requirement.
**Special:** Minors offered in all majors. Independent study. Internships. Graduate school at which undergraduates may take graduate-level courses. Preprofessional programs in art and design.. Member of Alliance of Independent Colleges of Art and Design (AICAD); exchange possible. Member of Cleveland Community of Higher Education. Teacher certification in elementary and secondary education. Study abroad in France.
**Honors:** Honors program.
**Academic Assistance:** Remedial reading, writing, and study skills. Nonremedial tutoring.
**ADMISSIONS. Academic basis for candidate selection** (in order of priority): Class rank, standardized test scores, school's recommendation, essay.
**Nonacademic basis for candidate selection:** Particular talent or ability is emphasized. Character and personality are important. Extracurricular participation is considered.
**Requirements:** Graduation from secondary school is required; GED is accepted. 15 units and the following program of study are recommended: 4 units of English, 4 units of math, 2 units of science, 1 unit of foreign language, 2 units of social studies, 2 units of academic electives. Minimum 2.0 GPA required; minimum combined SAT score of 800 (composite ACT score of 19) and rank in top half of secondary school class recommended. Portfolio required of art program applicants. SAT is recommended. ACT is recommended. SAT or ACT is required. Campus visit and interview recommended. Off-campus interviews available with an admissions representative.
**Procedure:** Take SAT or ACT by November of 12th year. Visit college for interview by January of 12th year. Suggest filing application by February. Application deadline is June. Notification of admission on rolling basis. Reply is required within two weeks of notification. $200 tuition deposit, refundable until May 1. $100 nonrefundable room deposit. Freshmen accepted for terms other than fall.
**Special programs:** Admission may be deferred one year. Credit and/or placement may be granted through CEEB Advanced Placement exams for scores of 3 or higher. Credit and/or placement may be granted through CLEP general and subject exams. Early decision program. In fall 1993, 4 applied for early decision and 4 were accepted. Deadline for applying for early decision is November 1.
**Transfer students:** Transfer students accepted for terms other than fall. In fall 1993, 40% of all new students were transfers into all classes. 102 transfer applications were received, 91 were accepted. Application deadline is June 1 for fall; December 1 for spring. Minimum 2.0 GPA required. Lowest course grade accepted is "C." Maximum number of transferable credits is 12 semester hours. At least 36 semester hours must be completed at the college to receive degree.
**Admissions contact:** Thomas W. Steffen, M.S., Director of Admissions. 216 421-7418.
**FINANCIAL AID. Available aid:** Pell grants, SEOG, state scholarships and grants, school scholarships and grants, private scholarships and grants, and academic merit scholarships. Perkins Loans (NDSL), PLUS, Stafford Loans (GSL), school loans, and SLS. Tuition Plan Inc. and AMS. Installment payment plan.
**Financial aid statistics:** Average amounts of aid awarded freshmen: Scholarships and grants, $9,000; loans, $2,625.
**Supporting data/closing dates:** FAFSA/FAF/FFS: Deadline is March 1. School's own aid application: Deadline is June 1. State aid form: Deadline is March 1. Income tax forms: Deadline is March 1. Notification of awards on rolling basis.
**Financial aid contact:** Michael Jacubenta, M.S., Director of Financial Aid. 216 421-7425.

## Cleveland Institute of Music

**Cleveland, OH 44106-1776** 216 791-5000

**1994-95 Costs.** Tuition: $13,650. Room: $2,935-$3,140. Board: $1,770-$1,970. Fees, books, misc. academic expenses (school's estimate): $375.
**Enrollment.** Undergraduates: 82 men, 99 women (full-time). Freshman class: 206 applicants, 93 accepted, 41 enrolled. Graduate enrollment: 70 men, 109 women.
**Test score averages/ranges.** N/A.
**Faculty.** 29 full-time; 74 part-time. 8% of faculty holds doctoral degree. Student/faculty ratio: 10 to 1.
**Selectivity rating.** N/A.

**PROFILE.** CIM, founded in 1920, is a private conservatory. Its campus is located in University Circle, five miles from downtown Cleveland.
**Accreditation:** NCACS. Professionally accredited by the National Association of Schools of Music.
**Religious orientation:** Cleveland Institute of Music is nonsectarian; no religious requirements.
**Library:** Collections totaling over 1,000,000 volumes, 10,000 periodical subscriptions, and 500,000 microform items.
**Athletic facilities:** Students at the conservatory have access to athletic facilities at Case Western Reserve U.
**STUDENT BODY. Undergraduate profile:** 20% are state residents; 14% are transfers. 5% Asian-American, 2% Black, 2% Hispanic, 1% Native American, 71% White, 19% Other. Average age of undergraduates is 20.
**Undergraduate achievement:** 98% of fall 1992 freshmen returned for fall 1993 term. 70% of entering class graduated. 85% of students who completed a degree program went on to graduate study within five years.
**Foreign students:** 34 students are from out of the country. Countries represented include Canada, China, Germany, Japan, Korea, and Taiwan; 27 in all.

**PROGRAMS OF STUDY. Degrees:** B.A.Mus.Ed., B.Mus., B.S.Mus.Ed.
**Majors:** Audio Recording, Brass Instruments, Classical Guitar, Composition, Eurhythmics, Harp, Harpsichord, Organ, Percussion Instruments, Piano, String Instruments, Theory, Voice, Woodwind Instruments.
**Requirements:** General education requirement.
**Academic regulations:** Minimum 2.0 GPA must be maintained.
**Special:** Optional minors offered in music history and literature, orchestral conducting, and liberal arts fields. The conservatory maintains a close relationship with the Cleveland Orchestra; 35 members of the orchestra are on the CIM faculty. Double majors. Dual degrees. Accelerated study. Pass/fail grading option. Graduate school at which undergraduates may take graduate-level courses.
**Honors:** Honor societies.

**ADMISSIONS. Academic basis for candidate selection** (in order of priority): Secondary school record, standardized test scores, class rank, essay, school's recommendation.
**Nonacademic basis for candidate selection:** Particular talent or ability is emphasized. Character and personality are important.
**Requirements:** Graduation from secondary school is required; GED is accepted. 16 units and the following program of study are recommended: 4 units of English, 3 units of math, 3 units of science, 3 units of foreign language, 3 units of social studies. Audition and special entrance exam required. SAT or ACT is required. Campus visit and interview recommended. No off-campus interviews.
**Procedure:** Take SAT or ACT by December of 12th year. Suggest filing application by December 1. Application deadline is January 15. Notification of admission by April 1. Reply is required by May 1. $250 tuition deposit, refundable until May 1. $200 nonrefundable room deposit. Freshmen accepted for terms other than fall.
**Special programs:** Admission may be deferred one semester. Credit and/or placement may be granted through CEEB Advanced Placement exams for scores of 4 or higher. Early entrance/early admission program. Concurrent enrollment program.
**Transfer students:** Transfer students accepted for terms other than fall. In fall 1993, 14% of all new students were transfers into all classes. 50 transfer applications were received, 25 were accepted. Application deadline is January 15 for fall; November 1 for spring. Lowest course grade accepted is "C."
**Admissions contact:** William Fay, Director of Admissions. 216 795-3107.

**FINANCIAL AID. Available aid:** Pell grants, SEOG, state scholarships and grants, school grants, private scholarships, and aid for undergraduate foreign students. Perkins Loans (NDSL), PLUS, Stafford Loans (GSL), state loans, school loans, and SLS. AMS.
**Financial aid statistics:** 35% of aid is not need-based. In 1993-94, 80% of all undergraduate applicants received aid; 90% of freshman applicants. Average amounts of aid awarded freshmen: Loans, $3,600.
**Supporting data/closing dates:** FAFSA/FAF: Deadline is March 1. School's own aid application: Deadline is March 1. Income tax forms: Deadline is May 1. Notification of awards on rolling basis.
**Financial aid contact:** Carol Peffer, Director of Financial Aid. 216 791-5000, extension 262.

8-28

## College of Mount St. Joseph

**Cincinnati, OH 45233-1672 513 244-4200**

**1994-95 Costs.** Tuition: $9,800. Room: $2,280. Board: $2,150. Fees, books, misc. academic expenses (school's estimate): $350.
**Enrollment.** Undergraduates: 365 men, 801 women (full-time). Freshman class: 798 applicants, 620 accepted, 238 enrolled. Graduate enrollment: 46 men, 127 women.
**Test score averages/ranges.** Average SAT scores: 440 verbal, 480 math. Range of SAT scores of middle 50%: 380-500 verbal, 400-550 math. Average ACT scores: 20 English, 23 math, 21 composite. Range of ACT scores of middle 50%: 18-24 English, 20-26 math.
**Faculty.** 83 full-time; 147 part-time. 49% of faculty holds doctoral degree. Student/faculty ratio: 15 to 1.
**Selectivity rating.** Less noncompetitive.

**PROFILE.** Mount St. Joseph, founded in 1920, is a private, church-affiliated, liberal arts college. Its 325-acre campus is located in Mount St. Joseph, seven miles from downtown Cincinnati.

**Accreditation:** NCACS. Professionally accredited by the American Medical Association (CAHEA), the National Association of Schools of Music, the National League for Nursing.
**Religious orientation:** College of Mount St. Joseph is affiliated with the Roman Catholic Church (Sisters of Charity); three credit hours of religion required.
**Library:** Collections totaling over 87,169 volumes, 733 periodical subscriptions, and 205,059 microform items.
**Special facilities/museums:** Art studio/gallery.
**Athletic facilities:** Aerobic fitness room, gymnasium, swimming pool, football, soccer, and softball fields, basketball, tennis, and volleyball courts, training and weight rooms.

**STUDENT BODY. Undergraduate profile:** 92% are state residents; 19% are transfers. 1% Asian-American, 6% Black, 1% Hispanic, 92% White. Average age of undergraduates is 22.
**Freshman profile:** 4% of freshmen who took SAT scored 600 or over on verbal, 9% scored 600 or over on math; 22% scored 500 or over on verbal, 40% scored 500 or over on math; 76% scored 400 or over on verbal, 87% scored 400 or over on math; 98% scored 300 or over on verbal, 97% scored 300 or over on math. 1% of freshmen who took ACT scored 30 or over on composite; 43% scored 24 or over on composite; 95% scored 18 or over on composite; 100% scored 12 or over on composite. 50% of accepted applicants took SAT; 85% took ACT. 60% of freshmen come from public schools.
**Undergraduate achievement:** 83% of fall 1992 freshmen returned for fall 1993 term. 66% of entering class graduated. 6% of students who completed a degree program went on to graduate study within one year.
**Foreign students:** 100 students are from out of the country. Countries represented include Japan, Korea, Taiwan, Thailand, and United Arab Emirates; 13 in all.

**PROGRAMS OF STUDY. Degrees:** B.A., B.F.A., B.S., B.S.Nurs.
**Majors:** Accounting, Art, Art Education, Biology, Business, Chemistry, Chemistry/Mathematics, Communication Arts, Computer Information, Elementary Education, English, Fine Arts, Gerontological Studies, Graphic Design, Health, History, Human Services, Humanities, Interior Design, Liberal Arts, Liberal Studies, Management, Management Communications, Management of Health Care Services, Mathematics, Mathematics with Computer Science, Medical Technology, Music, Natural Science, Nursing, Paralegal Studies, Physical Education, Religious Education, Religious Pastoral Ministry, Religious Studies, Social Work, Sociopsychology, Special Education, Women's Studies.
**Distribution of degrees:** The majors with the highest enrollment are business, education, and art; music has the lowest.
**Requirements:** General education requirement.
**Academic regulations:** Freshmen must maintain minimum 1.75 GPA; sophomores, juniors, seniors 1.9 GPA.
**Special:** Minors offered in most departments. Certification programs offered in graphic/interior design, gerontological studies, and paralegal studies. Associate's degrees offered. Self-designed majors. Double majors. Independent study. Pass/fail grading option. Internships. Cooperative education programs. Graduate school at which undergraduates may take graduate-level courses. Preprofessional programs in law, medicine, veterinary science, dentistry, optometry, art therapy, and podiatry. Member of Dayton-Miami Valley Consortium of Colleges and Universities and Greater Cincinnati Consortium of Colleges and Universities; cross-registration possible. Exchange programs with five other Seton Colleges. Teacher certification in early childhood, elementary, secondary, and special education. Certification in specific subject areas. Study abroad in England, Germany, Korea, and Spain. ROTC at Xavier U. AFROTC at U of Cincinnati.
**Honors:** Honors program.
**Academic Assistance:** Remedial reading, writing, math, and study skills. Nonremedial tutoring.

**STUDENT LIFE. Housing:** All freshmen and sophomores under age 21 must live on campus unless living with family. Coed dorms. Off-campus privately-owned housing. 30% of students live in college housing.
**Services and counseling/handicapped student services:** Placement services. Health service. Women's center. Day care. Counseling services for minority students. Personal counseling. Career and academic guidance services. Religious counseling. Physically disabled student services. Learning disabled program/services. Notetaking services. Tape recorders. Tutors. Reader services for the blind.
**Campus organizations:** Undergraduate student government. Student newspaper (Dateline, published once/month). Yearbook. Radio station. Glee club, orchestra, gospel choir, music club, ensembles, art club and exhibits, commuter council, residence hall councils, science society, nutrition club, nurses association, business and education groups, Social Work Action Team, 22 organizations in all.
**Religious organizations:** Campus Ministry.
**Minority/foreign student organizations:** Black Student Association. International Club.

**ATHLETICS. Physical education requirements:** Two courses of physical education required.
**Intercollegiate competition:** 20% of students participate. Baseball (M), basketball (W), football (M), softball (W), tennis (M,W), volleyball (W), wrestling (M). Member of NAIA.
**Intramural and club sports:** 20% of students participate. Intramural basketball, cross-country, flag football, indoor soccer, soccer, softball, track, volleyball. Men's club basketball, cross-country, indoor track. Women's club indoor track, soccer.

**ADMISSIONS. Academic basis for candidate selection** (in order of priority): Secondary school record, standardized test scores, class rank, school's recommendation, essay.
**Nonacademic basis for candidate selection:** Extracurricular participation, particular talent or ability, and geographical distribution are important. Character and personality and alumni/ae relationship are considered.
**Requirements:** Graduation from secondary school is recommended; GED is accepted. 18 units and the following program of study are required: 4 units of English, 2 units of math, 2 units of science including 1 unit of lab, 1 unit of social studies, 1 unit of history, 8 units of academic electives. Minimum composite ACT score of 19 (SAT scores of 400 verbal and 440 math), rank in top three-fifths of secondary school class, and minimum 2.25 GPA required. Chemistry required of science and nursing program applicants. Audition required of music program applicants. SAT or ACT is required. Campus visit recommended. Off-campus interviews available with an admissions representative.
**Procedure:** Take SAT or ACT by February of 12th year. Visit college for interview by March of 12th year. Application deadline is August 1. Notification of admission on rolling basis. Applicant must accept offer within 30 days of acceptance. $100 tuition deposit, refundable until May 1. Freshmen accepted for terms other than fall.
**Special programs:** Credit and/or placement may be granted through CEEB Advanced Placement exams for scores of 3 or higher. Credit may be granted through CLEP general and subject exams. Credit and placement may be granted through military and life experience. Early entrance/early admission program. Concurrent enrollment program.
**Transfer students:** Transfer students accepted for terms other than fall. In fall 1993, 19% of all new students were transfers into all classes. 106 transfer applications were received, 74 were accepted. Application deadline is August 1 for fall; January 1 for spring. Minimum 2.0 GPA required. Lowest course grade accepted is "C." At least 27 semester hours must be completed at the college to receive degree.
**Admissions contact:** Edward Eckel, M.Ed., Director of Admissions. 513 244-4531.

**FINANCIAL AID. Available aid:** Pell grants, SEOG, Federal Nursing Student Scholarships, state scholarships and grants, school scholarships and grants, private scholarships and grants, ROTC scholarships, academic merit scholarships, and athletic scholarships. Perkins Loans (NDSL), PLUS, Stafford Loans (GSL), NSL, and SLS. College payment plan.
**Financial aid statistics:** 15% of aid is not need-based. In 1993-94, 95% of all undergraduate applicants received aid; 95% of freshman applicants. Average amounts of aid awarded freshmen: Scholarships and grants, $3,800; loans, $2,000.
**Supporting data/closing dates:** FAFSA/FAF/FFS: Priority filing date is April 15. School's own aid application: Priority filing date is April 15. Notification of awards on rolling basis.

**Financial aid contact:** Kathryn Hake Kelly, M.B.A., Director of Financial Aid. 513 244-4418.

**STUDENT EMPLOYMENT.** College Work/Study Program. Institutional employment. 15% of full-time undergraduates work on campus during school year. Students may expect to earn an average of $1,600 during school year. Off-campus part-time employment opportunities rated "good."

**COMPUTER FACILITIES.** 60 IBM/IBM-compatible, Macintosh/Apple, and RISC-/UNIX-based microcomputers; 40 are networked. Students may access Digital minicomputer/mainframe systems. Client/LAN operating systems include Apple/Macintosh. Computer languages and software packages include BASIC, C++, COBOL, dBASE, Lotus 1-2-3, Microsoft Works, Multimate, PageMaker, Pascal, SPSS, WordPerfect; 500 in all. Computer facilities are available to all students.
**Fees:** None.
**Hours:** 8 AM-10 PM.

**GRADUATE CAREER DATA.** Graduate school percentages: 2% enter medical school. 4% enter graduate arts and sciences programs. Highest graduate school enrollments: U of Cincinnati, Miami U, Xavier U. 52% of graduates choose careers in business and industry. Companies and businesses that hire graduates: AT&T, Cincinnati Gas & Electric, General Electric, Gibson Greetings, Procter & Gamble, hospitals and schools, law firms.

**PROMINENT ALUMNI/AE.** Cathy Cola, assistant attorney general, Columbus, Ohio; Dr. Billmire, Cincinnati pediatrician, recognized for her work against child abuse; Nancy Noel, artist.

# The College of Wooster

**Wooster, OH 44691** **216 263-2000**

**1993-94 Costs.** Tuition: $15,425. Room: $2,050. Board: $2,400. Fees, books, misc. academic expenses (school's estimate): $450.
**Enrollment.** Undergraduates: 822 men, 864 women (full-time). Freshman class: 2,017 applicants, 1,711 accepted, 458 enrolled.
**Test score averages/ranges.** Average SAT scores: 510 verbal, 550 math. Range of SAT scores of middle 50%: 460-560 verbal, 480-600 math. Average ACT scores: 24 composite.
**Faculty.** 138 full-time; 33 part-time. 90% of faculty holds doctoral degree. Student/faculty ratio: 12 to 1.
**Selectivity rating.** Competitive.

**PROFILE.** The College of Wooster, founded in 1866, is a church-affiliated, liberal arts institution. Its 320-acre campus is located in Wooster, 60 miles southwest of Cleveland.

**Accreditation:** NCACS. Professionally accredited by the National Association of Schools of Music.
**Religious orientation:** The College of Wooster is affiliated with the Presbyterian Church; one semester of religion required.
**Library:** Collections totaling over 325,196 volumes, 2,060 periodical subscriptions, and 245,208 microform items.
**Special facilities/museums:** Art museum, language lab, on-campus nursery school, institute of politics.
**Athletic facilities:** Gymnasiums, stadium, track, baseball, field hockey, lacrosse, and soccer fields, basketball, racquetball, and tennis courts, golf course, swimming pool, weight room.

**STUDENT BODY. Undergraduate profile:** 36% are state residents; 6% are transfers. 1% Asian-American, 6% Black, 1% Hispanic, 85% White, 7% Other. Average age of undergraduates is 21.
**Freshman profile:** 3% of freshmen who took SAT scored 700 or over on verbal, 5% scored 700 or over on math; 20% scored 600 or over on verbal, 30% scored 600 or over on math; 55% scored 500 or over on verbal, 70% scored 500 or over on math; 91% scored 400 or over on verbal, 97% scored 400 or over on math; 100% scored 300 or over on verbal, 100% scored 300 or over on math. 81% of accepted applicants took SAT; 52% took ACT. 70% of freshmen come from public schools.
**Undergraduate achievement:** 84% of fall 1991 freshmen returned for fall 1992 term. 62% of entering class graduated. 30% of students who completed a degree program immediately went on to graduate study.
**Foreign students:** 140 students are from out of the country. Countries represented include China, India, Malaysia, Pakistan, and Sweden; 32 in all.

**PROGRAMS OF STUDY. Degrees:** B.A., B.Mus., B.Mus.Ed.
**Majors:** African Studies, Applied Music, Art, Art History, Biology, Black Studies, Business Economics, Chemical Physics, Chemistry, Classical Civilization, Classical Studies, Comparative Literature, Computer Science, Cultural Area Studies, East Asian Studies, Economics, English, French, Geology, German, Greek, History, International Relations, Latin, Latin American Studies, Mathematics, Middle East/the Islamic World, Modern Western Europe Studies, Music, Music Education, Music History/Literature, Music Theory/Composition, Music Therapy, Philosophy, Physical Education, Physics, Political Science, Psychology, Religious Studies, Russian Studies, Sociology, South Asia/India Studies, Spanish, Speech Communication, Studio Art, Theatre, Urban Studies.
**Distribution of degrees:** The majors with the highest enrollment are history, English, and sociology; Greek, Latin, and black studies have the lowest.
**Requirements:** General education requirement.
**Academic regulations:** Freshmen must maintain minimum 1.8 GPA; sophomores, 1.9 GPA; juniors, 2.0 GPA; seniors, 2.0 GPA.
**Special:** Minors offered in most majors. Interdepartmental and divisional majors. Comprehensive science major qualifies student to teach three sciences. Courses offered in archaeology, education, Hebrew, Italian, natural sciences, and Russian. Women's studies program. Self-designed majors. Double majors. Dual degrees. Independent study. Accelerated study. Pass/fail grading option. Internships. Cooperative education programs. Preprofessional programs in law, medicine, and dentistry. Combined bachelor's/master's programs in economics, math, and physics with U of Michigan. 3-2 law program with Columbia U. 3-2 engineering programs with Case Western Reserve U, U of Michigan, and Washington U. 3-2 forestry and environmental studies program with Duke U. 3-2 social work program, 3-3 nursing program, and seven-year dental program with Case Western Reserve U. 3-2 communicative disorders and rehabilitation counseling programs with Boston U. 3-4 architecture program with Washington U. Member of Great Lakes Colleges Association. Washington Semester and UN Semester. Arts Program in New York. Oak Ridge Science Semester (Tennessee). Philadelphia Urban Semester. Other off-campus study opportunities. Teacher certification in elementary and secondary education. Certification in specific subject areas. Study abroad in Austria, China, Colombia, France, Germany, Greece, India, Israel, Japan, the former Soviet Republics, Spain, the United Kingdom, and other countries.
**Honors:** Phi Beta Kappa.
**Academic Assistance:** Remedial reading, writing, math, and study skills. Nonremedial tutoring.

**STUDENT LIFE. Housing:** All students must live on campus. Coed, women's, and men's dorms. Sorority and fraternity housing. Off-campus privately-owned housing. 93% of students live in college housing.
**Social atmosphere:** The student newspaper reports, "The school provides the students with frequent parties. There are also many plays each year, both on campus and in the community. There is a good mixture of different people and it is a very friendly place for people to interact." On campus, student gathering spots are Mom's and the Lowry Student Center. Favorite hangouts off campus are the Street Cafe and the Underground. Some influential groups on campus are sectionalist clubs (local fraternities) and the Student Activities Board. Popular events during the school year are Homecoming, Winter Gala, and the Party on the Green.
**Services and counseling/handicapped student services:** Placement services. Health service. Counseling services for minority students. Birth control, personal, and psychological counseling. Career and academic guidance services. Religious counseling. Physically disabled student services. Learning disabled services. Tutors.
**Campus organizations:** Undergraduate student government. Student newspaper (Wooster Voice, published once/week). Literary magazine. Radio station. Band, orchestra, concert and jazz bands, mixed chorus, concert choir, gospel choir, dance company, Students for Peace through Action, Circle K, Model UN, debating, Lesbian/Gay Support Group, Society for Creative Anachronism, Environmental Concerns of Students, academic groups. Eight fraternities, one chapter house; eight sororities, no chapter houses. 20% of men join a fraternity. 15% of women join a sorority.
**Religious organizations:** Campus Christian Association, Newman Club, Jewish Student Association, Canterbury Club.
**Minority/foreign student organizations:** Black Student Association, Black Women's Organization, Black Forum, Harambee. International Student Association.

**ATHLETICS. Physical education requirements:** None.
**Intercollegiate competition:** 25% of students participate. Baseball (M), basketball (M,W), cheerleading (M,W), cross-country (M,W), diving (M,W), field hockey (W), football (M), golf (M), lacrosse (M,W), soccer (M,W), swimming (M,W), tennis (M,W), track (indoor) (M,W), track (outdoor) (M,W), track and field (indoor) (M,W), track and field (outdoor) (M,W), volleyball (W). Member of NCAA Division III, North Coast Athletic Conference.
**Intramural and club sports:** 70% of students participate. Intramural archery, badminton, bowling, cross-country, fencing, flag football, floor hockey, golf, racquetball, soccer, softball, swimming, tennis, volleyball, weight training. Men's club badminton, bowling, fencing, racquetball, softball, weight lifting. Women's club badminton, bowling, fencing, racquetball, softball, weight lifting.

**ADMISSIONS. Academic basis for candidate selection** (in order of priority): Secondary school record, standardized test scores, school's recommendation, essay, class rank.
**Nonacademic basis for candidate selection:** Character and personality and particular talent or ability are emphasized. Extracurricular participation and geographical distribution are important. Alumni/ae relationship is considered.
**Requirements:** Graduation from secondary school is required; GED is accepted. 16 units and the following program of study are required: 4 units of English, 3 units of math, 2 units of lab science, 2 units of foreign language, 3 units of social studies. SAT or ACT is required. ACH recommended. Campus visit and interview recommended. Off-campus interviews available with admissions and alumni representatives.
**Procedure:** Take SAT or ACT by January of 12th year. Visit college for interview by February of 12th year. Suggest filing application by February 15; no deadline. Notification of admission by April 1. Reply is required by May 1. $250 nonrefundable tuition deposit. Freshmen accepted for terms other than fall.
**Special programs:** Admission may be deferred one year. Credit and/or placement may be granted through CEEB Advanced Placement exams for scores of 4 or higher. Early decision program. In fall 1992, 111 applied for early decision and 97 were accepted. Deadlines for applying for early decision are December 1 and January 15. Early entrance/early admission program.
**Transfer students:** Transfer students accepted for terms other than fall. In fall 1992, 6% of all new students were transfers into all classes. 92 transfer applications were received, 65 were accepted. Application deadline is June 1 for fall; December 1 for spring. Minimum 2.5 GPA recommended. Lowest course grade accepted is "C." Maximum number of transferable credits is 64 semester hours. At least 16 courses must be completed at the college to receive degree.
**Admissions contact:** W A. Hayden Schilling, Ph.D., Dean of Admissions. 216 263-2322, 800-877-9905.

**FINANCIAL AID. Available aid:** Pell grants, SEOG, state grants, school scholarships and grants, private scholarships and grants, academic merit scholarships, and aid for undergraduate foreign students. Perkins Loans (NDSL), PLUS, Stafford Loans (GSL), school loans, and private loans. Tuition Plan Inc., Knight Tuition Plans, AMS, Tuition Management Systems, and deferred payment plan.
**Financial aid statistics:** 12% of aid is not need-based. In 1992-93, 98% of all undergraduate applicants received aid; 96% of freshman applicants. Average amounts of aid awarded freshmen: Scholarships and grants, $1,200; loans, $2,300.
**Supporting data/closing dates:** FAFSA/FAF: Priority filing date is February 15. Income tax forms: Accepted on rolling basis. Notification of awards begins March 1.
**Financial aid contact:** David B. Miller, Ph.D., Director of Financial Aid. 216 263-2317.

**STUDENT EMPLOYMENT.** College Work/Study Program. Institutional employment. 50% of full-time undergraduates work on campus during school year. Students may expect to earn an average of $900 during school year. Freshmen are discouraged from working during their first term. Off-campus part-time employment opportunities rated "excellent."

**COMPUTER FACILITIES.** 70 IBM/IBM-compatible and Macintosh/Apple microcomputers; 50 are networked. Students may access Digital minicomputer/mainframe systems, BITNET, Internet. Residence halls may be equipped with networked microcomputers. Client/LAN operating systems include Apple/Macintosh, LocalTalk/AppleTalk. Computer languages and software packages include BASIC, C, FORTRAN, MINITAB, Pascal, SPSS-X; 30 in all. Computer facilities are available to all students.
**Fees:** None.
**Hours:** 20 hours/day.

**GRADUATE CAREER DATA.** Graduate school percentages: 8% enter law school. 7% enter medical school. 1% enter dental school. 5% enter graduate business programs. 47% enter graduate arts and sciences programs. 3% enter theological school/seminary. Highest graduate school enrollments: Case Western Reserve U, Ohio State U, U of Washington at St. Louis. 34% of graduates choose careers in business and industry. Companies and businesses that hire graduates: Peace Corps, Andersen Consulting, Beacon Graphics.

**PROMINENT ALUMNI/AE.** Eric H. Boehm, founder, American Bibliographic Center; Arthur H. Compton, Nobel prize-winning physicist; Jane S. Abell Coon, U.S. ambassador to Bangladesh; Stephen R. Donaldson, best-selling fantasy author; Jerold K. Footlick, senior editor, *Newsweek*; Erie A. Mills, opera singer; Stanley C. Gault, chair/CEO, Goodyear; Helen Murry Free, president, American Chemical Society; Tim Smucker, chairman of board, J.M. Smucker Co.; Arthur Kropp, president, People for the American Way.

## Columbus College of Art and Design

**Columbus, OH 43215-3875** **614 224-9101**

**1994-95 Costs.** Tuition: $9,700. Room & board: $5,400. Fees, books, misc. academic expenses (school's estimate): $700.
**Enrollment.** Undergraduates: 724 men, 496 women (full-time). Freshman class: 714 applicants, 437 accepted, 300 enrolled.
**Test score averages/ranges.** Average SAT scores: 440 verbal, 440 math. Average ACT scores: 21 composite.
**Faculty.** 61 full-time; 47 part-time. 8% of faculty holds doctoral degree. Student/faculty ratio: 15 to 1.
**Selectivity rating.** Less competitive.

**PROFILE.** The Columbus College of Art and Design, founded in 1879, is a private institution. Programs are offered through the Divisions of Advertising Design, Retail Advertising, Industrial Design, Interior Design, Illustration, Fine Arts, and Photography. Its 15-acre campus, adjacent to the Columbus Museum of Art, is located near downtown Columbus.

**Accreditation:** NCACS. Professionally accredited by the National Association of Schools of Art and Design.
**Religious orientation:** Columbus College of Art and Design is nonsectarian; no religious requirements.
**Library:** Collections totaling over 36,387 volumes, 256 periodical subscriptions, and 9,119 microform items.
**Special facilities/museums:** Student art exhibition hall, gallery, auditorium, recreation center.

**STUDENT BODY. Undergraduate profile:** 65% are state residents; 19% are transfers. 2.5% Asian-American, 5.4% Black, 1.7% Hispanic, 1% Native American, 87% White, 2.4% Other. Average age of undergraduates is 21.
**Freshman profile:** Majority of accepted applicants took SAT.
**Undergraduate achievement:** 78% of fall 1992 freshmen returned for fall 1993 term. 60% of entering class graduated.
**Foreign students:** 56 students are from out of the country. Countries represented include England, Indonesia, Japan, Korea, Taiwan, and Thailand; 33 in all.

**PROGRAMS OF STUDY. Degrees:** B.F.A.
**Majors:** Advertising Design, Fine Arts, Illustration, Industrial Design, Interior Design, Photography, Retail Advertising.
**Distribution of degrees:** The majors with the highest enrollment are illustration, advertising design, and fine arts; photography, interior design, and retail advertising have the lowest.
**Requirements:** General education requirement.
**Academic regulations:** Minimum 2.0 GPA must be maintained.
**Special:** Numerous concentrations offered, including package, product, fashion, transportation, and furniture design; commercial, institutional, and environmental interior design; fashion, magazine, decorative, and three-dimensional illustration; black and white, color, film, and video photography; animation; visual communication; computer graphics; desktop publishing; display design copywriting; space planning; architectural signage; drawing, painting, sculpture, printmaking, ceramics, glassblowing, and papermaking; and art therapy. Foundation Year program provides art fundamentals. Double majors. Independent study. Accelerated study. Internships. Graduate school at which undergraduates may take graduate-level courses. Member of Higher Education Council of Columbus and National Portfolio Day Association.
**Academic Assistance:** Remedial reading and writing. Nonremedial tutoring.

**STUDENT LIFE. Housing:** All unmarried students under age 21 must live on campus unless living near campus with relatives. Coed dorms. School-owned/operated apartments. 20% of students live in college housing.
**Services and counseling/handicapped student services:** Personal counseling. Career and academic guidance services. Learning disabled services.
**Campus organizations:** Undergraduate student government. Student newspaper (Above Ground, published two times/month). Literary magazine. Soccer team, annual student art sale, special-interest groups, 5 organizations in all.
**Religious organizations:** Bible study group.
**Minority/foreign student organizations:** Black Student Alliance, Nontraditional Student Resource Group. International Student Club.

**ATHLETICS. Physical education requirements:** One semester of physical education required.

**ADMISSIONS. Academic basis for candidate selection** (in order of priority): Secondary school record, school's recommendation, class rank, standardized test scores.
**Nonacademic basis for candidate selection:** Particular talent or ability is important.
**Requirements:** Graduation from secondary school is required; GED is accepted. No specific distribution of secondary school units required. Minimum 2.0 GPA required. Portfolio required of art program applicants. SAT or ACT is recommended. Campus visit and interview recommended. Off-campus interviews available with an admissions representative.
**Procedure:** Notification of admission on rolling basis. $100 nonrefundable tuition deposit. $150 refundable room deposit. Freshmen accepted for terms other than fall.
**Special programs:** Admission may be deferred to be determined.
**Transfer students:** Transfer students accepted for terms other than fall. In fall 1993, 19% of all new students were transfers into all classes. 146 transfer applications were received, 83 were accepted. Minimum 2.0 GPA required. Lowest course grade accepted is "C." Maximum number of transferable credits is 85 semester hours. At least 60 semester hours must be completed at the college to receive degree.
**Admissions contact:** Thomas E. Green, Director of Admissions. 614 222-3261.

**FINANCIAL AID. Available aid:** Pell grants, SEOG, state grants, school scholarships, private scholarships and grants, and aid for undergraduate foreign students. Veteran scholarships. War Orphan scholarships. Perkins Loans (NDSL), PLUS, Stafford Loans (GSL), private loans, and SLS. Deferred payment plan. AMS payment plan.
**Financial aid statistics:** 10% of aid is not need-based. In 1993-94, 90% of all undergraduate applicants received aid; 70% of freshman applicants. Average amounts of aid awarded freshmen: Scholarships and grants, $13,000; loans, $2,500.
**Supporting data/closing dates:** FAFSA/FAF: Priority filing date is May 1; accepted on rolling basis. School's own aid application: Priority filing date is May 1; accepted on rolling basis. State aid form: Deadline is September. Income tax forms: Priority filing date is May 1; accepted on rolling basis. Notification of awards on rolling basis.
**Financial aid contact:** Anna Lyttle, Director of Financial Aid. 614 222-3275.

**STUDENT EMPLOYMENT.** College Work/Study Program. Institutional employment. Students may expect to earn an average of $1,636 during school year. Freshmen are discouraged from working during their first term. Off-campus part-time employment opportunities rated "excellent."

**COMPUTER FACILITIES.** 48 Macintosh/Apple microcomputers. Client/LAN operating systems include Apple/Macintosh. Computer languages and software packages include CADD, CAM, animation, desktop publishing, and graphics packages. Computer facilities are available to students enrolled in computer classes. Limited computer use available in library.
**Fees:** None.

**GRADUATE CAREER DATA.** Highest graduate school enrollments: Maryland Inst of Art, Ohio State U, Ohio U, Pratt Inst. Companies and businesses that hire graduates: Disney, Hallmark, The Limited, Gibson Greetings, Leo Burnett Advertising, Dave Ellies Industrial Designs, Fitch Richardson Smith, B. Altman, Marshall Fields, SCASS!, Women's Wear Daily.

**PROMINENT ALUMNI/AE.** Bob McCall, illustrator for NASA and the Smithsonian; Alice Schille, watercolorist; Dennis R. Williams, designer of bicentennial dollar.

8-29

## The Defiance College

**Defiance, OH 43512** **419 784-4010**

**1994-95 Costs.** Tuition: $10,850. Room & board: $3,670. Fees, books, misc. academic expenses (school's estimate): $500.
**Enrollment.** Undergraduates: 339 men, 306 women (full-time). Freshman class: 571 applicants, 461 accepted, 174 enrolled. Graduate enrollment: 7 men, 35 women.
**Test score averages/ranges.** Average SAT scores: 381 verbal, 438 math. Range of SAT scores of middle 50%: 320-440 verbal, 340-510 math. Average ACT scores: 21 composite. Range of ACT scores of middle 50%: 16-22 English, 16-21 math.
**Faculty.** 50 full-time; 21 part-time. 56% of faculty holds doctoral degree. Student/faculty ratio: 14 to 1.
**Selectivity rating.** Less competitive.

**PROFILE.** The Defiance College, founded in 1850, is a church-affiliated, liberal arts college. Its 150-acre campus is located in a residential area of Defiance, 50 miles from Toledo.

**Accreditation:** NCACS. Professionally accredited by the Council on Social Work Education.
**Religious orientation:** The Defiance College is affiliated with the United Church of Christ; no religious requirements.
**Library:** Collections totaling over 90,000 volumes, 481 periodical subscriptions, and 14,982 microform items.
**Special facilities/museums:** Art gallery, media center, Eisenhower archives room, curriculum resource center, Indian wars collection.
**Athletic facilities:** Gymnasium, outdoor athletic complex, weight lifting center, racquetball courts, indoor track.

**STUDENT BODY. Undergraduate profile:** 90% are state residents; 25% are transfers. 6% Black, 3% Hispanic, 88% White, 3% Other. Average age of undergraduates is 21.
**Freshman profile:** 6% of freshmen who took SAT scored 600 or over on math; 9% scored 500 or over on verbal, 32% scored 500 or over on math; 43% scored 400 or over on verbal,

58% scored 400 or over on math; 80% scored 300 or over on verbal, 100% scored 300 or over on math. 15% of accepted applicants took SAT; 92% took ACT.
**Undergraduate achievement:** 62% of fall 1992 freshmen returned for fall 1993 term. 35% of entering class graduated. 8% of students who completed a degree program immediately went on to graduate study.
**Foreign students:** 14 students are from out of the country. Countries represented include Ethiopia, Japan, Korea, and Thailand; six in all.

**PROGRAMS OF STUDY. Degrees:** B.A., B.S.
**Majors:** Accounting, Art, Biology, Business Administration/Management, Chemistry, Christian Education, Communication Arts, Comprehensive Social Studies, Computer/Information Sciences, Criminal Justice, Education, Elementary Education, English, Finance, General Business, History, Humanities, Kindergarten/Primary Education, Management, Marketing, Mathematics, Medical Technology, Multimedia Journalism, Museology, Music, Natural Systems, Physical Education, Psychology, Religion, Restoration Ecology, Secondary Education, Self-Designed Majors, Social Work, Sports Management, Wellness/Corporate Fitness.
**Distribution of degrees:** The majors with the highest enrollment are elementary education, criminal justice, and business administration; chemistry has the lowest.
**Requirements:** General education requirement.
**Academic regulations:** Freshmen must maintain minimum 1.8 GPA; sophomores, 1.9 GPA; juniors, 2.0 GPA; seniors, 2.0 GPA.
**Special:** Minors offered in athletic training and museology. Associate's degrees offered. Self-designed majors. Double majors. Independent study. Pass/fail grading option. Internships. Cooperative education programs. Preprofessional programs in law, medicine, veterinary science, dentistry, and theology. 3-1 medical technology programs with various hospitals. Teacher certification in elementary, secondary, and special education. Certification in specific subject areas. Study abroad possible. ROTC at Bowling Green State U.
**Honors:** Honor societies.
**Academic Assistance:** Remedial reading, writing, math, and study skills.

**ADMISSIONS. Academic basis for candidate selection** (in order of priority): Secondary school record, class rank, standardized test scores, essay, school's recommendation.
**Nonacademic basis for candidate selection:** Character and personality are important. Extracurricular participation, particular talent or ability, and alumni/ae relationship are considered.
**Requirements:** Graduation from secondary school is required; GED is accepted. No specific distribution of secondary school units required. Minimum composite ACT score of 18 (combined SAT score of 700), rank in top 60% of secondary school class, and minimum 2.0 GPA recommended. Conditional admission possible for applicants not meeting standard requirements. SAT or ACT is required. Campus visit and interview recommended. Off-campus interviews available with an admissions representative.
**Procedure:** Take SAT or ACT by June of 12th year. Visit college for interview by May of 12th year. Suggest filing application by March 1. Application deadline is August 1. Notification of admission on rolling basis. Reply is required by May 1 or within 30 days of acceptance. $150 tuition deposit, refundable until May 1. Freshmen accepted for terms other than fall.
**Special programs:** Admission may be deferred. Credit and/or placement may be granted through CEEB Advanced Placement exams for scores of 3 or higher. Credit and/or placement may be granted through CLEP general and subject exams. Early entrance/early admission program. Concurrent enrollment program.
**Transfer students:** Transfer students accepted for terms other than fall. In fall 1993, 25% of all new students were transfers into all classes. 111 transfer applications were received, 80 were accepted. Application deadline is August 1 for fall; December 20 for spring. Minimum 2.0 GPA recommended. Lowest course grade accepted is "C." Maximum number of transferable credits is 60 semester hours. At least 38 semester hours must be completed at the college to receive degree.
**Admissions contact:** Julie Waldron, Acting Director of Admission. 419 783-2330.

**FINANCIAL AID. Available aid:** Pell grants, SEOG, state scholarships and grants, school scholarships and grants, and academic merit scholarships. Perkins Loans (NDSL), PLUS, Stafford Loans (GSL), and SLS. Tuition Plan Inc., Knight Tuition Plans, AMS, and EFI Fund Management.
**Financial aid statistics:** 22% of aid is not need-based. Average amounts of aid awarded freshmen: Scholarships and grants, $5,000; loans, $2,625.
**Supporting data/closing dates:** FAFSA/FAF: Priority filing date is February 28. Income tax forms: Accepted on rolling basis. Notification of awards on rolling basis.
**Financial aid contact:** Son Ho, M.A., Director of Financial Aid. 419 783-2356.

# Denison University

**Granville, OH 43023** **614 587-0810**

**1993-94 Costs.** Tuition: $15,950. Room & board: $4,450. Fees, books, misc. academic expenses (school's estimate): $1,280.
**Enrollment.** Undergraduates: 862 men, 973 women (full-time). Freshman class: 2,762 applicants, 2,279 accepted, 535 enrolled.
**Test score averages/ranges.** Range of SAT scores of middle 50%: 460-570 verbal, 520-630 math. Range of ACT scores of middle 50%: 24-29 composite.
**Faculty.** 155 full-time; 10 part-time. 97% of faculty holds highest degree in specific field. Student/faculty ratio: 12 to 1.
**Selectivity rating.** Competitive.

**PROFILE.** Denison, founded in 1831, is a liberal arts university. Its 1,200-acre campus is located in Granville, 27 miles east of Columbus.

**Accreditation:** NCACS.
**Religious orientation:** Denison University is nonsectarian; no religious requirements.
**Library:** Collections totaling over 313,202 volumes, 1,174 periodical subscriptions, and 52,989 microform items.
**Special facilities/museums:** Burmese art collection, language lab, 500-acre biological reserve for scientific experimentation and research, observatory, high resolution spectrometer lab, nuclear magnetic resonance spectrometer, planetarium.
**Athletic facilities:** Gymnasium, field house, swimming pool, weight room, basketball, handball, racquetball, platform tennis, squash, and tennis courts, baseball, field hockey, football, lacrosse, practice, and soccer fields, track, dance studio.

**STUDENT BODY. Undergraduate profile:** 41% are state residents; 4% are transfers. 3% Asian-American, 4% Black, 2% Hispanic, 91% White. Average age of undergraduates is 20.
**Freshman profile:** 1% of freshmen who took SAT scored 700 or over on verbal, 5% scored 700 or over on math; 10% scored 600 or over on verbal, 28% scored 600 or over on math; 45% scored 500 or over on verbal, 74% scored 500 or over on math; 92% scored 400 or over on verbal, 96% scored 400 or over on math; 100% scored 300 or over on verbal, 100% scored 300 or over on math. 85% of accepted applicants took SAT; 58% took ACT. 68% of freshmen come from public schools.
**Undergraduate achievement:** 82% of fall 1992 freshmen returned for fall 1993 term. 75% of entering class graduated. 15% of students who completed a degree program immediately went on to graduate study.
**Foreign students:** 57 students are from out of the country. Countries represented include China, Germany, Japan, Spain, and Sri Lanka; 29 in all.

**PROGRAMS OF STUDY. Degrees:** B.A., B.F.A., B.S.
**Majors:** Art History, Astronomy, Biology, Black Studies, Chemistry, Cinema, Classical Studies, Communication, Computer/Information Sciences, Dance, East Asian Studies, Economics, Educational Studies, English, English Literature, Environmental Science, Environmental Studies, French, French Area Studies, Geology, German, History, Individualized Majors, International Studies, Latin American Studies, Mathematical Sciences, Microbiology, Music, Music Theory/Composition, Philosophy, Philosophy/Politics/Economics, Physical Education, Physics, Political Science, Psychology, Religion, Sociology/Anthropology, Spanish, Studio Art, Theatre, Women's Studies.
**Distribution of degrees:** The majors with the highest enrollment are economics, English, and history; black studies, women's studies, and music have the lowest.
**Requirements:** General education requirement.
**Academic regulations:** Minimum 2.0 GPA must be maintained.
**Special:** Minors offered in most majors. Concentrations within majors in astronomy, environmental studies, geophysics, international relations, and mass media. Freshman Studies Program. Honors Project in senior year earns eight credits toward graduation. Particular circumstances may allow substitution of comprehensive exams for final exams. Self-designed majors. Double majors. Independent study. Accelerated study. Pass/fail grading option. Internships. Graduate school at which undergraduates may take graduate-level courses. Preprofessional programs in law, medicine, dentistry, forestry, and engineering.. 4-3 dentistry program with Case Western Reserve U. 3-2 engineering programs with Case Western Reserve U, Columbia U, Rensselaer Polytech Inst, U of Rochester, and Washington U. 3-2 forestry and natural resources programs with Duke U and U of Michigan. 3-2 occupational therapy program with Washington U. Member of Great Lakes Colleges Association and Marine Science Education Consortium. Washington Semester and Sea Semester. Semester at Arts Program in New York, Newberry Library Program in the Humanities (Illinois), Oak Ridge Science Semester (Tennessee), and Philadelphia Urban Semester. Black College Exchange Program. Teacher certification in secondary education. Certification in specific subject areas. Exchange programs abroad in Asian, European, Latin American, and Middle Eastern countries. Junior Year Abroad.
**Honors:** Phi Beta Kappa. Honors program. Honor societies.
**Academic Assistance:** Nonremedial tutoring.

**STUDENT LIFE. Housing:** All freshmen, sophomores, juniors, and most seniors must live on campus unless living with family. Coed, women's, and men's dorms. Fraternity housing. School-owned/operated apartments. 97% of students live in college housing.
**Social atmosphere:** Favorite gathering spots include the Roast, the Villa, and the Manor House. Student Activities Committee, Greeks, and Denison Film Society influence student life. Homecoming (bonfire, parade, and gala), All-Campus Formal, and Halloween Party are popular social events. "Despite its semi-rural location, there is a lot to do at Denison," reports the editor of the student newspaper. "There are many on-campus activities every week." The majority of students stay on campus on weekends.
**Services and counseling/handicapped student services:** Placement services. Health service. Women's center. Counseling services for minority and older students. Birth control, personal, and psychological counseling. Career and academic guidance services. Religious counseling. Physically disabled student services. Learning disabled services. Notetaking services. Tape recorders. Reader services for the blind.
**Campus organizations:** Undergraduate student government. Student newspaper (Denisonian, published once/week). Literary magazine. Yearbook. Radio and TV stations. Choral groups, recitals, orchestra, band, dance recitals, theatre productions, women's group, recycling center, Amnesty International, departmental, political, service, and special-interest groups, 118 organizations in all. 11 fraternities, nine chapter houses; eight sororities, six chapter houses. 56% of men join a fraternity. 58% of women join a sorority.
**Religious organizations:** Hillel, Canterbury, Chapel Advisory Board, Newman Association.
**Minority/foreign student organizations:** Black Student Union. International Student Organization.

**ATHLETICS. Physical education requirements:** None.
**Intercollegiate competition:** 42% of students participate. Baseball (M), basketball (M,W), cross-country (M,W), diving (M,W), field hockey (W), football (M), golf (M), lacrosse (M,W), soccer (M,W), swimming (M,W), tennis (M,W), track (indoor) (M,W), track (outdoor) (M,W), track and field (indoor) (M,W), track and field (outdoor) (M,W), volleyball (W). Member of NCAA Division III, North Coast Athletic Conference.
**Intramural and club sports:** 70% of students participate. Intramural basketball, flag football, floor hockey, golf, platform tennis, racquetball, sand volleyball, soccer, softball, squash, tennis, ultimate frisbee, volleyball, wallyball. Men's club crew, equestrian sports, ice hockey, lacrosse, martial arts, outing, rugby, sailing, skeet and trap-shooting, soccer, squash, ultimate frisbee, volleyball. Women's club cheerleading, crew, equestrian sports, martial arts, outing, rugby, sailing, skeet and trap-shooting, soccer, softball, squash, ultimate frisbee.

**ADMISSIONS. Academic basis for candidate selection** (in order of priority): Secondary school record, standardized test scores, class rank, essay, school's recommendation.

**Nonacademic basis for candidate selection:** Character and personality and particular talent or ability are emphasized. Extracurricular participation and alumni/ae relationship are important. Geographical distribution is considered.
**Requirements:** Graduation from secondary school is required; GED is not accepted. 16 units required and the following program of study recommended: 4 units of English, 3 units of math, 3 units of science, 3 units of foreign language, 2 units of social studies, 1 unit of history. Minimum "B" average recommended. Some exceptions made by committee on admissions; special consideration to B.F.A. program applicants. Special attention given to recruitment, enrollment, and financial support of minority groups. SAT or ACT is required. ACH recommended. Campus visit and interview recommended. Off-campus interviews available with admissions and alumni representatives.
**Procedure:** Take SAT or ACT by December of 12th year. Visit college for interview by January 31 of 12th year. Suggest filing application by January. Application deadline is February 1. Notification of admission by April 1. Reply is required by May 1. $300 tuition deposit, refundable until May 1. Freshmen accepted for terms other than fall.
**Special programs:** Admission may be deferred one year. Credit and/or placement may be granted through CEEB Advanced Placement exams for scores of 4 or higher. Credit and/or placement may be granted through CLEP subject exams. Credit and placement may be granted through challenge exams. Early decision program. In fall 1993, 121 applied for early decision and 91 were accepted. Deadline for applying for early decision is January 1. Early entrance/early admission program. Concurrent enrollment program.
**Transfer students:** Transfer students accepted for terms other than fall. In fall 1993, 4% of all new students were transfers into all classes. 116 transfer applications were received, 58 were accepted. Application deadline is May 15 for fall; December 1 for spring. Minimum 2.75 GPA recommended. Lowest course grade accepted is "C." Maximum number of transferable semester hours is 67. At least 60 semester hours must be completed at the university to receive degree.
**Admissions contact:** Ms. Stuart R. Oremus, M.Ed., Director of Admissions. 800 336-4766.
**FINANCIAL AID. Available aid:** Pell grants, SEOG, state scholarships and grants, school scholarships and grants, private scholarships and grants, academic merit scholarships, and aid for undergraduate foreign students. Perkins Loans (NDSL), PLUS, Stafford Loans (GSL), school loans, private loans, and SLS. Knight Tuition Plans and deferred payment plan.
**Financial aid statistics:** 33% of aid is not need-based. In 1993-94, 89% of all undergraduate applicants received aid; 89% of freshman applicants. Average amounts of aid awarded freshmen: Scholarships and grants, $11,851; loans, $2,836.
**Supporting data/closing dates:** FAFSA/FAF/FFS: Priority filing date is March 1. Notification of awards begins April 1.
**Financial aid contact:** Lynn Gilbert, Director of Financial Aid. 614 587-6279.
**STUDENT EMPLOYMENT.** College Work/Study Program. Institutional employment. 40% of full-time undergraduates work on campus during school year. Students may expect to earn an average of $1,600 during school year. Off-campus part-time employment opportunities rated "poor."
**COMPUTER FACILITIES.** 160 IBM/IBM-compatible and Macintosh/Apple microcomputers; all are networked. Students may access AT&T, Digital, IBM, SUN minicomputer/mainframe systems, BITNET, Internet. Residence halls may be equipped with stand-alone microcomputers, networked microcomputers, networked terminals, modems. Client/LAN operating systems include Apple/Macintosh, LocalTalk/AppleTalk. 575 major computer languages and software packages available. Computer facilities are available to all students.
**Fees:** None.
**Hours:** 24 hours.
**GRADUATE CAREER DATA.** Graduate school percentages: 8% enter law school. 5% enter medical school. 1% enter dental school. 15% enter graduate business programs. 15% enter graduate arts and sciences programs. 1% enter theological school/seminary. 50% of graduates choose careers in business and industry. Companies and businesses that hire graduates: Anderson Consulting, Leo Burnett, Bank One, Chubb Insurance, Northern Trust.
**PROMINENT ALUMNI/AE.** Michael Eisner, president and CEO, Walt Disney Productions; Richard Lugar, U.S. senator, Indiana; Hal Holbrook, actor; Sara Fritz, television news correspondent.

## DeVry Institute of Technology

**Columbus, OH 43209** — **614 253-7291**

**1994-95 Costs.** Tuition: $5,962. Housing: None. Fees, books, misc. academic expenses (school's estimate): $580.
**Enrollment.** Undergraduates: 1,827 men, 425 women (full-time). Freshman class: 1,426 applicants, 1,295 accepted, 716 enrolled.
**Test score averages/ranges.** N/A.
**Faculty.** 60 full-time; 18 part-time. Student/faculty ratio: 37 to 1.
**Selectivity rating.** N/A.

**PROFILE.** DeVry/Columbus, founded in 1952, is a private institution specializing in electronics technology and computer information systems. It is a member of a network of technical institutes with nine campuses in the U.S. and two in Canada. Its 21-acre campus is located in Columbus.

**Accreditation:** NCACS. Professionally accredited by the Accreditation Board for Engineering and Technology.
**Religious orientation:** DeVry Institute of Technology is nonsectarian; no religious requirements.
**Library:** Collections totaling over 15,458 volumes, 180 periodical subscriptions, and 66,000 microform items.
**Athletic facilities:** Basketball court.
**STUDENT BODY. Undergraduate profile:** 56% are state residents; 49% are transfers. 2% Asian-American, 18% Black, 1% Hispanic, 79% White. Average age of undergraduates is 22.
**Undergraduate achievement:** 44% of fall 1992 freshmen returned for fall 1993 term. 32% of entering class graduated.
**Foreign students:** 21 students are from out of the country. Countries represented include Canada, Indonesia, Liberia, United Arab Emirates, and the former Yugoslav Republics; 11 in all.
**PROGRAMS OF STUDY. Degrees:** B.Acct., B.S.Bus.Oper., B.S.Comp.Info.Sys., B.S.Elec.Eng.Tech.
**Majors:** Accounting, Business Operations, Computer Information Systems, Electronics Engineering Technology.
**Distribution of degrees:** The majors with the highest enrollment are electronics engineering technology, computer information systems, and business operations.
**Requirements:** General education requirement.
**Academic regulations:** Minimum 2.0 GPA must be maintained.
**Special:** Associate's degrees offered. Accelerated study. Cooperative education programs. Graduate school at which undergraduates may take graduate-level courses. ROTC and AFROTC at Ohio State U.
**Honors:** Honor societies.
**Academic Assistance:** Nonremedial tutoring.
**STUDENT LIFE. Housing:** Commuter campus; no student housing.
**Services and counseling/handicapped student services:** Placement services. Career and academic guidance services. Physically disabled student services. Notetaking services. Reader services for the blind.
**Campus organizations:** Undergraduate student government. Student newspaper (Transmitter, published once/month). State band, Society of Women Engineers, Future Accounting Society, activities board, transfer student association, tae kwon do club, 8 organizations in all.
**Religious organizations:** DeVry Christian Association.
**Minority/foreign student organizations:** Black Students United.
**ATHLETICS. Physical education requirements:** None.
**Intramural and club sports:** Intramural basketball, billards, softball, volleyball.
**ADMISSIONS. Academic basis for candidate selection** (in order of priority): Standardized test scores.
**Requirements:** Graduation from secondary school is required; GED is accepted. No specific distribution of secondary school units required. All applicants must be at least 17 years of age on first day of classes. Minimum math SAT score of 400-480 (math ACT score of 16-18) required depending on program. SAT or ACT is recommended. Applicants not submitting SAT or ACT must pass DeVry entrance exam. Campus visit recommended. Off-campus interviews available with an admissions representative.
**Procedure:** Notification of admission on rolling basis. Reply is required by registration. $75 tuition deposit, refundable until beginning of classes. Freshmen accepted for terms other than fall.
**Special programs:** Admission may be deferred one year. Credit may be granted through CLEP subject exams and DANTES and challenge exams.
**Transfer students:** Transfer students accepted for terms other than fall. In fall 1993, 49% of all new students were transfers into all classes. Application deadline is rolling for fall; rolling for spring. Minimum 2.0 GPA required. Lowest course grade accepted is "C." Maximum number of transferable semester hours is 65% of total required for degree. At least 35% of total semester hours must be completed at the institute to receive degree.
**Admissions contact:** Richard Rodman, Director of Admissions. 614 253-1525.
**FINANCIAL AID. Available aid:** Pell grants, SEOG, state scholarships and grants, school scholarships, and academic merit scholarships. Perkins Loans (NDSL), PLUS, Stafford Loans (GSL), state loans, and SLS. EDUCARD Plan.
**Financial aid statistics:** In 1993-94, 83% of all undergraduate applicants received aid; 81% of freshman applicants.
**Supporting data/closing dates:** FAFSA: Accepted on rolling basis. Notification of awards on rolling basis.
**Financial aid contact:** Cynthia Price, Director of Financial Aid.
**STUDENT EMPLOYMENT.** College Work/Study Program. Institutional employment. 5% of full-time undergraduates work on campus during school year. Students may expect to earn an average of $4,420 during school year. Freshmen are discouraged from working during their first term. Off-campus part-time employment opportunities rated "excellent."
**COMPUTER FACILITIES.** 186 IBM/IBM-compatible microcomputers; all are networked. Students may access Hewlett-Packard, IBM minicomputer/mainframe systems. Client/LAN operating systems include DOS, UNIX/XENIX/AIX, Novell. Computer languages and software packages include CICS, COBOL, IMS, MicroFocus, OS/JCL, Pascal, RPG; database, graphics, spreadsheet, word processing packages; 12 in all. Computer facilities are available to all students.
**Fees:** Computer fee is included in tuition/fees.
**GRADUATE CAREER DATA.** 86% of graduates choose careers in business and industry. Companies and businesses that hire graduates: Nationwide Insurance, Defense Logistics Agency, Royal Appliance Manufacturing, Applied Materials.

9-7

## Dyke College

**Cleveland, OH 44115-1096** — **216 696-9000**

**1994-95 Costs.** Tuition: $12,000. Housing: None. Fees, books, misc. academic expenses (school's estimate): $650.
**Enrollment.** Undergraduates: 180 men, 404 women (full-time). Freshman class: 257 applicants, 230 accepted, 194 enrolled.
**Test score averages/ranges.** N/A.
**Faculty.** 32 full-time; 60 part-time. 18% of faculty holds highest degree in specific field. Student/faculty ratio: 16 to 1.
**Selectivity rating.** N/A.

**PROFILE.** Dyke, founded in 1848 is a private college of business. The campus is located in downtown Cleveland.

**Accreditation:** NCACS. Professionally accredited by the American Bar Association.
**Religious orientation:** Dyke College is nonsectarian; no religious requirements.

**Library:** Collections totaling over 16,000 volumes, 142 periodical subscriptions and 92 microform items.

**STUDENT BODY. Undergraduate profile:** 40% are transfers. 41% Black, 3% Hispanic, 45% White, 11% Other. Average age of undergraduates is 28.

**Freshman profile:** 96% of freshmen come from public schools.

**Undergraduate achievement:** 70% of fall 1991 freshmen returned for fall 1992 term. 48% of entering class graduated. 15% of students who completed a degree program immediately went on to graduate study.

**Foreign students:** Two students are from out of the country. Two countries represented in all.

**PROGRAMS OF STUDY. Degrees:** B.S.

**Majors:** Accounting, Business Administration, Economics/Finance, Health Services Management, Industrial Management, Information Processing, Management, Marketing, Office Systems Administration, Paralegal Education, Public Administration, Real Estate, Retail Merchandising, Social Science.

**Distribution of degrees:** The majors with the highest enrollment are accounting, management, and paralegal education; retail merchandising, real estate, and industrial management have the lowest.

**Requirements:** General education requirement.

**Academic regulations:** Freshmen must maintain minimum 1.667 GPA; sophomores, 1.833 GPA; juniors, 2.0 GPA; seniors, 2.0 GPA.

**Special:** External Degree and Accelerated Management Degree programs. Associate's degrees offered. Double majors. Independent study. Accelerated study. Internships. Cooperative education programs. Graduate school at which undergraduates may take graduate-level courses. Member of Cleveland Commission on Higher Education. ROTC at John Carroll U.

**Honors:** Honor societies.

**Academic Assistance:** Remedial reading, writing, math, and study skills. Nonremedial tutoring.

**ADMISSIONS. Academic basis for candidate selection** (in order of priority): Secondary school record, standardized test scores, class rank, school's recommendation, essay.

**Nonacademic basis for candidate selection:** Character and personality, extracurricular participation, and particular talent or ability are important.

**Requirements:** Graduation from secondary school is required; GED is accepted. 18 units and the following program of study are required: 4 units of English, 3 units of math, 2 units of science including 1 unit of lab, 3 units of social studies, 6 units of electives including 3 units of academic electives. Minimum composite ACT score of 18, rank in top half of secondary school class, and minimum 2.0 GPA recommended. Separate admissions procedures required of paralegal education program applicants. Developmental Education Program for applicants not normally admissible. ACT is required; SAT may be substituted. Campus visit required. Off-campus interviews available with an admissions representative.

**Procedure:** Take SAT or ACT by October of 12th year. Visit college for interview by March of 12th year. Suggest filing application by February 1. Application deadline is August 15. Notification of admission on rolling basis. No set date by which applicants must accept offer. Freshmen accepted for terms other than fall.

**Special programs:** Admission may be deferred one year. Credit and/or placement may be granted through CLEP general and subject exams. Credit and placement may be granted through ACT PEP and challenge exams and military and life experience. Early entrance/early admission program. Concurrent enrollment program.

**Transfer students:** Transfer students accepted for terms other than fall. In fall 1992, 40% of all new students were transfers into all classes. 170 transfer applications were received, 169 were accepted. Application deadline is September 1 for fall; January 3 for spring. Minimum 2.0 GPA recommended. Lowest course grade accepted is "C." SAT/ACT scores and both transcripts required for applicants with fewer than 24 semester hours or 36 quarter hours. Maximum number of transferable credits is 64 semester hours from a two-year school and 93 semester hours from a four-year school. At least 33 semester hours must be completed at the college to receive degree.

**Admissions contact:** Ronald A. Wendeln, Ph.D., Acting Director of Admissions. 216 696-9000, extension 800.

**FINANCIAL AID. Available aid:** Pell grants, SEOG, state scholarships and grants, school scholarships and grants, private scholarships and grants, ROTC scholarships, academic merit scholarships, and athletic scholarships. Perkins Loans (NDSL), PLUS, Stafford Loans (GSL), school loans, and SLS. Deferred payment plan.

**Financial aid statistics:** 10% of aid is not need-based. In 1992-93, 80% of all freshman applicants received aid. Average amounts of aid awarded freshmen: Scholarships and grants, $2,800; loans, $2,800.

**Supporting data/closing dates:** FAFSA: Deadline is in June. FAF/FFS: Priority filing date is July 1. School's own aid application: Accepted on rolling basis. State aid form: Deadline is September 30. Notification of awards on rolling basis.

**Financial aid contact:** James McMullen, M.A., Director of Financial Aid. 216 696-9000, extension 818.

8-28

# Franciscan University of Steubenville

Steubenville, OH 43952-6701 614 283-3771

**1993-94 Costs.** Tuition: $8,940. Room & board: $4,200. Fees, books, misc. academic expenses (school's estimate): $885.

**Enrollment.** Undergraduates: 534 men, 767 women (full-time). Freshman class: 553 applicants, 452 accepted, 228 enrolled. Graduate enrollment: 174 men, 184 women.

**Test score averages/ranges.** Average SAT scores: 488 verbal, 516 math. Range of SAT scores of middle 50%: 410-550 verbal, 440-590 math. Average ACT scores: 23 composite. Range of ACT scores of middle 50%: 20-26 composite.

**Faculty.** 80 full-time; 53 part-time. 71% of faculty holds doctoral degree. Student/faculty ratio: 16 to 1.

**Selectivity rating.** Competitive.

**PROFILE.** Franciscan University of Steubenville, founded in 1946, is a church-affiliated, liberal arts institution. Its 100-acre campus is located in Steubenville, 70 miles west of Pittsburgh.

**Accreditation:** NCACS. Professionally accredited by the National League for Nursing.

**Religious orientation:** Franciscan University of Steubenville is affiliated with the Roman Catholic Church (Franciscan Friars); two semesters of theology required.

**Library:** Collections totaling over 200,499 volumes, 800 periodical subscriptions, and 105,802 microform items.

**Special facilities/museums:** Computer center.

**Athletic facilities:** Athletic center.

**STUDENT BODY. Undergraduate profile:** 37% are state residents; 47% are transfers. 2.5% Asian-American, 1% Black, 4% Hispanic, .5% Native American, 84% White, 8% Other. Average age of undergraduates is 23.

**Freshman profile:** 2% of freshmen who took SAT scored 700 or over on verbal, 3% scored 700 or over on math; 14% scored 600 or over on verbal, 24% scored 600 or over on math; 48% scored 500 or over on verbal, 58% scored 500 or over on math; 82% scored 400 or over on verbal, 85% scored 400 or over on math; 97% scored 300 or over on verbal, 99% scored 300 or over on math. 63% of accepted applicants took SAT; 52% took ACT. 56% of freshmen come from public schools.

**Undergraduate achievement:** 41% of entering class graduated.

**Foreign students:** Countries represented include Canada, Honduras, Japan, Nigeria, and Trinidad; 21 in all.

**PROGRAMS OF STUDY. Degrees:** B.A., B.S.

**Majors:** Accounting, Biology, Business Administration, Chemistry, Communication, Computer Information Science, Computer Science, Criminal Justice, Drama, Economics, Education, Elementary Education, Engineering Science, English, Finance, French, History, Humanities/Catholic Culture, Journalism, Kindergarten Education, Literature, Management, Mathematical Science, Medical Technology, Mental Health/Human Services, Nursing, Philosophy, Political Science, Psychology, Secondary Education, Sociology, Special Education, Theology, TV/Radio.

**Distribution of degrees:** The majors with the highest enrollment are business administration, psychology, and theology/philosophy; engineering has the lowest.

**Requirements:** General education requirement.

**Academic regulations:** Minimum 2.0 GPA must be maintained.

**Special:** Minors offered in anthropology, human life issues, and music. Associate's degrees offered. Double majors. Internships. Cooperative education programs. Graduate school at which undergraduates may take graduate-level courses. Preprofessional programs in law, medicine, veterinary science, pharmacy, dentistry, theology, and optometry. Five-year bachelor's/M.B.A. program. Teacher certification in early childhood, elementary, secondary, and special education. Certification in specific subject areas. School operates a campus abroad in Austria where students spend one semester studying and traveling in Europe.

**Honors:** Honors program. Honor societies.

**Academic Assistance:** Nonremedial tutoring.

**STUDENT LIFE. Housing:** All unmarried students under age 23 must live on campus unless living with family. Women's and men's dorms. Off-campus privately-owned housing. 64% of students live in college housing.

**Social atmosphere:** On campus, Steubenville students gather at the Portuncula chapel, the J.C. Williams Center, and Finnegan Fieldhouse. Off campus, the Drover's Inn and Damon's Club are popular. The campus household system, intramural sports, Greeks, Knights of Columbus, and Works of Mercy are widely influential on student social life. Highlights of the school year include the annual Household Olympics, Spring Fling, coffeehouses, Battle of the Bands, a monthly Festival of Praise, and the March For Life in Washington, D.C. "FUS is a Catholic, Christian, and Franciscan university," reports the student newspaper. "We seek to balance our work and play." Integral to campus life is the household system, which provides "a unique peer-to-peer support system unrivaled by any other."

**Services and counseling/handicapped student services:** Placement services. Health service. Counseling services for veteran students. Personal and psychological counseling. Career and academic guidance services. Religious counseling. Physically disabled student services. Learning disabled services. Notetaking services. Tape recorders. Tutors. Reader services for the blind.

**Campus organizations:** Undergraduate student government. Student newspaper (Troubadour, published once/week). Yearbook. Musical groups, drama groups, Activities Board, accounting club, American Chemical Society, economics and language clubs, education association, engineering society, political science forum, 28 organizations in all. Three fraternities, no chapter houses; three sororities, no chapter houses. 5% of men join a fraternity. 5% of women join a sorority.

**Religious organizations:** Franciscan Youth Ministries, Human Life Concerns, Works of Mercy.

**Minority/foreign student organizations:** Hispanic group. International Student Organization.

**ATHLETICS. Physical education requirements:** None.

**Intercollegiate competition:** 9% of students participate. Member of Ohio Collegiate Soccer Conference.

**Intramural and club sports:** 50% of students participate. Intramural aerobics, badminton, basketball, billiards, cross-country, flag football, frisbee, racquetball, table tennis, tennis, volleyball, walleyball, weight lifting. Men's club baseball, soccer. Women's club soccer, volleyball.

**ADMISSIONS. Academic basis for candidate selection** (in order of priority): Secondary school record, standardized test scores, class rank, essay, school's recommendation.

**Nonacademic basis for candidate selection:** Character and personality, extracurricular participation, and particular talent or ability are considered.

**Requirements:** Graduation from secondary school is required; GED is accepted. 15 units and the following program of study are required: 4 units of English, 2 units of math, 2 units of science, 2 units of foreign language, 2 units of social studies, 3 units of academic electives. Additional units of science and mathematics recommended. Minimum combined SAT score of 850 (composite ACT score of 19), rank in top half of secondary school class, and minimum 2.4 GPA required. Conditional admission possible for applicants not meeting standard requirements. SAT or ACT is required. Campus visit and interview recommended. No off-campus interviews.

**Procedure:** Take SAT or ACT by October of 12th year. Visit college for interview by March 31 of 12th year. Application deadline is July 31. Notification of admission on rolling basis. Reply is required by August 15. $50 tuition deposit, refundable before June 1. $100 room deposit, refundable before June 1. Freshmen accepted for terms other than fall.
**Special programs:** Admission may be deferred one year. Credit and/or placement may be granted through CEEB Advanced Placement exams for scores of 3 or higher. Credit and/or placement may be granted through CLEP general and subject exams. Placement may be granted through challenge exams. Credit and placement may be granted through ACT PEP exams. Deadline for applying for early decision is August 1. Early entrance/early admission program.
**Transfer students:** Transfer students accepted for terms other than fall. In fall 1993, 47% of all new students were transfers into all classes. 542 transfer applications were received, 435 were accepted. Application deadline is July 31 for fall; December 31 for spring. Minimum 2.0 GPA required. Lowest course grade accepted is "C." At least 30 semester hours must be completed at the university to receive degree.
**Admissions contact:** Margaret Weber, Director of Admissions. 614 283-6226.

**FINANCIAL AID. Available aid:** Pell grants, SEOG, state scholarships and grants, school scholarships and grants, private scholarships and grants, and academic merit scholarships. Perkins Loans (NDSL), PLUS, Stafford Loans (GSL), state loans, school loans, and SLS. Tuition Plan Inc., AMS, and Tuition Management Systems.
**Financial aid statistics:** 20% of aid is not need-based. In 1993-94, 96% of all undergraduate applicants received aid; 96% of freshman applicants. Average amounts of aid awarded freshmen: Scholarships and grants, $2,000; loans, $2,625.
**Supporting data/closing dates:** FAFSA: Priority filing date is March 1. School's own aid application: Accepted on rolling basis. State aid form: Priority filing date is September 1; accepted on rolling basis. Notification of awards on rolling basis.
**Financial aid contact:** Ann Johnston, M.S., Director of Financial Aid. 614 283-6211.

**STUDENT EMPLOYMENT.** College Work/Study Program. Institutional employment. 55% of full-time undergraduates work on campus during school year. Students may expect to earn an average of $1,200 during school year. Off-campus part-time employment opportunities rated "fair."

**COMPUTER FACILITIES.** 50 IBM/IBM-compatible and Macintosh/Apple microcomputers; 5 are networked. Students may access Digital, IBM minicomputer/mainframe systems. Computer languages and software packages include BASIC, C, COBOL, FORTRAN, Pascal; database, spreadsheet, word processing programs. Priority use given to students enrolled in computer-applied courses.
**Fees:** $25 computer fee per semester hour; included in tuition/fees.
**Hours:** 9 AM-11 PM (M-F); 10 AM-9 PM (Sa); noon-5 PM (Su).

**PROMINENT ALUMNI/AE.** Don Donnell, president, Starvaggi Industries; Dr. Jess Young, M.D., president, Society of Vascular Medicine and Biology at the Cleveland Clinic; Orlando Schappa, president, American Industries and Resources.

## Franklin University

**Columbus, OH 43215** — **614 341-6237**

**1993-94 Costs.** Tuition: $4,576. Housing: None. Fees, books, misc. academic expenses (school's estimate): $635.
**Enrollment.** Undergraduates: 551 men, 593 women (full-time). Freshman class: 275 applicants, 275 accepted, 133 enrolled.
**Test score averages/ranges.** N/A.
**Faculty.** 46 full-time; 150 part-time. 23% of faculty holds doctoral degree. Student/faculty ratio: 20 to 1.
**Selectivity rating.** N/A.

**PROFILE.** Franklin, founded in 1902, is a private university. Programs are offered through the Colleges of Arts and Sciences, Business, and Technology. Its 13-acre campus is located in downtown Columbus.

**Accreditation:** NCACS. Professionally accredited by the Accreditation Board for Engineering and Technology, the National League for Nursing.
**Religious orientation:** Franklin University is nonsectarian; no religious requirements.
**Library:** Collections totaling over 83,458 volumes, 1,120 periodical subscriptions, and 143,735 microform items.
**Special facilities/museums:** Art gallery, media production studio, engineering technology lab.
**Athletic facilities:** Gymnasium.

**STUDENT BODY. Undergraduate profile:** 61% are transfers. 1% Asian-American, 13% Black, 82% White, 4% Other. Average age of undergraduates is 25.
**Freshman profile:** Majority of accepted applicants took ACT. 86% of freshmen come from public schools.
**Undergraduate achievement:** 39% of fall 1991 freshmen returned for fall 1992 term. 10% of entering class graduated.
**Foreign students:** 86 students are from out of the country. Countries represented include China, Indonesia, Japan, Korea, Taiwan, and United Arab Emirates; 35 in all.

**PROGRAMS OF STUDY. Degrees:** B.S., B.S.Nurs.
**Majors:** Accounting, Applied Communication, Banking, Business Management, Computer Management, Computer Science, Electronic Engineering Technology, Employee Assistance Counseling, Finance, Human Resources Management, Management Science, Marketing, Mechanical Engineering Technology, Nursing, Public Administration, Public Management, Real Estate.
**Distribution of degrees:** The majors with the highest enrollment are business management, accounting, and marketing; public management and public administration have the lowest.
**Requirements:** General education requirement.
**Academic regulations:** Freshmen must maintain minimum 1.1 GPA; sophomores, 1.5 GPA; juniors, 1.7 GPA; seniors, 2.0 GPA.
**Special:** Courses offered in anthropology, communications, economics, English, history, humanities, information processing, math, political science, psychology, science, and sociology. Associate's degrees offered. Double majors. Independent study. Internships. 2-2 programs offered. Member of Higher Education Council of Columbus; cross-registration possible with seven area colleges and universities. Semester at Sea. Exchange programs abroad in England (Richmond Coll) and other countries. ROTC. AFROTC at Ohio State U.
**Honors:** Honor societies.
**Academic Assistance:** Remedial reading, writing, math, and study skills.

**STUDENT LIFE. Housing:** Commuter campus; no student housing.
**Services and counseling/handicapped student services:** Placement services. Developmental Studies Division. Counseling services for minority and veteran students. Personal counseling. Career and academic guidance services. Physically disabled student services. Learning disabled services. Notetaking services. Tape recorders. Tutors. Reader services for the blind.
**Campus organizations:** Student newspaper (Almanac, published nine times/year). Drama and ski clubs, Collegiate Entrepreneurs, Nursing Student Council, Student Organization Board, Student Events and Activities Planning Board, departmental and special-interest groups, 18 organizations in all.
**Minority/foreign student organizations:** Black Student Union. International Student Organization.

**ATHLETICS. Physical education requirements:** None.
**Intercollegiate competition:** Soccer (M).
**Intramural and club sports:** Intramural basketball, bowling, soccer, softball, volleyball.

**ADMISSIONS.**
**Requirements:** Graduation from secondary school is required; GED is accepted. 3 units and the following program of study are recommended: 3 units of math. Open admissions policy. R.N. and separate admissions requirements required of nursing program applicants. ACT is recommended. Campus visit and interview recommended. Off-campus interviews available with an admissions representative.
**Procedure:** No set date by which applicants must accept offer. Freshmen accepted for terms other than fall.
**Special programs:** Admission may be deferred one year. Credit may be granted through CLEP general and subject exams, Regents College and ACT PEP exams, and military and life experience. Credit and placement may be granted through challenge exams. Early entrance/early admission program. Concurrent enrollment program.
**Transfer students:** Transfer students accepted for terms other than fall. In fall 1992, 61% of all new students were transfers into all classes. Open admissions for transfers. 827 transfer applications were received, 827 were accepted. Lowest course grade accepted is "C-." At least 30 semester hours must be completed at the university to receive degree.
**Admissions contact:** Kitty Miller, Director of Admissions. 614 341-6231.

**FINANCIAL AID. Available aid:** Pell grants, SEOG, state scholarships and grants, school scholarships, private scholarships, and academic merit scholarships. Perkins Loans (NDSL), PLUS, Stafford Loans (GSL), state loans, and SLS. Deferred payment plan. Installment payment plan.
**Financial aid statistics:** 42% of aid is not need-based. In 1992-93, 59% of all undergraduate applicants received aid; 73% of freshman applicants.
**Supporting data/closing dates:** FAFSA: Accepted on rolling basis. School's own aid application: Accepted on rolling basis. State aid form: Accepted on rolling basis. Notification of awards on rolling basis.
**Financial aid contact:** Kathy Fay, Director of Financial Aid. 614 341-6245.

**STUDENT EMPLOYMENT.** College Work/Study Program. Institutional employment. 2% of full-time undergraduates work on campus during school year. Students may expect to earn an average of $5,000 during school year. Off-campus part-time employment opportunities rated "excellent."

**COMPUTER FACILITIES.** IBM/IBM-compatible and Macintosh/Apple microcomputers; 96 are networked. Students may access Digital, IBM minicomputer/mainframe systems, Internet. Computer languages and software packages include Ada, BASIC, C, dBASE, FORTRAN, LISP, Lotus 1-2-3, Pascal, WordPerfect. Computer facilities are available to all students.
**Fees:** Computer fee is included in tuition/fees.
**Hours:** 7 AM-11 PM (M-Th); 8 AM-8 PM (F); 8 AM-7 PM (Sa); 1 PM-6 PM (Su).

**GRADUATE CAREER DATA.** Highest graduate school enrollments: Capital U, Ohio State U, Wright State U. 98% of graduates choose careers in business and industry.

**PROMINENT ALUMNI/AE.** John E. Fisher, insurance executive; Tod J. Ortlip, real estate developer.

## Heidelberg College

**Tiffin, OH 44883** — **419 448-2000**

**1994-95 Costs.** Tuition: $13,900. Room & board: $4,400. Fees, books, misc. academic expenses (school's estimate): $500.
**Enrollment.** Undergraduates: 507 men, 447 women (full-time). Freshman class: 953 applicants, 754 accepted, 232 enrolled. Graduate enrollment: 48 men, 126 women.
**Test score averages/ranges.** Average SAT scores: 420 verbal, 460 math. Average ACT scores: 21 composite.
**Faculty.** 73 full-time; 38 part-time. 75% of faculty holds doctoral degree. Student/faculty ratio: 13 to 1.
**Selectivity rating.** Competitive.

**PROFILE.** Heidelberg, founded in 1850, is a church-affiliated, liberal arts college. Its 110-acre campus is located 45 miles southeast of Toledo. Several campus buildings are listed in the National Register of Historic Places; campus architecture includes Greek Revival, Victorian Gothic, modern English Gothic, and international styles.

**Accreditation:** NCACS. Professionally accredited by the National Association of Schools of Music.

8-24

**Religious orientation:** Heidelberg College is affiliated with the United Church of Christ; two semesters of religion/theology required.
**Library:** Collections totaling over 193,205 volumes, 748 periodical subscriptions, and 88,100 microform items.
**Special facilities/museums:** Water quality lab, nature preserves.
**Athletic facilities:** Gymnasium, weight room, track, baseball, lacrosse, and softball fields, swimming pool, basketball, racquetball, tennis, and volleyball courts.

**STUDENT BODY. Undergraduate profile:** 82% are state residents; 7% are transfers. 14% Asian-American, 3% Black, 1% Hispanic, 82% White. Average age of undergraduates is 20.
**Freshman profile:** 10% of accepted applicants took SAT; 90% took ACT. 80% of freshmen come from public schools.
**Undergraduate achievement:** 78% of fall 1992 freshmen returned for fall 1993 term. 65% of entering class graduated. 21% of students who completed a degree program immediately went on to graduate study.
**Foreign students:** 107 students are from out of the country. Countries represented include China, Germany, Japan, Korea, Malaysia, and Thailand; 12 in all.

**PROGRAMS OF STUDY. Degrees:** A.B., B.Mus., B.S.
**Majors:** Accounting, Anthropology, Biology, Business Administration, Chemistry, Communication/Theatre Arts, Computer Information Systems, Computer Science, Economics, Elementary Education, English, Environmental Biology, German, Health/Physical Education, Health Services Management, History, International Studies, Management Science, Mathematics, Music, Music Education, Music Industry, Philosophy/Religion, Physics, Political Science, Psychology, Public Administration, Public Relations, Secondary Education, Spanish, Special Education, Sports Medicine, Water Resources Management.
**Distribution of degrees:** The majors with the highest enrollment are business, economics, communication/theatre arts, and education; chemistry and management science have the lowest.
**Requirements:** General education requirement.
**Academic regulations:** Minimum 2.5 GPA must be maintained.
**Special:** Courses offered in geology/geography, literature and fine arts, and non-Western cultures. Japanese language course through cooperation with State U of New York. Innovative College Studies Program offers seminar-type experience. Self-designed majors. Double majors. Dual degrees. Independent study. Accelerated study. Pass/fail grading option. Internships. Preprofessional programs in law, medicine, veterinary science, dentistry, and optometry. 3-2 engineering program with Case Western Reserve U. Cooperative programs in forestry with Duke U and in medical technology and nursing with Case Western Reserve U. Washington Semester. Teacher certification in elementary, secondary, and special education. Certification in specific subject areas. Study abroad in African, Asian, European, and Latin American countries. Caribbean biogeography on-site field work. ROTC and AFROTC at Bowling Green State U.
**Honors:** Honors program. Honor societies.
**Academic Assistance:** Remedial study skills. Nonremedial tutoring.

**ADMISSIONS. Academic basis for candidate selection** (in order of priority): Secondary school record, standardized test scores, class rank, school's recommendation, essay.
**Nonacademic basis for candidate selection:** Character and personality, extracurricular participation, and particular talent or ability are considered.
**Requirements:** Graduation from secondary school is required; GED is accepted. 24 units and the following program of study are recommended: 4 units of English, 4 units of math, 4 units of science including 1 unit of lab, 2 units of foreign language, 3 units of social studies, 2 units of history, 5 units of electives. Rank in top half of secondary school class and minimum 2.5 GPA recommended. Audition required of music program applicants. Vocal and instrumental audition required for placement in relevant areas. SAT or ACT is required. Campus visit and interview recommended. Off-campus interviews available with an admissions representative.
**Procedure:** Take SAT or ACT by April 1 of 12th year. Visit college for interview by June 1 of 12th year. Application deadline is June 30. Notification of admission on rolling basis. Reply is required within 30 days of notification. $100 tuition deposit, refundable until May 1. $100 room deposit, refundable until May 1. Freshmen accepted for terms other than fall.
**Special programs:** Admission may be deferred one year. Credit and/or placement may be granted through CEEB Advanced Placement exams for scores of 3 or higher. Credit and/or placement may be granted through CLEP general and subject exams. Credit and placement may be granted through Regents College, ACT PEP, DANTES, and challenge exams and military and life experience. Early entrance/early admission program. Concurrent enrollment program.
**Transfer students:** Transfer students accepted for terms other than fall. In fall 1993, 7% of all new students were transfers into all classes. 71 transfer applications were received, 59 were accepted. Application deadline is rolling for fall; rolling for spring. Minimum 2.0 GPA required. Lowest course grade accepted is "C." Maximum number of transferable credits is 30 semester hours from a two-year school and 90 semester hours from a four-year school. At least 30 semester hours must be completed at the college to receive degree.
**Admissions contact:** Stephen E. Eidson, Dean of Admission. 800 434-3352, 800 HEIDELBERG.

**FINANCIAL AID. Available aid:** Pell grants, SEOG, state grants, school scholarships and grants, private scholarships and grants, and academic merit scholarships. Perkins Loans (NDSL), PLUS, Stafford Loans (GSL), and SLS. Tuition Plan Inc., Education Plan Inc., and Knight Tuition Plans. College payment plans.
**Financial aid statistics:** 30% of aid is not need-based. In 1993-94, 82% of all undergraduate applicants received aid; 85% of freshman applicants. Average amounts of aid awarded freshmen: Scholarships and grants, $4,600; loans, $2,500.
**Supporting data/closing dates:** FAFSA/FAF/FFS: Priority filing date is April 1; accepted on rolling basis. State aid form. Notification of awards on rolling basis.
**Financial aid contact:** Juli Weininger, Director of Financial Aid. 419 448-2293.

# Hiram College

**Hiram, OH 44234** **216 569-3211**

**1994-95 Costs.** Tuition: $14,065. Room & board: $4,560. Fees, books, misc. academic expenses (school's estimate): $830.
**Enrollment.** Undergraduates: 408 men, 432 women (full-time). Freshman class: 922 applicants, 729 accepted, 244 enrolled.
**Test score averages/ranges.** Average SAT scores: 510 verbal, 540 math. Range of SAT scores of middle 50%: 430-560 verbal, 480-590 math. Average ACT scores: 24 English, 22 math, 25 composite. Range of ACT scores of middle 50%: 21-27 English, 20-25 math.
**Faculty.** 81 full-time. 95% of faculty holds highest degree in specific field. Student/faculty ratio: 12 to 1.
**Selectivity rating.** Competitive.

**PROFILE.** Hiram, founded in 1850, is a church-affiliated, liberal arts college. Its 245-acre campus is located in Hiram, 35 miles southeast of Cleveland.

**Accreditation:** NCACS. Professionally accredited by the National Association of Schools of Music, the National Council for Accreditation of Teacher Education.
**Religious orientation:** Hiram College is affiliated with the Christian Church (Disciples of Christ); no religious requirements.
**Library:** Collections totaling over 169,695 volumes, 826 periodical subscriptions, and 76,597 microform items.
**Special facilities/museums:** Psychology lab, language lab, international center, center for literature and medicine, fitness center, health center, observatory, electron microscope, two field stations for study and research.
**Athletic facilities:** Gymnasium, field house, baseball, football, intramural, soccer, and softball fields, track, basketball, racquetball, tennis, and volleyball courts, weight, sauna, fitness trail, Nordic skiing trail, swimming pool.

**STUDENT BODY. Undergraduate profile:** 80% are state residents; 12% are transfers. 1% Asian-American, 6% Black, 1% Hispanic, 92% White. Average age of undergraduates is 18.
**Freshman profile:** 4% of freshmen who took SAT scored 700 or over on math; 14% scored 600 or over on verbal, 24% scored 600 or over on math; 52% scored 500 or over on verbal, 64% scored 500 or over on math; 86% scored 400 or over on verbal, 94% scored 400 or over on math; 100% scored 300 or over on verbal, 100% scored 300 or over on math. 8% of freshmen who took ACT scored 30 or over on English, 5% scored 30 or over on math, 8% scored 30 or over on composite; 52% scored 24 or over on English, 41% scored 24 or over on math, 57% scored 24 or over on composite; 92% scored 18 or over on English, 89% scored 18 or over on math, 97% scored 18 or over on composite; 100% scored 12 or over on English, 100% scored 12 or over on math, 100% scored 12 or over on composite. 56% of accepted applicants took SAT; 88% took ACT.
**Undergraduate achievement:** 84% of fall 1992 freshmen returned for fall 1993 term. 75% of entering class graduated. 30% of students who completed a degree program went on to graduate study within one year.
**Foreign students:** 10 students are from out of the country. Countries represented include France, Germany, Italy, Japan, and Spain; seven in all.

**PROGRAMS OF STUDY. Degrees:** B.A.
**Majors:** Applied Physics, Art, Art History, Biology, Chemistry, Classical Studies, Communications, Comparative Arts, Computer Science, Economics, Elementary Education, English, French, German, History, International Economics/Management, Management, Mathematics, Music, Philosophy, Political Science, Psychobiology, Psychology, Religious Studies, Social Sciences, Sociology/Anthropology, Spanish, Theatre Arts.
**Requirements:** General education requirement.
**Academic regulations:** Minimum 2.00 GPA must be maintained.
**Special:** Minors offered in most majors and in environmental studies, exercise and sport science, photography, and writing. Self-designed majors. Double majors. Dual degrees. Independent study. Accelerated study. Pass/fail grading option. Internships. Preprofessional programs in law, medicine, veterinary science, pharmacy, dentistry, theology, optometry, engineering, and nursing. 3-2 business administration program with Washington U. 3-2 engineering programs with Case Western Reserve U and Washington U. 3-2 forestry and environmental management programs with Duke U. 3-2 international affairs and public administration programs with U of Pittsburgh. 3-2 physical therapy program with Cleveland State U. 3-4 nursing program with Case Western Reserve U. Member of East Central College Consortium. Washington Semester. Teacher certification in elementary, secondary, and special education. Certification in specific subject areas. Member of Institute for Asian Studies and Institute for European Studies. Exchange programs abroad in India (Mithibai Coll), Italy (John Cabot U), and Japan (Kansai U). Study abroad also in Australia, the Caribbean, Costa Rica, England, France, Germany, Ireland, Mexico, the former Soviet Republics, Spain, Switzerland, and Turkey.
**Honors:** Phi Beta Kappa. Honor societies.
**Academic Assistance:** Remedial writing, math, and study skills. Nonremedial tutoring.

**ADMISSIONS. Academic basis for candidate selection** (in order of priority): Secondary school record, standardized test scores, school's recommendation, essay, class rank.
**Nonacademic basis for candidate selection:** Character and personality and extracurricular participation are emphasized. Particular talent or ability is important. Geographical distribution and alumni/ae relationship are considered.
**Requirements:** Graduation from secondary school is recommended; GED is accepted. 16 units and the following program of study are required: 4 units of English, 3 units of math, 3 units of science including 2 units of lab, 1 unit of social studies, 2 units of history, 2 units of electives including 1 unit of academic electives. SAT or ACT is required. Three ACH exams (including English and math) may replace SAT or ACT. Campus visit and interview recommended. No off-campus interviews.

**Procedure:** Suggest filing application by March 1. Application deadline is April 15. Notification of admission on rolling basis. Reply is required by May 1. Freshmen accepted for terms other than fall.
**Special programs:** Admission may be deferred one year. Credit and/or placement may be granted through CEEB Advanced Placement exams for scores of 3 or higher. Credit and/or placement may be granted through CLEP subject exams. Credit may be granted through military experience. Placement may be granted through challenge exams. Early entrance/early admission program.
**Transfer students:** Transfer students accepted for terms other than fall. In fall 1993, 12% of all new students were transfers into all classes. 77 transfer applications were received, 53 were accepted. Application deadline is August 1 for fall; March 1 for spring. Minimum 2.5 GPA recommended. Lowest course grade accepted is "C." Maximum number of transferable quarter hours is 90. At least 90 quarter hours must be completed at the college to receive degree.
**Admissions contact:** Gary G. Craig, M.A., Dean of Admissions. 800 362-5280.

**FINANCIAL AID. Available aid:** Pell grants, SEOG, state scholarships and grants, school scholarships and grants, private scholarships and grants, and academic merit scholarships. Perkins Loans (NDSL), PLUS, Stafford Loans (GSL), school loans, and SLS. Tuition Plan Inc., AMS, and deferred payment plan.
**Financial aid statistics:** In 1993-94, 95% of all undergraduate applicants received aid; 90% of freshman applicants. Average amounts of aid awarded freshmen: Scholarships and grants, $8,250; loans, $2,334.
**Supporting data/closing dates:** FAFSA/FAF: Priority filing date is February 15; accepted on rolling basis. School's own aid application: Priority filing date is February 15; accepted on rolling basis. State aid form: Priority filing date is Febuary 15; accepted on rolling basis; deadline is September 1. Income tax forms: Priority filing date is February 15; accepted on rolling basis. Notification of awards on rolling basis.
**Financial aid contact:** Alan M. Donley, Director of Financial Aid. 216 569-5107.

## John Carroll University

**Cleveland, OH 44118 216 397-1886**

**1994-95 Costs.** Tuition: $11,700. Room & board: $5,550. Fees, books, misc. academic expenses (school's estimate): $600.
**Enrollment.** Undergraduates: 1,587 men, 1,583 women (full-time). Freshman class: 2,421 applicants, 2,109 accepted, 820 enrolled. Graduate enrollment: 316 men, 564 women.
**Test score averages/ranges.** Average SAT scores: 502 verbal, 561 math. Range of SAT scores of middle 50%: 460-580 verbal, 530-630 math. Average ACT scores: 22 English, 22 math, 23 composite. Range of ACT scores of middle 50%: 20-26 English, 19-24 math.
**Faculty.** 206 full-time; 131 part-time. 89% of faculty holds highest degree in specific field. Student/faculty ratio: 15 to 1.
**Selectivity rating.** Less competitive.

**PROFILE.** John Carroll, founded in 1886, is a church-affiliated, liberal arts university. Programs are offered through the College of Arts and Sciences, the School of Business, the Graduate School, and the Office of Continuing Education. Its 60-acre campus is located in a residential area, 10 miles from downtown Cleveland. Campus architecture is primarily Gothic in style.

**Accreditation:** NCACS. Professionally accredited by the American Assembly of Collegiate Schools of Business, the National Council for Accreditation of Teacher Education.
**Religious orientation:** John Carroll University is affiliated with the Roman Catholic Church (Society of Jesus); two semesters of religion required.
**Library:** Collections totaling over 533,899 volumes, 1,620 periodical subscriptions, and 164,737 microform items.
**Special facilities/museums:** International studies center, closed-circuit TV studio, broadcast archives.
**Athletic facilities:** Athletic fields, swimming pool, recreation center, gymnasium, wrestling room, baseball stadium.

**STUDENT BODY. Undergraduate profile:** 59% are state residents; 15% are transfers. 2% Asian-American, 5% Black, 1% Hispanic, 89% White, 3% Other. Average age of undergraduates is 20.
**Freshman profile:** 2% of freshmen who took SAT scored 700 or over on verbal, 8% scored 700 or over on math; 12% scored 600 or over on verbal, 41% scored 600 or over on math; 48% scored 500 or over on verbal, 81% scored 500 or over on math; 85% scored 400 or over on verbal, 99% scored 400 or over on math; 99% scored 300 or over on verbal, 100% scored 300 or over on math. 43% of accepted applicants took SAT; 57% took ACT. 48% of freshmen come from public schools.
**Undergraduate achievement:** 87% of fall 1992 freshmen returned for fall 1993 term. 62% of entering class graduated. 27% of students who completed a degree program immediately went on to graduate study.
**Foreign students:** 33 students are from out of the country. Countries represented include China, the Czech Republic, Israel, Japan, Russia, and Sudan; 15 in all.

**PROGRAMS OF STUDY. Degrees:** B.A., B.A.Classics, B.S., B.S.Bus.Admin., B.S.Econ.
**Majors:** Accountancy, Art History, Biology, Business Logistics, Chemistry, Classical Languages, Communications, Computer Science, Economics, Elementary Education, Engineering Physics/Electronics, English, Finance, French, German, Greek, History, Humanities, Latin, Management, Marketing, Mathematics, Mathematics Teaching, Philosophy, Physical Education, Physics, Political Science, Psychology, Religious Studies, Secondary Education, Sociology, Spanish, World Literature.
**Distribution of degrees:** The majors with the highest enrollment are communications, English, and psychology; physical education, religion, and physics/engineering physics have the lowest.
**Requirements:** General education requirement.
**Academic regulations:** Freshmen must maintain minimum 1.8 GPA; sophomores, juniors, seniors, 2.0 GPA.
**Special:** Minors offered in some majors and in the American political system, fine arts, foreign affairs, and probability/statistics. Interdisciplinary concentrations include environmental studies, gerontology, international economics/modern languages, neuroscience, sex/gender, and public administration/public policy. Some departments require comprehensive exam during senior year. Studies offered in Hebrew, Italian, Japanese, Russian, and Slovak. Self-designed majors. Double majors. Dual degrees. Independent study. Accelerated study. Pass/fail grading option. Internships. Cooperative education programs. Graduate school at which undergraduates may take graduate-level courses. Preprofessional programs in law, medicine, veterinary science, and dentistry. 2-2 engineering programs with Case Western Reserve U and U of Detroit. 3-3 nursing program with Case Western Reserve U. 3-2 engineering programs with Case Western Reserve U and Washington U. 2-3 engineering program with U of Detroit. Cooperative program with Notre Dame Coll leads to certification as teacher of the mildly retarded. Teacher certification in elementary and secondary education. Certification in specific subject areas. Exchange programs abroad in Japan (Nanzan U, Sophia U). Study abroad also in England, France, Germany, Italy, and Latin American countries. ROTC.
**Honors:** Honors program. Honor societies.
**Academic Assistance:** Nonremedial tutoring.

**STUDENT LIFE. Housing:** Students may live on or off campus. Coed, women's, and men's dorms. 65% of students live in college housing.
**Social atmosphere:** Social and cultural life on campus is something students have to generate on their own, reports the student newspaper. Popular events include campus mixers, Homecoming, and basketball and rugby games. Students meet at local bars and frequent area theatres.
**Services and counseling/handicapped student services:** Placement services. Health service. Counseling services for minority, military, and older students. Personal and psychological counseling. Career and academic guidance services. Religious counseling. Physically disabled student services. Learning disabled services. Tape recorders. Reader services for the blind.
**Campus organizations:** Undergraduate student government. Student newspaper (Carroll News, published once/week). Literary magazine. Yearbook. Radio station. Bands, jazz ensemble, brass choir, chorale, University Singers, debating, Little Theatre Society, radio station, military groups, Project GOLD, University Cultural Series, departmental, service, and special-interest groups, 92 organizations in all. 12 fraternities, no chapter houses; seven sororities, no chapter houses. 32% of men join a fraternity. 35% of women join a sorority.
**Religious organizations:** Christian Life Community, Knights of Columbus, Hillel Society.
**Minority/foreign student organizations:** Black United Students Association. International Student Association.

**ATHLETICS. Physical education requirements:** None.
**Intercollegiate competition:** 10% of students participate. Baseball (M), basketball (M,W), cheerleading (M,W), cross-country (M,W), diving (M,W), football (M), golf (M), soccer (M,W), softball (W), swimming (M,W), tennis (M,W), track (indoor) (M,W), track (outdoor) (M,W), track and field (indoor) (M,W), track and field (outdoor) (M,W), volleyball (W), wrestling (M). Member of NCAA Division III, Ohio Athletic Conference.
**Intramural and club sports:** 30% of students participate. Intramural basketball, flag football, racquetball, softball, volleyball, water polo, wrestling. Men's club ice hockey, lacrosse, riflery, rugby, volleyball. Women's club lacrosse.

**ADMISSIONS. Academic basis for candidate selection** (in order of priority): Secondary school record, standardized test scores, class rank, school's recommendation, essay.
**Nonacademic basis for candidate selection:** Character and personality and extracurricular participation are important. Particular talent or ability, geographical distribution, and alumni/ae relationship are considered.
**Requirements:** Graduation from secondary school is required; GED is accepted. 16 units required and the following program of study recommended: 4 units of English, 3 units of math, 2 units of science, 2 units of foreign language, 1 unit of social studies, 2 units of history, 1 unit of electives. SAT or ACT is required. Campus visit and interview recommended. Off-campus interviews available with admissions and alumni representatives.
**Procedure:** Take SAT or ACT by February of 12th year. Suggest filing application by March 15. Application deadline is June 1. Notification of admission on rolling basis. Reply is required by May 1. $100 tuition deposit, refundable until May 1. $100 room deposit, refundable until May 1. Freshmen accepted for terms other than fall.
**Special programs:** Admission may be deferred one year. Credit and/or placement may be granted through CEEB Advanced Placement exams for scores of 3 or higher. Credit and/or placement may be granted through CLEP general and subject exams. Credit and placement may be granted through DANTES exams. Early entrance/early admission program.
**Transfer students:** Transfer students accepted for terms other than fall. In fall 1993, 15% of all new students were transfers into all classes. 275 transfer applications were received, 210 were accepted. Application deadline is August 1 for fall; December 1 for spring. Minimum 2.0 GPA required. Lowest course grade accepted is "C." Maximum number of transferable credits is 64 semester hours. At least 30 semester hours must be completed at the university to receive degree.
**Admissions contact:** Laryn D. Runco, Director of Admission. 216 397-4294.

**FINANCIAL AID. Available aid:** Pell grants, SEOG, state scholarships and grants, school scholarships and grants, private scholarships and grants, ROTC scholarships, and academic merit scholarships. Perkins Loans (NDSL), PLUS, Stafford Loans (GSL), state loans, and SLS. Prepayment plan.
**Financial aid statistics:** 25% of aid is not need-based. In 1993-94, 93% of all undergraduate applicants received aid; 95% of freshman applicants. Average amounts of aid awarded freshmen: Scholarships and grants, $4,100; loans, $2,446.
**Supporting data/closing dates:** FAFSA: Priority filing date is March 1. State aid form: Accepted on rolling basis. Notification of awards on rolling basis.
**Financial aid contact:** John P. Sammon, M.A., Director of Financial Aid. 216 397-4248.

**STUDENT EMPLOYMENT.** College Work/Study Program. Institutional employment. 28% of full-time undergraduates work on campus during school year. Students may expect to earn an average of $1,000 during school year. Off-campus part-time employment opportunities rated "good."

**COMPUTER FACILITIES.** 94 IBM/IBM-compatible and Macintosh/Apple microcomputers; 68 are networked. Students may access Digital minicomputer/mainframe systems, BITNET, Internet. Residence halls may be equipped with networked microcomputers. Client/LAN operating systems include Apple/Macintosh, DOS, Novell. Computer languages and software packages include BASIC, C, COBOL, dBASE, FORTRAN, Lotus 1-2-3, MINITAB, Pascal, Quattro Pro, SAS, SPSS, WordPerfect. Computer facilities are available to all students.
**Fees:** None.
**Hours:** Some 24 hrs., some 8 AM-midn.

**GRADUATE CAREER DATA.** Graduate school percentages: 5% enter law school. 2% enter medical school. 1% enter dental school. 1% enter graduate business programs. 20% enter graduate arts and sciences programs. Highest graduate school enrollments: U of Akron, Case Western Reserve U, U of Cincinnati, Cleveland St U, Ohio State U, Ohio U. 55% of graduates choose careers in business and industry. Companies and businesses that hire graduates: Andersen Consulting, Cleveland Clinic, Coopers & Lybrand, Ernst & Young, National City Bank, Sherwin-Williams, local school systems.

**PROMINENT ALUMNI/AE.** Donald Shula, head coach, Miami Dolphins; John G. Breen, chairman of the board, Sherwin-Williams; Anthony M. Pilla, bishop, Diocese of Cleveland; Timothy J. Russert, vice-president, NBC News; Christine DeBlaey, president, DeMille Aircraft Corp.; Carl Walz, astronaut, member of 1993 Discovery space shuttle mission.

5-5

# Kent State University

**Kent, OH 44242-0001 216 672-2121**

**1994-95 Costs.** Tuition: $3,596 (state residents), $7,192 (out-of-state). Room: $1,984. Board: $1,410. Fees, books, misc. academic expenses (school's estimate): $500.

**Enrollment.** Undergraduates: 6,963 men, 9,068 women (full-time). Freshman class: 8,498 applicants, 7,226 accepted, 2,760 enrolled. Graduate enrollment: 1,748 men, 2,986 women.

**Test score averages/ranges.** Average SAT scores: 420 verbal, 458 math. Range of SAT scores of middle 50%: 360-480 verbal, 380-530 math. Average ACT scores: 20 English, 19 math, 21 composite. Range of ACT scores of middle 50%: 17-23 English, 16-22 math.

**Faculty.** 85% of faculty holds highest degree in specific field. Student/faculty ratio: 23 to 1.

**Selectivity rating.** Less competitive.

**PROFILE.** Kent State, founded in 1910, is a public, comprehensive university. Programs are offered through the Colleges of Arts and Sciences, Business Administration, Education, and Fine and Professional Arts and the Schools of Nursing and Physical Education, Recreation, and Dance. Its 1,223-acre campus is located in Kent, northeast of Akron.

**Accreditation:** NCACS. Professionally accredited by the Accreditation Board for Engineering and Technology, the Accrediting Council on Education in Journalism and Mass Communication, the American Assembly of Collegiate Schools of Business, the American Association for Counseling and Development, the American Dietetic Association, the American Library Association, the American Medical Association (CAHEA), the American Psychological Association, the American Speech-Language-Hearing Association, the Council on Rehabilitation Education, the National Architecture Accrediting Board, the National Association of Schools of Art and Design, the National Association of Schools of Music, the National Council for Accreditation of Teacher Education, the National League for Nursing.
**Religious orientation:** Kent State University is nonsectarian; no religious requirements.
**Library:** Collections totaling over 2,110,238 volumes, 10,700 periodical subscriptions, and 1,414,912 microform items.
**Special facilities/museums:** Fashion museum, herbarium, liquid crystal institute, planetarium, airport.
**Athletic facilities:** Gymnasiums, field house, stadium, tracks, golf courses, baseball, field hockey, football, intramural, rugby, soccer, and softball fields, ice rink, basketball, racquetball, tennis, and volleyball courts, swimming pools, gymnastics, weight, and wrestling rooms, fitness circuits, cross-country course.

**STUDENT BODY. Undergraduate profile:** 94% are state residents. 1% Asian-American, 6% Black, 1% Hispanic, 1% Native American, 90% White, 1% Other. Average age of undergraduates is 22.
**Freshman profile:** 1% of freshmen who took SAT scored 700 or over on math; 4% scored 600 or over on verbal, 9% scored 600 or over on math; 20% scored 500 or over on verbal, 37% scored 500 or over on math; 58% scored 400 or over on verbal, 72% scored 400 or over on math; 94% scored 300 or over on verbal, 96% scored 300 or over on math. 2% of freshmen who took ACT scored 30 or over on English, 1% scored 30 or over on math, 1% scored 30 or over on composite; 23% scored 24 or over on English, 14% scored 24 or over on math, 20% scored 24 or over on composite; 71% scored 18 or over on English, 64% scored 18 or over on math, 80% scored 18 or over on composite; 99% scored 12 or over on English, 100% scored 12 or over on math, 100% scored 12 or over on composite; 100% scored 6 or over on English. 36% of accepted applicants took SAT; 89% took ACT.
**Undergraduate achievement:** 74% of fall 1992 freshmen returned for fall 1993 term. 13% of entering class graduated.
**Foreign students:** Countries represented include Canada, China, India, Korea, Malaysia, and Taiwan; 65 in all.

**PROGRAMS OF STUDY. Degrees:** B.A., B.Arch., B.Bus.Admin., B.F.A., B.Gen.Studies, B.Mus., B.Mus.Ed., B.S., B.S.Ed., B.S.Nurs.
**Majors:** Accounting, Advertising, Aerospace Engineering Technology, Aerospace Flight Technology, Aerospace Management Technology, Airway Computer Sciences, American Studies, Anthropology, Architecture, Art Education, Art History, Biology, Botany, Business Management, Chemistry, Classical Humanities, Clinical Laboratory Sciences, Computational Mathematics, Computer Science within Business Organizations, Computer Systems Hardware/Physics, Conservation, Crafts, Criminal Justice Studies, Cytotechnology, Dance, Design/Crafts, Earth Science, Economics, Electronics Technology, English, Ethnic Heritage, Family/Consumer Studies, Fashion Design, Fashion Merchandising, Finance, French, Geography, Geology, German, Gerontology, Graphic Design, History, Hospitality Food Service Management, Human Resources Management, Individual/Family Studies, Industrial Design, Industrial Engineering Technology, Industrial Management, Instrumental Music, Integrated Life Sciences, Integrative Change, International Relations, Latin, Latin American Studies, Management Science, Manufacturing Technology, Marketing, Mathematics, Medical Technology, Music, Music Composition, Music Education, Music Theory, Musical Theatre, News, Nursing, Nutrition/Dietetics, Organ, Pan-African Studies, Philosophy, Photoillustration, Photojournalism, Physical Education, Physics, Piano, Political Science, Pre-Dentistry, Pre-Engineering, Pre-Fashion, Pre-Forestry, Pre-Interior Design, Pre-Journalism, Pre-Medicine, Pre-Natural Resources, Pre-Osteopathy, Pre-Pharmacy, Pre-Speech Pathology/Audiology, Pre-Telecommunications, Pre-Theatre, Pre-Veterinary, Psychology, Public Relations, Real Estate, Recreation/Leisure Services, Rhetoric/Communication, Russian, Sociology, Software Systems Analysis/Math, Soviet/East European Studies, Spanish, Speech Education, Speech Pathology/Audiology, Studio Art, Technology Education, Telecommunications, Theatre, Theoretical Computer Science/Math, Vocal Music, Zoology.
**Distribution of degrees:** The majors with the highest enrollment are elementary education, marketing, and nursing; Latin, botany, and crafts have the lowest.
**Requirements:** General education requirement.
**Academic regulations:** Minimum 2.0 GPA must be maintained.
**Special:** Minors offered in many majors. Experimental and Integrative Studies program. Affirmative action policy. Self-designed majors. Double majors. Dual degrees. Independent study. Pass/fail grading option. Internships. Cooperative education programs. Graduate school at which undergraduates may take graduate-level courses. Preprofessional programs in law, medicine, veterinary science, pharmacy, and dentistry. 2-2 programs with Cuyahoga Comm Coll. 3-1 program in clinical lab sciences with approved medical institutions. 3-2 forestry and international relations M.B.A. programs with Duke U and U of Michigan. Member of Northeastern Ohio Universities Consortium. Washington Semester. Exchange program with Northeastern Ohio U Coll of Medicine. Teacher certification in early childhood, elementary, secondary, special education, and vo-tech education. Certification in specific subject areas. Exchange programs abroad in Canada (Nova Scotia Coll of Art and Design), England (U of Leicester), France (U of Bordeaux), Israel (Haifa U), and the former Soviet Republics (Volograd State U). Study abroad also in Ireland, Italy, Mexico, Spain, and Switzerland. ROTC and AFROTC.
**Honors:** Honors program. Honor societies.
**Academic Assistance:** Remedial reading, writing, and math. Nonremedial tutoring.

**STUDENT LIFE. Housing:** All freshmen and sophomores under age 21 must live on campus unless living with family. Coed, women's, and men's dorms. Sorority and fraternity housing. Off-campus privately-owned housing. On-campus married-student housing. 33% of students live in college housing.
**Social atmosphere:** The student newspaper reports, "There is a great deal to become involved in both on and off campus for students, faculty, and staff with varying interests and concerns." Kent State has an active Greek system, and a campus programming board that books speakers, comedians, and concerts. There are also a number of minority organizations and religious groups. Students frequent the Student Center Plaza, the Hub, and the Gym Annex. Special events include the Black Squirrel Festival in September, Homecoming in October, and the May 4, 1970 Commemoration.
**Services and counseling/handicapped student services:** Placement services. Health service. Day care. Counseling services for older students. Personal and psychological counseling. Career and academic guidance services. Physically disabled student services. Learning disabled services. Tape recorders. Tutors. Reader services for the blind.
**Campus organizations:** Undergraduate student government. Student newspaper (Daily Kent Stater, published four times/week). Literary magazine. Radio and TV stations. Marching band, choir, Fashion Students Organization, International Film Society, Student Ambassadors, Women's Network, Gay/Lesbian Foundation, Total Grace, SNAP, Harambee, 270 organizations in all. 20 fraternities, 10 chapter houses; 12 sororities, seven chapter houses. 7% of men join a fraternity. 6% of women join a sorority.
**Religious organizations:** Campus Crusade for Christ, Chi Alpha Christian Fellowship, Hillel Jewish Student Board, Latter-Day Saint Student Association, United Christian Ministries, Christian Student Foundation.
**Minority/foreign student organizations:** Black United Students, Arab-American Association. Chinese, Indian, and Muslim groups.

**ATHLETICS. Physical education requirements:** None.
**Intercollegiate competition:** 5% of students participate. Baseball (M), basketball (M,W), cheerleading (M,W), cross-country (M,W), field hockey (W), football (M), golf (M), gymnastics (M,W), ice hockey (M), softball (W), track (indoor) (M,W), track (outdoor) (M,W), track and field (indoor) (M,W), track and field (outdoor) (M,W), volleyball (W), wrestling (M). Member of Mid-American Conference, NCAA Division I.
**Intramural and club sports:** 50% of students participate. Intramural badminton, basketball, floor hockey, football, golf, racquetball, road racing, rugby, soccer, softball, swimming, tennis, volleyball, Wiffle ball, wrestling. Men's club Alpine skiing, badminton, bowling, canoe/kayak, crew, cycling, diving, fencing, lacrosse, martial arts, racquetball, rugby, sailing, soccer, swimming, volleyball, wheelchair games, wrestling. Women's club Alpine skiing, bowling, canoe/kayak, crew, cycling, diving, fencing, martial arts, racquetball, sailing, soccer, swimming, volleyball, wheelchair games.

**ADMISSIONS. Academic basis for candidate selection** (in order of priority): Secondary school record, standardized test scores, class rank.
**Nonacademic basis for candidate selection:** Particular talent or ability is considered.
**Requirements:** Graduation from secondary school is required; GED is accepted. 16 units and the following program of study are recommended: 4 units of English, 3 units of math, 3 units of science, 2 units of foreign language, 3 units of social studies, 1 unit of electives. Minimum combined SAT score of 870 (composite ACT score of 21), rank in top half of secondary school class, and minimum 2.1 GPA recommended. Auditions required of dance, music, and theatre program applicants. Additional requirements for architecture, business, education, fashion design and fashion merchandising, flight, the honors college, interior design, nursing, and six-year M.D. program applicants. Conditional admission possible for applicants not meeting standard requirements. SAT or ACT is required. Campus visit recommended. No off-campus interviews.

**Procedure:** Take SAT or ACT by fall of 12th year. Suggest filing application by fall. Application deadline is March 15. Notification of admission on rolling basis. $100 room deposit, refundable until July 20. Freshmen accepted for terms other than fall.
**Special programs:** Admission may be deferred one year. Credit and/or placement may be granted through CEEB Advanced Placement exams for scores of 3 or higher. Credit may be granted through CLEP general and subject exams, DANTES and challenge exams. Concurrent enrollment program.
**Transfer students:** Transfer students accepted for terms other than fall. In fall 1993, 1,961 transfer applications were received, 1,149 were accepted. Application deadline is July 1 for fall; December 15 for spring. Minimum 2.0 GPA required. Lowest course grade accepted is "C." At least 32 semester hours must be completed at the university to receive degree.
**Admissions contact:** Charles Rickard, Director of Admissions. 216 672-2444.

**FINANCIAL AID. Available aid:** Pell grants, SEOG, state scholarships and grants, school scholarships and grants, private scholarships, and athletic scholarships. Perkins Loans (NDSL), PLUS, Stafford Loans (GSL), NSL, school loans, private loans, and SLS. Deferred payment plan.
**Financial aid statistics:** 16% of aid is not need-based. In 1994-95, 77% of all undergraduate applicants received aid. Average amounts of aid awarded freshmen: Scholarships and grants, $3,500.
**Supporting data/closing dates:** FAFSA/FAF: Priority filing date is February 15; accepted on rolling basis. State aid form. Notification of awards begins April 1.
**Financial aid contact:** Theodore Hallenbeck, Ph.D., Director of Financial Aid. 216 672-2972.

**STUDENT EMPLOYMENT.** College Work/Study Program. Institutional employment. 20% of full-time undergraduates work on campus during school year. Students may expect to earn an average of $2,000 during school year. Off-campus part-time employment opportunities rated "good."

**COMPUTER FACILITIES.** 3,500 IBM/IBM-compatible and Macintosh/Apple microcomputers; 500 are networked. Students may access Digital, IBM minicomputer/mainframe systems, BITNET, Internet. Residence halls may be equipped with stand-alone microcomputers. Computer languages and software packages include AOA, Assembler, C, COBOL, FORTRAN, LISP, MACRO, Pascal, PL/1, Prolog, SAS, SAS/ETS, SAS/Graph, SAS/PSP, SNOBOL, SPSS-X; 50 in all. Dormitory computer facilities restricted to dorm residents.
**Fees:** Computer fee is included in tuition/fees.
**Hours:** Correspond with building hours.

**PROMINENT ALUMNI/AE.** Oliver Ocasek and Robert Boggs, state senators; Michael Keaton, actor; Arsenio Hall, talk show host; John Kapioltas, CEO, Sheraton Worldwide; Julia Walsh, first woman president, American Stock Exchange; Jack Lambert, Thurman Munson, and Steve Stone, athletes; Beatrice Berry, talk show host.

8-28

# Kenyon College

**Gambier, OH 43022-9623 — 614 427-5000**

**1994-95 Costs.** Tuition: $19,850. Room: $1,640. Board: $2,050. Fees, books, misc. academic expenses (school's estimate): $780.
**Enrollment.** Undergraduates: 685 men, 760 women (full-time). Freshman class: 2,212 applicants, 1,538 accepted, 408 enrolled.
**Test score averages/ranges.** Average SAT scores: 560 verbal, 590 math. Range of SAT scores of middle 50%: 510-620 verbal, 540-640 math. Average ACT scores: 27 composite. Range of ACT scores of middle 50%: 25-29 composite.
**Faculty.** 122 full-time; 21 part-time. 96% of faculty holds highest degree in specific field. Student/faculty ratio: 10 to 1.
**Selectivity rating.** Highly competitive.

**PROFILE.** Kenyon, founded in 1824, is a church-affiliated, liberal arts college. Programs are offered through the Divisions of Fine Arts, Humanities, Natural Sciences, and Social Sciences. Its 600-acre campus is located 50 miles north of Columbus. Campus architecture is primarily Gothic in style.

**Accreditation:** NCACS.
**Religious orientation:** Kenyon College is affiliated with the Episcopal Church; no religious requirements.
**Library:** Collections totaling over 381,625 volumes, 1,400 periodical subscriptions, and 293,011 microform items.
**Special facilities/museums:** Art gallery.
**Athletic facilities:** Gymnasium, field house, swimming pool, stadium, basketball, racquetball, squash, tennis, and volleyball courts, tracks, baseball, field hockey, football, intramural, lacrosse, rugby, soccer, and softball fields, weight rooms, arena, stadium.

**STUDENT BODY. Undergraduate profile:** 25% are state residents; 4% are transfers. 5.2% Asian-American, 3.4% Black, 2.7% Hispanic, .1% Native American, 87.5% White, 1.1% Other. Average age of undergraduates is 20.
**Freshman profile:** 6% of freshmen who took SAT scored 700 or over on verbal, 9% scored 700 or over on math; 33% scored 600 or over on verbal, 43% scored 600 or over on math; 75% scored 500 or over on verbal, 91% scored 500 or over on math; 100% scored 400 or over on verbal, 100% scored 400 or over on math. 19% of freshmen who took ACT scored 30 or over on composite; 79% scored 24 or over on composite; 100% scored 18 or over on composite. 91% of accepted applicants took SAT; 51% took ACT. 63% of freshmen come from public schools.
**Undergraduate achievement:** 93% of fall 1992 freshmen returned for fall 1993 term. 85% of entering class graduated. 25% of students who completed a degree program immediately went on to graduate study.
**Foreign students:** 39 students are from out of the country. Countries represented include Canada, China, Costa Rica, Germany, Japan, and the United Kingdom; 22 in all.

**PROGRAMS OF STUDY. Degrees:** A.B.
**Majors:** Anthropology, Archaeology, Art, Art History, Biology, Chemistry, Classics, Drama, Economics, English, French Studies, German Studies, History, International Studies, Mathematics, Music, Philosophy, Physics, Political Science, Psychology, Religion, Russian Studies, Sociology, Spanish, Studio Art.
**Distribution of degrees:** The majors with the highest enrollment are English, history, and political science; philosophy and classics have the lowest.
**Requirements:** General education requirement.
**Academic regulations:** Minimum 2.0 GPA must be maintained.
**Special:** Four-course system. Integrated program in humane studies. Intensive Language Model method of teaching foreign languages. Courses offered in Dutch, Hebrew, Italian, Sanskrit, Asian studies, American studies, law/society, women/gender studies. Comprehensive exam in major required of seniors. Self-designed majors. Double majors. Dual degrees. Independent study. Accelerated study. Pass/fail grading option. Internships. Cooperative education programs. Preprofessional programs in law, medicine, veterinary science, dentistry, theology, engineering, business, and education. 3-2 engineering programs with Case Western Reserve U, Rensselaer Polytech Inst, and Washington U. 3-2 nursing program with Case Western Reserve U. Five-year double degree program option for students who wish to add a year of study in a particular area at a foreign or American institution. Member of Great Lakes College Association. Many GLCA semester-away programs. Exchange program abroad in Japan (Rikkyo U). Study abroad also in many other countries.
**Honors:** Phi Beta Kappa. Honors program. Honor societies.
**Academic Assistance:** Remedial writing, math, and study skills. Nonremedial tutoring.

**STUDENT LIFE. Housing:** All students must live on campus. Coed, women's, and men's dorms. School-owned/operated apartments. 100% of students live in college housing.
**Social atmosphere:** "Kenyon's cultural and social life is wildly introverted," reports the student newspaper. "With no proximity to a major or even minor city, Kenyon students turn to each other for their social activities. While the college attempts to provide interesting activities, small budgets prevent these events from gaining widespread interest." Favorite gathering spots tend to be the Atrium, the Village Inn, the Bookstore, and Ike's Restaurant. Greeks and numerous student organizations are popular on campus. Well-attended events on campus include the Gambier Folk Festival, Spring Riot, Summer Send-off, and swim meets.
**Services and counseling/handicapped student services:** Placement services. Health service. Women's center. Career services. Counseling services for minority students. Birth control, personal, and psychological counseling. Career and academic guidance services. Religious counseling. Physically disabled student services. Learning disabled services. Notetaking services. Tape recorders. Tutors. Reader services for the blind.
**Campus organizations:** Undergraduate student government. Student newspaper (Kenyon Collegian, published once/week). Literary magazine. Yearbook. Radio station. Music groups, dramatics society, debating, arts and crafts club, film and photography group, folklore club, media club, rock climbing club, sports and games clubs, outing club, literary societies, service and special-interest groups, 90 organizations in all. Nine fraternities, no chapter houses; one sorority, no chapter house. 25% of men join a fraternity. 2% of women join a sorority.
**Religious organizations:** Christian Fellowship, Christian Science Organization, Hillel, Catholic Student Organization, Society of Friends, Harcourt Parish, Fellowship of Christian Athletes, Zen group.
**Minority/foreign student organizations:** Black Student Union, Asian Students at Kenyon, ADELANTE. International Students at Kenyon (ISAK).

**ATHLETICS. Physical education requirements:** None.
**Intercollegiate competition:** 50% of students participate. Baseball (M), basketball (M,W), cross-country (M,W), diving (M,W), field hockey (W), football (M), golf (M), lacrosse (M,W), soccer (M,W), swimming (M,W), tennis (M,W), track and field (indoor) (M,W), track and field (outdoor) (M,W), volleyball (W). Member of NCAA Division III, North Coast Athletic Conference (NCAC).
**Intramural and club sports:** 60% of students participate. Intramural field goal kick, football, foul shooting, golf, hole-in-one, indoor soccer, racquetball, running, soccer, softball, tennis, volleyball. Men's club crew/rowing, fencing, horsemanship, ice hockey, martial arts, Nordic skiing, rugby, sailing, ultimate frisbee, volleyball, water polo. Women's club crew/rowing, fencing, horsemanship, martial arts, Nordic skiing, rugby, sailing, softball, ultimate frisbee.

**ADMISSIONS. Academic basis for candidate selection** (in order of priority): Secondary school record, class rank, standardized test scores, school's recommendation, essay.
**Nonacademic basis for candidate selection:** Character and personality and particular talent or ability are emphasized. Extracurricular participation and alumni/ae relationship are important. Geographical distribution is considered.
**Requirements:** Graduation from secondary school is required; GED is accepted. 20 units and the following program of study are required: 4 units of English, 3 units of math, 2 units of lab science, 2 units of foreign language, 1 unit of social studies, 1 unit of history, 7 units of electives including 4 units of academic electives. Minimum combined SAT score of 1100, rank in top quarter of secondary school class, and honors courses in secondary school recommended. SAT or ACT is required. Campus visit and interview recommended. Off-campus interviews available with admissions and alumni representatives.
**Procedure:** Take SAT or ACT by January of 12th year. Visit college for interview by February of 12th year. Application deadline is February 15. Notification of admission by April 1. Reply is required by May 1. $300 nonrefundable tuition deposit. Freshmen accepted for fall term only.
**Special programs:** Admission may be deferred one year. Credit and/or placement may be granted through CEEB Advanced Placement exams for scores of 3 or higher. Placement may be granted through challenge exams. Early decision program. In fall 1993, 162 applied for early decision and 115 were accepted. Deadline for applying for early decision is December 1 or February 1. Concurrent enrollment program.
**Transfer students:** Transfer students accepted for terms other than fall. In fall 1993, 4% of all new students were transfers into all classes. 55 transfer applications were received, 37 were accepted. Application deadline is April 1 for fall; November 15 for spring. Minimum 3.0 GPA recommended. Lowest course grade accepted is "C." Maximum number of transferable credits is 16 semester hours. At least 16 semester hours must be completed at the college to receive degree.

**Admissions contact:** John W. Anderson, M.Ed., Dean of Admissions. 614 427-5776, 800 848-2468.

**FINANCIAL AID. Available aid:** Pell grants, SEOG, state scholarships and grants, school scholarships and grants, private scholarships and grants, and academic merit scholarships. Perkins Loans (NDSL), PLUS, Stafford Loans (GSL), state loans, school loans, private loans, and SLS. Tuition Plan Inc., Knight Tuition Plans, and AMS. VISA/MasterCard.

**Financial aid statistics:** 18% of aid is not need-based. In 1993-94, 38% of all undergraduate applicants received aid; 80% of freshman applicants. Average amounts of aid awarded freshmen: Scholarships and grants, $10,020; loans, $3,400.

**Supporting data/closing dates:** FAFSA/FAF: Deadline is February 15. Income tax forms: Priority filing date is April 15. Notification of awards begins April 1.

**Financial aid contact:** Craig A. Daugherty, Director of Financial Aid. 614 427-5782.

**STUDENT EMPLOYMENT.** College Work/Study Program. Institutional employment. 40% of full-time undergraduates work on campus during school year. Students may expect to earn an average of $900 during school year. Off-campus part-time employment opportunities rated "poor."

**COMPUTER FACILITIES.** 300 IBM/IBM-compatible microcomputers; all are networked. Students may access Digital minicomputer/mainframe systems, Internet. Residence halls may be equipped with stand-alone microcomputers, networked terminals. Client/LAN operating systems include DOS, Novell. Computer languages and software packages include BASIC, C, FORTRAN, MINITAB, Pascal, SPSS SAS, WordPerfect, VAX Mail. Computer facilities are available to all students.

**Fees:** None.

**Hours:** 24 hours.

**GRADUATE CAREER DATA.** Graduate school percentages: 9% enter law school. 8% enter medical school. 14% enter graduate business programs. 38% enter graduate arts and sciences programs. 1% enter theological school/seminary. Highest graduate school enrollments: U of Chicago, U of Cincinnati, U of Michigan, U of Virginia, Columbia U, Johns Hopkins U, Ohio State U. 40% of graduates choose careers in business and industry. Companies and businesses that hire graduates: Chase Manhattan Bank, Chubb Inc., First National Bank of Chicago, Deloitte & Touche, Anderson Consulting, Morningstar, Teach for America.

**PROMINENT ALUMNI/AE.** Rutherford B. Hayes, U.S. President; Paul Newman, actor; Robert Lowell, poet; Peter Taylor, author; E.L. Doctorow, author; Carl Djerassi, chemist, developer of birth control pill; Olof Palme, former Prime Minister, Sweden; Jim Borgman, political cartoonist; Bill Watterson, cartoonist, "Calvin and Hobbes"; Richard Thomas, president, First National Bank of Chicago; William Knight, CEO, Nabisco.

## Lake Erie College

**Painesville, OH 44077** 216 352-3361

**1993-94 Costs.** Tuition: $9,600. Room: $2,200. Board: $2,000. Fees, books, misc. academic expenses (school's estimate): $600.

**Enrollment.** (Figures are for students on-campus.) Undergraduates: 71 men, 245 women (full-time). Freshman class: 110 applicants, 105 accepted, 45 enrolled. Graduate enrollment: 81 men, 78 women.

**Test score averages/ranges.** Average SAT scores: 430 verbal, 480 math. Range of SAT scores of middle 50%: 370-490 verbal, 430-490 math. Average ACT scores: 22 composite. Range of ACT scores of middle 50%: 20-24 composite.

**Faculty.** 30 full-time; 30 part-time. 75% of faculty holds doctoral degree. Student/faculty ratio: 13 to 1.

**Selectivity rating.** Less competitive.

**PROFILE.** Lake Erie is a private, liberal arts college. Founded as a seminary for women in 1856, it adopted coeducation in 1985. Its 57-acre campus is located in Painesville, 28 miles from Cleveland.

**Accreditation:** NCACS.

**Religious orientation:** Lake Erie College is nonsectarian; no religious requirements.

**Library:** Collections totaling over 89,232 volumes, 767 periodical subscriptions, and 8,091 microform items.

**Special facilities/museums:** Indian museum.

**Athletic facilities:** Swimming pool, gymnasium, weight room, outdoor track, tennis courts.

**STUDENT BODY. Undergraduate profile:** 83% are state residents; 67% are transfers. 1% Black, 96% White, 3% Other. Average age of undergraduates is 25.

**Freshman profile:** 6% of freshmen who took SAT scored 700 or over on math; 25% scored 500 or over on verbal, 25% scored 500 or over on math; 56% scored 400 or over on verbal, 87% scored 400 or over on math; 87% scored 300 or over on verbal, 100% scored 300 or over on math. 28% of freshmen who took ACT scored 24 or over on composite; 92% scored 18 or over on composite; 100% scored 12 or over on composite. 39% of accepted applicants took SAT; 61% took ACT.

**Undergraduate achievement:** 58% of fall 1991 freshmen returned for fall 1992 term. 33% of entering class graduated.

**Foreign students:** Seven students are from out of the country. Countries represented include Canada, Ecuador, Japan, Mexico, and Spain.

**PROGRAMS OF STUDY. Degrees:** B.A., B.F.A., B.S.

**Majors:** Accounting, Applied Environmental Management, Biology, Business Administration, Chemistry, Communications, Dance, Elementary Education, English, Equestrian Facility Management, Equestrian Teacher/Trainer, Equine Stud Farm Management, Fine Arts, Health Care, Individualized Academic Major, Legal Assistant, Modern Foreign Language, Music, Psychology, Social Science.

**Distribution of degrees:** The majors with the highest enrollment are business administration, accounting, and elementary education; dance and communications have the lowest.

**Requirements:** General education requirement.

**Academic regulations:** Minimum 2.0 GPA must be maintained.

**Special:** Minors offered in all majors. Self-designed majors. Double majors. Dual degrees. Independent study. Accelerated study. Pass/fail grading option. Internships. Graduate school at which undergraduates may take graduate-level courses. Preprofessional programs in medicine and veterinary science. Member of Cleveland Commission on Higher Education. Teacher certification in elementary education. Certification in specific subject areas. Study abroad in Australia, England, France, Germany, Italy, the Netherlands, and Spain.

**Honors:** Honor societies.

**Academic Assistance:** Remedial study skills. Nonremedial tutoring.

**ADMISSIONS. Academic basis for candidate selection** (in order of priority): Secondary school record, standardized test scores, class rank, school's recommendation, essay.

**Nonacademic basis for candidate selection:** Character and personality are important. Extracurricular participation and particular talent or ability are considered.

**Requirements:** Graduation from secondary school is required; GED is accepted. 17 units and the following program of study are required: 4 units of English, 3 units of math, 3 units of science including 2 units of lab, 2 units of foreign language, 3 units of social studies, 2 units of electives. Minimum composite ACT score of 20 (combined SAT score of 900) and minimum 2.75 GPA required. Portfolio, audition, or essay may be required of fine arts or language program applicants. Conditional admission possible for applicants not meeting standard requirements. ACT is required; SAT may be substituted. Campus visit and interview recommended. No off-campus interviews.

**Procedure:** Take SAT or ACT by October 1 of 12th year. Visit college for interview by November 1 of 12th year. Suggest filing application by March 1. Application deadline is August 1. Notification of admission on rolling basis. $150 tuition deposit, refundable until the first day of classes. Freshmen accepted for terms other than fall.

**Special programs:** Admission may be deferred one year. Credit and/or placement may be granted through CEEB Advanced Placement exams for scores of 4 or higher. Credit and/or placement may be granted through CLEP general and subject exams. Credit may be granted through military experience. Credit and placement may be granted through life experience. Early entrance/early admission program. Concurrent enrollment program.

**Transfer students:** Transfer students accepted for terms other than fall. In fall 1992, 67% of all new students were transfers into all classes. 141 transfer applications were received, 141 were accepted. Application deadline is August 1 for fall; December 1 for spring. Minimum 2.0 GPA required. Lowest course grade accepted is "C." Test scores and transcripts required of transfer applicants under 22. Maximum number of transferable credits is 64 semester hours from a two-year school and 96 semester hours from a four-year school. At least 32 semester hours must be completed at the college to receive degree.

**Admissions contact:** Phyliss Hammerstrom, M.A., Director of Admissions. 216 639-7879, 800 533-4996.

**FINANCIAL AID. Available aid:** Pell grants, SEOG, state scholarships and grants, school scholarships and grants, private scholarships and grants, academic merit scholarships, and athletic scholarships. Family tuition reduction for twins. Perkins Loans (NDSL), PLUS, Stafford Loans (GSL), state loans, school loans, and SLS.

**Financial aid statistics:** 3% of aid is not need-based. In 1992-93, 85% of all undergraduate applicants received aid; 83% of freshman applicants. Average amounts of aid awarded freshmen: Scholarships and grants, $5,470; loans, $2,701.

**Supporting data/closing dates:** FAFSA/FAF/FFS: Priority filing date is April 1; accepted on rolling basis. School's own aid application: Priority filing date is April 1; accepted on rolling basis. State aid form: Deadline is September 25. Income tax forms: Priority filing date is April 1; accepted on rolling basis. Notification of awards on rolling basis.

**Financial aid contact:** Michiale Schneider, M.Ed., Director of Financial Aid. 216 639-7815.

## Lourdes College

**Sylvania, OH 43560** 419 885-3211

**1994-95 Costs.** Tuition: $6,660. Housing: None. Fees, books, misc. academic expenses (school's estimate): $725.

**Enrollment.** Undergraduates: 74 men, 356 women (full-time).

**Test score averages/ranges.** N/A.

**Faculty.** 62 full-time; 64 part-time. Student/faculty ratio: 13 to 1.

**Selectivity rating.** N/A.

**PROFILE.** Lourdes College is a church-affiliated liberal arts college. Founded as a women's college in 1958, it became coeducational in 1972. Its 89-acre campus is located in Sylvania, 10 miles northwest of Toledo.

**Accreditation:** NCACS. Professionally accredited by the Council on Social Work Education, the National League for Nursing.

**Religious orientation:** Lourdes College is affiliated with the Roman Catholic Church; two semesters of religion/theology required.

**Library:** Collections totaling over 53,214 volumes, 375 periodical subscriptions, and 8,624 microform items.

**Special facilities/museums:** Art museum, on-campus laboratory classroom, planetarium, nature center.

**Athletic facilities:** Gymnasium.

**STUDENT BODY. Undergraduate profile:** 80% are state residents. .5% Asian-American, 7% Black, .5% Hispanic, 92% White. Average age of undergraduates is 32.

**Freshman profile:** 77% of freshmen come from public schools.

**Undergraduate achievement:** 84% of fall 1992 freshmen returned for fall 1993 term.

**Foreign students:** Nine students are from out of the country. Countries represented include China, Hungary, and Poland.

**PROGRAMS OF STUDY. Degrees:** B.A., B.A.Rel.St., B.Internat.Studies, B.S.Nurs.

**Majors:** Art, Art History, Business, Criminal Justice, Early Childhood, English, Gerontology, History, Nursing, Psychology, Religious Studies, Social Work, Sociology.

**Distribution of degrees:** The majors with the highest enrollment are business administration and nursing.

**Requirements:** General education requirement.

**Special:** Minors offered in most majors and in French, music, philosophy, therapeutic recreation, and women's studies. Associate's degrees offered. Self-designed majors. Double majors. Dual degrees. Independent study. Pass/fail grading option. Internships. Preprofessional programs in medicine and theology. Teacher certification in early childhood and elementary education.
**Honors:** Honor societies.
**Academic Assistance:** Remedial reading, writing, math, and study skills.

**ADMISSIONS.**
**Requirements:** Graduation from secondary school is recommended; GED is accepted. No specific distribution of secondary school units required. Portfolio required of art program applicants. Conditional admission possible for applicants not meeting standard requirements. SAT or ACT is required. Admissions interview recommended.
**Procedure:** Notification of admission on rolling basis. Freshmen accepted for terms other than fall.
**Special programs:** Credit may be granted through CEEB Advanced Placement for scores of 3 or higher. Credit may be granted through CLEP general and subject exams, Regents College, DANTES, and challenge exams, and military and life experience. Concurrent enrollment program.
**Transfer students:** Transfer students accepted for terms other than fall. Lowest course grade accepted is "C." Maximum number of transferable credits is 96 semester hours. At least 32 semester hours must be completed at the college to receive degree.
**Admissions contact:** Mary Ellen Briggs, M.S., Director of Admissions. 419 885-5291.

**FINANCIAL AID. Available aid:** Pell grants, SEOG, state grants, and school scholarships. Perkins Loans (NDSL), PLUS, Stafford Loans (GSL), NSL, private loans, and SLS.
**Financial aid statistics:** In 1993-94, 95% of all undergraduate applicants received aid; 5% of freshman applicants. Average amounts of aid awarded freshmen: Loans, $2,600.
**Supporting data/closing dates:** FAFSA: Priority filing date is March 1. School's own aid application: Priority filing date is March 1. Notification of awards begins April 1.
**Financial aid contact:** Clark Rebel, Ed.S., Director of Financial Aid. 419 885-5291.

8-28

## Malone College

**Canton, OH 44709** **216 471-8100**

**1994-95 Costs.** Tuition: $9,858. Room: $2,020. Board: $1,680. Fees, books, misc. academic expenses (school's estimate): $585.
**Enrollment.** Undergraduates: 680 men, 925 women (full-time). Freshman class: 874 applicants, 758 accepted, 434 enrolled. Graduate enrollment: 26 men, 100 women.
**Test score averages/ranges.** Average SAT scores: 433 verbal, 479 math. Range of SAT scores of middle 50%: 380-490 verbal, 410-560 math. Average ACT scores: 21 English, 20 math, 21 composite. Range of ACT scores of middle 50%: 18-24 English, 18-22 math.
**Faculty.** 70 full-time; 67 part-time. 44% of faculty holds highest degree in specific field. Student/faculty ratio: 13 to 1.
**Selectivity rating.** Competitive.

**PROFILE.** Malone, founded in 1892, is a church-affiliated, liberal arts college. Its 78-acre campus is located in Canton, 20 miles south of Akron.
**Accreditation:** NCACS. Professionally accredited by the Council on Social Work Education, the National League for Nursing.
**Religious orientation:** Malone College is affiliated with the Evangelical Friends Church (Eastern Region); three semesters of religion required.
**Library:** Collections totaling over 127,372 volumes, 1,094 periodical subscriptions, and 337,227 microform items.
**Special facilities/museums:** Child development center.
**Athletic facilities:** Athletic fields, gymnasium, weight room, tennis courts.

**STUDENT BODY. Undergraduate profile:** 95% are state residents; 15% are transfers. .5% Asian-American, 5% Black, .5% Hispanic, .5% Native American, 93% White, .5% Other. Average age of undergraduates is 23.
**Freshman profile:** 2% of freshmen who took SAT scored 700 or over on verbal; 9% scored 600 or over on verbal, 17% scored 600 or over on math; 26% scored 500 or over on verbal, 38% scored 500 or over on math; 68% scored 400 or over on verbal, 79% scored 400 or over on math; 91% scored 300 or over on verbal, 98% scored 300 or over on math. 21% of accepted applicants took SAT; 95% took ACT. 87% of freshmen come from public schools.
**Undergraduate achievement:** 69% of fall 1992 freshmen returned for fall 1993 term. 26% of entering class graduated. 7% of students who completed a degree program immediately went on to graduate study.
**Foreign students:** 11 students are from out of the country. Countries represented include Canada, Hong Kong, India, Ireland, Spain, and Taiwan; nine in all.

**PROGRAMS OF STUDY. Degrees:** B.A., B.S.Ed., B.S.Nurs.
**Majors:** Accounting, Art, Biology, Business Administration, Chemistry, Christian Ministries, Church Music, Commercial Music Technology, Communications Arts, Communications Comprehensive, Computer Science, Elementary Education, English, History, Liberal Arts, Management, Mathematics, Medical Technology, Music, Music Education, Nursing, Physical Education, Pre-Medicine, Psychology, Radiological Science, Science Comprehensive, Social Science, Social Studies Comprehensive, Social Work, Spanish, Special Education, Sports Science.
**Distribution of degrees:** The majors with the highest enrollment are management, elementary education, and business administration; radiological science, church music, and pre-medicine have the lowest.
**Requirements:** General education requirement.
**Academic regulations:** Minimum 2.0 GPA must be maintained.
**Special:** Area and international studies courses. Minors offered in some majors and in coaching. Associate's degrees offered. Self-designed majors. Double majors. Dual degrees. Independent study. Accelerated study. Internships. Cooperative education programs. Graduate school at which undergraduates may take graduate-level courses. Preprofessional programs in law, medicine, veterinary science, pharmacy, dentistry, engineering, nursing, and pre-seminary. 2-2 engineering programs with Kent State U, Ohio State U, and U of Akron. 3-1 medical technology programs with various hospitals. 3-2 pharmacy programs with Ohio State U and U of Cincinnati. Member of Christian College Consortium and Christian College Coalition. Washington Semester. Other semester-away programs available. Teacher certification in early childhood, elementary, secondary, and special education. Certification in specific subject areas. Study abroad in Costa Rica, Egypt, Guatemala, Kenya, and Russia.
**Honors:** Phi Beta Kappa. Honor societies.
**Academic Assistance:** Remedial study skills. Nonremedial tutoring.

**STUDENT LIFE. Housing:** All unmarried students under age 21 must live on campus unless living near campus with relatives. Women's and men's dorms. Off-campus married-student housing. 48% of students live in college housing.
**Social atmosphere:** According to the editor of the student newspaper, "There are always a lot of things going on on campus. Whether it's a social activity, club meeting or a concert, one can always find something to do. There are a lot of ways students can get involved in things on campus, and the many clubs and academic organizations try to accommodate as many students as possible." The Randell Campus Center is a favorite meeting place on campus. Off-campus, students like to go to the Players Guild and the Football Hall of Fame. Students Activities Committee, Habitat for Humanity, and a variety of clubs are influential groups on campus. Favorite events during the year tend to be sporting events, spring and fall plays, and numerous concerts.
**Services and counseling/handicapped student services:** Placement services. Health service. Day care. Counseling services for minority and older students. Personal and psychological counseling. Career and academic guidance services. Religious counseling. Physically disabled student services. Learning disabled services. Notetaking services. Tape recorders. Tutors. Reader services for the blind.
**Campus organizations:** Undergraduate student government. Student newspaper (Aviso, published twice/month). Literary magazine. Yearbook. Radio station. Chorale, women's ensemble, chamber singers, jazz band, symphonic band, flute ensemble, touring vocal and drama groups, Education Association, Ohio Music Teachers Association, student senate, Student Activities Committee, World Awareness and Social Issues Committee, 28 organizations in all.
**Religious organizations:** Spiritual Life Committee, Malone Nurses Christian Fellowship, Thursdays, World Christian Outreach, Bible study groups.
**Minority/foreign student organizations:** Unity Under Christ.

**ATHLETICS. Physical education requirements:** Two activity classes and one physical education course required.
**Intercollegiate competition:** 20% of students participate. Baseball (M), basketball (M,W), cheerleading (M,W), cross-country (M,W), golf (M), soccer (M), softball (W), tennis (M,W), track and field (indoor) (M,W), track and field (outdoor) (M,W), volleyball (W). Member of Mid-Ohio Intercollegiate Athletic Conference, NAIA, NCCAA.
**Intramural and club sports:** 50% of students participate. Intramural basketball, flag football, softball, tennis, volleyball.

**ADMISSIONS. Academic basis for candidate selection** (in order of priority): Secondary school record, standardized test scores, class rank, school's recommendation.
**Nonacademic basis for candidate selection:** Character and personality are emphasized. Alumni/ae relationship is important. Extracurricular participation and particular talent or ability are considered.
**Requirements:** Graduation from secondary school is required; GED is accepted. 16 units required and the following program of study recommended: 4 units of English, 3 units of math, 3 units of science, 2 units of foreign language, 3 units of social studies, 1 unit of electives. Minimum composite ACT score of 19 and minimum 2.5 GPA required. Additional units of science and math recommended of science and engineeering program applicants. Proof of math proficiency required of nursing program applicants. Audition required of music program applicants. Conditional admission possible for applicants not meeting standard requirements. ACT is required; SAT may be substituted. Campus visit and interview recommended. Off-campus interviews available with admissions and alumni representatives.
**Procedure:** Take SAT or ACT by December of 12th year. Visit college for interview by January of 12th year. Suggest filing application by November. Notification of admission on rolling basis. $100 nonrefundable tuition deposit. $50 nonrefundable room deposit. Freshmen accepted for terms other than fall.
**Special programs:** Admission may be deferred one year. Credit and/or placement may be granted through CEEB Advanced Placement exams for scores of 3 or higher. Credit and/or placement may be granted through CLEP general and subject exams. Credit and placement may be granted through Regents College, ACT PEP, DANTES, and challenge exams and military and life experience. Concurrent enrollment program.
**Transfer students:** Transfer students accepted for terms other than fall. In fall 1993, 15% of all new students were transfers into all classes. 179 transfer applications were received, 129 were accepted. Application deadline is rolling for fall; rolling for spring. Minimum 2.0 GPA required. Lowest course grade accepted is "C." At least 30 semester hours must be completed at the college to receive degree.
**Admissions contact:** Lee Sommers, Dean of Admissions. 216 471-8145.

**FINANCIAL AID. Available aid:** Pell grants, SEOG, state scholarships and grants, school scholarships and grants, private scholarships and grants, academic merit scholarships, and athletic scholarships. Perkins Loans (NDSL), PLUS, Stafford Loans (GSL), school loans, private loans, and SLS. Deferred payment plan and family tuition reduction. Institutional payment plan.
**Financial aid statistics:** 27% of aid is not need-based. In 1993-94, 79% of all undergraduate applicants received aid; 79% of freshman applicants. Average amounts of aid awarded freshmen: Scholarships and grants, $3,575; loans, $2,481.
**Supporting data/closing dates:** FAFSA: Priority filing date is March 31. School's own aid application: Priority filing date is March 31. Notification of awards on rolling basis.
**Financial aid contact:** Patty Little, Director of Financial Aid. 216 471-8159.

**STUDENT EMPLOYMENT.** College Work/Study Program. Institutional employment. 29% of full-time undergraduates work on campus during school year. Students may expect to earn an average of $1,300 during school year. Off-campus part-time employment opportunities rated "excellent."

**COMPUTER FACILITIES.** 50 IBM/IBM-compatible and Macintosh/Apple microcomputers. Students may access Digital minicomputer/mainframe systems, Internet. Client/LAN operating systems include Apple/Macintosh, DOS, LocalTalk/AppleTalk. Computer languages and software packages include BASIC, C, COBOL, FORTRAN, Lotus 1-2-3, MS Works, Pascal, PFS Write, WordPerfect. Computer facilities are available to all students.

**Hours:** 8 AM-10 PM (M-Th).

**GRADUATE CAREER DATA.** Graduate school percentages: 1% enter law school. 1% enter medical school. 1% enter graduate business programs. 4% enter graduate arts and sciences programs. 1% enter theological school/seminary. Highest graduate school enrollments: Kent State U, Case Western Reserve, U of Akron. Companies and businesses that hire graduates: Ernst & Young, Goodyear, Internal Revenue Service, Nationwide Insurance, Timken.

**PROMINENT ALUMNI/AE.** H. David Bryant, founder and president of Concerts of Prayer International; David P. Rawson, U.S. ambassador to Rwanda; Marian P. Lair, opera and musical theatre performer.

9-22

# Marietta College

**Marietta, OH 45750** **614 376-4600**

**1993-94 Costs.** Tuition: $13,170. Room: $1,950. Board: $1,820. Fees, books, misc. academic expenses (school's estimate): $900.

**Enrollment.** Undergraduates: 585 men, 508 women (full-time). Freshman class: 1,643 applicants, 983 accepted, 370 enrolled. Graduate enrollment: 13 men, 49 women.

**Test score averages/ranges.** Range of SAT scores of middle 50%: 430-540 verbal, 480-590 math. Range of ACT scores of middle 50%: 21-25 English, 20-25 math.

**Faculty.** 76 full-time; 34 part-time. 74% of faculty holds highest degree in specific field. Student/faculty ratio: 12 to 1.

**Selectivity rating.** More competitive.

**PROFILE.** Marietta, founded in 1835, is a private college. Its 60-acre campus is located in Marietta, 115 miles southwest of Columbus. The campus's oldest building, of Greek Revival design, is listed in the National Register of Historic Places.

**Accreditation:** NCACS. Professionally accredited by the Accreditation Board for Engineering and Technology.

**Religious orientation:** Marietta College is nonsectarian; no religious requirements.

**Library:** Collections totaling over 250,600 volumes, 935 periodical subscriptions, and 28,384 microform items.

**Special facilities/museums:** Mass media building, fine arts center, natural science field camp, operational oil wells, geology field station, observatory.

**Athletic facilities:** Field house, swimming pool, basketball, racquetball, and tennis courts, baseball, football, lacrosse, soccer, and softball fields, stadium, weight room, fitness center, golf driving range.

**STUDENT BODY. Undergraduate profile:** 57% are state residents; 14% are transfers. 1% Asian-American, 1% Black, 2% Hispanic, 94% White, 2% Other. Average age of undergraduates is 20.

**Freshman profile:** 2% of freshmen who took SAT scored 700 or over on math; 8% scored 600 or over on verbal, 22% scored 600 or over on math; 43% scored 500 or over on verbal, 66% scored 500 or over on math; 92% scored 400 or over on verbal, 95% scored 400 or over on math; 100% scored 300 or over on verbal, 100% scored 300 or over on math. 7% of freshmen who took ACT scored 30 or over on English, 3% scored 30 or over on math, 5% scored 30 or over on composite; 45% scored 24 or over on English, 38% scored 24 or over on math, 47% scored 24 or over on composite; 90% scored 18 or over on English, 94% scored 18 or over on math, 99% scored 18 or over on composite; 100% scored 12 or over on English, 100% scored 12 or over on math, 100% scored 12 or over on composite. 62% of accepted applicants took SAT; 61% took ACT.

**Undergraduate achievement:** 78% of fall 1992 freshmen returned for fall 1993 term. 65% of entering class graduated. 19% of students who completed a degree program immediately went on to graduate study.

**Foreign students:** 24 students are from out of the country. Countries represented include Canada, Japan, Kuwait, Taiwan, United Arab Emirates, and the United Kingdom; 11 in all.

**PROGRAMS OF STUDY. Degrees:** B.A., B.F.A., B.S., B.S.Petrol.Eng.

**Majors:** Accounting, Advertising, Art for the Professions, Biochemistry, Biology, Business Communications, Chemistry, Computer Information Systems, Computer Science, Drama, Economics, English, French, Geology, History, Human Resource Management, Industrial Engineering, International Business Management, Journalism, Management, Marketing, Mathematics, Music, Petroleum Engineering, Philosophy, Physics, Political Science/Government, Psychology, Radio/Television, Religion, Spanish, Speech, Sports Medicine, Studio Art.

**Distribution of degrees:** The majors with the highest enrollment are management, history, and political science; philosophy, religion, and mathematics have the lowest.

**Requirements:** General education requirement.

**Academic regulations:** Freshmen must maintain minimum 1.8 GPA; sophomores, juniors, seniors, 2.0 GPA.

**Special:** Minors offered in many majors and in Asian studies, coaching, English literature, entrepreneurship, finance, German, mass media, and women's studies. McDonough Leadership Program. Associate's degrees offered. Self-designed majors. Double majors. Dual degrees. Independent study. Accelerated study. Pass/fail grading option. Internships. Preprofessional programs in law, medicine, veterinary science, dentistry, and business. 3-2 engineering programs with Case Western Reserve U, Columbia U, U of Pennsylvania, and Washington U. 3-2 forestry and environmental studies program with Duke U. 3-3 nursing program with Case Western Reserve U. Member of East Central College Consortium. Washington Semester and Sea Semester. Teacher certification in early childhood, elementary, and secondary education. Certification in specific subject areas. Exchange program abroad in China. Study abroad also in European and other Asian countries.

**Honors:** Phi Beta Kappa. Honors program. Honor societies.

**Academic Assistance:** Remedial writing and math. Nonremedial tutoring.

**STUDENT LIFE. Housing:** All unmarried students under age 21 must live on campus unless living near campus with relatives. Coed, women's, and men's dorms. Sorority and fraternity housing. 84% of students live in college housing.

**Social atmosphere:** "Greeks have a lot of influence on campus social life although they comprise just 30 percent of the student body," reports the editor of the student newspaper. Popular events of the year include Doo Dah Day, "a big, campus-wide party held during spring Homecoming," Homecoming, and Winter Weekend. Students gather at The Pit, The Galley, The Townhouse, and Little John's.

**Services and counseling/handicapped student services:** Placement services. Health service. Counseling services for minority, military, and older students. Birth control, personal, and psychological counseling. Career and academic guidance services. Physically disabled student services. Learning disabled services. Tape recorders. Tutors.

**Campus organizations:** Undergraduate student government. Student newspaper (Marcolian, published once/week). Literary magazine. Yearbook. Radio and TV stations. College Singers, madrigal singers, concert band, jazz band, jazz/rock ensemble, intercollegiate play festivals, environmental awareness group, intercollegiate debating, tournaments, speech contests, Young Democrats, Young Republicans, service and special-interest groups, 100 organizations in all. Seven fraternities, all with chapter houses; four sororities, all with chapter houses. 35% of men join a fraternity. 37% of women join a sorority.

**Religious organizations:** Fellowship of Christian Athletes, Intervarsity Christian Fellowship.

**Minority/foreign student organizations:** Awareness Society. International Student Organization.

**ATHLETICS. Physical education requirements:** None.

**Intercollegiate competition:** 34% of students participate. Baseball (M), basketball (M,W), cheerleading (M,W), crew (M,W), football (M), golf (M), lacrosse (M), soccer (M,W), softball (W), tennis (M,W), volleyball (W). Member of NCAA Division III, Ohio Athletic Conference, USRA.

**Intramural and club sports:** 50% of students participate. Intramural basketball, soccer, softball, tennis, volleyball. Men's club crew, rugby. Women's club cheerleading, crew, lacrosse.

**ADMISSIONS. Academic basis for candidate selection** (in order of priority): Secondary school record, standardized test scores, school's recommendation, essay, class rank.

**Nonacademic basis for candidate selection:** Character and personality and alumni/ae relationship are emphasized. Extracurricular participation, particular talent or ability, and geographical distribution are important.

**Requirements:** Graduation from secondary school is required; GED is accepted. No specific distribution of secondary school units required. Specific GPA and courses required of sports medicine and petroleum engineering program applicants. Specific GPA and recommendations required of McDonough Leadership Program applicants. Summer Success and Fall Success programs for applicants not normally admissible. SAT or ACT is required. PSAT is recommended. Campus visit and interview recommended. Off-campus interviews available with admissions and alumni representatives.

**Procedure:** Take SAT or ACT by February of 12th year. Visit college for interview by May of 12th year. Suggest filing application by February. Application deadline is May. Notification of admission on rolling basis. Reply is required by May 1. $200 nonrefundable tuition deposit. Freshmen accepted for terms other than fall.

**Special programs:** Admission may be deferred one year. Credit and/or placement may be granted through CEEB Advanced Placement exams for scores of 3 or higher. Credit and/or placement may be granted through CLEP general and subject exams. Credit may be granted through challenge exams. Credit and placement may be granted through Regents College and DANTES exams and military and life experience. Early entrance/early admission program. Concurrent enrollment program.

**Transfer students:** Transfer students accepted for terms other than fall. In fall 1993, 14% of all new students were transfers into all classes. 198 transfer applications were received, 119 were accepted. Application deadline is July 15 for fall; December 15 for spring. Minimum 2.3 GPA required. Lowest course grade accepted is "C." At least 30 semester hours must be completed at the college to receive degree.

**Admissions contact:** Dennis R. DePerro, M.S., Dean of Admission and Financial Aid. 614 376-4600, 800 331-7896.

**FINANCIAL AID. Available aid:** Pell grants, SEOG, state scholarships and grants, school scholarships and grants, private grants, and academic merit scholarships. Perkins Loans (NDSL), PLUS, Stafford Loans (GSL), school loans, and SLS. Tuition Plan Inc. and deferred payment plan.

**Financial aid statistics:** 8% of aid is not need-based. In 1993-94, 98% of all undergraduate applicants received aid; 98% of freshman applicants. Average amounts of aid awarded freshmen: Scholarships and grants, $6,873; loans, $2,880.

**Supporting data/closing dates:** FAFSA/FAF: Deadline is May 1. State aid form: Deadline is September 24. Notification of awards begins March 15.

**Financial aid contact:** James Bauer, M.S., Associate Dean/Director of Financial Aid. 614 376-4712, 800 331-2709.

**STUDENT EMPLOYMENT.** College Work/Study Program. Institutional employment. 65% of full-time undergraduates work on campus during school year. Students may expect to earn an average of $1,100 during school year. Off-campus part-time employment opportunities rated "good."

**COMPUTER FACILITIES.** 150 IBM/IBM-compatible and Macintosh/Apple microcomputers; 9 are networked. Students may access Digital minicomputer/mainframe systems. Computer languages and software packages include Ada, BASIC, C, COBOL, dBASE, FORTRAN, Lotus 1-2-3, MacWrite, Mathematica, Microsoft Word, Modula 2, Pascal, RPG, SmallTalk, Turbo Pascal, Turbo Prolog, WordPerfect, WordStar. Computer facilities are available to all students.

**Hours:** 8 AM-midn.

**GRADUATE CAREER DATA.** Graduate school percentages: 1% enter law school. 2% enter medical school. 3% enter graduate business programs. 13% enter graduate arts and sciences programs. Highest graduate school enrollments: Ohio U, Ohio State U, West Virginia U. 52% of graduates choose careers in business and industry. Companies and businesses that hire graduates: Arthur Andersen, Ernst & Young, Marathon Oil.

**PROMINENT ALUMNI/AE.** Dr. Story Musgrave, astronaut, NASA space shuttle program; Kent Tekulve, baseball player, Pittsburgh Pirates; Gary Fitzgerald, president, Standard Oil; Gary Kott, writer/producer, "The Cosby Show"; John McCoy, CEO, Bank One; Charles Dawes, former Vice President of the U.S.

8-29

# Miami University

**Oxford, OH 45056 513 529-1809**

**1993-94 Costs.** Tuition: $3,931 (state residents), $7,030 (out-of-state). Room: $1,860. Board: $2,100. Fees, books, misc. academic expenses (school's estimate): $1,225.

**Enrollment.** Undergraduates: 6,353 men, 7,265 women (full-time). Freshman class: 9,239 applicants, 7,788 accepted, 3,290 enrolled. Graduate enrollment: 686 men, 1,107 women.

**Test score averages/ranges.** Range of SAT scores of middle 50%: 470-560 verbal, 540-640 math. Average ACT scores: 26 composite. Range of ACT scores of middle 50%: 23-27 composite.

**Faculty.** 764 full-time; 110 part-time. 88% of faculty holds highest degree in specific field. Student/faculty ratio: 20 to 1.

**Selectivity rating.** Highly competitive.

**PROFILE.** Miami, founded in 1809, is a comprehensive, public university. Programs are offered through the College of Arts and Science; Schools of Applied Science, Business Administration, Education and Allied Professions, Fine Arts, Interdisciplinary Studies; and the Graduate School. Its 1,921-acre campus is located in Oxford, 30 miles northwest of Cincinnati.

**Accreditation:** NCACS. Professionally accredited by the Accreditation Board for Engineering and Technology, the American Assembly of Collegiate Schools of Business, the American Dental Association, the American Home Economics Association, the American Society of Landscape Architects, the National Architecture Accrediting Board, the National Association of Schools of Art and Design, the National Association of Schools of Music, the National Council for Accreditation of Teacher Education, the National League for Nursing.
**Religious orientation:** Miami University is nonsectarian; no religious requirements.
**Library:** Collections totaling over 1,400,000 volumes, 7,264 periodical subscriptions, and 2,000,000 microform items.
**Special facilities/museums:** Geology, art, anthropology, and zoology museums, performing arts center, herbarium, environmental research center, 400-acre nature preserve, electron microscope center.
**Athletic facilities:** Gymnasiums, natatorium, recreation center with tennis, racquetball, and squash courts, artificial turf field.

**STUDENT BODY. Undergraduate profile:** 73% are state residents; 8% are transfers. 2% Asian-American, 3% Black, 1% Hispanic, 1% Native American, 93% White. Average age of undergraduates is 20.
**Freshman profile:** 2% of freshmen who took SAT scored 700 or over on verbal, 9% scored 700 or over on math; 14% scored 600 or over on verbal, 47% scored 600 or over on math; 60% scored 500 or over on verbal, 90% scored 500 or over on math; 98% scored 400 or over on verbal, 99% scored 400 or over on math; 100% scored 300 or over on verbal, 100% scored 300 or over on math. 52% of accepted applicants took SAT; 48% took ACT.
**Undergraduate achievement:** 97% of fall 1992 freshmen returned for fall 1993 term. 75% of entering class graduated. 52% of students who completed a degree program went on to graduate study.
**Foreign students:** 139 students are from out of the country. Countries represented include Canada, China, France, Hong Kong, India, and Japan; 54 in all.

**PROGRAMS OF STUDY. Degrees:** B.A., B.A.Internat.Studies, B.Env.Design, B.F.A., B.Mus., B.Phil., B.S., B.S.Appl.Sci., B.S.Bus., B.S.Ed., B.S.Fam./Cons.Sci., B.S.Nurs.
**Majors:** Accounting, American Studies, Anthropology, Art, Art Education, Athletic Training, Black World Studies, Botany, Business/Economics, Chemistry, Classical Humanities, Decision Science, Dietetics, Diplomacy/Foreign Affairs, Economics, Elementary Education, Engineering, Engineering Management, Engineering Physics, English, English/Creative Writing, English/Journalism, English/Literature, Environmental Design, Exercise Science, Finance, French, General Business, Geography, Geology, German, Greek, Health Appraisal/Enhancement, Health Education, History, History of Architecture/Art, Housing/Interior Design, Individual/Family Studies, Individualized Major, Interdisciplinary Studies, International Studies, Latin, Linguistics, Management Information Systems, Manufacturing Engineering, Marketing, Mass Communications, Mathematics, Mathematics/Statistics, Medical Technology, Microbiology, Music, Music Education, Music Performance, Nursing, Operations Management, Organizational Behavior/Management, Paper Science/Engineering, Personnel/Employment Relations Management, Philosophy, Physical Education, Physics, Political Science, Pre-Kindergarten Education, Psychology, Public Administration, Purchasing/Procurement Management, Religion, Retailing, Russian, Secondary Education, Sociology, Spanish, Special Education, Speech Communication, Speech Pathology/Audiology, Sport Organization, Statistics, Systems Analysis/Computer Science, Theatre, Urban/Regional Planning, Zoology.
**Distribution of degrees:** The majors with the highest enrollment are marketing, accountancy, and elementary education; linguistics and black world studies have the lowest.
**Requirements:** General education requirement.
**Academic regulations:** Freshmen must maintain minimum 1.7 GPA; sophomores, juniors, seniors, 2.0 GPA.
**Special:** Minors in all majors. Programs in American culture studies, black studies, comparative literature, gerontology, medieval studies, and women's studies. Courses offered in Chinese, Hebrew, Japanese, Italian, and Portuguese. Undergraduate Fellows program for seniors preparing for college teaching. Arts management option for art, business, music, physical education/dance, and theatre majors. Self-designed majors. Double majors. Dual degrees. Independent study. Pass/fail grading option. Internships. Cooperative education programs. Graduate school at which undergraduates may take graduate-level courses. Preprofessional programs in law, medicine, veterinary science, dentistry, engineering, and physical therapy. 3-1 medical technology programs with regional hospital affiliates. Arts-Professional arrangement: B.A. degree awarded after completing junior year and first year of professional school. 3-2 engineering programs with Case Western Reserve U and Columbia U. 3-2 forestry and environmental studies program with Duke U. Member of Greater Cincinnati Consortium of Colleges and Universities and of Dayton/Miami Valley Consortium. Semester-away architecture program in Alexandria, Va. Teacher certification in early childhood, elementary, secondary, and special education. Numerous exchange programs abroad. Study abroad also in Luxembourg. NROTC and AFROTC.
**Honors:** Phi Beta Kappa. Honors program. Honor societies.
**Academic Assistance:** Remedial reading, writing, math, and study skills. Nonremedial tutoring.

**STUDENT LIFE. Housing:** All freshmen must live on campus unless living with family. Coed, women's, and men's dorms. Fraternity housing. On-campus married-student housing. Sororities have suites in residence halls. 50% of students live in college housing.
**Social atmosphere:** The social scene is active, as Miami students both work and play hard. Students participate in the 300-plus organizations related to career, sports, political, community, or other special interests. The uptown scene is very much a "college town" atmosphere in the traditional sense, with pubs and restaurants catering primarily to the student body, featuring live music most nights in one haunt or another. There is a strong cohesive nature to the university community in which both the eccentric and conformist alike thrive.
**Services and counseling/handicapped student services:** Placement services. Health service. Women's center. Multicultural center. Counseling services for minority, military, veteran, and older students. Birth control, personal, and psychological counseling. Career and academic guidance services. Physically disabled student services. Learning disabled services. Notetaking services. Tape recorders. Reader services for the blind.
**Campus organizations:** Undergraduate student government. Student newspaper. Literary magazine. Yearbook. Radio and TV stations. Chorale, women's choral society, men's glee club, orchestra, marching band, debating, public speaking, theatre, community service, departmental and special-interest groups, 325 organizations in all. 28 fraternities, 26 chapter houses; 22 sororities, no chapter houses. 33% of men join a fraternity. 39% of women join a sorority.
**Religious organizations:** Bahai, Baptist Student Union, Campus Crusade for Christ, Campus Mission, Catholic Campus Ministry, Christian Science Organization, Christian Student Fellowship, Hillel, Intervarsity Christian Fellowship, Kappa Phi, Latter-Day Saints Student Association, Lutheran Campus Ministry, Muslim Student Association, Navigators, United Campus Ministry, Vineyard Christian Fellowship, Wesley Foundation.
**Minority/foreign student organizations:** Asian American Association, Black Student Action Association, Hispano American Association, Minority Graduate Student Association. Indian Student Association, International Club, Japanese Culture and Language Club, Korean Club.

**ATHLETICS. Physical education requirements:** None.
**Intercollegiate competition:** 9% of students participate. Baseball (M), basketball (M,W), cross-country (M,W), field hockey (W), football (M), golf (M), ice hockey (M), soccer (M), softball (W), swimming (M,W), tennis (M,W), track (indoor) (M,W), track and field (M,W), volleyball (W), wrestling (M). Member of CCHA, Mid-American Conference, NCAA Division I, NCAA Division I-A for football.
**Intramural and club sports:** Men's club archery, boxing, fencing, golf, gymnastics, horsemanship, ice hockey, lacrosse, martial arts, Nordic skiing, racquetball, rifle, rugby, sailing, soccer, squash, synchronized swimming, tennis, ultimate frisbee, volleyball, water polo, water skiing, weight lifting, wrestling. Women's club archery, field hockey, golf, gymnastics, horsemanship, sailing, soccer, tennis, ultimate frisbee, volleyball.

**ADMISSIONS. Academic basis for candidate selection** (in order of priority): Secondary school record, class rank, standardized test scores, school's recommendation, essay.
**Nonacademic basis for candidate selection:** Character and personality, extracurricular participation, particular talent or ability, and alumni/ae relationship are considered.
**Requirements:** Graduation from secondary school is required; GED is accepted. 16 units and the following program of study are recommended: 4 units of English, 3 units of math, 3 units of science, 2 units of foreign language, 3 units of social studies, 1 unit of history. Audition required of music and theatre program applicants. Interview required of architecture program applicants. Portfolio required of art program applicants. Academic Enhancement Program (AEP). SAT or ACT is required. Campus visit recommended. No off-campus interviews.
**Procedure:** Take SAT or ACT by winter of 12th year. Application deadline is January 31. Notification of admission by March 15. Reply is required by May 1. $70 nonrefundable tuition deposit. $100 room deposit, refundable until May 1. Freshmen accepted for terms other than fall.
**Special programs:** Credit may be granted through CEEB Advanced Placement for scores of 3 or higher. Credit may be granted through CLEP subject exams. Credit and placement may be granted through challenge exams. Early decision program. In fall 1993, 593 applied for early decision and 536 were accepted. Deadline for applying for early decision is November 1. Concurrent enrollment program.
**Transfer students:** Transfer students accepted for terms other than fall. In fall 1993, 8% of all new students were transfers into all classes. 678 transfer applications were received, 495 were accepted. Application deadline is May 1 for fall; November 15 for spring. Minimum 2.5 GPA recommended. Lowest course grade accepted is "C." Maximum number of transferable credits is 64 semester hours; 96 quarter hours. At least 32 semester hours must be completed at the university to receive degree.
**Admissions contact:** James S. McCoy, Ph.D., Dir. of Admissions/Asst. VP for Enrollment Mgmt.. 513 529-2531.

**FINANCIAL AID. Available aid:** Pell grants, SEOG, state scholarships and grants, school scholarships and grants, private scholarships and grants, ROTC scholarships, academic merit scholarships, and aid for undergraduate foreign students. Perkins Loans (NDSL), PLUS, Stafford Loans (GSL), state loans, school loans, private loans, and SLS. Fifth Third plan; academic scholarship program.
**Financial aid statistics:** 35% of aid is not need-based. In 1993-94, 80% of all undergraduate applicants received aid; 73% of freshman applicants. Average amounts of aid awarded freshmen: Scholarships and grants, $2,260; loans, $3,534.
**Supporting data/closing dates:** FAFSA: Priority filing date is February 15. Notification of awards begins mid-March.
**Financial aid contact:** Diane Stemper, M.A., Director of Student Financial Aid. 513 529-4734.

**STUDENT EMPLOYMENT.** College Work/Study Program. Institutional employment. 26% of full-time undergraduates work on campus during school year. Students may expect to earn an average of $946 during school year. Off-campus part-time employment opportunities rated "good."

**COMPUTER FACILITIES.** 450 IBM/IBM-compatible, Macintosh/Apple, and RISC-/UNIX-based microcomputers. Students may access Digital, IBM minicomputer/mainframe systems, BITNET, Internet. Residence halls may be equipped with stand-alone microcomputers, networked microcomputers, modems. Client/LAN operating systems include Apple/Macintosh, DOS, X-windows, LocalTalk/AppleTalk, Novell. 15 major computer languages and software packages available. Some computing labs restricted to certain majors.
**Fees:** None.
**Hours:** 8 AM-midn.

**GRADUATE CAREER DATA.** Graduate school percentages: 12% enter law school. 8% enter medical school. 9% enter graduate business programs. 19% enter theological school/seminary. 42% of graduates choose careers in business and industry. Companies and businesses that hire graduates: Big Six accounting firms, 5th Third Bank, Procter & Gamble, retailers.

**PROMINENT ALUMNI/AE.** John Smale, former chairman, Procter & Gamble; Benjamin Harrison, former president of the United States; Rita Dove, Pulitzer Prize-winning poet, U.S. poet laureate; Ernest Volwiler, past chairman, Abbott Labs, developer of topical anaesthetics.

8-28

## Mount Union College

**Alliance, OH 44601** **216 821-5320**

**1993-94 Costs.** Tuition: $11,670. Room: $1,400. Board: $2,130. Fees, books, misc. academic expenses (school's estimate): $1,150.
**Enrollment.** Undergraduates: 711 men, 642 women (full-time). Freshman class: 1,310 applicants, 1,086 accepted, 458 enrolled.
**Test score averages/ranges.** Average ACT scores: 24 composite. Range of ACT scores of middle 50%: 19-25 composite.
**Faculty.** 78 full-time; 14 part-time. 75% of faculty holds highest degree in specific field. Student/faculty ratio: 15 to 1.
**Selectivity rating.** Competitive.

**PROFILE.** Mount Union, founded in 1846, is a church-affiliated college. The 72-acre campus is situated in a residential section of Alliance, 78 miles south of Cleveland and 75 miles west of Pittsburgh.

**Accreditation:** NCACS. Professionally accredited by the National Association of Schools of Music.
**Religious orientation:** Mount Union College is affiliated with the United Methodist Church; two semesters of religion required.
**Library:** Collections totaling over 216,000 volumes, 800 periodical subscriptions, and 20,200 microform items.
**Special facilities/museums:** Art gallery, ecological center, observatory, educational media center.
**Athletic facilities:** Physical education building, tracks, basketball, racquetball, and tennis courts, swimming pool, baseball, intramural, and softball fields, gymnastics, weight, and wrestling rooms.

**STUDENT BODY. Undergraduate profile:** 85% are state residents; 10% are transfers. 2% Asian-American, 5% Black, 2% Hispanic, 1% Native American, 85% White, 5% Other. Average age of undergraduates is 20.
**Freshman profile:** 3% of freshmen who took ACT scored 30 or over on composite; 34% scored 24 or over on composite; 93% scored 18 or over on composite; 100% scored 12 or over on composite. 38% of accepted applicants took SAT; 83% took ACT. 88% of freshmen come from public schools.
**Undergraduate achievement:** 91% of fall 1992 freshmen returned for fall 1993 term. 66% of entering class graduated. 24% of students who completed a degree program immediately went on to graduate study.
**Foreign students:** 70 students are from out of the country. Countries represented include Indonesia, Japan, Malaysia, Singapore, Spain, and Thailand; 19 in all.

**PROGRAMS OF STUDY. Degrees:** B.A., B.Mus., B.Mus.Ed., B.S.
**Majors:** Accounting, American Studies, Art, Biology, Business Administration, Chemistry, Communications, Computer Science, Cytotechnology, Economics, Education, English, French, Geology, History, Information Systems, Interdisciplinary, International Business/Economics, Mathematics, Medical Technology, Music, Nonwestern Studies, Philosophy, Physical Education/Health, Physics/Astronomy, Political Science, Psychology, Religion, Sociology, Spanish, Speech, Sports Management, Sports Medicine, Theatre Arts.
**Distribution of degrees:** The majors with the highest enrollment are business, education, and biology; speech, American studies, and nonwestern studies have the lowest.
**Requirements:** General education requirement.
**Academic regulations:** Freshmen must maintain minimum 1.60 GPA; sophomores, 1.75 GPA; juniors, 1.90 GPA; seniors, 2.00 GPA.
**Special:** Minors offered in most majors. Self-designed majors. Double majors. Independent study. Internships. Cooperative education programs. Graduate school at which undergraduates may take graduate-level courses. Preprofessional programs in law, medicine, dentistry, theology, and engineering. 3-1 medical technology programs with approved schools of medical technology. Member of East Central College Consortium and Five-College Commission. Sea Semester. Teacher certification in elementary, secondary, and special education. Exchange program abroad in Japan (Balka Coll). Study abroad also in England and Hong Kong. ROTC and AFROTC at Kent State U.
**Honors:** Honors program.
**Academic Assistance:** Remedial reading, writing, math, and study skills. Nonremedial tutoring.

**STUDENT LIFE. Housing:** Students may live on or off campus. Women's and men's dorms. Fraternity housing. School-owned/operated apartments. 80% of students live in college housing.
**Social atmosphere:** The student newspaper reports, "Off-campus cultural life is very limited; most popular social events are planned by the Student Activities Council, Student Senate, or Greeks." Popular events include the Snow Carnival, Black Student Union activities, mixers, Comedy Club Night, Homecoming, and football games. On campus, students meet at the campus center, snack bar, and fraternity houses; off campus, they gather at the Bier Haus.
**Services and counseling/handicapped student services:** Placement services. Health service. Counseling services for minority students. Personal and psychological counseling. Career and academic guidance services. Religious counseling. Physically disabled student services. Learning disabled services.
**Campus organizations:** Undergraduate student government. Student newspaper (Dynamo, published once/week). Literary magazine. Yearbook. Radio station. Dance company, chorale, Mount Union Players, departmental, political, and service groups, 75 organizations in all. Five fraternities, four chapter houses; five sororities, four chapter houses. 40% of men join a fraternity. 40% of women join a sorority.
**Religious organizations:** Fellowship of Christian Athletes, Christian Science Organization, Christian Outreach, Kappa Phi, Little Flock, Newman Club, Sigma Theta Epsilon.
**Minority/foreign student organizations:** Black Student Union. International Student Association.

**ATHLETICS. Physical education requirements:** Two semesters of physical education required.
**Intercollegiate competition:** 40% of students participate. Baseball (M), basketball (M,W), cheerleading (W), cross-country (M,W), diving (M,W), football (M), golf (M), soccer (M,W), softball (W), swimming (M,W), tennis (M,W), track (indoor) (M,W), track (outdoor) (M,W), track and field (indoor) (M,W), track and field (outdoor) (M,W), volleyball (W), wrestling (M). Member of NCAA Division III, Ohio Athletic Conference.
**Intramural and club sports:** 30% of students participate. Intramural aerobics, badminton, basketball, bowling, racquetball, softball, volleyball, walleyball.

**ADMISSIONS. Academic basis for candidate selection** (in order of priority): Secondary school record, class rank, standardized test scores, essay, school's recommendation.
**Nonacademic basis for candidate selection:** Character and personality, extracurricular participation, particular talent or ability, geographical distribution, and alumni/ae relationship are important.
**Requirements:** Graduation from secondary school is required; GED is accepted. 15 units and the following program of study are recommended: 4 units of English, 3 units of math, 3 units of science, 2 units of foreign language, 3 units of social studies. Minimum composite ACT score of 18 (combined SAT score of 950), rank in top half of secondary school class, and minimum 2.0 GPA required. Interview may be required of marginal applicants. Audition required of music program applicants. Probationary admission possible for applicants not meeting standard requirements. SAT or ACT is required. Campus visit and interview recommended. Off-campus interviews available with an admissions representative.
**Procedure:** Take SAT or ACT by October of 12th year. Visit college for interview by May of 12th year. Suggest filing application by February. Application deadline is May. Notification of admission on rolling basis. No set date by which applicants must accept offer. $150 tuition deposit, refundable until May 1. $150 room deposit, refundable until May 1. Freshmen accepted for terms other than fall.
**Special programs:** Admission may be deferred one year. Credit and/or placement may be granted through CEEB Advanced Placement exams for scores of 3 or higher. Credit and/or placement may be granted through CLEP general and subject exams. Credit and placement may be granted through challenge exams, and military and life experience. Early entrance/early admission program. Concurrent enrollment program.
**Transfer students:** Transfer students accepted for terms other than fall. In fall 1993, 10% of all new students were transfers into all classes. 100 transfer applications were received, 70 were accepted. Application deadline is rolling for fall; rolling for spring. Lowest course grade accepted is "C." Maximum number of transferable credits is 75 semester hours. At least 45 semester hours must be completed at the college to receive degree.
**Admissions contact:** Greg King, M.Ed., Director of Admissions. 216 821-5320, extension 2594.

**FINANCIAL AID. Available aid:** Pell grants, SEOG, state scholarships and grants, school scholarships and grants, private scholarships, ROTC scholarships, academic merit scholarships, and aid for undergraduate foreign students. Perkins Loans (NDSL), PLUS, Stafford Loans (GSL), state loans, and SLS. Knight Tuition Plans and family tuition reduction. Monthly payment plan.
**Financial aid statistics:** 26% of aid is not need-based. In 1993-94, 97% of all undergraduate applicants received aid; 97% of freshman applicants. Average amounts of aid awarded freshmen: Scholarships and grants, $5,300; loans, $2,500.
**Supporting data/closing dates:** FAFSA/FAF/FFS: Accepted on rolling basis. School's own aid application: Accepted on rolling basis. State aid form: Deadline is September. Notification of awards begins March 1.
**Financial aid contact:** Sandra Pittenger, M.A., Director of Financial Aid. 216 821-5320, extension 2674.

**STUDENT EMPLOYMENT.** College Work/Study Program. Institutional employment. 70% of full-time undergraduates work on campus during school year. Students may expect to earn an average of $1,000 during school year. Off-campus part-time employment opportunities rated "fair."

**COMPUTER FACILITIES.** 130 IBM/IBM-compatible and Macintosh/Apple microcomputers. Students may access Hewlett-Packard minicomputer/mainframe systems. Computer languages and software packages include Ada, Assembler, BASIC, C, COBOL, FORTRAN, Pascal, Prolog; database, graphics, quantitative methods, spreadsheet, word processing packages. Computer facilities are available to all students.
**Fees:** None.
**Hours:** 8 AM-11 PM.

**GRADUATE CAREER DATA.** Graduate school percentages: 5% enter law school. 4% enter medical school. 1% enter dental school. 4% enter graduate business programs. 10% enter graduate arts and sciences programs. Highest graduate school enrollments: Akron U, Case Western Reserve U, Kent State U, Ohio State U. 35% of graduates choose careers in business and industry. Companies and businesses that hire graduates: Andersen Consulting, Ernest & Young; Hill, Barth, and King; Price Waterhouse.

**PROMINENT ALUMNI/AE.** Ralph Regula, congressman; Vince Marotta, inventor of "Mr. Coffee."

8-30

# Mount Vernon Nazarene College

**Mount Vernon, OH 43050** **614 397-1244**

**1993-94 Costs.** Tuition: $6,840. Room: $1,750. Board: $1,450. Fees, books, misc. academic expenses (school's estimate): $750.

**Enrollment.** Undergraduates: 479 men, 635 women (full-time). Freshman class: 510 applicants, 485 accepted, 334 enrolled. Graduate enrollment: 15 men, 1 woman.

**Test score averages/ranges.** Average ACT scores: 21 composite.

**Faculty.** 51 full-time; 18 part-time. 53% of faculty holds doctoral degree. Student/faculty ratio: 17 to 1.

**Selectivity rating.** Less competitive.

**PROFILE.** Mount Vernon Nazarene, founded in 1964, is a private, church-affiliated, liberal arts college. The academic organization of the college includes the Divisions of Business; Education and Physical Education; Fine Arts; Literature, Language, and Communication; Natural Sciences; Religion and Philosophy; and Social Sciences. Its 210-acre campus is located in Mount Vernon, 25 miles south of Mansfield.

**Accreditation:** NCACS.

**Religious orientation:** Mount Vernon Nazarene College is affiliated with the Church of the Nazarene; three semesters of religion/theology required.

**Library:** Collections totaling over 851,243 volumes, 526 periodical subscriptions, and 3,294 microform items.

**Special facilities/museums:** Art gallery, nature reserve, radio station.

**Athletic facilities:** Gymnasium, athletic training and weight rooms, tennis courts, softball and soccer fields.

**STUDENT BODY. Undergraduate profile:** 82% are state residents; 20% are transfers. 1% Asian-American, 1% Black, 97% White, 1% Other. Average age of undergraduates is 20.

**Freshman profile:** 99% of accepted applicants took ACT. 95% of freshmen come from public schools.

**Undergraduate achievement:** 76% of fall 1992 freshmen returned for fall 1993 term. 40% of entering class graduated. 22% of students who completed a degree program immediately went on to graduate study.

**Foreign students:** Nine students are from out of the country. Countries represented include Canada, Chile, India, Japan, Nicaragua, and Puerto Rico.

**PROGRAMS OF STUDY. Degrees:** B.A., B.Bus.Admin., B.S.

**Majors:** Accounting, Art, Athletic Training, Biology, Broadcasting, Business Administration, Chemistry, Christian Education, Church Music, Communication, Comprehensive Business Education, Comprehensive Education, Computer Science, Criminal Justice, Drama, Economics, Elementary Education, English, History, Home Economics, Information Processing, Kindergarten/Primary Education, Literature, Mathematics, Medical Technology, Music, Music Education, Music Performance, Office Administration, Philosophy/Humanities, Physical Education, Pre-Kindergarten Education, Pre-Seminary Studies, Psychology, Religion, Secondary Education, Secretarial Administration, Social Welfare, Sociology, Spanish, Special Education/Learning Disabilities, Speech/Drama.

**Distribution of degrees:** The majors with the highest enrollment are business, education, and social studies; Spanish, home economics, and physical education have the lowest.

**Requirements:** General education requirement.

**Academic regulations:** Freshmen must maintain minimum 1.8 GPA; sophomores, 1.9 GPA; juniors, 2.0 GPA; seniors, 2.0 GPA.

**Special:** Associate's degrees offered. Double majors. Independent study. Internships. Preprofessional programs in law, medicine, veterinary science, pharmacy, dentistry, theology, optometry, agriculture, engineering, nursing, and physical therapy. 2-2 nursing program with Capital U. Member of Christian Colleges Coalition, Council of Independent Colleges, and National Association of Independent Colleges and Universities. Washington Semester. Teacher certification in early childhood, elementary, secondary, and special education. Certification in specific subject areas. Study abroad in Asia, Israel, Mexico, and elsewhere. Spanish majors spend one semester at the U of Costa Rica.

**Honors:** Honors program.

**Academic Assistance:** Remedial reading, writing, math, and study skills. Nonremedial tutoring.

**STUDENT LIFE. Housing:** All unmarried students under age 21 must live on campus unless living near campus with relatives. Women's and men's dorms. School-owned/operated apartments. 68% of students live in college housing.

**Services and counseling/handicapped student services:** Health service. Counseling services for older students. Personal and psychological counseling. Career and academic guidance services. Religious counseling.

**Campus organizations:** Undergraduate student government. Student newspaper (Lakeholm Viewer). Yearbook. Radio station. Treble Singers, Singing Collegians, drama groups, Goliards, Spanish Club, Student Council, special-interest groups, 27 organizations in all.

**Religious organizations:** Fellowship of Christian Athletes, Koinonia, Living Witness, Mohican Ministries, Reaching Out.

**ATHLETICS. Physical education requirements:** Two semesters of physical education required.

**Intercollegiate competition:** 7% of students participate. Baseball (M), basketball (M,W), cheerleading (M,W), golf (M), soccer (M), softball (W), volleyball (W). Member of Mid-Ohio Conference, NAIA, NCCAA.

**Intramural and club sports:** 15% of students participate. Intramural basketball, flag football, softball, volleyball.

**ADMISSIONS. Academic basis for candidate selection** (in order of priority): Secondary school record, standardized test scores, school's recommendation, class rank, essay.

**Nonacademic basis for candidate selection:** Character and personality and extracurricular participation are considered.

**Requirements:** Graduation from secondary school is required; GED is accepted. 18 units and the following program of study are required: 3 units of English, 2 units of math, 1 unit of science, 2 units of social studies. Minimum composite ACT score of 15, rank in top two-thirds of secondary school class, and minimum 2.0 GPA required. College Experience Enhancement Program (CEEP) for applicants not meeting standard requirements. ACT is required. Campus visit recommended. Off-campus interviews available with an admissions representative.

**Procedure:** Take ACT by June of 12th year. Application deadline is August 15. Notification of admission on rolling basis. Reply is required by August 30. $40 nonrefundable room deposit. Freshmen accepted for terms other than fall.

**Special programs:** Admission may be deferred one year. Credit and/or placement may be granted through CEEB Advanced Placement exams for scores of 3 or higher. Credit and/or placement may be granted through CLEP general and subject exams. Credit may be granted through military experience. Concurrent enrollment program.

**Transfer students:** Transfer students accepted for terms other than fall. In fall 1993, 20% of all new students were transfers into all classes. 122 transfer applications were received, 97 were accepted. Application deadline is August 1 for fall; January 2 for spring. Minimum 2.0 GPA required. Lowest course grade accepted is "C." Maximum number of transferable credits is 64 semester hours. At least 30 must be completed at the college to receive degree.

**Admissions contact:** Bruce Oldham, M.A., Director of Admissions. 800 782-2435.

**FINANCIAL AID. Available aid:** Pell grants, SEOG, state scholarships and grants, school scholarships and grants, private scholarships and grants, academic merit scholarships, and athletic scholarships. Perkins Loans (NDSL), PLUS, Stafford Loans (GSL), state loans, private loans, and SLS. AMS and family tuition reduction.

**Financial aid statistics:** In 1993-94, 91% of all undergraduate applicants received aid; 98% of freshman applicants. Average amounts of aid awarded freshmen: Scholarships and grants, $1,856; loans, $2,625.

**Supporting data/closing dates:** FAFSA: Priority filing date is April 30. School's own aid application: Priority filing date is April 30; accepted on rolling basis. Income tax forms: Priority filing date is April 30; accepted on rolling basis. Notification of awards on rolling basis.

**Financial aid contact:** Joanne Bowman, Student Financial Planning. 800 782-2435.

**STUDENT EMPLOYMENT.** College Work/Study Program. Institutional employment. 28% of full-time undergraduates work on campus during school year. Students may expect to earn an average of $1,000 during school year. Off-campus part-time employment opportunities rated "good."

**COMPUTER FACILITIES.** 100 IBM/IBM-compatible and Macintosh/Apple microcomputers. Students may access Digital, SUN minicomputer/mainframe systems, Internet. Client/LAN operating systems include Apple/Macintosh, DOS, UNIX/XENIX/AIX, LocalTalk/AppleTalk, Novell. Computer languages and software packages include Assembly, C, COBOL, dBASE III & IV, FORTRAN, Lotus, Microsoft Word/DOS and Windows, Pascal, WordPerfect. Computer facilities are available to all students.

**Fees:** None.

**Hours:** 8 AM-11 PM.

**GRADUATE CAREER DATA.** Highest graduate school enrollments: Ohio State U, Nazarene Theological Seminary. 20% of graduates choose careers in business and industry. Companies and businesses that hire graduates: Cooper Industries.

**PROMINENT ALUMNI/AE.** Dr. James Radcliff, missionary doctor; Tim Belcher, professional baseball player; numerous leading pastors throughout the world.

8-29

# Muskingum College

**New Concord, OH 43762** **614 826-8211**

**1994-95 Costs.** Tuition: $13,240. Room: $1,634. Board: $2,280. Fees, books, misc. academic expenses (school's estimate): $780.

**Enrollment.** Undergraduates: 572 men, 542 women (full-time). Freshman class: 1,109 applicants, 922 accepted, 375 enrolled. Graduate enrollment: 10 men, 32 women.

**Test score averages/ranges.** Average SAT scores: 436 verbal, 490 math. Range of SAT scores of middle 50%: 370-490 verbal, 420-550 math. Average ACT scores: 21 English, 21 math, 22 composite. Range of ACT scores of middle 50%: 18-24 English, 18-23 math.

**Faculty.** 79 full-time; 37 part-time. 72% of faculty holds doctoral degree. Student/faculty ratio: 14 to 1.

**Selectivity rating.** Less competitive.

**PROFILE.** Muskingum, founded in 1837, is a private, church-affiliated, liberal arts college. Its 215-acre campus is located in New Concord, 80 miles east of Columbus.

**Accreditation:** NCACS. Professionally accredited by the National Association of Schools of Music.

**Religious orientation:** Muskingum College is affiliated with the United Presbyterian Church USA; two semesters of religion required.

**Library:** Collections totaling over 222,039 volumes, 647 periodical subscriptions, and 164,501 microform items.

**Special facilities/museums:** Art gallery, on-campus nursery school, electron microscope, 57-acre biology field station and mobile biology lab.

**Athletic facilities:** Gymnasiums, basketball, racquetball, and tennis courts, weight rooms, batting cage, swimming pool, baseball, football, soccer, and softball fields, track, stadium.

**STUDENT BODY. Undergraduate profile:** 85% are state residents; 11% are transfers. 1% Asian-American, 2% Black, 1% Hispanic, 1% Native American, 95% White. Average age of undergraduates is 20.

**Freshman profile:** 44% of accepted applicants took SAT; 86% took ACT. 91% of freshmen come from public schools.

**Undergraduate achievement:** 77% of fall 1992 freshmen returned for fall 1993 term. 48% of entering class graduated. 11% of students who completed a degree program immediately went on to graduate study.

**Foreign students:** 28 students are from out of the country. Countries represented include Canada, Hong Kong, India, Korea, and Spain; 11 in all.

**PROGRAMS OF STUDY. Degrees:** B.A., B.S.

**Majors:** Accounting, American Studies, Applied Music, Art, Biology, Business, Chemistry, Christian Education, Communication, Computing Science, Earth Science in Education, Economics, Elementary Education, English, Environmental Science, French, Geology, German, Health/Physical Education, History, Humanities, International Business, Mathematics, Music Education, Neuroscience, Philosophy, Physical Education, Physics, Political Science, Psychology, Public/International Affairs, Religion, Religion/Philosophy, Sociology, Spanish, Theatre.

**Distribution of degrees:** The majors with the highest enrollment are business, education, and history; philosophy, religion, and German have the lowest.

**Requirements:** General education requirement.

**Academic regulations:** Minimum 2.0 GPA must be maintained.

**Special:** Minors required of education majors. Minors offered in all single-subject areas. Courses offered in anthropology and Russian. Bridges To Careers program in administration, environmental studies, health care, journalism/information arts, public/international affairs, and social service. Merrill Palmer Institute programs for psychology and sociology majors. Self-designed majors. Double majors. Independent study. Pass/fail grading option. Internships. Preprofessional programs in law, medicine, veterinary science, pharmacy, dentistry, theology, and engineering. 3-1 medical technology program with Southeastern General Hospital (Cleveland). 3-3 nursing program and 3-2 engineering program with Case Western Reserve U. Member of East Central College Consortium. Washington Semester, UN Semester, and Sea Semester. Princeton Visiting Students Program (New Jersey). Critical Languages Program at Princeton for study of non-Western languages. Teacher certification in early childhood, elementary, secondary, and special education. Study abroad in Canada, France, Italy, Japan, Mexico, South Korea, and Spain. ROTC at Marietta Coll through Ohio U.

**Honors:** Phi Beta Kappa. Honor societies.

**Academic Assistance:** Nonremedial tutoring.

**STUDENT LIFE. Housing:** All freshmen and sophomores must live on campus unless living with family. Coed, women's, and men's dorms. Sorority and fraternity housing. School-owned/operated apartments. 82% of students live in college housing.

**Social atmosphere:** The student newspaper reports, "Social life here is very club-oriented. Over 60% of the campus (both male and female) are in social clubs. The off-campus bars are often too far to drive to." Greek organizations have a big influence on campus life. Special events include pledge parties, Homecoming, various dances, concerts, and parties. Students like to gather at the Bottom of the Center, the Party House, Zak's, Sharon's Cafe, Cliff Hangers, and the Western Pancake House (for late-night food).

**Services and counseling/handicapped student services:** Placement services. Health service. Counseling services for minority and older students. Birth control, personal, and psychological counseling. Career and academic guidance services. Religious counseling. Physically disabled student services. Learning disabled program/services. Notetaking services. Tape recorders. Tutors. Reader services for the blind.

**Campus organizations:** Undergraduate student government. Student newspaper (Black and Magenta, published once/week). Literary magazine. Yearbook. Radio and TV stations. Choral society, chorus, madrigal singers, concert and marching bands, jazz ensemble, orchestra, Muskingum Players, debating, Habitat for Humanity, Young Republicans, Interclub Council, activity planning board, women's group, 53 organizations in all. Four fraternities, all with chapter houses; four sororities, all with chapter houses. 65% of men join a fraternity. 45% of women join a sorority.

**Religious organizations:** Fellowship of Christian Athletes, Christian Fellowship.

**Minority/foreign student organizations:** Black Awareness Society. International Student Organization.

**ATHLETICS. Physical education requirements:** Three semesters of physical education required.

**Intercollegiate competition:** 65% of students participate. Baseball (M), basketball (M,W), cross-country (M,W), football (M), golf (M), soccer (M,W), softball (W), tennis (M,W), track (indoor) (M,W), track (outdoor) (M,W), track and field (indoor) (M,W), track and field (outdoor) (M,W), volleyball (W), wrestling (M). Member of NCAA Division III, Ohio Athletic Conference.

**Intramural and club sports:** 80% of students participate. Intramural basketball, flag football, racquetball, swimming, tennis, track, walleyball. Men's club rugby.

**ADMISSIONS. Academic basis for candidate selection** (in order of priority): Secondary school record, standardized test scores, class rank, school's recommendation, essay.

**Nonacademic basis for candidate selection:** Character and personality and extracurricular participation are important. Particular talent or ability and alumni/ae relationship are considered.

**Requirements:** Graduation from secondary school is required; GED is accepted. 15 units required and the following program of study recommended: 4 units of English, 3 units of math, 3 units of science, 2 units of foreign language, 2 units of social studies, 2 units of history. Minimum 2.3 GPA in college prep courses required. SAT or ACT is required. Campus visit and interview recommended. Off-campus interviews available with admissions and alumni representatives.

**Procedure:** Take SAT or ACT by April of 12th year. Suggest filing application by June 1. Application deadline is August 1. Notification of admission on rolling basis. Reply is required by May 1. $150 tuition deposit, refundable until May 1. Freshmen accepted for terms other than fall.

**Special programs:** Admission may be deferred one year. Credit and/or placement may be granted through CEEB Advanced Placement exams for scores of 3 or higher. Credit and/or placement may be granted through CLEP general and subject exams. Credit and placement may be granted through ACT PEP exams. Early entrance/early admission program. Concurrent enrollment program.

**Transfer students:** Transfer students accepted for terms other than fall. In fall 1993, 11% of all new students were transfers into all classes. 96 transfer applications were received, 70 were accepted. Application deadline is August 1 for fall; January 1 for spring. Minimum 2.0 GPA required. Lowest course grade accepted is "C." Maximum number of transferable credits is 93 semester hours. At least 48 semester hours must be completed at the college to receive degree.

**Admissions contact:** Teddi A. Joyce, Director of Admissions. 614 826-8137, 800 752-6082.

**FINANCIAL AID. Available aid:** Pell grants, SEOG, state scholarships and grants, school scholarships and grants, academic merit scholarships, and aid for undergraduate foreign students. Awards of Circumstance. Perkins Loans (NDSL), PLUS, Stafford Loans (GSL), school loans, and SLS. Tuition Plan Inc., Knight Tuition Plans, AMS, and deferred payment plan.

**Financial aid statistics:** 9% of aid is not need-based. In 1993-94, 97% of all undergraduate applicants received aid; 96% of freshman applicants. Average amounts of aid awarded freshmen: Scholarships and grants, $9,100; loans, $3,100.

**Supporting data/closing dates:** FAFSA/FAF/FFS: Priority filing date is March 1. School's own aid application: Priority filing date is March 1. State aid form: Deadline is September 25. Income tax forms. Notification of awards on rolling basis.

**Financial aid contact:** Jeff Zellers, Director of Financial Aid/Dean of Enrollment. 614 826-8139.

**STUDENT EMPLOYMENT.** College Work/Study Program. Institutional employment. 60% of full-time undergraduates work on campus during school year. Students may expect to earn an average of $800 during school year. Off-campus part-time employment opportunities rated "poor."

**COMPUTER FACILITIES.** 65 IBM/IBM-compatible, Macintosh/Apple, and RISC-/UNIX-based microcomputers; all are networked. Students may access Digital, Prime, SUN minicomputer/mainframe systems, Internet. Residence halls may be equipped with networked microcomputers. Client/LAN operating systems include Apple/Macintosh, DOS, UNIX/XENIX/AIX, X-windows, LocalTalk/AppleTalk. Computer languages and software packages include Assembly, BASIC, COBOL, FORTRAN, Lotus 1-2-3, Pascal, WordPerfect; 30 in all. Computer facilities are available to all students.

**Fees:** $150 computer fee per year.

**Hours:** 8:30 AM-midn.; 24 hours in residence halls.

**GRADUATE CAREER DATA.** Graduate school percentages: 3% enter law school. 2% enter medical school. 3% enter graduate business programs. 10% enter graduate arts and sciences programs. 1% enter theological school/seminary. Highest graduate school enrollments: Case Western Reserve U, Miami U, Ohio State U. 55% of graduates choose careers in business and industry. Companies and businesses that hire graduates: BancOhio, Nationwide, Ohio Bell, Prudential.

**PROMINENT ALUMNI/AE.** Philip Caldwell, former CEO, Ford Motor Co.; William Dentzer, CEO, The Depository Trust & Co.; John Glenn, U.S. Senator; Jack Hanna, director, Columbus Zoo; Alfred S. Warren, Jr., vice-president industrial relations, General Motors.

# Notre Dame College of Ohio

**South Euclid, OH 44121** **216 381-1680**

**1993-94 Costs.** Tuition: $7,200. Room & board: $3,690. Fees, books, misc. academic expenses (school's estimate): $680.

**Enrollment.** 377 women (full-time). Freshman class: 136 applicants, 107 accepted, 42 enrolled. Graduate enrollment: 44 women.

**Test score averages/ranges.** Average SAT scores: 443 verbal, 418 math. Range of SAT scores of middle 50%: 410-470 verbal, 360-380 math. Average ACT scores: 20 English, 18 math, 20 composite. Range of ACT scores of middle 50%: 17-22 composite.

**Faculty.** 33 full-time; 68 part-time. 61% of faculty holds doctoral degree. Student/faculty ratio: 10 to 1.

**Selectivity rating.** Competitive.

**PROFILE.** Notre Dame College of Ohio, founded in 1922, is a private, church-affiliated, liberal arts college for women. Its 53-acre campus, with architecture in a Tudor-Gothic style, is located in South Euclid, 15 miles from central Cleveland.

**Accreditation:** NCACS. Professionally accredited by the American Dietetic Association.

**Religious orientation:** Notre Dame College of Ohio is affiliated with the Roman Catholic Church; three semesters of theology required.

**Library:** Collections totaling over 88,476 volumes, 266 periodical subscriptions, and 10,183 microform items.

**Special facilities/museums:** Electron microscope.

**Athletic facilities:** Gymnasium, fitness center, swimming pool, tennis courts.

**STUDENT BODY. Undergraduate profile:** 99% are state residents. 1% Asian-American, 27% Black, 1% Hispanic, 61% White, 10% Other. Average age of undergraduates is 20.

**Freshman profile:** 14% of freshmen who took SAT scored 500 or over on verbal, 14% scored 500 or over on math; 78% scored 400 or over on verbal, 57% scored 400 or over on math; 85% scored 300 or over on verbal, 100% scored 300 or over on math. 6% of freshmen who took ACT scored 30 or over on English; 14% scored 24 or over on English, 14% scored 24 or over on math; 70% scored 18 or over on English, 53% scored 18 or over on math; 100% scored 12 or over on English, 95% scored 12 or over on math; 100% scored 6 or over on math. 20% of accepted applicants took SAT; 80% took ACT. 64% of freshmen come from public schools.

**Undergraduate achievement:** 64% of fall 1992 freshmen returned for fall 1993 term. 40% of entering class graduated. 14% of students who completed a degree program went on to graduate study within one year.

**Foreign students:** Five students are from out of the country. Countries represented include China and Kenya.

**PROGRAMS OF STUDY. Degrees:** B.A., B.S.

**Majors:** Accounting, Art, Biochemistry, Biology, Business Administration, Chemistry, Communications, Dietetics, Economics, Education, English, French, Graphic Commu-

nications, Human Resource Development, Management, Management/Financial Institutions, Marketing, Mathematics, Medical Technology, Nutrition, Pastoral Ministry, Political Science, Pre-Dentistry, Pre-Law, Pre-Medicine, Pre-Veterinary, Psychology, Social Sciences, Sociology, Spanish, Theology, Visual Arts Management.
**Distribution of degrees:** The majors with the highest enrollment are business, education, and English; biology, math, and social science have the lowest.
**Requirements:** General education requirement.
**Academic regulations:** Minimum 2.0 GPA must be maintained.
**Special:** Minors offered in many majors and in approximately 10 other fields. Associate's degrees offered. Double majors. Independent study. Pass/fail grading option. Cooperative education programs. Preprofessional programs in law, medicine, veterinary science, and dentistry. 3-2 engineering program with Case Western Reserve U. Member of Cleveland Commission on Higher Education. Cross-registration with Baldwin-Wallace Coll, Case Western Reserve U, Cleveland Inst of Art, Cleveland Inst of Music, Cleveland State U, Dyke Coll, John Carroll U, and Ursuline Coll. Teacher certification in early childhood, elementary, secondary, and special education. Certification in specific subject areas. Study abroad in France and Spain.
**Honors:** Honor societies.
**Academic Assistance:** Remedial reading, writing, math, and study skills. Nonremedial tutoring.
**ADMISSIONS. Academic basis for candidate selection** (in order of priority): Secondary school record, standardized test scores, class rank, essay, school's recommendation.
**Nonacademic basis for candidate selection:** Extracurricular participation is emphasized. Character and personality, particular talent or ability, and alumni/ae relationship are considered.
**Requirements:** Graduation from secondary school is required; GED is accepted. 15 units and the following program of study are required: 4 units of English, 2 units of math, 1 unit of lab science, 2 units of foreign language, 2 units of social studies, 4 units of academic electives. Minimum composite ACT score of 20 (combined SAT score of 850) and minimum 2.5 GPA required. Conditional admission possible for applicants not meeting standard requirements. SAT or ACT is required. Campus visit and interview recommended. Off-campus interviews available with an admissions representative.
**Procedure:** Take SAT or ACT by December of 12th year. Visit college for interview by September of 12th year. Application deadline is June 30. Notification of admission on rolling basis. Reply is required by July 15. $50 nonrefundable tuition deposit. $50 nonrefundable room deposit. Freshmen accepted for terms other than fall.
**Special programs:** Admission may be deferred one semester. Credit and/or placement may be granted through CEEB Advanced Placement exams for scores of 3 or higher. Credit and/or placement may be granted through CLEP general exams. Credit may be granted through life experience. Credit and placement may be granted through challenge exams. Early decision program. Deadline for applying for early decision is December 15. Concurrent enrollment program.
**Transfer students:** Transfer students accepted for terms other than fall. In fall 1993, 32 transfer applications were received, 25 were accepted. Application deadline is rolling for fall; rolling for spring. Minimum 2.5 GPA required. Lowest course grade accepted is "C." At least 32 semester hours must be completed at the college to receive degree.
**Admissions contact:** Karen Poelking, M.Ed., Dean of Admission and Records. 216 381-1680, extension 240.
**FINANCIAL AID. Available aid:** Pell grants, SEOG, state scholarships and grants, school scholarships and grants, private scholarships and grants, academic merit scholarships, and athletic scholarships. Perkins Loans (NDSL), PLUS, Stafford Loans (GSL), school loans, private loans, and SLS. AMS and Tuition Management Systems.
**Financial aid statistics:** 24% of aid is not need-based. In 1994-95, 85% of all undergraduate applicants received aid; 100% of freshman applicants. Average amounts of aid awarded freshmen: Scholarships and grants, $700; loans, $1,900.
**Supporting data/closing dates:** School's own aid application: Priority filing date is April 15. Notification of awards on rolling basis.
**Financial aid contact:** William Edmonson, M.A., Director of Financial Aid. 216 381-1680, extension 263.

5-11 8-31

## Oberlin College

**Oberlin, OH 44074 216 775-8121**

**1994-95 Costs.** Tuition: $19,670. Room: $2,920. Board: $2,900. Fees, books, misc. academic expenses (school's estimate): $699.
**Enrollment.** Undergraduates: 1,114 men, 1,469 women (full-time). Freshman class: 3,887 applicants, 2,472 accepted, 563 enrolled. Graduate enrollment: 6 men, 10 women.
**Test score averages/ranges.** Average SAT scores: 605 verbal, 633 math. Range of SAT scores of middle 50%: 550-650 verbal, 580-680 math. Average ACT scores: 28 composite. Range of ACT scores of middle 50%: 25-30 composite.
**Faculty.** 238 full-time; 39 part-time. 95% of faculty holds highest degree in specific field. Student/faculty ratio: 12 to 1.
**Selectivity rating.** Highly competitive.

**PROFILE.** Oberlin, founded in 1833, is a private college. Programs are offered through the College of Arts and Sciences and the Conservatory of Music. Its 440-acre campus, in Gothic architecture style, is located 34 miles southwest of Cleveland.

**Accreditation:** NCACS. Professionally accredited by the National Association of Schools of Art and Design, the National Association of Schools of Music.
**Religious orientation:** Oberlin College is nonsectarian; no religious requirements.
**Library:** Collections totaling over 1,033,183 volumes, 2,737 periodical subscriptions, and 275,000 microform items.
**Special facilities/museums:** Art museum, isotope lab, observatory.
**Athletic facilities:** Gymnasiums, basketball, racquetball, squash, tennis, and volleyball courts, swimming pools, baseball, field hockey, football, lacrosse, and soccer fields, tracks, fitness trail, free weight and Nautilus rooms, field house.

**STUDENT BODY. Undergraduate profile:** 10% are state residents; 8% are transfers. 9% Asian-American, 8% Black, 5% Hispanic, 77% White, 1% Other. Average age of undergraduates is 20.
**Freshman profile:** Majority of accepted applicants took SAT. 67% of freshmen come from public schools.
**Undergraduate achievement:** 90% of fall 1992 freshmen returned for fall 1993 term. 82% of entering class graduated. 75% of students who completed a degree program went on to graduate study within five years.
**Foreign students:** 175 students are from out of the country. Countries represented include Canada, China, India, Japan, and Pakistan; 40 in all.
**PROGRAMS OF STUDY. Degrees:** A.B., B.F.A.Mus., B.Mus.
**Majors:** Archaeological Studies, Art, Art History, Astronomy, Biochemistry, Biology, Black Studies, Chemistry, Classical Archaeology, Classics, Comparative Literature, Composition, Computer Science, Creative Writing, Dance, East Asian Studies, Economics, Electronic/Computer Music, English, Environmental Studies, Ethnomusicology, French, Geology, German, German Studies, Government, Historical Performance, History, Individual Interdisciplinary Major, Individual Major, Jazz Studies, Judaic/Near Eastern Studies, Latin American Studies, Law/Society, Mathematics, Music, Music Education, Music History, Music Performance, Music Theory, Neuroscience, Philosophy, Physics, Psychobiology, Psychology, Religion, Russian, Russian/Soviet Studies, Sociology/Anthropology, Spanish, Studio Art, Theatre, Third World Studies, Urban Studies, Women's Studies.
**Distribution of degrees:** The majors with the highest enrollment are English, history, and biology; classical archaeology, modern dance, and Judaic/Near Eastern studies have the lowest.
**Requirements:** General education requirement.
**Special:** Minors offered. African-American music offered as individual major. Programs in conservation of art and prearchitecture. Interdisciplinary programs in human development, interarts, and public service. Performance diplomas offered by conservatory. Participation in three January noncredit independent study periods required. Experimental College emphasizes self-education and group discussion; courses approved by faculty may be taken for credit on pass/fail basis. Self-designed majors. Double majors. Dual degrees. Independent study. Pass/fail grading option. Internships. Graduate school at which undergraduates may take graduate-level courses. Preprofessional programs in law, medicine, veterinary science, architecture, and business. 3-2 B.A./B.S. engineering programs with Case Western Reserve U, U of Pennsylvania, and Washington U. Five-year B.A./B.Mus. program. Member of Great Lakes Colleges Association. Arts Program in New York. Newberry Library Program in the Humanities (Illinois). Oak Ridge Science Semester (Tennessee). Philadelphia Urban Semester. Other off-campus study opportunities. Exchange programs with Fisk U, Gallaudet U, and Tougaloo Coll. Certification in specific subject areas. Study abroad in African countries, Austria, the Dominican Republic, England, France, Germany, India, Israel, Japan, Latin American countries, the Netherlands, Scotland, Spain, and Taiwan.
**Honors:** Phi Beta Kappa. Honors program. Honor societies.
**Academic Assistance:** Nonremedial tutoring.
**STUDENT LIFE. Housing:** All freshmen and sophomores must live on campus. Coed, women's, and men's dorms. Off-campus privately-owned housing. Off-campus married-student housing. Program housing, language houses, women's collective, student-run cooperatives. 75% of students live in college housing.
**Social atmosphere:** "Social life usually stems from small gatherings in dorms and off-campus houses," reports the student newspaper. "In addition, the disco, Rathskellar, and Tap House are very popular. Cooperative houses also organize social events." Popular campus events include "visiting blues, jazz, folk, and rock bands, Cleveland Symphony Orchestra concerts, the Midnight Madness basketball game. The most popular is the all-day Mayfair celebration in the spring, with bands, arts and crafts, the 'egg a Republican' contest, and food."
**Services and counseling/handicapped student services:** Placement services. Health service. Women's center. Reading and speech clinics. Developmental skills services. Counseling services for minority and veteran students. Birth control, personal, and psychological counseling. Career and academic guidance services. Religious counseling. Physically disabled student services. Notetaking services. Tape recorders. Reader services for the blind.
**Campus organizations:** Undergraduate student government. Student newspaper (Review, published once/week). Literary magazine. Yearbook. Radio station. Chapel choir, college choir, orchestra, Musical Union, modern dance group, repertory theatre, philosophy and social service magazines, political and special-interest groups, 110 organizations in all.
**Religious organizations:** Newman Community, Christian Fellowship, Voices for Christ, Hillel, Muslim student group.
**Minority/foreign student organizations:** Black and Latino student groups, Asian-American Alliance. International Student Organization.
**ATHLETICS. Physical education requirements:** None.
**Intercollegiate competition:** 15% of students participate. Baseball (M), basketball (M,W), cross-country (M,W), diving (M,W), field hockey (W), football (M), lacrosse (M,W), soccer (M,W), swimming (M,W), tennis (M,W), track (indoor) (M,W), track (outdoor) (M,W), track and field (indoor) (M,W), track and field (outdoor) (M,W), volleyball (W). Member of NCAA Division III, North Coast Athletic Conference.
**Intramural and club sports:** 55% of students participate. Intramural arm wrestling, badminton, basketball, billiards, bowling, floor hockey, football, inner-tube water polo, racquetball, running, soccer, softball, squash, table tennis, tennis, turkey trot, ultimate frisbee, volleyball, walleyball. Men's club fencing, frisbee, horsemanship, ice hockey, martial arts, rugby, squash, volleyball. Women's club fencing, frisbee, horsemanship, ice hockey, martial arts, rugby, softball, squash.
**ADMISSIONS. Academic basis for candidate selection** (in order of priority): Secondary school record, standardized test scores, school's recommendation, essay, class rank.
**Nonacademic basis for candidate selection:** Character and personality and extracurricular participation are emphasized. Particular talent or ability is important. Geographical distribution and alumni/ae relationship are considered.
**Requirements:** Graduation from secondary school is recommended; GED is accepted. 17 units and the following program of study are recommended: 4 units of English, 4 units of math, 3 units of lab science, 3 units of foreign language, 3 units of social studies. Audition required of music program applicants. SAT or ACT is required. ACH recommended.

Campus visit and interview recommended. Off-campus interviews available with an alumni representative.
**Procedure:** Take SAT or ACT by January of 12th year. Take ACH by January of 12th year. Visit college for interview by January 15 of 12th year. Application deadline is January 15. Notification of admission by April 1. Reply is required by May 1. $200 nonrefundable tuition deposit. Freshmen accepted for terms other than fall.
**Special programs:** Admission may be deferred one year. Credit and/or placement may be granted through CEEB Advanced Placement exams. Early decision program. In fall 1993, 198 applied for early decision and 162 were accepted. Deadline for applying for early decision is November 15 and January 2. Early entrance/early admission program. Concurrent enrollment program.
**Transfer students:** Transfer students accepted for terms other than fall. In fall 1993, 8% of all new students were transfers into all classes. 221 transfer applications were received, 145 were accepted. Application deadline is March 15 for fall; November 15 for spring. Minimum 3.0 GPA required. Lowest course grade accepted is "C-." Maximum number of transferable credits is 56 semester hours. At least 56 semester hours must be completed at the college to receive degree.
**Admissions contact:** Debra Chermonte, M.A., Director of Admissions. 216 775-8411.

**FINANCIAL AID. Available aid:** Pell grants, SEOG, state scholarships and grants, school scholarships and grants, private scholarships and grants, and academic merit scholarships. Perkins Loans (NDSL), PLUS, Stafford Loans (GSL), school loans, and SLS. Knight Tuition Plans and deferred payment plan.
**Financial aid statistics:** Average amounts of aid awarded freshmen: Loans, $3,670.
**Supporting data/closing dates:** FAFSA: Deadline is February 1. School's own aid application: Accepted on rolling basis. Notification of awards begins April 1.
**Financial aid contact:** Howard J. Thomas, M.A., Director of Financial Aid. 216 775-8142.

**STUDENT EMPLOYMENT.** College Work/Study Program. Institutional employment. 55% of full-time undergraduates work on campus during school year. Students may expect to earn an average of $1,450 during school year. Off-campus part-time employment opportunities rated "good."

**COMPUTER FACILITIES.** 250 IBM/IBM-compatible and Macintosh/Apple microcomputers. Residence halls may be equipped with stand-alone microcomputers, networked microcomputers, networked terminals, modems. Computer languages and software packages include BASIC, C, FORTRAN, Macro II, Pascal, SAS, Smartstar, SPSS-X, VAXMail. Computer facilities are available to all students.
**Fees:** None.
**Hours:** 8 AM-2 AM daily (library computers); 24 hours (dorm computers).

**PROMINENT ALUMNI/AE.** Erwin Griswold, former U.S. solicitor general, former dean of Harvard Law School; Roger Sperry, neurobiologist, educator; Johnetta Cole, president, Spelman Coll; William Goldman, novelist, screenwriter.

## Ohio Dominican College

**Columbus, OH 43219** **614 251-2741**

**1993-94 Costs.** Tuition: $7,730. Room & board: $4,090. Fees, books, misc. academic expenses (school's estimate): $600.
**Enrollment.** Undergraduates: 438 men, 626 women (full-time). Freshman class: 223 enrolled.
**Test score averages/ranges.** N/A.
**Faculty.** 53 full-time; 43 part-time. 47% of faculty holds doctoral degree. Student/faculty ratio: 15 to 1.
**Selectivity rating.** N/A.

**PROFILE.** Ohio Dominican is a church-affiliated, liberal arts college. Founded in 1911, it adopted coeducation in 1964. Its 46-acre campus is located four miles from downtown Columbus.

**Accreditation:** NCACS.
**Religious orientation:** Ohio Dominican College is affiliated with the Roman Catholic Church (Dominican Sisters); four semester hours of theology, four of philosophy, and four additional hours of either theology or philosophy required.
**Library:** Collections totaling over 154,000 volumes, 552 periodical subscriptions, and 5,545 microform items.
**Athletic facilities:** Gymnasium, baseball and softball fields, tennis courts.

**STUDENT BODY. Undergraduate profile:** 97% are state residents; 35% are transfers. 1% Asian-American, 13% Black, 2% Hispanic, 1% Native American, 72% White, 11% Other. Average age of undergraduates is 22.
**Freshman profile:** Majority of accepted applicants took ACT. 58% of freshmen come from public schools.
**Undergraduate achievement:** 11% of students who completed a degree program immediately went on to graduate study.
**Foreign students:** 170 students are from out of the country. Countries represented include Hong Kong, Indonesia, Japan, Korea, Taiwan, and Thailand; 20 in all.

**PROGRAMS OF STUDY. Degrees:** B.A., B.S., B.S.Ed.
**Majors:** Accounting, Art, Biology, Business Administration, Chemistry, Communication Arts, Computer Science, Criminal Justice, Cross-Discipline Studies, Economics, Elementary Education, English, Fashion Merchandising, Health Administration, History, Information Systems, International Business, Library/Information Systems, Mathematics, Philosophy, Physical Education, Political Science, Psychology, School Library Media Services, Secondary Education, Social Science, Social Welfare, Sociology, Spanish, Special Education, Teaching English as Second Language, Theology.
**Distribution of degrees:** The majors with the highest enrollment are business administration, accounting, and education; philosophy, economics, and sociology have the lowest.
**Requirements:** General education requirement.
**Academic regulations:** Minimum 2.0 GPA required for graduation.
**Special:** Courses offered in coaching, French, geography, German, gerontology, music, and physics. Associate's degrees offered. Self-designed majors. Double majors. Independent study. Internships. Member of Higher Education Council of Columbus. Washington Semester. Teacher certification in early childhood, elementary, secondary, and special education. Certification in specific subject areas. Study abroad available on an individual basis. ROTC, NROTC, and AFROTC at Ohio State U.
**Honors:** Honors program. Honor societies.
**Academic Assistance:** Remedial reading, writing, math, and study skills. Nonremedial tutoring.

**ADMISSIONS. Academic basis for candidate selection** (in order of priority): Secondary school record, standardized test scores, class rank, essay, school's recommendation.
**Nonacademic basis for candidate selection:** Character and personality and extracurricular participation are considered.
**Requirements:** Graduation from secondary school is required; GED is accepted. 16 units and the following program of study are required: 4 units of English, 3 units of math, 3 units of lab science, 3 units of foreign language, 3 units of social studies. Minimum 2.0 GPA required. Conditional admission possible for applicants not meeting standard requirements. SAT or ACT is required. Campus visit and interview required. Off-campus interviews available with an admissions representative.
**Procedure:** Take SAT or ACT by February of 12th year. Visit college for interview by April of 12th year. Suggest filing application by March. Application deadline is August 15. Notification of admission on rolling basis. No set date by which applicants must accept offer. $50 nonrefundable tuition deposit. $50 room deposit, refundable until classes begin. Freshmen accepted for terms other than fall.
**Special programs:** Admission may be deferred one year. Credit and/or placement may be granted through CEEB Advanced Placement exams for scores of 3 or higher. Credit may be granted through CLEP general exams, ACT PEP and DANTES exams, and life experience. Credit and/or placement may be granted through CLEP subject exams. Placement may be granted through challenge exams. Credit and placement may be granted through military experience. Concurrent enrollment program.
**Transfer students:** Transfer students accepted for terms other than fall. In fall 1993, 35% of all new students were transfers into all classes. Minimum 2.0 GPA recommended. Lowest course grade accepted is "C." Maximum number of transferable credits is 68 semester hours. At least 32 semester hours must be completed at the college to receive degree.
**Admissions contact:** Kathleen Groskopf-Coon, M.Ed., Director of Admissions. 614 251-4500.

**FINANCIAL AID. Available aid:** Pell grants, SEOG, state scholarships and grants, school scholarships and grants, private scholarships and grants, academic merit scholarships, and athletic scholarships. Perkins Loans (NDSL), PLUS, and Stafford Loans (GSL). AMS and deferred payment plan. Institutional Payment Plan.
**Supporting data/closing dates:** FAFSA/FAF/FFS: Deadline is June 1. Notification of awards begins in February.
**Financial aid contact:** Cindy Diller, Director of Financial Aid. 614 251-4640. 9-5

## Ohio Northern University

**Ada, OH 45810** **419 772-2260**

**1994-95 Costs.** Tuition: $15,990. Room & board: $4,080. Fees, books, misc. academic expenses (school's estimate): $500.
**Enrollment.** Undergraduates: 1,387 men, 1,182 women (full-time). Freshman class: 2,615 applicants, 2,448 accepted, 669 enrolled. Graduate enrollment: 274 men, 121 women.
**Test score averages/ranges.** Average SAT scores: 500 verbal, 560 math. Range of SAT scores of middle 50%: 400-600 verbal, 400-700 math. Average ACT scores: 23 English, 23 math, 24 composite. Range of ACT scores of middle 50%: 21-25 English, 21-25 math.
**Faculty.** 158 full-time; 20 part-time. 78% of faculty holds doctoral degree. Student/faculty ratio: 13 to 1.
**Selectivity rating.** More competitive.

**PROFILE.** Ohio Northern, founded in 1871, is a church-affiliated university. Programs are offered through the Colleges of Arts and Sciences, Business Administration, Engineering, Pharmacy and Allied Health Sciences, and Law. Its 260-acre campus is located in Ada, in northwestern Ohio.

**Accreditation:** NCACS. Professionally accredited by the Accreditation Board for Engineering and Technology, the American Bar Association, the American Council on Pharmaceutical Education, the Association of American Law Schools, the National Association of Schools of Music.
**Religious orientation:** Ohio Northern University is affiliated with the United Methodist Church; one term of religion/theology required.
**Library:** Collections totaling over 448,939 volumes, 4,192 periodical subscriptions, and 446,084 microform items.
**Special facilities/museums:** Art gallery, performing arts center, language lab.
**Athletic facilities:** Gymnasium, field house, basketball, handball, tennis, and volleyball courts, swimming pool, aerobics and weight rooms, fitness lab, athletic fields.

**STUDENT BODY. Undergraduate profile:** 79% are state residents; 10% are transfers. 2% Asian-American, 2% Black, 1% Hispanic, 93% White, 2% Other. Average age of undergraduates is 20.
**Freshman profile:** 7% of freshmen who took SAT scored 700 or over on math; 4% scored 600 or over on verbal, 27% scored 600 or over on math; 28% scored 500 or over on verbal, 67% scored 500 or over on math; 78% scored 400 or over on verbal, 93% scored 400 or over on math; 97% scored 300 or over on verbal, 100% scored 300 or over on math. 32% of accepted applicants took SAT; 68% took ACT. 82% of freshmen come from public schools.
**Undergraduate achievement:** 78% of fall 1992 freshmen returned for fall 1993 term. 29% of students who completed a degree program went on to graduate study within one year.

**Foreign students:** 55 students are from out of the country. Countries represented include India, Kuwait, Saudi Arabia, Singapore, Thailand, and United Arab Emirates; 20 in all.

**PROGRAMS OF STUDY. Degrees:** B.A., B.F.A., B.Mus., B.S., B.S.Bus.Admin., B.S.Civil Eng., B.S.Elec.Eng., B.S.M.T., B.S.Mech.Eng., B.S.Pharm.

**Majors:** Accounting, Art, Biochemistry, Biology, Chemistry, Civil Engineering, Communication Arts, Computer Science, Criminal Justice, Economics, Electrical Engineering, Elementary Education, English, English/Writing, Environmental Studies, Finance, French, Health Education, Health/Physical Education, History, Industrial Technology, International Studies, Management, Marketing, Mathematics, Mechanical Engineering, Medical Technology, Music, Music Composition, Music Education, Music Performance, Musical Theatre, Pharmacy, Philosophy, Philosophy/Religion, Physical Education, Physics, Political Science, Printmaking, Psychology, Religion, Sociology, Spanish, Speech, Sports Management, Sports Medicine, Theatre.

**Distribution of degrees:** The majors with the highest enrollment are pharmacy, mechanical engineering, and elementary education; physics, health, and music performance have the lowest.

**Requirements:** General education requirement.

**Academic regulations:** Minimum 2.0 GPA must be maintained.

**Special:** Minors offered in most majors and in arts/engineering, arts/pharmacy, German, and writing. Double majors. Dual degrees. Independent study. Accelerated study. Pass/fail grading option. Internships. Cooperative education programs. Preprofessional programs in law, medicine, veterinary science, dentistry, theology, and pre-physical therapy. Combined degree program in pharmacy/law. 2-2 programs in engineering and industrial technology. Member of Indiana Consortium for International Programs. Cincinnati Council of World Affairs. Teacher certification in elementary, secondary, and special education. Certification in specific subject areas. Exchange program abroad in Korea (Dankook U). Study abroad also in France, Japan, Scotland, and Wales. ROTC and AFROTC at Bowling Green State U.

**STUDENT LIFE. Housing:** All freshmen and sophomores must live on campus. Coed, women's, and men's dorms. Sorority and fraternity housing. Honors housing. 70% of students live in college housing.

**Social atmosphere:** The student newspaper reports, "Many people complain there is nothing to do here, and others find much to do. It's all what one makes of it." Among the most popular student activities are Tunes on the Tundra in spring, weekly movies, quarterly plays, sports, the winter concert, and the artists' series films. Favorite student gathering spots include the Reagle Beagle, the Northern Freeze, Lima Mall, Ohio Theatre, the White Bear Inn, and the Ada Theatre.

**Services and counseling/handicapped student services:** Placement services. Health service. Teacher placement service. Personal and psychological counseling. Career and academic guidance services. Learning disabled services.

**Campus organizations:** Undergraduate student government. Student newspaper (Northern Review, published once/week). Literary magazine. Yearbook. Radio and TV stations. Band, chorus/choir, instrumental ensembles, orchestra, debating, community service, departmental, and professional groups, 181 organizations in all. Eight fraternities, all with chapter houses; four sororities, all with chapter houses. 35% of men join a fraternity. 35% of women join a sorority.

**Religious organizations:** Chancel Singers, Chapel Committee, Fellowship of Christian Athletes, Unlimited Sharing, Son's Rays, Youth Outreach, Puppets Personified.

**Minority/foreign student organizations:** Black Student Union, Student National Pharmaceutical Association. World Student Organization.

**ATHLETICS. Physical education requirements:** Three terms of physical education required.

**Intercollegiate competition:** 30% of students participate. Baseball (M), basketball (M,W), cheerleading (M,W), cross-country (M,W), diving (M,W), football (M), golf (M), soccer (M,W), softball (W), swimming (M,W), tennis (M,W), track and field (indoor) (M,W), track and field (outdoor) (M,W), volleyball (W), wrestling (M). Member of NCAA Division III, Ohio Athletic Conference.

**Intramural and club sports:** 50% of students participate. Intramural basketball, billiards, bowling, flashball, football, handball, racquetball, softball, swimming, volleyball. Men's club rugby.

**ADMISSIONS. Academic basis for candidate selection** (in order of priority): Secondary school record, class rank, standardized test scores, school's recommendation.

**Nonacademic basis for candidate selection:** Particular talent or ability is important. Character and personality, extracurricular participation, and alumni/ae relationship are considered.

**Requirements:** Graduation from secondary school is required; GED is accepted. 16 units and the following program of study are required: 4 units of English, 2 units of math, 2 units of lab science, 2 units of social studies, 2 units of history, 4 units of electives including 2 units of academic electives. Minimum 2.5 GPA, minimum composite ACT score of 20, and rank in top half of secondary school class required. 4 units of math required of applicants to College of Engineering and College of Pharmacy. SAT or ACT is required. Campus visit and interview recommended. No off-campus interviews.

**Procedure:** Take SAT or ACT by December of 12th year. Visit college for interview by March 1 of 12th year. Suggest filing application by March 1. Application deadline is August 1. Notification of admission on rolling basis. Reply is requested within 30 days of notification. $200 tuition deposit, refundable until May 1. Freshmen accepted for terms other than fall.

**Special programs:** Admission may be deferred one year. Credit and/or placement may be granted through CEEB Advanced Placement exams for scores of 3 or higher. Credit and/or placement may be granted through CLEP general and subject exams. Credit and placement may be granted through challenge exams. Early entrance/early admission program. Concurrent enrollment program.

**Transfer students:** Transfer students accepted for terms other than fall. In fall 1993, 10% of all new students were transfers into all classes. 371 transfer applications were received, 138 were accepted. Application deadline is August 1. Minimum 2.0 GPA required. Lowest course grade accepted is "C." Maximum number of transferable credits is 137 quarter hours. At least 45 quarter hours must be completed at the university to receive degree.

**Admissions contact:** Karen P. Condeni, M.S.Ed., Dean of Admission and Financial Aid. 419 772-2260.

**FINANCIAL AID. Available aid:** Pell grants, SEOG, state scholarships and grants, school scholarships and grants, private scholarships and grants, ROTC scholarships, and academic merit scholarships. Perkins Loans (NDSL), PLUS, Stafford Loans (GSL), Health Professions Loans, school loans, private loans, and SLS. University discount plan.

**Financial aid statistics:** In 1993-94, 95% of all undergraduate applicants received aid; 99% of freshman applicants. Average amounts of aid awarded freshmen: Scholarships and grants, $6,500; loans, $2,500.

**Supporting data/closing dates:** FAFSA: Accepted on rolling basis. FAF/FFS: Priority filing date is May 1; accepted on rolling basis. School's own aid application: Priority filing date is May 1; accepted on rolling basis. State aid form: Accepted on rolling basis. Notification of awards on rolling basis.

**Financial aid contact:** Wendell Schick, M.B.A., Director of Financial Aid. 419 772-2272.

**STUDENT EMPLOYMENT.** College Work/Study Program. Institutional employment. 33% of full-time undergraduates work on campus during school year. Students may expect to earn an average of $1,100 during school year. Off-campus part-time employment opportunities rated "good."

**COMPUTER FACILITIES.** 724 IBM/IBM-compatible, Macintosh/Apple, and RISC-/UNIX-based microcomputers; 586 are networked. Students may access Data General minicomputer/mainframe systems, Internet. Residence halls may be equipped with stand-alone microcomputers, networked microcomputers. Client/LAN operating systems include Apple/Macintosh, DOS, OS/2, UNIX/XENIX/AIX, Microsoft. Computer languages and software packages include Ada, BASIC, C, COBOL, FORTRAN, LISP, Lotus 1-2-3, Maple, MINITAB, Pascal, SPSS-X, WordPerfect. Computer facilities are available to all students.

**Fees:** None.

**GRADUATE CAREER DATA.** Graduate school percentages: 15% enter law school. 18% enter medical school. 13% enter graduate business programs. 9% enter graduate arts and sciences programs. 4% enter theological school/seminary. Highest graduate school enrollments: Ohio Northern U, Ohio State U, Bowling Green State, U of Michigan, U of Toledo. 53% of graduates choose careers in business and industry. Companies and businesses that hire graduates: Cooper Ind., Marathon, Ernst & Young, Rite-Aid, Phar-Mor, DuPont, ODOT.

**PROMINENT ALUMNI/AE.** Anthony Celebrezze, judge; Michael DeWine, lt. governor, Ohio.

# Ohio State University–Columbus

**Columbus, OH 43210-1200** **614 292-OHIO**

**1993-94 Costs.** Tuition: $2,940 (state residents), $8,871 (out-of-state). Room & board: $4,071. Fees, books, misc. academic expenses (school's estimate): $450.

**Enrollment.** Undergraduates: 16,418 men, 14,621 women (full-time). Freshman class: 15,076 applicants, 12,860 accepted, 5,330 enrolled. Graduate enrollment: 5,206 men, 5,725 women.

**Test score averages/ranges.** Range of SAT scores of middle 50%: 400-530 verbal, 450-610 math. Range of ACT scores of middle 50%: 19-26 English, 19-26 math.

**Faculty.** 2,968 full-time; 822 part-time. 95% of faculty holds highest degree in specific field. Student/faculty ratio: 14 to 1.

**Selectivity rating.** Less competitive.

**PROFILE.** Ohio State-Columbus, founded in 1870, is a public, comprehensive university. Programs are offered through the Colleges of Agriculture, Arts and Sciences, the Arts, Biological Sciences, Business, Dentistry, Education, Engineering, Human Ecology, Humanities, Law, Mathematical and Physical Sciences, Medicine, Nursing, Optometry, Pharmacy, Social and Behavioral Sciences, and Social Work; the Schools of Allied Medical Professions, Architecture, Music, Natural Resources, and Public Policy and Management; and the University College. Its 3,303-acre campus is located in Columbus.

**Accreditation:** NCACS.

**Religious orientation:** Ohio State University-Columbus is nonsectarian; no religious requirements.

**Library:** Collections totaling over 4,693,081 volumes, 33,010 periodical subscriptions, and 3,700,774 microform items.

**Special facilities/museums:** Zoology museum, art and photography galleries, nuclear research reactor, electroscience lab, biomedical engineering center.

**Athletic facilities:** Ice rink, tracks, football stadium, baseball, field hockey, football, lacrosse, soccer, and softball fields, swimming pool, gymnastics and wrestling rooms, weight rooms, gymnasiums, basketball arena, tennis courts.

**STUDENT BODY. Undergraduate profile:** 95% are state residents; 27% are transfers. 4% Asian-American, 7% Black, 2% Hispanic, 83% White, 4% Other. Average age of undergraduates is 21.

**Freshman profile:** 1% of freshmen who took SAT scored 700 or over on verbal, 8% scored 700 or over on math; 12% scored 600 or over on verbal, 29% scored 600 or over on math; 36% scored 500 or over on verbal, 62% scored 500 or over on math; 75% scored 400 or over on verbal, 87% scored 400 or over on math; 96% scored 300 or over on verbal, 98% scored 300 or over on math. 50% of accepted applicants took SAT; 88% took ACT.

**Undergraduate achievement:** 81% of fall 1992 freshmen returned for fall 1993 term. 21% of entering class graduated. 25% of students who completed a degree program immediately went on to graduate study.

**Foreign students:** 1,106 students are from out of the country. Countries represented include China, India, Indonesia, Japan, Korea, and Taiwan; 84 in all.

**PROGRAMS OF STUDY. Degrees:** B.A., B.A.Ed., B.A.Journ., B.F.A., B.Mus., B.Mus.Ed., B.S., B.S.Aero./Astro.Eng., B.S.Agri., B.S.Agri.Eng., B.S.Arch., B.S.Bus.Admin., B.S.Chem.Eng., B.S.Civil Eng., B.S.Comp.Sci., B.S.Dent.Hyg., B.S.Ed., B.S.Elec.Eng., B.S.Food Sci., B.S.Hosp.Mgmt., B.S.Indust.Design, B.S.Mech.Eng., B.S.Metal.Eng., B.S.Min.Eng., B.S.Nurs., B.S.Pharm., B.S.Soc.Work, B.S.Surv./Topog.

**Majors:** Accounting, Actuarial Sciences, Aeronautical/Astronautical Engineering, Agribusiness/Applied Economics, Agricultural Communications, Agricultural Education, Agricultural Engineering, Agricultural Systems Management, Agronomy, Ancient History/Classics, Animal/Dairy/Poultry Science, Animal Science, Anthropology, Arabic, Architecture, Art, Art Education, Astronomy, Aviation, Aviation in Engineering, Biochemistry, Biology, Black Studies, Ceramic Engineering, Chemistry, Chinese, Circulation Technology, Civil Engineering, Classics, Communication, Community Health Education, Computer/Information Sciences, Construction Systems Management, Criminology/Criminal Justice, Dairy Science, Dance, Dental Hygiene, Drama/Theatre Education, Economics, Economics/Business, Economics Education, Electrical Engineering, Elementary Education, Engineering Physics, English, Entomology, Environmental Communications/Interpretation, Environmental Science, Exercise Science Education, Family Relations/Human Development, Family Resource Management, Finance, Fisheries Management, Food Business Management, Food Science/Nutrition, Forestry, French, Geography, Geography Education, Geological Sciences, German, Health Education, Hebrew, History, History Education, History of Art, Home Economics Education, Honors Contract, Horticulture, Hospitality Management, Human Nutrition/Food Management, Human Resources, Industrial/Systems Engineering, Information Systems, Interior Space Design, International Business Administration, International Studies, Islamic Studies, Italian, Japanese, Jazz Studies, Jewish Studies, Journalism, Landscape Architecture, Linguistics, Mapping and Land Information Science, Marketing, Materials Science/Engineering, Mathematical Sciences, Mathematics, Mechanical Engineering, Medical Communications, Medical Dietetics, Medical Illustration, Medical Records Administration, Medical Technology, Medieval/Renaissance Studies, Metallurgical Engineering, Microbiology, Modern Greek, Molecular Genetics, Music, Music Education, Music History, Natural Resources, Nursing, Nutrition, Occupational Therapy, Orchestral Instrument, Parks/Recreation/Tourism Administration, Personalized Study Program, Pharmacy, Philosophy, Physical Therapy, Physics, Physiological Optics, Plant Biology, Plant Health Management, Political Science, Political Science Education, Portuguese, Poultry Science, Product Design, Production/Operations Management, Psychology, Radiologic Technology, Real Estate/Urban Analysis, Religious Studies, Respiratory Therapy, Risk Management/Insurance, Slavic Languages/Literatures, Social Studies Education, Social Work, Sociology, Sociology/Psychology Education, Spanish, Special Education, Special Major, Speech/Communication Education, Speech/Hearing Science, Sport/Leisure Studies, Statistics, Surveying, Sustainable Resource Management, Technical Education/Training, Technology Education, Theatre, Theory/Composition, Transportation/Logistics, Urban Forestry, Visual Communication Design, Voice, Welding Engineering, Wildlife Management, Women's Studies, Zoology.

**Distribution of degrees:** The majors with the highest enrollment are accounting, psychology, and education.

**Requirements:** General education requirement.

**Academic regulations:** Minimum 2.00 GPA must be maintained.

**Special:** Minors offered in many majors and in American studies, avian biology, East Asian languages/literatures, city/regional planning, crop science, classical Greek, cognitive science, exercise science, folklore, family relations/human development, hotel management, family resource management, human nutrition, international economic/social development, international studies, life sciences, Latin, natural resources management, Persian, plant pathology, plant improvement, resource economics, production agriculture, soil resources, turf grass management, Romanian, restaurant management, Russian, Serbo-Croatian, Scandinavian, textiles/clothing, surveying/mapping, Turkish, and Yiddish. Associate's degrees offered. Self-designed majors. Double majors. Dual degrees. Independent study. Accelerated study. Pass/fail grading option. Internships. Cooperative education programs. Graduate school at which undergraduates may take graduate-level courses. Preprofessional programs in law, medicine, veterinary science, dentistry, and optometry. Combined-degree programs offered in dentistry, arts and sciences, business, medicine, and veterinary medicine. Semester-away programs on individual basis. Teacher certification in early childhood, elementary, secondary, special education, and vo-tech education. Certification in specific subject areas. Study abroad in Brazil, Canada, China, Denmark, the Dominican Republic, France, Germany, Mexico, the former Soviet Republics, Spain, Sweden, and the United Kingdom. ROTC, NROTC, and AFROTC.

**Honors:** Phi Beta Kappa. Honors program. Honor societies.

**Academic Assistance:** Remedial reading, writing, math, and study skills. Nonremedial tutoring.

**STUDENT LIFE. Housing:** All freshmen under age 19 must live on campus unless living with family. Coed and women's dorms. Sorority and fraternity housing. School-owned/operated apartments. On-campus married-student housing. Cooperative housing. 19% of students live in college housing.

**Services and counseling/handicapped student services:** Placement services. Health service. Women's center. Day care. Counseling services for minority, military, veteran, and older students. Birth control, personal, and psychological counseling. Career and academic guidance services. Religious counseling. Physically disabled student services. Learning disabled program/services. Notetaking services. Tape recorders. Tutors. Reader services for the blind.

**Campus organizations:** Undergraduate student government. Student newspaper (Lantern, published once/day). Yearbook. Radio and TV stations. Concert and marching bands, jazz ensemble, vocal groups, dance groups, theatre, Fashion Guild, Flight Team, Boot and Saddle club, Centurion Drill Team, State College Democrats, State College Republicans, Council of Exceptional Children, athletic, departmental, and professional groups, 600 organizations in all. 35 fraternities, all with chapter houses; 24 sororities, all with chapter houses. 10% of men join a fraternity. 11% of women join a sorority.

**Religious organizations:** Adventist Christian Fellowship, Baptist Student Union, Campus Bible Study, Campus Crusade for Christ, Fellowship for Christian Athletes, Intervarsity Christian Fellowship, Christian Community Fellowship, Capital Bible Studies, Lutheran Student Movement, Navigators, Nichiren Shoshu of America, Maranatha Christian Church, numerous other religious groups.

**Minority/foreign student organizations:** Women and Minority Advocates, United Black World Week Committee, Black Law Student Association, Black Engineering Council, Black Arts Society, Black Greek Council, Black Student Fellowship, Black Music Student Association, Hispanic group, other minority student groups. International Student Association, Asian, Chinese, Indonesian, Korean, Malaysian, Pakistan, Singapore, Taiwanese, Turkish, and Ukrainian groups, Campus Committee on Latin America, Central African Association, French club, Hellenic Student Association, Hermandad Latina.

**ATHLETICS. Physical education requirements:** None.

**Intercollegiate competition:** 2% of students participate. Baseball (M), basketball (M,W), cheerleading (M,W), cross-country (M,W), diving (M,W), fencing (M,W), field hockey (W), football (M), golf (M,W), gymnastics (M,W), ice hockey (M), lacrosse (M), riflery (M,W), soccer (M), softball (W), swimming (M,W), tennis (M,W), track (indoor) (M,W), track (outdoor) (M,W), track and field (indoor) (M,W), track and field (outdoor) (M,W), volleyball (M,W), wrestling (M). Member of Big 10 Conference, NCAA Division I.

**Intramural and club sports:** 90% of students participate. Intramural aerobics, archery, badminton, basketball, bowling, canoeing, crew, fencing, football, golf, gymnastics, handball, ice skating, martial arts, platform tennis, racquetball, rugby, sailing, softball, squash, swimming, table tennis, track, volleyball, water polo, weight lifting, wrestling. Men's club archery, bowling, canoe/kayak, cheerleading, crew, martial arts, rugby. Women's club archery, bowling, canoe/kayak, cheerleading, crew, martial arts.

**ADMISSIONS. Academic basis for candidate selection** (in order of priority): Secondary school record, class rank, standardized test scores, school's recommendation, essay.

**Nonacademic basis for candidate selection:** Particular talent or ability is important. Extracurricular participation and geographical distribution are considered.

**Requirements:** Graduation from secondary school is required; GED is accepted. 16 units and the following program of study are required: 4 units of English, 3 units of math, 2 units of lab science, 2 units of foreign language, 2 units of social studies, 2 units of electives including 1 unit of academic electives. Portfolio required of art program applicants. Audition required of music program applicants. Conditional admission possible for applicants not meeting standard requirements. SAT or ACT is required. Campus visit recommended. No off-campus interviews.

**Procedure:** Take SAT or ACT by October of 12th year. Application deadline is February 15. Notification of admission on rolling basis but no later than March 31. Reply is required by May 1. Nonrefundable $50 acceptance fee which is not applied toward tuition. $130 refundable room deposit. Admissions may be deferred for one year under special circumstances. Freshmen accepted for terms other than fall.

**Special programs:** Credit and/or placement may be granted through CEEB Advanced Placement exams for scores of 4 or higher. Credit may be granted through CLEP subject exams, DANTES exams, and military and life experience. Credit and placement may be granted through challenge exams. Early entrance/early admission program. Concurrent enrollment program.

**Transfer students:** Transfer students accepted for terms other than fall. In fall 1993, 27% of all new students were transfers into all classes. 4,811 transfer applications were received, 3,469 were accepted. Application deadline is June 25 for fall; February 1 for spring. Minimum 2.0 GPA required. Lowest course grade accepted is "C-." At least 45 quarter hours must be completed at the university to receive degree.

**Admissions contact:** James J. Mager, Ph.D., Director of Admissions and Financial Aid. 614 292-3980.

**FINANCIAL AID. Available aid:** Pell grants, SEOG, state scholarships and grants, school scholarships and grants, private scholarships and grants, ROTC scholarships, academic merit scholarships, and athletic scholarships. Perkins Loans (NDSL), PLUS, Stafford Loans (GSL), NSL, Health Professions Loans, school loans, private loans, and SLS. Tuition Plan Inc..

**Procedure:** Take SAT or ACT by October of 12th year. Suggest filing application by October 1. Application deadline is July 1. Notification of admission on rolling basis. Applicants must accept offer of admission by first day of term. Nonrefundable $50 acceptance fee which is not applied to tuition. Freshmen accepted for terms other than fall.

**Special programs:** Admission may be deferred one year. Credit and/or placement may be granted through CEEB Advanced Placement exams for scores of 3 or higher. Credit and/or placement may be granted through CLEP subject exams.

**Transfer students:** Transfer students accepted for terms other than fall. In fall 1993, 30% of all new students were transfers into all classes. 173 transfer applications were received, 160 were accepted. Application deadline is July 1. Minimum 2.0 GPA required. Lowest course grade accepted is "C-."

**Admissions contact:** Henry Thomas, M.A., Director of Admissions and Financial Aid. 419 755-4226.

**FINANCIAL AID. Available aid:** Pell grants, SEOG, state grants, school scholarships and grants, private scholarships and grants, ROTC scholarships, and academic merit scholarships. Perkins Loans (NDSL), PLUS, Stafford Loans (GSL), school loans, and SLS. Tuition Plan Inc..

**Supporting data/closing dates:** FAFSA: Priority filing date is February 15. School's own aid application: Priority filing date is February 15. Notification of awards on rolling basis.

**PROMINENT ALUMNI/AE.** Faye Wattleton, president, Planned Parenthood; Paul Flory, Nobel Prize-winning physicist; Archie Griffin, two-time Heisman trophy winner; Fred Sullivan, TV producer; James Thurber, author; Richard Lewis, comedian.

# Ohio State University–Lima

Lima, OH 45804 — 419 221-1641

**1993-94 Costs.** Tuition: $2,835 (state residents), $8,766 (out-of-state). Fees, books, misc. academic expenses (school's estimate): $507.

**Enrollment.** Undergraduates: 380 men, 511 women (full-time). Freshman class: 537 applicants, 526 accepted, 364 enrolled. Graduate enrollment: 17 men, 140 women.

**Test score averages/ranges.** Range of SAT scores of middle 50%: 393-468 verbal, 403-558 math. Range of ACT scores of middle 50%: 17-23 English, 17-23 math.

**Faculty.** 57 full-time; 35 part-time. 85% of faculty holds highest degree in specific field. Student/faculty ratio: 15 to 1.

**Selectivity rating.** Less competitive.

**PROFILE.** Ohio State-Lima, founded in 1960, is a public university focusing on elementary education. Its 565-acre campus is located in Lima, 80 miles south of Toledo.

**Accreditation:** NCACS. Professionally accredited by the National Council for Accreditation of Teacher Education.

**Religious orientation:** Ohio State University - Lima is nonsectarian; no religious requirements.
**Library:** Collections totaling over 82,054 volumes, 584 periodical subscriptions, and 8,703 microform items.
**Athletic facilities:** Gymnasium, baseball field, intramural field.

**STUDENT BODY. Undergraduate profile:** 26% are transfers. 1% Asian-American, 3% Black, 1% Hispanic, .5% Native American, 94% White, .5% Other. Average age of undergraduates is 22.
**Freshman profile:** 10% of freshmen who took SAT scored 600 or over on math; 24% scored 500 or over on verbal, 43% scored 500 or over on math; 76% scored 400 or over on verbal, 86% scored 400 or over on math; 100% scored 300 or over on verbal, 100% scored 300 or over on math. 6% of accepted applicants took SAT; 87% took ACT.
**Undergraduate achievement:** 51% of fall 1992 freshmen returned for fall 1993 term.

**PROGRAMS OF STUDY. Degrees:** B.S.Ed.
**Majors:** Elementary Education.
**Requirements:** General education requirement.
**Academic regulations:** Minimum 2.0 GPA must be maintained.
**Special:** Associate's degrees offered. Independent study. Pass/fail grading option. Graduate school at which undergraduates may take graduate-level courses. Teacher certification in early childhood and elementary education. Study abroad in China, England, France, Germany, Japan, the former Soviet Republics, and Spain. ROTC, NROTC, and AFROTC at Ohio State U at Columbus.
**Honors:** Honors program.
**Academic Assistance:** Remedial reading, writing, math, and study skills.

**ADMISSIONS. Academic basis for candidate selection** (in order of priority): Secondary school record, standardized test scores.
**Requirements:** Graduation from secondary school is required; GED is accepted. 15 units and the following program of study are required: 4 units of English, 3 units of math, 2 units of science including 1 unit of lab, 2 units of foreign language, 2 units of social studies, 2 units of academic electives. Electives should include 1 unit of fine arts. Admission for out-of-state applicants is competitive. Conditional admission possible for applicants not meeting standard requirements. ACT is required; SAT may be substituted. Campus visit recommended. No off-campus interviews.
**Procedure:** Take SAT or ACT by October of 12th year. Suggest filing application by February 15. Application deadline is July 1. Notification of admission on rolling basis. Nonrefundable $50 acceptance fee required. Freshmen accepted for terms other than fall.
**Special programs:** Credit and/or placement may be granted through CEEB Advanced Placement exams for scores of 3 or higher. Credit and/or placement may be granted through CLEP general and subject exams. Credit and placement may be granted through ACT PEP and challenge exams. Early entrance/early admission program. Concurrent enrollment program.
**Transfer students:** Transfer students accepted for terms other than fall. In fall 1993, 26% of all new students were transfers into all classes. 191 transfer applications were received, 157 were accepted. Application deadline is July 1 for fall; March 1 for spring. Minimum 2.0 GPA required. Lowest course grade accepted is "C-." At least 45 quarter hours must be completed at the university to receive degree.
**Admissions contact:** Cynthia Spiers, Director of Admissions. 419 221-1641, extension 264.

**FINANCIAL AID. Available aid:** Pell grants, SEOG, state scholarships and grants, school scholarships, private scholarships and grants, and academic merit scholarships. Perkins Loans (NDSL), PLUS, Stafford Loans (GSL), school loans, and SLS. Tuition Plan Inc..
**Supporting data/closing dates:** FAFSA: Priority filing date is February 15. School's own aid application: Priority filing date is February 15; accepted on rolling basis. Notification of awards begins April 1.
**Financial aid contact:** Gary D. Weaver, M.A., Director of Financial Aid. 419 221-1641, extension 299.

## Ohio State University–Mansfield

**Mansfield, OH 44906** — **419 755-4011**

**1993-94 Costs.** Tuition: $2,835 (state residents), $8,766 (out-of-state). Housing: None. Fees, books, misc. academic expenses (school's estimate): $450.
**Enrollment.** Undergraduates: 369 men, 503 women (full-time). Freshman class: 575 applicants, 554 accepted, 376 enrolled. Graduate enrollment: 23 men, 83 women.
**Test score averages/ranges.** Range of SAT scores of middle 50%: 363-503 verbal, 335-553 math. Range of ACT scores of middle 50%: 17-22 English, 17-22 math.
**Faculty.** 41 full-time; 31 part-time. 50% of faculty holds doctoral degree. Student/faculty ratio: 12 to 1.
**Selectivity rating.** Less competitive.

**PROFILE.** Ohio State-Mansfield, founded in 1958, is a public university focusing on elementary education. Its 600-acre campus is located in Mansfield, 60 miles southeast of Cleveland.

**Accreditation:** NCACS. Professionally accredited by the National Council for Accreditation of Teacher Education.
**Religious orientation:** Ohio State University-Mansfield is nonsectarian; no religious requirements.
**Library:** Collections totaling over 38,874 volumes, 410 periodical subscriptions, and 17,559 microform items.
**Special facilities/museums:** Art gallery, archives and reading room, elementary education suite.
**Athletic facilities:** Gymnasium, weight room, tennis courts, softball diamond, football fields.

**STUDENT BODY. Undergraduate profile:** 30% are transfers. 1% Asian-American, 3% Black, 1% Hispanic, 1% Native American, 91% White, 3% Other. Average age of undergraduates is 22.
**Freshman profile:** 7% of freshmen who took SAT scored 700 or over on math; 1% scored 600 or over on verbal, 10% scored 600 or over on math; 27% scored 500 or over on verbal, 39% scored 500 or over on math; 62% scored 400 or over on verbal, 58% scored 400 or over on math; 88% scored 300 or over on verbal, 90% scored 300 or over on math. 8% of accepted applicants took SAT; 86% took ACT.
**Undergraduate achievement:** 53% of fall 1992 freshmen returned for fall 1993 term.
**Foreign students:** One student is from out of the country.

**PROGRAMS OF STUDY. Degrees:** B.S.Ed.
**Majors:** Elementary Education.
**Requirements:** General education requirement.
**Academic regulations:** Minimum 2.0 GPA must be maintained.
**Special:** Associate's degrees offered. Double majors. Cooperative education programs. Teacher certification in early childhood and elementary education. Qualified undergraduate students may take graduate-level classes through Ohio State U at Columbus. Study abroad available through Ohio State U at Columbus. ROTC, NROTC, and AFROTC at Ohio State U at Columbus
**Honors:** Honors program.
**Academic Assistance:** Remedial math. Nonremedial tutoring.

**ADMISSIONS. Academic basis for candidate selection** (in order of priority): Secondary school record, standardized test scores, class rank, school's recommendation.
**Requirements:** Graduation from secondary school is required; GED is accepted. 15 units and the following program of study are required: 4 units of English, 3 units of math, 2 units of lab science, 2 units of foreign language, 2 units of social studies, 2 units of electives. Electives must include 1 unit of fine arts. Admission for out-of-state applicants is competitive. SAT or ACT is recommended. ACH recommended. Campus visit and interview recommended. No off-campus interviews.

## Ohio State University–Marion

**Marion, OH 43302** — **614 389-6786**

**1993-94 Costs.** Tuition: $2,835 (state residents), $8,766 (out-of-state). Housing: None. Fees, books, misc. academic expenses (school's estimate): $450.
**Enrollment.** Undergraduates: 381 men, 357 women (full-time). Freshman class: 490 applicants, 460 accepted, 293 enrolled. Graduate enrollment: 25 women.
**Test score averages/ranges.** Range of SAT scores of middle 50%: 360-445 verbal, 370-520 math. Range of ACT scores of middle 50%: 17-22 English, 16-21 math.
**Faculty.** 30 full-time; 45 part-time. 54% of faculty holds doctoral degree. Student/faculty ratio: 20 to 1.
**Selectivity rating.** Noncompetitive.

**PROFILE.** Ohio State-Marion, founded in 1958, is a public university focusing on elementary education. Its 180-acre campus is located in Marion, 50 miles north of Columbus.

**Accreditation:** NCACS. Professionally accredited by the National Council for Accreditation of Teacher Education.
**Religious orientation:** Ohio State University-Marion is nonsectarian; no religious requirements.
**Library:** Collections totaling over 36,764 volumes, 322 periodical subscriptions, and 2,906 microform items.
**Athletic facilities:** Gymnasium, swimming pool, athletic fields, weight room, indoor rock climbing wall.

**STUDENT BODY. Undergraduate profile:** 96% are state residents; 29% are transfers. 1% Asian-American, 7% Black, 2% Hispanic, 1% Native American, 88% White, 1% Other. Average age of undergraduates is 23.
**Freshman profile:** 3% of freshmen who took SAT scored 600 or over on verbal, 9% scored 600 or over on math; 15% scored 500 or over on verbal, 36% scored 500 or over on math; 59% scored 400 or over on verbal, 68% scored 400 or over on math; 97% scored 300 or over on verbal, 97% scored 300 or over on math. 12% of accepted applicants took SAT; 71% took ACT.
**Undergraduate achievement:** 50% of fall 1992 freshmen returned for fall 1993 term.

**PROGRAMS OF STUDY. Degrees:** B.S.Ed.
**Majors:** Elementary Education.
**Requirements:** General education requirement.
**Academic regulations:** Minimum 2.0 GPA must be maintained.
**Special:** Associate's degrees offered. Pass/fail grading option. Graduate school at which undergraduates may take graduate-level courses. Teacher certification in early childhood and elementary education. Study abroad in China, England, France, Germany, Japan, the former Soviet Republics, Spain, and other countries available through Ohio State U at Columbus. ROTC, NROTC, and AFROTC at Ohio State U at Columbus.
**Honors:** Honors program.
**Academic Assistance:** Remedial reading, writing, math, and study skills.

**ADMISSIONS.**
**Requirements:** Graduation from secondary school is recommended; GED is accepted. 15 units and the following program of study are required: 4 units of English, 3 units of math, 2 units of lab science, 2 units of foreign language, 2 units of social studies, 2 units of electives. Electives should include 1 unit of fine arts. Admission is competitive for out-of-state applicants. Conditional admission possible for applicants not meeting standard requirements. ACT is recommended; SAT may be substituted. No off-campus interviews.
**Procedure:** Take SAT or ACT by October of 12th year. Application deadline is July 1. Notification of admission on rolling basis. Nonrefundable $50 acceptance fee which is not applied to tuition. Freshmen accepted for terms other than fall.
**Special programs:** Credit and/or placement may be granted through CEEB Advanced Placement exams for scores of 3 or higher. Credit and/or placement may be granted through CLEP general and subject exams. Credit and placement may be granted through ACT PEP and challenge exams.

**Transfer students:** Transfer students accepted for terms other than fall. In fall 1993, 29% of all new students were transfers into all classes. 131 transfer applications were received, 117 were accepted. Application deadline is July 1. Minimum 2.0 GPA required. Lowest course grade accepted is "C-." At least 45 quarter hours must be completed at the university to receive degree.
**Admissions contact:** Becky Vanderlind, M.A., Admissions Officer. 614 389-2361.

**FINANCIAL AID. Available aid:** Pell grants, SEOG, state scholarships and grants, and private grants. Stafford Loans (GSL) and state loans. Tuition Plan Inc.
**Supporting data/closing dates:** FAFSA: Priority filing date is March 1. School's own aid application: Priority filing date is March 1. Notification of awards on rolling basis.
**Financial aid contact:** Dixie Strawser, M.A., Financial Aid Secretary. 614 389-2361.

# Ohio State University–Newark

**Newark, OH 43055** **614 366-3321**

**1993-94 Costs.** Tuition: $2,835 (state residents), $8,766 (out-of-state). Housing: None. Fees, books, misc. academic expenses (school's estimate): $507.
**Enrollment.** Undergraduates: 479 men, 658 women (full-time). Freshman class: 644 applicants, 616 accepted, 370 enrolled. Graduate enrollment: 7 men, 81 women.
**Test score averages/ranges.** Range of SAT scores of middle 50%: 370-510 verbal, 390-550 math. Range of ACT scores of middle 50%: 17-23 English, 16-22 math.
**Faculty.** 49 full-time; 61 part-time. 56% of faculty holds doctoral degree. Student/faculty ratio: 14 to 1.
**Selectivity rating.** Less competitive.

**PROFILE.** Ohio State-Newark, founded in 1957, is a public university focusing on education. Its 150-acre campus is located in Newark, 30 miles east of Columbus.

**Accreditation:** NCACS. Professionally accredited by the National Council for Accreditation of Teacher Education.
**Religious orientation:** Ohio State University-Newark is nonsectarian; no religious requirements.
**Library:** Collections totaling over 46,388 volumes, 427 periodical subscriptions, and 15,481 microform items.
**Athletic facilities:** Gymnasium with practice and game court, weight room, training room, softball fields, flag football field, tennis courts.

**STUDENT BODY. Undergraduate profile:** 90% are state residents; 23% are transfers. 1% Asian-American, 2% Black, 1% Hispanic, 1% Native American, 93% White, 2% Other. Average age of undergraduates is 22.
**Freshman profile:** 5% of freshmen who took SAT scored 700 or over on math; 3% scored 600 or over on verbal, 14% scored 600 or over on math; 28% scored 500 or over on verbal, 39% scored 500 or over on math; 66% scored 400 or over on verbal, 71% scored 400 or over on math; 95% scored 300 or over on verbal, 95% scored 300 or over on math. 21% of accepted applicants took SAT; 74% took ACT.
**Undergraduate achievement:** 54% of fall 1992 freshmen returned for fall 1993 term.
**Foreign students:** One student is from out of the country.

**PROGRAMS OF STUDY. Degrees:** B.S.Ed.
**Majors:** Education.
**Requirements:** General education requirement.
**Academic regulations:** Minimum 2.0 GPA must be maintained.
**Special:** Minors offered. Associate's degrees offered. Cooperative education programs. Graduate school at which undergraduates may take graduate-level courses. Semester-away programs available through Columbus campus. Teacher certification in elementary education. Study abroad available through Ohio St U at Columbus. ROTC, NROTC, and AFROTC at Ohio State U at Columbus.
**Honors:** Honors program. Honor societies.
**Academic Assistance:** Remedial reading, writing, math, and study skills. Nonremedial tutoring.

**STUDENT LIFE. Housing:** Commuter campus; no student housing.
**Services and counseling/handicapped student services:** Placement services. Day care. Counseling services for minority and older students. Personal counseling. Academic guidance services. Physically disabled student services. Learning disabled services. Note-taking services. Tape recorders. Tutors. Reader services for the blind.
**Campus organizations:** Undergraduate student government.
**Religious organizations:** Campus Ministry.
**Minority/foreign student organizations:** Minority student group.

**ATHLETICS. Physical education requirements:** None.
**Intercollegiate competition:** Member of Ohio Regional Campus Conference.
**Intramural and club sports:** Intramural aerobics, basketball, bowling, flag football, golf, racquetball, softball, tennis, volleyball, weight lifting. Men's club baseball, basketball, cheerleading, football, golf, lacrosse, tennis. Women's club baseball, basketball, cheerleading, golf, softball, tennis.

**ADMISSIONS. Academic basis for candidate selection** (in order of priority): Class rank, secondary school record.
**Nonacademic basis for candidate selection:** Extracurricular participation is emphasized. Particular talent or ability is important.
**Requirements:** Graduation from secondary school is required; GED is accepted. 15 units and the following program of study are required: 4 units of English, 3 units of math, 2 units of lab science, 2 units of foreign language, 2 units of social studies, 2 units of electives. Electives should include one unit of fine arts. Admission for out-of-state applicants is competitive. Conditional admission possible for applicants not meeting standard requirements. SAT or ACT is required. Campus visit and interview recommended. No off-campus interviews.
**Procedure:** Take SAT or ACT by October of 12th year. Suggest filing application by April 1. Application deadline is July 1. Notification of admission on rolling basis. Reply is required by May 1. Nonrefundable $50 acceptance fee which is not applied to tuition. Freshmen accepted for terms other than fall.
**Special programs:** Credit and/or placement may be granted through CEEB Advanced Placement exams for scores of 4 or higher. Credit and/or placement may be granted through CLEP general and subject exams. Placement may be granted through challenge exams. Concurrent enrollment program.
**Transfer students:** Transfer students accepted for terms other than fall. In fall 1993, 23% of all new students were transfers into all classes. 186 transfer applications were received, 161 were accepted. Application deadline is July 1 for fall; March 1 for spring. Minimum 2.0 GPA required. Lowest course grade accepted is "C." At least 45 credit hours must be completed at the university to receive degree.
**Admissions contact:** Ann Donahue, M.A., Director of Admissions. 614 366-9333.

**FINANCIAL AID. Available aid:** Pell grants, SEOG, state grants, school scholarships and grants, private scholarships, and academic merit scholarships. Perkins Loans (NDSL), PLUS, Stafford Loans (GSL), and SLS.
**Supporting data/closing dates:** FAFSA: Priority filing date is March 1; deadline is April 1. School's own aid application: Priority filing date is March 1; deadline is April 1. State aid form: Priority filing date is April 1. Notification of awards begins April 15.
**Financial aid contact:** Robert Noble, Financial Aid Coordinator. 614 366-9328.

**STUDENT EMPLOYMENT.** College Work/Study Program. Institutional employment. Students may expect to earn an average of $2,000 during school year. Off-campus part-time employment opportunities rated "good."

**COMPUTER FACILITIES.** 36 IBM/IBM-compatible and Macintosh/Apple microcomputers; all are networked. Computer languages and software packages include Pascal, PC-Write, several math packages. Computer facilities are available to all students.
**Fees:** None.
**Hours:** 8 AM-8 PM (M-F).
**Supporting data/closing dates:** FAFSA: Priority filing date is February 15. School's own aid application: Priority filing date is February 15. Notification of awards begins April 15.
**Financial aid contact:** James J. Mager, Ph.D., Director of Admissions and Financial Aid. 614 292-0300.

**STUDENT EMPLOYMENT.** College Work/Study Program. Institutional employment. 30% of full-time undergraduates work on campus during school year. Off-campus part-time employment opportunities rated "excellent."

**COMPUTER FACILITIES.** 1,110 IBM/IBM-compatible and Macintosh/Apple microcomputers; 1,000 are networked. Students may access Digital, Hewlett-Packard, IBM, SUN minicomputer/mainframe systems, BITNET, Internet. Residence halls may be equipped with networked microcomputers. Client/LAN operating systems include Apple/Macintosh. Computer languages and software packages include Assembler, FORTRAN, Mathematica, Pascal, SAS, SPSS; database, spreadsheet, word processing packages; 50 in all. Computer facilities are available to all students.
**Fees:** Varied computer fees charged by some departments.
**Hours:** 24 hours.

6-1 9-6

# Ohio University

**Athens, OH 45701-2979** **614 593-1000**

**1993-94 Costs.** Tuition: $3,370 (state residents), $7,250 (out-of-state). Room: $1,944. Board: $2,013. Fees, books, misc. academic expenses (school's estimate): $500.
**Enrollment.** Undergraduates: 6,831 men, 7,972 women (full-time). Freshman class: 11,023 applicants, 8,298 accepted, 3,183 enrolled. Graduate enrollment: 1,593 men, 1,295 women.
**Test score averages/ranges.** Average SAT scores: 473 verbal, 520 math. Range of SAT scores of middle 50%: 420-530 verbal, 460-580 math. Average ACT scores: 23 English, 22 math, 24 composite. Range of ACT scores of middle 50%: 21-26 English, 20-25 math.
**Faculty.** 786 full-time; 173 part-time. 87% of faculty holds highest degree in specific field. Student/faculty ratio: 18 to 1.
**Selectivity rating.** Competitive.

**PROFILE.** Ohio University, founded in 1804, is a public, comprehensive institution. Programs are offered through the Colleges of Arts and Sciences, Business Administration, Communication, Education, Engineering and Technology, Fine Arts, Health and Human Services, Osteopathic Medicine, Honors Tutorial, and University College. The main buildings on campus are of 19th century Georgian-style architecture, one of which has been designated a National Historic Landmark. The 1,300-acre campus is located in Athens, 75 miles southeast of Columbus.

**Accreditation:** NCACS. Professionally accredited by the Accreditation Board for Engineering and Technology, the Accrediting Council on Education in Journalism and Mass Communication, the American Assembly of Collegiate Schools of Business, the American Dietetic Association, the American Home Economics Association, the American Osteopathic Association, the American Physical Therapy Association, the American Psychological Association, the Council on Social Work Education, the Foundation for Interior Design Education Research, the National Association of Schools of Art and Design, the National Association of Schools of Music, the National Council for Accreditation of Teacher Education, the National League for Nursing.
**Religious orientation:** Ohio University is nonsectarian; no religious requirements.
**Library:** Collections totaling over 1,600,000 volumes, 11,083 periodical subscriptions, and 2,000,000 microform items.
**Special facilities/museums:** Museum of American art, innovation center, nuclear accelerator, electron microscope.
**Athletic facilities:** Gymnasiums, swimming pool, track, basketball, racquetball, volleyball court, athletic fields, weight rooms, fitness trails.

**STUDENT BODY. Undergraduate profile:** 87% are state residents; 13% are transfers. 1% Asian-American, 4% Black, 1% Hispanic, 1% Native American, 91% White, 2% Foreign national. Average age of undergraduates is 21.

**Freshman profile:** 1% of freshmen who took SAT scored 700 or over on verbal, 2% scored 700 or over on math; 7% scored 600 or over on verbal, 19% scored 600 or over on math; 37% scored 500 or over on verbal, 60% scored 500 or over on math; 85% scored 400 or over on verbal, 92% scored 400 or over on math; 99% scored 300 or over on verbal, 99% scored 300 or over on math. 5% of freshmen who took ACT scored 30 or over on English, 4% scored 30 or over on math, 4% scored 30 or over on composite; 48% scored 24 or over on English, 39% scored 24 or over on math, 47% scored 24 or over on composite; 93% scored 18 or over on English, 91% scored 18 or over on math, 97% scored 18 or over on composite; 100% scored 12 or over on English, 100% scored 12 or over on math, 100% scored 12 or over on composite. 53% of accepted applicants took SAT; 88% took ACT. 86% of freshmen come from public schools.
**Undergraduate achievement:** 86% of fall 1992 freshmen returned for fall 1993 term. 60% of entering class graduated. 28% of students who completed a degree program went on to graduate study within one year.
**Foreign students:** 424 students are from out of the country. Countries represented include Canada, Hong Kong, Japan, Korea, Malaysia, and Taiwan; 100 in all.

**PROGRAMS OF STUDY. Degrees:** A.B., B.Bus.Admin., B.Crim.Just., B.F.A., B.Mus., B.S., B.S.Airway Sci., B.S.Chem.Eng., B.S.Civil Eng., B.S.Comm., B.S.Elec.Eng., B.S.Env.Hlth., B.S.Hear./Speech Sci., B.S.Hlth., B.S.Indust.Sys.Eng., B.S.Indust.Tech., B.S.Journ., B.S.Mech.Eng., B.S.Nurs., B.S.Phys.Ed., B.S.Phys.Ther., B.S.Recr.Studies, B.Spec.Studies.
**Majors:** Accounting, Afro-American Studies, Airway Science, Anthropology, Art, Art Education, Biological Sciences, Bookkeeping/Basic Business, Business Administration, Business Economics, Business/Pre-Law, Chemical Engineering, Chemistry, Civil Engineering, Classical Languages, Communication, Communication Systems Management, Comprehensive Business Education, Computer Science, Creative Writing, Criminal Justice, Dance, Economics, Electrical Engineering, Elementary Education, Engineering Physics, English, Environmental/Plant Biology, Environmental Studies, Film, Finance, French, General Business, General Speech, Geography, Geological Sciences, German, Health Education, Health Sciences, Hearing/Speech, Hearing/Speech Science, History, Human/Consumer Sciences, Human Resource Management, Industrial/Systems Engineering, Industrial Technology, International Business, International Studies, Interpersonal Communication, Journalism, Latin, Linguistics, Management, Management Information Systems, Marketing, Mathematics, Mechanical Engineering, Microbiology, Modern Languages, Music, Music Education, Nursing, Operations, Philosophy, Physical Education, Physics, Political Science, Psychology, Recreation Studies, School Nursing, Science Education, Small Business Entrepreneurship, Social Studies Comprehensive, Social Work, Sociology, Spanish, Special Education, Specialized Studies, Sports Sciences, Telecommunications, Theatre, Visual Communication, Vocational Home Economics.
**Distribution of degrees:** The majors with the highest enrollment are biological sciences, journalism, and elementary education.
**Requirements:** General education requirement.
**Academic regulations:** Minimum 2.0 GPA must be maintained.
**Special:** Minors offered in most majors. Certificate programs offered in gerontology, international studies, political communication, and women's studies. Preparatory programs offered in dentistry, medicine, and veterinary science. Honors Tutorial College students typically finish degree in three years. Associate's degrees offered. Self-designed majors. Double majors. Dual degrees. Independent study. Accelerated study. Pass/fail grading option. Internships. Cooperative education programs. Graduate school at which undergraduates may take graduate-level courses. Preprofessional programs in law, medicine, veterinary science, pharmacy, dentistry, theology, optometry, and nursing. 2-3 natural resources program with U of Michigan. 2-3 forestry programs with Duke U and North Carolina State U. Member of Avionics Engineering Consortium. Teacher certification in early childhood, elementary, secondary, and special education. Certification in specific subject areas. Study abroad in over 50 countries, including Austria, Canada, England, France, Italy, Mexico, and Spain. ROTC and AFROTC.
**Honors:** Phi Beta Kappa. Honors program.
**Academic Assistance:** Remedial reading, writing, math, and study skills. Nonremedial tutoring.

**STUDENT LIFE. Housing:** All freshmen and sophomores must live on campus. Coed, women's, and men's dorms. Sorority and fraternity housing. School-owned/operated apartments. Off-campus privately-owned housing. Both on-campus and off-campus married-student housing. 60% of students live in college housing.
**Social atmosphere:** According to the Assistant Director of Admissions, "Fewer than 10 percent of our students leave campus on weekends. With over 250 clubs and organizations, numerous plays, concerts, and films, social life and cultural activities abound." Influential groups on campus include the University Program Council, the Ecology Club, and Greeks. The Front Room, Campus Coffee House, and War Memorial are popular on-campus hangouts; favorite off-campus bars and restaurants include the Pub, Pawpurrs, the Greenery, the CI, and Events. Halloween and Springfest are two of the year's most popular social events.
**Services and counseling/handicapped student services:** Placement services. Health service. Women's center. Day care. Counseling services for minority, military, veteran, and older students. Birth control, personal, and psychological counseling. Career and academic guidance services. Physically disabled student services. Learning disabled services. Tape recorders. Reader services for the blind.
**Campus organizations:** Undergraduate student government. Student newspaper (Post, published once/day). Literary magazine. Yearbook. Radio and TV stations. Musical and drama groups, dance groups, debating and speaking clubs, Athens Magazine, 338 organizations in all. 20 fraternities, no chapter houses; 14 sororities, no chapter houses. 18% of men join a fraternity. 21% of women join a sorority.
**Religious organizations:** Baptist Club, Bible Fellowship, Fellowship of Christian Athletes, Hillel Center, Newman Club, United Campus Ministry.
**Minority/foreign student organizations:** Black Student Union, Black Student Business Caucus, Black Student Prelaw/Premed Club, Communications Caucus. Foreign Student Club, International Understanding Club.

**ATHLETICS. Physical education requirements:** None.
**Intercollegiate competition:** 3% of students participate. Baseball (M), basketball (M,W), cheerleading (M,W), cross-country (M,W), diving (M,W), field hockey (W), football (M), golf (M), softball (W), swimming (M,W), track and field (indoor) (M,W), track and field (outdoor) (M,W), volleyball (W), wrestling (M). Member of Mid-America Conference, NCAA Division I.
**Intramural and club sports:** 78% of students participate. Intramural baseball, basketball, billiards, bocciball, bowling, broomball, cross-country, football, golf, horseshoes, racquetball, soccer, softball, swimming, table tennis, tennis, track, tug-o-war, volleyball, innertube water polo. Men's club boxing, cycling, horsemanship, ice hockey, juggling, lacrosse, martial arts, rugby, soccer, ultimate frisbee, volleyball, water polo, water skiing, weight lifting. Women's club cycling, figure skating, horsemanship, lacrosse, martial arts, rugby, soccer, ultimate frisbee, water skiing.

**ADMISSIONS. Academic basis for candidate selection** (in order of priority): Secondary school record, class rank, standardized test scores, school's recommendation.
**Nonacademic basis for candidate selection:** Particular talent or ability is important. Extracurricular participation and alumni/ae relationship are considered.
**Requirements:** Graduation from secondary school is required; GED is accepted. 17 units and the following program of study are recommended: 4 units of English, 3 units of math, 3 units of science, 2 units of foreign language, 3 units of social studies, 2 units of electives. Minimum composite ACT score of 21 (combined SAT score of 900) and rank in top three-tenths of secondary school class required. Portfolio required of art program applicants. Audition required of music program applicants. ACT is required; SAT may be substituted. Campus visit recommended. No off-campus interviews.
**Procedure:** Take SAT or ACT by January of 12th year. Visit college for interview by May 1 of 12th year. Application deadline is March 1. Notification of admission on rolling basis. Reply is required by May 1. $100 nonrefundable room deposit. Freshmen accepted for terms other than fall.
**Special programs:** Admission may be deferred one year. Credit and/or placement may be granted through CEEB Advanced Placement exams for scores of 3 or higher. Credit and/or placement may be granted through CLEP subject exams. Credit and placement may be granted through challenge exams and military and life experience. Early entrance/early admission program. Concurrent enrollment program.
**Transfer students:** Transfer students accepted for terms other than fall. In fall 1993, 13% of all new students were transfers into all classes. 1,309 transfer applications were received, 1,168 were accepted. Application deadline is June 1 for fall; March 1 for spring. Minimum 2.5 GPA required. Lowest course grade accepted is "C." At least 48 quarter hours must be completed at the university to receive degree.
**Admissions contact:** N. Kip Howard, M.A., Director of Admissions. 614 593-4100.

**FINANCIAL AID. Available aid:** Pell grants, SEOG, Federal Nursing Student Scholarships, state scholarships and grants, school scholarships and grants, private scholarships and grants, ROTC scholarships, academic merit scholarships, and athletic scholarships. Perkins Loans (NDSL), PLUS, Stafford Loans (GSL), NSL, state loans, and school loans. Tuition Plan Inc. and deferred payment plan.
**Financial aid statistics:** 42% of aid is not need-based. In 1992-93, 64% of all undergraduate applicants received aid; 78% of freshman applicants. Average amounts of aid awarded freshmen: Scholarships and grants, $2,200; loans, $2,625.
**Supporting data/closing dates:** FAFSA: Priority filing date is April 1; accepted on rolling basis. School's own aid application. State aid form: Priority filing date is June 1; accepted on rolling basis. Scholarship Application: Priority filing date is February 15. Notification of awards on rolling basis.
**Financial aid contact:** Carolyn Sabatino, M.S., Director of Financial Aid. 614 593-4141.

**STUDENT EMPLOYMENT.** College Work/Study Program. Institutional employment. 35% of full-time undergraduates work on campus during school year. Students may expect to earn an average of $1,100 during school year. Off-campus part-time employment opportunities rated "poor."

**COMPUTER FACILITIES.** 903 IBM/IBM-compatible and Macintosh/Apple microcomputers; 446 are networked. Students may access Digital, Hewlett-Packard, IBM, SUN minicomputer/mainframe systems, BITNET, Internet. Residence halls may be equipped with stand-alone microcomputers, networked microcomputers, networked terminals, modems. Client/LAN operating systems include Apple/Macintosh, DOS. All major computer languages and software packages available. Computer facilities are available to all students.
**Fees:** None.
**Hours:** 24 hours/day.

**GRADUATE CAREER DATA.** Graduate school percentages: 2% enter law school. 1% enter medical school. 1% enter dental school. 6% enter graduate business programs. 13% enter graduate arts and sciences programs. Highest graduate school enrollments: Ohio State U, Ohio U. 85% of graduates enter job market in field related to major within 6 months of graduation. 54% of graduates choose careers in business and industry. Companies and businesses that hire graduates: Dow Chemical, Ernst & Young, MCI, NCR, Price Waterhouse, Westinghouse.

**PROMINENT ALUMNI/AE.** George Voinovich, governor, Ohio; Clarence Page, columnist, *Chicago Tribune*; Richard Dean Anderson, actor, *MacGyver*.

8-28

# Ohio Wesleyan University

**Delaware, OH 43015** **614 369-4431**

**1994-95 Costs.** Tuition: $16,732. Room: $2,860. Board: $2,790. Fees, books, misc. academic expenses (school's estimate): $550.
**Enrollment.** Undergraduates: 871 men, 909 women (full-time). Freshman class: 2,190 applicants, 1,700 accepted, 458 enrolled.
**Test score averages/ranges.** Average SAT scores: 523 verbal, 580 math. Range of SAT scores of middle 50%: 480-580 verbal, 530-620 math. Average ACT scores: 24 English, 26 math, 25 composite. Range of ACT scores of middle 50%: 22-28 composite.
**Faculty.** 132 full-time; 35 part-time. 95% of faculty holds doctoral degree. Student/faculty ratio: 13 to 1.
**Selectivity rating.** More competitive.

**PROFILE.** Ohio Wesleyan, founded in 1842, is a church-affiliated, liberal arts university. Its 200-acre campus is located in Delaware, 24 miles north of Columbus.

**Accreditation:** NCACS. Professionally accredited by the National Association of Schools of Music, the National League for Nursing.
**Religious orientation:** Ohio Wesleyan University is affiliated with the United Methodist Church; no religious requirements.
**Library:** Collections totaling over 479,473 volumes, 1,061 periodical subscriptions, and 46,027 microform items.
**Special facilities/museums:** Observatory.
**Athletic facilities:** Gymnasium, basketball, handball, racquetball, squash, tennis, and volleyball courts, baseball, field hockey, football, lacrosse, and soccer fields, tracks, swimming pool, aerobics and weight rooms, stadium, field house, arena.

**STUDENT BODY. Undergraduate profile:** 49% are state residents; 4% are transfers. 2% Asian-American, 5% Black, 1% Hispanic, 1% Native American, 83% White, 8% Other. Average age of undergraduates is 20.
**Freshman profile:** 1% of freshmen who took SAT scored 700 or over on verbal, 12% scored 700 or over on math; 23% scored 600 or over on verbal, 44% scored 600 or over on math; 61% scored 500 or over on verbal, 86% scored 500 or over on math; 93% scored 400 or over on verbal, 99% scored 400 or over on math; 100% scored 300 or over on verbal, 100% scored 300 or over on math. 15% of freshmen who took ACT scored 30 or over on composite; 65% scored 24 or over on composite; 97% scored 18 or over on composite; 100% scored 12 or over on composite. 83% of accepted applicants took SAT; 56% took ACT. 72% of freshmen come from public schools.
**Undergraduate achievement:** 83% of fall 1992 freshmen returned for fall 1993 term. 72% of entering class graduated. 30% of students who completed a degree program immediately went on to graduate study.
**Foreign students:** 148 students are from out of the country. Countries represented include India, Japan, Malaysia, Mexico, and Pakistan; 50 in all.

**PROGRAMS OF STUDY. Degrees:** B.A., B.F.A., B.Mus., B.S.
**Majors:** Accounting, Anthropology, Art, Astronomy, Biochemistry, Black World, Botany/Bacteriology, Chemistry, Chemistry/Commerce, Classical Civilization, Computing Science, Economics/Management, Education, English, Environmental Science, Fine Arts, French, Genetics, Geology/Geography, German, History, Humanities/Classics, International Business Management, International Studies, Journalism/Broadcast Journalism, Mathematical Statistics, Microbiology, Music, Music Education, Philosophy, Physical Education, Physics, Politics/Government, Psychology, Religion, Sociology/Anthropology, Spanish, Theatre, Urban World, Women's Studies, Zoology.
**Distribution of degrees:** The majors with the highest enrollment are economics/management, politics/government, and biological sciences.
**Requirements:** General education requirement.
**Academic regulations:** Minimum 2.0 GPA must be maintained.
**Special:** Minors offered in sports/business, marketing/advertising, and political journalism. Self-designed majors. Double majors. Independent study. Accelerated study. Internships. Graduate school at which undergraduates may take graduate-level courses. Preprofessional programs in law, medicine, veterinary science, dentistry, and physical therapy. 3-2 engineering programs with Caltech, Case Western Reserve U, Georgia Tech, Ohio State U, Polytech U, and Rensselaer Polytech Inst. Member of Great Lakes Colleges Association. Washington Semester and UN Semester. Arts Program in New York. Newberry Library Program in the Humanities (Illinois). Oak Ridge Science Semester (Tennessee). Philadelphia Urban Semester. Other semester-away programs available. Exchange program with Spelman Coll. Teacher certification in early childhood, elementary, and secondary education. Study abroad in Germany, Japan, and other countries. AFROTC at Ohio State U at Columbus.
**Honors:** Phi Beta Kappa. Honors program. Honor societies.
**Academic Assistance:** Remedial writing. Nonremedial tutoring.

**STUDENT LIFE. Housing:** All unmarried students under age 21 must live on campus unless living near campus with relatives. Coed and women's dorms. Fraternity housing. School-owned/operated apartments. 94% of students live in college housing.
**Social atmosphere:** Students gather at fraternities on campus and at local bars and theatres off campus. According to the student newspaper, Greeks are the most influential group on campus. Favorite events are Homecoming, the President's Christmas Ball, soccer games, and fraternity parties.
**Services and counseling/handicapped student services:** Placement services. Health service. Women's center. Counseling services for minority students. Personal and psychological counseling. Career and academic guidance services. Religious counseling. Physically disabled student services. Learning disabled services. Tutors.
**Campus organizations:** Undergraduate student government. Student newspaper (Transcript, published once/week). Literary magazine. Yearbook. Radio and TV stations. Bands and ensembles, glee club, other singing groups, drama group, Orchesis, President's Club, Habitat for Humanity, tutoring group, film/performance/lecture series, departmental, professional, and special-interest groups, 110 organizations in all. 13 fraternities, 12 chapter houses; eight sororities, seven chapter houses. 50% of men join a fraternity. 40% of women join a sorority.
**Religious organizations:** Campus Ministry, Christian Fellowship, Hillel, Baptist, Buddhist, Catholic, and Methodist groups.
**Minority/foreign student organizations:** Sisters United, Student Union on Black Awareness, House of Black Culture, Alpha Kappa Alpha, Alpha Phi Alpha, Delta Sigma Theta, Omega Psi Phi. Horizons International, International House, Tauheed.

**ATHLETICS. Physical education requirements:** None.
**Intercollegiate competition:** 30% of students participate. Baseball (M), basketball (M,W), cheerleading (M,W), cross-country (M,W), diving (M,W), field hockey (W), football (M), golf (M), lacrosse (M,W), sailing (M,W), soccer (M,W), swimming (M,W), tennis (M,W), track (indoor) (M,W), track (outdoor) (M,W), track and field (indoor) (M,W), track and field (outdoor) (M,W), volleyball (W). Member of Great Lakes Conference, NCAA Division III, North Coast Athletic Conference.
**Intramural and club sports:** 73% of students participate. Intramural badminton, basketball, cross-country, flag football, golf, handball, indoor soccer, lacrosse, racquetball, soccer, softball, squash, swimming, tennis, volleyball.

**ADMISSIONS. Academic basis for candidate selection** (in order of priority): Secondary school record, school's recommendation, class rank, standardized test scores.
**Nonacademic basis for candidate selection:** Character and personality, extracurricular participation, particular talent or ability, and alumni/ae relationship are emphasized. Geographical distribution is important.
**Requirements:** Graduation from secondary school is required; GED is accepted. 16 units and the following program of study are recommended: 4 units of English, 3 units of math, 1 unit of science, 2 units of foreign language, 1 unit of social studies, 1 unit of history, 4 units of electives. Audition required of music program applicants. SAT or ACT is required. Campus visit and interview recommended. Off-campus interviews available with admissions and alumni representatives.
**Procedure:** Take SAT or ACT by mid-January of 12th year. Suggest filing application by February 1. Application deadline is March 1. Notification of admission by April 1. Reply is required by May 1. Freshmen accepted for terms other than fall.
**Special programs:** Admission may be deferred one year. Early decision program. Early action/notification program. In fall 1993, 288 applied for early decision and 275 were accepted. Deadline for applying for early decision is May 1.
**Transfer students:** Transfer students accepted for terms other than fall. In fall 1993, 4% of all new students were transfers into all classes. 63 transfer applications were received, 42 were accepted. Application deadline is July 30 for fall; December 1 for spring. Minimum 2.5 GPA recommended. Lowest course grade accepted is "C."
**Admissions contact:** Donald Bishop, Ph.D., Dean for Enrollment Management. 614 368-3020.

**FINANCIAL AID. Available aid:** Pell grants, SEOG, Federal Nursing Student Scholarships, state grants, school scholarships and grants, private scholarships, academic merit scholarships, and aid for undergraduate foreign students. AFROTC scholarships. Perkins Loans (NDSL), PLUS, Stafford Loans (GSL), Health Professions Loans, school loans, private loans, and SLS. Tuition Plan Inc., Knight Tuition Plans, and AMS.
**Financial aid statistics:** In 1993-94, 100% of all undergraduate applicants received aid; 100% of freshman applicants. Average amounts of aid awarded freshmen: Scholarships and grants, $9,500.
**Supporting data/closing dates:** FAFSA/FAF: Priority filing date is February 15; deadline is March 15. Income tax forms: Priority filing date is April 1; deadline is May 15. Notification of awards on rolling basis.
**Financial aid contact:** Pat Browne, Director of Financial Aid. 614 368-3050.

**STUDENT EMPLOYMENT.** College Work/Study Program. Institutional employment. 45% of full-time undergraduates work on campus during school year. Students may expect to earn an average of $1,200 during school year. Off-campus part-time employment opportunities rated "excellent."

**COMPUTER FACILITIES.** 130 IBM/IBM-compatible microcomputers; 110 are networked. Students may access Digital, IBM minicomputer/mainframe systems, BITNET, Internet. Residence halls may be equipped with networked microcomputers, networked terminals, modems. Client/LAN operating systems include Apple/Macintosh, DOS, UNIX/XENIX/AIX, Novell. Computer languages and software packages include BASIC, C, COBOL, FORTRAN, Pascal, SPSS; 10 in all. Computer facilities are available to all students.
**Fees:** Computer fee is included in tuition/fees.
**Hours:** 24 hours.

**GRADUATE CAREER DATA.** Graduate school percentages: 14% enter law school. 14% enter medical school. 6% enter dental school. 33% enter graduate business programs. 30% enter graduate arts and sciences programs. 3% enter theological school/seminary. Highest graduate school enrollments: Harvard U, Johns Hopkins U, Ohio State U, Stanford U, U of California at Berkeley, U of Michigan, U of Pennsylvania, U of Wisconsin. 60% of graduates choose careers in business and industry. Companies and businesses that hire graduates: Big Six accounting firms, General Electric, General Foods, Kidder Peabody.

**PROMINENT ALUMNI/AE.** Norman Vincent Peale, author/clergyman; Mary King, author; Bob Bauman, executive and CEO, Beecham Group; Ron Liebman, actor; Trish Van Devere, actress; Richard Gordon, real estate developer; Phillip Meek, senior vice-president, Capital Cities; Jim Berry, cartoonist; George Conrades, founder, Conrades-Riley Associates; Dr. David Smith, Smith Investments, Gordon Witkin, Sr., editor, *U.S. News and World Report.*

## Otterbein College

**Westerville, OH 43081** **800 488-8144**

**1994-95 Costs.** Tuition: $12,888. Room: $1,941. Board: $2,499. Fees, books, misc. academic expenses (school's estimate): $400.
**Enrollment.** Undergraduates: 649 men, 1,041 women (full-time). Freshman class: 1,535 applicants, 1,417 accepted, 416 enrolled. Graduate enrollment: 16 men, 103 women.
**Test score averages/ranges.** Average SAT scores: 453 verbal, 504 math. Average ACT scores: 22 English, 21 math, 22 composite.
**Faculty.** 130 full-time; 28 part-time. 64% of faculty holds doctoral degree. Student/faculty ratio: 13 to 1.
**Selectivity rating.** Less competitive.

**PROFILE.** Otterbein, founded in 1847, is a church-affiliated, liberal arts college. Its 70-acre campus is located in Westerville, five miles north of Columbus.

**Accreditation:** NCACS. Professionally accredited by the National Association of Schools of Music, the National Council for Accreditation of Teacher Education, the National League for Nursing.
**Religious orientation:** Otterbein College is affiliated with the United Methodist Church; two terms of religion required.
**Library:** Collections totaling over 188,047 volumes, 919 periodical subscriptions, and 140,357 microform items.

**Special facilities/museums:** Language lab, horse stable, observatory and planetarium, Celestron 8-inch and 14-inch telescopes.
**Athletic facilities:** Field house, baseball, football, soccer, and softball fields, badminton, basketball, handball, racquetball, tennis, and volleyball courts, aerobics and weight rooms, track.

**STUDENT BODY. Undergraduate profile:** 91% are state residents; 10% are transfers. 1% Asian-American, 4% Black, 1% Hispanic, 92% White, 2% Other. Average age of undergraduates is 21.
**Freshman profile:** 8% of freshmen who took SAT scored 600 or over on verbal, 9% scored 600 or over on math; 31% scored 500 or over on verbal, 46% scored 500 or over on math; 75% scored 400 or over on verbal, 76% scored 400 or over on math; 97% scored 300 or over on verbal, 90% scored 300 or over on math. 39% of accepted applicants took SAT; 73% took ACT.
**Undergraduate achievement:** 79% of fall 1991 freshmen returned for fall 1992 term. 74% of entering class graduated. 14% of students who completed a degree program immediately went on to graduate study.
**Foreign students:** 32 students are from out of the country. Countries represented include Hong Kong, Japan, Kenya, Nigeria, and Thailand; 24 in all.

**PROGRAMS OF STUDY. Degrees:** B.A., B.F.A., B.Mus.Ed., B.S., B.S.Ed., B.S.Nurs.
**Majors:** Accounting, Broadcasting, Business Administration, Business/Organizational Communication, Chemistry, Computer Science, Dance, Economics, Elementary Education, English, Environmental Science, Equine Science, French, Health Education, History, International Studies, Journalism, Life Sciences, Mathematics, Molecular Biology/Pre-Genetic Engineering, Music, Music Education, Musical Theatre, Nursing, Philosophy, Physical Education, Physics, Political Science, Psychology, Public Relations, Religion, Sociology, Spanish, Speech, Sports Medicine, Theatre, Visual Arts.
**Distribution of degrees:** The majors with the highest enrollment are business administration, elementary education, and business/organizational communication; religion, philosophy, and sociology have the lowest.
**Requirements:** General education requirement.
**Academic regulations:** Freshmen must maintain minimum 1.7 GPA; sophomores, juniors, seniors, 2.0 GPA.
**Special:** Minors offered in most majors. Courses offered in astronomy, geology, Greek, and radio/television. Integrative Studies program. Self-designed majors. Double majors. Independent study. Internships. Preprofessional programs in law, medicine, veterinary science, dentistry, and optometry. Member of East Central Colleges Consortium, Higher Education Council of Columbus, and Great Lakes Colleges Association. Washington Semester. Philadelphia Urban Semester. Exchange program with Alma Coll. Teacher certification in elementary and secondary education. Certification in specific subject areas. Exchange program abroad in France (U of Bourgogne). ROTC, NROTC, and AFROTC at Ohio State U.
**Honors:** Honors program. Honor societies.
**Academic Assistance:** Remedial study skills. Nonremedial tutoring.

**STUDENT LIFE. Housing:** All freshmen and sophomores must live on campus unless living with family within a 30-mile radius. Women's and men's dorms. Sorority and fraternity housing. 55% of students live in college housing.
**Social atmosphere:** The student newspaper reports, "Columbus is only 15 minutes away and offers many cultural, social, and professional opportunities." Popular on-campus gathering spots are the Roost, Campus Center Lounge, dormitory lounges, and the library. Off-campus hangouts include High Street bars in Columbus and Schneider's Bakery. Influential groups are Greeks, athletes, Otterbein Christian Fellowship, and the Baptist Student Union. Football and basketball games, Homecoming Mixer, Greek Rush, and the Artist Series are popular campus events.
**Services and counseling/handicapped student services:** Placement services. Health service. Counseling services for minority and older students. Birth control counseling. Career and academic guidance services. Physically disabled student services. Learning disabled services.
**Campus organizations:** Undergraduate student government. Student newspaper (Tan and Cardinal, published once/week). Literary magazine. Yearbook. Radio and TV stations. Marching, concert, and jazz bands, choir, show choir, Amnesty International, Campus Programming Board, 87 organizations in all. Seven fraternities, five chapter houses; six sororities, all with chapter houses. 50% of men join a fraternity. 50% of women join a sorority.
**Religious organizations:** Baptist Student Union, Christian Fellowship, Fellowship of Christian Athletes, Religious Activities Council, Serendipity.
**Minority/foreign student organizations:** African American Student Union, two minority fraternities. International Student Association.

**ATHLETICS. Physical education requirements:** Three terms of physical education required.
**Intercollegiate competition:** 35% of students participate. Baseball (M), basketball (M,W), cheerleading (M,W), cross-country (M,W), football (M), golf (M), soccer (M,W), softball (W), tennis (M,W), track (indoor) (M,W), track (outdoor) (M,W), track and field (indoor) (M,W), track and field (outdoor) (M,W), volleyball (W). Member of NCAA Division III, Ohio Athletic Conference.
**Intramural and club sports:** 30% of students participate. Intramural badminton, basketball, bowling, flag football, handball, putt-putt golf, racquetball, softball, tennis, volleyball. Men's club horsemanship, volleyball. Women's club horsemanship.

**ADMISSIONS. Academic basis for candidate selection** (in order of priority): Secondary school record, class rank, standardized test scores, school's recommendation.
**Nonacademic basis for candidate selection:** Character and personality, extracurricular participation, particular talent or ability, and alumni/ae relationship are considered.
**Requirements:** Graduation from secondary school is required; GED is accepted. 16 units and the following program of study are recommended: 4 units of English, 3 units of math, 3 units of science, 3 units of foreign language, 1 unit of social studies, 2 units of history. Minimum composite ACT score of 20 (combined SAT score of 860), rank in top half of secondary school class, and minimum 2.5 GPA recommended. Audition required of music program applicants. ACT is required; SAT may be substituted. Campus visit and interview recommended. No off-campus interviews.
**Procedure:** Take SAT or ACT by December of 12th year. Visit college for interview by February 15 of 12th year. Suggest filing application by December 31. Application deadline is April 20. Notification of admission on rolling basis. Reply is required by May 1. $100 nonrefundable tuition deposit. Freshmen accepted for terms other than fall.
**Special programs:** Admission may be deferred one year. Credit and/or placement may be granted through CEEB Advanced Placement exams for scores of 4 or higher. Credit and/or placement may be granted through CLEP general and subject exams. Credit and placement may be granted through ACT PEP and challenge exams. Concurrent enrollment program.
**Transfer students:** Transfer students accepted for terms other than fall. In fall 1993, 10% of all new students were transfers into all classes. 216 transfer applications were received, 149 were accepted. Application deadline is August 15 for fall; March 15 for spring. Minimum 2.5 GPA recommended. Lowest course grade accepted is "C." At least 60 quarter hours must be completed at the college to receive degree.
**Admissions contact:** Cass Johnson, M.A., Director of Admissions. 614 823-1500.

**FINANCIAL AID. Available aid:** Pell grants, SEOG, state grants, school scholarships and grants, private scholarships and grants, ROTC scholarships, and academic merit scholarships. Perkins Loans (NDSL), PLUS, Stafford Loans (GSL), and SLS. AMS and family tuition reduction. Monthly payment plan. Education Credit Corp. plan.
**Financial aid statistics:** In 1993-94, 70% of all undergraduate applicants received aid; 93% of freshman applicants. Average amounts of aid awarded freshmen: Scholarships and grants, $2,600; loans, $2,600.
**Supporting data/closing dates:** FAFSA/FAF: Priority filing date is March 1; deadline is April 15. Notification of awards on rolling basis.
**Financial aid contact:** Thomas V. Yarnell, Director of Financial Aid. 614 823-1502.

**STUDENT EMPLOYMENT.** College Work/Study Program. Institutional employment. 30% of full-time undergraduates work on campus during school year. Students may expect to earn an average of $1,000 during school year. Off-campus part-time employment opportunities rated "excellent."

**COMPUTER FACILITIES.** 102 IBM/IBM-compatible and Macintosh/Apple microcomputers; 45 are networked. Students may access IBM minicomputer/mainframe systems. Residence halls may be equipped with stand-alone microcomputers. Client/LAN operating systems include Apple/Macintosh, DOS. Computer languages and software packages include Ada, C, COBOL, FORTRAN, Microsoft Word, Pascal, SPSS, WordPerfect. Computer facilities are available to all students.
**Fees:** None.
**Hours:** 8 AM-midn. (M-Th); 9 AM-9 PM (F-Sa); 1 PM-11 PM (Su).

**GRADUATE CAREER DATA.** Graduate school percentages: 2% enter law school. 3% enter medical school. 2% enter graduate business programs. 6% enter graduate arts and sciences programs. Highest graduate school enrollments: Capital U Law Sch, Medical Coll of Ohio, Miami U, Ohio State U, Ohio U.

**PROMINENT ALUMNI/AE.** Alan E. Norris, judge, U.S. Circuit Court; David Graf, actor; Dee Hoty, Broadway actress; Stephen Spurgen, senior vice-president and director, Ketchum Public Relations; Belinda Berkowitz, psychologist; Wolfe G. Schmidt, president, Rubbermaid; Dr. David S. Yoh, director, Comprehensive Cancer Center, Ohio State U.

# Pontifical College Josephinum

**Columbus, OH 43235** — **614 885-5585**

**1994-95 Costs.** Tuition: $5,512. Room: $1,890. Board: $1,890. Fees, books, misc. academic expenses (school's estimate): $325.
**Enrollment.** 57 men (full-time). Freshman class: 6 applicants, 6 accepted, 6 enrolled. Graduate enrollment: 63 men, 5 women.
**Test score averages/ranges.** Average SAT scores: 340 verbal, 361 math. Average ACT scores: 18 English, 18 math, 18 composite.
**Faculty.** 9 full-time; 8 part-time. 46% of faculty holds doctoral degree. Student/faculty ratio: 3 to 1.
**Selectivity rating.** Noncompetitive.

**PROFILE.** Pontifical College Josephinum, founded in 1888, is a private, church-affiliated, liberal arts college. Its 96-acre campus is located 11 miles from downtown Columbus.

**Accreditation:** NCACS.
**Religious orientation:** Pontifical College Josephinum is affiliated with the Roman Catholic Church; eight semesters of religion required.
**Library:** Collections totaling over 98,000 volumes and 400 periodical subscriptions.
**Athletic facilities:** Gymnasium, swimming pool, athletic, soccer, and softball fields, tennis courts.

**STUDENT BODY. Undergraduate profile:** 33% are state residents; 53% are transfers. 5% Asian-American, 4% Black, 14% Hispanic, 77% White. Average age of undergraduates is 20.
**Freshman profile:** 10% of freshmen who took SAT scored 500 or over on verbal, 20% scored 500 or over on math; 20% scored 400 or over on verbal, 30% scored 400 or over on math; 40% scored 300 or over on verbal, 50% scored 300 or over on math. Majority of accepted applicants took SAT. 70% of freshmen come from public schools.
**Undergraduate achievement:** 66% of fall 1992 freshmen returned for fall 1993 term. 36% of entering class graduated. 100% of students who completed a degree program went on to graduate study within five years.
**Foreign students:** Two students are from out of the country.

**PROGRAMS OF STUDY. Degrees:** B.A.
**Majors:** English, History, Latin American Studies, Philosophy, Psychology, Religious Studies.
**Distribution of degrees:** The majors with the highest enrollment are philosophy and psychology.
**Academic regulations:** Freshmen must maintain minimum 1.8 GPA; sophomores, 1.9 GPA; juniors, 2.0 GPA; seniors, 2.0 GPA.

**Special:** Minor offered in classics. Courses offered in art, biblical Hebrew, French, German, math, music, science, sociology, and Spanish. Pastoral Formation Program, Personal Formation Program, and Spiritual Formation Program supplement academic offerings. Double majors. Independent study. Pass/fail grading option. Graduate school at which undergraduates may take graduate-level courses. Preprofessional programs in theology. Member of consortium with Trinity Lutheran Seminary and Methodist Theological School in Ohio.
**Academic Assistance:** Remedial writing. Nonremedial tutoring.

**ADMISSIONS. Academic basis for candidate selection** (in order of priority): Essay, secondary school record, school's recommendation, standardized test scores, class rank.
**Nonacademic basis for candidate selection:** Character and personality are important.
**Requirements:** Graduation from secondary school is required; GED is accepted. 16 units and the following program of study are required: 4 units of English, 2 units of math, 2 units of science, 4 units of social studies, 4 units of academic electives. SAT or ACT is required. Admissions interview recommended. Off-campus interviews available with an alumni representative.
**Procedure:** Take SAT or ACT by December of 12th year. Visit college for interview by March 15 of 12th year. Application deadline is August 15. Notification of admission on rolling basis. Reply is required one week after acceptance. Freshmen accepted for fall term only.
**Special programs:** Admission may be deferred. Credit and/or placement may be granted through CLEP general and subject exams.
**Transfer students:** Transfer students accepted for terms other than fall. In fall 1993, 53% of all new students were transfers into all classes. 16 transfer applications were received, 15 were accepted. Minimum 2.5 GPA required. Lowest course grade accepted is "C." At least 30 semester hours must be completed at the college to receive degree.
**Admissions contact:** Byron W. Thorsen, Ph.D., Registrar.

**FINANCIAL AID. Available aid:** Pell grants, SEOG, state grants, and private scholarships. Perkins Loans (NDSL), PLUS, and Stafford Loans (GSL).
**Financial aid statistics:** In 1993-94, 80% of all undergraduate applicants received aid; 80% of freshman applicants.
**Supporting data/closing dates:** FAFSA/FAF: Accepted on rolling basis. School's own aid application: Accepted on rolling basis. Notification of awards on rolling basis.
**Financial aid contact:** Linda Bryant, Director of Financial Aid.

# Shawnee State University

**Portsmouth, OH 45662** **614 354-3205**

**1993-94 Costs.** Tuition: $2,154 (state residents), $3,882 (out-of-state). Room & board: $4,113. Fees, books, misc. academic expenses (school's estimate): $875.
**Enrollment.** Undergraduates: 1,059 men, 1,670 women (full-time). Freshman class: 1,551 applicants, 1,551 accepted.
**Test score averages/ranges.** N/A.
**Faculty.** Student/faculty ratio: 14 to 1.
**Selectivity rating.** N/A.

**PROFILE.** Shawnee State, founded in 1986, is a public university. Its 50-acre campus is located in Portsmouth, 100 miles from Cincinnati.

**Accreditation:** NCACS. Professionally accredited by the American Dental Association, the American Medical Association (CAHEA).
**Religious orientation:** Shawnee State University is nonsectarian; no religious requirements.
**Library:** Collections totaling over 108,000 volumes, 1,000 periodical subscriptions, and 200,000 microform items.

**STUDENT BODY. Undergraduate profile:** 95% are state residents; 6% are transfers. 4% Black, 94% White, 2% Other.
**Freshman profile:** Majority of accepted applicants took ACT.
**Foreign students:** Nine students are from out of the country. Six countries represented in all.

**PROGRAMS OF STUDY. Degrees:** B.A., B.S.
**Majors:** Business Administration, Electrical/Computer Engineering Technology, English/Humanities, Mathematics, Natural Science, Plastics Engineering Technology, Social Science.
**Special:** Minors offered in computer technology, environmental science, and plastics engineering technology. Associate's degrees offered. Self-designed majors. Double majors. Dual degrees. Independent study. Pass/fail grading option. Preprofessional programs in law, medicine, veterinary science, pharmacy, dentistry, and optometry. 2-2 program in legal assisting/social science. Dual degree program in plastics engineering technology. Teacher certification in elementary education. Certification in specific subject areas. Exchange program abroad in Russia (Nizhny Novgorod State U).
**Honors:** Honors program. Honor societies.
**Academic Assistance:** Remedial reading, writing, math, and study skills. Nonremedial tutoring.

**STUDENT LIFE. Housing:** On-campus privately-owned housing.
**Social atmosphere:** Favorite hangouts include the student union, university center, Micklewaithe Lounge, Celeron Square, Sportsman's Bar, the Royal, Ramada Inn, and Ye Ole Lantern. Student groups with widespread influence include TKE, Delta Sigma Phi, Student Senate, and Student Programming Board. Annual Blood Donor Challenge, Parade of Clubs and Organizations, Comedy Night, Cinema Night, Monday Night Football, Volleyrock, SSU Classic, River Days, Scioto County Fair, and Dickens of a Christmas are popular events. "Social and cultural life, on and off campus, is an example of the quaint hometown feeling of middle-America," observes the student newspaper.
**Services and counseling/handicapped student services:** Placement services. Women's center. career planning, personal counseling Counseling services for minority, military, veteran, and older students. Personal and psychological counseling. Career and academic guidance services. Physically disabled student services. Learning disabled services. Notetaking services. Tape recorders. Tutors. Reader services for the blind.

**Campus organizations:** Undergraduate student government. Student newspaper (University Chronicle, published once/week). Literary magazine. Choir, Student Programming Board. Two fraternities, no chapter houses; one sorority, no chapter house.
**Religious organizations:** Campus ministry.
**Minority/foreign student organizations:** AHANA (minority student group).

**ATHLETICS. Physical education requirements:** None.

**ADMISSIONS. Requirements:** Graduation from secondary school is required; GED is accepted. 16 units and the following program of study are recommended: 4 units of English, 3 units of math, 3 units of science, 2 units of foreign language, 3 units of social studies, 1 unit of electives. Elective should be in the arts. Open admissions policy. Minimum GPA, specific coursework, and other requirements for health science program applicants. ACT is required; SAT may be substituted. Campus visit and interview recommended. No off-campus interviews.
**Procedure:** Application deadline is September. Notification of admission on rolling basis. Freshmen accepted for terms other than fall.
**Special programs:** Credit and/or placement may be granted through CEEB Advanced Placement exams for scores of 3 or higher. Credit and/or placement may be granted through CLEP subject exams. Credit and placement may be granted through DANTES and challenge exams and military experience. Concurrent enrollment program.
**Transfer students:** Transfer students accepted for terms other than fall. In fall 1993, 6% of all new students were transfers into all classes. 291 transfer applications were received, 291 were accepted. Application deadline is rolling for fall; rolling for spring. SAT/ACT scores required of applicants under 21 years of age. Lowest course grade accepted is "C."
**Admissions contact:** Rosemary K. Poston, M.A., Director of Admissions. 614 355-2221.

**FINANCIAL AID. Available aid:** Pell grants, SEOG, state scholarships and grants, school scholarships, private scholarships and grants, academic merit scholarships, and athletic scholarships. PLUS, Stafford Loans (GSL), Health Professions Loans, school loans, and SLS. State Nursing Loans. School's own payment plan.
**Financial aid statistics:** Average amounts of aid awarded freshmen: Loans, $1,900.
**Supporting data/closing dates:** FAFSA.
**Financial aid contact:** Eugene D. Wilson, M.A., Director of Financial Aid. 614 355-2237.

**STUDENT EMPLOYMENT.** College Work/Study Program. Institutional employment. 5% of full-time undergraduates work on campus during school year. Off-campus part-time employment opportunities rated "fair."

**COMPUTER FACILITIES.** IBM/IBM-compatible and Macintosh/Apple microcomputers. Computer facilities are available to all students.
**Fees:** None.

9-6

# Tiffin University

**Tiffin, OH 44883** **419 447-6442**

**1994-95 Costs.** Tuition: $7,600. Room & board: $3,800. Fees, books, misc. academic expenses (school's estimate): $600.
**Enrollment.** Undergraduates: 392 men, 270 women (full-time). Freshman class: 783 applicants, 734 accepted, 242 enrolled. Graduate enrollment: 35 men, 27 women.
**Test score averages/ranges.** Average SAT scores: 308 verbal, 372 math. Average ACT scores: 18 English, 18 math, 19 composite. Range of ACT scores of middle 50%: 15-20 English, 16-20 math.
**Faculty.** 27 full-time; 40 part-time. 65% of faculty holds highest degree in specific field. Student/faculty ratio: 19 to 1.
**Selectivity rating.** Noncompetitive.

**PROFILE.** Tiffin, founded in 1888, is a private university of business. Its 10-acre campus is located in Tiffin, 50 miles southeast of Toledo.

**Accreditation:** NCACS.
**Religious orientation:** Tiffin University is nonsectarian; no religious requirements.
**Library:** Collections totaling over 15,971 volumes, 105 periodical subscriptions, and 27,400 microform items.
**Special facilities/museums:** National criminal justice referral service microform department.
**Athletic facilities:** Gymnasium, student center, park, physical fitness center.

**STUDENT BODY. Undergraduate profile:** 91% are state residents; 20% are transfers. .1% Asian-American, 9% Black, 1% Hispanic, 86% White, 3.9% Other. Average age of undergraduates is 24.
**Freshman profile:** 7% of accepted applicants took SAT; 78% took ACT. 90% of freshmen come from public schools.
**Undergraduate achievement:** 56% of fall 1992 freshmen returned for fall 1993 term. 28% of entering class graduated. 6% of students who completed a degree program immediately went on to graduate study.
**Foreign students:** 29 students are from out of the country. Countries represented include the Bahamas, Canada, India, Jamaica, Japan, and Turkey; 18 in all.

**PROGRAMS OF STUDY. Degrees:** B.Bus.Admin., B.Crim.Just.
**Majors:** Accounting, Accounting/Information Systems, Administrative Management, Corrections, Economics/Finance, Forensic Psychology, Hospitality Management, Human Resource Management, Information Systems, International Business, Law Enforcement, Management, Management Information Systems, Managerial Studies, Marketing, Operations Management, Personal Computer Administration, Programming/Systems Analysis, Sports Management.
**Distribution of degrees:** The majors with the highest enrollment are management, accounting, and corrections; office management, computer information systems, and accounting/computer systems have the lowest.
**Requirements:** General education requirement.
**Academic regulations:** Freshmen must maintain minimum 1.7 GPA; sophomores, juniors, seniors, 2.0 GPA.
**Special:** Associate's degrees offered. Independent study. Internships. Study abroad in England.
**Honors:** Honor societies.

**Academic Assistance:** Remedial writing, math, and study skills. Nonremedial tutoring.

**ADMISSIONS. Academic basis for candidate selection** (in order of priority): Secondary school record, standardized test scores, class rank, school's recommendation, essay.
**Nonacademic basis for candidate selection:** Extracurricular participation is considered.
**Requirements:** Graduation from secondary school is required; GED is accepted. 16 units and the following program of study are recommended: 4 units of English, 3 units of math, 2 units of science, 2 units of social studies, 5 units of electives. Minimum composite ACT score of 18, rank in top half of secondary school class, and minimum 2.25 GPA recommended. Conditional admission possible for applicants not meeting standard requirements. ACT is recommended; SAT may be substituted. Campus visit and interview recommended. Off-campus interviews available with an admissions representative.
**Procedure:** Take SAT or ACT by June of 12th year. Visit college for interview by May of 12th year. Application deadline is August 1. Notification of admission on rolling basis. $50 tuition deposit, refundable until May 1. $100 room deposit, refundable until May 1. Freshmen accepted for terms other than fall.
**Special programs:** Admission may be deferred two semesters. Credit may be granted through CEEB Advanced Placement for scores of 5 or higher. Credit may be granted through CLEP general and subject exams. Placement may be granted through challenge exams. Credit and placement may be granted through life experience. Early entrance/early admission program. Concurrent enrollment program.
**Transfer students:** Transfer students accepted for terms other than fall. In fall 1993, 20% of all new students were transfers into all classes. 141 transfer applications were received, 125 were accepted. Application deadline is August 1 for fall; December 1 for spring. Minimum 1.8 GPA recommended. Lowest course grade accepted is "C." Maximum number of transferable credits is 60 semester hours from a two-year school and 90 semester hours from a four-year school. At least 30 semester hours must be completed at the university to receive degree.
**Admissions contact:** Kristine Boyle, Director of Admissions. 419 447-6443, 800 968-6446.

**FINANCIAL AID. Available aid:** Pell grants, SEOG, state scholarships and grants, school scholarships and grants, private scholarships and grants, academic merit scholarships, athletic scholarships, and aid for undergraduate foreign students. Perkins Loans (NDSL), PLUS, Stafford Loans (GSL), private loans, and SLS. Tuition Plan Inc. and AMS.
**Financial aid statistics:** 20% of aid is not need-based. In 1993-94, 96% of all undergraduate applicants received aid; 97% of freshman applicants. Average amounts of aid awarded freshmen: Scholarships and grants, $1,895; loans, $2,441.
**Supporting data/closing dates:** FAFSA: Priority filing date is March 31; deadline is May 1. State aid form: Deadline is in September. Notification of awards begins April 15.
**Financial aid contact:** Carol McDonnell, Director of Financial Aid. 419 447-6442, extension 215.

5-4 8-28

# The University of Akron

**Akron, OH 44325** **216 972-7111**

**1994-95 Costs.** Tuition: $3,198 (state residents), $7,642 (out-of-state). Room & board: $3,850. Fees, books, misc. academic expenses (school's estimate): $500.
**Enrollment.** Undergraduates: 8,790 men, 8,981 women (full-time). Freshman class: 6,477 applicants, 6,132 accepted, 3,278 enrolled. Graduate enrollment: 2,181 men, 2,143 women.
**Test score averages/ranges.** Average SAT scores: 412 verbal, 473 math. Range of SAT scores of middle 50%: 300-499 verbal, 400-599 math. Average ACT scores: 19 English, 19 math, 20 composite. Range of ACT scores of middle 50%: 16-25 English, 16-25 math.
**Faculty.** 836 full-time; 940 part-time. 63% of faculty holds doctoral degree. Student/faculty ratio: 20 to 1.
**Selectivity rating.** Noncompetitive.

**PROFILE.** The University of Akron is a public, multipurpose institution. It was founded as a private college in 1870, came under city control in 1913, and joined the state university system in 1967. Programs are offered through the Colleges of Business Administration, Education, Engineering, Fine and Applied Arts, Nursing, and Polymer Science and Polymer Engineering; Butchel College of Arts and Sciences; Community and Technical College; University College; and the School of Law. Its 162-acre campus of modern buildings is located within walking distance of downtown Akron.

**Accreditation:** NCACS. Professionally accredited by the Accreditation Board for Engineering and Technology, the American Assembly of Collegiate Schools of Business, the American Association for Counseling and Development, the American Dental Association, the American Medical Association (CAHEA), the American Speech-Language-Hearing Association, the Council on Social Work Education, the National Association of Schools of Art and Design, the National Association of Schools of Music, the National Council for Accreditation of Teacher Education, the National League for Nursing.
**Religious orientation:** The University of Akron is nonsectarian; no religious requirements.
**Library:** Collections totaling over 1,007,486 volumes, 8,186 periodical subscriptions, and 1,552,631 microform items.
**Special facilities/museums:** Performing arts hall, elementary school on campus, nursery center, language lab, speech and hearing center, nursing learning resource labs, institute of polymer science and engineering, chemical lab.
**Athletic facilities:** Gymnasiums, arena, swimming pool, basketball, tennis, and volleyball courts, bowling lanes, baseball, football, intramural, soccer, and softball fields, track.

**STUDENT BODY. Undergraduate profile:** 99% are state residents; 20% are transfers. 1% Asian-American, 8% Black, 1% Hispanic, 1% Native American, 86% White, 3% Other. Average age of undergraduates is 19.
**Freshman profile:** 2% of freshmen who took SAT scored 700 or over on math; 1% scored 600 or over on verbal, 17% scored 600 or over on math; 18% scored 500 or over on verbal, 44% scored 500 or over on math; 57% scored 400 or over on verbal, 72% scored 400 or over on math; 89% scored 300 or over on verbal, 94% scored 300 or over on math. 15% of accepted applicants took SAT; 70% took ACT.
**Undergraduate achievement:** 80% of fall 1991 freshmen returned for fall 1992 term.
**Foreign students:** 900 students are from out of the country. Countries represented include China, India, Malaysia, South Korea, and Taiwan; 85 in all.

**PROGRAMS OF STUDY. Degrees:** B.A., B.F.A., B.Mus., B.S., B.S.Bus.Admin., B.S.Cytotech., B.S.Ed., B.S.Eng., B.S.Labor Econ., B.S.M.T., B.S.Nurs.
**Majors:** Accounting, Advertising, Art, Biology, Business Administration, Chemical Engineering, Chemistry, Civil Engineering, Classics, Communication, Communicative Disorders, Computer Science, Construction Technology, Cytotechnology, Dance, Economics, Electrical Engineering, Elementary Education, English, Finance, Geography/Planning, Geology, History, Home Economics/Family Ecology, Humanities, Management, Marketing, Mathematical Sciences, Mechanical Engineering, Medical Technology, Modern Languages, Music, Natural Sciences, Nursing, Philosophy, Physical Education/Health Education, Physics, Political Science, Psychology, Secondary Education, Social Sciences, Social Work, Sociology, Special Education, Speech Pathology/Audiology, Technical Education, Theatre, Theatre Arts.
**Distribution of degrees:** The majors with the highest enrollment are accounting, electrical engineering, and elementary education.
**Requirements:** General education requirement.
**Academic regulations:** Minimum 2.0 GPA must be maintained.
**Special:** Associate's degrees offered. Dual degrees. Independent study. Accelerated study. Pass/fail grading option. Internships. Cooperative education programs. Graduate school at which undergraduates may take graduate-level courses. Preprofessional programs in law, medicine, veterinary science, pharmacy, and dentistry. 2-2 programs in electronic technology and mechanical technology. 2-3 program in construction technology. Combined five-year B.S./M.Eng. in biomedical engineering. Combined six-year B.S./M.D. program. Child-life specialist and respiratory therapist programs. Member of Northeastern Ohio Universities College of Medicine Consortium. Cooperative programs with Kent State U, U of Akron, and Youngstown State U. Teacher certification in early childhood, elementary, secondary, and special education. Study abroad in Australia, Belgium, Canada, China, England, France, Germany, Israel, Japan, Korea, Mexico, the Netherlands, Puerto Rico, Singapore, and Turkey. ROTC and AFROTC.
**Honors:** Honors program.
**Academic Assistance:** Remedial reading, writing, math, and study skills.

**STUDENT LIFE. Housing:** Students may live on or off campus. Coed, women's, and men's dorms. Sorority and fraternity housing. School-owned/operated apartments. 10% of students live in college housing.
**Social atmosphere:** UA is described as quite diverse. "Our campus, though the third largest in Ohio, is primarily a commuter school. Approximately 2,000 students live in residence halls on campus and an additional 6,000 live in off-campus housing. We are an urban campus, and downtown Akron is just several blocks away. Most of our students are working their way through school, which tends to make them more serious about their studies. We also have nearly a thousand international students. Nontraditional students dot our campus as well. UA truly is a school for someone who wants to do anything."
**Services and counseling/handicapped student services:** Placement services. Health service. Day care. Adult resource center. Counseling services for minority, veteran, and older students. Personal and psychological counseling. Career and academic guidance services. Physically disabled student services. Learning disabled services. Notetaking services. Tape recorders. Tutors. Reader services for the blind.
**Campus organizations:** Undergraduate student government. Student newspaper (Buchtelite, published twice/month). Yearbook. Radio and TV stations. Experimental dance ensemble, theatre, opera, gospel chorus, steel drum band, jazz ensemble, Student Toastmasters, departmental groups, 200 organizations in all. 16 fraternities, 13 chapter houses; 10 sororities, seven chapter houses. 10% of men join a fraternity. 5% of women join a sorority.
**Religious organizations:** ABC's of Salvation, AGAPE, Alpha Omega Christian Fraternity, Bahai Club, Baptist Student Union, Ecumenical Christian Association.
**Minority/foreign student organizations:** Black Law Student Association, Black United Students, Black Greek Council, National Society of Black Engineers. Association of Arab Students, Chinese Student Association, International Student Club, Nigerian Student Union, Palestine Club.

**ATHLETICS. Physical education requirements:** One semester of physical education required.
**Intercollegiate competition:** 2% of students participate. Baseball (M), basketball (M,W), cheerleading (M,W), cross-country (M,W), football (M), golf (M), riflery (M,W), soccer (M), softball (W), tennis (M,W), track (indoor) (M,W), track (outdoor) (M,W), track and field (indoor) (M,W), track and field (outdoor) (M,W), volleyball (W). Member of Mid-American Conference, NCAA Division I.
**Intramural and club sports:** 30% of students participate. Intramural basketball, cross-country, flag football, golf, inner-tube water polo, soccer, softball, swimming, track, volleyball, weight lifting, wrestling. Men's club Alpine skiing, cycling, lacrosse, martial arts. Women's club Alpine skiing, cycling, martial arts.

**ADMISSIONS. Academic basis for candidate selection** (in order of priority): Secondary school record, standardized test scores, class rank, school's recommendation, essay.
**Requirements:** Graduation from secondary school is required; GED is accepted. 15 units and the following program of study are recommended: 4 units of English, 3 units of math, 3 units of science, 2 units of foreign language, 3 units of social studies. Minimum composite ACT score of 20 (combined SAT score of 886) and minimum 2.8 GPA required of out-of-state applicants. Audition required of dance and music program applicants. Portfolio required of art program applicants. ACT is required; SAT may be substituted. Campus visit recommended. No off-campus interviews.
**Procedure:** Take SAT or ACT by October of 12th year. Visit college for interview by December of 12th year. Application deadline is August 12. Notification of admission on rolling basis. $150 nonrefundable room deposit. Freshmen accepted for terms other than fall.
**Special programs:** Admission may be deferred one semester. Credit may be granted through CEEB Advanced Placement for scores of 3 or higher. Credit may be granted through CLEP subject exams and military experience. Credit and placement may be granted through challenge exams. Concurrent enrollment program.
**Transfer students:** Transfer students accepted for terms other than fall. In fall 1992, 20% of all new students were transfers into all classes. 1,525 transfer applications were received, 1,081 were accepted. Application deadline is August 12 for fall; December 31 for

spring. Minimum 2.0 GPA required. Lowest course grade accepted is "C." Maximum number of transferable credits is 96 semester hours. At least 32 semester hours must be completed at the university to receive degree.

**Admissions contact:** Martha Booth, Senior Associate Director of Admissions. 216 972-7100.

**FINANCIAL AID. Available aid:** Pell grants, SEOG, state scholarships and grants, school scholarships, private scholarships, academic merit scholarships, and athletic scholarships. Perkins Loans (NDSL), PLUS, Stafford Loans (GSL), NSL, state loans, school loans, private loans, and SLS. Guaranteed tuition. University payment plan.

**Financial aid statistics:** In 1992-93, 74% of all undergraduate applicants received aid. Average amounts of aid awarded freshmen: Loans, $2,000.

**Supporting data/closing dates:** FAFSA/FAF: Priority filing date is March 15. State aid form: Deadline is September 28. Notification of awards begins April 15.

**Financial aid contact:** Robert D. Hahn, Director of Financial Aid. 216 972-7032.

**STUDENT EMPLOYMENT.** College Work/Study Program. Institutional employment. 25% of full-time undergraduates work on campus during school year. Students may expect to earn an average of $1,400 during school year. Off-campus part-time employment opportunities rated "good."

**COMPUTER FACILITIES.** 600 IBM/IBM-compatible, Macintosh/Apple, and RISC-/UNIX-based microcomputers. Computer languages and software packages include APL, Assembly, BMDP, C, COBOL, FORTRAN, Lotus 1-2-3, MacWrite, MacDraw, Pascal, PC-Write, R:BASE, SAS, SPSS, WordPerfect; 50 in all. Computer facilities are available to all students.

**Fees:** Computer fee is included in tuition/fees.

**Hours:** 7 AM-2 AM.

**PROMINENT ALUMNI/AE.** William Considine, president, Akron Children's Hospital; George Nanchoff, professional soccer player; Brig. Gen. Honeywill, U.S.A.F., special assistant for Strategic Defense Initiative; Janet Purnell, ex-member, U of Akron Board of Trustees; Steve Albrecht, president, ACME-CLICK; Charles Zodrow, president, Roadway, Inc.

# University of Cincinnati

**Cincinnati, OH 45221-0127** **513 556-0361**

**1994-95 Costs.** Tuition: $3,558 (state residents), $8,712 (out-of-state). Room & board: $4,263-$4,431. Fees, books, misc. academic expenses (school's estimate): $350.

**Enrollment.** Undergraduates: 5,672 men, 5,364 women (full-time). Freshman class: 10,644 applicants, 9,211 accepted, 4,663 enrolled. Graduate enrollment: 2,503 men, 2,557 women.

**Test score averages/ranges.** Average SAT scores: 460 verbal, 526 math. Range of SAT scores of middle 50%: 400-520 verbal, 450-600 math. Range of ACT scores of middle 50%: 20-26 composite.

**Faculty.** 966 full-time; 19 part-time. 78% of faculty holds highest degree in specific field. Student/faculty ratio: 14 to 1.

**Selectivity rating.** Less competitive.

**PROFILE.** The University of Cincinnati, founded in 1819, is a comprehensive, public institution. Programs are offered through the Colleges of Applied Science; Arts and Sciences; Business Administration; Design, Architecture, Art, and Planning; Education; Engineering; Evening and Continuing Education; Law; Medicine; Nursing and Health; and Pharmacy. Courses are also available through Clermont and Raymond Walters Colleges, the College-Conservatory of Music, the School of Social Work, and University College. Its 200-acre campus is located two miles from downtown Cincinnati.

**Accreditation:** NCACS.

**Religious orientation:** University of Cincinnati is nonsectarian; no religious requirements.

**Library:** Collections totaling over 1,947,773 volumes, 19,574 periodical subscriptions, and 2,691,444 microform items.

**Special facilities/museums:** Language lab, observatory, showboat.

**Athletic facilities:** Gymnasiums, field house, track, basketball, handball, racquetball, squash, tennis, and volleyball courts, swimming pool, weight rooms, baseball, football, intramural, soccer, and softball fields, bowling lanes, stadium.

**STUDENT BODY. Undergraduate profile:** 94% are state residents; 21% are transfers. 2% Asian-American, 10% Black, 1% Hispanic, 85% White, 2% Other. Average age of undergraduates is 22.

**Freshman profile:** 1% of freshmen who took SAT scored 700 or over on verbal, 5% scored 700 or over on math; 7% scored 600 or over on verbal, 28% scored 600 or over on math; 34% scored 500 or over on verbal, 61% scored 500 or over on math; 77% scored 400 or over on verbal, 89% scored 400 or over on math; 98% scored 300 or over on verbal, 99% scored 300 or over on math. 63% of accepted applicants took SAT; 86% took ACT.

**Undergraduate achievement:** 77% of fall 1992 freshmen returned for fall 1993 term.

**PROGRAMS OF STUDY. Degrees:** B.A., B.Arch., B.Bus.Admin., B.F.A., B.Gen.Studies, B.Mus., B.S., B.S.Design, B.S.Ed., B.S.Eng., B.S.Indust.Mgmt., B.S.Nurs., B.S.Pharm., B.S.Soc.Work, B.Urban Plan.

**Majors:** Accounting, Aerospace Engineering, Afro-American Studies, Anthropology, Architectural Engineering Technology, Architecture, Art Education, Art History, Asian Studies, Bassoon, Biochemistry, Biological Sciences, Broadcasting, Chemical Engineering, Chemistry, Civil Engineering, Clarinet, Classical Civilization, Classical Guitar, Classics, Communication Arts, Communication Disorders, Comparative Literature, Composition, Computer Engineering, Computer Science, Construction Management, Criminal Justice, Dance, Double Bass, Dramatic Performance, Early Childhood Education, Economics, Electrical Engineering, Electrical Engineering Technology, Elementary Education, Engineering Mechanics, English Literature, Euphonium, Fashion Design, Finance, Fine Arts, Fire/Industrial Safety Technology, Fire/Safety Engineering Technology, Flute, French, French Horn, French Studies, General Studies, Geography, Geology, German, German Studies, Graphic Design, Harp, Harpsichord, Health Education, Health Services Administration, History, Industrial Design, Industrial Engineering, Industrial Management, Information Systems, Interior Design, International Affairs, Jazz/Studio Music, Judaic Studies, Latin American Studies, Linguistics, Management, Marketing, Mathematical Sciences, Mechanical Engineering, Mechanical Engineering Technology, Medical Technology, Metallurgical Engineering, Music, Music Education, Music History, Music Theory, Musical Theatre, Nuclear Medicine Technology, Nuclear/Power Engineering, Nursing, Nutrition, Oboe, Operations Management, Orchestral Conducting, Organ, Percussion, Pharmacy, Philosophy, Physics, Piano, Political Science, Pre-Personnel/Industrial Relations, Psychology, Quantitative Analysis, Real Estate, Saxophone, Secondary Education, Social Work, Sociology, Spanish, Spanish Studies, Special Education, Theatre Design/Production, Trombone, Trumpet, Tuba, Urban Planning, Urban Studies/Administration, Viola, Violin, Violoncello, Voice.

**Distribution of degrees:** The majors with the highest enrollment are nursing, electrical engineering, and accounting; classical civilization and general studies have the lowest.

**Special:** Courses offered at Art Academy of Cincinnati and Hebrew Union Coll. Associate's degrees offered. Self-designed majors. Double majors. Dual degrees. Independent study. Pass/fail grading option. Internships. Cooperative education programs. Graduate school at which undergraduates may take graduate-level courses. Preprofessional programs in law, medicine, veterinary science, and dentistry. 2-2 engineering technology program. Member of Greater Cincinnati Consortium of Colleges. Washington Semester. Teacher certification in early childhood, elementary, secondary, and special education. Study abroad in England, Germany, Israel, Mexico, and Spain. ROTC and AFROTC.

**Honors:** Phi Beta Kappa. Honors program.

**Academic Assistance:** Nonremedial tutoring.

**STUDENT LIFE. Housing:** Coed, women's, and men's dorms. Sorority and fraternity housing. School-owned/operated apartments. 16% of students live in college housing.

**Services and counseling/handicapped student services:** Placement services. Health service. Women's center. Day care. Counseling services for minority, military, and veteran students. Birth control, personal, and psychological counseling. Career and academic guidance services.

**Campus organizations:** Undergraduate student government. Student newspaper (News Record, published twice/month). Literary magazine. Yearbook. Student Community Involvement, Showboat Majestic, special-interest groups. 24 fraternities, all with chapter houses; 11 sororities, all with chapter houses.

**Religious organizations:** African Campus Ministries, B'nai B'rith, Baptist Campus Ministries, Christian Student Fellowship, Hillel Foundation, Lutheran Campus Ministries, Newman Center, Wesley Foundation.

**Minority/foreign student organizations:** United Black Association.

**ATHLETICS. Physical education requirements:** None.

**Intercollegiate competition:** 2% of students participate. Baseball (M), basketball (M,W), cheerleading (M,W), cross-country (M,W), diving (M,W), football (M), golf (M,W), riflery (M,W), soccer (M,W), swimming (M,W), tennis (M,W), track and field (indoor) (M), track and field (outdoor) (M), volleyball (W). Member of Great Midwestern Conference, NCAA Division I, NCAA Division I-A for football.

**Intramural and club sports:** 40% of students participate. Intramural basketball, billiards, bowling, dance, foosball, football, free throw, golf, handball, indoor soccer, softball, squash, swimming, table tennis, tennis, track, tug-of-war, volleyball, walleyball, wrestling. Men's club bowling, crew, handball, sailing, volleyball. Women's club crew, sailing.

**ADMISSIONS. Academic basis for candidate selection** (in order of priority): Secondary school record, class rank, standardized test scores, school's recommendation.

**Nonacademic basis for candidate selection:** Character and personality and extracurricular participation are considered.

**Requirements:** Graduation from secondary school is recommended; GED accepted only for university's two-year colleges. 16 units and the following program of study are required: 4 units of English, 3 units of math, 2 units of science, 2 units of foreign language, 2 units of social studies, 2 units of academic electives. 1 unit of fine arts also required. Audition required of dance and music program applicants. Two or more years of college required of pharmacy program applicants. SAT or ACT is recommended. Campus visit and interview recommended.

**Procedure:** Take SAT or ACT by fall of 12th year. Visit college for interview by March 1 of 12th year. Suggest filing application by December 15; no deadline. Notification by March 1 on applications completed by January 1; within six to eight weeks for later applications. Reply is required by May 1 for applicants admitted by April 15. $75 refundable room deposit. Freshmen accepted for terms other than fall.

**Transfer students:** Transfer students accepted for terms other than fall. In fall 1993, 21% of all new students were transfers into all classes. 2,283 transfer applications were received, 1,525 were accepted. Lowest course grade accepted is "C."

**FINANCIAL AID. Available aid:** Pell grants, SEOG, Federal Nursing Student Scholarships, state scholarships and grants, school scholarships and grants, private scholarships and grants, ROTC scholarships, academic merit scholarships, athletic scholarships, and aid for undergraduate foreign students. Perkins Loans (NDSL), PLUS, Stafford Loans (GSL), NSL, school loans, and SLS. Tuition Plan Inc. and deferred payment plan. College Aid Plan.

**Financial aid statistics:** In 1993-94, 65% of all undergraduate applicants received aid.

**Supporting data/closing dates:** FAFSA/FAF/FFS: Accepted on rolling basis. Notification of awards on rolling basis.

**Financial aid contact:** James Williams, M.Ed., Director of Financial Aid. 513 556-6982.

**STUDENT EMPLOYMENT.** College Work/Study Program. Institutional employment. 30% of full-time undergraduates work on campus during school year. Students may expect to earn an average of $1,200 during school year. Freshmen are discouraged from working during their first term. Off-campus part-time employment opportunities rated "good."

**COMPUTER FACILITIES.** 1,500 IBM/IBM-compatible, Macintosh/Apple, and RISC-/UNIX-based microcomputers. Students may access Cray, Digital, IBM minicomputer/mainframe systems, Internet. Client/LAN operating systems include Apple/Macintosh, DOS, UNIX/XENIX/AIX, Windows NT, X-windows. Computer languages and software packages include BASIC, C, COBOL, FORTRAN, Pascal; statistical, general software packages. Microcomputers are available to all students; multi-user system is available only to students enrolled in computer courses.

# University of Dayton

Dayton, OH 45469-1660 513 229-1000

**1994-95 Costs.** Tuition: $11,380. Room: $2,160. Board: $2,060. Fees, books, misc. academic expenses (school's estimate): $1,250.
**Enrollment.** Undergraduates: 3,095 men, 2,804 women (full-time). Freshman class: 6,361 applicants, 5,293 accepted, 1,507 enrolled. Graduate enrollment: 1,805 men, 2,293 women.
**Test score averages/ranges.** Average SAT scores: 504 verbal, 578 math. Range of SAT scores of middle 50%: 940-1190 combined. Average ACT scores: 25 composite.
**Faculty.** 419 full-time; 394 part-time. 80% of faculty holds doctoral degree. Student/faculty ratio: 15 to 1.
**Selectivity rating.** Competitive.

**PROFILE.** The University of Dayton, founded in 1849, is a church-affiliated institution. Programs are offered through the College of Arts and Sciences and the Schools of Business Administration, Education, and Engineering. Its 76-acre campus is located in Dayton.

**Accreditation:** NCACS. Professionally accredited by the Accreditation Board for Engineering and Technology, the American Assembly of Collegiate Schools of Business, the American Bar Association, the Computing Sciences Accreditation Board, the National Association of Schools of Music, the National Council for Accreditation of Teacher Education.
**Religious orientation:** University of Dayton is affiliated with the Roman Catholic Church (Marianists); four semesters of religion/theology required.
**Library:** Collections totaling over 1,302,522 volumes, 3,089 periodical subscriptions, and 682,505 microform items.
**Special facilities/museums:** Student art gallery, information sciences center, young children's learning center.
**Athletic facilities:** Gymnasiums, swimming pool, badminton, basketball, handball, racquetball, squash, tennis, volleyball, and walleyball courts, exercise and weight rooms, flag football, soccer, and softball fields, track, conditioning center, field house.

**STUDENT BODY. Undergraduate profile:** 57% are state residents; 9% are transfers. 1.4% Asian-American, 3.8% Black, 1.9% Hispanic, .1% Native American, 91.1% White, 1.7% Other. Average age of undergraduates is 20.
**Freshman profile:** 55% of accepted applicants took SAT; 61% took ACT. 55% of freshmen come from public schools.
**Undergraduate achievement:** 86% of fall 1992 freshmen returned for fall 1993 term. 55% of entering class graduated.
**Foreign students:** 110 students are from out of the country. Countries represented include China, India, Indonesia, Jordan, Kuwait, and Taiwan; 44 in all.

**PROGRAMS OF STUDY. Degrees:** B.A., B.Chem.Eng., B.Civil Eng., B.Elec.Eng., B.F.A., B.Gen.Studies, B.Mech.Eng., B.Mus., B.S., B.S.Art Ed., B.S.Bus.Admin., B.S.Ed., B.S.Eng.Tech.
**Majors:** Accounting, American Studies, Art Education, Biochemistry, Biology, Chemical Engineering, Chemical Process Technology, Chemistry, Civil Engineering, Communication, Computer Information Systems, Computer Science, Criminal Justice, Economics, Education of the Handicapped, Electrical Engineering, Electronic Engineering Technology, Elementary Education, English, Environmental Engineering Technology, Exercise Science/Fitness Management, Finance, Fine Arts, General Studies, Geology, Health Education, Health Information Specialist, History, Human Ecology, Industrial Engineering Technology, Interior Design, International Studies, Kindergarten/Primary Education, Languages, Management, Management Information Systems, Manufacturing Engineering Technology, Marketing, Mathematics, Mechanical Engineering, Mechanical Engineering Technology, Music, Music Education, Music Performance, Music Theory/Composition, Music Therapy, Nuclear Medicine Technology, Philosophy, Photography, Physical Education, Physical Sciences, Physics, Physics/Computer Science, Political Science, Pre-Dentistry, Pre-Medicine, Psychology, Religious Studies, School Nurse/Health Educator, Secondary Education, Sociology, Special Education, Sports Management, Theatre, Visual Communication Design.
**Distribution of degrees:** The majors with the highest enrollment are communication, elementary education, and psychology; physics, languages, and religious studies have the lowest.
**Requirements:** General education requirement.
**Academic regulations:** Freshmen must maintain minimum 1.7 GPA; sophomores, 1.9 GPA; juniors, 2.0 GPA; seniors, 2.0 GPA.
**Special:** Minors offered in some majors and in anthropology, social work, and women's studies. Associate's degrees offered. Self-designed majors. Double majors. Dual degrees. Independent study. Pass/fail grading option. Internships. Cooperative education programs. Graduate school at which undergraduates may take graduate-level courses. Preprofessional programs in law, medicine, and dentistry. Five-year bachelor's/master's biology program. Member of Southwestern Ohio Council for Higher Education and Dayton-Miami Valley Consortium; cross-registration possible. Exchange programs with Chaminade U and St. Mary's U. Teacher certification in early childhood, elementary, secondary, and special education. Certification in specific subject areas. Study abroad in Austria, France, Germany (U of Augsburg), Italy, Spain, and the United Kingdom. ROTC. AFROTC at Wright State U.
**Honors:** Honors program. Honor societies.
**Academic Assistance:** Remedial reading, writing, and math. Nonremedial tutoring.

**STUDENT LIFE. Housing:** Women's and men's dorms. School-owned/operated apartments. Off-campus privately-owned housing. Suites. 78% of students live in college housing.
**Social atmosphere:** The student newspaper notes, "The university community does try its best to offer the students a variety of social/cultural opportunities/experiences." The Student Government Association, University Activities, campus ministry organizations, and the Greeks influence student social life. On-campus gathering spots include the Pub and Monk's Inn Coffeehouse. Off campus, students frequent Tim's, Alexander's, the Shed, Flannigan's, the Brown Jug, Walnut Hills, and the Oregon District in Dayton. Homecoming, Halloween, Christmas celebrations, St. Patrick's Day, Senior Ball, campus art series, and the Turnabout Dance highlight the school year.
**Services and counseling/handicapped student services:** Placement services. Health service. Women's center. Day care. Self-designed learning programs. Counseling services for minority and older students. Personal and psychological counseling. Career and academic guidance services. Religious counseling. Physically disabled student services. Learning disabled services.
**Campus organizations:** Undergraduate student government. Student newspaper (Flyer News, published twice/week). Literary magazine. Yearbook. Radio station. Vocal and instrumental ensembles, orchestra, concert and marching bands, jazz and pep bands, choir, gospel choir, organ recital series, experimental theatre, University Players, telecommunications group, debating, veterans club, Model UN, Amnesty International, Food Share, Big Brothers/Big Sisters, Youth Hospice, departmental and professional groups, 174 organizations in all. 13 fraternities, 12 chapter houses; 10 sororities, eight chapter houses. 17% of men join a fraternity. 21% of women join a sorority.
**Religious organizations:** Campus Crusade for Christ, Campus Ministry, Fellowship of Christian Athletes, S.A.R.E., Sodality.
**Minority/foreign student organizations:** Minority sororities and fraternities, Black Action Through Unity, Black Greek Council, National Society of Black Engineers. American International Association; Chinese, Irish, Latin American, and Muslim student groups.

**ATHLETICS. Physical education requirements:** None.
**Intercollegiate competition:** 7% of students participate. Baseball (M), basketball (M,W), cheerleading (M,W), cross-country (M,W), football (M), golf (M,W), soccer (M,W), softball (W), tennis (M,W), volleyball (W), water polo (M), wrestling (M). Member of Great Midwest Conference, NCAA Division I, NCAA Division I-AA for football, Pioneer Conference for football.
**Intramural and club sports:** 65% of students participate. Intramural basketball, billiards, bowling, cross-country, flag football, floor hockey, golf, inner-tube water polo, marksmanship, racquetball, soccer, softball, swimming, table tennis, tennis, ultimate frisbee, volleyball, walleyball, wrestling. Men's club crew, ice hockey, lacrosse, martial arts, rugby, soccer, track/field, ultimate frisbee, volleyball. Women's club crew, golf, lacrosse, martial arts, rugby, soccer, track/field, ultimate frisbee.

**ADMISSIONS. Academic basis for candidate selection** (in order of priority): Secondary school record, class rank, standardized test scores, school's recommendation, essay.
**Nonacademic basis for candidate selection:** Extracurricular participation and particular talent or ability are considered.
**Requirements:** Graduation from secondary school is required; GED is accepted. 18 units and the following program of study are recommended: 4 units of English, 3 units of math, 2 units of science, 2 units of foreign language, 3 units of social studies, 4 units of electives. Rank in top two-thirds of secondary school class recommended; minimum test scores and GPA vary depending on program. Completion of math courses through algebra II and trigonometry recommended for business administration, computer science, engineering, mathematics, and natural sciences program applicants. Audition required of music program applicants. Conditional admission possible for applicants not meeting standard requirements. SAT or ACT is required. Campus visit and interview recommended. Off-campus interviews available with an admissions representative.
**Procedure:** Take SAT or ACT by December of 12th year. Visit college for interview by January of 12th year. Notification of admission on rolling basis beginning in late October. Reply is required by date specified in letter of acceptance. $200 nonrefundable tuition deposit. Freshmen accepted for terms other than fall.
**Special programs:** Admission may be deferred one year. Credit and/or placement may be granted through CEEB Advanced Placement exams for scores of 4 or higher. Credit may be granted through CLEP general and subject exams. Early entrance/early admission program. Concurrent enrollment program.
**Transfer students:** Transfer students accepted for terms other than fall. In fall 1993, 9% of all new students were transfers into all classes. 544 transfer applications were received, 360 were accepted. Application deadline is rolling. Minimum 3.0 GPA required of engineering program applicants; 2.5 GPA of business and education program applicants; 2.0 of other applicants. SAT or ACT required of all transfer applicants under age 22. Lowest course grade accepted is "C." At least 54 semester hours must be completed at the university to receive degree.
**Admissions contact:** Myron H. Achbach, Director of Admissions. 513 229-4411.

**FINANCIAL AID. Available aid:** Pell grants, SEOG, state grants, school scholarships and grants, private scholarships and grants, ROTC scholarships, academic merit scholarships, athletic scholarships, and aid for undergraduate foreign students. Perkins Loans (NDSL), PLUS, Stafford Loans (GSL), state loans, school loans, private loans, and SLS. Knight Tuition Plans, AMS, deferred payment plan, and family tuition reduction.
**Financial aid statistics:** 40% of aid is not need-based. In 1993-94, 93% of all undergraduate applicants received aid; 89% of freshman applicants. Average amounts of aid awarded freshmen: Scholarships and grants, $4,500; loans, $3,207.
**Supporting data/closing dates:** FAFSA: Priority filing date is March 31. School's own aid application: Priority filing date is March 31. State aid form: Deadline varies by state. Income tax forms: Accepted on rolling basis. Notification of awards begins March 15.
**Financial aid contact:** Joyce J. Wilkins, Director of Financial Aid. 513 229-4311.

**STUDENT EMPLOYMENT.** College Work/Study Program. Institutional employment. 40% of full-time undergraduates work on campus during school year. Students may expect to earn an average of $1,200 during school year. Off-campus part-time employment opportunities rated "excellent."

**COMPUTER FACILITIES.** 420 IBM/IBM-compatible, Macintosh/Apple, and RISC-/UNIX-based microcomputers; all are networked. Students may access Digital minicomputer/mainframe systems, BITNET, Internet. Residence halls may be equipped with modems. Client/LAN operating systems include Apple/Macintosh, DOS, Microsoft, Novell. Computer languages and software packages include Auto CAD, BASIC, C, COBOL, Composer, dBASE, DBMS, Excelerator, FORTRAN, Harvard Graphics, Lotus 1-2-3, MAPLE, MathCAD, PageMaker, Paradox, PATRAN, Personal Designer, SAS, SCADA, SPSS, WordPerfect, WordStar. Computer facilities are available to all students.
**Fees:** $100 computer fee per year; included in tuition/fees.
**Hours:** 8 AM-midn.

**GRADUATE CAREER DATA.** Companies and businesses that hire graduates: Bank One, Dayton Power & Light Co., Fifth Third Bank, Lazarus, Mead Engineering.

**PROMINENT ALUMNI/AE.** Erma Bombeck, newspaper columnist and author; Charles Pedersen, Nobel Prize-winning chemist; Chuck Noll, head coach, Pittsburgh Steelers; Colombe M. Nicholas, president and CEO, Christian Dior.

# The University of Findlay

**Findlay, OH 45840-3695 419 422-8313**

**1993-94 Costs.** Tuition: $10,920. Room & board: $4,780. Fees, books, misc. academic expenses (school's estimate): $604.
**Enrollment.** Undergraduates: 2,178 (full-time). Freshman class: 2,165 applicants, 1,783 accepted, 412 enrolled. Graduate enrollment: 78.
**Test score averages/ranges.** Average SAT scores: 439 verbal, 473 math. Range of SAT scores of middle 50%: 370-500 verbal, 400-550 math. Average ACT scores: 20 English, 21 math, 20 composite. Range of ACT scores of middle 50%: 18-22 composite.
**Faculty.** 155 full-time; 100 part-time. 45% of faculty holds doctoral degree. Student/faculty ratio: 15 to 1.
**Selectivity rating.** Competitive.

**PROFILE.** Findlay, founded in 1882, is a church-affiliated, liberal arts university. Programs are offered through the Divisions of Business Administration, Fine Arts, Humanities, Mathematics and Computer Science, Natural Science, Social Science, and Teacher Education and the Centers for Bilingual Multicultural Studies and Equine Studies. Its 142-acre campus is located in Findlay, 45 miles south of Toledo.

**Accreditation:** NCACS. Professionally accredited by the National Council for Accreditation of Teacher Education.
**Religious orientation:** The University of Findlay is affiliated with the Churches of God (General Conference); one semester of religion required.
**Library:** Collections totaling over 122,600 volumes, 980 periodical subscriptions, and 90,400 microform items.
**Special facilities/museums:** Art gallery, planetarium.
**Athletic facilities:** Physical education center, swimming pool, exercise and weight rooms, track, tennis and racquetball courts.

**STUDENT BODY. Undergraduate profile:** 85% are state residents. 2% Asian-American, 6% Black, 2% Hispanic, 90% White. Average age of undergraduates is 20.
**Freshman profile:** 20% of accepted applicants took SAT; 80% took ACT. 80% of freshmen come from public schools.
**Undergraduate achievement:** 89% of fall 1992 freshmen returned for fall 1993 term. 45% of entering class graduated. 7% of students who completed a degree program immediately went on to graduate study.
**Foreign students:** 170 students are from out of the country. Countries represented include Japan, Jordan, Korea, Malaysia, Taiwan, and Thailand; 23 in all.

**PROGRAMS OF STUDY. Degrees:** B.A., B.S.
**Majors:** Accounting, Art, Art Education, Art Therapy, Athletic Training, Bilingual/Business, Bilingual Business Education, Bilingual/Multicultural Education, Biology, Business Education, Business Systems Analysis, Business Writing, Communication, Computer Science, Criminal Justice, Economics/Finance, Elementary Education, Engineering, English, Environmental/Hazardous Materials, Equestrian Studies, Equine Management, Health/Physical Education/Recreation, History, Management, Marketing, Mathematics/Computers/Science, Nature Interpretation, Nuclear Medical Technology, Philosophy, Physical Education, Political Science, Pre-Engineering, Pre-Medicine, Pre-Veterinary, Psychology, Religion, Religion/Christian Education/Philosophy, Science, Social Sciences, Social Work, Sociology, Spanish, Spanish/Business, Speech, Technical Writing, Theatre, Therapeutic Recreation.
**Distribution of degrees:** The majors with the highest enrollment are business, natural sciences, and education; religion and philosophy have the lowest.
**Requirements:** General education requirement.
**Academic regulations:** Freshmen must maintain minimum 1.7 GPA; sophomores, 1.8 GPA; juniors, 1.9 GPA; seniors, 1.9 GPA.
**Special:** Minors offered in many majors and in chemistry, fine arts, general science, gerontology, international studies, musical arts, teaching English as a second language, and writing. Courses offered in geography and geology. Students encouraged to work with advisers to develop programs of study best suited to personal needs and interests. Program may be interdisciplinary and may cross divisional lines. Portfolio program grants up to 90 credits toward bachelor's degree. Associate's degrees offered. Self-designed majors. Double majors. Independent study. Accelerated study. Pass/fail grading option. Internships. Cooperative education programs. Graduate school at which undergraduates may take graduate-level courses. Preprofessional programs in law, medicine, veterinary science, and engineering. 3-1 programs in medical technology and nuclear medicine technology. 3-2 engineering programs with U of Toledo and Washington U. Washington Semester. Teacher certification in elementary, secondary, special education, and bilingual/bicultural education. Certification in specific subject areas. Study abroad in several countries. AFROTC at Bowling Green State U.
**Honors:** Honors program. Honor societies.
**Academic Assistance:** Remedial reading, writing, math, and study skills. Nonremedial tutoring.

**STUDENT LIFE. Housing:** All students under age 22 must live on campus unless living with family. Women's and men's dorms. Sorority and fraternity housing. 68% of students live in college housing.
**Services and counseling/handicapped student services:** Placement services. Health service. Counseling services for minority and older students. Personal and psychological counseling. Career and academic guidance services. Learning disabled services.
**Campus organizations:** Undergraduate student government. Student newspaper (Pulse, published twice/month). Literary magazine. Radio station. Choir, jazz ensemble, drama group, deparmental and service groups, 33 organizations in all. Four fraternities, all with chapter houses; one sorority, with chapter house.
**Religious organizations:** Intervarsity Christian Fellowship.
**Minority/foreign student organizations:** Black Student Union. International Student Group.

**ATHLETICS. Physical education requirements:** None.
**Intercollegiate competition:** 30% of students participate. Baseball (M), basketball (M,W), cross-country (M,W), football (M), golf (M), soccer (M), softball (W), swimming (M,W), tennis (M,W), track (M,W), track (outdoor) (M,W), track and field (indoor) (M,W), track and field (outdoor) (M,W), volleyball (W), water polo (M), wrestling (M). Member of NAIA, NCAA Division III.
**Intramural and club sports:** 40% of students participate. Intramural basketball, softball, touch football, volleyball. Men's club field hockey, water polo. Women's club water polo.

**ADMISSIONS. Academic basis for candidate selection** (in order of priority): Secondary school record, class rank, standardized test scores, school's recommendation, essay.
**Nonacademic basis for candidate selection:** Character and personality, extracurricular participation, particular talent or ability, and alumni/ae relationship are considered.
**Requirements:** Graduation from secondary school is required; GED is accepted. 16 units and the following program of study are recommended: 4 units of English, 3 units of math, 3 units of science, 2 units of foreign language, 2 units of social studies, 1 unit of history, 1 unit of academic electives. Minimum composite ACT score of 18, rank in top half of secondary school class, and minimum 2.3 GPA recommended. Foundations Semester recommended for applicants not normally admissible; interviews required. ACT is required; SAT may be substituted. Campus visit and interview recommended. Off-campus interviews available with an admissions representative.
**Procedure:** Take SAT or ACT by fall of 12th year. Application deadline is August 1. Notification of admission by August 1. $100 tuition deposit, refundable until May 1. Freshmen accepted for terms other than fall.
**Special programs:** Admission may be deferred. Credit and/or placement may be granted through CEEB Advanced Placement exams for scores of 3 or higher. Credit may be granted through CLEP general and subject exams. Credit and placement may be granted through military and life experience. Early entrance/early admission program.
**Transfer students:** Transfer students accepted for terms other than fall. In fall 1993, 209 transfer applications were received. Application deadline is August 1 for fall; December 15 for spring. Minimum 2.0 GPA required. Lowest course grade accepted is "C." Maximum number of transferable credits is 90 semester hours. At least 30 semester hours must be completed at the university to receive degree.
**Admissions contact:** Mary Ellen Klein, Ph.D., Director of Admissions. 800 548-0932.

**FINANCIAL AID. Available aid:** Pell grants, SEOG, state scholarships and grants, school scholarships and grants, private scholarships and grants, academic merit scholarships, and athletic scholarships. Perkins Loans (NDSL), PLUS, Stafford Loans (GSL), and state loans. Family tuition reduction. Monthly payment plan.
**Financial aid statistics:** 20% of aid is not need-based. In 1993-94, 85% of all undergraduate applicants received aid; 85% of freshman applicants. Average amounts of aid awarded freshmen: Scholarships and grants, $3,300; loans, $2,200.
**Supporting data/closing dates:** FAFSA/FAF: Deadline is August 1. Notification of awards begins February 1.
**Financial aid contact:** Arman Habegger, M.A., Director of Financial Aid. 419 424-4791.

**STUDENT EMPLOYMENT.** College Work/Study Program. Institutional employment. 40% of full-time undergraduates work on campus during school year. Students may expect to earn an average of $1,000 during school year. Off-campus part-time employment opportunities rated "good."

**COMPUTER FACILITIES.** 104 IBM/IBM-compatible and Macintosh/Apple microcomputers; 63 are networked. Computer languages and software packages include BASIC, COBOL, FORTRAN, MacroAssembler, Pascal, RPG II. Computer facilities are available to all students.
**Fees:** None.

**GRADUATE CAREER DATA.** Highest graduate school enrollments: Ohio State U. 70% of graduates choose careers in business and industry.

**PROMINENT ALUMNI/AE.** Patrick Rooney, president, Cooper Tire.

# University of Rio Grande

**Rio Grande, OH 45674 614 245-5353**

**1993-94 Costs.** Tuition: $2,460 (state residents), $6,012 (out-of-state). Room & board: $3,555-$3,600. Fees, books, misc. academic expenses (school's estimate): $840.
**Enrollment.** Undergraduates: 763 men, 1,057 women (full-time). Freshman class: 908 applicants, 889 accepted, 648 enrolled. Graduate enrollment: 2 men, 111 women.
**Test score averages/ranges.** Average ACT scores: 19 English, 18 math, 19 composite. Range of ACT scores of middle 50%: 19-26 English, 19-26 math.
**Faculty.** 108 full-time; 22 part-time. 80% of faculty holds doctoral degree. Student/faculty ratio: 18 to 1.
**Selectivity rating.** Noncompetitive.

**PROFILE.** University of Rio Grande, founded in 1876, is a private institution. Programs are offered through the Colleges of Education, Health, and Physical Education, and Fine Arts Education; General Studies and Liberal Arts; Mathematics, Natural Sciences, and Computer Science; and Technology; the Holzer College of Nursing; and the Emerson E. Evans College of Business Management. Its 170-acre campus is located in Rio Grande, 80 miles south of Columbus.

**Accreditation:** NCACS. Professionally accredited by the American Medical Association (CAHEA), the National League for Nursing.
**Religious orientation:** University of Rio Grande is nonsectarian; no religious requirements.
**Library:** Collections totaling over 52,392 volumes, 650 periodical subscriptions, and 15,000 microform items.
**Special facilities/museums:** Archives of local and college history, art museum.

**Athletic facilities:** Gymnasium, swimming pool, weight room with Universal equipment, baseball, soccer, and softball fields, racquetball and tennis courts, track, cross-country course.

**STUDENT BODY. Undergraduate profile:** 96% are state residents; 10% are transfers. 3% Asian-American, 10% Black, 80% White, 7% Other. Average age of undergraduates is 23.
**Freshman profile:** 80% of accepted applicants took ACT. 80% of freshmen come from public schools.
**Undergraduate achievement:** 70% of fall 1992 freshmen returned for fall 1993 term. 60% of entering class graduated. 2% of students who completed a degree program immediately went on to graduate study.
**Foreign students:** 147 students are from out of the country. Countries represented include China, Japan, Korea, Morrocco, Philippines, and United Kingdom; 11 in all.

**PROGRAMS OF STUDY. Degrees:** B.S.
**Majors:** Accounting, American Studies, Art, Biology, Business Education, Business Management, Chemistry/Physics, Communications, Economics, Education, English, Fine Arts, History, Humanities, Industrial Technology, International Business, Marketing, Mathematics, Music Education, Physical Education, Social Science, Social Work, Sport/Exercise Studies.
**Distribution of degrees:** The majors with the highest enrollment are education, business management, and social sciences; chemistry and mathematics have the lowest.
**Requirements:** General education requirement.
**Academic regulations:** Freshmen must maintain minimum 1.8 GPA; sophomores, 1.9 GPA; juniors, 2.0 GPA; seniors, 2.0 GPA.
**Special:** Minors offered in some majors and in computer science, finance, general business, general science, political science, psychology, and sociology. Courses offered in banking, data processing, English as a Second Language, geology, journalism, music, natural science, philosophy/religion, Spanish, and theatre. Associate's degrees offered. Self-designed majors. Double majors. Dual degrees. Independent study. Pass/fail grading option. Internships. Graduate school at which undergraduates may take graduate-level courses. Preprofessional programs in law, medicine, veterinary science, pharmacy, dentistry, theology, optometry, engineering, library science, and social work. Washington Semester. Teacher certification in early childhood, elementary, secondary, special education, and vo-tech education. Certification in specific subject areas. Study abroad in Japan. ROTC.
**Honors:** Honors program. Honor societies.
**Academic Assistance:** Remedial reading, writing, math, and study skills. Nonremedial tutoring.

**STUDENT LIFE. Housing:** All unmarried students under age 23 must live on campus unless living with family. Coed, women's, and men's dorms. 31% of students live in college housing.
**Social atmosphere:** According to the editor of the student newspaper, the university has "a very active Student Programming Board. This group sponsors concerts and films on a weekly basis. The theatre program produces a play approximately every two weeks." Favorite student hangouts are the Student Center, the Fine and Performing Arts Center, and the Athletic Center. Social events include Homecoming, May Day, and basketball games.
**Services and counseling/handicapped student services:** Placement services. Health service. Day care. Counseling services for minority, military, veteran, and older students. Birth control, personal, and psychological counseling. Career and academic guidance services. Physically disabled student services. Learning disabled services. Notetaking services. Tape recorders. Tutors. Reader services for the blind.
**Campus organizations:** Undergraduate student government. Student newspaper (Smoke Signals, published once/week). Literary magazine. Yearbook. Radio station. Grande Chorale, choir, theatre, programming board, special-interest groups, 21 organizations in all. Five fraternities, no chapter houses; five sororities, no chapter houses. 25% of men join a fraternity. 25% of women join a sorority.
**Religious organizations:** Intervarsity Christian Fellowship.
**Minority/foreign student organizations:** Black Student Union. Foreign Student Organization.

**ATHLETICS. Physical education requirements:** Three terms of physical education required.
**Intercollegiate competition:** 9% of students participate. Baseball (M), basketball (M,W), cheerleading (W), cross-country (M,W), soccer (M), softball (W), track (indoor) (M,W), track (outdoor) (M,W), track and field (indoor) (M,W), track and field (outdoor) (M,W), volleyball (W). Member of Mid-Ohio Conference, NAIA.
**Intramural and club sports:** 18% of students participate. Intramural basketball, flag football, sand volleyball, softball, swimming, tennis, volleyball, wallyball. Men's club golf, tennis.

**ADMISSIONS. Academic basis for candidate selection** (in order of priority): Secondary school record, standardized test scores, class rank, essay, school's recommendation.
**Requirements:** Graduation from secondary school is required; GED is accepted. No specific distribution of secondary school units required. Minimum composite ACT score of 15 and minimum 2.0 GPA required. Minimum composite ACT score of 19 and biology, algebra, and chemistry required of nursing program applicants. Audition required of music program applicants. Summer remedial program for applicants not normally admissible. ACT is required. Campus visit and interview recommended. Off-campus interviews available with an admissions representative.
**Procedure:** Take ACT by October 30 of 12th year. Visit college for interview by February 28 of 12th year. Application deadline is July 1. Notification of admission on rolling basis. $200 nonrefundable room deposit. Freshmen accepted for terms other than fall.
**Special programs:** Admission may be deferred one quarter. Credit and/or placement may be granted through CEEB Advanced Placement exams for scores of 3 or higher. Credit may be granted through CLEP general and subject exams, challenge exams, and military and life experience. Early entrance/early admission program. Concurrent enrollment program.
**Transfer students:** Transfer students accepted for terms other than fall. In fall 1993, 10% of all new students were transfers into all classes. 49 transfer applications were received, 49 were accepted. Application deadline is August 1 for fall; January 15 for spring. Minimum 2.0 GPA recommended. Lowest course grade accepted is "D." At least 45 quarter hours must be completed at the university to receive degree.
**Admissions contact:** Mark F. Abell, M.Ed., Director of Admissions. 614 245-5353, extension 208.

**FINANCIAL AID. Available aid:** Pell grants, SEOG, Federal Nursing Student Scholarships, state scholarships and grants, school scholarships and grants, private scholarships and grants, ROTC scholarships, academic merit scholarships, athletic scholarships, and aid for undergraduate foreign students. Perkins Loans (NDSL), PLUS, Stafford Loans (GSL), NSL, state loans, school loans, and SLS. AMS.
**Financial aid statistics:** 25% of aid is not need-based. In 1993-94, 82% of all undergraduate applicants received aid; 70% of freshman applicants. Average amounts of aid awarded freshmen: Scholarships and grants, $900; loans, $1,250.
**Supporting data/closing dates:** FAFSA: Priority filing date is March 1; accepted on rolling basis. School's own aid application: Accepted on rolling basis. State aid form: Priority filing date is February 15.
**Financial aid contact:** Dr. John Hill, Ph.D., Director of Financial Aid. 614 245-5353, extension 218.

**STUDENT EMPLOYMENT.** College Work/Study Program. Institutional employment. 25% of full-time undergraduates work on campus during school year. Students may expect to earn an average of $1,500 during school year. Off-campus part-time employment opportunities rated "fair."

**COMPUTER FACILITIES.** 75 IBM/IBM-compatible and Macintosh/Apple microcomputers; 20 are networked. Computer languages and software packages include BASIC, COBOL, RPG II. Computer facilities are available to all students.
**Fees:** None.

**GRADUATE CAREER DATA.** Highest graduate school enrollments: Marshall U, Ohio State U, Ohio U. 40% of graduates choose careers in business and industry. Companies and businesses that hire graduates: Ashland Oil, Ernst & Young, Good Year, IBM, Internal Revenue Service.

**PROMINENT ALUMNI/AE.** Ronald Grover, president, Dunn & Bradstreet; Dr. John Evans, consulting scientist, Palo Alto Research Lab; John Hoyt, president, National Humane Society.

## The University of Toledo

**Toledo, OH 43606** **419 537-4242**

**1993-94 Costs.** Tuition: $3,236 (state residents), $7,758 (out-of-state). Room & board: $3,400. Fees, books, misc. academic expenses (school's estimate): $600.
**Enrollment.** Undergraduates: 7,652 men, 7,776 women (full-time). Freshman class: 7,345 applicants, 7,092 accepted, 3,600 enrolled. Graduate enrollment: 1,736 men, 1,654 women.
**Test score averages/ranges.** Average SAT scores: 434 verbal, 489 math. Range of SAT scores of middle 50%: 390-530 verbal, 430-610 math. Average ACT scores: 20 English, 20 math, 21 composite. Range of ACT scores of middle 50%: 18-24 English, 17-24 math.
**Faculty.** 565 full-time; 563 part-time. 88% of faculty holds doctoral degree. Student/faculty ratio: 19 to 1.
**Selectivity rating.** Noncompetitive.

**PROFILE.** The University of Toledo is a public institution. Founded in 1872, it joined the state system in 1967. Programs are offered through the Colleges of Arts and Sciences, Business Administration, Education, Engineering, and Pharmacy; University College; and the Graduate School. Its 305-acre campus is located in Toledo.
**Accreditation:** NCACS. Professionally accredited by the Accreditation Board for Engineering and Technology, the American Assembly of Collegiate Schools of Business, the American Bar Association, the American Council on Pharmaceutical Education, the American Medical Association (CAHEA), the American Physical Therapy Association, the National Association of Schools of Music, the National Council for Accreditation of Teacher Education, the National League for Nursing.
**Religious orientation:** The University of Toledo is nonsectarian; no religious requirements.
**Library:** Collections totaling over 1,558,864 volumes, 7,529 periodical subscriptions, and 1,477,497 microform items.
**Special facilities/museums:** Language lab, arboretum, planetariums, two observatories, electron microscope.
**Athletic facilities:** Field house, health education center, baseball, intramural, and softball fields, tracks, swimming pool.

**STUDENT BODY. Undergraduate profile:** 88% are state residents; 23% are transfers. 2% Asian-American, 7% Black, 2% Hispanic, 85% White, 4% Other. Average age of undergraduates is 22.
**Freshman profile:** 3% of freshmen who took SAT scored 700 or over on verbal, 11% scored 700 or over on math; 13% scored 600 or over on verbal, 29% scored 600 or over on math; 33% scored 500 or over on verbal, 58% scored 500 or over on math; 71% scored 400 or over on verbal, 82% scored 400 or over on math; 95% scored 300 or over on verbal, 98% scored 300 or over on math. 20% of accepted applicants took SAT; 79% took ACT.
**Undergraduate achievement:** 72% of fall 1992 freshmen returned for fall 1993 term.
**Foreign students:** 1,337 students are from out of the country. Countries represented include Indonesia, Jordan, Korea, Malaysia, Taiwan, and Thailand; 85 in all.

**PROGRAMS OF STUDY. Degrees:** B.A., B.Bus.Admin., B.Ed., B.Eng.Tech., B.F.A., B.Med.Tech., B.Mus., B.S., B.S.Admin., B.S.Chem.Eng., B.S.Civil Eng., B.S.Crim.Just., B.S.Elec.Eng., B.S.Hlth.Care Admin., B.S.Indust.Eng., B.S.Mech.Eng., B.S.Nurs., B.S.Pharm., B.S.Phys.Ther., B.S.Physics, B.Voc.Ed.
**Majors:** Accounting, Adaptive Physical Education, Administrative Services, Adult Liberal Studies, American Studies, Anthropology, Art, Art Education, Art History, Asian Studies, Biology, Biology Education, Business Education, Chemical Engineering, Chemistry, Chemistry Education, Civil Engineering, Classics, Communication, Communication Education, Community Health Education, Comparative Literature, Comprehensive Physical Education, Computer Science/Engineering, Computer Systems/Production Management, Criminal Justice, Deaf/Hard of Hearing, Early Childhood Education, Earth

Science Education, Economics, Educational Media, Electrical Engineering, Elementary Education, Engineering Physics, Engineering Technology, English, English Language Arts, European Studies, Exercise Science, Finance, French, French Education, General Studies, Geography/Planning, Geology, German, German Education, History, Human Performance, Humanities, Individualized Program, Industrial Engineering, Institutional Health Care Supervision, Interdisciplinary Major, International Relations, Latin American Studies, Latin Education, Learning/Behavior Disorders, Linguistics, Management, Marketing, Mathematics, Mathematics Education, Mechanical Engineering, Medical Technology, Mental Retardation/Educable, Multi-Handicapped Education, Music, Music Education, Nursing, Nursing Home Administration, Orthopedically Handicapped, Pharmacy, Philosophy, Physical Education, Physical Therapy, Physics, Political Science, Pre-Dentistry, Pre-Medicine, Psychology, Public Affairs/Community Services, Recreation/Leisure Education, School/Public Health, Social Sciences Education, Social Work, Sociology, Spanish, Spanish Education, Special Education, Special/Elementary Education, Speech Communication, Speech/Hearing Therapy, Theatre, Trainable Mentally Retarded, Visually Handicapped Education, Vocational Education, Women's Studies.

**Distribution of degrees:** The majors with the highest enrollment are business, engineering, and individualized programs; interdepartmental B.A., medical technology, and philosophy have the lowest.

**Requirements:** General education requirement.

**Academic regulations:** Minimum 2.0 GPA must be maintained.

**Special:** Associate's degrees offered. Self-designed majors. Double majors. Dual degrees. Independent study. Pass/fail grading option. Internships. Cooperative education programs. Graduate school at which undergraduates may take graduate-level courses. Preprofessional programs in law, medicine, and dentistry. 2-2 programs in criminal justice, engineering technologies, and law enforcement. Coll of Pharmacy has preprofessional program that admits freshmen; of these, top 80 students continue in professional division. 3-4 dental program with Case Western Reserve U. 3-4 medical program with Medical Coll of Ohio. Member of Central States Universities, Inc. and Consortium for Health Education in Northwest Ohio. Teacher certification in early childhood, elementary, secondary, and special education. Certification in specific subject areas. Study abroad possible in Australia, the Dominican Republic, England, France, Germany, Ireland, Japan, Mexico, Russia, Scotland, Spain, Trinidad, and Uganda. ROTC. AFROTC at Bowling Green State U.

**Honors:** Phi Beta Kappa. Honors program. Honor societies.

**Academic Assistance:** Remedial reading, writing, math, and study skills. Nonremedial tutoring.

**STUDENT LIFE. Housing:** Freshmen and sophomores must live on campus unless living with family. Coed and women's dorms. Sorority and fraternity housing. Off-campus privately-owned housing. Honors housing. 12% of students live in college housing.

**Social atmosphere:** According to the student newspaper, The University of Toledo has a "great social life and getting better all the time." Football and basketball games, Homecoming Week activities, Winter Week, Spring Week, and Spring Release are popular social events of the school year. Among the influential groups on campus are Greeks and the Student Government. Favorite student gathering spots include Angelo's Attic, the Orchard Inn, Nick and Jimmy's, the Pub, Charlie's Blind Pig, Arnie's, and Frankie's.

**Services and counseling/handicapped student services:** Placement services. Health service. Women's center. Day care. Counseling services for minority, military, veteran, and older students. Birth control, personal, and psychological counseling. Career and academic guidance services. Physically disabled student services. Learning disabled program/services. Notetaking services. Tape recorders. Tutors. Reader services for the blind.

**Campus organizations:** Undergraduate student government. Student newspaper (Collegian, published twice/week). Radio and TV stations. University and ROTC bands, Madrigal Singers, chorus, orchestra, theatre, departmental and special-interest groups, 216 organizations in all. 15 fraternities, 10 chapter houses; 10 sororities, six chapter houses. 10% of men join a fraternity. 10% of women join a sorority.

**Religious organizations:** Active Christians Today, Campus Bible Fellowship, Campus Christian Fellowship, Christian Life, Christian Student Fellowship, Hillel, Muslim student group, Newman Club, Gospel Choir, Campus Crusade for Christ.

**Minority/foreign student organizations:** Association for Advancement of African-American Women, Black Law Student Association, Black Student Union, Epsilon Delta Pi, Hispanic Law Student Association, MEChA, Society of Black Engineers, Society of Black Professionals, Chinese Student Union, Korean Student Association, Delta Phi Alpha. Arabic, Chinese, Egyptian, Korean, Hong Kong, Indian, Japanese, Malaysian, Pakistani, Palestinian, Singapore, and Venezuelan groups.

**ATHLETICS. Physical education requirements:** None.

**Intercollegiate competition:** 2% of students participate. Baseball (M), basketball (M,W), cheerleading (M,W), cross-country (M,W), football (M), golf (M), softball (W), swimming (M,W), tennis (M,W), track (indoor) (M,W), track (outdoor) (M,W), track and field (indoor) (M,W), track and field (outdoor) (M,W), volleyball (W), wrestling (M). Member of Mid-American Athletic Conference, NCAA Division I, NCAA Division I-A for football.

**Intramural and club sports:** Men's club Alpine skiing, bowling, crew, fencing, ice hockey, lacrosse, martial arts, racquetball, rifle, sailing, soccer, ultimate frisbee, volleyball. Women's club Alpine skiing, bowling, crew, fencing, field hockey, martial arts, racquetball, rifle, sailing, soccer, ultimate frisbee.

**ADMISSIONS. Academic basis for candidate selection** (in order of priority): Secondary school record, standardized test scores, class rank, school's recommendation, essay.

**Nonacademic basis for candidate selection:** Geographical distribution is important. Extracurricular participation, particular talent or ability, and alumni/ae relationship are considered.

**Requirements:** Graduation from secondary school is required; GED is accepted. 16 units and the following program of study are recommended: 4 units of English, 3 units of math, 3 units of science including 1 unit of lab, 3 units of foreign language, 2 units of social studies, 1 unit of history. Minimum composite ACT score of 18 (combined SAT scores of 900) recommended of in-state applicants; minimum composite ACT score of 21 (combined SAT score of 900) and minimum 2.0 GPA required of out-of-state applicants. 4 units of math and science required of engineering program applicants; 3 units of math required of business administration program applicants; 2 units of algebra and 1 unit of plane geometry required of applicants to other programs. Foreign language required of arts and sciences and secondary education program applicants; recommended for applicants to other programs. Audition required of music program applicants. Ohio residents with academic deficiencies may be admitted but must complete required secondary school units prior to sophomore year. ACT is required; SAT may be substituted. Campus visit and interview recommended. Off-campus interviews available with an admissions representative.

**Procedure:** Take SAT or ACT by November of 12th year. Visit college for interview by January of 12th year. Application deadline is one week prior to start of each quarter. Notification of admission on rolling basis. $100 room deposit, 40% of which is refundable until March 1. Freshmen accepted for terms other than fall.

**Special programs:** Admission may be deferred one year. Credit and/or placement may be granted through CEEB Advanced Placement exams for scores of 3 or higher. Credit and/or placement may be granted through CLEP general and subject exams. Credit and placement may be granted through life experience. Early entrance/early admission program. Concurrent enrollment program.

**Transfer students:** Transfer students accepted for terms other than fall. In fall 1993, 23% of all new students were transfers into all classes. 1,828 transfer applications were received, 1,666 were accepted. Application deadline is 7 days prior to start of quarter for fall; 7 days prior to start of quarter for spring. Minimum 2.0 GPA required. Lowest course grade accepted is "C." Maximum number of transferable credits is 141 quarter hours. At least 45 quarter hours must be completed at the university to receive degree.

**Admissions contact:** Richard J. Eastop, M.Ed., Dean of Admissions. 419 537-2696.

**FINANCIAL AID. Available aid:** Pell grants, SEOG, Federal Nursing Student Scholarships, state scholarships and grants, school scholarships and grants, private scholarships and grants, ROTC scholarships, academic merit scholarships, and athletic scholarships. Full-ride scholarships offered to National Merit, Achievement, and Hispanic finalists. Full-ride Presidential Scholarship. Perkins Loans (NDSL), PLUS, Stafford Loans (GSL), NSL, school loans, private loans, and SLS. Incremental Payment Plan (Ipp).

**Financial aid statistics:** 40% of aid is not need-based. In 1993-94, 59% of all undergraduate applicants received aid; 72% of freshman applicants. Average amounts of aid awarded freshmen: Scholarships and grants, $2,354; loans, $9,357.

**Supporting data/closing dates:** FAFSA: Priority filing date is April 1; accepted on rolling basis. School's own aid application: Priority filing date is April 1. State aid form: Accepted on rolling basis. Notification of awards on rolling basis.

**Financial aid contact:** Dr. Richard Lasko, Ph.D., Director of Financial Aid. 419 537-2056.

**STUDENT EMPLOYMENT.** College Work/Study Program. Institutional employment. 20% of full-time undergraduates work on campus during school year. Students may expect to earn an average of $3,060 during school year. Freshmen are discouraged from working during their first term. Off-campus part-time employment opportunities rated "good."

**COMPUTER FACILITIES.** 2,000 IBM/IBM-compatible and Macintosh/Apple microcomputers; 800 are networked. Students may access Digital, IBM minicomputer/mainframe systems, Internet. Residence halls may be equipped with stand-alone microcomputers, networked microcomputers. Client/LAN operating systems include OS/2, Novell. Computer languages and software packages include Ada, BASIC, COBOL, FORTRAN, MINITAB, OMNICALL, PL-I, RAMIS, SAS, SPSS-X; 69 in all. Computer facilities are available to all students.

**Fees:** None.

**Hours:** 8:30 AM-midn. (M-F); 8:30 AM-5 PM (Sa); 1 PM-midn. (Su).

**GRADUATE CAREER DATA.** 68% of graduates choose careers in business and industry. Companies and businesses that hire graduates: ALCOA, Dana Corp., FBI, Ford, Lilly, Ohio State U Hospital, Owens Corning, Owens-Illinois.

**PROMINENT ALUMNI/AE.** Howard C. Ansel, dean, Coll of Pharmacy, U of Georgia; Beverly W. Miller, president Western New England Coll; Andy Douglas, Ohio supreme court justice; Ivan W. Gorr, CEO, Cooper Tire & Rubber; John Snow, president and CEO, CSX Corp.; William Marohn, president, Whirpool Corp.; Andrew Fenady, television and movie producer, including *Gunsmoke*; Jean Gould, author; Hal B. Jennings, Jr., M.D., U.S. Army Surgeon General, 1969-1973.

8-22

# Urbana University

**Urbana, OH 43078** **513 652-1301**

**1994-95 Costs.** Tuition: $8,468. Room: $1,760. Board: $2,380. Fees, books, misc. academic expenses (school's estimate): $1,107.

**Enrollment.** Undergraduates: 476 men, 269 women (full-time). Freshman class: 318 applicants, 265 accepted, 132 enrolled.

**Test score averages/ranges.** Average SAT scores: 750 combined. Average ACT scores: 19 composite. Range of ACT scores of middle 50%: 17-21 composite.

**Faculty.** 34 full-time; 44 part-time. 62% of faculty holds doctoral degree. Student/faculty ratio: 14 to 1.

**Selectivity rating.** Less competitive.

**PROFILE.** Urbana, founded in 1850, is a private, church-affiliated, comprehensive university. Its 128-acre campus is located in Urbana, in west-central Ohio, 40 miles west of Columbus.

**Accreditation:** NCACS.

**Religious orientation:** Urbana University is affiliated with the General Convention of the Swedenborgian Church; no religious requirements.

**Library:** Collections totaling over 64,000 volumes, 300 periodical subscriptions, and 7,222 microform items.

**Special facilities/museums:** TV studio, rare book collection.

**Athletic facilities:** Gymnasium, racquetball and tennis courts, swimming pool, track, weight room, baseball and practice football fields.

**STUDENT BODY. Undergraduate profile:** 94% are state residents; 42% are transfers. 1% Asian-American, 25% Black, 1% Hispanic, 72% White, 1% Other. Average age of undergraduates is 20.

**Freshman profile:** 5% of accepted applicants took SAT; 95% took ACT. 97% of freshmen come from public schools.

**Undergraduate achievement:** 77% of fall 1992 freshmen returned for fall 1993 term. 26% of entering class graduated. 13% of students who completed a degree program immediately went on to graduate study.
**Foreign students:** 10 students are from out of the country. Countries represented include Canada, Japan, Kenya, Malaysia, and Taiwan.

**PROGRAMS OF STUDY. Degrees:** B.A., B.S., B.S.Bus.Admin., B.S.Ed.
**Majors:** Accounting, Athletic Training, Biology, Business Administration, Case Management, Chemistry, Child Services/Family Services, Communications, Comprehensive Science, Corrections, Economics, Elementary Education, English, Finance, General Business/Management, Health Care, Law Enforcement, Liberal Studies, Marketing, Middle School Education, Personnel Management, Philosophy/Religion, Physical Education, Psychology, Recreation, Secondary Education, Sociology.
**Distribution of degrees:** The majors with the highest enrollment are business administration, social sciences, and education; sciences, humanities, and recreation have the lowest.
**Requirements:** General education requirement.
**Academic regulations:** Freshmen must maintain minimum 1.7 GPA; sophomores, juniors, seniors, 2.0 GPA.
**Special:** Minors offered in some majors and in computer science and theatre; interdisciplinary minors offered. Associate's degrees offered. Self-designed majors. Double majors. Independent study. Accelerated study. Pass/fail grading option. Internships. Preprofessional programs in law, medicine, and dentistry. 2-2 business administration program with Miami-Jacobs Junior Coll. Member of Southwestern Ohio Council for Higher Education; cross-registration possible. Teacher certification in elementary, middle school, and secondary education. Certification in specific subject areas. AFROTC at Wright State U.
**Honors:** Honor societies.
**Academic Assistance:** Remedial reading, writing, math, and study skills. Nonremedial tutoring.

**ADMISSIONS. Academic basis for candidate selection** (in order of priority): Secondary school record, standardized test scores, class rank, essay, school's recommendation.
**Nonacademic basis for candidate selection:** Character and personality, extracurricular participation, particular talent or ability, and alumni/ae relationship are considered.
**Requirements:** Graduation from secondary school is required; GED is accepted. 16 units and the following program of study are recommended: 4 units of English, 3 units of math, 3 units of science, 2 units of foreign language, 2 units of social studies, 2 units of electives. Minimum composite ACT score of 19 (combined SAT score of 700) and minimum 2.2 GPA required. Teacher education program has separate admissions criteria. Compensatory Admission Program for applicants not normally admissible. SAT or ACT is required. Campus visit and interview recommended. Off-campus interviews available with an admissions representative.
**Procedure:** Notification of admission on rolling basis. $100 nonrefundable tuition deposit. $100 room deposit, refundable until beginning of classes. Freshmen accepted for terms other than fall.
**Special programs:** Admission may be deferred one year. Credit may be granted through CLEP general and subject exams, Regents College, ACT PEP, DANTES, and challenge exams, and military and life experience. Early entrance/early admission program. Concurrent enrollment program.
**Transfer students:** Transfer students accepted for terms other than fall. In fall 1993, 42% of all new students were transfers into all classes. 196 transfer applications were received, 144 were accepted. Application deadline is rolling for fall; rolling for spring. Minimum 2.0 GPA recommended. Lowest course grade accepted is "C." At least 30 semester hours must be completed at the university to receive degree.
**Admissions contact:** Lori Botkin-Carpenter, M.Ed., Director of Admissions. 513 652-1301, extension 356.

**FINANCIAL AID. Available aid:** Pell grants, SEOG, state scholarships and grants, school scholarships and grants, private scholarships and grants, academic merit scholarships, and athletic scholarships. Perkins Loans (NDSL), PLUS, Stafford Loans (GSL), state loans, and SLS. AMS, Tuition Management Systems, and deferred payment plan.
**Financial aid statistics:** 32% of aid is not need-based. In 1993-94, 100% of all undergraduate applicants received aid. Average amounts of aid awarded freshmen: Scholarships and grants, $1,600; loans, $2,625.
**Supporting data/closing dates:** FAFSA/FFS: Accepted on rolling basis. School's own aid application: Accepted on rolling basis. State aid form: Deadline varies by state. Priority filing date is May 1; deadline is September 24. Income tax forms: Accepted on rolling basis. Notification of awards on rolling basis.
**Financial aid contact:** Roberta J. Rabe, M.Ed., Director of Financial Aid. 513 652-1301, extension 355.

8-24

# Ursuline College

**Pepper Pike, OH 44124** **216 449-4200**

**1994-95 Costs.** Tuition: $9,600. Room & board: $4,500. Fees, books, misc. academic expenses (school's estimate): $690.
**Enrollment.** Undergraduates: 11 men, 609 women (full-time). Freshman class: 325 applicants, 260 accepted, 234 enrolled. Graduate enrollment: 10 men, 109 women.
**Test score averages/ranges.** Average SAT scores: 431 verbal, 444 math. Range of SAT scores of middle 50%: 380-470 verbal, 400-510 math. Average ACT scores: 20 English, 18 math, 20 composite. Range of ACT scores of middle 50%: 17-23 English, 15-20 math.
**Faculty.** 63 full-time; 64 part-time. 40% of faculty holds doctoral degree. Student/faculty ratio: 13 to 1.
**Selectivity rating.** Less competitive.

**PROFILE.** Ursuline, founded in 1871, is a church-affiliated, multipurpose college for women. Its 116-acre campus is located in Pepper Pike, 12 miles east of Cleveland.
**Accreditation:** NCACS. Professionally accredited by the National League for Nursing.
**Religious orientation:** Ursuline College is affiliated with the Roman Catholic Church; two semesters of religion/theology required.
**Library:** Collections totaling over 110,500 volumes and 600 periodical subscriptions.
**Special facilities/museums:** Art gallery, theatre, art studio.
**Athletic facilities:** Gymnasium, swimming pool, exercise room.

**STUDENT BODY. Undergraduate profile:** 98% are state residents; 39% are transfers. 1% Asian-American, 16% Black, 1% Hispanic, 82% White. Average age of undergraduates is 31.
**Freshman profile:** 3% of freshmen who took SAT scored 700 or over on verbal; 6% scored 600 or over on verbal; 16% scored 500 or over on verbal, 23% scored 500 or over on math; 56% scored 400 or over on verbal, 73% scored 400 or over on math; 96% scored 300 or over on verbal, 100% scored 300 or over on math. 3% of freshmen who took ACT scored 30 or over on English, 2% scored 30 or over on composite; 20% scored 24 or over on English, 3% scored 24 or over on math, 12% scored 24 or over on composite; 69% scored 18 or over on English, 47% scored 18 or over on math, 61% scored 18 or over on composite; 100% scored 12 or over on English, 96% scored 12 or over on math, 92% scored 12 or over on composite; 99% scored 6 or over on math, 100% scored 6 or over on composite. 41% of accepted applicants took SAT; 81% took ACT. 68% of freshmen come from public schools.
**Foreign students:** Eight students are from out of the country. Countries represented include China, El Salvador, Ghana, India, Lebanon, and Philippines.

**PROGRAMS OF STUDY. Degrees:** B.A., B.S.Nurs.
**Majors:** Accounting, American Studies, Art, Arts Management, Behavioral Sciences, Biology, Business Administration, Communication Arts, Cytotechnology, Elementary Education, English, Family Studies, Fashion Design, Fashion Merchandising, Health Services Management, History, Humanities, Interior Design, Long-term Care Administration, Mathematics, Nursing, Philosophy, Psychology, Public Relations, Religious Studies, Social Studies, Social Work, Sociology, Special Studies.
**Distribution of degrees:** The majors with the highest enrollment are nursing, business administration, and psychology; American studies, humanities, and arts management have the lowest.
**Requirements:** General education requirement.
**Academic regulations:** Minimum 2.0 GPA must be maintained.
**Special:** Self-designed majors. Double majors. Independent study. Pass/fail grading option. Internships. Cooperative education programs. Preprofessional programs in law and medicine. 3-2 podiatry program with Ohio Coll of Podiatric Medicine. 3-2 cytotechnology program with St. Luke's Health Center. Member of Cleveland Commission on Higher Education; cross-registration possible. Teacher certification in elementary, secondary, and special education.
**Academic Assistance:** Remedial reading, writing, math, and study skills. Nonremedial tutoring.

**ADMISSIONS. Academic basis for candidate selection** (in order of priority): Secondary school record, standardized test scores, class rank, school's recommendation, essay.
**Nonacademic basis for candidate selection:** Extracurricular participation and particular talent or ability are important. Character and personality and alumni/ae relationship are considered.
**Requirements:** Graduation from secondary school is required; GED is accepted. 18 units and the following program of study are recommended: 4 units of English, 3 units of math, 3 units of science, 2 units of foreign language, 3 units of social studies, 3 units of history. 1 unit of fine or performing arts and 1 unit of health or physical education also recommended. Minimum composite ACT score of 17 (combined SAT score of 900) and minimum 2.5 GPA recommended. Conditional admission possible for applicants not meeting standard requirements. SAT or ACT is required. Campus visit and interview recommended. Off-campus interviews available with an admissions representative.
**Procedure:** Notification of admission on rolling basis. Reply is required within one month of acceptance. $50 tuition deposit, refundable until May 1. $50 room deposit, refundable until May 1. Freshmen accepted for terms other than fall.
**Special programs:** Admission may be deferred. Credit and/or placement may be granted through CEEB Advanced Placement exams for scores of 3 or higher. Credit and/or placement may be granted through CLEP subject exams. Credit and placement may be granted through challenge exams and life experience. Early entrance/early admission program. Concurrent enrollment program.
**Transfer students:** Transfer students accepted for terms other than fall. In fall 1993, 39% of all new students were transfers into all classes. 92 transfer applications were received, 72 were accepted. Application deadline is rolling for fall; rolling for spring. Minimum 2.5 GPA recommended. Lowest course grade accepted is "C." Maximum number of transferable semester hours is 64 from two-year schools; unlimited from four-year schools. At least 30 semester hours, including half of requirements for major, must be completed at the college to receive B.A. degree; 49 semester hours for B.S.Nurs. degree.
**Admissions contact:** Dennis Giacomino, Director of Admissions. 216 449-4203.

**FINANCIAL AID. Available aid:** Pell grants, SEOG, state scholarships and grants, school scholarships and grants, private scholarships, ROTC scholarships, and academic merit scholarships. Perkins Loans (NDSL), PLUS, Stafford Loans (GSL), and school loans. AMS.
**Financial aid statistics:** 11% of aid is not need-based. In 1993-94, 95% of all undergraduate applicants received aid; 95% of freshman applicants.
**Supporting data/closing dates:** FAFSA/FAF: Priority filing date is March 1. School's own aid application: Priority filing date is March 1. State aid form: Priority filing date is March 1. Income tax forms: Priority filing date is March 1. Notification of awards begins March 1.
**Financial aid contact:** Mary Lynn Perri, Director of Financial Aid. 216 646-8329.

9-6

# Walsh University

**North Canton, OH 44720** **216 499-7090**

**1994-95 Costs.** Tuition: $7,710. Room & board: $3,930. Fees, books, misc. academic expenses (school's estimate): $800.
**Enrollment.** Undergraduates: 331 men, 480 women (full-time). Freshman class: 1,242 applicants, 795 accepted, 477 enrolled. Graduate enrollment: 66 men, 153 women.
**Test score averages/ranges.** Average ACT scores: 21 English, 20 math, 21 composite.
**Faculty.** 65 full-time; 48 part-time. 51% of faculty holds doctoral degree. Student/faculty ratio: 19 to 1.
**Selectivity rating.** Less competitive.

**PROFILE.** Walsh, founded in 1958, is a church-affiliated, liberal arts college. Its 58-acre campus is located in North Canton, 20 miles from Akron.

**Accreditation:** NCACS. Professionally accredited by the National League for Nursing.
**Religious orientation:** Walsh University is affiliated with the Roman Catholic Church; two semesters of theology required.
**Library:** Collections totaling over 115,000 volumes, 900 periodical subscriptions and 100 microform items.
**Athletic facilities:** Swimming pool, gymnasium, weight room, dance studio, all-weather track, baseball, football, soccer, and softball fields, tennis courts.
**STUDENT BODY. Undergraduate profile:** 99% are state residents; 35% are transfers. 7% Black, 1% Hispanic, 90% White, 2% Other. Average age of undergraduates is 27.
**Freshman profile:** 10% of freshmen who took ACT scored 30 or over on composite; 20% scored 24 or over on composite; 70% scored 18 or over on composite; 80% scored 12 or over on composite; 95% scored 6 or over on composite. 10% of accepted applicants took SAT; 90% took ACT. 75% of freshmen come from public schools.
**Undergraduate achievement:** 78% of fall 1992 freshmen returned for fall 1993 term.
**Foreign students:** 42 students are from out of the country. 11 countries represented in all.
**PROGRAMS OF STUDY. Degrees:** B.A., B.S., B.S.Nurs.
**Majors:** Accounting, Biology, Chemistry, Communication, Computer Science, Elementary Education, English, Finance, French, General Business, History, Interdisciplinary Studies, Latin American Business, Management, Marketing, Mathematics, Medical Technology, Nursing, Philosophy/Theology, Physical Education, Political Science, Psychology, Secondary Education, Sociology, Spanish, Special Education.
**Distribution of degrees:** The majors with the highest enrollment are business, nursing, and education.
**Requirements:** General education requirement.
**Academic regulations:** Freshmen must maintain minimum 1.75 GPA; sophomores, juniors, seniors, 2.00 GPA.
**Special:** Associate's degrees offered. Self-designed majors. Double majors. Dual degrees. Independent study. Accelerated study. Pass/fail grading option. Internships. Cooperative education programs. Graduate school at which undergraduates may take graduate-level courses. Preprofessional programs in law, medicine, veterinary science, pharmacy, dentistry, and optometry. 3-1 medical technology program with recognized hospital or medical center. 3-2 forestry/natural resources program with U of Michigan. 3-4 dentistry program with Case Western Reserve U. Teacher certification in early childhood, elementary, secondary, and special education. Study abroad possible.
**Honors:** Honors program.
**Academic Assistance:** Remedial reading, writing, math, and study skills. Nonremedial tutoring.
**ADMISSIONS. Academic basis for candidate selection** (in order of priority): Secondary school record, standardized test scores, essay, class rank, school's recommendation.
**Nonacademic basis for candidate selection:** Character and personality, extracurricular participation, particular talent or ability, and alumni/ae relationship are important.
**Requirements:** Graduation from secondary school is required; GED is accepted. 16 units and the following program of study are required: 4 units of English, 3 units of math, 3 units of science including 1 unit of lab, 2 units of foreign language, 3 units of social studies, 1 unit of academic electives. Minimum composite ACT score of 18 and minimum 2.5 GPA recommended. Summer enrichment program for applicants not normally admissible. ACT is required; SAT may be substituted. Campus visit and interview recommended. Off-campus interviews available with an admissions representative.
**Procedure:** Take SAT or ACT by February of 12th year. Notification of admission on rolling basis. Reply required by May 1. $125 tuition deposit, refundable until May 1. $100 room deposit, refundable until beginning of semester. Freshmen accepted for terms other than fall.
**Special programs:** Admission may be deferred four years. Placement may be granted through CEEB Advanced Placement exams for scores of 4 or higher. Credit and/or placement may be granted through CLEP general and subject exams. Credit and placement may be granted through life experience. Early entrance/early admission program. Concurrent enrollment program.
**Transfer students:** Transfer students accepted for terms other than fall. In fall 1993, 35% of all new students were transfers into all classes. 275 transfer applications were received, 239 were accepted. Application deadline is rolling for fall; rolling for spring. Minimum 2.0 GPA recommended. Lowest course grade accepted is "C." At least 30 semester hours must be completed at the university to receive degree.
**Admissions contact:** Doug Swartz, M.A., Director of Admissions. 216 499-7090, extension 171.
**FINANCIAL AID. Available aid:** Pell grants, SEOG, Federal Nursing Student Scholarships, state scholarships and grants, school scholarships and grants, private scholarships and grants, academic merit scholarships, athletic scholarships, and aid for undergraduate foreign students. Perkins Loans (NDSL), PLUS, Stafford Loans (GSL), NSL, and school loans. AMS. Installment payment plan.
**Financial aid statistics:** 45% of aid is not need-based. In 1993-94, 85% of all undergraduate applicants received aid; 85% of freshman applicants. Average amounts of aid awarded freshmen: Scholarships and grants, $1,200; loans, $1,100.
**Supporting data/closing dates:** FAFSA/FAF/FFS: Accepted on rolling basis; deadline is July 15. School's own aid application: Accepted on rolling basis; deadline is July 15. Scholarship Application: Accepted on rolling basis; deadline is July 15. Notification of awards on rolling basis.
**Financial aid contact:** Perie Brown, Director of Financial Aid. 800 362-9846. 8-25

# Wilmington College

**Wilmington, OH 45177** **513 382-6661**

**1994-95 Costs.** Tuition: $10,230. Room & board: $4,110. Fees, books, misc. academic expenses (school's estimate): $180.
**Enrollment.** Undergraduates: 464 men, 415 women (full-time). Freshman class: 706 applicants, 602 accepted, 225 enrolled.
**Test score averages/ranges.** Average ACT scores: 21 composite.
**Faculty.** 62 full-time; 4 part-time. 52% of faculty holds doctoral degree. Student/faculty ratio: 17 to 1.
**Selectivity rating.** Less competitive.

**PROFILE.** Wilmington, founded in 1870, is church-affiliated college. Its 65-acre campus is located in Wilmington, 30 miles southeast of Dayton.
**Accreditation:** NCACS.
**Religious orientation:** Wilmington College is affiliated with the Society of Friends; no religious requirements.
**Library:** Collections totaling over 100,145 volumes and 500 periodical subscriptions.
**Special facilities/museums:** Hiroshima-Nagasaki memorial collection and peace resource center, education lab, language lab, three farms, observatory, electron microscope.
**Athletic facilities:** Gymnasiums, racquetball, squash, and tennis courts, track, swimming pool, baseball, football, softball, and soccer fields.
**STUDENT BODY. Undergraduate profile:** 93% are state residents; 28% are transfers. 1% Asian-American, 3% Black, 1% Hispanic, 95% White. Average age of undergraduates is 19.
**Freshman profile:** 10% of accepted applicants took SAT; 90% took ACT. 95% of freshmen come from public schools.
**Undergraduate achievement:** 77% of fall 1991 freshmen returned for fall 1992 term. 50% of entering class graduated.
**Foreign students:** 26 students are from out of the country. Countries represented include Japan and Kenya; 14 in all.
**PROGRAMS OF STUDY. Degrees:** B.A., B.S.
**Majors:** Accounting, Agriculture, Athletic Training, Biology, Business Administration, Chemistry, Communication Arts, Computer Science, Criminal Justice, Education, English, History, Mathematics, Physical Education, Psychology, Religion/Philosophy, Social Work, Sociology, Spanish, Theatre.
**Distribution of degrees:** The majors with the highest enrollment are education and agriculture; English and chemistry have the lowest.
**Requirements:** General education requirement.
**Special:** Minors offered in all majors and in art, leadership, music, and political science. Interdepartmental programs. Certificate in applied peace studies. Self-designed majors. Double majors. Independent study. Pass/fail grading option. Internships. Preprofessional programs in law, medicine, veterinary science, dentistry, and theology. Member of Southwest Ohio Council for Higher Education; cross-registration possible. Washington Semester. Teacher certification in elementary and secondary education. Certification in specific subject areas. Study abroad in Austria, France, and Mexico.
**Academic Assistance:** Remedial reading, writing, math, and study skills. Nonremedial tutoring.
**ADMISSIONS. Academic basis for candidate selection** (in order of priority): Secondary school record, standardized test scores, class rank, school's recommendation.
**Nonacademic basis for candidate selection:** Character and personality are emphasized. Extracurricular participation is considered.
**Requirements:** Graduation from secondary school is required; GED is accepted. 16 units and the following program of study are required: 4 units of English, 2 units of math, 2 units of lab science. ACT is required; SAT may be substituted. Campus visit and interview recommended. No off-campus interviews.
**Procedure:** Take SAT or ACT by October of 12th year. Notification of admission on rolling basis. Reply is required by May 1. $100 nonrefundable tuition deposit. $100 room deposit, refundable until July 1. Freshmen accepted for terms other than fall.
**Special programs:** Admission may be deferred one year. Credit and/or placement may be granted through CEEB Advanced Placement exams for scores of 3 or higher. Credit and/or placement may be granted through CLEP general and subject exams. Credit may be granted through life experience. Credit and placement may be granted through challenge exams.
**Transfer students:** Transfer students accepted for terms other than fall. In fall 1993, 28% of all new students were transfers into all classes. Minimum 2.5 GPA required. Lowest course grade accepted is "C." Maximum number of transferable credits is 67 semester hours from a two-year school and 97 semester hours from a four-year school. At least 30 semester hours must be completed at the college to receive degree.
**Admissions contact:** Lawrence T. Lesick, Ph.D., Director of Admission. 513 382-6661, extension 260.
**FINANCIAL AID. Available aid:** Pell grants, SEOG, state scholarships and grants, school scholarships and grants, private scholarships and grants, and academic merit scholarships. Perkins Loans (NDSL), PLUS, Stafford Loans (GSL), school loans, private loans, and SLS. Tuition Plan Inc., Knight Tuition Plans, AMS, and deferred payment plan.
**Financial aid statistics:** In 1993-94, 91% of all freshman applicants received aid. Average amounts of aid awarded freshmen: Scholarships and grants, $3,603; loans, $3,041.
**Supporting data/closing dates:** FAFSA/FAF/FFS: Priority filing date is February 15; deadline is March 31. School's own aid application: Priority filing date is March 31. State aid form: Deadline is March 31. Notification of awards on rolling basis.
**Financial aid contact:** Linda Beals, Director of Financial Aid. 513 382-6661, extension 235.

8-24

# Wittenberg University

**Springfield, OH 45501** **513 327-6231**

**1994-95 Costs.** Tuition: $15,948. Room: $2,190. Board: $2,214. Fees, books, misc. academic expenses (school's estimate): $1,822.

**Enrollment.** Undergraduates: 989 men, 1,078 women (full-time). Freshman class: 2,062 applicants, 1,725 accepted, 595 enrolled.

**Test score averages/ranges.** Average SAT scores: 520 verbal, 574 math. Range of SAT scores of middle 50%: 470-570 verbal, 510-620 math. Average ACT scores: 24 English, 25 math, 24 composite. Range of ACT scores of middle 50%: 21-27 composite.

**Faculty.** 148 full-time; 25 part-time. 98% of faculty holds highest degree in specific field. Student/faculty ratio: 13 to 1.

**Selectivity rating.** More competitive.

**PROFILE.** Wittenberg, founded in 1845, is a church-affiliated, liberal arts university. Its 71-acre campus is located in Springfield, 25 miles northeast of Dayton.

**Accreditation:** NCACS. Professionally accredited by the American Medical Association (CAHEA), the National Association of Schools of Music, the National Council for Accreditation of Teacher Education.

**Religious orientation:** Wittenberg University is affiliated with the Evangelical Lutheran Church in America; one term of religion required.

**Library:** Collections totaling over 350,000 volumes, 1,500 periodical subscriptions, and 40,000 microform items.

**Special facilities/museums:** Language lab, electron microscope.

**Athletic facilities:** Gymnasiums, field house, stadium, track, swimming pool, weight room, basketball, racquetball, tennis, and volleyball courts, athletic fields.

**STUDENT BODY. Undergraduate profile:** 52% are state residents; 5% are transfers. 2% Asian-American, 6% Black, 2% Hispanic, 88% White, 2% Other. Average age of undergraduates is 20.

**Freshman profile:** 3% of freshmen who took SAT scored 700 or over on verbal, 6% scored 700 or over on math; 19% scored 600 or over on verbal, 37% scored 600 or over on math; 69% scored 500 or over on verbal, 82% scored 500 or over on math; 95% scored 400 or over on verbal, 98% scored 400 or over on math; 100% scored 300 or over on verbal, 100% scored 300 or over on math. 45% of accepted applicants took SAT; 55% took ACT. 80% of freshmen come from public schools.

**Undergraduate achievement:** 88% of fall 1992 freshmen returned for fall 1993 term. 75% of entering class graduated. 20% of students who completed a degree program went on to graduate study within one year.

**Foreign students:** 105 students are from out of the country. Countries represented include Japan, Latin America, Mexico, the Netherlands, and Sweden; 36 in all.

**PROGRAMS OF STUDY. Degrees:** B.A., B.F.A., B.Mus., B.Mus.Ed.

**Majors:** American Studies, Art, Biology, Business Administration, Chemistry, Computer Science, Earth Science, East Asian Studies, Economics, Education, English, French, Geography, Geology, German, History, Mathematics, Music, Music Education, Music Performance, Philosophy, Physics, Political Science, Psychology, Religion, Russian Studies, Sociology, Spanish, Theatre.

**Distribution of degrees:** The majors with the highest enrollment are business, biology, and psychology; geography, physics, and religion have the lowest.

**Requirements:** General education requirement.

**Academic regulations:** Minimum 2.0 GPA must be maintained.

**Special:** Minors offered in most majors and in global studies, urban studies, and women's studies. Courses offered in East Asian and Russian studies. Interdepartmental majors. Self-designed majors. Double majors. Dual degrees. Independent study. Accelerated study. Pass/fail grading option. Internships. Preprofessional programs in law, medicine, veterinary science, dentistry, theology, and optometry. Three-year program plus first year of professional school earns B.A. degree in absentia. 3-3 nursing program with Case Western Reserve U. 3-2 forestry and environmental studies program with Duke U. 3-2 engineering programs with Case Western Reserve U, Columbia U, Georgia Tech, and Washington U. Member of Southwestern Ohio College Consortium, Cincinnati Council on World Affairs, and International Educational Association of Ohio Colleges and Universities. Washington Semester. Teacher certification in elementary, secondary, and special education. Member of International Student Exchange Program (ISEP). Exchange programs abroad in China, England, Germany, Japan and Russia. Study abroad also in Australia, Austria, China, Denmark, France, Kenya, Mexico, Sweden, and other countries. Student teaching exchange programs offered. ROTC at Central State U. AFROTC at Wright State U.

**Honors:** Phi Beta Kappa. Honors program.

**Academic Assistance:** Nonremedial tutoring.

**STUDENT LIFE. Housing:** All freshmen and sophomores must live on campus. Coed and women's dorms. Sorority and fraternity housing. School-owned/operated apartments. Off-campus privately-owned housing. Off-campus married-student housing. Substance-free housing. 98% of students live in college housing.

**Social atmosphere:** The Pub, fraternity houses, area bars, and off-campus houses are the most frequented student gathering spots. Greeks, the Student Senate, athletes, the Union Board, and Concerned Black Students have widespread influence on student social life at Wittenberg. Greek activities, Union Board events, sports events, comedy nights, and the yearly concert are some of the highlights of the school year. "Since we are a small school, it's easy to make friends and find social events," reports the editor of the school newspaper. "There aren't many area bars, but there are many alternatives to parties, like Union Board cultural activities and sports."

**Services and counseling/handicapped student services:** Placement services. Health service. Women's center. Day care. Counseling services for minority, veteran, and older students. Birth control, personal, and psychological counseling. Career and academic guidance services. Religious counseling. Physically disabled student services. Learning disabled services. Tape recorders.

**Campus organizations:** Undergraduate student government. Student newspaper (Torch, published once/week). Literary magazine. Yearbook. Radio station. A cappella choir, annual opera, chapel and women's choir, chamber ensembles, symphonic band, drama group, intercollegiate debating, oratorical contests, Project Outreach, Habitat for Humanity, departmental groups. Seven fraternities, all with chapter houses; seven sororities, all with chapter houses. 30% of men join a fraternity. 47% of women join a sorority.

**Religious organizations:** Weaver Chapel Association, Newman Club, Hillel.

**Minority/foreign student organizations:** Concerned Black Students. American International Association.

**ATHLETICS. Physical education requirements:** Three terms of physical education required.

**Intercollegiate competition:** 30% of students participate. Baseball (M), basketball (M,W), cross-country (M,W), diving (M,W), field hockey (W), football (M), golf (M), lacrosse (M,W), soccer (M,W), softball (W), swimming (M,W), tennis (M,W), track and field (indoor) (M,W), track and field (outdoor) (M,W), volleyball (W). Member of NCAA Division III, North Coast Athletic Conference.

**Intramural and club sports:** 53% of students participate. Intramural badminton, basketball, billiards, flag football, floor hockey, frisbee golf, golf, indoor soccer, racquetball, relays, soccer, softball, table tennis, tennis, triathlon, volleyball, walleyball, Wiffle ball, wrestling. Men's club cheerleading, cycling, fencing, ice hockey, rugby, volleyball. Women's club cheerleading, cycling, fencing, golf, rugby.

**ADMISSIONS. Academic basis for candidate selection** (in order of priority): Secondary school record, class rank, standardized test scores, school's recommendation, essay.

**Nonacademic basis for candidate selection:** Character and personality are emphasized. Extracurricular participation, particular talent or ability, and alumni/ae relationship are important. Geographical distribution is considered.

**Requirements:** Graduation from secondary school is required; GED is not accepted. 16 units and the following program of study are required: 4 units of English, 3 units of math, 3 units of science, 3 units of foreign language, 3 units of social studies. Portfolio required of art program applicants. Audition required of music program applicants. Conditional admission possible for applicants not meeting standard requirements. SAT or ACT is required. ACH recommended. Campus visit and interview recommended. Off-campus interviews available with an admissions representative.

**Procedure:** Take SAT or ACT by January of 12th year. Take ACH by January of 12th year. Visit college for interview by March of 12th year. Suggest filing application by January 15. Application deadline is March 15. Notification of admission on rolling basis. Reply is required by May 1. $400 nonrefundable tuition deposit. Freshmen accepted for terms other than fall.

**Special programs:** Admission may be deferred one year. Credit and/or placement may be granted through CEEB Advanced Placement exams for scores of 5 or higher. Early decision program. In fall 1993, 60 applied for early decision and 48 were accepted. Deadline for applying for early decision is December 15. Early entrance/early admission program. Concurrent enrollment program.

**Transfer students:** Transfer students accepted for terms other than fall. In fall 1993, 5% of all new students were transfers into all classes. 80 transfer applications were received, 64 were accepted. Application deadline is August 1 for fall; December 1 for winter; March 1 for spring. Minimum 2.4 GPA recommended. Lowest course grade accepted is "C."

**Admissions contact:** Ken Benne, M.A., M.Div., Dean of Admissions. 800 677-7558.

**FINANCIAL AID. Available aid:** Pell grants, SEOG, state scholarships and grants, school scholarships and grants, private scholarships and grants, ROTC scholarships, academic merit scholarships, and aid for undergraduate foreign students. National Merit Scholarship. Perkins Loans (NDSL), PLUS, Stafford Loans (GSL), school loans, and private loans. Tuition Plan Inc., Knight Tuition Plans, deferred payment plan, and guaranteed tuition.

**Financial aid statistics:** 10% of aid is not need-based. In 1993-94, 95% of all undergraduate applicants received aid; 95% of freshman applicants. Average amounts of aid awarded freshmen: Scholarships and grants, $9,100; loans, $2,400.

**Supporting data/closing dates:** FAFSA/FAF/FFS: Priority filing date is March 15; accepted on rolling basis. Income tax forms: Accepted on rolling basis. Notification of awards on rolling basis.

**Financial aid contact:** Ray Kennelly, M.A., Director of Financial Aid.

**STUDENT EMPLOYMENT.** College Work/Study Program. Institutional employment. 50% of full-time undergraduates work on campus during school year. Students may expect to earn an average of $1,275 during school year. Off-campus part-time employment opportunities rated "good."

**COMPUTER FACILITIES.** 125 IBM/IBM-compatible and Macintosh/Apple microcomputers; 70 are networked. Students may access Digital minicomputer/mainframe systems, BITNET, Internet. Residence halls may be equipped with stand-alone microcomputers, networked microcomputers, networked terminals, modems. Client/LAN operating systems include Apple/Macintosh, DOS, X-windows, Banyan, DEC, LocalTalk/AppleTalk. Computer languages and software packages include BASIC, FORTRAN, LISP-C, MACRO, Pascal. Computer facilities are available to all students.

**Fees:** None.

**Hours:** 24 hours.

**GRADUATE CAREER DATA.** Graduate school percentages: 5% enter law school. 3% enter medical school. 1% enter dental school. 8% enter graduate business programs. 5% enter graduate arts and sciences programs. 3% enter theological school/seminary. Highest graduate school enrollments: Case Western Reserve U, Ohio State U. 25% of graduates choose careers in business and industry. Companies and businesses that hire graduates: Financial services companies.

**PROMINENT ALUMNI/AE.** Earl Morris, former president, American Bar Association.

6-1

# Wright State University

Dayton, OH 45435 513 873-3333

**1994-95 Costs.** Tuition: $3,238 (state residents), $6,476 (out-of-state). Room & board: $4,000. Fees, books, misc. academic expenses (school's estimate): $725.
**Enrollment.** Undergraduates: 4,508 men, 5,035 women (full-time). Freshman class: 4,298 applicants, 3,948 accepted, 2,091 enrolled. Graduate enrollment: 1,568 men, 2,302 women.
**Test score averages/ranges.** Range of SAT scores of middle 50%: 760-1040 combined. Range of ACT scores of middle 50%: 18-24 composite.
**Faculty.** 708 full-time; 22 part-time. 80% of faculty holds highest degree in specific field. Student/faculty ratio: 20 to 1.
**Selectivity rating.** Less competitive.

**PROFILE.** Wright State, founded in 1964, is a public, multipurpose university. Programs are offered through the Colleges of Business and Administration, Continuing and Community Education, Education and Human Services, Engineering and Computer Science, Liberal Arts, and Science and Mathematics and the Schools of Graduate Studies, Medicine, Nursing, and Professional Psychology. Its 645-acre campus is located in Dayton.

**Accreditation:** NCACS. Professionally accredited by the Accreditation Board for Engineering and Technology, the American Assembly of Collegiate Schools of Business, the American Medical Association (CAHEA), the Council on Social Work Education, the National Association of Schools of Music, the National Council for Accreditation of Teacher Education, the National League for Nursing.
**Religious orientation:** Wright State University is nonsectarian; no religious requirements.
**Library:** Collections totaling over 460,000 volumes, 4,151 periodical subscriptions, and 940,000 microform items.
**Special facilities/museums:** Center for Arts for the Disabled and Handicapped, Museum of Contemporary Art.
**Athletic facilities:** Gymnasium, swimming pool, basketball, racquetball, squash, tennis, and volleyball courts, baseball, soccer, and softball fields, weight room.
**STUDENT BODY. Undergraduate profile:** 99% are state residents; 32% are transfers. 2% Asian-American, 7% Black, 1% Hispanic, 88% White, 2% Other. Average age of undergraduates is 24.
**Freshman profile:** 39% of accepted applicants took SAT; 92% took ACT.
**Undergraduate achievement:** 66% of fall 1992 freshmen returned for fall 1993 term.
**Foreign students:** 104 students are from out of the country. Countries represented include Bangladesh, Canada, Japan, Jordan, Kuwait, and Pakistan; 46 in all.
**PROGRAMS OF STUDY. Degrees:** B.A., B.F.A., B.Mus., B.S., B.S.Civil Eng., B.S.Ed., B.S.Eng., B.S.M.T., B.S.Nurs.
**Majors:** Accountancy, Acting, Anthropology, Art/Art History, Biological Science Education, Biological Sciences, Biomedical Engineering, Business Economics, Chemistry, Chemistry Education, Classical Humanities, Communication Studies, Computer Engineering, Computer Science, Computer Science Education, Dance, Directing/Stage Management, Early Childhood Education, Earth Science Education, Economics, Electrical Engineering, Elementary Education, Engineering Physics, English, English Education, Environmental Health, Finance, Financial Services, French, Geography, Geological Science, Geological Sciences/Groundwater Technology, Geophysics/Geological Sciences, German, Greek, History, History Education, Human Factors Engineering, Human Resources Management, International Studies, Languages Education, Latin, Management, Management Information Systems, Marketing, Mass Communications, Materials Science/Engineering, Mathematics, Mathematics Education, Mechanical Engineering, Medical Technology, Moderately/Severely/Profoundly Handicapped Education, Modern Languages, Motion Picture History/Theory/Criticism, Motion Picture Production, Music, Music/Applied, Music Composition, Music Education, Music History/Literature, Music Theory, Nursing, Operations Management, Organizational Communication, Philosophy, Physical Education, Physics, Physics Education, Political Science, Psychology, Rehabilitation Education, Religion, Science Education, Selected Studies, Social/Industrial Communication, Social Sciences Comprehensive Education, Social Work, Sociology, Spanish, Special Education, Theatre Design/Technology, Theatre Studies, Urban Affairs, Visual Arts Education, Vocational Business Education.
**Distribution of degrees:** The majors with the highest enrollment are education, nursing, and accountancy; religion, classical humanities, and geography have the lowest.
**Requirements:** General education requirement.
**Academic regulations:** Minimum 2.0 GPA must be maintained.
**Special:** Minors offered in many majors and in African and African-American studies, health sciences, and statistics. Associate's degrees offered. Self-designed majors. Double majors. Internships. Cooperative education programs. Graduate school at which undergraduates may take graduate-level courses. Preprofessional programs in law, medicine, veterinary science, and dentistry. Member of Dayton-Miami Valley Consortium and Southwestern Ohio Council for Higher Education. Teacher certification in early childhood, elementary, secondary, and special education. Study abroad in Brazil, China, and Japan. ROTC and AFROTC.
**Honors:** Honors program. Honor societies.
**Academic Assistance:** Remedial reading, writing, math, and study skills.
**STUDENT LIFE. Housing:** Coed dorms. School-owned/operated apartments. Coed suite-style residence halls. 18% of students live in college housing.
**Social atmosphere:** "Since we're mostly a commuter campus, it's hard to get people to come back to campus for on-campus events," reports the student newspaper. Popular events include basketball, baseball, and soccer games, October and May Daze, and open houses. Greek-letter organizations are influential on campus. Off campus, students frequent Keller's Pub, McGuffy's, and the Oregon District. On campus, students gather at the Rathskeller.
**Services and counseling/handicapped student services:** Counseling services for minority, military, veteran, and older students. Birth control, personal, and psychological counseling. Career and academic guidance services. Religious counseling. Physically disabled student services. Notetaking services. Tape recorders. Tutors. Reader services for the blind.
**Campus organizations:** Undergraduate student government. Student newspaper (Guardian). Literary magazine. Radio and TV stations. Musical and drama groups, Activity Office, athletic, departmental, and special-interest groups, 160 organizations in all. 11 fraternities, no chapter houses; seven sororities, no chapter houses. 4% of men join a fraternity. 4% of women join a sorority.
**Religious organizations:** Baptist Student Union, Campus Bible Fellowship, Campus Crusade for Christ, Chinese Christian Fellowship, Christian Medical Society, Fellowship of Christian Students, Intervarsity Christian Fellowship, Latter-Day Saints Association, Muslim Student Association, Newman Club.
**Minority/foreign student organizations:** Association of Asian-American Student Association, Black Students, Black Student Union, NAACP, Phi Beta Sigma, black professional groups. International Student Association, Chinese, Indian, Korean, Pakistani, Taiwanese, and Turkish groups.
**ATHLETICS. Physical education requirements:** None.
**Intercollegiate competition:** 9% of students participate. Baseball (M), basketball (M,W), cross-country (M,W), diving (M,W), golf (M), soccer (M,W), softball (W), swimming (M,W), tennis (M,W), volleyball (W). Member of Mid-Continent Conference, NCAA Division I.
**Intramural and club sports:** 18% of students participate. Intramural basketball, flag football, golf, racquetball, soccer, softball, tennis, volleyball, wrestling.
**ADMISSIONS. Academic basis for candidate selection** (in order of priority): Secondary school record, standardized test scores, class rank.
**Nonacademic basis for candidate selection:** Character and personality, extracurricular participation, and particular talent or ability are considered.
**Requirements:** Graduation from secondary school is required; GED is accepted. 16 units and the following program of study are required: 4 units of English, 3 units of math, 3 units of lab science, 2 units of foreign language, 3 units of social studies, 1 unit of academic electives. Minimum composite ACT score of 17 (combined SAT score of 900), minimum 2.0 GPA, and college preparatory courses recommended of in-state applicants. Minimum composite ACT score of 20, minimum 2.5 GPA, and rank in top half of secondary school class recommended of out-of-state applicants. Audition required of theatre program applicants. ACT is required; SAT may be substituted. Campus visit recommended. No off-campus interviews.
**Procedure:** Take SAT or ACT by fall of 12th year. Suggest filing application by December 31. Application deadline is September 1. Notification of admission on rolling basis. $150 room deposit, refundable until May 1. $150 room deposit, partially refundable until 30 days prior to beginning of quarter. Freshmen accepted for terms other than fall.
**Special programs:** Admission may be deferred one year. Credit and/or placement may be granted through CEEB Advanced Placement exams for scores of 3 or higher. Credit and/or placement may be granted through CLEP subject exams. Credit may be granted through ACT PEP, DANTES, and challenge exams. Credit and placement may be granted through military experience. Concurrent enrollment program.
**Transfer students:** Transfer students accepted for terms other than fall. In fall 1993, 32% of all new students were transfers into all classes. 1,547 transfer applications were received, 1,321 were accepted. Minimum 2.0 GPA required. Lowest course grade accepted is "C." At least 45 quarter hours must be completed at the university to receive degree.
**Admissions contact:** Kenneth Davenport, M.S., Director of Admissions. 513 873-2211, 800 247-1770.
**FINANCIAL AID. Available aid:** Pell grants, SEOG, state grants, school scholarships, ROTC scholarships, academic merit scholarships, and athletic scholarships. Perkins Loans (NDSL), PLUS, Stafford Loans (GSL), NSL, school loans, private loans, and SLS. Deferred payment plan.
**Financial aid statistics:** 6% of aid is not need-based. In 1993-94, 92% of all undergraduate applicants received aid; 93% of freshman applicants. Average amounts of aid awarded freshmen: Scholarships and grants, $1,855.
**Supporting data/closing dates:** FAFSA: Priority filing date is March 1. School's own aid application: Priority filing date is April 1. State aid form: Priority filing date is September 30. Notification of awards begins April 15.
**Financial aid contact:** David Darr, Director of Financial Aid. 513 873-2321.
**STUDENT EMPLOYMENT.** College Work/Study Program. Institutional employment. Students may expect to earn an average of $3,000 during school year. Off-campus part-time employment opportunities rated "good."
**COMPUTER FACILITIES.** 300 IBM/IBM-compatible and Macintosh/Apple microcomputers. Students may access Digital, IBM minicomputer/mainframe systems. Computer languages and software packages include Ada, BASIC, COBOL, FORTRAN, LISP, Pascal, SAS; numerous software packages.
**Fees:** None.
**Hours:** 9 AM-1 AM (M-Th); 9 AM-10 PM (F); 9 AM-6 PM (Sa); noon-11 PM (Su).
**GRADUATE CAREER DATA.** Companies and businesses that hire graduates: Big Six accounting firms, U.S. government.

8-23

# Xavier University

Cincinnati, OH 45207-5311 513 745-3000

**1994-95 Costs.** Tuition: $11,520. Room & board: $4,960. Fees, books, misc. academic expenses (school's estimate): $500.
**Enrollment.** Undergraduates: 1,343 men, 1,506 women (full-time). Freshman class: 1,957 applicants, 1,803 accepted, 695 enrolled. Graduate enrollment: 1,114 men, 1,209 women.
**Test score averages/ranges.** Average SAT scores: 475 verbal, 521 math. Range of SAT scores of middle 50%: 420-540 verbal, 450-600 math. Average ACT scores: 24 composite. Range of ACT scores of middle 50%: 21-27 composite.
**Faculty.** 232 full-time; 210 part-time. 75% of faculty holds highest degree in specific field. Student/faculty ratio: 16 to 1.
**Selectivity rating.** Competitive.

**PROFILE.** Xavier is a church-affiliated, liberal arts university. It was founded as a seminary for men in 1831, gained university status in 1930, and became coeducational in 1969. Programs are offered through the Colleges of Arts and Sciences, Business Administration, and Social Sciences and the Graduate Programs Office. Its 85-acre campus is located in the city of Cincinnati.

**Accreditation:** NCACS. Professionally accredited by the American Medical Association (CAHEA), the Council on Social Work Education, the National League for Nursing.
**Religious orientation:** Xavier University is affiliated with the Roman Catholic Church (Society of Jesus); four semesters of theology required.
**Library:** Collections totaling over 350,000 volumes, 1,500 periodical subscriptions, and 450,750 microform items.
**Special facilities/museums:** Student-run art gallery, language lab, Montessori lab school, observatory.
**Athletic facilities:** Swimming pool, Nautilus/free weights room, racquetball courts, gymnasium, field house, athletic fields.

**STUDENT BODY. Undergraduate profile:** 70% are state residents; 25% are transfers. 2% Asian-American, 6% Black, 2% Hispanic, 1% Native American, 88% White, 1% Other. Average age of undergraduates is 25.
**Freshman profile:** 1% of freshmen who took SAT scored 700 or over on verbal, 5% scored 700 or over on math; 9% scored 600 or over on verbal, 26% scored 600 or over on math; 41% scored 500 or over on verbal, 59% scored 500 or over on math; 82% scored 400 or over on verbal, 87% scored 400 or over on math; 99% scored 300 or over on verbal, 99% scored 300 or over on math. 8% of freshmen who took ACT scored 30 or over on composite; 54% scored 24 or over on composite; 96% scored 18 or over on composite; 99% scored 12 or over on composite. 74% of accepted applicants took SAT; 81% took ACT.
**Undergraduate achievement:** 85% of fall 1992 freshmen returned for fall 1993 term. 53% of entering class graduated. 21% of students who completed a degree program immediately went on to graduate study.
**Foreign students:** 186 students are from out of the country. Countries represented include Colombia, India, Japan, Peru, and Thailand; 50 in all.

**PROGRAMS OF STUDY. Degrees:** B.A., B.F.A., B.S., B.S.Bus.Admin., B.S.Nurs.
**Majors:** Accounting, Advertising, Applied Biology, Applied Science, Art, Art Education, Athletic Training, Biology, Chemical Science, Chemistry, Classical Humanities, Classics, Communication Arts, Computer Science, Criminal Justice, Early Childhood Education, Economics, Education, Electronic Media, Elementary Education, English, Environmental Management, Finance, Fine Arts, Forestry, French, History, Human Resources, Information Systems, International Affairs, Management, Marketing, Mathematics, Medical Technology, Modern Language, Montessori Education, Music, Music Education, Natural Science, Nursing, Occupational Therapy, Organizational Communication, Philosophy, Physical Education/Health, Physics, Political Science, Pre-Medicine, Psychology, Public Relations, Radio/Television, Radiologic Technology, Secondary Education, Social Work, Sociology, Spanish, Special Education, Sport Marketing, Sports Management, Theology.
**Distribution of degrees:** The majors with the highest enrollment are liberal arts, marketing, and communications; physical education, music, and medical technology have the lowest.
**Requirements:** General education requirement.
**Academic regulations:** Freshmen must maintain minimum 1.75 GPA; sophomores, juniors, seniors, 2.0 GPA.
**Special:** Minors offered. Associate's degrees offered. Double majors. Internships. Graduate school at which undergraduates may take graduate-level courses. Preprofessional programs in law, medicine, pharmacy, dentistry, theology, optometry, engineering, and forestry. Four-year bachelor's/M.B.A. program. Cooperative dual-degree programs with first three years at Xavier include forestry with Duke U, engineering with U of Cincinnati, dentistry with Case Western Reserve U, and podiatry with Barry U and Ohio Coll of Podiatric Medicine. Member of Greater Cincinnati Consortium. Washington Semester. Teacher certification in early childhood, elementary, secondary, and special education. Certification in specific subject areas. Study abroad in Austria, Colombia, England, France, Greece, Italy, and Spain. ROTC. AFROTC at U of Cincinnati.
**Honors:** Honors program. Honor societies.
**Academic Assistance:** Remedial reading, writing, math, and study skills. Nonremedial tutoring.

**STUDENT LIFE. Housing:** All freshmen and sophomores living beyond a 35-mile radius must live on campus. Coed dorms. School-owned/operated apartments. Off-campus privately-owned housing. 49% of students live in college housing.
**Social atmosphere:** The basketball season, the Homecoming Dance, Spring Breakaway, Senior Week, and the Manresa Orientation Program are the most popular Xavier events. The Student Activities Council is the most influential group on campus. Xavier students spend free time at the Grill, the Down Under, Dana Gardens, and the Norwood Cafe. The student newspaper reports that the social atmosphere is "average at best...limited on weekends."
**Services and counseling/handicapped student services:** Placement services. Health service. Counseling services for minority and older students. Personal and psychological counseling. Career and academic guidance services. Religious counseling. Learning disabled services.
**Campus organizations:** Undergraduate student government. Student newspaper (NewsWire, published once/week). Literary magazine. Yearbook. Radio and TV stations. Instrumental and vocal groups, theatre, departmental, military, political, professional, special-interest, and women's groups, 100 organizations in all.
**Religious organizations:** Ministry Center, Peace and Justice Center programs.
**Minority/foreign student organizations:** Black Student Association, Minority Student Center. International Student Association.

**ATHLETICS. Physical education requirements:** None.
**Intercollegiate competition:** 12% of students participate. Baseball (M), basketball (M,W), cross-country (M,W), golf (M,W), riflery (M,W), soccer (M,W), swimming (M,W), tennis (M,W), volleyball (W). Member of Midwestern Collegiate Conference, NCAA Division I.
**Intramural and club sports:** 65% of students participate. Intramural aerobics, basketball, body works, fitness club, flag football, floor hockey, golf, inner-tube water polo, racquetball, sand volleyball, scuba, soccer, softball, swimming, table tennis, tennis, ultimate frisbee, walleyball, water aerobics, Wiffle ball, yoga. Men's club boxing, crew, cross-country, cycling, fencing, racquetball, rugby, sailing, wrestling. Women's club crew, cross-country, cycling, fencing, racquetball, sailing.

**ADMISSIONS. Academic basis for candidate selection** (in order of priority): Secondary school record, standardized test scores, school's recommendation, class rank.
**Nonacademic basis for candidate selection:** Extracurricular participation is important. Character and personality, particular talent or ability, and alumni/ae relationship are considered.
**Requirements:** Graduation from secondary school is required; GED is accepted. 15 units and the following program of study are required: 4 units of English, 2 units of math, 2 units of science, 2 units of foreign language, 3 units of social studies, 2 units of electives. Minimum composite ACT score of 20 (combined SAT score of 800) and minimum 2.4 GPA recommmended. Academic Bridge Program for applicants not normally admissible. SAT or ACT is required. Campus visit and interview recommended. Off-campus interviews available with an admissions representative.
**Procedure:** Take SAT or ACT by December of 12th year. Visit college for interview by February of 12th year. Suggest filing application by April 15; no deadline. Notification of admission on rolling basis. Reply is required by May 1. $50 tuition deposit, refundable until May 1. $100 room deposit, refundable until May 1. Freshmen accepted for terms other than fall.
**Special programs:** Admission may be deferred one year. Credit and/or placement may be granted through CEEB Advanced Placement exams for scores of 3 or higher. Credit and/or placement may be granted through CLEP general and subject exams. Concurrent enrollment program.
**Transfer students:** Transfer students accepted for terms other than fall. In fall 1993, 25% of all new students were transfers into all classes. 355 transfer applications were received, 283 were accepted. Application deadline is rolling for fall; rolling for spring. Minimum 2.0 GPA required. Lowest course grade accepted is "D." At least 30 semester hours must be completed at the university to receive degree.
**Admissions contact:** Jay Leiendecker, M.Ed., Director of Admissions. 513 745-3301.

**FINANCIAL AID. Available aid:** Pell grants, SEOG, state scholarships and grants, school scholarships and grants, private scholarships and grants, ROTC scholarships, academic merit scholarships, and athletic scholarships. Perkins Loans (NDSL), PLUS, Stafford Loans (GSL), NSL, state loans, school loans, private loans, and SLS. Deferred payment plan. 10-month payment plan.
**Financial aid statistics:** 40% of aid is not need-based. In 1993-94, 83% of all undergraduate applicants received aid; 87% of freshman applicants. Average amounts of aid awarded freshmen: Scholarships and grants, $3,500; loans, $2,625.
**Supporting data/closing dates:** FAFSA: Priority filing date is April 15. Notification of awards on rolling basis.
**Financial aid contact:** Paul Calme, M.A., Director of Financial Aid. 513 745-3142.

**STUDENT EMPLOYMENT.** College Work/Study Program. Institutional employment. 20% of full-time undergraduates work on campus during school year. Students may expect to earn an average of $1,300 during school year. Off-campus part-time employment opportunities rated "excellent."

**COMPUTER FACILITIES.** 425 IBM/IBM-compatible and Macintosh/Apple microcomputers; 75 are networked. Students may access Digital minicomputer/mainframe systems. Residence halls may be equipped with networked microcomputers. Client/LAN operating systems include Apple/Macintosh, DOS, Novell. Computer languages and software packages include Assembler, BASIC, C, COBOL, FORTRAN, MAS-11, Pascal, Powerhouse, REF-11, SAS, SPSS-X, 20-20, WordPerfect. Computer facilities are available to all students.
**Fees:** Computer fee is included in tuition/fees.
**Hours:** 8 AM-11 PM.

**GRADUATE CAREER DATA.** Graduate school percentages: 3% enter law school. 5% enter medical school. 2% enter graduate business programs. Highest graduate school enrollments: U of Cincinnati, U of Dayton, Ohio State U, Wright State U. 50% of graduates choose careers in business and industry. Companies and businesses that hire graduates: Accounting firms, IBM, Procter & Gamble, Xerox.

**PROMINENT ALUMNI/AE.** David Huhn, president, McAlpin's; Larry Lesser, CEO, E.W. Scripps; Joe Viviano, president/COO, Hershey Foods.

# Youngstown State University

**Youngstown, OH 44555-0001** **216 742-3000**

**1993-94 Costs.** Tuition: $2,742 (state residents), $5,082 (out-of-state). Room & board: $3,675. Fees, books, misc. academic expenses (school's estimate): $670.
**Enrollment.** Undergraduates: 4,816 men, 4,817 women (full-time). Freshman class: 3,297 applicants, 2,903 accepted, 2,157 enrolled. Graduate enrollment: 477 men, 729 women.
**Test score averages/ranges.** Average SAT scores: 411 verbal, 453 math. Average ACT scores: 19 English, 19 math, 20 composite.
**Faculty.** 459 full-time; 445 part-time. 71% of faculty holds doctoral degree. Student/faculty ratio: 20 to 1.
**Selectivity rating.** Less competitive.

**PROFILE.** Youngstown State is a public, multipurpose university. It was founded as a school of law in 1908, gained university status in 1955, and became a member of the state system of higher education in 1967. Programs are offered through the Colleges of Applied Science and Technology, Arts and Sciences, Fine and Performing Arts, and Medicine; the Schools of Business Administration, Education, and Engineering; and the Graduate School. Its 105-acre campus is located less than a mile from downtown Youngstown.

**Accreditation:** NCACS. Professionally accredited by the Accreditation Board for Engineering and Technology, the American Dental Association, the American Dietetic Association, the Committee on Allied Health Education and Accreditation, the National Association of Schools of Music, the National Council for Accreditation of Teacher Education, the National League for Nursing.

**Religious orientation:** Youngstown State University is nonsectarian; no religious requirements.
**Library:** Collections totaling over 805,796 volumes, 3,125 periodical subscriptions, and 1,012,937 microform items.
**Special facilities/museums:** Art museum, human services development center, engineering services center, planetarium, center for urban studies, industrial development center.
**Athletic facilities:** Gymnasiums, stadium, basketball, racquetball, and tennis courts, swimming pool, baseball, football, practice, and softball fields, track, weight room.
**STUDENT BODY. Undergraduate profile:** 92% are state residents; 19% are transfers. .5% Asian-American, 7.5% Black, 1.1% Hispanic, .2% Native American, 89.2% White, 1.5% Other. Average age of undergraduates is 25.
**Freshman profile:** 4% of freshmen who took SAT scored 700 or over on math; 7% scored 600 or over on verbal, 16% scored 600 or over on math; 21% scored 500 or over on verbal, 36% scored 500 or over on math; 52% scored 400 or over on verbal, 64% scored 400 or over on math; 89% scored 300 or over on verbal, 91% scored 300 or over on math. 3% of freshmen who took ACT scored 30 or over on English, 2% scored 30 or over on math, 3% scored 30 or over on composite; 20% scored 24 or over on English, 16% scored 24 or over on math, 19% scored 24 or over on composite; 63% scored 18 or over on English, 57% scored 18 or over on math, 71% scored 18 or over on composite; 97% scored 12 or over on English, 99% scored 12 or over on math, 100% scored 12 or over on composite; 100% scored 6 or over on English, 100% scored 6 or over on math. 10% of accepted applicants took SAT; 16% took ACT.
**Foreign students:** 191 students are from out of the country. Countries represented include India, Jordan, Lebanon, Pakistan, the former Soviet Republics, and the United Kingdom; 56 in all.
**PROGRAMS OF STUDY. Degrees:** A.B., B.Eng., B.F.A., B.Mus., B.S., B.S.Appl.Sci., B.S.Bus.Admin., B.S.Ed., B.S.Nurs.
**Majors:** Accounting, Accounting Technology, Advertising Art, Advertising/Public Relations, Allied Health, American Studies, Anthropology, Art History, Biology, Biology/Pre-Dental, Biology/Pre-Forestry, Biology/Pre-Medical, Black Studies, Business Management Technology, Chemical Engineering, Chemistry, Chemistry/Pre-Dentistry, Chemistry/Pre-Medicine, Civil Engineering, Civil Engineering Technology, Combined Science, Computer Information Systems, Computer Science, Court/Conference Reporting, Criminal Justice, Drafting/Design Technology, Earth Science, Economics, Electrical Engineering, Electrical Engineering Technology, Elementary Education, Elementary/Kindergarten Education, English, Fashion Retailing, Finance, Food/Nutrition, French, General Administration, Geography, Geology, German, Health Sciences, History, Home Economics Services, Human Performance/Exercise Science, Humanities, Industrial Engineering, Industrial Management, Industrial Marketing, Italian, Labor Relations, Labor Studies, Latin, Mall Management, Management, Marketing Management, Materials Engineering, Mathematics, Mechanical Engineering, Mechanical Engineering Technology, Music Education, Music History/Literature, Music/Performance, Music Theory/Composition, Office Services/Administration, Philosophy, Physics, Physics/Astronomy, Political Science, Pre-Law, Professional Writing/Editing, Psychology, Public Administration, Religious Studies, Retail Marketing, Russian, Secondary Education, Social Studies, Social Work, Sociology, Spanish, Special Education, Speech Communication, Studio Art, Telecommunications, Theatre.
**Distribution of degrees:** The majors with the highest enrollment are elementary education, accounting, and criminal justice; American studies, French, and earth science have the lowest.
**Requirements:** General education requirement.
**Academic regulations:** Minimum 2.0 GPA required for graduation.
**Special:** Biology and chemistry majors include options in dentistry, forestry, and medicine. Colleges of Applied Science and Technology, Education and Fine and Performing Arts include several concentrations. Interdisciplinary minors include environmental science, journalism, peace and conflict studies, women's studies. Individual curriculum programs also available. Associate's degrees offered. Self-designed majors. Double majors. Independent study. Accelerated study. Pass/fail grading option. Internships. Graduate school at which undergraduates may take graduate-level courses. Preprofessional programs in law, medicine, dentistry, and forestry. 2-2 programs in civil engineering technology, computer information systems, electrical engineering technology, and mechanical engineering technology. 3-2 forestry management program with Duke U. Six-year B.S./M.D. program. Member of Northeastern Ohio Universities College of Medicine. Teacher certification in elementary, secondary, special education, and vo-tech education. Certification in specific subject areas. Study abroad in France, Germany, Greece, Italy, Latin American countries, the former Soviet Republics, and Spain. ROTC.
**Honors:** Honors program. Honor societies.
**Academic Assistance:** Remedial reading, writing, math, and study skills. Nonremedial tutoring.
**STUDENT LIFE. Housing:** Students may live on or off campus. Coed and women's dorms. Sorority and fraternity housing. School-owned/operated apartments. Off-campus privately-owned housing. 3% of students live in college housing.
**Social atmosphere:** Students frequently congregate at Kilcawley Center, Cushwa Hall, and Beeghly Center. Among the groups with the most widespread influence on campus social life are the Student Democrats, the College Republicans, the student government, and the International Affairs Club. Homecoming is a big event on campus, as are football, baseball, and basketball games, plays, and other student activities. "There is not much to do in Youngstown," observes the editor of the student newspaper, "and it's hard to interest students in cultural events. Social lives are developed through student organizations and classes."
**Services and counseling/handicapped student services:** Placement services. Health service. Women's center. Counseling services for minority, military, veteran, and older students. Personal and psychological counseling. Career and academic guidance services. Physically disabled student services. Learning disabled services. Tutors. Reader services for the blind.
**Campus organizations:** Undergraduate student government. Student newspaper (Jambar, published twice/week). Literary magazine. Yearbook. Radio station. Chorus, jazz ensemble, Organization for Women's Equality, Students for Reproductive Freedom, Student Democrats, College Republicans, Students for a Healthier Planet, academic, cultural, and special-interest groups, 141 organizations in all. 10 fraternities, six chapter houses; seven sororities, three chapter houses. 4% of men join a fraternity. 3% of women join a sorority.
**Religious organizations:** Apostolic Christian Fellowship, Chi Alpha Christian Fellowship, Intervarsity Christian Fellowship, Voices of Praise.
**Minority/foreign student organizations:** Pan-African Student Union.
**ATHLETICS. Physical education requirements:** Three quarter hours of physical education required.
**Intercollegiate competition:** 4% of students participate. Baseball (M), basketball (M,W), cheerleading (M,W), cross-country (M,W), football (M), golf (M), softball (W), tennis (M,W), track and field (indoor) (M,W), track and field (outdoor) (M,W), volleyball (W). Member of Mid-Continent Conference, NCAA Division I, NCAA Division I-AA for football.
**Intramural and club sports:** 13% of students participate. Intramural arm wrestling, badminton, basketball, bowling, darts, flag football, floor hockey, golf, handball, horseshoes, indoor soccer, pickleball, racquetball, riflery, soccer, softball, squash, swimming, team fitness, tennis, turkey trot, track, volleyball, wallyball, water polo. Men's club cricket, cycling, soccer, volleyball. Women's club cricket, cycling, soccer, volleyball.
**ADMISSIONS. Academic basis for candidate selection** (in order of priority): Secondary school record, standardized test scores, class rank.
**Nonacademic basis for candidate selection:** Geographical distribution is considered.
**Requirements:** Graduation from secondary school is required; GED is accepted. 16 units and the following program of study are required: 4 units of English, 3 units of math, 1 unit of lab science, 2 units of foreign language, 1 unit of social studies, 1 unit of history, 1 unit of academic electives. 1 unit of fine/performing arts also required. Minimum composite ACT score of 15 (combined SAT score of 700) and rank in top two-thirds of secondary school class required of out-of-state applicants. Audition required of music program applicants. SAT or ACT is required. Campus visit recommended. No off-campus interviews.
**Procedure:** Take SAT or ACT by December of 12th year. Visit college for interview by December of 12th year. Application deadline is August 15. Notification of admission on rolling basis. No set date by which applicants must accept offer. $200 nonrefundable room deposit. Freshmen accepted for terms other than fall.
**Special programs:** Admission may be deferred one year. Credit and/or placement may be granted through CEEB Advanced Placement exams for scores of 3 or higher. Credit and/or placement may be granted through CLEP subject exams. Credit may be granted through ACT PEP exams and military experience. Credit and placement may be granted through challenge exams. Early decision program. In fall 1993, 615 applied for early decision and 599 were accepted. Deadline for applying for early decision is February 15. Early entrance/early admission program. Concurrent enrollment program.
**Transfer students:** Transfer students accepted for terms other than fall. In fall 1993, 19% of all new students were transfers into all classes. 786 transfer applications were received, 639 were accepted. Application deadline is August 15 for fall; February 15 for spring. Minimum 2.0 GPA required. Lowest course grade accepted is "C." At least 45 quarter hours must be completed at the university to receive degree.
**Admissions contact:** Harold Yiannaki, Ed.D., Director of Enrollment Services. 216 742-3150.
**FINANCIAL AID. Available aid:** Pell grants, SEOG, state scholarships and grants, school scholarships and grants, private scholarships and grants, ROTC scholarships, academic merit scholarships, and athletic scholarships. Perkins Loans (NDSL), PLUS, Stafford Loans (GSL), and SLS. Tuition Management Systems.
**Financial aid statistics:** 10% of aid is not need-based. In 1993-94, 65% of all undergraduate applicants received aid; 60% of freshman applicants. Average amounts of aid awarded freshmen: Scholarships and grants, $1,800; loans, $1,800.
**Supporting data/closing dates:** FAFSA: Priority filing date is April 1; accepted on rolling basis. School's own aid application: Deadline is April 1. State aid form: Priority filing date is April 1. Notification of awards begins June 1.
**Financial aid contact:** William T. Collins, Jr., M.B.A., Director of Financial Aid. 216 742-3505.
**STUDENT EMPLOYMENT.** College Work/Study Program. Institutional employment. 9% of full-time undergraduates work on campus during school year. Students may expect to earn an average of $1,520 during school year. Off-campus part-time employment opportunities rated "excellent."
**COMPUTER FACILITIES.** 1,700 IBM/IBM-compatible, Macintosh/Apple, and RISC-/UNIX-based microcomputers; 300 are networked. Students may access Cray, SUN minicomputer/mainframe systems, BITNET, Internet. Residence halls may be equipped with modems. Client/LAN operating systems include Apple/Macintosh, DOS, UNIX/XENIX/AIX, X-windows, Artisoft, LocalTalk/AppleTalk. Computer languages and software packages include Ada, C, COBOL, dBASE, FORTRAN, GPSS, SAS, SNOBOL, WordPerfect; 90 in all. Computer facilities are available to all students.
**Fees:** None.
**Hours:** 8 AM-midn. (M-Th); 8 AM-10 PM (F); 8 AM-4 PM (Sa).

# Oklahoma

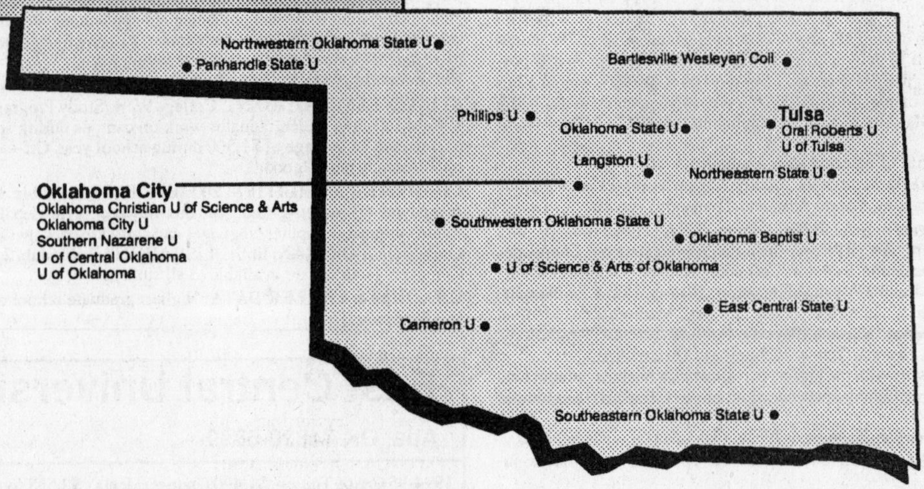


## Bartlesville Wesleyan College

**Bartlesville, OK 74006** **918 335-6200**

**1994-95 Costs.** Tuition: $6,450. Room: $1,500. Board: $1,800. Fees, books, misc. academic expenses (school's estimate): $500.
**Enrollment.** Undergraduates: 205 men, 303 women (full-time). Freshman class: 258 applicants, 187 accepted, 160 enrolled.
**Test score averages/ranges.** Average ACT scores: 21 composite.
**Faculty.** 40 full-time; 25 part-time. 28% of faculty holds doctoral degree. Student/faculty ratio: 14 to 1.
**Selectivity rating.** Competitive.

**PROFILE.** Bartlesville Wesleyan, founded in 1910, is a church-affiliated, liberal arts college. Its 36-acre campus is located in a residential section of Bartlesville.

**Accreditation:** NCACS.
**Religious orientation:** Bartlesville Wesleyan College is affiliated with the Wesleyan Church; nine semester hours of religion required.
**Library:** Collections totaling over 133,623 volumes and 262 periodical subscriptions.
**Special facilities/museums:** La Quinta Mansion.
**Athletic facilities:** Gymnasium, racquetball and tennis courts, weight room, baseball, football, and soccer fields.
**STUDENT BODY. Undergraduate profile:** 57% are state residents; 12% are transfers. 5% Asian-American, 4% Black, 3% Hispanic, 5% Native American, 82% White, 1% Other. Average age of undergraduates is 23.
**Freshman profile:** 32% of freshmen who took ACT scored 24 or over on composite; 74% scored 18 or over on composite; 100% scored 12 or over on composite. Majority of accepted applicants took ACT.
**Undergraduate achievement:** 68% of fall 1992 freshmen returned for fall 1993 term. 36% of entering class graduated.
**Foreign students:** 26 students are from out of the country. Countries represented include Antigua, Japan, and South Africa; five in all.
**PROGRAMS OF STUDY. Degrees:** B.A., B.S.
**Majors:** Accounting, Behavioral Science, Biblical Literature, Biology, Business Administration, Business Education, Chemistry, Communication, Computer Information Systems, Computer Science, Education, Elementary Education, English, General Science, History/Political Science, Management of Human Resources, Mathematics, Mathematics Education, Ministry, Missions, Natural Science, Office Administration, Physical Education, Religion, Science Education, Secondary Education, Social Science Education, Theology, Youth Ministries.
**Distribution of degrees:** The majors with the highest enrollment are business administration, management of human resources, and elementary education.
**Requirements:** General education requirement.
**Academic regulations:** Freshmen must maintain minimum 1.8 GPA; sophomores, juniors, seniors, 2.0 GPA.
**Special:** Associate's degrees offered. Double majors. Internships. Preprofessional programs in law, medicine, and theology. Washington Semester. Teacher certification in elementary and secondary education. Certification in specific subject areas. Study abroad in Costa Rica and England.
**Academic Assistance:** Remedial reading, writing, math, and study skills. Nonremedial tutoring.
**ADMISSIONS. Academic basis for candidate selection** (in order of priority): Secondary school record, standardized test scores, class rank, school's recommendation.
**Nonacademic basis for candidate selection:** Character and personality are emphasized. Extracurricular participation and particular talent or ability are important.
**Requirements:** Graduation from secondary school is recommended; GED is accepted. 16 units and the following program of study are required: 4 units of English, 2 units of math, 1 unit of lab science, 1 unit of social studies, 1 unit of history, 7 units of electives. Minimum composite ACT score of 18 (combined SAT score of 790), rank in top two-thirds of secondary school class, or minimum 2.0 GPA required. ACT is required; SAT may be substituted. Campus visit and interview recommended. Off-campus interviews available with an admissions representative.
**Procedure:** Take SAT or ACT by August of 12th year. Suggest filing application by May 1; no deadline. Notification of admission on rolling basis. No set date by which applicants must accept offer. $100 room deposit, refundable until early August. Freshmen accepted for terms other than fall.
**Special programs:** Admission may be deferred indefinitely. Credit may be granted through CEEB Advanced Placement, CLEP general and subject exams, ACT PEP exams, and military and life experience. Credit and placement may be granted through challenge exams. Concurrent enrollment program.
**Transfer students:** Transfer students accepted for terms other than fall. In fall 1993, 12% of all new students were transfers into all classes. 84 transfer applications were received, 72 were accepted. Application deadline is rolling for fall; rolling for spring. Minimum 2.0 GPA required. Lowest course grade accepted is "D." Maximum number of transferable credits is 65 semester hours from a two-year school and 96 semester hours from a four-year school. At least 24 semester hours must be completed at the college to receive degree.
**Admissions contact:** Bob Hubbard, Enrollment Services Administrator. 918 335-6219.
**FINANCIAL AID. Available aid:** Pell grants, SEOG, state scholarships and grants, school scholarships and grants, private scholarships, academic merit scholarships, athletic scholarships, and aid for undergraduate foreign students. Perkins Loans (NDSL), PLUS, Stafford Loans (GSL), and SLS. AMS and deferred payment plan.
**Financial aid statistics:** 33% of aid is not need-based. In 1993-94, 90% of all undergraduate applicants received aid; 90% of freshman applicants. Average amounts of aid awarded freshmen: Loans, $3,000.
**Supporting data/closing dates:** FAFSA: Accepted on rolling basis. School's own aid application: Priority filing date is May 1; accepted on rolling basis. Income tax forms: Accepted on rolling basis. Notification of awards on rolling basis.
**Financial aid contact:** Laura Parkes, Director of Financial Aid. 918 335-6219.

## Cameron University

**Lawton, OK 73505** **405 581-2230**

**1994-95 Costs.** Tuition: $1,500 (state residents), $3,500 (out-of-state). Room & board: $2,302. Fees, books, misc. academic expenses (school's estimate): $360.
**Enrollment.** Undergraduates: 1,471 men, 1,909 women (full-time). Freshman class: 1,288 applicants, 1,248 accepted, 912 enrolled. Graduate enrollment: 134 men, 221 women.
**Test score averages/ranges.** N/A.
**Faculty.** 192 full-time; 10 part-time. 51% of faculty holds doctoral degree. Student/faculty ratio: 28 to 1.
**Selectivity rating.** Noncompetitive.

**PROFILE.** Cameron is a public, comprehensive university. It was founded in 1908, became a four-year college in 1966, and gained university status in 1974. Programs are offered through the Division of Educational Outreach and the Schools of Business, Education and Behavioral Sciences, Fine Arts, Language Arts, and Mathematical and Applied Sciences. Its 160-acre campus is located in Lawton, 90 miles southwest of Oklahoma City.

**Accreditation:** NCACS. Professionally accredited by the National Association of Schools of Music, the National Council for Accreditation of Teacher Education, the National League for Nursing.
**Religious orientation:** Cameron University is nonsectarian; no religious requirements.
**Library:** Collections totaling over 229,895 volumes, 3,816 periodical subscriptions, and 370,969 microform items.
**Special facilities/museums:** Satellite labs.
**Athletic facilities:** Gymnasium; stadium; baseball, football, softball fields; tennis courts; swimming pool.

**STUDENT BODY. Undergraduate profile:** 99% are state residents; 13% are transfers. 2% Asian-American, 15% Black, 6% Hispanic, 4% Native American, 72% White, 1% Other. Average age of undergraduates is 25.

**Freshman profile:** 1% of freshmen who took ACT scored 30 or over on English, 1% scored 30 or over on math, 1% scored 30 or over on composite; 14% scored 24 or over on English, 10% scored 24 or over on math, 13% scored 24 or over on composite; 57% scored 18 or over on English, 50% scored 18 or over on math, 63% scored 18 or over on composite; 94% scored 12 or over on English, 94% scored 12 or over on math, 99% scored 12 or over on composite; 99% scored 6 or over on English, 98% scored 6 or over on math, 100% scored 6 or over on composite. Majority of accepted applicants took ACT. 91% of freshmen come from public schools.

**Undergraduate achievement:** 5% of entering class graduated.

**Foreign students:** 18 students are from out of the country. Countries represented include Canada, Colombia, Panama, Paraguay, Puerto Rico, and Thailand; 17 in all.

**PROGRAMS OF STUDY. Degrees:** B.A., B.Bus.Admin., B.F.A., B.M., B.S.

**Majors:** Accounting, Agriculture, Art, Biology, Business Administration, Chemistry, Communication, Computer Information Systems, Computer Science, Criminal Justice, Elementary Education, English, Health/Physical Education, History, Home Economics, Human Ecology/Home Economics, Interdisciplinary Studies, Mathematics, Medical Technology, Music, Natural Science, Nursing, Physics, Political Science, Psychology, Romance Languages, Sociology, Speech/Drama, Technology, Theatre Arts.

**Distribution of degrees:** The majors with the highest enrollment are business administration, elementary education, and health/physical education; physics, fine arts, and natural science have the lowest.

**Requirements:** General education requirement.

**Academic regulations:** Freshmen must maintain minimum 1.7 GPA; sophomores, juniors, seniors, 2.0 GPA.

**Special:** Minors offered in most majors. Associate's degrees offered. Self-designed majors. Double majors. Pass/fail grading option. Internships. Graduate school at which undergraduates may take graduate-level courses. Preprofessional programs in law, medicine, veterinary science, pharmacy, dentistry, and engineering. 3-1 medical technology program. Teacher certification in early childhood, elementary, and secondary education. ROTC.

**Honors:** Honors program.

**Academic Assistance:** Remedial reading, writing, math, and study skills. Nonremedial tutoring.

**STUDENT LIFE. Housing:** Students may live on or off campus. Women's and men's dorms. 1% of students live in college housing.

**Social atmosphere:** According to the editor of the student newspaper, "Cameron has mostly commuters with an average age of 27." Influential groups are the Aggie Club, ROTC, the Ebony Society, the newly formed Greek system, the debate team, and the student newspaper staff. The most popular events are Homecoming, Spring Fling, football and basketball games, Halloween activities, back-to-school dances, and stand-up comics. Favorite gathering spots are the Student Union, Central Mall, the residence halls, and nightclubs such as the Mad Dog Saloon and City Limits.

**Services and counseling/handicapped student services:** Placement services. Counseling services for minority, military, veteran, and older students. Personal counseling. Career and academic guidance services. Religious counseling. Physically disabled student services. Learning disabled services. Notetaking services. Reader services for the blind.

**Campus organizations:** Undergraduate student government. Student newspaper (Cameron Collegian, published once/week). Literary magazine. Yearbook. Radio station. Programming and Activities Council, Residence Hall Association, Greek Council, PLUS, Residence Life Conduct, 53 organizations in all. Two fraternities, no chapter houses; three sororities, no chapter houses. 4% of men join a fraternity. 6% of women join a sorority.

**Religious organizations:** Cameron Campus Ministry, Fellowship of Christian Athletes, Interfaith Council, Latter Day Saint's Student Association, Baptist Student Union.

**Minority/foreign student organizations:** Native American association, Kappa Alpha Psi, Intertribal Council, Alpha Phi Alpha, Delta Sigma Theta. International Club.

**ATHLETICS. Physical education requirements:** Four terms of physical education required.

**Intercollegiate competition:** 2% of students participate. Baseball (M), basketball (M,W), cheerleading (M,W), golf (M), softball (W), tennis (M,W), volleyball (W). Member of NCAA Division II.

**Intramural and club sports:** 30% of students participate. Intramural bowling, flag football, frisbee golf, golf, putt-putt golf, racquetball, soccer, softball, volleyball.

**ADMISSIONS. Academic basis for candidate selection** (in order of priority): Secondary school record, class rank, standardized test scores.

**Requirements:** Graduation from secondary school is required; GED is accepted. 11 units and the following program of study are required: 4 units of English, 3 units of math, 2 units of lab science, 2 units of history. Minimum composite ACT score of 19, or rank in the top 55% of secondary school class. Minimum 2.7 GPA required. Conditional admission possible for applicants not meeting standard requirements. ACT is required; SAT may be substituted. Campus visit recommended. No off-campus interviews.

**Procedure:** Take SAT or ACT by December of 12th year. Notification of admission on rolling basis. Freshmen accepted for terms other than fall.

**Special programs:** Credit and/or placement may be granted through CEEB Advanced Placement exams for scores of 3 or higher. Credit may be granted through CLEP general exams, ACT PEP exams, and military experience. Credit and/or placement may be granted through CLEP subject exams. Credit and placement may be granted through DANTES and challenge exams. Concurrent enrollment program.

**Transfer students:** Transfer students accepted for terms other than fall. In fall 1993, 13% of all new students were transfers into all classes. 461 transfer applications were received, 446 were accepted. Minimum 2.0 GPA required. Lowest course grade accepted is "D." Maximum number of transferable credits is 64 semester hours. At least 30 semester hours must be completed at the university to receive degree.

**Admissions contact:** Zoe DuRant, M.B.S., Director of Admissions. 405 581-2230.

**FINANCIAL AID. Available aid:** Pell grants, SEOG, Federal Nursing Student Scholarships, state grants, school scholarships, private scholarships, ROTC scholarships, academic merit scholarships, and athletic scholarships. Perkins Loans (NDSL), PLUS, Stafford Loans (GSL), and SLS.

**Financial aid statistics:** 10% of aid is not need-based. In 1993-94, 85% of all undergraduate applicants received aid; 78% of freshman applicants. Average amounts of aid awarded freshmen: Scholarships and grants, $800; loans, $2,000.

**Supporting data/closing dates:** FAFSA/FAF/FFS: Priority filing date is March 1; accepted on rolling basis. School's own aid application: Priority filing date is March 1; accepted on rolling basis. Income tax forms: Priority filing date is March 1; accepted on rolling basis. Notification of awards on rolling basis.

**Financial aid contact:** Caryn Pacheco, Director of Financial Aid. 405 581-2293.

**STUDENT EMPLOYMENT.** College Work/Study Program. Institutional employment. 12% of full-time undergraduates work on campus during school year. Students may expect to earn an average of $1,500 during school year. Off-campus part-time employment opportunities rated "good."

**COMPUTER FACILITIES.** 200 IBM/IBM-compatible and Macintosh/Apple microcomputers; 60 are networked. Students may access Hewlett-Packard minicomputer/mainframe systems. Computer languages and software packages include Ada, BMDP, BASIC, C, COBOL, FORTRAN, ImSL, LISP, MINITAB, Modula 2, Pascal, RPG II, SAS, SPSS. Computer facilities are available to all students.

**GRADUATE CAREER DATA.** Highest graduate school enrollments: Oklahoma State U, Oklahoma U.

# East Central University

**Ada, OK 74820-6899** **405 332-8000**

**1994-95 Costs.** Tuition: $1,490 (state residents), $3,553 (out-of-state). Room & board: $2,068. Fees, books, misc. academic expenses (school's estimate): $545.

**Enrollment.** Undergraduates: 1,376 men, 1,909 women (full-time). Freshman class: 909 applicants, 534 accepted, 499 enrolled. Graduate enrollment: 183 men, 394 women.

**Test score averages/ranges.** Average ACT scores: 20 English, 18 math, 20 composite.

**Faculty.** 157 full-time; 47 part-time. 61% of faculty holds doctoral degree. Student/faculty ratio: 25 to 1.

**Selectivity rating.** Competitive.

**PROFILE.** East Central, founded as a Normal school in 1909, is a public university. Programs are now offered through the Divisions of Applied Sciences; Arts and Letters; Health, Physical Education, and Recreation; and Social Sciences, and the Schools of Business, Education and Psychology, Mathematics and Sciences, and Graduate Studies. Its 140-acre campus is located in Ada, 90 miles from Oklahoma City.

**Accreditation:** NCACS. Professionally accredited by the National Council for Accreditation of Teacher Education, the National League for Nursing.

**Religious orientation:** East Central University is nonsectarian; no religious requirements.

**Library:** Collections totaling over 203,301 volumes, 1,300 periodical subscriptions, and 293,094 microform items.

**Athletic facilities:** Gymnasium, tennis courts, baseball, football, soccer, and softball fields, swimming pool, archery range, golf course, track, weight rooms, stadium, activity center.

**STUDENT BODY. Undergraduate profile:** 99% are state residents; 11% are transfers. 1% Asian-American, 3% Black, 1% Hispanic, 86% White, 9% Other. Average age of undergraduates is 25.

**Freshman profile:** 100% of accepted applicants took ACT. 99% of freshmen come from public schools.

**Undergraduate achievement:** 61% of fall 1992 freshmen returned for fall 1993 term.

**Foreign students:** 13 students are from out of the country. Countries represented include China, India, Korea, Malaysia, Nepal, and Taiwan; seven in all.

**PROGRAMS OF STUDY. Degrees:** B.A., B.Mus., B.S., B.S.Ed., B.Soc.Work.

**Majors:** Accounting, Adult Corrections, Aging, Allied Health, Architecture/Construction Technology, Art, Athletic Training, Biology, Business Administration, Business Education, Cartography, Chemistry, Computer Science, Counseling, Criminal Justice, Early Childhood Education, Electrical Engineering Technology, Elementary Education, Engineering Technology, English, Environmental Health, Environmental Management, Environmental Science, Fashion Merchandising, General Home Economics, Government, Health/Physical Education/Recreation, History, Home Economics, Human Resources, Industrial Education/Technology, Industrial Engineering Technology, Industrial Hygiene, Industrial Management, Instrumental Music, Interior Architecture, Juvenile Justice, Law Enforcement, Legal Studies, Literature, Mass Communications, Mathematics, Mathematics/Computer Science, Mathematics/General, Medical Records Administration, Medical Technology, News/Editorial, Nursing, Office Administration, Physical Education/Health, Physics, Piano, Psychology, Radio/Television, Services to the Deaf, Social Work, Sociology, Special Education, Speech, Speech Communication, Technology Education, Theatre, Vocal Music, Vocational Home Economics, Water/Wastewater Technology, Writing.

**Distribution of degrees:** The majors with the highest enrollment are business/accounting, nursing, and elementary education.

**Requirements:** General education requirement.

**Academic regulations:** Freshmen must maintain minimum 1.7 GPA; sophomores, juniors, seniors, 2.0 GPA.

**Special:** Minors offered in some majors and in communications, economics, ethnic studies, and journalism. Double majors. Dual degrees. Independent study. Internships. Graduate school at which undergraduates may take graduate-level courses. Preprofessional programs in law, medicine, veterinary science, dentistry, and physical therapy. Combined bachelor's/M.D. and bachelor's/dentistry programs. Exchange program with Westfield State Coll. Teacher certification in early childhood, elementary, secondary, and special education. ROTC.

**Honors:** Phi Beta Kappa. Honors program.

**Academic Assistance:** Remedial reading, writing, and math. Nonremedial tutoring.

**STUDENT LIFE. Housing:** Students may live on or off campus. Coed and women's dorms. School-owned/operated apartments. On-campus married-student housing. 50% of students live in college housing.
**Social atmosphere:** "Social life at East Central University consists of dancing at local clubs and attending sporting events," reports the student newspaper. "Greek organizations generally have their own gathering spots and social events." Popular areas for students to hang out are Wild Willy's, Bandana's, the Tiger's Den, and Wintersmith Park. Greeks, athletics, United Campus Ministries, and the Association of Black Students are influential organizations on campus. Some of the favorite events on campus are Homecoming, Greek Week, Don't Go Home This Weekend Weekend, Spring Fling, and the Pesagi Coronation.
**Services and counseling/handicapped student services:** Placement services. Health service. Day care. Counseling services for minority, military, veteran, and older students. Personal and psychological counseling. Career and academic guidance services. Physically disabled student services. Notetaking services. Reader services for the blind.
**Campus organizations:** Undergraduate student government. Student newspaper (Journal, published once/week). Yearbook. Choir, marching and jazz bands, small vocal groups, Association of Women Students, Federation of College Republicans, Young Democrats, Nursing Student Association, Student Education Association, departmental, political, and service groups. Four fraternities, all with chapter houses; three sororities, all with chapter houses. 9% of men join a fraternity. 10% of women join a sorority.
**Religious organizations:** Bahai Club, Baptist Student Union, Chi Alpha, Church of Christ Student Center, Fellowship of Christian Athletes, United Christian Student Center.
**Minority/foreign student organizations:** Black Student Union, Intertribal Council. International Student Association.

**ATHLETICS. Physical education requirements:** One semester of physical education required.
**Intercollegiate competition:** 9% of students participate. Baseball (M), basketball (M,W), football (M), golf (M), tennis (M,W), track (outdoor) (M). Member of NAIA, Oklahoma Intercollegiate Conference.
**Intramural and club sports:** 35% of students participate. Intramural basketball, bowling, football, softball, tennis, volleyball.

**ADMISSIONS. Academic basis for candidate selection** (in order of priority): Standardized test scores, secondary school record, class rank.
**Requirements:** Graduation from secondary school is required; GED is not accepted. No specific distribution of secondary school units required. Minimum composite ACT score of 19 or rank in top 55% of secondary school class and minimum 2.7 GPA required. Conditional admission possible for applicants not meeting standard requirements. ACT is required. Campus visit recommended. Off-campus interviews available with an admissions representative.
**Procedure:** Suggest filing application by May; no deadline. Notification of admission on rolling basis. No set date by which applicants must accept offer. $50 room deposit, refundable until two weeks before beginning of term. Freshmen accepted for terms other than fall.
**Special programs:** Credit may be granted through CLEP subject exams, ACT PEP, DANTES, and challenge exams, and military experience. Early entrance/early admission program. Concurrent enrollment program.
**Transfer students:** Transfer students accepted for terms other than fall. In fall 1993, 11% of all new students were transfers into all classes. 532 transfer applications were received, 524 were accepted. Application deadline is August for fall; January for spring. Minimum 2.0 GPA required. Lowest course grade accepted is "D." Maximum number of transferable credits is 64 semester hours from a two-year school and 94 semester hours from a four-year school. At least 30 semester hours must be completed at the university to receive degree.
**Admissions contact:** Pamla Armstrong, M.S.H.R., Director of Admissions. 405 332-8000, extension 234.

**FINANCIAL AID. Available aid:** Pell grants, SEOG, Federal Nursing Student Scholarships, state grants, school scholarships, private scholarships, ROTC scholarships, academic merit scholarships, and athletic scholarships. Perkins Loans (NDSL), PLUS, Stafford Loans (GSL), state loans, school loans, and SLS. Deferred payment plan.
**Financial aid statistics:** 15% of aid is not need-based. In 1993-94, 75% of all undergraduate applicants received aid; 75% of freshman applicants.
**Supporting data/closing dates:** FAFSA/FFS: Priority filing date is April 1. School's own aid application: Priority filing date is April 1. Notification of awards on rolling basis.
**Financial aid contact:** Cheryl Lyons, M.A., Director of Financial Aid. 405 332-8000, extension 243.

**STUDENT EMPLOYMENT.** College Work/Study Program. Institutional employment. 13% of full-time undergraduates work on campus during school year. Students may expect to earn an average of $1,600 during school year. Off-campus part-time employment opportunities rated "good."

**COMPUTER FACILITIES.** IBM/IBM-compatible and Macintosh/Apple microcomputers. Computer languages and software packages include Ada, BASIC, C, COBOL, FORTRAN, Pascal, SPL; filing, spreadsheet, word processing programs. Computer facilities are available to all students.

**PROMINENT ALUMNI/AE.** George Nigh, former governor of Oklahoma; Portia Isaacson, president, Isaacson, Inc.; Lyle Boren, U.S. congressman.

# Langston University

**Langston, OK 73050 — 405 466-2231**

**1993-94 Costs.** Tuition: $906 (state residents), $2,448 (out-of-state). Room: $896. Board: $1,484. Fees, books, misc. academic expenses (school's estimate): $569.
**Enrollment.** Undergraduates: 1,383 men, 2,029 women (full-time). Freshman class: 710 applicants, 397 accepted, 397 enrolled.
**Test score averages/ranges.** N/A.
**Faculty.** 95 full-time; 117 part-time. 55% of faculty holds doctoral degree. Student/faculty ratio: 24 to 1.
**Selectivity rating.** N/A.

**PROFILE.** Langston, founded in 1897, is a public, multipurpose university. Programs are offered through the Divisions of Allied Health, Applied Science, Arts and Sciences, Business, and Education and Behavioral Sciences. Its 40-acre campus is located in Langston, 42 miles north of Okalahoma City.

**Accreditation:** NCACS. Professionally accredited by the National Council for Accreditation of Teacher Education, the National League for Nursing.
**Religious orientation:** Langston University is nonsectarian; no religious requirements.
**Library:** Collections totaling over 160,000 volumes, 680 periodical subscriptions, and 3,175 microform items.
**Athletic facilities:** Athletic center, basketball courts, weight rooms, track, football field, gymnasium, stadium.

**STUDENT BODY. Undergraduate profile:** 62% are state residents. Average age of undergraduates is 20.
**Freshman profile:** 10% of accepted applicants took SAT; 90% took ACT.

**PROGRAMS OF STUDY. Degrees:** B.A., B.A.Ed., B.S., B.S.Ed.
**Majors:** Accounting, Agricultural Economics, Agriculture, Animal Science/Husbandry, Art, Art Education Method/Theory, Biology, Business/Commerce, Business/Commerce/Distribution, Business Management/Administration, Chemistry, Communication Media/Film/Radio/TV, Computer Information Sciences, Corrections, Criminal Justice, Dietetics/Human Nutritional Services, Dramatics/Theatre Arts, Drawing, Economics, Elementary Education, Engineering Technologies, English, Food/Nutrition/Dietetics, Gerontology, Health Care Administration, History, Home Economics, Home Economics Education, Industrial Arts, Liberal Arts/Sciences, Music/Liberal Arts, Nursing, Painting, Personnel Management, Physical Education/Recreation, Pre-Elementary Education, Psychology, Sculpture, Secondary Education, Secretarial Studies, Social Science Education, Social Sciences, Sociology, Special Education, Urban Studies, Vocational Home Economics, Vocational-Technical Education.
**Distribution of degrees:** The majors with the highest enrollment are accounting and education.
**Academic regulations:** Minimum 2.0 GPA required for graduation.
**Special:** Minors offered in all majors and in French, German, religion, and Spanish. Courses offered in philosophy and political science. Black studies program. Associate's degrees offered. Cooperative education programs. Preprofessional programs in law, library science, and social work. Cooperative nursing program leads to B.S. after completion of work at Langston and approved school of nursing. Teacher certification in elementary and secondary education. ROTC at Central State U.
**Academic Assistance:** Nonremedial tutoring.

**STUDENT LIFE. Housing:** Freshmen must live on campus. Women's and men's dorms. Sorority and fraternity housing. School-owned/operated apartments. Married-student housing. 60% of students live in college housing.
**Social atmosphere:** Social life at Langston is influenced by Phi Beta Sigma fraternity and other black Greek organizations. The most popular entertainment events include Homecoming and the "Thriller" talent show. On campus, students most often frequent the Hale Student Union. According to the editor of the student newspaper, "The cultural life includes seeing plays produced by Langston students, visiting nearby cities to attend concerts, learning the history of LU, and having general get-togethers."
**Services and counseling/handicapped student services:** Placement services. Health service. Upward Bound. Freshman development program. Reading laboratory. Career and academic guidance services.
**Campus organizations:** Undergraduate student government. Student newspaper. Yearbook. Choir and concert choir, debating, marching and concert bands, political clubs, special-interest groups, theatre productions. Four fraternities, no chapter houses; four sororities, no chapter houses. 10% of men join a fraternity. 15% of women join a sorority.
**Religious organizations:** Several religious groups.

**ATHLETICS. Physical education requirements:** Four credit hours of physical education required.
**Intercollegiate competition:** 3% of students participate. Basketball (M,W), football (M), track (indoor) (M,W), track (outdoor) (M,W), track and field (outdoor) (W). Member of NAIA, Oklahoma Intercollegiate Conference.
**Intramural and club sports:** 40% of students participate. Intramural basketball, flag football, softball, table tennis, track, volleyball.

**ADMISSIONS. Academic basis for candidate selection** (in order of priority): Secondary school record, class rank, school's recommendation, standardized test scores, essay.
**Requirements:** Graduation from secondary school is required; GED is accepted. No specific distribution of secondary school units required. Minimum composite ACT score of 12, rank in top three-quarters of secondary school class, or minimum 2.7 GPA required of state residents. Minimum composite ACT score of 14, rank in top half of secondary school class, or minimum 2.7 GPA required of out-of-state applicants. ACT is required; SAT may be substituted. No off-campus interviews.
**Procedure:** Application deadline is August 18. Notification of admission on rolling basis. Reply is required by May 1. Freshmen accepted for fall term only.
**Special programs:** Early entrance/early admission program. Concurrent enrollment program.
**Transfer students:** Transfer students accepted for terms other than fall. In fall 1992, 277 transfer applications were received, 183 were accepted. Application deadline is August 18 for fall; January 10 for spring. Minimum 2.0 GPA recommended. Lowest course grade accepted is "D."
**Admissions contact:** Ronald K. Smith, M.A., Director of Admissions and Records. 405 466-2231.

**FINANCIAL AID. Available aid:** Pell grants, SEOG, state scholarships, school scholarships and grants, private grants, and ROTC scholarships. Perkins Loans (NDSL), PLUS, Stafford Loans (GSL), NSL, state loans, and school loans. Deferred payment plan.
**Supporting data/closing dates:** FAFSA/FAF: Deadline is April 15. State aid form. Income tax forms. Notification of awards begins June 15.
**Financial aid contact:** Yvonne Maxwell, M.S., Director of Financial Aid.

**STUDENT EMPLOYMENT.** College Work/Study Program. Off-campus part-time employment opportunities rated "fair."

**COMPUTER FACILITIES.** 20 IBM/IBM-compatible microcomputers.

# Northeastern State University

**Tahlequah, OK 74464** **918 456-5511**

**1994-95 Costs.** Tuition: $1,407 (state residents), $3,200 (out-of-state). Room & board: $2,392. Fees, books, misc. academic expenses (school's estimate): $450.
**Enrollment.** Undergraduates: 2,400 men, 2,435 women (full-time). Freshman class: 1,120 applicants, 1,035 accepted, 851 enrolled. Graduate enrollment: 911 men, 1,000 women.
**Test score averages/ranges.** Average ACT scores: 22 composite.
**Faculty.** 270 full-time; 148 part-time. 60% of faculty holds doctoral degree. Student/faculty ratio: 20 to 1.
**Selectivity rating.** Less competitive.

**PROFILE.** Northeastern State is a public, comprehensive university. It was founded in 1846 as a result of a treaty between the U.S. and the Cherokee Nation to provide higher education for the Cherokees. Programs are offered through the Colleges of Arts and Sciences, Business Administration, Education, and Music, and the Schools of Community Service, Human Resource Management, and Library and Information Services. Its 425-acre campus is located in Denton, 39 miles north of Dallas.

**Accreditation:** NCACS. Professionally accredited by the National Council for Accreditation of Teacher Education.
**Religious orientation:** Northeastern State University is nonsectarian; no religious requirements.
**Library:** Collections totaling over 150,000 volumes.
**Athletic facilities:** Gymnasiums, field house, athletic fields, track.

**STUDENT BODY. Undergraduate profile:** 99% are state residents; 42% are transfers. 1% Asian-American, 3% Black, 1% Hispanic, 17% Native American, 78% White. Average age of undergraduates is 26.
**Freshman profile:** 100% of accepted applicants took ACT. 99% of freshmen come from public schools.

**PROGRAMS OF STUDY. Degrees:** B.A., B.Bus.Admin., B.S., B.S.Nurs.
**Majors:** Accounting, Administration of Allied Health Services, Art, Biology, Botany, Business Administration, Business Education, Chemistry, Cherokee Bilingual Education, Combined Instrumental/Vocal Music, Computer/Information Sciences, Criminal Justice, Early Childhood Education, Economics, Elementary Education, Engineering Physics, English, Finance, French, Geography, German, Health/Physical Education/Recreation, Health/Physical Education/Safety, History, Home Economics, Home Economics in Business, Indian Studies, Industrial Arts, Industrial Technology, Instrumental Music, Journalism, Learning Disabilities, Library Media, Management, Marketing, Mathematics, Medical Technology, Mental Retardation, Music, Nursing, Office Administration, Physics, Piano or Vocal Music, Psychology, Safety, Social Studies, Social Work, Sociology, Spanish, Special Education, Speech, Speech/Hearing Therapy, Speech Pathology/Audiology, Tourism Management, Vision Science, Zoology.
**Distribution of degrees:** The majors with the highest enrollment are education and business; the fine arts have the lowest.
**Requirements:** General education requirement.
**Academic regulations:** Freshmen must maintain minimum 1.7 GPA; sophomores, juniors, seniors, 2.0 GPA.
**Special:** Minors offered. Courses offered in ethnic studies, geology, philosophy, religious education, and tribal management. Certificate programs in accounting/general business, administration, building/construction technology, horticultural technology, police science, psychology, and secretrial training. Double majors. Dual degrees. Independent study. Internships. Cooperative education programs. Preprofessional programs in law, medicine, and dentistry. 2-2 nursing program. 3-1 medical technology program. Teacher certification in early childhood, elementary, secondary, and special education. ROTC.
**Academic Assistance:** Remedial reading, writing, and math. Nonremedial tutoring.

**STUDENT LIFE. Housing:** All unmarried students under age 21 must live on campus unless living near campus with relatives. Coed, women's, and men's dorms. Sorority and fraternity housing. School-owned/operated apartments. On-campus married-student housing. 30% of students live in college housing.
**Social atmosphere:** "Tahlequah is a small community set in the heart of the Cherokee Nation," reports the editor of the student newspaper. "We have the Illinois River about 5-10 miles out of town where, during the warm summer months, students can float either in canoes or inner tubes. We also have clubs not far from campus. During the spring semester, we have Kaleidoscope Week which provides entertainment for students." The most influential group is the Northeastern Activities Board, which sponsors ski trips, concerts, etc. Favorite events are football and basketball games, Tuesday night movies, and Homecoming Week. Students enjoy going to University Center on campus; off campus, it's Granny's Attic, Ned's, Ole El Paso, and the Hard Luck Cafe.
**Services and counseling/handicapped student services:** Placement services. Health service. Counseling services for minority and veteran students. Personal and psychological counseling. Academic guidance services. Learning disabled services.
**Campus organizations:** Undergraduate student government. Student newspaper. Yearbook. Drama group, debating, band, chorus, academic and service groups. Four fraternities, two chapter houses; three sororities, no chapter houses. 10% of men join a fraternity. 10% of women join a sorority.

**ATHLETICS. Physical education requirements:** Two semesters of physical education required.
**Intercollegiate competition:** 2% of students participate. Baseball (M), basketball (M,W), cheerleading (M,W), football (M), golf (M), soccer (M), softball (W), tennis (M,W), track (outdoor) (M), track and field (outdoor) (M). Member of NAIA, Oklahoma Intercollegiate Conference.
**Intramural and club sports:** 25% of students participate. Intramural basketball, bowling, flag football, softball, swimming, tennis, track.

**ADMISSIONS. Academic basis for candidate selection** (in order of priority): Standardized test scores, secondary school record, class rank, school's recommendation.
**Requirements:** Graduation from secondary school is required; GED is accepted. 15 units and the following program of study are required: 4 units of English, 3 units of math, 2 units of science, 2 units of foreign language, 2 units of social studies, 2 units of history. Minimum composite ACT score of 20 or rank in top half of secondary school class and minimum 2.7 GPA required. ACT is required. Campus visit recommended. Off-campus interviews available with an admissions representative.
**Procedure:** Take ACT by October of 12th year. Application deadline is August 1. Notification of admission on rolling basis. $50 nonrefundable room deposit. Freshmen accepted for terms other than fall.
**Special programs:** Credit may be granted through CEEB Advanced Placement for scores of 3 or higher. Credit may be granted through CLEP general and subject exams, challenge exams and military experience. Concurrent enrollment program.
**Transfer students:** Transfer students accepted for terms other than fall. In fall 1992, 42% of all new students were transfers into all classes. Application deadline is August 1 for fall; December 1 for spring. Minimum 2.0 GPA required. Lowest course grade accepted is "D." Maximum number of transferable credits is 63 semester hours. At least 30 semester hours must be completed at the university to receive degree.
**Admissions contact:** Dr. David J. Harbeck, Ph.D., Director of Admissions/Registrar.

**FINANCIAL AID. Available aid:** Pell grants, SEOG, and state scholarships and grants.
**Supporting data/closing dates:** FAFSA/FAF/FFS: Priority filing date is April 1. Notification of awards on rolling basis.
**Financial aid contact:** Peggy Carey, Director of Financial Aid.

**STUDENT EMPLOYMENT.** College Work/Study Program. Off-campus part-time employment opportunities rated "fair."

**COMPUTER FACILITIES.** 300 IBM/IBM-compatible microcomputers. Residence halls may be equipped with stand-alone microcomputers, networked microcomputers, networked terminals, modems. Computer facilities are available to all students.
**Fees:** None.

# Northwestern Oklahoma State University

**Alva, OK 73717** **405 327-1700**

**1993-94 Costs.** Tuition: $1,418 (state residents), $3,668 (out-of-state). Room & board: $1,956. Fees, books, misc. academic expenses (school's estimate): $400.
**Enrollment.** Undergraduates: 646 men, 845 women (full-time). Freshman class: 306 applicants, 289 accepted, 256 enrolled. Graduate enrollment: 99 men, 209 women.
**Test score averages/ranges.** Average ACT scores: 19 composite.
**Faculty.** 83 full-time; 32 part-time. 42% of faculty holds doctoral degree. Student/faculty ratio: 23 to 1.
**Selectivity rating.** Noncompetitive.

**PROFILE.** Northwestern Oklahoma State is a public, liberal arts university. Founded as a coeducational institution in 1897, it gained university status in 1974. Its 70-acre campus is located in Alva, northwest of Oklahoma City.

**Accreditation:** NCACS. Professionally accredited by the National Council for Accreditation of Teacher Education, the National League for Nursing.
**Religious orientation:** Northwestern Oklahoma State University is nonsectarian; no religious requirements.
**Library:** Collections totaling over 208,000 volumes, 1,407 periodical subscriptions, and 650,000 microform items.
**Special facilities/museums:** Natural history museum, instructional media center, TV production facility.
**Athletic facilities:** Gymnasiums, tennis courts, weight rooms, and softball fields.

**STUDENT BODY. Undergraduate profile:** 86% are state residents; 38% are transfers. 3% Black, 1.5% Hispanic, 2.5% Native American, 93% White. Average age of undergraduates is 24.
**Freshman profile:** 2% of freshmen who took ACT scored 30 or over on composite; 24% scored 24 or over on composite; 85% scored 18 or over on composite; 100% scored 12 or over on composite. 80% of accepted applicants took ACT.
**Undergraduate achievement:** 58% of fall 1992 freshmen returned for fall 1993 term. 14% of entering class graduated.
**Foreign students:** 10 students are from out of the country. Countries represented include China, Hong Kong, and Korea; six in all.

**PROGRAMS OF STUDY. Degrees:** B.A., B.A.Ed., B.Mus., B.Mus.Ed., B.S., B.S.Ed., B.S.Nurs.
**Majors:** Accounting, Agribusiness, Agricultural Ecology, Biology, Business Administration, Business Education, Chemistry, Computer Science, Conservation Law Enforcement, Economics, Elementary Education, English, Health/Physical Education, History, Home Economics, Law Enforcement, Library Science, Mass Communications, Mathematics, Medical Technology, Music, Natural Science, Nursing, Office Administration, Physical Education, Physics, Political Science, Psychology, Social Science, Social Work, Sociology, Special Education, Speech/Drama, Technology, Vocational Home Economics, Zoology.
**Distribution of degrees:** The majors with the highest enrollment are teacher education, business, and health sciences; library science, chemistry, and music have the lowest.
**Requirements:** General education requirement.
**Academic regulations:** Freshmen must maintain minimum 1.7 GPA; sophomores, juniors, seniors, 2.0 GPA.
**Special:** Minors offered in many majors and in agriculture, French, journalism, Spanish, and speech pathology. Double majors. Independent study. Graduate school at which undergraduates may take graduate-level courses. Preprofessional programs in law, medicine, veterinary science, pharmacy, dentistry, and optometry. 2-2 occupational therapy, physical therapy, and physician assistant programs with U of Oklahoma. 3-2 radiologic

technology program with U of Oklahoma. 3-2 engineering programs may be arranged. Teacher certification in early childhood, elementary, secondary, special education, vo-tech, and bilingual/bicultural education. Certification in specific subject areas.
**Honors:** Honors program. Honor societies.
**Academic Assistance:** Remedial reading, writing, math, and study skills. Nonremedial tutoring.

**STUDENT LIFE. Housing:** Students may live on or off campus. Women's and men's dorms. 31% of students live in college housing.
**Social atmosphere:** On campus, students congregate at the Campus Student Center. Off campus, the favored hang-out is the Nite Lite Bar and Dance Club. The Baptist Student Union and the Student Government Association are among the most influential groups on campus. Popular social events include Homecoming, Bahama Breakaway, the Ranger Rodeo, and the two basketball games against Southwestern Oklahoma State U, their biggest rival. "Alva is a small town with few recreational offerings," reports the editor of the student newspaper.
**Services and counseling/handicapped student services:** Placement services. Health service. Counseling services for minority and older students. Personal and psychological counseling. Career and academic guidance services. Physically disabled student services. Learning disabled services. Notetaking services. Tape recorders. Tutors. Reader services for the blind.
**Campus organizations:** Undergraduate student government. Student newspaper (Northwestern News, published once/week). Yearbook. Radio and TV stations. Men's and women's glee clubs, choir chamber singers, Soundsations, Castile Players, Young Democrats, Young Republicans, 34 organizations in all. Two fraternities, no chapter houses; one sorority, no chapter house.
**Religious organizations:** Baptist Student Union, Wesley Foundation, Chi Alpha, Bible Choir.
**Minority/foreign student organizations:** Black Student Alliance. International Student Organization.

**ATHLETICS. Physical education requirements:** Three semesters of physical education required.
**Intercollegiate competition:** Baseball (M), basketball (M,W), football (M), tennis (M,W), track (M).
**Intramural and club sports:** Intramural basketball, bowling, football, frisbee, racquetball, softball, swimming, track and field, volleyball, weight lifting.

**ADMISSIONS. Academic basis for candidate selection** (in order of priority): Secondary school record, standardized test scores, class rank.
**Nonacademic basis for candidate selection:** Extracurricular participation, particular talent or ability, and geographical distribution are considered.
**Requirements:** Graduation from secondary school is required; GED is accepted. 20 units and the following program of study are required: 4 units of English, 3 units of math, 2 units of lab science, 2 units of history, 4 units of academic electives. Minimum composite ACT score of 19 or rank in the top 50% of secondary school class and minimum 2.7 GPA required. Audition required of music program applicants. Conditional admission possible for applicants not meeting standard requirements. ACT is required; SAT may be substituted. Campus visit recommended. No off-campus interviews.
**Procedure:** Take SAT or ACT by August 1 of 12th year. Suggest filing application by June 1; no deadline. Notification of admission on rolling basis. No set date by which applicants must accept offer. $50 room deposit, refundable until August 15. Freshmen accepted for terms other than fall.
**Special programs:** Credit may be granted through CLEP subject exams and military experience. Credit and placement may be granted through challenge exams. Concurrent enrollment program.
**Transfer students:** Transfer students accepted for terms other than fall. In fall 1993, 38% of all new students were transfers into all classes. 188 transfer applications were received, 187 were accepted. Application deadline is by second week of classes for fall; by second week of classes for spring. Minimum 2.0 GPA required. Lowest course grade accepted is "D." Maximum number of transferable credits is 64 semester hours from a two-year school and 94 semester hours from a four-year school. At least 30 semester hours must be completed at the university to receive degree.
**Admissions contact:** Shirley Murrow, M.Ed., Director of Admissions. 405 327-1700, extension 213.

**FINANCIAL AID. Available aid:** Pell grants, SEOG, state scholarships and grants, private scholarships, academic merit scholarships, and athletic scholarships. Perkins Loans (NDSL), PLUS, Stafford Loans (GSL), school loans, and SLS.
**Financial aid statistics:** 10% of aid is not need-based. In 1993-94, 90% of all undergraduate applicants received aid; 85% of freshman applicants. Average amounts of aid awarded freshmen: Scholarships and grants, $800; loans, $2,625.
**Supporting data/closing dates:** FAFSA: Accepted on rolling basis. School's own aid application: Accepted on rolling basis. Notification of awards on rolling basis.
**Financial aid contact:** David Pecha, M.Ed., Director of Financial Aid. 405 327-1700, extension 252.

**STUDENT EMPLOYMENT.** College Work/Study Program. Institutional employment. 30% of full-time undergraduates work on campus during school year. Students may expect to earn an average of $2,040 during school year. Off-campus part-time employment opportunities rated "good."

**COMPUTER FACILITIES.** 90 IBM/IBM-compatible and Macintosh/Apple microcomputers; 40 are networked. Students may access Digital minicomputer/mainframe systems. Client/LAN operating systems include Apple/Macintosh, DOS, DEC, Novell. Computer languages and software packages include Ada, AppleWorks, Assembly, BASIC, C, COBOL, dBASE, FORTRAN, Lotus 1-2-3, Pascal, Poise, SPSS, WordPerfect. Computer facilities are available to all students.
**Fees:** $5 computer fee per student lab; included in tuition/fees.
**Hours:** 8 AM-8 PM.

**GRADUATE CAREER DATA.** Highest graduate school enrollments: Northwestern Oklahoma State U. Companies and businesses that hire graduates: Conoco, Halliburton, K mart.

**PROMINENT ALUMNI/AE.** Tom McDaniel, vice-president, Kerr-McGee; Lori Hansen, M.D., plastic surgeon; Mike Hargrove, baseball player, Texas Rangers and Cleveland Indians; Gary Horn, speech professor, Ferris State U.

# Oklahoma Baptist University

**Shawnee, OK 74801** **405 275-2850**

**1994-95 Costs.** Tuition: $5,390. Room: $1,350. Board: $1,790. Fees, books, misc. academic expenses (school's estimate): $1,170.
**Enrollment.** Undergraduates: 730 men, 981 women (full-time). Freshman class: 717 applicants, 681 accepted, 483 enrolled. Graduate enrollment: 11 men, 9 women.
**Test score averages/ranges.** Average ACT scores: 23 composite. Range of ACT scores of middle 50%: 20-26 composite.
**Faculty.** 107 full-time; 50 part-time. 63% of faculty holds doctoral degree. Student/faculty ratio: 14 to 1.
**Selectivity rating.** Less competitive.

**PROFILE.** Oklahoma Baptist, founded in 1910, is a church-affiliated university. Programs are offered through the Colleges of Arts and Sciences and Fine Arts and the Schools of Christian Service and Nursing. Its 125-acre campus is located in Shawnee, 35 miles east of Oklahoma City.

**Accreditation:** NCACS. Professionally accredited by the National Association of Schools of Music, the National Council for Accreditation of Teacher Education, the National League for Nursing.
**Religious orientation:** Oklahoma Baptist University is affiliated with the Southern Baptist Church (Baptist General Convention of Oklahoma); two semesters of religion required.
**Library:** Collections totaling over 120,000 volumes, 600 periodical subscriptions, and 300,000 microform items.
**Special facilities/museums:** Language lab, planetarium.
**Athletic facilities:** Sports complex with arena, basketball, racquetball, and tennis courts, swimming pool, all-weather track, soccer, softball and baseball fields.

**STUDENT BODY. Undergraduate profile:** 73% are state residents; 24% are transfers. .6% Asian-American, 4% Black, .8% Hispanic, 5.5% Native American, 88.5% White, .6% Other. Average age of undergraduates is 22.
**Freshman profile:** 20% of accepted applicants took SAT; 80% took ACT. 85% of freshmen come from public schools.
**Undergraduate achievement:** 79% of fall 1992 freshmen returned for fall 1993 term. 40% of students who completed a degree program immediately went on to graduate study.
**Foreign students:** 25 students are from out of the country. Countries represented include Brazil, Canada, China, Japan, Malaysia, and Mauritius; 23 in all.

**PROGRAMS OF STUDY. Degrees:** B.A., B.Bus.Admin., B.F.A., B.Human., B.Mus., B.Mus.Arts, B.Mus.Ed., B.S., B.S.Ed.
**Majors:** Accounting, Art, Art Education, Bible, Biology, Biology Education, Business Education, Chemistry, Chemistry Education, Child Care Administration, Children's Ministry, Christian Studies, Church Business Administration, Church Music, Combined Vocal/Instrumental Certificate, Communication/Theatre Arts Education, Computer/Information Sciences, Computer Science, Data Management, Early Childhood Education, Educational Ministry, Elementary Education, English, English Education, Ethics/Religion, Exercise Science, Family Development, Family Psychology, Finance/Banking, Foreign Missions, French, French Education, German, German Education, Health Care Administration, Health/Physical Education/Recreation, History, History of Religion, Home Missions, Humanities, Instrumental Music Education, Interdisciplinary, Interpersonal/Public Communication, Journalism, Management, Marketing, Mathematics, Mathematics Education, Multilingual Communication, Music Theory/Composition, Musical Arts, Natural Science, Nursing, Organ Education, Organ Performance, Pastoral Ministry, Philosophy, Physics, Physics Education, Piano Pedagogy, Piano Performance, Political Science, Pre-Physical Therapy, Psychology, Public Relations, Recreation Administration, Religion, Science Education, Social Science Education, Social Work, Sociology, Spanish, Spanish Education, Special Education, Studio Art, Telecommunication, Theatre, Theology, Voice Education, Voice Performance, Youth Minister.
**Requirements:** General education requirement.
**Academic regulations:** Freshmen must maintain minimum 1.75 GPA; sophomores, 1.90 GPA; juniors, 2.00 GPA; seniors, 2.00 GPA.
**Special:** Minors offered in most majors and in administrative services, anthropology, applied ministry, athletic coaching, broadcast news, church recreation, creative writing, general business, religious journalism, and teaching English as a foreign langugage. Courses offered in library science, photography, and statistics. Major emphasis in all approved teaching fields. Competency exams in writing and in major field required for graduation. GRE required in some programs. Associate's degrees offered. Self-designed majors. Double majors. Dual degrees. Independent study. Accelerated study. Pass/fail grading option. Internships. Cooperative education programs. Preprofessional programs in law, medicine, veterinary science, pharmacy, dentistry, theology, and optometry. 3-2 engineering programs with Oklahoma State U and U of Oklahoma. Other semester-away programs available. Exchange program with St. Gregory's Coll (Oklahoma). Teacher certification in early childhood, elementary, secondary, and special education. Exchange program abroad in Japan (Seinan Gakuin U). Study abroad also in Argentina, China, England, France, Hong Kong, Hungary, and Mexico.
**Honors:** Honors program. Honor societies.
**Academic Assistance:** Remedial reading, writing, math, and study skills. Nonremedial tutoring.

**STUDENT LIFE. Housing:** All students under age 21 with fewer than 56 semester hours or under age 20 with fewer than 88 semester hours must live on campus. Women's and men's dorms. School-owned/operated apartments. On-campus married-student housing. 50% of students live in college housing.

**Social atmosphere:** According to the editor of the student newspaper, "Social clubs (which are not fraternities or sororities–they're not allowed) like to pretend that they actually do things and serve a purpose. Actually, they tend to merely create cliques. Culturally, the music is good, and the theatre is good when the director is not too highly censored." Popular events are the Hanging of the Green/Feast of the Boar's Head, Freshman Follies and Dance, The Biggie, Homecoming, and basketball games. Students like to gather at the Geiger Center (the student union), Wood Science Building offices, the fishbowl of the library, Hardee's, The Kettle, and Shawnee Twin Lakes.
**Services and counseling/handicapped student services:** Placement services. Health service. Personal counseling. Career and academic guidance services. Religious counseling.
**Campus organizations:** Undergraduate student government. Student newspaper (Bison, published once/week). Yearbook. American Guild of Organists, symphonic band, chorale, men's and women's glee clubs, College Players, College Republicans, Student Nurses Association, departmental, political, and special-interest groups, 65 organizations in all. Five fraternities, no chapter houses; five sororities, no chapter houses. 15% of men join a fraternity. 17% of women join a sorority.
**Religious organizations:** Baptist Student Union, Campus Crusade for Christ, Fellowship of Christian Athletes.
**Minority/foreign student organizations:** Black Student Fellowship, Native American Heritage Association. International Student Union.

**ATHLETICS. Physical education requirements:** Two semesters of physical education required.
**Intercollegiate competition:** 4% of students participate. Baseball (M), basketball (M,W), cheerleading (M,W), cross-country (M,W), softball (W), tennis (M), track (outdoor) (M,W), track and field (indoor) (M,W), track and field (outdoor) (M,W). Member of NAIA, Sooner Athletic Conference.
**Intramural and club sports:** 1% of students participate. Intramural basketball, flag football, racquetball, tennis, volleyball, walleyball, water polo. Men's club racquetball, soccer. Women's club racquetball.

**ADMISSIONS. Academic basis for candidate selection** (in order of priority): Secondary school record, class rank, standardized test scores.
**Requirements:** Graduation from secondary school is required; GED is accepted. 14 units and the following program of study are recommended: 4 units of English, 2 units of math, 2 units of science, 2 units of foreign language, 2 units of social studies, 2 units of history. Minimum composite ACT score of 20 and rank in top half of secondary school class, or minimum 2.0 GPA, required. Minimum 2.5 GPA, interview, and special exam required of teacher education program applicants. Audition and special exam recommended of music program applicants. Portfolio recommended of art program applicants. Conditional admission possible for applicants not meeting standard requirements. SAT or ACT is required. Campus visit recommended. Off-campus interviews available with an admissions representative.
**Procedure:** Application deadline is August 15. Notification of admission on rolling basis. $75 tuition deposit, refundable until July 15. $50 room deposit, refundable until July 15. Freshmen accepted for terms other than fall.
**Special programs:** Credit and/or placement may be granted through CEEB Advanced Placement exams for scores of 3 or higher. Credit may be granted through CLEP subject exams, ACT PEP and challenge exams, and military experience. Concurrent enrollment program.
**Transfer students:** Transfer students accepted for terms other than fall. In fall 1993, 24% of all new students were transfers into all classes. 225 transfer applications were received, 200 were accepted. Minimum 2.0 GPA required. Lowest course grade accepted is "D." Maximum number of transferable credits is 64 semester hours. At least 33 semester hours must be completed at the university to receive degree.
**Admissions contact:** Jody Johnson, M.Ed., Dean of Admission. 405 878-2033.

**FINANCIAL AID. Available aid:** Pell grants, SEOG, state grants, school scholarships and grants, private scholarships and grants, academic merit scholarships, and athletic scholarships. Perkins Loans (NDSL), PLUS, Stafford Loans (GSL), school loans, and SLS. Semester installment plan.
**Financial aid statistics:** 52% of aid is not need-based. In 1993-94, 85% of all undergraduate applicants received aid; 85% of freshman applicants. Average amounts of aid awarded freshmen: Scholarships and grants, $2,500; loans, $1,800.
**Supporting data/closing dates:** FAFSA: Priority filing date is March 1. School's own aid application: Priority filing date is March 1. Income tax forms: Priority filing date is March 1. Notification of awards begins May 1.
**Financial aid contact:** Kay Vincent, Director of Financial Aid. 405 878-2016.

**STUDENT EMPLOYMENT.** College Work/Study Program. Institutional employment. 30% of full-time undergraduates work on campus during school year. Students may expect to earn an average of $1,000 during school year. Off-campus part-time employment opportunities rated "good."

**COMPUTER FACILITIES.** 135 IBM/IBM-compatible, Macintosh/Apple, and RISC-/UNIX-based microcomputers; all are networked. Students may access Hewlett-Packard minicomputer/mainframe systems, Internet. Client/LAN operating systems include Apple/Macintosh, DOS, UNIX/XENIX/AIX, Novell. Computer languages and software packages include BASIC, COBOL, dBASE, FORTRAN, Lotus 1-2-3, MacPaint, MacWrite, Paradox, Pascal, Quattro Pro, WordPerfect. Computer facilities are available to all students.
**Fees:** $10 computer fee per semester.
**Hours:** 76 hours/week.

**GRADUATE CAREER DATA.** Graduate school percentages: 6% enter law school. 2% enter medical school. 1% enter dental school. 7% enter graduate business programs. 10% enter graduate arts and sciences programs. 10% enter theological school/seminary. Highest graduate school enrollments: Baylor U, Oklahoma State U, North Texas State U, U of Oklahoma, Vanderbilt U. 17% of graduates choose careers in business and industry.

**PROMINENT ALUMNI/AE.** Bill Pogue, astronaut; Dr. Sunday Fadulu, medical researcher (sickle cell anemia); Mary Kathryne Timberlake MacKenzie, national president, Mortar Board.

# Oklahoma Christian University of Science and Arts

**Oklahoma City, OK 73136-1100 — 405 425-5000**

**1993-94 Costs.** Tuition: $5,580. Room & board: $2,950. Fees, books, misc. academic expenses (school's estimate): $520.
**Enrollment.** Undergraduates: 733 men, 686 women (full-time). Freshman class: 765 applicants, 754 accepted, 349 enrolled. 29 men.
**Test score averages/ranges.** Average ACT scores: 22 composite.
**Faculty.** 80 full-time; 44 part-time. 58% of faculty holds doctoral degree. Student/faculty ratio: 17 to 1.
**Selectivity rating.** Less competitive.

**PROFILE.** Oklahoma Christian, founded in 1950, is a church-affiliated university. Programs are offered through the Divisions of Behavioral and Social Sciences, Bible, Business, Communication and Fine Arts, Education, Language and Literature, Physical Education, and Science and Engineering. Its 200-acre campus is located in Oklahoma City.

**Accreditation:** NCACS. Professionally accredited by the Accreditation Board for Engineering and Technology, the National Council for Accreditation of Teacher Education.
**Religious orientation:** Oklahoma Christian University of Science and Arts is affiliated with the Church of Christ; 16 hours of religion required.
**Library:** Collections totaling over 110,000 volumes, 1,140 periodical subscriptions, and 153,773 microform items.
**Special facilities/museums:** Computerized center for economics education.
**Athletic facilities:** Gymnasiums, swimming pool, tennis courts, football, soccer, and softball fields, weight room.

**STUDENT BODY. Undergraduate profile:** 44% are state residents; 31% are transfers. 4% Asian-American, 5% Black, 2% Hispanic, 2% Native American, 87% White. Average age of undergraduates is 21.
**Freshman profile:** Majority of accepted applicants took ACT.
**Foreign students:** 90 students are from out of the country. Countries represented include Bahamas, Brazil, Canada, Hong Kong, and Japan; 33 in all.

**PROGRAMS OF STUDY. Degrees:** B.A., B.F.A., B.Mus.Ed., B.S., B.S.Ed.
**Majors:** Accounting, Advertising Design, Applied Music, Art, Bible, Bible/Ministry, Biochemistry, Biology, Business Administration, Business Administration/Pre-Law, Business Education, Chemistry, Computer Information Systems, Computer Science, Early Childhood Education, Early Childhood Education/Elementary Education, Electrical Engineering, Elementary Education, Engineering Physics, English, English Education, English/Pre-Law, English/Writing, Family Life, Finance, History, History/Pre-Law, Interior Design, Liberal Studies, Management, Marketing, Mass Communications, Mathematics, Mathematics/Computer Science, Mechanical Engineering, Medical Technology, Missions, Music, Music Education, Music Technique, Organizational Communication, Physical Education, Preaching, Psychology, Religious Education, Secondary Education, Social Studies, Social Work, Sociology, Spanish, Special Education, Special Education/Elementary Education, Speech Communication, Speech Education, Youth Ministry.
**Distribution of degrees:** The majors with the highest enrollment are science/engineering, business, and communications/fine arts.
**Requirements:** General education requirement.
**Academic regulations:** Freshmen must maintain minimum 1.60 GPA; sophomores, 1.80 GPA; juniors, 2.00 GPA; seniors, 2.00 GPA.
**Special:** Minors offered in all majors. Double majors. Dual degrees. Independent study. Internships. Graduate school at which undergraduates may take graduate-level courses. Preprofessional programs in law, medicine, and dentistry. Teacher certification in early childhood, elementary, secondary, and special education. Certification in specific subject areas. Exchange program abroad in Japan (Ibaraki Christian Coll). Study abroad also in Austria, Brazil, and Uraguay. ROTC at U of Central Oklahoma. AFROTC at U of Oklahoma.
**Honors:** Honor societies.
**Academic Assistance:** Remedial reading, writing, math, and study skills. Nonremedial tutoring.

**STUDENT LIFE. Housing:** All unmarried full-time students under age 23 with fewer than 123 credits must live on campus. Women's and men's dorms. On-campus married-student housing. 71% of students live in college housing.
**Services and counseling/handicapped student services:** Placement services. Health service. Counseling services for veteran students. Personal and psychological counseling. Career and academic guidance services. Religious counseling. Physically disabled student services. Notetaking services. Tape recorders.
**Campus organizations:** Undergraduate student government. Student newspaper (Talon, published once/week). Literary magazine. Yearbook. Radio station. Choir, chorale, chamber singers, symphonic and jazz bands, concert and stage bands, musicals, opera and drama workshops, Thalian Players, debating, Young Republicans, Young Democrats, service clubs.
**Religious organizations:** Gleaners, Harvesters, Outreach.

**ATHLETICS. Physical education requirements:** One term of physical education required.
**Intercollegiate competition:** 9% of students participate. Baseball (M), basketball (M,W), cheerleading (M,W), cross-country (M,W), soccer (M,W), tennis (M), track (indoor) (M,W), track (outdoor) (M,W), track and field (indoor) (M,W), track and field (outdoor) (M,W). Member of NAIA, Sooner Athletic Conference.
**Intramural and club sports:** 70% of students participate. Intramural basketball, bowling, diving, football, golf, pool, soccer, softball, swimming, table tennis, volleyball.

**ADMISSIONS. Nonacademic basis for candidate selection:** Character and personality are considered.
**Requirements:** Graduation from secondary school is recommended; GED is accepted. No specific distribution of secondary school units required. ACT is required; SAT may be substituted. Campus visit and interview recommended. Off-campus interviews available with an admissions representative.
**Procedure:** Notification of admission on rolling basis. $35 room deposit, refundable until July 15. Freshmen accepted for terms other than fall.
**Special programs:** Admission may be deferred. Credit may be granted through CEEB Advanced Placement for scores of 3 or higher. Credit may be granted through CLEP general and subject exams, DANTES and challenge exams, and military experience. Concurrent enrollment program.
**Transfer students:** Transfer students accepted for terms other than fall. In fall 1993, 31% of all new students were transfers into all classes. 318 transfer applications were received, 318 were accepted. Application deadline is rolling for fall; rolling for spring. Lowest course grade accepted is "D." Maximum number of transferable credits is 65 semester hours. At least 30 semester hours must be completed at the university to receive degree.
**Admissions contact:** Tom Clark, M.S., Vice President of Admissions/Marketing. 405 425-5050.

**FINANCIAL AID. Available aid:** Pell grants, SEOG, state grants, school scholarships and grants, private scholarships, academic merit scholarships, and athletic scholarships. Perkins Loans (NDSL), PLUS, Stafford Loans (GSL), and SLS. AMS, deferred payment plan, and family tuition reduction.
**Financial aid statistics:** 48% of aid is not need-based. In 1993-94, 85% of all undergraduate applicants received aid. Average amounts of aid awarded freshmen: Scholarships and grants, $1,825; loans, $2,600.
**Supporting data/closing dates:** FAFSA/FAF/FFS: Priority filing date is April 15. School's own aid application: Priority filing date is April 15; deadline is August 31. Notification of awards begins April 15.
**Financial aid contact:** D. Andy Carpenter, Director of Financial Aid. 405 425-5190.

**STUDENT EMPLOYMENT.** College Work/Study Program. Institutional employment. 40% of full-time undergraduates work on campus during school year. Students may expect to earn an average of $1,200 during school year. Off-campus part-time employment opportunities rated "excellent."

**COMPUTER FACILITIES.** 122 IBM/IBM-compatible and Macintosh/Apple microcomputers; 54 are networked. Students may access AT&T, Digital minicomputer/mainframe systems. Client/LAN operating systems include Apple/Macintosh, LocalTalk/AppleTalk. Computer languages and software packages include Ada, BASIC, C, COBOL, FORTRAN, LISP, Lotus 1-2-3, Pascal, Quattro, WordPerfect. Computer facilities are available to all students.
**Hours:** 8 AM-11 PM.

**GRADUATE CAREER DATA.** Highest graduate school enrollments: Abilene Christian U, Harding U, Oklahoma State U, U of Oklahoma. 50% of graduates choose careers in business and industry. Companies and businesses that hire graduates: Conoco, Haliburton, Loves, Phillips.

## Oklahoma City University

**Oklahoma City, OK 73106 — 405 521-5000**

**1993-94 Costs.** Tuition: $6,150. Room: $1,650. Board: $1,980. Fees, books, misc. academic expenses (school's estimate): $515.
**Enrollment.** Undergraduates: 426 men, 855 women (full-time). Freshman class: 1,277 applicants, 937 accepted, 370 enrolled. Graduate enrollment: 1,440 men, 761 women.
**Test score averages/ranges.** Average SAT scores: 501 verbal, 531 math. Average ACT scores: 22 English, 21 math, 23 composite.
**Faculty.** 157 full-time; 172 part-time. 60% of faculty holds doctoral degree. Student/faculty ratio: 21 to 1.
**Selectivity rating.** Less competitive.

**PROFILE.** Oklahoma City, founded in 1904, is a church-affiliated university. Programs are offered through the Divisions of Education, Humanities, Science and Mathematics, and Social Sciences; the Schools of Nursing and Graduate Studies; the Meinders School of Business; the Margaret E. Petree School of Music and Performing Arts; and the Wimberly School of Religion and Church Vocations. Its 64-acre campus is located in downtown Oklahoma City.
**Accreditation:** NCACS. Professionally accredited by the American Bar Association, the National Association of Schools of Music, the National League for Nursing.
**Religious orientation:** Oklahoma City University is affiliated with the Methodist Church; one semester of religion required.
**Library:** Collections totaling over 431,377 volumes, 4,036 periodical subscriptions, and 149,251 microform items.
**Special facilities/museums:** Art museum, audio-visual center, language lab.
**Athletic facilities:** Gymnasium, soccer, baseball, and softball fields, tennis courts.

**STUDENT BODY. Undergraduate profile:** 75% are state residents; 46% are transfers. 3% Asian-American, 4% Black, 1% Hispanic, 3% Native American, 56% White, 33% Other. Average age of undergraduates is 18.
**Freshman profile:** Majority of accepted applicants took ACT. 95% of freshmen come from public schools.
**Undergraduate achievement:** 74% of fall 1992 freshmen returned for fall 1993 term.
**Foreign students:** 640 students are from out of the country. Countries represented include China, India, Korea, Malaysia, Taiwan, and Thailand; 60 in all.

**PROGRAMS OF STUDY. Degrees:** B.A., B.F.A., B.Mus., B.Perf.Arts, B.S., B.S.Bus., B.S.Nurs.
**Majors:** Accounting, Art, Asian Studies, Biology, Business, Business Administration, Chemistry, Computer Science, Corrections, Dance, Early Childhood Education, Economics, Elementary Education, English, Finance, French, German, Health Education, History, Humanities, Information Systems, Management, Marketing, Mass Communications, Mathematics, Music, Music Education, Musical Theatre, Nursing, Orchestral Instrument, Organ, Philosophy, Philosophy/Religion, Physical Education, Physics, Piano, Political Science, Professional Law Enforcement, Psychology, Religion, Science, Sociology, Spanish, Speech/Theatre, Technical Education, Theory, Voice.
**Requirements:** General education requirement.
**Academic regulations:** Freshmen must maintain minimum 1.5 GPA; sophomores, 1.75 GPA; juniors, 2.25 GPA; seniors, 2.25 GPA.
**Special:** Self-designed majors. Double majors. Independent study. Pass/fail grading option. Internships. Graduate school at which undergraduates may take graduate-level courses. Preprofessional programs in law, medicine, and dentistry. Washington Semester. Exchange programs with American U, Drew U, and Hawaii Loa Coll. Teacher certification in early childhood, elementary, and secondary education. Study abroad in China, England, France, Germany, Mexico, and Russia. ROTC at U of Central Oklahoma. AFROTC at U of Oklahoma.
**Honors:** Honors program.
**Academic Assistance:** Remedial reading, writing, math, and study skills.

**STUDENT LIFE. Housing:** All unmarried students under age 23 must live on campus unless living with family. Coed, women's, and men's dorms. Fraternity housing. School-owned/operated apartments. Both on-campus and off-campus married-student housing. 20% of students live in college housing.
**Services and counseling/handicapped student services:** Placement services. Health service. Personal and psychological counseling. Career and academic guidance services. Religious counseling. Physically disabled student services. Learning disabled program/services. Notetaking services. Tape recorders. Tutors. Reader services for the blind.
**Campus organizations:** Undergraduate student government. Student newspaper (Campus, published once/week). Yearbook. TV station. Intrafraternity/Panhellenic Council, Surrey Singers, chamber choir, pep band, orchestra, Sierra Club, ski club, Association of Women Students, community service, departmental, political, and special-interest groups, 41 organizations in all. Three fraternities, all with chapter houses; three sororities, no chapter houses. 11% of men join a fraternity. 14% of women join a sorority.
**Religious organizations:** United Methodist Student Fellowship, National Methodist Sorority, United Methodist Student Movement, Baptist Student Union.
**Minority/foreign student organizations:** Black Student Union, Native American Organization. International Student Association, Chinese, Korean, Malaysian, Singaporean, and Thai groups.

**ATHLETICS. Physical education requirements:** One semester of physical education required.
**Intercollegiate competition:** 3% of students participate. Baseball (M), basketball (M,W), golf (M), soccer (M), softball (W), tennis (M,W). Member of NAIA, Sooner Athletic Conference.
**Intramural and club sports:** 3% of students participate. Intramural baseball, football, softball, volleyball.

**ADMISSIONS. Academic basis for candidate selection** (in order of priority): Secondary school record, standardized test scores, class rank, school's recommendation, essay.
**Nonacademic basis for candidate selection:** Particular talent or ability is emphasized. Character and personality are important. Extracurricular participation, geographical distribution, and alumni/ae relationship are considered.
**Requirements:** Graduation from secondary school is required; GED is accepted. 19 units and the following program of study are recommended: 4 units of English, 3 units of math, 3 units of science, 2 units of foreign language, 3 units of social studies, 4 units of electives. Minimum composite ACT score of 20 (combined SAT score of 900) and minimum 2.0 GPA required. Audition required of dance program applicants. Special programs for applicants not normally admissible. SAT or ACT is required. Campus visit and interview recommended. Off-campus interviews available with an admissions representative.
**Procedure:** Notification of admission on rolling basis. No set date by which applicants must accept offer. $80 room deposit, of which $60 is refundable. Freshmen accepted for terms other than fall.
**Special programs:** Admission may be deferred four semesters. Credit may be granted through CEEB Advanced Placement for scores of 3 or higher. Credit may be granted through CLEP subject exams. Early decision program. In fall 1993, two applied for early decision and two were accepted. Deadline for applying for early decision is rolling. Early entrance/early admission program. Concurrent enrollment program.
**Transfer students:** Transfer students accepted for terms other than fall. In fall 1993, 46% of all new students were transfers into all classes. 399 transfer applications were received, 299 were accepted. Application deadline is rolling for fall; rolling for spring. Minimum 2.0 GPA required. Lowest course grade accepted is "C." Maximum number of transferable credits is 90 semester hours. At least 15 semester hours must be completed at the university to receive degree.
**Admissions contact:** Keith Hackett, Dean of Admissions. 405 521-5050.

**FINANCIAL AID. Available aid:** Pell grants, SEOG, state scholarships and grants, school scholarships, private scholarships and grants, academic merit scholarships, athletic scholarships, and aid for undergraduate foreign students. Perkins Loans (NDSL), PLUS, Stafford Loans (GSL), NSL, school loans, private loans, and SLS. Deferred payment plan.
**Financial aid statistics:** 57% of aid is not need-based. In 1993-94, 96% of all undergraduate applicants received aid; 84% of freshman applicants. Average amounts of aid awarded freshmen: Scholarships and grants, $3,711; loans, $3,354.
**Supporting data/closing dates:** FAFSA. School's own aid application: Priority filing date is March 1. Income tax forms: Priority filing date is March 1. Notification of awards on rolling basis.
**Financial aid contact:** Vicki Hendrickson, Director of Financial Aid. 405 521-5211.

**STUDENT EMPLOYMENT.** College Work/Study Program. Institutional employment. 20% of full-time undergraduates work on campus during school year. Students may expect to earn an average of $1,815 during school year. Off-campus part-time employment opportunities rated "excellent."

**COMPUTER FACILITIES.** 90 IBM/IBM-compatible microcomputers. Students may access AT&T, Digital, NCR minicomputer/mainframe systems, BITNET, Internet. Residence halls may be equipped with networked microcomputers. Client/LAN operating sys-

tems include Apple/Macintosh, DOS, Windows NT, LocalTalk/AppleTalk, Novell. Computer languages and software packages include BASIC, C, C++, COBOL, Macro, Oracle, Pascal, SAS. Computer facilities are available to all students.
**Fees:** $30 computer fee per semester.
**Hours:** 8 AM-11:30 PM (M-F); 9 AM-10 PM (Sa); 1 PM-7 PM (Su).
**PROMINENT ALUMNI/AE.** Marian Opala and Yvonne Kauger, Oklahoma Supreme Court; Leona Mitchell, opera singer; Susan Powell, Miss America, 1981; Jayne Jayroe, Miss America, 1969.

# Oklahoma State University

**Stillwater, OK 74078** **405 744-5000**

**1993-94 Costs.** Tuition: $1,350 (state residents), $4,350 (out-of-state). Room & board: $3,200. Fees, books, misc. academic expenses (school's estimate): $872.
**Enrollment.** Undergraduates: 6,981 men, 5,849 women (full-time). Freshman class: 4,522 applicants, 3,913 accepted, 2,181 enrolled. Graduate enrollment: 2,439 men, 1,802 women.
**Test score averages/ranges.** Average ACT scores: 23 English, 23 math, 24 composite. Range of ACT scores of middle 50%: 20-26 English, 19-25 math.
**Faculty.** 609 full-time; 51 part-time. 80% of faculty holds doctoral degree. Student/faculty ratio: 24 to 1.
**Selectivity rating.** Competitive.

**PROFILE.** Oklahoma State, founded in 1890, is a public, comprehensive university. Programs are offered through the Colleges of Agriculture; Arts and Sciences; Business Administration; Education; Engineering, Architecture, and Technology; Home Economics; and Veterinary Medicine; and the Graduate College. Its 480-acre campus, with a modified Georgian architectural style, is located in Stillwater, 70 miles west of Tulsa.
**Accreditation:** NCACS. Professionally accredited by the American Assembly of Collegiate Schools of Business, the American Veterinary Medical Association, the National Association of Schools of Music.
**Religious orientation:** Oklahoma State University is nonsectarian; no religious requirements.
**Library:** Collections totaling over 1,625,000 volumes, 14,500 periodical subscriptions, and 2,620,000 microform items.
**Special facilities/museums:** Archaeology, art, history, and natural science museums; wellness center, laser research center.
**Athletic facilities:** Gymnasium, outdoor fields, swimming pool, stadium, handball, racquetball, squash, and tennis courts.
**STUDENT BODY. Undergraduate profile:** 85% are state residents; 41% are transfers. 2% Asian-American, 3% Black, 1% Hispanic, 6% Native American, 88% White. Average age of undergraduates is 22.
**Freshman profile:** Majority of accepted applicants took ACT.
**Undergraduate achievement:** 77% of fall 1992 freshmen returned for fall 1993 term. 16% of entering class graduated. 9% of students who completed a degree program immediately went on to graduate study.
**Foreign students:** 866 students are from out of the country. Countries represented include Indonesia, Japan, Korea, Malaysia, Pakistan, and Taiwan; 98 in all.
**PROGRAMS OF STUDY. Degrees:** B.A., B.Arch., B.Arch.Eng., B.F.A., B.Land.Arch., B.Mus., B.S.
**Majors:** Accounting, Aerospace Mechanical Engineering, Aerospace Studies, Agribusiness, Agricultural Communications, Agricultural Economics, Agricultural Education, Agricultural Engineering, Agronomy, Animal Science, Architecture, Art, Art Education, Aviation Science, Biochemistry, Biological Sciences, Botany, Cell/Molecular Biology, Chemical Engineering, Chemistry, Civil Engineering, Computing/Information Science, Construction Management Technology, Design, Economics, Electrical Engineering, Electronics Technology, Elementary Education, English, Entomology, Family Relations/Child Development, Finance, Fire Protection/Safety Technology, Foreign Languages, Forestry, French, General Agriculture, General Business, General Engineering, General Technology, Geography, Geology, German, Health, History, Horticulture/Landscape Architecture, Hotel/Restaurant Administration, Housing, Industrial Engineering/Management, International Business, Journalism, Journalism/Broadcasting, Leisure, Management, Management Information Systems, Management Science/Computer Systems, Manufacturing Technology, Marketing, Mathematics, Mechanical Design Technology, Mechanical Engineering, Mechanical Power Technology, Medical Technology, Merchandising, Microbiology, Military Science, Music, Music Education, Nutritional Sciences, Philosophy, Physical Education, Physics, Physiology, Political Science, Pre-Veterinary Medicine, Psychology, Russian Language/Literature, Secondary Education, Sociology, Spanish, Special Education, Speech, Speech Pathology, Statistics, Technical Education, Theatre, Trade/Industrial Education, University Studies, Wildlife/Fisheries Ecology, Zoology.
**Distribution of degrees:** The majors with the highest enrollment are marketing, elementary education, and accounting; botany and geology have the lowest.
**Requirements:** General education requirement.
**Academic regulations:** Freshmen must maintain minimum 1.7 GPA; sophomores, juniors, seniors, 2.0 GPA.
**Special:** Associate's degrees offered. Self-designed majors. Double majors. Independent study. Pass/fail grading option. Internships. Cooperative education programs. Graduate school at which undergraduates may take graduate-level courses. Preprofessional programs in law, medicine, veterinary science, osteopathy, journalism, social work, and health-related fields. 3-2 accounting program. Member of University Center at Tulsa. National Student Exchange. Semester at Sea. Teacher certification in early childhood, elementary, secondary, special education, vo-tech, and bilingual/bicultural education. Certification in specific subject areas. Branch campus in Kyoto, Japan. Study abroad also in Belgium, England, France, Germany, Japan, and Switzerland. ROTC and AFROTC.
**Honors:** Phi Beta Kappa. Honors program. Honor societies.
**Academic Assistance:** Remedial writing and math.
**STUDENT LIFE. Housing:** All unmarried freshmen under age 21 must live on campus. Coed, women's, and men's dorms. Sorority and fraternity housing. School-owned/operated apartments. Off-campus privately-owned housing. On-campus married-student housing. 22% of students live in college housing.
**Services and counseling/handicapped student services:** Placement services. Health service. Counseling services for minority students. Birth control, personal, and psychological counseling. Career and academic guidance services. Physically disabled student services. Learning disabled services. Notetaking services. Tape recorders. Reader services for the blind.
**Campus organizations:** Undergraduate student government. Student newspaper (O'Collegian, published once/day). Yearbook. Radio station. Concert and marching bands, varsity and pep bands, symphony orchestra, glee club, symphonic choir, women's choral club, debating and drama groups, departmental clubs, special-interest groups, 265 organizations in all. 25 fraternities, 23 chapter houses; 14 sororities, all with chapter houses. 18% of men join a fraternity. 16% of women join a sorority.
**Religious organizations:** Bahai, Baptist, Christian Science, Muslim, and Nazarene groups, Campus Crusade for Christ, Canterbury Association, Ministry for International Students.
**Minority/foreign student organizations:** Afro-American Organization, Native American, black, and Greek professional groups, Hispanic group, Minority Women's Association, NAACP. African, Arab, Chinese, Egyptian, Greek, Indonesian, Iranian, Korean, Lebanese, Thai, Turkish Venezuelan, Vietnamese, and other foreign student groups.
**ATHLETICS. Physical education requirements:** None.
**Intercollegiate competition:** 7% of students participate. Baseball (M), basketball (M,W), cross-country (M,W), football (M), golf (M,W), softball (W), tennis (M,W), track (indoor) (M,W), track and field (M,W), wrestling (M). Member of Big Eight Conference, NCAA Division I, NCAA Division I-A for football.
**Intramural and club sports:** Intramural archery, badminton, basketball, billiards, bowling, cross-country, fencing, flag football, floor hockey, free throw shooting, frisbee golf, golf, handball, inner-tube water polo, racquetball, soccer, softball, squash, swimming, table tennis, tennis, track, volleyball, weight lifting, wrestling. Men's club bowling, crew, cycling, fencing, lacrosse, martial arts, rodeo, rugby, sailing, scuba, soccer, volleyball. Women's club bowling, cycling, fencing, martial arts, rodeo, rugby, sailing, scuba, soccer, volleyball.
**ADMISSIONS. Academic basis for candidate selection** (in order of priority): Secondary school record, class rank, standardized test scores.
**Nonacademic basis for candidate selection:** Particular talent or ability is considered.
**Requirements:** Graduation from secondary school is required; GED is not accepted. 11 units and the following program of study are required: 4 units of English, 3 units of math, 2 units of lab science, 2 units of history. Minimum composite ACT score of 21 (combined SAT score of 990) or rank in top one-third of secondary school class and minimum 3.0 GPA required. Alternative programs possible for applicants not meeting standard requirements. ACT is required; SAT may be substituted. No off-campus interviews.
**Procedure:** Take SAT or ACT by December 1 of 12th year. Notification of admission on rolling basis. $40 refundable tuition deposit. $150 room deposit, refundable until July 1. Freshmen accepted for terms other than fall.
**Special programs:** Credit may be granted through CEEB Advanced Placement for scores of 3 or higher. Credit may be granted through CLEP subject exams, ACT PEP and DANTES exams, and military and life experience. Credit and placement may be granted through challenge exams. Concurrent enrollment program.
**Transfer students:** Transfer students accepted for terms other than fall. In fall 1993, 41% of all new students were transfers into all classes. 2,487 transfer applications were received, 2,097 were accepted. Application deadline is Friday before beginning of semester for fall; Friday before beginning of semester for spring. Minimum 2.0 GPA required. Lowest course grade accepted is "D." Maximum number of transferable credits is 60 semester hours from a two-year school and 90 semester hours from a four-year school. At least 30 semester hours must be completed at the university to receive degree.
**Admissions contact:** Norman Durham, Ph.D., Interim Director of Admissions. 405 744-6876.
**FINANCIAL AID. Available aid:** Pell grants, SEOG, state scholarships and grants, school scholarships and grants, private scholarships and grants, ROTC scholarships, academic merit scholarships, and athletic scholarships. Perkins Loans (NDSL), PLUS, Stafford Loans (GSL), school loans, and SLS. Deferred payment plan.
**Financial aid statistics:** 52% of aid is not need-based. In 1993, 92% of all undergraduate applicants received aid; 99% of freshman applicants. Average amounts of aid awarded freshmen: Scholarships and grants, $2,366; loans, $5,929.
**Supporting data/closing dates:** FAFSA: Priority filing date is March 1. Notification of awards on rolling basis.
**Financial aid contact:** Charles Bruce, Ph.D., Director of Financial Aid. 405 744-6604.
**STUDENT EMPLOYMENT.** College Work/Study Program. Institutional employment. 16% of full-time undergraduates work on campus during school year. Students may expect to earn an average of $1,958 during school year. Off-campus part-time employment opportunities rated "good."
**COMPUTER FACILITIES.** 500 IBM/IBM-compatible, Macintosh/Apple, and RISC-/UNIX-based microcomputers; 250 are networked. Students may access Digital, IBM, Sequent, SUN minicomputer/mainframe systems, BITNET, Internet. Residence halls may be equipped with stand-alone microcomputers, networked microcomputers, networked terminals, modems. Client/LAN operating systems include Apple/Macintosh, DOS, UNIX/XENIX/AIX, X-windows, LocalTalk/AppleTalk, Novell. Computer languages and software packages include Ada, Assembler, Excel, C, COBOL, FORTRAN, LISP, Lotus, MacPaint, MacWrite, Mathematica, Maple, Pascal, PL/1, Prolog, SAS, SPSS, Systat, WordPerfect. Computer facilities are available to all students.
**GRADUATE CAREER DATA.** 15% of graduates pursue further study at Oklahoma State U. At OSU, 2% enter graduate business programs, 3% enter graduate arts and sciences programs. 65% of graduates choose careers in business and industry. Companies and businesses that hire graduates: Arthur Andersen, Conoco, Phillips Petroleum.
**PROMINENT ALUMNI/AE.** T. Boone Pickens, petroleum/geology; M.B. Bud Seretean, publishing; Garth Brooks, musician.

# Oral Roberts University

Tulsa, OK 74171 918 495-6161

**1994-95 Costs.** Tuition: $7,950. Room & board: $3,994. Fees, books, misc. academic expenses (school's estimate): $680.

**Enrollment.** Undergraduates: 1,142 men, 1,491 women (full-time). Freshman class: 1,867 applicants, 1,100 accepted, 991 enrolled. Graduate enrollment: 262 men, 266 women.

**Test score averages/ranges.** Average SAT scores: 440 verbal, 460 math. Range of SAT scores of middle 50%: 370-510 verbal, 380-550 math. Average ACT scores: 21 English, 20 math, 21 composite. Range of ACT scores of middle 50%: 18-25 English, 16-23 math.

**Faculty.** 145 full-time; 35 part-time. 52% of faculty holds doctoral degree. Student/faculty ratio: 17 to 1.

**Selectivity rating.** Competitive.

**PROFILE.** Oral Roberts, founded in 1965, is a private, liberal arts university with religious affiliation. Its 400-acre campus is located in Tulsa.

**Accreditation:** NCACS. Professionally accredited by the Council on Social Work Education, the National Association of Schools of Music, the National League for Nursing.

**Religious orientation:** Oral Roberts University is an interdenominational Christian school; two semesters of religion required.

**Library:** Collections totaling over 685,000 volumes, 2,300 periodical subscriptions, and 200,000 microform items.

**Special facilities/museums:** Dial Access Information Retrieval System, programmed learning facilities, early learning center, TV production studio.

**Athletic facilities:** Aerobics center, basketball courts, flag football fields, tennis, squash, and racquetball courts, indoor and outdoor tracks, soccer fields, swimming pool, weight rooms.

**STUDENT BODY. Undergraduate profile:** 26% are state residents; 23% are transfers. 2% Asian-American, 26% Black, 4% Hispanic, 1% Native American, 58% White, 9% Other. Average age of undergraduates is 23.

**Freshman profile:** 1% of freshmen who took SAT scored 700 or over on verbal, 3% scored 700 or over on math; 7% scored 600 or over on verbal, 17% scored 600 or over on math; 34% scored 500 or over on verbal, 42% scored 500 or over on math; 69% scored 400 or over on verbal, 73% scored 400 or over on math; 93% scored 300 or over on verbal, 93% scored 300 or over on math. 6% of freshmen who took ACT scored 30 or over on English, 5% scored 30 or over on math, 3% scored 30 or over on composite; 38% scored 24 or over on English, 24% scored 24 or over on math, 23% scored 24 or over on composite; 78% scored 18 or over on English, 60% scored 18 or over on math, 65% scored 18 or over on composite; 97% scored 12 or over on English, 100% scored 12 or over on math, 98% scored 12 or over on composite; 100% scored 6 or over on English, 99% scored 6 or over on composite. 44% of accepted applicants took SAT; 48% took ACT.

**Undergraduate achievement:** 75% of fall 1991 freshmen returned for fall 1992 term. 26% of entering class graduated.

**Foreign students:** 207 students are from out of the country. Countries represented include Bahamas, Canada, Indonesia, Jamaica, Korea, and Singapore; 58 in all.

**PROGRAMS OF STUDY. Degrees:** B.A., B.A.Soc.Work, B.Mus., B.Mus.Ed., B.S., B.S.Eng., B.S.Nurs.

**Majors:** Accounting, Art Education, Biological Science Education, Biology, Biomedical Chemistry, Biomedical Engineering, Broadcast Design/Art, Business Administration, Business Education, Chemistry, Church Ministries/Christian Education, Church Ministries/Missions, Church Ministries/Music, Church Ministries/New Testament, Church Ministries/Pastoral Ministry, Commercial Art, Communication Arts, Computer Science, Drama, Drama/Television/Film Performance, Electrical Engineering, Elementary Education, Engineering/Computer Science, English Bible, English Education, English Literature, Finance, Foreign Language Education, French, German, Government, Health/Exercise Science, Health/Physical Education/Recreation, History, International Business, Liberal Arts, Management, Management Information Systems, Marine Biology, Marketing, Mathematics, Mathematics Education, Mechanical Engineering, Medical Technology, Music, Music Composition, Music Education, Music Performance, Nursing, Old Testament, Organizational/Interpersonal Communications, Physical Science Education, Physics, Psychology, Recreation Administration, Sacred Music, Social Studies Education, Social Work, Spanish, Speech/Drama Education, Studio Art, Telecommunication, Theological/Historical Studies.

**Distribution of degrees:** The majors with the highest enrollment are elementary education, telecommunications, and business/accounting.

**Requirements:** General education requirement.

**Academic regulations:** Freshmen must maintain minimum 1.5 GPA; sophomores, 1.5 GPA; juniors, 1.75 GPA; seniors, 2.0 GPA.

**Special:** Minors offered in many majors and in coaching, education, fine arts, Hebrew, humanities, journalism, pastoral care/counseling, preseminary, public relations/advertising, sociology, and writing. Four-year integrated program has academic, physical, and spiritual emphases. Elective interdisciplinary general studies courses. Senior paper required in most majors. Self-designed majors. Double majors. Dual degrees. Independent study. Pass/fail grading option. Internships. Cooperative education programs. Graduate school at which undergraduates may take graduate-level courses. Preprofessional programs in law, medicine, veterinary science, pharmacy, dentistry, theology, optometry, and physical therapy. 3-2 bachelor's/M.B.A. and bachelor's/M.A.Ed. programs. Washington Semester. Teacher certification in early childhood, elementary, secondary, and special education. Certification in specific subject areas. Study abroad in Central American, European, and South American countries. ROTC at U of Tulsa.

**Honors:** Honor societies.

**Academic Assistance:** Remedial reading, writing, math, and study skills. Nonremedial tutoring.

**STUDENT LIFE. Housing:** All unmarried students under age 21 must live on campus unless living near campus with relatives. Women's and men's dorms. School-owned/operated apartments. On-campus married-student housing. 75% of students live in college housing.

**Social atmosphere:** The editor of the student newspaper reports that there are many activities sponsored by the university. "The International Students' Organization is growing, 150 members now, and sponsors cultural dinners and programs. The Christian Service Council allows opportunity to get involved in community needs for the elderly, hungry, handicapped, in over 60 outreaches." Titan's basketball is popular, as are Homecoming, the Fall Gala, and Christian concerts. Students gather at The Depot, a campus eating spot. Off campus, they meet at Metro for ice cream and at Mazzio's.

**Services and counseling/handicapped student services:** Placement services. Day care. Counseling services for minority, military, veteran, and older students. Personal and psychological counseling. Career and academic guidance services. Religious counseling. Physically disabled student services. Learning disabled services. Notetaking services. Tape recorders. Tutors. Reader services for the blind.

**Campus organizations:** Undergraduate student government. Student newspaper (Oracle, published once/week). Literary magazine. Yearbook. Radio and TV stations. Art and opera guilds, Association for Ethnic Unity, College Republicans, karate club, societies for accounting and administrative management, Cybernaut Club, American Chemical Society, departmental groups.

**Religious organizations:** African Christian Fellowship, Bible Seminarian Fellowship, Ekklesia, Mission Club, Single Parent Fellowship.

**Minority/foreign student organizations:** International Student Organization.

**ATHLETICS. Physical education requirements:** Eight semesters of physical education required.

**Intercollegiate competition:** 4% of students participate. Baseball (M), basketball (M,W), cheerleading (M,W), cross-country (M,W), golf (M,W), soccer (M,W), tennis (M,W), track (indoor) (M,W), track (outdoor) (M,W), track and field (indoor) (M,W), track and field (outdoor) (M,W), volleyball (W). Member of NCAA I.

**Intramural and club sports:** 90% of students participate. Intramural basketball, football, golf, handball, racquetball, softball, tennis, volleyball. Men's club bowling. Women's club bowling.

**ADMISSIONS. Academic basis for candidate selection** (in order of priority): Standardized test scores, secondary school record, essay, class rank, school's recommendation.

**Nonacademic basis for candidate selection:** Character and personality, extracurricular participation, and particular talent or ability are emphasized. Alumni/ae relationship is important.

**Requirements:** Graduation from secondary school is required; GED is accepted. No specific distribution of secondary school units required. Minimum combined SAT score of 950, rank in top two-fifths of secondary school class, and minimum 2.6 GPA required. Audition required of music program applicants. Bridge Program for applicants not normally admissible. SAT or ACT is required. PSAT is recommended. Campus visit and interview recommended. Off-campus interviews available with an alumni representative.

**Procedure:** Take SAT or ACT by August 15 of 12th year. Visit college for interview by May of 12th year. Suggest filing application by April 1. Notification of admission on rolling basis. No set date by which applicants must accept offer. $125 tuition deposit, refundable until July 1. Freshmen accepted for terms other than fall.

**Special programs:** Admission may be deferred two years. Credit and/or placement may be granted through CEEB Advanced Placement exams for scores of 4 or higher. Credit may be granted through CLEP subject exams. Credit and placement may be granted through challenge exams and military experience. Early decision program. Early entrance/early admission program. Concurrent enrollment program.

**Transfer students:** Transfer students accepted for terms other than fall. In fall 1992, 23% of all new students were transfers into all classes. 465 transfer applications were received, 300 were accepted. Application deadline is rolling for fall; rolling for spring. Minimum 2.5 GPA recommended. Lowest course grade accepted is "C." Maximum number of transferable credits is 64 semester hours from a two-year school and 98 semester hours from a four-year school. At least 30 semester hours must be completed at the university to receive degree.

**Admissions contact:** Shawn Nichols, Director of Admissions. 918 495-6518.

**FINANCIAL AID. Available aid:** Pell grants, SEOG, state grants, school scholarships and grants, ROTC scholarships, academic merit scholarships, athletic scholarships, and aid for undergraduate foreign students. Exceptional Need Grant. Perkins Loans (NDSL), PLUS, Stafford Loans (GSL), state loans, school loans, and SLS. Guaranteed tuition. 10-payment installment plan.

**Financial aid statistics:** 18% of aid is not need-based. In 1992-93, 90% of all undergraduate applicants received aid; 80% of freshman applicants. Average amounts of aid awarded freshmen: Scholarships and grants, $1,300; loans, $2,250.

**Supporting data/closing dates:** FAFSA: Accepted on rolling basis. Income tax forms: Accepted on rolling basis. Notification of awards begins April 1.

**Financial aid contact:** William McFarland, Ph.D., Director of Financial Aid. 918 495-6510.

**STUDENT EMPLOYMENT.** College Work/Study Program. Institutional employment. 35% of full-time undergraduates work on campus during school year. Students may expect to earn an average of $1,500 during school year. Off-campus part-time employment opportunities rated "good."

**COMPUTER FACILITIES.** 25 IBM/IBM-compatible and Macintosh/Apple microcomputers. Students may access Data General, Digital, IBM minicomputer/mainframe systems. Client/LAN operating systems include UNIX/XENIX/AIX. Computer languages and software packages include C++, dBASE, Lotus 1-2-3, Turbo Pascal, WordPerfect; 20 in all. Computer facilities are available to all students.

**Fees:** $30 computer fee per semester.

**Hours:** 8 AM-10:30 PM (M-F); 9 AM-10:30 PM (Sa); 2 PM-10:30 PM (Su).

**GRADUATE CAREER DATA.** Companies and businesses that hire graduates: CBN, Electronic Data Systems, Ernst & Young, Lloyd Haskens Accounting.

**PROMINENT ALUMNI/AE.** Kenneth Copeland, evangelist; Carlton Pearson and Billy Joe Daugherty, pastor/evangelists; Terry Law, founder of Living Sound; Stephanie Boosahda, singer.

## Panhandle State University

**Goodwell, OK 73939** **405 349-2611**

**1994-95 Costs.** Tuition: $1,232 (state residents), $3,517 (out-of-state). Room: $600. Board: $1,200. Fees, books, misc. academic expenses (school's estimate): $163.
**Enrollment.** Undergraduates: 412 men, 437 women (full-time). Freshman class: 225 applicants, 200 accepted, 182 enrolled.
**Test score averages/ranges.** Average ACT scores: 18 English, 18 math, 19 composite. Range of ACT scores of middle 50%: 15-21 English, 15-20 math.
**Faculty.** 54 full-time; 24 part-time. 54% of faculty holds doctoral degree. Student/faculty ratio: 22 to 1.
**Selectivity rating.** Less competitive.

**PROFILE.** Panhandle State, founded in 1909, is a public university. Programs are offered through the Divisions of Agriculture, Business and Applied Arts, Education, Liberal Arts, and Mathematics and Science. It 120-acre campus is located in Goodwell, in northeastern Oklahoma.

**Accreditation:** NCACS. Professionally accredited by the National Council for Accreditation of Teacher Education.
**Religious orientation:** Panhandle State University is nonsectarian; no religious requirements.
**Library:** Collections totaling over 122,024 volumes, 512 periodical subscriptions, and 10,753 microform items.
**Special facilities/museums:** Art and natural history museums, language lab, agricultural research station, 960-acre farm, 1,200-acre range area.
**Athletic facilities:** Field house, tennis courts, golf course, weight room, football field, softball diamond.
**STUDENT BODY. Undergraduate profile:** 51% are state residents; 43% are transfers. 1% Asian-American, 3% Black, 6% Hispanic, 1% Native American, 89% White. Average age of undergraduates is 24.
**Freshman profile:** 1% of accepted applicants took SAT; 99% took ACT. 98% of freshmen come from public schools.
**Undergraduate achievement:** 50% of fall 1992 freshmen returned for fall 1993 term. 19% of entering class graduated.
**Foreign students:** Six students are from out of the country. Countries represented include Canada and Japan; four in all.
**PROGRAMS OF STUDY. Degrees:** B.A., B.Mus.Ed., B.S., B.Tech.
**Majors:** Accounting, Agribusiness, Agronomy, Animal Science, Biology, Business Administration, Business Education, Chemistry, Computer Science, Elementary Education, English, Health/Physical Education, History, Home Economics, Industrial Arts, Industrial/Business Management, Instruments, Mathematics, Medical Technology, Music, Music Education, Natural Science, Psychology, Recreation, Secretarial Science, Social Studies, Speech, Technology, Vocational Agricultural Education.
**Distribution of degrees:** The majors with the highest enrollment are agribusiness, elementary education, and business administration; natural science, chemistry, and history have the lowest.
**Requirements:** General education requirement.
**Academic regulations:** Freshmen must maintain minimum 1.70 GPA; sophomores, 1.70 GPA; juniors, 2.00 GPA; seniors, 2.00 GPA.
**Special:** Minors offered in some majors and in art, business management/marketing, driver/safety education, earth science, fashion merchandising, French, journalism, law enforcement, military science, political science, sociology, and Spanish. Associate's degrees offered. Double majors. Dual degrees. Preprofessional programs in law, veterinary science, pharmacy, dentistry, engineering, forestry, and medical fields. Teacher certification in early childhood, elementary, and secondary education.
**Academic Assistance:** Remedial reading, writing, math, and study skills. Nonremedial tutoring.
**ADMISSIONS. Academic basis for candidate selection** (in order of priority): Secondary school record, standardized test scores, class rank.
**Requirements:** Graduation from secondary school is recommended; GED is accepted. 20 units and the following program of study are required: 4 units of English, 3 units of math, 2 units of science, 2 units of history, 9 units of electives. Minimum composite ACT score of 15, rank in top two-thirds of secondary school class, and minimum 2.7 GPA required. Developmental classes for applicants with a composite ACT score of less than 18. ACT is required; SAT may be substituted. Campus visit and interview required. Off-campus interviews available with an admissions representative. No off-campus interviews.
**Procedure:** No set date by which applicants must accept offer. $100 refundable room deposit. Freshmen accepted for terms other than fall.
**Special programs:** Credit may be granted through CLEP subject exams, ACT PEP and challenge exams, and military experience. Early entrance/early admission program. Concurrent enrollment program.
**Transfer students:** Transfer students accepted for terms other than fall. In fall 1993, 43% of all new students were transfers into all classes. 201 transfer applications were received, 192 were accepted. Application deadline is rolling for fall; rolling for spring. Minimum 2.0 GPA recommended. Lowest course grade accepted is "D." At least 30 semester hours must be completed at the university to receive degree.
**Admissions contact:** Emma Schultz, M.A., Director of Admissions. 405 349-2611, extension 375.
**FINANCIAL AID. Available aid:** Pell grants, SEOG, state scholarships and grants, school scholarships, private scholarships, athletic scholarships, and aid for undergraduate foreign students. Perkins Loans (NDSL), PLUS, Stafford Loans (GSL), private loans, and SLS. Deferred payment plan.
**Financial aid statistics:** In 1993-94, 84% of all undergraduate applicants received aid; 77% of freshman applicants. Average amounts of aid awarded freshmen: Scholarships and grants, $700; loans, $2,625.
**Supporting data/closing dates:** FAFSA/FAF/FFS: Accepted on rolling basis. School's own aid application: Accepted on rolling basis. State aid form: Priority filing date is March 15; accepted on rolling basis. Income tax forms: Accepted on rolling basis. Notification of awards on rolling basis.
**Financial aid contact:** Mary Ellen Riley, Director of Financial Aid. 405 349-2611, extension 224.

## Phillips University

**Enid, OK 73701-6439** **405 237-4433**

**1993-94 Costs.** Tuition: $8,880. Room & board: $3,004. Fees, books, misc. academic expenses (school's estimate): $1,030.
**Enrollment.** Undergraduates: 292 men, 361 women (full-time). Freshman class: 690 applicants, 574 accepted, 172 enrolled. Graduate enrollment: 39 men, 35 women.
**Test score averages/ranges.** Average SAT scores: 424 verbal, 466 math. Range of SAT scores of middle 50%: 430-430 verbal, 470-470 math. Average ACT scores: 22 composite. Range of ACT scores of middle 50%: 21-21 composite.
**Faculty.** 43 full-time; 24 part-time. 72% of faculty holds doctoral degree. Student/faculty ratio: 13 to 1.
**Selectivity rating.** Less competitive.

**PROFILE.** Phillips University, founded in 1906, is a private, church-affiliated university. Programs are offered in the Divisions of Behavioral and Social Sciences; Business Administration; Education; Fine Arts; Language and Communication; Natural and Mathematical Sciences; and Religion, History, and Philosophy. Its 35-acre campus is located in Enid, 85 miles northwest of Oklahoma City.
**Accreditation:** NCACS. Professionally accredited by the National Association of Schools of Music, the National Council for Accreditation of Teacher Education.
**Religious orientation:** Phillips University is affiliated with the Christian Church (Disciples of Christ); nine semester hours of religion required.
**Library:** Collections totaling over 179,748 volumes, 913 periodical subscriptions, and 6,377 microform items.
**Special facilities/museums:** Art museum, field camp in San Juan Mountains of Colorado.
**Athletic facilities:** Basketball, racquetball, and tennis courts, weight room, baseball, soccer, and softball fields, golf course.
**STUDENT BODY. Undergraduate profile:** 67% are state residents; 21% are transfers. 2% Asian-American, 7% Black, 4% Hispanic, 3% Native American, 71% White, 13% Other. Average age of undergraduates is 21.
**Freshman profile:** 12% of freshmen who took SAT scored 600 or over on verbal, 8% scored 600 or over on math; 32% scored 500 or over on verbal, 41% scored 500 or over on math; 75% scored 400 or over on verbal, 76% scored 400 or over on math; 81% scored 300 or over on verbal, 88% scored 300 or over on math. 2% of freshmen who took ACT scored 30 or over on composite; 24% scored 24 or over on composite; 68% scored 18 or over on composite; 77% scored 12 or over on composite.
**Undergraduate achievement:** 56% of fall 1992 freshmen returned for fall 1993 term. 25% of entering class graduated. 18% of students who completed a degree program immediately went on to graduate study.
**Foreign students:** 61 students are from out of the country. Countries represented include Japan, Korea, Malaysia, Pakistan, Sweden, and Taiwan; 14 in all.
**PROGRAMS OF STUDY. Degrees:** B.A., B.F.A., B.Med.Tech., B.Mus.Ed., B.S., B.S.Bus.Admin., B.S.Ed., B.S.Mus.
**Majors:** Accounting, American Studies, Applied Mathematics/Computer Science, Applied Political Science, Applied Sociology, Art Education, Asian Studies, Aviation Management, Biology, Business Administration, Business Computing, Chemistry, Chemistry/Business, Christian Education, Communications, Economics, Elementary Education, English, Environmental Science, European Studies, Finance, French, Geology, Health/Physical Education/Recreation, History, Library Science, Management, Marketing, Mathematics, Medical Technology, Music, Music/Business Emphasis, Music Education, Philosophy, Political Science, Psychology, Religion, Resource Management, Secondary Education, Sociology, Spanish, Studio Art.
**Distribution of degrees:** The majors with the highest enrollment are business administration, education, and psychology.
**Requirements:** General education requirement.
**Academic regulations:** Freshmen must maintain minimum 1.8 GPA; sophomores, 1.9 GPA; juniors, 2.0 GPA; seniors, 2.0 GPA.
**Special:** Minors offered. Associate's degrees offered. Self-designed majors. Double majors. Dual degrees. Independent study. Accelerated study. Pass/fail grading option. Internships. Graduate school at which undergraduates may take graduate-level courses. Preprofessional programs in law, medicine, veterinary science, pharmacy, dentistry, theology, and optometry. 3-2 engineering program with Washington U. 3-3 theology program. Teacher certification in early childhood, elementary, and secondary education. Exchange programs abroad in Costa Rica, Germany, Japan, and Mexico.
**Honors:** Honors program.
**Academic Assistance:** Remedial reading, writing, math, and study skills. Nonremedial tutoring.
**ADMISSIONS. Academic basis for candidate selection** (in order of priority): Secondary school record, standardized test scores, class rank, essay, school's recommendation.
**Nonacademic basis for candidate selection:** Extracurricular participation is emphasized. Character and personality are important. Particular talent or ability and alumni/ae relationship are considered.
**Requirements:** Graduation from secondary school is required; GED is accepted. No specific distribution of secondary school units required. Minimum composite ACT score of 18 and minimum 2.75 GPA required; rank in top half of secondary school class recommended. Portfolio required of art program applicants. Audition required of music program applicants. Conditional admission possible for applicants not meeting standard requirements. SAT or ACT is required. Campus visit and interview recommended. Off-campus interviews available with an admissions representative.

**Procedure:** Take SAT or ACT by April 1 of 12th year. Visit college for interview by April 1 of 12th year. Suggest filing application by December 1. Application deadline is August 15. Notification of admission on rolling basis. Reply is required by August 15. $200 tuition deposit, refundable until May 1. $100 room deposit, refundable until July 1. Freshmen accepted for terms other than fall.
**Special programs:** Admission may be deferred one semester. Credit and/or placement may be granted through CEEB Advanced Placement exams for scores of 3 or higher. Placement may be granted through CLEP general exams, Regents College, ACT PEP, and DANTES exams. Credit and/or placement may be granted through CLEP subject exams. Credit may be granted through military experience. Credit and placement may be granted through challenge exams. Concurrent enrollment program.
**Transfer students:** Transfer students accepted for terms other than fall. In fall 1993, 21% of all new students were transfers into all classes. Application deadline is August 15 for fall; December 15 for spring. Minimum 2.0 GPA required. Lowest course grade accepted is "C." Applicants over age 22 do not have to submit SAT/ACT scores. Maximum number of transferable credits is 104 semester hours. At least 32 semester hours must be completed at the university to receive degree.
**Admissions contact:** Leigh Smith, M.A., Director of Admission. 405 237-4433, extension 203, 800 238-1185.
**FINANCIAL AID. Available aid:** Pell grants, SEOG, state scholarships and grants, school scholarships and grants, private scholarships and grants, academic merit scholarships, and athletic scholarships. Perkins Loans (NDSL), PLUS, Stafford Loans (GSL), school loans, and SLS. Institutional payment plan.
**Financial aid statistics:** 16% of aid is not need-based. In 1993-94, 100% of all undergraduate applicants received aid. Average amounts of aid awarded freshmen: Scholarships and grants, $5,247; loans, $3,606.
**Supporting data/closing dates:** FAFSA/FAF: Accepted on rolling basis. Notification of awards on rolling basis.
**Financial aid contact:** Kay Midkiff, Director of Financial Aid. 405 237-4433, ext. 201.

# Southeastern Oklahoma State University

Durant, OK 74701 405 924-0121

**1992-93 Costs.** Tuition: $1,373 (state residents), $3,330 (out-of-state). Room & board: $2,080. Fees, books, misc. academic expenses (school's estimate): $1,020.
**Enrollment.** Undergraduates: 1,420 men, 1,576 women (full-time). Freshman class: 772 applicants, 667 accepted, 536 enrolled. Graduate enrollment: 155 men, 293 women.
**Test score averages/ranges.** Average ACT scores: 19 English, 18 math, 20 composite.
**Faculty.** 152 full-time; 57 part-time. 55% of faculty holds doctoral degree. Student/faculty ratio: 20 to 1.
**Selectivity rating.** Less competitive.

**PROFILE.** Southeastern Oklahoma, founded in 1909, is a public, comprehensive university. Programs are offered through the Schools of Liberal Studies, Behavioral Studies, and Business and Industry. Its 170-acre campus is located in Durant, 90 miles north of Dallas.
**Accreditation:** NCACS. Professionally accredited by the National Association of Schools of Music, the National Council for Accreditation of Teacher Education.
**Religious orientation:** Southeastern Oklahoma State University is nonsectarian; no religious requirements.
**Library:** Collections totaling over 163,500 volumes, 1,150 periodical subscriptions, and 326,000 microform items.
**Athletic facilities:** Football stadium, swimming pool, basketball and tennis courts, baseball, soccer, and softball fields, gymnasiums, weight room, track.
**STUDENT BODY. Undergraduate profile:** 90% are state residents; 37% are transfers. 1% Asian-American, 4% Black, 1% Hispanic, 31% Native American, 61% White, 2% Other. Average age of undergraduates is 25.
**Freshman profile:** 1% of freshmen who took ACT scored 30 or over on composite; 17% scored 24 or over on composite; 70% scored 18 or over on composite; 99% scored 12 or over on composite; 100% scored 6 or over on composite. 98% of accepted applicants took ACT. 99% of freshmen come from public schools.
**Undergraduate achievement:** 61% of fall 1992 freshmen returned for fall 1993 term. 15% of entering class graduated.
**Foreign students:** 98 students are from out of the country. Countries represented include Bangladesh, China, Japan, Jordan, Pakistan, and Puerto Rico; 20 in all.
**PROGRAMS OF STUDY. Degrees:** B.A., B.Mus., B.S.
**Majors:** Accounting, Airframe/Power Plant, Art, Aviation, Biology, Business Administration, Business Education, Chemistry, Conservation, Criminal Justice, Economics, Electronics Technology, Elementary Education, English, Health/Physical Education, History, Information Systems, Management, Marketing, Mathematics, Medical Technology, Music, Physics, Political Science, Psychology, Recreation, Safety, Science, Secretarial Administration, Social Gerontology, Social Studies, Sociology, Technology Education, Theatre.
**Distribution of degrees:** The majors with the highest enrollment are elementary education, business administration, and health/physical education; music and technology education have the lowest.
**Requirements:** General education requirement.
**Academic regulations:** Freshmen must maintain minimum 1.7 GPA; sophomores, 1.7 GPA; juniors, 2.0 GPA; seniors, 2.0 GPA.
**Special:** Minors offered in most majors. Minor required in some majors in order to graduate. Biomedical sciences program encourages Native American, Black, and other minority students to pursue careers in this area. International studies program. Associate's degrees offered. Double majors. Independent study. Accelerated study. Graduate school at which undergraduates may take graduate-level courses. Preprofessional programs in law, veterinary science, engineering, and health fields. Teacher certification in early childhood, elementary, secondary, and special education.
**Honors:** Honor societies.
**Academic Assistance:** Remedial study skills. Nonremedial tutoring.
**STUDENT LIFE. Housing:** All freshmen must live on campus. Coed, women's, and men's dorms. School-owned/operated apartments. On-campus married-student housing. 15% of students live in college housing.
**Social atmosphere:** The SOSU coffee shop, Outlaw's, Calhoun's, and the Corner Bar & Grill are considered popular places for students. Some of the most influential groups on campus are Kappa Sigma, Baptist Student Union, Cardinal Key/Blue Key, Super Savage Leaders, and Student Government Association. Homecoming/Parent's Day, Hokey Day, Alcohol Awareness Week, SOSU vs. East Central U games, and Springfest are anticipated social events. Students usually go off campus for social activity and entertainment, reports the editor of the school newspaper. "Depending on the season, the lake is a popular place for college students. No matter what the season, there is partying and clubs."
**Services and counseling/handicapped student services:** Placement services. Health service. Counseling services for minority, military, and veteran students. Personal counseling. Career and academic guidance services. Learning disabled services.
**Campus organizations:** Undergraduate student government. Student newspaper (Southeastern, published once/week). Yearbook. Radio station. Choral groups, bands, music ensembles, University Players, debating, rodeo and martial arts clubs, Circle K, Young Democrats, College Republicans, 70 organizations in all. Five fraternities, no chapter houses; two sororities, no chapter houses. 10% of men join a fraternity. 5% of women join a sorority.
**Religious organizations:** Assemblies of God/Chi Alpha, Baptist Student Union, Church of Christ Bible Center, Fellowship of Christian Athletes, Wesley Foundation.
**Minority/foreign student organizations:** Black American Student Society, Native American Indian Council. International Student Club, Bangladesh and Pakistani groups.
**ATHLETICS. Physical education requirements:** Four semester hours of physical education required.
**Intercollegiate competition:** Baseball (M), basketball (M,W), cheerleading (M,W), cross-country (W), football (M), golf (M), tennis (M,W), track and field (outdoor) (M,W). Member of NAIA, OIC.
**Intramural and club sports:** Intramural racquetball, softball, tennis, touch football, volleyball. Men's club aviation, rodeo. Women's club aviation, rodeo.
**ADMISSIONS. Academic basis for candidate selection** (in order of priority): Standardized test scores, secondary school record, class rank, school's recommendation.
**Nonacademic basis for candidate selection:** Particular talent or ability is considered.
**Requirements:** Graduation from secondary school is required; GED is accepted. 20 units and the following program of study are required: 4 units of English, 3 units of math, 2 units of lab science, 2 units of history, 9 units of electives. Minimum composite ACT score of 19, or rank in top half of secondary school class and minimum 2.7 GPA required. ACT is required; SAT may be substituted. Campus visit recommended. No off-campus interviews.
**Procedure:** Take SAT or ACT by May of 12th year. Suggest filing application by June 1. Application deadline is August 10. Notification of admission on rolling basis. $50 refundable room deposit. Freshmen accepted for terms other than fall.
**Special programs:** Admission may be deferred. Credit and/or placement may be granted through CEEB Advanced Placement exams for scores of 3 or higher. Credit and/or placement may be granted through CLEP subject exams. Credit may be granted through challenge exams and military and life experience. Concurrent enrollment program.
**Transfer students:** Transfer students accepted for terms other than fall. In fall 1993, 37% of all new students were transfers into all classes. 549 transfer applications were received, 539 were accepted. Application deadline is August 10 for fall; January 5 for spring. Minimum 2.0 GPA required. Lowest course grade accepted is "C." Maximum number of transferable credits is 64 semester hours from a two-year school and 94 semester hours from a four-year school. At least 30 semester hours must be completed at the university to receive degree.
**Admissions contact:** Dr. Fred Stroup, Director of Admissions. 405 924-0121, extension 264.
**FINANCIAL AID. Available aid:** Pell grants, SEOG, state grants, school scholarships, private scholarships, academic merit scholarships, and athletic scholarships. Perkins Loans (NDSL), PLUS, Stafford Loans (GSL), and SLS.
**Financial aid statistics:** 15% of aid is not need-based. In 1993-94, 75% of all undergraduate applicants received aid; 60% of freshman applicants. Average amounts of aid awarded freshmen: Scholarships and grants, $1,200; loans, $2,000.
**Supporting data/closing dates:** FAFSA: Priority filing date is April 1. School's own aid application: Priority filing date is April 1. Income tax forms: Priority filing date is April 1. Notification of awards on rolling basis.
**Financial aid contact:** Sherry Foster, M.Ed., Director of Financial Aid. 405 924-0121, extension 406.
**STUDENT EMPLOYMENT.** College Work/Study Program. Institutional employment. 25% of full-time undergraduates work on campus during school year. Students may expect to earn an average of $1,000 during school year. Off-campus part-time employment opportunities rated "fair."
**COMPUTER FACILITIES.** IBM/IBM-compatible and Macintosh/Apple microcomputers. Computer languages and software packages include Ada, BASIC, C, COBOL, FORTRAN, LISP, Lotus 1-2-3, Oracle, Pascal, RPG, SimScript, SNOBOL, SPSS, WordPerfect. Computer facilities are available to all students.
**Hours:** 7 AM-midn.
**GRADUATE CAREER DATA.** Highest graduate school enrollments: U of North Texas, Oklahoma State U, U of Oklahoma. 40% of graduates choose careers in business and industry. Companies and businesses that hire graduates: Conoco, Texas Instruments.
**PROMINENT ALUMNI/AE.** Dr. Sam Pool, chief of medical science and research (physics), NASA; Dr. E.T. Dunlap, former chancellor, OSU higher education system; Reba McEntire, country/western singer; Dr. Jack Van Duren Hough, ear physician and researcher; Gen. Ira E. Eaker, former chief of staff, Army Air Force; Dennis Rodman, professional basketball player.

# Southern Nazarene University

**Bethany, OK 73008** **405 789-6400**

**1994-95 Costs.** Tuition: $5,684. Room & board: $3,602. Fees, books, misc. academic expenses (school's estimate): $748.
**Enrollment.** Undergraduates: 592 men, 732 women (full-time). Freshman class: 538 applicants, 538 accepted, 319 enrolled. Graduate enrollment: 76 men, 74 women.
**Test score averages/ranges.** Average ACT scores: 22 English, 19 math, 21 composite.
**Faculty.** 50 full-time; 51 part-time. 53% of faculty holds doctoral degree. Student/faculty ratio: 17 to 1.
**Selectivity rating.** Noncompetitive.

**PROFILE.** Southern Nazarene, founded in 1899, is a church-affiliated, comprehensive university. Programs are offered in the Colleges of Ministry and the Humanities, Professional and Social Studies, and Science and Health. Its 40-acre campus is located in Bethany, one mile from Oklahoma City.

**Accreditation:** NCACS. Professionally accredited by the National Council for Accreditation of Teacher Education, the National League for Nursing.
**Religious orientation:** Southern Nazarene University is affiliated with the Church of the Nazarene; three semesters of religion required.
**Library:** Collections totaling over 112,673 volumes, 667 periodical subscriptions, and 180,152 microform items.
**Special facilities/museums:** On-campus lab school, recital hall, concert grand piano, tracker pipe organ, seven-foot double French harpsichord, media center, cadaver lab, laser labs.
**Athletic facilities:** Swimming pool, gymnasiums, field hockey, football, and softball fields.
**STUDENT BODY. Undergraduate profile:** 69% are state residents; 23% are transfers. 1% Asian-American, 4% Black, 2% Hispanic, 1% Native American, 91% White, 1% Other. Average age of undergraduates is 21.
**Freshman profile:** Majority of accepted applicants took ACT. 90% of freshmen come from public schools.
**Undergraduate achievement:** 72% of fall 1992 freshmen returned for fall 1993 term. 25% of entering class graduated.
**Foreign students:** 28 students are from out of the country. Countries represented include Canada, Japan, Kenya, Korea, Mexico, and Russia; 18 in all.
**PROGRAMS OF STUDY. Degrees:** B.A., B.Mus.Ed., B.S.
**Majors:** Accounting, Art, Aviation/Business, Biology, Business, Business Administration, Business Education, Chemistry, Christian Education, Church Music, Computer Information Systems, Computer Science, Criminal Justice, Early Childhood Education, Economics, Education, Elementary Education, English, Environmental Science, Family Studies/Gerontology, Fitness/Wellness Management, Health, Health/Physical Education/Recreation, History, Home Economics, Human Relations, International Studies, Management, Management of Human Resources, Marketing, Mass Communication/Journalism, Mathematics, Modern Languages, Music, Music Business, Music Education, Music/Instrumental, Music/Keyboard, Music/Vocal, Nursing, Office Administration, Philosophy, Physics, Political Science, Psychology, Religion, Sociology, Spanish, Speech Communication.
**Distribution of degrees:** The majors with the highest enrollment are business, education, and religion; Spanish, art, and human relations have the lowest.
**Requirements:** General education requirement.
**Academic regulations:** Freshmen must maintain minimum 1.5 GPA; sophomores, 1.6 GPA; juniors, 1.8 GPA; seniors, 2.0 GPA.
**Special:** Minors offered. Undergraduate laser research program. Associate's degrees offered. Self-designed majors. Double majors. Dual degrees. Independent study. Pass/fail grading option. Internships. Graduate school at which undergraduates may take graduate-level courses. Preprofessional programs in law, medicine, veterinary science, pharmacy, dentistry, and theology. Member of Christian College Coalition. American Studies Program (Washington, D.C.), Los Angeles Film Studies Program. Teacher certification in early childhood, elementary, and secondary education. Certification in specific subject areas. Study abroad in Costa Rica and England; may be arranged in other countries. ROTC and AFROTC at U of Central Oklahoma and U of Oklahoma.
**Honors:** Phi Beta Kappa. Honor societies.
**Academic Assistance:** Remedial reading, writing, and math. Nonremedial tutoring.
**ADMISSIONS. Academic basis for candidate selection** (in order of priority): Standardized test scores, class rank, secondary school record.
**Nonacademic basis for candidate selection:** Character and personality, extracurricular participation, particular talent or ability, and alumni/ae relationship are emphasized.
**Requirements:** Graduation from secondary school is required; GED is accepted. 23 units and the following program of study are required: 4 units of English, 3 units of math, 2 units of lab science, 2 units of foreign language, 1 unit of social studies, 2 units of history, 7 units of electives. Minimum composite ACT score of 15 (combined SAT score of 700), rank in top half of secondary school class, and minimum 2.5 GPA required. Audition required of performing arts program applicants. Conditional admission possible for applicants not meeting standard requirements. ACT is required; SAT may be substituted. Campus visit and interview recommended. Off-campus interviews available with an admissions representative.
**Procedure:** Take SAT or ACT by June 15 of 12th year. Application deadline is August 15. Notification of admission on rolling basis. No set date by which applicants must accept offer. $50 tuition deposit, refundable until July 1. $50 room deposit, refundable until beginning of semester. Freshmen accepted for terms other than fall.
**Special programs:** Admission may be deferred one year. Credit and/or placement may be granted through CEEB Advanced Placement exams for scores of 3 or higher. Credit and/or placement may be granted through CLEP general exams. Credit may be granted through CLEP subject exams, DANTES and challenge exams, and military and life experience. Concurrent enrollment program.
**Transfer students:** Transfer students accepted for terms other than fall. In fall 1993, 23% of all new students were transfers into all classes. 184 transfer applications were received, 184 were accepted. Application deadline is August 15 for fall; January 2 for spring. Minimum 2.0 GPA recommended. Lowest course grade accepted is "D." Maximum number of transferable credits is 62 semester hours. At least 30 semester hours must be completed at the university to receive degree.
**Admissions contact:** Jeffrey Williamson, M.A., Director of Admissions. 405 491-6324.
**FINANCIAL AID. Available aid:** Pell grants, SEOG, Federal Nursing Student Scholarships, state scholarships and grants, school scholarships and grants, private scholarships and grants, ROTC scholarships, academic merit scholarships, and athletic scholarships. Perkins Loans (NDSL), PLUS, Stafford Loans (GSL), state loans, private loans, and SLS. 10-month payment plan.
**Financial aid statistics:** 20% of aid is not need-based. In 1993-94, 96% of all undergraduate applicants received aid; 96% of freshman applicants. Average amounts of aid awarded freshmen: Loans, $2,625.
**Supporting data/closing dates:** FAFSA: Priority filing date is March 1; accepted on rolling basis. Notification of awards on rolling basis.
**Financial aid contact:** Diana Lee, M.S., Director of Financial Aid. 405 491-6310.

# Southwestern Oklahoma State University

**Weatherford, OK 73096** **405 772-6611**

**1994-95 Costs.** Tuition: $1,224 (state residents), $3,395 (out-of-state). Room & board: $2,016. Fees, books, misc. academic expenses (school's estimate): $668.
**Enrollment.** Undergraduates: 1,815 men, 2,022 women (full-time). Freshman class: 1,041 applicants, 969 accepted, 826 enrolled. Graduate enrollment: 187 men, 380 women.
**Test score averages/ranges.** Average ACT scores: 20 English, 19 math, 20 composite. Range of ACT scores of middle 50%: 16-22 English, 15-21 math.
**Faculty.** 212 full-time; 19 part-time. 65% of faculty holds doctoral degree. Student/faculty ratio: 19 to 1.
**Selectivity rating.** Noncompetitive.

**PROFILE.** Southwestern Oklahoma State, founded in 1901, is a private, comprehensive university. Programs are offered through the Schools of Arts and Sciences, Business, Education, and Health Sciences and the Graduate School. Its 73-acre campus is located in Weatherford, 65 miles west of Oklahoma City.

**Accreditation:** NCACS. Professionally accredited by the Accrediting Bureau of Health Education Schools, the American Council on Pharmaceutical Education, the American Medical Association (CAHEA), the National Association of Schools of Music, the National Council for Accreditation of Teacher Education, the National League for Nursing.
**Religious orientation:** Southwestern Oklahoma State University is nonsectarian; no religious requirements.
**Library:** Collections totaling over 242,406 volumes, 1,518 periodical subscriptions, and 751,114 microform items.
**Special facilities/museums:** Writing lab.
**Athletic facilities:** Gymnasium, weight room, swimming pool, football, intramural, soccer, and softball fields, tennis courts.
**STUDENT BODY. Undergraduate profile:** 89% are state residents; 10% are transfers. 2% Asian-American, 3% Black, 2% Hispanic, 4% Native American, 89% White. Average age of undergraduates is 23.
**Freshman profile:** Majority of accepted applicants took ACT. 98% of freshmen come from public schools.
**Foreign students:** 42 students are from out of the country. Countries represented include Canada, Ethiopia, India, North Vietnam, Pakistan, and Zimbabwe; 26 in all.
**PROGRAMS OF STUDY. Degrees:** B.A., B.A.Ed., B.Commercial Art, B.Gen.Tech., B.Hlth.Info.Mgmt., B.Mus., B.Mus.Ed., B.Recr., B.S., B.S.Ed., B.S.Eng.Tech., B.S.Med.Tech., B.S.Nurs., B.S.Pharm.
**Majors:** Accounting, Administration of Health Care, Art, Art Education, Biological Sciences, Biophysics, Business Administration, Business Education, Chemistry, Commercial Art, Computer Science, Criminal Justice, Economics, Elementary Education, Engineering Physics, Engineering Technology, English, English Education, Finance, General Technology, Geography, Health Information Management, Health/Physical Education/Recreation, History, History Education, Home Economics, Housing/Interior Design, Information Processing Systems, Library Science, Management, Marketing, Mathematics, Mathematics Education, Medical Technology, Music, Music Education, Music Therapy, Natural Science Education, Nursing, Office Administration, Pharmacy, Physics, Political Science, Psychology, Recreational Leadership, Social Sciences Education, Sociology, Special Education, Speech/Drama Education, Speech/Theatre, Technology Education, Vocational Home Economics Education.
**Distribution of degrees:** The majors with the highest enrollment are pharmacy, elementary education, and accounting.
**Requirements:** General education requirement.
**Academic regulations:** Minimum 2.0 GPA must be maintained.
**Special:** Minors offered in agrimechanics, allied health, banking, communications, counseling, electronics, equestrian, fashion merchandising, drafting, gerontology, geology, human development/family life, journalism, math for business, physical sciences, Russian studies, social science, Spanish, and statistics. Certificate programs offered in clerical practice, commercial art, and secretarial science. Double majors. Independent study. Internships. Graduate school at which undergraduates may take graduate-level courses. Preprofessional programs in law, medicine, veterinary science, pharmacy, dentistry, optometry, dietetics, engineering, hotel/restaurant administratin, and physical therapy. Member of Academic Common Market, provided by Southern Regional Education Board. Teacher certification in early childhood, elementary, secondary, special education, and vo-tech education. Certification in specific subject areas. Exchange program abroad in France (the

Sorbonne, Stendahl U), Byelorusse (Language Inst in Minsk), and Russia (Music Conservatory in Rostov).
**Honors:** Honors program. Honor societies.
**Academic Assistance:** Remedial reading, writing, math, and study skills. Nonremedial tutoring.

**STUDENT LIFE. Housing:** Students may live on or off campus. Women's and men's dorms. Off-campus privately-owned housing. On-campus married-student housing. 25% of students live in college housing.
**Services and counseling/handicapped student services:** Placement services. Health service. Day care. Counseling services for minority and veteran students. Personal counseling. Career and academic guidance services.
**Campus organizations:** Undergraduate student government. Student newspaper (Southwestern, published once/week). Bands, choirs, competitive speech and debate, academic groups, 74 organizations in all. Three fraternities, one chapter house; three sororities, no chapter houses. 2% of men join a fraternity. 2% of women join a sorority.
**Religious organizations:** Baptist Student Union, Church of Christ Bible Chair, Wesley Foundation, Campus Crusade for Christ, Canterbury Association, Catholic Student Association, Chi Alpha Gamma Delta, Fellowship of Christian Athletes, Latter-Day Saints Student Organization.
**Minority/foreign student organizations:** Black Student Association, Native American club, Sombreros y Matillas. International Student Association.

**ATHLETICS. Physical education requirements:** Four semester hours of physical education required.
**Intercollegiate competition:** 3% of students participate. Baseball (M), basketball (M,W), football (M), golf (M), rodeo (M,W), tennis (M,W), track (M). Member of NAIA, Oklahoma Intercollegiate Conference.
**Intramural and club sports:** Intramural basketball, football, volleyball.

**ADMISSIONS. Academic basis for candidate selection** (in order of priority): Secondary school record, standardized test scores, class rank, school's recommendation.
**Requirements:** Graduation from secondary school is required; GED is accepted. 22 units and the following program of study are required: 4 units of English, 3 units of math, 2 units of lab science, 2 units of history, 9 units of electives. Minimum composite ACT score of 19, rank in top half of secondary school class, and minimum 2.7 GPA recommended. Interview required of pharmacy program applicants during sophomore year. Conditional admission possible for applicants not meeting standard requirements. ACT is required; SAT may be substituted. No off-campus interviews.
**Procedure:** Take SAT or ACT by March of 12th year. Suggest filing application by March. Application deadline is August. Notification of admission on rolling basis. $60 refundable room deposit. Freshmen accepted for terms other than fall.
**Special programs:** Admission may be deferred indefinitely. Credit may be granted through CLEP general and subject exams and DANTES exams. Early entrance/early admission program. Concurrent enrollment program.
**Transfer students:** Transfer students accepted for terms other than fall. In fall 1993, 10% of all new students were transfers into all classes. Application deadline is August for fall; January for spring. Minimum 2.0 GPA required. Lowest course grade accepted is "D." Maximum number of transferable credits is 64 semester hours. At least 30 semester hours must be completed at the university to receive degree.
**Admissions contact:** Bob Klaassen, M.S., Director of Admissions. 405 774-3777.

**FINANCIAL AID. Available aid:** Pell grants, SEOG, state scholarships and grants, school scholarships and grants, private scholarships and grants, academic merit scholarships, and athletic scholarships. Perkins Loans (NDSL), PLUS, Stafford Loans (GSL), state loans, and SLS.
**Financial aid statistics:** 22% of aid is not need-based. In 1993-94, 81% of all undergraduate applicants received aid; 88% of freshman applicants. Average amounts of aid awarded freshmen: Scholarships and grants, $642; loans, $1,123.
**Supporting data/closing dates:** FAFSA: Priority filing date is March 1. School's own aid application: Priority filing date is March 1. Notification of awards on rolling basis.
**Financial aid contact:** Larry Hollingsworth, Director of Financial Assistance. 405 774-3786.

**STUDENT EMPLOYMENT.** College Work/Study Program. Institutional employment. 13% of full-time undergraduates work on campus during school year. Students may expect to earn an average of $1,700 during school year. Off-campus part-time employment opportunities rated "fair."

**COMPUTER FACILITIES.** 120 IBM/IBM-compatible and Macintosh/Apple microcomputers; 64 are networked. Students may access Digital minicomputer/mainframe systems. Client/LAN operating systems include Apple/Macintosh, DOS, LocalTalk/AppleTalk, Novell. 15 major computer languages and software packages available. Computer facilities are available to all students.
**Hours:** Most labs open 8 AM-midn.

# University of Central Oklahoma

**Edmond, OK 73034** **405 341-2980**

**1993-94 Costs.** Tuition: $1,150 (state residents), $2,700 (out-of-state). Room & board: $2,100. Fees, books, misc. academic expenses (school's estimate): $550.
**Enrollment.** Undergraduates: 3,463 men, 4,293 women (full-time). Freshman class: 3,554 applicants, 3,430 accepted, 1,464 enrolled. Graduate enrollment: 1,381 men, 2,328 women.
**Test score averages/ranges.** Average ACT scores: 20 English, 19 math, 20 composite. Range of ACT scores of middle 50%: 17-23 English, 17-21 math.
**Faculty.** 395 full-time; 283 part-time. 51% of faculty holds doctoral degree. Student/faculty ratio: 23 to 1.
**Selectivity rating.** Less competitive.

**PROFILE.** The University of Central Oklahoma, founded in 1889, is a public, liberal arts institution; its name was changed from Central State University in 1991. Programs are offered through the Colleges of Business Administration, Education, Liberal Arts, and Mathematics and Science. Its 200-acre campus is located in Edmond, 12 miles from Oklahoma City. Campus buildings are predominantly contemporary in design.

**Accreditation:** NCACS. Professionally accredited by the National Council for Accreditation of Teacher Education, the National League for Nursing.
**Religious orientation:** University of Central Oklahoma is nonsectarian; no religious requirements.
**Library:** Collections totaling over 250,463 volumes, 2,735 periodical subscriptions, and 537,228 microform items.
**Special facilities/museums:** Art and history museums, archives.
**Athletic facilities:** Tennis and basketball courts, weight room, swimming pool, athletic fields.

**STUDENT BODY. Undergraduate profile:** 98% are state residents; 41% are transfers. 2% Asian-American, 7% Black, 1% Hispanic, 3% Native American, 82% White, 5% Other. Average age of undergraduates is 26.
**Freshman profile:** 3% of freshmen who took ACT scored 30 or over on English, 1% scored 30 or over on math, 1% scored 30 or over on composite; 27% scored 24 or over on English, 15% scored 24 or over on math, 20% scored 24 or over on composite; 79% scored 18 or over on English, 72% scored 18 or over on math, 85% scored 18 or over on composite; 100% scored 12 or over on English, 100% scored 12 or over on math, 100% scored 12 or over on composite. Majority of accepted applicants took ACT.
**Undergraduate achievement:** 47% of fall 1992 freshmen returned for fall 1993 term.
**Foreign students:** 672 students are from out of the country. Countries represented include India, Korea, Malaysia, Pakistan, Taiwan, and Thailand; 78 in all.

**PROGRAMS OF STUDY. Degrees:** B.A., B.A.Ed., B.Bus.Admin., B.Mus., B.Mus.Ed., B.S., B.S.Ed.
**Majors:** Accounting, Accounting/Computer Science, Actuarial Science, Advertising, Allied Health Education, Allied Health Education/Medical Institutions, Applied Communication, Applied Liberal Arts, Applied Mathematics, Art Education, Biochemistry, Biology, Biology/Computer Science, Biology Education, Broadcasting, Business Communication, Business/Economics, Business Education, Ceramics, Chemical Dependency, Chemistry, Chemistry Education, Commercial Art, Computer Science, Construction Technology, Construction Technology/General, Criminal Justice, Decision Sciences, Dietetics, Early Childhood Education, Economics, Economics/Computer Science, Elementary Education, Emotionally Disturbed, Engineering Physics, English, English Education, Family/Child Development, Fashion Merchandising, Finance, Fine Art, Food Management/Nutrition/General, Food Management/Nutrition/Management, Forensic Science, Formation Arts, French, French Education, Funeral Service, General Art, General Business, General Business/Computer Science, General History, General Journalism, General Political Science, Geography, Geography Education, German, German Education, Graphic Advertising Design, Graphic Arts, Health, Health Sciences, History Education, Home Economics Education, Hotel/Food Service Administration, Housing/Interior Design, Human Resource Management, Industrial Arts, Industrial Safety, Industrial Technology, Insurance, Journalism Education, Learning Disabilities, Liberal Arts/Sciences, Magazines, Management, Management/Computer Science, Marketing, Marketing/Computer Science, Marketing Education, Mathematics, Mathematics/Accounting, Mathematics/Computer Science, Mathematics/Economics/Statistics, Mathematics Education, Mathematics/Management, Mathematics/Marketing, Mathematics/Other Areas, Mathematics/Physics, Mathematics/Statistics, Medical Technology, Mental Retardation, Military Science, Municipal Management, Museum Training, Music Education/Instrumental, Music Education/Vocal, Music/Percussion, Music/Piano, Music/String, Music/Theatre, Music/Vocal, Music/Wind, Newspaper, Nursing, Office Administration, Oral Communication Education, Other Areas/Computer Science, Painting, Philosophy, Photographic Arts, Physical Education, Physical Education/Health, Physics/Computer Science, Physics Education, Physics/Graduate Study/Research, Physics/Health Science Professions, Physics/Industry/Technology, Physics/Solar Technology, Political Science Education, Pre-Dental, Pre-Engineering, Pre-Medical, Pre-Optometry, Pre-Pharmacy, Pre-Veterinary Medicine, Professional Writing, Promotion Management, Psychology, Psychology/Computer Science, Public Administration, Public Relations, Public School Nursing, Public Service, Purchasing/Materials Management, Real Estate, Retail Management, Safety Education, Sculpture, Social Studies Education, Sociology, Spanish, Spanish Education, Special Education, Speech, Speech/Language Pathology, Theatre, Trade/Industrial Education, Training/Development, Vocational Consumer Home Economics Education, Vocational Home Economics Education/Occupations.
**Distribution of degrees:** The majors with the highest enrollment are accounting, elementary education, and business administration.
**Requirements:** General education requirement.
**Academic regulations:** Freshmen must maintain minimum 1.7 GPA; sophomores, 1.7 GPA; juniors, 2.0 GPA; seniors, 2.0 GPA.
**Special:** Minors offered in most majors. Double majors. Independent study. Internships. Preprofessional programs in law, medicine, veterinary science, pharmacy, dentistry, optometry, engineering, and osteopathy. Teacher certification in early childhood, elementary, secondary, and special education. Certification in specific subject areas. ROTC.
**Honors:** Honors program. Honor societies.
**Academic Assistance:** Remedial reading and math.

**STUDENT LIFE. Housing:** All unmarried students under age 21 must live on campus unless living near campus with relatives. Women's and men's dorms. Sorority and fraternity housing. School-owned/operated apartments. On-campus married-student housing. 9% of students live in college housing.
**Services and counseling/handicapped student services:** Placement services. Health service. Day care. Counseling services for minority, military, and veteran students. Personal counseling. Physically disabled student services. Notetaking services. Reader services for the blind.
**Campus organizations:** Undergraduate student government. Student newspaper (Vista, published twice/week). Literary magazine. Yearbook. Radio and TV stations. Music and drama groups, gospel choir, Association of Women Students, Music Teachers Association, Gay/Lesbian Alliance, Cheer Team, pom pom squad, 119 organizations in all. Seven

fraternities, three chapter houses; five sororities, three chapter houses. 2% of men join a fraternity. 2% of women join a sorority.
**Religious organizations:** Baptist Student Union, Catholic Campus Ministry, Chi Alpha, Muslim Student Association, Wesley Foundation.
**Minority/foreign student organizations:** Black Student Association, First American Student Association. Chinese, Indian, Korean, Malaysian, Pakistani, and South Asian groups.

**ATHLETICS. Physical education requirements:** Two semesters of physical education required.
**Intercollegiate competition:** 2% of students participate. Baseball (M), basketball (M,W), cross-country (M,W), football (M), golf (M), softball (W), tennis (M,W), track (indoor) (M,W), track (outdoor) (M,W), track and field (indoor) (M,W), track and field (outdoor) (M,W), volleyball (W), wrestling (M). Member of Lone Star Conference, NCAA Division II.
**Intramural and club sports:** 2% of students participate. Intramural basketball, flag football, golf, softball, table tennis, volleyball, wrestling. Men's club bowling, rodeo, soccer. Women's club bowling, rodeo, soccer.

**ADMISSIONS. Academic basis for candidate selection** (in order of priority): Class rank, standardized test scores, secondary school record, school's recommendation.
**Nonacademic basis for candidate selection:** Particular talent or ability is considered.
**Requirements:** Graduation from secondary school is required; GED is accepted. 11 units and the following program of study are required: 4 units of English, 3 units of math, 2 units of lab science, 2 units of history. Minimum composite ACT score of 19 (combined SAT score of 870) or rank in top half of secondary school class and minimum 2.7 GPA required. Nursing, teacher education, funeral service, and music program applicants must meet additional requirements. Special Talent Waiver, Special Adult Admission, and Exceptional Student Admission programs for applicants not normally admissible. ACT is required; SAT may be substituted. Campus visit recommended. No off-campus interviews.
**Procedure:** Take SAT or ACT by February of 12th year. Suggest filing application by April; no deadline. Notification of admission on rolling basis. No set date by which applicants must accept offer. Freshmen accepted for terms other than fall.
**Special programs:** Admission may be deferred one semester. Credit may be granted through CLEP general and subject exams, ACT PEP, DANTES, and challenge exams, and military experience. Concurrent enrollment program.
**Transfer students:** Transfer students accepted for terms other than fall. In fall 1993, 41% of all new students were transfers into all classes. 3,617 transfer applications were received, 3,529 were accepted. Application deadline is August 16 for fall; January 3 for spring. Minimum 2.0 GPA required. Lowest course grade accepted is "D." Maximum number of transferable credits is 94 semester hours. At least 30 semester hours must be completed at the university to receive degree.
**Admissions contact:** Paul Patrick, M.A., Acting Registrar. 405 341-2980, extension 3366.

**FINANCIAL AID. Available aid:** Pell grants, SEOG, state scholarships and grants, school scholarships and grants, private scholarships, ROTC scholarships, academic merit scholarships, and athletic scholarships. Perkins Loans (NDSL), PLUS, Stafford Loans (GSL), state loans, school loans, private loans, and SLS.
**Financial aid statistics:** 58% of aid is not need-based.
**Supporting data/closing dates:** FAFSA/FAF/FFS: Priority filing date is April 1. School's own aid application: Priority filing date is April 1. Notification of awards on rolling basis.
**Financial aid contact:** Sheila Fugett, Director of Financial Aid. 405 341-2980, ext. 3336.

**STUDENT EMPLOYMENT.** College Work/Study Program. Institutional employment. 5% of full-time undergraduates work on campus during school year. Students may expect to earn an average of $2,500 during school year. Freshmen are discouraged from working during their first term. Off-campus part-time employment opportunities rated "excellent."

**COMPUTER FACILITIES.** 250 IBM/IBM-compatible and Macintosh/Apple microcomputers; all are networked. Students may access Digital, IBM minicomputer/mainframe systems. Residence halls may be equipped with networked microcomputers. Client/LAN operating systems include Apple/Macintosh, DOS, UNIX/XENIX/AIX, Banyan, DEC, LocalTalk/AppleTalk. Computer languages and software packages include Ada, BASIC, C, COBOL, FORTRAN, Lotus 1-2-3, Pascal, R BASE, WordPerfect; 15 in all. Computer facilities are available to all students.
**Hours:** 8 AM-10 PM (M-F); 10 AM-5 PM (Sa); 2 PM-10 PM (Su).

# University of Oklahoma

**Norman, OK 73019** **405 325-2151**

**1993-94 Costs.** Tuition: $1,628 (state residents), $4,977 (out-of-state). Room & board: $3,526. Fees, books, misc. academic expenses (school's estimate): $889.
**Enrollment.** Undergraduates: 6,753 men, 5,571 women (full-time). Freshman class: 4,743 applicants, 3,970 accepted, 2,233 enrolled. Graduate enrollment: 2,613 men, 2,235 women.
**Test score averages/ranges.** Average SAT scores: 1043 combined. Average ACT scores: 24 English, 23 math, 24 composite. Range of ACT scores of middle 50%: 21-27 composite.
**Faculty.** 828 full-time; 159 part-time. 83% of faculty holds doctoral degree.
**Selectivity rating.** Competitive.

**PROFILE.** The University of Oklahoma, founded in 1892, is a public, comprehensive institution. Programs are offered through the Colleges of Architecture, Arts and Sciences, Business Administration, Education, Engineering, Fine Arts, Geosciences, and Liberal Studies and the Graduate School. Its 2,695 acre campus is located in Norman, 15 miles south of Oklahoma City.

**Accreditation:** NCACS. Professionally accredited by the Accreditation Board for Engineering and Technology, the Accrediting Council on Education in Journalism and Mass Communication, the American Assembly of Collegiate Schools of Business, the American Bar Association, the American Council for Construction Education, the American Library Association, the American Psychological Association, the Association of American Law Schools, the Council on Social Work Education, the Foundation for Interior Design Education Research, the National Architecture Accrediting Board, the National Association of Schools of Music, the National Council for Accreditation of Teacher Education.
**Religious orientation:** University of Oklahoma is nonsectarian; no religious requirements.
**Library:** Collections totaling over 2,425,086 volumes, 17,440 periodical subscriptions, and 3,294,140 microform items.
**Special facilities/museums:** Museums of art and natural history, linguistics institute, institute of Asian affairs, biological field station, energy center.
**Athletic facilities:** Fitness center, swim complex, tennis courts.

**STUDENT BODY. Undergraduate profile:** 80% are state residents; 39% are transfers. 4.6% Asian-American, 7% Black, 2.8% Hispanic, 5.7% Native American, 74.2% White, 5.7% Other. Average age of undergraduates is 22.
**Freshman profile:** 8% of accepted applicants took SAT; 88% took ACT.
**Undergraduate achievement:** 77% of fall 1992 freshmen returned for fall 1993 term. 16% of entering class graduated.
**Foreign students:** 861 students are from out of the country. Countries represented include China, India, Malaysia, Pakistan, Singapore, and Taiwan; 68 in all.

**PROGRAMS OF STUDY. Degrees:** B.A., B.Acct., B.Arch., B.Bus.Admin., B.F.A., B.Lib.Studies, B.Mus., B.Mus.Ed., B.S.
**Majors:** Accounting, Advertising, Aerospace Engineering, Anthropology, Architecture, Art/General Fine Arts, Art History, Asian Studies, Astronomy, Astrophysics, Ballet Pedagogy, Ballet Performance, Botany, Broadcast News, Ceramics/Metal Design, Chemical Engineering, Chemical Engineering/Biotechnology, Chemistry, Civil Engineering, Civil Engineering/Pre-Architecture, Classics, Communication, Computer Science, Construction Science, Dance/General Fine Arts, Drama/General Fine Arts, Early Childhood Education, Economics, Electrical Engineering, Electrical Engineering/Computer Engineering, Electronic Media, Elementary Education, Engineering, Engineering Physics, English, Environmental Design, Environmental Engineering, Environmental Science, Ethics/Religion, European Studies, Film/Video Studies, Filmmaking/Photography/Video, Finance, Foreign Language Education, French, Geography, Geological Engineering, Geology, Geophysics, Geosciences, German, Health Studies, History, Individualized Majors, Industrial Engineering, Interior Design, International Business, Journalism/Mass Communications, Laboratory Technology, Language Arts Education, Large Systems Engineering, Latin American Studies, Letters, Linguistics, Management, Management Information Systems, Marketing, Mathematics, Mathematics Education, Mechanical Engineering, Meteorology, Microbiology, Modern Dance Pedagogy, Modern Dance Performance, Music, Music Composition, Music Education, Music Education/Instrumental, Music Education/Vocal, Music/General Fine Arts, Music Theatre Performance, News Communication, Organ, Painting/Printmaking, Petroleum Engineering, Petroleum Land Management, Philosophy, Physics, Piano, Piano Pedagogy, Political Science, Pre-Architecture, Pre-Medical Engineering, Professional Studies, Professional Writing, Psychology, Public Affairs/Administration, Public Relations, Real Estate, Russian, Russian Studies, Science Education, Social Studies Education, Social Work, Sociology, Spanish, Special Education, Sports Studies, Theatre, Visual Communications, Voice, Wind/Percussion/Strings, Zoology.
**Distribution of degrees:** The majors with the highest enrollment are management information system, marketing, and accounting.
**Requirements:** General education requirement.
**Academic regulations:** Freshmen must maintain minimum 1.7 GPA; sophomores, juniors, seniors, 2.0 GPA.
**Special:** Minors offered in many majors in College of Arts and Sciences, in geography and geology (College of Geosciences), and in women's studies. Entering freshmen enroll for at least two semesters in University Coll. Coll of Business Administration offers training for professional certification in numerous areas, including CPA. Self-designed majors. Dual degrees. Independent study. Pass/fail grading option. Internships. Cooperative education programs. Graduate school at which undergraduates may take graduate-level courses. Preprofessional programs in medicine, veterinary science, pharmacy, dentistry, theology, optometry, clinical dietetics, communication disorders, cytotechnology, dental hygiene, medical technology, nursing, occupational therapy, physical therapy, physician's assistant, radiologic technology, and respiratory therapy. Five-year bachelor's/M.B.A. program. Member of South Regional Educational Board and Academic Common Market. Teacher certification in early childhood, elementary, secondary, and special education. Certification in specific subject areas. Study abroad in over 19 countries. ROTC, NROTC, and AFROTC.
**Honors:** Phi Beta Kappa. Honors program. Honor societies.
**Academic Assistance:** Remedial reading and study skills. Nonremedial tutoring.

**STUDENT LIFE. Housing:** All unmarried students under age 20 or with fewer than 24 credit hours must live on campus unless living with family. Coed dorms. Sorority and fraternity housing. School-owned/operated apartments. On-campus married-student housing. 22% of students live in college housing.
**Social atmosphere:** "Norman is a relatively quiet community," reports the editor of the student newspaper, "but it is a community that is very responsive to the university and its students. The opportunity for entertainment and social life is select, but you can find almost anything you want to do. It's a great place to be." Popular events include home football and basketball games, concerts, Medieval Fair, and Sooner Scandals.
**Services and counseling/handicapped student services:** Placement services. Health service. Women's center. Day care. Counseling services for minority, veteran, and older students. Personal and psychological counseling. Career and academic guidance services. Physically disabled student services. Learning disabled services. Notetaking services. Reader services for the blind.
**Campus organizations:** Undergraduate student government. Student newspaper (Oklahoma Daily). Radio station. A cappella choir and chorus, quartets, glee clubs, orchestra, band, playhouse, studio theatre, debating, Model UN, Amnesty International, College Republicans, Young Democrats, Arnold Air Society, academic, service, and special-interest

groups, 271 organizations in all. 22 fraternities, 17 chapter houses; 15 sororities, 11 chapter houses. 19% of men join a fraternity. 17% of women join a sorority.
**Religious organizations:** African Christian Fellowship, Bahai Club, Baptist Student Union, Campus Crusade for Christ, Chi Alpha, Christians on Campus, Hillel Jewish Student Organization, Latter-Day Saints Student Association, Lutheran Student Fellowship, Muslim Student Association, United Ministry, Norman Youth Fellowship.
**Minority/foreign student organizations:** Asian-American Association, American Indian Association, Black Student Association, Hispanic-American Association, NAACP, Society of African-American Men. International Advisory Council, Arab, Bangladesh, Chinese, European, Hong Kong, Indian, Indonesian, Iranian, Japanese, Malaysian, Nepalese, Pakistani, Thai, Turkish, and Vietnamese groups.

**ATHLETICS. Physical education requirements:** None.
**Intercollegiate competition:** 6% of students participate. Baseball (M), basketball (M,W), cheerleading (M,W), cross-country (M,W), football (M), golf (M,W), gymnastics (M,W), softball (W), tennis (M,W), track (indoor) (M,W), track (outdoor) (M,W), track and field (indoor) (M,W), track and field (outdoor) (M,W), volleyball (W), wrestling (M). Member of Big Eight Conference, NCAA Division I.
**Intramural and club sports:** 45% of students participate. Intramural badminton, basketball, bowling, flag football, frisbee golf, fun run, golf, handball, horseshoes, inner-tube waterpolo, pickleball, putt-putt golf, racquetball, softball, swimming, table tennis, tennis, track/field, volleyball. Men's club aviation, badminton, cycling, fencing, karate, racquetball, rugby, sailing, soccer, triathlon, volleyball, water polo, weight lifting, wheelchair basketball, wind surfing. Women's club aviation, badminton, cycling, fencing, karate, racquetball, rugby, sailing, soccer, triathlon, volleyball, water polo, weight lifting, wheelchair basketball, wind surfing.

**ADMISSIONS. Academic basis for candidate selection** (in order of priority): Secondary school record, class rank, standardized test scores, essay, school's recommendation.
**Nonacademic basis for candidate selection:** Particular talent or ability is important. Character and personality and extracurricular participation are considered.
**Requirements:** Graduation from secondary school is required; GED is not accepted. 11 units and the following program of study are required: 4 units of English, 3 units of math, 2 units of lab science, 2 units of history. Minimum combined SAT score of 990 (composite ACT score of 21) or rank in top third of secondary school class and minimum 3.0 GPA required. Portfolio required of art program applicants. Audition required of music program applicants. Conditional admission possible for applicants not meeting standard requirements. SAT or ACT is required. Campus visit recommended. Off-campus interviews available with an admissions representative.
**Procedure:** Take SAT or ACT by October of 12th year. Suggest filing application by March 1; no deadline. Notification of admission on rolling basis. No set date by which applicants must accept offer. $20 nonrefundable room deposit. Freshmen accepted for terms other than fall.
**Special programs:** Admission may be deferred one year. Credit and/or placement may be granted through CEEB Advanced Placement exams for scores of 3 or higher. Credit and/or placement may be granted through CLEP subject exams. Credit and placement may be granted through ACT PEP, DANTES, and challenge exams and military experience. Early entrance/early admission program. Concurrent enrollment program.
**Transfer students:** Transfer students accepted for terms other than fall. In fall 1993, 39% of all new students were transfers into all classes. 2,766 transfer applications were received, 2,424 were accepted. Application deadline is rolling for fall; rolling for spring. Minimum 2.0 GPA required. Lowest course grade accepted is "D." Maximum number of transferable credits is 90 quarter hours; 64 semester hours. At least 30 semester hours must be completed at the university to receive degree.
**Admissions contact:** Marc Borish, M.Ed., Director of Admissions. 405 325-2251.

**FINANCIAL AID. Available aid:** Pell grants, SEOG, Federal Nursing Student Scholarships, state scholarships and grants, school scholarships and grants, private scholarships and grants, academic merit scholarships, and athletic scholarships. Institutional grants/scholarships. Perkins Loans (NDSL), PLUS, Stafford Loans (GSL), NSL, Health Professions Loans, school loans, private loans, and SLS. Institutional loans. Deferred payment plan.
**Financial aid statistics:** 32% of aid is not need-based. In 1993-94, 84% of all undergraduate applicants received aid; 86% of freshman applicants. Average amounts of aid awarded freshmen: Scholarships and grants, $3,450; loans, $3,504.
**Supporting data/closing dates:** FAFSA: Priority filing date is March 1. Notification of awards begins March 15.
**Financial aid contact:** Matt Hamilton, M.Hum.Rel., Director of Financial Aid. 405 325-4521.

**STUDENT EMPLOYMENT.** College Work/Study Program. Institutional employment. 10% of full-time undergraduates work on campus during school year. Students may expect to earn an average of $4,011 during school year. Off-campus part-time employment opportunities rated "good."

**COMPUTER FACILITIES.** 500 IBM/IBM-compatible, Macintosh/Apple, and RISC-/UNIX-based microcomputers; all are networked. Students may access Digital, IBM minicomputer/mainframe systems, BITNET, Internet. Residence halls may be equipped with stand-alone microcomputers, networked microcomputers, networked terminals. Client/LAN operating systems include Apple/Macintosh, DOS, OS/2, UNIX/XENIX/AIX, X-windows, DEC, LocalTalk/AppleTalk, Novell. Computer languages and software packages include C, COBOL, dBase, FORTRAN, Lotus 1-2-3, MS Excell, MS Word, Pascal, SAS WordPerfect. Computer facilities are available to all students.
**Fees:** Vary according to course and department.
**Hours:** 24 hours.

**GRADUATE CAREER DATA.** Companies and businesses that hire graduates: Big Six accounting firms, major energy companies.

**PROMINENT ALUMNI/AE.** Lawrence G. Rawl, president, Exxon; Alex Massad, senior vice-president, Mobil; William R. Howell, chairperson of the board, J.C. Penney; Carl Albert, former speaker, U.S. House of Representatives.

# University of Science and Arts of Oklahoma

**Chickasha, OK 73018 405 224-3140**

**1993-94 Costs.** Tuition: $1,376 (state residents), $3,520 (out-of-state). Room & board: $1,920. Fees, books, misc. academic expenses (school's estimate): $700.
**Enrollment.** Undergraduates: 395 men, 745 women (full-time). Freshman class: 438 applicants, 420 accepted, 360 enrolled.
**Test score averages/ranges.** N/A.
**Faculty.** 54 full-time; 20 part-time. 70% of faculty holds doctoral degree. Student/faculty ratio: 15 to 1.
**Selectivity rating.** N/A.

**PROFILE.** USAO is a public, liberal arts university. Founded in 1908, it adopted coeducation in 1965. Its 75-acre campus is locate in Chickasha, 40 miles southwest of Oklahoma City.

**Accreditation:** NCACS. Professionally accredited by the National Association of Schools of Music, the National Council for Accreditation of Teacher Education.
**Religious orientation:** University of Science and Arts of Oklahoma is nonsectarian; no religious requirements.
**Library:** Collections totaling over 90,000 volumes, 1,200 periodical subscriptions, and 6,000 microform items.
**Special facilities/museums:** Language labs, speech and hearing clinic, school for the deaf, university farm.
**Athletic facilities:** Gymnasium, indoor swimming pool, basketball and tennis courts, softball field, field house, community golf course.
**STUDENT BODY. Undergraduate profile:** 98% are state residents; 31% are transfers. 3% Black, 1% Hispanic, 10% Native American, 84% White, 2% Other. Average age of undergraduates is 29.
**Freshman profile:** 2% of accepted applicants took SAT; 98% took ACT. 99% of freshmen come from public schools.
**Undergraduate achievement:** 48% of fall 1992 freshmen returned for fall 1993 term. 25% of students who completed a degree program went on to graduate study within five years.
**Foreign students:** 34 students are from out of the country. Countries represented include Bangladesh, Hong Kong, India, Indonesia, Malaysia, and Taiwan; 10 in all.
**PROGRAMS OF STUDY. Degrees:** B.A., B.S.
**Majors:** Accounting, Administration, Art, Biology, Business, Chemistry, Communication, Computer Science, Deaf Education, Drama, Economics, Elementary Education, English, Health/Physical Education/Recreation, History, Home Economics, Indian Studies, Management, Mathematics, Medical Technology, Music, Natural Science, Physics, Political Science, Psychology, Sociology, Special Education/Learning Disabled, Speech Correction, Speech/Hearing Therapy.
**Distribution of degrees:** The majors with the highest enrollment are education, business, and computer science; Indian studies, physics, and natural science have the lowest.
**Requirements:** General education requirement.
**Academic regulations:** Minimum 2.2 GPA required for graduation.
**Special:** Minors offered in all major areas except education. One- or two-year certificate programs offered in business. Courses in earth/space science, geography, German, philosophy, and religion. Double majors. Independent study. Accelerated study. Graduate school at which undergraduates may take graduate-level courses. Preprofessional programs in law, medicine, veterinary science, pharmacy, dentistry, and nursing. 3-1 medical technology program. Teacher certification in early childhood, elementary, secondary, and special education.
**Honors:** Honors program.
**ADMISSIONS. Academic basis for candidate selection** (in order of priority): Standardized test scores, secondary school record, class rank.
**Requirements:** Graduation from secondary school is required; GED is accepted. 20 units and the following program of study are required: 4 units of English, 3 units of math, 2 units of lab science, 1 unit of social studies, 1 unit of history, 9 units of electives including 4 units of academic electives. Minimum composite ACT score of 19, rank in top one-half of secondary school class, and minimum 2.7 GPA required. Special summer entrance program for state residents who do not meet normal admissions criteria. ACT is required; SAT may be substituted. Campus visit and interview recommended. Off-campus interviews available with an admissions representative.
**Procedure:** Suggest filing application by July 1. Notification of admission on rolling basis. $35 nonrefundable room deposit. Freshmen accepted for terms other than fall.
**Special programs:** Credit may be granted through CLEP subject exams, ACT PEP, DANTES, and challenge exams and military experience. Concurrent enrollment program.
**Transfer students:** Transfer students accepted for terms other than fall. In fall 1993, 31% of all new students were transfers into all classes. 90 transfer applications were received, 79 were accepted. Application deadline is rolling for fall; rolling for spring. Minimum 2.2 GPA recommended. Lowest course grade accepted is "D" for general education courses, "C" in major. At least 30 quarter hours must be completed at the university to receive degree.
**Admissions contact:** Tim McElroy, Ed.D., Director of Admissions. 405 224-3140, extension 204.
**FINANCIAL AID. Available aid:** Pell grants, SEOG, state scholarships and grants, school scholarships, private scholarships, academic merit scholarships, and athletic scholarships. Tuition is waived every third term until graduation for in-state students who complete two consecutive terms and remain in continuous attendance with good academic standing. Perkins Loans (NDSL), PLUS, Stafford Loans (GSL), school loans, and SLS.

**Financial aid statistics:** Average amounts of aid awarded freshmen: Scholarships and grants, $1,500; loans, $1,300.
**Supporting data/closing dates:** FAFSA/FFS: Accepted on rolling basis. Income tax forms: Accepted on rolling basis. Notification of awards on rolling basis.
**Financial aid contact:** Gale Thorsen, M.A., Director of Financial Aid. 405 224-3140, extension 240.

# University of Tulsa

**Tulsa, OK 74104** **918 631-2000**

**1993-94 Costs.** Tuition: $9,995. Room & board: $3,958. Fees, books, misc. academic expenses (school's estimate): $750.
**Enrollment.** Undergraduates: 1,404 men, 1,532 women (full-time). Freshman class: 1,712 applicants, 1,557 accepted, 696 enrolled. Graduate enrollment: 855 men, 585 women.
**Test score averages/ranges.** Average SAT scores: 524 verbal, 575 math. Range of SAT scores of middle 50%: 450-580 verbal, 498-640 math. Average ACT scores: 24 English, 23 math, 24 composite. Range of ACT scores of middle 50%: 21-27 English, 19-26 math.
**Faculty.** 339 full-time; 115 part-time. 93% of faculty holds doctoral degree. Student/faculty ratio: 12 to 1.
**Selectivity rating.** Competitive.

**PROFILE.** The University of Tulsa, founded in 1894, is a private institution. Programs are offered through the Colleges of Arts and Sciences, Business Administration, Education, Engineering and Applied Sciences, and Nursing. Its 100-acre campus is located in Tulsa, 100 miles northeast of Oklahoma City.
**Accreditation:** NCACS. Professionally accredited by the Accreditation Board for Engineering and Technology, the American Assembly of Collegiate Schools of Business, the National Association of Schools of Music, the National Council for Accreditation of Teacher Education, the National League for Nursing.
**Religious orientation:** University of Tulsa is affiliated with the Presbyterian Church; no religious requirements.
**Library:** Collections totaling over 2,023,298 volumes, 3,421 periodical subscriptions, and 1,592,700 microform items.
**Special facilities/museums:** Art gallery, center for communicative disorders, charge-coupled camera microscope, electron microscopes.
**Athletic facilities:** Gymnasiums, weight rooms, swimming pool, racquetball, squash, tennis, and volleyball courts, dance studio, stadium, athletic fields.
**STUDENT BODY. Undergraduate profile:** 58% are state residents; 30% are transfers. 2% Asian-American, 6% Black, 2% Hispanic, 5% Native American, 74% White, 11% Other. Average age of undergraduates is 22.
**Freshman profile:** 3% of freshmen who took SAT scored 700 or over on verbal, 11% scored 700 or over on math; 20% scored 600 or over on verbal, 43% scored 600 or over on math; 66% scored 500 or over on verbal, 81% scored 500 or over on math; 93% scored 400 or over on verbal, 95% scored 400 or over on math; 100% scored 300 or over on verbal, 99% scored 300 or over on math. 25% of accepted applicants took SAT; 75% took ACT. 85% of freshmen come from public schools.
**Undergraduate achievement:** 80% of fall 1992 freshmen returned for fall 1993 term. 40% of entering class graduated.
**Foreign students:** 332 students are from out of the country. Countries represented include China, India, Indonesia, Malaysia, Saudi Arabia, and Venezuela; 61 in all.
**PROGRAMS OF STUDY. Degrees:** B.A., B.F.A., B.Mus., B.Mus.Ed., B.S., B.S.Bus. Admin., B.S.Nurs.
**Majors:** Accounting, Art, Athletic Training, Biological Sciences, Chemical Engineering, Chemistry, Communication, Computer Information Systems, Computer Science, Deaf Education, Economics, Education, Electrical Engineering, Engineering Physics, English, Environmental Policy, Finance, Foreign Languages, Geoscience, Geosciences, History, International Studies, Law/Society, Management, Management Information Systems, Marketing, Mathematics, Mechanical Engineering, Music, Musical Theatre, Nursing, Petroleum Engineering, Philosophy, Physics, Political Science, Psychology, Russian, Sociology, Speech/Language Pathology, Student-Designed Area of Concentration, Theatre.
**Distribution of degrees:** The majors with the highest enrollment are accounting, psychology, and communication; philosophy, musical theatre, and student-designed areas of concentration have the lowest.
**Requirements:** General education requirement.
**Academic regulations:** Minimum 2.0 GPA must be maintained.
**Special:** Minors offered in numerous fields. Minor required in College of Arts and Sciences. Self-designed majors. Double majors. Dual degrees. Independent study. Pass/fail grading option. Internships. Graduate school at which undergraduates may take graduate-level courses. Preprofessional programs in law, medicine, veterinary science, and dentistry. Five-year bachelor's/M.B.A. program. Washington Semester and Sea Semester. Teacher certification in elementary and secondary education. Certification in specific subject areas. Study abroad in Australia and African, Asian, and European countries. ROTC.
**Honors:** Phi Beta Kappa. Honors program. Honor societies.
**Academic Assistance:** Nonremedial tutoring.
**STUDENT LIFE. Housing:** All freshmen must live on campus unless living with family within a 20-mile radius. Coed, women's, and men's dorms. Sorority and fraternity housing. School-owned/operated apartments. 40% of students live in college housing.
**Social atmosphere:** According to the student newspaper, J.R.'s Place, the Hurricane Hut, and fraternity houses are popular hangouts at the University of Tulsa. Some of the prominent organizations on campus are Greeks, the Student Association, Residence Hall Association, and Campus Ministries. The Miss TU Pageant, air band contest, TU theatre productions, football games, and Homecoming are among the year's favorite events.
**Services and counseling/handicapped student services:** Placement services. Health service. Women's center. Counseling services for minority, military, veteran, and older students. Birth control, personal, and psychological counseling. Career and academic guidance services. Religious counseling. Physically disabled student services. Learning disabled services. Tutors.
**Campus organizations:** Undergraduate student government. Student newspaper (Collegian, published once/week). Literary magazine. Yearbook. Radio and TV stations. Bands, orchestras, ensembles, chorale, choir, opera theatre, theatre, Spirit Squad, Model UN, departmental, recreational, professional, and special-interest groups, 140 organizations in all. Seven fraternities, all with chapter houses; seven sororities, all with chapter houses. 21% of men join a fraternity. 22% of women join a sorority.
**Religious organizations:** Baptist Student Union, Campus Crusade for Christ, Catholic Center, Christian Science Organization, Church of Christ, Council for Religious Life, Jewish University Students of Tulsa, Latin American Christian Fellowship, Muslim student group, United Ministry Canterbury Center, Wesley Foundation.
**Minority/foreign student organizations:** Association of Black Collegians, African-American culture group, Coalition Against Apartheid, Hispanic Student Association, Native American group, Pan-African Student Association. Indonesian Student Union, International Friendship House, Malaysian Student Union, Norwegian Viking Club, Vietnamese group.
**ATHLETICS. Physical education requirements:** None.
**Intercollegiate competition:** 8% of students participate. Basketball (M), cheerleading (M,W), cross-country (M,W), football (M), golf (M,W), soccer (M,W), softball (W), tennis (M,W), track (indoor) (M,W), track (outdoor) (M,W), track and field (indoor) (M,W), track and field (outdoor) (M,W), volleyball (W). Member of Missouri Valley Conference, NCAA Division I-A.
**Intramural and club sports:** 80% of students participate. Intramural badminton, basketball, billiards, bowling, cross-country, flag football, frisbee golf, golf, horseshoes, racquetball, sand volleyball, soccer, softball, squash, swimming, table tennis, tennis, volleyball, walleyball. Men's club racquetball. Women's club racquetball.
**ADMISSIONS. Academic basis for candidate selection** (in order of priority): Secondary school record, class rank, standardized test scores, school's recommendation, essay.
**Nonacademic basis for candidate selection:** Character and personality and particular talent or ability are important. Extracurricular participation and alumni/ae relationship are considered.
**Requirements:** Graduation from secondary school is required; GED is accepted. 15 units and the following program of study are recommended: 4 units of English, 3 units of math, 3 units of science, 2 units of foreign language, 3 units of social studies. 4 units of mathematics required of engineering and physical sciences program applicants. Audition required of music and theatre program scholarship applicants. Portfolio required of art program scholarship applicants. SAT or ACT is required. Campus visit and interview recommended. Off-campus interviews available with an admissions representative.
**Procedure:** Take SAT or ACT by December of 12th year. Suggest filing application by March; no deadline. Notification of admission on rolling basis. Reply is required by May 1. $100 nonrefundable tuition deposit. $100 nonrefundable room deposit. Freshmen accepted for terms other than fall.
**Special programs:** Admission may be deferred one year. Credit and/or placement may be granted through CEEB Advanced Placement exams for scores of 4 or higher. Credit may be granted through CLEP general and subject exams. Credit and placement may be granted through DANTES and challenge exams. Early entrance/early admission program. Concurrent enrollment program.
**Transfer students:** Transfer students accepted for terms other than fall. In fall 1993, 30% of all new students were transfers into all classes. 679 transfer applications were received, 545 were accepted. Application deadline is rolling for fall; rolling for spring. Minimum 2.5 GPA recommended. Lowest course grade accepted is "C." Maximum number of transferable credits is 62 semester hours from a two-year school and 94 semester hours from a four-year school. At least 30 semester hours must be completed at the university to receive degree.
**Admissions contact:** John Corso, Dean of Admissions. 918 631-2307, 800 331-3050.
**FINANCIAL AID. Available aid:** Pell grants, SEOG, state scholarships and grants, school scholarships and grants, private scholarships and grants, ROTC scholarships, academic merit scholarships, and athletic scholarships. Perkins Loans (NDSL), PLUS, Stafford Loans (GSL), private loans, and SLS. Manufacturers Hanover tuition payment plan.
**Financial aid statistics:** 30% of aid is not need-based. In 1993-94, 95% of all undergraduate applicants received aid; 95% of freshman applicants. Average amounts of aid awarded freshmen: Scholarships and grants, $5,000; loans, $2,000.
**Supporting data/closing dates:** FAFSA: Priority filing date is April 1; accepted on rolling basis. School's own aid application: Priority filing date is April 1; accepted on rolling basis. Income tax forms: Priority filing date is April 1; accepted on rolling basis. Notification of awards begins March 1.
**Financial aid contact:** David Gruen, M.S., Director of Financial Aid. 918 631-2526.
**STUDENT EMPLOYMENT.** College Work/Study Program. Institutional employment. 40% of full-time undergraduates work on campus during school year. Students may expect to earn an average of $1,225 during school year. Off-campus part-time employment opportunities rated "excellent."
**COMPUTER FACILITIES.** 1,150 IBM/IBM-compatible and Macintosh/Apple microcomputers; 600 are networked. Students may access Digital minicomputer/mainframe systems, BITNET, Internet. Residence halls may be equipped with stand-alone microcomputers, networked microcomputers, networked terminals, modems. Computer languages and software packages include Ada, APL, Assembly, BASIC, BLISS, C, COBOL, FORTRAN, IFPS, ImSL, LINDO, MINITAB, PL/1, Pascal, SAS, SLAM, SPSS. Computer facilities are available to all students.
**Hours:** 24 hours.
**GRADUATE CAREER DATA.** Highest graduate school enrollments: Harvard U, Rice U, Tulane U, Washington U.
**PROMINENT ALUMNI/AE.** Rue McClanahan, actress on TV's "Golden Girls"; S.E. Hinton, author, *The Outsiders*; Linda Roark-Strummer, opera singer; Steve Largent, former Seattle Seahawks football player; Bob Losure, CNN correspondent.

# Oregon

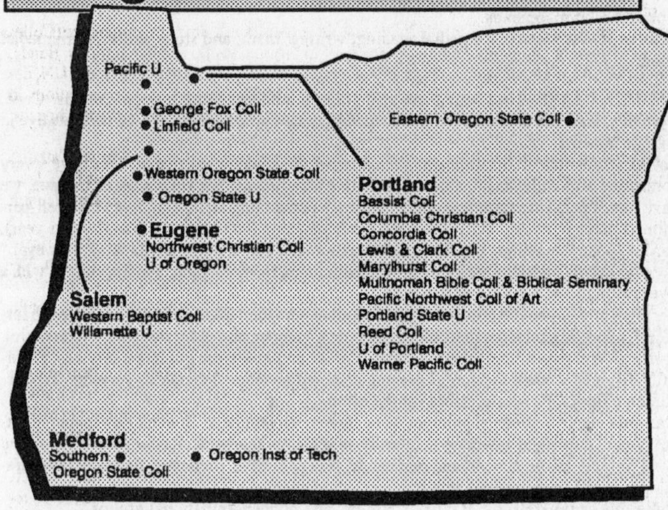


## Bassist College

**Portland, OR 97201** **503 228-6528**

**1994-95 Costs.** Tuition: $8,500. Room: $2,450-$3,950. No meal plan. Fees, books, misc. academic expenses (school's estimate): $2,000.
**Enrollment.** Undergraduates: 18 men, 115 women (full-time). Freshman class: 124 applicants, 124 accepted, 88 enrolled.
**Test score averages/ranges.** N/A.
**Faculty.** 10 full-time; 8 part-time. 11% of faculty holds doctoral degree. Student/faculty ratio: 12 to 1.
**Selectivity rating.** N/A.

**PROFILE.** Bassist, founded in 1963, is a private college of design. Its one-acre campus is located in downtown Portland.

**Accreditation:** NASC.
**Religious orientation:** Bassist College is nonsectarian; no religious requirements.
**Library:** Collections totaling over 21,059 volumes, and 6,959 periodical subscriptions.
**Special facilities/museums:** Computer-aided design lab, industrial sewing lab, industrial design lab.
**STUDENT BODY. Undergraduate profile:** 82% are state residents; 64% are transfers. 8% Asian-American, 2% Black, 2% Hispanic, 88% White. Average age of undergraduates is 28.
**Freshman profile:** 81% of freshmen come from public schools.
**Undergraduate achievement:** 73% of fall 1992 freshmen returned for fall 1993 term. 76% of entering class graduated. 20% of students who completed a degree program immediately went on to graduate study.
**Foreign students:** Six students are from out of the country. Countries represented include Canada, China, Indonesia, Japan, Korea, and Taiwan.
**PROGRAMS OF STUDY. Degrees:** B.Apparel Design, B.Indust.Design, B.Inter.Design, B.Retail Mgmt.
**Majors:** Apparel Design, Industrial Design, Interior Design, Retail Management.
**Distribution of degrees:** The majors with the highest enrollment are interior design, apparel design, and retail management.
**Requirements:** General education requirement.
**Academic regulations:** Minimum 2.0 GPA must be maintained.
**Special:** Associate's degrees offered. Independent study. Internships. Cooperative education programs.
**Academic Assistance:** Remedial writing. Nonremedial tutoring.
**ADMISSIONS. Academic basis for candidate selection** (in order of priority): Secondary school record, school's recommendation, standardized test scores, essay, class rank.
**Nonacademic basis for candidate selection:** Particular talent or ability is important. Character and personality and extracurricular participation are considered.
**Requirements:** Graduation from secondary school is required; GED is accepted. 14.5 units and the following program of study are recommended: 3 units of English, 2 units of math, 1.5 units of science including 1 unit of lab, 1 unit of foreign language, 3 units of social studies, 2 units of history, 3 units of electives. Minimum 2.25 GPA required; 2.75 GPA recommended. Portfolio recommended of design program applicants for challenging coursework. Conditional admission possible for applicants not meeting standard requirements. Campus visit and interview recommended. Off-campus interviews available with an admissions representative.
**Procedure:** Visit college for interview by June 1 of 12th year. Suggest filing application by June 1. Application deadline is September 1. Notification of admission on rolling basis. Applicant must accept offer of admission by first day of school. $200 nonrefundable tuition deposit. $100 room deposit, refundable until move-in date. Freshmen accepted for terms other than fall.
**Special programs:** Admission may be deferred one year. Credit may be granted through CEEB Advanced Placement for scores of 3 or higher. Credit may be granted through CLEP general and subject exams and DANTES exams. Credit and placement may be granted through challenge exams.
**Transfer students:** Transfer students accepted for terms other than fall. In fall 1993, 64% of all new students were transfers into all classes. 98 transfer applications were received, 98 were accepted. Application deadline is September 1. Minimum 2.0 GPA required. Lowest course grade accepted is "C." Maximum number of transferable credits is 125 quarter hours. At least 65 must be completed at the college to receive degree. At least one year of course work must be completed at the college to receive degree.
**Admissions contact:** Christina Billington, M.A., Registrar. 503 228-6528.
**FINANCIAL AID. Available aid:** Pell grants, SEOG, school scholarships and grants, private scholarships and grants, and academic merit scholarships. Perkins Loans (NDSL), PLUS, Stafford Loans (GSL), and SLS. Family tuition reduction. College 10-month payment plan.
**Financial aid statistics:** 31% of aid is not need-based. In 1993-94, 100% of all undergraduate applicants received aid. Average amounts of aid awarded freshmen: Scholarships and grants, $1,135; loans, $2,036.
**Supporting data/closing dates:** FAFSA: Accepted on rolling basis. School's own aid application: Accepted on rolling basis. Income tax forms: Accepted on rolling basis. Notification of awards begins June 15.
**Financial aid contact:** Robin Alton, Director of Financial Aid. 503 228-6528.

## Concordia College

**Portland, OR 97211** **503 288-9371**

**1994-95 Costs.** Tuition: $9,600. Room & board: $3,150. Fees, books, misc. academic expenses (school's estimate): $250.
**Enrollment.** Undergraduates: 369 men, 442 women (full-time). Freshman class: 299 applicants, 206 accepted, 81 enrolled.
**Test score averages/ranges.** Average SAT scores: 434 verbal, 466 math. Range of SAT scores of middle 50%: 370-480 verbal, 370-530 math. Average ACT scores: 19 composite.
**Faculty.** 41 full-time; 42 part-time. 52% of faculty holds doctoral degree. Student/faculty ratio: 20 to 1.
**Selectivity rating.** Less competitive.

**PROFILE.** Concordia is a church-affiliated college. Founded as a two-year college in 1905, it became a four-year college in 1977. Its 13-acre campus is located in a residential area of Portland.

**Accreditation:** NASC.
**Religious orientation:** Concordia College is affiliated with the Lutheran Church-Missouri Synod; 15 quarter hours of religion required.
**Library:** Collections totaling over 53,000 volumes, 426 periodical subscriptions, and 47,000 microform items.
**Special facilities/museums:** Apple Education Computer Lab, early childhood center.
**Athletic facilities:** Gymnasium, tennis courts, baseball and soccer fields, weight room.
**STUDENT BODY. Undergraduate profile:** 46% are state residents; 70% are transfers. 2% Asian-American, 2% Black, 1% Hispanic, 1% Native American, 68% White, 26% Other. Average age of undergraduates is 28.
**Freshman profile:** 2% of freshmen who took SAT scored 700 or over on verbal, 3% scored 700 or over on math; 9% scored 600 or over on verbal, 13% scored 600 or over on math; 22% scored 500 or over on verbal, 34% scored 500 or over on math; 63% scored 400 or over on verbal, 70% scored 400 or over on math; 100% scored 300 or over on verbal, 100% scored 300 or over on math. 75% of accepted applicants took SAT; 12% took ACT. 90% of freshmen come from public schools.
**Undergraduate achievement:** 55% of fall 1992 freshmen returned for fall 1993 term.
**Foreign students:** 85 students are from out of the country. Countries represented include Canada, Hong Kong, Indonesia, Japan, Korea, and Singapore; 12 in all.
**PROGRAMS OF STUDY. Degrees:** B.A., B.S.
**Majors:** Business Administration, Director of Christian Education, Elementary Education, Health Care Administration, Health Care Social Work, Liberal Arts, Pre-Seminary, Secondary Education, Social Work, Theological Studies.
**Distribution of degrees:** The majors with the highest enrollment are business administration, elementary education, and liberal arts.
**Requirements:** General education requirement.
**Academic regulations:** Freshmen must maintain minimum 1.5 GPA; sophomores, 1.8 GPA; juniors, 2.0 GPA; seniors, 2.0 GPA.
**Special:** Minors offered in all majors. Business administration major includes accounting, health care, international business, management, and marketing concentrations. Associate's degrees offered. Independent study. Accelerated study. Pass/fail grading option. Internships. Teacher certification in elementary and secondary education. Certification in specific subject areas. Exchange programs abroad in China (Guangxi Teachers Coll), Japan (Aichi Gakuin U, Japan Lutheran Coll and Seminary), and England (Oak Hill Coll).
**Honors:** Honor societies.
**Academic Assistance:** Nonremedial tutoring.
**ADMISSIONS. Academic basis for candidate selection** (in order of priority): Secondary school record, standardized test scores, school's recommendation, class rank, essay.
**Nonacademic basis for candidate selection:** Character and personality and particular talent or ability are emphasized. Extracurricular participation is important. Alumni/ae relationship is considered.
**Requirements:** Graduation from secondary school is required; GED is accepted. No specific distribution of secondary school units required. Minimum verbal SAT score of 400 and minimum 2.5 GPA required. Minimum 2.5 GPA with 2.75 in professional courses for student teaching required of teacher education program applicants. Conditional admis-

sion possible for applicants not meeting standard requirements. SAT is required. Campus visit and interview recommended.

**Procedure:** Take SAT by June of 12th year. Visit college for interview by June 1 of 12th year. Suggest filing application by June. Application deadline is September 1. Notification of admission on rolling basis. Reply is required by May 1 or within 30 days of acceptance. $100 tuition deposit, refundable until May 1. $100 nonrefundable room deposit. Freshmen accepted for terms other than fall.

**Special programs:** Admission may be deferred one year. Credit may be granted through CEEB Advanced Placement for scores of 3 or higher. Credit may be granted through CLEP general and subject exams, military and life experience. Early entrance/early admission program.

**Transfer students:** Transfer students accepted for terms other than fall. In fall 1993, 70% of all new students were transfers into all classes. 391 transfer applications were received, 267 were accepted. Application deadline is September 1 for fall; rolling for spring. Minimum 2.0 GPA required. Lowest course grade accepted is "D." At least 45 quarter hours must be completed at the college to receive degree.

**Admissions contact:** William H. Balke, Vice President for Student Services/Admissions. 503 280-8501.

**FINANCIAL AID. Available aid:** Pell grants, SEOG, state scholarships, school scholarships and grants, private scholarships and grants, academic merit scholarships, and athletic scholarships. Perkins Loans (NDSL), Stafford Loans (GSL), and SLS. Deferred payment plan.

**Financial aid statistics:** In 1993, 80% of all undergraduate applicants received aid; 90% of freshman applicants.

**Supporting data/closing dates:** FAFSA/FAF/FFS: Accepted on rolling basis. Notification of awards on rolling basis.

**Financial aid contact:** James Cullen, Director of Financial Aid. 503 288-8514.

# Eastern Oregon State College

**LaGrande, OR 97850** **503 962-3672**

**1994-95 Costs.** Tuition: $2,600. Room & board: $3,495. Fees, books, misc. academic expenses (school's estimate): $450.

**Enrollment.** Undergraduates: 802 men, 880 women (full-time). Freshman class: 595 applicants, 579 accepted, 622 enrolled. Graduate enrollment: 6 men, 13 women.

**Test score averages/ranges.** N/A.

**Faculty.** 127 full-time; 10 part-time. 50% of faculty holds doctoral degree. Student/faculty ratio: 10 to 1.

**Selectivity rating.** N/A.

**PROFILE.** Eastern Oregon State, founded as a teachers college in 1929, is a public college. Programs are offered through the Schools of Arts and Sciences and Professional Studies. Its 121-acre campus is located in the Grande Ronde Valley, between the Wallowa and Blue Mountains.

**Accreditation:** NASC. Professionally accredited by the National Council for Accreditation of Teacher Education.

**Religious orientation:** Eastern Oregon State College is nonsectarian; no religious requirements.

**Library:** Collections totaling over 116,590 volumes, 1,299 periodical subscriptions, and 59,929 microform items.

**Special facilities/museums:** Art gallery, archaeological museum, Indian education institute, on-campus elementary school.

**Athletic facilities:** Football stadium, gymnasiums, weight room, handball/racquetball courts, Olympic-sized pool, track, athletic fields.

**STUDENT BODY. Undergraduate profile:** 76% are state residents; 41% are transfers. 2% Asian-American, 1% Black, 2% Hispanic, 2% Native American, 88% White, 5% Other. Average age of undergraduates is 22.

**Freshman profile:** 92% of accepted applicants took SAT; 8% took ACT. 98% of freshmen come from public schools.

**Undergraduate achievement:** 52% of fall 1992 freshmen returned for fall 1993 term. 22% of entering class graduated.

**Foreign students:** 69 students are from out of the country. Countries represented include Canada, Hong Kong, Japan, Kenya, Malaysia, and Taiwan; 25 in all.

**PROGRAMS OF STUDY. Degrees:** B.A., B.S.

**Majors:** Agribusiness, Agricultural Economics, Anthropology/Sociology, Art, Biology, Business, Chemistry, Crop Science, Education, English, Fire Science, History, Liberal Studies, Mathematics, Music, Nursing, Physical Education/Health, Physics, Psychology, Rangeland Resources, Theatre Arts.

**Distribution of degrees:** The majors with the highest enrollment are education, business, and biology; psychology and music have the lowest.

**Requirements:** General education requirement.

**Academic regulations:** Minimum 2.0 GPA must be maintained.

**Special:** Minors offered in some majors and in coaching, economics, French, German, health, international studies, office administration, philosophy, physical education/health, political science, Spanish, and sports medicine. Ed Net offers off-campus programs. Associate's degrees offered. Self-designed majors. Double majors. Dual degrees. Independent study. Accelerated study. Pass/fail grading option. Internships. Cooperative education programs. Preprofessional programs in law, medicine, veterinary science, pharmacy, dentistry, theology, and optometry. 3-2 chemistry/engineering and physics/engineering programs with Oregon State U. Member of National Student Exchange (NSE). Teacher certification in early childhood, elementary, secondary, special education, and bilingual/bicultural education. Certification in specific subject areas. Study abroad in Ecuador, France, Germany, Hungary, Japan, Korea, Mexico, and Thailand.

**Honors:** Honor societies.

**Academic Assistance:** Remedial reading, writing, math, and study skills. Nonremedial tutoring.

**STUDENT LIFE. Housing:** First-year foreign students must live on campus. Coed, women's, and men's dorms. School-owned/operated apartments. 20% of students live in college housing.

**Social atmosphere:** According to the editor of the student newspaper, "We have a very concerned and enthusiastic student activities department. For such a small campus, we have lots of neat entertainment opportunities: a performing arts series, five very-well-performed plays per year, TGIF concerts, other concerts (including the Bangles this year), dances, poetry readings, etc. The off-campus social life is definitely lacking, however." Popular events include Oktoberfest, which includes Homecoming, and Springfest, with a river rafting race, a rodeo, and dances.

**Services and counseling/handicapped student services:** Placement services. Health service. Counseling services for minority, military, veteran, and older students. Birth control, personal, and psychological counseling. Career and academic guidance services. Physically disabled student services. Learning disabled services. Notetaking services. Tape recorders. Tutors. Reader services for the blind.

**Campus organizations:** Undergraduate student government. Student newspaper (Eastern Voice, published biweekly). Literary magazine. Yearbook. Radio station. Blue and Gold Singers, choir, concert and pep bands, jazz ensemble, orchestra, forensics club, drama group, 60 organizations in all.

**Religious organizations:** Baptist, Catholic, and nondenominational groups.

**Minority/foreign student organizations:** Black Student Union, Hispanic and Native American groups. International Relations Club, Japanese club.

**ATHLETICS. Physical education requirements:** None.

**Intercollegiate competition:** 3% of students participate. Alpine skiing (M,W), baseball (M), basketball (M,W), cross-country (M,W), football (M), Nordic skiing (M,W), rodeo (M,W), track (indoor) (M,W), track and field (M,W), volleyball (W). Member of Cascade Conference, Columbia Football League, NAIA, NCRA, Northwest Collegiate Ski Conference, USA Skiing Association.

**Intramural and club sports:** 2% of students participate. Intramural badminton, basketball, flag football, golf, racquetball, softball, swimming, tennis, volleyball. Men's club bowling, golf, soccer, swimming, tennis. Women's club bowling, soccer, swimming, tennis.

**ADMISSIONS. Academic basis for candidate selection** (in order of priority): Secondary school record, standardized test scores, school's recommendation, class rank, essay.

**Nonacademic basis for candidate selection:** Character and personality, extracurricular participation, particular talent or ability, and geographical distribution are considered.

**Requirements:** Graduation from secondary school is required; GED is accepted. 14 units and the following program of study are required: 4 units of English, 3 units of math, 2 units of science including 1 unit of lab, 3 units of social studies, 2 units of academic electives. Minimum 2.5 GPA required. Conditional admission possible for applicants not meeting standard requirements. 10-county special admission and adult special admission program for applicants not normally admissible. SAT is required; ACT may be substituted. Campus visit recommended. No off-campus interviews.

**Procedure:** Take SAT or ACT by June of 12th year. Visit college for interview by June of 12th year. Suggest filing application by August 1. Application deadline is September 22 for residents, April 1 for non-residents. Notification of admission on rolling basis. No set date by which applicants must accept offer. Deferment allowed with proof of receiving state aid. $25 nonrefundable room deposit. Freshmen accepted for terms other than fall.

**Special programs:** Credit may be granted through CEEB Advanced Placement, CLEP general and subject exams, DANTES and challenge exams, and military and life experience. Early decision program. In fall 1993, 45 applied for early decision and 40 were accepted. Early entrance/early admission program. Concurrent enrollment program.

**Transfer students:** Transfer students accepted for terms other than fall. In fall 1993, 41% of all new students were transfers into all classes. 529 transfer applications were received, 438 were accepted. Application deadline is August 1 for fall; January 1 for spring. Minimum 2.0 GPA required. Maximum number of transferable credits is 108 quarter hours. At least 45 quarter hours must be completed at the college to receive degree.

**Admissions contact:** Terral Schut, M.S., Director of Admissions. 800 452-8658.

**FINANCIAL AID. Available aid:** Pell grants, SEOG, state scholarships and grants, school scholarships, private scholarships and grants, academic merit scholarships, and athletic scholarships. Perkins Loans (NDSL), PLUS, Stafford Loans (GSL), private loans, and SLS. Deferred payment plan.

**Financial aid statistics:** 40% of aid is not need-based. In 1993-94, 80% of all undergraduate applicants received aid; 80% of freshman applicants.

**Supporting data/closing dates:** FAFSA: Deadline is January 31. Notification of awards begins April 1.

**Financial aid contact:** Jack Johnson, Director of Financial Aid. 503 962-3550.

**STUDENT EMPLOYMENT.** College Work/Study Program. Institutional employment. 20% of full-time undergraduates work on campus during school year. Students may expect to earn an average of $1,000 during school year. Off-campus part-time employment opportunities rated "fair."

**COMPUTER FACILITIES.** 75 IBM/IBM-compatible and Macintosh/Apple microcomputers. Students may access Bull, Sequent minicomputer/mainframe systems. Residence halls may be equipped with stand-alone microcomputers. Computer languages and software packages include BASIC, C, COBOL, FORTRAN, LISP, LOGO, Pascal, Prolog, WordPerfect, WordStar. Computer facilities are available to all students.

## George Fox College

**Newberg, OR 97132** **503 538-8383**

**1994-95 Costs.** Tuition: $12,500. Room & board: $4,130. Fees, books, misc. academic expenses (school's estimate): $540.
**Enrollment.** Undergraduates: 434 men, 608 women (full-time). Freshman class: 629 applicants, 551 accepted, 281 enrolled. Graduate enrollment: 107 men, 75 women.
**Test score averages/ranges.** Average SAT scores: 465 verbal, 484 math.
**Faculty.** 67 full-time; 62 part-time. 61% of faculty holds doctoral degree. Student/faculty ratio: 15 to 1.
**Selectivity rating.** Less competitive.

**PROFILE.** George Fox, founded in 1891, is a church-affiliated, liberal arts college. Its 60-acre campus is located on a wooded ravine in Newberg, 23 miles from Portland.

**Accreditation:** NASC. Professionally accredited by the National Association of Schools of Music.
**Religious orientation:** George Fox College is affiliated with the Society of Friends (Northwest Yearly Meeting); 10 semesters of religion required.
**Library:** Collections totaling over 91,000 volumes, 1,000 periodical subscriptions, and 2,000 microform items.
**Special facilities/museums:** Quaker museum, language lab, electron microscope.
**Athletic facilities:** Gymnasium, sports center, basketball, racquetball, and tennis courts, track, weight room, baseball, intramural, and softball fields.

**STUDENT BODY. Undergraduate profile:** 60% are state residents; 26% are transfers. 1% Asian-American, 2% Black, 2% Hispanic, 91% White, 4% Other. Average age of undergraduates is 20.
**Freshman profile:** 2% of freshmen who took SAT scored 700 or over on verbal, 5% scored 700 or over on math; 9% scored 600 or over on verbal, 16% scored 600 or over on math; 40% scored 500 or over on verbal, 47% scored 500 or over on math; 77% scored 400 or over on verbal, 79% scored 400 or over on math; 100% scored 300 or over on verbal, 100% scored 300 or over on math. Majority of accepted applicants took SAT. 85% of freshmen come from public schools.
**Undergraduate achievement:** 72% of fall 1991 freshmen returned for fall 1992 term. 39% of entering class graduated.
**Foreign students:** 49 students are from out of the country. Countries represented include Canada, Hong Kong, Japan, Korea, and Taiwan; 11 in all.

**PROGRAMS OF STUDY. Degrees:** B.A., B.S.
**Majors:** Biology, Biology Education, Chemistry, Christian Ministries, Church Music, Communication Arts, Computer/Information Sciences, Economics/Business, Elementary Education, Engineering, History, Home Economics, Home Economics/Business, Home Economics Education, Home Economics/Social Services, Integrated Science Education, International Studies, Language Arts Education, Liberal Arts, Literature, Mathematics, Mathematics Education, Music, Music Education, Music/Religion, Physical Education, Physical Education/Religion, Psychology, Religion, Science/Business, Social Services, Social Studies Education, Sociology, Telecommunication, Writing/Literature.
**Distribution of degrees:** The majors with the highest enrollment are elementary education, economics/business, and sociology; music, history, and religion have the lowest.
**Requirements:** General education requirement.
**Special:** Courses offered in art, Bible, geography, Greek, philosophy, physics, political science, Spanish. American and Latin American studies programs. Special programs in athletic training and telecommunications. Self-designed majors. Double majors. Dual degrees. Independent study. Pass/fail grading option. Internships. Cooperative education programs. Graduate school at which undergraduates may take graduate-level courses. Preprofessional programs in law, medicine, veterinary science, pharmacy, and dentistry. 3-2 engineering program with U of Portland. Member of Christian College Consortium and Christian College Coalition. Washington Semester. Exchange programs possible. Teacher certification in elementary and secondary education. Certification in specific subject areas. Study abroad in numerous countries (different each year).
**Honors:** Honors program.
**Academic Assistance:** Nonremedial tutoring.

**ADMISSIONS. Academic basis for candidate selection** (in order of priority): Secondary school record, standardized test scores, school's recommendation, essay, class rank.
**Nonacademic basis for candidate selection:** Character and personality are emphasized. Extracurricular participation is considered.
**Requirements:** Graduation from secondary school is required; GED is not accepted. No specific distribution of secondary school units required. Conditional admission possible for applicants not meeting standard requirements. SAT or ACT is required. Campus visit and interview recommended. Off-campus interviews available with admissions and alumni representatives.
**Procedure:** Take SAT or ACT by May of 12th year. Suggest filing application by May 1. Application deadline is July 15. Notification of admission is sent on rolling basis beginning in October. Reply is required by May 1 or within three weeks if notified after May 1. $100 tuition deposit, refundable until July 1. Freshmen accepted for terms other than fall.
**Special programs:** Admission may be deferred one year. Credit and/or placement may be granted through CEEB Advanced Placement exams for scores of 3 or higher. Credit and/or placement may be granted through CLEP general and subject exams. Placement may be granted through challenge exams. Credit and placement may be granted through military experience. Early entrance/early admission program. Concurrent enrollment program.
**Transfer students:** Transfer students accepted for terms other than fall. In fall 1992, 26% of all new students were transfers into all classes. 251 transfer applications were received, 224 were accepted. Application deadline is July 15 for fall; November 15 for spring. Minimum 2.3 GPA required. Lowest course grade accepted is "C-." Maximum number of transferable credits is 96 semester hours. At least 30 semester hours must be completed at the college to receive degree.
**Admissions contact:** Randall C. Comfort, Director of Admissions. 503 538-8383, extension 234.

**FINANCIAL AID. Available aid:** Pell grants, SEOG, state scholarships and grants, school scholarships and grants, private scholarships and grants, academic merit scholarships, athletic scholarships, and aid for undergraduate foreign students. Perkins Loans (NDSL), PLUS, Stafford Loans (GSL), and SLS. Deferred payment plan. Monthly budget plan.
**Financial aid statistics:** 40% of aid is not need-based. In 1992-93, 95% of all undergraduate applicants received aid; 89% of freshman applicants. Average amounts of aid awarded freshmen: Scholarships and grants, $4,576; loans, $2,370.
**Supporting data/closing dates:** FAFSA/FAF/FFS: Accepted on rolling basis. Notification of awards on rolling basis.
**Financial aid contact:** James Jackson, Director of Financial Aid. 503 538-8383, extension 240.

## Lewis & Clark College

**Portland, OR 97219-7899** **503 768-7188**

**1994-95 Costs.** Tuition: $15,800. Room & board: $4,789.
**Enrollment.** Undergraduates: 786 men, 977 women (full-time). Freshman class: 2,774 applicants, 2,092 accepted, 482 enrolled. Graduate enrollment: 596 men, 825 women.
**Test score averages/ranges.** Range of SAT scores of middle 50%: 490-590 verbal, 520-640 math. Range of ACT scores of middle 50%: 24-28 composite.
**Faculty.** 113 full-time; 27 part-time. 96% of faculty holds doctoral degree. Student/faculty ratio: 13 to 1.
**Selectivity rating.** More competitive.

**PROFILE.** Lewis and Clark, founded in 1867, is a church-affiliated college offering programs in the liberal arts and sciences and preprofessional areas. Its 130-acre campus was developed from a private estate, six miles from downtown Portland.

**Accreditation:** NASC. Professionally accredited by the National Association of Schools of Music, the National Council for Accreditation of Teacher Education.
**Religious orientation:** Lewis & Clark College is nonsectarian; no religious requirements.
**Library:** Collections totaling over 270,000 volumes, 1,880 periodical subscriptions, and 222,000 microform items.
**Special facilities/museums:** Art gallery, observatory, world music room.
**Athletic facilities:** Gymnasium, swimming pool, squash and tennis courts, weight room, baseball, football, and softball fields.

**STUDENT BODY. Undergraduate profile:** 27% are state residents; 16% are transfers. 10% Asian-American, 2% Black, 2% Hispanic, 1% Native American, 76% White, 9% Other. Average age of undergraduates is 19.
**Freshman profile:** 4% of freshmen who took SAT scored 700 or over on verbal, 9% scored 700 or over on math; 25% scored 600 or over on verbal, 40% scored 600 or over on math; 71% scored 500 or over on verbal, 85% scored 500 or over on math; 97% scored 400 or over on verbal, 98% scored 400 or over on math; 100% scored 300 or over on verbal, 100% scored 300 or over on math. 79% of accepted applicants took SAT; 33% took ACT. 74% of freshmen come from public schools.
**Undergraduate achievement:** 77% of fall 1992 freshmen returned for fall 1993 term. 61% of entering class graduated. 25% of students who completed a degree program went on to graduate study within one year.
**Foreign students:** 23 students are from out of the country. Countries represented include India, Indonesia, Japan, Korea, United Arab Emirates, and Venezuela; 45 in all.

**PROGRAMS OF STUDY. Degrees:** B.A.
**Majors:** Art, Biochemistry, Biology, Business, Chemistry, Communications, Computer Science/Mathematics, Economics, English, Foreign Languages/Literatures, French, German, History, International Affairs, Mathematics, Music, Natural Science, Philosophy, Physics, Political Science, Psychology, Religious Studies, Sociology/Anthropology, Spanish, Theatre.
**Distribution of degrees:** The majors with the highest enrollment are international affairs, psychology, and sociology/anthropology; music, chemistry, and religious studies have the lowest.
**Requirements:** General education requirement.
**Academic regulations:** Minimum 2.0 GPA must be maintained.
**Special:** Minors offered in many majors and in computer science, East Asian studies, education, gender studies, Latin American studies, political economy, Russian/East European studies, and Western European studies. Self-designed majors. Double majors. Independent study. Pass/fail grading option. Internships. Preprofessional programs in law, medicine, veterinary science, and dentistry. 3-2 and 4-2 engineering programs with Columbia U, Oregon Graduate Inst, U of Southern California, and Washington U. Washington Semester. New York Semester. Teacher certification in secondary and special education. Certification in specific subject areas. Study abroad in Argentina, China, France (U of Strasbourg), Germany (U of Munich), Hungary, India, Japan (Kyoto U), Russia, and approximately 15 other countries. Over half of all students participate.
**Honors:** Honors program. Honor societies.
**Academic Assistance:** Remedial writing, math, and study skills. Nonremedial tutoring.

**STUDENT LIFE. Housing:** All first-year students under age 21 must live on campus unless living with family. Coed and women's dorms. Off-campus privately-owned housing. 48% of students live in college housing.
**Social atmosphere:** "Most parties are organized by dorms or floors in dorms," reports the student newspaper, "plus there are a wide variety of off-campus parties. Student musicians playing at events is extremely popular." Influential groups at the college include SOFA (Students Organized For Activities), Sigma Phi Epsilon and Sigma Alpha Epsilon fraternities, and student musicians. Popular on-campus events include outdoor music concerts, Lip Syncs, rugby and football games, intramural championships, school plays, symposia, Homecoming, and the Photosynthesis Jam. Students like to gather at The Platform and Rusty Nail (student-run restaurants on campus), the library, the lower campus gardens, Templeton College Center, Fulton Pub, Chez Jose, and Buffalo Gap.

**Services and counseling/handicapped student services:** Placement services. Health service. Counseling services for minority and older students. Birth control, personal, and psychological counseling. Career and academic guidance services. Religious counseling. Physically disabled student services. Learning disabled services. Notetaking services. Tape recorders. Tutors.

**Campus organizations:** Undergraduate student government. Student newspaper (Pioneer Log, published once/week). Literary magazine. Yearbook. Radio and TV stations. Chorale, chorus, orchestra, jazz band, drama group, forensics, outdoor program, political, social service, and special-interest groups, 60 organizations in all. One fraternity, no chapter house. 1% of men join a fraternity.

**Religious organizations:** Bahai Club, Campus Crusade for Christ, Canterbury Club, Fellowship of Christian Athletes, Havrai Student Union, Roamin' Catholics.

**Minority/foreign student organizations:** Cultural awareness group (SUACA), Black Student Union (BSU), Hawaii Club. International Student Association.

**ATHLETICS. Physical education requirements:** One semester of physical education required.

**Intercollegiate competition:** 30% of students participate. Baseball (M), basketball (M,W), cross-country (M,W), football (M), golf (M), softball (W), swimming (M,W), tennis (M,W), track (outdoor) (M,W), track and field (outdoor) (M,W), volleyball (W). Member of NAIA, Northwest Conference of Independent Colleges.

**Intramural and club sports:** 25% of students participate. Intramural badminton, basketball, softball, swimming, tennis, volleyball. Men's club Alpine skiing, crew, fencing, lacrosse, martial arts, mountain biking, rugby, sailing, soccer, ultimate frisbee, volleyball. Women's club Alpine skiing, crew, fencing, lacrosse, martial arts, mountain biking, rugby, sailing, soccer, ultimate frisbee.

**ADMISSIONS. Academic basis for candidate selection** (in order of priority): Secondary school record, class rank, standardized test scores, essay, school's recommendation.

**Nonacademic basis for candidate selection:** Character and personality, particular talent or ability, geographical distribution, and alumni/ae relationship are important. Extracurricular participation is considered.

**Requirements:** Graduation from secondary school is required; GED is accepted. No specific distribution of secondary school units required. 1 unit of fine arts recommended. SAT or ACT is required. Campus visit and interview recommended. Off-campus interviews available with admissions and alumni representatives.

**Procedure:** Take SAT or ACT by January of 12th year. SAT or ACT required of all applicants except those choosing Portfolio Path admissions option; these applicants create their own portfolio of materials that they feel best demonstrate their academic strengths. Visit college for interview by March 1 of 12th year. Suggest filing application by February 1; no deadline. Notification of admission by April 1. Reply is required by May 1. $100 nonrefundable tuition deposit. $100 nonrefundable room deposit. Freshmen accepted for terms other than fall.

**Special programs:** Admission may be deferred one year. Credit and/or placement may be granted through CEEB Advanced Placement exams for scores of 4 or higher. Placement may be granted through challenge exams. Early decision program. In fall 1993, 39 applied for early decision and 36 were accepted. Deadline for applying for early decision is November 15. Deadline for applying for early action is December 15. Concurrent enrollment program.

**Transfer students:** Transfer students accepted for terms other than fall. In fall 1993, 16% of all new students were transfers into all classes. 319 transfer applications were received, 192 were accepted. Application deadline is February 1 for fall; December 1 for spring. Minimum 2.0 GPA required. Lowest course grade accepted is "C-." Maximum number of transferable credits is 68 semester hours. At least 60 semester hours must be completed at the college to receive degree.

**Admissions contact:** Michael B. Sexton, M.A., Dean of Admissions and Student Financial Services. 503 768-7040, 800 444-4111.

**FINANCIAL AID. Available aid:** Pell grants, SEOG, state scholarships and grants, school scholarships and grants, private scholarships and grants, academic merit scholarships, and aid for undergraduate foreign students. Perkins Loans (NDSL), PLUS, Stafford Loans (GSL), state loans, private loans, and SLS. Excel Loans. Alaska state loans. AMS and family tuition reduction. Major credit cards.

**Financial aid statistics:** 9% of aid is not need-based. In 1993-94, 91% of all undergraduate applicants received aid; 92% of freshman applicants. Average amounts of aid awarded freshmen: Scholarships and grants, $9,327; loans, $3,213.

**Supporting data/closing dates:** FAFSA: Priority filing date is February 15. School's own aid application: Priority filing date is February 15. Notification of awards begins April 1.

**Financial aid contact:** Ann Coker, M.Ed., Director of Financial Aid. 503 768-7090.

**STUDENT EMPLOYMENT.** College Work/Study Program. Institutional employment. 40% of full-time undergraduates work on campus during school year. Students may expect to earn an average of $1,330 during school year. Off-campus part-time employment opportunities rated "good."

**COMPUTER FACILITIES.** 150 IBM/IBM-compatible and Macintosh/Apple microcomputers; all are networked. Students may access SUN minicomputer/mainframe systems, Internet. Residence halls may be equipped with networked microcomputers. Client/LAN operating systems include Apple/Macintosh, DOS, UNIX/XENIX/AIX, LocalTalk/AppleTalk, Novell. Computer languages and software packages include Excel, FORTRAN, LISP, Lotus, Microsoft Word, Microsoft Works, Modula 2, Pascal, Perl, Prolog, SPSS, Stella. Computer facilities are available to all students.

**Hours:** 24 hours in library and dorms.

**GRADUATE CAREER DATA.** Graduate school percentages: 3% enter law school. 4% enter medical school. 1% enter dental school. 10% enter graduate business programs. 36% enter graduate arts and sciences programs. 1% enter theological school/seminary. Highest graduate school enrollments: Columbia U, Northwestern U, Oregon Health Sciences U, UC Berkeley. 46% of graduates choose careers in business and industry. Companies and businesses that hire graduates: General Mills, Nike.

**PROMINENT ALUMNI/AE.** Doug Tunnell, CBS News correspondent; Don Bonker, former U.S. congressman; Markie Post, actress; Earl Blumenauer, city councilman, Portland; Charles Blanchard, Arizona state senator; Lewis Sharp, director, Denver Art Museum; David Stumpf, chairman, department of neurology, Northwestern U Medical School.

# Linfield College

**McMinnville, OR 97128** 503 434-2200

**1993-94 Costs.** Tuition: $12,510. Room & board: $3,970. Fees, books, misc. academic expenses (school's estimate): $790.

**Enrollment.** Undergraduates: 702 men, 886 women (full-time). Freshman class: 1,561 applicants, 1,186 accepted, 451 enrolled. Graduate enrollment: 12 men, 18 women.

**Test score averages/ranges.** Average SAT scores: 495 verbal, 556 math. Range of SAT scores of middle 50%: 440-510 verbal, 560-630 math. Average ACT scores: 25 composite. Range of ACT scores of middle 50%: 24-29 composite.

**Faculty.** 122 full-time; 11 part-time. 91% of faculty holds doctoral degree. Student/faculty ratio: 13 to 1.

**Selectivity rating.** More competitive.

**PROFILE.** Linfield, founded in 1849, is a church-affiliated, liberal arts college. Its 100-acre campus is located in McMinnville, 38 miles southwest of Portland.

**Accreditation:** NASC. Professionally accredited by the National Association of Schools of Music, the National League for Nursing.

**Religious orientation:** Linfield College is affiliated with the American Baptist Church; one semester of religion required.

**Library:** Collections totaling over 135,000 volumes, 1,029 periodical subscriptions, and 116,363 microform items.

**Special facilities/museums:** Art gallery, anthropology museum, observatory, environmental field station, research institute, electron microscope, scanning auger microprobe spectrometer.

**Athletic facilities:** Sports complex, gymnasium, handball, racquetball courts, weight room, aerobics rooms, eight-lane swimming pool, year-round track, soccer, baseball, football, intramural fields.

**STUDENT BODY. Undergraduate profile:** 63% are state residents; 15% are transfers. 4% Asian-American, 1% Black, 2% Hispanic, 1% Native American, 85% White, 7% Other. Average age of undergraduates is 21.

**Freshman profile:** 14% of freshmen who took ACT scored 30 or over on composite; 67% scored 24 or over on composite; 95% scored 18 or over on composite; 100% scored 12 or over on composite. 89% of accepted applicants took SAT; 26% took ACT. 86% of freshmen come from public schools.

**Undergraduate achievement:** 78% of fall 1992 freshmen returned for fall 1993 term. 54% of entering class graduated. 23% of students who completed a degree program immediately went on to graduate study.

**Foreign students:** 82 students are from out of the country. Countries represented include China, France, Japan, Malaysia, Nepal, and United Arab Emirates; 28 in all.

**PROGRAMS OF STUDY. Degrees:** B.A., B.S., B.S.Nurs.

**Majors:** Accounting, Applied Physics, Art, Arts Management, Athletic Training, Biology, Business Information Systems, Chemistry, Communications, Computing Science, Creative Writing, Dramatic Arts, Economics/Business, Education, Elementary/Early Childhood Education, English, Exercise Science, Finance, French, General Science, German, Health, History, Liberal Arts, Mass Communications, Mathematics, Modern Languages, Music, Nursing, Philosophy, Physical Education, Physics, Political Science, Psychology, Religious Studies, Sociology/Anthropology, Spanish, Theatre.

**Distribution of degrees:** The majors with the highest enrollment are economics/business, liberal arts, and education; religious studies, creative writing, and philosophy have the lowest.

**Requirements:** General education requirement.

**Academic regulations:** Minimum 2.0 GPA must be maintained.

**Special:** Minors offered in most majors. Linfield Research Institute offers individual research opportunities and assistantships for undergraduates in biology, chemistry, math, physics, and psychology. Self-designed majors. Double majors. Independent study. Accelerated study. Pass/fail grading option. Internships. Graduate school at which undergraduates may take graduate-level courses. Preprofessional programs in law, medicine, engineering, and pre-forestry. 3-2 engineering programs with Oregon State U, U of Southern California, U of Washington, and Washington State U. 3-2 forestry program with Oregon State U. Oregon Independent Colleges Association. January travel program. Exchange program with all American Baptist-related colleges. Teacher certification in early childhood, elementary, and secondary education. Certification in specific subject areas. Sophomores may study abroad in Austria, Costa Rica, England, France, Japan, and Korea. Language majors must spend junior year abroad. AFROTC at U of Portland.

**Honors:** Honors program.

**Academic Assistance:** Remedial writing, math, and study skills. Nonremedial tutoring.

**STUDENT LIFE. Housing:** All students under age 21 and those with fewer than 93 credits must live on campus. Coed, women's, and men's dorms. Fraternity housing. School-owned/operated apartments. 67% of students live in college housing.

**Social atmosphere:** According to the student newspaper, "Everyone is deeply involved in some activity or even two. It's as central to the 'Linfield experience' as classes and residential life are." Most influential groups are the Campus Crusade for Christ, fraternities and sororities, Amnesty International, and Linfield Students for Peace (LISP). The Nobel Laureate Symposium draws top speakers from around the globe and Linfield football always proves popular. Traditionally, athletics have played a large role in the lives of Linfield students. Other popular events are Homecoming and the "Fly-Me Dance." Students like to gather at the Sports Complex, Jake's Deli, and The Deluxe.

**Services and counseling/handicapped student services:** Placement services. Health service. Women's center. Day care. Counseling services for minority, veteran, and older students. Birth control, personal, and psychological counseling. Career and academic guidance services. Religious counseling. Learning disabled services.

**Campus organizations:** Undergraduate student government. Student newspaper (Linews, published once/week). Literary magazine. Yearbook. Radio station. Choral groups, Art Student League, Little Theatre, outdoor club, College Companions, Students for Peace, Habitat for Humanity, academic and professional groups. Four fraternities, all with chapter houses; three sororities, no chapter houses. 25% of men join a fraternity. 35% of women join a sorority.
**Religious organizations:** Campus Ministry, Fellowship of Christian Athletes, Campus Crusade for Christ, Kyrios Singers, Young Life, Newman Club, Chaplain's Interns.
**Minority/foreign student organizations:** Hawaiian club, Upward Bound, Multicultural Student Union. International Club.
**ATHLETICS. Physical education requirements:** One semester of physical education required.
**Intercollegiate competition:** 30% of students participate. Baseball (M), basketball (M,W), cheerleading (W), cross-country (M,W), football (M), golf (M), soccer (M,W), softball (W), swimming (M,W), tennis (M,W), track (M), track (outdoor) (M,W), track and field (W), volleyball (W). Member of NAIA.
**Intramural and club sports:** Intramural basketball, football, racquetball, soccer, softball, tennis, volleyball. Men's club lacrosse, waterpolo. Women's club waterpolo.
**ADMISSIONS. Academic basis for candidate selection** (in order of priority): Secondary school record, school's recommendation, essay, standardized test scores, class rank.
**Nonacademic basis for candidate selection:** Extracurricular participation and geographical distribution are emphasized. Character and personality are important. Particular talent or ability and alumni/ae relationship are considered.
**Requirements:** Graduation from secondary school is required; GED is accepted. No specific distribution of secondary school units required. Minimum 2.5 GPA required. Special program for students not normally admissible. SAT or ACT is required. Campus visit and interview recommended.
**Procedure:** Take SAT or ACT by February 6 of 12th year. Suggest filing application by February 15; no deadline. Notification of admission by April 1. Reply is required by May 1. $300 tuition deposit, refundable until May 1. $200 tuition/room deposit, refundable until May 1. Freshmen accepted for terms other than fall.
**Special programs:** Admission may be deferred one year. Credit may be granted through CEEB Advanced Placement for scores of 4 or higher. Credit may be granted through CLEP general and subject exams, challenge exams, and military and life experience. Early decision program. Deadline for applying for early decision is January 15. Early entrance/early admission program. Concurrent enrollment program.
**Transfer students:** Transfer students accepted for terms other than fall. In fall 1993, 15% of all new students were transfers into all classes. 211 transfer applications were received, 116 were accepted. Application deadline is February 15 for fall; December 1 for spring. Minimum 2.5 GPA recommended. Lowest course grade accepted is "C." Maximum number of transferable credits is 72 semester hours. At least 30 semester hours must be completed at the college to receive degree.
**Admissions contact:** John W. Reed, Dean of Enrollment Services. 503 434-2213.
**FINANCIAL AID. Available aid:** Pell grants, SEOG, state grants, school scholarships and grants, private scholarships, academic merit scholarships, and aid for undergraduate foreign students. Perkins Loans (NDSL), PLUS, Stafford Loans (GSL), school loans, private loans, and SLS. AMS and family tuition reduction. institutional payment plans.
**Financial aid statistics:** 21% of aid is not need-based. In 1993-94, 95% of all undergraduate applicants received aid; 95% of freshman applicants. Average amounts of aid awarded freshmen: Scholarships and grants, $4,917; loans, $3,000.
**Supporting data/closing dates:** FAFSA/FAF/FFS: Priority filing date is February 1. Income tax forms: Accepted on rolling basis. Notification of awards begins April 1.
**Financial aid contact:** Dan Preston, M.S., Director of Financial Aid. 503 434-2225.
**STUDENT EMPLOYMENT.** College Work/Study Program. Institutional employment. 52% of full-time undergraduates work on campus during school year. Students may expect to earn an average of $1,000 during school year. Off-campus part-time employment opportunities rated "fair."
**COMPUTER FACILITIES.** 150 IBM/IBM-compatible and Macintosh/Apple microcomputers; 50 are networked. Students may access Sequent minicomputer/mainframe systems, Internet. Residence halls may be equipped with stand-alone microcomputers. Client/LAN operating systems include Apple/Macintosh, DOS, UNIX/XENIX/AIX, LocalTalk/AppleTalk. Computer languages and software packages include Assembler, C, Modula 2, Pascal. Computer facilities are available to all students.
**Hours:** 10 AM-midn. (M-Th); 10 AM-5 PM (F); noon-5 PM (Sa); noon-midn. (Su).
**GRADUATE CAREER DATA.** Graduate school percentages: 10% enter graduate business programs. 9% enter graduate arts and sciences programs. Highest graduate school enrollments: Oregon Health Sciences U, Oregon State U, Portland State U, U of Oregon, Willamette U. 60% of graduates choose careers in business and industry. Companies and businesses that hire graduates: Arthur Andersen, Evergreen Aviation, K mart, Nissho Iwai.
**PROMINENT ALUMNI/AE.** Henry Hwang, president, Far East National Bank; Roger Eigsti, president and CEO, Safeco Corp.; Dr. Robert Dow, neurologist; Roger Utter, supreme court justice, Washington; Ronald Paul, CEO, Battelle Memorial Institute.

## Marylhurst College

**Marylhurst, OR 97036** 503 636-8141

**1994-95 Costs.** Tuition: $8,055. Housing: None. Fees, books, misc. academic expenses (school's estimate): $45.
**Enrollment.** Undergraduates: 57 men, 175 women (full-time). Freshman class: 100 applicants, 100 accepted, 100 enrolled. Graduate enrollment: 64 men, 84 women.
**Test score averages/ranges.** N/A.
**Faculty.** 18 full-time; 250 part-time. 20% of faculty holds doctoral degree. Student/faculty ratio: 14 to 1.
**Selectivity rating.** N/A.

**PROFILE.** Marylhurst, founded in 1893, is a private, liberal arts college. Founded in 1893, it adopted coeducation in 1974. Its 68-acre campus is located in Marylhurst, 10 miles from Portland.
**Accreditation:** NASC. Professionally accredited by the National Association of Schools of Music.
**Religious orientation:** Marylhurst College is affiliated with the Roman Catholic Church; no religious requirements.
**Library:** Collections totaling over 128,000 volumes, 350 periodical subscriptions, and 4,520 microform items.
**STUDENT BODY. Undergraduate profile:** 99% are state residents. 1% Asian-American, 1% Black, 1% Hispanic, 1% Native American, 96% White.
**Foreign students:** 13 students are from out of the country. Four countries represented in all.
**PROGRAMS OF STUDY. Degrees:** B.A., B.F.A., B.Mus., B.S.
**Majors:** Art, Communication, Human Studies, Humanities, Interdisciplinary Studies, Management, Music, Pastoral Ministry, Science, Social Science.
**Distribution of degrees:** The majors with the highest enrollment are management, social science, and communication.
**Requirements:** General education requirement.
**Academic regulations:** Minimum 2.00 GPA required for graduation.
**Special:** Self-designed majors. Double majors. Dual degrees. Independent study. Pass/fail grading option. Internships. Graduate school at which undergraduates may take graduate-level courses.
**Academic Assistance:** Remedial writing and math. Nonremedial tutoring.
**ADMISSIONS. Requirements:** Graduation from secondary school is required; GED is accepted. No specific distribution of secondary school units required. Open admissions policy. No off-campus interviews.
**Procedure:** Notification of admission on rolling basis. Freshmen accepted for terms other than fall.
**Special programs:** Admission may be deferred. Credit may be granted through CLEP general and subject exams, Regents College, ACT PEP, DANTES, and challenge exams, and military and life experience.
**Transfer students:** Transfer students accepted for terms other than fall. Application deadline is rolling for fall; rolling for spring. Lowest course grade accepted is "C-." Maximum number of transferable credits is 135 quarter hours. At least 45 quarter hours must be completed at the college to receive degree.
**Admissions contact:** Keith Protonentis, M.S., Registrar. 503 636-8141.
**FINANCIAL AID. Available aid:** Pell grants, SEOG, state scholarships and grants, school scholarships and grants, and private scholarships and grants. Perkins Loans (NDSL), PLUS, Stafford Loans (GSL), school loans, private loans, and SLS. Deferred payment plan.
**Financial aid statistics:** 10% of aid is not need-based. In 1993-94, 67% of all undergraduate applicants received aid; 67% of freshman applicants. Average amounts of aid awarded freshmen: Scholarships and grants, $750; loans, $3,200.
**Supporting data/closing dates:** FAFSA: Accepted on rolling basis. School's own aid application: Deadline is May 31. Income tax forms: Accepted on rolling basis. Notification of awards on rolling basis.
**Financial aid contact:** Marlena McKee-Flores, M.S., Financial Aid Director. 503 636-8141, extension 314.

## Multnomah Bible College and Biblical Seminary

**Portland, OR 97220** 503 255-0332

**1994-95 Costs.** Tuition: $6,370. Room: $1,480. Board: $1,960. Fees, books, misc. academic expenses (school's estimate): $340.
**Enrollment.** Undergraduates: 268 men, 181 women (full-time). Freshman class: 452 applicants, 335 accepted, 236 enrolled. Graduate enrollment: 108 men, 46 women.
**Test score averages/ranges.** N/A.
**Faculty.** 26 full-time; 11 part-time. 49% of faculty holds doctoral degree. Student/faculty ratio: 22 to 1.
**Selectivity rating.** N/A.

**PROFILE.** Multnomah Bible College and Biblical Seminary, founded in 1936, is a private, church-affiliated, liberal arts college and seminary. Its 17-acre campus is located in Portland.
**Accreditation:** AABC.
**Religious orientation:** Multnomah Bible College and Biblical Seminary is a nondenominational Christian school; attendance at chapel four times/week required.
**Library:** Collections totaling over 58,657 volumes, 492 periodical subscriptions, and 6,404 microform items.
**Athletic facilities:** Gymnasium, weight room, off-campus athletic club.
**STUDENT BODY. Undergraduate profile:** 90% are state residents; 38% are transfers. 2% Asian-American, 1% Hispanic, 92% White, 5% Non-resident alien. Average age of undergraduates is 25.
**Undergraduate achievement:** 52% of fall 1992 freshmen returned for fall 1993 term.
**Foreign students:** 31 students are from out of the country. 18 countries represented in all.
**PROGRAMS OF STUDY. Degrees:** B.A.Bibl.Stud., B.S.Bibl.Stud.
**Majors:** Bible, Communication Studies, Educational Ministries, Intercultural Studies, Music Ministry, Pastoral Ministry, Women's Ministries, Youth Ministry.
**Requirements:** General education requirement.
**Academic regulations:** Minimum 2.0 GPA must be maintained.
**Special:** Minors offered in all majors and in biblical languages. Associate's degrees offered. Double majors. Internships. Preprofessional programs in theology.
**ADMISSIONS. Academic basis for candidate selection** (in order of priority): Standardized test scores, secondary school record, class rank, essay, school's recommendation.

**Nonacademic basis for candidate selection:** Character and personality are emphasized. Extracurricular participation is considered.
**Requirements:** Graduation from secondary school is required; GED is accepted. No specific distribution of secondary school units required. SAT is required. No off-campus interviews.
**Procedure:** Take SAT by March of 12th year. Application deadline is July 15. Notification of admission on rolling basis. Reply is required by July 1 or within 10 days of date specified in letter of acceptance. $100 reservation deposit refundable until August 1. Freshmen accepted for terms other than fall.
**Special programs:** Admission may be deferred one year. Credit and/or placement may be granted through CEEB Advanced Placement exams for scores of 3 or higher. Credit may be granted through CLEP general and subject exams.
**Transfer students:** Transfer students accepted for terms other than fall. In fall 1993, 38% of all new students were transfers into all classes. Application deadline is July 15 for fall; November 15 for spring. Minimum 2.0 GPA required. Lowest course grade accepted is "C." Maximum number of transferable credits is 64 semester hours from a two-year school and 96 semester hours from a four-year school. At least 32 semester hours must be completed at the college to receive degree.
**Admissions contact:** Joyce L. Kehoe, M.Ed., Director of Admissions. 503 255-0332, extension 373.

**FINANCIAL AID. Available aid:** Pell grants, SEOG, school scholarships and grants, private scholarships and grants, academic merit scholarships, and aid for undergraduate foreign students. PLUS, Stafford Loans (GSL), and SLS. EFI Fund Management and family tuition reduction.
**Financial aid statistics:** 30% of aid is not need-based. In 1993-94, 94% of all undergraduate applicants received aid; 95% of freshman applicants. Average amounts of aid awarded freshmen: Scholarships and grants, $2,450; loans, $2,350.
**Supporting data/closing dates:** FAFSA: Priority filing date is April 1. School's own aid application: Priority filing date is April 1. Notification of awards begins May 1.
**Financial aid contact:** David Allen, Director of Financial Aid. 503 255-0332, extension 335.

## Northwest Christian College

**Eugene, OR 97401** **503 343-1641**

**1994-95 Costs.** Tuition: $8,550. Room & board: $3,910. Fees, books, misc. academic expenses (school's estimate): $945.
**Enrollment.** Undergraduates: 113 men, 113 women (full-time). Freshman class: 196 applicants, 140 accepted, 93 enrolled. Graduate enrollment: 23 men, 28 women.
**Test score averages/ranges.** Average SAT scores: 450 verbal, 446 math.
**Faculty.** 9 full-time; 19 part-time. 80% of faculty holds doctoral degree. Student/faculty ratio: 14 to 1.
**Selectivity rating.** Less competitive.

**PROFILE.** Northwest Christian, founded in 1895, is a private, church-affiliated, liberal arts college. Its 10-acre campus, adjacent to the University of Oregon, is located in Eugene, south of Portland.

**Accreditation:** NASC.
**Religious orientation:** Northwest Christian College is an interdenominational Christian school; no religious requirements.
**Library:** Collections totaling over 57,024 volumes, 260 periodical subscriptions and 608 microform items.
**Special facilities/museums:** Museum of African, Oriental, American Indian, and pioneer artifacts, rare book and Bible collection, Northwest and Turnbull collections.
**Athletic facilities:** Gymnasium, athletic complex, swimming pool, weight room, basketball, racquetball, squash, and tennis courts.

**STUDENT BODY. Undergraduate profile:** 98% are state residents; 40% are transfers. 3% Asian-American, 1% Black, 2% Hispanic, 1% Native American, 92% White, 1% Other. Average age of undergraduates is 21.
**Freshman profile:** 6% of freshmen who took SAT scored 600 or over on verbal, 13% scored 600 or over on math; 31% scored 500 or over on verbal, 38% scored 500 or over on math; 60% scored 400 or over on verbal, 60% scored 400 or over on math; 91% scored 300 or over on verbal, 88% scored 300 or over on math. 98% of accepted applicants took SAT; 2% took ACT.
**Undergraduate achievement:** 65% of fall 1992 freshmen returned for fall 1993 term.
**Foreign students:** 21 students are from out of the country. Countries represented include China, Japan, Korea, Norway, Taiwan, and Tibet.

**PROGRAMS OF STUDY. Degrees:** B.A., B.Chris.Minist., B.S., B.Sacred Mus., B.Theol.
**Majors:** Asian Studies, Biblical Language/Interpretation, Biblical Studies, Biology, Christian Ministry, Computer Science, Cross-Cultural Ministry, Economics, Educational Ministry, English, General Science, Geography, Germanic Languages, History, Intercultural Studies, Interdisciplinary Studies, Management Communications, Mathematics, Music Ministry, Organizational Management, Pastoral Care/Counseling, Pastoral Ministry, Philosophy, Physics, Political Science, Pre-Business, Romance Languages, Russian, Sacred Music, Speech Communication, Telecommunications/Film, Theatre Arts, Theology, Youth Ministry/Leadership.
**Requirements:** General education requirement.
**Special:** Minors offered in many majors and in anthropology, biblical archaeology, biblical languages, psychology, sociology, and youth ministry. Double majors. Dual degrees. Internships. Graduate school at which undergraduates may take graduate-level courses. Preprofessional programs in law, medicine, business, journalism, and nursing. Study abroad in Israel. ROTC at U of Oregon.
**Academic Assistance:** Remedial reading, writing, and study skills. Nonremedial tutoring.

**ADMISSIONS. Academic basis for candidate selection** (in order of priority): Secondary school record, standardized test scores, class rank, school's recommendation.
**Nonacademic basis for candidate selection:** Character and personality, extracurricular participation, and alumni/ae relationship are considered.
**Requirements:** Graduation from secondary school is required; GED is accepted. No specific distribution of secondary school units required. Minimum 2.0 GPA required. SAT or ACT is required. Campus visit and interview recommended. Off-campus interviews available with an admissions representative.
**Procedure:** Take SAT or ACT by March of 12th year. Suggest filing application by March 1; no deadline. Notification of admission on rolling basis. No set date by which applicants must accept offer. $40 nonrefundable tuition deposit. $50 nonrefundable room deposit. Freshmen accepted for terms other than fall.
**Special programs:** Admission may be deferred three years. Credit and/or placement may be granted through CEEB Advanced Placement exams for scores of 3 or higher. Credit and/or placement may be granted through CLEP general and subject exams. Credit may be granted through military experience. Early decision program. Early entrance/early admission program. Concurrent enrollment program.
**Transfer students:** Transfer students accepted for terms other than fall. In fall 1993, 40% of all new students were transfers into all classes. Minimum 2.0 GPA required. Lowest course grade accepted is "C."
**Admissions contact:** Randolph P. Jones, Director of Admissions. 503 343-1641, extension 20.

**FINANCIAL AID. Available aid:** Pell grants, SEOG, state grants, private grants, academic merit scholarships, and aid for undergraduate foreign students. Aid for students from affiliated churches and dependents of ministers and missionaries. Perkins Loans (NDSL), PLUS, Stafford Loans (GSL), and private loans. Deferred payment plan. Full-year prepayment plan (3% discount).
**Financial aid statistics:** In 1993-94, 90% of all undergraduate applicants received aid. Average amounts of aid awarded freshmen: Scholarships and grants, $2,798; loans, $2,434.
**Supporting data/closing dates:** FAFSA: Priority filing date is February. School's own aid application: Priority filing date is March 1; deadline is March 1. Notification of awards on rolling basis.
**Financial aid contact:** Carrie Lecompte, Director of Financial Aid. 503 343-1641, extension 12.

## Oregon Institute of Technology

**Klamath Falls, OR 97601-8801** **503 885-1000**

**1994-95 Costs.** Tuition: $2,904 (state residents), $8,696 (out-of-state). Room & board: $3,800. Fees, books, misc. academic expenses (school's estimate): $700.
**Enrollment.** Undergraduates: 1,344 men, 889 women (full-time). Freshman class: 890 applicants, 620 accepted, 404 enrolled.
**Test score averages/ranges.** Average SAT scores: 424 verbal, 468 math. Range of SAT scores of middle 50%: 370-460 verbal, 390-530 math.
**Faculty.** 135 full-time; 40 part-time. 19% of faculty holds doctoral degree. Student/faculty ratio: 15 to 1.
**Selectivity rating.** Less competitive.

**PROFILE.** Oregon Institute of Technology, founded in 1947, is a public institution of technology. Its 173-acre campus is located in Klamath Falls, in south-central Oregon.

**Accreditation:** NASC. Professionally accredited by the Accreditation Board for Engineering and Technology, the American Dental Association, the American Medical Association (CAHEA), the National League for Nursing.
**Religious orientation:** Oregon Institute of Technology is nonsectarian; no religious requirements.
**Library:** Collections totaling over 100,583 volumes, 6,477 periodical subscriptions, and 89,815 microform items.
**Special facilities/museums:** Historical library.
**Athletic facilities:** Gymnasium, weight room, swimming pool, track, tennis courts, intramural, softball fields.

**STUDENT BODY. Undergraduate profile:** 92% are state residents. 5% Asian-American, 2% Black, 3% Hispanic, 3% Native American, 86% White, 1% Other. Average age of undergraduates is 25.
**Freshman profile:** 2% of freshmen who took SAT scored 700 or over on math; 4% scored 600 or over on verbal, 12% scored 600 or over on math; 18% scored 500 or over on verbal, 39% scored 500 or over on math; 61% scored 400 or over on verbal, 73% scored 400 or over on math; 96% scored 300 or over on verbal, 98% scored 300 or over on math. 80% of accepted applicants took SAT; 10% took ACT.
**Undergraduate achievement:** 70% of fall 1992 freshmen returned for fall 1993 term. 40% of entering class graduated. 2% of students who completed a degree program immediately went on to graduate study.
**Foreign students:** 29 students are from out of the country. Countries represented include Canada, China, Japan, Kuwait, Saudi Arabia, and Singapore; 17 in all.

**PROGRAMS OF STUDY. Degrees:** B.S.
**Majors:** Civil Engineering Technology, Computer Systems Engineering Technology, Dental Hygiene, Electronics Engineering Technology, Industrial Management, Information Technology Management, Laser Optical Engineering Technology, Manufacturing Engineering Technology, Mechanical Engineering Technology, Medical Imaging Technology, Nursing, Software Engineering Technology, Surveying.
**Distribution of degrees:** The majors with the highest enrollment are medical imaging technology, electronics engineering technology, and civil engineering technology; dental hygiene has the lowest.
**Requirements:** General education requirement.
**Academic regulations:** Minimum 2.0 GPA must be maintained.

**Special:** Associate's degrees offered. Dual degrees. Independent study. Internships. Cooperative education programs. 2-2 business technologies and engineering technologies programs. 3-1 medical imaging technology program. Exchange programs abroad in Japan (Muroran Inst and Musashi Inst). Study abroad also in China, England, France, Germany, and Hungary.

**Honors:** Honor societies.

**Academic Assistance:** Remedial reading, writing, math, and study skills. Nonremedial tutoring.

**STUDENT LIFE. Housing:** Students may live on or off campus. Coed, women's, and men's dorms. 13% of students live in college housing.

**Social atmosphere:** According to the editor of the student newspaper, "OIT is a haven for computer nerds (diode heads) and calculator jocks. It's a tough school, and a lot of intelligent people come here." Homecoming is considered the most popular social event of the year. Students like to gather at BJ's Tavern, Abby's Pizza Parlor, and the college union.

**Services and counseling/handicapped student services:** Placement services. Health service. Counseling services for minority, veteran, and older students. Birth control, personal, and psychological counseling. Career and academic guidance services. Physically disabled student services. Learning disabled services. Notetaking services. Tape recorders. Tutors. Reader services for the blind.

**Campus organizations:** Undergraduate student government. Student newspaper (Edge, published once/week). Radio station. Band, Game Players Alliance, Outdoor Program, Sailing and Social Club, Residence Hall Association, Outlaws, 41 organizations in all. Two fraternities, no chapter houses; one sorority, no chapter house. 1% of men join a fraternity. 1% of women join a sorority.

**Religious organizations:** Christian Fellowship, Latter-Day Saints Association, Newman Club.

**Minority/foreign student organizations:** African-American Club, Native American Club. International Club.

**ATHLETICS. Physical education requirements:** None.

**Intercollegiate competition:** 3% of students participate. Basketball (M), softball (W). Member of Cascade Athletic Conference, NAIA.

**Intramural and club sports:** 20% of students participate. Intramural basketball, bicycle, flag football, softball, track and field, ultimate frisbee, volleyball, waterpolo. Men's club Alpine skiing, crew, rodeo, rugby. Women's club Alpine skiing, crew.

**ADMISSIONS. Academic basis for candidate selection** (in order of priority): Secondary school record, standardized test scores, school's recommendation, class rank.

**Requirements:** Graduation from secondary school is required; GED is accepted. 15 units and the following program of study are required: 4 units of English, 3 units of math, 2 units of science, 3 units of social studies, 1 unit of history, 2 units of electives. Minimum combined SAT score of 890 (composite ACT score of 21) and minimum 2.5 GPA required of in-state applicants. Conditional admission possible for applicants not meeting standard requirements. SAT is required; ACT may be substituted. Campus visit recommended. Off-campus interviews available with admissions and alumni representatives.

**Procedure:** Take SAT or ACT by June of 12th year. Suggest filing application by July 1. Application deadline is September 15. Notification of admission on rolling basis. No set date by which applicants must accept offer. $50 refundable room deposit. Freshmen accepted for terms other than fall.

**Special programs:** Admission may be deferred indefinitely. Credit and/or placement may be granted through CEEB Advanced Placement exams for scores of 3 or higher. Credit may be granted through CLEP subject exams, DANTES, and challenge exams. Credit and placement may be granted through ACT PEP exams and military experience. Concurrent enrollment program.

**Transfer students:** Transfer students accepted for terms other than fall. Application deadline is September 15. Minimum 2.0 GPA required. Lowest course grade accepted is "C." Maximum number of transferable credits is 108 quarter hours. At least 45 quarter hours must be completed at the institute to receive degree.

**Admissions contact:** Barbara Kratochvil, M.A., Director of Admissions. 503 885-1150.

**FINANCIAL AID. Available aid:** Pell grants, SEOG, state scholarships and grants, school scholarships and grants, private scholarships and grants, academic merit scholarships, athletic scholarships, and aid for undergraduate foreign students. Perkins Loans (NDSL), PLUS, Stafford Loans (GSL), NSL, state loans, school loans, private loans, and SLS. Deferred payment plan.

**Financial aid statistics:** In 1993-94, 76% of all undergraduate applicants received aid; 60% of freshman applicants.

**Supporting data/closing dates:** FAFSA: Priority filing date is March 1; accepted on rolling basis. Notification of awards begins April 15.

**Financial aid contact:** John Huntley, M.Ed., Director of Financial Aid. 503 885-1280.

**STUDENT EMPLOYMENT.** College Work/Study Program. Institutional employment. 30% of full-time undergraduates work on campus during school year. Students may expect to earn an average of $1,000 during school year. Off-campus part-time employment opportunities rated "good."

**COMPUTER FACILITIES.** 650 IBM/IBM-compatible and Macintosh/Apple microcomputers; all are networked. Students may access Sequent minicomputer/mainframe systems. Residence halls may be equipped with networked microcomputers. Client/LAN operating systems include DOS, UNIX/XENIX/AIX. Computer languages and software packages include Ada, BASIC, C, COBOL, FORTRAN, LISP, Pascal; 200 in all. Computer facilities are available to all students.

**Hours:** 16 hours/day.

**GRADUATE CAREER DATA.** Graduate school percentages: 1% enter graduate business programs. 1% enter graduate arts and sciences programs. 70% of graduates choose careers in business and industry. Companies and businesses that hire graduates: Boeing, Hewlett-Packard, Intel, Merle West Medical Center, Microsoft, Washington State Department of Transportation.

# Pacific Northwest College of Art

**Portland, OR 97205** **503 226-4391**

**1994-95 Costs.** Tuition: $7,750. Housing: None. Fees, books, misc. academic expenses (school's estimate): $1,400.

**Enrollment.** Undergraduates: 100 men, 124 women (full-time). Freshman class: 181 applicants, 170 accepted, 103 enrolled.

**Test score averages/ranges.** N/A.

**Faculty.** 17 full-time; 21 part-time. 55% of faculty holds highest degree in specific field. Student/faculty ratio: 10 to 1.

**Selectivity rating.** Less competitive.

**PROFILE.** Pacific Northwest College of Art is a private college of the arts. The campus is located in one building in downtown Portland.

**Accreditation:** NASC. Professionally accredited by the National Association of Schools of Art and Design.

**Religious orientation:** Pacific Northwest College of Art is nonsectarian; no religious requirements.

**Library:** Collections totaling over 22,500 volumes, 82 periodical subscriptions, and 50,000 microform items.

**Special facilities/museums:** Portland art museum, type shop, darkrooms, bronze-casting foundry, variety of studios, film study center, computer lab.

**STUDENT BODY. Undergraduate profile:** 70% are state residents; 70% are transfers. 3% Asian-American, 1% Black, 2% Hispanic, 1% Native American, 85% White, 8% Other. Average age of undergraduates is 27.

**Freshman profile:** 13% of freshmen who took SAT scored 600 or over on verbal; 32% scored 500 or over on verbal, 33% scored 500 or over on math; 82% scored 400 or over on verbal, 71% scored 400 or over on math; 100% scored 300 or over on verbal, 100% scored 300 or over on math. Majority of accepted applicants took SAT.

**Undergraduate achievement:** 74% of fall 1992 freshmen returned for fall 1993 term. 16% of entering class graduated.

**Foreign students:** 17 students are from out of the country. Countries represented include Canada, Indonesia, Japan, Korea, Malaysia, and Taiwan; 10 in all.

**PROGRAMS OF STUDY. Degrees:** B.F.A.

**Majors:** Ceramics, Crafts, Drawing, Graphic Design, Illustration, Painting, Photography, Printmaking, Sculpture.

**Distribution of degrees:** The majors with the highest enrollment are painting, graphic design, and illustration; photography, ceramics, and sculpture have the lowest.

**Requirements:** General education requirement.

**Academic regulations:** Minimum 2.0 GPA must be maintained.

**Special:** Double majors. Independent study. Internships. Five-year B.A./B.F.A. program with Reed Coll. Member of Oregon Independent Colleges Association and Association of Independent Colleges of Art and Design (AICAD); exchanges available with AICAD members. Study abroad in France, Italy, or in any country with a NASAD-accredited program. Study abroad in England and Italy with Art Schools International (SACI).

**ADMISSIONS. Academic basis for candidate selection** (in order of priority): Secondary school record, essay.

**Nonacademic basis for candidate selection:** Particular talent or ability is emphasized. Extracurricular participation is important.

**Requirements:** Graduation from secondary school is required; GED is accepted. No specific distribution of secondary school units required. No specific distribution of secondary school units required. Drawing courses recommended. Portfolio required of all applicants. SAT or ACT is recommended. Campus visit and interview recommended. Off-campus interviews available with admissions and alumni representatives.

**Procedure:** Visit college for interview by March 1 of 12th year. Suggest filing application by April 1. Application deadline is August 15. Notification of admission on rolling basis. Reply is required by August 20. $100 tuition deposit, refundable until July 1. Freshmen accepted for terms other than fall.

**Special programs:** Admission may be deferred one year. Concurrent enrollment program.

**Transfer students:** Transfer students accepted for terms other than fall. In fall 1993, 70% of all new students were transfers into all classes. 121 transfer applications were received, 121 were accepted. Application deadline is August 15 for fall; December 1 for spring. Minimum 2.0 GPA required. Lowest course grade accepted is "C." At least 48 semester hours must be completed at the college to receive degree.

**Admissions contact:** Colin Page, Director of Admissions. 503 226-0462.

**FINANCIAL AID. Available aid:** Pell grants, SEOG, state grants, school grants, and academic merit scholarships. PLUS, Stafford Loans (GSL), and SLS. Deferred payment plan.

**Financial aid statistics:** 3% of aid is not need-based. In 1993-94, 98% of all undergraduate applicants received aid; 100% of freshman applicants. Average amounts of aid awarded freshmen: Scholarships and grants, $1,000; loans, $2,000.

**Supporting data/closing dates:** FAFSA: Priority filing date is April 1. School's own aid application: Priority filing date is April 1. Notification of awards begins June 22.

**Financial aid contact:** Fayne Griffiths, Director of Financial Aid. 503 266-4391.

# Pacific University

**Forest Grove, OR 97116** **503 357-6151**

**1994-95 Costs.** Tuition: $13,945. Room & board: $3,815. Fees, books, misc. academic expenses (school's estimate): $660.
**Enrollment.** Undergraduates: 368 men, 535 women (full-time). Freshman class: 943 applicants, 849 accepted, 288 enrolled. Graduate enrollment: 281.
**Test score averages/ranges.** Average SAT scores: 479 verbal, 542 math. Average ACT scores: 24 composite.
**Faculty.** 64 full-time; 56 part-time. 84% of faculty holds doctoral degree. Student/faculty ratio: 13 to 1.
**Selectivity rating.** Competitive.

**PROFILE.** Pacific University, founded in 1849, is a church-affiliated university. Programs are offered in the Colleges of Arts and Sciences and Optometry. Its 57-acre campus is located in Forest Grove, 25 miles west of Portland.

**Accreditation:** NASC. Professionally accredited by the American Optometric Association, the American Physical Therapy Association, the American Speech-Language-Hearing Association, the National Association of Schools of Music.
**Religious orientation:** Pacific University is a nondenominational Christian school; no religious requirements.
**Library:** Collections totaling over 149,700 volumes, 1,022 periodical subscriptions, and 28,307 microform items.
**Special facilities/museums:** State history museum, art museum, radio/TV production studios, media center, humanitarian center, politics/law forum, electron microscopes.
**Athletic facilities:** Athletic center, basketball, racquetball, and squash courts, field house, weight room, dance studio, saunas, wrestling facility, football field, swimming pool.

**STUDENT BODY. Undergraduate profile:** 51% are state residents; 30% are transfers. 16% Asian-American, 1% Black, 3% Hispanic, 2% Native American, 75% White, 3% Other. Average age of undergraduates is 20.
**Freshman profile:** 5% of freshmen who took SAT scored 700 or over on math; 5% scored 600 or over on verbal, 25% scored 600 or over on math; 33% scored 500 or over on verbal, 65% scored 500 or over on math; 79% scored 400 or over on verbal, 92% scored 400 or over on math; 100% scored 300 or over on verbal, 100% scored 300 or over on math. 6% of freshmen who took ACT scored 30 or over on composite; 45% scored 24 or over on composite; 99% scored 18 or over on composite; 100% scored 12 or over on composite. Majority of accepted applicants took SAT. 88% of freshmen come from public schools.
**Undergraduate achievement:** 71% of fall 1992 freshmen returned for fall 1993 term. 52% of entering class graduated.
**Foreign students:** 45 students are from out of the country. Countries represented include China, Japan, Korea, and Taiwan; 14 in all.

**PROGRAMS OF STUDY. Degrees:** B.A., B.Mus.Ed., B.S.
**Majors:** Applied Science, Art, Biology, Business Administration, Chemistry, Chinese, Communications, Computer Science, Creative Writing, Economics, Elementary Education, English, Environmental Science, Fine Arts, French, German, History, International Studies, Japanese, Journalism, Mathematics, Medical Technology, Modern Languages, Music, Occupational Therapy, Philosophy/Religion, Physical Education, Physical Therapy, Physics, Political Science, Psychology, Secondary Education, Social Work, Sociology, Spanish, Telecommunications, Theatre, Visual Science.
**Distribution of degrees:** The majors with the highest enrollment are health professions, business, and psychology; sociology, computer science, and philosophy have the lowest.
**Requirements:** General education requirement.
**Academic regulations:** Minimum 2.01 GPA must be maintained.
**Special:** Minors offered in all majors and in peace/conflict studies. Courses offered in dance, Eastern area studies, and Pacific Rim studies. Double majors. Independent study. Internships. Graduate school at which undergraduates may take graduate-level courses. Preprofessional programs in law, medicine, dentistry, optometry, and physical therapy. 3-2 engineering programs with Oregon Graduate Inst and Washington U. 3-2 applied physics program and 4-1 computer science program with Oregon Graduate Inst. 4-1 medical technology program with Oregon Health Sciences U. Member of Oregon Liberal Arts Placement Consortium and Oregon Independent College Foundation. Teacher certification in elementary and secondary education. Certification in specific subject areas. Exchange programs abroad in Austria (U of Vienna), England (U of London), France (Inst Catholique, the Sorbonne, U of Nice), Spain (U of Granada), and Wales (Trinity Coll). Study abroad also in China, Ecuador, Hong Kong, and Japan. ROTC at Portland State U.
**Honors:** Honors program. Honor societies.
**Academic Assistance:** Nonremedial tutoring.

**ADMISSIONS. Academic basis for candidate selection** (in order of priority): Secondary school record, standardized test scores, essay, school's recommendation, class rank.
**Nonacademic basis for candidate selection:** Character and personality are important. Extracurricular participation, particular talent or ability, and alumni/ae relationship are considered.
**Requirements:** Graduation from secondary school is required; GED is accepted. No specific distribution of secondary school units required. Minimum combined SAT score of 900 and minimum 3.0 GPA recommended. CBEST skills test required of education program applicants. Audition required of music program applicants. SAT is required; ACT may be substituted. ACH recommended. Campus visit and interview recommended. Off-campus interviews available with admissions and alumni representatives.
**Procedure:** Take SAT or ACT by January 31 of 12th year. Visit college for interview by March 1 of 12th year. Suggest filing application by March 1. Application deadline is June 1. Notification of admission on rolling basis. No set date by which applicants must accept offer. $200 tuition deposit, refundable until May 1. Freshmen accepted for terms other than fall.
**Special programs:** Admission may be deferred one year. Credit and/or placement may be granted through CEEB Advanced Placement exams for scores of 4 or higher. Credit and/or placement may be granted through CLEP general and subject exams. Credit and placement may be granted through challenge exams. Early entrance/early admission program.
**Transfer students:** Transfer students accepted for terms other than fall. In fall 1993, 30% of all new students were transfers into all classes. 233 transfer applications were received, 189 were accepted. Application deadline is June 1 for fall; January 5 for spring. Minimum 2.75 GPA recommended. Lowest course grade accepted is "C." At least 30 semester hours must be completed at the university to receive degree.
**Admissions contact:** Bart Howard, Dean of Admissions and Financial Aid. 800 677-6712.

**FINANCIAL AID. Available aid:** Pell grants, SEOG, state scholarships and grants, school scholarships and grants, private scholarships and grants, ROTC scholarships, and academic merit scholarships. Perkins Loans (NDSL), PLUS, Stafford Loans (GSL), Health Professions Loans, and SLS. Guaranteed tuition.
**Financial aid statistics:** In 1993-94, 90% of all undergraduate applicants received aid; 90% of freshman applicants. Average amounts of aid awarded freshmen: Scholarships and grants, $3,500; loans, $2,625.
**Supporting data/closing dates:** FAFSA: Priority filing date is March 1. Notification of awards begins March 1.
**Financial aid contact:** Ron Noborikawa, M.A., Director of Financial Aid. 503 359-2222, 800 635-0561.

# Portland State University

**Portland, OR 97207-0751** **503 725-4433**

**1993–94 Costs.** Tuition: $2,826 (state residents), $7,923 (out-of-state). Room & board: $4,365. Fees, books, misc. academic expenses (school's estimate): $750.
**Enrollment.** Undergraduates: 2,889 men, 2,879 women (full-time). Freshman class: 1,639 applicants, 1,574 accepted, 837 enrolled. Graduate enrollment: 1,916 men, 2,293 women.
**Test score averages/ranges.** Average SAT scores: 417 verbal, 481 math. Range of SAT scores of middle 50%: 350-480 verbal, 410-550 math. Average ACT scores: 22 composite. Range of ACT scores of middle 50%: 19-24 composite.
**Faculty.** 426 full-time undergraduate and graduate; 156 part-time undergraduate and graduate. 78% of faculty holds doctoral degree. Student/faculty ratio: 18 to 1.
**Selectivity rating.** Noncompetitive.

**PROFILE.** Portland State, founded in 1946, is a public, comprehensive university. Programs are offered through the College of Liberal Arts and Sciences and the Schools of Business Administration, Education, Engineering and Applied Science, Health and Physical Education, Performing Arts, Social Work, and Urban and Public Affairs. Its 49-acre urban campus is located in Portland.

**Accreditation:** NASC. Professionally accredited by the Accreditation Board for Engineering and Technology, the American Assembly of Collegiate Schools of Business, the American Speech-Language-Hearing Association, the Council on Social Work Education, the National Association of Schools of Music, the National Association of Schools of Public Affairs and Administration, the National Council for Accreditation of Teacher Education.
**Religious orientation:** Portland State University is nonsectarian; no religious requirements.
**Library:** Collections totaling over 930,693 volumes, 11,132 periodical subscriptions, and 1,919,542 microform items.
**Special facilities/museums:** Art galleries, audio-visual resources, classroom multimedia computer systems, learning lab, child development center.
**Athletic facilities:** Gymnasiums, handball, racquetball, squash, and tennis courts, swimming pool, weight room, circuit-training facility, city-owned facilities for baseball, football, golf, and track and field.

**STUDENT BODY. Undergraduate profile:** 87% are state residents; 52% are transfers. 10% Asian-American, 3% Black, 3% Hispanic, 2% Native American, 66% White, 16% Other. Average age of undergraduates is 24.
**Freshman profile:** 2% of freshmen who took SAT scored 700 or over on verbal, 2% scored 700 or over on math; 5% scored 600 or over on verbal, 14% scored 600 or over on math; 23% scored 500 or over on verbal, 43% scored 500 or over on math; 60% scored 400 or over on verbal, 79% scored 400 or over on math; 89% scored 300 or over on verbal, 98% scored 300 or over on math. 2% of freshmen who took ACT scored 30 or over on composite; 26% scored 24 or over on composite; 85% scored 18 or over on composite; 99% scored 12 or over on composite; 100% scored 6 or over on composite. Majority of accepted applicants took SAT.
**Undergraduate achievement:** 64% of fall 1992 freshmen returned for fall 1993 term. 6% of entering class graduated.

**PROGRAMS OF STUDY. Degrees:** B.A., B.Mus., B.S.
**Majors:** Accounting, Administration of Justice, Anthropology, Applied Linguistics, Art, Art/Applied Design, Art/Sculpture, Arts/Letters, Biology, Business Administration, Chemistry, Child/Family Studies, Civil Engineering, Computer Engineering, Computer Science, Economics, Electrical Engineering, English, Finance/Law, Foreign Languages, French, General Business, General Studies, Geography, Geology, German, Health Education, History, International Studies, Japanese, Management, Marketing, Mathematics, Mechanical Engineering, Music, Music Performance, Philosophy, Physics, Political Science, Psychology, Russian, Science, Social Science, Sociology, Spanish, Speech Communication, Theatre Arts.
**Distribution of degrees:** The majors with the highest enrollment are psychology, marketing, and management; physics, applied linguistics, and philosophy have the lowest.
**Requirements:** General education requirement.
**Academic regulation:** Minimum GPA required for students to remain off probation is 1.6 for 20-39 credits; 1.8 for 40-59 credits; 2.0 for 60+ credits. Minimum 2.0 GPA required for graduation.

**Special:** Minors offered in most majors and in art history, athletic training, black studies, Chinese, computer applications, graphic design, international economics, professional writing, urban studies, and women's studies. Certificate programs in black studies, Central European studies, international business studies, Hispanic and Latin American studies, Middle East studies, postbaccalaureate accounting, Teaching English as a Second Language, Teaching Japanese as a Foreign Language, urban studies, and women's studies. Participant in American Inst of Yemeni Studies. Self-designed majors. Double majors. Dual degrees. Independent study. Accelerated study. Pass/fail grading option. Internships. Cooperative education programs. Graduate school at which undergraduates may take graduate-level courses. Member of Berkeley Mathematical Sciences Research Institute, Malheur Field Station Consortium, and Western States Middle East Studies Consortium. Washington Semester. Exchange programs with Oregon State System of Higher Education and National Student Exchange Program. Teacher certification in elementary, secondary, and special education at the master's level only. Certification in specific subject areas. Study abroad in Argentina, Australia, Brazil, Chile, China, Costa Rica, Denmark, the Dominican Republic, Ecuador, France, Greece, Germany, Hungary, Italy, Japan, Mexico, South Korea, the former Soviet Republics, Spain, and the United Kingdom. ROTC. AFROTC at U of Portland.
**Honors:** Honors program. Honor societies.
**Academic Assistance:** Remedial writing, math, and study skills. Nonremedial tutoring.

**STUDENT LIFE. Housing:** Students may live on or off campus. Coed dorms. Sorority and fraternity housing. School-owned/operated apartments. Off-campus privately-owned housing. 10% of students live in college housing.
**Services and counseling/handicapped student services:** Placement services. Health service. Women's center. Day care. Counseling services for minority, military, veteran, and older students. Birth control, personal, and psychological counseling. Career and academic guidance services. Religious counseling. Physically disabled student services. Learning disabled services. Notetaking services. Tape recorders. Tutors. Reader services for the blind.
**Campus organizations:** Undergraduate student government. Student newspaper (Vanguard, published once/day). Literary magazine. Yearbook. Art exhibition committee, dance team, film/music committee, dance committee, Hawaii Student Association, outdoor program, popular music board, speakers board, Students with Disabilities Union, Women's Union Resource Center, 100 organizations in all. Five fraternities, three chapter houses; four sororities, three chapter houses. 1% of men join a fraternity. 1% of women join a sorority.
**Religious organizations:** Baptist Student Ministries, Campus Crusade for Christ, Muslim Student Association, Nichiren Shoshu Soka Gakkai, Christian World Outreach.
**Minority/foreign student organizations:** Black Cultural Affairs Board, United Indian Students in Higher Education, Association of African Students, La Raza. Organization for International Students, African, Cambodian, Chinese, Filipino, Japanese, Korean, Malaysian, Nigerian, Palestinian, and Vietnamese student groups.

**ATHLETICS. Physical education requirements:** One term of physical education required.
**Intercollegiate competition:** 10% of students participate. Baseball (M), basketball (W), cheerleading (W), cross-country (M,W), football (M), golf (M), soccer (M,W), tennis (W), track (outdoor) (M,W), track and field (outdoor) (M,W), volleyball (W), wrestling (M). Member of NCAA Division I for baseball, NCAA Division II, Pacific West Conference for basketball.
**Intramural and club sports:** 10% of students participate. Intramural basketball, bowling, fencing, handball, racquetball, skiing, soccer, softball, squash, swimming, table tennis, tennis, volleyball, water polo weight lifting. Men's club bowling, fencing, soccer, tennis, weight lifting. Women's club bowling, fencing, soccer, weight lifting.

**ADMISSIONS. Academic basis for candidate selection** (in order of priority): Secondary school record, standardized test scores.
**Requirements:** Graduation from secondary school is required; GED is accepted. 14 units and the following program of study are required: 4 units of English, 3 units of math, 2 units of science, 3 units of social studies, 2 units of academic electives. Minimum combined SAT score of 890 (composite ACT score of 21) and minimum 2.5 GPA required. EOP for applicants not normally admissible. Special Admission Program for applicants not normally admissible. SAT is required; ACT may be substituted. Campus visit and interview recommended. No off-campus interviews.
**Procedure:** Take SAT or ACT by January of 12th year. Application deadline is June 1 for fall; October 1 for winter; February 1 for spring. Notification of admission on rolling basis. Student must enroll within one calendar year or resubmit application and fee. $85-$270 refundable room deposit. Freshmen accepted for terms other than fall.
**Special programs:** Admission may be deferred one year. Credit and/or placement may be granted through CEEB Advanced Placement exams for scores of 3 or higher. Credit may be granted through CLEP general exams, challenge exams, and military experience. Credit and/or placement may be granted through CLEP subject exams. Early entrance/early admission program. Concurrent enrollment program.
**Transfer students:** Transfer students accepted for terms other than fall. In fall 1993, 52% of all new students were transfers into all classes. 2,140 transfer applications were received, 2,076 were accepted. Application deadline is June 1; October 1 for winter for fall; February 1 for spring. Minimum 2.0 GPA required of in-state transfers; 2.25 GPA required of out-of-state transfers. Lowest course grade accepted is "C." Maximum number of transferable credits is 108 quarter hours. At least 45 quarter hours must be completed at the university to receive degree.
**Admissions contact:** Jesse R. Welch, Director of Admissions. 503 725-3511.

**FINANCIAL AID. Available aid:** Pell grants, SEOG, state scholarships and grants, school scholarships and grants, private scholarships and grants, ROTC scholarships, academic merit scholarships, athletic scholarships, and aid for undergraduate foreign students. Underrepresented Minority Achievement Scholarship. Perkins Loans (NDSL), PLUS, Stafford Loans (GSL), and SLS. Deferred payment plan.
**Financial aid statistics:** 17% of aid is not need-based. In 1993-94, 83% of all undergraduate applicants received aid; 74% of freshman applicants. Average amounts of aid awarded freshmen: Scholarships and grants, $2,341; loans, $2,721.
**Supporting data/closing dates:** FAFSA: Accepted on rolling basis. School's own aid application: Accepted on rolling basis. Notification of awards on rolling basis.
**Financial aid contact:** John E. Anderson, Ph.D., Director of Financial Aid. 503 725-3461.

**STUDENT EMPLOYMENT.** College Work/Study Program. Institutional employment. 8% of full-time undergraduates work on campus during school year. Off-campus part-time employment opportunities rated "excellent."

**COMPUTER FACILITIES.** 200 IBM/IBM-compatible, Macintosh/Apple, and RISC-/UNIX-based microcomputers; 75 are networked. Students may access IBM, Sequent, SUN minicomputer/mainframe systems, BITNET, Internet. Client/LAN operating systems include Apple/Macintosh, DOS, UNIX/XENIX/AIX, X-windows, Novell. Computer languages and software packages include C, COBOL, FORTRAN, SAS, SPSS; 10 in all. Mainframe use restricted to those taking specific courses.
**Fees:** Computer fees vary.
**Hours:** 8 AM-10 PM.

**PROMINENT ALUMNI/AE.** Betty Roberts, first woman justice, Oregon Supreme Courts; Tom Trebelhorn, manager of Chicago Cubs; Lawrence Leighton Smith, music director, Louisville Symphony; A. Gary Ames, president/CEO, U.S. West Communications; John Callahan, syndicated cartoonist; Judith Hofer, president/CEO, Meier & Frank; Michael Schrunk, district attorney, Multnomah County.

# Reed College

**Portland, OR 97202** — **503 771-1112**

**1993-94 Costs.** Tuition: $19,100. Room: $2,560. Board: $2,670. Fees, books, misc. academic expenses (school's estimate): $300.
**Enrollment.** Undergraduates: 594 men, 605 women (full-time). Freshman class: 1,966 applicants, 1,436 accepted, 327 enrolled. Graduate enrollment: 7 men, 10 women.
**Test score averages/ranges.** Average SAT scores: 603 verbal, 632 math. Range of SAT scores of middle 50%: 550-660 verbal, 570-700 math. Average ACT scores: 30 composite.
**Faculty.** 105 full-time; 28 part-time. 80% of faculty holds doctoral degree. Student/faculty ratio: 9 to 1.
**Selectivity rating.** Highly competitive.

**PROFILE.** Reed, founded in 1909, is a private, multipurpose college. Programs are offered through the Divisions of the Arts; History and Social Sciences; Literature and Languages; Mathematics and Natural Sciences; and Philosophy, Education, Religion, and Psychology. Its 100-acre campus is located five miles from downtown Portland.

**Accreditation:** NASC.
**Religious orientation:** Reed College is nonsectarian; no religious requirements.
**Library:** Collections totaling over 354,995 volumes, 1,750 periodical subscriptions, and 146,179 microform items.
**Special facilities/museums:** Art gallery, studio art building, language lab, computerized music listening lab, nuclear research reactor.
**Athletic facilities:** Gymnasium, badminton, basketball, handball, racquetball, squash, tennis, and volleyball courts, weight room, swimming pool, rugby and soccer fields, martial arts room, dance studio.

**STUDENT BODY. Undergraduate profile:** 5% are state residents; 13% are transfers. 9% Asian-American, 1% Black, 4% Hispanic, 1% Native American, 76% White, 9% Other. Average age of undergraduates is 21.
**Freshman profile:** 12% of freshmen who took SAT scored 700 or over on verbal, 25% scored 700 or over on math; 60% scored 600 or over on verbal, 69% scored 600 or over on math; 90% scored 500 or over on verbal, 94% scored 500 or over on math; 100% scored 400 or over on verbal, 100% scored 400 or over on math. Majority of accepted applicants took SAT. 64% of freshmen come from public schools.
**Undergraduate achievement:** 90% of fall 1992 freshmen returned for fall 1993 term. 42% of entering class graduated. 33% of students who completed a degree program immediately went on to graduate study.
**Foreign students:** 51 students are from out of the country. Countries represented include China, India, Kenya, Korea, Pakistan, and the United Kingdom; 15 in all.

**PROGRAMS OF STUDY. Degrees:** B.A.
**Majors:** American Studies, Anthropology, Art, Biochemistry, Biology, Chemistry, Chinese Literature, Classics, Dance/Theatre, Economics, English Literature, French Literature, General Literature, German Literature, History, International Studies, Linguistics, Mathematics, Mathematics/Physics, Music, Philosophy, Physics, Political Science, Psychology, Religion, Russian Literature, Sociology, Spanish Literature, Theatre.
**Distribution of degrees:** The majors with the highest enrollment are biology, English, and history; Chinese, Spanish, and German have the lowest.
**Requirements:** General education requirement.
**Academic regulations:** Minimum 2.0 GPA required for graduation.
**Special:** Interdisciplinary study offered in many combinations of majors and in Judaic studies and medieval studies. Courses offered in creative writing, educational psychology, environmental/alternate biology, natural sciences, and Spanish. Three- and five-year programs may be arranged. Self-designed majors. Double majors. Dual degrees. Independent study. Accelerated study. Pass/fail grading option. Internships. Cooperative education programs. Preprofessional programs in medicine and veterinary science. Combined degree programs in applied physics, art, business, computer technology, electronic science, engineering, and environmental studies. Member of Pacific Northwest Independent Colleges. Exchange program with Howard U. Member of International Student Exchange Program (ISEP). Study abroad also in China, Costa Rica, France, Germany, India, Israel, Italy, former Soviet Republics, and the United Kingdom. ROTC at Portland State U.
**Honors:** Phi Beta Kappa.
**Academic Assistance:** Nonremedial tutoring.

**STUDENT LIFE. Housing:** Students may live on or off campus. Coed, women's, and men's dorms. School-owned/operated apartments. 50% of students live in college housing.
**Social atmosphere:** The Student Union, 7-11 (beer runs only), Cafe Lena, Dots, La Patisserie, and the Rimsky-Korsakov house are popular student gathering-spots. Groups with

widespread influence on Reed's social life include the Student Senate, the Lesbian, Gay, and Bisexual Student Union, the student newspaper, and student radio station. Concerts, the winter and spring formals, and the Rynn Faire weekend at the end of the school year are among the most popular on-campus events. "Portland is a great city, and Reed is the intellectual heart of the city," writes the editor of the student newspaper. "Coffeehouses abound, bringing in their wake some semblance of the form, if not the foundations, of culture."
**Services and counseling/handicapped student services:** Placement services. Health service. Women's center. Birth control, personal, and psychological counseling. Career and academic guidance services. Learning disabled services.
**Campus organizations:** Undergraduate student government. Student newspaper (Quest, published once/week). Literary magazine. Yearbook. Radio station. Choral groups, jazz band, orchestra, coffeehouse, drama workshop, community government, Educational Policy Committee, Lesbian/Gay/Bisexual Student Union, men's issues discussion group, 59 organizations in all.
**Religious organizations:** Christian Fellowship, Jewish Student Union.
**Minority/foreign student organizations:** Black Student Union, Asian House, Latino Student Union. Asian Student Union.

**ATHLETICS. Physical education requirements:** Three semesters of physical education required.
**Intercollegiate competition:** 15% of students participate.
**Intramural and club sports:** 15% of students participate. Intramural badminton, basketball, bowling, cricket, cycling, golf, handball, jogging, racquetball, rowing, sailing, softball, squash, tennis, ultimate frisbee, volleyball. Men's club basketball, crew, fencing, handball, rugby, sailing, soccer, softball, squash, ultimate frisbee, volleyball. Women's club crew, rugby, sailing, soccer, volleyball.

**ADMISSIONS. Academic basis for candidate selection** (in order of priority): Secondary school record, standardized test scores, essay, class rank, school's recommendation.
**Nonacademic basis for candidate selection:** Character and personality and alumni/ae relationship are considered.
**Requirements:** Graduation from secondary school is recommended; GED is accepted. 16 units and the following program of study are recommended: 4 units of English, 3 units of math, 2 units of science, 2 units of foreign language, 1 unit of social studies, 1 unit of history. SAT or ACT is required. ACH recommended. Campus visit and interview recommended. Off-campus interviews available with admissions and alumni representatives.
**Procedure:** Take SAT or ACT by January of 12th year. Take ACH by December of 12th year. Visit college for interview by February 1 of 12th year. Suggest filing application by December 1. Application deadline is February 1. Notification of admission by April 1. Reply is required by May 1. $300 nonrefundable tuition deposit. $100 nonrefundable room deposit. Freshmen accepted for terms other than fall.
**Special programs:** Admission may be deferred one year. Credit may be granted through CEEB Advanced Placement for scores of 4 or higher. Placement may be granted through challenge exams. Early decision program. In fall 1993, 150 applied for early decision and 107 were accepted. Deadline for applying for early decision is December 1. Early entrance/early admission program. Concurrent enrollment program.
**Transfer students:** Transfer students accepted for terms other than fall. In fall 1993, '3% of all new students were transfers into all classes. 270 transfer applications were received, 200 were accepted. Application deadline is April 1 for fall; December 1 for spring. Lowest course grade accepted is "C." At least 60 semester hours must be completed at the college to receive degree.
**Admissions contact:** Robert J. Mansueto, Dean of Admission. 503 777-7511, 800 547-4750.

**FINANCIAL AID. Available aid:** Pell grants, SEOG, school grants, and ROTC scholarships. Perkins Loans (NDSL), PLUS, Stafford Loans (GSL), school loans, and SLS. Tuition Plan Inc. and Knight Tuition Plans. Monthly Payment Plan.
**Financial aid statistics:** In 1993-94, 90% of all undergraduate applicants received aid; 73% of freshman applicants. Average amounts of aid awarded freshmen: Scholarships and grants, $12,000; loans, $2,600.
**Supporting data/closing dates:** FAFSA/FAF: Priority filing date is January 1; deadline is February 1. FFS: Priority filing date is February 1; deadline is March 1. School's own aid application: Priority filing date is January 1; deadline is February 1. Income tax forms: Priority filing date is May 1. Notification of awards begins April 1.
**Financial aid contact:** Richard Dent, Director of Financial Aid. 503 777-7223, extension 223.

**STUDENT EMPLOYMENT.** College Work/Study Program. Institutional employment. 65% of full-time undergraduates work on campus during school year. Students may expect to earn an average of $700 during school year. Off-campus part-time employment opportunities rated "good."

**COMPUTER FACILITIES.** 600 IBM/IBM-compatible and Macintosh/Apple microcomputers; all are networked. Students may access Digital, Hewlett-Packard, IBM, Sequent, SUN minicomputer/mainframe systems, Internet. Residence halls may be equipped with networked microcomputers. Client/LAN operating systems include Apple/Macintosh, LocalTalk/AppleTalk. Computer languages and software packages include Excel, Microsoft Word, Filemaker; 100 in all. Computer facilities are available to all students.
**Fees:** None.
**Hours:** 24 hours.

**GRADUATE CAREER DATA.** Graduate school percentages: 7% enter law school. 7% enter medical school. 4% enter graduate business programs. 15% enter graduate arts and sciences programs. Highest graduate school enrollments: Columbia U, Harvard U, Princeton U, Stanford U, Yale U. 12% of graduates choose careers in business and industry. Companies and businesses that hire graduates: Microsoft Corp., high-tech firms, law firms.

**PROMINENT ALUMNI/AE.** Howard Vollum, co-founder, Tectronix; Marchese Emilio Pucci, fashion designer, former member of Italian parliament; Barry Hansen, "Dr. Demento"; Robert Morris, sculptor; Gary S. Snyder, Pulitzer Prize-winning poet; Dr. Lendon Smith, pediatrician, author; J.E. Bud Clark, mayor of Portland; Barbara Ehrenreich, author.

# Southern Oregon State College

**Ashland, OR 97520** — **503 552-7672**

**1993-94 Costs.** Tuition: $2,823 (state residents), $7,812 (out-of-state). Room & board: $3,564. Fees, books, misc. academic expenses (school's estimate): $600.
**Enrollment.** Undergraduates: 1,568 men, 1,647 women (full-time). Freshman class: 1,421 applicants, 1,057 accepted, 749 enrolled. Graduate enrollment: 140 men, 213 women.
**Test score averages/ranges.** Average SAT scores: 442 verbal, 476 math. Average ACT scores: 23 English, 23 math, 25 composite.
**Faculty.** 202 full-time; 60 part-time. 78% of faculty holds highest degree in specific field. Student/faculty ratio: 18 to 1.
**Selectivity rating.** Less competitive.

**PROFILE.** Southern Oregon State, founded in 1869, is a public, multipurpose college. Programs are offered through the Schools of Business, Education and Psychology, Fine and Performing Arts, Health and Physical Education, Humanities, Nursing, Science and Mathematics, and Social Science and the Graduate School. Its 175-acre campus is located in Ashland, in southwestern Oregon.

**Accreditation:** NASC. Professionally accredited by the National Association of Schools of Music, the National Council for Accreditation of Teacher Education.
**Religious orientation:** Southern Oregon State College is nonsectarian; no religious requirements.
**Library:** Collections totaling over 265,000 volumes, 2,150 periodical subscriptions, and 650,000 microform items.
**Special facilities/museums:** Art and history museums, art galleries, on-campus preschool and kindergarten, National Guard armory, United States Wildlife Forensics Lab.
**Athletic facilities:** Gymnasiums, swimming pool, all-weather track, basketball, racquetball, and tennis courts, stadium, fitness center, dance studio, athletic fields.

**STUDENT BODY. Undergraduate profile:** 80% are state residents; 41% are transfers. 3% Asian-American, 1% Black, 3% Hispanic, 2% Native American, 91% White. Average age of undergraduates is 25.
**Freshman profile:** 90% of accepted applicants took SAT; 10% took ACT. 90% of freshmen come from public schools.
**Undergraduate achievement:** 57% of fall 1992 freshmen returned for fall 1993 term. 40% of students who completed a degree program went on to graduate study within five years.
**Foreign students:** 165 students are from out of the country. Countries represented include China, Japan, Korea, Latin American countries, and Mexico; 50 in all.

**PROGRAMS OF STUDY. Degrees:** B.A., B.F.A., B.S.
**Majors:** Accounting, Art, Biology, Business, Business/Accounting, Business Education, Business/Management, Business/Marketing, Chemistry, Chemistry/Business, Communication, Computer Science, Criminology, Economics, Elementary Education, English, General Studies, Geography, Geology, Health/Physical Education, History, Humanities, Interdisciplinary Studies, International Studies, Marketing, Mathematics, Music, Physics, Political Science, Pre-Law, Psychology, Science/Mathematics, Social Sciences, Sociology, Speech, Theatre Arts.
**Distribution of degrees:** The majors with the highest enrollment are business, social sciences, and psychology; mathematics and computer science have the lowest.
**Requirements:** General education requirement.
**Academic regulations:** Minimum 2.0 GPA must be maintained.
**Special:** Minors offered in most majors. Minors required of business majors. Associate's degrees offered. Double majors. Dual degrees. Independent study. Internships. Graduate school at which undergraduates may take graduate-level courses. Preprofessional programs in law, medicine, veterinary science, pharmacy, dentistry, optometry, chiropractic, dental hygiene, engineering, optics, physical therapy, and podiatry. Combined-degree programs in applied optics, optometry, and physical therapy with Pacific U; chiropractic program with Western States Chiropractic; dental hygiene, dental education, medical education, medical technology and nursing programs with Oregon Health Sciences U. Exchange programs with Coll of the Siskiyous and Coll of the Redwoods. Member of National Student Exchange (NSE). Teacher certification in early childhood, elementary, and secondary education. Exchange programs abroad in Mexico (U of Guanajuato) and Korea (Dankook U). Study abroad also in Europe.
**Honors:** Honors program.
**Academic Assistance:** Remedial writing and math.

**STUDENT LIFE. Housing:** All freshmen must live on campus unless living with family. Coed dorms. On-campus married-student housing. Special-interest halls, quiet halls, adult-student hall. Family housing. 25% of students live in college housing.
**Social atmosphere:** The student newspaper reports, "SOSC has an excellent Program Board that presents fine lectures and entertainment throughout the year, and a theatre and art museum on campus. Ashland has the world-class Shakespearean Festival that runs for nine months, the world-renowned Britt Music Festival each summer, and great skiing at nearby (15 miles) Mount Ashland. Many art galleries in Ashland, an 'artsy' town of about 16,000." Popular events on campus include monthly Southern Socials and Homecoming. Off campus, students frequent Omar's and The Pub.
**Services and counseling/handicapped student services:** Placement services. Health service. Women's center. Day care. Reading clinic. Counseling services for minority, military, veteran, and older students. Birth control, personal, and psychological counseling. Career and academic guidance services. Religious counseling. Physically disabled student services. Learning disabled services. Notetaking services. Tape recorders. Tutors. Reader services for the blind.
**Campus organizations:** Undergraduate student government. Student newspaper (Siskiyou, published once/week). Literary magazine. Yearbook. Radio station. Brass, concert, and swing choirs, chamber ensemble, symphony, vocal and instrumental jazz groups,

opera workshop, swimming and ski clubs, Outdoor Program (mountaineering), photography club.
**Religious organizations:** Campus Christian Ministry, Baptist Student Union, Campus Ambassadors, Campus Crusade for Christ, Newman Club.
**Minority/foreign student organizations:** Minority Student Program. International Student Club.

**ATHLETICS. Physical education requirements:** None.
**Intercollegiate competition:** 8% of students participate. Basketball (M,W), cheerleading (W), cross-country (M,W), football (M), golf (M,W), track and field (outdoor) (M,W), volleyball (W), wrestling (M). Member of Cascade Collegiate Conference, Columbia Football Association, Mount Hood League, NAIA.
**Intramural and club sports:** 25% of students participate. Intramural basketball, cross-country, rock climbing, rugby, soccer, softball, touch football, volleyball, water polo. Men's club football, golf, rock climbing, rugby, tennis, volleyball, water polo. Women's club cross-country, rock climbing, tennis, volleyball.

**ADMISSIONS. Academic basis for candidate selection** (in order of priority): Secondary school record, standardized test scores.
**Requirements:** Graduation from secondary school is required; GED is accepted. 14 units and the following program of study are required: 4 units of English, 3 units of math, 2 units of science, 3 units of social studies, 2 units of electives. Minimum combined SAT score of 900 (composite ACT score of 21) or minimum 2.75 GPA required. Additional course in math and science plus selected entrance exams required of nursing program applicants. Conditional admission possible for applicants not meeting standard requirements. SAT is required; ACT may be substituted. Campus visit and interview recommended. No off-campus interviews.
**Procedure:** Suggest filing application by June 1; no deadline. Notification of admission on rolling basis. Reply is required by registration date. $50 nonrefundable room deposit. Freshmen accepted for terms other than fall.
**Special programs:** Credit and/or placement may be granted through CEEB Advanced Placement exams for scores of 3 or higher. Credit and/or placement may be granted through CLEP general and subject exams. Early entrance/early admission program. Concurrent enrollment program.
**Transfer students:** Transfer students accepted for terms other than fall. In fall 1993, 41% of all new students were transfers into all classes. 985 transfer applications were received, 780 were accepted. Application deadline is rolling for fall; rolling for spring. Minimum 2.0 GPA required. Lowest course grade accepted is "C." Maximum number of transferable credits is 108 quarter hours. At least 45 quarter hours must be completed at the college to receive degree.
**Admissions contact:** Allen H. Blaszak, M.S., Director of Admissions. 503 552-6411.

**FINANCIAL AID. Available aid:** Pell grants, SEOG, state scholarships and grants, school scholarships, private scholarships, academic merit scholarships, athletic scholarships, and aid for undergraduate foreign students. Perkins Loans (NDSL), PLUS, Stafford Loans (GSL), NSL, state loans, school loans, private loans, and SLS. Deferred payment plan.
**Financial aid statistics:** 20% of aid is not need-based. In 1993-94, 70% of all undergraduate applicants received aid; 50% of freshman applicants. Average amounts of aid awarded freshmen: Scholarships and grants, $900; loans, $2,000.
**Supporting data/closing dates:** FAFSA: Priority filing date is February 1. Notification of awards begins in April.
**Financial aid contact:** Conney Alexander, M.S., Director of Financial Aid. 503 552-6161.

**STUDENT EMPLOYMENT.** College Work/Study Program. Institutional employment. 25% of full-time undergraduates work on campus during school year. Students may expect to earn an average of $1,100 during school year. Off-campus part-time employment opportunities rated "fair."

**COMPUTER FACILITIES.** 200 IBM/IBM-compatible and Macintosh/Apple microcomputers; 175 are networked. Students may access Digital minicomputer/mainframe systems, Internet. Client/LAN operating systems include Apple/Macintosh, DOS, OS/2, UNIX/XENIX/AIX, Windows NT, DEC, Novell. 36 major computer languages and software packages available. Computer facilities are available to all students.
**Fees:** None.
**Hours:** 8 AM-10 PM (M-F); 1 PM-5 PM (Sa-Su and holidays).

**GRADUATE CAREER DATA.** Highest graduate school enrollments: U of Oregon, other Oregon state universities. Companies and businesses that hire graduates: Retail companies, school districts, Arthur Andersen and other accounting firms.

# University of Oregon

**Eugene, OR 97403-1217** **503 346-3111**

**1994-95 Costs.** Tuition: $3,059 (state residents), $10,590 (out-of-state). Room & board: $3,800. Fees, books, misc. academic expenses (school's estimate): $570.
**Enrollment.** Undergraduates: 5,378 men, 5,736 women (full-time). Freshman class: 8,631 applicants, 7,079 accepted, 2,546 enrolled. Graduate enrollment: 1,733 men, 1,794 women.
**Test score averages/ranges.** Range of SAT scores of middle 50%: 440-570 verbal, 470-600 math.
**Faculty.** 762 full-time; 456 part-time. 80% of faculty holds doctoral degree. Student/faculty ratio: 18 to 1.
**Selectivity rating.** Competitive.

**PROFILE.** The University of Oregon, founded in 1872, is a public, comprehensive institution. Programs are offered through the Colleges of Arts and Sciences, Business Administration, Education, and Human Development and Performance and the Schools of Architecture and Allied Arts, Journalism, and Music. Its 250-acre campus is located in Eugene, south of Portland.
**Accreditation:** NASC. Professionally accredited by the Accrediting Council on Education in Journalism and Mass Communication, the American Assembly of Collegiate Schools of Business, the American Bar Association, the American Psychological Association, the American Society of Landscape Architects, the Association of American Law Schools, the Foundation for Interior Design Education Research, the National Architecture Accrediting Board, the National Association of Schools of Music, the National Association of Schools of Public Affairs and Administration, the National Council for Accreditation of Teacher Education, the National Recreation and Park Association.
**Religious orientation:** University of Oregon is nonsectarian; no religious requirements.
**Library:** Collections totaling over 2,000,000 volumes, 22,000 periodical subscriptions, and 1,700,000 microform items.
**Special facilities/museums:** Art, natural history, geology, anthropology, and law museums, research institutes, marine biology center, observatory.
**Athletic facilities:** Gymnasium, weight room, swimming pool, football, intramural, soccer, and softball fields, stadium, athletic center, basketball, racquetball, tennis, and volleyball courts, track and field complex.

**STUDENT BODY. Undergraduate profile:** 68% are state residents; 38% are transfers. 6% Asian-American, 2% Black, 3% Hispanic, 1% Native American, 72% White, 16% Other. Average age of undergraduates is 22.
**Freshman profile:** 1% of freshmen who took SAT scored 700 or over on verbal, 3% scored 700 or over on math; 11% scored 600 or over on verbal, 24% scored 600 or over on math; 43% scored 500 or over on verbal, 65% scored 500 or over on math; 85% scored 400 or over on verbal, 95% scored 400 or over on math; 99% scored 300 or over on verbal, 100% scored 300 or over on math. 97% of accepted applicants took SAT; 3% took ACT. 89% of freshmen come from public schools.
**Undergraduate achievement:** 83% of fall 1992 freshmen returned for fall 1993 term. 32% of entering class graduated.
**Foreign students:** 1,046 students are from out of the country. Countries represented include Canada, China, Indonesia, Japan, Singapore, and Taiwan; 83 in all.

**PROGRAMS OF STUDY. Degrees:** B.A., B.Arch., B.Bus.Admin., B.F.A., B.Inter.Arch., B.Land.Arch., B.Mus., B.Phys.Ed., B.S.
**Majors:** Accounting, Advertising, Anthropology, Architecture, Art History, Arts/Letters, Asian Studies, Biology, Business Statistics, Ceramics, Chemistry, Chinese, Classical Civilization, Classics, Communication Disorders, Comparative Literature, Computer Science, Dance, Decision Sciences, Economics, English, Exercise/Movement Science, Finance, Fine/Applied Arts, French, General Science, Geography, Geology, German, Greek, History, Independent Study, Interior Architecture, International Business, International Studies, Italian, Japanese, Journalism, Landscape Architecture, Latin, Linguistic Studies, Magazine Journalism, Management, Marketing, Mathematics, Metalsmithing/Jewelry, Music Composition, Music Education, Music Education/Choral, Music Education/Choral/Instrumental, Music Education/Instrumental, Music Merchandising, Music Performance/Instrumental, Music Performance/Keyboard, Music Performance/Voice, Music Theory, News/Editorial, Painting, Philosophy, Physics, Planning/Public Policy/Management, Political Science, Production/Operations Management, Psychology, Public Relations, Radio/Television, Recreation Tourism Management/Design, Religious Studies, Romance Languages, Russian, Sculpture, Sociology, Spanish, Theatre, Visual Design, Weaving.
**Distribution of degrees:** The majors with the highest enrollment are psychology, English, and finance; comparative literature, religious studies, and Italian have the lowest.
**Requirements:** General education requirement.
**Academic regulations:** Minimum 2.0 GPA must be maintained.
**Special:** Minors offered in many majors and in business administration, coaching, criminal justice, environmental studies, ethnic studies, historic preservation, leisure studies, linguistics, medieval studies, peace studies, Scandinavian, speech, and women's studies. Double majors. Independent study. Pass/fail grading option. Internships. Graduate school at which undergraduates may take graduate-level courses. Preprofessional programs in medicine, veterinary science, pharmacy, dentistry, and optometry. 3-2 engineering program with Oregon State U. Member of Western Interstate Commission for Higher Education (WICHE); exchange programs possible. Member of National Student Exchange (NSE). Teacher certification in special education. Study abroad in Australia, China, France, Germany, Italy, Japan, Mexico, the Netherlands, Norway, the former Soviet Republics, Spain, Sweden, and the United Kingdom; 35 programs in all. ROTC.
**Honors:** Phi Beta Kappa. Honors program. Honor societies.
**Academic Assistance:** Remedial reading, writing, math, and study skills. Nonremedial tutoring.

**STUDENT LIFE. Housing:** Students may live on or off campus. Coed, women's, and men's dorms. Sorority and fraternity housing. Both on-campus and off-campus married-student housing. 25% of students live in college housing.
**Social atmosphere:** According to the student newspaper, "The Greeks have a strong social network, but everyone else pretty much meets independently." Popular events include Greek Week, Student Orientation Week, and the Willamette Valley Folk Festival. Favorite off-campus spots include Guido's, Rennie's Landing, Old Taylor's, Max's, Confetti's, The Beanery, and Prince Puckler's.
**Services and counseling/handicapped student services:** Placement services. Health service. Women's center. Day care. Counseling services for minority, military, veteran, and older students. Birth control, personal, and psychological counseling. Career and academic guidance services. Physically disabled student services. Learning disabled services. Notetaking services. Tape recorders. Tutors. Reader services for the blind.
**Campus organizations:** Undergraduate student government. Student newspaper (Oregon Daily Emerald). Literary magazine. Radio station. Chorus, bands, symphony orchestra, drama group, concert dance group, debating and oratory, outdoor program, PIRG, Oregon Student Lobby, 64 organizations in all. 14 fraternities, all with chapter houses; 11 sororities, all with chapter houses. 20% of men join a fraternity. 22% of women join a sorority.
**Religious organizations:** Campus Interfaith Ministries, Jewish Student Association.
**Minority/foreign student organizations:** Asian/Pacific Island Student Union, Black Student Union, MEChA, Native American Student Union. International Student Association, Chinese, Muslim, and Singaporean student groups.

**ATHLETICS. Physical education requirements:** None.

**Intercollegiate competition:** 10% of students participate. Basketball (M,W), cheerleading (M,W), cross-country (M,W), football (M), golf (M,W), softball (W), tennis (M,W), track (outdoor) (M,W), track and field (indoor) (M), track and field (outdoor) (M,W), volleyball (W), wrestling (M). Member of NCAA Division I, NCAA Division I-A for football, Pacific 10 Conference.
**Intramural and club sports:** 43% of students participate. Intramural Alpine skiing, archery, baseball, basketball, crew, cross-country, diving, field hockey, flag football, golf, lacrosse, racquetball, soccer, softball, swimming, tennis, track and field, ultimate frisbee, volleyball, wrestling. Men's club Alpine skiing, bowling, crew, cycling, fencing, ice hockey, judo, lacrosse, ranger challenge, rugby, snowboarding, soccer, swimming, ultimate frisbee, volleyball, water polo. Women's club Alpine skiing, bowling, crew, cycling, fencing, ice hockey, judo, lacrosse, ranger challenge, rugby, snowboarding, soccer, swimming, ultimate frisbee, volleyball, water polo.
**ADMISSIONS. Academic basis for candidate selection** (in order of priority): Secondary school record, class rank, standardized test scores.
**Nonacademic basis for candidate selection:** Geographical distribution is considered.
**Requirements:** Graduation from secondary school is required; GED is accepted. 14 units and the following program of study are required: 4 units of English, 3 units of math, 2 units of science including 1 unit of lab, 3 units of social studies, 2 units of academic electives. Minimum 3.0 GPA required. Portfolio required of art program applicants. Audition required of music program applicants. Admission By Exception program for applicants not normally admissible. SAT or ACT is required. Campus visit and interview recommended. No off-campus interviews.
**Procedure:** Take SAT or ACT by January of 12th year. Application deadline is March 1. Notification of admission on rolling basis. Reply is required by May 1. $200 nonrefundable tuition deposit. $250 room deposit, refundable until July 1. Freshmen accepted for terms other than fall.
**Special programs:** Credit and/or placement may be granted through CEEB Advanced Placement exams for scores of 3 or higher. Credit may be granted through CLEP general and subject exams, DANTES and challenge exams, and military experience.
**Transfer students:** Transfer students accepted for terms other than fall. In fall 1993, 38% of all new students were transfers into all classes. 3,552 transfer applications were received, 2,480 were accepted. Application deadline is May 15 for fall; January 22 for spring. Minimum GPA required is 2.25 for residents, 2.50 for non-residents. Lowest course grade accepted is "D." SAT/ACT scores and both secondary school and college transcripts required of transfer applicants with fewer than 36 quarter hours. Maximum number of transferable credits is 108 quarter hours. At least 45 quarter hours must be completed at the university to receive degree.
**Admissions contact:** James R. Buch, M.A., Director of Admissions and Records. 503 346-3201.
**FINANCIAL AID. Available aid:** Pell grants, SEOG, state scholarships and grants, school scholarships and grants, ROTC scholarships, academic merit scholarships, and athletic scholarships. Perkins Loans (NDSL), PLUS, Stafford Loans (GSL), school loans, and SLS. Deferred payment plan.
**Financial aid statistics:** In 1993-94, 80% of all undergraduate applicants received aid; 55% of freshman applicants.
**Supporting data/closing dates:** FAFSA: Priority filing date is February 15. Notification of awards begins April 15.
**Financial aid contact:** Edmond Vignoul, Director of Financial Aid. 503 346-3211.
**STUDENT EMPLOYMENT.** College Work/Study Program. Institutional employment. 30% of full-time undergraduates work on campus during school year. Students may expect to earn an average of $1,000 during school year. Off-campus part-time employment opportunities rated "good."
**COMPUTER FACILITIES.** 1,000 IBM/IBM-compatible and Macintosh/Apple microcomputers. Students may access Digital minicomputer/mainframe systems, BITNET, Internet. Residence halls may be equipped with networked terminals. Computer languages and software packages include COBOL, FORTRAN, Pascal, SAS, SPSS; 18 in all. Computer facilities are available to all students.
**Hours:** 24 hours.

# University of Portland

**Portland, OR 97203-5798** **800 227-4568**

**1994-95 Costs.** Tuition: $12,040. Room: $1,750. Board: $2,470. Fees, books, misc. academic expenses (school's estimate): $680.
**Enrollment.** Undergraduates: 904 men, 1,137 women (full-time). Freshman class: 1,758 applicants, 1,485 accepted, 424 enrolled. Graduate enrollment: 214 men, 271 women.
**Test score averages/ranges.** Average SAT scores: 474 verbal, 527 math. Range of SAT scores of middle 50%: 450-499 verbal, 500-549 math.
**Faculty.** 127 full-time; 73 part-time. 90% of faculty holds doctoral degree. Student/faculty ratio: 17 to 1.
**Selectivity rating.** Competitive.

**PROFILE.** The University of Portland, founded in 1901, is a private, church-affiliated institution. Programs are offered through the College of Arts and Sciences; the Schools of Business Administration, Education, Engineering, and Nursing; and the Graduate School. Its 92-acre is located four miles from downtown Portland.
**Accreditation:** NASC. Professionally accredited by the Accreditation Board for Engineering and Technology, the American Assembly of Collegiate Schools of Business, the National League for Nursing.
**Religious orientation:** University of Portland is affiliated with the Roman Catholic Church (Congregation of the Holy Cross); three semesters of theology required.
**Library:** Collections totaling over 320,000 volumes, 1,500 periodical subscriptions, and 220,200 microform items.
**Special facilities/museums:** Art gallery, observatory.
**Athletic facilities:** Gymnasiums, swimming pool, weight rooms, tennis courts, athletic fields.
**STUDENT BODY. Undergraduate profile:** 55% are state residents; 32% are transfers. 7% Asian-American, 2% Black, 2% Hispanic, 1% Native American, 76% White, 12% Other. Average age of undergraduates is 19.
**Freshman profile:** 3% of freshmen who took SAT scored 700 or over on math; 8% scored 600 or over on verbal, 18% scored 600 or over on math; 34% scored 500 or over on verbal, 62% scored 500 or over on math; 77% scored 400 or over on verbal, 87% scored 400 or over on math; 92% scored 300 or over on verbal, 92% scored 300 or over on math. Majority of accepted applicants took SAT. 60% of freshmen come from public schools.
**Undergraduate achievement:** 76% of fall 1992 freshmen returned for fall 1993 term. 56% of entering class graduated.
**Foreign students:** 275 students are from out of the country. Countries represented include Canada, Indonesia, Japan, Saudi Arabia, Singapore, and Vietnam; 47 in all.
**PROGRAMS OF STUDY. Degrees:** B.A., B.A.Elem.Ed., B.A.Sec.Ed., B.Bus.Admin., B.Mus., B.Mus.Ed., B.S., B.S.Civil Eng., B.S.Elec.Eng., B.S.Eng.Mgmt., B.S.Eng.Sci., B.S.Mech.Eng., B.S.Nurs.
**Majors:** Accounting, Allied Health Science, Biology, Chemistry, Civil Engineering, Communications, Communications Management, Computer Applications Management, Com- puter Engineering, Computer Science, Drama, Electrical Engineering, Elementary Education, Engineering Chemistry, Engineering Management, Engineering Science, English, Finance, Health Care Management, History, Interdisciplinary Studies, Journalism, Management, Marketing, Mathematics, Mechanical Engineering, Modern Languages, Music, Music Education, Music Merchandising/Management, Nursing, Philosophy, Physics, Political Science, Pre-Law, Pre-Medicine, Psychology, Science Communication, Secondary Education, Social Service, Society/Justice, Sociology, Theatre Management, Theology.
**Distribution of degrees:** The majors with the highest enrollment are nursing, electrical engineering, and communications; music, science communication, and theatre management have the lowest.
**Requirements:** General education requirement.
**Academic regulations:** Minimum 2.0 GPA must be maintained.
**Special:** Minors offered in some majors and in fine arts, gerontology, Japan studies, and peace studies. Courses offered in religious education. Self-designed majors. Double majors. Dual degrees. Independent study. Internships. Graduate school at which undergraduates may take graduate-level courses. Preprofessional programs in law, medicine, pharmacy, dentistry, optometry, and physical therapy. Teacher certification in early childhood, elementary, secondary, and special education. Study abroad in Austria, England, France, Japan, and Spain. ROTC and AFROTC.
**Honors:** Honors program. Honor societies.
**Academic Assistance:** Nonremedial tutoring.
**STUDENT LIFE. Housing:** Students may live on or off campus. Coed, women's, and men's dorms. 62% of students live in college housing.
**Services and counseling/handicapped student services:** Placement services. Health service. Counseling services for minority, military, and older students. Personal and psychological counseling. Career and academic guidance services. Religious counseling.
**Campus organizations:** Undergraduate student government. Student newspaper (Beacon, published once/week). Literary magazine. Yearbook. Radio station. Musical and drama groups, Cultural Arts Board, outdoor education program, ski club, theatre groups, Community Action Program, Circle K, Volunteer Services, Women in Communications, Society of Women Engineers, 35 organizations in all. Three fraternities, no chapter houses; three sororities, one chapter house. 7% of men join a fraternity. 10% of women join a sorority.
**Religious organizations:** Campus Crusade for Christ, Campus Ministry.
**Minority/foreign student organizations:** Hawaiian Club. International Student Association, Chinese and Vietnamese groups.
**ATHLETICS. Physical education requirements:** None.
**Intercollegiate competition:** 10% of students participate. Baseball (M), basketball (M,W), cheerleading (W), cross-country (M,W), golf (M), soccer (M,W), tennis (M,W), track (outdoor) (M,W), track and field (indoor) (M,W), track and field (outdoor) (M,W), volleyball (W). Member of NCAA Division I, Pacific 10 Conference, West Coast Conference.
**Intramural and club sports:** 70% of students participate. Men's club rugby. Women's club rugby.
**ADMISSIONS. Academic basis for candidate selection** (in order of priority): Secondary school record, standardized test scores, school's recommendation, class rank, essay.
**Nonacademic basis for candidate selection:** Character and personality, extracurricular participation, particular talent or ability, geographical distribution, and alumni/ae relationship are emphasized.
**Requirements:** Graduation from secondary school is required; GED is accepted. 18 units and the following program of study are required: 4 units of English, 3 units of math, 2 units of science including 1 unit of lab, 2 units of foreign language, 3 units of social studies, 3 units of history. Minimum combined SAT score of 800 or minimum 2.6 GPA required. Minimum combined SAT score of 900 required of engineering, math, and science program applicants. SAT or ACT is required. Campus visit recommended. No off-campus interviews.
**Procedure:** Take SAT or ACT by December of 12th year. Suggest filing application by March 1. Application deadline is July 31. Notification of admission on rolling basis. No set date by which applicants must accept offer. $100 room deposit, refundable until June 1. Freshmen accepted for terms other than fall.
**Special programs:** Admission may be deferred one year. Credit may be granted through CEEB Advanced Placement for scores of 3 or higher. Placement may be granted through challenge exams.
**Transfer students:** Transfer students accepted for terms other than fall. In fall 1993, 32% of all new students were transfers into all classes. 661 transfer applications were received, 444 were accepted. Application deadline is July 31 for fall; December 15 for spring. Minimum 2.5 GPA required. Lowest course grade accepted is "C." Maximum number of transferable credits is 75 semester hours. At least 30 semester hours must be completed at the university to receive degree.
**Admissions contact:** Daniel B. Reilly, M.A., Director of Admissions. 503 283-7147.

**FINANCIAL AID. Available aid:** Pell grants, SEOG, state scholarships and grants, school scholarships and grants, private scholarships and grants, ROTC scholarships, academic merit scholarships, and athletic scholarships. Perkins Loans (NDSL), PLUS, Stafford Loans (GSL), NSL, private loans, and SLS. Knight Tuition Plans and deferred payment plan.
**Financial aid statistics:** In 1993-94, 80% of all undergraduate applicants received aid; 80% of freshman applicants. Average amounts of aid awarded freshmen: Scholarships and grants, $4,600; loans, $3,400.
**Supporting data/closing dates:** FAFSA: Priority filing date is March 15. School's own aid application: Priority filing date is March 15. Notification of awards begins April 10.
**Financial aid contact:** Rita Lambert, Director of Financial Aid. 503 283-7311.
**STUDENT EMPLOYMENT.** College Work/Study Program. Institutional employment. 39% of full-time undergraduates work on campus during school year. Students may expect to earn an average of $1,300 during school year. Off-campus part-time employment opportunities rated "good."
**COMPUTER FACILITIES.** 120 IBM/IBM-compatible and Macintosh/Apple microcomputers; all are networked. Students may access Digital minicomputer/mainframe systems. Client/LAN operating systems include Apple/Macintosh. Computer languages and software packages include Ada, Automata, C, Formal, FORTRAN, LISP, Pascal, Prolog, Smalltalk; artificial intelligence, data management, graphics, spreadsheet, statistical analysis, word processing programs. Computer facilities are available to all students.
**Hours:** 8 AM-11 PM.
**GRADUATE CAREER DATA.** Highest graduate school enrollments: Georgetown U, UC Berkeley, U of Notre Dame, U of Oregon, U of Washington. Companies and businesses that hire graduates: Arthur Andersen, Boeing, Good Samaritan Hospital, Nike, Xerox.
**PROMINENT ALUMNI/AE.** Ken Dayley, baseball pitcher, Toronto Blue Jays; John Emrick, CEO, Norm Thompson; Jack O'Neill, president, O'Neill Sportswear; Larry LaRocco, U.S. congressman, Idaho.

## Warner Pacific College

**Portland, OR 97215** — **503 775-4366**

**1994-95 Costs.** Tuition: $7,980. Room & board: $4,000. Fees, books, misc. academic expenses (school's estimate): $582.
**Enrollment.** Undergraduates: 198 men, 320 women (full-time). Freshman class: 112 applicants, 87 accepted, 53 enrolled. Graduate enrollment: 10 men, 1 women.
**Test score averages/ranges.** Average SAT scores: 415 verbal, 460 math. Range of SAT scores of middle 50%: 380-440 verbal, 380-530 math. Average ACT scores: 21 composite. Range of ACT scores of middle 50%: 20-22 composite.
**Faculty.** 33 full-time; 24 part-time. 41% of faculty holds doctoral degree. Student/faculty ratio: 15 to 1.
**Selectivity rating.** Less competitive.

**PROFILE.** Warner Pacific, founded in 1937, is a church-affiliated, liberal arts college. Its campus is located in Portland.
**Accreditation:** NASC.
**Religious orientation:** Warner Pacific College is affiliated with the Church of God; three semesters of religion required.
**Library:** Collections totaling over 42,210 volumes, 233 periodical subscriptions, and 1,195 microform items.
**Special facilities/museums:** Early learning center, electron microscopes.
**STUDENT BODY. Undergraduate profile:** 74% are state residents; 66% are transfers. 3% Asian-American, 3% Black, 1% Hispanic, 1% Native American, 83% White, 9% Other. Average age of undergraduates is 27.
**Freshman profile:** 7% of freshmen who took SAT scored 600 or over on verbal, 4% scored 600 or over on math; 14% scored 500 or over on verbal, 43% scored 500 or over on math; 64% scored 400 or over on verbal, 72% scored 400 or over on math; 89% scored 300 or over on verbal, 93% scored 300 or over on math. 10% of freshmen who took ACT scored 24 or over on composite; 80% scored 18 or over on composite; 100% scored 12 or over on composite. Majority of accepted applicants took SAT. 78% of freshmen come from public schools.
**Undergraduate achievement:** 79% of fall 1992 freshmen returned for fall 1993 term. 12% of entering class graduated.
**Foreign students:** 50 students are from out of the country. Countries represented include Canada, Hong Kong, Japan, Korea, Lebanon, and the former Soviet Republics; 11 in all.
**PROGRAMS OF STUDY. Degrees:** B.A., B.S.
**Majors:** American Studies, Biological Science, Business Administration, English, General Science, Health/Recreational Ministry, History, Human Development, Mathematics, Music Education, Music Ministry, Music Studies, Music Theory/Composition, Physical Education, Physical Science, Religion, Social Science, Sociology/Social Work.
**Distribution of degrees:** The majors with the highest enrollment are business administration, human development, and music education; mathematics and history have the lowest.
**Requirements:** General education requirement.
**Academic regulations:** Minimum 2.0 GPA must be maintained.
**Special:** Minors offered in most majors. Associate's degrees offered. Self-designed majors. Double majors. Independent study. Pass/fail grading option. Internships. Cooperative education programs. Graduate school at which undergraduates may take graduate-level courses. Preprofessional programs in medicine, veterinary science, pharmacy, dentistry, and theology. 3-2 nursing program with Linfield Coll. Member of Christian College Coalition and Oregon Independent College Coalition; exchange possible. Washington Semester. Hollywood semester. Exchange possible with Au Sable Inst of Environmental Studies (Michigan). Teacher certification in early childhood, elementary, and secondary education. Exchange programs abroad in Canada (Trinity Western U), England (Oxford U), and Ireland (Queens U). Study abroad also in Costa Rica, Egypt, Honduras, the former Soviet Republics, and the Ukraine. ROTC and AFROTC at Portland State U and U of Portland.
**Honors:** Honors program.
**Academic Assistance:** Nonremedial tutoring.
**ADMISSIONS. Academic basis for candidate selection** (in order of priority): Secondary school record, standardized test scores, class rank, essay.
**Nonacademic basis for candidate selection:** Character and personality are emphasized. Extracurricular participation and particular talent or ability are considered.
**Requirements:** Graduation from secondary school is required; GED is accepted. No specific distribution of secondary school units required. Minimum combined SAT score of 800 (composite ACT score of 20) and minimum 2.0 GPA required. Audition required of music program applicants. Conditional admission possible for applicants not meeting standard requirements. SAT is required; ACT may be substituted. ACH recommended. Campus visit and interview recommended. Off-campus interviews available with an admissions representative.
**Procedure:** Take SAT or ACT by June of 12th year. Visit college for interview by June of 12th year. Suggest filing application by June 1; no deadline. Notification of admission on rolling basis. Reply is recommended by June 1. Room deposit is fifty-percent refundable before August 1. Freshmen accepted for terms other than fall.
**Special programs:** Credit may be granted through CEEB Advanced Placement. Credit and/or placement may be granted through CLEP general and subject exams. Credit and placement may be granted through Regents College, ACT PEP, and challenge exams and military and life experience. Early decision program. Deadline for applying for early decision is December 15.
**Transfer students:** Transfer students accepted for terms other than fall. In fall 1993, 66% of all new students were transfers into all classes. 174 transfer applications were received, 140 were accepted. Minimum 2.0 GPA required. Lowest course grade accepted is "C." Maximum number of transferable credits is 72 semester hours. No limit on transferable credit hours from four-year institution. At least 30 credit hours must be completed at the college to receive degree.
**Admissions contact:** John Barber, M.A., Director of Admissions. 503 775-4366, extension 491, 800 582-7885.
**FINANCIAL AID. Available aid:** Pell grants, SEOG, state scholarships and grants, school scholarships and grants, private scholarships, academic merit scholarships, and aid for undergraduate foreign students. Perkins Loans (NDSL), PLUS, Stafford Loans (GSL), school loans, private loans, and SLS.
**Financial aid statistics:** In 1993-94, 75% of all undergraduate applicants received aid; 70% of freshman applicants. Average amounts of aid awarded freshmen: Scholarships and grants, $3,252; loans, $3,034.
**Supporting data/closing dates:** FAFSA/FAF/FFS: Priority filing date is May 1. School's own aid application: Priority filing date is May 1. Notification of awards on rolling basis.
**Financial aid contact:** Rick Weems, Director of Financial Aid. 503 775-4366, extension 541.

## Western Baptist College

**Salem, OR 97301-9392** — **503 581-8600**

**1994-95 Costs.** Tuition: $9,200. Room & board: $4,000. Fees, books, misc. academic expenses (school's estimate): $800.
**Enrollment.** Undergraduates: 229 men, 284 women (full-time). Freshman class: 263 applicants, 216 accepted, 121 enrolled.
**Test score averages/ranges.** Average SAT scores: 404 verbal, 429 math. Range of SAT scores of middle 50%: 400-500 verbal, 380-530 math.
**Faculty.** 23 full-time; 24 part-time. 19% of faculty holds doctoral degree. Student/faculty ratio: 15 to 1.
**Selectivity rating.** Competitive.

**PROFILE.** Western Baptist is a church-affiliated college. Founded in 1935 in Arizona, it moved to California before acquiring its present campus in 1969. The 100-acre campus is located in Salem, 45 miles south of Portland.
**Accreditation:** AABC, NASC.
**Religious orientation:** Western Baptist College is affiliated with the Baptist Church; 30 credit hours of religion/theology required.
**Library:** Collections totaling over 61,531 volumes, and 3,118 microform items.
**Athletic facilities:** Gymnasium, athletic fields, sports center.
**STUDENT BODY. Undergraduate profile:** 59% are state residents; 41% are transfers. 2% Asian-American, 1% Black, 2% Hispanic, 1% Native American, 92% White, 2% Other. Average age of undergraduates is 24.
**Freshman profile:** 4% of freshmen who took SAT scored 600 or over on verbal, 6% scored 600 or over on math; 18% scored 500 or over on verbal, 38% scored 500 or over on math; 62% scored 400 or over on verbal, 74% scored 400 or over on math; 93% scored 300 or over on verbal, 95% scored 300 or over on math. 90% of accepted applicants took SAT; 10% took ACT. 65% of freshmen come from public schools.
**Undergraduate achievement:** 56% of fall 1992 freshmen returned for fall 1993 term. 35% of entering class graduated.
**Foreign students:** Five students are from out of the country. Countries represented include Japan; four in all.
**PROGRAMS OF STUDY. Degrees:** B.A., B.S., B.Theol.
**Majors:** Accounting, Biblical Studies, Business Education, Elementary Education, English/Humanities, Family Studies, Finance, Intercultural Studies/Missions, Interdisciplinary Studies, Language Arts, Liberal Studies, Management, Management/Communication, Music, Music Education, Pastoral/Youth Ministries, Physical Education, Pre-Law, Psychology, Recreation/Leisure Services, Secondary Education, Social Science, Social Studies, Youth Work.
**Distribution of degrees:** The majors with the highest enrollment are education, psychology, and management; social science, finance, and biblical studies have the lowest.
**Requirements:** General education requirement.
**Academic regulations:** Minimum 2.0 GPA must be maintained.

**Special:** Minors offered. Associate's degrees offered. Double majors. Accelerated study. Internships. Preprofessional programs in law and theology. 3-3 biblical/theological studies program. Washington Semester. Other semester-away programs available. Teacher certification in elementary and secondary education. Certification in specific subject areas. Study abroad in Israel and Latin America. ROTC at Western Oregon State Coll. AFROTC at Oregon State U.
**Honors:** Honors program. Honor societies.
**Academic Assistance:** Nonremedial tutoring.

**ADMISSIONS. Academic basis for candidate selection** (in order of priority): Secondary school record, essay, standardized test scores, class rank, school's recommendation.
**Nonacademic basis for candidate selection:** Character and personality are emphasized. Extracurricular participation and particular talent or ability are considered.
**Requirements:** Graduation from secondary school is required; GED is accepted. No specific distribution of secondary school units required. Minimum 2.5 GPA required. Conditional admission possible for applicants not meeting standard requirements. SAT is required; ACT may be substituted. Campus visit and interview recommended. Off-campus interviews available with an admissions representative.
**Procedure:** Take SAT or ACT by July 1 of 12th year. Suggest filing application by March 1. Application deadline is August 15. Notification of admission on rolling basis. $150 tuition deposit, refundable until June 1. $100 room deposit, refundable until June 1. Freshmen accepted for terms other than fall.
**Special programs:** Admission may be deferred one year. Credit and/or placement may be granted through CEEB Advanced Placement exams for scores of 3 or higher. Credit and/or placement may be granted through CLEP general and subject exams. Credit and placement may be granted through DANTES and challenge exams, and military and life experience.
**Transfer students:** Transfer students accepted for terms other than fall. In fall 1993, 41% of all new students were transfers into all classes. 153 transfer applications were received, 110 were accepted. Application deadline is rolling for fall; rolling for spring. Minimum 2.0 GPA required. Lowest course grade accepted is "C." Maximum number of transferable credits is 96 semester hours. At least 32 semester hours must be completed at the college to receive degree.
**Admissions contact:** Palmer Muntz, M.Ed., Director of Admissions and Financial Aid. 503 375-7005.

**FINANCIAL AID. Available aid:** Pell grants, SEOG, state grants, school scholarships and grants, private scholarships and grants, ROTC scholarships, academic merit scholarships, and athletic scholarships. Perkins Loans (NDSL), PLUS, Stafford Loans (GSL), and SLS. Alaska state loans for Alaska residents. AMS. Prepayment discounts.
**Financial aid statistics:** 38% of aid is not need-based. In 1993-94, 99% of all undergraduate applicants received aid; 98% of freshman applicants. Average amounts of aid awarded freshmen: Scholarships and grants, $2,323; loans, $3,128.
**Supporting data/closing dates:** FAFSA: Priority filing date is February 15. School's own aid application: Priority filing date is February 15. Notification of awards on rolling basis.
**Financial aid contact:** Palmer Muntz, M.Ed., Director of Admissions and Financial Aid. 503 375-7006.

# Western Oregon State College

**Monmouth, OR 97361** **503 838-8000**

**1994-95 Costs.** Tuition: $2,790 (state residents), $7,770 (out-of-state). Room & board: $3,750. Fees, books, misc. academic expenses (school's estimate): $660.
**Enrollment.** Undergraduates: 1,523 men, 2,192 women (full-time). Freshman class: 1,438 applicants, 1,279 accepted, 695 enrolled. Graduate enrollment: 116 men, 168 women.
**Test score averages/ranges.** Average SAT scores: 429 verbal, 470 math.
**Faculty.** 131 full-time; 151 part-time. 79% of faculty holds doctoral degree. Student/faculty ratio: 30 to 1.
**Selectivity rating.** Less competitive.

**PROFILE.** Western Oregon State, founded in 1856, is a public college. Programs are offered through the Schools of Liberal Arts and Sciences and Education. Its 122-acre campus is located in Monmouth, 20 miles southwest of Salem.

**Accreditation:** NASC. Professionally accredited by the National Association of Schools of Music, the National Council for Accreditation of Teacher Education.
**Religious orientation:** Western Oregon State College is nonsectarian; no religious requirements.
**Library:** Collections totaling over 186,000 volumes, 1,680 periodical subscriptions, and 70,000 microform items.
**Special facilities/museums:** Arctic museum, Alaskan artifacts, natural history museum, Oregon Policy Academy, anatomy lab.
**Athletic facilities:** Gymnasiums, track, weight and wrestling rooms, baseball, football, intramural, soccer, and softball fields, swimming pools, handball, racquetball, tennis, and volleyball courts, dance studio, archery range.

**STUDENT BODY. Undergraduate profile:** 97% are state residents; 46% are transfers. 3.9% Asian-American, .8% Black, 3.1% Hispanic, 1.3% Native American, 86.6% White, 4.3% Other. Average age of undergraduates is 21.
**Freshman profile:** 95% of accepted applicants took SAT; 5% took ACT.
**Undergraduate achievement:** 65% of fall 1992 freshmen returned for fall 1993 term. 9% of students who completed a degree program went on to graduate study within one year.
**Foreign students:** 100 students are from out of the country. Countries represented include Japan and Pacific Rim countries; 27 in all.

**PROGRAMS OF STUDY. Degrees:** B.A., B.S.
**Majors:** American Sign Language/English Interpreting, Art, Biology, Business, Chemistry, Computer Science, Corrections, Economics, Elementary Education, English, Fire Services Administration, Geography, History, Humanities, Interdisciplinary Studies, International Studies, Law Enforcement, Mathematics, Music, Natural Science, Political Science, Psychology, Public Policy/Administration, Secondary Education, Social Sciences, Sociology, Spanish, Special Education, Speech Communication, The Arts, Theatre Arts.
**Distribution of degrees:** The majors with the highest enrollment are education, business, and psychology; interdisciplinary studies and mathematics have the lowest.
**Requirements:** General education requirement.
**Academic regulations:** Minimum 2.0 GPA must be maintained.
**Special:** Teaching majors offered in bilingual/multicultural, biology, educational media, French, German, health, integrated science, language arts, basic math, physical education, reading, Spanish, special education (handicapped learner, severely handicapped learner), and social studies. Associate's degrees offered. Self-designed majors. Double majors. Dual degrees. Independent study. Pass/fail grading option. Internships. Graduate school at which undergraduates may take graduate-level courses. Preprofessional programs in law, medicine, veterinary science, dentistry, occupational therapy, and physical therapy. Member of Oregon State System of Higher Education (OSSHE). Teacher certification in early childhood, elementary, secondary, special education, and bilingual/bicultural education. Certification in specific subject areas. Exchange programs abroad in China (Shaanxi Teachers U), Germany (U of Kassel), Japan (Saitama U), Taiwan (Shih Chien Coll), Tasmania (Tasmanian Inst of Tech), and Thailand (Mahidol U). Study abroad also in Ecuador, England, France, Hungary, and Mexico. ROTC. AFROTC at Oregon State U.
**Honors:** Phi Beta Kappa. Honors program.
**Academic Assistance:** Remedial reading, writing, math, and study skills. Nonremedial tutoring.

**STUDENT LIFE. Housing:** All freshmen must live on campus. Coed dorms. School-owned/operated apartments. Both on-campus and off-campus married-student housing. 66% of students live in college housing.
**Social atmosphere:** Favorite gathering places include Rustlers Bar and Grill, Werner College Center, and the Coffee Escape. Influential student groups include the multicultural student union, student media, and athletic teams. Popular events include the NAIA Tournament and lighting of the largest living Christmas tree on a college campus.
**Services and counseling/handicapped student services:** Placement services. Health service. Day care. Counseling services for minority, military, veteran, and older students. Birth control, personal, and psychological counseling. Career and academic guidance services. Physically disabled student services. Learning disabled program/services. Notetaking services. Reader services for the blind.
**Campus organizations:** Undergraduate student government. Student newspaper (Western Star, published once/week). Literary magazine. Yearbook. TV station. Choirs, bands, theatre group, dance group, group for the hearing impaired, group for reentering students, professional, service, and social groups, 50 organizations in all.
**Religious organizations:** Baptist Student Union, Lighthouse Christian Fellowship, Campus Ambassadors, Latter-Day Saints group, Navigators, Campus Ministry.
**Minority/foreign student organizations:** Multicultural Student Union. International Student Club, Multicultural Student Union, Chinese, Japanese, and Pacific Islander groups.

**ATHLETICS. Physical education requirements:** Five quarter hours of physical education required.
**Intercollegiate competition:** 11% of students participate. Baseball (M), basketball (M,W), cheerleading (M,W), cross-country (M,W), football (M), softball (W), track (indoor) (M,W), track (outdoor) (M,W), track and field (indoor) (M,W), track and field (outdoor) (M,W), volleyball (W). Member of Cascade Collegiate Conference, Columbia Football Association, NAIA.
**Intramural and club sports:** 27% of students participate. Intramural archery, basketball, billiards, bowling, flag football, golf, racquetball, running, soccer, softball, table tennis, tennis. Women's club soccer.

**ADMISSIONS. Academic basis for candidate selection** (in order of priority): Secondary school record, standardized test scores.
**Nonacademic basis for candidate selection:** Particular talent or ability is considered.
**Requirements:** Graduation from secondary school is required; GED is accepted. 14 units and the following program of study are required: 4 units of English, 3 units of math, 2 units of science including 1 unit of lab, 2 units of social studies, 1 unit of history, 2 units of academic electives. Minimum combined SAT score of 890 (composite ACT score of 21) and minimum 2.75 GPA required. SAT is required; ACT may be substituted. PSAT is recommended. ACH required. Campus visit recommended. No off-campus interviews.
**Procedure:** Take SAT or ACT by January of 12th year. Take ACH by January of 12th year. Notification of admission on rolling basis. Reply is required by July. $50 nonrefundable room deposit. Freshmen accepted for terms other than fall.
**Special programs:** Credit and/or placement may be granted through CEEB Advanced Placement exams for scores of 3 or higher. Credit and/or placement may be granted through CLEP general and subject exams. Credit and placement may be granted through DANTES and challenge exams and military experience. Concurrent enrollment program.
**Transfer students:** Transfer students accepted for terms other than fall. In fall 1993, 46% of all new students were transfers into all classes. 1,150 transfer applications were received, 985 were accepted. Application deadline is May 15 for fall; January 15 for spring. Minimum 2.0 GPA required. Lowest course grade accepted is "D." Maximum number of transferable credits is 108 quarter hours. At least 60 quarter hours must be completed at the college to receive degree.
**Admissions contact:** Craig A. Kolins, M.S.Ed., Director of Admissions. 503 838-8211.

**FINANCIAL AID. Available aid:** Pell grants, SEOG, state scholarships and grants, school scholarships, private scholarships and grants, ROTC scholarships, and academic merit scholarships. Perkins Loans (NDSL), PLUS, Stafford Loans (GSL), state loans, school loans, private loans, and SLS. Deferred payment plan.
**Financial aid statistics:** 60% of aid is not need-based. In 1993-94, 70% of all undergraduate applicants received aid; 60% of freshman applicants.
**Supporting data/closing dates:** FAFSA: Priority filing date is March 1. Income tax forms. Notification of awards begins in mid-April.
**Financial aid contact:** Michael Cihak, Ed.D., Director of Financial Aid. 503 838-8475.

**STUDENT EMPLOYMENT.** College Work/Study Program. Institutional employment. 20% of full-time undergraduates work on campus during school year. Students may ex-

pect to earn an average of $1,050 during school year. Off-campus part-time employment opportunities rated "fair."

**COMPUTER FACILITIES.** 140 IBM/IBM-compatible and Macintosh/Apple microcomputers; all are networked. Students may access IBM minicomputer/mainframe systems, BITNET, Internet. Residence halls may be equipped with stand-alone microcomputers, networked microcomputers, modems. Client/LAN operating systems include Apple/Macintosh, DOS, Windows NT, Microsoft, Novell. Computer languages and software packages include BASIC, COBOL, FORTRAN, Lotus 1-2-3, Pascal, word processing programs. Computer facilities are available to all students.

**PROMINENT ALUMNI/AE.** Edith Green, U.S. congresswoman; Kirk Matthews, broadcaster; Michael Holland, associate superintendent, Public Instruction; Hoyt Cupp, superintendent, Oregon State Penitentiary; Marvin and Rindy Ross, musicians.

## Willamette University

**Salem, OR 97301** — **503 370-6300**

**1993-94 Costs.** Tuition: $13,575. Room & board: $4,420. Fees, books, misc. academic expenses (school's estimate): $490.

**Enrollment.** Undergraduates: 712 men, 883 women (full-time). Freshman class: 1,658 applicants, 1,314 accepted, 396 enrolled. Graduate enrollment: 429 men, 268 women.

**Test score averages/ranges.** Average SAT scores: 525 verbal, 575 math. Range of SAT scores of middle 50%: 470-580 verbal, 520-630 math. Average ACT scores: 26 composite. Range of ACT scores of middle 50%: 23-28 composite.

**Faculty.** 108 full-time; 79 part-time. 90% of faculty holds doctoral degree. Student/faculty ratio: 14 to 1.

**Selectivity rating.** Highly competitive.

**PROFILE.** Willamette, founded in 1842, is a church-affiliated university. Programs are offered through the Colleges of Law and Liberal Arts and the Graduate School of Management. Its 57-acre campus is located in the center of Salem, 45 miles south of Portland.

**Accreditation:** NASC. Professionally accredited by the American Bar Association, the Association of American Law Schools, the National Association of Schools of Music.

**Religious orientation:** Willamette University is affiliated with the United Methodist Church; no religious requirements.

**Library:** Collections totaling over 226,000 volumes, 1,395 periodical subscriptions, and 7,000 microform items.

**Special facilities/museums:** Art gallery, history museum, U.S. Senator Mark Hatfield's collected papers, herbarium, Japanese and botanical gardens, electron microscope, spectrometer, telescope.

**Athletic facilities:** Basketball, handball, racquetball, and tennis courts, baseball and football stadiums, soccer complex, all-weather track, fitness/weight training room, aquatic facilities, field house, climbing wall.

**STUDENT BODY. Undergraduate profile:** 55% are state residents; 24% are transfers. 6% Asian-American, 3% Black, 2% Hispanic, 1% Native American, 88% White. Average age of undergraduates is 20.

**Freshman profile:** 2% of freshmen who took SAT scored 700 or over on verbal, 9% scored 700 or over on math; 20% scored 600 or over on verbal, 42% scored 600 or over on math; 62% scored 500 or over on verbal, 82% scored 500 or over on math; 96% scored 400 or over on verbal, 100% scored 400 or over on math; 100% scored 300 or over on verbal. 15% of freshmen who took ACT scored 30 or over on composite; 71% scored 24 or over on composite; 100% scored 18 or over on composite. Majority of accepted applicants took SAT. 90% of freshmen come from public schools.

**Undergraduate achievement:** 88% of fall 1992 freshmen returned for fall 1993 term. 70% of entering class graduated. 30% of students who completed a degree program immediately went on to graduate study.

**Foreign students:** 51 students are from out of the country. Countries represented include Canada, India, Indonesia, and Japan; 22 in all.

**PROGRAMS OF STUDY. Degrees:** B.A., B.Mus.Ed., B.Mus.Perf., B.Mus.Ther., B.S.

**Majors:** American Studies, Art, Asian Studies, Biology, British Studies, Business Economics, Chemistry, Computer Science, Economics, English, Environmental Science, French, French Studies, German, German Studies, Hispanic Studies, History, Humanities, International Studies, Mathematics, Music, Music Education, Music Performance, Music Therapy, Philosophy, Physical Education, Physics, Political Science, Psychology, Religious Studies, Sociology/Anthropology, Soviet Studies, Spanish, Speech, Theatre.

**Distribution of degrees:** The majors with the highest enrollment are economics, psychology, and politics; American studies, music, and theatre have the lowest.

**Requirements:** General education requirement.

**Academic regulations:** Minimum 2.0 GPA must be maintained.

**Special:** Minors offered in all majors and in classics, earth science, East Asian studies, Japanese, Russian, sociology, and women's studies. Double majors. Dual degrees. Independent study. Accelerated study. Pass/fail grading option. Internships. Graduate school at which undergraduates may take graduate-level courses. Preprofessional programs in law, medicine, veterinary science, dentistry, and physical therapy. 3-2 computer science programs with Oregon Graduate Center and U of Oregon. 3-2 forestry and environmental studies program with Duke U. 3-2 engineering programs with Columbia U, U of Southern California, and Washington U. 4-2 engineering program with Columbia U, U of Southern California, and Washington U. Washington Semester, UN Semester, and Sea Semester. Teacher certification in elementary and secondary education. Certification in specific subject areas. Exchange program abroad in Japan (Tokyo International U). Study abroad also in China, Ecuador, England, France, Germany, Korea, Spain, and Ukraine.

**Honors:** Honor societies.

**Academic Assistance:** Nonremedial tutoring.

**STUDENT LIFE. Housing:** All unmarried freshmen and sophomores under age 21 must live on campus unless living with family. Coed dorms. Sorority and fraternity housing. School-owned/operated apartments. Off-campus privately-owned housing. 75% of students live in college housing.

**Services and counseling/handicapped student services:** Placement services. Health service. Women's center. Counseling services for minority and older students. Birth control, personal, and psychological counseling. Career and academic guidance services. Religious counseling. Physically disabled student services. Learning disabled services. Notetaking services. Tape recorders. Tutors. Reader services for the blind.

**Campus organizations:** Undergraduate student government. Student newspaper (Collegian, published once/week). Literary magazine. Yearbook. Freshman glee club, chamber groups, choir, chorales, orchestra, band, theatre and dance groups, Willamette Outdoors, coffeehouse, Community Action Group, Gay and Lesbian Alliance, Off the Block, 80 organizations in all. Six fraternities, all with chapter houses; three sororities, all with chapter houses. 33% of men join a fraternity. 32% of women join a sorority.

**Religious organizations:** Campus Ambassadors, Fellowship of Christian Athletes, Intervarsity Christian Fellowship, Jewish Student Union, Latter-Day Saints Student Association, Newman Community.

**Minority/foreign student organizations:** American Indian Organization, Black Student Union, Hawaii Club, Unidos Por Fin. International Student Association.

**ATHLETICS. Physical education requirements:** None.

**Intercollegiate competition:** 30% of students participate. Baseball (M), basketball (M,W), cross-country (M,W), football (M), golf (M), lacrosse (M), soccer (M,W), softball (W), swimming (M,W), tennis (M,W), track (indoor) (M,W), track (outdoor) (M,W), track and field (indoor) (M,W), track and field (outdoor) (M,W), volleyball (W). Member of NAIA, Northwest Conference of Independent Colleges.

**Intramural and club sports:** 60% of students participate. Intramural badminton, basketball, cross-country, football, golf, pickleball, racquetball, soccer, softball, swimming, track, volleyball. Men's club rugby, water polo. Women's club water polo.

**ADMISSIONS. Academic basis for candidate selection** (in order of priority): Secondary school record, class rank, essay, standardized test scores, school's recommendation.

**Nonacademic basis for candidate selection:** Extracurricular participation and particular talent or ability are emphasized. Character and personality and geographical distribution are important. Alumni/ae relationship is considered.

**Requirements:** Graduation from secondary school is recommended; GED is accepted. 16 units and the following program of study are required: 4 units of English, 3 units of math, 3 units of science including 2 units of lab, 2 units of foreign language, 3 units of social studies. SAT or ACT is required. Campus visit and interview recommended. Off-campus interviews available with admissions and alumni representatives.

**Procedure:** Take SAT or ACT by November of 12th year. Visit college for interview by February 1 of 12th year. Suggest filing application by February 1; no deadline. Notification of admission by April 1. Reply is required by May 1. $200 nonrefundable tuition deposit. Freshmen accepted for terms other than fall.

**Special programs:** Admission may be deferred one year. Credit and placement may be granted through challenge exams. Early decision program. In fall 1993, 93 applied for early decision and 70 were accepted. Deadline for applying for early decision is December 1.

**Transfer students:** Transfer students accepted for terms other than fall. In fall 1993, 24% of all new students were transfers into all classes. 236 transfer applications were received, 166 were accepted. Application deadline is February 1 for fall; November 1 for spring. Minimum 3.0 GPA recommended. Lowest course grade accepted is "C." Maximum number of transferable credits is 60 semester hours. At least 64 semester hours must be completed at the university to receive degree.

**Admissions contact:** James M. Sumner, M.Ed., Dean of University Admissions. 503 370-6303.

**FINANCIAL AID. Available aid:** Pell grants, SEOG, state scholarships and grants, school scholarships and grants, private scholarships and grants, academic merit scholarships, and aid for undergraduate foreign students. Perkins Loans (NDSL), PLUS, Stafford Loans (GSL), state loans, private loans, and SLS. Tuition Plan Inc., Knight Tuition Plans, and deferred payment plan.

**Financial aid statistics:** 10% of aid is not need-based. In 1993-94, 100% of all undergraduate applicants received aid. Average amounts of aid awarded freshmen: Scholarships and grants, $6,000; loans, $4,500.

**Supporting data/closing dates:** FAFSA/FFS: Priority filing date is February 1. Notification of awards begins April 1.

**Financial aid contact:** James S. Woodland, M.Ed., Director of Financial Aid. 503 370-6273.

**STUDENT EMPLOYMENT.** College Work/Study Program. Institutional employment. 70% of full-time undergraduates work on campus during school year. Students may expect to earn an average of $1,200 during school year. Off-campus part-time employment opportunities rated "good."

**COMPUTER FACILITIES.** 95 IBM/IBM-compatible and Macintosh/Apple microcomputers; all are networked. Students may access SUN minicomputer/mainframe systems, BITNET, Internet. Computer languages and software packages include Assembly, BASIC, C, COBOL, FORTRAN, Lotus 1-2-3, Microsoft Word, Pascal, SimScript, SPSS, WordPerfect; 20 in all. Computer facilities are available to all students.

**Hours:** 24 hours.

**GRADUATE CAREER DATA.** Graduate school percentages: 20% enter law school. 15% enter medical school. 5% enter dental school. 20% enter graduate business programs. 10% enter graduate arts and sciences programs. 2% enter theological school/seminary. Highest graduate school enrollments: U of California, U of Oregon, U of Washington. 30% of graduates choose careers in business and industry. Companies and businesses that hire graduates: First Interstate Bank, Floating Point Systems, Hewlett-Packard, Textronix, U.S. Bancorp.

**PROMINENT ALUMNI/AE.** Mark Hatfield and Robert Packwood, U.S. senators; Robert Smith, U.S. congressman; Wallace Carson, Berkeley Lent, and J.R. Campbell, Oregon supreme court justices; Robert Sayre, U.S. ambassador; Gerald Pearson and Daryl Chapin, co-inventers of solar cell; Neil Hutchinson, flight director, NASA; William McDougall, former senior editor, *U.S. News & World Report*.

# Pennsylvania

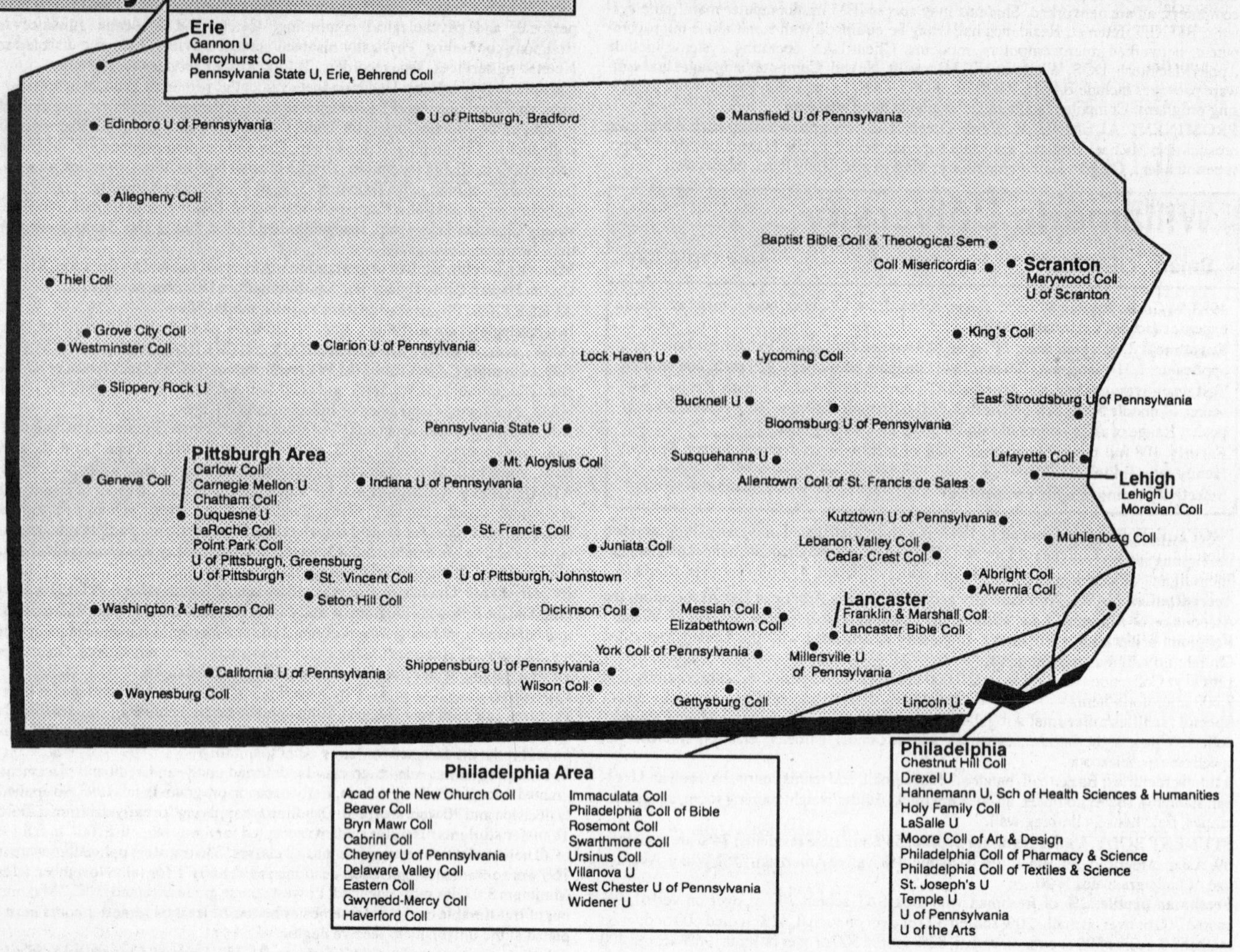


## Academy of the New Church College

**Bryn Athyn, PA 19009** **215 938-2543**

**1994-95 Costs.** Tuition: $3,408. Room & board: $3,351. Fees, books, misc. academic expenses (school's estimate): $1,082.
**Enrollment.** Undergraduates: 54 men, 51 women (full-time). Freshman class: 58 applicants, 55 accepted, 51 enrolled. Graduate enrollment: 5 men.
**Test score averages/ranges.** Average SAT scores: 471 verbal, 478 math.
**Faculty.** 20 full-time; 26 part-time. 35% of faculty holds doctoral degree. Student/faculty ratio: 8 to 1.
**Selectivity rating.** Less competitive.

**PROFILE.** Academy of the New Church, founded in 1876, is a church-affiliated college. Its 170-acre campus is located in Bryn Athyn, 15 miles from Philadelphia.

**Accreditation:** MSACS.
**Religious orientation:** Academy of the New Church College is affiliated with the General Church of the New Jerusalem (Swedenborgian); eight courses of religion required.
**Library:** Collections totaling over 100,000 volumes, 356 periodical subscriptions, and 3,000 microform items.
**Special facilities/museums:** Ancient and medieval history museums.
**Athletic facilities:** Field houses, tennis courts, athletic fields, fitness center/Nautilus room.

**STUDENT BODY. Undergraduate profile:** 45% are state residents. 3% Asian-American, 5% Black, 92% White. Average age of undergraduates is 19.
**Freshman profile:** 3% of freshmen who took SAT scored 700 or over on verbal, 3% scored 700 or over on math; 24% scored 600 or over on verbal, 26% scored 600 or over on math; 52% scored 500 or over on verbal, 59% scored 500 or over on math; 100% scored 400 or over on verbal, 100% scored 400 or over on math. 100% of accepted applicants took SAT. 29% of freshmen come from public schools.
**Undergraduate achievement:** 87% of fall 1992 freshmen returned for fall 1993 term.
**Foreign students:** 38 students are from out of the country. Countries represented include Australia, Canada, England, Korea, South Africa, and Sweden; 12 in all.

**PROGRAMS OF STUDY. Degrees:** B.A., B.S.
**Majors:** Education, Interdisciplinary Studies, Religion.
**Requirements:** General education requirement.
**Academic regulations:** Minimum 1.9 GPA must be maintained in general studies; 2.5 GPA required in area of specialization.
**Special:** Self-designed majors. Double majors. Independent study. Internships. Cooperative education programs. Preprofessional program in theology. Five-year B.S./M.Ed. program with Lehigh U. Teacher certification in elementary education.
**Academic Assistance:** Remedial study skills.

**ADMISSIONS. Academic basis for candidate selection** (in order of priority): Secondary school record, school's recommendation, essay, standardized test scores, class rank.
**Nonacademic basis for candidate selection:** Alumni/ae relationship is emphasized. Character and personality are important. Extracurricular participation and particular talent or ability are considered.
**Requirements:** Graduation from secondary school is required; GED is accepted. 16 units and the following program of study are recommended: 4 units of English, 3 units of math, 3 units of science, 2 units of foreign language, 3 units of social studies. Conditional admission possible for applicants not meeting standard requirements. SAT is required; ACT may be substituted. Campus visit and interview recommended. Off-campus interviews available with admissions and alumni representatives.
**Procedure:** Take SAT or ACT by December of 12th year. Visit college for interview by March 1 of 12th year. Application deadline is March 1. Notification of admission on rolling basis. No set date by which applicants must accept offer. $150 nonrefundable room deposit. Freshmen accepted for terms other than fall.
**Special programs:** Admission may be deferred one year. Credit and/or placement may be granted through CEEB Advanced Placement exams for scores of 4 or higher. Credit and/or placement may be granted through CLEP general and subject exams. Credit and placement may be granted through life experience. Early decision program. In fall 1993, seven applied for early decision and seven were accepted.
**Transfer students:** Transfer students accepted for terms other than fall. Application deadline is August 1 for fall; February 1 for spring. Minimum 1.9 GPA required. Lowest course grade accepted is "C-." Maximum number of transferable credits is 68 semester hours. At least 68 semester hours must be completed at the college to receive degree.
**Admissions contact:** Dan A. Synnestvedt, M.A., Director of Admissions. 215 938-2503.

**FINANCIAL AID. Available aid:** School scholarships and grants and private scholarships and grants. Private loans. Tuition Management Systems and deferred payment plan. Private nine-month payment plan.
**Financial aid statistics:** In 1993-94, 100% of all undergraduate applicants received aid. Average amounts of aid awarded freshmen: Scholarships and grants, $2,627; loans, $6,972.
**Supporting data/closing dates:** School's own aid application: Deadline is April 15. Notification of awards on rolling basis.
**Financial aid contact:** William R. Zeitz, Business Manager. 215 938-2635.

## Albright College

**Reading, PA 19612-5234 215 921-2381**

**1994-95 Costs.** Tuition: $15,595. Room: $2,400. Board: $2,000. Fees, books, misc. academic expenses (school's estimate): $460.
**Enrollment.** Undergraduates: 459 men, 514 women (full-time). Freshman class: 1,041 applicants, 841 accepted, 310 enrolled.
**Test score averages/ranges.** Range of SAT scores of middle 50%: 920-1100 combined. Range of ACT scores of middle 50%: 22-28 composite.
**Faculty.** 79 full-time; 45 part-time. 80% of faculty holds doctoral degree. Student/faculty ratio: 11 to 1.
**Selectivity rating.** Competitive.

**PROFILE.** Albright, founded in 1856, is a church-affiliated, liberal arts college. Its 110-acre campus is located at the edge of a residential section of Reading, 45 miles from Philadelphia.

**Accreditation:** MSACS.
**Religious orientation:** Albright College is affiliated with the United Methodist Church; no religious requirements.
**Library:** Collections totaling over 175,000 volumes, 1,002 periodical subscriptions, and 9,000 microform items.
**Special facilities/museums:** Art gallery, center for the arts, child development center, language labs, Mountain Meadows research station, TV/film studio, two electron microscopes.
**Athletic facilities:** Gymnasiums, badminton, basketball, racquetball, tennis, and volleyball courts, weight and wrestling rooms, batting cage, baseball, field hockey, football, soccer, and softball fields, tracks, swimming pool.
**STUDENT BODY. Undergraduate profile:** 53% are state residents; 13% are transfers. 3% Asian-American, 3% Black, 1% Hispanic, 1% Native American, 86% White, 6% Other.
**Freshman profile:** 92% of accepted applicants took SAT; 7% took ACT.
**Undergraduate achievement:** 89% of fall 1992 freshmen returned for fall 1993 term. 70% of entering class graduated. 50% of students who completed a degree program immediately went on to graduate study.
**Foreign students:** 70 students are from out of the country. Countries represented include Botswana, India, Japan, Pakistan, Peru, and Sri Lanka; 29 in all.
**PROGRAMS OF STUDY. Degrees:** B.A., B.S.
**Majors:** Accounting, American Civilization, Biochemistry, Biology, Business Administration, Chemistry, Computer Science, Cooperative Program in Forestry, Economics, English, Environmental Science, Family Studies, Finance, French, German, Government Service, History, International Business, Management, Marketing, Mathematics, Medical Technology, Philosophy, Political Science, Psychobiology, Psychology, Psychology/Business, Religion, Sociology, Spanish, Textiles/Design, Visual/Apparel Merchandising.
**Distribution of degrees:** The majors with the highest enrollment are business administration, biology, and psychology; American civilization, philosophy, and physics have the lowest.
**Requirements:** General education requirement.
**Academic regulations:** Freshmen must maintain minimum 1.7 GPA; sophomores, 1.9 GPA; juniors, 2.0 GPA; seniors, 2.0 GPA.
**Special:** Minors offered in art history, communications, computer information systems, music, and women's studies. ALPHA program for freshmen and sophomores who are undecided about major. Self-designed majors. Double majors. Independent study. Pass/fail grading option. Internships. Cooperative education programs. Preprofessional programs in law, medicine, veterinary science, and dentistry. 3-2 forestry and environmental studies program with Duke U. Washington Semester. Teacher certification in elementary and secondary education. Certification in specific subject areas. Study abroad possible.
**Honors:** Honors program.
**Academic Assistance:** Remedial study skills. Nonremedial tutoring.
**ADMISSIONS. Academic basis for candidate selection** (in order of priority): Secondary school record, class rank, standardized test scores, essay, school's recommendation.
**Nonacademic basis for candidate selection:** Character and personality and extracurricular participation are important. Particular talent or ability, geographical distribution, and alumni/ae relationship are considered.
**Requirements:** Graduation from secondary school is required; GED is accepted. No specific distribution of secondary school units required. SAT or ACT is required. ACH recommended. Campus visit and interview recommended. Off-campus interviews available with admissions and alumni representatives.
**Procedure:** Take SAT or ACT by December of 12th year. Visit college for interview by February of 12th year. Application deadline is February 15. Notification of admission on rolling basis. Reply is required by May 1. $200 nonrefundable tuition deposit. Freshmen accepted for terms other than fall.
**Special programs:** Admission may be deferred. Credit and/or placement may be granted through CEEB Advanced Placement exams for scores of 3 or higher. Credit may be granted through CLEP subject exams. Early entrance/early admission program.
**Transfer students:** Transfer students accepted for terms other than fall. In fall 1993, 13% of all new students were transfers into all classes. 80 transfer applications were received, 75 were accepted. Application deadline is August 15 for fall; December 15 for spring. Minimum 2.5 GPA required. Lowest course grade accepted is "D." Maximum number of transferable credits is 16 semester units. At least 16 semester units must be completed at the college to receive degree.
**Admissions contact:** William Stahler, Ph.D., Director of Admissions. 215 921-7512.
**FINANCIAL AID. Available aid:** Pell grants, SEOG, state scholarships and grants, school scholarships and grants, private scholarships and grants, and academic merit scholarships. Perkins Loans (NDSL), PLUS, Stafford Loans (GSL), NSL, and SLS. Tuition Management Systems and deferred payment plan.
**Financial aid statistics:** 8% of aid is not need-based. In 1993-94, 96% of all undergraduate applicants received aid; 96% of freshman applicants. Average amounts of aid awarded freshmen: Scholarships and grants, $4,600; loans, $2,433.
**Supporting data/closing dates:** FAFSA/FAF: Priority filing date is April 1. State aid form: Priority filing date is May 1. Income tax forms: Priority filing date is May 1. Notification of awards on rolling basis.
**Financial aid contact:** Joyce Frantz, Director of Financial Aid. 215 921-7515.

## Allegheny College

**Meadville, PA 16335 814 332-3100**

**1994-95 Costs.** Tuition: $17,080. Room: $2,280. Board: $2,160. Fees, books, misc. academic expenses (school's estimate): $660.
**Enrollment.** Undergraduates: 848 men, 898 women (full-time). Freshman class: 2,652 applicants, 1,900 accepted, 487 enrolled.
**Test score averages/ranges.** Range of SAT scores of middle 50%: 453-560 verbal, 520-630 math. Range of ACT scores of middle 50%: 22-27 composite.
**Faculty.** 161 full-time; 35 part-time. 91% of faculty holds highest degree in specific field. Student/faculty ratio: 11 to 1.
**Selectivity rating.** More competitive.

**PROFILE.** Allegheny is a church-affiliated, liberal arts college. It was founded in 1815, closed briefly in the 1830s, and began admitting women in 1870. Its 72-acre main campus and 465-acres of athletic/recreational lands are located in northwestern Pennsylvania.

**Accreditation:** MSACS.
**Religious orientation:** Allegheny College is affiliated with the United Methodist Church; no religious requirements.
**Library:** Collections totaling over 394,099 volumes, 1,065 periodical subscriptions, and 176,510 microform items.
**Special facilities/museums:** Art galleries, TV studio, observatory and planetarium, 285-acre environmental field station.
**Athletic facilities:** Gymnasium, field house, football stadium, track, basketball, racquetball, and tennis courts, swimming pool, lacrosse, rugby, soccer, and softball fields, weight room.
**STUDENT BODY. Undergraduate profile:** 53% are state residents; 3% are transfers. 2% Asian-American, 3% Black, 1% Hispanic, 91% White, 3% Foreign. Average age of undergraduates is 20.
**Freshman profile:** 1% of freshmen who took SAT scored 700 or over on verbal, 6% scored 700 or over on math; 14% scored 600 or over on verbal, 38% scored 600 or over on math; 57% scored 500 or over on verbal, 86% scored 500 or over on math; 94% scored 400 or over on verbal, 99% scored 400 or over on math; 99% scored 300 or over on verbal, 100% scored 300 or over on math. 7% of freshmen who took ACT scored 30 or over on composite; 67% scored 24 or over on composite; 98% scored 18 or over on composite; 100% scored 12 or over on composite. 87% of accepted applicants took SAT; 35% took ACT. 80% of freshmen come from public schools.
**Undergraduate achievement:** 88% of fall 1992 freshmen returned for fall 1993 term. 64% of entering class graduated. 30% of students who completed a degree program immediately went on to graduate study.
**Foreign students:** 57 students are from out of the country. Countries represented include India, Malaysia, Mexico, and Pakistan; 28 in all.
**PROGRAMS OF STUDY. Degrees:** B.A., B.S.
**Majors:** Art, Art History, Biochemistry, Biology, Chemistry, Classical Languages, Classics, Communication Arts, Computer Science, Economics, Education, English, Environmental Geology, Environmental Science, Environmental Studies, French, Geology, German, Greek, History, International Studies, Latin, Mass Communication, Mathematics, Music, Philosophy, Physics, Political Science, Psychology, Religious Studies, Rhetoric/Public Address, Russian, Sociology/Anthropology, Spanish, Theatre, Women's Studies.
**Distribution of degrees:** The majors with the highest enrollment are psychology, English, and economics; religious studies, music, and German have the lowest.
**Requirements:** General education requirement.
**Academic regulations:** Minimum 2.0 GPA must be maintained.
**Special:** Minors offered in most majors and in Black studies, Latin American/Caribbean studies. Summer research opportunities. Critical Languages Program in Arabic, Chinese, Japanese, and other languages. Preprofessional programs in law and health professions. Self-designed majors. Double majors. Dual degrees. Independent study. Accelerated study. Pass/fail grading option. Internships. Preprofessional programs in law, medicine, veterinary science, dentistry, and education. 3-2 cytotechnology, dental hygiene, diagnostic imaging, medical technology, nursing, and occupational therapy programs with Thomas Jefferson U. 3-2 nursing program with U of Rochester. 3-2 engineering programs with Case Western Reserve U, Columbia U, Duke U, U of Pittsburgh, and Washington U. 3-2 forestry and environmental studies program with Duke U. 3-2 forestry master's program with U of Michigan. 3-3 physical therapy master's program with Thomas Jefferson U. 3-4 doctoral nursing program with Case Western Reserve U. Member of American Collegiate Consortium. Washington Semester and Sea Semester. Appalachian Semester (Kentucky). Other semester-away programs available. Teacher certification in elementary and secondary education. Certification in specific subject areas. Exchange programs abroad in England (U of Sheffield), South Africa (U of Natal), and the former Soviet Republics. Study

abroad also in France, Germany, Spain, and other countries. ROTC at Edinboro U of Pennsylvania.
**Honors:** Phi Beta Kappa. Honor societies.
**Academic Assistance:** Remedial reading, writing, math, and study skills. Nonremedial tutoring.

**STUDENT LIFE. Housing:** All freshmen and sophomores must live on campus. Coed, women's, and men's dorms. Fraternity housing. School-owned/operated apartments. Off-campus privately-owned housing. 76% of students live in college housing.
**Social atmosphere:** According to the student newspaper, Allegheny provides "lots of diverse opportunities. You don't have to look for them. Greeks are being cracked down on and may not remain an entertainment opportunity for independents much longer. In the meantime, Greeks remain a very strong influence." Favorite gathering spots include McKinley's, Mulligan's, Mickey's, the library, and the post office.
**Services and counseling/handicapped student services:** Placement services. Health service. Graduate/professional school advising. Counseling services for minority and older students. Personal and psychological counseling. Career and academic guidance services. Religious counseling. Physically disabled student services. Learning disabled services. Tape recorders. Tutors.
**Campus organizations:** Undergraduate student government. Student newspaper (Campus, published once/week). Literary magazine. Yearbook. Radio and TV stations. Music, theatre, and dance groups, community service and special-interest groups, 112 organizations in all. Five fraternities, all with chapter houses; five sororities, no chapter houses. 25% of men join a fraternity. 30% of women join a sorority.
**Religious organizations:** Christian Outreach, Hillel, Newman Fellowship.
**Minority/foreign student organizations:** Advancement of Black Culture, Union Latina. International Club.

**ATHLETICS. Physical education requirements:** Five seven-week units of physical education required.
**Intercollegiate competition:** 34% of students participate. Baseball (M), basketball (M,W), cross-country (M,W), diving (M,W), football (M), golf (M), lacrosse (W), soccer (M,W), softball (W), swimming (M,W), tennis (M,W), track (indoor) (M,W), track (outdoor) (M,W), track and field (indoor) (M,W), track and field (outdoor) (M,W), volleyball (W). Member of NCAA Division III, North Coast Athletic Conference.
**Intramural and club sports:** 65% of students participate. Intramural basketball, football, floor hockey, golf, racquetball, soccer, softball, tennis, volleyball, cycling, climbing, bowling. Men's club cheerleading, fencing, ice hockey, lacrosse, rugby, volleyball. Women's club cheerleading, dance team, fencing.

**ADMISSIONS. Academic basis for candidate selection** (in order of priority): Secondary school record, class rank, standardized test scores, school's recommendation, essay.
**Nonacademic basis for candidate selection:** Character and personality are emphasized. Extracurricular participation and particular talent or ability are important. Geographical distribution and alumni/ae relationship are considered.
**Requirements:** Graduation from secondary school is required; GED is not accepted. 16 units and the following program of study are recommended: 4 units of English, 3 units of math, 3 units of science, 2 units of foreign language, 3 units of social studies, 1 unit of academic electives. Minimum 2.5 GPA and rank in top three-fifths of class recommended. Educational Enhancement Program for applicants not normally admissible. SAT or ACT is required. ACH recommended. Campus visit and interview recommended. Off-campus interviews available with admissions and alumni representatives.
**Procedure:** Take SAT or ACT by December of 12th year. Visit college for interview by February 15 of 12th year. Application deadline is February 15. Notification of admission by April 1. Reply is required by May 1. $200 nonrefundable tuition deposit. Freshmen accepted for terms other than fall.
**Special programs:** Admission may be deferred one year. Credit and/or placement may be granted through CEEB Advanced Placement exams for scores of 4 or higher. Credit and/or placement may be granted through CLEP general and subject exams. Early decision program. In fall 1993, 158 applied for early decision and 147 were accepted. Deadline for applying for early decision is November 30 (Plan I) or January 15 (Plan II). Early entrance/early admission program. Concurrent enrollment program.
**Transfer students:** Transfer students accepted for terms other than fall. In fall 1993, 3% of all new students were transfers into all classes. 77 transfer applications were received, 39 were accepted. Application deadline is July 1 for fall; November 1 for spring. Minimum 2.0 GPA required. Lowest course grade accepted is "C." Maximum number of transferable credits is 64 semester hours. At least 64 semester hours must be completed at the college to receive degree.
**Admissions contact:** Gayle W. Pollock, Director of Admissions. 814 332-4351, 800 521-5293.

**FINANCIAL AID. Available aid:** Pell grants, SEOG, state scholarships and grants, school scholarships and grants, private scholarships and grants, ROTC scholarships, academic merit scholarships, and aid for undergraduate foreign students. National Methodist Scholarships. National Science Foundation Research Careers for Minority Scholars Awards. Perkins Loans (NDSL), PLUS, Stafford Loans (GSL), state loans, school loans, private loans, and SLS. Tuition Plan Inc., AMS, and guaranteed tuition. Installment plan. One-year full payment discount plan.
**Financial aid statistics:** 29% of aid is not need-based. In 1993-94, 99% of all undergraduate applicants received aid; 99% of freshman applicants. Average amounts of aid awarded freshmen: Scholarships and grants, $11,221; loans, $4,211.
**Supporting data/closing dates:** FAFSA/FAF: Priority filing date is February 15. State aid form: Priority filing date is February 15. Income tax forms: Deadline is July 1. SAR: Deadline is July 1. Notification of awards begins April 1.
**Financial aid contact:** John C. Reynders, M.A.Ed., Director of Financial Aid. 814 332-2701, 800 835-7780.

**STUDENT EMPLOYMENT.** College Work/Study Program. Institutional employment. 65% of full-time undergraduates work on campus during school year. Students may expect to earn an average of $1,012 during school year. Off-campus part-time employment opportunities rated "fair."

**COMPUTER FACILITIES.** 250 IBM/IBM-compatible, Macintosh/Apple, and RISC-/UNIX-based microcomputers; 200 are networked. Students may access Hewlett-Packard, SUN minicomputer/mainframe systems, BITNET, Internet. Client/LAN operating systems include DOS, UNIX/XENIX/AIX. Computer languages and software packages include WordPerfect, Improv, Pascal, C, Lisp, Nextstep. Computer facilities are available to all students.
**Fees:** Computer fee is included in tuition/fees.
**Hours:** 24 hours.

**GRADUATE CAREER DATA.** Graduate school percentages: 5% enter law school. 5% enter medical school. 1% enter dental school. 2% enter graduate business programs. 12% enter graduate arts and sciences programs. Highest graduate school enrollments: Case Western Reserve U, Cornell U, Pennsylvania State U, Syracuse U, U of Pittsburgh. 29% of graduates choose careers in business and industry. Companies and businesses that hire graduates: Chubb Group, Federal-Mogul Corp., Society National Bank.

**PROMINENT ALUMNI/AE.** William McKinley, 25th U.S. president; Raymond P. Shafer, former Pennsylvania governor; David Hoag, chairman and CEO, LTV Corp.

# Allentown College of St. Francis de Sales

**Center Valley, PA 18034-9568** **215 282-1100**

**1994-95 Costs.** Tuition: $9,690. Room & board: $4,815. Fees, books, misc. academic expenses (school's estimate): $660.
**Enrollment.** Undergraduates: 436 men, 503 women (full-time). Freshman class: 1,179 applicants, 780 accepted, 291 enrolled.
**Test score averages/ranges.** Average SAT scores: 470 verbal, 515 math. Range of SAT scores of middle 50%: 410-520 verbal, 460-580 math.
**Faculty.** 68 full-time; 30 part-time. 65% of faculty holds doctoral degree. Student/faculty ratio: 13 to 1.
**Selectivity rating.** Less competitive.

**PROFILE.** Allentown is a church-affiliated, liberal arts college. Bachelor degree-granting classes began in 1965 and accreditation was granted in 1969. The 300-acre rural campus is in Center Valley, 50 miles from Philadelphia.

**Accreditation:** MSACS. Professionally accredited by the National League for Nursing.
**Religious orientation:** Allentown College of St. Francis de Sales is affiliated with the Roman Catholic Church (Oblates of St. Francis de Sales); three semesters of theology required.
**Library:** Collections totaling over 147,000 volumes, 1,000 periodical subscriptions, and 114,000 microform items.
**Special facilities/museums:** Performing arts center, language lab.
**Athletic facilities:** Gymnasium, fitness center, dance studio, batting cages, baseball, soccer, and softball fields, weight room, cross-country course, basketball and tennis courts.

**STUDENT BODY. Undergraduate profile:** 65% are state residents; 10% are transfers. 1% Asian-American, 3% Black, 2% Hispanic, 94% White. Average age of undergraduates is 19.
**Freshman profile:** 1% of freshmen who took SAT scored 700 or over on verbal, 2% scored 700 or over on math; 9% scored 600 or over on verbal, 19% scored 600 or over on math; 35% scored 500 or over on verbal, 56% scored 500 or over on math; 84% scored 400 or over on verbal, 94% scored 400 or over on math; 100% scored 300 or over on verbal, 100% scored 300 or over on math. 99% of accepted applicants took SAT; 1% took ACT. 40% of freshmen come from public schools.
**Undergraduate achievement:** 85% of fall 1992 freshmen returned for fall 1993 term. 53% of entering class graduated. 10% of students who completed a degree program immediately went on to graduate study.
**Foreign students:** 10 students are from out of the country. Countries represented include Bangladesh, China, Japan, Jordan, Scotland, and South Africa; eight in all.

**PROGRAMS OF STUDY. Degrees:** B.A., B.S., B.S.Nurs.
**Majors:** Accounting, Biology, Business, Business Communications, Chemistry, Computer Science, Criminal Justice, Dance, English/Communications, Finance, Foreign Languages/Multiple Emphasis, Liberal Studies, Management, Marketing, Mathematics, Nursing, Politics, Psychology, Sports Administration, Theatre, Theology.
**Distribution of degrees:** The majors with the highest enrollment are accounting, management, and marketing; theology and foreign languages have the lowest.
**Requirements:** General education requirement.
**Academic regulations:** Freshmen must maintain minimum 1.50 GPA; sophomores, 1.70 GPA; juniors, 1.90 GPA; seniors, 1.90 GPA.
**Special:** Minors offered in some majors and in American studies, dramatic literature, French, German, philosophy, Spanish, technical communication, and theatre design/technology. Courses offered in economics, German, Latin, linguistics, pastoral ministry, philosophy, and physical education. Double majors. Independent study. Pass/fail grading option. Internships. Graduate school at which undergraduates may take graduate-level courses. Preprofessional programs in law, medicine, veterinary science, dentistry, theology, and optometry. Member of Lehigh Valley Association of Independent Colleges; cross-registration possible. Washington Semester. Harrisburg Urban Semester. Teacher certification in secondary education. Certification in specific subject areas. Study abroad in England, France, Germany, Mexico, and Spain. ROTC at Lehigh U.
**Honors:** Honors program. Honor societies.
**Academic Assistance:** Remedial study skills. Nonremedial tutoring.

**ADMISSIONS. Academic basis for candidate selection** (in order of priority): Secondary school record, class rank, school's recommendation, standardized test scores, essay.
**Nonacademic basis for candidate selection:** Character and personality, extracurricular participation, particular talent or ability, and alumni/ae relationship are considered.
**Requirements:** Graduation from secondary school is required; GED is accepted. 12 units and the following program of study are required: 4 units of English, 2 units of math, 2 units of science including 1 unit of lab, 2 units of foreign language, 1 unit of social studies, 1 unit of history. Rank in top half of secondary school class and minimum 2.5 GPA required. Audition required of dance program applicants. Act 101 program for in-state applicants

not normally admissible. SAT is required; ACT may be substituted. Campus visit and interview recommended. No off-campus interviews.
**Procedure:** Take SAT or ACT by December of 12th year. Suggest filing application by March 15. Application deadline is August 1. Notification of admission on rolling basis. Reply is required by May 1. $100 nonrefundable tuition deposit. $100 room deposit, refundable until May 1. Freshmen accepted for terms other than fall.
**Special programs:** Admission may be deferred one year. Credit may be granted through CEEB Advanced Placement for scores of 3 or higher. Credit may be granted through CLEP general and subject exams. Credit and placement may be granted through challenge exams and military and life experience. Early entrance/early admission program. Concurrent enrollment program.
**Transfer students:** Transfer students accepted for terms other than fall. In fall 1993, 10% of all new students were transfers into all classes. 80 transfer applications were received, 55 were accepted. Application deadline is August 1 for fall; December 1 for spring. Minimum 2.0 GPA required. Lowest course grade accepted is "C-." Maximum number of transferable credits is 60 semester hours. At least 60 semester hours must be completed at the college to receive degree.
**Admissions contact:** Kathleen H. Link, M.B.A., Director of Admissions. 215 282-1100, extension 1277, 800 228-5114.

**FINANCIAL AID. Available aid:** Pell grants, SEOG, Federal Nursing Student Scholarships, state scholarships and grants, school scholarships and grants, private scholarships and grants, ROTC scholarships, and academic merit scholarships. Perkins Loans (NDSL), PLUS, Stafford Loans (GSL), NSL, private loans, and SLS. Deferred payment plan and family tuition reduction. MPP/HES Plan Trust.
**Financial aid statistics:** 15% of aid is not need-based. In 1993-94, 90% of all undergraduate applicants received aid; 90% of freshman applicants. Average amounts of aid awarded freshmen: Scholarships and grants, $4,500; loans, $2,625.
**Supporting data/closing dates:** FAFSA: Priority filing date is February 15; deadline is May 15. School's own aid application: Priority filing date is January 30; deadline is May 1. State aid form: Priority filing date is February 15; deadline is May 1. Notification of awards begins December 15.
**Financial aid contact:** Cate McIntyre, M.P.A., Director of Financial Aid. 215 282-1100, extension 1287.

# Alvernia College

**Reading, PA 19607** **215 796-8200**

**1994-95 Costs.** Tuition: $8,950. Room & board: $4,200. Fees, books, misc. academic expenses (school's estimate): $150.
**Enrollment.** Undergraduates: 291 men, 504 women (full-time). Freshman class: 707 applicants, 614 accepted, 283 enrolled.
**Test score averages/ranges.** Average SAT scores: 400 verbal, 420 math.
**Faculty.** 51 full-time; 55 part-time. 22% of faculty holds doctoral degree. Student/faculty ratio: 14 to 1.
**Selectivity rating.** Less competitive.

**PROFILE.** Alvernia is a church-affiliated college. Founded in 1961, it adopted coeducation ten years later. Its 85-acre campus is located in the Blue Mountain area of eastern Pennsylvania, 50 miles from Philadelphia.

**Accreditation:** MSACS. Professionally accredited by the American Physical Therapy Association, the National Council for Accreditation of Teacher Education, the National League for Nursing.
**Religious orientation:** Alvernia College is affiliated with the Roman Catholic Church (Bernardine Sisters of the Third Order of St. Francis); two semesters of theology required.
**Library:** Collections totaling over 61,395 volumes, 795 periodical subscriptions, and 1,441 microform items.
**Special facilities/museums:** Physical therapist assistant labs, nursing resource center.
**Athletic facilities:** Gymnasium, tennis, sand volleyball, and volleyball courts, baseball, soccer, and field hockey fields, fitness and weight rooms.

**STUDENT BODY. Undergraduate profile:** 85% are state residents; 40% are transfers. 1% Asian-American, 1% Black, 1% Hispanic, 97% White.
**Undergraduate achievement:** 85% of fall 1992 freshmen returned for fall 1993 term. 70% of entering class graduated. 2% of students who completed a degree program immediately went on to graduate study.
**Foreign students:** Six students are from out of the country. Five countries represented in all.

**PROGRAMS OF STUDY. Degrees:** B.A., B.S.
**Majors:** Accounting, Addiction Studies, Banking/Finance, Biochemistry, Biology, Biology/Medical Technology, Business Management/Administration, Chemistry, Chemistry/Medical Technology, Communication, Computer Science, Criminal Justice, Early Childhood Education, Elementary Education, English, General Science, General Studies, History, Marketing, Mathematics, Nursing, Political Science/Government, Psychology, Secondary Education, Social Studies, Social Work, Spanish, Theology/Philosophy.
**Distribution of degrees:** The majors with the highest enrollment are business, education, and criminal justice; theology, social work, and Spanish have the lowest.
**Requirements:** General education requirement.
**Academic regulations:** Freshmen must maintain minimum 1.75 GPA; sophomores, 1.80 GPA; juniors, 1.90 GPA; seniors, 2.0 GPA.
**Special:** Minors offered in some majors and in art, business communications, fine arts, foreign language, and physics. Associate's degrees offered. Double majors. Independent study. Pass/fail grading option. Internships. Preprofessional programs in law, medicine, veterinary science, dentistry, and ophthalmology. Washington Semester. Teacher certification in early childhood, elementary, and secondary education. Certification in specific subject areas. Study abroad possible.
**Academic Assistance:** Nonremedial tutoring.

**ADMISSIONS. Academic basis for candidate selection** (in order of priority): Secondary school record, class rank, standardized test scores, school's recommendation.
**Nonacademic basis for candidate selection:** Character and personality, extracurricular participation, and particular talent or ability are considered.
**Requirements:** Graduation from secondary school is required; GED is accepted. 16 units and the following program of study are required: 4 units of English, 2 units of math, 2 units of science including 1 unit of lab, 2 units of foreign language, 2 units of social studies, 4 units of academic electives. Minimum composite SAT score of 800, rank in top half of secondary school class, and 2.0 GPA required. PSB or NLN tests required of nursing program applicants. SAT is required; ACT may be substituted. Campus visit and interview recommended. No off-campus interviews.
**Procedure:** Take SAT or ACT by fall of 12th year. Visit college for interview by spring of 12th year. Suggest filing application by May 1. Application deadline is August 1. Notification of admission on rolling basis. Reply is required within four weeks of acceptance. $100 nonrefundable tuition deposit. $200 nonrefundable room deposit. Freshmen accepted for terms other than fall.
**Special programs:** Admission may be deferred one year. Credit and/or placement may be granted through CEEB Advanced Placement exams for scores of 4 or higher. Credit and/or placement may be granted through CLEP general and subject exams. Credit and placement may be granted through challenge exams and military and life experience. Early entrance/early admission program. Concurrent enrollment program.
**Transfer students:** Transfer students accepted for terms other than fall. In fall 1993, 40% of all new students were transfers into all classes. 248 transfer applications were received, 217 were accepted. Application deadline is August 1. Minimum 2.0 GPA required. Lowest course grade accepted is "C." Maximum number of transferable credits is 60 semester hours from a two-year school and 90 semester hours from a four-year school. At least 30 semester hours must be completed at the college to receive degree.
**Admissions contact:** Karin Allmendinger, Director of Admissions. 215 796-8200.

**FINANCIAL AID. Available aid:** Pell grants, SEOG, state scholarships and grants, school scholarships and grants, private scholarships, and academic merit scholarships. Perkins Loans (NDSL), PLUS, Stafford Loans (GSL), NSL, state loans, and SLS. O'Rourke Nursing Loans Installment Payment Plan.
**Financial aid statistics:** 5% of aid is not need-based. In 1993-94, 100% of all undergraduate applicants received aid. Average amounts of aid awarded freshmen: Scholarships and grants, $1,500.
**Supporting data/closing dates:** FAFSA. State aid form: Deadline is April 1. Notification of awards on rolling basis.
**Financial aid contact:** Vali G. Heist, Director of Financial Aid. 215 796-8215.

# Baptist Bible College and Theological Seminary

**Clarks Summit, PA 18411** **717 587-1172**

**1994-95 Costs.** Tuition: $5,820. Room: $1,522. Board: $2,320. Fees, books, misc. academic expenses (school's estimate): $786.
**Enrollment.** Undergraduates: 231 men, 261 women (full-time). Freshman class: 426 applicants, 332 accepted, 197 enrolled.
**Test score averages/ranges.** Average SAT scores: 445 verbal, 439 math. Average ACT scores: 20 composite.
**Faculty.** 22 full-time; 2 part-time. 25% of faculty holds doctoral degree. Student/faculty ratio: 14 to 1.
**Selectivity rating.** Less competitive.

**PROFILE.** Baptist Bible College is a church-affiliated institution. Founded in 1932, it received academic accreditation in 1969. Its 145-acre campus is located in Clarks Summit, seven miles from Scranton.

**Accreditation:** AABC, MSACS.
**Religious orientation:** Baptist Bible College and Theological Seminary is affiliated with the Baptist Church; eight semesters of religion required.
**Library:** Collections totaling over 76,000 volumes, 480 periodical subscriptions, and 3,315 microform items.
**Special facilities/museums:** Music museum.
**Athletic facilities:** Gymnasium, intramural, soccer, and softball fields, handball, racquetball, tennis, and volleyball courts, swimming pool, weight and wrestling rooms.

**STUDENT BODY. Undergraduate profile:** 30% are state residents; 34% are transfers.
**Freshman profile:** 55% of accepted applicants took SAT; 39% took ACT. 51% of freshmen come from public schools.
**Undergraduate achievement:** 73% of fall 1992 freshmen returned for fall 1993 term. 47% of entering class graduated. 30% of students who completed a degree program immediately went on to graduate study.

**PROGRAMS OF STUDY. Degrees:** B.S.Bible, B.Sacred Mus.
**Majors:** Bible, Elementary Education, Minister of Christian Education, Missions, Pastoral Studies, Pre-Counseling, Pre-Seminary, Secondary Education, Secretarial, Youth Ministries.
**Distribution of degrees:** The majors with the highest enrollment are pastoral studies, missions, and Christian education; general ministry, pre-counseling, and secretarial have the lowest.
**Requirements:** General education requirement.
**Academic regulations:** Minimum 2.0 GPA must be maintained.
**Special:** Diploma and certificate programs. Courses in communication skills, humanities and social science, natural science, physical education, and psychology. All students must take biblical studies, general studies, and Christian ministries courses. Associate's degrees offered. Independent study. Internships. Graduate school at which undergraduates may take graduate-level courses. Preprofessional programs in seminary studies. Teacher certi-

fication in elementary and secondary education. Study abroad in Israel and Peru. ROTC at U of Scranton.
**Honors:** Honor societies.

**ADMISSIONS. Academic basis for candidate selection** (in order of priority): Secondary school record, standardized test scores, school's recommendation, class rank.
**Nonacademic basis for candidate selection:** Character and personality are emphasized. Extracurricular participation and particular talent or ability are considered.
**Requirements:** Graduation from secondary school is required; GED is accepted. No specific distribution of secondary school units required. SAT or ACT is required. Campus visit and interview recommended. Off-campus interviews available with admissions and alumni representatives.
**Procedure:** Suggest filing application by May 1. Application deadline is August 15. Notification of admission on rolling basis. Reply is required within 30 days of notification. $75 room deposit, refundable until August 1. Freshmen accepted for terms other than fall.
**Special programs:** Admission may be deferred. Credit may be granted through CEEB Advanced Placement for scores of 3 or higher. Credit may be granted through CLEP general and subject exams. Early entrance/early admission program.
**Transfer students:** Transfer students accepted for terms other than fall. In fall 1993, 34% of all new students were transfers into all classes. 140 transfer applications were received, 106 were accepted. Lowest course grade accepted is "C."
**Admissions contact:** Glenn Amos, Director of Enrollment Management. 717 587-1172, extension 380.

**FINANCIAL AID. Available aid:** Pell grants, state scholarships and grants, school scholarships and grants, private scholarships, and academic merit scholarships. PLUS, Stafford Loans (GSL), state loans, private loans, and SLS. Tuition Plan Inc. and deferred payment plan.
**Financial aid statistics:** 31% of aid is not need-based. In 1993-94, 85% of all undergraduate applicants received aid. Average amounts of aid awarded freshmen: Loans, $2,455.
**Supporting data/closing dates:** FAFSA/FAF: Priority filing date is April 15. School's own aid application: Priority filing date is April 15. State aid form: Priority filing date is April 15. Income tax forms: Priority filing date is April 15. Notification of awards begins May 15.
**Financial aid contact:** Rob Ritz, M.S., Director of Financial Aid. 717 587-1172, extension 215.

# Beaver College

**Glenside, PA 19038-3295 215 572-2900**

**1993-94 Costs.** Tuition: $12,250. Room & board: $5,150. Fees, books, misc. academic expenses (school's estimate): $960.
**Enrollment.** Undergraduates: 222 men, 650 women (full-time). Freshman class: 1,163 applicants, 850 accepted, 348 enrolled. Graduate enrollment: 242 men, 747 women.
**Test score averages/ranges.** Average SAT scores: 460 verbal, 505 math. Range of SAT scores of middle 50%: 390-510 verbal, 430-550 math.
**Faculty.** 67 full-time; 138 part-time. 85% of faculty holds highest degree in specific field. Student/faculty ratio: 13 to 1.
**Selectivity rating.** Less competitive.

**PROFILE.** Beaver is a liberal arts college affiliated with the Presbyterian Church. Founded as the Beaver Female Seminary in 1853, it adopted coeducation in 1973. Its 35-acre campus is located in Glenside, 20 minutes from Philadelphia by train. The "Castle," a campus landmark, is fashioned after a medieval English manor.

**Accreditation:** MSACS. Professionally accredited by the American Assembly of Collegiate Schools of Business, the American Medical Association (CAHEA), the American Physical Therapy Association, the National Association of Schools of Art and Design.
**Religious orientation:** Beaver College is affiliated with the Presbyterian Church; no religious requirements.
**Library:** Collections totaling over 119,403 volumes, 668 periodical subscriptions, and 88,017 microform items.
**Special facilities/museums:** Art gallery, language lab, observatory.
**Athletic facilities:** Gymnasium, field hockey, lacrosse, soccer, and softball fields, basketball and tennis courts, recreation center.

**STUDENT BODY. Undergraduate profile:** 78% are state residents; 35% are transfers. 2% Asian-American, 9% Black, 2% Hispanic, 86% White, 1% Other. Average age of undergraduates is 23.
**Freshman profile:** 98% of accepted applicants took SAT. 70% of freshmen come from public schools.
**Undergraduate achievement:** 78% of fall 1992 freshmen returned for fall 1993 term. 71% of entering class graduated. 17% of students who completed a degree program went on to graduate study within one year.
**Foreign students:** 27 students are from out of the country. Countries represented include Ecuador, Italy, Panama, and Venezuela; 11 in all.

**PROGRAMS OF STUDY. Degrees:** B.A., B.F.A., B.S.
**Majors:** Accounting, Art, Art Education, Art History, Art Therapy, Artificial Intelligence/Cognitive Science, Biology, Business Administration, Ceramics, Chemistry, Chemistry/Business, Communications, Computer Science, Early Childhood/Elementary Education, Elementary/Special Education, English, Finance, Graphic Design, History, Interdepartmental Science, Interior Design, Management, Management Information Systems, Marketing, Mathematics, Metals/Jewelry, Painting, Philosophy, Photography, Political Science, Printmaking, Psychobiology, Psychology, Psychology/Personnel/Human Resources Management, Psychology/Special Education, Science Illustration, Secondary Education, Sociology, Special Education, Special Education/Early Child, Theatre Arts, Theatre Arts/English.
**Distribution of degrees:** The majors with the highest enrollment are biology and business administration; philosophy, history, and chemistry have the lowest.
**Requirements:** General education requirement.
**Academic regulations:** Freshmen must maintain minimum 1.75 GPA; sophomores, juniors, seniors, 2.0 GPA.
**Special:** Minors offered. Associate's degrees offered. Self-designed majors. Double majors. Dual degrees. Independent study. Accelerated study. Pass/fail grading option. Internships. Cooperative education programs. Graduate school at which undergraduates may take graduate-level courses. Preprofessional programs in law, medicine, veterinary science, dentistry, theology, optometry, and physical therapy. 3-2 engineering program with Columbia U. 4-2 physical therapy program. Seven-year optometry program with Pennsylvania Coll of Optometry. Washington Semester. Appalachian Semester (Kentucky). Philadelphia Urban Semester. Exchange program with U of Pennsylvania. Teacher certification in early childhood, elementary, secondary, and special education. Study abroad in Austria, England, Greece, Hungary, Ireland, Japan, and Mexico. ROTC at LaSalle U and Temple U.
**Honors:** Honors program.
**Academic Assistance:** Remedial reading, writing, math, and study skills. Nonremedial tutoring.

**ADMISSIONS. Academic basis for candidate selection** (in order of priority): Secondary school record, class rank, standardized test scores, school's recommendation, essay.
**Nonacademic basis for candidate selection:** Character and personality, extracurricular participation, and alumni/ae relationship are considered.
**Requirements:** Graduation from secondary school is required; GED is accepted. 16 units and the following program of study are recommended: 4 units of English, 3 units of math, 1 unit of science, 2 units of foreign language, 3 units of social studies, 3 units of electives. Portfolio recommended of art program applicants. Portfolio required of science illustration program applicants. Act 101 program for applicants not normally admissible. SAT is required; ACT may be substituted. Campus visit and interview recommended.
**Procedure:** Notification of admission on rolling basis. Reply is required by May 1. $75 nonrefundable tuition deposit. $125 nonrefundable room deposit. Freshmen accepted for terms other than fall.
**Special programs:** Admission may be deferred one year. Credit may be granted through CEEB Advanced Placement for scores of 3 or higher. Credit may be granted through CLEP general and subject exams, ACT PEP exams, and military experience. Early decision program. In fall 1993, 16 applied for early decision and 16 were accepted. Deadline for applying for early decision is October 15. Early entrance/early admission program. Concurrent enrollment program.
**Transfer students:** Transfer students accepted for terms other than fall. In fall 1993, 35% of all new students were transfers into all classes. 300 transfer applications were received, 206 were accepted. Application deadline is September 7 for fall; January 15 for spring. Minimum 2.5 GPA recommended. Lowest course grade accepted is "C-." Maximum number of transferable credits is 64 semester hours from a two-year school and 96 semester hours from a four-year school. At least 32 semester hours must be completed at the college to receive degree.
**Admissions contact:** Dennis L. Nostrand, M.Ed., V.P. for Enrollment Management. 215 572-2910.

**FINANCIAL AID. Available aid:** Pell grants, SEOG, state grants, school scholarships and grants, and academic merit scholarships. Perkins Loans (NDSL), PLUS, Stafford Loans (GSL), state loans, school loans, and SLS. Knight Tuition Plans. Installment payment plans.
**Financial aid statistics:** In 1993-94, 90% of all undergraduate applicants received aid; 90% of freshman applicants. Average amounts of aid awarded freshmen: Scholarships and grants, $11,042; loans, $2,625.
**Supporting data/closing dates:** FAFSA/FAF: Priority filing date is March 15; deadline is May 1. School's own aid application: Priority filing date is March 15; deadline is May 1. State aid form: Priority filing date is March 15; deadline is May 1. Income tax forms: Priority filing date is March 15; deadline is May 1. Notification of awards begins March 6.
**Financial aid contact:** Lois Roemmele, Director of Financial Aid. 215 572-2980.

# Bloomsburg University of Pennsylvania

**Bloomsburg, PA 17815 717 389-4000**

**1994-95 Costs.** Tuition: $3,086 (state residents), $8,270 (out-of-state). Room: $1,650. Board: $1,298. Fees, books, misc. academic expenses (school's estimate): $1,108.
**Enrollment.** Undergraduates: 2,249 men, 3,599 women (full-time). Freshman class: 6,773 applicants, 3,028 accepted, 1,025 enrolled. Graduate enrollment: 157 men, 425 women.
**Test score averages/ranges.** Average SAT scores: 465 verbal, 524 math.
**Faculty.** 369 full-time; 29 part-time. 61% of faculty holds doctoral degree. Student/faculty ratio: 19 to 1.
**Selectivity rating.** Competitive.

**PROFILE.** Bloomsburg is a public, multipurpose university. Founded in 1838, it gained university status in 1982. Programs are offered through the Colleges of Arts and Sciences, Professional Studies, and Business and the Schools of Graduate Studies and Extended Programs. Its 177-acre campus is located in the town of Bloomsburg, 80 miles northeast of Harrisburg.

**Accreditation:** MSACS. Professionally accredited by the Council on Social Work Education, the National Council for Accreditation of Teacher Education, the National League for Nursing.
**Religious orientation:** Bloomsburg University of Pennsylvania is nonsectarian; no religious requirements.
**Library:** Collections totaling over 341,402 volumes, 1,745 periodical subscriptions, and 1,751,790 microform items.
**Special facilities/museums:** Art gallery, language lab, TV studio, radio stations.

**STUDENT BODY. Undergraduate profile:** 90% are state residents; 21% are transfers. 1% Asian-American, 3% Black, 1% Hispanic, 95% White. Average age of undergraduates is 22.
**Freshman profile:** 1% of freshmen who took SAT scored 700 or over on math; 3% scored 600 or over on verbal, 15% scored 600 or over on math; 31% scored 500 or over on verbal, 66% scored 500 or over on math; 89% scored 400 or over on verbal, 98% scored 400 or over on math; 100% scored 300 or over on verbal, 100% scored 300 or over on math. Majority of accepted applicants took SAT. 86% of freshmen come from public schools.
**Undergraduate achievement:** 87% of fall 1992 freshmen returned for fall 1993 term. 37% of entering class graduated. 15% of students who completed a degree program went on to graduate study within one year.
**Foreign students:** 29 students are from out of the country. Countries represented include Bangladesh, China, England, Italy, Japan, and Scotland; 16 in all.

**PROGRAMS OF STUDY. Degrees:** B.A., B.S., B.S.Ed., B.S.Nurs., B.S.Office Admin.
**Majors:** Accounting, Adult Health, Anthropology, Art History, Biology, Business, Business Administration, Business Education, Chemistry, Clinical Chemistry, Comprehensive Social Studies, Computer/Information Sciences, Dramatic Arts, Early Childhood Education, Earth Science, Economics, Elementary Education, English, French, Geography, Geology, German, Health Physics, History, Humanities, Interpreting for the Hearing Impaired, Mass Communications, Mathematics, Medical Laboratory Technology, Music, Natural Science/Mathematics, Nursing, Office Supervision/Management, Philosophy, Physics, Political Economics, Political Science/Government, Psychology, Radiographic Medical Technology, Secondary Education, Social Sciences, Social Work, Sociology, Spanish, Special Education, Speech Correction/Audiology, Speech/Debate/Forensics, Studio Art.
**Distribution of degrees:** The majors with the highest enrollment are elementary education, business administration, and accounting; natural sciences, mathematics, and humanities have the lowest.
**Requirements:** General education requirement.
**Academic regulations:** Minimum 2.0 GPA required for graduation.
**Special:** Minors offered in some majors and in art studio. Certificate offered in journalism. Multidisciplinary studies in natural sciences/mathematics, social sciences, and humanities. Associate's degrees offered. Double majors. Independent study. Pass/fail grading option. Internships. Graduate school at which undergraduates may take graduate-level courses. Preprofessional programs in law, pharmacy, cytotechnology, occupational therapy, and physical therapy. 3-2 engineering program with Wilkes U and Pennsylvania State U. Member of Marine Science Consortium; off-campus study possible at Wallops Island, Va. Teacher certification in early childhood, elementary, and special education. Certification in specific subject areas. Study abroad in Australia, England, France, Germany, Ireland, Italy, Japan, Scotland, and other countries. ROTC. AFROTC at Wilkes U.
**Honors:** Honors program.
**Academic Assistance:** Remedial reading, writing, math, and study skills. Nonremedial tutoring.

**STUDENT LIFE. Housing:** All freshmen under age 21 must live on campus unless living with family. Women's and men's dorms. School-owned/operated apartments. Off-campus privately-owned housing. 43% of students live in college housing.
**Social atmosphere:** According to the editor of the student newspaper, "There are many cultural activities on and off campus in the form of fairs, theatre, and special performing groups. Social life is very active, though somewhat 'toned down' from previous years due to recent crackdowns on fraternity parties." Greeks still exert quite a strong influence, however. On campus, students enjoy going to Kehr Union, basketball courts, and the Schuylkill Lawn. Off campus, they spend time at Hess', Sal's, Good Ol' Days, and Lemon's Tavern. Favorite university events are the Bloomsburg Fair, Homecoming Weekend, the Renaissance Fair, and Greek Week.
**Services and counseling/handicapped student services:** Placement services. Health service. Day care. Counseling services for minority, veteran, and older students. Personal counseling. Career and academic guidance services. Physically disabled student services. Learning disabled services. Notetaking services. Tutors. Reader services for the blind.
**Campus organizations:** Undergraduate student government. Student newspaper (Voice, published weekly). Literary magazine. Yearbook. Radio and TV stations. Concert choir, madrigal singers, men's glee club, women's choral ensemble, band, chamber orchestra, Bloomsburg Players, forensic society, literary group, film society, 124 organizations in all. 10 fraternities, no chapter houses; 10 sororities, no chapter houses. 12% of men join a fraternity. 15% of women join a sorority.
**Religious organizations:** Christian Student Fellowship, Catholic Campus Ministry, Fellowship of Christian Athletes, Intervarsity Christian Fellowship, Protestant Campus Ministry, Hillel.
**Minority/foreign student organizations:** Association of Hispanic Students, Black Cultural Society. Third World Cultural Society.

**ATHLETICS. Physical education requirements:** Three semester hours of physical education required.
**Intercollegiate competition:** 15% of students participate. Baseball (M), basketball (M,W), cheerleading (M,W), cross-country (M,W), diving (M,W), field hockey (W), football (M), lacrosse (W), soccer (M,W), softball (W), swimming (M,W), tennis (M,W), track and field (outdoor) (M,W), wrestling (M). Member of Eastern Wrestling League, ECAC, NCAA Division II, NCAA Divison I for wrestling, Pennsylvania State Athletic Conference.
**Intramural and club sports:** Intramural hockey, lacrosse, rugby. Men's club Alpine skiing, billiards, bowling, cycling, fencing, tennis, ultimate frisbee, volleyball, weightlifting. Women's club Alpine skiing, billiards, bowling, cycling, fencing, tennis, ultimate frisbee, volleyball, weightlifting.

**ADMISSIONS. Academic basis for candidate selection** (in order of priority): Standardized test scores, secondary school record, class rank.
**Nonacademic basis for candidate selection:** Character and personality, extracurricular participation, and geographical distribution are considered.
**Requirements:** Graduation from secondary school is required; GED is accepted. 16 units and the following program of study are recommended: 4 units of English, 3 units of math, 3 units of science, 2 units of foreign language, 4 units of social studies. Minimum combined SAT score of 850, rank in top half of secondary school class, and minimum 2.5 GPA recommended. Applicants are admitted in one of the following academic categories: computer science, nursing, allied health sciences, arts and sciences, business administration, business education, interpreting for the deaf, teacher education, or undeclared. More selective requirements for nursing, communication disorders, and computer and information science programs. EOP for applicants not normally admissible. Act 101 program for applicants not normally admissible. SAT is required. Campus visit recommended. No off-campus interviews.
**Procedure:** Take SAT by December of 12th year. Suggest filing application by December 1; no deadline. Notification of admission on rolling basis. Reply is required by February 1 or within 30 days of acceptance. $100 room deposit, half of which is refundable. Freshmen accepted for terms other than fall.
**Special programs:** Credit and/or placement may be granted through CEEB Advanced Placement exams for scores of 3 or higher. Credit and/or placement may be granted through CLEP general and subject exams. Credit and placement may be granted through military and life experience. Early entrance/early admission program. Concurrent enrollment program.
**Transfer students:** Transfer students accepted for terms other than fall. In fall 1993, 21% of all new students were transfers into all classes. 1,183 transfer applications were received, 486 were accepted. Application deadline is March 15 for fall; October 15 for spring. Minimum 2.0 GPA required. Lowest course grade accepted is "C+." Maximum number of transferable credits is 64 semester hours from a two-year school and 96 semester hours from a four-year school. At least 32 of final 64 semester hours must be completed at the university to receive degree.
**Admissions contact:** Bernie Vinovrski, M.S./M.B.A., Director of Admissions. 717 389-4316.

**FINANCIAL AID. Available aid:** Pell grants, SEOG, state grants, school scholarships and grants, private scholarships, ROTC scholarships, academic merit scholarships, and athletic scholarships. Perkins Loans (NDSL), PLUS, and Stafford Loans (GSL).
**Supporting data/closing dates:** FAFSA: Deadline is March 15. PHEAA/PAIR: Deadline is March 15. Notification of awards on rolling basis.
**Financial aid contact:** Thomas Lyons, M.A., Director of Financial Aid. 717 389-4279.

**STUDENT EMPLOYMENT.** College Work/Study Program. Institutional employment. 28% of full-time undergraduates work on campus during school year. Students may expect to earn an average of $2,700 during school year. Off-campus part-time employment opportunities rated "fair."

**COMPUTER FACILITIES.** 250 IBM/IBM-compatible and Macintosh/Apple microcomputers. Students may access AT&T, UNISYS minicomputer/mainframe systems. Client/LAN operating systems include Apple/Macintosh, DOS. Computer languages and software packages include BMD/BMDP, C, COBOL, FORTRAN, PL/1, SPSS. Computer facilities are available to all students.
**Fees:** None.
**Hours:** 90 hours/week.

**GRADUATE CAREER DATA.** Highest graduate school enrollments: Dickinson Law School, Lehigh U, and Pennsylvania State U. Companies and businesses that hire graduates: Johns Hopkins, Peat Marwick, Prudential.

**PROMINENT ALUMNI/AE.** Chuck Daly, head basketball coach, 1992 U.S. Olympic basketball team.

# Bryn Mawr College

**Bryn Mawr, PA 19010-2899** **215 526-5000**

**1994-95 Costs.** Tuition: $18,165. Room & board: $6,750. Fees, books, misc. academic expenses (school's estimate): $880.
**Enrollment.** 1,093 women (full-time). Freshman class: 1,500 applicants, 825 accepted, 313 enrolled. Graduate enrollment: 116 men, 423 women.
**Test score averages/ranges.** Average SAT scores: 630 verbal, 630 math. Range of SAT scores of middle 50%: 570-670 verbal, 570-680 math.
**Faculty.** 137 full-time; 50 part-time. 99% of faculty holds doctoral degree. Student/faculty ratio: 9 to 1.
**Selectivity rating.** Highly competitive.

**PROFILE.** Bryn Mawr, founded in 1885, is a private, liberal arts college for women; its graduate schools became coeducational in 1930. Its 135-acre campus is located in Bryn Mawr, 11 miles west of Philadelphia.

**Accreditation:** MSACS.
**Religious orientation:** Bryn Mawr College is nonsectarian; no religious requirements.
**Library:** Collections totaling over 926,464 volumes, 1,958 periodical subscriptions, and 108,724 microform items.
**Special facilities/museums:** Museum of classical and Near Eastern archaeology, mineral collection, child study institute, on-campus nursery school, electron microscope.
**Athletic facilities:** Gymnasium, swimming pool, diving well, field hockey, rugby, and soccer fields, badminton, basketball, tennis, and volleyball courts, fencing and weight rooms.

**STUDENT BODY. Undergraduate profile:** 13% are state residents; 6% are transfers. 15.5% Asian-American, 5% Black, 4.4% Hispanic, .1% Native American, 68% White, 7% Other. Average age of undergraduates is 20.
**Freshman profile:** 13% of freshmen who took SAT scored 700 or over on verbal, 12% scored 700 or over on math; 59% scored 600 or over on verbal, 62% scored 600 or over on math; 94% scored 500 or over on verbal, 95% scored 500 or over on math; 99% scored 400 or over on verbal, 99% scored 400 or over on math; 100% scored 300 or over on verbal, 100% scored 300 or over on math. 99% of accepted applicants took SAT. 71% of freshmen come from public schools.
**Undergraduate achievement:** 96% of fall 1992 freshmen returned for fall 1993 term. 84% of entering class graduated. 30% of students who completed a degree program immediately went on to graduate study.

**Foreign students:** 126 students are from out of the country. Countries represented include Canada, Hong Kong, India, Japan, Kenya, and Korea; 51 in all.

**PROGRAMS OF STUDY. Degrees:** A.B., A.B./B.S., A.B./M.A., A.B./M.C.P.
**Majors:** Africana Studies, Anthropology, Astronomy, Biology, Chemistry, Chinese, Classical Languages, Classical/Near Eastern Archaeology, Classical Studies, Comparative Literature, Computer Science, Dance, East Asian Studies, Economics, English, Environmental Science, Feminist/Gender Studies, Fine Arts, French/French Studies, Geology, German/German Studies, Greek, Growth/Structure of Cities, Hebrew/Judaic Studies, Hispanic/Hispanic-American Studies, History, History of Art, Independent Major, International Economic Relations, Italian, Japanese, Latin, Mathematics, Music, Neural/Behavioral Studies, Peace Studies, Philosophy, Physics, Political Science, Psychology, Religion, Romance Languages, Russian, Sociology, Spanish, Theater.
**Distribution of degrees:** The majors with the highest enrollment are political science, English, and biology; classical languages, German, and romance languages have the lowest.
**Requirements:** General education requirement.
**Academic regulations:** Minimum 2.0 GPA required for graduation.
**Special:** Minors offered in all majors. Credit granted for creative work in art, dance, and music. Courses offered in performing arts and education. Interdepartmental courses. Self-scheduled exams. Self-designed majors. Double majors. Dual degrees. Independent study. Accelerated study. Pass/fail grading option. Graduate school at which undergraduates may take graduate-level courses. Preprofessional programs in medicine, veterinary science, and dentistry. 3-2 engineering program with U of Pennsylvania. Cross-registration with Haverford Coll, Swarthmore Coll, and U of Pennsylvania. Close academic, residential, and social cooperation with Haverford Coll. Exchange program with Spelman Coll. Teacher certification in secondary education. Certification in specific subject areas. Exchange program abroad in Japan (Tsuda Coll). Study abroad also in France, Germany, Italy, Russia, Spain, and many other countries. ROTC and AFROTC at U of Pennsylvania. NROTC at St. Joseph's U.
**Academic Assistance:** Remedial study skills. Nonremedial tutoring.

**STUDENT LIFE. Housing:** All freshmen must live on campus unless living with family. Coed and women's dorms. 95% of students live in college housing.
**Services and counseling/handicapped student services:** Placement services. Health service. Women's center. Day care. Counseling services for minority and older students. Birth control, personal, and psychological counseling. Career and academic guidance services. Religious counseling. Physically disabled student services. Notetaking services. Tape recorders. Tutors. Reader services for the blind.
**Campus organizations:** Undergraduate student government. Student newspaper (Bi-College News; Bryn Mawr College News). Literary magazine. Yearbook. Radio station. Chamber music ensemble, chorus, orchestra, debating, theatre workshop, dance group, outing and riding clubs, special-interest groups, 100 organizations in all.
**Religious organizations:** Catholic, Protestant, Jewish, and Islamic groups.
**Minority/foreign student organizations:** Color, Sisterhood, Muertes, Asian Student Association, Bisexual/Gay/Lesbian Alliance. International Student Association.

**ATHLETICS. Physical education requirements:** Two semesters of physical education required.
**Intercollegiate competition:** 17% of students participate. Badminton (W), basketball (W), cross-country (W), diving (W), field hockey (W), lacrosse (W), soccer (W), swimming (W), tennis (W), volleyball (W). Member of Centennial Conference, NCAA Division III, PAIAW, USCBA, USCBA, USFHA, USWLA.
**Intramural and club sports:** 2% of students participate. Intramural basketball, soccer, softball, volleyball. Women's club fencing, rugby, track/field, ultimate frisbee.

**ADMISSIONS. Academic basis for candidate selection** (in order of priority): Secondary school record, school's recommendation, standardized test scores, class rank, essay.
**Nonacademic basis for candidate selection:** Character and personality and particular talent or ability are important. Extracurricular participation, geographical distribution, and alumni/ae relationship are considered.
**Requirements:** Graduation from secondary school is recommended; GED is accepted. 16 units and the following program of study are required: 4 units of English, 3 units of math, 1 unit of lab science, 4 units of foreign language, 1 unit of history, 2 units of academic electives. SAT is required; ACT may be substituted. ACH required. Campus visit and interview recommended. Off-campus interviews available with admissions and alumni representatives.
**Procedure:** Take SAT or ACT by January of 12th year. Take ACH by January of 12th year. Visit college for interview by January of 12th year. Application deadline is January 15. Notification of admission by April 15. Reply is required by May 1. $200 nonrefundable room deposit. Freshmen accepted for fall term only.
**Special programs:** Admission may be deferred one year. Credit and/or placement may be granted through CEEB Advanced Placement exams for scores of 4 or higher. Credit and placement may be granted through challenge exams. Early decision program. In fall 1993, 157 applied for early decision and 79 were accepted. Deadline for applying for early decision is November 15. Early entrance/early admission program.
**Transfer students:** Transfer students accepted for terms other than fall. In fall 1993, 6% of all new students were transfers into all classes. 82 transfer applications were received, 30 were accepted. Application deadline is March 15 for fall; November 1 for spring. Minimum 3.0 GPA recommended. Lowest course grade accepted is "C." Maximum number of transferable semester hours is the equivalent of two years of course work. At least 24 semester hours must be completed at the college to receive degree.
**Admissions contact:** Elizabeth G. Vermey, M.A., Director of Admissions. 215 526-5152.

**FINANCIAL AID. Available aid:** Pell grants, SEOG, state scholarships and grants, school scholarships and grants, private scholarships and grants, ROTC scholarships, and aid for undergraduate foreign students. Perkins Loans (NDSL), PLUS, Stafford Loans (GSL), state loans, school loans, private loans, and SLS. Knight Tuition Plans, AMS, deferred payment plan, and guaranteed tuition. College Prepaid Tuition Plan. Prepaid Tuition Loan. Annual Tuition and Expenses Loan Program.
**Financial aid statistics:** In 1993-94, 49% of all undergraduate applicants received aid; 49% of freshman applicants. Average amounts of aid awarded freshmen: Scholarships and grants, $12,789; loans, $2,200.
**Supporting data/closing dates:** FAFSA. School's own aid application: Deadline is January 15. State aid form: Accepted on rolling basis. Income tax forms: Accepted on rolling basis. Special Circumstances Form. Notification of awards begins April 1.
**Financial aid contact:** Nancy Monnich, Director of Financial Aid. 215 526-5245.

**STUDENT EMPLOYMENT.** College Work/Study Program. Institutional employment. 75% of full-time undergraduates work on campus during school year. Students may expect to earn an average of $1,375 during school year. Off-campus part-time employment opportunities rated "good."

**COMPUTER FACILITIES.** 150 IBM/IBM-compatible, Macintosh/Apple, and RISC-/UNIX-based microcomputers; 125 are networked. Students may access Digital, SUN minicomputer/mainframe systems, Internet. Residence halls may be equipped with modems. Client/LAN operating systems include Apple/Macintosh, DOS, UNIX/XENIX/AIX. Computer languages and software packages include BASIC, C, Cricketgraph, Excel, FORTRAN, Microsoft Word, MINITAB, Paradox, Pascal, Quattro, SPSS, TST; 27 in all. Computer facilities are available to all students.
**Fees:** None.
**Hours:** 24 hours.

**GRADUATE CAREER DATA.** Graduate school percentages: 6% enter law school. 9% enter medical school. 2% enter graduate business programs. 18% enter graduate arts and sciences programs. Highest graduate school enrollments: Columbia U, Harvard U, Stanford U, UC Berkeley, U of Pennsylvania, U of Rochester. 14% of graduates choose careers in business and industry. Companies and businesses that hire graduates: banks, Bell Telephone, IBM.

**PROMINENT ALUMNI/AE.** Alice Rivlin, economist and Deputy Director OMB; Hannah Holborn Gray, president, U of Chicago; Anna Kisselgoff, dance critic, *New York Times*; Betsy Zubrow Cohen, banker; Candace Pert, neuroscientist; Katharine Hepburn, actress.

# Bucknell University

**Lewisburg, PA 17837 — 717 523-1271**

**1994-95 Costs.** Tuition: $18,440. Room: $2,545. Board: $2,205. Fees, books, misc. academic expenses (school's estimate): $610.
**Enrollment.** Undergraduates: 1,730 men, 1,596 women (full-time). Freshman class: 6,548 applicants, 3,813 accepted, 862 enrolled. Graduate enrollment: 128 men, 115 women.
**Test score averages/ranges.** Range of SAT scores of middle 50%: 510-590 verbal, 590-670 math.
**Faculty.** 241 full-time; 18 part-time. 95% of faculty holds doctoral degree. Student/faculty ratio: 13 to 1.
**Selectivity rating.** Highly competitive.

**PROFILE.** Bucknell, founded in 1846, is a private university. Programs are offered through the Colleges of Arts and Sciences and Engineering. Its 300-acre campus is located in Lewisburg, 55 miles from Harrisburg. Buildings on campus and in town retain 19th century architectural styles.

**Accreditation:** MSACS. Professionally accredited by the Accreditation Board for Engineering and Technology, the Computing Sciences Accreditation Board, the National Association of Schools of Music.
**Religious orientation:** Bucknell University is nonsectarian; no religious requirements.
**Library:** Collections totaling over 562,000 volumes, 2,294 periodical subscriptions, and 538,000 microform items.
**Special facilities/museums:** Art gallery, center for performing arts, poetry center, photography lab, observatory, 44-acre nature site, greenhouse, primate facility, gas chromatograph/mass spectrometer, nuclear magnetic resonance spectrometer.
**Athletic facilities:** Gymnasium, field house, swimming pool, stadium, tennis courts, golf course, athletic fields.

**STUDENT BODY. Undergraduate profile:** 33% are state residents; 5% are transfers. 3% Asian-American, 3% Black, 2% Hispanic, 1% Native American, 89% White, 2% Other. Average age of undergraduates is 20.
**Freshman profile:** 18% of freshmen who took SAT scored 700 or over on math; 21% scored 600 or over on verbal, 64% scored 600 or over on math; 73% scored 500 or over on verbal, 94% scored 500 or over on math; 97% scored 400 or over on verbal, 98% scored 400 or over on math; 98% scored 300 or over on verbal. 99% of accepted applicants took SAT; 1% took ACT. 68% of freshmen come from public schools.
**Undergraduate achievement:** 96% of fall 1992 freshmen returned for fall 1993 term. 85% of entering class graduated. 28% of students who completed a degree program immediately went on to graduate study.
**Foreign students:** 91 students are from out of the country. Countries represented include China, Greece, India, Japan, Pakistan, and the United Kingdom; 40 in all.

**PROGRAMS OF STUDY. Degrees:** B.A., B.Mus., B.S., B.S.Bus.Admin., B.S.Ed., B.S.Eng.
**Majors:** Accounting, Animal Behavior, Anthropology, Applied Music, Art, Art History, Biology, Cell Biology/Biochemistry, Chemical Engineering, Chemistry, Civil Engineering, Classics, Computer Engineering, Computer Science, Early Childhood Education, East Asian Studies, Economics, Educational Research, Electrical Engineering, Elementary Education, Engineering, English, Environmental Geology, Environmental Studies, French, Geography, Geology, German, History, International Relations, Japanese/East Asian Studies, Latin American Studies, Linguistics, Management, Management/Policy, Marketing, Mathematics, Mechanical Engineering, Mechanical Engineering/Management, Music, Music Education, Music History, Music Performance, Music Theory/Composition, Operations Research/Management Science, Personnel, Philosophy, Physics, Political Science, Psychology, Religion, Russian Studies, Secondary Education, Sociology, Spanish, Theatre/Drama, Women's Studies.

**Distribution of degrees:** The majors with the highest enrollment are economics, management, and political science; geography, classics, and Latin American studies have the lowest.
**Requirements:** General education requirement.
**Academic regulations:** Freshmen must maintain minimum 1.8 GPA; sophomores, 1.9 GPA; juniors, 2.0 GPA; seniors, 2.0 GPA.
**Special:** Minors offered in 60 fields. Student-planned interdisciplinary curriculum with flexible distribution and major guidelines. Classical arts in residence. Self-designed majors. Double majors. Dual degrees. Independent study. Graduate school at which undergraduates may take graduate-level courses. Preprofessional programs in law, medicine, veterinary science, and dentistry. Five-year B.S./M.S. biology, chemistry, engineering, and math programs. Five-year B.S./B.A. engineering/liberal arts program. Washington Semester and UN Semester. Teacher certification in early childhood, elementary, and secondary education. Certification in specific subject areas. Exchange programs abroad in England and France. Study abroad also in Australia, Belgium, Germany, Italy, Japan, Kenya, the Netherlands, Russia, Scotland, and Spain. ROTC.
**Honors:** Phi Beta Kappa. Honors program. Honor societies.
**Academic Assistance:** Nonremedial tutoring.

**STUDENT LIFE. Housing:** All unmarried students under age 21 must live on campus unless living near campus with relatives. Coed, women's, and men's dorms. Fraternity housing. Off-campus privately-owned housing. Off-campus married-student housing. 83% of students live in college housing.
**Social atmosphere:** According to the student newspaper, Bucknell students are a rowdy bunch, but "the University needs to come up with more social programs that students will participate in. In addition, more student social space is needed on campus." Greeks are very influential on student social life "for the time being" but "because University alcohol policy is much stricter now than in the past, parties are moving off campus to apartments." Popular events include House Party Weekend, Homecoming, the Performing Arts Series, and concerts (recently Squeeze and the Steve Miller Band). On campus, students gather at the Bison (sub shop) and the snack bar. Popular destinations off campus include the Bull Run Inn and Vennari's (pizza).
**Services and counseling/handicapped student services:** Placement services. Health service. Women's center. Counseling services for minority and military students. Birth control, personal, and psychological counseling. Career and academic guidance services. Religious counseling. Physically disabled student services. Learning disabled services. Tape recorders. Tutors. Reader services for the blind.
**Campus organizations:** Undergraduate student government. Student newspaper (Bucknellian, published once/week). Literary magazine. Yearbook. Radio station. Jazz and rock ensemble, debating, theatre, modern dance and outing groups, professional and service groups, Big Brothers/Big Sisters, volunteer services, student technical societies, 130 organizations in all. 12 fraternities, all with chapter houses; eight sororities, no chapter houses. 52% of men join a fraternity. 58% of women join a sorority.
**Religious organizations:** Christian Fellowship, Hillel, Eastern Orthodox Christian group, Catholic Campus Ministry, Chapel Committee, Newman Club.
**Minority/foreign student organizations:** NAACP, African-American Cultural Society, Cumbre Multicultural Center, Students for Asian Awareness. International Organization, Pakistan-India Association.

**ATHLETICS. Physical education requirements:** None.
**Intercollegiate competition:** 25% of students participate. Baseball (M), basketball (M,W), crew (M,W), cross-country (M,W), diving (M,W), field hockey (W), football (M), golf (M), lacrosse (M,W), soccer (M,W), softball (W), swimming (M,W), tennis (M,W), track (indoor) (M,W), track (outdoor) (M,W), track and field (indoor) (M,W), track and field (outdoor) (M,W), volleyball (W), water polo (M), wrestling (M). Member of East Coast Wrestling Association, ECAC, NCAA Division I, Patriot League.
**Intramural and club sports:** 50% of students participate. Intramural basketball, billiards, bowling, cross-country, field hockey, golf, handball, racquetball, softball, squash, swimming, table tennis, tennis, track and field, volleyball, weight lifting. Men's club Alpine skiing, cycling, ice hockey, lacrosse, rugby, sailing, squash, ultimate frisbee, volleyball. Women's club Alpine skiing, cycling, equestrian sports, golf, rugby, sailing, ultimate frisbee, water polo.

**ADMISSIONS. Academic basis for candidate selection** (in order of priority): Secondary school record, class rank, standardized test scores, school's recommendation, essay.
**Nonacademic basis for candidate selection:** Character and personality, extracurricular participation, particular talent or ability, and alumni/ae relationship are important. Geographical distribution is considered.
**Requirements:** Graduation from secondary school is required; GED is accepted. 16 units and the following program of study are required: 4 units of English, 3 units of math, 2 units of lab science, 2 units of foreign language, 2 units of social studies, 2 units of history, 1 unit of academic electives. Audition required of music program applicants. SAT is required; ACT may be substituted. Campus visit and interview recommended. Off-campus interviews available with an alumni representative.
**Procedure:** Take SAT or ACT by January of 12th year. Visit college for interview by January 15 of 12th year. Application deadline is January 1. Notification of admission by April 1. Reply is required by May 1. $200 nonrefundable tuition deposit. Freshmen accepted for fall term only.
**Special programs:** Admission may be deferred two years. Credit and/or placement may be granted through CEEB Advanced Placement exams for scores of 3 or higher. Placement may be granted through CLEP subject exams. Credit may be granted through challenge exams. Early decision program. In fall 1993, 436 applied for early decision and 290 were accepted. Deadline for applying for early decision is December 1. Early entrance/early admission program.
**Transfer students:** Transfer students accepted for terms other than fall. In fall 1992, 5% of all new students were transfers into all classes. 156 transfer applications were received, 79 were accepted. Application deadline is April 1 for fall; December 1 for spring. Minimum 2.5 GPA required. Lowest course grade accepted is "C." Maximum number of transferable credits is 80 semester hours. At least 48 semester hours must be completed at the university to receive degree.
**Admissions contact:** Mark D. Davies, M.S., Director of Admissions. 717 524-1101.

**FINANCIAL AID. Available aid:** Pell grants, SEOG, state scholarships and grants, school scholarships, private scholarships, and ROTC scholarships. Perkins Loans (NDSL), PLUS, Stafford Loans (GSL), state loans, and SLS. Higher Education Services Installment Payment Plan.
**Financial aid statistics:** In 1993-94, 47% of all undergraduate applicants received aid; 83% of freshman applicants. Average amounts of aid awarded freshmen: Scholarships and grants, $12,038; loans, $2,900.
**Supporting data/closing dates:** FAFSA: Priority filing date is February 15. FAF: Deadline is February 15. Notification of awards begins March 25.
**Financial aid contact:** Ronald T. Laszewski, M.Ed., Director of Financial Aid. 717 524-1331.

**STUDENT EMPLOYMENT.** College Work/Study Program. Institutional employment. 50% of full-time undergraduates work on campus during school year. Students may expect to earn an average of $1,500 during school year. Off-campus part-time employment opportunities rated "poor."

**COMPUTER FACILITIES.** 650 IBM/IBM-compatible and Macintosh/Apple microcomputers; 475 are networked. Students may access Bull, Digital, Hewlett-Packard, SUN minicomputer/mainframe systems, Internet. Residence halls may be equipped with stand-alone microcomputers, networked microcomputers, modems. 100 major computer languages and software packages available. Computer facilities are available to all students.
**Fees:** None.
**Hours:** 24 hours.

**GRADUATE CAREER DATA.** Graduate school percentages: 5% enter law school. 4% enter medical school. 1% enter dental school. 3% enter graduate business programs. 14% enter graduate arts and sciences programs. Highest graduate school enrollments: Cornell U, Harvard U, Pennsylvania State U. 40% of graduates choose careers in business and industry. Companies and businesses that hire graduates: Anderson Consulting, American Express, Big Six accounting firms, May Co.

**PROMINENT ALUMNI/AE.** Edward Herrmann and Ralph Waite, actors; Peter Diamandis, magazine publisher; Philip Roth, author; Susan J. Crawford, justice, U.S. Court of Military Appeals; Robert Andrews, congressman; Kenneth G. Langone, financier.

# Cabrini College

**Radnor, PA 19087-3699 — 215 971-8100**

**1993-94 Costs.** Tuition: $9,742. Room & board: $5,790. Fees, books, misc. academic expenses (school's estimate): $780.
**Enrollment.** Undergraduates: 326 men, 700 women (full-time). Freshman class: 547 applicants, 434 accepted, 161 enrolled. Graduate enrollment: 52 men, 331 women.
**Test score averages/ranges.** Average SAT scores: 438 verbal, 453 math. Range of SAT scores of middle 50%: 400-502 verbal, 400-499 math.
**Faculty.** 43 full-time; 83 part-time. 55% of faculty holds doctoral degree. Student/faculty ratio: 18 to 1.
**Selectivity rating.** Less competitive.

**PROFILE.** Cabrini, founded in 1957, is a church-affiliated college of liberal arts and sciences. Its 100-acre campus, once a country estate, is located in Radnor, 10 miles from Philadelphia; the original buildings were designed in the early 1900s.

**Accreditation:** MSACS.
**Religious orientation:** Cabrini College is affiliated with the Roman Catholic Church (Missionary Sisters of the Sacred Heart); no religious requirements.
**Library:** Collections totaling over 80,300 volumes, 400 periodical subscriptions, and 5,566 microform items.
**Special facilities/museums:** On-campus children's school.
**Athletic facilities:** Gymnasium, tennis courts, outdoor fields, fitness center with Universal equipment.

**STUDENT BODY. Undergraduate profile:** 73% are state residents; 37% are transfers. 1% Asian-American, 4% Black, 1% Hispanic, 93% White, 1% Other. Average age of undergraduates is 20.
**Freshman profile:** 1% of freshmen who took SAT scored 600 or over on verbal, 7% scored 600 or over on math; 23% scored 500 or over on verbal, 28% scored 500 or over on math; 71% scored 400 or over on verbal, 78% scored 400 or over on math; 99% scored 300 or over on verbal, 100% scored 300 or over on math. 97% of accepted applicants took SAT; 3% took ACT. 37% of freshmen come from public schools.
**Undergraduate achievement:** 78% of fall 1991 freshmen returned for fall 1992 term. 49% of entering class graduated.
**Foreign students:** Seven students are from out of the country. Countries represented include Brazil, Canada, Italy, Japan, Panama, and Spain.

**PROGRAMS OF STUDY. Degrees:** B.A., B.S., B.S.Ed., B.Soc.Work.
**Majors:** Accounting, American Studies, Arts Administration, Biology, Business Administration, Chemistry, Computer Information Science, Education, English, English/Communications, Fine Arts, French, History, Human Resources Management, Individualized Major, Marketing, Mathematics, Medical Technology, Organizational Management, Philosophy, Political Science, Psychology, Religion, Social Work, Sociology, Spanish.
**Distribution of degrees:** The majors with the highest enrollment are education, business, and communications; chemistry and foreign languages have the lowest.
**Requirements:** General education requirement.
**Academic regulations:** Minimum 2.0 GPA required for graduation.
**Special:** Minors offered in most majors and in graphic arts. Self-designed majors. Double majors. Dual degrees. Independent study. Accelerated study. Pass/fail grading option. Internships. Cooperative education programs. Graduate school at which undergraduates may take graduate-level courses. Preprofessional programs in law, medicine, pharmacy, nursing, and physical therapy. 2-2 programs with Philadelphia Coll of Pharmacy, Thomas Jefferson U, West Chester U, and Widener U. Exchange programs with Eastern Coll, Rosemont Coll, and Villanova U. Teacher certification in early childhood, elementary, second-

ary, and special education. Certification in specific subject areas. Study abroad in England, France, and Spain. ROTC at Valley Forge Military Academy.
**Honors:** Honors program. Honor societies.
**Academic Assistance:** Remedial reading, writing, math, and study skills. Nonremedial tutoring.

**ADMISSIONS. Academic basis for candidate selection** (in order of priority): Secondary school record, class rank, school's recommendation, standardized test scores, essay.
**Nonacademic basis for candidate selection:** Character and personality are important. Extracurricular participation, particular talent or ability, geographical distribution, and alumni/ae relationship are considered.
**Requirements:** Graduation from secondary school is recommended; GED is accepted. 17 units and the following program of study are required: 4 units of English, 3 units of math, 3 units of science, 2 units of foreign language, 3 units of social studies, 2 units of academic electives. Minimum combined SAT score of 900, rank in top half of secondary school class, and minimum 2.5 GPA recommended. EOP for applicants not normally admissible. Conditional admission possible for applicants not meeting standard requirements. Act 101 program for in-state applicants not normally admissible. SAT is required; ACT may be substituted. Campus visit and interview recommended. Off-campus interviews available with admissions and alumni representatives.
**Procedure:** Take SAT or ACT by November of 12th year. Visit college for interview by February of 12th year. Suggest filing application by December 31. Notification of admission on rolling basis. Reply is required by May 1. $150 tuition deposit, refundable until May 1. $250 room deposit, refundable until May 1. Freshmen accepted for terms other than fall.
**Special programs:** Admission may be deferred one year. Credit and/or placement may be granted through CEEB Advanced Placement exams for scores of 3 or higher. Credit and/or placement may be granted through CLEP subject exams. Credit may be granted through Regents College, ACT PEP, and DANTES exams and military experience. Placement may be granted through challenge exams. Credit and placement may be granted through life experience. Early entrance/early admission program. Concurrent enrollment program.
**Transfer students:** Transfer students accepted for terms other than fall. In fall 1992, 37% of all new students were transfers into all classes. 139 transfer applications were received, 102 were accepted. Application deadline is rolling for fall; rolling for spring. Minimum 2.2 GPA recommended. Lowest course grade accepted is "C." Maximum number of transferable credits is 78 semester hours. At least 45 semester hours must be completed at the college to receive degree.
**Admissions contact:** Nancy Gardner, Director of Admissions. 215 971-8552.

**FINANCIAL AID. Available aid:** Pell grants, SEOG, state scholarships, school scholarships and grants, private scholarships and grants, ROTC scholarships, and academic merit scholarships. Perkins Loans (NDSL), PLUS, Stafford Loans (GSL), state loans, and SLS. AMS and Tuition Management Systems.
**Financial aid statistics:** In 1992-93, 100% of all undergraduate applicants received aid. Average amounts of aid awarded freshmen: Scholarships and grants, $2,000; loans, $2,625.
**Supporting data/closing dates:** School's own aid application: Priority filing date is April 1; accepted on rolling basis. State aid form: Priority filing date is April 1. Income tax forms: Priority filing date is April 1. Notification of awards on rolling basis.
**Financial aid contact:** Elizabeth L. Cairns, M.S., Director of Financial Aid. 215 971-8240.

# California University of Pennsylvania

**California, PA 15419** **412 938-4000**

**1992-93 Costs.** Tuition: $2,828 (state residents), $6,122 (out-of-state). Room & board: $3,460. Fees, books, misc. academic expenses (school's estimate): $1,156.
**Enrollment.** Undergraduates: 2,464 men, 2,323 women (full-time). Freshman class: 2,746 applicants, 1,505 accepted, 1,028 enrolled. Graduate enrollment: 356 men, 522 women.
**Test score averages/ranges.** Average SAT scores: 385 verbal, 416 math. Range of SAT scores of middle 50%: 330-430 verbal, 350-460 math.
**Faculty.** 332 full-time; 53 part-time. 40% of faculty holds doctoral degree. Student/faculty ratio: 19 to 1.
**Selectivity rating.** Competitive.

**PROFILE.** California University of Pennsylvania, founded in 1852, is a public institution. Programs are offered through the Colleges of Liberal Arts, Science and Technology, and Education and the Graduate School. Its 143-acre campus is located in the town of California, 25 miles from Pittsburgh.

**Accreditation:** MSACS. Professionally accredited by the Council on Social Work Education, the National Council for Accreditation of Teacher Education, the National League for Nursing.
**Religious orientation:** California University of Pennsylvania is nonsectarian; no religious requirements.
**Library:** Collections totaling over 327,126 volumes, 1,788 periodical subscriptions, and 395,111 microform items.
**Special facilities/museums:** Art museum.
**Athletic facilities:** Stadium, baseball and softball fields, track, cross-country trail, weight and wrestling rooms, fitness center, tennis courts, bowling alley.

**STUDENT BODY. Undergraduate profile:** 95% are state residents; 29% are transfers. 1% Asian-American, 5% Black, 1% Hispanic, 1% Native American, 92% White. Average age of undergraduates is 24.
**Freshman profile:** 95% of accepted applicants took SAT.
**Undergraduate achievement:** 75% of fall 1991 freshmen returned for fall 1992 term. 23% of entering class graduated. 17% of students who completed a degree program immediately went on to graduate study.
**Foreign students:** 87 students are from out of the country. Countries represented include China, Germany, India, Japan, Russia, and Saudi Arabia; 41 in all.

**PROGRAMS OF STUDY. Degrees:** B.A., B.S., B.S.Ed., B.S.Nurs.
**Majors:** Accounting, Anthropology, Art, Arts in Human Services, Athletic Trainer, Biology, Business Administration, Business Economics, Chemistry, Community Service Personnel, Early Childhood Education, Earth Science, Economics, Elementary Education, Emphasis on Radio/Television, English, Environmental Studies, Finance, French, Geography, Geology, German, Gerontology, Graphic Communications Technology, History, Industrial Arts Education, Industrial Management Technology, Industrial Organizational Psychology, Industrial Technology, Interdisciplinary Major, Management, Marketing, Mathematics, Nursing, Philosophy, Physics, Political Science, Pre-Health Professions, Professional Writing, Psychology, Science/Technology, Secondary Education, Slavic/Eastern European Studies, Sociology, Soviet Studies, Spanish, Special Education, Speech, Speech Pathology/Audiology, Theatre.
**Distribution of degrees:** The majors with the highest enrollment are early childhood education, elementary education, and accounting.
**Requirements:** General education requirement.
**Academic regulations:** Freshmen must maintain minimum 1.75 GPA; sophomores, 1.85 GPA; juniors, 1.95 GPA; seniors, 2.0 GPA.
**Special:** Endorsement programs (available as an addition to another certification program) in driver's training, environmental education, and general science. Associate's degrees offered. Double majors. Dual degrees. Independent study. Accelerated study. Internships. Cooperative education programs. Graduate school at which undergraduates may take graduate-level courses. Preprofessional programs in law, medicine, veterinary science, pharmacy, dentistry, theology, optometry, and engineering. 3-2 engineering programs with Pennsylvania State U and U of Pittsburgh. Member of Pennsylvania State System of Higher Education. Member of National Student Exchange (NSE). Teacher certification in early childhood, elementary, secondary, and special education. Certification in specific subject areas. Study abroad in England, France, Germany, Italy, and Mexico. ROTC.
**Honors:** Honors program.
**Academic Assistance:** Remedial reading, writing, and math. Nonremedial tutoring.

**STUDENT LIFE. Housing:** Students may live on or off campus. Coed, women's, and men's dorms. Sorority and fraternity housing. Off-campus privately-owned housing. Off-campus married-student housing. 25% of students live in college housing.
**Services and counseling/handicapped student services:** Placement services. Health service. Women's center. Day care. Counseling services for minority, military, veteran, and older students. Birth control, personal, and psychological counseling. Career and academic guidance services. Religious counseling. Physically disabled student services. Learning disabled program/services. Notetaking services. Tape recorders. Tutors. Reader services for the blind.
**Campus organizations:** Undergraduate student government. Student newspaper (California Times). Literary magazine. Yearbook. Radio and TV stations. Band, choir, orchestra, drama group, debating, public speaking group, academic groups, service and special-interest groups, 60 organizations in all. Nine fraternities, all with chapter houses; seven sororities, all with chapter houses. 10% of men join a fraternity. 10% of women join a sorority.
**Religious organizations:** Unified Campus Ministry.
**Minority/foreign student organizations:** Black Action Group. International Student Organization.

**ATHLETICS. Physical education requirements:** Three semester hours of health/physical education required of students in School of Liberal Arts.
**Intercollegiate competition:** 35% of students participate. Basketball (M,W), cheerleading (M,W), cross-country (M,W), football (M), soccer (M,W), tennis (W), track (indoor) (M,W), track (outdoor) (M,W), track and field (indoor) (M,W), track and field (outdoor) (M,W), volleyball (W), wrestling (M). Member of ECAC, NCAA Division I for wrestling, NCAA Division II, Pennsylvania State Athletic Conference.
**Intramural and club sports:** 60% of students participate. Intramural badminton, basketball, rugby, softball, touch football, volleyball. Men's club rugby, volleyball. Women's club rugby, volleyball.

**ADMISSIONS. Academic basis for candidate selection** (in order of priority): Class rank, secondary school record, school's recommendation, standardized test scores.
**Nonacademic basis for candidate selection:** Extracurricular participation and particular talent or ability are important. Character and personality, geographical distribution, and alumni/ae relationship are considered.
**Requirements:** Graduation from secondary school is required; GED is accepted. 18 units required and the following program of study recommended: 4 units of English, 3 units of math, 2 units of science, 2 units of foreign language, 3 units of social studies, 1 unit of history, 3 units of electives. Minimum combined SAT score of 700, rank in top three-fifths of secondary school class, and minimum 2.0 GPA required. R.N. required of nursing program applicants. Act 101 program for in-state applicants not normally admissible. SAT is required; ACT may be substituted. Campus visit and interview recommended. Off-campus interviews available with admissions and alumni representatives.
**Procedure:** Take SAT or ACT by March of 12th year. Visit college for interview by March 1 of 12th year. Suggest filing application by March 1. Application deadline is August 1. Notification of admission on rolling basis. Reply is required by May 1. $75 nonrefundable tuition deposit. $100 room deposit, refundable until June 1. Freshmen accepted for terms other than fall.
**Special programs:** Admission may be deferred three years. Credit may be granted through CEEB Advanced Placement for scores of 3 or higher. Credit and/or placement may be granted through CLEP general and subject exams. Credit and placement may be granted through ACT PEP, DANTES, and challenge exams and military experience. Early decision program. In fall 1992, 110 applied for early decision and 90 were accepted. Deadline for applying for early decision is November 1. Early entrance/early admission program. Concurrent enrollment program.
**Transfer students:** Transfer students accepted for terms other than fall. In fall 1992, 29% of all new students were transfers into all classes. 870 transfer applications were received,

644 were accepted. Application deadline is August 1 for fall; December 1 for spring. Minimum 2.3 GPA required. Lowest course grade accepted is "C." Maximum number of transferable credits is 75 semester hours. At least 53 semester hours must be completed at the university to receive degree.
**Admissions contact:** Norman G. Hasbrouck, M.A., Dean of Admissions. 412 938-4404.

**FINANCIAL AID. Available aid:** Pell grants, SEOG, state scholarships and grants, school scholarships, private grants, ROTC scholarships, academic merit scholarships, athletic scholarships, and aid for undergraduate foreign students. Perkins Loans (NDSL), PLUS, Stafford Loans (GSL), state loans, school loans, and SLS. AMS.
**Financial aid statistics:** Average amounts of aid awarded freshmen: Scholarships and grants, $1,500; loans, $2,044.
**Supporting data/closing dates:** PHEAA: Priority filing date is April 1. Notification of awards on rolling basis.
**Financial aid contact:** Joyce Spencer, Acting Director of Financial Aid. 412 938-4415.

**STUDENT EMPLOYMENT.** College Work/Study Program. Institutional employment. 20% of full-time undergraduates work on campus during school year. Students may expect to earn an average of $1,000 during school year. Off-campus part-time employment opportunities rated "poor."

**COMPUTER FACILITIES.** 1,400 IBM/IBM-compatible and Macintosh/Apple microcomputers; 800 are networked. Students may access Digital minicomputer/mainframe systems, Internet. Computer languages and software packages include BASIC, C, COBOL, FORTRAN, Pascal; 30 in all. Computer facilities are available to all students.
**Fees:** None.
**Hours:** 8 AM-midn.

**GRADUATE CAREER DATA.** Graduate school percentages: 5% enter law school. 3% enter medical school. 2% enter dental school. 70% enter graduate business programs. 20% enter graduate arts and sciences programs. Highest graduate school enrollments: California U of Pennsylvania, Duquesne U, Ohio State U, U of Pittsburgh, West Virginia U. 50% of graduates choose careers in business and industry. Companies and businesses that hire graduates: Commonwealth of Pennsylvania, 84 Lumber, Mellon Bank, school districts, Westinghouse.

## Carlow College

**Pittsburgh, PA 15213** 412 578-6000

**1994-95 Costs.** Tuition: $9,826. Room & board: $4,434.
**Enrollment.** Undergraduates: 74 men, 733 women (full-time). Freshman class: 376 applicants, 306 accepted, 160 enrolled. Graduate enrollment: 43 women.
**Test score averages/ranges.** N/A.
**Faculty.** 57 full-time; 127 part-time. 34% of faculty holds highest degree in specific field. Student/faculty ratio: 12 to 1.
**Selectivity rating.** N/A.

**PROFILE.** Carlow, founded in 1929, is a church-affiliated, liberal arts college. Although it admits a small number of men, the college is primarily concerned with the education of women. Its 13-acre campus is located in the Oakland section of Pittsburgh, ten minutes from the downtown area, near the University of Pittsburgh and Carnegie Mellon University.

**Accreditation:** MSACS. Professionally accredited by the National League for Nursing.
**Religious orientation:** Carlow College is affiliated with the Roman Catholic Church (Sisters of Mercy); one semester of theology required.
**Library:** Collections totaling over 113,045 volumes, 441 periodical subscriptions, and 11,154 microform items.
**Special facilities/museums:** On-campus preschool and elementary school for education students, media center.
**Athletic facilities:** Gynmasium, dance room, swimming pool, fitness center.

**STUDENT BODY. Undergraduate profile:** 98% are state residents; 55% are transfers. 1% Asian-American, 10% Black, 1% Hispanic, 1% Native American, 87% White. Average age of undergraduates is 24.
**Freshman profile:** 86% of freshmen come from public schools.
**Undergraduate achievement:** 70% of fall 1992 freshmen returned for fall 1993 term. 42% of entering class graduated.
**Foreign students:** 25 students are from out of the country. Countries represented include China, India, Japan, Nigeria, Saudi Arabia, and South Africa; 15 in all.

**PROGRAMS OF STUDY. Degrees:** B.A., B.S., B.S.Nurs.
**Majors:** Accounting, Art, Art/Art History, Art Education, Biology, Business Management, Communication, Communication/Business Management, Comprehensive Social Studies, Early Childhood Education, Elementary Education, English, English/Business Management, Health Science, History, Independent Major, Information Management, Liberal Studies, Mathematics, Mathematics/Computer Science, Nursing, Philosophy, Psychology, Sociology/Anthropology, Special Education, Theology, Writing.
**Distribution of degrees:** The majors with the highest enrollment are nursing, communication/business, and business management; English/business management and special education have the lowest.
**Requirements:** General education requirement.
**Academic regulations:** Minimum 2.0 GPA required for graduation.
**Special:** Minors offered in several majors and in chemistry, computer science, French, media, ministry, political science, public leadership, social studies, Spanish, theatre, and women's studies. Certification offered in over 25 areas. Self-designed majors. Double majors. Independent study. Accelerated study. Pass/fail grading option. Internships. Graduate school at which undergraduates may take graduate-level courses. Preprofessional programs in law, medicine, veterinary science, pharmacy, dentistry, theology, optometry, osteopathic, physical therapy, and podiatry. Member of Pittsburgh Council on Higher Education; cross-registration possible. Teacher certification in early childhood, elementary, secondary, and special education. Certification in specific subject areas. Study abroad possible. ROTC at Carnegie Mellon U, Duquesne U, and U of Pittsburgh. NROTC at Carnegie Mellon U. AFROTC at Carnegie Mellon U and U of Pittsburgh.
**Honors:** Honors program. Honor societies.
**Academic Assistance:** Remedial reading, writing, math, and study skills. Nonremedial tutoring.

**ADMISSIONS. Academic basis for candidate selection** (in order of priority): Secondary school record, class rank, standardized test scores.
**Nonacademic basis for candidate selection:** Character and personality are emphasized. Extracurricular participation is important. Particular talent or ability and alumni/ae relationship are considered.
**Requirements:** Graduation from secondary school is required; GED is accepted. 18 units and the following program of study are required: 4 units of English, 3 units of math, 3 units of science, 8 units of electives. Rank in top two-fifths of secondary school class and minimum 3.0 GPA required. Portfolio required of art program applicants. SAT is required; ACT may be substituted. Campus visit and interview recommended. Off-campus interviews available with admissions and alumni representatives.
**Procedure:** Notification of admission within two weeks of receipt of completed application. Applicant must accept offer within four weeks of acceptance or upon receipt of financial aid offer. $100 nonrefundable tuition deposit. $100 room deposit, refundable until May 1. Freshmen accepted for terms other than fall.
**Special programs:** Admission may be deferred one year. Credit may be granted through CEEB Advanced Placement for scores of 3 or higher. Credit may be granted through CLEP general and subject exams, challenge exams, and life experience. Early decision program. Deadline for applying for early decision is September 30. Early entrance/early admission program.
**Transfer students:** Transfer students accepted for terms other than fall. In fall 1993, 55% of all new students were transfers into all classes. 251 transfer applications were received, 181 were accepted. Application deadline is rolling for fall; rolling for spring. Minimum 2.0 GPA required. Lowest course grade accepted is "C." At least 32 semester hours must be completed at the college to receive degree.
**Admissions contact:** Carol Descak, M.Ed., Director of Admissions. 412 578-6059, 800 333-CARLOW.

**FINANCIAL AID. Available aid:** Pell grants, SEOG, Federal Nursing Student Scholarships, state grants, school scholarships and grants, private scholarships and grants, academic merit scholarships, athletic scholarships, and aid for undergraduate foreign students. Perkins Loans (NDSL), PLUS, Stafford Loans (GSL), NSL, school loans, and SLS. AMS and deferred payment plan.
**Financial aid statistics:** 16% of aid is not need-based. In 1993-94, 89% of all undergraduate applicants received aid; 96% of freshman applicants. Average amounts of aid awarded freshmen: Scholarships and grants, $2,800; loans, $3,425.
**Supporting data/closing dates:** FAFSA: Priority filing date is May 1. School's own aid application: Priority filing date is May 1; accepted on rolling basis. State aid form: Priority filing date is May 1. Income tax forms: Priority filing date is May 1; accepted on rolling basis. Student Aid Report: Priority filing date is May 1. Notification of awards on rolling basis.
**Financial aid contact:** Natalie Wilson, Director of Financial Aid. 412 578-6058.

## Carnegie Mellon University

**Pittsburgh, PA 15213** 412 268-2000

**1994-95 Costs.** Tuition: $17,900. Room: $3,520. Board: $2,170. Fees, books, misc. academic expenses (school's estimate): $550.
**Enrollment.** Undergraduates: 2,960 men, 1,305 women (full-time). Freshman class: 8,720 applicants, 5,201 accepted, 1,259 enrolled. Graduate enrollment: 1,890 men, 813 women.
**Test score averages/ranges.** Range of SAT scores of middle 50%: 500-620 verbal, 610-730 math. Range of ACT scores of middle 50%: 23-29 English, 26-31 math.
**Faculty.** 552 full-time; 170 part-time. 86% of faculty holds doctoral degree. Student/faculty ratio: 8 to 1.
**Selectivity rating.** Highly competitive.

**PROFILE.** Carnegie Mellon, founded in 1900, is a private university. Programs are offered through the Carnegie Institute of Technology; the Colleges of Fine Arts and Humanities and Social Sciences; the Mellon College of Science; and the School of Industrial Management. Its 105-acre campus is located five miles from downtown Pittsburgh.

**Accreditation:** MSACS. Professionally accredited by the Accreditation Board for Engineering and Technology, the American Assembly of Collegiate Schools of Business, the National Architecture Accrediting Board, the National Association of Schools of Art and Design, the National Association of Schools of Music, the National Association of Schools of Public Affairs and Administration.
**Religious orientation:** Carnegie Mellon University is nonsectarian; no religious requirements.
**Library:** Collections totaling over 828,109 volumes, 3,727 periodical subscriptions, and 717,355 microform items.
**Special facilities/museums:** Art galleries, theatres, on-campus school, botanical institute, extensive lab facilities and equipment.
**Athletic facilities:** Gymnasiums, swimming pool, weight rooms, badminton, basketball, handball, racquetball, tennis, and volleyball courts, track, stadium, athletic fields, boat house, golf course.

**STUDENT BODY. Undergraduate profile:** 38% are state residents; 10% are transfers. 14% Asian-American, 3% Black, 3% Hispanic, 1% Native American, 56% White, 23% Other. Average age of undergraduates is 20.
**Freshman profile:** 98% of accepted applicants took SAT; 14% took ACT. 70% of freshmen come from public schools.

**Undergraduate achievement:** 88% of fall 1992 freshmen returned for fall 1993 term. 56% of entering class graduated. 28% of students who completed a degree program immediately went on to graduate study.
**Foreign students:** 131 students are from out of the country. Countries represented include Hong Kong, Japan, Malaysia, Singapore, South Korea, and Thailand; 67 in all.

**PROGRAMS OF STUDY. Degrees:** B.A., B.A.H., B.Arch., B.F.A., B.S.
**Majors:** Acting, Applied History, Applied Mathematics, Architecture, Art, Biochemistry, Biology, Biomedical Engineering, Chemical Engineering, Chemistry, Chemistry/Management, Civil Engineering, Cognitive Sciences, Colloids, Computational Linguistics, Computer Science Track, Creative Writing, Design, Directing, Drama, Drama/Design, Drama/Production, Economics, Electrical/Computer Engineering, Engineering/Public Policy, European Studies, Genetics, Graphic Communications Management, Graphic Design, History, Illustration, Industrial Design, Industrial Management, Information/Decision Systems, Interdisciplinary History, Literary/Cultural Studies, Logic/Computation, Managerial Economics, Manufacturing Engineering, Materials Science/Engineering, Mathematics, Mathematics/Computer Science, Mechanical Engineering, Modern Languages, Molecular Biology, Music, Music Composition, Music Education, Music Performance, Musical Instruments, Musical Theatre, Operations Research/Management Science, Painting, Philosophy, Physics, Policy/Management, Political Science, Polymer Science, Polymers/Surfaces, Pre-Health Professions, Printmaking, Professional Writing, Psychology, Rhetoric, Robotics, Scientific Computing/Engineering Systems, Scientific Instrumentation, Sculpture, Social/Decision Sciences, Statistics, Technical Writing/Editing, Voice.
**Distribution of degrees:** The majors with the highest enrollment are electrical/computer engineering, industrial management, and mathematics/computer science; statistics, philosophy, and mechanical engineering have the lowest.
**Requirements:** General education requirement.
**Academic regulations:** Freshmen must maintain minimum 1.75 GPA; sophomores, juniors, seniors, 2.00 GPA.
**Special:** Minors offered in architecture, art, ethics, European studies, film studies, gender studies, history of arts, industrial management, logic and computation, music, philosophy, product design, public management, social and cultural studies, statistics, theatre arts, and visual communications. Self-designed majors. Double majors. Dual degrees. Independent study. Accelerated study. Internships. Graduate school at which undergraduates may take graduate-level courses. Preprofessional programs in law, medicine, veterinary science, pharmacy, dentistry, and optometry. Five-year bachelor's/M.B.A. and bachelor's/M.P.M. programs. Member of Pittsburgh Council of Higher Education; cross-registration possible. Washington Semester. Certification in specific subject areas. Exchange programs abroad in Japan (Keio U), and Switzerland (Ecole Polytech). Study abroad also in Germany and Spain. ROTC, NROTC, and AFROTC.
**Honors:** Honors program. Honor societies.
**Academic Assistance:** Nonremedial tutoring.

**STUDENT LIFE. Housing:** All freshmen must live on campus. Coed, women's, and men's dorms. Sorority and fraternity housing. School-owned/operated apartments. 74% of students live in college housing.
**Social atmosphere:** According to the student newspaper, life on campus is "low-key during the week, powerful on weekends." The biggest event of the year is Spring Carnival, a weekend of concerts, dances, arcade amusements, and buggy races; other popular events include the Sweepstakes and the Greek Sing. Greeks and the Activities Board are influential in student life. On campus, students gather at Scotland Yard and Grey Matter. Popular local nightclubs include Harris's, the Holiday, Panther Hollow Inn, Graffiti, and the Electric Banana.
**Services and counseling/handicapped student services:** Placement services. Health service. Women's center. Day care. Counseling services for minority students. Birth control, personal, and psychological counseling. Career and academic guidance services. Religious counseling. Physically disabled student services. Notetaking services. Tape recorders.
**Campus organizations:** Undergraduate student government. Student newspaper (Tartan, published once/week). Literary magazine. Yearbook. Radio station. Musical, professional, and special-interest groups, 118 organizations in all. 14 fraternities, 12 chapter houses; four sororities, all with chapter houses. 25% of men join a fraternity. 14% of women join a sorority.
**Religious organizations:** Hillel, United Campus Ministry, Baptist, Byzantine Catholic, Episcopal, Lutheran, Mormon, Orthodox, Presbyterian, Roman Catholic, and Unitarian groups.
**Minority/foreign student organizations:** Carnegie Mellon Action Project, SPIRIT, Hispanic Student Organization. Asian, Chinese, Indian, and Korean groups.

**ATHLETICS. Physical education requirements:** None.
**Intercollegiate competition:** 19% of students participate. Basketball (M,W), cheerleading (M,W), cross-country (M,W), football (M), golf (M), riflery (M), soccer (M,W), swimming (M,W), tennis (M,W), track (indoor) (M,W), track (outdoor) (M,W), track and field (indoor) (M,W), track and field (outdoor) (M,W), volleyball (W). Member of NCAA Division III, University Athletic Association.
**Intramural and club sports:** 80% of students participate. Intramural badminton, basketball, bowling, chess, cross-country, darts, fencing, floor hockey, football, golf, pool, racquetball, soccer, softball, swimming, table tennis, tennis, touch football, track and field, triathlon, ultimate frisbee, volleyball, water polo, weight lifting, wrestling. Men's club baseball, crew, fencing, ice hockey, lacrosse, martial arts, rugby, ultimate frisbee. Women's club crew, fencing, lacrosse, martial arts, rugby, ultimate frisbee.

**ADMISSIONS. Academic basis for candidate selection** (in order of priority): Secondary school record, class rank, standardized test scores, school's recommendation, essay.
**Nonacademic basis for candidate selection:** Character and personality are emphasized. Particular talent or ability is important. Extracurricular participation, geographical distribution, and alumni/ae relationship are considered.
**Requirements:** Graduation from secondary school is required; GED is accepted. 16 units and the following programs of study are required: 4 English, 4 math, 1 chemistry, 1 physics, and 6 electives for Carnegie Inst of Tech (CIT); 4 English, 4 math, 1 chemistry, and 6 electives for Mellon Coll of Science; 4 English, 3 math, 1 science, and 8 electives for Coll of Humanities and Social Sciences (H&SS) and Sch of Industrial Management (IM); 4 English, 4 math, 1 physics, and 7 electives (2 units foreign language recommended) for Coll of Fine Arts (CFA) Department of Architecture; 4 English and 12 electives (2 units foreign language recommended) for CFA Department of Art, Drama, and Music; 4 English, 2 math, 1 science, and 9 electives for CFA Department of Design. Audition required of music and drama program applicants (acting and music theatre options). Portfolio required of art and drama program applicants (production option). Design projects required of design program applicants. Carnegie Mellon Action Program for applicants not normally admissible. SAT or ACT is required. ACH required. Campus visit and interview recommended. Off-campus interviews available with admissions and alumni representatives.
**Procedure:** Take SAT or ACT by February of 12th year. Take ACH by February of 12th year. Visit college for interview by February of 12th year. Application deadline is February 1. Notification of admission by April 15. Reply is required by May 1. $200 nonrefundable tuition deposit. Freshmen accepted for fall term only.
**Special programs:** Admission may be deferred one year. Credit and/or placement may be granted through CEEB Advanced Placement exams for scores of 5 or higher. Credit and placement may be granted through challenge exams. Early decision program. In fall 1993, 306 applied for early decision and 181 were accepted. Deadline for applying for early decision is December 1. Early entrance/early admission program. Concurrent enrollment program.
**Transfer students:** Transfer students accepted for terms other than fall. In fall 1993, 10% of all new students were transfers into all classes. 507 transfer applications were received, 181 were accepted. Application deadline is April 1 for fall; November 1 for spring. Minimum 3.3 GPA recommended. Lowest course grade accepted is "C." At least one academic year must be completed at the university to receive degree.
**Admissions contact:** Michael A. Steidel, M.S., Director of Admissions. 412 268-2082.

**FINANCIAL AID. Available aid:** Pell grants, SEOG, state scholarships and grants, school scholarships and grants, private scholarships and grants, ROTC scholarships, and academic merit scholarships. Perkins Loans (NDSL), PLUS, Stafford Loans (GSL), state loans, private loans, and SLS. Education Plan Inc., Knight Tuition Plans, AMS, and Tuition Management Systems.
**Financial aid statistics:** 10% of aid is not need-based. In 1993-94, 99% of all undergraduate applicants received aid; 99% of freshman applicants. Average amounts of aid awarded freshmen: Scholarships and grants, $11,254; loans, $3,193.
**Supporting data/closing dates:** FAFSA/FAF/FFS: Deadline is February 15. School's own aid application: Deadline is February 15. State aid form: Deadline is May 1. Income tax forms: Deadline is March 15. Notification of awards on rolling basis.
**Financial aid contact:** Linda M. Anderson, M.A., Director of Financial Aid. 412 268-2068.

**STUDENT EMPLOYMENT.** College Work/Study Program. Institutional employment. 65% of full-time undergraduates work on campus during school year. Students may expect to earn an average of $1,400 during school year. Off-campus part-time employment opportunities rated "good."

**COMPUTER FACILITIES.** 345 IBM/IBM-compatible, Macintosh/Apple, and RISC-/UNIX-based microcomputers; all are networked. Students may access IBM minicomputer/mainframe systems, Internet. Residence halls may be equipped with networked microcomputers, modems. Client/LAN operating systems include Apple/Macintosh, DOS, UNIX/XENIX/AIX, X-windows. Computer languages and software packages include C, C+, FORTRAN, LISP, Pascal. Computer facilities are available to all students.
**Fees:** None.

**GRADUATE CAREER DATA.** Highest graduate school enrollments: Harvard U, Illinois U, MIT, Stanford U, UC Berkely, Yale U. 90% of graduates choose careers in business and industry. Companies and businesses that hire graduates: IBM, Westinghouse, AT&T, General Motors, DuPont, General Electric.

**PROMINENT ALUMNI/AE.** Judith Resnick, electrical engineer and astronaut; Jack Klugman and George Peppard, actors; Stephen Bochco, producer/writer; Philip Pearlstein and Andy Warhol, artists; Holly Hunter and Shari Belafonte, actresses.

# Cedar Crest College

**Allentown, PA 18104-6196 215 437-4471**

**1994-95 Costs.** Tuition: $14,340. Room & board: $5,290. Fees, books, misc. academic expenses (school's estimate): $550.
**Enrollment.** Undergraduates: 18 men, 773 women (full-time). Freshman class: 776 applicants, 633 accepted, 198 enrolled.
**Test score averages/ranges.** Average SAT scores: 469 verbal, 489 math. Range of SAT scores of middle 50%: 380-500 verbal, 390-520 math.
**Faculty.** 64 full-time; 76 part-time. 56% of faculty holds doctoral degree. Student/faculty ratio: 12 to 1.
**Selectivity rating.** Less competitive.

**PROFILE.** Cedar Crest, founded in 1867, is a church-affiliated, liberal arts college for women. Its 84-acre campus, a designated arboretum, is located in a residential area of Allentown, 55 miles from Philadelphia.

**Accreditation:** MSACS. Professionally accredited by the American Bar Association, the American Medical Association (CAHEA), the Council on Social Work Education, the National League for Nursing.
**Religious orientation:** Cedar Crest College is an interdenominational Christian school; no religious requirements.
**Library:** Collections totaling over 318,887 volumes, 1,274 periodical subscriptions, and 30,344 microform items.
**Special facilities/museums:** Art gallery, theatre, arboretum, genetic engineering lab.
**Athletic facilities:** Gymnasium, exercise and weight rooms, dance studio, field hockey and lacrosse fields, fitness trail, badminton, basketball, tennis, and volleyball courts.
**STUDENT BODY. Undergraduate profile:** 83% are state residents; 25% are transfers. 2% Asian-American, 2% Black, 2% Hispanic, 93% White, 1% Other. Average age of undergraduates is 20.

**Freshman profile:** 1% of freshmen who took SAT scored 700 or over on verbal, 2% scored 700 or over on math; 8% scored 600 or over on verbal, 7% scored 600 or over on math; 33% scored 500 or over on verbal, 42% scored 500 or over on math; 77% scored 400 or over on verbal, 80% scored 400 or over on math; 100% scored 300 or over on verbal, 100% scored 300 or over on math. 99% of accepted applicants took SAT; 1% took ACT. 88% of freshmen come from public schools.

**Undergraduate achievement:** 77% of fall 1992 freshmen returned for fall 1993 term. 56% of entering class graduated. 15% of students who completed a degree program immediately went on to graduate study.

**Foreign students:** 49 students are from out of the country. Countries represented include China, India, Japan, South Africa, Taiwan, and Tanzania; 20 in all.

**PROGRAMS OF STUDY. Degrees:** B.A., B.S., B.S.Nurs.

**Majors:** Accounting, Art, Biochemistry, Biology, Business Administration, Chemistry, Communications Studies, Comparative Literature, Computer Science, Education, Engineering/Applied Science, English, Fine Arts, French, General Science, Genetic Engineering, German, History, International Languages, Liberal Studies, Mathematics, Medical Technology, Music, Nuclear Medicine, Nursing, Paralegal, Philosophy, Political Science, Pre-Law, Pre-Medical, Psychology, Public Administration, Religion, Social Work, Sociology, Spanish, Studio Art, Theatre/Speech.

**Distribution of degrees:** The majors with the highest enrollment are nursing, business administration, and psychology; computer science, Spanish, and chemistry have the lowest.

**Requirements:** General education requirement.

**Academic regulations:** Minimum 2.0 GPA must be maintained.

**Special:** Minors offered in some majors and in economics and religion. Certificates offered in accounting, computer science, gerontology, human resource management, international business, management leadership, marketing and retailing, merchandising and advertising, nuclear medicine, paralegal studies, and school/teacher aide. Certification programs in addictions counselor, elementary/secondary teacher, public school nurse, and social work. Self-designed majors. Double majors. Independent study. Pass/fail grading option. Internships. Preprofessional programs in law, medicine, veterinary science, pharmacy, and dentistry. 3-2 computer/information sciences, engineering, engineering/applied science, health systems management, and industrial management programs with Georgia Tech and Washington U. Member of Lehigh Valley Association of Independent Colleges. Washington Semester. Teacher certification in elementary and secondary education. Study abroad in various countries. ROTC at Lehigh U.

**Honors:** Honors program. Honor societies.

**Academic Assistance:** Remedial reading, writing, math, and study skills. Nonremedial tutoring.

**ADMISSIONS. Academic basis for candidate selection** (in order of priority): Secondary school record, standardized test scores, school's recommendation, class rank, essay.

**Nonacademic basis for candidate selection:** Character and personality are emphasized. Extracurricular participation is important. Particular talent or ability and alumni/ae relationship are considered.

**Requirements:** Graduation from secondary school is required; GED is accepted. 19 units and the following program of study are required: 4 units of English, 3 units of math, 2 units of lab science, 2 units of foreign language, 3 units of social studies, 3 units of history. Rank in top half of secondary school class and minimum 2.0 GPA recommended. Support Toward Educational Progress (STEP) program for applicants with academic deficiencies. SAT or ACT is required. Campus visit and interview recommended. Off-campus interviews available with admissions and alumni representatives.

**Procedure:** Take SAT or ACT by spring of 12th year. Visit college for interview by May of 12th year. Notification of admission on rolling basis. No set date by which applicants must accept offer. $200 tuition deposit, refundable until May 1. Freshmen accepted for terms other than fall.

**Special programs:** Admission may be deferred two years. Credit and/or placement may be granted through CEEB Advanced Placement exams for scores of 5 or higher. Credit and/or placement may be granted through CLEP general and subject exams. Credit may be granted through life experience. Credit and placement may be granted through challenge exams. Early entrance/early admission program. Concurrent enrollment program.

**Transfer students:** Transfer students accepted for terms other than fall. In fall 1993, 25% of all new students were transfers into all classes. 157 transfer applications were received, 124 were accepted. Application deadline is rolling for fall; rolling for spring. Minimum 2.0 GPA required. Lowest course grade accepted is "C." Maximum number of transferable credits is 60 semester hours from a two-year school and 90 semester hours from a four-year school. At least 30 semester hours must be completed at the college to receive degree.

**Admissions contact:** Cynthia Phillips, Director of Admissions. 215 740-3780.

**FINANCIAL AID. Available aid:** Pell grants, SEOG, state scholarships and grants, school scholarships and grants, private scholarships and grants, ROTC scholarships, academic merit scholarships, and aid for undergraduate foreign students. Perkins Loans (NDSL), PLUS, Stafford Loans (GSL), NSL, state loans, school loans, private loans, and SLS. AMS, Tuition Management Systems, deferred payment plan, and family tuition reduction. Advanced Education Services

**Financial aid statistics:** 15% of aid is not need-based. In 1993-94, 100% of all undergraduate applicants received aid. Average amounts of aid awarded freshmen: Scholarships and grants, $7,474; loans, $2,625.

**Supporting data/closing dates:** FAFSA. School's own aid application: Accepted on rolling basis. State aid form: Accepted on rolling basis. Income tax forms: Accepted on rolling basis. Notification of awards on rolling basis.

**Financial aid contact:** Judith Neyhart, M.A., Director of Financial Aid. 215 740-3785.

# Chatham College

**Pittsburgh, PA 15232** **412 365-1100**

**1994-95 Costs.** Tuition: $13,550. Room & board: $5,440. Fees, books, misc. academic expenses (school's estimate): $550.

**Enrollment.** 469 women (full-time). Freshman class: 212 applicants, 197 accepted, 91 enrolled. Graduate enrollment: 2 women.

**Test score averages/ranges.** Average SAT scores: 491 verbal, 481 math. Range of SAT scores of middle 50%: 420-550 verbal, 400-560 math. Average ACT scores: 24 English, 22 math, 22 composite. Range of ACT scores of middle 50%: 21-27 English, 18-23 math.

**Faculty.** 43 full-time; 31 part-time. 93% of faculty holds doctoral degree. Student/faculty ratio: 9 to 1.

**Selectivity rating.** Less competitive.

**PROFILE.** Chatham, founded in 1869, is a private, liberal arts college for women. Its 32-acre campus is located in a residential area, eight miles from downtown Pittsburgh. Several mansions in the neighborhood serve as student dormitories.

**Accreditation:** MSACS.

**Religious orientation:** Chatham College is nonsectarian; no religious requirements.

**Library:** Collections totaling over 130,000 volumes, 600 periodical subscriptions and 500 microform items.

**Special facilities/museums:** Museum, center for student development, media center.

**Athletic facilities:** Gymnasium, badminton, basketball, platform tennis, tennis, and volleyball courts, dance studio, weight room, swimming pool, bowling lanes, athletic field.

**STUDENT BODY. Undergraduate profile:** 87% are state residents; 29% are transfers. 1% Asian-American, 7% Black, 1% Hispanic, 88% White, 3% Other. Average age of undergraduates is 21.

**Freshman profile:** 2% of freshmen who took SAT scored 700 or over on verbal, 1% scored 700 or over on math; 14% scored 600 or over on verbal, 11% scored 600 or over on math; 40% scored 500 or over on verbal, 37% scored 500 or over on math; 80% scored 400 or over on verbal, 77% scored 400 or over on math; 98% scored 300 or over on verbal, 99% scored 300 or over on math. 5% of freshmen who took ACT scored 30 or over on English, 5% scored 30 or over on math, 5% scored 30 or over on composite; 53% scored 24 or over on English, 22% scored 24 or over on math, 38% scored 24 or over on composite; 79% scored 18 or over on English, 64% scored 18 or over on math, 75% scored 18 or over on composite; 100% scored 12 or over on English, 100% scored 12 or over on math, 100% scored 12 or over on composite. 86% of accepted applicants took SAT; 14% took ACT.

**Undergraduate achievement:** 77% of fall 1992 freshmen returned for fall 1993 term. 42% of entering class graduated. 28% of students who completed a degree program went on to graduate study within one year.

**Foreign students:** Four students are from out of the country. Countries represented include India, Japan, and the former Soviet Republics.

**PROGRAMS OF STUDY. Degrees:** B.A., B.S.

**Majors:** Accounting, Administration of Justice, Arts Management, Biology, Chemistry, Communication, Economics, Education, English, Environmental Studies, European Studies, French, History, Human Services Administration, Information Science, International Business, International Studies, Management, Mathematics, Music, Philosophy/Religion, Political Science, Psychology, Spanish, Theatre, Visual Arts, Women's Studies.

**Distribution of degrees:** The majors with the highest enrollment are communication, psychology, and history; music, Spanish, and French have the lowest.

**Requirements:** General education requirement.

**Academic regulations:** Freshmen must maintain minimum 1.8 GPA; sophomores, juniors, seniors, 2.0 GPA.

**Special:** Minors offered in most majors. Programs in African/Africal American studies, dance, and writing. Self-designed majors. Double majors. Independent study. Pass/fail grading option. Internships. Cooperative education programs. Preprofessional programs in law, medicine, veterinary science, dentistry, physical therapy, and occupational therapy. 3-1 engineering program with the Medical Coll of Pennsylvania. 3-2 engineering programs with Carnegie-Mellon U, Pennsylvania St U, Washington U. Member of the Pittsburgh Council of Higher Education; cross-registration possible. Washington Semester. Teacher certification in early childhood, elementary, and secondary education. Certification in specific subject areas. Study abroad in Belize, Ireland, Morocco, and the United Kingdom. ROTC and AFROTC at U of Pittsburgh. NROTC at Carnegie Mellon U.

**Honors:** Phi Beta Kappa. Honor societies.

**Academic Assistance:** Remedial reading, writing, math, and study skills. Nonremedial tutoring.

**ADMISSIONS. Academic basis for candidate selection** (in order of priority): Secondary school record, essay, standardized test scores, school's recommendation, class rank.

**Nonacademic basis for candidate selection:** Particular talent or ability is emphasized. Extracurricular participation is important. Character and personality are considered.

**Requirements:** Graduation from secondary school is recommended; GED is accepted. 16 units and the following program of study are recommended: 4 units of English, 3 units of math, 3 units of science, 2 units of foreign language, 3 units of social studies, 1 unit of electives. Minimum combined SAT score of 900 (composite ACT score of 20), rank in top two-fifths of secondary school class, and minimum 2.5 GPA recommended. Conditional admission possible for applicants not meeting standard requirements. Act 101 program for in-state applicants not normally admissible. SAT or ACT is required. Campus visit recommended. Off-campus interviews available with admissions and alumni representatives.

**Procedure:** Take SAT or ACT by January of 12th year. Suggest filing application by March 31; no deadline. Notification of admission on rolling basis. Reply is required within

30 days of notification or by May 1. $100 nonrefundable tuition deposit. $100 nonrefundable room deposit. Freshmen accepted for terms other than fall.
**Special programs:** Admission may be deferred one year. Credit and/or placement may be granted through CEEB Advanced Placement exams for scores of 4 or higher. Credit may be granted through CLEP general exams and life experience. Credit and placement may be granted through challenge exams and military experience. Concurrent enrollment program.
**Transfer students:** Transfer students accepted for terms other than fall. In fall 1993, 29% of all new students were transfers into all classes. 113 transfer applications were received, 101 were accepted. Application deadline is rolling for fall; rolling for spring. Minimum 2.0 GPA required. Lowest course grade accepted is "C." Maximum number of transferable credits is 22 course units. At least 14 course units (7 per year) must be completed at the college to receive degree.
**Admissions contact:** Suellen Ofe, M.A., Dean of Admissions/Financial Aid. 412 365-1290, 800 837-1290.
**FINANCIAL AID. Available aid:** Pell grants, SEOG, state grants, school scholarships and grants, private scholarships, academic merit scholarships, and aid for undergraduate foreign students. Perkins Loans (NDSL), PLUS, Stafford Loans (GSL), and SLS. Knight Tuition Plans and AMS. Higher Education Services. Institutional payment plan.
**Financial aid statistics:** 28% of aid is not need-based. In 1993-94, 98% of all undergraduate applicants received aid; 100% of freshman applicants. Average amounts of aid awarded freshmen: Scholarships and grants, $8,843; loans, $3,220.
**Supporting data/closing dates:** FAFSA: Priority filing date is February 1; accepted on rolling basis. School's own aid application: Priority filing date is February 1; accepted on rolling basis. Income tax forms: Priority filing date is April 15; accepted on rolling basis. Notification of awards on rolling basis.
**Financial aid contact:** Patty Hladio, M.S., Director of Financial Aid. 412 365-1292.

## Chestnut Hill College

**Philadelphia, PA 19118-2695 — 215 248-7000**

**1994-95 Costs.** Tuition: $10,335. Room & board: $5,015. Fees, books, misc. academic expenses (school's estimate): $960.
**Enrollment.** 556 women (full-time). Freshman class: 337 applicants, 250 accepted, 134 enrolled. Graduate enrollment: 83 men, 357 women.
**Test score averages/ranges.** Average SAT scores: 493 verbal, 480 math.
**Faculty.** 61 full-time; 59 part-time. 69% of faculty holds highest degree in specific field. Student/faculty ratio: 9 to 1.
**Selectivity rating.** Less competitive.

**PROFILE.** Chestnut Hill is a private, liberal arts college. Founded as a college for women in 1924, it remains primarily dedicated to the education of women, although men are now admitted through the Continuing Division. Its 45-acre campus is located in Chestnut Hill, a residential area of Philadelphia.

**Accreditation:** MSACS.
**Religious orientation:** Chestnut Hill College is affiliated with the Roman Catholic Church (Sisters of St. Joseph); six semester hours of religion required.
**Library:** Collections totaling over 135,554 volumes, 1,220 periodical subscriptions, and 1,427 microform items.
**Special facilities/museums:** Archival museum, rare book collection, Irish literature collection, observatory, planetarium.
**Athletic facilities:** Gymnasium, tennis courts, swimming pool, weight room, field hockey, lacrosse, and softball fields.
**STUDENT BODY. Undergraduate profile:** 77% are state residents; 5% are transfers. 3% Asian-American, 10% Black, 7% Hispanic, 80% White. Average age of undergraduates is 20.
**Freshman profile:** 1% of freshmen who took SAT scored 700 or over on verbal, 1% scored 700 or over on math; 10% scored 600 or over on verbal, 14% scored 600 or over on math; 46% scored 500 or over on verbal, 55% scored 500 or over on math; 86% scored 400 or over on verbal, 87% scored 400 or over on math; 100% scored 300 or over on verbal, 100% scored 300 or over on math. 96% of accepted applicants took SAT. 50% of freshmen come from public schools.
**Undergraduate achievement:** 83% of fall 1991 freshmen returned for fall 1992 term. 64% of entering class graduated. 13% of students who completed a degree program immediately went on to graduate study.
**Foreign students:** 36 students are from out of the country. Countries represented include Indonesia, Japan, Kenya, Korea, Pakistan, and Sweden; 13 in all.
**PROGRAMS OF STUDY. Degrees:** B.A., B.S.
**Majors:** Accounting, Art History, Biochemistry, Biology, Business Administration, Chemistry, Classical Civilization, Computer/Mathematical Sciences, Early Childhood Education, Economics, Elementary Education, English, Fine Arts, French, German, History, Marketing, Mathematical Sciences, Molecular Biology, Music, Music Education, Political Science, Psychology, Sociology, Spanish, Studio Art.
**Distribution of degrees:** The majors with the highest enrollment are elementary education, English, and psychology; mathematical sciences and Spanish have the lowest.
**Requirements:** General education requirement.
**Academic regulations:** Freshmen must maintain minimum 1.75 GPA; sophomores, juniors, seniors, 2.0 GPA.
**Special:** Complementary career preparation programs for students in all majors offered in international studies, mass media communications, and women in management. Informal monthly luncheons conducted by faculty on significant topics of academic, intellectual, national, or international interest. Associate's degrees offered. Self-designed majors. Double majors. Dual degrees. Independent study. Accelerated study. Pass/fail grading option. Internships. Cooperative education programs. Graduate school at which undergraduates may take graduate-level courses. Preprofessional programs in medicine, veterinary science, and dentistry. 2-2 medical technology program with Thomas Jefferson U. Bachelor's/doctoral program with Pennsylvania Coll of Podiatric Medicine. Member of Sisters of St. Joseph College Consortium. Teacher certification in early childhood, elementary, and secondary education. Study abroad in England, France, Germany, Japan, and Spain. ROTC at LaSalle U.
**Honors:** Honors program. Honor societies.
**Academic Assistance:** Remedial writing and math.
**ADMISSIONS. Academic basis for candidate selection** (in order of priority): Secondary school record, class rank, standardized test scores, school's recommendation, essay.
**Nonacademic basis for candidate selection:** Character and personality and extracurricular participation are emphasized. Particular talent or ability and alumni/ae relationship are considered.
**Requirements:** Graduation from secondary school is required; GED is not accepted. 16 units and the following program of study are required: 4 units of English, 3 units of math, 3 units of science, 2 units of foreign language, 4 units of social studies. Minimum combined SAT score of 950, rank in top two-fifths of secondary school class, and minimum 3.0 GPA recommended. Portfolio recommended of studio art program applicants. Audition required of music program applicants. Act 101 program for in-state applicants not normally admissible. SAT or ACT is required. Campus visit and interview recommended. Off-campus interviews available with an admissions representative.
**Procedure:** Take SAT or ACT by November of 12th year. Visit college for interview by March of 12th year. Suggest filing application by March 1; no deadline. Notification of admission on rolling basis. Reply is required by May 1. $100 tuition deposit, refundable until May 1. $100 room deposit, refundable until May 1. Freshmen accepted for terms other than fall.
**Special programs:** Admission may be deferred one year. Credit and/or placement may be granted through CEEB Advanced Placement exams for scores of 3 or higher. Credit may be granted through CLEP general and subject exams and life experience. Early entrance/early admission program. Concurrent enrollment program.
**Transfer students:** Transfer students accepted for terms other than fall. In fall 1992, 5% of all new students were transfers into all classes. 55 transfer applications were received, 36 were accepted. Application deadline is March 15 if applying for aid; rolling for others. Minimum 2.5 GPA required. Lowest course grade accepted is "C." Maximum number of transferable credits is 60 semester hours. At least 60 semester hours must be completed at the college to receive degree.
**Admissions contact:** Margaret Anne Birtwistle, S.S.J., M.S., Director of Admissions/Assistant Dean. 215 248-7001.
**FINANCIAL AID. Available aid:** Pell grants, SEOG, state grants, and academic merit scholarships. Perkins Loans (NDSL), PLUS, Stafford Loans (GSL), and SLS.
**Financial aid statistics:** 30% of aid is not need-based. In 1991-92, 70% of all undergraduate applicants received aid; 72% of freshman applicants. Average amounts of aid awarded freshmen: Loans, $2,100.
**Supporting data/closing dates:** FAFSA/FAF/FFS: Priority filing date is March 15. School's own aid application: Priority filing date is March 15. State aid form: Priority filing date is March 15. Income tax forms: Priority filing date is March 15. Notification of awards on rolling basis.
**Financial aid contact:** Laura Rucinski, M.S., Director of Financial Planning. 215 248-7101.

## Cheyney University of Pennsylvania

**Cheyney, PA 19319 — 215 399-2000**

**1993-94 Costs.** Tuition: $6,478 (state residents), $9,872 (out-of-state). Room & board: $3,340. Fees, books, misc. academic expenses (school's estimate): $545.
**Enrollment.** Undergraduates: 449 men, 462 women (full-time). Freshman class: 1,104 applicants, 767 accepted, 287 enrolled. Graduate enrollment: 98 men, 226 women.
**Test score averages/ranges.** N/A.
**Faculty.** 93 full-time; 16 part-time. 52% of faculty holds doctoral degree. Student/faculty ratio: 14 to 1.
**Selectivity rating.** N/A.

**PROFILE.** Cheyney, founded in 1837, is a public, historically black university. Programs are offered through the Departments of Arts and Sciences, Education, and Technical and Applied Sciences. Its 275-acre campus is located 24 miles west of Philadelphia.

**Accreditation:** MSACS. Professionally accredited by the National Council for Accreditation of Teacher Education.
**Religious orientation:** Cheyney University of Pennsylvania is nonsectarian; no religious requirements.
**Library:** Collections totaling over 237,780 volumes, 655 periodical subscriptions, and 517,955 microform items.
**Special facilities/museums:** Afro-American history/culture collection, planetarium, weather station, satellite communication network.
**Athletic facilities:** Gymnasiums, basketball and tennis courts, football, soccer, and softball fields, indoor pool, stadium, weight rooms.
**STUDENT BODY. Undergraduate profile:** 79% are state residents; 20% are transfers. .4% Asian-American, 97% Black, 1.3% Hispanic, .3% Native American, 1% White. Average age of undergraduates is 21.
**Freshman profile:** 93% of accepted applicants took SAT; 2% took ACT. 90% of freshmen come from public schools.
**Undergraduate achievement:** 12% of students who completed a degree program immediately went on to graduate study.
**Foreign students:** 12 students are from out of the country. Countries represented include Bermuda, Jamaica, Korea, Nigeria, Taiwan, and Zimabwe; nine in all.
**PROGRAMS OF STUDY. Degrees:** B.A., B.S., B.S.Ed.

**Majors:** Art, Biology, Broadcast Communication Technology, Business Administration, Chemistry, Clothing/Textiles, Communication Arts, Computer/Information Sciences, Dietetics, Early Childhood Education, Elementary Education, English, General Science, Geography, History, Home Economics, Hotel/Restaurant/Institutional Management, Industrial Management, Industrial Technology, Mathematics, Medical Technology, Music, Music Merchandising, Political Science, Psychology, Recreation, Secondary Education, Social Relations, Social Sciences, Special Education, Technology Education, Theatre Arts.
**Distribution of degrees:** The majors with the highest enrollment are business administration, education, and social relations; geography, industrial management, and home economics have the lowest.
**Requirements:** General education requirement.
**Academic regulations:** Freshmen must maintain minimum 1.6 GPA; sophomores, 1.75 GPA; juniors, 1.85 GPA; seniors, 2.0 GPA.
**Special:** Areas of concentration offered in some majors. Courses in design/merchandising and guidance/counseling. Seminars and special-topic courses. Field experience in art and community health. Associate's degrees offered. Double majors. Dual degrees. Independent study. Pass/fail grading option. Cooperative education programs. Graduate school at which undergraduates may take graduate-level courses. Member of Allied Health Careers Opportunity Program, Cheyney-Lincoln-Temple Cluster, and Compact for Lifelong Educational Opportunities. Teacher certification in elementary, secondary, and special education. Certification in specific subject areas. ROTC.
**Honors:** Honor societies.
**Academic Assistance:** Remedial reading, writing, math, and study skills. Nonremedial tutoring.
**ADMISSIONS. Academic basis for candidate selection** (in order of priority): Secondary school record, standardized test scores, essay, class rank, school's recommendation.
**Nonacademic basis for candidate selection:** Extracurricular participation, particular talent or ability, and geographical distribution are considered.
**Requirements:** Graduation from secondary school is required; GED is accepted. 17 units and the following program of study are recommended: 4 units of English, 3 units of math, 2 units of science, 1 unit of social studies, 2 units of history, 5 units of electives. Minimum combined SAT score of 650 and minimum 2.0 GPA required; others may be considered on an individual basis. Act 101 program for in-state applicants not normally admissible; Freshman Studies Program for out-of-state applicants not normally admissible. SAT is required; ACT may be substituted. Campus visit and interview recommended. Off-campus interviews available with an admissions representative.
**Procedure:** Take SAT or ACT by October 31 of 12th year. Visit college for interview by October 31 of 12th year. Suggest filing application by June 30; no deadline. Notification of admission on rolling basis. Reply is required within 30 days of acceptance. $35 nonrefundable tuition deposit. $100 refundable room deposit. Freshmen accepted for terms other than fall.
**Special programs:** Credit may be granted through CLEP general and subject exams. Credit and placement may be granted through challenge exams and military and life experience. Early decision program. Deadline for applying for early decision is November 30. Early entrance/early admission program.
**Transfer students:** Transfer students accepted for terms other than fall. In fall 1993, 20% of all new students were transfers into all classes. 166 transfer applications were received, 107 were accepted. Application deadline is June 30 for fall; November 15 for spring. Minimum 2.0 GPA recommended. Lowest course grade accepted is "C." At least 30 semester hours must be completed at the university to receive degree.
**Admissions contact:** Sharon Cannon, M.A., Director of Admissions. 800 CHEYNEY, 800 223-3608.
**FINANCIAL AID. Available aid:** Pell grants, SEOG, state scholarships and grants, school scholarships and grants, private scholarships and grants, academic merit scholarships, and athletic scholarships. Perkins Loans (NDSL), PLUS, Stafford Loans (GSL), state loans, and SLS. AMS and Tuition Management Systems.
**Financial aid statistics:** 4% of aid is not need-based. In 1994-95, 93% of all undergraduate applicants received aid; 87% of freshman applicants. Average amounts of aid awarded freshmen: Scholarships and grants, $2,450; loans, $2,625.
**Supporting data/closing dates:** FAFSA: Priority filing date is April 1. State aid form: Priority filing date is May 1. Income tax forms: Priority filing date is April 1. Notification of awards on rolling basis.
**Financial aid contact:** James Brown, M.Ed., Director of Financial Aid. 215 399-2302.

## Clarion University of Pennsylvania

**Clarion, PA 16214** **814 226-2000**

**1993-94 Costs.** Tuition: $2,954 (state residents), $7,352 (out-of-state). Room: $1,610. Board: $1,176. Fees, books, misc. academic expenses (school's estimate): $1,625.
**Enrollment.** Undergraduates: 1,969 men, 2,859 women (full-time). Freshman class: 2,740 applicants, 2,497 accepted, 1,188 enrolled. Graduate enrollment: 142 men, 306 women.
**Test score averages/ranges.** Average SAT scores: 412 verbal, 448 math. Range of SAT scores of middle 50%: 400-500 verbal, 400-500 math.
**Faculty.** 333 full-time; 33 part-time. 55% of faculty holds doctoral degree. Student/faculty ratio: 19 to 1.
**Selectivity rating.** Less competitive.

**PROFILE.** Clarion, founded in 1867, is a public university. Programs are offered through the Colleges of Arts and Sciences, Business Administration, Communication and Computer Information Science, Education and Human Services, Graduate Studies and Continuing Education, and Library Science and the School of Nursing. Its 99-acre campus is located in a mountainous area 85 miles northeast of Pittsburgh.
**Accreditation:** MSACS. Professionally accredited by the American Speech-Language-Hearing Association, the National Council for Accreditation of Teacher Education, the National League for Nursing.
**Religious orientation:** Clarion University of Pennsylvania is nonsectarian; no religious requirements.
**Library:** Collections totaling over 362,962 volumes, 1,689 periodical subscriptions, and 2,885 microform items.
**Special facilities/museums:** Planetarium.
**STUDENT BODY. Undergraduate profile:** 95% are state residents; 23% are transfers. 1% Asian-American, 2% Black, 1% Hispanic, 1% Native American, 94% White, 1% Other. Average age of undergraduates is 22.
**Freshman profile:** 2% of freshmen who took SAT scored 600 or over on verbal, 4% scored 600 or over on math; 11% scored 500 or over on verbal, 24% scored 500 or over on math; 46% scored 400 or over on verbal, 58% scored 400 or over on math; 79% scored 300 or over on verbal, 81% scored 300 or over on math. Majority of accepted applicants took SAT.
**Undergraduate achievement:** 72% of fall 1992 freshmen returned for fall 1993 term. 29% of entering class graduated. 11% of students who completed a degree program immediately went on to graduate study.
**PROGRAMS OF STUDY. Degrees:** B.A., B.F.A., B.Mus., B.S., B.S.Bus.Admin., B.S.Ed., B.S.Nurs.
**Majors:** Accounting, Anthropology, Art, Biology, Biotechnology, Chemistry, Communication, Computer Science, Early Childhood Education, Earth Science, Economics, Elementary Education, English, Finance, General Studies, Geography, German, History, Humanities, Industrial Relations, Library Science, Management, Management/Library Science, Marketing, Mathematics, Medical Technology, Music Education, Music Merchandising, Music Performance, Natural Sciences, Nursing, Philosophy, Physics, Political Science, Psychology, Real Estate, Rehabilitative Sciences, Secondary Education, Social Sciences, Sociology, Sociology/Psychology, Spanish, Special Education, Speech Communication, Speech Communication/Theatre, Speech Pathology/Audiology, Theatre.
**Distribution of degrees:** The majors with the highest enrollment are communication, elementary education, and marketing.
**Requirements:** General education requirement.
**Academic regulations:** Minimum 2.00 GPA must be maintained. Minimum 2.5 GPA required in College of Business Administration and College of Education and Human Services.
**Special:** Minors offered in many majors and in computer information sciences, international business, and women's studies. Associate's degrees offered. Self-designed majors. Double majors. Internships. Graduate school at which undergraduates may take graduate-level courses. Preprofessional programs in law, medicine, veterinary science, pharmacy, dentistry, theology, and optometry. 3-2 engineering programs with Case Western Reserve U and U of Pittsburgh. Five-year B.S.B.A./M.B.A. program. Polymer science/chemistry program with U of Akron. Bachelor's/doctoral degree program in biology with Pennsylvania State U. Member of Conference on Medieval and Renaissance Cultures. Washington Semester. Teacher certification in early childhood, elementary, secondary, and special education. Certification in specific subject areas. Member of International Student Exchange Program (ISEP).
**Honors:** Honors program. Honor societies.
**Academic Assistance:** Remedial reading, writing, math, and study skills. Nonremedial tutoring.
**STUDENT LIFE. Housing:** Students may live on or off campus. Coed, women's, and men's dorms. 33% of students live in college housing.
**Social atmosphere:** Students gather at the Gemmell Student Center and at local bars. The student senate and Greeks are influential groups on campus. The Autumn Leaf Festival is the most popular event of the year, followed closely by the Battle of the Bands and the Spring Concert. According to the student newspaper, "The town of Clarion offers little in the way of social or cultural opportunities. The campus offers more, but the students seem uninterested in participating. Off-campus life generally revolves around the house-party scene and the bar scene."
**Services and counseling/handicapped student services:** Placement services. Health service. Day care. Counseling services for minority, veteran, and older students. Birth control, personal, and psychological counseling. Career and academic guidance services. Religious counseling. Physically disabled student services. Learning disabled services. Notetaking services. Tape recorders. Tutors. Reader services for the blind.
**Campus organizations:** Undergraduate student government. Student newspaper (Clarion Call, published once/week). Literary magazine. Yearbook. Radio and TV stations. Musical groups, coffeehouse, College Players, Black Arts Festival, debating, lecture series, handicapped awareness group, health careers club, American Marketing Association, university center board, 120 organizations in all. 13 fraternities, six chapter houses; 10 sororities, seven chapter houses. 18% of men join a fraternity. 14% of women join a sorority.
**Religious organizations:** Fellowship of Christian Athletes, Koinonia Christian Fellowship, United Campus Ministry, Newman Association, Jewish Student Association, Muslim Student Association.
**Minority/foreign student organizations:** Black Student Union, minority fraternities/sororities. International Student Association.
**ATHLETICS. Physical education requirements:** Two semesters of physical education required.
**Intercollegiate competition:** 5% of students participate. Baseball (M), basketball (M,W), cheerleading (M), cross-country (M,W), diving (M,W), football (M), golf (M), softball (W), swimming (M,W), tennis (W), track (M,W), volleyball (W), wrestling (M). Member of Eastern Wrestling League, NCAA Division I for wrestling, NCAA Division II, Pennsylvania State Athletic Conference.
**ADMISSIONS. Academic basis for candidate selection** (in order of priority): Secondary school record, class rank, standardized test scores, school's recommendation, essay.
**Nonacademic basis for candidate selection:** Particular talent or ability is considered.
**Requirements:** Graduation from secondary school is required; GED is accepted. 16 units and the following program of study are required: 4 units of English, 2 units of math, 2 units of science including 1 unit of lab, 4 units of social studies, 3 units of history. 3 units of social studies, 1 unit of chemistry ("C" or better), 1 unit of biology ("C" or better), and 1 unit

of algebra or higher, taken within five years of high school graduation, required of applicants to nursing program. NLN pre-entrance test also required of nursing program applicants. Portfolio required of art program applicants. Audition required of music program applicants. EOP for applicants not normally admissible. Summer Start Program and Academic Support Program for applicants not normally admissible. SAT or ACT is required. Campus visit and interview recommended. Off-campus interviews available with an admissions representative.
**Procedure:** Take SAT or ACT by December of 12th year. Visit college for interview by January of 12th year. Suggest filing application by October 1. Application deadline is August 1. Notification of admission on rolling basis. Applicants must accept offer of admission by May 1 if accepted before April 1. $50 nonrefundable tuition deposit. $75 nonrefundable room deposit. Freshmen accepted for terms other than fall.
**Special programs:** Admission may be deferred two years. Credit and/or placement may be granted through CEEB Advanced Placement exams for scores of 3 or higher. Credit and/or placement may be granted through CLEP general and subject exams. Credit and placement may be granted through DANTES and challenge exams and military and life experience. Early decision program. Deadline for applying for early decision is October. Early entrance/early admission program. Concurrent enrollment program.
**Transfer students:** Transfer students accepted for terms other than fall. In fall 1993, 23% of all new students were transfers into all classes. 730 transfer applications were received, 650 were accepted. Application deadline is July for fall; November for spring. Minimum 2.0 GPA required. Lowest course grade accepted is "C." Maximum number of transferable credits is 64 semester hours from a two-year school and 83 semester hours from a four-year school. At least 45 semester hours must be completed at the university to receive degree.
**Admissions contact:** John S. Shropshire, Dean of Enrollment Management and Academic Records. 814 226-2306.

**FINANCIAL AID. Available aid:** Pell grants, SEOG, state scholarships and grants, school scholarships, private scholarships and grants, academic merit scholarships, and athletic scholarships. Health Professions Scholarships. Perkins Loans (NDSL), PLUS, Stafford Loans (GSL), and SLS. AMS. Installment Payment Plan.
**Financial aid statistics:** In 1993-94, 72% of all undergraduate applicants received aid; 90% of freshman applicants. Average amounts of aid awarded freshmen: Scholarships and grants, $1,673; loans, $2,300.
**Supporting data/closing dates:** State aid form: Deadline is May 1. Notification of awards begins June 1.
**Financial aid contact:** Kenneth Grugel, M.A., Director of Financial Aid. 814 226-2315.

**STUDENT EMPLOYMENT.** College Work/Study Program. Institutional employment. 17% of full-time undergraduates work on campus during school year. Students may expect to earn an average of $1,200 during school year. Freshmen are discouraged from working during their first term. Off-campus part-time employment opportunities rated "fair."

**COMPUTER FACILITIES.** 175 IBM/IBM-compatible and Macintosh/Apple microcomputers; 125 are networked. Students may access Digital minicomputer/mainframe systems. Residence halls may be equipped with stand-alone microcomputers. Client/LAN operating systems include Apple/Macintosh, DOS. Computer languages and software packages include Ada, BASIC, C, COBOL, dBASE, FORTRAN, Lotus 1-2-3, PageMaker, Pascal, PL/1, Prolog, R:BASE, RPG, Turbo C, Turbo Prolog, WordPerfect. Computer facilities are available to all students.
**Fees:** Computer fee is included in tuition/fees.
**Hours:** 9 AM-midn. in computer labs; 24 hours in dorms.

**GRADUATE CAREER DATA.** Highest graduate school enrollments: Clarion U of Pennsylvania, Pennsylvania State U, U of Pittsburgh.

**PROMINENT ALUMNI/AE.** Charles R. Alexander, judge; Audrey Sadar Hall, physician; Lawrence Ianni, university chancellor.

# College Misericordia

**Dallas, PA 18612** **717 674-6400**

**1993-94 Costs.** Tuition: $9,960. Room & board: $5,360. Fees, books, misc. academic expenses (school's estimate): $1,000.
**Enrollment.** Undergraduates: 228 men, 710 women (full-time). Freshman class: 1,428 applicants, 883 accepted, 323 enrolled. Graduate enrollment: 33 men, 99 women.
**Test score averages/ranges.** Average SAT scores: 440 verbal, 460 math.
**Faculty.** 62 full-time; 58 part-time. 26% of faculty holds doctoral degree. Student/faculty ratio: 14 to 1.
**Selectivity rating.** Competitive.

**PROFILE.** College Misericordia, founded in 1924, is a private, church-affiliated, liberal arts college. Its 100-acre campus is located in Dallas, northeast of Wilkes-Barre.

**Accreditation:** MSACS. Professionally accredited by the American Medical Association (CAHEA), the Council on Social Work Education, the National League for Nursing.
**Religious orientation:** College Misericordia is affiliated with the Roman Catholic Church; two semesters of religion/theology required.
**Library:** Collections totaling over 95,000 volumes, 762 periodical subscriptions, and 3,900 microform items.
**Special facilities/museums:** On-campus nursery school and retirement center.
**Athletic facilities:** Indoor swimming pool, baseball, field hockey, soccer, and softball fields, racquetball and tennis courts, gymnasium, indoor track, weight room, fitness trail.

**STUDENT BODY. Undergraduate profile:** 82% are state residents. 1% Black, 1% Hispanic, 98% White. Average age of undergraduates is 21.
**Freshman profile:** 2% of freshmen who took SAT scored 700 or over on verbal, 3% scored 700 or over on math; 6% scored 600 or over on verbal, 9% scored 600 or over on math; 41% scored 500 or over on verbal, 49% scored 500 or over on math; 95% scored 400 or over on verbal, 96% scored 400 or over on math; 100% scored 300 or over on verbal, 100% scored 300 or over on math. 95% of accepted applicants took SAT; 5% took ACT. 40% of freshmen come from public schools.
**Undergraduate achievement:** 80% of fall 1992 freshmen returned for fall 1993 term. 80% of entering class graduated. 12% of students who completed a degree program went on to graduate study within five years.
**Foreign students:** 12 students are from out of the country. Five countries represented in all.

**PROGRAMS OF STUDY. Degrees:** B.A., B.S., B.S.Nurs., B.S.Occup.Ther., B.Soc.Work.
**Majors:** Accounting, Biology, Business Administration, Business Information Systems, Chemistry, Computer Science, Early Childhood Education, Elementary Education, English, General Studies, History, Liberal Studies, Mathematics, Mathematics/Computer Science, Medical Technology, Nursing, Occupational Therapy, Physical Therapy, Psychology, Radiography, Secondary Education, Social Work, Special Education.
**Distribution of degrees:** The majors with the highest enrollment are occupational therapy, business administration, and nursing.
**Requirements:** General education requirement.
**Academic regulations:** Minimum 2.5 GPA required for graduation.
**Special:** Minors offered in some majors and in child welfare, gerontology, management, philosophy, political science and government, religious studies, Russian area studies, and writing. Self-designed majors. Double majors. Dual degrees. Independent study. Accelerated study. Internships. Cooperative education programs. Graduate school at which undergraduates may take graduate-level courses. Preprofessional programs in law, medicine, veterinary science, and dentistry. Five-year bachelor's/master's degree programs in art, music, and other fields with U of Scranton. Five-year M.Soc.Work program with Marywood Coll. Member of Northeastern Pennsylvania Independent Colleges. Cross-registration with King's Coll. Teacher certification in early childhood, elementary, and special education. Study abroad in England. ROTC at U of Scranton. AFROTC at Wilkes Coll.
**Honors:** Honors program.
**Academic Assistance:** Remedial math. Nonremedial tutoring.

**ADMISSIONS. Academic basis for candidate selection** (in order of priority): Class rank, secondary school record, standardized test scores, school's recommendation.
**Nonacademic basis for candidate selection:** Character and personality and alumni/ae relationship are emphasized. Particular talent or ability is important. Extracurricular participation is considered.
**Requirements:** Graduation from secondary school is required; GED is accepted. No specific distribution of secondary school units required. Chemistry or biology recommended of nursing program applicants. Chemistry recommended of occupational therapy program applicants. Biology and physics recommended of radiologic technology program applicants. Trigonometry, chemistry, and biology recommended of premedicine program applicants. SAT is required; ACT may be substituted. Campus visit and interview recommended. Off-campus interviews available with an admissions representative.
**Procedure:** Take SAT or ACT by January of 12th year. Visit college for interview by June of 12th year. Notification of admission on rolling basis. Reply is required by May 1. $50 nonrefundable tuition deposit. $50 nonrefundable room deposit. Freshmen accepted for terms other than fall.
**Special programs:** Admission may be deferred two months. Credit and/or placement may be granted through CEEB Advanced Placement exams for scores of 3 or higher. Credit and/or placement may be granted through CLEP general and subject exams.
**Transfer students:** Transfer students accepted for terms other than fall. In fall 1993, 356 transfer applications were received, 164 were accepted. Application deadline is August 1 for fall; January 1 for spring. Minimum 2.0 GPA required. Lowest course grade accepted is "C." Maximum number of transferable credits is 60 semester hours from a two-year school and 90 semester hours from a four-year school. At least 30 semester hours must be completed at the college to receive degree.
**Admissions contact:** Michael Joseph, Director of Admissions. 717 675-4449.

**FINANCIAL AID. Available aid:** Pell grants, SEOG, Federal Nursing Student Scholarships, school scholarships and grants, private scholarships and grants, and academic merit scholarships. Perkins Loans (NDSL), PLUS, Stafford Loans (GSL), NSL, state loans, and SLS. AMS.
**Financial aid statistics:** 20% of aid is not need-based. Average amounts of aid awarded freshmen: Scholarships and grants, $3,450; loans, $2,286.
**Supporting data/closing dates:** FAFSA/FAF: Priority filing date is March 1. State aid form: Priority filing date is March 1. Notification of awards on rolling basis.
**Financial aid contact:** Jane Dessoye, Director of Financial Aid. 717 674-6280.

# Delaware Valley College

**Doylestown, PA 18901** **215 345-1500**

**1993-94 Costs.** Tuition: $11,645. Room: $2,100. Board: $2,685. Fees, books, misc. academic expenses (school's estimate): $400.
**Enrollment.** Undergraduates: 759 men, 621 women (full-time). Freshman class: 1,383 applicants, 1,199 accepted, 435 enrolled.
**Test score averages/ranges.** Average SAT scores: 423 verbal, 477 math. Range of SAT scores of middle 50%: 390-480 verbal, 420-530 math.
**Faculty.** 74 full-time; 32 part-time. 54% of faculty holds doctoral degree. Student/faculty ratio: 16 to 1.
**Selectivity rating.** Less competitive.

**PROFILE.** Delaware Valley, founded in 1896, is a private college. Its 725-acre campus is located in central Bucks County, 20 miles north of Philadelphia.

**Accreditation:** MSACS.
**Religious orientation:** Delaware Valley College is nonsectarian; no religious requirements.
**Library:** Collections totaling over 73,110 volumes, 603 periodical subscriptions, and 50,554 microform items.
**Special facilities/museums:** Dairy processing plant, greenhouse and nursery lab complex, poultry diagnostic lab, arboretum, equine facilities, 850-acre farm, tissue culture lab.

**Athletic facilities:** Gymnasiums, track, baseball, field hockey, lacrosse, soccer, and softball fields, basketball and tennis courts, weight room, football stadium, cross-country course, lake, equestrian facilities.

**STUDENT BODY. Undergraduate profile:** 70% are state residents; 22% are transfers. 1% Asian-American, 2% Black, 1% Hispanic, 96% White. Average age of undergraduates is 21.
**Freshman profile:** 1% of freshmen who took SAT scored 700 or over on math; 3% scored 600 or over on verbal, 9% scored 600 or over on math; 22% scored 500 or over on verbal, 40% scored 500 or over on math; 75% scored 400 or over on verbal, 83% scored 400 or over on math; 99% scored 300 or over on verbal, 99% scored 300 or over on math. 98% of accepted applicants took SAT; 2% took ACT. 87% of freshmen come from public schools.
**Undergraduate achievement:** 78% of fall 1992 freshmen returned for fall 1993 term. 46% of entering class graduated. 15% of students who completed a degree program went on to graduate study within one year.
**Foreign students:** 17 students are from out of the country. Countries represented include Japan, Spain, Sweden, and Venezuela; nine in all.

**PROGRAMS OF STUDY. Degrees:** B.A., B.S.
**Majors:** Agribusiness, Agronomy/Environmental Science, Animal Science, Biology, Business Administration, Chemistry, Computer Information Systems Management, Criminal Justice Administration, Dairy Science, English, Equine Sciences, Food Science/Management, Horticulture, Mathematics, Ornamental Horticulture/Environmental Design, Secondary Education.
**Distribution of degrees:** The majors with the highest enrollment are business administration, ornamental horticulture/environmental design, and animal science; horticulture and chemistry have the lowest.
**Requirements:** General education requirement.
**Academic regulations:** Minimum 2.0 GPA must be maintained.
**Special:** Minors offered in all majors. Courses offered in art history, drama, economics, French, history, humanities, math, music, physical education, physics, political science, psychology, sociology, Spanish, speech, and studio art. Each student completes 24-week work experience in area of specialization. Associate's degrees offered. Double majors. Dual degrees. Independent study. Accelerated study. Internships. Cooperative education programs. Preprofessional programs in law, medicine, veterinary science, dentistry, and optometry. Teacher certification in secondary education. Certification in specific subject areas. ROTC at Temple U.
**Honors:** Honors program. Honor societies.
**Academic Assistance:** Remedial reading, writing, math, and study skills. Nonremedial tutoring.

**STUDENT LIFE. Housing:** Students may live on or off campus. Coed, women's, and men's dorms. 70% of students live in college housing.
**Social atmosphere:** Students gather at The Pub, Lake Archer, Lake Helena, and Peace Valley Park. Influential student groups include the student government, Alpha Phi Omega, and the school yearbook, newspaper, and radio station. Sporting events, Homecoming, and Agriculture Days, a festival showcasing the educational benefits of agriculture, are popular campus events.
**Services and counseling/handicapped student services:** Placement services. Health service. Counseling services for minority students. Personal and psychological counseling. Career and academic guidance services. Physically disabled student services. Learning disabled services. Notetaking services.
**Campus organizations:** Undergraduate student government. Student newspaper (Ram-Pages, published once/two weeks). Literary magazine. Yearbook. Radio station. Chorale, band, Circle K, Environmental Awareness Club, Apiary Society, Future Farmers of America, Volunteer Corps, 40 organizations in all.
**Religious organizations:** Hillel, Christian Fellowship, Newman Club.
**Minority/foreign student organizations:** Minority Leadership Coalition. International Student Association.

**ATHLETICS. Physical education requirements:** Two semesters of physical education required.
**Intercollegiate competition:** 45% of students participate. Baseball (M), basketball (M,W), cheerleading (W), cross-country (M,W), field hockey (W), football (M), golf (M), horsemanship (M,W), soccer (M), softball (W), track (indoor) (M,W), track (outdoor) (M,W), track and field (indoor) (M,W), track and field (outdoor) (M,W), volleyball (W), wrestling (M). Member of ECAC, Mid-Atlantic Conference, NCAA Division III.
**Intramural and club sports:** 70% of students participate. Intramural basketball, bowling, floor hockey, softball, tennis, touch football, turkey trot, volleyball, weight lifting. Men's club lacrosse. Women's club soccer.

**ADMISSIONS. Academic basis for candidate selection** (in order of priority): Secondary school record, class rank, standardized test scores, school's recommendation, essay.
**Nonacademic basis for candidate selection:** Character and personality, extracurricular participation, and particular talent or ability are important. Alumni/ae relationship is considered.
**Requirements:** Graduation from secondary school is recommended; GED is accepted. 15 units and the following program of study are required: 3 units of English, 2 units of math, 2 units of lab science, 2 units of social studies, 6 units of electives. Minimum 2.0 GPA required. Act 101 program for in-state applicants not normally admissible. SAT or ACT is required. Campus visit and interview recommended. Off-campus interviews available with an admissions representative.
**Procedure:** Take SAT or ACT by November of 12th year. Visit college for interview by April of 12th year. Application deadline is August 1. Notification of admission on rolling basis. Reply is required by August 20. $400 tuition deposit, refundable until May 1. $300 room deposit, refundable until May 1. Freshmen accepted for terms other than fall.
**Special programs:** Admission may be deferred one year. Credit and/or placement may be granted through CEEB Advanced Placement exams for scores of 3 or higher. Credit may be granted through CLEP general and subject exams. Early entrance/early admission program.
**Transfer students:** Transfer students accepted for terms other than fall. In fall 1993, 22% of all new students were transfers into all classes. 255 transfer applications were received, 126 were accepted. Application deadline is August 15 for fall; January 15 for spring. Minimum 2.0 GPA required. Lowest course grade accepted is "C." Maximum number of transferable credits is 78 semester hours. At least 48 semester hours must be completed at the college to receive degree.
**Admissions contact:** Stephen W. Zenko, Director of Admissions. 215 345-1500, extension 2211.

**FINANCIAL AID. Available aid:** Pell grants, SEOG, state scholarships and grants, school scholarships and grants, private scholarships and grants, and academic merit scholarships. Perkins Loans (NDSL), PLUS, Stafford Loans (GSL), state loans, private loans, and SLS. AMS.
**Financial aid statistics:** 32% of aid is not need-based. In 1993-94, 72% of all undergraduate applicants received aid; 71% of freshman applicants. Average amounts of aid awarded freshmen: Scholarships and grants, $4,700; loans, $2,625.
**Supporting data/closing dates:** FAFSA: Priority filing date is April 1; accepted on rolling basis. State aid form: Priority filing date is April 1; accepted on rolling basis. Income tax forms: Priority filing date is April 1. Notification of awards on rolling basis.
**Financial aid contact:** Robert Sauer, M.Ed., Director of Financial Aid. 215 345-1500, extension 2272.

**STUDENT EMPLOYMENT.** College Work/Study Program. Institutional employment. 22% of full-time undergraduates work on campus during school year. Students may expect to earn an average of $1,500 during school year. Off-campus part-time employment opportunities rated "excellent."

**COMPUTER FACILITIES.** 52 IBM/IBM-compatible and Macintosh/Apple microcomputers; 36 are networked. Client/LAN operating systems include Windows NT, Novell. Computer languages and software packages include Assembler, BASIC, COBOL, FORTRAN, Pascal, Quattro, WordPerfect. Computer facilities are available to all students.
**Fees:** None.
**Hours:** 8:30 AM-10 PM.

**GRADUATE CAREER DATA.** Graduate school percentages: 2% enter medical school. 1% enter graduate business programs. 5% enter graduate arts and sciences programs. 1% enter theological school/seminary. Highest graduate school enrollments: U of Illinois, Michigan State U, Pennsylvania State U, U of Pennsylvania, U of Virginia. 80% of graduates choose careers in business and industry. Companies and businesses that hire graduates: Agway, federal government, Merck, SmithKline.

# Dickinson College

**Carlisle, PA 17013-2896 717 243-5121**

**1994-95 Costs.** Tuition: $18,700. Room: $2,600. Board: $2,400. Fees, books, misc. academic expenses (school's estimate): $720.
**Enrollment.** Undergraduates: 805 men, 1,084 women (full-time). Freshman class: 3,014 applicants, 2,539 accepted, 487 enrolled.
**Test score averages/ranges.** Range of SAT scores of middle 50%: 490-580 verbal, 520-620 math.
**Faculty.** 154 full-time; 32 part-time. 99% of faculty holds highest degree in specific field. Student/faculty ratio: 11 to 1.
**Selectivity rating.** More competitive.

**PROFILE.** Dickinson, founded in 1773, is a private, liberal arts college. Its 196-acre campus is located in Carlisle, 18 miles from Harrisburg. The oldest campus building, completed in 1804, is a registered National Historic Landmark.

**Accreditation:** MSACS.
**Religious orientation:** Dickinson College is nonsectarian; no religious requirements.
**Library:** Collections totaling over 540,463 volumes, 1,699 periodical subscriptions, and 157,411 microform items.
**Special facilities/museums:** Art gallery, center for the arts, planetarium, observatory, scanning electron microscope.
**Athletic facilities:** Gymnasium, field house, track, badminton, basketball, racquetball, squash, tennis, and volleyball courts, indoor golf, batting cages, swimming pool, diving well, weight rooms, athletic fields, dance studio.

**STUDENT BODY. Undergraduate profile:** 41% are state residents; 2% are transfers. 3% Asian-American, 2% Black, 2% Hispanic, .1% Native American, 92.9% White. Average age of undergraduates is 20.
**Freshman profile:** 99% of accepted applicants took SAT; 1% took ACT. 68% of freshmen come from public schools.
**Undergraduate achievement:** 87% of fall 1992 freshmen returned for fall 1993 term. 83% of entering class graduated. 25% of students who completed a degree program immediately went on to graduate study.
**Foreign students:** 68 students are from out of the country. Countries represented include England, France, Germany, Japan, Korea, and Russia; 38 in all.

**PROGRAMS OF STUDY. Degrees:** B.A., B.S.
**Majors:** American Studies, Anthropology, Biology, Chemistry, Computer Science, Dramatic Arts, East Asian Studies, Economics, English, Fine Arts, French, Geology, German, Greek, History, International Studies, Italian Studies, Judaic Studies, Latin, Mathematics, Music, Philosophy, Physics, Policy Studies, Political Science, Psychology, Religion, Russian, Russian Area Studies, Sociology, Spanish.
**Distribution of degrees:** The majors with the highest enrollment are political science, English, and foreign languages; Judaic studies, Greek, and Italian studies have the lowest.
**Requirements:** General education requirement.
**Academic regulations:** Freshmen must maintain minimum 1.75 GPA; sophomores, juniors, seniors, 2.0 GPA.
**Special:** Minors offered in all departments. Certification programs in environmental, Latin American, and women's studies. Self-designed majors. Double majors. Independent study. Accelerated study. Pass/fail grading option. Internships. Preprofessional programs in law, medicine, dentistry, and optometry. 3-2 engineering programs with Case Western Reserve U, Rensselaer Polytech Inst, and U of Pennsylvania. Member of Central Pennsylvania Consortium of Colleges; cross-registration possible. Washington Semester. Appala-

chian Semester (Kentucky). Asian studies program with U of Pennsylvania. Teacher certification in secondary education. Certification in specific subject areas. Member of International Student Exchange Program (ISEP). Study abroad in China, Cameroon, England, France, Germany, Italy, Japan, Russia, Spain, and other countries. ROTC.
**Honors:** Phi Beta Kappa. Honors program. Honor societies.
**Academic Assistance:** Nonremedial tutoring.

**STUDENT LIFE. Housing:** All freshmen must live on campus. Coed, women's, and men's dorms. Sorority and fraternity housing. Language and arts houses. 90% of students live in college housing.
**Services and counseling/handicapped student services:** Placement services. Health service. Women's center. Day care. Writing center. Guidance testing. Counseling services for minority, veteran, and older students. Birth control, personal, and psychological counseling. Career and academic guidance services. Religious counseling. Physically disabled student services. Learning disabled services. Notetaking services. Tape recorders. Tutors. Reader services for the blind.
**Campus organizations:** Undergraduate student government. Student newspaper (Dickinsonian, published once/week). Literary magazine. Yearbook. Radio station. Choir, orchestra, ensembles, drama groups, dance theatre, Big Brothers/Big Sisters, debating, Women's Center, literary societies, Young Democrats, Young Republicans, 136 organizations in all. Nine fraternities, seven chapter houses; five sororities, two chapter houses. 30% of men join a fraternity. 40% of women join a sorority.
**Religious organizations:** Catholic Campus Ministries, Episcopal Campus Ministry, Hillel, Interfaith, Christian Fellowship, Lutheran Campus Ministry, Society of Friends, United Methodist Campus Ministry.
**Minority/foreign student organizations:** African-American Society, Society of Hispanic Students. International Club, Korean Student Organization, Multicultural House, East Asian, Latin American, Russian, Spanish, French, and German clubs.

**ATHLETICS. Physical education requirements:** Six semesters of physical education required.
**Intercollegiate competition:** 30% of students participate. Baseball (M), basketball (M,W), cross-country (M,W), field hockey (W), football (M), golf (M), lacrosse (M,W), soccer (M,W), softball (W), swimming (M,W), tennis (M,W), track (indoor) (M,W), track (outdoor) (M,W), track and field (indoor) (M,W), track and field (outdoor) (M,W), volleyball (W). Member of Centennial Conference, ECAC, NCAA Division III.
**Intramural and club sports:** 65% of students participate. Intramural basketball, flag football, ice hockey, indoor soccer, racquetball, rugby, running, skiing, soccer, squash, swimming, tennis, volleyball. Men's club Alpine skiing, bowling, cycling, ice hockey, rugby, squash, weight lifting. Women's club Alpine skiing, bowling, cheerleading, cycling, rugby, squash, weight lifting.

**ADMISSIONS. Academic basis for candidate selection** (in order of priority): Secondary school record, school's recommendation, standardized test scores, class rank, essay.
**Nonacademic basis for candidate selection:** Character and personality are emphasized. Extracurricular participation is important. Particular talent or ability, geographical distribution, and alumni/ae relationship are considered.
**Requirements:** Graduation from secondary school is required; GED is accepted. 16 units and the following program of study are required: 4 units of English, 3 units of math, 3 units of science, 2 units of foreign language, 2 units of social studies, 2 units of electives. SAT or ACT is required. Campus visit and interview recommended. Off-campus interviews available with admissions and alumni representatives.
**Procedure:** Take SAT or ACT by January of 12th year. Application deadline is February 20. Notification of admission by March 30. Reply is required by May 1. $200 nonrefundable tuition deposit. Freshmen accepted for terms other than fall.
**Special programs:** Admission may be deferred one year. Credit and/or placement may be granted through CEEB Advanced Placement exams for scores of 4 or higher. Placement may be granted through challenge exams. Early decision program. In fall 1993, 170 applied for early decision and 153 were accepted. Deadline for applying for early decision is December 15 (Plan I) and February 1 (Plan II). Early entrance/early admission program. Concurrent enrollment program.
**Transfer students:** Transfer students accepted for terms other than fall. In fall 1993, 2% of all new students were transfers into all classes. 143 transfer applications were received, 105 were accepted. Application deadline is June 1 for fall; December 1 for spring. Minimum 2.5 GPA required. Lowest course grade accepted is "C." Maximum number of transferable credits is 17 courses. At least 17 courses must be completed at the college to receive degree.
**Admissions contact:** J. Larry Mench, M.A., Dean of Admissions and Enrollment. 717 245-1231.

**FINANCIAL AID. Available aid:** Pell grants, SEOG, state scholarships and grants, school scholarships and grants, private scholarships and grants, ROTC scholarships, academic merit scholarships, and aid for undergraduate foreign students. Perkins Loans (NDSL), PLUS, Stafford Loans (GSL), state loans, school loans, private loans, and SLS. Tuition Plan Inc., Knight Tuition Plans, and AMS. Dickinson Financing System. Mellon Bank Edu-Check.
**Financial aid statistics:** In 1993-94, 76% of all undergraduate applicants received aid; 74% of freshman applicants. Average amounts of aid awarded freshmen: Scholarships and grants, $9,228; loans, $2,694.
**Supporting data/closing dates:** FAFSA/FAF: Priority filing date is February 15. State aid form: Priority filing date is February 15. Income tax forms: Priority filing date is February 15. Notification of awards begins March 30.
**Financial aid contact:** Donald V. Raley, M.A., Director of Financial Aid. 717 245-1308.

**STUDENT EMPLOYMENT.** College Work/Study Program. Institutional employment. 60% of full-time undergraduates work on campus during school year. Students may expect to earn an average of $710 during school year. Off-campus part-time employment opportunities rated "good."

**COMPUTER FACILITIES.** 202 IBM/IBM-compatible and Macintosh/Apple microcomputers; 154 are networked. Students may access Digital, SUN minicomputer/mainframe systems, Internet. Residence halls may be equipped with modems. Client/LAN operating systems include Apple/Macintosh, DOS, UNIX/XENIX/AIX, LocalTalk/ AppleTalk, Novell. Computer languages and software packages include AutoCAD, BASIC, C, COBOL, Dreams, FORTRAN, Kermit, LISP, Lotus 1-2-3, MINITAB, Pacerlink, Pascal, SPSS-X, WordPerfect. Computer facilities are available to all students.
**Fees:** None.
**Hours:** 24 hours.

**GRADUATE CAREER DATA.** Graduate school percentages: 13% enter law school. 4% enter medical school. 1% enter dental school. 10% enter graduate business programs. 30% enter graduate arts and sciences programs. Highest graduate school enrollments: American U, Dickinson Sch of Law, George Washington U, New York U, Rutgers U, Temple U, Pennsylvania State U, U of Pennsylvania, U of Pittsburgh, U of Virginia. 43% of graduates choose careers in business and industry. Companies and businesses that hire graduates: American Management Systems, Arthur Andersen, Bankers Trust, Chubb Insurance, Merck, J.P. Morgan.

**PROMINENT ALUMNI/AE.** James Buchanan, 15th President of the United States; Roger B. Taney, U.S. Supreme Court justice (1836-1864); John Curley, editor of *USA Today* and CEO of Gannett; Spencer Fullerton Baird, founder, Smithsonian Institution; James Shepley, former chairperson of the board, Time, Inc.; Stuart Pankin, actor; Rosie O'Donnell, actress/comedian.

# Drexel University

**Philadelphia, PA 19104** **215 895-2000**

**1993-94 Costs.** Tuition: $11,654. Room: $3,390-$4,008. Board: $2,426. Fees, books, misc. academic expenses (school's estimate): $1,817.
**Enrollment.** Undergraduates: 3,838 men, 1,809 women (full-time). Freshman class: 3,501 applicants, 2,960 accepted, 1,129 enrolled. Graduate enrollment: 2,086 men, 1,031 women.
**Test score averages/ranges.** Average SAT scores: 469 verbal, 553 math. Range of SAT scores of middle 50%: 410-530 verbal, 480-630 math.
**Faculty.** 422 full-time; 425 part-time. 93% of faculty holds doctoral degree. Student/ faculty ratio: 15 to 1.
**Selectivity rating.** Competitive.

**PROFILE.** Drexel, founded in 1891, is a private university. Programs are offered through the Colleges of Arts and Sciences, Business Administration, Engineering, and Information Studies and Nesbitt College of Design Arts. Its 40-acre campus is located in the University City area of West Philadelphia.

**Accreditation:** MSACS. Professionally accredited by the Accreditation Board for Engineering and Technology, the American Assembly of Collegiate Schools of Business, the American Dietetic Association, the American Home Economics Association, the American Library Association, the Foundation for Interior Design Education Research, the National Architecture Accrediting Board.
**Religious orientation:** Drexel University is nonsectarian; no religious requirements.
**Library:** Collections totaling over 493,537 volumes and 3,435 periodical subscriptions.
**Special facilities/museums:** Art museum, theatre, audio-visual center, TV studio, recreational center, center for automation technology, engineering center.
**Athletic facilities:** Dance studio, badminton, basketball, racquetball, squash, tennis, and volleyball courts, swimming pool, diving pool, bowling lanes, baseball, lacrosse, soccer, softball, and touch football fields, weight and wrestling rooms, sauna.

**STUDENT BODY. Undergraduate profile:** 75% are state residents; 4% are transfers. 15% Asian-American, 13% Black, 3% Hispanic, 1% Native American, 66% White, 2% Other. Average age of undergraduates is 22.
**Freshman profile:** 1% of freshmen who took SAT scored 700 or over on verbal, 8% scored 700 or over on math; 7% scored 600 or over on verbal, 31% scored 600 or over on math; 33% scored 500 or over on verbal, 69% scored 500 or over on math; 80% scored 400 or over on verbal, 95% scored 400 or over on math; 96% scored 300 or over on verbal, 100% scored 300 or over on math. 100% of accepted applicants took SAT. 60% of freshmen come from public schools.
**Undergraduate achievement:** 76% of fall 1992 freshmen returned for fall 1993 term. 57% of entering class graduated.
**Foreign students:** 761 students are from out of the country. Countries represented include China, Hong Kong, India, South Korea, Taiwan, and Vietnam; 94 in all.

**PROGRAMS OF STUDY. Degrees:** B.Arch., B.S., B.S.Arch.Eng., B.S.Bus.Admin., B.S.Chem.Eng., B.S.Civil Eng., B.S.Commerce/Eng., B.S.Elec.Eng., B.S.Info.Sci., B.S.Mat.Eng., B.S.Mech.Eng.
**Majors:** Accounting, Applied Philosophy, Appropriate Technology, Architectural Engineering, Architecture, Biological Sciences, Chemical Engineering, Chemistry, Civil Engineering, Commerce/Engineering, Computer Science, Construction Management, Corporate Communication, Design/Merchandising, Economics, Electrical/Computer Engineering, Environmental Science, Fashion Design, Finance, General Business, General Information Systems, Graphic Design, History/Politics, Hotel/Restaurant/Institutional Management, Human Resource Management, Industrial Engineering, Information Systems Analysis/Development, Information Systems Applications, Information Systems Concepts, Interior Design, International Area Studies, International Business, Literature, Management of Information Systems, Marketing, Materials Engineering, Mathematics, Mechanical Engineering, Music, Nutrition/Food Science, Operations Management, Photography, Physics, Printing Technology, Psychology, Psychology/Sociology/Anthropology, Sociology, Teacher Preparation, Technical/Science Communication, Unified Science.
**Distribution of degrees:** The majors with the highest enrollment are electrical engineering, computer science, and design/merchandising; sociology, engineering science, and technical/science communication have the lowest.
**Requirements:** General education requirement.
**Special:** All students participate in Drexel Cooperative Plan, a five-year work/study program combining practical industry experience with classroom learning; between three

and seven terms of student's five years are spent employed off campus. Double majors. Dual degrees. Independent study. Accelerated study. Pass/fail grading option. Cooperative education programs. Graduate school at which undergraduates may take graduate-level courses. Preprofessional programs in law, medicine, veterinary science, and dentistry. 3-3 engineering programs with Eastern Mennonite Coll, Indiana U of Pennsylvania, and Lincoln U. Teacher certification in elementary and secondary education. Study abroad in China, England, Japan, Latin American countries, the former Soviet Republics, and other countries. ROTC. NROTC at U of Pennsylvania. AFROTC at St. Joseph's U.
**Honors:** Honors program.
**Academic Assistance:** Remedial reading, writing, math, and study skills.

**STUDENT LIFE. Housing:** Students may live on or off campus. Coed dorms. Sorority and fraternity housing. 45% of students live in college housing.
**Social atmosphere:** According to the editor of the student newspaper, students gather at fraternity houses, New Deck Tavern, Carney's Pub, and the Triangle offices. Fraternities and the Triangle paper are influential groups on campus. Social events are "the Block Party, International Food Festival, basketball games, and reading the Triangle every Friday."
**Services and counseling/handicapped student services:** Placement services. Counseling services for minority and older students. Personal and psychological counseling. Career guidance services. Religious counseling. Physically disabled student services. Learning disabled services. Notetaking services. Tape recorders. Reader services for the blind.
**Campus organizations:** Undergraduate student government. Student newspaper (Triangle, published once/week). Literary magazine. Yearbook. Radio and TV stations. Band, orchestra, glee club, Varsity Singers, drama club, Amnesty International, Commuter Coalition, College Republicans, 67 organizations in all. 13 fraternities, 11 chapter houses; five sororities, no chapter houses. 17% of men join a fraternity. 12% of women join a sorority.
**Religious organizations:** Christian Fellowship, Hillel.
**Minority/foreign student organizations:** NAACP, Black Student Union, Black Accountants Association, Society of Minority Engineers, Latin American Organization. International Student Association, Cambodian and Chinese groups, Cultural Club.

**ATHLETICS. Physical education requirements:** Three terms of physical education required.
**Intercollegiate competition:** 8% of students participate. Baseball (M), basketball (M,W), crew (M), cross-country (M,W), diving (M,W), field hockey (W), golf (M), lacrosse (M,W), soccer (M,W), softball (W), swimming (M,W), tennis (M,W), track (indoor) (M), track (outdoor) (M), track and field (indoor) (M), track and field (outdoor) (M), volleyball (W), wrestling (M). Member of East Coast Wrestling Association, ECAC, NCAA Division I, North Atlantic Conference, PAIAW, Philadelphia Soccer 7.
**Intramural and club sports:** 25% of students participate. Intramural badminton, basketball, bowling, flag football, racquetball, softball, squash, table tennis, tennis, volleyball, water polo, weight lifting, wrestling. Men's club bowling, cheerleading, fencing, ice hockey, martial arts, sailing, rugby, volleyball. Women's club cheerleading, crew, fencing.

**ADMISSIONS. Academic basis for candidate selection** (in order of priority): Secondary school record, standardized test scores, essay, school's recommendation, class rank.
**Nonacademic basis for candidate selection:** Character and personality, extracurricular participation, and particular talent or ability are important. Alumni/ae relationship is considered.
**Requirements:** Graduation from secondary school is recommended; GED is accepted. 16 units and the following program of study are recommended: 4 units of English, 3 units of math, 1 unit of science, 1 unit of social studies, 7 units of electives. Elective units must be in English, history, math, science, social science, foreign language, or mechanical drawing. Ability and academic promise of applicant of primary importance. Foreign language recommended. One additional unit in both math and science required of applicants to Coll of Engineering, Coll of Science, and for commerce and engineering curriculum offered by Coll of Business and Administration. Three ACH (English composition, math level I and II, and science) required of applicants submitting SAT and applying to Coll of Engineering and Science or to commerce and engineering curriculum of Coll of Business and Administration. SAT or ACT is required. Campus visit and interview recommended. No off-campus interviews.
**Procedure:** Take SAT or ACT by March 1 of 12th year. Suggest filing application by January 1. Application deadline is May 1. Notification of admission on rolling basis. Reply is required by May 1. $100 nonrefundable tuition deposit. $100 nonrefundable room deposit. Freshmen accepted for terms other than fall.
**Special programs:** Admission may be deferred. Credit and/or placement may be granted through CEEB Advanced Placement exams for scores of 4 or higher. Credit and placement may be granted through challenge exams. Early decision program. In fall 1992, 150 applied for early decision and 105 were accepted. Deadline for applying for early decision is November 15. Early entrance/early admission program. Concurrent enrollment program.
**Transfer students:** Transfer students accepted for terms other than fall. In fall 1993, 4% of all new students were transfers into all classes. 694 transfer applications were received, 548 were accepted. Application deadline is rolling for fall; rolling for spring. Minimum 2.5 GPA required. Lowest course grade accepted is "C." Maximum number of transferable credits is 142 quarter hours. At least 45 quarter hours must be completed at the university to receive degree.
**Admissions contact:** John E. Russel, Ph.D., Director of Admissions. 215 895-2400.

**FINANCIAL AID. Available aid:** Pell grants, SEOG, state scholarships and grants, school scholarships and grants, private scholarships and grants, ROTC scholarships, academic merit scholarships, and athletic scholarships. Perkins Loans (NDSL), PLUS, Stafford Loans (GSL), state loans, school loans, private loans, and SLS. Higher Education Services, Inc.
**Financial aid statistics:** 2% of aid is not need-based. In 1993-94, 87% of all undergraduate applicants received aid; 76% of freshman applicants. Average amounts of aid awarded freshmen: Scholarships and grants, $3,367; loans, $3,242.
**Supporting data/closing dates:** State aid form: Deadline is May 1. Notification of awards on rolling basis.
**Financial aid contact:** Nicholas Flocco, Director of Financial Aid. 215 895-2536.

**STUDENT EMPLOYMENT.** College Work/Study Program. Freshmen are discouraged from working during their first term. Off-campus part-time employment opportunities rated "excellent."

**COMPUTER FACILITIES.** 600 IBM/IBM-compatible and Macintosh/Apple microcomputers; 300 are networked. Students may access AT&T, IBM, Prime minicomputer/mainframe systems, BITNET, Internet. Residence halls may be equipped with stand-alone microcomputers. Client/LAN operating systems include Apple/Macintosh, LocalTalk/AppleTalk. Computer languages and software packages include Excel, Filemaker Pro, MacWrite; 150 in all. Computer facilities are available to all students.
**Fees:** None.
**Hours:** 24 hours.

**GRADUATE CAREER DATA.** Companies and businesses that hire graduates: General Electric, IBM.

**PROMINENT ALUMNI/AE.** James P. Bagian, astronaut; Susan O. Seidelman, filmmaker; Dr. George Ullrich, theoretic physicist, deputy director, Defense Nuclear Agency.

## Duquesne University

**Pittsburgh, PA 15282** **412 396-6220**

**1992-93 Costs.** Tuition: $9,840. Room & board: $4,875. Fees, books, misc. academic expenses (school's estimate): $890.
**Enrollment.** Undergraduates: 1,887 men, 2,361 women (full-time). Freshman class: 3,320 applicants, 2,374 accepted, 1,029 enrolled. Graduate enrollment: 1,407 men, 1,805 women.
**Test score averages/ranges.** Range of SAT scores of middle 50%: 420-550 verbal, 450-570 math. Range of ACT scores of middle 50%: 21-25 composite.
**Faculty.** 337 full-time; 301 part-time. 89% of faculty holds doctoral degree. Student/faculty ratio: 16 to 1.
**Selectivity rating.** Less competitive.

**PROFILE.** Duquesne, founded in 1878, is a church-affiliated university. Programs are offered through the College of Liberal Arts and Sciences; the Graduate School of Liberal Arts and Sciences; and the Schools of Business and Administration, Education, Law, Music, Nursing, and Pharmacy. Its 39-acre campus overlooks downtown Pittsburgh.

**Accreditation:** MSACS. Professionally accredited by the American Assembly of Collegiate Schools of Business, the American Medical Association (CAHEA), the National Association of Schools of Music, the National Council for Accreditation of Teacher Education, the National League for Nursing.
**Religious orientation:** Duquesne University is affiliated with the Roman Catholic Church (Holy Ghost Fathers); Six semester hours of theology and philosophy required.
**Library:** Collections totaling over 626,184 volumes, 5,532 periodical subscriptions, and 379,244 microform items.
**Special facilities/museums:** Center for study in existential phenomenological psychology, electron microscope, Kurzweil 250 digital keyboard.
**Athletic facilities:** Recreation center, basketball, handball, racquetball, and tennis courts, athletic and football fields, gymnasiums, aerobics and weight rooms.

**STUDENT BODY. Undergraduate profile:** 83% are state residents; 21% are transfers. 2% Asian-American, 4% Black, 1% Hispanic, 93% White. Average age of undergraduates is 21.
**Freshman profile:** 98% of accepted applicants took SAT; 2% took ACT. 65% of freshmen come from public schools.
**Undergraduate achievement:** 89% of fall 1991 freshmen returned for fall 1992 term. 71% of entering class graduated. 12% of students who completed a degree program immediately went on to graduate study.
**Foreign students:** 148 students are from out of the country. Countries represented include China, India, Indonesia, Japan, Nigeria, and Taiwan; 72 in all.

**PROGRAMS OF STUDY. Degrees:** B.A., B.Mus., B.S., B.S.Bus.Admin., B.S.Ed., B.S.Nurs., B.S.Pharm.
**Majors:** Accounting, Advertising, American Literature, Athletic Training, Biochemistry, Biology, Chemistry, Classics, Computer/Information Sciences, Conservatory Music, Cooperative Program in Engineering, Early Childhood Education, Economics, Elementary Education, English, English Literature, Finance, French, German, Greek, Guitar, Health Records Administration, History, International Business Management, International Relations, Jazz Performance, Journalism, Latin, Law Administration, Logistics, Management, Management Information Systems, Marketing, Mathematics, Media Arts, Music Education, Music Therapy, Nursing, Occupational Therapy, Orchestral Instruments, Organ, Perfusion Technology, Pharmacy, Philosophy, Physical Therapy, Physician's Assistant, Physics, Piano, Political Science/Government, Psychology, Public Relations, Quantitative Methods, Real Estate, Sacred Music, Secondary Education, Sociology, Sound Recording Technology, Spanish, Special Education, Speech Communication/Theatre, Theology, Voice, World Literature.
**Distribution of degrees:** The majors with the highest enrollment are management, pharmacy, and secondary education; French and economics have the lowest.
**Requirements:** General education requirement.
**Academic regulations:** Minimum 2.0 GPA must be maintained.
**Special:** Research projects for science majors. Double majors. Independent study. Accelerated study. Internships. Cooperative education programs. Graduate school at which undergraduates may take graduate-level courses. Preprofessional programs in law, medicine, veterinary science, and dentistry. Early admissions program with Pennsylvania Medical Coll. 3-3 law program. 3-2 engineering programs with Case Western Reserve U and Florida Inst of Tech. Member of Pittsburgh Council on Higher Education; cross-registration possible. Washington Semester. Teacher certification in elementary, secondary, and special education. Certification in specific subject areas. Study abroad possible in Belgium, France, Germany, Italy, and Spain. ROTC. AFROTC at U of Pittsburgh.

**Honors:** Phi Beta Kappa. Honors program. Honor societies.
**Academic Assistance:** Remedial reading, writing, math, and study skills. Nonremedial tutoring.

**STUDENT LIFE. Housing:** All freshmen must live on campus unless living with family. Coed and women's dorms. Fraternity housing. On-campus, privately owned apartments. 46% of students live in college housing.
**Social atmosphere:** The O and Zelda's are student hotspots. Student Government, Campus Ministry, and Greeks influence student life.
**Services and counseling/handicapped student services:** Placement services. Health service. Day care. Counseling services for minority, veteran, and older students. Personal and psychological counseling. Career and academic guidance services. Religious counseling. Physically disabled student services. Learning disabled services. Tape recorders. Tutors. Reader services for the blind.
**Campus organizations:** Undergraduate student government. Student newspaper (Duquesne Duke, published once/week). Literary magazine. Yearbook. Radio station. Choral groups, music ensembles, orchestra, dance and theatre groups, debating, Union Program Board, Model UN, 97 organizations in all. Eight fraternities, no chapter houses; eight sororities, no chapter houses. 15% of men join a fraternity. 17% of women join a sorority.
**Religious organizations:** Campus Ministry.
**Minority/foreign student organizations:** Black Student Union, Esquire Social Club. International Student Organization.

**ATHLETICS. Physical education requirements:** None.
**Intercollegiate competition:** 10% of students participate. Baseball (M), basketball (M,W), cheerleading (W), crew (M,W), cross-country (M,W), diving (M,W), football (M), golf (M), riflery (M,W), swimming (M,W), tennis (M,W), track (indoor) (M,W), track (outdoor) (M,W), track and field (indoor) (M,W), track and field (outdoor) (M,W), volleyball (W), wrestling (M). Member of Atlantic 10, ECAC, NCAA Division I, NCAA Division I-AA for football.
**Intramural and club sports:** 40% of students participate. Intramural basketball, flag football, racquetball, pool, softball, street hockey, tennis, volleyball, water polo. Men's club crew, ice hockey, soccer. Women's club cheerleading, crew, soccer.

**ADMISSIONS. Academic basis for candidate selection** (in order of priority): Secondary school record, class rank, standardized test scores, school's recommendation, essay.
**Nonacademic basis for candidate selection:** Particular talent or ability is emphasized. Character and personality and extracurricular participation are important. Geographical distribution and alumni/ae relationship are considered.
**Requirements:** Graduation from secondary school is required; GED is accepted. No specific distribution of secondary school units required. 16 secondary school units required, including 4 units of English, 8 units chosen from math, science, foreign language, and social studies, and 4 units of academic electives. Minimum combined SAT score of 800, rank in top three-fifths of secondary school class, and minimum 2.5 GPA recommended. Interviews required of nursing program applicants. Audition required of music program applicants. Conditional admission possible for applicants not meeting standard requirements. SAT is required; ACT may be substituted. Campus visit and interview recommended. Off-campus interviews available with admissions and alumni representatives.
**Procedure:** Take SAT or ACT by January of 12th year. Visit college for interview by February of 12th year. Application deadline is July 1. Notification of admission on rolling basis. Reply is required by May 1. $100 nonrefundable tuition deposit. $150 nonrefundable room deposit. Freshmen accepted for terms other than fall.
**Special programs:** Admission may be deferred one year. Credit and/or placement may be granted through CEEB Advanced Placement exams for scores of 3 or higher. Credit may be granted through CLEP general and subject exams, ACT PEP, DANTES, and challenge exams, and military and life experience. Early decision program. Deadline for applying for early decision is November 15. Early entrance/early admission program.
**Transfer students:** Transfer students accepted for terms other than fall. In fall 1992, 21% of all new students were transfers into all classes. 823 transfer applications were received, 424 were accepted. Application deadline is July 1 for fall; December 1 for spring. Minimum 2.0 GPA required. Lowest course grade accepted is "C." Maximum number of transferable credits is 90 semester hours. At least 30 semester hours must be completed at the university to receive degree.
**Admissions contact:** Thomas Schaefer, C.S.S.P., Director of Admissions. 412 396-6220.

**FINANCIAL AID. Available aid:** Pell grants, SEOG, state scholarships and grants, school scholarships and grants, private scholarships and grants, ROTC scholarships, academic merit scholarships, athletic scholarships, and aid for undergraduate foreign students. Perkins Loans (NDSL), PLUS, Stafford Loans (GSL), NSL, Health Professions Loans, state loans, and SLS. Tuition Plan Inc. and Knight Tuition Plans.
**Financial aid statistics:** 38% of aid is not need-based. In 1992-93, 78% of all undergraduate applicants received aid; 60% of freshman applicants. Average amounts of aid awarded freshmen: Scholarships and grants, $5,000; loans, $2,000.
**Supporting data/closing dates:** FAFSA/FAF: Deadline is May 1. School's own aid application: Deadline is May 1. State aid form: Priority filing date is May 1. Notification of awards on rolling basis.
**Financial aid contact:** Frank Dutkovich, Jr., Director of Financial Aid. 412 396-6607.

**STUDENT EMPLOYMENT.** College Work/Study Program. Institutional employment. 11% of full-time undergraduates work on campus during school year. Students may expect to earn an average of $1,900 during school year. Off-campus part-time employment opportunities rated "good."

**COMPUTER FACILITIES.** 350 IBM/IBM-compatible, Macintosh/Apple, and RISC-/UNIX-based microcomputers. Students may access Digital, SUN minicomputer/mainframe systems. Computer languages and software packages include BASIC, C, COBOL, dBASE, e-mail, FORTRAN, LISP, Lotus 1-2-3, Pascal, SPSS, WordPerfect. Computer facilities are available to all students.
**Fees:** None.
**Hours:** 24 hours.

**GRADUATE CAREER DATA.** Graduate school percentages: 8% enter law school. 2% enter medical school. 12% enter graduate business programs. 26% enter graduate arts and sciences programs. Highest graduate school enrollments: Dickinson Coll, Duquesne U, U of Pittsburgh. Companies and businesses that hire graduates: ALCOA, Big Six accounting firms, Chubb Insurance, Equibank, Federated Investors, First Jersey Securities, Mellon Bank, Westinghouse.

**PROMINENT ALUMNI/AE.** Art Rooney, owner, Pittsburgh Steelers; Bobby Vinton, recording artist; Sheila Tate, vice-president, Burson-Marstellar; Sid Federbusch, producer, NBC News; Robert DePalma, chief financial officer and vice-president, Rockwell International.

# East Stroudsburg University of Pennsylvania

**East Stroudsburg, PA 18301** **717 424-3211**

**1993-94 Costs.** Tuition: $2,954 (state residents), $7,352 (out-of-state). Room: $2,100. Board: $1,125. Fees, books, misc. academic expenses (school's estimate): $1,210.
**Enrollment.** Undergraduates: 1,728 men, 2,144 women (full-time). Freshman class: 4,472 applicants, 2,055 accepted, 641 enrolled. Graduate enrollment: 280 men, 508 women.
**Test score averages/ranges.** Average SAT scores: 430 verbal, 483 math. Range of SAT scores of middle 50%: 380-470 verbal, 430-530 math.
**Faculty.** 260 full-time; 13 part-time. 62% of faculty holds doctoral degree. Student/faculty ratio: 20 to 1.
**Selectivity rating.** Competitive.

**PROFILE.** East Stroudsburg, founded as a Normal school in 1893, is a public university. Programs are offered through the Schools of Arts and Sciences, Professional Studies, and Health Sciences and Physical Education. Its 183-acre campus is located in the foothills of the Pocono Mountains.

**Accreditation:** MSACS. Professionally accredited by the National League for Nursing.
**Religious orientation:** East Stroudsburg University of Pennsylvania is nonsectarian; no religious requirements.
**Library:** Collections totaling over 319,589 volumes, 3,368 periodical subscriptions, and 1,113,730 microform items.
**Special facilities/museums:** Natural history museum, human performance lab, TV production studios, 52-acre student-owned/operated recreation area and wildlife sanctuary, observatory, electron microscopes.
**Athletic facilities:** Stadium; field house, tracks, gymnasium, baseball, field hockey, football, lacrosse, soccer, and softball fields, swimming pools.

**STUDENT BODY. Undergraduate profile:** 77% are state residents; 41% are transfers. 1% Asian-American, 2% Black, 2% Hispanic, 94% White, 1% Other. Average age of undergraduates is 20.
**Freshman profile:** 1% of freshmen who took SAT scored 700 or over on math; 2% scored 600 or over on verbal, 8% scored 600 or over on math; 15% scored 500 or over on verbal, 45% scored 500 or over on math; 71% scored 400 or over on verbal, 87% scored 400 or over on math; 99% scored 300 or over on verbal, 100% scored 300 or over on math. 97% of accepted applicants took SAT.
**Undergraduate achievement:** 75% of fall 1991 freshmen returned for fall 1992 term. 25% of entering class graduated.
**Foreign students:** 43 students are from out of the country. Countries represented include Brazil, China, Cyprus, England, India, and Mexico; 29 in all.

**PROGRAMS OF STUDY. Degrees:** B.A., B.S.
**Majors:** Allied Health, Art, Biology, Biology/Chemistry, Chemistry, Communication Studies, Communications Technology, Computer Science, Early Childhood, Economics, Elementary Education, Engineering, English, Environmental Studies, Fine Arts, French, Geography, German, Health Education, Health/Physical Education, History, Hospitality Management, Marine Science, Mathematics, Medical Technology, Music, Nursing, Pharmacy, Philosophy, Physical Education, Physics, Podiatric Medicine, Political Science, Psychology, Recreation/Leisure Studies, Rehabilitation Services, Secondary Education, Social Studies, Sociology/Anthropology, Spanish, Special Education, Speech Communication, Speech Pathology/Audiology, Theatre.
**Distribution of degrees:** The majors with the highest enrollment are elementary education, physical education, and hospitality management; philosophy, music, and geography have the lowest.
**Requirements:** General education requirement.
**Academic regulations:** Minimum 2.0 GPA must be maintained.
**Special:** Associate's degrees offered. Self-designed majors. Independent study. Internships. Graduate school at which undergraduates may take graduate-level courses. Preprofessional programs in medicine and pharmacy. 3-2 engineering programs with Pennsylvania State U and U of Pittsburgh. Six-year pharmacy transfer program with Temple U. Podiatric medicine transfer program with Pennsylvania Coll of Podiatric Medicine. Physical therapy transfer program with Hahnemann U. Member of Marine Science Consortium; off-campus study possible at Wallops Island, Va. Member of National Student Exchange (NSE). Teacher certification in early childhood, elementary, secondary, and special education. Certification in specific subject areas. Exchange program abroad in England (U of Leeds). ROTC. AFROTC at Lehigh U.
**Honors:** Honors program. Honor societies.
**Academic Assistance:** Remedial reading, writing, math, and study skills. Nonremedial tutoring.

**STUDENT LIFE. Housing:** All freshmen must live on campus. Coed, women's, and men's dorms. Fraternity housing. School-owned/operated apartments. 44% of students live in college housing.

**Social atmosphere:** "ESU is a suitcase college, so weekend social life is limited on and off campus," reports the student newspaper. "The university does sponsor art exhibits, concerts, and plays on some weekends." Influential groups on campus include the Greeks, the United Campus Ministry, and athletes. Favorite off-campus destinations include the fraternity and sports houses, Rudy's, Flood's, the Holiday Inn, Marita's, and the Pocono Grand Hotel. On campus, students gather at the Student Center. Popular yearly events include Springfest (bands and games), Earth Day, Dance Marathon, Convocations Series, and One Night Stand (weekly performers).

**Services and counseling/handicapped student services:** Placement services. Health service. Women's center. Day care. Counseling services for minority, military, and older students. Birth control, personal, and psychological counseling. Career and academic guidance services. Religious counseling. Physically disabled student services. Learning disabled services. Notetaking services. Tape recorders. Tutors. Reader services for the blind.

**Campus organizations:** Undergraduate student government. Student newspaper (Stroud Courier, published once/week). Literary magazine. Yearbook. Radio station. Choir, madrigal singers, jazz ensemble, concert and pep bands, folk music club, children's theatre, summer theatre, Stage II, forensic club, service fraternities, programming council, 56 organizations in all. 10 fraternities, two chapter houses; seven sororities, no chapter houses. 10% of men join a fraternity.

**Religious organizations:** Fellowship of Christian Athletes, Newman Club, United Campus Ministry, Christian Fellowship.

**Minority/foreign student organizations:** Black Student Association, Latin American Association. International Students Organization.

**ATHLETICS. Physical education requirements:** Three semesters of physical education required.

**Intercollegiate competition:** 10% of students participate. Baseball (M), basketball (M,W), cross-country (M,W), field hockey (W), football (M), lacrosse (W), soccer (M,W), softball (W), tennis (M,W), track (indoor) (M,W), track (outdoor) (M,W), track and field (indoor) (M,W), track and field (outdoor) (M,W), volleyball (M,W), wrestling (M). Member of ECAC, NCAA Division I for wrestling, NCAA Division II, Pennsylvania State Athletic Conference.

**Intramural and club sports:** 17% of students participate. Intramural basketball, soccer, softball, touch football, volleyball. Men's club diving, golf, ice hockey, lacrosse, rugby, weight lifting. Women's club diving, weight lifting.

**ADMISSIONS. Academic basis for candidate selection** (in order of priority): Secondary school record, class rank, standardized test scores, school's recommendation.

**Nonacademic basis for candidate selection:** Character and personality, extracurricular participation, particular talent or ability, and alumni/ae relationship are considered.

**Requirements:** Graduation from secondary school is required; GED is accepted. No specific distribution of secondary school units required. Minimum math SAT score of 500 required of computer science applicants. Act 101 program for in-state applicants not normally admissible. Summer Intensive Study Program and June/January Freshman Program for applicants not normally admissible. SAT or ACT is required. No off-campus interviews.

**Procedure:** Take SAT or ACT by January of 12th year. Application deadline is March 1. Notification of admission by March 1. Reply is required by April 2. $100 nonrefundable tuition deposit. $50 nonrefundable room deposit. Freshmen accepted for terms other than fall.

**Special programs:** Credit and/or placement may be granted through CEEB Advanced Placement exams for scores of 3 or higher. Credit and/or placement may be granted through CLEP general and subject exams.

**Transfer students:** Transfer students accepted for terms other than fall. In fall 1992, 41% of all new students were transfers into all classes. 1,192 transfer applications were received, 810 were accepted. Application deadline is June 4 for fall; December 11 for spring. Minimum 2.3 GPA required. Lowest course grade accepted is "C." Maximum number of transferable credits is 96 semester hours. At least 32 semester hours must be completed at the university to receive degree.

**Admissions contact:** Alan T. Chesterton, M.A., Director of Admissions. 717 424-3542.

**FINANCIAL AID. Available aid:** Pell grants, SEOG, state scholarships and grants, school scholarships and grants, private scholarships and grants, ROTC scholarships, academic merit scholarships, and athletic scholarships. Perkins Loans (NDSL), PLUS, Stafford Loans (GSL), state loans, and SLS. AMS.

**Financial aid statistics:** In 1992-93, 90% of all undergraduate applicants received aid; 90% of freshman applicants. Average amounts of aid awarded freshmen: Loans, $2,600.

**Supporting data/closing dates:** School's own aid application: Deadline is March 15. State aid form: Deadline is March 15. Notification of awards begins May 1.

**Financial aid contact:** Georgia Prell, Director of Financial Aid. 717 424-3340.

**STUDENT EMPLOYMENT.** College Work/Study Program. Institutional employment. 25% of full-time undergraduates work on campus during school year. Students may expect to earn an average of $1,275 during school year. Off-campus part-time employment opportunities rated "good."

**COMPUTER FACILITIES.** 150 IBM/IBM-compatible and Macintosh/Apple microcomputers; 70 are networked. Students may access Digital minicomputer/mainframe systems. Computer languages and software packages include Ada, MINITAB, Pascal, SAS, SNOBOL, WordPerfect. Computer facilities are available to all students.

**Fees:** None.

# Eastern College

**St. Davids, PA 19087-3696 215 341-5800**

**1994-95 Costs.** Tuition: $11,120. Room: $2,130. Board: $2,400. Fees, books, misc. academic expenses (school's estimate): $1,418.
**Enrollment.** Undergraduates: 423 men, 634 women (full-time). Freshman class: 690 applicants, 530 accepted, 250 enrolled. Graduate enrollment: 187 men, 243 women.
**Test score averages/ranges.** Average SAT scores: 452 verbal, 479 math. Average ACT scores: 22 composite.
**Faculty.** 56 full-time; 92 part-time. 38% of faculty holds doctoral degree. Student/faculty ratio: 12 to 1.
**Selectivity rating.** Less competitive.

**PROFILE.** Eastern, founded in 1952, is a church-affiliated college of arts and sciences. Its 107-acre campus is located on five former estates, 19 miles from Philadelphia.

**Accreditation:** MSACS. Professionally accredited by the Council on Social Work Education, the National League for Nursing.

**Religious orientation:** Eastern College is affiliated with the American Baptist Church; two semesters of religion required.

**Library:** Collections totaling over 111,416 volumes, 969 periodical subscriptions, and 257,618 microform items.

**Special facilities/museums:** Planetarium.

**Athletic facilities:** Gymnasium, basketball and tennis courts, weight room, outdoor swimming pool, track, baseball, field hockey, lacrosse, soccer, and softball fields, fitness trail.

**STUDENT BODY. Undergraduate profile:** 69% are state residents; 33% are transfers. 2% Asian-American, 11% Black, 2% Hispanic, 1% Native American, 69% White, 15% Other. Average age of undergraduates is 26.

**Freshman profile:** 1% of freshmen who took SAT scored 700 or over on math; 5% scored 600 or over on verbal, 14% scored 600 or over on math; 31% scored 500 or over on verbal, 44% scored 500 or over on math; 72% scored 400 or over on verbal, 72% scored 400 or over on math; 87% scored 300 or over on verbal, 90% scored 300 or over on math. 40% of freshmen who took ACT scored 24 or over on composite; 80% scored 18 or over on composite; 100% scored 12 or over on composite. 96% of accepted applicants took SAT; 2% took ACT.

**Undergraduate achievement:** 73% of fall 1992 freshmen returned for fall 1993 term. 9% of students who completed a degree program immediately went on to graduate study.

**Foreign students:** Eight students are from out of the country. Countries represented include China, Haiti, India, Indonesia, and South Korea; six in all.

**PROGRAMS OF STUDY. Degrees:** B.A., B.S., B.S.Nurs., B.Soc.Work.

**Majors:** Art History, Astronomy, Bible Studies, Biology, Business Administration, Chemistry, Communications, Communications Education, Elementary Education, English Education, English/Literature, English/Writing, French, Health/Physical Education, History, Mathematics, Medical Technology, Music, Nursing, Organizational Management, Philosophy, Political Science, Psychology, Religion/Philosophy, School Health Services, Secondary Education, Social Work, Sociology, Spanish, Studio Art, Youth Ministry.

**Distribution of degrees:** The majors with the highest enrollment are organizational management, nursing, and elementary education; communications, English/writing, and Biblical studies have the lowest.

**Requirements:** General education requirement.

**Academic regulations:** Freshmen must maintain minimum 1.67 GPA; sophomores, 1.75 GPA; juniors, 1.9 GPA; seniors, 2.0 GPA.

**Special:** Minors offered in many majors and in American history, European history, fine arts, gerontology, health science, language, Latin American studies, missions, physical education, religion, and social welfare. Associate's degrees offered. Self-designed majors. Double majors. Independent study. Accelerated study. Pass/fail grading option. Internships. Graduate school at which undergraduates may take graduate-level courses. Preprofessional programs in medicine, dentistry, nursing, occupational therapy, and physical therapy. 3-1 medical technology program with Bryn Mawr Hospital. Member of Christian College Coalition. Cross-registration with Cabrini Coll and Rosemont Coll. Course work possible through Eastern Baptist Theological Seminary. American Studies Program (Washington, D.C.), Argonne Science Semester (Illinois), AuSable Inst of Environmental Studies Program (Michigan), and Oregon Extension Program. Exchange programs with Goshen Coll and other American Baptist colleges. Teacher certification in early childhood, elementary, secondary, and special education. Certification in specific subject areas. Study abroad possible. ROTC at Valley Forge Military Junior Coll. AFROTC at St. Joseph's U.

**Honors:** Honors program. Honor societies.

**Academic Assistance:** Remedial reading, writing, math, and study skills. Nonremedial tutoring.

**STUDENT LIFE. Housing:** All unmarried students under age 21 must live on campus unless living near campus with relatives. Coed dorms. School-owned/operated apartments. 39% of students live in college housing.

**Social atmosphere:** Students gather on campus at the Lower Walton Lounge, the Keal Guffin Lounge, the gym, the McInnis Auditorium for chapel, and the Mariott Dining Hall. Christian groups, athletes, the Black Student League, the Student Government Association, and music and theatre arts groups influence campus life. Popular events on campus include chapel service, Convocation, the Spring Banquet, the Variety Show, basketball games, and get-togethers at the Coffee House. "The Student Activities Board offers various social activities, and Eastern's location is ideal. Philadelphia is a 20-minute train ride away, so many students go into the city for entertainment. However, a majority of students go home on weekends and the campus can feel deserted. Those who stay usually find their own entertainment, however," reports the student newspaper.

**Services and counseling/handicapped student services:** Placement services. Health service. Counseling services for minority, veteran, and older students. Birth control, personal, and psychological counseling. Career and academic guidance services. Religious counseling. Physically disabled student services.

**Campus organizations:** Undergraduate student government. Student newspaper (Waltonian, published biweekly). Literary magazine. Yearbook. Radio station. Stage band, touring choir, Habitat for Humanity, 60 organizations in all.

**Religious organizations:** Clown and prison ministries, Evangelicals for Social Action, Fellowship of Christian Athletes, Turning Point gospel team, World Concerns Task Force, Young Life, Angels of Harmony, Crossways.

**Minority/foreign student organizations:** Black Student League, Hispanic Caucus. International Student Club.

**ATHLETICS. Physical education requirements:** One semester of physical education required.

**Intercollegiate competition:** 35% of students participate. Baseball (M), basketball (M,W), cheerleading (M,W), cross-country (M,W), field hockey (W), lacrosse (W), soccer (M,W), softball (W), tennis (M,W), volleyball (W). Member of NCAA Division III, NCCAA, PAC.

**Intramural and club sports:** 45% of students participate. Intramural bowling, basketball, flag football, golf, table tennis, tennis, volleyball. Men's club volleyball.

**ADMISSIONS. Academic basis for candidate selection** (in order of priority): Secondary school record, class rank, standardized test scores, essay, school's recommendation.

**Nonacademic basis for candidate selection:** Character and personality, extracurricular participation, and particular talent or ability are important.

**Requirements:** Graduation from secondary school is required; GED is accepted. No specific distribution of secondary school units required. Associate's degree or diploma in nursing and Nursing Mobility Profile required of B.S.N. program applicants. R.N. required of nursing program applicants. SAT is required; ACT may be substituted. Campus visit and interview recommended. Off-campus interviews available with an admissions representative.

**Procedure:** Suggest filing application by December; no deadline. Take SAT/ACT as soon as possible in the 12th year. Notification of admission on rolling basis. No set date by which applicants must accept offer. $150 tuition deposit, refundable until May 1. Freshmen accepted for terms other than fall.

**Special programs:** Admission may be deferred. Credit and/or placement may be granted through CEEB Advanced Placement exams for scores of 3 or higher. Credit and/or placement may be granted through CLEP subject exams. Credit and placement may be granted through ACT PEP and DANTES exams and military and life experience. Early entrance/early admission program. Concurrent enrollment program.

**Transfer students:** Transfer students accepted for terms other than fall. In fall 1993, 33% of all new students were transfers into all classes. 172 transfer applications were received, 103 were accepted. Application deadline is rolling for fall; rolling for spring. Minimum 2.0 GPA required. Lowest course grade accepted is "C." At least 30 semester hours must be completed at the college to receive degree.

**Admissions contact:** Stephen Mark Seymour, Director of Admissions. 215 341-5967.

**FINANCIAL AID. Available aid:** Pell grants, SEOG, state scholarships and grants, school scholarships and grants, private scholarships and grants, and academic merit scholarships. Perkins Loans (NDSL), PLUS, Stafford Loans (GSL), and SLS. Deferred payment plan. College payment plans.

**Financial aid statistics:** In 1993-94, 85% of all undergraduate applicants received aid; 58% of freshman applicants.

**Supporting data/closing dates:** FAFSA/FAF/FFS: Accepted on rolling basis; deadline is May. School's own aid application: Accepted on rolling basis. State aid form: Accepted on rolling basis. Income tax forms: Priority filing date is August 15; accepted on rolling basis. Financial Aid Transcripts from transfers: Accepted on rolling basis. Notification of awards on rolling basis.

**Financial aid contact:** Carolyn Brody, Acting Director of Financial Aid. 215 341-5842.

**STUDENT EMPLOYMENT.** College Work/Study Program. Institutional employment. 15% of full-time undergraduates work on campus during school year. Students may expect to earn an average of $900 during school year. Off-campus part-time employment opportunities rated "fair."

**COMPUTER FACILITIES.** 56 IBM/IBM-compatible microcomputers; 39 are networked. Client/LAN operating systems include Artisoft, LocalTalk/AppleTalk. Computer languages and software packages include C++, Paradox, Quattro Pro, WordPerfect; 15 in all. Computer facilities are available to all students.

**Fees:** $45 computer fee per course; included in tuition/fees.

**Hours:** 9 AM-10 PM (M-Th, Sa); 9 AM-9 PM (F); 2 PM-10 PM (Su).

**GRADUATE CAREER DATA.** Graduate school percentages: 1% enter law school. 2% enter medical school. 1% enter graduate business programs. 10% enter graduate arts and sciences programs. 1% enter theological school/seminary. 13% of graduates choose careers in business and industry.

**PROMINENT ALUMNI/AE.** Charles Blum, specialist in international relations; Judith LaDrew, assistant to president, United Technologies.

# Edinboro University of Pennsylvania

**Edinboro, PA 16444** **814 732-2000**

**1993-94 Costs.** Tuition: $2,954 (state residents), $7,352 (out-of-state). Room: $1,760. Board: $1,890. Fees, books, misc. academic expenses (school's estimate): $1,077.

**Enrollment.** Undergraduates: 2,751 men, 3,567 women (full-time). Freshman class: 4,419 applicants, 3,074 accepted, 1,349 enrolled. Graduate enrollment: 147 men, 448 women.

**Test score averages/ranges.** N/A.

**Faculty.** 392 full-time; 14 part-time. 56% of faculty holds highest degree in specific field. Student/faculty ratio: 17 to 1.

**Selectivity rating.** N/A.

**PROFILE.** Edinboro, founded in 1857, is a public university. Its 585-acre campus is located in Edinboro, 18 miles from Erie.

**Accreditation:** MSACS. Professionally accredited by the American Dietetic Association, the Council on Social Work Education, the National League for Nursing.

**Religious orientation:** Edinboro University of Pennsylvania is nonsectarian; no religious requirements.

**Library:** Collections totaling over 412,081 volumes, 2,175 periodical subscriptions, and 1,234,416 microform items.

**Special facilities/museums:** Art galleries, biology museum, on-campus preschool/early elementary school, TV studio, planetarium, solar observatory, robotics lab.

**Athletic facilities:** Field house, gymnasium.

**STUDENT BODY. Undergraduate profile:** 88% are state residents; 21% are transfers. 1% Asian-American, 4% Black, 92% White, 3% Other. Average age of undergraduates is 22.

**Undergraduate achievement:** 72% of fall 1992 freshmen returned for fall 1993 term.

**Foreign students:** 177 students are from out of the country. Countries represented include Bangladesh, China, Hong Kong, India, Japan, and Pakistan; 41 in all.

**PROGRAMS OF STUDY. Degrees:** B.A., B.F.A., B.S., B.S.Ed.

**Majors:** Anthropology, Art Education, Art History, Biology, Black Studies/Social Science, Business Administration/Accounting, Business Administration/Administration, Ceramics/Crafts, Chemistry, Chemistry Education, Cinema/Applied Media Arts, Communication, Communications/Applied Media Arts, Computer Science, Criminal Justice, Drama, Drawing/Crafts, Earth Sciences, Economics, Elementary/Early Childhood Education, Elementary Education, Elementary/Special Education, English/Literature, English/Writing, Environmental Science/Biology, Environmental Science/Earth Science, Environmental Studies/Geography, Foreign Language, French, French Education, General Studies, Geography, Geology, German, German Education, Graphics/Applied Media Arts, Health/Physical Education, History, Humanities, Industrial Biochemistry, Industrial Trades Leadership, Jewelry/Metalry/Crafts, Mathematics, Medical Technology, Multimedia/Crafts, Music, Natural Science/Mathematics, Nuclear Medicine Technology, Nursing, Nutrition, Painting/Crafts, Philosophy, Photography/Applied Media Arts, Physics, Political Science, Pre-Dental, Pre-Law, Pre-Law/Social Science, Pre-Medical, Pre-Pharmacy, Pre-Veterinary, Printmaking/Crafts, Psychology, Russian, School Dental Hygiene, Sculpture/Crafts, Secondary Biology Education, Secondary Earth/Space Education, Secondary English Education, Secondary General Science Education, Secondary Mathematics Education, Secondary Physics Education, Secondary Social Studies Education, Social Science, Social Work, Sociology, Spanish, Spanish Education, Special Education, Special Education/Elementary, Specialized Studies, Speech/Hearing Disorders, Textile Design/Crafts, Weaving/Fibers/Crafts.

**Distribution of degrees:** The majors with the highest enrollment are elementary education, business administration, and speech communication; anthropology, philosophy, and foreign language have the lowest.

**Requirements:** General education requirement.

**Academic regulations:** Freshmen must maintain minimum 1.67 GPA; sophomores, 1.85 GPA; juniors, 2.00 GPA; seniors, 2.00 GPA.

**Special:** Minors offered in many majors and in approximately 15 other fields. Associate's degrees offered. Self-designed majors. Independent study. Accelerated study. Pass/fail grading option. Internships. Graduate school at which undergraduates may take graduate-level courses. Preprofessional programs in law, medicine, veterinary science, pharmacy, and dentistry. 3-2 engineering programs with Case Western Reserve U, Pennsylvania State U, and U of Pittsburgh. Member of Marine Science Consortium; off-campus study possible at Wallops Island, Va. Washington Semester. Teacher certification in early childhood, elementary, secondary, and special education. Study abroad in China, England, Italy, Morocco, Pakistan, Poland, the former Soviet Republics, and Thailand. ROTC.

**Honors:** Honors program. Honor societies.

**Academic Assistance:** Remedial reading, writing, math, and study skills. Nonremedial tutoring.

**STUDENT LIFE. Housing:** All freshmen must live on campus. Coed, women's, and men's dorms. Off-campus married-student housing. Honors housing. 37% of students live in college housing.

**Social atmosphere:** The student newspaper reports, "EUP was once included on Playboy's notorious Top Ten Party Schools list. The university still rocks on the weekends (and even on Thursdays), but a new president and recent enrollment surges have caused EUP to become recognized as a more respected academic institution." To some extent, Greeks have a significant amount of influence on campus life. Other influential groups on campus are the football and wrestling teams, the Student Government Association, The Spectator, and WFSE-FM campus radio station. Favorite activities which keep students entertained

throughout the year include Homecoming, Greek Week, SGA concert, Edinboro-Gannon University basketball game, and the Edinboro-Slippery Rock football game.
**Services and counseling/handicapped student services:** Placement services. Health service. Day care. Counseling services for minority, veteran, and older students. Birth control, personal, and psychological counseling. Career and academic guidance services. Religious counseling. Physically disabled student services. Learning disabled program/services. Tape recorders. Tutors. Reader services for the blind.
**Campus organizations:** Undergraduate student government. Student newspaper (Spectator, published once/week). Yearbook. Radio station. Numerous musical groups, University Players, children's theatre, Art League, Circle K, peace center, chess and karate clubs, 85 organizations in all. Seven fraternities, no chapter houses; five sororities, no chapter houses. 10% of men join a fraternity. 15% of women join a sorority.
**Religious organizations:** Campus Ministry, Christian Fellowship, Newman Student Association, New Beginnings, Celebration, Fellowship of Christian Athletes, Prophets Bible Study.
**Minority/foreign student organizations:** Minority Students United, United Voices of Edinboro. International Student Association.

**ATHLETICS. Physical education requirements:** Three semester hours of physical education required.
**Intercollegiate competition:** Baseball (M), basketball (M,W), cross-country (M,W), football (M), gymnastics (W), riflery (M), soccer (M), softball (W), swimming (M,W), tennis (M,W), track (M,W), volleyball (M,W), wrestling (M). Member of ECAC, NCAA Division I for wrestling, NCAA Division II, Pennsylvania State Athletic Conference.
**Intramural and club sports:** Intramural baseball, basketball, cross-country, football, golf, handball, racquetball, softball, swimming, tennis, track, volleyball, wrestling.

**ADMISSIONS. Academic basis for candidate selection** (in order of priority): Secondary school record, class rank, school's recommendation, standardized test scores.
**Nonacademic basis for candidate selection:** Character and personality, extracurricular participation, and particular talent or ability are considered.
**Requirements:** Graduation from secondary school is required; GED is accepted. No specific distribution of secondary school units required. Audition required of music program applicants. Trial Admission Program (TAP) and Act 101 program for applicants not normally admissible. SAT is required; ACT may be substituted. Admissions interview recommended. Off-campus interviews available with an admissions representative.
**Procedure:** Take SAT or ACT by January of 12th year. Notification of admission on rolling basis. Reply is required within 30 days of acceptance. $100 nonrefundable tuition deposit. Freshmen accepted for terms other than fall.
**Special programs:** Admission may be deferred. Credit and/or placement may be granted through CEEB Advanced Placement exams for scores of 4 or higher. Credit and/or placement may be granted through CLEP general and subject exams. Credit and placement may be granted through challenge exams and military experience. Early entrance/early admission program. Concurrent enrollment program.
**Transfer students:** Transfer students accepted for terms other than fall. In fall 1993, 21% of all new students were transfers into all classes. 921 transfer applications were received, 583 were accepted. Application deadline is rolling for fall; rolling for spring. Minimum 2.0 GPA required. Lowest course grade accepted is "C." Maximum number of transferable credits is 96 semester hours. At least 32 semester hours must be completed at the university to receive degree.
**Admissions contact:** Terrence Carlin, M.Ed., Director of Admissions. 800 626-2203.

**FINANCIAL AID. Available aid:** Pell grants, SEOG, state scholarships and grants, school scholarships and grants, private scholarships, ROTC scholarships, academic merit scholarships, athletic scholarships, and aid for undergraduate foreign students. Perkins Loans (NDSL), PLUS, Stafford Loans (GSL), NSL, and state loans. AMS and Tuition Management Systems.
**Financial aid statistics:** 17% of aid is not need-based. Average amounts of aid awarded freshmen: Scholarships and grants, $1,700; loans, $2,400.
**Supporting data/closing dates:** FAFSA: Deadline is May 1. Notification of awards begins July 15.
**Financial aid contact:** Kenneth Brandt, M.Ed., Director of Financial Aid. 814 732-2821.

**STUDENT EMPLOYMENT.** College Work/Study Program. Institutional employment. 25% of full-time undergraduates work on campus during school year. Students may expect to earn an average of $1,200 during school year. Off-campus part-time employment opportunities rated "fair."

**COMPUTER FACILITIES.** 163 IBM/IBM-compatible and Macintosh/Apple microcomputers; 104 are networked. Students may access Digital minicomputer/mainframe systems, BITNET, Internet. Client/LAN operating systems include Apple/Macintosh, DOS, OS/2. Computer languages and software packages include Assembly, BASIC, C, COBOL, Excel, FORTRAN, Hyper Card, Lotus 1-2-3, Microsoft Works, Pascal, RPG II, Super Paint, WordPerfect. Computer facilities are available to all students.
**Fees:** None.
**Hours:** 7:45 AM-11 PM (M-F); 9 AM-5 PM (Sa); 1 PM-9 PM (Su).

# Elizabethtown College

**Elizabethtown, PA 17022 — 717 361-1000**

**1993-94 Costs.** Tuition: $13,200. Room: $2,150. Board: $2,100. Fees, books, misc. academic expenses (school's estimate): $900.

**Enrollment.** Undergraduates: 504 men, 981 women (full-time). Freshman class: 2,417 applicants, 1,843 accepted, 426 enrolled.

**Test score averages/ranges.** Average SAT scores: 492 verbal, 546 math. Range of SAT scores of middle 50%: 440-540 verbal, 490-600 math.

**Faculty.** 105 full-time; 42 part-time. 70% of faculty holds doctoral degree. Student/faculty ratio: 14 to 1.

**Selectivity rating.** Competitive.

**PROFILE.** Elizabethtown College, founded in 1899, is a church-affiliated, liberal arts institution. Its 180-acre campus is located in Elizabethtown, 20 miles from Harrisburg.
**Accreditation:** MSACS. Professionally accredited by the American Medical Association (CAHEA), the Association of Collegiate Business Schools and Programs, the Council on Social Work Education, the National Association of Schools of Music.
**Religious orientation:** Elizabethtown College is affiliated with the Church of the Brethren; no religious requirements.
**Library:** Collections totaling over 156,694 volumes, 1,100 periodical subscriptions, and 100,485 microform items.
**Special facilities/museums:** Art gallery, meetinghouse/center for Anabaptist and Pietist studies, nuclear magnetic resonance spectrometer, scanning electron microscope, microspectrometer, liquid scintillation counter, vacuum atmospheric lab system.
**Athletic facilities:** Gymnasium, swimming pool, racquetball, tennis, and volleyball courts, baseball, soccer, softball fields.

**STUDENT BODY. Undergraduate profile:** 62% are state residents; 7% are transfers. 2% Asian-American, 2% Black, 1% Hispanic, 95% White. Average age of undergraduates is 20.
**Freshman profile:** 1% of freshmen who took SAT scored 700 or over on verbal, 4% scored 700 or over on math; 8% scored 600 or over on verbal, 26% scored 600 or over on math; 46% scored 500 or over on verbal, 72% scored 500 or over on math; 92% scored 400 or over on verbal, 95% scored 400 or over on math; 100% scored 300 or over on verbal, 99% scored 300 or over on math. 99% of accepted applicants took SAT; 1% took ACT.
**Undergraduate achievement:** 81% of fall 1992 freshmen returned for fall 1993 term. 56% of entering class graduated. 16% of students who completed a degree program immediately went on to graduate study.
**Foreign students:** 34 students are from out of the country. Countries represented include Brazil, Indonesia, Japan, Netherlands, Russia, and Zambia; 19 in all.

**PROGRAMS OF STUDY. Degrees:** B.A., B.S.
**Majors:** Accounting, Biochemistry, Biology, Business Administration, Chemical Physics, Chemistry, Chemistry Management, Communications, Computer Engineering, Computer Science, Early Childhood Education, Economics, Elementary Education, Engineering, Engineering Physics, English, Environmental Science, French, German, History, Industrial Engineering, International Business, Mathematics, Medical Technology, Music, Music Education, Music Therapy, Occupational Therapy, Philosophy, Physics, Political Science, Psychology, Religious Studies, Secondary Education, Social Work, Sociology/Anthropology, Spanish.
**Distribution of degrees:** The majors with the highest enrollment are business administration, education, and communications; philosophy, religious studies, and sociology/anthropology have the lowest.
**Requirements:** General education requirement.
**Academic regulations:** Freshmen must maintain minimum 1.8 GPA; sophomores, 1.9 GPA; juniors, 1.95 GPA; seniors, 2.0 GPA.
**Special:** 52 minors or concentrations offered. Double majors. Dual degrees. Independent study. Pass/fail grading option. Internships. Preprofessional programs in law, medicine, veterinary science, dentistry, theology, optometry, forestry, and physical therapy. 2-3 M.S. program in physical therapy and 2-2 B.S. program in allied health with Thomas Jefferson U. 3-2 forestry and environmental management program with Duke U. 3-2 engineering program with Pennsylvania State U. Capital Semester Program. Teacher certification in early childhood, elementary, and secondary education. Certification in specific subject areas. Exchange programs abroad in China (Dalian Inst), Ecuador (U of Azuay), England (Cheltenham and Gloucester Coll of Higher Education), France (U of Nancy, U of Strasbourg), Germany (Phillips U), Greece (LaVerne Coll of Athens), Japan (Hokusei Gakuen U), and Spain (U of Barcelona).
**Honors:** Honor societies.
**Academic Assistance:** Remedial reading, writing, math, and study skills. Nonremedial tutoring.

**STUDENT LIFE. Housing:** All unmarried students must live on campus unless living with family. Coed, women's, and men's dorms. School-owned/operated apartments. Off-campus privately-owned housing. 90% of students live in college housing.
**Social atmosphere:** The Roost, the Jay's Nest, Wolgemuths, Mookies, and B & T are favorite hang-outs. The Activities Planning Board, Inter-Varsity Christian Fellowship, and soccer players influence campus life. Homecoming, Thanksgiving, TGIS (Spring weekend), and weekly "Wednesday at 10" lectures are popular social/cultural events. "E'town students work hard at their studies but also value extra-curricular activities," according to the editor of the student newspaper. "Almost all are involved in something. Weekends feature two college-wide dances, plus a weekly night club. The campus cultivates the sense of being friendly, like a family."
**Services and counseling/handicapped student services:** Placement services. Health service. Counseling services for older students. Personal and psychological counseling. Career and academic guidance services. Religious counseling. Physically disabled student services. Tape recorders. Tutors.
**Campus organizations:** Undergraduate student government. Student newspaper (Etownian, published once/week). Literary magazine. Yearbook. Radio and TV stations. Choirs, orchestra, bands, theatre, Activities Planning Board, outdoors club, Amnesty International, Circle K, Habitat for Humanity, departmental clubs, 50 organizations in all.
**Religious organizations:** Brethren Fellowship, Campus Fellowship, Hillel, Newman Club, Student Outreach Ministry.
**Minority/foreign student organizations:** African American Cultural Society, STEP. International Club.

**ATHLETICS. Physical education requirements:** Three semesters of physical education required.
**Intercollegiate competition:** 40% of students participate. Baseball (M), basketball (M,W), cheerleading (W), cross-country (M,W), field hockey (W), golf (M), soccer (M,W), softball (W), swimming (M,W), tennis (M,W), volleyball (W), wrestling (M). Member of Middle Atlantic Conference, NCAA Division III.
**Intramural and club sports:** 75% of students participate. Intramural badminton, basketball, soccer, racquetball, softball, tennis, touch football, volleyball. Men's club track and field, volleyball. Women's club track and field.

**ADMISSIONS. Academic basis for candidate selection** (in order of priority): Secondary school record, class rank, standardized test scores, school's recommendation, essay.
**Nonacademic basis for candidate selection:** Extracurricular participation is important. Character and personality, particular talent or ability, geographical distribution, and alumni/ae relationship are considered.
**Requirements:** Graduation from secondary school is required; GED is accepted. 18 units and the following program of study are recommended: 4 units of English, 3 units of math, 2 units of foreign language, 2 units of social studies. Minimum combined SAT score of 950, rank in top quarter of secondary school class, and minimum 2.5 GPA recommended. Interviews required of occupational therapy program applicants. Audition required of music program applicants. Special advising for applicants not normally admissible. SAT or ACT is required. Campus visit and interview recommended. No off-campus interviews.
**Procedure:** Take SAT or ACT by December of 12th year. Visit college for interview by February of 12th year. Suggest filing application by March 1. Notification of admission begins in November. Reply is required by May 1. $200 tuition deposit, refundable until February 15. Freshmen accepted for terms other than fall.
**Special programs:** Admission may be deferred one year. Credit and/or placement may be granted through CEEB Advanced Placement exams for scores of 3 or higher. Credit and/or placement may be granted through CLEP general and subject exams. Credit may be granted through life experience. Credit and placement may be granted through Regents College, DANTES, and challenge exams. Early entrance/early admission program. Concurrent enrollment program.
**Transfer students:** Transfer students accepted for terms other than fall. In fall 1993, 7% of all new students were transfers into all classes. 125 transfer applications were received, 77 were accepted. Application deadline is rolling for fall; rolling for spring. Minimum 2.5 GPA recommended. Lowest course grade accepted is "C." Maximum number of transferable credits is 64 semester hours from two-year schools; unlimited from four-year schools. At least 30 semester hours must be completed at the college to receive degree.
**Admissions contact:** Ronald D. Potier, Director of Admissions. 717 361-1400.

**FINANCIAL AID. Available aid:** Pell grants, SEOG, state scholarships and grants, school scholarships and grants, private scholarships and grants, academic merit scholarships, and aid for undergraduate foreign students. Perkins Loans (NDSL), PLUS, Stafford Loans (GSL), state loans, private loans, and SLS. Tuition Plan Inc., Knight Tuition Plans, AMS, and family tuition reduction.
**Financial aid statistics:** 23% of aid is not need-based. In 1993-94, 98% of all undergraduate applicants received aid; 98% of freshman applicants. Average amounts of aid awarded freshmen: Scholarships and grants, $6,450; loans, $3,675.
**Supporting data/closing dates:** FAFSA: Priority filing date is March 1; accepted on rolling basis; deadline is April 1. School's own aid application: Priority filing date is March 1; deadline is April 1. Income tax forms: Priority filing date is March 1; accepted on rolling basis; deadline is April 1. Notification of awards on rolling basis.
**Financial aid contact:** Gordon McK. Bateman, M.S., Director of Financial Aid. 717 361-1404.

**STUDENT EMPLOYMENT.** College Work/Study Program. Institutional employment. 60% of full-time undergraduates work on campus during school year. Students may expect to earn an average of $73 during school year. Off-campus part-time employment opportunities rated "fair."

**COMPUTER FACILITIES.** 150 IBM/IBM-compatible and Macintosh/Apple microcomputers; 75 are networked. Students may access Digital, SUN minicomputer/mainframe systems, Internet. Client/LAN operating systems include Apple/Macintosh, DOS, UNIX/XENIX/AIX, LocalTalk/AppleTalk, Novell. Computer languages and software packages include ADA, BASIC, C, COBOL, dBASE, FORTRAN, Lotus 1-2-3, MINITAB, PageMaker, Pascal, SPSS-X, Windows, WordPerfect. Computer facilities are available to all students.
**Fees:** None.
**Hours:** 24 hours (mainframe); 8 AM-midn. (PC's).

**GRADUATE CAREER DATA.** Graduate school percentages: 11% enter law school. 9% enter medical school. 12% enter graduate business programs. 55% enter graduate arts and sciences programs. 2% enter theological school/seminary. Highest graduate school enrollments: Carnegie Mellon U, Dickinson U Law School, U of Maryland, Pennsylvania State U College of Medicine, Villanova U. Companies and businesses that hire graduates: Coopers & Lybrand, Ernst & Young, HERCO EDS, AMP, Commonwealth of Pennsylvania.

**PROMINENT ALUMNI/AE.** W. Ernest Lefever, founder and Senior Fellow for Ethics and Public Policy Center in Washington, DC; William Foster, former basketball coach for Duke U; John West, Washington, D.C. attorney and law clerk for Supreme Court Justice William Brennan.

# Franklin & Marshall College

**Lancaster, PA 17604-3003 717 291-3911**

**1994-95 Costs.** Tuition: $20,960. Room & board: $3,980. Fees, books, misc. academic expenses (school's estimate): $590.

**Enrollment.** Undergraduates: 972 men, 836 women (full-time). Freshman class: 3,270 applicants, 2,120 accepted, 508 enrolled.

**Test score averages/ranges.** Range of SAT scores of middle 50%: 500-600 verbal, 560-660 math. Average ACT scores: 26 composite.

**Faculty.** 157 full-time; 14 part-time. 94% of faculty holds highest degree in specific field. Student/faculty ratio: 11 to 1.

**Selectivity rating.** Highly competitive.

**PROFILE.** Franklin & Marshall, founded in 1787, is a private, liberal arts college. Its 125-acre campus is located in a residential area of Lancaster, 60 miles west of Philadelphia.

**Accreditation:** MSACS.
**Religious orientation:** Franklin & Marshall College is nonsectarian; no religious requirements.
**Library:** Collections totaling over 345,000 volumes, 1,703 periodical subscriptions, and 250,000 microform items.
**Special facilities/museums:** Art gallery, natural history museums, bronze casting foundry, retail sales complex, psychology and language labs, TV and radio station, observatory/planetarium.
**Athletic facilities:** Gymnasiums, tennis courts, swimming pool, ice rink, athletic fields, tracks, weight rooms, wrestling room, baseball stadium, climbing wall, aerobic center.

**STUDENT BODY. Undergraduate profile:** 33% are state residents; 2% are transfers. 6% Asian-American, 3% Black, 3% Hispanic, 82% White, 6% Other. Average age of undergraduates is 20.
**Freshman profile:** 94% of accepted applicants took SAT; 9% took ACT. 56% of freshmen come from public schools.
**Undergraduate achievement:** 95% of fall 1992 freshmen returned for fall 1993 term. 83% of entering class graduated. 34% of students who completed a degree program immediately went on to graduate study.
**Foreign students:** 106 students are from out of the country. Countries represented include China, Great Britain, India, Russia, Sri Lanka, and Turkey; 50 in all.

**PROGRAMS OF STUDY. Degrees:** B.A.
**Majors:** American Studies, Anthropology, Art, Biology, Biology/Psychology, Business Administration, Chemistry, Classics, Drama, Economics, English, French, Geosciences, German, Government, Greek, History, Latin, Mathematics, Music, Neuroscience, Philosophy, Physics, Psychology, Religious Studies, Sociology, Spanish, Special Studies.
**Distribution of degrees:** The majors with the highest enrollment are government, business administration, and English; German, religious studies, and biology/psychology have the lowest.
**Requirements:** General education requirement.
**Academic regulations:** Freshmen must maintain minimum 1.60 GPA; sophomores, 1.80 GPA; juniors, 1.90 GPA; seniors, 2.00 GPA.
**Special:** Minors offered in all majors and in Asian studies, astronomy, computer science, dance, environmental studies, Italian, Judaic studies, Russian, science/technology/society, and women's studies. Third World studies and writing programs. Archaeological and geological field work. Self-designed majors. Double majors. Independent study. Pass/fail grading option. Internships. Preprofessional programs in law, medicine, veterinary science, dentistry, and optometry. 3-2 forestry and environmental studies program with Duke U. 3-2 engineering programs with Case Western Reserve U, Columbia U, Georgia Tech, Rensselaer Polytech Inst, U of Pennsylvania, and Washington U. Member of Central Pennsylvania Consortium; cross-registration possible. Washington Semester and Sea Semester. Arts Program in New York. National Theatre Institute Semester (Connecticut). Shape of Two Cities program (New York/Paris). Exchange program abroad in Japan (Tohoku Gakiun U). Study abroad also in various countries worldwide.
**Honors:** Phi Beta Kappa. Honor societies.
**Academic Assistance:** Nonremedial tutoring.

**STUDENT LIFE. Housing:** All freshmen and sophomores must live on campus unless living with family. Coed dorms. School-owned/operated apartments. Off-campus privately-owned housing. 74% of students live in college housing.
**Social atmosphere:** On campus, students gather at Ben's Underground and The Common Ground. Off campus, students head for Brendee's Town Tavern and Hildy's Bar. Influential campus groups include Greeks, theatre groups, the student government, and the student newspaper and radio station. Students enjoy Homecoming, Spring Arts Weekend, and men's and women's sporting events. "Students often say that at F&M you work hard and party hard. There are fraternity parties almost every weekend, but there are also a lot of other campus activities--concerts, musicals, films, and plays," reports the student newspaper.
**Services and counseling/handicapped student services:** Placement services. Health service. Women's center. Counseling services for minority and older students. Birth control, personal, and psychological counseling. Career and academic guidance services. Religious counseling.
**Campus organizations:** Undergraduate student government. Student newspaper (College Reporter, published once/week). Literary magazine. Yearbook. Radio and TV stations. Poor Richards (singing group), chamber singers, F&M Players, entertainment committee, student arts council, Environmental Action Alliance, Habitat for Humanity, Coalition for Choice, Right-to-Life Advocates, Peace Forum, Teach for America, Voices for Women, gay/lesbian group, chess club, martial arts group, 112 organizations in all. Nine fraternities, seven chapter houses; three sororities, one chapter house. 45% of men join a fraternity. 30% of women join a sorority.
**Religious organizations:** Catholic Campus Community, Christian Fellowship, Buddhist, HinduPrayer, Christian Science Organization, Hillel, Nural-Islam, Orthodox Christian Fellowship.
**Minority/foreign student organizations:** Black Student Union, Association of Spanish Cultures. International Club, East Asian Society.

**ATHLETICS. Physical education requirements:** None.
**Intercollegiate competition:** 25% of students participate. Baseball (M), basketball (M,W), cross-country (M,W), field hockey (W), football (M), golf (M,W), lacrosse (M,W), soccer (M,W), softball (W), squash (M,W), swimming (M,W), tennis (M,W), track (indoor) (M,W), track (outdoor) (M,W), track and field (indoor) (M,W), track and field (outdoor) (M,W), volleyball (W), wrestling (M). Member of Centennial Conference, Eastern Intercollegiate Wrestling Association, ECAC, NCAA Division I for wrestling, NCAA Division III.
**Intramural and club sports:** 65% of students participate. Intramural bowling, soccer, softball, squash, swimming, tennis, touch football, track, volleyball. Men's club cheerleading, crew, fencing, ice hockey, racqetball, rugby, volleyball. Women's club cheerleading, crew, fencing, rugby.

**ADMISSIONS. Academic basis for candidate selection** (in order of priority): Secondary school record, class rank, school's recommendation, standardized test scores, essay.
**Nonacademic basis for candidate selection:** Extracurricular participation is emphasized. Character and personality and particular talent or ability are important. Geographical distribution and alumni/ae relationship are considered.

**Requirements:** Graduation from secondary school is required; GED is accepted. 16 units and the following program of study are recommended: 4 units of English, 4 units of math, 3 units of science, 3 units of foreign language, 3 units of social studies. Portfolios, auditions, and interviews recommended for demonstration of special skills or talent. SAT or ACT is required. ACH recommended. Campus visit and interview recommended. Off-campus interviews available with an admissions representative.
**Procedure:** Take SAT or ACT by December of 12th year. Take ACH by January of 12th year. Visit college for interview by February of 12th year. Application deadline is February 1. Notification of admission by April 1. Reply is required by May 1. $200 nonrefundable tuition deposit. Freshmen accepted for terms other than fall.
**Special programs:** Admission may be deferred one year. Credit and/or placement may be granted through CEEB Advanced Placement exams for scores of 4 or higher. Credit and/or placement may be granted through CLEP subject exams. Credit and placement may be granted through challenge exams. Early decision program. In fall 1993, 174 applied for early decision and 124 were accepted. Deadline for applying for early decision is January 15. Early entrance/early admission program.
**Transfer students:** Transfer students accepted for terms other than fall. In fall 1993, 2% of all new students were transfers into all classes. 45 transfer applications were received, 27 were accepted. Application deadline is May 15 for fall; December 1 for spring. Minimum 3.0 GPA recommended. Lowest course grade accepted is "C." Maximum number of transferable credits is 64 semester hours. At least 64 semester hours must be completed at the college to receive degree.
**Admissions contact:** Peter Van Buskirk, Dean of Admissions. 717 291-3951.

**FINANCIAL AID. Available aid:** Pell grants, SEOG, state scholarships and grants, school scholarships and grants, private scholarships and grants, ROTC scholarships, academic merit scholarships, and aid for undergraduate foreign students. Perkins Loans (NDSL), PLUS, Stafford Loans (GSL), state loans, school loans, private loans, and SLS. Tuition Plan Inc., Knight Tuition Plans, AMS, and Tuition Management Systems.
**Financial aid statistics:** 5% of aid is not need-based. In 1993-94, 47% of all freshman applicants received aid. Average amounts of aid awarded freshmen: Scholarships and grants, $15,467; loans, $2,625.
**Supporting data/closing dates:** FAFSA/FAF: Priority filing date is February 1. State aid form: Priority filing date is February 1. Income tax forms: Priority filing date is April 15. Notification of awards begins March 24.
**Financial aid contact:** Suzanne Schlager, Director of Financial Aid. 717 291-3991.

**STUDENT EMPLOYMENT.** College Work/Study Program. Institutional employment. 41% of full-time undergraduates work on campus during school year. Students may expect to earn an average of $1,350 during school year. Off-campus part-time employment opportunities rated "good."

**COMPUTER FACILITIES.** 70 Macintosh/Apple microcomputers; 60 are networked. Students may access Digital minicomputer/mainframe systems, BITNET, Internet. Residence halls may be equipped with networked microcomputers. Client/LAN operating systems include Apple/Macintosh. Computer languages and software packages include BASIC, COBOL, Excel, FORTRAN, SAS, SPSS. Computer facilities are available to all students.
**Fees:** Computer fee is included in tuition/fees.
**Hours:** 16 hours/day.

**GRADUATE CAREER DATA.** Graduate school percentages: 10% enter law school. 8% enter medical school. 1% enter dental school. 3% enter graduate business programs. 10% enter graduate arts and sciences programs. 2% enter theological school/seminary. Highest graduate school enrollments: Columbia U, Johns Hopkins U, Temple U, U of Pennsylvania, Yale U. 41% of graduates choose careers in business and industry. Companies and businesses that hire graduates: Chubb, Arthur Andersen, Coopers & Lybrand, Ernst & Young, KPMG Peat Marwick.

**PROMINENT ALUMNI/AE.** William H. Gray, president, United Negro College Fund and former U.S. representative; Roy Scheider and Treat Williams, actors; James Lapine, Pulitzer Prize winning playwright; Dr. Paul Knappenberger, president, Adler Planetarium.

# Gannon University

**Erie, PA 16541** — **814 871-7000**

**1994-95 Costs.** Tuition (1993-94): $10,350 per year (humanities, education, science, business); $10,970 (engineering, health sciences). Room: $2,340. Board: $1,940. Fees, books, misc. academic expenses (school's estimate): $598.
**Enrollment.** Undergraduates: 1,299 men, 1,394 women (full-time). Freshman class: 2,464 applicants, 1,908 accepted, 678 enrolled. Graduate enrollment: 228 men, 369 women.
**Test score averages/ranges.** Average SAT scores: 464 verbal, 518 math. Range of SAT scores of middle 50%: 400-510 verbal, 450-570 math. Average ACT scores: 23 composite. Range of ACT scores of middle 50%: 20-25 composite.
**Faculty.** 203 full-time; 128 part-time. 51% of faculty holds highest degree in specific field. Student/faculty ratio: 13 to 1.
**Selectivity rating.** Less competitive.

**PROFILE.** Gannon is a church-affiliated, liberal arts university. It was founded as a two-year college in 1933, became a four-year institution in 1941, and gained university status in 1979. Its 18-acre campus is located in downtown Erie, close to the south shore of Lake Erie.

**Accreditation:** MSACS. Professionally accredited by the Accreditation Board for Engineering and Technology, the American Bar Association, the American Dietetic Association, the American Medical Association (CAHEA), the Council on Social Work Education, the National League for Nursing.
**Religious orientation:** Gannon University is affiliated with the Roman Catholic Church (Diocese of Erie); six credits of religion/theology required.
**Library:** Collections totaling over 211,234 volumes, 1,335 periodical subscriptions, and 308,595 microform items.
**Special facilities/museums:** Historical museum, planetarium, electron microscope, laser and spectrographic labs, metallurgy institute, computer-integrated manufacturing facilities.
**Athletic facilities:** Gymnasium, basketball, handball, racquetball, tennis, and volleyball courts, tracks, swimming pool, football field.

**STUDENT BODY. Undergraduate profile:** 80% are state residents; 17% are transfers. 1.4% Asian-American, 3.7% Black, .9% Hispanic, .3% Native American, 92.4% White, 1.3% Other. Average age of undergraduates is 21.
**Freshman profile:** 1% of freshmen who took SAT scored 700 or over on verbal, 2% scored 700 or over on math; 5% scored 600 or over on verbal, 13% scored 600 or over on math; 25% scored 500 or over on verbal, 46% scored 500 or over on math; 68% scored 400 or over on verbal, 80% scored 400 or over on math; 96% scored 300 or over on verbal, 99% scored 300 or over on math. 1% of freshmen who took ACT scored 30 or over on composite; 36% scored 24 or over on composite; 94% scored 18 or over on composite; 100% scored 12 or over on composite. 89% of accepted applicants took SAT; 4% took ACT.
**Undergraduate achievement:** 79% of fall 1992 freshmen returned for fall 1993 term.
**Foreign students:** 40 students are from out of the country. Countries represented include the Bahamas, Canada, Kuwait, Malaysia, the Netherlands, and Russia; 17 in all.

**PROGRAMS OF STUDY. Degrees:** B.A., B.Elec.Eng., B.Eng.Tech., B.Mech.Eng., B.S., B.S.Nurs.
**Majors:** Accounting, Administrative Studies, Anthropology, Art, Art Education, Arts/Humanities, Biology, Chemistry, Communication Arts, Communication/English, Computer Science, Criminal Justice, Dietetics, Early Childhood Education, Earth Science, Economics, Electrical Engineering, Electrical Engineering Technology, Elementary Education, English, Finance, Foreign Language/International Business, Foreign Language/International Studies, Foreign Language/Literature, Foreign Language/Teaching, History, Human Services, Industrial Distribution, Industrial Management, Legal Assistant, Liberal Arts, Management, Management Information Systems, Marketing, Mathematics, Mechanical Engineering, Mechanical Engineering Technology, Medical Technology, Mental Health Counseling, Mortuary Science, Optometry, Philosophy, Physician Assistant, Physics, Podiatric Medicine, Political Science, Professional Nursing, Professional Writing, Psychology, Respiratory Care, Science, Social Science, Social Work, Sociology, Special Education, Teacher Trainee, Technical Studies, Theatre/Communication Arts, Theology, Therapeutic Recreation.
**Distribution of degrees:** The majors with the highest enrollment are professional nursing, engineering, and biology; special education has the lowest.
**Requirements:** General education requirement.
**Academic regulations:** Minimum 2.0 GPA must be maintained.
**Special:** Minor offered in gerontology. Associate's degrees offered. Double majors. Dual degrees. Independent study. Pass/fail grading option. Internships. Cooperative education programs. Graduate school at which undergraduates may take graduate-level courses. Preprofessional programs in law, medicine, veterinary science, pharmacy, dentistry, optometry, osteopathy, podiatry, and physical therapy. Combined chemical engineering programs with U of Akron, U of Detroit, and U of Pittsburgh. Combined mortuary science programs with accredited schools. Washington Semester and Sea Semester. Teacher certification in early childhood, elementary, secondary, and special education. Certification in specific subject areas. Study abroad possible. ROTC.
**Honors:** Honors program. Honor societies.
**Academic Assistance:** Remedial writing, math, and study skills. Nonremedial tutoring.

**STUDENT LIFE. Housing:** All freshmen and sophomores must live on campus. Women's and men's dorms. Sorority and fraternity housing. School-owned/operated apartments. Off-campus privately-owned housing. 37% of students live in college housing.
**Social atmosphere:** According to the student newspaper, influential groups on campus include the Activities Programming Board, the Campus Ministry, the Student Government, the basketball team, and fraternities. Some of the most popular events of the year are basketball games, the Homecoming Dance, and Winter Carnival. Students gather at various bars (Antler's, the Shaggy Dog, Park Place) and at the Student Activities Center. Fraternity parties are popular.
**Services and counseling/handicapped student services:** Placement services. Health service. Women's center. Counseling services for minority, veteran, and older students. Personal and psychological counseling. Career and academic guidance services. Religious counseling. Physically disabled student services. Learning disabled program/services. Notetaking services. Tutors. Reader services for the blind.
**Campus organizations:** Undergraduate student government. Student newspaper (Gannon Knight, published once/week). Literary magazine. Yearbook. Radio and TV stations. Glee club, ROTC and pep bands, drama club, debating, international relations club, Model UN, ski and karate clubs, departmental groups, 57 organizations in all. Seven fraternities, all with chapter houses; five sororities, one chapter house. 20% of men join a fraternity. 5% of women join a sorority.
**Religious organizations:** Campus Ministry, Center for Social Concerns, Cornerstone Christian Fellowship, Pax Christi.
**Minority/foreign student organizations:** Minority Student Union, Delta Sigma Theta. International Student Association.

**ATHLETICS. Physical education requirements:** Six semester hours of physical education required.
**Intercollegiate competition:** 15% of students participate. Baseball (M), basketball (M,W), cheerleading (M,W), cross-country (M,W), diving (M,W), football (M), golf (M), soccer (M,W), softball (W), swimming (M,W), tennis (M,W), volleyball (W), wrestling (M). Member of ECAC, NCAA Division II.
**Intramural and club sports:** 60% of students participate. Intramural basketball, bowling, flag football, free throw, golf, handball, indoor soccer, racquetball, soccer, softball, swimming, table tennis, tennis, volleyball, walleyball, water polo, Wiffle ball, wrestling. Men's club cheerleading, ice hockey, volleyball. Women's club cheerleading.

**ADMISSIONS. Academic basis for candidate selection** (in order of priority): Secondary school record, standardized test scores, class rank, school's recommendation, essay.

**Nonacademic basis for candidate selection:** Character and personality are important. Extracurricular participation and alumni/ae relationship are considered.
**Requirements:** Graduation from secondary school is recommended; GED is accepted. 15 units and the following program of study are required: 4 units of English, 3 units of math, 2 units of science, 2 units of foreign language, 4 units of social studies. Rank in top half of secondary school class and minimum 2.5 GPA required; minimum required test scores vary by program. EOP for applicants not normally admissible. Conditional admission possible for applicants not meeting standard requirements. General Studies Program for applicants not normally admissible. SAT is required; ACT may be substituted. Campus visit and interview recommended. No off-campus interviews.
**Procedure:** Take SAT or ACT by December of 12th year. Notification of admission on rolling basis. $100 nonrefundable tuition deposit. $100 nonrefundable room deposit. Freshmen accepted for terms other than fall.
**Special programs:** Admission may be deferred one year. Credit and/or placement may be granted through CEEB Advanced Placement exams for scores of 3 or higher. Credit and/or placement may be granted through CLEP general and subject exams. Credit and placement may be granted through challenge exams.
**Transfer students:** Transfer students accepted for terms other than fall. In fall 1993, 17% of all new students were transfers into all classes. 463 transfer applications were received, 314 were accepted. Application deadline is rolling for fall; rolling for spring. Minimum 2.0 GPA required. Lowest course grade accepted is "C." Maximum number of transferable credits is 64 semester hours from a two-year school and 70 semester hours from a four-year school. At least 30 semester hours must be completed at the university to receive degree.
**Admissions contact:** Joyce Scheid-Gilman, M.P.A., Director of Freshman Admissions and Transfer. 800 GANNON-U.

**FINANCIAL AID. Available aid:** Pell grants, SEOG, state grants, school scholarships and grants, ROTC scholarships, academic merit scholarships, and athletic scholarships. Perkins Loans (NDSL), PLUS, Stafford Loans (GSL), NSL, state loans, and SLS. AMS and deferred payment plan.
**Financial aid statistics:** 28% of aid is not need-based. Average amounts of aid awarded freshmen: Scholarships and grants, $3,236; loans, $2,500.
**Supporting data/closing dates:** School's own aid application: Priority filing date is February 1. State aid form: Priority filing date is March 15; deadline is May 1. Notification of awards on rolling basis.
**Financial aid contact:** James Treiber, M.Ed., Director of Financial Aid. 814 871-7337.

**STUDENT EMPLOYMENT.** College Work/Study Program. Institutional employment. 24% of full-time undergraduates work on campus during school year. Students may expect to earn an average of $1,200 during school year. Off-campus part-time employment opportunities rated "good."

**COMPUTER FACILITIES.** 250 IBM/IBM-compatible and Macintosh/Apple microcomputers; 14 are networked. Students may access Digital, IBM minicomputer/mainframe systems, Internet. Client/LAN operating systems include DOS, Novell. Computer languages and software packages include BASIC, COBOL, COMPASS, FORTRAN, Lotus 1-2-3, MINITAB, RPG, SPSS-X, WordPerfect. Computer facilities are available to all students.
**Fees:** None.
**Hours:** 9 AM-midn. (M-F); 12 AM-6 PM (Sa).

**PROMINENT ALUMNI/AE.** Art Gunther, president, PepsiCo; David C. Kozak, professor of public policy, National War Coll; Robert H. Morosky, former president, The Limited; James R. Boris, president and CEO, Kemper Securities; William C. Springer, president and CEO, H.J. Heinz USA.

# Geneva College

**Beaver Falls, PA 15010** — **412 846-5100**

**1993-94 Costs.** Tuition: $8,810. Room & board: $4,220. Fees, books, misc. academic expenses (school's estimate): $540.
**Enrollment.** Undergraduates: 654 men, 652 women (full-time). Freshman class: 624 applicants, 534 accepted, 237 enrolled. Graduate enrollment: 13 men, 30 women.
**Test score averages/ranges.** Average SAT scores: 460 verbal, 502 math. Range of SAT scores of middle 50%: 400-500 verbal, 560-430 math. Average ACT scores: 22 composite.
**Faculty.** 51 full-time; 51 part-time. 66% of faculty holds doctoral degree. Student/faculty ratio: 18 to 1.
**Selectivity rating.** Less competitive.

**PROFILE.** Geneva, founded in 1848, is a church-affiliated, liberal arts college. Its 55-acre campus is located in a residential area of Beaver Falls, 45 miles northwest of Pittsburgh.
**Accreditation:** MSACS.
**Religious orientation:** Geneva College is affiliated with the Reformed Presbyterian Church of North America; three semesters of religion required.
**Library:** Collections totaling over 149,482 volumes, 737 periodical subscriptions, and 77,717 microform items.
**Special facilities/museums:** Language lab, center for industrial heritage.
**Athletic facilities:** Gymnasium, field house, athletic fields, stadium, tennis courts, weight room, bowling lanes.

**STUDENT BODY. Undergraduate profile:** 74% are state residents; 32% are transfers. 1% Asian-American, 3% Black, 96% White. Average age of undergraduates is 20.
**Freshman profile:** 1% of freshmen who took SAT scored 700 or over on verbal, 2% scored 700 or over on math; 8% scored 600 or over on verbal, 18% scored 600 or over on math; 33% scored 500 or over on verbal, 48% scored 500 or over on math; 78% scored 400 or over on verbal, 87% scored 400 or over on math; 99% scored 300 or over on verbal, 99% scored 300 or over on math. 89% of accepted applicants took SAT. 80% of freshmen come from public schools.
**Undergraduate achievement:** 77% of fall 1992 freshmen returned for fall 1993 term. 39% of entering class graduated. 20% of students who completed a degree program immediately went on to graduate study.
**Foreign students:** 31 students are from out of the country. Countries represented include Canada, the Dominican Republic, Kenya, Korea, Russia, and Taiwan; 16 in all.

**PROGRAMS OF STUDY. Degrees:** B.A., B.S., B.S.Bus.Admin., B.S.Ed., B.S.Eng., B.S.Indust.Eng.
**Majors:** Accounting, Applied Mathematics, Applied Music, Aviation/Business Administration, Biblical Studies, Biology, Broadcasting, Business, Business Education, Chemical Engineering, Chemistry, Christian Ministries, Civil Engineering, Communications, Computer Science, Counseling, Electrical Engineering, Elementary Education, Engineering, English, General Science, History, Human Resource Management, Independent Major, Industrial Engineering, Latin American Business, Mathematics, Mechanical Engineering, Music, Music Business, Music Education, Philosophy, Physics, Political Science, Psychology, Sociology, Spanish, Speech Communication, Speech Pathology, Writing.
**Distribution of degrees:** The majors with the highest enrollment are business administration and education; physics and Latin-American business have the lowest.
**Requirements:** General education requirement.
**Academic regulations:** Minimum 2.00 GPA required for graduation.
**Special:** Minors offered in many majors and in Christian school teaching, data analysis, data processing, oral communication in business/industry, public administration, public relations, social work, theatre, and visual communication. Associate's degrees offered. Self-designed majors. Double majors. Dual degrees. Independent study. Pass/fail grading option. Internships. Cooperative education programs. Preprofessional programs in law, medicine, theology, and psychology. 1-2-1 and 2-2 A.A.S./B.S.B.A. aviation/business programs with Comm Coll of Beaver County. 2-2 and 3-2 nursing programs with U of Rochester. 3-1 medical technology programs with three hospitals. 3-1 cardiovascular technology program with Fairfax (Virginia) Hospital. Member of Christian College Coalition. American Studies Program (Washington, D.C.). AuSable Inst of Environmental Studies Program (Michigan). Teacher certification in elementary and secondary education. Study abroad in England, France, and Latin American countries.
**Honors:** Honors program. Honor societies.
**Academic Assistance:** Remedial reading, math, and study skills. Nonremedial tutoring.

**STUDENT LIFE. Housing:** All unmarried, full-time students under age 25 must live on campus unless living with family. Women's and men's dorms. School-owned houses. 60% of students live in college housing.
**Social atmosphere:** According to the student newspaper, "There is usually something to do if you have extra time, and it is not always school–sponsored activities. The rec room, sports, and just socializing are always possibilities." Popular gathering spots on campus are The Brig, the recreation room, the library, and the Eat 'n Park, located downtown. Influential groups on campus include the Student Senate, the Activities Planning Board, and Sunday Night Fellowship. Among the favorite campus events are football and basketball games, the annual Midnight Breakfast, Homecoming, and The Big Event.
**Services and counseling/handicapped student services:** Placement services. Health service. Day care. Counseling services for minority students. Personal and psychological counseling. Career and academic guidance services. Religious counseling. Physically disabled student services. Learning disabled services. Notetaking services.
**Campus organizations:** Undergraduate student government. Student newspaper (Cabinet, published once/week). Literary magazine. Yearbook. Radio and TV stations. Concert and stage band, marching band, wind and brass ensembles, touring choir, drama group, debating, engineering quarterly, departmental groups, special-interest groups.
**Religious organizations:** Community Youth Movement for Christ, Fellowship of Christian Athletes, Bible study group, Sunday Night Fellowship, Spiritual Affairs Committee, Student Missions Fellowship, student outreach ministries, youth ministries program.
**Minority/foreign student organizations:** African-American Christian Cultural Society. International Student Organization.

**ATHLETICS. Physical education requirements:** Two semesters of physical education required.
**Intercollegiate competition:** 30% of students participate. Baseball (M), basketball (M,W), cross-country (M,W), football (M), soccer (M,W), softball (W), tennis (M,W), track (indoor) (M,W), track (outdoor) (M,W), track and field (indoor) (M,W), track and field (outdoor) (M,W), volleyball (W). Member of Mid States Footbal Association, NAIA, NCCAA.
**Intramural and club sports:** 75% of students participate. Intramural basketball, bowling, football, floor hockey, racquetball, soccer, softball, tennis, volleyball. Men's club rugby, volleyball.

**ADMISSIONS. Academic basis for candidate selection** (in order of priority): Secondary school record, class rank, standardized test scores, essay, school's recommendation.
**Nonacademic basis for candidate selection:** Character and personality are emphasized. Extracurricular participation and particular talent or ability are important. Alumni/ae relationship is considered.
**Requirements:** Graduation from secondary school is recommended; GED is accepted. 16 units and the following program of study are required: 4 units of English, 2 units of math, 1 unit of science, 2 units of foreign language, 3 units of social studies, 4 units of electives. Rank in top half of secondary school class and minimum "C+" average recommended. Summer Developmental Program and Limited Hours Acceptance Program for applicants not normally admissible. SAT or ACT is required. Campus visit and interview recommended. Off-campus interviews available with admissions and alumni representatives.
**Procedure:** Take SAT or ACT by December of 12th year. Visit college for interview by December of 12th year. Acceptance notification on rolling basis, usually within two weeks of completion of file. Reply is required by date specified in letter of acceptance. $25 nonrefundable tuition deposit. $75 room deposit, refundable until August 15. Freshmen accepted for terms other than fall.
**Special programs:** Admission may be deferred one year. Credit and/or placement may be granted through CEEB Advanced Placement exams for scores of 3 or higher. Credit and/or placement may be granted through CLEP general and subject exams. Credit may be granted through military experience. Credit and placement may be granted through life experience. Early entrance/early admission program. Concurrent enrollment program.
**Transfer students:** Transfer students accepted for terms other than fall. In fall 1993, 32% of all new students were transfers into all classes. 186 transfer applications were received,

165 were accepted. Application deadline is rolling for fall; rolling for spring. Minimum 2.0 GPA required. Lowest course grade accepted is "D." Maximum number of transferable credits is 64 semester hours. At least 48 semester hours must be completed at the college to receive degree.
**Admissions contact:** William J. Katip, Ph.D., Vice President for Enrollment Management. 800 847-8255, 800 847-2428.
**FINANCIAL AID. Available aid:** Pell grants, SEOG, state scholarships and grants, school scholarships and grants, private scholarships and grants, academic merit scholarships, and athletic scholarships. Perkins Loans (NDSL), PLUS, Stafford Loans (GSL), state loans, private loans, and SLS. Advanced Education Service.
**Financial aid statistics:** In 1993-94, 93% of all undergraduate applicants received aid; 93% of freshman applicants. Average amounts of aid awarded freshmen: Scholarships and grants, $1,500; loans, $3,100.
**Supporting data/closing dates:** FAFSA: Priority filing date is April 15. School's own aid application: Accepted on rolling basis. Notification of awards on rolling basis.
**Financial aid contact:** Timothy Russell, M.Div., Director of Financial Aid. 412 847-6530.
**STUDENT EMPLOYMENT.** College Work/Study Program. Institutional employment. 50% of full-time undergraduates work on campus during school year. Students may expect to earn an average of $750 during school year. Off-campus part-time employment opportunities rated "fair."
**COMPUTER FACILITIES.** 50 IBM/IBM-compatible microcomputers; 30 are networked. Students may access Digital minicomputer/mainframe systems. Client/LAN operating systems include DOS, X-windows, Novell. Computer languages and software packages include Assembler, BASIC, C, COBOL, dBASE, FORTRAN, Lotus 1-2-3, Pascal, WordPerfect. Computer facilities are available to all students.
**Fees:** None.
**Hours:** 8 AM-11 PM (M-Sa).
**GRADUATE CAREER DATA.** Highest graduate school enrollments: Duquesne U, George Washington U, Michigan State U, Ohio Northern U, U of Pittsburgh, Youngstown St U. Companies and businesses that hire graduates: Public school systems.
**PROMINENT ALUMNI/AE.** George Lewis Arnold, operational analyst, Lockheed.

# Gettysburg College

**Gettysburg, PA 17325-1484 — 717 337-6000**

**1994-95 Costs.** Tuition: $19,964. Room: $2,180. Board: $2,148. Fees, books, misc. academic expenses (school's estimate): $590.
**Enrollment.** Undergraduates: 950 men, 950 women (full-time). Freshman class: 3,596 applicants, 2,450 accepted, 575 enrolled.
**Test score averages/ranges.** Range of SAT scores of middle 50%: 500-580 verbal, 550-640 math. Range of ACT scores of middle 50%: 24-28 composite.
**Faculty.** 154 full-time; 39 part-time. 91% of faculty holds doctoral degree. Student/faculty ratio: 12 to 1.
**Selectivity rating.** Highly competitive.

**PROFILE.** Gettysburg, founded in 1832, is a church-affiliated, liberal arts college. Its 200-acre campus is located three blocks from the center of the town of Gettysburg. The campus administration building is listed with the National Register of Historic Places.
**Accreditation:** MSACS.
**Religious orientation:** Gettysburg College is affiliated with the Lutheran Church; one semester of religion required.
**Library:** Collections totaling over 330,000 volumes, 1,350 periodical subscriptions, and 35,000 microform items.
**Special facilities/museums:** Art gallery, language lab, fine and performing arts facilities, planetarium and observatory, electron microscopes, NMR spectrometer.
**Athletic facilities:** Gymnasiums, swimming pool, field house, tennis courts, athletic fields, stadium.
**STUDENT BODY. Undergraduate profile:** 25% are state residents; 5% are transfers. 4% Asian-American, 3% Black, 2% Hispanic, 90% White, 1% Other. Average age of undergraduates is 20.
**Freshman profile:** Majority of accepted applicants took SAT. 80% of freshmen come from public schools.
**Undergraduate achievement:** 90% of fall 1991 freshmen returned for fall 1992 term. 76% of entering class graduated. 33% of students who completed a degree program immediately went on to graduate study.
**Foreign students:** 49 students are from out of the country. Countries represented include Brazil, Canada, France, India, Japan, and Mexico; 35 in all.
**PROGRAMS OF STUDY. Degrees:** B.A., B.S.
**Majors:** Art, Biology, Business Administration/Management, Chemistry, Classical Studies, Computer Studies, Economics, English, French, German, Greek, Health/Physical Education, History, Latin, Mathematics, Music, Philosophy, Physics, Political Science, Psychology, Religion, Sociology/Anthropology, Spanish, Theatre Arts.
**Distribution of degrees:** The majors with the highest enrollment are business administration/management, political science, and history; Greek, Latin, and religion have the lowest.
**Requirements:** General education requirement.
**Academic regulations:** Minimum 2.0 GPA must be maintained.
**Special:** Minors offered. Courses in astronomy and speech. Seminars and directed reading in most departments, primarily for seniors; senior scholars seminars on contemporary issues. Comprehensive exam may be required in major field. Grades may be reduced in all courses for poor writing. Asian studies program in cooperation with U of Pennsylvania. Off-campus marine lab study. Certified public accounting preparation for all states. Self-designed majors. Double majors. Dual degrees. Independent study. Accelerated study. Pass/fail grading option. Internships. Preprofessional programs in law, medicine, veterinary science, and dentistry. 3-2 engineering programs with Pennsylvania State U, Rensselaer Polytech Inst, and Washington U. 3-2 forestry and environmental studies program with Duke U. Member of Central Pennsylvania Consortium. Cross-registration with Lutheran Theological Seminary. Washington Semester, UN Semester, and Sea Semester. Exchange programs with Dickinson Coll and Franklin & Marshall Coll. Teacher certification in elementary and secondary education. Certification in specific subject areas. Study abroad in Colombia, France, Germany, India, Japan, Spain, the United Kingdom, and other countries.
**Honors:** Phi Beta Kappa. Honors program.
**Academic Assistance:** Nonremedial tutoring.
**STUDENT LIFE. Housing:** All first-year students must live on campus. Coed, women's, and men's dorms. Fraternity housing. School-owned/operated apartments. Special-interest housing. 85% of students live in college housing.
**Social atmosphere:** Favorite student gathering spots include fraternity houses, the Towne Tavern, J.D.'s Pub, Marvelous Marv's, and Tavern on the Village. Greeks and athletes are influential groups on campus. Popular annual events include football and lacrosse games, Homecoming, Alumni Weekend, Springfest, the Black Student Union Talent Show, the Halloween Concert, the spring concert, the fall magician, and lectures and speeches by guest speakers. "Social life peaks on Thursday and Saturday nights, when the fraternity parties commence. The college provides many different cultural activities, but needs to work on attracting more non-white students," comments the student newspaper.
**Services and counseling/handicapped student services:** Placement services. Health service. Women's center. Writing Center. Intercultural resource center. Counseling services for minority and military students. Birth control, personal, and psychological counseling. Career and academic guidance services. Religious counseling.
**Campus organizations:** Undergraduate student government. Student newspaper (Gettysburgian, published once/week). Literary magazine. Yearbook. Radio and TV stations. Choirs, orchestra. 12 fraternities, all with chapter houses; seven sororities, no chapter houses. 55% of men join a fraternity. 45% of women join a sorority.
**Religious organizations:** Catholic Council, Chapel Council, Fellowship of Christian Athletes, Hillel, Intervarsity Christian Fellowship.
**Minority/foreign student organizations:** Black Student Union. International Student Group.
**ATHLETICS. Physical education requirements:** 1-1/2 years of physical education required.
**Intercollegiate competition:** 35% of students participate. Baseball (M), basketball (M,W), cheerleading (M,W), cross-country (M,W), field hockey (W), football (M), golf (M), lacrosse (M,W), soccer (M,W), softball (W), swimming (M,W), tennis (M,W), track (indoor) (M,W), track (outdoor) (M,W), track and field (indoor) (M,W), track and field (outdoor) (M,W), volleyball (W), wrestling (M). Member of Centennial Conference, ECAC, NCAA Division III.
**Intramural and club sports:** 80% of students participate. Intramural boxing, cycling, ice hockey, martial arts, rugby. Men's club boxing, cycling, ice hockey, martial arts, rugby, volleyball. Women's club cycling, martial arts, rugby.
**ADMISSIONS. Academic basis for candidate selection** (in order of priority): Secondary school record, class rank, standardized test scores, school's recommendation, essay.
**Nonacademic basis for candidate selection:** Character and personality and particular talent or ability are important. Extracurricular participation, geographical distribution, and alumni/ae relationship are considered.
**Requirements:** Graduation from secondary school is required; GED is accepted. No specific distribution of secondary school units required. Participation in accelerated, enriched, and advanced courses desirable. Auditions and interviews required of art and music program applicants. SAT or ACT is required. ACH recommended. Campus visit and interview recommended. No off-campus interviews.
**Procedure:** Take SAT or ACT by January of 12th year. Take ACH by January of 12th year. Visit college for interview by February 1 of 12th year. Suggest filing application by fall. Application deadline is February 15. Notification of acceptance in early April. Reply is required by May 1. $200 nonrefundable tuition deposit. Freshmen accepted for terms other than fall.
**Special programs:** Admission may be deferred. Credit and/or placement may be granted through CEEB Advanced Placement exams for scores of 4 or higher. Early decision program. In fall 1992, 159 applied for early decision and 88 were accepted. Deadline for applying for early decision is February 1. Early entrance/early admission program.
**Transfer students:** Transfer students accepted for terms other than fall. In fall 1992, 5% of all new students were transfers into all classes. 113 transfer applications were received, 39 were accepted. Application deadline is February 15 for fall; December 1 for spring. Minimum 2.0 GPA required. Lowest course grade accepted is "C."
**Admissions contact:** Delwin K. Gustafson, J.D., Dean of Admissions. 717 337-6100, 800 431-0803.
**FINANCIAL AID. Available aid:** Pell grants, SEOG, state scholarships and grants, school scholarships and grants, private scholarships and grants, academic merit scholarships, and aid for undergraduate foreign students. Perkins Loans (NDSL), PLUS, Stafford Loans (GSL), state loans, school loans, private loans, and SLS. Tuition Plan Inc., Knight Tuition Plans, and AMS. Higher Education Services.
**Financial aid statistics:** In 1992-93, 95% of all undergraduate applicants received aid; 95% of freshman applicants. Average amounts of aid awarded freshmen: Scholarships and grants, $9,450; loans, $2,200.
**Supporting data/closing dates:** FAFSA/FAF/FFS: Deadline is February 1. State aid form: Accepted on rolling basis.
**Financial aid contact:** Ronald Shunk, M.Ed., Director of Financial Aid. 717 337-6611.
**STUDENT EMPLOYMENT.** College Work/Study Program. Institutional employment. 35% of full-time undergraduates work on campus during school year. Students may expect to earn an average of $900 during school year. Off-campus part-time employment opportunities rated "good."
**COMPUTER FACILITIES.** 225 IBM/IBM-compatible, Macintosh/Apple, and RISC-/UNIX-based microcomputers; all are networked. Students may access Digital, SUN minicomputer/mainframe systems, BITNET, Internet. Residence halls may be equipped with stand-alone microcomputers, networked microcomputers, networked terminals, modems. Client/LAN operating systems include Apple/Macintosh. 250 major computer languages and software packages available. Computer facilities are available to all students.
**Fees:** Computer fee is included in tuition/fees.

**Hours:** 24 hours.
**GRADUATE CAREER DATA.** Graduate school percentages: 7% enter law school. 5% enter medical school. 1% enter dental school. 5% enter graduate business programs. 17% enter graduate arts and sciences programs. Highest graduate school enrollments: Dickinson Sch of Law, George Washington U, Peabody Conservatory of Music, Pennsylvania State U, U of Pennsylvania, U of Virginia. 40% of graduates choose careers in business and industry. Companies and businesses that hire graduates: Aetna Life and Casualty Insurance Co., Arthur Andersen, AT&T, Eastman Kodak, Maryland National Bank, Merck & Co., Procter & Gamble, U.S. Gypsum.
**PROMINENT ALUMNI/AE.** Dr. Alexander Astin, educator and researcher; Carol Bellamy, former New York City council president; Frederick Fielding, attorney, former chief counsel to the President; Robert Hosking, president, CBS radio; Dr. Norman Rasmussen, nuclear engineer, recipient of Fermi prize; Jennifer Stone, head athletic trainer, U.S. Olympic Training Center.

# Grove City College

**Grove City, PA 16127 412 458-2000**

**1994-95 Costs.** Tuition: $5,224. Room & board: $3,048. Fees, books, misc. academic expenses (school's estimate): $1,175.
**Enrollment.** Undergraduates: 1,123 men, 1,090 women (full-time). Freshman class: 2,491 applicants, 1,109 accepted, 573 enrolled.
**Test score averages/ranges.** Average SAT scores: 537 verbal, 607 math. Range of SAT scores of middle 50%: 500-600 verbal, 560-660 math. Average ACT scores: 27 composite. Range of ACT scores of middle 50%: 24-27 composite.
**Faculty.** 108 full-time; 35 part-time. 66% of faculty holds doctoral degree. Student/faculty ratio: 20 to 1.
**Selectivity rating.** Highly competitive.

**PROFILE.** Grove City, founded in 1876, is a church-affiliated college of liberal arts and sciences. Its 150-acre campus is located near the center of Grove City, about 60 miles north of Pittsburgh.

**Accreditation:** MSACS. Professionally accredited by the Accreditation Board for Engineering and Technology.
**Religious orientation:** Grove City College is affiliated with the Presbyterian Church USA; no religious requirements.
**Library:** Collections totaling over 169,000 volumes, 1,200 periodical subscriptions, and 244,000 microform items.
**Special facilities/museums:** Fine arts center, language lab, on-campus preschool, technological learning center.
**Athletic facilities:** Field house, 400-meter track, bowling alleys, basketball arena, natatorium, racquetball and tennis courts, baseball, football, and softball fields, intramural rooms, pits and runways for jumping and pole vaulting.
**STUDENT BODY. Undergraduate profile:** 64% are state residents; 6% are transfers. 1% Black, 1% Hispanic, 96% White, 2% Other. Average age of undergraduates is 20.
**Freshman profile:** 2% of freshmen who took SAT scored 700 or over on verbal, 13% scored 700 or over on math; 20% scored 600 or over on verbal, 58% scored 600 or over on math; 72% scored 500 or over on verbal, 93% scored 500 or over on math; 97% scored 400 or over on verbal, 99% scored 400 or over on math; 100% scored 300 or over on verbal, 100% scored 300 or over on math. 21% of freshmen who took ACT scored 30 or over on composite; 87% scored 24 or over on composite; 100% scored 18 or over on composite. 93% of accepted applicants took SAT; 34% took ACT. 90% of freshmen come from public schools.
**Undergraduate achievement:** 88% of fall 1992 freshmen returned for fall 1993 term. 70% of entering class graduated. 15% of students who completed a degree program immediately went on to graduate study.
**Foreign students:** 28 students are from out of the country. Countries represented include China, Japan, Korea, and Sri Lanka; 16 in all.
**PROGRAMS OF STUDY. Degrees:** B.A., B.Mus., B.S., B.S.Elec.Eng., B.S.Mech.Eng.
**Majors:** Accounting, Applied Physics, Biochemistry, Biology, Business Administration/Management, Chemistry, Christian Ministries, Communications, Computers, Economics, Electrical Engineering, Elementary Education, English Education, Financial Management, French, History, International Studies/Business, Literature, Marketing, Mathematics, Mechanical Engineering, Molecular Biology, Music, Music Education, Philosophy, Political Science/Government, Pre-Health, Pre-Dental, Pre-Law, Pre-Medical, Pre-Theology, Pre-Veterinary, Psychology, Religion, Spanish.
**Distribution of degrees:** The majors with the highest enrollment are business administration, elementary education, and engineering; Spanish has the lowest.
**Requirements:** General education requirement.
**Academic regulations:** Minimum 2.00 GPA must be maintained.
**Special:** All students must complete 38-50 credit hours of general education courses with emphasis in the humanities, social sciences, quantitative and logical reasoning, natural sciences (with labs), and foreign language. Self-designed majors. Double majors. Independent study. Internships. Preprofessional programs in law, medicine, veterinary science, dentistry, theology, and health. Washington Semester. Teacher certification in elementary and secondary education. Certification in specific subject areas. Study abroad possible.
**Honors:** Honor societies.
**Academic Assistance:** Remedial writing and study skills. Nonremedial tutoring.
**STUDENT LIFE. Housing:** All unmarried students under age 21 must live on campus unless living with family. Women's and men's dorms. 88% of students live in college housing.
**Social atmosphere:** The student union, dorm rec rooms, bookstore/cafe, and Taco Bell are favorite hang-outs. Christian fellowship groups, Student Government Association, musical groups, athletes, housing groups, fraternities, and sororities have widespread influence on campus life. Popular social events are Tri-Rho Extravaganza, talent shows, Faculty Follies, Homecoming, Grove Aid, plays, square dancing, ice skating, and Parents Weekend. Even though Grove City College is not in the social hub of the state, students are creative about how they spend their free time, according to the editor of the student newspaper. Student Government Association plans events for weekends when other groups have not scheduled big events. "People play games and watch TV in their rooms. When there's nothing else to do, you can always find lots of people in the Student Union."
**Services and counseling/handicapped student services:** Placement services. Health service. Counseling services for minority students. Personal counseling. Career and academic guidance services. Religious counseling. Physically disabled student services. Tutors.
**Campus organizations:** Undergraduate student government. Student newspaper (Collegian, published once/week). Yearbook. Radio station. Chapel choir, touring choir, New Grace Singers, orchestra, band, creative writing journal groups, drama fraternity, men's/women's governing boards, student court, synchronized swimming club, outing club, Homecoming Committee, Parent's Weekend Committee, departmental groups, 126 organizations in all. Six fraternities, no chapter houses; nine sororities, no chapter houses. 28% of men join a fraternity. 50% of women join a sorority.
**Religious organizations:** Clowns for Christ, Fellowship of Christian Athletes, Intervarsity Missions Fellowship, New Life, Newman Club, Young Life, Polk Christian Outreach, Religious Activities Committee, Revelation Bookstore, Salt Company, Warriors for Christ.
**Minority/foreign student organizations:** International Student Club.
**ATHLETICS. Physical education requirements:** Two semester of physical education required.
**Intercollegiate competition:** 7% of students participate. Baseball (M), basketball (M,W), cross-country (M,W), football (M), golf (M), soccer (M), softball (W), swimming (M), tennis (M,W), track (M), track and field (W), volleyball (W). Member of NCAA Division III, President's Conference, Women's Keystone Conference.
**Intramural and club sports:** 1% of students participate.
**ADMISSIONS. Academic basis for candidate selection** (in order of priority): Class rank, secondary school record, standardized test scores, essay, school's recommendation.
**Nonacademic basis for candidate selection:** Character and personality are emphasized. Extracurricular participation and particular talent or ability are important. Geographical distribution and alumni/ae relationship are considered.
**Requirements:** Graduation from secondary school is required; GED is accepted. 16 units and the following program of study are required: 4 units of English, 3 units of math, 2 units of science including 1 unit of lab, 3 units of foreign language, 2 units of social studies, 1 unit of history, 1 unit of academic electives. 4 units of math (including trigonometry) and 3 units of lab science required of engineering, math, and sciences program applicants. Audition required of music program applicants. SAT or ACT is required. Campus visit and interview recommended. No off-campus interviews.
**Procedure:** Take SAT or ACT by November of 12th year. Visit college for interview by February of 12th year. Suggest filing application by November 15. Application deadline is February 15. Notification of admission by March 15. Reply is required by May 1. $100 nonrefundable tuition deposit. Freshmen accepted for terms other than fall.
**Special programs:** Admission may be deferred one year. Credit and/or placement may be granted through CEEB Advanced Placement exams for scores of 3 or higher. Credit and/or placement may be granted through CLEP subject exams. Early decision program. In fall 1993, 597 applied for early decision and 322 were accepted. Deadline for applying for early decision is November 15. Early entrance/early admission program. Concurrent enrollment program.
**Transfer students:** Transfer students accepted for terms other than fall. In fall 1993, 6% of all new students were transfers into all classes. 231 transfer applications were received, 49 were accepted. Application deadline is August 1 for fall; January 1 for spring. Minimum 2.0 GPA required. Lowest course grade accepted is "C." There is no limit to the number of credits that may be transferred. At least 32 semester hours must be completed at the college to receive degree.
**Admissions contact:** Jeffrey C. Mincey, M.Ed., Director of Admissions. 412 458-2100.
**FINANCIAL AID. Available aid:** State scholarships and grants, school scholarships and grants, private scholarships and grants, academic merit scholarships, and aid for undergraduate foreign students. PLUS, Stafford Loans (GSL), state loans, school loans, private loans, and SLS.
**Financial aid statistics:** 37% of aid is not need-based. In 1993-94, 85% of all undergraduate applicants received aid; 75% of freshman applicants. Average amounts of aid awarded freshmen: Scholarships and grants, $2,328; loans, $3,208.
**Supporting data/closing dates:** FAFSA/FAF: Priority filing date is March 15. School's own aid application: Priority filing date is May 1. Notification of awards begins June 1.
**Financial aid contact:** Anne P. Bowne, M.A., Director of Financial Aid. 412 458-2163.
**STUDENT EMPLOYMENT.** Institutional employment. 35% of full-time undergraduates work on campus during school year. Students may expect to earn an average of $534 during school year. Off-campus part-time employment opportunities rated "fair."
**COMPUTER FACILITIES.** 155 IBM/IBM-compatible and Macintosh/Apple microcomputers; 110 are networked. Students may access Digital, SUN minicomputer/mainframe systems. Client/LAN operating systems include Apple/Macintosh, DOS, LocalTalk/AppleTalk, Novell. Computer languages and software packages include Ada, BASIC, C, COBOL, DataTrieve, dBASE, DBMS, FMS, FORTRAN, Lotus 1-2-3, Max Macro, Microsoft Word, Microsoft Works, Pascal, PL/1, RDB. Computer facilities are available to all students.
**Fees:** None.
**Hours:** 8:30 AM-1 AM (M-F); 8:30 AM-5 PM (Sa); 2 PM-1 AM (Su).
**GRADUATE CAREER DATA.** Graduate school percentages: 2% enter law school. 2% enter medical school. 2% enter graduate business programs. 6% enter graduate arts and sciences programs. 1% enter theological school/seminary. Highest graduate school enrollments: Carnegie Mellon U, Case Western Reserve U, Dickinson Law School, Duquesne U, Pennsylvania State U, U of Pittsburgh, Purdue U, West Virginia U. 40% of graduates choose careers in business and industry. Companies and businesses that hire graduates: ALCOA, Armstrong World Industries, Big Six accounting firms, Deluxe Checks, Dietrich Industries, Mellon Bank, Pittsburgh National Bank.

**PROMINENT ALUMNI/AE.** J. Howard Pew, president, Sun Oil Co.; James P. Passilla, vice-president, Walt Disney Productions; R. Heath Larry, president, National Association of Manufacturers; C. Fred Fetterolf, president, ALCOA; Dr. David L. Morrison, president, ITT Research Institute; J. Paul Sticht, president, R.J. Reynolds, Inc. (1973-78).

# Gwynedd-Mercy College

**Gwynedd Valley, PA 19437** **215 646-7300**

**1993-94 Costs.** Tuition: $10,200. Room & board: $5,250. Fees, books, misc. academic expenses (school's estimate): $600.

**Enrollment.** Undergraduates: 136 men, 580 women (full-time). Freshman class: 380 applicants, 237 accepted, 104 enrolled. Graduate enrollment: 10 men, 152 women.

**Test score averages/ranges.** Average SAT scores: 470 verbal, 500 math. Range of SAT scores of middle 50%: 450-470 verbal, 480-500 math.

**Faculty.** 86 full-time; 82 part-time. 29% of faculty holds doctoral degree. Student/faculty ratio: 11 to 1.

**Selectivity rating.** Competitive.

**PROFILE.** Gwynedd-Mercy is a church-affiliated college. It was founded as a junior college for women in 1948, became a four-year college in 1963, and adopted coeduation in 1973. Its 315-acre campus is located northwest of Philadelphia.

**Accreditation:** MSACS. Professionally accredited by the American Medical Association (CAHEA), the National League for Nursing.
**Religious orientation:** Gwynedd-Mercy College is affiliated with the Roman Catholic Church (Religious Sisters of Mercy); Two semesters of religion/theology required of B.A./B.S. students; one semester required of A.A./A.S. students.
**Library:** Collections totaling over 93,600 volumes, 766 periodical subscriptions and 79 microform items.
**Special facilities/museums:** Center for creative studies, nursery school for early childhood education majors.
**Athletic facilities:** Gymnasium, basketball, racquetball, tennis, and walleyball courts, sauna, swimming pool, aerobics and weight rooms, outdoor recreation areas.

**STUDENT BODY. Undergraduate profile:** 97% are state residents; 80% are transfers. 5.3% Asian-American, 3.6% Black, 1.6% Hispanic, .3% Native American, 89.2% White. Average age of undergraduates is 29.
**Freshman profile:** 1% of freshmen who took SAT scored 700 or over on verbal, 1% scored 700 or over on math; 8% scored 600 or over on verbal, 11% scored 600 or over on math; 31% scored 500 or over on verbal, 43% scored 500 or over on math; 74% scored 400 or over on verbal, 85% scored 400 or over on math; 95% scored 300 or over on verbal, 99% scored 300 or over on math. Majority of accepted applicants took SAT. 45% of freshmen come from public schools.
**Undergraduate achievement:** 85% of fall 1992 freshmen returned for fall 1993 term. 81% of entering class graduated.
**Foreign students:** 66 students are from out of the country. Countries represented include Colombia, Ireland, Japan, Korea, Saudi Arabia, and United Arab Emirates; 19 in all.

**PROGRAMS OF STUDY. Degrees:** B.A., B.Hlth.Sci., B.S.
**Majors:** Accounting, Biology, Business Administration, Business Education, Computer Information Systems, Early Childhood Education, Elementary Education, English, Gerontology, Health Science, History, Mathematics, Mathematics/Computers, Medical Technology, Nursing, Psychology, Secondary Education, Sociology, Special Education.
**Distribution of degrees:** The majors with the highest enrollment are education, business, and nursing; sociology, mathematics, and business education have the lowest.
**Requirements:** General education requirement.
**Academic regulations:** Freshmen must maintain minimum 1.8 GPA; sophomores, juniors, seniors, 2.0 GPA.
**Special:** Minors offered in some majors and in communications, computer science, finance, health administration, literature, management, marketing, media, personnel/human services, public relations/communications, and theatre. Certificate programs in athletic training, computer and information systems, education, gerontology, radiation therapy, and respiratory care. Courses offered in art, chemistry, German, music, nutrition, pharmacology, philosophy, physical education, physics, political science, religious studies, social science, and Spanish. Associate's degrees offered. Double majors. Dual degrees. Pass/fail grading option. Internships. Preprofessional programs in medicine, veterinary science, and dentistry. Teacher certification in early childhood, elementary, secondary, and special education. Certification in specific subject areas. ROTC at U of Pennsylvania.
**Honors:** Honor societies.
**Academic Assistance:** Remedial reading, writing, and math.

**ADMISSIONS. Academic basis for candidate selection** (in order of priority): Secondary school record, standardized test scores, class rank, school's recommendation.
**Nonacademic basis for candidate selection:** Extracurricular participation and alumni/ae relationship are considered.
**Requirements:** Graduation from secondary school is required; GED is accepted. 16 units and the following program of study are required: 4 units of English, 3 units of math, 3 units of science including 1 unit of lab, 2 units of foreign language, 1 unit of history, 3 units of academic electives. Minimum combined SAT score of 800 required; rank in top third of secondary school class recommended. Chemistry required of biology, cardiovascular technology, and nursing program applicants. Physics required of radiation therapy technology program applicants. Chemistry or physics required of respiratory care program applicants. SAT is required; ACT may be substituted. Campus visit and interview recommended. No off-campus interviews.
**Procedure:** Take SAT or ACT by December of 12th year. Visit college for interview by March of 12th year. Notification of admission on rolling basis. $100 nonrefundable tuition deposit. $100 room deposit, refundable until August 31. Freshmen accepted for terms other than fall.
**Special programs:** Admission may be deferred one year. Credit may be granted through CEEB Advanced Placement for scores of 3 or higher. Credit may be granted through CLEP general and subject exams, Regents College, ACT PEP, and challenge exams, and military and life experience. Early entrance/early admission program. Concurrent enrollment program.
**Transfer students:** Transfer students accepted for terms other than fall. In fall 1993, 80% of all new students were transfers into all classes. 614 transfer applications were received, 528 were accepted. Application deadline is August 1 for fall; December 1 for spring. Minimum 2.0 GPA required. Lowest course grade accepted is "C." Maximum number of transferable credits is 34 semester hours from a two-year school and 65 semester hours from a four-year school. 60 semester hours must be completed at the college to receive B.A./B.S. degree; 30 semester hours must be completed at the college to receive A.A./A.S. degree.
**Admissions contact:** Marjorie DeSimone, M.A., Dean of Admissions. 215 641-5510, 800 DIAL-GMC.

**FINANCIAL AID. Available aid:** Pell grants, SEOG, Federal Nursing Student Scholarships, state scholarships and grants, school scholarships and grants, private scholarships and grants, and academic merit scholarships. Perkins Loans (NDSL), PLUS, Stafford Loans (GSL), NSL, state loans, private loans, and SLS. AMS.
**Financial aid statistics:** 5% of aid is not need-based. In 1993-94, 97% of all undergraduate applicants received aid; 96% of freshman applicants. Average amounts of aid awarded freshmen: Scholarships and grants, $7,610; loans, $3,451.
**Supporting data/closing dates:** FAFSA/FAF: Priority filing date is February 20. School's own aid application: Priority filing date is March 15. State aid form: Priority filing date is February 20. Income tax forms: Priority filing date is March 15; accepted on rolling basis. Notification of awards begins March 15.
**Financial aid contact:** Sr. Barbara Kaufmann, M.A., Financial Aid Officer. 215 641-5570.

# Hahnemann University, School of Health Sciences and Humanities

**Philadelphia, PA 19102-1192** **215 762-7000**

**1993-94 Costs.** Tuition: $8,550. Room: $4,800. Fees, books, misc. academic expenses (school's estimate): $860.

**Enrollment.** Freshman class: 2,143 applicants, 551 accepted, 441 enrolled.

**Test score averages/ranges.** Average SAT scores: 380 verbal, 406 math.

**Faculty.** 165 full-time; 265 part-time. 47% of faculty holds doctoral degree. Student/faculty ratio: 2 to 1.

**Selectivity rating.** Less competitive.

**PROFILE.** Hahnemann, founded in 1848, is a private college of allied health professions. Programs are offered through the Schools of Allied Health Professions and Medicine and the Graduate School. Its campus is located in downtown Philadelphia.

**Accreditation:** MSACS. Professionally accredited by the American Medical Association (CAHEA), the American Physical Therapy Association, the National League for Nursing.
**Religious orientation:** Hahnemann University, School of Health Sciences and Humanities is nonsectarian; no religious requirements.
**Library:** Collections totaling over 90,000 volumes, 1,500 periodical subscriptions, and 362 microform items.
**Special facilities/museums:** Anatomy museum, science institute, Hahnemann U Hospital.
**Athletic facilities:** On-campus fitness center, YMCA facility off-campus with swimming pool, racquetball and handball courts, weight room.

**STUDENT BODY. Undergraduate profile:** 75% are state residents. 5% Asian-American, 17% Black, 3% Hispanic, 1% Native American, 70% White, 4% Other. Average age of undergraduates is 29.
**Freshman profile:** 25% of accepted applicants took SAT.
**Undergraduate achievement:** 90% of fall 1992 freshmen returned for fall 1993 term.
**Foreign students:** Eight students are from out of the country. Countries represented include Canada, India, Jamaica, Thailand, the Philippines, and the United Kingdom.

**PROGRAMS OF STUDY. Degrees:** B.S.
**Majors:** Cardiovascular Perfusion, Emergency Medical Services, Health Sciences/Society, Humanities/Social Sciences, Medical Technology, Mental Health Technology, Nursing, Occupational/Environmental Health, Physical Therapist Assistant, Physician Assistant, Radiologic Technology.
**Distribution of degrees:** The majors with the highest enrollment are physician assistant, mental health technology, and nursing; health sciences/society and medical technology have the lowest.
**Requirements:** General education requirement.
**Academic regulations:** Minimum 2.0 GPA required for graduation.
**Special:** Associate's degrees offered. Independent study. Pass/fail grading option. Cooperative education programs. Graduate school at which undergraduates may take graduate-level courses. Preprofessional programs in medicine and physical therapy.
**Honors:** Honor societies.
**Academic Assistance:** Remedial reading, writing, math, and study skills. Nonremedial tutoring.

**ADMISSIONS. Academic basis for candidate selection** (in order of priority): Secondary school record, class rank, school's recommendation, standardized test scores, essay.
**Nonacademic basis for candidate selection:** Character and personality are important. Extracurricular participation, particular talent or ability, and alumni/ae relationship are considered.
**Requirements:** Graduation from secondary school is recommended; GED is accepted. 16 units and the following program of study are required: 4 units of English, 2 units of math, 2 units of lab science, 3 units of social studies, 5 units of electives. Minimum 2.0 GPA re-

quired. Applicants entering directly from secondary school must complete associate's degree program in appropriate area before beginning bachelor's program. R.N. required of nursing program applicants. Academic Enrichment Services (Act 101) and Health Education and Related Training (HEART) programs for applicants not normally admissible. SAT or ACT is required. Campus visit recommended. No off-campus interviews.
**Procedure:** Take SAT or ACT by March 1 of 12th year. Suggest filing application by January 31; no deadline. Notification of admission on rolling basis. Reply is required within 20 days of acceptance. $100 nonrefundable tuition deposit. Freshmen accepted for fall term only.
**Special programs:** Admission may be deferred one year. Credit may be granted through CLEP general and subject exams and ACT PEP exams. Placement may be granted through challenge exams.
**Transfer students:** Transfer students accepted for fall term only. Application deadline is rolling. Minimum 2.0 GPA required. Lowest course grade accepted is "C." Maximum number of transferable credits is 30 semester hours.
**Admissions contact:** Londa Tuzi, Director of Admissions. 215 762-8288.

**FINANCIAL AID. Available aid:** Pell grants, SEOG, state scholarships and grants, school scholarships, and private grants. Perkins Loans (NDSL), PLUS, Stafford Loans (GSL), Health Professions Loans, school loans, and SLS. Deferred payment plan.
**Supporting data/closing dates:** FAFSA/FAF/FFS: Priority filing date is May 1; deadline is May 31. Notification of awards begins July 5.
**Financial aid contact:** James Ianuzzi, Director of Financial Aid. 215 762-7739.

# Haverford College

**Haverford, PA 19041-1392 — 610 896-1000**

**1994-95 Costs.** Tuition: $18,833. Room: $3,400. Board: $2,835. Fees, books, misc. academic expenses (school's estimate): $867.
**Enrollment.** Undergraduates: 563 men, 521 women (full-time). Freshman class: 2,128 applicants, 927 accepted, 294 enrolled.
**Test score averages/ranges.** Range of SAT scores of middle 50%: 580-660 verbal, 620-720 math.
**Faculty.** 97 full-time; 12 part-time. 99% of faculty holds highest degree in specific field. Student/faculty ratio: 11 to 1.
**Selectivity rating.** Most competitive.

**PROFILE.** Haverford, founded in 1833, is a college of the liberal arts and sciences. Its 216-acre campus is located in the village of Haverford, 30 miles from Philadelphia.
**Accreditation:** MSACS.
**Religious orientation:** Haverford College is nonsectarian; no religious requirements.
**Library:** Collections totaling over 400,000 volumes, 1,170 periodical subscriptions, and 65,000 microform items.
**Special facilities/museums:** Rare book and manuscript collections. Art gallery, center for cross-cultural study of religion, observatory, two electron microscopes, NMR spectrometer. Campus designated as an arboretum.
**Athletic facilities:** Gymnasium, field house, basketball, squash, tennis, and volleyball courts, fencing, martial arts, weight lifting, and wrestling rooms, indoor and outdoor tracks, batting cage, athletic fields.
**STUDENT BODY. Undergraduate profile:** 21% are state residents; 1% are transfers. 9% Asian-American, 5% Black, 4% Hispanic, 82% White. Average age of undergraduates is 19.
**Freshman profile:** 100% of accepted applicants took SAT. 60% of freshmen come from public schools.
**Undergraduate achievement:** 99% of fall 1992 freshmen returned for fall 1993 term. 83% of entering class graduated. 29% of students who completed a degree program immediately went on to graduate study.
**Foreign students:** 28 students are from out of the country. 17 countries represented in all.
**PROGRAMS OF STUDY. Degrees:** B.A., B.S.
**Majors:** Anthropology, Archaeology, Astronomy, Biology, Chemistry, Classical Civilizations, Classical Tradition, Classics, Comparative Literature, East Asian Studies, Economics, English, Fine Arts, French, Geology, German, Greek/Latin, Growth/Structure of Cities, History, History of Art, History of Religion, Italian, Mathematics, Music, Philosophy, Physics, Political Science, Psychology, Religion, Russian, Sociology/Anthropology, Spanish.
**Distribution of degrees:** The majors with the highest enrollment are biology, political science, and English; astronomy and geology have the lowest.
**Requirements:** General education requirement.
**Academic regulations:** Minimum 2.0 GPA required for graduation.
**Special:** Concentrations offered in African studies, biochemistry/biophysics, computer science, East Asian studies, gender studies, inter-cultural studies, Latin American and Iberian studies, and peace studies. Offerings under Academic Flexibility Program include reduced course load, graduation in more or less than four years, enrichment and independent study (thesis program), and term-away-from-Haverford. Over 100 distinguished visitors and lecturers come to the campus each year. Self-designed majors. Double majors. Dual degrees. Independent study. Accelerated study. Pass/fail grading option. Internships. Preprofessional programs in law and medicine. Archaeology, geology, growth/structure of cities, history of art, history of religion, and Italian offered in cooperation with Bryn Mawr Coll. 3-2 engineering program with U of Pennsylvania. Cross-registration with Bryn Mawr Coll, Swarthmore Coll, and U of Pennsylvania. Haverford Coll and Bryn Mawr Coll form a bi-college community; students may major, take courses, reside, and eat at either campus. Exchange programs with Claremont McKenna Coll and Spelman Coll. Teacher certification in secondary education. 48 approved study-abroad programs in 29 countries.
**Honors:** Phi Beta Kappa. Honor societies.
**Academic Assistance:** Nonremedial tutoring.
**STUDENT LIFE. Housing:** All freshmen must live on campus. Coed dorms. School-owned/operated apartments. 96% of students live in college housing.
**Social atmosphere:** "Not a 'party' school, although parties are held Thursday through Saturday. It's a do-it-yourself situation; smallish parties are the norm. The campus is small, but Philly is one-half hour by train, and the possibilities there are endless." On campus, students like to frequent the 3 Seasons (a movie theatre that shows VCR movies and sells popcorn), The Cafe (for espresso, cheesecake, and live music), and the Coop (a social/study dining center alternative). Off campus, they head for Al. E. Gator's, Lee's Hoagie House, Roache's, and The Rusty Nail. Popular events include Haverfest, Snowball (a formal dance in December), soccer and basketball games (especially the soccer game against Swarthmore), and the Suitcase Party in February.
**Services and counseling/handicapped student services:** Placement services. Health service. Women's center. Counseling services for minority and older students. Birth control, personal, and psychological counseling. Career and academic guidance services. Religious counseling. Physically disabled student services. Learning disabled services.
**Campus organizations:** Undergraduate student government. Student newspaper (Bi-College News, published once/week). Literary magazine. Yearbook. Radio station. Choruses, orchestra, ensemble group, cafe, community service program, debating, drama group, film series, humor magazine, environmental action club, political groups, women's groups, Bisexual/Gay/Lesbian Alliance, 50 organizations in all.
**Religious organizations:** Hillel, Christian Fellowship, Newman Association, Quaker Activities Committee.
**Minority/foreign student organizations:** Black Student League, Puerto Rican Students at Haverford, Asian Student Association. International Club.
**ATHLETICS. Physical education requirements:** Three semesters of physical education required.
**Intercollegiate competition:** 60% of students participate. Baseball (M), basketball (M,W), cricket (M), cross-country (M,W), fencing (M,W), field hockey (W), lacrosse (M,W), soccer (M,W), softball (W), squash (M,W), tennis (M,W), track (indoor) (M,W), track (outdoor) (M,W), track and field (indoor) (M,W), track and field (outdoor) (M,W), volleyball (W), wrestling (M). Member of Centennial Conference, Middle Atlantic College Fencing Association, NCAA Division III, Philadelphia Association of Intercollegiate Athletics for Women.
**Intramural and club sports:** 90% of students participate. Intramural badminton, basketball, cycling, floor hockey, golf, rugby, running, soccer, softball, squash, swimming, tennis, ultimate frisbee, volleyball, weight training. Men's club cycling, ice hockey, rugby, sailing, swimming, ultimate frisbee, volleyball, water polo. Women's club cycling, ice hockey, rugby, sailing, softball, swimming, ultimate frisbee, water polo.
**ADMISSIONS. Academic basis for candidate selection** (in order of priority): Secondary school record, class rank, school's recommendation, standardized test scores, essay.
**Nonacademic basis for candidate selection:** Character and personality and extracurricular participation are emphasized. Alumni/ae relationship is important. Particular talent or ability and geographical distribution are considered.
**Requirements:** Graduation from secondary school is required; GED is accepted. 12 units and the following program of study are required: 4 units of English, 3 units of math, 1 unit of lab science, 3 units of foreign language, 1 unit of social studies. SAT is required. ACH required. Campus visit and interview recommended. Off-campus interviews available with an alumni representative.
**Procedure:** Take SAT by January 15 of 12th year. Take ACH by January 15 of 12th year. Visit college for interview by January 15 of 12th year. (Interview is required of applicants living within 150 miles of the college.) Application deadline is January 15. Notification of admission by April 15. Reply is required by May 1. Freshmen accepted for fall term only.
**Special programs:** Admission may be deferred one year. Credit and/or placement may be granted through CEEB Advanced Placement exams for scores of 4 or higher. Placement may be granted through challenge exams. Early decision program. In fall 1993, 94 applied for early decision and 58 were accepted. Deadline for applying for early decision is November 15. Early entrance/early admission program.
**Transfer students:** Transfer students accepted for fall term only. In fall 1993, 1% of all new students were transfers into all classes. 116 transfer applications were received, 7 were accepted. Application deadline is March 31. Minimum 3.0 GPA required. Lowest course grade accepted is "C." Maximum number of transferable credits is 64 semester hours. At least 64 semester hours must be completed at the college to receive degree.
**Admissions contact:** Delsie Z. Phillips, M.A., Director of Admissions. 610 896-1350.
**FINANCIAL AID. Available aid:** Pell grants, SEOG, state grants, school grants, and aid for undergraduate foreign students. Perkins Loans (NDSL), PLUS, Stafford Loans (GSL), school loans, and SLS. Knight Tuition Plans and AMS.
**Financial aid statistics:** Average amounts of aid awarded freshmen: Scholarships and grants, $11,452; loans, $2,110.
**Supporting data/closing dates:** FAFSA/FAF/FFS: Deadline is January 31. School's own aid application: Deadline is January 31. State aid form. Income tax forms. Notification of awards begins April 15.
**Financial aid contact:** David J. Hoy, Director of Financial Aid. 610 896-1350.
**STUDENT EMPLOYMENT.** College Work/Study Program. Institutional employment. Students may expect to earn an average of $1,226 during school year. Off-campus part-time employment opportunities rated "good."
**COMPUTER FACILITIES.** 80 IBM/IBM-compatible and Macintosh/Apple microcomputers; all are networked. Students may access Digital, SUN minicomputer/mainframe systems, Internet. Residence halls may be equipped with networked microcomputers. Client/LAN operating systems include Apple/Macintosh, DOS, LocalTalk/Apple Talk. Computer languages and software packages include BASIC, C, Excel, Fetch, Filemaker, FORTRAN, FTP, Gopher, Microsoft Word, Pascal, Statistica, Telnet. Computer facilities are available to all students.
**Hours:** 9 AM-midn. (M-F); 1 PM-5 PM (Sa); 1 PM-midn. (Su).
**GRADUATE CAREER DATA.** Graduate school percentages: 5% enter law school. 7% enter medical school. 1% enter graduate business programs. 16% enter graduate arts and sciences programs. 20% of graduates choose careers in business and industry.
**PROMINENT ALUMNI/AE.** John Whitehead, former assistant secretary of state; Juan Williams, author, *Eyes on the Prize*, and reporter, *Washington Post;* Jerry Levin, president and CEO, *Time Warner;* Andrew Lewis, CEO, Union-Pacific Railroad; Joseph Taylor, Nobel Prize winner, physics.

## Holy Family College

**Philadelphia, PA 19114** **215 637-7700**

**1994-95 Costs.** Tuition: $9,000. Housing: None. Fees, books, misc. academic expenses (school's estimate): $500.
**Enrollment.** Undergraduates: 282 men, 863 women (full-time). Freshman class: 622 applicants, 354 accepted, 169 enrolled. Graduate enrollment: 58 men, 194 women.
**Test score averages/ranges.** Range of SAT scores of middle 50%: 423-481 verbal, 444-512 math.
**Faculty.** 83 full-time; 153 part-time. 43% of faculty holds doctoral degree. Student/faculty ratio: 12 to 1.
**Selectivity rating.** Competitive.

**PROFILE.** Holy Family is a church-affiliated college. Founded in 1954, it adopted coeducation in 1971. Its 47-acre campus is located in northeast Philadelphia.

**Accreditation:** MSACS. Professionally accredited by the American Assembly of Collegiate Schools of Business, the Council on Social Work Education, the National League for Nursing.
**Religious orientation:** Holy Family College is affiliated with the Roman Catholic Church; three semesters of religion/theology required of Catholic students.
**Library:** Collections totaling over 110,332 volumes, 509 periodical subscriptions, and 1,273 microform items.
**Special facilities/museums:** On-campus nursery school, language lab.
**Athletic facilities:** Basketball, racquetball, and volleyball courts, soccer and softball fields.
**STUDENT BODY. Undergraduate profile:** 95% are state residents; 49% are transfers. 2% Asian-American, 2% Black, 2% Hispanic, 94% White. Average age of undergraduates is 21.
**Freshman profile:** 85% of accepted applicants took SAT. 21% of freshmen come from public schools.
**Undergraduate achievement:** 86% of fall 1992 freshmen returned for fall 1993 term. 48% of entering class graduated. 67% of students who completed a degree program went on to graduate study within five years.
**Foreign students:** Nine students are from out of the country. Countries represented include Cyprus, India, Italy, Nigeria, Pakistan, and Poland.
**PROGRAMS OF STUDY. Degrees:** B.A., B.S., B.S.Nurs.
**Majors:** Accounting, Art, Biochemistry, Biology, Business French, Business Spanish, Chemistry, Criminal Justice, Early Childhood Education, Economics, Elementary Education, English/Communications/Literature, Fire Science Administration, French, History, Humanities, International Business Management, Management Information Systems, Marketing/Management, Mathematics, Medical Technology, Nursing, Psychobiology, Psychology, Psychology for Business, Religious Studies, Social Work, Sociology, Spanish, Special Education.
**Distribution of degrees:** The majors with the highest enrollment are nursing, elementary education, and business; art, French, and sociology have the lowest.
**Requirements:** General education requirement.
**Academic regulations:** Freshmen must maintain minimum 1.80 GPA; sophomores, 1.90 GPA; juniors, 2.00 GPA; seniors, 2.00 GPA.
**Special:** Associate's degrees offered. Double majors. Dual degrees. Independent study. Accelerated study. Pass/fail grading option. Internships. Cooperative education programs. Graduate school at which undergraduates may take graduate-level courses. Preprofessional programs in law, medicine, veterinary science, pharmacy, dentistry, and optometry. Teacher certification in early childhood, elementary, secondary, and special education. Certification in specific subject areas. Study abroad possible.
**Academic Assistance:** Remedial reading, writing, and study skills.
**ADMISSIONS. Academic basis for candidate selection** (in order of priority): Class rank, secondary school record, standardized test scores, school's recommendation, essay.
**Nonacademic basis for candidate selection:** Character and personality, extracurricular participation, particular talent or ability, geographical distribution, and alumni/ae relationship are considered.
**Requirements:** Graduation from secondary school is required; GED is accepted. 16 units and the following program of study are required: 4 units of English, 2 units of math, 2 units of science including 1 unit of lab, 2 units of foreign language, 2 units of social studies, 2 units of history, 2 units of electives. Rank in top three-fifths of secondary school class required; rank in top two-fifths recommended. Alternative Admissions Program for applicants not normally admissible. SAT or ACT is required. Campus visit and interview recommended. No off-campus interviews.
**Procedure:** Take SAT or ACT by March of 12th year. Visit college for interview by February of 12th year. Suggest filing application by January 31. Application deadline is July 1. Notification of admission on rolling basis. Reply is required by May 1. $200 nonrefundable tuition deposit. Freshmen accepted for terms other than fall.
**Special programs:** Admission may be deferred one year. Credit and/or placement may be granted through CEEB Advanced Placement exams for scores of 3 or higher. Credit and/or placement may be granted through CLEP subject exams. Credit and placement may be granted through ACT PEP, DANTES, and challenge exams and military and life experience. Early entrance/early admission program. Concurrent enrollment program.
**Transfer students:** Transfer students accepted for terms other than fall. In fall 1993, 49% of all new students were transfers into all classes. 482 transfer applications were received, 252 were accepted. Application deadline is July 1 for fall; December 1 for spring. Minimum 2.5 GPA required. Lowest course grade accepted is "C." Maximum number of transferable credits is 75 semester hours. At least 45 semester hours must be completed at the college to receive degree.
**Admissions contact:** Mott Linn, Ed.D., Director of Admissions. 215 637-3050.
**FINANCIAL AID. Available aid:** Pell grants, SEOG, Federal Nursing Student Scholarships, state scholarships and grants, school scholarships and grants, private scholarships and grants, academic merit scholarships, and athletic scholarships. Perkins Loans (NDSL), PLUS, Stafford Loans (GSL), NSL, Health Professions Loans, state loans, private loans, and SLS. Deferred payment plan.
**Financial aid statistics:** 10% of aid is not need-based. In 1993-94, 88% of all undergraduate applicants received aid; 88% of freshman applicants. Average amounts of aid awarded freshmen: Scholarships and grants, $2,200; loans, $2,500.
**Supporting data/closing dates:** FAFSA/FAF: Deadline is June 1. School's own aid application: Accepted on rolling basis. State aid form: Deadline is February 15. Notification of awards on rolling basis.
**Financial aid contact:** Anna Raffaele, Director of Financial Aid. 215 637-5538.

## Immaculata College

**Immaculata, PA 19345** **215 647-4400**

**1994-95 Costs.** Tuition: $10,000. Room & board: $5,454. Fees, books, misc. academic expenses (school's estimate): $680.
**Enrollment.** Undergraduates: 15 men, 479 women (full-time). Freshman class: 311 applicants, 253 accepted, 148 enrolled. Graduate enrollment: 80 men, 467 women.
**Test score averages/ranges.** Average SAT scores: 470 verbal, 460 math.
**Faculty.** 61 full-time; 406 part-time. 56% of faculty holds doctoral degree. Student/faculty ratio: 8 to 1.
**Selectivity rating.** Less competitive.

**PROFILE.** Immaculata, founded in 1920, is a church-affiliated, liberal arts college. Although predominantly a women's college, men may enroll in the evening division and graduate programs. Its 373-acre campus overlooks Chester Valley and is located on Philadelphia's Main Line, about 20 miles from the city.

**Accreditation:** MSACS. Professionally accredited by the American Dietetic Association, the National Association of Schools of Music.
**Religious orientation:** Immaculata College is affiliated with the Roman Catholic Church; three semesters of theology required of Catholic students.
**Library:** Collections totaling over 160,000 volumes, 650 periodical subscriptions, and 7,500 microform items.
**Special facilities/museums:** On-campus early childhood school.
**Athletic facilities:** Gymnasiums, swimming pool, field hockey and softball fields, tennis courts, weight room, jogging trail.
**STUDENT BODY. Undergraduate profile:** 76% are state residents; 10% are transfers. 3% Asian-American, 5% Black, 4% Hispanic, 85% White, 3% Other. Average age of undergraduates is 20.
**Freshman profile:** 3% of freshmen who took SAT scored 600 or over on verbal, 1% scored 600 or over on math; 34% scored 500 or over on verbal, 29% scored 500 or over on math; 86% scored 400 or over on verbal, 79% scored 400 or over on math; 99% scored 300 or over on verbal, 99% scored 300 or over on math. 99% of accepted applicants took SAT. 50% of freshmen come from public schools.
**Undergraduate achievement:** 75% of fall 1992 freshmen returned for fall 1993 term. 66% of entering class graduated. 25% of students who completed a degree program went on to graduate study within one year.
**Foreign students:** 80 students are from out of the country. Countries represented include China, Japan, Kenya, Mexico, Taiwan, and Venezuela; 26 in all.
**PROGRAMS OF STUDY. Degrees:** B.A., B.Mus., B.S., B.S.Nurs.
**Majors:** Accounting, Biology, Biology/Chemistry, Biology/Psychology, Business Administration/Management, Chemistry, Dietetics, Economics, English, Fashion Merchandising, Food Service Management, French, German, History, Home Economics Education, International Business, International Studies, Mathematics, Mathematics/Computer Science, Mathematics/Physics, Music, Music Therapy, Psychology, Sociology, Spanish, Spanish/Psychology, Spanish/Sociology.
**Distribution of degrees:** The majors with the highest enrollment are psychology, economics, and English; sociology and mathematics have the lowest.
**Requirements:** General education requirement.
**Academic regulations:** Freshmen must maintain minimum 1.7 GPA; sophomores, juniors, seniors, 2.0 GPA.
**Special:** Minors offered in most majors and in art, computer science, Italian, and Russian. Law Enforcement Advancement Program (LEAP) prepares students academically and professionally for careers in corrections, probation, parole, court, or police work. Associate's degrees offered. Self-designed majors. Double majors. Accelerated study. Pass/fail grading option. Internships. Preprofessional programs in law, medicine, veterinary science, dentistry, theology, and optometry. Teacher certification in early childhood, elementary, secondary, and bilingual/bicultural education. Certification in specific subject areas. Study abroad in England, France, Germany, Italy, Mexico, and Spain.
**Honors:** Honors program. Honor societies.
**Academic Assistance:** Remedial reading, writing, math, and study skills. Nonremedial tutoring.
**ADMISSIONS. Academic basis for candidate selection** (in order of priority): Secondary school record, class rank, standardized test scores, school's recommendation, essay.
**Nonacademic basis for candidate selection:** Extracurricular participation is important. Character and personality, particular talent or ability, and alumni/ae relationship are considered.
**Requirements:** Graduation from secondary school is required; GED is accepted. 19 units and the following program of study are required: 4 units of English, 2 units of math, 2 units of science including 1 unit of lab, 2 units of foreign language, 3 units of social studies, 1 unit of history, 5 units of electives including 4 units of academic electives. Minimum SAT scores of 400 in both verbal and math, rank in top three-fifths of secondary school class, and minimum 2.3 GPA required. Audition required of music program applicants. R.N. required of nursing program applicants. SAT is required; ACT may be substituted. ACH recommended. Campus visit and interview recommended. Off-campus interviews available with an admissions representative.
**Procedure:** Take SAT or ACT by December 15 of 12th year. Take ACH by March 15 of 12th year. Visit college for interview by February 15 of 12th year. Suggest filing applica-

tion by February 15. Application deadline is June 15. Notification of admission on rolling basis. Reply is required by May 1. $100 nonrefundable tuition deposit. Freshmen accepted for terms other than fall.
**Special programs:** Admission may be deferred one year. Credit and/or placement may be granted through CEEB Advanced Placement exams for scores of 3 or higher. Credit and/or placement may be granted through CLEP general exams. Credit may be granted through CLEP subject exams and challenge exams. Early entrance/early admission program. Concurrent enrollment program.
**Transfer students:** Transfer students accepted for terms other than fall. In fall 1993, 10% of all new students were transfers into all classes. 103 transfer applications were received, 81 were accepted. Application deadline is June 1 for fall; December 1 for spring. Minimum 2.5 GPA recommended. Lowest course grade accepted is "C." Maximum number of transferable credits is 64 semester hours. At least 36 semester hours must be completed at the college to receive degree.
**Admissions contact:** James P. Sullivan, M.B.A., Director of Admission. 215 296-9067.

**FINANCIAL AID. Available aid:** Pell grants, SEOG, Federal Nursing Student Scholarships, state scholarships and grants, school scholarships and grants, private scholarships and grants, and academic merit scholarships. Perkins Loans (NDSL), PLUS, Stafford Loans (GSL), NSL, state loans, private loans, and SLS. AMS, deferred payment plan, and family tuition reduction.
**Financial aid statistics:** 25% of aid is not need-based. In 1993-94, 82% of all undergraduate applicants received aid. Average amounts of aid awarded freshmen: Scholarships and grants, $2,500; loans, $2,000.
**Supporting data/closing dates:** School's own aid application: Priority filing date is March 15; accepted on rolling basis. State aid form: Priority filing date is March 15; accepted on rolling basis. Income tax forms: Accepted on rolling basis. Notification of awards begins March 1.
**Financial aid contact:** Beverly Yager, M.A., Director of Financial Aid. 215 647-4400.

## Indiana University of Pennsylvania

**Indiana, PA 15705-1088 412 357-2100**

**1994-95 Costs.** Tuition: $2,954 (state residents), $7,352 (out-of-state). Room & board: $2,834. Fees, books, misc. academic expenses (school's estimate): $1,085.
**Enrollment.** Undergraduates: 5,041 men, 6,334 women (full-time). Freshman class: 6,373 applicants, 3,264 accepted, 1,625 enrolled. Graduate enrollment: 594 men, 961 women.
**Test score averages/ranges.** Average SAT scores: 444 verbal, 495 math. Range of SAT scores of middle 50%: 415-500 verbal, 466-516 math.
**Faculty.** 722 full-time; 86 part-time. 76% of faculty holds doctoral degree. Student/faculty ratio: 19 to 1.
**Selectivity rating.** Competitive.

**PROFILE.** Indiana University of Pennsylvania, founded in 1875, is a public, comprehensive institution. Programs are offered through the Colleges of Business, Education, Fine Arts, Health Sciences, Human Ecology, Humanities and Social Sciences, and Natural Sciences and Mathematics and the School of Continuing Education. Its 200-acre campus is located in western Pennsylvania, 65 miles from Pittsburgh.

**Accreditation:** MSACS. Professionally accredited by the American Home Economics Association, the American Medical Association (CAHEA), the National Association of Schools of Music, the National Council for Accreditation of Teacher Education, the National League for Nursing.
**Religious orientation:** Indiana University of Pennsylvania is nonsectarian; no religious requirements.
**Library:** Collections totaling over 600,000 volumes, 4,500 periodical subscriptions, and 1,700,000 microform items.
**Special facilities/museums:** Art museum, natural history museum, on-campus elementary school, lodge, farm, co-generation plant.
**Athletic facilities:** Field house, gymnasiums, swimming pools, training room, dance studio, tennis courts, weight room.

**STUDENT BODY. Undergraduate profile:** 96% are state residents. 1% Asian-American, 5% Black, 1% Hispanic, 90% White, 3% Other. Average age of undergraduates is 20.
**Freshman profile:** 1% of freshmen who took SAT scored 700 or over on math; 4% scored 600 or over on verbal, 12% scored 600 or over on math; 26% scored 500 or over on verbal, 54% scored 500 or over on math; 83% scored 400 or over on verbal, 92% scored 400 or over on math; 100% scored 300 or over on verbal, 100% scored 300 or over on math. 99% of accepted applicants took SAT; 1% took ACT. 91% of freshmen come from public schools.
**Undergraduate achievement:** 82% of fall 1992 freshmen returned for fall 1993 term. 67% of entering class graduated. 12% of students who completed a degree program went on to graduate study within one year.
**Foreign students:** 369 students are from out of the country. Countries represented include Bangladesh, China, Japan, Malaysia, Pakistan, and Thailand; 69 in all.

**PROGRAMS OF STUDY. Degrees:** B.A., B.F.A., B.S., B.S.Ed.
**Majors:** Accounting, Anthropology, Applied Mathematics, Art Education, Art Performance, Biochemistry, Biology, Business Education, Chemistry, Child Development/Family Relations, Communications Media, Community Services, Computer/Information Sciences, Consumer Affairs, Consumer Services, Criminology, Dietetics, Distributive Education, Early Childhood Education, Earth Science, Economics, Education of the Deaf/Hearing Impaired, Elementary Education, English, Environmental Health, Exceptional Education, Family Medicine, Fashion Merchandising, Finance, Food Sciences/Human Nutrition, Food Service Management, Foreign Languages, French, General Business, General Management, General Science, Geography, Geology, Geoscience, German, Government/Public Service, Health/Physical Education, History, Hotel/Restaurant/Institutional Management, Human Resource Management, Interior Design/Housing, International Studies, Journalism, Management Information Systems, Marketing, Mathematics, Medical Technology, Music Education, Music Performance, Natural Science, Nursing, Nutrition Education, Office Administration, Philosophy, Physical Education/Sport, Physics, Physics/Mathematics, Political Science/Government, Psychology, Regional Planning, Rehabilitation, Respiratory Therapy, Safety Sciences, Social Services/Applied Sociology, Social Studies, Sociology, Spanish, Speech, Speech Pathology, Theatre, Theatre/Performance/Technical Design, Vocational Education.
**Distribution of degrees:** The majors with the highest enrollment are elementary education, marketing, and accounting; music performance, nutrition education, and government/public service have the lowest.
**Requirements:** General education requirement.
**Academic regulations:** Freshmen must maintain minimum 1.8 GPA; sophomores, juniors, seniors, 2.0 GPA.
**Special:** Minors offered in all departments. Branch campuses at Kittanning and Punxsutawney offer one- and two-year programs. Self-designed majors. Double majors. Independent study. Accelerated study. Pass/fail grading option. Internships. Graduate school at which undergraduates may take graduate-level courses. Preprofessional programs in law, medicine, veterinary science, optometry, engineering, and podiatry. 2-2 engineering program with U of Pittsburgh. 3-2 engineering program with Drexel U. 3-2 forestry and environmental studies program with Duke U. Optometry program with Pennsylvania Coll of Optometry. Podiatry program with Pennsylvania Coll of Podiatry. Member of Marine Science Consortium; off-campus study possible at Wallops Island, Va. Washington Semester. Member of National Student Exchange (NSE). Teacher certification in early childhood, elementary, secondary, and special education. Study abroad in 34 countries. ROTC.
**Honors:** Honors program.
**Academic Assistance:** Remedial reading, writing, math, and study skills. Nonremedial tutoring.

**STUDENT LIFE. Housing:** Students may live on or off campus. Coed, women's, and men's dorms. Fraternity housing. 33% of students live in college housing.
**Services and counseling/handicapped student services:** Placement services. Health service. Day care. Counseling services for minority, military, veteran, and older students. Birth control, personal, and psychological counseling. Career and academic guidance services. Physically disabled student services. Learning disabled services. Notetaking services. Tape recorders. Tutors. Reader services for the blind.
**Campus organizations:** Undergraduate student government. Student newspaper (Penn, published three times/week). Literary magazine. Yearbook. Radio and TV stations. Choral and instrumental ensembles, jazz bands, Residence Hall Association, athletic, departmental, service, and special-interest groups, 180 organizations in all. 20 fraternities, 16 chapter houses; 17 sororities, no chapter houses. 17% of men join a fraternity. 15% of women join a sorority.
**Religious organizations:** Foundation for Buddhism, Chi Alpha Fellowship, Deseret Club, Navigators, Intervarsity Christian Fellowship, IUP Alive, Unity Christian Campus Ministry, Newman Center, Campus Crusade for Christ, Time Out, Lutheran Student Movement, Maranatha, Muslim Student Association.
**Minority/foreign student organizations:** Black Greek Council, Black Student League, Future Black Professionals. International Student Club, Chinese Student Association.

**ATHLETICS. Physical education requirements:** None.
**Intercollegiate competition:** 5% of students participate. Baseball (M), basketball (M,W), cross-country (M,W), field hockey (W), football (M), golf (M), gymnastics (W), softball (W), swimming (M,W), tennis (W), track (indoor) (M,W), track (outdoor) (M,W), track and field (indoor) (M,W), track and field (outdoor) (M,W), volleyball (W). Member of ECAC, NCAA Division II, Pennsylvania State Athletic Conference.
**Intramural and club sports:** 50% of students participate. Intramural archery, badminton, basketball, billards, bowling, cross-country, flag football, foul throw, golf, horseshoes, parcourse, racquetball, softball, speed football, swimming, table tennis, tennis, track, tug-of-war, volleyball, walleyball, water polo, wrestling. Men's club Alpine skiing, badminton, cycling, equestrian sports, fencing, ice hockey, orienteering, racquetball, rifle, rugby, soccer, tae kwon do, volleyball. Women's club Alpine skiing, badminton, cycling, equestrian sports, fencing, ice hockey, orienteering, racquetball, rifle, volleyball.

**ADMISSIONS. Academic basis for candidate selection** (in order of priority): Secondary school record, class rank, standardized test scores, school's recommendation, essay.
**Nonacademic basis for candidate selection:** Character and personality, extracurricular participation, and particular talent or ability are considered.
**Requirements:** Graduation from secondary school is required; GED is accepted. No specific distribution of secondary school units required. Portfolio required of art program applicants. Audition required of music program applicants. Learning Assistance Program and ACT 101 for in-state applicants not normally admissible. Educational Development Services for minority applicants. Special admissions program for veterans. SAT is required; ACT may be substituted. Campus visit recommended. No off-campus interviews.
**Procedure:** Take SAT or ACT by November of 12th year. Suggest filing application by December 31; no deadline. Notification of admission on rolling basis. Reply is required by April 15. Freshmen accepted for terms other than fall.
**Special programs:** Admission may be deferred one year. Credit may be granted through CEEB Advanced Placement for scores of 3 or higher. Credit may be granted through CLEP general and subject exams, ACT PEP exams, and military and life experience. Early decision program. Deadline for applying for early decision is October 15. Early entrance/early admission program. Concurrent enrollment program.
**Transfer students:** Transfer students accepted for terms other than fall. In fall 1993, 1,346 transfer applications were received, 1,007 were accepted. Application deadline is February 1 for fall; November 1 for spring. Minimum 2.0 GPA required. Lowest course grade accepted is "C." At least 45 semester hours must be completed at the university to receive degree.
**Admissions contact:** William Nunn, M.Ed., Dean of Admissions. 412 357-2230, 800 442-6830.

**FINANCIAL AID. Available aid:** Pell grants, SEOG, state scholarships and grants, school scholarships, private scholarships and grants, ROTC scholarships, academic merit

scholarships, and athletic scholarships. Perkins Loans (NDSL), PLUS, Stafford Loans (GSL), state loans, and SLS. Installment payment plan.
**Financial aid statistics:** In 1993-94, 85% of all undergraduate applicants received aid; 85% of freshman applicants. Average amounts of aid awarded freshmen: Scholarships and grants, $2,000; loans, $2,500.
**Supporting data/closing dates:** FAFSA: Priority filing date is May 1; deadline is May 1. Notification of awards begins June 15.
**Financial aid contact:** Frederick Joseph, M.Ed., Director of Financial Aid. 412 357-2218.
**STUDENT EMPLOYMENT.** College Work/Study Program. Institutional employment. 26% of full-time undergraduates work on campus during school year. Students may expect to earn an average of $1,200 during school year. Off-campus part-time employment opportunities rated "good."
**COMPUTER FACILITIES.** 3,000 IBM/IBM-compatible, Macintosh/Apple, and RISC-/UNIX-based microcomputers. Students may access Digital minicomputer/mainframe systems, BITNET, Internet, CompuServe. Residence halls may be equipped with networked microcomputers, networked terminals, modems. Client/LAN operating systems include Apple/Macintosh, DOS, UNIX/XENIX/AIX, Novell. Computer languages and software packages include APL, BMDP, BASIC, C, COBOL, dBASE III+, FORTRAN, LISP, Lotus 1-2-3, Natural/ADABAS, Pascal, RPG, SAS, SPSS, SPITBOL, TEXT, WordPerfect; 33 in all. Computer facilities are available to all students.
**Fees:** None.
**Hours:** Facilities open 8 AM-midn.; 24-hour access through remote terminals.
**PROMINENT ALUMNI/AE.** Robert Cook, chairperson and CEO, V.M. Software; Charlotte Cooper, CEO, Standard Offset Printing; Joseph Laposata, general, U.S. Army; Daniel Barry, vice-president, Orion; Dr. Richard Ferguson, president, American College Testing; Robin Litton, ABC News special events.

# Juniata College

Huntingdon, PA 16652-2119 814 643-4310

**1994-95 Costs.** Tuition: $14,850. Room: $2,250. Board: $2,210. Fees, books, misc. academic expenses (school's estimate): $1,000.
**Enrollment.** Undergraduates: 502 men, 573 women (full-time). Freshman class: 1,005 applicants, 859 accepted, 298 enrolled.
**Test score averages/ranges.** Average SAT scores: 509 verbal, 558 math. Range of SAT scores of middle 50%: 990-1140 combined. Average ACT scores: 26 composite. Range of ACT scores of middle 50%: 21-29 composite.
**Faculty.** 75 full-time; 29 part-time. 94% of faculty holds highest degree in specific field. Student/faculty ratio: 13 to 1.
**Selectivity rating.** More competitive.

**PROFILE.** Juniata, founded in 1876, is a church-affiliated, liberal arts college. Its 100-acre campus, 180-acre nature preserve, and 365-acre environmental studies field are located in Huntingdon.

**Accreditation:** MSACS. Professionally accredited by the Council on Social Work Education.
**Religious orientation:** Juniata College is nonsectarian; no religious requirements.
**Library:** Collection totaling over 208,000 volumes, periodicals, and microforms.
**Special facilities/museums:** Art gallery, early childhood development center, human interaction lab, environmental field station, nature preserve, observatory, electron microscopes, nuclear magnetic resonance spectrometers.
**Athletic facilities:** Sports/recreation complex, track, athletic fields, natatorium, sauna, courts for all sports, outdoor facilities for all sports; camping, hiking, skiing, hunting, fishing, and swimming nearby.
**STUDENT BODY. Undergraduate profile:** 75% are state residents; 7% are transfers. 2% Asian-American, 1% Black, 2% Hispanic, 94% White, 1% Other. Average age of undergraduates is 20.
**Freshman profile:** 1% of freshmen who took SAT scored 700 or over on verbal, 2% scored 700 or over on math; 13% scored 600 or over on verbal, 26% scored 600 or over on math; 49% scored 500 or over on verbal, 77% scored 500 or over on math; 94% scored 400 or over on verbal, 96% scored 400 or over on math; 100% scored 300 or over on verbal, 100% scored 300 or over on math. 3% of freshmen who took ACT scored 30 or over on composite; 41% scored 24 or over on composite; 85% scored 18 or over on composite; 100% scored 12 or over on composite. 90% of accepted applicants took SAT; 18% took ACT. 80% of freshmen come from public schools.
**Undergraduate achievement:** 92% of fall 1992 freshmen returned for fall 1993 term. 71% of entering class graduated. 34% of students who completed a degree program went on to graduate study within one year.
**Foreign students:** 40 students are from out of the country. 16 countries represented in all.
**PROGRAMS OF STUDY. Degrees:** B.A., B.S.
**Majors:** Accounting, Allied Health Professions, Anthropology, Art, Biochemistry, Biology, Biophysics, Business Administration/Management, Business/Computers, Chemistry, Communications, Computer/Information Sciences, Criminology, Early Childhood Education, Ecology/Environmental Science, Economics, Education, Educational Psychology, Elementary Education, English, Finance, Fine Arts, Foreign Languages/Multiple Emphasis, Forestry, French, Geology, German, History, Humanities, International Studies, Liberal Arts, Marketing, Mathematics, Medical Laboratory Technologies, Music, Natural Science, Peace/Conflict Studies, Personnel, Philosophy, Physics, Political Science/Government, Pre-Dentistry, Pre-Engineering, Pre-Forestry, Pre-Law, Pre-Medicine, Pre-Ministry, Pre-Pharmacy, Pre-Podiatry, Pre-Veterinary, Production/Operations Management, Psychology, Public Administration, Religion, Religious Education, Russian, Secondary Education, Social Sciences, Social Work, Sociology, Spanish.
**Distribution of degrees:** The majors with the highest enrollment are biology, education, and economics.
**Requirements:** General education requirement.
**Academic regulations:** Minimum 2.0 GPA must be maintained.
**Special:** Traditional majors are replaced by Programs of Emphasis designed by each student with help from two faculty advisers. Students may combine established offerings for dual preparation, create a variety of career options, or explore a number of vocational interests before final design; many programs are interdisciplinary and include independent study, tutorials, and research experience. Courses offered in Chinese and Japanese. Double majors. Dual degrees. Independent study. Pass/fail grading option. Internships. Cooperative education programs. Preprofessional programs in law, medicine, veterinary science, pharmacy, dentistry, theology, and optometry. 2-2 dental hygiene, medical technology, nursing, occupational therapy, physical therapy, and radiologic technology programs with Thomas Jefferson U. 3-1 medical technology program with Abington Memorial, Altoona, and Lancaster General Hospitals and Princeton Medical Center. 3-2 engineering programs with Clarkson U, Columbia U, Georgia Tech, Pennsylvania State U, and Washington U. 3-2 forestry and environmental studies program with Duke U. 3-4 accelerated medicine program with Pennsylvania Coll of Podiatric Medicine. 3-2 and 2-2 nursing programs with Columbia U, Johns Hopkins U, and Thomas Jefferson U. 3-2 occupational therapy programs with Boston U, Thomas Jefferson U, and Washington U. 3-1, 3-2, and 3-3 allied health programs with Thomas Jefferson U. 4-2 physical therapy program with Hahnemann U. 3-3 law program with Duquesne U. Washington Semester. Philadelphia Urban Semester. Marine Science Semester. Exchange program with Duke U for marine biology only. Teacher certification in early childhood, elementary, and secondary education. Certification in specific subject areas. Exchange programs abroad in China (Dalian Inst of Foreign Muenster), Ecuador (U of Azuay), England (Cheltenham and Gloucester Coll of Higher Education, Humberside Polytech, U of Leeds), France (U of Lille, U of Nancy, U of Strasbourg), Germany (U of Marburg, U of Languages), Greece (Laverne Coll of Athens), Japan (Hokusei Gakuen U, Kansai Gaidai U), Mexico (U of Las Americas), and Spain (U of Barcelona).
**Honors:** Honors program.
**Academic Assistance:** Remedial study skills. Nonremedial tutoring.
**STUDENT LIFE. Housing:** All unmarried students under age 21 must live on campus unless living near campus with relatives. Coed and women's dorms. School-owned/operated apartments. Off-campus privately-owned housing. 95% of students live in college housing.
**Social atmosphere:** According to the editor of the student newspaper, there are many cultural events at Juniata all year-round, and students can usually find something to do socially during the week and on weekends. Students enjoy special events such as the Madrigal Dinner, Mountain Day, Spring Fest, Presidential Ball, All Class Night, and Mud Volleyball. Students like to gather at the Tote (equivalent to the Student Union), J.T.'s, and Dave's.
**Services and counseling/handicapped student services:** Placement services. Health service. Counseling services for older students. Birth control, personal, and psychological counseling. Career and academic guidance services. Religious counseling. Physically disabled student services. Notetaking services. Tape recorders. Reader services for the blind.
**Campus organizations:** Undergraduate student government. Student newspaper (Juniatian, published once/week). Literary magazine. Yearbook. Radio station. Choir, band, instrumental ensembles, Juniata Players, Programming Board, Residence Hall Association, outing club, women's group, professional, service, and special-interest groups, 60 organizations in all.
**Religious organizations:** Campus Ministry Board, Deputation Club, Jewish Student Association, Catholic Council.
**Minority/foreign student organizations:** African-American Student Association, multicultural organization. International Club.
**ATHLETICS. Physical education requirements:** None.
**Intercollegiate competition:** 50% of students participate. Baseball (M), basketball (M,W), cheerleading (M,W), cross-country (M,W), field hockey (W), football (M), golf (M), soccer (M), softball (W), swimming (M,W), tennis (M,W), track (outdoor) (M,W), volleyball (M,W), wrestling (M). Member of Middle Atlantic Conference, NCAA Division III.
**Intramural and club sports:** 85% of students participate. Intramural basketball, racquetball, tennis, volleyball, walleyball. Men's club Alpine skiing, indoor track, lacrosse, martial arts, racquetball, rugby, skeet and trapshooting, soccer, weight lifting. Women's club Alpine skiing, indoor track, lacrosse, martial arts, rugby.
**ADMISSIONS. Academic basis for candidate selection** (in order of priority): Secondary school record, class rank, standardized test scores, essay, school's recommendation.
**Nonacademic basis for candidate selection:** Character and personality, extracurricular participation, particular talent or ability, geographical distribution, and alumni/ae relationship are considered.
**Requirements:** Graduation from secondary school is required; GED is accepted. 16 units and the following program of study are required: 4 units of English, 3 units of math, 3 units of science including 2 units of lab, 2 units of foreign language, 4 units of social studies. Minimum combined SAT score of 1000 and minimum 3.0 GPA recommended. Conditional admission possible for applicants not meeting standard requirements. SAT or ACT is required. PSAT is recommended. Campus visit and interview recommended. Off-campus interviews available with admissions and alumni representatives.
**Procedure:** Take SAT or ACT by fall of 12th year. Visit college for interview by March of 12th year. Application deadline is March 1. Acceptance notification on rolling basis after December 15. Reply is required by May 1. $200 nonrefundable tuition deposit. Freshmen accepted for terms other than fall.
**Special programs:** Admission may be deferred two semesters. Credit and/or placement may be granted through CEEB Advanced Placement exams for scores of 4 or higher. Early decision program. In fall 1993, 67 applied for early decision and 62 were accepted. Deadline for applying for early decision is November 15. Early entrance/early admission program. Concurrent enrollment program.
**Transfer students:** Transfer students accepted for terms other than fall. In fall 1993, 7% of all new students were transfers into all classes. 65 transfer applications were received, 47 were accepted. Application deadline is July 1 for fall; December 1 for spring. Minimum 2.5 GPA recommended. Lowest course grade accepted is "C-." Maximum number of transferable credits is 60 semester hours. At least 30 semester hours must be completed at the college to receive degree.
**Admissions contact:** Carlton E. Surbeck III, M.S., Director of Admission. 814 643-4310, extension 420.

**FINANCIAL AID. Available aid:** Pell grants, SEOG, state grants, school scholarships and grants, private scholarships and grants, academic merit scholarships, and aid for undergraduate foreign students. Perkins Loans (NDSL), PLUS, Stafford Loans (GSL), state loans, and school loans. Knight Tuition Plans and Tuition Management Systems. Tuition exchange with other private colleges and universities employee families.
**Financial aid statistics:** 15% of aid is not need-based. In 1993-94, 75% of all undergraduate applicants received aid; 79% of freshman applicants. Average amounts of aid awarded freshmen: Scholarships and grants, $8,871; loans, $2,735.
**Supporting data/closing dates:** FAFSA/FAF: Priority filing date is March 1. State aid form: Priority filing date is March 1. Notification of awards on rolling basis.
**Financial aid contact:** Randall S. Rennell, M.A., Director of Financial Aid. 814 643-4310, extension 242.

**STUDENT EMPLOYMENT.** College Work/Study Program. Institutional employment. 55% of full-time undergraduates work on campus during school year. Students may expect to earn an average of $700 during school year. Off-campus part-time employment opportunities rated "poor."

**COMPUTER FACILITIES.** 60 IBM/IBM-compatible, Macintosh/Apple, and RISC-/UNIX-based microcomputers; 15 are networked. Students may access Digital, IBM minicomputer/mainframe systems, Internet. Computer languages and software packages include Ada, APL, BASIC, C, COBOL, dBASE, FORTRAN, LISP, Lotus 1-2-3, Modula 2, Pascal, PL/1, Prolog, 20/20, WordPerfect; 24 in all. Computer facilities are available to all students.
**Fees:** None.
**Hours:** 18.5 hours/day.

**GRADUATE CAREER DATA.** Graduate school percentages: 8% enter law school. 21% enter medical school. 10% enter dental school. 4% enter graduate business programs. 20% enter graduate arts and sciences programs. 2% enter theological school/seminary. Highest graduate school enrollments: Pennsylvania State U, U of Pennsylvania. 40% of graduates choose careers in business and industry. Companies and businesses that hire graduates: Corning Glass, Electronic Data Systems, Hess Department Stores, Johns Hopkins U, Meridan Bank, National Cancer Institute.

**PROMINENT ALUMNI/AE.** Dr. Charles C. Ellis, distinguished lecturer, Georgetown U; Dr. Vince Sarni, chairperson of the board, Pittsburgh Plate Glass; Dr. Peter C. Marzio, executive director, Museum of Fine Arts; Charles R. Knox, head coach, L.A. Rams; Dr. Bruce Davis, executive administrator, Academy of Motion Picture Arts and Sciences.

# King's College

**Wilkes-Barre, PA 18711** **717 826-5900**

**1994-95 Costs.** Tuition: $10,910. Room: $2,410. Board: $2,750. Fees, books, misc. academic expenses (school's estimate): $1,300.
**Enrollment.** Undergraduates: 916 men, 855 women (full-time). Freshman class: 1,456 applicants, 1,053 accepted, 381 enrolled. Graduate enrollment: 28 men, 24 women.
**Test score averages/ranges.** Average SAT scores: 466 verbal, 512 math. Range of SAT scores of middle 50%: 419-517 verbal, 456-578 math.
**Faculty.** 97 full-time; 74 part-time. 68% of faculty holds highest degree in specific field. Student/faculty ratio: 17 to 1.
**Selectivity rating.** Less competitive.

**PROFILE.** King's College is a church-affiliated, liberal arts institution. Founded as a men's college in 1946, it adopted coeducation in 1970. Its 15-acre campus is located in a residential area of Wilkes-Barre.

**Accreditation:** MSACS. Professionally accredited by the American Medical Association (CAHEA).
**Religious orientation:** King's College is affiliated with the Roman Catholic Church (Congregation of the Holy Cross); two semesters of theology required.
**Library:** Collections totaling over 145,481 volumes, 760 periodical subscriptions, and 432,580 microform items.
**Special facilities/museums:** Electron microscope, robotics lab.
**Athletic facilities:** Gymnasium, swimming pool, aerobics, fitness, and wrestling rooms, basketball, racquetball, tennis, and volleyball courts, sauna, rifle range, baseball, field hockey, football, soccer, and softball fields.

**STUDENT BODY. Undergraduate profile:** 72% are state residents; 26% are transfers. 1.3% Asian-American, 1.5% Black, .7% Hispanic, .2% Native American, 95.2% White, 1.1% Other. Average age of undergraduates is 20.
**Freshman profile:** 1% of freshmen who took SAT scored 700 or over on verbal, 2% scored 700 or over on math; 5% scored 600 or over on verbal, 18% scored 600 or over on math; 32% scored 500 or over on verbal, 56% scored 500 or over on math; 87% scored 400 or over on verbal, 93% scored 400 or over on math; 100% scored 300 or over on verbal, 100% scored 300 or over on math. 89% of accepted applicants took SAT. 63% of freshmen come from public schools.
**Undergraduate achievement:** 85% of fall 1992 freshmen returned for fall 1993 term. 66% of entering class graduated. 12% of students who completed a degree program immediately went on to graduate study.
**Foreign students:** 10 students are from out of the country. Countries represented include Bahamas, Bulgaria, Japan, Russia, Spain, and Sri Lanka.

**PROGRAMS OF STUDY. Degrees:** B.A., B.S.
**Majors:** Accounting, Biology, Business Administration, Chemistry, Communications, Computer/Information Systems, Computer Science, Criminal Justice, Economics, Elementary Education, English, Finance, French, General Science, Gerontology, Health Care Management, History, Human Resources Management, International Business, Management Information Systems, Marketing, Mathematics, Medical Technology, Philosophy, Physician Assistant, Physics, Political Science, Psychology, Sociology, Spanish, Theatre, Theology.
**Distribution of degrees:** The majors with the highest enrollment are accounting, communications, and criminal justice; philosophy, general science, and physics have the lowest.
**Requirements:** General education requirement.
**Academic regulations:** Minimum 2.00 GPA must be maintained.
**Special:** Minors offered in most majors. Unorthodox major program. Courses offered in career decision-making. Special program in urban studies. Associate's degrees offered. Double majors. Independent study. Accelerated study. Pass/fail grading option. Internships. Cooperative education programs. Preprofessional programs in law, medicine, veterinary science, pharmacy, dentistry, theology, and optometry. Member of Northeast Pennsylvania Independent Colleges (NEPIC). Washington Semester. Teacher certification in early childhood, elementary, secondary, and special education. Certification in specific subject areas. Study abroad in England. ROTC. AFROTC at Wilkes U.
**Honors:** Honors program. Honor societies.
**Academic Assistance:** Remedial study skills. Nonremedial tutoring.

**STUDENT LIFE. Housing:** All freshmen and sophomores under age 21 must live on campus unless living with family. Women's and men's dorms. School-owned/operated apartments. Off-campus privately-owned housing. 39% of students live in college housing.
**Services and counseling/handicapped student services:** Placement services. Health service. Counseling services for minority, veteran, and older students. Personal and psychological counseling. Career and academic guidance services. Religious counseling. Physically disabled student services. Learning disabled services. Tape recorders. Tutors.
**Campus organizations:** Undergraduate student government. Student newspaper (Crown, published biweekly). Literary magazine. Yearbook. Radio station. Blood Council, Emergency Response Team, Jazz/Rock Ensemble, King's Singers, King's Players, Politics Society, debating, Big Brothers/Big Sisters, Amnesty International, Circle K, athletic, departmental, and special-interest groups, 50 organizations in all.
**Religious organizations:** Campus Ministry, Knights of Columbus.
**Minority/foreign student organizations:** International Club.

**ATHLETICS. Physical education requirements:** None.
**Intercollegiate competition:** 30% of students participate. Baseball (M), basketball (M,W), cheerleading (M,W), cross-country (M,W), field hockey (W), football (M), golf (M), riflery (M,W), soccer (M,W), softball (W), swimming (M,W), tennis (M,W), volleyball (W), wrestling (M). Member of ECAC, Middle Atlantic Conference, NCAA Division III.
**Intramural and club sports:** 65% of students participate. Intramural basketball, bowling, flag football, racquetball, riflery, street hockey. Men's club volleyball.

**ADMISSIONS. Academic basis for candidate selection** (in order of priority): Secondary school record, class rank, standardized test scores, school's recommendation, essay.
**Nonacademic basis for candidate selection:** Character and personality are emphasized. Extracurricular participation, particular talent or ability, geographical distribution, and alumni/ae relationship are important.
**Requirements:** Graduation from secondary school is recommended; GED is accepted. 17 units are required and the following program of study recommended: 4 units of English, 3 units of math, 2 units of science, 2 units of foreign language, 3 units of social studies, 3 units of history. EOP for applicants not normally admissible. Conditional admission possible for applicants not meeting standard requirements. Act 101 program for in-state applicants not normally admissible. SAT or ACT is required. PSAT is recommended. ACH recommended. Campus visit and interview recommended. Off-campus interviews available with an admissions representative.
**Procedure:** Take SAT or ACT by November of 12th year. Visit college for interview by March 1 of 12th year. Notification of admission on rolling basis. Reply is required by May 1. $100 nonrefundable tuition deposit. $100 nonrefundable room deposit. Freshmen accepted for terms other than fall.
**Special programs:** Admission may be deferred two years. Credit and/or placement may be granted through CLEP general and subject exams. Credit and placement may be granted through challenge exams and military experience. Early decision program. In fall 1993, 31 applied for early decision and 31 were accepted. Deadline for applying for early decision is September 1. Early entrance/early admission program. Concurrent enrollment program.
**Transfer students:** Transfer students accepted for terms other than fall. In fall 1993, 26% of all new students were transfers into all classes. 239 transfer applications were received, 194 were accepted. Application deadline is August 15 for fall; January 10 for spring. Minimum 2.0 GPA recommended. Lowest course grade accepted is "C." Maximum number of transferable credits is 60 semester hours. At least 60 semester hours must be completed at the college to receive degree.
**Admissions contact:** Daniel Conry, M.A., Dean of Admissions. 717 826-5858, 800 955-5777.

**FINANCIAL AID. Available aid:** Pell grants, SEOG, state scholarships and grants, school scholarships and grants, private scholarships and grants, ROTC scholarships, academic merit scholarships, and aid for undergraduate foreign students. Perkins Loans (NDSL), PLUS, Stafford Loans (GSL), state loans, private loans, and SLS. Tuition Plan Inc., Knight Tuition Plans, AMS, Tuition Management Systems, and deferred payment plan.
**Financial aid statistics:** 20% of aid is not need-based. In 1993-94, 76% of all undergraduate applicants received aid; 88% of freshman applicants. Average amounts of aid awarded freshmen: Scholarships and grants, $5,290; loans, $3,010.
**Supporting data/closing dates:** FAFSA: Priority filing date is March 1; accepted on rolling basis. School's own aid application: Priority filing date is March 1; accepted on rolling basis. State aid form: Priority filing date is March 1; deadline is May 1. Income tax forms: Priority filing date is March 1; accepted on rolling basis. Notification of awards on rolling basis.
**Financial aid contact:** Henry Chance, M.S., Director of Financial Aid. 717 826-5668.

**STUDENT EMPLOYMENT.** College Work/Study Program. Institutional employment. 24% of full-time undergraduates work on campus during school year. Students may expect to earn an average of $1,250 during school year. Off-campus part-time employment opportunities rated "good."

**COMPUTER FACILITIES.** 220 IBM/IBM-compatible and Macintosh/Apple microcomputers; 140 are networked. Students may access IBM minicomputer/mainframe sys-

tems, Internet. Residence halls may be equipped with networked microcomputers. Client/LAN operating systems include Apple/Macintosh, LocalTalk/AppleTalk, Novell. Computer languages and software packages include Assembler, C, COBOL, Excel, FORTRAN, Foxpro, Pascal, PL/1, RPG 400, SAS, SPSS, SQL, VASM, Windows. Computer facilities are available to all students.
**Fees:** Computer fee is included in tuition/fees.
**Hours:** 8 AM-11 PM (M-F); 9 AM-6 PM (Sa); 1 PM-midn. (Su); 24 hours in residence halls.

**GRADUATE CAREER DATA.** Graduate school percentages: 1% enter law school. 2% enter medical school. 2% enter graduate business programs. 7% enter graduate arts and sciences programs. Highest graduate school enrollments: Bloomsburg U, Duquesne U, Ithaca Coll, King's Coll, Notre Dame U, SUNY at Binghamton, Temple U, U of Pennsylvania, U of Pittsburgh, Seton Hall Coll, Thomas Jefferson U, Villanova U. 60% of graduates choose careers in business and industry. Companies and businesses that hire graduates: Big Six accounting firms, Blue Cross/Blue Shield, Borg Warner, C-TEC, FDIC, Ingersoll Rand, Litton Industries, Metlife Prudential.

**PROMINENT ALUMNI/AE.** Mary Beth Backof, partner, Price-Waterhouse; The Honorable Joseph J. Farnun, federal judge, State of Delaware; Stanley Benjamin, M.D., surgeon and clinical instructor, Georgetown Medical School.

# Kutztown University of Pennsylvania

**Kutztown, PA 19530** **215 683-4000**

**1994-95 Costs.** Tuition: $3,086 (state residents), $7,720 (out-of-state). Room: $2,000. Board: $1,000. Fees, books, misc. academic expenses (school's estimate): $1,113-$1,190.
**Enrollment.** Undergraduates: 2,594 men, 3,367 women (full-time). Freshman class: 5,095 applicants, 3,033 accepted, 1,304 enrolled. Graduate enrollment: 233 men, 674 women.
**Test score averages/ranges.** Average SAT scores: 450 verbal, 580 math.
**Faculty.** 333 full-time. 50% of faculty holds highest degree in specific field. Student/faculty ratio: 20 to 1.
**Selectivity rating.** More competitive.

**PROFILE.** Kutztown is a public university. It was founded as a teacher training school in 1866, became a state college in 1960, and gained university status in 1983. Programs are offered through the Colleges of Business, Education, Graduate Studies, Liberal Arts and Sciences, and Visual and Performing Arts. Its 325-acre campus is located in Kutztown, midway between Reading and Allentown.

**Accreditation:** MSACS. Professionally accredited by the National Council for Accreditation of Teacher Education, the National League for Nursing.
**Religious orientation:** Kutztown University of Pennsylvania is nonsectarian; no religious requirements.
**Library:** Collections totaling over 409,432 volumes, 2,015 periodical subscriptions, and 1,138,515 microform items.
**Special facilities/museums:** Art gallery, cartography lab, planetarium, artificial intelligence center, seismograph. Day care center.
**Athletic facilities:** Field house, weight room, swimming pool, fitness center, track, athletic fields, team locker rooms, sports medicine center.

**STUDENT BODY. Undergraduate profile:** 86% are state residents. 1% Asian-American, 3% Black, 2% Hispanic, 1% Native American, 93% White. Average age of undergraduates is 20.
**Freshman profile:** 96% of freshmen come from public schools.
**Undergraduate achievement:** 77% of fall 1992 freshmen returned for fall 1993 term.
**Foreign students:** 135 students are from out of the country. 30 countries represented in all.

**PROGRAMS OF STUDY. Degrees:** B.A., B.F.A., B.S., B.S.Bus.Admin., B.S.Ed., B.S.Nurs.
**Majors:** Accounting, American Studies, Anthropology, Art Education, Biology, Business Economics, Chemistry, Communication Design, Computer/Information Sciences, Crafts, Criminal Justice, Early Childhood Education, Economics, Elementary Education, English, Environmental Science, Finance, French, General Business, General Studies, Geography, Geology, German, History, International Business, Library Science, Management, Marine Science, Marketing, Mathematics, Medical Technology, Music, Nursing, Philosophy, Physics, Physics/Engineering, Political Science, Psychology, Public Administration, Related Arts, Russian, Russian/Slavic Studies, Secondary Education, Social Welfare, Sociology, Spanish, Special Education, Speech, Speech Communication, Studio Art, Telecommunications, Theatre.
**Distribution of degrees:** The majors with the highest enrollment are education, telecommunications, and communication design.
**Requirements:** General education requirement.
**Academic regulations:** Freshmen must maintain minimum 1.65 GPA; sophomores, 1.8 GPA; juniors, 1.9 GPA; seniors, 2.0 GPA.
**Special:** Self-designed majors. Double majors. Independent study. Accelerated study. Pass/fail grading option. Internships. Graduate school at which undergraduates may take graduate-level courses. 3-2 engineering program with Pennsylvania State U. Member of Marine Science Consortium and Pennsylvania State System of Higher Education. Teacher certification in early childhood, elementary, secondary, and special education. Certification in specific subject areas. Exchange programs abroad in Costa Rica, Denmark, England, Germany, Puerto Rico, Russia, Scotland, and Spain.
**Honors:** Honors program. Honor societies.
**Academic Assistance:** Remedial reading, math, and study skills.

**STUDENT LIFE. Housing:** Coed, women's, and men's dorms. 50% of students live in college housing.
**Social atmosphere:** According to the editor of the student newspaper, "Kutztown is a school characterized by a very strong, culturally diverse campus with a moderate size of 8,000 students, with social and cultural events to suit almost everyone's taste." Favorite gathering spots for students are Backstreets (a dance club), Dr. Robert's Pub, Snuzzle's Pub, the Strand movie theatre, and the North Student Center Lounge. The most influential groups on campus are the Student Government and the student newspaper staff. Popular yearly happenings are the Beer Fest, the fall Homecoming, Earth Day, and Hunger Day.
**Services and counseling/handicapped student services:** Placement services. Health service. Women's center. Day care. Counseling services for minority, veteran, and older students. Birth control, personal, and psychological counseling. Career and academic guidance services. Physically disabled student services. Learning disabled services. Tape recorders. Reader services for the blind.
**Campus organizations:** Undergraduate student government. Student newspaper (Keystone, published once/week). Literary magazine. Yearbook. Radio and TV stations. Orchestra, concert, marching, and jazz bands, choral groups, dance group, drama club, Keystonnaires, Readers Theatre, debate club, computer club, outing club, nontraditional student group, Women's Action Group, social service group, 90 organizations in all. Six fraternities, no chapter houses; four sororities, no chapter houses. 4% of men join a fraternity. 4% of women join a sorority.
**Religious organizations:** Intervarsity Christian Fellowship, Newman Association.
**Minority/foreign student organizations:** Black Student Union, Latino Student Association, Minority Achievement Coalition, NAACP. International Student Organization.

**ATHLETICS. Physical education requirements:** Two semesters of physical education required.
**Intercollegiate competition:** 10% of students participate. Baseball (M), basketball (M,W), cheerleading (M,W), cross-country (M,W), field hockey (W), football (M), soccer (M,W), softball (W), swimming (M,W), tennis (M,W), track (indoor) (M,W), track (outdoor) (M,W), track and field (indoor) (M,W), track and field (outdoor) (M,W), volleyball (W), wrestling (M). Member of ECAC, NCAA Division II, Pennsylvania State Athletic Conference.
**Intramural and club sports:** 50% of students participate. Intramural aerobics, basketball, flag football, golf, softball, tennis, volleyball. Men's club equestrian sports, ice hockey, karate, lacrosse, rugby, volleyball, water polo. Women's club equestrian sports, karate, lacrosse, volleyball, water polo.

**ADMISSIONS. Academic basis for candidate selection** (in order of priority): Secondary school record, class rank, standardized test scores, school's recommendation, essay.
**Nonacademic basis for candidate selection:** Character and personality, extracurricular participation, and particular talent or ability are emphasized. Alumni/ae relationship is considered.
**Requirements:** Graduation from secondary school is required; GED is accepted. 16 units and the following program of study are recommended: 4 units of English, 3 units of math, 2 units of science, 2 units of foreign language, 2 units of social studies, 2 units of history, 1 unit of electives. Rank in top half of secondary school class and minimum grade average of "B" required. Admission to a special curriculum may require additional proof of ability. Campus visit and interview recommended. No off-campus interviews.
**Procedure:** Take SAT or ACT by fall of 12th year. Suggest filing application by January 1; no deadline. Notification of admission on rolling basis. Reply is required by May 1. $100 nonrefundable tuition deposit. $125 room deposit, refundable until May 1. Freshmen accepted for terms other than fall.
**Special programs:** Credit and/or placement may be granted through CEEB Advanced Placement exams for scores of 3 or higher. Credit and/or placement may be granted through CLEP general and subject exams. Credit and placement may be granted through challenge exams. Early entrance/early admission program. Concurrent enrollment program.
**Transfer students:** Transfer students accepted for terms other than fall. Application deadline is rolling for fall; rolling for spring. Minimum 2.0 GPA required. Lowest course grade accepted is "C." Maximum number of transferable credits is 64 semester hours. At least 33 semester hours must be completed at the university to receive degree.
**Admissions contact:** George E. McKinley, M.Mus., Director of Admissions. 215 683-4060.

**FINANCIAL AID. Available aid:** Pell grants, SEOG, state grants, school scholarships, ROTC scholarships, and athletic scholarships. Perkins Loans (NDSL), PLUS, Stafford Loans (GSL), state loans, and SLS. AMS and deferred payment plan.
**Financial aid statistics:** 40% of aid is not need-based. Average amounts of aid awarded freshmen: Scholarships and grants, $575; loans, $2,625.
**Supporting data/closing dates:** FAFSA: Priority filing date is March 15. State aid form: Priority filing date is March 15. Notification of awards begins April.

**STUDENT EMPLOYMENT.** College Work/Study Program. Institutional employment. 10% of full-time undergraduates work on campus during school year. Students may expect to earn an average of $1,600 during school year. Off-campus part-time employment opportunities rated "excellent."

**COMPUTER FACILITIES.** 652 IBM/IBM-compatible and Macintosh/Apple microcomputers; 325 are networked. Students may access UNISYS minicomputer/mainframe systems. Client/LAN operating systems include UNIX/XENIX/AIX, Novell. Computer languages and software packages include over 1,300 computer languages and software programs. Computer facilities are available to all students.
**Fees:** None.

# Lafayette College

**Easton, PA 18042-1770** **215 250-5000**

**1994-95 Costs.** Tuition: $18,730. Room: $3,000. Board: $2,740. Fees, books, misc. academic expenses (school's estimate): $675.
**Enrollment.** Undergraduates: 1,116 men, 902 women (full-time). Freshman class: 4,010 applicants, 2,387 accepted, 572 enrolled.
**Test score averages/ranges.** Range of SAT scores of middle 50%: 470-570 verbal, 560-680 math.
**Faculty.** 175 full-time; 53 part-time. 96% of faculty holds doctoral degree. Student/faculty ratio: 11 to 1.
**Selectivity rating.** Highly competitive.

**PROFILE.** Lafayette is a church-affiliated, liberal arts college. Founded as a men's college in 1826, it adopted coeducation in 1970. Its 110-acre campus is located in Easton, 60 miles north of Philadelphia.

**Accreditation:** MSACS. Professionally accredited by the Accreditation Board for Engineering and Technology.
**Religious orientation:** Lafayette College is affiliated with the United Presbyterian Church; no religious requirements.
**Library:** Collections totaling over 438,911 volumes, 1,807 periodical subscriptions, and 105,949 microform items.
**Special facilities/museums:** Art and geological museums, center for the arts, engineering labs, INSTRON materials testing machine, electron microscopes, transform nuclear magnetic resonance spectrometer, computerized gas chromatograph/mass spectrometer.
**Athletic facilities:** Gymnasiums, swimming pools, field house, athletic fields.

**STUDENT BODY. Undergraduate profile:** 25% are state residents; 7% are transfers. 2% Asian-American, 4% Black, 3% Hispanic, 1% Native American, 82% White, 8% Other. Average age of undergraduates is 20.
**Freshman profile:** 100% of accepted applicants took SAT. 64% of freshmen come from public schools.
**Undergraduate achievement:** 94% of fall 1992 freshmen returned for fall 1993 term. 81% of entering class graduated. 25% of students who completed a degree program immediately went on to graduate study.
**Foreign students:** 140 students are from out of the country. Countries represented include Brazil, India, Japan, Pakistan, Spain, and Sri Lanka; 40 in all.

**PROGRAMS OF STUDY. Degrees:** B.A., B.S.
**Majors:** American Civilization, Anthropology/Sociology, Art, Biochemistry, Biology, Chemical Engineering, Chemistry, Civil Engineering, Computer Science, Economics/Business, Electrical Engineering, Engineering, English, Environmental Science, French, Geology, German, Government/Law, History, International Affairs, Mathematics, Mathematics/Economics, Mechanical Engineering, Music History/Theory, Philosophy, Physics, Psychology, Religion, Russian, Spanish.
**Distribution of degrees:** The majors with the highest enrollment are economics/business, biology, and English; music and religion have the lowest.
**Requirements:** General education requirement.
**Academic regulations:** Minimum 1.8 GPA must be maintained.
**Special:** Minors offered in many majors and in black studies, classical languages/civilization, East Asian studies, ethics, health care/society, Jewish studies, technology studies, and women's studies. B.A. option in engineering. Course clusters for special areas of study. Self-designed majors. Double majors. Dual degrees. Independent study. Accelerated study. Pass/fail grading option. Internships. Preprofessional programs in law, medicine, and architecture. Five-year B.A./B.S. or dual B.S. degree programs. Member of Lehigh Valley Association of Independent Colleges; cross-registration possible. Washington Semester and Sea Semester. Exchange program with American U. Study abroad in Austria, Belgium, England, France, Germany, Ireland, Israel, Italy, Russia, Scotland, and Switzerland. ROTC at Lehigh U.
**Honors:** Phi Beta Kappa. Honors program. Honor societies.
**Academic Assistance:** Remedial study skills. Nonremedial tutoring.

**STUDENT LIFE. Housing:** All students must live on campus unless special permission is granted. Coed, women's, and men's dorms. Sorority and fraternity housing. School-owned/operated apartments. Off-campus privately-owned housing. 98% of students live in college housing.
**Social atmosphere:** Students gather at the College Hill Tavern, the Farinon College Center, and fraternities. Greeks and the Lafayette Activities Forum influence campus life. The most popular events on campus are All-college Day and the Lafayette vs. Lehigh football game. According to the editor of the student newspaper, students strike a "perfect balance" between work and play. "Lafayette students are motivated in both studies and social life, but our work is finished before we go out. We have many social and cultural events every weekend; the Lafayette Activities Forum, fraternities, and the Cultural Center always have busy schedules."
**Services and counseling/handicapped student services:** Placement services. Health service. Women's center. Birth control, personal, and psychological counseling. Career and academic guidance services. Religious counseling. Physically disabled student services. Learning disabled services. Notetaking services. Tape recorders. Reader services for the blind.
**Campus organizations:** Undergraduate student government. Student newspaper (Lafayette, published once/week). Literary magazine. Yearbook. Radio station. Jazz club, chorus, chorale, orchestra, concert band, drama group, College Democrats, College Republicans, Big Brothers/Big Sisters, Circle K, Hands Together, environmental group, outing club, academic and special-interest groups, 100 organizations in all. 12 fraternities, all with chapter houses; six sororities, all with chapter houses. 50% of men join a fraternity. 70% of women join a sorority.
**Religious organizations:** Christian Fellowship, Hillel Society, Newman Society, Muslim Student Association.
**Minority/foreign student organizations:** Association of Black Collegians, Brothers of Lafayette, Black Women's Support Group. International Student Association, East Asian Club, SALSA, ASIA, Latin American Club.

**ATHLETICS. Physical education requirements:** None.
**Intercollegiate competition:** 30% of students participate. Baseball (M), basketball (M,W), cheerleading (M,W), cross-country (M,W), diving (M,W), fencing (M,W), field hockey (W), football (M), golf (M), lacrosse (M,W), soccer (M,W), softball (W), swimming (M,W), tennis (M,W), track (indoor) (M,W), track (outdoor) (M,W), track and field (indoor) (M,W), track and field (outdoor) (M,W), volleyball (W). Member of ECAC, NCAA Division I, NCAA Division I-AA for football, Patriot League.
**Intramural and club sports:** 60% of students participate. Intramural badminton, basketball, billiards, bowling, cross-country, flag football, racquetball, soccer, softball, squash, swimming, table tennis, tennis, track, ultimate frisbee, volleyball, wrestling. Men's club Alpine skiing, bowling, cheerleading, crew, cricket, martial arts, racquetball, rugby, sailing, squash, ultimate frisbee, volleyball, weight lifting, wrestling. Women's club bowling, cheerleading, crew, rugby.

**ADMISSIONS. Academic basis for candidate selection** (in order of priority): Secondary school record, school's recommendation, standardized test scores, class rank, essay.
**Nonacademic basis for candidate selection:** Character and personality and extracurricular participation are important. Particular talent or ability, geographical distribution, and alumni/ae relationship are considered.
**Requirements:** Graduation from secondary school is required; GED is not accepted. 13 units and the following program of study are required: 4 units of English, 3 units of math, 2 units of lab science, 2 units of foreign language. SAT is required; ACT may be substituted. ACH recommended. Campus visit and interview recommended. Off-campus interviews available with admissions and alumni representatives.
**Procedure:** Take SAT or ACT by January of 12th year. Take ACH by January of 12th year. Visit college for interview by January 31 of 12th year. Suggest filing application by January 15; no deadline. Notification of admission by April 1. Reply is required by May 1. $300 nonrefundable tuition deposit. $100 room deposit, refundable until July 15. Freshmen accepted for fall term only.
**Special programs:** Admission may be deferred one year. Credit and/or placement may be granted through CEEB Advanced Placement exams for scores of 3 or higher. Early decision program. In fall 1993, 213 applied for early decision and 100 were accepted. Deadline for applying for early decision is January 15 through February 15. Early entrance/early admission program. Concurrent enrollment program.
**Transfer students:** Transfer students accepted for terms other than fall. In fall 1993, 7% of all new students were transfers into all classes. 128 transfer applications were received, 40 were accepted. Application deadline is June 1 for fall; December 1 for spring. Minimum 3.0 GPA recommended. Lowest course grade accepted is "C." Maximum number of transferable credits is 60 semester hours. At least 60 semester hours must be completed at the college to receive degree.
**Admissions contact:** G. Gary Ripple, M.Ed., Ph.D., Director of Admissions. 215 250-5100.

**FINANCIAL AID. Available aid:** Pell grants, SEOG, state scholarships and grants, school scholarships and grants, private scholarships and grants, ROTC scholarships, academic merit scholarships, athletic scholarships, and aid for undergraduate foreign students. Perkins Loans (NDSL), PLUS, Stafford Loans (GSL), state loans, school loans, private loans, and SLS. Tuition Plan Inc., Knight Tuition Plans, AMS, deferred payment plan, and guaranteed tuition.
**Financial aid statistics:** 1% of aid is not need-based. In 1993-94, 95% of all undergraduate applicants received aid; 93% of freshman applicants. Average amounts of aid awarded freshmen: Scholarships and grants, $11,953; loans, $3,152.
**Supporting data/closing dates:** FAFSA/FAF: Priority filing date is February 15. School's own aid application: Priority filing date is February 15. State aid form: Accepted on rolling basis. Income tax forms: Priority filing date is May 1. Notification of awards begins March 18.
**Financial aid contact:** Barry W. McCarty, M.A., Director of Student Financial Aid. 215 250-5055.

**STUDENT EMPLOYMENT.** College Work/Study Program. Institutional employment. 54% of full-time undergraduates work on campus during school year. Students may expect to earn an average of $850 during school year. Off-campus part-time employment opportunities rated "good."

**COMPUTER FACILITIES.** 250 IBM/IBM-compatible and Macintosh/Apple microcomputers; 190 are networked. Students may access Digital, IBM minicomputer/mainframe systems, BITNET, Internet. Residence halls may be equipped with modems. Client/LAN operating systems include Apple/Macintosh, DOS. Computer languages and software packages include APL, BASIC, C, COBOL, dBASE, FORTRAN, Informix, MINITAB, PageMaker, Paradox, Pascal, Quattro, SAS, SPSS, Windows, WordPerfect; 150 in all. Computer facilities are available to all students.
**Fees:** Computer fee is included in tuition/fees.
**Hours:** 24 hours.

**GRADUATE CAREER DATA.** Graduate school percentages: 7% enter law school. 5% enter medical school. 1% enter dental school. Highest graduate school enrollments: American U, George Washington U, Georgetown U, Medical Coll of Pennsylvania, New York Law Sch, Pennsylvania State U, Villanova U. Companies and businesses that hire graduates: Air Products & Chemicals, Arthur Andersen, General Electric, Merck, Procter & Gamble, Prudential Insurance.

**PROMINENT ALUMNI/AE.** William E. Simon, former secretary, U.S. Department of the Treasury; Robert B. Meyner, former governor of New Jersey; Dominique Lapierre, historian and author; Fred M. Kirby II, chairperson of the board, Allegheny Corp.; Robert Smith, U.S. senator; George L. Schaefer, Hollywood producer and director.

# Lancaster Bible College

**Lancaster, PA 17601 717 569-7071**

**1994-95 Costs.** Tuition: $7,360. Room: $1,360. Board: $2,040. Fees, books, misc. academic expenses (school's estimate): $735.
**Enrollment.** Undergraduates: 166 men, 180 women (full-time). Freshman class: 122 applicants, 120 accepted, 91 enrolled.
**Test score averages/ranges.** Average ACT scores: 21 English, 18 math, 20 composite. Range of ACT scores of middle 50%: 17-25 English, 15-21 math.
**Faculty.** 21 full-time; 18 part-time. 36% of faculty holds doctoral degree. Student/faculty ratio: 16 to 1.
**Selectivity rating.** Less competitive.

**PROFILE.** Lancaster Bible, founded in 1933, is a college with religious orientation. Its 36-acre campus is located in Lancaster, 60 miles from Philadelphia.

**Accreditation:** AABC, MSACS.
**Religious orientation:** Lancaster Bible College is a nondenominational Christian school; eight semesters of religion/theology required.
**Library:** Collections totaling over 44,761 volumes, 321 periodical subscriptions, and 1,383 microform items.
**Athletic facilities:** Baseball field, soccer fields, tennis courts, gymnasium.

**STUDENT BODY. Undergraduate profile:** 72% are state residents; 38% are transfers. 2% Asian-American, 3% Black, 1% Hispanic, 1% Native American, 92% White, 1% Other. Average age of undergraduates is 22.
**Freshman profile:** 1% of freshmen who took ACT scored 30 or over on English, 2% scored 30 or over on math; 30% scored 24 or over on English, 9% scored 24 or over on math, 19% scored 24 or over on composite; 62% scored 18 or over on English, 46% scored 18 or over on math, 65% scored 18 or over on composite; 81% scored 12 or over on English, 82% scored 12 or over on math, 83% scored 12 or over on composite; 84% scored 6 or over on English, 84% scored 6 or over on math, 84% scored 6 or over on composite. 79% of accepted applicants took ACT. 66% of freshmen come from public schools.
**Undergraduate achievement:** 62% of fall 1992 freshmen returned for fall 1993 term. 20% of entering class graduated. 50% of students who completed a degree program went on to graduate study within five years.
**Foreign students:** Seven students are from out of the country. Countries represented include Chile, Japan, Kenya, and Vietnam; five in all.

**PROGRAMS OF STUDY. Degrees:** B.S.Bible
**Majors:** Bible.
**Requirements:** General education requirement.
**Academic regulations:** Freshmen must maintain minimum 1.5 GPA; sophomores, 1.75 GPA; juniors, 1.9 GPA; seniors, 2.0 GPA.
**Special:** Professional programs offered in counseling, education, computer ministries, missions, church music, pastoral studies, secretarial studies, and youth ministry. Associate's degrees offered. Independent study. Accelerated study. Internships. Cooperative education programs. Preprofessional programs in theology. Teacher certification in early childhood and elementary education. Study abroad in Israel.
**Academic Assistance:** Remedial study skills.

**ADMISSIONS. Academic basis for candidate selection** (in order of priority): Secondary school record, school's recommendation, class rank, essay, standardized test scores.
**Nonacademic basis for candidate selection:** Character and personality are emphasized. Extracurricular participation is considered.
**Requirements:** Graduation from secondary school is required; GED is accepted. No specific distribution of secondary school units required. Minimum composite ACT score of 17, rank in top half of secondary school class, and minimum 2.0 GPA recommended. ACT is recommended. Campus visit and interview recommended. No off-campus interviews.
**Procedure:** Suggest filing application by May; no deadline. Notification of admission on rolling basis. No set date by which applicants must accept offer. $50 nonrefundable tuition deposit. Freshmen accepted for terms other than fall.
**Special programs:** Admission may be deferred. Credit may be granted through CEEB Advanced Placement for scores of 3 or higher. Credit may be granted through CLEP subject exams, DANTES and challenge exams, and military experience. Early decision program. In fall 1993, five applied for early decision and five were accepted. Early entrance/early admission program. Concurrent enrollment program.
**Transfer students:** Transfer students accepted for terms other than fall. In fall 1993, 38% of all new students were transfers into all classes. 78 transfer applications were received, 72 were accepted. Application deadline is rolling for fall; rolling for spring. Minimum 2.0 GPA recommended. Lowest course grade accepted is "C." Maximum number of transferable credits is 90 semester hours. At least 24 semester hours must be completed at the college to receive degree.
**Admissions contact:** Joanne M. Roper, Director of Admissions. 717 560-8271.

**FINANCIAL AID. Available aid:** Pell grants, SEOG, state scholarships and grants, school scholarships, private scholarships, academic merit scholarships, and aid for undergraduate foreign students. Perkins Loans (NDSL), PLUS, Stafford Loans (GSL), state loans, and SLS. Deferred payment plan.
**Financial aid statistics:** 53% of aid is not need-based. In 1993-94, 88% of all undergraduate applicants received aid; 75% of freshman applicants. Average amounts of aid awarded freshmen: Scholarships and grants, $3,000; loans, $2,625.
**Supporting data/closing dates:** FAFSA. School's own aid application: Accepted on rolling basis. PHEAA: Deadline is May 1. Notification of awards on rolling basis.
**Financial aid contact:** Deb Clark, M.A.C.E., Director of Financial Aid. 717 569-7071.

# LaRoche College

**Pittsburgh, PA 15237 412 367-9300**

**1993-94 Costs.** Tuition: $8,422. Room: $2,726. Board: $1,829. Fees, books, misc. academic expenses (school's estimate): $860.
**Enrollment.** Undergraduates: 258 men, 392 women (full-time). Freshman class: 361 applicants, 349 accepted, 185 enrolled. Graduate enrollment: 71 men, 273 women.
**Test score averages/ranges.** Average SAT scores: 390 verbal, 410 math. Range of SAT scores of middle 50%: 350-490 verbal, 400-500 math.
**Faculty.** 44 full-time; 79 part-time. 70% of faculty holds highest degree in specific field. Student/faculty ratio: 19 to 1.
**Selectivity rating.** Less competitive.

**PROFILE.** LaRoche, founded in 1963, is a private, liberal arts college. Programs are offered through the Divisions of Administration and Management; Graphics, Design, and Communication; Humanities; Natural and Health-Related Sciences; and Social Sciences. Its 160-acre campus is located in a residential area of Pittsburgh.

**Accreditation:** MSACS. Professionally accredited by the Foundation for Interior Design Education Research, the National Association of Schools of Art and Design, the National League for Nursing. Numerous professional accreditations.
**Religious orientation:** LaRoche College is affiliated with the Roman Catholic Church (Sisters of Divine Providence); no religious requirements.
**Library:** Collections totaling over 66,000 volumes, 700 periodical subscriptions and 125 microform items.
**Special facilities/museums:** Art gallery, design complex and studios, learning center, Apple Macintosh computer graphics lab, darkroom and lighting studios, fully-equipped science labs.
**Athletic facilities:** Gymnasium, baseball, soccer, and softball fields, training and weight rooms, racquetball courts, indoor track.

**STUDENT BODY. Undergraduate profile:** 88% are state residents; 40% are transfers. 1% Asian-American, 2% Black, 1% Hispanic, 95% White, 1% Other. Average age of undergraduates is 22.
**Freshman profile:** 2% of freshmen who took SAT scored 600 or over on math; 11% scored 500 or over on verbal, 16% scored 500 or over on math; 37% scored 400 or over on verbal, 55% scored 400 or over on math; 84% scored 300 or over on verbal, 90% scored 300 or over on math. 95% of accepted applicants took SAT; 2% took ACT.
**Undergraduate achievement:** 77% of fall 1992 freshmen returned for fall 1993 term. 35% of entering class graduated. 32% of students who completed a degree program went on to graduate study within five years.
**Foreign students:** 30 students are from out of the country. Countries represented include Bosnia, Croatia, Japan, the Dominican Republic, and the Ukraine.

**PROGRAMS OF STUDY. Degrees:** B.A., B.S., B.S.Nurs.
**Majors:** Accounting, Administration/Management, Biology, Chemistry, Chemistry/Management, Communication, Computer Information Systems, English Language/Literature, English/Writing, Finance, Graphic Arts, Graphic Design, History, Human Services, Interior Design, International Business Management, Medical Technology, Natural Sciences, Nursing, Psychobiology, Psychology, Radiography, Religious Education, Religious Studies, Respiratory Therapy, Science Education, Sociology.
**Distribution of degrees:** The majors with the highest enrollment are administration/management, nursing, and graphic design; English, biology, and chemistry have the lowest.
**Requirements:** General education requirement.
**Academic regulations:** Freshmen must maintain minimum 1.80 GPA; sophomores, juniors, seniors, 2.00 GPA.
**Special:** Minors offered in some majors and in gerontology, humanities, mathematics, and philosophy. Double majors. Independent study. Pass/fail grading option. Internships. Graduate school at which undergraduates may take graduate-level courses. Preprofessional programs in law, medicine, veterinary science, and dentistry. Member of Pittsburgh Council of Higher Education; cross-registration possible. Washington Semester. Teacher certification in secondary education. Certification in specific subject areas. ROTC at U of Pittsburgh. AFROTC at Duquesne U.
**Honors:** Honors program. Honor societies.
**Academic Assistance:** Remedial reading, writing, math, and study skills. Nonremedial tutoring.

**ADMISSIONS. Academic basis for candidate selection** (in order of priority): Secondary school record, class rank, standardized test scores, school's recommendation.
**Nonacademic basis for candidate selection:** Particular talent or ability is important. Character and personality, extracurricular participation, and alumni/ae relationship are considered.
**Requirements:** Graduation from secondary school is required; GED is accepted. 16 units and the following program of study are recommended: 2 units of foreign language, 2 units of history. Minimum combined SAT score of 800, rank in top half of secondary school class, and minimum 2.0 GPA recommended. Portfolio required of design program transfer applicants. R.N. required of nursing program applicants. Act 101 program for in-state applicants not normally admissible. Developmental Pre-Session summer program for applicants not normally admissible. SAT is required; ACT may be substituted. PSAT is recommended. Campus visit and interview recommended. Off-campus interviews available with an admissions representative.
**Procedure:** Take SAT or ACT by November of 12th year. Visit college for interview by March 31 of 12th year. Suggest filing application by April 1; no deadline. Notification of admission on rolling basis. Reply is required by May 1. $100 nonrefundable tuition deposit. $100 nonrefundable room deposit. Freshmen accepted for terms other than fall.

**Special programs:** Admission may be deferred one year. Credit and/or placement may be granted through CEEB Advanced Placement exams for scores of 4 or higher. Credit may be granted through CLEP general and subject exams, challenge exams, and military and life experience. Credit and placement may be granted through ACT PEP and DANTES exams. Early entrance/early admission program.
**Transfer students:** Transfer students accepted for terms other than fall. In fall 1993, 40% of all new students were transfers into all classes. 131 transfer applications were received, 124 were accepted. Application deadline is September 1 for fall; January 1 for spring. Minimum 2.0 GPA recommended. Lowest course grade accepted is "C." Maximum number of transferable credits is 60 semester hours from a two-year school and 90 semester hours from a four-year school. At least 30 semester hours must be completed at the college to receive degree.
**Admissions contact:** Barry Duerr, M.A., Director of Admissions. 412 367-9241.

**FINANCIAL AID. Available aid:** Pell grants, SEOG, state grants, school scholarships and grants, private scholarships, academic merit scholarships, athletic scholarships, and aid for undergraduate foreign students. Perkins Loans (NDSL), PLUS, Stafford Loans (GSL), school loans, private loans, and SLS. Family tuition reduction.
**Financial aid statistics:** In 1993-94, 92% of all undergraduate applicants received aid; 93% of freshman applicants. Average amounts of aid awarded freshmen: Scholarships and grants, $3,700; loans, $2,200.
**Supporting data/closing dates:** FAFSA: Priority filing date is May 1. State aid form: Priority filing date is May 1. PHEAA: Deadline is May 1. Notification of awards on rolling basis.
**Financial aid contact:** Michael Bertonaschi, Director of Financial Aid. 412 367-9300.

# LaSalle University

**Philadelphia, PA 19141-1199 215 951-1000**

**1993-94 Costs.** Tuition: $11,510. Room & board: $5,430. Fees, books, misc. academic expenses (school's estimate): $300.
**Enrollment.** Undergraduates: 1,380 men, 1,375 women (full-time). Freshman class: 2,798 applicants, 1,804 accepted, 660 enrolled. Graduate enrollment: 590 men, 700 women.
**Test score averages/ranges.** Average SAT scores: 490 verbal, 560 math. Range of SAT scores of middle 50%: 450-540 verbal, 480-590 math.
**Faculty.** 220 full-time; 103 part-time. 89% of faculty holds doctoral degree. Student/faculty ratio: 13 to 1.
**Selectivity rating.** Competitive.

**PROFILE.** LaSalle, founded in 1863, is a church-affiliated university. Programs are offered through the Schools of Arts and Sciences and Business Administration. Its 120-acre campus is located in a residential area of Philadelphia. Campus architecture ranges from Gothic to modern design.

**Accreditation:** MSACS. Professionally accredited by the Council on Social Work Education, the National League for Nursing.
**Religious orientation:** LaSalle University is affiliated with the Roman Catholic Church (Christian Brothers); three semesters of religion required.
**Library:** Collections totaling over 345,000 volumes, 1,650 periodical subscriptions, and 19,101 microform items.
**Special facilities/museums:** Art museum, Japanese tea house, language lab, child development center, urban studies center.
**Athletic facilities:** Baseball, football, and soccer fields, swimming pool, outdoor and indoor tracks, basketball and tennis court, gymnasium, weight room, fitness center, stadium.

**STUDENT BODY. Undergraduate profile:** 60% are state residents; 16% are transfers. 4% Asian-American, 5% Black, 3% Hispanic, 87% White, 1% Other. Average age of undergraduates is 20.
**Freshman profile:** 5% of freshmen who took SAT scored 700 or over on verbal, 10% scored 700 or over on math; 15% scored 600 or over on verbal, 28% scored 600 or over on math; 54% scored 500 or over on verbal, 80% scored 500 or over on math; 100% scored 400 or over on verbal, 100% scored 400 or over on math. 99% of accepted applicants took SAT; 1% took ACT. 40% of freshmen come from public schools.
**Undergraduate achievement:** 88% of fall 1992 freshmen returned for fall 1993 term. 80% of entering class graduated. 17% of students who completed a degree program went on to graduate study within one year.
**Foreign students:** 120 students are from out of the country. Countries represented include China, India, Japan, the Philippines, and Venezuela; 25 in all.

**PROGRAMS OF STUDY. Degrees:** B.A., B.S., B.S.Nurs., B.Soc.Work.
**Majors:** Accounting, Art History/Appreciation, Biochemistry, Biology, Chemistry, Classical Languages, Communication Arts, Computer/Information Sciences, Criminal Justice, Economics, Elementary Education, English, Environmental Science, Finance, French, Geology, German, History, International Studies, Italian, Management, Marketing, Mathematics, Military Science, Modern Languages, Music, Nursing, Personnel/Labor Relations, Philosophy, Physics, Political Science/Government, Portuguese, Psychology, Public Administration, Quantitative Analysis, Religion, Russian, Secondary Education, Social Work, Sociology, Spanish, Special Education, Special Options, Writing.
**Distribution of degrees:** The majors with the highest enrollment are nursing and communication arts; physics, mathematics, and philosophy/religion have the lowest.
**Requirements:** General education requirement.
**Academic regulations:** Freshmen must maintain minimum 1.50 GPA; sophomores, 1.75 GPA; juniors, 2.00 GPA; seniors, 2.00 GPA.
**Special:** Minors offered in environmental science, health care administration, information systems, international studies, risk management, urban studies, and women studies. Self-designed majors. Double majors. Dual degrees. Independent study. Accelerated study. Pass/fail grading option. Internships. Cooperative education programs. Graduate school at which undergraduates may take graduate-level courses. Preprofessional programs in law, medicine, veterinary science, pharmacy, dentistry, theology, and optometry. 2-2 and 2-3 allied health programs with Thomas Jefferson U. Exchange program and cross-registration with Chestnut Hill Coll. Teacher certification in elementary, secondary, and special education. Certification in specific subject areas. Exchange programs abroad in Spain (U of Madrid) and Switzerland (U of Fribourg). ROTC and NROTC at U of Pennsylvania. AFROTC at St. Joseph's U.
**Honors:** Honors program. Honor societies.
**Academic Assistance:** Remedial writing. Nonremedial tutoring.

**STUDENT LIFE. Housing:** Students may live on or off campus. Coed dorms. School-owned/operated apartments. 65% of students live in college housing.
**Social atmosphere:** According to the editor of the student newspaper, "LaSalle does not offer a great deal of social options. The immediate campus is fun, but it is not wise to venture into the surrounding neighborhood. Most students drive to center city clubs at night or attend off-campus parties." Influential groups are the Greeks, who throw great parties, and athletes. Students gather at an on-campus nonalcoholic club called Backstage/Intermissions for snacks; off campus, it's Trocadero and Flannery's. Popular events include the Explorers basketball games (Big 5), Spring Fling weekend, Greek Week, and the Charlie Awards, a festival of short films produced by students each semester.
**Services and counseling/handicapped student services:** Placement services. Health service. Day care. Counseling services for minority, veteran, and older students. Personal and psychological counseling. Career and academic guidance services. Religious counseling. Physically disabled student services. Learning disabled services. Tutors.
**Campus organizations:** Undergraduate student government. Student newspaper (Collegian, published once/week). Literary magazine. Yearbook. Radio and TV stations. LaSalle Singers, jazz/pep bands, ROTC band, pep club, chorale, debating, The Masque, Residence Council, Community Service Corps, Homeless Committee, peace and justice group, departmental groups, special-interest groups, 106 organizations in all. Eight fraternities, two chapter houses; six sororities, no chapter houses. 13% of men join a fraternity. 12% of women join a sorority.
**Religious organizations:** Campus Ministry, Hillel.
**Minority/foreign student organizations:** African-American Students League, POWER. Asian Intercultural Association.

**ATHLETICS. Physical education requirements:** None.
**Intercollegiate competition:** Baseball (M), basketball (M,W), cheerleading (M,W), crew (M,W), cross-country (M,W), diving (M,W), field hockey (W), golf (M), soccer (M,W), softball (W), swimming (M,W), tennis (M,W), track (indoor) (M,W), track (outdoor) (M,W), track and field (indoor) (M,W), track and field (outdoor) (M,W), volleyball (W), wrestling (M). Member of ECAC, Metro Atlantic Athletic Conference, NCAA Division I.
**Intramural and club sports:** Intramural basketball, football, road racing, soccer, softball, tennis, volleyball.

**ADMISSIONS. Academic basis for candidate selection** (in order of priority): Secondary school record, class rank, standardized test scores, essay, school's recommendation.
**Nonacademic basis for candidate selection:** Extracurricular participation is important. Character and personality, particular talent or ability, and alumni/ae relationship are considered.
**Requirements:** Graduation from secondary school is required; GED is accepted. 16 units and the following program of study are required: 4 units of English, 3 units of math, 1 unit of lab science, 2 units of foreign language, 1 unit of history, 5 units of academic electives. Rank in top half of secondary school class and minimum "C" average recommended. Open admissions policy for women over age 25 and for veterans. Conditional admission possible for applicants not meeting standard requirements. Act 101 Academic Discovery Program for in-state applicants not normally admissible. SAT is required; ACT may be substituted. ACH recommended. Campus visit and interview recommended. Off-campus interviews available with an admissions representative.
**Procedure:** Take SAT or ACT by fall of 12th year. Take ACH by fall of 12th year. Visit college for interview by fall of 12th year. Notification of admission on rolling basis. Reply is required no later than one month before start of classes. $100 nonrefundable tuition deposit. $100 room deposit, refundable until June 15. Freshmen accepted for terms other than fall.
**Special programs:** Admission may be deferred one year. Credit and/or placement may be granted through CEEB Advanced Placement exams for scores of 3 or higher. Credit may be granted through CLEP general and subject exams. Credit may be granted through DANTES exams and military experience. Credit and placement may be granted through ACT PEP exams. Concurrent enrollment program.
**Transfer students:** Transfer students accepted for terms other than fall. In fall 1993, 16% of all new students were transfers into all classes. 490 transfer applications were received, 330 were accepted. Application deadline is August 15 for fall; December 15 for spring. Minimum 2.5 GPA recommended. Lowest course grade accepted is "C." Maximum number of transferable credits is 70 semester hours. At least 50 semester hours must be completed at the university to receive degree.
**Admissions contact:** Br. Gerald Fitzgerald, F.S.C., M.B.A., Director of Admissions. 215 951-1500.

**FINANCIAL AID. Available aid:** Pell grants, SEOG, state grants, school scholarships and grants, private scholarships and grants, ROTC scholarships, academic merit scholarships, and athletic scholarships. Perkins Loans (NDSL), PLUS, Stafford Loans (GSL), and SLS. Knight Tuition Plans, AMS, and deferred payment plan.
**Financial aid statistics:** 42% of aid is not need-based. In 1993-94, 90% of all undergraduate applicants received aid; 77% of freshman applicants. Average amounts of aid awarded freshmen: Scholarships and grants, $5,200; loans, $2,570.
**Supporting data/closing dates:** FAFSA/FAF: Deadline is February 15. State aid form: Deadline is February 15. Income tax forms: Deadline is February 15. Notification of awards begins April 1.
**Financial aid contact:** Wendy McLaughlin, M.A., Director of Financial Aid. 215 951-1070.

**STUDENT EMPLOYMENT.** College Work/Study Program. Institutional employment. 25% of full-time undergraduates work on campus during school year. Students may expect to earn an average of $2,000 during school year. Freshmen are discouraged from working during their first term. Off-campus part-time employment opportunities rated "excellent."

**COMPUTER FACILITIES.** 220 IBM/IBM-compatible microcomputers; 110 are networked. Students may access Hewlett-Packard, IBM, Prime minicomputer/mainframe systems. Residence halls may be equipped with modems. Computer languages and software packages include dBASE, Lotus 1-2-3, Microsoft Word; 10 in all. Computer facilities are available to all students.
**Fees:** Computer fee is included in tuition/fees.
**Hours:** 8 AM-11 PM (M-F); 9 AM-7 PM (Sa); noon-7 PM (Su).

**GRADUATE CAREER DATA.** Graduate school percentages: 4% enter law school. 3% enter medical school. 2% enter dental school. 4% enter graduate business programs. 6% enter graduate arts and sciences programs. Highest graduate school enrollments: Georgetown U, U of Notre Dame, U of Pennsylvania. 55% of graduates choose careers in business and industry. Companies and businesses that hire graduates: Big Six accounting firms, IBM.

**PROMINENT ALUMNI/AE.** Charles Fuller, author of screenplay for *A Soldier's Story*; Nicholas Giordano, president, Philadelphia Stock Exchange; Dennis Cunningham, drama critic, CBS; Gen. William Burns, chief of staff, U.S. Army; Joseph Luecke, CEO, Kemper Insurance; Peter Boyle, actor; John Potts, chief of staff, Massachusetts General Hospital.

## Lebanon Valley College

**Annville, PA 17003** **717 867-6100**

**1994-95 Costs.** Tuition: $13,850. Room & board: $4,755. Fees, books, misc. academic expenses (school's estimate): $795.
**Enrollment.** Undergraduates: 498 men, 467 women (full-time). Freshman class: 1,548 applicants, 1,169 accepted, 372 enrolled. Graduate enrollment: 138 men, 75 women.
**Test score averages/ranges.** Average SAT scores: 467 verbal, 521 math.
**Faculty.** 66 full-time; 23 part-time. 80% of faculty holds doctoral degree. Student/faculty ratio: 14 to 1.
**Selectivity rating.** Less competitive.

**PROFILE.** Lebanon Valley, founded in 1866, is a church-affiliated, liberal arts college. Its 200-acre campus is located in Annville, 85 miles from Philadelphia.

**Accreditation:** MSACS. Professionally accredited by the National Association of Schools of Music.
**Religious orientation:** Lebanon Valley College is affiliated with the United Methodist Church; two semesters of religion required.
**Library:** Collections totaling over 131,040 volumes, 730 periodical subscriptions and 579 microform items.
**Special facilities/museums:** Electric pianos, sound recording studio, electron microscope, scanning electron microscope, Fourier transform infrared spectrometer, atomic absorption spectrophotometer, nuclear magnetic resonance spectrometer.
**Athletic facilities:** Football stadium, gymnasium, sports arena, field house, swimming pool, basketball, racquetball, squash, tennis, volleyball, and walleyball courts, sauna, weight and wrestling rooms, tracks, baseball, field hockey, and soccer fields.

**STUDENT BODY. Undergraduate profile:** 79% are state residents; 13% are transfers. 1% Asian-American, 1% Black, 1% Hispanic, 94% White, 3% Other. Average age of undergraduates is 18.
**Freshman profile:** 4% of freshmen who took SAT scored 700 or over on math; 7% scored 600 or over on verbal, 19% scored 600 or over on math; 35% scored 500 or over on verbal, 58% scored 500 or over on math; 77% scored 400 or over on verbal, 89% scored 400 or over on math; 100% scored 300 or over on verbal, 100% scored 300 or over on math. Majority of accepted applicants took SAT. 87% of freshmen come from public schools.
**Undergraduate achievement:** 80% of fall 1992 freshmen returned for fall 1993 term. 59% of entering class graduated. 15% of students who completed a degree program immediately went on to graduate study.
**Foreign students:** 21 students are from out of the country. Countries represented include India, Japan, Korea, Malaysia, Nepal, and Sierra Leone; 12 in all.

**PROGRAMS OF STUDY. Degrees:** B.A., B.S., B.S.Chem., B.S.Med.Tech.
**Majors:** Accounting, Actuarial Sciences, Administration for Health Care Personnel, Allied Health, American Studies, Applied Computer Science, Biochemistry, Biology, Chemistry, Computer Science, Economics, Elementary Education, Engineering, English, Foreign Languages, Forestry/Environmental Studies, French, General Studies, German, History, Hotel Management, Individualized Majors, International Business Management, Management, Mathematics, Medical Technology, Music, Music Education, Music Performance, Philosophy, Physics, Political Science, Psychobiology, Psychology, Religion, Sociology, Sound Recording Technology, Spanish.
**Distribution of degrees:** The majors with the highest enrollment are management, elementary education, and psychology and biology; American studies, French, and religion/philosophy have the lowest.
**Requirements:** General education requirement.
**Academic regulations:** Freshmen must maintain minimum 1.6 GPA; sophomores, 1.7 GPA; juniors, 1.9 GPA; seniors, 2.0 GPA.
**Special:** Minors offered in all majors and in art. Courses offered in computer programming, geography, Greek, and Latin. College participates in Presidential Leadership Program developed for secondary school students, college students, middle management, and chief executive officers. Associate's degrees offered. Self-designed majors. Double majors. Dual degrees. Independent study. Accelerated study. Pass/fail grading option. Internships. Cooperative education programs. Preprofessional programs in law, medicine, veterinary science, pharmacy, dentistry, theology, and optometry. 2-2 programs in cytotechnology, medical technology, nursing, occupational therapy, radiologic technology, and diagnostic technology with Thomas Jefferson U. 3-1 medical technology program. 3-2 forestry and environmental studies program with Duke U. 3-2 engineering programs with Case Western Reserve U, U of Pennsylvania, and Widener U. 2-3 physical therapy program with Thomas Jefferson U. Washington Semester. Teacher certification in elementary and secondary education. Certification in specific subject areas. Study abroad in over 45 countries. ROTC.
**Honors:** Honors program.
**Academic Assistance:** Remedial study skills. Nonremedial tutoring.

**ADMISSIONS. Academic basis for candidate selection** (in order of priority): Secondary school record, class rank, standardized test scores, school's recommendation.
**Nonacademic basis for candidate selection:** Particular talent or ability is emphasized. Character and personality are important. Extracurricular participation and alumni/ae relationship are considered.
**Requirements:** Graduation from secondary school is required; GED is accepted. 16 units and the following program of study are required: 4 units of English, 3 units of math, 2 units of lab science, 2 units of foreign language, 2 units of social studies, 1 unit of history, 2 units of electives. Minimum combined SAT score of 950, rank in top two-fifths of secondary school class, and minimum 2.7 GPA recommended. Audition required of music program applicants. Conditional admission possible for applicants not meeting standard requirements. SAT is required; ACT may be substituted. Campus visit and interview recommended. Off-campus interviews available with an admissions representative.
**Procedure:** Take SAT or ACT by January of 12th year. Visit college for interview by March 1 of 12th year. Notification of admission on rolling basis. Reply is required by May 1. $200 nonrefundable tuition deposit. Freshmen accepted for terms other than fall.
**Special programs:** Admission may be deferred one year. Credit and/or placement may be granted through CEEB Advanced Placement exams for scores of 3 or higher. Credit and/or placement may be granted through CLEP general and subject exams. Credit and placement may be granted through military and life experience. Early entrance/early admission program. Concurrent enrollment program.
**Transfer students:** Transfer students accepted for terms other than fall. In fall 1993, 13% of all new students were transfers into all classes. 125 transfer applications were received, 98 were accepted. Application deadline is rolling for fall; rolling for spring. Minimum 2.0 GPA required. Lowest course grade accepted is "C." Maximum number of transferable credits is 60 semester hours from a two-year school and 90 semester hours from a four-year school. At least 30 semester hours must be completed at the college to receive degree.
**Admissions contact:** William J. Brown, Jr., M.B.A., Dean of Admission and Financial Aid. 800 445-6181.

**FINANCIAL AID. Available aid:** Pell grants, SEOG, state scholarships and grants, school scholarships and grants, private scholarships and grants, and ROTC scholarships. Perkins Loans (NDSL), PLUS, Stafford Loans (GSL), state loans, school loans, and private loans. AMS and deferred payment plan. Institutional Payment Plan.
**Financial aid statistics:** 29% of aid is not need-based. In 1993-94, 98% of all undergraduate applicants received aid; 97% of freshman applicants. Average amounts of aid awarded freshmen: Scholarships and grants, $5,679; loans, $3,100.
**Supporting data/closing dates:** School's own aid application: Accepted on rolling basis. State aid form: Priority filing date is March; accepted on rolling basis. Income tax forms: Accepted on rolling basis. Notification of awards on rolling basis.

## Lehigh University

**Bethlehem, PA 18015-3035** **215 758-3000**

**1993-94 Costs.** Tuition: $17,750. Room & board: $5,500. Fees, books, misc. academic expenses (school's estimate): $600. (Required fees for engineering students: $250.)
**Enrollment.** Undergraduates: 2,748 men, 1,548 women (full-time). Freshman class: 6,397 applicants, 4,424 accepted, 1,095 enrolled. Graduate enrollment: 1,201 men, 812 women.
**Test score averages/ranges.** Range of SAT scores of middle 50%: 480-580 verbal, 590-690 math.
**Faculty.** 413 full-time; 90 part-time. 98% of faculty holds highest degree in specific field. Student/faculty ratio: 12 to 1.
**Selectivity rating.** Highly competitive.

**PROFILE.** Lehigh, founded in 1865, is a private university. Programs are offered through the College of Arts and Science, Business and Economics, Education, and Engineering and Physical Sciences and the Graduate School. Its 1,600-acre campus is located in Bethlehem, 60 miles from Philadelphia.

**Accreditation:** MSACS. Professionally accredited by the Accreditation Board for Engineering and Technology, the American Assembly of Collegiate Schools of Business, the National Association of Schools of Theatre, the National Council for Accreditation of Teacher Education.
**Religious orientation:** Lehigh University is nonsectarian; no religious requirements.
**Library:** Collections totaling over 1,063,462 volumes, and 10,110 microform items.
**Special facilities/museums:** Marine lab (Stone Harbor, N.J.), electron optical labs, electron microscope, civil engineering lab, particle accelerator.
**Athletic facilities:** Gymnasium, field house, swimming pools, basketball, squash, tennis, and volleyball courts, weight room, tracks, baseball, field hockey, football, lacrosse, soccer, and softball fields, wrestling room, fitness center, cross-country course.

**STUDENT BODY. Undergraduate profile:** 32% are state residents; 2% are transfers. 5% Asian-American, 3% Black, 2% Hispanic, .1% Native American, 87% White, 2.9% Other. Average age of undergraduates is 20.
**Freshman profile:** 1% of freshmen who took SAT scored 700 or over on verbal, 18% scored 700 or over on math; 15% scored 600 or over on verbal, 67% scored 600 or over on math; 62% scored 500 or over on verbal, 96% scored 500 or over on math; 94% scored 400 or over on verbal, 100% scored 400 or over on math; 100% scored 300 or over on verbal. Majority of accepted applicants took SAT. 70% of freshmen come from public schools.
**Undergraduate achievement:** 92% of fall 1992 freshmen returned for fall 1993 term. 74% of entering class graduated. 23% of students who completed a degree program immediately went on to graduate study.
**Foreign students:** 133 students are from out of the country. Countries represented include Canada, Japan, Korea, Malaysia, Thailand, and Venezuela; 67 in all.

**PROGRAMS OF STUDY. Degrees:** B.A., B.S.

**Majors:** Accounting, African American Studies, American Studies, Anthropology, Applied Science, Architecture, Art, Behavioral and Evolutionary Bioscience, Behavioral Neuroscience, Biochemistry, Biology, Chemical Engineering, Chemistry, Civil Engineering, Classical Civilization, Classics, Cognitive Sciences, Computer Engineering, Computer Science, East Asian Studies, Economics, Electrical Engineering, Engineering Mechanics, Engineering Physics, English, Environment and Society, Environmental Science, Environmental Science/Resource Management, Finance, French, Fundamental Sciences, Geological Sciences, Geology, Geophysics, German, Government, History, Industrial Engineering, International Careers, International Relations, Journalism, Journalism/Science Writing, Management, Marketing, Materials Science/Engineering, Mathematics, Mechanical Engineering, Molecular Biology, Music, Natural Science, Philosophy, Physics, Pre-Dental Science, Pre-Medical Science, Psychology, Religious Studies, Russian, Science/Technology/Society, Social Relations, Sociology/Social Psychology, Spanish, Statistics, Theatre, Urban Studies.

**Distribution of degrees:** The majors with the highest enrollment are accounting, finance, and civil engineering; classics, music, and cognitive science have the lowest.

**Requirements:** General education requirement.

**Academic regulations:** Freshmen must maintain minimum 1.7 GPA; sophomores, 1.8 GPA; juniors, 2.0 GPA; seniors, 2.0 GPA.

**Special:** Minors offered in most majors and in education, interpersonal behavior, Jewish studies, Latin American studies, law/legal institutions, Russian studies, and women's studies. Investment lab for students in College of Business and Economics. Self-designed majors. Double majors. Dual degrees. Independent study. Accelerated study. Pass/fail grading option. Internships. Cooperative education programs. Graduate school at which undergraduates may take graduate-level courses. Preprofessional programs in medicine and dentistry. 3-2 engineering/business and engineering/liberal arts programs. Five-year teacher-preparation program. Six-year B.A./M.D. program with Medical Coll of Pennsylvania. Seven-year B.A./D.D.S. program with U of Pennsylvania Dental Sch. Member of Lehigh Valley Association of Independent Colleges; cross-registration possible. Member of Ben Franklin Partnership Consortium and Advanced Technology Center. Washington Semester. Philadelphia Urban Semester. Teacher certification in elementary, secondary, and special education. Certification in specific subject areas. Exchange programs abroad in England (London Scl of Economics and Political Science, University Coll of London, U of Kent, U of Manchester, U of York), France (Ecole Superieure, U Paul Valery), Scotland (U of Edinburgh), and the former Soviet Republics. Study abroad also in Australia, Austria, Belgium, Chile, China, Germany, Greece, Hong Kong, Ireland, Israel, Italy, Japan, Korea, Singapore, Spain, and Taiwan. ROTC and AFROTC.

**Honors:** Phi Beta Kappa. Honors program. Honor societies.

**Academic Assistance:** Remedial reading, writing, math, and study skills. Nonremedial tutoring.

**STUDENT LIFE. Housing:** Students may live on or off campus. Coed dorms. Sorority and fraternity housing. School-owned/operated apartments. On-campus married-student housing. 75% of students live in college housing.

**Social atmosphere:** The student newspaper reports that social and cultural life at Lehigh "traditionally centers around Greeks, but many more interests are being accommodated of late, with new clubs and events." Popular events on campus include the Lehigh-Lafayette Weekend, Greek Week, and football, basketball, and wrestling matches. Favorite off-campus gathering spots include the Tally Ho, Uncle Manny's, Bloomer's, Leon's, and the Funhouse.

**Services and counseling/handicapped student services:** Placement services. Health service. Women's center. Day care. Wellness Center. Alcohol and Drug Office. Counseling services for minority students. Birth control, personal, and psychological counseling. Career and academic guidance services. Religious counseling. Physically disabled student services. Learning disabled services. Notetaking services. Tape recorders. Tutors. Reader services for the blind.

**Campus organizations:** Undergraduate student government. Student newspaper (Brown & White, published twice/week). Literary magazine. Yearbook. Radio station. Choir, gospel choir, choral union, pep, marching, and concert bands, jazz ensemble, Dancin', College Republicans, College Democrats, special-interest groups, 165 organizations in all. 28 fraternities, all with chapter houses; eight sororities, all with chapter houses. 51% of men join a fraternity. 47% of women join a sorority.

**Religious organizations:** Christian Fellowship, Hillel, Newman Council, Navigators, Campus Ministry, Fellowship of Christian Athletes, Mustard Seed Fellowship.

**Minority/foreign student organizations:** Black Student Union, Society of Black Engineers, SALSA, Society of Ebony Men. International Club, Asian, Chinese, French, Indian, Korean, Russian, and Spanish clubs.

**ATHLETICS. Physical education requirements:** None.

**Intercollegiate competition:** 25% of students participate. Baseball (M), basketball (M,W), cheerleading (M,W), cross-country (M,W), diving (M,W), field hockey (W), football (M), golf (M), lacrosse (M,W), soccer (M,W), softball (W), swimming (M,W), tennis (M,W), track (indoor) (M,W), track (outdoor) (M,W), track and field (indoor) (M,W), track and field (outdoor) (M,W), volleyball (W), wrestling (M). Member of Eastern Intercollegiate Wrestling Association, NCAA Division I, NCAA Division I-AA for football, Patriot League.

**Intramural and club sports:** 83% of students participate. Intramural archery, baseball, basketball, cross-country, floor hockey, football, golf, Nordic skiing, soccer, softball, swimming, table tennis, tennis, track, wrestling. Men's club boxing, crew, ice hockey, Nordic skiing, rugby, volleyball. Women's club crew, golf, Nordic skiing.

**ADMISSIONS. Academic basis for candidate selection** (in order of priority): Secondary school record, class rank, standardized test scores, school's recommendation, essay.

**Nonacademic basis for candidate selection:** Extracurricular participation is emphasized. Character and personality and particular talent or ability are important. Geographical distribution and alumni/ae relationship are considered.

**Requirements:** Graduation from secondary school is required; GED is not accepted. 16 units and the following program of study are required: 4 units of English, 4 units of math, 2 units of foreign language, 6 units of academic electives. Electives should be chosen from foreign languages, sciences, and social studies. Chemistry and math through trigonometry required of engineering program applicants. Conditional admission possible for applicants not meeting standard requirements. SAT or ACT is required. ACH recommended. Campus visit and interview recommended. No off-campus interviews.

**Procedure:** Take SAT or ACT by January of 12th year. Take ACH by June of 12th year. Visit college for interview by February 15 of 12th year. Suggest filing application by January 1. Application deadline is February 15. Notification of admission by April 1. Reply is required by May 1. $100 nonrefundable tuition deposit. $200 nonrefundable room deposit. Freshmen accepted for terms other than fall.

**Special programs:** Admission may be deferred one year. Credit and/or placement may be granted through CEEB Advanced Placement exams for scores of 4 or higher. Credit and placement may be granted through challenge exams. Early decision program. In fall 1993, 363 applied for early decision and 288 were accepted. Deadline for applying for early decision is December 1 or January 15. Early entrance/early admission program. Concurrent enrollment program.

**Transfer students:** Transfer students accepted for terms other than fall. In fall 1993, 2% of all new students were transfers into all classes. 219 transfer applications were received, 90 were accepted. Application deadline is June 1 (priority filing date: April 1) for fall; November 1 for spring. Minimum 3.0 GPA required. Lowest course grade accepted is "C." At least 30 semester hours must be completed at the university to receive degree.

**Admissions contact:** Patricia Boig, Director of Admissions. 215 758-3100.

**FINANCIAL AID. Available aid:** Pell grants, SEOG, state scholarships and grants, school scholarships and grants, private scholarships and grants, ROTC scholarships, academic merit scholarships, and athletic scholarships. Perkins Loans (NDSL), PLUS, Stafford Loans (GSL), state loans, school loans, private loans, and SLS. Knight Tuition Plans. Institutional 10-Month Installment Plan.

**Financial aid statistics:** 2% of aid is not need-based. In 1993-94, 95% of all undergraduate applicants received aid; 83% of freshman applicants. Average amounts of aid awarded freshmen: Scholarships and grants, $10,833; loans, $3,405.

**Supporting data/closing dates:** FAFSA: Priority filing date is February 15. FAF: Priority filing date is February 5. School's own aid application: Priority filing date is February 15. State aid form: Deadline is May 1. Income tax forms: Accepted on rolling basis. Notification of awards begins March 23.

**Financial aid contact:** William Stanford, Director of Financial Aid. 215 758-3181.

**STUDENT EMPLOYMENT.** College Work/Study Program. Institutional employment. 28% of full-time undergraduates work on campus during school year. Students may expect to earn an average of $800 during school year. Off-campus part-time employment opportunities rated "fair."

**COMPUTER FACILITIES.** 317 IBM/IBM-compatible and Macintosh/Apple microcomputers; 312 are networked. Students may access IBM minicomputer/mainframe systems, Internet. Residence halls may be equipped with modems. Client/LAN operating systems include Apple/Macintosh, DOS, UNIX/XENIX/AIX, X-windows, Novell. Computer languages and software packages include BASIC, C, COBOL, FORTRAN, Pascal, Prolog, WordPerfect. Computer facilities are available to all students.

**Fees:** None.

**Hours:** 24 hours.

**GRADUATE CAREER DATA.** Graduate school percentages: 19% enter law school. 15% enter medical school. 1% enter dental school. 6% enter graduate business programs. 56% enter graduate arts and sciences programs. Highest graduate school enrollments: UC Berkeley, Columbia U, Harvard U, Medical Coll of Pennsylvania, U Michigan, New York U Law Sch, U Pennsylvania. 58% of graduates choose careers in business and industry. Companies and businesses that hire graduates: IBM, General Electric, AT&T, Price Waterhouse, Arthur Andersen.

**PROMINENT ALUMNI/AE.** Lee Iacocca, chairperson, Chrysler Corp.; Roger Penske, president, Penske Corp.; Dexter Baker, CEO, Air Products & Chemicals Corp.; Terry Hart, astronaut.

# Lock Haven University of Pennsylvania

**Lock Haven, PA 17745** **717 893-2011**

**1993-94 Costs.** Tuition: $2,728 (state residents), $6,122 (out-of-state). Room & board: $3,524. Fees, books, misc. academic expenses (school's estimate): $1,032.

**Enrollment.** Undergraduates: 1,633 men, 2,054 women (full-time). Freshman class: 4,058 applicants, 2,049 accepted, 684 enrolled. Graduate enrollment: 1 man, 2 women.

**Test score averages/ranges.** Average SAT scores: 980 combined.

**Faculty.** 185 full-time; 41 part-time. 54% of faculty holds doctoral degree. Student/faculty ratio: 21 to 1.

**Selectivity rating.** Competitive.

**PROFILE.** Lock Haven is a public university. Founded as a Normal school in 1870, it gained university status in 1983. Its 135-acre campus is located in Lock Haven, 30 miles west of Williamsport and 70 miles north of Harrisburg.

**Accreditation:** MSACS. Professionally accredited by the Council on Social Work Education, the National Council for Accreditation of Teacher Education.

**Religious orientation:** Lock Haven University of Pennsylvania is nonsectarian; no religious requirements.

**Library:** Collections totaling over 344,716 volumes, 1,598 periodical subscriptions, and 508,122 microform items.

**Special facilities/museums:** Model UN with translation capabilities, color TV studio, computerized theatre lighting, planetarium.

**Athletic facilities:** Gymnasiums, swimming pool, equipment rooms, saunas, weight rooms, basketball arena, exercise/dance studio, wrestling gym, Nautilus facility, basketball, racquetball, tennis and volleyball courts, athletic fields, field house with press box and broadcast facilities, stadium with football field and all-weather track.

**STUDENT BODY. Undergraduate profile:** 82% are state residents; 18% are transfers. 1% Asian-American, 3% Black, 1% Hispanic, 95% White. Average age of undergraduates is 20.

**Freshman profile:** 1% of freshmen who took SAT scored 700 or over on math; 2% scored 600 or over on verbal, 14% scored 600 or over on math; 28% scored 500 or over on verbal, 58% scored 500 or over on math; 84% scored 400 or over on verbal, 96% scored 400 or over on math; 98% scored 300 or over on verbal, 98% scored 300 or over on math. 98% of accepted applicants took SAT; 2% took ACT.

**Undergraduate achievement:** 80% of fall 1992 freshmen returned for fall 1993 term. 40% of entering class graduated. 14% of students who completed a degree program immediately went on to graduate study.

**Foreign students:** 118 students are from out of the country. Countries represented include China, England, India, Ireland, Japan, and Sri Lanka; 40 in all.

**PROGRAMS OF STUDY. Degrees:** B.A., B.S., B.S.Ed.

**Majors:** Art, Athletic Training, Biology, Business Computer Science, Business Management Science, Chemistry, Chemistry/Biology, Cooperative Program in Engineering, Early Childhood Education, Economics, Education, Elementary Education, Elementary Library Science, English, Environmental Biology, Fine Arts, Foreign Languages, French, General Studies, Geography, German, Health/Physical Education, Health Sciences, History, Humanities, International Studies, Journalism/Media Studies, Latin American Studies, Management Science, Mathematical/Computer Sciences, Mathematics, Medical Technology, Music, Natural Science, Philosophy, Physics, Political Science/Government, Pre-Dentistry, Pre-Medicine, Pre-Pharmacy, Pre-Physical Therapy, Pre-Veterinary, Psychology, Recreation, Secondary Communications, Secondary Education, Social Sciences, Social Work, Sociology, Spanish, Special Education, Speech Communications, Sports Medicine, Theatre.

**Distribution of degrees:** The majors with the highest enrollment are education, health sciences, and journalism/media studies.

**Requirements:** General education requirement.

**Academic regulations:** Freshmen must maintain minimum 1.5 GPA; sophomores, 1.7 GPA; juniors, 2.0 GPA; seniors, 2.0 GPA.

**Special:** Special degree program in chemistry/biology leads to certification in medical technology. Associate's degrees offered. Self-designed majors. Double majors. Dual degrees. Independent study. Accelerated study. Pass/fail grading option. Cooperative education programs. Graduate school at which undergraduates may take graduate-level courses. Preprofessional programs in law, medicine, veterinary science, pharmacy, dentistry, and physical therapy. Combined degree programs in music with Clarion U and Millersville U. 3-2 engineering program with Pennsylvania State U. Member of Pennsylvania Consortium for International Education. Teacher certification in early childhood, elementary, secondary, and special education. Certification in specific subject areas. Study abroad in Australia, China, England, Germany, Japan, Mexico, Poland, Scotland, the former Yugoslav Republics, and other countries. ROTC.

**Honors:** Honors program. Honor societies.

**Academic Assistance:** Remedial reading, writing, math, and study skills. Nonremedial tutoring.

**STUDENT LIFE. Housing:** All freshmen must live on campus unless living with family. Coed and women's dorms. 42% of students live in college housing.

**Services and counseling/handicapped student services:** Health service. Counseling services for minority, military, veteran, and older students. Birth control, personal, and psychological counseling. Career and academic guidance services. Religious counseling. Physically disabled student services. Learning disabled program/services. Notetaking services. Tape recorders. Tutors. Reader services for the blind.

**Campus organizations:** Undergraduate student government. Student newspaper (Eagle Eye, published once/week). Literary magazine. Radio and TV stations. Ensembles, community orchestra, band, choir, Readers Theatre, Children's Theatre, Theatre Workshop, University Players, Circle K, Wilderness Club, academic, professional, and special-interest groups, 70 organizations in all. Seven fraternities, five chapter houses; four sororities, no chapter houses. 11% of men join a fraternity. 8% of women join a sorority.

**Religious organizations:** Fellowship of Christian Athletes, Newman Community.

**Minority/foreign student organizations:** Black Action Society. International Student Organization.

**ATHLETICS. Physical education requirements:** Three credits of physical education required.

**Intercollegiate competition:** 11% of students participate. Baseball (M), basketball (M,W), cross-country (M,W), diving (W), field hockey (W), football (M), golf (M), lacrosse (W), soccer (M), softball (W), swimming (W), tennis (M,W), track (indoor) (M,W), track (outdoor) (M,W), track and field (M,W), track and field (indoor) (M,W), volleyball (W), wrestling (M). Member of ECAC, NCAA Division I for wrestling, NCAA Division II, Pennsylvania State Athletic Conference.

**Intramural and club sports:** 28% of students participate. Intramural basketball, flag football, floor hockey, softball, volleyball, wrestling. Men's club cheerleading, ice hockey. Women's club cheerleading, soccer.

**ADMISSIONS. Academic basis for candidate selection** (in order of priority): Secondary school record, class rank, standardized test scores, school's recommendation, essay.

**Nonacademic basis for candidate selection:** Particular talent or ability is emphasized. Character and personality and extracurricular participation are important. Alumni/ae relationship is considered.

**Requirements:** Graduation from secondary school is required; GED is accepted. 18 units and the following program of study are required: 4 units of English, 3 units of math, 3 units of science including 2 units of lab, 2 units of foreign language, 1 unit of social studies, 3 units of history. Additional units of mathematics and science recommended. Minimum combined SAT score of 980, rank in top two-fifths of secondary school class, and college preparatory program recommended. Interview required of nursing and social work program applicants. Audition required of music program applicants. EOP for applicants not normally admissible. SAT or ACT is required. Campus visit recommended. No off-campus interviews.

**Procedure:** Take SAT or ACT by November of 12th year. Take ACH by November of 12th year. Suggest filing application by fall. Notification of admission on rolling basis. Reply is required by March 1. $100 nonrefundable tuition deposit. $100 nonrefundable tuition/room deposit. Freshmen accepted for terms other than fall.

**Special programs:** Admission may be deferred one year. Credit and/or placement may be granted through CEEB Advanced Placement exams for scores of 3 or higher. Credit and/or placement may be granted through CLEP general and subject exams. Credit may be granted through military and life experience. Credit and placement may be granted through challenge exams. Early entrance/early admission program.

**Transfer students:** Transfer students accepted for terms other than fall. In fall 1993, 18% of all new students were transfers into all classes. 635 transfer applications were received, 274 were accepted. Application deadline is June 15 for fall; December 1 for spring. Minimum 2.0 GPA required. Lowest course grade accepted is "C." Maximum number of transferable credits is 64 semester hours. At least 32 semester hours must be completed at the university to receive degree.

**Admissions contact:** Joseph A. Coldren, M.Ed., Director of Admissions. 717 893-2027.

**FINANCIAL AID. Available aid:** Pell grants, state scholarships and grants, school scholarships, private scholarships, ROTC scholarships, academic merit scholarships, athletic scholarships, and aid for undergraduate foreign students. Perkins Loans (NDSL), PLUS, Stafford Loans (GSL), and state loans. Tuition Management Systems and deferred payment plan.

**Financial aid statistics:** Average amounts of aid awarded freshmen: Scholarships and grants, $1,200; loans, $1,800.

**Supporting data/closing dates:** FAFSA/FAF: Priority filing date is April 15. School's own aid application: Priority filing date is April 15. State aid form: Priority filing date is April 15. Notification of awards on rolling basis.

**Financial aid contact:** William Irwin, Ph.D., Director of Financial Aid. 717 893-2344.

**STUDENT EMPLOYMENT.** College Work/Study Program. Institutional employment. 25% of full-time undergraduates work on campus during school year. Students may expect to earn an average of $1,000 during school year. Off-campus part-time employment opportunities rated "good."

**COMPUTER FACILITIES.** 125 IBM/IBM-compatible and Macintosh/Apple microcomputers; all are networked. Residence halls may be equipped with networked microcomputers. Computer languages and software packages include Assembler, BASIC, C, COBOL, FORTRAN, LISP, Pascal, PL/1, SNOBOL. Computer facilities are available to all students.

**Fees:** Computer fee is included in tuition/fees.

**Hours:** 8 AM-11 PM daily.

**GRADUATE CAREER DATA.** Highest graduate school enrollments: Penn State U, U of Pennsylvania, Temple U.

**PROMINENT ALUMNI/AE.** Timothy Davey, director of operations, New York Jets; John Brouse, marketing vice-president, Pennsylvania Blue Shield; Gary Littimer, chief of infectious diseases, Williamsport and Divine Hospitals.

## Lycoming College

**Williamsport, PA 17701-5192** — **800 345-3920**

**1994-95 Costs.** Tuition: $13,900. Room & board: $4,300. Fees, books, misc. academic expenses (school's estimate): $800.

**Enrollment.** Undergraduates: 642 men, 721 women (full-time). Freshman class: 1,286 applicants, 1,005 accepted, 363 enrolled.

**Test score averages/ranges.** Average SAT scores: 450 verbal, 500 math. Range of SAT scores of middle 50%: 400-510 verbal, 430-560 math. Average ACT scores: 21 composite. Range of ACT scores of middle 50%: 18-22 composite.

**Faculty.** 94 full-time; 19 part-time. 87% of faculty holds highest degree in specific field. Student/faculty ratio: 14 to 1.

**Selectivity rating.** Less competitive.

**PROFILE.** Lycoming, founded in 1812, is a church-affiliated, liberal arts college. Its 35-acre campus is located near downtown Williamsport, 200 miles from Philadelphia. Most campus buildings have been constructed since 1950.

**Accreditation:** MSACS. Professionally accredited by the National League for Nursing.

**Religious orientation:** Lycoming College is affiliated with the United Methodist Church; no religious requirements.

**Library:** Collections totaling over 165,000 volumes, 1,069 periodical subscriptions, and 1,756 microform items.

**Special facilities/museums:** Language lab, nursing skills lab, tissue culture lab, TV studio, planetarium.

**Athletic facilities:** Gymnasium, swimming pool, basketball and tennis courts, weight rooms, field hockey, football, and soccer fields, sauna.

**STUDENT BODY. Undergraduate profile:** 77% are state residents; 15% are transfers. 1% Asian-American, 2% Black, 1% Hispanic, 95% White, 1% Other. Average age of undergraduates is 21.

**Freshman profile:** 1% of freshmen who took SAT scored 700 or over on verbal, 1% scored 700 or over on math; 7% scored 600 or over on verbal, 13% scored 600 or over on math; 29% scored 500 or over on verbal, 48% scored 500 or over on math; 77% scored 400 or over on verbal, 88% scored 400 or over on math; 100% scored 300 or over on verbal, 100% scored 300 or over on math. 92% of accepted applicants took SAT; 8% took ACT. 75% of freshmen come from public schools.

**Undergraduate achievement:** 84% of fall 1992 freshmen returned for fall 1993 term. 58% of entering class graduated. 11% of students who completed a degree program immediately went on to graduate study.

**Foreign students:** 24 students are from out of the country. Countries represented include China, India, and Sierra Leone; 14 in all.

**PROGRAMS OF STUDY. Degrees:** B.A., B.F.A., B.S.Nurs.

**Majors:** Accounting, American Studies, Art History, Art Studio, Astronomy, Biology, Business Administration, Chemistry, Computer Science, Criminal Justice, Economics,

English, French, German, History, International Studies, Literature, Mass Communications, Mathematics, Music, Near East Culture/Archaeology, Nursing, Philosophy, Physics, Political Science, Psychology, Religion, Sculpture, Sociology/Anthropology, Spanish, Theatre.
**Distribution of degrees:** The majors with the highest enrollment are business administration, psychology, and biology; Near-east culture, Spanish, and astronomy have the lowest.
**Requirements:** General education requirement.
**Academic regulations:** Freshmen must maintain minimum 1.8 GPA; sophomores, juniors, seniors, 2.0 GPA.
**Special:** Minors offered in most majors and in foreign languages, literature, and math sciences. Courses offered in creative writing, earth science, education, Greek, law, speech, and statistics. Combined curriculum in business and psychology. Optional May term offers additional courses and opportunities for independent study, acceleration, and remedial work. Scholars Program permits increased independent and interdisciplinary study. Self-designed majors. Double majors. Independent study. Accelerated study. Internships. Cooperative education programs. Preprofessional programs in law, medicine, veterinary science, and dentistry. 3-1 medical technology program with five hospitals. 3-4 podiatry program with Pennsylvania Coll of Podiatric Medicine. 3-4 optometry program with Pennsylvania Coll of Optometry. 3-2 engineering program with Pennsylvania State U. 3-2 forestry and environmental studies program with Duke U. Washington Semester and UN Semester. Exchange programs with Bloomsburg U, Bucknell U, Lock Haven U, Mansfield U, Pennsylvania Coll of Tech, and Susquehanna U. Teacher certification in elementary and secondary education. Certification in specific subject areas. Study abroad in England, France, Germany, and Spain. ROTC at Bucknell U.
**Honors:** Honors program. Honor societies.
**Academic Assistance:** Remedial reading, writing, and math. Nonremedial tutoring.

**STUDENT LIFE. Housing:** All unmarried students under age 23 must live on campus unless living with family. Coed, women's, and men's dorms. 73% of students live in college housing.
**Social atmosphere:** According to the editor of the student newspaper, popular on-campus gathering spots include Greek floors, Pennington and Burchfield Lounges, the library, and the cafeteria. Some of the off-campus hang outs are area night clubs, pizza parlors, the mall, and movie theaters. Greeks, the school choir, the Student Association, and the Lycourier are influential groups on campus. Favorite campus events include plays, opera performances, concerts, and football games.
**Services and counseling/handicapped student services:** Placement services. Personal and psychological counseling. Career and academic guidance services. Physically disabled student services. Learning disabled services. Notetaking services. Tape recorders. Reader services for the blind.
**Campus organizations:** Undergraduate student government. Student newspaper (Lycourier, published once/week). Literary magazine. Yearbook. Radio station. Band, a cappella choir, drama group, artist and lecture series, language clubs, special-interest groups, 41 organizations in all. Five fraternities, no chapter houses; four sororities, no chapter houses. 31% of men join a fraternity. 27% of women join a sorority.
**Religious organizations:** Catholic Council, Chapel Fellowship, Campus Ministry.
**Minority/foreign student organizations:** Multicultural Awareness Organization.

**ATHLETICS. Physical education requirements:** Two semesters of physical education required.
**Intercollegiate competition:** 33% of students participate. Basketball (M,W), cheerleading (W), cross-country (M,W), field hockey (W), football (M), golf (M,W), soccer (M), softball (W), swimming (M,W), tennis (M,W), track and field (outdoor) (M,W), volleyball (W), wrestling (M). Member of Middle Atlantic Conference, NCAA Division III.
**Intramural and club sports:** 75% of students participate. Intramural basketball, football, softball, volleyball, water polo, wrestling.

**ADMISSIONS. Academic basis for candidate selection** (in order of priority): Secondary school record, class rank, standardized test scores, school's recommendation, essay.
**Nonacademic basis for candidate selection:** Character and personality are emphasized. Extracurricular participation and particular talent or ability are important. Alumni/ae relationship is considered.
**Requirements:** Graduation from secondary school is required; GED is accepted. 16 units and the following program of study are required: 4 units of English, 3 units of math, 2 units of lab science, 2 units of foreign language, 3 units of social studies, 2 units of academic electives. Minimum combined SAT score of 850 (composite ACT score of 18), rank in top half of secondary school class, and minimum 2.5 GPA recommended. SAT or ACT is required. Campus visit and interview recommended. Off-campus interviews available with admissions and alumni representatives.
**Procedure:** Take SAT or ACT by February 1 of 12th year. Application deadline is April 1. Notification of admission on rolling basis. Reply is required by May 1. $100 tuition deposit, refundable until May 1. $100 room deposit, refundable until May 1. Freshmen accepted for terms other than fall.
**Special programs:** Admission may be deferred one year. Credit and/or placement may be granted through CEEB Advanced Placement exams for scores of 3 or higher. Credit and/or placement may be granted through CLEP general and subject exams. Early entrance/early admission program. Concurrent enrollment program.
**Transfer students:** Transfer students accepted for terms other than fall. In fall 1993, 15% of all new students were transfers into all classes. 186 transfer applications were received, 151 were accepted. Application deadline is April 1 for fall; December 15 for spring. Minimum 2.0 GPA required. Lowest course grade accepted is "C." Maximum number of transferable credits is 64 semester hours from a two-year school and 96 semester hours from a four-year school. At least 32 semester hours must be completed at the college to receive degree.
**Admissions contact:** James Spencer, Dean of Admissions and Financial Aid. 717 321-4026.

**FINANCIAL AID. Available aid:** Pell grants, SEOG, state grants, school scholarships and grants, private scholarships and grants, ROTC scholarships, academic merit scholarships, and aid for undergraduate foreign students. Perkins Loans (NDSL), PLUS, Stafford Loans (GSL), state loans, school loans, private loans, and SLS. AMS.
**Financial aid statistics:** 21% of aid is not need-based. In 1993-94, 80% of all undergraduate applicants received aid; 80% of freshman applicants. Average amounts of aid awarded freshmen: Scholarships and grants, $8,173; loans, $3,013.
**Supporting data/closing dates:** FAFSA: Priority filing date is April 15. School's own aid application: Priority filing date is April 1. State aid form: Priority filing date is April 1. Income tax forms: Priority filing date is May 1; accepted on rolling basis. Notification of awards begins March.
**Financial aid contact:** James Lakis, Director of Financial Aid. 717 321-4040.

**STUDENT EMPLOYMENT.** College Work/Study Program. Institutional employment. 23% of full-time undergraduates work on campus during school year. Students may expect to earn an average of $800 during school year. Off-campus part-time employment opportunities rated "good."

**COMPUTER FACILITIES.** 150 IBM/IBM-compatible and Macintosh/Apple microcomputers; 85 are networked. Students may access IBM minicomputer/mainframe systems. Computer languages and software packages include BASIC, BMDP, C, COBOL, FORTRAN, Lotus 1-2-3, Pascal, VP-Planner, WordPerfect. Computer facilities are available to all students.
**Fees:** Computer fee is included in tuition/fees.
**Hours:** 8 AM-midn.

**GRADUATE CAREER DATA.** Graduate school percentages: 3% enter law school. 2% enter medical school. 1% enter dental school. 1% enter graduate business programs. 3% enter graduate arts and sciences programs. 1% enter theological school/seminary. Highest graduate school enrollments: Dickinson Law Sch, Pennsylvania State U, Syracuse U, Temple U, U of Pennsylvania. 50% of graduates choose careers in business and industry.

# Mansfield University of Pennsylvania

**Mansfield, PA 16933** **717 662-4000**

**1993-94 Costs.** Tuition: $3,028 (state residents), $7,070 (out-of-state). Room: $1,588. Board: $1,400. Fees, books, misc. academic expenses (school's estimate): $1,150.
**Enrollment.** Undergraduates: 1,248 men, 1,643 women (full-time). Freshman class: 2,453 applicants, 1,566 accepted, 845 enrolled. Graduate enrollment: 74 men, 258 women.
**Test score averages/ranges.** Average SAT scores: 439 verbal, 481 math.
**Faculty.** 178 full-time; 11 part-time. 48% of faculty holds doctoral degree. Student/faculty ratio: 18 to 1.
**Selectivity rating.** Competitive.

**PROFILE.** Mansfield is a public, multipurpose university. It was founded in 1857, became a state teachers college in 1927, and gained university status 1983. Its 200-acre campus is located in Mansfield, 30 miles south of Elmira, N.Y.

**Accreditation:** MSACS. Professionally accredited by the American Dietetic Association, the Council on Social Work Education, the National Association of Schools of Music, the National Council for Accreditation of Teacher Education.
**Religious orientation:** Mansfield University of Pennsylvania is nonsectarian; no religious requirements.
**Library:** Collections totaling over 221,188 volumes, 2,180 periodical subscriptions, and 708,736 microform items.
**Special facilities/museums:** Science museum, two art galleries, animal collection, planetarium, solar collector.
**Athletic facilities:** Gymnasium, field house, basketball, racquetball, and tennis courts, baseball, football, and soccer fields, swimming pool, weight rooms, saunas.

**STUDENT BODY. Undergraduate profile:** 81% are state residents. 1% Asian-American, 4% Black, 94% White, 1% Other. Average age of undergraduates is 20.
**Freshman profile:** Majority of accepted applicants took SAT.
**Undergraduate achievement:** 78% of fall 1992 freshmen returned for fall 1993 term. 76% of entering class graduated. 25% of students who completed a degree program went on to graduate study within five years.
**Foreign students:** 45 students are from out of the country. Countries represented include Canada, India, Japan, Korea, Sri Lanka, and Zimbabwe; 19 in all.

**PROGRAMS OF STUDY. Degrees:** B.A., B.Mus., B.S.
**Majors:** Art Education, Art History, Biology, Business Administration, Chemistry, Communication, Computer Science, Criminal Justice Administration, Earth/Space Sciences, Economics, Education, Elementary Education, English, Fashion Merchandising, Fisheries, General Studies, Geography, History, Information Processing, Mathematics, Medical Technology, Music, Music Education, Music Merchandising, Music Therapy, Nursing, Philosophy, Physics, Physics/Mathematics, Political Science, Psychology, Psychology/Human Relations/Personnel Administration, Social Studies, Sociology/Social Work, Spanish, Special Education, Speech, Studio Art, Theatre Arts Management, Travel/Tourism.
**Distribution of degrees:** The majors with the highest enrollment are elementary education, criminal justice, and business administration; art history, studio art, and theatre arts management have the lowest.
**Requirements:** General education requirement.
**Academic regulations:** Minimum 2.0 GPA required for graduation.
**Special:** Associate's degrees offered. Self-designed majors. Double majors. Independent study. Accelerated study. Pass/fail grading option. Internships. Graduate school at which undergraduates may take graduate-level courses. 3-2 engineering programs with George Washington U, Georgia Tech, Pennsylvania State U, and U of Pittsburgh. Member of College Center of the Finger Lakes. Off-campus study opportunities possible. Teacher certification in early childhood, elementary, secondary, and special education.
**Honors:** Honors program. Honor societies.

**Academic Assistance:** Remedial reading, writing, math, and study skills. Nonremedial tutoring.

**STUDENT LIFE. Housing:** All students with fewer than 96 credits must live on campus. Coed, women's, and men's dorms. 64% of students live in college housing.

**Social atmosphere:** "Our school is very tight-knit and great to be a part of," reports the student newspaper. "Most of the campus is involved in one or more organizations. It's a great place to be! The Greek organizations have widespread influence on student social life, as well as the athletes and Black Student Union, which sponsors many dances on campus. The campus radio station, WXMU, also influences campus life. The most popular on-campus gathering spots are Zanzibar, our award-winning nonalcoholic bar, and Memorial Hall, our student union building. For off-campus action, students flock to Lambda Chi Alpha, Sigma Tau Gamma, or Tau Kappa Epsilon."

**Services and counseling/handicapped student services:** Placement services. Health service. Women's center. Counseling services for minority, military, veteran, and older students. Birth control, personal, and psychological counseling. Career and academic guidance services. Learning disabled services.

**Campus organizations:** Undergraduate student government. Student newspaper (Flashlight, published once/week). Yearbook. Radio and TV stations. Band, jazz band, chorus, instrumental ensembles, chamber singers, opera workshop, debating, drama group, Activities Council, academic groups, special-interest groups, 100 organizations in all. Eight fraternities, four chapter houses; four sororities, no chapter houses. 18% of men join a fraternity. 13% of women join a sorority.

**Religious organizations:** Campus Christian Fellowship, United Campus Ministry, Kappa Phi.

**Minority/foreign student organizations:** Black Student Union. International Student Association.

**ATHLETICS. Physical education requirements:** One semester of physical education required.

**Intercollegiate competition:** 10% of students participate. Baseball (M), basketball (M,W), cheerleading (M,W), cross-country (M,W), diving (W), field hockey (W), football (M), softball (W), swimming (W), track (indoor) (M,W), track (outdoor) (M,W), track and field (indoor) (M,W), track and field (outdoor) (M,W), wrestling (M). Member of ECAC, NCAA Division II, Pennsylvania State Athletic Conference.

**Intramural and club sports:** 50% of students participate. Intramural aerobics, basketball, flag football, softball, swimming, tennis, volleyball. Men's club martial arts, Nordic skiing, soccer, tennis, weight lifting. Women's club martial arts, Nordic skiing, tennis, weight lifting.

**ADMISSIONS. Academic basis for candidate selection** (in order of priority): Secondary school record, class rank, school's recommendation, standardized test scores, essay.

**Nonacademic basis for candidate selection:** Particular talent or ability is important. Character and personality, extracurricular participation, and geographical distribution are considered.

**Requirements:** Graduation from secondary school is required; GED is accepted. 21 units and the following program of study are required: 4 units of English, 2 units of math, 3 units of science including 2 units of lab, 2 units of foreign language, 3 units of social studies, 3 units of history, 6 units of academic electives. Minimum combined SAT score of 800, rank in top three-fifths of secondary school class, and minimum 2.0 GPA required. Biology, chemistry, and algebra required of nursing program applicants. Portfolio required of art program applicants. Audition required of music program applicants. EOP for applicants not normally admissible. SAT or ACT is required. Campus visit and interview recommended. No off-campus interviews.

**Procedure:** Take SAT or ACT by December of 12th year. Visit college for interview by December of 12th year. Suggest filing application by December. Application deadline is June. Notification of admission on rolling basis. Reply is required by March 1. $150 nonrefundable tuition deposit. Freshmen accepted for terms other than fall.

**Special programs:** Admission may be deferred one year. Credit and/or placement may be granted through CEEB Advanced Placement exams for scores of 3 or higher. Credit and/or placement may be granted through CLEP subject exams. Credit and placement may be granted through challenge exams and military experience. Early entrance/early admission program. Concurrent enrollment program.

**Transfer students:** Transfer students accepted for terms other than fall. In fall 1993, 589 transfer applications were received, 427 were accepted. Application deadline is December 5 for fall; May 15 for spring. Minimum 2.0 GPA required. Lowest course grade accepted is "C." Maximum number of transferable credits is 67 semester hours. At least 32 semester hours must be completed at the university to receive degree.

**Admissions contact:** John J. Abplanalp, M.S., Director of Admissions. 717 662-4243.

**FINANCIAL AID. Available aid:** Pell grants, SEOG, state scholarships and grants, school scholarships, private scholarships, ROTC scholarships, academic merit scholarships, athletic scholarships, and aid for undergraduate foreign students. Perkins Loans (NDSL), PLUS, Stafford Loans (GSL), state loans, and SLS. AMS, Tuition Management Systems, and deferred payment plan.

**Financial aid statistics:** In 1993-94, 75% of all undergraduate applicants received aid; 78% of freshman applicants. Average amounts of aid awarded freshmen: Loans, $2,000.

**Supporting data/closing dates:** FAFSA. School's own aid application: Deadline is April 15. State aid form: Priority filing date is March 15; deadline is May 1. PHEAU: Priority filing date is March 15; deadline is May 1. Notification of awards begins April/May.

**Financial aid contact:** Christopher Vaughn, M.S., Director of Financial Aid. 717 662-4129.

**STUDENT EMPLOYMENT.** College Work/Study Program. Institutional employment. 25% of full-time undergraduates work on campus during school year. Students may expect to earn an average of $900 during school year. Off-campus part-time employment opportunities rated "fair."

**COMPUTER FACILITIES.** 100 IBM/IBM-compatible microcomputers. Students may access IBM minicomputer/mainframe systems. Residence halls may be equipped with stand-alone microcomputers. Computer languages and software packages include BASIC, COBOL, FORTRAN, Lotus 1-2-3, MINITAB, Pascal, Quattro, SAS, WordPerfect. Computer facilities are available to all students.

**Fees:** None.

**Hours:** 24 hours (one lab); 8 AM-10 PM (most others).

**GRADUATE CAREER DATA.** Highest graduate school enrollments: Pennsylvania State U, U of Pittsburg, Temple U. 50% of graduates choose careers in business and industry. Companies and businesses that hire graduates: GTE, IBM, federal and state governments, schools.

# Marywood College

**Scranton, PA 185091598 — 717 348-6211**

**1994-95 Costs.** Tuition: $10,240. Room & board: $4,300. Fees, books, misc. academic expenses (school's estimate): $850.

**Enrollment.** Undergraduates: 287 men, 1,165 women (full-time). Freshman class: 1,064 applicants, 826 accepted, 323 enrolled. Graduate enrollment: 291 men, 872 women.

**Test score averages/ranges.** Average SAT scores: 449 verbal, 470 math. Range of SAT scores of middle 50%: 400-500 verbal, 410-510 math.

**Faculty.** 102 full-time; 41 part-time. 57% of faculty holds doctoral degree. Student/faculty ratio: 16 to 1.

**Selectivity rating.** Less competitive.

**PROFILE.** Marywood is a church-affiliated, liberal arts college. Founded as a college for women in 1915, it adopted coeducation in 1980. Undergraduate programs are offered through the residential school for women and the nonresidential, coeducational school; graduate programs are also offered. Its 180-acre campus is located in Scranton, 120 miles north of Philadelphia.

**Accreditation:** MSACS. Professionally accredited by the American Bar Association, the American Dietetic Association, the Council on Social Work Education, the National Association of Schools of Art and Design, the National Association of Schools of Music, the National Council for Accreditation of Teacher Education, the National League for Nursing.

**Religious orientation:** Marywood College is affiliated with the Roman Catholic Church (Sisters of the Immaculate Heart of Mary); three semesters of religion required.

**Library:** Collections totaling over 198,425 volumes, 1,114 periodical subscriptions, and 213,881 microform items.

**Special facilities/museums:** Two art galleries, museum, electronic learning labs, communications center, instructional media lab, interactive video lab, computerized editing facility, psychology/education research lab, science multi-media lab, language lab, center for justice and peace, on-campus preschool and day care.

**Athletic facilities:** Gymnasium, swimming pool, tennis/racquetball courts, weight room, one outdoor all-purpose field.

**STUDENT BODY. Undergraduate profile:** 79% are state residents; 36% are transfers. 1.2% Asian-American, .9% Black, 1.7% Hispanic, .1% Native American, 95.5% White, .6% Other. Average age of undergraduates is 22.

**Freshman profile:** 4% of freshmen who took SAT scored 600 or over on verbal, 6% scored 600 or over on math; 24% scored 500 or over on verbal, 33% scored 500 or over on math; 73% scored 400 or over on verbal, 79% scored 400 or over on math; 93% scored 300 or over on verbal, 92% scored 300 or over on math. 80% of accepted applicants took SAT; 1% took ACT. 82% of freshmen come from public schools.

**Undergraduate achievement:** 76% of fall 1992 freshmen returned for fall 1993 term. 38% of entering class graduated. 17% of students who completed a degree program immediately went on to graduate study.

**Foreign students:** 11 students are from out of the country. Countries represented include Africa, China, Hong Kong, Indonesia, Japan, and Singapore; 10 in all.

**PROGRAMS OF STUDY. Degrees:** B.A., B.F.A., B.Mus., B.S., B.S.Nurs., B.Soc.Work.

**Majors:** Accounting, Advertising/Public Relations, Art Administration, Art Education, Arts Administration/Music, Biology, Biology/Secondary Education, Business Administration/Finance, Business Administration/Management, Business Administration/Marketing, Business Computer Information Systems, Ceramics, Church Music, Communication Arts/Secondary Education, Communication Disorders, Comprehensive Social Science, Comprehensive Social Science/Criminal Justice, Comprehensive Social Science/History, Comprehensive Social Science/Public Administration, Comprehensive Social Science/Secondary Education, Comprehensive Social Studies/Sociology, Design/Photography, Dietetics, Elementary Education/Art, Elementary Education/Communication Arts, Elementary Education/Communication Disorders, Elementary Education/Deaf Education, Elementary Education/Early Childhood, Elementary Education/English, Elementary Education/Foreign Language, Elementary Education/Health and Physical Education, Elementary Education/Math, Elementary Education/Music, Elementary Education/Psychology, Elementary Education/Religion Studies, Elementary Education/Science, Elementary Education/Social Science, Elementary Education/Special Education, English, English Secondary Education, Environmental Science, Environmental Studies, French, French/Secondary Education, General Science/Secondary Education, General Studies, Graphic Design, Health/Physical Education, Health/Physical Education/Athletic Training, Health/Physical Education/Physical Activity, Health Services Administration, Home Economics Education, Hotel/Restaurant Management, Illustration Design, Interior Design, International Business, Legal Assistant, Mathematics, Mathematics/Secondary Education, Medical Technology, Music Education, Music Performance, Music Therapy, Nursing, Nursing/Pre-Service, Painting, Performing Arts, Performing Arts/Music/Theatre, Psychology, Psychology/Clinical Practice, Radio/Television, Religious Studies, Retailing/Fashion Merchandising, Sculpture, Social Work, Sociology, Spanish, Spanish/Secondary Education, Special Education, Speech, Theatre.

**Distribution of degrees:** The majors with the highest enrollment are elementary education, business administration, and accounting; environmental science, French, and religious studies have the lowest.

**Requirements:** General education requirement.

**Academic regulations:** Minimum 2.0 GPA must be maintained.

**Special:** Minors offered in all majors. Associate's degrees offered. Self-designed majors. Double majors. Dual degrees. Independent study. Internships. Cooperative education pro-

grams. Graduate school at which undergraduates may take graduate-level courses. Preprofessional programs in law, medicine, veterinary science, and dentistry. Semester at Fashion Inst of Tech. Exchange program with Lock Haven U. Teacher certification in early childhood, elementary, secondary, and special education. Certification in specific subject areas. Study abroad in Canada, England, France, Mexico, and Spain. Student teaching abroad. AFROTC at Wilkes U.
**Honors:** Honors program. Honor societies.
**Academic Assistance:** Remedial reading, writing, math, and study skills. Nonremedial tutoring.

**STUDENT LIFE. Housing:** Coed, women's, and men's dorms. School-owned/operated apartments. Off-campus privately-owned housing. Special-interest housing. 31% of students live in college housing.
**Social atmosphere:** Students gather at The Woods and The 1st Stop, on-campus snack shops. Students also frequent off-campus bars such as Mickey Gannon's, Sal's, and Heil's. The student government oversees all on-campus events and has the most influence on campus life. Favorite campus events include Spring Fling, Homecoming, and the annual Symphony Ball. The student newspaper reports, "Off-campus life in Scranton allows for a multitude of activity, especially for students over age 21. With so many colleges in Scranton and Wilkes-Barre, you're never bored."
**Services and counseling/handicapped student services:** Placement services. Health service. Day care. Counseling services for minority and older students. Personal and psychological counseling. Career and academic guidance services. Religious counseling. Physically disabled student services. Learning disabled services. Notetaking services. Tape recorders. Tutors. Reader services for the blind.
**Campus organizations:** Undergraduate student government. Student newspaper (Woodword, published once/month). Literary magazine. Yearbook. Radio and TV stations. Choir, St. Cecilia Music Society, Marywood Players, International Performing Arts Society, Scriblerus Club, Circle K, Volunteers in Action, ski, karate, and swim clubs, Student Pugwash Society, student arts magazine, environmental club, multicultural club, philosophy club, Academic Honors Program publication, departmental, professional, and special-interest groups, 41 organizations in all.
**Religious organizations:** Campus Ministry.
**Minority/foreign student organizations:** Multicultural Club. International Students.

**ATHLETICS. Physical education requirements:** Two semesters of physical education required.
**Intercollegiate competition:** Basketball (W), field hockey (W), softball (W), tennis (W), volleyball (W). Member of Eastern States Athletic Conference, NCAA Division III.
**Intramural and club sports:** Intramural basketball, racquetball, tennis, volleyball.

**ADMISSIONS. Academic basis for candidate selection** (in order of priority): Secondary school record, class rank, standardized test scores, school's recommendation, essay.
**Nonacademic basis for candidate selection:** Character and personality, extracurricular participation, particular talent or ability, and alumni/ae relationship are considered.
**Requirements:** Graduation from secondary school is recommended; GED is accepted. 16 units and the following program of study are required: 4 units of English, 2 units of math, 1 unit of lab science, 3 units of social studies, 6 units of academic electives. Minimum combined SAT score of 770, rank in top half of secondary school class, and minimum 2.5 GPA recommended. Minimum combined SAT score of 850 (composite ACT score of 20) required of nursing program applicants. Minimum combined SAT score of 850 (composite ACT score of 21) required of education and special education program applicants. Portfolio required of art program applicants. Audition required of music program applicants. Academic Modified Program and Act 101 program for applicants not normally admissible. SAT is required; ACT may be substituted. Campus visit and interview recommended. No off-campus interviews.
**Procedure:** Take SAT or ACT by May 1 of 12th year. Visit college for interview by May 1 of 12th year. Suggest filing application by May 1. Notification of admission on rolling basis. Reply is required by May 1. $100 tuition deposit, refundable until May 1. $200 room deposit, refundable until May 1. Freshmen accepted for terms other than fall.
**Special programs:** Admission may be deferred two years. Credit and/or placement may be granted through CEEB Advanced Placement exams for scores of 3 or higher. Credit may be granted through CLEP general and subject exams, ACT PEP and DANTES exams, and military and life experience. Credit and placement may be granted through challenge exams. Early entrance/early admission program. Concurrent enrollment program.
**Transfer students:** Transfer students accepted for terms other than fall. In fall 1993, 36% of all new students were transfers into all classes. 321 transfer applications were received, 256 were accepted. Application deadline is rolling for fall; rolling for spring. Minimum 2.5 GPA required. Lowest course grade accepted is "C." At least 60 semester hours must be completed at the college to receive degree.
**Admissions contact:** Fred R. Brooks, Jr., M.Div., Director of Admissions. 717 348-6234.

**FINANCIAL AID. Available aid:** Pell grants, SEOG, state scholarships and grants, school scholarships and grants, private scholarships and grants, ROTC scholarships, academic merit scholarships, and aid for undergraduate foreign students. Perkins Loans (NDSL), PLUS, Stafford Loans (GSL), state loans, private loans, and SLS. Tuition Plan Inc., Knight Tuition Plans, AMS, Tuition Management Systems, deferred payment plan, and family tuition reduction.
**Financial aid statistics:** 25% of aid is not need-based. In 1993-94, 85% of all undergraduate applicants received aid; 90% of freshman applicants. Average amounts of aid awarded freshmen: Scholarships and grants, $5,000; loans, $2,625.
**Supporting data/closing dates:** FAFSA: Priority filing date is February 15. School's own aid application: Priority filing date is February 15. Income tax forms: Priority filing date is April 15. Notification of awards begins March 1.
**Financial aid contact:** Stanley Skrutski, M.S., Director of Financial Aid. 717 348-6225.

**STUDENT EMPLOYMENT.** College Work/Study Program. Institutional employment. 24% of full-time undergraduates work on campus during school year. Students may expect to earn an average of $900 during school year. Off-campus part-time employment opportunities rated "good."

**COMPUTER FACILITIES.** 300 IBM/IBM-compatible and Macintosh/Apple microcomputers; 106 are networked. Students may access Digital minicomputer/mainframe systems, BITNET, Internet. Residence halls may be equipped with stand-alone microcomputers, modems. Client/LAN operating systems include Apple/Macintosh, DOS, Windows NT, DEC, LocalTalk/AppleTalk, Microsoft, Novell. 1,000 major computer languages and software packages available. Computer facilities are available to all students.
**Fees:** $45 computer fee per course.
**Hours:** 8 AM-10 PM (M-F); 8 AM-5 PM (Sa); 1 PM-10 PM (Su); 24 hours in residence halls.

**GRADUATE CAREER DATA.** Graduate school percentages: 5% enter law school. 3% enter medical school. 5% enter graduate business programs. 75% enter graduate arts and sciences programs. Highest graduate school enrollments: Bloomsburg U of Pennsylvania, Edinboro U of Pennsylvania, SUNY at Binghamton, Marywood College, U of Scranton. 75% of graduates choose careers in business and industry. Companies and businesses that hire graduates: Aetna, American Restaurant Association, Dunn & Bradstreet, Emery Worldwide, IBM, K mart, Macy's, Marriott, Mellon Bank, Metropolitan Life, RCA, Talbots, U.S. Army, health centers, schools.

**PROMINENT ALUMNI/AE.** Dr. Judith Tama, network vice president of engineering services, AT&T; Ann Giordano, vice president, Digital Corp.; Ann Bender Dufficy, New York Supreme Court Justice.

# Mercyhurst College

**Erie, PA 16546** **814 824-2200**

**1994-95 Costs.** Tuition: $9,813. Room & board: $4,050. Fees, books, misc. academic expenses (school's estimate): $1,538.
**Enrollment.** Undergraduates: 764 men, 1,066 women (full-time). Freshman class: 1,545 applicants, 1,043 accepted, 397 enrolled. Graduate enrollment: 33 men, 46 women.
**Test score averages/ranges.** Average SAT scores: 457 verbal, 506 math. Range of SAT scores of middle 50%: 426-532 verbal, 470-556 math. Average ACT scores: 21 English, 24 math, 23 composite. Range of ACT scores of middle 50%: 20-24 English, 20-26 math.
**Faculty.** 101 full-time; 53 part-time. 63% of faculty holds highest degree in specific field. Student/faculty ratio: 17 to 1.
**Selectivity rating.** Less competitive.

**PROFILE.** Mercyhurst, founded in 1926, is a private, church-affiliated college. In addition to baccalaureate degrees in the liberal arts, career, and preprofessional areas, Mercyhurst confers master's degrees. Its 75-acre campus is located in Erie, 100 miles southwest of Buffalo, N.Y.

**Accreditation:** MSACS. Professionally accredited by the American Dental Association, the American Dietetic Association, the Council on Social Work Education, the National Athletic Trainers Association.
**Religious orientation:** Mercyhurst College is affiliated with the Roman Catholic Church (Sisters of Mercy); One course in religion required.
**Library:** Collections totaling over 140,613 volumes, 825 periodical subscriptions, and 42,000 microform items.
**Special facilities/museums:** Art gallery, college-owned restaurant for hotel/restaurant management department, observatory, archaeology lab.
**Athletic facilities:** Gymnasium, ice rink, baseball, football, and soccer fields, Nautilus center, crew tanks.

**STUDENT BODY. Undergraduate profile:** 64% are state residents; 19% are transfers. 1% Asian-American, 8% Black, 2% Hispanic, 1% Native American, 84% White, 4% Other. Average age of undergraduates is 23.
**Freshman profile:** Majority of accepted applicants took SAT. 65% of freshmen come from public schools.
**Undergraduate achievement:** 78% of fall 1992 freshmen returned for fall 1993 term. 53% of entering class graduated. 17% of students who completed a degree program went on to graduate study within one year.
**Foreign students:** 169 students are from out of the country. Countries represented include Canada, England, Ireland, and Japan; 17 in all.

**PROGRAMS OF STUDY. Degrees:** B.A., B.Mus., B.S.Nurs.
**Majors:** Accounting, Advertising/Public Relations, Anthropology/Archaeology, Art, Art Therapy, Biology, Broadcasting, Business Administration, Business/Chemistry, Business Education, Business/Finance, Business Management/Organizational Science, Business/Sports Management, Chemistry, Communication, Computer Management Information Systems, Criminal Justice, Dance, Dietetics, Early Childhood Education, Elementary Education, Engineering, English, English Education, Environmental Science, Fashion Merchandising, Food Sciences/Human Nutrition, Geology, History, History/Research/Intelligence Analyst Program, Hotel/Restaurant/Institutional Management, Human Ecology/Home Economics, Interior Design, Journalism, Mathematics, Mathematics Education, Medical Technology, Music, Music Education, Music Theory/Composition, Nutrition/Food, Piano, Political Science, Psychology, Religious Education, Risk Management/Insurance, Secondary Education, Social Science Education, Social Work, Sociology, Special Education, Sports Medicine, Voice.
**Distribution of degrees:** The majors with the highest enrollment are business, natural sciences, and music.
**Requirements:** General education requirement.
**Academic regulations:** Freshmen must maintain minimum 1.8 GPA; sophomores, juniors, seniors, 2.0 GPA.
**Special:** Minors offered in most majors and in earth/space science, environmental studies, gerontology, housing/interior design, philosophy, religious studies, textiles/clothing, theatre arts, and writing. Associate's degrees offered. Self-designed majors. Double majors. Independent study. Accelerated study. Pass/fail grading option. Internships. Cooperative education programs. Graduate school at which undergraduates may take graduate-level courses. Preprofessional programs in law, medicine, veterinary science, pharmacy, and dentistry. 3-2 engineering program. Washington Semester. Exchange programs with Gannon U and U of Pittsburgh. Teacher certification in early childhood, elementary, sec-

ondary, and special education. Certification in specific subject areas. Study abroad in England, Ireland, and Mexico. ROTC at Gannon U.
**Honors:** Honors program. Honor societies.
**Academic Assistance:** Remedial reading, writing, math, and study skills. Nonremedial tutoring.

**STUDENT LIFE. Housing:** All freshmen and sophomores must live on campus unless living with family. Women's and men's dorms. School-owned/operated apartments. 78% of students live in college housing.
**Social atmosphere:** On campus, students gather at the student union and Garvey Park. Off campus, students frequent Herman's Tavern and The Shaggy Dog. Groups with a considerable influence on campus social life include the Student Activities Committee, the hockey team, and residents of townhouses. Spring Activity Weekend is a big event on campus. Other popular activities include hockey games, the SAC coffeehouse, formals, films for discussion, and townhouse parties. "Cultural life is expanding through a newly revived coffeehouse which welcomes amateur entertainment and intellectual, social discussion," comments the editor of the student newspaper. "However, social life is strained on weekends due to strict policies under the resident director. Many seek nightlife on the streets of Erie, although on-campus parties are sometimes successful."
**Services and counseling/handicapped student services:** Placement services. Health service. Women's center. Day care. Counseling services for minority, military, veteran, and older students. Personal and psychological counseling. Career and academic guidance services. Religious counseling. Physically disabled student services. Learning disabled program/services. Notetaking services. Tape recorders. Tutors.
**Campus organizations:** Undergraduate student government. Student newspaper (Merciad, published once/week). Literary magazine. Yearbook. Radio station. Folk choir, chorus, debating, special-interest groups, 31 organizations in all.
**Religious organizations:** Campus Ministry.
**Minority/foreign student organizations:** Association of Black Collegians. International Student Association.

**ATHLETICS. Physical education requirements:** None.
**Intercollegiate competition:** 20% of students participate. Baseball (M), basketball (M,W), cheerleading (M,W), crew (M,W), cross-country (M,W), football (M), golf (M), ice hockey (M), soccer (M,W), softball (W), tennis (M,W), volleyball (W). Member of ECAC, NCAA Division II, NCAA Division III for football and ice hockey.
**Intramural and club sports:** 10% of students participate. Intramural basketball, bowling, football, golf, hockey, soccer, softball, volleyball. Men's club cycling, volleyball.

**ADMISSIONS. Academic basis for candidate selection** (in order of priority): Secondary school record, school's recommendation, essay, class rank, standardized test scores.
**Nonacademic basis for candidate selection:** Character and personality are emphasized. Extracurricular participation and particular talent or ability are important. Geographical distribution and alumni/ae relationship are considered.
**Requirements:** Graduation from secondary school is required; GED is accepted. 18 units and the following program of study are recommended: 4 units of English, 3 units of math, 3 units of science including 1 unit of lab, 2 units of foreign language, 1 unit of social studies, 2 units of history, 2 units of electives. Minimum combined SAT score of 800, rank in top half of secondary school class, or minimum 2.5 GPA recommended. Portfolio required of art program applicants. Audition required of music program applicants. Conditional admission possible for applicants not meeting standard requirements. Foundations Program for applicants not normally admissible. SAT or ACT is required. Campus visit and interview recommended. Off-campus interviews available with an admissions representative.
**Procedure:** Take SAT or ACT by January of 12th year. Take ACH by March of 12th year. Visit college for interview by April of 12th year. Notification of admission is sent on rolling basis beginning January 15. Reply is required by May 1. $200 nonrefundable tuition deposit. $200 nonrefundable room deposit. Freshmen accepted for terms other than fall.
**Special programs:** Admission may be deferred one year. Credit and/or placement may be granted through CEEB Advanced Placement exams for scores of 3 or higher. Credit and/or placement may be granted through CLEP general and subject exams. Credit and placement may be granted through ACT PEP and challenge exams and military and life experience. Concurrent enrollment program.
**Transfer students:** Transfer students accepted for terms other than fall. In fall 1993, 19% of all new students were transfers into all classes. 282 transfer applications were received, 205 were accepted. Application deadline is rolling for fall; rolling for spring. Minimum 2.0 GPA required. Lowest course grade accepted is "C." Maximum number of transferable credits is 75 semester hours. At least 45 semester hours must be completed at the college to receive degree.
**Admissions contact:** Andrew Roth, M.B.A., Dean of Enrollment Services. 814 824-2202.

**FINANCIAL AID. Available aid:** Pell grants, SEOG, Federal Nursing Student Scholarships, state scholarships and grants, school scholarships and grants, private scholarships and grants, ROTC scholarships, academic merit scholarships, athletic scholarships, and aid for undergraduate foreign students. Perkins Loans (NDSL), PLUS, Stafford Loans (GSL), state loans, school loans, private loans, and SLS. AMS, deferred payment plan, and family tuition reduction.
**Financial aid statistics:** 17% of aid is not need-based. In 1993-94, 100% of all undergraduate applicants received aid. Average amounts of aid awarded freshmen: Scholarships and grants, $4,000; loans, $2,000.
**Supporting data/closing dates:** School's own aid application: Accepted on rolling basis. State aid form: Accepted on rolling basis. Income tax forms: Accepted on rolling basis. Notification of awards on rolling basis.
**Financial aid contact:** Catherine Crawford, M.A., Director of Financial Aid. 814 824-2287.

**STUDENT EMPLOYMENT.** College Work/Study Program. Institutional employment. 65% of full-time undergraduates work on campus during school year. Students may expect to earn an average of $750 during school year. Off-campus part-time employment opportunities rated "good."

**COMPUTER FACILITIES.** 150 IBM/IBM-compatible and Macintosh/Apple microcomputers; 120 are networked. Students may access Hewlett-Packard minicomputer/mainframe systems. Residence halls may be equipped with networked microcomputers. Computer languages and software packages include BASIC, COBOL, FORTRAN, Lotus 1-2-3, Pascal, SPSS, WordPerfect. Computer facilities are available to all students.
**Fees:** None.

**GRADUATE CAREER DATA.** Graduate school percentages: 2% enter law school. 2% enter medical school. 2% enter dental school. 2% enter graduate business programs. 9% enter graduate arts and sciences programs. Highest graduate school enrollments: Case Western Reserve U, Pennsylvania State U, U of Pittsburgh. 28% of graduates choose careers in business and industry. Companies and businesses that hire graduates: Arthur Andersen, Hyatt, Marriott, Diocese of Erie.

**PROMINENT ALUMNI/AE.** Linda Colvin-Rhodes, secretary for aging, state of Pennsylvania; Joyce Savocchio, mayor, Erie; Joe Necastro, treasurer, *U.S. News & World Report*.

# Messiah College

**Grantham, PA 17027-0800 — 717 766-2511**

**1994-95 Costs.** Tuition: $10,300. Room & board: $5,070. Fees, books, misc. academic expenses (school's estimate): $585.
**Enrollment.** Undergraduates: 911 men, 1,347 women (full-time). Freshman class: 1,742 applicants, 1,382 accepted, 607 enrolled.
**Test score averages/ranges.** Average SAT scores: 509 verbal, 555 math. Range of SAT scores of middle 50%: 450-550 verbal, 470-610 math. Average ACT scores: 22 English, 25 math, 24 composite. Range of ACT scores of middle 50%: 21-27 English, 25-29 math.
**Faculty.** 152 full-time; 65 part-time. 68% of faculty holds doctoral degree. Student/faculty ratio: 15 to 1.
**Selectivity rating.** More competitive.

**PROFILE.** Messiah, founded in 1909, is a private, church-affiliated, liberal arts college. Its 300-acre campus in located in Grantham, 10 miles southwest of Harrisburg.
**Accreditation:** MSACS. Professionally accredited by the American Dietetic Association, the National Association of Schools of Music, the National League for Nursing.
**Religious orientation:** Messiah College is affiliated with the Brethren in Christ Church; 18 semester hours of religion required.
**Library:** Collections totaling over 180,000 volumes, 500 periodical subscriptions, and 5,000 microform items.
**Special facilities/museums:** Museum archives, natural science museum, on-campus preschool and elementary school.
**Athletic facilities:** Gymnasium, natatorium, racquetball and tennis courts, athletic fields, sports arena, field house, weight rooms.

**STUDENT BODY. Undergraduate profile:** 53% are state residents; 19% are transfers. 3% Asian-American, 4% Black, 3% Hispanic, 88% White, 2% Other. Average age of undergraduates is 19.
**Freshman profile:** 1% of freshmen who took SAT scored 700 or over on verbal, 7% scored 700 or over on math; 15% scored 600 or over on verbal, 38% scored 600 or over on math; 59% scored 500 or over on verbal, 84% scored 500 or over on math; 99% scored 400 or over on verbal, 99% scored 400 or over on math; 100% scored 300 or over on verbal, 100% scored 300 or over on math. 95% of accepted applicants took SAT; 5% took ACT. 76% of freshmen come from public schools.
**Undergraduate achievement:** 86% of fall 1992 freshmen returned for fall 1993 term. 64% of entering class graduated. 12% of students who completed a degree program immediately went on to graduate study.
**Foreign students:** 52 students are from out of the country. Countries represented include Canada, China, Japan, Kenya, Zambia, and Zimbabwe; 21 in all.

**PROGRAMS OF STUDY. Degrees:** B.A., B.S.
**Majors:** Accounting, Art, Behavioral Science, Bible, Biochemistry, Biology, Business Administration, Business Information Systems, Chemistry, Christian Education, Christian Ministries, Communication, Computer Science, Dietetics, Early Childhood, Economics, Education, Elementary Education, Engineering, English, Family Studies, French, German, Health/Physical Education, History, Home Economics, Human Resource Management, Humanities, International Business, Journalism, Marketing, Mathematics, Medical Technology, Music, Music/Christian Education, Natural Science, Nursing, Physical Education, Physics, Political Science, Pre-Dental, Pre-Law, Pre-Medical, Pre-Ministry, Pre-Occupational Therapy, Pre-Physical Therapy, Pre-Veterinary, Psychology, Radio/TV/Film, Religion, Social Studies, Social Work, Sociology, Spanish, Sports Medicine, Theatre.
**Distribution of degrees:** The majors with the highest enrollment are business, mathematics, and education; home economics and music have the lowest.
**Requirements:** General education requirement.
**Academic regulations:** Freshmen must maintain minimum 1.8 GPA; sophomores, 1.8 GPA; juniors, 2.0 GPA; seniors, 2.0 GPA.
**Special:** Two-year certificate programs offered in religious studies and retail management. Courses offered in Greek. Self-designed majors. Double majors. Independent study. Accelerated study. Pass/fail grading option. Internships. Graduate school at which undergraduates may take graduate-level courses. Preprofessional programs in medicine, veterinary science, dentistry, theology, occupational therapy, and physical therapy. Member of Christian College Consortium. Washington Semester. Teacher certification in early childhood, elementary, and secondary education. Study abroad in China, England, France, Germany, Kenya, and Spain.
**Academic Assistance:** Remedial reading, writing, math, and study skills.

**STUDENT LIFE. Housing:** All first-year students must live on campus. Women's and men's dorms. School-owned/operated apartments. 92% of students live in college housing.
**Social atmosphere:** According to the student newspaper, "Although there is an attempt to bring cultured figures to the campus (we have many distinguished figures visit and several first-rate art shows) the social life on campus is lacking somewhat, as the rules do not permit dancing and male/female visitation restrictions exist after certain hours." The student association is influential on campus. Favorite gathering spots include the Student Center

Snack Shoppe and the library. Off campus, students congregate at the White Mountain Creamery, Pizza Hut, the Ground Round, and the Gingerbread Man. Homecoming, the King's Tournament, the Spring Special, and theatre productions are all popular events.

**Services and counseling/handicapped student services:** Placement services. Health service. Counseling services for minority and veteran students. Personal and psychological counseling. Career and academic guidance services. Religious counseling.

**Campus organizations:** Undergraduate student government. Student newspaper (Swinging Bridge). Literary magazine. Yearbook. Radio station. Choral society, instrumental ensembles, Platform Arts Society, camera and outing clubs, cultural series.

**Religious organizations:** Gospel Team, Music Ministries.

**Minority/foreign student organizations:** Black Student Union. Cultural Awareness Club.

**ATHLETICS. Physical education requirements:** Three semesters of physical education required.

**Intercollegiate competition:** 16% of students participate. Baseball (M), basketball (M,W), cheerleading (M,W), cross-country (M,W), field hockey (W), golf (M), soccer (M,W), softball (W), tennis (M,W), track (outdoor) (M,W), volleyball (W), wrestling (M). Member of ECAC, Middle Atlantic Conference, NCAA Division III.

**Intramural and club sports:** 43% of students participate. Intramural badminton, basketball, bowling, cross-country, floor hockey, flag football, soccer, softball, table tennis, volleyball. Men's club lacrosse, volleyball. Women's club lacrosse.

**ADMISSIONS. Academic basis for candidate selection** (in order of priority): Secondary school record, class rank, standardized test scores, school's recommendation, essay.

**Nonacademic basis for candidate selection:** Character and personality are emphasized. Extracurricular participation is important. Particular talent or ability is considered.

**Requirements:** Graduation from secondary school is required; GED is not accepted. 16 units and the following program of study are required: 4 units of English, 2 units of math, 2 units of lab science, 2 units of foreign language, 2 units of social studies, 2 units of electives. Minimum combined SAT score of 850 (composite ACT score of 19), rank in top half of secondary school class, and minimum "C+" average required. Audition required of music program applicants. Conditional admission possible for applicants not meeting standard requirements. SAT or ACT is required. Campus visit and interview recommended. Off-campus interviews available with an admissions representative.

**Procedure:** Take SAT or ACT by February 1 of 12th year. Visit college for interview by March 1 of 12th year. Suggest filing application by March 1. Application deadline is April 1. Notification of admission on rolling basis. Reply is required within 30 days of acceptance. $100 room deposit, refundable until May 1. Freshmen accepted for terms other than fall.

**Special programs:** Admission may be deferred. Credit and/or placement may be granted through CEEB Advanced Placement exams for scores of 3 or higher. Credit and/or placement may be granted through CLEP general and subject exams. Placement may be granted through challenge exams.

**Transfer students:** Transfer students accepted for terms other than fall. In fall 1993, 19% of all new students were transfers into all classes. 311 transfer applications were received, 202 were accepted. Application deadline is December 1 for fall; July 1 for spring. Minimum 2.0 GPA required. Lowest course grade accepted is "C." Maximum number of transferable credits is 60 semester hours. At least 60 semester hours must be completed at the college to receive degree.

**Admissions contact:** Ron E. Long, M.A., Vice President. 717 691-6000.

**FINANCIAL AID. Available aid:** Pell grants, SEOG, state scholarships and grants, school scholarships and grants, private scholarships and grants, academic merit scholarships, and aid for undergraduate foreign students. Perkins Loans (NDSL), PLUS, Stafford Loans (GSL), NSL, state loans, school loans, private loans, and SLS. Family tuition reduction. Institutional monthly payment plan.

**Financial aid statistics:** 40% of aid is not need-based. In 1993-94, 86% of all undergraduate applicants received aid; 87% of freshman applicants. Average amounts of aid awarded freshmen: Scholarships and grants, $5,250; loans, $2,500.

**Supporting data/closing dates:** FAFSA/FAF/FFS: Deadline is April 1. School's own aid application: Deadline is April 1. State aid form: Deadline is April 1. Notification of awards on rolling basis.

**Financial aid contact:** Greg Gearhart, M.A., Director of Financial Aid. 717 691-6007.

**STUDENT EMPLOYMENT.** College Work/Study Program. Institutional employment. 42% of full-time undergraduates work on campus during school year. Students may expect to earn an average of $1,500 during school year. Off-campus part-time employment opportunities rated "good."

**COMPUTER FACILITIES.** 750 IBM/IBM-compatible and Macintosh/Apple microcomputers; 500 are networked. Students may access Digital minicomputer/mainframe systems, Internet. Residence halls may be equipped with networked microcomputers. Client/LAN operating systems include Apple/Macintosh, DOS, Windows NT. Computer facilities are available to all students.

**Fees:** None.

**Hours:** 24 hours.

**GRADUATE CAREER DATA.** Graduate school percentages: 2% enter law school. 2% enter medical school. 1% enter dental school. 3% enter graduate business programs. 2% enter graduate arts and sciences programs. 1% enter theological school/seminary. 20% of graduates choose careers in business and industry.

# Millersville University of Pennsylvania

**Millersville, PA 17551-0302 — 717 872-3011**

**1993-94 Costs.** Tuition: $2,912 (state residents), $7,653 (out-of-state). Room & board: $3,620. Fees, books, misc. academic expenses (school's estimate): $1,246.

**Enrollment.** Undergraduates: 2,205 men, 3,148 women (full-time). Freshman class: 6,137 applicants, 2,996 accepted, 1,017 enrolled. Graduate enrollment: 198 men, 566 women.

**Test score averages/ranges.** Average SAT scores: 489 verbal, 534 math.

**Faculty.** 325 full-time; 77 part-time. 71% of faculty holds doctoral degree. Student/faculty ratio: 18 to 1.

**Selectivity rating.** More competitive.

**PROFILE.** Millersville, founded in 1855, is a public, liberal arts university. Its 225-acre campus is located in Millersville, four miles south of Lancaster.

**Accreditation:** MSACS. Professionally accredited by the American Medical Association (CAHEA), the Council on Social Work Education, the National Association of Schools of Music, the National Council for Accreditation of Teacher Education, the National League for Nursing.

**Religious orientation:** Millersville University of Pennsylvania is nonsectarian; no religious requirements.

**Library:** Collections totaling over 454,482 volumes, 1,745 periodical subscriptions, and 401,511 microform items.

**Special facilities/museums:** Art galleries, early childhood education lab school, language lab, extensive inventory of scientific and technological instrumentation.

**Athletic facilities:** Gymnasiums, swimming pools, tennis courts, softball fields.

**STUDENT BODY. Undergraduate profile:** 92% are state residents; 20% are transfers. 2% Asian-American, 5% Black, 1% Hispanic, 92% White. Average age of undergraduates is 22.

**Freshman profile:** 2% of freshmen who took SAT scored 700 or over on math; 6% scored 600 or over on verbal, 19% scored 600 or over on math; 43% scored 500 or over on verbal, 72% scored 500 or over on math; 94% scored 400 or over on verbal, 98% scored 400 or over on math; 100% scored 300 or over on verbal, 100% scored 300 or over on math. 87% of accepted applicants took SAT.

**Undergraduate achievement:** 87% of fall 1991 freshmen returned for fall 1992 term. 40% of entering class graduated.

**Foreign students:** 75 students are from out of the country. Countries represented include China, Germany, India, Japan, Kenya, and Sweden; 36 in all.

**PROGRAMS OF STUDY. Degrees:** B.A., B.F.A., B.S., B.S.Ed., B.S.Nurs.

**Majors:** Accounting, Acting, Actuarial Science/Statistics, Anthropology, Art, Art Education, Biochemistry, Biology, Biotechnology, Broadcasting, Business Administration, Chemistry, Chemistry/Cooperative Engineering, Commercial Art, Comparative Literature, Computer Science, Early Childhood Education, Earth Science, East Asian Studies, Economics, Elementary Education, Engineering, English, English as a Second Language, Environmental Biology, Finance, French, Geography, Geology, German, Greek, History, Industrial Technology, International Studies, Journalism, Latin, Latin American Studies, Linguistics, Marine Biology, Marketing, Mathematics, Medical Technology, Meteorology, Music, Music Education, Nursing, Occupational Safety/Hygiene Management, Oceanography, Philosophy, Physics, Physics/Computer Engineering, Physics/Cooperative Engineering, Political Science, Pre-Podiatry, Psychology, Public Relations, Respiratory Therapy, Russian, Secondary Education, Social Studies, Social Work, Sociology, Spanish, Special Education, Speech Communications, Technical Theatre, Technology Education.

**Distribution of degrees:** The majors with the highest enrollment are elementary education, business administration, and psychology; meteorology, French, and philosophy have the lowest.

**Requirements:** General education requirement.

**Academic regulations:** Freshmen must maintain minimum 1.75 GPA; sophomores, juniors, seniors, 2.0 GPA.

**Special:** Minors offered in most majors and in American literature, art history, athletic coaching, British literature, criminal justice, engineering physics, film/literature, gerontology, management, studio art, theatre, and writing. Course offered in speech/drama. Teaching intern program. Associate's degrees offered. Double majors. Dual degrees. Independent study. Accelerated study. Pass/fail grading option. Internships. Cooperative education programs. Graduate school at which undergraduates may take graduate-level courses. Preprofessional programs in law, medicine, optometry, and podiatry. 3-2 engineering programs with Pennsylvania State U and U of Pennsylvania. Member of Marine Science Consortium; off-campus study possible at Wallops Island, Va. Exchange program with Franklin & Marshall Coll. Teacher certification in early childhood, elementary, secondary, and special education. Certification in specific subject areas. Study abroad in England (Humberside Coll), Germany (Philipps U), and Japan (Aiche U). ROTC.

**Honors:** Honors program. Honor societies.

**Academic Assistance:** Remedial reading, writing, math, and study skills. Nonremedial tutoring.

**STUDENT LIFE. Housing:** All freshmen must live on campus unless living with family. Coed, women's, and men's dorms. School-owned/operated apartments. 40% of students live in college housing.

**Social atmosphere:** The student newspaper describes Millersville as having a "rather quiet, rural atmosphere. It may be difficult to go to Lancaster and/or out in general without a car. The social life is somewhat limited, but expanding. There are a variety of national and local Greek organizations, at least three church groups, and a dramatics organization which does a 'Saturday Night Special' in addition to regular plays and musicals. Culturally, we have had Victor Borge and the Pittsburgh Philharmonic, the Ballet Theatre of Monte Carlo, the Netherlands Dance Theatre, and National Players productions of *Amadeus* and *Dracula*." Favorite off-campus spots include the House of Pizza, the Sugar Bowl, and the Park City Mall.

**Services and counseling/handicapped student services:** Placement services. Health service. Day care. Counseling services for minority, military, veteran, and older students. Birth control, personal, and psychological counseling. Career and academic guidance services. Religious counseling. Physically disabled student services. Learning disabled services. Notetaking services. Tape recorders. Tutors. Reader services for the blind.

**Campus organizations:** Undergraduate student government. Student newspaper (Snapper, published once/week). Literary magazine. Yearbook. Radio station. Music theatre, choral music group, marching band, gospel choir, madrigal singers, men's chorus, jazz ensemble, pep and symphonic bands, chamber ensemble, Circle K, College Republicans, outing club, academic, athletic, professional, service, and special-interest groups, 100 organizations in all. 13 fraternities, no chapter houses; 12 sororities, no chapter houses. 10% of men join a fraternity. 10% of women join a sorority.

**Religious organizations:** Brothers & Sisters in Christ, Campus Crusade for Christ, Black Campus Ministry, Newman Association, Hillel, Intervarsity Christian Fellowship.

**Minority/foreign student organizations:** Black Student Union, Black Greek Council. International Relations Club, French Circle, Japanese Culture Club, German and Spanish clubs.

**ATHLETICS. Physical education requirements:** Three credit hours of physical education required.

**Intercollegiate competition:** 20% of students participate. Baseball (M), basketball (M,W), cheerleading (M,W), cross-country (M,W), diving (W), field hockey (W), football (M), golf (M), lacrosse (W), soccer (M), softball (W), swimming (W), tennis (M,W), track (indoor) (M,W), track (outdoor) (M,W), track and field (indoor) (M,W), track and field (outdoor) (M,W), volleyball (W), wrestling (M). Member of ECAC, NCAA Division I for wrestling, NCAA Division II, PSAC.

**Intramural and club sports:** 50% of students participate. Intramural badminton, basketball, cross-country, flag football, foul-shooting contest, frisbee, home run derby, hot-shot contest, racquetball, sand volleyball, soccer, softball, street hockey, table tennis, tennis, track, volleyball, walleyball. Men's club archery, bicycling, bowling, fencing, folk dancing, ice hockey, lacrosse, martial arts, rugby, volleyball, water polo. Women's club archery, bicycling, bowling, dance, fencing, folk dancing, martial arts, synchronized swimming, water polo.

**ADMISSIONS. Academic basis for candidate selection** (in order of priority): Class rank, secondary school record, standardized test scores, school's recommendation.

**Nonacademic basis for candidate selection:** Character and personality are important. Extracurricular participation, particular talent or ability, and alumni/ae relationship are considered.

**Requirements:** Graduation from secondary school is required; GED is accepted. 14 units and the following program of study are required: 4 units of English, 3 units of math, 2 units of science including 1 unit of lab, 4 units of social studies. Minimum combined SAT score of 900 and rank in top two-fifths of secondary school class recommended. Portfolio required of art program applicants. Audition required of music program applicants. EOP for applicants not normally admissible. SAT is required; ACT may be substituted. Campus visit and interview recommended. Off-campus interviews available with admissions and alumni representatives.

**Procedure:** Take SAT or ACT by July of 12th year. Visit college for interview by February of 12th year. Suggest filing application by November; no deadline. Notification of admission on rolling basis. Reply is required by April 1. $75 tuition deposit, refundable until first full day of scheduled classes. $125 room deposit, refundable due to illness or compulsory military service only. Freshmen accepted for terms other than fall.

**Special programs:** Admission may be deferred one year. Credit and/or placement may be granted through CEEB Advanced Placement exams for scores of 3 or higher. Credit may be granted through CLEP general and subject exams. Credit may be granted through ACT PEP exams and military experience. Credit and placement may be granted through challenge exams. Early entrance/early admission program. Concurrent enrollment program.

**Transfer students:** Transfer students accepted for terms other than fall. In fall 1992, 20% of all new students were transfers into all classes. 980 transfer applications were received, 416 were accepted. Application deadline is rolling for fall; rolling for spring. Minimum 2.5 GPA required. Lowest course grade accepted is "C." Maximum number of transferable credits is 60 semester hours from a two-year school and 90 semester hours from a four-year school. At least 30 semester hours must be completed at the university to receive degree.

**Admissions contact:** Darrell Davis, M.S., Director of Admissions. 717 872-3371.

**FINANCIAL AID. Available aid:** Pell grants, SEOG, state scholarships and grants, school scholarships and grants, private scholarships and grants, ROTC scholarships, academic merit scholarships, and athletic scholarships. Perkins Loans (NDSL), PLUS, Stafford Loans (GSL), state loans, private loans, and SLS. Millersville Installment Payment Plan.

**Financial aid statistics:** 49% of aid is not need-based. In 1992-93, 87% of all undergraduate applicants received aid; 80% of freshman applicants. Average amounts of aid awarded freshmen: Scholarships and grants, $1,200; loans, $1,500.

**Supporting data/closing dates:** School's own aid application: Deadline is May 1. State aid form: Deadline is May 1. Income tax forms: Accepted on rolling basis. Notification of awards begins June 1.

**Financial aid contact:** Gene R. Wise, M.S., Director of Financial Aid. 717 872-3026.

**STUDENT EMPLOYMENT.** College Work/Study Program. Institutional employment. 20% of full-time undergraduates work on campus during school year. Students may expect to earn an average of $1,200 during school year. Off-campus part-time employment opportunities rated "excellent."

**COMPUTER FACILITIES.** 287 IBM/IBM-compatible and Macintosh/Apple microcomputers; 129 are networked. Students may access Digital, IBM, SUN minicomputer/mainframe systems, BITNET, Internet. Residence halls may be equipped with stand-alone microcomputers. Client/LAN operating systems include Apple/Macintosh, LocalTalk/AppleTalk. Computer languages and software packages include BASIC, C, COBOL, dBASE, Excel, FORTRAN, ImSL, Lotus 1-2-3, Microsoft Works, MINITAB, Modula 2, Pascal, SAS, SPSS-X, WordPerfect; 48 in all. Computer facilities are available to all students.

**Fees:** None.

**Hours:** 8 AM-11 PM (M-F); noon-5 PM (Sa); 2 PM-10 PM (Su).

**PROMINENT ALUMNI/AE.** Robert Walker, U.S. congressman; Louise Herr, judge, Lancaster County Court of Common Pleas; Tony Ward, photographer; David Aston-Reese, actor; Joan M. Detz, author and speech writer; J. Freeland Chryst, CEO, the Jay Group.

# Moore College of Art and Design

**Philadelphia, PA 19103 — 215 568-4515**

**1994-95 Costs.** Tuition: $14,017. Room & board: $5,143. Fees, books, misc. academic expenses (school's estimate): $1,000.

**Enrollment.** 330 women (full-time). Freshman class: 286 applicants, 228 accepted, 100 enrolled.

**Test score averages/ranges.** Average SAT scores: 420 verbal, 410 math.

**Faculty.** 35 full-time; 35 part-time. 9% of faculty holds highest degree in specific field. Student/faculty ratio: 10 to 1.

**Selectivity rating.** N/A.

**PROFILE.** Moore College of Art, founded in 1844, is a private college. Its two-acre campus is located in downtown Philadelphia.

**Accreditation:** MSACS. Professionally accredited by the Foundation for Interior Design Education Research, the National Association of Schools of Art and Design.

**Religious orientation:** Moore College of Art and Design is nonsectarian; no religious requirements.

**Library:** Collections totaling over 36,000 volumes, 227 periodical subscriptions, 195 microform items, 73,000 slides, 1,500 recordings, picture files, and exhibition catalogs.

**Special facilities/museums:** Art galleries.

**Athletic facilities:** Fitness center.

**STUDENT BODY. Undergraduate profile:** 70% are state residents; 21% are transfers. 11% Asian-American, 11% Black, 7% Hispanic, 71% White. Average age of undergraduates is 21.

**Freshman profile:** 2% of freshmen who took SAT scored 700 or over on math; 5% scored 600 or over on verbal, 6% scored 600 or over on math; 29% scored 500 or over on verbal, 21% scored 500 or over on math; 76% scored 400 or over on verbal, 66% scored 400 or over on math; 98% scored 300 or over on verbal, 100% scored 300 or over on math. 90% of accepted applicants took SAT. 80% of freshmen come from public schools.

**Undergraduate achievement:** 85% of fall 1992 freshmen returned for fall 1993 term. 75% of entering class graduated. 10% of students who completed a degree program went on to graduate study within five years.

**Foreign students:** 35 students are from out of the country. Countries represented include Hong Kong, Indonesia, Japan, Korea, Singapore, and Taiwan; 10 in all.

**PROGRAMS OF STUDY. Degrees:** B.F.A.

**Majors:** Ceramics, Fashion Design, Fashion Illustration, Graphic Design, Illustration, Interior Design, Jewelry/Metalsmithing, Painting, Printmaking, Sculpture, Textile Design.

**Distribution of degrees:** The majors with the highest enrollment are fine arts and graphic design.

**Requirements:** General education requirement.

**Academic regulations:** Minimum 2.0 GPA required for graduation.

**Special:** Minors offered in art history and art teaching certification. Self-designed majors. Double majors. Independent study. Pass/fail grading option. Internships. Cooperative education programs. Graduate school at which undergraduates may take graduate-level courses. Member of Association of Independent Colleges of Art & Design (AICAD); exchange possible through Mobility Program. Teacher certification in elementary and secondary education. Study abroad in France and Italy.

**Academic Assistance:** Remedial writing. Nonremedial tutoring.

**ADMISSIONS. Academic basis for candidate selection** (in order of priority): Secondary school record, school's recommendation, standardized test scores, class rank.

**Nonacademic basis for candidate selection:** Particular talent or ability is emphasized. Character and personality are important. Extracurricular participation is considered.

**Requirements:** Graduation from secondary school is required; GED is accepted. 16 units and the following program of study are recommended: 4 units of English, 2 units of math, 2 units of science, 2 units of social studies. Portfolio required of all applicants. SAT is required; ACT may be substituted. Campus visit and interview recommended. Off-campus interviews available with an admissions representative.

**Procedure:** Take SAT or ACT by December of 12th year. Visit college for interview by April 1 of 12th year. Suggest filing application by March 1; no deadline. Notification of admission on rolling basis. $200 tuition deposit, refundable until May 1. $200 room deposit, refundable until May 1. Freshmen accepted for fall term only.

**Special programs:** Admission may be deferred two years. Credit may be granted through CEEB Advanced Placement for scores of 4 or higher. Placement may be granted through CLEP general exams. Credit may be granted through CLEP subject exams. Early decision program. In fall 1993, 40 applied for early decision and 30 were accepted. Deadline for applying for early decision is December 15. Early entrance/early admission program.

**Transfer students:** Transfer students accepted for terms other than fall. In fall 1993, 21% of all new students were transfers into all classes. 52 transfer applications were received, 40 were accepted. Application deadline is August 15 for fall; January 1 for spring. Minimum 2.0 GPA required. Lowest course grade accepted is "C." Maximum number of transferable credits is 60 semester hours from a two-year school and 72 semester hours from a four-year school. At least 30 semester hours must be completed at the college to receive degree.

**Admissions contact:** Claire E. Gallicano, Director of Admissions. 215 568-4515.

**FINANCIAL AID. Available aid:** Pell grants, SEOG, state scholarships and grants, school scholarships and grants, private scholarships and grants, academic merit scholarships, and aid for undergraduate foreign students. Perkins Loans (NDSL), PLUS, and Stafford Loans (GSL). Tuition Management Systems and family tuition reduction.
**Financial aid statistics:** Average amounts of aid awarded freshmen: Scholarships and grants, $2,000; loans, $2,600.
**Supporting data/closing dates:** FAFSA/FAF/FFS: Priority filing date is April 1. School's own aid application: Accepted on rolling basis. State aid form: Deadline is May 1. Notification of awards on rolling basis.
**Financial aid contact:** Mary Wright, Director of Financial Aid. 215 568-4515.

# Moravian College

**Bethlehem, PA 18018** **215 861-1300**

**1994-95 Costs.** Tuition: $14,990. Room: $2,600. Board: $2,130. Fees, books, misc. academic expenses (school's estimate): $680.
**Enrollment.** Undergraduates: 566 men, 560 women (full-time). Freshman class: 1,232 applicants, 955 accepted, 303 enrolled. Graduate enrollment: 114 men, 72 women.
**Test score averages/ranges.** Range of SAT scores of middle 50%: 440-540 verbal, 490-580 math. Average ACT scores: 23 composite. Range of ACT scores of middle 50%: 22-26 composite.
**Faculty.** 79 full-time; 45 part-time. 91% of faculty holds highest degree in specific field. Student/faculty ratio: 14 to 1.
**Selectivity rating.** Competitive.

**PROFILE.** Moravian, founded in 1742, is a church-affiliated, liberal arts college. Its 60-acre campus is located in Bethlehem, 15 miles east of Allentown.

**Accreditation:** MSACS. Professionally accredited by the American Medical Association (CAHEA).
**Religious orientation:** Moravian College is affiliated with the Moravian Church; One semester of religion required of most students.
**Library:** Collections totaling over 225,000 volumes, 1,200 periodical subscriptions, and 3,537 microform items.
**Special facilities/museums:** Art gallery, music and art center, language lab.
**Athletic facilities:** Gymnasiums, basketball, tennis, badminton, and volleyball courts, weight rooms, baseball, football, and softball fields, track.

**STUDENT BODY. Undergraduate profile:** 52% are state residents; 21% are transfers. 1% Asian-American, 1% Black, 2% Hispanic, 94% White, 2% Other. Average age of undergraduates is 20.
**Freshman profile:** 2% of freshmen who took SAT scored 700 or over on math; 8% scored 600 or over on verbal, 20% scored 600 or over on math; 38% scored 500 or over on verbal, 65% scored 500 or over on math; 95% scored 400 or over on verbal, 98% scored 400 or over on math; 100% scored 300 or over on verbal, 100% scored 300 or over on math. 95% of accepted applicants took SAT; 5% took ACT. 74% of freshmen come from public schools.
**Undergraduate achievement:** 87% of fall 1992 freshmen returned for fall 1993 term. 70% of entering class graduated. 15% of students who completed a degree program immediately went on to graduate study.
**Foreign students:** 20 students are from out of the country. Countries represented include China, the Czech Republic, India, Slovakia, and Spain; 15 in all.

**PROGRAMS OF STUDY. Degrees:** B.A., B.Mus., B.S.
**Majors:** Accounting, Art, Art History/Criticism, Biology, Chemistry, Church Music, Classics, Computer Science, Criminal Justice, Economics, Elementary Education, Engineering, English, English Literature/Language, Experimental Psychology, French, Geology, German, Graphic Design, History, Information Systems, International Management, Journalism, Management, Mathematics, Medical Technology, Music, Music Education, Music Theory/Composition, Natural Resources Management, Performance, Philosophy, Physics, Political Science, Psychology, Religion, Science Education, Social Sciences, Sociology, Spanish, Theatre.
**Distribution of degrees:** The majors with the highest enrollment are management, psychology, and English; religion, philosophy, and classics have the lowest.
**Requirements:** General education requirement.
**Academic regulations:** Freshmen must maintain minimum 1.35 GPA; sophomores, 1.7 GPA; juniors, 1.8 GPA; seniors, 1.8 GPA.
**Special:** Minors offered in some majors and in earth science, education, Greek, and Latin. Self-designed majors. Double majors. Independent study. Internships. Cooperative education programs. Preprofessional programs in law, medicine, veterinary science, dentistry, and theology. 3-2 engineering programs with Lafayette Coll, Lehigh U, U of Pennsylvania, and Washington U. 3-2 natural resources management program with Duke U. 3-2 occupational therapy program with Washington U. Member of Lehigh Valley Association of Independent Colleges; cross-registration possible. Washington Semester. Teacher certification in elementary and secondary education. Certification in specific subject areas. Exchange program abroad in England (Oxford U). Study abroad also in France, Germany, and Spain. AFROTC at Lehigh U.
**Honors:** Honors program. Honor societies.
**Academic Assistance:** Nonremedial tutoring.

**STUDENT LIFE. Housing:** All freshmen must live on campus unless living with family; upperclassmen must obtain permission to live off campus. Coed, women's, and men's dorms. Sorority and fraternity housing. School-owned/operated apartments. School-owned/operated townhouses. 86% of students live in college housing.
**Social atmosphere:** Favorite off-campus gathering spots include the Tally Ho, Ripper's Pub, Casey's, and the Old Brewery Tavern. On campus, "there is always an open frat. Two Left Feet is a nonalcoholic dance club popular with commuter and resident students," reports the student newspaper. Popular campus events include Sigma Phi Omega's Halloween Dance, Homecoming, the Moravian vs. Muhlenberg football game, the St. Patrick's Day Party, and Senior Farewell.
**Services and counseling/handicapped student services:** Placement services. Health service. Counseling services for minority, military, veteran, and older students. Birth control, personal, and psychological counseling. Career and academic guidance services. Religious counseling. Physically disabled student services. Reader services for the blind.
**Campus organizations:** Undergraduate student government. Student newspaper (Comenian, published once/week). Literary magazine. Yearbook. Radio station. Choir, orchestra, jazz group, string ensemble, film society, modern dance group, departmental, service, and special-interest groups, 60 organizations in all. Two fraternities, all with chapter houses; three sororities, all with chapter houses. 25% of men join a fraternity. 25% of women join a sorority.
**Religious organizations:** Intervarsity Christian Fellowship, Fellowship of Christian Athletes, Hillel Society, Newman Association, Religious Life Council.
**Minority/foreign student organizations:** Black Student Union. International Club.

**ATHLETICS. Physical education requirements:** Four half-semesters of physical education required.
**Intercollegiate competition:** 40% of students participate. Baseball (M), basketball (M,W), cheerleading (M,W), cross-country (M,W), field hockey (W), football (M), golf (M,W), soccer (M), softball (W), tennis (M,W), track (indoor) (M,W), track (outdoor) (M,W), track and field (indoor) (M,W), track and field (outdoor) (M,W), volleyball (W), wrestling (M). Member of ECAC, Middle Atlantic States Collegiate Athletic Conference, NCAA Division III.
**Intramural and club sports:** 60% of students participate. Intramural basketball, field hockey, flag football, racquetball, softball, street hockey, tennis, touch football, volleyball. Men's club horsemanship, ice hockey, lacrosse. Women's club cheerleading, horsemanship, lacrosse.

**ADMISSIONS. Academic basis for candidate selection** (in order of priority): Secondary school record, standardized test scores, class rank, school's recommendation, essay.
**Nonacademic basis for candidate selection:** Character and personality and extracurricular participation are emphasized. Particular talent or ability, geographical distribution, and alumni/ae relationship are considered.
**Requirements:** Graduation from secondary school is required; GED is accepted. 16 units and the following program of study are required: 4 units of English, 3 units of math, 2 units of lab science, 2 units of foreign language, 4 units of social studies, 1 unit of academic electives. Minimum combined SAT score of 950 and rank in top half of secondary school class recommended. Audition required of music program applicants. SAT is required; ACT may be substituted. ACH recommended. Campus visit and interview recommended. Off-campus interviews available with admissions and alumni representatives.
**Procedure:** Take SAT or ACT by January of 12th year. Visit college for interview by March of 12th year. Suggest filing application by January. Application deadline is March 1. Notification of admission by March 15. Reply is required by May 1. $200 nonrefundable tuition deposit. Freshmen accepted for terms other than fall.
**Special programs:** Admission may be deferred one year. Credit and/or placement may be granted through CEEB Advanced Placement exams for scores of 3 or higher. Credit may be granted through CLEP general and subject exams, challenge exams, and military experience. Early decision program. In fall 1993, 70 applied for early decision and 55 were accepted. Deadline for applying for early decision is December 15. Early entrance/early admission program. Concurrent enrollment program.
**Transfer students:** Transfer students accepted for terms other than fall. In fall 1993, 21% of all new students were transfers into all classes. 150 transfer applications were received, 116 were accepted. Application deadline is July 31 for fall; January 15 for spring. Minimum 2.5 GPA recommended. Lowest course grade accepted is "C-." Maximum number of transferable credits is 64 semester hours from a two-year school and 94 semester hours from a four-year school. At least 30 semester hours must be completed at the college to receive degree.
**Admissions contact:** Bernard J. Story, Director of Admissions. 215 861-1320.

**FINANCIAL AID. Available aid:** Pell grants, SEOG, state scholarships and grants, school scholarships and grants, private scholarships and grants, ROTC scholarships, academic merit scholarships, and aid for undergraduate foreign students. Perkins Loans (NDSL), PLUS, Stafford Loans (GSL), state loans, school loans, private loans, and SLS. Knight Tuition Plans, AMS, and Tuition Management Systems.
**Financial aid statistics:** 15% of aid is not need-based. In 1993-94, 97% of all freshman applicants received aid. Average amounts of aid awarded freshmen: Scholarships and grants, $8,091; loans, $3,101.
**Supporting data/closing dates:** FAFSA/FAF: Priority filing date is February 15. School's own aid application: Priority filing date is February 15. State aid form: Priority filing date is February 15; deadline is May 1. Income tax forms: Deadline is February 15. Student loan applications: Priority filing date is May 1. Notification of awards begins March 15.
**Financial aid contact:** Susan Hoffmeier, Director of Financial Aid. 215 861-1330.

**STUDENT EMPLOYMENT.** College Work/Study Program. Institutional employment. 46% of full-time undergraduates work on campus during school year. Students may expect to earn an average of $784 during school year. Off-campus part-time employment opportunities rated "good."

**COMPUTER FACILITIES.** 100 IBM/IBM-compatible and Macintosh/Apple microcomputers; 40 are networked. Students may access SUN minicomputer/mainframe systems, Internet. Client/LAN operating systems include Apple/Macintosh, LocalTalk/AppleTalk. Computer languages and software packages include Assembly, BASIC, C, COBOL, FORTRAN, Framemaker, Mathematica, Modula 2, Pascal, Prolog, Small Talk; 20 in all. Computer facilities are available to all students.
**Fees:** None.
**Hours:** 8 AM-midn. (M-Th); 8 AM-10 PM (F); 10 AM-10 PM (Sa); 1 PM-midn. (Su).

**GRADUATE CAREER DATA.** Graduate school percentages: 2% enter law school. 3% enter medical school. 1% enter dental school. 1% enter graduate business programs. 9% enter graduate arts and sciences programs. 1% enter theological school/seminary. Highest graduate school enrollments: Lehigh U. Companies and businesses that hire graduates: AT&T, Air Products, Merck.

**PROMINENT ALUMNI/AE.** Dr. Frank Rauscher, senior vice-president, American Cancer Society; Hugh Connell, executive vice-president, J. Walter Thompson; Judge William Hutchison, U.S. Court of Appeals; Lt. Gen. Bernhard Mittemeyer, surgeon general, U.S. Army.

## Mount Aloysius College

**Cresson, PA 16630** **814 886-4131**

**1993-94 Costs.** Tuition: $7,580; $9,300 (nursing). Room: $1,510. Board: $1,980. Fees, books, misc. academic expenses (school's estimate): $700.
**Enrollment.** Undergraduates: 295 men, 736 women (full-time). Freshman class: 1,092 applicants, 732 accepted, 505 enrolled.
**Test score averages/ranges.** Average SAT scores: 400 verbal, 350 math.
**Faculty.** 40 full-time; 48 part-time. 17% of faculty holds doctoral degree. Student/faculty ratio: 13 to 1.
**Selectivity rating.** Less competitive.

**PROFILE.** Mount Aloysius is a private, church-affiliated college. Its 125-acre campus is located in Cresson, 12 miles from Altoona.

**Accreditation:** MSACS. Professionally accredited by the American Medical Association (CAHEA), the National League for Nursing.
**Religious orientation:** Mount Aloysius College is affiliated with the Roman Catholic Church (Religious Sisters of Mercy); one course of religion/theology required.
**Library:** Collections totaling over 47,200 volumes, 270 periodical subscriptions and 73 microform items.
**Athletic facilities:** Gymnasium, health and fitness center.

**STUDENT BODY. Undergraduate profile:** 99% are state residents; 12% are transfers. 1% Asian-American, 3% Black, 3% Hispanic, 93% White. Average age of undergraduates is 25.
**Freshman profile:** 1% of freshmen who took SAT scored 600 or over on verbal, 2% scored 600 or over on math; 8% scored 500 or over on verbal, 13% scored 500 or over on math; 33% scored 400 or over on verbal, 39% scored 400 or over on math; 79% scored 300 or over on verbal, 87% scored 300 or over on math. 17% of freshmen who took ACT scored 24 or over on composite; 34% scored 18 or over on composite; 92% scored 12 or over on composite; 100% scored 6 or over on composite. 50% of accepted applicants took SAT; 2% took ACT.
**Undergraduate achievement:** 55% of fall 1991 freshmen returned for fall 1992 term. 70% of entering class graduated.
**Foreign students:** 15 students are from out of the country. Countries represented include Barbados, Canada, England, Grenada, Jamaica, and the West Indies; seven in all.

**PROGRAMS OF STUDY. Degrees:** B.A., B.S.
**Majors:** Nursing, Professional Studies, Public Administration.
**Distribution of degrees:** The major with the highest enrollment is nursing; public administration has the lowest.
**Requirements:** General education requirement.
**Academic regulations:** Minimum 2.0 GPA must be maintained.
**Special:** Associate's degrees offered. Internships. 2-2 A.S./B.S. nursing program.
**Honors:** Honor societies.
**Academic Assistance:** Remedial reading, writing, math, and study skills. Nonremedial tutoring.

**STUDENT LIFE. Housing:** Students may live on or off campus. Women's and men's dorms. 10% of students live in college housing.
**Services and counseling/handicapped student services:** Day care. Counseling services for veteran students. Personal counseling. Career and academic guidance services. Religious counseling. Physically disabled student services. Learning disabled services.
**Campus organizations:** Undergraduate student government. Yearbook. Theatre company, deaf and interpreter clubs, BACCHUS, academic and athletic groups.
**Religious organizations:** Campus Ministry.

**ATHLETICS. Physical education requirements:** None.
**Intercollegiate competition:** 2% of students participate. Basketball (M,W). Member of NJCAA Division I.
**Intramural and club sports:** 10% of students participate. Intramural basketball, football, softball, volleyball.

**ADMISSIONS. Academic basis for candidate selection** (in order of priority): Standardized test scores, secondary school record, class rank, school's recommendation, essay.
**Nonacademic basis for candidate selection:** Character and personality and particular talent or ability are important. Extracurricular participation is considered.
**Requirements:** Graduation from secondary school is required; GED is accepted. 21 units and the following program of study are required: 4 units of English, 3 units of math, 3 units of science, 3 units of social studies, 5 units of electives. All applicants must meet state's secondary school graduation requirements. Interview is required of some medical program applicants. Conditional admission possible for applicants not meeting standard requirements. SAT or ACT is required. Campus visit recommended.
**Procedure:** Notification of admission on rolling basis. $100 tuition deposit, refundable until May 1. Freshmen accepted for terms other than fall.
**Special programs:** Admission may be deferred three semesters. Credit may be granted through CLEP subject exams. Credit and placement may be granted through challenge exams.
**Transfer students:** Transfer students accepted for terms other than fall. In fall 1993, 12% of all new students were transfers into all classes. Application deadline is rolling for fall; rolling for spring. SAT or ACT required of all transfer applicants out of secondary school five years or less. Minimum 2.0 GPA required. Lowest course grade accepted is "C." Maximum number of transferable credits is 30 semester hours from a two-year school and 60 semester hours from a four-year school. At least 30 semester hours must be completed at the college to receive degree.
**Admissions contact:** Sylvia Ghezzi Hirsch, Dean of Enrollment Management. 814 886-8480.

**FINANCIAL AID. Available aid:** Pell grants, SEOG, state grants, school grants, and athletic scholarships. Perkins Loans (NDSL), PLUS, Stafford Loans (GSL), and SLS.
**Supporting data/closing dates:** State aid form: Priority filing date is May 1; accepted on rolling basis.
**Financial aid contact:** Valerie J. Quay, Director of Financial Aid. 814 886-2521.

**STUDENT EMPLOYMENT.** College Work/Study Program. Off-campus part-time employment opportunities rated "poor."

**COMPUTER FACILITIES.** 45 IBM/IBM-compatible microcomputers; 15 are networked. Client/LAN operating systems include DOS. Computer languages and software packages include COBOL, Lotus 1-2-3, WordPerfect. Computer facilities are available to all students.
**Fees:** None.
**Hours:** 8 AM-9 PM.

## Muhlenberg College

**Allentown, PA 18104-5586** **215 821-3100**

**1993-94 Costs.** Tuition: $16,385. Room & board: $4,410. Fees, books, misc. academic expenses (school's estimate): $350.
**Enrollment.** Undergraduates: 762 men, 879 women (full-time). Freshman class: 2,455 applicants, 1,903 accepted, 470 enrolled.
**Test score averages/ranges.** Average SAT scores: 508 verbal, 567 math. Range of SAT scores of middle 50%: 435-583 verbal, 491-643 math. Average ACT scores: 24 composite. Range of ACT scores of middle 50%: 23-26 composite.
**Faculty.** 110 full-time; 51 part-time. 87% of faculty holds highest degree in specific field. Student/faculty ratio: 13 to 1.
**Selectivity rating.** Competitive.

**PROFILE.** Muhlenberg, founded in 1848, is a private, church-affiliated, liberal arts college. Its 75-acre campus, including among its buildings a neo-Gothic chapel, is located in Allentown, 55 miles north of Philadelphia.

**Accreditation:** MSACS.
**Religious orientation:** Muhlenberg College is affiliated with the Evangelical Lutheran Church in America; one semester of religion required.
**Library:** Collections totaling over 308,400 volumes, 1,290 periodical subscriptions, and 20,000 microform items.
**Special facilities/museums:** Art gallery, biology museum, greenhouse, mainstage theatre, recital hall, 20-foot boat for marine studies, 38-acre environmental field station, two electron microscopes.
**Athletic facilities:** Swimming pool, basketball, racquetball, squash, and tennis courts, field house, track, weight room, gymnasium, football stadium, sports center.

**STUDENT BODY. Undergraduate profile:** 36% are state residents; 5% are transfers. 4% Asian-American, 2% Black, 2% Hispanic, 90% White, 2% Other. Average age of undergraduates is 20.
**Freshman profile:** 1% of freshmen who took SAT scored 700 or over on verbal, 4% scored 700 or over on math; 11% scored 600 or over on verbal, 36% scored 600 or over on math; 49% scored 500 or over on verbal, 76% scored 500 or over on math; 87% scored 400 or over on verbal, 90% scored 400 or over on math; 91% scored 300 or over on verbal, 91% scored 300 or over on math. 97% of accepted applicants took SAT; 3% took ACT. 66% of freshmen come from public schools.
**Undergraduate achievement:** 91% of fall 1991 freshmen returned for fall 1992 term. 79% of entering class graduated. 29% of students who completed a degree program immediately went on to graduate study.
**Foreign students:** 21 students are from out of the country. Countries represented include Australia, the Czech Republic, Japan, Namibia, Slovakia, the former Soviet Republics, and the United Kingdom; 14 in all.

**PROGRAMS OF STUDY. Degrees:** B.A., B.S.
**Majors:** Accounting, American Studies, Art, Biology, Business Administration, Chemistry, Classics, Communications Studies, Computer Science, Drama, Economics, English, Entrepreneurial Studies, French, German, Greek, History, History/Government, Human Resources Administration, Information Science, International Studies, Latin, Mathematics, Music, Natural Science, Philosophy, Philosophy/Political Thought, Physics, Political Economy, Political Science/Government, Political Science/History, Psychology, Religion, Russian/Slavic Studies, Social Sciences, Social Work, Sociology, Spanish.
**Distribution of degrees:** The majors with the highest enrollment are psychology, biology, and business administration; classics, information science, and social science have the lowest.
**Requirements:** General education requirement.
**Academic regulations:** Freshmen must maintain minimum 1.5 GPA; sophomores, 1.7 GPA; juniors, 1.9 GPA; seniors, 2.0 GPA.
**Special:** Minors offered in most majors and in anthropology, computer and information science, and foreign language. Concentrations available in African American, Asian, environmental, Latin American, and women's studies, and aging and gerontology. Associate's degrees offered. Self-designed majors. Double majors. Dual degrees. Independent study. Accelerated study. Pass/fail grading option. Internships. Cooperative education programs. Preprofessional programs in law, medicine, veterinary science, pharmacy, dentistry, theology, and optometry. 3-2 nursing program with Columbia U. 3-2 engineering programs with Columbia U and Washington U. 3-2 forestry and environmental studies program with Duke U. 3-4 dentistry program with U of Pennsylvania Sch of Dental Medicine. 4-4 medical school program with Hahnemann U. Member of Lehigh Valley Association of Independent Colleges. Washington Semester. London Semester. Teacher certification in elementary and secondary education. Certification in specific subject areas. Member of International Student Exchange Program (ISEP). Exchange program abroad in Australia, Austria, Belgium, France, Germany, Ireland, Israel, Japan, Latin America, Poland, the former Soviet Republics, Spain, Sweden, and the United Kingdom. ROTC at Lehigh U.
**Honors:** Phi Beta Kappa. Honors program. Honor societies.

**STUDENT LIFE. Housing:** All freshmen must live on campus. Coed and women's dorms. Sorority and fraternity housing. School-owned/operated apartments. 96% of students live in college housing.
**Social atmosphere:** "Social life is suffering," reports the student newspaper, but "the cultural life is great; plenty of speakers, plays, shows, and acts in the Red Door." Homecoming, the Muhlenberg/Moravian football game, Spring Fever Weekend, Theatre Association plays, Parents Weekend, and Candlelight Services are among the year's special events; Campus Security, the Muhlenberg Weekly, Greeks, the Activities Council, the Student Council, and WMUH have widespread influence on the student body.
**Services and counseling/handicapped student services:** Placement services. Health service. Counseling services for minority students. Birth control, personal, and psychological counseling. Career and academic guidance services. Religious counseling. Physically disabled student services. Learning disabled services. Notetaking services. Tutors.
**Campus organizations:** Undergraduate student government. Student newspaper (Muhlenberg Weekly). Literary magazine. Yearbook. Radio station. Band, wind ensemble, choir, jazz ensemble, opera group, debating, Theatre Association, arts festival, art magazine, modern dance club, Habitat for Humanity, Amnesty International, Alliance for Progressive Action, environmental action group, Gay Student Union, cheerleaders, activities council, pre-law society, forensics club, first aid corps, social issues club, 80 organizations in all. Six fraternities, five chapter houses; four sororities, three chapter houses. 55% of men join a fraternity. 50% of women join a sorority.
**Religious organizations:** Hillel, Lutheran Student Movement, Newman Association, Christian Fellowship, Interfaith Council.
**Minority/foreign student organizations:** Black Student Association, Women of Color Support Group. International Student Association, Culture Club.

**ATHLETICS. Physical education requirements:** Four quarters of physical education required.
**Intercollegiate competition:** 25% of students participate. Baseball (M), basketball (M,W), cheerleading (M,W), cross-country (M,W), field hockey (W), football (M), golf (M), lacrosse (W), soccer (M,W), softball (W), tennis (M,W), track (outdoor) (M,W), track and field (indoor) (M,W), track and field (outdoor) (M,W), volleyball (W), wrestling (M). Member of Centennial Conference, ECAC, NCAA Division III.
**Intramural and club sports:** 75% of students participate. Intramural cross-country, soccer, softball, touch football, track, volleyball, walleyball, water polo. Men's club lacrosse, rugby, ultimate frisbee, volleyball. Women's club ultimate frisbee.

**ADMISSIONS. Academic basis for candidate selection** (in order of priority): Secondary school record, class rank, standardized test scores, essay, school's recommendation.
**Nonacademic basis for candidate selection:** Extracurricular participation is emphasized. Character and personality and particular talent or ability are important. Geographical distribution and alumni/ae relationship are considered.
**Requirements:** Graduation from secondary school is required; GED is accepted. 16 units and the following program of study are required: 4 units of English, 3 units of math, 2 units of science, 2 units of foreign language, 2 units of history, 2 units of electives. SAT or ACT is required. Campus visit and interview recommended. Off-campus interviews available with an admissions representative.
**Procedure:** Take SAT or ACT by January of 12th year. Take ACH by January of 12th year. Visit college for interview by January of 12th year. Application deadline is February 15. Notification of admission by April 1. Reply is required by May 1. $400 tuition deposit, refundable until May 1. Freshmen accepted for terms other than fall.
**Special programs:** Admission may be deferred one year. Credit and/or placement may be granted through CEEB Advanced Placement exams for scores of 4 or higher. Credit may be granted through CLEP subject exams. Credit and placement may be granted through challenge exams. Early decision program. In fall 1992, 160 applied for early decision and 138 were accepted. Deadline for applying for early decision is January 15. Early entrance/early admission program.
**Transfer students:** Transfer students accepted for terms other than fall. In fall 1992, 5% of all new students were transfers into all classes. 76 transfer applications were received, 49 were accepted. Application deadline is June 1 for fall; December 1 for spring. Minimum 2.5 GPA recommended. Lowest course grade accepted is "C." Maximum number of transferable courses is 17. At least 17 courses must be completed at Muhlenberg to receive degree.
**Admissions contact:** Christopher Hooker-Haring, Director of Admissions. 215 821-3200.

**FINANCIAL AID. Available aid:** Pell grants, SEOG, state scholarships and grants, school scholarships and grants, private scholarships and grants, ROTC scholarships, academic merit scholarships, and aid for undergraduate foreign students. Perkins Loans (NDSL), PLUS, Stafford Loans (GSL), state loans, private loans, and SLS. Tuition Plan Inc., Knight Tuition Plans, and AMS.
**Financial aid statistics:** 7% of aid is not need-based. In 1992-93, 89% of all undergraduate applicants received aid; 89% of freshman applicants. Average amounts of aid awarded freshmen: Scholarships and grants, $7,854; loans, $3,000.
**Supporting data/closing dates:** FAFSA/FAF: Deadline is February 15. School's own aid application: Priority filing date is January 15; deadline is February 15. State aid form: Deadline is February 15. Income tax forms: Deadline is April 15. Notification of awards begins April 1.
**Financial aid contact:** Charles Colton, M.A., Director of Financial Aid. 215 821-3175.

**STUDENT EMPLOYMENT.** College Work/Study Program. Institutional employment. 32% of full-time undergraduates work on campus during school year. Students may expect to earn an average of $1,000 during school year. Off-campus part-time employment opportunities rated "fair."

**COMPUTER FACILITIES.** 250 IBM/IBM-compatible and Macintosh/Apple microcomputers; 125 are networked. Students may access AT&T, Hewlett-Packard minicomputer/mainframe systems. Computer languages and software packages include ADA, COBOL, dBASE, FORTRAN, Lotus 1-2-3, Microsoft Word, MINITAB, Modula 2, Pascal, R:BASE, SPSS-X, Turbo C, Turbo Pascal. Computer facilities are available to all students.
**Fees:** None.
**Hours:** 9 AM-midn (M-Th); 9 AM-5 PM (F); 1 PM-5 PM (Sa); 1 PM-midn. (Su).

**GRADUATE CAREER DATA.** Graduate school percentages: 6% enter law school. 8% enter medical school. 2% enter dental school. 1% enter graduate business programs. 11% enter graduate arts and sciences programs. 1% enter theological school/seminary. Highest graduate school enrollments: American U, Boston C, Columbia U, Georgetown U, Hahnemann U, Lehigh U, New York U, Pennsylvania State U, Syracuse U, Temple U, Thomas Jefferson Medical Coll, U of Pennsylvania. 45% of graduates choose careers in business and industry. Companies and businesses that hire graduates: AT&T, Air Products & Chemicals, Chase Manhattan Bank, Deloitte & Touche, Dun & Bradstreet, Prudential Insurance, Rodale Press, Sony.

**PROMINENT ALUMNI/AE.** James Skidmore, CEO, Science Management; Theodore T. Lithgow, president, Mercken's Chocolate, division of Nabisco; Daniel Hosage, president and CEO, Davox Communication; Dr. Alan DeCherney, physician, Yale U; Dr. Karen H. Antman, associate professor, Harvard Medical School.

4-26 8-23

## Pennsylvania State University

**University Park, PA 16802 814 865-4700**

**1993-94 Costs.** Tuition: $4,752 (state residents), $10,100 (out-of-state). Room & board: $3,930. Fees, books, misc. academic expenses (school's estimate): $560.
**Enrollment.** Undergraduates: 16,253 men, 12,685 women (full-time). Freshman class: 19,315 applicants, 10,344 accepted, 3,450 enrolled. Graduate enrollment: 3,810 men, 2,885 women.
**Test score averages/ranges.** Average SAT scores: 506 verbal, 591 math. Range of SAT scores of middle 50%: 450-560 verbal, 530-651 math.
**Faculty.** 2,540 full-time; 327 part-time. 88% of faculty holds doctoral degree. Student/faculty ratio: 19 to 1.
**Selectivity rating.** More competitive.

**PROFILE.** Pennsylvania State, founded in 1855, is a public, comprehensive university. Programs are offered through the Colleges of Agriculture, Arts and Architecture, Business Administration, Earth and Mineral Sciences, Education, Engineering, Health and Human Development, Liberal Arts, and Science and the School of Communications. Its 5,013-acre campus is located in University Park, 70 miles northwest of Harrisburg.

**Accreditation:** MSACS. Professionally accredited by the Accreditation Board for Engineering and Technology, the Accrediting Commission on Education for Health Services Administration, the Accrediting Council on Education in Journalism and Mass Communication, the American Assembly of Collegiate Schools of Business, the American Dietetic Association, the American Psychological Association, the American Society of Landscape Architects, the American Speech-Language-Hearing Association, the Council on Rehabilitation Education, the Council on Social Work Education, the National Architecture Accrediting Board, the National Association of Schools of Art and Design, the National Association of Schools of Music, the National Council for Accreditation of Teacher Education, the National League for Nursing, the National Recreation and Park Association, the Society of American Foresters.
**Religious orientation:** Pennsylvania State University is nonsectarian; no religious requirements.
**Library:** Collections totaling over 2,357,961 volumes, 27,336 periodical subscriptions, and 2,265,898 microform items.
**Special facilities/museums:** Museums, several theatres, language labs, weather station, nuclear reactor.
**Athletic facilities:** Stadium, golf courses, ice skating rinks, natatorium, outdoor track, indoor sports complex/field house, intramural building with weight training room, wrestling room, basketball gymnasiums, jogging track, and racquet-sport tennis courts, recreation building with multiple courts, bowling lanes, rifle range, athletic fields.

**STUDENT BODY. Undergraduate profile:** 82% are state residents; 10% are transfers. 4% Asian-American, 3% Black, 2% Hispanic, 1% Native American, 86% White, 4% Foreign. Average age of undergraduates is 21.
**Freshman profile:** 2% of freshmen who took SAT scored 700 or over on verbal, 12% scored 700 or over on math; 15% scored 600 or over on verbal, 49% scored 600 or over on math; 55% scored 500 or over on verbal, 86% scored 500 or over on math; 93% scored 400 or over on verbal, 98% scored 400 or over on math; 99% scored 300 or over on verbal, 100% scored 300 or over on math. 94% of accepted applicants took SAT; 5% took ACT.
**Undergraduate achievement:** 84% of fall 1992 freshmen returned for fall 1993 term. 33% of entering class graduated.
**Foreign students:** 1,809 students are from out of the country. Countries represented include China, India, Japan, Korea, and Taiwan.

**PROGRAMS OF STUDY. Degrees:** B.A., B.Arch., B.Arch.Eng., B.F.A., B.Mus., B.Phil., B.S.
**Majors:** Accounting, Accounting/International Business, Actuarial Science, Administration of Justice, Adult Education, Advertising, Aerospace Engineering, African American Studies, Agricultural Business Management, Agricultural Economics/Rural Sociology, Agricultural Education, Agricultural Engineering, Agricultural Science, Agricultural Systems Management/Technology, Agronomy, American Studies, Animal Bioscience, Architectural Engineering, Architecture, Art, Art Education, Art History, Astronomy/Astrophysics, Biochemistry, Biology, Broadcast/Cable, Business Logistics, Business Logistics/International Business, Ceramic Science/Engineering, Chemical Engineering, Chemistry, Civil Engineering, Classics, Communication Disorders, Comparative Literature, Computer Engineering, Computer Science, Counseling Psychology, Counselor Education, Curriculum/Supervision, Dairy/Animal Science, Early Childhood Education, Earth/Mineral Sciences/Liberal Arts, Earth Sciences, East Asian Studies, Economics, Economics/International Business, Educational Administration, Educational Psychology, Educational Theory/Policy, Electrical Engineering, Elementary/Kindergarten Education, Engineering/Liberal Arts, Engineering Science, English, Entomology, Environmental Resource Management, Exercise/Sport Science, Film/Video, Finance, Finance/International Business, Food Science, Forest Science, French, Fuel Science, General Anthropology, General Arts/Sciences, Geography, Geosciences, German, Health Education,

Health Policy/Administration, Higher Education, History, Home Economics Education, Horticulture, Hotel/Restaurant/Institutional Management, Human Development/Family Studies, Industrial Engineering, Instructional Systems, Insurance, Insurance/International Business, Integrative Arts, International Politics, Italian, Journalism, Labor/Industrial Relations, Landscape Architecture, Landscape Contracting, Language/Literacy Education, Latin American Studies, Leisure Studies, Liberal Arts/Earth/Mineral Sciences, Liberal Arts/Engineering, Management, Management Information Systems, Management/International Business, Marketing, Marketing/International Business, Mass Communications, Mathematics, Mathematics Education, Mechanical Engineering, Medieval Studies, Metals Science/Engineering, Meteorology, Microbiology, Mineral Economics, Mining Engineering, Molecular/Cell Biology, Music, Music Education, Nuclear Engineering, Nursing, Nutrition, Operations Management, Operations Management/International Business, Petroleum/Natural Gas Engineering, Philosophy, Physics, Plant Science, Political Science, Polymer Science, Poultry Technology/Management, Pre-Law, Pre-Medical/Medical Science, Pre-Medicine, Psychology, Public Service, Quantitative Business Analysis, Real Estate, Real Estate/International Business, Rehabilitation Education, Religious Studies, Russian, School Psychology, Science Education, Secondary Education, Social Studies Education, Social Work, Sociology, Soil Science, Spanish, Special Education, Speech Communication, Theatre Arts, Vocational Industrial Education, Wildlife/Fisheries Science, Women's Studies, Wood Products.

**Distribution of degrees:** The majors with the highest enrollment are elementary education, accounting, and marketing; medieval studies, religion, and wood products have the lowest.

**Requirements:** General education requirement.

**Academic regulations:** Minimum 2.0 GPA must be maintained.

**Special:** Minors offered in some majors and in agricultural mechanization technology, anthropology, bioengineering, business/liberal arts, Chinese, dance, extension education, Greek, humanities, international agriculture, Japanese, Latin, legal environment of business, Middle East studies, Pennsylvania studies, Russian area studies, science/technology/society, and technical writing. Associate's degrees offered. Self-designed majors. Double majors. Dual degrees. Independent study. Pass/fail grading option. Internships. Cooperative education programs. Graduate school at which undergraduates may take graduate-level courses. Preprofessional programs in law, medicine, veterinary science, and dentistry. 3-2 dual degree programs between liberal arts and either engineering or earth and mineral sciences with many colleges and universities. Six-year combined medical program with Thomas Jefferson U. Member of Marine Science Consortium; off-campus study possible at Wallops Island, Va. Teacher certification in early childhood, elementary, secondary, special education, and vo-tech education. Certification in specific subject areas. Study abroad in Australia, Costa Rica, Egypt, England, France, Germany, Greece, Israel, Italy, Japan, Kenya, the Netherlands, Puerto Rico, and Spain. ROTC, NROTC, and AFROTC.

**Honors:** Phi Beta Kappa. Honors program. Honor societies.

**Academic Assistance:** Remedial reading, writing, math, and study skills. Nonremedial tutoring.

**STUDENT LIFE. Housing:** All unmarried, nonveteran freshmen under age 21 must live on campus unless living with family. Women's and men's dorms. Fraternity housing. School-owned/operated apartments. On-campus married-student housing. Sorority housing in dormitories. Language and special-interest housing. 39% of students live in college housing.

**Social atmosphere:** According to the editor of the student newspaper, "Penn State, for better or worse, is known as a party/football school for undergraduates and a research school for graduates. Greeks are very big; there are 5,000 students and more than 50 fraternities and 20 sororities." Penn State football games are among the most popular social events, with more than 85,000 people attending. The Central Pennsylvania Festival of the Arts, held in the summer, is also popular. Favorite student gathering spots are the Student Union Building, the HUB, the All-American Rathskeller, and the Gingerbread Man.

**Services and counseling/handicapped student services:** Placement services. Health service. Women's center. Day care. Testing service, speech and hearing clinic, reading center. Counseling services for minority, military, veteran, and older students. Birth control, personal, and psychological counseling. Career and academic guidance services. Physically disabled student services. Learning disabled services. Notetaking services. Tape recorders. Tutors. Reader services for the blind.

**Campus organizations:** Undergraduate student government. Student newspaper (Daily Collegian). Literary magazine. Yearbook. Radio station. Chorus, orchestra, jazz club, glee club, debating, Thespians, athletic, departmental, and special-interest groups, 415 organizations in all. 55 fraternities, all with chapter houses; 25 sororities, no chapter houses. 14% of men join a fraternity. 17% of women join a sorority.

**Minority/foreign student organizations:** Numerous religious, minority, and foreign student groups.

**ATHLETICS. Physical education requirements:** Three semesters of physical education required.

**Intercollegiate competition:** 3% of students participate. Baseball (M), basketball (M,W), cheerleading (M,W), cross-country (M,W), diving (M,W), fencing (M,W), field hockey (W), football (M), golf (M,W), gymnastics (M,W), lacrosse (M,W), soccer (M), softball (W), swimming (M,W), tennis (M,W), track and field (indoor) (M,W), track and field (outdoor) (M,W), volleyball (M,W), wrestling (M). Member of Atlantic-10, ECAC, NCAA Division I.

**Intramural and club sports:** 1% of students participate. Intramural badminton, basketball, bowling, field hockey, flag football, golf, handball, racquetball, soccer, softball, squash, swimming, tennis, track, volleyball, wrestling, cross-country.

**ADMISSIONS. Academic basis for candidate selection** (in order of priority): Secondary school record, standardized test scores.

**Nonacademic basis for candidate selection:** Extracurricular participation, geographical distribution, and alumni/ae relationship are considered.

**Requirements:** Graduation from secondary school is required; GED is accepted. 15 units and the following program of study are required: 4 units of English, 3 units of math, 3 units of science. Requirements vary by college division and program. In general, 4 units of English, 3 units of math, 3 units of science, and 5 units of arts, humanities, and social studies are required. In addition, 2 units of a single foreign language are recommended. EOP for applicants not normally admissible. Developmental Year Program for applicants not normally admissible. SAT is required; ACT may be substituted. No off-campus interviews.

**Procedure:** Take SAT by Spring of 11th year. Suggest filing application by November 30. Notification of admission on rolling basis. Reply is required by March 1 or within two weeks of acceptance. $75 nonrefundable tuition deposit. $100 room deposit, refundable until mid-July. Freshmen accepted for terms other than fall.

**Special programs:** Credit may be granted through CEEB Advanced Placement for scores of 3 or higher. Credit may be granted through CLEP general and subject exams.

**Transfer students:** Transfer students accepted for terms other than fall. In fall 1993, 10% of all new students were transfers into all classes. 1,700 transfer applications were received, 645 were accepted. Application deadline is November 30 for fall; October 15 for spring. Minimum 2.0 GPA required. Lowest course grade accepted is "C." At least 36 of final 60 semester hours must be completed at Penn State to receive degree.

**Admissions contact:** John J. Romano, Ph.D., Associate Provost. 814 865-5471.

**FINANCIAL AID. Available aid:** Pell grants, SEOG, state scholarships and grants, school scholarships and grants, private scholarships and grants, ROTC scholarships, academic merit scholarships, and athletic scholarships. Perkins Loans (NDSL), PLUS, Stafford Loans (GSL), state loans, school loans, private loans, and SLS. Deferred payment plan.

**Financial aid statistics:** Average amounts of aid awarded freshmen: Scholarships and grants, $2,592; loans, $3,193.

**Supporting data/closing dates:** FAFSA: Priority filing date is February 15. State aid form: Priority filing date is early January; accepted on rolling basis. Notification of awards on rolling basis.

**Financial aid contact:** Anna M. Griswold, M.A., Director of Financial Aid. 814 865-6301.

**STUDENT EMPLOYMENT.** College Work/Study Program. Institutional employment. 29% of full-time undergraduates work on campus during school year. Students may expect to earn an average of $1,168 during school year. Off-campus part-time employment opportunities rated "good."

**COMPUTER FACILITIES.** 1,922 IBM/IBM-compatible, Macintosh/Apple, and RISC-/UNIX-based microcomputers. Students may access IBM minicomputer/mainframe systems, BITNET, Internet. Residence halls may be equipped with stand-alone microcomputers, modems. Client/LAN operating systems include Apple/Macintosh, DOS, UNIX/XENIX/AIX. Numerous computer languages and software packages available. Computer facilities are available to all students.

**Fees:** $70 computer fee per academic year; included in tuition/fees.

**Hours:** 24 hours.

**GRADUATE CAREER DATA.** Companies and businesses that hire graduates: IBM, Procter & Gamble, U.S. Government, Westinghouse.

**PROMINENT ALUMNI/AE.** Guion Bluford and Paul Weitz, astronauts; David Jones, national editor, *New York Times*; William Schreyer, CEO, Merrill Lynch; Rachel Newman, editor, *Country Living* magazine; Stanley Latham, film producer.

# Pennsylvania State University, Erie, The Behrend College

**Erie, PA 16563-0105 814 898-6000**

**1993-94 Costs.** Tuition: $4,752 (state residents), $10,100 (out-of-state). Room & board: $3,930. Fees, books, misc. academic expenses (school's estimate): $560.

**Enrollment.** Undergraduates: 1,510 men, 844 women (full-time). Freshman class: 2,902 applicants, 2,048 accepted, 544 enrolled. Graduate enrollment: 95 men, 71 women.

**Test score averages/ranges.** Average SAT scores: 446 verbal, 510 math. Range of SAT scores of middle 50%: 390-491 verbal, 450-570 math.

**Faculty.** 135 full-time; 77 part-time. 85% of faculty holds doctoral degree. Student/faculty ratio: 18 to 1.

**Selectivity rating.** Less competitive.

**PROFILE.** Pennsylvania State at Erie, The Behrend College, founded in 1948, is a public university. Programs are offered through the Divisions of Humanities and Social Sciences; Science, Engineering, and Technology; and Undergraduate Studies and the School of Business. Its 700-acre campus is located 10 miles from downtown Erie.

**Accreditation:** MSACS. Professionally accredited by the Accreditation Board for Engineering and Technology.

**Religious orientation:** Pennsylvania State University, Erie, The Behrend College is nonsectarian; no religious requirements.

**Library:** Collections totaling over 74,636 volumes, 919 periodical subscriptions, and 35,460 microform items.

**Special facilities/museums:** Observatory, plastics lab.

**Athletic facilities:** Gymnasium, weight room, intramural and varsity fields, lighted tennis courts, ski slope, Nordic ski trails.

**STUDENT BODY. Undergraduate profile:** 94% are state residents; 5% are transfers. 2% Asian-American, 4% Black, 1% Hispanic, 1% Native American, 92% White. Average age of undergraduates is 21.

**Freshman profile:** 1% of freshmen who took SAT scored 700 or over on math; 3% scored 600 or over on verbal, 19% scored 600 or over on math; 24% scored 500 or over on verbal, 57% scored 500 or over on math; 74% scored 400 or over on verbal, 90% scored 400 or over on math; 98% scored 300 or over on verbal, 100% scored 300 or over on math. 91% of accepted applicants took SAT; 9% took ACT.

**Undergraduate achievement:** 84% of fall 1992 freshmen returned for fall 1993 term. 33% of entering class graduated.

**Foreign students:** Two students are from out of the country.

**PROGRAMS OF STUDY. Degrees:** B.A., B.S.
**Majors:** Accounting, Biology, Business Economics, Business/Liberal Arts/Sciences, Chemistry, Communication, Economics, Electrical Engineering Technology, Engineering, English, General Arts/Sciences, History, Management, Management Information Systems, Mathematics, Mechanical Engineering Technology, Physics, Plastics Engineering Technology, Political Science, Psychology, Science.
**Distribution of degrees:** The majors with the highest enrollment are business administration, accounting, and general engineering; general arts/sciences, physics, and chemistry have the lowest.
**Requirements:** General education requirement.
**Academic regulations:** Minimum 2.0 GPA must be maintained.
**Special:** Minors offered in some majors. Associate's degrees offered. Self-designed majors. Double majors. Dual degrees. Independent study. Pass/fail grading option. Internships. Cooperative education programs. Preprofessional programs in law and medicine. Study abroad in Australia, Egypt, England, France, Germany, Greece, Israel, Italy, Japan, Kenya, the Netherlands, Puerto Rico, Spain, and Costa Rica.
**Honors:** Honors program. Honor societies.
**Academic Assistance:** Remedial reading, writing, math, and study skills. Nonremedial tutoring.

**STUDENT LIFE. Housing:** Students may live on or off campus. Coed dorms. School-owned/operated apartments. 41% of students live in college housing.
**Social atmosphere:** Students frequent The Gorge, Bruno's, Felix's, Jimmy Z's Timeout Tavern, Sherlock's, The Park Place, and the Millcreek Mall. Greeks, athletes, the student newspaper and radio station, and student government influence life on campus. Popular events include basketball games, the Snow Ball, Greek formals, Rush Week, and Homecoming. The student newspaper reports, "Most students of age go off campus for their partying. Shopping at the mall is also a big thing."
**Services and counseling/handicapped student services:** Placement services. Health service. Women's center. Day care. Counseling services for minority, veteran, and older students. Birth control, personal, and psychological counseling. Career and academic guidance services. Physically disabled student services. Learning disabled services. Notetaking services. Tape recorders. Tutors. Reader services for the blind.
**Campus organizations:** Undergraduate student government. Student newspaper (Collegian, published once/week). Literary magazine. Yearbook. Radio station. Music society, pep band, Adventurers Guild, Round Table Society, Women Today, SADD, Winterfest, science fiction/fantasy club, athletic, departmental, and special-interest groups, 67 organizations in all. Six fraternities, two chapter houses; four sororities, no chapter houses. 10% of men join a fraternity. 8% of women join a sorority.
**Religious organizations:** Newman Association, Intervarsity Christian Fellowship, Protestant Campus Ministry.
**Minority/foreign student organizations:** Association of Black Collegians, Society of Black Engineers, Organization of Latin American Students. Asian Student Organization.

**ATHLETICS. Physical education requirements:** Three semesters of physical education required.
**Intercollegiate competition:** 5% of students participate. Baseball (M), basketball (M,W), cheerleading (M,W), golf (M), soccer (M), softball (W), tennis (M,W), volleyball (W). Member of ECAC, NCAA Division III.
**Intramural and club sports:** 48% of students participate. Intramural badminton, basketball, billiards, flag football, golf, soccer, softball, tennis, volleyball. Men's club volleyball.

**ADMISSIONS. Academic basis for candidate selection** (in order of priority): Secondary school record, standardized test scores.
**Nonacademic basis for candidate selection:** Extracurricular participation, geographical distribution, and alumni/ae relationship are considered.
**Requirements:** Graduation from secondary school is required; GED is accepted. 15 units and the following program of study are required: 4 units of English, 3 units of math, 3 units of science, 5 units of social studies. EOP for applicants not normally admissible. SAT is required; ACT may be substituted. No off-campus interviews.
**Procedure:** Take SAT/ACT by May of 11th year. Suggest filing application by November 30; no deadline. Notification of admission on rolling basis. Reply is required by March 1 or within two weeks of acceptance. $75 nonrefundable tuition deposit. $75 room deposit, refundable until mid-July. Freshmen accepted for terms other than fall.
**Special programs:** Credit may be granted through CEEB Advanced Placement for scores of 3 or higher. Credit may be granted through CLEP general and subject exams.
**Transfer students:** Transfer students accepted for terms other than fall. In fall 1993, 5% of all new students were transfers into all classes. 185 transfer applications were received, 133 were accepted. Application deadline is November 30 for fall; October 15 for spring. Minimum 2.0 GPA required. Lowest course grade accepted is "C." 36 semester hours out of the last 60 must be completed at the university to receive degree.
**Admissions contact:** Mary-Ellen Madigan, M.A., Director of Admissions. 814 898-6100.

**FINANCIAL AID. Available aid:** Pell grants, SEOG, state scholarships and grants, school scholarships and grants, private scholarships and grants, and academic merit scholarships. Perkins Loans (NDSL), PLUS, Stafford Loans (GSL), state loans, school loans, private loans, and SLS. Deferred payment plan.
**Financial aid statistics:** Average amounts of aid awarded freshmen: Scholarships and grants, $2,449; loans, $3,015.
**Supporting data/closing dates:** FAFSA: Priority filing date is February 15. State aid form: Priority filing date is early January. Notification of awards on rolling basis.
**Financial aid contact:** Kate Delfino, M.A., Director of Financial Aid. 814 898-6162.

**STUDENT EMPLOYMENT.** College Work/Study Program. Institutional employment. 21% of full-time undergraduates work on campus during school year. Students may expect to earn an average of $1,082 during school year. Off-campus part-time employment opportunities rated "good."

**COMPUTER FACILITIES.** IBM/IBM-compatible, Macintosh/Apple, and RISC/UNIX-based microcomputers. Students may access Digital, IBM minicomputer/mainframe systems, BITNET, Internet. Client/LAN operating systems include Apple/Macintosh, DOS, OS/2, UNIX/XENIX/AIX, DEC. Computer languages and software packages include Ada, Assembler, C, COBOL, FORTRAN, PL/1, REXX; 108 in all. Computer facilities are available to all students.
**Fees:** $70 computer fee per year; included in tuition/fees.
**Hours:** 8 AM-midn. (M-Th); 8 AM-5 PM (F); 8 AM-10 PM (Sa); noon-midn. (Su).

**GRADUATE CAREER DATA.** Companies and businesses that hire graduates: IBM, Internal Revenue Service, Pennsylvania Department of Transportation, AT&T, General Electric, Big Six accounting firms.

**PROMINENT ALUMNI/AE.** Richard J. Fasenmeyer, CEO, RJF International Corp.; Edward P. Junker, III, vice chairman, PNC Bank N.A.; Raymond L. McGarvey, CEO, Country Fair, Inc.

## Philadelphia College of Bible

**Langhorne, PA 19047-2992 215 752-5800**

**1994-95 Costs.** Tuition: $7,370. Room: $2,000. Board: $2,280. Fees, books, misc. academic expenses (school's estimate): $560.
**Enrollment.** Undergraduates: 315 men, 317 women (full-time). Freshman class: 307 applicants, 298 accepted, 260 enrolled. Graduate enrollment: 58 men, 50 women.
**Test score averages/ranges.** Average SAT scores: 454 verbal, 494 math. Average ACT scores: 22 English, 19 math, 21 composite.
**Faculty.** 49 full-time; 24 part-time. Student/faculty ratio: 16 to 1.
**Selectivity rating.** Competitive.

**PROFILE.** Philadelphia College of Bible, founded in 1913, is a private college with religious orientation. Its 110-acre wooded campus is located in Langhorne, northeast of Philadelphia.

**Accreditation:** AABC, MSACS. Professionally accredited by the Council on Social Work Education, the National Association of Schools of Music.
**Religious orientation:** Philadelphia College of Bible is a nondenominational Christian school; 51 credits of Bible and theological courses required.
**Library:** Collections totaling over 66,512 volumes, 480 periodical subscriptions, and 18,255 microform items.
**Athletic facilities:** Gymnasium, sand volleyball and tennis courts, baseball, field hockey, soccer, and softball fields, cross-country course.

**STUDENT BODY. Undergraduate profile:** 86% are state residents; 20% are transfers. 3% Asian-American, 8% Black, 2% Hispanic, 79% White, 8% Other. Average age of undergraduates is 24.
**Freshman profile:** 1% of freshmen who took SAT scored 700 or over on verbal, 1% scored 700 or over on math; 5% scored 600 or over on verbal, 17% scored 600 or over on math; 32% scored 500 or over on verbal, 53% scored 500 or over on math; 73% scored 400 or over on verbal, 77% scored 400 or over on math; 95% scored 300 or over on verbal, 99% scored 300 or over on math. 60% of accepted applicants took SAT; 4% took ACT.
**Undergraduate achievement:** 75% of fall 1991 freshmen returned for fall 1992 term. 40% of entering class graduated. 30% of students who completed a degree program went on to graduate study within one year.
**Foreign students:** 37 students are from out of the country. Countries represented include Canada, Germany, Jamaica, Kenya, Korea, and Uganda; 18 in all.

**PROGRAMS OF STUDY. Degrees:** B.Mus., B.S., B.S.Ed., B.Soc.Work.
**Majors:** Bible Studies, Elementary Education, Music, Social Work.
**Distribution of degrees:** The majors with the highest enrollment are Bible studies, elementary education, and music.
**Requirements:** General education requirement.
**Academic regulations:** Minimum 2.0 GPA must be maintained.
**Special:** Minors offered in Christian education, communication, missions, music, pastoral studies, social work, and teacher education. Classroom study complemented by required field experience of about 100 hours. Associate's degrees offered. Dual degrees. Independent study. Accelerated study. Internships. Preprofessional programs in theology. 2-2 B.S./A.A. program with Bucks County Community Coll. One-year intensive Bible and Christian Life program at college's Wisconsin Wilderness Campus. Teacher certification in elementary and secondary education. Study abroad in Israel.
**Honors:** Honor societies.
**Academic Assistance:** Remedial reading, writing, math, and study skills. Nonremedial tutoring.

**ADMISSIONS. Academic basis for candidate selection** (in order of priority): Secondary school record, standardized test scores, essay, school's recommendation, class rank.
**Nonacademic basis for candidate selection:** Character and personality are emphasized. Extracurricular participation and particular talent or ability are important. Alumni/ae relationship is considered.
**Requirements:** Graduation from secondary school is required; GED is accepted. 15 units required and the following program of study recommended: 4 units of English, 1 unit of math, 2 units of science, 2 units of foreign language, 3 units of social studies, 3 units of electives. Minimum combined SAT score of 800 and minimum 2.0 GPA recommended. Audition required of music program applicants. EXCEL program for applicants not normally admissible. SAT or ACT is required. Campus visit and interview recommended. Off-campus interviews available with an admissions representative.
**Procedure:** Take SAT or ACT by fall of 12th year. Visit college for interview by April of 12th year. Suggest filing application by December. Application deadline is August. Notification of admission on rolling basis. No set date by which applicants must accept offer. $100 tuition deposit, refundable until May 1. $50 room deposit, refundable until May 1. Freshmen accepted for terms other than fall.
**Special programs:** Admission may be deferred one year. Credit and/or placement may be granted through CEEB Advanced Placement exams for scores of 3 or higher. Credit and/or placement may be granted through CLEP general and subject exams. Credit may be granted through military and life experience. Early decision program. In fall 1992, 14 applied for early decision and 14 were accepted. Early entrance/early admission program.
**Transfer students:** Transfer students accepted for terms other than fall. In fall 1992, 20% of all new students were transfers into all classes. Application deadline is rolling for fall; rolling for spring. Minimum 2.0 GPA. Lowest course grade accepted is "C." Maximum

number of transferable credits is 68 semester hours. At least 60 semester hours must be completed at the college to receive degree.
**Admissions contact:** Frances Emmons, Director of Admissions. 215 752-5800.

**FINANCIAL AID. Available aid:** Pell grants, SEOG, state scholarships and grants, school scholarships, private scholarships and grants, and academic merit scholarships. PLUS, Stafford Loans (GSL), and SLS. AMS. Institutional payment plan.
**Financial aid statistics:** 51% of aid is not need-based. In 1992-93, 95% of all undergraduate applicants received aid; 95% of freshman applicants. Average amounts of aid awarded freshmen: Scholarships and grants, $1,191; loans, $2,481.
**Supporting data/closing dates:** FAFSA/FAF: Deadline is May 1. State aid form: Priority filing date is May 1. Income tax forms: Accepted on rolling basis. Notification of awards on rolling basis.
**Financial aid contact:** Travis Roy, Director of Financial Aid. 215 752-5800.

## Philadelphia College of Pharmacy and Science

**Philadelphia, PA 19104-4495 215 596-8800**

**1993-94 Costs.** Tuition: $10,600. Room & board: $4,200. Fees, books, misc. academic expenses (school's estimate): $750.
**Enrollment.** Undergraduates: 671 men, 1,046 women (full-time). Freshman class: 1,374 applicants, 843 accepted, 392 enrolled. Graduate enrollment: 57 men, 96 women.
**Test score averages/ranges.** Average SAT scores: 476 verbal, 570 math.
**Faculty.** 158 full-time; 40 part-time. 64% of faculty holds doctoral degree. Student/faculty ratio: 13 to 1.
**Selectivity rating.** More competitive.

**PROFILE.** The Philadelphia College of Pharmacy and Science is a private college of pharmacy and health sciences. Its 12-acre campus is located in Philadelphia.

**Accreditation:** MSACS. Professionally accredited by the American Council on Pharmaceutical Education.
**Religious orientation:** Philadelphia College of Pharmacy and Science is nonsectarian; no religious requirements.
**Library:** Collections totaling over 55,000 volumes, 890 periodical subscriptions, and 28,107 microform items.
**Special facilities/museums:** Pharmacy museum, electron microscope.
**Athletic facilities:** Gymnasium, weight room, rifle range.

**STUDENT BODY. Undergraduate profile:** 68% are state residents; 15% are transfers. 17% Asian-American, 4% Black, .5% Hispanic, 78% White, .5% Other. Average age of undergraduates is 20.
**Freshman profile:** 1% of freshmen who took SAT scored 700 or over on verbal, 3% scored 700 or over on math; 7% scored 600 or over on verbal, 30% scored 600 or over on math; 38% scored 500 or over on verbal, 81% scored 500 or over on math; 92% scored 400 or over on verbal, 99% scored 400 or over on math; 98% scored 300 or over on verbal. 95% of accepted applicants took SAT; 1% took ACT. 72% of freshmen come from public schools.
**Undergraduate achievement:** 91% of fall 1992 freshmen returned for fall 1993 term. 13% of entering class graduated. 98% of students who completed a degree program immediately went on to graduate study.
**Foreign students:** 35 students are from out of the country. Eight countries represented in all.

**PROGRAMS OF STUDY. Degrees:** B.S.
**Majors:** Biochemistry, Biology, Chemistry, Medical Technology, Microbiology, Pharmaceutical Chemistry, Pharmacology/Toxicology, Pharmacy, Physical Therapy.
**Distribution of degrees:** The majors with the highest enrollment are pharmacy, physical therapy, and biology; microbiology, medical technology, and pharmacology/toxicology have the lowest.
**Requirements:** General education requirement.
**Academic regulations:** Minimum 2.0 GPA must be maintained.
**Special:** Minors offered in communications, economics, humanities, mathematics, and psychology/sociology. Courses offered in American studies, English, German, history, pharmacy administration/practice, philosophy, physical education, and physics. Internships. Graduate school at which undergraduates may take graduate-level courses. Preprofessional programs in medicine. Six-year B.S.Pharm./M.B.A. program with Drexel U. College maintains active relationships with seven area clinical teaching facilities. Member of University City Science Center Corporation, a research-lab complex. Certification in specific subject areas. ROTC at U of Pennsylvania.
**Academic Assistance:** Remedial writing and study skills.

**STUDENT LIFE. Housing:** All freshmen must live on campus unless living with family. Coed dorms. Fraternity housing. Off-campus privately-owned housing. Apartment-like suites in some dorms. 36% of students live in college housing.
**Services and counseling/handicapped student services:** Placement services. Health service. Counseling services for minority and military students. Personal and psychological counseling. Career and academic guidance services. Physically disabled student services. Tape recorders. Tutors.
**Campus organizations:** Undergraduate student government. Student newspaper (Panacea, published twice/semester). Literary magazine. Yearbook. Choral and drama groups, professional associations, Megabyte computer operators club, chess and photography clubs, investment club, 28 organizations in all. Five fraternities, all with chapter houses; three sororities, no chapter houses. 21% of men join a fraternity. 18% of women join a sorority.
**Religious organizations:** Agape Christian Fellowship, Hillel, Newman Club.
**Minority/foreign student organizations:** Black Academic Achievement Society, Oriental Student Association. International Student Association.

**ATHLETICS. Physical education requirements:** Two semesters of physical education required.
**Intercollegiate competition:** 4% of students participate. Baseball (M), basketball (M,W), cross-country (M,W), golf (M,W), riflery (M,W), softball (M,W), tennis (M,W), volleyball (M,W). Member of NAIA, PAIAW.
**Intramural and club sports:** 5% of students participate. Intramural archery, basketball, bowling, chess, darts, foul shooting, frisbee, pool, riflery, softball, table tennis, volleyball. Men's club cheerleading.

**ADMISSIONS. Academic basis for candidate selection** (in order of priority): Secondary school record, class rank, standardized test scores, essay, school's recommendation.
**Nonacademic basis for candidate selection:** Character and personality are important. Extracurricular participation, particular talent or ability, and alumni/ae relationship are considered.
**Requirements:** Graduation from secondary school is required; GED is accepted. 16 units and the following program of study are required: 4 units of English, 3 units of math, 3 units of science including 2 units of lab, 2 units of social studies, 4 units of academic electives. Minimum combined SAT score of 950 and rank in top two-fifths of secondary school class or minimum 3.0 GPA required. 20 hours of volunteer/work experience required of physical therapy program applicants. PREP program for applicants not normally admissible. SAT is required. ACH recommended. Campus visit and interview recommended. No off-campus interviews.
**Procedure:** Take SAT by December 15 of 12th year. Suggest filing application by January. Application deadline is August 1. Notification of admission on rolling basis. Reply is required by April 15. $150 nonrefundable tuition deposit. $145 room deposit, refundable until August 1. Freshmen accepted for fall term only.
**Special programs:** Admission may be deferred one year. Credit may be granted through CEEB Advanced Placement for scores of 3 or higher. Credit and/or placement may be granted through CLEP general and subject exams. Placement may be granted through challenge exams. Early entrance/early admission program. Concurrent enrollment program.
**Transfer students:** Transfer students accepted for fall term only. In fall 1993, 15% of all new students were transfers into all classes. 1,020 transfer applications were received, 107 were accepted. Application deadline is January 15. Minimum 3.0 GPA required. Lowest course grade accepted is "C." Maximum number of transferable credits is 64 semester hours. At least 64 semester hours must be completed at the college to receive degree.
**Admissions contact:** Louis L. Hegyes, Director of Admissions. 215 596-8810.

**FINANCIAL AID. Available aid:** Pell grants, SEOG, state scholarships and grants, school scholarships and grants, private scholarships and grants, ROTC scholarships, academic merit scholarships, athletic scholarships, and aid for undergraduate foreign students. Perkins Loans (NDSL), PLUS, Stafford Loans (GSL), Health Professions Loans, state loans, school loans, private loans, and SLS. Knight Tuition Plans, AMS, and deferred payment plan.
**Financial aid statistics:** 12% of aid is not need-based. In 1993-94, 80% of all undergraduate applicants received aid; 82% of freshman applicants. Average amounts of aid awarded freshmen: Loans, $2,000.
**Supporting data/closing dates:** School's own aid application: Priority filing date is March 15; deadline is April 1. State aid form: Priority filing date is March 15. Notification of awards begins April 15.
**Financial aid contact:** Beverly Hayden, M.L.A., Director of Financial Aid. 215 596-8894.

**STUDENT EMPLOYMENT.** College Work/Study Program. Institutional employment. 12% of full-time undergraduates work on campus during school year. Students may expect to earn an average of $1,000 during school year. Freshmen are discouraged from working during their first term. Off-campus part-time employment opportunities rated "poor."

**COMPUTER FACILITIES.** 34 IBM/IBM-compatible and Macintosh/Apple microcomputers. Students may access Prime minicomputer/mainframe systems. Client/LAN operating systems include Apple/Macintosh. Computer facilities are available to all students.
**Fees:** None.

**GRADUATE CAREER DATA.** Graduate school percentages: 94% enter medical school. 2% enter graduate business programs. 2% enter graduate arts and sciences programs. 30% of graduates choose careers in business and industry.

**PROMINENT ALUMNI/AE.** Dr. Eli Lilly, founder, Eli Lilly Co.; Gerard Rorer, board chairperson, the Rorer Group; John Wyeth, founder, Wyeth Labs; William Warner, founder, Warner-Lambert.

## Philadelphia College of Textiles and Science

**Philadelphia, PA 19144 215 951-2700**

**1993-94 Costs.** Tuition: $10,914. Room & board: $4,982. Fees, books, misc. academic expenses (school's estimate): $640.
**Enrollment.** Undergraduates: 587 men, 1,077 women (full-time). Freshman class: 2,042 applicants, 1,673 accepted, 605 enrolled. Graduate enrollment: 335 men, 256 women.
**Test score averages/ranges.** Average SAT scores: 450 verbal, 500 math.
**Faculty.** 90 full-time; 23 part-time. 52% of faculty holds highest degree in specific field. Student/faculty ratio: 16 to 1.
**Selectivity rating.** Less competitive.

**PROFILE.** Philadelphia College of Textiles and Science, founded in 1884, is a private college of textiles and related sciences. Its 100-acre campus is eight miles northwest of downtown Philadelphia.

**Accreditation:** MSACS.
**Religious orientation:** Philadelphia College of Textiles and Science is nonsectarian; no religious requirements.
**Library:** Collections totaling over 80,000 volumes, 1,800 periodical subscriptions, and 5,500 microform items.
**Special facilities/museums:** Design center and museum, photography lab, TV studio, textile product testing and production lab. Fabric collection of 1,400,000 samples.
**Athletic facilities:** Gymnasiums, baseball and soccer fields, tennis courts, weight room.

**STUDENT BODY. Undergraduate profile:** 60% are state residents; 22% are transfers. 3% Asian-American, 10% Black, 2% Hispanic, 81% White, 4% Other. Average age of undergraduates is 20.
**Freshman profile:** 1% of freshmen who took SAT scored 700 or over on verbal, 2% scored 700 or over on math; 3% scored 600 or over on verbal, 12% scored 600 or over on math; 20% scored 500 or over on verbal, 44% scored 500 or over on math; 67% scored 400 or over on verbal, 82% scored 400 or over on math; 94% scored 300 or over on verbal, 95% scored 300 or over on math. 98% of accepted applicants took SAT; 2% took ACT.
**Undergraduate achievement:** 70% of fall 1992 freshmen returned for fall 1993 term. 43% of entering class graduated. 4% of students who completed a degree program immediately went on to graduate study.
**Foreign students:** 130 students are from out of the country. Countries represented include Colombia, India, Japan, Korea, Pakistan, and Taiwan; 46 in all.

**PROGRAMS OF STUDY. Degrees:** B.Arch., B.S.
**Majors:** Accounting, Applied Mathematics, Architecture, Biochemistry, Biology, Chemistry, Chemistry/Applied Science, Computer Science, Environmental Science, Fashion Apparel Management, Fashion Design, Fashion Merchandising, Finance, Human Resource Management, Interior Design, International Business, Management, Management Information Systems, Marketing, Polymer Science, Polymer/Textile Chemistry, Product/Brand Management, Psychology, Small Business/Entrepreneurship, Textile Design, Textile Engineering, Textile Technology.
**Distribution of degrees:** The majors with the highest enrollment are marketing, fashion merchandising, and fashion design; polymer/textile chemistry, biochemistry, and chemistry have the lowest.
**Requirements:** General education requirement.
**Academic regulations:** Minimum 2.0 GPA must be maintained.
**Special:** Minors offered in some majors and in apparel management, apparel marketing, economics, finance, history, human resource management, literature, organizational behavior, political science, quantitative methods, real estate, sociology, and textiles. College offers B.S. curriculum for registered nurses. Courses offered in audio-visual, business administration, photography, physical education, and physics/biological science. Co-op programs in Washington, D.C., New York, and Philadelphia. Associate's degrees offered. Double majors. Dual degrees. Independent study. Pass/fail grading option. Internships. Cooperative education programs. Graduate school at which undergraduates may take graduate-level courses. Preprofessional programs in law, medicine, veterinary science, and dentistry. Exchange programs abroad in England (London Coll of Fashion) and Scotland (Scottish Coll of Textiles). Study abroad also in France, Germany, Japan, Spain, and other countries.
**Honors:** Honors program.
**Academic Assistance:** Remedial reading, writing, math, and study skills. Nonremedial tutoring.

**STUDENT LIFE. Housing:** Students may live on or off campus. Coed, women's, and men's dorms. School-owned/operated apartments. Townhouses. Honors housing. 50% of students live in college housing.
**Social atmosphere:** According to the editor of the student newspaper, "Because the school is so close to center city, going out to clubs and bars is much more popular than on-campus activities. The college is small and many go home on the weekend." Favorite on-campus spots to go are the Student Center, the Ram's Head Inn, and Hughes Gym. Off campus, students head for the Saloonery, Charlie's Place, Carney's, Grape Street Pub, and Chubby's. Influential groups include athletes and some fraternities. Favorite college events are Homecoming, the Senior Banquet, Welcome Week, and Spring Week.
**Services and counseling/handicapped student services:** Placement services. Health service. Personal and psychological counseling. Career and academic guidance services. Physically disabled student services. Learning disabled services. Notetaking services. Tape recorders. Reader services for the blind.
**Campus organizations:** Undergraduate student government. Student newspaper (Text, published bimonthly). Literary magazine. Yearbook. Radio station. Drama Guild, Special Olympics, Inter-Residence Council, Student/Alumni Association, Programming Board, Fashion Industry Association, Textile Engineering Society, sun and ski club, photo club, cheerleaders, 40 organizations in all. Two fraternities, no chapter houses; two sororities, no chapter houses.
**Religious organizations:** Christian Fellowship, Hillel, Newman Club.
**Minority/foreign student organizations:** Black Awareness Society. International Student Organization.

**ATHLETICS. Physical education requirements:** Two semesters of physical education required.
**Intercollegiate competition:** 23% of students participate. Baseball (M,W), basketball (M,W), cheerleading (M,W), field hockey (W), golf (M), lacrosse (W), soccer (M,W), softball (W), tennis (M,W). Member of ECAC, Mid-East Conference, NCAA Division I for men's soccer, NCAA Division II, New York Collegiate Athletic Conference, PAIAW.
**Intramural and club sports:** 40% of students participate. Intramural aerobics, basketball, flag football, floor hockey, indoor soccer, softball, table tennis, volleyball. Men's club volleyball.

**ADMISSIONS. Academic basis for candidate selection** (in order of priority): Secondary school record, class rank, standardized test scores, school's recommendation, essay.
**Nonacademic basis for candidate selection:** Character and personality, extracurricular participation, and particular talent or ability are emphasized. Alumni/ae relationship is considered.
**Requirements:** Graduation from secondary school is required; GED is accepted. 14 units and the following program of study are required: 4 units of English, 3 units of math, 2 units of lab science, 3 units of social studies. Minimum combined SAT score of 700, rank in top half of secondary school class, and minimum 2.5 GPA required. EXCEL program for applicants not normally admissible. SAT or ACT is required. PSAT is recommended. Campus visit and interview recommended. No off-campus interviews.
**Procedure:** Take SAT or ACT by April of 12th year. Visit college for interview by February of 12th year. Suggest filing application by December 1. Notification of admission on rolling basis. Reply is required within three weeks of acceptance. $200 nonrefundable tuition deposit. $250 nonrefundable room deposit. Freshmen accepted for terms other than fall.
**Special programs:** Admission may be deferred one year. Credit and/or placement may be granted through CEEB Advanced Placement exams for scores of 3 or higher. Credit and/or placement may be granted through CLEP general and subject exams. Credit and placement may be granted through ACT PEP, DANTES, and challenge exams and military and life experience. Concurrent enrollment program.
**Transfer students:** Transfer students accepted for terms other than fall. In fall 1993, 22% of all new students were transfers into all classes. 314 transfer applications were received, 264 were accepted. Application deadline is August 15 for fall; January 11 for spring. Minimum 2.5 GPA required. Lowest course grade accepted is "C." At least 60 semester hours must be completed at the college to receive degree.
**Admissions contact:** David B. Conway, M.A., Dean of Admissions. 215 951-2800.

**FINANCIAL AID. Available aid:** Pell grants, SEOG, state scholarships and grants, school scholarships and grants, private scholarships and grants, academic merit scholarships, and athletic scholarships. Perkins Loans (NDSL), PLUS, Stafford Loans (GSL), state loans, and SLS. AMS. Higher Educational Services.
**Financial aid statistics:** 22% of aid is not need-based. In 1993-94, 95% of all undergraduate applicants received aid; 90% of freshman applicants. Average amounts of aid awarded freshmen: Scholarships and grants, $5,350; loans, $3,417.
**Supporting data/closing dates:** FAFSA/FAF: Priority filing date is April 15. School's own aid application: Priority filing date is April 15; accepted on rolling basis. State aid form: Priority filing date is April 15. Income tax forms: Priority filing date is April 15. Notification of awards on rolling basis.
**Financial aid contact:** Lisa J. Cooper, Director of Financial Aid. 215 951-2940.

**STUDENT EMPLOYMENT.** College Work/Study Program. Institutional employment. 27% of full-time undergraduates work on campus during school year. Students may expect to earn an average of $1,000 during school year. Off-campus part-time employment opportunities rated "good."

**COMPUTER FACILITIES.** 120 IBM/IBM-compatible and Macintosh/Apple microcomputers; 50 are networked. Students may access AT&T, Digital, IBM minicomputer/mainframe systems, Internet. Client/LAN operating systems include Apple/Macintosh, DOS, UNIX/XENIX/AIX, Windows NT, Microsoft, Novell. Computer languages and software packages include Ada, BASIC, C, COBOL, dBASE, FORTRAN, GPSS, IFPS, LINDO, Lotus 1-2-3, Macsyma, MATHLAB, MINITAB, Pascal, PFS:Write, Prolog, Quattro, SPSS-X, VAX Assembler, WordPerfect. Computer facilities are available to all students.
**Fees:** None.
**Hours:** 84 hours/week.

**GRADUATE CAREER DATA.** Highest graduate school enrollments: Clemson U, Inst of Textile Tech, Philadelphia Coll of Textiles and Science, U of Pennsylvania, Villanova U. Companies and businesses that hire graduates: Ann Taylor, Arthur Andersen, Millikin & Co., Strawbridge & Clothier, The Gap.

# Point Park College

**Pittsburgh, PA 15222** **412 391-4100**

**1994-95 Costs.** Tuition: $9,700. Room & board: $4,830. Fees, books, misc. academic expenses (school's estimate): $750.
**Enrollment.** Undergraduates: 494 men, 679 women (full-time). Freshman class: 875 applicants, 744 accepted, 207 enrolled. Graduate enrollment: 43 men, 51 women.
**Test score averages/ranges.** Average SAT scores: 418 verbal, 424 math. Range of SAT scores of middle 50%: 370-480 verbal, 360-490 math. Average ACT scores: 21 composite.
**Faculty.** 74 full-time; 134 part-time. 44% of faculty holds highest degree in specific field. Student/faculty ratio: 13 to 1.
**Selectivity rating.** Less competitive.

**PROFILE.** Point Park, founded in 1960, is a private, multipurpose college. The campus includes dormitory, administration, and classroom buildings and a theatre complex in downtown Pittsburgh.

**Accreditation:** MSACS. Professionally accredited by the Accreditation Board for Engineering and Technology.
**Religious orientation:** Point Park College is nonsectarian; no religious requirements.
**Library:** Collections totaling over 123,496 volumes, 571 periodical subscriptions, and 27,734 microform items.
**Special facilities/museums:** Pittsburgh Playhouse, on-campus day care center and elementary school, engineering technology labs, television and radio studios.
**Athletic facilities:** Gymnasium (local), health and recreation center.

**STUDENT BODY. Undergraduate profile:** 80% are state residents; 45% are transfers. 10% Black, 1% Hispanic, 84% White, 5% Other. Average age of undergraduates is 23.

**Freshman profile:** 1% of freshmen who took SAT scored 600 or over on verbal, 2% scored 600 or over on math; 16% scored 500 or over on verbal, 22% scored 500 or over on math; 61% scored 400 or over on verbal, 64% scored 400 or over on math; 95% scored 300 or over on verbal, 92% scored 300 or over on math. 98% of accepted applicants took SAT.

**Undergraduate achievement:** 68% of fall 1992 freshmen returned for fall 1993 term. 15% of students who completed a degree program went on to graduate study within one year.

**Foreign students:** 133 students are from out of the country. Countries represented include Curacao, Japan, Korea, Saudi Arabia, Thailand, and Turkey; 36 in all.

**PROGRAMS OF STUDY. Degrees:** B.A., B.F.A., B.S.

**Majors:** Accounting, Applied Arts, Applied History, Arts Management, Behavioral Science, Biological Sciences, Business Management, Civil Engineering Technology, Computer Science, Dance, Early Childhood Education, Electrical Engineering Technology, Elementary Education, English, Environmental Protection Science, Fashion Marketing, Film/Video Production, Funeral Service, General Studies, Health Services, Human Resource Management, International Studies, Journalism/Communications, Legal Studies, Management Services, Mathematics Education, Mechanical Engineering Technology, Political Science, Psychology, Public Administration, Secondary Education, Theatre Arts.

**Distribution of degrees:** The majors with the highest enrollment are business management, electrical engineering technology, and journalism/communications; general studies and general science have the lowest.

**Requirements:** General education requirement.

**Academic regulations:** Freshmen must maintain minimum 1.5 GPA; sophomores, 1.8 GPA; juniors, 2.0 GPA; seniors, 2.0 GPA.

**Special:** Minors offered in most majors. Capstone Programs in applied arts, general studies, health services, hotel/restaurant management, human resources management, international studies, legal studies, management services, photography, and visual arts and design. Associate's degrees offered. Self-designed majors. Double majors. Dual degrees. Independent study. Accelerated study. Pass/fail grading option. Internships. Cooperative education programs. Graduate school at which undergraduates may take graduate-level courses. Preprofessional programs in law and health-related areas. 2-2 film/video production program with Pittsburgh Filmmakers. 3-1 mortuary science program with Pittsburgh Inst of Mortuary Science. Member of Pittsburgh Council on Higher Education and Western Pennsylvania Council of Higher Education; cross-registration possible. Exchange program with Art Inst of Pittsburgh. Teacher certification in early childhood, elementary, and secondary education. Certification in specific subject areas. ROTC at Duquesne U. AFROTC at U of Pittsburgh.

**Academic Assistance:** Remedial reading, writing, and math. Nonremedial tutoring.

**STUDENT LIFE. Housing:** Students may live on or off campus. Coed dorms. On-campus married-student housing. Female-only floor, quiet study floors. 31% of students live in college housing.

**Social atmosphere:** As reported by the student newspaper, "Downtown Pittsburgh has much to offer a student who seeks something to do: eat, shop, drink, get a job, entertainment. Buses go everywhere so you're not 'stuck' downtown. More than half of the students are commuters. Many have apartment parties. Many are foreign students who hold International Nights which introduce everyone to their culture, food, games, etc. The United Student Government sponsors semiformal dances, SnoBall, and Spring Fling. The Student Development Office holds a Welcome Week cruise on a clipper ship on Pittsburgh's waterways."

**Services and counseling/handicapped student services:** Placement services. Health service. Day care. Counseling services for minority and veteran students. Birth control, personal, and psychological counseling. Career and academic guidance services. Religious counseling. Physically disabled student services. Learning disabled services. Notetaking services. Tape recorders. Reader services for the blind.

**Campus organizations:** Undergraduate student government. Student newspaper (Globe, published once/week). Literary magazine. Radio and TV stations. Point Park Singers, drama and dance groups, veterans organization, advertising, photography, media, and outdoor adventure clubs, departmental, professional, and special interest groups. Two fraternities, no chapter houses; four sororities, no chapter houses. 2% of men join a fraternity. 2% of women join a sorority.

**Religious organizations:** Campus Ministry.

**Minority/foreign student organizations:** BASICS (black student group). International Club.

**ATHLETICS. Physical education requirements:** None.

**Intercollegiate competition:** 1% of students participate. Baseball (M), basketball (M,W), cheerleading (M), soccer (M), softball (W), volleyball (W). Member of NAIA.

**Intramural and club sports:** 1% of students participate. Intramural basketball, billiards, flag football, floor hockey, soccer, tennis, volleyball, weight lifting.

**ADMISSIONS. Academic basis for candidate selection** (in order of priority): Secondary school record, class rank, standardized test scores, school's recommendation, essay.

**Nonacademic basis for candidate selection:** Character and personality, extracurricular participation, and particular talent or ability are considered.

**Requirements:** Graduation from secondary school is required; GED is accepted. 16 units and the following program of study are recommended: 4 units of English, 2 units of math, 3 units of science, 4 units of history, 3 units of electives. Audition required of dance and theatre program applicants. Program for Academic Success for applicants not normally admissible. SAT or ACT is required. Campus visit and interview recommended. Off-campus interviews available with an admissions representative.

**Procedure:** Take SAT or ACT by March 1 of 12th year. Visit college for interview by April of 12th year. Suggest filing application by October; no deadline. Notification of admission on rolling basis. Reply is required by May 1. $150 nonrefundable tuition deposit. $50 nonrefundable room deposit. Freshmen accepted for terms other than fall.

**Special programs:** Admission may be deferred one year. Credit and/or placement may be granted through CEEB Advanced Placement exams for scores of 3 or higher. Credit and/or placement may be granted through CLEP general and subject exams. Credit and placement may be granted through DANTES and challenge exams and military and life experience. Early entrance/early admission program. Concurrent enrollment program.

**Transfer students:** Transfer students accepted for terms other than fall. In fall 1993, 45% of all new students were transfers into all classes. 504 transfer applications were received, 419 were accepted. Application deadline is rolling for fall; rolling for spring. Minimum 2.0 GPA recommended. Lowest course grade accepted is "C." Maximum number of transferable credits is 70 semester hours from a two-year school and 90 semester hours from a four-year school. At least 30 semester hours must be completed at the college to receive degree.

**Admissions contact:** Terrance R. Kizina, M.S., Director of Admissions. 412 392-3430, 800 321-0129.

**FINANCIAL AID. Available aid:** Pell grants, SEOG, state scholarships and grants, school scholarships and grants, private scholarships and grants, ROTC scholarships, academic merit scholarships, athletic scholarships, and aid for undergraduate foreign students. Perkins Loans (NDSL), PLUS, Stafford Loans (GSL), state loans, and private loans. Deferred payment plan and family tuition reduction.

**Financial aid statistics:** 19% of aid is not need-based. In 1993-94, 94% of all freshman applicants received aid. Average amounts of aid awarded freshmen: Scholarships and grants, $3,620; loans, $2,957.

**Supporting data/closing dates:** School's own aid application: Accepted on rolling basis. State aid form: Priority filing date is May 1. Notification of awards on rolling basis.

**Financial aid contact:** Deidre Smith, M.B.A., Director of Financial Aid. 412 392-3930.

**STUDENT EMPLOYMENT.** College Work/Study Program. Institutional employment. 27% of full-time undergraduates work on campus during school year. Students may expect to earn an average of $873 during school year. Off-campus part-time employment opportunities rated "good."

**COMPUTER FACILITIES.** 81 IBM/IBM-compatible and Macintosh/Apple microcomputers; 40 are networked. Students may access AT&T, Hewlett-Packard minicomputer/mainframe systems. Client/LAN operating systems include Apple/Macintosh, DOS, UNIX/XENIX/AIX, X-windows. Computer languages and software packages include C, C++, COBOL, dBASE, Excel, FORTRAN, Harvard Graphics, Lotus, Microsoft Word, Pascal, Turbo Pascal, WordPerfect. Computer facilities are available to all students.

**Fees:** $65 computer fee per course; included in tuition/fees.

**Hours:** 24 hours for lab; 80 hours/week for mainframes.

**GRADUATE CAREER DATA.** Graduate school percentages: 12% enter graduate arts and sciences programs. Highest graduate school enrollments: Duquesne U, U of Pittsburgh. Companies and businesses that hire graduates: Duquesne Light Co., Mellon Bank, Westinghouse.

**PROMINENT ALUMNI/AE.** Dennis Miller, comedian; Thomas Golanski, president and CEO, First Seneca Bank; Nancy Bromall, partner, KPMG Peat Marwick; Flo Lacy, actress, *Evita*.

# Robert Morris College

**Coraopolis, PA 15108-1189 — 412 262-8200**

**1994-95 Costs.** Tuition: $6,540. Room & board: $4,326. Fees, books, misc. academic expenses (school's estimate): $1,200.

**Enrollment.** Undergraduates: 1,371 men, 1,250 women (full-time). Freshman class: 907 applicants, 771 accepted, 387 enrolled. Graduate enrollment: 575 men, 343 women.

**Test score averages/ranges.** Average SAT scores: 396 verbal, 451 math. Range of SAT scores of middle 50%: 380-480 verbal, 400-510 math.

**Faculty.** 129 full-time; 219 part-time. 59% of faculty holds doctoral degree. Student/faculty ratio: 21 to 1.

**Selectivity rating.** Less competitive.

**PROFILE.** Robert Morris, founded in 1921, is a private college focusing on business-related areas. Its 238-acre campus is located in Coraopolis, west of downtown Pittsburgh.

**Accreditation:** MSACS.

**Religious orientation:** Robert Morris College is nonsectarian; no religious requirements.

**Library:** Collections totaling over 120,832 volumes, 836 periodical subscriptions, and 276,525 microform items.

**Athletic facilities:** Gymnasiums, athletic fields, basketball, tennis, and volleyball courts, track.

**STUDENT BODY. Undergraduate profile:** 95% are state residents; 44% are transfers. .5% Asian-American, 4.9% Black, .4% Hispanic, .1% Native American, 93.3% White, .8% Other. Average age of undergraduates is 23.

**Freshman profile:** 2% of freshmen who took SAT scored 700 or over on math; 2% scored 600 or over on verbal, 7% scored 600 or over on math; 10% scored 500 or over on verbal, 34% scored 500 or over on math; 50% scored 400 or over on verbal, 71% scored 400 or over on math; 91% scored 300 or over on verbal, 94% scored 300 or over on math. Majority of accepted applicants took SAT.

**Undergraduate achievement:** 82% of fall 1992 freshmen returned for fall 1993 term.

**Foreign students:** 36 students are from out of the country. Countries represented include Canada, China, and India; 16 in all.

**PROGRAMS OF STUDY. Degrees:** B.A., B.S.Bus.Admin.

**Majors:** Accounting, Administrative Management, Aviation Management, Business Teacher Education, Communication, Communications Education, Communications Management, Computer Information Systems, Economics, English, English Education, Finance, Finance/Economics, Health Services Management, Hospitality Management, Human Resource Management, Logistics Management, Management, Marketing, Sport Management.

**Distribution of degrees:** The majors with the highest enrollment are accounting, management, and marketing; logistics and economics have the lowest.

**Requirements:** General education requirement.

**Academic regulations:** Minimum 2.0 GPA must be maintained.
**Special:** Minors offered in accounting, business administration, international studies, and quantitative business analysis. Courses offered in drama and fine arts. Associate's degrees offered. Double majors. Independent study. Accelerated study. Pass/fail grading option. Internships. Cooperative education programs. Member of Pittsburgh Council on Higher Education. Teacher certification in secondary education. Certification in specific subject areas. Exchange program abroad in Australia (Victoria Coll). ROTC at Duquesne U. AFROTC at U of Pittsburgh.
**Honors:** Honor societies.
**Academic Assistance:** Remedial reading, writing, math, and study skills. Nonremedial tutoring.

**STUDENT LIFE. Housing:** Women's and men's dorms. 30% of students live in college housing.
**Social atmosphere:** According to the editor of the student newspaper, "Most social life orients around Greek organizations. Most people shy away from involvement in different organizations." Popular gathering spots on campus are the Student Union Snack Bar and fraternity houses. Basketball games, "Snowball" Formal, Friday Night Pub, and the Muscular Dystrophy Dance Marathon are among the year's favorite events.
**Services and counseling/handicapped student services:** Placement services. Health service. Counseling services for veteran and older students. Birth control, personal, and psychological counseling. Career and academic guidance services. Physically disabled student services. Learning disabled services. Notetaking services. Tape recorders. Tutors. Reader services for the blind.
**Campus organizations:** Undergraduate student government. Student newspaper (Minuteman, published bimonthly). Literary magazine. Yearbook. TV station. Music choral, pep band, dance and drill team, theatre group, cheerleaders, Rotaract International, ski club, political groups, 35 organizations in all. Four fraternities, no chapter houses; six sororities, no chapter houses. 15% of men join a fraternity. 5% of women join a sorority.
**Religious organizations:** Chi Alpha.
**Minority/foreign student organizations:** Minority Student Organization, Minority Business Student Association, National Association of Black Accountants. International Student Association.

**ATHLETICS. Physical education requirements:** Two semesters of physical education required.
**Intercollegiate competition:** 3% of students participate. Basketball (M,W), cheerleading (M,W), cross-country (M,W), football (M), golf (M), soccer (M,W), softball (W), tennis (M,W), track and field (indoor) (M,W), track and field (outdoor) (M,W), volleyball (W). Member of ECAC, NCAA Division I, Northeast Athletic Conference.
**Intramural and club sports:** 15% of students participate. Intramural basketball, boxing, football, softball, team handball, tennis, volleyball. Men's club bowling, volleyball. Women's club bowling.

**ADMISSIONS. Academic basis for candidate selection** (in order of priority): Secondary school record, standardized test scores, class rank, school's recommendation.
**Nonacademic basis for candidate selection:** Character and personality, extracurricular participation, particular talent or ability, geographical distribution, and alumni/ae relationship are considered.
**Requirements:** Graduation from secondary school is required; GED is accepted. 16 units and the following program of study are required: 4 units of English, 3 units of math, 2 units of science, 3 units of social studies, 1 unit of history, 3 units of electives. Minimum combined SAT score of 750 and minimum 2.0 GPA required. Minimum combined SAT score of 900 (composite ACT score of 21) and minimum 2.5 GPA required of accounting, finance, and secondary teaching certification program applicants. Conditional admission possible for applicants not meeting standard requirements. Guided Studies Program and Act 101 program for applicants not normally admissible. SAT is recommended; ACT may be substituted. Campus visit and interview recommended. Off-campus interviews available with an admissions representative.
**Procedure:** Take SAT or ACT by December of 12th year. Notification of admission on rolling basis. No set date by which applicants must accept offer. $100 tuition deposit, refundable until May 1. $100 room deposit, refundable until May 1. Freshmen accepted for terms other than fall.
**Special programs:** Admission may be deferred two semesters. Credit and/or placement may be granted through CEEB Advanced Placement exams for scores of 3 or higher. Credit and/or placement may be granted through CLEP general and subject exams. Credit and placement may be granted through ACT PEP, DANTES, and challenge exams and military experience. Early entrance/early admission program. Concurrent enrollment program.
**Transfer students:** Transfer students accepted for terms other than fall. In fall 1993, 44% of all new students were transfers into all classes. 599 transfer applications were received, 514 were accepted. Application deadline is rolling for fall; rolling for spring. Minimum 2.0 GPA required. Lowest course grade accepted is "C." Maximum number of transferable credits is 69 semester hours from a two-year school and 90 semester hours from a four-year school. At least 30 semester hours must be completed at the college to receive degree.
**Admissions contact:** James R. Welsh, Dean of Admissions. 412 262-8206, 800 762-0097.

**FINANCIAL AID. Available aid:** Pell grants, SEOG, state scholarships and grants, school scholarships and grants, private scholarships and grants, ROTC scholarships, academic merit scholarships, athletic scholarships, and United Negro College Fund. Perkins Loans (NDSL), PLUS, Stafford Loans (GSL), state loans, private loans, and SLS. Tuition Plan Inc., Knight Tuition Plans, AMS, deferred payment plan, and family tuition reduction.
**Financial aid statistics:** 21% of aid is not need-based. In 1993-94, 84% of all undergraduate applicants received aid; 75% of freshman applicants. Average amounts of aid awarded freshmen: Scholarships and grants, $3,883; loans, $2,828.
**Supporting data/closing dates:** FAFSA: Priority filing date is March 1; deadline is May 1. School's own aid application: Priority filing date is March 1; deadline is May 1. State aid form: Priority filing date is March 1; deadline is May 1. Income tax forms: Priority filing date is March 1; deadline is May 1. Notification of awards begins April 1.
**Financial aid contact:** Douglas Mahler, M.A., Director of Financial Aid. 412 262-8209.

**STUDENT EMPLOYMENT.** College Work/Study Program. Institutional employment. 8% of full-time undergraduates work on campus during school year. Students may expect to earn an average of $1,200 during school year. Off-campus part-time employment opportunities rated "good."

**COMPUTER FACILITIES.** 350 IBM/IBM-compatible microcomputers; all are networked. Students may access IBM minicomputer/mainframe systems. Client/LAN operating systems include DOS, Novell. Computer languages and software packages include BASIC, C, CICS, COBOL, dBASE, FORTRAN, Lotus 1-2-3, MUMPS, Pascal, SQL, WordPerfect. Computer facilities are available to all students.
**Fees:** Computer fee is included in tuition/fees.
**Hours:** 8 AM-midn.

**GRADUATE CAREER DATA.** Highest graduate school enrollments: Robert Morris Coll, U of Pittsburgh. 95% of graduates choose careers in business and industry. Companies and businesses that hire graduates: Price Waterhouse, Federated Investors, Mellon Bank, Deloitte & Touche.

**PROMINENT ALUMNI/AE.** David M. Roderick, CEO, USX; Clifford Barton, CEO, U.S. Bank Corp.; William Coyne, U.S. congressman.

# Rosemont College

**Rosemont, PA 19010** **215 527-0200**

**1993-94 Costs.** Tuition: $10,700. Room & board: $5,700. Fees, books, misc. academic expenses (school's estimate): $1,075.
**Enrollment.** 500 women (full-time). Freshman class: 350 applicants, 250 accepted, 121 enrolled. Graduate enrollment: 26 men, 58 women.
**Test score averages/ranges.** Average SAT scores: 505 verbal, 502 math.
**Faculty.** 43 full-time; 47 part-time. 75% of faculty holds highest degree in specific field. Student/faculty ratio: 10 to 1.
**Selectivity rating.** Competitive.

**PROFILE.** Rosemont, founded in 1921, is a private, church-affiliated, liberal arts college for women; qualified men offered admission to graduate program. Programs are offered in the Divisions of Arts; Business; English, Theatre, and Classics; Foreign Language and Literature; Humanities; Natural Science and Mathematics; and Social Science. Its 56-acre campus, located on the Renaissance-style, former Sinnott Estate in Rosemont.

**Accreditation:** MSACS.
**Religious orientation:** Rosemont College is affiliated with the Roman Catholic Church; two semesters of religion required.
**Library:** Collections totaling over 150,500 volumes, 550 periodical subscriptions, and 25,000 microform items.
**Athletic facilities:** Gymnasium, Nautilus and weight room, field hockey and softball fields, tennis courts.

**STUDENT BODY. Undergraduate profile:** 55% are state residents; 25% are transfers. 4% Asian-American, 4% Black, 2% Hispanic, 90% White.
**Freshman profile:** 10% of freshmen who took SAT scored 600 or over on verbal, 12% scored 600 or over on math; 50% scored 500 or over on verbal, 49% scored 500 or over on math; 85% scored 400 or over on verbal, 89% scored 400 or over on math; 100% scored 300 or over on verbal, 100% scored 300 or over on math. 99% of accepted applicants took SAT. 40% of freshmen come from public schools.
**Undergraduate achievement:** 85% of fall 1992 freshmen returned for fall 1993 term. 65% of entering class graduated. 20% of students who completed a degree program went on to graduate study within four years.

**PROGRAMS OF STUDY. Degrees:** B.A., B.F.A., B.S.
**Majors:** American Studies, Art History/Appreciation, Biology, Business, Business/Accounting, Chemistry, Economics, English, French, German, History, Humanities, Italian Studies, Mathematics, Philosophy, Political Science/Government, Psychology, Religious Studies, Social Sciences, Sociology, Spanish, Studio Art.
**Distribution of degrees:** The majors with the highest enrollment are English, psychology, and business.
**Requirements:** General education requirement.
**Academic regulations:** Minimum 2.0 GPA required for graduation.
**Special:** Self-designed majors. Double majors. Independent study. Accelerated study. Pass/fail grading option. Internships. Preprofessional programs in law and medicine. Washington Semester. Exchange programs with Villanova U and seven design schools. Teacher certification in early childhood, elementary, and secondary education. Study abroad possible.
**Honors:** Honors program. Honor societies.
**Academic Assistance:** Nonremedial tutoring.

**ADMISSIONS. Academic basis for candidate selection** (in order of priority): Secondary school record, class rank, standardized test scores, school's recommendation, essay.
**Nonacademic basis for candidate selection:** Character and personality are emphasized. Extracurricular participation is important. Particular talent or ability and alumni/ae relationship are considered.
**Requirements:** Graduation from secondary school is required; GED is accepted. 17 units and the following program of study are required: 4 units of English, 2 units of math, 2 units of lab science, 2 units of foreign language, 2 units of social studies, 5 units of academic electives. Conditional admission possible for applicants not meeting standard requirements. SAT is required. Campus visit and interview recommended. Off-campus interviews available with an admissions representative.
**Procedure:** Notification of admission on rolling basis. No set date by which applicants must accept offer. $300 nonrefundable tuition deposit. Freshmen accepted for terms other than fall.
**Special programs:** Admission may be deferred one year. Credit and/or placement may be granted through CEEB Advanced Placement exams for scores of 3 or higher. Placement may be granted through CLEP general exams. Early entrance/early admission program.

**Transfer students:** Transfer students accepted for terms other than fall. In fall 1993, 25% of all new students were transfers into all classes. Application deadline is August 1 for fall; January 1 for spring. Minimum 2.5 GPA required. Lowest course grade accepted is "C." At least 60 semester hours must be completed at the college to receive degree.
**Admissions contact:** Linda S. de Simone, Ed.D., Director of Enrollment Management. 215 526-2966.

**FINANCIAL AID. Available aid:** Pell grants, SEOG, state scholarships and grants, school scholarships and grants, private scholarships and grants, and academic merit scholarships. Perkins Loans (NDSL), PLUS, Stafford Loans (GSL), state loans, private loans, and SLS. Tuition Management Systems and family tuition reduction.
**Financial aid statistics:** 20% of aid is not need-based. In 1993-94, 85% of all undergraduate applicants received aid; 90% of freshman applicants. Average amounts of aid awarded freshmen: Scholarships and grants, $4,500; loans, $2,600.
**Supporting data/closing dates:** FAFSA/FAF: Priority filing date is February 15; accepted on rolling basis. State aid form: Priority filing date is February 15; accepted on rolling basis; deadline is May 1. Income tax forms: Priority filing date is March 1; accepted on rolling basis. Notification of awards begins April 1.
**Financial aid contact:** Kristan Harrington, Director of Financial Aid. 215 526-2966.

# Saint Francis College

**Loretto, PA 15940** **814 472-3000**

**1993-94 Costs.** Tuition: $10,304. Room & board: $4,720. Fees, books, misc. academic expenses (school's estimate): $1,170.
**Enrollment.** Undergraduates: 541 men, 595 women (full-time). Freshman class: 981 applicants, 775 accepted, 308 enrolled. Graduate enrollment: 159 men, 213 women.
**Test score averages/ranges.** Average SAT scores: 460 verbal, 520 math. Range of SAT scores of middle 50%: 410-530 verbal, 420-580 math.
**Faculty.** 67 full-time; 26 part-time. 69% of faculty holds highest degree in specific field. Student/faculty ratio: 15 to 1.
**Selectivity rating.** Less competitive.

**PROFILE.** Saint Francis College of Pennsylvania, founded in 1847, is a church-affiliated college of liberal arts and sciences. Its 600-acre campus is located in Loretto, 90 miles east of Pittsburgh.

**Accreditation:** MSACS. Professionally accredited by the American Medical Association (CAHEA), the Council on Social Work Education, the National League for Nursing.
**Religious orientation:** Saint Francis College is affiliated with the Roman Catholic Church (Franciscan Order); Two semesters each of religion and theology required.
**Library:** Collections totaling over 172,000 volumes, 757 periodical subscriptions and 79 microform items.
**Special facilities/museums:** Art museum, elementary-level library for education majors, physician assistant practice facilities, cadaver lab.
**Athletic facilities:** Athletic center, tennis courts, stadium, athletic fields, golf course, lake.

**STUDENT BODY. Undergraduate profile:** 73% are state residents; 24% are transfers. 1% Asian-American, 2% Black, 1% Hispanic, 95% White, 1% Other. Average age of undergraduates is 21.
**Freshman profile:** 3% of freshmen who took SAT scored 700 or over on math; 3% scored 600 or over on verbal, 17% scored 600 or over on math; 25% scored 500 or over on verbal, 45% scored 500 or over on math; 67% scored 400 or over on verbal, 88% scored 400 or over on math; 97% scored 300 or over on verbal, 100% scored 300 or over on math. 92% of accepted applicants took SAT; 2% took ACT. 73% of freshmen come from public schools.
**Undergraduate achievement:** 77% of fall 1991 freshmen returned for fall 1992 term. 53% of entering class graduated. 16% of students who completed a degree program immediately went on to graduate study.
**Foreign students:** Four students are from out of the country. Countries represented include Canada, India, Kuwait, and South Africa.

**PROGRAMS OF STUDY. Degrees:** B.A., B.S., B.S.Nurs., B.Soc.Work.
**Majors:** Accounting, American Studies, Biology, Chemistry, Computer Science, Economics, Elementary Education, English/Communications, French, History, International Business/Modern Language, Management, Mathematics, Medical Technology, Nursing, Philosophy, Physical Therapy, Physician Assistant, Podiatric Science, Political Science, Pre-Dentistry, Pre-Engineering, Pre-Environmental Management, Pre-Forestry, Pre-Law, Pre-Medicine, Pre-Optometry, Pre-Veterinary, Psychology, Public Administration/Government Service, Religious Studies, Secondary Education, Social Work, Sociology, Spanish.
**Distribution of degrees:** The majors with the highest enrollment are management, accounting, and elementary education; economics, chemistry, and political science have the lowest.
**Requirements:** General education requirement.
**Academic regulations:** Freshmen must maintain minimum 1.75 GPA; sophomores, 1.90 GPA; juniors, 2.00 GPA; seniors, 2.00 GPA.
**Special:** Minors offered. Concentrations in anthropology, communications, computer science, criminal justice, environmental science, finance, fine arts (art, music, theatre), international business, journalism, management information systems, marine biology, marketing, personnel management, and public relations. Self-designed majors. Double majors. Dual degrees. Independent study. Accelerated study. Internships. Graduate school at which undergraduates may take graduate-level courses. Preprofessional programs in law, medicine, veterinary science, dentistry, and optometry. 4-1 personnel administration/industrial relations program. 3-2 engineering programs with Clarkson U, Pennsylvania State U, and U of Pittsburgh. 3-2 forestry and environmental management program with Duke U. Member of Marine Science Consortium; off-campus study possible at Wallops Island, Va. Washington Semester. Teacher certification in elementary and secondary education. Certification in specific subject areas. Study abroad in numerous countries. ROTC at Indiana U of Pennsylvania.
**Honors:** Honors program. Honor societies.
**Academic Assistance:** Remedial reading, writing, math, and study skills. Nonremedial tutoring.

**STUDENT LIFE. Housing:** All students under age 21 must live on campus unless living with family. Women's and men's dorms. Sorority and fraternity housing. On-campus married-student housing. 65% of students live in college housing.
**Social atmosphere:** The student newspaper reports, "We are a very small campus, and a very united one. Because we are way up in the mountains, the students love to create their own fun like sledding down hills on the food trays from the cafeteria. Basketball is a big sport on campus that gets a lot of student support. Home games are exciting and tons of fun! Many of the students at St. Francis spend their time up at the fraternities and sororities on the weekends. Students also enjoy hanging out at the John F. Kennedy Student Center. The hangout off campus is the only bar in Loretto, Spanky's; they have fantastic food and great disc jockeys."
**Services and counseling/handicapped student services:** Placement services. Health service. Counseling services for veteran students. Personal and psychological counseling. Career and academic guidance services. Religious counseling.
**Campus organizations:** Undergraduate student government. Student newspaper (Loretto, published biweekly). Literary magazine. Yearbook. Radio station. SFC Singers, New Theatre, Adopt-a-Grandparent, College Entrepreneurs, Big Brothers/Big Sisters, ski club, cheerleaders, academic, service, and special-interest groups, 45 organizations in all. Three fraternities, all with chapter houses; three sororities, all with chapter houses. 15% of men join a fraternity. 15% of women join a sorority.
**Religious organizations:** Campus Ministry, Secular Franciscans, Knights of Columbus.
**Minority/foreign student organizations:** Multicultural Awareness Society.

**ATHLETICS. Physical education requirements:** None.
**Intercollegiate competition:** 25% of students participate. Basketball (M,W), cross-country (M,W), football (M), golf (M,W), soccer (M,W), softball (W), swimming (W), tennis (M,W), track (outdoor) (M,W), track and field (outdoor) (M,W), volleyball (M,W). Member of NCAA Division I, NCAA Division I-AA for football, Northeast Athletic Conference.
**Intramural and club sports:** 68% of students participate. Intramural basketball, flag football, floor hockey, golf, Nordic skiing, soccer, softball, tennis, volleyball. Men's club cheerleading. Women's club cheerleading.

**ADMISSIONS. Academic basis for candidate selection** (in order of priority): Secondary school record, class rank, standardized test scores, school's recommendation, essay.
**Nonacademic basis for candidate selection:** Extracurricular participation is important. Character and personality, particular talent or ability, geographical distribution, and alumni/ae relationship are considered.
**Requirements:** Graduation from secondary school is required; GED is accepted. 16 units and the following program of study are required: 4 units of English, 2 units of math, 1 unit of lab science, 2 units of social studies, 7 units of academic electives. Minimum combined SAT score of 900, rank in top half of secondary school class, and minimum 3.0 GPA recommended. 4 units of math and 2 units of lab science required of math and science applicants. Act 101 program for applicants not normally admissible. SAT or ACT is required. Campus visit and interview recommended. Off-campus interviews available with an admissions representative.
**Procedure:** Take SAT or ACT by March of 12th year. Visit college for interview by May of 12th year. Suggest filing application by December 1. Application deadline is August 1. Notification of admission on rolling basis. Reply is required by May 1. $100 tuition deposit, refundable until May 1. $100 room deposit, refundable until May 1. Freshmen accepted for terms other than fall.
**Special programs:** Admission may be deferred one year. Credit and/or placement may be granted through CEEB Advanced Placement exams for scores of 4 or higher. Credit and/or placement may be granted through CLEP subject exams. Placement may be granted through challenge exams and military experience. Early entrance/early admission program.
**Transfer students:** Transfer students accepted for terms other than fall. In fall 1992, 24% of all new students were transfers into all classes. 302 transfer applications were received, 167 were accepted. Application deadline is August 1 for fall; December 1 for spring. Minimum 2.0 GPA required. Lowest course grade accepted is "C." Maximum number of transferable credits is 64 semester hours. At least 64 semester hours must be completed at the college to receive degree.
**Admissions contact:** Gerard J. Rooney, M.A., Dean of Admissions. 814 472-3000, 800 457-6300 (in Pennsylvania), 800 342-5732 (in other states).

**FINANCIAL AID. Available aid:** Pell grants, SEOG, state scholarships and grants, school scholarships and grants, private scholarships and grants, academic merit scholarships, and athletic scholarships. Perkins Loans (NDSL), PLUS, Stafford Loans (GSL), state loans, school loans, and SLS. AMS and deferred payment plan.
**Financial aid statistics:** 23% of aid is not need-based. In 1992-93, 89% of all undergraduate applicants received aid; 94% of freshman applicants. Average amounts of aid awarded freshmen: Scholarships and grants, $7,900; loans, $3,050.
**Supporting data/closing dates:** FAFSA/FAF/FFS: Priority filing date is May 1. School's own aid application: Priority filing date is May 1. State aid form: Priority filing date is May 1. Income tax forms: Priority filing date is May 1. Notification of awards on rolling basis.
**Financial aid contact:** Patricia Loughran, M.A., Director of Student Financial Aid. 814 472-3010.

**STUDENT EMPLOYMENT.** College Work/Study Program. Institutional employment. 48% of full-time undergraduates work on campus during school year. Students may expect to earn an average of $750 during school year. Off-campus part-time employment opportunities rated "fair."

**COMPUTER FACILITIES.** 40 IBM/IBM-compatible and Macintosh/Apple microcomputers; all are networked. Residence halls may be equipped with stand-alone microcomputers. Computer languages and software packages include Assembler, BASIC, COBOL, dBASE, FORTRAN, MINITAB, Pascal, SuperCalc, WordPerfect. Computer facilities are available to all students.

**Fees:** None.
**Hours:** 8 AM-11 PM.

**GRADUATE CAREER DATA.** Graduate school percentages: 1% enter law school. 2% enter medical school. 1% enter dental school. 3% enter graduate business programs. 6% enter graduate arts and sciences programs.

**PROMINENT ALUMNI/AE.** Charles M. Schwab, steel industry executive; Maurice Stokes, professional basketball player.

# Saint Joseph's University

**Philadelphia, PA 19131** **610 660-1000**

**1994-95 Costs.** Tuition: $12,650. Room & board: $6,150. Fees, books, misc. academic expenses (school's estimate): $800.

**Enrollment.** Undergraduates: 1,159 men, 1,314 women (full-time). Freshman class: 2,519 applicants, 2,003 accepted, 760 enrolled. Graduate enrollment: 1,417 men, 1,705 women.

**Test score averages/ranges.** Average SAT scores: 497 verbal, 544 math. Range of SAT scores of middle 50%: 450-550 verbal, 490-590 math.

**Faculty.** 155 full-time; 200 part-time. 89% of faculty holds doctoral degree. Student/faculty ratio: 16 to 1.

**Selectivity rating.** Competitive.

**PROFILE.** Saint Joseph's, founded in 1851, is a private, church-affiliated university. Programs are offered through the Colleges of Arts and Sciences and Business and Administration and the University College. Its 60-acre campus is located in western Philadelphia.

**Accreditation:** MSACS.
**Religious orientation:** Saint Joseph's University is affiliated with the Roman Catholic Church (Society of Jesus); three semesters of theology required.
**Library:** Collections totaling over 310,000 volumes, 1,800 periodical subscriptions, and 700,000 microform items.
**Special facilities/museums:** Brazilian institute, faith and justice institute, food marketing academy.
**Athletic facilities:** Basketball, racquetball, tennis, and volleyball courts, tracks, swimming pool, weight room, field hockey, football, intramural, lacrosse, rugby, soccer, and softball fields, hockey rink, field house, fitness center.

**STUDENT BODY. Undergraduate profile:** 54% are state residents; 13% are transfers. 3% Asian-American, 4% Black, 2% Hispanic, 87% White, 4% Other. Average age of undergraduates is 20.
**Freshman profile:** 98% of accepted applicants took SAT; 2% took ACT. 26% of freshmen come from public schools.
**Undergraduate achievement:** 83% of fall 1992 freshmen returned for fall 1993 term. 69% of entering class graduated. 22% of students who completed a degree program immediately went on to graduate study.
**Foreign students:** 224 students are from out of the country. Countries represented include Brazil, China, Ecuador, England, Ireland, and Japan; 65 in all.

**PROGRAMS OF STUDY. Degrees:** B.A., B.S.
**Majors:** Accounting, Biology, Chemistry, Computer Science, Criminal Justice, Economics, Elementary Education, English, Finance, Fine/Performing Arts, Food Marketing, French, German, Health Services Administration, History, Human Services Administration, Humanities, Information Systems, Interdisciplinary Studies, International Relations, Labor Studies, Management, Marketing, Mathematics, Pharmaceutical Marketing, Philosophy, Physics, Politics, Psychology, Public Administration, Purchasing, Sociology, Spanish, Theology.
**Distribution of degrees:** The majors with the highest enrollment are marketing, food marketing, and English; German, Spanish, and French have the lowest.
**Requirements:** General education requirement.
**Academic regulations:** Freshmen must maintain minimum 1.6 GPA; sophomores, 1.8 GPA; juniors, 2.0 GPA; seniors, 2.0 GPA.
**Special:** Minors offered in all majors. Undeclared majors possible in business administration and food marketing, humanities and social sciences, natural sciences, and math. Programs in American, European, Latin American, and medieval studies. Courses offered in classics, education, Italian, Japanese, and Portuguese. Institute of Latin American Studies offers four years of specialized undergraduate study in government and business with field work. Associate's degrees offered. Self-designed majors. Double majors. Independent study. Internships. Cooperative education programs. Graduate school at which undergraduates may take graduate-level courses. Preprofessional programs in law, medicine, and dentistry. Five-year B.S./M.S. international marketing and psychology programs. Washington Semester. Member of Jesuit Student Exchange Program. Teacher certification in elementary and secondary education. Certification in specific subject areas. Study abroad in Canada, England, France, Ireland, Japan, and Mexico. AFROTC. ROTC and NROTC at U of Pennsylvania.
**Honors:** Honors program. Honor societies.
**Academic Assistance:** Remedial study skills. Nonremedial tutoring.

**STUDENT LIFE. Housing:** Students may live on or off campus. Coed, women's, and men's dorms. School-owned/operated apartments. 55% of students live in college housing.
**Social atmosphere:** According to the editor of the student newspaper, the social life of the university is becoming more and more influenced by the Greeks. Other influential groups are the newspaper staff and the Campion Center Union Board. Students like to hang out at the Student Center and go to Cavanaugh's, off campus. Most popular events of the year include the big basketball game between St. Joe's and Villanova, the Hand-in-Hand Festival for the Mentally Handicapped, Spring Fling, and the Thanksgiving Dinner Dance, a volunteer program for the elderly.
**Services and counseling/handicapped student services:** Placement services. Health service. Women's center. Personal and psychological counseling. Career and academic guidance services. Religious counseling. Learning disabled services.
**Campus organizations:** Undergraduate student government. Student newspaper (Hawk, published once/week). Literary magazine. Yearbook. Radio station. Glee club, chorus, band, debating, dance troupe, drama group, Community Action Program, Amnesty International, departmental groups, 60 organizations in all. Four fraternities, no chapter houses; three sororities, no chapter houses. 25% of men join a fraternity. 25% of women join a sorority.
**Religious organizations:** Campus Ministry, Bread for the World, Hand-in-Hand Service Organization, Pro-Life Organization.
**Minority/foreign student organizations:** Black Awareness Society. International Student Association.

**ATHLETICS. Physical education requirements:** None.
**Intercollegiate competition:** 16% of students participate. Baseball (M), basketball (M,W), cheerleading (M,W), crew (M,W), cross-country (M,W), field hockey (W), golf (M), lacrosse (M,W), soccer (M), softball (W), tennis (M,W), track (indoor) (M,W), track (outdoor) (M,W), track and field (indoor) (M,W), track and field (outdoor) (M,W). Member of Atlantic 10 Conference, ECAC, NCAA Division I.
**Intramural and club sports:** 75% of students participate. Intramural basketball, football, golf, racquetball, soccer, volleyball. Men's club ice hockey, rugby, swimming, volleyball. Women's club swimming.

**ADMISSIONS. Academic basis for candidate selection** (in order of priority): Secondary school record, class rank, standardized test scores, school's recommendation, essay.
**Nonacademic basis for candidate selection:** Extracurricular participation is important. Character and personality, particular talent or ability, geographical distribution, and alumni/ae relationship are considered.
**Requirements:** Graduation from secondary school is required; GED is not accepted. 12 units and the following program of study are required: 4 units of English, 3 units of math, 2 units of science, 2 units of foreign language, 1 unit of social studies. Rank in top two-fifths of secondary school class and minimum "B" average recommended. SAT is required; ACT may be substituted. Campus visit and interview recommended. No off-campus interviews.
**Procedure:** Take SAT or ACT by December of 12th year. Visit college for interview by March 1 of 12th year. Suggest filing application by January 1. Application deadline is March 1. Notification of admission on rolling basis. Reply is required by May 1. $100 nonrefundable tuition deposit. $100 nonrefundable room deposit. $225 room deposit, $125 of which is refundable upon withdrawal from residence hall or upon graduation. Freshmen accepted for terms other than fall.
**Special programs:** Admission may be deferred one year. Credit and/or placement may be granted through CEEB Advanced Placement exams for scores of 4 or higher. Early decision program. Deadline for applying for early decision is on rolling basis. Early entrance/early admission program.
**Transfer students:** Transfer students accepted for terms other than fall. In fall 1993, 13% of all new students were transfers into all classes. 282 transfer applications were received, 174 were accepted. Application deadline is July 1 for fall; December 1 for spring. Minimum 2.5 GPA required. Lowest course grade accepted is "C." Maximum number of transferable credits is 60 semester hours. At least 60 semester hours must be completed at the university to receive degree.
**Admissions contact:** John Sullivan, Director of Admissions. 610 660-1300.

**FINANCIAL AID. Available aid:** Pell grants, SEOG, state scholarships and grants, school scholarships and grants, private scholarships and grants, ROTC scholarships, academic merit scholarships, and athletic scholarships. Perkins Loans (NDSL), PLUS, Stafford Loans (GSL), state loans, and SLS. Knights of Columbus loans, Commercial loans. Tuition Plan Inc. Installment payment plan, SJU payment plan.
**Financial aid statistics:** 25% of aid is not need-based. In 1993-94, 100% of all undergraduate applicants received aid. Average amounts of aid awarded freshmen: Scholarships and grants, $8,258; loans, $3,750.
**Supporting data/closing dates:** FAFSA: Priority filing date is March 11. School's own aid application: Deadline is February 15. State aid form: Deadline is March 1. Income tax forms: Deadline is February 15. Notification of awards begins March 15.
**Financial aid contact:** John A. Pergolin, M.A., Director of Financial Aid. 610 660-1340.

**STUDENT EMPLOYMENT.** College Work/Study Program. Institutional employment. 10% of full-time undergraduates work on campus during school year. Students may expect to earn an average of $900 during school year. Off-campus part-time employment opportunities rated "good."

**COMPUTER FACILITIES.** 200 IBM/IBM-compatible and Macintosh/Apple microcomputers; all are networked. Students may access SUN minicomputer/mainframe systems, Internet. Residence halls may be equipped with networked microcomputers, modems. Client/LAN operating systems include Apple/Macintosh, DOS, UNIX/XENIX/AIX, Windows NT, X-windows, LocalTalk/AppleTalk, Microsoft, Novell. Computer languages and software packages include Ada, Assembler, BASIC, C, COBOL, FORTRAN, LISP, Pascal, Prolog; database, financial, spreadsheet, word processing programs; 72 in all. Computer facilities are available to all students.
**Fees:** Computer fee is included in tuition/fees.
**Hours:** 13 hours/day (M-F); eight hours/day (Sa-Su).

**GRADUATE CAREER DATA.** Graduate school percentages: 5% enter law school. 3% enter medical school. 2% enter dental school. 6% enter graduate business programs. 6% enter graduate arts and sciences programs. Highest graduate school enrollments: Georgetown U, Pennsylvania State U, Temple U, Thomas Jefferson U, U of Delaware, U of Pennsylvania, Villanova U. 55% of graduates choose careers in business and industry. Companies and businesses that hire graduates: Andersen Consulting, Chase Manhattan, Coopers & Lybrand, Deloitte & Touche, Kraft, Pillsbury, Vanguard.

**PROMINENT ALUMNI/AE.** Rosemary Greco, president, Fidelity Bank; William J. Byron, S.J., president, Catholic U; James E. Dougherty, U.S. representative to UN Advisory Board on Disarmament; Michael C. Mallowe, senior editor, *Philadelphia Magazine*; James Lynam, coach, Washington Bullets.

# Saint Vincent College

**Latrobe, PA 15650-2690** **412 539-9761**

**1993-94 Costs.** Tuition: $10,168. Room: $1,712. Board: $2,054. Fees, books, misc. academic expenses (school's estimate): $650.
**Enrollment.** Undergraduates: 533 men, 502 women (full-time). Freshman class: 700 applicants, 595 accepted, 278 enrolled.
**Test score averages/ranges.** Range of SAT scores of middle 50%: 410-520 verbal, 430-560 math.
**Faculty.** 75 full-time; 30 part-time. 68% of faculty holds highest degree in specific field. Student/faculty ratio: 15 to 1.
**Selectivity rating.** Less competitive.

**PROFILE.** Saint Vincent is a private, church-affiliated, liberal arts college. Founded in 1846 as a college for men, it adopted coeducation in 1983. Its 100-acre campus is located in Latrobe, 35 miles east of Pittsburgh.

**Accreditation:** MSACS.
**Religious orientation:** Saint Vincent College is affiliated with the Roman Catholic Church (Benedictine Order); three semesters of religion required.
**Library:** Collections totaling over 247,034 volumes, 856 periodical subscriptions, and 78,476 microform items.
**Special facilities/museums:** Art gallery, life sciences research center, spectrophotometer, spectrometer, physiograph work stations, data acquisition work station, planetarium, observatory, radio telescope.
**Athletic facilities:** Gymnasium, weight room, bowling lanes, basketball and tennis courts, aerobics room, baseball, football, soccer, and softball fields, swimming pool.

**STUDENT BODY. Undergraduate profile:** 89% are state residents; 15% are transfers. 1% Asian-American, 2% Black, 1% Hispanic, 1% Native American, 95% White. Average age of undergraduates is 20.
**Freshman profile:** 1% of freshmen who took SAT scored 700 or over on verbal, 3% scored 700 or over on math; 7% scored 600 or over on verbal, 20% scored 600 or over on math; 35% scored 500 or over on verbal, 55% scored 500 or over on math; 81% scored 400 or over on verbal, 87% scored 400 or over on math; 99% scored 300 or over on verbal, 100% scored 300 or over on math. 97% of accepted applicants took SAT; 3% took ACT. 68% of freshmen come from public schools.
**Undergraduate achievement:** 90% of fall 1992 freshmen returned for fall 1993 term. 60% of entering class graduated. 25% of students who completed a degree program went on to graduate study.
**Foreign students:** Nine students are from out of the country. Countries represented include Ecuador, Greece, India, Japan, Panama, and Thailand; eight in all.

**PROGRAMS OF STUDY. Degrees:** B.A., B.F.A., B.S.
**Majors:** Accounting, Applied Physics, Art, Art Education, Art/Graphic Design, Art/Photography, Art/Studio, Art Therapy, Art/Visual Arts, Biochemistry, Biology, Business Administration, Chemistry, Child Care, Communication, Computing/Information Science, Consumer Service, Economics, English, Environmental Studies, Fashion Merchandising, Finance, Food Service Management, Foreign Languages, French, History, Home Economics, Interior Design, Liberal Arts, Management, Mathematics, Medical Technology, Music, Music Education, Music Performance, Philosophy, Physics, Physics Education, Political Science, Pre-Engineering, Psychology, Religious Education, Religious Studies, Retail Merchandising, Sacred Music, Social Work, Sociology, Spanish, Theatre, Visual Arts Management.
**Distribution of degrees:** The majors with the highest enrollment are psychology, accounting, and political science; art/graphic design and fashion merchandising have the lowest.
**Requirements:** General education requirement.
**Academic regulations:** Minimum 2.0 GPA must be maintained.
**Special:** Minors offered in most majors. Self-designed majors. Double majors. Dual degrees. Independent study. Accelerated study. Pass/fail grading option. Internships. Cooperative education programs. Preprofessional programs in law, medicine, veterinary science, pharmacy, dentistry, theology, optometry, and physical therapy. 3-4 podiatry programs with Ohio Coll of Podiatric Medicine and Pennsylvania Coll of Podiatric Medicine. 3-2 engineering programs with Boston U, Pennsylvania State U, and U of Pittsburgh. Washington Semester. Teacher certification in early childhood, elementary, and secondary education. Exchange program abroad in Taiwan (Fu Jen Catholic U). Study abroad also in Austria, England, France, Mexico, the Netherlands, Spain, Wales, and other countries. AFROTC at U of Pittsburgh (main campus).
**Honors:** Honors program. Honor societies.
**Academic Assistance:** Nonremedial tutoring.

**ADMISSIONS. Academic basis for candidate selection** (in order of priority): Secondary school record, class rank, standardized test scores, school's recommendation, essay.
**Nonacademic basis for candidate selection:** Character and personality are important. Extracurricular participation, particular talent or ability, and alumni/ae relationship are considered.
**Requirements:** Graduation from secondary school is required; GED is accepted. 15 units and the following program of study are required: 4 units of English, 2 units of math, 1 unit of lab science, 2 units of foreign language, 3 units of social studies, 3 units of electives. Audition required of theatre program applicants. 1 unit each of plane geometry, algebra, and physics and 1/2 unit of trigonometry required of engineering program applicants. Portfolio required of art program applicants. Audition required of music program applicants. Conditional admission possible for applicants not meeting standard requirements. SAT is required; ACT may be substituted. Campus visit and interview recommended. No off-campus interviews.
**Procedure:** Take SAT or ACT by November of 12th year. Suggest filing application by February 1. Application deadline is May 1. Notification of admission on rolling basis. Reply is required by May 1. $75 nonrefundable tuition deposit. $75 nonrefundable room deposit. Freshmen accepted for terms other than fall.
**Special programs:** Admission may be deferred one year. Credit may be granted through CEEB Advanced Placement for scores of 3 or higher. Credit may be granted through CLEP general and subject exams, ACT PEP and challenge exams. Credit and placement may be granted through DANTES exams and military and life experience. Early entrance/early admission program. Concurrent enrollment program.
**Transfer students:** Transfer students accepted for terms other than fall. In fall 1993, 15% of all new students were transfers into all classes. 94 transfer applications were received, 69 were accepted. Application deadline is May 1 for fall; December 1 for spring. Minimum 2.5 GPA recommended. Lowest course grade accepted is "C." Maximum number of transferable credits is 62 semeter hours from a two-year school and 90 semester hours from a four-year school. At least 34 semester hours must be completed at the college to receive degree.
**Admissions contact:** Rev. Earl J. Henry, O.S.B., M.Div., Dean of Admissions and Financial Aid. 412 537-4540.

**FINANCIAL AID. Available aid:** Pell grants, SEOG, state scholarships and grants, school scholarships and grants, ROTC scholarships, academic merit scholarships, athletic scholarships, and aid for undergraduate foreign students. Perkins Loans (NDSL), PLUS, Stafford Loans (GSL), and SLS. AMS and Tuition Management Systems.
**Financial aid statistics:** 27% of aid is not need-based. In 1993-94, 100% of all undergraduate applicants received aid; 83% of freshman applicants. Average amounts of aid awarded freshmen: Scholarships and grants, $3,000; loans, $2,513.
**Supporting data/closing dates:** FAFSA: Priority filing date is March 1; deadline is May 1. Income tax forms: Accepted on rolling basis. Notification of awards on rolling basis.
**Financial aid contact:** Rev. Earl J. Henry, O.S.B., M.Div., Dean of Admissions and Financial Aid. 412 537-4540.

# Seton Hill College

**Greensburg, PA 15601-1599** **412 834-2200**

**1993-94 Costs.** Tuition: $10,240. Fees, books, misc. academic expenses (school's estimate): $350.
**Enrollment.** Undergraduates: 47 men, 705 women (full-time). Freshman class: 936 applicants, 560 accepted, 197 enrolled.
**Test score averages/ranges.** Range of SAT scores of middle 50%: 400-520 verbal, 400-530 math.
**Faculty.** 55 full-time; 52 part-time. 67% of faculty holds doctoral degree. Student/faculty ratio: 12 to 1.
**Selectivity rating.** Competitive.

**PROFILE.** Seton Hill, founded in 1883, is a private, church-affiliated, liberal arts college for women; qualified men admitted only to the School of Fine Arts. Its 200-acre campus, including buildings of Victorian architectural style, is located in Greensburg, 30 miles east of Pittsburgh.

**Accreditation:** MSACS. Professionally accredited by the American Dietetic Association, the National Association of Schools of Music.
**Religious orientation:** Seton Hill College is affiliated with the Roman Catholic Church (Sisters of Charity); two semesters of theology required.
**Library:** Collections totaling over 101,000 volumes, 530 periodical subscriptions, and 4,600 microform items.
**Special facilities/museums:** Art gallery, concert hall, theatre, nursery school, kindergarten, microcomputer lab.
**Athletic facilities:** Gymnasium, weight room, swimming pool, tennis courts, fitness trail, soccer and softball fields.

**STUDENT BODY. Undergraduate profile:** 80% are state residents; 18% are transfers. 3% Asian-American, 6% Black, 5% Hispanic, 85% White, 1% Other. Average age of undergraduates is 20.
**Freshman profile:** 8% of freshmen who took SAT scored 600 or over on verbal, 11% scored 600 or over on math; 32% scored 500 or over on verbal, 37% scored 500 or over on math; 79% scored 400 or over on verbal, 77% scored 400 or over on math; 95% scored 300 or over on verbal, 95% scored 300 or over on math. 95% of accepted applicants took SAT; 2% took ACT. 80% of freshmen come from public schools.
**Undergraduate achievement:** 72% of fall 1992 freshmen returned for fall 1993 term. 51% of entering class graduated. 22% of students who completed a degree program immediately went on to graduate study.
**Foreign students:** 17 students are from out of the country. Countries represented include China, India, and Japan; seven in all.

**PROGRAMS OF STUDY. Degrees:** B.A., B.F.A., B.Mus., B.S., B.Soc.Work.
**Majors:** Abused Land Management, Accounting, Actuarial Science, Art, Art Education, Art History, Art Therapy, Biochemistry, Biology, Business Administration, Chemistry, Child Care, Communication, Computer Science, Data Management, Dietetics, Early Childhood Education, Economics, Education, Elementary Education, Engineering, English, Entrepreneurship, Family Studies, Fashion Merchandising, Finance, Food Service Management, French, Graphic Design, History, Home Economics, Home Economics Education, Interior Design, International Organization/Management, Journalism, Management, Mathematics, Medical Technology, Music, Music Education, Nursing, Philosophy, Photography, Physics, Political Science, Psychology, Religious Studies/Theology, Retailing Management, Sacred Music, Secondary Education, Social Work, Sociology, Spanish, Theatre, Visual Arts/Theatre.
**Distribution of degrees:** The majors with the highest enrollment are psychology and management; accounting and social work have the lowest.
**Requirements:** General education requirement.
**Academic regulations:** Minimum 2.0 GPA must be maintained.
**Special:** Minors offered in all majors and in women's studies. Self-designed majors. Double majors. Dual degrees. Independent study. Accelerated study. Pass/fail grading option. Internships. Cooperative education programs. Preprofessional programs in law,

medicine, veterinary science, dentistry, optometry, and podiatry. 2-2 nursing program with Catholic U. 3-2 engineering programs with Georgia Tech, Pennsylvania State U, and U of Pittsburgh. Washington Semester and UN Semester. Exchange programs with Saint Vincent Coll and U of Pittsburgh at Greensburg. Teacher certification in early childhood, elementary, and secondary education. Certification in specific subject areas. Exchange programs abroad in China (Nanjing U) and Japan (Nanzan Junior Coll). Study abroad also in numerous countries. ROTC at U of Pittsburgh at Greensburg.

**Honors:** Honors program. Honor societies.

**Academic Assistance:** Remedial writing, math, and study skills. Nonremedial tutoring.

**ADMISSIONS. Academic basis for candidate selection** (in order of priority): Secondary school record, school's recommendation, standardized test scores, class rank, essay.

**Nonacademic basis for candidate selection:** Character and personality and particular talent or ability are important. Extracurricular participation, geographical distribution, and alumni/ae relationship are considered.

**Requirements:** Graduation from secondary school is required; GED is accepted. 15 units and the following program of study are required: 4 units of English, 2 units of math, 1 unit of science, 2 units of foreign language, 2 units of social studies, 4 units of academic electives. Audition required of theatre program applicants. Portfolio required of art program applicants. Audition required of music program applicants. Act 101 program and Summer Opportunity Program for applicants not normally admissible. SAT or ACT is required. Campus visit and interview recommended. Off-campus interviews available with admissions and alumni representatives.

**Procedure:** Take SAT or ACT by fall of 12th year. Suggest filing application by May 1. Application deadline is August 15. Notification of admission on rolling basis. July 31 (fall); November 30 (spring). $100 tuition deposit, refundable until May 1. Freshmen accepted for terms other than fall.

**Special programs:** Admission may be deferred one year. Credit and/or placement may be granted through CEEB Advanced Placement exams for scores of 3 or higher. Credit and/or placement may be granted through CLEP general and subject exams. Credit and placement may be granted through DANTES and challenge exams and military and life experience. Early entrance/early admission program.

**Transfer students:** Transfer students accepted for terms other than fall. In fall 1993, 18% of all new students were transfers into all classes. 95 transfer applications were received, 83 were accepted. Application deadline is August 1 for fall; January 1 for spring. Minimum 2.0 GPA required. Lowest course grade accepted is "C." Maximum number of transferable credits is 80 semester hours. At least 48 semester hours must be completed at the college to receive degree.

**FINANCIAL AID. Available aid:** Pell grants, SEOG, state scholarships and grants, school scholarships and grants, private scholarships and grants, academic merit scholarships, athletic scholarships, and aid for undergraduate foreign students. Perkins Loans (NDSL), PLUS, Stafford Loans (GSL), state loans, school loans, private loans, and SLS. Knight Tuition Plans and Tuition Management Systems. Seton Hill Installment Plan.

**Financial aid statistics:** 21% of aid is not need-based. In 1993-94, 98% of all undergraduate applicants received aid; 100% of freshman applicants. Average amounts of aid awarded freshmen: Scholarships and grants, $3,500; loans, $2,300.

**Supporting data/closing dates:** FAFSA: Accepted on rolling basis. School's own aid application: Accepted on rolling basis. State aid form: Deadline is May 1. Income tax forms: Accepted on rolling basis. Notification of awards on rolling basis.

**Financial aid contact:** Sr. Mary Philip Aaron, Director of Financial Aid. 412 838-4293.

# Shippensburg University of Pennsylvania

**Shippensburg, PA 17257** **717 532-9121**

**1993-94 Costs.** Tuition: $2,956 (state residents), $7,352 (out-of-state). Room: $1,826. Board: $1,522. Fees, books, misc. academic expenses (school's estimate): $977.

**Enrollment.** Undergraduates: 2,462 men, 2,797 women (full-time). Freshman class: 5,416 applicants, 3,281 accepted, 1,144 enrolled. Graduate enrollment: 410 men, 520 women.

**Test score averages/ranges.** Average SAT scores: 468 verbal, 529 math. Range of SAT scores of middle 50%: 420-500 verbal, 570-480 math.

**Faculty.** 307 full-time; 23 part-time. 80% of faculty holds highest degree in specific field. Student/faculty ratio: 18 to 1.

**Selectivity rating.** Competitive.

**PROFILE.** Shippensburg, founded in 1871, is a public, comprehensive university. Programs are offered through the Colleges of Arts and Sciences, Business, and Education and Human Services. The oldest building on campus, dating from 1871, is registered as a National Historic Landmark. Its 200-acre campus is located in Shippensburg, 50 miles southwest of Harrisburg.

**Accreditation:** MSACS. Professionally accredited by the American Assembly of Collegiate Schools of Business, the Council on Social Work Education, the National Council for Accreditation of Teacher Education.

**Religious orientation:** Shippensburg University of Pennsylvania is nonsectarian; no religious requirements.

**Library:** Collections totaling over 425,325 volumes, 1,727 periodical subscriptions, and 1,503,166 microform items.

**Special facilities/museums:** Fashion archives, art gallery, vertebrate museum, on-campus elementary school, public service centers in arts/humanities, government, and management, planetarium, electron microscope, NMR spectrometer.

**Athletic facilities:** Gymnasium, field house, golf course, intramural fields.

**STUDENT BODY. Undergraduate profile:** 91% are state residents; 16% are transfers. 1% Asian-American, 3% Black, 1% Hispanic, 95% White. Average age of undergraduates is 20.

**Freshman profile:** 1% of freshmen who took SAT scored 700 or over on math; 3% scored 600 or over on verbal, 16% scored 600 or over on math; 32% scored 500 or over on verbal, 70% scored 500 or over on math; 87% scored 400 or over on verbal, 99% scored 400 or over on math; 100% scored 300 or over on verbal, 100% scored 300 or over on math. 98% of accepted applicants took SAT. 89% of freshmen come from public schools.

**Undergraduate achievement:** 83% of fall 1992 freshmen returned for fall 1993 term. 45% of entering class graduated. 15% of students who completed a degree program went on to graduate study within one year.

**Foreign students:** 33 students are from out of the country. Countries represented include China, England, India, Israel, and Kenya; 21 in all.

**PROGRAMS OF STUDY. Degrees:** B.A., B.S., B.S.Bus.Admin., B.S.Ed.

**Majors:** Accounting, Applied Physics, Art, Biology, Business Education, Business Information Systems, Chemistry, Communication Arts, Communications/Journalism, Comprehensive Social Studies/Economics, Comprehensive Social Studies/Geography, Comprehensive Social Studies/History, Comprehensive Social Studies/Political Science, Comprehensive Social Studies/Psychology, Comprehensive Social Studies/Sociology, Computer Science, Criminal Justice, Earth Science, Economics, Elementary Education, English, Finance, French, Geoenvironmental Studies, Geography, German, Government, History, Interdisciplinary Arts, Management, Management Science, Marketing, Mathematics, Medical Technology, Office Administration, Physics, Psychology, Public Administration, Real Estate, Social Work, Sociology, Spanish, Speech Communications, Transportation/Logistics, Urban Studies.

**Distribution of degrees:** The majors with the highest enrollment are teacher education, criminal justice, and accounting; transportation/logistics, physics, and economics have the lowest.

**Requirements:** General education requirement.

**Academic regulations:** Minimum 2.0 GPA must be maintained.

**Special:** Minors offered in some majors and in anthropology, coaching, early childhood education, gerontology, music, philosophy, reading education, speech, and women's studies. Double majors. Independent study. Pass/fail grading option. Internships. Graduate school at which undergraduates may take graduate-level courses. Preprofessional programs in law, medicine, veterinary science, pharmacy, dentistry, optometry, physical therapy, and podiatry. 3-2 engineering programs with U of Maryland and Pennsylvania State U. Member of Marine Science Consortium; off-campus study possible at Wallops Island, Va. Member of Pennsylvania Consortium for International Education. Washington Semester. Exchange programs with Art Inst of Philadelphia, Art Inst of Pittsburgh, six other design schools, and Wilson Coll. Visiting Student Program. Teacher certification in early childhood, elementary, secondary, and special education. Certification in specific subject areas. Exchange program abroad in England. Study abroad also in France, Germany, Spain, and other countries. ROTC.

**Honors:** Honors program. Honor societies.

**Academic Assistance:** Remedial reading, writing, math, and study skills. Nonremedial tutoring.

**STUDENT LIFE. Housing:** Students may live on or off campus. Coed, women's, and men's dorms. School-owned/operated apartments. 43% of students live in college housing.

**Social atmosphere:** According to the editor of the student newspaper, "The community does not offer a serious social climate aside from bars and restaurants. On-campus activities are seldom, but more are planned every month, and the situation is improving." The Greeks and the Activities Program Board (senate committee) have the most influence on campus. Popular events around the university include Homecoming, rock concerts held each semester, and Shenanigans, a nonalcoholic dance held weekly. Favorite gathering place for students on campus is the Cumberland Union Building. Off campus, they head for Wilo's and Gingerbread (two local bars), and Duck Pond.

**Services and counseling/handicapped student services:** Placement services. Health service. Women's center. Day care. Counseling services for minority, veteran, and older students. Personal and psychological counseling. Career and academic guidance services. Physically disabled student services. Learning disabled services. Notetaking services. Tape recorders. Tutors. Reader services for the blind.

**Campus organizations:** Undergraduate student government. Student newspaper (Slate, published once/week). Literary magazine. Yearbook. Radio and TV stations. Choirs, bands, ensembles, orchestra, drama group, dance troupe, outing club, nontraditional student group, Big Brother/Big Sister, special-interest and volunteer groups, 156 organizations in all. 13 fraternities, one chapter house; 11 sororities, no chapter houses. 15% of men join a fraternity. 15% of women join a sorority.

**Religious organizations:** United Campus Ministry, Black Campus Ministry, Catholic Campus Ministry, Christian Fellowship, Jewish Student Organization, Brothers & Sisters in Christ, Fellowship of Christian Athletes.

**Minority/foreign student organizations:** Afro-American Organization, Latino Club, Black Greek organizations. International Student Organization.

**ATHLETICS. Physical education requirements:** None.

**Intercollegiate competition:** 1% of students participate. Baseball (M), basketball (M,W), cheerleading (M), cross-country (M,W), diving (M), field hockey (W), football (M), lacrosse (M,W), soccer (M), softball (W), swimming (M,W), track and field (indoor) (M,W), track and field (outdoor) (M,W), volleyball (M,W), wrestling (M). Member of ECAC, NCAA Division II, Pennsylvania State Athletic Conference.

**Intramural and club sports:** 1% of students participate. Intramural aerobics, basketball, billiards, bowling, boxing, cross-country, golf, handball, lacrosse, rugby, softball, street hockey, swimming, table tennis, tennis, track, volleyball, water aerobics, wrestling. Men's club bowling, boxing, lacrosse, rugby, tennis. Women's club rugby, soccer.

**ADMISSIONS. Academic basis for candidate selection** (in order of priority): Secondary school record, class rank, standardized test scores, school's recommendation.

**Nonacademic basis for candidate selection:** Character and personality, extracurricular participation, and particular talent or ability are considered.

**Requirements:** Graduation from secondary school is required; GED is accepted. 20 units and the following program of study are recommended: 4 units of English, 3 units of math, 3 units of science, 2 units of foreign language, 2 units of social studies, 2 units of history, 2 units of electives. Act 101 program for in-state applicants not normally admissible. SAT is

required; ACT may be substituted. Campus visit recommended. No off-campus interviews.
**Procedure:** Take SAT or ACT by fall of 12th year. Suggest filing application by February 1; no deadline. Notification of admission on rolling basis. Reply is required by March 1 or within four weeks. $75 nonrefundable tuition deposit. $100 nonrefundable room deposit. Freshmen accepted for terms other than fall.
**Special programs:** Admission may be deferred one semester. Credit and/or placement may be granted through CEEB Advanced Placement exams for scores of 3 or higher. Credit and/or placement may be granted through CLEP general and subject exams. Placement may be granted through challenge exams. Early entrance/early admission program. Concurrent enrollment program.
**Transfer students:** Transfer students accepted for terms other than fall. In fall 1993, 16% of all new students were transfers into all classes. 938 transfer applications were received, 664 were accepted. Minimum 2.2 GPA required. Lowest course grade accepted is "C." Maximum number of transferable credits is 60 semester hours from a two-year school and 75 semester hours from a four-year school. At least 45 semester hours must be completed at the university to receive degree.
**Admissions contact:** Joseph G. Cretella, M.S., Dean of Admissions. 717 532-1231.

**FINANCIAL AID. Available aid:** Pell grants, SEOG, state scholarships and grants, school scholarships, private scholarships and grants, ROTC scholarships, academic merit scholarships, athletic scholarships, and aid for undergraduate foreign students. Perkins Loans (NDSL), PLUS, Stafford Loans (GSL), school loans, private loans, and SLS. Prepayment plan.
**Financial aid statistics:** 77% of aid is not need-based. In 1993-94, 84% of all undergraduate applicants received aid; 81% of freshman applicants. Average amounts of aid awarded freshmen: Scholarships and grants, $1,272; loans, $2,091.
**Supporting data/closing dates:** FAFSA/FAF/FFS: Priority filing date is May 1. School's own aid application: Priority filing date is May 1. State aid form: Deadline is May 1. Notification of awards on rolling basis.
**Financial aid contact:** Thomas Moriarty, M.S., Director of Financial Aid. 717 532-1131.

**STUDENT EMPLOYMENT.** College Work/Study Program. Institutional employment. 17% of full-time undergraduates work on campus during school year. Off-campus part-time employment opportunities rated "fair."

**COMPUTER FACILITIES.** 200 IBM/IBM-compatible and Macintosh/Apple microcomputers; 150 are networked. Students may access Digital, UNISYS minicomputer/mainframe systems, BITNET, Internet. Residence halls may be equipped with networked terminals. Computer languages and software packages include BASIC, C, COBOL, dBASE, FORTRAN, Oracle, Pascal, SAS, SPSS. Computer facilities are available to all students.
**Hours:** 15 hours/day.

**GRADUATE CAREER DATA.** Highest graduate school enrollments: Pennsylvania State U, Shippensburg U, Villanova U. Companies and businesses that hire graduates: Financial institutions, school districts, government.

**PROMINENT ALUMNI/AE.** Dean Koontz, author; Dr. Edwin Zechman, president and CEO, Children's Hospital, Pittsburgh; Dr. Samuel Kirkpatrick, president, U of Texas at San Antonio.

5-7 8-28

# Slippery Rock University of Pennsylvania

**Slippery Rock, PA 16057 — 412 738-2800**

**1993-94 Costs.** Tuition: $2,920 (state residents), $7,650 (out-of-state). Room: $1,762. Board: $1,602. Fees, books, misc. academic expenses (school's estimate): $1,190.
**Enrollment.** Undergraduates: 2,752 men, 3,265 women (full-time). Freshman class: 4,690 applicants, 2,785 accepted, 1,208 enrolled. Graduate enrollment: 247 men, 506 women.
**Test score averages/ranges.** Average SAT scores: 429 verbal, 474 math.
**Faculty.** 392 full-time; 23 part-time. 64% of faculty holds doctoral degree. Student/faculty ratio: 20 to 1.
**Selectivity rating.** Competitive.

**PROFILE.** Slippery Rock, founded in 1889, is a public, comprehensive university. Programs are offered through the Colleges of Arts and Sciences, Education and Human Service Professions, and Information Science and Business Administration, and the Graduate School. Its 650-acre campus is located in Slippery Rock, 50 miles north of Pittsburgh.

**Accreditation:** MSACS. Professionally accredited by the American Physical Therapy Association, the Council on Social Work Education, the National Association of Schools of Music, the National Council for Accreditation of Teacher Education, the National League for Nursing, the National Recreation and Park Association.
**Religious orientation:** Slippery Rock University of Pennsylvania is nonsectarian; no religious requirements.
**Library:** Collections totaling over 767,220 volumes, 1,649 periodical subscriptions, and 1,074,422 microform items.
**Special facilities/museums:** Special education school for student teachers, physical therapy clinic, microvideo system, planetarium, electron microscope.
**Athletic facilities:** Field house, weight room, swimming pool, indoor/outdoor track, basketball, racquetball, tennis, and volleyball courts.

**STUDENT BODY. Undergraduate profile:** 89% are state residents; 32% are transfers. 4% Black, 93% White, 3% Other. Average age of undergraduates is 21.
**Freshman profile:** 90% of accepted applicants took SAT; 20% took ACT. 83% of freshmen come from public schools.
**Undergraduate achievement:** 83% of fall 1991 freshmen returned for fall 1992 term. 56% of entering class graduated. 11% of students who completed a degree program immediately went on to graduate study.
**Foreign students:** 180 students are from out of the country. Countries represented include Denmark, England, Japan, Korea, Malaysia, and Sri Lanka; 60 in all.

**PROGRAMS OF STUDY. Degrees:** B.A., B.F.A., B.Mus., B.S., B.S.Bus.Admin., B.S.Ed., B.S.Mus.Ed., B.S.Nurs.
**Majors:** Accounting, Anthropology, Applied Science, Art, Biology, Chemistry, Communication, Computer Science, Cytotechnology, Dance, Economics, Elementary Education, English, Environmental Education, Environmental Science, Environmental Studies, Finance, French, Geography, Geology, German, Health Education, Health Science, History, Information Systems, International Business, Management, Marketing, Mathematics, Medical Technology, Music, Music Education, Music Therapy, Nursing, Occupational Health/Safety Management, Parks/Recreation, Philosophy, Physical Education, Physics, Political Science, Psychology, Public Administration, Secondary Education, Social Work, Sociology, Spanish, Special Education, Theatre.
**Distribution of degrees:** The majors with the highest enrollment are elementary education, allied health, and secondary education; anthropology and music therapy have the lowest.
**Requirements:** General education requirement.
**Academic regulations:** Minimum 2.0 GPA must be maintained.
**Special:** Minors offered in most majors and in cartography, gerontology, meteorology, Russian, and women's studies. Paramedical programs. Artist-in-residence series. Double majors. Independent study. Pass/fail grading option. Internships. Graduate school at which undergraduates may take graduate-level courses. Preprofessional programs in law, medicine, veterinary science, pharmacy, dentistry, optometry, engineering, physical therapy, and podiatry. 3-2 engineering program with Pennsylvania State U. Member of Marine Science Consortium; off-campus study possible at Wallops Island, Va. Washington Semester. Teacher certification in early childhood, elementary, secondary, and special education. Certification in specific subject areas. Study abroad in Austria, Canada, China, the Czech Republic, England, France, Germany, Hungary, Iceland, Italy, Japan, Korea, Mexico, Russia, Scotland, Slovakia, and Spain. ROTC.
**Honors:** Honors program. Honor societies.
**Academic Assistance:** Remedial writing, math, and study skills. Nonremedial tutoring.

**STUDENT LIFE. Housing:** Students may live on or off campus. Coed, women's, and men's dorms. 35% of students live in college housing.
**Social atmosphere:** According to the editor of the student newspaper, "We are considered a 'dry' town because there are no bars, and sometimes this limits the amount of social gatherings and events for those students who are 21 and even those who are older." Greeks, athletes, and the Student Government Association tend to be among the most influential groups on campus. Homecoming, the rugby tournament, and Spring Weekend are some of the most popular annual events. Students hang out at frat houses, the Keister apartment complex, Night People's Place, the University Union, and the Shed.
**Services and counseling/handicapped student services:** Placement services. Health service. Women's center. Day care. Counseling services for minority, military, veteran, and older students. Personal and psychological counseling. Academic guidance services. Physically disabled student services. Learning disabled services. Notetaking services. Tape recorders. Tutors.
**Campus organizations:** Undergraduate student government. Student newspaper (Rocket, published once/week). Literary magazine. Yearbook. Radio and TV stations. Chamber singers, choir, gospel choir, jazz ensemble, concert band, orchestra, dance theatre, Amnesty International, SADD, Special Olympics Club, Circle K, Alternative Lifestyles Union, Planet Keepers, Outing Club, National Organization for Women, 120 organizations in all. 10 fraternities, two chapter houses; eight sororities, no chapter houses. 10% of men join a fraternity. 10% of women join a sorority.
**Religious organizations:** Campus Crusade for Christ, Muslim Student Association, New Life Christian Fellowship.
**Minority/foreign student organizations:** Black Action Society, Black Student Life/Awareness, minority fraternity and sorority. International Student Organization.

**ATHLETICS. Physical education requirements:** Two semesters of physical education required.
**Intercollegiate competition:** 25% of students participate. Baseball (M), basketball (M,W), cheerleading (M,W), cross-country (M,W), field hockey (W), football (M), golf (M), soccer (M), swimming (M,W), tennis (M,W), track (indoor) (M,W), track (outdoor) (M,W), track and field (indoor) (M,W), track and field (outdoor) (M,W), volleyball (W), water polo (M), wrestling (M). Member of NCAA Division I for water polo and wrestling, NCAA Division II, PSAC.
**Intramural and club sports:** 45% of students participate. Intramural basketball, flag football, gymnastics, soccer, street hockey, volleyball. Men's club ice hockey, lacrosse, rugby, volleyball. Women's club rugby.

**ADMISSIONS. Academic basis for candidate selection** (in order of priority): Secondary school record, class rank, standardized test scores, school's recommendation, essay.
**Nonacademic basis for candidate selection:** Geographical distribution is emphasized. Character and personality are important. Extracurricular participation, particular talent or ability, and alumni/ae relationship are considered.
**Requirements:** Graduation from secondary school is recommended; GED is accepted. 17 units and the following program of study are recommended: 4 units of English, 3 units of math, 3 units of science, 2 units of foreign language, 2 units of social studies, 1 unit of history, 2 units of electives. Audition required of music program applicants. R.N. required of nursing program applicants. Act 101 program for applicants not normally admissible. ACT is required; SAT may be substituted. Campus visit and interview recommended. No off-campus interviews.
**Procedure:** Take SAT or ACT by December 1 of 12th year. Visit college for interview by April of 12th year. Suggest filing application by February 1. Application deadline is May 1. Notification of admission on rolling basis. Reply is required by May 1. $125 nonrefundable tuition deposit. $140 room deposit, refundable until June 15. Freshmen accepted for terms other than fall.
**Special programs:** Admission may be deferred one year. Credit may be granted through CEEB Advanced Placement for scores of 3 or higher. Credit may be granted through CLEP general and subject exams, DANTES exams, and military experience. Credit and placement may be granted through challenge exams. Early decision program. In fall 1992,

25 applied for early decision and 23 were accepted. Deadline for applying for early decision is May 1. Early entrance/early admission program. Concurrent enrollment program.
**Transfer students:** Transfer students accepted for terms other than fall. In fall 1992, 32% of all new students were transfers into all classes. 1,204 transfer applications were received, 798 were accepted. Application deadline is March 15 for fall; November 1 for spring. Minimum 2.5 GPA required. Lowest course grade accepted is "C." Maximum number of transferable credits is 67 semester hours from a two-year school and 98 semester hours from a four-year school. At least 36 semester hours must be completed at the university to receive degree.
**Admissions contact:** David A. Collins, M.Ed., Director of Admissions. 412 738-2015.

**FINANCIAL AID. Available aid:** Pell grants, SEOG, state scholarships and grants, school scholarships, private scholarships and grants, ROTC scholarships, academic merit scholarships, athletic scholarships, and aid for undergraduate foreign students. Perkins Loans (NDSL), PLUS, Stafford Loans (GSL), state loans, and SLS. Deferred payment plan.
**Financial aid statistics:** 37% of aid is not need-based. In 1992-93, 80% of all undergraduate applicants received aid; 80% of freshman applicants. Average amounts of aid awarded freshmen: Scholarships and grants, $1,500; loans, $2,000.
**Supporting data/closing dates:** State aid form: Priority filing date is May 1. PHEAA: Priority filing date is May 1. Notification of awards on rolling basis.
**Financial aid contact:** Dale Ekas, M.S., Director of Financial Aid. 412 738-2044.

**STUDENT EMPLOYMENT.** College Work/Study Program. Institutional employment. 15% of full-time undergraduates work on campus during school year. Students may expect to earn an average of $800 during school year. Off-campus part-time employment opportunities rated "poor."

**COMPUTER FACILITIES.** 280 IBM/IBM-compatible and Macintosh/Apple microcomputers; 90 are networked. Students may access Digital, IBM, Prime minicomputer/mainframe systems, BITNET, Internet. Residence halls may be equipped with stand-alone microcomputers, networked terminals. Computer languages and software packages include Ada, BASIC, C, COBOL, dBASE, FORTRAN, LISP, Lotus 1-2-3, MINITAB, Pascal, PL/1, SAS, Shazam, SPSS-X, SuperCalc, Symphony, WordPerfect. Computer facilities are available to all students.
**Hours:** 8 AM-midn. (M-F); 8 AM-4 PM (Sa); 4 PM-midn. (Su).

**GRADUATE CAREER DATA.** Highest graduate school enrollments: Indiana U of Pennsylvania, Slippery Rock U, U of Pittsburgh. 38% of graduates choose careers in business and industry. Companies and businesses that hire graduates: Deloitte & Touche, Eveready Battery, J.C. Penney.

**PROMINENT ALUMNI/AE.** Robert Hanna, president, Thrift Drug; Dr. Linda Rose, author and professor, West Virginia U; Dr. Russell Wright, osteopath and member of U.S. Olympic Committee; Anthony Daniels, director, FBI Training Division; Dr. Richard Rose, president, Rochester Institute of Technology; Dr. Oswald Ndanga, deputy secretary of foreign affairs, Zimbabwe.

# Susquehanna University

**Selinsgrove, PA 17870** **717 374-0101**

**1993-94 Costs.** Tuition: $15,310. Room & board: $4,370. Fees, books, misc. academic expenses (school's estimate): $670.
**Enrollment.** Undergraduates: 713 men, 738 women (full-time). Freshman class: 2,096 applicants, 1,512 accepted, 465 enrolled.
**Test score averages/ranges.** Range of SAT scores of middle 50%: 450-570 verbal, 510-610 math.
**Faculty.** 99 full-time; 42 part-time. 87% of faculty holds doctoral degree. Student/faculty ratio: 14 to 1.
**Selectivity rating.** Competitive.

**PROFILE.** Susquehanna, founded in 1858, is a private, church-affiliated university. Programs are offered through the Schools of Arts and Sciences, Fine Arts and Communications, and Business. Its 190-acre campus is located in Selinsgrove, 50 miles north of Harrisburg.

**Accreditation:** MSACS. Professionally accredited by the American Assembly of Collegiate Schools of Business, the National Association of Schools of Music.
**Religious orientation:** Susquehanna University is affiliated with the Evangelical Lutheran Church in America (Upper Susquehanna Synod); no religious requirements.
**Library:** Collections totaling over 212,000 volumes, 1,400 periodical subscriptions, and 92,700 microform items.
**Special facilities/museums:** Art gallery, auditorium, child development center, foreign language broadcast system, teaching theatre, greenhouse, rare book room, ecological field station, electron microscope, reflecting telescope, fluorescent microscopes.
**Athletic facilities:** Gymnasiums, swimming pool, baseball, rugby, soccer, and softball fields, sauna, tennis and volleyball courts, track.

**STUDENT BODY. Undergraduate profile:** 57% are state residents; 6% are transfers. 2% Asian-American, 2% Black, 1% Hispanic, 95% White. Average age of undergraduates is 20.
**Freshman profile:** 1% of freshmen who took SAT scored 700 or over on verbal, 3% scored 700 or over on math; 11% scored 600 or over on verbal, 25% scored 600 or over on math; 44% scored 500 or over on verbal, 75% scored 500 or over on math; 94% scored 400 or over on verbal, 98% scored 400 or over on math; 100% scored 300 or over on verbal, 100% scored 300 or over on math. 98% of accepted applicants took SAT; 1% took ACT. 85% of freshmen come from public schools.
**Undergraduate achievement:** 90% of fall 1992 freshmen returned for fall 1993 term. 67% of entering class graduated. 19% of students who completed a degree program immediately went on to graduate study.
**Foreign students:** 22 students are from out of the country. Countries represented include Germany, India, Japan, Malaysia, Namibia, and Russia; 12 in all.

**PROGRAMS OF STUDY. Degrees:** B.A., B.Mus., B.S.
**Majors:** Accounting, Art, Art History, Biochemistry, Biology, Business Administration, Chemistry, Church Music, Classics, Communication/Theatre Arts, Computer Science, Economics, Elementary Education, English, Environmental Science, French, Geoscience, German, Greek, History, Information Systems, International Studies, Latin, Mathematics, Music, Philosophy, Physics, Political Science, Psychology, Religion, Sociology, Spanish.
**Distribution of degrees:** The majors with the highest enrollment are business, communications/theatre arts, and English; art, philosophy, and church music have the lowest.
**Requirements:** General education requirement.
**Academic regulations:** Freshmen must maintain minimum 1.9 GPA; sophomores, juniors, seniors, 2.0 GPA.
**Special:** Minors offered in most majors and in actuarial science, arts administration, athletic training, composing, European studies, film, finance, global management, human resource management, international business/foreign language, international politics, international economics/political relations, legal studies, management science, marketing, music criticism, music theoretical studies, non-Western studies, operations management, public relations, studio art, studio recording, urban studies, women's studies, and writing. Associate's degrees offered. Self-designed majors. Double majors. Dual degrees. Independent study. Accelerated study. Pass/fail grading option. Internships. Preprofessional programs in law, medicine, veterinary science, dentistry, theology, and optometry. 3-2 engineering programs with Pennsylvania State U and U of Pennsylvania. 3-2 forestry and environmental studies program with Duke U. Member of American Collegiate Consortium for East-West Cultural and Academic Exchange, Association of College Libraries of Central Pennsylvania, Keystone Colleges Consortium, and Lutheran College Consortium. Washington Semester and UN Semester. Appalachian Semester (Kentucky), Philadelphia Urban Semester, Washington Center for Internships. Exchange possible with Bucknell U. Teacher certification in early childhood, elementary, and secondary education. Certification in specific subject areas. Exchange programs abroad in Germany (Konstanz U), Japan (Senshu U), and Russia (Yaroslavl U). Study abroad also in Australia, Austria, China, Denmark, England, France, Mexico, Singapore, Spain, and many other countries. ROTC at Bucknell U.
**Honors:** Honors program. Honor societies.
**Academic Assistance:** Nonremedial tutoring.

**STUDENT LIFE. Housing:** All unmarried students under age 21 must live on campus unless living near campus with relatives. Coed, women's, and men's dorms. Sorority and fraternity housing. Off-campus privately-owned housing. Volunteer service houses. 85% of students live in college housing.
**Social atmosphere:** According to the student newspaper, "The surrounding community is rather rural, so most events are held on campus. Many lectures and musical performances are held throughout the week, with theatrical performances and dances being sponsored during the weekends. Spring Weekend is the most popular event of the year. It includes several bands, magicians, mimes, comedians, picnic meals, dances, and an overall carnival atmosphere. About a third of the students belong to Greek organizations. Intervarsity Christian Fellowship also has many members. Many students gather at Charlie's on the weekends, or the Crusader Castle throughout the week. Off-campus spots include White Mountain Creamery and the Tavern."
**Services and counseling/handicapped student services:** Placement services. Health service. Women's center. Day care. Counseling services for minority, veteran, and older students. Birth control, personal, and psychological counseling. Career and academic guidance services. Religious counseling. Physically disabled student services. Learning disabled services. Tape recorders. Tutors.
**Campus organizations:** Undergraduate student government. Student newspaper (Crusader, published once/week). Literary magazine. Yearbook. Radio station. Choir, chamber singers, orchestra, wind ensemble, jazz ensemble, theatre, outing club, photography club, Student Environmental Action Coalition, Student Association for Cultural Awareness, National Organization for Women, Amnesty International, Sexual Diversity Awareness Coalition, Habitat for Humanity, Global Concerns Club, 100 organizations in all. Four fraternities, all with chapter houses; four sororities, all with chapter houses. 28% of men join a fraternity. 28% of women join a sorority.
**Religious organizations:** Intervarsity Christian Fellowship, Chapel Council, Catholic Campus Ministry.
**Minority/foreign student organizations:** Black Student Union. International Club.

**ATHLETICS. Physical education requirements:** Two semesters of physical education required.
**Intercollegiate competition:** 32% of students participate. Baseball (M), basketball (M), cheerleading (W), crew (M,W), cross-country (M,W), field hockey (W), football (M), golf (M), lacrosse (W), soccer (M), swimming (M,W), tennis (M,W), track (indoor) (M,W), track (outdoor) (M,W), track and field (indoor) (M,W), track and field (outdoor) (M,W), wrestling (M). Member of Middle Atlantic States Collegiate Athletic Conference, NCAA Division III.
**Intramural and club sports:** 32% of students participate. Intramural basketball, bowling, crew, field events, ice hockey, road racing, rugby, table tennis, touch football, volleyball, weight lifting. Men's club crew, ice hockey, lacrosse, rugby, volleyball, weight lifting. Women's club crew, soccer.

**ADMISSIONS. Academic basis for candidate selection** (in order of priority): Secondary school record, class rank, standardized test scores, school's recommendation, essay.
**Nonacademic basis for candidate selection:** Character and personality, extracurricular participation, and particular talent or ability are important. Geographical distribution and alumni/ae relationship are considered.
**Requirements:** Graduation from secondary school is required; GED is accepted. 18 units and the following program of study are required: 4 units of English, 3 units of math, 3 units of science including 2 units of lab, 2 units of foreign language, 1 unit of history, 3 units of electives including 2 units of academic electives. SAT or ACT, or two writing samples, required of applicants ranked in top fifth of secondary school class; SAT or ACT required of all other applicants. Rank in top fifth of secondary school class and minimum 3.0 GPA recommended. Portfolio required of art program applicants. Audition required of music program applicants. Conditional admission possible for applicants not meeting standard requirements. Act 101 program for in-state applicants not normally admissible. SAT is re-

quired; ACT may be substituted. ACH recommended. Campus visit and interview recommended. Off-campus interviews available with admissions and alumni representatives.

**Procedure:** Take SAT or ACT by December of 12th year. Take ACH by January of 12th year. Visit college for interview by March 15 of 12th year. Suggest filing application by December 15. Application deadline is March 15. Notification of admission on rolling basis. Reply is required by May 1. $200 nonrefundable tuition deposit. Freshmen accepted for terms other than fall.

**Special programs:** Admission may be deferred one semester. Credit and/or placement may be granted through CEEB Advanced Placement exams for scores of 4 or higher. Credit and/or placement may be granted through CLEP general and subject exams. Placement may be granted through challenge exams. Early decision program. In fall 1993, 131 applied for early decision and 93 were accepted. Deadline for applying for early decision is December 15. Early entrance/early admission program. Concurrent enrollment program.

**Transfer students:** Transfer students accepted for terms other than fall. In fall 1993, 6% of all new students were transfers into all classes. 115 transfer applications were received, 58 were accepted. Application deadline is July 1 for fall; December 1 for spring. Minimum 2.5 GPA required. Lowest course grade accepted is "C." Maximum number of transferable credits is 64 semester hours. At least 64 semester hours must be completed at the university to receive degree.

**Admissions contact:** J. Richard Ziegler, Director of Admissions. 717 372-4260, 800 326-9672.

**FINANCIAL AID. Available aid:** Pell grants, SEOG, state scholarships and grants, school scholarships and grants, private scholarships and grants, ROTC scholarships, academic merit scholarships, and aid for undergraduate foreign students. Perkins Loans (NDSL), PLUS, Stafford Loans (GSL), state loans, school loans, private loans, and SLS. AMS.

**Financial aid statistics:** 20% of aid is not need-based. In 1993-94, 85% of all undergraduate applicants received aid; 90% of freshman applicants. Average amounts of aid awarded freshmen: Scholarships and grants, $9,000; loans, $2,625.

**Supporting data/closing dates:** FAFSA/FAF: Priority filing date is March 15; deadline is May 1. State aid form: Priority filing date is March 15; deadline is May 1. Income tax forms: Priority filing date is March 15; deadline is May 1. Notification of awards on rolling basis.

**Financial aid contact:** Helen S. Nunn, M.A., Director of Financial Aid. 717 372-4450.

**STUDENT EMPLOYMENT.** College Work/Study Program. Institutional employment. 60% of full-time undergraduates work on campus during school year. Students may expect to earn an average of $1,000 during school year. Off-campus part-time employment opportunities rated "good."

**COMPUTER FACILITIES.** 106 IBM/IBM-compatible and Macintosh/Apple microcomputers; all are networked. Students may access Hewlett-Packard, SUN minicomputer/mainframe systems, BITNET, Internet, CompuServe. Residence halls may be equipped with networked microcomputers. Client/LAN operating systems include Apple/Macintosh, DOS, Microsoft. Computer languages and software packages include Assembly, C, COBOL, dBASE, Excel, FoxPro, Harvard Graphics, Lotus 1-2-3, Microsoft Word, PageMaker, Pascal, SAS, SPSS, WordPerfect; 80 in all. Computer facilities are available to all students.

**Fees:** $180 computer fee per year; included in tuition/fees.

**Hours:** 24-hours.

**GRADUATE CAREER DATA.** Graduate school percentages: 3% enter law school. 1% enter medical school. 1% enter dental school. 2% enter graduate business programs. 10% enter graduate arts and sciences programs. 1% enter theological school/seminary. Highest graduate school enrollments: Cornell U, Dickinson Sch of Law, Georgetown U, Hahnemann Sch of Medicine, Hershey Medical Center, Pennsylvania State U, Rutgers U, Syracuse U, Temple U. 71% of graduates choose careers in business and industry. Companies and businesses that hire graduates: Arthur Andersen, Continental, Hewlett-Packard, AMP.

**PROMINENT ALUMNI/AE.** Claude A. Buss, diplomat, historian, professor emeritus of history, Stanford U; Roger M. Blough, late chairman of the board and CEO, U.S. Steel Corporation; Samuel D. Ross, president and CEO, Pennsylvania Blue Shield; Nicholas A. Lopardo, president and CEO, State Street Global Advisors; Mary T. Coughlin, vice-president, Morgan Stanley Asset Management, Inc.

# Swarthmore College

**Swarthmore, PA 19081 215 328-8000**

**1993-94 Costs.** Tuition: $18,292. Room & board: $6,300. Fees, books, misc. academic expenses (school's estimate): $690.

**Enrollment.** Undergraduates: 695 men, 692 women (full-time). Freshman class: 3,203 applicants, 1,255 accepted, 413 enrolled.

**Test score averages/ranges.** Range of SAT scores of middle 50%: 580-690 verbal, 630-720 math.

**Faculty.** 146 full-time; 25 part-time. 95% of faculty holds doctoral degree. Student/faculty ratio: 9 to 1.

**Selectivity rating.** Most competitive.

**PROFILE.** Swarthmore, founded in 1864, is a private, liberal arts college. Its 300-acre campus is located in Swarthmore, 10 miles from downtown Philadelphia.

**Accreditation:** MSACS. Professionally accredited by the Accreditation Board for Engineering and Technology.

**Religious orientation:** Swarthmore College is nonsectarian; no religious requirements.

**Library:** Collections totaling over 776,000 volumes, 2,300 periodical subscriptions, and 6,800 microform items.

**Special facilities/museums:** Art gallery, music library, language lab, performing arts center, observatory.

**Athletic facilities:** Playing fields, field house, swimming pool, squash and tennis courts, tracks, Nautilius and free weight rooms, jogging trails.

**STUDENT BODY. Undergraduate profile:** 10% are state residents; 4% are transfers. 11% Asian-American, 5% Black, 5% Hispanic, 75% White, 4% Other. Average age of undergraduates is 19.

**Freshman profile:** 23% of freshmen who took SAT scored 700 or over on verbal, 45% scored 700 or over on math; 72% scored 600 or over on verbal, 86% scored 600 or over on math; 94% scored 500 or over on verbal, 98% scored 500 or over on math; 100% scored 400 or over on verbal, 100% scored 400 or over on math. 100% of accepted applicants took SAT. 65% of freshmen come from public schools.

**Undergraduate achievement:** 98% of fall 1992 freshmen returned for fall 1993 term. 87% of entering class graduated. 33% of students who completed a degree program immediately went on to graduate study.

**Foreign students:** 76 students are from out of the country. Countries represented include Canada, France, Ghana, Greece, Pakistan, and Singapore; 40 in all.

**PROGRAMS OF STUDY. Degrees:** A.B., B.S.Eng.

**Majors:** Ancient History, Art, Art History, Astronomy, Biology, Chemistry, Civil Engineering, Computer Engineering, Economics, Electrical Engineering, Engineering, English Literature, Environmental Studies, French, German, Greek, History, International Relations, Latin, Linguistics, Literature, Mathematics, Mechanical Engineering, Medieval Studies, Music, Philosophy, Physics, Political Science, Psychology, Public Policy, Religion, Russian, Sociology/Anthropology, Spanish, Theatre/Dramatics.

**Distribution of degrees:** The majors with the highest enrollment are English, economics, and biology.

**Requirements:** General education requirement.

**Academic regulations:** Minimum 2.00 GPA required for graduation.

**Special:** Self-designed majors. Double majors. Dual degrees. Independent study. Pass/fail grading option. Internships. Graduate school at which undergraduates may take graduate-level courses. Preprofessional programs in law and medicine. Cooperation with Bryn Mawr Coll, Haverford Coll, and U of Pennsylvania enables students to take courses at other colleges without additional expense. Exchange programs with Brandeis U, Harvey Mudd Coll, Middlebury Coll, Mills Coll, Pomona Coll, Rice U, and Tufts U. Teacher certification in secondary education. Study abroad in France, Ghana, Spain, and other countries. NROTC at U of Pennsylvania.

**Honors:** Phi Beta Kappa. Honors program.

**Academic Assistance:** Nonremedial tutoring.

**STUDENT LIFE. Housing:** All freshmen must live on campus. Coed, women's, and men's dorms. Off-campus married-student housing. Special-interest housing. 92% of students live in college housing.

**Services and counseling/handicapped student services:** Placement services. Health service. Women's center. Day care. Counseling services for minority students. Birth control, personal, and psychological counseling. Career and academic guidance services. Religious counseling. Physically disabled student services. Tape recorders. Reader services for the blind.

**Campus organizations:** Undergraduate student government. Student newspaper (Phoenix, published once/week). Literary magazine. Yearbook. Radio station. Chamber music groups, chorus, folk, rock, and jazz festivals, madrigal groups, jazz band, orchestra, drama, and workshop productions, debating, modern and folk dance groups, outing clubs, community tutoring, other community service activities, Social Committee, political groups, special-interest groups, 90 organizations in all. Two fraternities, all with chapter houses. 5% of men join a fraternity.

**Religious organizations:** Several religious groups.

**Minority/foreign student organizations:** Black Cultural Center, Asian Organization, Hispanic Organization for Latino Awareness. International Club.

**ATHLETICS. Physical education requirements:** Two semesters of physical education required.

**Intercollegiate competition:** 35% of students participate. Badminton (M,W), baseball (M), basketball (M,W), cross-country (M,W), field hockey (W), football (M), golf (M), lacrosse (M,W), soccer (M,W), softball (W), swimming (M,W), tennis (M,W), track and field (indoor) (M,W), track and field (outdoor) (M,W), volleyball (W), wrestling (M). Member of Centennial Conference, NCAA Division III.

**Intramural and club sports:** 60% of students participate. Intramural basketball, soccer, softball, ultimate frisbee, volleyball. Men's club badminton, martial arts, rugby, sailing, squash, ultimate frisbee, volleyball. Women's club cheerleading, martial arts, rugby, sailing, squash, ultimate frisbee.

**ADMISSIONS. Academic basis for candidate selection** (in order of priority): Secondary school record, school's recommendation, essay, standardized test scores.

**Nonacademic basis for candidate selection:** Character and personality, extracurricular participation, particular talent or ability, and alumni/ae relationship are important. Geographical distribution is considered.

**Requirements:** Graduation from secondary school is required; GED is not accepted. No specific distribution of secondary school units required. Strong preparation in English and 4 units of foreign language recommended. Other units should be chosen from natural science and math, history and social studies, and literature, art, and music. SAT or ACT is required. ACH required. Campus visit and interview recommended. Off-campus interviews available with an alumni representative.

**Procedure:** Take SAT or ACT by December of 12th year. Take ACH by December of 12th year. Visit college for interview by February 1 of 12th year. Suggest filing application by fall. Application deadline is January 1. Notification of admission by April 15. Reply is required by May 1. $100 nonrefundable tuition deposit. Freshmen accepted for fall term only.

**Special programs:** Admission may be deferred one year. Credit and/or placement may be granted through CEEB Advanced Placement exams for scores of 4 or higher. Placement may be granted through challenge exams. Early decision program. In fall 1993, 214 applied for early decision and 103 were accepted. Deadline for applying for early decision is November 15 for fall.

**Transfer students:** Transfer students accepted for terms other than fall. In fall 1993, 4% of all new students were transfers into all classes. 145 transfer applications were received, 36 were accepted. Application deadline is April 15 for fall; November 15 for spring. Minimum 3.0 GPA required. Lowest course grade accepted is "C." Maximum number of transferable credits is the equivalent of four semesters of course work. At least four semesters must be completed at the college to receive degree.

**Admissions contact:** Carl Wartenburg, M.Div., Dean of Admissions. 215 328-8300.

**FINANCIAL AID. Available aid:** Pell grants, SEOG, state scholarships and grants, school scholarships and grants, and aid for undergraduate foreign students. Perkins Loans (NDSL), PLUS, Stafford Loans (GSL), state loans, and school loans. Tuition Plan Inc. and deferred payment plan.

**Financial aid statistics:** Average amounts of aid awarded freshmen: Scholarships and grants, $13,500; loans, $2,460.

**Supporting data/closing dates:** FAFSA/FAF: Deadline is February 1. School's own aid application: Deadline is February 1. Income tax forms: Deadline is February 1. Divorced/Separated Parents Statement: Deadline is February 1. Notification of awards on rolling basis.

**Financial aid contact:** Laura Talbot, Director of Financial Aid. 215 328-8358.

**STUDENT EMPLOYMENT.** College Work/Study Program. Institutional employment. 70% of full-time undergraduates work on campus during school year. Students may expect to earn an average of $1,050 during school year. Off-campus part-time employment opportunities rated "fair."

**COMPUTER FACILITIES.** 125 Macintosh/Apple microcomputers. Students may access Digital minicomputer/mainframe systems, Internet. Residence halls may be equipped with networked microcomputers. Client/LAN operating systems include Apple/Macintosh, UNIX/XENIX/AIX, LocalTalk/AppleTalk. Computer languages and software packages include WordPerfect. Computer facilities are available to all students.

**Fees:** None.

**GRADUATE CAREER DATA.** Graduate school percentages: 9% enter law school. 7% enter medical school. 9% enter graduate business programs. 50% of graduates choose careers in business and industry.

**PROMINENT ALUMNI/AE.** James Michener, author; Michael Dukakis, former governor, Massachusetts; Molly Yard, founder, National Organization for Women.

## Temple University

**Philadelphia, PA 19122-1803 215 204-7000**

**1993-94 Costs.** Tuition: $5,086 (state residents), $9,662 (out-of-state). Room & board: $5,062. Fees, books, misc. academic expenses (school's estimate): $640.

**Enrollment.** Undergraduates: 7,387 men, 8,070 women (full-time). Freshman class: 8,848 applicants, 5,680 accepted, 2,491 enrolled. Graduate enrollment: 5,368 men, 5,648 women.

**Test score averages/ranges.** Average SAT scores: 455 verbal, 508 math. Range of SAT scores of middle 50%: 412-511 verbal, 457-564 math.

**Faculty.** 1,698 full-time; 849 part-time. 86% of faculty holds doctoral degree. Student/faculty ratio: 12 to 1.

**Selectivity rating.** Competitive.

**PROFILE.** Temple, founded in 1884, is a public, comprehensive university. Programs are offered through the Colleges of Allied Health Professions; Arts and Sciences; Education; Engineering, Computer Sciences, and Architecture; Health, Physical Education, Recreation, and Dance; Music; the Department of Landscape Architecture and Horticulture; the Graduate School; and the Schools of Art, Communications and Theater, Dentistry, Law, Medicine, Pharmacy, and Social Administration. Its 82-acre main campus is located in the center of Philadelphia.

**Accreditation:** MSACS. Professionally accredited by the American Assembly of Collegiate Schools of Business, the American Council on Pharmaceutical Education, the American Dental Association, the American Medical Association (CAHEA), the American Speech-Language-Hearing Association, the National Association of Schools of Art and Design, the National Association of Schools of Music, the National Council for Accreditation of Teacher Education.

**Religious orientation:** Temple University is nonsectarian; no religious requirements.

**Library:** Collections totaling over 2,100,000 volumes, 15,600 periodical subscriptions, and 1,600,000 microform items.

**Athletic facilities:** Gymnasiums, weight rooms, swimming pools, racquetball and tennis courts, track, grass and astroturf fields, stadium complex.

**STUDENT BODY. Undergraduate profile:** 80% are state residents; 48% are transfers. 12% Asian-American, 19% Black, 3% Hispanic, .2% Native American, 64% White, .8% Other.

**Freshman profile:** 2% of freshmen who took SAT scored 700 or over on math; 4% scored 600 or over on verbal, 14% scored 600 or over on math; 28% scored 500 or over on verbal, 54% scored 500 or over on math; 81% scored 400 or over on verbal, 93% scored 400 or over on math; 97% scored 300 or over on verbal, 100% scored 300 or over on math. 98% of accepted applicants took SAT; 2% took ACT. 63% of freshmen come from public schools.

**Foreign students:** 561 students are from out of the country. Countries represented include India, Jamaica, Japan, Russia, South Korea, and Vietnam; 77 in all.

**PROGRAMS OF STUDY. Degrees:** B.A., B.Arch., B.Bus.Admin., B.F.A., B.Mus., B.S., B.S.Ed., B.S.Eng., B.Soc.Work.

**Majors:** Accounting, Actuarial Sciences, African-American Studies, American Studies, Anthropology, Architecture, Art, Art Education, Art History, Asian Studies, Biochemistry, Biology, Business Administration, Business Law, Ceramics/Glass, Chemistry, Civil/Construction Engineering Technology, Civil Engineering, Classics, Computer/Information Sciences, Criminal Justice, Dance, Early Childhood Education, Economics, Electrical Engineering, Electrical Engineering Technology, Elementary Education, English, Environmental Engineering Technology, Finance, French, Geography, Geology, German, Graphic Design, Health Education, Health Information Management, Hebrew, History, Horticulture, Industrial Relations/Organizational Behavior, Insurance/Risk, International Business Administration, Italian, Jazz/Commercial Music, Journalism, Landscape Architecture, Linguistics, Management, Marketing, Mathematical Economics, Mathematics, Mechanical Engineering, Mechanical Engineering Technology, Metalsmithing, Music, Music Composition, Music Education, Music History, Music Performance, Music Theory, Music Therapy, Nursing, Occupational Therapy, Painting, Pharmacy, Philosophy, Photography, Physical Education, Physics, Political Science, Printmaking, Psychology, Radio/Television/Film, Real Estate, Recreation/Leisure Studies, Religion, Rhetoric/Communication, Russian, Sculpture, Secondary Education, Social Welfare, Sociology, Spanish, Speech/Language/Hearing, Statistics, Theatre, Urban Studies, Vocational Education, Weaving, Women's Studies.

**Distribution of degrees:** The majors with the highest enrollment are business administration, radio/television/film, and accounting; Hebrew, Russian, and classics have the lowest.

**Requirements:** General education requirement.

**Academic regulations:** Minimum 2.0 GPA required for graduation.

**Special:** Associate's degrees in most majors and in horticulture and landscape design at Ambler campus. Double majors. Independent study. Pass/fail grading option. Internships. Cooperative education programs. Graduate school at which undergraduates may take graduate-level courses. Preprofessional programs in law, medicine, pharmacy, and dentistry. 3-3 physical therapy program. Teacher certification in early childhood, elementary, secondary, special education, and vo-tech education. Study abroad in England, France, Italy, and Japan. ROTC. NROTC at U of Pennsylvania. AFROTC at St. Joseph's U.

**Honors:** Phi Beta Kappa. Honors program.

**Academic Assistance:** Remedial reading, writing, math, and study skills. Nonremedial tutoring.

**STUDENT LIFE. Housing:** Students may live on or off campus. Coed dorms. School-owned/operated apartments. 10% of students live in college housing.

**Social atmosphere:** "Temple has a wonderfully eclectic, multi-cultural, and diverse student population," reports the student newspaper. "Perenially volatile and aware, there is never a dull moment concerning topical events." On campus, students gather at Crossroads, Saladalley, and the Diamond Club. Favorite hangouts off campus include Tina's Crazy Corner and The Twist Bar. Campus Crusade for Christ, African Student Union, White Student Union, and Students United for Education are prominent groups on campus. Popular campus events include Spring Fling, Cherry and White Day, and the Annual Broad Street Sit-In.

**Services and counseling/handicapped student services:** Placement services. Day care. Counseling services for veteran and older students. Personal and psychological counseling. Career and academic guidance services. Religious counseling. Physically disabled student services. Learning disabled services. Notetaking services. Tape recorders. Tutors. Reader services for the blind.

**Campus organizations:** Undergraduate student government. Student newspaper (Temple News, published once/day). Literary magazine. Yearbook. Radio station. Concert choir, chorus, orchestra, jazz ensemble, marching and concert bands, theatre, business, professional, and special-interest groups, 143 organizations in all. 13 fraternities, no chapter houses; seven sororities, no chapter houses. 7% of men join a fraternity. 3% of women join a sorority.

**Religious organizations:** Campus Crusade for Christ, Church and World Institute, Hillel, Newman Center.

**Minority/foreign student organizations:** Black Law Student Association. Arab, Chinese, Iranian, Muslim, and Nigerian groups.

**ATHLETICS. Physical education requirements:** None.

**Intercollegiate competition:** 25% of students participate. Baseball (M), basketball (M,W), cheerleading (M,W), crew (M,W), fencing (W), field hockey (W), football (M), golf (M), gymnastics (M,W), lacrosse (W), soccer (M,W), softball (W), tennis (M,W), track (indoor) (M,W), track (outdoor) (M,W), track and field (indoor) (M,W), track and field (outdoor) (M,W), volleyball (W). Member of Atlantic 10, Big East Conference, ECAC, NCAA Division I, NCAA Division I-A for football.

**Intramural and club sports:** 50% of students participate. Intramural badminton, basketball, bowling, flag football, floor hockey, indoor soccer, inner-tube water polo, running, racquetball, soccer, softball, swimming, tennis, volleyball, weight lifting, Wiffle ball. Men's club bowling, cycling, martial arts, rugby, volleyball, weight lifting, wheelchair basketball. Women's club bowling, cycling, martial arts, weight lifting.

**ADMISSIONS. Academic basis for candidate selection** (in order of priority): Secondary school record, class rank, standardized test scores, essay, school's recommendation.

**Nonacademic basis for candidate selection:** Particular talent or ability is emphasized. Extracurricular participation and alumni/ae relationship are considered.

**Requirements:** Graduation from secondary school is required; GED is accepted. 16 units and the following program of study are required: 4 units of English, 2 units of math, 1 unit of lab science, 2 units of foreign language, 1 unit of social studies, 6 units of academic electives. At least 12 of these units should have been completed in last three years. Additional math and foreign language units strongly recommended. Audition required of dance and music program applicants. Portfolio required of art program applicants. Special Recruitment and Admissions Program for applicants not normally admissible. SAT or ACT is required. Campus visit and interview recommended. No off-campus interviews.

**Procedure:** Take SAT or ACT by May of 12th year. Suggest filing application by fall. Application deadline is June 15. Notification of admission on rolling basis. Reply is required by May 1. $50 nonrefundable tuition deposit. $250 nonrefundable room deposit. Freshmen accepted for terms other than fall.

**Special programs:** Credit may be granted through CEEB Advanced Placement for scores of 3 or higher. Credit may be granted through CLEP general and subject exams, ACT PEP and DANTES exams, and military and life experience. Credit and placement may be granted through challenge exams. Early entrance/early admission program.

**Transfer students:** Transfer students accepted for terms other than fall. In fall 1993, 48% of all new students were transfers into all classes. 4,778 transfer applications were received, 3,328 were accepted. Application deadline is June 15 for fall; November 15 for

spring. Minimum 2.0 GPA required. Lowest course grade accepted is "C-." Maximum number of transferable credits is 64 semester hours. At least 30 semester hours must be completed at the university to receive degree.
**Admissions contact:** Randy H. Miller, Director of Admissions. 215 204-7200.

**FINANCIAL AID. Available aid:** Pell grants, SEOG, state scholarships and grants, school scholarships and grants, ROTC scholarships, academic merit scholarships, and athletic scholarships. Perkins Loans (NDSL), PLUS, Stafford Loans (GSL), NSL, Health Professions Loans, and SLS. Temple Easy Payment Plan (TEPP). Temple Installment Payment Plan (TIPP).
**Financial aid statistics:** In 1993-94, 71% of all undergraduate applicants received aid; 68% of freshman applicants.
**Supporting data/closing dates:** School's own aid application. State aid form. Notification of awards begins in February.
**Financial aid contact:** John F. Morris, Director of Financial Aid. 215 204-1492.

**STUDENT EMPLOYMENT.** College Work/Study Program. Institutional employment. Students may expect to earn an average of $1,500 during school year. Off-campus part-time employment opportunities rated "good."

**COMPUTER FACILITIES.** 1,500 IBM/IBM-compatible, Macintosh/Apple, and RISC-/UNIX-based microcomputers. Students may access Digital, IBM minicomputer/mainframe systems, Internet. Residence halls may be equipped with stand-alone microcomputers, networked microcomputers. Client/LAN operating systems include Apple/Macintosh, DOS, OS/2, UNIX/XENIX/AIX, LocalTalk/AppleTalk, Novell. Computer languages and software packages include Assembler, BMDP, C, COBOL, FORTRAN, LISP, Pascal, SAS, SNOBOL, SPSS. Computer facilities are available to all students.
**Fees:** $15 computer fee per class.
**Hours:** 24 hours for mainframes; 9 AM-10 PM for microcomputers.

**PROMINENT ALUMNI/AE.** Bill Cosby, comedian and actor; Bob Saget, TV actor; Joseph Boyle, president, American Medical Association.

# Thiel College

**Greenville, PA 16125** **412 589-2000**

**1994-95 Costs.** Tuition: $11,072. Room & board: $4,970. Fees, books, misc. academic expenses (school's estimate): $840.
**Enrollment.** Undergraduates: 379 men, 428 women (full-time). Freshman class: 1,160 applicants, 960 accepted, 253 enrolled.
**Test score averages/ranges.** Average SAT scores: 407 verbal, 440 math. Average ACT scores: 20 composite. Range of ACT scores of middle 50%: 18-23 composite.
**Faculty.** 62 full-time; 34 part-time. 65% of faculty holds doctoral degree. Student/faculty ratio: 11 to 1.
**Selectivity rating.** Less competitive.

**PROFILE.** Thiel, founded in 1866, is a private, church-affiliated college. Its 135-acre campus is located in Greenville, 80 miles north of Pittsburgh.

**Accreditation:** MSACS. Professionally accredited by the National League for Nursing.
**Religious orientation:** Thiel College is affiliated with the Evangelical Lutheran Church in America; three semester hours of religion required.
**Library:** Collections totaling over 133,083 volumes, 480 periodical subscriptions, and 22,000 microform items.
**Special facilities/museums:** Art gallery, language lab, center for lifelong learning, center for productive retirement, enterprise institute.
**Athletic facilities:** Gymnasiums, basketball, tennis, and volleyball courts, track, swimming pool, weight rooms, baseball, and soccer fields.

**STUDENT BODY. Undergraduate profile:** 84% are state residents; 17% are transfers. 3% Asian-American, 4% Black, 1% Hispanic, 92% White. Average age of undergraduates is 20.
**Freshman profile:** 2% of freshmen who took SAT scored 700 or over on math; 3% scored 600 or over on verbal, 8% scored 600 or over on math; 20% scored 500 or over on verbal, 28% scored 500 or over on math; 60% scored 400 or over on verbal, 70% scored 400 or over on math; 93% scored 300 or over on verbal, 95% scored 300 or over on math. 1% of freshmen who took ACT scored 30 or over on composite; 8% scored 24 or over on composite; 79% scored 18 or over on composite; 100% scored 12 or over on composite. 74% of accepted applicants took SAT; 16% took ACT. 88% of freshmen come from public schools.
**Undergraduate achievement:** 81% of fall 1992 freshmen returned for fall 1993 term. 47% of entering class graduated. 5% of students who completed a degree program immediately went on to graduate study.
**Foreign students:** 24 students are from out of the country. Countries represented include Japan, Korea, and Russia; seven in all.

**PROGRAMS OF STUDY. Degrees:** B.A., B.S.Nurs.
**Majors:** Accounting, Actuarial Studies, Art, Biology, Biology/Forestry, Business Administration, Business Communication, Chemistry, Communication, Computer Science, Conservation Biology, Cytotechnology, English, Environmental Science, French, General Studies, Geology/Earth Science, History, International Business, Management Information Science, Mathematics, Medical Technology, Nursing, Parish Education, Philosophy, Physics, Political Science, Pre-Engineering Chemistry, Pre-Engineering Computer, Pre-Engineering Mathematics, Pre-Engineering Physics, Psychology, Religion, Respiratory Care, Sociology, Spanish, Speech/Hearing Science.
**Distribution of degrees:** The majors with the highest enrollment are business administration, accounting, and nursing; geology, parish education, and philosophy have the lowest.
**Requirements:** General education requirement.
**Academic regulations:** Minimum 2.0 GPA must be maintained.
**Special:** Minors offered in most majors and in art, church music, economics, German, gerontology, international studies, and theatre arts. Courses offered in communication arts, drawing, education, and geography. Global Perspectives Program. Associate's degrees offered. Double majors. Dual degrees. Independent study. Internships. Cooperative education programs. Preprofessional programs in law, medicine, veterinary science, pharmacy, dentistry, theology, and physical therapy. 2-2 commercial art program with Art Inst of Pittsburgh. 3-2 engineering program with Case Western Reserve U, Pittsburgh Inst of Mortuary Science, and U of Pittsburgh. 3-2 forestry and environmental studies program with Duke U. Washington Semester. Teacher certification in elementary and secondary education. Certification in specific subject areas. Exchange programs abroad in Korea (EWHA U) and Mexico. Study abroad also in France, Germany, and Spain.
**Honors:** Honors program. Honor societies.
**Academic Assistance:** Remedial reading, writing, math, and study skills. Nonremedial tutoring.

**ADMISSIONS. Academic basis for candidate selection** (in order of priority): Secondary school record, class rank, standardized test scores, school's recommendation, essay.
**Nonacademic basis for candidate selection:** Character and personality and particular talent or ability are important. Extracurricular participation and alumni/ae relationship are considered.
**Requirements:** Graduation from secondary school is required; GED is accepted. 16 units and the following program of study are recommended: 4 units of English, 2 units of math, 2 units of science, 2 units of foreign language, 3 units of social studies, 3 units of electives. Minimum combined SAT score of 800 (composite ACT score of 20), rank in top three-fifths of secondary school class, and minimum 2.0 GPA recommended. Biology, chemistry, and algebra II required of nursing program applicants. Physics program applicants must be ready to begin calculus sequence in first semester of freshman year; secondary school physics recommended. TAP program for applicants not normally admissible. SAT or ACT is recommended. Campus visit and interview recommended. Off-campus interviews available with an admissions representative.
**Procedure:** Take ACH by April 1 of 12th year. Suggest filing application by May 1. Notification of admission on rolling basis. Reply is required by August 15. Freshmen accepted for terms other than fall.
**Special programs:** Admission may be deferred one year. Credit and/or placement may be granted through CEEB Advanced Placement exams for scores of 3 or higher. Credit and/or placement may be granted through CLEP general and subject exams. Credit and placement may be granted through ACT PEP, DANTES, and challenge exams and military and life experience. Concurrent enrollment program.
**Transfer students:** Transfer students accepted for terms other than fall. In fall 1993, 17% of all new students were transfers into all classes. 129 transfer applications were received, 97 were accepted. Minimum 2.0 GPA required. Lowest course grade accepted is "C." Maximum number of transferable credits is 64 semester hours from a two-year school and 94 semester hours from a four-year school. At least 30 semester hours must be completed at the college to receive degree.
**Admissions contact:** David J. Rhodes, Director of Admissions. 412 589-2345.

**FINANCIAL AID. Available aid:** Pell grants, SEOG, state scholarships and grants, school scholarships and grants, private scholarships and grants, and academic merit scholarships. Perkins Loans (NDSL), PLUS, Stafford Loans (GSL), NSL, school loans, private loans, and SLS. Tuition Plan Inc., AMS, and family tuition reduction.
**Financial aid statistics:** 14% of aid is not need-based. In 1993-94, 94% of all undergraduate applicants received aid; 98% of freshman applicants. Average amounts of aid awarded freshmen: Scholarships and grants, $3,800; loans, $3,200.
**Supporting data/closing dates:** FAFSA/FAF: Priority filing date is March 1. State aid form: Priority filing date is May 1; accepted on rolling basis. Institutional Aid Form (in lieu of state form). Notification of awards on rolling basis.
**Financial aid contact:** Cynthia Farrell, Director of Financial Aid. 412 589-2250.

# The University of the Arts

**Philadelphia, PA 19102** **215 875-4800**

**1993-94 Costs.** Tuition: $11,900. Room: $3,750. Fees, books, misc. academic expenses (school's estimate): $1,500.
**Enrollment.** Undergraduates: 592 men, 614 women (full-time). Freshman class: 1,276 applicants, 805 accepted, 385 enrolled. Graduate enrollment: 27 men, 87 women.
**Test score averages/ranges.** Average SAT scores: 434 verbal, 435 math.
**Faculty.** 85 full-time; 209 part-time. 9% of faculty holds doctoral degree. Student/faculty ratio: 9 to 1.
**Selectivity rating.** Less competitive.

**PROFILE.** The University of the Arts, founded in 1876, is a private institution of the visual and performing arts. The university includes the Philadelphia College of Art and Design and the Philadelphia College of Performing Arts. Its facilities are located in Philadelphia's city center.

**Accreditation:** MSACS. Professionally accredited by the National Association of Schools of Art and Design, the National Association of Schools of Music.
**Religious orientation:** The University of the Arts is nonsectarian; no religious requirements.
**Library:** Collections totaling over 100,992 volumes, 395 periodical subscriptions and 461 microform items.
**Special facilities/museums:** Departmental galleries, theatres, electronic media labs, computer-aided product design lab, laser scanner lab, video editing studio, Oxberry animation stand, center for publication arts, recording studio, analog and digital electronic music studios, music calligraphy lab.

**STUDENT BODY. Undergraduate profile:** 50% are state residents; 36% are transfers. 4% Asian-American, 10% Black, 3% Hispanic, 78% White, 5% Non-resident Alien. Average age of undergraduates is 21.
**Freshman profile:** 3% of freshmen who took SAT scored 600 or over on verbal, 4% scored 600 or over on math; 26% scored 500 or over on verbal, 27% scored 500 or over on math; 65% scored 400 or over on verbal, 60% scored 400 or over on math; 91% scored 300

or over on verbal, 91% scored 300 or over on math. 90% of accepted applicants took SAT. 78% of freshmen come from public schools.
**Undergraduate achievement:** 84% of fall 1991 freshmen returned for fall 1992 term. 43% of entering class graduated.
**Foreign students:** 63 students are from out of the country. Countries represented include Canada, Japan, Korea, Taiwan, and Venezuela; 20 in all.
**PROGRAMS OF STUDY. Degrees:** B.F.A., B.Mus., B.S.
**Majors:** Animation, Architectural Studies, Ballet, Bassoon, Cello, Ceramics, Clarinet, Classical Guitar, Double Bass, Electric Bass, Fibers, Film, Film/Animation, Flute, French Horn, Graphic Design, Harp, Illustration, Industrial Design, Jazz Dance, Jazz Guitar, Metals, Modern Dance, Music Composition, Music Theory, Musical Theater, Oboe, Opera, Organ, Painting/Drawing, Percussion, Photography, Piano, Printmaking, Sculpture, Theatre/Acting, Trombone, Trumpet, Tuba, Viola, Violin, Voice, Wood.
**Distribution of degrees:** The majors with the highest enrollment are illustration, theatre/acting, and industrial design.
**Requirements:** General education requirement.
**Academic regulations:** Minimum 2.0 GPA must be maintained.
**Special:** Associate's degrees offered. Independent study. Pass/fail grading option. Internships. Graduate school at which undergraduates may take graduate-level courses. B.Mus./M.A.T. program. Member of East Coast Consortium of Art Schools and Alliance of Independent Colleges of Art; exchange possible. Certification in specific subject areas. Exchange programs abroad in Canada (Nova Scotia Coll of Art and Design), England (Brighton Polytech, Ravensbourne Coll of Design), France (Parsons Sch of Design), Italy (Tyler Sch of Art), and Japan (Tokyo Sch of Art).
**Academic Assistance:** Remedial reading, writing, math, and study skills.
**STUDENT LIFE. Housing:** Freshmen must live on campus unless living with family. School-owned/operated apartments. 11% of students live in college housing.
**Social atmosphere:** According to the admissions office, "Student life is an extension of commitment to the students' professional development in the visual and performing arts." Popular among students are "exhibitions and performances in the Shubert Theater, which is owned by the university." Popular student gathering spots include "Philadelphia restaurants, the Academy of Music, the Philadelphia Museum of Art, and artists' and musicians' studios."
**Services and counseling/handicapped student services:** Placement services. Health service. Counseling services for minority and older students. Birth control, personal, and psychological counseling. Career and academic guidance services. Physically disabled student services. Learning disabled services. Notetaking services. Tape recorders. Tutors.
**Campus organizations:** Undergraduate student government. Choral groups, jazz band, music ensembles, musical theatre, orchestra, Arts Council, Society for Ecological Education.
**Religious organizations:** Artists Christian Fellowship.
**Minority/foreign student organizations:** Afro-American Student Union. International Student Club.
**ATHLETICS. Physical education requirements:** None.
**Intramural and club sports:** 10% of students participate. Intramural volleyball.
**ADMISSIONS. Academic basis for candidate selection** (in order of priority): Secondary school record, class rank, standardized test scores, essay, school's recommendation.
**Nonacademic basis for candidate selection:** Character and personality and particular talent or ability are important. Extracurricular participation, geographical distribution, and alumni/ae relationship are considered.
**Requirements:** Graduation from secondary school is required; GED is accepted. 14 units and the following program of study are required: 4 units of English, 2 units of math, 2 units of science, 1 unit of social studies. Portfolio required of art program applicants. Audition required of music program applicants. Act 101 program for applicants not normally admissible. SAT is required; ACT may be substituted. Campus visit and interview recommended. Off-campus interviews available with an admissions representative.
**Procedure:** Take SAT or ACT by January of 12th year. Visit college for interview by March of 12th year. Suggest filing application by March 15; no deadline. Notification of admission on rolling basis. Reply is required within three weeks of acceptance. $200 tuition deposit, refundable until May 1. $100 nonrefundable room deposit. Freshmen accepted for terms other than fall.
**Special programs:** Admission may be deferred one year. Credit and/or placement may be granted through CEEB Advanced Placement exams for scores of 4 or higher. Credit and/or placement may be granted through CLEP general and subject exams. Credit and placement may be granted through challenge exams. Early entrance/early admission program.
**Transfer students:** Transfer students accepted for terms other than fall. In fall 1992, 36% of all new students were transfers into all classes. 901 transfer applications were received, 265 were accepted. Application deadline is rolling for fall; rolling for spring. Minimum 2.0 GPA recommended. Lowest course grade accepted is "C." Maximum number of transferable credits is 84 semester hours. At least 48 semester hours must be completed at the university to receive degree.
**Admissions contact:** Barbara Elliott, Director of Admissions. 215 875-4808.
**FINANCIAL AID. Available aid:** Pell grants, SEOG, state scholarships and grants, school scholarships and grants, and academic merit scholarships. Talent scholarships. Perkins Loans (NDSL), PLUS, Stafford Loans (GSL), state loans, school loans, and SLS. AMS, Tuition Management Systems, and family tuition reduction.
**Financial aid statistics:** 7% of aid is not need-based. Average amounts of aid awarded freshmen: Scholarships and grants, $3,250; loans, $2,625.
**Supporting data/closing dates:** FAFSA/FAF: Priority filing date is February 15; accepted on rolling basis. APSGFSA: Priority filing date is February 15; accepted on rolling basis. Notification of awards on rolling basis.
**Financial aid contact:** John Musto, Director of Financial Aid. 215 875-4858.
**STUDENT EMPLOYMENT.** College Work/Study Program. Institutional employment. 22% of full-time undergraduates work on campus during school year. Students may expect to earn an average of $1,250 during school year. Freshmen are discouraged from working during their first term. Off-campus part-time employment opportunities rated "fair."
**COMPUTER FACILITIES.** 82 Macintosh/Apple microcomputers. Students may access minicomputer/mainframe systems. Residence halls may be equipped with stand-alone microcomputers. Computer languages and software packages include Aldus PageMaker, FreeHand, Hypertalk, Microsoft Word, Photoshop, Picturepress, QuarkXPress, SuperMac Pixelpaint Pro, SuperPaint; 15 in all. Computer facilities are available to all students.
**Fees:** $15 computer fee per semester.
**Hours:** 8:30 AM-2 AM.
**GRADUATE CAREER DATA.** Companies and businesses that hire graduates: Industrial and graphic design companies.
**PROMINENT ALUMNI/AE.** Andre Watts, pianist; Michael Ludwig, violinist, Philadelphia Orchestra; Judith Jamison, dancer.

# University of Pennsylvania

**Philadelphia, PA 19104** **215 898-5000**

**1994-95 Costs.** Tuition: $17,020. Room: $3,700. Board: $3,570. Fees, books, misc. academic expenses (school's estimate): $2,356.
**Enrollment.** Undergraduates: 5,313 men, 4,125 women (full-time). Freshman class: 12,394 applicants, 5,232 accepted, 2,464 enrolled. Graduate enrollment: 4,421 men, 4,228 women.
**Test score averages/ranges.** Average SAT scores: 599 verbal, 670 math. Range of SAT scores of middle 50%: 540-650 verbal, 650-740 math. Average ACT scores: 28 English, 29 math, 29 composite. Range of ACT scores of middle 50%: 25-30 English, 26-31 math.
**Faculty.** 1,912 full-time; 2,297 part-time. 99% of faculty holds doctoral degree. Student/faculty ratio: 5 to 1.
**Selectivity rating.** Most competitive.

**PROFILE.** The University of Pennsylvania, founded in 1740, is a private, comprehensive institution. Programs are offered through the Colleges of Arts and Sciences and Engineering and Applied Sciences; the School of Nursing; and the Wharton School of Business. Its 260-acre campus is two miles from downtown Philadelphia.
**Accreditation:** MSACS. Professionally accredited by the Accreditation Board for Engineering and Technology, the American Assembly of Collegiate Schools of Business, the National Architecture Accrediting Board, the National Council for Accreditation of Teacher Education.
**Religious orientation:** University of Pennsylvania is nonsectarian; no religious requirements.
**Library:** Collections totaling over 4,099,648 volumes, 33,024 periodical subscriptions, and 2,600,000 microform items.
**Special facilities/museums:** Art gallery, anthropology museum, institute for contemporary art, language lab, large animal research center, primate research center, arboretum, observatory, wind tunnel, electron microscope.
**Athletic facilities:** Gymnasiums, swimming pools, basketball, squash, and tennis courts, athletic fields, basketball arena, dance studio, Nautilus center, ice rink, palestra.
**STUDENT BODY. Undergraduate profile:** 22% are state residents; 11% are transfers. 15% Asian-American, 7% Black, 3% Hispanic, 66% White, 9% Other. Average age of undergraduates is 20.
**Freshman profile:** 99% of accepted applicants took SAT; 13% took ACT. 60% of freshmen come from public schools.
**Undergraduate achievement:** 97% of fall 1992 freshmen returned for fall 1993 term. 83% of entering class graduated. 26% of students who completed a degree program immediately went on to graduate study.
**Foreign students:** 851 students are from out of the country. Countries represented include Canada, Hong Kong, India, Japan, Malaysia, and Pakistan; 85 in all.
**PROGRAMS OF STUDY. Degrees:** B.A., B.Appl.Sci., B.S., B.S.Econ., B.S.Eng., B.S.Nurs.
**Majors:** Accounting, Actuarial Sciences, American Civilization, Anthropology, Astronomy, Biochemistry, Bioengineering, Biology, Biophysics, Chemical Engineering, Chemistry, Civil/Urban Engineering, Communications, Computer Science, Decision Sciences, Design of Environment, Economics, Electrical Engineering/Science, Elementary Education, English, Environmental Studies, Finance, Fine Arts, Folklore/Folklife, French, History, History of Art, History/Sociology of Science, Insurance, International Relations, Italian, Linguistics, Management, Management/Technology, Marketing, Mathematics, Mechanical/Applied Mechanics, Metallurgy/Materials Science, Multinational Enterprise, Music, Natural Science, Nursing, Oriental Studies, Philosophy, Physics, Political Science, Psychology, Religious Science, Religious Studies, Slavic Languages/Literatures, Social Science/History, Spanish, Systems Science/Engineering, Theatre Arts, Transportation, Urban Studies.
**Distribution of degrees:** The majors with the highest enrollment are banking/finance, history, and English.
**Requirements:** General education requirement.
**Academic regulations:** Minimum 2.0 GPA must be maintained.
**Special:** Minors offered in all majors. U of Pennsylvania has a "one university" approach where undergraduates may draw on all the resources of the university, including research, graduate, and professional schools. Flexible interdisciplinary programs of varying lengths open to all students. Associate's degrees offered. Self-designed majors. Double majors. Dual degrees. Independent study. Accelerated study. Pass/fail grading option. Internships. Graduate school at which undergraduates may take graduate-level courses. Preprofessional programs in law, medicine, veterinary science, dentistry, theology, city and regional planning, foreign service, and government. Four-year B.A./M.A. program in museum curatorship. Combined dentistry program. 3-4 degree program with Sch of Veterinary Medicine. Architecture program in cooperation with Graduate Sch of Fine Arts leads to B.Arch. or B.A. 3-2 liberal arts/engineering program. Member of consortium with Bryn Mawr Coll, Haverford Coll, and Swarthmore Coll. Teacher certification in elementary education. Certification in specific subject areas. Exchange programs abroad in France (U of Bordeaux, U of Dijon, U of Lyons), Scotland (U of Edinburgh), and Switzerland (U of

Lausanne). Study abroad also in Belgium, China, the Czech Republic, England, Germany, Italy, Japan, Mexico, Nigeria, Russia, Slovakia, Spain, Sri Lanka, Taiwan. ROTC and NROTC. AFROTC at St. Joseph's U.
**Honors:** Phi Beta Kappa. Honors program. Honor societies.
**Academic Assistance:** Nonremedial tutoring.

**STUDENT LIFE. Housing:** Students may live on or off campus. Coed dorms. Sorority and fraternity housing. School-owned/operated apartments. Off-campus privately-owned housing. On-campus married-student housing. 71% of students live in college housing.
**Social atmosphere:** "It is impossible to qualify such a diverse social life," reports the student newspaper, "but in general there seems to be something for everyone at U Penn, from local bars to downtown Philadelphia. Greeks are influential on campus, but stricter alcohol regulations have decentralized social life around bars and apartments." Popular events on campus include Spring Fling (a three-day carnival), football and basketball games, and a wide variety of student performances. On campus, students gather at the Palladium, Houston Hall (student center), and fraternity houses; off campus, favorite spots include Smoke's (a "jock bar"), student apartments, Billy Bob's (an all-night restaurant), and Philadelphia.
**Services and counseling/handicapped student services:** Placement services. Health service. Women's center. Counseling services for minority and older students. Birth control, personal, and psychological counseling. Career and academic guidance services. Religious counseling. Physically disabled student services. Learning disabled services. Notetaking services. Tape recorders. Tutors. Reader services for the blind.
**Campus organizations:** Undergraduate student government. Student newspaper (Daily Pennsylvanian). Literary magazine. Yearbook. Radio and TV stations. Choral society, marching and concert bands, debating, academic and departmental groups, 250 organizations in all. 29 fraternities, 26 chapter houses; 14 sororities, nine chapter houses. 33% of men join a fraternity. 32% of women join a sorority.
**Religious organizations:** Hillel, Newman Center, Christian Fellowship.
**Minority/foreign student organizations:** Black Student League, United Minority Council, MEChA, ACELA. Caribbean, Chinese, Japanese, Korean, pan-African, and Vietnamese groups.

**ATHLETICS. Physical education requirements:** None.
**Intercollegiate competition:** 15% of students participate. Baseball (M), basketball (M,W), cheerleading (M,W), crew (M,W), cross-country (M,W), diving (M,W), fencing (M,W), field hockey (W), football (M), golf (M), gymnastics (W), lacrosse (M,W), soccer (M,W), softball (W), squash (M,W), swimming (M,W), tennis (M,W), track (indoor) (M,W), track (outdoor) (M,W), track and field (indoor) (M,W), track and field (outdoor) (M,W), volleyball (W), wrestling (M). Member of ECAC, Ivy League, NCAA Division I, NCAA Division I-AA for football.
**Intramural and club sports:** 15% of students participate. Intramural basketball, football, soccer, softball, squash, swimming, tennis, track, volleyball, wrestling. Men's club aikido, badminton, baseball, cricket, frisbee, gymnastics, ice hockey, ice skating, jujitsu, karate, lacrosse, rugby, sailing, ski racing, tae kwon do, tennis, volleyball, water polo. Women's club equestrian sports, frisbee, ice hockey, rugby, synchronized swimming, tennis.

**ADMISSIONS. Academic basis for candidate selection** (in order of priority): Secondary school record, class rank, standardized test scores, school's recommendation, essay.
**Nonacademic basis for candidate selection:** Character and personality, extracurricular participation, and alumni/ae relationship are emphasized. Particular talent or ability and geographical distribution are important.
**Requirements:** Graduation from secondary school is recommended; GED is not accepted. 17 units and the following program of study are recommended: 4 units of English, 3 units of math, 3 units of science including 2 units of lab, 3 units of foreign language, 2 units of social studies, 2 units of history. Rigorous, well-rounded academic preparation expected. Math level I or II ACH required of business and engineering program applicants. SAT or ACT is required. ACH required. Campus visit and interview recommended. Off-campus interviews available with an alumni representative.
**Procedure:** Take SAT or ACT by December of 12th year. Take ACH by December of 12th year. Application deadline is January 1. Notification of admission by early April. Reply is required by May 1. $50 nonrefundable tuition deposit. Freshmen accepted for fall term only.
**Special programs:** Admission may be deferred one year. Credit and/or placement may be granted through CEEB Advanced Placement exams for scores of 4 or higher. Early decision program. In fall 1993, 1,386 applied for early decision and 886 were accepted. Deadline for applying for early decision is November 1. Early entrance/early admission program. Concurrent enrollment program.
**Transfer students:** Transfer students accepted for terms other than fall. In fall 1993, 11% of all new students were transfers into all classes. 1,249 transfer applications were received, 415 were accepted. Application deadline is April 1 for fall; October 15 for spring. Minimum 3.5 GPA recommended. Lowest course grade accepted is "C." Maximum number of transferable credits is 16 course units. 16 to 20 course units (half of degree program) must be completed at the university to receive degree.
**Admissions contact:** Willis J. Stetson, Jr., M.Ed., Dean of Admissions. 215 898-7507.

**FINANCIAL AID. Available aid:** Pell grants, SEOG, state scholarships and grants, school scholarships and grants, private scholarships and grants, ROTC scholarships, and aid for undergraduate foreign students. Perkins Loans (NDSL), PLUS, Stafford Loans (GSL), NSL, state loans, school loans, private loans, and SLS. AMS, deferred payment plan, and guaranteed tuition. Credit line.
**Financial aid statistics:** In 1993-94, 82% of all undergraduate applicants received aid; 81% of freshman applicants. Average amounts of aid awarded freshmen: Scholarships and grants, $12,930; loans, $3,473.
**Supporting data/closing dates:** FAFSA: Priority filing date is February 15. School's own aid application: Priority filing date is January 1. Income tax forms: Priority filing date is June 1. Notification of awards begins April 3.
**Financial aid contact:** William Schilling, Director of Financial Aid. 215 898-1988.

**STUDENT EMPLOYMENT.** College Work/Study Program. Institutional employment. 47% of full-time undergraduates work on campus during school year. Students may expect to earn an average of $1,270 during school year. Off-campus part-time employment opportunities rated "good."

**COMPUTER FACILITIES.** 450 IBM/IBM-compatible and Macintosh/Apple microcomputers. Students may access Digital, IBM minicomputer/mainframe systems, BITNET, Internet. Residence halls may be equipped with stand-alone microcomputers, networked microcomputers, networked terminals. Client/LAN operating systems include Apple/Macintosh, DOS, OS/2, UNIX/XENIX/AIX, Windows NT, X-windows, Artisoft, Banyan, DEC, LocalTalk/AppleTalk, Novell. Computer languages and software packages include programming languages; charting, database, graphics, spreadsheet, word processing packages. Computer facilities are available to all students.
**Fees:** None.
**Hours:** 24 hours.

**GRADUATE CAREER DATA.** Highest graduate school enrollments: UC Berkeley, Chicago U, Columbia U, Harvard U, New York U, Princeton U, Stanford U, U of Pennsylvania, Yale U. 45% of graduates choose careers in business and industry. Companies and businesses that hire graduates: Andersen Consulting, Children's Hospital, Goldman-Sachs, General Electric, Hospital of U of Penn, Merrill Lynch, Peace Corps, Procter & Gamble.

**PROMINENT ALUMNI/AE.** Ezra Pound and William Carlos Williams, poets; Louis Kahn, architect; William Brennan, former U.S. Supreme Court justice; Walter Annenberg, newspaper executive and ambassador to Great Britain; Charles Addams, cartoonist; Harold Prince, Broadway producer; Saul Steinberg, chairperson and CEO, Reliance Group Holdings.

# University of Pittsburgh at Bradford

**Bradford, PA 16701-2898** **800 872-1787**

**1994-95 Costs.** Tuition: $4,964 (state residents), $10,800 (out-of-state). Room & board: $4,030. Fees, books, misc. academic expenses (school's estimate): $900.
**Enrollment.** Undergraduates: 372 men, 464 women (full-time). Freshman class: 687 applicants, 620 accepted, 345 enrolled.
**Test score averages/ranges.** Average SAT scores: 437 verbal, 483 math. Range of SAT scores of middle 50%: 850-1150 combined.
**Faculty.** 64 full-time; 25 part-time. 80% of faculty holds doctoral degree. Student/faculty ratio: 14 to 1.
**Selectivity rating.** Less competitive.

**PROFILE.** U Pittsburgh at Bradford, founded in 1963, is a public, liberal arts university. Its 125-acre campus is located in Bradford, 79 miles south of Buffalo.

**Accreditation:** MSACS.
**Religious orientation:** University of Pittsburgh at Bradford is nonsectarian; no religious requirements.
**Library:** Collections totaling over 100,000 volumes, 650 periodical subscriptions, and 27,000 microform items.
**Special facilities/museums:** Sports medicine and rehabilitative therapy clinic.
**Athletic facilities:** Sports center, gymnasium, badminton, basketball, handball, tennis, and volleyball courts, fitness and weight rooms, baseball, football, soccer, and softball fields.

**STUDENT BODY. Undergraduate profile:** 87% are state residents; 21% are transfers. 2% Asian-American, 8% Black, 1% Hispanic, 89% White. Average age of undergraduates is 20.
**Freshman profile:** Majority of accepted applicants took SAT.
**Undergraduate achievement:** 65% of fall 1992 freshmen returned for fall 1993 term. 25% of entering class graduated. 20% of students who completed a degree program went on to graduate study within one year.

**PROGRAMS OF STUDY. Degrees:** B.A., B.S., B.S.Nurs.
**Majors:** American Studies, Anthropology/Human Relations, Biology, Business/Management, Chemical Engineering, Chemistry, Civil Engineering, Communication, Computer Science, Creative Writing, Economics, Education, Electrical/Computer Engineering, Elementary Education, Engineering, English, Environmental Health, General Science, Geology, History, Human Relations, Industrial Engineering, Literature, Mathematics, Mechanical Engineering, Nursing, Physical Sciences, Political Science/Government, Psychology, Public Administration, Public Relations, Secondary Education, Social Sciences, Sociology/Human Relations, Writing.
**Distribution of degrees:** The majors with the highest enrollment are business/management, human relations, and psychology; economics, mathematics, and writing have the lowest.
**Requirements:** General education requirement.
**Academic regulations:** Freshmen must maintain minimum 1.75 GPA; sophomores, juniors, seniors, 2.0 GPA.
**Special:** Minors offered in some majors and in accounting, administration of justice, archaeology, art, comparative literature, computer information systems, international studies, philosophy, and theatre. Courses offered in fine arts, French, German, humanities, music, philosophy, physical education, physics, Spanish, and speech/theatre. Associate's degrees offered. Self-designed majors. Double majors. Pass/fail grading option. Internships. Cooperative education programs. Preprofessional programs in law, medicine, veterinary science, pharmacy, dentistry, and optometry. Combined-degree programs in dentistry, engineering, and pharmacy with main campus of U of Pittsburgh. Combined-degree optometry program with Pennsylvania Sch of Optometry. Cross-registration with other U of Pittsburgh campuses. Sea Semester. Teacher certification in elementary and secondary education. Study abroad in England, France, Germany, Italy, Japan, and Spain. ROTC at St. Bonaventure U.
**Honors:** Honor societies.
**Academic Assistance:** Remedial reading, writing, and math. Nonremedial tutoring.

**ADMISSIONS. Academic basis for candidate selection** (in order of priority): Secondary school record, class rank, school's recommendation, standardized test scores, essay.

**Nonacademic basis for candidate selection:** Character and personality and extracurricular participation are emphasized. Particular talent or ability is considered.

**Requirements:** Graduation from secondary school is required; GED is accepted. 15 units and the following program of study are required: 4 units of English, 2 units of math, 2 units of science including 1 unit of lab, 2 units of social studies, 1 unit of history, 3 units of electives. Minimum combined SAT score of 900, rank in top two-fifths of secondary school class, and minimum 3.0 GPA recommended. 2 units of algebra, 1/2 unit of trigonometry, 1 unit of chemistry, and 1 unit of physics required of engineering program applicants. Conditional admission possible for applicants not meeting standard requirements. SAT or ACT is required. Campus visit and interview recommended. No off-campus interviews.

**Procedure:** Take SAT or ACT by March 1 of 12th year. Visit college for interview by April 1 of 12th year. Application deadline is July 1. Notification of admission on rolling basis. Reply is required by May 1. $100 nonrefundable tuition deposit. $125 nonrefundable room deposit. Freshmen accepted for terms other than fall.

**Special programs:** Admission may be deferred one year. Credit and/or placement may be granted through CEEB Advanced Placement exams for scores of 3 or higher. Credit and/or placement may be granted through CLEP general and subject exams. Placement may be granted through challenge exams. Early entrance/early admission program.

**Transfer students:** Transfer students accepted for terms other than fall. In fall 1993, 21% of all new students were transfers into all classes. 118 transfer applications were received, 101 were accepted. Application deadline is rolling for fall; rolling for spring. Minimum 2.0 GPA required. Lowest course grade accepted is "C." Maximum number of transferable credits is 60 semester hours. At least 30 semester hours must be completed at the university to receive degree.

**Admissions contact:** Philip J. Alletto, M.Ed., Director of Admissions and Financial Aid. 814 362-7555.

**FINANCIAL AID. Available aid:** Pell grants, SEOG, state scholarships and grants, school scholarships and grants, private scholarships, ROTC scholarships, academic merit scholarships, and athletic scholarships. Perkins Loans (NDSL), PLUS, Stafford Loans (GSL), state loans, and SLS. Deferred payment plan.

**Financial aid statistics:** 29% of aid is not need-based. In 1993-94, 97% of all undergraduate applicants received aid; 97% of freshman applicants. Average amounts of aid awarded freshmen: Scholarships and grants, $2,100; loans, $2,300.

**Supporting data/closing dates:** FAFSA: Priority filing date is March 1. Notification of awards on rolling basis.

**Financial aid contact:** Tammie Hannon, Assistant Director of Financial Aid. 814 362-7555.

## University of Pittsburgh, Greensburg

**Greensburg, PA 15601-5898 412 837-7040**

**1994-95 Costs.** Tuition: $4,990 (state residents), $10,748 (out-of-state). Room & board: $3,800. Fees, books, misc. academic expenses (school's estimate): $900.

**Enrollment.** Undergraduates: 517 men, 539 women (full-time). Freshman class: 906 applicants, 718 accepted, 328 enrolled.

**Test score averages/ranges.** Average SAT scores: 420 verbal, 470 math. Range of SAT scores of middle 50%: 400-499 verbal, 400-499 math.

**Faculty.** 59 full-time; 30 part-time. 70% of faculty holds doctoral degree. Student/faculty ratio: 18 to 1.

**Selectivity rating.** Less competitive.

**PROFILE.** The University of Pittsburgh at Greensburg, founded in 1963, is a private, liberal arts university. Its 165-acre campus is located in Greensburg, 30 miles from Pittsburgh.

**Accreditation:** MSACS.

**Religious orientation:** University of Pittsburgh, Greensburg is nonsectarian; no religious requirements.

**Library:** Collections totaling over 69,103 volumes, 401 periodical subscriptions, and 7,693 microform items.

**STUDENT BODY. Undergraduate profile:** 99% are state residents; 23% are transfers. 1% Asian-American, 1% Black, 98% White. Average age of undergraduates is 20.

**Freshman profile:** 2% of freshmen who took SAT scored 700 or over on math; 3% scored 600 or over on verbal, 12% scored 600 or over on math; 22% scored 500 or over on verbal, 41% scored 500 or over on math; 74% scored 400 or over on verbal, 77% scored 400 or over on math; 100% scored 300 or over on verbal, 100% scored 300 or over on math. 100% of accepted applicants took SAT. 92% of freshmen come from public schools.

**Undergraduate achievement:** 72% of fall 1992 freshmen returned for fall 1993 term. 57% of entering class graduated.

**PROGRAMS OF STUDY. Degrees:** B.A., B.S.

**Majors:** Accounting, Administration of Justice, Biology, English Literature, English Writing, Humanities, Information Sciences/Systems, Management, Mathematics, Natural Sciences, Political Science/Government, Psychology, Social Sciences.

**Distribution of degrees:** The majors with the highest enrollment are psychology, accounting, and management; information science, political science, and math have the lowest.

**Requirements:** General education requirement.

**Academic regulations:** Minimum 2.0 GPA must be maintained.

**Special:** Minor offered in Gerontology. Self-designed majors. Double majors. Independent study. Accelerated study. Pass/fail grading option. Internships. Washington Semester and Sea Semester. ROTC and AFROTC at the Pittsburgh campus.

**Honors:** Honor societies.

**Academic Assistance:** Remedial reading, writing, math, and study skills. Nonremedial tutoring.

**STUDENT LIFE. Housing:** Coed dorms. School-owned/operated apartments. 20% of students live in college housing.

**Social atmosphere:** Popular gathering spots include the student center snack bar, library, lounge, computer center, local malls, and restuarants. Student Government and Activities Board influence student life. Intramural sports, monthly "Mixers," Sunday evening movies, sporting events, and performances by the National Shakespeare Company are popular social/cultural events. "A small campus means a closeness that you don't get at larger schools," reports the editor of the student newspaper. "The small class sizes allow for friendships to develop not only between students, but also between students and faculty."

**Services and counseling/handicapped student services:** Placement services. Health service. Counseling services for minority students. Personal and psychological counseling. Career and academic guidance services. Physically disabled student services. Learning disabled services. Notetaking services. Tape recorders. Tutors.

**Campus organizations:** Undergraduate student government. Student newspaper (Perspectives, published once/month). Literary magazine. Circle K, Ambassadors, debating, writers' group, chess club, academic groups, ski club, 20 organizations in all.

**Minority/foreign student organizations:** Organization for Black Awareness.

**ATHLETICS. Physical education requirements:** None.

**ADMISSIONS. Academic basis for candidate selection** (in order of priority): Secondary school record, class rank, standardized test scores, school's recommendation, essay.

**Nonacademic basis for candidate selection:** Character and personality, extracurricular participation, particular talent or ability, and alumni/ae relationship are considered.

**Requirements:** Graduation from secondary school is required; GED is accepted. 15 units and the following program of study are required: 4 units of English, 2 units of math, 1 unit of lab science, 3 units of foreign language, 2 units of social studies, 3 units of academic electives. Minimum 2.5 GPA required. College Skills Program for applicants not normally admissible. SAT is required; ACT may be substituted. Campus visit and interview recommended. No off-campus interviews.

**Procedure:** Suggest filing application by May 1. Application deadline is August 1. Notification of admission on rolling basis. Reply required by May 1 or within 15 days of acceptance. $100 nonrefundable tuition deposit. $125 nonrefundable room deposit. Freshmen accepted for terms other than fall.

**Special programs:** Admission may be deferred one year. Credit and/or placement may be granted through CEEB Advanced Placement exams for scores of 4 or higher. Credit may be granted through CLEP general exams. Credit and placement may be granted through challenge exams. Early entrance/early admission program. Concurrent enrollment program.

**Transfer students:** Transfer students accepted for terms other than fall. In fall 1993, 23% of all new students were transfers into all classes. 155 transfer applications were received, 118 were accepted. Application deadline is August 1 for fall; December 1 for spring. Minimum 2.0 GPA required. Lowest course grade accepted is "C." Maximum number of transferable credits is 90 semester hours. At least 30 semester hours must be completed at the university to receive degree.

**Admissions contact:** Larry J. Whatule, Ph.D., Director of Admissions and Financial Aid. 412 836-9880.

**FINANCIAL AID. Available aid:** Pell grants, SEOG, state grants, school scholarships, and private scholarships. Perkins Loans (NDSL), PLUS, Stafford Loans (GSL), and SLS. Deferred payment plan.

**Financial aid statistics:** 1% of aid is not need-based. In 1993-94, 75% of all undergraduate applicants received aid; 90% of freshman applicants. Average amounts of aid awarded freshmen: Scholarships and grants, $950; loans, $2,600.

**Supporting data/closing dates:** FAFSA: Priority filing date is April 1. School's own aid application: Deadline is April 1. State aid form: Deadline is May 1. Income tax forms: Priority filing date is April 1. Notification of awards begins April 1.

**Financial aid contact:** Larry J. Whatule, Ph.D., Director of Admissions and Financial Aid. 412 836-9880.

**STUDENT EMPLOYMENT.** College Work/Study Program. Institutional employment. 7% of full-time undergraduates work on campus during school year. Students may expect to earn an average of $1,300 during school year. Off-campus part-time employment opportunities rated "good."

**COMPUTER FACILITIES.** 47 IBM/IBM-compatible, Macintosh/Apple, and RISC-/UNIX-based microcomputers; all are networked. Students may access Digital, IBM minicomputer/mainframe systems, BITNET, Internet. Client/LAN operating systems include Apple/Macintosh, DOS, UNIX/XENIX/AIX, LocalTalk/AppleTalk, Novell. Computer languages and software packages include BASIC, C, COBOL, FORTRAN, NeXT, Pascal. Computer facilities are available to all students.

**Fees:** $110 computer fee per term.

**Hours:** 9 AM-midn. (M-Th); 9 AM-7PM (F); 9 AM-5 PM (Sa-Su).

**GRADUATE CAREER DATA.** Highest graduate school enrollments: Indiana U of Pennsylvania, U of Pittsburgh.

# University of Pittsburgh at Johnstown

**Johnstown, PA 15904** **814 269-7000**

**1993-94 Costs.** Tuition: $4,750 (state residents), $10,272 (out-of-state). Room & board: $3,702. Fees, books, misc. academic expenses (school's estimate): $1,062.
**Enrollment.** Undergraduates: 1,264 men, 1,240 women (full-time). Freshman class: 1,767 applicants, 1,229 accepted, 612 enrolled.
**Test score averages/ranges.** Range of SAT scores of middle 50%: 430-520 verbal, 470-570 math.
**Faculty.** 141 full-time; 46 part-time. 68% of faculty holds highest degree in specific field. Student/faculty ratio: 20 to 1.
**Selectivity rating.** Less competitive.

**PROFILE.** U Pittsburgh at Johnstown, founded in 1927, is a public, liberal arts university. Its 635-acre campus is located in Johnstown, 70 miles from Pittsburgh.

**Accreditation:** MSACS. Professionally accredited by the Accreditation Board for Engineering and Technology.
**Religious orientation:** University of Pittsburgh at Johnstown is nonsectarian; no religious requirements.
**Library:** Collections totaling over 130,173 volumes, 638 periodical subscriptions, and 16,249 microform items.
**Special facilities/museums:** Performing arts center, language lab.
**Athletic facilities:** Gymnasium, basketball and tennis courts, weight and wrestling rooms, swimming pool, dance studio, athletic fields, sports center.

**STUDENT BODY. Undergraduate profile:** 98% are state residents; 27% are transfers. 2% Black, 97% White, 1% Other. Average age of undergraduates is 19.
**Freshman profile:** 99% of accepted applicants took SAT; 1% took ACT. 89% of freshmen come from public schools.
**Undergraduate achievement:** 70% of fall 1992 freshmen returned for fall 1993 term. 71% of entering class graduated. 9% of students who completed a degree program immediately went on to graduate study.
**Foreign students:** One student is from out of the country.

**PROGRAMS OF STUDY. Degrees:** B.A., B.S.
**Majors:** Accounting, American Studies, Biology, Business, Chemistry, Civil Engineering Technology, Communication/Theatre, Computer Science, Creative Writing, Ecology, Economics, Electrical Engineering Technology, Elementary Education, English Literature, Finance, Geography, Geology, History, Humanities, Journalism, Management, Mathematics, Mechanical Engineering Technology, Natural Sciences, Political Science, Psychology, Secondary Education, Social Sciences, Sociology, Writing.
**Distribution of degrees:** The majors with the highest enrollment are business, elementary education, and biology; social sciences, economics, and mathematics have the lowest.
**Requirements:** General education requirement.
**Academic regulations:** Minimum 2.0 GPA must be maintained.
**Special:** Minors offered in many majors and in Ancient Greek, French, German, Italian, Latin, land surveying, physics, philosophy, and Spanish. Certificate program in international studies. Associate's degrees offered. Self-designed majors. Double majors. Dual degrees. Accelerated study. Internships. Preprofessional programs in law, medicine, veterinary science, pharmacy, dentistry, theology, optometry, and physical therapy. 3-1 medical technology program. Member of Pittsburgh Council on Higher Education. Washington Semester and Sea Semester. Teacher certification in elementary and secondary education. Certification in specific subject areas. Study abroad in Asian countries, the United Kingdom, and other European countries.
**Honors:** Honor societies.
**Academic Assistance:** Nonremedial tutoring.

**STUDENT LIFE. Housing:** Students may live on or off campus. Women's and men's dorms. Sorority and fraternity housing. School-owned/operated apartments. Small-group "lodges." 62% of students live in college housing.
**Social atmosphere:** According to the student newspaper, "The alcohol policy is strictly enforced–no one under 21 may drink on campus. There are countless other events (dances, films, comedy shows) held on campus to accommodate students because of the alcohol policy." The Greeks have widespread influence on campus. On campus, students frequent Chaser's Pub and the Gameroom; Gingerbread Man and Conzattis are off-campus spots. Homecoming, Greek Week, women's basketball, and wrestling are all popular campus events.
**Services and counseling/handicapped student services:** Health service. Counseling services for minority, veteran, and older students. Personal and psychological counseling. Career and academic guidance services. Religious counseling.
**Campus organizations:** Undergraduate student government. Student newspaper (Advocate, published once/week). Literary magazine. Yearbook. Radio station. Choir, band, dance ensemble, theatre, academic, political, and special-interest groups, 75 organizations in all. Five fraternities, all with chapter houses; five sororities, all with chapter houses. 15% of men join a fraternity. 16% of women join a sorority.
**Religious organizations:** Newman Student Association, Time-Out Christian Fellowship, Mu Upsilon Mu.
**Minority/foreign student organizations:** Black Action Society.

**ATHLETICS. Physical education requirements:** Two physical education classes per eight terms required of engineering technology majors.
**Intercollegiate competition:** 10% of students participate. Baseball (M), basketball (M,W), cheerleading (W), cross-country (W), soccer (M), track (indoor) (W), track (outdoor) (W), track and field (indoor) (W), track and field (outdoor) (W), volleyball (W), wrestling (M). Member of Mideast Women's Basketball Conference, NCAA Division II, Pennsylvania Wrestling Conference, West Pennsylvania Soccer League.
**Intramural and club sports:** 50% of students participate. Intramural baseball, basketball, billiards, cross-country, darts, hockey, power lifting, softball, street hockey, swimming, tennis, touch football, track, volleyball, water basketball, water polo, water volleyball. Men's club ice hockey, martial arts, rugby, skiing, swimming. Women's club martial arts, soccer, skiing, swimming.

**ADMISSIONS. Academic basis for candidate selection** (in order of priority): Secondary school record, class rank, standardized test scores, essay, school's recommendation.
**Nonacademic basis for candidate selection:** Character and personality, extracurricular participation, particular talent or ability, and alumni/ae relationship are considered.
**Requirements:** Graduation from secondary school is required; GED is accepted. 15 units and the following program of study are required: 4 units of English, 3 units of math, 1 unit of lab science, 2 units of foreign language, 4 units of social studies. Geometry, trigonometry, chemistry, and physics required of engineering program applicants. R.N. required of nursing program applicants. Conditional admission possible for applicants not meeting standard requirements. SAT or ACT is required. Campus visit and interview recommended. No off-campus interviews.
**Procedure:** Take SAT or ACT by November of 12th year. Visit college for interview by April of 12th year. Suggest filing application by March 1; no deadline. Notification of admission on rolling basis. Reply is required by May 1. $100 nonrefundable tuition deposit. Freshmen accepted for terms other than fall.
**Special programs:** Admission may be deferred one year. Credit and/or placement may be granted through CEEB Advanced Placement exams for scores of 3 or higher. Credit and/or placement may be granted through CLEP general exams. Early entrance/early admission program. Concurrent enrollment program.
**Transfer students:** Transfer students accepted for terms other than fall. In fall 1993, 27% of all new students were transfers into all classes. 396 transfer applications were received, 288 were accepted. Application deadline is April 1 for fall; December 1 for spring. Minimum 2.5 GPA recommended. Lowest course grade accepted is "C." Maximum number of transferable credits is 60 semester hours from a two-year school and 90 semester hours from a four-year school. At least 30 semester hours must be completed at the college to receive degree.
**Admissions contact:** Thomas J. Wonders, Director of Admissions and Financial Aid. 814 269-7050.

**FINANCIAL AID. Available aid:** Pell grants, SEOG, state grants, school scholarships, private scholarships, academic merit scholarships, and athletic scholarships. Perkins Loans (NDSL), PLUS, Stafford Loans (GSL), state loans, private loans, and SLS. Deferred payment plan.
**Financial aid statistics:** 18% of aid is not need-based. In 1993-94, 83% of all undergraduate applicants received aid; 84% of freshman applicants. Average amounts of aid awarded freshmen: Scholarships and grants, $1,549; loans, $2,328.
**Supporting data/closing dates:** FAFSA: Priority filing date is April 1. State aid form: Priority filing date is April 1. Notification of awards on rolling basis.
**Financial aid contact:** Thomas J. Wonders, Director of Admissions and Financial Aid. 814 269-7045.

**STUDENT EMPLOYMENT.** College Work/Study Program. Institutional employment. 10% of full-time undergraduates work on campus during school year. Students may expect to earn an average of $1,275 during school year. Off-campus part-time employment opportunities rated "good."

**COMPUTER FACILITIES.** 193 IBM/IBM-compatible and Macintosh/Apple microcomputers; 137 are networked. Students may access AT&T, Digital minicomputer/mainframe systems, BITNET, Internet. Client/LAN operating systems include Apple/Macintosh, DOS, OS/2, UNIX/XENIX/AIX, Windows NT, LocalTalk/AppleTalk, Novell. Computer languages and software packages include C, FORTRAN, Lotus, Microsoft Word, PageMaker, PASCAL, WordPerfect, Works. Computer facilities are available to all students.
**Fees:** $110 computer fee per term; included in tuition/fees.
**Hours:** 9 AM-11 PM.

**GRADUATE CAREER DATA.** Graduate school percentages: 1% enter law school. 1% enter medical school. 1% enter dental school. 1% enter graduate business programs. 5% enter graduate arts and sciences programs. Highest graduate school enrollments: Indiana U of Pennsylvania, Pennsylvania State U, U of Pittsburgh.

# University of Pittsburgh, Pittsburgh Campus

**Pittsburgh, PA 15260** **412 624-4141**

**1992-93 Costs.** Tuition: $4,546 (state residents), $9,690 (out-of-state). Room: $2,528. Board: $1,602. Fees, books, misc. academic expenses (school's estimate): $776.
**Enrollment.** Undergraduates: 6,835 men, 6,520 women (full-time). Freshman class: 9,014 applicants, 6,884 accepted, 2,456 enrolled. Graduate enrollment: 5,064 men, 4,876 women.
**Test score averages/ranges.** Range of SAT scores of middle 50%: 420-520 verbal, 480-590 math.
**Faculty.** 2,756 full-time; 556 part-time. 90% of faculty holds highest degree in specific field. Student/faculty ratio: 16 to 1.
**Selectivity rating.** Competitive.

**PROFILE.** U Pittsburgh, founded in 1787, is a public, comprehensive university. Programs are offered in the Colleges of Arts and Sciences and General Studies; the Schools of Education, Engineering, Health Related Professions, Library and Information Science, Nursing, and Social Work; and the Graduate School of Public Health. Its 132-acre campus is located in Pittsburgh.

**Accreditation:** MSACS. Professionally accredited by the Accreditation Board for Engineering and Technology, the American Assembly of Collegiate Schools of Business, the American Council on Pharmaceutical Education, the American Dietetic Association, the

American Medical Association (CAHEA), the American Physical Therapy Association, the Council on Social Work Education, the National League for Nursing.
**Religious orientation:** University of Pittsburgh, Pittsburgh Campus is nonsectarian; no religious requirements.
**Library:** Collections totaling over 3,042,043 volumes, 21,508 periodical subscriptions, and 2,796,902 microform items.
**Special facilities/museums:** Stephen Foster Memorial, observatory.
**Athletic facilities:** Stadium, athletic hall, field house, swimming pools, basketball, handball, racquetball, squash, tennis, and volleyball courts, weight rooms, multipurpose field.

**STUDENT BODY. Undergraduate profile:** 90% are state residents; 31% are transfers. 2% Asian-American, 8% Black, 1% Hispanic, 1% Native American, 88% White. Average age of undergraduates is 23.
**Freshman profile:** 98% of accepted applicants took SAT.
**Undergraduate achievement:** 84% of fall 1991 freshmen returned for fall 1992 term. 38% of students who completed a degree program immediately went on to graduate study.
**Foreign students:** 193 students are from out of the country. Countries represented include China, India, Japan, Korea, Saudi Arabia, and Taiwan; 46 in all.

**PROGRAMS OF STUDY. Degrees:** B.A., B.A.Soc.Work, B.Phil., B.S., B.S.Eng., B.S.Nurs., B.S.Pharm.
**Majors:** Administration, Administration of Justice, Anthropology, Applied Mathematics, Architectural Studies, Biological Sciences, Biological Sciences/Biochemistry/Biophysics, Biological Sciences/Ecology/Evolution, Biological Sciences/Microbiology, Black Studies, Business, Business/Accounting, Chemical Engineering, Chemistry, Child Development/Child Care, Chinese, Civil Engineering, Classics, Clinical Dietetics/Nutrition, Communication, Communication/Science, Computer Science, Economics, Electrical Engineering, Engineering Physics, English, English Literature, English Writing, Film Studies, Fine Arts, French, Geology, German, Health Information Management, Health/Physical/Recreation Education, Health Services, History, History/Philosophy of Science, Humanities Area, Industrial Engineering, Information Science, Italian, Japanese, Legal Studies, Liberal Studies, Linguistics, Materials Science/Engineering, Mathematics, Mathematics/Computer Science, Mathematics/Economics, Mathematics/Philosophy, Mathematics/Psychology, Mathematics/Sociology, Mechanical Engineering, Media Communications, Medical Technology, Metallurgical Engineering, Music, Natural Sciences Area, Neuroscience, Nursing, Occupational Therapy, Pharmacy, Philosophy, Physics, Physics/Astronomy, Polish, Political Science, Politics/Philosophy, Psychology, Public Administration, Religious Studies, Rhetoric/Communication, Russian, Social Sciences Area, Social Work, Sociology, Spanish, Statistics, Studio Arts, Theatre Arts, Urban Studies, Vocational Education/Business, Vocational Education/Distributive, Vocational Education/Industrial.
**Distribution of degrees:** The majors with the highest enrollment are business, psychology, and communication; engineering physics, linguistics, and religious studies have the lowest.
**Requirements:** General education requirement.
**Academic regulations:** Minimum 2.0 GPA must be maintained.
**Special:** Minors offered in all majors. After completing requirements, College of Arts and Sciences students may transfer to the Schools of Education, Health and Rehabilitation Sciences, Library and Information Science, Pharmacy, or Social Work for bachelor's degrees. University Honors College offers honors course work to qualified undergraduates, who may be considered for candidacy for B.Phil. degrees. Self-designed majors. Double majors. Dual degrees. Independent study. Internships. Cooperative education programs. Graduate school at which undergraduates may take graduate-level courses. 3-2 liberal arts/engineering program. Member of Pittsburgh Council on Higher Education; cross-registration possible. Washington Semester and Sea Semester. Teacher certification in early childhood, elementary, special education, and vo-tech education. Certification in specific subject areas. Study abroad in African countries, Asian countries, Germany, the United Kingdom, other European countries, and Latin American countries. ROTC, NROTC, and AFROTC.
**Honors:** Phi Beta Kappa. Honors program. Honor societies.
**Academic Assistance:** Remedial reading, writing, math, and study skills. Nonremedial tutoring.

**STUDENT LIFE. Housing:** Students may live on or off campus. Coed and women's dorms. Sorority and fraternity housing. School-owned/operated apartments. 33% of students live in college housing.
**Social atmosphere:** "As a major metropolitan university, Pitt is able to partake in a plethora of urban activities, centered in the Oakland section of the city," reports the student newspaper. "But at the university itself, Pitt sports always take precedence." Popular events at Pitt include the Big East Basketball Tournament, Pitt vs. Penn State football, Again Days, Greek Week, and Black History Month. Favorite off-campus spots include Hemingway's Cafe and Dave & Andy's Ice Cream.
**Services and counseling/handicapped student services:** Placement services. Health service. Women's center. Counseling services for minority, military, veteran, and older students. Birth control, personal, and psychological counseling. Career and academic guidance services. Physically disabled student services. Learning disabled services. Notetaking services. Tutors. Reader services for the blind.
**Campus organizations:** Undergraduate student government. Student newspaper (Pitt News, published four times/week). Yearbook. Radio station. Chapel choir, women's choral ensemble, men's glee club, jazz ensemble, dance ensemble, Amnesty International, Model UN, University Democrats, College Republicans, Friends of Animals, chess club, Society for Creative Anachronism, science fiction groups, Bisexual/Gay/Lesbian Alliance, Campus Women's Organization, athletic, departmental, professional, service, social, and special-interest groups, 320 organizations in all. 22 fraternities, 13 chapter houses; 14 sororities, two chapter houses. 14% of men join a fraternity. 9% of women join a sorority.
**Religious organizations:** Ambassadors for Christ, Baptist Campus Ministry, B'nai B'rith Hillel, Campus Crusade for Christ, Christian Student Fellowship, Newman Oratory Student Organization, Orthodox Christian Fellowship, Some of God's Children, University Christian Outreach.
**Minority/foreign student organizations:** Black Action Society. International Student Organization, Asian, Caribbean, French, German, Hellenic, Indonesian, Italian, Iranian, Japanese, Korean, Latin American, Saudi Arabian, Slavic, Slovak, Turkish, Ukrainian, and Vietnamese groups.

**ATHLETICS. Physical education requirements:** None.
**Intercollegiate competition:** 3% of students participate. Baseball (M), basketball (M,W), cross-country (M,W), diving (M,W), football (M), gymnastics (M,W), soccer (M), swimming (M,W), tennis (M,W), track (indoor) (M,W), track (outdoor) (M,W), track and field (indoor) (M,W), track and field (outdoor) (M,W), volleyball (W), wrestling (M). Member of Big East Conference, Eastern Wrestling League, ECAC, NCAA Division I.
**Intramural and club sports:** 65% of students participate. Men's club archery, cheerleading, crew, golf, horsemanship, ice hockey, martial arts, rifle, rugby, ultimate frisbee, volleyball, water skiing, weight lifting. Women's club archery, cheerleading, horsemanship, lacrosse, ultimate frisbee, water skiing.

**ADMISSIONS. Academic basis for candidate selection** (in order of priority): Secondary school record, class rank, standardized test scores, school's recommendation, essay.
**Nonacademic basis for candidate selection:** Character and personality, extracurricular participation, particular talent or ability, and alumni/ae relationship are considered.
**Requirements:** Graduation from secondary school is required; GED is accepted. 15 units and the following program of study are required: 4 units of English, 3 units of math, 3 units of lab science, 1 unit of social studies, 4 units of academic electives. Audition required of music program applicants. University Challenge for Excellence Program and Summer Transitional Education Program (Coll of Arts and Sciences) and Pitt Engineering Impact Program (Sch of Engineering) for applicants not normally admissible. SAT or ACT is required. Campus visit and interview recommended. Off-campus interviews available with an admissions representative.
**Procedure:** Take SAT or ACT by December of 12th year. Notification of admission on rolling basis. Reply is required by May 1 or within two weeks of acceptance. $100 nonrefundable tuition deposit. No housing deposit, but accommodations guaranteed to students who pay tuition deposit by March 1. Freshmen accepted for terms other than fall.
**Special programs:** Admission may be deferred two years. Credit and/or placement may be granted through CEEB Advanced Placement exams for scores of 3 or higher. Credit and/or placement may be granted through CLEP general exams. Credit and placement may be granted through DANTES and challenge exams. Early entrance/early admission program. Concurrent enrollment program.
**Transfer students:** Transfer students accepted for terms other than fall. In fall 1992, 31% of all new students were transfers into all classes. 1,759 transfer applications were received, 1,628 were accepted. Application deadline is rolling for fall; rolling for spring. Lowest course grade accepted is "C." Maximum number of transferable credits varies by program. Final 30 credits, including half of credits for major, must be completed at the university to receive degree.
**Admissions contact:** Betsy A. Porter, Ph.D., Director of Admissions and Financial Aid. 412 624-PITT.

**FINANCIAL AID. Available aid:** Pell grants, SEOG, state grants, school scholarships and grants, private scholarships, ROTC scholarships, academic merit scholarships, and athletic scholarships. Perkins Loans (NDSL), PLUS, Stafford Loans (GSL), NSL, Health Professions Loans, state loans, school loans, and SLS. Deferred payment plan.
**Financial aid statistics:** 16% of aid is not need-based. In 1992-93, 74% of all undergraduate applicants received aid; 74% of freshman applicants. Average amounts of aid awarded freshmen: Scholarships and grants, $3,500; loans, $3,500.
**Supporting data/closing dates:** FAFSA/FAF: Priority filing date is March 1. School's own aid application: Priority filing date is March 1. State aid form: Priority filing date is May 1. Income tax forms: Priority filing date is March 1. Notification of awards on rolling basis.
**Financial aid contact:** Betsy A. Porter, Ph.D., Director of Admissions and Financial Aid. 412 624-PITT.

**STUDENT EMPLOYMENT.** College Work/Study Program. Institutional employment. Off-campus part-time employment opportunities rated "good."

**COMPUTER FACILITIES.** 600 IBM/IBM-compatible and Macintosh/Apple microcomputers; all are networked. Students may access Digital minicomputer/mainframe systems, BITNET, Internet. Residence halls may be equipped with networked microcomputers. Computer languages and software packages include Ada, AutoCAD, COBOL, Cricket Graph, dBASE, Excel, FORTRAN 77, Kermit, LISP, Lotus 1-2-3, Microsoft Word, Modula 3 PageMaker, Paradox, Pascal, Prolog, WordPerfect. Computer facilities are available to all students.
**Fees:** $110 computer fee per term.

**GRADUATE CAREER DATA.** Graduate school percentages: 3% enter law school. 2% enter medical school. 1% enter dental school. 5% enter graduate business programs. 22% enter graduate arts and sciences programs. Highest graduate school enrollments: Duquesne U, U of Pittsburgh, West Virginia U. 56% of graduates choose careers in business and industry. Companies and businesses that hire graduates: General Motors, Rite Aid, Thrift Drug, Westinghouse.

**PROMINENT ALUMNI/AE.** Gene Kelly, actor; Lorin Maazel, musical director, Pittsburgh Symphony; Dan Marino, quarterback, Miami Dolphins.

# University of Scranton

**Scranton, PA 18510-4699** **717 941-7400**

**1993-94 Costs.** Tuition: $10,720. Room: $3,076. Board: $2,380. Fees, books, misc. academic expenses (school's estimate): $1,370.
**Enrollment.** Undergraduates: 1,791 men, 1,948 women (full-time). Freshman class: 4,471 applicants, 2,942 accepted, 910 enrolled. Graduate enrollment: 337 men, 420 women.
**Test score averages/ranges.** Average SAT scores: 504 verbal, 556 math. Range of SAT scores of middle 50%: 450-550 verbal, 510-610 math.
**Faculty.** 249 full-time; 146 part-time. 78% of faculty holds doctoral degree. Student/faculty ratio: 14 to 1.
**Selectivity rating.** Competitive.

**PROFILE.** The University of Scranton is a church-affiliated, comprehensive institution. Founded in 1888, it adopted coeducation in 1970. Its 50-acre campus is located in Scranton, 75 miles north of Allentown.

**Accreditation:** MSACS. Professionally accredited by the American Physical Therapy Association, the National Council for Accreditation of Teacher Education, the National League for Nursing.
**Religious orientation:** University of Scranton is affiliated with the Roman Catholic Church (Society of Jesus); two semesters of theology required.
**Library:** Collections totaling over 310,910 volumes, 2,022 periodical subscriptions, and 280,802 microform items.
**Special facilities/museums:** Art gallery, fine arts facility, theatre, center for music groups, language lab, electron microscope, greenhouse.
**Athletic facilities:** Swimming pools, sports courts, aerobics and weight lifting rooms, basketball, racquetball, street hockey, tennis, and volleyball courts, soccer and intramural playing fields.

**STUDENT BODY. Undergraduate profile:** 7% are transfers. 2% Asian-American, 1% Black, 1% Hispanic, 94% White, 2% Other. Average age of undergraduates is 20.
**Freshman profile:** 1% of freshmen who took SAT scored 700 or over on verbal, 4% scored 700 or over on math; 12% scored 600 or over on verbal, 30% scored 600 or over on math; 56% scored 500 or over on verbal, 86% scored 500 or over on math; 99% scored 400 or over on verbal, 100% scored 400 or over on math; 100% scored 300 or over on verbal. 99% of accepted applicants took SAT; 1% took ACT. 51% of freshmen come from public schools.
**Undergraduate achievement:** 92% of fall 1992 freshmen returned for fall 1993 term. 75% of entering class graduated. 25% of students who completed a degree program immediately went on to graduate study.
**Foreign students:** 42 students are from out of the country. Countries represented include India, Ireland, Japan, Pakistan, and Russia; 20 in all.

**PROGRAMS OF STUDY. Degrees:** B.A., B.S.
**Majors:** Accounting, Biochemistry, Biology, Biophysics, Chemistry, Chemistry/Business, Chemistry/Computer Science, Classical Languages, Communication, Computer Information Systems, Computer Science, Criminal Justice, Economics, Electronics/Business, Electronics Engineering, Elementary Education, English, Environmental Science, Finance, Gerontology, Health Administration, History, Human Services, International Language/Business, International Studies, Management, Marketing, Mathematics, Medical Technology, Modern Languages, Neuroscience, Occupational Therapy, Philosophy, Physical Therapy, Physics, Political Science, Production/Operations Management, Psychology, Public Administration/Public Affairs, Secondary Education, Sociology, Theology/Religious Studies.
**Distribution of degrees:** The majors with the highest enrollment are biology, accounting, and communication; theology, biophysics, and gerontology have the lowest.
**Requirements:** General education requirement.
**Academic regulations:** Minimum 2.0 GPA must be maintained.
**Special:** Minors offered in most majors and in fine arts, foreign language and theatre. Self-designed majors. Double majors. Independent study. Accelerated study. Pass/fail grading option. Internships. Graduate school at which undergraduates may take graduate-level courses. Preprofessional programs in law, medicine, veterinary science, dentistry, and optometry. 2-2 and 2-3 engineering programs with U of Detroit Mercy and Widener U. Five-year master's programs in biochemistry, business, chemistry, English, human services, and physics. Four-year master's programs in biochemistry, chemistry, and history. Washington Semester, UN Semester, and Sea Semester. Exchange program with any of 27 other U.S. Jesuit colleges and universities. Teacher certification in elementary and secondary education. Certification in specific subject areas. Study abroad possible. ROTC. AFROTC at Wilkes U.
**Honors:** Honors program. Honor societies.
**Academic Assistance:** Remedial reading, writing, and study skills. Nonremedial tutoring.

**STUDENT LIFE. Housing:** All freshmen must live on campus unless living with family. Coed, women's, and men's dorms. Off-campus privately-owned housing. Theme houses. 60% of students live in college housing.
**Social atmosphere:** Popular places to gather are the Student Union, Mulberry Street Inn, O'Toole's Tavern, and Cockeyed Oscar's. Influential groups on campus include intramural sports, Campus Ministry, and counseling organizations. Concerts, basketball games, and political speaking engagements are among the well-attended events during the year.
**Services and counseling/handicapped student services:** Placement services. Health service. Counseling services for minority and older students. Personal and psychological counseling. Career and academic guidance services. Religious counseling. Physically disabled student services. Learning disabled services. Notetaking services. Tutors.
**Campus organizations:** Undergraduate student government. Student newspaper (Aquinas, published once/week). Literary magazine. Yearbook. Radio station. Concert, jazz, pep, and pit bands, University Singers, debating, aviation, photography, horticulture, and ski clubs, People Help People, Big Brothers/Big Sisters, Campus Democrats, College Republicans, historical and science journals, departmental groups, 63 organizations in all.
**Religious organizations:** Campus Ministry, Students for Social Justice, Students for Life, Knights of Columbus, Collegiate Volunteers Program, Intervarsity Christian Fellowship.
**Minority/foreign student organizations:** Afro-American Club. International Student Association, India Club, Gaelic Society.

**ATHLETICS. Physical education requirements:** Four semesters of physical education required.
**Intercollegiate competition:** 20% of students participate. Baseball (M), basketball (M,W), cheerleading (M,W), cross-country (M,W), field hockey (W), golf (M), ice hockey (M), lacrosse (M), soccer (M,W), softball (W), swimming (M,W), tennis (M,W), volleyball (W), wrestling (M). Member of ECAC, Middle Atlantic Conference, NCAA Division III.
**Intramural and club sports:** 75% of students participate. Intramural basketball, cross-country, football, golf, softball, swimming, tennis, volleyball, walleyball, wrestling. Men's club Alpine skiing, crew, cycling, rugby, track/field, volleyball. Women's club Alpine skiing, crew, cycling, lacrosse, rugby, track/field.

**ADMISSIONS. Academic basis for candidate selection** (in order of priority): Secondary school record, class rank, standardized test scores, school's recommendation, essay.
**Nonacademic basis for candidate selection:** Character and personality, extracurricular participation, and alumni/ae relationship are considered.
**Requirements:** Graduation from secondary school is required; GED is accepted. 18 units and the following program of study are required: 4 units of English, 3 units of math, 3 units of science, 2 units of foreign language, 2 units of social studies, 2 units of history, 2 units of electives. Rank in top two-fifths of secondary school class and minimum 3.0 GPA recommended. Clinical observation required for physical therapy and occupational therapy program applicants. SAT is required; ACT may be substituted. Campus visit and interview recommended. No off-campus interviews.
**Procedure:** Take SAT or ACT by December of 12th year. Suggest filing application by February 1. Application deadline is March 1. Notification of admission on rolling basis. Reply is required by May 1. $100 nonrefundable tuition deposit. $100 nonrefundable room deposit. Freshmen accepted for terms other than fall.
**Special programs:** Admission may be deferred one year. Credit and/or placement may be granted through CEEB Advanced Placement exams for scores of 3 or higher. Credit and/or placement may be granted through CLEP general and subject exams. Credit and placement may be granted through ACT PEP and DANTES exams and military and life experience. Early entrance/early admission program.
**Transfer students:** Transfer students accepted for terms other than fall. In fall 1993, 7% of all new students were transfers into all classes. 267 transfer applications were received, 193 were accepted. Application deadline is July 1 for fall; December 15 for spring. Minimum 2.5 GPA required. Lowest course grade accepted is "C." Maximum number of transferable credits is 60 semester hours. At least 63 semester hours must be completed at the university to receive degree.
**Admissions contact:** Rev. Bernard R. McIlhenny, S.J., M.A., Dean of Admissions. 717 941-7540.

**FINANCIAL AID. Available aid:** Pell grants, SEOG, state scholarships and grants, school scholarships and grants, private scholarships and grants, ROTC scholarships, and academic merit scholarships. Perkins Loans (NDSL), PLUS, Stafford Loans (GSL), state loans, private loans, and SLS. AMS and family tuition reduction.
**Financial aid statistics:** 30% of aid is not need-based. In 1993-94, 95% of all undergraduate applicants received aid; 95% of freshman applicants. Average amounts of aid awarded freshmen: Scholarships and grants, $4,400; loans, $2,800.
**Supporting data/closing dates:** FAFSA: Priority filing date is February 15. School's own aid application: Priority filing date is February 15. Notification of awards begins March 15.
**Financial aid contact:** William R. Burke, M.B.A., Director of Financial Aid. 717 941-7700.

**STUDENT EMPLOYMENT.** College Work/Study Program. Institutional employment. 16% of full-time undergraduates work on campus during school year. Students may expect to earn an average of $800 during school year. Off-campus part-time employment opportunities rated "good."

**COMPUTER FACILITIES.** 300 IBM/IBM-compatible, Macintosh/Apple, and RISC-/UNIX-based microcomputers; all are networked. Students may access Digital, SUN minicomputer/mainframe systems, Internet. Residence halls may be equipped with networked microcomputers, modems. Client/LAN operating systems include Apple/Macintosh, DOS, UNIX/XENIX/AIX, LocalTalk/AppleTalk, Novell. Computer languages and software packages include Ada, C, COBOL, dBASE, Excel, FORTRAN, Hypercard, LISP, Lotus 1-2-3, MacDraw, Macro, Modula 2, Oracle, PageMaker, Pascal, SAS, SPSS, WordPerfect; 84 in all. Computer facilities are available to all students.
**Fees:** Computer fee is included in tuition/fees.
**Hours:** 24 hours.

**GRADUATE CAREER DATA.** Graduate school percentages: 6% enter law school. 8% enter medical school. 1% enter dental school. 2% enter graduate business programs. 7% enter graduate arts and sciences programs. 1% enter theological school/seminary. Highest graduate school enrollments: Cornell U, Fordham U, Georgetown U, Pennsylvania State U, Rutgers U, Syracuse U, Thomas Jefferson U, U of Pennsylvania, U of Pittsburgh, Villanova U. Companies and businesses that hire graduates: AT&T, Coopers & Lybrand, IBM, KPMG Peat Marwick, Prudential-Bache.

**PROMINENT ALUMNI/AE.** Glenn Lunney, chief engineer, Apollo moon flight; Gene Gibbons, UPI White House correspondent; Eugene Cardinal O'Boyle, retired Archbishop of Washington; Michael Egan, retired chief justice, Pennsylvania supreme court; Jason Miller, playwright, author, and actor.

# Ursinus College

**Collegeville, PA 19426** **215 489-4111**

**1993-94 Costs.** Tuition: $14,100. Room & board: $4,900. Fees, books, misc. academic expenses (school's estimate): $115.
**Enrollment.** Undergraduates: 553 men, 578 women (full-time). Freshman class: 1,399 applicants, 1,026 accepted, 308 enrolled.
**Test score averages/ranges.** Average SAT scores: 512 verbal, 567 math. Range of SAT scores of middle 50%: 460-560 verbal, 520-620 math.
**Faculty.** 93 full-time; 27 part-time. 75% of faculty holds doctoral degree. Student/faculty ratio: 12 to 1.
**Selectivity rating.** More competitive.

**PROFILE.** Ursinus is a church-affiliated college of arts and sciences. Founded in 1869, it adopted coeducation in 1881. Its 140-acre campus is located in Collegeville, 30 miles northwest of Philadelphia.

**Accreditation:** MSACS.
**Religious orientation:** Ursinus College is affiliated with the United Church of Christ; no religious requirements.

**Library:** Collections totaling over 185,000 volumes, 900 periodical subscriptions, and 155,000 microform items.
**Special facilities/museums:** Art museum, language labs, telescope, electron microscope.
**Athletic facilities:** Field house, natatorium, basketball, racquetball, squash, and tennis courts, track, weight and wrestling rooms, dance studio, baseball, football, intramural, and softball fields.

**STUDENT BODY. Undergraduate profile:** 65% are state residents; 2% are transfers. 3% Asian-American, 3% Black, 2% Hispanic, 88% White, 4% Other. Average age of undergraduates is 19.
**Freshman profile:** 1% of freshmen who took SAT scored 700 or over on verbal, 3% scored 700 or over on math; 13% scored 600 or over on verbal, 38% scored 600 or over on math; 58% scored 500 or over on verbal, 86% scored 500 or over on math; 96% scored 400 or over on verbal, 99% scored 400 or over on math; 100% scored 300 or over on verbal, 100% scored 300 or over on math. 96% of accepted applicants took SAT; 4% took ACT. 75% of freshmen come from public schools.
**Undergraduate achievement:** 92% of fall 1992 freshmen returned for fall 1993 term. 75% of entering class graduated. 25% of students who completed a degree program immediately went on to graduate study.
**Foreign students:** 14 students are from out of the country. Countries represented include China, England, India, Japan, Spain, and Sri Lanka; 11 in all.

**PROGRAMS OF STUDY. Degrees:** B.A., B.S.
**Majors:** Anthropology/Sociology, Biology, Chemistry, Classical Studies, Communication Arts, Computer Science, Economics/Business Administration, English, French, German, Health/Physical Education/Recreation, History, International Relations, Mathematics, Modern Languages, Philosophy/Religion, Physics, Politics, Psychology, Spanish.
**Distribution of degrees:** The majors with the highest enrollment are biology, economics, and English; philosophy/religion, anthropology/sociology, and Classical studies have the lowest.
**Requirements:** General education requirement.
**Academic regulations:** Minimum 2.0 GPA must be maintained.
**Special:** Minors offered in approximately 40 fields. Courses offered in astronomy, education, fine arts, geography, geology, and music. Study of Japanese language beginning at intermediate level. East Asian and Latin American studies programs. Pennsylvania German studies program during summer. Self-designed majors. Double majors. Dual degrees. Independent study. Accelerated study. Internships. Graduate school at which undergraduates may take graduate-level courses. Preprofessional programs in law, medicine, veterinary science, and dentistry. 3-2 engineering programs with Georgia Tech, U of Pennsylvania, U of Southern California. Washington Semester and Sea Semester. Teacher certification in secondary education. Certification in specific subject areas. Exchange program abroad in Japan (Tohoku Gakuin U). Study abroad also in England, France, Germany, and Spain.
**Honors:** Phi Beta Kappa. Honors program. Honor societies.
**Academic Assistance:** Nonremedial tutoring.

**STUDENT LIFE. Housing:** All students must live on campus unless living with family. Coed, women's, and men's dorms. 90% of students live in college housing.
**Social atmosphere:** The Java Trench, Reimert, Wisner, South Street, and the Trappe are favorite gathering spots. Intervarsity Christian Fellowship, Hillel, Greeks, and the Grizzly influence student life. Homecoming, football games, field hockey, dances, comedians, musicians, and guest speakers are popular social/sports/cultural events. "Very small school, everyone is pretty close with many people," reports the editor of the student newspaper. "Family-like, everyone also knows everyone's business. Very sociable, very hardworking, and intelligent student body."
**Services and counseling/handicapped student services:** Placement services. Health service. Counseling services for minority students. Personal and psychological counseling. Career and academic guidance services. Religious counseling. Physically disabled student services.
**Campus organizations:** Undergraduate student government. Student newspaper (Grizzly, published once/week). Literary magazine. Yearbook. Radio and TV stations. Concert band, choir, Meistersingers, madrigal group, drama productions, academic, athletic, social, and special-interest groups. Nine fraternities, no chapter houses; five sororities, no chapter houses. 40% of men join a fraternity. 35% of women join a sorority.
**Religious organizations:** Fellowship of Christian Athletes, Intervarsity Christian Fellowship, Hillel, Newman Society.
**Minority/foreign student organizations:** Minority Student Union.

**ATHLETICS. Physical education requirements:** Two semesters of physical education required.
**Intercollegiate competition:** 50% of students participate. Baseball (M), basketball (M), cross-country (M,W), field hockey (W), football (M), golf (M), gymnastics (W), lacrosse (W), soccer (M), softball (W), swimming (M,W), tennis (M,W), track (indoor) (M,W), track (outdoor) (M,W), track and field (indoor) (M,W), track and field (outdoor) (M,W), volleyball (W), wrestling (M). Member of Centennial Football Conference, EAIAW, ECAC, NCAA Division I for field hockey, NCAA Division III, PAIAW.
**Intramural and club sports:** 60% of students participate. Intramural basketball, dancing, fishing, softball, table tennis, tennis, touch football, track, volleyball, water polo. Men's club Alpine skiing, cheerleading, cycling, fencing, lacrosse, racquetball, sailing, volleyball. Women's club Alpine skiing, cheerleading, cycling, fencing, racquetball, sailing.

**ADMISSIONS. Academic basis for candidate selection** (in order of priority): Secondary school record, standardized test scores, class rank, school's recommendation, essay.
**Nonacademic basis for candidate selection:** Extracurricular participation and particular talent or ability are emphasized. Alumni/ae relationship is important. Character and personality and geographical distribution are considered.
**Requirements:** Graduation from secondary school is required; GED is accepted. 20 units recommended and the following program of study required: 4 units of English, 3 units of math, 1 unit of science, 2 units of foreign language, 1 unit of social studies, 3.5 units of academic electives. SAT is required; ACT may be substituted. ACH recommended. Campus visit and interview recommended. No off-campus interviews.
**Procedure:** Take SAT or ACT by January of 12th year. Take ACH by January of 12th year. Visit college for interview by February 15 of 12th year. Application deadline is February 15. Acceptance notification by April 1. Reply is required by May 1. $250 nonrefundable tuition deposit. Freshmen accepted for terms other than fall.
**Special programs:** Admission may be deferred one year. Credit and/or placement may be granted through CEEB Advanced Placement exams for scores of 4 or higher. Credit may be granted through CLEP subject exams. Early decision program. In fall 1993, 98 applied for early decision and 80 were accepted. Deadline for applying for early decision is December 15. Early entrance/early admission program. Concurrent enrollment program.
**Transfer students:** Transfer students accepted for terms other than fall. In fall 1993, 2% of all new students were transfers into all classes. 70 transfer applications were received, 25 were accepted. Application deadline is August 1 for fall; December 1 for spring. Minimum 2.5 GPA required. Lowest course grade accepted is "C." Maximum number of transferable credits is 64 semester hours. At least 64 semester hours must be completed at the college to receive degree.
**Admissions contact:** Richard G. DiFeliciantonio, M.A., Dean of Admissions.

**FINANCIAL AID. Available aid:** Pell grants, SEOG, state grants, school scholarships and grants, academic merit scholarships, and aid for undergraduate foreign students. Perkins Loans (NDSL), PLUS, Stafford Loans (GSL), state loans, and private loans. Knight Tuition Plans.
**Financial aid statistics:** 10% of aid is not need-based. In 1993-94, 97% of all undergraduate applicants received aid; 98% of freshman applicants. Average amounts of aid awarded freshmen: Scholarships and grants, $9,059; loans, $3,512.
**Supporting data/closing dates:** FAFSA: Priority filing date is February 15. FAF: Deadline is February 15. State aid form: Deadline is February 15. Notification of awards begins April 1.
**Financial aid contact:** Mary Frances Waite, M.Ed., Director of Financial Aid.

**STUDENT EMPLOYMENT.** College Work/Study Program. Institutional employment. 50% of full-time undergraduates work on campus during school year. Students may expect to earn an average of $1,000 during school year. Off-campus part-time employment opportunities rated "good."

**COMPUTER FACILITIES.** 150 IBM/IBM-compatible and Macintosh/Apple microcomputers; 120 are networked. Students may access Digital minicomputer/mainframe systems, BITNET, Internet. Residence halls may be equipped with stand-alone microcomputers, networked microcomputers. Client/LAN operating systems include Apple/Macintosh, DOS. Computer languages and software packages include BASIC, C, COBOL, FORTRAN, ImSL, LISP, Lotus 1-2-3, Pascal, Prolog, SAS, VMS, other word processing programs. Computer facilities are available to all students.
**Fees:** None.
**Hours:** 8 AM-1 AM.

**GRADUATE CAREER DATA.** Graduate school percentages: 2% enter law school. 7% enter medical school. 1% enter dental school. 1% enter graduate business programs. 12% enter graduate arts and sciences programs. Highest graduate school enrollments: Penn State U, Temple U, U of Pennsylvania. 36% of graduates choose careers in business and industry.

**PROMINENT ALUMNI/AE.** Gerald M. Edelman, Nobel laureate in medicine, 1972.

# Villanova University

**Villanova, PA 19085** **610 519-4500**

**1994-95 Costs.** Tuition: $15,905 (average of arts and commerce and finance, science and nursing, and engineering tuitions). Room: $3,680. Board: $3,170. Fees, books, misc. academic expenses (school's estimate): $960.

**Enrollment.** Undergraduates: 3,052 men, 3,102 women (full-time). Freshman class: 7,759 applicants, 5,588 accepted, 1,535 enrolled. Graduate enrollment: 1,265 men, 1,216 women.

**Test score averages/ranges.** Range of SAT scores of middle 50%: 470-570 verbal, 550-640 math.

**Faculty.** 540 full-time; 346 part-time. 88% of faculty holds highest degree in specific field. Student/faculty ratio: 12 to 1.

**Selectivity rating.** More competitive.

**PROFILE.** Villanova, founded in 1842, is a private, church-affiliated, comprehensive university. Programs are offered through the Colleges of Commerce and Finance, Engineering, Liberal Arts and Sciences, and Nursing and the School of Law. Its 240-acre campus is located in Villanova, 12 miles west of Philadelphia.

**Accreditation:** MSACS. Professionally accredited by the Accreditation Board for Engineering and Technology, the American Assembly of Collegiate Schools of Business, the National League for Nursing.
**Religious orientation:** Villanova University is affiliated with the Roman Catholic Church (the Augustinians); two semesters of religion required.
**Library:** Collections totaling over 629,000 volumes, 2,805 periodical subscriptions, and 1,456 microform items.
**Special facilities/museums:** Augustinian historical museum, two observatories, planetarium.
**Athletic facilities:** Gymnasiums, field house, swimming pools, track, basketball, racquetball, tennis, and volleyball courts, weight rooms, stadiums, athletic fields, sports pavilion.

**STUDENT BODY. Undergraduate profile:** 28% are state residents; 7% are transfers. 4% Asian-American, 3% Black, 2% Hispanic, 89% White, 2% Other. Average age of undergraduates is 20.
**Freshman profile:** 1% of freshmen who took SAT scored 700 or over on verbal, 10% scored 700 or over on math; 15% scored 600 or over on verbal, 47% scored 600 or over on math; 64% scored 500 or over on verbal, 92% scored 500 or over on math; 99% scored 400 or over on verbal, 100% scored 400 or over on math; 100% scored 300 or over on verbal. 99% of accepted applicants took SAT; 1% took ACT. 50% of freshmen come from public schools.

**Undergraduate achievement:** 94% of fall 1992 freshmen returned for fall 1993 term. 84% of entering class graduated. 13% of students who completed a degree program immediately went on to graduate study.
**Foreign students:** 60 students are from out of the country. Countries represented include Canada, China, the Dominican Republic, India, Panama, and the United Kingdom; 45 in all.

**PROGRAMS OF STUDY. Degrees:** B.A., B.Chem.Eng., B.Civil Eng., B.Elec.Eng., B.Eng., B.Mech.Eng., B.S., B.S.Bus.Admin., B.S.Nurs.
**Majors:** Accountancy, Art/Art History, Astronomy/Astrophysics, Biology, Business Administration, Chemical Engineering, Chemistry, Civil Engineering, Classical Studies, Communication Arts, Computer Engineering, Computer Science, Economics, Electrical Engineering, English, Finance, French, General Studies, Geography, German, History, Honors Program, Human Services, Liberal Studies, Marketing, Mathematics, Mechanical Engineering, Nursing, Philosophy, Physics, Political Science, Psychology, Religious Studies, Secondary Education, Sociology, Spanish, Special Education.
**Distribution of degrees:** The majors with the highest enrollment are accounting, nursing, and finance; German, religious studies, and classical studies have the lowest.
**Requirements:** General education requirement.
**Academic regulations:** Freshmen must maintain minimum 1.6 GPA; sophomores, 1.75 GPA; juniors, 1.8 GPA; seniors, 2.0 GPA.
**Special:** Students who select General Program may concentrate in Arabic, biological chemistry, criminal justice, elementary education, ethnic studies, geography, Irish studies, Latin American studies, meteorology, peace and justice, planetarium education and management, and special education. Associate's degrees offered. Double majors. Dual degrees. Independent study. Pass/fail grading option. Internships. Graduate school at which undergraduates may take graduate-level courses. Preprofessional programs in law, medicine, veterinary science, dentistry, optometry, physical therapy, and occupational therapy. 3-4 M.D. program with the Medical Coll of Pennsylvania. 3-4 pre-dental program with U of Pennsylvania. 3-4 pre-optometry program with Pennsylvania Coll of Optometry. M.S. physical therapy, occupational therapy, diagnostic imaging, cytotechnology, and medical technology programs with Thomas Jefferson U. Cross-registration with Cabrini Coll and Rosemont Coll. Washington Semester. Exchange programs with Fordham U, Georgetown U, and U of Notre Dame. Teacher certification in elementary, secondary, and special education. Certification in specific subject areas. Study abroad possible in Asian, European, Latin American, and Middle Eastern countries. ROTC and NROTC. AFROTC at Saint Joseph's U.
**Honors:** Phi Beta Kappa. Honors program. Honor societies.
**Academic Assistance:** Remedial reading. Nonremedial tutoring.

**STUDENT LIFE. Housing:** Coed, women's, and men's dorms. 54% of students live in college housing.
**Social atmosphere:** "Villanova tries to offer a wide variety of programs," reports the student newspaper. "There are over 120 student activities." Most influential of the student organizations are the Greeks. The big events of the year are the Special Olympics, Balloon Day, Radiation Day, and Senior Week. Villanova basketball is especially popular. On campus, students frequent Dougherty Hall and the Connelly Center. Favorite off-campus nightspots include Kelly's and Minella's Diner.
**Services and counseling/handicapped student services:** Placement services. Health service. Counseling services for minority, military, veteran, and older students. Personal and psychological counseling. Career and academic guidance services. Religious counseling. Physically disabled student services. Learning disabled services. Tape recorders.
**Campus organizations:** Undergraduate student government. Student newspaper (Villanovan, published once/week). Literary magazine. Yearbook. Radio station. Community service activities, concert and marching bands, orchestra, drama group, Free University, debating, Political Union, Student Union, professional societies, Special Olympics, 150 organizations in all. 14 fraternities, no chapter houses; eight sororities, no chapter houses. 30% of men join a fraternity. 48% of women join a sorority.
**Religious organizations:** Campus Ministry.
**Minority/foreign student organizations:** Black Cultural Society, Arab and Islamic associations, other minority groups. Eight foreign student clubs.

**ATHLETICS. Physical education requirements:** None.
**Intercollegiate competition:** 13% of students participate. Baseball (M), basketball (M,W), cheerleading (M,W), cross-country (M,W), diving (M,W), field hockey (W), football (M), golf (M), ice hockey (M), lacrosse (M,W), soccer (M,W), softball (W), swimming (M,W), tennis (M,W), track (indoor) (M,W), track (outdoor) (M,W), track and field (indoor) (M,W), track and field (outdoor) (M,W), volleyball (W), water polo (M). Member of Big East Conference, Big Five Conference, Eastern Collegiate Athletic Conference, NCAA Division I, NCAA Division I-AA for football, Yankee Conference.
**Intramural and club sports:** 46% of students participate. Intramural aerobics, basketball, field hockey, flag football, inner-tube water polo, soccer, softball, volleyball. Men's club baseball, crew, karate, rugby, volleyball. Women's club crew, karate.

**ADMISSIONS. Academic basis for candidate selection** (in order of priority): Secondary school record, class rank, standardized test scores, school's recommendation, essay.
**Nonacademic basis for candidate selection:** Character and personality, extracurricular participation, particular talent or ability, geographical distribution, and alumni/ae relationship are considered.
**Requirements:** Graduation from secondary school is required; GED is accepted. 16 units and the following program of study are required: 4 units of English, 3 units of math, 2 units of lab science, 2 units of foreign language, 1 unit of social studies, 2 units of history, 2 units of academic electives. CEEB Achievement Test in foreign language required of applicants to College of Arts and Sciences only. Interviews required of pre-dental, pre-optometry, allied health, and accelerated medical school program applicants. Act 101 program for in-state applicants not meeting standard requirements. SAT is required; ACT may be substituted. ACH required. Campus visit recommended. No off-campus interviews.
**Procedure:** Take SAT or ACT by November of 12th year. Take ACH by June of 12th year. Visit college for interview by January 15 of 12th year. Suggest filing application by December 15. Application deadline is January 15. Notification of admission by April 1. Reply is required by May 1. $250 nonrefundable tuition deposit. $150 refundable room deposit. Freshmen accepted for fall term only.
**Special programs:** Admission may be deferred one year. Credit and/or placement may be granted through CEEB Advanced Placement exams for scores of 4 or higher. Credit and/or placement may be granted through CLEP subject exams. Credit may be granted through challenge exams. Early decision program. In fall 1993, 1,245 applied for early decision and 1,052 were accepted. Deadline for applying for early decision is December 15. Early entrance/early admission program.
**Transfer students:** Transfer students accepted for terms other than fall. In fall 1993, 7% of all new students were transfers into all classes. 405 transfer applications were received, 254 were accepted. Application deadline is July 15 for fall; November 15 for spring. Minimum 3.0 GPA required for transfer applicants to the College of Arts and Sciences; minimum 2.5 GPA required for transfer applicants to nursing, engineering, and commerce/finance programs. Lowest course grade accepted is "C." Maximum number of transferable credits is 60 semester hours. At least 62 semester hours must be completed at the university to receive degree.
**Admissions contact:** Stephen R. Merritt, Director of Undergraduate Admissions. 610 519-7599, 800 338-7927.

**FINANCIAL AID. Available aid:** Pell grants, SEOG, state scholarships and grants, school scholarships and grants, private scholarships and grants, ROTC scholarships, academic merit scholarships, and athletic scholarships. Perkins Loans (NDSL), PLUS, Stafford Loans (GSL), NSL, state loans, private loans, and SLS. Tuition Plan Inc., AMS, and Tuition Management Systems.
**Financial aid statistics:** 30% of aid is not need-based. In 1993-94, 90% of all undergraduate applicants received aid; 87% of freshman applicants. Average amounts of aid awarded freshmen: Scholarships and grants, $7,933; loans, $4,227.
**Supporting data/closing dates:** FAFSA/FAF: Priority filing date is February 15. School's own aid application: Priority filing date is March 15. Income tax forms: Priority filing date is March 15. Notification of awards begins April 1.
**Financial aid contact:** George J. Walter, M.S., Director of Financial Assistance. 610 519-4010.

**STUDENT EMPLOYMENT.** College Work/Study Program. Institutional employment. 24% of full-time undergraduates work on campus during school year. Students may expect to earn an average of $1,500 during school year. Off-campus part-time employment opportunities rated "excellent."

**COMPUTER FACILITIES.** 1,000 IBM/IBM-compatible and Macintosh/Apple microcomputers; all are networked. Students may access Digital, IBM, SUN minicomputer/mainframe systems. Client/LAN operating systems include Apple/Macintosh, DOS, OS/2, UNIX/XENIX/AIX, Windows NT, Novell. Computer languages and software packages include Assembler, COBOL, FORTRAN, Pascal, PL/1; 20 in all. Computer facilities are available to all students.
**Fees:** Computer fee is included in tuition/fees.
**Hours:** 24 hours.

**GRADUATE CAREER DATA.** Graduate school percentages: 5% enter law school. 2% enter medical school. 1% enter dental school. 1% enter graduate business programs. 7% enter graduate arts and sciences programs. Highest graduate school enrollments: New York U, U of Pennsylvania, Seton Hall, Temple U, Villanova U, U of Virginia. 38% of graduates choose careers in business and industry. Companies and businesses that hire graduates: Chase Manhattan, General Electric, U.S. government, U.S. Navy.

**PROMINENT ALUMNI/AE.** Paul X. Kelly, former commandant, U.S. Marine Corps; Hon. Robert N.C. Nix, Pennsylvania supreme court chief justice; Hazel Johnson, former brigadier general, U.S. Army Nursing Corps; Capt. Andrew M. Allen, USMC, NASA astronaut; Ed Pinckney, Boston Celtics; Thomas G. Labrecque, president, Chase Manhattan Bank; Harold Pressley, Sacramento Kings.

# Washington and Jefferson College

**Washington, PA 15301** 412 222-4400

**1994-95 Costs.** Tuition: $16,260. Room: $1,935. Board: $2,070. Fees, books, misc. academic expenses (school's estimate): $780.
**Enrollment.** Undergraduates: 603 men, 507 women (full-time). Freshman class: 1,308 applicants, 1,000 accepted, 332 enrolled.
**Test score averages/ranges.** Range of SAT scores of middle 50%: 940-1170 combined. Range of ACT scores of middle 50%: 20-25 composite.
**Faculty.** 86 full-time; 24 part-time. 91% of faculty holds doctoral degree. Student/faculty ratio: 11 to 1.
**Selectivity rating.** Competitive.

**PROFILE.** Washington and Jefferson is a private, liberal arts college. Tracing its origin to three schools established between 1781 and 1787, it was founded as a college for men by 1869 and became coeducational in 1970. Its 35-acre campus is located in Washington, 30 miles southwest of Pittsburgh.

**Accreditation:** MSACS.
**Religious orientation:** Washington and Jefferson College is nonsectarian; no religious requirements.
**Library:** Collections totaling over 195,000 volumes, 750 periodical subscriptions, and 5,400 microform items.
**Special facilities/museums:** Language lab, spectrometers, isolator lab, X-ray diffraction unit, neuropsychology lab, atomic absorption unit, refrigerated centrifuge.
**Athletic facilities:** Gymnasiums, stadium, baseball, football, lacrosse, soccer, and softball fields.

**STUDENT BODY. Undergraduate profile:** 68% are state residents; 5% are transfers. 2% Asian-American, 6% Black, 1% Hispanic, 90% White, 1% Other. Average age of undergraduates is 20.

**Freshman profile:** 1% of freshmen who took SAT scored 700 or over on verbal, 2% scored 700 or over on math; 11% scored 600 or over on verbal, 22% scored 600 or over on math; 59% scored 500 or over on verbal, 67% scored 500 or over on math; 95% scored 400 or over on verbal, 94% scored 400 or over on math; 100% scored 300 or over on verbal, 100% scored 300 or over on math. 85% of accepted applicants took SAT; 15% took ACT. 75% of freshmen come from public schools.
**Undergraduate achievement:** 94% of fall 1992 freshmen returned for fall 1993 term. 84% of entering class graduated. 60% of students who completed a degree program went on to graduate study within one year.
**Foreign students:** 10 students are from out of the country. Countries represented include Canada, England, Iran, Italy, Japan, and Korea.

**PROGRAMS OF STUDY. Degrees:** B.A.
**Majors:** Accounting, Art, Art History, Biology, Business, Chemistry, Economics, English, French, German, History, Industrial Chemistry/Management, Mathematics, Mathematics/Computer Science, Philosophy, Physics, Political Science, Psychology, Sociology, Spanish.
**Distribution of degrees:** The majors with the highest enrollment are business, biology, and accounting; French, German, and philosophy have the lowest.
**Requirements:** General education requirement.
**Academic regulations:** Minimum 2.0 GPA must be maintained.
**Special:** Minors offered in most majors and in business administration, music, and religious studies. Courses offered in astronomy, communications (journalism, speech), earth and space science, education, geology, human resource management, Latin, music, religion, and Russian. Entrepreneurial Studies Program. Self-designed majors. Double majors. Independent study. Pass/fail grading option. Internships. Preprofessional programs in law, medicine, veterinary science, pharmacy, dentistry, theology, optometry, prephysical therapy, and pre-podiatry. 3-2 engineering programs with Case Western Reserve U and Washington U. 3-4 podiatry program with Pennsylvania Coll of Podiatry. 3-4 optometry program with Pennsylvania Coll of Optometry. Washington Semester. Teacher certification in secondary education. Certification in specific subject areas. Study abroad in England (Royal Hollaway Coll of the U of London). ROTC at Duquesne U.
**Honors:** Phi Beta Kappa. Honor societies.
**Academic Assistance:** Nonremedial tutoring.

**STUDENT LIFE. Housing:** All students must live on campus unless living with family. Coed, women's, and men's dorms. Fraternity housing. School-owned/operated apartments. 95% of students live in college housing.
**Services and counseling/handicapped student services:** Placement services. Health service. Counseling services for minority, military, and veteran students. Personal counseling. Career and academic guidance services. Religious counseling. Physically disabled student services. Tape recorders. Reader services for the blind.
**Campus organizations:** Undergraduate student government. Student newspaper (Red & Black, published once/week). Literary magazine. Yearbook. Radio station. Choir, wind ensemble, pep band, coffeehouse, literary and theatre groups, debating, Interfraternity Council, Panhellenic Council, academic, departmental, and special-interest groups, 87 organizations in all. 10 fraternities, all with chapter houses; four sororities, no chapter houses. 53% of men join a fraternity. 67% of women join a sorority.
**Religious organizations:** Hillel, Newman Association, Student Christian Association.
**Minority/foreign student organizations:** Cultural Awareness Support Group, Black Student Union.

**ATHLETICS. Physical education requirements:** Two semesters of physical education required.
**Intercollegiate competition:** 33% of students participate. Baseball (M), basketball (M,W), cheerleading (M,W), cross-country (M,W), football (M), golf (M), soccer (M,W), softball (W), swimming (M,W), tennis (M,W), track (outdoor) (M,W), track and field (outdoor) (M,W), volleyball (W), wrestling (M). Member of NCAA Division III, President's Athletic Conference.
**Intramural and club sports:** 70% of students participate. Intramural basketball, flag football, racquetball, softball, swimming, tennis, volleyball, wrestling. Men's club lacrosse.

**ADMISSIONS. Academic basis for candidate selection** (in order of priority): Class rank, secondary school record, standardized test scores, school's recommendation, essay.
**Nonacademic basis for candidate selection:** Character and personality, extracurricular participation, and particular talent or ability are emphasized. Alumni/ae relationship is important.
**Requirements:** Graduation from secondary school is required; GED is accepted. 15 units and the following program of study are required: 3 units of English, 3 units of math, 1 unit of science, 2 units of foreign language, 6 units of academic electives. Electives should be chosen from general science, biology, physics, chemistry, math, and social science. Two units in some other area may be acceptable. Conditional admission possible for applicants not meeting standard requirements. SAT or ACT is required. ACH required. Campus visit and interview recommended. Off-campus interviews available with admissions and alumni representatives.
**Procedure:** Take SAT or ACT by January of 12th year. Take ACH by June of 12th year. Visit college for interview by May of 12th year. Application deadline is March 1. Acceptance notification on rolling basis beginning February 1. Reply is required by May 1. $200 nonrefundable tuition deposit. Freshmen accepted for terms other than fall.
**Special programs:** Admission may be deferred one year. Credit and/or placement may be granted through CEEB Advanced Placement exams for scores of 3 or higher. Credit and/or placement may be granted through CLEP general and subject exams. Placement may be granted through challenge exams. Early decision program. In fall 1993, 35 applied for early decision and 30 were accepted. Deadline for applying for early decision is November 1. Early entrance/early admission program. Concurrent enrollment program.
**Transfer students:** Transfer students accepted for terms other than fall. In fall 1993, 5% of all new students were transfers into all classes. 76 transfer applications were received, 45 were accepted. Application deadline is September 1 for fall; February 1 for spring. Minimum 2.5 GPA recommended. Lowest course grade accepted is "C." Maximum number of transferable credits is 18 courses. At least 18 courses must be completed at the college to receive degree.

**Admissions contact:** Thomas P. O'Connor, M.Ed., Director of Admissions. 412 223-6025.

**FINANCIAL AID. Available aid:** Pell grants, SEOG, state scholarships and grants, school scholarships and grants, private scholarships and grants, and academic merit scholarships. Perkins Loans (NDSL), PLUS, Stafford Loans (GSL), state loans, school loans, and SLS. Tuition Plan Inc., AMS, and Tuition Management Systems.
**Financial aid statistics:** 15% of aid is not need-based. In 1993-94, 70% of all undergraduate applicants received aid; 73% of freshman applicants. Average amounts of aid awarded freshmen: Loans, $2,625.
**Supporting data/closing dates:** FAFSA/FAF: Deadline is March 15. State aid form: Deadline is March 15. Notification of awards begins February 1.
**Financial aid contact:** Richard H. Soudan, Director of Financial Aid. 412 223-6019.

**STUDENT EMPLOYMENT.** College Work/Study Program. Institutional employment. 20% of full-time undergraduates work on campus during school year. Students may expect to earn an average of $1,000 during school year. Freshmen are discouraged from working during their first term. Off-campus part-time employment opportunities rated "good."

**COMPUTER FACILITIES.** 155 IBM/IBM-compatible, Macintosh/Apple, and RISC-/UNIX-based microcomputers; 132 are networked. Students may access Digital, IBM minicomputer/mainframe systems, Internet. Computer languages and software packages include BASIC, COBOL, dBASE, DIBOL, FORTRAN, Lotus 1-2-3, Microsoft DOS, Turbo Pascal, VisiCalc, WordPerfect, WordStar; 20 in all. Computer facilities are available to all students.
**Fees:** None.
**Hours:** 2 PM-midn.

**GRADUATE CAREER DATA.** Graduate school percentages: 17% enter law school. 20% enter medical school. 5% enter graduate business programs. 16% enter graduate arts and sciences programs. Highest graduate school enrollments: Carnegie Mellon U, Case Western Reserve U, Emory U, George Washington U, Georgetown U, Hahnemann U, Pennsylvania State U, U of North Carolina, U of Pennsylvania, U of Pittsburgh, U of Virginia, West Virginia U, Coll of William & Mary, Yale U. Companies and businesses that hire graduates: ALCOA, Arthur Andersen, Coca-Cola, Colgate-Palmolive, Coopers & Lybrand, IBM, Hershey, ITT, Integra Bank, Internal Revenue Service, Xerox, Eastman Kodak, Mellon Bank, PPG Industries, AT&T.

**PROMINENT ALUMNI/AE.** John Reed, president and CEO, Citibank; Robert Elliot, president and CEO, Levitz Furniture; Ronald Sandmeyer, president, Sandmeyer Steel; Robert Ivie, president and CEO, Guild Wineries; John J. Coury, president, American Medical Association.

# Waynesburg College

**Waynesburg, PA 15370** **412 627-8191**

**1994-95 Costs.** Tuition: $8,840. Room: $1,800. Board: $1,820. Fees, books, misc. academic expenses (school's estimate): $720.
**Enrollment.** Undergraduates: 552 men, 728 women (full-time). Freshman class: 1,190 applicants, 978 accepted, 324 enrolled. Graduate enrollment: 22 men, 13 women.
**Test score averages/ranges.** N/A.
**Faculty.** 67 full-time; 42 part-time. 61% of faculty holds highest degree in specific field. Student/faculty ratio: 16 to 1.
**Selectivity rating.** N/A.

**PROFILE.** Waynesburg, founded in 1849, is a church-affiliated college. Its 30-acre campus and 174-acre farm are located in Waynesburg, 60 miles from Pittsburgh.

**Accreditation:** MSACS. Professionally accredited by the National League for Nursing.
**Religious orientation:** Waynesburg College is affiliated with the Presbyterian Church USA; no religious requirements.
**Library:** Collections totaling over 100,000 volumes, 550 periodical subscriptions, and 5,327 microform items.
**Special facilities/museums:** Geology, biology, archaeology, and ceramics museum, arboretum, 174-acre farm.

**STUDENT BODY. Undergraduate profile:** 89% are state residents; 21% are transfers. 4% Black, 1% Hispanic, 94% White, 1% Other. Average age of undergraduates is 21.
**Freshman profile:** 97% of freshmen come from public schools.
**Undergraduate achievement:** 77% of fall 1992 freshmen returned for fall 1993 term. 47% of entering class graduated. 18% of students who completed a degree program went on to graduate study within six months.
**Foreign students:** 11 students are from out of the country. Countries represented include the Bahamas, Japan, Korea, New Guinea, Pakistan, and Thailand; 11 in all.

**PROGRAMS OF STUDY. Degrees:** B.A., B.S., B.S.Bus.Admin., B.S.Nurs.
**Majors:** Accounting, Biology, Chemistry, Communications/Electronic Media, Computer Science, Criminal Justice Administration, Economics, Elementary Education, English, Finance, History, Management, Marketing, Mathematics Education, Medical Technology, Mine Management, Nursing, Political Science, Professional Writing, Psychology, Public Service Administration, Small Business Management, Social Sciences, Sports Information Broadcasting, Sports Medicine, Visual Arts/Visual Communications.
**Distribution of degrees:** The majors with the highest enrollment are nursing and education; economics, mine management, and medical technology have the lowest.
**Requirements:** General education requirement.
**Academic regulations:** Minimum 2.0 GPA must be maintained.
**Special:** Minors offered in many majors and in applied mathematics, business administration, and philosophy. Courses offered in art, drama, government, music, physical education, physics, public speaking, religion, and secretarial science. Associate's degrees offered. Double majors. Independent study. Pass/fail grading option. Internships. Preprofessional programs in law, medicine, veterinary science, dentistry, and theology. 3-1 medical technology programs with Montefiore and West Penn Hospitals. 3-2 engi-

neering programs with Case Western Reserve U, Pennsylvania State U, and Washington U. Teacher certification in elementary and secondary education. Certification in specific subject areas. Study abroad possible.
**Honors:** Honors program. Honor societies.
**Academic Assistance:** Remedial reading, math, and study skills.

**STUDENT LIFE. Housing:** All freshmen, sophomores, and juniors must live on campus. Coed, women's, and men's dorms. Fraternity housing. Off-campus privately-owned housing. 47% of students live in college housing.
**Services and counseling/handicapped student services:** Placement services. Health service. Prematriculation tests for freshmen on personality, interests, and aptitudes. Counseling services for minority and older students. Personal and psychological counseling. Career and academic guidance services. Religious counseling. Learning disabled services.
**Campus organizations:** Undergraduate student government. Student newspaper (Yellow Jacket, published once/month). Literary magazine. Yearbook. Radio and TV stations. Concert, jazz, and pep bands, mixed chorus, drama group, dance club, women's association, color guard, ski club, departmental, professional, and service groups, 25 organizations in all. Two fraternities, one chapter house; three sororities, no chapter houses. 9% of men join a fraternity. 12% of women join a sorority.
**Religious organizations:** Christian Fellowship, Fellowship of Christian Athletes, Convocation-Chapel Hour, Residence Hall Bible Studies, Newman Club.
**Minority/foreign student organizations:** Black Student Union. International Student Organization.

**ATHLETICS. Physical education requirements:** One semester of physical education required.
**Intercollegiate competition:** 4% of students participate. Baseball (M), basketball (M), football (M), golf (M), softball (W), tennis (M), track (M), volleyball (W), wrestling (M). Member of NAIA.
**Intramural and club sports:** 2% of students participate.

**ADMISSIONS. Academic basis for candidate selection** (in order of priority): Secondary school record, class rank, school's recommendation, essay, standardized test scores.
**Nonacademic basis for candidate selection:** Extracurricular participation is emphasized. Character and personality, particular talent or ability, and alumni/ae relationship are considered.
**Requirements:** Graduation from secondary school is required; GED is accepted. 16 units and the following program of study are recommended: 4 units of English, 2 units of math, 2 units of science, 2 units of social studies, 6 units of electives. Rank in top half of class and minimum 3.0 GPA required. Conditional admission possible for applicants not meeting standard requirements. Act 101 program and Academic Support Service for applicants not normally admissible. SAT or ACT is recommended. Campus visit and interview recommended. Off-campus interviews available with an admissions representative.
**Procedure:** Notification of admission on rolling basis. Reply is required by date specified in letter of acceptance. $50 tuition deposit, half of which is refundable until August 4. $50 room deposit, half of which is refundable until August 4. Freshmen accepted for terms other than fall.
**Special programs:** Credit and/or placement may be granted through CEEB Advanced Placement exams for scores of 3 or higher. Credit may be granted through CLEP general exams. Credit and/or placement may be granted through CLEP subject exams. Credit and placement may be granted through Regents College, ACT PEP, DANTES, and challenge exams and military and life experience. Early entrance/early admission program. Concurrent enrollment program.
**Transfer students:** Transfer students accepted for terms other than fall. In fall 1993, 21% of all new students were transfers into all classes. 150 transfer applications were received, 145 were accepted. Application deadline is rolling for fall; rolling for spring. Minimum 2.0 GPA required. Lowest course grade accepted is "C." Maximum number of transferable credits is 60 semester hours. At least 45 semester hours must be completed at the college to receive degree.
**Admissions contact:** Robin L. Moore, M.B.A., Director of Admissions. 412 852-3248, 800 225-7393.

**FINANCIAL AID. Available aid:** Pell grants, SEOG, state scholarships and grants, school scholarships and grants, private scholarships, ROTC scholarships, and academic merit scholarships. Perkins Loans (NDSL), PLUS, Stafford Loans (GSL), NSL, state loans, school loans, and SLS. AMS and Tuition Management Systems.
**Financial aid statistics:** 2% of aid is not need-based. In 1993-94, 87% of all undergraduate applicants received aid; 90% of freshman applicants. Average amounts of aid awarded freshmen: Scholarships and grants, $5,740; loans, $2,267.
**Supporting data/closing dates:** FAFSA/FAF/FFS: Priority filing date is March 15. School's own aid application: Priority filing date is March 15. State aid form: Deadline is May 1. Income tax forms: Priority filing date is March 1. Notification of awards on rolling basis.
**Financial aid contact:** Karen Pratz, M.B.A., Director of Financial Aid. 412 852-3227.

**STUDENT EMPLOYMENT.** College Work/Study Program. Institutional employment. 17% of full-time undergraduates work on campus during school year. Students may expect to earn an average of $700 during school year. Off-campus part-time employment opportunities rated "fair."

**COMPUTER FACILITIES.** 250 IBM/IBM-compatible and Macintosh/Apple microcomputers. Students may access Digital minicomputer/mainframe systems. Client/LAN operating systems include Apple/Macintosh, DOS, Novell. Computer languages and software packages include BASIC, COBOL, dBASE, FORTRAN, Lotus 1-2-3, Pascal, PFS, WordPerfect, Write. Computer facilities are available to all students.
**Fees:** None.
**Hours:** 8:30 AM-10 PM.

**GRADUATE CAREER DATA.** Highest graduate school enrollments: Duquesne U, U of Pittsburgh, Waynesburg Coll, West Virginia U.

**PROMINENT ALUMNI/AE.** William E. Morrow, executive secretary, U.S. Department of Labor; Edward J. Evans, president, Comdisco Disaster Recovery Systems; W. Robert Stover, president, Western Temporary Services, Inc; Barbara Thompson Howell, editor, *Time*, Inc.

# West Chester University of Pennsylvania

**West Chester, PA 19383** **215 436-1000**

**1993-94 Costs.** Tuition: $2,954 (state residents), $7,352 (out-of-state). Room & board: $3,988. Fees, books, misc. academic expenses (school's estimate): $1,000.
**Enrollment.** Undergraduates: 2,912 men, 4,572 women (full-time). Freshman class: 6,502 applicants, 3,539 accepted, 1,391 enrolled. Graduate enrollment: 649 men, 1,956 women.
**Test score averages/ranges.** Average SAT scores: 450 verbal, 495 math. Range of SAT scores of middle 50%: 410-480 verbal, 450-550 math.
**Faculty.** 539 full-time; 131 part-time. 61% of faculty holds doctoral degree. Student/faculty ratio: 18 to 1.
**Selectivity rating.** Competitive.

**PROFILE.** West Chester is a public, multipurpose university. Founded as a state Normal school in 1871, it became a state college in 1960, and gained university status in 1983. Programs are offered through the College of Arts and Sciences and the Schools of Business and Public Affairs, Education, Health Sciences, and Music. Its 388-acre campus is located in West Chester, 25 miles west of Philadelphia.

**Accreditation:** MSACS. Professionally accredited by the Council on Social Work Education, the National Council for Accreditation of Teacher Education, the National League for Nursing.
**Religious orientation:** West Chester University of Pennsylvania is nonsectarian; no religious requirements.
**Library:** Collections totaling over 499,157 volumes, 2,912 periodical subscriptions, and 1,010,579 microform items.
**Special facilities/museums:** Art gallery, center for governmental and community affairs, herbarium, music library.
**Athletic facilities:** Swimming pools, indoor/outdoor track, tennis courts, basketball field house, field hockey, softball, and soccer fields, baseball and football stadium, gymnasiums.

**STUDENT BODY. Undergraduate profile:** 81% are state residents; 36% are transfers. 2% Asian-American, 7% Black, 1% Hispanic, 90% White. Average age of undergraduates is 21.
**Freshman profile:** 1% of freshmen who took SAT scored 700 or over on math; 3% scored 600 or over on verbal, 10% scored 600 or over on math; 26% scored 500 or over on verbal, 49% scored 500 or over on math; 77% scored 400 or over on verbal, 88% scored 400 or over on math; 96% scored 300 or over on verbal, 97% scored 300 or over on math. Majority of accepted applicants took SAT. 77% of freshmen come from public schools.
**Undergraduate achievement:** 83% of fall 1992 freshmen returned for fall 1993 term. 25% of entering class graduated. 17% of students who completed a degree program immediately went on to graduate study.
**Foreign students:** 25 students are from out of the country. Countries represented include Finland, France, Germany, India, Japan, and Russia; nine in all.

**PROGRAMS OF STUDY. Degrees:** B.A., B.F.A., B.Mus., B.S., B.S./R.N., B.S.Ed., B.S.Nurs.
**Majors:** Accounting, American Studies, Anthropology, Anthropology/Sociology, Art, Athletic Training, Biology/Cellular/Molecular, Business/Economics, Business Management, Communication, Communication Disorders, Comparative Literature, Computer Science, Criminal Justice, Early Childhood Education, Earth Science, Economics, Elementary Education, Engineering, English, English Literature, Fine Arts, French, Geography, German, Health, Health Education, History, Latin, Liberal/General Studies, Marketing, Mathematics, Mathematics/Computer Studies, Music Composition, Music Education, Music History, Music Performance, Nursing, Philosophy, Physical Education, Physics, Political Science, Political Science/Public Administration, Psychology, Public Health/Environmental, Public Health/Nutrition, Religious Studies, Russian, Secondary Education, Social Studies, Social Work, Sociology, Spanish, Special Education, Speech Correction, Theatre Arts.
**Distribution of degrees:** The majors with the highest enrollment are elementary education, physical education, and criminal justice; physics, instrumental music, and latin have the lowest.
**Requirements:** General education requirement.
**Academic regulations:** Freshmen must maintain minimum 1.8 GPA; sophomores, juniors, seniors, 2.0 GPA (on a 4.33 scale).
**Special:** Minors offered in approximately 56 fields. Certificate programs in athletic coaching, athletic training, driver education and safe living, environmental (outdoor) education, ethnic studies, outdoor recreation pursuits, and women's studies. Associate's degrees offered. Self-designed majors. Double majors. Independent study. Accelerated study. Pass/fail grading option. Internships. Graduate school at which undergraduates may take graduate-level courses. Preprofessional programs in law, medicine, veterinary science, pharmacy, dentistry, theology, and optometry. 3-2 physics/engineering program with Pennsylvania State U. Member of National Student Exchange (NSE). Teacher certification in early childhood, elementary, secondary, and special education. Certification in specific subject areas. Exchange programs abroad in France (U of Montpellier) and Wales (U of Wales). Study abroad also in Austria, China, and other countries. ROTC at Widener U. AFROTC at St. Joseph's U.
**Honors:** Honors program. Honor societies.
**Academic Assistance:** Remedial reading, writing, math, and study skills. Nonremedial tutoring.

**STUDENT LIFE. Housing:** Students may live on or off campus. Coed and women's dorms. International and honors housing. 29% of students live in college housing.
**Social atmosphere:** According to the student newspaper, WCU is a "beautiful campus offering both an urban and rural setting. Athletic facilities are located on South Campus,

which is more of a rural setting (30 minutes from Philadelphia)." The paper also reports, "Athletics are very important to the university. Our football team and women's field hockey teams are nationally ranked every year." Popular social events include the WCU vs. Delaware football game and tailgate party, the annual airband contest, and Spring Weekend.

**Services and counseling/handicapped student services:** Placement services. Health service. Women's center. Day care. Personal and psychological counseling. Career and academic guidance services. Physically disabled student services. Learning disabled services. Tape recorders. Tutors.

**Campus organizations:** Undergraduate student government. Student newspaper (Quad, published once/week). Literary magazine. Yearbook. Radio and TV stations. Concert and chamber choirs, choruses, instrumental ensembles, jazz group, three bands, string orchestra, theatre group, Little Theatre, forensics, debating, film and concert series, lecture series, service groups, 171 organizations in all. 15 fraternities, no chapter houses; 11 sororities, no chapter houses. 10% of men join a fraternity. 10% of women join a sorority.

**Religious organizations:** Several religious groups.

**Minority/foreign student organizations:** Black Student Union, Hispanic Student Union. International Student Association.

**ATHLETICS. Physical education requirements:** Two semesters of physical education required.

**Intercollegiate competition:** 5% of students participate. Baseball (M), basketball (M,W), cross-country (M,W), diving (M,W), field hockey (W), football (M), golf (M), gymnastics (W), lacrosse (M,W), soccer (M,W), softball (W), swimming (M,W), tennis (M,W), track (outdoor) (M,W), track and field (indoor) (M,W), track and field (outdoor) (M,W), volleyball (W). Member of ECAC, NCAA Division I for baseball and field hockey, NCAA Division II, PAIAW, Pennsylvania State Athletic Conference.

**Intramural and club sports:** 50% of students participate. Intramural basketball, floor hockey, golf, softball, tennis, volleyball. Men's club Alpine skiing, cheerleading, fencing, horsemanship, ice hockey, martial arts, rugby, water polo. Women's club Alpine skiing, cheerleading, fencing, horsemanship, martial arts, soccer, water polo.

**ADMISSIONS. Academic basis for candidate selection** (in order of priority): Secondary school record, class rank, standardized test scores, essay, school's recommendation.

**Nonacademic basis for candidate selection:** Character and personality, extracurricular participation, particular talent or ability, geographical distribution, and alumni/ae relationship are considered.

**Requirements:** Graduation from secondary school is required; GED is accepted. 21 units and the following program of study are recommended: 4 units of English, 3 units of math, 3 units of science, 2 units of foreign language, 4 units of social studies, 2 units of history. 11 secondary school units required. Minimum combined SAT score of 900, rank in top three-fifths of secondary school class, and minimum 3.0 GPA recommended. Interview required of premedical and athletic training program applicants. Audition required of music program applicants. Academic Development Program for applicants not normally admissible. SAT is required; ACT may be substituted. Campus visit recommended. No off-campus interviews.

**Procedure:** Take SAT or ACT by November of 12th year. Suggest filing application by December 1. Notification of admission on rolling basis. Reply is required by date specified in letter of acceptance. $100 nonrefundable tuition deposit. $100 nonrefundable room deposit. Freshmen accepted for terms other than fall.

**Special programs:** Admission may be deferred one semester. Credit and/or placement may be granted through CEEB Advanced Placement exams for scores of 3 or higher. Credit and/or placement may be granted through CLEP subject exams. Credit and placement may be granted through challenge exams and military and life experience. Early entrance/early admission program.

**Transfer students:** Transfer students accepted for terms other than fall. In fall 1993, 36% of all new students were transfers into all classes. 2,444 transfer applications were received, 1,282 were accepted. Application deadline is August 1 for fall; December 1 for spring. Minimum 2.0 GPA required. Lowest course grade accepted is "D." Maximum number of transferable credits is 98 semester hours. At least 30 semester hours must be completed at the university to receive degree.

**Admissions contact:** Marsha L. Haug, M.S., Director of Admissions. 215 436-3411.

**FINANCIAL AID. Available aid:** Pell grants, SEOG, state scholarships and grants, school scholarships, private scholarships, ROTC scholarships, academic merit scholarships, and athletic scholarships. Perkins Loans (NDSL), PLUS, Stafford Loans (GSL), NSL, state loans, school loans, and SLS. Deferred payment plan.

**Financial aid statistics:** 10% of aid is not need-based. In 1993-94, 95% of all undergraduate applicants received aid; 58% of freshman applicants. Average amounts of aid awarded freshmen: Scholarships and grants, $2,139; loans, $3,000.

**Supporting data/closing dates:** FAFSA: Priority filing date is March 15. State aid form: Priority filing date is March 15; deadline is May 1. Notification of awards begins April 15.

**Financial aid contact:** Mr. Dana Parker, M.B.A., Director of Financial Aid. 215 436-2627.

**STUDENT EMPLOYMENT.** College Work/Study Program. Institutional employment. 8% of full-time undergraduates work on campus during school year. Students may expect to earn an average of $1,725 during school year. Off-campus part-time employment opportunities rated "excellent."

**COMPUTER FACILITIES.** 2,000 IBM/IBM-compatible, Macintosh/Apple, and RISC-/UNIX-based microcomputers; 1,500 are networked. Students may access Digital, IBM minicomputer/mainframe systems, BITNET, Internet. Residence halls may be equipped with networked microcomputers. Client/LAN operating systems include Banyan. Computer languages and software packages include APL-PC, Access, Assembler, BASIC, COBOL, dBASE, Excel, FORTRAN, GPSS-PC, LISP, Lotus 1-2-3, MINITAB, Modula, MSWord, Pascal, PC-File, PC-Write, Powerpaint, Quick BASIC, SAS, SAS/GRAPH, SPSS-X, Turbo Pascal, VP-Planner, WordPerfect, WordStar. Computer facilities are available to all students.

**Fees:** None.

**Hours:** 8 AM-midn.

**GRADUATE CAREER DATA.** Highest graduate school enrollments: Pennsylvania State U, Temple U, Thomas Jefferson U, U of Delaware, U of Pennsylvania. Companies and businesses that hire graduates: Hewlett-Packard, John Hancock Insurance, Meridian, UNISYS.

**PROMINENT ALUMNI/AE.** George Wackenhut, CEO, Wackenhut Securities; Jim Holt, regional director; U.S. Secret Service; Curt Weldon, U.S. congressman; Patricia Morinelli, executive vice-president for productions, Radio City Music Hall; Dr. Clarence Alston, director, National Health Service Corps' Family Health Center; John Nolan, vice-president, CIGNA Corp.

## Westminster College

**New Wilmington, PA 16172** — **412 946-8761**

**1994-95 Costs.** Tuition: $12,660. Room: $1,635. Board: $1,980. Fees, books, misc. academic expenses (school's estimate): $685.

**Enrollment.** Undergraduates: 616 men, 795 women (full-time). Freshman class: 995 applicants, 868 accepted, 377 enrolled. Graduate enrollment: 36 men, 65 women.

**Test score averages/ranges.** Average SAT scores: 470 verbal, 520 math. Range of SAT scores of middle 50%: 420-520 verbal, 460-570 math. Average ACT scores: 24 composite.

**Faculty.** 94 full-time; 24 part-time. 78% of faculty holds highest degree in specific field. Student/faculty ratio: 16 to 1.

**Selectivity rating.** Less competitive.

**PROFILE.** Westminster, founded in 1852, is a church-affiliated, liberal arts college. Its 300-acre campus is located in New Wilmington, 65 miles north of Pittsburgh.

**Accreditation:** MSACS. Professionally accredited by the National Association of Schools of Music.

**Religious orientation:** Westminster College is affiliated with the Presbyterian Church USA; one semester of religion required.

**Library:** Collections totaling over 220,000 volumes, 1,000 periodical subscriptions, and 100 microform items.

**Special facilities/museums:** On-campus preschool, Moeller pipe organs, planetarium, observatory, electron microscopes, X-ray diffractor, spectrometer.

**Athletic facilities:** Fieldhouse, football and softball fields, tennis courts.

**STUDENT BODY. Undergraduate profile:** 76% are state residents; 10% are transfers. 1% Asian-American, 1.5% Black, .3% Hispanic, .1% Native American, 97% White, .1% Other. Average age of undergraduates is 20.

**Freshman profile:** 1% of freshmen who took SAT scored 700 or over on verbal, 1% scored 700 or over on math; 8% scored 600 or over on verbal, 19% scored 600 or over on math; 38% scored 500 or over on verbal, 62% scored 500 or over on math; 83% scored 400 or over on verbal, 93% scored 400 or over on math; 100% scored 300 or over on verbal, 100% scored 300 or over on math. 91% of accepted applicants took SAT; 45% took ACT. 70% of freshmen come from public schools.

**Undergraduate achievement:** 89% of fall 1992 freshmen returned for fall 1993 term. 69% of entering class graduated. 19% of students who completed a degree program went on to graduate study within one year.

**Foreign students:** One student is from out of the country.

**PROGRAMS OF STUDY. Degrees:** B.A., B.Mus., B.S.

**Majors:** Accounting, Applied Music, Art, Art Education, Biology, Broadcast Communications, Business Administration, Chemistry, Christian Education, Church Music, Computer Information Systems, Computer Science, Criminal Justice, Economics, Elementary Education, English, Environmental Science, Finance/Marketing, French, German, History, Industrial Relations, Intercultural Studies, International Economics/Business, International Politics, Latin, Management, Management Sciences, Mathematics, Molecular Biology, Music, Music Education, Organizational Behavior, Philosophy, Physics, Political Science, Psychobiology, Psychology, Public Relations, Religion, Sociology, Spanish, Theatre.

**Distribution of degrees:** The majors with the highest enrollment are business administration, elementary education, and history; theatre, Spanish, and philosophy have the lowest.

**Requirements:** General education requirement.

**Academic regulations:** Freshmen must maintain minimum 1.7 GPA; sophomores, 1.8 GPA; juniors, 1.9 GPA; seniors, 2.0 GPA.

**Special:** Minors offered in all majors except business. Interdisciplinary programs in many majors and in information arts and Western Civilization. "Quest" interdisciplinary humanities program includes internships. Self-designed majors. Double majors. Independent study. Accelerated study. Pass/fail grading option. Internships. Graduate school at which undergraduates may take graduate-level courses. Preprofessional programs in law, medicine, veterinary science, pharmacy, dentistry, theology, optometry, and physical therapy. 3-2 engineering programs with Case Western Reserve U, Pennsylvania State U, and Washington U. Member of East Central College Consortium. Washington Semester and Sea Semester. Exchange programs with other 4-1-4 calendar schools. Teacher certification in elementary and secondary education. Certification in specific subject areas. Exchange programs abroad in Chile, France, Germany, and Spain. Study abroad may be arranged in other countries.

**Honors:** Honors program. Honor societies.

**Academic Assistance:** Remedial reading and writing. Nonremedial tutoring.

**STUDENT LIFE. Housing:** All unmarried students under age 21 must live on campus unless living near campus with relatives. Women's and men's dorms. Fraternity housing. 90% of students live in college housing.

**Social atmosphere:** Popular on-campus gathering spots include fraternity houses, the student union, and the campus pub; students gather off-campus at Seafood Express and Quaker Steak & Lube. According to the editor of the school newspaper, the most influential groups on campus are Christian organizations and the Greeks. The most popular events of the year are football and basketball games, Homecoming, Greek Week, and intramural softball and Razzle football games. "Socially, fraternities provide the greatest amount of activity; culturally, there's not much happening, but Pittsburgh is close for concerts and museums," reports the Holcad student newspaper.

**Services and counseling/handicapped student services:** Placement services. Health service. Counseling services for minority students. Personal and psychological counseling. Career and academic guidance services. Religious counseling. Physically disabled student services. Notetaking services. Tape recorders. Tutors.
**Campus organizations:** Undergraduate student government. Student newspaper (Holcad, published once/week). Literary magazine. Yearbook. Radio and TV stations. Concert and vesper choirs, band, orchestra, film series, theatre, dance theatre, film series, art league, scuba club, outing club, Students in Action Who Value the Environment, programming committee, academic and departmental groups, 85 organizations in all. Five fraternities, all with chapter houses; five sororities, no chapter houses. 60% of men join a fraternity. 45% of women join a sorority.
**Religious organizations:** Bible study group, Coalition, Fellowship of Christian Athletes, Habitat for Humanity, InterVarsity.
**Minority/foreign student organizations:** Black Student Union, Cultural Awareness Series.

**ATHLETICS. Physical education requirements:** Four semesters of physical education required.
**Intercollegiate competition:** Baseball (M), basketball (M,W), cheerleading (W), cross-country (M,W), football (M), golf (M), horsemanship (M,W), soccer (M), softball (W), swimming (M,W), tennis (M,W), track (indoor) (M,W), track (outdoor) (M,W), track and field (indoor) (M,W), track and field (outdoor) (M,W), volleyball (W). Member of NAIA.
**Intramural and club sports:** Intramural basketball, soccer, softball, touch football, volleyball. Men's club racquetball, rugby, volleyball. Women's club soccer.

**ADMISSIONS. Academic basis for candidate selection** (in order of priority): Secondary school record, class rank, standardized test scores, school's recommendation, essay.
**Nonacademic basis for candidate selection:** Character and personality and extracurricular participation are important. Particular talent or ability, geographical distribution, and alumni/ae relationship are considered.
**Requirements:** Graduation from secondary school is required; GED is accepted. 18 units and the following program of study are required: 4 units of English, 3 units of math, 2 units of lab science, 2 units of foreign language, 3 units of social studies, 1 unit of history, 3 units of academic electives. Conditional admission possible for applicants not meeting standard requirements. SAT or ACT is required. Campus visit and interview recommended. No off-campus interviews.
**Procedure:** Take SAT or ACT by December of 12th year. Visit college for interview by April 1 of 12th year. Application deadline is April 15. Notification of admission on rolling basis. Reply is required by May 1. $100 nonrefundable tuition deposit. Freshmen accepted for terms other than fall.
**Special programs:** Admission may be deferred one year. Credit and/or placement may be granted through CEEB Advanced Placement exams for scores of 4 or higher. Credit and/or placement may be granted through CLEP general and subject exams. Credit and placement may be granted through challenge exams and life experience. Early entrance/early admission program. Concurrent enrollment program.
**Transfer students:** Transfer students accepted for terms other than fall. In fall 1993, 10% of all new students were transfers into all classes. 82 transfer applications were received, 60 were accepted. Application deadline is August 1 for fall; January 1 for spring. Minimum 2.0 GPA required. Lowest course grade accepted is "C." Maximum number of transferable credits is 84 semester hours. At least 42 semester hours must be completed at the college to receive degree.
**Admissions contact:** Richard Dana Paul, M.Ed., Director of Admissions. 412 946-7100, 800 942-8033.

**FINANCIAL AID. Available aid:** Pell grants, SEOG, state scholarships and grants, school scholarships and grants, private scholarships and grants, academic merit scholarships, athletic scholarships, and aid for undergraduate foreign students. Perkins Loans (NDSL), PLUS, Stafford Loans (GSL), and SLS. AMS and Tuition Management Systems.
**Financial aid statistics:** 26% of aid is not need-based. In 1993-94, 83% of all undergraduate applicants received aid; 77% of freshman applicants. Average amounts of aid awarded freshmen: Scholarships and grants, $6,700; loans, $3,100.
**Supporting data/closing dates:** FAFSA: Priority filing date is May 1; accepted on rolling basis. FAF: Priority filing date is May 1. School's own aid application: Priority filing date is May 1; accepted on rolling basis. State aid form: Priority filing date is May 1. Income tax forms: Accepted on rolling basis. W-2: Accepted on rolling basis. Notification of awards on rolling basis.
**Financial aid contact:** Robert A. Latta, M.Ed., Director of Financial Aid. 412 946-7102.

**STUDENT EMPLOYMENT.** College Work/Study Program. Institutional employment. 27% of full-time undergraduates work on campus during school year. Students may expect to earn an average of $1,300 during school year. Freshmen are discouraged from working during their first term. Off-campus part-time employment opportunities rated "poor."

**COMPUTER FACILITIES.** 140 IBM/IBM-compatible, Macintosh/Apple, and RISC-/UNIX-based microcomputers; 55 are networked. Students may access Digital minicomputer/mainframe systems, Internet. Residence halls may be equipped with modems. Client/LAN operating systems include OS/2. Computer languages and software packages include BASIC, COBOL, dBASE, FORTRAN, LISP, Lotus 1-2-3, Mathematica, MINITAB, Pascal, PC-Write, Quick BASIC, SAS, SPSS-X, Turbo Pascal, WordPerfect. Computer facilities are available to all students.
**Fees:** None.
**Hours:** 8 AM-11 PM.

**GRADUATE CAREER DATA.** Graduate school percentages: 3% enter law school. 3% enter medical school. 2% enter graduate business programs. Highest graduate school enrollments: Case Western Reserve U, Pennsylvania State U, U of Pittsburgh. 55% of graduates choose careers in business and industry. Companies and businesses that hire graduates: Aetna, Deloitte & Touche, H.J. Heinz, IBM, Integra, LTV Steel, Mellon Bank, PPG, USX, Westinghouse.

**PROMINENT ALUMNI/AE.** Donald Wiley, senior vice-president, H.J. Heinz; Wende Logan-Younge, breast cancer researcher; William Dembaugh, vocalist, New York City Opera; Scott McLuckey, NASA astronaut; Bob Braunlich, unit manager, ABC; Andrew McKelvey, developer of telephone marketing programs; Rich Dalrymple, director of public relations, Dallas Cowboys.

# Widener University

**Chester, PA 19013** — **610 499-4000**

**1994-95 Costs.** Tuition: $12,350. Room & board: $5,370. Fees, books, misc. academic expenses (school's estimate): $500.
**Enrollment.** Undergraduates: 1,110 men, 1,015 women (full-time). Freshman class: 2,040 applicants, 1,279 accepted, 502 enrolled. Graduate enrollment: 873 men, 1,226 women.
**Test score averages/ranges.** Average SAT scores: 466 verbal, 491 math.
**Faculty.** 146 full-time; 81 part-time. 92% of faculty holds highest degree in specific field. Student/faculty ratio: 12 to 1.
**Selectivity rating.** Competitive.

**PROFILE.** Widener, founded in 1821, is a private, comprehensive university. Programs are offered through the College of Arts and Sciences; the Schools of Engineering, Hotel and Restaurant Management, Management, Nursing, and Law; and University College. Its 120-acre main campus is located in Chester, 10 miles from Philadelphia.
**Accreditation:** MSACS. Professionally accredited by the Accreditation Board for Engineering and Technology, the American Bar Association, the American Psychological Association, the Council on Social Work Education, the National League for Nursing.
**Religious orientation:** Widener University is nonsectarian; no religious requirements.
**Library:** Collections totaling over 211,237 volumes, 2,310 periodical subscriptions, 106,791 microform items, 2,700 recordings, and 1,200 slides. Law library of 10,000 volumes.
**Special facilities/museums:** Art museum, restaurant lab, child development center education lab, recording studio, commercial graphics lab.
**Athletic facilities:** Gymnasium, swimming pool, weight room, exercise room, training room, basketball, racquetball, squash, and tennis courts, indoor and outdoor tracks, football stadium, athletic fields.

**STUDENT BODY. Undergraduate profile:** 53% are state residents; 32% are transfers. 3.6% Asian-American, 11.2% Black, 2.2% Hispanic, 79% White, 4% Other. Average age of undergraduates is 21.
**Freshman profile:** 1% of freshmen who took SAT scored 700 or over on verbal, 4% scored 700 or over on math; 8% scored 600 or over on verbal, 19% scored 600 or over on math; 32% scored 500 or over on verbal, 51% scored 500 or over on math; 88% scored 400 or over on verbal, 93% scored 400 or over on math; 100% scored 300 or over on verbal, 99% scored 300 or over on math. 99% of accepted applicants took SAT. 51% of freshmen come from public schools.
**Undergraduate achievement:** 90% of fall 1992 freshmen returned for fall 1993 term. 49% of entering class graduated. 12% of students who completed a degree program immediately went on to graduate study.
**Foreign students:** 83 students are from out of the country. Countries represented include India, Japan, Malaysia, Taiwan, Turkey, and Ukraine; 42 in all.

**PROGRAMS OF STUDY. Degrees:** B.A., B.S., B.S.Nurs., B.Soc.Work.
**Majors:** Accounting, Allied Health, Behavioral Science, Biology, Business Administration, Chemical Engineering, Chemistry, Chemistry Management, Civil Engineering, Computer Science, Criminal Justice, Economics, Electrical Engineering, Engineering, English, History, Hotel/Restaurant Management, Humanities, Industrial/Management Engineering, Information Systems, International Business, Liberal Studies, Management, Management Information Systems, Mathematics, Mechanical Engineering, Media Studies, Modern Languages, Nursing, Office Administration, Physics, Political Science, Psychology, Science Administration, Science Education, Social Work, Sociology, Technical/Industrial Administration.
**Distribution of degrees:** The majors with the highest enrollment are management, hotel management, and nursing; chemistry, mathematics, and behavioral science have the lowest.
**Requirements:** General education requirement.
**Academic regulations:** Minimum 2.0 GPA required for graduation.
**Special:** Delaware campus includes the Widener School of Law and the part-time/evening University College–Delaware. Exploratory studies program for students who are undecided about major. Advanced language program offers 24 semester hours of intensive instruction. Music and education certification available. Harrisburg campus includes branch of the Law School and graduate programs from the School of Nursing. Associate's degrees offered. Self-designed majors. Double majors. Dual degrees. Independent study. Accelerated study. Pass/fail grading option. Internships. Cooperative education programs. Graduate school at which undergraduates may take graduate-level courses. Preprofessional programs in law, medicine, pharmacy, dentistry, optometry, physical therapy, and podiatry. 3-3 programs with Philadelphia Coll of Optometry, Philadelphia Coll of Osteopathic Medicine, and Philadelphia Coll of Podiatry; 3-3 B.S./M.S. in D.T.; M.B.A./M.D. with Jefferson Medical Coll. Member of Independent Colleges, Ben Franklin Partnership Consortium of Academic Clinical Coordinators of Physical Theraphy Education, Academic Administrator Group of American Physical Theraphy Association. Washington Semester. Exchange programs with Swarthmore Coll, American U. Teacher certification in early childhood, elementary, and secondary education. Certification in specific subject areas. Study abroad in Belgium, England, Ireland, Italy, Scotland, and Switzerland. ROTC. AFROTC at St. Joseph's U.
**Honors:** Honors program. Honor societies.
**Academic Assistance:** Remedial writing, math, and study skills. Nonremedial tutoring.

**STUDENT LIFE. Housing:** All unmarried, nonveteran freshmen and sophomores under age 24 must live on campus unless living with family. Coed, women's, and men's dorms. Sorority and fraternity housing. School-owned/operated apartments. Special-interest housing. 60% of students live in college housing.
**Social atmosphere:** "Widener is a diverse campus in regards to tastes in music and manners of life," reports the editor of the student newspaper. "This diversity leads itself to the students getting to know a variety of people. Almost 25% of the community is Greek, so Greek life plays a major part. During the week, the Student Activities Office runs pro-

grams for all students including movies, committee meetings, comedians, magicians, hypnotists, etc. Weekends signal sporting events, The Metro (a student-run, school-sponsored night club), and studying in the library." Popular events during the year include Homecoming, Greek Week, and Spring Week.

**Services and counseling/handicapped student services:** Placement services. Health service. Counseling services for minority, military, veteran, and older students. Personal and psychological counseling. Career and academic guidance services. Learning disabled services.

**Campus organizations:** Undergraduate student government. Student newspaper (Dome, published once/week). Literary magazine. Yearbook. Radio station. Annual international festival, drama club, publications, chorale, varsity and other bands, wind, jazz, and brass ensembles, academic and social clubs, special-interest groups, 92 organizations in all. Eight fraternities, all with chapter houses; four sororities, two chapter houses. 28% of men join a fraternity. 18% of women join a sorority.

**Religious organizations:** Christian Fellowship, Fellowship of Christian Athletes, Hillel, Newman Apostolate.

**Minority/foreign student organizations:** Black Student Union. Modern language club, International Club, La sociedad Hispanica, Vietnamese student club.

**ATHLETICS. Physical education requirements:** Two semesters of physical education required.

**Intercollegiate competition:** 30% of students participate. Baseball (M), basketball (M,W), cheerleading (W), cross-country (M,W), field hockey (W), football (M), golf (M), lacrosse (M,W), soccer (M), softball (W), squash (M), swimming (M,W), tennis (M,W), track and field (indoor) (M,W), track and field (outdoor) (M,W), volleyball (W). Member of ECAC, Middle Atlantic States Collegiate Athletic Conference, NCAA Division III.

**Intramural and club sports:** 50% of students participate. Intramural basketball, flag football, floor hockey, frisbee football, indoor soccer, softball, squash, volleyball. Men's club volleyball. Women's club soccer.

**ADMISSIONS. Academic basis for candidate selection** (in order of priority): Secondary school record, class rank, standardized test scores, school's recommendation, essay.

**Nonacademic basis for candidate selection:** Character and personality, extracurricular participation, particular talent or ability, and alumni/ae relationship are considered.

**Requirements:** Graduation from secondary school is required; GED is accepted. 16 units and the following program of study are recommended: 4 units of English, 3 units of math, 3 units of science, 2 units of foreign language, 2 units of social studies, 2 units of history, 2 units of electives. Minimum SAT scores of 400 in both verbal and math, rank in top half of secondary school class, and minimum 2.5 GPA recommended. Audition required for music program scholarships. Summer preparatory program for applicants not normally admissible. SAT is required; ACT may be substituted. ACH recommended. Campus visit and interview recommended. Off-campus interviews available with an admissions representative.

**Procedure:** Take SAT or ACT by December of 12th year. Take ACH by November of 12th year. Visit college for interview by March of 12th year. Application deadline is April 1. Notification of admission on rolling basis. Reply is required by May 1. $100 nonrefundable tuition deposit. $100 nonrefundable room deposit. Freshmen accepted for terms other than fall.

**Special programs:** Admission may be deferred two years. Credit and/or placement may be granted through CEEB Advanced Placement exams for scores of 3 or higher. Credit may be granted through CLEP subject exams. Early entrance/early admission program. Concurrent enrollment program.

**Transfer students:** Transfer students accepted for terms other than fall. In fall 1993, 32% of all new students were transfers into all classes. 670 transfer applications were received, 583 were accepted. Application deadline is July 1 for fall; December 1 for spring. Minimum 2.0 GPA required. Lowest course grade accepted is "C." Maximum number of transferable credits is 60 semester hours from a two-year school and 80 semester hours from a four-year school. At least 45 semester hours must be completed at the university to receive degree.

**Admissions contact:** Michael L. Mahoney, Ed.D., Director of Admissions. 610 499-4126.

**FINANCIAL AID. Available aid:** Pell grants, SEOG, state scholarships and grants, school scholarships and grants, private scholarships and grants, ROTC scholarships, and academic merit scholarships. Perkins Loans (NDSL), PLUS, Stafford Loans (GSL), state loans, and SLS. Institutional tuition payment plan.

**Financial aid statistics:** 24% of aid is not need-based. In 1993-94, 93% of all undergraduate applicants received aid; 92% of freshman applicants. Average amounts of aid awarded freshmen: Scholarships and grants, $5,200; loans, $2,543.

**Supporting data/closing dates:** FAFSA: Priority filing date is March 1. School's own aid application: Priority filing date is March 1. Income tax forms: Priority filing date is March 1; accepted on rolling basis. Notification of awards on rolling basis.

**Financial aid contact:** Ethel Desmarais, M.Ed., Director of Financial Aid. 610 499-4168.

**STUDENT EMPLOYMENT.** College Work/Study Program. Institutional employment. 21% of full-time undergraduates work on campus during school year. Students may expect to earn an average of $900 during school year. Off-campus part-time employment opportunities rated "good."

**COMPUTER FACILITIES.** 187 IBM/IBM-compatible and Macintosh/Apple microcomputers; all are networked. Students may access CDC Cyber, Digital, SUN minicomputer/mainframe systems, Internet. Client/LAN operating systems include DOS, UNIX/XENIX/AIX, Novell. Computer languages and software packages include C++, COBOL, FORTRAN, LISP, Pascal. Computer facilities are available to all students.

**Fees:** None.

**Hours:** 8 AM-midn. (Longer hours during exam periods.)

**GRADUATE CAREER DATA.** Graduate school percentages: 5% enter law school. 3% enter medical school. 2% enter dental school. 14% enter graduate business programs. 3% enter graduate arts and sciences programs. Highest graduate school enrollments: Bryn Mawr Coll, U of Delaware, Drexel U, U of Pennsylvania, Villanova U, Widener U. 82% of graduates choose careers in business and industry. Companies and businesses that hire graduates: ARA Services, Boeing, Coopers & Lybrand, DuPont, KPMG Peat Marwick, Marriott, Scott Paper.

**PROMINENT ALUMNI/AE.** Leslie Quick, CEO, Quick and Riley; Cecil B. DeMille, movie producer; Bill ("White Shoes") Johnson, NFL football player.

# Wilson College

**Chambersburg, PA 17201-1285 717 264-4141**

**1994-95 Costs.** Tuition: $11,428. Room & board: $5,084. Fees, books, misc. academic expenses (school's estimate): $568.

**Enrollment.** 160 women (full-time). Freshman class: 134 applicants, 111 accepted, 39 enrolled.

**Test score averages/ranges.** Average SAT scores: 462 verbal, 469 math. Range of SAT scores of middle 50%: 400-530 verbal, 400-560 math.

**Faculty.** 35 full-time; 6 part-time. 77% of faculty holds doctoral degree. Student/faculty ratio: 5 to 1.

**Selectivity rating.** Less competitive.

**PROFILE.** Wilson, founded in 1869, is a church-affiliated college for women. Its 260-acre campus is located in Chambersburg, 55 miles southwest of Harrisburg.

**Accreditation:** MSACS. Professionally accredited by the American Veterinary Medical Association.

**Religious orientation:** Wilson College is affiliated with the Presbyterian Church; no religious requirements.

**Library:** Collections totaling over 159,846 volumes, 393 periodical subscriptions, and 11,703 microform items.

**Special facilities/museums:** Art gallery, natural history museum, electron microscope.

**Athletic facilities:** Gymnasiums, swimming pool, basketball and tennis courts, athletic fields, weight room, archery range, bowling alley.

**STUDENT BODY. Undergraduate profile:** 61% are state residents; 20% are transfers. 4% Asian-American, 92% White, 4% Other. Average age of undergraduates is 20.

**Freshman profile:** 11% of freshmen who took SAT scored 600 or over on verbal, 13% scored 600 or over on math; 33% scored 500 or over on verbal, 46% scored 500 or over on math; 72% scored 400 or over on verbal, 76% scored 400 or over on math; 96% scored 300 or over on verbal, 100% scored 300 or over on math. Majority of accepted applicants took SAT. 94% of freshmen come from public schools.

**Undergraduate achievement:** 68% of fall 1992 freshmen returned for fall 1993 term. 57% of entering class graduated. 18% of students who completed a degree program immediately went on to graduate study.

**Foreign students:** 11 students are from out of the country. Countries represented include Japan, Sri Lanka, and Thailand.

**PROGRAMS OF STUDY. Degrees:** B.A., B.S.

**Majors:** Behavioral Sciences, Biology, Business/Economics, Chemistry, Communications, Elementary Education, English, Equestrian Studies, Fine Arts, Foreign Languages, History/Political Science, International Studies, Mathematics, Philosophy/Religion, Psychobiology, Veterinary Medical Technology.

**Distribution of degrees:** The majors with the highest enrollment are biology, veterinary medical technology, and business/economics; chemistry, communications, and English have the lowest.

**Requirements:** General education requirement.

**Academic regulations:** Freshmen must maintain minimum 1.6 GPA; sophomores, 1.7 GPA; juniors, 1.85 GPA; seniors, 2.0 GPA.

**Special:** Numerous minors offered. Associate's degrees offered. Self-designed majors. Independent study. Pass/fail grading option. Internships. Preprofessional programs in law, medicine, veterinary science, and dentistry. 2-2 B.S./M.S. computer science program with Shippensburg U. 3-2 nursing program with U of Pennsylvania. 4-2 B.S./D.M.D. biodental program with U of Pennsylvania. Medical technology programs with affiliated hospitals. Washington Semester and UN Semester. Exchange programs with Gettysburg Coll and Shippensburg U. Teacher certification in elementary and secondary education. Certification in specific subject areas. Exchange program abroad in Japan (Aichi Shukutoku U). Study abroad also in other countries. ROTC at Shippensburg U.

**Academic Assistance:** Remedial study skills. Nonremedial tutoring.

**ADMISSIONS. Academic basis for candidate selection** (in order of priority): Secondary school record, standardized test scores, essay, school's recommendation, class rank.

**Nonacademic basis for candidate selection:** Character and personality are emphasized. Extracurricular participation, particular talent or ability, and alumni/ae relationship are considered.

**Requirements:** Graduation from secondary school is required; GED is accepted. 15 units and the following program of study are recommended: 4 units of English, 3 units of math, 2 units of science, 2 units of foreign language, 4 units of history. Minimum combined SAT score of 900, rank in top half of secondary school class, and minimum 2.5 GPA recommended. Conditional admission possible for applicants not meeting standard requirements. SAT is required; ACT may be substituted. Campus visit and interview recommended. Off-campus interviews available with an admissions representative.

**Procedure:** Visit college for interview by February of 12th year. Suggest filing application by March 1. Application deadline is July 1. Notification of admission on rolling basis. Reply is required by May 1. $200 nonrefundable tuition deposit. $50 nonrefundable room deposit. Freshmen accepted for terms other than fall.

**Special programs:** Admission may be deferred one year. Credit and/or placement may be granted through CEEB Advanced Placement exams for scores of 4 or higher. Credit and/or placement may be granted through CLEP general and subject exams. Credit may be granted through life experience. Early entrance/early admission program.

**Transfer students:** Transfer students accepted for terms other than fall. In fall 1993, 20% of all new students were transfers into all classes. 24 transfer applications were received, 20 were accepted. Application deadline is July 1 for fall; January 1 for spring. Minimum 2.0 GPA required. Lowest course grade accepted is "C." Maximum number of transferable credits is 22 course credits. At least 14 course credits must be completed at the college to receive degree.

**Admissions contact:** Karen Jewell, Director of Admissions. 717 264-4141, extension 223, 225.

**FINANCIAL AID. Available aid:** Pell grants, SEOG, state scholarships and grants, school scholarships and grants, private scholarships and grants, ROTC scholarships, academic merit scholarships, and aid for undergraduate foreign students. Perkins Loans (NDSL), PLUS, Stafford Loans (GSL), state loans, school loans, private loans, and SLS. Guaranteed tuition. School's own monthly payment plan.

**Financial aid statistics:** 21% of aid is not need-based. In 1993-94, 98% of all undergraduate applicants received aid; 98% of freshman applicants. Average amounts of aid awarded freshmen: Scholarships and grants, $1,885; loans, $1,927.

**Supporting data/closing dates:** FAFSA: Priority filing date is April 30; accepted on rolling basis. School's own aid application: Priority filing date is April 30; accepted on rolling basis. State aid form. Notification of awards on rolling basis.

**Financial aid contact:** Ruth K. Cramer, Director of Financial Aid. 717 264-4141, extension 224, 227.

## York College of Pennsylvania

**York, PA 17403-3426 717 846-7788**

**1994-95 Costs.** Tuition: $4,990. Room: $1,725. Board: $1,835. Fees, books, misc. academic expenses (school's estimate): $725.

**Enrollment.** Undergraduates: 1,254 men, 1,734 women (full-time). Freshman class: 2,989 applicants, 1,855 accepted, 691 enrolled. Graduate enrollment: 67 men, 36 women.

**Test score averages/ranges.** Range of SAT scores of middle 50%: 440-530 verbal, 480-570 math.

**Faculty.** 130 full-time; 180 part-time. 75% of faculty holds doctoral degree. Student/faculty ratio: 19 to 1.

**Selectivity rating.** Competitive.

**PROFILE.** York is a private, liberal arts college. It was founded as an academy in 1787, merged with York Collegiate Institute in 1929, became a two-year college in 1941, and gained four-year status in 1968. Its 80-acre campus is located in the city of York, 45 miles north of Baltimore.

**Accreditation:** MSACS. Professionally accredited by the American Medical Association (CAHEA), the National League for Nursing.

**Religious orientation:** York College of Pennsylvania is nonsectarian; no religious requirements.

**Library:** Collections totaling over 300,000 volumes, 1,400 periodical subscriptions, and 500,000 microform items.

**Special facilities/museums:** Museum, telecommunications center, science and foreign language labs.

**Athletic facilities:** Swimming pool, gymnasiums, athletic fields, track, weight rooms, tennis courts.

**STUDENT BODY. Undergraduate profile:** 61% are state residents; 19% are transfers. 1% Asian-American, 2% Black, 1% Hispanic, 95% White, 1% Other. Average age of undergraduates is 21.

**Freshman profile:** 1% of freshmen who took SAT scored 700 or over on verbal, 2% scored 700 or over on math; 11% scored 600 or over on verbal, 17% scored 600 or over on math; 51% scored 500 or over on verbal, 73% scored 500 or over on math; 96% scored 400 or over on verbal, 99% scored 400 or over on math; 100% scored 300 or over on verbal, 100% scored 300 or over on math. 99% of accepted applicants took SAT; 1% took ACT. 82% of freshmen come from public schools.

**Undergraduate achievement:** 81% of fall 1992 freshmen returned for fall 1993 term. 65% of entering class graduated. 19% of students who completed a degree program immediately went on to graduate study.

**Foreign students:** 29 students are from out of the country. Countries represented include Canada, England, India, Japan, Kenya, and Spain; 19 in all.

**PROGRAMS OF STUDY. Degrees:** B.A., B.S.

**Majors:** Accounting, Art, Behavioral Science, Biology, Chemistry, Community/Therapeutic Recreation, Computer Information Systems, Criminal Justice, Economics/Finance, Elementary Education, Engineering Management, English, English Education, Health Records Administration, History, Humanities, Latin American Studies, Long-term Care Administration, Management, Marketing, Mathematics, Medical Technology, Music, Nuclear Medicine Technology, Nursing, Office Administration, Physical Science, Political Science, Psychology, Respiratory Therapy, Secondary Education, Social Studies Education, Sociology, Speech Communications.

**Distribution of degrees:** The majors with the highest enrollment are management, elementary education, and nursing.

**Requirements:** General education requirement.

**Academic regulations:** Freshmen must maintain minimum 1.7 GPA; sophomores, juniors, seniors, 2.0 GPA.

**Special:** Minors offered in all majors. Associate's degrees offered. Double majors. Independent study. Pass/fail grading option. Internships. Preprofessional programs in law, medicine, and veterinary science. 3-2 mechanical engineering program with Columbia U. Wallops Island Marine Biology consortium. Washington Semester. Exchange program with American U. Teacher certification in early childhood, elementary, and secondary education. Exchange program abroad in England (Coll of Ripon and York St. John).

**Honors:** Honors program. Honor societies.

**Academic Assistance:** Remedial writing, math, and study skills. Nonremedial tutoring.

**STUDENT LIFE. Housing:** Students may live on or off campus. Coed, women's, and men's dorms. Sorority housing. School-owned/operated apartments. 45% of students live in college housing.

**Social atmosphere:** Hotspots for students include Murph's Study Hall, Fat Daddy's, the Gingerbread Man, York Galleria Mall, and Broolyn Alley Depot. Greeks are influential in student social life. Popular social events include Greek Week, Winter Formals, Spring Festival, and Mr. & Miss YCP Contest. "It's definitely what the student makes it," reports the student newspaper. "There aren't many options in the York area, especially if you are under 21 or opposed to drinking alcohol. A car is a must for any activities."

**Services and counseling/handicapped student services:** Placement services. Health service. Counseling services for minority, veteran, and older students. Birth control, personal, and psychological counseling. Career and academic guidance services. Religious counseling. Physically disabled student services. Tape recorders. Reader services for the blind.

**Campus organizations:** Undergraduate student government. Student newspaper (Spartan, published once/week). Literary magazine. Yearbook. Radio and TV stations. Choir, madrigal singers, stage band, theatre group, debating, Circle K, recycling committee, alcohol/drug education committee, departmental groups, special-interest groups, 70 organizations in all. 10 fraternities, no chapter houses; nine sororities, no chapter houses. 25% of men join a fraternity. 20% of women join a sorority.

**Religious organizations:** Catholic Campus Ministry, Intervarsity Christian Fellowship, Hillel, Christian Life Fellowship.

**Minority/foreign student organizations:** Black Student Union. International Student Club.

**ATHLETICS. Physical education requirements:** Four semesters of physical education required.

**Intercollegiate competition:** 10% of students participate. Baseball (M), basketball (M,W), cheerleading (W), cross-country (M), field hockey (W), golf (M), soccer (M), softball (W), swimming (M,W), tennis (M,W), track and field (outdoor) (M), volleyball (W), wrestling (M). Member of Capital Athletic Conference, NCAA Division III.

**Intramural and club sports:** 60% of students participate. Intramural basketball, flag football, floor hockey, soccer, softball, tennis, volleyball, water polo. Men's club lacrosse, rugby. Women's club soccer.

**ADMISSIONS. Academic basis for candidate selection** (in order of priority): Secondary school record, class rank, standardized test scores, school's recommendation, essay.

**Nonacademic basis for candidate selection:** Particular talent or ability is emphasized. Character and personality are important. Extracurricular participation and alumni/ae relationship are considered.

**Requirements:** Graduation from secondary school is required; GED is accepted. 15 units and the following program of study are required: 4 units of English, 3 units of math, 2 units of lab science, 2 units of foreign language, 3 units of social studies, 1 unit of electives. Minimum combined SAT score of 870, rank in top three-fifths of secondary school class, and minimum 2.5 GPA required. Audition required of music program applicants. SAT or ACT is required. PSAT is recommended. Campus visit and interview recommended. No off-campus interviews.

**Procedure:** Take SAT or ACT by March 1 of 12th year. Visit college for interview by March 1 of 12th year. Suggest filing application by March 1; no deadline. Notification of admission on rolling basis. No set date by which applicants must accept offer. $100 tuition deposit, refundable until April 15. $100 room deposit, refundable until April 15. Freshmen accepted for terms other than fall.

**Special programs:** Admission may be deferred one year. Credit may be granted through CEEB Advanced Placement for scores of 3 or higher. Credit may be granted through CLEP general and subject exams, Regents College, ACT PEP, DANTES, and challenge exams, and military and life experience. Early entrance/early admission program. Concurrent enrollment program.

**Transfer students:** Transfer students accepted for terms other than fall. In fall 1993, 19% of all new students were transfers into all classes. 548 transfer applications were received, 345 were accepted. Application deadline is rolling for fall; rolling for spring. Minimum 2.5 GPA recommended. Lowest course grade accepted is "C." Maximum number of transferable credits is 75 semester hours. At least 30 semester hours must be completed at the college to receive degree.

**Admissions contact:** Nancy Spataro, Director of Admissions. 717 849-1600.

**FINANCIAL AID. Available aid:** Pell grants, SEOG, Federal Nursing Student Scholarships, state scholarships and grants, school scholarships and grants, private scholarships and grants, academic merit scholarships, and aid for undergraduate foreign students. Perkins Loans (NDSL), PLUS, Stafford Loans (GSL), NSL, state loans, school loans, private loans, and SLS. AMS. Educational Financing Group. Installment Payment Plan.

**Financial aid statistics:** 25% of aid is not need-based. In 1993-94, 68% of all undergraduate applicants received aid; 80% of freshman applicants. Average amounts of aid awarded freshmen: Scholarships and grants, $2,680; loans, $3,095.

**Supporting data/closing dates:** FAFSA/FAF/FFS: Accepted on rolling basis. School's own aid application: Accepted on rolling basis. State aid form: Accepted on rolling basis. Notification of awards on rolling basis.

**Financial aid contact:** Calvin Williams, Director of Financial Aid. 717 846-7788, extension 226.

**STUDENT EMPLOYMENT.** College Work/Study Program. Institutional employment. 10% of full-time undergraduates work on campus during school year. Students may expect to earn an average of $1,500 during school year. Off-campus part-time employment opportunities rated "excellent."

**COMPUTER FACILITIES.** 120 IBM/IBM-compatible and Macintosh/Apple microcomputers; 25 are networked. Students may access Digital minicomputer/mainframe systems, Internet. Client/LAN operating systems include Apple/Macintosh, DOS, OS/2, X-windows, DEC. Computer languages and software packages include Design CAD, MINITAB, PageMaker, Paradox, Quattro Pro, SimScript, SPSS-X, Twin, WordPerfect, XBB, computer art, graphics, accounting, spreadsheet packages; 140 in all. Computer facilities are available to all students.

**Fees:** Computer fee is included in tuition/fees.

**Hours:** 120 hours/week.

**GRADUATE CAREER DATA.** Highest graduate school enrollments: Johns Hopkins U, Pennsylvania State U, Temple U, Towson U, U of Baltimore, U of Maryland, U of Pennsylvania, Villanova U. 39% of graduates choose careers in business and industry. Companies and businesses that hire graduates: Amp, AT&T, BMY-Combat Systems, Caterpillar, IBM, Wyeth-Ayerst, York Hospital.

# Rhode Island

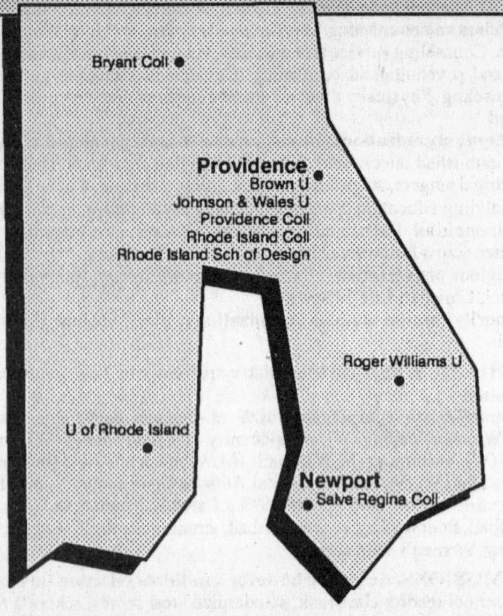


## Brown University

**Providence, RI 02912** **401 863-1000**

**1994-95 Costs.** Tuition: $19,528. Room: $3,574. Board: $2,352. Fees, books, misc. academic expenses (school's estimate): $1,220.

**Enrollment.** Undergraduates: 2,762 men, 2,881 women (full-time). Freshman class: 12,587 applicants, 3,239 accepted, 1,466 enrolled. Graduate enrollment: 935 men, 728 women.

**Test score averages/ranges.** Average SAT scores: 610 verbal, 670 math. Range of SAT scores of middle 50%: 560-680 verbal, 630-730 math. Average ACT scores: 31 composite.

**Faculty.** 551 full-time; 138 part-time. 98% of faculty holds doctoral degree. Student/faculty ratio: 9 to 1.

**Selectivity rating.** Most competitive.

**PROFILE.** Brown, founded in 1764, is a private, Ivy League, liberal arts university. Programs are offered through the College, the Graduate School, and the Program of Medicine. Its 146-acre campus is located in Providence, 45 miles from Boston.

**Accreditation:** NEASC. Professionally accredited by the Accreditation Board for Engineering and Technology.
**Religious orientation:** Brown University is nonsectarian; no religious requirements.
**Library:** Collections totaling over 2,500,000 volumes, 15,090 periodical subscriptions, and 1,000,000 microform items.
**Special facilities/museums:** Art gallery, anthropology museum, language lab, information technology center.
**Athletic facilities:** Gymnasium, basketball, racquetball, squash, tennis, and volleyball courts, swimming center, weight rooms, ice rink, athletic fields.

**STUDENT BODY. Undergraduate profile:** 3% are state residents; 7% are transfers. 14% Asian-American, 6% Black, 5% Hispanic, 1% Native American, 67% White, 7% Other. Average age of undergraduates is 19.
**Freshman profile:** 9% of freshmen who took SAT scored 700 or over on verbal, 32% scored 700 or over on math; 44% scored 600 or over on verbal, 69% scored 600 or over on math; 77% scored 500 or over on verbal, 91% scored 500 or over on math; 93% scored 400 or over on verbal, 98% scored 400 or over on math; 98% scored 300 or over on verbal, 100% scored 300 or over on math. 89% of accepted applicants took SAT; 11% took ACT. 80% of freshmen come from public schools.
**Undergraduate achievement:** 97% of fall 1992 freshmen returned for fall 1993 term. 80% of entering class graduated. 30% of students who completed a degree program immediately went on to graduate study.
**Foreign students:** 415 students are from out of the country. Countries represented include Canada, England, France, Greece, Hong Kong, and Singapore; 63 in all.

**PROGRAMS OF STUDY. Degrees:** A.B., S.B.
**Majors:** African-American Studies, American Civilization, Ancient/Medieval Culture, Ancient Studies, Anthropology, Applied Mathematics, Applied Mathematics/Biomedical Science, Applied Mathematics/Computer Science, Applied Mathematics/Economics, Applied Mathematics/Psychology, Aquatic Biology, Art, Biochemistry, Bioelectrical Engineering, Biological/Medical Sciences, Biomedical Engineering, Biomedical Ethics, Biophysics, Chemistry, Chinese, Classics, Cognitive Science, Comparative Literature, Computer Science, Computer Technology, Economics, Educational Studies, Energy Studies, Engineering, English, Environmental Studies, Ethics/Political Philosophy, French Studies, Geological Sciences, German, Greek, Health/Society, Hispanic Studies, History, Human Biology, International Relations, Italian Studies, Judaic Studies, Latin, Latin American Studies, Linguistics, Literature, Literature/Society, Logic/Philosophy of Science, Mathematics, Medieval Studies, Music, Neural Science, Operations Research, Organizational Behavior, Philosophy, Physics, Political Science, Portuguese/Brazilian Studies, Psycholinguistics, Psychology, Religious Studies, Renaissance Studies, Russian Language/Literature, Russian Studies, Semiotics, Sociology, Theatre Arts, Urban Studies, Women's Studies.
**Distribution of degrees:** The majors with the highest enrollment are biological sciences, history, and engineering; French studies, geological sciences, and physics have the lowest.
**Special:** Self-designed majors. Double majors. Dual degrees. Independent study. Accelerated study. Pass/fail grading option. Internships. Graduate school at which undergraduates may take graduate-level courses. Five-year A.B./M.A., A.B./Sc.B., and Sc.B./M.S. programs. Eight-year continuum in medicine. Member of Ivy League Consortium and COFHE. Exchange programs with Dartmouth Medical Sch, Rhode Island Sch of Design, and Tougaloo Coll. Teacher certification in secondary education. Study abroad in Barbados, Brazil, China, Denmark, Egypt, England, France, Germany, Hong Kong, India, Italy, Japan, Korea, Mexico, Nigeria, Poland, Sweden, and Tanzania. ROTC at Providence Coll.
**Honors:** Phi Beta Kappa. Honors program.
**Academic Assistance:** Nonremedial tutoring.

**STUDENT LIFE. Housing:** All freshmen, sophomores, and juniors must live on campus. Coed and women's dorms. Sorority and fraternity housing. School-owned/operated apartments. Graduate student housing. Language and cooperative houses. Social dorms. 85% of students live in college housing.
**Social atmosphere:** According to the student newspaper, "Social life is very strong and well-integrated into campus life." Popular social events held during the year include Spring Weekend and Homecoming Weekend. On campus, students meet at the university's snack bars, the Blueroom, and the Underground pub. Off campus, Brown students frequent Oliver's.
**Services and counseling/handicapped student services:** Placement services. Health service. Women's center. Day care. Counseling services for minority and older students. Birth control, personal, and psychological counseling. Career and academic guidance services. Physically disabled student services. Learning disabled services. Notetaking services. Tape recorders. Tutors. Reader services for the blind.
**Campus organizations:** Undergraduate student government. Student newspaper (Brown Daily Herald). Literary magazine. Yearbook. Radio and TV stations. Chorus, orchestra, jazz band, a cappella singing groups, ballroom dance club, drama groups, Community Outreach, political groups, 240 organizations in all. 11 fraternities, all with chapter houses; two sororities, all with chapter houses. 12% of men join a fraternity. 2% of women join a sorority.
**Religious organizations:** Numerous religious groups.
**Minority/foreign student organizations:** African Students Association, Latin-American Student Organization, Asian-American Students Association, Native Americans at Brown, Third World Center. International Student Organization.

**ATHLETICS. Physical education requirements:** None.
**Intercollegiate competition:** 20% of students participate. Baseball (M), basketball (M,W), crew (M,W), cross-country (M,W), diving (M,W), fencing (M,W), field hockey (W), football (M), golf (M), gymnastics (W), ice hockey (M,W), lacrosse (M,W), soccer (M,W), softball (W), squash (M,W), swimming (M,W), tennis (M,W), track and field (indoor) (M,W), track and field (outdoor) (M,W), volleyball (W), water polo (M), wrestling (M). Member of ECAC, Ivy League, NCAA Division I, NCAA Division I-AA for football.
**Intramural and club sports:** 40% of students participate. Intramural basketball, ice hockey, soccer, softball, street hockey, tennis, touch football, ultimate frisbee, volleyball. Men's club Alpine skiing, cheerleading, fencing, golf, horsemanship, martial arts, Nordic skiing, rugby, sailing, ultimate frisbee, volleyball, water polo. Women's club Alpine skiing, cheerleading, fencing, golf, horsemanship, martial arts, Nordic skiing, rugby, sailing, ultimate frisbee, water polo.

**ADMISSIONS. Academic basis for candidate selection** (in order of priority): Secondary school record, school's recommendation, class rank, essay, standardized test scores.
**Nonacademic basis for candidate selection:** Character and personality are emphasized. Extracurricular participation and particular talent or ability are important. Geographical distribution and alumni/ae relationship are considered.
**Requirements:** Graduation from secondary school is required; GED is not accepted. 16 units and the following program of study are required: 4 units of English, 3 units of math, 3 units of science including 2 units of lab, 3 units of foreign language, 2 units of history, 1 unit of academic elective. Slightly different distributions of units required of applicants to Sc.B. program and eight-year liberal arts/medical education program. SAT is required; ACT may be substituted. ACH required. Campus visit recommended. Off-campus interviews available with an alumni representative.
**Procedure:** Take SAT or ACT by January of 12th year. Take ACH by January of 12th year. Application deadline is January 1. Notification of admission by April 1. Reply is required by May 1. Freshmen accepted for terms other than fall.
**Special programs:** Admission may be deferred one year. Placement may be granted through CEEB Advanced Placement exams for scores of 4 or higher. Early decision program. In fall 1993, 1,928 applied for early decision and 544 were accepted. Deadline for applying for early decision is November 1. Early entrance/early admission program.
**Transfer students:** Transfer students accepted for terms other than fall. In fall 1993, 7% of all new students were transfers into all classes. 639 transfer applications were received, 176 were accepted. Application deadline is April 1 for fall; April 1 of previous year for spring. Lowest course grade accepted is "C." Maximum number of transferable courses is 15. At least 15 courses must be completed at the university to receive degree.
**Admissions contact:** Eric Widmer, Ph.D., Dean of Admission and Financial Aid. 401 863-2378.

**FINANCIAL AID. Available aid:** Pell grants, SEOG, state scholarships and grants, school scholarships and grants, private scholarships and grants, and aid for undergraduate foreign students. Perkins Loans (NDSL), PLUS, Stafford Loans (GSL), school loans, and SLS. Knight Tuition Plans and deferred payment plan.
**Financial aid statistics:** Average amounts of aid awarded freshmen: Scholarships and grants, $10,313; loans, $3,200.
**Supporting data/closing dates:** FAFSA/FAF/FFS: Deadline is February 1. School's own aid application: Deadline is January 1. State aid form: Deadline is February 1. Income tax forms: Deadline is April 15. Notification of awards begins April 2.
**Financial aid contact:** Fernando de Necochea, Director of Financial Aid. 401 863-2721.

**STUDENT EMPLOYMENT.** College Work/Study Program. Institutional employment. 55% of full-time undergraduates work on campus during school year. Students may expect to earn an average of $1,600 during school year. Off-campus part-time employment opportunities rated "good."

**COMPUTER FACILITIES.** 300 IBM/IBM-compatible and Macintosh/Apple microcomputers; all are networked. Students may access IBM, SUN minicomputer/mainframe systems, BITNET, Internet. Residence halls may be equipped with modems. Client/LAN operating systems include Apple/Macintosh, DOS, OS/2, LocalTalk/AppleTalk, Microsoft, Novell. Numerous computer languages and software programs available. Computer facilities are available to all students.
**Fees:** None.
**Hours:** 24 hours.

**GRADUATE CAREER DATA.** Graduate school percentages: 10% enter law school. 10% enter medical school. 1% enter graduate business programs. 9% enter graduate arts and sciences programs.

**PROMINENT ALUMNI/AE.** Thomas Watson, Jr., former CEO, IBM; John Sculley III, former president/CEO, Apple Computers; Charles Evans Hughes, lawyer; Ted Turner, entertainment industry; John F. Kennedy, Jr., lawyer.

# Bryant College

**Smithfield, RI 02917-1285 — 401 232-6000**

**1994-95 Costs.** Tuition: $12,600. Room: $3,640. Board: $2,670. Fees, books, misc. academic expenses (school's estimate): $500.
**Enrollment.** Undergraduates: 1,472 men, 1,084 women (full-time). Freshman class: 2,221 applicants, 1,775 accepted, 631 enrolled. Graduate enrollment: 413 men, 282 women.
**Test score averages/ranges.** Average SAT scores: 450 verbal, 540 math. Range of SAT scores of middle 50%: 400-480 verbal, 480-580 math. Average ACT scores: 22 English, 24 math, 23 composite.
**Faculty.** 135 full-time; 77 part-time. 84% of faculty holds doctoral degree. Student/faculty ratio: 19 to 1.
**Selectivity rating.** Less competitive.

**PROFILE.** Bryant, founded in 1863, is private college of business studies. Its 387-acre campus is located in Smithfield, 12 miles from Providence.

**Accreditation:** NEASC.
**Religious orientation:** Bryant College is nonsectarian; no religious requirements.
**Library:** Collections totaling over 129,249 volumes, 1,376 periodical subscriptions, and 16,606 microform items.
**Special facilities/museums:** Technology center.
**Athletic facilities:** Gymnasium, basketball, racquetball, tennis, and volleyball courts, athletic fields, fitness center, track, swimming pool, cross-country trails, golf putting green and practice tee.

**STUDENT BODY. Undergraduate profile:** 16% are state residents; 20% are transfers. 2% Asian-American, 1.8% Black, 2.2% Hispanic, .2% Native American, 91.3% White, 2.5% Other. Average age of undergraduates is 20.
**Freshman profile:** 2% of freshmen who took SAT scored 700 or over on math; 2% scored 600 or over on verbal, 21% scored 600 or over on math; 22% scored 500 or over on verbal, 69% scored 500 or over on math; 79% scored 400 or over on verbal, 98% scored 400 or over on math; 100% scored 300 or over on verbal, 100% scored 300 or over on math. 95% of accepted applicants took SAT; 5% took ACT. 77% of freshmen come from public schools.
**Undergraduate achievement:** 85% of fall 1992 freshmen returned for fall 1993 term. 73% of entering class graduated. 5% of students who completed a degree program went on to graduate study within one year.
**Foreign students:** 59 students are from out of the country. Countries represented include Ecuador, Hong Kong, Malaysia, Sweden, the former Yugoslav Republics, and the United Kingdom; 37 in all.

**PROGRAMS OF STUDY. Degrees:** B.A., B.S.Bus.Admin.
**Majors:** Accounting, Applied Actuarial Mathematics, Communications, Computer Information Systems, Economics, English, Finance, History, International Studies, Management, Marketing.
**Distribution of degrees:** The majors with the highest enrollment are management, accounting, and finance; applied actuarial mathematics, economics, and communications have the lowest.
**Requirements:** General education requirement.
**Academic regulations:** Juniors must maintain minimum 2.0 GPA; seniors, 2.0 GPA.
**Special:** Associate's degrees offered. Double majors. Independent study. Accelerated study. Internships. Five-year B.S./M.B.A. program. Sea Semester. Exchange programs abroad in Austria (U of Salzburg), China (Peking U), England (City of London Polytech, U of London-London Sch of Economics), and Russia (Leningrad Polytech Inst). Study abroad also in Australia, Canada, France, Germany, Israel, Italy, Korea, Spain, and Switzerland. ROTC.
**Honors:** Honors program. Honor societies.
**Academic Assistance:** Remedial reading, writing, math, and study skills. Nonremedial tutoring.

**STUDENT LIFE. Housing:** Students may live on or off campus. Coed and women's dorms. Sorority and fraternity housing. School-owned/operated apartments. Graduate housing. 82% of students live in college housing.
**Social atmosphere:** According to the editor of the student newspaper, students like to hang out at dorms one and two, the Rotunda, Kirby's Pub, and Country Comfort. The most influential groups on campus are the newspaper staff, the Greeks, and the Student Senate. Annual events enjoyed by students are Spring Weekend, Un-Homecoming Weekend, and Northern Rhode Island Special Olympics.
**Services and counseling/handicapped student services:** Placement services. Health service. Counseling services for minority students. Personal and psychological counseling. Career and academic guidance services. Religious counseling. Physically disabled student services. Learning disabled services. Notetaking services. Tape recorders. Tutors. Reader services for the blind.
**Campus organizations:** Undergraduate student government. Student newspaper (Archway, published once/week). Yearbook. Radio station. Bryant Players, dance club, Big Sisters, Hunger Coalition, SADD, environmental action club, programming board, Commuter Connection, Student Alumni Association, adventure club, athletic, academic, professional, and special-interest groups, 61 organizations in all. Nine fraternities, no chapter houses; five sororities, no chapter houses. 20% of men join a fraternity. 18% of women join a sorority.
**Religious organizations:** Hillel, Newman Club.
**Minority/foreign student organizations:** Multicultural Student Union. International Student Organization.

**ATHLETICS. Physical education requirements:** None.
**Intercollegiate competition:** 11% of students participate. Baseball (M), basketball (M,W), cheerleading (W), cross-country (M,W), golf (M,W), soccer (M,W), softball (W), tennis (M,W), track (outdoor) (M,W), track and field (outdoor) (M,W), volleyball (W). Member of ECAC, NCAA Division II, Northeast 10.
**Intramural and club sports:** 90% of students participate. Intramural basketball, flag football, floor hockey, indoor soccer, racquetball, softball, tennis, volleyball. Men's club Alpine skiing, bowling, ice hockey, lacrosse, martial arts, racquetball, rugby, ultimate frisbee, volleyball. Women's club Alpine skiing, field hockey, frisbee, martial arts, racquetball, rugby, volleyball.

**ADMISSIONS. Academic basis for candidate selection** (in order of priority): Secondary school record, standardized test scores, class rank, school's recommendation, essay.
**Nonacademic basis for candidate selection:** Extracurricular participation is emphasized. Particular talent or ability and geographical distribution are important. Character and personality and alumni/ae relationship are considered.
**Requirements:** Graduation from secondary school is required; GED is accepted. 16 units and the following program of study are required: 4 units of English, 3 units of math, 1 unit of lab science, 2 units of social studies, 6 units of electives. EOP for applicants not normally admissible. SAT or ACT is required. Campus visit and interview recommended. No off-campus interviews.
**Procedure:** Take SAT or ACT by January of 12th year. Notification of admission on rolling basis. Reply is required by May 1. $100 nonrefundable tuition deposit. $100 nonrefundable room deposit. Freshmen accepted for terms other than fall.
**Special programs:** Admission may be deferred one year. Credit and/or placement may be granted through CEEB Advanced Placement exams for scores of 3 or higher. Credit may be granted through DANTES and challenge exams, and military experience. Early decision program. In fall 1993, 97 applied for early decision and 91 were accepted. Deadline for applying for early decision is November 15. Early entrance/early admission program.
**Transfer students:** Transfer students accepted for terms other than fall. In fall 1993, 20% of all new students were transfers into all classes. 334 transfer applications were received, 275 were accepted. Application deadline is rolling for fall; rolling for spring. Minimum 2.0 GPA required. Lowest course grade accepted is "C." Maximum number of transferable credits is 60 semester hours from a two-year school and 90 semester hours from a four-year school. At least 30 semester hours must be completed at the college to receive degree.
**Admissions contact:** Roy A. Nelson, M.A., Director of Admission. 401 232-6100, 800 622-7001.

**FINANCIAL AID. Available aid:** Pell grants, SEOG, state scholarships and grants, school scholarships and grants, private scholarships and grants, ROTC scholarships, academic merit scholarships, and athletic scholarships. Perkins Loans (NDSL), PLUS, Stafford Loans (GSL), state loans, school loans, private loans, and SLS. AMS, family tuition reduction, and guaranteed tuition.
**Financial aid statistics:** 10% of aid is not need-based. In 1993-94, 83% of all undergraduate applicants received aid; 68% of freshman applicants. Average amounts of aid awarded freshmen: Scholarships and grants, $6,745; loans, $2,625.
**Supporting data/closing dates:** FAFSA/FAF: Priority filing date is February 15. School's own aid application: Priority filing date is February 15. Income tax forms: Priority filing date is May 1. Notification of awards begins in March.
**Financial aid contact:** James C. Dorian, M.B.A., Director of Financial Aid. 401 232-6020, 800 248-4036.

**STUDENT EMPLOYMENT.** College Work/Study Program. Institutional employment. 33% of full-time undergraduates work on campus during school year. Students may expect to earn an average of $1,200 during school year. Off-campus part-time employment opportunities rated "fair."

**COMPUTER FACILITIES.** 200 IBM/IBM-compatible and Macintosh/Apple microcomputers; all are networked. Students may access Digital minicomputer/mainframe systems, Internet. Residence halls may be equipped with networked microcomputers. Client/LAN operating systems include Novell. Computer languages and software packages include BASIC, C, COBOL, Corel Draw, dBASE, FORTRAN, Harvard Graphics, Lotus 1-2-3, Minitab, Paradox, Pascal, PC-Write, Peach Tree, Quattro, Q & A, Real World Accounting, Twin, WordPerfect; 100 in all. Computer facilities are available to all students.
**Fees:** Computer fee is included in tuition/fees.
**Hours:** 7 AM-midnight.

**GRADUATE CAREER DATA.** Graduate school percentages: 2% enter law school. 3% enter graduate business programs. Highest graduate school enrollments: Bentley Coll, Bryant Coll, U of Hartford, New England Sch of Law. 96% of graduates choose careers in business and industry. Companies and businesses that hire graduates: Big Six accounting firms, Fleet Bank, Metropolitan Life, Pratt & Whitney, State Street Bank, T.J. Maxx, Toys R Us, Travelers.

**PROMINENT ALUMNI/AE.** Mary D. Decelles, partner-in-charge, KPMG Peat Marwick; Raymond Iannetta, chairman, Key-Tech, Inc.; Joseph Lemieux, president/CEO, Owens Illinois, Inc.

# Johnson & Wales University

**Providence, RI 02903** **401 456-1000**

**1993-94 Costs.** Tuition: $9,216. Room & board: $4,485. Fees, books, misc. academic expenses (school's estimate): $600.
**Enrollment.** Undergraduates: 3,848 men, 3,131 women (full-time). Freshman class: 14,545 applicants, 12,403 accepted, 2,467 enrolled. Graduate enrollment: 211 men, 173 women.
**Test score averages/ranges.** Average SAT scores: 400 verbal, 420 math.
**Faculty.** 164 full-time; 99 part-time. 5% of faculty holds highest degree in specific field.
**Selectivity rating.** Less competitive.

**PROFILE.** Johnson & Wales, founded in 1914, is a private university. Programs are offered in Business, Food Service, Hospitality, Secretarial, and Teacher Education. Its 100-acre campus is located in Providence.

**Accreditation:** CCA-ACICS.
**Religious orientation:** Johnson & Wales University is nonsectarian; no religious requirements.
**Library:** Collections totaling over 28,242 volumes, 350 periodical subscriptions, and 14,500 microform items.
**Special facilities/museums:** Data processing, retail, hotel, restaurant, and travel centers, secretarial science lab.
**Athletic facilities:** Gymnasiums, swimming pools, racquetball and squash courts, weight rooms, fitness centers.

**STUDENT BODY. Undergraduate profile:** 16% are state residents; 21% are transfers. 2% Asian-American, 10% Black, 5% Hispanic, 78% White, 5% Other. Average age of undergraduates is 20.
**Freshman profile:** 65% of accepted applicants took SAT. 80% of freshmen come from public schools.
**Undergraduate achievement:** 72% of fall 1992 freshmen returned for fall 1993 term. 54% of students who completed a degree program immediately went on to graduate study.
**Foreign students:** 200 students are from out of the country. Countries represented include China, India, Japan, Taiwan, Thailand, and the Netherland Antilles; 77 in all.

**PROGRAMS OF STUDY. Degrees:** B.S.
**Majors:** Accounting, Administrative Management, Advertising Communication, Court Reporting, Culinary Arts, Electronic Engineering Technology, Equestrian Arts, Equine Business Management, Equine Studies, Fashion Merchandising, Food Marketing, Food Service Management, Health Care/Hospitality Management, Hospitality Management, Hospitality Sales/Meeting Management, Hotel/Restaurant/Institutional Management, Information Science, Management, Marketing, Pastry Arts, Retail Merchandise Management, Travel/Tourism Management, Travel/Tourism Marketing.
**Distribution of degrees:** The major with the highest enrollment is culinary arts; accounting has the lowest.
**Academic regulations:** Minimum 2.0 GPA must be maintained.
**Special:** Associate's degrees offered. Double majors. Internships. Cooperative education programs. Certification in specific subject areas. Cooperative education program with Dellecurio Hotels (Switzerland). Exchange program abroad in Ireland (Galway Tech Coll). Study abroad also in Austria, England, France, Holland, Hungary, and Israel. ROTC at Providence Coll.
**Honors:** Honors program. Honor societies.
**Academic Assistance:** Remedial math and study skills. Nonremedial tutoring.

**STUDENT LIFE. Housing:** Unmarried freshmen under age 21 must live on campus unless living with family. Coed and women's dorms. 39% of students live in college housing.
**Social atmosphere:** Students report that the art museum, theatres, and nightspots in Providence offer excellent cultural opportunities. The university sponsors dances as well as concerts featuring national headliners. Favorite gathering spots include the City Club, a university-sponsored nonalcoholic nightclub, JW Maxwell's, the Recess Pub, Mama Mia's, and the Culinary Arts Center Gym. Popular campus events include Spring Weekend, Parents Weekend, Mocktail Weekend, the Battle of the Dorms, and the annual Concert on Rocky Point Park.
**Services and counseling/handicapped student services:** Placement services. Women's center. Counseling services for minority and older students. Personal and psychological counseling. Career and academic guidance services. Physically disabled student services. Learning disabled services. Notetaking services. Tape recorders. Tutors. Reader services for the blind.
**Campus organizations:** Student newspaper (Campus Herald, published once/week). Yearbook. Cake decorating, ice sculpture, and wine tasting clubs, drama group, film committee, fashion show club, Future Homemakers of America, Student Alumni Association, Lifesigns, nutrition club, ski club, 62 organizations in all. 10 fraternities, no chapter houses; nine sororities, no chapter houses. 11% of men join a fraternity. 7% of women join a sorority.
**Religious organizations:** Hillel, Christian Student Club.
**Minority/foreign student organizations:** Black Student Union. International Club, Asian Student Association.

**ATHLETICS. Physical education requirements:** None.
**Intercollegiate competition:** 4% of students participate.
**Intramural and club sports:** 8% of students participate. Intramural basketball, flag football, floor hockey, soccer, softball, volleyball. Men's club baseball, basketball, cheerleading, golf, ice hockey, soccer, tennis, volleyball. Women's club basketball, cheerleading, golf, soccer, softball, tennis, volleyball.

**ADMISSIONS. Academic basis for candidate selection** (in order of priority): Secondary school record, class rank, standardized test scores, school's recommendation, essay.
**Nonacademic basis for candidate selection:** Character and personality are important. Extracurricular participation, particular talent or ability, and alumni/ae relationship are considered.
**Requirements:** Graduation from secondary school is required; GED is accepted. 9 units and the following program of study are recommended: 4 units of English, 2 units of math, 1 unit of science, 2 units of social studies. Rank in top three-quarters of secondary class recommended. SAT is recommended; ACT may be substituted. Campus visit and interview recommended. Off-campus interviews available with an admissions representative.
**Procedure:** Notification of admission on rolling basis. No set date by which candidate must accept offer. $100 refundable tuition deposit. $100 refundable room deposit. Freshmen accepted for terms other than fall.
**Special programs:** Admission may be deferred one year. Credit and/or placement may be granted through CEEB Advanced Placement exams for scores of 3 or higher. Credit and/or placement may be granted through CLEP general and subject exams. Credit and placement may be granted through life experience. Early entrance/early admission program. Concurrent enrollment program.
**Transfer students:** Transfer students accepted for terms other than fall. In fall 1993, 21% of all new students were transfers into all classes. 1,102 transfer applications were received, 964 were accepted. Application deadline is rolling for fall; rolling for spring. Minimum 2.0 GPA recommended. Lowest course grade accepted is "C." Maximum number of transferable credits is 30 quarter hours from a two-year school and 90 quarter hours from a four-year school. At least 10 quarter hours must be completed at the university to receive degree.
**Admissions contact:** Marie McGovern/William Priante, Director of Business Admissions/Director of Culinary Admissions: 800 343-2565.

**FINANCIAL AID. Available aid:** Pell grants, SEOG, state scholarships and grants, school scholarships and grants, and private scholarships and grants. Perkins Loans (NDSL), PLUS, Stafford Loans (GSL), and SLS. AMS, family tuition reduction, and guaranteed tuition.
**Financial aid statistics:** 23% of aid is not need-based. In 1993-94, 98% of all undergraduate applicants received aid; 98% of freshman applicants. Average amounts of aid awarded freshmen: Scholarships and grants, $1,823; loans, $2,344.
**Supporting data/closing dates:** FAFSA/FAF/FFS: Accepted on rolling basis. School's own aid application. Notification of awards begins March 1.
**Financial aid contact:** Annette Cataldo, Director of Financial Services. 401 456-1040.

**STUDENT EMPLOYMENT.** College Work/Study Program. Institutional employment. Freshmen are discouraged from working during their first term. Off-campus part-time employment opportunities rated "good."

**COMPUTER FACILITIES.** 120 IBM/IBM-compatible microcomputers. Students may access IBM, NCR minicomputer/mainframe systems. Computer languages and software packages include COBOL, dBASE, Grammatik, Lotus 1-2-3, Pascal, RPG, Windows, WordPerfect. Computer facilities are available to all students.
**Fees:** None.
**Hours:** 7 AM-10 PM.

**GRADUATE CAREER DATA.** Highest graduate school enrollments: U of Connecticut, Florida International U, Johnson & Wales U, U of Nevada at Las Vegas. 50% of graduates choose careers in business and industry. Companies and businesses that hire graduates: Professional Food Service Mgt., Gilbert Robinson, Marriot Corp., Walt Disney World, Hyatt Hotels, Harrah's/Holiday Corp., Caesar's Corp., Kinney Corp.; travel agencies, restaurants, and retail stores.

# Providence College

**Providence, RI 02918** **401 865-1000**

**1993-94 Costs.** Tuition: $13,500. Room: $2,800. Board: $3,100. Fees, books, misc. academic expenses (school's estimate): $710.
**Enrollment.** Undergraduates: 1,648 men, 1,964 women (full-time). Freshman class: 5,138 applicants, 3,346 accepted, 973 enrolled. Graduate enrollment: 285 men, 506 women.
**Test score averages/ranges.** Average SAT scores: 502 verbal, 559 math. Range of SAT scores of middle 50%: 450-540 verbal, 500-600 math. Average ACT scores: 23 English, 25 math, 24 composite.
**Faculty.** 257 full-time; 55 part-time. 74% of faculty holds doctoral degree. Student/faculty ratio: 14 to 1.
**Selectivity rating.** Competitive.

**PROFILE.** Providence is a church-affiliated, liberal arts college. Founded in 1917, it adopted coeducation in 1971. Its 105-acre campus is located in downtown Providence.

**Accreditation:** NEASC. Professionally accredited by the Council on Social Work Education, the National Council for Accreditation of Teacher Education.
**Religious orientation:** Providence College is affiliated with the Roman Catholic Church (Dominican Fathers); two semesters of religion required.
**Library:** Collections totaling over 307,655 volumes, 1,950 periodical subscriptions, and 25,709 microform items.
**Special facilities/museums:** Art gallery, theatre, science center complex, language labs.
**Athletic facilities:** Recreation center, basketball, racquetball, tennis, and volleyball courts, gymnasium, swimming pool, track, weight room, ice rink, baseball and soccer fields.

**STUDENT BODY. Undergraduate profile:** 14% are state residents; 7% are transfers. 2% Asian-American, 4% Black, 3% Hispanic, 90% White, 1% Other. Average age of undergraduates is 20.
**Freshman profile:** 2% of freshmen who took SAT scored 700 or over on math; 7% scored 600 or over on verbal, 25% scored 600 or over on math; 46% scored 500 or over on verbal, 75% scored 500 or over on math; 100% scored 400 or over on verbal, 100% scored 400 or over on math. 1% of freshmen who took ACT scored 30 or over on English, 6% scored 30 or over on math, 2% scored 30 or over on composite; 39% scored 24 or over on English,

38% scored 24 or over on math, 45% scored 24 or over on composite; 99% scored 18 or over on English, 94% scored 18 or over on math, 92% scored 18 or over on composite; 100% scored 12 or over on English, 100% scored 12 or over on math, 100% scored 12 or over on composite. 98% of accepted applicants took SAT; 7% took ACT. 62% of freshmen come from public schools.
**Undergraduate achievement:** 96% of fall 1992 freshmen returned for fall 1993 term. 95% of entering class graduated.
**Foreign students:** 29 students are from out of the country. Countries represented include Canada, Ecuador, England, Ireland, Japan, and Switzerland; 16 in all.

**PROGRAMS OF STUDY. Degrees:** B.A., B.S.
**Majors:** Accountancy, American Studies, Art, Art History, Biology, Business, Chemistry, Clinical Chemistry, Computer Science, Economics, English, Finance, General Social Studies, Health Policy/Management, History, Humanities, Instrumentation/Computation, Latin American Studies, Management, Marketing, Mathematics, Modern Languages, Music, Philosophy, Political Science, Psychology, Secondary Education, Sociology/Social Work, Special/Elementary Education, Systems Science/Engineering, Theatre Arts, Theology.
**Distribution of degrees:** The majors with the highest enrollment are business, English, and history; theatre arts, music, and Latin American studies have the lowest.
**Requirements:** General education requirement.
**Academic regulations:** Freshmen must maintain minimum 1.6 GPA; sophomores, 1.8 GPA; juniors, 2.0 GPA; seniors, 2.0 GPA.
**Special:** Minors offered in many majors and in anthropology and religious studies. Accelerated course work and tutorials for underclass students; emphasis on research during academic year and summer for upperclass students. Four-year individualized program in engineering systems science. Concentration in public administration. Early Identification Program with Brown U Medical Sch. Honors program and five-year M.B.A. also offered. Self-designed majors. Double majors. Dual degrees. Independent study. Accelerated study. Pass/fail grading option. Internships. Graduate school at which undergraduates may take graduate-level courses. Preprofessional programs in law, medicine, dentistry, and optometry. 3-2 engineering programs with Columbia U and Washington U. Five-year M.B.A. program. Teacher certification in elementary, secondary, and special education. Certification in specific subject areas. Exchange programs abroad in England (Blackfriars/Oxford U), Japan (Kansai-Gaidai U), and Switzerland (U of Fribourg). Study abroad also in Australia, Canada, France, Ireland, Italy, and Spain. ROTC.
**Honors:** Honors program. Honor societies.
**Academic Assistance:** Nonremedial tutoring.

**STUDENT LIFE. Housing:** All freshmen and sophomores must live on campus. Women's and men's dorms. School-owned/operated apartments. Off-campus privately-owned housing. 67% of students live in college housing.
**Services and counseling/handicapped student services:** Placement services. Health service. Counseling services for minority, military, and older students. Personal and psychological counseling. Career and academic guidance services. Religious counseling. Physically disabled student services. Learning disabled services. Notetaking services. Tape recorders. Tutors. Reader services for the blind.
**Campus organizations:** Undergraduate student government. Student newspaper (Cowl, published once/week). Literary magazine. Yearbook. Radio station. Band, chorus, theatre, dance team, debating, literary, accounting and business societies, athletic clubs, Friars Club, Young Democrats, Young Republicans, Big Brothers/Big Sisters, PC Pride, Pre-law Society, Student Congress, Board of Programmers, Social Work Alliance, Amnesty International, Environmental & Wildlife Club, 63 organizations in all.
**Religious organizations:** Knights of Columbus, Pastoral Council.
**Minority/foreign student organizations:** Afro-American Society, Board of Multicultural Student Affairs, NAACP, Students Organized Against Racism. International Club.

**ATHLETICS. Physical education requirements:** None.
**Intercollegiate competition:** 10% of students participate. Baseball (M), basketball (M,W), cheerleading (M,W), cross-country (M,W), diving (M,W), field hockey (W), golf (M), ice hockey (M,W), lacrosse (M), soccer (M,W), softball (W), swimming (M,W), tennis (M,W), track (indoor) (M,W), track (outdoor) (M,W), track and field (indoor) (M,W), track and field (outdoor) (M,W), volleyball (W). Member of Big East Conference, ECAC, Hockey East, NCAA Division I.
**Intramural and club sports:** 60% of students participate. Intramural basketball, field hockey, flag football, ice hockey, inner-tube water polo, running, soccer, softball, street hockey, tennis, ultimate frisbee, volleyball, walleyball, Wiffle ball. Men's club rugby, volleyball. Women's club rugby.

**ADMISSIONS. Academic basis for candidate selection** (in order of priority): Secondary school record, standardized test scores, class rank, essay, school's recommendation.
**Nonacademic basis for candidate selection:** Character and personality and extracurricular participation are emphasized. Particular talent or ability is important. Geographical distribution and alumni/ae relationship are considered.
**Requirements:** Graduation from secondary school is required; GED is not accepted. 18 units and the following program of study are required: 4 units of English, 2 units of math, 2 units of lab science, 3 units of foreign language, 2 units of social studies, 1 unit of history, 4 units of electives. SAT scores of 510 verbal and 550 math (composite ACT score of 25), rank in top third of secondary school class, and minimum 3.0 GPA recommended. 4 units of math and science recommended of biology, chemistry, and pre-engineering program applicants. SAT or ACT is required. ACH recommended. Campus visit and interview recommended. No off-campus interviews.
**Procedure:** Take SAT or ACT by January of 12th year. Take ACH by December of 12th year. Visit college for interview by February 1 of 12th year. Suggest filing application by January 15. Application deadline is February 1. Notification of admission by April 1. Reply is required by May 1. $300 nonrefundable tuition deposit. Freshmen accepted for terms other than fall.
**Special programs:** Admission may be deferred one year. Credit may be granted through CEEB Advanced Placement for scores of 4 or higher. Credit may be granted through CLEP general and subject exams. Early decision program. In fall 1993, 467 applied for early decision and 274 were accepted. Deadline for applying for early decision is December 15. Early entrance/early admission program.
**Transfer students:** Transfer students accepted for terms other than fall. In fall 1993, 7% of all new students were transfers into all classes. 260 transfer applications were received, 162 were accepted. Application deadline is March 15 for fall; December 15 for spring. Minimum 3.0 GPA recommended. Lowest course grade accepted is "C." Maximum number of transferable credits is 56 credits. At least 60 credits must be completed at the college to receive degree.
**Admissions contact:** Michael G. Backes, M.A., Dean of Admissions. 401 865-2535.

**FINANCIAL AID. Available aid:** Pell grants, SEOG, state scholarships, school scholarships and grants, private scholarships and grants, ROTC scholarships, academic merit scholarships, and athletic scholarships. Perkins Loans (NDSL), PLUS, Stafford Loans (GSL), and SLS. Family tuition reduction. Tuition Payment Agreement.
**Financial aid statistics:** 1% of aid is not need-based. In 1993-94, 100% of all undergraduate applicants received aid. Average amounts of aid awarded freshmen: Scholarships and grants, $7,500; loans, $3,625.
**Supporting data/closing dates:** FAFSA/FAF/FFS: Deadline is February 15. Income tax forms: Deadline is May 15. Notification of awards begins April 1.
**Financial aid contact:** Herbert J. D'Arcy, Jr., M.A., Executive Director of Financial Aid. 401 865-2286.

**STUDENT EMPLOYMENT.** College Work/Study Program. Institutional employment. 35% of full-time undergraduates work on campus during school year. Students may expect to earn an average of $1,600 during school year. Off-campus part-time employment opportunities rated "good."

**COMPUTER FACILITIES.** 85 IBM/IBM-compatible and RISC-/UNIX-based microcomputers. Client/LAN operating systems include Apple/Macintosh, DOS. Computer languages and software packages include BASIC, C, Chip, COBOL, dBASE, Designer, FORTRAN, Lotus 1-2-3, Manuscript Manager, Modern Physics, Natural Science, NewWord, Pathfinder, Peachtree/Turbo Tax, Pascal, Pro3D, SPSS, Systat, Turbo Pascal, SuperCalc II, WordPerfect. Computer facilities are available to all students.
**Fees:** Computer fee is included in tuition/fees.
**Hours:** Noon-midn. (Su); 8 AM-midn. (M-Th); 8 AM-4 PM (F); 9 AM-5 PM (Sa).

**GRADUATE CAREER DATA.** Graduate school percentages: 8% enter law school. 3% enter medical school. 1% enter dental school. 4% enter graduate business programs. 12% enter graduate arts and sciences programs. Companies and businesses that hire graduates: Big Six accounting firms, Chase Manhattan Bank, Fleet Bank, Marriott Corporation, Sara Lee Foods, Stouffer Foods.

**PROMINENT ALUMNI/AE.** John Quinn, editor, *USA Today*; Christopher Dodd, U.S. senator, Connecticut; Dr. Robert Gallo, AIDS researcher, National Cancer Institute; Raymond Flynn, mayor of Boston; Archbishop Thomas Kelly; John Bowab, Broadway producer.

# Rhode Island College

**Providence, RI 02908** **401 456-8000**

**1994-95 Costs.** Tuition: $2,367 (state residents), $6,697 (out-of-state). Room & board: $5,230. Fees, books, misc. academic expenses (school's estimate): $933.
**Enrollment.** Freshman class: 2,310 applicants, 1,767 accepted, 950 enrolled.
**Test score averages/ranges.** Average SAT scores: 411 verbal, 450 math.
**Faculty.** 376 full-time. 72% of faculty holds doctoral degree. Student/faculty ratio: 18 to 1.
**Selectivity rating.** Competitive.

**PROFILE.** Rhode Island College, founded in 1854, is a public, multipurpose institution. Its 125-acre campus is located in a residential area of Providence.

**Accreditation:** NEASC. Professionally accredited by the Council on Social Work Education, the National Association of Schools of Art and Design, the National Association of Schools of Music, the National Council for Accreditation of Teacher Education, the National League for Nursing.
**Religious orientation:** Rhode Island College is nonsectarian; no religious requirements.
**Library:** Collections totaling over 339,582 volumes, 2,094 periodical subscriptions, and 686,633 microform items.
**Special facilities/museums:** Art gallery, curriculum resource center, center for economic education, on-campus elementary school, closed-circuit TV studios.
**Athletic facilities:** Gymnasium, weight room, basketball, tennis, and volleyball courts, swimming pool, baseball, soccer, and softball field, indoor and outdoor tracks.

**STUDENT BODY. Undergraduate profile:** 90% are state residents; 41% are transfers. 1% Asian-American, 3% Black, 3% Hispanic, 93% White. Average age of undergraduates is 20.
**Freshman profile:** 5% of freshmen who took SAT scored 600 or over on verbal, 5% scored 600 or over on math; 17% scored 500 or over on verbal, 28% scored 500 or over on math; 57% scored 400 or over on verbal, 65% scored 400 or over on math; 92% scored 300 or over on verbal, 95% scored 300 or over on math. 100% of accepted applicants took SAT.
**Undergraduate achievement:** 76% of fall 1992 freshmen returned for fall 1993 term. 20% of entering class graduated. 12% of students who completed a degree program immediately went on to graduate study.

**PROGRAMS OF STUDY. Degrees:** B.A., B.A.Just.Studies, B.F.A., B.Gen.Studies, B.Mus.Perf., B.S., B.Soc.Work.
**Majors:** African/Afro-American Studies, Anthropology, Anthropology/Public Archaeology, Art, Art Education, Art History, Biology, Business, Chemistry, Classical Area Studies, Communication/Theatre, Communications, Computer Science, Economics, Elementary Education, Elementary Education/Special Education, English, Film Studies, French, General Science, General Studies, Geography, Health Education, History, Industrial Arts Education, Justice Studies, Labor Studies, Latin American Studies, Management, Mathematics, Medical Technology, Medieval/Renaissance Studies, Music, Music Education, Music Performance, Nursing, Philosophy, Physical Education, Physical Education/Recreation, Physical Science, Physics, Political Science, Political Science/Public Administration,

Psychology, Radiologic Technology, Social Science, Social Work, Sociology, Spanish, Theatre, Urban Studies, Vocational Industrial Education, Women's Studies.
**Distribution of degrees:** The majors with the highest enrollment are psychology, education, and nursing; labor studies, urban studies, and physics have the lowest.
**Requirements:** General education requirement.
**Academic regulations:** Freshmen must maintain minimum 1.75 GPA; sophomores, 1.9 GPA; juniors, 2.0 GPA; seniors, 2.0 GPA.
**Special:** Minors offered in most majors and in dance, Portuguese, and recreation. Self-designed majors. Double majors. Dual degrees. Independent study. Accelerated study. Internships. Cooperative education programs. Graduate school at which undergraduates may take graduate-level courses. Preprofessional programs in law, medicine, veterinary science, dentistry, and optometry. 2-2 and 3-2 occupational therapy programs with Washington U. 3-2 physical therapy program with U of Rhode Island. Cross-registration with Comm Coll of Rhode Island, Providence Coll, and U of Rhode Island. Member of National Student Exchange (NSE). Teacher certification in early childhood, elementary, secondary, special education, vo-tech, and bilingual/bicultural education. Study abroad possible. ROTC at Providence Coll.
**Honors:** Phi Beta Kappa. Honors program.
**Academic Assistance:** Nonremedial tutoring.

**STUDENT LIFE. Housing:** Students may live on or off campus. Coed, women's, and men's dorms. 20% of students live in college housing.
**Social atmosphere:** According to the editor of the student newspaper, "RIC is largely a commuter school. Many of the on-campus events are aimed at the resident population. Although many of the students do not live on campus, there are over 50 student organizations on campus." Popular gathering spots on and around campus are the Donovan Dining Center, The Coffeehouse, Thayer Street, Spat's, and Penguin's. Influential groups on campus include the Student Community Government Inc., Rhode Island Campus Programming, and the Campus Center. A favorite event on campus is RIC-END which is a week-long series of events sponsored by many student organizations.
**Services and counseling/handicapped student services:** Placement services. Health service. Women's center. Day care. Counseling services for minority, military, veteran, and older students. Birth control, personal, and psychological counseling. Career and academic guidance services. Religious counseling. Physically disabled student services. Learning disabled services. Notetaking services. Tape recorders.
**Campus organizations:** Undergraduate student government. Student newspaper (Anchor, published once/week). Yearbook. Radio station. Choir, jazz and wind ensembles, coffeehouse, rathskeller, dance company, theatre, performing arts and lecture series, chess club, handicapped student group, Amnesty International, athletic and departmental groups, service and special-interest groups. Two fraternities, no chapter houses; one sorority, no chapter house. 1% of men join a fraternity. 1% of women join a sorority.
**Religious organizations:** Christian Fellowship, Hillel.
**Minority/foreign student organizations:** Latin American Student Organization, Harambee, Asian Student Association. VISA.

**ATHLETICS. Physical education requirements:** None.
**Intercollegiate competition:** 5% of students participate. Baseball (M), basketball (M,W), cross-country (M,W), gymnastics (W), soccer (M), softball (W), tennis (M,W), track (outdoor) (M,W), track and field (indoor) (M,W), track and field (outdoor) (M,W), volleyball (W), wrestling (M). Member of ECAC, Little East Conference, National Collegiate Gymnastic Association, NCAA Division III, New England College Athletic Conference.
**Intramural and club sports:** 25% of students participate. Intramural basketball, floor hockey, softball, touch football, volleyball, Wiffle ball. Men's club golf, rugby. Women's club golf, rugby.

**ADMISSIONS. Academic basis for candidate selection** (in order of priority): Secondary school record, class rank, school's recommendation, standardized test scores, essay.
**Nonacademic basis for candidate selection:** Particular talent or ability is important. Character and personality, extracurricular participation, and alumni/ae relationship are considered.
**Requirements:** Graduation from secondary school is required; GED is accepted. 18 units and the following program of study are required: 4 units of English, 3 units of math, 2 units of lab science, 2 units of foreign language, 1 unit of social studies, 1 unit of history, 5 units of academic electives. Rank in top half of secondary school class recommended. Education, fine arts, nursing, and social work program applicants must file separate applications after being admitted to the college. Portfolio required of art program applicants. Audition required of music program applicants. Conditional admission possible for applicants not meeting standard requirements. Preparatory Enrollment Program for applicants not normally admissible. Performance-Based Admission for adult freshmen. SAT is required. PSAT is recommended. ACH recommended. No off-campus interviews.
**Procedure:** Take SAT by December of 12th year. Application deadline is May 1. Notification of admission on rolling basis. Reply is required by May 1 or by date specified in letter of acceptance. $50 nonrefundable tuition deposit. $50 nonrefundable room deposit. Freshmen accepted for terms other than fall.
**Special programs:** Admission may be deferred one year. Credit and/or placement may be granted through CEEB Advanced Placement exams for scores of 3 or higher. Credit and/or placement may be granted through CLEP general and subject exams. Placement may be granted through challenge exams. Credit and placement may be granted through ACT PEP and DANTES exams, and military and life experience. Concurrent enrollment program.
**Transfer students:** Transfer students accepted for terms other than fall. In fall 1993, 41% of all new students were transfers into all classes. 1,136 transfer applications were received, 949 were accepted. Application deadline is June 1 for fall; November 15 for spring. Minimum 2.0 GPA required. Lowest course grade accepted is "C-." Maximum number of transferable credits is 90 semester hours. At least 30 semester hours must be completed at the college to receive degree.
**Admissions contact:** William H. Hurry, Jr., M.S.Ed., Dean of Admissions and Financial Aid. 401 456-8234.

**FINANCIAL AID. Available aid:** Pell grants, SEOG, Federal Nursing Student Scholarships, state scholarships and grants, school scholarships and grants, private scholarships and grants, ROTC scholarships, and academic merit scholarships. Talent awards. Perkins Loans (NDSL), PLUS, Stafford Loans (GSL), NSL, and SLS. Deferred payment plan.
**Financial aid statistics:** Average amounts of aid awarded freshmen: Scholarships and grants, $3,500; loans, $1,800.
**Supporting data/closing dates:** FAFSA/FAF: Deadline is March 1. State aid form: Deadline is March 1. Income tax forms: Accepted on rolling basis. Notification of awards on rolling basis.
**Financial aid contact:** William H. Hurry, Jr., M.S.Ed., Dean of Admissions and Financial Aid. 401 456-8033.

**STUDENT EMPLOYMENT.** College Work/Study Program. Institutional employment. 15% of full-time undergraduates work on campus during school year. Students may expect to earn an average of $1,500 during school year. Off-campus part-time employment opportunities rated "good."

**COMPUTER FACILITIES.** IBM/IBM-compatible and Macintosh/Apple microcomputers. Students may access Digital, IBM minicomputer/mainframe systems. Computer languages and software packages include BASIC, C, COBOL, FORTRAN, LISP, Pascal, PPC.
**Fees:** None.
**Hours:** 24 hours (DEC VAX); 8 AM-10 PM (IBM); 8 AM-midn. (microcomputers).

**GRADUATE CAREER DATA.** Graduate school percentages: 1% enter law school. 1% enter medical school. 2% enter graduate business programs. 8% enter graduate arts and sciences programs. 38% of graduates choose careers in business and industry.

# Rhode Island School of Design

**Providence, RI 02903 — 401 454-6100**

**1994-95 Costs.** Tuition: $16,684. Room: $3,318. Board: $3,354. Fees, books, misc. academic expenses (school's estimate): $1,290.
**Enrollment.** Undergraduates: 840 men, 1,004 women (full-time). Freshman class: 1,412 applicants, 842 accepted, 379 enrolled. Graduate enrollment: 64 men, 82 women.
**Test score averages/ranges.** Average SAT scores: 508 verbal, 551 math.
**Faculty.** 122 full-time; 201 part-time. 71% of faculty holds highest degree in specific field. Student/faculty ratio: 12 to 1.
**Selectivity rating.** More competitive.

**PROFILE.** RISD, founded in 1877, is a private institute of the arts. Its urban campus of Victorian architectural style is located in a residential section of Providence.

**Accreditation:** NEASC. Professionally accredited by the American Society of Landscape Architects, the Foundation for Interior Design Education Research, the National Architecture Accrediting Board, the National Association of Schools of Art and Design.
**Religious orientation:** Rhode Island School of Design is nonsectarian; no religious requirements.
**Library:** Collections totaling over 80,000 volumes and 360 periodical subscriptions.
**Special facilities/museums:** Art museum with over 45 galleries, extensive facilities for glassblowing, metalsmithing, lithography, sculpture, painting, and other art disciplines, nature lab.
**Athletic facilities:** Swimming pool and athletic facilities at Brown U.

**STUDENT BODY. Undergraduate profile:** 8% are state residents; 30% are transfers. 7% Asian-American, 2% Black, 2% Hispanic, 1% Native American, 65% White, 23% Other. Average age of undergraduates is 23.
**Freshman profile:** 2% of freshmen who took SAT scored 700 or over on verbal, 9% scored 700 or over on math; 14% scored 600 or over on verbal, 33% scored 600 or over on math; 53% scored 500 or over on verbal, 72% scored 500 or over on math; 82% scored 400 or over on verbal, 94% scored 400 or over on math; 94% scored 300 or over on verbal, 100% scored 300 or over on math. 98% of accepted applicants took SAT; 1% took ACT. 60% of freshmen come from public schools.
**Undergraduate achievement:** 94% of fall 1992 freshmen returned for fall 1993 term. 5% of students who completed a degree program went on to graduate study within one year.
**Foreign students:** 204 students are from out of the country. Countries represented include Canada, Colombia, Hong Kong, Japan, Korea, and Venezula; 48 in all.

**PROGRAMS OF STUDY. Degrees:** B.Arch., B.F.A., B.Graph.Design, B.Indust.Design, B.Inter.Arch., B.Land.Arch.
**Majors:** Apparel Design, Architecture, Ceramics, Film/Video, Furniture Design, Glass, Graphic Design, Illustration, Industrial Design, Interior Architecture, Jewelry/Metals, Landscape Architecture, Painting, Photography, Printmaking, Sculpture, Textiles.
**Distribution of degrees:** The majors with the highest enrollment are illustration, architecture, and graphic design; glass, jewelry/metals, and ceramics have the lowest.
**Requirements:** General education requirement.
**Academic regulations:** Freshmen must maintain minimum 1.8 GPA; sophomores, juniors, seniors, 2.0 GPA.
**Special:** Division of Liberal Arts offers courses in art history, English, and special studies including science, social sciences, and philosophy. Freshman foundation courses. Seniors complete major projects. Independent study. Internships. Five-year architectural, industrial design, and graphic design programs. Reciprocal arrangement with Brown U allows RISD students to enroll in classes and use athletic facilities. Mobility program with 12 U.S. art colleges. Teacher certification in elementary and secondary education. Certification in specific subject areas. Exchange programs abroad in England (Newcastle Upon Tyne, Trent Polytech, Winchester Art Sch), Estonia (Tallinn U), France (Les Ateliers, Speos), the Netherlands (Academie Minerva, Academie St. Joost), New Zealand (U of Canterbury), Scotland (Glasgow Sch of Art), Spain (Elisava Escola de Disseny), Sweden, and Switzerland (Eidgenossische Tech Hochschule). Study abroad also in Mexico.

**STUDENT LIFE. Housing:** All unmarried freshmen under age 21 must live on campus unless living with family. Coed dorms. School-owned/operated apartments. 33% of students live in college housing.

**Social atmosphere:** According to the editor of the student newspaper, "People are basically introverts here at RISD, in their own worlds. Each person has a different view of the world, which makes this place so interesting." Popular on-campus spots are the Carr Haus, the Tap Room, and the Pit. Off campus, students gather at the Living Room, 33 Doyle, Mutt's, and Thayer Street. Special social events include the President's Ball, Awareness Week, gallery openings, and hockey games.
**Services and counseling/handicapped student services:** Health service. Counseling services for minority students. Personal and psychological counseling. Career and academic guidance services. Physically disabled student services. Learning disabled services. Note-taking services. Tape recorders. Reader services for the blind.
**Campus organizations:** Undergraduate student government. Student newspaper (Independent). Yearbook. Camera and ceramics clubs, dance and textile clubs, environmental awareness group, film society, outing club, theater group, 60 organizations in all.
**Religious organizations:** Christian Fellowship, Hillel, Newman Association.
**Minority/foreign student organizations:** Artists for Awareness, United Students. International Student Club.

**ATHLETICS. Physical education requirements:** None.
**Intramural and club sports:** 70% of students participate. Intramural aerobic dance, volleyball, weight lifting. Men's club basketball, hockey, soccer, softball, volleyball. Women's club basketball, hockey, soccer, softball, volleyball.

**ADMISSIONS. Academic basis for candidate selection** (in order of priority): Secondary school record, essay, class rank, standardized test scores, school's recommendation.
**Nonacademic basis for candidate selection:** Particular talent or ability is emphasized. Character and personality, extracurricular participation, geographical distribution, and alumni/ae relationship are considered.
**Requirements:** Graduation from secondary school is required; GED is accepted. No specific distribution of secondary school units required. College-preparatory program with courses in studio art and art history strongly recommended. Portfolio required of art program applicants; optional for architectural program applicants. SAT is required; ACT may be substituted. No off-campus interviews.
**Procedure:** Take SAT or ACT by December 31 of 12th year. Suggest filing application by January 21. Application deadline is February 15. Notification of admission by April 1. Reply is required by May 1. $300 nonrefundable tuition deposit. $175 nonrefundable room deposit. Freshmen accepted for terms other than fall.
**Special programs:** Admission may be deferred one year. Credit and/or placement may be granted through CEEB Advanced Placement exams for scores of 4 or higher. Early entrance/early admission program.
**Transfer students:** Transfer students accepted for terms other than fall. In fall 1993, 30% of all new students were transfers into all classes. 480 transfer applications were received, 245 were accepted. Application deadline is March 31 for fall; November 25 for spring. Lowest course grade accepted is "C." Maximum number of transferable credits is 60 semester hours. At least 66 semester hours must be completed at the art school to receive degree.
**Admissions contact:** Edward E. Newhall, Director of Admissions. 401 454-6300.

**FINANCIAL AID. Available aid:** Pell grants, SEOG, state scholarships and grants, school scholarships and grants, and private scholarships and grants. Arts Recognition Talent Search and Trustees Scholarships. Perkins Loans (NDSL), PLUS, Stafford Loans (GSL), and SLS. Knight Tuition Plans, Tuition Management Systems, and deferred payment plan.
**Financial aid statistics:** In 1993-94, 91% of all undergraduate applicants received aid; 87% of freshman applicants. Average amounts of aid awarded freshmen: Scholarships and grants, $8,212; loans, $2,625.
**Supporting data/closing dates:** FAFSA/FAF: Deadline is February 15. Notification of awards begins April 1.
**Financial aid contact:** Peter Riefler, M.A., M.B.A., Director of Financial Aid. 401 454-6636.

**STUDENT EMPLOYMENT.** College Work/Study Program. Institutional employment. 57% of full-time undergraduates work on campus during school year. Students may expect to earn an average of $1,100 during school year. Freshmen are discouraged from working during their first term. Off-campus part-time employment opportunities rated "good."

**COMPUTER FACILITIES.** 163 IBM/IBM-compatible and Macintosh/Apple microcomputers; 80 are networked. Students may access Internet. Residence halls may be equipped with networked microcomputers. Client/LAN operating systems include Apple/Macintosh, DOS, LocalTalk/AppleTalk. Computer languages and software packages include Apple-based computer languages, CAD languages, Omega modeling and animation, digitizing/scanning software/hardware, video export and import capabilities; 50 in all. Computer facilities are available to all students.
**Fees:** None.
**Hours:** 9 AM-midn.

**GRADUATE CAREER DATA.** Highest graduate school enrollments: Cornell U, Cranbrook Academy of Art, Michigan State U, Yale U.

# Roger Williams University

**Bristol, RI 02809** **401 253-1040**

**1994-95 Costs.** Tuition: $12,520. Room: $3,060. Board: $2,990. Fees, books, misc. academic expenses (school's estimate): $1,155. (Studio fee for architecture students: $1,430.)
**Enrollment.** Undergraduates: 1,159 men, 952 women (full-time). Freshman class: 3,291 applicants, 2,751 accepted, 676 enrolled.
**Test score averages/ranges.** Average SAT scores: 861 combined. Range of SAT scores of middle 50%: 400-440 verbal, 450-490 math.
**Faculty.** 108 full-time; 66 part-time. 65% of faculty holds highest degree in specific field. Student/faculty ratio: 19 to 1.
**Selectivity rating.** Competitive.

**PROFILE.** Roger Williams, founded in 1948, is a private university. Programs are offered through the Schools of Architecture, Business, Engineering, Fine Arts, Humanities, Natural Science, Mathematics, and Open School. Its 80-acre campus is located in Bristol.
**Accreditation:** NEASC. Professionally accredited by the Accreditation Board for Engineering and Technology, the National Architecture Accrediting Board, the National Council for Accreditation of Teacher Education.
**Religious orientation:** Roger Williams University is nonsectarian; no religious requirements.
**Library:** Collections totaling over 117,800 volumes, 1,220 periodical subscriptions, and 18,300 microform items.
**Athletic facilities:** Baseball and softball fields, rugby and lacrosse fields, horse stables and course, gymnasium, basketball, tennis, beach volleyball, and volleyball courts, exercise and weight rooms, athletic fields.

**STUDENT BODY. Undergraduate profile:** 15% are state residents; 10% are transfers. 2% Asian-American, 1% Black, 2% Hispanic, 92% White, 3% Other. Average age of undergraduates is 20.
**Freshman profile:** 87% of accepted applicants took SAT; 30% took ACT. 70% of freshmen come from public schools.
**Undergraduate achievement:** 75% of fall 1992 freshmen returned for fall 1993 term. 46% of entering class graduated. 15% of students who completed a degree program went on to graduate study within two years.
**Foreign students:** 134 students are from out of the country. Countries represented include Ecuador, Indonesia, Japan, Korea, Thailand, and Venezuela; 43 in all.

**PROGRAMS OF STUDY. Degrees:** B.A., B.Arch., B.F.A., B.S.
**Majors:** Accounting, Administration of Justice, Architecture, Art, Biology, Business Administration, Chemistry, Communications, Computer Information Systems, Computer Science, Construction Science, Creative Writing, Dance, Engineering, Environmental Engineering Science, Historic Preservation, History, Management, Marine Biology, Marketing, Mathematics, Paralegal Studies, Philosophy, Political Studies, Psychology, Theatre.
**Distribution of degrees:** The majors with the highest enrollment are business administration, architecture, and psychology; mathematics has the lowest.
**Requirements:** General education requirement.
**Academic regulations:** Freshmen must maintain minimum 1.4 GPA; sophomores, 1.8 GPA; juniors, 2.0 GPA; seniors, 2.0 GPA.
**Special:** Minors offered in American studies, anthropology, art history, film studies, horticulture, landscape architecture, music, religious studies, social work, and sociology. Associate's degrees offered. Self-designed majors. Double majors. Independent study. Pass/fail grading option. Internships. Cooperative education programs. Graduate school at which undergraduates may take graduate-level courses. Preprofessional programs in medicine, veterinary science, and dentistry. Five-year architecture program. 3-2 engineering program with Syracuse U. Environmental science and forestry program with SUNY Coll of Environmental Science and Forestry. Teacher certification in early childhood and elementary education. Exchange program abroad in Russia (Moscow Linguistic U). Study abroad also in China, England, Greece, and Jamaica. ROTC at Providence Coll.
**Honors:** Honor societies.
**Academic Assistance:** Remedial reading, writing, math, and study skills. Nonremedial tutoring.

**STUDENT LIFE. Housing:** Students may live on or off campus. Coed dorms. School-owned/operated apartments. 65% of students live in college housing.
**Services and counseling/handicapped student services:** Placement services. Health service. Counseling services for veteran students. Personal and psychological counseling. Career and academic guidance services. Physically disabled student services. Learning disabled services. Tape recorders. Tutors. Reader services for the blind.
**Campus organizations:** Undergraduate student government. Student newspaper (Messenger, published twice/month). Literary magazine. Yearbook. Radio station. Jazz band, chorus, Stage Company, architectural, business, and various engineering groups, rugby and windsurfing clubs, Elizabethan Society, environmental club, volunteer center, 42 organizations in all.
**Religious organizations:** Jewish Student Club, Hillel, Christian Fellowship.
**Minority/foreign student organizations:** Minority affairs committee. International Student Club.

**ATHLETICS. Physical education requirements:** None.
**Intercollegiate competition:** 18% of students participate. Baseball (M), basketball (M,W), cheerleading (M,W), cross-country (M,W), golf (M), horsemanship (M,W), ice hockey (M), lacrosse (M), sailing (M,W), soccer (M,W), softball (W), tennis (M,W), volleyball (M,W), wrestling (M). Member of Commonwealth Coast Conference, ECAC, NCAA Division III, New England Club Football Conference, New England College Conference Wrestling Association, Pilgrim League, RIAIAW.
**Intramural and club sports:** 26% of students participate. Intramural basketball, beach volleyball, flag football, floor hockey, indoor soccer, softball, tennis, volleyball, Wiffle ball. Men's club biking, cheerleading, crew, equestrian sports, Greco wrestling, karate, mountain biking, power lifting, rock climbing, rod and gun, rugby, surfing, track. Women's club cheerleading, crew, equestrian sports, karate, lacrosse, mountain biking, rock climbing, rod and gun, surfing, track.

**ADMISSIONS. Academic basis for candidate selection** (in order of priority): Secondary school record, class rank, standardized test scores, essay, school's recommendation.
**Nonacademic basis for candidate selection:** Character and personality, extracurricular participation, particular talent or ability, geographical distribution, and alumni/ae relationship are important.
**Requirements:** Graduation from secondary school is required; GED is accepted. 16 units and the following program of study are required: 4 units of English, 2 units of math, 2 units of science, 2 units of social studies, 2 units of history, 4 units of electives. Additional secondary school units recommended in math, science, and social studies. Portfolio required of architecture and art program applicants. SAT or ACT is required. Campus visit and interview recommended. Off-campus interviews available with an admissions representative.
**Procedure:** Take SAT or ACT by December of 12th year. Visit college for interview by January of 12th year. Application deadline is February 1. Notification of admission on rol-

ling basis. Reply is required by May 1. $100 tuition deposit, refundable until May 1. $200 room deposit, refundable until May 1. Freshmen accepted for terms other than fall.
**Special programs:** Admission may be deferred one year. Credit and/or placement may be granted through CEEB Advanced Placement exams for scores of 3 or higher. Credit and/or placement may be granted through CLEP general and subject exams. Credit and placement may be granted through challenge exams, and military and life experience. Early entrance/early admission program. Concurrent enrollment program.
**Transfer students:** Transfer students accepted for terms other than fall. In fall 1993, 10% of all new students were transfers into all classes. 150 transfer applications were received, 100 were accepted. Application deadline is rolling for fall; rolling for spring. Minimum 2.0 GPA required. Lowest course grade accepted is "C-." Maximum number of transferable credits is 60 semester hours from a two-year school and 90 semester hours from a four-year school. At least 30 semester hours must be completed at the university to receive degree.
**Admissions contact:** William B. Galloway, M.A., Dean of Admissions. 401 254-3500.

**FINANCIAL AID. Available aid:** Pell grants, SEOG, state scholarships and grants, school scholarships and grants, private scholarships and grants, and academic merit scholarships. Perkins Loans (NDSL), PLUS, Stafford Loans (GSL), private loans, and SLS.
**Financial aid statistics:** 1% of aid is not need-based. In 1993-94, 86% of all undergraduate applicants received aid; 83% of freshman applicants. Average amounts of aid awarded freshmen: Scholarships and grants, $5,300; loans, $2,800.
**Supporting data/closing dates:** FAFSA: Priority filing date is March 1. School's own aid application: Priority filing date is March 1. Income tax forms: Priority filing date is April 15. Notification of awards begins March 20.
**Financial aid contact:** Lynn Fawthrop, Director of Financial Aid. 401 254-3100.

**STUDENT EMPLOYMENT.** College Work/Study Program. 25% of full-time undergraduates work on campus during school year. Students may expect to earn an average of $1,600 during school year. Off-campus part-time employment opportunities rated "good."

**COMPUTER FACILITIES.** 125 IBM/IBM-compatible and Macintosh/Apple microcomputers; 75 are networked. Students may access Data General minicomputer/mainframe systems, Internet, CompuServe. Residence halls may be equipped with stand-alone microcomputers. Computer languages and software packages include APL, Assembler, BASIC, C, COBOL, FORTRAN, LISP, Pascal, PL/1, RPG, SAS, SPSS; software programs. Computer facilities are available to all students.
**Fees:** Computer fee is included in tuition/fees.
**Hours:** 100 hours/week.

**GRADUATE CAREER DATA.** Graduate school percentages: 1% enter law school. 2% enter medical school. 1% enter dental school. 4% enter graduate business programs. 4% enter graduate arts and sciences programs. Highest graduate school enrollments: Brown U, U of Massachusetts, U of Rhode Island. 80% of graduates choose careers in business and industry. Companies and businesses that hire graduates: Aetna, Eastern Utilities, Raytheon.

# Salve Regina University

**Newport, RI 02840-4192** **401 847-6650**

**1994-95 Costs.** Tuition: $14,200. Room & board: $6,500. Fees, books, misc. academic expenses (school's estimate): $500.
**Enrollment.** Undergraduates: 449 men, 1,026 women (full-time). Freshman class: 1,353 applicants, 1,259 accepted, 400 enrolled. Graduate enrollment: 263 men, 321 women.
**Test score averages/ranges.** N/A.
**Faculty.** 114 full-time; 98 part-time. 80% of faculty holds highest degree in specific field. Student/faculty ratio: 14 to 1.
**Selectivity rating.** N/A.

**PROFILE.** Salve Regina, founded in 1934, is a private, church-affiliated, liberal arts university. Its 65-acre campus, situated among Newport's turn-of-the-century summer estates listed with the National Register of Historic Places, is located in Newport, 35 miles from Providence.

**Accreditation:** NEASC. Professionally accredited by the Council on Social Work Education, the National Association of Schools of Art and Design, the National League for Nursing.
**Religious orientation:** Salve Regina University is affiliated with the Roman Catholic Church (Religious Sisters of Mercy); nine semester hours of religion/theology required.
**Library:** Collections totaling over 83,624 volumes, 1,250 periodical subscriptions, and 11,208 microform items.
**Special facilities/museums:** Language labs.
**Athletic facilities:** Gymnasium, swimming pool, basketball and tennis courts, track, baseball, practice, soccer, and softball fields.

**STUDENT BODY. Undergraduate profile:** 22% are state residents; 20% are transfers. 1% Asian-American, 1% Black, 2% Hispanic, 95% White, 1% Other. Average age of undergraduates is 20.
**Undergraduate achievement:** 95% of fall 1991 freshmen returned for fall 1992 term. 80% of entering class graduated. 56% of students who completed a degree program immediately went on to graduate study.
**Foreign students:** Nine students are from out of the country. Countries represented include Colombia, the Dominican Republic, Germany, India, Ireland, and Kenya.

**PROGRAMS OF STUDY. Degrees:** B.A., B.Arts/Sci., B.Gen.Studies, B.S.
**Majors:** Accounting, Administration of Justice, American Studies, Anthropology, Art, Biology, Chemistry, Economics, Elementary Education, English, French, History, Information Systems Science, Language, Management, Mathematical Sciences, Medical Technology, Music, Nursing, Philosophy, Politics, Psychology, Religious Studies, Secondary Education, Social Work, Sociology, Spanish, Special Education, Theatre.
**Distribution of degrees:** The majors with the highest enrollment are management, elementary education, and administration of justice; religious studies, music, and general studies have the lowest.
**Requirements:** General education requirement.
**Academic regulations:** Minimum 2.0 GPA must be maintained.
**Special:** Minors offered in most majors and in computer science and geography. Associate's degrees offered. Double majors. Dual degrees. Independent study. Accelerated study. Pass/fail grading option. Internships. Graduate school at which undergraduates may take graduate-level courses. Preprofessional programs in law and medicine. 4-1 B.A./M.S. program in administration of justice. Other combined degree programs in accounting, economics, health services administration, history, management, and politics. Teacher certification in elementary, secondary, and special education. Certification in specific subject areas. Exchange program abroad in England (Trinity All Saints Coll). Study abroad also in Austria, France, Germany, Hungary, Ireland, Italy, Kenya, Mexico, Poland, Spain, and Switzerland. ROTC at Providence Coll and U of Rhode Island.
**Honors:** Honors program. Honor societies.
**Academic Assistance:** Remedial reading, writing, math, and study skills. Nonremedial tutoring.

**STUDENT LIFE. Housing:** Students may live on or off campus. Women's and men's dorms. 50% of students live in college housing.
**Social atmosphere:** Students gather on campus at O'Hare Academic Center, Wakehurst Campus Center, and Miley Hall. Off campus, students often head to Maximillian's or to the Brick Alley Pub and Restaurant. Influential campus groups include Sigma Phi Sigma honor society, the Student Life Senate, and the Activities Office. Students enjoy a number of special events on campus, including football games, Octoberfest Weekend, Welcome Back Weekend, the Special Olympics, the Winter Semi-formal, Spring Weekend, Parents' Weekend, and shows by Frank Santos, hypnotist.
**Services and counseling/handicapped student services:** Placement services. Health service. Counseling services for minority, military, veteran, and older students. Personal and psychological counseling. Career and academic guidance services. Religious counseling. Physically disabled student services. Learning disabled services. Notetaking services. Tutors. Reader services for the blind.
**Campus organizations:** Undergraduate student government. Student newspaper (What's Going On?, published biweekly). Yearbook. Choral groups, art club, drama groups, accounting and administration clubs, Arete Society (history), athletics club, band, community service groups, Council for Exceptional Children, French club, hockey and ice skating clubs, weight lifting club, Student Nurse Association, medical technology club, economics and finance club, Association for Computer Machinery, 16 organizations in all.
**Religious organizations:** Campus Ministry.

**ATHLETICS. Physical education requirements:** None.
**Intercollegiate competition:** 15% of students participate. Baseball (M), basketball (M,W), cross-country (M), field hockey (W), football (M), golf (M,W), ice hockey (M), soccer (M,W), softball (M,W), tennis (M,W), track (indoor) (M,W), track (outdoor) (M,W), track and field (indoor) (M,W), track and field (outdoor) (M,W). Member of Commonwealth Coast Conference, ECAC, NCAA Division III.
**Intramural and club sports:** 60% of students participate. Intramural aerobics, badminton, basketball, field hockey, flag football, racquetball, softball, tennis, volleyball. Men's club sailing. Women's club sailing.

**ADMISSIONS. Academic basis for candidate selection** (in order of priority): Secondary school record, class rank, school's recommendation, essay, standardized test scores.
**Nonacademic basis for candidate selection:** Character and personality and particular talent or ability are important. Extracurricular participation and alumni/ae relationship are considered.
**Requirements:** Graduation from secondary school is required; GED is accepted. 16 units and the following program of study are recommended: 4 units of English, 3 units of math, 2 units of science, 2 units of foreign language, 1 unit of history, 4 units of electives. SAT is required; ACT may be substituted. Campus visit and interview recommended. No off-campus interviews.
**Procedure:** Take SAT or ACT by January of 12th year. Notification of admission on rolling basis. Reply is required by May 1. $100 nonrefundable tuition deposit. $200 room deposit, refundable until June 30. Freshmen accepted for terms other than fall.
**Special programs:** Admission may be deferred one year. Credit and/or placement may be granted through CEEB Advanced Placement exams for scores of 3 or higher. Credit may be granted through CLEP general and subject exams, Regents College, ACT PEP, DANTES, and challenge exams. Credit and placement may be granted through military and life experience. Early decision program. In fall 1992, 20 applied for early decision and 11 were accepted. Deadline for applying for early decision is November 15. Concurrent enrollment program.
**Transfer students:** Transfer students accepted for terms other than fall. In fall 1992, 20% of all new students were transfers into all classes. 286 transfer applications were received, 225 were accepted. Application deadline is rolling for fall; rolling for spring. Minimum 2.5 GPA recommended. Lowest course grade accepted is "C." Maximum number of transferable credits is 92 semester hours. At least 36 semester hours must be completed at the university to receive degree.
**Admissions contact:** Sr. Roselina McKillop, R.S.M., M.A., Dean of Admissions. 401 847-6650, extension 2334.

**FINANCIAL AID. Available aid:** Pell grants, SEOG, state scholarships and grants, school scholarships and grants, and private scholarships and grants. Perkins Loans (NDSL), PLUS, Stafford Loans (GSL), NSL, state loans, school loans, private loans, and SLS. Knight Tuition Plans, AMS, Tuition Management Systems, deferred payment plan, and family tuition reduction.
**Financial aid statistics:** In 1992-93, 85% of all undergraduate applicants received aid; 90% of freshman applicants. Average amounts of aid awarded freshmen: Scholarships and grants, $5,750; loans, $3,620.
**Supporting data/closing dates:** FAFSA/FAF/FFS: Deadline is March 1. School's own aid application: Deadline is March 1. State aid form: Deadline is March 1. Income tax forms: Deadline is March 1. Notification of awards begins in March.
**Financial aid contact:** Lucille Flanagan, M.A., Director of Financial Aid. 401 847-6650, extension 2901.

**STUDENT EMPLOYMENT.** College Work/Study Program. Institutional employment. 25% of full-time undergraduates work on campus during school year. Students may expect to earn an average of $1,200 during school year. Off-campus part-time employment opportunities rated "fair."

**COMPUTER FACILITIES.** 77 IBM/IBM-compatible and Macintosh/Apple microcomputers; all are networked. Students may access IBM minicomputer/mainframe systems. Computer languages and software packages include BASIC, COBOL, dBASE, FORTRAN, Lotus 1-2-3, Pascal; graphics, statistical, word processing programs; 30 in all. Computer facilities are available to all students.
**Fees:** Computer fee is included in tuition/fees.
**Hours:** 8 AM-midn. (M-F); 10 AM-6 PM (Sa-Su).

**GRADUATE CAREER DATA.** Graduate school percentages: 10% enter law school. 5% enter medical school. 3% enter dental school. 25% enter graduate business programs. 10% enter graduate arts and sciences programs. 2% enter theological school/seminary. Highest graduate school enrollments: Brown U, Harvard U, Notre Dame, Rhode Island Coll, U of Rhode Island. 80% of graduates choose careers in business and industry. Companies and businesses that hire graduates: FBI, Miriam Hospital, Providence School Department, Prudential Insurance, Rhode Island Hospital, Yale-New Haven Hospital.

**PROMINENT ALUMNI/AE.** Kathleen Connell, secretary of state, Rhode Island; Arlene Violet, former attorney general, Rhode Island.

## University of Rhode Island

**Kingston, RI 02881** — **401 792-1000**

**1994-95 Costs.** Tuition: $3,140 (state residents), $10,166 (out-of-state). Room: $3,000. Board: $2,370. Fees, books, misc. academic expenses (school's estimate): $2,037.

**Enrollment.** Undergraduates: 4,232 men, 4,662 women (full-time). Freshman class: 9,642 applicants, 7,750 accepted, 1,968 enrolled. Graduate enrollment: 1,599 men, 1,976 women.

**Test score averages/ranges.** Average SAT scores: 449 verbal, 515 math. Range of SAT scores of middle 50%: 400-490 verbal, 450-560 math. Average ACT scores: 23 composite.

**Faculty.** 695 full-time; 22 part-time. 87% of faculty holds doctoral degree. Student/faculty ratio: 16 to 1.

**Selectivity rating.** Less competitive.

**PROFILE.** URI, founded in 1892, is a public, comprehensive university. Programs are offered through the Colleges of Arts and Sciences, Business Administration, Continuing Education, Engineering, Human Science and Services, Nursing, Pharmacy, and Resource Development. Its 1,200-acre campus is located in Kingston, 30 miles south of Providence.

**Accreditation:** NEASC. Professionally accredited by the Accreditation Board for Engineering and Technology, the American Assembly of Collegiate Schools of Business, the American Council on Pharmaceutical Education, the American Dental Association, the American Psychological Association, the American Speech-Language-Hearing Association, the National Association of Schools of Music, the National League for Nursing.
**Religious orientation:** University of Rhode Island is nonsectarian; no religious requirements.
**Library:** Collections totaling over 1,019,000 volumes, 9,759 periodical subscriptions, and 1,313,000 microform items.
**Special facilities/museums:** Child development center, human performance lab, robotics center.
**Athletic facilities:** Gymnasiums, badminton, basketball, tennis, and volleyball courts, dance studio, baseball, football, intramural, soccer, and softball fields, golf course, weight rooms, sauna, tracks, swimming pools, fitness center.

**STUDENT BODY. Undergraduate profile:** 54% are state residents; 22% are transfers. 3% Asian-American, 3% Black, 2% Hispanic, 1% Native American, 79% White, 12% Other. Average age of undergraduates is 20.
**Freshman profile:** 1% of freshmen who took SAT scored 700 or over on verbal, 2% scored 700 or over on math; 4% scored 600 or over on verbal, 16% scored 600 or over on math; 23% scored 500 or over on verbal, 60% scored 500 or over on math; 79% scored 400 or over on verbal, 95% scored 400 or over on math; 99% scored 300 or over on verbal, 100% scored 300 or over on math. 95% of accepted applicants took SAT; 5% took ACT. 80% of freshmen come from public schools.
**Undergraduate achievement:** 75% of fall 1992 freshmen returned for fall 1993 term. 40% of entering class graduated.
**Foreign students:** 40 students are from out of the country. Countries represented include Cyprus, Hong Kong, India, Malaysia, Norway, and Pakistan; 72 in all.

**PROGRAMS OF STUDY. Degrees:** B.A., B.F.A., B.Gen.Studies, B.Land.Arch., B.Mus., B.S.
**Majors:** Accounting, Animal Science/Technology, Anthropology, Aquaculture/Fish Technology, Art, Biology, Botany, Chemical Engineering, Chemical/Ocean Engineering, Chemistry, Civil Engineering, Classical Studies, Clinical Laboratory Sciences, Communication Studies, Communicative Disorders, Comparative Literature, Computer Engineering, Computer Science, Consumer Affairs, Dental Hygiene, Dietetics, Economics, Electrical Engineering, Elementary Education, English, Environmental Management, Finance, Food Science/Nutrition, French, General Business Administration, Geology, German, History, Home Economics, Human Development/Family Studies, Human Science/Services, Industrial Engineering, Italian, Journalism, Landscape Architecture, Latin American Studies, Linguistics, Management, Management Information Systems, Marine Affairs, Marketing, Materials Engineering, Mathematics, Mechanical Engineering, Microbiology, Music, Nursing, Ocean Engineering, Pharmacy, Philosophy, Physical Education, Physics, Plant Science/Technology, Political Science, Psychology, Resource Economics/Commerce, Russian, Secondary Education, Sociology, Soil/Water Science, Spanish, Textile Marketing, Textiles/Fashion Merchandising/Design, Theatre, Urban Affairs, Urban Horticulture/Turfgrass Management, Wildlife Biology/Management, Women's Studies, Zoology.
**Distribution of degrees:** The majors with the highest enrollment are psychology, communications, and political science; comparative literature has the lowest.
**Requirements:** General education requirement.
**Academic regulations:** Minimum 2.0 GPA required for graduation.
**Special:** Minors offered in all majors. Interdisciplinary programs in consumer affairs, gerontology, New England studies, special populations, and women's studies. Associate's degrees offered. Double majors. Dual degrees. Independent study. Pass/fail grading option. Internships. Cooperative education programs. Graduate school at which undergraduates may take graduate-level courses. Preprofessional programs in law, medicine, veterinary science, and dentistry. B.S./M.S. physical therapy program; B.S. Engineering/B.A. German program. Member of New England Regional Student Program. Washington Semester. Member of National Student Exchange (NSE). Teacher certification in early childhood, elementary, and secondary education. Certification in specific subject areas. Study abroad in Canada, England, France, Germany, Italy, Japan, Spain, and other countries. ROTC.
**Honors:** Phi Beta Kappa. Honors program.
**Academic Assistance:** Remedial reading and writing. Nonremedial tutoring.

**STUDENT LIFE. Housing:** Students may live on or off campus. Coed and women's dorms. Sorority and fraternity housing. School-owned/operated apartments. Off-campus privately-owned housing. On-campus married-student housing. 48% of students live in college housing.
**Social atmosphere:** The Union, Fraternity houses, dance clubs, bars, and pool halls are hot spots for students to go. The Greeks are influential in student life. Homecoming and Rush week are popular social events.
**Services and counseling/handicapped student services:** Placement services. Health service. Women's center. Day care. Counseling services for minority students. Birth control, personal, and psychological counseling. Career and academic guidance services. Religious counseling. Physically disabled student services. Learning disabled services. Notetaking services. Tape recorders. Tutors. Reader services for the blind.
**Campus organizations:** Undergraduate student government. Student newspaper (The Good 5-Cent Cigar, published once/day). Literary magazine. Yearbook. Radio and TV stations. Chorus, band, orchestra, theatre, debating, lectures, art programs, student-run businesses, older-student association, student entertainment committee, 88 organizations in all. 17 fraternities, 14 chapter houses; eight sororities, seven chapter houses. 18% of men join a fraternity. 14% of women join a sorority.
**Religious organizations:** Catholic Student Association, Campus Crusade for Christ, Hillel, Intervarsity Christian Fellowship, Navigators.
**Minority/foreign student organizations:** Minority Student Center, Minority Coalition, UHURU SASA, Native American group, LASA. International Student Association, Asian, Chinese, Latin American, Taiwanese, and Vietnamese groups.

**ATHLETICS. Physical education requirements:** None.
**Intercollegiate competition:** 10% of students participate. Basketball (M,W), cross-country (M,W), diving (M,W), field hockey (W), football (M), golf (M), gymnastics (W), soccer (M,W), softball (W), swimming (M,W), tennis (M,W), track (indoor) (M,W), track (outdoor) (M,W), track and field (indoor) (M,W), track and field (outdoor) (M,W), volleyball (W). Member of Atlantic 10, ECAC, NCAA Division I, NCAA Division I-AA for football, Yankee Conference.
**Intramural and club sports:** 60% of students participate. Intramural badminton, basketball, beach volleyball, cross-country, flag football, floor hockey, inner-tube basketball, inner-tube water polo, pickleball, soccer, softball, tennis, volleyball, Wiffle ball. Men's club Alpine skiing, crew, cricket, cycling, equestrian sports, fencing, ice hockey, lacrosse, rugby, sailing, volleyball, water polo. Women's club Alpine skiing, crew, cycling, equestrian sports, fencing, lacrosse, rugby, sailing, water polo.

**ADMISSIONS. Academic basis for candidate selection** (in order of priority): Secondary school record, standardized test scores, class rank, school's recommendation, essay.
**Nonacademic basis for candidate selection:** Particular talent or ability, geographical distribution, and alumni/ae relationship are important. Character and personality and extracurricular participation are considered.
**Requirements:** Graduation from secondary school is required; GED is accepted. 18 units and the following program of study are required: 4 units of English, 3 units of math, 2 units of lab science, 2 units of foreign language, 2 units of social studies, 5 units of academic electives. Average combined SAT score of 1000, rank in top third of secondary school class, and minimum "B" average recommended. 4 units of math and 1 unit each of chemistry and physics required of engineering program applicants. Audition required of music program applicants. Talent Development Program for in-state applicants not normally admissible. SAT or ACT is required. Campus visit and interview recommended. Off-campus interviews available with an alumni representative.
**Procedure:** Take SAT or ACT by January of 12th year. Visit college for interview by December of 12th year. Suggest filing application by November 1. Application deadline is March 1. Notification of admission on rolling basis. Reply is required by May 1. $150 tuition deposit for in-state students, $300 for out-of-state; 50% of each deposit is refundable until June 1. $100 nonrefundable room deposit. Freshmen accepted for terms other than fall.
**Special programs:** Credit and/or placement may be granted through CEEB Advanced Placement exams for scores of 3 or higher. Credit and/or placement may be granted through CLEP subject exams. Credit and placement may be granted through challenge exams and military experience. Early entrance/early admission program. Concurrent enrollment program.
**Transfer students:** Transfer students accepted for terms other than fall. In fall 1993, 22% of all new students were transfers into all classes. 1,668 transfer applications were received, 1,083 were accepted. Application deadline is March 1 for fall; November 1 for spring. Minimum 2.6 GPA recommended. Lowest course grade accepted is "C." At least 24 quarter hours must be completed at the university to receive degree.
**Admissions contact:** David G. Taggart, M.Ed., Dean of Admissions and Financial Aid. 401 792-9800.

**FINANCIAL AID. Available aid:** Pell grants, SEOG, Federal Nursing Student Scholarships, state scholarships and grants, school scholarships and grants, private scholarships

and grants, ROTC scholarships, academic merit scholarships, athletic scholarships, and aid for undergraduate foreign students. Talent Development Grants. Perkins Loans (NDSL), PLUS, Stafford Loans (GSL), NSL, Health Professions Loans, state loans, school loans, private loans, and SLS. Tuition Plan Inc. and AMS.

**Financial aid statistics:** 2% of aid is not need-based. In 1993-94, 82% of all undergraduate applicants received aid; 75% of freshman applicants.

**Supporting data/closing dates:** FAFSA/FAF: Priority filing date is January 1; deadline is March 1. Notification of awards on rolling basis.

**Financial aid contact:** Horace J. Amaral, Jr., M.A., Assistant Dean of Financial Aid. 401 792-2314.

**STUDENT EMPLOYMENT.** College Work/Study Program. Institutional employment. 11% of full-time undergraduates work on campus during school year. Students may expect to earn an average of $1,000 during school year. Off-campus part-time employment opportunities rated "good."

**COMPUTER FACILITIES.** 500 IBM/IBM-compatible, Macintosh/Apple, and RISC-/UNIX-based microcomputers. Students may access Digital, IBM, SUN minicomputer/mainframe systems, BITNET, Internet. Client/LAN operating systems include Apple/Macintosh, LocalTalk/AppleTalk. Computer languages and software packages include Assembler, C, COBOL, FOCUS, FORTRAN, MINITAB, Pascal, PL/1, SAS, SPSS, SQL; 50 in all. Computer facilities are available to all students.

**Fees:** None.

**Hours:** 24 hours.

**GRADUATE CAREER DATA.** Highest graduate school enrollments: U of Rhode Island. Companies and businesses that hire graduates: Big Six accounting firms.

**PROMINENT ALUMNI/AE.** Robert L. Crandall, president, American Airlines; Ann Hood, novelist; Robert D. Ballard, oceanographer and leader of *Titanic* exploration; J.T. Walsh, actor.

# South Carolina

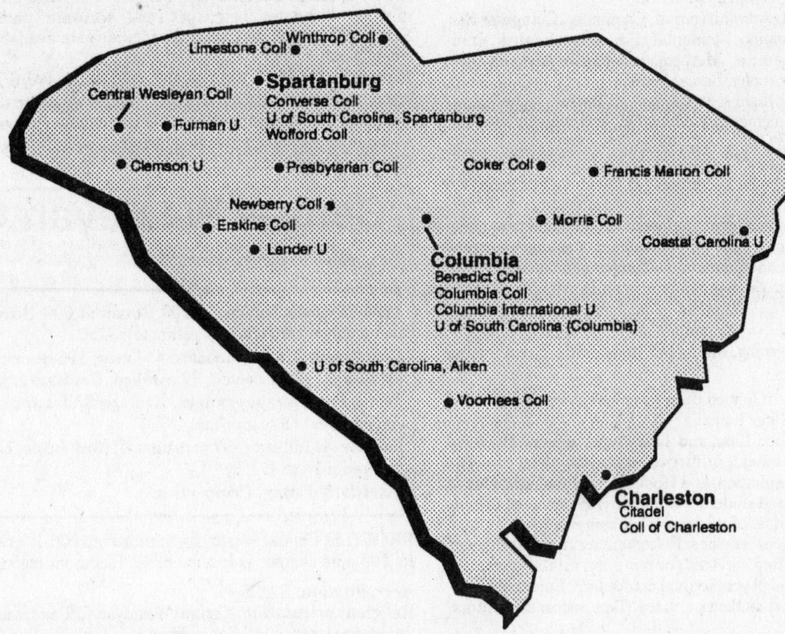


## Anderson College

**Anderson, SC 29621** **803 231-2000**

**1994-95 Costs.** Tuition: $8,026. Room: $2,086. Board: $2,086. Fees, books, misc. academic expenses (school's estimate): $1,362.
**Enrollment.** Freshman class: 732 applicants, 635 accepted, 274 enrolled.
**Test score averages/ranges.** Average SAT scores: 770 combined.
**Faculty.** Student/faculty ratio: 17 to 1.
**Selectivity rating.** Less competitive.

**PROFILE.** Anderson is a private, church-affiliated, liberal arts college. Founded in 1911, it adopted coeducation in 1930. Its 32-acre campus is located in the town of Anderson, 20 miles from Greenville.

**Accreditation:** SACS.
**Religious orientation:** Anderson College is affiliated with the Baptist Church; two semesters of religion/theology required.
**Athletic facilities:** Gymnasium, racquetball and tennis courts, soccer and softball fields, weight room.

**STUDENT BODY. Undergraduate profile:** 77% are state residents; 16% are transfers. 1% Asian-American, 18% Black, 81% White.
**Freshman profile:** 95% of accepted applicants took SAT; 5% took ACT.
**Undergraduate achievement:** 55% of fall 1992 freshmen returned for fall 1993 term.
**Foreign students:** 52 students are from out of the country. Countries represented include Jamaica, Japan, Kuwait, and the West Indies; 22 in all.

**PROGRAMS OF STUDY. Degrees:** B.A., B.Mus.Ed., B.S.
**Majors:** Art, Biology, Business, Communications, Elementary Education, English, Liberal Studies, Music, Music Education, Physical Education, Psychology.
**Distribution of degrees:** The majors with the highest enrollment are business and elementary education.
**Requirements:** General education requirement.
**Academic regulations:** Freshmen must maintain minimum 1.5 GPA; sophomores, 1.7 GPA; juniors, 1.9 GPA; seniors, 2.0 GPA.
**Special:** Associate's degrees offered. Independent study. Pass/fail grading option. Internships. Preprofessional programs in law, medicine, pharmacy, dentistry, agriculture, allied health, computer science, engineering, forestry, medical technician, nursing, and social science. Teacher certification in elementary and secondary education. Certification in specific subject areas. ROTC. AFROTC at Clemson U.
**Honors:** Honors program. Honor societies.
**Academic Assistance:** Remedial reading, writing, math, and study skills. Nonremedial tutoring.

**ADMISSIONS. Academic basis for candidate selection** (in order of priority): Secondary school record, standardized test scores, class rank, school's recommendation.
**Nonacademic basis for candidate selection:** Character and personality are important. Extracurricular participation and particular talent or ability are considered.
**Requirements:** Graduation from secondary school is required; GED is accepted. No specific distribution of secondary school units required. Minimum combined SAT score of 700 and minimum 2.0 GPA required. Conditional admission possible for applicants not meeting standard requirements. SAT is required; ACT may be substituted. Campus visit recommended. Off-campus interviews available with an admissions representative.
**Procedure:** Take SAT or ACT by April of 12th year. Notification of admission on rolling basis. Reply is required by August 15. $25 tuition deposit, refundable until June 1. $50 room deposit, refundable until June 1. Freshmen accepted for terms other than fall.
**Special programs:** Admission may be deferred one semester. Credit and/or placement may be granted through CEEB Advanced Placement exams for scores of 3 or higher. Credit and/or placement may be granted through CLEP subject exams. Credit and placement may be granted through challenge exams. Early entrance/early admission program. Concurrent enrollment program.
**Transfer students:** Transfer students accepted for terms other than fall. In fall 1993, 16% of all new students were transfers into all classes. 182 transfer applications were received, 181 were accepted. Application deadline is August 15 for fall; January 1 for spring. Minimum 2.0 GPA required. Lowest course grade accepted is "D."
**Admissions contact:** Carl D. Lockman, Director of Admissions. 803 231-2030.

**FINANCIAL AID. Available aid:** Pell grants, SEOG, state scholarships and grants, school scholarships and grants, private scholarships and grants, academic merit scholarships, and athletic scholarships. Perkins Loans (NDSL), PLUS, Stafford Loans (GSL), and school loans. Family tuition reduction. College tuition plan.
**Supporting data/closing dates:** FAFSA/FAF/FFS: Accepted on rolling basis. School's own aid application: Accepted on rolling basis. State aid form: Accepted on rolling basis. Notification of awards begins March 15.
**Financial aid contact:** Jim Owens, Director of Financial Aid. 803 231-2073.

## Benedict College

**Columbia, SC 29204** **803 256-4220**

**1992-93 Costs.** Tuition: $5,084. Room & board: $2,892. Fees, books, misc. academic expenses (school's estimate): $1,015.
**Enrollment.** Undergraduates: 424 men, 860 women (full-time). Freshman class: 1,158 applicants, 798 accepted, 251 enrolled.
**Test score averages/ranges.** Average ACT scores: 21 composite.
**Faculty.** 81 full-time; 19 part-time. 41% of faculty holds doctoral degree. Student/faculty ratio: 14 to 1.
**Selectivity rating.** Highly competitive.

**PROFILE.** Benedict, founded in 1870, is a private, liberal arts college. Its 20-acre campus is located in Columbia.

**Accreditation:** SACS. Professionally accredited by the Council on Social Work Education.
**Religious orientation:** Benedict College is affiliated with the Baptist Church; two semesters of religion required.
**Library:** Collections totaling over 134,167 volumes, 415 periodical subscriptions, and 5,142 microform items.
**Special facilities/museums:** Language lab.
**Athletic facilities:** Gymnasium, swimming pool, tennis courts, weight room.

**STUDENT BODY. Undergraduate profile:** 85% are state residents; 2% are transfers. 97% Black, 3% Other. Average age of undergraduates is 21.
**Freshman profile:** 20% of freshmen who took SAT scored 700 or over on verbal, 20% scored 700 or over on math; 70% scored 600 or over on verbal, 70% scored 600 or over on

math; 100% scored 500 or over on verbal, 100% scored 500 or over on math. 30% of accepted applicants took SAT; 20% took ACT. 100% of freshmen come from public schools.
**Foreign students:** 45 students are from out of the country. Countries represented include the Bahamas, Jamaica, Kuwait, Lebanon, Nigeria, and Saudi Arabia; eight in all.

**PROGRAMS OF STUDY. Degrees:** B.A., B.S., B.Soc.Work.
**Majors:** Accounting, Art, Biology, Business Administration, Chemistry, Computer Science, Criminal Justice, Early Childhood Education, Elementary Education, English, Environmental Health Science, History, Management, Mathematics, Media Arts, Physics, Political Science, Recreation, Religion/Philosophy, Social Work.
**Distribution of degrees:** The majors with the highest enrollment are business administration, criminal justice, and social work; art, elementary education, and physics have the lowest.
**Requirements:** General education requirement.
**Academic regulations:** Freshmen must maintain minimum 1.5 GPA; sophomores, 1.6 GPA; juniors, 1.8 GPA; seniors, 1.9 GPA.
**Special:** Dual degrees. Independent study. Internships. Cooperative education programs. Preprofessional programs in medicine, dentistry, and allied health. 3-2 engineering programs with Georgia Tech, Southern Tech Inst, and Clemson U. Teacher certification in early childhood, elementary, and secondary education. Study abroad in Mexico. ROTC. AFROTC at U of South Carolina.
**Honors:** Honors program. Honor societies.
**Academic Assistance:** Remedial reading, writing, math, and study skills. Nonremedial tutoring.

**STUDENT LIFE. Housing:** All students must live on campus unless living with family. Women's dorms. 80% of students live in college housing.
**Social atmosphere:** The College Corner, Food Lion, and Five Points area are the most popular student gathering spots. Greeks are a major influence on student social life. The annual basketball tournament, Springfest, Coronation, and Homecoming are highlights of the school year. Movies, the student center, and student lounge provide some opportunities for social and cultural life at Benedict; most of it is found off campus.
**Services and counseling/handicapped student services:** Placement services. Health service. Day care. Freshman seminars. Counseling services for minority, military, veteran, and older students. Birth control, personal, and psychological counseling. Career and academic guidance services. Physically disabled student services. Tape recorders. Tutors. Reader services for the blind.
**Campus organizations:** Undergraduate student government. Student newspaper (Benedict Tiger, published once/month). Yearbook. Choir, concert band, gospel choir, drama club, departmental clubs, service societies, special-interest groups, 29 organizations in all. Four fraternities, no chapter houses; four sororities, no chapter houses. 5% of men join a fraternity. 8% of women join a sorority.
**Religious organizations:** Pretheological Association.
**Minority/foreign student organizations:** Foreign Student Association.

**ATHLETICS. Physical education requirements:** Two credit hours of physical education required.
**Intercollegiate competition:** 1% of students participate. Baseball (M), basketball (M,W), softball (W), track and field (M,W), volleyball (W). Member of EIAC Conference, NAIA.
**Intramural and club sports:** Intramural baseball, basketball.

**ADMISSIONS. Academic basis for candidate selection** (in order of priority): Secondary school record, class rank, standardized test scores, school's recommendation, essay.
**Nonacademic basis for candidate selection:** Extracurricular participation and geographical distribution are emphasized. Character and personality, particular talent or ability, and alumni/ae relationship are important.
**Requirements:** Graduation from secondary school is required; GED is accepted. 20 units and the following program of study are recommended: 4 units of English, 3 units of math, 2 units of science, 4 units of social studies, 7 units of electives. SAT or ACT is required. Campus visit recommended. Off-campus interviews available with admissions and alumni representatives.
**Procedure:** Take SAT or ACT by February of 12th year. Visit college for interview by April 15 of 12th year. Notification of admission on rolling basis. Reply is required within 30 days of notification. $50 nonrefundable tuition deposit. $50 room deposit, refundable until August 15. Freshmen accepted for terms other than fall.
**Special programs:** Admission may be deferred three years. Credit and/or placement may be granted through CLEP general exams. Credit may be granted through CLEP subject exams, DANTES exams, and military and life experience. Placement may be granted through challenge exams. Early decision program. In fall 1992, 17 applied for early decision and 17 were accepted. Deadline for applying for early decision is August. Early entrance/early admission program. Concurrent enrollment program.
**Transfer students:** Transfer students accepted for terms other than fall. In fall 1993, 2% of all new students were transfers into all classes. 109 transfer applications were received, 42 were accepted. Application deadline is rolling for fall; rolling for spring. Minimum 2.0 GPA required. Lowest course grade accepted is "C." Maximum number of transferable credits is 90 semester hours. At least 30 semester hours must be completed at the college to receive degree.
**Admissions contact:** LeRoy Brown, Ph.D., Director of Enrollment Management. 803 253-5143, 800 868-6598.

**FINANCIAL AID. Available aid:** Pell grants, SEOG, state grants, school scholarships and grants, private scholarships, ROTC scholarships, academic merit scholarships, athletic scholarships, and United Negro College Fund. Perkins Loans (NDSL), PLUS, Stafford Loans (GSL), and SLS. Deferred payment plan.
**Financial aid statistics:** 98% of aid is not need-based. In 1993-94, 88% of all undergraduate applicants received aid; 90% of freshman applicants. Average amounts of aid awarded freshmen: Scholarships and grants, $6,000.
**Supporting data/closing dates:** FAFSA/FAF/FFS: Priority filing date is May 30. School's own aid application: Priority filing date is May 30; accepted on rolling basis. State aid form: Priority filing date is May 30; accepted on rolling basis.
**Financial aid contact:** Shelia Brown, Director of Financial Aid. 803 253-5105.

**STUDENT EMPLOYMENT.** College Work/Study Program. Institutional employment. 65% of full-time undergraduates work on campus during school year. Students may expect to earn an average of $1,200 during school year. Off-campus part-time employment opportunities rated "good."

**COMPUTER FACILITIES.** 140 IBM/IBM-compatible and Macintosh/Apple microcomputers; 60 are networked. Students may access Digital minicomputer/mainframe systems. Residence halls may be equipped with stand-alone microcomputers, networked terminals. Computer languages and software packages include BASIC, COBOL, FORTRAN, STAT II. Computer facilities are available to all students.
**Fees:** None.
**Hours:** 7:30 AM-11 PM (M-Th); 7:30 AM-6 PM (F); 2 PM-5 PM (Sa-Su).

**GRADUATE CAREER DATA.** Highest graduate school enrollments: Atlanta U, Ohio State U, U of South Carolina. 14% of graduates choose careers in business and industry. Companies and businesses that hire graduates: Equitable Life, IBM, Michelin Tire, South Carolina Electric and Gas Co.

# Central Wesleyan College

**Central, SC 29630** **803 639-2453**

**1994-95 Costs.** Tuition: $8,300. Room: $1,000. Board: $2,080. Fees, books, misc. academic expenses (school's estimate): $250.
**Enrollment.** Undergraduates: 454 men, 516 women (full-time). Freshman class: 141 applicants, 121 accepted, 79 enrolled. Graduate enrollment: 44 men, 36 women.
**Test score averages/ranges.** Average SAT scores: 398 verbal, 426 math. Average ACT scores: 18 composite.
**Faculty.** 42 full-time; 97 part-time. 61% of faculty holds doctoral degree. Student/faculty ratio: 14 to 1.
**Selectivity rating.** Competitive.

**PROFILE.** Central Wesleyan, founded in 1906, is a church-affiliated, liberal arts college. Its 190-acre campus is located in the Piedmont region, near the Blue Ridge Mountains.

**Accreditation:** SACS.
**Religious orientation:** Central Wesleyan College is affiliated with the Wesleyan Church; three semesters of religion required.
**Library:** Collections totaling over 72,453 volumes, 389 periodical subscriptions and 300 microform items.

**STUDENT BODY. Undergraduate profile:** 86% are state residents; 38% are transfers. 13% Black, 85% White, 2% Other.
**Freshman profile:** 4% of freshmen who took SAT scored 600 or over on math; 15% scored 500 or over on verbal, 21% scored 500 or over on math; 43% scored 400 or over on verbal, 64% scored 400 or over on math; 85% scored 300 or over on verbal, 95% scored 300 or over on math. 92% of accepted applicants took SAT; 8% took ACT. 80% of freshmen come from public schools.
**Undergraduate achievement:** 56% of fall 1991 freshmen returned for fall 1992 term. 33% of entering class graduated.
**Foreign students:** Four students are from out of the country. Countries represented include Canada, the Cayman Islands, Ireland, and Korea.

**PROGRAMS OF STUDY. Degrees:** B.A., B.S.
**Majors:** Accounting, Bible, Biology, Business Administration, Chemistry, Chemistry Education, Christian Education, Church Music, Criminal Justice, Elementary Education, English, History, Management of Human Resources, Mathematics, Medical Technology, Mental Retardation/Learning Disabilities Education, Music, Music Education, New Testament Greek, Nursing, Physical Education, Psychology, Recreation, Religion, Social Studies, Special Education, Theology, Youth/Music.
**Distribution of degrees:** The majors with the highest enrollment are business administration, elementary education, and management of human resources; medical technology, nursing, and chemistry have the lowest.
**Requirements:** General education requirement.
**Academic regulations:** Freshmen must maintain minimum 1.6 GPA; sophomores, juniors, seniors, 2.0 GPA.
**Special:** Minors offered in some majors and in computer information systems, finance/economics, management, music, and youth ministry. Associate's degrees offered. Double majors. Independent study. Cooperative education programs. Preprofessional programs in law, medicine, and dentistry. Cooperative nursing program with Clemson U. Member of Christian College Coalition. American Studies Program (Washington, D.C.). Exchange program with Clemson U. Teacher certification in early childhood, elementary, secondary, and special education. Certification in specific subject areas. Exchange programs abroad in Costa Rica and England. ROTC and AFROTC at Clemson U.
**Honors:** Honors program. Honor societies.
**Academic Assistance:** Remedial reading, writing, math, and study skills.

**ADMISSIONS. Academic basis for candidate selection** (in order of priority): Secondary school record, class rank, school's recommendation, standardized test scores.
**Nonacademic basis for candidate selection:** Character and personality are emphasized. Particular talent or ability is considered.
**Requirements:** Graduation from secondary school is required; GED is accepted. 10 units and the following program of study are recommended: 4 units of English, 2 units of math, 2 units of science, 2 units of social studies. Minimum combined SAT score of 740, rank in top half of secondary school class, and minimum 2.0 GPA required. Conditional admission possible for applicants not meeting standard requirements. SAT or ACT is required. Campus visit and interview recommended. Off-campus interviews available with an admissions representative.
**Procedure:** Take SAT or ACT by June of 12th year. Suggest filing application by April 15. Application deadline is August 15. Notification of admission on rolling basis. Reply is required by May 1. $100 room deposit, refundable until August 1. Freshmen accepted for terms other than fall.
**Special programs:** Admission may be deferred. Credit may be granted through CEEB Advanced Placement for scores of 4 or higher. Credit may be granted through CLEP general exams. Early entrance/early admission program. Concurrent enrollment program.

**Transfer students:** Transfer students accepted for terms other than fall. In fall 1992, 38% of all new students were transfers into all classes. 65 transfer applications were received, 59 were accepted. Application deadline is August 15 for fall; January 15 for spring. Minimum 2.0 GPA recommended. Lowest course grade accepted is "1.6." Maximum number of transferable credits is 68 semester hours. At least 32 semester hours must be completed at the college to receive degree.
**Admissions contact:** Tim Wilkerson, Dean of Enrollment Management. 800 289-1CWC.
**FINANCIAL AID. Available aid:** Pell grants, SEOG, state scholarships and grants, school scholarships and grants, private scholarships and grants, ROTC scholarships, academic merit scholarships, athletic scholarships, and aid for undergraduate foreign students. Perkins Loans (NDSL), PLUS, Stafford Loans (GSL), state loans, and SLS. Institutional payment plan.
**Financial aid statistics:** 25% of aid is not need-based. In 1992-93, 98% of all undergraduate applicants received aid; 98% of freshman applicants. Average amounts of aid awarded freshmen: Scholarships and grants, $2,000; loans, $1,400.
**Supporting data/closing dates:** School's own aid application: Priority filing date is April 15; accepted on rolling basis. State aid form: Priority filing date is March 1; deadline is April 15. SINGLEFILE: Priority filing date is April 15; accepted on rolling basis. Notification of awards on rolling basis.
**Financial aid contact:** Debbie Hamilton, Director of Financial Aid. 800 289-1CWC.

## The Citadel

**Charleston, SC 29409** **803 792-5230**

**1993-94 Costs.** Tuition: $2,805 (state residents), $6,804 (out-of-state). Room & board: $3,094. Fees, books, misc. academic expenses (school's estimate): $950.
**Enrollment.** 1,934 men (full-time). Freshman class: 1,500 applicants, 1,280 accepted, 629 enrolled.
**Test score averages/ranges.** Average SAT scores: 462 verbal, 514 math. Average ACT scores: 22 composite.
**Faculty.** 160 full-time; 25 part-time. 90% of faculty holds highest degree in specific field. Student/faculty ratio: 13 to 1.
**Selectivity rating.** Less competitive.

**PROFILE.** The Citadel, founded in 1842, is a public, liberal arts, military college. Its 130-acre campus is located in Charleston.

**Accreditation:** SACS. Professionally accredited by the Accreditation Board for Engineering and Technology, the National Council for Accreditation of Teacher Education.
**Religious orientation:** The Citadel is nonsectarian; no religious requirements.
**Library:** Collections totaling over 141,000 volumes, 250 periodical subscriptions, and 5,000 microform items.
**Special facilities/museums:** Language lab, military history museum.
**Athletic facilities:** Field house, racquetball and tennis courts, swimming pool, training, weight, and wrestling rooms, batting cage, gymnasium, stadium.
**STUDENT BODY. Undergraduate profile:** 49% are state residents; 6% are transfers. 2% Asian-American, 7% Black, 1% Hispanic, 89% White, 1% Other. Average age of undergraduates is 20.
**Freshman profile:** 2% of freshmen who took SAT scored 700 or over on math; 5% scored 600 or over on verbal, 13% scored 600 or over on math; 28% scored 500 or over on verbal, 57% scored 500 or over on math; 80% scored 400 or over on verbal, 95% scored 400 or over on math; 100% scored 300 or over on verbal, 100% scored 300 or over on math. 90% of accepted applicants took SAT; 5% took ACT.
**Undergraduate achievement:** 73% of fall 1991 freshmen returned for fall 1992 term. 65% of entering class graduated.
**Foreign students:** 32 students are from out of the country. Countries represented include Canada, Japan, Jordan, Panama, Taiwan, and Thailand; 11 in all.
**PROGRAMS OF STUDY. Degrees:** B.A., B.S., B.S.Bus.Admin., B.S.Eng.
**Majors:** Biology, Business Administration, Chemistry, Civil Engineering, Computer Science, Education, Electrical Engineering, English, History, Mathematics, Modern Languages, Physical Education, Physics, Political Science, Psychology.
**Distribution of degrees:** The majors with the highest enrollment are business administration, political science, and biology; computer science, chemistry, and physics have the lowest.
**Requirements:** General education requirement.
**Academic regulations:** Minimum 2.0 GPA required for graduation.
**Special:** The Citadel is a liberal arts military college. Cadets are required to complete four years of ROTC; entrance into military service is optional. Courses offered in anthropology, fine arts, geology, philosopy, and sociology. Preprofessional programs in law and medicine. Teacher certification in secondary and special education. Summer study abroad programs in France and Spain. ROTC, NROTC, and AFROTC.
**Honors:** Honors program. Honor societies.
**Academic Assistance:** Nonremedial tutoring.
**STUDENT LIFE. Housing:** All students in Corps of Cadets must live on campus. Men's dorms. 100% of students live in college housing.
**Social atmosphere:** "During the week, Cadets are more or less restricted to campus," reports the student newspaper. "There is no social life during the week. On weekends everyone is allowed out and the thing that everyone does most is party." Popular gathering spots on campus are Mark Clark Hall and the Social Activities Center. An influential group on campus is the Cadet-Chain of Command. Favorite events during the year are large parties, the fine arts film series, and football and basketball games.
**Services and counseling/handicapped student services:** Placement services. Health service. Counseling services for military students. Personal and psychological counseling. Career and academic guidance services. Religious counseling. Learning disabled services.
**Campus organizations:** Undergraduate student government. Student newspaper (Brigadier, published twice/month). Literary magazine. Yearbook. Bagpipers, band, orchestra, gospel and protestant choirs, chorale, Corps of Cadets, departmental and political groups, drama group professional groups, Original 13, service organizations, special-interest groups.
**Religious organizations:** Several religious organizations.
**Minority/foreign student organizations:** Afro-American Society.
**ATHLETICS. Physical education requirements:** Two semesters of physical education required.
**Intercollegiate competition:** 40% of students participate. Baseball (M), basketball (M), cheerleading (M), cross-country (M), football (M), golf (M), riflery (M), soccer (M), tennis (M), track (indoor) (M), track (outdoor) (M), track and field (indoor) (M), track and field (outdoor) (M), wrestling (M). Member of NCAA Division I, NCAA Division I-AA for football, Southern Conference.
**Intramural and club sports:** 95% of students participate. Intramural lacrosse, pistol, rugby, sailing. Men's club bowling, boxing, crew, cycling, fencing, gymnastics, lacrosse, parachute, rifle, rugby, sailing.
**ADMISSIONS. Academic basis for candidate selection** (in order of priority): Secondary school record, standardized test scores, class rank, school's recommendation.
**Nonacademic basis for candidate selection:** Character and personality and extracurricular participation are emphasized. Particular talent or ability and alumni/ae relationship are important.
**Requirements:** Graduation from secondary school is required; GED is not accepted. 18 units and the following program of study are required: 4 units of English, 3 units of math, 2 units of lab science, 2 units of foreign language, 2 units of social studies, 1 unit of history, 2 units of electives including 3 units of academic electives. Minimum combined SAT score of 800 required. All applicants must pass physical exam. SAT is required; ACT may be substituted. ACH recommended. Campus visit and interview recommended. No off-campus interviews.
**Procedure:** Take SAT or ACT by May of 12th year. Take ACH by July of 12th year. Visit college for interview by May of 12th year. Notification of admission on rolling basis. Reply is required within 15 days of notification. $150 room deposit, refundable until June 1. Freshmen accepted for fall term only.
**Special programs:** Credit and/or placement may be granted through CLEP subject exams. Credit and placement may be granted through challenge exams.
**Transfer students:** Transfer students accepted for fall term only. In fall 1992, 6% of all new students were transfers into all classes. 91 transfer applications were received, 54 were accepted. Application deadline is May. Minimum 2.5 GPA required. Lowest course grade accepted is "C." Maximum number of transferable credits is 60 semester hours.
**Admissions contact:** Lt. Col. Wallace I. West, Director of Admissions. 800 868-1842.
**FINANCIAL AID. Available aid:** Pell grants, SEOG, state scholarships, school scholarships and grants, private scholarships, ROTC scholarships, academic merit scholarships, and athletic scholarships. Perkins Loans (NDSL), PLUS, Stafford Loans (GSL), state loans, school loans, private loans, and SLS. Tuition Plan Inc., Education Plan Inc., Knight Tuition Plans, and AMS. 10-month payment plan.
**Financial aid statistics:** 30% of aid is not need-based. In 1992-93, 80% of all undergraduate applicants received aid; 80% of freshman applicants. Average amounts of aid awarded freshmen: Scholarships and grants, $1,000; loans, $2,000.
**Supporting data/closing dates:** Income tax forms: Deadline is March 15. Federal Form: Priority filing date is March 15; accepted on rolling basis. Notification of awards begins in March.
**Financial aid contact:** Maj. H. Fuller, Director of Financial Aid. 803 792-5187.
**STUDENT EMPLOYMENT.** College Work/Study Program. Institutional employment. 10% of full-time undergraduates work on campus during school year. Students may expect to earn an average of $800 during school year. Freshmen are discouraged from working during their first term. Off-campus part-time employment opportunities rated "good."
**COMPUTER FACILITIES.** 250 IBM/IBM-compatible and Macintosh/Apple microcomputers; 200 are networked. Students may access Digital minicomputer/mainframe systems. Residence halls may be equipped with stand-alone microcomputers, networked microcomputers, networked terminals. Computer languages and software packages include Ada, BASIC, C, COBOL, dBASE, FORTRAN, LISP, Lotus 1-2-3, MINITAB, Pascal, SPSS, WordPerfect; 25 in all. Computer facilities are available to all students.
**Fees:** None.
**Hours:** 24 hours.
**GRADUATE CAREER DATA.** Highest graduate school enrollments: Medical U of South Carolina, U of South Carolina. 56% of graduates choose careers in business and industry.
**PROMINENT ALUMNI/AE.** Pat Conroy, author; Ernest F. Hollings, U.S. senator, South Carolina; John C. West, former governor of South Carolina and ambassador to Saudi Arabia; Alva H. Chapman, former chairperson, Knight Ridder Publishing; Tandy C. Rice, president, Top Billing International; Dr. Harvey W. Schiller, executive director, United States Olympic Committee.

## Clemson University

**Clemson, SC 29634-5124** **803 656-3311**

**1993-94 Costs.** Tuition: $2,853 (state residents), $7,794 (out-of-state). Room: $1,200-$2,200. Board: $1,638. Fees, books, misc. academic expenses (school's estimate): $700.
**Enrollment.** Undergraduates: 6,599 men, 5,156 women (full-time). Freshman class: 8,065 applicants, 5,257 accepted. Graduate enrollment: 2,179 men, 1,910 women.
**Test score averages/ranges.** Range of SAT scores of middle 50%: 430-530 verbal, 510-620 math.
**Faculty.** 1,101 full-time; 167 part-time. 75% of faculty holds doctoral degree. Student/faculty ratio: 17 to 1.
**Selectivity rating.** More competitive.

**PROFILE.** Clemson, founded in 1889, is a public university. Programs are offered through the Colleges of Agricultural Sciences, Architecture, Commerce and Industry,

Education, Engineering, Forest and Recreation Resources, Liberal Arts, Nursing, and Sciences. Its 600-acre campus is located in Clemson, 55 miles from Greenville-Spartanburg.

**Accreditation:** SACS. Professionally accredited by the Accreditation Board for Engineering and Technology, the National Architecture Accrediting Board, the National League for Nursing, the Society of American Foresters.
**Religious orientation:** Clemson University is nonsectarian; no religious requirements.
**Library:** Collections totaling over 1,485,000 volumes, 6,900 periodical subscriptions, and 218,674 microform items.
**Athletic facilities:** Indoor track, indoor tennis courts, swimming pool, cross-country course.

**STUDENT BODY. Undergraduate profile:** 72% are state residents; 17% are transfers. 1% Asian-American, 9% Black, 88% White, 2% Other. Average age of undergraduates is 20.
**Freshman profile:** 100% of accepted applicants took SAT; 1% took ACT. 80% of freshmen come from public schools.
**Undergraduate achievement:** 87% of fall 1992 freshmen returned for fall 1993 term. 39% of entering class graduated. 20% of students who completed a degree program immediately went on to graduate study.
**Foreign students:** 115 students are from out of the country. Countries represented include Canada, India, Jamaica, Mexico, Pakistan, and the United Kingdom; 22 in all.

**PROGRAMS OF STUDY. Degrees:** B.A., B.F.A., B.Land.Arch., B.S., B.S.Nurs.
**Majors:** Accounting, Agricultural Economics/Rural Sociology, Agricultural Education, Agricultural Engineering, Agricultural Mechanization/Business, Animal Industries, Architecture, Biochemistry, Biological Sciences, Building Science/Management, Ceramic Engineering, Chemical Engineering, Chemistry, Civil Engineering, Computer Engineering, Computer Information Systems, Computer Science, Design, Early Childhood, Economics, Electrical Engineering, Elementary Education, Engineering Analysis, English, Entomology, Financial Management, Food Science, Forest Products, Forest Resource Management, Geology, Graphic Communications, Health Science, History, Industrial Education, Industrial Engineering, Industrial Management, Language/International Trade, Management, Marketing, Mathematical Sciences, Mechanical Engineering, Medical Technology, Microbiology, Modern Languages, Nursing, Packaging Science, Parks/Recreation/Tourist Management, Philosophy, Physics, Plant Sciences, Political Science, Pre-Pharmacy, Pre-Physical Therapy, Psychology, Science Teaching, Secondary Education, Sociology, Special Education, Speech/Communication Studies, Textile Chemistry, Textile Science.
**Distribution of degrees:** The majors with the highest enrollment are management, financial management, and marketing; plant pathology, foreign languages, and entomology have the lowest.
**Requirements:** General education requirement.
**Academic regulations:** Freshmen must maintain minimum 1.6 GPA; sophomores, 1.87 GPA; juniors, 1.98 GPA; seniors, 2.0 GPA.
**Special:** Minors offered in most majors. Double majors. Independent study. Internships. Cooperative education programs. Graduate school at which undergraduates may take graduate-level courses. Preprofessional programs in law, medicine, veterinary science, pharmacy, and dentistry. 2-2 physical therapy program. 2-3 pharmacy program. Teacher certification in early childhood, elementary, secondary, special education, and vo-tech education. Certification in specific subject areas. Study abroad in Germany, Italy, Mexico, Spain, and the United Kingdom. ROTC and AFROTC.
**Honors:** Honors program. Honor societies.
**Academic Assistance:** Remedial reading, writing, and study skills.

**STUDENT LIFE. Housing:** Students may live on or off campus. Coed, women's, and men's dorms. Sorority and fraternity housing. School-owned/operated apartments. On-campus married-student housing. 52% of students live in college housing.
**Services and counseling/handicapped student services:** Placement services. Health service. Counseling services for minority, military, veteran, and older students. Birth control, personal, and psychological counseling. Career and academic guidance services. Physically disabled student services. Learning disabled services. Notetaking services. Tape recorders. Tutors. Reader services for the blind.
**Campus organizations:** Undergraduate student government. Student newspaper (Tiger, published once/week). Literary magazine. Yearbook. Radio station. Marching and pep bands, chorus and gospel choir, theatre group, departmental, service, and special-interest groups, 250 organizations in all. 19 fraternities, no chapter houses; 13 sororities, no chapter houses. 15% of men join a fraternity. 26% of women join a sorority.
**Religious organizations:** B'nai B'rith, Baptist Student Union, Campus Crusade for Christ, Catholic Student Association, Fellowship of Christian Athletes, Lutheran Student Movement.
**Minority/foreign student organizations:** Society of Black Engineers, Pan-Greek Council, Minority Council. International Student Association, International Student Council.

**ATHLETICS. Physical education requirements:** None.
**Intercollegiate competition:** 7% of students participate. Baseball (M), basketball (M,W), cross-country (M,W), diving (M,W), football (M), golf (M), soccer (M), swimming (M,W), tennis (M,W), track (indoor) (M,W), track (outdoor) (M,W), track and field (indoor) (M,W), track and field (outdoor) (M,W), volleyball (W), wrestling (M). Member of Atlantic Coast Conference, NCAA Division I, NCAA Division I-A for football.

**ADMISSIONS. Academic basis for candidate selection** (in order of priority): Class rank, secondary school record, standardized test scores, school's recommendation, essay.
**Nonacademic basis for candidate selection:** Alumni/ae relationship is emphasized. Character and personality and geographical distribution are considered.
**Requirements:** Graduation from secondary school is required; GED is accepted. 14 units and the following program of study are required: 4 units of English, 3 units of math, 2 units of lab science, 2 units of foreign language, 3 units of social studies. Minimum combined SAT score of 950, rank in top quarter of secondary school class, and minimum 2.5 GPA recommended. Interview required of architecture program applicants. Choice of major is incorporated into admissions decision due to enrollment pressures in certain areas. Portfolio required of art program applicants. SAT is required; ACT may be substituted. ACH required. Campus visit recommended. No off-campus interviews.
**Procedure:** Take SAT or ACT by December of 12th year. Take ACH by May of 12th year. Notification of admission on rolling basis. Reply is required within two weeks of acceptance; extension of deadline may be granted until May 1 upon written request. Tuition deposit is partially refundable until June 1. Freshmen accepted for terms other than fall.
**Special programs:** Credit and/or placement may be granted through CEEB Advanced Placement exams for scores of 3 or higher. Credit and/or placement may be granted through CLEP subject exams. Credit may be granted through challenge exams. Early entrance/early admission program.
**Transfer students:** Transfer students accepted for terms other than fall. In fall 1993, 17% of all new students were transfers into all classes. 1,470 transfer applications were received, 672 were accepted. Minimum 2.5 GPA recommended. Lowest course grade accepted is "C." At least 30 semester hours must be completed at the university to receive degree.
**Admissions contact:** Michael R. Heintze, Ph.D., Director of Admissions. 803 656-2287.

**FINANCIAL AID. Available aid:** Pell grants, SEOG, state grants, school scholarships and grants, private scholarships and grants, ROTC scholarships, academic merit scholarships, and athletic scholarships. Perkins Loans (NDSL), PLUS, Stafford Loans (GSL), private loans, and SLS. Tuition Plan Inc. and Knight Tuition Plans.
**Financial aid statistics:** 49% of aid is not need-based. In 1993-94, 84% of all undergraduate applicants received aid; 80% of freshman applicants. Average amounts of aid awarded freshmen: Scholarships and grants, $3,300; loans, $1,750.
**Supporting data/closing dates:** FAFSA: Priority filing date is April 1. School's own aid application: Priority filing date is April. Notification of awards begins May 1.
**Financial aid contact:** Marvin Carmichael, M.Ed., Director of Financial Aid. 803 656-2280.

**STUDENT EMPLOYMENT.** College Work/Study Program. Institutional employment. 25% of full-time undergraduates work on campus during school year. Students may expect to earn an average of $1,100 during school year. Off-campus part-time employment opportunities rated "good."

**COMPUTER FACILITIES.** 1,000 IBM/IBM-compatible and Macintosh/Apple microcomputers. Students may access minicomputer/mainframe systems. Numerous computer languages and software packages available. Computer facilities are available to all students.
**Fees:** None.
**Hours:** 24 hours.

**GRADUATE CAREER DATA.** Highest graduate school enrollments: U of South Carolina Medical Sch and Law Sch. 80% of graduates choose careers in business and industry. Companies and businesses that hire graduates: AT&T, DuPont, IBM, Milliken, NCNB.

**PROMINENT ALUMNI/AE.** Strom Thurmond, U.S. senator; Harvey B. Gantt, architect and former mayor of Charlotte, N.C.

# Coastal Carolina University

**Conway, SC, SC 29526** **803 448-1481**

**1994-95 Costs.** Tuition: $2,470 (state residents), $6,280 (out-of-state). Room: $2,370. Board: $1,300. Fees, books, misc. academic expenses (school's estimate): $450.
**Enrollment.** Undergraduates: 1,513 men, 1,690 women (full-time). Freshman class: 1,854 applicants, 1,391 accepted, 756 enrolled. Graduate enrollment: 31 men, 228 women.
**Test score averages/ranges.** Average SAT scores: 449 verbal, 495 math. Range of SAT scores of middle 50%: 350-450 verbal, 400-560 math. Average ACT scores: 20 composite.
**Faculty.** 179 full-time; 70 part-time. 74% of faculty holds doctoral degree. Student/faculty ratio: 18 to 1.
**Selectivity rating.** Less competitive.

**PROFILE.** Coastal Carolina University, founded in 1954, is a public, comprehensive university. Its 208-acre campus is located in Conway, nine miles from Myrtle Beach.

**Accreditation:** SACS.
**Religious orientation:** Coastal Carolina University is nonsectarian; no religious requirements.
**Library:** Collections totaling over 153,949 volumes, 978 periodical subscriptions, and 28,647 microform items.
**Special facilities/museums:** Off-campus marine research lab.
**Athletic facilities:** Gymnasium, baseball and soccer fields, weight room, racquetball and tennis courts, swimming pool.

**STUDENT BODY. Undergraduate profile:** 73% are state residents; 23% are transfers. 1% Asian-American, 7% Black, 1% Hispanic, 1% Native American, 90% White. Average age of undergraduates is 21.
**Freshman profile:** 1% of freshmen who took SAT scored 600 or over on verbal, 6% scored 600 or over on math; 12% scored 500 or over on verbal, 32% scored 500 or over on math; 59% scored 400 or over on verbal, 79% scored 400 or over on math; 96% scored 300 or over on verbal, 99% scored 300 or over on math. 17% of freshmen who took ACT scored 24 or over on composite; 79% scored 18 or over on composite; 100% scored 12 or over on composite. 86% of accepted applicants took SAT; 14% took ACT. 92% of freshmen come from public schools.
**Undergraduate achievement:** 65% of fall 1992 freshmen returned for fall 1993 term. 17% of entering class graduated.
**Foreign students:** 73 students are from out of the country. Countries represented include Canada, France, Iceland, Japan, Sweden, and the United Kingdom; 25 in all.

**PROGRAMS OF STUDY. Degrees:** B.A., B.S.
**Majors:** Accounting, Applied Mathematics, Art Studio, Biology, Computer Science, Dramatic Arts, Early Childhood Education, Elementary Education, English, Finance, History, Interdisciplinary Studies, Management, Marine Science, Marketing, Physical Education, Political Science, Psychology, Secondary Education, Sociology.

**Distribution of degrees:** The majors with the highest enrollment are elementary education, management, and marketing; math and art studio have the lowest.
**Requirements:** General education requirement.
**Academic regulations:** Minimum 2.0 GPA must be maintained.
**Special:** Minors offered in many majors and in business administration, chemistry, French, German, international studies, mathematics, music, philosophy, Spanish, and theatre/speech. Self-designed majors. Double majors. Independent study. Pass/fail grading option. Internships. Graduate school at which undergraduates may take graduate-level courses. Preprofessional programs in law, medicine, veterinary science, pharmacy, dentistry, and theology. Teacher certification in early childhood, elementary, and secondary education. Certification in specific subject areas. Study abroad in England and France.
**Honors:** Phi Beta Kappa. Honors program. Honor societies.
**Academic Assistance:** Remedial writing and math. Nonremedial tutoring.

**STUDENT LIFE. Housing:** Students may live on or off campus. Coed dorms. 12% of students live in college housing.
**Social atmosphere:** Favorite student hangouts include Ibby's (a coffee house), Club Zero (an alternative club), Shamrock's (a bar), the Trestle (a restaurant), and Perkins (a coffee shop). Greeks, Amnesty International, the African-American Association, and STAR (Students Taking Active Responsibility, a community service organization) are influential groups on campus. Students enjoy UN Day, Karaoke Night, the AIDS three-on-three basketball tournament, Cultural Explosion, and soccer games. The student newspaper reports that although the school's student population has increased dramatically in recent years, the number of student activities and organizations has helped maintain a personal atmosphere on campus.
**Services and counseling/handicapped student services:** Placement services. Counseling services for minority, veteran, and older students. Personal and psychological counseling. Career and academic guidance services.
**Campus organizations:** Undergraduate student government. Student newspaper (Chanticleer, published biweekly). Literary magazine. Yearbook. Choir, music ensembles, pep band, musical theatre, drama club, literary groups, Spring Arts Festival, Campus Union, 48 organizations in all. Four fraternities, no chapter houses; five sororities, no chapter houses. 7% of men join a fraternity. 6% of women join a sorority.
**Religious organizations:** Baptist Student Union, Campus Crusade for Christ, Fellowship of Christian Athletes, Neuman Club.
**Minority/foreign student organizations:** Afro-American Society. International Student Club.

**ATHLETICS. Physical education requirements:** None.
**Intercollegiate competition:** 5% of students participate. Baseball (M), basketball (M,W), cheerleading (M,W), cross-country (M,W), golf (M,W), soccer (M), softball (W), tennis (M,W), track (outdoor) (M,W), volleyball (W). Member of Big South Athletic Conference, NCAA Division I.
**Intramural and club sports:** 10% of students participate. Intramural basketball, bowling, flag football, frisbee golf, golf, racquetball, running, softball, tennis, triathlon, volleyball, walking, walleyball, water polo.

**ADMISSIONS. Academic basis for candidate selection** (in order of priority): Class rank, secondary school record, standardized test scores, school's recommendation.
**Nonacademic basis for candidate selection:** Geographical distribution is considered.
**Requirements:** Graduation from secondary school is required; GED is accepted. 17 units and the following program of study are required: 4 units of English, 3 units of math, 2 units of lab science, 2 units of foreign language, 3 units of social studies, 1 unit of history, 2 units of electives including 1 unit of academic electives. Minimum 1.75 GPA and minimum combined SAT score of 650 required of in-state applicants; minimum combined SAT score of 700 required of out-of-state applicants. Conditional admission possible for applicants not meeting standard requirements. SAT or ACT is required. Campus visit and interview recommended. Off-campus interviews available with admissions and alumni representatives.
**Procedure:** Take SAT or ACT by May of 12th year. Suggest filing application by August 15; no deadline. Notification of admission on rolling basis. No set date by which applicants must accept offer. $100 nonrefundable room deposit. Freshmen accepted for terms other than fall.
**Special programs:** Admission may be deferred one year. Credit may be granted through CEEB Advanced Placement for scores of 3 or higher. Credit may be granted through CLEP subject exams, challenge exams, and military experience. Concurrent enrollment program.
**Transfer students:** Transfer students accepted for terms other than fall. In fall 1993, 23% of all new students were transfers into all classes. 839 transfer applications were received, 598 were accepted. Application deadline is August 15 for fall; December 15 for spring. Minimum 2.0 GPA recommended. Lowest course grade accepted is "C." Maximum number of transferable credits is 90 semester hours. At least 30 semester hours must be completed at the university to receive degree.
**Admissions contact:** Timothy McCormick, M.A.S., Director of Admissions. 800 277-7000.

**FINANCIAL AID. Available aid:** Pell grants, SEOG, state scholarships, school scholarships, private scholarships, academic merit scholarships, and athletic scholarships. Perkins Loans (NDSL), PLUS, Stafford Loans (GSL), state loans, and SLS. Tuition Plan Inc.
**Financial aid statistics:** 53% of aid is not need-based. In 1993-94, 58% of all undergraduate applicants received aid.
**Supporting data/closing dates:** School's own aid application: Priority filing date is April 1. Notification of awards on rolling basis.
**Financial aid contact:** Mollie Bethea-Floyd, M.Ed., Director of Financial Aid. 803 349-2313.

**STUDENT EMPLOYMENT.** College Work/Study Program. Institutional employment. 1% of full-time undergraduates work on campus during school year. Students may expect to earn an average of $2,000 during school year. Off-campus part-time employment opportunities rated "excellent."

**COMPUTER FACILITIES.** 625 IBM/IBM-compatible and Macintosh/Apple microcomputers; 250 are networked. Students may access Digital, IBM minicomputer/mainframe systems, Internet. Client/LAN operating systems include Apple/Macintosh, DOS, Novell. Computer languages and software packages include BASIC, COBOL, dBASE, FORTRAN, Lotus 1-2-3, Pascal, PC-Calc, PC-Write, WordPerfect; 100 in all. Computer facilities are available to all students.
**Fees:** None.
**Hours:** 8:30 AM-11 PM.

**GRADUATE CAREER DATA.** Highest graduate school enrollments: Medical U of South Carolina, U of South Carolina. Companies and businesses that hire graduates: Horry County School District, Waccamaw Corp.

**PROMINENT ALUMNI/AE.** Billy Alford, chairperson, Horry County Higher Education Commission; Ruthie Kearns, vice-president of administration, Coastal Federal Savings & Loan; Fran Gilbert, vice-president of administration, Canal Industries.

# Coker College

**Hartsville, SC 29550** **803 383-8000**

**1994-95 Costs.** Tuition: $9,888. Room: $2,670. Board: $1,846. Fees, books, misc. academic expenses (school's estimate): $850.
**Enrollment.** Undergraduates: 284 men, 406 women (full-time). Freshman class: 411 applicants, 303 accepted, 165 enrolled.
**Test score averages/ranges.** Average SAT scores: 431 verbal, 469 math. Range of SAT scores of middle 50%: 370-470 verbal, 420-540 math. Average ACT scores: 20 composite.
**Faculty.** 47 full-time; 42 part-time. 76% of faculty holds highest degree in specific field. Student/faculty ratio: 9 to 1.
**Selectivity rating.** Less competitive.

**PROFILE.** Coker, founded in 1908, is a private, liberal arts college. Its 15-acre campus is located in Hartsville, 70 miles from Columbia.

**Accreditation:** SACS. Professionally accredited by the National Association of Schools of Music.
**Religious orientation:** Coker College is nonsectarian; no religious requirements.
**Library:** Collections totaling over 80,000 volumes, 390 periodical subscriptions, and 1,400 microform items.
**Special facilities/museums:** Art gallery, botanical gardens, graduate-level science equipment.
**Athletic facilities:** Swimming pool, gymnasium, exercise and weight rooms, dance studio, baseball, soccer, and softball fields, tennis courts.

**STUDENT BODY. Undergraduate profile:** 87% are state residents; 17% are transfers. 31% Black, 1% Hispanic, 66% White, 2% Other. Average age of undergraduates is 27.
**Freshman profile:** 8% of freshmen who took SAT scored 600 or over on verbal, 5% scored 600 or over on math; 21% scored 500 or over on verbal, 38% scored 500 or over on math; 63% scored 400 or over on verbal, 82% scored 400 or over on math; 98% scored 300 or over on verbal, 99% scored 300 or over on math. 87% of accepted applicants took SAT; 13% took ACT. 85% of freshmen come from public schools.
**Undergraduate achievement:** 81% of fall 1992 freshmen returned for fall 1993 term. 48% of entering class graduated. 16% of students who completed a degree program immediately went on to graduate study.
**Foreign students:** 12 students are from out of the country. Countries represented include Canada, England, Ireland, Japan, Trinidad, and Venezuela.

**PROGRAMS OF STUDY. Degrees:** B.A., B.S.
**Majors:** Art, Art Education, Biology, Business Administration, Chemistry, Communications, Dance, Drama, Early Childhood Education, Elementary Education, English, French, History, Individualized Major, Mathematics, Medical Technology, Music, Music Education, Physical Education, Political Science, Psychology, Religion, Social Science, Sociology, Spanish.
**Distribution of degrees:** The majors with the highest enrollment are business administration, elementary/early childhood education, and social science; medical technology, French, and political science have the lowest.
**Requirements:** General education requirement.
**Academic regulations:** Freshmen must maintain minimum 1.5 GPA; sophomores, 1.7 GPA; juniors, 1.9 GPA; seniors, 2.0 GPA.
**Special:** Minors offered in some majors and in American history, coaching, computer science, English education, European history, and international studies. Concentrations offered in accounting, counseling, criminology, exercise science, finance, fine arts, graphic design, marketing management, operations management, organ, photography, physical fitness, piano, professional writing, social work, sports communication, sports management, teacher education. Self-designed majors. Double majors. Independent study. Accelerated study. Pass/fail grading option. Internships. Cooperative education programs. Graduate school at which undergraduates may take graduate-level courses. Preprofessional programs in law, medicine, veterinary science, pharmacy, dentistry, theology, and optometry. Combined-degree program in medical technology. Washington Semester. Arts study programs. Teacher certification in early childhood, elementary, and secondary education. Certification in specific subject areas. Study abroad in China, England, France, Japan (Daito Bunka U), the Netherlands, Portugal, Russia, and Spain.
**Honors:** Honors program. Honor societies.
**Academic Assistance:** Remedial writing, math, and study skills. Nonremedial tutoring.

**ADMISSIONS. Academic basis for candidate selection** (in order of priority): Secondary school record, class rank, standardized test scores, school's recommendation, essay.
**Nonacademic basis for candidate selection:** Character and personality are important. Extracurricular participation, particular talent or ability, and alumni/ae relationship are considered.
**Requirements:** Graduation from secondary school is required; GED is accepted. 20 units and the following program of study are required: 4 units of English, 3 units of math, 2 units of science, 2 units of history, 9 units of electives. Minimum combined ACT score of 20 (combined SAT score of 850), rank in top half of secondary school class, and minimum 2.0 GPA required. Audition required of dance and music program applicants. Portfolio required of art program applicants. Conditional admission possible for applicants not meet-

ing standard requirements. SAT or ACT is required. PSAT is recommended. Campus visit and interview recommended. Off-campus interviews available with an admissions representative.
**Procedure:** Take SAT or ACT by March of 12th year. Visit college for interview by May of 12th year. Suggest filing application by March 1; no deadline. Notification of admission on rolling basis. $50 tuition deposit, refundable until May 1. $75 room deposit, refundable until May 1. Freshmen accepted for terms other than fall.
**Special programs:** Admission may be deferred one year. Credit and/or placement may be granted through CEEB Advanced Placement exams for scores of 3 or higher. Credit and/or placement may be granted through CLEP general and subject exams. Credit may be granted through military experience. Credit and placement may be granted through DANTES and challenge exams. Early entrance/early admission program. Concurrent enrollment program.
**Transfer students:** Transfer students accepted for terms other than fall. In fall 1993, 17% of all new students were transfers into all classes. 34 transfer applications were received, 34 were accepted. Application deadline is August 1 for fall; December 15 for spring. Minimum 2.0 GPA required. Lowest course grade accepted is "C." Maximum number of transferable credits is 64 semester hours from a two-year school and 90 semester hours from a four-year school. At least 30 semester hours must be completed at the college to receive degree.
**Admissions contact:** Stephen B. Terry, Ed.D., Vice-President for Enrollment Management. 803 383-8050.

**FINANCIAL AID. Available aid:** Pell grants, SEOG, state scholarships and grants, school scholarships and grants, private scholarships and grants, academic merit scholarships, athletic scholarships, and aid for undergraduate foreign students. Perkins Loans (NDSL), PLUS, Stafford Loans (GSL), state loans, private loans, and SLS. Knight Tuition Plans and AMS.
**Financial aid statistics:** 18% of aid is not need-based. In 1993-94, 95% of all undergraduate applicants received aid; 90% of freshman applicants. Average amounts of aid awarded freshmen: Scholarships and grants, $4,300; loans, $2,200.
**Supporting data/closing dates:** FAFSA: Priority filing date is March 15; accepted on rolling basis. Notification of awards on rolling basis.
**Financial aid contact:** Hal Lewis, B.S., Director of Financial Aid. 803 383-8055.

## College of Charleston

**Charleston, SC 29424** **803 792-5500**

**1994-95 Costs.** Tuition: $3,100 (state residents), $6,200 (out-of-state). Room & board: $3,460. Fees, books, misc. academic expenses (school's estimate): $666.
**Enrollment.** Undergraduates: 2,466 men, 4,030 women (full-time). Freshman class: 4,516 applicants, 2,793 accepted, 1,129 enrolled. Graduate enrollment: 154 men, 1,685 women.
**Test score averages/ranges.** Average SAT scores: 483 verbal, 526 math. Range of SAT scores of middle 50%: 430-520 verbal, 480-570 math. Average ACT scores: 21 composite. Range of ACT scores of middle 50%: 20-24 composite.
**Faculty.** 313 full-time; 225 part-time. 86% of faculty holds highest degree in specific field. Student/faculty ratio: 20 to 1.
**Selectivity rating.** Competitive.

**PROFILE.** The College of Charleston, founded in 1770, is a public, liberal arts institution. Its 52-acre campus, located in the center of Charleston, contains many pre-Civil War buildings.

**Accreditation:** SACS. Professionally accredited by the American Assembly of Collegiate Schools of Business.
**Religious orientation:** College of Charleston is nonsectarian; no religious requirements.
**Library:** Collections totaling over 325,767 volumes, 2,681 periodical subscriptions, and 580,073 microform items.
**Special facilities/museums:** Art gallery, broadcast museum, early childhood development center, African American history and culture institute, observatory, marine sciences station.
**Athletic facilities:** Gymnasium, baseball, football, intramural, rugby, soccer, and softball fields, marina, badminton, basketball, handball, racquetball, squash, tennis, and volleyball courts, gymnastics and weight rooms, swimming pool.
**STUDENT BODY. Undergraduate profile:** 81% are state residents; 45% are transfers. 1% Asian-American, 6% Black, 1% Hispanic, 89% White, 3% Other. Average age of undergraduates is 22.
**Freshman profile:** 2% of freshmen who took SAT scored 700 or over on math; 7% scored 600 or over on verbal, 17% scored 600 or over on math; 37% scored 500 or over on verbal, 66% scored 500 or over on math; 93% scored 400 or over on verbal, 98% scored 400 or over on math; 100% scored 300 or over on verbal, 100% scored 300 or over on math. 92% of accepted applicants took SAT; 8% took ACT. 75% of freshmen come from public schools.
**Undergraduate achievement:** 82% of fall 1991 freshmen returned for fall 1992 term. 37% of entering class graduated. 33% of students who completed a degree program immediately went on to graduate study.
**Foreign students:** 132 students are from out of the country. Countries represented include Brazil, Canada, France, Germany, Japan, and the Netherlands; 58 in all.
**PROGRAMS OF STUDY. Degrees:** A.B., B.A., B.S., B.S.Dent., B.S.Med.
**Majors:** Accounting, Anthropology, Art History, Biochemistry, Biology, Business Administration, Chemistry, Classical Studies, Communications, Computer Science, Economics, Elementary Education, English, Fine Arts, French, Geology, German, History, Marine Biology, Mathematics, Music, Philosophy, Physical Education/Health, Physics, Political Science, Psychology, Sociology, Spanish, Special Education, Studio Art, Theatre, Urban Studies.
**Distribution of degrees:** The majors with the highest enrollment are business administration, elementary education, and biology; classical studies, German, and accounting have the lowest.
**Requirements:** General education requirement.
**Academic regulations:** Freshmen must maintain minimum 1.5 GPA; sophomores, 1.8 GPA; juniors, 2.0 GPA; seniors, 2.0 GPA.
**Special:** Minors offered in all majors and in African studies, American studies, intermodal transportation, international studies, Jewish studies, and women's studies. Double majors. Independent study. Accelerated study. Pass/fail grading option. Internships. Cooperative education programs. Graduate school at which undergraduates may take graduate-level courses. Preprofessional programs in law, medicine, veterinary science, pharmacy, and dentistry. 3-2 and 2-2 engineering programs with Case Western Reserve U, Clemson U, Georgia Tech, and Washington U. 2-2 nursing program with Medical U of South Carolina. 3-1 program with accredited dental or medical school leads to B.S. in dentistry or medicine. Five-year B.S./M.S. program in biometry with Medical U of South Carolina. Member of Charleston Higher Education Consortium. Washington Semester and Sea Semester. Member of National Student Exchange (NSE). Teacher certification in early childhood, elementary, secondary, and special education. Certification in specific subject areas. Member of International Student Exchange Program (ISEP). Exchange programs abroad in Japan (Kansai U) and Scotland (St. Andrews U). AFROTC at Charleston Southern U.
**Honors:** Honors program. Honor societies.
**Academic Assistance:** Remedial reading, writing, math, and study skills. Nonremedial tutoring.
**STUDENT LIFE. Housing:** Students may live on or off campus. Coed, women's, and men's dorms. Sorority and fraternity housing. 22% of students live in college housing.
**Services and counseling/handicapped student services:** Placement services. Health service. Day care. Counseling services for minority, veteran, and older students. Birth control, personal, and psychological counseling. Career and academic guidance services. Religious counseling. Physically disabled student services. Learning disabled services. Notetaking services. Tape recorders. Tutors. Reader services for the blind.
**Campus organizations:** Undergraduate student government. Student newspaper (Cougar Pause, published biweekly). Literary magazine. Yearbook. Fine Arts Singers, Madrigal Singers, Center Stage, concert band, concert choir, wind symphony, jazz, film, and video clubs, literary societies, premedical and prelegal societies, activities board, commuter student organization, State Student Legislature, political, sports, and service groups, 120 organizations in all. 11 fraternities, seven chapter houses; 10 sororities, six chapter houses. 15% of men join a fraternity. 15% of women join a sorority.
**Religious organizations:** Bahai Club, Baptist Student Union, Campus Crusade for Christ, Catholic Student Union, Fellowship of Christian Athletes.
**Minority/foreign student organizations:** Black Student Association, Student Union for Minority Affairs. International Club.
**ATHLETICS. Physical education requirements:** None.
**Intercollegiate competition:** 9% of students participate. Baseball (M), basketball (M,W), cheerleading (M,W), cross-country (M,W), diving (M,W), golf (M,W), horsemanship (M,W), sailing (M,W), soccer (M,W), softball (W), swimming (M,W), tennis (M,W), volleyball (W). Member of NCAA Division I, Trans America Athletic Conference.
**Intramural and club sports:** 29% of students participate. Intramural badminton, basketball, flag football, indoor soccer, racquetball, soccer, softball, tennis, volleyball, water polo. Men's club crew. Women's club crew.
**ADMISSIONS. Academic basis for candidate selection** (in order of priority): Secondary school record, class rank, standardized test scores, school's recommendation, essay.
**Nonacademic basis for candidate selection:** Character and personality, extracurricular participation, and particular talent or ability are considered.
**Requirements:** Graduation from secondary school is recommended; GED is accepted. No specific distribution of secondary school units required. Conditional admission possible for applicants not meeting standard requirements. SAT or ACT is required. Campus visit and interview recommended. No off-campus interviews.
**Procedure:** Take SAT or ACT by fall of 12th year. Visit college for interview by spring of 12th year. Suggest filing application by January. Application deadline is July 1. Notification of admission on rolling basis. Reply is required by May 1. $100 tuition deposit, refundable until May 1. $250 room deposit, refundable until May 1. Freshmen accepted for terms other than fall.
**Special programs:** Admission may be deferred one semester. Credit and/or placement may be granted through CEEB Advanced Placement exams for scores of 3 or higher. Credit and/or placement may be granted through CLEP subject exams. Credit and placement may be granted through challenge exams. Concurrent enrollment program.
**Transfer students:** Transfer students accepted for terms other than fall. In fall 1992, 45% of all new students were transfers into all classes. 1,653 transfer applications were received, 1,360 were accepted. Application deadline is July 1 for fall; December 1 for spring. Minimum 2.3 GPA required. Lowest course grade accepted is "C." Maximum number of transferable credits is 92 semester hours. At least 30 semester hours must be completed at the college to receive degree.
**Admissions contact:** Donald Burkard, M.S., Dean of Admissions and Continuing Education. 803 792-5670.

**FINANCIAL AID. Available aid:** Pell grants, SEOG, state scholarships and grants, school scholarships and grants, private scholarships and grants, ROTC scholarships, academic merit scholarships, and athletic scholarships. Perkins Loans (NDSL), PLUS, Stafford Loans (GSL), state loans, school loans, private loans, and SLS.
**Financial aid statistics:** In 1992-93, 72% of all undergraduate applicants received aid; 68% of freshman applicants. Average amounts of aid awarded freshmen: Scholarships and grants, $1,240; loans, $2,000.
**Supporting data/closing dates:** FAFSA/FAF/FFS: Priority filing date is April 15. School's own aid application: Priority filing date is April 15. Notification of awards begins June 1.
**Financial aid contact:** Donald Griggs, M.Ed., Director of Financial Aid. 803 792-5540.
**STUDENT EMPLOYMENT.** College Work/Study Program. Institutional employment. 17% of full-time undergraduates work on campus during school year. Students may expect to earn an average of $1,600 during school year. Off-campus part-time employment opportunities rated "good."

**COMPUTER FACILITIES.** 400 IBM/IBM-compatible and Macintosh/Apple microcomputers; all are networked. Residence halls may be equipped with stand-alone microcomputers. Computer languages and software packages include Assembler, BASIC, C, COBOL, dBASE, FORTRAN, LISP, Lotus 1-2-3, Pascal, Prolog, Unify, WordPerfect; 100 in all. Computer facilities are available to all students.
**Fees:** $25 computer fee per semester.
**Hours:** 8 AM-11 PM (M-Th); 8 AM-5 PM (F); 10 AM-5 PM (Sa).
**GRADUATE CAREER DATA.** Graduate school percentages: 3% enter law school. 2% enter medical school. 1% enter dental school. 3% enter graduate business programs. 15% enter graduate arts and sciences programs. Highest graduate school enrollments: Medical U of South Carolina, U of South Carolina Law Sch. 36% of graduates choose careers in business and industry.
**PROMINENT ALUMNI/AE.** Robert Mills, architect (Washington Monument); John C. Fremont, explorer and solder; Basil Gildersleeve, classical scholar; James B. Edwards, former U.S. secretary of energy and former governor of South Carolina.

# Columbia International University

**Columbia, SC 29230** 800 777-2227

**1994-95 Costs.** Tuition: $6,650. Room: $1,620. Board: $1,950. Fees, books, misc. academic expenses (school's estimate): $1,000.
**Enrollment.** Undergraduates: 208 men, 168 women (full-time). Freshman class: 308 applicants, 254 accepted, 158 enrolled. Graduate enrollment: 10 men, 38 women.
**Test score averages/ranges.** Average SAT scores: 475 verbal, 430 math. Average ACT scores: 20 composite. Range of ACT scores of middle 50%: 16-20 composite.
**Faculty.** 22 full-time; 7 part-time. 56% of faculty holds doctoral degree. Student/faculty ratio: 17 to 1.
**Selectivity rating.** Less competitive.

**PROFILE.** Columbia Bible, founded in 1923, is a college with religious orientation. Its 450-acre campus is located eight miles from downtown Columbia.

**Accreditation:** AABC, SACS.
**Religious orientation:** Columbia Bible College is a nondenominational Christian school; no religious requirements.
**Library:** Collections totaling over 84,361 volumes, 725 periodical subscriptions, and 35,000 microform items.
**Athletic facilities:** Basketball and tennis courts, volleyball courts, athletic field, weight room, gymnasium.
**STUDENT BODY. Undergraduate profile:** 33% are state residents; 40% are transfers. 1% Asian-American, 6% Black, 1% Hispanic, 1% Native American, 86% White, 5% Other. Average age of undergraduates is 24.
**Freshman profile:** 9% of freshmen who took ACT scored 30 or over on composite; 18% scored 24 or over on composite; 27% scored 18 or over on composite; 91% scored 12 or over on composite; 100% scored 6 or over on composite. 84% of accepted applicants took SAT; 16% took ACT.
**Undergraduate achievement:** 72% of fall 1992 freshmen returned for fall 1993 term. 47% of entering class graduated.
**Foreign students:** 31 students are from out of the country. Countries represented include Canada, Germany, Japan, Malaysia, New Zealand, and Palau; 21 in all.
**PROGRAMS OF STUDY. Degrees:** B.A., B.S.
**Majors:** Bible, Bible Teaching, Biblical Languages, Biblical Studies, Church Ministries, Elementary Education, Humanities, Intercultural Studies, Music, Pastoral Ministries, Psychology, Youth Ministries.
**Distribution of degrees:** The majors with the highest enrollment are Bible and Bible/elementary education.
**Requirements:** General education requirement.
**Academic regulations:** Minimum 2.0 GPA must be maintained.
**Special:** Minors offered in most majors. All bachelor degree programs include major in Bible. Associate's degrees offered. Double majors. Independent study. Graduate school at which undergraduates may take graduate-level courses. Teacher certification in early childhood and elementary education. Study abroad in Israel.
**Academic Assistance:** Nonremedial tutoring.
**ADMISSIONS. Academic basis for candidate selection** (in order of priority): Secondary school record, standardized test scores, class rank, school's recommendation.
**Nonacademic basis for candidate selection:** Character and personality are emphasized. Particular talent or ability is important. Extracurricular participation and alumni/ae relationship are considered.
**Requirements:** Graduation from secondary school is required; GED is accepted. No specific distribution of secondary school units required. Minimum SAT score of 420 verbal and 420 math (composite ACT score of 18) and 2.0 GPA required. SAT is required; ACT may be substituted. Campus visit recommended. No off-campus interviews.
**Procedure:** Notification of admission on rolling basis. $100 tuition deposit, refundable until May 15. $75 room deposit, refundable until May 15. Freshmen accepted for terms other than fall.
**Special programs:** Admission may be deferred one year. Credit may be granted through CLEP general and subject exams.
**Transfer students:** Transfer students accepted for terms other than fall. In fall 1993, 40% of all new students were transfers into all classes. 111 transfer applications were received, 92 were accepted. Minimum 2.0 GPA required. Lowest course grade accepted is "C." Maximum number of transferable credits is 96 semester hours. At least 32 semester hours must be completed at the college to receive degree.
**Admissions contact:** Frank J. Bedell, Director of Recruitment. 800 777-2227, extension 3024.

**FINANCIAL AID. Available aid:** Pell grants, SEOG, state grants, school scholarships and grants, private scholarships and grants, and aid for undergraduate foreign students. Minority funding. PLUS, Stafford Loans (GSL), state loans, and SLS. Tuition Management Systems.
**Financial aid statistics:** 3% of aid is not need-based. In 1993-94, 67% of all undergraduate applicants received aid; 80% of freshman applicants. Average amounts of aid awarded freshmen: Scholarships and grants, $1,352; loans, $2,625.
**Supporting data/closing dates:** FAFSA: Priority filing date is February 15. Notification of awards on rolling basis.
**Financial aid contact:** Rich Heath, M.A., Director of Financial Aid. 800 777-2227, extension 3036.

# Columbia College

**Columbia, SC 29203** 803 786-3012

**1994-95 Costs.** Tuition: $10,425. Room & board: $3,975. Fees, books, misc. academic expenses (school's estimate): $500.
**Enrollment.** 968 women (full-time). Freshman class: 737 applicants, 614 accepted, 242 enrolled.
**Test score averages/ranges.** Average SAT scores: 413 verbal, 438 math.
**Faculty.** 70 full-time; 6 part-time. 62% of faculty holds doctoral degree. Student/faculty ratio: 14 to 1.
**Selectivity rating.** Less competitive.

**PROFILE.** Columbia, founded in 1854, is a church-affiliated college for women. Its 32-acre campus is located on the north side of Columbia.

**Accreditation:** SACS. Professionally accredited by the Council on Social Work Education, the National Association of Schools of Music, the National Council for Accreditation of Teacher Education.
**Religious orientation:** Columbia College is affiliated with the United Methodist Church; two semesters of religion required.
**Library:** Collections totaling over 132,321 volumes, 651 periodical subscriptions, and 11,435 microform items.
**Special facilities/museums:** Language lab, corrective speech pathology clinic.
**Athletic facilities:** Gymnasium, swimming pool, health/fitness lab, tennis courts, athletic field.
**STUDENT BODY. Undergraduate profile:** 93% are state residents; 26% are transfers. 1% Asian-American, 20% Black, 1% Hispanic, 78% White. Average age of undergraduates is 20.
**Freshman profile:** Majority of accepted applicants took SAT.
**Undergraduate achievement:** 75% of fall 1992 freshmen returned for fall 1993 term. 46% of entering class graduated. 25% of students who completed a degree program immediately went on to graduate study.
**Foreign students:** Five students are from out of the country. Countries represented include Japan and Korea.
**PROGRAMS OF STUDY. Degrees:** B.A., B.F.A., B.Mus.
**Majors:** Accounting, Applied Music, Art, Biology, Business Administration, Chemistry, Christian Education, Corrective Speech Pathology, Dance, Early Childhood Education, Elementary Education, French, History, Mathematics, Medical Technology, Music, Music Education, Natural Science, Political Science, Pre-Law, Pre-Medical, Psychology, Public Affairs, Religion, Social Work, Sociology, Spanish, Special Education.
**Distribution of degrees:** The majors with the highest enrollment are elementary education, business administration, and public affairs; church music, health services, and religion have the lowest.
**Requirements:** General education requirement.
**Academic regulations:** Minimum 2.0 GPA must be maintained.
**Special:** Self-designed majors. Double majors. Independent study. Pass/fail grading option. Internships. Cooperative education programs. Preprofessional programs in law and medicine. Teacher certification in early childhood, elementary, secondary, and special education. Study abroad in France, Germany, and Spain. ROTC, NROTC, and AFROTC at U of South Carolina.
**Honors:** Honors program.
**Academic Assistance:** Remedial reading, writing, and math. Nonremedial tutoring.
**ADMISSIONS. Academic basis for candidate selection** (in order of priority): Secondary school record, standardized test scores, school's recommendation, class rank, essay.
**Nonacademic basis for candidate selection:** Character and personality, extracurricular participation, and particular talent or ability are considered.
**Requirements:** Graduation from secondary school is required; GED is accepted. 16 units and the following program of study are recommended: 4 units of English, 3 units of math, 2 units of science, 2 units of foreign language, 2 units of social studies, 2 units of history, 1 unit of electives. College-preparatory courses strongly recommended. SAT or ACT is required. PSAT is recommended. Campus visit and interview recommended. Off-campus interviews available with an admissions representative.
**Procedure:** Take SAT or ACT by December of 12th year. Notification of admission on rolling basis. Reply is required as soon as possible, preferably within one month of acceptance. $100 tuition deposit, refundable until May 1. $100 room deposit, refundable until May 1. Freshmen accepted for terms other than fall.
**Special programs:** Admission may be deferred one year. Credit and/or placement may be granted through CEEB Advanced Placement exams for scores of 3 or higher. Credit and/or placement may be granted through CLEP general and subject exams. Credit and placement may be granted through challenge exams. Early entrance/early admission program. Concurrent enrollment program.
**Transfer students:** Transfer students accepted for terms other than fall. In fall 1993, 26% of all new students were transfers into all classes. 198 transfer applications were received, 160 were accepted. Application deadline is August 15 for fall; December 1 for spring. Minimum 2.0 GPA required. Lowest course grade accepted is "C." Maximum number of

transferable credits is 72 semester hours. At least 30 semester hours must be completed at the college to receive degree.
**Admissions contact:** J. Joseph Mitchell, Ed.D., Vice President, Enrollment Management. 803 786-3871.

**FINANCIAL AID. Available aid:** Pell grants, SEOG, state grants, school scholarships and grants, private scholarships and grants, academic merit scholarships, and athletic scholarships. Perkins Loans (NDSL), PLUS, Stafford Loans (GSL), and SLS. Tuition Plan Inc. and AMS. College payment plan.
**Financial aid statistics:** 20% of aid is not need-based. In 1993-94, 98% of all undergraduate applicants received aid; 98% of freshman applicants. Average amounts of aid awarded freshmen: Scholarships and grants, $5,635; loans, $2,600.
**Supporting data/closing dates:** FAFSA: Accepted on rolling basis. Notification of awards on rolling basis.
**Financial aid contact:** Doris Harrell, Assistant Vice President and Director of Financial Aid. 803 786-3644.

## Converse College

**Spartanburg, SC 29302** **803 596-9000**

**1994-95 Costs.** Tuition: $12,050. Room & board: $3,700. Fees, books, misc. academic expenses (school's estimate): $650.
**Enrollment.** 660 women (full-time). Freshman class: 440 applicants, 407 accepted, 149 enrolled. 366 women.
**Test score averages/ranges.** Average SAT scores: 1050 combined.
**Faculty.** 88 full-time; 8 part-time. 65% of faculty holds doctoral degree. Student/faculty ratio: 9 to 1.
**Selectivity rating.** Competitive.

**PROFILE.** Converse, founded in 1889, is a private, liberal arts college for women. Its 70-acre campus is located in downtown Spartanburg, near the Blue Ridge Mountains.

**Accreditation:** SACS. Professionally accredited by the National Association of Schools of Music.
**Religious orientation:** Converse College is nonsectarian; no religious requirements.
**Library:** Collections totaling over 140,000 volumes, 689 periodical subscriptions, and 10,500 microform items.
**Special facilities/museums:** Language lab.
**Athletic facilities:** Gymnasium, weight room, tennis courts, swimming pool, bowling lanes, dance studio, field hockey and soccer fields.

**STUDENT BODY. Undergraduate profile:** 59% are state residents; 10% are transfers. 2% Asian-American, 6% Black, 2% Hispanic, 88% White, 2% Other. Average age of undergraduates is 20.
**Freshman profile:** 70% of freshmen come from public schools.
**Undergraduate achievement:** 72% of fall 1992 freshmen returned for fall 1993 term. 58% of entering class graduated. 27% of students who completed a degree program went on to graduate study within five years.
**Foreign students:** 17 students are from out of the country. Countries represented include Japan, South Africa, and United Arab Emirates; six in all.

**PROGRAMS OF STUDY. Degrees:** B.A., B.F.A., B.Mus.
**Majors:** Accounting, Art, Biology, Business Administration, Chemistry, Composition, Comprehensive Science, Early Childhood Education, Economics, Education of the Hearing Impaired, Education of the Mentally Retarded, Elementary Education, Emotionally Handicapped, English, French, History, Interior Design, Learning Disabilities, Mathematics, Modern Foreign Languages, Music Education, Music History/Literature, Music Theory, Performance, Piano Pedagogy, Politics, Psychology, Religion, Sociology, Spanish, Special Education, Theatre.
**Distribution of degrees:** The majors with the highest enrollment are education, business, and applied art; theater, art history, and accounting have the lowest.
**Requirements:** General education requirement.
**Academic regulations:** Minimum 2.0 GPA required for graduation.
**Special:** Minors offered in all majors. Career internships include archival administration, arts management, criminal justice, inner city service, interior design, journalism/media, and urban planning; individual internships may be arranged. Double majors. Independent study. Accelerated study. Internships. Graduate school at which undergraduates may take graduate-level courses. Preprofessional programs in law, medicine, veterinary science, pharmacy, dentistry, theology, and optometry. 2-2 nursing program with Medical U of South Carolina. Exchange program with Wofford Coll. Teacher certification in early childhood, elementary, secondary, and special education. Study abroad in England, France, Latin American countries, and Spain. ROTC at Wofford Coll.
**Honors:** Honors program. Honor societies.
**Academic Assistance:** Remedial reading and study skills. Nonremedial tutoring.

**ADMISSIONS. Academic basis for candidate selection** (in order of priority): Secondary school record, standardized test scores, school's recommendation, class rank.
**Nonacademic basis for candidate selection:** Character and personality, extracurricular participation, and particular talent or ability are considered.
**Requirements:** Graduation from secondary school is required; GED is accepted. 16 units and the following program of study are required: 4 units of English, 3 units of math, 2 units of science including 1 unit of lab, 2 units of foreign language, 2 units of social studies, 1 unit of history, 2 units of academic electives. Audition required of music program applicants. SAT or ACT is required. Campus visit and interview recommended. Off-campus interviews available with an admissions representative.
**Procedure:** Take SAT or ACT by December of 12th year. Suggest filing application by February 1. Notification of admission on rolling basis. Reply is required by May 1. $300 nonrefundable tuition deposit. Freshmen accepted for terms other than fall.
**Special programs:** Admission may be deferred one year. Credit may be granted through CEEB Advanced Placement for scores of 3 or higher. Credit may be granted through CLEP general and subject exams. Early entrance/early admission program. Concurrent enrollment program.
**Transfer students:** Transfer students accepted for terms other than fall. In fall 1993, 10% of all new students were transfers into all classes. 32 transfer applications were received, 26 were accepted. Application deadline is rolling for fall; rolling for spring. Minimum 2.0 GPA required. Lowest course grade accepted is "C." At least 42 semester hours must be completed at the college to receive degree.
**Admissions contact:** Martha E. Rogers, M.A., Ph.D., Director of Admissions. 803 596-9040.

**FINANCIAL AID. Available aid:** Pell grants, SEOG, state grants, school scholarships and grants, private scholarships, academic merit scholarships, and athletic scholarships. Music scholarship applicants must audition on campus or provide tape recordings. Perkins Loans (NDSL), PLUS, Stafford Loans (GSL), state loans, school loans, and SLS. Tuition Plan Inc. and Knight Tuition Plans.
**Financial aid statistics:** 50% of aid is not need-based.
**Supporting data/closing dates:** FAFSA/FAF/FFS: Priority filing date is March 1. School's own aid application: Deadline is March 1. State aid form: Priority filing date is March 1. Notification of awards on rolling basis.
**Financial aid contact:** Margaret P. Collins, M.Ed., Director of Financial Aid. 803 596-9019.

## Erskine College

**Due West, SC 29639** **803 379-2131**

**1993-94 Costs.** Tuition: $9,995. Room & board: $3,680. Fees, books, misc. academic expenses (school's estimate): $1,130.
**Enrollment.** Undergraduates: 228 men, 304 women (full-time). Freshman class: 659 applicants, 557 accepted, 167 enrolled. Graduate enrollment: 145 men, 8 women.
**Test score averages/ranges.** Average SAT scores: 482 verbal, 532 math. Range of SAT scores of middle 50%: 410-550 verbal, 470-590 math.
**Faculty.** 40 full-time; 13 part-time. 83% of faculty holds doctoral degree. Student/faculty ratio: 13 to 1.
**Selectivity rating.** More competitive.

**PROFILE.** Erskine, founded in 1839, is a church-affiliated, liberal arts college. Its 85-acre campus is located in Due West, 45 miles from Greenville. Several antebellum buildings on campus are listed with the National Register of Historic Places.

**Accreditation:** SACS.
**Religious orientation:** Erskine College is affiliated with the Associate Reformed Presbyterian Church; two semesters of religion required.
**Library:** Collections totaling over 215,000 volumes, 1,065 periodical subscriptions, and 74,938 microform items.
**Athletic facilities:** Physical activities center, baseball, intramural, soccer, and softball fields, racquetball and tennis courts, gymnasiums, dance studio, fitness, and weight rooms, swimming pool.

**STUDENT BODY. Undergraduate profile:** 73% are state residents; 9% are transfers. 4% Black, 1% Hispanic, 94% White, 1% Other. Average age of undergraduates is 20.
**Freshman profile:** 1% of freshmen who took SAT scored 700 or over on verbal, 2% scored 700 or over on math; 15% scored 600 or over on verbal, 23% scored 600 or over on math; 42% scored 500 or over on verbal, 62% scored 500 or over on math; 80% scored 400 or over on verbal, 96% scored 400 or over on math; 100% scored 300 or over on verbal, 100% scored 300 or over on math. Majority of accepted applicants took SAT. 90% of freshmen come from public schools.
**Undergraduate achievement:** 81% of fall 1992 freshmen returned for fall 1993 term. 54% of entering class graduated.
**Foreign students:** Six students are from out of the country. Countries represented include Canada, India, Italy, Jamaica, Japan, and Trinidad.

**PROGRAMS OF STUDY. Degrees:** B.A., B.S.
**Majors:** Behavioral Science, Bible, Biology, Business Administration, Chemistry, Christian Education, Early Childhood Education, Elementary Education, English, French, History, Mathematics, Music, Music Education, Natural Science, Physical Education, Physics, Psychology, Spanish, Special Education, Sports Management.
**Distribution of degrees:** The majors with the highest enrollment are business, history, and biology; natural science, special education, and sports management have the lowest.
**Requirements:** General education requirement.
**Academic regulations:** Freshmen must maintain minimum 1.7 GPA; sophomores, 1.8 GPA; juniors, 1.9 GPA; seniors, 2.0 GPA.
**Special:** Minors offered in most majors and in American history, European history, religion, philosophy, economics, secondary education, recreation, and computer science. Certification offered in athletic training. Double majors. Dual degrees. Independent study. Pass/fail grading option. Internships. Cooperative education programs. Preprofessional programs in law, medicine, veterinary science, pharmacy, dentistry, theology, and ministry. 3-1 medical technology program with certified hospital. 3-2 engineering programs with Clemson U and Georgia Tech. 3-1 and 3-2 allied health programs with Medical U of South Carolina. Exchange programs with numerous 4-1-4 colleges during January term. Teacher certification in early childhood, elementary, secondary, and special education. Certification in specific subject areas. Study abroad in England, France, and Scotland.
**Honors:** Honor societies.
**Academic Assistance:** Nonremedial tutoring.

**ADMISSIONS. Academic basis for candidate selection** (in order of priority): Secondary school record, standardized test scores, school's recommendation, class rank.
**Nonacademic basis for candidate selection:** Character and personality, extracurricular participation, and particular talent or ability are important. Alumni/ae relationship is considered.
**Requirements:** Graduation from secondary school is recommended; GED is accepted. 16 units and the following program of study are required: 4 units of English, 2 units of math, 2

units of science, 2 units of foreign language, 1 unit of social studies, 1 unit of history, 4 units of academic electives. SAT is required; ACT may be substituted. PSAT is recommended. Campus visit and interview recommended. No off-campus interviews.
**Procedure:** Take SAT or ACT by October of 12th year. Visit college for interview by January of 12th year. Suggest filing application by fall. Application deadline is August 15. Notification of admission on rolling basis. Reply is required by May 1. $100 tuition deposit, refundable until May 1. $150 room deposit, refundable until May 1. Freshmen accepted for terms other than fall.
**Special programs:** Admission may be deferred one year. Credit and/or placement may be granted through CEEB Advanced Placement exams for scores of 3 or higher. Credit may be granted through CLEP subject exams, DANTES, and challenge exams. Early entrance/early admission program. Concurrent enrollment program.
**Transfer students:** Transfer students accepted for terms other than fall. In fall 1993, 9% of all new students were transfers into all classes. 47 transfer applications were received, 27 were accepted. Application deadline is rolling for fall; rolling for spring. Minimum 2.0 GPA required. Lowest course grade accepted is "C." Maximum number of transferable credits is 64 semester hours. At least 60 semester hours must be completed at the college to receive degree.
**Admissions contact:** Dorothy J. Carter, Director of Admissions and Financial Aid. 803 379-8838.

**FINANCIAL AID. Available aid:** Pell grants, SEOG, state scholarships and grants, school scholarships and grants, private scholarships and grants, academic merit scholarships, athletic scholarships, and aid for undergraduate foreign students. Perkins Loans (NDSL), PLUS, Stafford Loans (GSL), school loans, private loans, and SLS. Tuition Plan Inc. Institutional payment plan.
**Financial aid statistics:** 22% of aid is not need-based. In 1993-94, 97% of all undergraduate applicants received aid; 92% of freshman applicants. Average amounts of aid awarded freshmen: Scholarships and grants, $7,700; loans, $2,590.
**Supporting data/closing dates:** FAFSA: Priority filing date is February 15. School's own aid application: Priority filing date is February 15. Income tax forms: Priority filing date is February 15. Notification of awards on rolling basis.
**Financial aid contact:** Dorothy J. Carter, Director of Admissions and Financial Aid. 803 379-8832.

# Francis Marion University

**Florence, SC 29501-0547** **803 661-1362**

**1994-95 Costs.** Tuition: $2,800 (state residents), $5,600 (out-of-state). Room: $1,480. Board: $1,599. Fees, books, misc. academic expenses (school's estimate): $400.
**Enrollment.** Undergraduates: 1,463 men, 1,758 women (full-time). Freshman class: 1,801 applicants, 1,655 accepted. Graduate enrollment: 87 men, 356 women.
**Test score averages/ranges.** N/A.
**Faculty.** 166 full-time; 50 part-time. 75% of faculty holds doctoral degree. Student/faculty ratio: 20 to 1.
**Selectivity rating.** N/A.

**PROFILE.** Francis Marion is a public university. Founded as a college in 1970, it gained university status in 1992. Its 309-acre campus is located seven miles east of Florence.

**Accreditation:** SACS.
**Religious orientation:** Francis Marion University is nonsectarian; no religious requirements.
**Library:** Collections totaling over 233,156 volumes, 1,724 periodical subscriptions, and 75,077 microform items.
**Special facilities/museums:** Media center, planetarium, observatory.
**Athletic facilities:** Gymnasium, swimming pool, racquetball courts, weight room and fitness center, lighted baseball complex, tennis courts, track, soccer and softball fields, intramural fields.

**STUDENT BODY. Undergraduate profile:** 96% are state residents; 25% are transfers. 22% Black, 76% White, 2% Other. Average age of undergraduates is 22.
**Freshman profile:** 95% of accepted applicants took SAT. 85% of freshmen come from public schools.
**Undergraduate achievement:** 69% of fall 1992 freshmen returned for fall 1993 term.
**Foreign students:** 23 students are from out of the country. Countries represented include Canada, Germany, Trinidad, the United Kingdom, and Zimbabwe; 12 in all.

**PROGRAMS OF STUDY. Degrees:** B.A., B.Bus.Admin., B.Gen.Studies, B.S.
**Majors:** Accounting, Art, Art Education, Biology, Business Administration, Business Economics, Chemistry, Civil Engineering Technology, Computer Information Systems, Computer Science, Early Childhood Education, Economics, Electronic Engineering Technology, Elementary Education, English, Finance, French, Geography, Health Physics, History, Management, Marketing, Mathematics, Medical Technology, Physics, Political Science, Psychology, Sociology, Spanish, Theatre.
**Distribution of degrees:** The majors with the highest enrollment are elementary education, political science, and biology; geography and theatre have the lowest.
**Requirements:** General education requirement.
**Academic regulations:** Minimum 1.9 GPA must be maintained.
**Special:** Minors offered in many majors and in environmental studies, German, mass communications, philosophy, and physical education (coaching). Courses offered in astronomy, journalism, music, and speech. Double majors. Dual degrees. Independent study. Accelerated study. Internships. Cooperative education programs. Graduate school at which undergraduates may take graduate-level courses. Preprofessional programs in law, medicine, veterinary science, pharmacy, dentistry, and nursing. 2-2 forestry program with Clemson U. 2-2 nursing program with Medical U of South Carolina. 3-1 medical technology program. 3-1 philosophy, religion, and mass communications programs with other schools. 3-2 engineering program with Clemson U. Teacher certification in early childhood, elementary, and secondary education. Certification in specific subject areas. ROTC.
**Honors:** Honors program. Honor societies.
**Academic Assistance:** Remedial writing, math, and study skills.

**STUDENT LIFE. Housing:** Coed dorms. School-owned/operated apartments. 29% of students live in college housing.
**Social atmosphere:** "The students are some of the friendliest around," reports the student newspaper. "You could poll anyone who's ever visited FMC and he or she would express our closeness." The Greeks are dominant, and there are some Christian groups. Off campus, students frequent Patriot Place (student apartments off campus), College Station (restaurant/game room), Appleby's (seven miles away in town), Chuck's, Carrie Nation's, Apple Annie's, and Venus. On campus, students meet at the college center gameroom, swimming pool, workout room, and "the ever-popular Commons." Attendance is high at intramurals and basketball games.
**Services and counseling/handicapped student services:** Placement services. Health service. Counseling services for minority, military, veteran, and older students. Career and academic guidance services. Physically disabled student services. Learning disabled services. Notetaking services. Tape recorders. Reader services for the blind.
**Campus organizations:** Undergraduate student government. Student newspaper (Campus Crier, published once/week). Literary magazine. Chorus, FMU theatre, cheerleaders, academic, political, service, and special-interest groups. Eight fraternities, three chapter houses; six sororities, no chapter houses. 13% of men join a fraternity. 9% of women join a sorority.
**Religious organizations:** Baptist Student Union, Episcopal College Churchmen, Fellowship of Christian Athletes, Lutheran Student Association, Campus Crusade for Christ.
**Minority/foreign student organizations:** Minority Student Association, NAACP. International Student Association.

**ATHLETICS. Physical education requirements:** None.
**Intercollegiate competition:** 5% of students participate. Baseball (M), basketball (M,W), cheerleading (M,W), cross-country (M,W), golf (M), soccer (M), softball (W), tennis (M,W), track (outdoor) (M,W), track and field (outdoor) (M), volleyball (W). Member of NCAA Division II, Peach Belt Athletic Conference.
**Intramural and club sports:** 25% of students participate. Intramural badminton, basketball, bowling, flag football, golf, racquetball, soccer, softball, swimming, table tennis, tennis, track and field, volleyball.

**ADMISSIONS. Academic basis for candidate selection** (in order of priority): Secondary school record, standardized test scores, class rank, school's recommendation.
**Requirements:** Graduation from secondary school is required; GED is accepted. 16 units and the following program of study are required: 4 units of English, 3 units of math, 2 units of lab science, 2 units of foreign language, 2 units of social studies, 1 unit of history, 2 units of academic electives. Electives should include 1 unit of physical education or ROTC, 1 unit of advanced math or computer science, or 1 unit of world history, world geography, or Western civilization. Minimum combined SAT score of 900 and rank in top half of secondary school class recommended. SAT is required; ACT may be substituted. Campus visit recommended. No off-campus interviews.
**Procedure:** Take SAT or ACT by December of 12th year. Notification of admission on rolling basis. $150 room deposit, refundable until May 1. Freshmen accepted for terms other than fall.
**Special programs:** Admission may be deferred. Credit may be granted through CEEB Advanced Placement for scores of 3 or higher. Credit may be granted through CLEP subject exams and military experience. Credit and placement may be granted through challenge exams. Early entrance/early admission program. Concurrent enrollment program.
**Transfer students:** Transfer students accepted for terms other than fall. In fall 1993, 25% of all new students were transfers into all classes. 446 transfer applications were received, 352 were accepted. Minimum 2.0 GPA required. Lowest course grade accepted is "C." Maximum number of transferable credits is 65 semester hours. At least 30 semester hours must be completed at the university to receive degree.
**Admissions contact:** Marvin W. Lynch, M.A., Director of Admissions. 803 661-1231.

**FINANCIAL AID. Available aid:** Pell grants, SEOG, state scholarships and grants, school scholarships, private scholarships and grants, ROTC scholarships, academic merit scholarships, and athletic scholarships. Perkins Loans (NDSL), PLUS, Stafford Loans (GSL), state loans, private loans, and SLS.
**Financial aid statistics:** 40% of aid is not need-based. In 1993-94, 75% of all undergraduate applicants received aid.
**Supporting data/closing dates:** FAFSA: Priority filing date is March 1. School's own aid application: Priority filing date is March 1. Scholarship application: Priority filing date is March 1. Notification of awards on rolling basis.
**Financial aid contact:** H. Scott Brown, M.Ed., Director of Financial Aid. 803 661-1190.

**STUDENT EMPLOYMENT.** College Work/Study Program. Institutional employment. 18% of full-time undergraduates work on campus during school year. Students may expect to earn an average of $705 during school year. Freshmen are discouraged from working during their first term. Off-campus part-time employment opportunities rated "excellent."

**COMPUTER FACILITIES.** 170 IBM/IBM-compatible microcomputers; 141 are networked. Students may access Digital, IBM minicomputer/mainframe systems, Internet. Residence halls may be equipped with stand-alone microcomputers. Client/LAN operating systems include Apple/Macintosh, DOS, UNIX/XENIX/AIX, DEC, Novell. Computer languages and software packages include Assembler, Assist, Bank Street Writer, BASIC, COBOL, FORTRAN, MicroStat, MicroUse, Paradox, Pascal, PL/1, PsychoStat, QuattroPro, RPG, SAS, SPSS, WordPerfect, WordStar. Computer facilities are available to all students.
**Fees:** Computer fee is included in tuition/fees.
**Hours:** 8 AM-11 PM (M-Th); 8 AM-5 PM (F); 1 PM-5 PM (Sa); 3 PM-11 PM (Su).

# Furman University

**Greenville, SC 29613** **803 294-2185**

**1994-95 Costs.** Tuition: $13,440. Room: $2,096. Board: $1,952. Fees, books, misc. academic expenses (school's estimate): $734.
**Enrollment.** Undergraduates: 1,171 men, 1,375 women (full-time). Freshman class: 2,161 applicants, 1,951 accepted, 687 enrolled. Graduate enrollment: 65 men, 230 women.
**Test score averages/ranges.** Range of SAT scores of middle 50%: 470-580 verbal, 520-640 math. Range of ACT scores of middle 50%: 23-27 composite.
**Faculty.** 185 full-time; 13 part-time. 89% of faculty holds doctoral degree. Student/faculty ratio: 12 to 1.
**Selectivity rating.** Highly competitive.

**PROFILE.** Furman, founded in 1826, is a non-sectarian, liberal arts university. Its 750-acre campus, five miles from Greenville, is located at the foot of Paris Mountain.

**Accreditation:** SACS. Professionally accredited by the National Association of Schools of Music.
**Religious orientation:** Furman University is nonsectarian; one semester of religion/theology required.
**Library:** Collections totaling over 350,289 volumes, 1,514 periodical subscriptions, and 556,924 microform items.
**Special facilities/museums:** Visual arts gallery and teaching facility, language lab.
**Athletic facilities:** Gymnasium, swimming pool, golf course, tennis and volleyball courts, football, practice, soccer, and softball fields, track.

**STUDENT BODY. Undergraduate profile:** 33% are state residents; 6% are transfers. 1% Asian-American, 3% Black, 1% Hispanic, 95% White. Average age of undergraduates is 20.
**Freshman profile:** 4% of freshmen who took SAT scored 700 or over on verbal, 11% scored 700 or over on math; 23% scored 600 or over on verbal, 44% scored 600 or over on math; 61% scored 500 or over on verbal, 84% scored 500 or over on math; 97% scored 400 or over on verbal, 99% scored 400 or over on math; 100% scored 300 or over on verbal, 100% scored 300 or over on math. 14% of freshmen who took ACT scored 30 or over on composite; 69% scored 24 or over on composite; 100% scored 18 or over on composite. 97% of accepted applicants took SAT; 32% took ACT. 75% of freshmen come from public schools.
**Undergraduate achievement:** 92% of fall 1992 freshmen returned for fall 1993 term. 82% of entering class graduated. 40% of students who completed a degree program immediately went on to graduate study.
**Foreign students:** 34 students are from out of the country. Countries represented include Belgium, Bulgaria, Finland, Japan, Peru, and Venezuela; 20 in all.

**PROGRAMS OF STUDY. Degrees:** B.A., B.Gen.Studies, B.Mus., B.S.
**Majors:** Accounting, Art, Asian Studies, Biology, Business Administration, Chemistry, Church Music, Computer Science, Computer Science/Mathematics, Computing/Business, Drama, Economics, Education, English, French, Geology, German, Greek, Health/Exercise Science, History, Individualized Curriculum, Latin, Mathematics, Music, Music Education, Music Performance, Music Theory, Philosophy, Physics, Piano Pedagogy, Political Science, Pre-Engineering, Psychology, Religion, Sociology, Spanish, Urban Studies.
**Distribution of degrees:** The majors with the highest enrollment are business administration, political science, and education; urban studies, Greek, and Latin have the lowest.
**Requirements:** General education requirement.
**Academic regulations:** Minimum 2.0 GPA required for graduation.
**Special:** Self-designed majors. Double majors. Dual degrees. Independent study. Pass/fail grading option. Internships. Preprofessional programs in law, medicine, veterinary science, pharmacy, dentistry, and theology. 3-1 programs may be arranged in dentistry, forestry, law, medical technology, medicine, physical therapy, religious studies, and social service. 3-2 engineering programs with Auburn U, Clemson U, Georgia Tech, and North Carolina State U. 3-2 forestry program with Duke U. Member of Southern Consortium with 19 private selective institutions in the South; member of Associated Colleges of the South with 13 private, liberal arts colleges. Washington Semester. Teacher certification in early childhood, elementary, secondary, and special education. Study abroad in Belgium, Costa Rica, Ecuador, Egypt, France, Germany, Greece, Israel, Italy, Japan, Kenya, Russia, Spain, and the United Kingdom. ROTC.
**Honors:** Phi Beta Kappa.
**Academic Assistance:** Nonremedial tutoring.

**STUDENT LIFE. Housing:** Unmarried freshmen and sophomores must live on campus unless living with family. Coed, women's, and men's dorms. Off-campus privately-owned housing. 65% of students live in college housing.
**Social atmosphere:** Popular places to congregate at Furman include Al's Pump House, The Manor, FUSAB movies, local restaurants, and malls. Greeks, Christian groups, athletes, musical organizations, Student Government, and the Student Activities Board are among the influential groups on campus. Some favorite campus events of the year are Homecoming, concerts, football games, Beach Weekend, Raft Regatta, and the Fall Flamingo.
**Services and counseling/handicapped student services:** Placement services. Health service. Counseling services for minority students. Personal and psychological counseling. Career and academic guidance services. Religious counseling. Physically disabled student services. Notetaking services. Tape recorders. Tutors. Reader services for the blind.
**Campus organizations:** Undergraduate student government. Student newspaper (Paladin, published once/week). Literary magazine. Yearbook. Radio station. Band, symphony orchestra, string ensemble, concert choir, University Singers, Theatre Guild, Collegiate Educational Service Corps, departmental, professional, and special-interest groups, 121 organizations in all. Eight fraternities, no chapter houses; seven sororities, no chapter houses. 32% of men join a fraternity. 30% of women join a sorority.
**Religious organizations:** Baptist Student Union, Canterbury, Fellowship of Christian Athletes, Intervarsity Christian Fellowship, Lutheran Student Association, Newman Club, Wesley Foundation, Presbyterian Westminster Fellowship, Worldwide Discipleship Association, Young Life, Greek Orthodox Young Adult League, Furman U Gospel Ensemble, Habitat for Humanity.
**Minority/foreign student organizations:** Student League for Black Culture. Foreign Student Association.

**ATHLETICS. Physical education requirements:** One semester of physical education required.
**Intercollegiate competition:** 13% of students participate. Baseball (M), basketball (M,W), cheerleading (M,W), cross-country (M,W), football (M), golf (M,W), soccer (M,W), softball (W), tennis (M,W), track (indoor) (W), track (outdoor) (M,W), volleyball (W). Member of NCAA Division I, NCAA Division I-AA for football, Southern Athletic Conference.
**Intramural and club sports:** 40% of students participate. Intramural badminton, baseball, basketball, bowling, crew, flag football, golf, lacrosse, racquetball, soccer, softball, swimming, table tennis, tennis, volleyball, wrestling. Men's club bowling, crew, lacrosse, racquetball, softball, tennis, wrestling. Women's club bowling, crew, soccer, softball, tennis.

**ADMISSIONS. Academic basis for candidate selection** (in order of priority): Secondary school record, standardized test scores, class rank, essay.
**Nonacademic basis for candidate selection:** Character and personality, extracurricular participation, particular talent or ability, and alumni/ae relationship are considered.
**Requirements:** Graduation from secondary school is required; GED is not accepted. No specific distribution of secondary school units required. Minimum 3.0 GPA recommended. Portfolio required of art program applicants. SAT or ACT is required. PSAT is recommended. Campus visit recommended. No off-campus interviews.
**Procedure:** Take SAT or ACT by November of 12th year. Application deadline is February 1. Notification of admission by March 15. Reply is required by May 1. $100 nonrefundable tuition deposit. $100 nonrefundable room deposit. Freshmen accepted for fall term only.
**Special programs:** Credit and/or placement may be granted through CEEB Advanced Placement exams for scores of 4 or higher. Early decision program. In fall 1993, 510 applied for early decision and 367 were accepted. Deadline for applying for early decision is December 1. Early entrance/early admission program.
**Transfer students:** Transfer students accepted for terms other than fall. In fall 1993, 6% of all new students were transfers into all classes. 122 transfer applications were received, 92 were accepted. Application deadline is February 1 for fall; December 1 for spring. SAT/ACT scores required of transfer applicants with fewer than 30 semester hours. Minimum 3.0 GPA required. Lowest course grade accepted is "C." Maximum number of transferable credits is 64 semester hours. At least 64 semester hours must be completed at the university to receive degree.
**Admissions contact:** J. Carey Thompson, M.Ed., Director of Admissions. 803 294-2034.

**FINANCIAL AID. Available aid:** Pell grants, SEOG, state scholarships and grants, school scholarships and grants, private scholarships and grants, ROTC scholarships, academic merit scholarships, athletic scholarships, and aid for undergraduate foreign students. Perkins Loans (NDSL), PLUS, Stafford Loans (GSL), state loans, school loans, private loans, and SLS. Knight Tuition Plans.
**Financial aid statistics:** 40% of aid is not need-based. In 1993-94, 56% of all freshman applicants received aid. Average amounts of aid awarded freshmen: Scholarships and grants, $8,500; loans, $2,600.
**Supporting data/closing dates:** FAFSA/FAF/FFS: Deadline is February 1. School's own aid application: Deadline is February 1. State aid form: Priority filing date is February 1; accepted on rolling basis; deadline is June 30. Notification of awards begins March 15.
**Financial aid contact:** Lynda Sayer, Director of Financial Aid. 803 294-2204.

**STUDENT EMPLOYMENT.** College Work/Study Program. Institutional employment. 28% of full-time undergraduates work on campus during school year. Students may expect to earn an average of $1,200 during school year. Off-campus part-time employment opportunities rated "good."

**COMPUTER FACILITIES.** 100 IBM/IBM-compatible and Macintosh/Apple microcomputers; all are networked. Students may access Digital, Hewlett-Packard, SUN minicomputer/mainframe systems, BITNET, Internet. Client/LAN operating systems include Apple/Macintosh, DOS, UNIX/XENIX/AIX, X-windows, LocalTalk/AppleTalk, Microsoft. Computer languages and software packages include BASIC, C, COBOL, DINE, Excel, FORTRAN, Pascal, SPSS, Word for Windows. Computer facilities are available to all students.
**Fees:** None.
**Hours:** 8 AM-midn.

**GRADUATE CAREER DATA.** Graduate school percentages: 5% enter law school. 3% enter medical school. 1% enter dental school. 2% enter graduate business programs. 24% enter graduate arts and sciences programs. 2% enter theological school/seminary. Highest graduate school enrollments: Emory U, Georgia State U, U of Florida, U of Georgia, U of North Carolina at Chapel Hill, U of South Carolina. Companies and businesses that hire graduates: retail, accounting, insurance, and financial firms.

**PROMINENT ALUMNI/AE.** Charles Townes, Nobel Prize-winner in physics; Richard Riley, U.S. Secretary of Education and former governor, South Carolina; David Garrett, chairperson of the board, Delta Airlines; Betsy King, Beth Daniel, and Dottie Mochrie, professional golfers; Herman Lay, former chairperson, PepsiCo and Frito-Lay; Clement Haynesworth, federal judge.

# Lander University

**Greenwood, SC 29649** **803 229-8400**

**1993-94 Costs.** Tuition: $3,220 (state residents), $4,598 (out-of-state). Room & board: $2,960. Fees, books, misc. academic expenses (school's estimate): $550.
**Enrollment.** Undergraduates: 735 men, 1,339 women (full-time). Freshman class: 1,166 applicants, 1,009 accepted, 510 enrolled. Graduate enrollment: 67 men, 278 women.
**Test score averages/ranges.** N/A.
**Faculty.** 127 full-time; 39 part-time. 64% of faculty holds doctoral degree. Student/faculty ratio: 16 to 1.
**Selectivity rating.** N/A.

**PROFILE.** Lander, founded in 1872, is a public, liberal arts university. Its 100-acre campus is located in Greenwood, in the Piedmont region of South Carolina.

**Accreditation:** SACS. Professionally accredited by the National League for Nursing.
**Religious orientation:** Lander University is nonsectarian; no religious requirements.
**Library:** Collections totaling over 232,371 volumes, 1,067 periodical subscriptions, and 79,146 microform items.
**Special facilities/museums:** Art gallery, continuing education center, media center, electronic piano instruction facility, amphitheatre.
**Athletic facilities:** Gymnasium, tennis courts, softball and soccer fields.

**STUDENT BODY. Undergraduate profile:** 95% are state residents; 27% are transfers. 18% Black, 80% White, 2% Other. Average age of undergraduates is 22.
**Freshman profile:** 95% of freshmen come from public schools.
**Undergraduate achievement:** 65% of fall 1992 freshmen returned for fall 1993 term. 19% of entering class graduated.
**Foreign students:** 31 students are from out of the country. Countries represented include Bolivia, France, Japan, Sweden, and Trinidad; 19 in all.

**PROGRAMS OF STUDY. Degrees:** B.A., B.S.
**Majors:** Art, Biology, Business Administration, Chemistry, Computer Science, Early Childhood Education, Elementary Education, English, Health/Physical Education/Recreation, History, Interdisciplinary Studies, Mathematics, Medical Technology, Music, Music Education, Nursing, Political Science, Psychology, Sociology, Speech/Theatre.
**Distribution of degrees:** The majors with the highest enrollment are business administration, elementary and early childhood education, and sociology; French and medical technology have the lowest.
**Requirements:** General education requirement.
**Special:** Minors offered in most majors. Courses offered in dance, developmental reading, writing, math, German, philosophy/religion, and Spanish. Self-designed majors. Double majors. Dual degrees. Cooperative education programs. Graduate school at which undergraduates may take graduate-level courses. Preprofessional programs in law, medicine, veterinary science, pharmacy, and dentistry. 3-2 dual engineering program with Clemson U. Washington Semester. M.B.A. from Clemson U offered on Lander U campus. Teacher certification in early childhood, elementary, secondary, and special education. Certification in specific subject areas. Study abroad in England. ROTC.
**Academic Assistance:** Remedial reading, writing, math, and study skills. Nonremedial tutoring.

**STUDENT LIFE. Housing:** Students may live on or off campus. Women's and men's dorms. Sorority and fraternity housing. 40% of students live in college housing.
**Services and counseling/handicapped student services:** Placement services. Health service. Counseling services for minority, military, and veteran students. Personal counseling. Career and academic guidance services. Physically disabled student services. Learning disabled services. Notetaking services. Tape recorders. Tutors.
**Campus organizations:** Undergraduate student government. Student newspaper (Forum, published bimonthly). Lander Singers, jazz ensemble, dance and theatre groups, Art Alliance, Ground Zero for Peace, 55 organizations in all. Five fraternities, three chapter houses; six sororities, two chapter houses. 20% of men join a fraternity. 30% of women join a sorority.
**Religious organizations:** Baptist Student Union, Bible Study, Fellowship of Christian Athletes, Sigma Iota Chi.
**Minority/foreign student organizations:** Minorities on the Move, minority fraternities/sororities. International Student Organization.

**ATHLETICS. Physical education requirements:** Two semesters of physical education required.
**Intercollegiate competition:** 5% of students participate. Basketball (M,W), cross-country (M,W), soccer (M), softball (W), tennis (M,W). Member of NCAA Division II, Peach Belt Athletic Conference.
**Intramural and club sports:** 2% of students participate. Intramural basketball, bowling, flag football, soccer, softball, tennis, volleyball.

**ADMISSIONS. Academic basis for candidate selection** (in order of priority): Secondary school record, class rank, standardized test scores, school's recommendation.
**Nonacademic basis for candidate selection:** Extracurricular participation and particular talent or ability are considered.
**Requirements:** Graduation from secondary school is required; GED is accepted. 16 units and the following program of study are required: 4 units of English, 3 units of math, 2 units of lab science, 2 units of foreign language, 2 units of social studies, 1 unit of history, 2 units of electives. Rank in top half of secondary school class required. Academic Support Center Advisement Program for applicants not normally admissible. SAT or ACT is required. Campus visit and interview recommended. Off-campus interviews available with an admissions representative.
**Procedure:** Take SAT or ACT by September of 12th year. Visit college for interview by September of 12th year. Suggest filing application by November; no deadline. Notification of admission on rolling basis. No set date by which applicants must accept offer. $75 room deposit, refundable until July 1. Freshmen accepted for terms other than fall.
**Special programs:** Admission may be deferred one year. Credit may be granted through CEEB Advanced Placement for scores of 3 or higher. Credit may be granted through CLEP subject exams and military experience. Early entrance/early admission program. Concurrent enrollment program.
**Transfer students:** Transfer students accepted for terms other than fall. In fall 1993, 27% of all new students were transfers into all classes. 469 transfer applications were received. Application deadline is August 7 for fall; December 11 for spring. Minimum 2.0 GPA required. Lowest course grade accepted is "C." Maximum number of transferable credits is 64 semester hours from a two-year school and 90 semester hours from a four-year school. At least 30 semester hours must be completed at the university to receive degree.
**Admissions contact:** Jacquelyn DeVore Roark, M.Ed., Director of Admissions. 803 229-8307, 800 768-3600.

**FINANCIAL AID. Available aid:** Pell grants, SEOG, school scholarships and grants, private scholarships and grants, ROTC scholarships, academic merit scholarships, and athletic scholarships. Perkins Loans (NDSL), PLUS, Stafford Loans (GSL), private loans, and SLS. Tuition Plan Inc. and AMS.
**Financial aid statistics:** 33% of aid is not need-based. In 1993-94, 68% of all undergraduate applicants received aid; 72% of freshman applicants. Average amounts of aid awarded freshmen: Scholarships and grants, $610; loans, $2,317.
**Supporting data/closing dates:** FAFSA: Priority filing date is April 15. Notification of awards begins June 1.
**Financial aid contact:** Ian M. Hubbard, Director of Financial Aid. 803 229-8340.

**STUDENT EMPLOYMENT.** College Work/Study Program. Institutional employment. 12% of full-time undergraduates work on campus during school year. Students may expect to earn an average of $900 during school year. Off-campus part-time employment opportunities rated "excellent."

**COMPUTER FACILITIES.** 90 IBM/IBM-compatible and Macintosh/Apple microcomputers; 15 are networked. Students may access IBM minicomputer/mainframe systems, BITNET, Internet. Client/LAN operating systems include OS/2. Computer languages and software packages include C, COBOL, Excel, FORTRAN, Microsoft, Pascal, ProfWrite, WordPerfect; 62 in all. Computer facilities are available to all students.
**Fees:** $10 computer fee per course; included in tuition/fees.
**Hours:** 8 AM-11 PM.

**GRADUATE CAREER DATA.** Graduate school percentages: 2% enter law school. 9% enter graduate business programs. Highest graduate school enrollments: Clemson U, U of South Carolina.

# Limestone College

**Gaffney, SC 29340** **803 489-7151**

**1994-95 Costs.** Tuition: $7,600. Room: $1,800. Board: $1,800. Fees, books, misc. academic expenses (school's estimate): $500.
**Enrollment.** Undergraduates: 170 men, 180 women (full-time). Freshman class: 424 applicants, 313 accepted, 136 enrolled. Graduate enrollment: 31.
**Test score averages/ranges.** Average SAT scores: 360 verbal, 390 math.
**Faculty.** 26 full-time; 15 part-time. 44% of faculty holds highest degree in specific field. Student/faculty ratio: 10 to 1.
**Selectivity rating.** Less competitive.

**PROFILE.** Limestone, founded in 1845, is a private, liberal arts college. Its 115-acre campus is located in Gaffney, 50 miles from Charlotte, N.C.

**Accreditation:** SACS.
**Religious orientation:** Limestone College is nonsectarian; two semesters of religion/theology required.
**Library:** Collections totaling over 89,000 volumes, 554 periodical subscriptions and 900 microform items.
**Special facilities/museums:** Language lab, observatory.
**Athletic facilities:** Gymnasium, swimming pool, track, baseball, soccer, and softball fields, tennis courts.

**STUDENT BODY. Undergraduate profile:** 80% are state residents; 25% are transfers. 31% Black, 1% Hispanic, 68% White. Average age of undergraduates is 19.
**Freshman profile:** 4% of freshmen who took SAT scored 600 or over on math; 4% scored 500 or over on verbal, 13% scored 500 or over on math; 37% scored 400 or over on verbal, 48% scored 400 or over on math; 82% scored 300 or over on verbal, 93% scored 300 or over on math. 97% of accepted applicants took SAT; 3% took ACT. 95% of freshmen come from public schools.
**Undergraduate achievement:** 60% of fall 1992 freshmen returned for fall 1993 term. 50% of entering class graduated. 5% of students who completed a degree program went on to graduate study within five years.
**Foreign students:** Seven students are from out of the country. Countries represented include Australia and Japan.

**PROGRAMS OF STUDY. Degrees:** B.A., B.S.
**Majors:** Applied Music, Art, Art Education, Biology, Business Administration, Computer Science, Elementary Education, English, Guidance/Counseling, History, Mathematics, Music Education, Physical Education, Psychology, Social Work.
**Distribution of degrees:** The majors with the highest enrollment are business administration, elementary education, and computer science.
**Requirements:** General education requirement.
**Special:** Associate's degrees offered. Self-designed majors. Double majors. Dual degrees. Independent study. Internships. Graduate school at which undergraduates may take graduate-level courses. Preprofessional programs in law, medicine, and dentistry. Teacher certification in elementary and secondary education. Certification in specific subject areas.
**Honors:** Honors program.
**Academic Assistance:** Remedial reading, writing, math, and study skills.

**ADMISSIONS. Academic basis for candidate selection** (in order of priority): Secondary school record, class rank, standardized test scores.

**Nonacademic basis for candidate selection:** Character and personality and particular talent or ability are important. Extracurricular participation is considered.
**Requirements:** Graduation from secondary school is required; GED is accepted. No specific distribution of secondary school units required. Minimum combined SAT score of 700 and minimum 2.0 GPA required. Portfolio required of art program applicants. Audition required of music program applicants. Conditional admission possible for applicants not meeting standard requirements. SAT or ACT is required. Campus visit and interview recommended. Off-campus interviews available with an admissions representative.
**Procedure:** Take SAT or ACT by December of 12th year. Suggest filing application by February 1; no deadline. Notification of admission on rolling basis. $50 tuition deposit, refundable until April 30. $50 room deposit, refundable until April 30. Freshmen accepted for terms other than fall.
**Special programs:** Admission may be deferred one year. Credit may be granted through CEEB Advanced Placement for scores of 3 or higher. Credit may be granted through CLEP general and subject exams.
**Transfer students:** Transfer students accepted for terms other than fall. In fall 1993, 25% of all new students were transfers into all classes. 111 transfer applications were received, 90 were accepted. Minimum 2.0 GPA recommended. Lowest course grade accepted is "C." Maximum number of transferable credits is 64 semester hours. At least 30 semester hours must be completed at the college to receive degree.
**Admissions contact:** Sherri Horton, Director of Admissions. 803 489-7151, extension 554.

**FINANCIAL AID. Available aid:** Pell grants, SEOG, state scholarships and grants, school scholarships and grants, private scholarships and grants, academic merit scholarships, and athletic scholarships. Perkins Loans (NDSL), PLUS, Stafford Loans (GSL), state loans, private loans, and SLS. AMS, Tuition Management Systems, and deferred payment plan. IPP.
**Financial aid statistics:** Average amounts of aid awarded freshmen: Scholarships and grants, $1,500; loans, $2,625.
**Supporting data/closing dates:** FAFSA/FAF: Priority filing date is February 1. School's own aid application: Priority filing date is February 1. Notification of awards on rolling basis.
**Financial aid contact:** Virgina Hickey, Director of Financial Aid. 803 489-7151, extension 595.

## Morris College

**Sumter, SC 29150-3599** **803 775-9371**

**1994-95 Costs.** Tuition: $4,515. Room & board: $2,550. Fees, books, misc. academic expenses (school's estimate): $915.
**Enrollment.** Undergraduates: 329 men, 597 women (full-time). Freshman class: 882 applicants, 730 accepted, 330 enrolled.
**Test score averages/ranges.** N/A.
**Faculty.** 46 full-time; 11 part-time. 42% of faculty holds doctoral degree. Student/faculty ratio: 16 to 1.
**Selectivity rating.** N/A.

**PROFILE.** Morris, founded in 1908, is a private, church-affiliated, historically black college. Programs are offered through the Divisions of Business Administration; Education; General Studies; Humanities; Natural Sciences and Mathematics; and Social Sciences, History, and Pre-Law Studies. Its 34-acre campus is located in Sumter, east of Columbia.

**Accreditation:** SACS.
**Religious orientation:** Morris College is affiliated with the Baptist Church; two semesters of religion required.
**Library:** Collections totaling over 93,248 volumes, 697 periodical subscriptions, and 136,633 microform items.
**Special facilities/museums:** Satellite, commercial radio station.
**Athletic facilities:** Gymnasium, athletic field.

**STUDENT BODY. Undergraduate profile:** 91% are state residents; 7% are transfers. 100% Black. Average age of undergraduates is 21.
**Freshman profile:** 98% of freshmen come from public schools.
**Undergraduate achievement:** 57% of fall 1992 freshmen returned for fall 1993 term. 13% of entering class graduated. 10% of students who completed a degree program immediately went on to graduate study.

**PROGRAMS OF STUDY. Degrees:** B.A., B.F.A., B.S., B.S.Ed.
**Majors:** Biology, Biology Teaching, Business Administration, Community Health, Criminal Justice, Early Childhood Education, Elementary Education, English, English Education, Fine Arts, History, History Education, Liberal Studies, Liberal/Technical Studies, Mathematics, Mathematics Education, Political Science/History, Recreation Administration, Religious Education, Social Studies, Social Studies Education, Sociology.
**Distribution of degrees:** The majors with the highest enrollment are business administration, sociology, and liberal studies; early childhood education, history, and religious education have the lowest.
**Requirements:** General education requirement.
**Academic regulations:** Freshmen must maintain minimum 1.2 GPA; sophomores, 1.5 GPA; juniors, 1.7 GPA; seniors, 2.0 GPA.
**Special:** Minors offered in some majors and in gerontology, international relations, media arts, minority studies, and music. Liberal and technical studies major is for technical or vocational program graduates. Courses in chemistry, economics, French, humanities, philosophy, and speech and theatre. Division of General Studies. Double majors. Internships. Cooperative education programs. Preprofessional programs in law, medicine, veterinary science, pharmacy, dentistry, and nursing. Teacher certification in early childhood, elementary, and secondary education. Certification in specific subject areas. ROTC.
**Honors:** Honors program. Honor societies.

**Academic Assistance:** Remedial reading, writing, math, and study skills. Nonremedial tutoring.

**ADMISSIONS. Academic basis for candidate selection** (in order of priority): Secondary school record, school's recommendation, standardized test scores, class rank.
**Nonacademic basis for candidate selection:** Character and personality are emphasized. Extracurricular participation, particular talent or ability, and alumni/ae relationship are considered.
**Requirements:** Graduation from secondary school is required; GED is accepted. 20 units and the following program of study are required: 4 units of English, 3 units of math, 2 units of science, 2 units of social studies, 1 unit of history, 8 units of electives including 7 units of academic electives. Completion of 60 credit hours (with minimum 2.5 GPA) and qualifying grade on the EEE required for admission to Teacher Education program. SAT or ACT is recommended. Campus visit and interview recommended. Off-campus interviews available with an admissions representative.
**Procedure:** Take SAT or ACT by January of 12th year. Notification of admission on rolling basis. No set date by which applicants must accept offer. $25 room deposit, refundable when student leaves housing. Freshmen accepted for terms other than fall.
**Special programs:** Admission may be deferred one semester. Credit may be granted through CLEP general and subject exams and military experience.
**Transfer students:** Transfer students accepted for terms other than fall. In fall 1993, 7% of all new students were transfers into all classes. 140 transfer applications were received, 63 were accepted. Application deadline is rolling for fall; rolling for spring. Minimum 2.0 GPA required. Lowest course grade accepted is "C." Maximum number of transferable credits is 94 semester hours. At least 30 semester hours must be completed at the college to receive degree.
**Admissions contact:** Queen W. Spann, M.Ed., Admissions and Records Officer. 803 775-9371, extension 225.

**FINANCIAL AID. Available aid:** Pell grants, SEOG, state scholarships and grants, school scholarships and grants, private scholarships and grants, ROTC scholarships, academic merit scholarships, athletic scholarships, and United Negro College Fund. Perkins Loans (NDSL), PLUS, Stafford Loans (GSL), state loans, private loans, and SLS.
**Financial aid statistics:** 1% of aid is not need-based. In 1993-94, 93% of all undergraduate applicants received aid; 95% of freshman applicants. Average amounts of aid awarded freshmen: Scholarships and grants, $3,190; loans, $2,625.
**Supporting data/closing dates:** FAFSA/FAF/FFS: Priority filing date is March 30. School's own aid application: Priority filing date is March 30. State aid form: Priority filing date is March 30. Income tax forms: Priority filing date is March 30. Notification of awards on rolling basis.
**Financial aid contact:** Sandra S. Gibson, M.Ed., Director of Financial Aid. 803 775-9371, extension 238.

## Newberry College

**Newberry, SC 29108** **800 845-4955**

**1994-95 Costs.** Tuition: $10,194. Room & board: $2,600. Fees, books, misc. academic expenses (school's estimate): $500.
**Enrollment.** Undergraduates: 310 men, 309 women (full-time). Freshman class: 872 applicants, 796 accepted, 198 enrolled.
**Test score averages/ranges.** Average SAT scores: 409 verbal, 459 math.
**Faculty.** 43 full-time; 22 part-time. 54% of faculty holds doctoral degree. Student/faculty ratio: 13 to 1.
**Selectivity rating.** Less competitive.

**PROFILE.** Newberry, founded in 1856, is a private, church-affiliated, liberal arts college. Its 60-acre campus is located in Newberry, 40 miles northwest of Columbia.

**Accreditation:** SACS. Professionally accredited by the National Association of Schools of Music, the National Council for Accreditation of Teacher Education.
**Religious orientation:** Newberry College is affiliated with the Evangelical Lutheran Church in America; two semesters of religion required.
**Library:** Collections totaling over 82,379 volumes and 359 periodical subscriptions.
**Athletic facilities:** Gymnasium, arena, athletic fields, handball courts, weight room, swimming pool.

**STUDENT BODY. Undergraduate profile:** 83% are state residents; 20% are transfers. 17% Black, 1% Hispanic, 82% White. Average age of undergraduates is 19.
**Freshman profile:** Majority of accepted applicants took SAT. 98% of freshmen come from public schools.
**Undergraduate achievement:** 77% of fall 1992 freshmen returned for fall 1993 term.

**PROGRAMS OF STUDY. Degrees:** B.A., B.Mus., B.Mus.Ed., B.S.
**Majors:** Accounting, Applied Music, Art, Arts Management, Biology, Business Administration, Business Administration/Chemistry, Business Administration/Computer Science, Business Administration/Industrial Safety, Chemistry, Church Music, Computer Science/Mathematics, Early Childhood Education, Economics, Elementary Education, English, Foreign Languages, French, History, International Government/Commerce, Mathematics, Medical Technology, Music, Music Education, Music Literature, Music Theory, Organ, Physical Education, Piano, Political Science, Religion/Philosophy, Sociology, Spanish, Speech, Theatre, Voice.
**Distribution of degrees:** The majors with the highest enrollment are business administration, English, and political science; Spanish, theatre/speech, and religion/philosophy have the lowest.
**Requirements:** General education requirement.
**Special:** Minors offered in some majors and in athletic training, coaching, communications, education, physics, psychology, and safety/health. Double majors. Dual degrees. Independent study. Internships. Preprofessional programs in law, medicine, pharmacy, dentistry, theology, forestry, and nursing. 3-2 forestry program with Duke U. Combined-degree computer science, engineering, management science, and physics programs with Georgia Tech. Combined-degree engineering program with Clemson U. Combined-

degree allied health program with Medical U of South Carolina. Teacher certification in early childhood, elementary, and secondary education. Study abroad in England, Mexico, the Netherlands, and Wales. ROTC.
**Honors:** Honor societies.
**Academic Assistance:** Nonremedial tutoring.

**ADMISSIONS. Academic basis for candidate selection** (in order of priority): Secondary school record, class rank, standardized test scores, school's recommendation.
**Nonacademic basis for candidate selection:** Character and personality and extracurricular participation are emphasized.
**Requirements:** Graduation from secondary school is required; GED is accepted. No specific distribution of secondary school units required. Audition required of music program applicants. SAT or ACT is required. Campus visit and interview recommended. Off-campus interviews available with admissions and alumni representatives.
**Procedure:** Take SAT or ACT by December of 12th year. Visit college for interview by March of 12th year. Suggest filing application by March. Application deadline is August. Notification of admission on rolling basis. $50 tuition deposit, refundable until June 1. $50 room deposit, refundable until June 1. Freshmen accepted for terms other than fall.
**Special programs:** Credit and/or placement may be granted through CEEB Advanced Placement exams for scores of 3 or higher. Credit may be granted through CLEP general exams and DANTES exams. Credit and/or placement may be granted through CLEP subject exams. Credit and placement may be granted through military experience. Early decision program. Early entrance/early admission program. Concurrent enrollment program.
**Transfer students:** Transfer students accepted for terms other than fall. In fall 1993, 20% of all new students were transfers into all classes. 102 transfer applications were received, 70 were accepted. Lowest course grade accepted is "C." Maximum number of transferable credits is 72 semester hours. At least 30 semester hours must be completed at the college to receive degree.
**Admissions contact:** John Ryder, M.Ed., Director of Admissions. 800 845-4955.

**FINANCIAL AID. Available aid:** Pell grants, SEOG, state scholarships and grants, school scholarships and grants, private scholarships and grants, ROTC scholarships, academic merit scholarships, and athletic scholarships. Perkins Loans (NDSL), PLUS, Stafford Loans (GSL), school loans, private loans, and SLS. Knight Tuition Plans. 10-month payment plan.
**Financial aid statistics:** In 1993-94, 95% of all undergraduate applicants received aid; 95% of freshman applicants. Average amounts of aid awarded freshmen: Scholarships and grants, $5,000; loans, $2,200.
**Supporting data/closing dates:** FAFSA/FAF/FFS: Priority filing date is May 1. School's own aid application: Priority filing date is May; deadline is August 1. State aid form: Priority filing date is April 15. Income tax forms: Priority filing date is May 1. Notification of awards on rolling basis.
**Financial aid contact:** Sean Van Pallardt, M.A., Ed.D., Director of Financial Aid. 800 845-4955.

# Presbyterian College

**Clinton, SC 29325** **800 476-7272**

**1994-95 Costs.** Tuition: $11,859. Room: $1,711. Board: $1,924. Fees, books, misc. academic expenses (school's estimate): $1,446.
**Enrollment.** Undergraduates: 581 men, 582 women (full-time). Freshman class: 1,083 applicants, 831 accepted, 302 enrolled.
**Test score averages/ranges.** Average SAT scores: 530 verbal, 570 math. Range of SAT scores of middle 50%: 500-560 verbal, 540-600 math. Average ACT scores: 26 English, 28 math, 27 composite. Range of ACT scores of middle 50%: 24-30 composite.
**Faculty.** 75 full-time; 16 part-time. 90% of faculty holds doctoral degree. Student/faculty ratio: 15 to 1.
**Selectivity rating.** Highly competitive.

**PROFILE.** Presbyterian, founded in 1880, is a private, church-affiliated, liberal arts college. Its 212-acre campus is locate in Clinton, 30 miles south of Greenville.

**Accreditation:** SACS. Professionally accredited by the American Assembly of Collegiate Schools of Business.
**Religious orientation:** Presbyterian College is an interdenominational Christian school; two semesters of religion required.
**Library:** Collections totaling over 140,000 volumes, 750 periodical subscriptions, and 4,500 microform items.
**Special facilities/museums:** Art gallery, recital hall, media center, marine/ecological center, scanning and transmission electron microscopes, visible spectrophotometer.
**Athletic facilities:** Field house, gymnasium, basketball, racquetball, tennis, and volleyball courts, fitness and weight rooms, swimming pool, intramural, soccer, and softball fields.

**STUDENT BODY. Undergraduate profile:** 46% are state residents; 2% are transfers. 1% Asian-American, 5% Black, 1% Hispanic, 93% White. Average age of undergraduates is 19.
**Freshman profile:** 4% of freshmen who took SAT scored 700 or over on verbal, 7% scored 700 or over on math; 22% scored 600 or over on verbal, 33% scored 600 or over on math; 70% scored 500 or over on verbal, 90% scored 500 or over on math; 99% scored 400 or over on verbal, 99% scored 400 or over on math; 100% scored 300 or over on verbal, 100% scored 300 or over on math. 75% of accepted applicants took SAT; 25% took ACT. 70% of freshmen come from public schools.
**Undergraduate achievement:** 90% of fall 1992 freshmen returned for fall 1993 term. 77% of entering class graduated. 40% of students who completed a degree program immediately went on to graduate study.
**Foreign students:** Eight students are from out of the country. Countries represented include Argentina, Bulgaria, China, France, Nicaragua, and Spain; eight in all.

**PROGRAMS OF STUDY. Degrees:** B.A., B.S.
**Majors:** Accounting, Art, Biology, Business Administration, Chemistry, Economics, Elementary Education, English, Fine Arts, French, German, History, Mathematics, Modern Foreign Languages, Music, Music Education, Philosophy/Religion, Physics, Political Science, Psychology, Religion, Social Studies, Sociology, Spanish, Special Education, Theatre Arts.
**Distribution of degrees:** The majors with the highest enrollment are economics/business administration, biology, and English; Spanish, fine arts, and visual arts have the lowest.
**Requirements:** General education requirement.
**Academic regulations:** Freshmen must maintain minimum 1.5 GPA; sophomores, 1.75 GPA; juniors, 2.0 GPA; seniors, 2.0 GPA.
**Special:** Minors offered in all majors and in computer science, international studies, journalism, media studies, physical education, secondary education, and teacher certification. Courses offered in Greek and speech. Cultural Enrichment program. Program in applied ethics and in media studies. Double majors. Dual degrees. Independent study. Accelerated study. Pass/fail grading option. Internships. Preprofessional programs in law, medicine, veterinary science, pharmacy, dentistry, and theology. 3-2 engineering programs with Auburn U, Clemson U, Mercer U, and Vanderbilt U. 3-2 forestry and environmental studies program with Duke U. Combined-degree religion program with Presbyterian Sch of Christian Education. Member of South Carolina Consortium for International Studies. Washington Semester and Sea Semester. Teacher certification in elementary, secondary, and special education. Certification in specific subject areas. Exchange programs abroad in England (Oxford U) and Finland (Turku U). Ecology study/research tours to Alaska, Argentina, Australia, African countries, Chile, the Czech Republic/Slovakia, the Galapagos Islands, Greece, Hungary, Indonesia, Poland, Russia, Scotland, and Thailand. Study abroad also in Austria, China, France, Grenada, India, Japan, Mexico, the Netherlands, Portugal, Spain, and Wales. ROTC.
**Honors:** Honors program. Honor societies.
**Academic Assistance:** Nonremedial tutoring.

**STUDENT LIFE. Housing:** All unmarried students under age 21 must live on campus unless living near campus with relatives. Women's and men's dorms. Fraternity housing. Off-campus married-student housing. 88% of students live in college housing.
**Services and counseling/handicapped student services:** Placement services. Health service. Counseling services for minority students. Personal and psychological counseling. Career and academic guidance services. Religious counseling. Physically disabled student services. Learning disabled services. Notetaking services. Tape recorders.
**Campus organizations:** Undergraduate student government. Student newspaper (Blue Stocking, published biweekly). Literary magazine. Yearbook. Radio station. Choir, madrigal singers, chamber music ensemble, drama productions, literary journal, Amnesty International, Habitat for Humanity, Volunteer Services Program, Young Democrats, Young Republicans, Student Union Board, 39 organizations in all. Nine fraternities, six chapter houses; three sororities, all with chapter houses. 44% of men join a fraternity. 41% of women join a sorority.
**Religious organizations:** Canterbury Club, Newman Club, Fellowship of Christian Athletes, Baptist Student Union, Regnuh, Westminster Fellowship.
**Minority/foreign student organizations:** Minority Student Union, Fellowship Choir, Underground Social Club.

**ATHLETICS. Physical education requirements:** Two semesters of physical education required.
**Intercollegiate competition:** 33% of students participate. Baseball (M), basketball (M,W), cheerleading (M,W), football (M), golf (M), soccer (M,W), tennis (M,W), track and field (outdoor) (M), volleyball (W). Member of NCAA Division II, South Atlantic Conference.
**Intramural and club sports:** 80% of students participate. Intramural basketball, soccer, softball, table tennis, tennis, touch football, volleyball.

**ADMISSIONS. Academic basis for candidate selection** (in order of priority): Secondary school record, standardized test scores, class rank, school's recommendation, essay.
**Nonacademic basis for candidate selection:** Character and personality are important. Extracurricular participation, particular talent or ability, and alumni/ae relationship are considered.
**Requirements:** Graduation from secondary school is required; GED is accepted. 20 units and the following program of study are required: 4 units of English, 3 units of math, 2 units of lab science, 2 units of foreign language, 2 units of social studies, 2 units of history, 3 units of electives. SAT or ACT is required. PSAT is recommended. Campus visit and interview recommended. No off-campus interviews.
**Procedure:** Take SAT or ACT by October of 12th year. Visit college for interview by March of 12th year. Suggest filing application by April 1. Application deadline is June 1. Notification of admission on rolling basis. Reply is required by May 1. $200 tuition deposit, refundable until May 1. Freshmen accepted for terms other than fall.
**Special programs:** Admission may be deferred one semester. Credit and/or placement may be granted through CEEB Advanced Placement exams for scores of 3 or higher. Placement may be granted through CLEP general exams and challenge exams. Credit and/or placement may be granted through CLEP subject exams. Credit may be granted through military experience. Early entrance/early admission program. Concurrent enrollment program.
**Transfer students:** Transfer students accepted for terms other than fall. In fall 1993, 2% of all new students were transfers into all classes. 70 transfer applications were received, 34 were accepted. Application deadline is July 1 for fall; December 1 for spring. Minimum 2.5 GPA recommended. Lowest course grade accepted is "C." Maximum number of transferable credits is 45 semester hours from a two-year school and 68 semester hours from a four-year school. At least 24 semester hours must be completed at the college to receive degree.
**Admissions contact:** Margaret Williamson, M.S., Vice President for Enrollment/Dean of Admissions. 803 833-8230.

**FINANCIAL AID. Available aid:** Pell grants, SEOG, state grants, school scholarships and grants, private scholarships and grants, ROTC scholarships, academic merit scholarships, athletic scholarships, and aid for undergraduate foreign students. Perkins Loans (NDSL), PLUS, Stafford Loans (GSL), school loans, private loans, and SLS. Tuition Plan Inc., Knight Tuition Plans, and EFI Fund Management. 10-month payment plan.

**Financial aid statistics:** 40% of aid is not need-based. In 1993-94, 90% of all undergraduate applicants received aid; 79% of freshman applicants. Average amounts of aid awarded freshmen: Scholarships and grants, $5,560; loans, $3,048.
**Supporting data/closing dates:** FAFSA: Priority filing date is March 1. Notification of awards begins March 1.
**Financial aid contact:** Judi Gillespie, Director of Financial Aid. 803 833-8287.

**STUDENT EMPLOYMENT.** College Work/Study Program. Institutional employment. 25% of full-time undergraduates work on campus during school year. Students may expect to earn an average of $650 during school year. Off-campus part-time employment opportunities rated "fair."

**COMPUTER FACILITIES.** 100 IBM/IBM-compatible, Macintosh/Apple, and RISC-/UNIX-based microcomputers; all are networked. Students may access Prime minicomputer/mainframe systems, Internet. Client/LAN operating systems include Apple/Macintosh, DOS, UNIX/XENIX/AIX, Windows NT. Computer languages and software packages include BASIC, COBOL, FORTRAN, LISP, Lotus 1-2-3, MINITAB, Pascal, RPG II, SimScript. Computer facilities are available to all students.
**Fees:** Computer fee is included in tuition/fees.
**Hours:** 7 AM-12 AM.

**GRADUATE CAREER DATA.** Graduate school percentages: 8% enter law school. 9% enter medical school. 3% enter dental school. 7% enter graduate business programs. 8% enter graduate arts and sciences programs. 1% enter theological school/seminary. Highest graduate school enrollments: Duke U, Cornell U, Emory U, Johns Hopkins U, U of Georgia, U of North Carolina at Chapel Hill, U of South Carolina, Wake Forest U, Vanderbilt U. 60% of graduates choose careers in business and industry. Companies and businesses that hire graduates: Delta Airlines, First Union, Milliken, Multimedia, Nations Bank, Pitney-Bowes.

**PROMINENT ALUMNI/AE.** Douglas Kiker, NBC News correspondent; Albert F. Sloan, chairperson of the board, Lance, Inc.; Bennett Brown, chairperson and CEO, NationsBank; Walter Newton Wells, editor, *International Herald Tribune*, Paris; Charles B. MacDonald, military historian and author, *The Sounds of Trumpets;* Carlos Emmanuel, financial minister, Ecuador; Harry S. Dent, U.S. presidential counsel; Gen. Christian Patte, director of logistics, NATO.

## University of South Carolina at Aiken

**Aiken, SC 29801** 803 648-6851

**1994-95 Costs.** Tuition: $2,320 (state residents), $5,800 (out-of-state). Room: $1,700. Board: $1,500. Fees, books, misc. academic expenses (school's estimate): $520.
**Enrollment.** Undergraduates: 759 men, 1,193 women (full-time). Freshman class: 848 applicants, 560 accepted, 277 enrolled.
**Test score averages/ranges.** Average SAT scores: 413 verbal, 473 math.
**Faculty.** 110 full-time; 122 part-time. 69% of faculty holds doctoral degree. Student/faculty ratio: 15 to 1.
**Selectivity rating.** Less competitive.

**PROFILE.** USC–Aiken, founded in 1961, is a public, comprehensive university. Its 144-acre campus is located in Aiken, 15 miles from Augusta, Ga.

**Accreditation:** SACS. Professionally accredited by the Association of Collegiate Business Schools and Programs, the National League for Nursing.
**Religious orientation:** University of South Carolina at Aiken is nonsectarian; no religious requirements.
**Library:** Collections totaling over 120,444 volumes, 1,418 periodical subscriptions, and 19,180 microform items.
**Special facilities/museums:** Center for fine and performing arts, science education center.
**Athletic facilities:** Gymnasium, basketball, tennis, and volleyball courts, track, baseball, soccer, and softball fields, aerobics and weight rooms.

**STUDENT BODY. Undergraduate profile:** 85% are state residents; 23% are transfers. 1% Asian-American, 15% Black, 1% Hispanic, 82% White, 1% Other. Average age of undergraduates is 26.
**Freshman profile:** 1% of freshmen who took SAT scored 700 or over on math; 2% scored 600 or over on verbal, 9% scored 600 or over on math; 12% scored 500 or over on verbal, 38% scored 500 or over on math; 55% scored 400 or over on verbal, 79% scored 400 or over on math; 98% scored 300 or over on verbal, 99% scored 300 or over on math. 89% of accepted applicants took SAT; 11% took ACT. 98% of freshmen come from public schools.
**Undergraduate achievement:** 50% of fall 1992 freshmen returned for fall 1993 term.
**Foreign students:** 12 students are from out of the country. Countries represented include Canada and El Salvador; eight in all.

**PROGRAMS OF STUDY. Degrees:** B.A., B.A.Ed., B.A.Interdis.Studies, B.S., B.S.Bus., B.S.Ed., B.S.Interdis.Studies, B.S.Nurs.
**Majors:** Accounting, Allied Health, Anthropology, Art, Biology, Business Administration, Chemistry, Early Childhood Education, Economics, Education, Elementary Education, Engineering, English Language/Literature, Finance, French, Geography, Geology, German, History, Interdisciplinary Studies, International Studies, Journalism, Management, Marketing, Mathematics/Computer Science, Media Arts, Music, Nursing, Philosophy, Physical Education, Physics, Plant Sciences, Political Science, Psychology, Religious Studies, Secondary Education, Sociology, Spanish, Theatre/Speech.
**Distribution of degrees:** The majors with the highest enrollment are business administration, education, and nursing; mathematics/computer science, chemistry, and English have the lowest.
**Requirements:** General education requirement.
**Academic regulations:** Freshmen must maintain minimum 1.2 GPA; sophomores, 1.6 GPA; juniors, 2.0 GPA; seniors, 2.0 GPA.
**Special:** Minors offered in many majors. Courses offered in astronomy, criminal justice, and humanities. Associate's degrees offered. Self-designed majors. Double majors. Independent study. Accelerated study. Pass/fail grading option. Internships. Cooperative education programs. Graduate school at which undergraduates may take graduate-level courses. Preprofessional programs in law, medicine, veterinary science, and dentistry. 2-2 engineering program and combined-degree pharmacy program with U of South Carolina at Columbia. Teacher certification in early childhood, elementary, and secondary education. Certification in specific subject areas. ROTC.
**Honors:** Honors program.
**Academic Assistance:** Remedial reading, writing, math, and study skills. Nonremedial tutoring.

**STUDENT LIFE. Housing:** Students may live on or off campus. On-campus privately owned/operated apartments. 12% of students live in college housing.
**Social atmosphere:** Students tend to gather at the Student Activities Center, Rambler's, Chevy's, the Alley, and Newberry's. Phi Mu, TKE, AASA, SGA, PUB, and the Pacer Times have widespread influence on campus. According to the editor of the student newspaper, "The Aiken campus is usually considered the most beautiful in the USC system. The student body is very diverse and most are commuters."
**Services and counseling/handicapped student services:** Placement services. Day care. Counseling services for minority and veteran students. Personal and psychological counseling. Career and academic guidance services. Physically disabled student services. Learning disabled services. Notetaking services. Tape recorders. Tutors. Reader services for the blind.
**Campus organizations:** Undergraduate student government. Student newspaper (Pacer Times, published once/week). Literary magazine. Yearbook. Radio station. Chorus, gospel choir, music club, drama group, Artist Union, Student Alumni Association, Pacesetters, Broken Ink, College Republicans, Pacer Union Board. Two fraternities, no chapter houses; two sororities, no chapter houses. 1% of men join a fraternity. 1% of women join a sorority.
**Religious organizations:** Campus Crusade for Christ, Baptist Student Union.
**Minority/foreign student organizations:** Minority Affairs. International Club.

**ATHLETICS. Physical education requirements:** None.
**Intercollegiate competition:** 5% of students participate. Baseball (M), basketball (M,W), cheerleading (W), cross-country (M,W), golf (M), soccer (M), softball (W), tennis (M), volleyball (W). Member of NCAA Division II, Peach Belt Athletic Conference.
**Intramural and club sports:** 17% of students participate. Intramural basketball, flag football, pool, softball, table tennis, tennis, volleyball, Wiffle ball. Men's club cheerleading. Women's club cheerleading.

**ADMISSIONS. Academic basis for candidate selection** (in order of priority): Standardized test scores, secondary school record, class rank, school's recommendation, essay.
**Nonacademic basis for candidate selection:** Character and personality, extracurricular participation, and particular talent or ability are considered.
**Requirements:** Graduation from secondary school is required; GED is not accepted. 16 units and the following program of study are required: 4 units of English, 3 units of math, 2 units of lab science, 2 units of foreign language, 3 units of social studies, 1 unit of history, 1 unit of electives. Minimum combined SAT score of 700 (composite ACT score of 17) required. R.N. required of nursing program applicants. Conditional admission possible for applicants not meeting standard requirements. SAT is required; ACT may be substituted. Campus visit and interview recommended. No off-campus interviews.
**Procedure:** Take SAT or ACT by November of 12th year. Visit college for interview by December 1 of 12th year. Suggest filing application by January 1. Application deadline is August 1. Notification of admission on rolling basis. Reply is required by May 1. $150 nonrefundable room deposit. Freshmen accepted for terms other than fall.
**Special programs:** Admission may be deferred one year. Credit may be granted through CEEB Advanced Placement for scores of 3 or higher. Credit may be granted through CLEP subject exams, DANTES and challenge exams, and military experience. Early entrance/early admission program. Concurrent enrollment program.
**Transfer students:** Transfer students accepted for terms other than fall. In fall 1993, 23% of all new students were transfers into all classes. 640 transfer applications were received, 434 were accepted. Application deadline is August 1 for fall; December 1 for spring. Minimum 2.0 GPA required. Lowest course grade accepted is "C." Maximum number of transferable credits is 90 semester hours. At least 30 semester hours must be completed at the university to receive degree.
**Admissions contact:** Randy R. Duckett, M.A., Director of Admissions. 803 648-6851, extension 3272.

**FINANCIAL AID. Available aid:** Pell grants, SEOG, state scholarships, school scholarships, private scholarships, academic merit scholarships, and athletic scholarships. Perkins Loans (NDSL), PLUS, Stafford Loans (GSL), and private loans. Deferred payment plan.
**Financial aid statistics:** 20% of aid is not need-based. In 1993-94, 65% of all undergraduate applicants received aid; 43% of freshman applicants. Average amounts of aid awarded freshmen: Scholarships and grants, $1,500.
**Supporting data/closing dates:** FAFSA: Priority filing date is March. School's own aid application: Priority filing date is March 15. Notification of awards on rolling basis.
**Financial aid contact:** Glenn Shumpert, M.Ed., Director of Financial Aid. 803 648-6851, extension 3433.

**STUDENT EMPLOYMENT.** College Work/Study Program. Institutional employment. 22% of full-time undergraduates work on campus during school year. Students may expect to earn an average of $1,500 during school year. Off-campus part-time employment opportunities rated "excellent."

**COMPUTER FACILITIES.** 100 IBM/IBM-compatible and Macintosh/Apple microcomputers; 25 are networked. Students may access IBM minicomputer/mainframe systems. Client/LAN operating systems include Apple/Macintosh. Computer languages and software packages include BASIC, COBOL, FORTRAN, Lotus 1-2-3, Pascal, PC-File, SAS, SPSS, WordStar. Computer facilities are available to all students.
**Fees:** None.
**Hours:** 24 hours.

**GRADUATE CAREER DATA.** Highest graduate school enrollments: U of South Carolina. 30% of graduates choose careers in business and industry. Companies and businesses that hire graduates: Milliken, Savannah River site, banks, hospitals in Aiken and Augusta, Ga., school districts.

**PROMINENT ALUMNI/AE.** Rob Matwick, director of public relations, Houston Astros.

# University of South Carolina (Columbia)

**Columbia, SC 29208** **803 777-7000**

**1994-95 Costs.** Tuition: $3,090 (state residents), $7,808 (out-of-state). Room & board: $3,522. Fees, books, misc. academic expenses (school's estimate): $500.

**Enrollment.** Undergraduates: 5,950 men, 6,644 women (full-time). Freshman class: 7,693 applicants, 5,813 accepted, 2,328 enrolled. Graduate enrollment: 4,152 men, 6,497 women.

**Test score averages/ranges.** Average SAT scores: 465 verbal, 520 math. Range of SAT scores of middle 50%: 400-520 verbal, 460-580 math. Average ACT scores: 22 English, 22 math, 22 composite. Range of ACT scores of middle 50%: 19-25 English, 19-25 math.

**Faculty.** 1,429 full-time. 83% of faculty holds doctoral degree. Student/faculty ratio: 16 to 1.

**Selectivity rating.** Less competitive.

**PROFILE.** USC–Columbia, founded in 1801, is a public, comprehensive university. Programs are offered through the Colleges of Applied Professional Sciences, Business Administration, Criminal Justice, Engineering, Health, Humanities and Social Sciences, Journalism, Nursing, Pharmacy, and Science and Mathematics. Its 242-acre campus, including a pre-Civil War portion of the Columbia campus listed on the National Register of Historic Places, is located in Columbia, in central South Carolina.

**Accreditation:** SACS. Professionally accredited by the Accreditation Board for Engineering and Technology, the Accrediting Council on Education in Journalism and Mass Communication, the American Assembly of Collegiate Schools of Business, the American Bar Association, the American Council on Pharmaceutical Education, the Association of American Law Schools, the Council on Education for Public Health, the Council on Rehabilitation Education, the Council on Social Work Education, the Liaison Committee on Medical Education, the National Association of Schools of Music, the National Association of Schools of Public Affairs and Administration, the National Council for Accreditation of Teacher Education, the National League for Nursing.

**Religious orientation:** University of South Carolina (Columbia) is nonsectarian; no religious requirements.

**Library:** Collections totaling over 2,600,000 volumes, 19,232 periodical subscriptions, and 3,900,000 microform items.

**Special facilities/museums:** Art, movie, and geological museums/archives, nuclear magnetic resonance facility, electron microscopy center.

**Athletic facilities:** Physical education center, track, football stadium, baseball field, basketball arena.

**STUDENT BODY. Undergraduate profile:** 83% are state residents; 25% are transfers. 3% Asian-American, 17% Black, 1% Hispanic, 77% White, 2% Other. Average age of undergraduates is 19.

**Freshman profile:** 1% of freshmen who took SAT scored 700 or over on verbal, 4% scored 700 or over on math; 9% scored 600 or over on verbal, 21% scored 600 or over on math; 35% scored 500 or over on verbal, 60% scored 500 or over on math; 78% scored 400 or over on verbal, 93% scored 400 or over on math; 99% scored 300 or over on verbal, 100% scored 300 or over on math. 6% of freshmen who took ACT scored 30 or over on English, 1% scored 30 or over on math, 5% scored 30 or over on composite; 42% scored 24 or over on English, 37% scored 24 or over on math, 40% scored 24 or over on composite; 85% scored 18 or over on English, 83% scored 18 or over on math, 89% scored 18 or over on composite; 100% scored 12 or over on English, 100% scored 12 or over on math, 100% scored 12 or over on composite. 99% of accepted applicants took SAT; 1% took ACT. 80% of freshmen come from public schools.

**Undergraduate achievement:** 81% of fall 1992 freshmen returned for fall 1993 term. 34% of entering class graduated.

**Foreign students:** 329 students are from out of the country. Countries represented include Canada, China, India, South Korea, Taiwan, and the United Kingdom; 124 in all.

**PROGRAMS OF STUDY. Degrees:** B.A., B.A.Interdis.Studies, B.A.Journ., B.A.Phys.Ed., B.Appl.Sci., B.F.A., B.Media Arts, B.Mus., B.S., B.S.Bus.Admin., B.S.Chem., B.S.Eng., B.S.Interdis.Studies, B.S.Med.Tech., B.S.Nurs., B.S.Pharm., B.S.Phys.Ed.

**Majors:** Accounting, Advertising/Public Relations, Afro-American Studies, Anthropology, Art Education, Art History, Biology, Broadcasting, Business Economics, Chemical Engineering, Chemistry, Civil Engineering, Classical Studies, Computer Engineering, Computer Science, Contemporary European Studies, Criminal Justice, Economics, Electrical Engineering, English, Exercise Science, Experimental Psychology, Finance, French, Geography, Geology, Geophysics, German, Greek, History, Hotel/Restaurant/Tourism Management, Insurance/Economic Security, Interdisciplinary Studies, International Studies, Italian, Latin, Latin American Studies, Management, Management Science, Marine Science, Marketing, Mass Media Telecommunications, Mathematics, Mechanical Engineering, Media Arts, Medical Technology, Music, Music Education, Music Performance/Composition, Music Theory/History, News/Editorial, Nursing, Office Administration, Pharmaceutical Science, Pharmacy, Philosophy, Physical Education, Physics, Political Science, Real Estate, Religious Studies, Retailing, Sociology, Spanish, Sports Administration, Statistics, Studio Art, Theatre/Speech.

**Distribution of degrees:** The majors with the highest enrollment are business, journalism, and engineering; philosophy, foreign languages, and computer science have the lowest.

**Requirements:** General education requirement.

**Special:** Minor required for graduation in some majors. Minors offered in most majors and in comparative literature, social work, South Carolina studies, and Southern studies. Double majors. Dual degrees. Independent study. Pass/fail grading option. Internships. Cooperative education programs. Graduate school at which undergraduates may take graduate-level courses. Preprofessional programs in law, medicine, veterinary science, dentistry, theology, optometry, and podiatry. 3-2 engineering program. Five-year pharmacy program. Member of National Student Exchange (NSE). Teacher certification in early childhood, elementary, and secondary education. Member of International Student Exchange Program (ISEP). Exchange programs abroad in England (U of Kent, U of Warwick). ROTC, NROTC, and AFROTC.

**Honors:** Honors program.

**Academic Assistance:** Remedial reading, writing, math, and study skills. Nonremedial tutoring.

**STUDENT LIFE. Housing:** Freshmen must live on campus. Coed, women's, and men's dorms. Sorority and fraternity housing. School-owned/operated apartments. On-campus married-student housing. 42% of students live in college housing.

**Social atmosphere:** Football and basketball games, especially against Clemson U, are particularly popular events on campus. Groups with the greatest social influence on campus include Greeks, athletes, members of student government, the staff of the newspaper, the Carolina Program Union, and the Baptist Student Union and other Christian organizations. Favorite nightspots in the area include Crazy Zack's, Yesterday's, Pappy's, Rockaway's, Zanadu, the Parthenon, and California Dreamin'. According to the student newspaper, the new, higher drinking age has resulted in more private parties.

**Services and counseling/handicapped student services:** Placement services. Health service. Women's center. Day care. Counseling services for minority, military, veteran, and older students. Birth control, personal, and psychological counseling. Career and academic guidance services. Religious counseling. Physically disabled student services. Learning disabled services. Notetaking services. Tape recorders. Tutors. Reader services for the blind.

**Campus organizations:** Undergraduate student government. Student newspaper (Gamecock, published three times/week). Literary magazine. Yearbook. Radio station. Band, chorus, debate, and drama societies, 234 organizations in all. 20 fraternities, 14 chapter houses; 14 sororities, 10 chapter houses. 14% of men join a fraternity. 14% of women join a sorority.

**Religious organizations:** Several religious groups.

**Minority/foreign student organizations:** Association of Afro-American Students, Asian-American Association. Numerous foreign student groups.

**ATHLETICS. Physical education requirements:** None.

**Intercollegiate competition:** Baseball (M), basketball (M,W), cheerleading (M,W), cross-country (M,W), diving (M,W), football (M), golf (M,W), soccer (M), softball (W), swimming (M,W), tennis (M,W), track and field (indoor) (M), track and field (outdoor) (M), volleyball (W). Member of NCAA Division I, Southeastern Conference.

**Intramural and club sports:** Intramural basketball, bowling, field hockey, flag football, frisbee, golf, indoor soccer, racquetball, soccer, softball, table tennis, tennis, volleyball, water polo. Men's club bowling, equestrian sports, fencing, flying, frisbee, karate, lacrosse, martial arts, mountaineering, racquetball, rugby, sailing, scuba, water skiing, weight lifting, wrestling. Women's club bowling, equestrian sports, fencing, lacrosse, martial arts, racquetball, sailing, soccer, water skiing, weight lifting.

**ADMISSIONS. Academic basis for candidate selection** (in order of priority): Secondary school record, standardized test scores, class rank, school's recommendation.

**Nonacademic basis for candidate selection:** Particular talent or ability is considered.

**Requirements:** Graduation from secondary school is required; GED is accepted. 16 units and the following program of study are required: 4 units of English, 3 units of math, 2 units of lab science, 2 units of foreign language, 2 units of social studies, 1 unit of American history, 2 units of electives including 1 unit of academic electives. Minimum 2.0 GPA or 16 secondary school units required. Opportunity Scholars Program for in-state applicants not normally admissible. SAT or ACT is required. No off-campus interviews.

**Procedure:** Take SAT or ACT by November of 12th year. Suggest filing application by December 25; no deadline. Notification of admission on rolling basis. No set date by which applicants must accept offer. $100 room deposit, refundable until July 1, partially refundable after July 1. Freshmen accepted for terms other than fall.

**Special programs:** Credit and/or placement may be granted through CEEB Advanced Placement exams for scores of 3 or higher. Credit may be granted through CLEP subject exams, DANTES exams, and military experience. Credit and placement may be granted through challenge exams. Concurrent enrollment program.

**Transfer students:** Transfer students accepted for terms other than fall. In fall 1993, 25% of all new students were transfers into all classes. 2,752 transfer applications were received, 1,627 were accepted. Application deadline is August 1 for fall; December 1 for spring. Minimum 2.0 GPA required of applicants from four-year schools; minimum 2.5 GPA from two-year schools. SAT or ACT scores required of business and engineering program applicants. Lowest course grade accepted is "C." Maximum number of transferable credits is 76 semester hours from a two-year school and 90 semester hours from a four-year school. At least 30 semester hours must be completed at the university to receive degree.

**Admissions contact:** Terry L. Davis, M.Ed., Director of Admissions. 803 777-7700, 800 868-5872.

**FINANCIAL AID. Available aid:** Pell grants, SEOG, Federal Nursing Student Scholarships, school scholarships, private scholarships and grants, ROTC scholarships, academic merit scholarships, and athletic scholarships. Perkins Loans (NDSL), PLUS, Stafford Loans (GSL), NSL, Health Professions Loans, private loans, and SLS. Tuition Plan Inc., AMS, and deferred payment plan.

**Financial aid statistics:** 10% of aid is not need-based. In 1993-94, 60% of all undergraduate applicants received aid; 70% of freshman applicants. Average amounts of aid awarded freshmen: Scholarships and grants, $2,500; loans, $2,625.

**Supporting data/closing dates:** FAFSA: Priority filing date is April 15; accepted on rolling basis. FAF/FFS: Priority filing date is April 15. School's own aid application: Priority filing date is April 15; accepted on rolling basis. Notification of awards begins May 15.

**Financial aid contact:** John F. Bannister, M.A., Director of Financial Aid and Scholarships. 803 777-8134.

**STUDENT EMPLOYMENT.** College Work/Study Program. Institutional employment. 8% of full-time undergraduates work on campus during school year. Students may expect to earn an average of $1,300 during school year. Off-campus part-time employment opportunities rated "excellent."

**COMPUTER FACILITIES.** 800 IBM/IBM-compatible and Macintosh/Apple microcomputers. Students may access AT&T, Digital, IBM, SUN minicomputer/mainframe systems, BITNET, Internet. Residence halls may be equipped with stand-alone microcomputers, networked microcomputers, networked terminals, modems. Client/LAN operating systems include UNIX/XENIX/AIX. Numerous computer languages and software packages available. Computer facilities are available to all students.
**Fees:** Computer fee is included in tuition/fees.

**GRADUATE CAREER DATA.** 77% of graduates choose careers in business and industry. Companies and businesses that hire graduates: Arthur Andersen, C&S/Sovran Bank, DuPont, NCR, NationsBank.

**PROMINENT ALUMNI/AE.** John E. Swearingen, chairperson/CEO, Continental Illinois Bank, and retired chairperson, Standard Oil of Indiana; Daniel Reeves, head coach/general manager, New York Giants; Joseph Bernardin, archbishop, Chicago; Alex English, professional basketball player; Edward L. Addison, CEO, Southern Co.; Ira Koger, real estate developer; Leeza Gibbons, *Entertainment Tonight*.

## University of South Carolina at Spartanburg

**Spartanburg, SC 29303** **803 599-2000**

**1994-95 Costs.** Tuition: $2,320 (state residents), $5,800 (out-of-state). Housing: None. Fees, books, misc. academic expenses (school's estimate): $425.
**Enrollment.** Undergraduates: 831 men, 1,376 women (full-time). Freshman class: 885 applicants, 553 accepted, 381 enrolled.
**Test score averages/ranges.** Average SAT scores: 411 verbal, 459 math.
**Faculty.** 162 full-time; 71 part-time. 42% of faculty holds doctoral degree. Student/faculty ratio: 14 to 1.
**Selectivity rating.** Competitive.

**PROFILE.** USC–Spartanburg, founded in 1967, is a public, multipurpose university. Programs are offered through the Schools of Business Administration, Education, Humanities and Sciences, and Nursing. Its 298-acre campus is located in Spartanburg, 93 miles northeast of Columbia.

**Accreditation:** SACS. Professionally accredited by the National League for Nursing.
**Religious orientation:** University of South Carolina at Spartanburg is nonsectarian; no religious requirements.
**Library:** Collections totaling over 107,905 volumes, 1,200 periodical subscriptions, and 18,518 microform items.
**Special facilities/museums:** Performing arts theatre, on-campus nursery school, electron microscope.
**Athletic facilities:** Gymnasium, tennis courts, baseball, soccer, and softball fields.

**STUDENT BODY. Undergraduate profile:** 94% are state residents; 42% are transfers. 1% Asian-American, 12% Black, 1% Hispanic, 85% White, 1% Other. Average age of undergraduates is 22.
**Freshman profile:** 3% of freshmen who took SAT scored 600 or over on verbal, 6% scored 600 or over on math; 14% scored 500 or over on verbal, 35% scored 500 or over on math; 55% scored 400 or over on verbal, 77% scored 400 or over on math; 96% scored 300 or over on verbal, 98% scored 300 or over on math. 89% of accepted applicants took SAT; 2% took ACT.
**Undergraduate achievement:** 66% of fall 1992 freshmen returned for fall 1993 term. 13% of entering class graduated.
**Foreign students:** 31 students are from out of the country. Countries represented include Canada, Peru, South Africa, Spain, and the United Kingdom; 15 in all.

**PROGRAMS OF STUDY. Degrees:** B.A., B.S.
**Majors:** Accounting, Biology, Business Administration, Chemistry, Communications, Computer Science, Criminal Justice, Early Childhood Education, Economics, Education, Elementary Education, English, Finance, French, History, Interdisciplinary Studies, Management, Marketing, Mathematics, Middle School Education, Nursing, Physical Education, Political Science/Public Administration, Psychology, Secondary Education, Sociology, Spanish.
**Distribution of degrees:** The major with the highest enrollment is business administration.
**Requirements:** General education requirement.
**Academic regulations:** Freshmen must maintain minimum 1.5 GPA; sophomores, 1.5 GPA; juniors, 2.0 GPA; seniors, 2.0 GPA.
**Special:** Associate's degrees offered. Self-designed majors. Double majors. Independent study. Pass/fail grading option. Preprofessional programs in law, medicine, pharmacy, dentistry, and optometry. Member of Greenville Technical College Consortium. Exchange program with Wofford Coll. Teacher certification in early childhood, elementary, and secondary education. Summer study abroad in France and Germany. ROTC.
**Academic Assistance:** Nonremedial tutoring.

**STUDENT LIFE. Housing:** Commuter campus; no student housing.
**Social atmosphere:** The Greek community and the Campus Activities Board influence student social life. Eagerly anticipated social/sporting events include Shoestring Player's performances, musicals, and homecoming. Even though it is a commuter campus, students do enjoy a lively social life. The student newspaper reports, "Social life on campus is fairly active. We enjoy live events every week, great comedians, and such acts."
**Services and counseling/handicapped student services:** Placement services. Health service. Women's center. Day care. Counseling services for minority, veteran, and older students. Personal counseling. Career and academic guidance services.
**Campus organizations:** Undergraduate student government. Student newspaper (Carolinian, published once/week). Literary magazine. Yearbook. Jazz and pep bands, University Singers, gospel choir, chorus, Shoestring Players, outdoor and jogging clubs, 46 organizations in all. Two fraternities, no chapter houses; two sororities, no chapter houses. 4% of men join a fraternity. 5% of women join a sorority.
**Religious organizations:** Baptist Student Union, Campus Crusade for Christ.
**Minority/foreign student organizations:** Afro-American Association, United Students. International Association.

**ATHLETICS. Physical education requirements:** None.
**Intercollegiate competition:** 4% of students participate. Baseball (M), basketball (M,W), cheerleading (M,W), cross-country (M,W), soccer (M), softball (W), tennis (M,W), volleyball (W). Member of NCAA Division II, Peach Belt Athletic Conference.
**Intramural and club sports:** 51% of students participate. Intramural basketball, bowling, flag football, fun run, golf, racquetball, soccer, softball, table tennis, tennis, volleyball, walleyball, weight lifting. Men's club baseball, basketball, rugby. Women's club basketball.

**ADMISSIONS. Academic basis for candidate selection** (in order of priority): Secondary school record, standardized test scores, class rank.
**Requirements:** Graduation from secondary school is required; GED is accepted. 20 units and the following program of study are required: 4 units of English, 3 units of math, 2 units of lab science, 2 units of foreign language, 2 units of social studies, 1 unit of history, 5 units of electives including 1 unit of academic electives. Minimum combined SAT score of 700 (composite ACT score of 18) and minimum 2.0 GPA required. SAT is required; ACT may be substituted. Campus visit and interview recommended. No off-campus interviews.
**Procedure:** Application deadline is August 10. Notification of admission on rolling basis. No set date by which applicants must accept offer. $150 nonrefundable room deposit. Freshmen accepted for terms other than fall.
**Special programs:** Admission may be deferred one year. Credit and/or placement may be granted through CEEB Advanced Placement exams for scores of 3 or higher. Credit may be granted through CLEP subject exams, ACT PEP, DANTES, and challenge exams, and military experience. Concurrent enrollment program.
**Transfer students:** Transfer students accepted for terms other than fall. In fall 1993, 42% of all new students were transfers into all classes. 783 transfer applications were received, 589 were accepted. Application deadline is rolling for fall; rolling for spring. Minimum 2.0 GPA required. Lowest course grade accepted is "C." Maximum number of transferable credits is 90 semester hours. At least 30 semester hours must be completed at the university to receive degree.
**Admissions contact:** Donette Stewart, Director of Admissions. 803 599-2246.

**FINANCIAL AID. Available aid:** Pell grants, SEOG, school scholarships and grants, private scholarships and grants, ROTC scholarships, academic merit scholarships, and athletic scholarships. Perkins Loans (NDSL), PLUS, Stafford Loans (GSL), NSL, and SLS.
**Financial aid statistics:** 25% of aid is not need-based. In 1993-94, 88% of all undergraduate applicants received aid; 84% of freshman applicants.
**Supporting data/closing dates:** FAFSA/FAF/FFS: Priority filing date is April 1; deadline is July 1. School's own aid application: Priority filing date is April 1; deadline is July 1. Notification of awards on rolling basis.
**Financial aid contact:** Donna Hawkins, Director of Financial Aid. 803 599-2340.

**STUDENT EMPLOYMENT.** College Work/Study Program. Institutional employment. Students may expect to earn an average of $1,600 during school year. Off-campus part-time employment opportunities rated "good."

**COMPUTER FACILITIES.** 142 IBM/IBM-compatible and Macintosh/Apple microcomputers. Computer languages and software packages include BASIC, C, COBOL, dBASE IV, Lotus 1-2-3, Modula 2, Pascal, PL/1, Quattro, SAS, WordPerfect, Windows, WordStar; 15 in all. Computer facilities are available to all students.
**Fees:** None.
**Hours:** 8:30 AM-10 PM (M-Th); 8:30 AM-5 PM (F); 9 AM-5 PM (Sa); 2 PM-6 PM (Su).

## Voorhees College

**Denmark, SC 29042** **803 793-3351**

**1993-94 Costs.** Tuition: $3,950. Room & board: $2,522. Fees, books, misc. academic expenses (school's estimate): $750.
**Enrollment.** Undergraduates: 298 men, 405 women (full-time). Freshman class: 1,465 applicants, 1,006 accepted, 188 enrolled.
**Test score averages/ranges.** Average SAT scores: 320 verbal, 350 math.
**Faculty.** 47 full-time; 2 part-time. 40% of faculty holds doctoral degree. Student/faculty ratio: 20 to 1.
**Selectivity rating.** Less competitive.

**PROFILE.** Voorhees, founded in 1897, is a church-affiliated, historically black college. Its 350-acre campus is located in Denmark, 55 miles south of Columbia.

**Accreditation:** SACS.
**Religious orientation:** Voorhees College is affiliated with the Episcopal Church; one semester of religion/theology required.
**Library:** Collections totaling over 110,000 volumes and 400 periodical subscriptions.
**Special facilities/museums:** Archives.
**Athletic facilities:** Gymnasium, baseball and softball fields, tennis courts, track and field.

**STUDENT BODY. Undergraduate profile:** 75% are state residents; 12% are transfers. 98% Black, 1% Hispanic, 1% White. Average age of undergraduates is 19.
**Freshman profile:** 2% of freshmen who took SAT scored 500 or over on verbal, 2% scored 500 or over on math; 17% scored 400 or over on verbal, 12% scored 400 or over on math; 52% scored 300 or over on verbal, 52% scored 300 or over on math. 70% of accepted applicants took SAT; 5% took ACT. 95% of freshmen come from public schools.
**Undergraduate achievement:** 58% of fall 1992 freshmen returned for fall 1993 term. 35% of entering class graduated. 10% of students who completed a degree program immediately went on to graduate study.

**Foreign students:** Two students are from out of the country. Countries represented include Bangladesh and Liberia.

**PROGRAMS OF STUDY. Degrees:** B.A., B.S.
**Majors:** Accounting, Biology, Business Administration, Computer Science, Criminal Justice, English, Health/Recreation, Mathematics, Organizational Management, Political Science, Sociology.
**Distribution of degrees:** The majors with the highest enrollment are sociology, criminal justice, and business administration; English, mathematics, and political science have the lowest.
**Requirements:** General education requirement.
**Academic regulations:** Freshmen must maintain minimum 1.5 GPA; sophomores, 1.75 GPA; juniors, 2.0 GPA; seniors, 2.0 GPA.
**Special:** Voorhees Management Institute and Saturday/evening classes available. Internships. Cooperative education programs. Preprofessional programs in law, medicine, engineering, and nursing. 2-3 nursing program with Clemson U. 2-3 engineering programs with Clemson U and U of South Carolina. ROTC at South Carolina State U.
**Honors:** Honors program. Honor societies.
**Academic Assistance:** Remedial reading, writing, math, and study skills.

**ADMISSIONS. Academic basis for candidate selection** (in order of priority): Secondary school record, class rank, school's recommendation, standardized test scores, essay.
**Nonacademic basis for candidate selection:** Character and personality are emphasized. Particular talent or ability is important. Extracurricular participation is considered.
**Requirements:** Graduation from secondary school is required; GED is accepted. 20 units and the following program of study are required: 4 units of English, 3 units of math, 2 units of science, 2 units of foreign language, 1 unit of social studies, 1 unit of history, 7 units of electives. Automatic acceptance to applicants with minimum combined SAT score of 600 (composite ACT score of 16) and minimum 2.0 GPA. Conditional admission possible for applicants not meeting standard requirements. Excel Program for applicants not normally admissible. SAT or ACT is recommended. Campus visit and interview recommended. Off-campus interviews available with admissions and alumni representatives.
**Procedure:** Take SAT or ACT by May of 12th year. Visit college for interview by May of 12th year. Suggest filing application by April 1. Application deadline is August 1. Notification of admission on rolling basis. Reply is required by August 16. $250 tuition deposit, refundable until July 15. $25 nonrefundable room deposit. Freshmen accepted for terms other than fall.
**Special programs:** Admission may be deferred one year. Credit may be granted through CEEB Advanced Placement for scores of 3 or higher. Credit and/or placement may be granted through CLEP general and subject exams. Credit may be granted through life experience. Credit and placement may be granted through challenge exams and military experience.
**Transfer students:** Transfer students accepted for terms other than fall. In fall 1993, 12% of all new students were transfers into all classes. 65 transfer applications were received, 50 were accepted. Application deadline is rolling for fall; rolling for spring. Minimum 2.0 GPA recommended. Lowest course grade accepted is "C." Maximum number of transferable credits is 100 credits. At least 33 credits must be completed at the college to receive degree.
**Admissions contact:** Samuel Blackwell, M.Ed., Director of Admissions. 803 793-3351, extension 7301.

**FINANCIAL AID. Available aid:** Pell grants, SEOG, state grants, school scholarships and grants, private scholarships, ROTC scholarships, academic merit scholarships, and United Negro College Fund. Perkins Loans (NDSL), PLUS, and Stafford Loans (GSL). Deferred payment plan.
**Financial aid statistics:** 15% of aid is not need-based. In 1993-94, 98% of all undergraduate applicants received aid; 98% of freshman applicants. Average amounts of aid awarded freshmen: Scholarships and grants, $2,300; loans, $2,625.
**Supporting data/closing dates:** FAFSA/FAF/FFS: Priority filing date is April 15; accepted on rolling basis. School's own aid application: Priority filing date is April 15; deadline is August 15. State aid form: Priority filing date is January 30; deadline is June 30. Income tax forms: Priority filing date is January 31; deadline is April 15. Notification of awards begins April 30.
**Financial aid contact:** Lavenia Freeman, M.Ed., Director of Financial Aid. 803 793-3351, extension 7290.

# Winthrop University

**Rock Hill, SC 29733** **803 323-2211**

**1993-94 Costs.** Tuition: $3,400 (state residents), $6,000 (out-of-state). Room & board: $3,255. Fees, books, misc. academic expenses (school's estimate): $485.
**Enrollment.** Undergraduates: 1,094 men, 2,301 women (full-time). Freshman class: 2,320 applicants, 1,805 accepted, 769 enrolled. Graduate enrollment: 307 men, 735 women.
**Test score averages/ranges.** Average SAT scores: 470 verbal, 516 math. Range of SAT scores of middle 50%: 410-520 verbal, 460-570 math. Average ACT scores: 18 composite. Range of ACT scores of middle 50%: 16-20 composite.
**Faculty.** 297 full-time; 123 part-time. 91% of faculty holds highest degree in specific field. Student/faculty ratio: 18 to 1.
**Selectivity rating.** Less competitive.

**PROFILE.** Winthrop is a public college. Founded in 1886 as a teacher training school for women, it adopted coeducation in 1974. Programs are offered through the College of Arts and Sciences and the Schools of Business Administration, Education, and Visual and Performing Arts. Its 400-acre campus is located in Rock Hill, 25 miles south of Charlotte, N.C.

**Accreditation:** SACS. Professionally accredited by the American Assembly of Collegiate Schools of Business, the Computing Sciences Accreditation Board, the Council on Social Work Education, the Foundation for Interior Design Education Research, the National Association of Schools of Art and Design, the National Association of Schools of Music, the National Council for Accreditation of Teacher Education.
**Religious orientation:** Winthrop University is nonsectarian; no religious requirements.
**Library:** Collections totaling over 357,110 volumes, 70,037 periodical subscriptions, and 1,026,572 microform items.
**Special facilities/museums:** Art gallery, on-campus nursery and kindergarten.
**Athletic facilities:** Gymnasiums, football, soccer, and softball fields, handball, racquetball, and tennis courts, swimming pool, weight rooms, dance studios, golf course, lake.

**STUDENT BODY. Undergraduate profile:** 86% are state residents; 32% are transfers. 1% Asian-American, 20% Black, 1% Hispanic, 76% White, 2% Foreign. Average age of undergraduates is 22.
**Freshman profile:** 1% of freshmen who took SAT scored 700 or over on verbal, 3% scored 700 or over on math; 9% scored 600 or over on verbal, 18% scored 600 or over on math; 35% scored 500 or over on verbal, 58% scored 500 or over on math; 82% scored 400 or over on verbal, 94% scored 400 or over on math; 100% scored 300 or over on verbal, 100% scored 300 or over on math. 85% of accepted applicants took SAT; 15% took ACT.
**Undergraduate achievement:** 75% of fall 1992 freshmen returned for fall 1993 term. 23% of entering class graduated. 19% of students who completed a degree program immediately went on to graduate study.
**Foreign students:** 121 students are from out of the country. Countries represented include Canada, France, Japan, Spain, and Thailand; 42 in all.

**PROGRAMS OF STUDY. Degrees:** B.A., B.F.A., B.Mus., B.Mus.Ed., B.S., B.Soc.Work
**Majors:** Art, Art History, Biology, Business Administration, Business Education, Ceramics, Chemistry, Choral Music Education, Computer Science, Dance, Distributive Education, Early Childhood Education, Elementary Education, English, Graphic Design, History, Home Economics, Home Economics Education, Human Nutrition, Instrumental Music Education, Interior Design, Mass Communications, Mathematics, Medical Technology, Modern Languages, Music, Music Performance, Painting, Philosophy/Religion, Photography, Physical Education, Political Science, Printmaking, Psychology, Science Communications, Sculpture, Social Work, Sociology, Special Education, Speech, Studio Art, Theatre.
**Distribution of degrees:** The majors with the highest enrollment are business administration, elementary education, and mass communication; distributive education, home economics education, and music/choral education have the lowest.
**Requirements:** General education requirement.
**Academic regulations:** Freshmen must maintain minimum 1.4 GPA; sophomores, 1.6 GPA; juniors, 1.9 GPA; seniors, 2.0 GPA.
**Special:** Minor required. Minors offered in some majors and in over 15 other fields. Double majors. Independent study. Pass/fail grading option. Internships. Cooperative education programs. Graduate school at which undergraduates may take graduate-level courses. Preprofessional programs in law, medicine, veterinary science, dentistry, engineering, and nursing. 2-2 engineering program with U of South Carolina at Columbia. Member of Charlotte Area Educational Consortium. Member of National Student Exchange (NSE). Teacher certification in early childhood, elementary, secondary, special education, and vo-tech education. Certification in specific subject areas. Exchange programs abroad in China (Shanghai U), France, and Malawi (U of Malawi). Study abroad also in Australia, Chile, Costa Rica, Denmark, Egypt, England, India, Ireland, Mexico, the Netherlands, Peru, Poland, Scotland, and Spain.
**Honors:** Honors program. Honor societies.

**STUDENT LIFE. Housing:** Students may live on or off campus. Coed, women's, and men's dorms. School-owned/operated apartments. 47% of students live in college housing.
**Social atmosphere:** According to the editor of the student newspaper, "Most students migrate home on weekends. High points (of social life) are during the week. The school has instituted 'cultural events' to bring in symphonies, etc." On campus, students meet at Dinkins Student Union; off campus, bars such as Crazy Zack's and Scandals are popular destinations. Some popular events on campus include Homecoming, plays, band concerts, Greek Week, and Halloween Happening. Greeks and Christian groups are influential on campus.
**Services and counseling/handicapped student services:** Placement services. Health service. Counseling services for minority, veteran, and older students. Birth control, personal, and psychological counseling. Career and academic guidance services. Religious counseling.
**Campus organizations:** Undergraduate student government. Student newspaper (Johnsonian, published once/week). Literary magazine. Yearbook. Chorale, glee club, Jazz Voices, symphonic band, Model UN, SADD, Circle K, Big Brothers/Big Sisters, Action for Food, theatre, dance theatre, cheerleading, Eaglettes, Winthrop Ambassadors, 120 organizations in all. 10 fraternities, six chapter houses; nine sororities, five chapter houses. 14% of men join a fraternity. 16% of women join a sorority.
**Religious organizations:** Abundant Life in Christ, Bahai Club, Baptist Student Union, Campus Baptist Young Women, Fellowship of Christian Athletes, International Friendship Ministries, Latter-Day Saints Student Association, Lutheran/Episcopal Campus Ministry, Newman Community, Reformed University Fellowship, Wesley Foundation, Westminster Fellowship.
**Minority/foreign student organizations:** Black Greek Association, Ebonites, NAACP, SORAW (peer mentoring program). International Club.

**ATHLETICS. Physical education requirements:** None.
**Intercollegiate competition:** 4% of students participate. Baseball (M), basketball (M,W), cheerleading (M,W), cross-country (M,W), golf (M,W), soccer (M), softball (W), tennis (M,W), track (outdoor) (M,W), volleyball (W). Member of Big South Conference, NCAA Division I.
**Intramural and club sports:** 30% of students participate. Intramural aerobics, badminton, basketball, cross-country, flag football, golf, racquetball, soccer, softball, swimming, tennis, ultimate frisbee, volleyball, weight lifting.

**ADMISSIONS. Academic basis for candidate selection** (in order of priority): Secondary school record, class rank, standardized test scores, school's recommendation, essay.
**Nonacademic basis for candidate selection:** Extracurricular participation, particular talent or ability, and geographical distribution are important. Character and personality are considered.

**Requirements:** Graduation from secondary school is required; GED is accepted. 16 units and the following program of study are required: 4 units of English, 3 units of math, 2 units of lab science, 2 units of foreign language, 2 units of social studies, 1 unit of history, 1 unit of academic electives. Audition required of music program applicants. Summer Term Education Preparation (STEP) and Learning Excellent Academic Practices (LEAP) for applicants not normally admissible. SAT is required; ACT may be substituted. Campus visit recommended. No off-campus interviews.
**Procedure:** Take SAT or ACT by March of 12th year. Suggest filing application by November 1. Application deadline is May 1. Notification of admission sent out on 21st of each month from November to May. Reply is required by May 1. $50 nonrefundable tuition deposit. $100 room deposit, refundable until June 1 (Fall) or December 1 (Spring). Freshmen accepted for terms other than fall.
**Special programs:** Admission may be deferred one year. Credit may be granted through CEEB Advanced Placement for scores of 3 or higher. Credit may be granted through CLEP subject exams and military experience. Early entrance/early admission program. Concurrent enrollment program.
**Transfer students:** Transfer students accepted for terms other than fall. In fall 1993, 32% of all new students were transfers into all classes. 671 transfer applications were received, 514 were accepted. Application deadline is June 1 for fall; January 1 for spring. Minimum 2.2 GPA required. Lowest course grade accepted is "C." Maximum number of transferable credits is 65 semester hours from a two-year school and 94 semester hours from a four-year school. At least 30 semester hours must be completed at the university to receive degree.
**Admissions contact:** Deborah Barber, M.Ed., Associate Director of Admissions. 803 323-2191.

**FINANCIAL AID. Available aid:** Pell grants, SEOG, private scholarships, academic merit scholarships, and athletic scholarships. Perkins Loans (NDSL), PLUS, Stafford Loans (GSL), and SLS. AMS.
**Financial aid statistics:** 37% of aid is not need-based. In 1993-94, 58% of all undergraduate applicants received aid; 75% of freshman applicants. Average amounts of aid awarded freshmen: Scholarships and grants, $3,060; loans, $1,300.
**Supporting data/closing dates:** FAFSA: Priority filing date is March 1; accepted on rolling basis. School's own aid application: Priority filing date is May 1. Notification of awards on rolling basis.
**Financial aid contact:** Dia Frierson, M.A., Director of Financial Aid. 803 323-2189.

**STUDENT EMPLOYMENT.** College Work/Study Program. Institutional employment. 26% of full-time undergraduates work on campus during school year. Students may expect to earn an average of $1,632 during school year. Off-campus part-time employment opportunities rated "excellent."

**COMPUTER FACILITIES.** 250 IBM/IBM-compatible, Macintosh/Apple, and RISC-/UNIX-based microcomputers; 200 are networked. Students may access Digital, IBM, SUN minicomputer/mainframe systems, BITNET, Internet. Client/LAN operating systems include Apple/Macintosh, DOS, OS/2, UNIX/XENIX/AIX, Windows NT, X-windows, DEC, LocalTalk/AppleTalk, Novell. Computer languages and software packages include Ada, BASIC, C, COBOL, dBASE, FORTRAN, Harvard Graphics, LISP, Lotus 1-2-3, Pascal, PL/1, Quattro Pro, SAS, SPSS, Turbo Pascal, Word, WordPerfect, WordStar, Works; 350 in all. Computer facilities are available to all students.
**Fees:** Computer fee is included in tuition/fees.
**Hours:** 8 AM-11 PM (M-Th); 8 AM-4 PM (F); noon-4 PM (Sa); noon-9 PM (Su).

**GRADUATE CAREER DATA.** Graduate school percentages: 1% enter law school. 2% enter medical school. 8% enter graduate business programs. 9% enter graduate arts and sciences programs. Highest graduate school enrollments: Furman U, U of South Carolina, Winthrop U. 49% of graduates choose careers in business and industry.

**PROMINENT ALUMNI/AE.** Ida Crawford Stewart, vice president, Estee Lauder; Andie McDowell, model and actress; Cecily Truett, producer of children's TV program, "Reading Rainbow."

# Wofford College

**Spartanburg, SC 29303-3663** **803 597-4000**

**1993-94 Costs.** Tuition: $11,480. Room & board: $4,150. Fees, books, misc. academic expenses (school's estimate): $350.
**Enrollment.** Undergraduates: 627 men, 432 women (full-time). Freshman class: 1,565 applicants, 935 accepted, 273 enrolled.
**Test score averages/ranges.** Average SAT scores: 517 verbal, 564 math. Range of SAT scores of middle 50%: 980-1190 combined. Average ACT scores: 24 composite. Range of ACT scores of middle 50%: 22-26 composite.
**Faculty.** 69 full-time; 27 part-time. 92% of faculty holds highest degree in specific field. Student/faculty ratio: 14 to 1.
**Selectivity rating.** More competitive.

**PROFILE.** Wofford is a church-affiliated, liberal arts college. Founded as a men's college in 1854, it adopted coeducation in 1971. Its 100-acre campus is located in Spartanburg, 65 miles southwest of Charlotte, N.C.

**Accreditation:** SACS.
**Religious orientation:** Wofford College is affiliated with the United Methodist Church; one semester of religion required.
**Library:** Collections totaling over 165,676 volumes, 641 periodical subscriptions, and 60,354 microform items.
**Special facilities/museums:** Art gallery, technological research center, planetarium, satellite earth station.
**Athletic facilities:** Gymnasiums; handball, racquetball, tennis courts; weight room; baseball, football, intramural fields.

**STUDENT BODY. Undergraduate profile:** 71% are state residents; 8% are transfers. 2% Asian-American, 8% Black, 89% White, 1% Other. Average age of undergraduates is 21.
**Freshman profile:** 3% of freshmen who took SAT scored 700 or over on verbal, 6% scored 700 or over on math; 19% scored 600 or over on verbal, 36% scored 600 or over on math; 53% scored 500 or over on verbal, 81% scored 500 or over on math; 94% scored 400 or over on verbal, 98% scored 400 or over on math; 100% scored 300 or over on verbal, 100% scored 300 or over on math. 98% of accepted applicants took SAT; 20% took ACT. 72% of freshmen come from public schools.
**Undergraduate achievement:** 91% of fall 1992 freshmen returned for fall 1993 term. 72% of entering class graduated. 31% of students who completed a degree program immediately went on to graduate study.
**Foreign students:** Nine students are from out of the country. Nine countries represented in all.

**PROGRAMS OF STUDY. Degrees:** B.A., B.S.
**Majors:** Accounting, Art History, Biology, Business Economics, Chemistry, Computer Science/Mathematics, Economics, English Language/Literature, Finance, Foreign Languages, French, German, Government, History, Humanities, Intercultural Studies, Mathematics, Philosophy, Physics, Political Economy/Philosophy, Psychology, Religion, Sociology, Spanish.
**Distribution of degrees:** The majors with the highest enrollment are biology, English, and business economics; German, intercultural studies, and humanities have the lowest.
**Requirements:** General education requirement.
**Academic regulations:** Freshmen must maintain minimum 1.6 GPA; sophomores, 1.8 GPA; juniors, 1.9 GPA; seniors, 2.0 GPA.
**Special:** Courses offered in art, education, geography, geology, Greek, music, and physical education. Self-designed majors. Double majors. Independent study. Accelerated study. Pass/fail grading option. Internships. Cooperative education programs. Preprofessional programs in law, medicine, veterinary science, dentistry, and theology. 3-2 engineering programs with Columbia U and Georgia Tech. Member of American Institute for Foreign Studies, Council for International Education Exchange, and Institute of European Studies. Off-campus study opportunities during January interim. Teacher certification in secondary education. Certification in specific subject areas. Exchange program abroad in Canada (U of Quebec). Study abroad also in Austria, Belize, Brazil, China, Costa Rica, the Dominican Republic, France, Germany, Guatemala, Indonesia, Italy, Nicaragua, Poland, Russia, Singapore, Spain, the United Kingdom, and other countries. Presidential International Program gives one student each year financial support to study and travel in developing nations of the world for one year. ROTC.
**Honors:** Phi Beta Kappa.
**Academic Assistance:** Remedial writing. Nonremedial tutoring.

**STUDENT LIFE. Housing:** Students may live off campus if permission is obtained. Women's and men's dorms. 81% of students live in college housing.
**Social atmosphere:** Students often gather at fraternity houses and at the Campus Life Building. Greeks, athletes, and the Social Affairs Committee are influential on campus. Popular campus events include Homecoming, the Greek Games during Spring Weekend, and football games. "Spartanburg is not exactly a college town, and there's not an awful lot to do off-campus. On campus, the Student Affairs Office is making improvements in social life, trying to sponsor more activities," comments the editor of the student newspaper.
**Services and counseling/handicapped student services:** Placement services. Health service. Counseling services for minority students. Birth control and personal counseling. Career and academic guidance services. Religious counseling. Physically disabled student services. Notetaking services. Tutors. Reader services for the blind.
**Campus organizations:** Undergraduate student government. Student newspaper (Old Gold & Black, published once/week). Literary magazine. Yearbook. Concert choir, gospel choir, glee club, pep band, Women's Ensemble, dance team, Theatre Workshop, Scabbard and Blade, College Bowl Team, College Republicans, Young Democrats, debating, fencing, rifle team, cycling club, Campus Union. Eight fraternities, six chapter houses; three sororities, one chapter house. 50% of men join a fraternity. 58% of women join a sorority.
**Religious organizations:** Baptist Student Union, Fellowship of Christian Athletes, Pre-Ministerial Society, Wesley Fellowship.
**Minority/foreign student organizations:** African-American Student Association, African-American Gospel choir, minority fraternities/sororities.

**ATHLETICS. Physical education requirements:** Two semesters of physical education required.
**Intercollegiate competition:** 8% of students participate. Baseball (M), basketball (M,W), cross-country (M,W), football (M), golf (M), soccer (M), tennis (M,W), volleyball (W). Member of Independent, NCAA Division II.
**Intramural and club sports:** 2% of students participate. Intramural basketball, blitz ball, racquetball, soccer, softball, touch football, volleyball. Men's club cheerleading, fencing, rifle. Women's club cheerleading, fencing.

**ADMISSIONS. Academic basis for candidate selection** (in order of priority): Secondary school record, class rank, standardized test scores, essay, school's recommendation.
**Nonacademic basis for candidate selection:** Character and personality and extracurricular participation are important. Particular talent or ability, geographical distribution, and alumni/ae relationship are considered.
**Requirements:** Graduation from secondary school is required; GED is accepted. 16 units and the following program of study are recommended: 4 units of English, 4 units of math, 3 units of lab science, 2 units of foreign language, 2 units of social studies, 1 unit of academic electives. Minimum combined SAT score of 900 recommended. SAT or ACT is required. PSAT is recommended. Campus visit and interview recommended. Off-campus interviews available with admissions and alumni representatives.
**Procedure:** Take SAT or ACT by November of 12th year. Visit college for interview by November of 12th year. Suggest filing application by December 1. Application deadline is February 1. Notification of admission on December 15 and March 15. Reply is required by May 1. $150 nonrefundable tuition deposit. $50 nonrefundable room deposit. Freshmen accepted for terms other than fall.
**Special programs:** Admission may be deferred. Credit and/or placement may be granted through CEEB Advanced Placement exams for scores of 3 or higher. Credit and/or

placement may be granted through CLEP subject exams. Credit and placement may be granted through DANTES exams and military experience. Early entrance/early admission program. Concurrent enrollment program.

**Transfer students:** Transfer students accepted for terms other than fall. In fall 1993, 8% of all new students were transfers into all classes. Application deadline is February 1 for fall; rolling for spring. Minimum 3.0 GPA required of applicants from two-year schools; 2.5 GPA from four-year schools. Lowest course grade accepted is "C." Maximum number of transferable credits is 62 semester hours from a two-year school and 90 semester hours from a four-year school. At least 30 semester hours must be completed at the college to receive degree.

**Admissions contact:** Charles H. Gray, M.A., Director of Admissions. 803 597-4130.

**FINANCIAL AID. Available aid:** Pell grants, SEOG, state scholarships and grants, school scholarships and grants, private scholarships and grants, ROTC scholarships, academic merit scholarships, and athletic scholarships. Perkins Loans (NDSL), PLUS, Stafford Loans (GSL), private loans, and SLS. Tuition Plan Inc. and Knight Tuition Plans.

**Financial aid statistics:** 49% of aid is not need-based. In 1993-94, 78% of all undergraduate applicants received aid; 70% of freshman applicants. Average amounts of aid awarded freshmen: Scholarships and grants, $7,438; loans, $3,366.

**Supporting data/closing dates:** FAFSA/FAF: Priority filing date is March 15. School's own aid application: Deadline is March 15. State aid form: Deadline is June 30. Notification of awards begins in March.

**Financial aid contact:** Susan S. McCrackin, Director of Financial Aid. 803 597-4160.

**STUDENT EMPLOYMENT.** College Work/Study Program. Institutional employment. 40% of full-time undergraduates work on campus during school year. Students may expect to earn an average of $1,200 during school year. Off-campus part-time employment opportunities rated "excellent."

**COMPUTER FACILITIES.** 63 IBM/IBM-compatible and Macintosh/Apple microcomputers. Students may access Digital minicomputer/mainframe systems. Computer languages and software packages include Ada, BASIC, C, COBOL, FORTRAN, Macro, Pascal. Computer facilities are available to all students.

**Fees:** None.

**Hours:** 8:30 AM-10:30 PM (M-Th); 8:30 AM-5 PM (F); 2 PM-10:30 PM (Su); hours vary in some locations.

**GRADUATE CAREER DATA.** Graduate school percentages: 6% enter law school. 6% enter medical school. 3% enter dental school. 4% enter graduate business programs. 5% enter graduate arts and sciences programs. 3% enter theological school/seminary. Highest graduate school enrollments: Medical U of South Carolina, U of South Carolina. 38% of graduates choose careers in business and industry. Companies and businesses that hire graduates: federal government, major banks, U.S. military.

**PROMINENT ALUMNI/AE.** T. Milton Rhodes, former president of the American Council for the Arts, general manager of the Spoleto Festival, USA; Jerome J. Richardson, CEO, Flagstar Companies, Inc. and the Carolina Panthers NFL franchise; William H. Willimon, Dean of the Chapel at Duke U, author.

# South Dakota

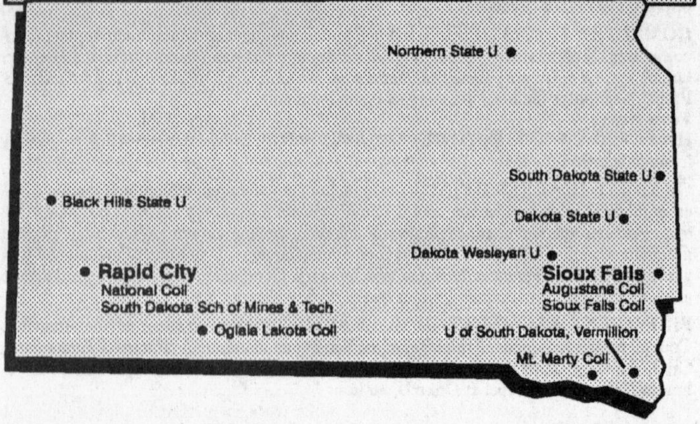


## Augustana College

**Sioux Falls, SD 57197** **605 336-0770**

**1993-94 Costs.** Tuition: $10,300. Room: $1,560. Board: $1,560. Fees, books, misc. academic expenses (school's estimate): $600.
**Enrollment.** Undergraduates: 558 men, 934 women (full-time). Freshman class: 731 applicants, 694 accepted, 394 enrolled. Graduate enrollment: 10 men, 29 women.
**Test score averages/ranges.** Average ACT scores: 23 composite.
**Faculty.** 131 full-time; 25 part-time. 66% of faculty holds doctoral degree. Student/faculty ratio: 14 to 1.
**Selectivity rating.** Less competitive.

**PROFILE.** Augustana, founded in 1860, is a church-related, liberal arts college. Its 110-acre campus is located in Sioux Falls, 15 miles from the western borders of Minnesota and Iowa.

**Accreditation:** NCACS. Professionally accredited by the American Medical Association (CAHEA), the Council on Social Work Education, the National Association of Schools of Music, the National Council for Accreditation of Teacher Education, the National League for Nursing.
**Religious orientation:** Augustana College is affiliated with the Evangelical Lutheran Church in America; two semesters of religion required.
**Special facilities/museums:** Language lab, community organization and area development center, western studies center.
**Athletic facilities:** Gymnasium, baseball and softball fields, outdoor track, tennis courts.

**STUDENT BODY. Undergraduate profile:** 55% are state residents; 27% are transfers. 1% Asian-American, 1% Black, 1% Native American, 97% White. Average age of undergraduates is 20.
**Freshman profile:** Majority of accepted applicants took ACT. 95% of freshmen come from public schools.
**Undergraduate achievement:** 78% of fall 1991 freshmen returned for fall 1992 term. 49% of entering class graduated. 22% of students who completed a degree program immediately went on to graduate study.
**Foreign students:** 64 students are from out of the country. Countries represented include Germany, Japan, Korea, Norway, and Singapore; 22 in all.

**PROGRAMS OF STUDY. Degrees:** B.A.
**Majors:** Accounting, Art, Biological Chemistry, Biology, Business Administration, Chemistry, Communication/Business, Communication/Theatre, Computer Science, Early Childhood Education, Economics, Education, Education of the Hearing Impaired, Elementary Education, Engineering Physics, English, Fitness Management, French, German, Government/International Affairs, Greek, Health/Hospital Services Administration, History, Journalism, Management Information Systems, Mathematics, Medical Technology, Music, Music Education, Nursing, Philosophy, Physical Education, Physics, Planning, Psychology, Religion, Social Studies Teaching, Social Work/Community Development, Sociology, Spanish, Special Education, Speech Education, Theology.
**Distribution of degrees:** The majors with the highest enrollment are business, nursing, and elementary education; Greek, philosophy, and Spanish have the lowest.
**Requirements:** General education requirement.
**Academic regulations:** Freshmen must maintain minimum 1.66 GPA; sophomores, 1.66 GPA; juniors, 1.76 GPA; seniors, 1.91 GPA.
**Special:** Programs offered in aviation administration, biophysics, environmental studies, gender studies, gerontology/geriatics, and Russian/Soviet area studies. Associate's degrees offered. Self-designed majors. Double majors. Independent study. Pass/fail grading option. Internships. Graduate school at which undergraduates may take graduate-level courses. Numerous preprofessional programs. 2-2, 3-2, and 4-2 engineering programs. B.A./M.Div. program with North American Baptist Seminary. Cross-registration with Sioux Falls Coll and North American Baptist Seminary. Living/learning semester in Minneapolis Modern Cities area. San Francisco Studies Term. Teacher certification in elementary, secondary, and special education. Exchange program abroad in Germany (Schiller International U). Study abroad also in Scandinavian and South American countries.
**Academic Assistance:** Nonremedial tutoring.

**STUDENT LIFE. Housing:** All freshmen and sophomores must live on campus unless living with family. Coed dorms. On-campus married-student housing. Special-interest housing. 67% of students live in college housing.
**Services and counseling/handicapped student services:** Placement services. Health service. Day care. Counseling services for veteran and older students. Personal counseling. Career and academic guidance services. Physically disabled student services. Learning disabled services. Tape recorders. Reader services for the blind.
**Campus organizations:** Undergraduate student government. Student newspaper (Mirror, published once/week). Literary magazine. Yearbook. Radio station. Brass ensemble, Northlanders, concert and varsity bands, chamber orchestra, women's chorus, college and chapel choirs, Young Democrats, College Republicans, volunteer and tutoring groups, debating, drama club, professional groups, special-interest groups. One fraternity, no chapter house; two sororities, no chapter houses. 1% of men join a fraternity. 1% of women join a sorority.
**Religious organizations:** Christian Fellowship, College Congregation and Outreach, Fellowship of Christian Athletes.
**Minority/foreign student organizations:** Native American Council, United Black Cultural Association. International Student Club.

**ATHLETICS. Physical education requirements:** Two semester of physical education required.
**Intercollegiate competition:** 15% of students participate. Baseball (M), basketball (M,W), cheerleading (M,W), football (M), softball (W), tennis (M,W), track (indoor) (M,W), track (outdoor) (M,W), track and field (indoor) (M,W), track and field (outdoor) (M,W), volleyball (W), wrestling (M). Member of NCAA Division II, North Central Conference.
**Intramural and club sports:** 40% of students participate. Intramural badminton, basketball, dance aerobics, flag football, free-throw, golf, home run derby, horseback riding, Nerf football, racquetball, running, sand volleyball, soccer, softball, table tennis, tennis, triathlon, volleyball, walleyball, water aerobics, water basketball, Wiffle ball, wrestling. Men's club fencing, golf, martial arts, soccer, volleyball. Women's club fencing, golf, martial arts, soccer.

**ADMISSIONS. Academic basis for candidate selection** (in order of priority): Secondary school record, standardized test scores, school's recommendation, class rank.
**Nonacademic basis for candidate selection:** Extracurricular participation is emphasized. Character and personality are important. Alumni/ae relationship is considered.
**Requirements:** Graduation from secondary school is required; GED is accepted. No specific distribution of secondary school units required. Rank in top half of secondary school class required; minimum composite ACT score of 23 recommended. ACT is required; SAT may be substituted. Campus visit and interview recommended. Off-campus interviews available with an admissions representative.
**Procedure:** Take SAT or ACT by April of 12th year. Application deadline is March 1. Acceptance notification on rolling basis; by February 15 for nursing. Reply is required by May 1. $150 nonrefundable tuition deposit. $100 room deposit, refundable until July 15. Freshmen accepted for terms other than fall.
**Special programs:** Admission may be deferred one year. Credit and/or placement may be granted through CEEB Advanced Placement exams for scores of 3 or higher. Credit and/or placement may be granted through CLEP general and subject exams. Credit and placement may be granted through challenge exams and military and life experience. Concurrent enrollment program.
**Transfer students:** Transfer students accepted for terms other than fall. In fall 1992, 27% of all new students were transfers into all classes. 238 transfer applications were received, 219 were accepted. Application deadline is August 15 for fall; January 15 for spring. Minimum 2.0 GPA required. Lowest course grade accepted is "C." Maximum number of semester hours that may be transferred is 65 from two-year schools, unlimited from four-year schools. At least 30 semester hours must be completed at the college to receive degree.
**Admissions contact:** Susan Bies, Director of Admissions. 605 336-5516.

**FINANCIAL AID. Available aid:** Pell grants, SEOG, Federal Nursing Student Scholarships, state scholarships and grants, school scholarships and grants, private scholarships and grants, academic merit scholarships, athletic scholarships, and aid for undergraduate foreign students. Perkins Loans (NDSL), PLUS, Stafford Loans (GSL), NSL, and SLS. AMS, family tuition reduction, and guaranteed tuition.
**Financial aid statistics:** In 1992-93, 88% of all undergraduate applicants received aid; 91% of freshman applicants.
**Supporting data/closing dates:** FAFSA/FAF/FFS: Priority filing date is March 1. EAC: Priority filing date is March 1. Notification of awards on rolling basis.
**Financial aid contact:** F. Eugene Linton, Director of Financial Aid. 605 336-5217.

**STUDENT EMPLOYMENT.** College Work/Study Program. Institutional employment. 48% of full-time undergraduates work on campus during school year. Students may expect to earn an average of $700 during school year. Off-campus part-time employment opportunities rated "excellent."

**COMPUTER FACILITIES.** 110 IBM/IBM-compatible and Macintosh/Apple microcomputers. Students may access IBM minicomputer/mainframe systems, Internet. Residence halls may be equipped with stand-alone microcomputers. Client/LAN operating systems include Novell. Computer languages and software packages include BASIC, C, CAI, COBOL, FORTRAN, Pascal, SPSS, Word Pro. Computer facilities are available to all students.
**Fees:** None.
**Hours:** 24 hours.

**GRADUATE CAREER DATA.** Graduate school percentages: 10% enter law school. 5% enter medical school. 1% enter dental school. 10% enter graduate business programs. 5% enter graduate arts and sciences programs. 5% enter theological school/seminary. Highest graduate school enrollments: Creighton U, U of Iowa, U of Minnesota, U of Nebraska, U of South Dakota. 30% of graduates choose careers in business and industry. Companies and businesses that hire graduates: Citibank, Federated Insurance, Lutheran Brotherhood, Minnesota Mutual Insurance, Norwest Bancorp, State Farm Insurance.

**PROMINENT ALUMNI/AE.** Mary Hart, anchor, *Entertainment Tonight*; Dr. Robert M. Berdah, president, U of Texas at Austin.

# Black Hills State University

**Spearfish, SD 57799** 605 642-6011

**1994-95 Costs.** Tuition: $1,411 (state residents), $3,437 (out-of-state). Room: $1,264. Board: $1,449. Fees, books, misc. academic expenses (school's estimate): $1,471.
**Enrollment.** Undergraduates: 1,171 men, 1,632 women (full-time). Freshman class: 938 applicants, 938 accepted, 588 enrolled. Graduate enrollment: 18 men, 49 women.
**Test score averages/ranges.** Average ACT scores: 19 composite.
**Faculty.** 103 full-time; 8 part-time. 63% of faculty holds highest degree in specific field. Student/faculty ratio: 24 to 1.
**Selectivity rating.** Noncompetitive.

**PROFILE.** Black Hills State is a public university. It was founded in 1883, became a four-year institution in 1924, and gained university status in 1989. Its 123-acre campus is located in Spearfish, 47 miles from Rapid City.

**Accreditation:** NCACS. Professionally accredited by the National Association of Schools of Music, the National Council for Accreditation of Teacher Education.
**Religious orientation:** Black Hills State University is nonsectarian; no religious requirements.
**Library:** Collections totaling over 211,000 volumes, 598 periodical subscriptions, and 355,000 microform items.
**Special facilities/museums:** Art galleries, museum collections, western historical studies library, center for Indian studies, center for advancement and study of tourism, small business institute.
**Athletic facilities:** Swimming pool, basketball, tennis, and volleyball courts, tracks, football, soccer, and softball fields, aerobics, combatives, fitness, and weight rooms, rodeo arena.

**STUDENT BODY. Undergraduate profile:** 72% are state residents; 25% are transfers. 1% Asian-American, 1% Black, 1% Hispanic, 2% Native American, 95% White. Average age of undergraduates is 26.
**Freshman profile:** 95% of accepted applicants took ACT.
**Undergraduate achievement:** 45% of fall 1992 freshmen returned for fall 1993 term. 23% of entering class graduated. 10% of students who completed a degree program immediately went on to graduate study.
**Foreign students:** 14 students are from out of the country. 12 countries represented in all.

**PROGRAMS OF STUDY. Degrees:** B.A., B.S., B.S.Ed.
**Majors:** Accounting/Business, Art, Biology, Business Administration/Business Education, Chemistry, Commercial Art, Communications, Elementary Education, English, History, Human Services, Industrial Technology, Library Media, Marketing, Mass Communications, Mathematics, Music, Office Administration, Outdoor Education, Physical Education, Physical Science, Physical Wellness, Political Science, Pre-Physical Therapy, Psychology, Social Science, Sociology, Spanish, Special Education, Speech, Tourism, Travel Industry Management.
**Distribution of degrees:** The majors with the highest enrollment are elementary education, business administration, and social sciences; mathematics, physical science, and communications have the lowest.
**Requirements:** General education requirement.
**Academic regulations:** Minimum 2.0 GPA must be maintained.
**Special:** Minors offered in most majors. Associate's degrees offered in administration assistance, communication arts, drafting technology, radio/television operations, and travel industry management. Associate's degrees offered. Independent study. Pass/fail grading option. Internships. Graduate school at which undergraduates may take graduate-level courses. Preprofessional programs in law. Teacher certification in early childhood, elementary, secondary, and special education. Certification in specific subject areas. ROTC.
**Honors:** Honor societies.
**Academic Assistance:** Remedial reading, writing, and math. Nonremedial tutoring.

**STUDENT LIFE. Housing:** All freshmen must live on campus unless living with family. Coed, women's, and men's dorms. 25% of students live in college housing.
**Social atmosphere:** On campus, students congregate at the Student Union. Favorite off-campus haunts include the Back Porch Lounge, Breakaway Billiards, and the Bay Leaf Cafe. Student groups with a strong influence on campus life include student ambassadors, peer assistance groups, and the student activities committee. Among the most popular events of the school year are Homecoming and the BHSU vs. SDSM&T (South Dakota School of Mines & Technology) football and basketball games. "Spearfish, SD, is a tourist area, and there are many attractions in the Black Hills for students to visit," observes the editor of the student newspaper. "Hiking, skiing, boating, mountain biking and motorcycle touring are also very popular here."
**Services and counseling/handicapped student services:** Placement services. Health service. Day care. Counseling services for minority, military, veteran, and older students. Personal and psychological counseling. Career and academic guidance services. Religious counseling. Physically disabled student services. Learning disabled services. Notetaking services. Tutors.
**Campus organizations:** Undergraduate student government. Student newspaper (Today, published once/week). Yearbook. Radio station. Choir, jazz band, instrumental groups, debating, graphics magazine, Student Activities Committee, BACCHUS, Young Democrats, Young Republicans, Interhall Council, service and special-interest groups, 55 organizations in all. One fraternity, no chapter house; one sorority, no chapter house. 2% of men join a fraternity. 2% of women join a sorority.
**Religious organizations:** Fellowship of Christian Athletes, United Ministries in Higher Education.
**Minority/foreign student organizations:** Native American student group.

**ATHLETICS. Physical education requirements:** Two semesters of physical education required.
**Intercollegiate competition:** 7% of students participate. Basketball (M,W), cross-country (M,W), football (M), track (indoor) (M,W), track (outdoor) (M,W), track and field (indoor) (M,W), track and field (outdoor) (M,W), volleyball (W). Member of NAIA, SDIC.
**Intramural and club sports:** 35% of students participate. Intramural aerobics, archery, badminton, basketball, bowling, darts, flag football, free throw, golf, inner-tube water polo, miniature golf, racquetball, sand volleyball, softball, swimming, table tennis, track and field, turkey trot, volleyball, wrestling, wrist wrestling. Men's club rodeo. Women's club cheerleading, rodeo.

**ADMISSIONS. Academic basis for candidate selection** (in order of priority): Secondary school record, class rank, standardized test scores.
**Requirements:** Graduation from secondary school is required; GED is accepted. 14 units and the following program of study are required: 4 units of English, 3 units of math, 2 units of lab science, 3 units of social studies, 2 units of academic electives. Minimum composite ACT score of 20, rank in top two-thirds of secondary school class, or minimum 2.0 GPA required. Conditional admission possible for applicants not meeting standard requirements. ACT is required; SAT may be substituted. Campus visit recommended. Off-campus interviews available with an admissions representative.
**Procedure:** Take SAT or ACT by October of 12th year. Suggest filing application by September 1. Notification of admission on rolling basis. Reply is required by September 1. $100 room deposit, refundable until two weeks prior to beginning of term. Freshmen accepted for terms other than fall.
**Special programs:** Credit and/or placement may be granted through CEEB Advanced Placement exams for scores of 4 or higher. Credit and/or placement may be granted through CLEP general and subject exams. Placement may be granted through military and life experience. Credit and placement may be granted through DANTES exams. Concurrent enrollment program.
**Transfer students:** Transfer students accepted for terms other than fall. In fall 1993, 25% of all new students were transfers into all classes. 686 transfer applications were received, 686 were accepted. Application deadline is September 1 for fall; January 5 for spring. Minimum 2.0 GPA required. Lowest course grade accepted is "D." Maximum number of transferable credits is 64 semester hours from a two-year school and 96 semester hours from a four-year school. At least 32 semester hours must be completed at the university to receive degree.
**Admissions contact:** April Meeker, Director of Admissions. 605 642-6343.

**FINANCIAL AID. Available aid:** Pell grants, SEOG, state grants, school scholarships, private scholarships, ROTC scholarships, and athletic scholarships. Perkins Loans (NDSL), PLUS, Stafford Loans (GSL), and SLS. AMS.
**Financial aid statistics:** 15% of aid is not need-based. In 1993-94, 75% of all undergraduate applicants received aid; 79% of freshman applicants. Average amounts of aid awarded freshmen: Scholarships and grants, $926; loans, $2,234.
**Supporting data/closing dates:** FAFSA/FAF/FFS: Priority filing date is April 1; accepted on rolling basis. PHEAA, EAC: Priority filing date is April 1. Notification of awards on rolling basis.
**Financial aid contact:** John Gritts, Director of Financial Aid. 605 642-6253.

**STUDENT EMPLOYMENT.** College Work/Study Program. Institutional employment. 20% of full-time undergraduates work on campus during school year. Students may expect to earn an average of $1,532 during school year. Off-campus part-time employment opportunities rated "fair."

**COMPUTER FACILITIES.** 400 IBM/IBM-compatible and Macintosh/Apple microcomputers; 20 are networked. Students may access IBM minicomputer/mainframe systems. Residence halls may be equipped with stand-alone microcomputers, networked microcomputers. Computer languages and software packages include Appleworks, Assembler, BASIC, COBOL, DisplayWrite, Lotus 1-2-3, PC- File, PL/1, PSS, Quattro, WordHandler, WordPerfect, various instructional software programs. Computer facilities are available to all students.
**Fees:** None.
**Hours:** Labs open until 10 PM (M-F); 24 hours in dorms.

**GRADUATE CAREER DATA.** Graduate school percentages: 2% enter law school. 3% enter medical school. 2% enter dental school. 3% enter graduate business programs. Highest graduate school enrollments: South Dakota State U, U of South Dakota. 35% of graduates choose careers in business and industry. Companies and businesses that hire graduates: school districts

**PROMINENT ALUMNI/AE.** Roland Dolly, U.S. Department of Agriculture; Roger Tellinghuizen, attorney general, South Dakota; Richard Roach, coach, Buffalo Bills; Paul Roach, athletic director, U of Wyoming; Raghbir Bhathal, owner, Raj Manufacturing.

# Dakota State University

**Madison, SD 57042** 605 256-5139

**1994-95 Costs.** Tuition: $1,230 (state residents), $3,000 (out-of-state). Room: $593. Board: $646. Fees, books, misc. academic expenses (school's estimate): $1,370.
**Enrollment.** Undergraduates: 418 men, 565 women (full-time). Freshman class: 910 applicants, 828 accepted, 715 enrolled.
**Test score averages/ranges.** Average ACT scores: 18 English, 19 math, 20 composite.
**Faculty.** 54 full-time; 5 part-time. 41% of faculty holds doctoral degree. Student/faculty ratio: 18 to 1.
**Selectivity rating.** Less competitive.

**PROFILE.** Dakota State, founded in 1881 as a Normal school, is a public university. Programs are offered through the Divisions of Business and Information Systems, Liberal Arts, Science and Mathematics, and Teacher Education. Its 40-acre campus is located four blocks from Madison's business district.

**Accreditation:** NCACS. Professionally accredited by the American Medical Association (CAHEA), the National Council for Accreditation of Teacher Education.

**Religious orientation:** Dakota State University is nonsectarian; no religious requirements.
**Library:** Collections totaling over 100,000 volumes, 644 periodical subscriptions, and 4,000 microform items.
**Special facilities/museums:** Natural history museum.
**Athletic facilities:** Gymnasium, sand volleyball courts, track, weight room, wellness center.
**STUDENT BODY. Undergraduate profile:** 86% are state residents; 10% are transfers. 1% Asian-American, 1% Black, 98% White. Average age of undergraduates is 23.
**Freshman profile:** 85% of accepted applicants took ACT. 94% of freshmen come from public schools.
**Undergraduate achievement:** 7% of students who completed a degree program immediately went on to graduate study.
**Foreign students:** Eight students are from out of the country. Countries represented include China, Japan, Jordan, Korea, Kuwait, and Nepal.
**PROGRAMS OF STUDY. Degrees:** B.Bus.Admin., B.S., B.S.Ed.
**Majors:** Applied Business, Art, Business, Business Administration, Computer Education, Computer Science, Early Childhood Education, Elementary Education, Elementary Education/Special Learning and Behavioral Problems, English, English for Information Systems, French, Gifted Education, Information Systems, Junior High/Middle School Language Arts, Marketing Education, Mathematics, Mathematics for Information Systems, Medical Records Administration, Music, Natural Science, Physical Sciences, Respiratory Care, Science, Secondary Education, Social Science, Spanish, Special Education, Special Learning/Behavioral Problems, Vocational/Technical Education.
**Distribution of degrees:** The majors with the highest enrollment are business administration, education, and information systems; mathematics, respiratory care, and social science have the lowest.
**Requirements:** General education requirement.
**Academic regulations:** Minimum 2.0 GPA must be maintained.
**Special:** Minors offered in some majors and in business education, biology, chemistry, health/physical education/coaching, history, physics, social systems, speech communication, and theatre. Associate's degrees offered. Double majors. Dual degrees. Independent study. Internships. Cooperative education programs. Preprofessional programs in law and medicine. Teacher certification in early childhood, elementary, secondary, special education, and vo-tech education. Study abroad in England. AFROTC at South Dakota State U.
**Honors:** Phi Beta Kappa. Honors program. Honor societies.
**Academic Assistance:** Remedial reading, writing, math, and study skills.
**ADMISSIONS. Academic basis for candidate selection** (in order of priority): Secondary school record, standardized test scores, class rank, school's recommendation, essay.
**Requirements:** Graduation from secondary school is recommended; GED is accepted. 20 units and the following program of study are required: 4 units of English, 2 units of math, 2 units of lab science, 3 units of social studies, 1.5 units of electives including .5 units of academic electives. Minimum composite ACT score of 20, rank in top two-thirds of secondary school class, or minimum 2.0 GPA required. Conditional admission possible for applicants not meeting standard requirements. ACT is recommended. ACT is required; SAT may be substituted. Campus visit recommended. No off-campus interviews.
**Procedure:** Take SAT or ACT by April of 12th year. Notification of admission on rolling basis. $50 nonrefundable room deposit. Freshmen accepted for terms other than fall.
**Special programs:** Admission may be deferred. Credit and/or placement may be granted through CEEB Advanced Placement exams for scores of 4 or higher. Credit and/or placement may be granted through CLEP general and subject exams. Credit may be granted through military experience. Credit and placement may be granted through Regents College exams. Concurrent enrollment program.
**Transfer students:** Transfer students accepted for terms other than fall. In fall 1993, 10% of all new students were transfers into all classes. 505 transfer applications were received, 481 were accepted. Application deadline is two weeks after beginning of semester for fall; two weeks after beginning of semester for spring. SAT/ACT scores required of transfers applying within three years of secondary school graduation. Minimum 2.0 GPA required. Lowest course grade accepted is "D." At least 32 semester hours must be completed at the university to receive degree.
**Admissions contact:** Mark G. Weiss, Director of Admissions. 605 256-5139.
**FINANCIAL AID. Available aid:** Pell grants, SEOG, state scholarships and grants, school scholarships, private scholarships, academic merit scholarships, and athletic scholarships. Perkins Loans (NDSL), PLUS, Stafford Loans (GSL), and SLS. AMS.
**Financial aid statistics:** In 1993-94, 85% of all undergraduate applicants received aid; 75% of freshman applicants. Average amounts of aid awarded freshmen: Scholarships and grants, $400; loans, $1,659.
**Supporting data/closing dates:** FAFSA/FAF/FFS: Priority filing date is March 1. PHEAA/EAC: Priority filing date is March 1. Notification of awards on rolling basis.
**Financial aid contact:** Rosie Jamison, Director of Financial Aid. 605 256-5152.

## Dakota Wesleyan University

**Mitchell, SD 57301** **605 995-2660**

**1993-94 Costs.** Tuition: $7,110. Room & board: $2,660. Fees, books, misc. academic expenses (school's estimate): $550.
**Enrollment.** Undergraduates: 236 men, 286 women (full-time). Freshman class: 335 applicants, 286 accepted, 118 enrolled.
**Test score averages/ranges.** Average ACT scores: 19 English, 19 math, 20 composite.
**Faculty.** 39 full-time; 40 part-time. 34% of faculty holds doctoral degree. Student/faculty ratio: 15 to 1.
**Selectivity rating.** Competitive.

**PROFILE.** Dakota Wesleyan, founded in 1885, is a church-affiliated, liberal arts college. Its 40-acre campus is located in Mitchell, 60 miles from Sioux Falls.
**Accreditation:** NCACS. Professionally accredited by the National League for Nursing.
**Religious orientation:** Dakota Wesleyan University is affiliated with the Methodist Church; no religious requirements.
**Library:** Collections totaling over 65,000 volumes, 412 periodical subscriptions, and 12,000 microform items.
**Athletic facilities:** Gymnasium, weight room, exercise room, racquetball court, indoor track.
**STUDENT BODY. Undergraduate profile:** 87% are state residents; 11% are transfers. 1% Black, 1% Hispanic, 5% Native American, 93% White. Average age of undergraduates is 24.
**Freshman profile:** 96% of accepted applicants took ACT. 98% of freshmen come from public schools.
**Undergraduate achievement:** 49% of fall 1992 freshmen returned for fall 1993 term. 42% of entering class graduated. 3% of students who completed a degree program immediately went on to graduate study.
**Foreign students:** Three students are from out of the country. Countries represented include Canada and Japan; three in all.
**PROGRAMS OF STUDY. Degrees:** B.A.
**Majors:** American Indian Studies, Art, Biology, Business Administration, Communication/Theatre, Community Recreation, Economics, Education, English, Fine Arts, Health/Physical Education/Recreation, History, Human Services, Mathematics, Medical Technology, Nursing, Philosophy, Psychology, Religion, Social Studies, Sociology.
**Distribution of degrees:** The majors with the highest enrollment are business, nursing, and education; economics, religion, and philosophy have the lowest.
**Requirements:** General education requirement.
**Academic regulations:** Freshmen must maintain minimum 1.6 GPA; sophomores, 1.8 GPA; juniors, 2.0 GPA; seniors, 2.0 GPA.
**Special:** Minors offered in all majors and in athletic training, chemistry, computer science, criminal justice, languages, nursing, and physics. Associate's degrees offered. Double majors. Independent study. Pass/fail grading option. Internships. Graduate school at which undergraduates may take graduate-level courses. Preprofessional programs in law, medicine, veterinary science, dentistry, theology, optometry, and physical therapy. Teacher certification in elementary and secondary education. Certification in specific subject areas.
**Honors:** Honors program.
**Academic Assistance:** Remedial reading, writing, math, and study skills. Nonremedial tutoring.
**ADMISSIONS. Academic basis for candidate selection** (in order of priority): Secondary school record, standardized test scores, class rank, school's recommendation.
**Nonacademic basis for candidate selection:** Character and personality, extracurricular participation, particular talent or ability, and alumni/ae relationship are considered.
**Requirements:** Graduation from secondary school is required; GED is accepted. No specific distribution of secondary school units required. Minimum composite ACT score of 18 and minimum 2.0 GPA required; rank in top half of secondary school class recommended. ACT is required; SAT may be substituted. Campus visit and interview recommended. Off-campus interviews available with an admissions representative.
**Procedure:** Take SAT or ACT by April of 12th year. Suggest filing application by March. Application deadline is August. Notification of admission on rolling basis. Reply is required within 30 days of acceptance. $50 tuition deposit, refundable until May 1. $50 room deposit, refundable until May 1. Freshmen accepted for terms other than fall.
**Special programs:** Admission may be deferred one year. Credit and/or placement may be granted through CEEB Advanced Placement exams for scores of 3 or higher. Credit and/or placement may be granted through CLEP general and subject exams. Credit and placement may be granted through DANTES and challenge exams and military and life experience. Concurrent enrollment program.
**Transfer students:** Transfer students accepted for terms other than fall. In fall 1993, 11% of all new students were transfers into all classes. 135 transfer applications were received, 114 were accepted. Application deadline is August 30 for fall; January 10 for spring. Minimum 2.0 GPA required. Lowest course grade accepted is "D." Maximum number of transferable semester hours is half of total required for degree. At least 30 semester hours must be completed at the university to receive degree.
**Admissions contact:** Melinda Larson, Director of Admission. 800 333-8506, 605 995-2650.
**FINANCIAL AID. Available aid:** Pell grants, SEOG, state grants, school scholarships and grants, academic merit scholarships, athletic scholarships, and aid for undergraduate foreign students. Perkins Loans (NDSL), PLUS, Stafford Loans (GSL), private loans, and SLS. Tuition Plan Inc., AMS, and deferred payment plan.
**Financial aid statistics:** 24% of aid is not need-based. In 1993-94, 100% of all undergraduate applicants received aid. Average amounts of aid awarded freshmen: Scholarships and grants, $2,029; loans, $3,998.
**Supporting data/closing dates:** FAFSA: Priority filing date is March 1. Notification of awards begins March 15.
**Financial aid contact:** Deb Henriksen, Director of Financial Aid. 605 995-2654.

## Mount Marty College

**Yankton, SD 57078** **800 658-4552**

**1994-95 Costs.** Tuition: $6,844. Room & board: $2,980. Fees, books, misc. academic expenses (school's estimate): $3,166.
**Enrollment.** Undergraduates: 196 men, 446 women (full-time). Freshman class: 279 applicants, 276 accepted, 126 enrolled. Graduate enrollment: 22 men, 23 women.
**Test score averages/ranges.** N/A.
**Faculty.** 37 full-time; 37 part-time. 34% of faculty holds doctoral degree. Student/faculty ratio: 12 to 1.
**Selectivity rating.** Less competitive.

**PROFILE.** Mount Marty, a private, church-affiliated, liberal arts college. Its 80-acre campus is located in Yankton, 30 miles south of Sioux Falls.

**Accreditation:** NCACS. Professionally accredited by the American Dietetic Association, the National League for Nursing.

**Religious orientation:** Mount Marty College is affiliated with the Roman Catholic Church; nine credit hours of religion/theology required.

**Library:** Collections totaling over 77,000 volumes, 600 periodical subscriptions, and 8,000 microform items.

**Special facilities/museums:** Day care center, hospital for clinical practice, student health lab.

**Athletic facilities:** Gymnasium, weight room, swimming pool, basketball, racquetball, and tennis courts, baseball, football, and softball fields, track.

**STUDENT BODY. Undergraduate profile:** 60% are state residents. 1% Black, 2% Native American, 96% White, 1% Other. Average age of undergraduates is 23.

**Freshman profile:** 1% of freshmen who took ACT scored 30 or over on English; 30% scored 24 or over on English, 17% scored 24 or over on math, 26% scored 24 or over on composite; 73% scored 18 or over on English, 69% scored 18 or over on math, 80% scored 18 or over on composite; 98% scored 12 or over on English, 100% scored 12 or over on math, 99% scored 12 or over on composite; 100% scored 6 or over on English, 100% scored 6 or over on composite. Majority of accepted applicants took ACT. 82% of freshmen come from public schools.

**Undergraduate achievement:** 69% of fall 1992 freshmen returned for fall 1993 term. 3% of students who completed a degree program immediately went on to graduate study.

**Foreign students:** Nine students are from out of the country. Countries represented include Canada and Korea; five in all.

**PROGRAMS OF STUDY. Degrees:** B.A., B.S., B.S.Nurs.

**Majors:** Accounting, Biology, Business Administration, Chemistry, English, Health Care Administration, Health/Physical Education, Mass Communications, Mathematical Sciences, Medical Technology, Music, Nursing, Nutrition/Food Science, Religious Education, Religious Studies/Philosophy, Selected Studies, Social Sciences, Teacher Education.

**Distribution of degrees:** The majors with the highest enrollment are nursing, business, and education; music, communication arts, and English/journalism have the lowest.

**Requirements:** General education requirement.

**Academic regulations:** Minimum 2.0 GPA must be maintained.

**Special:** Minors offered in most majors. Associate's degrees offered. Self-designed majors. Double majors. Pass/fail grading option. Internships. Preprofessional programs in law, medicine, veterinary science, pharmacy, dentistry, optometry, chiropractic, engineering, and physical therapy. 3-2 engineering program with Georgia Tech. 3-1-3 program with Northwestern Coll of Chiropractic. Member of Colleges of Mid-America Consortium. Teacher certification in elementary, secondary, and special education. ROTC at U of South Dakota.

**Academic Assistance:** Remedial writing and math.

**ADMISSIONS. Academic basis for candidate selection** (in order of priority): Secondary school record, standardized test scores, class rank, school's recommendation, essay.

**Nonacademic basis for candidate selection:** Extracurricular participation, particular talent or ability, and alumni/ae relationship are considered.

**Requirements:** Graduation from secondary school is required; GED is accepted. No specific distribution of secondary school units required. Probationary admission possible for applicants not meeting standard requirements. SAT or ACT is required. Campus visit and interview recommended. Off-campus interviews available with admissions and alumni representatives.

**Procedure:** Take SAT or ACT by December 1 of 12th year. Visit college for interview by February 1 of 12th year. Suggest filing application by February 1. Application deadline is September 1. Notification of admission on rolling basis. $50 tuition deposit, refundable until June 1. $50 room deposit, refundable until June 1. Freshmen accepted for terms other than fall.

**Special programs:** Admission may be deferred one year. Credit may be granted through CEEB Advanced Placement, CLEP subject exams, Regents College, ACT PEP, and DANTES exams, and military and life experience. Credit and placement may be granted through challenge exams. Concurrent enrollment program.

**Transfer students:** Transfer students accepted for terms other than fall. In fall 1993, 120 transfer applications were received, 116 were accepted. Application deadline is September 1 for fall; January 25 for spring. Minimum 2.0 GPA required. Lowest course grade accepted is "C." At least 60 credits must be completed at the college to receive degree.

**Admissions contact:** Paula Tacke, Director of Admissions. 800 658-4552.

**FINANCIAL AID. Available aid:** Pell grants, SEOG, Federal Nursing Student Scholarships, state scholarships and grants, school scholarships and grants, private scholarships and grants, ROTC scholarships, academic merit scholarships, athletic scholarships, and aid for undergraduate foreign students. Perkins Loans (NDSL), PLUS, Stafford Loans (GSL), NSL, state loans, school loans, private loans, and SLS. Tuition Plan Inc. and family tuition reduction.

**Financial aid statistics:** 21% of aid is not need-based. In 1993-94, 95% of all undergraduate applicants received aid; 94% of freshman applicants. Average amounts of aid awarded freshmen: Loans, $2,200.

**Supporting data/closing dates:** FAFSA/FAF/FFS: Accepted on rolling basis. School's own aid application: Accepted on rolling basis. State aid form: Accepted on rolling basis. Notification of awards on rolling basis.

**Financial aid contact:** Ken Kocer, Director of Financial Aid. 800 658-4552.

# National College

**Rapid City, SD 57701** **605 394-4800**

**1993-94 Costs.** Tuition: $7,440. Room & board: $3,180. Fees, books, misc. academic expenses (school's estimate): $875.

**Enrollment.** Undergraduates: 161 men, 232 women (full-time). Freshman class: 450 applicants, 420 accepted, 49 enrolled.

**Test score averages/ranges.** Average ACT scores: 17 composite.

**Faculty.** 16 full-time; 24 part-time. 20% of faculty holds doctoral degree. Student/faculty ratio: 13 to 1.

**Selectivity rating.** Noncompetitive.

**PROFILE.** National, founded in 1941, is a private, upper-division college. offering undergraduate programs in the areas of business, health, and technology. The academic organization includes the divisions of Allied Health, Arts and Sciences, Business, and Computer Information Systems and Technology. Its seven and one-half-acre campus is located in Rapid City.

**Accreditation:** NCACS. Professionally accredited by the Accrediting Bureau of Health Education Schools, the American Veterinary Medical Association.

**Religious orientation:** National College is nonsectarian; no religious requirements.

**Library:** Collections totaling over 35,900 volumes, 213 periodical subscriptions and 27 microform items.

**Special facilities/museums:** Medical lab, animal health care center, medical assistant room.

**Athletic facilities:** Gynmasium, weight room, rodeo arena.

**STUDENT BODY. Undergraduate profile:** 54% are state residents; 30% are transfers. 2% Asian-American, 3% Black, 5% Hispanic, 15% Native American, 75% White.

**Freshman profile:** Majority of accepted applicants took ACT.

**Undergraduate achievement:** 52% of fall 1992 freshmen returned for fall 1993 term. 28% of entering class graduated. 7% of students who completed a degree program went on to graduate study within five years.

**Foreign students:** 80 students are from out of the country. Countries represented include Japan

**PROGRAMS OF STUDY. Degrees:** B.S.

**Majors:** Accounting, Applied Management, Business Administration, Computer Information Systems, Management, Marketing, Paralegal, Travel/Tourism Management.

**Distribution of degrees:** The majors with the highest enrollment are business administration, accounting, and travel/tourism.

**Requirements:** General education requirement.

**Academic regulations:** Freshmen must maintain minimum 1.10 GPA; sophomores, 1.40 GPA; juniors, 1.50 GPA; seniors, 2.0 GPA.

**Special:** Diploma programs. Courses offered in applied management, English, German, Japanese, history, math, psychology, sociology, Spanish, and veterinary technology. Teacher recertification/renewal classes. Associate's degrees offered. Double majors. Independent study. Accelerated study. Internships. Cooperative education programs. ROTC at South Dakota Sch of Mines and Tech.

**Academic Assistance:** Remedial reading, writing, math, and study skills. Nonremedial tutoring.

**ADMISSIONS. Requirements:** Graduation from secondary school is required; GED is accepted. No specific distribution of secondary school units required. Open admission to graduates of accredited secondary schools. Remedial program for applicants not normally admissible. ACT is recommended; SAT may be substituted. Campus visit and interview recommended. Off-campus interviews available with an admissions representative.

**Procedure:** Application deadline is September 1. Notification of admission on rolling basis. $70 room deposit, refundable until 30 days prior to start of classes. Freshmen accepted for terms other than fall.

**Special programs:** Admission may be deferred one year. Credit and/or placement may be granted through CEEB Advanced Placement exams for scores of 3 or higher. Credit and/or placement may be granted through CLEP general and subject exams. Credit may be granted through military and life experience. Placement may be granted through challenge exams. Credit and placement may be granted through ACT PEP and DANTES exams.

**Transfer students:** Transfer students accepted for terms other than fall. In fall 1993, 30% of all new students were transfers into all classes. 200 transfer applications were received, 193 were accepted. Application deadline is September 1 for fall; March 1 for spring. Minimum 2.0 GPA required. Lowest course grade accepted is "C." Maximum number of transferable quarter hours is 144. At least 48 quarter hours must be completed at the college to receive degree.

**Admissions contact:** C. Robert Allen, Vice President for Admissions. 605 394-4827.

**FINANCIAL AID. Available aid:** School scholarships and grants, private scholarships and grants, athletic scholarships, and aid for undergraduate foreign students. In-house payment plan.

**Financial aid statistics:** Average amounts of aid awarded freshmen: Scholarships and grants, $2,500; loans, $3,160.

**Supporting data/closing dates:** FAFSA: Priority filing date is March 1; accepted on rolling basis. FAF/FFS: Accepted on rolling basis. School's own aid application: Priority filing date is March 1. Notification of awards on rolling basis.

**Financial aid contact:** Cheryl Schunneman, Director of Financial Aid. 605 394-4880.

# Northern State University

**Aberdeen, SD 57401** **605 622-3011**

**1993-94 Costs.** Tuition: $1,370 (state residents), $3,042 (out-of-state). Room: $1,074. Board: $991. Fees, books, misc. academic expenses (school's estimate): $1,122.
**Enrollment.** Undergraduates: 978 men, 1,223 women (full-time). Freshman class: 1,050 applicants, 1,022 accepted, 671 enrolled. Graduate enrollment: 84 men, 126 women.
**Test score averages/ranges.** Average ACT scores: 20 English, 19 math, 20 composite.
**Faculty.** 128 full-time; 15 part-time. 80% of faculty holds highest degree in specific field. Student/faculty ratio: 19 to 1.
**Selectivity rating.** Noncompetitive.

**PROFILE.** Northern State, founded in 1901, is a public, liberal arts university. Its 52-acre campus is located in Aberdeen, north of Sioux Falls.

**Accreditation:** NCACS. Professionally accredited by the National Association of Schools of Music, the National Council for Accreditation of Teacher Education.
**Religious orientation:** Northern State University is nonsectarian; no religious requirements.
**Library:** Collections totaling over 1,520,750 volumes, 939 periodical subscriptions, and 87,640 microform items.
**Special facilities/museums:** Art galleries.
**Athletic facilities:** Swimming pool, weight room, basketball, handball, racquetball, and tennis courts, athletic fields.
**STUDENT BODY. Undergraduate profile:** 97% are state residents; 21% are transfers. 3% Native American, 96% White, 1% Other. Average age of undergraduates is 22.
**Freshman profile:** 95% of accepted applicants took ACT.
**Undergraduate achievement:** 70% of fall 1992 freshmen returned for fall 1993 term. 50% of entering class graduated. 10% of students who completed a degree program immediately went on to graduate study.
**Foreign students:** 23 students are from out of the country. Countries represented include Canada, China, Japan, and Sweden; six in all.
**PROGRAMS OF STUDY. Degrees:** B.A., B.Mus.Ed., B.S., B.S.Ed.
**Majors:** Art, Biology, Business, Business Education, Chemistry, Communication Disorders, Community Services, Distributive Education, Drama/Speech, Economics, Elementary Education, English, Environmental Science, French, German, Health/Physical Education, History, Industrial Management, Industrial Technology, Industrial Technology Education, International Business, Mathematics, Medical Technology, Music, Office Administration, Physical Education, Political Science, Psychology, Recreation, Social Science for Teachers, Sociology, Spanish, Special Education, Speech.
**Distribution of degrees:** The majors with the highest enrollment are business management, elementary education, and secondary education.
**Requirements:** General education requirement.
**Academic regulations:** Freshmen must maintain minimum 2.0 GPA; sophomores, 2.2 GPA; juniors, 2.5 GPA; seniors, 2.5 GPA.
**Special:** Minors offered in many majors and in over 20 other fields. Associate's degrees offered. Double majors. Dual degrees. Independent study. Pass/fail grading option. Internships. Graduate school at which undergraduates may take graduate-level courses. Preprofessional programs in law, medicine, veterinary science, dentistry, physical therapy, and health sciences. Bachelor's/M.B.A. program with U of South Dakota. Member of National Student Exchange (NSE), Western Undergraduate Exchange. Teacher certification in early childhood, elementary, secondary, special education, and vo-tech education. Study abroad in England.
**Honors:** Honors program. Honor societies.
**Academic Assistance:** Remedial reading, writing, and math. Nonremedial tutoring.
**STUDENT LIFE. Housing:** All unmarried students under age 21 must live on campus unless living near campus with relatives. Coed, women's, and men's dorms. 33% of students live in college housing.
**Social atmosphere:** The Den, Dry Dock, and residence hall lobbies are popular on-campus gathering spots. Favorite off-campus haunts include Aquinas Catholic Center, Hardee's, Perkins, Millstone, and bars such as Zoo, Lager's Inn, Last Chance, and On the Rocks. Residence Halls, athletes, non-traditional students, University Programming Council, CHOICES, and the Native American Student Association influence social life. Special schoolyear events include Greek Week, Homecoming, I Hate Winter Weekend, and Spring Fling. According to the student newspaper, students are generally conservative and homogenous, but surprisingly tolerant. Non-traditional students make up over 40 percent of the student body.
**Services and counseling/handicapped student services:** Health service. Day care. Counseling services for veteran students. Personal counseling. Career and academic guidance services. Physically disabled student services. Learning disabled services. Reader services for the blind.
**Campus organizations:** Undergraduate student government. Student newspaper (Exponent, published once/two weeks). Yearbook. TV station. Choir, chamber singers, orchestra, bands, ensembles, Masquers, Fine Arts Society, Circle K, Collegiate 4-H, College Republicans, Young Democrats, 63 organizations in all.
**Religious organizations:** Newman Club, United Ministries.
**Minority/foreign student organizations:** Native American Club, Nontraditional Student Organization. International Club.
**ATHLETICS. Physical education requirements:** Four credits of physical education required.
**Intercollegiate competition:** 14% of students participate. Baseball (M), basketball (M,W), cheerleading (M,W), cross-country (M,W), football (M), golf (M,W), softball (W), tennis (M,W), track (indoor) (M,W), track (outdoor) (M,W), track and field (indoor) (M,W), track and field (outdoor) (M,W), volleyball (W), wrestling (M). Member of NAIA, Northern Intercollegiate Conference, Northern Sun Conference.
**Intramural and club sports:** 40% of students participate. Intramural basketball, racquetball, softball, touch football, volleyball.
**ADMISSIONS. Academic basis for candidate selection** (in order of priority): Secondary school record, class rank, standardized test scores, school's recommendation, essay.
**Nonacademic basis for candidate selection:** Extracurricular participation and particular talent or ability are considered.
**Requirements:** Graduation from secondary school is required; GED is accepted. 13 units and the following program of study are required: 4 units of English, 3 units of social studies, 3 units of mathematics or science, 1 unit of academic electives. Minimum composite ACT score of 20, rank in top two-thirds of secondary school class, and minimum 2.0 GPA required. Conditional admission possible for applicants not meeting standard requirements. ACT is required; SAT may be substituted. Campus visit recommended. No off-campus interviews.
**Procedure:** Take SAT or ACT by October of 12th year. Notification of admission on rolling basis. No set date by which applicants must accept offer. $50 room deposit, refundable until August 1. Freshmen accepted for terms other than fall.
**Special programs:** Admission may be deferred one year. Credit may be granted through CEEB Advanced Placement for scores of 3 or higher. Credit may be granted through CLEP general and subject exams. Concurrent enrollment program.
**Transfer students:** Transfer students accepted for terms other than fall. In fall 1993, 21% of all new students were transfers into all classes. 201 transfer applications were received, 190 were accepted. Application deadline is rolling for fall; rolling for spring. Minimum 2.0 GPA required. Lowest course grade accepted is "C." At least 128 must be completed at the university to receive degree.
**Admissions contact:** Steve Ochsner, Director of Admissions. 605 622-2544.
**FINANCIAL AID. Available aid:** Pell grants, SEOG, state scholarships and grants, school scholarships, private scholarships and grants, academic merit scholarships, athletic scholarships, and aid for undergraduate foreign students. Perkins Loans (NDSL), PLUS, Stafford Loans (GSL), school loans, private loans, and SLS. AMS.
**Financial aid statistics:** 16% of aid is not need-based. In 1993-94, 79% of all undergraduate applicants received aid; 79% of freshman applicants. Average amounts of aid awarded freshmen: Scholarships and grants, $1,637; loans, $2,603.
**Supporting data/closing dates:** FAFSA: Priority filing date is March 1. Notification of awards begins May.
**Financial aid contact:** Sharon Kienow, Director of Financial Aid. 605 622-2640.
**STUDENT EMPLOYMENT.** College Work/Study Program. Institutional employment. 25% of full-time undergraduates work on campus during school year. Students may expect to earn an average of $1,200 during school year. Off-campus part-time employment opportunities rated "excellent."
**COMPUTER FACILITIES.** 500 IBM/IBM-compatible and Macintosh/Apple microcomputers; 30 are networked. Students may access IBM minicomputer/mainframe systems, BITNET. Residence halls may be equipped with stand-alone microcomputers. Computer languages and software packages include BASIC, COBOL, dBASE, Enable, FORTRAN, Lotus 1-2-3, Pascal, RPG, SuperCalc, SuperWriter, WordPerfect; 1,000 in all. Computer facilities are available to all students.
**Fees:** None.
**Hours:** 8 AM-11 PM (M-Th); 8 AM-5 PM (F); 1 PM-5 PM (Sa); 2 PM-10 PM (Su).
**GRADUATE CAREER DATA.** Graduate school percentages: 20% enter graduate arts and sciences programs. Companies and businesses that hire graduates: schools and agencies.

# Oglala Lakota College

**Kyle, SD 57752** **605 455-2321**

**1994-95 Costs.** Tuition: $5,700. Housing: None. Fees, books, misc. academic expenses (school's estimate): $140.
**Enrollment.** Undergraduates: 353 (full-time). Freshman class: 254 enrolled. Graduate enrollment: 71.
**Test score averages/ranges.** N/A.
**Faculty.** 31 full-time; 67 part-time. Student/faculty ratio: 10 to 1.
**Selectivity rating.** N/A.

**PROFILE.** Oglala Lakota, founded in 1971, is a public, historically Native American college. Its campus is in Kyle on the Oglala Sioux reservation, 88 miles from Rapid City.

**Accreditation:** NCACS.
**Religious orientation:** Oglala Lakota College is nonsectarian; no religious requirements.
**Library:** Collections totaling over 29,250 volumes, 179 periodical subscriptions and 160 microform items.
**STUDENT BODY. Undergraduate profile:** 98% Native American, 2% White.
**Undergraduate achievement:** 50% of entering class graduated.
**PROGRAMS OF STUDY. Degrees:** B.S.
**Majors:** Business Administration, Early Childhood, Education, Elementary Education, Human Services.
**Requirements:** General education requirement.
**Special:** Minors offered in bilingual education, small business management, special education, and tribal management. Organic gardening program. Associate's degrees offered. Double majors. Dual degrees. Independent study. Pass/fail grading option. Internships. Cooperative education programs. Preprofessional programs in law. Member of American Indian Higher Education Consortium. Teacher certification in early childhood, special education, vo-tech, and bilingual/bicultural education. Certification in specific subject areas. Study abroad in Germany.
**Honors:** Honors program.
**ADMISSIONS. Academic basis for candidate selection** (in order of priority): Secondary school record.
**Nonacademic basis for candidate selection:** Geographical distribution is considered.
**Requirements:** Graduation from secondary school is required; GED is accepted. No specific distribution of secondary school units required. No off-campus interviews.

**Procedure:** Notification of admission by January 25. Reply is required by registration. $15 tuition deposit, refundable until February 5. Freshmen accepted for terms other than fall.
**Special programs:** Placement may be granted through challenge exams and life experience. Early entrance/early admission program. Concurrent enrollment program.
**Transfer students:** Transfer students accepted for terms other than fall. Application deadline is August 25 for fall; January 21 for spring.
**Admissions contact:** Ms. Walean Herman, Director of Admissions. 605 455-2321, extension 226.

**FINANCIAL AID. Available aid:** Pell grants, school scholarships, private scholarships, and academic merit scholarships. Family tuition reduction and guaranteed tuition.
**Financial aid statistics:** In 1992-93, 65% of all freshman applicants received aid.
**Supporting data/closing dates:** School's own aid application. Income tax forms.
**Financial aid contact:** Elizabeth Big Crow, Director of Financial Aid. 605 455-2321, extensions 245, 227.

# Sioux Falls College

**Sioux Falls, SD 57105-1699 605 331-5000**

**1994-95 Costs.** Tuition: $8,990. Room: $1,290. Board: $1,800. Fees, books, misc. academic expenses (school's estimate): $400.
**Enrollment.** Undergraduates: 271 men, 343 women (full-time). Freshman class: 437 applicants, 400 accepted, 250 enrolled. Graduate enrollment: 20 men, 46 women.
**Test score averages/ranges.** Average ACT scores: 21 composite.
**Faculty.** 37 full-time; 32 part-time. 65% of faculty holds highest degree in specific field. Student/faculty ratio: 16 to 1.
**Selectivity rating.** Competitive.

**PROFILE.** Sioux Falls, founded in 1883, is a private, church-affiliated, multipurpose college. Its 20-acre campus is located in Sioux Falls.

**Accreditation:** NCACS. Professionally accredited by the Council on Social Work Education, the National Council for Accreditation of Teacher Education.
**Religious orientation:** Sioux Falls College is affiliated with the American Baptist Churches in the U.S.A.; two semesters of religion required.
**Library:** Collections totaling over 75,000 volumes and 450 periodical subscriptions.
**Special facilities/museums:** Education curriculum lab, physiology lab, autoclave for research in diagnostic medicine.
**Athletic facilities:** Basketball, racquetball, tennis, and volleyball courts, batting cage, football field, gymnasium, track, and weight room.

**STUDENT BODY. Undergraduate profile:** 72% are state residents; 30% are transfers. 1% Asian-American, 1% Black, 97% White, 1% Other. Average age of undergraduates is 21.
**Freshman profile:** 82% of accepted applicants took ACT. 95% of freshmen come from public schools.
**Undergraduate achievement:** 45% of fall 1992 freshmen returned for fall 1993 term. 20% of entering class graduated. 15% of students who completed a degree program went on to graduate study within one year.
**Foreign students:** 11 students are from out of the country. Countries represented include African countries, Canada, India, Japan, and Mongolia; eight in all.

**PROGRAMS OF STUDY. Degrees:** B.A., B.S.
**Majors:** Applied Mathematics, Applied Science, Art, Biology, Business Administration, Chemistry, Computer Information Systems, Computer Science, Elementary Education, English, Exercise Science, Health/Physical Education, History, Humanities, Interdisciplinary, Mass Communications, Mathematics, Medical Technology, Music, Music Education, Office Administration, Political Science/History, Psychology, Public Accounting, Radiologic Technology, Religious Studies, Social Sciences, Social Work, Sociology, Speech Communication/Theatre, Wellness/Fitness Leadership, Wellness Program Management.
**Distribution of degrees:** The majors with the highest enrollment are business administration, education, and social science/psychology; art, sociology, and speech communication/theatre have the lowest.
**Requirements:** General education requirement.
**Academic regulations:** Freshmen must maintain minimum 1.5 GPA; sophomores, 1.75 GPA; juniors, 2.0 GPA; seniors, 2.0 GPA.
**Special:** Minors offered as concentrations within majors. Self-designed majors. Double majors. Independent study. Pass/fail grading option. Internships. Graduate school at which undergraduates may take graduate-level courses. Preprofessional programs in law, medicine, veterinary science, and theology. 2-2 program with North American Baptist Coll (Edmonton, Alberta, Canada). B.A/M.Div. program with North American Baptist Seminary. 3-2 engineering program with South Dakota State U. Member of Colleges of Mid-America Consortium, Christian College Coalition. Washington Semester. Interim study program with travel or attendance at another college on same 4-1-4 schedule. Teacher certification in early childhood, elementary, secondary, and special education. Certification in specific subject areas. Exchange program abroad in Japan (Kansai Gaidai). Study abroad also in China.
**Honors:** Honors program. Honor societies.
**Academic Assistance:** Remedial writing and math. Nonremedial tutoring.

**ADMISSIONS. Academic basis for candidate selection** (in order of priority): Secondary school record, standardized test scores, school's recommendation, class rank.
**Nonacademic basis for candidate selection:** Character and personality are emphasized. Extracurricular participation is important. Particular talent or ability is considered.
**Requirements:** Graduation from secondary school is required; GED is accepted. No specific distribution of secondary school units required. Minimum composite ACT score of 19 (combined SAT score of 850), rank in top half of secondary school class, or minimum 2.0 GPA recommended. Portfolio recommended of art program applicants. Audition recommended of music program applicants. Conditional admission possible for applicants not meeting standard requirements. SAT or ACT is required. Campus visit and interview recommended. Off-campus interviews available with an admissions representative.
**Procedure:** Notification of admission on rolling basis. $100 room deposit, refundable until 30 days prior to beginning of semester. Freshmen accepted for terms other than fall.
**Special programs:** Admission may be deferred. Credit and/or placement may be granted through CEEB Advanced Placement exams for scores of 4 or higher. Credit and/or placement may be granted through CLEP general and subject exams. Credit and placement may be granted through life experience. Early entrance/early admission program. Concurrent enrollment program.
**Transfer students:** Transfer students accepted for terms other than fall. In fall 1993, 30% of all new students were transfers into all classes. 52 transfer applications were received, 52 were accepted. Application deadline is rolling for fall; rolling for spring. Minimum 2.0 GPA recommended. Lowest course grade accepted is "D." Maximum number of transferable credits is 98 semester hours. At least 30 semester hours must be completed at the college to receive degree.
**Admissions contact:** Susan Reese, Director of Admissions. 605 331-6600.

**FINANCIAL AID. Available aid:** Pell grants, SEOG, state scholarships and grants, school scholarships and grants, private scholarships and grants, academic merit scholarships, and athletic scholarships. Perkins Loans (NDSL), PLUS, Stafford Loans (GSL), and SLS.
**Financial aid statistics:** 20% of aid is not need-based. In 1993-94, 94% of all undergraduate applicants received aid; 83% of freshman applicants. Average amounts of aid awarded freshmen: Scholarships and grants, $2,213; loans, $3,260.
**Supporting data/closing dates:** FAFSA/FAF/FFS: Priority filing date is April 1. School's own aid application: Priority filing date is April 1. State aid form: Priority filing date is April 1. Notification of awards begins April 1.
**Financial aid contact:** Patricia Ziegler, Director of Financial Aid. 605 331-6623.

# South Dakota School of Mines and Technology

**Rapid City, SD 57701-3995 605 394-2511**

**1994-95 Costs.** Tuition: $1,545 (state residents), $4,049 (out-of-state). Room: $1,200. Board: $1,700. Fees, books, misc. academic expenses (school's estimate): $1,962.
**Enrollment.** Undergraduates: 1,241 men, 450 women (full-time). Freshman class: 462 applicants, 410 accepted, 366 enrolled. Graduate enrollment: 213 men, 33 women.
**Test score averages/ranges.** Average ACT scores: 22 English, 27 math, 25 composite.
**Faculty.** 114 full-time; 17 part-time. 78% of faculty holds doctoral degree. Student/faculty ratio: 16 to 1.
**Selectivity rating.** Competitive.

**PROFILE.** The South Dakota School of Mines, founded in 1885, is a public institution of engineering and related sciences. Its 120-acre campus is located in Rapid City, in southwestern South Dakota.

**Accreditation:** NCACS. Professionally accredited by the Accreditation Board for Engineering and Technology.
**Religious orientation:** South Dakota School of Mines and Technology is nonsectarian; no religious requirements.
**Library:** Collections totaling over 106,000 volumes, 961 periodical subscriptions, and 194,414 microform items.
**Special facilities/museums:** Museum of geology and paleontology, electron microscope, engineering/mining experiment station, atmospheric science and other research institutes.
**Athletic facilities:** Gymnasiums, basketball, racquetball, squash, and volleyball courts, football and softball fields, dance, exercise, and weight rooms, swimming pool, all-weather track.

**STUDENT BODY. Undergraduate profile:** 82% are state residents; 32% are transfers. 1% Asian-American, 2% Black, 1% Hispanic, 1% Native American, 88% White, 7% Other. Average age of undergraduates is 24.
**Freshman profile:** 5% of freshmen who took ACT scored 30 or over on composite; 42% scored 24 or over on composite; 88% scored 18 or over on composite; 98% scored 12 or over on composite; 100% scored 6 or over on composite. 5% of accepted applicants took SAT; 95% took ACT. 95% of freshmen come from public schools.
**Undergraduate achievement:** 70% of fall 1992 freshmen returned for fall 1993 term. 37% of entering class graduated. 12% of students who completed a degree program immediately went on to graduate study.
**Foreign students:** 84 students are from out of the country. Countries represented include China, Norway, and Pakistan; 14 in all.

**PROGRAMS OF STUDY. Degrees:** B.S.
**Majors:** Chemical Engineering, Chemistry, Civil Engineering, Computer Engineering, Computer Science, Electrical Engineering, Geological Engineering, Geology, Industrial Engineering, Interdisciplinary Science, Mathematics, Mechanical Engineering, Metallurgical Engineering, Mining Engineering, Physics.
**Distribution of degrees:** The majors with the highest enrollment are mechanical engineering, electrical engineering, and civil engineering; physics, geology, and mathematics have the lowest.
**Requirements:** General education requirement.
**Academic regulations:** Freshmen must maintain minimum 1.8 GPA; sophomores, juniors, seniors, 2.0 GPA.

**Special:** Minors offered in all areas of science. Engineering students must take courses in humanities and social sciences. Program of transfer studies offered. College hosts seminars, lectures, conferences, and workshops. Double majors. Cooperative education programs. Graduate school at which undergraduates may take graduate-level courses. Preprofessional programs in medicine. ROTC.
**Academic Assistance:** Remedial study skills. Nonremedial tutoring.

**STUDENT LIFE. Housing:** All freshmen and sophomores must live on campus. Women's and men's dorms. Sorority and fraternity housing. Off-campus privately-owned housing. 25% of students live in college housing.
**Services and counseling/handicapped student services:** Placement services. Counseling services for military students. Personal counseling. Career and academic guidance services. Physically disabled student services. Learning disabled services.
**Campus organizations:** Undergraduate student government. Student newspaper (Tech, published once/month). Radio station. Drama and ski clubs, Singing Engineers, Master Chorale, jazz band, flying and martial arts clubs, Circle K. Four fraternities, all with chapter houses; two sororities, all with chapter houses. 20% of men join a fraternity. 19% of women join a sorority.
**Religious organizations:** Intervarsity Christian Fellowship, United Ministries in Higher Education, Lutheran Campus Ministry.
**Minority/foreign student organizations:** International Student Association, Association of Norwegian Students Abroad.

**ATHLETICS. Physical education requirements:** Two semesters of physical education required.
**Intercollegiate competition:** 7% of students participate. Basketball (M,W), cross-country (M,W), football (M), track (indoor) (M,W), track (outdoor) (M,W), track and field (indoor) (M,W), track and field (outdoor) (M,W), volleyball (W). Member of NAIA, SDIC.
**Intramural and club sports:** 30% of students participate. Intramural basketball, flag football, golf, softball, volleyball. Men's club cheerleading, martial arts, soccer. Women's club cheerleading, martial arts.

**ADMISSIONS. Academic basis for candidate selection** (in order of priority): Secondary school record, class rank, standardized test scores.
**Requirements:** Graduation from secondary school is required; GED is accepted. No specific distribution of secondary school units required. Minimum composite ACT score of 22 or rank in top half of secondary school class required of in-state applicants; minimum composite ACT score of 23 or rank in top half of secondary school class required of out-of-state applicants. ACT is required; SAT may be substituted. Campus visit recommended. No off-campus interviews.
**Procedure:** Take SAT or ACT by October of 12th year. Visit college for interview by January of 12th year. Notification of admission on rolling basis. $60 room deposit, refundable until August 1. Freshmen accepted for terms other than fall.
**Special programs:** Credit and/or placement may be granted through CEEB Advanced Placement exams for scores of 4 or higher. Credit and/or placement may be granted through CLEP general and subject exams. Credit and placement may be granted through challenge exams and military and life experience. Concurrent enrollment program.
**Transfer students:** Transfer students accepted for terms other than fall. In fall 1993, 32% of all new students were transfers into all classes. 302 transfer applications were received, 290 were accepted. Application deadline is August 15 for fall; December 15 for spring. Minimum 2.0 GPA required. Lowest course grade accepted is "C." Maximum number of transferable credits is 98 semester hours. At least 32 semester hours must be completed at the college to receive degree.
**Admissions contact:** Gary A. Bjordal, M.A., Director of Admissions. 605 394-2400.

**FINANCIAL AID. Available aid:** Pell grants, SEOG, state scholarships and grants, school scholarships, private scholarships, ROTC scholarships, academic merit scholarships, and athletic scholarships. Perkins Loans (NDSL), PLUS, Stafford Loans (GSL), and SLS. AMS.
**Financial aid statistics:** 20% of aid is not need-based. In 1993-94, 98% of all undergraduate applicants received aid; 96% of freshman applicants. Average amounts of aid awarded freshmen: Scholarships and grants, $543; loans, $2,600.
**Supporting data/closing dates:** FAFSA: Priority filing date is April 15. State aid form: Priority filing date is April 15; accepted on rolling basis. Notification of awards begins April 15.
**Financial aid contact:** Sharon Colombe, M.A., Director of Financial Aid. 605 394-2274.

**STUDENT EMPLOYMENT.** College Work/Study Program. Institutional employment. 24% of full-time undergraduates work on campus during school year. Students may expect to earn an average of $1,800 during school year. Off-campus part-time employment opportunities rated "good."

**COMPUTER FACILITIES.** 310 IBM/IBM-compatible microcomputers; all are networked. Students may access CDC Cyber minicomputer/mainframe systems. Residence halls may be equipped with stand-alone microcomputers. Computer languages and software packages include Assembly, BASIC, BMDP, C, COBOL, FORTRAN, LISP, Pascal, SPSS. Computer facilities are available to all students.
**Fees:** Computer fee is included in tuition/fees.
**Hours:** 24 hours/day.

**GRADUATE CAREER DATA.** Graduate school percentages: 1% enter law school. 1% enter medical school. 2% enter graduate business programs. Highest graduate school enrollments: Arizona State U, Iowa State U, MIT, South Dakota Sch of Mines and Tech, U of Colorado, U of South Dakota. 80% of graduates choose careers in business and industry. Companies and businesses that hire graduates: Boeing, Cargill, Dow Chemical, DuPont, Texas Instruments, Dow Corning, Exxon, John Deere, Shell Oil.

**PROMINENT ALUMNI/AE.** Frank Richardson, president, Shell Oil; Thomas Bolger, CEO, Bell Atlantic.

# South Dakota State University

**Brookings, SD 57007** **605 688-4121**

**1994-95 Costs.** Tuition: $1,432 (state, Minnesota, and Wyoming residents), $3,800 (out-of-state). Room & board: $2,080. Fees, books, misc. academic expenses (school's estimate): $1,340.
**Enrollment.** Undergraduates: 3,708 men, 3,292 women (full-time). Freshman class: 2,807 applicants, 2,589 accepted, 1,717 enrolled. Graduate enrollment: 663 men, 770 women.
**Test score averages/ranges.** Average ACT scores: 23 composite.
**Faculty.** 510 full-time; 49 part-time. 75% of faculty holds doctoral degree. Student/faculty ratio: 17 to 1.
**Selectivity rating.** Less competitive.

**PROFILE.** South Dakota State, founded in 1881, is a public, comprehensive university. Programs are offered through the Colleges of Agriculture, Arts and Sciences, Education, Engineering, Home Economics, Nursing, Pharmacy, and the Graduate School. Its 220-acre campus is located in Brookings, 50 miles from Sioux Falls.
**Accreditation:** NCACS. Professionally accredited by the Accreditation Board for Engineering and Technology, the Accrediting Council on Education in Journalism and Mass Communication, the American Council on Pharmaceutical Education, the American Dietetic Association, the American Home Economics Association, the National Association of Schools of Music, the National Council for Accreditation of Teacher Education, the National League for Nursing.
**Religious orientation:** South Dakota State University is nonsectarian; no religious requirements.
**Library:** Collections totaling over 700,000 volumes, 3,500 periodical subscriptions, and 558,101 microform items.
**Special facilities/museums:** Art museum, agricultural heritage museum, bio-stress lab, electron microscope.
**Athletic facilities:** Physical education center, swimming pool, indoor track, weight and wrestling rooms, dance studios, field house, basketball, racquetball, and tennis courts, wellness facility.
**STUDENT BODY. Undergraduate profile:** 75% are state residents; 34% are transfers. 1% Asian-American, 1% Black, 1% Native American, 97% White. Average age of undergraduates is 19.
**Freshman profile:** 90% of accepted applicants took ACT. 95% of freshmen come from public schools.
**Undergraduate achievement:** 80% of fall 1992 freshmen returned for fall 1993 term.
**Foreign students:** 261 students are from out of the country. Countries represented include Bangladesh, China, India, Korea, Malaysia, and Pakistan; 44 in all.
**PROGRAMS OF STUDY. Degrees:** B.A., B.Mus.Ed., B.S., B.S.Tech.
**Majors:** Agricultural Business, Agricultural Economics, Agricultural Education, Agricultural Engineering, Agricultural Extension, Agricultural Journalism, Agronomy, Animal Science, Art, Athletic Training, Biochemistry, Biology, Botany, Chemistry, Civil Engineering, Clinical Lab Technology, Communication Studies/Theatre, Computer Science, Consumer Affairs, Dairy Manufacturing, Dairy Production, Dairy Science, Economics, Education, Electrical Engineering, Electronics Engineering Technology, Engineering Physics, English, Environmental Management, Food/Bio-Materials Engineering, General Agriculture, General Studies, Geography, German, Health/Physical Education/Recreation, History, Home Economics Education, Horticulture, Hotel/Restaurant/Institution Management, Human Development/Child/Family Studies, Interior Design, Journalism, Landscape Design, Mathematics, Mechanical Engineering, Mechanized Agriculture, Microbiology, Music, Music Education, Music Merchandising, Nursing, Nutrition/Food Science, Park Management, Physics, Plant Pathology, Political Science, Pre-Veterinary Science, Printing Education, Printing Journalism, Printing Management, Psychological Services, Public Recreation, Range Science, Rural Sociology, Sociology, Spanish, Textiles/Clothing, Wildlife/Fisheries Science, Zoology.
**Distribution of degrees:** The majors with the highest enrollment are nursing, economics, and sociology; physics, public recreation, and music have the lowest.
**Requirements:** General education requirement.
**Academic regulations:** Freshmen must maintain minimum 1.5 GPA; sophomores, 1.7 GPA; juniors, 1.8 GPA; seniors, 1.9 GPA.
**Special:** Minors offered. Associate's degrees offered. Double majors. Independent study. Pass/fail grading option. Internships. Cooperative education programs. Graduate school at which undergraduates may take graduate-level courses. Preprofessional programs in law, medicine, veterinary science, dentistry, theology, optometry, chiropractic, mortuary science, and physical therapy. Six-year Pharm.D. program. Semester at Fashion Inst of Tech for home economics majors. Exchange programs with Black Hills State U and Dakota State U for elementary education and with U of South Dakota for criminal justice. Member of National Student Exchange (NSE). Teacher certification in early childhood and secondary education. Certification in specific subject areas. ROTC and AFROTC.
**Honors:** Honors program. Honor societies.

**STUDENT LIFE. Housing:** All students out of secondary school less than two years must live on campus unless living with family. Coed dorms. Sorority and fraternity housing. School-owned/operated apartments. On-campus married-student housing. 40% of students live in college housing.
**Social atmosphere:** According to the student newspaper, "SDSU is the social and cultural center of Brookings. When school is in session, the town doubles in size." The influential groups on campus include Greeks, varsity athletes, the university program council, the Students Association Senate, the newspaper staff, and the theatre department. The most popular events of the year include Hobo Day (Homecoming), games with the U of South Dakota, basketball games, Spring Fling, Binnewies Bash, International Day, Dance for

Dystrophy, and the Jackrabbit Stampede. On-campus hangouts are Jack's Place, a deli, and the Grand Market Place cafeteria. Off campus, students frequent Jim's Tap.
**Services and counseling/handicapped student services:** Placement services. Health service. Counseling services for veteran students. Personal counseling. Career and academic guidance services. Learning disabled services.
**Campus organizations:** Undergraduate student government. Student newspaper (Collegian, published once/week). Yearbook. Radio and TV stations. Concert and marching bands, chorus, other singing groups, orchestra, debating, oratory group, Young Democrats, Young Republicans, 160 organizations in all. Five fraternities, four chapter houses; three sororities, two chapter houses. 4% of men join a fraternity. 3% of women join a sorority.
**Religious organizations:** Baptist Student Union, Campus Crusade for Christ, Catholic Campus Parish, University Lutheran Center, United Ministries, Moslem Student Association, other religious groups.
**Minority/foreign student organizations:** International Relations Club, African, Arab, Iranian, Latin American, Malaysian, and Palestinian groups.
**ATHLETICS. Physical education requirements:** Two semesters of physical education required.
**Intercollegiate competition:** 19% of students participate. Baseball (M), basketball (M,W), cross-country (M,W), diving (M,W), football (M), golf (M,W), softball (W), swimming (M,W), tennis (M,W), track (indoor) (M,W), track (outdoor) (M,W), track and field (indoor) (M,W), track and field (outdoor) (M,W), volleyball (W), wrestling (M). Member of NCAA Division II, North Central Conference.
**Intramural and club sports:** 70% of students participate. Intramural aerobics, badminton, basketball, broom hockey, dance, fencing, flag football, football, golf, ice hockey, racquetball, softball, snow softball, tennis, track and field, volleyball, water polo, wrestling. Men's club archery, badminton, dance, fencing, ice hockey, karate, rugby, soccer, tae kwon do, tennis, weight lifting. Women's club archery, badminton, dance, fencing, tae kwon do, tennis, weight lifting.
**ADMISSIONS. Academic basis for candidate selection** (in order of priority): Secondary school record, standardized test scores, class rank.
**Nonacademic basis for candidate selection:** Particular talent or ability is considered.
**Requirements:** Graduation from secondary school is required; GED is accepted. 13 units and the following program of study are required: 4 units of English, 2 units of math, 2 units of lab science, 3 units of social studies. 1 additional year of math or science with lab required. 1/2 unit each of fine arts and computer science also required. Applicants not achieving grade of "C" in listed courses must meet one of the following standards: Minimum composite ACT score of 22 for South Dakota and Minnesota applicants (minimum score of 23 for others) or rank in top half of secondary school class. Audition required of music program applicants. Conditional admission possible for applicants not meeting standard requirements. ACT is required. Campus visit and interview recommended. No off-campus interviews.
**Procedure:** Take ACT by December of 12th year. Visit college for interview by January of 12th year. Suggest filing application by January. Application deadline is August 15. Notification of admission on rolling basis. Reply is required by beginning of term. $50 room deposit, refundable until June 30. Freshmen accepted for terms other than fall.
**Special programs:** Admission may be deferred one year. Credit may be granted through CEEB Advanced Placement for scores of 3 or higher. Credit may be granted through CLEP general exams, ACT PEP, DANTES, and challenge exams, and military experience. Credit and/or placement may be granted through CLEP subject exams. Concurrent enrollment program.
**Transfer students:** Transfer students accepted for terms other than fall. In fall 1993, 34% of all new students were transfers into all classes. 995 transfer applications were received, 859 were accepted. Application deadline is August 15 for fall; January 7 for spring. ACT required of applicants who are under age 21. Minimum 2.0 GPA required. Lowest course grade accepted is "C." Maximum number of transferable credits is 64 semester hours from two-year schools. At least 32 semester hours must be completed at the university to receive degree.
**Admissions contact:** Tracy Welsh, Acting Director of Admissions. 605 688-4121.
**FINANCIAL AID. Available aid:** Pell grants, SEOG, Federal Nursing Student Scholarships, state scholarships and grants, school scholarships and grants, private scholarships and grants, ROTC scholarships, academic merit scholarships, and athletic scholarships. Perkins Loans (NDSL), PLUS, Stafford Loans (GSL), NSL, Health Professions Loans, state loans, school loans, private loans, and SLS. AMS and Tuition Management Systems.
**Financial aid statistics:** 6% of aid is not need-based. In 1993-94, 92% of all undergraduate applicants received aid; 94% of freshman applicants. Average amounts of aid awarded freshmen: Scholarships and grants, $1,736; loans, $1,890.
**Supporting data/closing dates:** FAFSA/FAF/FFS: Priority filing date is March 15; accepted on rolling basis. Educational Assistance Corp. form: Priority filing date is March 15; accepted on rolling basis. Notification of awards begins April 12.
**Financial aid contact:** Jay A. Larsen, Director of Financial Aids. 605 688-4695.
**STUDENT EMPLOYMENT.** College Work/Study Program. Institutional employment. 10% of full-time undergraduates work on campus during school year. Students may expect to earn an average of $1,100 during school year. Off-campus part-time employment opportunities rated "excellent."
**COMPUTER FACILITIES.** 204 IBM/IBM-compatible and Macintosh/Apple microcomputers; 150 are networked. Computer languages and software packages include Assembly, BASIC, C, COBOL, FORTRAN, LISP, Pascal, PL/1; compiling, database, spreadsheet, word processing programs. Computer facilities are available to all students.
**Fees:** Computer fee is included in tuition/fees.
**GRADUATE CAREER DATA.** Highest graduate school enrollments: South Dakota State U, U of South Dakota.
**PROMINENT ALUMNI/AE.** William F. DuDuy, four-star general, U.S. Army; George Hamm, president, U of Texas at Tyler; Stephen F. Briggs, engineer; Alvin Shock, president, Nordica International; Palmer "Pete" Retzlaff, NFL MVP in 1965; Nels Hanson, agronomist; Theodore Schultz, Nobel Prize-winning economist; Eugene Amdahl, physics engineer.

# University of South Dakota at Vermillion

**Vermillion, SD 57069 — 605 677-5011**

**1994-95 Costs.** Tuition: $1,454 (state residents), $3,811 (out-of-state). Room: $1,208. Board: $1,464. Fees, books, misc. academic expenses (school's estimate): $2,542.
**Enrollment.** Undergraduates: 2,584 men, 3,278 women (full-time). Freshman class: 2,160 applicants, 2,031 accepted, 1,268 enrolled. Graduate enrollment: 764 men, 991 women.
**Test score averages/ranges.** Average ACT scores: 21 English, 21 math, 22 composite. Range of ACT scores of middle 50%: 18-23 English, 17-23 math.
**Faculty.** 77% of faculty holds doctoral degree. Student/faculty ratio: 17 to 1.
**Selectivity rating.** Less competitive.

**PROFILE.** University of South Dakota-Vermillion, founded in 1862, is a public, comprehensive institution. Programs are offered through the Colleges of Arts and Sciences and Fine Arts; the Schools of Business, Education, Law, and Medicine; and the Graduate School. Its 216-acre campus is located in Vermillion, 40 miles northwest of Sioux City, Iowa.

**Accreditation:** NCACS. Professionally accredited by the American Assembly of Collegiate Schools of Business, the American Dental Association, the American Psychological Association, the American Speech-Language-Hearing Association, the Council on Social Work Education, the National Association of Schools of Art and Design, the National Association of Schools of Music, the National Association of Schools of Theatre, the National Council for Accreditation of Teacher Education, the National League for Nursing.
**Religious orientation:** University of South Dakota at Vermillion is nonsectarian; no religious requirements.
**Library:** Collections totaling over 445,215 volumes and 2,687 periodical subscriptions.
**Special facilities/museums:** Art galleries, fine arts center, natural history museum, music museum, business research bureau, center for developmental disabilities, American Indian studies institute, archaeology lab, human factors lab, social science research institute, telecommunication center, governmental research bureau.
**Athletic facilities:** Swimming pool, basketball, tennis, and volleyball courts, baseball, soccer, and softball fields, track.

**STUDENT BODY. Undergraduate profile:** 74% are state residents; 24% are transfers. 5% Asian-American, 1% Black, .5% Hispanic, 3% Native American, 93% White, 2% Other.
**Freshman profile:** Majority of accepted applicants took ACT. 93% of freshmen come from public schools.
**Undergraduate achievement:** 72% of fall 1992 freshmen returned for fall 1993 term.
**Foreign students:** 94 students are from out of the country. Countries represented include China, Germany, India, Korea, Malaysia, and Turkey; 47 in all.

**PROGRAMS OF STUDY. Degrees:** B.A., B.F.A., B.Lib.Studies, B.Mus., B.S.
**Majors:** Accounting, Alcohol/Drug Abuse, Anesthesia, Anthropology, Applied Music, Art, Biology, Botany, Business Management, Chemistry, Classical Humanities, Classics, Communication, Communication Disorders, Computer Science, Criminal Justice, Dental Hygiene, Earth Science, Economics, Elementary Education, English, Fisheries Biology, French, German, Greek, Health Services Administration, History, Latin, Liberal Studies, Mass Communication, Mathematics, Medical Technology, Music, Philosophy, Physical Education, Physician Assistant Studies, Physics, Political Science, Psychology, Public Recreation, Secondary Education, Social Work, Sociology, Spanish, Special Education, Statistics, Theatre.
**Distribution of degrees:** The majors with the highest enrollment are biology and psychology.
**Requirements:** General education requirement.
**Academic regulations:** Freshmen must maintain minimum 1.65 GPA; sophomores, 1.8 GPA; juniors, 1.9 GPA; seniors, 2.0 GPA.
**Special:** Minors offered. Minor required in some majors in order to graduate. Preparation for American Foreign Service. Associate's degrees offered. Self-designed majors. Double majors. Dual degrees. Independent study. Accelerated study. Pass/fail grading option. Internships. Graduate school at which undergraduates may take graduate-level courses. Preprofessional programs in law, medicine, veterinary science, dentistry, theology, optometry, engineering, occupational therapy, osteopathy, and physical therapy. 3-2 accounting program. Member of National Student Exchange (NSE). Teacher certification in elementary, secondary, and special education. Certification in specific subject areas. Exchange programs abroad in France (U of Orleans) and Germany (U of Oldenburg). ROTC.
**Honors:** Phi Beta Kappa. Honors program.
**Academic Assistance:** Remedial reading, writing, math, and study skills. Nonremedial tutoring.

**STUDENT LIFE. Housing:** All unmarried students under age 21 must live on campus unless living near campus with relatives. Coed and women's dorms. Sorority and fraternity housing. School-owned/operated apartments. 27% of students live in college housing.
**Services and counseling/handicapped student services:** Placement services. Health service. Day care. Counseling services for minority, veteran, and older students. Birth control, personal, and psychological counseling. Career and academic guidance services. Religious counseling. Physically disabled student services. Learning disabled services. Tape recorders. Tutors. Reader services for the blind.
**Campus organizations:** Undergraduate student government. Student newspaper (Volante, published once/week). Literary magazine. Yearbook. Radio and TV stations. Chorus, band, orchestra, Adopt-a-Grandparent Program, debating, Student Ambassadors, Strollers, Dakota Days Committee, College Republicans, Young Democrats, 108 orga-

nizations in all. Eight fraternities, all with chapter houses; five sororities, all with chapter houses. 15% of men join a fraternity. 15% of women join a sorority.
**Religious organizations:** Various religious groups.
**Minority/foreign student organizations:** Students for Civil and Human Rights, Tiospaye Council. International Student Club, Chinese Student Friendship Association.

**ATHLETICS. Physical education requirements:** None.
**Intercollegiate competition:** 19% of students participate. Baseball (M), basketball (M,W), cheerleading (M,W), cross-country (M,W), diving (M,W), football (M), softball (W), swimming (M,W), tennis (M,W), track (indoor) (M,W), track (outdoor) (M,W), track and field (indoor) (M,W), track and field (outdoor) (M,W), volleyball (W). Member of NCAA Division II, North Central Intercollegiate Athletic Conference.
**Intramural and club sports:** 62% of students participate. Intramural badminton, basketball, bowling, cross-country, cycling, flag football, golf, racquetball, soccer, softball, swimming, table tennis, tennis, track and field, trapshooting, volleyball, wrestling. Men's club fencing, hockey, rugby, soccer, tae kwon do. Women's club fencing, soccer, tae kwon do.

**ADMISSIONS. Academic basis for candidate selection** (in order of priority): Secondary school record, class rank, standardized test scores.
**Nonacademic basis for candidate selection:** Character and personality, extracurricular participation, and particular talent or ability are considered.
**Requirements:** Graduation from secondary school is recommended; GED is accepted. 13 units and the following program of study are required: 4 units of English, 2 units of math, 2 units of lab science, 3 units of social studies, 1 unit of academic electives. Computer science, fine arts, and foreign language recommended. Minimum composite ACT score of 22 or rank in top half of secondary school class recommended of in-state applicants; minimum composite ACT score of 23 or rank in top half of secondary school class recommended of out-of-state applicants. Special applications required of nursing, dental hygiene, and physician assistant program applicants. Conditional admission possible for applicants not meeting standard requirements. ACT is required; SAT may be substituted. PSAT is recommended. Campus visit recommended. No off-campus interviews.
**Procedure:** Take SAT or ACT by June of 12th year. Suggest filing application by January 1; no deadline. Notification of admission on rolling basis. $100 room deposit, refundable until June 30. Freshmen accepted for terms other than fall.
**Special programs:** Credit and/or placement may be granted through CEEB Advanced Placement exams for scores of 3 or higher. Credit and/or placement may be granted through CLEP subject exams. Credit may be granted through military experience. Credit and placement may be granted through DANTES and challenge exams. Concurrent enrollment program.
**Transfer students:** Transfer students accepted for terms other than fall. In fall 1993, 24% of all new students were transfers into all classes. 897 transfer applications were received, 643 were accepted. Application deadline is August 15 for fall; December 31 for spring. Minimum 2.0 GPA required. Lowest course grade accepted is "D." Maximum number of transferable credits is 64 semester hours. At least 30 semester hours must be completed at the university to receive degree.
**Admissions contact:** David Lorenz, M.P.A., Associate Dean of Students/Director of Admissions. 605 677-5434.

**FINANCIAL AID. Available aid:** Pell grants, SEOG, state scholarships and grants, school scholarships, private scholarships and grants, ROTC scholarships, academic merit scholarships, and athletic scholarships. Perkins Loans (NDSL), PLUS, Stafford Loans (GSL), NSL, Health Professions Loans, private loans, and SLS. AMS.
**Financial aid statistics:** 20% of aid is not need-based. In 1993-94, 85% of all undergraduate applicants received aid; 85% of freshman applicants. Average amounts of aid awarded freshmen: Scholarships and grants, $1,000; loans, $2,500.
**Supporting data/closing dates:** FAFSA: Priority filing date is February 15; accepted on rolling basis. FAF/FFS: Priority filing date is February 15. Notification of awards on rolling basis.
**Financial aid contact:** Clarence Shoemaker, M.S., Director of Financial Aid. 605 677-5446.

**STUDENT EMPLOYMENT.** College Work/Study Program. Institutional employment. 34% of full-time undergraduates work on campus during school year. Students may expect to earn an average of $1,700 during school year. Off-campus part-time employment opportunities rated "fair."

**COMPUTER FACILITIES.** 1,000 IBM/IBM-compatible and Macintosh/Apple microcomputers; 200 are networked. Students may access Digital, IBM, SUN minicomputer/mainframe systems, Internet. Residence halls may be equipped with stand-alone microcomputers. Client/LAN operating systems include Apple/Macintosh, DOS, OS/2, UNIX/XENIX/AIX, LocalTalk/AppleTalk, Novell. Computer languages and software packages include BASIC A, dBASE, GW Basic, Hyper Card, Lexus, Lotus 1-2-3, Minitab, Nexus, Pascal, Turbo Pascal, WordPerfect. Computer facilities are available to all students.
**Fees:** Computer fee is included in tuition/fees.

**PROMINENT ALUMNI/AE.** Tom Brokaw, NBC news anchor; Pat O'Brien, CBS sports commentator; Ernest O. Lawrence, Nobel prize winner (1939).

# Tennessee

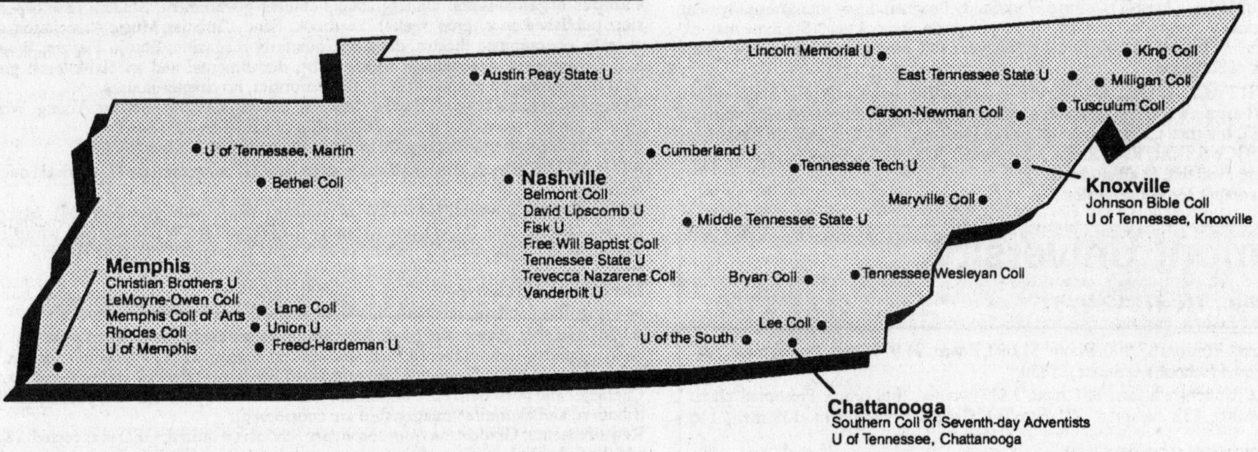


## Austin Peay State University

**Clarksville, TN 37044** **615 648-7011**

**1994-95 Costs.** Tuition: $1,700 (state residents), $5,869 (out-of-state). Room: $1,390. Board: $1,258. Fees, books, misc. academic expenses (school's estimate): $646.
**Enrollment.** Undergraduates: 1,769 men, 2,739 women (full-time). Freshman class: 1,492 applicants, 1,229 accepted, 640 enrolled. Graduate enrollment: 110 men, 303 women.
**Test score averages/ranges.** Average ACT scores: 20 composite.
**Faculty.** 212 full-time; 200 part-time. 69% of faculty holds doctoral degree. Student/faculty ratio: 18 to 1.
**Selectivity rating.** Less competitive.

**PROFILE.** Austin Peay State, founded in 1927, is a public, comprehensive university. The 470-acre campus is located in Clarksville, 25 miles northwest of Nashville.

**Accreditation:** SACS. Professionally accredited by the Council on Social Work Education, the National Association of Schools of Music, the National Council for Accreditation of Teacher Education, the National League for Nursing.
**Religious orientation:** Austin Peay State University is nonsectarian; no religious requirements.
**Library:** Collections totaling over 3,787 volumes, 2,178 periodical subscriptions, and 22,400 microform items.
**Special facilities/museums:** Art museum, biology museum, language lab, demonstration farm.
**Athletic facilities:** Field house, tennis courts, track, baseball, intramural, soccer, and softball fields, golf range, swimming pool.

**STUDENT BODY. Undergraduate profile:** 91% are state residents; 35% are transfers. 2% Asian-American, 20% Black, 3% Hispanic, 74% White, 1% Other. Average age of undergraduates is 25.
**Freshman profile:** 95% of freshmen come from public schools.
**Undergraduate achievement:** 67% of fall 1992 freshmen returned for fall 1993 term. 10% of entering class graduated.
**Foreign students:** 30 students are from out of the country. Countries represented include Australia, Canada, India, Japan, Sri Lanka, and Sweden; 10 in all.

**PROGRAMS OF STUDY. Degrees:** B.A., B.Bus.Admin., B.F.A., B.S., B.S.Ed., B.S.Nurs.
**Majors:** Accounting, Advertising Design, Agriculture, Art, Art Education, Biology, Business, Business Administration, Business Education, Chemistry, Communication, Computer Science, Economics, Education, Elementary Education, English, Fine Arts, French, Geology, Graphics, Health, Health/Physical Education, History, Industrial Technology, Management, Marketing, Mathematics, Music, Music Education, Nursing, Painting, Philosophy, Physical Education, Physics, Political Science, Psychology, Sculpture, Secretarial, Social Work, Sociology, Special Education, Speech/Theatre.
**Distribution of degrees:** The majors with the highest enrollment are business, management, elementary education, and nursing; philosophy and physics have the lowest.
**Requirements:** General education requirement.
**Academic regulations:** Freshmen must maintain minimum 1.5 GPA; sophomores, 1.8 GPA; juniors, 1.9 GPA; seniors, 2.0 GPA.
**Special:** Minors offered in all majors and in black studies, geography, military science, photography, and women's studies. Associate's degrees offered. Double majors. Independent study. Pass/fail grading option. Internships. Cooperative education programs. Graduate school at which undergraduates may take graduate-level courses. Preprofessional programs in law, medicine, veterinary science, pharmacy, dentistry, optometry, dental hygiene, engineering, forestry, and physical therapy. Teacher certification in early childhood, elementary, secondary, and special education. Certification in specific subject areas. Study abroad in Mexico and the United Kingdom. ROTC.
**Honors:** Honors program. Honor societies.
**Academic Assistance:** Remedial reading, writing, math, and study skills.

**STUDENT LIFE. Housing:** All unmarried students under age 21 must live on campus unless living near campus with relatives. Coed, women's, and men's dorms. On-campus married-student housing. 21% of students live in college housing.
**Social atmosphere:** The social and cultural opportunities in Clarksville are limited, reports the student newspaper. Favorite meeting spots include O'Charly's, the university center, the Brary tavern, and the Rockuegas dance club. Popular campus events include Homecoming and concerts; Greeks and athletes are influential.
**Services and counseling/handicapped student services:** Placement services. Health service. Day care. Counseling services for minority and veteran students. Birth control, personal, and psychological counseling. Career and academic guidance services. Physically disabled student services. Learning disabled services. Reader services for the blind.
**Campus organizations:** Undergraduate student government. Student newspaper (All State, published once/week). Literary magazine. Radio station. Brass and clarinet choir, choir, madrigal singers, concert, stage, and marching bands, orchestra, Playhouse, departmental groups, professional societies, special-interest groups, 89 organizations in all. Eight fraternities, four chapter houses; six sororities, no chapter houses. 8% of men join a fraternity. 7% of women join a sorority.
**Religious organizations:** Baptist Student Union, Fellowship of Christian Athletes, Campus Crusade for Christ, Laurel Wreath, Wesley Fellowship, Newman Club.
**Minority/foreign student organizations:** Stomp, University Connections, African American Student Group, FOCUS. International Student Organization, FLAGS.

**ATHLETICS. Physical education requirements:** Two semesters of physical education required.
**Intercollegiate competition:** 2% of students participate. Baseball (M), basketball (M,W), cheerleading (M,W), cross-country (M,W), football (M), golf (M), softball (W), tennis (M,W), track (W), track and field (indoor) (W), track and field (outdoor) (W), volleyball (W). Member of NCAA Division I, NCAA Division I-AA for football, Ohio Valley Conference.
**Intramural and club sports:** Intramural aerobics, basketball, flag football, jogging, physical fitness, racquetball, softball, swimming, tennis, track, volleyball, weight lifting. Men's club soccer.

**ADMISSIONS. Academic basis for candidate selection** (in order of priority): Secondary school record, standardized test scores, school's recommendation, class rank.
**Nonacademic basis for candidate selection:** Extracurricular participation, particular talent or ability, and alumni/ae relationship are considered.
**Requirements:** Graduation from secondary school is recommended; GED is accepted. 14 units and the following program of study are required: 4 units of English, 3 units of math, 2 units of science including 1 unit of lab, 2 units of foreign language, 1 unit of social studies, 1 unit of history, 1 unit of visual/performing arts. Minimum composite ACT score of 19 (minimum combined SAT score of 720) or minimum 2.75 GPA required. Freshman applicants missing one or two units may be admitted if they have a minimum composite ACT score of 21, minimum combined SAT score of 810, or minimum GPA of 2.85. SAT or ACT is required. Campus visit recommended. Off-campus interviews available with an admissions representative.
**Procedure:** Take SAT or ACT by April of 12th year. Application deadline is August 1. Notification of admission on rolling basis. $100 room deposit, refundable until August 1. Freshmen accepted in terms other than fall.
**Special programs:** Credit may be granted through CEEB Advanced Placement for scores of 3 or higher. Credit may be granted through CLEP general and subject exams, and military experience. Early entrance/early admission program. Concurrent enrollment program.
**Transfer students:** Transfer students accepted for terms other than fall. In fall 1992, 35% of all new students were transfers into all classes. 829 transfer applications were received, 425 were accepted. Application deadline is August 1 for fall; December 10 for spring. Lowest course grade accepted is "D." At least 24 semester hours must be completed at the university to receive degree.
**Admissions contact:** Charles McCorkle, M.A., Director of Admissions. 615 648-7661, 800 844-2778.

**FINANCIAL AID. Available aid:** Pell grants, SEOG, state scholarships and grants, school scholarships, private scholarships and grants, ROTC scholarships, academic merit scholarships, athletic scholarships, and aid for undergraduate foreign students. Perkins Loans (NDSL), PLUS, Stafford Loans (GSL), and SLS.
**Financial aid statistics:** 35% of aid is not need-based.

**Supporting data/closing dates:** FAFSA/FAF/FFS: Priority filing date is April 1. State aid form: Deadline is July 1. Notification of awards begins May 1.
**Financial aid contact:** Darolyn Porter, M.A., Director of Student Financial Aid. 615 648-7907.

**STUDENT EMPLOYMENT.** College Work/Study Program. Institutional employment. 10% of full-time undergraduates work on campus during school year. Students may expect to earn an average of $1,400 during school year. Off-campus part-time employment opportunities rated "good."

**COMPUTER FACILITIES.** 451 IBM/IBM-compatible and Macintosh/Apple microcomputers; 41 are networked. Students may access Digital minicomputer/mainframe systems, BITNET, Internet. Computer languages and software packages include Assembler, C, COBOL, FOCUS, FORTRAN, Lotus 1-2-3, Pascal, RPG, SPSS, WordPerfect. Computer facilities are available to all students.
**Fees:** $12 computer fee per semester.

# Belmont University

**Nashville, TN 37212-3757** **615 383-7001**

**1994-95 Costs.** Tuition: $7,800. Room: $1,690. Board: $1,974. Fees, books, misc. academic expenses (school's estimate): $850.
**Enrollment.** Undergraduates: 851 men, 1,113 women (full-time). Freshman class: 1,069 applicants, 832 accepted, 371 enrolled. Graduate enrollment: 138 men, 146 women.
**Test score averages/ranges.** Average SAT scores: 487 verbal, 507 math. Range of SAT scores of middle 50%: 410-550 verbal, 450-570 math. Average ACT scores: 23 composite. Range of ACT scores of middle 50%: 21-26 composite.
**Faculty.** 128 full-time; 133 part-time. 58% of faculty holds doctoral degree. Student/faculty ratio: 10 to 1.
**Selectivity rating.** Less competitive.

**PROFILE.** Belmont, founded in 1951, is a church-affiliated college. Its 34-acre campus is located in southeast Nashville.

**Accreditation:** SACS. Professionally accredited by the National Association of Schools of Music, the National League for Nursing.
**Religious orientation:** Belmont University is affiliated with the Southern Baptist Church (Tennessee Baptist Convention); two semesters of religion required.
**Library:** Collections totaling over 135,000 volumes, and 1,800 periodical subscriptions.
**Special facilities/museums:** Language lab, recording studio.
**Athletic facilities:** Student center, gymnasium, swimming pool, track, racquetball and tennis courts, athletic field.

**STUDENT BODY. Undergraduate profile:** 66% are state residents; 65% are transfers. 1% Asian-American, 3% Black, 93% White, 3% Other. Average age of undergraduates is 22.
**Freshman profile:** 1% of freshmen who took SAT scored 700 or over on math; 13% scored 600 or over on verbal, 17% scored 600 or over on math; 54% scored 500 or over on verbal, 56% scored 500 or over on math; 80% scored 400 or over on verbal, 90% scored 400 or over on math; 100% scored 300 or over on verbal, 99% scored 300 or over on math. 4% of freshmen who took ACT scored 30 or over on composite; 45% scored 24 or over on composite; 98% scored 18 or over on composite; 100% scored 12 or over on composite. Majority of accepted applicants took ACT.
**Undergraduate achievement:** 66% of fall 1992 freshmen returned for fall 1993 term. 34% of entering class graduated.
**Foreign students:** 174 students are from out of the country. 46 countries represented in all.

**PROGRAMS OF STUDY. Degrees:** B.A., B.Bus.Admin., B.Mus., B.S., B.S.Nurs.
**Majors:** Accounting, Art, Behavioral Science, Biblical Languages, Biology, Business Administration, Business Education, Chemistry, Church Music, Commercial Music, Communication Arts, Computer Science, Criminal Justice, Economics, Elementary Education, English, Finance, Health, Health Care Administration, History, Hospitality Business, Imaging Technology, Information Systems Management, International Studies, Management, Management Science, Marketing, Mathematics, Music, Music Business, Music Education, Music Performance, Office Administration, Philosophy, Physical Education, Physics, Piano Pedagogy, Political Science, Psychology, Religion, Science Education, Secondary Education, Social Work.
**Distribution of degrees:** The majors with the highest enrollment are business and music business; English and mathematics have the lowest.
**Requirements:** General education requirement.
**Academic regulations:** Minimum 2.0 GPA must be maintained.
**Special:** Minors offered in most majors. Associate's degrees offered. Double majors. Independent study. Internships. Preprofessional programs in law, medicine, veterinary science, pharmacy, dentistry, theology, and optometry. 3-1 medical technology and imaging technology programs with Vanderbilt U. 3-2 engineering programs with Auburn U, Georgia Tech, and U of Tennessee at Knoxville. Washington Semester. Teacher certification in early childhood, elementary, and secondary education. Study abroad in England, France, Germany, and Russia. ROTC and NROTC at Vanderbilt U. AFROTC at Tennessee State U.
**Honors:** Honors program.

**STUDENT LIFE. Housing:** All freshmen from outside of Nashville must live on campus. Women's and men's dorms. School-owned/operated apartments. Off-campus married-student housing. International House. 30% of students live in college housing.
**Social atmosphere:** According to the editor of the student newspaper, "A little bit of creativity, initiative, and leadership ability can go a long way." Most students are commuters, and there are not many activities on campus, so much of student social life is off campus. Most influential groups on campus include the Student Government Association, music groups, the newspaper staff, and the Baptist Student Union. Favorite events are basketball games, T-N-T Week, the Masquerade Ball, the Spring Gala, and the Christmas Dance. On-campus gathering spots are the Student Center courtyard and dorm lobbies. Off campus, students head for Obie's Pizza, Dalt's, the West End Cooker, Fountain Square, the Spaghetti Factory, the San Antonio Taco Company, and Bob and Ian's Bed and Breakfast.
**Services and counseling/handicapped student services:** Placement services. Health service. Personal counseling. Academic guidance services.
**Campus organizations:** Undergraduate student government. Student newspaper (Vision, published once/three weeks). Yearbook. Band, Christian Music Association, choir, chorale, opera/music theatre, debating, quarterly magazine, Studio Players, Women's Self-Government Association, social clubs, departmental and special-interest groups. Two fraternities, no chapter houses; two sororities, no chapter houses.
**Religious organizations:** Baptist Student Union, Campus Baptist Young Women, church-related vocational group, Fellowship of Christian Athletes.
**Minority/foreign student organizations:** International Student Society.

**ATHLETICS. Physical education requirements:** Four semesters of physical education required.
**Intercollegiate competition:** 12% of students participate. Baseball (M), basketball (M,W), cheerleading (M,W), cross-country (M,W), golf (M,W), soccer (M), softball (W), tennis (M,W), volleyball (W). Member of NAIA, Tennessee Collegiate Athletic Conference.
**Intramural and club sports:** 20% of students participate. Intramural basketball, billiards, bowling, flag football, racquetball, soccer, softball, table tennis, tennis.

**ADMISSIONS. Academic basis for candidate selection** (in order of priority): Class rank, secondary school record, standardized test scores, school's recommendation.
**Nonacademic basis for candidate selection:** Particular talent or ability is emphasized. Character and personality are important. Extracurricular participation, geographical distribution, and alumni/ae relationship are considered.
**Requirements:** Graduation from secondary school is required; GED is accepted. 18 units and the following program of study are required: 4 units of English, 3 units of math. Additional secondary school units should be in science, foreign language, social studies, and history. Minimum composite ACT score of 20 (combined SAT score of 800), rank in top half of secondary school class, and minimum 2.0 GPA required. General studies approval required of music, music business, and nursing program applicants. Audition required of music program applicants. Opportunity Admission program for applicants not normally admissible. SAT is required; ACT may be substituted. Campus visit and interview recommended. Off-campus interviews available with an admissions representative.
**Procedure:** Take SAT or ACT by May of 12th year. Suggest filing application by April 30. Application deadline is August 1. Notification of admission on rolling basis. Reply is required by August 1. $150 nonrefundable tuition deposit. $100 nonrefundable room deposit. Freshmen accepted in terms other than fall.
**Special programs:** Admission may be deferred one year. Credit and/or placement may be granted through CEEB Advanced Placement exams. Early entrance/early admission program. Concurrent enrollment program.
**Transfer students:** Transfer students accepted for terms other than fall. In fall 1993, 65% of all new students were transfers into all classes. Application deadline is August 1 for fall; December 31 for spring. Minimum 2.0 GPA required. Lowest course grade accepted is "C." At least 30 semester hours must be completed at the university to receive degree.
**Admissions contact:** Kathryn H. Baugher, M.A., Dean of Admissions. 615 385-6785.

**FINANCIAL AID. Available aid:** Pell grants, SEOG, state grants, school scholarships and grants, private scholarships and grants, ROTC scholarships, academic merit scholarships, athletic scholarships, and aid for undergraduate foreign students. Perkins Loans (NDSL), PLUS, Stafford Loans (GSL), NSL, state loans, school loans, private loans, and SLS. Tuition Plan Inc. and AMS.
**Supporting data/closing dates:** FAFSA: Priority filing date is March 15. School's own aid application: Priority filing date is March 15. State aid form: Priority filing date is March 15. Notification of awards on rolling basis.
**Financial aid contact:** Claude Pressnell, M.A., Financial Aid Director. 615 385-6403.

**STUDENT EMPLOYMENT.** College Work/Study Program. Institutional employment. 10% of full-time undergraduates work on campus during school year. Students may expect to earn an average of $1,000 during school year. Off-campus part-time employment opportunities rated "excellent."

**COMPUTER FACILITIES.** 200 IBM/IBM-compatible and Macintosh/Apple microcomputers. Students may access Digital minicomputer/mainframe systems, Internet. Client/LAN operating systems include Apple/Macintosh, DOS, LocalTalk/AppleTalk. Computer languages and software packages include Ada, BASIC, COBOL, FORTRAN, Pascal. Computer facilities are available to all students.
**Fees:** None.

# Bethel College

**McKenzie, TN 38201** **901 352-1000**

**1994-95 Costs.** Tuition: $6,735. Room & board: $3,003. Fees, books, misc. academic expenses (school's estimate): $500.
**Enrollment.** Undergraduates: 125 men, 222 women (full-time). Freshman class: 525 applicants, 499 accepted, 181 enrolled. Graduate enrollment: 10 men, 30 women.
**Test score averages/ranges.** Average SAT scores: 820 combined. Average ACT scores: 19 composite.
**Faculty.** 28 full-time; 17 part-time. 55% of faculty holds doctoral degree. Student/faculty ratio: 12 to 1.
**Selectivity rating.** Noncompetitive.

**PROFILE.** Bethel, founded in 1842, is a church-affiliated, liberal arts college. Its 100-acre campus is located in McKenzie, 120 miles from Memphis.

**Accreditation:** SACS.
**Religious orientation:** Bethel College is affiliated with the Cumberland Presbyterian Church; two terms of religion required.
**Library:** Collections totaling over 60,000 volumes, 300 periodical subscriptions, and 1,500 microform items.
**Athletic facilities:** Field house, baseball, flag football, and softball fields, swimming pool, gymnasium, tennis courts, weight room.

**STUDENT BODY. Undergraduate profile:** 84% are state residents; 5% are transfers. 14% Black, 1% Hispanic, 1% Native American, 84% White. Average age of undergraduates is 20.
**Freshman profile:** 10% of accepted applicants took SAT; 90% took ACT.
**Undergraduate achievement:** 85% of fall 1992 freshmen returned for fall 1993 term. 60% of entering class graduated. 15% of students who completed a degree program went on to graduate study within five years.
**PROGRAMS OF STUDY. Degrees:** B.A., B.S.
**Majors:** Accounting, Applied Mathematics, Biology, Business Administration, Christian Education, Computer Science, Elementary Education, Engineering, English, General Business, Natural Science, Religion, Secondary Education, Social Sciences, Written Communication.
**Distribution of degrees:** The majors with the highest enrollment are business administration, education, and applied mathematics.
**Requirements:** General education requirement.
**Academic regulations:** Minimum 2.0 GPA must be maintained.
**Special:** Minors offered in many majors and in chemistry, economics, health, history, mathematics, music, philosophy, physical education, physics, psychology, sociology, and speech and theatre. Self-designed majors. Double majors. Accelerated study. Pass/fail grading option. Internships. Preprofessional programs in medicine, pharmacy, dentistry, optometry, cytotechnology, dental hygiene, medical technology, nursing, physical therapy, radiology, and seminary. 3-2 engineering program with Tennessee Tech U. Teacher certification in early childhood, elementary, secondary, and special education.
**Honors:** Honors program. Honor societies.
**Academic Assistance:** Remedial writing and math. Nonremedial tutoring.
**ADMISSIONS. Academic basis for candidate selection** (in order of priority): Secondary school record, standardized test scores, class rank, school's recommendation.
**Nonacademic basis for candidate selection:** Character and personality, extracurricular participation, particular talent or ability, and alumni/ae relationship are considered.
**Requirements:** Graduation from secondary school is required; GED is accepted. 14 units and the following program of study are recommended: 4 units of English, 2 units of math, 2 units of science, 1 unit of foreign language, 2 units of social studies, 3 units of electives. Conditional admission possible for applicants not meeting standard requirements. ACT is required. Campus visit and interview recommended. Off-campus interviews available with an admissions representative.
**Procedure:** Take ACT by January of 12th year. Visit college for interview by March of 12th year. Suggest filing application by May 1. Application deadline is September 15. Notification of admission on rolling basis. Reply is required by registration. $100 nonrefundable tuition deposit. Freshmen accepted in terms other than fall.
**Special programs:** Admission may be deferred. Credit and/or placement may be granted through CEEB Advanced Placement exams for scores of 3 or higher. Credit and/or placement may be granted through CLEP general and subject exams. Early entrance/early admission program.
**Transfer students:** Transfer students accepted for terms other than fall. In fall 1993, 5% of all new students were transfers into all classes. 21 transfer applications were received, 21 were accepted. Lowest course grade accepted is "C-." Maximum number of transferable credits is 64 semester hours.
**Admissions contact:** Joseph S. Rigell, Assistant to the President for Admissions.
**FINANCIAL AID. Available aid:** Pell grants, SEOG, state grants, school scholarships, private scholarships, academic merit scholarships, and athletic scholarships. Valedictorian/salutatorian scholarships. Presidential, ministerial, and Bob Hope honor scholarships. Music scholarships. Perkins Loans (NDSL), PLUS, Stafford Loans (GSL), and SLS. Deferred payment plan.
**Financial aid statistics:** 50% of aid is not need-based. In 1993-94, 100% of all undergraduate applicants received aid. Average amounts of aid awarded freshmen: Scholarships and grants, $2,500; loans, $2,400.
**Supporting data/closing dates:** FAFSA: Priority filing date is February 15. FAF/FFS: Deadline is June 1. School's own aid application: Accepted on rolling basis. Notification of awards on rolling basis.
**Financial aid contact:** Laura Bateman, Director of Financial Aid.

# Bryan College

**Dayton, TN 37321-7000 — 615 775-2041**

**1994-95 Costs.** Tuition: $8,140. Room: $1,750. Board: $2,200. Fees, books, misc. academic expenses (school's estimate): $740.
**Enrollment.** Undergraduates: 193 men, 217 women (full-time). Freshman class: 440 applicants, 271 accepted, 99 enrolled.
**Test score averages/ranges.** Average SAT scores: 453 verbal, 471 math. Average ACT scores: 23 composite.
**Faculty.** 28 full-time; 24 part-time. 67% of faculty holds doctoral degree. Student/faculty ratio: 14 to 1.
**Selectivity rating.** Less competitive.

**PROFILE.** Bryan, founded in 1930, is a liberal arts college with religious orientation. Its 100-acre campus is located in Dayton, 38 miles north of Chattanooga.

**Accreditation:** SACS.
**Religious orientation:** Bryan College is an interdenominational Christian school; 16 semesters of religion required.
**Library:** Collections totaling over 66,627 volumes, 300 periodical subscriptions, and 12,179 microform items.
**Special facilities/museums:** Natural science museum.
**Athletic facilities:** Gymnasium, swimming pool, tennis courts, athletic fields.
**STUDENT BODY. Undergraduate profile:** 32% are state residents; 37% are transfers. 1% Asian-American, 2% Black, 1% Hispanic, 96% White. Average age of undergraduates is 20.
**Freshman profile:** 4% of freshmen who took SAT scored 700 or over on math; 6% scored 600 or over on verbal, 13% scored 600 or over on math; 31% scored 500 or over on verbal, 43% scored 500 or over on math; 74% scored 400 or over on verbal, 83% scored 400 or over on math; 96% scored 300 or over on verbal, 94% scored 300 or over on math. 5% of freshmen who took ACT scored 30 or over on composite; 39% scored 24 or over on composite; 97% scored 18 or over on composite; 100% scored 12 or over on composite. 50% of accepted applicants took SAT; 64% took ACT.
**Undergraduate achievement:** 67% of fall 1992 freshmen returned for fall 1993 term. 35% of entering class graduated.
**Foreign students:** 14 students are from out of the country. Countries represented include Chile, Japan, Mexico, Russia, Scotland, and Zimbabwe; 10 in all.
**PROGRAMS OF STUDY. Degrees:** B.A., B.S.
**Majors:** Accounting, Bible, Biology, Business Administration, Chemistry Education, Christian Education, Communication Arts, Elementary Education, English, History, Individualized Major, Liberal Arts, Mathematics/Computer Science, Mathematics Education, Music, Organizational Management, Psychology.
**Distribution of degrees:** The majors with the highest enrollment are English, psychology, and elementary education; history, communication arts, and Christian education have the lowest.
**Requirements:** General education requirement.
**Academic regulations:** Freshmen must maintain minimum 1.5 GPA; sophomores, 1.75 GPA; juniors, 2.0 GPA; seniors, 2.0 GPA.
**Special:** Minors offered in some majors and in computer science, counseling, French, Greek, literature, mathematical sciences, physical education, Spanish, writing, and youth ministry. Associate's degrees offered. Self-designed majors. Double majors. Independent study. Internships. Preprofessional programs in law, medicine, veterinary science, dentistry, and theology. Washington Semester. Latin American Studies Program. Teacher certification in early childhood, elementary, and secondary education. Certification in specific subject areas.
**Academic Assistance:** Remedial reading, writing, math, and study skills.
**ADMISSIONS. Academic basis for candidate selection** (in order of priority): Secondary school record, standardized test scores, school's recommendation, class rank.
**Nonacademic basis for candidate selection:** Character and personality are emphasized. Extracurricular participation, particular talent or ability, and alumni/ae relationship are considered.
**Requirements:** Graduation from secondary school is required; GED is accepted. 20 units and the following program of study are recommended: 4 units of English, 3 units of math, 3 units of science, 2 units of foreign language, 3 units of social studies. Minimum composite ACT score of 18 (combined SAT score of 700) and 2.5 GPA, or minimum composite ACT score of 20 (combined SAT score of 800) and 2.0 GPA required. Conditional admission possible for applicants not meeting standard requirements. ACT is required; SAT may be substituted. Campus visit and interview recommended. Off-campus interviews available with an admissions representative.
**Procedure:** Take SAT or ACT by fall of 12th year. Visit college for interview by spring of 12th year. Application deadline is July 31. Notification of admission on rolling basis. Reply is required by May 1. $100 tuition deposit, refundable until May 1. Freshmen accepted in terms other than fall.
**Special programs:** Admission may be deferred two years. Credit and/or placement may be granted through CEEB Advanced Placement exams for scores of 3 or higher. Credit may be granted through CLEP subject exams and military experience. Credit and placement may be granted through DANTES and challenge exams. Early entrance/early admission program. Concurrent enrollment program.
**Transfer students:** Transfer students accepted for terms other than fall. In fall 1993, 37% of all new students were transfers into all classes. Application deadline is July 31 for fall; November 1 for spring. Minimum 2.0 GPA required. Lowest course grade accepted is "C-." Maximum number of transferable credits is 64 semester hours from a two-year school and 93 semester hours from a four-year school. At least 31 semester hours must be completed at the college to receive degree.
**Admissions contact:** Thomas A. Shaw, Director of Admissions. 615 775-2041, extension 204, 800 277-9522.
**FINANCIAL AID. Available aid:** Pell grants, SEOG, state scholarships and grants, school scholarships and grants, private scholarships and grants, academic merit scholarships, and athletic scholarships. Perkins Loans (NDSL), PLUS, Stafford Loans (GSL), school loans, and SLS. Deferred payment plan.
**Financial aid statistics:** 20% of aid is not need-based. In 1993-94, 95% of all undergraduate applicants received aid; 92% of freshman applicants. Average amounts of aid awarded freshmen: Scholarships and grants, $1,200; loans, $3,500.
**Supporting data/closing dates:** FAFSA/FAF/FFS: Priority filing date is April 1. School's own aid application: Priority filing date is May 1. State aid form: Priority filing date is March 1. Notification of awards on rolling basis.
**Financial aid contact:** Timothy J. Hostetler, Director of Financial Aid. 615 775-2041, extension 224.

# Carson-Newman College

**Jefferson City, TN 37760 — 615 475-9061**

**1993-94 Costs.** Tuition: $7,400. Room: $1,200. Board: $1,800. Fees, books, misc. academic expenses (school's estimate): $1,350.
**Enrollment.** Undergraduates: 785 men, 984 women (full-time). Freshman class: 1,130 applicants, 960 accepted, 460 enrolled. Graduate enrollment: 21 men, 88 women.
**Test score averages/ranges.** Average ACT scores: 23 composite. Range of ACT scores of middle 50%: 20-25 composite.
**Faculty.** 115 full-time; 67 part-time. 60% of faculty holds doctoral degree. Student/faculty ratio: 13 to 1.
**Selectivity rating.** Less competitive.

**PROFILE.** Carson-Newman, founded in 1851, is a church-affiliated college. Its 25-acre campus is located in Jefferson City, 30 miles east of Knoxville. Most campus buildings were constructed within the last 25 years.

**Accreditation:** SACS. Professionally accredited by the American Home Economics Association, the National Association of Schools of Art and Design, the National Association of Schools of Music, the National Council for Accreditation of Teacher Education, the National League for Nursing.
**Religious orientation:** Carson-Newman College is affiliated with the Baptist Church; two semesters of religion required.
**Library:** Collections totaling over 180,000 volumes, 1,000 periodical subscriptions, and 183,999 microform items.
**Special facilities/museums:** Art galleries, Appalachian history museum, home management house, language lab.
**Athletic facilities:** Field house, gymnasium, weight room, basketball, racquetball, tennis, and volleyball courts, baseball, soccer, and softball fields, swimming pool.
**STUDENT BODY. Undergraduate profile:** 69% are state residents; 31% are transfers. 1% Asian-American, 6.5% Black, 1% Hispanic, 91.5% White. Average age of undergraduates is 21.
**Freshman profile:** 44% of accepted applicants took SAT; 98% took ACT.
**Undergraduate achievement:** 71% of fall 1992 freshmen returned for fall 1993 term. 56% of entering class graduated.
**Foreign students:** Six students are from out of the country. Countries represented include Canada, China, and Uganda; five in all.
**PROGRAMS OF STUDY. Degrees:** B.A., B.Mus., B.S., B.S.Nurs.
**Majors:** Accounting, Art, Biology, Business Administration, Business Economics, Chemistry, Church Music, Church Recreation, Communication Arts, Data Processing, Early Childhood Education, Elementary Education, English, French, General Business Management, General Studies, German, History, Home Economics, Human Services, Instrumental Performance, Leisure Services, Mathematics, Music, Music Education, Nursing, Organ/Piano, Philosophy, Photography, Physical Education/Health/Recreation, Physics, Piano Pedagogy, Political Science, Psychology, Religion, Sociology, Spanish, Special Education, Voice.
**Distribution of degrees:** The majors with the highest enrollment are communication arts, psychology, and biology; music, philosophy, and Spanish have the lowest.
**Requirements:** General education requirement.
**Academic regulations:** Minimum 2.0 GPA must be maintained.
**Special:** Courses offered in geography, geology, and Greek. Fox Fire Program for teachers in Appalachia. Associate's degrees offered. Self-designed majors. Double majors. Dual degrees. Independent study. Internships. Preprofessional programs in law, medicine, veterinary science, pharmacy, dentistry, theology, and optometry. 3-1 medical technology programs with approved professional schools. 3-2 engineering programs with Georgia Tech and U of Tennessee. Washington Semester. Teacher certification in early childhood, elementary, secondary, and special education. Certification in specific subject areas. Study abroad in England, France, and Spain. Chinese Cross-Cultural Exchange program. ROTC.
**Honors:** Honors program. Honor societies.
**Academic Assistance:** Remedial reading, writing, math, and study skills. Nonremedial tutoring.
**STUDENT LIFE. Housing:** All unmarried students under age 20 must live on campus unless living with family. Women's and men's dorms. Both on-campus and off-campus married-student housing. 55% of students live in college housing.
**Services and counseling/handicapped student services:** Placement services. Health service. Counseling services for minority, military, veteran, and older students. Birth control, personal, and psychological counseling. Career and academic guidance services. Religious counseling. Learning disabled services.
**Campus organizations:** Undergraduate student government. Student newspaper (Orange and Blue). Literary magazine. Yearbook. TV station. Musical organizations, concert-lecture series, film society, debating, departmental, social, and special-interest groups, 30 organizations in all. Two fraternities, no chapter houses; two sororities, no chapter houses. 10% of men join a fraternity. 15% of women join a sorority.
**Religious organizations:** Baptist Student Union, Fellowship of Christian Athletes.
**Minority/foreign student organizations:** Black Cultural Society.
**ATHLETICS. Physical education requirements:** None.
**Intercollegiate competition:** 19% of students participate. Baseball (M), basketball (M,W), cross-country (M,W), football (M), golf (M), soccer (M,W), softball (W), tennis (M,W), track and field (outdoor) (M,W), volleyball (W), wrestling (M). Member of NAIA, NCAA II, SAC-8.
**Intramural and club sports:** 35% of students participate. Intramural baseball, basketball, billiards, flag football, softball, table tennis, tennis, volleyball. Men's club cheerleading, swimming. Women's club cheerleading, swimming.
**ADMISSIONS. Academic basis for candidate selection** (in order of priority): Secondary school record, standardized test scores, class rank, school's recommendation.
**Nonacademic basis for candidate selection:** Alumni/ae relationship is important. Character and personality, extracurricular participation, and particular talent or ability are considered.
**Requirements:** Graduation from secondary school is required; GED is accepted. 20 units and the following program of study are required: 4 units of English, 2 units of math, 3 units of science including 1 unit of lab, 1 unit of social studies, 2 units of history, 7 units of electives. Minimum composite ACT score of 19, rank in top half of secondary school class, and minimum 2.0 GPA required. Portfolio required of art program applicants. Audition required of music program applicants. Developmental Education program for applicants not normally admissible. ACT is required; SAT may be substituted. Campus visit and interview recommended. Off-campus interviews available with an admissions representative.
**Procedure:** Take SAT or ACT by May of 12th year. Suggest filing application by December 1. Application deadline is August 1. Notification of admission on rolling basis. Reply is required by August 1. $100 tuition deposit, refundable until May 1. Freshmen accepted in terms other than fall.
**Special programs:** Admission may be deferred one year. Credit may be granted through CEEB Advanced Placement for scores of 4 or higher. Credit may be granted through CLEP general and subject exams, ACT PEP and challenge exams, and military and life experience. Early entrance/early admission program. Concurrent enrollment program.
**Transfer students:** Transfer students accepted for terms other than fall. In fall 1992, 31% of all new students were transfers into all classes. 313 transfer applications were received, 239 were accepted. Application deadline is August 1 for fall; December 1 for spring. Minimum 2.0 GPA required. Lowest course grade accepted is "D." At least 60 semester hours must be completed at the college by transfers from two-year schools; 45 semester hours by other transfer students.
**Admissions contact:** Sheryl Gray, M.S., Director of Admissions. 615 471-3223.
**FINANCIAL AID. Available aid:** Pell grants, SEOG, state scholarships and grants, school scholarships and grants, private scholarships, ROTC scholarships, academic merit scholarships, and athletic scholarships. Perkins Loans (NDSL), PLUS, Stafford Loans (GSL), NSL, state loans, private loans, and SLS. AMS.
**Financial aid statistics:** 40% of aid is not need-based. In 1993-94, 92% of all undergraduate applicants received aid; 96% of freshman applicants. Average amounts of aid awarded freshmen: Scholarships and grants, $2,200; loans, $2,400.
**Supporting data/closing dates:** FAFSA/FAF/FFS: Deadline is April 15. School's own aid application: Deadline is April 15. Income tax forms: Priority filing date is April 15. Notification of awards begins in January.
**Financial aid contact:** Don Elia, M.S., Director of Financial Aid. 615 471-3247.
**STUDENT EMPLOYMENT.** College Work/Study Program. Institutional employment. 30% of full-time undergraduates work on campus during school year. Students may expect to earn an average of $800 during school year. Off-campus part-time employment opportunities rated "good."
**COMPUTER FACILITIES.** 100 IBM/IBM-compatible and Macintosh/Apple microcomputers; all are networked. Residence halls may be equipped with networked microcomputers. Computer languages and software packages include BASIC, COBOL, dBASE, FORTRAN, Lotus 1-2-3, Pascal, R:BASE, RPG, WordPerfect. Computer facilities are available to all students.
**Fees:** $12 computer fee per semester.
**Hours:** 2 PM-10 PM.
**GRADUATE CAREER DATA.** Highest graduate school enrollments: U of Tennessee at Knoxville, U of Tennessee at Memphis, Vanderbilt U. 30% of graduates choose careers in business and industry. Companies and businesses that hire graduates: Dollywood, IBM.
**PROMINENT ALUMNI/AE.** Mary McDonald, composer; Sylvia Lane, editor, *Winston-Salem Journal.*

# Christian Brothers University

**Memphis, TN 38104** **901 722-0200**

**1994-95 Costs.** Tuition: $9,300. Room & board: $3,170. Fees, books, misc. academic expenses (school's estimate): $620.

**Enrollment.** Undergraduates: 602 men, 431 women (full-time). Freshman class: 889 applicants, 694 accepted, 323 enrolled. Graduate enrollment: 208.

**Test score averages/ranges.** Average SAT scores: 448 verbal, 502 math. Average ACT scores: 23 composite.

**Faculty.** 142 full-time; 43 part-time. 75% of faculty holds doctoral degree. Student/faculty ratio: 12 to 1.

**Selectivity rating.** Less competitive.

**PROFILE.** Christian Brothers is church-affiliated university. Founded in 1871, it gained university status in 1990. Programs are offered through the Schools of the Arts, Business Administration, Engineering, and Sciences. Its 60-acre campus is located four miles from downtown Memphis.

**Accreditation:** SACS. Professionally accredited by the Accreditation Board for Engineering and Technology.
**Religious orientation:** Christian Brothers University is affiliated with the Roman Catholic Church (Christian Brothers); two semesters of religion required.
**Library:** Collections totaling over 91,830 volumes, 582 periodical subscriptions, and 4,000 microform items.
**Special facilities/museums:** Telecommunication and information systems center, engineering graphics lab.
**Athletic facilities:** Gymnasium, weight room, field house, track, swimming pool, baseball and soccer fields, basketball, handball, racquetball, and tennis courts.
**STUDENT BODY. Undergraduate profile:** 77% are state residents; 30% are transfers. 14% Black, 82% White, 4% Other. Average age of undergraduates is 24.
**Freshman profile:** Majority of accepted applicants took ACT. 68% of freshmen come from public schools.
**Undergraduate achievement:** 74% of fall 1991 freshmen returned for fall 1992 term. 46% of entering class graduated. 18% of students who completed a degree program went on to graduate study within one year.
**Foreign students:** 40 students are from out of the country. Countries represented include Hong Kong, India, Malaysia, Mexico, Nicaragua, and Panama; 19 in all.
**PROGRAMS OF STUDY. Degrees:** B.A., B.S.
**Majors:** Accounting, Biology, Business Administration, Chemical Engineering, Chemistry, Civil Engineering, Computer Science, Economics/Finance, Electrical Engineering, Engineering Physics, English, English for Corporate Communications/Management, General Business, History, Human Development, Journalism, Management, Marketing, Mathematics, Mechanical Engineering, Medical Technology, Natural Science, Performing Arts, Physics, Pre-Health Professional Programs, Psychology, Religion/Philosophy, Telecommunications Management, Theatre, Theatre/Art, Theatre/Music.
**Distribution of degrees:** The majors with the highest enrollment are accounting, management, and electrical engineering; physics and religion/philosophy have the lowest.
**Requirements:** General education requirement.
**Academic regulations:** Freshmen must maintain minimum 1.5 GPA; sophomores, 1.7 GPA; juniors, 2.0 GPA; seniors, 2.0 GPA.

**Special:** Minors offered in most majors and in American studies, computer information systems, foreign languages, peace studies, political science, prelaw studies, public relations, and sociology. Double majors. Independent study. Accelerated study. Internships. Preprofessional programs in law, medicine, veterinary science, pharmacy, dentistry, theology, optometry, and nursing. Nursing program with St. Joseph Hospital. Member of Greater Memphis Consortium. Teacher certification in elementary and secondary education. Certification in specific subject areas. ROTC, NROTC, and AFROTC at Memphis State U.
**Honors:** Honors program.
**Academic Assistance:** Remedial reading, writing, and math. Nonremedial tutoring.

**STUDENT LIFE. Housing:** All freshmen outside of Shelby County must live on campus. Women's and men's dorms. School-owned/operated apartments. 35% of students live in college housing.
**Services and counseling/handicapped student services:** Placement services. Health service. Personal and psychological counseling. Career and academic guidance services. Religious counseling. Physically disabled student services. Tape recorders. Tutors.
**Campus organizations:** Undergraduate student government. Student newspaper (Cannon, published twice/month). Literary magazine. Yearbook. Christian Brothers Singers, concert chorus, jazz/pep band, Theatre Guild, cheerleading, College Republicans, Chemical Engineering Society, Liberal Arts Association, Knights of Columbus, martial arts club, radio club, Society of Women Engineers, 48 organizations in all. Four fraternities, no chapter houses; three sororities, no chapter houses. 24% of men join a fraternity. 20% of women join a sorority.
**Religious organizations:** Baptist Student Union, Peace Fellowship, Search, Students for Christian Community.
**Minority/foreign student organizations:** Black Student Association, National Society of Black Engineers. International Club.

**ATHLETICS. Physical education requirements:** Two semesters of physical education required.
**Intercollegiate competition:** 10% of students participate. Baseball (M), basketball (M,W), soccer (M,W), tennis (M,W), volleyball (W). Member of NAIA, Tennessee Collegiate Athletic Conference.
**Intramural and club sports:** 30% of students participate. Intramural basketball, flag football, golf, soccer, softball, swimming, table tennis, tennis, track, tug-o-war, volleyball.

**ADMISSIONS. Academic basis for candidate selection** (in order of priority): Standardized test scores, secondary school record, class rank, school's recommendation, essay.
**Nonacademic basis for candidate selection:** Character and personality, extracurricular participation, and alumni/ae relationship are considered.
**Requirements:** Graduation from secondary school is required; GED is accepted. No specific distribution of secondary school units required. Minimum composite ACT score of 20 (combined SAT score of 830) and minimum 2.0 GPA required. Conditional admission possible for applicants not meeting standard requirements. ACT is required; SAT may be substituted. Campus visit and interview recommended. Off-campus interviews available with admissions and alumni representatives.
**Procedure:** Take SAT or ACT by February of 12th year. Visit college for interview by May of 12th year. Suggest filing application by January 1. Application deadline is July 15. Notification of admission on rolling basis. Reply is required by May 1. $250 tuition deposit, refundable until May 1. $100 room deposit, refundable until May 1. Freshmen accepted in terms other than fall.
**Special programs:** Credit and/or placement may be granted through CEEB Advanced Placement exams for scores of 4 or higher. Credit and/or placement may be granted through CLEP general and subject exams. Credit and placement may be granted through challenge exams. Concurrent enrollment program.
**Transfer students:** Transfer students accepted for terms other than fall. In fall 1992, 30% of all new students were transfers into all classes. 209 transfer applications were received, 158 were accepted. Application deadline is July 15 for fall; January 1 for spring. Minimum 2.5 GPA required. Lowest course grade accepted is "C." At least 30 semester hours must be completed at the university to receive degree.
**Admissions contact:** Director of Admissions. 901 722-0205.

**FINANCIAL AID. Available aid:** Pell grants, SEOG, state scholarships and grants, school scholarships and grants, private scholarships and grants, ROTC scholarships, academic merit scholarships, and athletic scholarships. Perkins Loans (NDSL), PLUS, Stafford Loans (GSL), state loans, school loans, private loans, and SLS. Deferred payment plan and family tuition reduction. Twelve-month payment plan.
**Financial aid statistics:** 27% of aid is not need-based. Average amounts of aid awarded freshmen: Scholarships and grants, $2,655.
**Supporting data/closing dates:** FAFSA/FAF/FFS: Priority filing date is April 1; accepted on rolling basis. Income tax forms: Accepted on rolling basis. Notification of awards on rolling basis.
**Financial aid contact:** Sandi Mayo, Director of Financial Aid. 901 722-0305.

**STUDENT EMPLOYMENT.** College Work/Study Program. Institutional employment. 40% of full-time undergraduates work on campus during school year. Students may expect to earn an average of $800 during school year. Off-campus part-time employment opportunities rated "excellent."

**COMPUTER FACILITIES.** 138 IBM/IBM-compatible and Macintosh/Apple microcomputers; 48 are networked. Students may access Digital minicomputer/mainframe systems. Computer languages and software packages include Assembler, BASIC, C, COBOL, FORTRAN, LISP, Pascal; 22 in all. Computer facilities are available to all students.
**Fees:** Computer fee is included in tuition/fees.
**Hours:** 7:30 AM-midn. (M-Th); 7:30 AM-4:30 PM (F); 9:30 AM-5 PM (Sa); 4 PM-midn. (Su).

**GRADUATE CAREER DATA.** Highest graduate school enrollments: Memphis State U, U of Tennessee at Chattanooga, U of Tennessee at Knoxville. Companies and businesses that hire graduates: Federal Express, Shell Oil, Procter & Gamble, McDonnell Douglas, DuPont, IBM, Ford Aerospace and Communications, Ford Motor, RCA, General Electric, Dow Corning Wright, Xerox.

**PROMINENT ALUMNI/AE.** Dr. C. Paul Robinson, U.S. ambassador, nuclear test talks in Geneva; Dr. Michael Steffan, resident, Mayo Clinic; Hank Pelligrin, former vice-president, Schering Plough; Joe Birch, anchor, WMC-TV; William B. Plough, president, Plough Enterprises; James J. Tenge, vice-president, Federal Reserve Bank; Jack Benware, finance director, Archdiocese of Chicago.

## Cumberland University

**Lebanon, TN 37087** **615 444-2562**

**1993-94 Costs.** Tuition: $5,500. Room & board: $3,100. Fees, books, misc. academic expenses (school's estimate): $505.
**Enrollment.** Freshman class: 315 applicants, 300 accepted, 233 enrolled. Graduate enrollment: 50.
**Test score averages/ranges.** N/A.
**Faculty.** 50 full-time; 25 part-time. 40% of faculty holds doctoral degree. Student/faculty ratio: 15 to 1.
**Selectivity rating.** N/A.

**PROFILE.** Cumberland, founded in 1842, is a private, liberal arts university. Its 40-acre campus is located in the town of Lebanon, 25 miles from Nashville.

**Accreditation:** SACS.
**Religious orientation:** Cumberland University is nonsectarian; no religious requirements.
**Library:** Collections totaling over 100,000 volumes, 100 periodical subscriptions and 100 microform items.
**Athletic facilities:** Recreation center, gymnasium, softball complex.

**STUDENT BODY. Undergraduate profile:** 90% are state residents; 7% are transfers. 7% Black, 92% White, 1% Other. Average age of undergraduates is 20.
**Freshman profile:** Majority of accepted applicants took ACT. 88% of freshmen come from public schools.
**Undergraduate achievement:** 50% of fall 1992 freshmen returned for fall 1993 term. 33% of entering class graduated. 10% of students who completed a degree program immediately went on to graduate study.

**PROGRAMS OF STUDY. Degrees:** B.A., B.S.
**Majors:** Business Administration, Education, Social Sciences.
**Requirements:** General education requirement.
**Academic regulations:** Freshmen must maintain minimum 1.5 GPA; sophomores, 1.8 GPA; juniors, 2.0 GPA; seniors, 2.0 GPA.
**Special:** Minors offered in most majors and in computer science and mathematics. Associate's degrees offered. Double majors. Independent study. Cooperative education programs. Preprofessional programs in law, medicine, pharmacy, and dentistry. Teacher certification in early childhood, elementary, and secondary education.
**Honors:** Honors program. Honor societies.
**Academic Assistance:** Remedial reading, writing, math, and study skills.

**ADMISSIONS. Academic basis for candidate selection** (in order of priority): Standardized test scores, secondary school record, class rank, school's recommendation, essay.
**Nonacademic basis for candidate selection:** Character and personality are emphasized. Extracurricular participation and particular talent or ability are important. Alumni/ae relationship is considered.
**Requirements:** Graduation from secondary school is required; GED is accepted. 14 units and the following program of study are recommended: 4 units of English, 4 units of math, 2 units of science, 2 units of social studies, 2 units of history. Minimum composite ACT score of 20, rank in the top tenth of secondary school class, and minimum 2.0 GPA recommended. ACT is required; SAT may be substituted. Campus visit and interview recommended. Off-campus interviews available with an admissions representative.
**Procedure:** Take SAT or ACT by February of 12th year. Visit college for interview by March of 12th year. Suggest filing application by March 1. Notification of admission on rolling basis. $50 nonrefundable room deposit. Freshmen accepted in terms other than fall.
**Special programs:** Credit may be granted through CEEB Advanced Placement for scores of 3 or higher. Credit may be granted through CLEP general and subject exams, DANTES exams, and military and life experience. Placement may be granted through challenge exams. Concurrent enrollment program.
**Transfer students:** Transfer students accepted for fall term. In fall 1993, 7% of all new students were transfers into all classes. 100 transfer applications were received, 90 were accepted. Application deadline is March for fall; November for spring. Minimum 2.0 GPA. Lowest course grade accepted is "C." Maximum number of transferable credits is 70 semester hours. At least 30 semester hours must be completed at the university to receive degree.
**Admissions contact:** Charlie Gregory, M.A.Ed., Dean of Admissions. 615 444-2562.

**FINANCIAL AID. Available aid:** Pell grants, SEOG, state scholarships and grants, school scholarships and grants, private scholarships and grants, academic merit scholarships, and athletic scholarships. Perkins Loans (NDSL), PLUS, Stafford Loans (GSL), and SLS. AMS.
**Financial aid statistics:** 35% of aid is not need-based. In 1993-94, 79% of all undergraduate applicants received aid; 82% of freshman applicants. Average amounts of aid awarded freshmen: Scholarships and grants, $1,000; loans, $2,625.
**Supporting data/closing dates:** FAFSA/FFS: Accepted on rolling basis. School's own aid application: Priority filing date is May 1. Notification of awards begins May 1.
**Financial aid contact:** Lana Suite, Director of Financial Aid. 615 444-2562.

# David Lipscomb University

**Nashville, TN 37204-3951** **615 269-1000**

**1993-94 Costs.** Tuition: $5,340. Room & board: $3,190. Fees, books, misc. academic expenses (school's estimate): $1,445.
**Enrollment.** Undergraduates: 947 men, 986 women (full-time). Freshman class: 1,239 applicants, 872 accepted, 611 enrolled. Graduate enrollment: 72 men, 9 women.
**Test score averages/ranges.** Average SAT scores: 540 verbal, 450 math. Average ACT scores: 22 English, 25 math, 23 composite.
**Faculty.** 97 full-time; 87 part-time. 76% of faculty holds doctoral degree. Student/faculty ratio: 16 to 1.
**Selectivity rating.** Less competitive.

**PROFILE.** David Lipscomb, founded in 1891, is a church-affiliated, liberal arts university. Its 65-acre campus is located in a residential area of Nashville.

**Accreditation:** SACS. Professionally accredited by the American Dental Association, the Council on Social Work Education, the National Association of Schools of Music, the National Council for Accreditation of Teacher Education.
**Religious orientation:** David Lipscomb University is affiliated with the Church of Christ; religion course required each semester.
**Library:** Collections totaling over 184,509 volumes, 940 periodical subscriptions, and 93,779 microform items.
**Special facilities/museums:** On-campus elementary, middle, and secondary schools.
**Athletic facilities:** Gymnasium, activities center, weight room, swimming pool, athletic field.
**STUDENT BODY. Undergraduate profile:** 51% are state residents; 20% are transfers. 1% Asian-American, 5% Black, 1% Hispanic, 1% Native American, 90% White, 2% Other. Average age of undergraduates is 19.
**Freshman profile:** 2% of freshmen who took SAT scored 700 or over on verbal, 4% scored 700 or over on math; 20% scored 600 or over on verbal, 34% scored 600 or over on math; 48% scored 500 or over on verbal, 70% scored 500 or over on math; 84% scored 400 or over on verbal, 90% scored 400 or over on math; 96% scored 300 or over on verbal, 100% scored 300 or over on math. 14% of freshmen who took ACT scored 30 or over on composite; 54% scored 24 or over on composite; 97% scored 18 or over on composite; 100% scored 12 or over on composite. 18% of accepted applicants took SAT; 82% took ACT. 34% of freshmen come from public schools.
**Undergraduate achievement:** 80% of fall 1992 freshmen returned for fall 1993 term. 56% of entering class graduated.
**Foreign students:** 42 students are from out of the country. Countries represented include Canada, Iran, Japan, Korea, and Nigeria; 19 in all.
**PROGRAMS OF STUDY. Degrees:** B.A., B.S.
**Majors:** Accounting, American Studies, Applied Chemistry, Applied Music, Art, Art/Advertising, Bible, Biblical Languages, Biochemistry, Biology, Computer Information Systems, Computer Science, Dietetics, Elementary Education, Engineering Physics, Engineering Science, English, Fashion Merchandising, Finance/Economics, Food Systems Management, French, German, Government/Public Administration, Health/Physical Education, History, History/Communication, History/Political Science, Home Economics, Management, Marketing, Mass Communication, Mathematics, Missions, Music, Office Management, Physics, Political Science, Political Science/Communication, Pre-Forestry, Pre-Law, Pre-Medicine, Pre-Nursing, Pre-Wildlife Biology, Professional Chemistry, Psychology, Public Relations, Social Studies, Social Work, Sociology, Spanish, Speech Communication, Studio Art, Urban Studies.
**Distribution of degrees:** The majors with the highest enrollment are accounting, marketing, and pre-medicine; German and sociology have the lowest.
**Requirements:** General education requirement.
**Academic regulations:** Minimum 2.0 GPA must be maintained.
**Special:** Minors offered in many majors and in business distributive, church history, church music, coaching, food/nutrition, Greek, health, Hebrew, interior design, journalism, modern language distributive, philosophy, and social welfare. Self-designed majors. Double majors. Dual degrees. Independent study. Accelerated study. Pass/fail grading option. Internships. Cooperative education programs. Graduate school at which undergraduates may take graduate-level courses. Preprofessional programs in law, medicine, veterinary science, pharmacy, dentistry, and nursing. 3-1 nursing program with Vanderbilt U. 3-2 engineering programs with Auburn U, Georgia Tech, Tennessee Tech U, U of Tennessee at Knoxville, and Vanderbilt U. Teacher certification in elementary and secondary education. Study abroad in France with Toulouse Overseas Program (TOP). Study abroad also in Germany and Mexico. ROTC and NROTC at Vanderbilt U. AFROTC at Tennessee State U.
**Honors:** Honors program. Honor societies.
**Academic Assistance:** Remedial reading, writing, math, and study skills. Nonremedial tutoring.
**STUDENT LIFE. Housing:** All students under age 22 must live on campus unless living with family. 65% of students live in college housing.
**Social atmosphere:** The student newspaper reports that, "Because our enrollment is around 2,300, we are a fairly close-knit school. Social life for the most part centers upon social clubs (Lipscomb's version of fraternities and sororities). We have a very fine drama department which produces a Homecoming musical and four one-act plays each year. Off campus, some students enjoy seeing plays and hearing the symphony at the Tennessee Performing Arts Center in Nashville."
**Services and counseling/handicapped student services:** Placement services. Health service. Counseling services for minority students. Personal and psychological counseling. Career and academic guidance services. Religious counseling. Learning disabled services.
**Campus organizations:** Undergraduate student government. Student newspapers (Lipscomb News Quarterly; Babbler, published twice/month,). Yearbook. Radio and TV stations. A cappella choir, chorale, freshman chorus, concert band, ensembles, drama productions, Circle K, national professional clubs, special-interest groups, 50 organizations in all. Seven fraternities, 15 chapter houses; eight sororities, no chapter houses. 19% of men join a fraternity. 17% of women join a sorority.
**Religious organizations:** Project Good News.
**ATHLETICS. Physical education requirements:** Two semesters of physical education required.
**Intercollegiate competition:** 1% of students participate. Baseball (M), basketball (M,W), cheerleading (W), cross-country (M,W), golf (M), soccer (M), tennis (M,W), track (outdoor) (M), track and field (outdoor) (M), volleyball (W). Member of NAIA, Tennessee Collegiate Athletic Conference.
**Intramural and club sports:** 55% of students participate. Intramural basketball, football, racquetball, softball, tennis, volleyball.
**ADMISSIONS. Academic basis for candidate selection** (in order of priority): Standardized test scores, secondary school record, class rank, essay, school's recommendation.
**Nonacademic basis for candidate selection:** Extracurricular participation and particular talent or ability are emphasized. Character and personality and geographical distribution are important. Alumni/ae relationship is considered.
**Requirements:** Graduation from secondary school is required; GED is accepted. 16 units and the following program of study are required: 4 units of English, 2 units of math, 2 units of science, 2 units of foreign language, 2 units of social studies, 2 units of history, 2 units of academic electives. Portfolio required of art program applicants. Audition required of music program applicants. Conditional admission possible for applicants not meeting standard requirements. SAT or ACT is required. Campus visit and interview recommended. Off-campus interviews available with admissions and alumni representatives.
**Procedure:** Take SAT or ACT by April 15 of 12th year. Visit college for interview by February 28 of 12th year. Suggest filing application by November 15. Application deadline is August 1. Notification of admission is sent to priority applicants by January 1; to other applicants on rolling basis after January 1. Reply is required by May 1. Nonrefundable tuition deposit, $1,000 for boarding students, $500 for day students, required at registration. $50 nonrefundable room deposit. Freshmen accepted in terms other than fall.
**Special programs:** Credit and/or placement may be granted through CEEB Advanced Placement exams for scores of 3 or higher. Credit and/or placement may be granted through CLEP general and subject exams. Credit and placement may be granted through DANTES and challenge exams, and military experience. Early decision program. Deadline for applying for early decision is November 15. Early entrance/early admission program.
**Transfer students:** Transfer students accepted for terms other than fall. In fall 1993, 20% of all new students were transfers into all classes. 264 transfer applications were received, 222 were accepted. Application deadline is July 15 for fall; January 7 for spring. Lowest course grade accepted is "C." Maximum number of transferable credits is 67 semester hours. At least 30 semester hours must be completed at the university to receive degree.
**Admissions contact:** Wade Sandrell, Director of Admissions and Retention. 615 269-1776.
**FINANCIAL AID. Available aid:** Pell grants, SEOG, state scholarships and grants, school scholarships and grants, private scholarships and grants, ROTC scholarships, academic merit scholarships, and athletic scholarships. Perkins Loans (NDSL), PLUS, Stafford Loans (GSL), state loans, school loans, private loans, and SLS. Tuition Plan Inc.
**Financial aid statistics:** 40% of aid is not need-based. In 1993-94, 87% of all undergraduate applicants received aid. Average amounts of aid awarded freshmen: Scholarships and grants, $1,000; loans, $1,500.
**Supporting data/closing dates:** FAFSA/FAF/FFS: Priority filing date is April 15. School's own aid application: Priority filing date is April 15. Notification of awards begins February 15.
**Financial aid contact:** Jerry Masterson, Assistant V.P. of Student Aid. 615 269-1791.
**STUDENT EMPLOYMENT.** College Work/Study Program. Institutional employment. 38% of full-time undergraduates work on campus during school year. Students may expect to earn an average of $800 during school year. Off-campus part-time employment opportunities rated "excellent."
**COMPUTER FACILITIES.** 280 IBM/IBM-compatible and Macintosh/Apple microcomputers; all are networked. Students may access AT&T, Bull, CDC Cyber, Cray, Data General, Digital, Hewlett-Packard, IBM, NCR, Prime, Pyramid, Sequent, SUN, UNISYS minicomputer/mainframe systems, BITNET, Internet, CompuServe. Residence halls may be equipped with stand-alone microcomputers, networked microcomputers, modems. Client/LAN operating systems include Apple/Macintosh, DOS, UNIX/XENIX/AIX, Windows NT, DEC, LocalTalk/AppleTalk, Microsoft, Novell. Computer languages and software packages include Ada, BASIC, C, CAI, CAS, COBOL, DISSPLA, FORTRAN, LISP, MINITAB, Pascal, Poise, SPSS-X; 28 in all. Computer facilities are available to all students.
**Fees:** None.
**Hours:** 6 AM-midn.; 24 hours in dormitories.

# East Tennessee State University

**Johnson City, TN 37614-0002** **615 929-4112**

**1993-94 Costs.** Tuition: $1,540 (state residents), $5,156 (out-of-state). Room: $1,440. Board: $1,368. Fees, books, misc. academic expenses (school's estimate): $470.
**Enrollment.** Undergraduates: 3,276 men, 4,434 women (full-time). Freshman class: 3,633 applicants, 3,033 accepted, 1,637 enrolled. Graduate enrollment: 707 men, 981 women.
**Test score averages/ranges.** Average SAT scores: 420 verbal, 450 math. Average ACT scores: 21 English, 19 math, 21 composite. Range of ACT scores of middle 50%: 19-26 English, 19-26 math.
**Faculty.** 464 full-time; 165 part-time. 65% of faculty holds doctoral degree. Student/faculty ratio: 23 to 1.
**Selectivity rating.** Competitive.

**PROFILE.** East Tennessee State, founded in 1911, is a public university. Programs are offered through the Colleges of Arts and Sciences, Business, Education, and Medicine; the Schools of Applied Science and Technology, Nursing, Public and Allied Health; and the Graduate School. Its 360-acre campus is located in Johnson City.

**Accreditation:** SACS. Professionally accredited by the American Assembly of Collegiate Schools of Business, the American Dental Association, the American Dietetic Association, the Council on Social Work Education, the National Association of Schools of Art and Design, the National Association of Schools of Music, the National Council for Accreditation of Teacher Education, the National League for Nursing.
**Religious orientation:** East Tennessee State University is nonsectarian; no religious requirements.
**Library:** Collections totaling over 523,956 volumes, 3,499 periodical subscriptions, and 1,238,610 microform items.
**Special facilities/museums:** Regional history museum, art gallery, archives of Appalachia, planetarium.
**Athletic facilities:** Gymnasium, swimming pool, basketball, racquetball, tennis, and volleyball courts, conditioning and weight rooms, track, fitness trail, baseball, football, intramural, soccer, and softball fields, rifle range.

**STUDENT BODY. Undergraduate profile:** 84% are state residents; 26% are transfers. 4% Black, 92% White, 4% Other. Average age of undergraduates is 22.
**Freshman profile:** 1% of accepted applicants took SAT; 75% took ACT. 95% of freshmen come from public schools.
**Undergraduate achievement:** 73% of fall 1991 freshmen returned for fall 1992 term. 43% of entering class graduated.
**Foreign students:** 45 students are from out of the country. Countries represented include Canada, China, Ethiopia, India, Kenya, and Taiwan; 17 in all.

**PROGRAMS OF STUDY. Degrees:** B.A., B.Bus.Admin., B.Ed., B.F.A., B.Mus.Ed., B.S., B.S.Env.Hlth., B.S.M.T., B.S.Nurs., B.Soc.Work.
**Majors:** Accounting, Art, Biology, Business Education, Chemical Physics, Chemistry, Computer/Information Sciences, Criminal Justice, Economics, Engineering Technology, English, Environmental Health, Finance, Foreign Languages, General Science, Geography, Geology, Health Education, History, Home Economics, Humanities, Industrial Arts Education, Industrial Arts/Technology, Industrial Technology, Interdisciplinary Studies, Law Enforcement, Management, Marketing, Mass Communications, Mathematics, Medical Technology, Microbiology, Music, Music Education, Nursing, Philosophy, Physical Education, Physics, Political Science, Psychology, Social Services, Social Work, Sociology, Special Education, Speech, Speech/Hearing.
**Distribution of degrees:** The majors with the highest enrollment are education, management, and marketing; philosophy, physics, and chemistry have the lowest.
**Requirements:** General education requirement.
**Academic regulations:** Minimum 2.0 GPA must be maintained.
**Special:** Minors available in most majors. Associate's degrees offered. Double majors. Cooperative education programs. Graduate school at which undergraduates may take graduate-level courses. Preprofessional programs in law, medicine, veterinary science, pharmacy, dentistry, and optometry. 2-2 and 3-2 engineering programs. 3-1 medical technology program with Holston Valley Community Hospital Sch of Medical Tech (Kingsport). 3-1 programs also in dentistry, engineering, and forestry. Premedical/medical program with ETSU's Quilten-Dishner Coll of Medicine; students are admitted after freshman year and graduate with B.S or M.D. Teacher certification in early childhood, elementary, secondary, and special education. Study abroad in England, France, Scotland, and Spain. ROTC.
**Academic Assistance:** Remedial reading, writing, math, and study skills. Nonremedial tutoring.

**STUDENT LIFE. Housing:** Students may live on or off campus. Women's and men's dorms. Fraternity housing. On-campus married-student housing. 30% of students live in college housing.
**Social atmosphere:** Popular on-campus gathering spots are The Cave, the restaurant in the Student Center, and the Games Room. Off campus, students tend to hang out at Cheers, Bennigan's, Poor Richard's, Quarterback's, and Richard's A's. Among the influential groups on campus are the Greeks, Campus Crusade for Christ, and the Campus Activities Board. Some of the favorite events during the school year are Homecoming and basketball games.
**Services and counseling/handicapped student services:** Placement services. Health service. Counseling services for minority, military, veteran, and older students. Birth control, personal, and psychological counseling. Career and academic guidance services. Religious counseling. Physically disabled student services. Learning disabled services. Tutors. Reader services for the blind.
**Campus organizations:** Undergraduate student government. Student newspaper (East Tennessean, published once/week). Literary magazine. Yearbook. Radio station. Band, choir, madrigal group, brass and woodwind ensembles, men's and women's choruses, stage band, theatre, debating, Young Americans for Freedom. Eight fraternities, six chapter houses; five sororities, no chapter houses. 5% of men join a fraternity. 4% of women join a sorority.
**Religious organizations:** Bahai Association, Baptist Student Union, Campus Crusade for Christ, Catholic Campus Ministry, Christian Student Fellowship, Christians in Action, Episcopal Ministry, Fellowship of Christian Athletes, Intervarsity Christian Fellowship, Presbyterian Ministry, Real Life, Rock Christian Campus Fellowship, Wesley Foundation, Young Life, Spirit and Life Training.
**Minority/foreign student organizations:** Black Affairs. International Student Organization.

**ATHLETICS. Physical education requirements:** Two semesters of physical education required.
**Intercollegiate competition:** 3% of students participate. Baseball (M), basketball (M,W), cheerleading (M,W), cross-country (M,W), football (M), golf (M,W), tennis (M,W), track (indoor) (M,W), track (outdoor) (M,W), track and field (indoor) (M,W), track and field (outdoor) (M,W), volleyball (W). Member of NCAA Division I, NCAA Division I-AA for football, Southern Conference.
**Intramural and club sports:** Intramural archery, badminton, baseball, basketball, bowling, cycling, golf, handball, martial arts, racquetball, rifle, soccer, softball, swimming, tennis, track, volleyball, weight lifting, Wiffle ball. Men's club soccer.

**ADMISSIONS. Academic basis for candidate selection** (in order of priority): Secondary school record, standardized test scores, class rank, essay, school's recommendation.
**Requirements:** Graduation from secondary school is required; GED is accepted. 15 units and the following program of study are required: 4 units of English, 3 units of math, 2 units of science including 1 unit of lab, 2 units of foreign language, 1 unit of social studies, 1 unit of history, 1 unit of visual/performing arts, 1 unit of academic electives. Minimum composite ACT score of 19 or minimum 2.3 GPA required. Additional secondary school units and interviews required of dental hygiene, allied health, and nursing program applicants. ACT is required; SAT may be substituted. Campus visit and interview recommended. Off-campus interviews available with an admissions representative.
**Procedure:** Take SAT or ACT by December of 12th year. Suggest filing application by July 1; no deadline. Notification of admission on rolling basis. No set date by which applicants must accept offer. $35 refundable room deposit. Freshmen accepted in terms other than fall.
**Special programs:** Admission may be deferred one year. Credit may be granted through CEEB Advanced Placement for scores of 3 or higher. Credit may be granted through CLEP general and subject exams, and DANTES exams. Credit and placement may be granted through ACT PEP and challenge exams, and military experience. Early entrance/early admission program. Concurrent enrollment program.
**Transfer students:** Transfer students accepted for terms other than fall. In fall 1992, 26% of all new students were transfers into all classes. 1,532 transfer applications were received, 1,051 were accepted. Application deadline is August 1 for fall; December 1 for spring. Minimum 2.0 GPA required. Lowest course grade accepted is "C." At least 34 semester hours must be completed at the university to receive degree.
**Admissions contact:** Nancy Dishner, Ed.D., Dean of Admissions and Enrollment Management. 615 929-4213.

**FINANCIAL AID. Available aid:** Pell grants, SEOG, Federal Nursing Student Scholarships, state scholarships and grants, school scholarships and grants, private scholarships and grants, ROTC scholarships, academic merit scholarships, and athletic scholarships. Perkins Loans (NDSL), PLUS, Stafford Loans (GSL), state loans, school loans, private loans, and SLS.
**Financial aid statistics:** 20% of aid is not need-based. In 1992-93, 85% of all undergraduate applicants received aid; 80% of freshman applicants. Average amounts of aid awarded freshmen: Scholarships and grants, $1,000; loans, $2,600.
**Supporting data/closing dates:** FAFSA/FAF/FFS: Priority filing date is July 1. Notification of awards on rolling basis.
**Financial aid contact:** Linda Clemons, M.A., Director of Financial Aid. 615 929-4313.

**STUDENT EMPLOYMENT.** College Work/Study Program. Institutional employment. 6% of full-time undergraduates work on campus during school year. Students may expect to earn an average of $1,200 during school year. Off-campus part-time employment opportunities rated "good."

**COMPUTER FACILITIES.** 300 IBM/IBM-compatible and Macintosh/Apple microcomputers; 110 are networked. Students may access Digital, IBM minicomputer/mainframe systems, BITNET. Computer languages and software packages include Ada, APL, Assembler, BASIC, BMDP, C, COBOL, Easytrieve, FORTRAN, MINITAB, Pascal, PL/1, Plot II, Romance, RPG, SAS, SPSS-X; 25 in all. Computer facilities are available to all students.
**Fees:** None.
**Hours:** 8 AM-2 AM.

**PROMINENT ALUMNI/AE.** Oliver B. Revell, executive assistant director of investigations, FBI; Teresa Bowers Parker, star of Broadway plays; Felix Lowe, director, Smithsonian Institution Press; Dr. Clyde H. Farnsworth, Jr., director, Federal Reserve Bank operations.

# Fisk University

**Nashville, TN 37208** 615 329-8500

**1993-94 Costs.** Tuition: $9,950. Room & board: $3,690. Fees, books, misc. academic expenses (school's estimate): $400.
**Enrollment.** N/A.
**Test score averages/ranges.** N/A.
**Faculty.** 52 full-time; 25 part-time. 70% of faculty holds doctoral degree. Student/faculty ratio: 9 to 1.
**Selectivity rating.** N/A.

**PROFILE.** Fisk, founded in 1867, is a church-affiliated, liberal arts university. Its 40-acre campus, listed with the National Register of Historical Landmarks, is located on a hill overlooking downtown Nashville.

**Accreditation:** SACS. Professionally accredited by the National Association of Schools of Music.
**Religious orientation:** Fisk University is a nondenominational Christian school; no religious requirements.
**Library:** Collections totaling over 186,174 volumes, 595 periodical subscriptions, and 4,270 microform items.
**Special facilities/museums:** Speech and language labs.
**Athletic facilities:** Gymnasium, weight room, recreation room, football and softball fields.

**STUDENT BODY.**

**PROGRAMS OF STUDY. Degrees:** B.A., B.Mus., B.S.
**Majors:** Accounting, Art, Biology, Chemistry, Computer Science, Dramatics/Speech, Economics, English, Finance, French, History, Management, Mathematics, Music, Music Education, Physics, Political Science, Psychology, Religious/Philosophical Studies, Sociology, Spanish.
**Distribution of degrees:** The majors with the highest enrollment are chemistry, psychology, and political science.
**Requirements:** General education requirement.
**Special:** Self-designed majors. Double majors. Independent study. Pass/fail grading option. Internships. Graduate school at which undergraduates may take graduate-level

courses. Preprofessional programs in law, medicine, pharmacy, dentistry, mass communication media, and theological studies. 2-2 medical technology and nursing programs with Rush-Presbyterian-St. Luke's Medical Center (Chicago). Five-year B.A./M.B.A. management program and five-year B.A./B.S. or B.A./B.Eng. science and engineering program with Vanderbilt U. Dual-degree pharmacy program with Howard U. Nashville area college consortium offers cross-registration at Meharry Medical Coll, Scarritt Coll for Christian Workers, and Vanderbilt U. Oak Ridge Science Semester (Tennessee). Exchange programs with numerous colleges. Teacher certification in secondary education. Study abroad in England. ROTC and NROTC at Vanderbilt U. AFROTC at Tennessee State U.

**Honors:** Phi Beta Kappa. Honors program.
**Academic Assistance:** Nonremedial tutoring.

**STUDENT LIFE. Housing:** All students not normally living in Nashville must live on campus unless excused. Women's and men's dorms. 92% of students live in college housing.
**Services and counseling/handicapped student services:** Placement services. Health service. One-semester orientation course for new students. Birth control, personal, and psychological counseling. Career and academic guidance services.
**Campus organizations:** Undergraduate student government. Student newspaper. Literary magazine. Yearbook. Radio station. Stagecrafters, university choir, Modern Mass Choir, Jubilee Singers, jazz ensemble, Orchesis Dance Club, departmental and special-interest groups. Four fraternities, no chapter houses; four sororities, no chapter houses.
**Religious organizations:** Several religious groups.
**Minority/foreign student organizations:** Foreign student club, International Student Association.

**ATHLETICS. Physical education requirements:** None.
**Intercollegiate competition:** 9% of students participate. Baseball (M), basketball (M,W), cross-country (M,W), tennis (M,W), track (W), track and field (indoor) (M), track and field (outdoor) (M), volleyball (W). Member of CAC, NCAA Division III, WIAC.
**Intramural and club sports:** 3% of students participate. Intramural badminton, basketball, golf, softball, table tennis, tennis, volleyball.

**ADMISSIONS. Academic basis for candidate selection** (in order of priority): Secondary school record, class rank, standardized test scores, school's recommendation, essay.
**Nonacademic basis for candidate selection:** Character and personality are important. Extracurricular participation, particular talent or ability, and alumni/ae relationship are considered.
**Requirements:** Graduation from secondary school is required; GED is accepted. 15 units and the following program of study are recommended: 4 units of English, 2 units of math, 1 unit of science, 1 unit of foreign language, 1 unit of history, 6 units of electives. Electives should be in fields relating to intended major. Math units must be algebra and plane geometry. ACH is considered; if taken, English composition should be included. Several years of applied music (preferably piano) and participation (as performer and listener) in various musical activities required of music program applicants. SAT or ACT is required. Campus visit recommended. No off-campus interviews.
**Procedure:** Take SAT or ACT by December of 12th year. Application deadline is June 15. Notification of admission on rolling basis. $100 nonrefundable tuition deposit. Freshmen accepted in terms other than fall.
**Special programs:** Credit and/or placement may be granted through CEEB Advanced Placement exams for scores of 4 or higher. Credit and/or placement may be granted through CLEP general and subject exams. Early entrance/early admission program.
**Transfer students:** Transfer students accepted for terms other than fall. Application deadline is June 15 for fall; November 1 for spring. Minimum 2.0 GPA required. Lowest course grade accepted is "C."
**Admissions contact:** Harrison F. DeShields, M.A., Director of Admissions. 615 329-8666.

**FINANCIAL AID. Available aid:** Pell grants, SEOG, state grants, school scholarships and grants, academic merit scholarships, and United Negro College Fund. Awards granted on basis of scholarly potential, need, leadership, character, achievement, and promise in some special field. Perkins Loans (NDSL), PLUS, and Stafford Loans (GSL).
**Financial aid statistics:** In 1992-93, 60% of all undergraduate applicants received aid.
**Supporting data/closing dates:** FAFSA/FAF: Deadline is April 1. Student Eligibility Report. Notification of awards on rolling basis.
**Financial aid contact:** Annette Miller, Director of Financial Aid. 615 329-8735.

**STUDENT EMPLOYMENT.** College Work/Study Program.

## Free Will Baptist Bible College

**Nashville, TN 37205-2498** — **615 383-1340**

**1993-94 Costs.** Tuition: $3,520. Room: $1,150. Board: $1,830. Fees, books, misc. academic expenses (school's estimate): $844.
**Enrollment.** Undergraduates: 146 men, 120 women (full-time). Freshman class: 93 applicants, 84 accepted, 78 enrolled.
**Test score averages/ranges.** Average ACT scores: 19 composite. Range of ACT scores of middle 50%: 16-21 composite.
**Faculty.** 17 full-time; 8 part-time. 28% of faculty holds doctoral degree. Student/faculty ratio: 12 to 1.
**Selectivity rating.** Less competitive.

**PROFILE.** Free Will Baptist Bible, founded in 1942, is a church-affiliated college. Its 10-acre campus is located in a residential area several miles from downtown Nashville.

**Accreditation:** AABC.
**Religious orientation:** Free Will Baptist Bible College is affiliated with the National Association of Free Will Baptists; 30 semester hours of theology required.
**Library:** Collections totaling over 55,295 volumes, 3,168 periodical subscriptions, and 1,382 microform items.
**Athletic facilities:** Gymnasium, swimming pool, tennis courts.

**STUDENT BODY. Undergraduate profile:** 30% are state residents; 32% are transfers. 1% Hispanic, 98% White, 1% Other. Average age of undergraduates is 21.
**Freshman profile:** 100% of accepted applicants took ACT.
**Undergraduate achievement:** 64% of fall 1991 freshmen returned for fall 1992 term. 13% of entering class graduated. 5% of students who completed a degree program went on to graduate study within five years.
**Foreign students:** Five students are from out of the country. Countries represented include Canada and the Ivory Coast; four in all.

**PROGRAMS OF STUDY. Degrees:** B.A., B.S.
**Majors:** Bible, Business Administration, Christian Education, Church Music, Church Music/Christian Education, Elementary Education, English, Human Development, Missions, Music Education, Pastoral Training, Physical Education, Secondary Education.
**Requirements:** General education requirement.
**Special:** Minors offered in some majors and in music, foundations of education, and psychology. All bachelor's degree programs include a major (30–40 hours) in Bible/Christian Doctrine. Where first major is Bible, student may opt to take second major instead of minor. Associate's degrees offered. Double majors. Internships. Teacher certification in early childhood, elementary, and secondary education. Certification in specific subject areas. ROTC at Vanderbilt U. AFROTC at Tennessee State U.

**ADMISSIONS. Academic basis for candidate selection** (in order of priority): Secondary school record, standardized test scores, class rank.
**Nonacademic basis for candidate selection:** Character and personality are emphasized.
**Requirements:** Graduation from secondary school is required; GED is accepted. No specific distribution of secondary school units required. ACT is required. Campus visit and interview recommended. Off-campus interviews available with an alumni representative.
**Procedure:** Take ACT by spring of 12th year. Suggest filing application by April 15; no deadline. Notification of admission on rolling basis. $50 room deposit, refundable until five days before semester begins. Freshmen accepted in terms other than fall.
**Special programs:** Admission may be deferred one year. Credit and/or placement may be granted through CEEB Advanced Placement exams for scores of 4 or higher. Credit and/or placement may be granted through CLEP general and subject exams. Credit may be granted through military experience. Credit and placement may be granted through ACT PEP, DANTES, and challenge exams.
**Transfer students:** Transfer students accepted for terms other than fall. In fall 1992, 32% of all new students were transfers into all classes. Application deadline is April 15 for fall; September 15 for spring. Lowest course grade accepted is "D." At least 30 semester hours must be completed at the college to receive degree.
**Admissions contact:** Charles E. Hampton, Ph.D., Director of Admissions. 615 383-1346, extension 2232.

**FINANCIAL AID. Available aid:** Pell grants, SEOG, school scholarships, and private scholarships and grants. PLUS, Stafford Loans (GSL), school loans, and SLS. Deferred payment plan. Spouse tuition reduction plan.
**Financial aid statistics:** 1% of aid is not need-based. In 1992-93, 92% of all undergraduate applicants received aid; 90% of freshman applicants. Average amounts of aid awarded freshmen: Scholarships and grants, $890; loans, $1,162.
**Supporting data/closing dates:** FAFSA/FAF/FFS: Priority filing date is April 15; accepted on rolling basis. School's own aid application: Priority filing date is April 15; accepted on rolling basis. Notification of awards on rolling basis.
**Financial aid contact:** Peggy N. Hampton, Director of Financial Aid. 615 383-1346, extension 2250.

## Freed-Hardeman University

**Henderson, TN 38340** — **901 989-6000**

**1994-95 Costs.** Tuition: $5,500. Room: $1,590. Board: $1,740. Fees, books, misc. academic expenses (school's estimate): $1,170.
**Enrollment.** Undergraduates: 1,174 (full-time). Freshman class: 895 applicants, 548 accepted, 312 enrolled. Graduate enrollment: 65 men, 72 women.
**Test score averages/ranges.** Average SAT scores: 458 verbal, 485 math. Average ACT scores: 20 English, 17 math, 22 composite.
**Faculty.** 92 full-time; 10 part-time. 54% of faculty holds doctoral degree. Student/faculty ratio: 16 to 1.
**Selectivity rating.** Less competitive.

**PROFILE.** Freed-Hardeman is a church-affiliated university. Founded in 1869, it gained university status in 1991. Its 95-acre campus is located in Henderson, 13 miles from Jackson.

**Accreditation:** SACS. Professionally accredited by the Council on Social Work Education, the National Council for Accreditation of Teacher Education.
**Religious orientation:** Freed-Hardeman University is affiliated with the Church of Christ; eight semesters of religion required.
**Library:** Collections totaling over 135,000 volumes, 864 periodical subscriptions, and 5,279 microform items.
**Special facilities/museums:** Child development lab, nursery school.
**Athletic facilities:** Gymnasiums, game and weight rooms, swimming pool, track, baseball and softball fields, tennis courts.

**STUDENT BODY. Undergraduate profile:** 47% are state residents; 27% are transfers. 1% Asian-American, 4% Black, 93% White, 2% Other. Average age of undergraduates is 20.
**Freshman profile:** 3% of freshmen who took SAT scored 700 or over on math; 10% scored 600 or over on verbal, 10% scored 600 or over on math; 34% scored 500 or over on verbal, 45% scored 500 or over on math; 69% scored 400 or over on verbal, 83% scored 400 or over on math; 97% scored 300 or over on verbal, 97% scored 300 or over on math. 1% of freshmen who took ACT scored 30 or over on English, 3% scored 30 or over on math, 3% scored 30 or over on composite; 21% scored 24 or over on English, 15% scored 24 or over on math, 21% scored 24 or over on composite; 69% scored 18 or over on Eng-

lish, 47% scored 18 or over on math, 59% scored 18 or over on composite; 92% scored 12 or over on English, 68% scored 12 or over on math, 86% scored 12 or over on composite; 99% scored 6 or over on English, 92% scored 6 or over on math, 100% scored 6 or over on composite. Majority of accepted applicants took ACT.
**Undergraduate achievement:** 75% of fall 1992 freshmen returned for fall 1993 term. 43% of entering class graduated.
**Foreign students:** 29 students are from out of the country. Countries represented include India, Jamaica, Nigeria, South Korea, Taiwan, and Venezuela; 14 in all.

**PROGRAMS OF STUDY. Degrees:** B.A., B.Bus.Admin., B.S., B.Soc.Work.
**Majors:** American Studies, Art, Arts/Humanities, Bible, Biology, Business Administration, Chemistry, Communication, Elementary Education, English, History, Home Economics/Family Studies, Mathematics, Mathematics/Natural Sciences, Missions, Music, Physical Education, Physical Science, Psychology, Secondary Education, Social/Behavioral Sciences, Social Work, Theatre, World Culture.
**Distribution of degrees:** The majors with the highest enrollment are business administration, education, and Bible; art, missions, and American studies have the lowest.
**Requirements:** General education requirement.
**Academic regulations:** Freshmen must maintain minimum 1.6 GPA; sophomores, 1.8 GPA; juniors, 2.0 GPA; seniors, 2.0 GPA.
**Special:** Minors offered in many majors and in biblical languages, child studies, computer science, family studies, fashion merchandising, fine arts, French, gerontology, Greek, health, housing/home furnishings, information science, interior design, music theater, New Testament, nutrition/health, philosophy, preaching, sociology, and youth ministry. Self-designed majors. Double majors. Independent study. Pass/fail grading option. Internships. Graduate school at which undergraduates may take graduate-level courses. Preprofessional programs in law, medicine, veterinary science, pharmacy, dentistry, and engineering. 3-1 medical technology program with Baptist Memorial Hospital. 3-2 engineering programs with Auburn U, Georgia Tech, Memphis State U, Oklahoma Christian U of Arts and Sciences, Tennessee Tech U, U of Tennessee, and Vanderbilt U. Member of West Tennessee Librarian Consortium. Teacher certification in early childhood, elementary, secondary, and special education. Certification in specific subject areas. Study abroad in Italy.
**Honors:** Honors program. Honor societies.
**Academic Assistance:** Remedial reading, math, and study skills. Nonremedial tutoring.

**STUDENT LIFE. Housing:** All unmarried students under age 23 must live on campus unless living with family. Women's and men's dorms. Off-campus privately-owned housing. 73% of students live in college housing.
**Social atmosphere:** "Most social life centers around the campus," reports the student newspaper. "Freed-Hardeman is like a close-knit family. There are always movies, devotionals, ballgames, or plays each weekend." The Student Alumni Association plans campuswide events throughout the year. The most popular event of the year is Makin' Music, a musical showcase extravaganza held each spring. Favorite off-campus gathering spots include the mall in Jackson, the local Dairy Queen, Chickasaw State Park, and the Mid-South Youth Camp.
**Services and counseling/handicapped student services:** Placement services. Health service. Day care. Counseling services for veteran and older students. Personal and psychological counseling. Career and academic guidance services. Religious counseling. Physically disabled student services. Learning disabled services. Tape recorders. Tutors.
**Campus organizations:** Undergraduate student government. Student newspaper (Belltower, published twice/month). Yearbook. Radio and TV stations. Band, chorus, Sunshine Singers, quartets, trios, art guild, Thespians, cheerleading, Pied Pipers, communication and business clubs, SNEA, Young Democrats, College Republicans, 45 organizations in all.
**Religious organizations:** Evangelism Forum, Preachers Club, Preachers' Wives Club, Totalife.
**Minority/foreign student organizations:** International Club.

**ATHLETICS. Physical education requirements:** Two semesters of physical education required.
**Intercollegiate competition:** 9% of students participate. Baseball (M), basketball (M,W), cheerleading (W), golf (M), softball (W), tennis (M,W), volleyball (W). Member of NAIA, Tennessee Collegiate Athletic Conference.
**Intramural and club sports:** 55% of students participate. Intramural badminton, basketball, bowling, cross-country, flag football, golf, pickleball, softball, tennis, volleyball. Men's club soccer.

**ADMISSIONS. Academic basis for candidate selection** (in order of priority): Secondary school record, standardized test scores, school's recommendation.
**Nonacademic basis for candidate selection:** Character and personality are emphasized. Extracurricular participation is important. Particular talent or ability is considered.
**Requirements:** Graduation from secondary school is required; GED is accepted. 20 units and the following program of study are recommended: 4 units of English, 2 units of math, 2 units of science, 2 units of social studies, 10 units of electives. Minimum composite ACT score of 19 and minimum 2.25 GPA required. Conditional admission possible for applicants not meeting standard requirements. ACT is required; SAT may be substituted. Campus visit and interview recommended. Off-campus interviews available with an admissions representative.
**Procedure:** Take SAT or ACT by December of 12th year. Visit college for interview by April of 12th year. Suggest filing application by March 1; no deadline. Notification of admission on rolling basis. Reply is required prior to registration. $50 room deposit, refundable until 30 days prior to enrolling. After February 1, room deposit is $75. Freshmen accepted in terms other than fall.
**Special programs:** Admission may be deferred two years. Credit may be granted through CLEP general and subject exams, and military experience. Early entrance/early admission program. Concurrent enrollment program.
**Transfer students:** Transfer students accepted for terms other than fall. In fall 1993, 27% of all new students were transfers into all classes. 247 transfer applications were received, 162 were accepted. Application deadline is September 1 for fall; January 10 for spring. Minimum 2.0 GPA required. Lowest course grade accepted is "D." Maximum number of transferable credits is 66 semester hours from a two-year school and 100 semester hours from a four-year school. At least 33 semester hours must be completed at the university to receive degree.
**Admissions contact:** Paul Pinckley, M.A., Director of Admissions. 800 FHU-FHU1, 800 348-3481.

**FINANCIAL AID. Available aid:** Pell grants, SEOG, state scholarships and grants, school scholarships, private scholarships, academic merit scholarships, athletic scholarships, and aid for undergraduate foreign students. Perkins Loans (NDSL), PLUS, Stafford Loans (GSL), private loans, and SLS. Tuition Plan Inc. Monthly payment plan.
**Financial aid statistics:** 30% of aid is not need-based. In 1992-93, 80% of all undergraduate applicants received aid; 80% of freshman applicants. Average amounts of aid awarded freshmen: Scholarships and grants, $1,000; loans, $1,800.
**Supporting data/closing dates:** FAFSA/FAF/FFS: Priority filing date is April 1. Notification of awards on rolling basis.
**Financial aid contact:** Doris Maness, Director of Financial Aid. 800 FHU-FHU1, 800 348-3481.

**STUDENT EMPLOYMENT.** College Work/Study Program. Institutional employment. 40% of full-time undergraduates work on campus during school year. Students may expect to earn an average of $1,000 during school year. Off-campus part-time employment opportunities rated "fair."

**COMPUTER FACILITIES.** Macintosh/Apple microcomputers. Students may access Digital minicomputer/mainframe systems. Client/LAN operating systems include Apple/Macintosh, DOS, DEC, Microsoft. Computer languages and software packages include BASIC, C, COBOL, DataTrieve, DECalc, DECGraph, FORTRAN, LISP, Pascal, Prolog, RDB, SPSS-X. Computer facilities are available to all students.
**Fees:** $45 computer fee per semester.
**Hours:** 8 AM-10 PM (M-F); noon-6 PM (Su).

**GRADUATE CAREER DATA.** Highest graduate school enrollments: Harding U, Memphis State U, U of Tennessee. 40% of graduates choose careers in business and industry. Companies and businesses that hire graduates: American Cancer Society, Holiday Inn.

# Johnson Bible College

**Knoxville, TN 37998** **615 573-4517**

**1994-95 Costs.** Tuition: $3,800. Room & board: $3,030. Fees, books, misc. academic expenses (school's estimate): $1,150.
**Enrollment.** Undergraduates: 233 men, 172 women (full-time). Freshman class: 164 applicants, 134 accepted, 103 enrolled. Graduate enrollment: 54 men, 1 woman.
**Test score averages/ranges.** Average ACT scores: 21 composite. Range of ACT scores of middle 50%: 18-24 composite.
**Faculty.** 18 full-time; 9 part-time. 50% of faculty holds doctoral degree. Student/faculty ratio: 20 to 1.
**Selectivity rating.** Less competitive.

**PROFILE.** Johnson Bible, founded in 1893, is a church-affiliated college. Its 350-acre campus is located outside the city of Knoxville.

**Accreditation:** AABC, SACS.
**Religious orientation:** Johnson Bible College is affiliated with the Christian Church; eight semesters of theology required.
**Library:** Collections totaling over 77,755 volumes, 352 periodical subscriptions, and 13,423 microform items.
**Athletic facilities:** Gymnasiums, basketball, racquetball, and tennis courts, swimming pool, soccer and softball fields, swimming pool.

**STUDENT BODY. Undergraduate profile:** 18% are state residents; 26% are transfers. 1% Black, 1% Hispanic, 98% White.
**Freshman profile:** 95% of accepted applicants took ACT.
**Undergraduate achievement:** 63% of fall 1992 freshmen returned for fall 1993 term. 35% of entering class graduated. 21% of students who completed a degree program went on to graduate study within five years.
**Foreign students:** Eight students are from out of the country. Countries represented include Australia, China, Haiti, Mexico, Romania, and Spain; seven in all.

**PROGRAMS OF STUDY. Degrees:** B.A., B.S.
**Majors:** Bible, Bible/Church Music, Bible/Teacher Education.
**Requirements:** General education requirement.
**Academic regulations:** Freshmen must maintain minimum 1.5 GPA; sophomores, juniors, seniors, 2.0 GPA.
**Special:** Minors offered in Christian education, counseling, deaf missions, missions, preaching, preschool/daycare skills, teaching English to speakers of other languages, telecommunications, and youth ministry. Associate's degrees offered. Double majors. Internships. Graduate school at which undergraduates may take graduate-level courses. Teacher certification in early childhood and elementary education.
**Academic Assistance:** Remedial reading, writing, math, and study skills.

**ADMISSIONS. Academic basis for candidate selection** (in order of priority): Class rank, standardized test scores, secondary school record.
**Nonacademic basis for candidate selection:** Character and personality are emphasized. Particular talent or ability is considered.
**Requirements:** Graduation from secondary school is required; GED is accepted. 16 units required and the following program of study recommended: 4 units of English, 2 units of math, 2 units of science, 2 units of foreign language, 2 units of social studies, 2 units of history, 2 units of electives. Minimum composite ACT score of 14 and rank in top eighth of secondary school class required. Minimum composite ACT score of 19 required of teacher education program applicants. Audition required of music program applicants. Conditional admission possible for applicants not meeting standard requirements. ACT is required. Campus visit and interview recommended. Off-campus interviews available with an admissions representative.
**Procedure:** Take ACT by June of 12th year. Suggest filing application by April 1; no deadline. Notification of admission on rolling basis. $50 room deposit, refundable by August 1 Freshmen accepted in terms other than fall.

**Special programs:** Admission may be deferred two years. Credit may be granted through CLEP general and subject exams, and military experience. Placement may be granted through challenge exams.
**Transfer students:** Transfer students accepted for terms other than fall. In fall 1993, 26% of all new students were transfers into all classes. 67 transfer applications were received, 49 were accepted. Application deadline is July 1 for fall; December 1 for spring. Lowest course grade accepted is "C." Maximum number of transferable credits is 100 semester hours. At least 30 semester hours must be completed at the college to receive degree.
**Admissions contact:** Larry Green, Director of Admissions. 615 573-4517, extension 2233.
**FINANCIAL AID. Available aid:** Pell grants, SEOG, state scholarships and grants, school scholarships, private scholarships and grants, academic merit scholarships, and aid for undergraduate foreign students. PLUS, Stafford Loans (GSL), state loans, school loans, private loans, and SLS. Deferred payment plan.
**Financial aid statistics:** 25% of aid is not need-based. In 1993-94, 98% of all undergraduate applicants received aid; 98% of freshman applicants. Average amounts of aid awarded freshmen: Scholarships and grants, $1,000; loans, $2,365.
**Supporting data/closing dates:** FAFSA: Priority filing date is July 1; accepted on rolling basis. School's own aid application: Priority filing date is May 1. State aid form: Priority filing date is April 1. Income tax forms: Accepted on rolling basis. Notification of awards on rolling basis.
**Financial aid contact:** Dick Smelser, Director of Financial Aid. 615 573-4517, extension 2314.

## King College

**Bristol, TN 37620** **615 968-1187**

**1994-95 Costs.** Tuition: $8,664. Room & board: $3,350. Fees, books, misc. academic expenses (school's estimate): $1,300.
**Enrollment.** Undergraduates: 233 men, 276 women (full-time). Freshman class: 355 applicants, 300 accepted, 142 enrolled.
**Test score averages/ranges.** Average SAT scores: 473 verbal, 521 math. Range of SAT scores of middle 50%: 420-530 verbal, 450-610 math. Average ACT scores: 22 English, 22 math, 23 composite. Range of ACT scores of middle 50%: 21-26 English, 20-23 math.
**Faculty.** 42 full-time; 23 part-time. 62% of faculty holds doctoral degree. Student/faculty ratio: 13 to 1.
**Selectivity rating.** Less competitive.

**PROFILE.** King College, founded in 1867, is a church-affiliated, liberal arts institution. Its 135-acre campus is located two miles from the center of Bristol, in the foothills of the Appalachians.

**Accreditation:** SACS.
**Religious orientation:** King College is affiliated with the Presbyterian Church; four semesters of religion required.
**Library:** Collections totaling over 95,006 volumes, 630 periodical subscriptions, and 44,000 microform items.
**Special facilities/museums:** Electron microscope, observatory with two reflecting telescopes, solar telescope.
**Athletic facilities:** Gymnasium, weight room, indoor swimming pool, baseball and soccer fields, fitness trail, tennis courts.
**STUDENT BODY. Undergraduate profile:** 37% are state residents; 22% are transfers. 1% Asian-American, 1% Black, 1% Hispanic, 97% White. Average age of undergraduates is 21.
**Freshman profile:** 1% of freshmen who took SAT scored 700 or over on verbal, 3% scored 700 or over on math; 9% scored 600 or over on verbal, 27% scored 600 or over on math; 35% scored 500 or over on verbal, 58% scored 500 or over on math; 81% scored 400 or over on verbal, 90% scored 400 or over on math; 99% scored 300 or over on verbal, 100% scored 300 or over on math. 49% of accepted applicants took SAT; 51% took ACT. 95% of freshmen come from public schools.
**Undergraduate achievement:** 76% of fall 1992 freshmen returned for fall 1993 term. 28% of entering class graduated.
**Foreign students:** 35 students are from out of the country. Countries represented include China, Japan, Puerto Rico, South Korea, Taiwan, and Venezuela; 15 in all.
**PROGRAMS OF STUDY. Degrees:** B.A., B.S., B.S.Med.Tech.
**Majors:** Applied Science/Mathematics, Behavioral Science, Bible/Religion, Biology, Chemistry, Economics/Business Administration, English, Fine Arts, French, History, Mathematics, Medical Technology, Modern Languages, Physics, Political Science, Psychology, Spanish.
**Distribution of degrees:** The majors with the highest enrollment are economics/business administration, English, and psychology; fine arts, modern languages, and Bible/religion have the lowest.
**Requirements:** General education requirement.
**Academic regulations:** Freshmen must maintain minimum 1.6 GPA; sophomores, 1.8 GPA; juniors, 2.0 GPA; seniors, 2.0 GPA.
**Special:** Minors offered in most majors and in music and philosophy. Double majors. Dual degrees. Independent study. Accelerated study. Internships. Cooperative education programs. Graduate school at which undergraduates may take graduate-level courses. Preprofessional programs in law, medicine, pharmacy, dentistry, and theology. 2-2 nursing program. 3-1 medical technology programs with Vanderbilt U and Holston Valley Hospital. 3-2 engineering dual degree programs with Georgia Tech, U of Maryland, and U of Tennessee. 3-2 applied science and math program. Member of Christian College Coalition and Council of Independent Colleges. Washington Semester. Teacher certification in elementary and secondary education. Study abroad in Africa, Costa Rica, France, Germany, Israel, Italy, the Netherlands, Russia, Spain, and the United Kingdom. Latin American Studies program. ROTC at East Tennessee State U.
**Honors:** Honors program. Honor societies.
**Academic Assistance:** Nonremedial tutoring.
**ADMISSIONS. Academic basis for candidate selection** (in order of priority): Secondary school record, standardized test scores, essay, class rank, school's recommendation.
**Nonacademic basis for candidate selection:** Character and personality are important. Extracurricular participation and particular talent or ability are considered.
**Requirements:** Graduation from secondary school is required; GED is accepted. 16 units and the following program of study are required: 4 units of English, 3 units of math, 1 unit of science, 2 units of foreign language, 1 unit of social studies, 1 unit of history, 4 units of academic electives. Minimum 2.4 GPA and minimum composite ACT score of 22 (combined SAT score of 900) required. SAT or ACT is required. PSAT is recommended. Campus visit and interview recommended. Off-campus interviews available with an admissions representative.
**Procedure:** Take SAT or ACT by February of 12th year. Visit college for interview by March of 12th year. Suggest filing application by August 1. Application deadline is August 1. Notification of admission on rolling basis. Reply is required by August 15. $100 tuition deposit, refundable until May 1. $50 room deposit, refundable until May 1. Freshmen accepted in terms other than fall.
**Special programs:** Admission may be deferred one semester. Credit and/or placement may be granted through CEEB Advanced Placement exams for scores of 4 or higher. Credit may be granted through CLEP general and subject exams, and challenge exams. Early entrance/early admission program. Concurrent enrollment program.
**Transfer students:** Transfer students accepted for terms other than fall. In fall 1993, 22% of all new students were transfers into all classes. 74 transfer applications were received, 67 were accepted. Minimum 2.0 GPA required. Lowest course grade accepted is "C." Maximum number of transferable credits is 65 semester hours from a two-year school and 74 semester hours from a four-year school. At least 50 semester hours must be completed at the college to receive degree.
**Admissions contact:** Roger Kieffer, M.S., Dean of Enrollment Management. 615 968-1787.
**FINANCIAL AID. Available aid:** Pell grants, SEOG, state scholarships and grants, school scholarships and grants, private scholarships and grants, ROTC scholarships, academic merit scholarships, and athletic scholarships. Perkins Loans (NDSL), PLUS, Stafford Loans (GSL), state loans, school loans, and SLS. Deferred payment plan.
**Financial aid statistics:** 30% of aid is not need-based. In 1993-94, 92% of all undergraduate applicants received aid; 92% of freshman applicants. Average amounts of aid awarded freshmen: Scholarships and grants, $4,332; loans, $2,300.
**Supporting data/closing dates:** FAFSA: Priority filing date is March 1. School's own aid application: Priority filing date is March 1; accepted on rolling basis. Notification of awards on rolling basis.
**Financial aid contact:** Mildred Greeson, B.S., Director of Financial Aid. 615 652-4725.

## Lane College

**Jackson, TN 38301** **901 426-7500**

**1993-94 Costs.** Tuition: $4,416. Room & board: $2,862. Fees, books, misc. academic expenses (school's estimate): $850.
**Enrollment.** Undergraduates: 397 men, 347 women (full-time). Freshman class: 577 applicants, 260 enrolled.
**Test score averages/ranges.** Average ACT scores: 15 English, 13 math, 15 composite.
**Faculty.** 38 full-time; 1 part-time. 33% of faculty holds doctoral degree. Student/faculty ratio: 13 to 1.
**Selectivity rating.** Noncompetitive.

**PROFILE.** Lane, founded in 1882, is a church-affiliated, liberal arts college. Its 15-acre campus is located in Jackson, in western Tennessee.
**Accreditation:** SACS.
**Religious orientation:** Lane College is affiliated with the Christian Methodist Episcopal Church; attendance at religious activities recommended.
**Library:** Collections totaling over 6,643 volumes, 206 periodical subscriptions, and 9,203 microform items.
**Athletic facilities:** Field house, swimming pool, weight room, track, baseball and football fields.
**STUDENT BODY. Undergraduate profile:** 57% are state residents; 21% are transfers. 100% Black.
**Freshman profile:** 25% of freshmen who took ACT scored 18 or over on English, 18% scored 18 or over on math, 20% scored 18 or over on composite; 94% scored 12 or over on English, 85% scored 12 or over on math, 89% scored 12 or over on composite; 92% scored 6 or over on math, 94% scored 6 or over on composite. Majority of accepted applicants took ACT. 97% of freshmen come from public schools.
**Undergraduate achievement:** 63% of fall 1992 freshmen returned for fall 1993 term. 11% of entering class graduated.
**Foreign students:** One student is from out of the country.
**PROGRAMS OF STUDY. Degrees:** B.A., B.S.
**Majors:** Administration, Biology, Business, Chemistry, Communications, Computer Science, Criminal Justice, Elementary Education, Engineering, English, History, International Studies, Mathematics, Music, Physical Education/Health, Religion, Social Justice, Sociology.
**Distribution of degrees:** The majors with the highest enrollment are business, elementary education, and communications; music, religion, and history have the lowest.
**Academic regulations:** Freshmen must maintain minimum 1.25 GPA; sophomores, 1.5 GPA; juniors, 1.75 GPA; seniors, 2.0 GPA.
**Special:** Minors offered in most majors. Courses offered in art, art appreciation, drama, economics, French, geography, music appreciation, professional education, psychology, political science, reading, secondary education, science, social welfare, and speech. Undergraduate Program Examination required of all seniors. Cooperative education programs. Graduate school at which undergraduates may take graduate-level courses. Preprofessional programs in law and medicine. 2-3 engineering program with Tennessee State U. Teacher certification in elementary and secondary education. Certification in specific subject areas.

**Academic Assistance:** Remedial reading, writing, math, and study skills. Nonremedial tutoring.

**ADMISSIONS. Academic basis for candidate selection** (in order of priority): Secondary school record, standardized test scores, school's recommendation, class rank.

**Nonacademic basis for candidate selection:** Character and personality are emphasized. Extracurricular participation, particular talent or ability, and alumni/ae relationship are considered.

**Requirements:** Graduation from secondary school is required; GED is accepted. 15 units and the following program of study are required: 4 units of English, 2 units of math, 2 units of science, 1 unit of foreign language, 2 units of social studies. Center for Academic Skills Development for applicants not normally admissible. ACT is required; SAT may be substituted. Campus visit recommended. No off-campus interviews.

**Procedure:** Take SAT or ACT by December of 12th year. Suggest filing application by May 15. Application deadline is August 1. Notification of admission on rolling basis. Reply is required by June 15. $50 refundable room deposit. Freshmen accepted in terms other than fall.

**Special programs:** Admission may be deferred one year. Credit and/or placement may be granted through CEEB Advanced Placement exams for scores of 3 or higher. Credit and/or placement may be granted through CLEP general and subject exams. Credit may be granted through military experience. Placement may be granted through challenge exams.

**Transfer students:** Transfer students accepted for terms other than fall. In fall 1993, 21% of all new students were transfers into all classes. 128 transfer applications were received, 100 were accepted. Application deadline is August 1 for fall; December 15 for spring. Lowest course grade accepted is "C." Maximum number of transferable credits is 68 semester hours from a two-year school and 92 semester hours from a four-year school. At least 124 semester hours must be completed at the college to receive degree.

**Admissions contact:** Karen R. Winston, Director of Admissions. 901 426-4532, 800 960-7533.

**FINANCIAL AID. Available aid:** Pell grants, SEOG, state grants, school scholarships, private scholarships, and United Negro College Fund. Perkins Loans (NDSL), PLUS, and Stafford Loans (GSL).

**Financial aid statistics:** 5% of aid is not need-based. In 1993-94, 97% of all undergraduate applicants received aid; 95% of freshman applicants. Average amounts of aid awarded freshmen: Scholarships and grants, $2,400; loans, $2,000.

**Supporting data/closing dates:** FAFSA: Priority filing date is July 1. FAF/FFS: Deadline is July 1.

**Financial aid contact:** Michael Roberts, M.B.A., Director of Financial Aid.

# Lee College

**Cleveland, TN 37311** — **615 472-2111**

**1993-94 Costs.** Tuition: $4,560. Room & board: $3,160. Fees, books, misc. academic expenses (school's estimate): $675.

**Enrollment.** Undergraduates: 869 men, 923 women (full-time). Freshman class: 1,159 applicants, 839 accepted, 731 enrolled.

**Test score averages/ranges.** N/A.

**Faculty.** 88 full-time; 69 part-time. 50% of faculty holds doctoral degree. Student/faculty ratio: 19 to 1.

**Selectivity rating.** N/A.

**PROFILE.** Lee College, founded in 1918, is a church-affiliated institution. Programs are offered through the Departments of Behavioral and Social Sciences, Bible and Christian Ministries, Business, Education, Language Arts, Music and Fine Arts, Natural Sciences and Mathematics, and Continuing Education. Its 37-acre campus is located in Cleveland.

**Accreditation:** SACS.

**Religious orientation:** Lee College is affiliated with the Church of God; six semesters of religion required.

**Library:** Collections totaling over 126,392 volumes, 330 periodical subscriptions, and 20,278 microform items.

**Athletic facilities:** Gymnasium, fitness and weight rooms, soccer and softball fields, racquetball and tennis courts, arena, game room.

**STUDENT BODY. Undergraduate profile:** 19% are state residents; 33% are transfers. 2% Asian-American, 6% Black, 5% Hispanic, 1% Native American, 86% White. Average age of undergraduates is 22.

**Freshman profile:** 35% of accepted applicants took SAT; 65% took ACT.

**Undergraduate achievement:** 60% of fall 1991 freshmen returned for fall 1992 term. 22% of entering class graduated.

**Foreign students:** 61 students are from out of the country. Countries represented include the Bahamas, Canada, Germany, Jamaica, Japan, and Taiwan; 27 in all.

**PROGRAMS OF STUDY. Degrees:** B.A., B.Mus.Ed., B.S.

**Majors:** Accounting, Biblical Education, Biological Science, Business Administration, Chemistry, Christian Education, Communication, Computer Information Systems, Elementary Education, General Business, Health/Physical Education, History, Intercultural Studies, Mathematics, Modern Foreign Languages, Music, Music Education, Natural Science, Psychology, Secondary Education, Social Science, Sociology.

**Requirements:** General education requirement.

**Academic regulations:** Freshmen must maintain minimum 1.5 GPA; sophomores, 1.7 GPA; juniors, 1.9 GPA; seniors, 2.0 GPA.

**Special:** Double majors. Independent study. Accelerated study. Internships. Graduate school at which undergraduates may take graduate-level courses. Preprofessional programs in law, medicine, veterinary science, pharmacy, dentistry, theology, optometry, nursing, physical therapy, and social work. 3-1 medical technology program. Washington Semester. Teacher certification in early childhood, elementary, secondary, and special education. Study abroad in China, England, and Germany.

**Honors:** Honor societies.

**Academic Assistance:** Remedial reading, writing, math, and study skills. Nonremedial tutoring.

**STUDENT LIFE. Housing:** All unmarried students under age 21 must live on campus unless living near campus with relatives. Women's and men's dorms. Off-campus married-student housing. 63% of students live in college housing.

**Social atmosphere:** Students gather at the Student Center, the Hamilton Place Mall, and Denny's. Greek organizations, musical groups, and basketball players influence campus life. Popular events include the Block Party, Sadie Hawkins Day, Masquerade on the Mall, the Christmas tree lighting, Saint Patrick's Day, and Cotton Club and Friday Night Live events. According to the student newspaper, "Lee has a small, friendly campus, so it is easy to get to know people. Many students spend time between classes socializing on the pedestrian mall. On weekends, Chattanooga becomes popular because of the short commute. Lee also has a great spiritual atmosphere."

**Services and counseling/handicapped student services:** Placement services. Health service. Counseling services for minority and veteran students. Personal and psychological counseling. Career and academic guidance services. Religious counseling. Learning disabled services.

**Campus organizations:** Undergraduate student government. Student newspaper (Collegian, published once/month). Literary magazine. Yearbook. Radio station. Bands, choir, Lee Singers, music drama workshop, academic, service, and special-interest groups, 44 organizations in all. Three fraternities, no chapter houses; two sororities, no chapter houses.

**Religious organizations:** Missions Club, Pioneers for Christ, Ministerial Association.

**ATHLETICS. Physical education requirements:** Two semesters of physical education required.

**Intercollegiate competition:** 7% of students participate. Basketball (M,W), cheerleading (W), cross-country (M,W), golf (M), soccer (M,W), softball (W), tennis (M,W), volleyball (W). Member of NAIA, Tennessee-Virginia Athletic Conference.

**Intramural and club sports:** 60% of students participate. Intramural badminton, basketball, flag football, racquetball, soccer, softball, table tennis, volleyball. Men's club volleyball.

**ADMISSIONS. Academic basis for candidate selection** (in order of priority): Secondary school record, standardized test scores, class rank, school's recommendation.

**Nonacademic basis for candidate selection:** Character and personality are important. Extracurricular participation, particular talent or ability, and alumni/ae relationship are considered.

**Requirements:** Graduation from secondary school is required; GED is accepted. No specific distribution of secondary school units required. College Prep curriculum is preferable. Minimum composite ACT score of 17 and minimum 2.0 GPA required. Audition required of music program applicants. ACT is required; SAT may be substituted. Campus visit and interview recommended. No off-campus interviews.

**Procedure:** Take SAT or ACT by July of 12th year. Suggest filing application by April 15; no deadline. Notification of admission on rolling basis. No set date by which applicants must accept offer. $100 room deposit, refundable until 30 days before registration. Freshmen accepted in terms other than fall.

**Special programs:** Admission may be deferred two semesters. Credit and/or placement may be granted through CEEB Advanced Placement exams for scores of 3 or higher. Credit and/or placement may be granted through CLEP general exams. Concurrent enrollment program.

**Transfer students:** Transfer students accepted for terms other than fall. In fall 1992, 33% of all new students were transfers into all classes. 295 transfer applications were received, 275 were accepted. Minimum 2.0 GPA required. Lowest course grade accepted is "C." Maximum number of transferable credits is 32 semester hours. At least 30 semester hours must be completed at the college to receive degree.

**Admissions contact:** Gary T. Ray, M.Ed., Director of Admissions. 615 478-7316.

**FINANCIAL AID. Available aid:** Pell grants, SEOG, state scholarships and grants, school scholarships, academic merit scholarships, and athletic scholarships. Perkins Loans (NDSL), PLUS, Stafford Loans (GSL), state loans, school loans, and SLS. AMS and family tuition reduction.

**Financial aid statistics:** 83% of aid is not need-based. In 1992-93, 90% of all undergraduate applicants received aid; 85% of freshman applicants.

**Supporting data/closing dates:** FAFSA/FAF/FFS: Priority filing date is April 15. School's own aid application: Priority filing date is April 15. Notification of awards on rolling basis.

**Financial aid contact:** Michael Ellis, Director of Financial Aid. 615 478-7330.

**STUDENT EMPLOYMENT.** College Work/Study Program. Institutional employment. 11% of full-time undergraduates work on campus during school year. Students may expect to earn an average of $1,360 during school year. Freshmen are discouraged from working during their first term. Off-campus part-time employment opportunities rated "fair."

**COMPUTER FACILITIES.** 123 IBM/IBM-compatible and Macintosh/Apple microcomputers; 104 are networked. Residence halls may be equipped with networked microcomputers. Computer languages and software packages include Apple Writer, BASIC, COBOL, Lotus 1-2-3, WordStar. Computer facilities are available to all students.

**Fees:** $25 computer fee per semester.

**Hours:** 8 AM-7 PM.

**PROMINENT ALUMNI/AE.** Paul Conn, president, Lee Coll; Jim Golden, lawyer and recent congressional candidate; Sharlinda Beach Turner, medical director for Southeast region, Tennessee Department of Public Health and Environment.

# LeMoyne-Owen College

**Memphis, TN 38126** — **901 774-9090**

**1993-94 Costs.** Tuition: $4,200. Room: $1,800. Board: $1,800.

**Enrollment.** Undergraduates: 480 men, 720 women (full-time). Freshman class: 1,043 applicants, 874 accepted, 401 enrolled. Graduate enrollment: 80 men, 70 women.

**Test score averages/ranges.** N/A.

**Faculty.** 44 full-time; 8 part-time. 60% of faculty holds doctoral degree. Student/faculty ratio: 16 to 1.

**Selectivity rating.** N/A.

**PROFILE.** LeMoyne-Owen is a church-affiliated, liberal arts college. It is the product of the 1968 merger of two traditionally black institutions. Its 15-acre campus is located in South Memphis.

**Accreditation:** SACS.
**Religious orientation:** LeMoyne-Owen College is affiliated with the United Church of Christ and Missionary Baptist Church; four semesters of religion required.
**Library:** Collections totaling over 90,231 volumes and 216 periodical subscriptions.
**Special facilities/museums:** Museum/gallery, language lab.
**Athletic facilities:** Gymnasium.

**STUDENT BODY. Undergraduate profile:** 90% are state residents; 25% are transfers. 96% Black, 1% White, 3% Other. Average age of undergraduates is 18.
**Freshman profile:** 10% of accepted applicants took SAT; 90% took ACT. 95% of freshmen come from public schools.
**Undergraduate achievement:** 60% of fall 1991 freshmen returned for fall 1992 term. 50% of entering class graduated. 35% of students who completed a degree program went on to graduate study within five years.
**Foreign students:** Countries represented include Iran and Nigeria.

**PROGRAMS OF STUDY. Degrees:** B.A., B.Bus.Admin., B.S.
**Majors:** Accounting, Art, Biochemistry, Business Administration, Chemistry, Computer Science, Economics, English, Health/Physical Education/Recreation, History, Humanities, Mathematics, Natural Science, Philosophy, Political Science, Pre-Dentistry, Pre-Medicine, Pre-Nursing, Pre-Physical Therapy, Social Work, Sociology.
**Distribution of degrees:** The majors with the highest enrollment are business, math, and science; English and history have the lowest.
**Requirements:** General education requirement.
**Academic regulations:** Minimum 2.0 GPA must be maintained.
**Special:** Self-designed majors. Double majors. Dual degrees. Independent study. Accelerated study. Internships. Cooperative education programs. Graduate school at which undergraduates may take graduate-level courses. Preprofessional programs in law, medicine, veterinary science, pharmacy, dentistry, and optometry. Dual degree program in English. 3-2 engineering program with Tuskegee U. Member of Greater Memphis Consortium; cross-registration possible. Teacher certification in elementary and secondary education. Certification in specific subject areas. Study abroad in Europe. ROTC, NROTC, and AFROTC at Memphis State U.
**Honors:** Honors program. Honor societies.
**Academic Assistance:** Remedial reading, writing, math, and study skills. Nonremedial tutoring.

**ADMISSIONS. Academic basis for candidate selection** (in order of priority): Secondary school record, standardized test scores, school's recommendation, class rank.
**Nonacademic basis for candidate selection:** Character and personality and extracurricular participation are important. Particular talent or ability is considered.
**Requirements:** Graduation from secondary school is recommended; GED is accepted. 20 secondary school units are required: Special Services Program for applicants not normally admissible. ACT is required; SAT may be substituted. Campus visit recommended. Off-campus interviews available with an alumni representative.
**Procedure:** Take SAT or ACT by fall of 12th year. Visit college for interview by March 15 of 12th year. Application deadline is June 15. Notification of admission on rolling basis. No set date by which applicants must accept offer. $100 nonrefundable room deposit. Freshmen accepted in terms other than fall.
**Special programs:** Credit and/or placement may be granted through CEEB Advanced Placement exams. Credit and/or placement may be granted through CLEP general and subject exams. Placement may be granted through challenge exams. Early decision program. In fall 1992, 45 applied for early decision and 40 were accepted. Deadline for applying for early decision is March 15. Early entrance/early admission program. Concurrent enrollment program.
**Transfer students:** Transfer students accepted for terms other than fall. In fall 1992, 25% of all new students were transfers into all classes. 105 transfer applications were received, 87 were accepted. Minimum 2.0 GPA required. Lowest course grade accepted is "C." At least 30 semester hours must be completed at the college to receive degree.
**Admissions contact:** Dr. Marie Milam, Ed.D., Director of Admissions. 901 942-7302.

**FINANCIAL AID. Available aid:** Pell grants, SEOG, school scholarships, private scholarships, ROTC scholarships, academic merit scholarships, athletic scholarships, and United Negro College Fund. Perkins Loans (NDSL), Stafford Loans (GSL), school loans, private loans, and SLS. Deferred payment plan.
**Financial aid statistics:** In 1992-93, 85% of all undergraduate applicants received aid. Average amounts of aid awarded freshmen: Scholarships and grants, $1,500; loans, $2,000.
**Supporting data/closing dates:** FAFSA/FAF/FFS: Deadline is July 15. Notification of awards on rolling basis.
**Financial aid contact:** Stephanie Larry, M.A., Director of Financial Aid. 901 942-7313.

# Lincoln Memorial University

**Harrogate, TN 37752** **615 869-3611**

**1994-95 Costs.** Tuition: $5,950. Room & board: $2,860. Fees, books, misc. academic expenses (school's estimate): $520.
**Enrollment.** Undergraduates: 382 men, 543 women (full-time). Freshman class: 787 applicants, 562 accepted, 363 enrolled. Graduate enrollment: 111 men, 263 women.
**Test score averages/ranges.** Average ACT scores: 23 English, 19 math, 22 composite. Range of ACT scores of middle 50%: 20-25 English, 17-24 math.
**Faculty.** 69 full-time; 44 part-time. 70% of faculty holds highest degree in specific field. Student/faculty ratio: 14 to 1.
**Selectivity rating.** Less competitive.

**PROFILE.** Lincoln Memorial, founded in 1897, is a private, liberal arts university. Its 1,000-acre campus is located in Harrogate, 55 miles north of Knoxville.

**Accreditation:** SACS. Professionally accredited by the American Medical Association (CAHEA), the American Veterinary Medical Association, the National League for Nursing.
**Religious orientation:** Lincoln Memorial University is nonsectarian; no religious requirements.
**Library:** Collections totaling over 126,000 volumes, 600 periodical subscriptions, and 60,000 microform items.
**Special facilities/museums:** Civil War museum, including collection of Abraham Lincoln memorabilia (over 6,000 books, paintings, manuscripts), two radio stations, television station.
**Athletic facilities:** Gymnasium, natatorium, tennis courts, athletic, baseball, soccer, and softball fields, arena.

**STUDENT BODY. Undergraduate profile:** 57% are state residents; 31% are transfers. 1% Asian-American, 3% Black, 1% Hispanic, 91% White, 4% Other. Average age of undergraduates is 23.
**Freshman profile:** 20% of accepted applicants took SAT; 80% took ACT. 87% of freshmen come from public schools.
**Undergraduate achievement:** 71% of fall 1992 freshmen returned for fall 1993 term. 45% of entering class graduated. 35% of students who completed a degree program went on to graduate study within two years.
**Foreign students:** 80 students are from out of the country. Countries represented include Canada, Japan, Korea, Sweden, Taiwan, and United Kingdom; 16 in all.

**PROGRAMS OF STUDY. Degrees:** B.A., B.Bus.Admin., B.S., B.S.Nurs.
**Majors:** Accounting, Athletic Training, Biology, Business Education, Business Management, Chemistry, Communications, Computer Science, Elementary Education, English, Environmental Science, Finance/Economics, Health, History, Marketing, Mathematics, Medical Technology, Nursing, Psychology, Publications Design, Social Work, Sport Management, Veterinary Technology, Visual Arts, Wildlife Management.
**Distribution of degrees:** The majors with the highest enrollment are elementary education, accounting, and biology; visual arts and medical technology have the lowest.
**Requirements:** General education requirement.
**Academic regulations:** Minimum 2.0 GPA must be maintained.
**Special:** Associate's degrees offered. Double majors. Independent study. Accelerated study. Internships. Graduate school at which undergraduates may take graduate-level courses. Preprofessional programs in law, medicine, veterinary science, pharmacy, dentistry, optometry, and physical therapy. Teacher certification in early childhood, elementary, and secondary education. Certification in specific subject areas.
**Honors:** Honors program. Honor societies.
**Academic Assistance:** Remedial reading, writing, math, and study skills.

**ADMISSIONS. Academic basis for candidate selection** (in order of priority): Secondary school record, standardized test scores, school's recommendation, class rank, essay.
**Nonacademic basis for candidate selection:** Character and personality are important. Extracurricular participation, particular talent or ability, and alumni/ae relationship are considered.
**Requirements:** Graduation from secondary school is recommended; GED is accepted. 20 units and the following program of study are required: 4 units of English, 2 units of math, 2 units of science including 1 unit of lab, 2 units of social studies, 1 unit of history, 8 units of electives. Minimum composite ACT score of 19 and minimum 2.3 GPA required. Conditional admission possible for applicants not meeting standard requirements. ACT is required; SAT may be substituted. Campus visit and interview recommended. No off-campus interviews.
**Procedure:** Take SAT or ACT by December 15 of 12th year. Suggest filing application by March 1. Application deadline is June 1. Notification of admission on rolling basis. $50 tuition deposit, refundable until June 1. $50 room deposit, refundable until August 1. Freshmen accepted in terms other than fall.
**Special programs:** Credit may be granted through CEEB Advanced Placement for scores of 4 or higher. Credit may be granted through CLEP general and subject exams, ACT PEP and DANTES exams, and military and life experience. Early entrance/early admission program. Concurrent enrollment program.
**Transfer students:** Transfer students accepted for terms other than fall. In fall 1993, 31% of all new students were transfers into all classes. 343 transfer applications were received, 286 were accepted. Application deadline is June 1 for fall; December 1 for spring. Minimum 2.0 GPA required. Lowest course grade accepted is "C." Maximum number of transferable credits is 64 semester hours. At least 30 semester hours must be completed at the university to receive degree.
**Admissions contact:** Conrad Daniels, Dean of Admissions. 615 869-6280.

**FINANCIAL AID. Available aid:** Pell grants, SEOG, state scholarships and grants, school scholarships and grants, private scholarships and grants, ROTC scholarships, academic merit scholarships, and athletic scholarships. Perkins Loans (NDSL), PLUS, Stafford Loans (GSL), state loans, school loans, and SLS. AMS and deferred payment plan.
**Financial aid statistics:** 40% of aid is not need-based. In 1993-94, 80% of all undergraduate applicants received aid; 80% of freshman applicants.
**Supporting data/closing dates:** FAFSA/FAF/FFS: Priority filing date is March 1; accepted on rolling basis. School's own aid application: Priority filing date is March 1. Income tax forms: Priority filing date is March 1; accepted on rolling basis. Notification of awards on rolling basis.
**Financial aid contact:** Greg Winkler, M.B.A., Director of Financial Aid. 615 869-6336.

# Maryville College

**Maryville, TN 37801** **615 981-8092**

**1994-95 Costs.** Tuition: $11,200. Room: $1,998. Board: $2,210. Fees, books, misc. academic expenses (school's estimate): $650.

**Enrollment.** Undergraduates: 313 men, 310 women (full-time). Freshman class: 1,094 applicants, 888 accepted, 176 enrolled.

**Test score averages/ranges.** Average SAT scores: 448 verbal, 505 math. Range of SAT scores of middle 50%: 390-520 verbal, 430-560 math. Average ACT scores: 22 English, 22 math, 23 composite. Range of ACT scores of middle 50%: 20-25 English, 19-25 math.

**Faculty.** 50 full-time; 31 part-time. 80% of faculty holds doctoral degree. Student/faculty ratio: 13 to 1.

**Selectivity rating.** Less competitive.

**PROFILE.** Maryville, founded in 1819, is a church-affiliated, liberal arts college. Its 370-acre campus is located in Maryville, 15 miles south of Knoxville.

**Accreditation:** SACS. Professionally accredited by the National Association of Schools of Music.
**Religious orientation:** Maryville College is affiliated with the Presbyterian Church; one semester of religion required.
**Library:** Collections totaling over 108,500 volumes, 625 periodical subscriptions, and 3,626 microform items.
**Special facilities/museums:** Art gallery, language lab.
**Athletic facilities:** Gymnasium, baseball, football, soccer, and softball fields, basketball, racquetball, tennis, and volleyball courts, weight room, swimming pool, batting cage, climbing wall.

**STUDENT BODY. Undergraduate profile:** 64% are state residents; 21% are transfers. .7% Asian-American, 5.1% Black, 1% Hispanic, .2% Native American, 87% White, 6% Other. Average age of undergraduates is 20.
**Freshman profile:** 1% of freshmen who took SAT scored 700 or over on math; 8% scored 600 or over on verbal, 21% scored 600 or over on math; 29% scored 500 or over on verbal, 51% scored 500 or over on math; 69% scored 400 or over on verbal, 85% scored 400 or over on math; 99% scored 300 or over on verbal, 100% scored 300 or over on math. 49% of accepted applicants took SAT; 80% took ACT. 95% of freshmen come from public schools.
**Undergraduate achievement:** 65% of fall 1992 freshmen returned for fall 1993 term. 29% of entering class graduated. 18% of students who completed a degree program immediately went on to graduate study.
**Foreign students:** 54 students are from out of the country. Countries represented include African countries, China, Japan, Korea, South American countries, and Spain; 18 in all.

**PROGRAMS OF STUDY. Degrees:** B.A., B.Mus., B.S.
**Majors:** Art, Biology, Business, Chemistry, Church Music, Computer Science/Business, Computer Science/Mathematics, Economics, Elementary Education, Engineering, English, History, International Studies, Management, Mathematics, Music Education, Music Performance, Music Theatre, Nursing, Physical Education, Political Science, Pre-Professional Physical Therapy, Psychology, Religion, Sign Language/Interpreting, Sociology.
**Distribution of degrees:** The majors with the highest enrollment are elementary education, business, and management; art, music, and religion have the lowest.
**Requirements:** General education requirement.
**Academic regulations:** Freshmen must maintain minimum 1.0 GPA; sophomores, 1.3 GPA; juniors, 1.6 GPA; seniors, 1.9 GPA.
**Special:** Minors offered in accounting, American studies, German, medieval studies, philosophy, physics, and sociology. Self-designed majors. Double majors. Dual degrees. Independent study. Accelerated study. Pass/fail grading option. Internships. Graduate school at which undergraduates may take graduate-level courses. Preprofessional programs in law and medicine. 2-2 nursing programs with U of Tennessee at Knoxville and Vanderbilt U. 3-2 M.B.A. program with U of Tennessee. 3-2 engineering programs with Georgia Tech and U of Tennessee. Member of Appalachian College Program. Washington Semester. Teacher certification in elementary and secondary education. Exchange programs abroad in Japan (Chuo U, Kansai U) and Korea (Han Nam U, Honsei U). Study abroad also in African, Latin American, and Western European countries.
**Honors:** Honors program.
**Academic Assistance:** Remedial study skills. Nonremedial tutoring.

**ADMISSIONS. Academic basis for candidate selection** (in order of priority): Secondary school record, standardized test scores, school's recommendation, class rank.
**Nonacademic basis for candidate selection:** Extracurricular participation, particular talent or ability, and alumni/ae relationship are important. Character and personality are considered.
**Requirements:** Graduation from secondary school is required; GED is accepted. 15 units and the following program of study are required: 4 units of English, 2 units of math, 1 unit of lab science, 1 unit of social studies, 7 units of electives including 5 units of academic electives. Electives should be chosen from math (excluding general math and arithmetic), science, social studies, foreign language, Bible, and music theory. Portfolio required of art program applicants. Audition required of music program applicants. Conditional admission possible for applicants not meeting standard requirements. SAT or ACT is required. Campus visit and interview recommended. Off-campus interviews available with an admissions representative.
**Procedure:** Take SAT or ACT by December of 12th year. Take ACH by December of 12th year. Visit college for interview by May of 12th year. Suggest filing application by April; no deadline. Notification of admission on rolling basis. Reply is required within 30 days of acceptance. $200 tuition deposit, refundable until May 1. Freshmen accepted in terms other than fall.
**Special programs:** Admission may be deferred one year. Credit and/or placement may be granted through CEEB Advanced Placement exams for scores of 3 or higher. Credit and/or placement may be granted through CLEP general and subject exams. Credit and placement may be granted through challenge exams. Early entrance/early admission program. Concurrent enrollment program.
**Transfer students:** Transfer students accepted for terms other than fall. In fall 1993, 21% of all new students were transfers into all classes. 144 transfer applications were received, 85 were accepted. Application deadline is rolling for fall; rolling for spring. Minimum 2.5 GPA required. Lowest course grade accepted is "C." At least 32 semester hours must be completed at the college to receive degree.
**Admissions contact:** Donna F. Libby, M.A., Vice President of Admissions and Enrollment. 615 981-8092, 800 597-2687.

**FINANCIAL AID. Available aid:** Pell grants, SEOG, state scholarships and grants, school scholarships and grants, private scholarships and grants, and academic merit scholarships. Perkins Loans (NDSL), PLUS, Stafford Loans (GSL), state loans, and SLS. Knight Tuition Plans, AMS, and Tuition Management Systems.
**Financial aid statistics:** 8% of aid is not need-based. In 1993-94, 84% of all undergraduate applicants received aid; 97% of freshman applicants. Average amounts of aid awarded freshmen: Scholarships and grants, $5,657; loans, $4,217.
**Supporting data/closing dates:** FAFSA: Priority filing date is April 1. FAF/FFS: Priority filing date is April 1; accepted on rolling basis. School's own aid application: Priority filing date is April 1; accepted on rolling basis. State aid form: Priority filing date is February 28; deadline is May 1. Income tax forms: Priority filing date is April 1; accepted on rolling basis. Notification of awards on rolling basis.
**Financial aid contact:** Ventia Jones, Director of Financial Aid. 615 981-8100.

# Memphis College of Art

**Memphis, TN 38104** **901 726-4085**

**1993-94 Costs.** Tuition: $8,950. Room: $2,950. Fees, books, misc. academic expenses (school's estimate): $1,040.

**Enrollment.** Undergraduates: 131 men, 78 women (full-time). Freshman class: 153 applicants, 130 accepted, 61 enrolled. Graduate enrollment: 9 men, 22 women.

**Test score averages/ranges.** Average SAT scores: 378 verbal, 450 math. Average ACT scores: 20 English, 18 math, 19 composite.

**Faculty.** 16 full-time; 28 part-time. Student/faculty ratio: 10 to 1.

**Selectivity rating.** N/A.

**PROFILE.** The Memphis College of Art, founded in 1936, is a public college. Its 200-acre campus is located in Overton Park.

**Accreditation:** SACS. Professionally accredited by the National Association of Schools of Art and Design.
**Religious orientation:** Memphis College of Art is nonsectarian; no religious requirements.
**Library:** Collections totaling over 14,000 volumes and 80 periodical subscriptions.
**Special facilities/museums:** Art museum, numerous galleries for student exhibition. Computer writing lab.
**Athletic facilities:** Golf and volleyball facilities.

**STUDENT BODY. Undergraduate profile:** 55% are state residents; 20% are transfers. 1% Asian-American, 14% Black, 1% Hispanic, 1% Native American, 78% White, 5% Other. Average age of undergraduates is 24.
**Freshman profile:** 17% of accepted applicants took SAT; 83% took ACT. 85% of freshmen come from public schools.
**Undergraduate achievement:** 65% of fall 1991 freshmen returned for fall 1992 term. 45% of entering class graduated.
**Foreign students:** Eight students are from out of the country. Countries represented include Canada, China, India, Japan, Malaysia, and Pakistan; seven in all.

**PROGRAMS OF STUDY. Degrees:** B.F.A.
**Majors:** Decorative Design, Graphic Design, Illustration, Painting, Printmaking, Sculpture.
**Distribution of degrees:** The majors with the highest enrollment are graphic design, illustration, and painting; printmaking has the lowest.
**Requirements:** General education requirement.
**Academic regulations:** Freshmen must maintain minimum 1.5 GPA; sophomores, 1.75 GPA; juniors, 2.0 GPA; seniors, 2.0 GPA.
**Special:** Minors offered in photography and computer imaging. Curriculum consists of four basic components: the Liberal Studies courses satisfy general education requirements; the Foundation Program develops basic visual arts skills, vocabulary, and principles, and must be completed in student's freshman and sophomore years; the Emphasis Studio element, in which the student concentrates on one specific discipline beyond the intermediate level, is a beginning toward specialization but does not constitute a major in the academic sense; and Elective Studios constitute the majority of studio courses and may continue the specialization begun in the Emphasis Studio phase. Courses in computer design and visual exploration required. Double majors. Independent study. Accelerated study. Internships. Cooperative education programs. Graduate school at which undergraduates may take graduate-level courses. Member of Greater Memphis Area Consortium and Alliance of Independent Colleges of Art and Design (AICAD). New York Studies Program. Exchange possible with other AICAD consortium schools.
**Academic Assistance:** Remedial study skills.

**ADMISSIONS. Academic basis for candidate selection** (in order of priority): Secondary school record, essay, school's recommendation, class rank, standardized test scores.
**Nonacademic basis for candidate selection:** Particular talent or ability is emphasized. Character and personality and extracurricular participation are important.
**Requirements:** Graduation from secondary school is required; GED is accepted. No specific distribution of secondary school units required. Portfolio of 10-20 pieces of best and most recent original work required; samples should display skill in several areas with variety of subject matter and media. Work may be presented in original form or in slide format. Presentation of portfolio at personal interview recommended. Minimum composite ACT score of 16 recommended. One point is added to admissions score if applicant has a minimum composite ACT score of 23 or minimum combined SAT score of 1050; one point is subtracted if composite ACT score is 15 or below or combined SAT score is 650 or below.

Conditional admission possible for applicants not meeting standard requirements. SAT or ACT is required. Campus visit and interview recommended. Off-campus interviews available with an admissions representative.
**Procedure:** Take SAT or ACT by February of 12th year. Suggest filing application by June 15. Application deadline is August 15. Notification of admission on rolling basis. No set date by which applicants must accept offer. $100 nonrefundable tuition deposit. Freshmen accepted in terms other than fall.
**Special programs:** Admission may be deferred one year. Credit and/or placement may be granted through CEEB Advanced Placement exams for scores of 3 or higher. Credit and/or placement may be granted through CLEP general and subject exams. Credit and placement may be granted through life experience. Early entrance/early admission program. Concurrent enrollment program.
**Transfer students:** Transfer students accepted for terms other than fall. In fall 1992, 20% of all new students were transfers into all classes. 76 transfer applications were received, 70 were accepted. Application deadline is rolling for fall; rolling for spring. Lowest course grade accepted is "C." Maximum number of transferable credits is 81 semester hours. At least 30 semester hours must be completed at the college to receive degree.
**Admissions contact:** Susan Miller, B.F.A., Director of Admissions. 800 727-1088.

**FINANCIAL AID. Available aid:** Pell grants, SEOG, state grants, school scholarships, private scholarships, academic merit scholarships, and aid for undergraduate foreign students. Perkins Loans (NDSL), PLUS, Stafford Loans (GSL), and SLS.
**Financial aid statistics:** In 1992-93, 85% of all undergraduate applicants received aid. Average amounts of aid awarded freshmen: Scholarships and grants, $1,800; loans, $2,625.
**Supporting data/closing dates:** FAFSA/FAF/FFS: Priority filing date is April 1. School's own aid application: Priority filing date is April 1; accepted on rolling basis. Notification of awards on rolling basis.
**Financial aid contact:** Beth Hoffman, Director of Financial Aid. 901 726-4085.

# Middle Tennessee State University

**Murfreesboro, TN 37132** **615 898-2300**

**1993-94 Costs.** Tuition: $1,480 (state residents), $5,082 (out-of-state). Room: $1,240. Board: $866. Fees, books, misc. academic expenses (school's estimate): $507.
**Enrollment.** Undergraduates: 5,959 men, 6,582 women (full-time). Freshman class: 4,587 applicants, 3,423 accepted, 2,132 enrolled. Graduate enrollment: 805 men, 1,152 women.
**Test score averages/ranges.** Average ACT scores: 20 composite.
**Faculty.** 677 full-time; 200 part-time. 63% of faculty holds highest degree in specific field. Student/faculty ratio: 20 to 1.
**Selectivity rating.** Less competitive.

**PROFILE.** Middle Tennessee State, founded in 1911, is a comprehensive, public university. Programs are offered through the Schools of Basic and Applied Sciences, Business, Education, Liberal Arts and Mass Communications. Its 500-acre campus is located in Murfreesboro, 30 miles southeast of Nashville.

**Accreditation:** SACS. Professionally accredited by the American Assembly of Collegiate Schools of Business, the Council on Social Work Education, the National Council for Accreditation of Teacher Education, the National League for Nursing.
**Religious orientation:** Middle Tennessee State University is nonsectarian; no religious requirements.
**Library:** Collections totaling over 518,000 volumes, 3,600 periodical subscriptions, and 842,000 microform items.
**Special facilities/museums:** On-campus nursery school, kindergarten, elementary school, radio/TV/photography mobile production lab, state-of-the-art recording studios.
**Athletic facilities:** Athletic center, basketball, handball, and tennis courts, gymnasiums, dance studios, track, athletic fields, swimming pool.

**STUDENT BODY. Undergraduate profile:** 95% are state residents; 45% are transfers. 2% Asian-American, 10% Black, 1% Hispanic, 87% White. Average age of undergraduates is 25.
**Freshman profile:** 3% of accepted applicants took SAT; 97% took ACT.
**Undergraduate achievement:** 40% of entering class graduated.
**Foreign students:** 325 students are from out of the country. Countries represented include China, India, Japan, Laos, Taiwan, and Thailand; 67 in all.

**PROGRAMS OF STUDY. Degrees:** B.A., B.Bus.Admin., B.F.A., B.Mus., B.S., B.S.Nurs., B.Soc.Work, B.Univ.Studies.
**Majors:** Accounting, Accounting/Information Systems, Advertising, Aerospace, Agribusiness, Animal Science, Art, Art Education, Audio, Biology, Broadcast Journalism, Broadcast Management, Broadcast Production, Business Administration, Business Education, Chemistry, Computer Science, Criminal Justice Administration, Digital Imaging, Distributive Education, Early Childhood Education, Economics, Elementary Education, English, Environmental Science/Technology, Fashion Merchandising, Finance, Foods/Nutrition, Foreign Languages, General Science, Geoscience, Graphic Communication, Health Education, History, Home Economics, Human Development/Family Life, Industrial Education, Industrial Technology, Interior Design, International Relations, Journalism, Management, Marketing, Mathematics, Medical Technology, Music, Nursing, Office Management, Philosophy, Photography, Physical Education, Physics, Plant/Soil Science, Political Science, Pre-Dental Hygiene, Pre-Dentistry, Pre-Medical Records Administration, Pre-Medicine, Pre-Nursing, Pre-Pharmacy, Pre-Physical Therapy, Pre-Veterinary, Psychology, Public Relations, Radio, Recording Industry Management, Recreation, Social Studies, Social Work, Sociology, Special Education, Speech/Theatre, Video, Vocational Home Economics Education.
**Requirements:** General education requirement.
**Academic regulations:** Freshmen must maintain minimum 1.5 GPA; sophomores, 1.8 GPA; juniors, 1.8 GPA; seniors, 2.0 GPA.
**Special:** Minors offered in many majors and in athletic coaching, business/economics for journalism, dance, driver safety education, earth science, information systems, insurance, library services, music arts, music education, music industry, religion, remote sensing, secondary education, speech/hearing therapy, urban planning, and interdisciplinary areas. Historic preservation program. Associate's degrees offered. Double majors. Dual degrees. Independent study. Accelerated study. Pass/fail grading option. Internships. Cooperative education programs. Graduate school at which undergraduates may take graduate-level courses. Preprofessional programs in law, medicine, veterinary science, pharmacy, dentistry, optometry, agricultural engineering, architecture, dental hygiene, engineering, medical records administration, nursing, occupational therapy, physical therapy, and radiologic technology. 3-2 engineering program with Tennessee Tech U. Member of consortium with Tennessee State U. Teacher certification in early childhood, elementary, secondary, special education, and vo-tech education. Study abroad in England and France. ROTC. AFROTC at Tennessee State U.
**Honors:** Honors program.
**Academic Assistance:** Remedial reading, writing, math, and study skills. Nonremedial tutoring.

**STUDENT LIFE. Housing:** Students may live on or off campus. Women's and men's dorms. School-owned/operated apartments. On-campus married-student housing. 30% of students live in college housing.
**Social atmosphere:** According to the student newspaper, "A lot of people at MTSU go home on weekends. Our town is basically dead on weekends." Influential groups on campus include the various Greek organizations, Christian groups (Baptist, Methodist, Presbyterian), service sororities and fraternities, and student bands. Popular campus events include Homecoming, basketball games, concerts, and movies. Favorite student gathering spots include the University Center Grill, Trotter's, Deli Junction, Mainstreet, and the Campus Pub.
**Services and counseling/handicapped student services:** Placement services. Health service. Women's center. Day care. Counseling services for minority, military, veteran, and older students. Birth control, personal, and psychological counseling. Career and academic guidance services. Physically disabled student services. Learning disabled services. Notetaking services. Tape recorders. Tutors. Reader services for the blind.
**Campus organizations:** Undergraduate student government. Student newspaper (Sidelines, published twice/week). Literary magazine. Yearbook. Radio and TV stations. Theatre, opera workshop, several instrumental groups, debating, professional and special-interest groups, 140 organizations in all. 13 fraternities, seven chapter houses; nine sororities, no chapter houses. 1% of men join a fraternity. 1% of women join a sorority.
**Religious organizations:** Bahai Faith, Baptist Student Union, Bible Study Group, Buddhist Discussion Group, Canterbury Club, Catholic Center, Crusade for Christ International, Fellowship of Christian Athletes, Followers Fellowship, Moslem Organization, Nondenominational Fellowship.
**Minority/foreign student organizations:** United Students Organization, Arab, Chinese, Indian, and Nigerian student groups.

**ATHLETICS. Physical education requirements:** Four semesters of physical education required.
**Intercollegiate competition:** 5% of students participate. Baseball (M), basketball (M,W), cross-country (M,W), football (M), golf (M), softball (W), tennis (M,W), track and field (indoor) (M,W), track and field (outdoor) (M,W), volleyball (W). Member of NCAA Division I, NCAA Division I-AA for football, Ohio Valley Conference.

**ADMISSIONS. Academic basis for candidate selection** (in order of priority): Secondary school record, standardized test scores, class rank.
**Requirements:** Graduation from secondary school is required; GED is accepted. 13 units and the following program of study are required: 4 units of English, 3 units of math, 2 units of science including 1 unit of lab, 2 units of foreign language, 1 unit of social studies, 1 unit of history. Minimum composite ACT score of 20 or minimum 2.8 GPA required. Variations of required secondary school units permitted only by applicants with minimum composite ACT score of 26. ACT required of in-state applicants; out-of-state applicants may submit SAT or ACT. Campus visit and interview recommended.
**Procedure:** Take SAT or ACT by December of 12th year. Application deadline is July 1. Notification of admission on rolling basis. $125 refundable room deposit. Freshmen accepted in terms other than fall.
**Special programs:** Admission may be deferred one year. Credit may be granted through CEEB Advanced Placement for scores of 3 or higher. Credit may be granted through CLEP general and subject exams, ACT PEP and challenge exams, and military experience. Early entrance/early admission program.
**Transfer students:** Transfer students accepted for terms other than fall. In fall 1993, 45% of all new students were transfers into all classes. 3,129 transfer applications were received, 2,348 were accepted. Application deadline is July 1 for fall; December 1 for spring. Minimum 2.0 GPA required. At least 30 semester hours must be completed at the university to receive degree.
**Admissions contact:** Lynn Palmer, M.Ed., Director of Admissions. 615 898-2111.

**FINANCIAL AID. Available aid:** Pell grants, SEOG, Federal Nursing Student Scholarships, state scholarships and grants, school scholarships and grants, private scholarships and grants, ROTC scholarships, academic merit scholarships, athletic scholarships, and aid for undergraduate foreign students. Perkins Loans (NDSL), PLUS, Stafford Loans (GSL), NSL, state loans, school loans, private loans, and SLS.
**Financial aid statistics:** 20% of aid is not need-based. In 1993-94, 55% of all freshman applicants received aid. Average amounts of aid awarded freshmen: Scholarships and grants, $1,612.
**Supporting data/closing dates:** FAFSA: Priority filing date is March 15. FAF/FFS: Priority filing date is March 15; accepted on rolling basis. School's own aid application: Priority filing date is March 15. Notification of awards begins May 15.
**Financial aid contact:** Robert Wrenn, Ed.S., Director of Financial Aid. 615 898-2830.

**STUDENT EMPLOYMENT.** College Work/Study Program. Institutional employment. 13% of full-time undergraduates work on campus during school year. Students may expect to earn an average of $1,200 during school year. Off-campus part-time employment opportunities rated "excellent."

**COMPUTER FACILITIES.** 200 IBM/IBM-compatible and Macintosh/Apple microcomputers; 100 are networked. Students may access Digital minicomputer/mainframe systems, BITNET, Internet. Residence halls may be equipped with stand-alone microcomputers. Client/LAN operating systems include Apple/Macintosh, DOS. Computer

languages and software packages include Assembler, C, COBOL, FOCUS, FORTRAN, Pascal. Computer facilities are available to all students.
**Fees:** None.
**Hours:** 8 AM-11 PM for some; 24 hours for others.

**PROMINENT ALUMNI/AE.** James McGill Buchanan, Nobel Prize-winning economist; Albert Gore, Sr., former U.S. senator; Gen. George Stoler, U.S. Army.

# Milligan College

**Milligan College, TN 37682** **615 461-8700**

**1994-95 Costs.** Tuition: $7,500. Room: $1,500. Board: $1,600. Fees, books, misc. academic expenses (school's estimate): $690.
**Enrollment.** Undergraduates: 291 men, 449 women (full-time). Freshman class: 382 applicants, 255 accepted, 188 enrolled. Graduate enrollment: 35 men, 44 women.
**Test score averages/ranges.** Average SAT scores: 475 verbal, 521 math. Average ACT scores: 21 English, 20 math, 22 composite.
**Faculty.** 46 full-time; 19 part-time. 65% of faculty holds highest degree in specific field. Student/faculty ratio: 14 to 1.
**Selectivity rating.** Competitive.

**PROFILE.** Milligan, founded in 1881, is a private, church-affiliated, liberal arts college. Its 135-acre campus is located in Milligan College, three miles southeast of Johnson City.

**Accreditation:** SACS. Professionally accredited by the National Council for Accreditation of Teacher Education.
**Religious orientation:** Milligan College is a nondenominational Christian school; three semesters of religion required.
**Library:** Collections totaling over 75,493 volumes, 553 periodical subscriptions, and 12,000 microform items.
**Athletic facilities:** Field house, swimming pool, baseball, soccer, and softball fields, tennis courts.

**STUDENT BODY. Undergraduate profile:** 30% are state residents; 24% are transfers. 1% Asian-American, 1% Black, 1% Hispanic, 1% Native American, 95% White, 1% Other. Average age of undergraduates is 21.
**Freshman profile:** 1% of freshmen who took SAT scored 700 or over on verbal, 7% scored 700 or over on math; 10% scored 600 or over on verbal, 27% scored 600 or over on math; 43% scored 500 or over on verbal, 61% scored 500 or over on math; 79% scored 400 or over on verbal, 85% scored 400 or over on math; 96% scored 300 or over on verbal, 97% scored 300 or over on math. 15% of freshmen who took ACT scored 30 or over on English, 9% scored 30 or over on math, 6% scored 30 or over on composite; 30% scored 24 or over on English, 20% scored 24 or over on math, 29% scored 24 or over on composite; 66% scored 18 or over on English, 54% scored 18 or over on math, 64% scored 18 or over on composite; 94% scored 12 or over on English, 90% scored 12 or over on math, 93% scored 12 or over on composite; 100% scored 6 or over on English, 100% scored 6 or over on math, 100% scored 6 or over on composite. 70% of accepted applicants took SAT; 55% took ACT. 80% of freshmen come from public schools.
**Undergraduate achievement:** 71% of fall 1992 freshmen returned for fall 1993 term. 43% of entering class graduated.
**Foreign students:** Eight students are from out of the country. Countries represented include Canada, Ghana, Indonesia, Japan, and the Philippines; six in all.

**PROGRAMS OF STUDY. Degrees:** B.A., B.S.
**Majors:** Accounting, Bible, Biology, Business Administration, Chemistry, Christian Education, Communications, Computer Science, Elementary Education, English, Family Ministry, Fine Arts, Health Care Administration, Health/Physical Education, History, Human Relations, Humanities, Legal Assisting, Mathematics, Missions, Music, Nursing, Office Administration, Organizational Management, Psychology, Social Agencies, Sociology, Youth Leadership, Youth Ministry.
**Distribution of degrees:** The majors with the highest enrollment are business administration, biology, and accounting; sociology, humanities, and Christian ministries have the lowest.
**Requirements:** General education requirement.
**Academic regulations:** Minimum 2.0 GPA must be maintained.
**Special:** Minors available in most majors and in French and German. Courses in art, government, Greek, Hebrew, physics, Spanish, and speech. College aims to introduce biblical data into content of each course. Double majors. Dual degrees. Independent study. Internships. Graduate school at which undergraduates may take graduate-level courses. Preprofessional programs in law, medicine, veterinary science, pharmacy, dentistry, and theology. 2-2 medical technology program with Western Carolina U. 3-1 prelaw and premedicine programs may be arranged. 3-2 engineering program with Georgia Tech. Member of Appalachian College Assessment Consortium. Washington Semester. Teacher certification in early childhood, elementary, secondary, and special education. Certification in specific subject areas. Study abroad in England. ROTC at East Tennessee State U.
**Academic Assistance:** Remedial reading, writing, and math. Nonremedial tutoring.

**ADMISSIONS. Academic basis for candidate selection** (in order of priority): Secondary school record, standardized test scores, class rank, school's recommendation.
**Nonacademic basis for candidate selection:** Character and personality are emphasized. Extracurricular participation is considered.
**Requirements:** Graduation from secondary school is required; GED is accepted. No specific distribution of secondary school units required. Minimum composite ACT score of 19 (combined SAT score of 900), minimum 3.0 GPA, and church and secondary school references required. Audition or tape required of music program applicants. SAT or ACT is required. Campus visit and interview recommended. Off-campus interviews available with an admissions representative.
**Procedure:** Take SAT or ACT by spring of 12th year. Visit college for interview by spring of 12th year. Application deadline is August 1. Notification of admission on rolling basis. $50 tuition deposit, refundable until May 1. $150 room deposit, refundable until May 1. Freshmen accepted in terms other than fall.
**Special programs:** Admission may be deferred one year. Credit may be granted through CEEB Advanced Placement for scores of 3 or higher. Credit may be granted through CLEP general and subject exams, DANTES exams, and life experience. Placement may be granted through challenge exams. Early entrance/early admission program.
**Transfer students:** Transfer students accepted for terms other than fall. In fall 1993, 24% of all new students were transfers into all classes. 92 transfer applications were received, 79 were accepted. Application deadline is August 1 for fall; December 1 for spring. Minimum 2.0 GPA required. Lowest course grade accepted is "C." At least 30 semester hours must be completed at the college to receive degree.
**Admissions contact:** Michael Johnson, Director of Admissions. 615 461-8730.

**FINANCIAL AID. Available aid:** Pell grants, SEOG, state grants, school scholarships, private scholarships and grants, academic merit scholarships, and athletic scholarships. Grant for nursing students. Perkins Loans (NDSL), PLUS, Stafford Loans (GSL), school loans, and SLS. AMS.
**Financial aid statistics:** 10% of aid is not need-based. In 1993-94, 90% of all undergraduate applicants received aid; 90% of freshman applicants. Average amounts of aid awarded freshmen: Scholarships and grants, $1,500.
**Supporting data/closing dates:** FAFSA: Priority filing date is April 1; accepted on rolling basis. FAF/FFS: Priority filing date is April 1. School's own aid application: Priority filing date is April 1; accepted on rolling basis. State aid form: Priority filing date is April 1; accepted on rolling basis. Income tax forms: Priority filing date is April 1; accepted on rolling basis. Notification of awards on rolling basis.
**Financial aid contact:** Nancy Beverly, Director of Financial Aid. 615 461-8713.

# Rhodes College

**Memphis, TN 38112** **901 726-3000**

**1994-95 Costs.** Tuition: $15,200. Room: $2,696. Board: $2,072. Fees, books, misc. academic expenses (school's estimate): $708.
**Enrollment.** Undergraduates: 605 men, 731 women (full-time). Freshman class: 2,302 applicants, 1,831 accepted, 391 enrolled. 5 men.
**Test score averages/ranges.** Range of SAT scores of middle 50%: 520-620 verbal, 570-680 math. Range of ACT scores of middle 50%: 25-30 composite.
**Faculty.** 115 full-time; 32 part-time. 99% of faculty holds highest degree in specific field. Student/faculty ratio: 12 to 1.
**Selectivity rating.** Highly competitive.

**PROFILE.** Rhodes is a church-affiliated college of arts and sciences. Founded in 1848, it adopted coeducation in 1916. Its 100-acre campus, with Gothic architectural style, is located in a residential area of Memphis.

**Accreditation:** SACS.
**Religious orientation:** Rhodes College is affiliated with the Presbyterian Church; four courses of religion, philosophy, or Western history required to complete core curriculum.
**Library:** Collections totaling over 230,000 volumes, 1,160 periodical subscriptions, and 35,000 microform items.
**Special facilities/museums:** Art gallery, anthropology museum, two reflecting telescopes, electron microscopes, cell culture lab, nuclear magnetic resonance instrument.
**Athletic facilities:** Gymnasiums, racquetball and tennis courts, weight rooms, swimming pool, baseball, football, multipurpose, and soccer fields.

**STUDENT BODY. Undergraduate profile:** 33% are state residents; 5% are transfers. 3% Asian-American, 5% Black, 92% White. Average age of undergraduates is 21.
**Freshman profile:** 7% of freshmen who took SAT scored 700 or over on verbal, 18% scored 700 or over on math; 41% scored 600 or over on verbal, 61% scored 600 or over on math; 86% scored 500 or over on verbal, 94% scored 500 or over on math; 100% scored 400 or over on verbal, 100% scored 400 or over on math. 27% of freshmen who took ACT scored 30 or over on English, 19% scored 30 or over on math, 32% scored 30 or over on composite; 85% scored 24 or over on English, 70% scored 24 or over on math, 93% scored 24 or over on composite; 99% scored 18 or over on English, 98% scored 18 or over on math, 100% scored 18 or over on composite; 100% scored 12 or over on English, 100% scored 12 or over on math. 74% of accepted applicants took SAT; 70% took ACT. 65% of freshmen come from public schools.
**Undergraduate achievement:** 86% of fall 1992 freshmen returned for fall 1993 term. 73% of entering class graduated. 36% of students who completed a degree program went on to graduate study within one year.
**Foreign students:** 45 students are from out of the country. Countries represented include Argentina, Belgium, Germany, India, Japan, and Pakistan; 16 in all.

**PROGRAMS OF STUDY. Degrees:** B.A., B.S.
**Majors:** Anthropology/Sociology, Art, Biology, Business Administration, Chemical Biology, Chemistry, Classics, Computer Science/Mathematics, Economics, Economics/Mathematics, English, French, German, History, Instrumental Music, International Studies, Latin American Cultural Studies, Mathematics, Music, Philosophy, Physics, Political Science, Psychology, Religious Studies, Russian/Soviet Cultural Studies, Spanish, Theatre/Media Arts, Urban Studies.
**Distribution of degrees:** The majors with the highest enrollment are psychology, English, and business administration.
**Requirements:** General education requirement.
**Academic regulations:** Freshmen must maintain minimum 1.6 GPA; sophomores, 1.8 GPA; juniors, 2.0 GPA; seniors, 2.0 GPA.
**Special:** Minors offered in most majors and in American, Asian, and women's studies. Self-designed majors. Double majors. Dual degrees. Independent study. Accelerated study. Pass/fail grading option. Internships. Graduate school at which undergraduates may take graduate-level courses. Preprofessional programs in law, medicine, veterinary science, pharmacy, and dentistry. Member of Associated Colleges of the South, Consortium for a Strong Minority Presence in Liberal Arts Colleges, Higher Education Data-sharing Consortium, PEW Science Consortium, and Southern Consortium on College Admissions. Washington Semester. Teacher certification in secondary education. Certification in specific subject areas. Exchange program abroad in Germany (U of Tubingen).

Study abroad also in Austria, England, France, Israel, Japan, Latin America, Mexico, and Spain. ROTC and AFROTC at Memphis State U.
**Honors:** Phi Beta Kappa. Honors program. Honor societies.
**Academic Assistance:** Nonremedial tutoring.

**STUDENT LIFE. Housing:** Students may live on or off campus. Women's and men's dorms. 77% of students live in college housing.
**Social atmosphere:** "The social life is good if you're a Greek," reports the student newspaper, "but if you are an independent, the city of Memphis offers off-campus entertainment. Memphis brings cultural events here such as the Ramses the Great exhibit, Broadway shows, symphony concerts, opera, art openings, etc." Popular campus events include the Rhodes Jazzfest, the Reggae-oriented Rites of Spring, and the Interfraternity Council/Panhellenic formal. "Alex's Tavern, just down Jackson Avenue, is the off-campus place to be. Lots of smoke, but a good place to mingle."
**Services and counseling/handicapped student services:** Placement services. Health service. Writing workshop. Counseling services for minority, veteran, and older students. Birth control, personal, and psychological counseling. Career and academic guidance services. Religious counseling. Physically disabled student services. Notetaking services. Tape recorders. Tutors.
**Campus organizations:** Undergraduate student government. Student newspaper (Sou'wester, published once/week). Literary magazine. Yearbook. Rhodes Singers, pep band, orchestra, drama groups, honor council, social regulations council, American Chemical Society, health professions group, philosophy club, College Bowl, Model UN, BACCHUS, academic journal, social and political groups, departmental organizations, 70 organizations in all. Six fraternities, all with chapter houses; seven sororities, four chapter houses. 58% of men join a fraternity. 57% of women join a sorority.
**Religious organizations:** Baptist Student Union, Fellowship of Christian Athletes, Catholic Student Association, Jewish Fellowship, Religion Commission.
**Minority/foreign student organizations:** Black Student Association. International House, All Students Interested in Asia.

**ATHLETICS. Physical education requirements:** Three half-semester courses of physical education required.
**Intercollegiate competition:** 21% of students participate. Baseball (M), basketball (M,W), cross-country (M,W), football (M), golf (M), soccer (M,W), tennis (M,W), track (outdoor) (M,W), track and field (outdoor) (M,W), volleyball (W). Member of College Athletic Conference, NCAA Division III, Southern Collegiate Athletic Conference.
**Intramural and club sports:** 37% of students participate. Intramural basketball, flag football, frisbee, oof ball, racquetball, softball, table tennis, tennis, volleyball, water polo. Men's club cheerleading, horsemanship, lacrosse, rugby. Women's club cheerleading, horsemanship.

**ADMISSIONS. Academic basis for candidate selection** (in order of priority): Secondary school record, class rank, standardized test scores, school's recommendation, essay.
**Nonacademic basis for candidate selection:** Character and personality are emphasized. Extracurricular participation, particular talent or ability, geographical distribution, and alumni/ae relationship are important.
**Requirements:** Graduation from secondary school is required; GED is accepted. 16 units and the following program of study are required: 4 units of English, 3 units of math, 2 units of foreign language. 2 units of social studies or history recommended. Minor program deviations may be accepted from applicants of superior ability. SAT or ACT is required. Campus visit and interview recommended. Off-campus interviews available with an admissions representative.
**Procedure:** Take SAT or ACT by December of 12th year. Visit college for interview by February 1 of 12th year. Suggest filing application by February 1; no deadline. Notification of admission by April 1. Reply is required by May 1. $200 nonrefundable tuition deposit. $200 nonrefundable room deposit. Freshmen accepted in terms other than fall.
**Special programs:** Admission may be deferred one year. Credit and/or placement may be granted through CEEB Advanced Placement exams for scores of 4 or higher. Early decision program. In fall 1993, 48 applied for early decision and 38 were accepted. Deadline for applying for early decision is November 15. Early entrance/early admission program. Concurrent enrollment program.
**Transfer students:** Transfer students accepted for terms other than fall. In fall 1993, 5% of all new students were transfers into all classes. 96 transfer applications were received, 44 were accepted. Application deadline is February 1 for fall; December 1 for spring. Minimum 2.5 GPA. Lowest course grade accepted is "C." Maximum number of transferable credits is 56 semester hours. At least 56 semester hours must be completed at the college to receive degree.
**Admissions contact:** David J. Wottle, Dean of Admissions and Financial Aid. 901 726-3700, 800 844-5969.

**FINANCIAL AID. Available aid:** Pell grants, SEOG, state scholarships and grants, school scholarships and grants, private scholarships and grants, ROTC scholarships, academic merit scholarships, and aid for undergraduate foreign students. Perkins Loans (NDSL), PLUS, Stafford Loans (GSL), state loans, school loans, private loans, and SLS. Guaranteed Access to Education (GATE) loans, Presbyterian Church student loans. Tuition Plan Inc., Education Plan Inc., and Knight Tuition Plans. Insured Tuition Payment Plan.
**Financial aid statistics:** 31% of aid is not need-based. In 1993-94, 99% of all undergraduate applicants received aid; 100% of freshman applicants. Average amounts of aid awarded freshmen: Scholarships and grants, $7,920; loans, $3,043.
**Supporting data/closing dates:** FAFSA/FAF: Priority filing date is March 1. School's own aid application: Priority filing date is March 1. Income tax forms: Priority filing date is March 1. Notification of awards on rolling basis.
**Financial aid contact:** Art Weeden, M.Ed., Dean of Financial Aid. 901 726-3810.

**STUDENT EMPLOYMENT.** College Work/Study Program. Institutional employment. 31% of full-time undergraduates work on campus during school year. Students may expect to earn an average of $1,068 during school year. Off-campus part-time employment opportunities rated "good."

**COMPUTER FACILITIES.** 110 Macintosh/Apple microcomputers; 100 are networked. Students may access Digital, SUN minicomputer/mainframe systems, BITNET, Internet. Client/LAN operating systems include Apple/Macintosh, LocalTalk/AppleTalk. Computer languages and software packages include Atlas Pro, BASIC, C, COBOL, EQS, Excel, FORTRAN, Lotus 1-2-3, MINITAB, MAPLE, Mathematica, Pascal, REF-11, SAS, SIGI, SPSS, Stella, SuperPaint, Systat, TEX, TSP, 20/20, WordPerfect, Works. Computer facilities are available to all students.
**Fees:** None.
**Hours:** 24 hours for most systems.

**GRADUATE CAREER DATA.** Graduate school percentages: 6% enter law school. 8% enter medical school. 1% enter dental school. 2% enter graduate business programs. 18% enter graduate arts and sciences programs. 1% enter theological school/seminary. Highest graduate school enrollments: Columbia U, Emory U, Johns Hopkins U, U of Tennessee at Memphis, Vanderbilt U. 56% of graduates choose careers in business and industry. Companies and businesses that hire graduates: IBM, Federal Express, Merrill Lynch, Holiday Corp., Schering Plough, IRS, Exxon, AT&T.

**PROMINENT ALUMNI/AE.** J. David Alexander, former president, Pomona Coll; Abe Fortas, former U.S. Supreme Court nominee; Anne Howard Bailey, Emmy Award-winning writer and editor; Hilton McConnico, filmmaker; Melanie Smith, Olympic gold-medal equestrienne; John Bryan, CEO, Sara Lee; Dixie Carter, actress, "Designing Women."

# Southern College of Seventh-day Adventists

**Collegedale, TN 37315-0370 — 615 238-2111**

**1994-95 Costs.** Tuition: $8,414. Room: $1,530. Board: $1,966. Fees, books, misc. academic expenses (school's estimate): $529.
**Enrollment.** Undergraduates: 577 men, 691 women (full-time). Freshman class: 790 applicants, 768 accepted, 470 enrolled.
**Test score averages/ranges.** Average ACT scores: 22 English, 20 math, 22 composite.
**Faculty.** 90 full-time; 5 part-time. 49% of faculty holds doctoral degree. Student/faculty ratio: 14 to 1.
**Selectivity rating.** Less competitive.

**PROFILE.** Southern College, founded in 1892, is a church-affiliated, liberal arts college. Its 1,000-acre campus is located in Collegedale, 18 miles northeast of Chattanooga.

**Accreditation:** SACS. Professionally accredited by the National Council for Accreditation of Teacher Education, the National League for Nursing.
**Religious orientation:** Southern College is affiliated with the Seventh-day Adventist Church; four semesters of religion required.
**Library:** Collections totaling over 100,653 volumes, 950 periodical subscriptions and 157 microform items.
**Special facilities/museums:** Lincoln museum, Tracker Organ.
**Athletic facilities:** Swimming pool, gymnasium, weight rooms, racquetball and tennis courts, track, playing fields, golf course, sailing facilities.

**STUDENT BODY. Undergraduate profile:** 21% are state residents; 9% are transfers. 4% Asian-American, 6% Black, 8% Hispanic, 1% Native American, 81% White. Average age of undergraduates is 21.
**Freshman profile:** Majority of accepted applicants took ACT. 13% of freshmen come from public schools.
**Undergraduate achievement:** 60% of fall 1992 freshmen returned for fall 1993 term. 36% of entering class graduated. 40% of students who completed a degree program immediately went on to graduate study.
**Foreign students:** 110 students are from out of the country. Countries represented include Canada, Indonesia, Jamaica, the Philippines, and South Africa; 42 in all.

**PROGRAMS OF STUDY. Degrees:** B.A., B.Bus.Admin., B.Mus., B.S., B.Soc.Work.
**Majors:** Behavioral Science, Biology, Business Administration, Business Education, Chemistry, Communication, Communication Design, Computer Science, Elementary Education, English, French, German, Health/Physical Education/Recreation, Health Sciences, History, International Studies, Long-term Health Care, Management, Marketing, Mathematics, Medical Science, Medical Technology, Music, Music Education, Nursing, Physics, Psychology, Religion, Social Work, Spanish, Theology.
**Distribution of degrees:** The majors with the highest enrollment are nursing, business, and biology; physics, foreign languages, and mathematics have the lowest.
**Requirements:** General education requirement.
**Academic regulations:** Freshmen must maintain minimum 2.0 GPA; sophomores, 2.0 GPA; juniors, 2.0 GPA; seniors, 2.25 GPA.
**Special:** Minors offered in many majors and in advertising, art, biblical languages, broadcast journalism, journalism, office administration, political economy, public relations, sales, sociology, and technology. One-year certificate programs in auto body repair, clerical skills, and food service technology. Associate's degrees offered. Double majors. Dual degrees. Internships. Preprofessional programs in law, medicine, veterinary science, pharmacy, dentistry, and optometry. 2-2 engineering program with Walla Walla Coll. 3-2 prephysical therapy program with Andrews U and Loma Linda U. Teacher certification in elementary and secondary education. Certification in specific subject areas. Study abroad in Austria, France, and Spain.
**Honors:** Honors program. Honor societies.
**Academic Assistance:** Remedial reading, math, and study skills.

**STUDENT LIFE. Housing:** All unmarried students under age 23 must live on campus. Women's and men's dorms. On-campus married-student housing. 90% of students live in college housing.
**Social atmosphere:** The editor of the student newspaper writes that the campus social life is "improved over past years but still needs help." The social atmosphere is influenced by Christian groups, "pseudo-Greeks," and "preppies." Popular events include basketball games and banquets, such as the Valentine's Day Banquet. Favorite hangouts are the Hamilton Place Mall and K.R. Place (cafe).
**Services and counseling/handicapped student services:** Placement services. Health service. Personal and psychological counseling. Career and academic guidance services. Religious counseling. Physically disabled student services. Learning disabled services. Tutors.

**Campus organizations:** Undergraduate student government. Student newspaper (Accent, published six times/year). Yearbook. Radio station. Orchestra, band, choirs, men's chorus, academic and recreational groups, social clubs, special-interest groups.
**Religious organizations:** Youth Ministries.

**ATHLETICS. Physical education requirements:** Two semesters of physical education required.
**Intramural and club sports:** 65% of students participate. Intramural badminton, basketball, cycling, flag football, floor hockey, golf, gymnastics, racquetball, soccer, softball, swimming, tennis, triathlon, volleyball.

**ADMISSIONS. Academic basis for candidate selection** (in order of priority): Secondary school record, standardized test scores, school's recommendation, class rank.
**Nonacademic basis for candidate selection:** Character and personality and alumni/ae relationship are considered.
**Requirements:** Graduation from secondary school is required; GED is accepted. 13 units and the following program of study are required: 4 units of English, 2 units of math, 2 units of science including 1 unit of lab, 2 units of history, 1 unit of academic electives. Minimum 2.0 GPA required. Conditional admission possible for applicants not meeting standard requirements. ACT is required. Campus visit and interview recommended. Off-campus interviews available with an admissions representative.
**Procedure:** Take ACT by December 15 of 12th year. Visit college for interview by April of 12th year. Suggest filing application by April 1. Application deadline is August 1. Notification of admission on rolling basis. $1850 tuition deposit, refundable until August 20. $100 room deposit, refundable until August 20. Freshmen accepted in terms other than fall.
**Special programs:** Admission may be deferred one year. Credit may be granted through CEEB Advanced Placement for scores of 3 or higher. Credit may be granted through CLEP subject exams and challenge exams. Deadline for applying for early decision is August 1. Early entrance/early admission program. Concurrent enrollment program.
**Transfer students:** Transfer students accepted for terms other than fall. In fall 1993, 9% of all new students were transfers into all classes. Application deadline is August 1 for fall; December 1 for spring. Minimum 2.0 GPA required. Lowest course grade accepted is "C-." Maximum number of transferable credits is 94 semester hours. At least 30 semester hours must be completed at the college to receive degree.
**Admissions contact:** Ronald M. Barrow, Ph.D., Vice President for Admissions and College Relations. 615 238-2844.

**FINANCIAL AID. Available aid:** Pell grants, SEOG, state grants, school scholarships, private scholarships, and academic merit scholarships. Perkins Loans (NDSL), PLUS, Stafford Loans (GSL), NSL, school loans, private loans, and SLS. Tuition Plan Inc., AMS, deferred payment plan, family tuition reduction, and guaranteed tuition.
**Financial aid statistics:** In 1993-94, 96% of all undergraduate applicants received aid; 92% of freshman applicants. Average amounts of aid awarded freshmen: Scholarships and grants, $2,000; loans, $2,900.
**Supporting data/closing dates:** FAFSA/FAF/FFS: Priority filing date is May 1. School's own aid application: Priority filing date is June 1. Notification of awards on rolling basis.
**Financial aid contact:** Kenneth Norton, M.A., Director of Financial Aid. 615 238-2834.

**STUDENT EMPLOYMENT.** College Work/Study Program. Institutional employment. 66% of full-time undergraduates work on campus during school year. Students may expect to earn an average of $1,200 during school year. Off-campus part-time employment opportunities rated "good."

**COMPUTER FACILITIES.** 150 IBM/IBM-compatible and Macintosh/Apple microcomputers; 30 are networked. Students may access Hewlett-Packard minicomputer/mainframe systems. Computer languages and software packages include BASIC, COBOL, dBASE, FORTRAN, Lotus 1-2-3, Pascal, WordPerfect. Computer facilities are available to all students.
**Fees:** None.

**GRADUATE CAREER DATA.** Highest graduate school enrollments: Andrews U, Loma Linda U. 20% of graduates choose careers in business and industry. Companies and businesses that hire graduates: Health Systems, McKee Baking Co.

**PROMINENT ALUMNI/AE.** O.D. McKee, chairperson of the board, McKee Baking Co.; Ellsworth McKee, president, McKee Baking Co.; Denzil McMeilus, president, McMeilus Corp.

## Tennessee State University

**Nashville, TN 37203** **615 320-3214**

**1993-94 Costs.** Tuition: $1,706 (state residents), $8,408 (out-of-state). Room: $1,420. Board: $1,300. Fees, books, misc. academic expenses (school's estimate): $1,700.
**Enrollment.** Undergraduates: 1,928 men, 2,855 women (full-time). Freshman class: 4,013 applicants, 3,151 accepted, 783 enrolled. Graduate enrollment: 426 men, 808 women.
**Test score averages/ranges.** Average ACT scores: 20 composite.
**Faculty.** 294 full-time. 58% of faculty holds doctoral degree. Student/faculty ratio: 25 to 1.
**Selectivity rating.** Less competitive.

**PROFILE.** Tennessee State, founded in 1912, is a public, historically black university. Programs are offered through the Schools of Agriculture and Home Economics, Allied Health Professions, Arts and Sciences, Business, Education, Engineering and Technology, Nursing, and the Graduate School. Its 465-acre main campus is located north of the center of Nashville.

**Accreditation:** SACS. Professionally accredited by the Accreditation Board for Engineering and Technology, the American Home Economics Association, the American Medical Association (CAHEA), the Council on Social Work Education, the National Association of Schools of Music, the National Council for Accreditation of Teacher Education.
**Religious orientation:** Tennessee State University is nonsectarian; no religious requirements.
**Library:** Collections totaling over 420,463 volumes, 1,775 periodical subscriptions, and 657,532 microform items.
**Athletic facilities:** Sports complex.

**STUDENT BODY. Undergraduate profile:** 79% are state residents; 20% are transfers. 1% Asian-American, 62% Black, 1% Hispanic, 35% White, 1% Other. Average age of undergraduates is 25.
**Freshman profile:** 10% of accepted applicants took SAT; 90% took ACT. 90% of freshmen come from public schools.
**Foreign students:** 115 students are from out of the country. Countries represented include the Bahamas, Canada, Jordan, Kuwait, Nigeria, and Saudi Arabia; 38 in all.

**PROGRAMS OF STUDY. Degrees:** B.A., B.Bus.Admin., B.S., B.S.Nurs.
**Majors:** Accounting, Aeronautical/Industrial Technology, African Studies, Agricultural Sciences, Architectural Engineering, Art, Arts/Sciences, Biology, Business Administration, Business Education, Cardiorespiratory Care Sciences, Chemistry, Civil Engineering, Criminal Justice, Dental Hygiene, Early Childhood Education, Economics, Electrical Engineering, Finance, Foreign Languages, General Home Economics, General Interdisciplinary Studies, Health Care Administration/Planning, Health/Physical Education/Recreation Education, History/Geography/Political Science, Home Economics Education, Language/Literature/Philosophy, Mechanical Engineering, Medical Records Administration, Medical Technology, Music, Nursing, Occupational Therapy, Office Management, Physical Therapy, Physics/Mathematics/Computer Science, Psychology, Respiratory Therapy, Social Work/Sociology, Special Education, Speech Communication/ Theatre, Speech Pathology/ Audiology.
**Special:** Minors offered. Internships. Preprofessional programs in medicine, veterinary science, dentistry, occupational theraphy, physical therapy, and social work. 2-2 pre-dentistry and 3-2 pre-medicine programs with Meharry Medical Coll. 3-1 medical technology program offered in cooperation with local hospitals. Natural science courses offered at Gulf Coast Research Lab. Teacher certification in elementary, secondary, and special education. Certification in specific subject areas. AFROTC. ROTC and NROTC at Vanderbilt U.
**Honors:** Phi Beta Kappa. Honors program.
**Academic Assistance:** Remedial reading, writing, math, and study skills.

**STUDENT LIFE. Housing:** Students may live on or off campus. Women's and men's dorms. 25% of students live in college housing.
**Services and counseling/handicapped student services:** Placement services. Health service. Day care. Counseling services for minority and veteran students. Birth control, personal, and psychological counseling. Career and academic guidance services.
**Campus organizations:** Undergraduate student government. Student newspaper (Meter). Yearbook. Radio station. String ensembles, concert singers, concert and marching bands, choir, jazz group, children's theatre, Players Guild, debate society, athletic, departmental, service, and special-interest groups. Four fraternities, no chapter houses; four sororities, no chapter houses. 1% of men join a fraternity. 1% of women join a sorority.
**Religious organizations:** Student Christian Association, Baptist Club, Catholic Club.

**ATHLETICS. Physical education requirements:** Two semesters of physical education required.
**Intercollegiate competition:** Baseball (M), basketball (M,W), cheerleading (M,W), cross-country (M,W), football (M), golf (M), tennis (M,W), track and field (indoor) (W), track and field (outdoor) (W), volleyball (W). Member of NCAA Division I, NCAA Division I-AA for football, Ohio Valley Conference.
**Intramural and club sports:** Intramural basketball.

**ADMISSIONS. Academic basis for candidate selection** (in order of priority): Secondary school record, standardized test scores, class rank, school's recommendation, essay.
**Nonacademic basis for candidate selection:** Character and personality, particular talent or ability, and alumni/ae relationship are considered.
**Requirements:** Graduation from secondary school is required; GED is accepted. 14 units and the following program of study are required: 4 units of English, 3 units of math, 2 units of science including 1 unit of lab, 2 units of foreign language, 1 unit of social studies, 1 unit of history, 1 unit of visual/performing arts. Minimum composite ACT score of 19 and minimum 2.25 GPA required of in-state applicants; minimum composite ACT score of 19 and minimum 2.5 GPA required of out-of-state applicants. Developmental studies program for applicants not normally admissible. ACT is required; SAT may be substituted. No off-campus interviews.
**Procedure:** Take SAT or ACT by November of 12th year. Application deadline is August 1. Notification of admission on rolling basis. No set date by which applicants must accept offer. $50 nonrefundable room deposit. Freshmen accepted in terms other than fall.
**Special programs:** Credit may be granted through CEEB Advanced Placement for scores of 4 or higher. Credit may be granted through CLEP subject exams, DANTES and challenge exams, and military experience. Placement may be granted through ACT PEP exams.
**Transfer students:** Transfer students accepted for terms other than fall. In fall 1993, 20% of all new students were transfers into all classes. 883 transfer applications were received, 803 were accepted. Application deadline is August 1 for fall; December 1 for spring. Minimum 2.0 GPA required. Lowest course grade accepted is "C." At least 60 semester hours must be completed at the university to receive degree.
**Admissions contact:** Carmelia Taylor, Ed.D., Interim Dean of Admissions and Records. 615 320-3725.

**FINANCIAL AID. Available aid:** Pell grants, SEOG, state grants, school scholarships and grants, private scholarships and grants, ROTC scholarships, academic merit scholarships, athletic scholarships, aid for undergraduate foreign students, and United Negro College Fund. Perkins Loans (NDSL), Stafford Loans (GSL), and school loans.
**Financial aid statistics:** In 1993-94, 75% of all undergraduate applicants received aid; 75% of freshman applicants. Average amounts of aid awarded freshmen: Scholarships and grants, $400.
**Supporting data/closing dates:** FAFSA/FAF/FFS: Priority filing date is April 1. School's own aid application: Priority filing date is April 1. Notification of awards on rolling basis.
**Financial aid contact:** Wilson Lee, Jr, M.S., M.P.A., Director of Financial Aid. 615 320-3750.

**STUDENT EMPLOYMENT.** College Work/Study Program. Institutional employment. 20% of full-time undergraduates work on campus during school year. Students may

expect to earn an average of $900 during school year. Off-campus part-time employment opportunities rated "excellent."

**COMPUTER FACILITIES.** 300 IBM/IBM-compatible microcomputers; 150 are networked. Students may access Digital minicomputer/mainframe systems. Client/LAN operating systems include DOS, Microsoft. Computer languages and software packages include BASIC, COBOL, FORTRAN, SAS, SPSS. Computer facilities are available to all students.
**Fees:** None.
**Hours:** 8 AM-10 PM.

# Tennessee Technological University

**Cookeville, TN 38505** **615 372-3101**

**1994-95 Costs.** Tuition: $1,710 (state residents), $5,492 (out-of-state). Room & board: $3,480. Fees, books, misc. academic expenses (school's estimate): $330.
**Enrollment.** Undergraduates: 3,547 men, 2,914 women (full-time). Freshman class: 2,594 applicants, 2,542 accepted, 1,336 enrolled. Graduate enrollment: 449 men, 521 women.
**Test score averages/ranges.** Average ACT scores: 22 composite. Range of ACT scores of middle 50%: 20-25 composite.
**Faculty.** 379 full-time; 115 part-time. 84% of faculty holds highest degree in specific field. Student/faculty ratio: 20 to 1.
**Selectivity rating.** Less competitive.

**PROFILE.** Tennessee Tech, founded in 1915, is a public, multipurpose university. Programs are offered through the Appalachian Center for Crafts; the Colleges of Arts and Sciences, Business Administration, Education, and Engineering; the Graduate School; and the Schools of Agriculture, Home Economics, and Nursing. Its 235-acre campus is located in Cookeville, 80 miles east of Nashville.

**Accreditation:** SACS. Professionally accredited by the Accreditation Board for Engineering and Technology, the American Assembly of Collegiate Schools of Business, the National Association of Schools of Music, the National Council for Accreditation of Teacher Education, the National League for Nursing.
**Religious orientation:** Tennessee Technological University is nonsectarian; no religious requirements.
**Library:** Collections totaling over 282,875 volumes, 3,050 periodical subscriptions, and 1,069,000 microform items.
**Special facilities/museums:** 550-acre biological research station on reservoir, 300-acre farm lab, electric power center.
**Athletic facilities:** Gymnasium, fitness center, swimming pool, racquetball and tennis courts, track, athletic fields.

**STUDENT BODY. Undergraduate profile:** 96% are state residents; 8% are transfers. 3% Asian-American, 3% Black, 1% Hispanic, 1% Native American, 92% White. Average age of undergraduates is 21.
**Freshman profile:** 4% of freshmen who took ACT scored 30 or over on composite; 39% scored 24 or over on composite; 90% scored 18 or over on composite; 100% scored 12 or over on composite. 100% of accepted applicants took ACT. 98% of freshmen come from public schools.
**Undergraduate achievement:** 65% of fall 1992 freshmen returned for fall 1993 term. 10% of entering class graduated. 15% of students who completed a degree program immediately went on to graduate study.
**Foreign students:** 238 students are from out of the country. Countries represented include Canada, China, India, Indonesia, Japan, and Malaysia; 52 in all.

**PROGRAMS OF STUDY. Degrees:** B.A., B.Bus.Admin., B.F.A., B.S.
**Majors:** Accounting, Acoustics, Aerospace, Agribusiness Economics, Agricultural Education, Agricultural Engineering Technology, Agricultural Sciences, Agronomy, Animal Science, Art Education, Biology, Business Management, Chemical Engineering, Chemistry, Child Care Services, Child/Family Science, Civil Engineering, Clothing Merchandising, Computer/Information Sciences, Computers/Digital Systems, Crafts, Criminal Justice, Decision Sciences, Design/Mechanical Systems, Early Childhood Education, Economics, Electrical/Communications Engineering, Elementary Education, Energy Conversion, English, English/Journalism, Environmental Engineering, Finance, Fine Arts, Food/Nutrition/Dietetics, Food Services, French, Geology, German, Health/Physical Education, History, Home Economics, Home Economics Education, Horticulture, Human Environment/Housing, Industrial Engineering, Industrial Technology Management/Supervision, Instrumental Music, Interior Design, Management Information Systems, Marketing, Material Science, Mathematics, Mechanical Engineering, Mechanical Engineering/Control Systems, Mechanical Engineering/Environmental, Metal Casting, Metals Manufacturing, Music Therapy, Networks/Control Systems, Nuclear Systems, Nursing, Occupational Home Economics, Performance/Pedagogy, Personnel/Labor Relations, Physical Phenomena, Physics, Planning/Municipal Engineering, Plant Sciences, Political Science, Power Systems/Energy Conversion, Production/Operations Management, Psychology, Secondary Education, Sociology, Soil Science, Spanish, Special Education, Structural Engineering, Structural Mechanics, Technical Communications, Textiles/Clothing, Transportation Engineering, Vocal/General Music, Wildlife/Fisheries.
**Distribution of degrees:** The majors with the highest enrollment are electrical engineering, business management, and civil engineering; home economics, agriculture, and nursing have the lowest.
**Requirements:** General education requirement.
**Academic regulations:** Minimum 2.0 GPA required for graduation.
**Special:** Minors offered in all majors and in military science. Associate's degrees offered. Double majors. Dual degrees. Cooperative education programs. Graduate school at which undergraduates may take graduate-level courses. Preprofessional programs in law, medicine, veterinary science, pharmacy, dentistry, and optometry. Member of consortium with the Biological Research Station. Teacher certification in early childhood, elementary, secondary, and special education. Certification in specific subject areas. Study abroad possible. ROTC.
**Honors:** Honors program.
**Academic Assistance:** Remedial reading, writing, math, and study skills.

**STUDENT LIFE. Housing:** All freshmen and sophomores must live on campus. Women's and men's dorms. Fraternity housing. School-owned/operated apartments. On-campus married-student housing. 40% of students live in college housing.
**Social atmosphere:** The student newspaper reports, "Tennessee Tech is not known as a party school, and Cookeville is not a large, cultural city. But for the student who wants a rich social and cultural life, opportunities do exist." Both Greek and Christian groups influence student social life. The most popular social events of the year are Homecoming, Greek Week, Spring Fling, and all athletic contests against "arch rival" Middle Tennessee State U. Many students often make outings to Center Hill Lake, Burgess Falls, and Window Cliffs. Popular nightspots include Bud's, John's, and Grady's.
**Services and counseling/handicapped student services:** Placement services. Health service. Day care. Counseling services for minority, military, veteran, and older students. Birth control, personal, and psychological counseling. Career and academic guidance services. Religious counseling. Physically disabled student services. Learning disabled services. Notetaking services. Tape recorders. Tutors. Reader services for the blind.
**Campus organizations:** Undergraduate student government. Student newspaper (Oracle, published once/week). Literary magazine. Yearbook. Radio and TV stations. Bands, stage bands, chorus, choir, orchestra, Tech Troubadours and Players, 166 organizations in all. 16 fraternities, 14 chapter houses; six sororities, no chapter houses. 18% of men join a fraternity. 12% of women join a sorority.
**Religious organizations:** Baptist Student Union, Fellowship of Christian Athletes, Intervarsity Christian Fellowship, Jewish, Lutheran, and Muslim groups, Latter-Day Saints Student Association, Presbyterian Student Association, University Christian Student Center, Wesley Foundation.
**Minority/foreign student organizations:** Black Student Organization, minority fraternities/sororities. Indian Association, Chinese Student Club.

**ATHLETICS. Physical education requirements:** Two semesters of physical education required.
**Intercollegiate competition:** 2% of students participate. Baseball (M), basketball (M,W), cheerleading (M,W), cross-country (M,W), football (M), golf (M,W), riflery (M,W), softball (W), tennis (M,W), track (indoor) (W), track (outdoor) (W), volleyball (W). Member of NCAA Division I, NCAA Division I-AA for football, Ohio Valley Conference.
**Intramural and club sports:** 80% of students participate. Intramural basketball, bowling, football, golf, soccer, softball, tennis, volleyball, wrestling. Men's club rugby.

**ADMISSIONS. Academic basis for candidate selection** (in order of priority): Secondary school record, standardized test scores, school's recommendation, class rank.
**Requirements:** Graduation from secondary school is required; GED is accepted. 13 units and the following program of study are required: 4 units of English, 3 units of math, 2 units of science including 1 unit of lab, 2 units of foreign language, 1 unit of social studies, 1 unit of history. Minimum composite ACT score of 19 and minimum 2.35 GPA recommended. ACT is required. Campus visit and interview recommended. Off-campus interviews available with an admissions representative.
**Procedure:** Suggest filing application by March 1. Application deadline is September 1. Notification of admission on rolling basis. Reply is required by August 1. $25 refundable room deposit. Freshmen accepted in terms other than fall.
**Special programs:** Admission may be deferred one year. Credit and/or placement may be granted through CEEB Advanced Placement exams and CLEP subject exams. Credit may be granted through military experience. Concurrent enrollment program.
**Transfer students:** Transfer students accepted for terms other than fall. In fall 1993, 8% of all new students were transfers into all classes. Application deadline is August 15 for fall; January 6 for spring. Minimum 2.0 GPA required. Lowest course grade accepted is "D." At least 2 semesters must be completed at the university to receive degree.
**Admissions contact:** James C. Perry, Ph.D., Director of Admissions. 615 372-3888, 800 255-8881.

**FINANCIAL AID. Available aid:** Pell grants, SEOG, state scholarships and grants, school scholarships and grants, private scholarships and grants, ROTC scholarships, academic merit scholarships, and athletic scholarships. Perkins Loans (NDSL), PLUS, Stafford Loans (GSL), NSL, state loans, school loans, private loans, and SLS. Deferred payment plan.
**Financial aid statistics:** 10% of aid is not need-based. In 1993-94, 65% of all undergraduate applicants received aid; 75% of freshman applicants. Average amounts of aid awarded freshmen: Scholarships and grants, $1,100; loans, $1,900.
**Supporting data/closing dates:** FAFSA/FFS: Priority filing date is March 15; accepted on rolling basis. Income tax forms: Priority filing date is March 15; accepted on rolling basis.
**Financial aid contact:** Raymond L. Holbrook, Ph.D., Director of Financial Aid. 615 372-3073.

**STUDENT EMPLOYMENT.** College Work/Study Program. Institutional employment. 18% of full-time undergraduates work on campus during school year. Students may expect to earn an average of $1,150 during school year. Off-campus part-time employment opportunities rated "good."

**COMPUTER FACILITIES.** 150 IBM/IBM-compatible and Macintosh/Apple microcomputers. Students may access Digital minicomputer/mainframe systems, Internet. Residence halls may be equipped with networked microcomputers. Client/LAN operating systems include Apple/Macintosh, DOS. Computer languages and software packages include BASIC, COBOL, FORTRAN, Pascal. Computer facilities are available to all students.
**Fees:** $1 computer fee per credit hour; included in tuition/fees.
**Hours:** 24 hours.

**GRADUATE CAREER DATA.** Highest graduate school enrollments: U of Tennessee, Tennessee Tech U, Vanderbilt U. 50% of graduates choose careers in business and industry.

**PROMINENT ALUMNI/AE.** William M. Leech, attorney general, state of Tennessee; James R. McKinney, former speaker of the house, state of Tennessee; Carl W. Stiener, commanding general, 82nd Airborne Division; Ronnie C. Marston, president, Hospice Corp. of America; Thurman D. Rodgers, lieutenant general, the Pentagon; Martha Olson, senior vice-president, First American Corp.

# Tennessee Wesleyan College

**Athens, TN 37371-0040** **615 745-7504**

**1994-95 Costs.** Tuition: $7,070. Room: $1,500. Board: $2,140. Fees, books, misc. academic expenses (school's estimate): $440.
**Enrollment.** Undergraduates: 227 men, 175 women (full-time). Freshman class: 228 applicants, 217 accepted, 99 enrolled.
**Test score averages/ranges.** Average SAT scores: 810 combined. Average ACT scores: 19 composite.
**Faculty.** 34 full-time; 21 part-time. 59% of faculty holds doctoral degree. Student/faculty ratio: 17 to 1.
**Selectivity rating.** Noncompetitive.

**PROFILE.** Tennessee Wesleyan, founded in 1857, is a private, church-affiliated college. Its 40-acre campus is located in Athens, 60 miles southwest of Knoxville.

**Accreditation:** SACS.
**Religious orientation:** Tennessee Wesleyan College is affiliated with the United Methodist Church; two semesters of religion required.
**Library:** Collections totaling over 87,827 volumes, 407 periodical subscriptions, and 6,392 microform items.
**Special facilities/museums:** Old college museum.
**Athletic facilities:** Gymnasium, athletic complex, athletic fields.

**STUDENT BODY. Undergraduate profile:** 79% are state residents; 62% are transfers. 1% Asian-American, 11% Black, 1% Hispanic, 1% Native American, 83% White, 3% Other. Average age of undergraduates is 24.
**Freshman profile:** 31% of accepted applicants took SAT; 69% took ACT. 98% of freshmen come from public schools.
**Undergraduate achievement:** 69% of fall 1992 freshmen returned for fall 1993 term.
**Foreign students:** 35 students are from out of the country. Countries represented include Japan, Korea, Peru, Russia, the United Kingdom, and Venezuela; 13 in all.

**PROGRAMS OF STUDY. Degrees:** B.A., B.Appl.Sci., B.Mus.Ed., B.S.
**Majors:** Accounting, Behavioral Science, Biology, Business Administration, Chemistry, Church Music, Church Vocations, English, English/Mass Communications, Health/Physical Education, History, Human Services, Mathematics, Music, Music Education, Physical Education, Pre-Seminary, Psychology.
**Distribution of degrees:** The majors with the highest enrollment are business and education.
**Requirements:** General education requirement.
**Academic regulations:** Freshmen must maintain minimum 1.5 GPA; sophomores, 1.8 GPA; juniors, 2.0 GPA; seniors, 2.0 GPA.
**Special:** Minors offered in all majors. Teacher licensure available. Self-designed majors. Double majors. Dual degrees. Graduate school at which undergraduates may take graduate-level courses. Preprofessional programs in law, medicine, veterinary science, pharmacy, dentistry, theology, and optometry. 3-2 program in physical therapy. Member of Appalachian Colleges Consortium. Teacher certification in early childhood, elementary, and secondary education. Certification in specific subject areas. Exchange program abroad in Japan (Nagasaki Wesleyan Junior Coll). Study abroad also in England (Wosthills Coll).
**Honors:** Honors program. Honor societies.
**Academic Assistance:** Remedial reading, writing, and math.

**ADMISSIONS. Academic basis for candidate selection** (in order of priority): Secondary school record, standardized test scores, school's recommendation, class rank.
**Nonacademic basis for candidate selection:** Character and personality, extracurricular participation, and particular talent or ability are emphasized. Geographical distribution and alumni/ae relationship are considered.
**Requirements:** Graduation from secondary school is required; GED is accepted. 16 units and the following program of study are recommended: 4 units of English, 2 units of math, 2 units of science, 2 units of foreign language, 1 unit of social studies, 1 unit of history, 4 units of electives. Minimum 2.0 GPA required; minimum composite ACT score of 17 and rank in top half of secondary school class recommended. Audition required of music program applicants. ACT is required; SAT may be substituted. Campus visit and interview recommended. Off-campus interviews available with an admissions representative.
**Procedure:** Suggest filing application by February 15; no deadline. Notification of admission on rolling basis. Freshmen accepted in terms other than fall.
**Special programs:** Admission may be deferred one year. Credit may be granted through CEEB Advanced Placement for scores of 3 or higher. Credit may be granted through CLEP general and subject exams, challenge exams, and military experience. Concurrent enrollment program.
**Transfer students:** Transfer students accepted for terms other than fall. In fall 1993, 62% of all new students were transfers into all classes. 202 transfer applications were received, 190 were accepted. Application deadline is July 31 for fall; November 30 for spring. Minimum 2.0 GPA required. Lowest course grade accepted is "D." Maximum number of transferable credits is 73 semester hours. At least 30 semester hours must be completed at the college to receive degree.
**Admissions contact:** Lynne Henderson, M.Ed., Director of Admissions. 615 745-5872.

**FINANCIAL AID. Available aid:** Pell grants, SEOG, state scholarships and grants, school scholarships and grants, private scholarships, academic merit scholarships, and athletic scholarships. Perkins Loans (NDSL), PLUS, Stafford Loans (GSL), and SLS. Tuition Plan Inc., AMS, and deferred payment plan.
**Financial aid statistics:** 30% of aid is not need-based. In 1993-94, 65% of all undergraduate applicants received aid; 99% of freshman applicants. Average amounts of aid awarded freshmen: Scholarships and grants, $3,497; loans, $1,900.
**Supporting data/closing dates:** FAFSA: Priority filing date is March 1. School's own aid application: Priority filing date is April 15; deadline is July 31. Income tax forms: Priority filing date is April 15. Notification of awards on rolling basis.
**Financial aid contact:** Edna Simpson, Director of Financial Aid. 615 745-7504, extension 209.

# Trevecca Nazarene College

**Nashville, TN 37210** **615 248-1200**

**1994-95 Costs.** Tuition: $6,656. Room: $1,310. Board: $1,966. Fees, books, misc. academic expenses (school's estimate): $880.
**Enrollment.** Undergraduates: 343 men, 418 women (full-time). Freshman class: 235 applicants, 235 accepted, 155 enrolled. Graduate enrollment: 126 men, 258 women.
**Test score averages/ranges.** Average ACT scores: 19 composite.
**Faculty.** 53 full-time; 18 part-time. 54% of faculty holds doctoral degree. Student/faculty ratio: 16 to 1.
**Selectivity rating.** Noncompetitive.

**PROFILE.** Trevecca Nazarene is a church-affiliated, liberal arts college. Founded in 1901, it moved to its present site in 1935. The main campus is in the southeast section of Nashville, overlooking the downtown district.

**Accreditation:** SACS. Professionally accredited by the American Medical Association (CAHEA), the National Association of Schools of Music.
**Religious orientation:** Trevecca Nazarene College is affiliated with the Church of the Nazarene; 12 semester hours of religion/theology required.
**Library:** Collections totaling over 154,232 volumes.
**Athletic facilities:** Gymnasium, track, baseball, football, intramural, and soccer fields, aerobics and weight rooms, swimming pool, racquetball and tennis courts.

**STUDENT BODY. Undergraduate profile:** 52% are state residents; 35% are transfers. 19% Black, 78% White, 3% Other.
**Freshman profile:** 93% of freshmen come from public schools.
**Undergraduate achievement:** 64% of fall 1992 freshmen returned for fall 1993 term. 46% of entering class graduated.
**Foreign students:** 20 students are from out of the country. Countries represented include Canada and Sweden; five in all.

**PROGRAMS OF STUDY. Degrees:** B.A., B.S.
**Majors:** Accounting, Allied Health, Behavioral Science, Biology, Business Administration, Business Education, Chemistry, Christian Education, Church Music, Communication, Communications/Human Resources, Computer Information Systems, Cross-Cultural Communication, Drama, Early Childhood Education, Elementary Education, Elementary/Special Education, English, English/Speech Education, Fitness Management, General Science, Health, History, Management, Mass Communication, Mathematics, Medical Technology, Music, Music Business, Music Education, Office Administration, Pastoral Ministry, Philosophy, Physical Education, Physician Assistant, Political Science, Pre-Seminary, Psychology, Religion, Religious Studies, Social Sciences, Social Studies, Social Welfare, Special Education, Speech, Youth Ministry, Youth/Music Ministry.
**Distribution of degrees:** The majors with the highest enrollment are religion, physician assistant, and business administration.
**Requirements:** General education requirement.
**Academic regulations:** Freshmen must maintain minimum 1.6 GPA; sophomores, 1.8 GPA; juniors, 1.95 GPA; seniors, 2.0 GPA.
**Special:** Minors offered in many majors and in economics, education, human relations, journalism, religion/philosophy, and social/behavioral sciences. Courses offered in anthropology, art, athletic training, French, geography, German, and Spanish. Associate's degrees offered. Double majors. Preprofessional programs in law, medicine, pharmacy, dentistry, and engineering. 2-2 medical technology program with area hospitals. 2-2 nursing program with MidAmerica Nazarene Coll. Teacher certification in elementary and secondary education. Certification in specific subject areas. ROTC and NROTC at Vanderbilt U. AFROTC at Tennessee State U.
**Honors:** Honors program. Honor societies.
**Academic Assistance:** Remedial reading, writing, math, and study skills. Nonremedial tutoring.

**ADMISSIONS.**
**Requirements:** Graduation from secondary school is required; GED is accepted. 11 units and the following program of study are recommended: 4 units of English, 2 units of math, 1 unit of science, 2 units of foreign language, 2 units of social studies. Interview required of medical technology, physician assistant, and teacher education program applicants. Audition required of music program applicants. Academic Enrichment Program for applicants not normally admissible. ACT is required; SAT may be substituted. Campus visit and interview recommended. Off-campus interviews available with an admissions representative.
**Procedure:** Notification of admission on rolling basis. $20 room deposit, refundable until August 20. Freshmen accepted in terms other than fall.
**Special programs:** Admission may be deferred. Credit may be granted through CEEB Advanced Placement for scores of 3 or higher. Credit may be granted through CLEP general and subject exams. Early entrance/early admission program. Concurrent enrollment program.
**Transfer students:** Transfer students accepted for terms other than fall. In fall 1993, 35% of all new students were transfers into all classes. 305 transfer applications were received, 305 were accepted. Application deadline is rolling for fall; rolling for spring. Lowest course grade accepted is "D." At least 30 semester hours must be completed at the college to receive degree.
**Admissions contact:** Mr. Jan R. Forman, M.A., Dean of Enrollment Services. 615 248-1320.

**FINANCIAL AID. Available aid:** Pell grants, SEOG, state scholarships and grants, school scholarships, private scholarships, academic merit scholarships, and athletic scholarships. Perkins Loans (NDSL), PLUS, Stafford Loans (GSL), private loans, and SLS. Tuition Plan Inc.
**Financial aid statistics:** 18% of aid is not need-based. In 1993-94, 95% of all undergraduate applicants received aid; 87% of freshman applicants. Average amounts of aid awarded freshmen: Scholarships and grants, $200; loans, $2,590.
**Supporting data/closing dates:** Notification of awards on rolling basis.
**Financial aid contact:** Everett Holmes, M.S., Director of Financial Aid. 615 248-1242.

# Tusculum College

**Greeneville, TN 37743** **615 636-7300**

**1994-95 Costs.** Tuition: $7,700. Room & board: $3,300. Fees, books, misc. academic expenses (school's estimate): $500.
**Enrollment.** Undergraduates: 547 men, 597 women (full-time). Freshman class: 438 applicants, 372 accepted, 145 enrolled. Graduate enrollment: 53 men, 68 women.
**Test score averages/ranges.** Average SAT scores: 364 verbal, 428 math. Average ACT scores: 19 composite.
**Faculty.** 27 full-time. 70% of faculty holds doctoral degree. Student/faculty ratio: 15 to 1.
**Selectivity rating.** Less competitive.

**PROFILE.** Tusculum, founded in 1794, is a private, church-affiliated college of arts and sciences. Its 142-acre campus is located in Greeneville, 70 miles from Knoxville.

**Accreditation:** SACS.
**Religious orientation:** Tusculum College is affiliated with the Presbyterian Church USA; no religious requirements.
**Library:** Collections totaling over 70,500 volumes, 500 periodical subscriptions, and 141,613 microform items.
**Special facilities/museums:** Andrew Johnson library.
**Athletic facilities:** Gymnasium, swimming pool, tennis courts, baseball, football, practice, soccer, and softball fields.

**STUDENT BODY. Undergraduate profile:** 76% are state residents; 24% are transfers. 7% Black, 1% Hispanic, 91% White, 1% Other. Average age of undergraduates is 29.
**Freshman profile:** 1% of freshmen who took SAT scored 600 or over on verbal, 4% scored 600 or over on math; 6% scored 500 or over on verbal, 22% scored 500 or over on math; 35% scored 400 or over on verbal, 61% scored 400 or over on math; 78% scored 300 or over on verbal, 99% scored 300 or over on math. 2% of freshmen who took ACT scored 30 or over on English, 1% scored 30 or over on math, 1% scored 30 or over on composite; 20% scored 24 or over on English, 9% scored 24 or over on math, 6% scored 24 or over on composite; 55% scored 18 or over on English, 53% scored 18 or over on math, 62% scored 18 or over on composite; 98% scored 12 or over on English, 100% scored 12 or over on math, 100% scored 12 or over on composite; 100% scored 6 or over on English. 38% of accepted applicants took SAT; 62% took ACT.
**Undergraduate achievement:** 80% of fall 1992 freshmen returned for fall 1993 term. 43% of entering class graduated. 10% of students who completed a degree program immediately went on to graduate study.
**Foreign students:** Nine students are from out of the country. Countries represented include England, Japan, Korea, and Russia; five in all.

**PROGRAMS OF STUDY. Degrees:** B.A., B.S.
**Majors:** Biology, Computer Science, Creative Arts, Elementary Education, English, Environmental Science, History, Human Growth/Learning, Management, Mass Communications, Museum Studies, Physical Education, Psychology, Secondary Education, Special Education.
**Distribution of degrees:** The majors with the highest enrollment are education and psychology; creative arts and biology have the lowest.
**Requirements:** General education requirement.
**Academic regulations:** Freshmen must maintain minimum 1.75 GPA; sophomores, juniors, seniors, 2.00 GPA.
**Special:** Minors offered in several majors and in business administration, chemistry, French, math, and Spanish. Double majors. Independent study. Internships. Preprofessional programs in law, medicine, veterinary science, and dentistry. Combined degree program in medical technology. Teacher certification in elementary, secondary, and special education. Certification in specific subject areas. Study abroad in Costa Rica (U Latina).
**Honors:** Honor societies.
**Academic Assistance:** Remedial reading, writing, math, and study skills.

**ADMISSIONS. Academic basis for candidate selection** (in order of priority): Secondary school record, standardized test scores, class rank, essay, school's recommendation.
**Nonacademic basis for candidate selection:** Character and personality, extracurricular participation, particular talent or ability, and alumni/ae relationship are considered.
**Requirements:** Graduation from secondary school is required; GED is accepted. 14 units and the following program of study are recommended: 4 units of English, 3 units of math, 2 units of science, 2 units of foreign language, 1 unit of social studies, 1 unit of history, 1 unit of elective. Minimum composite ACT score of 20 (combined SAT score of 800), rank in top half of secondary school class, and minimum 2.0 GPA in academic core required. Conditional admission possible for applicants not meeting standard requirements. ACT is required; SAT may be substituted. Campus visit and interview recommended. Off-campus interviews available with an admissions representative.
**Procedure:** Take SAT or ACT by October of 12th year. Visit college for interview by May of 12th year. Suggest filing application by November; no deadline. Notification of admission on rolling basis. Reply is required by May 1. $50 tuition deposit, refundable until May 1. $100 room deposit, refundable until May 1. Freshmen accepted in terms other than fall.
**Special programs:** Admission may be deferred one year. Credit may be granted through CEEB Advanced Placement for scores of 3 or higher. Credit may be granted through CLEP general and subject exams, DANTES exams, and military and life experience. Early entrance/early admission program.
**Transfer students:** Transfer students accepted for terms other than fall. In fall 1993, 24% of all new students were transfers into all classes. 66 transfer applications were received, 56 were accepted. Application deadline is rolling for fall; rolling for spring. Minimum 2.0 GPA recommended. Lowest course grade accepted is "D." At least 30 semester hours must be completed at the college to receive degree.
**Admissions contact:** Mark A. Stokes, M.A., Vice President for Students/Auxiliary Services. 615 636-7312.

**FINANCIAL AID. Available aid:** Pell grants, SEOG, state grants, private scholarships, academic merit scholarships, and athletic scholarships. Perkins Loans (NDSL), PLUS, Stafford Loans (GSL), and SLS. Tuition Plan Inc.
**Financial aid statistics:** 19% of aid is not need-based. In 1993-94, 98% of all undergraduate applicants received aid; 98% of freshman applicants. Average amounts of aid awarded freshmen: Scholarships and grants, $3,849; loans, $4,334.
**Supporting data/closing dates:** FAFSA/FFS: Priority filing date is April 1. Income tax forms: Priority filing date is April 1. Notification of awards on rolling basis.
**Financial aid contact:** Diane Keasling, Director of Financial Aid. 615 636-7312.

# Union University

**Jackson, TN 38305-3697** **901 668-1818**

**1994-95 Costs.** Tuition: $5,790. Room & board: $2,600. Fees, books, misc. academic expenses (school's estimate): $600.
**Enrollment.** Undergraduates: 549 men, 988 women (full-time). Freshman class: 875 applicants, 543 accepted, 443 enrolled. Graduate enrollment: 19 men, 58 women.
**Test score averages/ranges.** Average ACT scores: 23 composite.
**Faculty.** 93 full-time; 59 part-time. 53% of faculty holds doctoral degree. Student/faculty ratio: 13 to 1.
**Selectivity rating.** Less competitive.

**PROFILE.** Union, founded in 1823, is a private, church-affiliated university. Its 150-acre campus is located in Jackson, 75 miles west of Memphis.

**Accreditation:** SACS. Professionally accredited by the National Association of Schools of Music, the National League for Nursing.
**Religious orientation:** Union University is affiliated with the Southern Baptist Church; two semesters of religion required.
**Library:** Collections totaling over 110,641 volumes, 1,200 periodical subscriptions, and 45,971 microform items.
**Special facilities/museums:** Elementary education lab, TV communications truck, nursing/health assessment lab.
**Athletic facilities:** Two gymnasiums, swimming pool, tennis courts, softball, baseball, and soccer fields.

**STUDENT BODY. Undergraduate profile:** 80% are state residents; 28% are transfers. 6% Black, 93% White, 1% Other. Average age of undergraduates is 20.
**Freshman profile:** Majority of accepted applicants took ACT.
**Undergraduate achievement:** 76% of fall 1992 freshmen returned for fall 1993 term. 54% of entering class graduated. 37% of students who completed a degree program immediately went on to graduate study.
**Foreign students:** 14 students are from out of the country. Countries represented include Canada; 10 in all.

**PROGRAMS OF STUDY. Degrees:** B.A., B.Mus., B.S., B.S.Bus.Admin., B.S.Nurs.
**Majors:** Accounting, Art, Biology, Business Administration, Chemical Physics, Chemistry, Communication Arts, Computer/Information Sciences, Economics/Finance, Elementary Education, English, English/Journalism, French, Greek, History, Instrumental Music, Management/Marketing, Mathematics, Medical Technology, Music Education, Music Literature, Nursing, Philosophy, Physical Education/Health, Psychology, Religion, Sacred Music, Social Sciences, Social Work, Sociology, Spanish, Voice.
**Distribution of degrees:** The majors with the highest enrollment are nursing, elementary education, and management/marketing; chemical physics, foreign languages, and voice have the lowest.
**Requirements:** General education requirement.
**Special:** Minors offered in some majors and in business education, physics, political science, secondary education, and speech. Double majors. Dual degrees. Independent study. Accelerated study. Internships. Cooperative education programs. Graduate school at which undergraduates may take graduate-level courses. Preprofessional programs in law, medicine, veterinary science, pharmacy, dentistry, optometry, and engineering. 3-2 engineering program with Tennessee Tech U. Member of Christian College Coalition. American Studies Program, AuSable Inst of Environmental Studies Program, Latin American Studies Program, Oxford Summer Sch Program. Other programs also available. Teacher certification in early childhood, elementary, secondary, and special education. Certification in specific subject areas.
**Honors:** Honors program.
**Academic Assistance:** Nonremedial tutoring.

**STUDENT LIFE. Housing:** All unmarried students under age 21 must live on campus unless living near campus with relatives. Women's and men's dorms. On-campus married-student housing. 50% of students live in college housing.
**Social atmosphere:** The student newspaper reports, "Students' social activities range from going with a group to a movie or basketball game, taking a date to the play, to just talking with friends in the commons. Both on and off campus, a variety of activities are available." Influential student groups include the Baptist Student Union, Greek organizations, and the Student Activities Council. Popular events include basketball games, Homecoming in December, Christian concerts, productions of the theatre department, and All-Sing. Off campus, students frequent fast-food restaurants, the mall, and local movie theaters.
**Services and counseling/handicapped student services:** Placement services. Health service. Counseling services for minority, veteran, and older students. Personal counseling. Career and academic guidance services. Religious counseling. Physically disabled student services. Tape recorders. Tutors.
**Campus organizations:** Undergraduate student government. Student newspaper (Cardinal & Cream, published twice/month). Literary magazine. Yearbook. Choir, chorale, symphonic and pep bands, musical ensembles, speech club, drama club, Student Nurses Association, Prelegal Society, Student Foundation, Prexy Club. Three fraternities, two chapter houses; three sororities, two chapter houses. 28% of men join a fraternity. 23% of women join a sorority.
**Religious organizations:** Baptist Student Union, Black Christian Fellowship.
**Minority/foreign student organizations:** International Student Organization.

**ATHLETICS. Physical education requirements:** Two semesters of physical education required.

**Intercollegiate competition:** Baseball (M), basketball (M,W), golf (M), tennis (M,W). Member of NAIA, NCAA.
**Intramural and club sports:** Intramural basketball, bowling, cross-country, football, golf, soccer, softball, swimming, table tennis, tennis, volleyball.

**ADMISSIONS. Academic basis for candidate selection** (in order of priority): Standardized test scores, secondary school record, class rank, school's recommendation, essay.
**Nonacademic basis for candidate selection:** Character and personality are emphasized. Extracurricular participation is important. Particular talent or ability and alumni/ae relationship are considered.
**Requirements:** Graduation from secondary school is required; GED is accepted. 14 units and the following program of study are required: 4 units of English, 3 units of math, 4 units of science, 3 units of social studies. Minimum composite ACT score of 20, rank in top half of secondary school class, and minimum 2.5 GPA required. Audition required of music program applicants who apply for scholarships. Portfolio required of art program applicants. R.N. required of nursing program applicants. SAT or ACT is required. Campus visit and interview recommended. No off-campus interviews.
**Procedure:** Take SAT or ACT by October of 12th year. Visit college for interview by December of 12th year. Suggest filing application by October 15. Application deadline is August 1. Notification of admission on rolling basis. Reply is required within 30 days of acceptance. $25 tuition deposit, refundable partially until June 1. $50 room deposit, refundable partially until June 1. Freshmen accepted in terms other than fall.
**Special programs:** Credit and/or placement may be granted through CEEB Advanced Placement exams for scores of 3 or higher. Credit may be granted through CLEP subject exams. Credit and placement may be granted through ACT PEP and DANTES exams and military experience. Early entrance/early admission program. Concurrent enrollment program.
**Transfer students:** Transfer students accepted for terms other than fall. In fall 1993, 28% of all new students were transfers into all classes. 527 transfer applications were received, 326 were accepted. Application deadline is August 15 for fall; February 1 for spring. Minimum 2.0 GPA required. Lowest course grade accepted is "D." Maximum number of transferable credits is 72 semester hours. At least 32 semester hours must be completed at the university to receive degree.
**Admissions contact:** Carroll W. Griffin, Director of Admissions. 901 661-5000, 800 338-6466.

**FINANCIAL AID. Available aid:** Pell grants, SEOG, state grants, school scholarships, private grants, academic merit scholarships, and athletic scholarships. Perkins Loans (NDSL), PLUS, Stafford Loans (GSL), and SLS.
**Financial aid statistics:** 42% of aid is not need-based. In 1993-94, 83% of all undergraduate applicants received aid; 78% of freshman applicants. Average amounts of aid awarded freshmen: Scholarships and grants, $3,800; loans, $1,700.
**Supporting data/closing dates:** FAFSA/FAF/FFS: Priority filing date is April 1; deadline is May 15. School's own aid application: Priority filing date is April 1. Income tax forms: Priority filing date is April 1; deadline is May 15. Notification of awards begins May 1.
**Financial aid contact:** Donald R. Morris, M.S., Director of Financial Aid. 901 661-5015.

**STUDENT EMPLOYMENT.** College Work/Study Program. Institutional employment. 15% of full-time undergraduates work on campus during school year. Students may expect to earn an average of $1,000 during school year. Off-campus part-time employment opportunities rated "excellent."

**COMPUTER FACILITIES.** 85 IBM/IBM-compatible and Macintosh/Apple microcomputers. Computer languages and software packages include BASIC, COBOL, dBASE III+, FORTRAN 77, Lotus 1-2-3, Pascal, Prolog, RPG, WordPerfect. Computer facilities are available to all students.
**Fees:** $15 computer fee per semester.
**Hours:** 8 AM-11 PM (M-Th); 8 AM-5 PM (F); 10 AM-4 PM (Sa).

**GRADUATE CAREER DATA.** Highest graduate school enrollments: Memphis State U, New Orleans Baptist Seminary, Southern Baptist Seminary, U of Tennessee at Knoxville, U of Kentucky. 60% of graduates choose careers in business and industry. Companies and businesses that hire graduates: Ernst & Young, IFC, Nike, Quaker Oats, Porter Cable, Procter & Gamble.

**PROMINENT ALUMNI/AE.** John Dancy, U.S. Senate correspondent, NBC; Luis Ortiz, baseball player, Boston Red Sox; Mrs. Albert Gore, Sr., politician.

# University of Memphis

**Memphis, TN 38152** — **901 678-2000**

**1993-94 Costs.** Tuition: $1,858 (state residents), $5,640 (out-of-state). Room: $1,420-$2,760. Board: $1,450. Fees, books, misc. academic expenses (school's estimate): $563.
**Enrollment.** Undergraduates: 4,955 men, 5,666 women (full-time). Freshman class: 3,921 applicants, 2,557 accepted, 1,691 enrolled. Graduate enrollment: 2,135 men, 2,753 women.
**Test score averages/ranges.** Average ACT scores: 23 English, 21 math, 22 composite. Range of ACT scores of middle 50%: 20-25 English, 17-22 math.
**Faculty.** 755 full-time; 415 part-time. 75% of faculty holds doctoral degree. Student/faculty ratio: 20 to 1.
**Selectivity rating.** Less competitive.

**PROFILE.** The University of Memphis, founded in 1912, is a comprehensive, public university. It changed its name from Memphis State University in 1994. Its 310-acre campus, 275-acre campus, and 625-acre farm are located in Memphis.
**Accreditation:** SACS. Professionally accredited by the Accreditation Board for Engineering and Technology, the Accrediting Council on Education in Journalism and Mass Communication, the American Assembly of Collegiate Schools of Business, the American Association for Counseling and Development, the American Bar Association, the American Dietetic Association, the American Home Economics Association, the American Psychological Association, the American Speech-Language-Hearing Association, the Council on Rehabilitation Education, the Council on Social Work Education, the National Association of Schools of Art and Design, the National Association of Schools of Music, the National Association of Schools of Public Affairs and Administration, the National Council for Accreditation of Teacher Education, the National League for Nursing.
**Religious orientation:** U of Memphis is nonsectarian; no religious requirements.
**Library:** Collections totaling over 1,138,952 volumes, 12,239 periodical subscriptions, and 3,062,580 microform items.
**Special facilities/museums:** Indian museum and village, music archive, center for study of higher education, center for river studies, center for research on women, center for earthquake research and information, biological field station.
**Athletic facilities:** Indoor and outdoor swimming pools, diving well, gymnasiums, handball/racquetball and tennis courts, weight training and wrestling rooms, sauna and steam rooms, all-weather track with auxiliary field.

**STUDENT BODY. Undergraduate profile:** 92% are state residents; 7% are transfers. 2.5% Asian-American, 22.5% Black, 1% Hispanic, 74% White. Average age of undergraduates is 25.
**Freshman profile:** 66% of accepted applicants took ACT. 81% of freshmen come from public schools.
**Undergraduate achievement:** 85% of fall 1992 freshmen returned for fall 1993 term.
**Foreign students:** 787 students are from out of the country. Countries represented include Canada, China, India, Malaysia, Taiwan, and Vietnam; 74 in all.

**PROGRAMS OF STUDY. Degrees:** B.A., B.F.A., B.Lib.Studies, B.Mus., B.Prof.Studies, B.S., B.S.Chem., B.S.Civil Eng., B.S.Ed., B.S.Elec.Eng., B.S.Home Econ., B.S.Mech.Eng., B.S.Med.Tech., B.S.Nurs., B.S.Tech.
**Majors:** Accounting, Anthropology, Architectural Technology, Art, Art History, Biology, Business Economics, Chemistry, Civil Engineering, Commercial Music, Computer Science, Computer Systems Technology, Criminal Justice, Decision Sciences, Early Childhood Education, Economics, Educational Services, Electrical Engineering, Electronics Technology, Elementary Education, English, Finance, Financial Services, Foreign Languages, Geography, Health/Safety, History, Home Economics, Individual Studies, International Business, International Relations, Journalism, Legal Assistant, Management, Management Information Systems, Manufacturing Technology, Marketing, Mathematical Sciences, Mechanical Engineering, Medical Technology, Music, Nursing, Philosophy, Physical Education, Physical Science, Physics, Political Science, Pre-Professional Programs, Psychology, Real Estate, Recreation/Park Administration, Rehabilitation Education, Risk Management/Insurance, Sales/Marketing, Social Work, Sociology, Special Education, Theatre, Theatre/Communications Arts, Transportation/Distribution.
**Distribution of degrees:** The majors with the highest enrollment are finance, management, and accounting; physics, economics, and anthropology have the lowest.
**Academic regulations:** Freshmen must maintain minimum 1.4 GPA; sophomores, 1.7 GPA; juniors, 1.9 GPA; seniors, 2.0 GPA.
**Special:** Minors offered in many majors and in accountancy, black studies, coaching, legal thought/liberal arts, photography, preprofessional business administration, public administration, recreation, religion in society, safety, surveying, technology, and women's studies. Courses offered in Greek, Italian, and library science. Judaic studies program. Double majors. Dual degrees. Independent study. Pass/fail grading option. Internships. Cooperative education programs. Graduate school at which undergraduates may take graduate-level courses. Preprofessional programs in law, medicine, veterinary science, pharmacy, dentistry, optometry, cytotechnology, dental hygiene, medical records administration, nursing, physical therapy, and podiatry. Member of Academic Common Market. Exchange programs with over 90 schools. Teacher certification in early childhood, elementary, and special education. Certification in specific subject areas. Exchange programs abroad in Australia (Deacon U), China (Hwazhong Normal U), and France (Polytech de Lille). Study abroad also in Costa Rica, Germany, and Spain. Member of International Student Exchange Program (ISEP), Council on International Educational Exchange Program (CIEE), and Institute of International Education. ROTC, NROTC, and AFROTC.
**Honors:** Phi Beta Kappa. Honors program. Honor societies.
**Academic Assistance:** Remedial reading, writing, math, and study skills. Nonremedial tutoring.

**STUDENT LIFE. Housing:** Students may live on or off campus. Women's and men's dorms. Fraternity housing. School-owned/operated apartments. On-campus married-student housing. 14% of students live in college housing.
**Services and counseling/handicapped student services:** Placement services. Health service. Women's center. Day care. Counseling services for minority, military, veteran, and older students. Personal and psychological counseling. Career and academic guidance services. Physically disabled student services. Learning disabled program/services. Notetaking services. Tape recorders. Tutors. Reader services for the blind.
**Campus organizations:** Undergraduate student government. Student newspaper (Helmsman, published four times/week). Literary magazine. Yearbook. Radio station. University Singers, gospel choir, orchestra, bands, experimental theatre, creative writing club, Campus Democrats, Society for Creative Anachronism, interior design association, service and special-interest groups, 196 organizations in all. 16 fraternities, 12 chapter houses; 12 sororities, no chapter houses. 8% of men join a fraternity. 6% of women join a sorority.
**Religious organizations:** Bahai Student Association, Baptist Student Union, Barth House (Episcopalian), Campus Crusade for Christ, Catholic Student Center, Christian Science Organization, Christian Student Center, Interfaith Council, Jewish Student Union, Latter-Day Saints Student Organization, Lutheran Student Association, Muslim Student Association, Navigators, United Students for Christ.
**Minority/foreign student organizations:** Black Student Association, Black Studies Club, Society of Minority Engineers, NAACP College Chapter, Panhellenic Council. International Student Association; Chinese, Indian, Korean, and Malaysian student groups.

**ATHLETICS. Physical education requirements:** Four semesters of physical education required.
**Intercollegiate competition:** 1% of students participate. Baseball (M), basketball (M,W), cheerleading (M,W), cross-country (M,W), football (M), golf (M,W), handball (M,W), racquetball (M,W), riflery (M,W), soccer (M), tennis (M,W), track (indoor) (M,W), track (outdoor) (M,W), track and field (indoor) (M,W), track and field (outdoor) (M,W), volleyball (W). Member of Great Midwest conference, NCAA Division I, NCAA Division I-A for football.

**Intramural and club sports:** 17% of students participate. Intramural basketball, bowling, fencing, football, handball, karate, racquetball, rugby, softball, swimming, table tennis, tennis, track, tug-of-war, turkey trot, volleyball, weight lifting, wrestling.

**ADMISSIONS. Academic basis for candidate selection** (in order of priority): Secondary school record, standardized test scores.

**Requirements:** Graduation from secondary school is required; GED is accepted. 14 units and the following program of study are required: 4 units of English, 3 units of math, 2 units of science including 1 unit of lab, 2 units of foreign language, 1 unit of social studies, 1 unit of history. Minimum composite ACT score of 19 and minimum 2.0 GPA required; minimum composite ACT score of 20 and minimum 3.0 GPA recommended. Alternative Admissions program for applicants not normally admissible. ACT is required; SAT may be substituted. No off-campus interviews.

**Procedure:** Application deadline is August 1. Notification of admission on rolling basis. $100 refundable room deposit. Freshmen accepted in terms other than fall.

**Special programs:** Credit may be granted through CEEB Advanced Placement for scores of 3 or higher. Credit may be granted through CLEP subject exams, DANTES exams, and military and life experience. Credit and placement may be granted through challenge exams. Early entrance/early admission program. Concurrent enrollment program.

**Transfer students:** Transfer students accepted for terms other than fall. In fall 1993, 7% of all new students were transfers into all classes. 3,383 transfer applications were received, 2,434 were accepted. Application deadline is August 1 for fall; December 1 for spring. Minimum 2.0 GPA required. Lowest course grade accepted is "C." At least 33 semester hours must be completed at the university to receive degree.

**Admissions contact:** David Wallace, M.S., Director of Admissions. 901 678-2101.

**FINANCIAL AID. Available aid:** Pell grants, SEOG, Federal Nursing Student Scholarships, state scholarships and grants, school scholarships and grants, ROTC scholarships, academic merit scholarships, and athletic scholarships. Perkins Loans (NDSL), PLUS, Stafford Loans (GSL), NSL, Health Professions Loans, state loans, school loans, private loans, and SLS. Tuition Plan Inc.

**Financial aid statistics:** 61% of aid is not need-based.

**Supporting data/closing dates:** FAFSA/FFS: Priority filing date is April 1. School's own aid application: Priority filing date is April 1. Income tax forms: Priority filing date is April 1. Notification of awards begins June 1.

**Financial aid contact:** Allen J. Hammond, M.A., Dean of Student Aid. 901 678-2303.

**STUDENT EMPLOYMENT.** College Work/Study Program. Institutional employment. 7% of full-time undergraduates work on campus during school year. Students may expect to earn an average of $2,200 during school year. Off-campus part-time employment opportunities rated "excellent."

**COMPUTER FACILITIES.** 2,000 IBM/IBM-compatible and Macintosh/Apple microcomputers. Students may access Digital minicomputer/mainframe systems, BITNET, Internet. Residence halls may be equipped with stand-alone microcomputers, networked terminals, modems. Computer languages and software packages include BASIC, BMDP, C, COBOL, DOS, FOCUS, FORTRAN, ImSL, MapMaker, MINITAB, Pascal, SIR, SPSS, Versaterm; 43 in all. Computer facilities are available to all students.

**Fees:** Computer fee is included in tuition/fees.

**Hours:** 24 hours in one lab.

**GRADUATE CAREER DATA.** Highest graduate school enrollments: U of Arkansas, U of Memphis, U of Mississippi, U of Tennessee at Knoxville, U of Tennessee at Memphis Medical Sch. Companies and businesses that hire graduates: Baptist and Methodist Hospitals, Federal Express, International Paper, Memphis Board of Education, Memphis State University, Shelby County Board of Education.

**PROMINENT ALUMNI/AE.** William B. Dunavant, Jr., International Cotton; Ronald Terry, chairperson and CEO, First Tennessee National Corp.; Dr. Willie Herenton, mayor of Memphis; Dixie Carter, actress; Pat Kerr Tigret, international fashion designer; William M. Morris, Jr., mayor, Shelby County, Tenn.

# University of the South

**Sewanee, TN 37383-1000** **615 598-1000**

**1994-95 Costs.** Tuition: $15,350. Room & board: $4,080. Fees, books, misc. academic expenses (school's estimate): $625.

**Enrollment.** Undergraduates: 577 men, 552 women (full-time). Freshman class: 1,445 applicants, 966 accepted, 326 enrolled. Graduate enrollment: 49 men, 28 women.

**Test score averages/ranges.** Average SAT scores: 557 verbal, 601 math. Range of SAT scores of middle 50%: 500-620 verbal, 550-650 math. Average ACT scores: 27 composite. Range of ACT scores of middle 50%: 25-29 composite.

**Faculty.** 101 full-time; 15 part-time. 94% of faculty holds highest degree in specific field. Student/faculty ratio: 11 to 1.

**Selectivity rating.** Highly competitive.

**PROFILE.** The University of the South, founded in 1857, is a church-affiliated, liberal arts university. Programs are offered through the College of Arts and Sciences and the School of Theology. Its 10,000-acre campus is located in Sewanee, 50 miles from Chattanooga.

**Accreditation:** SACS.

**Religious orientation:** University of the South is affiliated with the Episcopal Church; one semester of religion required.

**Library:** Collections totaling over 433,820 volumes, 2,724 periodical subscriptions, and 199,683 microform items.

**Special facilities/museums:** Art gallery, observatory, keyboard collection.

**Athletic facilities:** Gymnasiums, swimming pool, basketball, handball, racquetball, indoor and outdoor tennis courts, weight room, athletic fields, golf course, riding stables.

**STUDENT BODY. Undergraduate profile:** 20% are state residents; 7% are transfers. .5% Asian-American, 3% Black, .5% Hispanic, 93% White, 3% Other. Average age of undergraduates is 20.

**Freshman profile:** 79% of accepted applicants took SAT; 57% took ACT. 54% of freshmen come from public schools.

**Undergraduate achievement:** 95% of fall 1992 freshmen returned for fall 1993 term. 87% of entering class graduated. 38% of students who completed a degree program immediately went on to graduate study.

**Foreign students:** Three students are from out of the country.

**PROGRAMS OF STUDY. Degrees:** B.A., B.S.

**Majors:** American Studies, Anthropology, Biology, Chemistry, Comparative Literature, Computer Science/Mathematics, Economics, Engineering, English, Fine Arts, French, Geology, German, German Studies, Greek, History, Latin, Mathematics, Medieval Studies, Music, Natural Resources, Philosophy, Physics, Political Science, Psychology, Religion, Russian, Russian/Soviet Studies, Social Science/Foreign Language, Spanish, Theatre Arts/Speech, Third World Studies.

**Distribution of degrees:** The majors with the highest enrollment are English, political science, and psychology; comparative literature, Greek, and Russian have the lowest.

**Requirements:** General education requirement.

**Academic regulations:** Freshmen must maintain minimum 1.2 GPA; sophomores, 1.6 GPA; juniors, 1,8 GPA; seniors, 1.9 GPA.

**Special:** Self-designed majors. Double majors. Independent study. Accelerated study. Pass/fail grading option. Internships. Graduate school at which undergraduates may take graduate-level courses. Preprofessional programs in law, medicine, veterinary science, dentistry, religious vocation, and Peace Corps. 3-2 engineering programs with Columbia U, Georgia Tech, Rensselaer Polytech Inst, Vanderbilt U, and Washington U. 3-2 environmental science programs with Duke U and Yale U. Member of Appalachian Colleges Association, Associated Colleges of the South, Association of Episcopal Colleges, Leadership South, Minority Faculty Registry, Southern University Conference, Tennessee College Association, and Tennessee's Independent Colleges and Universities. Oak Ridge Science Semester (Tennessee). Summer island ecology program on St. Catherine's Island, Ga. Tonya Internships in Public Affairs and Economics. Teacher certification in secondary education. Exchange programs abroad in England (Oxford U, Rhodes Coll), Germany (U of Bamberg, Federation of German American Clubs), Japan (Rikkyo U, Nanzan U), and Spain (U of Madrid). Study abroad also in Austria, France, Italy, Liberia, and Singapore.

**Honors:** Phi Beta Kappa. Honors program. Honor societies.

**STUDENT LIFE. Housing:** All students must live on campus; exceptions granted. Two-year residency required of all students. Coed, women's, and men's dorms. School-owned/operated apartments. Off-campus privately-owned housing. Both on-campus and off-campus married-student housing. 95% of students live in college housing.

**Social atmosphere:** According to the editor of the student newspaper, there is "an extraordinarily unified and gracious way of life" at the University of the South. The university has a surprisingly active social and cultural life, given its relative isolation, with a performing arts series that brings in nationally known performers. Fraternities and sororities are strong, and football games and party weekends in fall, mid-winter, and spring are popular social events. On campus, students frequent the Tiger Bay Pub, and off campus, they head for Shenanigan's in the village.

**Services and counseling/handicapped student services:** Placement services. Health service. Women's center. Day care. Counseling services for minority students. Birth control, personal, and psychological counseling. Career and academic guidance services. Religious counseling. Physically disabled student services. Learning disabled services. Notetaking services. Tape recorders. Reader services for the blind.

**Campus organizations:** Undergraduate student government. Student newspaper (Sewanee Purple, published twice/month). Literary magazine. Yearbook. Radio station. Art Forum, choir, orchestra, economics and forestry groups, chess club, Arcadians, Big Brothers/Big Sisters, BACCHUS, Headstart, AWARE, Student Women's Council, Waste Not, Sounds of Silence, 110 organizations in all. 18 fraternities, 11 chapter houses; seven sororities, no chapter houses. 62% of men join a fraternity. 65% of women join a sorority.

**Religious organizations:** Acolytes Guild, Campus Crusade for Christ, Chapel Council, Chapel Outreach, Fellowship of Christian Athletes, Sewanee Canterbury Club, Sewanee Catholic Community, Student Christian Fellowship.

**Minority/foreign student organizations:** Cross Cultural Understanding group, Black Student Union. International Club.

**ATHLETICS. Physical education requirements:** Two semesters of physical education required.

**Intercollegiate competition:** 45% of students participate. Baseball (M), basketball (M,W), cross-country (M,W), diving (M,W), field hockey (W), football (M), golf (M), soccer (M,W), softball (W), swimming (M,W), tennis (M,W), track (outdoor) (M,W), track and field (outdoor) (M,W), volleyball (W). Member of NCAA Division III, Southern Collegiate Athletic Conference.

**Intramural and club sports:** 70% of students participate. Intramural basketball, cross-country, golf, indoor soccer, racquetball, soccer, softball, swimming, tennis, touch football, track and field, ultimate frisbee, volleyball. Men's club Alpine skiing, canoe, crew, cycling, fencing, handball, horsemanship, lacrosse, rugby. Women's club Alpine skiing, canoe, cheerleading, crew, cycling, horsemanship, lacrosse.

**ADMISSIONS. Academic basis for candidate selection** (in order of priority): Secondary school record, standardized test scores, class rank, school's recommendation, essay.

**Nonacademic basis for candidate selection:** Character and personality and extracurricular participation are important. Particular talent or ability, geographical distribution, and alumni/ae relationship are considered.

**Requirements:** Graduation from secondary school is recommended; GED is accepted. 18 units and the following program of study are required: 4 units of English, 3 units of math, 2 units of science including 1 unit of lab, 2 units of foreign language, 2 units of social studies, 2 units of history, 2 units of academic electives. Conditional admission possible for applicants not meeting standard requirements. SAT or ACT is required. PSAT is recommended. Campus visit and interview recommended. No off-campus interviews.

**Procedure:** Take SAT or ACT by fall of 12th year. Visit college for interview by fall of 12th year. Suggest filing application by February 1; no deadline. Notification of admission by April 1. Reply is required by May 1. $300 nonrefundable tuition deposit. Freshmen accepted in terms other than fall.

**Special programs:** Admission may be deferred one year. Credit and/or placement may be granted through CEEB Advanced Placement exams for scores of 4 or higher. Early decision program. In fall 1993, 99 applied for early decision and 81 were accepted. Deadline for applying for early decision is November 15.

**Transfer students:** Transfer students accepted for terms other than fall. In fall 1993, 7% of all new students were transfers into all classes. 77 transfer applications were received, 36 were accepted. Application deadline is April 1 for fall; December 1 for spring. Minimum 3.0 GPA recommended. Lowest course grade accepted is "C." Maximum number of transferable credits is 60 semester hours. At least 60 semester hours must be completed at the university to receive degree.

**Admissions contact:** Robert M. Hedrick, M.Ed., Director of Admission. 615 598-1238, 800-522-2234.

**FINANCIAL AID. Available aid:** Pell grants, SEOG, state scholarships and grants, school scholarships and grants, private scholarships and grants, academic merit scholarships, and aid for undergraduate foreign students. Perkins Loans (NDSL), PLUS, Stafford Loans (GSL), state loans, school loans, private loans, and SLS. Tuition Plan Inc. and Knight Tuition Plans. Institutional payment plans.

**Financial aid statistics:** 10% of aid is not need-based. In 1993-94, 85% of all undergraduate applicants received aid; 78% of freshman applicants. Average amounts of aid awarded freshmen: Scholarships and grants, $9,035; loans, $2,328.

**Supporting data/closing dates:** FAFSA/FAF/FFS: Priority filing date is March 1. School's own aid application: Priority filing date is March 1. Income tax forms: Accepted on rolling basis. Notification of awards begins April 1.

**Financial aid contact:** David R. Gelinas, M.A., Director of Financial Aid. 615 598-1312.

**STUDENT EMPLOYMENT.** College Work/Study Program. Institutional employment. 37% of full-time undergraduates work on campus during school year. Students may expect to earn an average of $1,000 during school year. Off-campus part-time employment opportunities rated "fair."

**COMPUTER FACILITIES.** 65 Macintosh/Apple microcomputers; all are networked. Students may access Hewlett-Packard minicomputer/mainframe systems, Internet. Client/LAN operating systems include Apple/Macintosh, LocalTalk/AppleTalk, Microsoft. Computer languages and software packages include Assembler, BASIC, C, COBOL, Cricket Graph, Excel, FORTRAN, LISP, MacDraw, MacPaint, Microsoft Word, Pascal, Prolog, SPSS, Statworks; 30 in all. Computer facilities are available to all students.

**Fees:** None.

**Hours:** 24 hours.

**GRADUATE CAREER DATA.** Graduate school percentages: 15% enter law school. 13% enter medical school. 1% enter dental school. 5% enter graduate business programs. 20% enter graduate arts and sciences programs. 1% enter theological school/seminary. Highest graduate school enrollments: U of Alabama, Duke U, U of Tennessee, Yale U. 62% of graduates choose careers in business and industry. Companies and businesses that hire graduates: First Union Bank, Macy's, Provident Insurance.

**PROMINENT ALUMNI/AE.** John Woods, chairperson of the board, AmSouth Bank; Rear Adm. Bill Studeman, deputy director, CIA; Edwin Williamson, legal advisor to State Department; Sam Pickering, professor, author; Howard Baker, former U.S. senator.

# University of Tennessee at Chattanooga

**Chattanooga, TN 37403** **615 755-4111**

**1993-94 Costs.** Tuition: $1,670 (state residents), $5,270 (out-of-state). Room: $1,678. Board: $1,750. Fees, books, misc. academic expenses (school's estimate): $600.

**Enrollment.** Undergraduates: 2,511 men, 2,848 women (full-time). Freshman class: 2,091 applicants, 1,338 accepted, 991 enrolled. Graduate enrollment: 544 men, 664 women.

**Test score averages/ranges.** Average ACT scores: 22 composite.

**Faculty.** 292 full-time; 203 part-time. 78% of faculty holds highest degree in specific field. Student/faculty ratio: 17 to 1.

**Selectivity rating.** Less competitive.

**PROFILE.** U Tennessee at Chattanooga is a public, comprehensive university. Founded as a church-affiliated university in 1886, it became part of the state university system in 1969. Programs are offered through the College of Arts and Sciences and Health and Human Services and the Schools of Business Administration, Education, Engineering, and Nursing. Its 96-campus is located near the urban center of Chattanooga.

**Accreditation:** SACS. Professionally accredited by the Accreditation Board for Engineering and Technology, the American Assembly of Collegiate Schools of Business, the American Physical Therapy Association, the Council on Social Work Education, the National Association of Schools of Art and Design, the National Association of Schools of Music, the National Council for Accreditation of Teacher Education, the National League for Nursing.

**Religious orientation:** University of Tennessee at Chattanooga is nonsectarian; no religious requirements.

**Library:** Collections totaling over 424,272 volumes, 3,018 periodical subscriptions, and 1,083,505 microform items.

**Special facilities/museums:** Data processing center, observatory, scanning electron microscope.

**Athletic facilities:** Athletic fields, gymnasium, arena, weight room, basketball, racquetball, and tennis courts, swimming pool.

**STUDENT BODY. Undergraduate profile:** 90% are state residents; 9% are transfers. 3% Asian-American, 10% Black, 1% Hispanic, 1% Native American, 85% White. Average age of undergraduates is 24.

**Freshman profile:** 15% of accepted applicants took SAT; 85% took ACT.

**Undergraduate achievement:** 74% of fall 1992 freshmen returned for fall 1993 term.

**Foreign students:** 97 students are from out of the country. Countries represented include China, India, Jordan, Taiwan, Thailand, and the United Kingdom; 44 in all.

**PROGRAMS OF STUDY. Degrees:** B.A., B.F.A., B.Mus., B.S., B.S.Eng., B.S.Nurs., B.S.Phys.Ther., B.S.Soc.Work.

**Majors:** American Studies, Applied Mathematics, Art, Biology, Business Administration, Chemistry, Communication, Computer Science, Criminal Justice, Early Childhood Education, Economics, Elementary Education, Engineering, Engineering Management, English/American Language/Literature, Environmental Studies, French, Geology, Greek/Latin, History, Home Economics, Human Services, Humanities, Latin, Mathematics, Medical Technology, Music, Music Education, Nursing, Philosophy/Religion, Physical Therapy, Physics, Political Science, Psychology, Secondary Education, Social Work, Sociology/Anthropology, Spanish, Special Education, Theatre/Speech.

**Distribution of degrees:** The majors with the highest enrollment are business administration, engineering, and psychology.

**Requirements:** General education requirement.

**Academic regulations:** Minimum 2.0 GPA required for graduation.

**Special:** Minors offered. Concentrations offered in many majors. Double majors. Independent study. Internships. Cooperative education programs. Graduate school at which undergraduates may take graduate-level courses. Preprofessional programs in veterinary science, pharmacy, nursing, physical therapy, and social work. 3-1 and 3-2 engineering programs with Georgia Tech and U of Tennessee at Knoxville. Teacher certification in early childhood, elementary, secondary, and special education. Study abroad in England. ROTC.

**Honors:** Phi Beta Kappa. Honors program. Honor societies.

**Academic Assistance:** Remedial reading, writing, math, and study skills. Nonremedial tutoring.

**STUDENT LIFE. Housing:** Students may live on or off campus. Coed dorms. School-owned/operated apartments. 14% of students live in college housing.

**Social atmosphere:** "Most of the student body lives off campus, therefore on-campus events are limited," reports the student newspaper. "But with the activities and an enterprising student body, social life at UTC can be described as fun." Popular places to go are The Stone Lion, David's, Yesterday's, Brew and Cue, and the Pickle Barrel. "Greeks are popular and active. Student Government is very active as well as the Association for Campus Entertainment. We have a number of religious groups who are also active." The university has a good basketball team with a big following and an international film festival. This year, SGA has organized many campus-wide parties.

**Services and counseling/handicapped student services:** Placement services. Health service. Day care. Counseling services for military and veteran students. Career guidance services. Physically disabled student services. Learning disabled program/services. Note-taking services. Tape recorders. Tutors. Reader services for the blind.

**Campus organizations:** Undergraduate student government. Student newspaper (Echo, published once/week). Literary magazine. Yearbook. Radio station. Choir and other singing groups, concert and marching bands, jazz band, orchestra, ensembles, opera workshop, theatre, 130 organizations in all. Six fraternities, all with chapter houses; six sororities, no chapter houses. 20% of men join a fraternity. 20% of women join a sorority.

**Religious organizations:** Baptist, Catholic, Christian Science, Church of Christ, Disciples of Christ, Episcopal, Jewish, Lutheran, Methodist, and Seventh-day Adventist groups.

**Minority/foreign student organizations:** Black Student Association. International Student Association.

**ATHLETICS. Physical education requirements:** Two semesters of physical education required.

**Intercollegiate competition:** 5% of students participate. Basketball (M,W), cheerleading (M,W), cross-country (M,W), football (M), golf (M), softball (W), tennis (M,W), track (indoor) (M,W), track (outdoor) (M,W), track and field (indoor) (M,W), track and field (outdoor) (M,W), volleyball (W), wrestling (M). Member of NCAA Division I, NCAA Division I-AA for football, Southern Conference.

**Intramural and club sports:** 15% of students participate. Intramural basketball, flag football, racquetball, soccer, volleyball. Men's club crew, soccer. Women's club crew, soccer.

**ADMISSIONS. Academic basis for candidate selection** (in order of priority): Standardized test scores, secondary school record, class rank, school's recommendation.

**Nonacademic basis for candidate selection:** Particular talent or ability is emphasized. Extracurricular participation is important. Alumni/ae relationship is considered.

**Requirements:** Graduation from secondary school is recommended; GED is accepted. No specific distribution of secondary school units required. Minimum composite ACT score of 20 (combined SAT score of 900) and minimum 2.75 GPA required. Additional units in science and math recommended of engineering program applicants. ACT is required; SAT may be substituted. Campus visit and interview recommended. Off-campus interviews available with admissions and alumni representatives.

**Procedure:** Take SAT or ACT by January 1 of 12th year. Suggest filing application by January 1; no deadline. Notification of admission on rolling basis. $75 room deposit, refundable until July 1. Freshmen accepted in terms other than fall.

**Special programs:** Credit and/or placement may be granted through CEEB Advanced Placement exams for scores of 3 or higher. Credit may be granted through CLEP general and subject exams, and life experience. Early entrance/early admission program. Concurrent enrollment program.

**Transfer students:** Transfer students accepted for terms other than fall. In fall 1993, 9% of all new students were transfers into all classes. 1,352 transfer applications were received, 1,033 were accepted. Minimum 2.0 GPA required. Lowest course grade accepted is "D." At least 30 semester hours must be completed at the university to receive degree.

**Admissions contact:** Patsy Reynolds, M.Ed., Director of Admissions. 615 755-4662.

**FINANCIAL AID. Available aid:** Pell grants, SEOG, state scholarships and grants, school scholarships and grants, private scholarships and grants, ROTC scholarships, academic merit scholarships, athletic scholarships, and aid for undergraduate foreign students. Perkins Loans (NDSL), PLUS, Stafford Loans (GSL), state loans, and school loans. University prepayment plan.

**Financial aid statistics:** 30% of aid is not need-based. In 1993-94, 80% of all undergraduate applicants received aid; 78% of freshman applicants. Average amounts of aid awarded freshmen: Scholarships and grants, $1,075.

**Supporting data/closing dates:** FAFSA: Priority filing date is April 1. FAF/FFS: Priority filing date is March 1. School's own aid application: Priority filing date is April 1. Income tax forms: Priority filing date is April 1. Verification form: Priority filing date is April 1. Notification of awards on rolling basis.
**Financial aid contact:** Joel Harrell, M.P.P.A., Director of Financial Aid. 615 755-4677.

**STUDENT EMPLOYMENT.** College Work/Study Program. Institutional employment. Students may expect to earn an average of $1,650 during school year. Off-campus part-time employment opportunities rated "excellent."

**COMPUTER FACILITIES.** 110 IBM/IBM-compatible and Macintosh/Apple microcomputers. Students may access Hewlett-Packard minicomputer/mainframe systems. Computer facilities are available to all students.
**Fees:** None.

# University of Tennessee, Knoxville

**Knoxville, TN 37996-0230** **615 974-1000**

**1993-94 Costs.** Tuition: $1,982 (state residents), $5,762 (out-of-state). Room & board: $3,262. Fees, books, misc. academic expenses (school's estimate): $760.
**Enrollment.** Undergraduates: 8,662 men, 7,687 women (full-time). Freshman class: 7,473 applicants, 5,372 accepted, 3,013 enrolled. Graduate enrollment: 3,110 men, 3,103 women.
**Test score averages/ranges.** Average SAT scores: 468 verbal, 525 math. Range of SAT scores of middle 50%: 410-530 verbal, 460-590 math. Average ACT scores: 23 composite. Range of ACT scores of middle 50%: 21-26 composite.
**Faculty.** 1,152 full-time; 39 part-time. 86% of faculty holds doctoral degree. Student/faculty ratio: 17 to 1.
**Selectivity rating.** Less competitive.

**PROFILE.** U Tennessee at Knoxville is a public, comprehensive university. Founded as a private college in 1794, it became the first campus of the University of Tennessee in 1879. Programs are offered through the Colleges of Agriculture, Business Administration, Communications, Education, Engineering, Human Ecology, Law, Liberal Arts, Nursing, Social Work, and Veterinary Medicine; the Graduate School of Library and Information Science; and the Schools of Architecture and Planning. Its 417-acre campus is located in Knoxville.

**Accreditation:** SACS. Numerous professional accreditations.
**Religious orientation:** University of Tennessee, Knoxville is nonsectarian; no religious requirements.
**Library:** Collections totaling over 2,104,865 volumes, 14,037 periodical subscriptions, and 1,956,384 microform items.
**Special facilities/museums:** Comprehensive museum of anthropology, archaeology, art, geology, natural history, and medicine, theatre-in-the-round, child development lab, livestock farms, robotics research center, electron microscope.
**Athletic facilities:** Sports complex, tennis courts, athletic fields, tracks, swimming pools.

**STUDENT BODY. Undergraduate profile:** 82% are state residents; 29% are transfers. 1.7% Asian-American, 5.4% Black, .6% Hispanic, 92.1% White, .2% Other. Average age of undergraduates is 23.
**Freshman profile:** 1% of freshmen who took SAT scored 700 or over on verbal, 5% scored 700 or over on math; 9% scored 600 or over on verbal, 23% scored 600 or over on math; 37% scored 500 or over on verbal, 62% scored 500 or over on math; 79% scored 400 or over on verbal, 90% scored 400 or over on math; 98% scored 300 or over on verbal, 99% scored 300 or over on math. 45% of accepted applicants took SAT; 86% took ACT.
**Undergraduate achievement:** 81% of fall 1992 freshmen returned for fall 1993 term.
**Foreign students:** 370 students are from out of the country. Countries represented include China, Hong Kong, India, Japan, Malaysia, and the United Kingdom; 64 in all.

**PROGRAMS OF STUDY. Degrees:** B.A., B.Arch., B.F.A., B.Mus., B.S.
**Majors:** Accounting, Advertising, Aerospace Engineering, Agricultural Economics/Business, Agricultural Education, Agricultural Engineering, Animal Science, Anthropology, Architecture, Art Education, Art History, Audiology/Speech Pathology, Biochemistry, Biology, Botany, Broadcasting, Business/Marketing Education, Chemical Engineering, Chemistry, Child/Family Studies, Civil Engineering, Classics, College Scholars Program, Computer Science, Cultural Studies, Curriculum/Instruction, Economics, Electrical/Computer Engineering, Elementary Education, Engineering Physics, Engineering Science/Mechanics, English, English Education, Finance, Food Technology/Science, Forestry, French, General Business, Geography, Geology, German, Graphic Design/Illustration, Greek, Health Education, History, Home Economics Education, Hotel/Restaurant Administration, Human Performance/Sport Studies, Individualized Majors, Industrial Arts Education, Industrial Engineering, Interior Design, Italian, Journalism, Language/World Business, Latin, Management, Marketing, Materials Science/Engineering, Mathematics, Mechanical Engineering, Medical Technology, Microbiology, Music, Music Education, Nuclear Engineering, Nursing, Nutrition/Food Science, Ornamental Horticulture/Landscape Design, Philosophy, Physics, Plant/Soil Science, Political Science, Pre-Professional Programs, Pre-Teaching, Psychology, Public Administration, Recreation/Leisure Studies, Religious Studies, Retail/Consumer Sciences, Russian, Social Work, Sociology, Spanish, Special Education, Speech Communications, Statistics, Studio Art, Theatre, Transportation/Logistics, Wildlife/Fisheries Science, Zoology.
**Distribution of degrees:** The majors with the highest enrollment are psychology, accounting, and transportation/logistics; health education and art education have the lowest.
**Requirements:** General education requirement.
**Academic regulations:** Minimum 2.0 GPA must be maintained.
**Special:** Minors offered in numerous areas. Self-designed majors. Double majors. Dual degrees. Independent study. Pass/fail grading option. Internships. Cooperative education programs. Graduate school at which undergraduates may take graduate-level courses. Preprofessional programs in law, medicine, veterinary science, pharmacy, dentistry, optometry, business administration, cytotechnology, dental hygiene, medical technology, and medical records administration. 3-2 B.A/M.B.A. program. Combined-degree physical therapy programs with U of Tennessee at Chattanooga and Memphis. Member of National Student Exchange (NSE). Teacher certification in early childhood, elementary, secondary, special education, and vo-tech education. Certification in specific subject areas. Member of International Student Exchange Program (ISEP). Study abroad in over 30 countries. ROTC and AFROTC.
**Honors:** Phi Beta Kappa. Honors program.
**Academic Assistance:** Nonremedial tutoring.

**STUDENT LIFE. Housing:** All freshmen must live on campus unless living with family. Coed, women's, and men's dorms. Fraternity housing. School-owned/operated apartments. Off-campus married-student housing. University has approximately 1,690 units of rental property available. 35% of students live in college housing.
**Services and counseling/handicapped student services:** Placement services. Health service. Women's center. Counseling services for minority, military, veteran, and older students. Personal and psychological counseling. Career and academic guidance services. Religious counseling. Physically disabled student services. Learning disabled services. Notetaking services. Tape recorders. Reader services for the blind.
**Campus organizations:** Undergraduate student government. Student newspaper (Daily Beacon). Literary magazine. Yearbook. Radio station. Chorus, concert and marching bands, concert choir, women's chorale, symphony orchestra, opera workshop, theatre-in-the-round, departmental and political groups, special-interest groups, 300 organizations in all. 26 fraternities, 23 chapter houses; 19 sororities, no chapter houses. 11% of men join a fraternity. 14% of women join a sorority.
**Religious organizations:** Campus Crusade for Christ, Fellowship of Christian Athletes, other religious groups.
**Minority/foreign student organizations:** Black cultural programming club, National Society of Black Engineers, Association of Black Communicators, NAACP, Anti-Apartheid Coalition of Tennessee. Several foreign student groups.

**ATHLETICS. Physical education requirements:** None.
**Intercollegiate competition:** 4% of students participate. Baseball (M), basketball (M,W), cheerleading (M,W), cross-country (M,W), diving (M,W), football (M), golf (M,W), swimming (M,W), tennis (M,W), track and field (indoor) (M,W), track and field (outdoor) (M,W), volleyball (W). Member of NCAA Division I, Southeastern Conference.
**Intramural and club sports:** 1% of students participate. Men's club basketball, bowling, canoe, cheerleading, crew, fencing, football, golf, gymnastics, horsemanship, ice hockey, lacrosse, martial arts, Nordic skiing, racquetball, rugby, sailing, soccer, softball, volleyball, water polo, water skiing, weight lifting. Women's club basketball, bowling, canoe, cheerleading, crew, fencing, football, golf, gymnastics, horsemanship, martial arts, Nordic skiing, racquetball, sailing, soccer, softball, water polo, water skiing, weight lifting.

**ADMISSIONS. Academic basis for candidate selection** (in order of priority): Secondary school record, standardized test scores, essay, school's recommendation.
**Nonacademic basis for candidate selection:** Extracurricular participation, particular talent or ability, and alumni/ae relationship are considered.
**Requirements:** Graduation from secondary school is required; GED is accepted. 14 units and the following program of study are required: 4 units of English, 3 units of math, 2 units of science including 1 unit of lab, 2 units of foreign language, 1 unit of social studies, 1 unit of history, 1 unit of visual/performing arts. Minimum composite ACT score of 18 and minimum 2.0 GPA required of in-state applicants; minimum composite ACT score of 18 and minimum 2.25 GPA required of out-of-state applicants. Additional units in math required of architecture and engineering program applicants. Audition required of music program applicants. SAT or ACT is required. Campus visit and interview recommended. No off-campus interviews.
**Procedure:** Take SAT or ACT by November of 12th year. Visit college for interview by March of 12th year. Application deadline is July 1. Notification of admission on rolling basis. No set date by which applicants must accept offer. $100 nonrefundable room deposit. Freshmen accepted in terms other than fall.
**Special programs:** Admission may be deferred one year. Credit may be granted through CEEB Advanced Placement for scores of 3 or higher. Credit may be granted through CLEP general and subject exams, and military experience. Credit and placement may be granted through challenge exams. Early entrance/early admission program. Concurrent enrollment program.
**Transfer students:** Transfer students accepted for terms other than fall. In fall 1993, 29% of all new students were transfers into all classes. 2,501 transfer applications were received, 1,836 were accepted. Application deadline is July 1 for fall; November 1 for spring. Minimum 2.0 GPA required. Lowest course grade accepted is "C." Maximum number of transferable credits is 60 semester hours from a two-year school and 90 semester hours from a four-year school. At least 30 semester hours must be completed at the university to receive degree.
**Admissions contact:** Gordon Stanley, Ph.D., Director of Admissions. 615 974-2184.

**FINANCIAL AID. Available aid:** Pell grants, SEOG, state scholarships and grants, school scholarships, private scholarships, ROTC scholarships, academic merit scholarships, athletic scholarships, and aid for undergraduate foreign students. Perkins Loans (NDSL), PLUS, Stafford Loans (GSL), state loans, school loans, private loans, and SLS. Deferred payment plan. Prepayment plan.
**Financial aid statistics:** In 1993-94, 81% of all undergraduate applicants received aid. Average amounts of aid awarded freshmen: Scholarships and grants, $2,270; loans, $2,635.
**Supporting data/closing dates:** FAFSA/FAF/FFS: Priority filing date is February 14; accepted on rolling basis. State aid form: Priority filing date is February 14; accepted on rolling basis. Notification of awards begins April 1.
**Financial aid contact:** John Mays, Director of Financial Aid. 615 974-3131.

**STUDENT EMPLOYMENT.** College Work/Study Program. Institutional employment. Students may expect to earn an average of $2,000 during school year. Off-campus part-time employment opportunities rated "fair."

**COMPUTER FACILITIES.** 1,500 IBM/IBM-compatible and Macintosh/Apple microcomputers. Students may access Data General, Digital, Hewlett-Packard, IBM minicomputer/mainframe systems, BITNET, Internet. Residence halls may be equipped with stand-alone microcomputers, networked microcomputers, networked terminals. Client/LAN operating systems include Apple/Macintosh, LocalTalk/AppleTalk, Novell. 100 major computer languages and software packages available. Computer facilities are available to all students.
**Hours:** 20 hours/day (microcomputers); 24 hours (terminals).

**PROMINENT ALUMNI/AE.** Howard Baker, former U.S. senator; Chris Whittle, publishing executive; David Keith, actor; William Stokely, food industrialist; Delores Ziegler, mezzo-soprano; Willie Gault and Tim McGee, professional football players; Lindsey Nelson, sportscaster; Clarence Brown, film director.

# University of Tennessee at Martin

**Martin, TN 38238** **901 587-7777**

**1993-94 Costs.** Tuition: $1,810 (state residents), $5,590 (out-of-state). Room: $1,430. Board: $1,250-$1,390. Fees, books, misc. academic expenses (school's estimate): $500.
**Enrollment.** Undergraduates: 2,123 men, 2,546 women (full-time). Freshman class: 1,600 applicants, 1,350 accepted, 1,123 enrolled. Graduate enrollment: 57 men, 145 women.
**Test score averages/ranges.** Average ACT scores: 21 English, 20 math, 21 composite.
**Faculty.** 213 full-time; 50 part-time. 70% of faculty holds doctoral degree. Student/faculty ratio: 20 to 1.
**Selectivity rating.** Less competitive.

**PROFILE.** U Tennessee at Martin is a public university. Founded as a church-affiliated institute in 1900, it became a public, two-year college in 1927 and gained its present status in 1967. Programs are offered through the Division of Fine and Performing Arts and the Schools of Agriculture and Home Economics, Arts and Sciences, Business Administration, Education, and Engineering Technology and Engineering. Its 250-acre campus is located in Martin, 125 miles northeast of Memphis.

**Accreditation:** SACS. Professionally accredited by the American Assembly of Collegiate Schools of Business, the National Association of Schools of Music, the National Council for Accreditation of Teacher Education, the National League for Nursing.
**Religious orientation:** University of Tennessee at Martin is nonsectarian; no religious requirements.
**Library:** Collections totaling over 288,969 volumes, 1,651 periodical subscriptions, and 400,213 microform items.
**Special facilities/museums:** Archive museum.
**Athletic facilities:** Basketball, racquetball, and tennis courts, baseball, football, and softball fields, track, field house, golf driving and rifle ranges, swimming pool, weight room.

**STUDENT BODY. Undergraduate profile:** 97% are state residents; 10% are transfers. 15% Black, 84% White, 1% Other. Average age of undergraduates is 24.
**Freshman profile:** 95% of accepted applicants took ACT. 92% of freshmen come from public schools.
**Undergraduate achievement:** 67% of fall 1992 freshmen returned for fall 1993 term.
**Foreign students:** 190 students are from out of the country. Countries represented include Brazil, Canada, India, Japan, Korea, and Sweden; 38 in all.

**PROGRAMS OF STUDY. Degrees:** B.A., B.S.
**Majors:** Accounting, Administrative Management, Agricultural Business, Agricultural Education, Agricultural Sciences, Agriculture, Animal Science, Art Education, Biology, Broadcasting, Business, Chemistry, Civil Engineering, Communication, Computer/Information Sciences, Criminal Justice, Data Systems Management, Dietetics, Earth/Space Sciences, Economics, Electrical Engineering, Elementary Education, English, Finance, French, Geography, Geology, Geoscience, History, Home Economics, Home Economics/Business, Home Economics Education, Individualized Majors, International Business, Journalism/Mass Communications, Management, Marketing, Mathematics, Mechanical Engineering, Music, Music Education, Nursing, Office Administration, Parks/Recreation Management, Performance, Plant Sciences, Political Science/Government, Psychology, Public Administration, Radio/Television, Science/Dental, Science/Medical, Science/Pharmacy, Secondary Education, Social Work, Sociology, Soil Science, Soil/Water Conservation, Spanish, Wildlife Biology.
**Distribution of degrees:** The majors with the highest enrollment are marketing, management, and criminal justice; French, Spanish, and geoscience have the lowest.
**Requirements:** General education requirement.
**Special:** Sch of Business Administration offers one- and two-year secretarial science programs, cooperative education programs, and accountant internship. Dept of Engineering and Engineering Technology offers two-year transfer programs in aerospace, chemical, civil, electrical, industrial, mechanical, metallurgical, and nuclear engineering and in physics and science. Self-designed majors. Double majors. Dual degrees. Independent study. Accelerated study. Pass/fail grading option. Internships. Cooperative education programs. Preprofessional programs in law, medicine, veterinary science, pharmacy, dentistry, optometry, medical records, teaching, and physical therapy. Teacher certification in early childhood, elementary, secondary, and special education. Exchange program abroad in Japan (Hirosaki U). ROTC.
**Honors:** Phi Beta Kappa. Honors program.
**Academic Assistance:** Remedial reading and math.

**STUDENT LIFE. Housing:** All freshmen must live on campus unless living with family. Coed, women's, and men's dorms. Fraternity housing. Off-campus married-student housing. 65% of students live in college housing.
**Social atmosphere:** According to the student newspaper, "UTM has a very strong fine arts department which gets much support from the community. Students manage to make their own fun. UTM has many different groups of people, so there is something for everyone. The Greeks have a strong influence on social life, more so than any other group. The independents also have a strong influence." Favorite off-campus nightspots include Cadillac's, the Pub, and Cheer's. The University Center is a popular place to congregate on campus.
**Services and counseling/handicapped student services:** Counseling services for minority, veteran, and older students. Birth control, personal, and psychological counseling. Career and academic guidance services. Religious counseling. Physically disabled student services. Learning disabled program/services. Notetaking services. Tape recorders. Tutors. Reader services for the blind.
**Campus organizations:** Undergraduate student government. Student newspaper (Pacer, published once/week). Literary magazine. Yearbook. Radio and TV stations. Choir, several choruses and bands, opera workshop, vocal and instrumental ensembles, Vanguard Theatre, National Organization for Women, Young Democrats, Young Republicans, Young Americans for Freedom, athletic, departmental, service, and special-interest groups. 12 fraternities, 10 chapter houses; nine sororities, no chapter houses. 15% of men join a fraternity. 15% of women join a sorority.
**Religious organizations:** Baptist, Catholic, Church of Christ, Episcopal, Methodist, Muslim, and Presbyterian groups.
**Minority/foreign student organizations:** Minority Student Association, AKA, black student organization, Delta Sigma Theta, Minority Student Association. Korean, Malyasian, and Polynesian groups.

**ATHLETICS. Physical education requirements:** None.
**Intercollegiate competition:** 1% of students participate. Baseball (M), basketball (M,W), cross-country (M,W), football (M), golf (M), riflery (M,W), softball (W), tennis (M,W), track and field (indoor) (W), track and field (outdoor) (W), volleyball (W). Member of NCAA Division I, Ohio Valley Conference.
**Intramural and club sports:** 24% of students participate. Intramural basketball, flag football, racquetball, softball, tennis, volleyball.

**ADMISSIONS. Academic basis for candidate selection** (in order of priority): Secondary school record, standardized test scores, class rank, essay, school's recommendation.
**Nonacademic basis for candidate selection:** Character and personality are emphasized. Extracurricular participation and particular talent or ability are important.
**Requirements:** Graduation from secondary school is required; GED is accepted. 15 units and the following program of study are required: 4 units of English, 3 units of math, 2 units of science including 1 unit of lab, 2 units of foreign language, 1 unit of social studies, 1 unit of history, 1 unit of fine or performing arts, 1 unit of electives. Minimum composite ACT score of 19 and minimum 2.25 GPA required or minimum composite ACT score of 16 and minimum 2.6 GPA required. ACT is required; SAT may be substituted. Campus visit recommended. Off-campus interviews available with admissions and alumni representatives.
**Procedure:** Take SAT or ACT by October of 12th year. Visit college for interview by February of 12th year. Suggest filing application by July 1. Application deadline is August 1. Notification of admission on rolling basis. $50 room deposit, refundable until July 1. Freshmen accepted in terms other than fall.
**Special programs:** Credit may be granted through CEEB Advanced Placement for scores of 3 or higher. Credit may be granted through CLEP general and subject exams. Credit and placement may be granted through challenge exams. Early decision program. In fall 1993, 5 applied for early decision and 4 were accepted. Deadline for applying for early decision is within two weeks of notification. Early entrance/early admission program. Concurrent enrollment program.
**Transfer students:** Transfer students accepted for terms other than fall. In fall 1993, 10% of all new students were transfers into all classes. 504 transfer applications were received, 435 were accepted. Application deadline is two weeks prior to beginning of semester for fall; two weeks prior to beginning of semester for spring. Minimum 2.0 GPA required. Lowest course grade accepted is "D." At least 30 semester hours must be completed at the university to receive degree.
**Admissions contact:** Judy Rayburn, M.S., Director of Admissions. 901 587-7020.

**FINANCIAL AID. Available aid:** Pell grants, SEOG, state scholarships and grants, school scholarships, private scholarships, ROTC scholarships, academic merit scholarships, and athletic scholarships. Perkins Loans (NDSL), PLUS, Stafford Loans (GSL), and SLS. Deferred payment plan.
**Financial aid statistics:** In 1993-94, 70% of all undergraduate applicants received aid; 65% of freshman applicants. Average amounts of aid awarded freshmen: Scholarships and grants, $2,225; loans, $2,337.
**Supporting data/closing dates:** FAFSA/FAF/FFS: Priority filing date is March 1. Notification of awards on rolling basis.
**Financial aid contact:** Randal Hall, M.S., Director of Financial Aid. 901 587-7040.

**STUDENT EMPLOYMENT.** College Work/Study Program. Institutional employment. 60% of full-time undergraduates work on campus during school year. Off-campus part-time employment opportunities rated "excellent."

**COMPUTER FACILITIES.** 56 IBM/IBM-compatible and Macintosh/Apple microcomputers. Students may access Digital, IBM minicomputer/mainframe systems. Computer languages and software packages include ADL, ASSIST, FORTRAN, KERMIT, PL/C, Poise, SPSS-H, TODO, WATBOL, WATFIV. Computer facilities are available to all students.

**GRADUATE CAREER DATA.** Highest graduate school enrollments: U of Tennessee at Knoxville. 45% of graduates choose careers in business and industry. Companies and businesses that hire graduates: Goodyear, Chrysler, banks.

**PROMINENT ALUMNI/AE.** Margaret Perry, chancellor, U of Tennessee at Martin; Ed Jones, U.S. congressman; Pat Head Summitt, head of women's basketball, U of Tennessee at Knoxville; Dr. Dwight Clark, heart surgeon.

# Vanderbilt University

**Nashville, TN 37203-1700** **615 322-7311**

**1994-95 Costs.** Tuition: $17,865. Room: $4,132. Board: $2,393. Fees, books, misc. academic expenses (school's estimate): $884.
**Enrollment.** Undergraduates: 3,005 men, 2,647 women (full-time). Freshman class: 7,791 applicants, 4,690 accepted, 1,499 enrolled. Graduate enrollment: 2,196 men, 2,005 women.
**Test score averages/ranges.** Average SAT scores: 559 verbal, 640 math. Range of SAT scores of middle 50%: 510-610 verbal, 590-690 math. Average ACT scores: 28 composite. Range of ACT scores of middle 50%: 26-30 composite.
**Faculty.** 616 full-time; 202 part-time. 98% of faculty holds highest degree in specific field. Student/faculty ratio: 8 to 1.
**Selectivity rating.** Highly competitive.

**PROFILE.** Vanderbilt, founded in 1873, is a private university. Programs are offered through the College of Arts and Science, the School of Engineering, the Peabody College, the Blair School of Music, and the Graduate School of Management. Its 330-acre campus is located in the University Center section of Nashville.
**Accreditation:** SACS. Professionally accredited by the Accreditation Board for Engineering and Technology, the American Assembly of Collegiate Schools of Business, the American Bar Association, the American Dietetic Association, the American Library Association, the American Medical Association (CAHEA), the American Psychological Association, the American Speech-Language-Hearing Association, the Association of American Law Schools, the Association of Theological Schools in the United States and Canada, the National Association of Schools of Music, the National Council for Accreditation of Teacher Education, the National League for Nursing.
**Religious orientation:** Vanderbilt University is nonsectarian; no religious requirements.
**Library:** Collections totaling over 2,085,652 volumes, 16,357 periodical subscriptions, and 150,064 microform items.
**Special facilities/museums:** Art galleries, center for research on education and human development, multimedia classrooms, teaching center, observatories, free-electron laser, electron microscope.
**Athletic facilities:** Gymnasium, basketball, racquetball, and tennis courts, swimming pool, aerobics and weight rooms, track, mountain climbing wall, softball fields.
**STUDENT BODY. Undergraduate profile:** 15% are state residents; 6% are transfers. 5% Asian-American, 4% Black, 2% Hispanic, 1% Native American, 85% White, 3% Other. Average age of undergraduates is 19.
**Freshman profile:** 94% of accepted applicants took SAT; 50% took ACT. 60% of freshmen come from public schools.
**Undergraduate achievement:** 89% of fall 1992 freshmen returned for fall 1993 term. 74% of entering class graduated. 74% of students who completed a degree program went on to graduate study within two years.
**PROGRAMS OF STUDY. Degrees:** B.A., B.Eng., B.Mus., B.S.
**Majors:** African-American Studies, American Studies, Anthropology, Biology, Biomedical Engineering, Chemical Engineering, Chemistry, Civil/Environmental Engineering, Classical Languages, Classics, Cognitive Studies, Communication, Composition/Theory, Computer Science, Early Childhood Education, East Asian Studies, Economics, Electrical Engineering, Elementary Education, Engineering Science, English, European Studies, Fine Arts, French, Geology, German, History, Human/Organizational Development, Latin American/Iberian Studies, Mathematics, Mechanical Engineering, Molecular Biology, Musical Arts, Performance, Philosophy, Physics, Physics/Astronomy, Political Science, Portuguese, Psychology, Public Policy Studies, Religious Studies, Russian, Secondary Education, Sociology, Spanish, Special Education, Theatre.
**Distribution of degrees:** The majors with the highest enrollment are human development, English, and economics.
**Requirements:** General education requirement.
**Academic regulations:** Freshmen must maintain minimum 1.8 GPA; sophomores, 1.9 GPA; juniors, 2.0 GPA; seniors, 2.0 GPA.
**Special:** Minors offered in many majors and in approximately 25 other fields. Self-designed majors. Double majors. Dual degrees. Independent study. Accelerated study. Pass/fail grading option. Internships. Graduate school at which undergraduates may take graduate-level courses. Preprofessional programs in law, medicine, dentistry, and nursing. 3-2 engineering/liberal arts program. Bachelor's/M.B.A., M.D., or other graduate or professional degree through Senior-in-Absentia program. NASA's Tennessee Space Grant Consortium, Intercollegiate Center for Classical Studies in Rome, Consortium of University Transportation Centers. Washington Semester. Exchange programs with Fisk U, Howard U, and Meharry Medical Coll. Teacher certification in early childhood, elementary, secondary, and special education. Certification in specific subject areas. Exchange programs abroad in England (U of Leeds), Germany (U of Regensburg), and Israel (U of Tel Aviv). Study abroad also in China, France, Italy, Japan, and Spain. ROTC and NROTC. AFROTC at Tennessee State U.
**Honors:** Phi Beta Kappa. Honors program. Honor societies.
**Academic Assistance:** Nonremedial tutoring.
**STUDENT LIFE. Housing:** All unmarried students must live on campus except those from Davidson County. Coed, women's, and men's dorms. Sorority and fraternity housing. School-owned/operated apartments. 86% of students live in college housing.
**Social atmosphere:** Popular student gathering spots include Exit/In, The Pub, fraternity row, Alumni Lawn, Branscomb Library, and Nashville bars. Greeks, the Concert Committee, Reformed University Fellowship, and McGill Hall are among the most influential groups on campus. Students particularly enjoy the annual Rites of Spring celebration, Homecoming, football games, and Greekfest. The student newspaper reports that fraternities dominate campus life while bars, concerts, and Nashville's country music industry provide off-campus amusement.
**Services and counseling/handicapped student services:** Placement services. Health service. Women's center. Day care. Study skills courses. Counseling services for minority, military, veteran, and older students. Birth control, personal, and psychological counseling. Career and academic guidance services. Physically disabled student services. Learning disabled services. Notetaking services. Tape recorders. Tutors. Reader services for the blind.
**Campus organizations:** Undergraduate student government. Student newspaper (Vanderbilt Hustler, published twice/week). Literary magazine. Yearbook. Radio and TV stations. Bands, orchestra, choir, dance group, theatre and video production groups, debating, Amnesty International, Habitat for Humanity, Prison Project, Association for Disability Advocacy, Office of Gay, Lesbian, and Bisexual Concerns, College Democrats, College Republicans, 247 organizations in all. 17 fraternities, 14 chapter houses; 12 sororities, 10 chapter houses. 36% of men join a fraternity. 54% of women join a sorority.
**Religious organizations:** Campus Crusade for Christ, Fellowship of Christian Athletes, Intervarsity Christian Fellowship, Baptist Student Union, Bahai Club, Latter-Day Saints Student Association, Jewish Student Union, Muslim Student Association, Orthodox Christian Fellowship, Presbyterian Student Union, Catholic Community, United Methodist Wesley Foundation, Officer Christian Fellowship, St. Augustine's Episcopal Chapel.
**Minority/foreign student organizations:** Black Student Alliance, Asian-American Student Association, Hispanic Student Association, NAACP, Undergraduate Indian Students Association, Black Greek Council, National Society of Black Engineers, Black American Law Students, Racial Environment Project. African, Arab, Chinese, European, Indian, Japanese, Taiwanese, and Turkish student groups, American Field Service, International Awareness Committee.
**ATHLETICS. Physical education requirements:** None.
**Intercollegiate competition:** Baseball (M), basketball (M,W), cross-country (M,W), football (M), golf (M,W), soccer (M,W), tennis (M,W), track (indoor) (W), track (outdoor) (W). Member of NCAA Division I, Southeastern Conference.
**Intramural and club sports:** Intramural badminton, basketball, bowling, cycling, darts, flag football, frisbee, golf, horseshoes, inner-tube water basketball, inner-tube water polo, pocket billiards, racquetball, soccer, softball, squash, swimming, table tennis, tennis, track and field, volleyball, walleyball, weight lifting, wrestling. Men's club cycling, equestrian sports, fencing, field hockey, ice hockey, judo, lacrosse, rifle, rowing, rugby, sailing, skiing, squash, swimming, tae kwon do, track, volleyball, water polo. Women's club cycling, equestrian sports, fencing, field hockey, ice hockey, judo, lacrosse, rifle, rowing, sailing, skiing, squash, tae know do, volleyball, water polo.
**ADMISSIONS. Academic basis for candidate selection** (in order of priority): Secondary school record, standardized test scores, school's recommendation, class rank, essay.
**Nonacademic basis for candidate selection:** Character and personality and particular talent or ability are important. Extracurricular participation and alumni/ae relationship are considered.
**Requirements:** Graduation from secondary school is recommended; GED is accepted. 20 units and the following program of study are recommended: 4 units of English, 4 units of math, 3 units of science, 4 units of foreign language, 3 units of social studies, 2 units of electives. Additional unit requirements vary by school. Audition required of music program applicants. SAT is required; ACT may be substituted. ACH required. Campus visit recommended. Off-campus interviews available with an alumni representative.
**Procedure:** Take SAT or ACT by December of 12th year. Take ACH by January of 12th year. Suggest filing application by January 15; no deadline. Notification of admission by April 1. Reply is required by May 1. $200 nonrefundable tuition deposit. Freshmen accepted for terms other than fall.
**Special programs:** Admission may be deferred one year. Credit and/or placement may be granted through CEEB Advanced Placement exams. Credit and placement may be granted through challenge exams. Early decision program. In fall 1993, 297 applied for early decision and 148 were accepted. Deadline for applying for early decision is November 1. Early entrance/early admission program. Concurrent enrollment program.
**Transfer students:** Transfer students accepted for terms other than fall. In fall 1993, 6% of all new students were transfers into all classes. 300 transfer applications were received, 169 were accepted. Application deadline is February 1 for fall; November 15 for spring. Lowest course grade accepted is "C-." At least 60 semester hours must be completed at the university to receive degree.
**Admissions contact:** Neill F. Sanders, Ph.D., Dean of Admissions. 615 322-2561.
**FINANCIAL AID. Available aid:** Pell grants, SEOG, state scholarships and grants, school scholarships and grants, private scholarships and grants, ROTC scholarships, academic merit scholarships, and athletic scholarships. Perkins Loans (NDSL), PLUS, Stafford Loans (GSL), state loans, school loans, private loans, and SLS. Knight Tuition Plans and guaranteed tuition.
**Financial aid statistics:** 37% of aid is not need-based. In 1993-94, 95% of all undergraduate applicants received aid; 91% of freshman applicants. Average amounts of aid awarded freshmen: Scholarships and grants, $11,998; loans, $3,921.
**Supporting data/closing dates:** FAFSA/FAF/FFS: Priority filing date is February 15. School's own aid application: Priority filing date is February 15. State aid form: Priority filing date is February 15. Income tax forms: Accepted on rolling basis. Notification of awards on rolling basis.
**Financial aid contact:** David D. Mohning, Ph.D., Director of Financial Aid. 615 322-3591.
**STUDENT EMPLOYMENT.** College Work/Study Program. Institutional employment. 29% of full-time undergraduates work on campus during school year. Students may expect to earn an average of $1,239 during school year. Off-campus part-time employment opportunities rated "good."
**COMPUTER FACILITIES.** 400 IBM/IBM-compatible and Macintosh/Apple microcomputers; all are networked. Students may access Digital, IBM minicomputer/mainframe systems, BITNET, Internet. Client/LAN operating systems include Apple/Macintosh, LocalTalk/AppleTalk. 54 major computer languages and software packages available. Computer facilities are available to all students.
**Hours:** 24 hours in some locations.
**GRADUATE CAREER DATA.** Graduate school percentages: 13% enter law school. 11% enter medical/dental school. 10% enter graduate business programs. 18% enter graduate arts and sciences programs. 1% enter theological school/seminary. Highest graduate school enrollments: Duke U, Emory U, Vanderbilt U. 60% of graduates choose careers in business and industry. Companies and businesses that hire graduates: Andersen Consulting, International Paper, Merrill Lynch, Procter & Gamble, Shearson Lehman Brothers, Tenneco Gas, Westinghouse.
**PROMINENT ALUMNI/AE.** Robert Penn Warren, Pulitzer Prize-winning author; William Bain, president, Bain and Co.; Michael Ainsley, president and CEO, Sotheby's; Tom Schulman, award-winning screenwriter of *Dead Poet's Society.*

# Texas

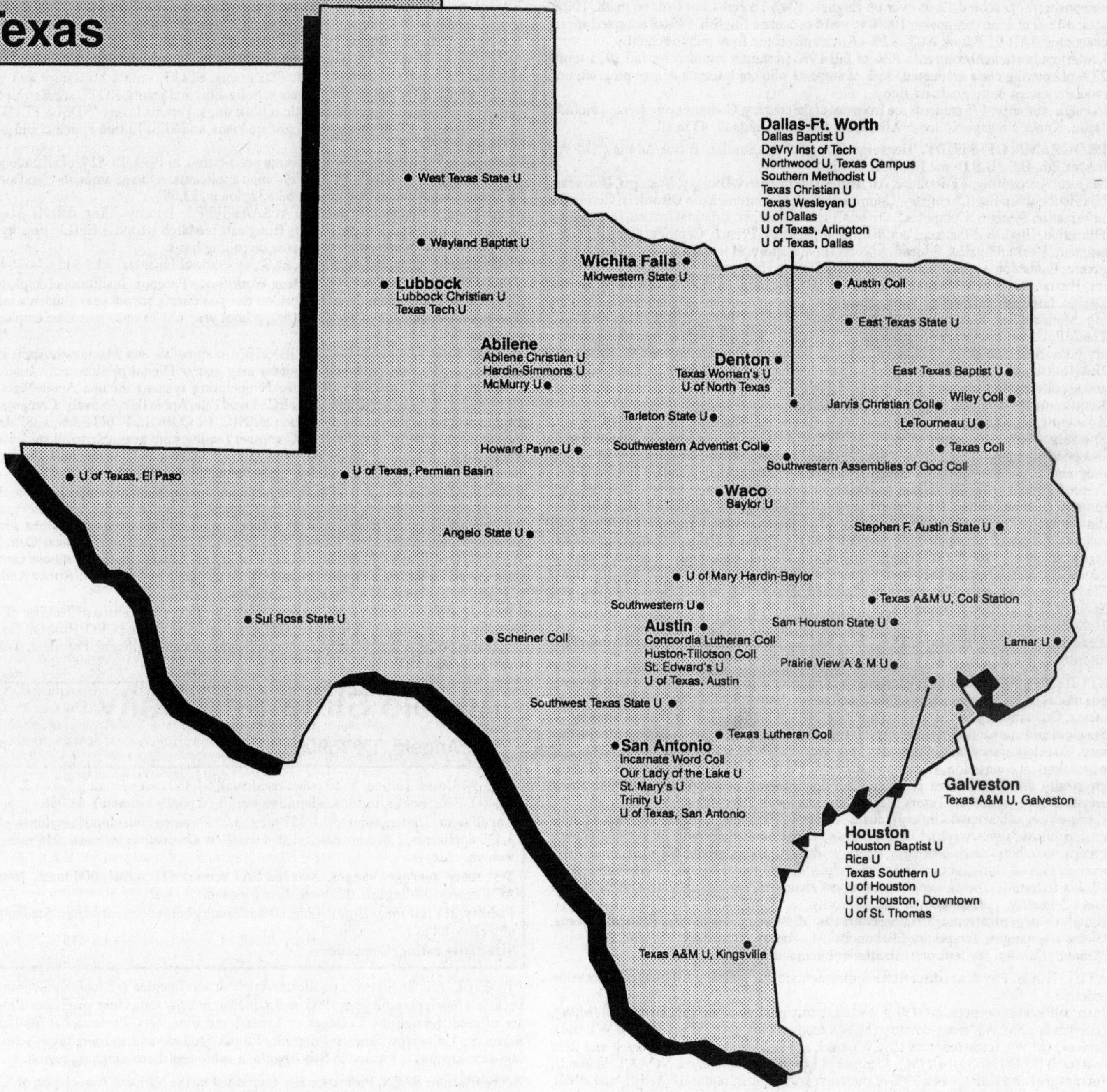


## Abilene Christian University

**Abilene, TX 79699-8465** **915 674-2000**

**1994-95 Costs.** Tuition: $7,440. Room & board: $3,100. Fees, books, misc. academic expenses (school's estimate): $600.

**Enrollment.** Undergraduates: 1,439 men, 1,450 women (full-time). Freshman class: 1,381 applicants, 1,379 accepted, 856 enrolled. Graduate enrollment: 406 men, 278 women.

**Test score averages/ranges.** Average SAT scores: 440 verbal, 495 math. Range of SAT scores of middle 50%: 376-500 verbal, 410-570 math. Average ACT scores: 22 English, 20 math, 21 composite. Range of ACT scores of middle 50%: 18-25 English, 18-23 math.

**Faculty.** 157 full-time; 77 part-time. 76% of faculty holds doctoral degree. Student/faculty ratio: 18 to 1.

**Selectivity rating.** Less competitive.

**PROFILE.** Abilene Christian is a church-affiliated university. It was founded in 1906, became a senior college in 1919, and gained university status in 1976. Programs are offered through the Colleges of Liberal and Fine Arts, Natural and Applied Sciences, Biblical Studies, Professional Studies, and Business Administration; the Graduate School; and the School of Nursing. Its 208-acre campus is located in Abilene, 150 miles west of Fort Worth.

**Accreditation:** SACS. Professionally accredited by the Association of Collegiate Business Schools and Programs, the Council on Social Work Education, the National Association of Schools of Music, the National League for Nursing.

**Religious orientation:** Abilene Christian University is affiliated with the Church of Christ; five semesters of religion required.

**Library:** Collections totaling over 551,382 volumes, 2,347 periodical subscriptions, and 785,266 microform items.

**Special facilities/museums:** Museum of university's history, biblical restoration studies center, voice institute, demonstration farm and ranch, observatory.

**Athletic facilities:** Gymnasium, basketball, handball, racquetball, tennis, and volleyball courts, swimming pool, baseball, football, and soccer fields, track, golf course, weight room.

**STUDENT BODY. Undergraduate profile:** 69% are state residents; 12% are transfers. 3% Asian-American, 4% Black, 4% Hispanic, 1% Native American, 83% White, 5% Other. Average age of undergraduates is 23.

**Freshman profile:** 2% of freshmen who took SAT scored 700 or over on verbal, 4% scored 700 or over on math; 9% scored 600 or over on verbal, 16% scored 600 or over on math; 29% scored 500 or over on verbal, 36% scored 500 or over on math; 60% scored 400 or over on verbal, 68% scored 400 or over on math; 91% scored 300 or over on verbal, 97% scored 300 or over on math. 7% of freshmen who took ACT scored 30 or over on English, 3% scored 30 or over on math, 5% scored 30 or over on composite; 34% scored 24 or over on English, 23% scored 24 or over on math, 28% scored 24 or over on composite; 80%

scored 18 or over on English, 75% scored 18 or over on math, 84% scored 18 or over on composite; 97% scored 12 or over on English, 100% scored 12 or over on math, 100% scored 12 or over on composite; 100% scored 6 or over on English. 54% of accepted applicants took SAT; 95% took ACT. 92% of freshmen come from public schools.
**Undergraduate achievement:** 70% of fall 1992 freshmen returned for fall 1993 term. 27% of entering class graduated. 36% of students who completed a degree program immediately went on to graduate study.
**Foreign students:** 175 students are from out of the country. Countries represented include Japan, Korea, Singapore, South Africa, Taiwan, and Thailand; 43 in all.

**PROGRAMS OF STUDY. Degrees:** B.A., B.Appl.Studies, B.Bus.Admin., B.F.A., B.Mus.Ed., B.S., B.S.Home Econ., B.S.Nurs.
**Majors:** Accounting, Agriculture, Art, Bible, Biochemistry, Biology, Business, Business/International Studies, Chemistry, Communication, Communication Disorders, Computer Information Systems, Computer Science, Corporate Fitness, Criminal Justice, Elementary Education, English, Finance, Food/Nutrition/Dietetics, French, Geology, German, Government, Health/Physical Education/Recreation, History, Home Economics, Home Economics Education, Home Economics/Family Studies, Human Development/Family Studies, Human Resources Management, Industrial Education, Instrumental Music, Interior Design, International Studies, Journalism/Mass Communications, Management, Marketing, Mathematics, Medical Technology, Music, Nursing, Physical Education, Physics, Piano, Political Science, Pre-Engineering, Psychology, Recreation Management, Secondary Education, Social Work, Spanish, Special Education, Theatre, Voice.
**Distribution of degrees:** The majors with the highest enrollment are education, biology, and accounting; art and home economics have the lowest.
**Requirements:** General education requirement.
**Academic regulations:** Minimum 2.0 GPA must be maintained.
**Special:** Associate's degrees offered. Self-designed majors. Double majors. Dual degrees. Independent study. Accelerated study. Pass/fail grading option. Cooperative education programs. Graduate school at which undergraduates may take graduate-level courses. Preprofessional programs in law, medicine, veterinary science, pharmacy, dentistry, optometry, and engineering. Cooperative programs in geology and criminal justice with Hardin-Simmons U. Other three-year cooperative programs with approved professional schools. 3-2 electrical engineering program with U of Texas at Dallas. Member of Tri-College Consortium. Teacher certification in early childhood, elementary, secondary, special education, and bilingual/bicultural education. Certification in specific subject areas. Study abroad in Australia, Belgium, England, France, Germany, Greece, Japan, and Spain. ROTC at Hardin-Simmons U.
**Honors:** Honors program. Honor societies.
**Academic Assistance:** Remedial reading, writing, math, and study skills. Nonremedial tutoring.

**STUDENT LIFE. Housing:** All unmarried freshmen and sophomores must live on campus unless living with family. Women's and men's dorms. School-owned/operated apartments. On-campus married-student housing. 34% of students live in college housing.
**Services and counseling/handicapped student services:** Placement services. Health service. Counseling services for minority, military, veteran, and older students. Personal and psychological counseling. Career and academic guidance services. Religious counseling. Physically disabled student services. Learning disabled program/services. Notetaking services. Tape recorders. Tutors. Reader services for the blind.
**Campus organizations:** Undergraduate student government. Student newspaper (Optimist, published twice/week). Literary magazine. Yearbook. Radio and TV stations. Choral groups, marching band, orchestra, opera workshop, drama group, debating, men's and women's social clubs, literary and service clubs, departmental groups, 75 organizations in all. Six fraternities, no chapter houses; seven sororities, no chapter houses. 10% of men join a fraternity. 11% of women join a sorority.
**Religious organizations:** Mission Outreach, Missionary Apprentice Resource Corps, Global Campaigns, Temporary Institutional Missionary Experience.
**Minority/foreign student organizations:** International Student Club.

**ATHLETICS. Physical education requirements:** Four semesters of physical education required.
**Intercollegiate competition:** 1% of students participate. Baseball (M), basketball (M,W), cheerleading (M,W), cross-country (M,W), football (M), golf (M), tennis (M,W), track (indoor) (M,W), track (outdoor) (M,W), track and field (indoor) (M,W), track and field (outdoor) (M,W), volleyball (W). Member of Lone Star Conference, NCAA Division II.
**Intramural and club sports:** 33% of students participate. Intramural baseball, basketball, cross-country, flag football, softball.

**ADMISSIONS. Academic basis for candidate selection** (in order of priority): Secondary school record, school's recommendation, standardized test scores, class rank, essay.
**Nonacademic basis for candidate selection:** Character and personality and extracurricular participation are emphasized. Particular talent or ability is important.
**Requirements:** Graduation from secondary school is required; GED is accepted. 21 units and the following program of study are required: 4 units of English, 1 unit of math, 2 units of lab science, 1 unit of social studies, 1 unit of history, 10 units of academic electives. Rank in top three-quarters of secondary school class and minimum 2.0 GPA required. Conditional admission possible for applicants not meeting standard requirements. ACT is required; SAT may be substituted. ACH recommended. Campus visit and interview recommended. Off-campus interviews available with an admissions representative.
**Procedure:** Take SAT or ACT by October of 12th year. Take ACH by October of 12th year. Suggest filing application by February 1. Notification of admission on rolling basis. No set date by which applicants must accept offer. $100 room deposit, refundable until six weeks before beginning of term. Freshmen accepted for terms other than fall.
**Special programs:** Admission may be deferred one year. Credit may be granted through CEEB Advanced Placement for scores of 3 or higher. Credit and/or placement may be granted through CLEP subject exams. Credit may be granted through military experience. Credit and placement may be granted through challenge exams. Early decision program. In fall 1993, 10 applied for early decision and 10 were accepted. Deadline for applying for early decision is January 1. Early entrance/early admission program. Concurrent enrollment program.
**Transfer students:** Transfer students accepted for terms other than fall. In fall 1993, 12% of all new students were transfers into all classes. 219 transfer applications were received, 174 were accepted. Application deadline is rolling for fall; rolling for spring. Minimum 2.0 GPA recommended. Lowest course grade accepted is "D." Maximum number of transferable credits is 64 semester hours. At least 24 semester hours must be completed at the university to receive degree.
**Admissions contact:** Don King, M.S., Director of Admissions. 915 674-2653.

**FINANCIAL AID. Available aid:** Pell grants, SEOG, state scholarships and grants, school scholarships and grants, private scholarships and grants, ROTC scholarships, academic merit scholarships, and athletic scholarships. Perkins Loans (NDSL), PLUS, Stafford Loans (GSL), NSL, state loans, private loans, and SLS. Tuition Plan Inc. and guaranteed tuition.
**Financial aid statistics:** 47% of aid is not need-based. In 1994-95, 82% of all undergraduate applicants received aid; 78% of freshman applicants. Average amounts of aid awarded freshmen: Scholarships and grants, $3,832; loans, $3,681.
**Supporting data/closing dates:** FAFSA/FAF/FFS: Priority filing date is March 1. School's own aid application: Priority filing date is March 1. SINGLEFILE: Priority filing date is March 1. Notification of awards on rolling basis.
**Financial aid contact:** Don Hilton, M.S., Director of Financial Aid. 915 674-2643.

**STUDENT EMPLOYMENT.** College Work/Study Program. Institutional employment. 20% of full-time undergraduates work on campus during school year. Students may expect to earn an average of $1,526 during school year. Off-campus part-time employment opportunities rated "good."

**COMPUTER FACILITIES.** 675 IBM/IBM-compatible and Macintosh/Apple microcomputers; 350 are networked. Students may access Digital minicomputer/mainframe systems, BITNET, Internet. Client/LAN operating systems include Apple/Macintosh, DOS, OS/2, UNIX/XENIX/AIX, DEC, LocalTalk/AppleTalk, Novell. Computer languages and software packages include BASIC, C, COBOL, FORTRAN, LISP, Oracle, Pascal, SPSS, 20/20, WordPerfect. Computer facilities are available to all students.
**Fees:** None.
**Hours:** 24 hours for some facilities; eight hours/day for others.

**GRADUATE CAREER DATA.** Graduate school percentages: 3% enter law school. 11% enter graduate business programs. 4% enter medical or dental school. 13% enter graduate arts and sciences programs. 4% enter theological school/seminary. Highest graduate school enrollments: Baylor Dental Sch, Emory U, Southwestern Medical Coll, Texas A&M U, U of Illinois, U of Oklahoma, U of Texas. 22% of graduates choose careers in business and industry. Companies and businesses that hire graduates: Arthur Andersen, Coopers & Lybrand, Dow Chemical, Pennzoil.

**PROMINENT ALUMNI/AE.** Louie Welch, president of Houston Chamber of Commerce and former mayor of Houston; C.E. Cornutt, Exec. VP and CEO, Hunt Oil Co.; Gerald Turner, Chancellor, U of Mississippi; J. MacDonald Williams, President, Trammel Crow and Co.

# Angelo State University

## San Angelo, TX 76909

**1993-94 Costs.** Tuition: $720 (state residents), $4,860 (out-of-state). Room & board: $3,490. Fees, books, misc. academic expenses (school's estimate): $1,056.
**Enrollment.** Undergraduates: 1,937 men, 2,257 women (full-time). Freshman class: 3,535 applicants, 1,825 accepted, 1,054 enrolled. Graduate enrollment: 216 men, 294 women.
**Test score averages/ranges.** Average SAT scores: 441 verbal, 500 math. Average ACT scores: 23 English, 22 math, 23 composite.
**Faculty.** 211 full-time; 29 part-time. 60% of faculty holds doctoral degree. Student/faculty ratio: 24 to 1.
**Selectivity rating.** Competitive.

**PROFILE.** Angelo State is a public university. It was founded as a junior college in 1928, became a four-year college in 1965, and gained university status four years later. Programs are offered through the Colleges of Liberal and Fine Arts, Professional Studies, and Sciences; University Studies Program; Ethnic Studies; and the Graduate School. Its 268-acre campus is located in San Angelo, a cattle and sheep ranching region.

**Accreditation:** SACS. Professionally accredited by the National Association of Schools of Music, the National League for Nursing.
**Religious orientation:** Angelo State University is nonsectarian; no religious requirements.
**Library:** Collections totaling over 462,000 volumes, 2,401 periodical subscriptions, and 227,110 microform items.
**Special facilities/museums:** Planetarium.
**Athletic facilities:** Gymnasium, swimming pool, track, multi-sports complex.

**STUDENT BODY. Undergraduate profile:** 96% are state residents; 10% are transfers. 1% Asian-American, 4% Black, 13% Hispanic, 80% White, 2% Other. Average age of undergraduates is 22.
**Freshman profile:** 1% of freshmen who took SAT scored 700 or over on verbal, 2% scored 700 or over on math; 6% scored 600 or over on verbal, 17% scored 600 or over on math; 25% scored 500 or over on verbal, 50% scored 500 or over on math; 66% scored 400 or over on verbal, 89% scored 400 or over on math; 97% scored 300 or over on verbal, 100% scored 300 or over on math. 51% of accepted applicants took SAT; 49% took ACT. 95% of freshmen come from public schools.
**Undergraduate achievement:** 63% of fall 1991 freshmen returned for fall 1992 term.
**Foreign students:** 81 students are from out of the country. Countries represented include Germany, India, and Thailand; 23 in all.

**PROGRAMS OF STUDY. Degrees:** B.A., B.Bus.Admin., B.Mus., B.S., B.S.Nurs.
**Majors:** Accounting, Animal Science, Art, Biology, Business Administration, Chemistry, Computer Science, Drama, Economics, Elementary Education, English, Finance, French, Geology, Government, History, Instrumental Music Education, Journalism, Kinesiology, Management, Marketing, Mathematics, Medical Technology, Music, Nursing, Physical Education, Physics, Psychology, Sociology, Spanish, Speech, Vocal Music Education.

**Requirements:** General education requirement.

**Academic regulations:** Minimum 2.0 GPA must be maintained.

**Special:** Courses offered in agriculture, German, linguistics, philosophy, and range/wildlife management. Associate's degrees offered. Self-designed majors. Independent study. Graduate school at which undergraduates may take graduate-level courses. Preprofessional programs in law, medicine, veterinary science, pharmacy, dentistry, and engineering. 3-1 medical technology program. 3-2 engineering program with U of Texas at El Paso. Member of Texas International Education Consortium. Teacher certification in early childhood, elementary, secondary, special education, and bilingual/bicultural education. Study abroad in Western European countries. AFROTC.

**Honors:** Honor societies.

**Academic Assistance:** Nonremedial tutoring.

**STUDENT LIFE. Housing:** Unmarried undergraduates with course loads of nine or more semester hours must live on campus unless other arrangements are approved. Women's and men's dorms. School-owned/operated apartments. On-campus married-student housing. 50% of students live in college housing.

**Services and counseling/handicapped student services:** Placement services. Health service. Counseling services for minority, military, and veteran students. Personal and psychological counseling. Career and academic guidance services. Learning disabled services.

**Campus organizations:** Student newspaper (Rampage, published once/week). Yearbook. Band, Angelettes, Choral Singers Association, drama group, Residence Hall Association, service and special-interest groups, 75 organizations in all. Three fraternities, no chapter houses; three sororities, no chapter houses. 3% of men join a fraternity. 1% of women join a sorority.

**Religious organizations:** Baptist Student Union, Christian Campus Center, United Campus Ministries, Newman Center, Theta Lambda, Campus Crusade for Christ.

**Minority/foreign student organizations:** Mexican American association, Striving for Success (black group). International Student Association.

**ATHLETICS. Physical education requirements:** Two semester hours of physical education required.

**Intercollegiate competition:** 3% of students participate. Basketball (M,W), cross-country (M,W), football (M), track (outdoor) (M,W), volleyball (W). Member of Lone Star Conference, NCAA Division II.

**Intramural and club sports:** 16% of students participate. Intramural basketball, flag football, soccer, softball, volleyball. Men's club volleyball.

**ADMISSIONS. Academic basis for candidate selection** (in order of priority): Class rank, standardized test scores, secondary school record, school's recommendation.

**Requirements:** Graduation from secondary school is required; GED is accepted. No specific distribution of secondary school units required. No minimum SAT or ACT scores required of graduates of accredited secondary schools who rank in top quarter of secondary school class; minimum composite ACT score of 17 (combined SAT score of 700) required of those in second quarter; minimum composite ACT score of 23 (combined SAT score of 920) required of those in third quarter; minimum composite ACT score of 30 (combined SAT score of 1200) required of those in fourth quarter. Students not normally admissible may be admitted by earning a "C" average in summer school. SAT or ACT is required. Campus visit and interview recommended. No off-campus interviews.

**Procedure:** Application deadline is August 19. Notification of admission on rolling basis. No set date by which applicants must accept offer. $60 room deposit, refundable until July 15. Freshmen accepted for terms other than fall.

**Special programs:** Admission may be deferred indefinitely. Credit may be granted through CLEP general and subject exams, DANTES, and challenge exams. Early decision program. Early entrance/early admission program. Concurrent enrollment program.

**Transfer students:** Transfer students accepted for terms other than fall. In fall 1992, 10% of all new students were transfers into all classes. 876 transfer applications were received, 623 were accepted. Application deadline is two weeks prior to registration for fall; two weeks prior to registration for spring. Minimum 2.0 GPA required. Maximum number of transferable credits is 66 semester hours. At least 30 semester hours must be completed at the university to receive degree.

**Admissions contact:** Lorri Morris, Assistant Director of Admissions. 915 942-2041.

**FINANCIAL AID. Available aid:** Pell grants, SEOG, school scholarships, private scholarships, ROTC scholarships, academic merit scholarships, and athletic scholarships. Perkins Loans (NDSL), Stafford Loans (GSL), state loans, school loans, and private loans. Housing installment plan.

**Supporting data/closing dates:** FAFSA/FAF/FFS: Priority filing date is July 15. School's own aid application: Deadline is July 15. State aid form: Deadline is July 15. Income tax forms: Deadline is July 15. Notification of awards begins May 15.

**Financial aid contact:** James B. Parker, Director of Financial Aid. 915 942-2246.

**STUDENT EMPLOYMENT.** College Work/Study Program. Institutional employment. 38% of full-time undergraduates work on campus during school year. Students may expect to earn an average of $2,040 during school year. Freshmen are discouraged from working during their first term. Off-campus part-time employment opportunities rated "good."

**COMPUTER FACILITIES.** 250 IBM/IBM-compatible and Macintosh/Apple microcomputers; 30 are networked. Students may access IBM minicomputer/mainframe systems. Residence halls may be equipped with networked terminals. Computer languages and software packages include Assembler, COBOL, dBASE, FORTRAN, Lotus 1-2-3, WordPerfect. Computer facilities are available to all students.

**Fees:** $3 computer fee per semester hour.

**Hours:** 8 AM-midn.

**GRADUATE CAREER DATA.** Graduate school percentages: 2% enter law school. 2% enter medical school. 1% enter dental school. 9% enter graduate business programs.

# Austin College

**Sherman, TX 75090-4440 — 903 813-2000**

**1994-95 Costs.** Tuition: $11,280. Room: $1,875. Board: $2,467. Fees, books, misc. academic expenses (school's estimate): $525.

**Enrollment.** Undergraduates: 542 men, 576 women (full-time). Freshman class: 948 applicants, 798 accepted, 295 enrolled. Graduate enrollment: 7 men, 29 women.

**Test score averages/ranges.** Average SAT scores: 495 verbal, 501 math. Range of SAT scores of middle 50%: 440-560 verbal, 500-610 math. Average ACT scores: 24 composite. Range of ACT scores of middle 50%: 21-27 composite.

**Faculty.** 84 full-time; 15 part-time. 95% of faculty holds highest degree in specific field. Student/faculty ratio: 14 to 1.

**Selectivity rating.** Less competitive.

**PROFILE.** Austin, founded in 1849, is a church-affiliated, liberal arts college. Its 60-acre campus is located in Sherman, 60 miles north of Dallas, near the Oklahoma state line.

**Accreditation:** SACS.

**Religious orientation:** Austin College is affiliated with the Presbyterian Church USA; no religious requirements.

**Library:** Collections totaling over 385,005 volumes, 943 periodical subscriptions, and 134,040 microform items.

**Special facilities/museums:** Tissue culture facility.

**Athletic facilities:** Gymnasiums, natatorium, basketball, racquetball, tennis, and volleyball courts, weight room, baseball, football, intramural, and soccer fields, dance studio, stadium, track.

**STUDENT BODY. Undergraduate profile:** 91% are state residents; 17% are transfers. 5% Asian-American, 5% Black, 9% Hispanic, 1% Native American, 78% White, 2% Other. Average age of undergraduates is 20.

**Freshman profile:** 2% of freshmen who took SAT scored 700 or over on verbal, 8% scored 700 or over on math; 14% scored 600 or over on verbal, 31% scored 600 or over on math; 49% scored 500 or over on verbal, 76% scored 500 or over on math; 88% scored 400 or over on verbal, 97% scored 400 or over on math; 100% scored 300 or over on verbal, 100% scored 300 or over on math. 95% of accepted applicants took SAT; 47% took ACT. 90% of freshmen come from public schools.

**Undergraduate achievement:** 81% of fall 1992 freshmen returned for fall 1993 term. 61% of entering class graduated. 34% of students who completed a degree program immediately went on to graduate study.

**Foreign students:** 25 students are from out of the country. Countries represented include France, Germany, India, Japan, and Mexico; 16 in all.

**PROGRAMS OF STUDY. Degrees:** B.A.

**Majors:** American Studies, Art, Biology, Business Administration, Chemistry, Classics, Communication Arts, Computer Science, Economics, Education, English, French, German, History, Interdisciplinary Studies, International Studies, Latin American Studies, Mathematics/Computer Studies, Music, Philosophy, Physical Education, Physics, Political Science, Psychology, Religion, Sociology, Spanish.

**Distribution of degrees:** The majors with the highest enrollment are biology, psychology, and business administration; religion, classics, and music have the lowest.

**Requirements:** General education requirement.

**Academic regulations:** Minimum 2.0 GPA must be maintained.

**Special:** Self-designed majors. Double majors. Dual degrees. Independent study. Pass/fail grading option. Internships. Graduate school at which undergraduates may take graduate-level courses. Preprofessional programs in law, medicine, dentistry, and theology. 3-2 engineering programs with Texas A&M U, U of Texas at Austin, U of Texas at Dallas, and Washington U. Washington Semester. Teacher certification in elementary and secondary education. Study abroad also in Europe, Far Eastern and Latin American countries, and Mexico.

**Honors:** Honors program. Honor societies.

**Academic Assistance:** Nonremedial tutoring.

**STUDENT LIFE. Housing:** All unmarried freshmen and sophomores under age 21 must live on campus unless living with family. Coed, women's, and men's dorms. School-owned/operated apartments. 67% of students live in college housing.

**Social atmosphere:** The most popular on-campus haunt is the AC Pub in the Student Union, where students gather before, between, and after classes. Off-campus, students meet at Calhoun's, a local country-western dance club. Greeks make up about 40% of the student population and offer most of the social activity on campus. The Campus Activities Board also exerts an influence on social life by sponsoring many on-campus activities. Popular events of the school year include Springfest, intermural sporting events, and the Roo Games (big messy sports events with stupid games: "major fun!"). "For a highly academic school, there is a lot of social activity," observes the editor of the school newspaper, "and it is really easy to meet people since it is such a small friendly school." Despite the limited cultural life in Sherman, students have access to the museums, theatres, and concerts of nearby Dallas.

**Services and counseling/handicapped student services:** Placement services. Health service. Birth control, personal, and psychological counseling. Career and academic guidance services. Religious counseling.

**Campus organizations:** Undergraduate student government. Student newspaper (Austin College Observer, published once/two weeks). Literary magazine. Yearbook. A cappella choir, instrumental ensembles, Sherman symphony, Circle K, BACCHUS, martial arts club, Amnesty International, environmental organization, Young Democrats, 56 organizations in all. Nine fraternities, no chapter houses; six sororities, no chapter houses. 19% of men join a fraternity. 21% of women join a sorority.

**Religious organizations:** Baptist Student Union, Fellowship of Christian Athletes, Intervarsity Christian Fellowship, Wesley Fellowship.

**Minority/foreign student organizations:** Black Expressions, Los Amigos. Students International Organization.

**ATHLETICS. Physical education requirements:** One semester of physical education required.

**Intercollegiate competition:** 20% of students participate. Baseball (M), basketball (M,W), diving (M,W), football (M), golf (M), soccer (M), swimming (M,W), tennis (M,W), track (outdoor) (M,W), track and field (outdoor) (M,W), volleyball (W). Member of NAIA, Texas Intercollegiate Athletic Association.

**Intramural and club sports:** 65% of students participate. Intramural flag football, racquetball, softball, swimming, tennis, volleyball. Men's club lacrosse.

**ADMISSIONS. Academic basis for candidate selection** (in order of priority): Secondary school record, class rank, standardized test scores, school's recommendation, essay.

**Nonacademic basis for candidate selection:** Character and personality and extracurricular participation are important. Particular talent or ability and alumni/ae relationship are considered.

**Requirements:** Graduation from secondary school is required; GED is accepted. 15 units and the following program of study are recommended: 4 units of English, 3 units of math, 3 units of science, 2 units of foreign language, 2 units of social studies, 1 unit of electives. Additional units of mathematics and foreign language highly recommended. SAT or ACT is required. Campus visit and interview recommended. Off-campus interviews available with an admissions representative.

**Procedure:** Take SAT or ACT by March 1 of 12th year. Visit college for interview by April 30 of 12th year. Suggest filing application by December 1. Application deadline is March 15. Notification of acceptance in December, February, and April. Reply is required by May 1. $200 tuition deposit, refundable until May 1. Freshmen accepted for terms other than fall.

**Special programs:** Admission may be deferred one year. Credit may be granted through CEEB Advanced Placement for scores of 4 or higher. Credit may be granted through CLEP general and subject exams. Early entrance/early admission program. Concurrent enrollment program.

**Transfer students:** Transfer students accepted for terms other than fall. In fall 1993, 17% of all new students were transfers into all classes. 124 transfer applications were received, 81 were accepted. Application deadline is August 1 for fall; January 10 for spring. Minimum 2.0 GPA required. Lowest course grade accepted is "C." Maximum number of transferable credits is 68 quarter hours. At least 17 course credits must be completed at the college to receive degree.

**Admissions contact:** Rodney Oto, Dean of Admissions and Financial Aid. 800 442-5363.

**FINANCIAL AID. Available aid:** Pell grants, SEOG, state grants, school scholarships and grants, private scholarships, and academic merit scholarships. Perkins Loans (NDSL), PLUS, Stafford Loans (GSL), school loans, and SLS. Family tuition reduction.

**Financial aid statistics:** 23% of aid is not need-based. In 1993-94, 94% of all undergraduate applicants received aid; 93% of freshman applicants. Average amounts of aid awarded freshmen: Scholarships and grants, $5,326; loans, $3,382.

**Supporting data/closing dates:** FAFSA/FAF: Priority filing date is May 1; accepted on rolling basis. School's own aid application: Priority filing date is May 1; accepted on rolling basis. Notification of awards on rolling basis.

**Financial aid contact:** Jimmy Trammell, Director of Financial Aid. 800 442-5363.

**STUDENT EMPLOYMENT.** College Work/Study Program. Institutional employment. 35% of full-time undergraduates work on campus during school year. Students may expect to earn an average of $1,300 during school year. Off-campus part-time employment opportunities rated "good."

**COMPUTER FACILITIES.** 58 IBM/IBM-compatible, Macintosh/Apple, and RISC-/UNIX-based microcomputers. Students may access Digital, NCR, SUN minicomputer/mainframe systems, Internet. Residence halls may be equipped with stand-alone microcomputers, networked microcomputers. Client/LAN operating systems include Apple/Macintosh, DOS, UNIX/XENIX/AIX, X-windows, LocalTalk/AppleTalk, Microsoft, Novell. Computer languages and software packages include AmiPro, C++, Excel, FORTRAN, Lotus 1-2-3, Mathematica, PageMaker, Pascal, SPSS/WIN, Word, WordPerfect, X Windows. Computer facilities are available to all students.

**Hours:** 24 hours in some locations.

**GRADUATE CAREER DATA.** Graduate school percentages: 5% enter law school. 7% enter medical school. 4% enter graduate business programs. Highest graduate school enrollments: Baylor U, Texas A&M U, U of North Texas, U of Texas at Austin. 48% of graduates choose careers in business and industry. Companies and businesses that hire graduates: Electronic Data Systems, State Farm Insurance, Texas Instruments.

**PROMINENT ALUMNI/AE.** Clifford Grum, president, Temple-Inland; James I. McCord, winner of Templeton Prize, head of Princeton Seminary; David Easterly, publisher, *Atlanta Constitution*; Bob Wood, Jr., president, Occidental Crude Sales; Steve Schlosstein, author; George Livings, opera singer; Patricia McClurg, director, National Council of Churches.

# Baylor University

**Waco, TX 76798** **817 755-1011**

**1994-95 Costs.** Tuition: $6,960. Room: $1,740. Board: $2,295. Fees, books, misc. academic expenses (school's estimate): $1,240.

**Enrollment.** Undergraduates: 4,446 men, 5,473 women (full-time). Freshman class: 2,433 enrolled. Graduate enrollment: 998 men, 793 women.

**Test score averages/ranges.** Range of SAT scores of middle 50%: 430-540 verbal, 500-620 math. Range of ACT scores of middle 50%: 20-26 English, 19-24 math.

**Faculty.** 603 full-time; 66 part-time. Student/faculty ratio: 16 to 1.

**Selectivity rating.** More competitive.

**PROFILE.** Baylor, founded in 1845, is a church-affiliated university. Programs are offered through the College of Arts and Sciences; the Hankamer School of Business; the Schools of Education, Law, Music, and Nursing; and the Graduate School. Its 428-acre campus is located in a residential area of Waco. The university also operates a medical school in Dallas.

**Accreditation:** SACS. Professionally accredited by the Accreditation Board for Engineering and Technology, the American Assembly of Collegiate Schools of Business, the Council on Social Work Education, the National Association of Schools of Music, the National Council for Accreditation of Teacher Education, the National League for Nursing.

**Religious orientation:** Baylor University is affiliated with the Baptist Church; six semester hours of religion required.

**Library:** Collections totaling over 51,510,561 volumes, 9,171 periodical subscriptions, and 1,013,639 microform items.

**Special facilities/museums:** Language labs, natural science museum, environmental studies lab, high definition television.

**Athletic facilities:** Facilities and equipment for badminton, baseball, basketball, cross-country, football, golf, indoor track, lacrosse, martial arts, racquetball, sailing, skeet, soccer, softball, swimming, tennis, track and field, volleyball, water skiing, and weight lifting.

**STUDENT BODY. Undergraduate profile:** 78% are state residents; 16% are transfers. 6% Asian-American, 4% Black, 7% Hispanic, 83% White. Average age of undergraduates is 21.

**Freshman profile:** 63% of accepted applicants took SAT; 37% took ACT.

**Undergraduate achievement:** 85% of fall 1992 freshmen returned for fall 1993 term. 43% of entering class graduated.

**Foreign students:** 403 students are from out of the country. 69 countries represented in all.

**PROGRAMS OF STUDY. Degrees:** B.A., B.Bus.Admin., B.F.A., B.Mech.Eng., B.Mus., B.Mus.Ed., B.S., B.S.Avia.Sci., B.S.Ed., B.S.Eng., B.S.Home Econ., B.S.Nurs.

**Majors:** Accounting, Acting, Administrative Information Systems, American Studies, Anthropology, Applied Music, Archaeology, Architecture, Art, Art History, Asian Studies, Aviation Sciences, Basic Business, Biblical/Related Languages, Biology, Business Administration, Business Broadcasting, Business Journalism, Chemistry, Child/Family Studies, Choral Music, Church Music, Church Recreation, Classics, Communication Disorders, Communication Specialist, Composition, Computer Information Systems, Computer Science, Dentistry, Design/Directing, Dietetics, Earth Science, Economics, Education, Elementary Education, Engineering, English, Entrepreneurship, Environmental Studies, Fashion Design, Fashion Merchandising, Finance, Financial Services/Planning, Foreign Service, Forestry, French, General Home Economics, Geology, Geophysics, German, Greek, Health, Health/Fitness Studies, Health Science, History, Human Performance/Recreation, Human Resources Management, Instrumental Music, Insurance, Interdisciplinary Studies, Interior Design, International Business, Journalism, Latin, Latin American Studies, Law, Life/Earth Science, Management, Marketing, Mathematical Sciences, Mathematics, Medical Technology/Biology, Medicine, Museum Studies, Music, Music History/Literature, Neuroscience, Nursing, Operations Management, Optometry, Pedagogy, Philosophy, Physical Education, Physical Science, Physics, Political Science, Professional Writing, Psychology, Public Administration, Quantitative Business Analysis, Real Estate, Recreation, Regional/Urban Studies, Religion, Russian, Science, Secondary Education, Slavic Studies, Social Studies, Social Work, Sociology, Spanish, Speech Communication, Speech Communications, Speech/Language Therapy, Studio Art, Telecommunication, Theater Arts, Theatre Arts, Theory, University Scholars.

**Distribution of degrees:** The majors with the highest enrollment are biology, interdisciplinary studies/education, and accounting.

**Requirements:** General education requirement.

**Academic regulations:** Minimum 2.0 GPA required for graduation.

**Special:** Minors offered in most majors and in numerous other fields. Self-designed majors. Double majors. Dual degrees. Independent study. Accelerated study. Pass/fail grading option. Internships. Graduate school at which undergraduates may take graduate-level courses. Preprofessional programs in law, medicine, dentistry, and optometry. B.B.A./J.D., B.B.A./M.Tax, and M.B.A./M.D. programs. 3-2 forestry and environmental studies program with Duke U. 3-4 architecture program with Washington U. B.A./J.D. program. Teacher certification in early childhood, elementary, secondary, and special education. Certification in specific subject areas. Study abroad in Australia, Canada, China, England, Hong Kong, Indonesia, Japan, Korea, Mexico, South Africa, the former Soviet Republics, and Thailand. AFROTC.

**Honors:** Phi Beta Kappa. Honors program.

**Academic Assistance:** Remedial reading, writing, and study skills. Nonremedial tutoring.

**STUDENT LIFE. Housing:** Students may live on or off campus. Women's and men's dorms. Married-student housing. 30% of students live in college housing.

**Social atmosphere:** According to the student newspaper, "Diverse social activities are a strong undercurrent at a school that stresses a family environment. Baptist dictates do not surmount social events similar to those at other universities. A wide range of campus organizations have influence on the social life: Greeks, Alpha Phi Omega service fraternity, international organizations such as the Russian Club, and business fraternities." Favorite student gathering spots include Health Camp, J.T. McCord's, Bill Daniel Student Center, Waco Elite Cafe, Austin's, and the 25th Street Theater.

**Services and counseling/handicapped student services:** Placement services. Health service. Counseling services for minority, military, veteran, and older students. Personal and psychological counseling. Career and academic guidance services. Religious counseling. Learning disabled services.

**Campus organizations:** Undergraduate student government. Student newspaper (Lariat, published once/day). Literary magazine. Yearbook. Radio station. Childhood Education International, International Business Association, social work organization, Women in Communication, Union Program committees, College Republicans, Young Democrats, Arnold Air Society, Medieval and Renaissance Society, academic, recreational, and special-interest groups, 158 organizations in all. 16 fraternities, no chapter houses; 13 sororities, no chapter houses. 20% of men join a fraternity. 25% of women join a sorority.

**Religious organizations:** Baptist Student Union, Canterbury Association, Catholic Student Center, Christian Science Fellowship, Fellowship of Christian Athletes, Greek Council for Christ, Intervarsity Christian Fellowship, Lutheran Student Fellowship, Wesley Foundation, Campus Crusade for Christ, Navigators.

**Minority/foreign student organizations:** Black Students at Baylor, Hispanic Culture Association, Oriental Student Association. Foreign Affairs Association, International

Club, Indian Subcontinent Student Association, Chinese Student Association, Nihon Club.

**ATHLETICS. Physical education requirements:** Four semesters of physical education and/or health and personal effectiveness required.
**Intercollegiate competition:** Baseball (M), basketball (M,W), cross-country (M,W), cycling (M,W), football (M), golf (M,W), tennis (M,W), track (indoor) (M,W), track (outdoor) (M,W), track and field (indoor) (M,W), track and field (outdoor) (M,W), volleyball (W). Member of CFA, NCAA Division I, NCAA Division I-A for football, Southwest Athletic Conference.
**Intramural and club sports:** Intramural badminton, basketball, bowling, cross-country, football, golf, lacrosse, martial arts, racquetball, sailing, skeet, soccer, softball, swimming, tennis, track and field, volleyball, water skiing, weight lifting. Men's club badminton, cycling, karate, lacrosse, sailing, soccer, volleyball, waterskiing. Women's club badminton, cycling, karate, sailing, soccer, volleyball, waterskiing.

**ADMISSIONS. Academic basis for candidate selection** (in order of priority): Class rank, standardized test scores, secondary school record, school's recommendation, essay.
**Nonacademic basis for candidate selection:** Character and personality are important. Extracurricular participation, particular talent or ability, geographical distribution, and alumni/ae relationship are considered.
**Requirements:** Graduation from secondary school is required; GED is accepted. 17 units and the following program of study are required: 4 units of English, 3 units of math, 2 units of lab science, 2 units of history, 6 units of electives including 2 units of academic electives. Minimum combined SAT score of 1000 (composite ACT score of 21) and rank in top half of secondary school class recommended. Portfolio required of art program applicants. Audition required of music program applicants. Conditional admission possible for applicants not meeting standard requirements. SAT or ACT is required. Campus visit and interview recommended. No off-campus interviews.
**Procedure:** Take SAT or ACT by December of 12th year. Suggest filing application by March 1; no deadline. Notification of admission on rolling basis. Applicant must accept offer of admission by May 1 and make a deposit of $100. Freshmen accepted for terms other than fall.
**Special programs:** Credit may be granted through CEEB Advanced Placement for scores of 3 or higher. Credit may be granted through CLEP subject exams, DANTES and challenge exams. Early entrance/early admission program.
**Transfer students:** Transfer students accepted for terms other than fall. In fall 1993, 16% of all new students were transfers into all classes. SAT/ACT scores, secondary school, and college transcripts required of transfer applicants with fewer than 30 semester hours. Minimum 2.5 GPA required. Lowest course grade accepted is "C." Maximum number of transferable credits is 70 semester hours. At least 60 semester hours must be completed at the university to receive degree.
**Admissions contact:** Diana M. Ramey, M.Ed., Director of Admissions. 817 755-1811.

**FINANCIAL AID. Available aid:** Pell grants, SEOG, state scholarships and grants, school scholarships and grants, private scholarships and grants, ROTC scholarships, academic merit scholarships, athletic scholarships, and aid for undergraduate foreign students. Perkins Loans (NDSL), PLUS, Stafford Loans (GSL), NSL, state loans, school loans, private loans, and SLS. Tuition Plan Inc.
**Financial aid statistics:** 40% of aid is not need-based. In 1993-94, 100% of all undergraduate applicants received aid. Average amounts of aid awarded freshmen: Scholarships and grants, $3,573; loans, $3,697.
**Supporting data/closing dates:** FAFSA: Priority filing date is May 1. School's own aid application: Priority filing date is May 1. Notification of awards on rolling basis.
**Financial aid contact:** Jeannette Armour, Director of Financial Aid. 817 755-2611.

**STUDENT EMPLOYMENT.** College Work/Study Program. Institutional employment. 16% of full-time undergraduates work on campus during school year. Students may expect to earn an average of $1,006 during school year. Off-campus part-time employment opportunities rated "good."

**COMPUTER FACILITIES.** 634 IBM/IBM-compatible, Macintosh/Apple, and RISC-/UNIX-based microcomputers; all are networked. Students may access AT&T, Digital, IBM minicomputer/mainframe systems, BITNET, Internet. Residence halls may be equipped with networked microcomputers. Client/LAN operating systems include Apple/Macintosh, DOS, UNIX/XENIX/AIX, LocalTalk/AppleTalk, Novell. 47 major computer languages and software packages available. Computer facilities are available to all students.
**Fees:** None.

# Concordia Lutheran College

**Austin, TX 78705** **512 452-7661**

**1994-95 Costs.** Tuition: $3,450. Room & board: $1,900. Fees, books, misc. academic expenses (school's estimate): $640.
**Enrollment.** Undergraduates: 243 men, 291 women (full-time). Freshman class: 232 applicants, 201 accepted, 111 enrolled.
**Test score averages/ranges.** Average SAT scores: 400 verbal, 466 math. Average ACT scores: 20 English, 20 math, 20 composite.
**Faculty.** 42 full-time; 18 part-time. 82% of faculty holds doctoral degree. Student/faculty ratio: 15 to 1.
**Selectivity rating.** Less competitive.

**PROFILE.** Concordia Lutheran is a private, church-affiliated, liberal arts college. Founded in 1951, it became coeducational in 1955. Its 20-acre campus is located in Austin, 79 miles from San Antonio.

**Accreditation:** SACS.
**Religious orientation:** Concordia Lutheran College is affiliated with the Lutheran Church (Missouri Synod); four semesters of religion/theology required.
**Library:** Collections totaling over 60,000 volumes, 8,349 periodical subscriptions, and 26,689 microform items.
**Athletic facilities:** Gymnasium, racquetball and tennis courts, weight room, athletic field.

**STUDENT BODY. Undergraduate profile:** 90% are state residents; 40% are transfers. 1% Asian-American, 9% Black, 9% Hispanic, 81% White. Average age of undergraduates is 23.
**Freshman profile:** 55% of accepted applicants took SAT; 45% took ACT. 85% of freshmen come from public schools.
**Undergraduate achievement:** 83% of fall 1992 freshmen returned for fall 1993 term. 39% of entering class graduated.
**Foreign students:** 10 students are from out of the country. Countries represented include Mexico, Nigeria, Peru, and South Korea; five in all.

**PROGRAMS OF STUDY. Degrees:** B.A.
**Majors:** Accounting, Behavioral Sciences, Business Management, Church Music, Communication, Education, English, Environmental Science, Liberal Arts, Mexican-American Studies, Pre-Seminary, Spanish.
**Distribution of degrees:** The majors with the highest enrollment are education, business, and communication; Spanish, Mexican-American studies, and church music have the lowest.
**Requirements:** General education requirement.
**Academic regulations:** Minimum 2.0 GPA must be maintained.
**Special:** Minors offered in most majors and in mathematics. Associate's degrees offered. Double majors. Independent study. Internships. Graduate school at which undergraduates may take graduate-level courses. Preprofessional programs in law, medicine, dentistry, and theology. Teacher certification in early childhood, elementary, and secondary education. Certification in specific subject areas. Study abroad in England and Mexico. ROTC and AFROTC at U of Texas.
**Honors:** Phi Beta Kappa. Honor societies.
**Academic Assistance:** Remedial reading, writing, and math. Nonremedial tutoring.

**ADMISSIONS. Academic basis for candidate selection** (in order of priority): Standardized test scores, class rank, secondary school record, school's recommendation, essay.
**Nonacademic basis for candidate selection:** Character and personality, extracurricular participation, and particular talent or ability are important. Alumni/ae relationship is considered.
**Requirements:** Graduation from secondary school is required; GED is accepted. No specific distribution of secondary school units required. Combined SAT score of 750 (composite ACT score of 17), rank in top half of secondary school class, and minimum 2.5 GPA recommended. Conditional admission possible for applicants not meeting standard requirements. SAT or ACT is required. Campus visit recommended. No off-campus interviews.
**Procedure:** Take SAT or ACT by December of 12th year. Visit college for interview by April of 12th year. Suggest filing application by April 15. Application deadline is August 15. Notification of admission on rolling basis. Reply is required by August 15. $100 nonrefundable room deposit. Freshmen accepted for terms other than fall.
**Special programs:** Admission may be deferred one year. Credit and/or placement may be granted through CEEB Advanced Placement exams for scores of 3 or higher. Credit and/or placement may be granted through CLEP general and subject exams. Credit and placement may be granted through DANTES exams and military and life experience. Early decision program. Concurrent enrollment program.
**Transfer students:** Transfer students accepted for terms other than fall. In fall 1993, 40% of all new students were transfers into all classes. 150 transfer applications were received, 125 were accepted. Application deadline is August 15 for fall; January 10 for spring. Minimum 2.0 GPA required. Lowest course grade accepted is "C." At least 30 semester hours must be completed at the college to receive degree.
**Admissions contact:** Kurt Senske, M.A., J.D., Director of Recruitment and Registration. 800 285-4CLC.

**FINANCIAL AID. Available aid:** Pell grants, SEOG, school scholarships and grants, private scholarships, academic merit scholarships, and athletic scholarships. PLUS, Stafford Loans (GSL), state loans, and SLS. Deferred payment plan.
**Financial aid statistics:** 45% of aid is not need-based. In 1993-94, 90% of all undergraduate applicants received aid; 90% of freshman applicants. Average amounts of aid awarded freshmen: Scholarships and grants, $3,500; loans, $2,200.
**Supporting data/closing dates:** FAFSA: Priority filing date is April 15; deadline is August 1. School's own aid application: Priority filing date is April 15. Notification of awards on rolling basis.
**Financial aid contact:** Lynette Heckmann, Director of Financial Assistance. 800 285-4CLC.

# Dallas Baptist University

**Dallas, TX 75211-9800** **214 331-8311**

**1994-95 Costs.** Tuition: $6,360. Room: $1,330. Board: $1,830. Fees, books, misc. academic expenses (school's estimate): $630.
**Enrollment.** Undergraduates: 430 men, 418 women (full-time). Freshman class: 360 applicants, 314 accepted, 155 enrolled. Graduate enrollment: 235 men, 178 women.
**Test score averages/ranges.** Average SAT scores: 435 verbal, 497 math. Range of SAT scores of middle 50%: 370-500 verbal, 430-560 math. Average ACT scores: 22 composite. Range of ACT scores of middle 50%: 19-25 composite.
**Faculty.** 61 full-time; 114 part-time. 51% of faculty holds doctoral degree. Student/faculty ratio: 17 to 1.
**Selectivity rating.** Less competitive.

**PROFILE.** Dallas Baptist, founded in 1898, is a church-affiliated, liberal arts university. Its 200-acre campus is located 13 miles from downtown Dallas.

**Accreditation:** SACS. Professionally accredited by the National League for Nursing.

**Religious orientation:** Dallas Baptist University is affiliated with the Southern Baptist Church; four semesters of religion required.
**Library:** Collections totaling over 523,993 volumes, 496 periodical subscriptions, and 314,602 microform items.
**Special facilities/museums:** On-campus elementary school.
**Athletic facilities:** Gymnasium, weight room, track, football and soccer fields, basketball, tennis, and volleyball courts, swimming pool, golf driving range.
**STUDENT BODY. Undergraduate profile:** 92% are state residents. 4% Asian-American, 18% Black, 6% Hispanic, 66% White, 6% Other. Average age of undergraduates is 21.
**Freshman profile:** 2% of freshmen who took SAT scored 700 or over on math; 2% scored 600 or over on verbal, 12% scored 600 or over on math; 20% scored 500 or over on verbal, 33% scored 500 or over on math; 43% scored 400 or over on verbal, 56% scored 400 or over on math; 65% scored 300 or over on verbal, 66% scored 300 or over on math. 2% of freshmen who took ACT scored 30 or over on composite; 17% scored 24 or over on composite; 42% scored 18 or over on composite; 51% scored 12 or over on composite. 67% of accepted applicants took SAT; 50% took ACT. 81% of freshmen come from public schools.
**Foreign students:** 161 students are from out of the country. Countries represented include Hong Kong, Indonesia, Korea, Malaysia, Taiwan, and Thailand; 26 in all.
**PROGRAMS OF STUDY. Degrees:** B.A., B.A.Bus.Admin., B.Appl.Arts/Sci., B.Bus.Admin., B.Mus., B.Mus.Ed., B.S.
**Majors:** Accounting, Accounting/Information Science, Aviation Management, Biblical Studies, Biology, Business Administration, Church Music, Computer Science, Computer Systems Management, Counseling, Criminal Justice, Economics, English, Finance, Fine Arts, General Studies, History, Management, Marketing, Mathematics, Multidisciplinary Studies, Music, Pastoral Ministries, Physical Education, Political Science, Psychology, Religious Education, Social Services, Sociology.
**Distribution of degrees:** The majors with the highest enrollment are business administration, general studies, and computer science; mathematics and music performance have the lowest.
**Requirements:** General education requirement.
**Academic regulations:** Minimum 2.00 GPA must be maintained.
**Special:** Minors offered in chemistry and physics. Associate's degrees offered. Double majors. Graduate school at which undergraduates may take graduate-level courses. Preprofessional programs in law, medicine, pharmacy, dentistry, optometry, occupational therapy, physical therapy, and podiatry. Washington Semester. Teacher certification in early childhood, elementary, and secondary education. Certification in specific subject areas. Study abroad in England (Oxford U). ROTC at U of Texas at Arlington. AFROTC at Texas Christian U.
**Honors:** Honor societies.
**ADMISSIONS. Academic basis for candidate selection** (in order of priority): Essay, class rank, standardized test scores, secondary school record.
**Nonacademic basis for candidate selection:** Character and personality are emphasized. Extracurricular participation and particular talent or ability are considered.
**Requirements:** Graduation from secondary school is required; GED is accepted. 16 units and the following program of study are recommended: 4 units of English, 3 units of math, 2 units of science, 2 units of foreign language, 3 units of social studies, 2 units of history. SAT or ACT is required. Campus visit and interview recommended. Off-campus interviews available with an admissions representative.
**Procedure:** Take SAT or ACT by June of 12th year. Visit college for interview by August of 12th year. Suggest filing application by January 15; deadline is the first day of semester. Notification of admission on rolling basis. No set date by which applicants must accept offer. $100 room deposit, refundable until one month prior to registration. Freshmen accepted for terms other than fall.
**Special programs:** Admission may be deferred one year. Credit may be granted through CEEB Advanced Placement for scores of 3 or higher. Credit may be granted through CLEP subject exams and life experience. Concurrent enrollment program.
**Transfer students:** Transfer students accepted for terms other than fall. In fall 1993, 281 transfer applications were received, 234 were accepted. Application deadline is rolling for fall; rolling for spring. Minimum 2.0 GPA required. Lowest course grade accepted is "C." Maximum number of transferable credits is 66 semester hours. At least 30 semester hours must be completed at the university to receive degree.
**Admissions contact:** John Plotts, Director of Admissions. 214 333-5360.
**FINANCIAL AID. Available aid:** Pell grants, SEOG, state scholarships and grants, school scholarships, private scholarships and grants, ROTC scholarships, academic merit scholarships, and athletic scholarships. Perkins Loans (NDSL), PLUS, Stafford Loans (GSL), state loans, school loans, private loans, and SLS. Deferred payment plan.
**Financial aid statistics:** 36% of aid is not need-based. In 1993-94, 75% of all undergraduate applicants received aid; 98% of freshman applicants. Average amounts of aid awarded freshmen: Scholarships and grants, $3,612; loans, $2,877.
**Supporting data/closing dates:** FAFSA/FAF/FFS: Priority filing date is May 1. School's own aid application: Priority filing date is May 1. State aid form: Priority filing date is May 1. Income tax forms: Priority filing date is May 1. Notification of awards on rolling basis.
**Financial aid contact:** Eric Mehringer, Assistant Vice President for Financial Affairs. 214 333-5363.

## DeVry Institute of Technology

**Irving, TX 75063** **214 258-6767**

**1994-95 Costs.** Tuition: $5,962. Housing: None. Fees, books, misc. academic expenses (school's estimate): $580.
**Enrollment.** Undergraduates: 1,149 men, 265 women (full-time). Freshman class: 1,038 applicants, 963 accepted, 568 enrolled.
**Test score averages/ranges.** N/A.
**Faculty.** 55 full-time; 45 part-time. Student/faculty ratio: 22 to 1.
**Selectivity rating.** N/A.

**PROFILE.** DeVry/Dallas, founded in 1969, is a private institution specializing in electronics technology and computer information systems. It is a member of a network of technical institutes with nine campuses in the U.S. and two in Canada. Its 10-acre campus is located in the Las Colinas area of Irving.

**Accreditation:** NCACS. Professionally accredited by the Accreditation Board for Engineering and Technology.
**Religious orientation:** DeVry Institute of Technology is nonsectarian; no religious requirements.
**Library:** Collections totaling over 7,800 volumes, 200 periodical subscriptions, and 1,346 microform items.
**Athletic facilities:** Volleyball court, softball field.

**STUDENT BODY. Undergraduate profile:** 81% are state residents; 67% are transfers. 5% Asian-American, 24% Black, 14% Hispanic, 1% Native American, 54% White, 2% Other. Average age of undergraduates is 25.
**Undergraduate achievement:** 48% of fall 1992 freshmen returned for fall 1993 term. 29% of entering class graduated.
**Foreign students:** 53 students are from out of the country. Countries represented include Hong Kong, Indonesia, Kenya, Taiwan, Thailand, and Turkey; 20 in all.

**PROGRAMS OF STUDY. Degrees:** B.S.Acct., B.S.Bus.Oper., B.S.Comp.Info.Sys., B.S.Elec.Eng.Tech.
**Majors:** Accounting, Business Operations, Computer Information Systems, Electronic Engineering Technology.
**Distribution of degrees:** The majors with the highest enrollment are electronic engineering technology, computer information systems, and business operations.
**Requirements:** General education requirement.
**Academic regulations:** Minimum 2.0 GPA must be maintained.
**Special:** Associate's degrees offered. Accelerated study. Cooperative education programs.
**Honors:** Honor societies.
**Academic Assistance:** Nonremedial tutoring.

**STUDENT LIFE. Housing:** Commuter campus; no student housing.
**Services and counseling/handicapped student services:** Placement services. Career and academic guidance services. Physically disabled student services. Notetaking services. Reader services for the blind.
**Campus organizations:** Undergraduate student government. Student newspaper (Current Flow, published once/month). Business, data processing, electronics, accounting, and engineering groups, chess club, Toastmasters, 10 organizations in all.
**Religious organizations:** Mannafest.
**Minority/foreign student organizations:** Society of Hispanic Professional Engineers, National Society for Black Engineers. Vietnamese Student Association.

**ATHLETICS. Physical education requirements:** None.
**Intramural and club sports:** Intramural basketball, football, softball, table tennis, volleyball.

**ADMISSIONS. Academic basis for candidate selection** (in order of priority): Standardized test scores.
**Requirements:** Graduation from secondary school is required; GED is accepted. No specific distribution of secondary school units required. Applicants not submitting SAT or ACT must pass DeVry entrance exam. SAT or ACT is recommended. Campus visit recommended. Off-campus interviews available with an admissions representative.
**Procedure:** Notification of admission on rolling basis. Reply is required by registration. $75 tuition deposit, refundable until beginning of classes. Freshmen accepted for terms other than fall.
**Special programs:** Admission may be deferred one year. Credit may be granted through CLEP subject exams, DANTES and challenge exams.
**Transfer students:** Transfer students accepted for terms other than fall. In fall 1993, 67% of all new students were transfers into all classes. Application deadline is rolling for fall; rolling for spring. Minimum 2.0 GPA required. Lowest course grade accepted is "C." Maximum number of transferable semester hours is 65% of total required for degree. At least 35% of total semester hours must be completed at the institute to receive degree.
**Admissions contact:** Danny Millan, Director of Admissions. 214 258-6330.

**FINANCIAL AID. Available aid:** Pell grants, SEOG, state scholarships and grants, school scholarships, and academic merit scholarships. Perkins Loans (NDSL), PLUS, Stafford Loans (GSL), state loans, and SLS. EDUCARD Plan.
**Financial aid statistics:** In 1993-94, 82% of all undergraduate applicants received aid; 80% of freshman applicants.
**Supporting data/closing dates:** FAFSA: Accepted on rolling basis. Notification of awards on rolling basis.
**Financial aid contact:** Laura Myers, Director of Financial Aid.

**STUDENT EMPLOYMENT.** College Work/Study Program. Institutional employment. 6% of full-time undergraduates work on campus during school year. Students may expect to earn an average of $5,244 during school year. Freshmen are discouraged from working during their first term. Off-campus part-time employment opportunities rated "good."

**COMPUTER FACILITIES.** 189 IBM/IBM-compatible microcomputers; 40 are networked. Students may access Hewlett-Packard, IBM minicomputer/mainframe systems. Client/LAN operating systems include DOS, UNIX/XENIX/AIX, Windows NT, Novell. 25 major computer languages and software packages available. Computer facilities are available to all students.
**Fees:** Computer fee is included in tuition/fees.
**Hours:** 7 AM-10 PM (M-Th); 7 AM-6 PM (F).

**GRADUATE CAREER DATA.** 89% of graduates choose careers in business and industry. Companies and businesses that hire graduates: Lear Siegler, Sante Fe Applied Materials, US Sprint.

## East Texas Baptist University

**Marshall, TX 75670** **903 935-7963**

**1994-95 Costs.** Tuition: $4,950. Room: $1,040. Board: $1,530. Fees, books, misc. academic expenses (school's estimate): $920.
**Enrollment.** Undergraduates: 459 men, 585 women (full-time). Freshman class: 612 applicants, 574 accepted, 257 enrolled. Graduate enrollment: 11 men, 6 women.
**Test score averages/ranges.** Range of ACT scores of middle 50%: 18-24 English, 16-22 math.
**Faculty.** 42 full-time; 25 part-time. 72% of faculty holds doctoral degree. Student/faculty ratio: 17 to 1.
**Selectivity rating.** Competitive.

**PROFILE.** East Texas Baptist, founded in 1912, is a church-affiliated, liberal arts university. Its 193-acre campus is located 10 blocks from downtown Marshall.

**Accreditation:** SACS. Professionally accredited by the National Association of Schools of Music.
**Religious orientation:** East Texas Baptist University is affiliated with the Southern Baptist Convention; three semesters of religion required.
**Library:** Collections totaling over 105,171 volumes, 557 periodical subscriptions, and 2,739 microform items.
**Special facilities/museums:** Electronic music lab.
**Athletic facilities:** Gymnasium, tennis courts, baseball, intramural, softball, and soccer fields.

**STUDENT BODY. Undergraduate profile:** 92% are state residents. 1% Asian-American, 10% Black, 3% Hispanic, 84% White, 2% Other. Average age of undergraduates is 22.
**Freshman profile:** 5% of freshmen who took ACT scored 30 or over on English, 2% scored 30 or over on math, 2% scored 30 or over on composite; 31% scored 24 or over on English, 16% scored 24 or over on math, 26% scored 24 or over on composite; 70% scored 18 or over on English, 61% scored 18 or over on math, 74% scored 18 or over on composite; 96% scored 12 or over on English, 100% scored 12 or over on math, 100% scored 12 or over on composite; 100% scored 6 or over on English. Majority of accepted applicants took ACT. 98% of freshmen come from public schools.
**Undergraduate achievement:** 65% of fall 1991 freshmen returned for fall 1992 term.
**Foreign students:** 43 students are from out of the country. Countries represented include China, Japan, and Mexico; 17 in all.

**PROGRAMS OF STUDY. Degrees:** B.A., B.Appl.Sci., B.Bus.Admin., B.Mus., B.S., B.S.Ed.
**Majors:** Accounting, Behavioral Sciences, Biology, Business Information Systems, Chemistry, Christian Ministry, Church Careers, Computer Information Systems, Elementary Education, English, General Business, History, Management, Mathematical Sciences, Medical Technology, Ministry Careers, Music Education, Nursing, Physical Education, Psychology, Religion, Sacred Music, Sociology, Spanish, Speech Communication, Theatre Arts.
**Distribution of degrees:** The majors with the highest enrollment are education, business, and religion; theatre arts, Spanish, and history have the lowest.
**Requirements:** General education requirement.
**Academic regulations:** Freshmen must maintain minimum 1.5 GPA; sophomores, 1.75 GPA; juniors, 2.0 GPA; seniors, 2.0 GPA.
**Special:** Minors offered in most majors and in administrative systems/services, allied health, computer science, economics/finance, legal assistant studies, marketing, music, political science, preprofessional legal studies, reading, and social sciences. Students are encouraged to choose a career cluster when selecting major and minor. Courses in art, Greek, physics. Associate's degrees offered. Double majors. Independent study. Accelerated study. Internships. Graduate school at which undergraduates may take graduate-level courses. Preprofessional programs in law, medicine, veterinary science, pharmacy, dentistry, theology, and optometry. Teacher certification in elementary and secondary education. Certification in specific subject areas. ROTC at Louisiana State U at Shreveport.
**Honors:** Honors program. Honor societies.
**Academic Assistance:** Remedial writing and math. Nonremedial tutoring.

**ADMISSIONS. Academic basis for candidate selection** (in order of priority): Standardized test scores, class rank, secondary school record, school's recommendation.
**Nonacademic basis for candidate selection:** Character and personality are emphasized. Extracurricular participation is important. Particular talent or ability is considered.
**Requirements:** Graduation from secondary school is recommended; GED is accepted. 16 units and the following program of study are required: 4 units of English, 2 units of math, 2 units of lab science, 2 units of social studies, 6 units of academic electives. Minimum composite ACT score of 18 or rank in top half of secondary school class and Texas Academic Skills Program (TASP) test required of all applicants. Conditional admission possible for applicants not meeting standard requirements. ACT is required; SAT may be substituted. Campus visit and interview recommended. Off-campus interviews available with an admissions representative.
**Procedure:** Take SAT or ACT by fall of 12th year. Visit college for interview by spring of 12th year. Notification of admission on rolling basis. $50 room deposit, refundable until August 1. Freshmen accepted for terms other than fall.
**Special programs:** Admission may be deferred one year. Credit and/or placement may be granted through CEEB Advanced Placement exams for scores of 3 or higher. Credit and/or placement may be granted through CLEP subject exams. Credit may be granted through military and life experience. Credit and placement may be granted through challenge exams.
**Transfer students:** Transfer students accepted for terms other than fall. Application deadline is 30 days prior to start of term for fall; 30 days prior to start of term for spring. Minimum 2.0 GPA required. Lowest course grade accepted is "D." Maximum number of transferable credits is 67 semester hours from a two-year school and 72 semester hours from a four-year school. At least 36 semester hours must be completed at the university to receive degree.
**Admissions contact:** Mike Davis, Director of Admissions. 903 935-7963, extension 225.

**FINANCIAL AID. Available aid:** Pell grants, SEOG, state grants, school scholarships, private scholarships and grants, academic merit scholarships, athletic scholarships, and aid for undergraduate foreign students. Perkins Loans (NDSL), PLUS, Stafford Loans (GSL), state loans, school loans, and SLS.
**Financial aid statistics:** 64% of aid is not need-based.
**Supporting data/closing dates:** FAFSA/FAF/FFS: Priority filing date is June 1. School's own aid application: Priority filing date is June 1. State aid form: Priority filing date is June 1. Notification of awards begins in March.
**Financial aid contact:** Betty McCrary, Director of Financial Aid. 903 935-7963, extension 216.

## East Texas State University

**Commerce, TX 75429** **214 886-5081**

**1993-94 Costs.** Tuition: $1,400 (state residents), $4,600 (out-of-state). Room & board: $3,300. Fees, books, misc. academic expenses (school's estimate): $400.
**Enrollment.** Undergraduates: 1,808 men, 2,337 women (full-time). Freshman class: 2,088 applicants, 1,387 accepted, 772 enrolled. Graduate enrollment: 1,130 men, 1,729 women.
**Test score averages/ranges.** Average SAT scores: 873 combined. Average ACT scores: 21 composite.
**Faculty.** 212 full-time; 148 part-time. 76% of faculty holds doctoral degree. Student/faculty ratio: 21 to 1.
**Selectivity rating.** Less competitive.

**PROFILE.** East Texas State, founded in 1889, is a public university. Programs are offered through the Colleges of Arts and Sciences, Business and Technology, and Education; the Graduate School; and the Division of Continuing Education. Its 140-acre main campus is located in Commerce, 60 miles northeast of Dallas.

**Accreditation:** SACS. Professionally accredited by the American Assembly of Collegiate Schools of Business, the Council on Social Work Education, the National Association of Schools of Music, the National Council for Accreditation of Teacher Education.
**Religious orientation:** East Texas State University is nonsectarian; no religious requirements.
**Library:** Collections totaling over 674,918 volumes, 2,131 periodical subscriptions, and 448,188 microform items.
**Special facilities/museums:** Electronic music studio, electronic piano lab.
**Athletic facilities:** Athletic practice fields, field house, gymnasium.

**STUDENT BODY. Undergraduate profile:** 24% are transfers. 1% Asian-American, 12% Black, 3% Hispanic, 1% Native American, 81% White, 2% Other.
**Freshman profile:** 54% of accepted applicants took SAT; 46% took ACT. 81% of freshmen come from public schools.
**Undergraduate achievement:** 60% of fall 1991 freshmen returned for fall 1992 term. 8% of entering class graduated. 28% of students who completed a degree program went on to graduate study within five years.
**Foreign students:** Countries represented include China, India, Nigeria, Pakistan, and Thailand; 38 in all.

**PROGRAMS OF STUDY. Degrees:** B.A., B.A.Crim.Just., B.A.Interdis.Studies, B.Bus.Admin., B.Comp.Info.Sys., B.F.A., B.Mus., B.Mus.Ed., B.S., B.S.Crim.Just., B.S.Interdis.Studies, B.Soc.Work.
**Majors:** Accounting, Agricultural Science, Agricultural Sciences/Technology, Animal Science, Art, Biological Sciences, Broad Field Science, Broad Field Social Studies, Business Administration, Chemistry, Communication Arts, Computer Information Systems, Computer Science, Construction Engineering Technology, Counseling/Guidance, Criminal Justice, Earth Sciences, Economics, English, Finance, French, General Business, Geography, Health, History, Industry/Technology, Interdisciplinary Studies, Journalism, Kinesiology/Sport Studies, Management Information Systems, Manufacturing Engineering Technology, Marketing, Mathematics, Music, Music Performance, Occupational Resources/Applied Technology, Office Management, Personnel/Human Resources Management, Photography, Physics, Political Science, Printing, Production/Operations Management, Professional Accounting, Radio/Television, Social Work, Sociology, Spanish, Speech Communication, Theatre.
**Distribution of degrees:** The majors with the highest enrollment is business.
**Requirements:** General education requirement.
**Academic regulations:** Minimum 2.0 GPA must be maintained.
**Special:** Major and minor, broad-field major, or two majors required of all majors except music and criminal justice. One-year secretarial certificate program. Asian, ethnic, Latin American, and Russian/East European studies programs. Courses offered in Bible, Latin, library and information science, philosophy, and Russian. Self-designed majors. Double majors. Independent study. Accelerated study. Pass/fail grading option. Internships. Graduate school at which undergraduates may take graduate-level courses. Preprofessional programs in law, medicine, veterinary science, pharmacy, dentistry, theology, optometry, engineering, nursing, seminary, medical records, medical technology, osteopathy, and physician's assistant. Member of the North Texas Federation Program. Teacher certification in early childhood, elementary, secondary, and special education. Study abroad in England.
**Honors:** Phi Beta Kappa. Honors program.
**Academic Assistance:** Nonremedial tutoring.

**STUDENT LIFE. Housing:** All freshmen must live on campus. Coed, women's, and men's dorms. Sorority and fraternity housing. School-owned/operated apartments. On-campus married-student housing. 17% of students live in college housing.
**Social atmosphere:** On campus, students congregate at the Memorial Student Center and the Zeppa Center. Favorite off-campus hangouts include R&P Junction and Little Bit O' Country. Among the groups having the most influence on campus social life are Greeks,

the New Birth Gospel Chorale, the student senate, and the Non-traditional Students' Organization. The Feast of Carols and the Five Star Series are big events on campus. Also popular are football games, step shows, and University Playhouse performances. "Social and cultural life is squelched," comments the editor of the student newspaper. "There are clear divisions between social groups drawn across age, ethnic and racial boundaries. There is racial tension. Politics, often dirty, are the key factors in getting results. It's the good ol' boy system here."
**Services and counseling/handicapped student services:** Placement services. Health service. Day care. Communication and mathematics skills centers. Counseling services for minority and veteran students. Birth control, personal, and psychological counseling. Career and academic guidance services. Religious counseling. Physically disabled student services. Learning disabled services.
**Campus organizations:** Undergraduate student government. Student newspaper (East Texan, published once/week). Radio and TV stations. Band, orchestra, brass choir, choir, chorale, opera ensemble, drama group, debating, Young Democrats, Young Republicans, service and special-interest groups, 96 organizations in all. 10 fraternities, four chapter houses; eight sororities, five chapter houses. 7% of men join a fraternity. 15% of women join a sorority.
**Religious organizations:** Several religious groups.
**Minority/foreign student organizations:** Afro-American Student Society.

**ATHLETICS. Physical education requirements:** Four semesters of physical education required.
**Intercollegiate competition:** 2% of students participate. Basketball (M,W), cross-country (M,W), football (M), golf (M), track and field (outdoor) (M,W), volleyball (W). Member of Lone Star Conference, NCAA Division II.
**Intramural and club sports:** 66% of students participate. Intramural archery, badminton, basketball, billiards, bowling, flag football, horseshoes, racquetball, table tennis, tennis, track and field, soccer, softball, swimming, volleyball, water polo.

**ADMISSIONS. Academic basis for candidate selection** (in order of priority): Standardized test scores, secondary school record, class rank, school's recommendation.
**Nonacademic basis for candidate selection:** Character and personality, extracurricular participation, geographical distribution, and alumni/ae relationship are important. Particular talent or ability is considered.
**Requirements:** Graduation from secondary school is required; GED is accepted. No specific distribution of secondary school units required. Open admissions policy for in-state applicants with minimum composite ACT score of 20 (combined SAT score of 800) or secondary school record indicating probability of attaining "C" average in college. Computer science courses required of business administration and education program applicants. Academic remediation program for applicants not normally admissible. SAT or ACT is required. Campus visit and interview recommended. No off-campus interviews.
**Procedure:** Take SAT or ACT by February of 12th year. Application deadline is August 15. Notification of admission on rolling basis. No set date by which applicants must accept offer. $50 room deposit, refundable until August 1. Freshmen accepted for terms other than fall.
**Special programs:** Credit and/or placement may be granted through CEEB Advanced Placement exams for scores of 3 or higher. Credit may be granted through CLEP general and subject exams, DANTES and challenge exams, and military experience. Early decision program. Concurrent enrollment program.
**Transfer students:** Transfer students accepted for terms other than fall. In fall 1992, 24% of all new students were transfers into all classes. 942 transfer applications were received, 798 were accepted. Application deadline is August 15 for fall; January 8 for spring. Minimum 2.0 GPA required. Lowest course grade accepted is "D." At least 30 semester hours must be completed at the university to receive degree.
**Admissions contact:** Suzanne K. Woodley, Assistant Director of Admissions. 214 886-5081.

**FINANCIAL AID. Available aid:** Pell grants, SEOG, state scholarships and grants, school scholarships, private scholarships, academic merit scholarships, and athletic scholarships. Perkins Loans (NDSL), PLUS, Stafford Loans (GSL), school loans, and SLS. Installment plan.
**Supporting data/closing dates:** FAFSA/FAF/FFS: Priority filing date is May 1; accepted on rolling basis. Notification of awards on rolling basis.
**Financial aid contact:** John Patton, M.B.A., Director of Financial Aid. 214 886-5096.

**STUDENT EMPLOYMENT.** College Work/Study Program. Institutional employment. 14% of full-time undergraduates work on campus during school year. Students may expect to earn an average of $1,900 during school year. Off-campus part-time employment opportunities rated "poor."

**COMPUTER FACILITIES.** 100 IBM/IBM-compatible microcomputers. Computer languages and software packages include Ada, Assembly, C, COBOL, dBase, FORTRAN, Microsoft Word, Pascal, PL/1, SAS, SPSS. Computer facilities are available to all students.
**Fees:** None.
**Hours:** 24 hours.

# Hardin-Simmons University

**Abilene, TX 79698** **915 670-1000**

**1994-95 Costs.** Tuition: $6,300. Room & board: $2,980. Fees, books, misc. academic expenses (school's estimate): $1,180.
**Enrollment.** Undergraduates: 649 men, 716 women (full-time). Freshman class: 467 applicants, 424 accepted, 350 enrolled. Graduate enrollment: 93 men, 182 women.
**Test score averages/ranges.** Average SAT scores: 470 verbal, 510 math. Range of SAT scores of middle 50%: 400-499 verbal, 500-599 math. Average ACT scores: 22 English, 20 math, 22 composite. Range of ACT scores of middle 50%: 19-25 composite.
**Faculty.** 101 full-time; 41 part-time. 76% of faculty holds highest degree in specific field. Student/faculty ratio: 18 to 1.
**Selectivity rating.** Less competitive.

**PROFILE.** Hardin-Simmons, founded in 1891, is a church-affiliated, comprehensive university. Programs are offered through the College of Arts and Sciences and the Schools of Business and Finance, Education, Music, Nursing, and Theology. Its 40-acre campus is located in Abilene, 150 miles west of Dallas/Fort Worth.
**Accreditation:** SACS. Professionally accredited by the Council on Social Work Education, the National Association of Schools of Music, the National League for Nursing.
**Religious orientation:** Hardin-Simmons University is affiliated with the Baptist Church; two semesters of theology required.
**Library:** Collections totaling over 411,025 volumes, 986 periodical subscriptions, and 18,061 microform items.
**Special facilities/museums:** Art center, observatory with 14-inch telescope.
**Athletic facilities:** Gymnasium, basketball, racquetball, tennis, and volleyball courts, weight rooms, soccer and softball fields, swimming pools, human performance laboratory, bowling alleys, track, steam rooms.

**STUDENT BODY. Undergraduate profile:** 93% are state residents; 27% are transfers. 1% Asian-American, 5% Black, 9% Hispanic, 83% White, 2% Other. Average age of undergraduates is 26.
**Freshman profile:** 1% of freshmen who took SAT scored 700 or over on verbal, 2% scored 700 or over on math; 9% scored 600 or over on verbal, 21% scored 600 or over on math; 34% scored 500 or over on verbal, 53% scored 500 or over on math; 75% scored 400 or over on verbal, 88% scored 400 or over on math; 98% scored 300 or over on verbal, 99% scored 300 or over on math. 64% of accepted applicants took SAT; 74% took ACT. 97% of freshmen come from public schools.
**Undergraduate achievement:** 60% of fall 1992 freshmen returned for fall 1993 term. 21% of entering class graduated.
**Foreign students:** 10 students are from out of the country. Countries represented include Brazil, Canada, Malaysia, Nigeria, Uzbekistan, and the West Indies; nine in all.

**PROGRAMS OF STUDY. Degrees:** B.A., B.Behav.Sci., B.Bus.Admin., B.Mus., B.S., B.S.Nurs.
**Majors:** Accounting, Agriculture, Applied Music, Applied Theology, Art, Art Education, Bible, Bilingual Education, Biology, Business Administration, Chemistry, Church Ministry, Church Music, Communication, Computer Science, Counseling/Human Development, Earth Science, Education/Business Administration, Education/Computer Information Systems, Education/Physical Science, Education/Social Studies, Elementary Education, English, Exercise Science, Finance, French, Geology, German, History, Journalism, Management, Marketing, Mass Communication, Mathematics, Medical Technology, Music, Music Business, Music Education, Music Theory/Composition, Nursing, Philosophy, Physical Education, Physics, Police Science/Administration, Political Science, Pre-Dentistry, Pre-Medicine, Probation/Parole, Psychology, Public Communication, Reading, Secondary Education, Social Work, Sociology, Spanish, Speech Communication, Speech Pathology/Audiology, Theatre.
**Distribution of degrees:** The majors with the highest enrollment are elementary education, psychology, and nursing; Spanish, music business, and theatre have the lowest.
**Requirements:** General education requirement.
**Academic regulations:** Freshmen must maintain minimum 1.6 GPA; sophomores, 1.8 GPA; juniors, 2.0 GPA; seniors, 2.0 GPA.
**Special:** Associate's degrees offered. Double majors. Independent study. Internships. Graduate school at which undergraduates may take graduate-level courses. Preprofessional programs in law, medicine, pharmacy, dentistry, and theology. 3-1 dentistry, medical technology, and medicine programs. Member of consortium with Abilene Intercollegiate School of Nursing. Teacher certification in early childhood, elementary, secondary, and bilingual/bicultural education. Certification in specific subject areas. Study abroad in Uzbekistan (Tashkent State U), England, Israel, and Mexico. ROTC.
**Honors:** Honor societies.
**Academic Assistance:** Remedial writing and math. Nonremedial tutoring.

**STUDENT LIFE. Housing:** All unmarried undergraduates must live on campus. Women's and men's dorms. Off-campus married-student housing. 41% of students live in college housing.
**Social atmosphere:** Favorite student gathering spots include the Stairs, Moody Center, the Pond, and the Abilene Mall. Greeks (Theta Alpha Zeta, Sigma Delta, and Mu Kappa) and the Fellowship of Christian Athletes have a widespread influence on campus social life. Popular events include Homecoming, May Day, the Christmas party, as well as pep rallies and soccer, football, and basketball games.
**Services and counseling/handicapped student services:** Placement services. Health service. Counseling services for veteran students. Personal and psychological counseling. Career and academic guidance services.
**Campus organizations:** Undergraduate student government. Student newspaper (Brand, published once/week). Yearbook. Concert choir, chorale, cowboy band, stage band, university band, film series, rodeo association, University Players, departmental, social, and special-interest groups, 50 organizations in all. Four fraternities, no chapter houses; four sororities, no chapter houses. 15% of men join a fraternity. 15% of women join a sorority.
**Religious organizations:** Baptist Student Union.
**Minority/foreign student organizations:** Black Student Fellowship, Latin American Club, United Mexican-American Student Collegiates for Racial Harmony. International Club.

**ATHLETICS. Physical education requirements:** Four semesters of physical education required.
**Intercollegiate competition:** 15% of students participate. Baseball (M), basketball (M), cheerleading (M,W), football (M), golf (M), soccer (M,W), tennis (M,W), volleyball (M). Member of NAIA, NCAA Division II, NCAA Division III for football, Texas Intercollegiate Athletic Association.
**Intramural and club sports:** 50% of students participate. Intramural badminton, basketball, bowling, flag football, golf, racquetball, softball, tennis, volleyball, Wiffle ball.

**ADMISSIONS. Academic basis for candidate selection** (in order of priority): Standardized test scores, class rank, secondary school record, school's recommendation.
**Nonacademic basis for candidate selection:** Character and personality, extracurricular participation, and particular talent or ability are considered.
**Requirements:** Graduation from secondary school is required; GED is accepted. 16 units and the following program of study are required: 3 units of English, 2 units of math, 2 units

of science, 2 units of social studies, 7 units of electives including 4 units of academic electives. Minimum composite ACT score of 19 (combined SAT score of 860), or minimum composite ACT score of 18 (combined SAT score of 810) and rank in top half of secondary school class required. Conditional admission possible for applicants not meeting standard requirements. SAT or ACT is required. Campus visit and interview recommended. Off-campus interviews available with an admissions representative.
**Procedure:** Take SAT or ACT by spring of 12th year. Notification of admission on rolling basis. Applicant must accept offer of admission 30 days prior to start of term. $100 room deposit, refundable until one month prior to start of term. Freshmen accepted for terms other than fall.
**Special programs:** Admission may be deferred one year. Credit and/or placement may be granted through CEEB Advanced Placement exams for scores of 3 or higher. Credit and/or placement may be granted through CLEP general and subject exams. Credit may be granted through military experience. Credit and placement may be granted through challenge exams. Early decision program. Early entrance/early admission program. Concurrent enrollment program.
**Transfer students:** Transfer students accepted for terms other than fall. In fall 1993, 27% of all new students were transfers into all classes. 187 transfer applications were received, 163 were accepted. Application deadline is 30 days prior to start of term for fall; 30 days prior to start of term for spring. Minimum 2.0 GPA required. Lowest course grade accepted is "C." Maximum number of transferable credits is 66 semester hours from a two-year school and 94 semester hours from a four-year school. At least 30 semester hours must be completed at the university to receive degree.
**Admissions contact:** Laura Moore, M.Ed., Director of Admissions. 915 670-1206.

**FINANCIAL AID. Available aid:** Pell grants, SEOG, Federal Nursing Student Scholarships, state scholarships and grants, school scholarships and grants, private scholarships and grants, ROTC scholarships, and academic merit scholarships. Perkins Loans (NDSL), PLUS, Stafford Loans (GSL), NSL, state loans, and SLS. E-Z Payment Plan.
**Financial aid statistics:** 45% of aid is not need-based. In 1993-94, 96% of all undergraduate applicants received aid; 92% of freshman applicants. Average amounts of aid awarded freshmen: Scholarships and grants, $2,909; loans, $2,285.
**Supporting data/closing dates:** FAFSA: Priority filing date is March 15. School's own aid application: Priority filing date is March 15; accepted on rolling basis. Notification of awards on rolling basis.
**Financial aid contact:** Fran Strange, M.H.R., M.Ed., Director of Financial Aid. 915 670-1331.

**STUDENT EMPLOYMENT.** College Work/Study Program. Institutional employment. 45% of full-time undergraduates work on campus during school year. Students may expect to earn an average of $1,700 during school year. Off-campus part-time employment opportunities rated "good."

**COMPUTER FACILITIES.** 125 IBM/IBM-compatible and Macintosh/Apple microcomputers. Students may access IBM minicomputer/mainframe systems. Computer languages and software packages include BASIC, COBOL, FORTRAN, Lotus 1-2-3, Pascal, SPSS, WordPerfect. Computer facilities are available to all students.
**Fees:** None.
**Hours:** 8 AM-11 PM (M-F); 9 AM-5 PM (Sa); 1 PM-6 PM (Su).

**PROMINENT ALUMNI/AE.** Charles Tandy, anesthesiologist; Glenn Burroughs, former president, Sun Oil Co.

# Houston Baptist University

**Houston, TX 77074** **713 774-7661**

**1994-95 Costs.** Tuition: $7,200. Room & board: $2,835. Fees, books, misc. academic expenses (school's estimate): $200.
**Enrollment.** Undergraduates: 467 men, 811 women (full-time). Freshman class: 459 applicants, 314 accepted, 199 enrolled. Graduate enrollment: 189 men, 311 women.
**Test score averages/ranges.** Average SAT scores: 460 verbal, 521 math.
**Faculty.** 118 full-time; 21 part-time. 61% of faculty holds doctoral degree. Student/faculty ratio: 17 to 1.
**Selectivity rating.** Less competitive.

**PROFILE.** Houston Baptist, founded in in 1960, is a church-affiliated university. Programs are offered through the Smith College of General Studies and the Colleges of Business and Economics, Education and Behavioral Studies, Fine Arts, Humanities, and Science and Health Professions. Its 100-acre campus is located in southwest Houston.

**Accreditation:** SACS. Professionally accredited by the National League for Nursing.
**Religious orientation:** Houston Baptist University is affiliated with the Southern Baptist Church (Baptist General Convention of Texas); three terms of theology required.
**Library:** Collections totaling over 20,080 volumes, 966 periodical subscriptions, and 134,970 microform items.
**Special facilities/museums:** Museum of architecture/decorative arts, language lab, research center.
**Athletic facilities:** Gymnasium, tennis courts, track, weight room, football, baseball, softball, and soccer fields.

**STUDENT BODY. Undergraduate profile:** 98% are state residents; 41% are transfers. 18% Asian-American, 10% Black, 9% Hispanic, 60% White, 3% Other. Average age of undergraduates is 21.
**Freshman profile:** 6% of freshmen who took SAT scored 700 or over on math; 7% scored 600 or over on verbal, 28% scored 600 or over on math; 31% scored 500 or over on verbal, 54% scored 500 or over on math; 78% scored 400 or over on verbal, 89% scored 400 or over on math; 98% scored 300 or over on verbal, 98% scored 300 or over on math. 87% of accepted applicants took SAT; 13% took ACT.
**Undergraduate achievement:** 59% of fall 1991 freshmen returned for fall 1992 term. 32% of entering class graduated. 15% of students who completed a degree program went on to graduate study within five years.
**Foreign students:** 54 students are from out of the country. 31 countries represented in all.

**PROGRAMS OF STUDY. Degrees:** B.A., B.Bus.Admin., B.Mus., B.S., B.S.Med.Tech., B.S.Nurs.
**Majors:** Accounting, Art, Art Education, Bilingual Education, Biology, Chemistry, Child Development, Christianity, Church Music, Computer Information Systems, Early Childhood Education, Economics, Elementary Education, English, Finance, French, Generic Special Education, History, Management, Marketing, Mass Media, Mathematics, Medical Technology, Music, Music Education, Music Performance, Nuclear Medical Technology, Nursing, Physical Education, Physics, Political Science, Psychology, Recreation, Sacred Music, Social Work, Sociology, Spanish, Speech.
**Distribution of degrees:** The majors with the highest enrollment are biology, accounting, and chemistry.
**Requirements:** General education requirement.
**Special:** Two majors required. Courses offered in German, Greek, philosophy, and secondary education. Double majors. Independent study. Pass/fail grading option. Internships. Preprofessional programs in medicine, dentistry, theology, engineering, health fields, and medical technology. 3-1 nuclear medicine technology program with Baylor Coll of Medicine. 3-1 medical technology program with approved schools of medical technology. Two- and three-year transfer programs in nutrition/dietetics, optometry, pharmacy, physician's assistant, and physical therapy. Teacher certification in early childhood, elementary, secondary, and special education. Exchange program abroad in England (Shakespeare Inst). Study abroad also in Israel, Jordan, and Mexico. ROTC and NROTC at Rice U.

**STUDENT LIFE. Housing:** All student athletes must live on campus. Women's and men's dorms. School-owned/operated apartments. 15% of students live in college housing.
**Services and counseling/handicapped student services:** Placement services. Health service. Personal counseling. Academic guidance services.
**Campus organizations:** Undergraduate student government. Student newspaper (Collegian, published once/month). Yearbook. TV station. Art guild, drama groups, marketing, finance, and accounting groups, Symposium, Young Democrats, Young Republicans, Society of Physics Students, special-interest groups. Three fraternities, no chapter houses; three sororities, no chapter houses. 13% of men join a fraternity. 20% of women join a sorority.
**Religious organizations:** Christian Life on Campus, Fellowship of Christian Athletes.
**Minority/foreign student organizations:** International Friends.

**ATHLETICS. Physical education requirements:** Two terms of physical education required.
**Intercollegiate competition:** 5% of students participate. Baseball (M), basketball (M), softball (W), volleyball (W). Member of NAIA.
**Intramural and club sports:** 20% of students participate. Intramural badminton, flag football, golf, kickball, miniature golf, soccer, softball, table tennis, tennis, track, volleyball.

**ADMISSIONS. Academic basis for candidate selection** (in order of priority): Standardized test scores, secondary school record, class rank, school's recommendation, essay.
**Nonacademic basis for candidate selection:** Character and personality, extracurricular participation, particular talent or ability, and alumni/ae relationship are considered.
**Requirements:** Graduation from secondary school is required; GED is accepted. No specific distribution of secondary school units required. No minimum test scores required of applicants in top quarter of secondary school class; minimum combined SAT score of 900 with minimum 400 verbal (composite ACT score of 20), rank in top half of secondary school class, and minimum 2.0 GPA required of others. Conditional admission possible for applicants not meeting standard requirements. SAT or ACT is required. Campus visit and interview recommended. No off-campus interviews.
**Procedure:** Take SAT or ACT by December of 12th year. Visit college for interview by March 31 of 12th year. Application deadline is August 1. Notification of admission on rolling basis. $100 nonrefundable tuition deposit. $100 nonrefundable room deposit. Freshmen accepted for terms other than fall.
**Special programs:** Credit may be granted through CEEB Advanced Placement for scores of 3 or higher. Credit may be granted through CLEP general and subject exams. Early entrance/early admission program.
**Transfer students:** Transfer students accepted for terms other than fall. In fall 1992, 41% of all new students were transfers into all classes. 924 transfer applications were received, 436 were accepted. Application deadline is August 1 for fall; March 1 for spring. Minimum 2.0 GPA required. Lowest course grade accepted is "C." Maximum number of transferable credits is 64 semester hours. At least 24 semester hours must be completed at the university to receive degree.
**Admissions contact:** R. Philip Kimrey, M.R.E., Director of Admissions. 713 995-3210, 800 969-3210.

**FINANCIAL AID. Available aid:** Pell grants, SEOG, state grants, school scholarships and grants, private scholarships and grants, academic merit scholarships, and athletic scholarships. TEG/SSIG. Aid for ministerial students. Perkins Loans (NDSL), PLUS, Stafford Loans (GSL), and SLS. Tuition Plan Inc.
**Financial aid statistics:** Average amounts of aid awarded freshmen: Scholarships and grants, $1,400; loans, $1,800.
**Supporting data/closing dates:** FAFSA/FAF: Deadline is May 1. School's own aid application: Accepted on rolling basis. Income tax forms: Accepted on rolling basis. Notification of awards on rolling basis.
**Financial aid contact:** Ken Rogers, Director of Financial Aid. 713 995-3204.

**STUDENT EMPLOYMENT.** College Work/Study Program. Institutional employment. 15% of full-time undergraduates work on campus during school year. Students may expect to earn an average of $1,000 during school year. Off-campus part-time employment opportunities rated "excellent."

**COMPUTER FACILITIES.** 22 IBM/IBM-compatible and Macintosh/Apple microcomputers. Students may access Prime minicomputer/mainframe systems. Computer languages and software packages include BASIC, COBOL; word processing, spreadsheet, database programs. Computer facilities are available to all students.
**Fees:** None.
**Hours:** 8 AM-10 PM.

# Howard Payne University

**Brownwood, TX 76801** **915 646-2502**

**1993-94 Costs.** Tuition: $4,830. Room & board: $2,982. Fees, books, misc. academic expenses (school's estimate): $685.
**Enrollment.** Undergraduates: 649 men, 561 women (full-time). Freshman class: 516 applicants, 454 accepted, 322 enrolled.
**Test score averages/ranges.** Average SAT scores: 405 verbal, 458 math. Range of SAT scores of middle 50%: 350-460 verbal, 380-520 math. Average ACT scores: 20 English, 20 math, 20 composite. Range of ACT scores of middle 50%: 17-22 English, 17-21 math.
**Faculty.** 84 full-time; 24 part-time. 59% of faculty holds doctoral degree. Student/faculty ratio: 15 to 1.
**Selectivity rating.** Less competitive.

**PROFILE.** Howard Payne, founded in 1889, is a church-affiliated, liberal arts university. Programs are offered through the College of Arts and Sciences and the Schools of Business Administration, Christianity, Education, Music, and Social Sciences. Its 30-acre campus is located near the business district of Brownwood, in central Texas.

**Accreditation:** SACS. Professionally accredited by the National Association of Schools of Music.
**Religious orientation:** Howard Payne University is affiliated with the Southern Baptist Church; two semesters of religion required.
**Library:** Collections totaling over 120,000 volumes, 862 periodical subscriptions, and 28,600 microform items.
**Special facilities/museums:** Douglas MacArthur museum.
**Athletic facilities:** Gymnasium, weight room, swimming pool, bowling alley, coliseum, football stadium, racquetball and tennis courts, intramural field.

**STUDENT BODY. Undergraduate profile:** 97% are state residents; 7% are transfers. 1% Asian-American, 6% Black, 8% Hispanic, 1% Native American, 83% White, 1% Other. Average age of undergraduates is 19.
**Freshman profile:** 1% of freshmen who took SAT scored 700 or over on verbal, 1% scored 700 or over on math; 3% scored 600 or over on verbal, 13% scored 600 or over on math; 15% scored 500 or over on verbal, 38% scored 500 or over on math; 53% scored 400 or over on verbal, 69% scored 400 or over on math; 90% scored 300 or over on verbal, 96% scored 300 or over on math. 5% of freshmen who took ACT scored 24 or over on English, 5% scored 24 or over on math, 4% scored 24 or over on composite; 65% scored 18 or over on English, 60% scored 18 or over on math, 69% scored 18 or over on composite; 98% scored 12 or over on English, 100% scored 12 or over on math, 100% scored 12 or over on composite; 100% scored 6 or over on English. 50% of accepted applicants took SAT; 50% took ACT. 98% of freshmen come from public schools.
**Undergraduate achievement:** 66% of fall 1992 freshmen returned for fall 1993 term. 10% of students who completed a degree program immediately went on to graduate study.
**Foreign students:** 15 students are from out of the country. Countries represented include Colombia, Mexico, and Taiwan.

**PROGRAMS OF STUDY. Degrees:** B.A., B.Appl.Arts/Sci., B.Bus.Admin., B.Mus., B.Mus.Ed., B.S.
**Majors:** Academy of Freedom, Accounting, Applied Art, Applied Music, Bible, Biblical Languages, Biology, Business Management, Chemistry, Church Music, Communication, Computer Science, Economics/Finance, Education/All Levels, Elementary Education, English, History, Marketing, Mathematics, Medical Technology, Music, Music Education, Philosophy, Physical Education, Political Science, Practical Theology, Psychology, Religious Education, Secondary Education, Social Work, Sociology, Spanish, Theatre Arts.
**Distribution of degrees:** The majors with the highest enrollment are business, education, and Bible; communication and art have the lowest.
**Requirements:** General education requirement.
**Academic regulations:** Minimum 2.00 GPA required for graduation.
**Special:** Minors offered in many majors and in French, international business, journalism, physics, preaching/evangelism, radio/TV, real estate, and secretarial training. Courses offered in geography, geology, and interdisciplinary studies. Double majors. Pass/fail grading option. Internships. Cooperative education programs. Preprofessional programs in law, medicine, veterinary science, dentistry, nursing, and medical technology. Teacher certification in early childhood, elementary, and secondary education. Certification in specific subject areas. ROTC at Abilene Christian U.
**Honors:** Honors program. Honor societies.
**Academic Assistance:** Remedial reading, writing, math, and study skills. Nonremedial tutoring.

**STUDENT LIFE. Housing:** All freshmen and sophomores must live on campus. Women's and men's dorms. Both on-campus and off-campus married-student housing. 47% of students live in college housing.
**Social atmosphere:** The student newspaper reports, "HPU is owned by the Baptist General Convention of Texas, so the Baptist Student Union is a major influence here. All activities are within the Christian guidelines. Intramural teams are more influential than Greeks, and you're known by the team you're on." On campus, students gather at the Student Union Building and the gym, and at Mims Auditorium for movies. Favorite off-campus spots include "Suspension Bridge" and Mr. Gatti's Pizza. Popular campus events include "Fall Fling (no class, outdoor games, barbecue), Spring Fling (same), Homecoming, Fall Revival, the Junior/Senior Prom Banquet, and Stinger Daze for recruiting students."
**Services and counseling/handicapped student services:** Placement services. Health service. Diagnostic testing service. Counseling services for veteran and older students. Personal and psychological counseling. Career and academic guidance services. Religious counseling. Physically disabled student services.
**Campus organizations:** Undergraduate student government. Student newspaper (Yellow Jacket, published once/week). Literary magazine. Yearbook. Radio and TV stations. HBU Players, Jubilation Brass, yell-leaders, Student Senate. Eight fraternities, no chapter houses; four sororities, no chapter houses. 12% of men join a fraternity. 18% of women join a sorority.
**Religious organizations:** Baptist Student Union, Fellowship of Christian Athletes, Ministerial Association, Ministerial Wives Association.
**Minority/foreign student organizations:** Students for Spanish Missions. International Club.

**ATHLETICS. Physical education requirements:** Two semesters of physical education required.
**Intercollegiate competition:** 25% of students participate. Baseball (M), basketball (M,W), cheerleading (M,W), cross-country (M,W), football (M), golf (M), tennis (M,W), track and field (indoor) (M,W), track and field (outdoor) (M,W), volleyball (W). Member of NAIA, Texas Intercollegiate Athletic Association.
**Intramural and club sports:** 85% of students participate. Intramural basketball, flag football, softball, volleyball. Men's club soccer, volleyball.

**ADMISSIONS. Academic basis for candidate selection** (in order of priority): Standardized test scores, secondary school record, class rank, school's recommendation.
**Nonacademic basis for candidate selection:** Character and personality are emphasized. Extracurricular participation is important. Particular talent or ability and geographical distribution are considered.
**Requirements:** Graduation from secondary school is required; GED is accepted. 15 units required and the following program of study is recommended: 3 units of English, 2 units of math, 1 unit of social studies. Remaining credits must be chosen from list approved by Texas Education Agency. Minimum composite ACT score of 19 (combined SAT score of 830), rank in top half of secondary school class, and minimum "B" average required. One semester of Foundations of University Life Program required of applicants not normally admissible. ACT is required; SAT may be substituted. PSAT is recommended. Campus visit recommended. Off-campus interviews available with an admissions representative.
**Procedure:** Take SAT or ACT by June of 12th year. Application deadline is August 1. Notification of admission on rolling basis. $100 refundable room deposit. Freshmen accepted for terms other than fall.
**Special programs:** Admission may be deferred one year. Credit may be granted through CEEB Advanced Placement. Credit may be granted through CLEP subject exams, ACT PEP, DANTES, and challenge exams, and military and life experience. Early entrance/early admission program. Concurrent enrollment program.
**Transfer students:** Transfer students accepted for terms other than fall. In fall 1993, 7% of all new students were transfers into all classes. Application deadline is August 1 for fall; January 1 for spring. Minimum 2.0 GPA required. Lowest course grade accepted is "D." Maximum number of transferable credits is 66 credits from a two-year school and 104 credits from a four-year school. At least 32 credits must be completed at the university to receive degree.
**Admissions contact:** Veta Young, Director of Admissions. 800 950-8468.

**FINANCIAL AID. Available aid:** Pell grants, SEOG, state scholarships and grants, school scholarships, private scholarships, ROTC scholarships, academic merit scholarships, and aid for undergraduate foreign students. Departmental scholarships. Perkins Loans (NDSL), PLUS, Stafford Loans (GSL), state loans, school loans, private loans, and SLS. Deferred payment plan. Installment payment plan.
**Financial aid statistics:** 45% of aid is not need-based. In 1993-94, 85% of all undergraduate applicants received aid. Average amounts of aid awarded freshmen: Scholarships and grants, $5,000.
**Supporting data/closing dates:** FAFSA/FFS: Priority filing date is May 1. School's own aid application: Priority filing date is May 1. Income tax forms: Priority filing date is May 1. Notification of awards on rolling basis.
**Financial aid contact:** Glenda Huff, Director of Financial Aid. 915 643-7806.

**STUDENT EMPLOYMENT.** College Work/Study Program. 20% of full-time undergraduates work on campus during school year. Students may expect to earn an average of $1,700 during school year. Off-campus part-time employment opportunities rated "excellent."

**COMPUTER FACILITIES.** 63 IBM/IBM-compatible microcomputers; all are networked. Client/LAN operating systems include Apple/Macintosh, DOS, Novell. Computer languages and software packages include Assembly, BASIC, C, COBOL, Database Toolbox, DeskMate, Eureka, FORTRAN, LISP, Prolog, The Slover, Turbo Pascal. Computer facilities are available to all students.
**Fees:** $25 computer fee per semester.
**Hours:** 8 AM-10 PM (M-F).

# Huston-Tillotson College

**Austin, TX 78702** **512 505-3000**

**1994-95 Costs.** Tuition: $4,500. Room: $1,560. Board: $1,911. Fees, books, misc. academic expenses (school's estimate): $1,180.
**Enrollment.** Undergraduates: 213 men, 242 women (full-time). Freshman class: 261 applicants, 159 accepted, 114 enrolled.
**Test score averages/ranges.** Average SAT scores: 786 combined. Average ACT scores: 16 composite.
**Faculty.** 40 full-time; 11 part-time. 43% of faculty holds doctoral degree. Student/faculty ratio: 13 to 1.
**Selectivity rating.** Less competitive.

**PROFILE.** Huston-Tillotson is a church-affiliated college. It was formed by the 1952 merger of Tillotson College (founded in 1877) and Samuel Huston College (founded in 1876). Its 23-acre campus is located one mile from downtown Austin.

**Accreditation:** SACS.
**Religious orientation:** Huston-Tillotson College is an interdenominational Christian school; no religious requirements.
**Library:** Collections totaling over 77,575 volumes, 320 periodical subscriptions, and 52,476 microform items.

**Athletic facilities:** Gymnasium, tennis court, athletic field.

**STUDENT BODY. Undergraduate profile:** 88% are state residents; 14% are transfers. 5.7% Asian-American, 78.3% Black, 6.9% Hispanic, 1.3% White, 7.8% Other. Average age of undergraduates is 21.

**Freshman profile:** Majority of accepted applicants took SAT. 85% of freshmen come from public schools.

**Undergraduate achievement:** 55% of fall 1992 freshmen returned for fall 1993 term. 18% of students who completed a degree program immediately went on to graduate study.

**Foreign students:** 73 students are from out of the country. Countries represented include Bahrain, Indonesia, Iran, Morocco, Nigeria, and Saudi Arabia; 15 in all.

**PROGRAMS OF STUDY. Degrees:** B.A., B.S.

**Majors:** Accounting, Biology, Business Administration, Chemistry, Computer Science, English, Government, Marketing, Mass Communication, Mathematics, Music, Physical Education/Recreation, Sociology, Teacher Education.

**Distribution of degrees:** The majors with the highest enrollment are business administration, accounting, and physical education; marketing, chemistry, and English have the lowest.

**Requirements:** General education requirement.

**Academic regulations:** Freshmen must maintain minimum 1.5 GPA; sophomores, 1.65 GPA; juniors, 1.75 GPA; seniors, 1.90 GPA.

**Special:** Minors offered in all majors. Courses offered in African-American studies, economics, finance, hospitality management, history, international studies, philosophy, psychology, and religion. Double majors. Independent study. Internships. Cooperative education programs. Preprofessional programs in law, medicine, dentistry, and nursing. 2-2 allied health program with Texas Tech U. 3-2 engineering program with Prairie View A&M U. Semester-away programs possible. Teacher certification in early childhood, elementary, secondary, and special education. Study abroad possible.

**Honors:** Honors program. Honor societies.

**Academic Assistance:** Remedial reading, writing, math, and study skills. Nonremedial tutoring.

**ADMISSIONS. Academic basis for candidate selection** (in order of priority): Standardized test scores, secondary school record, class rank, school's recommendation, essay.

**Nonacademic basis for candidate selection:** Alumni/ae relationship is important. Character and personality, extracurricular participation, and particular talent or ability are considered.

**Requirements:** Graduation from secondary school is required; GED is accepted. 18 units and the following program of study are required: 4 units of English, 3 units of math, 2 units of lab science, 2 units of social studies, 6 units of electives. Minimum combined SAT score of 700 recommended. Audition required of music scholarship program applicants. SAT or ACT is required. Campus visit and interview recommended.

**Procedure:** Application deadline is March 1. Notification of admission on rolling basis. Reply is required by May 1 or within two weeks of acceptance. $125 room deposit, refundable upon leaving the college. Freshmen accepted for terms other than fall.

**Special programs:** Admission may be deferred two semesters. Credit may be granted through CEEB Advanced Placement and CLEP subject exams. Early entrance/early admission program. Concurrent enrollment program.

**Transfer students:** Transfer students accepted for terms other than fall. In fall 1993, 14% of all new students were transfers into all classes. 70 transfer applications were received, 53 were accepted. Application deadline is March 1 for fall; December 1 for spring. Minimum 2.0 GPA required. Lowest course grade accepted is "D." Maximum number of transferable credits is 66 semester hours from a two-year school and 96 semester hours from a four-year school. At least 30 semester hours must be completed at the college to receive degree.

**Admissions contact:** Donnie J. Scott, Director of Admissions. 512 505-3027, extensions 3028, 3029.

**FINANCIAL AID. Available aid:** Pell grants, SEOG, state grants, school scholarships, academic merit scholarships, aid for undergraduate foreign students, and United Negro College Fund. Perkins Loans (NDSL), PLUS, Stafford Loans (GSL), school loans, and SLS. AMS, Tuition Management Systems, and deferred payment plan.

**Financial aid statistics:** In 1993-94, 85% of all undergraduate applicants received aid; 95% of freshman applicants. Average amounts of aid awarded freshmen: Loans, $2,625.

**Supporting data/closing dates:** FAFSA/FAF/FFS: Priority filing date is May 1. School's own aid application: Priority filing date is May 1. State aid form: Priority filing date is May 1. Income tax forms: Priority filing date is May 1. Notification of awards on rolling basis.

**Financial aid contact:** Jackie Wilson, Director of Financial Aid. 512 505-3030, extensions 3026, 3031.

# Incarnate Word College

## San Antonio, TX 78209-6397 210 828-1261

**1994-95 Costs.** Tuition: $8,840. Room: $2,640. Board: $2,047. Fees, books, misc. academic expenses (school's estimate): $940.

**Enrollment.** Undergraduates: 486 men, 1,199 women (full-time). Freshman class: 1,358 applicants, 1,099 accepted, 506 enrolled. Graduate enrollment: 217 men, 349 women.

**Test score averages/ranges.** Average SAT scores: 441 verbal, 480 math. Average ACT scores: 21 composite.

**Faculty.** 138 full-time; 76 part-time. 49% of faculty holds doctoral degree. Student/faculty ratio: 13 to 1.

**Selectivity rating.** Less competitive.

**PROFILE.** Incarnate Word, founded in 1881, is a church-affiliated, liberal arts college. Its 56-acre campus, including a villa listed with the National Register of Historic Places, is located on a former estate.

**Accreditation:** SACS. Professionally accredited by the American Medical Association (CAHEA), the National Council for Accreditation of Teacher Education, the National League for Nursing.

**Religious orientation:** Incarnate Word College is affiliated with the Roman Catholic Church; one semester of religion required.

**Library:** Collections totaling over 167,500 volumes, 1,145 periodical subscriptions, and 22,155 microform items.

**Special facilities/museums:** Black box theatre, language labs, wellness center, archaeological dig sites, electron microscope.

**Athletic facilities:** Gymnasiums, weight room, swimming pool, jacuzzi, sauna, baseball, soccer, and softball fields, basketball, racquetball, and tennis courts, track, fitness trail.

**STUDENT BODY. Undergraduate profile:** 95% are state residents. 1% Asian-American, 7% Black, 52% Hispanic, 1% Native American, 36% White, 3% Other. Average age of undergraduates is 23.

**Freshman profile:** 1% of freshmen who took SAT scored 700 or over on verbal, 1% scored 700 or over on math; 2% scored 600 or over on verbal, 5% scored 600 or over on math; 11% scored 500 or over on verbal, 27% scored 500 or over on math; 45% scored 400 or over on verbal, 60% scored 400 or over on math; 87% scored 300 or over on verbal, 93% scored 300 or over on math. 1% of freshmen who took ACT scored 30 or over on composite; 10% scored 24 or over on composite; 63% scored 18 or over on composite; 99% scored 12 or over on composite; 100% scored 6 or over on composite. 75% of accepted applicants took SAT; 45% took ACT. 80% of freshmen come from public schools.

**Undergraduate achievement:** 75% of fall 1992 freshmen returned for fall 1993 term. 58% of entering class graduated. 60% of students who completed a degree program went on to graduate study within five years.

**PROGRAMS OF STUDY. Degrees:** B.A., B.Bus.Admin., B.S., B.S.Nurs.

**Majors:** Accounting, Art, Banking/Finance, Biology, Chemistry, Child Psychology, Communication Arts, Early Childhood Education, Elementary Education, English, Fashion Design, Fashion Merchandising, General Business, History, Hotel/Restaurant Management, Interior Design, International Business, Management, Management Information Systems, Marketing, Mathematics, Medical Technology, Music, Music Education, Music Theory, Native America Studies, Nuclear Medicine Science, Nursing, Nutrition, Philosophy, Physical Education, Politics, Psychology, Religious Studies, Sociology, Spanish, Special Education, Speech, Theatre Arts.

**Distribution of degrees:** The majors with the highest enrollment are business, nursing, and education; history/politics, music, and philosophy have the lowest.

**Requirements:** General education requirement.

**Academic regulations:** Minimum 2.0 GPA must be maintained.

**Special:** Minors offered. Courses offered in dance, physical science, and physics. Senior seminar. Double majors. Independent study. Internships. Preprofessional programs in law, medicine, veterinary science, and dentistry. 3-4 dentistry program with U of Texas Health Science Center. Teacher certification in early childhood, elementary, secondary, and special education. Exchange program abroad in Japan (Kumamoto U). Study abroad also in Brazil, England, and Italy. ROTC at Trinity U.

**Honors:** Phi Beta Kappa. Honor societies.

**Academic Assistance:** Remedial reading, writing, and math. Nonremedial tutoring.

**STUDENT LIFE. Housing:** Students may live on or off campus. Coed, women's, and men's dorms. School-owned/operated apartments. 17% of students live in college housing.

**Social atmosphere:** Popular campus events at Incarnate Word include the Goblin Harvest Food Drive, the Christmas Social, theatre productions, and productions of the Nutcracker and Joffrey Ballets. Influential student groups include the student government and athletes, especially soccer players. Students gather at the coffee shop and Marian Hall.

**Services and counseling/handicapped student services:** Placement services. Health service. Counseling services for minority, military, veteran, and older students. Personal and psychological counseling. Career and academic guidance services. Religious counseling.

**Campus organizations:** Undergraduate student government. Student newspaper (Logos, published eight times/year). Alpha Phi Omega, Alpha Kappa Phi, Student Ambassadors Association, Student Nursing Association, art group, Animals Crusade, Spanish Club, Society of Interior Designers, 25 organizations in all. Two sororities, no chapter houses. 5% of women join a sorority.

**Religious organizations:** Campus Ministry.

**Minority/foreign student organizations:** Black Student Organization. International Student Organization.

**ATHLETICS. Physical education requirements:** Two semesters of physical education required.

**Intercollegiate competition:** 10% of students participate. Baseball (M), basketball (M,W), cheerleading (M,W), cross-country (M,W), golf (M,W), soccer (M,W), softball (W), tennis (M,W), volleyball (W). Member of Heart of Texas, NAIA.

**Intramural and club sports:** 15% of students participate. Intramural basketball, billiards, bowling, bungee jumping, flag football, floor hockey, golf, miniature golf, paintball, sand volleyball, softball, ultimate frisbee, volleyball, walleyball, water volleyball.

**ADMISSIONS. Academic basis for candidate selection** (in order of priority): Secondary school record, class rank, standardized test scores, essay.

**Nonacademic basis for candidate selection:** Particular talent or ability is important. Character and personality and extracurricular participation are considered.

**Requirements:** Graduation from secondary school is required; GED is accepted. 16 units and the following program of study are required: 4 units of English, 2 units of math, 2 units of science, 2 units of foreign language, 2 units of social studies, 2 units of history, 2 units of academic electives. Minimum composite ACT score of 20 (combined SAT score of 800), rank in top half of secondary school class, and minimum 2.0 GPA required. Science prerequisites and minimum 2.5 GPA required of nursing program applicants. TASP Test and minimum 2.5 GPA required of education program applicants. Conditional admission possible for applicants not meeting standard requirements. SAT or ACT is required. Campus visit and interview recommended. Off-campus interviews available with an admissions representative.

**Procedure:** Take SAT or ACT by March of 12th year. Take ACH by November of 12th year. Notification of admission on rolling basis. Reply is required by August 31. $100 tuition deposit, refundable until May 1. $100 room deposit, refundable until June 1. Freshmen accepted for terms other than fall.

**Special programs:** Admission may be deferred one year. Placement may be granted through CEEB Advanced Placement exams. Credit may be granted through CLEP subject exams, Regents College, ACT PEP, and DANTES exams, and military experience. Place-

ment may be granted through challenge exams. Early entrance/early admission program. Concurrent enrollment program.
**Transfer students:** Transfer students accepted for terms other than fall. Application deadline is August 15 for fall; January 10 for spring. Minimum 2.5 GPA required. Lowest course grade accepted is "D." Maximum number of transferable credits is 92 semester hours.
**Admissions contact:** Sr. Sally Mitchell, Ed.S., Dean of Enrollment. 210 829-6005, 800 749-9673.

**FINANCIAL AID. Available aid:** Pell grants, SEOG, school scholarships and grants, academic merit scholarships, and athletic scholarships. Stafford Loans (GSL). AMS and deferred payment plan.
**Financial aid statistics:** 40% of aid is not need-based. In 1993-94, 98% of all undergraduate applicants received aid; 99% of freshman applicants. Average amounts of aid awarded freshmen: Scholarships and grants, $2,106; loans, $5,906.
**Supporting data/closing dates:** FAFSA/FAF: Priority filing date is March 1. Income tax forms: Accepted on rolling basis. Notification of awards on rolling basis.
**Financial aid contact:** Diana M. Perez, Director of Financial Aid. 210 829-6008.

**STUDENT EMPLOYMENT.** College Work/Study Program. Institutional employment. 26% of full-time undergraduates work on campus during school year. Students may expect to earn an average of $1,800 during school year. Off-campus part-time employment opportunities rated "good."

**COMPUTER FACILITIES.** 65 IBM/IBM-compatible and Macintosh/Apple microcomputers; 50 are networked. Computer languages and software packages include BASIC, COBOL, dBASE, FISCAL, Harvard Graphics, Lotus 1-2-3, Quattro Pro, Quick C, SPSS, WordPerfect; 10 in all. Computer facilities are available to all students.
**Fees:** $20 computer fee per course; included in tuition/fees.
**Hours:** 7:30 AM-10:30 PM.

**GRADUATE CAREER DATA.** Graduate school percentages: 6% enter law school. 5% enter medical school. 1% enter dental school. 30% enter graduate business programs. 8% enter graduate arts and sciences programs. 7% enter theological school/seminary. Highest graduate school enrollments: Incarnate Word Coll, U of Texas at Austin, U of Texas at San Antonio. 63% of graduates choose careers in business and industry.

**PROMINENT ALUMNI/AE.** Lillian Dunlap and Madeline Parks, first and second women generals in the U.S. Armed Services; Dr. Sunny Stephens, specialist in spina bifida; Jesse Borrego, actor; Lucy Killea, California state senator; Rosemary Deason, St. Louis judge.

# Jarvis Christian College

**Hawkins, TX 75765** — **903 769-2174**

**1994-95 Costs.** Tuition: $3,750. Room & board: $3,060. Fees, books, misc. academic expenses (school's estimate): $860.
**Enrollment.** Undergraduates: 203 men, 278 women (full-time).
**Test score averages/ranges.** Average SAT scores: 294 verbal, 320 math. Average ACT scores: 10 English, 7 math, 11 composite.
**Faculty.** 35 full-time; 7 part-time. 60% of faculty holds doctoral degree. Student/faculty ratio: 14 to 1.
**Selectivity rating.** Noncompetitive.

**PROFILE.** Jarvis Christian, founded in 1912, is a church-affiliated, liberal arts college. Its 250-acre campus is located in Hawkins, 100 miles southeast of Dallas.

**Accreditation:** SACS.
**Religious orientation:** Jarvis Christian College is affiliated with the Disciples of Christ Church; two semesters of religion required.
**Library:** Collections totaling over 80,000 volumes, 472 periodical subscriptions, and 2,598 microform items.
**Special facilities/museums:** Language lab, media center, observatory, electron microscope.
**Athletic facilities:** Gymnasium, fitness lab, swimming pool, baseball and softball fields, weight room, tennis courts.

**STUDENT BODY. Undergraduate profile:** 79% are state residents. 99% Black, 1% White. Average age of undergraduates is 18.
**Freshman profile:** 1% of freshmen who took SAT scored 500 or over on math; 9% scored 400 or over on verbal, 15% scored 400 or over on math; 43% scored 300 or over on verbal, 66% scored 300 or over on math. Majority of accepted applicants took ACT. 100% of freshmen come from public schools.
**Undergraduate achievement:** 79% of fall 1992 freshmen returned for fall 1993 term. 22% of entering class graduated. 10% of students who completed a degree program went on to graduate study within one year.

**PROGRAMS OF STUDY. Degrees:** B.A., B.Bus.Admin., B.S.
**Majors:** Biology, Business Administration, Chemistry, English, History, Human Performance, Mathematics, Music, Reading, Religion, Sociology, Special Education.
**Distribution of degrees:** The majors with the highest enrollment are accounting, management, and history; chemistry, biology, and physical education have the lowest.
**Requirements:** General education requirement.
**Academic regulations:** Minimum 2.0 GPA must be maintained.
**Special:** Minors offered in all majors and in accounting, art, computer science, management, marketing, political science, psychology, reading, special education, and speech. Double majors. Dual degrees. Accelerated study. Cooperative education programs. Preprofessional programs in law and medicine. 3-2 law program with St. John's Sch of Law. 3-2 engineering program with U of Texas at Arlington. Black Executive Exchange Program. UNCF Premedical Summer Program with Fisk U. Biomedical Sciences Program of Meharry Medical Coll. Brookhaven Semester Program in New York. Teacher certification in elementary and secondary education.
**Honors:** Phi Beta Kappa. Honors program. Honor societies.
**Academic Assistance:** Remedial reading, writing, math, and study skills. Nonremedial tutoring.

**ADMISSIONS. Academic basis for candidate selection** (in order of priority): Secondary school record, school's recommendation, class rank, standardized test scores.
**Nonacademic basis for candidate selection:** Character and personality are emphasized. Particular talent or ability and alumni/ae relationship are important. Extracurricular participation is considered.
**Requirements:** Graduation from secondary school is recommended; GED is accepted. 16 units and the following program of study are required: 3 units of English, 2 units of math, 1 unit of science, 3 units of social studies, 7 units of academic electives. Open admissions. Students entering education program must achieve a satisfactory level of performance on TASP Skills Test as established by the State Board of Education. ACT is required; SAT may be substituted. Campus visit and interview recommended. Off-campus interviews available with an admissions representative.
**Procedure:** Take SAT or ACT by May 1 of 12th year. Visit college for interview by August of 12th year. Suggest filing application by April 1. Application deadline is August 1. Notification of admission on rolling basis. Reply is required by August 15. $30 room deposit, refundable until August 15. Freshmen accepted for terms other than fall.
**Special programs:** Credit may be granted through CLEP general and subject exams and military experience. Placement may be granted through challenge exams.
**Transfer students:** Transfer students accepted for terms other than fall. Application deadline is August 1 for fall; December 1 for spring. Minimum 2.0 GPA recommended. Maximum number of transferable credits is 65 semester hours. At least 59 semester hours must be completed at the college to receive degree.
**Admissions contact:** Anetha Francis, Director of Admissions. 903 769-2174, extension 733.

**FINANCIAL AID. Available aid:** Pell grants, SEOG, state scholarships and grants, school scholarships, private scholarships, and United Negro College Fund. Vocational Rehabilitation Grants. Perkins Loans (NDSL), PLUS, and Stafford Loans (GSL). Deferred payment plan.
**Financial aid statistics:** In 1993-94, 98% of all undergraduate applicants received aid; 98% of freshman applicants. Average amounts of aid awarded freshmen: Scholarships and grants, $1,000; loans, $2,250.
**Supporting data/closing dates:** FAFSA: Priority filing date is January 1; deadline is April 15. School's own aid application: Priority filing date is January 1; deadline is July 1. Income tax forms: Priority filing date is April 15; accepted on rolling basis. Notification of awards on rolling basis.
**Financial aid contact:** Harold Abney, Director of Financial Aid. 903 769-2174, extension 741.

# Lamar University

**Beaumont, TX 77710** — **409 880-8345**

**1994-95 Costs.** Tuition: $672 (state residents), $3,888 (out-of-state). Room & board: $1,300. Fees, books, misc. academic expenses (school's estimate): $1,080.
**Enrollment.** Undergraduates: 4,098 men, 4,114 women (full-time). Freshman class: 2,924 applicants, 2,459 accepted, 1,305 enrolled. Graduate enrollment: 6,020.
**Test score averages/ranges.** Average SAT scores: 379 verbal, 415 math.
**Faculty.** 475 full-time; 250 part-time. 61% of faculty holds highest degree in specific field. Student/faculty ratio: 25 to 1.
**Selectivity rating.** Less competitive.

**PROFILE.** Lamar, founded in 1923, is a public, multipurpose university. Programs are offered through the Colleges of Arts and Sciences, Business, Education and Human Development, Engineering, Fine Arts and Communication, Graduate Studies, Health and Behavioral Sciences, and Technical Arts. Its 250-acre campus is located in Beaumont, 90 miles from Houston.

**Accreditation:** SACS. Professionally accredited by the Accreditation Board for Engineering and Technology, the American Assembly of Collegiate Schools of Business, the American Dietetic Association, the American Medical Association (CAHEA), the National League for Nursing.
**Religious orientation:** Lamar University is nonsectarian; no religious requirements.
**Library:** Collections totaling over 900,000 volumes, 2,800 periodical subscriptions, and 222,975 microform items.
**Special facilities/museums:** Museum.
**Athletic facilities:** Gymnasium, racquetball and tennis courts, swimming pools, weight rooms, stadiums, track, softball fields.

**STUDENT BODY. Undergraduate profile:** 96% are state residents. 1% Asian-American, 16% Black, 3% Hispanic, 1% Native American, 78% White, 1% Other. Average age of undergraduates is 25.
**Freshman profile:** Majority of accepted applicants took SAT. 96% of freshmen come from public schools.
**Undergraduate achievement:** 59% of fall 1992 freshmen returned for fall 1993 term. 19% of entering class graduated.

**PROGRAMS OF STUDY. Degrees:** B.A., B.Appl.Arts/Sci., B.Bus.Admin., B.F.A., B.Gen.Studies, B.Mus., B.S., B.Soc.Work.
**Majors:** Accounting, Art, Biology, Chemical Engineering, Chemistry, Civil Engineering, Computer Science, Criminal Justice, Dance, Economics, Electrical Engineering, Elementary Education, Energy Resources Management, Engineering, Engineering Technology, English, Environmental Science, Family/Community Services, Fashion Retailing/Merchandising, Finance, Fine Arts, Food Service/Dietetics, French, General Business, General Home Economics, General Studies, Geology, Government, Graphic Arts, Health Education, History, Home Economics Education, Industrial Engineering, Industrial Technology, Instrumental Music, Interior Design, Management, Marketing, Mass Communications, Mathematical Sciences, Mathematics, Mechanical Engineering, Medical Technology, Music, Music Education, Music Theory/Composition, Nursing, Oceano-

graphic Technology, Office Administration, Physical Education, Physics, Piano/Organ, Psychology, Secondary Education, Social Work, Sociology, Spanish, Special Education, Speech, Strings, Studio Art, Vocal Music.
**Requirements:** General education requirement.
**Academic regulations:** Minimum 2.0 GPA required for graduation.
**Special:** Minors offered. Courses offered in anthropology, Bible/religious education, German, Italian, and philosophy. Associate's degrees offered. Pass/fail grading option. Internships. Cooperative education programs. Preprofessional programs in medicine, veterinary science, pharmacy, and dentistry. 3-1 programs in medicine or dentistry. 3-2 pharmacy programs with Texas Southern U and U of Houston. Teacher certification in early childhood, elementary, secondary, special education, and vo-tech education. Study abroad in England, France, and Italy. ROTC.
**Honors:** Honors program.
**Academic Assistance:** Remedial reading, writing, math, and study skills. Nonremedial tutoring.

**STUDENT LIFE. Housing:** Women's and men's dorms. Sorority and fraternity housing. School-owned/operated apartments. 9% of students live in college housing.
**Services and counseling/handicapped student services:** Placement services. Health service. Day care. Counseling services for veteran and older students. Birth control, personal, and psychological counseling. Career and academic guidance services. Religious counseling. Physically disabled student services. Learning disabled services. Notetaking services. Tape recorders. Tutors. Reader services for the blind.
**Campus organizations:** Undergraduate student government. Student newspaper (University Press, published twice/week). Radio and TV stations. 120 registered organizations. 11 fraternities, three chapter houses; eight sororities, four chapter houses. 5% of men join a fraternity. 5% of women join a sorority.
**Religious organizations:** Baptist, Catholic, Lutheran, and Methodist groups.
**Minority/foreign student organizations:** Black Student Union, Society of Black Engineers.

**ATHLETICS. Physical education requirements:** Two semesters of physical education required.
**Intercollegiate competition:** 2% of students participate. Baseball (M), basketball (M,W), cheerleading (M,W), cross-country (M,W), golf (M,W), tennis (M,W), track and field (indoor) (M,W), track and field (outdoor) (M,W), volleyball (W). Member of NCAA Division I, Sun Belt Conference.
**Intramural and club sports:** 5% of students participate. Intramural badminton, basketball, flag football, golf, racquetball, soccer, softball, swimming, table tennis, tennis, track, volleyball, weight lifting. Men's club soccer, volleyball. Women's club soccer.

**ADMISSIONS. Academic basis for candidate selection** (in order of priority): Secondary school record, class rank, standardized test scores.
**Requirements:** Graduation from secondary school is required; GED is accepted. 16 units and the following program of study are recommended: 4 units of English, 3 units of math, 2 units of science, 2.5 units of social studies. Rank in top two-thirds of secondary school class or minimum combined SAT score of 700 required of graduates of non-accredited secondary schools. 2 units of algebra, 1/2 unit of trigonometry, 1 unit of chemistry, and 1 unit of physics required of engineering program applicants. Special application, health exam, and letters of recommendation required of nursing and allied health program applicants. Conditional admission possible for applicants not meeting standard requirements. SAT is required; ACT may be substituted. No off-campus interviews.
**Procedure:** Take SAT or ACT by May 1 of 12th year. Application deadline is August 1. Notification of admission on rolling basis. Reply is required by May 1. $100 room deposit, refundable until three weeks before registration. Freshmen accepted for terms other than fall.
**Special programs:** Admission may be deferred. Credit and/or placement may be granted through CEEB Advanced Placement exams for scores of 3 or higher. Credit may be granted through CLEP subject exams, ACT PEP, and challenge exams. Early decision program. Early entrance/early admission program. Concurrent enrollment program.
**Transfer students:** Transfer students accepted for terms other than fall. Minimum 2.0 GPA required. Lowest course grade accepted is "D." Maximum number of transferable credits is 66 semester hours. At least 64 semester hours must be completed at the university to receive degree.
**Admissions contact:** Jim Rush, M.A., Director of Admissions. 800 458-7558.

**FINANCIAL AID. Available aid:** Pell grants, SEOG, state grants, school scholarships, private scholarships, ROTC scholarships, academic merit scholarships, and athletic scholarships. Perkins Loans (NDSL), Stafford Loans (GSL), state loans, school loans, and SLS. Tuition Plan Inc. and Education Plan Inc.
**Financial aid statistics:** 14% of aid is not need-based.
**Supporting data/closing dates:** FAFSA/FAF/FFS: Deadline is April 1. School's own aid application: Deadline is April 1. Income tax forms: Deadline is April 1. Notification of awards on rolling basis.
**Financial aid contact:** Ralynn Castete, M.A., Director of Financial Aid. 409 880-8454.

**STUDENT EMPLOYMENT.** College Work/Study Program. Institutional employment. 10% of full-time undergraduates work on campus during school year. Students may expect to earn an average of $4,000 during school year. Off-campus part-time employment opportunities rated "good."

**COMPUTER FACILITIES.** 120 IBM/IBM-compatible and Macintosh/Apple microcomputers. Students may access Bull minicomputer/mainframe systems. Residence halls may be equipped with stand-alone microcomputers. Computer languages and software packages include COBOL, FORTRAN, Pascal, Prolog, SAS, SPSS. Computer facilities are available to all students.
**Fees:** $30 computer fee per semester; included in tuition/fees.
**Hours:** 8 AM-10 PM.

# LeTourneau University

**Longview, TX 75607** **903 753-0231**

**1994-95 Costs.** Tuition: $8,840. Room & board: $4,240. Fees, books, misc. academic expenses (school's estimate): $420.
**Enrollment.** Undergraduates: 1,204 men, 541 women (full-time). Freshman class: 483 applicants, 418 accepted, 204 enrolled. Graduate enrollment: 128.
**Test score averages/ranges.** Average SAT scores: 491 verbal, 552 math. Average ACT scores: 24 composite.
**Faculty.** 49 full-time; 65 part-time. 63% of faculty holds doctoral degree. Student/faculty ratio: 16 to 1.
**Selectivity rating.** Competitive.

**PROFILE.** LeTourneau is a university with religious orientation. It was founded as a technical institute in 1946, became a four-year college in 1961, and gained university status in 1989. Its 162-acre campus is located in the East Texas community of Longview, 120 miles from Dallas.

**Accreditation:** SACS. Professionally accredited by the Accreditation Board for Engineering and Technology.
**Religious orientation:** LeTourneau University is an interdenominational Christian school; four semesters of theology required.
**Library:** Collections totaling over 98,641 volumes, 435 periodical subscriptions, and 38,520 microform items.
**Special facilities/museums:** Longview Citizens Resource Center.
**Athletic facilities:** Gymnasium, athletic fields.

**STUDENT BODY. Undergraduate profile:** 25% are state residents; 21% are transfers. 1% Asian-American, 4% Black, 2% Hispanic, 1% Native American, 87% White, 5% Other. Average age of undergraduates is 24.
**Freshman profile:** 2% of freshmen who took SAT scored 700 or over on verbal, 12% scored 700 or over on math; 17% scored 600 or over on verbal, 42% scored 600 or over on math; 48% scored 500 or over on verbal, 68% scored 500 or over on math; 82% scored 400 or over on verbal, 92% scored 400 or over on math; 100% scored 300 or over on verbal, 99% scored 300 or over on math. 53% of accepted applicants took SAT; 47% took ACT. 56% of freshmen come from public schools.
**Undergraduate achievement:** 64% of fall 1992 freshmen returned for fall 1993 term. 27% of entering class graduated.
**Foreign students:** 51 students are from out of the country. Countries represented include the Bahamas, Brazil, Canada, Guatemala, Kenya, and Tanzania; 24 in all.

**PROGRAMS OF STUDY. Degrees:** B.A., B.S.
**Majors:** Accounting, Aviation Technology, Biblical Studies, Biology, Business Administration, Business Administration/Marketing, Chemistry, Computer Science/Engineering, Computer Science/Engineering Technology, Electrical Engineering, Electrical Engineering Technology, Engineering, English, History/Government, Industrial Management, Mathematics, Mechanical Engineering, Mechanical Engineering Technology, Medical Technology, Physical Education, Psychology, Secondary Education, Welding Engineering, Welding Engineering Technology.
**Distribution of degrees:** The majors with the highest enrollment are business, aviation technology, and electrical engineering; biblical studies and math have the lowest.
**Requirements:** General education requirement.
**Special:** Minors offered in some majors and in several other fields. Certificates offered in automotive technology and technical design (drafting). Courses offered in anthropology, Koine Greek, philosophy, physics, sociology, and Spanish. Seminars in many departments. Flight training possible. Associate's degrees offered. Double majors. Internships. Cooperative education programs. Preprofessional programs in law, medicine, veterinary science, and dentistry. Member of Christian College Coalition. Washington Semester. Teacher certification in secondary education. Certification in specific subject areas. Travel-study programs in various countries.
**Honors:** Honors program.
**Academic Assistance:** Remedial reading, math, and study skills. Nonremedial tutoring.

**ADMISSIONS. Academic basis for candidate selection** (in order of priority): Secondary school record, standardized test scores, class rank, essay, school's recommendation.
**Nonacademic basis for candidate selection:** Character and personality are emphasized. Extracurricular participation and particular talent or ability are important. Alumni/ae relationship is considered.
**Requirements:** Graduation from secondary school is required; GED is accepted. 16 units and the following program of study are required: 4 units of English, 2 units of math, 1 unit of science, 2 units of social studies, 7 units of academic electives. Minimum composite ACT score of 20 (combined SAT score of 800), rank in top half of secondary school class, and minimum 2.0 GPA required. Giant Step summer program for applicants not normally admissible. SAT or ACT is required. Campus visit and interview recommended. Off-campus interviews available with an admissions representative.
**Procedure:** Take SAT or ACT by December of 12th year. Notification of admission on rolling basis. Reply is required by August 1. $100 tuition deposit, refundable until June 1. Freshmen accepted for terms other than fall.
**Special programs:** Admission may be deferred two years. Credit and/or placement may be granted through CEEB Advanced Placement exams for scores of 3 or higher. Credit and/or placement may be granted through CLEP subject exams. Placement may be granted through challenge exams and military experience. Credit and placement may be granted through Regents College exams. Early entrance/early admission program. Concurrent enrollment program.
**Transfer students:** Transfer students accepted for terms other than fall. In fall 1993, 21% of all new students were transfers into all classes. 203 transfer applications were received,

174 were accepted. Minimum 2.0 GPA required. Lowest course grade accepted is "C." At least 30 semester hours must be completed at the university to receive degree.
**Admissions contact:** Howard Wilson, Dean of Enrollment. 903 753-0231, extension 240.

**FINANCIAL AID. Available aid:** Pell grants, SEOG, state grants, school scholarships and grants, private scholarships and grants, academic merit scholarships, athletic scholarships, and aid for undergraduate foreign students. Perkins Loans (NDSL), PLUS, Stafford Loans (GSL), school loans, private loans, and SLS. Deferred payment plan. Interest-free 12-month payment plan.
**Financial aid statistics:** 5% of aid is not need-based. In 1993-94, 81% of all undergraduate applicants received aid; 76% of freshman applicants. Average amounts of aid awarded freshmen: Scholarships and grants, $1,500; loans, $2,800.
**Supporting data/closing dates:** FAFSA: Priority filing date is February 15; deadline is August 1. Notification of awards on rolling basis.
**Financial aid contact:** Bill Rusk, M.Ed., Director of Financial Aid. 903 753-0231, extension 234.

# Lubbock Christian University

**Lubbock, TX 79407 806 796-8800**

**1994-95 Costs.** Tuition: $6,600. Room & board: $2,800. Fees, books, misc. academic expenses (school's estimate): $600.
**Enrollment.** Undergraduates: 386 men, 482 women (full-time). Freshman class: 450 applicants, 430 accepted, 225 enrolled. Graduate enrollment: 2 men, 16 women.
**Test score averages/ranges.** Average ACT scores: 21 composite.
**Faculty.** 50 full-time; 50 part-time. 56% of faculty holds doctoral degree. Student/faculty ratio: 15 to 1.
**Selectivity rating.** Noncompetitive.

**PROFILE.** Lubbock Christian is a church-affiliated, liberal arts college. Founded in 1957 as a junior college, it became a senior college in 1972. Programs are offered through the Colleges of Liberal Arts and Professional Studies. Its 40-acre campus is located in Lubbock.

**Accreditation:** SACS.
**Religious orientation:** Lubbock Christian University is affiliated with the Church of Christ; 14 hours of biblical studies required.
**Library:** Collections totaling over 75,605 volumes.
**Special facilities/museums:** Two farms totaling 450 acres.
**Athletic facilities:** Field house, badminton, basketball/volleyball, and tennis courts, baseball, football, and softball fields, indoor and outdoor tracks.

**STUDENT BODY. Undergraduate profile:** 65% are state residents. 2% Asian-American, 4% Black, 7% Hispanic, 1% Native American, 84% White, 2% Other. Average age of undergraduates is 20.
**Freshman profile:** Majority of accepted applicants took ACT.
**Undergraduate achievement:** 53% of fall 1992 freshmen returned for fall 1993 term. 26% of entering class graduated.

**PROGRAMS OF STUDY. Degrees:** B.A., B.S., B.S.Ed.
**Majors:** Accounting, Agriculture, Art, Bible, Biblical Languages, Biology, Business Administration, Business Communication, Chemistry, Computer Science, Education, English, Finance, General Studies, History, Home Economics, Mathematics, Missions, Music, Physical Education, Reading Education, Religious Counseling, Social Work, Sociology, Spanish, Speech, Youth Ministry.
**Distribution of degrees:** The majors with the highest enrollment are education and business; chemistry and agriculture have the lowest.
**Requirements:** General education requirement.
**Special:** Education minors offered in numerous areas. Guaranteed Education Program allows students who cannot find suitable employment in their major field within two years of graduation to return to university and earn tuition-free second degree. Associate's degrees offered. Pass/fail grading option. Graduate school at which undergraduates may take graduate-level courses. Preprofessional programs in law, medicine, forestry, computer science, and engineering. Combined degree computer science, engineering, medical technology, occupational therapy, and physical therapy programs with Texas Tech U. Cross-registration with South Plains Coll and Texas Tech U. Teacher certification in elementary and secondary education. ROTC and AFROTC at Texas Tech U.
**Academic Assistance:** Remedial reading, writing, and math. Nonremedial tutoring.

**ADMISSIONS. Academic basis for candidate selection** (in order of priority): Standardized test scores, secondary school record, class rank, school's recommendation.
**Nonacademic basis for candidate selection:** Character and personality are emphasized. Extracurricular participation is important. Particular talent or ability is considered.
**Requirements:** Graduation from secondary school is required; GED is accepted. No specific distribution of secondary school units required. ACT is required; SAT may be substituted. Campus visit and interview recommended. Off-campus interviews available with admissions and alumni representatives.
**Procedure:** Take SAT or ACT by June of 12th year. Visit college for interview by June of 12th year. Notification of admission on rolling basis. $75 room deposit, refundable up to 30 days before registration. Freshmen accepted for terms other than fall.
**Special programs:** Admission may be deferred. Credit and/or placement may be granted through CEEB Advanced Placement exams for scores of 3 or higher. Credit and/or placement may be granted through CLEP general and subject exams. Credit and placement may be granted through challenge exams. Early entrance/early admission program. Concurrent enrollment program.
**Transfer students:** Transfer students accepted for terms other than fall. Application deadline is August 15 for fall; January 1 for spring. Lowest course grade accepted is "C." At least 30 semester hours must be completed at the university to receive degree.
**Admissions contact:** Steven German, M.B.A., Dean of Admissions. 806 796-8800, extension 260.

**FINANCIAL AID. Available aid:** Pell grants, SEOG, state grants, school scholarships and grants, private scholarships and grants, academic merit scholarships, and athletic scholarships. Perkins Loans (NDSL), PLUS, Stafford Loans (GSL), state loans, private loans, and SLS. Tuition Plan Inc., deferred payment plan, and family tuition reduction. Monthly payment plan.
**Supporting data/closing dates:** FAFSA/FFS: Priority filing date is July 15. School's own aid application: Priority filing date is July 15. State aid form: Priority filing date is July 15. Income tax forms: Priority filing date is July 15. Notification of awards on rolling basis.
**Financial aid contact:** Marcus Wilson, Director of Financial Aid. 806 796-8800, extension 267.

# McMurry University

**Abilene, TX 79697 915 691-6200**

**1992-93 Costs.** Tuition: $6,150. Room: $1,650. Board: $1,480. Fees, books, misc. academic expenses (school's estimate): $440.
**Enrollment.** Undergraduates: 388 men, 492 women (full-time). Freshman class: 578 applicants, 411 accepted, 187 enrolled.
**Test score averages/ranges.** Average SAT scores: 408 verbal, 500 math. Range of SAT scores of middle 50%: 340-470 verbal, 430-580 math. Average ACT scores: 21 English, 20 math, 21 composite. Range of ACT scores of middle 50%: 17-24 English, 18-23 math.
**Faculty.** 90 full-time; 62 part-time. 61% of faculty holds doctoral degree. Student/faculty ratio: 13 to 1.
**Selectivity rating.** Competitive.

**PROFILE.** McMurry is a church-affiliated, liberal arts university. Founded in 1921, it gained university status in 1990. Programs are offered in the Divisions of Business Administration, Fine and Applied Arts, Education, Science and Mathematics, Social Sciences, and Humanities. Its 50-acre campus is located in Abilene, in north central Texas.

**Accreditation:** SACS. Professionally accredited by the National League for Nursing.
**Religious orientation:** McMurry University is affiliated with the United Methodist Church; two semesters of religion required.
**Library:** Collections totaling over 137,000 volumes, 615 periodical subscriptions and 410 microform items.
**Athletic facilities:** Football stadium, basketball courts, field house, gymnasiums, swimming pool, track, practice fields.

**STUDENT BODY. Undergraduate profile:** 94% are state residents; 36% are transfers. 1% Asian-American, 10% Black, 8% Hispanic, 1% Native American, 79% White, 1% Other. Average age of undergraduates is 24.
**Freshman profile:** 8% of freshmen who took SAT scored 700 or over on math; 2% scored 600 or over on verbal, 23% scored 600 or over on math; 18% scored 500 or over on verbal, 50% scored 500 or over on math; 57% scored 400 or over on verbal, 86% scored 400 or over on math; 91% scored 300 or over on verbal, 100% scored 300 or over on math. 1% of freshmen who took ACT scored 30 or over on English, 2% scored 30 or over on math, 1% scored 30 or over on composite; 31% scored 24 or over on English, 17% scored 24 or over on math, 27% scored 24 or over on composite; 75% scored 18 or over on English, 79% scored 18 or over on math, 82% scored 18 or over on composite; 100% scored 12 or over on English, 100% scored 12 or over on math, 100% scored 12 or over on composite. 41% of accepted applicants took SAT; 59% took ACT. 96% of freshmen come from public schools.
**Undergraduate achievement:** 60% of fall 1992 freshmen returned for fall 1993 term. 24% of entering class graduated. 12% of students who completed a degree program immediately went on to graduate study.
**Foreign students:** Four students are from out of the country.

**PROGRAMS OF STUDY. Degrees:** B.A., B.Bus.Admin., B.F.A., B.Mus., B.Mus.Ed., B.S., B.S.Mult.Studies, B.S.Nurs.
**Majors:** Accounting, Applied Mathematics/Computer Science, Art, Athletic Training, Banking/Finance, Bilingual Education, Biology, Business Administration, Business Education, Chemistry, Church Music, Communication, Computer Information Systems, Computer Science, Criminal Justice/Human Services, Economics, Elementary Education, English, Finance, General Business, History, Instrumental Performance, Management, Marketing, Mathematics, Medical Technology, Music, Music Education, Natural Science, Nursing, Office Administration, Organ, Paralegal Studies, Philosophy, Physical Education, Piano, Political Science, Psychology, Religion, Secondary Education, Sociology, Spanish, Theatre, Voice.
**Distribution of degrees:** The majors with the highest enrollment are education, business, and sociology; philosophy, political science, and music have the lowest.
**Requirements:** General education requirement.
**Academic regulations:** Freshmen must maintain minimum 1.7 GPA; sophomores, 1.8 GPA; juniors, 2.0 GPA; seniors, 2.0 GPA.
**Special:** Minors offered in French, geology, German, media studies, physics, and public relations. Courses offered in geography, Greek, journalism, and Latin. Associate's degrees offered. Double majors. Accelerated study. Internships. Cooperative education programs. Preprofessional programs in law, medicine, veterinary science, pharmacy, dentistry, engineering, licensed athletic training, and physical therapy. 2-2 human services and criminal justice program. 3-1 medical technology program. Member of consortium with Abilene Christian U and Hardin-Simmons U. Teacher certification in elementary, secondary, and bilingual/bicultural education. Certification in specific subject areas. Study abroad in many countries. ROTC at Hardin-Simmons U.
**Honors:** Honors program. Honor societies.
**Academic Assistance:** Remedial reading, writing, math, and study skills. Nonremedial tutoring.

**ADMISSIONS. Academic basis for candidate selection** (in order of priority): Class rank, standardized test scores, secondary school record, school's recommendation, essay.

**Nonacademic basis for candidate selection:** Character and personality, extracurricular participation, particular talent or ability, geographical distribution, and alumni/ae relationship are considered.
**Requirements:** Graduation from secondary school is required; GED is accepted. 16 units and the following program of study are required: 4 units of English, 3 units of math, 2 units of lab science, 2 units of foreign language, 3 units of social studies. Minimum composite ACT score of 19 (combined SAT score of 780), rank in top half of secondary school class, and minimum 2.0 GPA required. Conditional admission possible for applicants not meeting standard requirements. ACT is required; SAT may be substituted. Campus visit and interview recommended. Off-campus interviews available with admissions and alumni representatives.
**Procedure:** Take SAT or ACT by January of 12th year. Visit college for interview by spring of 12th year. Suggest filing application by March 15. Application deadline is August 15. Notification of admission on rolling basis. Reply is required by June 1. $100 tuition deposit, refundable until June 1. $100 room deposit, refundable until June 1. Freshmen accepted for terms other than fall.
**Special programs:** Admission may be deferred one year. Credit and/or placement may be granted through CEEB Advanced Placement exams for scores of 3 or higher. Credit and/or placement may be granted through CLEP subject exams. Credit may be granted through military experience. Credit and placement may be granted through ACT PEP, DANTES, and challenge exams. Early entrance/early admission program. Concurrent enrollment program.
**Transfer students:** Transfer students accepted for terms other than fall. In fall 1993, 36% of all new students were transfers into all classes. 206 transfer applications were received, 124 were accepted. Application deadline is August 15 for fall; December 15 for spring. Minimum 2.0 GPA required. Lowest course grade accepted is "C." Maximum number of transferable credits is 66 semester hours from a two-year school and 96 semester hours from a four-year school. At least 30 semester hours must be completed at the university to receive degree.
**Admissions contact:** Becki Bryant, Director of Admissions. 800 477-0077, 915 691-6402.

**FINANCIAL AID. Available aid:** Pell grants, SEOG, state grants, school scholarships and grants, private scholarships and grants, ROTC scholarships, academic merit scholarships, and aid for undergraduate foreign students. Perkins Loans (NDSL), PLUS, Stafford Loans (GSL), state loans, private loans, and SLS. Tuition Plan Inc. and AMS.
**Financial aid statistics:** 45% of aid is not need-based. In 1993-94, 95% of all undergraduate applicants received aid; 93% of freshman applicants. Average amounts of aid awarded freshmen: Scholarships and grants, $4,673; loans, $2,323.
**Supporting data/closing dates:** FAFSA: Priority filing date is March 15. School's own aid application: Priority filing date is March 15; accepted on rolling basis. Notification of awards on rolling basis.
**Financial aid contact:** Mary Swanson, Director of Financial Aid. 800 477-0077, 915 691-6213.

# Midwestern State University

**Wichita Falls, TX 76308** 817 689-4000

**1994-95 Costs.** Tuition: $1,666 (state residents), $5,746 (out-of-state). Room & board: $3,120. Fees, books, misc. academic expenses (school's estimate): $780.
**Enrollment.** Undergraduates: 1,568 men, 1,836 women (full-time). Freshman class: 1,597 applicants, 1,125 accepted, 751 enrolled. Graduate enrollment: 299 men, 357 women.
**Test score averages/ranges.** Average SAT scores: 390 verbal, 453 math. Average ACT scores: 19 English, 19 math, 20 composite.
**Faculty.** 169 full-time; 126 part-time. 67% of faculty holds doctoral degree. Student/faculty ratio: 20 to 1.
**Selectivity rating.** Competitive.

**PROFILE.** Midwestern State, founded in 1922, is a public, liberal arts university. Its 172-acre campus is located in Wichita Falls.

**Accreditation:** SACS. Professionally accredited by the American Dental Association, the American Medical Association (CAHEA), the National Association of Schools of Music, the National Council for Accreditation of Teacher Education, the National League for Nursing.
**Religious orientation:** Midwestern State University is nonsectarian; no religious requirements.
**Library:** Collections totaling over 340,808 volumes, 900 periodical subscriptions, and 667,648 microform items.
**Special facilities/museums:** Language lab.
**Athletic facilities:** Gymnasiums, basketball, sand volleyball, and tennis courts, weight room, swimming pool, football practice, intramural, soccer, and softball fields, stadium, track, lake.

**STUDENT BODY. Undergraduate profile:** 96% are state residents; 9% are transfers. 2% Asian-American, 6% Black, 6% Hispanic, 1% Native American, 85% White. Average age of undergraduates is 24.
**Freshman profile:** 55% of accepted applicants took SAT; 59% took ACT.
**Undergraduate achievement:** 63% of fall 1992 freshmen returned for fall 1993 term.
**Foreign students:** 75 students are from out of the country. Countries represented include India, Italy, Japan, Mexico, Sudan, and Taiwan; 30 in all.

**PROGRAMS OF STUDY. Degrees:** B.A., B.Appl.Arts/Sci., B.Bus.Admin., B.F.A., B.Mus., B.S., B.S.Crim.Just., B.S.Dent.Hyg., B.S.Interdis.Studies, B.S.Med.Tech., B.S.Nurs., B.S.Radiol.Sci., B.Soc.Work.
**Majors:** Accounting, Applied Arts/Sciences, Art, Art Education, Biology, Biology/Wildlife Ecology, Business Education, Chemical Technology, Chemistry, Computer Science, Criminal Justice, Dental Hygiene, Economics, Education, Electronics Technology, Engineering Technology, English, English Language Arts, Finance, General Business, Geology, Geology/Geophysics, Geology/Petroleum, Health Fitness Management, History, Humanities, Management, Management Science, Marketing, Mass Communications, Mathematics, Medical Technology, Music, Music Education, Nursing, Physical Science, Political Science, Pre-Business, Pre-Dentistry, Pre-Engineering, Pre-Law, Pre-Medicine, Pre-Pharmacy, Pre-Physical Therapy, Pre-Veterinary, Psychology, Radiologic Technology, Social Work, Sociology, Spanish, Sport/Exercise Science, Teacher Certification, Theatre.
**Distribution of degrees:** The majors with the highest enrollment are applied arts/sciences, criminal justice, and management; general business and geology have the lowest.
**Requirements:** General education requirement.
**Academic regulations:** Freshmen must maintain minimum 1.7 GPA; sophomores, juniors, seniors, 2.0 GPA.
**Special:** Major and minor required in most degree programs. Bachelor of Applied Arts and Sciences program for students with occupational or technical skills. Courses offered in engineering drawing, French, geography, and German; courses in biblical history and literature taught off campus in centers provided by churches. Associate's degrees offered. Double majors. Dual degrees. Internships. Graduate school at which undergraduates may take graduate-level courses. Preprofessional programs in law, medicine, veterinary science, pharmacy, dentistry, optometry, engineering, and physical therapy. Member of Texas Consortium for Educational Telecommunications. Teacher certification in early childhood, elementary, secondary, and special education. Certification in specific subject areas. Exchange program abroad in Mexico (Monterrey Inst of Tech and Higher Education). Study abroad also in England.
**Honors:** Honors program. Honor societies.
**Academic Assistance:** Remedial reading, writing, and math. Nonremedial tutoring.

**STUDENT LIFE. Housing:** All unmarried students under age 21 must live on campus unless living near campus with relatives. Women's and men's dorms. Fraternity housing. School-owned/operated apartments. 12% of students live in college housing.
**Social atmosphere:** "This is basically a nontraditional school," reports the editor of the student newspaper. "Most of the student body lives off campus and is over the age of 25." The most popular campus activity is "America's Greatest College Weekend," a Homecoming in April. "Students frequent any number of the clubs and bars in town, including Baba Lu's, Sundance, Stardust, Stetson's, and Bennigan's."
**Services and counseling/handicapped student services:** Placement services. Health service. Counseling services for minority, military, veteran, and older students. Birth control, personal, and psychological counseling. Career and academic guidance services. Physically disabled student services. Learning disabled services. Notetaking services. Tape recorders. Tutors. Reader services for the blind.
**Campus organizations:** Undergraduate student government. Student newspaper (Wichitan, published once/week). Literary magazine. Yearbook. TV station. Choir, chorale, concert and symphonic bands, Writers Circle, artist lecture series, academic, political, and service groups, 77 organizations in all. Six fraternities, four chapter houses; four sororities, no chapter houses. 13% of men join a fraternity. 10% of women join a sorority.
**Religious organizations:** Bahai Club, Baptist Student Union, Catholic Campus Ministries, Church of Christ Student Center, College Life, Latter-Day Saints Association, United Campus Ministries, Wesley Foundation.
**Minority/foreign student organizations:** Black Student Union, NAACP, Organization of Hispanic Students. International Student Association.

**ATHLETICS. Physical education requirements:** Two semesters of physical education required.
**Intercollegiate competition:** 8% of students participate. Basketball (M,W), cheerleading (M,W), football (M), golf (M), soccer (M), tennis (M,W), track and field (outdoor) (M,W), volleyball (W). Member of NAIA, Texas Intercollegiate Athletics Association.
**Intramural and club sports:** 25% of students participate. Intramural archery, badminton, basketball, billiards, bowling, darts, flag football, frisbee golf, miniature golf, soccer, table tennis, tennis. Men's club baseball, cycling.

**ADMISSIONS. Academic basis for candidate selection** (in order of priority): Standardized test scores, class rank, secondary school record.
**Requirements:** Graduation from secondary school is required; GED is accepted. No specific distribution of secondary school units required. Minimum composite ACT score of 20 (combined SAT score of 800) or rank in top two-fifths of secondary school class required. Conditional admission possible for applicants not meeting standard requirements. SAT or ACT is required. Campus visit and interview recommended.
**Procedure:** Application deadline is August 7. Notification of admission on rolling basis. No set date by which applicants must accept offer. $100 refundable room deposit. Freshmen accepted for terms other than fall.
**Special programs:** Credit and/or placement may be granted through CEEB Advanced Placement exams for scores of 3 or higher. Credit and/or placement may be granted through CLEP subject exams. Credit and placement may be granted through DANTES and challenge exams and military and life experience. Early decision program. In fall 1993, applied for early decision. Concurrent enrollment program.
**Transfer students:** Transfer students accepted for terms other than fall. In fall 1993, 9% of all new students were transfers into all classes. 944 transfer applications were received, 929 were accepted. Application deadline is August 7 for fall; December 15 for spring. Lowest course grade accepted is "D." Maximum number of transferable credits is 66 semester hours from two-year schools.
**Admissions contact:** Billye J. Tims, M.Ed., Director of Admissions. 817 689-4321.

**FINANCIAL AID. Available aid:** Pell grants, SEOG, state grants, school grants, and private grants. Perkins Loans (NDSL), PLUS, Stafford Loans (GSL), state loans, school loans, private loans, and SLS. Deferred payment plan.
**Financial aid statistics:** 8% of aid is not need-based.
**Supporting data/closing dates:** FAFSA/FAF/FFS: Priority filing date is April 1. School's own aid application: Priority filing date is April 1; accepted on rolling basis. Income tax forms: Accepted on rolling basis. Notification of awards on rolling basis.
**Financial aid contact:** Judy Simmons, Director of Financial Aid. 817 689-4214.

**STUDENT EMPLOYMENT.** College Work/Study Program. Institutional employment. 5% of full-time undergraduates work on campus during school year. Students may expect to earn an average of $1,800 during school year. Off-campus part-time employment opportunities rated "good."

**COMPUTER FACILITIES.** 220 IBM/IBM-compatible and Macintosh/Apple microcomputers; 157 are networked. Students may access Digital, IBM minicomputer/mainframe systems. Residence halls may be equipped with networked microcomputers. Client/LAN operating systems include Apple/Macintosh, DOS, Novell. Computer languages and software packages include Ada, BASIC, C, COBOL, dBASE, Enable, FORTRAN, Lotus 1-2-3, Pascal, RPG II, Twin, WordPerfect. Computer facilities are available to all students.
**Fees:** $3 computer fee per semester hour; included in tuition/fees.
**Hours:** 9 AM-10 PM.

**PROMINENT ALUMNI/AE.** Marilyn Aboussie, judge, Texas Court of Appeals; William Dean, cardiologist; Jim Bowen, vice-president, M.D. Anderson.

## Northwood University–Texas Campus

**Cedar Hill, TX 75104** **214 291-1541**

**1993-94 Costs.** Tuition: $8,592. Room & board: $4,095. Fees, books, misc. academic expenses (school's estimate): $575.
**Enrollment.** Undergraduates: 160 men, 123 women (full-time). Freshman class: 236 applicants, 236 accepted, 71 enrolled.
**Test score averages/ranges.** Average SAT scores: 880 combined. Average ACT scores: 18 composite.
**Faculty.** 13 full-time; 7 part-time. 16% of faculty holds doctoral degree. Student/faculty ratio: 17 to 1.
**Selectivity rating.** Less competitive.

**PROFILE.** Northwood University, founded as Northwood Institute in 1959, is a private, management-related college. Its 350-acre campus is located in Cedar Hill, 10 miles from Dallas.

**Accreditation:** NCACS.
**Religious orientation:** Northwood University-Texas Campus is nonsectarian; no religious requirements.
**Library:** Collections totaling over 16,000 volumes and 110 periodical subscriptions.
**Athletic facilities:** Outdoor swimming pool, baseball and volleyball facilities, basketball and tennis courts.

**STUDENT BODY. Undergraduate profile:** 75% are state residents; 50% are transfers. 7% Black, 12% Hispanic, 3% Native American, 78% White. Average age of undergraduates is 21.
**Freshman profile:** Majority of accepted applicants took SAT. 93% of freshmen come from public schools.
**Undergraduate achievement:** 81% of fall 1992 freshmen returned for fall 1993 term.
**Foreign students:** 33 students are from out of the country. Countries represented include the Bahamas, Canada, Germany, India, and the Netherlands.

**PROGRAMS OF STUDY. Degrees:** B.Bus.Admin.
**Majors:** Automotive Marketing/Management, Business Management, Management/Marketing.
**Requirements:** General education requirement.
**Special:** Minors offered include advertising, automotive aftermarket management, automotive management, business management, fashion marketing/merchandising, hotel/restaurant management, language arts, and social studies. Double majors. Dual degrees. Independent study. Internships. Cooperative education programs. 2-2 programs with Dallas/Fort Worth Comm Coll. 3-1 programs with Dallas Comm Coll. Study abroad in England, France, Germany, Greece, and Italy. NROTC at Naval Air Station in Grand Prairie.
**Honors:** Honors program.
**Academic Assistance:** Nonremedial tutoring.

**ADMISSIONS. Academic basis for candidate selection** (in order of priority): Secondary school record, standardized test scores, school's recommendation, class rank.
**Nonacademic basis for candidate selection:** Particular talent or ability is emphasized. Character and personality, extracurricular participation, geographical distribution, and alumni/ae relationship are considered.
**Requirements:** Graduation from secondary school is required; GED is accepted. 16 units required and the following program of study is recommended: 4 units of English, 3 units of math, 2 units of science, 1 unit of social studies. "C" average required. Courses in business and involvement in business clubs recommended. Conditional admission possible for applicants not meeting standard requirements. ACT is required; SAT may be substituted. Campus visit and interview recommended. Off-campus interviews available with an admissions representative.
**Procedure:** Take SAT or ACT by May 31 of 12th year. Visit college for interview by August of 12th year. Application deadline is September 1. Notification of admission on rolling basis. $50 nonrefundable tuition deposit. $50 refundable room deposit. Freshmen accepted for terms other than fall.
**Special programs:** Admission may be deferred. Credit may be granted through CLEP subject exams.
**Transfer students:** Transfer students accepted for terms other than fall. In fall 1993, 50% of all new students were transfers into all classes. 110 transfer applications were received, 109 were accepted. Minimum 2.0 GPA recommended. Lowest course grade accepted is "C."
**Admissions contact:** James R. Hickerson, Director of Admissions. 214 291-1541, 800 927-9663.

**FINANCIAL AID. Available aid:** Pell grants, SEOG, school scholarships and grants, private scholarships and grants, academic merit scholarships, and athletic scholarships. Perkins Loans (NDSL), PLUS, Stafford Loans (GSL), and SLS. Tuition Plan Inc. and deferred payment plan.
**Financial aid statistics:** In 1993-94, 82% of all undergraduate applicants received aid.
**Supporting data/closing dates:** FAFSA/FAF/FFS: Priority filing date is February 15; deadline is September 1. Notification of awards on rolling basis.
**Financial aid contact:** Carol Witthoft, Director of Financial Aid. 214 291-1541, extension 427.

## Our Lady of the Lake University

**San Antonio, TX 78207-4689** **210 434-6711**

**1994-95 Costs.** Tuition: $8,530. Room: $2,020. Board: $1,624. Fees, books, misc. academic expenses (school's estimate): $750.
**Enrollment.** Undergraduates: 285 men, 928 women (full-time). Freshman class: 1,975 applicants, 1,290 accepted, 319 enrolled. Graduate enrollment: 240 men, 595 women.
**Test score averages/ranges.** Average SAT scores: 406 verbal, 429 math.
**Faculty.** 95 full-time; 76 part-time. 57% of faculty holds doctoral degree. Student/faculty ratio: 17 to 1.
**Selectivity rating.** Noncompetitive.

**PROFILE.** Our Lady of the Lake is a church-affiliated, liberal arts university. Founded as a women's college in 1911, it adopted coeducation in 1968. Programs are offered through the College of Arts and Sciences and the Schools of Business and Public Administration, Education and Clinical Studies, and Social Service. The primary campus buildings are Victorian Gothic architectural style. Its 75-acre campus is located in northwest San Antonio.

**Accreditation:** SACS. Professionally accredited by the American Speech-Language-Hearing Association, the Council on Social Work Education.
**Religious orientation:** Our Lady of the Lake University is affiliated with the Roman Catholic Church (Sisters of Divine Providence); no religious requirements.
**Library:** Collections totaling over 266,000 volumes.
**Special facilities/museums:** Lab school for children with language and learning disabilities, elementary demonstration school, intercultural institute for training and research, language lab.

**STUDENT BODY. Undergraduate profile:** 99% are state residents. 1% Asian-American, 6% Black, 48% Hispanic, 37% White, 8% Other. Average age of undergraduates is 24.
**Freshman profile:** Majority of accepted applicants took SAT. 83% of freshmen come from public schools.
**Undergraduate achievement:** 33% of entering class graduated.
**Foreign students:** 13 students are from out of the country. Countries represented include Japan, Mexico, and Taiwan; seven in all.

**PROGRAMS OF STUDY. Degrees:** B.A., B.Appl.Sci., B.Bus.Admin., B.S., B.Soc.Work.
**Majors:** Accounting, American Studies, Art, Bilingual Elementary Education, Biology, Chemistry, Communication Arts, Elementary Education, English, Fashion Merchandising, Fine Arts, Human Resources, Human Sciences, Liberal Studies, Management, Marketing Management, Mathematics, Medical Technology, Music, Natural Science, Philosophy, Psychology, Public Administration, Religious Studies, Secondary Education, Social Studies, Social Work, Spanish, Special Education, Speech/Drama, Speech Pathology.
**Distribution of degrees:** The majors with the highest enrollment are business and liberal studies.
**Requirements:** General education requirement.
**Academic regulations:** Minimum 1.75 GPA must be maintained.
**Special:** Minors offered. Certificate programs in criminal justice and office administration. Self-designed practicums. Courses offered in analytical studies, geography, history, intercultural studies, and political science. Double majors. Independent study. Pass/fail grading option. Internships. Graduate school at which undergraduates may take graduate-level courses. Preprofessional programs in law, medicine, medical technology, nursing, and social work. 3-2 program in engineering. Cross-registration with Incarnate Word Coll and St. Mary's U. Teacher certification in elementary, secondary, and bilingual/bicultural education. ROTC at Saint Mary's U.

**STUDENT LIFE. Housing:** Coed, women's, and men's dorms. 14% of students live in college housing.
**Social atmosphere:** According to the editor of the student newspaper, "San Antonio has lots to offer students including sports, symphony, theater, and clubs. On campus, we really don't have that much." Weekly informal dances ("Thursdays") and intramural sports tournaments are among the popular events on campus. Students congregate on campus at the student union building and the cafeteria. Off campus, they meet at Taco Cabana.
**Services and counseling/handicapped student services:** Placement services. Testing service appraises abilities, deficiencies, aptitudes, and personality attributes. Personal counseling. Career and academic guidance services.
**Campus organizations:** Undergraduate student government. Student newspaper (Steeplechase). Music and drama clubs, departmental and professional groups.
**Religious organizations:** CARE Campus Ministry.

**ATHLETICS. Physical education requirements:** None.
**Intercollegiate competition:** 5% of students participate.
**Intramural and club sports:** Intramural basketball, flag football, sailing, soccer, softball, swimming, table tennis, tennis, volleyball, weight lifting.

**ADMISSIONS. Academic basis for candidate selection** (in order of priority): Secondary school record, standardized test scores, class rank.
**Nonacademic basis for candidate selection:** Character and personality and extracurricular participation are important. Geographical distribution and alumni/ae relationship are considered.
**Requirements:** Graduation from secondary school is required; GED is accepted. 16 units and the following program of study are required: 4 units of English, 2 units of math, 2 units

of science, 2 units of foreign language, 2 units of social studies, 4 units of academic electives. Additional units may be required of applicants to some departments and particular majors. Conditional admission possible for applicants not meeting standard requirements. Deficiencies in math may be removed by completing precollege course in math department. Applicants considered for provisional admission must demonstrate compensatory features and undertake developmental work. SAT or ACT is required. Off-campus interviews available with an admissions representative.
**Procedure:** Take SAT or ACT by December of 12th year. Application deadline is August 15. Notification of admission as soon as all credentials have been evaluated. Reply is required by May 1. $100 room deposit, refundable upon moving off campus. Freshmen accepted for terms other than fall.
**Special programs:** Credit and/or placement may be granted through CEEB Advanced Placement exams for scores of 3 or higher. Credit may be granted through CLEP general and subject exams and life experience. Placement may be granted through challenge exams. Early decision program. Concurrent enrollment program.
**Transfer students:** Transfer students accepted for terms other than fall. Lowest course grade accepted is "D."
**Admissions contact:** Loretta Schlegel, Director of Admissions. 210 434-6711, extension 314.
**FINANCIAL AID. Available aid:** Pell grants, SEOG, state scholarships and grants, school scholarships and grants, private scholarships and grants, and aid for undergraduate foreign students. Perkins Loans (NDSL) and Stafford Loans (GSL).
**Supporting data/closing dates:** FAFSA/FAF: Deadline is April 15. Notification of awards on rolling basis.
**Financial aid contact:** Juan Gacia, Director of Financial Aid. 210 434-6711, extensión 319.
**STUDENT EMPLOYMENT.** College Work/Study Program. 30% of full-time undergraduates work on campus during school year. Students may expect to earn an average of $1,050 during school year. Off-campus part-time employment opportunities rated "excellent."
**COMPUTER FACILITIES.** 125 IBM/IBM-compatible microcomputers. Students may access Digital minicomputer/mainframe systems. Computer languages and software packages include Assembler, BASIC, C, COBOL, Datashare, FORTRAN, LISP, Pascal, PL/1, RPG II. Computer facilities are available to all students.
**Fees:** None.

## Prairie View A&M University

**Prairie View, TX 77446** 409 857-3311

**1993-94 Costs.** Tuition: $1,537 (state residents), $5,616 (out-of-state). Room & board: $2,521-$4,561. Fees, books, misc. academic expenses (school's estimate): $900.
**Enrollment.** Undergraduates: 2,243 men, 2,157 women (full-time). Freshman class: 3,107 applicants, 2,634 accepted, 1,097 enrolled. Graduate enrollment: 231 men, 455 women.
**Test score averages/ranges.** Average SAT scores: 367 verbal, 393 math. Average ACT scores: 15 composite.
**Faculty.** 267 full-time; 36 part-time. 38% of faculty holds doctoral degree. Student/faculty ratio: 25 to 1.
**Selectivity rating.** Less competitive.

**PROFILE.** Prairie View A&M, founded in 1876, is a public university. Programs are offered through the Colleges of Applied Sciences and Engineering Technology, Arts and Sciences, Business, Education, Engineering, and Nursing. Its 1,440-acre campus is located in Prairie View, 45 miles from Houston.
**Accreditation:** SACS. Professionally accredited by the Accreditation Board for Engineering and Technology, the American Home Economics Association, the National League for Nursing.
**Religious orientation:** Prairie View A&M University is nonsectarian; no religious requirements.
**Library:** Collections totaling over 240,117 volumes, 1,557 periodical subscriptions, and 261,318 microform items.
**Athletic facilities:** Health, physical education, and recreation building, baseball, football, and softball fields, golf course, tennis courts, track/field, jogging trail.
**STUDENT BODY. Undergraduate profile:** 87% are state residents; 24% are transfers. 1% Asian-American, 85% Black, 2% Hispanic, 8% White, 4% Other. Average age of undergraduates is 23.
**Freshman profile:** 1% of freshmen who took SAT scored 700 or over on verbal, 1% scored 700 or over on math; 3% scored 600 or over on verbal, 5% scored 600 or over on math; 13% scored 500 or over on verbal, 25% scored 500 or over on math; 46% scored 400 or over on verbal, 54% scored 400 or over on math; 84% scored 300 or over on verbal, 85% scored 300 or over on math. Majority of accepted applicants took SAT.
**Undergraduate achievement:** 60% of fall 1991 freshmen returned for fall 1992 term. 20% of students who completed a degree program immediately went on to graduate study.
**Foreign students:** 330 students are from out of the country. Countries represented include the Bahamas, Ghana, Iran, Jamaica, Liberia, and Nigeria; 46 in all.
**PROGRAMS OF STUDY. Degrees:** B.A., B.A.Soc.Work, B.Bus.Admin., B.F.A., B.S., B.S.Elec.Eng., B.S.Mech.Eng., B.S.Nurs.
**Majors:** Accounting, Administrative Information Systems, Advertising Art, Agri-Agronomy, Agricultural Economics, Agricultural Engineering, Agriculture, Agriculture/Human Resources, Animal Science, Applied Music, Applied Music-Percussion, Applied Music-Piano, Applied Music-Saxophone, Applied Music-Trombone, Applied Music-Trumpet, Applied Music-Voice, Architecture, Biology, Business, Chemical Engineering, Chemistry, Civil Engineering, Communication/Journalism, Communication-Radio/TV, Communications, Computer-Aided Drafting/Design, Computer Engineering Technology, Computer Science, Drama, Economics, Electrical Engineering, Electrical Engineering Technology, English, Family/Community Service, Finance, General Business Administration, Geography, History, Human Development/the Family, Human Nutrition/Food, Human Performance, Industrial Technology, Interdisciplinary, Law Enforcement, Management, Marketing, Mathematics, Mechanical Engineering, Mechanical Engineering Technology, Medical Technology, Merchandising/Design, Music, Nursing/Clinical, Nursing/Preclinical, Physics, Political Science, Psychology, Social Work, Sociology, Spanish, Speech.
**Distribution of degrees:** The majors with the highest enrollment are engineering, business, and nursing.
**Requirements:** General education requirement.
**Academic regulations:** Minimum 2.0 GPA must be maintained.
**Special:** Minors offered in most majors. Benjamin Banneker Honors College, a residential college, prepares selected students in the applied and natural sciences for future graduate and professional studies. Independent study. Internships. Cooperative education programs. Graduate school at which undergraduates may take graduate-level courses. Teacher certification in early childhood, secondary, and special education. ROTC and NROTC.
**Honors:** Honors program.
**Academic Assistance:** Remedial reading, writing, math, and study skills. Nonremedial tutoring.
**STUDENT LIFE. Housing:** All students must live on campus unless living with family within a 60-mile radius of campus. Women's and men's dorms. 75% of students live in college housing.
**Social atmosphere:** According to the editor of the student newspaper, "The most popular on-campus spot is Alumni Hall. If there is someone you're looking for or just finding out where the party will be that night, Alumni Hall is the place to go. Omega Psi Phi fraternity influences student social life. When they party, the entire campus parties. Many students look forward to Homecoming Week."
**Services and counseling/handicapped student services:** Placement services. Health service. Counseling services for minority, military, and veteran students. Birth control and personal counseling. Career and academic guidance services. Religious counseling.
**Campus organizations:** Undergraduate student government. Student newspaper (Panther). Yearbook. Radio station. Symphonic, jazz, and marching bands, choirs, drama group, forensic club, rodeo club, professional groups, 22 organizations in all. Four fraternities, no chapter houses; four sororities, no chapter houses. 8% of men join a fraternity. 8% of women join a sorority.
**Religious organizations:** Baptist Student Movement, Catholic and Moslem groups.
**Minority/foreign student organizations:** CHISPAS. Bahamian, Jamaican, and Nigerian student groups.
**ATHLETICS. Physical education requirements:** Four semesters of physical education required.
**Intercollegiate competition:** 4% of students participate. Baseball (M), basketball (M,W), cross-country (M,W), football (M), golf (M), tennis (M), track (indoor) (M,W), track (outdoor) (M,W), track and field (indoor) (M,W), track and field (outdoor) (M,W), volleyball (W). Member of NAIA, NCAA Division I-AA, Southwestern Athletic Conference.
**Intramural and club sports:** 30% of students participate. Intramural basketball, football, softball, tennis, volleyball.
**ADMISSIONS. Academic basis for candidate selection** (in order of priority): Secondary school record, standardized test scores, class rank, school's recommendation, essay.
**Nonacademic basis for candidate selection:** Character and personality are important. Extracurricular participation, particular talent or ability, and alumni/ae relationship are considered.
**Requirements:** Graduation from secondary school is required; GED is accepted. 16 units and the following program of study are required: 4 units of English, 3 units of math, 3 units of science, 2 units of social studies, 4 units of academic electives. Minimum combined SAT score of 700 (composite ACT score of 18), rank in top half of secondary school class, and minimum 2.0 GPA required. Conditional admission possible for applicants not meeting standard requirements. SAT or ACT is required. Campus visit recommended. Off-campus interviews available with admissions and alumni representatives.
**Procedure:** Notification of admission on rolling basis. $200 refundable room deposit. Freshmen accepted for terms other than fall.
**Special programs:** Admission may be deferred one year. Credit and/or placement may be granted through CEEB Advanced Placement exams for scores of 3 or higher. Credit and/or placement may be granted through CLEP general exams. Placement may be granted through challenge exams. Early decision program. Early entrance/early admission program. Concurrent enrollment program.
**Transfer students:** Transfer students accepted for terms other than fall. In fall 1992, 24% of all new students were transfers into all classes. 542 transfer applications were received, 336 were accepted. Application deadline is rolling for fall; rolling for spring. Minimum 2.0 GPA required. Lowest course grade accepted is "C." Maximum number of transferable credits is 90 semester hours.
**Admissions contact:** Robert Ford, M.S., Director of Admissions & Records. 409 857-2618, 409 857-2626.
**FINANCIAL AID. Available aid:** Pell grants, SEOG, state scholarships and grants, school scholarships and grants, private scholarships, and academic merit scholarships. Perkins Loans (NDSL), PLUS, Stafford Loans (GSL), state loans, and SLS.
**Financial aid statistics:** 25% of aid is not need-based. In 1992-93, 80% of all undergraduate applicants received aid; 80% of freshman applicants. Average amounts of aid awarded freshmen: Scholarships and grants, $4,000; loans, $2,625.
**Supporting data/closing dates:** School's own aid application: Accepted on rolling basis. Income tax forms: Priority filing date is May 1. Notification of awards on rolling basis.
**Financial aid contact:** A.D. James, Jr., M.S., Director of Financial Aid. 409 857-2424.
**STUDENT EMPLOYMENT.** College Work/Study Program. Institutional employment. 30% of full-time undergraduates work on campus during school year. Students may expect to earn an average of $3,000 during school year. Off-campus part-time employment opportunities rated "poor."
**COMPUTER FACILITIES.** IBM/IBM-compatible microcomputers. Computer languages and software packages include COBOL, dBASE, FORTRAN, FreeStyle, Lotus 1-2-3. Computer facilities are available to all students.
**Hours:** 9 AM-10 PM (M-F).

**GRADUATE CAREER DATA.** Graduate school percentages: 2% enter law school. 3% enter medical school. 1% enter dental school. 15% enter graduate business programs. 7% enter graduate arts and sciences programs. Highest graduate school enrollments: Prairie View A&M U, Texas A&M U, U of Houston. 32% of graduates choose careers in business and industry.

**PROMINENT ALUMNI/AE.** Craig Washington, state senator; Gen. Julius W. Becton, Jr. U.S. Army (retired).

## Rice University

**Houston, TX 77251** 713 527-8101

**1994-95 Costs.** Tuition: $10,400. Room & board: $5,725. Fees, books, misc. academic expenses (school's estimate): $900.

**Enrollment.** Undergraduates: 1,661 men, 1,036 women (full-time). Freshman class: 6,033 applicants, 1,262 accepted, 639 enrolled. Graduate enrollment: 909 men, 473 women.

**Test score averages/ranges.** Range of SAT scores of middle 50%: 580-702 verbal, 657-757 math.

**Faculty.** 421 full-time; 123 part-time. 95% of faculty holds doctoral degree. Student/faculty ratio: 9 to 1.

**Selectivity rating.** Most competitive.

**PROFILE.** Rice, founded in 1912, is a private, comprehensive university. Programs are offered through the Schools of Architecture, Humanities, and Social Services; the George R. Brown School of Engineering; the Jesse H. Jones School of Administration; the Shepherd School of Music; and the Wiess School of Natural Sciences. Its 300-acre campus is located three miles from Houston.

**Accreditation:** SACS. Professionally accredited by the Accreditation Board for Engineering and Technology, the National Architecture Accrediting Board.

**Religious orientation:** Rice University is nonsectarian; no religious requirements.

**Library:** Collections totaling over 1,500,000 volumes, 13,100 periodical subscriptions, and 1,800,000 microform items.

**Special facilities/museums:** Art gallery, museum, media center, language labs, NASA equipment for students enrolled in space physics courses.

**Athletic facilities:** Football stadium, swimming pool, basketball, handball, racquetball, squash, tennis, and volleyball courts, baseball, football, soccer, and softball fields, track, weight room.

**STUDENT BODY. Undergraduate profile:** 47% are state residents; 5% are transfers. 9% Asian-American, 6% Black, 6% Hispanic, 1% Native American, 78% White. Average age of undergraduates is 20.

**Freshman profile:** 100% of accepted applicants took SAT. 90% of freshmen come from public schools.

**Foreign students:** 11 students are from out of the country. Countries represented include China, Cyprus, Mexico, Singapore, and Sweden; nine in all.

**PROGRAMS OF STUDY. Degrees:** B.A., B.Arch., B.F.A., B.Mus., B.S.

**Majors:** Ancient Mediterranean Cultures, Anthropology, Architecture, Art/Art History, Behavioral Science, Biochemistry, Biology, Chemical Engineering, Chemical Physics, Chemistry, Civil Engineering, Classics, Cognitive Sciences, Computer Science, Ecology/Evolutionary Biology, Economics, Electrical/Computer Engineering, Engineering, English, Environmental Science Engineering, French, Geology/Geophysics, German, Health/Physical Education, History, Linguistics, Managerial Studies, Materials Science, Mathematical Sciences, Mathematics, Mechanical/Materials Science Engineering, Music, Philosophy, Physics, Policy Studies, Political Science, Psychology, Religious Studies, Russian, Sociology, Spanish, Statistics, Studio Art.

**Distribution of degrees:** The majors with the highest enrollment are political science, English, and engineering; geophysics, statistics, and cognitive science have the lowest.

**Academic regulations:** Minimum 1.67 GPA must be maintained.

**Special:** University has eight residential colleges, each with its own cultural, social, and athletic programs. Self-designed majors. Double majors. Dual degrees. Independent study. Pass/fail grading option. Internships. Graduate school at which undergraduates may take graduate-level courses. Preprofessional programs in dentistry, health-related sciences, and business. Eight-year medical program with Baylor Coll of Medicine. Five-year bachelor's/M.B.A program with the Rice-Jones Sch of Business. 3-3 law program with Columbia U. Member of Southern Consortium and COFHE. Washington Semester. Exchange program with Swarthmore Coll. Teacher certification in secondary education. Certification in specific subject areas. Exchange programs abroad in England (Cambridge U, U of Lancaster). Study abroad also in Africa, Austria, France, the former Soviet Republics, and other countries. NROTC. ROTC at U of Houston.

**Honors:** Phi Beta Kappa. Honors program.

**Academic Assistance:** Nonremedial tutoring.

**STUDENT LIFE. Housing:** Students may live on or off campus. Coed dorms. 70% of students live in college housing.

**Social atmosphere:** Hot spots on and off campus include the Pub, Valhalla, Taco Cabana, House of Pies, Red Square, and Emo's. Student Government, student media, and religious groups influence campus life. Popular social events include formal dances, theme parties, and dorm parties. Eighty percent of the students live on campus.

**Services and counseling/handicapped student services:** Placement services. Health service. Counseling services for minority students. Personal and psychological counseling. Career and academic guidance services. Religious counseling.

**Campus organizations:** Undergraduate student government. Student newspaper (Rice Thresher, published once/week). Literary magazine. Yearbook. Radio station. Band, orchestral and choral groups, drama club, debating, special-interest groups, 90 organizations in all.

**Religious organizations:** Baptist Student Union, Campus Crusade, Hillel, Intervarsity Christian Fellowship.

**Minority/foreign student organizations:** Black Student Union, Chinese Student Union, Mexican-American Organization. International Student Association.

**ATHLETICS. Physical education requirements:** Two semesters of physical education required.

**Intercollegiate competition:** 15% of students participate. Baseball (M), basketball (M,W), cheerleading (M,W), cross-country (M,W), football (M), golf (M), swimming (M,W), tennis (M,W), track (indoor) (M,W), track (outdoor) (M,W), track and field (indoor) (M,W), track and field (outdoor) (M,W), volleyball (W). Member of NCAA Division I, Southwest Athletic Conference.

**Intramural and club sports:** 90% of students participate. Intramural basketball, flag football, racquetball, rowing, soccer, softball, squash swimming, tennis, track, volleyball. Men's club bowling, crew, cycling, fencing, lacrosse, rugby, sailing, soccer. Women's club bowling, cycling, fencing, soccer.

**ADMISSIONS. Academic basis for candidate selection** (in order of priority): Secondary school record, standardized test scores, school's recommendation, essay, class rank.

**Nonacademic basis for candidate selection:** Character and personality and extracurricular participation are emphasized. Particular talent or ability is important. Geographical distribution and alumni/ae relationship are considered.

**Requirements:** Graduation from secondary school is required; GED is accepted. 16 units and the following program of study are required: 4 units of English, 3 units of math, 2 units of lab science, 2 units of foreign language, 2 units of social studies, 3 units of academic electives. Chemistry, physics, trigonometry, and further advanced mathematics required of science and engineering program applicants. Audition and theory test required of music program applicants. Portfolio strongly recommended of architecture program applicants. Conditional admission possible for applicants not meeting standard requirements. SAT is required. ACH required. Campus visit and interview recommended. Off-campus interviews available with an alumni representative.

**Procedure:** Take SAT by January 23 of 12th year. Take ACH by January 23 of 12th year. Visit college for interview by January 15 of 12th year. Application deadline is January 2. Notification of admission by April 1. Reply is required by May 1. $100 refundable tuition deposit. $50 refundable room deposit. Freshmen accepted for fall term only.

**Special programs:** Admission may be deferred one year. Credit may be granted through CEEB Advanced Placement for scores of 3 or higher. Credit and/or placement may be granted through CLEP subject exams. Credit and placement may be granted through challenge exams and military experience. Early decision program. In fall 1991, 196 applied for early decision and 82 were accepted. Deadline for applying for early decision is November 1. Early entrance/early admission program. Concurrent enrollment program.

**Transfer students:** Transfer students accepted for terms other than fall. In fall 1991, 5% of all new students were transfers into all classes. 587 transfer applications were received, 51 were accepted. Application deadline is April 1 for fall; November 1 for spring. Minimum 3.2 GPA required. Lowest course grade accepted is "C." At least 60 semester hours must be completed at the university to receive degree.

**Admissions contact:** Julie M. Browning, Director of Admissions. 713 527-4036.

**FINANCIAL AID. Available aid:** Pell grants, SEOG, state scholarships and grants, school scholarships and grants, private scholarships and grants, ROTC scholarships, academic merit scholarships, and athletic scholarships. Perkins Loans (NDSL), PLUS, Stafford Loans (GSL), state loans, school loans, private loans, and SLS. Knight Tuition Plans and deferred payment plan.

**Financial aid statistics:** 60% of aid is not need-based.

**Supporting data/closing dates:** FAFSA/FAF: Accepted on rolling basis. School's own aid application: Accepted on rolling basis. Income tax forms: Accepted on rolling basis.

**Financial aid contact:** David Hunt, M.S., Director of Financial Aid. 713 527-4958.

**STUDENT EMPLOYMENT.** College Work/Study Program. Institutional employment. 60% of full-time undergraduates work on campus during school year. Students may expect to earn an average of $1,250 during school year. Off-campus part-time employment opportunities rated "excellent."

**COMPUTER FACILITIES.** 60 IBM/IBM-compatible and Macintosh/Apple microcomputers. Residence halls may be equipped with networked terminals. Computer languages and software packages include APL, COBOL, FORTRAN, Pascal; numerous accounting, graphics, word processing programs. Some terminals are limited to specific majors.

**Hours:** 24 hours.

**GRADUATE CAREER DATA.** Graduate school percentages: 10% enter law school. 8% enter medical school. 3% enter graduate business programs. 26% enter graduate arts and sciences programs. Highest graduate school enrollments: Baylor Coll of Medicine, Carnegie Mellon U, Cornell U, Harvard U, Johns Hopkins U, MIT, Rice U, Stanford U, UC Berkeley, U of Texas. 40% of graduates choose careers in business and industry. Companies and businesses that hire graduates: Arthur Andersen, Dow Chemical, Ernst and Young, Exxon, IBM, McKenzie & Co., Texas Instruments.

**PROMINENT ALUMNI/AE.** E. Fay Jones, architect; Larry McMurtry, author; Robert Woodrow Wilson, physicist and Nobel Prize laureate.

## St. Edward's University

**Austin, TX 78704** 512 448-8400

**1994-95 Costs.** Tuition: $9,428. Room & board: $3,750-$4,150. Fees, books, misc. academic expenses (school's estimate): $600.

**Enrollment.** Undergraduates: 730 men, 1,002 women (full-time). Freshman class: 1,272 applicants, 1,012 accepted, 375 enrolled. Graduate enrollment: 237 men, 202 women.

**Test score averages/ranges.** Average SAT scores: 438 verbal, 483 math. Range of SAT scores of middle 50%: 380-500 verbal, 430-540 math. Average ACT scores: 22 English, 21 math, 22 composite. Range of ACT scores of middle 50%: 19-23 English, 17-22 math.

**Faculty.** 83 full-time; 134 part-time. 47% of faculty holds doctoral degree. Student/faculty ratio: 16 to 1.

**Selectivity rating.** Less competitive.

**PROFILE.** St. Edward's, founded in 1885, is a church-affiliated, liberal arts university. Its 180-acre campus is located in Austin, 80 miles northeast of San Antonio.

**Accreditation:** SACS. Professionally accredited by the American Assembly of Collegiate Schools of Business, the Council on Social Work Education.
**Religious orientation:** St. Edward's University is affiliated with the Roman Catholic Church; no religious requirements.
**Library:** Collections totaling over 150,000 volumes, 1,135 periodical subscriptions, and 6,000 microform items.
**Special facilities/museums:** Fine arts building, photography labs.
**Athletic facilities:** Swimming pool, track, basketball and racquetball courts, football, soccer, and, softball fields, weight room.

**STUDENT BODY. Undergraduate profile:** 96% are state residents; 35% are transfers. 1.9% Asian-American, 4.4% Black, 25.4% Hispanic, .4% Native American, 62.2% White, 5.7% Other. Average age of undergraduates is 23.
**Freshman profile:** 86% of accepted applicants took SAT; 57% took ACT. 76% of freshmen come from public schools.
**Undergraduate achievement:** 70% of fall 1992 freshmen returned for fall 1993 term. 20% of entering class graduated.
**Foreign students:** 112 students are from out of the country. Countries represented include Bahrain, Germany, Mexico, Peru, Taiwan, and Thailand; 45 in all.

**PROGRAMS OF STUDY. Degrees:** B.A., B.Bus.Admin., B.Lib.Studies, B.S.
**Majors:** Accounting, Art, Biology, Chemistry, Communications, Computer Information Science, Computer Science, Criminal Justice, Economics, English Literature, English Writing, Finance, Health/Recreation/Sports Management, History, International Studies, Language Arts, Liberal Studies, Management, Marketing, Mathematics, Philosophy, Photocommunications, Political Science, Psychology, Religious Studies, Social Studies, Social Work, Sociology, Spanish/International Business, Spanish/Liberal Arts, Theatre Arts.
**Distribution of degrees:** The majors with the highest enrollment are management, finance, and criminal justice; social studies, philosophy, and computer information science have the lowest.
**Requirements:** General education requirement.
**Academic regulations:** Minimum 2.0 GPA must be maintained.
**Special:** Minors offered in most majors and in gerontology, Hispanic relations, music, and Spanish. Courses offered in dance, French, geology, linguistics, and philosophy. Certification in gerontology. Global studies program. Research and Critical Missions course explores critical societal problems; required of juniors and seniors. Double majors. Independent study. Pass/fail grading option. Internships. Cooperative education programs. Preprofessional programs in law, medicine, veterinary science, pharmacy, dentistry, theology, and optometry. Teacher certification in elementary, secondary, and bilingual/bicultural education. Certification in specific subject areas. Member of International Student Exchange Program (ISEP). ROTC, NROTC, and AFROTC at U of Texas at Austin.
**Honors:** Honors program. Honor societies.
**Academic Assistance:** Remedial reading, writing, math, and study skills. Nonremedial tutoring.

**STUDENT LIFE. Housing:** All unmarried freshmen out of secondary school less than one year must live on campus unless living with family. Coed, women's, and men's dorms. 17% of students live in college housing.
**Social atmosphere:** The student newspaper reports, "St. Edward's is a very small commuter college that has very little on-campus activity. We try, but the participation is not good. Off-campus social life usually takes place at parties or downtown nightclubs." Favorite hang outs include the Courtyard and the Student Center. Campus Ministry, Student Government, Young Republicans, and the Student Activities Council are prominent organizations on campus. Popular campus events are basketball games, the Formal, semi formal balls, and Killer Bees concerts.
**Services and counseling/handicapped student services:** Placement services. Health service. Counseling services for veteran and older students. Personal and psychological counseling. Career and academic guidance services. Religious counseling. Physically disabled student services. Learning disabled services. Notetaking services. Tape recorders. Tutors. Reader services for the blind.
**Campus organizations:** Undergraduate student government. Student newspaper (Hilltop Views, published once/two weeks). Literary magazine. Choral groups, speaker series, volunteer program, student activities council, academic and special-interest groups, 38 organizations in all.
**Religious organizations:** Campus Ministry, Pax Christi.
**Minority/foreign student organizations:** Hispanic Student Association. International Club.

**ATHLETICS. Physical education requirements:** None.
**Intercollegiate competition:** 10% of students participate. Baseball (M), basketball (M,W), golf (M), soccer (M,W), softball (W), tennis (M,W), volleyball (W). Member of Heart of Texas Conference, NAIA.
**Intramural and club sports:** 20% of students participate. Intramural basketball, flag football, golf, racquetball, softball, tennis, ultimate frisbee, volleyball, walleyball.

**ADMISSIONS. Academic basis for candidate selection** (in order of priority): Class rank, standardized test scores, secondary school record, school's recommendation.
**Nonacademic basis for candidate selection:** Character and personality, extracurricular participation, particular talent or ability, and alumni/ae relationship are considered.
**Requirements:** Graduation from secondary school is required; GED is accepted. 11 units and the following program of study are required: 4 units of English, 3 units of math, 2 units of science, 2 units of social studies. Minimum combined SAT score of 800 (composite ACT score of 17) and rank in top half of secondary school class recommended. SAT or ACT is required. Campus visit and interview recommended. Off-campus interviews available with an admissions representative.
**Procedure:** Take SAT or ACT by fall of 12th year. Notification of admission on rolling basis. No set date by which applicants must accept offer. $100 refundable room deposit. Freshmen accepted for terms other than fall.
**Special programs:** Admission may be deferred one year. Credit and/or placement may be granted through CEEB Advanced Placement exams for scores of 3 or higher. Credit and/or placement may be granted through CLEP general and subject exams. Credit and placement may be granted through challenge exams and military and life experience. Early entrance/early admission program.
**Transfer students:** Transfer students accepted for terms other than fall. In fall 1993, 35% of all new students were transfers into all classes. 544 transfer applications were received, 446 were accepted. Application deadline is August 1 for fall; December 1 for spring. Minimum 2.0 GPA required. Lowest course grade accepted is "C." Maximum number of transferable credits is 60 semester hours from a two-year school and 90 semester hours from a four-year school. At least 30 semester hours must be completed at the university to receive degree.
**Admissions contact:** Megan Murphy, Director of Admissions. 512 448-8500.

**FINANCIAL AID. Available aid:** Pell grants, SEOG, state scholarships and grants, school scholarships and grants, private scholarships and grants, academic merit scholarships, and athletic scholarships. Perkins Loans (NDSL), PLUS, Stafford Loans (GSL), state loans, private loans, and SLS. Tuition Plan Inc., AMS, and deferred payment plan.
**Financial aid statistics:** 10% of aid is not need-based. In 1992-93, 99% of all undergraduate applicants received aid; 97% of freshman applicants. Average amounts of aid awarded freshmen: Loans, $2,600.
**Supporting data/closing dates:** FAFSA/FAF/FFS: Priority filing date is March 1; deadline is August 15. School's own aid application: Priority filing date is March 1; deadline is August 15. Notification of awards on rolling basis.
**Financial aid contact:** Doris Constantine, Director of Financial Aid. 512 448-8520.

**STUDENT EMPLOYMENT.** College Work/Study Program. Institutional employment. 27% of full-time undergraduates work on campus during school year. Students may expect to earn an average of $2,000 during school year. Off-campus part-time employment opportunities rated "excellent."

**COMPUTER FACILITIES.** 116 IBM/IBM-compatible and Macintosh/Apple microcomputers; 100 are networked. Students may access Hewlett-Packard minicomputer/mainframe systems, Internet. Residence halls may be equipped with stand-alone microcomputers. Client/LAN operating systems include Apple/Macintosh, DOS, OS/2, UNIX/XENIX/AIX, Windows NT, X-windows. Computer languages and software packages include Assembler, C, COBOL, FORTRAN, Hyper Card, Lotus 1-2-3, Microsoft Works, Pascal, Tool Book. Computer facilities are available to all students.
**Fees:** $40 computer science course fee.
**Hours:** 8 AM-11 PM (M-Th); 8 AM-6 PM (F); 2 PM-9 PM (Sa-Su).

# St. Mary's University

**San Antonio, TX 78228-8503 210 436-3011**

**1994-95 Costs.** Tuition: $8,678. Room: $1,950. Board: $1,350. Fees, books, misc. academic expenses (school's estimate): $1,030.
**Enrollment.** Undergraduates: 917 men, 1,232 women (full-time). Freshman class: 1,243 applicants, 1,020 accepted, 412 enrolled. Graduate enrollment: 809 men, 753 women.
**Test score averages/ranges.** Average SAT scores: 454 verbal, 516 math. Range of SAT scores of middle 50%: 400-510 verbal, 460-560 math. Average ACT scores: 21 English, 21 math, 22 composite. Range of ACT scores of middle 50%: 19-23 English, 20-23 math.
**Faculty.** 115 full-time; 79 part-time. 93% of faculty holds doctoral degree. Student/faculty ratio: 15 to 1.
**Selectivity rating.** Less competitive.

**PROFILE.** St. Mary's, founded in 1852, is a private, church-affiliated university. Programs are offered through the Schools of Business and Administration; Humanities and Social Sciences; Science, Engineering, and Technology; Law; the Department of Engineering; and the Graduate School. Its 135-acre campus is located in San Antonio.

**Accreditation:** SACS. Professionally accredited by the Accreditation Board for Engineering and Technology, the National Association of Schools of Music.
**Religious orientation:** St. Mary's University is affiliated with the Roman Catholic Church (Marianist Order); two semesters of theology required.
**Library:** Collections totaling over 335,000 volumes, 1,160 periodical subscriptions, and 76,000 microform items.
**Special facilities/museums:** Language lab.
**Athletic facilities:** Gymnasium, weight room, baseball, soccer, and softball fields, track, swimming pool, tennis courts.

**STUDENT BODY. Undergraduate profile:** 91% are state residents; 33% are transfers. 3% Asian/Pacific Island, 3.3% Black, 64% Hispanic, .2% Native American, 27.9% White, 1.6% Other. Average age of undergraduates is 20.
**Freshman profile:** 1% of freshmen who took SAT scored 700 or over on verbal, 3% scored 700 or over on math; 6% scored 600 or over on verbal, 17% scored 600 or over on math; 30% scored 500 or over on verbal, 60% scored 500 or over on math; 73% scored 400 or over on verbal, 95% scored 400 or over on math; 99% scored 300 or over on verbal, 100% scored 300 or over on math. 77% of accepted applicants took SAT; 58% took ACT. 86% of freshmen come from public schools.
**Undergraduate achievement:** 92% of fall 1992 freshmen returned for fall 1993 term. 50% of entering class graduated.
**Foreign students:** 109 students are from out of the country. Countries represented include India, Italy, Japan, Mexico, Peru, and Thailand; 34 in all.

**PROGRAMS OF STUDY. Degrees:** B.A., B.Appl.Sci., B.Bus.Admin., B.S.
**Majors:** Accounting, Applied Physics, Biochemistry, Biology, Chemistry, Computer/Information Sciences, Computer Science, Computer Science/Applied Statistics, Computer Science/Engineering, Corporate Financial Management, Economics, Electrical Engineering, Engineering Science, English, English/Communication Arts, Entrepreneurial Studies, Exercise/Sports Science, Financial Services/Risk Management, French, Geology, History, Human Resources Management, Industrial Engineering, Information Services Management, International Business Management, International Relations, Latin

American Studies, Marketing Management, Mathematics, Multinational Organization Studies, Music, Philosophy, Physics, Political Science, Pre-Veterinary Medicine Studies, Psychology, Public Justice, Sociology, Spanish, Speech, Theology.
**Distribution of degrees:** The majors with the highest enrollment are biological sciences, accounting, and political science; speech, earth science, and theology have the lowest.
**Requirements:** General education requirement.
**Academic regulations:** Freshmen must maintain minimum 1.7 GPA; sophomores, juniors, seniors, 2.0 GPA.
**Special:** Minors offered in most majors and in art, business administration, engineering, German, international public careers, military science, peace/justice studies, pre-law, public careers, and substance abuse. Concentration offered in biotechnology. Nondepartmental courses offered to enrich academic skills. Servicepersons' Opportunity College. Evening Studies Division. Health career opportunity program (minority summer enrichment). Minority access to research careers. Double majors. Independent study. Accelerated study. Pass/fail grading option. Internships. Graduate school at which undergraduates may take graduate-level courses. Preprofessional programs in law, medicine, veterinary science, pharmacy, dentistry, and medical technology. Five-year B.A./M.A. program. Seven-year B.A./D.D.S. program. Washington Semester. Exchange programs in Hawaii (Chaminade U) and Ohio. Teacher certification in elementary and secondary education. Certification in specific subject areas. Study abroad in Austria, England, Mexico, and Spain. ROTC.
**Honors:** Honors program. Honor societies.
**Academic Assistance:** Nonremedial tutoring.

**STUDENT LIFE. Housing:** All freshmen must live on campus unless living with family. Coed, women's, and men's dorms. 43% of students live in college housing.
**Social atmosphere:** St. Mary's has a good community spirit, reports the student newspaper. Greeks are the most socially influential group on campus, and the university has an outstanding basketball program. The biggest event of the year is the Fiesta Oyster Bake, a citywide celebration held on campus. On campus, students meet at the Student Sub and the Quad. Off campus, they frequent Boko Maru and Fatso's.
**Services and counseling/handicapped student services:** Placement services. Health service. Counseling services for minority, military, veteran, and older students. Birth control, personal, and psychological counseling. Career and academic guidance services. Learning disabled services.
**Campus organizations:** Undergraduate student government. Student newspaper (Rattler, published twice/month). English Guild, concert choir, jazz band, vocal jazz ensemble, spirit band, activities and entertainment organizations, academic, political, and professional groups, 57 organizations in all. Five fraternities, no chapter houses; four sororities, no chapter houses. 16% of men join a fraternity. 16% of women join a sorority.
**Religious organizations:** Campus Ministry, Christian Life Community, Fellowship of Christian Athletes.
**Minority/foreign student organizations:** Black Student Union, Mexican-American Students Association. International Student Association.

**ATHLETICS. Physical education requirements:** None.
**Intercollegiate competition:** 7% of students participate. Baseball (M), basketball (M,W), golf (M), soccer (M,W), softball (W), tennis (M,W), volleyball (W). Member of Heart of Texas Conference, NAIA.
**Intramural and club sports:** 40% of students participate. Intramural basketball, flag football, indoor soccer, sand volleyball, softball, table tennis, tennis, volleyball, water basketball.

**ADMISSIONS. Academic basis for candidate selection** (in order of priority): Secondary school record, standardized test scores, class rank, school's recommendation, essay.
**Nonacademic basis for candidate selection:** Character and personality are emphasized. Extracurricular participation is important. Particular talent or ability is considered.
**Requirements:** Graduation from secondary school is required; GED is accepted. 16 units and the following program of study are required: 4 units of English, 3 units of math, 2 units of lab science, 2 units of foreign language, 2 units of social studies, 3 units of academic electives. Rank in top 50th percentile nationally on SAT or ACT and rank in top half of secondary school class required. 4 units of mathematics (including trigonometry and analysis) recommended of biology, chemistry, engineering, geology, and physics program applicants. Academic preparation program for applicants not normally admissible. SAT or ACT is required. Campus visit and interview recommended. Off-campus interviews available with an admissions representative.
**Procedure:** Take SAT or ACT by February of 12th year. Visit college for interview by March 1 of 12th year. Suggest filing application by March 1. Application deadline is August 15. Notification of admission on rolling basis. Reply is required by May 1. $100 nonrefundable tuition deposit. $100 room deposit, refundable until June 1. Freshmen accepted for terms other than fall.
**Special programs:** Admission may be deferred two years. Credit and/or placement may be granted through CEEB Advanced Placement exams for scores of 3 or higher. Credit and/or placement may be granted through CLEP general and subject exams. Credit may be granted through military experience. Credit and placement may be granted through ACT PEP, DANTES, and challenge exams. Early entrance/early admission program. Concurrent enrollment program.
**Transfer students:** Transfer students accepted for terms other than fall. In fall 1993, 33% of all new students were transfers into all classes. 452 transfer applications were received, 325 were accepted. Application deadline is August 15 for fall; December 15 for spring. Minimum 2.5 GPA required. Lowest course grade accepted is "C." Maximum number of transferable credits is 66 semester hours from a two-year school and 90 semester hours from a four-year school. At least 30 semester hours must be completed at the university to receive degree.
**Admissions contact:** Richard Castillo, M.A., Director of Admissions. 210 436-3126.

**FINANCIAL AID. Available aid:** Pell grants, SEOG, state scholarships and grants, school scholarships and grants, private scholarships and grants, ROTC scholarships, academic merit scholarships, and athletic scholarships. Perkins Loans (NDSL), PLUS, Stafford Loans (GSL), state loans, and SLS. ACCESS loans. Tuition Plan Inc., AMS, deferred payment plan, and guaranteed tuition.
**Financial aid statistics:** 10% of aid is not need-based. In 1993-94, 79% of all undergraduate applicants received aid; 83% of freshman applicants. Average amounts of aid awarded freshmen: Scholarships and grants, $2,786; loans, $3,000.
**Supporting data/closing dates:** FAFSA/FAF: Priority filing date is March 1. School's own aid application: Priority filing date is March 1. Notification of awards begins February 1.
**Financial aid contact:** David R. Krause, M.S., Director of Financial Aid. 210 436-3141.

**STUDENT EMPLOYMENT.** College Work/Study Program. Institutional employment. 32% of full-time undergraduates work on campus during school year. Students may expect to earn an average of $1,425 during school year. Off-campus part-time employment opportunities rated "excellent."

**COMPUTER FACILITIES.** 75 IBM/IBM-compatible and Macintosh/Apple microcomputers; all are networked. Students may access Digital minicomputer/mainframe systems, BITNET, Internet. Residence halls may be equipped with stand-alone microcomputers. Client/LAN operating systems include Apple/Macintosh, DOS, UNIX/XENIX/AIX, Windows NT, Novell. Computer languages and software packages include Ada, APL, BASIC, C, COBOL, COGNOS, GURU, LISP, PL1, Pascal, Power House, SAS, SPS; 20 in all. Computer facilities are available to all students.
**Fees:** $30 computer fee per semester.
**Hours:** 24 hours.

**PROMINENT ALUMNI/AE.** Henry B. Gonzalez and Eligio de la Garza, U.S. congressmen; Martin L. Duggan, editor, St. Louis Globe-Democrat; Dr. Giovanni Fazio, director, Smithsonian Observatory, Harvard U; Lt. General William H. Schneider, commander, Fifth Army (retired); B.F. Biaggini, CEO (retired), Southern Pacific Railroad.

# Sam Houston State University

**Huntsville, TX 77341** **409 294-1111**

**1994-95 Costs.** Tuition: $780 (state residents), $4,860 (out-of-state). Room & board: $2,970. Fees, books, misc. academic expenses (school's estimate): $756.
**Enrollment.** Undergraduates: 4,216 men, 4,682 women (full-time). Freshman class: 4,839 applicants, 3,549 accepted, 1,677 enrolled. Graduate enrollment: 591 men, 1,069 women.
**Test score averages/ranges.** Average ACT scores: 20 composite. Range of ACT scores of middle 50%: 17-23 composite.
**Faculty.** 435 full-time; 21 part-time. 64% of faculty holds highest degree in specific field. Student/faculty ratio: 24 to 1.
**Selectivity rating.** Less competitive.

**PROFILE.** Sam Houston State, founded in 1879, is a public, comprehensive university. Programs are offered through the Colleges of Applied Arts and Sciences, Business Administration, Education, Fine Arts, Humanities, and Science and the Institute of Corrections and Behavioral Sciences. The campus, marked by the classic antebellum architecture of Austin Hall, is located in Huntsville, 70 miles from Houston.

**Accreditation:** SACS. Professionally accredited by the National Association of Schools of Music, the National Council for Accreditation of Teacher Education.
**Religious orientation:** Sam Houston State University is nonsectarian; no religious requirements.
**Library:** Collections totaling over 766,350 volumes, 3,111 periodical subscriptions, and 864,379 microform items.
**Special facilities/museums:** Sam Houston Memorial Museum, on-campus elementary school, communications center for photography, radio, TV, and film, agricultural complex and university farm.
**Athletic facilities:** Gymnasium, weight room, track, basketball and tennis courts, swimming pool, football stadium, baseball and softball fields.

**STUDENT BODY. Undergraduate profile:** 97% are state residents; 46% are transfers. 2% Asian-American, 11% Black, 7% Hispanic, 80% White. Average age of undergraduates is 24.
**Freshman profile:** 57% of accepted applicants took SAT; 43% took ACT.
**Undergraduate achievement:** 68% of fall 1992 freshmen returned for fall 1993 term.
**Foreign students:** 147 students are from out of the country. Countries represented include China, India, Japan, Pakistan, and Thailand; 41 in all.

**PROGRAMS OF STUDY. Degrees:** B.A., B.A.Teach., B.Appl.Arts/Sci., B.Bus.Admin., B.F.A., B.Mus., B.Mus.Ed., B.S.
**Majors:** Accounting, Advertising/Graphic Design, Agricultural Business, Agricultural Education, Agricultural Mechanization, Agriculture, American History, Animal Science, Applied Instrumental, Applied Vocal, Art, Art Education, Bible, Biology, Business Education, Chemistry, Clinical Education, Commercial Plant Management, Computing Science, Crafts, Criminal Justice, Criminology/Corrections, Dance, Drama, Economics, Education, Electricity/Electronics, Elementary Education, English, Environmental Science, European History, Fashion Merchandising, Finance, Food Science/Nutrition, Food Service Management, Foreign Languages, French, General Business Administration, Geography, Geoscience, German, Government, Health Education, History, Home Economics, Horticultural/Crop Science, Humanities, Industrial Design/Development, Industrial Education, Industrial Technology, Interior Design, Journalism, Latin American History, Law Enforcement/Police Science, Library Science, Management, Marketing, Mathematics, Medical Technology, Military Science, Music, Music Literature, Music Theory/Composition, Newspaper Production, Office Administration, Painting, Photography, Photoplate Making, Physical Education, Physics, Printing, Printmaking, Production/Manufacturing, Psychology, Radio/Television/Film, Sales/Distribution, Sales/Estimating, Sculpture, Secondary Education, Social Rehabilitation/Social Services, Sociology, Spanish, Speech, Speech Pathology/Audiology, Studio Art, Trade/Industrial Education, Vocational Education, Vocational Home Economics Education.

**Requirements:** General education requirement.

**Academic regulations:** Minimum 2.0 GPA must be maintained.

**Special:** Minors offered in most majors and in philosophy. Programs in ethnic, black, and Mexican-American studies; in American, European, and Latin American area studies; and in wildlife and physical sciences. Criminal Justice Center provides internships and graduate programs, national and international symposia, and facilities and funding for research and publication. Center for Agriculture Education and Rural Redevelopment (U.S. AID-sponsored) for foreign students. Self-designed majors. Double majors. Graduate school at which undergraduates may take graduate-level courses. Preprofessional programs in law, medicine, veterinary science, pharmacy, dentistry, theology, dental hygiene, engineering, nursing, physical therapy, and seminary. 3-2 engineering program with Texas A&M U. Teacher certification in elementary and secondary education. ROTC.

**Honors:** Honors program. Honor societies.

**Academic Assistance:** Remedial writing and math. Nonremedial tutoring.

**STUDENT LIFE. Housing:** All freshmen must live on campus. Coed, women's, and men's dorms. Sorority and fraternity housing. School-owned/operated apartments. Both on-campus and off-campus married-student housing. 40% of students live in college housing.

**Social atmosphere:** According to the student newspaper, "The university serves the Houston area, therefore many students return to the city on the weekends. Houston is only about 70 miles south. Those who remain enjoy the thick east Texas pine landscape. There are many active Greek organizations on campus as well as many religious associations that are quite active." Popular events include the Texas Department of Correction's rodeo, the Renaissance Festival in Plantersville, and the Walker County Fair.

**Services and counseling/handicapped student services:** Placement services. Health service. Personal and psychological counseling. Career and academic guidance services. Physically disabled student services. Notetaking services. Tape recorders. Reader services for the blind.

**Campus organizations:** Undergraduate student government. Student newspaper (Houstonian, published twice/week). Literary magazine. Yearbook. Radio and TV stations. Drama, musical, political, service, and special-interest groups. 14 fraternities, no chapter houses; nine sororities, no chapter houses.

**Religious organizations:** Numerous religious groups.

**Minority/foreign student organizations:** Numerous minority student groups.

**ATHLETICS. Physical education requirements:** Two semesters of physical education required.

**Intercollegiate competition:** 3% of students participate. Baseball (M), basketball (M,W), cheerleading (M,W), cross-country (M,W), football (M), golf (M), softball (W), tennis (W), track and field (indoor) (M,W), track and field (outdoor) (M,W), volleyball (W). Member of NCAA Division I, NCAA Division I-AA for football, Southland Conference.

**Intramural and club sports:** 50% of students participate. Intramural badminton, basketball, flag football, frisbee, golf, pickleball, racquetball, soccer, softball, swimming, tennis, track, triathlon, volleyball, walleyball, water polo, wrestling. Men's club cycling, gymnastics, lacrosse, rodeo, rugby, soccer. Women's club cycling, gymnastics, rodeo.

**ADMISSIONS. Academic basis for candidate selection** (in order of priority): Standardized test scores, class rank, secondary school record, school's recommendation.

**Requirements:** Graduation from secondary school is required; GED is accepted. 16 units and the following program of study are recommended: 4 units of English, 2 units of math, 2 units of science, 2 units of social studies, 6 units of electives. Minimum combined SAT score of 900 (composite ACT score of 21) or rank in top half of secondary school class required. Interview required of applicants not meeting standard requirements. SAT or ACT is required. Campus visit recommended. No off-campus interviews.

**Procedure:** Take SAT or ACT by May of 12th year. Suggest filing application one month before registration date; no deadline. Notification of admission on rolling basis. $75 room deposit, refundable until six weeks before beginning of term. Freshmen accepted for terms other than fall.

**Special programs:** Admission may be deferred. Credit and/or placement may be granted through CEEB Advanced Placement exams for scores of 3 or higher. Credit may be granted through CLEP subject exams. Credit and placement may be granted through military experience. Early decision program. Early entrance/early admission program. Concurrent enrollment program.

**Transfer students:** Transfer students accepted for terms other than fall. In fall 1993, 46% of all new students were transfers into all classes. 2,664 transfer applications were received, 1,963 were accepted. Application deadline is open for fall; open for spring. Minimum 2.0 GPA required. Lowest course grade accepted is "D." Maximum number of transferable credits is 60 semester hours. At least 30 semester hours must be completed at the university to receive degree.

**Admissions contact:** Joey Chandler, Director of Admissions. 409 294-1056.

**FINANCIAL AID. Available aid:** Pell grants, SEOG, state scholarships and grants, school grants, private scholarships, ROTC scholarships, and aid for undergraduate foreign students. Perkins Loans (NDSL), PLUS, Stafford Loans (GSL), state loans, school loans, private loans, and SLS. Tuition Plan Inc. United Student Aid Fund, Inc.

**Supporting data/closing dates:** FAFSA/FAF/FSS: Accepted on rolling basis. Notification of awards on rolling basis.

**Financial aid contact:** Jess Davis, Director of Financial Aid. 409 294-1724.

**STUDENT EMPLOYMENT.** College Work/Study Program. Institutional employment. 10% of full-time undergraduates work on campus during school year. Students may expect to earn an average of $1,500 during school year. Off-campus part-time employment opportunities rated "good."

**COMPUTER FACILITIES.** 249 IBM/IBM-compatible and Macintosh/Apple microcomputers; all are networked. Computer facilities are available to all students.

**Fees:** $30 computer fee per semester; included in tuition/fees.

**Hours:** Some labs open 24 hours.

# Schreiner College

**Kerrville, TX 78028** 210 896-5411

**1994-95 Costs.** Tuition: $8,955. Room: $2,810. Board: $3,090. Fees, books, misc. academic expenses (school's estimate): $540.

**Enrollment.** Undergraduates: 256 men, 265 women (full-time). Freshman class: 558 applicants, 435 accepted, 111 enrolled.

**Test score averages/ranges.** Average SAT scores: 410 verbal, 470 math. Range of SAT scores of middle 50%: 350-460 verbal, 400-540 math. Average ACT scores: 22 English, 22 math, 22 composite. Range of ACT scores of middle 50%: 18-25 English, 18-25 math.

**Faculty.** 38 full-time; 20 part-time. 63% of faculty holds doctoral degree. Student/faculty ratio: 13 to 1.

**Selectivity rating.** Competitive.

**PROFILE.** Schreiner is a private, church-affiliated, liberal arts college. Founded in 1917, it adopted coeducation in 1932. Its 175-acre campus is located in Kerrville, 60 miles northwest of San Antonio.

**Accreditation:** SACS.

**Religious orientation:** Schreiner College is affiliated with the Presbyterian Church USA; no religious requirements.

**Library:** Collections totaling over 70,000 volumes, 400 periodical subscriptions, and 1,700 microform items.

**Athletic facilities:** Gymnasium, basketball, racquetball, tennis, and volleyball courts, baseball, intramural, soccer, and softball fields, swimming pool, track, weight room, driving range.

**STUDENT BODY. Undergraduate profile:** 95% are state residents; 30% are transfers. Average age of undergraduates is 21.

**Freshman profile:** 61% of accepted applicants took SAT; 49% took ACT. 80% of freshmen come from public schools.

**Undergraduate achievement:** 52% of fall 1992 freshmen returned for fall 1993 term. 30% of entering class graduated. 10% of students who completed a degree program immediately went on to graduate study.

**Foreign students:** 35 students are from out of the country. Countries represented include Indonesia, Japan, Malaysia, Mexico, Singapore, and Taiwan; 13 in all.

**PROGRAMS OF STUDY. Degrees:** B.A., B.Bus.Admin., B.Gen.Studies.

**Majors:** Accounting, Art, Biochemistry, Biology, Business Administration, English, Exercise Science, Finance, General Studies, History, Humanities, Marketing, Mathematics, Philosophy, Pre-Professional Studies, Psychology, Real Estate, Religion, Secondary Teacher Certification.

**Distribution of degrees:** The majors with the highest enrollment are business administration, mathematics, and psychology; philosophy has the lowest.

**Requirements:** General education requirement.

**Academic regulations:** Freshmen must maintain minimum 1.5 GPA; sophomores, 1.8 GPA; juniors, 2.0 GPA; seniors, 2.0 GPA.

**Special:** Minors offered in all majors. Associate's degrees offered. Double majors. Independent study. Internships. Preprofessional programs in law, medicine, veterinary science, pharmacy, dentistry, theology, and optometry. 3-2 engineering programs with U of Texas and Texas A&M U. Teacher certification in elementary and secondary education. Certification in specific subject areas. Exchange program abroad in Japan (Nagasaki Wesleyan Coll).

**Honors:** Honors program. Honor societies.

**Academic Assistance:** Remedial reading, writing, math, and study skills. Nonremedial tutoring.

**ADMISSIONS. Academic basis for candidate selection** (in order of priority): Secondary school record, standardized test scores, class rank, school's recommendation.

**Nonacademic basis for candidate selection:** Extracurricular participation is emphasized. Character and personality are important. Particular talent or ability is considered.

**Requirements:** Graduation from secondary school is required; GED is accepted. No specific distribution of secondary school units required. Minimum SAT scores of 400 in both verbal and math (composite ACT score of 20), rank in top half of secondary school class, and minimum 2.0 GPA recommended. SAT or ACT is required. Campus visit and interview recommended. Off-campus interviews available with an admissions representative.

**Procedure:** Take SAT or ACT by June of 12th year. Suggest filing application by February. Application deadline is August 15. Notification of admission on rolling basis. Reply is required by May 1 or within 30 days of acceptance. $100 room deposit, refundable until May 1. Freshmen accepted for terms other than fall.

**Special programs:** Admission may be deferred one year. Credit and/or placement may be granted through CEEB Advanced Placement exams for scores of 3 or higher. Credit and placement may be granted through challenge exams. Early entrance/early admission program. Concurrent enrollment program.

**Transfer students:** Transfer students accepted for terms other than fall. In fall 1993, 30% of all new students were transfers into all classes. 153 transfer applications were received, 96 were accepted. Application deadline is August 15 for fall; January 10 for spring. Minimum 2.0 GPA recommended. Lowest course grade accepted is "C." Maximum number of transferable credits is 90 semester hours. At least 30 semester hours must be completed at the college to receive degree.

**Admissions contact:** Sandy Speed, Director of Admissions. 800 343-4919.

**FINANCIAL AID. Available aid:** Pell grants, SEOG, state scholarships and grants, school scholarships and grants, private scholarships and grants, academic merit scholarships, and athletic scholarships. PLUS, Stafford Loans (GSL), state loans, private loans, and SLS. Institutional payment plan.

**Financial aid statistics:** In 1993-94, 97% of all undergraduate applicants received aid; 96% of freshman applicants. Average amounts of aid awarded freshmen: Scholarships and grants, $7,367; loans, $2,507.
**Supporting data/closing dates:** FAFSA/FAF/FFS: Accepted on rolling basis. Notification of awards on rolling basis.
**Financial aid contact:** Pat Mitchell, Director of Financial Aid. 800 343-4919.

# Southern Methodist University

**Dallas, TX 75275** **214 768-2000**

**1994-95 Costs.** Tuition: $12,772. Room: $2,426. Board: $2,652. Fees, books, misc. academic expenses (school's estimate): $1,200.
**Enrollment.** Undergraduates: 2,356 men, 2,536 women (full-time). Freshman class: 4,301 applicants, 3,455 accepted, 1,166 enrolled. Graduate enrollment: 2,298 men, 1,354 women.
**Test score averages/ranges.** Range of SAT scores of middle 50%: 940-1160 combined. Range of ACT scores of middle 50%: 22-27 composite.
**Faculty.** 483 full-time; 157 part-time. 85% of faculty holds highest degree in specific field. Student/faculty ratio: 13 to 1.
**Selectivity rating.** Competitive.

**PROFILE.** SMU, founded in 1911, is a church-affiliated, comprehensive university. Programs are offered through the Dedman College; the Meadow School of the Arts; the Edwin L. Cox School of Business; the Perkins School of Theology; and the Schools of Engineering and Applied Science and Law. Its 163-acre, suburban campus is located in Dallas.

**Accreditation:** SACS. Professionally accredited by the Accreditation Board for Engineering and Technology, the American Assembly of Collegiate Schools of Business, the American Bar Association, the Association of American Law Schools, the Association of Theological Schools, the National Association of Schools of Dance, the National Association of Schools of Music.
**Religious orientation:** Southern Methodist University is affiliated with the United Methodist Church; no religious requirements.
**Library:** Collections totaling over 2,800,507 volumes, 5,727 periodical subscriptions, and 1,388,495 microform items.
**Special facilities/museums:** Art and natural history museums, southwest film/video archives, sculpture garden, performing arts theatres, pollen analysis and geothermal labs, electron microbe lab, microscopy lab, seismological observatory, TV studio.
**Athletic facilities:** Coliseum, track, natatorium, stadium, athletic fields, tennis courts.

**STUDENT BODY. Undergraduate profile:** 58% are state residents; 20% are transfers. 5% Asian-American, 5% Black, 7% Hispanic, 1% Native American, 79% White, 3% Other. Average age of undergraduates is 21.
**Freshman profile:** 94% of accepted applicants took SAT; 54% took ACT. 68% of freshmen come from public schools.
**Undergraduate achievement:** 82% of fall 1992 freshmen returned for fall 1993 term. 58% of entering class graduated.
**Foreign students:** 144 students are from out of the country. Countries represented include Australia, Canada, Japan, Mexico, Singapore, and South Africa; 57 in all.

**PROGRAMS OF STUDY. Degrees:** B.A., B.Bus.Admin., B.F.A., B.Human., B.Mus., B.S., B.Soc.Sci.
**Majors:** Accounting, Advertising, African-American Studies, Anthropology, Art, Art History, Biochemistry, Biology, Broadcast News, Business Administration, Chemistry, Cinematography, Communication Arts, Computer Engineering, Computer Science, Dance, Economics, Economics/Finance, Economics/Systems Analysis, Electrical Engineering, English, English/Creative Writing, Environmental Geology, Finance, Foreign Language/Literature, French, Geological Sciences, Geology, Geophysics, German, German Studies, History, Humanities, Individual Studies in Liberal Arts, International Studies, Italian Area Studies, Journalism, Latin American Studies, Management Information Systems, Management Science/Engineering Management, Marketing, Mathematics, Mechanical Engineering, Mexican-American Studies, Music, Music Education, Music Performance, Music Theory/Composition, Music Therapy, News/Editorial, Organizational Behavior, Philosophy, Physics, Piano Pedagogy, Political Science, Psychology, Public Relations, Real Estate, Religious Studies, Russian, Russian Area Studies, Social Sciences, Sociology, Spanish, Statistics, Studio Art, Television/Radio, Theatre.
**Distribution of degrees:** The majors with the highest enrollment are general business, psychology, and advertising; ethnic/Mexican-American studies, Italian area studies, and statistical science have the lowest.
**Requirements:** General education requirement.
**Academic regulations:** Minimum 2.0 GPA must be maintained.
**Special:** Minors offered in many majors and in Asian studies, education, medieval studies, and women's studies. All freshmen take one to two years of basic liberal arts before entering one of the degree-granting undergraduate schools. Summer study and research facility at Taos, N.M. Self-designed majors. Double majors. Dual degrees. Independent study. Pass/fail grading option. Internships. Cooperative education programs. Graduate school at which undergraduates may take graduate-level courses. Preprofessional programs in law, medicine, veterinary science, and dentistry. Comined B.A./B.S. program in music and computer science. 3-2 bachelor's/M.B.A. program. Member of Higher Education Data Sharing Consortium. Teacher certification in elementary and secondary education. Certification in specific subject areas. Exchange program abroad in Japan. Study abroad in Austria, Denmark, England, France, Italy, Mexico, Russia, and Spain. ROTC at U of Texas at Arlington. AFROTC at U of North Texas.
**Honors:** Phi Beta Kappa. Honors program. Honor societies.
**Academic Assistance:** Nonremedial tutoring.

**STUDENT LIFE. Housing:** All first-year students must live on campus unless living with family. Coed, women's, and men's dorms. Sorority and fraternity housing. School-owned/operated apartments. Off-campus privately-owned housing. Both on-campus and off-campus married-student housing. 45% of students live in college housing.
**Services and counseling/handicapped student services:** Placement services. Health service. Women's center. Day care. Counseling services for minority and older students. Birth control, personal, and psychological counseling. Career and academic guidance services. Religious counseling. Physically disabled student services. Learning disabled services. Notetaking services. Tape recorders. Tutors.
**Campus organizations:** Undergraduate student government. Student newspaper (Daily Campus). Literary magazine. Yearbook. Radio and TV stations. Band, choir, choral group, debating, drama group, Women's Interest Coalition, College Republicans, Young Democrats, Amnesty International, academic, service, and special-interest groups, 151 organizations in all. 15 fraternities, 14 chapter houses; 11 sororities, all with chapter houses. 44% of men join a fraternity. 51% of women join a sorority.
**Religious organizations:** Bahai Club, Baptist Student Union, Campus Crusade for Christ, Catholic Campus Ministry, Christian Science Organization, Fellowship of Christian Athletes, Jewish Student Association/Hillel, Muslim Student Association, Ponies of Christ, United Methodist Campus Ministry.
**Minority/foreign student organizations:** Association of Black Students, College Hispanic-American Students, Native American Indian Intertribal Student Council. International Student Organization, Chinese, East Asian, Hong Kong, Indian, Iranian, Japanese, Korean, and Turkish groups.

**ATHLETICS. Physical education requirements:** Two non-credit classes in the CHOICES Wellness Program required for graduation.
**Intercollegiate competition:** 4% of students participate. Basketball (M,W), cross-country (M,W), diving (M,W), football (M), golf (M,W), soccer (M,W), swimming (M,W), tennis (M,W), track (indoor) (M), track and field (M,W). Member of NCAA Division I, NCAA Division I-A for football, Southwest Conference.
**Intramural and club sports:** Men's club baseball, crew, cycling, fencing, ice hockey, lacrosse, polo, rugby, sailing, volleyball. Women's club crew, cycling, fencing, polo, sailing, volleyball.

**ADMISSIONS.**
**Nonacademic basis for candidate selection:** Extracurricular participation and particular talent or ability are important. Character and personality and alumni/ae relationship are considered.
**Requirements:** Graduation from secondary school is required; GED is accepted. 15 units and the following program of study are required: 4 units of English, 3 units of math, 3 units of science including 1 unit of lab, 2 units of foreign language, 3 units of social studies. Audition required of music and performing arts program applicants. Portfolio recommended of art scholarship applicants. SAT or ACT is required. Campus visit recommended. Off-campus interviews available with admissions and alumni representatives.
**Procedure:** Take SAT or ACT by December of 12th year. Suggest filing application by January 15. Application deadline is April 1. Notification of admission by March 15. Reply is required by May 1. $400 nonrefundable tuition/room deposit. Freshmen accepted for terms other than fall.
**Special programs:** Admission may be deferred one semester. Credit may be granted through CEEB Advanced Placement for scores of 4 or higher. Credit may be granted through CLEP subject exams. Early decision program. In fall 1993, 752 applied for early decision and 657 were accepted. Deadline for applying for early decision is November 1.
**Transfer students:** Transfer students accepted for terms other than fall. In fall 1993, 20% of all new students were transfers into all classes. 616 transfer applications were received, 488 were accepted. Application deadline is June 1 for fall; December 1 for spring. Minimum 2.5 GPA recommended. Lowest course grade accepted is "C-." At least 60 semester hours must be completed at the university to receive degree.
**Admissions contact:** Ron W. Moss, M.Ed., Director of Admission and Enrollment Management. 214 768-2058, 800 323-0672.

**FINANCIAL AID. Available aid:** Pell grants, SEOG, state grants, school scholarships and grants, private scholarships and grants, ROTC scholarships, academic merit scholarships, and athletic scholarships. Perkins Loans (NDSL), PLUS, Stafford Loans (GSL), state loans, school loans, private loans, and SLS. Deferred payment plan. Deferred and installment payment plans.
**Financial aid statistics:** 32% of aid is not need-based. In 1993-94, 69% of all undergraduate applicants received aid; 100% of freshman applicants. Average amounts of aid awarded freshmen: Scholarships and grants, $8,556; loans, $5,829.
**Supporting data/closing dates:** FAFSA/FAF: Priority filing date is February 1. School's own aid application: Priority filing date is February 1. Notification of awards begins March 15.
**Financial aid contact:** Michael Novak, M.A., Director of Financial Aid. 214 768-3417, 214 SMU-3417.

**STUDENT EMPLOYMENT.** College Work/Study Program. Institutional employment. 19% of full-time undergraduates work on campus during school year. Students may expect to earn an average of $2,000 during school year. Off-campus part-time employment opportunities rated "good."

**COMPUTER FACILITIES.** 500 IBM/IBM-compatible, Macintosh/Apple, and RISC-/UNIX-based microcomputers; 250 are networked. Students may access Digital, IBM, SUN minicomputer/mainframe systems, Internet. Residence halls may be equipped with stand-alone microcomputers, networked microcomputers. Client/LAN operating systems include Apple/Macintosh, DOS, OS/2, UNIX/XENIX/AIX, Windows NT, X-windows, DEC, LocalTalk/AppleTalk, Microsoft, Novell. Numerous computer languages and programs available. Computer facilities are available to all students.
**Fees:** Computer fee is included in tuition/fees.
**Hours:** 24 hours.

**PROMINENT ALUMNI/AE.** Kathy Bates, Academy Award-winning actress; James W. Cronin, Nobel laureate in physics; Roy Huffington, former U.S. Ambassador to Austria; Robert Dennard, inventor of the dynamic random access memory (DRAM) chip.

# Southwest Texas State University

San Marcos, TX 78666-5709 512 245-2111

**1994-95 Costs.** Tuition: $780 (state residents), $4,860 (out-of-state). Room & board: $4,286. Fees, books, misc. academic expenses (school's estimate): $1,344.
**Enrollment.** Undergraduates: 6,857 men, 7,693 women (full-time). Freshman class: 8,532 applicants, 5,316 accepted, 2,421 enrolled. Graduate enrollment: 1,216 men, 1,589 women.
**Test score averages/ranges.** Average SAT scores: 425 verbal, 481 math. Average ACT scores: 22 composite.
**Faculty.** 662 full-time; 240 part-time. 80% of faculty holds highest degree in specific field. Student/faculty ratio: 22 to 1.
**Selectivity rating.** Competitive.

**PROFILE.** Southwest Texas State, founded in 1899, is a public, comprehensive university. Its 1,091-acre campus is located in San Marcos, 30 miles from Austin.

**Accreditation:** SACS. Professionally accredited by the Accrediting Commission on Education for Health Services Administration, the American Home Economics Association, the American Medical Association (CAHEA), the American Speech-Language-Hearing Association, the Council on Social Work Education, the Foundation for Interior Design Education Research, the National Association of Schools of Music, the National Association of Schools of Public Affairs and Administration.
**Religious orientation:** Southwest Texas State University is nonsectarian; no religious requirements.
**Library:** Collections totaling over 965,373 volumes, and 1,373,034 microform items.
**Special facilities/museums:** Child development center, aquifer research center, southwest writers' collection, working ranch.
**Athletic facilities:** Swimming pool, weight room, basketball, handball, racquetball, and tennis courts, baseball, football, soccer, and softball fields, golf course, canoeing/rowing facilities.

**STUDENT BODY. Undergraduate profile:** 98% are state residents; 36% are transfers. 1% Asian-American, 6% Black, 17% Hispanic, 75% White, 1% Other. Average age of undergraduates is 23.
**Freshman profile:** 65% of accepted applicants took SAT; 35% took ACT. 95% of freshmen come from public schools.
**Undergraduate achievement:** 64% of fall 1992 freshmen returned for fall 1993 term. 12% of entering class graduated.
**Foreign students:** 409 students are from out of the country. Countries represented include Canada, China, Hong Kong, India, Iran, and Taiwan; 61 in all.

**PROGRAMS OF STUDY. Degrees:** B.A., B.A.Internat.Studies, B.Agri., B.Appl.Arts/Sci., B.Appl.Soc., B.Bus.Admin., B.Exer./Sports Sci., B.F.A., B.Hlth./Wellness Promo., B.Mus., B.S., B.S.Comm.Disorders, B.S.Crim.Just., B.S.Hlth.Prof., B.S.Home Econ., B.S.Med.Rec.Admin., B.S.Med.Tech., B.S.Recr., B.S.Resp.Care, B.S.Tech., B.Soc.Work.
**Majors:** Accounting, Administrative Science, Agricultural Business, Agricultural Journalism, Agricultural Mechanization, Allied Health Education, Animal Science, Anthropology, Applied Arts/Sciences, Applied/Physical Geography, Applied Sociology, Aquatic Biology, Art, Asian Studies, Athletic Training, Biology, Botany, Cartography/Photogrammetry, Chemistry, Commercial Art, Communication Disorders, Computer Information Systems, Computer Science, Consumer Science, Criminal Justice, Criminal Justice/Corrections, Criminal Justice/Law Enforcement, Economics, Engineering Technology, English, European Studies, Exercise/Sports Science, Family/Child Development, Fashion Merchandising/Clothing/Textiles, Finance, French, General Physiology, Geography, German, Health Care Administration, Health/Fitness Management, Health/Wellness Promotion, History, Home Economics, Horticulture, Industrial Technology, Inter-American Studies, Interior Design, International Relations, International Studies, Journalism, Long-term Health Care Administration, Management, Marine Biology, Marketing, Mass Communications, Mathematics, Medical Record Administration, Medical Technology, Microbiology, Middle Eastern/African Studies, Music, Music/Performance, Music/Piano Pedagogy, Musical Theatre, Nutrition/Foods, Philosophy, Physics, Plant/Soil Science, Political Science, Political Science/Public Administration, Production Management, Psychology, Range Management, Recreational Administration, Resource/Environmental Studies, Respiratory Care, Social Work, Sociology, Spanish, Speech Communication, Studio Art, Theatre Arts, Urban/Regional Planning, Wildlife Biology, Zoology.
**Distribution of degrees:** The majors with the highest enrollment are business, interdisciplinary studies, and psychology; Asian studies, agricultural science, and biology teacher education have the lowest.
**Requirements:** General education requirement.
**Academic regulations:** Minimum 2.0 GPA must be maintained.
**Special:** Minor required in some majors for graduation. Minors offered in most majors. Associate's degrees offered. Double majors. Dual degrees. Pass/fail grading option. Internships. Graduate school at which undergraduates may take graduate-level courses. Preprofessional programs in law, medicine, veterinary science, pharmacy, dentistry, occupational therapy, and pre-physical therapy. 3-2 engineering programs with Texas A&M U and U of Texas at Austin. Member of Texas London consortium and Council of International Educational Exchange. Teacher certification in early childhood, elementary, secondary, special education, vo-tech, and bilingual/bicultural education. Certification in specific subject areas. Study abroad in Belize, Costa Rica, France, Germany, Greece, Italy, Japan, Mexico, Puerto Rico, Saudi Arabia, Spain, the United Kingdom, and Yemen. ROTC and AFROTC.
**Honors:** Honors program. Honor societies.
**Academic Assistance:** Remedial reading, writing, math, and study skills. Nonremedial tutoring.

**STUDENT LIFE. Housing:** All students under age 21 with fewer than 60 semester hours must live on campus. Coed, women's, and men's dorms. School-owned/operated apartments. On-campus married-student housing. 25% of students live in college housing.
**Social atmosphere:** Favorite gathering spots on campus include the Quad, the LBJ Student Center, and Sewell Park. Off campus, students frequent bars and dance clubs in downtown San Marcos. Greeks influence campus social life. Homecoming, the Chilypiad, and Sunsplash Sunday are favorite student events. "Many SWT students commute from San Antonio and Austin. The campus is very beautiful with rolling hills and trees. Because of personalized attention from faculty and the friendliness of the students, the university has a small sense to it in spite of the large student population," reports the Daily University Star.
**Services and counseling/handicapped student services:** Placement services. Health service. Counseling services for minority, military, veteran, and older students. Birth control, personal, and psychological counseling. Career and academic guidance services. Physically disabled student services. Learning disabled services. Notetaking services. Tutors. Reader services for the blind.
**Campus organizations:** Undergraduate student government. Student newspaper (The Daily University Star). Literary magazine. Yearbook. Radio station. Band, chorus, a cappella choir, theatre and dance clubs, departmental, professional, service, and special-interest groups, 200 organizations in all. 21 fraternities, no chapter houses; 10 sororities, no chapter houses. 8% of men join a fraternity. 8% of women join a sorority.
**Religious organizations:** Baptist Student Union, Campus Crusade for Christ, Canterbury Association, Chi Alpha Christian Fellowship, Christians in Action, Fellowship of Christian Athletes, Catholic, Christian Science, Episcopal, Jewish, Latter-Day Saints, Lutheran, Methodist, and Muslim groups.
**Minority/foreign student organizations:** Black Student Alliance, Mexican-American Association, minority professional groups. International Student Association, International Studies Club.

**ATHLETICS. Physical education requirements:** Two semesters of physical education required.
**Intercollegiate competition:** 3% of students participate. Baseball (M), basketball (M,W), cross-country (M,W), football (M), golf (M), softball (W), tennis (M,W), track (indoor) (M), track (outdoor) (M), track and field (indoor) (M,W), track and field (outdoor) (M,W), volleyball (W). Member of NCAA Division I, Southland Conference.
**Intramural and club sports:** 7% of students participate. Men's club lacrosse, rodeo, rugby. Women's club gymnastics.

**ADMISSIONS. Academic basis for candidate selection** (in order of priority): Standardized test scores, class rank, secondary school record.
**Requirements:** Graduation from secondary school is required; GED is accepted. No specific distribution of secondary school units required. No minimum SAT or ACT score required of applicants ranking in top tenth of secondary school class; minimum combined SAT score of 800 (composite ACT score of 20) required of applicants ranking in next 15%; minimum combined SAT score of 900 (composite ACT score of 22) required of applicants ranking in second quarter; minimum combined SAT score of 1100 (composite ACT score of 26) required of applicants ranking in third quarter; minimum combined SAT score of 1200 (composite ACT score of 29) required of applicants ranking in fourth quarter. Audition required of sound recording technology program applicants. SAT or ACT is required. PSAT is recommended. Campus visit recommended. No off-campus interviews.
**Procedure:** Take SAT or ACT by October of 12th year. Application deadline is July 1. Notification of admission on rolling basis. $100 room deposit, refundable until July 1. Freshmen accepted for terms other than fall.
**Special programs:** Credit may be granted through CEEB Advanced Placement for scores of 3 or higher. Credit may be granted through CLEP general and subject exams, challenge exams, and military and life experience. Early entrance/early admission program. Concurrent enrollment program.
**Transfer students:** Transfer students accepted for terms other than fall. In fall 1993, 36% of all new students were transfers into all classes. 3,653 transfer applications were received, 2,623 were accepted. Application deadline is July 1 for fall; December 1 for spring. Minimum 2.25 GPA required. Lowest course grade accepted is "C." Maximum number of transferable credits is 66 semester hours. At least 30 semester hours must be completed at the university to receive degree.
**Admissions contact:** Fernando Yarrito, Director of Admissions. 512 245-2364.

**FINANCIAL AID. Available aid:** Pell grants, SEOG, state scholarships and grants, school scholarships, private scholarships, ROTC scholarships, academic merit scholarships, and athletic scholarships. Perkins Loans (NDSL), PLUS, Stafford Loans (GSL), and state loans. Installment payment plan.
**Financial aid statistics:** 5% of aid is not need-based. In 1993-94, 52% of all undergraduate applicants received aid; 91% of freshman applicants. Average amounts of aid awarded freshmen: Scholarships and grants, $1,562; loans, $2,369.
**Supporting data/closing dates:** FAFSA/FAF/FFS: Deadline is April 1. Income tax forms: Accepted on rolling basis. IVF: Accepted on rolling basis. Notification of awards on rolling basis.
**Financial aid contact:** Mariko Gomez, M.P.A., Director of Student Financial Aid. 512 245-2315.

**STUDENT EMPLOYMENT.** College Work/Study Program. Institutional employment. 20% of full-time undergraduates work on campus during school year. Students may expect to earn an average of $3,000 during school year. Off-campus part-time employment opportunities rated "good."

**COMPUTER FACILITIES.** 2,080 IBM/IBM-compatible and Macintosh/Apple microcomputers; 400 are networked. Students may access Digital minicomputer/mainframe systems, BITNET, Internet. Residence halls may be equipped with stand-alone microcomputers, modems. Client/LAN operating systems include Apple/Macintosh, DOS, DEC. Computer languages and software packages include Ada, C, COBOL, DBM, FORTRAN, Pascal, SAS, SPSS; spreadsheet, word processing programs; 100 in all. Computer facilities are available to all students.
**Fees:** $2 computer fee per credit hour.

**PROMINENT ALUMNI/AE.** Lyndon B. Johnson, 36th President of the United States; George Strait, country singer; Thomas Carter, actor; Tomas Rivera, educator; Emory Bellard, football coach.

# Southwestern Adventist College

**Keene, TX 76059** **817 645-3921**

**1994-95 Costs.** Tuition: $7,528. Room & board: $3,736. Fees, books, misc. academic expenses (school's estimate): $500.
**Enrollment.** Undergraduates: 301 men, 319 women (full-time). Freshman class: 422 applicants, 318 accepted, 186 enrolled. Graduate enrollment: 2 men, 8 women.
**Test score averages/ranges.** Average SAT scores: 395 verbal, 419 math. Range of SAT scores of middle 50%: 320-470 verbal, 330-510 math. Average ACT scores: 21 English, 19 math, 21 composite. Range of ACT scores of middle 50%: 17-26 English, 16-23 math.
**Faculty.** 48 full-time; 18 part-time. 48% of faculty holds doctoral degree. Student/faculty ratio: 14 to 1.
**Selectivity rating.** Less competitive.

**PROFILE.** Southwestern Adventist, founded in 1893, is a church-affiliated, multipurpose college. Its 150-acre campus is located in Keene, 30 miles south of Fort Worth.

**Accreditation:** SACS. Professionally accredited by the National League for Nursing.
**Religious orientation:** Southwestern Adventist College is affiliated with the Seventh-day Adventist Church; four semesters of religion required.
**Library:** Collections totaling over 98,570 volumes, 452 periodical subscriptions, and 338,729 microform items.
**Special facilities/museums:** Language lab, biology museum, observatory, historical museum.
**Athletic facilities:** Swimming pool, racquetball and tennis courts, athletic fields, weight room, aerobics room, gymnasium.
**STUDENT BODY. Undergraduate profile:** 53% are state residents; 39% are transfers. 3% Asian-American, 10% Black, 14% Hispanic, 1% Native American, 65% White, 7% Other. Average age of undergraduates is 26.
**Freshman profile:** 1% of freshmen who took SAT scored 700 or over on verbal, 1% scored 700 or over on math; 4% scored 600 or over on verbal, 7% scored 600 or over on math; 22% scored 500 or over on verbal, 27% scored 500 or over on math; 47% scored 400 or over on verbal, 56% scored 400 or over on math; 81% scored 300 or over on verbal, 85% scored 300 or over on math. 5% of freshmen who took ACT scored 30 or over on English, 3% scored 30 or over on math, 4% scored 30 or over on composite; 31% scored 24 or over on English, 15% scored 24 or over on math, 29% scored 24 or over on composite; 72% scored 18 or over on English, 60% scored 18 or over on math, 75% scored 18 or over on composite; 95% scored 12 or over on English, 100% scored 12 or over on math, 100% scored 12 or over on composite; 100% scored 6 or over on English. 58% of accepted applicants took SAT; 44% took ACT. 20% of freshmen come from public schools.
**Undergraduate achievement:** 62% of fall 1992 freshmen returned for fall 1993 term. 33% of entering class graduated.
**Foreign students:** 71 students are from out of the country. Countries represented include the Bahamas, Canada, Honduras, Mexico, Panama, and the former Soviet Republics; 32 in all.
**PROGRAMS OF STUDY. Degrees:** B.A., B.Bus.Admin., B.S., B.Soc.Work.
**Majors:** Accounting, Biology, Biostatistics, Broadcasting, Business Administration, Chemistry, Computer Information Systems, Computer Science, Corporate Communications, Elementary Education, English, Health Arts, Health Fitness, History, International Affairs, Journalism, Long-term Health Care, Management, Mathematical Physics, Mathematics, Medical Technology, Nursing, Office Administration, Office Information Systems, Physics, Psychology, Religion, Social Sciences, Social Work, Theology.
**Distribution of degrees:** The majors with the highest enrollment are business administration, nursing, and elementary education.
**Requirements:** General education requirement.
**Academic regulations:** Freshmen must maintain minimum 1.5 GPA; sophomores, 1.65 GPA; juniors, 1.85 GPA; seniors, 2.0 GPA.
**Special:** Minors offered in most majors and in biblical languages, community health, music, Spanish, and speech. Courses offered in geography and political science. Bible instructor training and preministerial programs. Associate's degrees offered. Self-designed majors. Double majors. Independent study. Internships. Cooperative education programs. Graduate school at which undergraduates may take graduate-level courses. Preprofessional programs in medicine. 2-2 nursing program. 3-1 nursing program. Teacher certification in early childhood, elementary, and secondary education. Certification in specific subject areas. Study abroad in Austria, France, and Spain.
**Honors:** Honors program.
**Academic Assistance:** Nonremedial tutoring.
**ADMISSIONS. Academic basis for candidate selection** (in order of priority): Secondary school record, standardized test scores, class rank, school's recommendation.
**Nonacademic basis for candidate selection:** Character and personality are emphasized.
**Requirements:** Graduation from secondary school is required; GED is accepted. 16 units required and the following program of study recommended: 3 units of English, 2 units of math, 2 units of science, 2 units of foreign language, 2 units of social studies. Open admissions policy. Minimum 2.8 GPA and "C" in 2 units of math, 1 unit of biology, and 1 unit of chemistry required of nursing program applicants. Special programs for applicants not normally admissible. SAT is required; ACT may be substituted. Campus visit recommended. No off-campus interviews.
**Procedure:** Take SAT or ACT by May of 12th year. Notification of admission on rolling basis. $50 refundable room deposit. Freshmen accepted for terms other than fall.
**Special programs:** Admission may be deferred three years. Credit may be granted through CLEP general and subject exams. Credit and placement may be granted through challenge exams and military and life experience.
**Transfer students:** Transfer students accepted for terms other than fall. In fall 1993, 39% of all new students were transfers into all classes. 201 transfer applications were received, 164 were accepted. Application deadline is rolling for fall; rolling for spring. Minimum 2.0 GPA recommended. Lowest course grade accepted is "C." At least 30 semester hours must be completed at the college to receive degree.
**Admissions contact:** Victor Brown, M.A., Enrollment Vice President. 817 645-3921, extension 252.
**FINANCIAL AID. Available aid:** Pell grants, SEOG, state scholarships and grants, school scholarships, private scholarships and grants, academic merit scholarships, and aid for undergraduate foreign students. Perkins Loans (NDSL), PLUS, Stafford Loans (GSL), state loans, private loans, and SLS. Family tuition reduction. Cash payment. Bank financing. Contract with college.
**Financial aid statistics:** 22% of aid is not need-based. In 1993-94, 87% of all undergraduate applicants received aid; 86% of freshman applicants. Average amounts of aid awarded freshmen: Scholarships and grants, $1,000; loans, $2,625.
**Supporting data/closing dates:** FAFSA: Priority filing date is March 15. School's own aid application: Priority filing date is March 15. Income tax forms: Priority filing date is March 15. Notification of awards begins in early spring.
**Financial aid contact:** Patty Norwood, Director of Financial Aid. 817 645-3921, extension 223.

# Southwestern Assemblies of God College

**Waxahachie, TX 75165** **214 937-4010**

**1994-95 Costs.** Tuition: $2,990. Room & board: $3,090. Fees, books, misc. academic expenses (school's estimate): $750.
**Enrollment.** Undergraduates: 384 men, 345 women (full-time). Freshman class: 217 applicants, 217 accepted, 174 enrolled.
**Test score averages/ranges.** Average SAT scores: 418 verbal, 463 math. Range of SAT scores of middle 50%: 380-450 verbal, 370-530 math. Average ACT scores: 20 English, 17 math, 20 composite. Range of ACT scores of middle 50%: 18-24 English, 19-32 math.
**Faculty.** 18 full-time; 14 part-time. 47% of faculty holds doctoral degree. Student/faculty ratio: 32 to 1.
**Selectivity rating.** Noncompetitive.

**PROFILE.** Southwestern Assemblies of God, founded in 1931, is a church-affiliated, multipurpose college. Its 70-acre campus is located in Waxahachie, 15 miles south of downtown Dallas.

**Accreditation:** AABC, SACS.
**Religious orientation:** Southwestern Assemblies of God College is affiliated with the Assemblies of God; 10 semesters of religion/theology required.
**Library:** Collections totaling over 110,000 volumes, 550 periodical subscriptions, and 1,106 microform items.
**Athletic facilities:** Gymnasium, weight room, tennis courts, baseball and football fields, beach volleyball pit.
**STUDENT BODY. Undergraduate profile:** 70% are state residents; 51% are transfers. 1% Asian-American, 2% Black, 10% Hispanic, 1% Native American, 85% White, 1% Other. Average age of undergraduates is 25.
**Freshman profile:** 2% of freshmen who took SAT scored 700 or over on verbal; 4% scored 600 or over on verbal, 15% scored 600 or over on math; 21% scored 500 or over on verbal, 39% scored 500 or over on math; 55% scored 400 or over on verbal, 68% scored 400 or over on math; 92% scored 300 or over on verbal, 97% scored 300 or over on math. 19% of accepted applicants took SAT; 81% took ACT. 90% of freshmen come from public schools.
**Undergraduate achievement:** 53% of fall 1992 freshmen returned for fall 1993 term. 26% of entering class graduated.
**Foreign students:** 10 students are from out of the country. Countries represented include Canada, China, Korea, Malaysia, Mexico, and Nigeria.
**PROGRAMS OF STUDY. Degrees:** B.A., B.Career Arts, B.Church Admin., B.S.
**Majors:** Business, Children's Ministries, Christian Education, Church Business Administration, Church School Administration, Counseling, Elementary Education, Missions, Music, Pastoral Ministry, Youth Ministries.
**Distribution of degrees:** The majors with the highest enrollment are pastoral ministry, elementary education, and business; Christian school administration has the lowest.
**Requirements:** General education requirement.
**Academic regulations:** Freshmen must maintain minimum 1.50 GPA; sophomores, 1.75 GPA; juniors, 2.0 GPA; seniors, 2.0 GPA.
**Special:** Programs offered in applied music, child development, psychology, religion, science, and theology. Associate's degrees offered. Double majors. Independent study. Preprofessional programs in theology, business, and elementary education. Teacher certification in elementary education. Certification in specific subject areas.
**Honors:** Honor societies.
**Academic Assistance:** Remedial reading, writing, and study skills.
**ADMISSIONS. Academic basis for candidate selection** (in order of priority): Secondary school record, essay, standardized test scores, school's recommendation.
**Nonacademic basis for candidate selection:** Character and personality are emphasized. Extracurricular participation and particular talent or ability are considered.
**Requirements:** Graduation from secondary school is required; GED is accepted. No specific distribution of secondary school units required. Conditional admission possible for applicants not meeting standard requirements. SAT or ACT is required. Campus visit and interview recommended. No off-campus interviews.
**Procedure:** Suggest filing application by July 1; no deadline. Notification of admission on rolling basis. $25 nonrefundable room deposit. Freshmen accepted for terms other than fall.

**Special programs:** Admission may be deferred one year. Credit may be granted through CLEP general and subject exams, Regents College and challenge exams, and military and life experience. Concurrent enrollment program.
**Transfer students:** Transfer students accepted for terms other than fall. In fall 1993, 51% of all new students were transfers into all classes. 249 transfer applications were received, 248 were accepted. Application deadline is rolling for fall; rolling for spring. Minimum 2.0 GPA recommended. Lowest course grade accepted is "C." Maximum number of transferable credits is 96 semester hours. At least 30 semester hours must be completed at the college to receive degree.
**Admissions contact:** Greg Dufrene, Registrar. 214 937-4010, extension 116.
**FINANCIAL AID. Available aid:** Pell grants, SEOG, state grants, school scholarships and grants, private scholarships, and academic merit scholarships. Perkins Loans (NDSL), PLUS, Stafford Loans (GSL), state loans, private loans, and SLS. Deferred payment plan.
**Financial aid statistics:** 10% of aid is not need-based. In 1993-94, 95% of all undergraduate applicants received aid; 95% of freshman applicants. Average amounts of aid awarded freshmen: Scholarships and grants, $750; loans, $2,625.
**Supporting data/closing dates:** FAFSA/FAF/FFS: Priority filing date is March 1; accepted on rolling basis. School's own aid application: Priority filing date is March 1; accepted on rolling basis. State aid form: Priority filing date is March 1; accepted on rolling basis. Income tax forms: Priority filing date is May 1; accepted on rolling basis. Notification of awards on rolling basis.
**Financial aid contact:** Myrna Wyckoff, Director of Financial Aid. 214 937-4010, extension 122.

## Southwestern University

**Georgetown, TX 78626** **512 863-6511**

**1994-95 Costs.** Tuition: $11,850. Room: $2,150. Board: $2,525. Fees, books, misc. academic expenses (school's estimate): $600.
**Enrollment.** Undergraduates: 508 men, 669 women (full-time). Freshman class: 1,244 applicants, 912 accepted, 352 enrolled.
**Test score averages/ranges.** Range of SAT scores of middle 50%: 470-580 verbal, 520-640 math. Range of ACT scores of middle 50%: 23-28 composite.
**Faculty.** 87 full-time; 48 part-time. 90% of faculty holds doctoral degree. Student/faculty ratio: 12 to 1.
**Selectivity rating.** Highly competitive.

**PROFILE.** Southwestern, founded in 1840, is a church-affiliated university of liberal arts and sciences. Its 500-acre campus is located in Georgetown, 28 miles north of Austin.

**Accreditation:** SACS. Professionally accredited by the National Association of Schools of Music.
**Religious orientation:** Southwestern University is affiliated with the United Methodist Church; one semester of religion required.
**Library:** Collections totaling over 243,833 volumes, 1,292 periodical subscriptions, and 27,244 microform items.
**Athletic facilities:** Gymnasiums, golf course, basketball, racquetball, tennis, and volleyball courts, weight room, swimming pool, baseball, intramural, and soccer fields.

**STUDENT BODY. Undergraduate profile:** 89% are state residents; 9% are transfers. 4% Asian-American, 3% Black, 13% Hispanic, 78% White, 2% Other. Average age of undergraduates is 20.
**Freshman profile:** 2% of freshmen who took SAT scored 700 or over on verbal, 9% scored 700 or over on math; 20% scored 600 or over on verbal, 42% scored 600 or over on math; 62% scored 500 or over on verbal, 85% scored 500 or over on math; 97% scored 400 or over on verbal, 99% scored 400 or over on math; 100% scored 300 or over on verbal. 97% of accepted applicants took SAT; 51% took ACT. 85% of freshmen come from public schools.
**Undergraduate achievement:** 86% of fall 1992 freshmen returned for fall 1993 term. 31% of students who completed a degree program immediately went on to graduate study.
**Foreign students:** 26 students are from out of the country. Countries represented include Canada, France, Germany, Japan, Mexico, and Sweden; 15 in all.

**PROGRAMS OF STUDY. Degrees:** B.A., B.F.A., B.Mus., B.S.
**Majors:** Accounting, American Studies, Animal Behavior, Art, Biology, Business, Chemistry, Child Study/Language Development, Classics, Communication, Computer Science, Economics, English, French, German, History, International Studies, Kinesiology, Latin, Mathematics, Music, Philosophy, Physics, Political Science, Psychology, Religion, Sociology, Spanish, Theatre, Women's Studies.
**Distribution of degrees:** The majors with the highest enrollment are biology, business, and communication; Latin and German have the lowest.
**Requirements:** General education requirement.
**Academic regulations:** Freshmen must maintain minimum 1.6 GPA; sophomores, juniors, seniors, 2.0 GPA.
**Special:** Minors offered in most majors and in art history, dance, Greek, sacred music, and studio art. Courses in linguistics. Self-designed majors. Double majors. Dual degrees. Independent study. Internships. Preprofessional programs in law, medicine, veterinary science, dentistry, theology, and optometry. 3-2 engineering programs with Arizona State U, Texas A&M U, U of Texas at Austin, and Washington U. Member of Associated Colleges of the South. Washington Semester. Teacher certification in early childhood, elementary, secondary, and special education. Certification in specific subject areas. Member of International Student Exchange Program (ISEP).
**Honors:** Honors program. Honor societies.
**Academic Assistance:** Nonremedial tutoring.

**STUDENT LIFE. Housing:** All freshman not living near campus with relatives. Coed, women's, and men's dorms. Fraternity housing. 75% of students live in college housing.
**Social atmosphere:** The Student Union is the most popular on-campus gathering spot. Off campus, students head for Kirby Lane and Whataburger. Groups with the most widespread influence on campus social life include Alpha Phi Omega (a co-ed service fraternity), several Greek organizations, and the University Program Council. Mall Ball and basketball games are the most popular events of the school year. According to the editor of the student newspaper, both social and cultural life are "limited since the school and the town are quite small."
**Services and counseling/handicapped student services:** Placement services. Health service. Women's center. Counseling services for minority students. Personal and psychological counseling. Career and academic guidance services. Religious counseling.
**Campus organizations:** Undergraduate student government. Student newspaper (Megaphone, published once/week). Literary magazine. Yearbook. Chorales, a cappella and jazz swing choirs, bands, orchestra, opera theatre, Mask and Wig Players, Young Democrats, Young Republicans, 87 organizations in all. Four fraternities, all with chapter houses; four sororities, no chapter houses. 38% of men join a fraternity. 38% of women join a sorority.
**Religious organizations:** Baptist Student Union, Catholic Youth Activity, Christian Fellowship, Methodist Youth Fellowship, Upward Bound.
**Minority/foreign student organizations:** Ebony, Mexican-American Student Association.

**ATHLETICS. Physical education requirements:** Two semesters of physical education required.
**Intercollegiate competition:** 12% of students participate. Baseball (M), basketball (M,W), cross-country (M,W), golf (M,W), soccer (M,W), tennis (M,W), volleyball (W). Member of NCAA Division III, Southern Collegiate Athletic Conference.
**Intramural and club sports:** 80% of students participate. Intramural basketball, billiards, bowling, flag football, golf, inner-tube water polo, racquetball,soccer, softball, swimming, tennis, track/field, ultimate frisbee, volleyball, walleyball, weight lifting. Men's club fencing, lacrosse, volleyball. Women's club fencing.

**ADMISSIONS. Academic basis for candidate selection** (in order of priority): Secondary school record, class rank, standardized test scores, essay, school's recommendation.
**Nonacademic basis for candidate selection:** Character and personality, extracurricular participation, particular talent or ability, geographical distribution, and alumni/ae relationship are considered.
**Requirements:** Graduation from secondary school is required; GED is accepted. 17 units and the following program of study are recommended: 4 units of English, 4 units of math, 3 units of science including 2 units of lab, 2 units of foreign language, 2 units of social studies, 1 unit of history, 1 unit of academic electives. Audition required of music and theatre program applicants. Portfolio required of art program applicants. SAT is required; ACT may be substituted. Campus visit and interview recommended. Off-campus interviews available with admissions and alumni representatives.
**Procedure:** Take SAT or ACT by December of 12th year. Visit college for interview by January of 12th year. Suggest filing application by January 1. Application deadline is February 15. Notification of admission by April 1. Reply is required by May 1. $100 nonrefundable tuition deposit. $100 nonrefundable room deposit. Freshmen accepted for terms other than fall.
**Special programs:** Admission may be deferred one year. Credit and/or placement may be granted through CEEB Advanced Placement exams for scores of 4 or higher. Credit and/or placement may be granted through CLEP subject exams. Credit and placement may be granted through challenge exams. Early decision program. In fall 1993, 167 applied for early decision and 132 were accepted. Deadline for applying for early decision is November 1 and January 1. Early entrance/early admission program. Concurrent enrollment program.
**Transfer students:** Transfer students accepted for terms other than fall. In fall 1993, 9% of all new students were transfers into all classes. 107 transfer applications were received, 59 were accepted. Application deadline is June 1 for fall; December 1 for spring. Minimum 3.0 GPA recommended. Lowest course grade accepted is "C." Maximum number of transferable credits is 90 semester hours. At least 30 semester hours must be completed at the university to receive degree.
**Admissions contact:** John W. Lind, M.A., Vice-President for Enrollment Management. 512 863-1200, 800 252-3166.

**FINANCIAL AID. Available aid:** Pell grants, SEOG, state grants, school scholarships and grants, private scholarships and grants, academic merit scholarships, and aid for undergraduate foreign students. Perkins Loans (NDSL), PLUS, Stafford Loans (GSL), state loans, school loans, private loans, and SLS. Knight Tuition Plans and AMS. Cost Stabilization Plan.
**Financial aid statistics:** 23% of aid is not need-based. In 1993-94, 92% of all undergraduate applicants received aid; 88% of freshman applicants. Average amounts of aid awarded freshmen: Scholarships and grants, $7,427; loans, $2,716.
**Supporting data/closing dates:** FAFSA: Priority filing date is March 1; deadline is March 15. School's own aid application: Deadline is March 15. Notification of awards on rolling basis.
**Financial aid contact:** Sonje Johnson, Director of Financial Aid. 512 863-1259.

**STUDENT EMPLOYMENT.** College Work/Study Program. Institutional employment. 41% of full-time undergraduates work on campus during school year. Students may expect to earn an average of $1,400 during school year. Off-campus part-time employment opportunities rated "good."

**COMPUTER FACILITIES.** 170 IBM/IBM-compatible and Macintosh/Apple microcomputers; 30 are networked. Students may access Sequent minicomputer/mainframe systems, BITNET, Internet. Residence halls may be equipped with stand-alone microcomputers. Client/LAN operating systems include Apple/Macintosh. Computer languages and software packages include APL, Assembler, BASIC, C, COBOL, FORTRAN, ImSL, INGRES, LISP, Oracle, Pascal, SSPS. Computer facilities are available to all students.
**Fees:** None.
**Hours:** 8 AM-midn. in labs; 24 hours in residence halls.

**GRADUATE CAREER DATA.** Graduate school percentages: 5% enter law school. 7% enter medical school. 1% enter dental school. 5% enter graduate business programs. 11% enter graduate arts and sciences programs. 2% enter theological school/seminary. Highest graduate school enrollments: U of Texas at Austin. 35% of graduates choose careers in business and industry.

**PROMINENT ALUMNI/AE.** Ernesto Nieto, founder and executive director, National Hispanic Institute; Ann Cochran, civil court judge, Houston; Joseph Sneed, judge, U.S. Court of Appeals, San Francisco.

## Stephen F. Austin State University

**Nacogdoches, TX 75962-3051** **409 568-2011**

**1993-94 Costs.** Tuition: $780 (state residents), $4,860 (out-of-state). Room & board: $3,602. Fees, books, misc. academic expenses (school's estimate): $985.
**Enrollment.** Undergraduates: 4,499 men, 5,352 women (full-time). Freshman class: 5,965 applicants, 4,453 accepted, 2,272 enrolled. Graduate enrollment: 627 men, 726 women.
**Test score averages/ranges.** Average SAT scores: 413 verbal, 467 math. Average ACT scores: 21 composite.
**Faculty.** 412 full-time; 275 part-time. 70% of faculty holds highest degree in specific field. Student/faculty ratio: 21 to 1.
**Selectivity rating.** Less competitive.

**PROFILE.** Stephen F. Austin State, founded in 1923, is a public, comprehensive university. Programs are offered through the Schools of Applied Arts and Sciences, Business, Education, Fine Arts, Forestry, Liberal Arts, and Sciences and Mathematics. Its 430-acre campus is located in Nacogdoches, north of Houston.

**Accreditation:** SACS. Professionally accredited by the American Assembly of Collegiate Schools of Business, the American Home Economics Association, the Council on Social Work Education, the National Association of Schools of Music, the National Council for Accreditation of Teacher Education, the Society of American Foresters.
**Religious orientation:** Stephen F. Austin State University is nonsectarian; no religious requirements.
**Library:** Collections totaling over 571,216 volumes, 3,995 periodical subscriptions, and 640,986 microform items.
**Special facilities/museums:** Language lab, farms of 200 and 280 acres, experimental forest, museum.
**Athletic facilities:** Indoor/outdoor swimming pool, basketball, handball, and tennis courts, softball and football fields, weight room, archery range, all-weather track.

**STUDENT BODY. Undergraduate profile:** 99% are state residents; 40% are transfers. 1% Asian-American, 6% Black, 3% Hispanic, 1% Native American, 89% White. Average age of undergraduates is 20.
**Freshman profile:** 1% of freshmen who took SAT scored 700 or over on verbal, 1% scored 700 or over on math; 3% scored 600 or over on verbal, 7% scored 600 or over on math; 14% scored 500 or over on verbal, 39% scored 500 or over on math; 57% scored 400 or over on verbal, 80% scored 400 or over on math; 100% scored 300 or over on verbal, 100% scored 300 or over on math. 3% of freshmen who took ACT scored 30 or over on composite; 38% scored 24 or over on composite; 90% scored 18 or over on composite; 100% scored 12 or over on composite. 70% of accepted applicants took SAT; 50% took ACT. 95% of freshmen come from public schools.
**Undergraduate achievement:** 64% of fall 1992 freshmen returned for fall 1993 term. 40% of entering class graduated. 15% of students who completed a degree program went on to graduate study within five years.
**Foreign students:** 12 students are from out of the country. Eight countries represented in all.

**PROGRAMS OF STUDY. Degrees:** B.A., B.Appl.Arts/Sci., B.Bus.Admin., B.F.A., B.Mus., B.S., B.S.Agri., B.S.Ed., B.S.Forestry, B.S.Home Econ., B.S.Nurs., B.S.Rehab., B.Soc.Work.
**Majors:** Accounting, Agriculture, Applied Arts/Sciences, Art, Biology, Business/Data Processing, Chemistry, Communication, Computer Science, Criminal Justice, Economics, Elementary Education, English, Environmental Science, Finance, Forest Game Management, Forest Management, Forest Range Management, Forest Recreation Management, Forestry, General Business, Geography, Geology, Health/Physical Education, History, Home Economics, Management, Marketing, Mathematical Statistics, Modern Languages, Music, Nursing, Office Administration, Philosophy, Physics, Political Science, Psychology, Secondary Education, Social Work, Sociology, Special Education, Theatre.
**Distribution of degrees:** The majors with the highest enrollment are business, education, and liberal arts; forestry, applied arts/sciences, and fine arts have the lowest.
**Requirements:** General education requirement.
**Academic regulations:** Minimum 2.0 GPA required for graduation.
**Special:** Minors offered in most majors and in anthropology, dance, and photography. Double majors. Graduate school at which undergraduates may take graduate-level courses. Preprofessional programs in pharmacy, dentistry, architecture, engineering, hospital administration, medical fields, nursing, and physical therapy. Teacher certification in early childhood, elementary, secondary, special education, and bilingual/bicultural education. ROTC.
**Honors:** Phi Beta Kappa.
**Academic Assistance:** Remedial reading, writing, math, and study skills. Nonremedial tutoring.

**STUDENT LIFE. Housing:** All unmarried students under age 21 must live on campus unless living near campus with relatives. Coed, women's, and men's dorms. School-owned/operated apartments. On-campus married-student housing. 35% of students live in college housing.
**Services and counseling/handicapped student services:** Placement services. Health service. Counseling services for minority, military, veteran, and older students. Personal and psychological counseling. Career and academic guidance services. Physically disabled student services. Learning disabled services. Notetaking services. Tape recorders. Tutors. Reader services for the blind.
**Campus organizations:** Undergraduate student government. Student newspaper (Pine Log, published biweekly). Yearbook. Radio and TV stations. Drama and musical groups, political and service organizations. 16 fraternities, 12 chapter houses; nine sororities, six chapter houses. 11% of men join a fraternity. 11% of women join a sorority.
**Religious organizations:** Religious groups.
**Minority/foreign student organizations:** Minority organizations.

**ATHLETICS. Physical education requirements:** Four credits/semester of physical education required.
**Intercollegiate competition:** 4% of students participate. Baseball (M), basketball (M,W), cheerleading (M,W), cross-country (M,W), football (M), golf (M), softball (W), track (outdoor) (M,W), track and field (indoor) (M,W), volleyball (W). Member of NCAA Division I, NCAA Division I-AA for football, Southland Conference.
**Intramural and club sports:** Intramural archery, badminton, basketball, flag football, golf, handball, racquetball, softball, swimming, tennis, track/field, volleyball, weight lifting, wrestling.

**ADMISSIONS. Academic basis for candidate selection** (in order of priority): Class rank, standardized test scores, secondary school record.
**Requirements:** Graduation from secondary school is required; GED is not accepted. No specific distribution of secondary school units required. Minimum composite ACT score of 19 (combined SAT score of 800) and rank in top half of secondary school class or minimum composite ACT score of 21 (combined SAT score of 900) and rank in the top sixty percent of secondary school class required. Prep program. ACT is required; SAT may be substituted. Campus visit and interview recommended. No off-campus interviews.
**Procedure:** Take SAT or ACT by June of 12th year. Suggest filing application by April 1; no deadline. Notification of admission on rolling basis. $50 room deposit, refundable until July 15. Freshmen accepted for terms other than fall.
**Special programs:** Admission may be deferred one semester. Credit and/or placement may be granted through CEEB Advanced Placement exams for scores of 3 or higher. Credit and placement may be granted through challenge exams and military and life experience. Early entrance/early admission program. Concurrent enrollment program.
**Transfer students:** Transfer students accepted for terms other than fall. In fall 1993, 40% of all new students were transfers into all classes. 2,608 transfer applications were received. Application deadline is April 1 for fall; November 15 for spring. Minimum 2.0 GPA required. Lowest course grade accepted is "D." At least 42 semester hours must be completed at the university to receive degree.
**Admissions contact:** Dennis Jones, Ph.D., Senior Associate for Admissions and Records. 409 568-2504.

**FINANCIAL AID. Available aid:** Pell grants, SEOG, state scholarships and grants, school scholarships, private scholarships, ROTC scholarships, academic merit scholarships, and athletic scholarships. Perkins Loans (NDSL), PLUS, Stafford Loans (GSL), state loans, school loans, and SLS. Tuition Plan Inc.
**Financial aid statistics:** 37% of aid is not need-based. In 1993-94, 78% of all undergraduate applicants received aid; 51% of freshman applicants.
**Supporting data/closing dates:** FAFSA: Priority filing date is June 1. School's own aid application: Priority filing date is June 1. Income tax forms: Accepted on rolling basis. Notification of awards on rolling basis.
**Financial aid contact:** Bob Lawson, Senior Associate for Financial Aid. 409 568-2403.

**STUDENT EMPLOYMENT.** College Work/Study Program. Institutional employment. 10% of full-time undergraduates work on campus during school year. Students may expect to earn an average of $2,500 during school year. Freshmen are discouraged from working during their first term. Off-campus part-time employment opportunities rated "fair."

**COMPUTER FACILITIES.** 1,400 IBM/IBM-compatible and Macintosh/Apple microcomputers; 250 are networked. Students may access Digital, IBM, SUN minicomputer/mainframe systems, BITNET, Internet. Residence halls may be equipped with stand-alone microcomputers, networked terminals, modems. Computer facilities are available to all students.
**Fees:** None.

## Sul Ross State University

**Alpine, TX 79832** **915 837-8011**

**1993-94 Costs.** Tuition: $624 (state residents), $3,888 (out-of-state). Room: $1,350. Board: $1,570. Fees, books, misc. academic expenses (school's estimate): $1,050.
**Enrollment.** Undergraduates: 726 men, 651 women (full-time). Freshman class: 293 enrolled. Graduate enrollment: 269 men, 284 women.
**Test score averages/ranges.** Average SAT scores: 340 verbal, 380 math. Range of SAT scores of middle 50%: 280-380 verbal, 330-440 math. Average ACT scores: 17 English, 16 math, 17 composite. Range of ACT scores of middle 50%: 13-19 English, 14-18 math.
**Faculty.** 74 full-time; 11 part-time. 67% of faculty holds highest degree in specific field. Student/faculty ratio: 20 to 1.
**Selectivity rating.** Noncompetitive.

**PROFILE.** Sul Ross State, founded in 1920, is a public, comprehensive university. Programs are offered through the Divisions of Business Administration, Fine Arts, Liberal Arts, Range Animal Science, Science, and Teacher Education, and the Graduate School. Its 600-acre campus is located in the Alpine, southeast of El Paso.

**Accreditation:** SACS. Professionally accredited by the American Veterinary Medical Association.
**Religious orientation:** Sul Ross State University is nonsectarian; no religious requirements.
**Library:** Collections totaling over 244,000 volumes, 1,950 periodical subscriptions, and 399,443 microform items.

**Special facilities/museums:** Museum, range animal science ranch, planetarium, observatory, scanning electron microscope, automated electron probe microanalyzer, computer controlled x-ray fluorescence analyzer.
**Athletic facilities:** Field house, weight room, gymnasium, baseball and football fields, track, swimming pool.

**STUDENT BODY. Undergraduate profile:** 98% are state residents; 38% are transfers. 3% Black, 39% Hispanic, 56% White, 2% Other. Average age of undergraduates is 24.
**Freshman profile:** 44% of accepted applicants took SAT; 63% took ACT. 98% of freshmen come from public schools.
**Undergraduate achievement:** 41% of fall 1991 freshmen returned for fall 1992 term. 6% of entering class graduated.
**Foreign students:** Nine students are from out of the country. Countries represented include Argentina, China, Guatemala, Japan, Mexico, and Qatar; eight in all.

**PROGRAMS OF STUDY. Degrees:** B.A., B.Bus.Admin., B.F.A., B.S.
**Majors:** Accounting, Animal Health Management, Animal Science, Art, Biology, Business Administration, Business Administration/Accounting, Business Administration/Finance, Business Administration/Marketing, Business Administration/Off Systems, Chemistry, Communication, Criminal Justice, Education, English, Geology, History, Industrial Technology, Interdisciplinary Studies, Kinesiology/Sports, Marketing, Mathematics, Meat Industry Management, Music, Political Science, Psychology, Range/Equine Science, Range Science/Agribusiness, Range/Wildlife Management, Social Science, Spanish, Theatre.
**Distribution of degrees:** The majors with the highest enrollment are education and business administration; chemistry, geology, and political science have the lowest.
**Requirements:** General education requirement.
**Academic regulations:** Minimum 2.0 GPA must be maintained.
**Special:** Minors offered in all majors except interdisciplinary studies and in computer science, economics, physics, and sociology. One-year certificate program in vocational nursing; two-year programs in animal health, farrier, and meat technologies. Courses offered in astronomy, Bible, bilingual education, geography, journalism, linguistics, and philosophy. Associate's degrees offered. Internships. Graduate school at which undergraduates may take graduate-level courses. Preprofessional programs in law, medicine, veterinary science, pharmacy, and dentistry. Teacher certification in early childhood, elementary, secondary, special education, and bilingual/bicultural education. Certification in specific subject areas. Study-travel program in Europe.
**Honors:** Honor societies.
**Academic Assistance:** Remedial reading, writing, math, and study skills. Nonremedial tutoring.

**STUDENT LIFE. Housing:** All students under age 20 with less than 45 semester hours completed must live on campus unless living with family. Coed and men's dorms. School-owned/operated apartments. On-campus married-student housing. 34% of students live in college housing.
**Social atmosphere:** According to the student newspaper, "SRSU is located in a small town ranching area, two hours form Big Bend National Park. There is not much organized activity, but local bars are popular and students who love the mountains, desert, and outdoor activities thrive here." Students tend to hang out at the University Center, Terlingua, and the Alpine Civic Center. The Non-Traditional Students Association, Program Council, and the Student Association Senate are influential groups on campus. Some of the favorite events during the school year include Homecoming, basketball games, summer outdoor theatre, and NIRA rodeo.
**Services and counseling/handicapped student services:** Placement services. Health service. Personal and psychological counseling. Career and academic guidance services. Learning disabled services.
**Campus organizations:** Undergraduate student government. Student newspaper (Skyline, published once/week). Literary magazine. Yearbook. Stage and concert bands, orchestra, concert choir, drama, student council, Freshmen Leadership Program, College Republicans, Circle K, Hammer and Anvil, Law Student Association, Press Club, range and wildlife, music, and biology clubs, Sachems Society, 42 organizations in all.
**Religious organizations:** Baptist Student Center, Methodist Student Center, Newman Club.
**Minority/foreign student organizations:** Black Student's Association. International Student Association.

**ATHLETICS. Physical education requirements:** Two semesters of physical education required.
**Intercollegiate competition:** 10% of students participate. Baseball (M), basketball (M,W), cheerleading (M,W), football (M), tennis (M,W), track and field (outdoor) (M,W), volleyball (W). Member of NAIA, Texas Intercollegiate Athletic Association.
**Intramural and club sports:** 30% of students participate. Intramural basketball, flag football, soccer, softball, volleyball.

**ADMISSIONS. Academic basis for candidate selection** (in order of priority): Class rank, standardized test scores, secondary school record.
**Requirements:** Graduation from secondary school is required; GED is accepted. 21 units and the following program of study are required: 4 units of English, 3 units of math, 2 units of science, 1 unit of social studies, 2 units of history, 9 units of academic electives. Minimum combined SAT score of 800 (composite ACT score of 20) or rank in top half of secondary school class required. Conditional admission possible for applicants not meeting standard requirements. SAT or ACT is required. Campus visit and interview recommended. Off-campus interviews available with an admissions representative.
**Procedure:** Take SAT or ACT by spring of 12th year. Visit college for interview by spring of 12th year. Suggest filing application by July 31. Notification of admission on rolling basis. No set date by which applicants must accept offer. $75 room deposit, refundable until August 1. Freshmen accepted for terms other than fall.
**Special programs:** Admission may be deferred one semester. Credit may be granted through CEEB Advanced Placement for scores of 3 or higher. Credit may be granted through CLEP general and subject exams, DANTES and challenge exams, and military experience. Early entrance/early admission program.
**Transfer students:** Transfer students accepted for terms other than fall. In fall 1992, 38% of all new students were transfers into all classes. Minimum 2.0 GPA required. Lowest course grade accepted is "D." Maximum number of transferable credits is 66 semester credit hours. At least 33 semester credit hours must be completed at the university to receive degree.
**Admissions contact:** Dorothy M. Leavitt, M.A., Director of Admissions. 915 837-8052.

**FINANCIAL AID. Available aid:** Pell grants, SEOG, state scholarships and grants, school scholarships, private scholarships, and academic merit scholarships. Perkins Loans (NDSL), PLUS, Stafford Loans (GSL), state loans, school loans, and SLS. Deferred payment plan.
**Supporting data/closing dates:** FAFSA/FAF/FFS: Priority filing date is May 1; accepted on rolling basis. Notification of awards on rolling basis.
**Financial aid contact:** Kathy Hibbert, M.A., Director of Financial Aid. 915 837-8055.

**STUDENT EMPLOYMENT.** College Work/Study Program. Institutional employment. 20% of full-time undergraduates work on campus during school year. Students may expect to earn an average of $2,000 during school year. Off-campus part-time employment opportunities rated "fair."

**COMPUTER FACILITIES.** 80 IBM/IBM-compatible microcomputers; 52 are networked. Computer languages and software packages include BASIC, C, dBASE, FORTRAN, Pascal, SPSS, SuperCalc, WordPerfect. Computer facilities are available to all students.
**Fees:** $18 computer fee per semester.
**Hours:** 8 AM-midn. (M-Th).

**PROMINENT ALUMNI/AE.** Dan Blocker, actor; Norm Cash, professional baseball player; Albert Bustamante, U.S. congressman; Alan Ludden, television personality.

# Tarleton State University

**Stephenville, TX 76402 — 817 968-9000**

**1994-95 Costs.** Tuition: $840 (state residents), $5,130 (out-of-state). Room: $1,192-$1,774. Board: $1,214-$1,366. Fees, books, misc. academic expenses (school's estimate): $1,390.
**Enrollment.** Undergraduates: 2,520 men, 2,339 women (full-time). Freshman class: 1,175 applicants, 1,075 accepted, 997 enrolled. Graduate enrollment: 336 men, 489 women.
**Test score averages/ranges.** Average SAT scores: 390 verbal, 440 math. Range of SAT scores of middle 50%: 340-440 verbal, 380-510 math. Average ACT scores: 19 English, 19 math, 19 composite. Range of ACT scores of middle 50%: 17-22 English, 17-20 math.
**Faculty.** 219 full-time; 4 part-time. 62% of faculty holds highest degree in specific field. Student/faculty ratio: 21 to 1.
**Selectivity rating.** Less competitive.

**PROFILE.** Tarleton State, founded in 1899, is a public university. Programs are offered through the Colleges of Agriculture and Technology, Arts and Sciences, Business Administration, Education and Fine Arts, and Graduate Studies. Its 123-acre campus is located in Stephenville, in north-central Texas, 65 miles southwest of Fort Worth.

**Accreditation:** SACS. Professionally accredited by the Council on Social Work Education, the National Association of Schools of Music.
**Religious orientation:** Tarleton State University is nonsectarian; no religious requirements.
**Library:** Collections totaling over 225,000 volumes, 2,000 periodical subscriptions, and 550,000 microform items.
**Athletic facilities:** Gymnasium, swimming pool, basketball, racquetball, and tennis courts, weight room.

**STUDENT BODY. Undergraduate profile:** 99% are state residents; 12% are transfers. 1% Asian-American, 3% Black, 4% Hispanic, 92% White. Average age of undergraduates is 20.
**Freshman profile:** 1% of freshmen who took SAT scored 600 or over on verbal, 5% scored 600 or over on math; 9% scored 500 or over on verbal, 26% scored 500 or over on math; 40% scored 400 or over on verbal, 67% scored 400 or over on math; 90% scored 300 or over on verbal, 97% scored 300 or over on math. 55% of accepted applicants took SAT; 50% took ACT. 99% of freshmen come from public schools.
**Undergraduate achievement:** 55% of fall 1992 freshmen returned for fall 1993 term.
**Foreign students:** 23 students are from out of the country. Countries represented include the Bahamas, China, Germany, Mexico, and Thailand; 10 in all.

**PROGRAMS OF STUDY. Degrees:** B.A., B.Appl.Arts/Sci., B.Bus.Admin., B.F.A., B.Mus., B.S., B.Soc.Work.
**Majors:** Accounting, Agribusiness, Agricultural Economics, Agricultural Services/Development, Agriculture, Animal Production, Animal Science, Art, Biology, Business Education, Chemistry, Computer Information Systems, Criminal Justice, Distribution/Marketing, Earth Science, Economics, English, Exercise/Sports Studies, Fashion Merchandising, Finance, General Agriculture, General Business, General Management, Geology, Government, History, Home Economics, Horse Production/Management, Horticulture/Landscape Management, Human Resources Management, Hydrology/Water Resources, Industrial Major, Industrial Technology, Interdisciplinary Studies, Law Enforcement, Marketing, Mathematics, Mechanized Agriculture, Medical Technology, Music, Music Education, Physics, Plant/Soil Science, Range/Range Management, Social Work, Sociology, Spanish, Speech Communication, Technical Major, Theatre, Vocational Home Economics Education.
**Distribution of degrees:** The majors with the highest enrollment are agricultural services/development, interdisciplinary studies, and exercise/sports studies; chemistry, mathematics, and fashion merchandising have the lowest.
**Requirements:** General education requirement.
**Academic regulations:** Freshmen must maintain minimum 1.75 GPA; sophomores, 1.75 GPA; juniors, 2.0 GPA; seniors, 2.0 GPA.
**Special:** Minors offered in all majors. Associate's degrees offered. Double majors. Dual degrees. Graduate school at which undergraduates may take graduate-level courses. Pre-

professional programs in law, medicine, veterinary science, pharmacy, dentistry, and physical therapy. Cross-registration possible with other institutions. Teacher certification in early childhood, elementary, secondary, special education, and vo-tech education. Certification in specific subject areas. ROTC.

**Honors:** Phi Beta Kappa. Honors program. Honor societies.

**Academic Assistance:** Remedial reading, writing, math, and study skills. Nonremedial tutoring.

**STUDENT LIFE. Housing:** All unmarried students under age 21 with fewer than 45 hours must live on campus unless living with family. Coed, women's, and men's dorms. School-owned/operated apartments. 22% of students live in college housing.

**Social atmosphere:** "Tarleton, often referred to as Texas' best-kept secret, is a place for everybody," according to the student newspaper. The Student Center, The Cave, The Dodge House and Boztocks are popular places to hang out. Influential organizations are the Purple Poo, Greeks, Student Government, and Minority Affairs. Football games, the Cowboy Christmas Ball, NIRA rodeo, Fall and Spring concerts, and the Chili Cookoff are among the year's favorite events.

**Services and counseling/handicapped student services:** Placement services. Health service. Day care. Counseling services for minority and veteran students. Personal and psychological counseling. Career and academic guidance services. Religious counseling. Physically disabled student services. Learning disabled services. Notetaking services. Tutors. Reader services for the blind.

**Campus organizations:** Undergraduate student government. Student newspaper (J-Tac, published once/week). Literary magazine. Yearbook. Music organzations, departmental, professional, social, and spirit-interest groups, 104 organizations in all. Five fraternities, no chapter houses; three sororities, no chapter houses. 7% of men join a fraternity. 5% of women join a sorority.

**Religious organizations:** Baptist Student Union, Catholics on Campus, Church of Christ group, Fellowship of Christian Athletes, Lutheran Student Fellowship, Wesley Foundation, Fellowship of Christian Cowboys, Full Gospel Fellowship, Latter-Day Saints Students Association.

**Minority/foreign student organizations:** Los Tejonas de Tarleton, Alpha Phi Alpha, United Black Students Association. Chinese Student Association.

**ATHLETICS. Physical education requirements:** Two semesters of physical education required.

**Intercollegiate competition:** 6% of students participate. Baseball (M), basketball (M,W), cross-country (M,W), football (M), golf (M), tennis (M,W), track and field (outdoor) (M,W), volleyball (W). Member of Lone Star Conference, NCAA Division II.

**Intramural and club sports:** 43% of students participate. Intramural archery, basketball, billiards, fishing, flag football, golf, racquetball, rodeo, softball, tennis, volleyball.

**ADMISSIONS. Academic basis for candidate selection** (in order of priority): Standardized test scores, class rank.

**Requirements:** Graduation from secondary school is recommended; GED is accepted. 19 units and the following program of study recommended: 4 units of English, 3 units of math, 2 units of science, 2 units of social studies, 1 unit of history, 7 units of electives, including 2 units of academic electives. Minimum combined SAT score of 800 (or composite ACT score of 18), or advanced secondary school program, or rank in top half of secondary school class required. SAT or ACT is required. Campus visit recommended. No off-campus interviews.

**Procedure:** Suggest filing application by August 1; no deadline. Notification of admission on rolling basis. No set date by which applicants must accept offer. $100 room deposit, refundable until July 15. Freshmen accepted for terms other than fall.

**Special programs:** Credit may be granted through CEEB Advanced Placement for scores of 3 or higher. Credit may be granted through CLEP subject exams, challenge exams, and military and life experience. Early decision program. Deadline for applying for early decision is April 1. Early entrance/early admission program. Concurrent enrollment program.

**Transfer students:** Transfer students accepted for terms other than fall. In fall 1993, 12% of all new students were transfers into all classes. 927 transfer applications were received, 851 were accepted. Application deadline is August 5 for fall; January 9 for spring. Maximum number of transferable credits is 72 semester hours. At least 30 semester hours must be completed at the university to receive degree.

**Admissions contact:** Gail Mayfield, Director of Admissions. 817 968-9125.

**FINANCIAL AID. Available aid:** Pell grants, SEOG, state scholarships and grants, and private scholarships. Perkins Loans (NDSL), PLUS, Stafford Loans (GSL), state loans, and SLS.

**Financial aid statistics:** In 1993-94, 60% of all undergraduate applicants received aid; 30% of freshman applicants. Average amounts of aid awarded freshmen: Scholarships and grants, $1,000; loans, $2,625.

**Supporting data/closing dates:** FAFSA/FAF/FFS: Priority filing date is May 1. Notification of awards on rolling basis.

**Financial aid contact:** F.H. "Skip" Landis, Ph.D., Director of Financial Aid. 817 968-9070.

**STUDENT EMPLOYMENT.** College Work/Study Program. Institutional employment. 9% of full-time undergraduates work on campus during school year. Students may expect to earn an average of $3,000 during school year. Off-campus part-time employment opportunities rated "good."

**COMPUTER FACILITIES.** 118 IBM/IBM-compatible and Macintosh/Apple microcomputers. Students may access CDC Cyber minicomputer/mainframe systems, Internet. Computer languages and software packages include Assembler, C, COBOL, dBASE, Lotus 1-2-3, Pascal, WordPerfect. Computer facilities are available to all students.

**Fees:** $3 computer fee per hour.

**Hours:** 8 AM-10 PM (M-Th); 8 AM-5 PM (F).

# Texas A&M University, College Station

**College Station, TX 77843-1265 409 845-3211**

**1994-95 Costs.** Tuition: $840 (state residents), $5,130 (out-of-state). Room: $1,640. Board: $1,772. Fees, books, misc. academic expenses (school's estimate): $1,007.

**Enrollment.** Undergraduates: 17,627 men, 14,016 women (full-time). Freshman class: 14,474 applicants, 10,519 accepted, 6,392 enrolled. Graduate enrollment: 4,992 men, 2,432 women.

**Test score averages/ranges.** Average SAT scores: 491 verbal, 578 math. Range of SAT scores of middle 50%: 430-550 verbal, 510-640 math. Average ACT scores: 24 English, 25 math, 25 composite. Range of ACT scores of middle 50%: 21-27 English, 22-28 math.

**Faculty.** 1,939 full-time; 543 part-time. 84% of faculty holds doctoral degree. Student/faculty ratio: 17 to 1.

**Selectivity rating.** More competitive.

**PROFILE.** Texas A&M at College Station, founded in 1876, is a public, comprehensive university. Programs are offered through the Colleges of Agriculture, Architecture and Environmental Design, Business Administration, Education, Engineering, Geosciences, Liberal Arts, Medicine, Science, and Veterinary Medicine. Its 5,142-acre campus is located in College Station, 90 miles northwest of Houston.

**Accreditation:** SACS. Numerous professional accreditations.

**Religious orientation:** Texas A&M University, College Station is nonsectarian; no religious requirements.

**Library:** Collections totaling over 2,200,000 volumes, 13,000 periodical subscriptions, and 4,300,000 microform items.

**Special facilities/museums:** Art galleries, cyclotron, nuclear reactor, electron microscope, demonstration oil wells, super collider.

**Athletic facilities:** Field house, sports centers, athletic fields, tracks, swimming pools, basketball, handball, racquetball, tennis, and volleyball courts, rifle range, fitness trails, golf course, bowling lanes.

**STUDENT BODY. Undergraduate profile:** 94% are state residents; 24% are transfers. 4% Asian-American, 3% Black, 9% Hispanic, 82% White, 2% Other.

**Freshman profile:** 1% of freshmen who took SAT scored 700 or over on verbal, 11% scored 700 or over on math; 13% scored 600 or over on verbal, 43% scored 600 or over on math; 46% scored 500 or over on verbal, 82% scored 500 or over on math; 87% scored 400 or over on verbal, 98% scored 400 or over on math; 99% scored 300 or over on verbal, 100% scored 300 or over on math. 10% of freshmen who took ACT scored 30 or over on English, 15% scored 30 or over on math, 10% scored 30 or over on composite; 60% scored 24 or over on English, 60% scored 24 or over on math, 65% scored 24 or over on composite; 95% scored 18 or over on English, 97% scored 18 or over on math, 99% scored 18 or over on composite; 100% scored 12 or over on English, 100% scored 12 or over on math, 100% scored 12 or over on composite. 91% of accepted applicants took SAT; 51% took ACT. 92% of freshmen come from public schools.

**Undergraduate achievement:** 86% of fall 1992 freshmen returned for fall 1993 term. 24% of entering class graduated.

**Foreign students:** 536 students are from out of the country. Countries represented include China, India, Korea, Mexico, and Taiwan; 111 in all.

**PROGRAMS OF STUDY. Degrees:** B.A., B.Bus.Admin., B.Env.Design, B.Land.Arch., B.S.

**Majors:** Accounting, Aerospace Engineering, Agribusiness, Agricultural Development, Agricultural Economics, Agricultural Engineering, Agricultural Journalism, Agricultural Science, Agricultural Statistics, Agricultural Systems Management, Agronomy, Animal Science, Anthropology, Applied Mathematical Sciences, Basic Medical Science, Biochemistry, Bioengineering, Bioenvironmental Sciences, Biology, Biomedical Science, Botany, Business Analysis, Chemical Engineering, Chemistry, Civil Engineering, Computer Engineering, Computer Science, Computer Science/Engineering, Construction Science, Dairy Science, Earth Science, Economics, Electrical Engineering, Engineering Technology, English, Entomology, Environmental Design, Finance, Floriculture, Food Science/Technology, Forestry, French, Genetics, Geography, Geology, Geophysics, German, Health, History, Horticulture, Industrial Distribution, Industrial Education, Industrial Engineering, Interdisciplinary Studies, International Studies, Journalism, Kinesiology, Landscape Architecture, Management, Marine Biology, Marine Engineering, Marine Fisheries, Marine Sciences, Marine Transportation, Maritime Administration, Maritime Systems Engineering, Marketing, Mathematics, Mechanical Engineering, Meteorology, Microbiology, Modern Languages, Molecular/Cell Biology, Nuclear Engineering, Ocean Engineering, Petroleum Engineering, Philosophy, Physical Education, Physics, Plant/Soil Science, Political Science, Poultry Science, Psychology, Radiological Health Engineering, Range Science, Recreation/Parks, Scientific Nutrition, Sociology, Spanish, Speech Communication, Theatre Arts, Tourism, Veterinary Science, Wildlife/Fisheries Science, Zoology.

**Distribution of degrees:** The majors with the highest enrollment are accounting and psychology; entomology, marine engineering, and geophysics have the lowest.

**Requirements:** General education requirement.

**Academic regulations:** Minimum 2.0 GPA must be maintained.

**Special:** Minors required for graduation in all Liberal Arts programs. Students enrolled in Colleges of Liberal Arts, Geosciences, and Science may take engineering courses with approval of respective Deans. Double majors. Dual degrees. Independent study. Pass/fail grading option. Internships. Cooperative education programs. Graduate school at which undergraduates may take graduate-level courses. Preprofessional programs in law, medi-

cine, veterinary science, pharmacy, dentistry, theology, and optometry. 3-2 engineering program with Sam Houston State U. Exchange programs. Teacher certification in early childhood, elementary, secondary, special education, vo-tech, and bilingual/bicultural education. Study abroad in Belgium, Denmark, France, Germany, Mexico, Sweden, Switzerland, Taiwan, Turkey, and the United Kingdom. ROTC, NROTC, and AFROTC.
**Honors:** Honors program. Honor societies.
**Academic Assistance:** Remedial reading, writing, math, and study skills. Nonremedial tutoring.

**STUDENT LIFE. Housing:** Limited housing available. Freshmen receive priority. Coed, women's, and men's dorms. Sorority and fraternity housing. School-owned/operated apartments. On-campus married-student housing. 28% of students live in college housing.
**Social atmosphere:** Favorite gathering places include the clubs and resturants on the Northside strip: Duddley's Draw, the Dixie Chicken, and the Dry Bean Saloon. Football games are very popular, especially with rival U of Texas. "Being located in a small town surrounded by farms and the like have brought a definite country influence to A&M," reports the editor of the student newspaper. "However, with more students coming from big cities, the country influence is softening. Still, the campus holds to what is considered traditional Texas culture. Happily, that is also changing to include other cultures that do not find themselves within that culture."
**Services and counseling/handicapped student services:** Placement services. Health service. Counseling services for minority, military, veteran, and older students. Birth control, personal, and psychological counseling. Career and academic guidance services. Physically disabled student services. Learning disabled services. Notetaking services. Tape recorders. Tutors. Reader services for the blind.
**Campus organizations:** Undergraduate student government. Student newspaper (Battalion, published once/day). Yearbook. Radio and TV stations. Aggie Band, Singing Cadets, drama, debating, 708 organizations in all. 32 fraternities, 27 chapter houses; 15 sororities, 11 chapter houses. 10% of men join a fraternity. 12% of women join a sorority.
**Religious organizations:** Association of Baptist Students, Bahai club, Baptist Student Union, Campus Crusade for Christ, Christian Science Organization, Faith in Action, Hillel Club of the B'nai B'rith, Intervarsity Christian Fellowship.
**Minority/foreign student organizations:** Black Awareness Committee, Hispanic Journalists Association, Voices of Praise, Minority Liberal Arts Society, Minority Medical Students, U-Act. International Student Association, Malaysians in Aggieland, the Norsemen, Arab, Bolivian, Canadian, Indian, Japanese, Peruvian, Taiwanese, and Turkish student groups.

**ATHLETICS. Physical education requirements:** Four semesters of physical education required.
**Intercollegiate competition:** 7% of students participate. Baseball (M), basketball (M,W), cross-country (M,W), diving (M,W), football (M), golf (M,W), riflery (M,W), soccer (W), softball (W), swimming (M,W), tennis (M,W), track (indoor) (M,W), track (outdoor) (M,W), track and field (indoor) (M,W), track and field (outdoor) (M,W), volleyball (W). Member of NCAA Division I, Southwest Athletic Conference.
**Intramural and club sports:** 40% of students participate. Men's club Alpine skiing, archery, bowling, boxing, canoeing, cheerleading, cycling, fencing, field hockey, gymnastics, handball, horsemanship, lacrosse, martial arts, Nordic skiing, polo, racquetball, rifle, rodeo, rugby, sailing, soccer, softball, squash, ultimate frisbee, volleyball, water polo, water skiing, weight lifting, wrestling. Women's club Alpine skiing, archery, bowling, canoeing, cheerleading, crew, cycling, fencing, field hockey, gymnastics, handball, horsemanship, lacrosse, martial arts, Nordic skiing, polo, racquetball, rifle, rodeo, rugby, sailing, soccer, ultimate frisbee, volleyball, water polo, water skiing, weight lifting, wrestling.

**ADMISSIONS. Academic basis for candidate selection** (in order of priority): Secondary school record, class rank, standardized test scores.
**Nonacademic basis for candidate selection:** Extracurricular participation is emphasized. Character and personality, particular talent or ability, and alumni/ae relationship are considered.
**Requirements:** Graduation from secondary school is required; GED is not accepted. 16 units and the following program of study are required: 4 units of English, 3.5 units of math, 2 units of lab science, 2.5 units of social studies, 4 units of academic electives. Admission based on secondary school class rank, test scores, and secondary school record. Texas applicants are given priority. Conditional admission possible for applicants not meeting standard requirements. SAT or ACT is required. ACH recommended. Campus visit recommended.
**Procedure:** Take SAT or ACT by December of 12th year. Take ACH by May of 12th year. Suggest filing application by February 1. Application deadline is March 1. Notification of admission on rolling basis. Reply is required by May 1. $200 room deposit, refundable until May 1. Freshmen accepted for terms other than fall.
**Special programs:** Admission may be deferred one year. Credit may be granted through CEEB Advanced Placement for scores of 3 or higher. Credit may be granted through CLEP subject exams, ACT PEP and DANTES exams, and military experience. Credit and placement may be granted through challenge exams. Early entrance/early admission program. Concurrent enrollment program.
**Transfer students:** Transfer students accepted for terms other than fall. In fall 1993, 24% of all new students were transfers into all classes. 4,212 transfer applications were received, 2,698 were accepted. Application deadline is March 1 for fall; November 1 for spring. Minimum 2.0 GPA required. Lowest course grade accepted is "D." At least 30 semester hours must be completed at the university to receive degree.
**Admissions contact:** Gary R. Engelgau, M.A., M.B.A., Executive Director of Admissions. 409 845-3741.

**FINANCIAL AID. Available aid:** Pell grants, SEOG, state scholarships and grants, school scholarships and grants, ROTC scholarships, academic merit scholarships, athletic scholarships, and aid for undergraduate foreign students. Two-year transfer scholarship. Perkins Loans (NDSL), PLUS, Stafford Loans (GSL), Health Professions Loans, state loans, school loans, and SLS. Deferred payment plan.
**Financial aid statistics:** 68% of aid is not need-based. In 1993-94, 86% of all undergraduate applicants received aid; 79% of freshman applicants. Average amounts of aid awarded freshmen: Scholarships and grants, $3,725; loans, $3,205.
**Supporting data/closing dates:** FAFSA/FAF/FFS: Priority filing date is April 15. School's own aid application: Priority filing date is April 15. State aid form: Priority filing date is April 15. Notification of awards begins May 1.
**Financial aid contact:** Don Engelage, M.A., Director of Financial Aid. 409 845-3236.

**STUDENT EMPLOYMENT.** College Work/Study Program. Institutional employment. 22% of full-time undergraduates work on campus during school year. Students may expect to earn an average of $1,740 during school year. Off-campus part-time employment opportunities rated "good."

**COMPUTER FACILITIES.** 1,017 IBM/IBM-compatible and Macintosh/Apple microcomputers; 500 are networked. Students may access Cray, Digital, IBM minicomputer/mainframe systems, BITNET, Internet. Residence halls may be equipped with networked terminals. Client/LAN operating systems include UNIX/XENIX/AIX. Computer languages and software packages include C, COBOL, FORTRAN, LISP, SAS, SPSS, UNIX. Computer facilities are available to all students.
**Fees:** $5 computer fee per credit hour; included in tuition/fees.
**Hours:** 24 hours.

**PROMINENT ALUMNI/AE.** Henry Cisneros, Secretary of Housing and Urban Development; Marvin Runyon, Postmaster General; Gerald Garcia, editor, *The Houston Post*; Tom DeFrank, White House correspondent, *Newsweek*; Lyle Lovett, singer and actor.

# Texas A&M University at Galveston

**Galveston, TX 77553** **409 740-4400**

**1994-95 Costs.** Tuition: $800 (state residents), $3,800 (out-of-state). Room & board: $3,378. Fees, books, misc. academic expenses (school's estimate): $1,500.
**Enrollment.** Undergraduates: 654 men, 497 women (full-time). Freshman class: 680 applicants, 537 accepted, 189 enrolled.
**Test score averages/ranges.** Average SAT scores: 456 verbal, 532 math. Average ACT scores: 22 English, 23 math, 23 composite.
**Faculty.** 56 full-time; 43 part-time. 64% of faculty holds doctoral degree. Student/faculty ratio: 14 to 1.
**Selectivity rating.** Less competitive.

**PROFILE.** Texas A&M at Galveston, founded in 1962, is a public university of marine- and maritime-related areas. Its 100-acre campus is located on the harbor in Galveston, on the Gulf Coast 50 miles southwest of Houston.

**Accreditation:** SACS. Professionally accredited by the Accreditation Board for Engineering and Technology.
**Religious orientation:** Texas A&M University at Galveston is nonsectarian; no religious requirements.
**Library:** Collections totaling over 44,686 volumes, 802 periodical subscriptions, and 52,984 microform items.
**Special facilities/museums:** Several boats and ships.
**Athletic facilities:** Tennis and volleyball courts, swimming pool, football and multi-purpose fields, weight room.

**STUDENT BODY. Undergraduate profile:** 68% are state residents; 55% are transfers. 1% Asian-American, 2% Black, 7% Hispanic, 1% Native American, 88% White, 1% Other. Average age of undergraduates is 21.
**Freshman profile:** Majority of accepted applicants took SAT.
**Undergraduate achievement:** 63% of fall 1991 freshmen returned for fall 1992 term. 8% of entering class graduated.
**Foreign students:** 12 students are from out of the country. Countries represented include Malaysia, Panama, and Saudi Arabia; 11 in all.

**PROGRAMS OF STUDY. Degrees:** B.S.
**Majors:** Marine Biology, Marine Engineering, Marine Fisheries, Marine Sciences, Marine Transportation, Maritime Administration, Maritime Systems Engineering.
**Distribution of degrees:** The majors with the highest enrollment are marine biology and maritime administration.
**Requirements:** General education requirement.
**Academic regulations:** Minimum 2.0 GPA must be maintained.
**Special:** Options offered in marine biology, marine engineering, marine sciences, and marine transportation; training leads to qualification for U.S. Coast Guard license as third mate or third assistant engineer. Classes are held at Mitchell Campus on Pelican Island and at Fort Crockett Campus on Galveston Island. Training ship serves as floating classroom, lab, and dorm for Summer School at Sea Program, which allows recent secondary school graduates to earn credit while assisting crew in maintaining and operating ship. Double majors. Pass/fail grading option. Sea Semester. NROTC.
**Academic Assistance:** Remedial reading, writing, and math. Nonremedial tutoring.

**STUDENT LIFE. Housing:** All unmarried, nonveteran students must live on campus unless living with family in Galveston County. Coed dorms. 49% of students live in college housing.
**Social atmosphere:** According to the editor of the student newspaper, Texas A&M is a relatively small school (around 975 students), it is very personal; everyone gets to know each other, including the professors. Off campus, Galveston is very diverse for culture and history. Influential groups at A&M include the Student Senate, the Sail Club, the Surf Club, and the Student Life Organization. Favorite events on campus are the Halloween Party, Christmas Ball, Mardi Gras (at Galveston), Dickens on the Strand, Spring Break, Surf Contest, and Springfest. Students like to gather at the Mary Moody Student Center, the Old Galveston Club, and Yaga's Cafe.
**Services and counseling/handicapped student services:** Placement services. Health service. Counseling services for minority and veteran students. Personal counseling. Career and academic guidance services.

**Campus organizations:** Undergraduate student government. Student newspaper (Nautilus, published once/week). Literary magazine. Yearbook. Dorm association, outdoor recreation club, professional engineering society, diving and sailing clubs, sportsmen's club, Student Advisory Committee, Corps of Cadets Drill Team, 25 organizations in all.
**Religious organizations:** United Methodist Ministry.
**Minority/foreign student organizations:** Hispanic student club.

**ATHLETICS. Physical education requirements:** None.
**Intercollegiate competition:** 4% of students participate. Volleyball (M,W).
**Intramural and club sports:** 8% of students participate. Intramural basketball, flag football, softball, volleyball. Men's club lacrosse, sailing.

**ADMISSIONS. Academic basis for candidate selection** (in order of priority): Secondary school record, class rank, standardized test scores.
**Requirements:** Graduation from secondary school is required; GED is accepted. 18 units and the following program of study are required: 4 units of English, 3.5 units of math, 2 units of lab science, 2 units of foreign language, 2.5 units of social studies, 4 units of electives including 2 units of academic electives. Minimum combined SAT score of 1000 and rank in top quarter of secondary school class required. SAT or ACT is required. ACH recommended. Campus visit recommended. No off-campus interviews.
**Procedure:** Take SAT or ACT by May 1 of 12th year. Suggest filing application by July 1. Application deadline is September 1. Notification of admission on rolling basis. No set date by which applicants must accept offer. $200 room deposit, refundable until July 1. Freshmen accepted for terms other than fall.
**Special programs:** Admission may be deferred one year. Credit may be granted through CEEB Advanced Placement for scores of 4 or higher. Credit may be granted through CLEP subject exams, challenge exams, and military experience.
**Transfer students:** Transfer students accepted for terms other than fall. In fall 1992, 55% of all new students were transfers into all classes. 405 transfer applications were received, 285 were accepted. Application deadline is September 1 for fall; January 10 for spring. Minimum 2.25 GPA required. Lowest course grade accepted is "D." Maximum number of transferable credits is 66 semester hours. At least 30 semester hours must be completed at the university to receive degree.
**Admissions contact:** Su-Zan Harper, M.A., Admissions and Records Officer. 409 740-4415.

**FINANCIAL AID. Available aid:** Pell grants, SEOG, state scholarships and grants, school scholarships and grants, private scholarships, ROTC scholarships, and academic merit scholarships. Perkins Loans (NDSL), PLUS, Stafford Loans (GSL), state loans, private loans, and SLS.
**Financial aid statistics:** 15% of aid is not need-based. In 1992-93, 48% of all undergraduate applicants received aid; 54% of freshman applicants. Average amounts of aid awarded freshmen: Scholarships and grants, $1,240; loans, $2,700.
**Supporting data/closing dates:** FAFSA/FAF/FFS: Priority filing date is April 1. School's own aid application: Priority filing date is April 1. SAR: Priority filing date is April 1. Notification of awards begins April 15.
**Financial aid contact:** Stephen G. Peterson, Director of Financial Aid. 409 740-4417.

**STUDENT EMPLOYMENT.** College Work/Study Program. Institutional employment. 25% of full-time undergraduates work on campus during school year. Students may expect to earn an average of $850 during school year. Off-campus part-time employment opportunities rated "good."

**COMPUTER FACILITIES.** 75 IBM/IBM-compatible and Macintosh/Apple microcomputers. Students may access Prime minicomputer/mainframe systems. Residence halls may be equipped with modems. Computer languages and software packages include BASIC, C, COBOL, FORTRAN; CAD-CAM, publishing, spreadsheet, word processing programs. Computer facilities are available to all students.
**Fees:** $3 computer fee per semester hour; included in tuition/fees.

# Texas A&M University–Kingsville

**Kingsville, TX 78363** — **512 595-2111**

**1993-94 Costs.** Tuition: $1,092 (state residents), $4,356 (out-of-state). Room & board: $3,000. Fees, books, misc. academic expenses (school's estimate): $500.
**Enrollment.** Undergraduates: 2,302 men, 2,120 women (full-time). Freshman class: 2,047 applicants, 1,196 accepted, 977 enrolled. Graduate enrollment: 565 men, 609 women.
**Test score averages/ranges.** Average ACT scores: 17 composite.
**Faculty.** 83% of faculty holds highest degree in specific field. Student/faculty ratio: 18 to 1.
**Selectivity rating.** Less competitive.

**PROFILE.** Texas A&M at Kingsville is a public, comprehensive university. Founded as a teachers college in 1925, it gained its present status in 1967. Programs are offered through the Colleges of Agriculture and Home Economics, Arts and Sciences, Business Administration, Education, Engineering, and Graduate Studies. Its 250-acre main campus is located in Kingsville, 40 miles southwest of Corpus Christi.

**Accreditation:** SACS. Professionally accredited by the Accreditation Board for Engineering and Technology, the National Association of Schools of Music, the National Council for Accreditation of Teacher Education.
**Religious orientation:** Texas A&M University-Kingsville is nonsectarian; no religious requirements.
**Library:** Collections totaling over 461,408 volumes, 2,117 periodical subscriptions, and 253,667 microform items.
**Special facilities/museums:** History and art museum, deer research facility, citrus research center, college farm, biology/marine science site, robotics lab, planetarium, electron microscope.
**Athletic facilities:** Physical education center, swimming pool, bowling alley, football stadium, track, athletic fields, tennis courts.

**STUDENT BODY. Undergraduate profile:** 99% are state residents. 1% Asian-American, 3% Black, 68% Hispanic, 26% White, 2% Other. Average age of undergraduates is 21.
**Freshman profile:** Majority of accepted applicants took ACT.
**Undergraduate achievement:** 52% of fall 1992 freshmen returned for fall 1993 term. 38% of entering class graduated.
**Foreign students:** 262 students are from out of the country. Countries represented include Bangladesh, China, India, Japan, Mexico, and Qatar; 47 in all.

**PROGRAMS OF STUDY. Degrees:** B.A., B.Appl.Arts/Sci., B.Bus.Admin., B.F.A., B.Mus., B.S.
**Majors:** Accounting, Agribusiness, Agricultural Education, Animal Science, Applied Music, Art, Biology, Chemical Engineering, Chemistry, Civil Engineering, Communication, Communication Disorders, Computer Information Systems, Computer Science, Dietetics, Electrical Engineering, Engineering/Business, English, Fashion Merchandising, Finance, General Business Administration, Geography, Geology, History, Home Economics, Industrial Technology, Interior Design, International Business, Management, Marketing, Mathematics, Mechanical Engineering, Music Education, Natural Gas Engineering, Physics, Plant/Soil Science, Political Science, Psychology, Public Administration, Range/Wildlife Management, Real Estate, Restaurant Food Management, Sociology, Spanish, Theatre Arts.
**Distribution of degrees:** The majors with the highest enrollment are general business administration and psychology; applied arts and sciences and industrial technology have the lowest.
**Requirements:** General education requirement.
**Academic regulations:** Minimum 2.0 GPA must be maintained.
**Special:** Minors offered. Double majors. Internships. Cooperative education programs. Graduate school at which undergraduates may take graduate-level courses. Preprofessional programs in law, medicine, veterinary science, pharmacy, and dentistry. Teacher certification in early childhood, elementary, secondary, special education, and bilingual/bicultural education. Certification in specific subject areas. Study abroad in Mexico. ROTC.
**Honors:** Honor societies.
**Academic Assistance:** Remedial study skills. Nonremedial tutoring.

**STUDENT LIFE. Housing:** All unmarried students under age 21 with fewer than 60 semester hours must live on campus unless living with family. Coed, women's, and men's dorms. On-campus married-student housing. 19% of students live in college housing.
**Social atmosphere:** The university has "a quiet campus," according to one student. Favorite activities include football games, Homecoming, and trips to Gulf of Mexico beaches and Corpus Christi. Religious organizations are among the influential student groups on campus.
**Services and counseling/handicapped student services:** Placement services. Health service. Day care. Counseling services for minority, military, veteran, and older students. Birth control, personal, and psychological counseling. Career and academic guidance services. Physically disabled student services. Learning disabled services. Notetaking services. Tape recorders. Tutors. Reader services for the blind.
**Campus organizations:** Undergraduate student government. Student newspaper (South Texan, published once/week). Radio station. Band, mariachi group, theatre, Footlights Club, amateur radio club, horsemanship association, rodeo club, Young Democrats, Young Republicans, departmental groups. Six fraternities, three chapter houses; three sororities, no chapter houses.
**Religious organizations:** Christian Fellowship, Baptist, Catholic, Latter-Day Saints, and Muslim groups.
**Minority/foreign student organizations:** Black and Hispanic groups. Chinese, Indian, Malaysian, Nigerian, and Pakistani groups.

**ATHLETICS. Physical education requirements:** Four semesters of physical education required.
**Intercollegiate competition:** 2% of students participate. Baseball (M), basketball (M,W), cross-country (M,W), football (M), track and field (outdoor) (M,W), volleyball (W). Member of Lone Star Conference, NCAA Division II.
**Intramural and club sports:** Intramural basketball, bench press, bowling, cross-country, cycling, fencing, football, racquetball, soccer, softball, swimming, tennis, track and field, volleyball.

**ADMISSIONS. Academic basis for candidate selection** (in order of priority): Standardized test scores, class rank, secondary school record.
**Nonacademic basis for candidate selection:** Character and personality, extracurricular participation, and particular talent or ability are considered.
**Requirements:** Graduation from secondary school is recommended; GED is accepted. 21 units and the following program of study are required: 4 units of English, 2 units of math, 2 units of lab science, 2 units of social studies, 2 units of history, 9 units of electives. Minimum composite ACT score of 21 or rank in top quarter of secondary school class required. 4 units of math (2 algebra, 1 geometry, 1 precalculus) and 3 units of science required of engineering program applicants. Conditional admission possible for applicants not meeting standard requirements. SAT or ACT is required. Campus visit and interview recommended. Off-campus interviews available with an admissions representative.
**Procedure:** Take SAT or ACT by December of 12th year. Visit college for interview by March of 12th year. Suggest filing application by March; no deadline. Notification of admission on rolling basis. $100 refundable room deposit. Freshmen accepted for terms other than fall.
**Special programs:** Admission may be deferred two years. Credit may be granted through CEEB Advanced Placement for scores of 3 or higher. Credit and/or placement may be granted through CLEP subject exams. Credit may be granted through military experience. Credit and placement may be granted through challenge exams. Early entrance/early admission program. Concurrent enrollment program.
**Transfer students:** Transfer students accepted for terms other than fall. Application deadline is fourth class day of term for fall; fourth class day of term for spring. Minimum 2.0 GPA required. Lowest course grade accepted is "D." At least 30 semester hours must be completed at the university to receive degree.
**Admissions contact:** Joe Estrada, M.A., Director of Admissions. 512 595-2315.

**FINANCIAL AID. Available aid:** Pell grants, SEOG, state scholarships, school scholarships, private scholarships, ROTC scholarships, academic merit scholarships, and athletic scholarships. Perkins Loans (NDSL), PLUS, Stafford Loans (GSL), state loans, school loans, and SLS. Tuition Plan Inc.
**Financial aid statistics:** 10% of aid is not need-based. In 1993-94, 70% of all undergraduate applicants received aid; 70% of freshman applicants.
**Supporting data/closing dates:** FAFSA/FAF: Deadline is May 15. Income tax forms: Deadline is May 15. Notification of awards on rolling basis.
**Financial aid contact:** Arturo Pecos, M.A., Director of Financial Aid. 512 595-3911.

**STUDENT EMPLOYMENT.** College Work/Study Program. Institutional employment. Students may expect to earn an average of $999 during school year. Off-campus part-time employment opportunities rated "fair."

**COMPUTER FACILITIES.** 868 IBM/IBM-compatible and Macintosh/Apple microcomputers. Students may access IBM minicomputer/mainframe systems, BITNET, Internet, CompuServe. Client/LAN operating systems include Apple/Macintosh, DOS, OS/2, UNIX/XENIX/AIX, X-windows, Artisoft. Computer languages and software packages include C, COBOL, dBASE, FORTRAN, Pascal, Quattro, SAS, WordPerfect; 100 in all. Computer facilities are available to all students.
**Fees:** $5 computer fee per semester; included in tuition/fees.
**Hours:** Engineering lab: 7:30 AM-11 PM (M-F); 7:30 AM-7 PM (Sa); 12 PM-1 AM (Su). Other labs have varying hours.

**GRADUATE CAREER DATA.** Highest graduate school enrollments: Corpus Christi State U, North Texas State U, Texas A&M U, U of Texas at Edinburg. Companies and businesses that hire graduates: AMOCO, Exxon, K mart, Pillsbury, Shell Oil, U.S. Army Material Command, U.S. Department of Agriculture, U.S. Navy.

**PROMINENT ALUMNI/AE.** William Stevens, president, Exxon; Jim Hill, broadcaster; Armando Hinojosa, sculptor, named official state artist of Texas in 1983.

# Texas Christian University

**Fort Worth, TX 76129 — 817 921-7000**

**1994-95 Costs.** Tuition: $8,490. Room: $1,920. Board: $1,400. Fees, books, misc. academic expenses (school's estimate): $1,640.
**Enrollment.** Undergraduates: 2,103 men, 2,961 women (full-time). Freshman class: 4,095 applicants, 3,079 accepted, 1,195 enrolled. Graduate enrollment: 575 men, 523 women.
**Test score averages/ranges.** Range of SAT scores of middle 50%: 420-540 verbal, 460-600 math. Range of ACT scores of middle 50%: 21-27 composite.
**Faculty.** 322 full-time; 172 part-time. 93% of faculty holds highest degree in specific field. Student/faculty ratio: 14 to 1.
**Selectivity rating.** Competitive.

**PROFILE.** Texas Christian, founded in 1873, is a private, church-affiliated university. Programs are offered through the Colleges of Arts and Sciences, Fine Arts and Communication, and Nursing and the Schools of Business and Education. Its 237-acre campus is located three miles from downtown Fort Worth.

**Accreditation:** SACS. Professionally accredited by the Accrediting Council on Education in Journalism and Mass Communication, the American Assembly of Collegiate Schools of Business, the American Dietetic Association, the American Speech-Language-Hearing Association, the Association of Theological Schools, the Computing Sciences Accreditation Board, the Council on Social Work Education, the Foundation for Interior Design Education Research, the National Association of Schools of Music, the National Athletic Trainers Association, the National League for Nursing.
**Religious orientation:** Texas Christian University is affiliated with the Christian Church (Disciples of Christ); three semester hours of religion required.
**Library:** Collections totaling over 744,824 volumes, 3,637 periodical subscriptions, and 440,997 microform items.
**Special facilities/museums:** Tandy film library, language lab, TV studios, computer labs, Moncrief Meteorite collection.
**Athletic facilities:** Gymnasium, swimming pool, weight room, track, basketball, handball, racquetball, and tennis courts, athletic fields.

**STUDENT BODY. Undergraduate profile:** 74% are state residents; 19% are transfers. 2% Asian-American, 3% Black, 5% Hispanic, 86% White, 4% Other. Average age of undergraduates is 21.
**Freshman profile:** Majority of accepted applicants took SAT. 88% of freshmen come from public schools.
**Undergraduate achievement:** 79% of fall 1992 freshmen returned for fall 1993 term. 37% of entering class graduated. 21% of students who completed a degree program went on to graduate study within one year.
**Foreign students:** 203 students are from out of the country. Countries represented include Canada, China, Germany, Japan, Mexico, and Taiwan; 63 in all.

**PROGRAMS OF STUDY. Degrees:** B.A., B.Bus.Admin., B.F.A., B.Gen.Studies, B.Mus., B.Mus.Ed., B.S., B.S.Ed., B.S.Nurs., B.S.Phys.Ed.
**Majors:** Accounting, Art Education, Art History, Astronomy/Physics, Ballet, Ballet/Modern Dance, Biochemistry, Biology, Broadcast Journalism, Chemistry, Child Studies, Church Music, Communication Graphics, Communication in Human Relations, Computer Science, Coordinated Dietetics, Criminal Justice, Economics, Engineering, English, Environmental Earth Resources, Environmental Science, Fashion, Fashion Design, Fashion Merchandising, Fashion Promotion, Finance, Finance/Real Estate, Fitness Promotion, Food Management, French, General Studies, Geology, Habilitation of the Deaf, History, Instruction of Exceptional Students, Interior Design, Interior Merchandising, Journalism, Language Studies, Latin American Studies, Liberal Studies, Management, Marketing, Mathematics, Medical Technology, Modern Dance, Movement Science, Music, Music Education, Music History, Music Performance, Music Theory/Composition, Neuroscience, News/Editorial Journalism, Nursing, Nutrition, Philosophy, Physical Education, Physics, Piano Pedagogy, Political Science, Psychology, Public Relations/Advertising, Radio/Television/Film, Religion, Social Work, Sociology, Spanish, Speech Communication, Speech/Language Pathology, Sports/Recreational Leadership, Studio Art, Theatre Arts, Theatre/Television.
**Distribution of degrees:** The majors with the highest enrollment are psychology, marketing, and public relations/advertising; biochemistry, neuroscience, and Latin American studies have the lowest.
**Requirements:** General education requirement.
**Academic regulations:** Minimum 2.0 GPA required for graduation.
**Special:** Minors offered in some majors and in anthropology, art, Asian studies, classical studies, combined science, communication disorders, general business, German, Japanese, nutrition/dietetics, and Russian. Students may take minor or electives outside of their own school. Premajor program of advising through Center for Academic Services. Nine-month ranch management certificate programs with practical study on ranches in the Southwest. Artistic Diploma. Performer's Certificate in piano. Graduate Performer's Certificate in piano. Double majors. Dual degrees. Independent study. Accelerated study. Pass/fail grading option. Internships. Graduate school at which undergraduates may take graduate-level courses. Preprofessional programs in law, medicine, veterinary science, dentistry, optometry, osteopathy, and podiatry. 3-2 occupational therapy and engineering programs with Washington U. 3-2 M.B.A. program. Member of Southern Consortium and Higher Education Data Sharing (HEDS) Consortium. Washington Semester. Teacher certification in early childhood, elementary, secondary, and special education. Certification in specific subject areas. Study abroad in Australia, Austria, Costa Rica, the Czech Republic, England, France, Germany, Hungary, Indonesia, Italy, Japan, Mexico, Russia, Singapore, Slovakia, Spain, and Thailand. Exchange programs available in England and Mexico. ROTC and AFROTC.
**Honors:** Phi Beta Kappa. Honors program.
**Academic Assistance:** Nonremedial tutoring.

**STUDENT LIFE. Housing:** All unmarried freshmen under age 21 must live on campus unless living with family. Coed, women's, and men's dorms. Sorority and fraternity housing. 52% of students live in college housing.
**Social atmosphere:** The student newspaper reports that Greeks are active on campus. Campus-wide events include Hunger Week, "a week dedicated to hunger education and fund-raising that involves almost every campus organization." On campus, students frequent the Student Center Lounge and The Pit. Favorite off-campus spots include The University Pub and The Oui.
**Services and counseling/handicapped student services:** Placement services. Health service. Counseling services for minority, military, veteran, and older students. Birth control, personal, and psychological counseling. Career and academic guidance services. Religious counseling. Physically disabled student services. Learning disabled services. Tape recorders. Tutors. Reader services for the blind.
**Campus organizations:** Undergraduate student government. Student newspaper (Daily Skiff, published four times/week). Literary magazine. Yearbook. Radio and TV stations. A cappella and chapel choirs, band, stage band, lab band, string quartet, symphony orchestra, departmental, professional, and special-interest groups. 10 fraternities, eight chapter houses; 12 sororities, 10 chapter houses. 28% of men join a fraternity. 38% of women join a sorority.
**Religious organizations:** Baptist Student Union, Campus Crusade for Christ, Canterbury, Christian Science Organization, Disciple Student Network, Fellowship of Christian Athletes, Fellowship of Presbyterian Students, Catholic Community, Jewish Association, Wesley Foundation, Young Life.
**Minority/foreign student organizations:** Black Student Caucus, Korean American Student Association, Native American Student Association, Organization of Latin American Students, United Asian Community. Host Family Program, International Student Organization.

**ATHLETICS. Physical education requirements:** Two semester hours of physical education required.
**Intercollegiate competition:** 11% of students participate. Baseball (M), basketball (M,W), cross-country (M,W), diving (M,W), football (M), golf (M,W), riflery (W), soccer (M,W), swimming (M,W), tennis (M,W), track and field (indoor) (M,W), track and field (outdoor) (M,W). Member of NCAA Division I, Southwest Athletic Conference.
**Intramural and club sports:** Intramural basketball, field hockey, flag football, lacrosse, rugby, soccer, softball, track. Men's club fencing, high adventure, tae kwon do, volleyball, water polo, water skiing. Women's club lacrosse, volleyball.

**ADMISSIONS. Academic basis for candidate selection** (in order of priority): Secondary school record, class rank, standardized test scores, school's recommendation, essay.
**Nonacademic basis for candidate selection:** Character and personality and extracurricular participation are important. Particular talent or ability and alumni/ae relationship are considered.
**Requirements:** Graduation from secondary school is required; GED is not accepted. 15 units and the following program of study are required: 4 units of English, 3 units of math, 3 units of science including 1 unit of lab, 2 units of foreign language, 3 units of social studies. SAT is required; ACT may be substituted. Campus visit and interview recommended. Off-campus interviews available with an admissions representative.
**Procedure:** Take SAT or ACT by December of 12th year. Visit college for interview by February 15 of 12th year. Application deadline is February 15. Notification of admission by April 1. Reply is required by May 1. $125 nonrefundable tuition deposit. $100 room deposit, refundable until June 1. Freshmen accepted for terms other than fall.
**Special programs:** Admission may be deferred one year. Credit and/or placement may be granted through CEEB Advanced Placement exams for scores of 3 or higher. Credit may be granted through CLEP general exams, DANTES exams, and military experience. Credit and/or placement may be granted through CLEP subject exams. Credit and placement may be granted through challenge exams. Concurrent enrollment program.
**Transfer students:** Transfer students accepted for terms other than fall. In fall 1993, 19% of all new students were transfers into all classes. 723 transfer applications were received, 546 were accepted. Application deadline is August 1 for fall; December 1 for spring. Minimum 2.5 GPA recommended. Lowest course grade accepted is "C." Maximum number of transferable credits is 66 semester hours. At least 63 semester hours must be completed at the university to receive degree.

**Admissions contact:** Leo Munson, M.S., Dean of Admissions. 817 921-7490.

**FINANCIAL AID. Available aid:** Pell grants, SEOG, Federal Nursing Student Scholarships, state scholarships and grants, school scholarships and grants, private scholarships and grants, ROTC scholarships, academic merit scholarships, athletic scholarships, and aid for undergraduate foreign students. Church-related scholarships. Fine Arts Talent Scholarships. Extended education grants. Employee grants. Perkins Loans (NDSL), PLUS, Stafford Loans (GSL), NSL, state loans, school loans, private loans, and SLS. Tuition Plan Inc. and AMS. Institutional payment plan.
**Financial aid statistics:** 50% of aid is not need-based. In 1993-94, 60% of all undergraduate applicants received aid; 91% of freshman applicants. Average amounts of aid awarded freshmen: Scholarships and grants, $3,500; loans, $2,672.
**Supporting data/closing dates:** FAFSA: Priority filing date is May 1. Income tax forms: Priority filing date is May 1. Notification of awards begins April 2.
**Financial aid contact:** Emma Baker, M.S., Director of Financial Aid. 817 921-7858.

**STUDENT EMPLOYMENT.** College Work/Study Program. Institutional employment. 23% of full-time undergraduates work on campus during school year. Students may expect to earn an average of $1,500 during school year. Off-campus part-time employment opportunities rated "good."

**COMPUTER FACILITIES.** 324 IBM/IBM-compatible and Macintosh/Apple microcomputers; 300 are networked. Students may access Digital, IBM, SUN minicomputer/mainframe systems, BITNET, Internet. Residence halls may be equipped with networked microcomputers, networked terminals. Client/LAN operating systems include Apple/Macintosh, DOS, DEC, LocalTalk/AppleTalk. Computer languages and software packages include Ada, Autocad, BASIC, BMDP, C, COBOL, CompuStat, FORTRAN, Harvard Graphics, Lotus, MINITAB, PageMaker, Paradox, Pascal, SAS, SPSS, WordPerfect, Works; 35 in all. Computer facilities are available to all students.
**Fees:** None.

**GRADUATE CAREER DATA.** Graduate school percentages: 14% enter law school. 17% enter medical school. 13% enter graduate business programs.

**PROMINENT ALUMNI/AE.** John Roach, CEO, Tandy Corp.; Roger King, chief personnel officer, PepsiCo; Dr. James Cash, Jr., professor, Harvard U; Betty Lynn Buckley, actress; Bob Lilly, professional football player; Bob Shieffer, journalist.

# Texas College

**Tyler, TX 75702** **903 593-8311**

**1994-95 Costs.** Tuition: $3,500. Room: $900. Board: $1,530. Fees, books, misc. academic expenses (school's estimate): $820.
**Enrollment.** Undergraduates: 296 men, 247 women (full-time). Freshman class: 225 applicants, 205 accepted, 198 enrolled.
**Test score averages/ranges.** N/A.
**Faculty.** 25 full-time; 5 part-time. 54% of faculty holds doctoral degree. Student/faculty ratio: 15 to 1.
**Selectivity rating.** N/A.

**PROFILE.** Texas College, founded in 1894, is a private, church-affiliated, historically black college. Its 66-acre campus is located in Tyler, 100 miles east of Dallas.

**Accreditation:** SACS.
**Religious orientation:** Texas College is affiliated with the Christian Methodist Episcopal Church; two semesters of religion required.
**Library:** Collections totaling over 80,492 volumes, 130 periodical subscriptions, and 24,513 microform items.
**Special facilities/museums:** On-campus preschool for elementary education majors.
**Athletic facilities:** Gymnasium, athletic fields.

**STUDENT BODY. Undergraduate profile:** 74% are state residents; 6% are transfers. 99% Black, 1% Other. Average age of undergraduates is 20.
**Freshman profile:** 98% of freshmen come from public schools.
**Undergraduate achievement:** 67% of fall 1991 freshmen returned for fall 1992 term. 40% of entering class graduated. 70% of students who completed a degree program went on to graduate study within five years.
**Foreign students:** 24 students are from out of the country.

**PROGRAMS OF STUDY. Degrees:** B.A., B.S.
**Majors:** Art, Biology, Business Administration, Business Education, Computer Science, Elementary Education, English, General Science, History, Mathematics, Music, Physical Education, Political Science, Social Science, Social Work, Sociology.
**Distribution of degrees:** The majors with the highest enrollment are business administration, biology, and physical education; elementary education, music, and English have the lowest.
**Academic regulations:** Minimum 2.0 GPA required for graduation.
**Special:** Minors offered in several majors. Double majors. Preprofessional programs in law, medicine, and dentistry. Teacher certification in early childhood, elementary, and secondary education.
**Academic Assistance:** Nonremedial tutoring.

**ADMISSIONS. Academic basis for candidate selection** (in order of priority): Secondary school record, standardized test scores, class rank, school's recommendation, essay.
**Nonacademic basis for candidate selection:** Character and personality and particular talent or ability are important. Extracurricular participation is considered.
**Requirements:** Graduation from secondary school is required; GED is accepted. 16 units and the following program of study are required: 4 units of English, 2 units of math, 2 units of lab science, 2 units of history, 6 units of academic electives. Academic Reinforcement Lab required of applicants not normally admissible who have ACT score below 10. Campus visit and interview recommended.
**Procedure:** Take SAT or ACT by November of 12th year. Application deadline is August 15. Notification of admission on rolling basis. Freshmen accepted for terms other than fall.
**Special programs:** Admission may be deferred one year. Early entrance/early admission program.
**Transfer students:** Transfer students accepted for terms other than fall. In fall 1992, 6% of all new students were transfers into all classes. 42 transfer applications were received, 40 were accepted. Application deadline is August 15 for fall; December 15 for spring. Minimum 2.0 GPA recommended. Lowest course grade accepted is "C." At least 30 semester hours must be completed at the college to receive degree.
**Admissions contact:** J.B. Derrick, M.B.A., Director of Enrollment Management. 903 593-8311, extension 224.

**FINANCIAL AID. Available aid:** Pell grants, SEOG, academic merit scholarships, and athletic scholarships. Perkins Loans (NDSL) and SLS. Deferred payment plan.
**Supporting data/closing dates:** FAFSA/FAF/FFS: Deadline is May 31. Notification of awards on rolling basis.
**Financial aid contact:** Peggy Taylor, Financial Aid Officer. 903 593-8311, extensions 278, 279.

# Texas Lutheran College

**Seguin, TX 78155** **512 372-8000**

**1994-95 Costs.** Tuition: $7,850. Room: $1,490. Board: $1,920. Fees, books, misc. academic expenses (school's estimate): $850.
**Enrollment.** Undergraduates: 357 men, 538 women (full-time). Freshman class: 533 applicants, 460 accepted, 215 enrolled.
**Test score averages/ranges.** Average SAT scores: 436 verbal, 498 math. Range of SAT scores of middle 50%: 370-490 verbal, 430-550 math. Average ACT scores: 22 English, 21 math, 22 composite. Range of ACT scores of middle 50%: 19-26 English, 19-26 math.
**Faculty.** 65 full-time; 26 part-time. 61% of faculty holds doctoral degree. Student/faculty ratio: 13 to 1.
**Selectivity rating.** Less competitive.

**PROFILE.** Texas Lutheran, founded in 1891, is a private, church-affiliated college. Its 148-acre campus is located in Seguin, 35 miles east of Austin.

**Accreditation:** SACS. Professionally accredited by the Association of Collegiate Business Schools and Programs.
**Religious orientation:** Texas Lutheran College is affiliated with the Evangelical Lutheran Church in America; two semesters of religion required.
**Library:** Collections totaling over 92,175 volumes, 710 periodical subscriptions, and 60,881 microform items.
**Special facilities/museums:** Language lab, Mexican-American studies center, geological museum.
**Athletic facilities:** Gymnasiums, basketball, racquetball, and tennis courts, swimming pools, aerobics, training, and weight rooms, golf course, fitness trail, baseball, soccer, and softball fields.

**STUDENT BODY. Undergraduate profile:** 87% are state residents; 21% are transfers. 1% Asian-American, 3% Black, 13% Hispanic, 1% Native American, 77% White, 5% Foreign national. Average age of undergraduates is 22.
**Freshman profile:** 3% of freshmen who took SAT scored 700 or over on math; 4% scored 600 or over on verbal, 17% scored 600 or over on math; 24% scored 500 or over on verbal, 51% scored 500 or over on math; 68% scored 400 or over on verbal, 86% scored 400 or over on math; 95% scored 300 or over on verbal, 98% scored 300 or over on math. 6% of freshmen who took ACT scored 30 or over on English, 4% scored 30 or over on math, 3% scored 30 or over on composite; 41% scored 24 or over on English, 37% scored 24 or over on math, 38% scored 24 or over on composite; 85% scored 18 or over on English, 82% scored 18 or over on math, 86% scored 18 or over on composite; 98% scored 12 or over on English, 98% scored 12 or over on math, 100% scored 12 or over on composite; 99% scored 6 or over on English, 99% scored 6 or over on math. 83% of accepted applicants took SAT; 58% took ACT. 88% of freshmen come from public schools.
**Undergraduate achievement:** 76% of fall 1992 freshmen returned for fall 1993 term. 29% of entering class graduated. 22% of students who completed a degree program immediately went on to graduate study.
**Foreign students:** 44 students are from out of the country. Countries represented include England, France, Norway, Sierra Leone, Taiwan, and Tanzania; 13 in all.

**PROGRAMS OF STUDY. Degrees:** B.A., B.Bus.Admin., B.S.
**Majors:** Art, Biology, Business Administration, Chemistry, Communication Arts, Computer Science, Computer Systems Management, Economics, English, German, History, Interdisciplinary Studies, Kinesiology, Mathematics, Music, Philosophy, Physics, Political Science, Psychology, Social Work, Sociology, Spanish, Theology.
**Requirements:** General education requirement.
**Special:** Double majors. Independent study. Internships. Preprofessional programs in law, medicine, veterinary science, pharmacy, dentistry, theology, and optometry. Washington Semester. Teacher certification in early childhood, elementary, and secondary education. Certification in specific subject areas. Member of International Student Exchange Program (ISEP). Exchange program abroad in Germany (U of Bonn). Study abroad also in Brazil, Ecuador, and Japan. AFROTC at Southwest Texas State U.
**Honors:** Honors program. Honor societies.
**Academic Assistance:** Remedial study skills. Nonremedial tutoring.

**ADMISSIONS. Academic basis for candidate selection** (in order of priority): Class rank, secondary school record, standardized test scores, school's recommendation, essay.
**Requirements:** Graduation from secondary school is required; GED is accepted. 21 units and the following program of study are recommended: 4 units of English, 3 units of math, 3 units of science including 2 units of lab, 2 units of foreign language, 3 units of social studies, 3 units of electives. Minimum combined SAT score of 800 (composite ACT score of 18) and rank in top half of secondary school class recommended. SAT or ACT is required. PSAT is recommended. Campus visit and interview recommended. No off-campus interviews.

**Procedure:** Take SAT or ACT by May of 12th year. Visit college for interview by May 1 of 12th year. Suggest filing application by January 1. Application deadline is August 15. Notification of admission on rolling basis. $100 tuition deposit, refundable until May 1. Freshmen accepted for terms other than fall.

**Special programs:** Admission may be deferred one year. Credit and/or placement may be granted through CEEB Advanced Placement exams for scores of 3 or higher. Credit and/or placement may be granted through CLEP general and subject exams. Credit may be granted through military experience. Placement may be granted through DANTES exams. Credit and placement may be granted through challenge exams. Concurrent enrollment program.

**Transfer students:** Transfer students accepted for terms other than fall. In fall 1993, 21% of all new students were transfers into all classes. 114 transfer applications were received, 89 were accepted. Application deadline is August 1 for fall; December 1 for spring. Minimum 2.0 GPA required. Lowest course grade accepted is "D." Maximum number of transferable credits is 66 semester hours. At least 30 semester hours must be completed at the college to receive degree.

**Admissions contact:** Jennifer Brewer Ehlers, M.Ed., Director of Admissions. 512 372-8050.

**FINANCIAL AID. Available aid:** Pell grants, SEOG, state grants, school scholarships and grants, private scholarships and grants, academic merit scholarships, and athletic scholarships. Perkins Loans (NDSL), PLUS, Stafford Loans (GSL), state loans, and SLS. Deferred payment plan.

**Financial aid statistics:** 42% of aid is not need-based. In 1993-94, 95% of all undergraduate applicants received aid; 85% of freshman applicants. Average amounts of aid awarded freshmen: Scholarships and grants, $4,520; loans, $4,941.

**Supporting data/closing dates:** FAFSA/FAF: Priority filing date is March 1; accepted on rolling basis; deadline is May 1. FFS: Accepted on rolling basis. School's own aid application: Priority filing date is February 1; accepted on rolling basis; deadline is April 1. Income tax forms: Accepted on rolling basis. Notification of awards on rolling basis.

**Financial aid contact:** Carol Hamilton, M.A., Director of Financial Aid. 512 372-8075.

# Texas Southern University

**Houston, TX 77004** **713 527-7011**

**1993-94 Costs.** Tuition: $1,082 (state residents), $4,346 (out-of-state). Room & board: $3,360. Fees, books, misc. academic expenses (school's estimate): $1,100.

**Enrollment.** Undergraduates: 2,515 men, 4,173 women (full-time). Freshman class: 3,234 applicants, 932 accepted, 2,071 enrolled. Graduate enrollment: 817 men, 1,072 women.

**Test score averages/ranges.** N/A.

**Faculty.** 376 full-time; 139 part-time. 60% of faculty holds doctoral degree. Student/faculty ratio: 20 to 1.

**Selectivity rating.** N/A.

**PROFILE.** Texas Southern, founded in 1947, is a public, historically black university. Programs are offered through the Colleges of Arts and Sciences, Education, and Pharmacy and Health Sciences; the Graduate School; and the Schools of Business, Law, and Technology. Its 118-acre campus is located in Houston.

**Accreditation:** SACS. Professionally accredited by the American Bar Association, the American Council on Pharmaceutical Education, the National Council for Accreditation of Teacher Education.

**Religious orientation:** Texas Southern University is nonsectarian; no religious requirements.

**Library:** Collections totaling over 747,785 volumes, 2,398 periodical subscriptions, and 349,969 microform items.

**Special facilities/museums:** Excellence in education center, hunger and world peace center, minority institute reserve center.

**Athletic facilities:** Gymnasiums, athletic complex, tennis courts.

**STUDENT BODY. Undergraduate profile:** 90% are state residents; 12% are transfers. 1% Asian-American, 78% Black, 4% Hispanic, 1% Native American, 4% White, 12% Other. Average age of undergraduates is 27.

**Freshman profile:** 90% of freshmen come from public schools.

**Undergraduate achievement:** 50% of fall 1992 freshmen returned for fall 1993 term. 9% of entering class graduated. 25% of students who completed a degree program immediately went on to graduate study.

**Foreign students:** 290 students are from out of the country. Countries represented include Bangladesh, Hong Kong, Iraq, Nigeria, Saudi Arabia, and Thailand; 40 in all.

**PROGRAMS OF STUDY. Degrees:** B.A.Ed., B.Bus.Admin., B.F.A., B.S.Comp.Sci., B.S.Ed., B.S.Home Econ., B.S.Indust.Tech., B.S.Med.Tech., B.S.Pharm., B.S.Phys.Ther., B.S.Pub.Aff.

**Majors:** Accounting, Administration of Justice, Art, Bilingual Education, Biology, Business, Business Education, Chemistry, Communications, Computer Science, Dietetics, Early Childhood Education, Economics, Education, English, French, Health Administration, Health Education, History, Home Economics, Housing Management, Industrial Education, Industrial Technology, Journalism, Law, Mathematics, Medical Records Administration, Medical Technology, Music, Music Education, Office Administration, Pharmacy, Physical Education, Physical Therapy, Physics, Political Science, Psychology, Public Affairs, Public Services, Respiratory Therapy, Social Work, Sociology, Spanish, Speech Communication, Speech Disorders, Technology, Telecommunications, Theatre/Cinema, Transportation.

**Distribution of degrees:** The majors with the highest enrollment are business, pharmacy, and accounting; art and history have the lowest.

**Requirements:** General education requirement.

**Academic regulations:** Freshmen must maintain minimum 1.5 GPA; sophomores, 1.75 GPA; juniors, 2.0 GPA; seniors, 2.0 GPA.

**Special:** Two-year certificate programs offered. Dual degrees. Cooperative education programs. Preprofessional programs in medicine and dentistry. B.A. in several areas of engineering with Rice U. M.P.A./J.D. and M.B.A./J.D. programs. Teacher certification in early childhood, elementary, secondary, and special education.

**Honors:** Honors program.

**Academic Assistance:** Remedial reading, writing, math, and study skills.

**STUDENT LIFE. Housing:** All freshmen and sophomores must live on campus unless living with family. Women's and men's dorms. Athletic housing.

**Social atmosphere:** Popular gathering spots for students include the student center, nearby fast food restaurants, and a few nearby soul food cafeterias. Spring Festival and Homecoming Week are among the most popular events of the school year.

**Services and counseling/handicapped student services:** Placement services. Health service. Counseling services for veteran students. Psychological counseling. Academic guidance services. Religious counseling.

**Campus organizations:** Undergraduate student government. Student newspaper (TSU Herald, published bimonthly). Yearbook. Radio station. Concert choir, marching band, stage band, debating, theatre. Four fraternities, no chapter houses; four sororities, no chapter houses. 15% of men join a fraternity. 15% of women join a sorority.

**Religious organizations:** United Ministries.

**Minority/foreign student organizations:** Hispanic Student Association. International Student Organization, Nigerian Student Association.

**ATHLETICS. Physical education requirements:** Two semesters of physical education required.

**Intercollegiate competition:** 3% of students participate. Baseball (M), basketball (M,W), cross-country (M,W), football (M), golf (M,W), tennis (M,W), track (indoor) (M,W), track (outdoor) (M,W), track and field (indoor) (M,W), track and field (outdoor) (M,W), volleyball (W). Member of NCAA Division I-AA, Southwestern Athletic Conference.

**Intramural and club sports:** 45% of students participate. Intramural basketball, pool, skating, softball, tennis, touch football, volleyball. Women's club cheerleading.

**ADMISSIONS. Academic basis for candidate selection** (in order of priority): Secondary school record, class rank, standardized test scores, essay, school's recommendation.

**Nonacademic basis for candidate selection:** Character and personality are emphasized. Extracurricular participation is important. Particular talent or ability and alumni/ae relationship are considered.

**Requirements:** Graduation from secondary school is recommended; GED is accepted. 15 units and the following program of study are recommended: 4 units of English, 2 units of math, 2 units of science, 2 units of social studies. Conditional admission possible for applicants not meeting standard requirements. SAT or ACT is required. No off-campus interviews.

**Procedure:** Take SAT or ACT by spring of 12th year. Suggest filing application by June 15. Application deadline is August 9. by August 31. $126 room deposit, refundable until July 15 for fall; December 20 for spring. Freshmen accepted for terms other than fall.

**Special programs:** Admission may be deferred one year. Credit may be granted through CLEP subject exams and military experience. Concurrent enrollment program.

**Transfer students:** Transfer students accepted for terms other than fall. In fall 1993, 12% of all new students were transfers into all classes. 819 transfer applications were received, 819 were accepted. Application deadline is August 7 for fall; December 18 for spring. Minimum 2.0 GPA recommended. Lowest course grade accepted is "D." At least 124 semester hours must be completed at the university to receive degree.

**Admissions contact:** Audrey Pearsall, M.B.A., Admissions Coordinator. 713 527-7070.

**FINANCIAL AID. Available aid:** Pell grants, SEOG, state scholarships and grants, school scholarships and grants, private scholarships, academic merit scholarships, athletic scholarships, and aid for undergraduate foreign students. PLUS, Stafford Loans (GSL), state loans, school loans, and SLS.

**Financial aid statistics:** In 1993-94, 80% of all undergraduate applicants received aid; 75% of freshman applicants. Average amounts of aid awarded freshmen: Scholarships and grants, $4,000; loans, $2,625.

**Supporting data/closing dates:** FAFSA/FAF/FFS: Deadline is May 1. School's own aid application: Priority filing date is May 1. Income tax forms: Priority filing date is May 1. ACT: Priority filing date is May 1. Notification of awards on rolling basis.

**Financial aid contact:** Yancy Beavers, M.S., Director of Financial Aid. 713 527-7530.

**STUDENT EMPLOYMENT.** College Work/Study Program. Institutional employment. 50% of full-time undergraduates work on campus during school year. Students may expect to earn an average of $2,000 during school year. Off-campus part-time employment opportunities rated "good."

**COMPUTER FACILITIES.** IBM/IBM-compatible and Macintosh/Apple microcomputers. Computer languages and software packages include Assembler, BASIC, C-Calc, COBOL, Cufs, DataTrieve, FORTRAN, Poise, RDB, SB-5, Words-11. Computer facilities are available to all students.

**Fees:** $15 computer fee per semester; included in tuition/fees.

**Hours:** 8 AM-11 PM; 24-hour access with modem.

**GRADUATE CAREER DATA.** Graduate school percentages: 10% enter law school. 2% enter medical school. 1% enter dental school. 20% enter graduate business programs. 55% enter graduate arts and sciences programs. 5% enter theological school/seminary. 20% of graduates choose careers in business and industry.

**PROMINENT ALUMNI/AE.** Barbara Jordan, U.S. congresswoman; G. Mickey Leland and Craig Washington, U.S. congressman.

# Texas Tech University

Lubbock, TX 79409 806 742-2011

**1994-95 Costs.** Tuition: $780 (state residents), $4,860 (out-of-state). Room & board: $3,688. Fees, books, misc. academic expenses (school's estimate): $1,300.
**Enrollment.** Undergraduates: 9,148 men, 7,637 women (full-time). Freshman class: 6,334 applicants, 5,051 accepted, 2,957 enrolled. Graduate enrollment: 2,520 men, 1,922 women.
**Test score averages/ranges.** Average SAT scores: 439 verbal, 507 math. Range of SAT scores of middle 50%: 390-490 verbal, 450-570 math. Average ACT scores: 22 English, 22 math, 22 composite. Range of ACT scores of middle 50%: 19-25 English, 20-25 math.
**Faculty.** 695 full-time; 124 part-time. 87% of faculty holds highest degree in specific field. Student/faculty ratio: 18 to 1.
**Selectivity rating.** Less competitive.

**PROFILE.** Texas Tech, founded in 1923, is a public, comprehensive university. Programs are offered through the Colleges of Agricultural Sciences, Architecture, Arts and Sciences, Business Administration, Education, Engineering, and Home Economics and the Health Sciences Center. Its 1,839-acre campus is located in Lubbock.

**Accreditation:** SACS. Professionally accredited by the Accreditation Board for Engineering and Technology, the Accrediting Council on Education in Journalism and Mass Communication, the American Assembly of Collegiate Schools of Business, the American Bar Association, the American Dietetic Association, the American Home Economics Association, the American Psychological Association, the American Society of Landscape Architects, the American Speech-Language-Hearing Association, the Council on Rehabilitation Education, the Council on Social Work Education, the Foundation for Interior Design Education Research, the National Architecture Accrediting Board, the National Association of Schools of Art and Design, the National Association of Schools of Music, the National Association of Schools of Public Affairs and Administration, the National Association of Schools of Theatre, the National Council for Accreditation of Teacher Education, the National Recreation and Park Association.
**Religious orientation:** Texas Tech University is nonsectarian; no religious requirements.
**Library:** Collections totaling over 1,200,000 volumes, 8,000 periodical subscriptions, and 800,000 microform items.
**Special facilities/museums:** Museum, child development center, textile research center, agricultural research center, planetarium, arid and semi-arid land studies center, ranching heritage center, seismological observatory.
**Athletic facilities:** Track, basketball and racquetball courts, soccer and softball fields, cross-country and golf courses, gymnastics facilities, stadium, swimming pool, recreation center.

**STUDENT BODY. Undergraduate profile:** 94% are state residents; 39% are transfers. 2% Asian-American, 3% Black, 10% Hispanic, 84% White, 1% Other. Average age of undergraduates is 21.
**Freshman profile:** 1% of freshmen who took SAT scored 700 or over on verbal, 3% scored 700 or over on math; 5% scored 600 or over on verbal, 17% scored 600 or over on math; 23% scored 500 or over on verbal, 54% scored 500 or over on math; 72% scored 400 or over on verbal, 89% scored 400 or over on math; 98% scored 300 or over on verbal, 99% scored 300 or over on math. 4% of freshmen who took ACT scored 30 or over on English, 4% scored 30 or over on math, 3% scored 30 or over on composite; 35% scored 24 or over on English, 32% scored 24 or over on math, 34% scored 24 or over on composite; 86% scored 18 or over on English, 87% scored 18 or over on math, 94% scored 18 or over on composite; 99% scored 12 or over on English, 100% scored 12 or over on math, 100% scored 12 or over on composite; 100% scored 6 or over on English. Majority of accepted applicants took SAT.
**Undergraduate achievement:** 76% of fall 1992 freshmen returned for fall 1993 term. 12% of entering class graduated.
**Foreign students:** 191 students are from out of the country. Countries represented include China, India, Korea, Malaysia, Mexico, and Pakistan; 92 in all.

**PROGRAMS OF STUDY. Degrees:** B.A., B.Arch., B.Bus.Admin., B.F.A., B.Gen.Studies, B.Inter.Design, B.Land.Arch., B.Mus., B.S., B.S.Agri.Eng., B.S.Chem.Eng., B.S.Civil Eng., B.S.Elec.Eng., B.S.Eng., B.S.Eng.Physics, B.S.Eng.Tech., B.S.Home Econ., B.S.Indust.Eng., B.S.Internat.Econ., B.S.Internat.Trade, B.S.Mech.Eng., B.S.Petrol.Eng., B.S.Rest./Hotel/Inst.Mgmt., B.S.Speech/Hear.Sci., B.S.Tech., B.S.Textile Eng., B.S.Textile Tech./Mgmt.
**Majors:** Accounting, Administration, Advertising, Agricultural Communications, Agricultural Economics, Agricultural Systems Management, Agronomy, Agronomy Industry Management, Agronomy Science, Animal Business, Animal Production, Animal Science, Anthropology, Architectural Design, Architectural History, Architecture, Architecture/Civil Engineering, Architecture/Urban Design, Art, Art History, Athletic Training, Biochemistry, Biology, Botany, Broadcast Journalism, Cell/Molecular Biology, Chemical Engineering, Chemistry, Civil Engineering, Clothing/Textiles, Communication Studies, Computer Science, Construction Technology, Consumer Studies/Management, Crops, Dance, Design Communication, Dietetics, Early Childhood, Economics, Electrical Engineering, Electrical Technology, Engineering Physics, Engineering Technology, English, Entomology, Environmental Design, Environmental Engineering, Exercise/Sports Science, Family Financial Planning, Family Studies, Fashion Design, Finance, Food/Nutrition, Food Technology, French, General Business Administration, General Studies, Geography, Geology, Geophysics, Geoscience, German, Hearing Impairment, History, Home Economics, Horticulture, Horticulture Industry Management, Horticulture Science, Housing/Interiors, Human Development, Industrial Engineering, Interdisciplinary Agriculture, Interior Design, Journalism, Landscape Architecture, Latin, Latin American Area Studies, Management, Management Information Systems, Marketing, Mathematics, Mechanical Engineering, Mechanical Technology, Merchandising, Microbiology, Multidisciplinary Sciences, Multidisciplinary Studies, Music, Music Composition, Music History/Literature, Music Theory, News/Editorial Journalism, Office Systems Technology, Performance, Petroleum Engineering, Petroleum Land Management, Philosophy, Photocommunications, Physics, Political Science, Psychology, Public Relations, Range Management, Recreation/Leisure Services, Restaurant/Hotel Institutional Management, Russian Language/Area Studies, Social Work, Sociology, Spanish, Speech/Hearing Sciences, Structural Architecture, Studio Art, Telecommunications, Textile Engineering, Textile Technology/Management, Theatre Arts, Wildlife Habitat, Wildlife Management, Zoology.
**Distribution of degrees:** The majors with the highest enrollment are marketing and restaurant/hotel institutional management.
**Requirements:** General education requirement.
**Academic regulations:** Minimum 2.0 GPA must be maintained.
**Special:** Minors offered include comparative literature, computer science, environmental studies, ethnic studies, humanities, international studies, linguistics, and urban studies. Self-designed majors. Double majors. Dual degrees. Independent study. Accelerated study. Pass/fail grading option. Internships. Graduate school at which undergraduates may take graduate-level courses. Preprofessional programs in law, medicine, veterinary science, pharmacy, dentistry, and optometry. Teacher certification in early childhood, elementary, secondary, special education, vo-tech, and bilingual/bicultural education. ROTC and AFROTC.
**Honors:** Phi Beta Kappa. Honors program.
**Academic Assistance:** Remedial reading, writing, math, and study skills. Nonremedial tutoring.

**STUDENT LIFE. Housing:** Coed, women's, and men's dorms. 21% of students live in college housing.
**Social atmosphere:** The editor of the student newspaper reports, "On campus, the emphasis is placed on getting a quality education. Off campus, students have found creative ways to entertain themselves in Lubbock." Popular campus activities include the Carol of Lights, Pikefest, the Fiji Olympics, SWC basketball, and intramurals. The popular on-campus meeting spot is the University Center. Off campus, students frequent J. Patrick O'Malley's, the Planet, and Fast 'n' Cool.
**Services and counseling/handicapped student services:** Placement services. Health service. Walk-in clinic. Counseling services for minority, military, and older students. Personal and psychological counseling. Career and academic guidance services. Physically disabled student services. Learning disabled services. Tutors. Reader services for the blind.
**Campus organizations:** Undergraduate student government. Student newspaper (University Daily). Literary magazine. Yearbook. Radio and TV stations. Choir, madrigal singers, marching and concert bands, orchestra, stage bands, theatre, musical theatre, opera theatre, debating, 293 organizations in all. 26 fraternities, 22 chapter houses; 15 sororities, 12 chapter houses. 16% of men join a fraternity. 18% of women join a sorority.
**Religious organizations:** Canterbury Association, Baptist Student Union, Campus Crusade for Christ, Catholic Student Association, Christian Fellowship, Christian Science Organization, Intervarsity Christian Fellowship, University Ministries, Wesley Foundation.
**Minority/foreign student organizations:** 27 minority student groups. Eight foreign student groups.

**ATHLETICS. Physical education requirements:** Two semester hours of physical education required; band or ROTC may be substituted.
**Intercollegiate competition:** 3% of students participate. Baseball (M), basketball (M,W), cross-country (M,W), football (M), golf (M,W), tennis (M,W), track (indoor) (M,W), track (outdoor) (M,W), track and field (indoor) (M,W), track and field (outdoor) (M,W), volleyball (W). Member of NCAA Division I, NCAA Division I-A for football, Southwest Athletic Conference.
**Intramural and club sports:** 35% of students participate. Intramural archery, badminton, basketball, darts, decathlon, disc golf, flag football, golf, homerun contest, indoor soccer, inner-tube water basketball, inner-tube water polo, pool, racquetball, slow-pitch softball, soccer, squash, swimming, table tennis, tennis, track and field, trap and skeet, volleyball, walleyball. Men's club bowling, cricket, cycling, fencing, lacrosse, martial arts, pistol, polo, racquetball, rifle, rock climbing, rodeo, rugby, soccer, volleyball, weight lifting, wrestling. Women's club bowling, cycling, fencing, martial arts, pistol, polo, racquetball, rifle, rock climbing, rodeo, soccer, weight lifting.

**ADMISSIONS. Academic basis for candidate selection** (in order of priority): Standardized test scores, class rank, secondary school record.
**Requirements:** Graduation from secondary school is required; GED is not accepted. 17 units and the following program of study are required: 4 units of English, 3 units of math, 2 units of lab science, 2.5 units of social studies, 3.5 units of academic electives. Applicants meeting one of the following standards are assured of admission: rank in top tenth of secondary school class; rank in top quarter with minimum combined SAT score of 900 (composite ACT score of 22); rank in second quarter with minimum combined SAT score of 1100 (composite ACT score of 27); or rank in bottom half with minimum combined SAT score of 1200 (composite ACT score of 29). Others may be admitted as space permits. Conditional admission possible for applicants not meeting standard requirements. SAT or ACT is required. Campus visit recommended. No off-campus interviews.
**Procedure:** Take SAT or ACT by April of 12th year. Application deadline is August 15. Notification of admission on rolling basis. $60 room deposit, refundable until July 1. Additional $100 deposit due by August 1; refunds sometimes given after that date. Freshmen accepted for terms other than fall.
**Special programs:** Credit and/or placement may be granted through CEEB Advanced Placement exams. Credit and/or placement may be granted through CLEP general and subject exams. Credit and placement may be granted through challenge exams. Early decision program. Concurrent enrollment program.
**Transfer students:** Transfer students accepted for terms other than fall. In fall 1993, 39% of all new students were transfers into all classes. 2,812 transfer applications were received, 2,290 were accepted. Application deadline is 30 days prior to beginning of term for fall; 30 days prior to beginning of term for spring. Minimum 2.0 GPA required. Lowest course grade accepted is "C." At least 30 semester hours must be completed at the university to receive degree.
**Admissions contact:** Gene Medley, Ph.D., Director of Admissions. 806 742-3661.

**FINANCIAL AID. Available aid:** Pell grants, SEOG, state scholarships and grants, private grants, and athletic scholarships. Perkins Loans (NDSL), PLUS, and Stafford Loans (GSL). Institutional payment plan.
**Financial aid statistics:** 20% of aid is not need-based. In 1993-94, 80% of all freshman applicants received aid. Average amounts of aid awarded freshmen: Scholarships and grants, $400; loans, $2,000.
**Supporting data/closing dates:** FAFSA/FAF/FFS: Priority filing date is March 1. Income tax forms: Priority filing date is March 1. Notification of awards on rolling basis.
**Financial aid contact:** Ronny Barnes, Ph.D., Director of Financial Aid. 806 742-3681.
**STUDENT EMPLOYMENT.** College Work/Study Program. Institutional employment. 30% of full-time undergraduates work on campus during school year. Students may expect to earn an average of $2,000 during school year. Off-campus part-time employment opportunities rated "excellent."
**COMPUTER FACILITIES.** IBM/IBM-compatible and Macintosh/Apple microcomputers. Students may access Digital, IBM, SUN minicomputer/mainframe systems, BITNET, Internet. Client/LAN operating systems include Apple/Macintosh, DOS. Computer facilities are available to all students.
**Fees:** $3 computer fee per semester hour.
**Hours:** General access facilities open approximately 120 hours/week.
**PROMINENT ALUMNI/AE.** Edward Whitacre, vice-president and chief financial officer, Southwestern Bell; Ernest Gloyna, dean of engineering, U of Texas; James Johnson, former president, GTE; Preston Smith, former governor of Texas.

## Texas Wesleyan University

**Fort Worth, TX 76105-1536 — 817 531-4444**

**1994-95 Costs.** Tuition: $6,400. Room: $1,068. Board: $1,930. Fees, books, misc. academic expenses (school's estimate): $890.
**Enrollment.** Undergraduates: 470 men, 734 women (full-time). Freshman class: 592 applicants, 501 accepted, 279 enrolled. Graduate enrollment: 260 men, 581 women.
**Test score averages/ranges.** Average SAT scores: 415 verbal, 420 math. Range of SAT scores of middle 50%: 790-1020 combined. Average ACT scores: 20 composite. Range of ACT scores of middle 50%: 18-23 composite.
**Faculty.** 85 full-time; 32 part-time. 77% of faculty holds doctoral degree. Student/faculty ratio: 17 to 1.
**Selectivity rating.** Competitive.

**PROFILE.** Texas Wesleyan, founded in 1891, is a private, church-affiliated college. Programs are offered in the Schools of Business, Education, Fine Arts, and Science and Humanities. Its 74-acre campus is located four miles southeast of downtown Fort Worth.

**Accreditation:** SACS.
**Religious orientation:** Texas Wesleyan University is affiliated with the United Methodist Church; two semesters of religion required.
**Library:** Collections totaling over 205,000 volumes, 1,511 periodical subscriptions, and 314,000 microform items.
**Special facilities/museums:** Art gallery.
**Athletic facilities:** Gymnasium, swimming pool, weight room, tennis courts, athletic fields.
**STUDENT BODY. Undergraduate profile:** 95% are state residents; 53% are transfers. 1% Asian-American, 13% Black, 13% Hispanic, 1% Native American, 69% White, 3% Other. Average age of undergraduates is 26.
**Freshman profile:** 4% of freshmen who took SAT scored 600 or over on verbal, 10% scored 600 or over on math; 22% scored 500 or over on verbal, 36% scored 500 or over on math; 61% scored 400 or over on verbal, 76% scored 400 or over on math; 93% scored 300 or over on verbal, 97% scored 300 or over on math. 1% of freshmen who took ACT scored 30 or over on composite; 16% scored 24 or over on composite; 75% scored 18 or over on composite; 100% scored 12 or over on composite. 76% of accepted applicants took SAT; 24% took ACT. 90% of freshmen come from public schools.
**Undergraduate achievement:** 64% of fall 1992 freshmen returned for fall 1993 term. 36% of entering class graduated. 15% of students who completed a degree program immediately went on to graduate study.
**Foreign students:** 52 students are from out of the country.
**PROGRAMS OF STUDY. Degrees:** B.A., B.Bus.Admin., B.Mus.Ed., B.S.
**Majors:** Accounting, Art, Bilingual Education, Biology, Business Administration, Business Education, Business Psychology, Chemistry, Christian Education, Computer Science, Criminal Justice, Early Childhood Education, Economics/Finance, Elementary Education, English, History, Humanities/Religion, Information Resources Management, International Business Administration, Management, Marketing, Mass Communications, Mathematics, Music, Music Education, Physical Education, Political Science, Psychology, Reading, Religion, Secondary Education, Social Science, Spanish, Sports Management, Theatre Arts.
**Distribution of degrees:** The majors with the highest enrollment are business, education, and psychology.
**Requirements:** General education requirement.
**Academic regulations:** Freshmen must maintain minimum 1.7 GPA; sophomores, 1.8 GPA; juniors, 1.9 GPA; seniors, 2.0 GPA.
**Special:** Minors offered in all majors and in Bible, economics, French, philosophy, and physics. Courses offered in geology, German, humanities, and office administration. Business majors take comprehensive examinations in senior year; music majors in sophomore and senior years. Students participate in off-campus mentorships with respected professionals in the community. Double majors. Dual degrees. Pass/fail grading option. Internships. Graduate school at which undergraduates may take graduate-level courses. Preprofessional programs in law, medicine, dentistry, theology, and optometry. 3-2 engineering programs with Case Western Reserve U, Southern Methodist U, U of Texas, Vanderbilt U, and Washington U. Teacher certification in early childhood, elementary, secondary, and bilingual/bicultural education. Certification in specific subject areas. Study abroad in Costa Rica, England, Ireland, Mexico, and Russia. ROTC and AFROTC at Texas Christian U.
**Academic Assistance:** Remedial writing, math, and study skills.
**ADMISSIONS. Academic basis for candidate selection** (in order of priority): Secondary school record, class rank, standardized test scores, essay, school's recommendation.
**Nonacademic basis for candidate selection:** Extracurricular participation is important. Character and personality and particular talent or ability are considered.
**Requirements:** Graduation from secondary school is recommended; GED is accepted. 17 units and the following program of study are recommended: 4 units of English, 4 units of math, 3 units of science, 2 units of foreign language, 2 units of social studies, 1 unit of history, 5 units of electives. Minimum combined SAT score of 800 (composite ACT score of 18), rank in top half of secondary school class, and minimum 2.0 GPA required. Portfolio required of art program applicants. Audition required of music program applicants. Conditional admission possible for applicants not meeting standard requirements. SAT or ACT is required. Campus visit and interview recommended. Off-campus interviews available with an admissions representative.
**Procedure:** Suggest filing application by January 15. Application deadline is August 15. Notification of admission on rolling basis. No set date by which applicants must accept offer. $100 tuition deposit, refundable until May 1. $100 room deposit, refundable until July 15. Freshmen accepted for terms other than fall.
**Special programs:** Credit and/or placement may be granted through CEEB Advanced Placement exams for scores of 3 or higher. Credit and/or placement may be granted through CLEP general and subject exams. Concurrent enrollment program.
**Transfer students:** Transfer students accepted for terms other than fall. In fall 1993, 53% of all new students were transfers into all classes. 562 transfer applications were received, 360 were accepted. Application deadline is one week prior to registration for fall; one week prior to registration for spring. Minimum 2.0 GPA required. Lowest course grade accepted is "D." Maximum number of transferable credits is 72 semester hours. At least 30 semester hours must be completed at the university to receive degree.
**Admissions contact:** David Voskuil, Vice President of Enrollment Management. 817 531-4422.
**FINANCIAL AID. Available aid:** Pell grants, SEOG, state grants, school scholarships and grants, private scholarships, academic merit scholarships, and athletic scholarships. Religious affiliated scholarships PLUS, Stafford Loans (GSL), state loans, private loans, and SLS. Tuition Plan Inc., Knight Tuition Plans, AMS, and deferred payment plan.
**Financial aid statistics:** 48% of aid is not need-based. In 1993-94, 85% of all undergraduate applicants received aid; 89% of freshman applicants. Average amounts of aid awarded freshmen: Scholarships and grants, $2,637; loans, $2,000.
**Supporting data/closing dates:** FAFSA: Priority filing date is April 1. School's own aid application: Priority filing date is April 1; accepted on rolling basis. State aid form: Priority filing date is April 1; accepted on rolling basis. Notification of awards begins January 1.
**Financial aid contact:** Marie Ferrier, Director of Financial Aid. 817 531-4420.

## Texas Woman's University

**Denton, TX 76204 — 817 898-2000**

**1993-94 Costs.** Tuition: $1,472 (state residents), $5,612 (out-of-state). Room & board: $2,938. Fees, books, misc. academic expenses (school's estimate): $450.
**Enrollment.** Undergraduates: 161 men, 3,630 women (full-time). Freshman class: 989 applicants, 777 accepted, 474 enrolled. Graduate enrollment: 529 men, 3,421 women.
**Test score averages/ranges.** Range of SAT scores of middle 50%: 320-440 verbal, 350-480 math. Range of ACT scores of middle 50%: 16-21 composite.
**Faculty.** 321 full-time; 85 part-time. 66% of faculty holds doctoral degree.
**Selectivity rating.** Less competitive.

**PROFILE.** Texas Woman's, founded in 1901, is a public, comprehensive university for women; qualified men admitted to the health sciences and graduate programs. Programs are offered through the University General Division, the Institute for Health Sciences, and the Graduate School. Its 270-acre main campus is located in Denton, 38 miles north of Dallas-Fort Worth.

**Accreditation:** SACS. Professionally accredited by the American Dental Association, the American Dietetic Association, the American Medical Association (CAHEA), the National Association of Schools of Music, the National Council for Accreditation of Teacher Education, the National League for Nursing.
**Religious orientation:** Texas Woman's University is nonsectarian; no religious requirements.
**Library:** Collections totaling over 776,747 volumes, 3,072 periodical subscriptions, and 640,735 microform items.
**Special facilities/museums:** Museum, radiation lab, language lab, lab nursery school, radio and TV studio.
**Athletic facilities:** Gymnasium, tennis courts, swimming pools, archery range, track, fitness room, golf course.
**STUDENT BODY. Undergraduate profile:** 97% are state residents; 49% are transfers. 2% Asian-American, 14% Black, 8% Hispanic, 1% Native American, 73% White, 2% International. Average age of undergraduates is 25.
**Freshman profile:** 1% of freshmen who took SAT scored 700 or over on math; 2% scored 600 or over on verbal, 5% scored 600 or over on math; 11% scored 500 or over on verbal, 23% scored 500 or over on math; 45% scored 400 or over on verbal, 60% scored 400 or over on math; 84% scored 300 or over on verbal, 92% scored 300 or over on math. 10% of freshmen who took ACT scored 24 or over on composite; 68% scored 18 or over on composite; 100% scored 12 or over on composite. Majority of accepted applicants took SAT.
**Undergraduate achievement:** 62% of fall 1992 freshmen returned for fall 1993 term. 17% of entering class graduated.
**Foreign students:** 112 students are from out of the country. Countries represented include China, Iran, Mexico, Nigeria, and Taiwan; 70 in all.
**PROGRAMS OF STUDY. Degrees:** B.A., B.Bus.Admin., B.F.A., B.S., B.Soc.Work.

**Majors:** Accounting, Advertising, Applied Music, Art, Art History, Biology, Business, Business Administration, Ceramics, Chemistry, Child Development, Clothing/Costume Design, Clothing/Fashion Merchandising, Communication Sciences, Community Health, Computer Science, Consumer Sciences, Criminal Justice, Dance, Dental Hygiene, Design, Drama, Economics, English, Fibers/Printed Textiles, Food/Nutrition in Business/ Industry, Government, Government Service, History, Home Economics, Human Biology, Interdisciplinary Studies, Jewelry/Metalsmithing, Kinesiology, Library Science, Management, Marketing, Mass Communications, Mathematics, Medical Technology, Music, Music Therapy, Nursing, Nutrition, Occupational Therapy, Painting, Pedagogy, Photography/Printmaking/Drawing, Psychology, Sculpture, Secretarial Administration, Social Work, Sociology, Spanish, Studio Art, Textiles/Clothing.

**Distribution of degrees:** The majors with the highest enrollment are nursing, interdisciplinary studies, and business administration.

**Requirements:** General education requirement.

**Academic regulations:** Freshmen must maintain minimum 1.4 GPA; sophomores, 1.7 GPA; juniors, 2.0 GPA; seniors, 2.0 GPA.

**Special:** Minors offered in many majors. Double majors. Dual degrees. Internships. Cooperative education programs. Graduate school at which undergraduates may take graduate-level courses. Preprofessional programs in law, medicine, and dentistry. 3-2 engineering program with U of Texas at Dallas. Member of consortium with East Texas State U and U of North Texas. Teacher certification in early childhood, elementary, secondary, and special education. Certification in specific subject areas. Exchange program abroad in Japan (Baiko Jo Gaquin, Mukogawa Women's U). ROTC at U of Texas - Arlington. AFROTC at U of North Texas.

**Honors:** Honors program.

**Academic Assistance:** Remedial reading, writing, math, and study skills. Nonremedial tutoring.

**STUDENT LIFE. Housing:** All full-time, unmarried undergraduates under age 21 with fewer than 60 semester hours of credit must live on campus unless living with family. Coed and women's dorms. On-campus married-student housing. 13% of students live in college housing.

**Social atmosphere:** Popular gathering spots on campus include the Garden Room and the Underground; popular off-campus spots are Rick's Place, the State Club, Muther's, and Rip Rocks. Influential campus groups include the Student Organization for Activities Programming (SOAP), Professional Business Women, Greeks, and athletes. Popular campus events include Fundango, Fiesta, Parent/Family Days, sporting events, the Redbud Awards Festival, Homecoming, and concerts sponsored by the Student Organization for Activities Programming. According to the student newspaper, students come from many cultures and backgrounds, so campus life is diverse: "Our campus has multi-cultural students, commuter students, and non-traditional students, so TWU has something for everyone."

**Services and counseling/handicapped student services:** Placement services. Health service. Day care. Counseling services for minority, veteran, and older students. Birth control, personal, and psychological counseling. Career and academic guidance services. Physically disabled student services. Learning disabled services. Tape recorders. Reader services for the blind.

**Campus organizations:** Undergraduate student government. Student newspaper (Lass-O). Chorus, choir, gospel and dance team, theatre, folk and literary groups, academic, social, and special-interest groups, 62 organizations in all. Five sororities, no chapter houses. 3% of women join a sorority.

**Religious organizations:** Baptist Student Union, Catholic Campus Community, Lutheran Student Fellowship, United Methodist Campus Ministry.

**Minority/foreign student organizations:** African American Student Alliance, Hispanic Organization for Leadership and Advancement, NAACP. Chinese Student Association.

**ATHLETICS. Physical education requirements:** Four semesters of physical education required.

**Intercollegiate competition:** Basketball (W), gymnastics (W), tennis (W), volleyball (W). Member of Lone Star Conference, NCAA Division II.

**Intramural and club sports:** 10% of students participate. Intramural badminton, basketball, billiards, bowling, flag football, golf, martial arts, soccer, softball, table tennis, tennis, volleyball.

**ADMISSIONS. Academic basis for candidate selection** (in order of priority): Secondary school record, standardized test scores.

**Requirements:** Graduation from secondary school is required; GED is accepted. 15 units and the following program of study are required: 3 units of English, 2 units of math, 2 units of lab science, 2 units of social studies, 6 units of academic electives. Minimum composite ACT score of 14 (combined SAT score of 630) and minimum 2.0 GPA recommended. Minimum 2.8 overall GPA required of occupational therapy program applicants. Portfolio required of art program applicants. Audition required of music program applicants. Conditional admission possible for applicants not meeting standard requirements. Application for nondegree status possible. SAT or ACT is required. PSAT is recommended. Campus visit recommended. Off-campus interviews available with admissions and alumni representatives.

**Procedure:** Take SAT or ACT by October of 12th year. Suggest filing application by March. Application deadline is July 15. Notification of admission on rolling basis. $75 nonrefundable room deposit. Freshmen accepted for terms other than fall.

**Special programs:** Admission may be deferred one year. Credit and/or placement may be granted through CEEB Advanced Placement exams for scores of 3 or higher. Credit and/or placement may be granted through CLEP general and subject exams. Credit may be granted through military experience. Credit and placement may be granted through challenge exams and life experience. Early decision program. Deadline for applying for early decision is April 1. Early entrance/early admission program. Concurrent enrollment program.

**Transfer students:** Transfer students accepted for terms other than fall. In fall 1993, 49% of all new students were transfers into all classes. 1,778 transfer applications were received, 1,428 were accepted. Application deadline is July 15 for fall; December 1 for spring. Minimum 2.0 GPA required. Lowest course grade accepted is "D." Maximum number of transferable credits is 72 semester hours. At least 30 semester hours must be completed at the university to receive degree.

**Admissions contact:** Cynthia Johnson, M.A., Director of Undergraduate Admissions. 817 898-3040.

**FINANCIAL AID. Available aid:** Pell grants, SEOG, state grants, school scholarships, private scholarships, academic merit scholarships, and athletic scholarships. Perkins Loans (NDSL), PLUS, Stafford Loans (GSL), NSL, state loans, school loans, and SLS. Installment Option Plan.

**Financial aid statistics:** 32% of aid is not need-based. In 1992-93, 57% of all undergraduate applicants received aid; 46% of freshman applicants. Average amounts of aid awarded freshmen: Scholarships and grants, $1,479; loans, $2,501.

**Supporting data/closing dates:** FAFSA: Priority filing date is April 1. School's own aid application: Deadline is April 1. Notification of awards on rolling basis.

**Financial aid contact:** Governor Jackson, M.B.A., Director of Financial Aid. 817 898-3050.

**STUDENT EMPLOYMENT.** College Work/Study Program. Institutional employment. 10% of full-time undergraduates work on campus during school year. Students may expect to earn an average of $1,960 during school year. Off-campus part-time employment opportunities rated "good."

**COMPUTER FACILITIES.** 250 IBM/IBM-compatible and Macintosh/Apple microcomputers; 200 are networked. Students may access Data General, Digital minicomputer/ mainframe systems, BITNET, Internet. Residence halls may be equipped with stand-alone microcomputers, networked terminals. Client/LAN operating systems include Apple/ Macintosh, DOS, LocalTalk/AppleTalk, Novell. Computer languages and software packages include BASIC, BMDP, COBOL, FORTRAN, Harvard Graphics, Lotus 1-2-3, MS Works, Pascal, SPSS-X, Word, WordPerfect; communications, data management, graphics, spreadsheet, word processing packages. Computer facilities are available to all students.

**Fees:** $50 computer fee per semester.

**Hours:** 24-hour modem access; 8 AM-10 PM in some labs; 8 AM-midn. in others.

# Trinity University

**San Antonio, TX 78212-7200** **210 736-7011**

**1994-95 Costs.** Tuition: $12,240. Room & board: $4,950. Fees, books, misc. academic expenses (school's estimate): $644.

**Enrollment.** Undergraduates: 1,032 men, 1,075 women (full-time). Freshman class: 2,425 applicants, 1,818 accepted, 601 enrolled. Graduate enrollment: 107 men, 150 women.

**Test score averages/ranges.** Average SAT scores: 575 verbal, 635 math. Range of SAT scores of middle 50%: 575-625 verbal, 595-695 math. Average ACT scores: 27 English, 27 math, 28 composite.

**Faculty.** 224 full-time; 46 part-time. 95% of faculty holds doctoral degree. Student/ faculty ratio: 10 to 1.

**Selectivity rating.** Highly competitive.

**PROFILE.** Trinity, founded in 1869, is a private, church-affiliated university of liberal arts and sciences. Its 113-acre campus is located in San Antonio.

**Accreditation:** SACS. Professionally accredited by the Accreditation Board for Engineering and Technology, the National Association of Schools of Music, the National Council for Accreditation of Teacher Education.

**Religious orientation:** Trinity University is affiliated with the Presbyterian Church USA; no religious requirements.

**Library:** Collections totaling over 740,388 volumes, 2,464 periodical subscriptions, and 258,839 microform items.

**STUDENT BODY. Undergraduate profile:** 63% are state residents; 5% are transfers. 8% Asian-American, 2% Black, 8% Hispanic, .3% Native American, 81.7% White. Average age of undergraduates is 20.

**Freshman profile:** 3% of freshmen who took SAT scored 700 or over on verbal, 20% scored 700 or over on math; 34% scored 600 or over on verbal, 64% scored 600 or over on math; 82% scored 500 or over on verbal, 95% scored 500 or over on math; 99% scored 400 or over on verbal, 99% scored 400 or over on math; 100% scored 300 or over on verbal, 100% scored 300 or over on math. 95% of accepted applicants took SAT; 46% took ACT. 82% of freshmen come from public schools.

**Undergraduate achievement:** 82% of fall 1992 freshmen returned for fall 1993 term. 65% of entering class graduated. 48% of students who completed a degree program immediately went on to graduate study.

**Foreign students:** 35 students are from out of the country. Countries represented include Brazil, Saudi Arabia, and Singapore; 22 in all.

**PROGRAMS OF STUDY. Degrees:** B.A., B.Mus., B.S.

**Majors:** Anthropology, Art, Art History, Biochemistry, Biology, Business Administration, Chemistry, Classical Studies, Communication, Computer Sciences, Earth Science, Economics, Education, Engineering Science, English, Environmental Studies, Geology, History, International Studies, Mathematics, Modern Languages, Music, Philosophy, Physics, Political Science, Psychology, Religion, Sociology, Speech/Drama, Urban Administration.

**Distribution of degrees:** The majors with the highest enrollment are business administration, economics, and English; biochemistry, classical studies, and urban studies have the lowest.

**Requirements:** General education requirement.

**Academic regulations:** Minimum 2.0 GPA must be maintained.

**Special:** Interdisciplinary minors offered in cognitive science, communication management, environmental studies, linguistics, medieval studies, and women's studies. Double majors. Dual degrees. Independent study. Pass/fail grading option. Internships. Cooperative education programs. Graduate school at which undergraduates may take graduate-level courses. Preprofessional programs in law, medicine, veterinary science, dentistry, and theology. Five-year B.A./M.A.T. and M.S.Acct programs. Washington Semester. Teacher certification in elementary and secondary education. Certification in specific subject areas. Study abroad in England, France, Germany, Italy, Japan, the Netherlands, and Spain. ROTC and AFROTC at U of Texas at San Antonio.

**Honors:** Phi Beta Kappa. Honors program. Honor societies.
**Academic Assistance:** Nonremedial tutoring.

**STUDENT LIFE. Housing:** All unmarried freshmen, sophomores, and juniors must live on campus unless living with family. Coed, women's, and men's dorms. 75% of students live in college housing.
**Social atmosphere:** Greeks, athletes, and the Student Association are among the influential groups on campus. Popular campus events include Homecoming, Parents Weekend, and home sporting events.
**Services and counseling/handicapped student services:** Placement services. Health service. Counseling services for minority students. Personal and psychological counseling. Career and academic guidance services. Religious counseling. Physically disabled student services. Tape recorders. Reader services for the blind.
**Campus organizations:** Undergraduate student government. Student newspaper (Trinitonian, published once/week). Literary magazine. Yearbook. Radio station. Choir, orchestra, band, jazz band, community service program, film committee, theatre, Young Democrats, Young Republicans, special-interest groups. Six fraternities, no chapter houses; six sororities, no chapter houses. 30% of men join a fraternity. 33% of women join a sorority.
**Religious organizations:** Catholic, Baptist, Methodist, and Jewish groups.
**Minority/foreign student organizations:** Black Student Association, Hispanic Student Association. Foreign Student Association.

**ATHLETICS. Physical education requirements:** None.
**Intercollegiate competition:** 13% of students participate. Baseball (M), basketball (M,W), cheerleading (M,W), cross-country (M,W), diving (M,W), football (M), golf (M), soccer (M,W), softball (W), swimming (M,W), tennis (M,W), track (outdoor) (M,W), track and field (outdoor) (M,W), volleyball (W). Member of NCAA Division III, Southern Collegiate Athletic Conference.
**Intramural and club sports:** 65% of students participate. Intramural baseball, basketball, bowling, cross-country, football, racquetball, softball, swimming, tennis, track, volleyball. Men's club cycling, fencing, lacrosse, volleyball. Women's club fencing, lacrosse.

**ADMISSIONS. Academic basis for candidate selection** (in order of priority): Secondary school record, class rank, standardized test scores, essay, school's recommendation.
**Nonacademic basis for candidate selection:** Character and personality and extracurricular participation are emphasized. Particular talent or ability is important. Geographical distribution and alumni/ae relationship are considered.
**Requirements:** Graduation from secondary school is required; GED is accepted. 16 units and the following program of study are required: 4 units of English, 3 units of math, 2 units of lab science, 2 units of foreign language, 2 units of social studies, 3 units of academic electives. Conditional admission possible for applicants not meeting standard requirements. SAT is required; ACT may be substituted. Campus visit and interview recommended. Off-campus interviews available with admissions and alumni representatives.
**Procedure:** Take SAT or ACT by November of 12th year. Visit college for interview by February 1 of 12th year. Application deadline is February 1. Notification of admission by April 1. Reply is required by May 1. $100 tuition deposit, refundable until May 1. $200 room deposit, refundable until May 1. Freshmen accepted for terms other than fall.
**Special programs:** Admission may be deferred one year. Credit and/or placement may be granted through CEEB Advanced Placement exams for scores of 4 or higher. Early decision program. In fall 1993, 133 applied for early decision and 102 were accepted. Deadline for applying for early decision is November 15. Early entrance/early admission program. Concurrent enrollment program.
**Transfer students:** Transfer students accepted for terms other than fall. In fall 1993, 5% of all new students were transfers into all classes. 94 transfer applications were received, 56 were accepted. Notification of admission begins February 1 for fall; November 1 for spring. Minimum 2.5 GPA recommended. Lowest course grade accepted is "C-." Maximum number of transferable credits is 64 semester hours. At least 60 semester hours must be completed at the university to receive degree.
**Admissions contact:** George Boyd, Ph.D., Acting Director of Admissions. 210 736-7207, 800 TRINITY.

**FINANCIAL AID. Available aid:** Pell grants, SEOG, state grants, school scholarships and grants, private scholarships and grants, ROTC scholarships, and academic merit scholarships. Perkins Loans (NDSL), PLUS, Stafford Loans (GSL), school loans, private loans, and SLS. Deferred payment plan and guaranteed tuition. Average amount of financial aid package awarded freshmen: $8,173.
**Supporting data/closing dates:** FAFSA/FAF: Deadline is February 1. School's own aid application: Deadline is February 1. Income tax forms: Deadline is February 1. Notification of awards begins April 1.
**Financial aid contact:** Estelle Frerichs, M.A., Director of Financial Aid. 210 736-8315.

**STUDENT EMPLOYMENT.** College Work/Study Program. Institutional employment. 25% of full-time undergraduates work on campus during school year. Students may expect to earn an average of $1,250 during school year. Freshmen are discouraged from working during their first term. Off-campus part-time employment opportunities rated "good."

**COMPUTER FACILITIES.** 600 IBM/IBM-compatible, Macintosh/Apple, and RISC-/UNIX-based microcomputers; 300 are networked. Students may access IBM, SUN minicomputer/mainframe systems. Computer languages and software packages include C, COBOL, FORTRAN, Pascal; 25 in all. Computer facilities are available to all students.
**Fees:** Computer fee is included in tuition/fees.
**Hours:** 24 hours.

**GRADUATE CAREER DATA.** Graduate school percentages: 10% enter law school. 5% enter medical school. 1% enter graduate business programs. 25% enter graduate arts and sciences programs. 1% enter theological school/seminary. Highest graduate school enrollments: Duke U, Harvard U, Stanford U, Texas A&M U, U of Texas. 40% of graduates choose careers in business and industry. Companies and businesses that hire graduates: Dow Chemical, Ernst & Young, IBM.

**PROMINENT ALUMNI/AE.** Daniel C. Morales, attorney general, Texas; Herbert H. Reynolds, president, Baylor U; Maj. Gen. William K. Suter, judge advocate general, U.S. Army.

# University of Dallas

**Irving, TX 75062-4799 — 214 721-5000**

**1993-94 Costs.** Tuition: $10,150. Room: $2,550. Board: $2,133. Fees, books, misc. academic expenses (school's estimate): $650.
**Enrollment.** Undergraduates: 494 men, 564 women (full-time). Freshman class: 680 applicants, 585 accepted, 246 enrolled. Graduate enrollment: 1,082 men, 688 women.
**Test score averages/ranges.** Average SAT scores: 550 verbal, 593 math. Range of SAT scores of middle 50%: 490-590 verbal, 530-650 math. Average ACT scores: 26 English, 25 math, 26 composite. Range of ACT scores of middle 50%: 25-28 English, 24-27 math.
**Faculty.** 86 full-time; 31 part-time. 95% of faculty holds highest degree in specific field. Student/faculty ratio: 20 to 1.
**Selectivity rating.** Highly competitive.

**PROFILE.** The University of Dallas, founded in 1910, is a church-affiliated, liberal arts institution. Programs are offered through the College of Liberal Arts, the Graduate School, and the Graduate School of Management. Its 744-acre campus is located in Irving, on the northwest boundary of Dallas. The Braniff Memorial Tower is the university's landmark.

**Accreditation:** SACS.
**Religious orientation:** University of Dallas is affiliated with the Roman Catholic Church; two semesters of theology required.
**Library:** Collections totaling over 288,566 volumes, 1,022 periodical subscriptions, and 75,416 microform items.
**Special facilities/museums:** Art gallery, language lab, observatory, science lab, computer lab.
**Athletic facilities:** Swimming pool, fencing, table tennis, and weight rooms, gymnasium, badminton, basketball, tennis, and volleyball courts, baseball, rugby, soccer, and softball fields.

**STUDENT BODY. Undergraduate profile:** 65% are state residents; 8% are transfers. 10% Asian-American, 1% Black, 13% Hispanic, 1% Native American, 71% White, 4% Other. Average age of undergraduates is 21.
**Freshman profile:** 4% of freshmen who took SAT scored 700 or over on verbal, 8% scored 700 or over on math; 25% scored 600 or over on verbal, 43% scored 600 or over on math; 74% scored 500 or over on verbal, 85% scored 500 or over on math; 99% scored 400 or over on verbal, 99% scored 400 or over on math; 100% scored 300 or over on verbal, 100% scored 300 or over on math. 18% of freshmen who took ACT scored 30 or over on English, 14% scored 30 or over on math, 19% scored 30 or over on composite; 79% scored 24 or over on English, 65% scored 24 or over on math, 76% scored 24 or over on composite; 100% scored 18 or over on English, 98% scored 18 or over on math, 100% scored 18 or over on composite; 100% scored 12 or over on math. 85% of accepted applicants took SAT; 56% took ACT.
**Undergraduate achievement:** 84% of fall 1992 freshmen returned for fall 1993 term. 46% of entering class graduated. 60% of students who completed a degree program went on to graduate study within five years.
**Foreign students:** 37 students are from out of the country. Countries represented include El Salvador, Japan, Mexico, Pakistan, Syria, and Taiwan; 22 in all.

**PROGRAMS OF STUDY. Degrees:** B.A., B.S.
**Majors:** Art, Art History, Biochemistry, Biology, Chemistry, Classics, Drama, Economics, Education, English, French, German, History, Mathematics, Philosophy, Physics, Politics, Psychology, Spanish, Theology.
**Distribution of degrees:** The majors with the highest enrollment are politics, English, and psychology; secondary education, mathematics, and German have the lowest.
**Requirements:** General education requirement.
**Academic regulations:** Freshmen must maintain minimum 1.0 GPA; sophomores, 1.3 GPA; juniors, 1.66 GPA; seniors, 2.0 GPA.
**Special:** Concentrations offered in Business Leaders of Tomorrow, computer science, Christian contemplative tradition, foreign language/area studies, international studies, journalism, and Medieval and Renaissance studies. Self-designed majors. Double majors. Dual degrees. Independent study. Internships. Graduate school at which undergraduates may take graduate-level courses. Preprofessional programs in law, medicine, dentistry, theology, architecture, business, counseling and psychology, engineering, and physical therapy. 3-1 medical technology and physical therapy programs. Five-year bachelor's/M.B.A. program. 3-2 engineering programs. 3-2 architecture program. Member of Association for Higher Education. Washington Semester. Rome, and Cuernavaca, Mexico. Exchange programs with over 20 schools. Teacher certification in art, elementary and secondary education. Certification in specific subject areas. Study abroad in Italy. ROTC at U of Texas at Arlington. AFROTC at U of North Texas.
**Honors:** Phi Beta Kappa. Honor societies.
**Academic Assistance:** Remedial writing and math. Nonremedial tutoring.

**STUDENT LIFE. Housing:** All freshmen and sophomores under age 21 must live on campus unless living with family. Coed, women's, and men's dorms. School-owned/operated apartments. 61% of students live in college housing.
**Social atmosphere:** According to the student newspaper, "Much of the social life at UD is on campus. A majority of the students live on campus and study. Students take their classes seriously, because they truly desire to learn the greater truth, but they manage to also become a family of close friends in their common journey." One of the popular places to gather on campus is the Cappuccino Bar. Numerous Catholic groups and the Enviornmental Awareness Group are influential organizations on campus. Groundhog Day, the Rome semester, Charity Week, and the Dallas Year Events are among the favorite events of the school year.
**Services and counseling/handicapped student services:** Placement services. Health service. Personal and psychological counseling. Career and academic guidance services.

Religious counseling. Physically disabled student services. Notetaking services. Tape recorders. Tutors. Reader services for the blind.
**Campus organizations:** Undergraduate student government. Student newspaper (University News, published once/week). Literary magazine. Yearbook. Chorus, madrigal group, pep band, drama group, film series, Charity Week, math club, tutoring program, Spring Olympics, departmental, social, and special-interest groups, 43 organizations in all.
**Minority/foreign student organizations:** African Awareness Culture Committee. International Student Association, Chinese, German, Indonesian, Japanese, Korean, Spanish, Thai, and Turkish groups.

**ATHLETICS. Physical education requirements:** None.
**Intercollegiate competition:** 18% of students participate. Basketball (M,W), golf (M), tennis (M,W), volleyball (W). Member of NAIA, Texas Intercollegiate Athletic Association.
**Intramural and club sports:** 65% of students participate. Intramural basketball, flag football, soccer, softball, tennis, volleyball, water polo. Men's club cheerleading, cross-country, fencing, rugby, sailing, soccer. Women's club cheerleading, cross-country, fencing, sailing, soccer.

**ADMISSIONS. Academic basis for candidate selection** (in order of priority): Secondary school record, class rank, standardized test scores, essay, school's recommendation.
**Nonacademic basis for candidate selection:** Character and personality are important. Extracurricular participation, particular talent or ability, geographical distribution, and alumni/ae relationship are considered.
**Requirements:** Graduation from secondary school is recommended; GED is accepted. 14 units and the following program of study are required: 4 units of English, 3 units of math, 3 units of science, 2 units of foreign language, 2 units of social studies. Minimum 2.5 GPA recommended. Conditional admission possible for applicants not meeting standard requirements. SAT or ACT is required. Campus visit and interview recommended. Off-campus interviews available with an admissions representative.
**Procedure:** Take SAT or ACT by December 1 of 12th year. Suggest filing application by December 1. Application deadline is February 1. Deadline of early admission is January 15; regular admission is March 15. Reply is required by May 1. $100 tuition deposit, refundable until May 1. Freshmen accepted for terms other than fall.
**Special programs:** Admission may be deferred one year. Credit and/or placement may be granted through CEEB Advanced Placement exams for scores of 3 or higher. Placement may be granted through military experience. Early entrance/early admission program.
**Transfer students:** Transfer students accepted for terms other than fall. In fall 1993, 8% of all new students were transfers into all classes. 129 transfer applications were received, 115 were accepted. Application deadline is April 1 through July 1 for fall; December 1 for spring. Minimum 2.5 GPA required. Lowest course grade accepted is "C." Maximum number of transferable credits is 60 semester hours. At least 30 advanced semester credits must be completed at the university to receive degree.
**Admissions contact:** Christopher Lydon, Director of Admissions/Financial Aid. 214 721-5266.

**FINANCIAL AID. Available aid:** Pell grants, SEOG, state scholarships and grants, school scholarships and grants, private scholarships and grants, ROTC scholarships, and academic merit scholarships. Perkins Loans (NDSL), PLUS, Stafford Loans (GSL), state loans, and SLS. AMS and family tuition reduction. U Dallas payment plan.
**Financial aid statistics:** 10% of aid is not need-based. In 1993-94, 100% of all undergraduate applicants received aid. Average amounts of aid awarded freshmen: Scholarships and grants, $6,777; loans, $3,468.
**Supporting data/closing dates:** FAFSA: Priority filing date is March 1. School's own aid application: Priority filing date is March 1. Financial aid transcripts: Priority filing date is March 1. Notification of awards on rolling basis.
**Financial aid contact:** Kenneth Covington, Director of Financial Aid. 214 721-5266.

**STUDENT EMPLOYMENT.** College Work/Study Program. Institutional employment. 40% of full-time undergraduates work on campus during school year. Students may expect to earn an average of $1,800 during school year. Off-campus part-time employment opportunities rated "good."

**COMPUTER FACILITIES.** 119 IBM/IBM-compatible and Macintosh/Apple microcomputers. Client/LAN operating systems include DOS. Computer facilities are available to all students.
**Fees:** $10 computer fee per semester.
**Hours:** 8 AM-10 PM.

**GRADUATE CAREER DATA.** Graduate school percentages: 6% enter law school. 10% enter medical school. 10% enter graduate business programs. 23% enter graduate arts and sciences programs. Highest graduate school enrollments: U of Dallas, U of St. Thomas, U of Texas at Austin. 49% of graduates choose careers in business and industry. Companies and businesses that hire graduates: GTE, MCI, Texas Instruments.

**PROMINENT ALUMNI/AE.** Terrance Larsen, chairman, Core States Financial Corp.; Jo Ann Shoaf Gasper, president, Franklin Park Assoc. Ltd.; Ignacio Salinas, Jr., San Diego Mayor Pro Tem.

# University of Houston

**Houston, TX 77204-2161 713 749-1101**

**1994-95 Costs.** Tuition: $840 (state residents), $4,920 (out-of-state). Room: $2,600. Board: $2,200. Fees, books, misc. academic expenses (school's estimate): $1,126.
**Enrollment.** Undergraduates: 7,867 men, 7,603 women (full-time). Freshman class: 6,530 applicants, 3,946 accepted, 2,363 enrolled. Graduate enrollment: 4,204 men, 3,605 women.
**Test score averages/ranges.** Average SAT scores: 465 verbal, 535 math.
**Faculty.** 907 full-time; 1,373 part-time. 92% of faculty holds highest degree in specific field. Student/faculty ratio: 20 to 1.
**Selectivity rating.** Competitive.

**PROFILE.** The University of Houston, founded in 1927, is a public institution. Programs are offered through the Colleges of Architecture, Business Administration, Education, Engineering, Hotel and Restaurant Management, Humanities and Fine Arts, Natural Sciences and Mathematics, Optometry, Pharmacy, Social Sciences, and Technology; the Graduate School of Social Work; and the UH Law Center. Its 556-acre campus is located in a residential area, three miles from downtown Houston.

**Accreditation:** SACS.
**Religious orientation:** University of Houston is nonsectarian; no religious requirements.
**Library:** Collections totaling over 1,562,001 volumes, 19,942 periodical subscriptions, and 3,001,026 microform items.
**Special facilities/museums:** Art gallery, language lab, human development and lab school, University Hilton (staffed in part by students in College of Hotel and Restaurant Management), opera studio.
**Athletic facilities:** Gymnasiums, field house, arena, track, baseball, football, soccer, and softball fields, basketball, racquetball, and tennis courts, swimming pools.

**STUDENT BODY. Undergraduate profile:** 85% are state residents; 13% are transfers. 11% Asian-American, 8% Black, 11% Hispanic, 1% Native American, 63% White, 6% Other. Average age of undergraduates is 24.
**Freshman profile:** 1% of freshmen who took SAT scored 700 or over on verbal, 5% scored 700 or over on math; 9% scored 600 or over on verbal, 26% scored 600 or over on math; 33% scored 500 or over on verbal, 66% scored 500 or over on math; 82% scored 400 or over on verbal, 94% scored 400 or over on math; 98% scored 300 or over on verbal, 99% scored 300 or over on math. Majority of accepted applicants took SAT.
**Foreign students:** 911 students are from out of the country. Countries represented include China, Hong Kong, India, Malysia, Pakistan, and Taiwan; 100 in all.

**PROGRAMS OF STUDY. Degrees:** B.A., B.Acct., B.Arch., B.Bus.Admin., B.F.A., B.Mus., B.S., B.S.Chem.Eng., B.S.Ed., B.S.Elec.Eng., B.S.Indust.Eng., B.S.Mech.Eng., B.S.Pharm., B.S.Tech.
**Majors:** Accountancy, Accounting, Anthropology, Architecture, Architecture/Environmental Design, Art, Art History, Biochemical/Biophysical Sciences, Biology, Biology/Medical Technology, Biology/Pre-Dental, Biology/Pre-Medical, Biology/Pre-Nuclear Medicine Technology, Biology/Pre-Nursing, Biology/Pre-Physical Therapy, Biology/Pre-Veterinary Medicine, Business Administration Teacher Education, Business Basic Teacher Education, Business Secretarial Teacher Education, Ceramics, Chemical Engineering, Chemistry, Civil Engineering, Classical Studies, Communication Disorders, Computer Drafting Design Technology, Computer Engineering Technology, Computer Science/Systems Science Option, Construction Management Technology, Consumer/Home Economics Education, Consumer Sciences/Merchandising, Control Systems Technology, Drama, Economics, Economics/Business Administration, Electrical Engineering, Electrical Power Technology, Electronics Technology, Elementary School Teacher Education, Engineering, English, English/Language Arts Teacher Education, Finance, French, General Science Teacher Education, Geology, Geophysics, German, German Area Studies, Graphic Communications, Health, Health Teacher Education, History, Hotel/Restaurant Management, Human Development/Family Studies, Human Nutrition/Foods, Humanities/Fine Arts, Industrial Arts Teacher Education, Industrial Distribution Technology, Industrial Education, Industrial Engineering, Industrial Supervision Technology, Interdisciplinary Studies, Jewelry/Metalsmithing, Journalism, Kinesiology, Latin Teacher Education, Life/Earth Science Teacher Education, Management Information Systems, Manufacturing Systems Technology, Marketing, Marketing/Distributive Education, Mathematics, Mathematics/Applied Analysis Option, Mathematics/Statistics, Mechanical Engineering, Music, Music Composition, Music Performance, Music Theory, Natural Science/Mathematics, Operations Management, Organizational Behavior/Management, Pharmacy, Philosophy, Physical Education, Physical Science Teacher Education, Physics, Physics/Geophysics Option, Political Science, Pre-Law, Pre-Optometry, Pre-Pharmacy, Psychology, Quantitative Management Science, Radio/Television, Russian Studies, Secondary Education, Social Sciences, Sociology, Spanish, Speech Communication, Surveying/Mapping Technology, Technical Education, Training/Development.
**Requirements:** General education requirement.
**Academic regulations:** Minimum 2.0 GPA must be maintained.
**Special:** Minors offered. Self-designed majors. Double majors. Independent study. Accelerated study. Internships. Cooperative education programs. Graduate school at which undergraduates may take graduate-level courses. Preprofessional programs in law, medicine, and dentistry. Member of Southeast Texas Consortium and Western Name Exchange. Teacher certification in early childhood, elementary, secondary, and special education. Study abroad in England, France, Mexico, and Spain. ROTC and NROTC.
**Honors:** Phi Beta Kappa. Honors program. Honor societies.
**Academic Assistance:** Remedial reading, writing, math, and study skills. Nonremedial tutoring.

**STUDENT LIFE. Housing:** Students may live on or off-campus. Coed dorms. Sorority and fraternity housing. School-owned/operated apartments. Both on-campus and off-campus married-student housing. Handicapped student housing. 8% of students live in college housing.
**Services and counseling/handicapped student services:** Health service. Day care. Legal counseling. International student adviser. Counseling services for minority, military, veteran, and older students. Birth control, personal, and psychological counseling. Career and academic guidance services. Religious counseling. Learning disabled services.
**Campus organizations:** Undergraduate student government. Student newspaper (Daily Cougar, published four times/week). Literary magazine. Yearbook. Radio and TV stations. Band, chorus, orchestra, academic, political, professional, and special-interest groups, 200 organizations in all. 17 fraternities, no chapter houses; 10 sororities, no chapter houses.
**Religious organizations:** Numerous religious groups.
**Minority/foreign student organizations:** Numerous minority student groups. Numerous foreign student groups.

**ATHLETICS. Physical education requirements:** Two semesters of physical education required.
**Intercollegiate competition:** 1% of students participate. Baseball (M), basketball (M,W), cheerleading (M,W), cross-country (M,W), diving (W), football (M), golf (M), swimming (W), tennis (W), track (indoor) (M,W), track (outdoor) (M,W), track and field (indoor)

(M,W), track and field (outdoor) (M,W), volleyball (W). Member of NCAA Division I, Southwest Conference.
**Intramural and club sports:** 35% of students participate. Intramural badminton, basketball, flag football, golf, handball, hockey, racquetball, soccer, softball, tennis, walleyball. Men's club bowling, rugby, soccer. Women's club bowling.

**ADMISSIONS. Academic basis for candidate selection** (in order of priority): Class rank, standardized test scores.
**Nonacademic basis for candidate selection:** Extracurricular participation and particular talent or ability are considered.
**Requirements:** Graduation from secondary school is required; GED is accepted. 12 units and the following program of study are required: 4 units of English, 3 units of math, 2 units of lab science, 3 units of social studies. Foreign language is recommended. Class rank determines minimum SAT or ACT scores required; generally ranges from combined SAT score of 800 (composite ACT score of 19) for applicants in top quarter of secondary school class to combined SAT score of 1100 (composite ACT score of 27) for those in bottom quarter. Minimum SAT verbal score of 400 (ACT English score of 19) required of all applicants. Chemistry ACH required of engineering program applicants in place of foreign language ACH. Audition required of music program applicants. Conditional admission possible for applicants not meeting standard requirements. SAT or ACT is required. ACH recommended. Campus visit recommended. No off-campus interviews.
**Procedure:** Take SAT or ACT by June of 12th year. Take ACH by June of 12th year. Visit college for interview by May 1 of 12th year. Suggest filing application by May 1; no deadline. Notification of admission on rolling basis. $250 room deposit, refundable until August 1. Freshmen accepted for terms other than fall.
**Special programs:** Credit may be granted through CLEP general and subject exams and military experience. Credit and placement may be granted through challenge exams. Early decision program. Early entrance/early admission program. Concurrent enrollment program.
**Transfer students:** Transfer students accepted for terms other than fall. In fall 1992, 13% of all new students were transfers into all classes. 4,545 transfer applications were received, 4,170 were accepted. Application deadline is June 14 for fall; October 21 for spring. Minimum 2.0 GPA recommended. Lowest course grade accepted is "C." Maximum number of transferable credits is 66 semester hours. At least 30 semester hours must be completed at the university to receive degree.
**Admissions contact:** Rob Sheinkopf, Ed.D., Director of Admissions. 713 743-1010.

**FINANCIAL AID. Available aid:** Pell grants, SEOG, state scholarships and grants, school scholarships and grants, private scholarships and grants, ROTC scholarships, academic merit scholarships, athletic scholarships, and aid for undergraduate foreign students. Perkins Loans (NDSL), PLUS, Stafford Loans (GSL), Health Professions Loans, state loans, school loans, private loans, and SLS. Deferred payment plan.
**Financial aid statistics:** 10% of aid is not need-based. In 1992-93, 39% of all undergraduate applicants received aid. Average amounts of aid awarded freshmen: Scholarships and grants, $1,160; loans, $1,486.
**Supporting data/closing dates:** FAFSA/FAF/FFS: Priority filing date is April 1; accepted on rolling basis. Income tax forms: Priority filing date is April 1; accepted on rolling basis. Notification of awards begins in June.
**Financial aid contact:** Robert Sheridan, Director of Financial Aid. 713 749-1582.

**STUDENT EMPLOYMENT.** College Work/Study Program. Institutional employment. 25% of full-time undergraduates work on campus during school year. Students may expect to earn an average of $1,800 during school year. Off-campus part-time employment opportunities rated "excellent."

**COMPUTER FACILITIES.** IBM/IBM-compatible and Macintosh/Apple microcomputers. Computer languages and software packages include Ada, Ada Base, CAD/CAM, COBOL, dBASE, FORTRAN, ImSL, Pascal, SIZE, SPSS. Computer facilities are available to all students.
**Fees:** $30 computer fee per semester.
**Hours:** 24 hours.

**PROMINENT ALUMNI/AE.** Cindy Pickins, actress; Rod Canion, founder, Compaq Computers; Kathy Whitmire, former mayor, Houston; Tom Jarriel, ABC newsman; Akeem Olajuwon, NBA player.

# University of Houston–Downtown

**Houston, TX 77002** **713 221-8000**

**1993-94 Costs.** Tuition: $576 (state residents), $3,888 (out-of-state). Housing: None. Fees, books, misc. academic expenses (school's estimate): $1,078.
**Enrollment.** Undergraduates: 1,680 men, 1,622 women (full-time). Freshman class: 1,250 enrolled.
**Test score averages/ranges.** N/A.
**Faculty.** 60 full-time; 40 part-time. 82% of faculty holds doctoral degree. Student/faculty ratio: 20 to 1.
**Selectivity rating.** N/A.

**PROFILE.** The University of Houston–Downtown, founded in 1942, is a public university. Programs are offered through the Divisions of Arts and Sciences and Business and Technology. Its two-building campus is located at the edge of Houston's business district.

**Accreditation:** SACS. Professionally accredited by the Accreditation Board for Engineering and Technology.
**Religious orientation:** University of Houston-Downtown is nonsectarian; no religious requirements.
**Library:** Collections totaling over 160,000 volumes, 1,450 periodical subscriptions, and 30,000 microform items.
**Special facilities/museums:** Art gallery.
**Athletic facilities:** Students may use University of Houston central campus facilities.

**STUDENT BODY. Undergraduate profile:** 45% are transfers. 11% Asian-American, 23% Black, 27% Hispanic, 35% White, 4% Other. Average age of undergraduates is 24.
**Undergraduate achievement:** 40% of fall 1991 freshmen returned for fall 1992 term.
**Foreign students:** 187 students are from out of the country. Countries represented include Hong Kong, Indonesia, Japan, Pakistan, Taiwan, and Turkey; 55 in all.

**PROGRAMS OF STUDY. Degrees:** B.A., B.Bus.Admin., B.Gen.Studies, B.S.
**Majors:** Accounting, Administrative Services Management, Applied Mathematics, Applied Microbiology, Applied Physics, Biological/Physical Sciences, Computer Information Systems, Computer Science, Criminal Justice, Electrical/Electronics Design, Engineering Design, Financial Institutions, General Business, General Studies, Humanities, Industrial Chemistry, Petroleum Land Management, Process/Piping Design, Professional Writing, Purchasing/Material Management, Quantitative Methods, Real Estate, Social Sciences, Structural Analysis/Design.
**Distribution of degrees:** The majors with the highest enrollment are accounting and criminal justice; quantitative methods, process/piping design, and structural analysis/design have the lowest.
**Requirements:** General education requirement.
**Academic regulations:** Minimum 2.0 GPA must be maintained.
**Special:** Boston Medical Program. Self-designed majors. Double majors. Independent study. Internships. Preprofessional programs in law, medicine, veterinary science, pharmacy, dentistry, optometry, and nursing. Combined-degree programs in dental hygiene, medical technology, nuclear medicine, nursing, nutrition, occupational therapy, and optometry with Baylor Coll of Medicine and U of Texas Sch of Allied Health Sciences. ROTC at U of Houston at Central Park. NROTC at Rice U.
**Academic Assistance:** Remedial reading, writing, math, and study skills.

**STUDENT LIFE. Housing:** Commuter campus; no student housing.
**Services and counseling/handicapped student services:** Placement services. Health service. Counseling services for minority and veteran students. Birth control, personal, and psychological counseling. Career and academic guidance services. Physically disabled student services. Learning disabled services. Tape recorders. Tutors. Reader services for the blind.
**Campus organizations:** Undergraduate student government. Student newspaper (Dateline, published bimonthly). Literary magazine. Choir, program council, Council of Organizations, Student Ambassadors, professional groups, 120 organizations in all. One sorority, no chapter house.
**Religious organizations:** Campus Christians.
**Minority/foreign student organizations:** Black Student Union, Latin American Student Services Organization, Chinese Student Association, Vietnamese Student Association, Philippine Association of College Enthusiasts, Indo-Pak Student Association. International Student Organization.

**ATHLETICS. Physical education requirements:** None.
**Intramural and club sports:** Intramural badminton, basketball, bowling, flag football, golf, jogging, racquetball, soccer, softball, superstars competitions, table tennis, tennis, volleyball. Men's club soccer.

**ADMISSIONS.**
**Requirements:** Graduation from secondary school is required; GED is accepted. No specific distribution of secondary school units required. SAT or ACT is recommended. Campus visit recommended. No off-campus interviews.
**Procedure:** Suggest filing application by July. Application deadline is August. Notification of admission on rolling basis. No set date by which applicants must accept offer. Freshmen accepted for terms other than fall.
**Special programs:** Admission may be deferred. Credit may be granted through CLEP subject exams, DANTES and challenge exams. Early decision program. Early entrance/early admission program. Concurrent enrollment program.
**Transfer students:** Transfer students accepted for terms other than fall. In fall 1992, 45% of all new students were transfers into all classes. 829 transfer applications were received, 829 were accepted. Application deadline is the Friday before regular registration for fall; the Friday before regular registration for spring. Minimum 2.0 GPA recommended. Lowest course grade accepted is "C-." Maximum number of transferable credits is 66 semester hours. At least 30 semester hours must be completed at the university to receive degree.
**Admissions contact:** Ron Petrie, M.A., Director of Admissions. 713 221-8533.

**FINANCIAL AID. Available aid:** Pell grants, SEOG, state scholarships and grants, school scholarships, private scholarships, ROTC scholarships, and academic merit scholarships. Stafford Loans (GSL), state loans, school loans, and SLS. Deferred payment plan.
**Financial aid statistics:** In 1992-93, 25% of all freshman applicants received aid.
**Supporting data/closing dates:** FAFSA/FAF/FFS: Priority filing date is June 1. School's own aid application: Priority filing date is June 1; accepted on rolling basis. Notification of awards on rolling basis.
**Financial aid contact:** Marilyn Allen, Director of Financial Aid. 713 221-8041.

**STUDENT EMPLOYMENT.** College Work/Study Program. Institutional employment. 15% of full-time undergraduates work on campus during school year. Students may expect to earn an average of $2,500 during school year. Off-campus part-time employment opportunities rated "excellent."

**COMPUTER FACILITIES.** 200 IBM/IBM-compatible and Macintosh/Apple microcomputers. Students may access Digital minicomputer/mainframe systems. Computer languages and software packages include BASIC, COBOL, FORTRAN, Pascal, PL/1; business, database, language, spreadsheet, statistical, word processing packages. Computer facilities are available to all students.
**Fees:** Computer fee is included in tuition/fees.
**Hours:** 8 AM-10 PM (M-Th); 8 AM-5 PM (F-Sa); 10 AM-5 PM (Su).

## University of Mary Hardin-Baylor

**Belton, TX 76513** **817 939-8642**

**1994-95 Costs.** Tuition: $5,550. Room & board: $3,106. Fees, books, misc. academic expenses (school's estimate): $1,060.
**Enrollment.** Undergraduates: 497 men, 990 women (full-time). Freshman class: 309 applicants, 304 accepted, 259 enrolled. Graduate enrollment: 69 men, 162 women.
**Test score averages/ranges.** Average SAT scores: 21 combined.
**Faculty.** 86 full-time; 53 part-time. 52% of faculty holds doctoral degree. Student/faculty ratio: 22 to 1.
**Selectivity rating.** Noncompetitive.

**PROFILE.** The University of Mary Hardin-Baylor, founded in 1845, is a church-affiliated, liberal arts university. Programs are offered through the Colleges of Arts and Sciences and the Schools of Business, Creative Arts, Nursing, and Education. Its 100-acre campus is located in Belton, in central Texas, 60 miles north of Austin.

**Accreditation:** SACS. Professionally accredited by the National League for Nursing.
**Religious orientation:** University of Mary Hardin-Baylor is affiliated with the Southern Baptist Church (Baptist General Convention of Texas); two semesters of religion required.
**Library:** Collections totaling over 96,330 volumes, 830 periodical subscriptions, and 27,749 microform items.
**Special facilities/museums:** Child development center, language lab, language institute.
**Athletic facilities:** Gymnasium, indoor and outdoor swimming pools, recreational field.

**STUDENT BODY. Undergraduate profile:** 88% are state residents; 19% are transfers. 1% Asian-American, 7% Black, 9% Hispanic, 78% White, 5% Other. Average age of undergraduates is 23.
**Freshman profile:** 2% of freshmen who took ACT scored 30 or over on composite; 28% scored 24 or over on composite; 82% scored 18 or over on composite; 99% scored 12 or over on composite; 100% scored 6 or over on composite. Majority of accepted applicants took ACT. 92% of freshmen come from public schools.
**Foreign students:** 120 students are from out of the country. Countries represented include China, Japan, Korea, Mexico, Taiwan, and Venezuela; 35 in all.

**PROGRAMS OF STUDY. Degrees:** B.A., B.Bus.Admin., B.F.A., B.Gen.Studies, B.Gen.Tech., B.Mus., B.S., B.S.Nurs., B.S.Soc.Work.
**Majors:** Accounting, Administrative Office Management, Art, Behavioral Science, Biology, Business, Business Administration, Chemistry, Church Music, Computer Information Systems, Computer Science, Economics/Finance, Elementary Education, English, General Studies, General Technology, Health/Physical Education, History, Human Resources Management, Information Science, Management, Marketing, Mathematics, Medical Technology, Music Education, Music Performance/Pedagogy, Nursing, Political Science, Psychology, Recreation, Religion, Social Work, Sociology, Spanish, Special Education/General, Speech.
**Distribution of degrees:** The majors with the highest enrollment are education, social sciences, and nursing.
**Requirements:** General education requirement.
**Academic regulations:** Freshmen must maintain minimum 1.5 GPA; sophomores, 1.7 GPA; juniors, 1.9 GPA; seniors, 2.0 GPA.
**Special:** Minors offered in most majors and in drama, French, and German. Courses offered in driver education and physics. Double majors. Independent study. Internships. Graduate school at which undergraduates may take graduate-level courses. Preprofessional programs in law, medicine, veterinary science, pharmacy, dentistry, theology, and optometry. 3-1 medical technology program with Scott and White Hospital. Tuition exchange progam with other participating universities. Teacher certification in early childhood, elementary, secondary, and special education. AFROTC at Baylor U.
**Honors:** Honors program. Honor societies.
**Academic Assistance:** Remedial reading, writing, math, and study skills. Nonremedial tutoring.

**ADMISSIONS. Academic basis for candidate selection** (in order of priority): Standardized test scores, secondary school record, class rank, school's recommendation, essay.
**Nonacademic basis for candidate selection:** Character and personality are important. Extracurricular participation and particular talent or ability are considered.
**Requirements:** Graduation from secondary school is required; GED is accepted. 15 units and the following program of study are required: 3 units of English, 2 units of math, 2 units of social studies. Minimum composite ACT score of 18 (combined SAT score of 740) and rank in top half of secondary school class required. Conditional admission possible for applicants not meeting standard requirements. ACT is required; SAT may be substituted. Campus visit and interview recommended. Off-campus interviews available with an admissions representative.
**Procedure:** Take SAT or ACT by July of 12th year. Suggest filing application by July 1. Application deadline is August 1. Notification of admission on rolling basis. $35 nonrefundable tuition deposit. $100 room deposit, refundable until August 1. Freshmen accepted for terms other than fall.
**Special programs:** Admission may be deferred one semester. Credit and/or placement may be granted through CEEB Advanced Placement exams for scores of 3 or higher. Credit and/or placement may be granted through CLEP general and subject exams. Credit may be granted through military experience. Credit and placement may be granted through DANTES and challenge exams. Early entrance/early admission program. Concurrent enrollment program.
**Transfer students:** Transfer students accepted for terms other than fall. In fall 1993, 19% of all new students were transfers into all classes. 355 transfer applications were received, 349 were accepted. Application deadline is August 1. Minimum 2.0 GPA required. Lowest course grade accepted is "C." Maximum number of transferable credits is 66 semester hours. At least one-quarter of total semester hours must be completed at the university to receive degree.
**Admissions contact:** Bobby Johnson, Director of Admissions. 817 939-4520.

**FINANCIAL AID. Available aid:** Pell grants, SEOG, Federal Nursing Student Scholarships, state scholarships and grants, school scholarships and grants, private scholarships and grants, academic merit scholarships, athletic scholarships, and aid for undergraduate foreign students. Perkins Loans (NDSL), PLUS, Stafford Loans (GSL), state loans, and SLS. Tuition Plan Inc., AMS, and deferred payment plan.
**Financial aid statistics:** 25% of aid is not need-based. In 1993-94, 78% of all undergraduate applicants received aid; 95% of freshman applicants. Average amounts of aid awarded freshmen: Scholarships and grants, $2,600; loans, $2,018.
**Supporting data/closing dates:** FAFSA/FAF/FFS: Priority filing date is June 1. School's own aid application: Priority filing date is June 1. State aid form: Accepted on rolling basis. Income tax forms: Accepted on rolling basis. Notification of awards begins May 1.
**Financial aid contact:** Ron Brown, Director of Financial Aid. 817 939-4515.

## University of North Texas

**Denton, TX 76203-3797** **817 565-2000**

**1993-94 Costs.** Tuition: $1,196 (state residents), $4,508 (out-of-state). Room & board: $3,510. Fees, books, misc. academic expenses (school's estimate): $600.
**Enrollment.** Undergraduates: 9,592 men, 10,041 women (full-time). Freshman class: 3,489 applicants, 3,078 accepted, 2,049 enrolled. Graduate enrollment: 3,034 men, 3,766 women.
**Test score averages/ranges.** Average SAT scores: 462 verbal, 517 math. Average ACT scores: 23 composite.
**Faculty.** 782 full-time. 80% of faculty holds doctoral degree. Student/faculty ratio: 18 to 1.
**Selectivity rating.** Less competitive.

**PROFILE.** The University of North Texas, founded in 1890, is a public, comprehensive institution. Programs are offered through the Colleges of Arts and Sciences, Business Administration, Education, and Music; the Schools of Community Service, Human Resource Management, Library and Information Sciences; and the Graduate School. Its 425-acre campus is located in Denton, 39 miles from Dallas.

**Accreditation:** SACS. Professionally accredited by the Accrediting Council on Education in Journalism and Mass Communication, the American Assembly of Collegiate Schools of Business, the American Library Association, the American Psychological Association, the American Speech-Language-Hearing Association, the Council on Rehabilitation Education, the Council on Social Work Education, the Foundation for Interior Design Education Research, the National Association of Schools of Music, the National Association of Schools of Public Affairs and Administration, the National Council for Accreditation of Teacher Education, the National Recreation and Park Association.
**Religious orientation:** University of North Texas is nonsectarian; no religious requirements.
**Library:** Collections totaling over 1,154,168 volumes, 7,582 periodical subscriptions, and 2,605,887 microform items.
**Special facilities/museums:** Laser facilities.
**Athletic facilities:** Golf course, weight-training room, swimming pools, indoor aquatics area, gymnasiums, handball, racquetball, and tennis courts, coliseum, track.

**STUDENT BODY. Undergraduate profile:** 95% are state residents; 51% are transfers. 2% Asian-American, 6% Black, 5% Hispanic, 82% White, 5% Other. Average age of undergraduates is 21.
**Freshman profile:** 68% of accepted applicants took SAT; 26% took ACT.
**Undergraduate achievement:** 70% of fall 1991 freshmen returned for fall 1992 term. 10% of entering class graduated.
**Foreign students:** 910 students are from out of the country. Countries represented include China, Hong Kong, India, Japan, South Korea, and Taiwan; 102 in all.

**PROGRAMS OF STUDY. Degrees:** B.A., B.Appl.Arts/Sci., B.Bus.Admin., B.F.A., B.Mus., B.S., B.S.Bio., B.S.Biochem., B.S.Chem., B.S.Econ., B.S.Eng.Tech., B.S.Hosp.Mgmt., B.S.Math., B.S.Med.Tech., B.S.Physics, B.Soc.Work.
**Majors:** Accounting, Accounting Control Systems, Advertising Design, Anthropology, Applied Arts/Sciences, Art, Art History, Biology, Biology/Chemistry, Business Computer/Information Systems, Business Economics, Chemistry, Child Development, Choral Music, Composition, Computer Science, Counseling Associate Studies, Criminal Justice, Cytotechnology, Dance, Drama, Drawing/Painting, Economics, Emergency Administration Planning/Rehabilitation Studies, Engineering Technology, English, Entrepreneurship, Fashion Design, Finance/Banking, French, General Business, General Crafts, General Music, General Studies, Geography, German, Health Promotion, History, Hotel/Restaurant Management, Housing/Home Furnishings Management, Human Resource Management, Information Science, Instrumental Music, Insurance, Interdisciplinary Studies, Interior Design, Jazz Studies, Journalism, Kinesiology, Leisure Studies, Library Science, Marketing, Mathematics, Medical Technology, Music, Music History/Literature, Music Performance, Music Theory, Occupational Training and Development, Personnel/Industrial Relations, Personnel Management/Organizational Behavior, Philosophy, Photography, Physics, Piano Pedagogy, Political Science, Printmaking, Production/Operations Management, Psychology, Public Address/Communication, Radio/Television/Film, Real Estate, Recreation, Sculpture, Social Sciences, Social Work, Sociology, Spanish, Speech/Language Pathology/Audiology, Strategic Management, Studies in Aging, Visual Arts Studies.
**Distribution of degrees:** The majors with the highest enrollment are marketing, management, and elementary education; studies in aging, library science, and philosophy have the lowest.
**Requirements:** General education requirement.
**Academic regulations:** Freshmen must maintain minimum 1.8 GPA; sophomores, juniors, seniors, 2.0 GPA.

**Special:** Minors offered. Courses offered in Asian and women's studies. Self-designed majors. Double majors. Dual degrees. Pass/fail grading option. Internships. Graduate school at which undergraduates may take graduate-level courses. Preprofessional programs in law, medicine, dentistry, theology, allied health fields, engineering, library science, nursing, and physical therapy. 3-1 medical technology program with any American Medical Association-approved school of medical technology. 3-1 classic combination program. Five-year bachelor's/master's accounting program. Teacher certification in early childhood, elementary, secondary, special education, vo-tech, and bilingual/bicultural education. Member of International Student Exchange Program (ISEP). ROTC and AFROTC.
**Honors:** Honors program. Honor societies.
**Academic Assistance:** Remedial reading, writing, math, and study skills. Nonremedial tutoring.

**STUDENT LIFE. Housing:** All students with fewer than 30 credit hours must live on campus. Coed and women's dorms. School-owned/operated apartments. 14% of students live in college housing.
**Services and counseling/handicapped student services:** Placement services. Health service. Counseling services for minority, military, veteran, and older students. Birth control, personal, and psychological counseling. Career and academic guidance services. Religious counseling. Physically disabled student services. Learning disabled services. Notetaking services. Tape recorders. Tutors. Reader services for the blind.
**Campus organizations:** Undergraduate student government. Student newspaper (North Texas Daily). Yearbook. Radio and TV stations. A cappella choir, chorus, bands, orchestra, debating, radio/TV club, University Players, 210 organizations in all. 18 fraternities, 10 chapter houses; 10 sororities, no chapter houses. 5% of men join a fraternity. 5% of women join a sorority.
**Religious organizations:** Numerous religious groups.
**Minority/foreign student organizations:** Numerous minority student groups. Numerous foreign student groups.

**ATHLETICS. Physical education requirements:** Four credit hours of physical education required.
**Intercollegiate competition:** 1% of students participate. Basketball (M,W), cheerleading (M,W), cross-country (M,W), football (M), golf (M,W), soccer (M), tennis (M,W), track (indoor) (M,W), track (outdoor) (M,W), track and field (indoor) (M,W), track and field (outdoor) (M,W), volleyball (W). Member of NCAA Division I, NCAA Division I-AA for football, Southland Conference, Sunbelt Conference for men's soccer.
**Intramural and club sports:** 20% of students participate. Intramural badminton, baseball, billiards, bowling, cycling, fencing, frisbee, gymnastics, martial arts, racquetball, sailing, soccer, volleyball. Men's club badminton, baseball, billiards, bowling, cricket, cycling, fencing, gymnastics, martial arts, power lifting, racquetball, sailing, ultimate frisbee, volleyball, weight lifting, wrestling. Women's club badminton, billiards, bowling, cricket, cycling, fencing, gymnastics, martial arts, power lifting, racquetball, sailing, soccer, ultimate frisbee, weight lifting, wrestling.

**ADMISSIONS. Academic basis for candidate selection** (in order of priority): Standardized test scores, class rank.
**Requirements:** Graduation from secondary school is required; GED is not accepted. No specific distribution of secondary school units required. SAT or ACT scores required of applicants in top tenth of secondary school class; no minimum scores required. Minimum combined SAT score of 800 (composite ACT score of 19) required of those in remainder of top quarter. Minimum combined SAT score of 900 (composite ACT score of 21) required of those in second quarter. Minimum combined SAT score of 1000 (composite ACT score of 24) required of those in third quarter. Minimum combined SAT score of 1100 (composite ACT score of 27) required of those in bottom quarter. Audition required of music program applicants. SAT or ACT is required. Campus visit recommended. No off-campus interviews.
**Procedure:** Take SAT or ACT by March of 12th year. Suggest filing application by February. Application deadline is June 15. Notification of admission on rolling basis. $300 room deposit, refundable until July 1. Freshmen accepted for terms other than fall.
**Special programs:** Credit and/or placement may be granted through CEEB Advanced Placement exams for scores of 3 or higher. Credit and/or placement may be granted through CLEP subject exams. Credit may be granted through military experience. Credit and placement may be granted through DANTES and challenge exams. Early entrance/early admission program. Concurrent enrollment program.
**Transfer students:** Transfer students accepted for terms other than fall. In fall 1992, 51% of all new students were transfers into all classes. 6,409 transfer applications were received, 4,035 were accepted. Application deadline is June 15 for fall; December 1 for spring. Lowest course grade accepted is "D." Maximum number of transferable credits is 66 semester hours. At least 30 semester hours must be completed at the university to receive degree.
**Admissions contact:** Don Palermo, M.A., Director of Admissions. 817 565-2681.

**FINANCIAL AID. Available aid:** Pell grants, SEOG, state scholarships and grants, school scholarships, private scholarships and grants, ROTC scholarships, academic merit scholarships, and athletic scholarships. Perkins Loans (NDSL), PLUS, Stafford Loans (GSL), school loans, and SLS. Deferred payment plan.
**Financial aid statistics:** 15% of aid is not need-based. In 1992-93, 70% of all undergraduate applicants received aid; 70% of freshman applicants. Average amounts of aid awarded freshmen: Scholarships and grants, $1,200; loans, $2,625.
**Supporting data/closing dates:** FAFSA: Priority filing date is April 1. Notification of awards begins July 1.
**Financial aid contact:** Carolyn Cunningham, M.B.Ed., Director of Financial Aid. 817 565-2016.

**STUDENT EMPLOYMENT.** College Work/Study Program. Institutional employment. 50% of full-time undergraduates work on campus during school year. Students may expect to earn an average of $6,500 during school year. Freshmen are discouraged from working during their first term. Off-campus part-time employment opportunities rated "good."

**COMPUTER FACILITIES.** IBM/IBM-compatible and Macintosh/Apple microcomputers. Students may access Digital minicomputer/mainframe systems, BITNET, Internet. Computer languages and software packages include BMDP, COBOL, MINITAB, SAS, SPSS; several thousand in all. Some computers are restricted for use by students in specific programs.
**Fees:** None.

**PROMINENT ALUMNI/AE.** Shirley Cothran Barrett, 1975 Miss America; Larry McMurtry, Pulitzer Prize-winning writer; Phyllis George, 1971 Miss America, television personality.

# University of St. Thomas

**Houston, TX 77006** **713 522-7911**

**1993-94 Costs.** Tuition: $8,550. Room: $1,000. Board: $835. Fees, books, misc. academic expenses (school's estimate): $298.
**Enrollment.** Undergraduates: 339 men, 656 women (full-time). Freshman class: 347 applicants, 328 accepted, 192 enrolled. Graduate enrollment: 471 men, 410 women.
**Test score averages/ranges.** Average SAT scores: 500 verbal, 560 math. Range of SAT scores of middle 50%: 410-500 verbal, 510-600 math. Average ACT scores: 25 composite. Range of ACT scores of middle 50%: 21-25 composite.
**Faculty.** 85 full-time; 75 part-time. 80% of faculty holds highest degree in specific field.
**Selectivity rating.** More Competitive.

**PROFILE.** The University of St. Thomas, founded in 1947, is a private, church-affiliated, liberal arts university. Its 20-acre campus is located in downtown Houston.

**Accreditation:** SACS.
**Religious orientation:** University of St. Thomas is affiliated with the Roman Catholic Church (Basilian Fathers); three semesters of religion required.
**Library:** Collections totaling over 181,570 volumes, 792 periodical subscriptions, and 47,609 microform items.
**Special facilities/museums:** Learning resource center, institute for storm research.
**Athletic facilities:** Gymnasium, basketball, racquetball, tennis, and volleyball courts, weight room.

**STUDENT BODY. Undergraduate profile:** 98% are state residents. 6% Asian-American, 6% Black, 17% Hispanic, 1% Native American, 63% White, 7% Other. Average age of undergraduates is 25.
**Freshman profile:** Majority of accepted applicants took SAT.
**Undergraduate achievement:** 72% of fall 1992 freshmen returned for fall 1993 term. 18% of entering class graduated.
**Foreign students:** 20 students are from out of the country. Countries represented include Indonesia, Mexico, Pakistan, Taiwan, Thailand, and Turkey; 15 in all.

**PROGRAMS OF STUDY. Degrees:** B.A., B.Bus.Admin., B.S.
**Majors:** Accounting, Biology, Business Administration, Chemistry, Communication, Computer Information Systems, Drama, Economics/Business, Education, English, Fine Arts, French, General Studies, History, International Studies, Legal Studies, Liberal Arts, Mathematics, Music, Paralegal Studies, Philosophy, Political Science, Psychology, Religious Education, Spanish, Theology.
**Distribution of degrees:** The majors with the highest enrollment are business administration, psychology, and accounting; French and music have the lowest.
**Requirements:** General education requirement.
**Academic regulations:** Freshmen must maintain minimum 1.68 GPA; sophomores, juniors, seniors, 2.0 GPA.
**Special:** Minors offered in most majors and in physics and sociology. Double majors. Dual degrees. Independent study. Internships. Cooperative education programs. Graduate school at which undergraduates may take graduate-level courses. Preprofessional programs in law, medicine, dentistry, and medical technology. 2-2 nutrition/dietetics and physical therapy programs with U of Texas Sch of Allied Health Sciences. 3-2 engineering program with U of Houston and U of Notre Dame. Member of Houston Inter-University Consortium for International Studies. Teacher certification in early childhood, elementary, secondary, special education, and bilingual/bicultural education. Exchange programs abroad in England and France. Study abroad also in China, Costa Rica, the Dominican Republic, Hungary, Israel, Japan, Mexico, Poland, and Spain. ROTC at U of Houston. NROTC at Rice U.
**Honors:** Honors program. Honor societies.
**Academic Assistance:** Remedial reading and writing. Nonremedial tutoring.

**ADMISSIONS. Academic basis for candidate selection** (in order of priority): Secondary school record, class rank, standardized test scores, school's recommendation, essay.
**Nonacademic basis for candidate selection:** Character and personality and particular talent or ability are important. Extracurricular participation is considered.
**Requirements:** Graduation from secondary school is required; GED is accepted. 16 units and the following program of study are required: 4 units of English, 3 units of math, 2 units of science, 2 units of foreign language, 1 unit of social studies, 1 unit of history, 1 unit of academic electives. Minimum combined SAT score of 900 (composite ACT score of 21) and rank in top half of secondary school class recommended. Audition required of music program applicants. Conditional admission possible for applicants not meeting standard requirements. SAT or ACT is required. ACH recommended. Campus visit and interview recommended. Off-campus interviews available with an admissions representative.
**Procedure:** Take SAT or ACT by June of 12th year. Suggest filing application by March 1. Notification of admission on rolling basis. $100 nonrefundable tuition deposit. $200 room deposit, refundable until June 1. Freshmen accepted for terms other than fall.
**Special programs:** Admission may be deferred one year. Credit may be granted through CEEB Advanced Placement for scores of 3 or higher. Credit may be granted through CLEP subject exams. Placement may be granted through challenge exams. Early entrance/early admission program. Concurrent enrollment program.
**Transfer students:** Transfer students accepted for terms other than fall. In fall 1993, 439 transfer applications were received, 362 were accepted. Application deadline is March 1 (priority). Minimum 2.0 GPA required. Lowest course grade accepted is "C." Maximum

number of transferable credits is 90 semester hours. At least 36 semester hours must be completed at the university to receive degree.
**Admissions contact:** Elsie Biron, Director of Admissions. 713 522-7911, extension 3500.

**FINANCIAL AID. Available aid:** Pell grants, SEOG, state scholarships and grants, school scholarships and grants, and academic merit scholarships. Perkins Loans (NDSL), PLUS, Stafford Loans (GSL), state loans, and SLS. Tuition Plan Inc., AMS, and deferred payment plan.
**Financial aid statistics:** 35% of aid is not need-based. In 1993-94, 60% of all undergraduate applicants received aid; 49% of freshman applicants. Average amounts of aid awarded freshmen: Scholarships and grants, $3,000; loans, $1,500.
**Supporting data/closing dates:** FAFSA/FAF/FFS: Priority filing date is March 1; accepted on rolling basis. School's own aid application: Priority filing date is March 1. Income tax forms: Priority filing date is March 1. Financial aid transcripts: Accepted on rolling basis. Notification of awards on rolling basis.
**Financial aid contact:** Claudia Carlson, M.B.A., Director of Financial Aid. 713 522-7911, extension 2170.

# University of Texas at Arlington

**Arlington, TX 76019** **817 273-2011**

**1994-95 Costs.** Tuition: $1,374 (state residents), $5,454 (out-of-state). Room: $1,180-$1,340. Fees, books, misc. academic expenses (school's estimate): $1,094.
**Enrollment.** Undergraduates: 5,704 men, 5,261 women (full-time). Freshman class: 3,281 applicants, 2,411 accepted, 1,475 enrolled. Graduate enrollment: 2,502 men, 1,851 women.
**Test score averages/ranges.** Average SAT scores: 427 verbal, 491 math. Range of SAT scores of middle 50%: 380-490 verbal, 440-550 math. Average ACT scores: 21 English, 21 math, 21 composite. Range of ACT scores of middle 50%: 20-25 English, 19-24 math.
**Faculty.** 555 full-time; 326 part-time. 84% of faculty holds doctoral degree. Student/faculty ratio: 28 to 1.
**Selectivity rating.** Less competitive.

**PROFILE.** U Texas at Arlington is a public, comprehensive university. Founded as a private college in 1895, it gained university status and became part of the state system in 1965. Programs are offered through the Center for Professional Teacher Education; the Colleges of Business Administration, Engineering, Liberal Arts, and Science; the Graduate School; the Graduate School of Social Work; the Institute of Urban Studies; and the Schools of Architecture and Environmental Design and Nursing. Its 348-acre campus is located in Arlington, in the heart of the Dallas-Fort Worth metropolitan area.

**Accreditation:** SACS. Professionally accredited by the Accreditation Board for Engineering and Technology, the American Assembly of Collegiate Schools of Business, the Council on Social Work Education, the Foundation for Interior Design Education Research, the National Architecture Accrediting Board, the National Association of Schools of Music, the National League for Nursing.
**Religious orientation:** University of Texas at Arlington is nonsectarian; no religious requirements.
**Library:** Collections totaling over 913,745 volumes, 8,035 periodical subscriptions, and 1,436,983 microform items.
**Special facilities/museums:** Cartographic history library, Comanche Peak collection, government publications and maps collection, minority cultures collection, library of Texan and Mexican war material.
**Athletic facilities:** Swimming pool, baseball, intramural, soccer, and softball fields, gymnasiums, weight rooms, track, basketball, tennis, and volleyball courts, stadium.

**STUDENT BODY. Undergraduate profile:** 96% are state residents; 72% are transfers. 9% Asian-American, 9% Black, 7% Hispanic, 1% Native American, 72% White, 2% Other. Average age of undergraduates is 26.
**Freshman profile:** 1% of freshmen who took SAT scored 700 or over on verbal, 2% scored 700 or over on math; 5% scored 600 or over on verbal, 15% scored 600 or over on math; 23% scored 500 or over on verbal, 46% scored 500 or over on math; 62% scored 400 or over on verbal, 83% scored 400 or over on math; 94% scored 300 or over on verbal, 99% scored 300 or over on math. 70% of accepted applicants took SAT; 30% took ACT. 85% of freshmen come from public schools.
**Undergraduate achievement:** 64% of fall 1992 freshmen returned for fall 1993 term. 17% of entering class graduated.
**Foreign students:** 430 students are from out of the country. Countries represented include China, Hong Kong, India, Pakistan, South Korea, and Thailand; 81 in all.

**PROGRAMS OF STUDY. Degrees:** B.A., B.Bus.Admin., B.F.A., B.Mus., B.S., B.Soc.Work.
**Majors:** Accounting, Aerospace Engineering, Anthropology, Architecture, Art, Biochemistry, Biology, Broadcasting Communication, Business Administration, Chemistry, Civil Engineering, Classical Studies, Computer Science/Engineering, Criminology/Criminal Justice, Economics, Electrical Engineering, English, Exercise/Sports/Health Studies, Finance, French, Geology, German, History, Industrial Engineering, Information Systems, Interdisciplinary Studies, Interior Design, Journalism, Management, Management Science, Marketing, Mathematics, Mechanical Engineering, Medical Technology, Microbiology, Music, Nursing, Philosophy, Physics, Political Science, Psychology, Real Estate, Russian, Social Work, Sociology, Spanish, Speech, Theatre Arts.
**Distribution of degrees:** The majors with the highest enrollment are business, nursing, and electrical engineering; art, anthropology, and philosophy have the lowest.
**Requirements:** General education requirement.
**Academic regulations:** Minimum 2.0 GPA must be maintained.
**Special:** Minors offered in some majors and in dance, military science, women's studies, and writing. Televised instruction to selected industrial sites in Dallas-Ft. Worth area through North Texas Association for Higher Education. Double majors. Pass/fail grading option. Internships. Cooperative education programs. Graduate school at which undergraduates may take graduate-level courses. Preprofessional programs in law, medicine, veterinary science, pharmacy, and dentistry. 4-2 architecture program. Teacher certification in early childhood, elementary, secondary, and bilingual/bicultural education. Certification in specific subject areas. Study abroad in Austria, China, Eastern Europe, England, France, Germany, Mexico, Norway, the former Soviet Republics, and Spain. ROTC. AFROTC at Texas Christian U.
**Honors:** Honors program. Honor societies.
**Academic Assistance:** Remedial writing and math. Nonremedial tutoring.

**STUDENT LIFE. Housing:** All unmarried freshmen must live on campus unless living with family. Coed, women's, and men's dorms. Sorority and fraternity housing. School-owned/operated apartments. 8% of students live in college housing.
**Services and counseling/handicapped student services:** Placement services. Health service. Day care. Counseling services for minority, military, veteran, and older students. Birth control, personal, and psychological counseling. Career and academic guidance services. Physically disabled student services. Learning disabled services. Notetaking services. Tape recorders. Tutors. Reader services for the blind.
**Campus organizations:** Undergraduate student government. Student newspaper (Shorthorn, published four times/week). Literary magazine. TV station. Orchestras, ensembles, singing groups, concert band, political, professional, recreational, social, and special-interest groups, 232 organizations in all. 15 fraternities, 13 chapter houses; nine sororities, seven chapter houses. 5% of men join a fraternity. 5% of women join a sorority.
**Religious organizations:** Hillel, Muslim Student Association, Christian organizations.
**Minority/foreign student organizations:** African Studies Committee, NAACP, Mexican-American Association, Sociedad Hispanica, other minority groups. Bengali, Brazilian, Chinese, Indonesian, Japanese, Pakistani, and Vietnamese student groups.

**ATHLETICS. Physical education requirements:** Four semesters of physical education required.
**Intercollegiate competition:** 4% of students participate. Baseball (M), basketball (M,W), cross-country (M,W), golf (M), softball (W), tennis (M,W), track (indoor) (M,W), track (outdoor) (M,W), track and field (indoor) (M,W), track and field (outdoor) (M,W), volleyball (W). Member of NCAA Division I, Southland Conference.
**Intramural and club sports:** 28% of students participate. Intramural basketball, dodgeball, flag football, golf, soccer, softball, swimming, tennis, volleyball. Men's club bowling, cheerleading, martial arts, racquetball, rugby, soccer, water skiing. Women's club bowling, cheerleading, martial arts, racquetball, rugby, soccer, water skiing.

**ADMISSIONS. Academic basis for candidate selection** (in order of priority): Secondary school record, class rank, standardized test scores, school's recommendation.
**Requirements:** Graduation from secondary school is required; GED is not accepted. 20 units and the following program of study are required: 4 units of English, 2 units of math, 2 units of science, 2 units of foreign language, 3 units of social studies, 7 units of academic electives. Additional math or science units may make up for deficiencies in foreign language units. Additional admissions requirements for architecture, engineering, and mathematics program applicants. Conditional admission possible for applicants not meeting standard requirements. SAT or ACT is required. Campus visit recommended. No off-campus interviews.
**Procedure:** Take SAT or ACT by May 1 of 12th year. Application deadline is August 1. Notification of admission on rolling basis. $50 room deposit, refundable in special circumstances. Freshmen accepted for terms other than fall.
**Special programs:** Credit may be granted through CEEB Advanced Placement for scores of 3 or higher. Credit may be granted through CLEP subject exams and challenge exams. Early entrance/early admission program. Concurrent enrollment program.
**Transfer students:** Transfer students accepted for terms other than fall. In fall 1993, 72% of all new students were transfers into all classes. 6,035 transfer applications were received, 4,313 were accepted. Application deadline is August 1 for fall; December 1 for spring. Minimum 2.0 GPA required. Lowest course grade accepted is "C." Maximum number of transferable credits is 72 semester hours. At least 30 semester hours must be completed at the university to receive degree.
**Admissions contact:** R. Zack Prince, M.A., Director of Admissions. 817 273-2118.

**FINANCIAL AID. Available aid:** Pell grants, SEOG, state scholarships and grants, school scholarships and grants, private scholarships and grants, ROTC scholarships, academic merit scholarships, athletic scholarships, and aid for undergraduate foreign students. Perkins Loans (NDSL), PLUS, Stafford Loans (GSL), state loans, school loans, private loans, and SLS. Deferred payment plan.
**Financial aid statistics:** 20% of aid is not need-based. In 1993-94, 80% of all undergraduate applicants received aid; 80% of freshman applicants. Average amounts of aid awarded freshmen: Scholarships and grants, $1,000; loans, $1,800.
**Supporting data/closing dates:** FAFSA: Priority filing date is June 1. School's own aid application: Priority filing date is June 1. Income tax forms: Priority filing date is June 1. Notification of awards on rolling basis.
**Financial aid contact:** Judy Schneider, M.B.A., Director of Financial Aid. 817 273-3561.

**STUDENT EMPLOYMENT.** College Work/Study Program. Institutional employment. 5% of full-time undergraduates work on campus during school year. Students may expect to earn an average of $3,000 during school year. Off-campus part-time employment opportunities rated "excellent."

**COMPUTER FACILITIES.** IBM/IBM-compatible, Macintosh/Apple, and RISC-/UNIX-based microcomputers. Students may access Digital, Hewlett-Packard, IBM, NCR, Sequent, SUN minicomputer/mainframe systems. Client/LAN operating systems include Apple/Macintosh, DOS, OS/2, UNIX/XENIX/AIX, X-windows, Artisoft, Banyan, DEC, LocalTalk/AppleTalk, Novell. Computer facilities are available to all students.
**Fees:** $5–$40 per course using computer.
**Hours:** 18 hours/day.

## University of Texas at Austin

Austin, TX 78712-1157 512 471-3434

**1994-95 Costs.** Tuition: $676 (state residents), $4,200 (out-of-state). Room & board: $3,600. Fees, books, misc. academic expenses (school's estimate): $1,434.
**Enrollment.** Undergraduates: 15,770 men, 14,247 women (full-time). Freshman class: 14,772 applicants, 9,572 accepted, 5,329 enrolled. Graduate enrollment: 7,559 men, 5,790 women.
**Test score averages/ranges.** Average SAT scores: 523 verbal, 603 math. Range of SAT scores of middle 50%: 460-580 verbal, 540-670 math. Average ACT scores: 25 English, 25 math, 25 composite. Range of ACT scores of middle 50%: 22-28 English, 22-28 math.
**Faculty.** 2,161 full-time; 181 part-time. 92% of faculty holds highest degree in specific field. Student/faculty ratio: 19 to 1.
**Selectivity rating.** Highly competitive.

**PROFILE.** U Texas at Austin, founded in 1883, is a public, comprehensive university. Programs are offered through the Colleges of Business Administration, Communication, Education, Engineering, Fine Arts, Liberal Arts, Natural Sciences, and Pharmacy; the Graduate School, including the Graduate School of Library and Information Science; and the Schools of Architecture, Law, Nursing, Public Affairs, and Social Work. Its 300-acre urban campus is located in Austin.

**Accreditation:** SACS. Professionally accredited by the Accreditation Board for Engineering and Technology, the Accrediting Council on Education in Journalism and Mass Communication, the American Assembly of Collegiate Schools of Business, the American Bar Association, the American Council on Pharmaceutical Education, the American Dietetic Association, the American Library Association, the American Psychological Association, the American Speech-Language-Hearing Association, the Council on Social Work Education, the National Architecture Accrediting Board, the National Association of Schools of Music, the National Council for Accreditation of Teacher Education, the National League for Nursing.
**Religious orientation:** University of Texas at Austin is nonsectarian; no religious requirements.
**Library:** Collections totaling over 6,800,000 volumes, 51,338 periodical subscriptions, and 4,900,000 microform items.
**Special facilities/museums:** Art gallery, Lyndon Baines Johnson library/museum, performing arts center, Texas Memorial museum, humanities research center.
**Athletic facilities:** Swimming center, gymnasiums, tennis courts, stadium, intramural fields.

**STUDENT BODY. Undergraduate profile:** 95% are state residents; 21% are transfers. 10% Asian-American, 4% Black, 14% Hispanic, 1% Native American, 67% White, 4% Other. Average age of undergraduates is 22.
**Freshman profile:** 3% of freshmen who took SAT scored 700 or over on verbal, 17% scored 700 or over on math; 22% scored 600 or over on verbal, 53% scored 600 or over on math; 61% scored 500 or over on verbal, 89% scored 500 or over on math; 93% scored 400 or over on verbal, 99% scored 400 or over on math; 99% scored 300 or over on verbal, 100% scored 300 or over on math. 10% of freshmen who took ACT scored 30 or over on English, 16% scored 30 or over on math; 65% scored 24 or over on English, 65% scored 24 or over on math; 96% scored 18 or over on English, 98% scored 18 or over on math; 100% scored 12 or over on English, 100% scored 12 or over on math. Majority of accepted applicants took SAT.
**Undergraduate achievement:** 87% of fall 1992 freshmen returned for fall 1993 term. 30% of entering class graduated.
**Foreign students:** 1,342 students are from out of the country. Countries represented include China, Hong Kong, India, Korea, Mexico, and Taiwan; 107 in all.

**PROGRAMS OF STUDY. Degrees:** B.A., B.Arch., B.Bus.Admin., B.F.A., B.Journ., B.Mus., B.S., B.S.Nurs., B.Soc.Work.
**Majors:** Accounting, Advertising, Aerospace Engineering, American Studies, Anthropology, Applied Learning/Development, Applied Music, Aquatic Biology, Archaeological Studies, Architectural Engineering, Architectural Studies, Architecture, Art History, Asian Studies, Astronomy, Biochemistry, Biology, Botany, Chemical Engineering, Chemistry, Child Development/Family Relations, Civil Engineering, Classics, Communication Sciences/Disorders, Computer Science, Czech, Dance, Design, Dietetics, Drama, Drama Production, Economics, Electrical Engineering, Engineering Route to Business, English, Ethnic Studies, Finance, French, General Business, Geography, Geological Sciences, Geophysics, German, Government, Greek, Health Promotion/Fitness, Hebrew, History, Home Economics, Humanities, Interior Design, International Business, Italian, Journalism, Kinesiology, Latin, Latin American Studies, Linguistics, Management, Management Information Systems, Marketing, Mathematics, Mechanical Engineering, Medical Technology, Microbiology, Middle Eastern Studies, Molecular Biology, Music, Music Composition, Music Literature, Music Studies, Music Theory, Nursing, Nutrition, Oriental/African Languages/Literatures, Petroleum Engineering, Pharmacy, Philosophy, Physics, Portuguese, Psychology, Radio/Television/Film, Russian, Scandinavian, Social Work, Sociology, Soviet/East European Studies, Spanish, Speech, Studio Art, Textiles/Apparel, Theatre Studies, Visual Art Studies, Youth/Community Studies, Zoology.
**Requirements:** General education requirement.
**Academic regulations:** Minimum 2.0 GPA required for graduation.
**Special:** Minors offered in most majors. Interdisciplinary options in College of Engineering including biomedical engineering, engineering management, environmental quality, materials science and engineering. Plan II honors program offered. Self-designed majors. Double majors. Dual degrees. Independent study. Accelerated study. Pass/fail grading option. Internships. Cooperative education programs. Graduate school at which undergraduates may take graduate-level courses. Preprofessional programs in law, medicine, veterinary science, and dentistry. 3-1 medical technology programs with U of Texas Health Science Centers. Bachelor's/M.P.A. and bachelor's/Pharm.D. programs. Teacher certification in elementary, secondary, special education, and bilingual/bicultural education. Certification in specific subject areas. Study abroad in Argentina, Australia, Austria, Brazil, Chile, China, the Commonwealth of Independent States, Costa Rica, the Czech Republic, Denmark, the Dominican Republic, Ecuador, England, France, Germany, Ghana, Israel, Italy, Japan, Morocco, the Netherlands, Singapore, Southeast Asia, South Africa, Spain, Taiwan and Venezuela. Internships in Hungary and Poland. ROTC, NROTC, and AFROTC.
**Honors:** Phi Beta Kappa. Honors program. Honor societies.
**Academic Assistance:** Remedial reading, writing, math, and study skills. Nonremedial tutoring.

**STUDENT LIFE. Housing:** Students may live on or off campus. Coed, women's, and men's dorms. School-owned/operated apartments. 13% of students live in college housing.
**Services and counseling/handicapped student services:** Placement services. Health service. Day care. Counseling services for minority students. Personal and psychological counseling. Career guidance services. Physically disabled student services. Learning disabled services. Notetaking services. Reader services for the blind.
**Campus organizations:** Undergraduate student government. Student newspaper (Daily Texan). Literary magazine. Yearbook. Radio and TV stations. Star Trek Fan Club, bungee jumpers, ballroom dance society, drama and musical groups, academic, athletic, political, professional, recreational, service, and social groups, 600 organizations in all. 28 fraternities, all with chapter houses; 15 sororities, all with chapter houses. 14% of men join a fraternity. 14% of women join a sorority.
**Religious organizations:** Bahai Association, Baptist Student Union, Buddhist Association, Campus Crusade for Christ, Chinese Bible Study, Hillel, Intervarsity Christian Fellowship, Korean Christian Fellowship, Lutheran Campus Ministry, Muslim Student Association, Orthodox Christian Fellowship, Pagan Student Alliance.
**Minority/foreign student organizations:** 32 African American groups, 23 Hispanic groups, 44 Asian American groups, Native American group. Over 30 foreign student groups.

**ATHLETICS. Physical education requirements:** None.
**Intercollegiate competition:** 7% of students participate. Baseball (M), basketball (M,W), cross-country (M,W), diving (M,W), football (M), golf (M,W), soccer (W), softball (W), swimming (M,W), tennis (M,W), track (indoor) (M,W), track (outdoor) (M,W), track and field (indoor) (M,W), track and field (outdoor) (M,W), volleyball (W). Member of NCAA Division I, NCAA Division I-A for football, Southwest Conference.
**Intramural and club sports:** 81% of students participate. Intramural badminton, backpacking, basketball, canoeing, eight-ball, fencing, football, golf, handball, hiking, innertube water polo, kayaking, racquetball, rifle, rock climbing, skiing, soccer, softball, squash, swimming, table tennis, tennis, track, triathlon, volleyball, walleyball, weight lifting. Men's club aerobics, aikido, archery, badminton, ballet folklorico, ballroom dance, bowling, crew, csardas, cycling, dance, equestrian sports, fencing, floor hockey, frisbee, gymnastics, handball, judo, karate, kendo, lacrosse, power lifting, racquetball, rifle, road-running, rugby, sailing, shotokan, soccer, table tennis, tae kwon do, tennis, triathlon, tukong moosul, volleyball, water polo, water skiing, wrestling. Women's club aerobics, aikido, archery, badminton, ballet folklorico, ballroom dance, bowling, crew, csardas, cycling, dance, equestrian sports, fencing, gymnastics, handball, judo, karate, kendo, power lifting, racquetball, rifle, road-running, sailing, shotokan, soccer, table tennis, tae kwon do, tennis, triathlon, tukong moosul, volleyball, water polo, water skiing.

**ADMISSIONS. Academic basis for candidate selection** (in order of priority): Standardized test scores, class rank, secondary school record, school's recommendation, essay.
**Nonacademic basis for candidate selection:** Particular talent or ability is emphasized. Character and personality and extracurricular participation are considered.
**Requirements:** Graduation from secondary school is required; GED is accepted. 15.5 units and the following program of study are required: 4 units of English, 3 units of math, 2 units of lab science, 2 units of foreign language, 3 units of social studies, 1.5 units of academic electives. In-state applicants who rank in top tenth of secondary school class may be admitted with minimun combined SAT score of 900 (composite ACT score of 22); those in next 15% must have minimum combined SAT score of 1050 (composite ACT score of 25); those in second quarter must have minimum combined SAT score of 1150 (composite ACT score of 28). Minimum combined SAT score of 1200 (composite ACT score of 29) and rank in top quarter of secondary school class required of out-of-state applicants. Audition required of music program applicants. Conditional admission possible for in-state applicants not meeting standard requirements. SAT or ACT is required. ACH required. Campus visit recommended. Off-campus interviews available with an alumni representative.
**Procedure:** Take SAT or ACT by October of 12th year. Take ACH by March of 12th year. Suggest filing application by March 1; no deadline. Notification of admission on rolling basis. No set date by which applicants must accept offer. $100 nonrefundable room deposit. Freshmen accepted for terms other than fall.
**Special programs:** Credit and/or placement may be granted through CEEB Advanced Placement exams for scores of 2 or higher. Credit may be granted through CLEP general exams. Credit and/or placement may be granted through CLEP subject exams. Credit and placement may be granted through DANTES and challenge exams. Concurrent enrollment program.
**Transfer students:** Transfer students accepted for terms other than fall. In fall 1993, 21% of all new students were transfers into all classes. 6,004 transfer applications were received, 2,853 were accepted. Application deadline is March 1 for fall; October 1 for spring. Minimum 3.0 GPA required. Lowest course grade accepted is "C." At least 30 semester hours must be completed at the university to receive degree.
**Admissions contact:** Shirley F. Binder, M.Ed., Director of Admissions. 512 471-7601.

**FINANCIAL AID. Available aid:** Pell grants, SEOG, state scholarships and grants, school scholarships and grants, private scholarships, ROTC scholarships, academic merit scholarships, and athletic scholarships. Perkins Loans (NDSL), PLUS, Stafford Loans (GSL), NSL, Health Professions Loans, state loans, private loans, and SLS. Installment payment plans.
**Financial aid statistics:** 55% of aid is not need-based. In 1993-94, 100% of all undergraduate applicants received aid. Average amounts of aid awarded freshmen: Scholarships and grants, $2,400; loans, $2,100.
**Supporting data/closing dates:** FAFSA: Priority filing date is April 1. AFSA: Priority filing date is March 1; accepted on rolling basis. Notification of awards on rolling basis.

**Financial aid contact:** Patricia Stewart-Harris, M.A., Director of Financial Aid. 512 475-6282.

**STUDENT EMPLOYMENT.** College Work/Study Program. Institutional employment. 20% of full-time undergraduates work on campus during school year. Students may expect to earn an average of $1,975 during school year. Off-campus part-time employment opportunities rated "good."

**COMPUTER FACILITIES.** 10,000 IBM/IBM-compatible and Macintosh/Apple microcomputers. Students may access Cray, Digital, IBM minicomputer/mainframe systems, Internet. Residence halls may be equipped with stand-alone microcomputers, networked microcomputers, networked terminals, modems. 191 major computer languages and software packages available. Computer facilities are available to all students.
**Fees:** $6 computer fee per semester hour.

**PROMINENT ALUMNI/AE.** Alan Bean and Robert Crippen, astronauts; Denton Cooley, heart surgeon; Barbara Jordan, former legislator; Walter Cronkite and Bill Moyers, journalists; Tom Landry, coach, Dallas Cowboys; Ilya Prigogine and Steven Weinberg, physicists; Barbara Conrad, Metropolitan Opera star; John Connally, former Texas governor and U.S. secretary of treasury.

# University of Texas at Dallas

**Richardson, TX 75083-0688 214 690-2111**

**1993-94 Costs.** Tuition: $1,222 (state residents), $4,486 (out-of-state). Housing: None. Fees, books, misc. academic expenses (school's estimate): $626.
**Enrollment.** Undergraduates: 945 men, 936 women (full-time). Freshman class: 369 applicants, 211 accepted, 97 enrolled. Graduate enrollment: 2,442 men, 1,710 women.
**Test score averages/ranges.** Average SAT scores: 500 verbal, 612 math. Range of SAT scores of middle 50%: 440-510 verbal, 560-660 math. Average ACT scores: 26 composite. Range of ACT scores of middle 50%: 24-29 composite.
**Faculty.** 219 full-time; 104 part-time. 95% of faculty holds highest degree in specific field. Student/faculty ratio: 19 to 1.
**Selectivity rating.** Highly competitive.

**PROFILE.** U Texas at Dallas, founded in 1969, is a public, comprehensive university. Programs are offered through the Schools of Arts and Humanities, Engineering and Computer Science, General Studies, Human Development, Management, Natural Sciences and Mathematics, and Social Sciences. Its 417-acre campus is located in Richardson, 17 miles north of the center of Dallas.

**Accreditation:** SACS. Professionally accredited by the Accreditation Board for Engineering and Technology, the American Speech-Language-Hearing Association.
**Religious orientation:** University of Texas at Dallas is nonsectarian; no religious requirements.
**Library:** Collections totaling over 474,576 volumes, 2,630 periodical subscriptions, and 1,570,878 microform items.
**Athletic facilities:** Physical instruction building, basketball, jogging track, racquetball, soccer and softball fields, squash, and tennis courts, volleyball court, weight room.

**STUDENT BODY. Undergraduate profile:** 99% are state residents; 98% are transfers. 7% Asian-American, 6% Black, 6% Hispanic, 79% White, 2% Other. Average age of undergraduates is 29.
**Freshman profile:** 2% of freshmen who took SAT scored 700 or over on verbal, 14% scored 700 or over on math; 13% scored 600 or over on verbal, 53% scored 600 or over on math; 50% scored 500 or over on verbal, 92% scored 500 or over on math; 90% scored 400 or over on verbal, 97% scored 400 or over on math; 95% scored 300 or over on verbal. 5% of freshmen who took ACT scored 30 or over on composite; 20% scored 24 or over on composite; 27% scored 18 or over on composite. 97% of accepted applicants took SAT; 27% took ACT. 93% of freshmen come from public schools.
**Undergraduate achievement:** 52% of fall 1991 freshmen returned for fall 1992 term.
**Foreign students:** 58 students are from out of the country. Countries represented include Bangladesh, China, Hong Kong, India, South Korea, and Taiwan; 57 in all.

**PROGRAMS OF STUDY. Degrees:** B.A., B.S., B.S.Elec.Eng.
**Majors:** Accounting, American Studies, Applied Mathematics, Arts/Humanities, Arts/Performance, Biology, Business Administration, Chemistry, Cognitive Science, Computer Science, Economics/Finance, Electrical Engineering, Electrical Engineering/Microelectronics, Electrical Engineering/Telecommunications, Geosciences, Government/Politics, Historical Studies, Interdisciplinary Studies, Literary Studies, Mathematical Sciences, Physics, Psychology, Sociology, Speech/Language Pathology/Audiology, Statistics.
**Distribution of degrees:** The majors with the highest enrollment are business administration, interdisciplinary studies, and economics/finance; arts/humanities, geosciences, and chemistry have the lowest.
**Requirements:** General education requirement.
**Academic regulations:** Minimum 2.0 GPA must be maintained.
**Special:** Self-designed majors. Double majors. Dual degrees. Independent study. Accelerated study. Internships. Graduate school at which undergraduates may take graduate-level courses. 3-2 electrical engineering program. Five-year bachelor's/master's programs in accounting, biology, business administration, communication disorders, computer science, interdisciplinary studies, and public affairs. Member of Academic Common Market and Association for Higher Education of North Texas. Teacher certification in secondary education. Certification in specific subject areas. Study abroad in Russia. ROTC at U of Texas at Arlington. AFROTC at U of North Texas.
**Honors:** Honor societies.
**Academic Assistance:** Remedial reading, writing, math, and study skills. Nonremedial tutoring.

**STUDENT LIFE. Housing:** No university-owned housing, but there are 400 privately owned/operated apartments on campus, housing 7% of students.
**Social atmosphere:** Popular gathering spots include the student union, the Green Pit, and Waterview Park Clubhouse. Among the most influential campus organizations are the Student Government Association, the Student Union Activities and Advisory Board, Greeks, and Freshman Services. Schoolyear highlights include Casino Night, Santa Bash, Welcome Week, Welcome Back Party/Chili Cook Off, International Week, "Take It On the Road," the A&H Film Series, Juneteenth, African American History Month, Hispanic Month, and sporting events such as the College Bowl. According to the university development specialist," UTD has a diverse student population with a high percentage of graduate students and commuters. The activities and programs reflect this diversity by offering activities that are directed to specific student groups as well as the general campus population."
**Services and counseling/handicapped student services:** Placement services. Health service. Day care. Counseling services for minority, veteran, and older students. Birth control, personal, and psychological counseling. Career and academic guidance services. Physically disabled student services. Learning disabled services. Notetaking services. Tape recorders. Tutors. Reader services for the blind.
**Campus organizations:** Undergraduate student government. Student newspaper (Mercury, published twice/month). Literary magazine. Speaking Scholars/Toastmasters, academic and special-interest groups, 41 organizations in all. One fraternity, no chapter house; one sorority, no chapter house.
**Religious organizations:** Bahai Club, Baptist Student Union, Buddhism study group.
**Minority/foreign student organizations:** African-American Student Association, Campus Hispanic Association, Multi-Cultural Association. Chinese, Indian, and Korean groups.

**ATHLETICS. Physical education requirements:** None.
**Intercollegiate competition:** 1% of students participate. Soccer (M,W). Member of NAIA.
**Intramural and club sports:** 12% of students participate. Intramural basketball, billiards, chess, flag football, golf, racquetball, softball, squash, table tennis, tennis, volleyball. Men's club pistol, frisbee. Women's club pistol, frisbee.

**ADMISSIONS. Academic basis for candidate selection** (in order of priority): Class rank, standardized test scores, secondary school record.
**Nonacademic basis for candidate selection:** Particular talent or ability is considered.
**Requirements:** Graduation from secondary school is required; GED is not accepted. 17.5 units and the following program of study are required: 4 units of English, 3.5 units of math, 3 units of lab science, 2 units of foreign language, 3 units of social studies, 2 units of academic electives. Rank in top tenth of secondary school class, or rank in top half of secondary school class with minimum combined SAT score of 1000 (composite ACT score of 24) required of in-state applicants. Minimum combined SAT score of 1200 (composite ACT score of 29) and rank in top quarter of secondary school class required of out-of-state applicants. SAT is required; ACT may be substituted. Campus visit recommended. No off-campus interviews.
**Procedure:** Take SAT or ACT by January of 12th year. Suggest filing application by March. Notification of admission on rolling basis. Reply is required by registration. Freshmen accepted for fall term only.
**Special programs:** Admission may be deferred one year. Credit may be granted through CEEB Advanced Placement for scores of 4 or higher. Credit may be granted through CLEP subject exams and DANTES exams. Concurrent enrollment program.
**Transfer students:** Transfer students accepted for terms other than fall. In fall 1992, 98% of all new students were transfers into all classes. Application deadline is rolling for fall; rolling for spring. Minimum 3.0 GPA required for up to 54 transferable semester hours; 2.5 GPA for computer science and engineering program applicants with more than 54 transferable semester hours; 2.0 GPA for other applicants with more than 54 transferable semester hours. Lowest course grade accepted is "C." No limit on number of transferable credit hours. At least 30 semester hours must be completed at the university to receive degree.
**Admissions contact:** Barry Samsula, M.A., Director of Admissions. 214 690-2294, 214 690-2341 (recording).

**FINANCIAL AID. Available aid:** Pell grants, SEOG, state scholarships and grants, school scholarships and grants, private scholarships and grants, academic merit scholarships, and aid for undergraduate foreign students. Perkins Loans (NDSL), PLUS, Stafford Loans (GSL), state loans, school loans, and SLS. Deferred payment plan.
**Financial aid statistics:** 27% of aid is not need-based. In 1992-93, 82% of all undergraduate applicants received aid; 73% of freshman applicants. Average amounts of aid awarded freshmen: Scholarships and grants, $1,675; loans, $1,457.
**Supporting data/closing dates:** FAFSA: Priority filing date is May 1; deadline is November 1. School's own aid application: Priority filing date is May 1; deadline is November 1. Income tax forms: Priority filing date is May 1; deadline is November 1. Notification of awards on rolling basis.
**Financial aid contact:** Michael O'Rear, M.S., Director of Financial Aid. 214 690-2941.

**STUDENT EMPLOYMENT.** College Work/Study Program. Institutional employment. 3% of full-time undergraduates work on campus during school year. Students may expect to earn an average of $3,200 during school year. Off-campus part-time employment opportunities rated "excellent."

**COMPUTER FACILITIES.** 165 IBM/IBM-compatible, Macintosh/Apple, and RISC-/UNIX-based microcomputers; all are networked. Students may access IBM, SUN minicomputer/mainframe systems, BITNET, Internet. All major languages and packages available. Computer facilities are available to all students.
**Fees:** $45 computer fee per semester.
**Hours:** 8 AM-midn.; 24-hour dial-in and terminal access.

**GRADUATE CAREER DATA.** Companies and businesses that hire graduates: Alatel, EDS, Northern Telecom, Rockwell, Texas Instruments.

**PROMINENT ALUMNI/AE.** Tracy Rowlett, local news anchor and broadcast journalist; Kathy Kushner, fellow, Hudson Institute; Dr. H.B. Puksoy, specialist on Soviet nationalities and Harvard U professor.

## University of Texas at El Paso

**El Paso, TX 79968** **915 747-5000**

**1994-95 Costs.** Tuition: $840 (state residents), $5,130 (out-of-state). Room: $1,750. Board: $1,200-$1,800. Fees, books, misc. academic expenses (school's estimate): $640.

**Enrollment.** Undergraduates: 4,577 men, 5,081 women (full-time). Freshman class: 3,441 applicants, 2,946 accepted, 2,248 enrolled. Graduate enrollment: 1,245 men, 1,369 women.

**Test score averages/ranges.** Average SAT scores: 371 verbal, 424 math. Average ACT scores: 18 English, 18 math, 18 composite.

**Faculty.** 397 full-time; 354 part-time. 90% of faculty holds doctoral degree. Student/faculty ratio: 24 to 1.

**Selectivity rating.** Less competitive.

**PROFILE.** U Texas at El Paso, founded in 1913, is a public university. Programs are offered through the Colleges of Business Administration, Education, Engineering, Liberal Arts, Nursing and Allied Health, and Science. Its 330-acre campus is located in El Paso.

**Accreditation:** SACS. Professionally accredited by the Accreditation Board for Engineering and Technology, the American Assembly of Collegiate Schools of Business, the American Medical Association (CAHEA), the National Association of Schools of Music, the National Council for Accreditation of Teacher Education, the National League for Nursing.
**Religious orientation:** University of Texas at El Paso is nonsectarian; no religious requirements.
**Library:** Collections totaling over 922,977 volumes, and 1,050,036 microform items.
**Special facilities/museums:** Cross-cultural ethnic study center, natural history and cultural museum, solar pond and solar house, electron microscope, atmospheric and acoustic research lab, seismic observatory.
**Athletic facilities:** Football stadium, gymnasium, track, athletic fields, swimming pool, basketball, racquetball, tennis, and volleyball courts.

**STUDENT BODY. Undergraduate profile:** 97% are state residents; 43% are transfers. 1% Asian-American, 3% Black, 65% Hispanic, 24% White, 7% Other. Average age of undergraduates is 24.
**Freshman profile:** 40% of accepted applicants took SAT; 30% took ACT. 95% of freshmen come from public schools.
**Undergraduate achievement:** 64% of fall 1991 freshmen returned for fall 1992 term.
**Foreign students:** 961 students are from out of the country. Countries represented include China, Germany, Honduras, India, Malaysia, and Mexico; 51 in all.

**PROGRAMS OF STUDY. Degrees:** B.A., B.Bus.Admin., B.F.A., B.Interdis.Studies, B.Mus., B.S., B.Soc.Work.
**Majors:** Accounting, Allied Health, Anthropology, Applied Mathematics, Art, Biological Sciences, Botany, Broadcasting, Ceramics, Chemistry, Chicano Studies, Civil Engineering, Commercial Banking, Communication, Community Health Work, Computer Information Systems, Computer Science, Creative Writing, Criminal Justice, Drawing, Economics, Electrical Engineering, English, Finance, French, Geological Sciences, Geophysics, German, Graphic Design, Health Care Administration, Health Science Education, History, Industrial Engineering, Journalism, Latin American Studies, Linguistics, Literature, Management, Marketing, Mathematics, Mechanical Engineering, Medical Technology, Metallurgical Engineering, Metals, Microbiology, Music, Music Performance, Music Theory/Composition, Nursing, Painting, Philosophy, Physics, Political Science, Printmaking, Psychology, Real Estate, Sculpture, Social Work, Sociology, Spanish, Speech, Speech/Language Pathology, Statistics, Studio Art, Theatre Arts, Zoology.
**Distribution of degrees:** The majors with the highest enrollment are nursing, accounting, and criminal justice; sociology, theatre arts, and economics have the lowest.
**Requirements:** General education requirement.
**Academic regulations:** Minimum 2.0 GPA must be maintained.
**Special:** Minors offered. Courses offered in black, Soviet/East European, and women's studies. Cooperative Student Trainee program at White Sands Missile Range in New Mexico for engineering, math, and physics program students. Inter-American science and humanities program for Spanish-speaking international students. Independent study. Pass/fail grading option. Graduate school at which undergraduates may take graduate-level courses. Preprofessional programs in law and medicine. Teacher certification in early childhood, elementary, secondary, special education, and bilingual/bicultural education. ROTC and AFROTC.
**Honors:** Honors program.
**Academic Assistance:** Remedial reading, writing, math, and study skills. Nonremedial tutoring.

**STUDENT LIFE. Housing:** Students may live on or off campus. Coed dorms. On-campus married-student housing. 2% of students live in college housing.
**Social atmosphere:** Popular gathering spots at UTEP are the Union Plaza, College station, and the Surf Club. Influential organizations on campus include the Mexican Student Union, the Baptist Student Union, Greeks, and the Student Association. Homecoming, the John Hancock Bowl, Rush Week, and basketball games are among the year's favorite events.
**Services and counseling/handicapped student services:** Placement services. Health service. Women's center. Day care. Counseling services for minority, military, veteran, and older students. Birth control, personal, and psychological counseling. Career and academic guidance services. Religious counseling. Physically disabled student services. Learning disabled services. Notetaking services. Tape recorders. Reader services for the blind.
**Campus organizations:** Undergraduate student government. Student newspaper (Prospector, published twice/week). Literary magazine. Artists Fair, film and arts series, chorale, chorus, orchestra, marching band, chamber ensembles, guitar and jazz ensembles, civic ballet and opera, University Players, Lyceum series, forensics team, cultural, political, professional, service, and special-interest groups. Six fraternities, no chapter houses; four sororities, no chapter houses.
**Religious organizations:** Moslem Student Organization, other religious groups.
**Minority/foreign student organizations:** Bilalian (black) Organization, Chicano prelaw group, MEChA, National Chicano Health Association. Chinese Student Organization.

**ATHLETICS. Physical education requirements:** None.
**Intercollegiate competition:** 5% of students participate. Basketball (M,W), cross-country (M,W), football (M), golf (M,W), riflery (M), tennis (M,W), track and field (indoor) (M,W), track and field (outdoor) (M,W), volleyball (W). Member of NCAA Division I, NCCSA, Western Athletic Conference.
**Intramural and club sports:** 5% of students participate. Intramural basketball, flag football, racquetball, softball, tennis, volleyball. Men's club cheerleading, cycling, fencing, soccer, wrestling. Women's club cheerleading, cycling, fencing, gymnastics.

**ADMISSIONS. Academic basis for candidate selection** (in order of priority): Class rank, secondary school record, standardized test scores.
**Requirements:** Graduation from secondary school is recommended; GED is accepted. 16 units and the following program of study are recommended: 4 units of English, 3 units of math, 3 units of science, 2 units of foreign language, 3 units of social studies, 2.5 units of history. No minimum SAT/ACT requirements for applicants in first quarter of secondary school class; minimum combined SAT score of 700 (composite ACT score of 15) required of applicants in second quarter; minimum combined SAT score of 800 (composite ACT score of 18) required of applicants in bottom half. 2 units of algebra, 1 unit of geometry, 1/2 unit of trigonometry, and minimum SAT score of 500 in math required of engineering program applicants. Provisional admission possible for in-state applicants not meeting standard requirements. Spanish-speaking applicants may submit PAA. SAT or ACT is required. Campus visit recommended. Off-campus interviews available with an admissions representative.
**Procedure:** Notification of admission on rolling basis. Freshmen accepted for terms other than fall.
**Special programs:** Admission may be deferred one year. Credit may be granted through CLEP general and subject exams. Early decision program. Deadline for applying for early decision is July 1. Early entrance/early admission program. Concurrent enrollment program.
**Transfer students:** Transfer students accepted for terms other than fall. In fall 1992, 43% of all new students were transfers into all classes. 1,658 transfer applications were received, 1,301 were accepted. Application deadline is July 1 for fall; November 15 for spring. Minimum 2.0 GPA required. Lowest course grade accepted is "D." Maximum number of transferable credits is 66 semester hours. At least 30 semester hours must be completed at the university to receive degree.
**Admissions contact:** Diana Guerrero, M.S., Director of Admissions. 915 747-5576.

**FINANCIAL AID. Available aid:** Pell grants, SEOG, Federal Nursing Student Scholarships, state scholarships and grants, school scholarships, private scholarships, ROTC scholarships, academic merit scholarships, athletic scholarships, and aid for undergraduate foreign students. Perkins Loans (NDSL), PLUS, Stafford Loans (GSL), state loans, school loans, and SLS. Deferred payment plan. Quarterly payment plan.
**Financial aid statistics:** In 1992-93, 82% of all undergraduate applicants received aid; 73% of freshman applicants. Average amounts of aid awarded freshmen: Scholarships and grants, $793; loans, $2,500.
**Supporting data/closing dates:** FAFSA/FAF/FFS: Priority filing date is March 15. School's own aid application: Priority filing date is March 15. Income tax forms: Priority filing date is March 15. Financial Aid Transcript: Priority filing date is March 15. Notification of awards begins June 1.
**Financial aid contact:** Linda A. Gonzalez-Hensgen, Director of Financial Aid. 915 747-5204.

**STUDENT EMPLOYMENT.** College Work/Study Program. Institutional employment. 37% of full-time undergraduates work on campus during school year. Students may expect to earn an average of $3,200 during school year. Off-campus part-time employment opportunities rated "good."

**COMPUTER FACILITIES.** IBM/IBM-compatible and Macintosh/Apple microcomputers. Students may access IBM minicomputer/mainframe systems. Computer languages and software packages include BASIC, COBOL, FORTRAN, RPG. Computer facilities are available to all students.
**Fees:** $10 computer fee per credit hour.

## University of Texas of the Permian Basin

**Odessa, TX 79762** **915 367-2011**

**1993-94 Costs.** Tuition: $1,234 (state residents), $5,268 (out-of-state). Room: $1,800.

**Enrollment.** Undergraduates: 269 men, 550 women (full-time). Freshman class: 211 applicants, 184 accepted, 95 enrolled. Graduate enrollment: 270 men, 446 women.

**Test score averages/ranges.** Average SAT scores: 834 combined.

**Faculty.** 65 full-time; 40 part-time. 60% of faculty holds doctoral degree. Student/faculty ratio: 18 to 1.

**Selectivity rating.** Less competitive.

**PROFILE.** U Texas of the Permian Basin, founded in 1969, is a public university. Programs are offered through the Divisions of Behavioral Science and Physical Education, Business Administration, Education, Humanities and Fine Arts, and Science and Engineering. Its 600-acre campus is located in Odessa, south of Lubbock.

**Accreditation:** SACS.
**Religious orientation:** University of Texas of the Permian Basin is nonsectarian; no religious requirements.
**Library:** Collections totaling over 236,876 volumes, 824 periodical subscriptions, and 321,108 microform items.

**Special facilities/museums:** Art institute.
**Athletic facilities:** Swimming pool, basketball, handball, racquetball, tennis, and volleyball courts, gymnasiums, exercise and weight rooms.

**STUDENT BODY. Undergraduate profile:** 99% are state residents; 100% are transfers. 3% Black, 13% Hispanic, 82% White, 2% Other. Average age of undergraduates is 30.
**Undergraduate achievement:** 2% of students who completed a degree program immediately went on to graduate study.
**Foreign students:** 29 students are from out of the country. Countries represented include India, Malaysia, Nigeria, Qatar, Taiwan, and Thailand; eight in all.

**PROGRAMS OF STUDY. Degrees:** B.A., B.Bus.Admin., B.S.
**Majors:** Accountancy/Information Systems, Art, Chemistry, Computer Science, Criminal Justice, Economics, Engineering, Finance, Geology, History, Kinesiology, Life Sciences, Management, Marketing, Mass Communications, Mathematics, Political Science, Psychology, Sociology, Spanish.
**Distribution of degrees:** The majors with the highest enrollment are history, psychology, and accounting/information systems; control engineering, economics, and mathematics have the lowest.
**Requirements:** General education requirement.
**Academic regulations:** Juniors must maintain minimum 2.0 GPA; seniors, 2.0 GPA.
**Special:** Double majors. Graduate school at which undergraduates may take graduate-level courses. Preprofessional programs in medicine. Teacher certification in early childhood, elementary, secondary, and bilingual/bicultural education. Certification in specific subject areas.
**Academic Assistance:** Remedial reading, writing, math, and study skills. Nonremedial tutoring.

**ADMISSIONS. Academic basis for candidate selection** (in order of priority): College GOA, college course distribution.
**Requirements:** Graduation from secondary school is recommended; GED is accepted. 20 units and the following program of study are required: 4 units of English, 3 units of math, 2 units of science, 2 units of foreign language, 2 units of social studies, 1 unit of history, 6 units of electives. Portfolio required of art program applicants. SAT or ACT is required. Campus visit recommended. No off-campus interviews. All students enter as transfers.
**Procedure:** Notification of admission on rolling basis. Suggest filing application no later than 60 days before registration. Require filing application by the 12th class day. No set date by which applicants must accept offer. Students accepted in terms other than fall.
**Special programs:** Admission may be deferred one year. Credit and/or placement may be granted through CEEB Advanced Placement exams for scores of 3 or higher.
**Transfer students:** Transfer students accepted for terms other than fall.
**Admissions contact:** Vickie Gomez, M.A., Director of Admissions. 915 367-2210.

**FINANCIAL AID. Available aid:** Pell grants, SEOG, state scholarships and grants, school scholarships, private scholarships and grants, and academic merit scholarships. PLUS, Stafford Loans (GSL), and SLS. Deferred payment plan.
**Financial aid statistics:** 25% of aid is not need-based. In 1992-93, 60% of all undergraduate applicants received aid; 85% of freshman applicants. Average amounts of aid awarded freshmen: Scholarships and grants, $1,200; loans, $2,625.
**Supporting data/closing dates:** FAFSA/FAF/FFS: Priority filing date is May 1; accepted on rolling basis. School's own aid application: Priority filing date is June 1; accepted on rolling basis. Income tax forms: Priority filing date is May 1; accepted on rolling basis. Financial Aid Transcript: Accepted on rolling basis. Notification of awards on rolling basis.
**Financial aid contact:** Richard Renshaw, M.A., Director of Financial Aid. 915 367-2354.

## University of Texas at San Antonio

**San Antonio, TX 78249** **210 691-4011**

**1993-94 Costs.** Tuition: $624 (state residents), $3,888 (out-of-state). Room: $2,052. Board: $2,080. Fees, books, misc. academic expenses (school's estimate): $1,166.
**Enrollment.** Undergraduates: 4,472 men, 4,903 women (full-time). Freshman class: 3,993 applicants, 3,106 accepted, 1,656 enrolled. Graduate enrollment: 1,093 men, 1,172 women.
**Test score averages/ranges.** Average SAT scores: 415 verbal, 473 math. Average ACT scores: 21 English, 20 math, 21 composite.
**Faculty.** 99% of faculty holds highest degree in specific field. Student/faculty ratio: 26 to 1.
**Selectivity rating.** Competitive.

**PROFILE.** U Texas at San Antonio, founded in 1969, is a public, comprehensive university. Programs are offered through the Colleges of Business, Fine Arts and Humanities, Sciences and Engineering, and Social and Behavioral Sciences. Its 600-acre campus is located 16 miles northwest of downtown San Antonio.

**Accreditation:** SACS. Professionally accredited by the Accreditation Board for Engineering and Technology, the American Assembly of Collegiate Schools of Business, the National Association of Schools of Music.
**Religious orientation:** University of Texas at San Antonio is nonsectarian; no religious requirements.
**Library:** Collections totaling over 431,740 volumes, 2,550 periodical subscriptions, and 404,460 microform items.
**Special facilities/museums:** Art gallery, audio-visual center.
**Athletic facilities:** Tennis courts, all-weather track, gymnasiums, volleyball courts, weight areas, intramural football fields.

**STUDENT BODY. Undergraduate profile:** 98% are state residents; 11% are transfers. 3% Asian-American, 3% Black, 35% Hispanic, 1% Native American, 57% White, 1% Other. Average age of undergraduates is 25.
**Freshman profile:** 75% of accepted applicants took SAT; 25% took ACT. 95% of freshmen come from public schools.
**Undergraduate achievement:** 90% of fall 1992 freshmen returned for fall 1993 term.
**Foreign students:** 352 students are from out of the country. Countries represented include Canada, China, Indonesia, Mexico, South Vietnam, and Taiwan; 55 in all.

**PROGRAMS OF STUDY. Degrees:** B.A., B.Bus.Admin., B.F.A., B.Mus., B.Mus.Studies, B.S.
**Majors:** Accounting, American Studies, Anthropology, Applied Physics, Architectural Design, Art, Art/Design, Biology, Building Management, Business, Chemistry, Civil Engineering, Criminal Justice, Early Childhood Education, Economics, Education, Electrical Engineering, Elementary Education, English, Environmental Science, Finance, French, Geography, German, Health Education, History, Humanities, Industrial Management, Information Systems, Interior Design, International Business, Kinesiology/Health, Management, Marketing, Mathematics, Mathematics/Computer Science/Systems Design, Mechanical Engineering, Medical Technology, Music, Music Education, Natural Resources, Occupational Therapy, Personnel/Human Resource Management, Physical Therapy, Political Science, Psychology, Public Administration, Sociology, Spanish.
**Distribution of degrees:** The majors with the highest enrollment are accounting, management, and education; French, German, and American studies have the lowest.
**Requirements:** General education requirement.
**Academic regulations:** Minimum 2.0 GPA must be maintained.
**Special:** Courses offered in art history and criticism, astronomy, bicultural/bilingual studies, business law, classics, comparative studies in humanities, communication, curriculum and instruction, educational psychology (special education), English as a Second Language, linguistics, military science, philosophy, Russian, and social science. Double majors. Dual degrees. Independent study. Pass/fail grading option. Internships. Graduate school at which undergraduates may take graduate-level courses. Preprofessional programs in law, medicine, and dentistry. 2-2 medical technology, occupational therapy, and physical therapy programs with U of Texas Health Science Center at San Antonio. Teacher certification in early childhood, elementary, secondary, special education, and bilingual/bicultural education. Study abroad in England. ROTC and AFROTC.
**Honors:** Honors program. Honor societies.
**Academic Assistance:** Remedial reading, writing, math, and study skills. Nonremedial tutoring.

**STUDENT LIFE. Housing:** Students may live on or off campus. Coed dorms. School-owned/operated apartments. 8% of students live in college housing.
**Social atmosphere:** Popular student gathering spots include Hills and Dales, Sunova Beach, Riverwalk, and Malibu. Among the groups with a widespread influence on campus social life are Greeks, athletes, student government, and the campus activities board. The most popular events of the school year are the BestFest, UTSA Fest, Homecoming, NIOSA, and Folklife. "This school has a reputation as a commuter school," the editor of the student newspaper comments. "Therefore, there are few people who are involved in the social and cultural life of this campus. However, the Greeks on campus have been developing strongly, and other students are starting to attend campus events, contributing to a growing campus life."
**Services and counseling/handicapped student services:** Placement services. Health service. Counseling services for minority, military, veteran, and older students. Personal and psychological counseling. Career and academic guidance services. Physically disabled student services. Learning disabled services. Notetaking services. Tape recorders. Tutors. Reader services for the blind.
**Campus organizations:** Undergraduate student government. Student newspaper (Paisano, published once/week). Yearbook. Madrigal Singers, concert choir, chorus, wind ensemble, chamber orchestra, jazz ensemble, symphonic and marching bands, political, service, social, and special-interest groups, 112 organizations in all. Nine fraternities, no chapter houses; three sororities, no chapter houses.
**Religious organizations:** Baptist Student Union, Campus Ministry, Catholic Student Association, Latter-Day Saints Association.
**Minority/foreign student organizations:** Black Student Alliance, MEChA. International Student Organization, Japanese and Vietnamese groups.

**ATHLETICS. Physical education requirements:** None.
**Intercollegiate competition:** Baseball (M), basketball (M,W), cheerleading (M,W), cross-country (M,W), golf (M), softball (W), tennis (M,W), track (indoor) (M,W), track (outdoor) (M,W), track and field (indoor) (M,W), track and field (outdoor) (M,W), volleyball (W). Member of NCAA Division I, Southland Conference.
**Intramural and club sports:** 20% of students participate. Intramural badminton, basketball, flag football, softball, table tennis, tennis, volleyball.

**ADMISSIONS. Academic basis for candidate selection** (in order of priority): Class rank, standardized test scores.
**Requirements:** Graduation from secondary school is required; GED is accepted. 14 units and the following program of study are recommended: 4 units of English, 3 units of math, 2 units of science, 2 units of foreign language, 2 units of social studies, 1 unit of electives. SAT or ACT is required. No minimum SAT/ACT scores required of in-state applicants in top tenth of secondary school class; minimum combined SAT score of 700 (composite ACT score of 18) required of applicants in remainder of top quarter; minimum combined SAT score of 750 (composite ACT score of 19) required of applicants in second quarter; minimum combined SAT score of 800 (composite ACT score of 21) required of applicants in third quarter; and minimum combined SAT score of 850 (composite ACT score of 22) required of applicants in bottom quarter. Rank in top half of secondary school with corresponding SAT/ACT scores required of out-of-state applicants. Provisional admission possible for in-state applicants not meeting standard requirements. Campus visit recommended. No off-campus interviews.
**Procedure:** Take SAT or ACT by June 1 of 12th year. Application deadline is July 1. Notification of admission on rolling basis. No set date by which applicants must accept offer. $100 room deposit, refundable until August 1. Freshmen accepted for terms other than fall.
**Special programs:** Credit may be granted through CEEB Advanced Placement for scores of 3 or higher. Credit may be granted through CLEP general and subject exams, ACT PEP, and challenge exams. Concurrent enrollment program.

**Transfer students:** Transfer students accepted for terms other than fall. In fall 1993, 11% of all new students were transfers into all classes. 4,733 transfer applications were received, 3,928 were accepted. Application deadline is July 1 for fall; December 1 for spring. Minimum 2.0 GPA required. Lowest course grade accepted is "D." Maximum number of transferable credits is 66 semester hours. At least 30 semester hours must be completed at the university to receive degree.
**Admissions contact:** John H. Brown, Ed.D., Director of Admissions and Registrar. 210 691-4530.

**FINANCIAL AID. Available aid:** Pell grants, SEOG, state scholarships and grants, school scholarships and grants, private scholarships and grants, ROTC scholarships, academic merit scholarships, and athletic scholarships. Perkins Loans (NDSL), PLUS, Stafford Loans (GSL), and SLS. Deferred payment plan.
**Supporting data/closing dates:** FAFSA/FAF: Priority filing date is March 31. School's own aid application: Priority filing date is March 31. Notification of awards on rolling basis.

**STUDENT EMPLOYMENT.** College Work/Study Program. Institutional employment. 5% of full-time undergraduates work on campus during school year. Students may expect to earn an average of $3,000 during school year. Off-campus part-time employment opportunities rated "good."

**COMPUTER FACILITIES.** 120 IBM/IBM-compatible and Macintosh/Apple microcomputers; all are networked. Students may access Digital, IBM minicomputer/mainframe systems, BITNET, Internet. Residence halls may be equipped with modems. Computer languages and software packages include Ada, C, FORTRAN, LISP, Pascal, PL/1, SAS, SPSS. Computer facilities are available to all students.
**Fees:** $3 computer fee per semester hour.
**Hours:** 24 hours.

**GRADUATE CAREER DATA.** Highest graduate school enrollments: U of Texas at Austin, U of Texas at San Antonio.

## Wayland Baptist University

**Plainview, TX 79072** **806 296-5521**

**1994-95 Costs.** Tuition: $5,626. Room & board: $3,121. Fees, books, misc. academic expenses (school's estimate): $2,405.
**Enrollment.** Undergraduates: 228 men, 409 women (full-time). Freshman class: 279 applicants, 243 accepted, 300 enrolled. Graduate enrollment: 6 men, 28 women.
**Test score averages/ranges.** Average SAT scores: 830 combined. Average ACT scores: 19 composite.
**Faculty.** 64 full-time; 20 part-time. 47% of faculty holds doctoral degree. Student/faculty ratio: 15 to 1.
**Selectivity rating.** Less competitive.

**PROFILE.** Wayland Baptist, founded in 1908, is a church-affiliated, multipurpose university. Programs are offered in the Divisions of Business; Christian Communication Arts; Education; Health, Physical Education, and Recreation; Languages and Literature; Mathematics and Sciences; Religion and Philosophy; and Social Sciences; and the Vocational and Technical Division. Its 80-acre campus is located in Plainview, 45 miles north of Lubbock.

**Accreditation:** SACS.
**Religious orientation:** Wayland Baptist University is affiliated with the Southern Baptist Convention; two semesters of religion required.
**Library:** Collections totaling over 136,067 volumes, 760 periodical subscriptions, and 75,275 microform items.
**Special facilities/museums:** Child development center for early childhood observation, language lab, regional history museum.
**Athletic facilities:** Gymnasium, fitness and weight rooms, racquetball court, track, intramural football and softball fields, YMCA swimming pool.

**STUDENT BODY. Undergraduate profile:** 87% are state residents; 22% are transfers. 1% Asian-American, 6% Black, 23% Hispanic, 69% White, 1% Other.
**Freshman profile:** 20% of accepted applicants took SAT; 80% took ACT.
**Undergraduate achievement:** 67% of fall 1992 freshmen returned for fall 1993 term. 50% of students who completed a degree program went on to graduate study within five years.
**Foreign students:** 15 students are from out of the country. Countries represented include Bahamas, Brazil, Colombia, Jamaica, Taiwan, and Trinidad; nine in all.

**PROGRAMS OF STUDY. Degrees:** B.A., B.Bus.Admin., B.Mus., B.S., B.S.Occup.Ed.
**Majors:** Art, Biology, Business Administration, Chemistry, Church Music, Composite Science, Education, English, History, Life/Earth Science, Mass Communications, Mathematics, Multidisciplinary Study, Music, Music Education, Philosophy, Physical Education, Physical Sciences, Political Science, Psychology, Religion, Religious Education, Social Sciences, Theatre, Vocational Education.
**Distribution of degrees:** The majors with the highest enrollment are multidisciplinary studies, business administration, and psychology; art, composite science, and music education have the lowest.
**Requirements:** General education requirement.
**Academic regulations:** Minimum 2.0 GPA must be maintained.
**Special:** Minors offered in all majors and in accounting, Christian leadership, coaching, computer business information systems, criminal justice, early childhood, earth science, finance, German, health administration, management, marketing, recreation, sociology, and Spanish. Courses offered in Greek. Seniors must take GRE. Associate's degrees offered. Double majors. Dual degrees. Independent study. Internships. Cooperative education programs. Graduate school at which undergraduates may take graduate-level courses. Preprofessional programs in law, medicine, veterinary science, pharmacy, dentistry, theology, optometry, business, engineering, nursing, and physical/occupational therapy. 3-2 engineering/math program with Texas Tech U. Teacher certification in early childhood, elementary, secondary, and vo-tech education.
**Honors:** Phi Beta Kappa. Honors program. Honor societies.
**Academic Assistance:** Remedial reading, writing, and math. Nonremedial tutoring.

**ADMISSIONS. Academic basis for candidate selection** (in order of priority): Secondary school record, class rank, standardized test scores.
**Nonacademic basis for candidate selection:** Character and personality are important.
**Requirements:** Graduation from secondary school is required; GED is accepted. 15 units and the following program of study are required: 3 units of English, 2 units of math, 1 unit of science, 2 units of social studies, 7 units of academic electives. 2 units of foreign language strongly recommended. Minimum composite ACT score of 18, rank in top third of secondary school class, and minimum 2.0 GPA required. Conditional admission possible for applicants not meeting standard requirements. ACT is required; SAT may be substituted. Campus visit and interview recommended. Off-campus interviews available with an admissions representative.
**Procedure:** Take SAT or ACT by May of 12th year. Visit college for interview by May of 12th year. Application deadline is August 1. Notification of admission on rolling basis. $50 room deposit, refundable until August 1. Freshmen accepted for terms other than fall.
**Special programs:** Credit may be granted through CEEB Advanced Placement for scores of 3 or higher. Credit may be granted through CLEP general and subject exams, DANTES and challenge exams, and military and life experience.
**Transfer students:** Transfer students accepted for terms other than fall. In fall 1993, 22% of all new students were transfers into all classes. 75 transfer applications were received, 74 were accepted. Application deadline is August 1 for fall; January 1 for spring. Minimum 2.0 GPA recommended. Lowest course grade accepted is "C." Maximum number of transferable credits is 94 semester hours. At least 30 semester hours must be completed at the university to receive degree.
**Admissions contact:** Claude Lusk, M.B.A., Director of Admissions. 806 296-4709.

**FINANCIAL AID. Available aid:** Pell grants, SEOG, state scholarships and grants, school scholarships, private scholarships, academic merit scholarships, athletic scholarships, and aid for undergraduate foreign students. Perkins Loans (NDSL), PLUS, Stafford Loans (GSL), state loans, private loans, and SLS. Tuition Plan Inc. and AMS.
**Financial aid statistics:** 18% of aid is not need-based. In 1993-94, 95% of all undergraduate applicants received aid; 85% of freshman applicants. Average amounts of aid awarded freshmen: Scholarships and grants, $5,000; loans, $2,625.
**Supporting data/closing dates:** FAFSA: Priority filing date is June 1. School's own aid application: Priority filing date is June 1. TEG: Priority filing date is June 1. Notification of awards on rolling basis.
**Financial aid contact:** Harold Whitis, Director of Financial Aid. 806 296-4713.

## West Texas State University

**Canyon, TX 79016** **806 656-0111**

**1993-94 Costs.** Tuition: $576 (state residents), $3,888 (out-of-state). Room & board: $2,700. Fees, books, misc. academic expenses (school's estimate): $1,440.
**Enrollment.** Undergraduates: 1,778 men, 1,843 women (full-time). Freshman class: 1,824 applicants, 1,425 accepted, 884 enrolled. Graduate enrollment: 521 men, 738 women.
**Test score averages/ranges.** N/A.
**Faculty.** 182 full-time; 137 part-time. 56% of faculty holds doctoral degree. Student/faculty ratio: 19 to 1.
**Selectivity rating.** N/A.

**PROFILE.** West Texas State, founded in 1909, is a public, comprehensive university. Programs are offered through the Colleges of Agriculture, Business, Education and Social Sciences, Fine Arts and Humanities, Natural Sciences, and Nursing. Its 135-acre main campus and ranch and farm of approximately 2,600 acres are located in Canyon, 15 miles south of Amarillo.

**Accreditation:** SACS. Professionally accredited by the Council on Social Work Education, the National Association of Schools of Music, the National Council for Accreditation of Teacher Education, the National League for Nursing.
**Religious orientation:** West Texas State University is nonsectarian; no religious requirements.
**Library:** Collections totaling over 270,000 volumes, and 26,291 microform items.
**Special facilities/museums:** Regional history museum.
**Athletic facilities:** Field house, basketball, racquetball, and tennis courts, tracks, swimming pool, baseball and softball fields.

**STUDENT BODY. Undergraduate profile:** 92% are state residents; 10% are transfers. 1% Asian-American, 3% Black, 6% Hispanic, 89% White, 1% Other. Average age of undergraduates is 24.
**Freshman profile:** 86% of freshmen come from public schools.
**Undergraduate achievement:** 62% of fall 1991 freshmen returned for fall 1992 term. 37% of entering class graduated.

**PROGRAMS OF STUDY. Degrees:** B.A., B.Appl.Arts/Sci., B.Bus.Admin., B.Bus.Ed., B.F.A., B.Gen.Studies, B.Mus., B.Mus.Ed., B.S., B.S.Med.Tech., B.S.Nurs.
**Majors:** Accounting, Administrative Services, Agricultural Business/Economics, Agricultural Communications, Agriculture, Animal Science, Art, Biological Sciences, Biology, Biomedical Science, Building Construction, Business, Business Education, Chemistry, Computer/Information Systems, Computer Science, Criminal Justice Administration, Dance, Economics, Elementary Education, Engineering Mathematics, Engineering Technology, English, Environmental Science, Finance, Geography, Geology, Graphic Design, Health/Physical Education, History, Journalism, Liberal Arts/Dentistry, Liberal Arts/Law, Liberal Arts/Medicine, Management, Marketing, Mathematics, Medical Technology, Music, Music Education, Music/Instrumental, Music Performance, Music Therapy, Music/Vocal, Musical Theatre, Nursing, Physics, Plant Sciences, Political Science, Psychology, Public Administration, Radio/Television, Recreation, Secondary Education, Social Sciences, Social Work, Sociology, Spanish, Special Education, Speech, Studio Art, Theatre.

**Distribution of degrees:** The majors with the highest enrollment are education, business, and nursing.
**Requirements:** General education requirement.
**Special:** Double majors. Independent study. Internships. Graduate school at which undergraduates may take graduate-level courses. Preprofessional programs in law, medicine, veterinary science, pharmacy, and dentistry. Teacher certification in early childhood, elementary, secondary, and special education.
**Honors:** Honors program.

**STUDENT LIFE. Housing:** All unmarried students under age 21 must live on campus unless living near campus with relatives. Coed, women's, and men's dorms. 31% of students live in college housing.
**Social atmosphere:** According to the editor of the student newspaper, "Social life is somewhat limited at WTSU unless you are part of an organization, mainly because of geography. Amarillo and Lubbock are the only cities with more than 25,000 population within 100 miles and the only ones of more than 100,000 within 250 miles. Some campus groups assume that they have influence, but outside of them, influence is paid little attention." The Student Activities Council sponsors movies and dances, and popular events include theatre department productions, the football and basketball games, and intramural sports. On campus, students head for the Activities Center and SUB. Off campus, there are several restaurants and nightclubs in Amarillo, 20 miles to the north.
**Services and counseling/handicapped student services:** Placement services. Health service. Counseling services for military, veteran, and older students. Birth control, personal, and psychological counseling. Career and academic guidance services. Learning disabled services.
**Campus organizations:** Undergraduate student government. Student newspaper. Yearbook. Sinfonia, other musical groups, Buffalo Masquers, Young Democrats, Young Republicans, athletic, departmental, service, and special-interest groups. Six fraternities, no chapter houses; three sororities, no chapter houses. 12% of men join a fraternity. 8% of women join a sorority.
**Religious organizations:** Several religious groups.
**Minority/foreign student organizations:** SABU, Mexican-American Association.

**ATHLETICS. Physical education requirements:** Two semesters of physical education required; ROTC or band may be substituted.
**Intercollegiate competition:** 5% of students participate. Baseball (M), basketball (M,W), cheerleading (M,W), cross-country (M,W), football (M), soccer (M), tennis (M,W), volleyball (W). Member of Lone Star Conference, NCAA Division II.
**Intramural and club sports:** 5% of students participate. Intramural badminton, baseball, billiards, bowling, flag football, frisbee golf, golf, handball, horseshoes, pickleball, racquetball, sand volleyball, softball, table tennis, tennis, volleyball. Men's club aikido, bowling, fitness club, golf, raquetball, swimming, volleyball, rodeo. Women's club aikido, bowling, fitness club, golf, racquetball, swimming, volleyball, rodeo.

**ADMISSIONS. Academic basis for candidate selection** (in order of priority): Secondary school record, class rank, standardized test scores, essay, school's recommendation.
**Requirements:** Graduation from secondary school is required; GED is accepted. 20 units and the following program of study are recommended: 4 units of English, 3 units of math, 2 units of science, 2 units of foreign language, 2 units of social studies, 2 units of history, 9 units of electives. Portfolio required of art program applicants. Audition required of music program applicants. SAT or ACT is required. No off-campus interviews.
**Procedure:** Take SAT or ACT by fall of 12th year. Application deadline is August 1. Notification of admission on rolling basis. $100 room deposit, refundable until August 1. Freshmen accepted for terms other than fall.
**Special programs:** Credit may be granted through CEEB Advanced Placement for scores of 3 or higher. Credit may be granted through CLEP subject exams, challenge exams, and military experience. Early entrance/early admission program. Concurrent enrollment program.
**Transfer students:** Transfer students accepted for terms other than fall. In fall 1992, 10% of all new students were transfers into all classes. 1,062 transfer applications were received, 851 were accepted. Application deadline is August 15 for fall; January 15 for spring. Minimum 2.0 GPA required. Lowest course grade accepted is "C." Maximum number of transferable credits is 66 semester hours. At least 36 semester hours must be completed at the university to receive degree.
**Admissions contact:** Lila Vars, Director of Admissions. 806 656-2541.

**FINANCIAL AID. Available aid:** Pell grants, SEOG, Federal Nursing Student Scholarships, state scholarships and grants, and school scholarships. Perkins Loans (NDSL), PLUS, Stafford Loans (GSL), NSL, and school loans.
**Supporting data/closing dates:** FAFSA/FFS: Accepted on rolling basis.
**Financial aid contact:** Lynda Tinsley, Director of Student Financial Aid. 806 656-3911.

**STUDENT EMPLOYMENT.** College Work/Study Program. 30% of full-time undergraduates work on campus during school year. Students may expect to earn an average of $1,600 during school year. Off-campus part-time employment opportunities rated "good."

**COMPUTER FACILITIES.** IBM/IBM-compatible microcomputers. Students may access Prime minicomputer/mainframe systems. Residence halls may be equipped with networked terminals. Computer facilities are available to all students.
**Fees:** $3 computer fee per semester hour.
**Hours:** 8 AM-11 PM.

# Wiley College

**Marshall, TX 75670** **903 927-3000**

**1993-94 Costs.** Tuition: $6,618. Room: $2,436. Board: $2,908. Fees, books, misc. academic expenses (school's estimate): $696.
**Enrollment.** Undergraduates: 250 men, 250 women (full-time). Freshman class: 323 applicants, 310 accepted, 181 enrolled.
**Test score averages/ranges.** Average SAT scores: 450 verbal, 400 math. Average ACT scores: 12 composite.
**Faculty.** 27 full-time; 10 part-time. 65% of faculty holds doctoral degree. Student/faculty ratio: 15 to 1.
**Selectivity rating.** Noncompetitive.

**PROFILE.** Wiley, founded in 1873, is a church-affiliated, historically black college. Its 63-acre campus is located in Marshall, in northeastern Texas, 38 miles west of Shreveport, La.
**Accreditation:** SACS.
**Religious orientation:** Wiley College is affiliated with the United Methodist Church; one semester of religion required.
**Library:** Collections totaling over 80,000 volumes.

**STUDENT BODY. Undergraduate profile:** 80% are state residents; 20% are transfers. 99% Black, 1% White. Average age of undergraduates is 18.
**Freshman profile:** 99% of freshmen come from public schools.
**Undergraduate achievement:** 75% of fall 1991 freshmen returned for fall 1992 term. 75% of entering class graduated. 15% of students who completed a degree program went on to graduate study within five years.
**Foreign students:** 20 students are from out of the country. Three countries represented in all.

**PROGRAMS OF STUDY. Degrees:** B.A., B.S.
**Majors:** Biology, Business/Economics, Business Education, Chemistry, Communications, Computer Science, Elementary Education, English, History, Hotel/Restaurant Management, Mathematics, Music, Nursing Home Administration, Office Administration, Physical Education, Physics, Religion/Philosophy, Social Science, Sociology.
**Distribution of degrees:** The majors with the highest enrollment are computer science and hotel/restaurant management; mathematics and religion/philosophy have the lowest.
**Requirements:** General education requirement.
**Academic regulations:** Minimum 2.0 GPA required for graduation.
**Special:** Minors offered in most majors and in accounting and business administration. Associate's degrees offered. Dual degrees. Independent study. Accelerated study. Pass/fail grading option. Preprofessional programs in law, medicine, dentistry, and nursing. Teacher certification in early childhood, elementary, and secondary education.
**Honors:** Honors program.
**Academic Assistance:** Nonremedial tutoring.

**ADMISSIONS. Academic basis for candidate selection** (in order of priority): Class rank, standardized test scores, secondary school record, school's recommendation.
**Nonacademic basis for candidate selection:** Character and personality are emphasized. Particular talent or ability is considered.
**Requirements:** Graduation from secondary school is required; GED is accepted. No specific distribution of secondary school units required. Minimum 2.0 GPA required. Audition required of music program applicants. Basic Studies Lab for applicants not normally admissible. SAT or ACT is required. Admissions interview recommended. Off-campus interviews available with admissions and alumni representatives.
**Procedure:** Take SAT or ACT by January 15 of 12th year. Visit college for interview by March 1 of 12th year. Application deadline is March 1. Notification of admission on rolling basis. Reply is required by May 1. $300 refundable tuition deposit. $50 nonrefundable room deposit. Freshmen accepted for terms other than fall.
**Special programs:** Admission may be deferred. Early decision program. In fall 1992, 40 applied for early decision and 30 were accepted. Early entrance/early admission program. Concurrent enrollment program.
**Transfer students:** Transfer students accepted for terms other than fall. In fall 1992, 20% of all new students were transfers into all classes. 75 transfer applications were received, 70 were accepted. Application deadline is rolling for fall; rolling for spring. Minimum 2.0 GPA required. Lowest course grade accepted is "C." At least 30 semester hours must be completed at the college to receive degree.
**Admissions contact:** Lee Marcus Roberts, Director of Admissions and Recruitment. 903 927-3311.

**FINANCIAL AID. Available aid:** Pell grants, SEOG, state scholarships and grants, school scholarships, private scholarships and grants, academic merit scholarships, and United Negro College Fund. Perkins Loans (NDSL), Stafford Loans (GSL), private loans, and SLS. Deferred payment plan.
**Supporting data/closing dates:** FAFSA/FAF/FFS: Accepted on rolling basis. Income tax forms: Accepted on rolling basis. Notification of awards on rolling basis.
**Financial aid contact:** Rachel Else, Director of Financial Aid. 903 927-3217.

# Utah

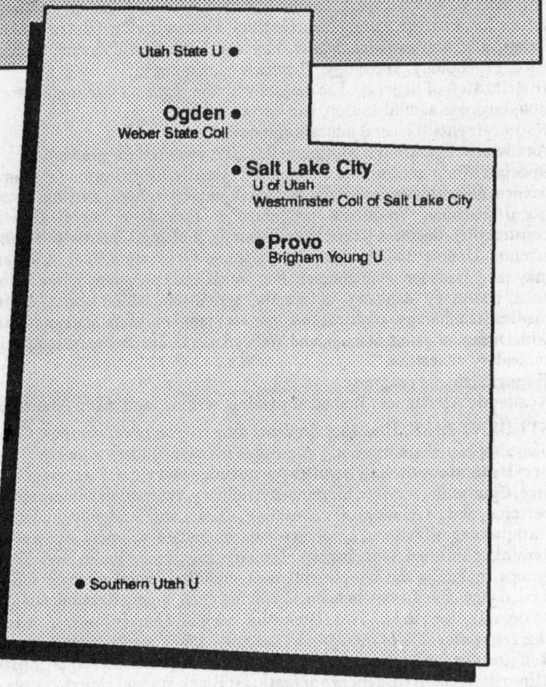


## Brigham Young University

**Provo, UT 84602** **801 378-4636**

**1993-94 Costs.** $2,340 (Latter-Day Saints members); $3,510 (others) per year. Room & board: $3,450. Fees, books, misc. academic expenses (school's estimate): $630.
**Enrollment.** Undergraduates: 13,062 men, 13,316 women (full-time). Freshman class: 7,316 applicants, 5,152 accepted, 4,291 enrolled. Graduate enrollment: 1,843 men, 1,083 women.
**Test score averages/ranges.** Average ACT scores: 26 English, 26 math, 27 composite. Range of ACT scores of middle 50%: 24-30 English, 23-29 math.
**Faculty.** 1,339 full-time; 321 part-time. 79% of faculty holds doctoral degree. Student/faculty ratio: 24 to 1.
**Selectivity rating.** Highly competitive.

**PROFILE.** Brigham Young, founded in 1875, is a church-affiliated university of liberal arts and sciences. Its 638-acre campus is located in Provo, 45 miles south of Salt Lake City.

**Accreditation:** NASC, WASC. Professionally accredited by the Accreditation Board for Engineering and Technology, the Accrediting Council on Education in Journalism and Mass Communication, the American Assembly of Collegiate Schools of Business, the American Bar Association, the American Medical Association (CAHEA), the American Psychological Association, the American Speech-Language-Hearing Association, the American Veterinary Medical Association, the Association of American Law Schools, the Council on Social Work Education, the National Association of Schools of Music, the National Council for Accreditation of Teacher Education, the National League for Nursing.
**Religious orientation:** Brigham Young University is affiliated with the Church of Jesus Christ of Latter-Day Saints; 14 credits of religion and theology required.
**Library:** Collections totaling over 2,262,029 volumes, 17,698 periodical subscriptions, and 2,006,215 microform items.
**Special facilities/museums:** Art, peoples/cultures, life science, and earth science museums, film studio, on-campus nursery school, language research center, dairy, poultry, and agricultural farms, seismography equipment, electron microscope.
**Athletic facilities:** Swimming pools, tennis and racquetball courts, softball and football fields, volleyball and basketball courts, weight rooms.

**STUDENT BODY. Undergraduate profile:** 32% are state residents; 22% are transfers. 1.4% Asian-American, .7% Black, 1.3% Hispanic, .6% Native American, 91% White, 5% Other. Average age of undergraduates is 22.
**Freshman profile:** 20% of freshmen who took ACT scored 30 or over on English, 21% scored 30 or over on math, 22% scored 30 or over on composite; 78% scored 24 or over on English, 70% scored 24 or over on math, 82% scored 24 or over on composite; 99% scored 18 or over on English, 98% scored 18 or over on math, 99% scored 18 or over on composite; 100% scored 12 or over on English, 100% scored 12 or over on math, 100% scored 12 or over on composite. 100% of accepted applicants took ACT.
**Undergraduate achievement:** The majority of male BYU students leave after their freshman year to serve two-year missions. They return for their sophomore year after the two-year break. 80% of starting freshman eventually return for their sophomore year. 25% of students who completed a degree program immediately went on to graduate study.
**Foreign students:** 1,210 students are from out of the country. Countries represented include Canada, China, England, Hong Kong, Japan, and Mexico; 101 in all.

**PROGRAMS OF STUDY. Degrees:** B.A., B.F.A., B.Indep.Studies, B.Mus., B.S.
**Majors:** Accounting, Advertising/Public Relations, Agricultural Economics, Agronomy, American Studies, Animal Science, Anthropology, Anthropology Teaching, Applied Physics, Art Education, Art History, Art Studio, Asian Studies, Athletic Training, Ballet, Botany, Broadcasting, Building Construction, Business Management, Canadian Studies, Cartography, Chemical Engineering, Chemistry, Chinese, Civil Engineering, Clothing/Textiles, Communications Disorders, Comparative Literature, Computer Science, Dance Specialization, Dance Sports Composite, Design, Design Engineering Technology, Early Childhood Education, Earth Science Teaching, Economics, Electrical Engineering, Electronics Engineering Technology, Elementary Education, Engineering Geology, English, English Composite Teaching, English Teaching, Entomology, European Studies, Family/Community History Studies, Family Living, Family Sciences, Fashion Design, Fashion Merchandising, Film, Food Science/Nutrition, French, French Teaching, Geography, Geography/Resource Management, Geography Teaching, Geology, German, German Teaching, Graphic Design, Greek, Health Teaching, History, Home Economics Education, Horticulture, Human Development, Humanities, Humanities Teaching, Independent Studies, Industrial Arts Teacher Education, Industrial Design, Industrial Education, Information Management, Interior Design, International Relations, Italian, Japanese, Journalism, Korean, Latin, Latin American Studies, Latin Teaching, Linguistics, Manufacturing Engineering Technology, Mathematics, Mathematics Education, Mechanical Engineering, Medical Technology, Microbiology, Music, Music Composition/Theory, Music Education, Music Pedagogy, Music Performance, Music Theatre, Near Eastern Studies, Nursing, Organizational Behavior, Philosophy, Photography, Physical Education, Physical Plant Administration, Physics, Political Science, Portuguese, Professional Dance, Professional Sociology, Psychology, Psychology Teaching, Range Science, Range Science/Agribusiness, Range Science/Range Resources, Range Science/Wildlife/Range Resources, Recreation Management/Youth Leadership, Russian, Russian Teaching, Secondary Education, Social Work, Sociology, Sociology Teaching, Spanish, Spanish Teaching, Spanish Translation, Special Education, Speech Communication, Statistics, Statistics/Computer Science, Theatre Arts Education, Travel/Tourism, Zoology.
**Distribution of degrees:** The majors with the highest enrollment are business management, elementary education, and communications disorders; food science/nutrition and Latin have the lowest.
**Requirements:** General education requirement.
**Academic regulations:** Minimum 2.0 GPA must be maintained.
**Special:** Minors offered in most majors. Courses offered in biblical and Middle Eastern languages, Danish, Native American studies, and Swedish. Associate's degrees offered. Double majors. Independent study. Internships. Cooperative education programs. Graduate school at which undergraduates may take graduate-level courses. Preprofessional programs in law, medicine, veterinary science, pharmacy, dentistry, and optometry. Washington Semester. Teacher certification in early childhood, elementary, secondary, special education, vo-tech, and bilingual/bicultural education. Certification in specific subject areas. International service projects. Study abroad in Austria, Chile, China, England, France, Israel, Japan, Korea, Mexico, Russia, Spain, and Taiwan. ROTC and AFROTC.
**Honors:** Honors program.
**Academic Assistance:** Remedial reading, writing, math, and study skills. Nonremedial tutoring.

**STUDENT LIFE. Housing:** Students may live on or off campus. Women's and men's dorms. On-campus married-student housing. 23% of students live in college housing.
**Social atmosphere:** Favorite student gathering spots include Mama's Cafe, Atticus Books, Provo Smith's, and the Maeser Building. The Student Service Organization, the Voice (a prominent women's organization), and the College Democrats are all influential on campus. Students enjoy attending football games, hiking, camping, and skiing in the nearby mountains, and attending exhibitions at the Brigham Young Museum of Art. According to the student newspaper, many students find enjoyable activities off campus: "The best social and cultural life can be found in Salt Lake. When people want to dance they go to The Bay; to shop, they go to Crossroads Plaza; for the symphony, to Abravanel; and for plays they go to the Sundance Theatre."
**Services and counseling/handicapped student services:** Placement services. Health service. Women's center. Counseling services for minority and older students. Personal and psychological counseling. Career and academic guidance services. Physically disabled student services. Reader services for the blind.
**Campus organizations:** Undergraduate student government. Student newspaper (Daily Universe). Literary magazine. Radio and TV stations. A cappella choir, dance groups, debating, service and special-interest groups, 200 organizations in all.
**Religious organizations:** Baptist Student Union, Moslem Student Union, Catholic Newman Club.
**Minority/foreign student organizations:** Polynesian Club, Tribe of Many Feathers, Black Student Association, Latin American Club, African Student Association. International Student Association, many foreign student groups.

**ATHLETICS. Physical education requirements:** 1.5 credits of physical education required.
**Intercollegiate competition:** 5% of students participate. Baseball (M), basketball (M,W), cross-country (M,W), diving (M,W), football (M), golf (M,W), gymnastics (M,W), skiing (W), swimming (M,W), tennis (M,W), track (indoor) (M,W), track (outdoor) (M,W), track and field (M,W), track and field (indoor) (M,W), track and field (outdoor) (M,W), volleyball (M,W), wrestling (M). Member of HCAC, NCAA Division I, NCAA Division I-A for football, Western Athletic Conference.
**Intramural and club sports:** Intramural archery, badminton, basketball, bowling, cross-country, fencing, field hockey, football, golf, handball, lacrosse, racquetball, rugby, skiing, soccer, softball, table tennis, tennis, volleyball, wrestling. Men's club fencing, lacrosse, racquetball, rugby, weight lifting. Women's club fencing, racquetball, softball.

**ADMISSIONS. Academic basis for candidate selection** (in order of priority): Secondary school record, standardized test scores, essay, school's recommendation, class rank.
**Nonacademic basis for candidate selection:** Character and personality are important. Extracurricular participation and particular talent or ability are considered.
**Requirements:** Graduation from secondary school is required; GED is accepted. 16 units and the following program of study are recommended: 4 units of English, 4 units of math, 2 units of science, 2 units of foreign language, 2 units of history, 2 units of literature. Minimum ACT score of 20 and minimum 3.0 GPA recommended. Completion of core classes

and minimum 2.85 GPA required of business and accounting program applicants. ACT is required.
**Procedure:** Take ACT by December of 12th year. Application deadline is February 15. Notification of admission on rolling basis. $150 room deposit, of which $100 is refundable until May 1. Freshmen accepted for terms other than fall.
**Special programs:** Admission may be deferred for LDS mission work. Credit and/or placement may be granted through CEEB Advanced Placement exams for scores of 3 or higher. Credit and/or placement may be granted through CLEP general exams. Credit and placement may be granted through challenge exams and military experience. Early entrance/early admission program. Concurrent enrollment program.
**Transfer students:** Transfer students accepted for terms other than fall. In fall 1993, 22% of all new students were transfers into all classes. 2,421 transfer applications were received, 1,305 were accepted. Application deadline is March 15 for fall; October 1 for spring. Minimum 3.0 GPA recommended. Lowest course grade accepted is "C-." At least 30 semester hours must be completed at the university to receive degree.
**Admissions contact:** Jeff Tanner, M.A., Associate Dean of Admissions and Records. 801 378-2500.

**FINANCIAL AID. Available aid:** Pell grants, school scholarships and grants, private scholarships, ROTC scholarships, academic merit scholarships, and athletic scholarships. PLUS, Stafford Loans (GSL), school loans, and SLS.
**Financial aid statistics:** In 1993-94, 93% of all undergraduate applicants received aid.
**Supporting data/closing dates:** FAFSA: Priority filing date is March 1. School's own aid application: Priority filing date is March 1. Notification of awards on rolling basis.
**Financial aid contact:** Ford Stevenson, M.A., Director of Financial Aid. 801 378-4104.

**STUDENT EMPLOYMENT.** Institutional employment. 35% of full-time undergraduates work on campus during school year. Students may expect to earn an average of $2,900 during school year. Off-campus part-time employment opportunities rated "good."

**COMPUTER FACILITIES.** 3,100 IBM/IBM-compatible, Macintosh/Apple, and RISC-/UNIX-based microcomputers. Students may access AT&T, Digital, Hewlett-Packard, IBM, SUN minicomputer/mainframe systems, Internet. Residence halls may be equipped with stand-alone microcomputers, networked microcomputers. Client/LAN operating systems include Apple/Macintosh, DOS, OS/2, UNIX/XENIX/AIX, X-windows, LocalTalk/AppleTalk, Novell. Computer languages and software packages include BASIC, BLISS, C, COBOL, DataTrieve, FORTRAN, IMSL, Lotus 1-2-3, Pascal, PL/1, SAS, SPSS, WordPerfect; graphics, simulation text prep, publishing programs. Computer facilities are available to all students.
**Fees:** None.
**Hours:** 24 hours, six days/week.

**GRADUATE CAREER DATA.** 34% of graduates choose careers in business and industry. Companies and businesses that hire graduates: Boeing, Ernst & Young, Price Waterhouse, WordPerfect.

**PROMINENT ALUMNI/AE.** Ezra Taft Benson, president of LDS Church, former U.S. secretary of agriculture; Virginia Cutler, national leader in consumer affairs; Philo T. Farnsworth, contributor to creation of TV; James C. Fletcher, former chief, NASA; Orrin G. Hatch, U.S. senator.

# Southern Utah University

**Cedar City, UT 84720** **801 586-7700**

**1994-95 Costs.** Tuition: $1,308 (state residents), $5,238 (out-of-state). Room: $1,080. Board: $1,665. Fees, books, misc. academic expenses (school's estimate): $1,140.
**Enrollment.** Undergraduates: 1,604 men, 1,828 women (full-time). Freshman class: 1,685 applicants, 1,649 accepted, 856 enrolled. Graduate enrollment: 30 men, 40 women.
**Test score averages/ranges.** Average ACT scores: 21 composite.
**Faculty.** 157 full-time; 43 part-time. 50% of faculty holds doctoral degree. Student/faculty ratio: 22 to 1.
**Selectivity rating.** Noncompetitive.

**PROFILE.** Southern Utah is a public, comprehensive university. It was founded in 1897, adopted coeducation in 1987, and gained university status in 1991. Programs are offered through the Schools of Arts and Letters; Business, Communication, and Technology; Education; and Science. Its 105-acre campus is located in Cedar City, in southwestern Utah.

**Accreditation:** NASC. Professionally accredited by the Council on Social Work Education, the National Council for Accreditation of Teacher Education.
**Religious orientation:** Southern Utah University is nonsectarian; no religious requirements.
**Library:** Collections totaling over 195,324 volumes, 1,191 periodical subscriptions, and 549,046 microform items.
**Special facilities/museums:** Art gallery, natural history museum, farm and ranch, TV studio.
**Athletic facilities:** Gymnasium, swimming pool, baseball, football, and softball fields, basketball arena.

**STUDENT BODY. Undergraduate profile:** 92% are state residents; 37% are transfers. 1% Black, 1% Hispanic, 4% Native American, 93% White, 1% Other. Average age of undergraduates is 23.
**Freshman profile:** 2% of accepted applicants took SAT; 98% took ACT. 95% of freshmen come from public schools.
**Foreign students:** 35 students are from out of the country. Five countries represented in all.

**PROGRAMS OF STUDY. Degrees:** B.A., B.S.
**Majors:** Accounting, Art, Biological Sciences, Botany, Business Administration, Business Education, Chemistry, Communication, Communication/Theatre Arts, Elementary Education, English, Family Life, Geology, History, Industrial Arts, Industrial Technology, Languages, Mathematics, Music, Physical Education, Physical Sciences, Political Science, Psychology, Sociology, Theatre Arts, Zoology.
**Distribution of degrees:** The majors with the highest enrollment are elementary education, business administration, and accounting.
**Requirements:** General education requirement.
**Academic regulations:** Minimum 2.0 GPA required for graduation.
**Special:** Minor in computer information systems. Certification programs in clerical, electronics, gerontology, industrial technical, nursery school, nursing, secretarial, and vocational teaching. Vocational programs in agriculture, automotive studies, building construction, business (clerical, secretarial), drafting, electronics technology, and police science. Double majors. Accelerated study. Graduate school at which undergraduates may take graduate-level courses. Preprofessional programs in medicine, veterinary science, pharmacy, dentistry, optometry, agriculture, allied health, engineering, forestry, medical technology, physical therapy, and range/wildlife sciences. Exchange programs with Dixie Coll, Utah State U, and Weber State U. Teacher certification in elementary and secondary education.
**Honors:** Honors program.
**Academic Assistance:** Remedial reading, writing, and math. Nonremedial tutoring.

**STUDENT LIFE. Housing:** Students may live on or off campus. Coed dorms. School-owned/operated apartments. On-campus married-student housing.
**Services and counseling/handicapped student services:** Placement services. Health service. Counseling services for minority, military, veteran, and older students. Birth control, personal, and psychological counseling. Career and academic guidance services.
**Campus organizations:** Undergraduate student government. Student newspaper (Thunderbird, published twice/week). Literary magazine. Radio and TV stations. Choral groups, marching and symphonic bands, orchestra, small ensembles, Shakespearean Festival, dance club, forensics team, skydiving club, Young Republicans, Young Democrats, 35 organizations in all. Two fraternities, all with chapter houses; two sororities, all with chapter houses. 1% of men join a fraternity. 1% of women join a sorority.
**Religious organizations:** Latter-Day Saints Association, Youth Christian Society.
**Minority/foreign student organizations:** Black Student Union, Native American Union. Multicultural Center.

**ATHLETICS. Physical education requirements:** Two terms of physical education required.
**Intercollegiate competition:** 3% of students participate. Baseball (M), basketball (M,W), cheerleading (M,W), cross-country (M,W), football (M), golf (M), gymnastics (W), softball (W), track (indoor) (M,W), track (outdoor) (M,W). Member of NCAA Division I.
**Intramural and club sports:** 1% of students participate. Intramural basketball, flag football, racquetball, soccer, softball, volleyball.

**ADMISSIONS. Academic basis for candidate selection** (in order of priority): Secondary school record, standardized test scores.
**Requirements:** Graduation from secondary school is required; GED is accepted. 11 units and the following program of study are recommended: 4 units of English, 3 units of math, 2 units of science including 1 unit of lab, 1 unit of social studies, 1 unit of history. Applicants must be graduates of accredited secondary schools whose ACT scores and GPA meet required admissions index. Nursing program applicants must apply through Weber State U. ACT is required; SAT may be substituted. Campus visit recommended. No off-campus interviews.
**Procedure:** Notification of admission on rolling basis. Reply is required by July 1. $100 room deposit, $85 of which is refundable. Freshmen accepted for terms other than fall.
**Special programs:** Admission may be deferred. Credit and/or placement may be granted through CEEB Advanced Placement exams for scores of 3 or higher. Credit and/or placement may be granted through CLEP general and subject exams. Early decision program. Early entrance/early admission program. Concurrent enrollment program.
**Transfer students:** Transfer students accepted for terms other than fall. In fall 1993, 37% of all new students were transfers into all classes. 885 transfer applications were received, 862 were accepted. Application deadline is July 1 for fall; December 1 for winter; March 1 for spring. Minimum 2.0 GPA required. Lowest course grade accepted is "C." At least 30 quarter hours must be completed at the university to receive degree.
**Admissions contact:** Dale S. Orton, Director of Admissions. 801 586-7740.

**FINANCIAL AID. Available aid:** Pell grants, SEOG, state scholarships and grants, school scholarships and grants, private scholarships, athletic scholarships, and aid for undergraduate foreign students. Perkins Loans (NDSL), PLUS, Stafford Loans (GSL), school loans, and SLS. Deferred payment plan.
**Financial aid statistics:** Average amounts of aid awarded freshmen: Scholarships and grants, $1,949; loans, $2,400.
**Supporting data/closing dates:** FAFSA: Accepted on rolling basis. Notification of awards on rolling basis.
**Financial aid contact:** Rex Mitchie, Director of Financial Aid. 801 586-7735.

**STUDENT EMPLOYMENT.** College Work/Study Program. Institutional employment. 32% of full-time undergraduates work on campus during school year. Students may expect to earn an average of $1,500 during school year. Off-campus part-time employment opportunities rated "fair."

**COMPUTER FACILITIES.** IBM/IBM-compatible and Macintosh/Apple microcomputers. Students may access Digital minicomputer/mainframe systems. Computer languages and software packages include BASIC, COBOL, dBASE, FORTRAN, Pascal; database, spreadsheet, word processing programs. Computer facilities are available to all students.
**Fees:** $10 computer fee per quarter.
**Hours:** 7 AM-11 PM.

**GRADUATE CAREER DATA.** Graduate school percentages: 2% enter law school. 3% enter medical school. Highest graduate school enrollments: Utah State U, U of Utah. 25% of graduates choose careers in business and industry. Companies and businesses that hire graduates: education districts from Arizona, California, Nevada, and Utah; Xerox.

# University of Utah

**Salt Lake City, UT 84112** **801 581-7200**

**1994-95 Costs.** Tuition: $1,954 (state residents), $6,857 (out-of-state). Room: $1,479. Board: $2,386. Fees, books, misc. academic expenses (school's estimate): $1,285.
**Enrollment.** Undergraduates: 7,801 men, 6,040 women (full-time). Freshman class: 4,856 applicants, 4,353 accepted, 2,287 enrolled. Graduate enrollment: 2,883 men, 1,907 women.
**Test score averages/ranges.** Average SAT scores: 480 verbal, 538 math. Range of SAT scores of middle 50%: 420-540 verbal, 460-610 math. Average ACT scores: 23 English, 22 math, 23 composite. Range of ACT scores of middle 50%: 20-26 English, 19-25 math.
**Faculty.** 1,463 full-time. 98% of faculty holds highest degree in specific field. Student/faculty ratio: 15 to 1.
**Selectivity rating.** Less competitive.

**PROFILE.** The University of Utah, founded in 1850, is a public institution. Programs are offered through the Colleges of Business, Engineering, Fine Arts, Health, Humanities, Law, Medicine, Mines and Earth Sciences, Nursing, Pharmacy, Science, Social and Behavioral Sciences and the Graduate Schools of Architecture, Business, Education, and Social Work. Its 1,500 campus is located in Salt Lake City.
**Accreditation:** NASC. Numerous professional accreditations.
**Religious orientation:** University of Utah is nonsectarian; no religious requirements.
**Library:** Collections totaling over 2,158,252 volumes, 16,531 periodical subscriptions, and 3,096,495 microform items.
**Special facilities/museums:** Museums of natural history and fine arts, government institute, environmental biological research facilities, human genetics lab.
**Athletic facilities:** Gymnasiums, basketball, tennis, and volleyball courts, track, athletic fields, stadium, field house.
**STUDENT BODY. Undergraduate profile:** 91% are state residents; 44% are transfers. 3% Asian-American, 1% Black, 3% Hispanic, 1% Native American, 82% White, 10% Other. Average age of undergraduates is 25.
**Freshman profile:** 2% of freshmen who took SAT scored 700 or over on verbal, 8% scored 700 or over on math; 15% scored 600 or over on verbal, 31% scored 600 or over on math; 44% scored 500 or over on verbal, 64% scored 500 or over on math; 81% scored 400 or over on verbal, 89% scored 400 or over on math; 96% scored 300 or over on verbal, 99% scored 300 or over on math. 7% of freshmen who took ACT scored 30 or over on English, 8% scored 30 or over on math, 9% scored 30 or over on composite; 47% scored 24 or over on English, 39% scored 24 or over on math, 47% scored 24 or over on composite; 89% scored 18 or over on English, 87% scored 18 or over on math, 94% scored 18 or over on composite; 100% scored 12 or over on English, 100% scored 12 or over on math, 100% scored 12 or over on composite. 19% of accepted applicants took SAT; 90% took ACT. 95% of freshmen come from public schools.
**Undergraduate achievement:** 62% of fall 1992 freshmen returned for fall 1993 term. 27% of students who completed a degree program immediately went on to graduate study.
**Foreign students:** 853 students are from out of the country. Countries represented include Canada, China, India, Japan, Korea, and Taiwan; 99 in all.
**PROGRAMS OF STUDY. Degrees:** B.A., B.F.A., B.Mus., B.S., B.Univ.Studies.
**Majors:** Accounting, Anthropology, Architecture, Art, Art History, Asian Studies, Ballet, Biology, Business Administration, Chemical/Fuels Engineering, Chemistry, Civil Engineering, Classics, Communication Disorders, Communication Skills, Computer Engineering, Computer Science, Consumer Studies/Family Economics, Economics, Electrical Engineering, Elementary Education, English, Environment/Behavior, Exercise/Sports Science, Film Studies, Finance, French, Geography, Geological Engineering, Geology/Geophysics, German, Health Education, History, Human Development/Family Studies, Linguistics, Management, Marketing, Mass Communication, Materials Science Engineering, Mathematics, Mechanical Engineering, Medical Biology, Metallurgical Engineering, Meteorology, Middle Eastern Studies, Mining Engineering, Modern Dance, Music, Nursing, Pharmacy, Philosophy, Physical Therapy, Physics, Political Science, Psychology, Recreation/Leisure, Russian, Social Science, Sociology, Spanish, Speech Communication, Theatre, Urban Planning.
**Distribution of degrees:** The majors with the highest enrollment are psychology, political science, and accounting; communication skills, geophysics, and geological engineering have the lowest.
**Requirements:** General education requirement.
**Academic regulations:** Minimum 2.0 GPA must be maintained.
**Special:** Minors offered in most majors. Self-designed majors. Double majors. Dual degrees. Independent study. Accelerated study. Pass/fail grading option. Internships. Cooperative education programs. Graduate school at which undergraduates may take graduate-level courses. Preprofessional programs in law, medicine, pharmacy, and dentistry. 3-2 law/M.B.A. program. Member of Western Interstate Commission for Higher Education (WICHE). Member of National Student Exchange (NSE) and Western Undergraduate Exchange (WUE). Teacher certification in elementary, secondary, and special education. Member of International Student Exchange Program (ISEP). ROTC, NROTC, and AFROTC.
**Honors:** Phi Beta Kappa. Honors program.
**Academic Assistance:** Remedial reading, writing, math, and study skills. Nonremedial tutoring.
**STUDENT LIFE. Housing:** Students may live on or off campus. Women's and men's dorms. Sorority and fraternity housing. School-owned/operated apartments. On-campus married-student housing. 10% of students live in college housing.
**Social atmosphere:** Popular gathering-places are the Port-O-Call Social Club, Bar-X, Lumpy's Social Club, and The Pie. Greeks, the football team, and the bar scene have a strong influence on student social life. Fraternity parties, Utah Jazz basketball games, rock concerts, football and basketball games are well-attended.
**Services and counseling/handicapped student services:** Placement services. Health service. Women's center. Counseling services for minority, military, veteran, and older students. Birth control, personal, and psychological counseling. Career and academic guidance services. Religious counseling. Physically disabled student services. Learning disabled program/services. Notetaking services. Tape recorders. Tutors. Reader services for the blind.
**Campus organizations:** Undergraduate student government. Student newspaper (Daily Utah Chronicle). Literary magazine. Radio and TV stations. Ballet and modern dance, chamber music ensembles, chorus, chorale, Opera Workshop, concert, marching, and pep bands, cheerleaders, drill team, experimental theatre workshop, Young People's Theatre, debating, departmental, professional, service, and special-interest groups. 12 fraternities, all with chapter houses; seven sororities, six chapter houses. 6% of men join a fraternity. 6% of women join a sorority.
**Religious organizations:** Groups for all major religions.
**ATHLETICS. Physical education requirements:** None.
**Intercollegiate competition:** 3% of students participate. Alpine skiing (M,W), baseball (M), basketball (M,W), cross-country (M,W), diving (M,W), football (M), golf (M), gymnastics (W), Nordic skiing (M,W), softball (W), swimming (M,W), tennis (M,W), track and field (indoor) (M,W), track and field (outdoor) (M,W), volleyball (W). Member of NCAA Division I-A, Western Athletic Conference.
**Intramural and club sports:** Intramural basketball, bowling, flag football, floor hockey, golf, racquetball, skiing, soccer, softball, squash, swimming, table tennis, tennis, triathlon, volleyball, wrestling, walleyball. Men's club bowling, lacrosse, rugby, skiing, soccer, volleyball. Women's club bowling, skiing, soccer, volleyball.
**ADMISSIONS. Academic basis for candidate selection** (in order of priority): Secondary school record, standardized test scores, school's recommendation, class rank.
**Nonacademic basis for candidate selection:** Extracurricular participation and particular talent or ability are considered.
**Requirements:** Graduation from secondary school is required; GED is accepted. 15 units and the following program of study are required: 4 units of English, 2 units of math, 2 units of science including 1 unit of lab, 2 units of foreign language, 1 unit of history, 4 units of academic electives. Math units should be selected from geometry, intermediate algebra, trigonometry, and calculus. Acceptable admissions index (combination of ACT/GPA) required. Audition required of ballet program applicants. Portfolio required of art program applicants. EOP for applicants not normally admissible. Conditional admission possible for applicants not meeting standard requirements. ACT is required; SAT may be substituted. No off-campus interviews.
**Procedure:** Suggest filing application by February 15. Application deadline is July 1. Acceptance notification on rolling basis, usually within two weeks of completion of file. No set date by which applicants must accept offer. $75 room deposit, refundable until August 1. Freshmen accepted for terms other than fall.
**Special programs:** Admission may be deferred one year. Credit and/or placement may be granted through CEEB Advanced Placement exams for scores of 3 or higher. Credit may be granted through CLEP subject exams and military experience. Credit and placement may be granted through challenge exams. Early entrance/early admission program. Concurrent enrollment program.
**Transfer students:** Transfer students accepted for terms other than fall. In fall 1993, 44% of all new students were transfers into all classes. 2,596 transfer applications were received, 2,277 were accepted. Application deadline is July 1 for fall; February 15 for spring. Minimum 2.5 GPA required. Lowest course grade accepted is "C." At least 45 quarter hours must be completed at the university to receive degree.
**Admissions contact:** Stayner Landward, D.S.W., Director of Admissions. 801 581-7281.
**FINANCIAL AID. Available aid:** Pell grants, SEOG, Federal Nursing Student Scholarships, state scholarships and grants, school scholarships, private scholarships and grants, ROTC scholarships, academic merit scholarships, athletic scholarships, and aid for undergraduate foreign students. Perkins Loans (NDSL), PLUS, Stafford Loans (GSL), NSL, Health Professions Loans, school loans, private loans, and SLS.
**Financial aid statistics:** 3% of aid is not need-based. In 1993-94, 95% of all undergraduate applicants received aid; 95% of freshman applicants.
**Supporting data/closing dates:** FAFSA: Priority filing date is February 15. School's own aid application: Priority filing date is February 15. Notification of awards begins in May.
**Financial aid contact:** Harold Weight, M.S., Director of Financial Aid. 801 581-6211.
**STUDENT EMPLOYMENT.** College Work/Study Program. Institutional employment. Off-campus part-time employment opportunities rated "excellent."
**COMPUTER FACILITIES.** 800 IBM/IBM-compatible and Macintosh/Apple microcomputers; all are networked. Students may access IBM minicomputer/mainframe systems, BITNET, Internet, CompuServe. Residence halls may be equipped with networked microcomputers. Client/LAN operating systems include Apple/Macintosh, DOS, OS/2, UNIX/XENIX/AIX, Windows NT, X-windows, Novell. All major languages and software packages available. Computer facilities are available to all students.
**Fees:** $5 plus $3 per credit hour.
**Hours:** 8 AM-10 PM.

# Utah State University

**Logan, UT 84322-1600** **801 750-1000**

**1994-95 Costs.** Tuition: $1,878 (state residents), $5,523 (out-of-state). Room & board: $3,105. Fees, books, misc. academic expenses (school's estimate): $705.
**Enrollment.** Undergraduates: 6,614 men, 5,411 women (full-time). Freshman class: 3,961 applicants, 3,591 accepted, 2,192 enrolled. Graduate enrollment: 1,638 men, 1,152 women.
**Test score averages/ranges.** Average SAT scores: 433 verbal, 514 math. Average ACT scores: 22 English, 20 math, 22 composite. Range of ACT scores of middle 50%: 19-26 English, 19-26 math.
**Faculty.** 726 full-time; 33 part-time. Student/faculty ratio: 19 to 1.
**Selectivity rating.** Less competitive.

**PROFILE.** Utah State, founded in 1888, is a public, comprehensive university. Programs are offered through the Colleges of Agriculture; Business; Education; Engineering; Family Life; Humanities, Arts, and Social Sciences; Natural Resources; and Science; and the Schools of Accountancy and Graduate Studies. Its 332-acre campus is located in Logan, 80 miles north of Salt Lake City.

**Accreditation:** NASC. Professionally accredited by the Accreditation Board for Engineering and Technology, the American Dietetic Association, the American Home Economics Association, the American Society of Landscape Architects, the Council on Rehabilitation Education, the Council on Social Work Education, the National Council for Accreditation of Teacher Education, the National League for Nursing, the Society of American Foresters.
**Religious orientation:** Utah State University is nonsectarian; no religious requirements.
**Library:** Collections totaling over 846,767 volumes, 6,205 periodical subscriptions, and 1,680,970 microform items.
**Special facilities/museums:** Art gallery, agricultural and engineering experiment station, water research lab, wildlife and fishery research unit, on-campus school, intermountain herbarium, electron microscope, space dynamics lab.
**Athletic facilities:** Field house, gymnastic and wrestling facilities, track, athletic fields, swimming pools, basketball and volleyball courts, weight room.

**STUDENT BODY. Undergraduate profile:** 87% are state residents; 38% are transfers. 2% Asian-American, 1% Black, 1% Hispanic, 1% Native American, 88% White, 7% Other. Average age of undergraduates is 24.
**Freshman profile:** 17% of freshmen who took ACT scored 30 or over on English, 10% scored 30 or over on math, 15% scored 30 or over on composite; 52% scored 24 or over on English, 38% scored 24 or over on math, 50% scored 24 or over on composite; 74% scored 18 or over on English, 60% scored 18 or over on math, 76% scored 18 or over on composite; 100% scored 12 or over on English, 100% scored 12 or over on math, 100% scored 12 or over on composite. 2% of accepted applicants took SAT; 98% took ACT. 98% of freshmen come from public schools.
**Undergraduate achievement:** 62% of fall 1992 freshmen returned for fall 1993 term. 58% of entering class graduated.
**Foreign students:** 515 students are from out of the country. Countries represented include China, India, Japan, Korea, and Taiwan; 79 in all.

**PROGRAMS OF STUDY. Degrees:** B.A., B.F.A., B.Land.Arch., B.Mus., B.S.
**Majors:** Agribusiness, Agricultural Economics, Agricultural Education, Agricultural/Irrigation Engineering, Agricultural Systems Technology, American Studies, Animal Science, Anthropology, Applied Biology, Applied Statistics, Art, Biology, Bioveterinary Science, Chemistry, Communicative Disorders, Computer Science, Dairy Science, Dance, Early Childhood Education, Economics, Electrical Engineering, Elementary Education, English, Environmental Studies, Family/Human Development, Fisheries/Wildlife, Forestry, French, General Business, General Family Life, Geography, Geology, German, Health Education, History, Home Economics Education, Household Economics/Management, Industrial Teacher Education, Industrial Technology/Aerospace, Industrial Technology/Electronics/Computer, International Agriculture, Journalism, Landscape Architecture/Environmental Planning, Liberal Arts, Management, Mathematics, Mathematics Education, Medical Technology, Music, Music Therapy, Nutrition/Food Science, Parks/Recreation, Personnel/Human Resources Management, Personnel/Industrial Relations, Philosophy, Physical Education, Physics, Plant Science, Political Science, Pre-Accounting, Pre-Administrative Systems, Pre-Business Administration, Pre-Business Education, Pre-Civil Engineering, Pre-Dental Biology, Pre-Finance, Pre-Law, Pre-Marketing, Pre-Marketing Education, Pre-Medical Biology, Pre-Production Management, Psychology, Public Health, Range Science, Recreation Resource Management, Secondary Education, Social Work, Sociology, Soil Science/Biometeorology, Spanish, Special Education, Theatre Arts, Watershed Science.
**Requirements:** General education requirement.
**Academic regulations:** Minimum 2.2 GPA required for graduation.
**Special:** Minors offered. Noncredit courses offered in clothing, English, finance, food, marriage, and mathematics. Vocational educational programs in agriculture, secretarial, and welding. Nondegree programs, area studies, and women's studies. Associate's degrees offered. Self-designed majors. Double majors. Dual degrees. Independent study. Pass/fail grading option. Internships. Cooperative education programs. Graduate school at which undergraduates may take graduate-level courses. Preprofessional programs in law, medicine, veterinary science, and dentistry. Member of Energy Impact Consortium. Member of Western Undergraduate Exchange. Teacher certification in early childhood, elementary, secondary, and special education. Certification in specific subject areas. Member of International Student Exchange Program (ISEP). Study abroad also in France, Germany, Korea, Mexico, and the former Soviet Republics. ROTC and AFROTC.
**Honors:** Honors program. Honor societies.
**Academic Assistance:** Remedial reading, writing, math, and study skills. Nonremedial tutoring.

**STUDENT LIFE. Housing:** Students may live on or off campus. Women's and men's dorms. School-owned/operated apartments. On-campus married-student housing.
**Services and counseling/handicapped student services:** Placement services. Health service. Women's center. Day care. Counseling services for minority, military, veteran, and older students. Birth control and personal counseling. Career and academic guidance services. Physically disabled student services. Learning disabled services. Notetaking services.
**Campus organizations:** Undergraduate student government. Student newspaper (Statesman, published three times/week). Literary magazine. Radio and TV stations. Band, orchestra, choral groups, music clubs, concert series, Old Lyric Repertory Company, U.S. Children's Theatre, USU Gamers, ballroom dance club, martial arts groups, Art Guild, Amnesty International, College Republicans, Gay and Lesbian Alliance, Circle K, Partners Program, Society for Creative Anachronism, academic and professional groups, 120 organizations in all. Eight fraternities, six chapter houses; three sororities, all with chapter houses. 5% of men join a fraternity. 5% of women join a sorority.
**Religious organizations:** Baptist Campus Ministries, Christian Fellowship, Lambda Delta Sigma, Latter-Day Saints Association, Lutheran Student Association, Newman Club, Sigma Gamma Chi.
**Minority/foreign student organizations:** Black Collegiate Association, Hispanic Student Union. International Council, United Southeast Asia Association.

**ATHLETICS. Physical education requirements:** None.
**Intercollegiate competition:** 7% of students participate. Basketball (M), cross-country (M,W), football (M), golf (M), gymnastics (W), softball (W), tennis (M,W), track (indoor) (M,W), track (outdoor) (M,W), track and field (indoor) (M,W), track and field (outdoor) (M,W), volleyball (W). Member of Big West Conference, NCAA Division I, NCAA Division I-A for football, NCSA.
**Intramural and club sports:** 20% of students participate. Intramural baseball, flag football, rifle, rodeo, rugby, skiing, soccer, softball, swimming, tennis. Men's club Alpine skiing, baseball, bowling, cheerleading, cycling, rifle, rodeo, rugby, soccer, softball, tennis. Women's club Alpine skiing, bowling, cheerleading, cycling, rifle, rodeo, soccer, tennis.

**ADMISSIONS. Academic basis for candidate selection** (in order of priority): Secondary school record, standardized test scores, class rank, school's recommendation.
**Requirements:** Graduation from secondary school is required; GED is accepted. 18 units and the following program of study are required: 4 units of English, 2.5 units of math, 2 units of science including 1 unit of lab, 3 units of social studies. Minimum composite ACT score of 20 and minimum 2.6 GPA required. General registration policy for applicants not meeting standard requirements. SAT or ACT is required. Campus visit recommended. Off-campus interviews available with an admissions representative.
**Procedure:** Take SAT or ACT by fall of 12th year. Application deadline is July 1. Notification of admission on rolling basis. No set date by which applicants must accept offer. $125 room deposit, refundable until July 1. Freshmen accepted for terms other than fall.
**Special programs:** Admission may be deferred one year. Credit and/or placement may be granted through CEEB Advanced Placement exams for scores of 3 or higher. Credit and/or placement may be granted through CLEP general exams. Placement may be granted through challenge exams and life experience. Credit and placement may be granted through DANTES exams and military experience. Early decision program. Deadline for applying for early decision is July 1. Early entrance/early admission program. Concurrent enrollment program.
**Transfer students:** Transfer students accepted for terms other than fall. In fall 1993, 38% of all new students were transfers into all classes. 2,308 transfer applications were received, 1,923 were accepted. Application deadline is 90 days before beginning of term for fall; 60 days before beginning of term for spring. Minimum 2.2 GPA required. Lowest course grade accepted is "C." Maximum number of transferable credits is 120 quarter hours. At least 60 quarter hours must be completed at the university to receive degree.
**Admissions contact:** J. Rodney Clark, M.S., Director of Admissions. 801 750-1096.

**FINANCIAL AID. Available aid:** Pell grants, SEOG, state scholarships and grants, school scholarships, private scholarships and grants, ROTC scholarships, academic merit scholarships, and athletic scholarships. Perkins Loans (NDSL), PLUS, Stafford Loans (GSL), school loans, and SLS. Deferred payment plan.
**Supporting data/closing dates:** FAFSA/FAF/FFS: Priority filing date is March 15; accepted on rolling basis. School's own aid application: Priority filing date is March 15. Income tax forms: Priority filing date is March 15; accepted on rolling basis. Notification of awards begins in May.
**Financial aid contact:** Vicki Atkinson, M.S., Director of Financial Aid. 801 750-1023.

**STUDENT EMPLOYMENT.** College Work/Study Program. Institutional employment. 20% of full-time undergraduates work on campus during school year. Students may expect to earn an average of $3,000 during school year. Off-campus part-time employment opportunities rated "good."

**COMPUTER FACILITIES.** 890 IBM/IBM-compatible and Macintosh/Apple microcomputers. Students may access Digital, IBM minicomputer/mainframe systems, BITNET, Internet. Residence halls may be equipped with stand-alone microcomputers, networked microcomputers. Client/LAN operating systems include Apple/Macintosh. Computer languages and software packages include BASIC, C, Pascal. Computer facilities are available to all students.
**Fees:** $2 computer fee per quarter hour; included in tuition/fees.
**Hours:** Some available 24 hours.

# Weber State University

**Ogden, UT 84408** **801 626-6000**

**1994-95 Costs.** Tuition: $1,836 (state residents), $5,607 (out-of-state). Room & board: $5,570. Fees, books, misc. academic expenses (school's estimate): $1,082.
**Enrollment.** Undergraduates: 4,251 men, 4,563 women (full-time). Freshman class: 6,913 applicants, 6,738 accepted, 2,099 enrolled. Graduate enrollment: 77 men, 79 women.
**Test score averages/ranges.** Average ACT scores: 19 English, 19 math, 19 composite.
**Faculty.** 444 full-time; 13 part-time. 61% of faculty holds doctoral degree. Student/faculty ratio: 21 to 1.
**Selectivity rating.** Noncompetitive.

**PROFILE.** Weber State is a public, comprehensive university. Founded in 1889, it gained university status in 1991. Programs are offered through the Schools of Allied Health Sciences, Business and Economics, Education, Humanities, Natural Sciences, Social Sciences, and Technology. Its 375-acre campus is located in Ogden, 35 miles from Salt Lake City.

**Accreditation:** NASC. Professionally accredited by the American Assembly of Collegiate Schools of Business, the American Dental Association, the American Medical Association (CAHEA), the Council on Social Work Education, the National Council for Accreditation of Teacher Education, the National League for Nursing.
**Religious orientation:** Weber State University is nonsectarian; no religious requirements.
**Library:** Collections totaling over 344,918 volumes, 2,778 periodical subscriptions, and 1,483,822 microform items.
**Special facilities/museums:** Language lab, TV studio, computer-assisted writing lab, natural science museum, herbarium, planetarium.

**Athletic facilities:** Gymnasium, stadium, swimming pool, tennis courts, weight room, softball field, tracks, bowling center.

**STUDENT BODY. Undergraduate profile:** 93% are state residents. 2% Asian-American, 1% Black, 2% Hispanic, 1% Native American, 92% White, 2% Other. Average age of undergraduates is 26.
**Freshman profile:** 4% of accepted applicants took SAT; 86% took ACT.
**Undergraduate achievement:** 52% of fall 1991 freshmen returned for fall 1992 term. 26% of students who completed a degree program went on to graduate study within five years.
**Foreign students:** 286 students are from out of the country. Countries represented include Canada, China, Japan, Saudi Arabia, Taiwan, and Thailand; 27 in all.

**PROGRAMS OF STUDY. Degrees:** B.A., B.F.A., B.Integ.Studies, B.S.
**Majors:** Accounting, Administrative Systems, Art, Automotive Technology, Botany, Business Administration, Chemistry, Child Development, Clinical Laboratory Sciences, Communication, Computer Information Systems, Computer Science, Criminal Justice, Early Childhood Education, Economics, Electronic Engineering Technology, Elementary Education, English, Family Studies, Foreign Languages, Geography, Geology, Gerontology, Health Administrative Services, History, Lifestyle Management, Logistics, Manufacturing Engineering Technology, Mathematics, Mechanical Engineering Technology, Microbiology, Music, Nursing, Physical Education Teaching, Physics, Political Science, Psychology, Social Work, Sociology, Technical Sales, Telecommunications Administration, Theatre Arts, Visual Arts, Zoology.
**Distribution of degrees:** The majors with the highest enrollment are education, electronic engineering technology, and accounting.
**Requirements:** General education requirement.
**Academic regulations:** Freshmen must maintain minimum 2.0 GPA; sophomores, 2.0 GPA; juniors, 2.5 GPA; seniors, 2.5 GPA.
**Special:** Minors offered in most majors and in aerospace studies, anthropology, Asian studies, athletic coaching, business education, community/occupational health education, dance, fashion merchandising, health education, interior design, Latin American studies, legal studies, military science, naval science, philosophy, photography, recreation education, and special education. Associate's degrees offered. Self-designed majors. Double majors. Independent study. Pass/fail grading option. Internships. Graduate school at which undergraduates may take graduate-level courses. Preprofessional programs in law, medicine, veterinary science, pharmacy, dentistry, agriculture, engineering, forestry, range management, and wildlife management. Teacher certification in early childhood, elementary, secondary, and special education. Study abroad in England, Germany, Mexico, and Spain. ROTC. NROTC and AFROTC at U of Utah.
**Honors:** Phi Beta Kappa. Honors program.
**Academic Assistance:** Remedial reading, writing, math, and study skills. Nonremedial tutoring.

**STUDENT LIFE. Housing:** Students may live on or off campus. Coed, women's, and men's dorms. 4% of students live in college housing.
**Social atmosphere:** As reported by the student newspaper, "WSU has a very strong cultural center with the Utah Symphony and Ballet West performing often. The social life is relaxed, but seems somewhat in tune with the Mormon culture. No 'heavy' partying. Fun activities, for example, dances and concerts, are well attended." Popular campus activities include basketball games, theatre productions, Homecoming, Sunfest (a week during spring quarter full of activities), pops concerts, and the Dessert Series (featuring jazz groups, comedians, etc.). Influential student groups include various Greek organizations and the LDSSA (Mormon) student group.
**Services and counseling/handicapped student services:** Placement services. Health service. Women's center. Day care available off campus. Counseling services for minority, military, veteran, and older students. Birth control, personal, and psychological counseling. Career and academic guidance services. Religious counseling. Physically disabled student services. Notetaking services. Tape recorders. Tutors. Reader services for the blind.
**Campus organizations:** Undergraduate student government. Student newspaper (Sign Post, published once/week). Literary magazine. Radio station. Chantonelles, drama groups, Office of Cultural Affairs, political, service, and special-interest groups, 80 organizations in all. Four fraternities, no chapter houses; three sororities, no chapter houses. 1% of men join a fraternity. 1% of women join a sorority.
**Religious organizations:** Baptist Student Union, Christian Crusade for Christ, Latter-Day Saint Student Association, Methodist group, Newman Center.
**Minority/foreign student organizations:** Black Scholars United, Hispanic Student Union, Native American Council. International Club.

**ATHLETICS. Physical education requirements:** Three credit hours of physical education required.
**Intercollegiate competition:** 4% of students participate. Basketball (M,W), cheerleading (M,W), cross-country (M,W), football (M), golf (M,W), tennis (M,W), track (indoor) (M,W), track (outdoor) (M,W), track and field (indoor) (M,W), track and field (outdoor) (M,W), volleyball (W). Member of Big Sky Athletic Conference, NCAA Division I, NCAA Division I-AA for football, NCSA.
**Intramural and club sports:** Intramural badminton, basketball, billiards, body building, bowling, cross-country, football, golf, Nordic skiing, pickleball, power lifting, racquetball, soccer, softball, swimming, table tennis, tennis, triathlon, volleyball, walleyball, water polo, wrist wrestling. Men's club soccer. Women's club soccer.

**ADMISSIONS. Academic basis for candidate selection** (in order of priority): Secondary school record, standardized test scores.
**Requirements:** Graduation from secondary school is required; GED is accepted. No specific distribution of secondary school units required. Interview required of dental hygiene, nursing, and all health profession program applicants. ACT is required; SAT may be substituted. Campus visit recommended. No off-campus interviews.
**Procedure:** Take ACT or SAT by February of 12th year. Suggest filing application by February 1. Application deadline is July 1. Notification of admission on rolling basis. $90 refundable room deposit. Freshmen accepted for terms other than fall.
**Special programs:** Admission may be deferred. Credit may be granted through CEEB Advanced Placement for scores of 3 or higher. Credit may be granted through CLEP general and subject exams, and military experience. Placement may be granted through challenge exams. Early decision program. Early entrance/early admission program. Concurrent enrollment program.
**Transfer students:** Transfer students accepted for terms other than fall. Application deadline is July 1 for fall; 30 days prior to beginning of term for spring. Minimum 2.25 GPA required. Lowest course grade accepted is "C." At least 45 quarter hours must be completed at the university to receive degree.
**Admissions contact:** L. Winslow Hurst, Ph.D., Director of Admissions. 801 626-6743.

**FINANCIAL AID. Available aid:** Pell grants, SEOG, Federal Nursing Student Scholarships, state scholarships and grants, school scholarships, private scholarships and grants, ROTC scholarships, academic merit scholarships, and athletic scholarships. Perkins Loans (NDSL), PLUS, Stafford Loans (GSL), NSL, school loans, and SLS.
**Financial aid statistics:** Average amounts of aid awarded freshmen: Scholarships and grants, $738; loans, $290.
**Supporting data/closing dates:** FAFSA/FAF/FFS: Priority filing date is April 1; accepted on rolling basis. Notification of awards on rolling basis.
**Financial aid contact:** Richard Effiong, M.B.A., Director of Financial Aid. 801 626-6581.

**STUDENT EMPLOYMENT.** College Work/Study Program. Institutional employment. Off-campus part-time employment opportunities rated "good."

**COMPUTER FACILITIES.** 473 IBM/IBM-compatible and Macintosh/Apple microcomputers. Students may access Digital minicomputer/mainframe systems. Computer languages and software packages include APL, Assembly, BASIC, C, COBOL, FORTRAN, LISP, Pascal, PL/I. Computer facilities are available to all students.
**Fees:** $4 computer fee per quarter; included in tuition/fees.

**GRADUATE CAREER DATA.** Graduate school percentages: 4% enter law school. 4% enter medical school. 4% enter graduate business programs. Highest graduate school enrollments: Brigham Young U, U of Utah, Utah State U. 13% of graduates choose careers in business and industry.

**PROMINENT ALUMNI/AE.** Jay Williard Marriott, founder, Marriott Hotels and Restaurants; Noland D. Archibald, president, Black and Decker; Mark Evans Austad, former ambassador to Denmark and Norway.

# Westminster College of Salt Lake City

**Salt Lake City, UT 84105** 801 484-7651

**1994-95 Costs.** Tuition: $8,820. Room & board: $4,050. Fees, books, misc. academic expenses (school's estimate): $660.
**Enrollment.** Undergraduates: 335 men, 671 women (full-time). Freshman class: 917 applicants, 720 accepted, 213 enrolled. Graduate enrollment: 201 men, 193 women.
**Test score averages/ranges.** Average SAT scores: 466 verbal, 486 math. Average ACT scores: 23 composite.
**Faculty.** 92 full-time; 113 part-time. 83% of faculty holds highest degree in specific field. Student/faculty ratio: 17 to 1.
**Selectivity rating.** Less competitive.

**PROFILE.** Westminster College, founded in 1875, is a private institution. Programs are offered in the Schools of Arts and Sciences, Business, and Nursing and Health Science. Its 27-acre campus is located two miles from downtown Salt Lake City.

**Accreditation:** NASC. Professionally accredited by the National League for Nursing.
**Religious orientation:** Westminster College of Salt Lake City is nonsectarian; no religious requirements.
**Library:** Collections totaling over 74,500 volumes, 350 periodical subscriptions, and 3,500 microform items.

**STUDENT BODY. Undergraduate profile:** 94% are state residents; 44% are transfers. 2% Asian-American, 1% Black, 4% Hispanic, 1% Native American, 92% White. Average age of undergraduates is 29.
**Freshman profile:** Majority of accepted applicants took ACT.
**Undergraduate achievement:** 66% of fall 1991 freshmen returned for fall 1992 term. 27% of entering class graduated.
**Foreign students:** 13 students are from out of the country. Countries represented include China, Indonesia, Iran, Japan, Taiwan, and Thailand.

**PROGRAMS OF STUDY. Degrees:** B.A., B.S.
**Majors:** Accounting, Art, Aviation, Biology, Business, Chemistry, Communication, Computer Science, Economics, Education, English, Finance, History, Human/Organizational Development, International Business, Management, Marketing, Mathematics, Nursing, Philosophy, Physics, Pre-Dental, Pre-Law, Pre-Medicine, Psychology, Social Sciences, Sociology.
**Distribution of degrees:** The majors with the highest enrollment are accounting, psychology, and nursing; history, physics, and philosophy have the lowest.
**Requirements:** General education requirement.
**Academic regulations:** Minimum 2.0 GPA must be maintained.
**Special:** Self-designed majors. Double majors. Dual degrees. Independent study. Pass/fail grading option. Internships. Preprofessional programs in law, medicine, and dentistry. Teacher certification in early childhood, elementary, secondary, and bilingual/bicultural education. Certification in specific subject areas. ROTC, NROTC, and AFROTC at U of Utah.
**Honors:** Honors program.
**Academic Assistance:** Remedial reading, writing, math, and study skills. Nonremedial tutoring.

**ADMISSIONS. Academic basis for candidate selection** (in order of priority): Secondary school record, standardized test scores, class rank, school's recommendation, essay.
**Nonacademic basis for candidate selection:** Particular talent or ability is important. Character and personality and alumni/ae relationship are considered.

**Requirements:** Graduation from secondary school is required; GED is accepted. No specific distribution of secondary school units required. SAT or ACT is required. Campus visit and interview recommended. Off-campus interviews available with an admissions representative.

**Procedure:** Take SAT or ACT by December of 12th year. Notification of admission on rolling basis. $100 refundable tuition deposit. $50 refundable room deposit. Freshmen accepted for terms other than fall.

**Special programs:** Admission may be deferred one year. Credit may be granted through CEEB Advanced Placement for scores of 3 or higher. Credit may be granted through CLEP general and subject exams, and military and life experience. Placement may be granted through ACT PEP exams. Credit and placement may be granted through DANTES exams. Early entrance/early admission program. Concurrent enrollment program.

**Transfer students:** Transfer students accepted for terms other than fall. In fall 1993, 44% of all new students were transfers into all classes. 621 transfer applications were received, 492 were accepted. Both secondary school and college transcripts required for transfer applicants with fewer than 60 semester hours. Minimum 2.0 GPA recommended. Lowest course grade accepted is "C-." Maximum number of transferable credits is 94 semester hours. At least 30 semester hours must be completed at the college to receive degree.

**Admissions contact:** Craig Green, Vice President for Enrollment Management. 801 488-4200, 800 748-4753.

**FINANCIAL AID. Available aid:** Pell grants, SEOG, state scholarships and grants, school scholarships and grants, private scholarships and grants, ROTC scholarships, academic merit scholarships, and athletic scholarships. Perkins Loans (NDSL), PLUS, Stafford Loans (GSL), school loans, and SLS. Deferred payment plan. Installment payment plans.

**Financial aid statistics:** 31% of aid is not need-based. In 1993-94, 72% of all undergraduate applicants received aid; 56% of freshman applicants. Average amounts of aid awarded freshmen: Loans, $2,500.

**Supporting data/closing dates:** FAFSA/FAF/FFS: Accepted on rolling basis. Income tax forms: Accepted on rolling basis. Notification of awards on rolling basis.

**Financial aid contact:** Ruth Henneman, Director of Financial Aid. 801 488-4104.

# Vermont

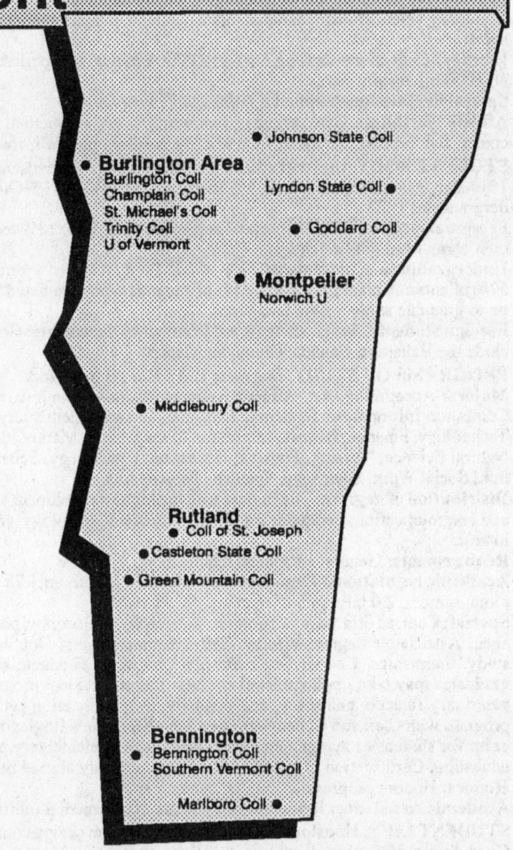


## Bennington College

**Bennington, VT 05201** **802 442-5401**

**1994-95 Costs.** Comprehensive fee for tuition, room, and board: $25,800 per year.
**Enrollment.** Undergraduates: 184 men, 275 women (full-time). Freshman class: 589 applicants, 365 accepted, 141 enrolled. Graduate enrollment: 34 men, 33 women.
**Test score averages/ranges.** Average SAT scores: 565 verbal, 551 math. Range of SAT scores of middle 50%: 520-620 verbal, 500-600 math. Average ACT scores: 25 composite. Range of ACT scores of middle 50%: 22-22 English, 29-29 math.
**Faculty.** 57 full-time; 21 part-time. 59% of faculty holds highest degree in specific field. Student/faculty ratio: 7 to 1.
**Selectivity rating.** More competitive.

**PROFILE.** Bennington, founded in 1932, is a private, liberal arts college. Its 550-acre campus is located on a former farm in the Green Mountains and includes original farm buildings converted to classrooms and studios.

**Accreditation:** NEASC.
**Religious orientation:** Bennington College is nonsectarian; no religious requirements.
**Library:** Collections totaling over 114,689 volumes, 580 periodical subscriptions, and 6,075 microform items.
**Special facilities/museums:** Visual and performing arts center, early childhood center.
**Athletic facilities:** Tennis courts, soccer field, outdoor basketball and volleyball courts, weight room.

**STUDENT BODY. Undergraduate profile:** 4% are state residents. 9% Asian-American, 7% Black, 2% Hispanic, 80% White, 2% Other.
**Freshman profile:** 95% of accepted applicants took SAT; 1% took ACT.
**Undergraduate achievement:** 85% of fall 1992 freshmen returned for fall 1993 term. 62% of entering class graduated. 60% of students who completed a degree program went on to graduate study within five years.
**Foreign students:** 37 students are from out of the country. Countries represented include China, England, France, Ghana, Sweden, and Switzerland; 19 in all.

**PROGRAMS OF STUDY. Degrees:** B.A.
**Majors:** Acoustics, Acting, Anthropology, Architecture, Art History, Audio/Visual, Biological Sciences/Pre-Med, Black Music, Ceramics, Chamber Music, Choreography, Composition, Design, Directing, Drawing, Early Childhood Development, Economics, Electronic Instrument Building, Ensembles, Environmental Sciences, Foreign Languages/Multiple Emphasis, Graphics, History, Improvisation, Instruments, Literature, Mathematics/Computers, Music History/Aesthetics, Painting, Performance, Philosophy, Photography, Physical Sciences, Political Science, Pre-Law, Psychology, Sculpture, Writing.
**Distribution of degrees:** The majors with the highest enrollment are literature and languages, interdivisional majors, and visual arts; dance, music, and natural sciences have the lowest.
**Requirements:** General education requirement.
**Special:** Students design own programs within college's educational guidelines and are required to develop a plan that includes work in four of the seven divisions during first two years; one year's work beyond the introductory level in two divisions must be completed by graduation; all work is evaluated by student's department. Self-designed majors. Double majors. Independent study. Pass/fail grading option. Internships. Preprofessional programs in law, medicine, and veterinary science. Postbaccalaureate premedical and allied health sciences program for students seeking preparatory work for health-related graduate school. M.F.A. offered in dance, writing, music, and visual arts. Combined B.A./M.S. in early childhood development and elementary education with Bank Street Coll of Education (New York). Member of Consortium of Vermont Colleges. Off-campus study opportunities available at the Sch for Field Studies (science), the British American Drama Academy in London (theatre design) and Jacob's Pillow in the Berkshires (dance). Teacher certification in early childhood education. Study abroad in Amesterdam, England, France, Germany, and other countries.
**Academic Assistance:** Remedial reading and writing. Nonremedial tutoring.

**STUDENT LIFE. Housing:** All unmarried students under age 21 must live on campus unless living near campus with relatives. Coed dorms. School-owned/operated apartments. Off-campus privately-owned housing. 100% of students live in college housing.
**Social atmosphere:** Popular gathering spots on and off campus include the Cafe, the Pig, the Brasserie, Blue Ben Diner, Yoshi's, the Commons, Man of Kent, and Up for Breakfast. Among the highlights of the schoolyear are music and dance concerts, student drama productions, Sunfest, the "Dress to Get Laid" Party (voted #1 college party of the year), the "Sucking in the '70s" party, the "'80s" party, visiting lecturers, Transvestite Night, the Senior Ball, and Personal Services Auction. "Every type of person imaginable attends Bennington. We all get along," reports the editor of the student newspaper. "It's a place where everyone and everything is accepted."
**Services and counseling/handicapped student services:** Placement services. Health service. Day care. Birth control, personal, and psychological counseling. Career and academic guidance services.
**Campus organizations:** Undergraduate student government. Student newspaper (Bennington Voice, five times/term). Literary magazine. "College Week" campus calendar, chamber music and choral groups, orchestra, drama and dance productions, student-managed cafe, Student Educational Policies Committee, tutoring program, women's issues study group.

**ATHLETICS. Physical education requirements:** None.
**Intramural and club sports:** Intramural basketball, cycling, judo, soccer, softball, tennis, volleyball. Men's club soccer, volleyball. Women's club soccer, volleyball.

**ADMISSIONS. Academic basis for candidate selection** (in order of priority): Essay, secondary school record, school's recommendation, class rank, standardized test scores.
**Nonacademic basis for candidate selection:** Character and personality and particular talent or ability are emphasized. Extracurricular participation is important.
**Requirements:** Graduation from secondary school is required; GED is accepted. 21 units and the following program of study are recommended: 4 units of English, 4 units of math, 3 units of science, 4 units of foreign language, 3 units of social studies, 3 units of history. SAT or ACT is required. Campus visit recommended. Off-campus interviews available with admissions and alumni representatives.
**Procedure:** Take SAT or ACT by December of 12th year. Visit college for interview by December of 12th year. Application deadline is January 1. Acceptance notification by end of March. Reply is required by May 1. $250 nonrefundable tuition deposit. Freshmen accepted for terms other than fall.
**Special programs:** Admission may be deferred one year. Placement may be granted through CEEB Advanced Placement exams. Early decision program. In fall 1993, 18 applied for early decision and 12 were accepted. Deadline for applying for early decision is November 15. Early entrance/early admission program.
**Transfer students:** Transfer students accepted for terms other than fall. In fall 1993, 71 transfer applications were received, 54 were accepted. Application deadline is April 1 for fall; January 1 for spring. Lowest course grade accepted is "C." At least two years must be completed at the college to receive degree.
**Admissions contact:** Karen Kristof, Director of Admissions. 800 833-6845.

**FINANCIAL AID. Available aid:** Pell grants, SEOG, state scholarships and grants, school scholarships and grants, private scholarships and grants, academic merit scholarships, and aid for undergraduate foreign students. PLUS, Stafford Loans (GSL), school loans, and SLS. AMS, Tuition Management Systems, and deferred payment plan. College's own monthly payment plan.
**Financial aid statistics:** In 1993-94, 100% of all undergraduate applicants received aid; 100% of freshman applicants. Average amounts of aid awarded freshmen: Scholarships and grants, $14,000; loans, $2,350.
**Supporting data/closing dates:** FAFSA/FAF: Priority filing date is February 1; deadline is March 1. School's own aid application: Priority filing date is February 1; deadline is March 1. Income tax forms: Priority filing date is February 1. Notification of awards begins in mid-March.
**Financial aid contact:** Meg Woolmington, Director of Financial Aid. 802 442-5401, extension 315.

**STUDENT EMPLOYMENT.** College Work/Study Program. Institutional employment. 65% of full-time undergraduates work on campus during school year. Students may expect to earn an average of $925 during school year. Off-campus part-time employment opportunities rated "fair."

**COMPUTER FACILITIES.** 18 IBM/IBM-compatible and Macintosh/Apple microcomputers. Computer languages and software packages include BASIC, C, FORTH, FORTRAN, LOGO, Pascal, Turbo Pascal. Computer facilities are available to all students.
**Fees:** None.
**Hours:** 24 hours.

**PROMINENT ALUMNI/AE.** Andrea Dworkin, essayist; Helen Frankenthaler, painter; Alan Arkin, actor.

# Burlington College

**Burlington, VT 05401** **802 862-9616**

**1993-94 Costs.** Tuition: $7,500. Housing: None. Fees, books, misc. academic expenses (school's estimate): $945.
**Enrollment.** Undergraduates: 31 men, 38 women (full-time). Freshman class: 45 applicants, 39 accepted, 37 enrolled.
**Test score averages/ranges.** N/A.
**Faculty.** 66 part-time. 12% of faculty holds doctoral degree. Student/faculty ratio: 4 to 1.
**Selectivity rating.** N/A.

**PROFILE.** Burlington, founded in 1972, is a private college offering programs based on individualized study. The college is located in a renovated, turn-of-the-century building in the city of Burlington.
**Accreditation:** NEASC.
**Religious orientation:** Burlington College is nonsectarian; no religious requirements.
**Library:** Collections totaling over 50,000 volumes, 375 periodical subscriptions, and 43,000 microform items.
**STUDENT BODY. Undergraduate profile:** 85% are state residents; 35% are transfers. 1% Asian-American, 5% Black, 3% Hispanic, 2% Native American, 89% White. Average age of undergraduates is 31.
**Freshman profile:** 85% of freshmen come from public schools.
**Undergraduate achievement:** 59% of fall 1992 freshmen returned for fall 1993 term. 37% of students who completed a degree program went on to graduate study within two years.
**PROGRAMS OF STUDY. Degrees:** B.A.
**Majors:** Feminist Studies, Fine Arts, Human Services, Humanities, Psychology, Student-Designed Major, Transpersonal Psychology.
**Requirements:** General education requirement. Students must achieve at least a 75% ratio of courses attempted/completed to remain in good academic standing.
**Special:** Minors offered in all majors. Degree options in Individualized Majors (course-oriented) and Contract-Based Learning (independent study). Associate's degrees offered. Self-designed majors. Double majors. Independent study. Pass/fail grading option. Internships. Graduate school at which undergraduates may take graduate-level courses. Member of Consortium of Vermont Colleges.
**Academic Assistance:** Remedial reading, writing, math, and study skills. Nonremedial tutoring.
**ADMISSIONS. Academic basis for candidate selection** (in order of priority): Secondary school record.
**Nonacademic basis for candidate selection:** Character and personality are emphasized. Particular talent or ability is considered.
**Requirements:** Graduation from secondary school is recommended; GED is accepted. No specific distribution of secondary school units required. Open admissions policy. Minimum 60 college credits required for Independent Degree Program (IDP). Campus visit recommended. Off-campus interviews available with an admissions representative.
**Procedure:** Suggest filing application by July 1. Application deadline is August 20. Notification of admission on rolling basis. Applicant must accept offer prior to start of semester. Freshmen accepted for terms other than fall.
**Special programs:** Admission may be deferred one year. Placement may be granted through CEEB Advanced Placement exams. Credit and/or placement may be granted through CLEP general and subject exams. Placement may be granted through challenge exams. Credit and placement may be granted through Regents College, ACT PEP, and DANTES exams and military and life experience.
**Transfer students:** Transfer students accepted for terms other than fall. In fall 1993, 35% of all new students were transfers into all classes. 56 transfer applications were received, 48 were accepted. Application deadline is August 20 for fall; January 10 for spring. Lowest course grade accepted is "C-." Maximum number of transferable credits is 90 semester hours. At least 30 semester hours must be completed at the college to receive degree.
**Admissions contact:** Nancy Wilson, Director of Admissions. 802 862-9616.
**FINANCIAL AID. Available aid:** Pell grants, SEOG, state grants, school scholarships and grants, private scholarships and grants, and academic merit scholarships. Perkins Loans (NDSL), PLUS, Stafford Loans (GSL), school loans, and SLS. Deferred payment plan.
**Financial aid statistics:** Average amounts of aid awarded freshmen: Scholarships and grants, $500; loans, $2,622.
**Supporting data/closing dates:** FAFSA/FAF/FFS: Accepted on rolling basis. School's own aid application: Accepted on rolling basis. State aid form: Accepted on rolling basis. Income tax forms: Accepted on rolling basis. Notification of awards on rolling basis.
**Financial aid contact:** Marcia Vance, M.A., Director of Financial Aid. 802 862-9616.

# Castleton State College

**Castleton, VT 05735** **802 468-5611**

**1993-94 Costs.** Tuition: $3,168 (state residents), $7,328 (out-of-state). Room & board: $4,640. Fees, books, misc. academic expenses (school's estimate): $988.
**Enrollment.** Undergraduates: 758 men, 808 women (full-time). Freshman class: 1,254 applicants, 940 accepted, 382 enrolled. Graduate enrollment: 66 men, 154 women.
**Test score averages/ranges.** Average SAT scores: 416 verbal, 459 math. Average ACT scores: 21 composite.
**Faculty.** 88 full-time; 77 part-time. 82% of faculty holds highest degree in specific field. Student/faculty ratio: 15 to 1.
**Selectivity rating.** Less competitive.

**PROFILE.** Castleton State, founded in 1787, is a public college. Its 130-acre campus is located in the small town of Castleton, 12 miles west of Rutland.
**Accreditation:** NEASC. Professionally accredited by the Council on Social Work Education, the National League for Nursing.
**Religious orientation:** Castleton State College is nonsectarian; no religious requirements.
**Library:** Collections totaling over 110,000 volumes, 657 periodical subscriptions, and 400,000 microform items.
**Special facilities/museums:** Language lab, observatory.
**Athletic facilities:** Gymnasiums, swimming pool, racquetball, handball, and tennis courts, flag football, lacrosse, field hockey, softball, baseball, soccer, and rugby fields.
**STUDENT BODY. Undergraduate profile:** 63% are state residents; 31% are transfers. 1% Asian-American, 1% Black, 1% Hispanic, 96% White, 1% Other. Average age of undergraduates is 22.
**Freshman profile:** 87% of accepted applicants took SAT; 13% took ACT. 80% of freshmen come from public schools.
**Undergraduate achievement:** 71% of fall 1992 freshmen returned for fall 1993 term. 57% of entering class graduated. 25% of students who completed a degree program went on to graduate study within five years.
**Foreign students:** Seven students are from out of the country. Countries represented include the Bahamas, Canada, China, and Japan.
**PROGRAMS OF STUDY. Degrees:** B.A., B.S., B.Soc.Work.
**Majors:** Accounting, Art, Athletic Trainer, Business Administration, Communication, Computer Information Systems, Criminal Justice, Elementary Education, Exercise Technology, Finance, History, Literature, Management, Marketing, Mathematics, Music, Natural Science, Nursing, Physical Education, Psychology, Science, Secondary Education, Social Work, Sociology, Spanish, Theatre Arts.
**Distribution of degrees:** The majors with the highest enrollment are business, education, and communication; computer information systems, sociology, and theatre arts have the lowest.
**Requirements:** General education requirement.
**Academic regulations:** Freshmen must maintain minimum 1.75 GPA; sophomores, juniors, seniors, 2.0 GPA.
**Special:** Courses offered in economics, geography, philosophy, physics, and political science. Associate's degrees offered. Self-designed majors. Double majors. Independent study. Internships. Cooperative education programs. Graduate school at which undergraduates may take graduate-level courses. Preprofessional programs in law, medicine, veterinary science, pharmacy, and dentistry. 3-2 engineering program and 4-1 M.B.A. program with Clarkson U. Sea Semester. Member of New England Regional Student Program for student exchange. Teacher certification in elementary, secondary, and special education. Certification in specific subject areas. Study abroad in 17 countries.
**Honors:** Honors program.
**Academic Assistance:** Remedial study skills. Nonremedial tutoring.
**STUDENT LIFE. Housing:** All students must live on campus unless living with family. Coed dorms. 55% of students live in college housing.
**Social atmosphere:** Influential groups on campus include athletic organizations and the Social Committee. Among the highlights of the school year are the Ray Boston Beach Party, Semi-Formal Dance, all basketball games, and the Air Band Competition. Students hang out at the Campus Center, the Dog, the Library, and the Snack Bar.
**Services and counseling/handicapped student services:** Placement services. Health service. Counseling services for older students. Birth control, personal, and psychological counseling. Career and academic guidance services. Physically disabled student services. Learning disabled services. Notetaking services. Reader services for the blind.
**Campus organizations:** Undergraduate student government. Student newspaper (Spartan, published twice/week). Literary magazine. Yearbook. Radio station. Chorus, wind ensembles, dance group, Castleton Players, community forum, folk club, concert and lecture program, departmental, service, and special-interest groups, 51 organizations in all.
**Religious organizations:** Acts IV (Christian Fellowship).
**Minority/foreign student organizations:** African American Students. International Club.
**ATHLETICS. Physical education requirements:** None.
**Intercollegiate competition:** 4% of students participate. Baseball (M), basketball (M,W), cross-country (M,W), lacrosse (M,W), soccer (M,W), softball (W), tennis (M,W). Member of ECAC, Laurie D. Cox League, Mayflower Conference, NAIA, NCAA Division III.
**Intramural and club sports:** 40% of students participate. Intramural badminton, basketball, cross-country running, flag football, floor hockey, foul shooting, handball, racquetball, rugby, soccer, superstars, swimming, table tennis, ultimate frisbee, volleyball. Men's club biathlon, cheerleading, cycling, freestyle skiing, rugby, Nordic skiing, swimming, volleyball. Women's club biathlon, cheerleading, cycling, freestyle skiing, Nordic skiing, swimming, volleyball.
**ADMISSIONS. Academic basis for candidate selection** (in order of priority): Secondary school record, school's recommendation, class rank, essay, standardized test scores.
**Nonacademic basis for candidate selection:** Character and personality are emphasized. Extracurricular participation is important. Particular talent or ability, geographical distribution, and alumni/ae relationship are considered.
**Requirements:** Graduation from secondary school is recommended; GED is accepted. 16 units and the following program of study are recommended: 4 units of English, 3 units of math, 2 units of science, 2 units of foreign language, 3 units of social studies, 2 units of electives. Minimum combined SAT score of 900, rank in top half of secondary school class, and minimum 2.7 GPA required. STEP program for first-generation college applicants not normally admissible. SAT is required; ACT may be substituted. Campus visit and interview recommended. No off-campus interviews.
**Procedure:** Take SAT or ACT by December of 12th year. Visit college for interview by March 15 of 12th year. Notification of admission on rolling basis. Reply is required by May 1 if notified before May; within 10 days if notified after May 1. $300 nonrefundable tuition deposit. Freshmen accepted for terms other than fall.
**Special programs:** Admission may be deferred one year. Credit may be granted through CEEB Advanced Placement for scores of 3 or higher. Credit may be granted through CLEP general and subject exams. Credit may be granted through ACT PEP exams and

military and life experience. Early entrance/early admission program. Concurrent enrollment program.
**Transfer students:** Transfer students accepted for terms other than fall. In fall 1993, 31% of all new students were transfers into all classes. 303 transfer applications were received, 259 were accepted. Application deadline is rolling for fall; rolling for spring. Minimum 2.0 GPA required. Lowest course grade accepted is "C." At least 30 semester hours must be completed at the college to receive degree.
**Admissions contact:** Gary Fallis, M.Ed., Director of Admissions. 802 468-5611.
**FINANCIAL AID. Available aid:** Pell grants, SEOG, state scholarships and grants, school scholarships and grants, private scholarships and grants, academic merit scholarships, and aid for undergraduate foreign students. Perkins Loans (NDSL), PLUS, Stafford Loans (GSL), NSL, state loans, private loans, and SLS. AMS and deferred payment plan. Credit card payment. Installment Plan.
**Financial aid statistics:** Average amounts of aid awarded freshmen: Scholarships and grants, $1,980; loans, $3,369.
**Supporting data/closing dates:** FAFSA: Priority filing date is March 15; accepted on rolling basis. Income tax forms: Accepted on rolling basis. Notification of awards begins April 15.
**Financial aid contact:** Ken Moulton, M.A., Director of Financial Aid. 802 468-5611.
**STUDENT EMPLOYMENT.** College Work/Study Program. Institutional employment. 31% of full-time undergraduates work on campus during school year. Students may expect to earn an average of $1,200 during school year. Off-campus part-time employment opportunities rated "good."
**COMPUTER FACILITIES.** 190 IBM/IBM-compatible and Macintosh/Apple microcomputers; 50 are networked. Students may access Digital minicomputer/mainframe systems. Residence halls may be equipped with stand-alone microcomputers. Computer languages and software packages include BASIC, COBOL, FORTRAN, MINITAB, Pascal, SPSS-X. Computer facilities are available to all students.
**Fees:** None.
**Hours:** 87 hours/week.

# Champlain College

**Burlington, VT 05402-0670 — 802 658-0800**

**1994-95 Costs.** Tuition: $8,195. Room: $3,505. Board: $2,415. Fees, books, misc. academic expenses (school's estimate): $475.
**Enrollment.** Undergraduates: 505 men, 746 women (full-time). Freshman class: 1,402 applicants, 878 accepted, 762 enrolled.
**Test score averages/ranges.** N/A.
**Faculty.** 60 full-time; 39 part-time. 100% of faculty holds highest degree in specific field. Student/faculty ratio: 16 to 1.
**Selectivity rating.** Less competitive.

**PROFILE.** Champlain is a private college offering business and management programs. Founded in 1878, it adopted coeducation in 1900. Its 19-acre campus is located in the town of Burlington, 39 miles from Montpelier.
**Accreditation:** NEASC. Professionally accredited by the Accreditation Board for Engineering and Technology.
**Religious orientation:** Champlain College is nonsectarian; no religious requirements.
**Library:** Collections totaling over 33,000 volumes, 1,100 periodical subscriptions, and 1,100 microform items.
**Athletic facilities:** Burlington YMCA, auditorium, park.
**STUDENT BODY. Undergraduate profile:** 80% are state residents; 15% are transfers. 2% Black, 1% Hispanic, 1% Native American, 95% White, 1% Other. Average age of undergraduates is 20.
**Freshman profile:** 2% of freshmen who took SAT scored 600 or over on verbal, 3% scored 600 or over on math; 8% scored 500 or over on verbal, 15% scored 500 or over on math; 36% scored 400 or over on verbal, 47% scored 400 or over on math; 85% scored 300 or over on verbal, 87% scored 300 or over on math. 60% of accepted applicants took SAT. 90% of freshmen come from public schools.
**Undergraduate achievement:** 70% of fall 1992 freshmen returned for fall 1993 term. 69% of entering class graduated. 20% of students who completed a degree program immediately went on to graduate study.
**Foreign students:** 50 students are from out of the country. Countries represented include Canada, China, France, Japan, Thailand, and the United Kingdom; nine in all.
**PROGRAMS OF STUDY. Degrees:** B.S.
**Majors:** Accounting, Business Management, Computer Information Systems, Early Childhood Education, General Business, Hotel/Restaurant Management, Law Enforcement, Marketing/Retail Management, Office Administration, Paralegal, Social Service.
**Distribution of degrees:** The majors with the highest enrollment are accounting and business management.
**Academic regulations:** Minimum 2.0 GPA must be maintained.
**Special:** Minors and/or certificates offered in accounting, computer information systems, office computing skills, office skills, and secretarial. Associate's degrees offered. Internships. Cooperative education programs. Member of Northern Vermont Consortium. Teacher certification in early childhood education. ROTC at U of Vermont. NROTC at Norwich U. AFROTC at St. Michael's Coll.
**Academic Assistance:** Remedial reading, writing, math, and study skills. Nonremedial tutoring.
**STUDENT LIFE. Housing:** Students may live on or off campus. Women's and men's dorms. Off-campus privately-owned housing. 36% of students live in college housing.
**Social atmosphere:** On campus, students gather at the student lounge and the Courtyard Cafe. Off campus, students head for downtown Burlington, area ski resorts, and Burlington night spots for dancing and socializing. The Student Activities Committee, the Champlain College Players, and the Resident Student Community Volunteers influence life on campus. Among the highlights of the schoolyear are the Champlain Beaver basketball games, the Christmas Dance, International Day, student plays, and the spring Travel & Tourism student trip. "Students enjoy the benefits of living in a city with five colleges, but also enjoy easy access to Lake Champlain (for boating, fishing, wind surfing, and skating) and to the Green and Adirondack Mountains (for skiing, hiking, camping, and snowshoeing)," comments Champlain Today.
**Services and counseling/handicapped student services:** Placement services. Health service. Day care. Peer tutoring. Counseling services for older students. Personal counseling. Career and academic guidance services. Physically disabled student services. Learning disabled services. Notetaking services.
**Campus organizations:** Undergraduate student government. Student newspaper (Champlain Today, published four times/year). Yearbook. Outing club, residence hall programs, theatre group, academic groups, 20 organizations in all.
**Minority/foreign student organizations:** Cultural Diversity Committee. International Club.
**ATHLETICS. Physical education requirements:** None.
**Intercollegiate competition:** 10% of students participate. Alpine skiing (M,W), basketball (M), cheerleading (M,W), golf (M), soccer (M,W), softball (W). Member of NJCAA III.
**Intramural and club sports:** 20% of students participate. Intramural aerobics, basketball, biking, hiking, indoor soccer, Alpine skiing, volleyball, weight/fitness training.
**ADMISSIONS. Academic basis for candidate selection** (in order of priority): Secondary school record, essay, school's recommendation, standardized test scores, class rank.
**Nonacademic basis for candidate selection:** Character and personality, extracurricular participation, and particular talent or ability are considered.
**Requirements:** Graduation from secondary school is required; GED is accepted. 18 units and the following program of study are required: 4 units of English, 1 unit of lab science, 4 units of social studies, 1 unit of history. Minimum 2.0 GPA recommended. Some programs have specific requirements. SAT is recommended; ACT may be substituted. ACH recommended. Campus visit and interview recommended. Off-campus interviews available with an admissions representative.
**Procedure:** Application deadline is August. Notification of admission on rolling basis. No set date by which applicants must accept offer. $150 tuition deposit, refundable until May 1. $50 room deposit, refundable until May 1. Freshmen accepted for terms other than fall.
**Special programs:** Admission may be deferred one year. Credit and/or placement may be granted through CEEB Advanced Placement exams for scores of 3 or higher. Credit may be granted through CLEP general and subject exams and through ACT PEP and DANTES exams. Credit and placement may be granted through challenge exams and military experience. Concurrent enrollment program.
**Transfer students:** Transfer students accepted for terms other than fall. In fall 1993, 15% of all new students were transfers into all classes. Application deadline is rolling for fall; rolling for spring. Minimum 2.0 GPA recommended. Lowest course grade accepted is "C." Maximum number of transferable credits is 30 semester hours from a two-year school and 60 semester hours from a four-year school. At least 60 semester hours must be completed at the college to receive degree.
**Admissions contact:** Josephine Churchill, M.Ed., Director of Admissions. 802 860-2727.
**FINANCIAL AID. Available aid:** Pell grants, SEOG, state scholarships and grants, school scholarships and grants, and athletic scholarships. Perkins Loans (NDSL), PLUS, Stafford Loans (GSL), state loans, school loans, and SLS. Tuition Management Systems and family tuition reduction.
**Financial aid statistics:** In 1993-94, 90% of all undergraduate applicants received aid; 90% of freshman applicants.
**Supporting data/closing dates:** FAFSA/FAF/FFS: Priority filing date is May 1; accepted on rolling basis. School's own aid application: Priority filing date is May 1; deadline is rolling. State aid form: Priority filing date is March 1; accepted on rolling basis. Income tax forms: Accepted on rolling basis. Notification of awards on rolling basis.
**Financial aid contact:** David Myette, M.S., Director of Financial Aid. 802 860-2730.
**STUDENT EMPLOYMENT.** College Work/Study Program. Institutional employment. 13% of full-time undergraduates work on campus during school year. Students may expect to earn an average of $1,500 during school year. Off-campus part-time employment opportunities rated "excellent."
**COMPUTER FACILITIES.** 100 IBM/IBM-compatible microcomputers; all are networked. Students may access IBM minicomputer/mainframe systems, Internet. Residence halls may be equipped with networked microcomputers. Client/LAN operating systems include DOS, Windows NT, Novell. Computer languages and software packages include C, COBOL, CPTyping, dBASE, Harvard Graphics, Lotus 1-2-3, PageMaker, Pascal, Quattro Pro, RPG, WordPerfect; 15 in all. Computer facilities are available to all students.
**GRADUATE CAREER DATA.** 40% of graduates choose careers in business and industry. Companies and businesses that hire graduates: Major accounting firms.

# College of St. Joseph

**Rutland, VT 05701 — 802 773-5900**

**1994-95 Costs.** Tuition: $8,300. Room & board: $4,650. Fees, books, misc. academic expenses (school's estimate): $550.
**Enrollment.** Undergraduates: 75 men, 125 women (full-time). Freshman class: 132 applicants, 127 accepted, 42 enrolled. Graduate enrollment: 25 men, 80 women.
**Test score averages/ranges.** Average SAT scores: 384 verbal, 413 math.
**Faculty.** 15 full-time; 30 part-time. 44% of faculty holds doctoral degree. Student/faculty ratio: 14 to 1.
**Selectivity rating.** Noncompetitive.

**PROFILE.** The College of St. Joseph, founded in 1950, is a private, church-affiliated, liberal arts college. Its 99-acre campus is located in Rutland, 66 miles from Burlington.
**Accreditation:** NEASC.
**Religious orientation:** College of St. Joseph is affiliated with the Roman Catholic Church; nine credits of religion required.

**Library:** Collections totaling over 44,547 volumes, 224 periodical subscriptions, and 1,006 microform items.
**Athletic facilities:** Gymnasium, weight room, cross-country ski trails, outside skating rink, soccer and softball fields.
**STUDENT BODY. Undergraduate profile:** 59% are state residents; 34% are transfers. 1% Asian-American, 1% Black, 1% Hispanic, 1% Native American, 94% White, 2% Other. Average age of undergraduates is 22.
**Freshman profile:** 3% of freshmen who took SAT scored 600 or over on math; 7% scored 500 or over on verbal, 18% scored 500 or over on math; 40% scored 400 or over on verbal, 51% scored 400 or over on math; 85% scored 300 or over on verbal, 87% scored 300 or over on math. Majority of accepted applicants took SAT. 89% of freshmen come from public schools.
**Undergraduate achievement:** 68% of fall 1992 freshmen returned for fall 1993 term. 51% of entering class graduated. 2% of students who completed a degree program immediately went on to graduate study.
**PROGRAMS OF STUDY. Degrees:** B.A., B.S.
**Majors:** Accounting, American Studies, Business, Business Management, Computer Information Systems Management, Early Childhood Education, Elementary Education, English, History, Human Services, Liberal Studies, Political Science, Pre-Law, Psychology, Secondary Education Certification, Special Education.
**Distribution of degrees:** The majors with the highest enrollment are business, liberal studies, and education; political science and American studies have the lowest.
**Requirements:** General education requirement.
**Academic regulations:** Minimum 2.0 GPA must be maintained.
**Special:** Minors offered in business, English, history, human services, political science, and psychology. Associate's degrees offered. Double majors. Independent study. Accelerated study. Internships. Graduate school at which undergraduates may take graduate-level courses. Preprofessional programs in law. Member of Consortium of Vermont Colleges and New England Catholic College Consortium. Independent study. Teacher certification in early childhood, elementary, secondary, and special education. Certification in specific subject areas. Study abroad possible through other colleges and universities.
**Honors:** Honor societies.
**Academic Assistance:** Remedial reading, writing, math, and study skills. Nonremedial tutoring.
**ADMISSIONS. Academic basis for candidate selection** (in order of priority): Secondary school record, class rank, essay, school's recommendation, standardized test scores.
**Nonacademic basis for candidate selection:** Character and personality are emphasized. Extracurricular participation and alumni/ae relationship are important. Particular talent or ability is considered.
**Requirements:** Graduation from secondary school is required; GED is accepted. 16 units and the following program of study are required: 4 units of English, 3 units of math, 2 units of science including 1 unit of lab, 1 unit of social studies, 1 unit of history, 5 units of academic electives. Minimum combined SAT score of 800, rank in top half of secondary school class, and minimum 2.0 GPA required. Conditional admission possible for applicants not meeting standard requirements. SAT or ACT is required. Campus visit and interview recommended. Off-campus interviews available with an admissions representative.
**Procedure:** Take SAT or ACT by March of 12th year. Suggest filing application by March 1; no deadline. Notification of admission on rolling basis. Reply is required by May 1. $200 tuition deposit, refundable until May 1. $300 refundable room deposit. Freshmen accepted for terms other than fall.
**Special programs:** Admission may be deferred one year. Placement may be granted through CEEB Advanced Placement exams for scores of 4 or higher. Placement may be granted through CLEP general exams. Credit and/or placement may be granted through CLEP subject exams. Credit and placement may be granted through Regents College, ACT PEP, DANTES, and challenge exams and military and life experience. Early entrance/early admission program. Concurrent enrollment program.
**Transfer students:** Transfer students accepted for terms other than fall. In fall 1993, 34% of all new students were transfers into all classes. 44 transfer applications were received, 44 were accepted. Application deadline is rolling for fall; rolling for spring. Minimum 2.0 GPA required. Lowest course grade accepted is "C." Maximum number of transferable credits is 97 semester hours. At least 30 semester hours must be completed at the college to receive degree.
**Admissions contact:** Carl N. Tichenor, M.Ed., Dean of Admissions. 802 773-5905.
**FINANCIAL AID. Available aid:** Pell grants, SEOG, state scholarships and grants, school scholarships and grants, private scholarships and grants, academic merit scholarships, and athletic scholarships. Perkins Loans (NDSL), PLUS, Stafford Loans (GSL), private loans, and SLS. Four-payment installment plan.
**Financial aid statistics:** In 1993-94, 98% of all undergraduate applicants received aid; 98% of freshman applicants. Average amounts of aid awarded freshmen: Scholarships and grants, $3,345; loans, $3,243.
**Supporting data/closing dates:** FAFSA: Priority filing date is March 1; accepted on rolling basis. State aid form: Priority filing date is March 1. Income tax forms: Priority filing date is March 1. Notification of awards on rolling basis.
**Financial aid contact:** Winifred Grace, Director of Financial Aid. 802 773-5900, ext 218.

## Goddard College

**Plainfield, VT 05667** 802 454-8311

**1993-94 Costs.** Tuition: $13,400. Room & board: $4,520. Fees, books, misc. academic expenses (school's estimate): $470.
**Enrollment.** Undergraduates: 90 men, 135 women (full-time). Freshman class: 94 applicants, 82 accepted, 49 enrolled. Graduate enrollment: 132.
**Test score averages/ranges.** Average SAT scores: 473 verbal, 464 math.
**Faculty.** 50% of faculty holds doctoral degree. Student/faculty ratio: 10 to 1.
**Selectivity rating.** Less competitive.

**PROFILE.** Goddard, founded in 1938, is a private college of liberal and practical arts. Its 220-acre campus, located on a former farm estate, is ten miles from Montpelier.
**Accreditation:** NEASC.
**Religious orientation:** Goddard College is nonsectarian; no religious requirements.
**Library:** Collections totaling over 70,000 volumes and 130 periodical subscriptions.
**STUDENT BODY. Undergraduate profile:** 10% are state residents; 55% are transfers. Average age of undergraduates is 22.
**Freshman profile:** 95% of freshmen come from public schools.
**Foreign students:** One student is from out of the country.
**PROGRAMS OF STUDY. Degrees:** B.A.
**Majors:** Individualized Majors.
**Special:** Double majors. Independent study. Pass/fail grading option. Internships. Cooperative education programs. Graduate school at which undergraduates may take graduate-level courses. Exchange program with Inst for Social Ecology, Sterling Coll, and Woodbury Coll. Teacher certification in early childhood, elementary, and secondary education. Study abroad in several countries.
**STUDENT LIFE. Housing:** Students may live on or off campus. Coed and women's dorms. 90% of students live in college housing.
**Services and counseling/handicapped student services:** Placement services. Women's center. Day care. Each student meets weekly with faculty adviser. Personal and psychological counseling. Academic guidance services.
**Campus organizations:** Undergraduate student government. Student newspaper. Literary magazine. Radio station. Gay/Lesbian/Bisexual Alliance, Women's Center.
**ATHLETICS. Physical education requirements:** None.
**ADMISSIONS. Academic basis for candidate selection** (in order of priority): Essay, school's recommendation, secondary school record, standardized test scores.
**Nonacademic basis for candidate selection:** Character and personality and extracurricular participation are emphasized. Particular talent or ability is important.
**Requirements:** Graduation from secondary school is required; GED is accepted. No specific distribution of secondary school units required. SAT is recommended. Campus visit recommended. Off-campus interviews available with an admissions representative.
**Procedure:** Take SAT or ACT by January of 12th year. Notification of admission on rolling basis. $250 tuition deposit, refundable until May 1 or November 15. Freshmen accepted for terms other than fall.
**Special programs:** Admission may be deferred one semester. Credit and/or placement may be granted through CLEP general and subject exams. Credit and placement may be granted through Regents College, ACT PEP, DANTES, and challenge exams and military and life experience.
**Transfer students:** Transfer students accepted for terms other than fall. 55% of all new students were transfers into all classes. Lowest course grade accepted is "C." Maximum number of transferable credits is 90 semester hours. At least 30 semester hours must be completed at the college to receive degree.
**Admissions contact:** Peter S. Burns, Director of Admissions. 800 468-4888.
**FINANCIAL AID. Available aid:** Pell grants, SEOG, state scholarships and grants, school grants, and private scholarships. Perkins Loans (NDSL), PLUS, Stafford Loans (GSL), school loans, private loans, and SLS. Knight Tuition Plans and AMS. Extended payment plan.
**Financial aid statistics:** In 1993-94, 70% of all undergraduate applicants received aid; 70% of freshman applicants.
**Supporting data/closing dates:** FAFSA/FAF/FFS: Accepted on rolling basis. Notification of awards on rolling basis.
**Financial aid contact:** Manuel O'Neill, M.A., Director of Financial Aid. 802 454-8311.
**STUDENT EMPLOYMENT.** College Work/Study Program. Off-campus part-time employment opportunities rated "good."
**COMPUTER FACILITIES.** IBM/IBM-compatible and Macintosh/Apple microcomputers. Computer facilities are available to all students.
**Fees:** None.

## Green Mountain College

**Poultney, VT 05764** 802 287-9313

**1994-95 Costs.** Tuition: $11,750. Room & board: $2,880. Fees, books, misc. academic expenses (school's estimate): $900.
**Enrollment.** Undergraduates: 291 men, 300 women (full-time). Freshman class: 850 applicants, 640 accepted, 200 enrolled.
**Test score averages/ranges.** Average SAT scores: 440 verbal, 440 math. Average ACT scores: 20 composite.
**Faculty.** 36 full-time; 17 part-time. 85% of faculty holds highest degree in specific field. Student/faculty ratio: 14 to 1.
**Selectivity rating.** Less competitive.

**PROFILE.** Green Mountain, founded in 1834, is a private college offering specialized programs in the fields of business and education. Its 155-acre campus is located in Poultney, 20 miles from Rutland.
**Accreditation:** NEASC. Professionally accredited by the National Recreation and Park Association.
**Religious orientation:** Green Mountain College is nonsectarian; no religious requirements.
**Library:** Collections totaling over 60,000 volumes, 245 periodical subscriptions, and 10,000 microform items.
**Athletic facilities:** Gymnasium, swimming pool, weight room, dance room, athletic fields.
**STUDENT BODY. Undergraduate profile:** 8% are state residents; 14% are transfers. 2% Asian-American, 2% Black, 1% Hispanic, 93% White, 2% Other. Average age of undergraduates is 19.

**Freshman profile:** 1% of freshmen who took SAT scored 700 or over on verbal, 1% scored 700 or over on math; 2% scored 600 or over on verbal, 4% scored 600 or over on math; 21% scored 500 or over on verbal, 19% scored 500 or over on math; 62% scored 400 or over on verbal, 65% scored 400 or over on math; 98% scored 300 or over on verbal, 97% scored 300 or over on math. 86% of accepted applicants took SAT; 14% took ACT. 60% of freshmen come from public schools.
**Undergraduate achievement:** 75% of fall 1992 freshmen returned for fall 1993 term. 65% of entering class graduated. 21% of students who completed a degree program went on to graduate study within three years.
**Foreign students:** 25 students are from out of the country. Countries represented include Canada, Ireland, Japan, and Norway; 12 in all.

**PROGRAMS OF STUDY. Degrees:** B.A., B.F.A., B.S.
**Majors:** Behavioral Science, Business Management, Elementary Education, English, Fine Arts, Leisure Resource Facilities Management, Liberal Studies, Recreation, Special Education, Therapeutic Recreation.
**Distribution of degrees:** The majors with the highest enrollment are elementary education, fine arts, and liberal studies; therapeutic recreation and English have the lowest.
**Requirements:** General education requirement.
**Academic regulations:** Freshmen must maintain minimum 1.7 GPA; sophomores, 1.8 GPA; juniors, 1.9 GPA; seniors, 2.0 GPA (on a 2.6 scale).
**Special:** Minors offered in accounting, economics, English, finance, gerontology, management, marketing, recreation, theatre, and therapeutic recreation. Associate's degrees offered. Double majors. Dual degrees. Independent study. Accelerated study. Internships. Preprofessional programs in law and medicine. Member of Consortium of Vermont Colleges. Teacher certification in elementary and special education. Study abroad in Canada, England, France, Ireland, Italy, and Japan.
**Honors:** Phi Beta Kappa. Honor societies.
**Academic Assistance:** Remedial reading, writing, math, and study skills.

**ADMISSIONS. Academic basis for candidate selection** (in order of priority): Secondary school record, standardized test scores, class rank, essay, school's recommendation.
**Nonacademic basis for candidate selection:** Character and personality and extracurricular participation are emphasized. Particular talent or ability is important. Geographical distribution and alumni/ae relationship are considered.
**Requirements:** Graduation from secondary school is required; GED is accepted. 16 units and the following program of study are required: 4 units of English, 2 units of math, 2 units of science including 1 unit of lab, 1 unit of social studies, 1 unit of history, 6 units of academic electives. Minimum combined SAT score of 850-950 (composite ACT score of 19-20) and minimum 2.5 GPA recommended. Conditional admission possible for applicants not meeting standard requirements. SAT is required; ACT may be substituted. Campus visit and interview recommended. Off-campus interviews available with admissions and alumni representatives.
**Procedure:** Take SAT or ACT by December of 12th year. Visit college for interview by February of 12th year. Suggest filing application by January; no deadline. Notification on rolling basis, beginning three or four weeks after completion of file. Reply is required by May 1. $300 tuition deposit, refundable until May 1. Freshmen accepted for terms other than fall.
**Special programs:** Admission may be deferred two years. Credit may be granted through CEEB Advanced Placement for scores of 4 or higher. Credit may be granted through CLEP general and subject exams. Early decision program. In fall 1993, 28 applied for early decision and 22 were accepted. Deadline for applying for early decision is November 1. Early entrance/early admission program.
**Transfer students:** Transfer students accepted for terms other than fall. In fall 1993, 14% of all new students were transfers into all classes. 60 transfer applications were received, 40 were accepted. Application deadline is rolling for fall; rolling for spring. Minimum 2.5 GPA recommended. Lowest course grade accepted is "C." Maximum number of transferable credits is 90 semester hours. At least 30 semester hours must be completed at the college to receive degree.
**Admissions contact:** Kevin M.R. Mayne, M.B.A., Vice President for External Affairs and Admissions. 800 776-6675.

**FINANCIAL AID. Available aid:** Pell grants, SEOG, state scholarships and grants, school scholarships and grants, private scholarships and grants, academic merit scholarships, and athletic scholarships. Perkins Loans (NDSL), PLUS, Stafford Loans (GSL), state loans, private loans, and SLS. Knight Tuition Plans.
**Financial aid statistics:** 22% of aid is not need-based. In 1993-94, 52% of all undergraduate applicants received aid; 52% of freshman applicants. Average amounts of aid awarded freshmen: Scholarships and grants, $4,000; loans, $2,625.
**Supporting data/closing dates:** FAFSA/FAF/FFS: Deadline is April 1. State aid form: Priority filing date is February 15. Income tax forms: Priority filing date is February 15. Notification of awards on rolling basis.
**Financial aid contact:** Richard Hendrickson, Director of Financial Aid. 802 287-9313.

# Johnson State College

**Johnson, VT 05656** **802 635-2356**

**1994-95 Costs.** Tuition: $3,168 (state residents), $7,320 (out-of-state). Room & board: $4,640. Fees, books, misc. academic expenses (school's estimate): $1,220.
**Enrollment.** Undergraduates: 639 men, 587 women (full-time). Freshman class: 833 applicants, 669 accepted, 277 enrolled. Graduate enrollment: 33 men, 61 women.
**Test score averages/ranges.** N/A.
**Faculty.** 64 full-time; 76 part-time. 84% of faculty holds doctoral degree. Student/faculty ratio: 16 to 1.
**Selectivity rating.** Less competitive.

**PROFILE.** Johnson State, founded in 1828, is a public, multipurpose college. Its 350-acre campus is located in Johnson, 40 miles from Burlington.
**Accreditation:** NEASC.
**Religious orientation:** Johnson State College is nonsectarian; no religious requirements.
**Library:** Collections totaling over 93,000 volumes, 450 periodical subscriptions, and 7,500 microform items.
**Special facilities/museums:** Art gallery, visual arts center, child development center, human performance lab, 1,000-acre nature preserve.
**Athletic facilities:** Gymnasiums, athletic fields, Nordic ski trails, human performance lab, aerobics and weight rooms, swimmig pool, racquetball and tennis courts.

**STUDENT BODY. Undergraduate profile:** 60% are state residents. 1% Asian-American, 1% Black, 1% Hispanic, 1% Native American, 96% White. Average age of undergraduates is 19.
**Freshman profile:** 1% of freshmen who took SAT scored 600 or over on verbal, 2% scored 600 or over on math; 11% scored 500 or over on verbal, 23% scored 500 or over on math; 100% scored 400 or over on verbal, 100% scored 400 or over on math.
**Foreign students:** 17 students are from out of the country. Eight countries represented in all.

**PROGRAMS OF STUDY. Degrees:** B.A., B.F.A., B.S.
**Majors:** Anthropology/Sociology, Anthropology/Sociology with Human Services, Art, Business Management, Early Childhood Education, Ecology, Education, Elementary Education, Environmental Science, Environmental Studies, Government, Health Sciences, Hotel Hospitality Management/Services, Management Information Systems, Mathematics, Music, Physical Education, Psychology, Reading, Secondary Education, Studio Arts, Theatre, Writing.
**Distribution of degrees:** The major with the highest enrollment is education.
**Requirements:** General education requirement.
**Special:** Associate's degrees offered. Double majors. Dual degrees. Independent study. Accelerated study. Pass/fail grading option. Internships. 2-2 nursing program with U of Vermont. Member of Consortium of Vermont Colleges. New England/Quebec exchange program. Teacher certification in elementary, secondary, and special education. Certification in specific subject areas. Exchange program abroad in England (U of London). Study abroad also in Canada.
**Academic Assistance:** Remedial reading, writing, and math. Nonremedial tutoring.

**STUDENT LIFE. Housing:** Unmarried freshmen and sophomores must live on campus; exceptions possible. Coed dorms. On-campus married-student housing. Theme housing. Alcohol-free housing. Freshman housing. International housing. 35% of students live in college housing.
**Social atmosphere:** Favorite off-campus gathering spots for Johnson State students include the Rusty Nail in Stowe, the Long Trail Tavern in Johnson, and Hilary's in Morrisville. Influential student groups include the College Republicans, the Student Association Steering Committee, the rugby club, the college radio station, and the student newspaper staff.
**Services and counseling/handicapped student services:** Health service. Day care. Counseling services for minority, military, veteran, and older students. Birth control, personal, and psychological counseling. Career and academic guidance services. Learning disabled services.
**Campus organizations:** Undergraduate student government. Student newspaper (Basement Medicine). Literary magazine. Yearbook. Radio station. Dance ensemble, film committee, jazz ensemble, theatre, College Republicans, athletic, departmental, service, and special-interest groups.
**Religious organizations:** Several religious groups.
**Minority/foreign student organizations:** International Student Club.

**ATHLETICS. Physical education requirements:** None.
**Intercollegiate competition:** 5% of students participate. Alpine skiing (M,W), baseball (M), basketball (M,W), cheerleading (W), cross-country (M,W), Nordic skiing (M,W), soccer (M,W), softball (W), tennis (M,W). Member of Eastern Intercollegiate Ski Association, NAIA, NCAA Division III, New England Intercollegiate Soccer League.
**Intramural and club sports:** 3% of students participate. Intramural basketball, floor hockey, football, racquetball, soccer, volleyball, walleyball. Men's club hockey, rugby, volleyball. Women's club rugby, volleyball.

**ADMISSIONS. Academic basis for candidate selection** (in order of priority): Secondary school record, class rank, school's recommendation, standardized test scores.
**Nonacademic basis for candidate selection:** Character and personality are emphasized. Extracurricular participation is important. Particular talent or ability and alumni/ae relationship are considered.
**Requirements:** Graduation from secondary school is required; GED is accepted. 16 units and the following program of study are required: 4 units of English, 3 units of math, 2 units of science including 1 unit of lab, 2 units of social studies, 2 units of history, 3 units of academic electives. Applicants who rank in top half of secondary school class with "C+" average and have good recommendations generally accepted. Provisional admission possible for applicants not meeting standard requirements. Summer PROVE program provides remedial courses, special skills instruction, tutoring, and other support services. SAT is required; ACT may be substituted. Campus visit and interview recommended.
**Procedure:** Acceptance notification on rolling basis, about two weeks after receipt of all credentials. Reply is required by May 1. $200 nonrefundable tuition deposit. Freshmen accepted for terms other than fall.
**Special programs:** Admission may be deferred one semester. Credit and/or placement may be granted through CEEB Advanced Placement exams for scores of 3 or higher. Credit and/or placement may be granted through CLEP subject exams. Credit may be granted through ACT PEP exams. Early entrance/early admission program.
**Transfer students:** Transfer students accepted for terms other than fall. Application deadline is rolling for fall; rolling for spring. Minimum 2.0 GPA required. Lowest course grade accepted is "C." At least 30 semester hours must be completed at the college to receive degree.
**Admissions contact:** John Henry, Director of Admissions. 802 635-2356, extension 219.

**FINANCIAL AID. Available aid:** Pell grants, SEOG, state scholarships and grants, school scholarships and grants, private grants, and academic merit scholarships. Member of New England Regional Student Program; tuition discounts possible for New England students in some programs. Perkins Loans (NDSL), PLUS, Stafford Loans (GSL), and SLS. AMS, deferred payment plan, and family tuition reduction.

**Financial aid statistics:** 2% of aid is not need-based. In 1993-94, 65% of all undergraduate applicants received aid; 60% of freshman applicants. Average amounts of aid awarded freshmen: Scholarships and grants, $630; loans, $2,550.
**Supporting data/closing dates:** FAFSA: Priority filing date is March 1; accepted on rolling basis. State aid form: Priority filing date is March 1; accepted on rolling basis. Notification of awards on rolling basis.
**Financial aid contact:** Penny Howrigan, Director of Financial Aid. 802 635-2356, extension 380.

**STUDENT EMPLOYMENT.** College Work/Study Program. Institutional employment. 65% of full-time undergraduates work on campus during school year. Students may expect to earn an average of $1,650 during school year. Off-campus part-time employment opportunities rated "good."

**COMPUTER FACILITIES.** 95 IBM/IBM-compatible and Macintosh/Apple microcomputers. Computer languages and software packages include BASIC, COBOL, dBASE, FORTRAN, Lotus 1-2-3, Pascal, Word, WordPerfect, WordStar. Computer facilities are available to all students.
**Fees:** None.
**Hours:** 9 AM-11 PM.

# Lyndon State College

**Lyndonville, VT 05851-0919 — 802 626-9371**

**1994-95 Costs.** Tuition: $3,294 (state residents), $7,612 (out-of-state). Room & board: $4,640. Fees, books, misc. academic expenses (school's estimate): $1,109.
**Enrollment.** Undergraduates: 505 men, 454 women (full-time). Freshman class: 778 applicants, 702 accepted, 367 enrolled. Graduate enrollment: 12 men, 57 women.
**Test score averages/ranges.** Average SAT scores: 475 verbal, 475 math.
**Faculty.** 58 full-time; 78 part-time. 47% of faculty holds doctoral degree. Student/faculty ratio: 17 to 1.
**Selectivity rating.** Less competitive.

**PROFILE.** Lyndon State, founded in 1911, is a public, multipurpose college. Its 175-acre campus is located in Lyndonville, 85 miles from Burlington.

**Accreditation:** NEASC.
**Religious orientation:** Lyndon State College is nonsectarian; no religious requirements.
**Library:** Collections totaling over 70,000 volumes, 500 periodical subscriptions, and 10,000 microform items.
**Special facilities/museums:** Museum of college history, weather satellite.
**Athletic facilities:** Gymnasiums, basketball, racquetball, squash, and tennis courts, swimming pool, training and weight rooms, soccer and softball fields, cross-country running and skiing trails.

**STUDENT BODY. Undergraduate profile:** 60% are state residents; 30% are transfers. 99% White, 1% Other. Average age of undergraduates is 20.
**Freshman profile:** 97% of accepted applicants took SAT; 1% took ACT.
**Undergraduate achievement:** 80% of fall 1992 freshmen returned for fall 1993 term.

**PROGRAMS OF STUDY. Degrees:** B.A., B.S.
**Majors:** Accounting, Business Administration, Communication Arts/Sciences, Computer Science, Elementary Education, English, Human Services/Counseling, Interdisciplinary Studies, Meteorology, Outdoor Education/Recreation, Physical Education, Psychology, Radio Broadcast, Science, Secondary Education, Ski Resort/Commercial Recreation Management, Small Business Management/Entrepreneurship, Social Science, Special Education, Visual Design.
**Distribution of degrees:** The majors with the highest enrollment are communication, business, and psychology; interdisciplinary studies and computer science have the lowest.
**Requirements.** General education requirement.
**Academic regulations:** Minimum 2.0 GPA must be maintained.
**Special:** Minors offered in biology, business, English, geology, math, music, philosophy, physical education (coaching), physics, psychology, and social science. Associate's degrees offered. Double majors. Independent study. Internships. Cooperative education programs. Member of Vermont College Consortium. Semester-away study programs in England and Nova Scotia. Teacher certification in early childhood, elementary, secondary, and special education. Certification in specific subject areas.
**Academic Assistance:** Remedial writing and math. Nonremedial tutoring.

**ADMISSIONS. Academic basis for candidate selection** (in order of priority): Secondary school record, essay, school's recommendation, standardized test scores, class rank.
**Nonacademic basis for candidate selection:** Character and personality and extracurricular participation are important.
**Requirements:** Graduation from secondary school is required; GED is accepted. 14 units and the following program of study are required: 4 units of English, 2 units of math, 2 units of lab science, 2 units of foreign language, 1 unit of social studies, 1 unit of history. Minimum combined SAT score of 900, rank in top half of secondary school class, or minimum 2.0 GPA recommended. SAT is required. Campus visit and interview recommended. No off-campus interviews.
**Procedure:** Take SAT by December 1 of 12th year. Visit college for interview by May 1 of 12th year. Notification of admission on rolling basis. Reply is required by May 1. $100 nonrefundable tuition deposit. $125 room deposit, refundable until July 1. Freshmen accepted for terms other than fall.
**Special programs:** Admission may be deferred one year. Credit and/or placement may be granted through CEEB Advanced Placement exams for scores of 3 or higher. Placement may be granted through CLEP general exams. Credit and/or placement may be granted through CLEP subject exams. Placement may be granted through challenge exams. Credit and placement may be granted through Regents College, ACT PEP, and DANTES exams and military and life experience.
**Transfer students:** Transfer students accepted for terms other than fall. In fall 1993, 30% of all new students were transfers into all classes. 157 transfer applications were received, 133 were accepted. Application deadline is rolling for fall; rolling for spring. Minimum 2.0 GPA required. Lowest course grade accepted is "C." At least 30 of the final 39 credit hours must be completed at the college to receive degree.
**Admissions contact:** Russell S. Powden, Jr., Ed.M., Director of Admissions. 802 626-9371, extension 113.

**FINANCIAL AID. Available aid:** Pell grants, SEOG, state grants, school scholarships, and ROTC scholarships. Perkins Loans (NDSL), PLUS, Stafford Loans (GSL), and state loans. AMS and family tuition reduction.
**Financial aid statistics:** Average amounts of aid awarded freshmen: Loans, $2,228.
**Supporting data/closing dates:** FAFSA: Deadline is March 15. School's own aid application: Deadline is March 15. State aid form: Priority filing date is March 1; accepted on rolling basis. Income tax forms: Priority filing date is March 1; accepted on rolling basis. Notification of awards on rolling basis.
**Financial aid contact:** Tanya Bradley, Director of Financial Aid. 802 626-9371, extension 218.

# Marlboro College

**Marlboro, VT 05344 — 802 257-4333**

**1994-95 Costs.** Tuition: $17,175. Room & board: $5,680. Fees, books, misc. academic expenses (school's estimate): $850.
**Enrollment.** Undergraduates: 127 men, 131 women (full-time). Freshman class: 251 applicants, 168 accepted, 74 enrolled.
**Test score averages/ranges.** Average SAT scores: 541 verbal, 531 math. Range of SAT scores of middle 50%: 530-570 verbal, 500-540 math.
**Faculty.** 32 full-time; 6 part-time. 70% of faculty holds doctoral degree. Student/faculty ratio: 8 to 1.
**Selectivity rating.** Competitive.

**PROFILE.** Marlboro, founded in 1947, is a private, liberal arts college. Its 400-acre campus is located in Marlboro, 10 miles north of Brattleboro.

**Accreditation:** NEASC.
**Religious orientation:** Marlboro College is nonsectarian; no religious requirements.
**Library:** Collections totaling over 57,000 volumes, 192 periodical subscriptions, and 6,555 microform items.
**Special facilities/museums:** Art gallery, theatre, dance studio, observatory.
**Athletic facilities:** Sauna, weight room, soccer field, extensive trail system. Structured outdoor program offered with instruction in canoeing, kayaking, rock climbing, backpacking, skiing, and leadership skills.

**STUDENT BODY. Undergraduate profile:** 20% are state residents; 24% are transfers. 1% Black, 2% Hispanic, 1% Native American, 96% White. Average age of undergraduates is 21.
**Freshman profile:** 95% of accepted applicants took SAT; 5% took ACT. 68% of freshmen come from public schools.
**Undergraduate achievement:** 80% of fall 1992 freshmen returned for fall 1993 term. 45% of entering class graduated. 60% of students who completed a degree program went on to graduate study.
**Foreign students:** Eight students are from out of the country. Countries represented include Canada, China, England, France, Japan, and Switzerland; seven in all.

**PROGRAMS OF STUDY. Degrees:** B.A., B.Interdis.Studies, B.S.
**Majors:** American Studies, Anthropology, Astronomy, Biochemistry, Biology, Chemistry, Classics, Computer Science, Creative Writing, Dance, Economics, Environmental Science, History, History of Art, History of Film, History of Music, Language, Literature, Mathematics, Music, Painting/Drawing, Philosophy, Physics, Politics, Pottery, Psychology, Religion, Sculpture, Sociology, Theatre, Woodworking, World Studies.
**Academic regulations:** Minimum 2.0 GPA must be maintained.
**Special:** Each student designs own Plan of Concentration for junior and senior years in conjunction with one or more faculty sponsors; several feature field trips for credit. Man, State, and Society program on global area studies brings in a series of scholars who present an interdisciplinary perspective of a specific cultural area (one area per semester). Desert biology trip. World Studies Program; student arranges a 10-month internship in country of choice. Writing requirement. Oral exams. Self-designed majors. Double majors. Dual degrees. Independent study. Accelerated study. Internships. Cooperative education programs. Graduate school at which undergraduates may take graduate-level courses. Preprofessional programs in law, medicine, veterinary science, dentistry, and theology. Member of Consortium of Vermont Colleges. College is affiliated with Brattleboro Music Center; credit is given for individual instrumental instruction and other classes. Teacher certification in early childhood, elementary, and secondary education. Certification in specific subject areas. Study abroad offered in Bali, Botswana, Ireland, the former Soviet Republics, Spain, Tunisia, and other countries through the World Studies program.
**Honors:** Honors program.
**Academic Assistance:** Nonremedial tutoring.

**ADMISSIONS. Academic basis for candidate selection** (in order of priority): Secondary school record, essay, school's recommendation, class rank, standardized test scores.
**Nonacademic basis for candidate selection:** Character and personality, extracurricular participation, and particular talent or ability are important.
**Requirements:** Graduation from secondary school is required; GED is accepted. No specific distribution of secondary school units required. Minimum combined SAT score of 1000 and minimum secondary school average of 85 recommended. SAT is required; ACT may be substituted. Campus visit recommended. Off-campus interviews available with admissions and alumni representatives.
**Procedure:** Take SAT or ACT by October of 12th year. Visit college for interview by March 1 of 12th year. Suggest filing application by December 1. Notification of admission on rolling basis. Reply is required by May 1. $300 nonrefundable tuition deposit. Freshmen accepted for terms other than fall.
**Special programs:** Admission may be deferred one year. Credit may be granted through CEEB Advanced Placement for scores of 4 or higher. Credit may be granted through CLEP general and subject exams and through military experience. Credit and placement

may be granted through Regents College exams. Early decision program. In fall 1992, 16 applied for early decision and 14 were accepted. Deadline for applying for early decision is December 1. Early entrance/early admission program. Concurrent enrollment program.
**Transfer students:** Transfer students accepted for terms other than fall. In fall 1993, 24% of all new students were transfers into all classes. 60 transfer applications were received, 45 were accepted. Application deadline is rolling for fall; rolling for spring. Minimum 2.0 GPA required. Lowest course grade accepted is "C." Maximum number of transferable credits is 60 semester hours from a two-year school and 90 semester hours from a four-year school. At least 30 semester hours must be completed at the college to receive degree.
**Admissions contact:** Wayne R. Wood, Director of Admissions. 802 257-4333, extension 230, 800 343-0049.

**FINANCIAL AID. Available aid:** Pell grants, SEOG, state scholarships and grants, school grants, private grants, and aid for undergraduate foreign students. Perkins Loans (NDSL), PLUS, Stafford Loans (GSL), state loans, school loans, private loans, and SLS. Tuition Plan Inc., Education Plan Inc., Knight Tuition Plans, AMS, and Tuition Management Systems.
**Financial aid statistics:** In 1993-94, 70% of all undergraduate applicants received aid; 75% of freshman applicants. Average amounts of aid awarded freshmen: Scholarships and grants, $7,000; loans, $2,625.
**Supporting data/closing dates:** FAFSA/FAF: Priority filing date is March 1. School's own aid application: Priority filing date is March 1. State aid form: Priority filing date is March 1; deadline is April 1. Income tax forms: Priority filing date is March 1. Notification of awards begins April 1.
**Financial aid contact:** Mary Greene, Director of Financial Aid. 802 257-4333, extension 212, 800 343-0049.

## Middlebury College

**Middlebury, VT 05753-6002 802 388-3711**

**1994-95 Costs.** Comprehensive fee, tuition, room, and board: $25,750 per year.
**Enrollment.** Undergraduates: 980 men, 980 women (full-time). Freshman class: 3,456 applicants, 1,171 accepted, 446 enrolled.
**Test score averages/ranges.** Range of SAT scores of middle 50%: 1180-1350 combined. Range of ACT scores of middle 50%: 27-30 composite.
**Faculty.** 181 full-time; 40 part-time. 95% of faculty holds doctoral degree. Student/faculty ratio: 11 to 1.
**Selectivity rating.** Most competitive.

**PROFILE.** Middlebury, founded in 1800, is a private, liberal arts college. Its 350-acre campus is located in Middlebury, 40 miles south of Burlington.

**Accreditation:** NEASC.
**Religious orientation:** Middlebury College is nonsectarian; no religious requirements.
**Library:** Collections totaling over 703,262 volumes, 2,006 periodical subscriptions, and 236,999 microform items.
**Special facilities/museums:** Art museum, theatre, language lab, observatory, electron microscope.
**Athletic facilities:** Athletic fields, intramural fields, field houses, fitness center, gymnasium, swimming pool, golf course, Alpine and Nordic ski center (Snow Bowl), outdoor/indoor tennis courts, trail, platform diving facilities.
**STUDENT BODY. Undergraduate profile:** 4% are state residents. 3% Asian-American, 2% Black, 3% Hispanic, 1% Native American, 89% White, 2% Other. Average age of undergraduates is 20.
**Freshman profile:** 7% of freshmen who took SAT scored 700 or over on verbal, 27% scored 700 or over on math; 62% scored 600 or over on verbal, 82% scored 600 or over on math; 93% scored 500 or over on verbal, 98% scored 500 or over on math; 100% scored 400 or over on verbal, 100% scored 400 or over on math. Majority of accepted applicants took SAT. 55% of freshmen come from public schools.
**Undergraduate achievement:** 97% of fall 1992 freshmen returned for fall 1993 term. 95% of entering class graduated. 35% of students who completed a degree program immediately went on to graduate study.
**Foreign students:** 212 students are from out of the country. Countries represented include Bulgaria, Canada, China, Germany, India, and the United Kingdom; 65 in all.
**PROGRAMS OF STUDY. Degrees:** A.B.
**Majors:** American Civilization, American Literature, Art, Biology, Biology/Chemistry, Chemistry, Chinese, Classical Studies, Classics, Computer Science, East Asian Studies, Economics, English, Environmental Studies, Film/Video, French, Geography, Geology, German, History, Independent Scholar, International Major, International Politics/Economics, Italian, Literary Studies, Mathematics/Computer Studies, Molecular Biology, Music, Philosophy, Physics, Political Science/Government, Psychology, Religion, Russian, Russian/Soviet Studies, Sociology/Anthropology, Spanish, Theatre/Dance, Women's Studies.
**Distribution of degrees:** The majors with the highest enrollment are English, history, and economics; music, Chinese, and classics have the lowest.
**Requirements:** General education requirement.
**Special:** Self-designed majors. Double majors. Dual degrees. Independent study. Accelerated study. Internships. Graduate school at which undergraduates may take graduate-level courses. Preprofessional programs in law, medicine, veterinary science, and dentistry. 3-2 B.A./M.S. program in forestry and environmental management with Duke U. Students may arrange similar programs in all major fields with any approved graduate school, including law, dentistry, medicine, and veterinary medicine. Early Assurance Program with medical schools of Dartmouth Coll, U of Rochester, and Tufts U and with Medical Coll of Pennsylvania. Early Entry Program for M.B.A. with U of Chicago. Member of American Collegiate Consortium. Washington Semester. Williams-Mystic Seaport Semester (Connecticut), other off-campus study opportunities. Semester exchange program with Swarthmore Coll. Interim exchange programs with Berea Coll, MIT, and Saint Olaf's Coll. Teacher certification in elementary and secondary education. Middlebury Schools Abroad in Florence, Madrid, Mainz, Moscow, Paris, and Oxford. Study abroad possible in other countries.
**Honors:** Phi Beta Kappa. Honors program.
**Academic Assistance:** Nonremedial tutoring.
**STUDENT LIFE. Housing:** All students must live on campus. Coed dorms. 98% of students live in college housing.
**Services and counseling/handicapped student services:** Placement services. Health service. Women's center. Counseling services for minority students. Personal and psychological counseling. Career and academic guidance services. Religious counseling. Physically disabled student services. Learning disabled services.
**Campus organizations:** Undergraduate student government. Student newspaper (Campus, published once/week). Literary magazine. Yearbook. Radio station. Film, musical, and visual arts groups, Carillonneurs, mountain and outing club, pottery studio, darkrooms, Judicial Board, Activities Board, environmental groups, volunteer community service groups, political groups, radio and movie clubs, Gay/Lesbian/Bisexual Alliance, 98 organizations in all.
**Religious organizations:** Christian Fellowship, Christian Science Organization, Hillel, Interfaith Council, Islamic Society.
**Minority/foreign student organizations:** African American Alliance, Hispanic-American League, Latin American and Spanish group. International Student Organization, East Asian, French, German, Greek, Italian, and Russian groups.
**ATHLETICS. Physical education requirements:** Two courses of physical education required.
**Intercollegiate competition:** 6% of students participate. Alpine skiing (M,W), baseball (M), basketball (M,W), cross-country (M,W), diving (M,W), field hockey (W), football (M), golf (M,W), ice hockey (M,W), lacrosse (M,W), Nordic skiing (M,W), soccer (M,W), squash (W), swimming (M,W), tennis (M,W), track (outdoor) (M,W), track and field (M,W), track and field (outdoor) (M,W). Member of ECAC, NCAA Division III, New England Small College Athletic Conference.
**Intramural and club sports:** 3% of students participate. Intramural sports for men and women include over 20 sports each. Men's club cycling, indoor track, martial arts, polo, rugby, squash, ultimate frisbee, volleyball, water polo. Women's club cycling, horsemanship, indoor track, rugby, ultimate frisbee, volleyball.
**ADMISSIONS. Academic basis for candidate selection** (in order of priority): Secondary school record, class rank, school's recommendation, standardized test scores, essay.
**Nonacademic basis for candidate selection:** Character and personality, extracurricular participation, and particular talent or ability are emphasized. Geographical distribution and alumni/ae relationship are considered.
**Requirements:** Graduation from secondary school is recommended; GED is accepted. 18 units and the following program of study are recommended: 4 units of English, 4 units of math, 3 units of science, 4 units of foreign language, 3 units of social studies. One of the following options is required: SAT and three ACH (including English composition), five ACH (including English composition or English composition with essay), or ACT. Minority and rural outreach recruiting programs for applicants not normally admissible. Campus visit and interview recommended. Off-campus interviews available with an alumni representative.
**Procedure:** Take SAT or ACT by January of 12th year. Take ACH by January of 12th year. Visit college for interview by January 1 of 12th year. Suggest filing application by December 15. Application deadline is December 25 for Part I; January 1 for Part II. Notification of admission by April 10. Reply is required by May 1. $200 nonrefundable tuition deposit. Freshmen accepted for terms other than fall.
**Special programs:** Admission may be deferred two years. Credit and/or placement may be granted through CEEB Advanced Placement exams for scores of 5 or higher. Placement may be granted through challenge exams. Early decision program. In fall 1993, 358 applied for early decision and 134 were accepted. Deadline for applying for early decision is November 15. Early entrance/early admission program.
**Transfer students:** Transfer students accepted for fall term only. In fall 1993, less than 1% of all new students were transfers into all classes. 150 transfer applications were received, 6 were accepted. Application deadline is March 1. Minimum 3.0 GPA required. Lowest course grade accepted is "B." Maximum number of transferable credits is 18 courses. At least 18 courses must be completed at the college to receive degree.
**Admissions contact:** Geoffrey R. Smith, M.Ed., Director of Admissions. 802 388-3711, extension 5153.

**FINANCIAL AID. Available aid:** Pell grants, SEOG, state scholarships and grants, school scholarships and grants, private scholarships and grants, and aid for undergraduate foreign students. Perkins Loans (NDSL), PLUS, Stafford Loans (GSL), school loans, and SLS. Knight Tuition Plans and AMS.
**Financial aid statistics:** In 1993-94, 88% of all undergraduate applicants received aid; 78% of freshman applicants. Average amounts of aid awarded freshmen: Scholarships and grants, $14,088; loans, $2,300.
**Supporting data/closing dates:** FAFSA/FAF: Deadline is January 15. School's own aid application: Deadline is January 15. Income tax forms: Accepted on rolling basis; deadline is January 15. Notification of awards begins in April.
**Financial aid contact:** Bob Donaghey, M.A., Director of Financial Aid. 802 388-3711, extension 5158.

**STUDENT EMPLOYMENT.** College Work/Study Program. Institutional employment. 60% of full-time undergraduates work on campus during school year. Students may expect to earn an average of $700 during school year. Off-campus part-time employment opportunities rated "good."

**COMPUTER FACILITIES.** 150 IBM/IBM-compatible and Macintosh/Apple microcomputers. Students may access Digital, SUN minicomputer/mainframe systems, BITNET, Internet. Residence halls may be equipped with networked microcomputers, modems. Computer languages and software packages include Assembler, BASIC, C, FORTRAN, LISP, Modula 2, Pascal; database, statistical, word processing programs. Computer facilities are available to all students.
**Fees:** Computer fee is included in tuition/fees.
**Hours:** 24 hours.

**PROMINENT ALUMNI/AE.** Ron Brown, secretary of commerce; Frank Sesno, Cable News Network anchor; Claire Gargalli, vice chair, Diversified Search Cos.; Abigail Alling, member of Biosphere II; Jane Bryant Quinn, columnist.

## Norwich University

**Northfield, VT 05663** **802 485-2000**

**1993-94 Costs.** Tuition: $13,460. Room & board: $5,270. Fees, books, misc. academic expenses (school's estimate): $2,250.

**Enrollment.** Undergraduates: 1,352 men, 500 women (full-time). Freshman class: 1,741 applicants, 1,588 accepted, 613 enrolled. Graduate enrollment: 136 men, 233 women.

**Test score averages/ranges.** Average SAT scores: 460 verbal, 500 math. Average ACT scores: 23 composite.

**Faculty.** 100 full-time; 35 part-time. 66% of faculty holds doctoral degree. Student/faculty ratio: 14 to 1.

**Selectivity rating.** Less competitive.

**PROFILE.** Norwich, including the Military College of Vermont and Vermont College, is a private, multipurpose university. Founded in 1819, it adopted coeducation in 1972. The Military College of Vermont, in Northfield, is a coeducational Corps of Cadets organized on a military model. Vermont College, in Montpelier, is a coeducational, undergraduate, nonmilitary college. The two campuses are 12 miles apart and total 1,150 acres.

**Accreditation:** NEASC. Professionally accredited by the Accreditation Board for Engineering and Technology, the Association of Collegiate Business Schools and Programs, the National League for Nursing.
**Religious orientation:** Norwich University is nonsectarian; no religious requirements.
**Library:** Collections totaling over 300,000 volumes, 1,300 periodical subscriptions, and 75,000 microform items.
**Special facilities/museums:** Military museum, language lab.
**Athletic facilities:** Sports center, field house, gymnasium, armory, rifle range, track, aerobics, weight training, and wrestling rooms, swimming pool, hockey arena, basketball, racquetball, squash, and tennis courts, on-campus ski area, climbing wall.

**STUDENT BODY. Undergraduate profile:** 20% are state residents; 6% are transfers. 3% Asian-American, 2% Black, 3% Hispanic, 1% Native American, 91% White. Average age of undergraduates is 19.
**Freshman profile:** 1% of freshmen who took SAT scored 700 or over on verbal, 1% scored 700 or over on math; 7% scored 600 or over on verbal, 11% scored 600 or over on math; 27% scored 500 or over on verbal, 47% scored 500 or over on math; 73% scored 400 or over on verbal, 83% scored 400 or over on math; 98% scored 300 or over on verbal, 98% scored 300 or over on math. 80% of accepted applicants took SAT; 20% took ACT. 65% of freshmen come from public schools.
**Undergraduate achievement:** 75% of fall 1992 freshmen returned for fall 1993 term. 60% of entering class graduated. 20% of students who completed a degree program went on to graduate study within one year.
**Foreign students:** 12 students are from out of the country. Countries represented include Canada, China/Taiwan, Malaysia, Puerto Rico, Russia, and Thailand; 13 in all.

**PROGRAMS OF STUDY. Degrees:** B.A., B.Arch., B.S.
**Majors:** Accounting, Architecture, Biology, Chemistry, Civil Engineering, Communications, Computer Engineering, Computer/Information Sciences, Computer Science/Engineering Technology, Computer Science/Mathematics, Criminal Justice, Economics, Electrical Engineering, Engineering, English, Environmental Engineering Technology, History, International Studies, Marketing/Management, Mathematics, Mechanical Engineering, Medical Technology, Nursing, Physical Education, Physics, Political Science, Psychology, Sports Medicine.
**Distribution of degrees:** The majors with the highest enrollment are engineering, criminal justice, and nursing.
**Requirements:** General education requirement.
**Academic regulations:** Freshmen must maintain minimum 1.45 GPA; sophomores, 1.85 GPA; juniors, 2.0 GPA; seniors, 2.0 GPA.
**Special:** Minors offered in some majors and in business administration, engineering science, finance, human services, and management. Interdepartmental minor in computer science studies. Marine Corps commissioning (Platoon Leader Corps). Students may join Corps of Cadets and live in military environment. Associate's degrees offered. Self-designed majors. Double majors. Dual degrees. Independent study. Accelerated study. Internships. Cooperative education programs. Graduate school at which undergraduates may take graduate-level courses. Preprofessional programs in law, medicine, veterinary science, and dentistry. 2-2 nursing program. Study abroad in England, France, and Germany. ROTC, NROTC, and AFROTC.
**Honors:** Honors program. Honor societies.
**Academic Assistance:** Remedial reading, writing, math, and study skills. Nonremedial tutoring.

**STUDENT LIFE. Housing:** All Corps of Cadet students must live on campus. Coed dorms. 90% of students live in college housing.
**Services and counseling/handicapped student services:** Placement services. Health service. Counseling services for minority, military, veteran, and older students. Personal and psychological counseling. Career and academic guidance services. Religious counseling. Physically disabled student services. Learning disabled services. Tape recorders.
**Campus organizations:** Undergraduate student government. Student newspaper (Guidon, published once/month). Literary magazine. Yearbook. Radio station. Cable television show. Choir, ensembles, orchestra, regimental and stage bands, symphonic band, mountain rescue team, parachute club, Doc Martin club, athletic, departmental, service, and special-interest groups, 45 organizations in all.
**Minority/foreign student organizations:** International Student Organization.

**ATHLETICS. Physical education requirements:** None.
**Intercollegiate competition:** 47% of students participate. Alpine skiing (M,W), baseball (M), basketball (M,W), cross-country (M,W), diving (M,W), football (M), golf (M), ice hockey (M), lacrosse (M), riflery (M,W), soccer (M,W), softball (W), swimming (M,W), tennis (M), track (indoor) (M,W), track (outdoor) (M,W), track and field (indoor) (M,W), track and field (outdoor) (M,W), wrestling (M). Member of Constitution Athletic Conference, Cox Lacrosse League, ECAC, Freedom Football Conference, NCAA Division III, Northeast Women's Athletic Conference.
**Intramural and club sports:** 60% of students participate. Intramural basketball, flag football, frisbee football, hockey, soccer, softball, swimming, track and field. Men's club cheerleading, cycling, fencing, martial arts, rugby, sailing, volleyball, weightlifting. Women's club cheerleading, cycling, fencing, martial arts, rugby, volleyball.

**ADMISSIONS. Academic basis for candidate selection** (in order of priority): Secondary school record, standardized test scores, class rank, school's recommendation, essay.
**Nonacademic basis for candidate selection:** Extracurricular participation and particular talent or ability are emphasized. Character and personality are important. Alumni/ae relationship is considered.
**Requirements:** Graduation from secondary school is required; GED is accepted. 18 units and the following program of study are required: 4 units of English, 3 units of math, 2 units of science, 2 units of foreign language, 2 units of social studies, 1 unit of history, 4 units of academic electives. Trigonometry or pre-calculus required of engineering program applicants. Lab chemistry and physics required of chemistry, engineering, math, and physics program applicants. SAT or ACT is required. ACH recommended. Campus visit and interview recommended. Off-campus interviews available with admissions and alumni representatives.
**Procedure:** Take SAT or ACT by March of 12th year. Visit college for interview by spring of 12th year. Suggest filing application by winter. Notification of admission on rolling basis. Reply is required by May 1. $250 nonrefundable tuition deposit. Freshmen accepted for terms other than fall.
**Special programs:** Admission may be deferred one year. Credit and/or placement may be granted through CEEB Advanced Placement exams for scores of 3 or higher. Credit may be granted through CLEP general and subject exams and through military experience. Placement may be granted through challenge exams. Early decision program. In fall 1992, 50 applied for early decision and 40 were accepted. Deadline for applying for early decision is November 15.
**Transfer students:** Transfer students accepted for terms other than fall. In fall 1992, 6% of all new students were transfers into all classes. 294 transfer applications were received, 260 were accepted. Application deadline is rolling for fall; rolling for spring. Minimum 2.0 GPA required. Lowest course grade accepted is "C-." Maximum number of transferable credits is 60 semester hours. At least 60 semester hours must be completed at the university to receive degree.
**Admissions contact:** Frank Griffis, Director of Admissions and Marketing. 800 468-6679.

**FINANCIAL AID. Available aid:** Pell grants, SEOG, state scholarships and grants, school scholarships and grants, private scholarships, ROTC scholarships, academic merit scholarships, and aid for undergraduate foreign students. Perkins Loans (NDSL), PLUS, Stafford Loans (GSL), school loans, private loans, and SLS. Tuition Plan Inc., Knight Tuition Plans, AMS, and deferred payment plan.
**Financial aid statistics:** 20% of aid is not need-based. In 1993-94, 80% of all undergraduate applicants received aid; 89% of freshman applicants. Average amounts of aid awarded freshmen: Scholarships and grants, $5,600; loans, $3,900.
**Supporting data/closing dates:** FAFSA/FAF/FFS: Priority filing date is March 1; accepted on rolling basis. Notification of awards on rolling basis.
**Financial aid contact:** Karen Waring, M.Ed., Director of Financial Aid. 800 468-6679.

**STUDENT EMPLOYMENT.** College Work/Study Program. Institutional employment. 46% of full-time undergraduates work on campus during school year. Students may expect to earn an average of $1,200 during school year. Off-campus part-time employment opportunities rated "good."

**COMPUTER FACILITIES.** 200 IBM/IBM-compatible and Macintosh/Apple microcomputers. Students may access Digital minicomputer/mainframe systems, BITNET, Internet. Computer languages and software packages include Ada, BASIC, C, FORTRAN, Pascal; 100 in all. Computer facilities are available to all students.
**Fees:** None.
**Hours:** 6 AM-2 AM.

**GRADUATE CAREER DATA.** 20% of graduates choose careers in business and industry. Companies and businesses that hire graduates: DEC, Raytheon, state of Vermont, federal government.

**PROMINENT ALUMNI/AE.** Pierson Mapes, president, NBC Television; Gen. Gordon Sullivan, chief of staff, U.S. Army; Fred Bertrand, chairperson and CEO, National Life Insurance Co. of Vermont; Brig. Gen. Robert F. McDermott, USAF (ret), chairperson and CEO, United Services Automobile Association.

## Saint Michael's College

**Colchester, VT 05439** **802 654-2000**

**1994-95 Costs.** Tuition: $13,030. Room: $3,550. Board: $2,310. Fees, books, misc. academic expenses (school's estimate): $585.

**Enrollment.** Undergraduates: 812 men, 903 women (full-time). Freshman class: 1,910 applicants, 1,380 accepted, 463 enrolled. Graduate enrollment: 220 men, 445 women.

**Test score averages/ranges.** Range of SAT scores of middle 50%: 440-544 verbal, 482-594 math.

**Faculty.** 121 full-time; 53 part-time. 89% of faculty holds highest degree in specific field. Student/faculty ratio: 14 to 1.

**Selectivity rating.** Competitive.

**PROFILE.** Saint Michael's is a church-affiliated college of liberal arts and sciences. Founded in 1904, it adopted coeducation in 1970. Its 400-acre campus is located in Colchester, three miles from Burlington.

**Accreditation:** NEASC.
**Religious orientation:** Saint Michael's College is affiliated with the Roman Catholic Church; two semesters of religion required.
**Library:** Collections totaling over 170,550 volumes, 1,390 periodical subscriptions, and 25,000 microform items.
**Special facilities/museums:** Language lab, observatory.
**Athletic facilities:** Sports center including basketball and volleyball courts, swimming pool, weight room, outdoor tennis courts, cross-country skiing and running trail, playing fields.

**STUDENT BODY. Undergraduate profile:** 16% are state residents; 15% are transfers. 1% Asian-American, 2% Black, 92% White, 5% Other. Average age of undergraduates is 21.
**Freshman profile:** 1% of freshmen who took SAT scored 700 or over on math; 4% scored 600 or over on verbal, 16% scored 600 or over on math; 35% scored 500 or over on verbal, 64% scored 500 or over on math; 100% scored 400 or over on verbal, 100% scored 400 or over on math. 92% of accepted applicants took SAT; 8% took ACT. 67% of freshmen come from public schools.
**Undergraduate achievement:** 87% of fall 1992 freshmen returned for fall 1993 term. 71% of entering class graduated. 14% of students who completed a degree program immediately went on to graduate study.
**Foreign students:** 60 students are from out of the country. Countries represented include Costa Rica, Guatemala, Japan, Panama, Thailand, and Venezuela.

**PROGRAMS OF STUDY. Degrees:** B.A., B.S.
**Majors:** Accounting, American Studies, Art, Biochemistry, Biology, Business Administration, Chemistry, Classics, Computer Science, Drama, Economics, Elementary Education, English Literature, Environmental Science, Fine Arts, French, History, Journalism, Mathematics, Modern Languages, Music, Philosophy, Physics, Political Science, Psychology, Religious Studies, Sociology, Spanish.
**Distribution of degrees:** The majors with the highest enrollment are business administration, psychology, and English literature; classics, chemistry, and biochemistry have the lowest.
**Requirements:** General education requirement.
**Academic regulations:** Freshmen must maintain minimum 1.6 GPA; sophomores, 1.8 GPA; juniors, 2.0 GPA; seniors, 2.0 GPA.
**Special:** Minors offered in most majors. Courses offered in German, humanities, Italian, and speech. English as a Second Language program. Self-designed majors. Double majors. Independent study. Internships. Preprofessional programs in law, medicine, dentistry, and optometry. 3-2 engineering program with Clarkson U and U of Vermont. Five-year B.S./M.B.A. program with Clarkson U. Washington Semester and Sea Semester. Exchange program with Xavier U. Teacher certification in elementary and secondary education. Certification in specific subject areas. Member of the Northeast Consortium for Study Abroad. Exchange programs abroad in England (Bath Coll of Higher Education) and Japan (Kansai Gaidai U). Study abroad also in Australia, Austria, Egypt, France, Greece, Ireland, Kenya, Nepal, the Netherlands, Norway, Spain, and Zimbabwe. ROTC at U of Vermont. AFROTC at Norwich U.
**Honors:** Honors program. Honor societies.
**Academic Assistance:** Remedial study skills. Nonremedial tutoring.

**STUDENT LIFE. Housing:** All unmarried students under age 21 must live on campus unless living near campus with relatives. Coed, women's, and men's dorms. School-owned/operated apartments. 90% of students live in college housing.
**Services and counseling/handicapped student services:** Placement services. Health service. Day care. Counseling services for minority students. Personal counseling. Career and academic guidance services. Religious counseling. Physically disabled student services. Learning disabled services.
**Campus organizations:** Undergraduate student government. Student newspaper (Defender, published once/week). Literary magazine. Yearbook. Radio station. Choir, wind and jazz ensembles, liturgical folk group, drama group, Big Brothers/Big Sisters, Student Center Governing Board, rathskeller, outing club, Volunteer Ambulance and Fire Squad, Knights of Columbus, Amnesty International, environmental/recycling groups, professional and special-interest groups, 36 organizations in all.
**Religious organizations:** Campus Ministry, Mobilization of Volunteer Efforts, LEAP.
**Minority/foreign student organizations:** Diversity Coalition, Martin Luther King Society.

**ATHLETICS. Physical education requirements:** None.
**Intercollegiate competition:** 5% of students participate. Baseball (M), basketball (M,W), cross-country (M,W), field hockey (W), golf (M), ice hockey (M), lacrosse (M,W), skiing (M,W), soccer (M,W), softball (W), swimming (M,W), tennis (M,W), volleyball (W). Member of ECAC, Mideast Conference, NCAA Division II, NECAC, Northeast 10.
**Intramural and club sports:** 2% of students participate. Intramural basketball, cross-country, poly-hockey, soccer, softball, swimming, tennis, track and field, ultimate frisbee, volleyball.

**ADMISSIONS. Academic basis for candidate selection** (in order of priority): Secondary school record, class rank, school's recommendation, standardized test scores, essay.
**Nonacademic basis for candidate selection:** Character and personality, extracurricular participation, particular talent or ability, geographical distribution, and alumni/ae relationship are considered.
**Requirements:** Graduation from secondary school is required; GED is accepted. 16 units and the following program of study are required: 4 units of English, 3 units of math, 3 units of science including 2 units of lab, 2 units of foreign language, 2 units of social studies, 2 units of history. Minimum combined SAT score of 960, rank in top third of secondary school class, and minimum 3.0 GPA recommended. Physics recommended of science program applicants. SAT is required; ACT may be substituted. Campus visit and interview recommended. Off-campus interviews available with an alumni representative.
**Procedure:** Take SAT or ACT by February 15 of 12th year. Visit college for interview by February 15 of 12th year. Suggest filing application by November 15. Application deadline is February 15. Notification of admission by April 2. Reply is required by May 1. $300 tuition deposit, refundable before May 1. $300 nonrefundable tuition/room deposit. Freshmen accepted for terms other than fall.
**Special programs:** Admission may be deferred one year. Credit and/or placement may be granted through CEEB Advanced Placement exams for scores of 4 or higher. Credit and/or placement may be granted through CLEP general and subject exams. Early decision program. Deadline for applying for early decision is November 15. Concurrent enrollment program.
**Transfer students:** Transfer students accepted for terms other than fall. In fall 1993, 15% of all new students were transfers into all classes. 156 transfer applications were received, 107 were accepted. Application deadline is February 15 for fall; November 1 for spring. Minimum 3.0 GPA recommended. Lowest course grade accepted is "C-." At least 30 semester hours must be completed at the college to receive degree.
**Admissions contact:** Jerry E. Flanagan, M.Ed., Dean of Admissions. 802 654-3000, 800 762-8000.

**FINANCIAL AID. Available aid:** Pell grants, SEOG, state scholarships and grants, school scholarships and grants, private scholarships and grants, academic merit scholarships, athletic scholarships, and aid for undergraduate foreign students. Perkins Loans (NDSL), PLUS, Stafford Loans (GSL), and SLS. Tuition Plan Inc., Knight Tuition Plans, AMS, and family tuition reduction.
**Financial aid statistics:** 13% of aid is not need-based. In 1993-94, 97% of all undergraduate applicants received aid; 97% of freshman applicants. Average amounts of aid awarded freshmen: Scholarships and grants, $7,500; loans, $3,300.
**Supporting data/closing dates:** FAFSA: Priority filing date is March 15. School's own aid application: Priority filing date is March 15. Income tax forms: Priority filing date is March 15. Notification of awards on rolling basis.
**Financial aid contact:** Nelberta Lunde, M.S.A., Director of Financial Aid. 802 654-2379.

**STUDENT EMPLOYMENT.** College Work/Study Program. Institutional employment. 40% of full-time undergraduates work on campus during school year. Students may expect to earn an average of $1,000 during school year. Off-campus part-time employment opportunities rated "good."

**COMPUTER FACILITIES.** 175 IBM/IBM-compatible microcomputers; all are networked. Students may access Digital minicomputer/mainframe systems, BITNET. Computer languages and software packages include Ada, BASIC, C, COBOL, Harvard Graphics, INGRES, Lotus 1-2-3, Paradox, Pascal, Quattro Pro, SPSS-X, WordPerfect; 15 in all. Computer facilities are available to all students.
**Fees:** None.
**Hours:** 8 AM-11 PM.

**GRADUATE CAREER DATA.** Graduate school percentages: 7% enter law school. 2% enter medical school. 1% enter graduate business programs. 12% enter graduate arts and sciences programs. Highest graduate school enrollments: Babson Coll, Boston Coll, Clarkson U, George Washington U Law Sch, Suffolk U Law Sch, U of Vermont. 30% of graduates choose careers in business and industry. Companies and businesses that hire graduates: accounting firms, hotels, financial industry, schools, social service agencies.

**PROMINENT ALUMNI/AE.** Patrick Leahy, U.S. senator; Robert White, former ambassador to El Salvador; Tom Freston, president and CEO, MTV; Moses Anderson, S.S.E., auxilliary bishop of Detroit.

# Southern Vermont College

**Bennington, VT 05201** **802 442-5427**

**1994-95 Costs.** Tuition: $8,940. Room & board: $4,514. Fees, books, misc. academic expenses (school's estimate): $730.
**Enrollment.** Undergraduates: 222 men, 196 women (full-time). Freshman class: 520 applicants, 204 accepted, 186 enrolled.
**Test score averages/ranges.** Average SAT scores: 409 verbal, 394 math.
**Faculty.** 25 full-time; 33 part-time. 19% of faculty holds doctoral degree. Student/faculty ratio: 18 to 1.
**Selectivity rating.** Competitive.

**PROFILE.** Southern Vermont, founded in 1926, is a private, liberal arts college. Its 371-acre campus is located in Bennington, 40 miles from Albany, N.Y. The main campus building is in the style of a 14th–century English-Norman manor house.

**Accreditation:** NEASC.
**Religious orientation:** Southern Vermont College is nonsectarian; no religious requirements.
**Library:** Collections totaling over 25,000 volumes, 287 periodical subscriptions and 3 microform items.
**Athletic facilities:** Gymnasium, weight room, basketball, tennis, and volleyball courts, aerobics room, baseball, soccer, and softball fields, batting cage.

**STUDENT BODY. Undergraduate profile:** 45% are state residents; 23% are transfers. 1% Asian-American, 1% Black, 1% Hispanic, 96% White, 1% Other. Average age of undergraduates is 20.
**Freshman profile:** Majority of accepted applicants took SAT. 85% of freshmen come from public schools.
**Undergraduate achievement:** 64% of fall 1992 freshmen returned for fall 1993 term. 14% of entering class graduated. 8% of students who completed a degree program immediately went on to graduate study.
**Foreign students:** Two students are from out of the country. Countries represented include Japan.

**PROGRAMS OF STUDY. Degrees:** B.A., B.S.
**Majors:** Accounting, Business Management, Child Care Management, Communications, Criminal Justice, English, Environmental Studies, Gerontology Management, Liberal Arts, Liberal Arts Management, Nursing, Private Security, Social Work.
**Distribution of degrees:** The majors with the highest enrollment are business management, criminal justice, and environmental studies.
**Requirements:** General education requirement.

**Academic regulations:** Freshmen must maintain minimum 1.75 GPA; sophomores, juniors, seniors, 2.0 GPA.
**Special:** Minors offered in most majors and in human services. Students are encouraged to combine classroom theory with practical work positions. Credit granted for television courses presented in association with Public Broadcasting Service and National University Consortium. Associate's degrees offered. Self-designed majors. Double majors. Dual degrees. Independent study. Internships. Cooperative education programs. Preprofessional programs in law. Study abroad in England (Oxford U).
**Honors:** Honors program.
**Academic Assistance:** Remedial reading, writing, math, and study skills. Nonremedial tutoring.
**ADMISSIONS. Academic basis for candidate selection** (in order of priority): Secondary school record, class rank, school's recommendation, essay.
**Nonacademic basis for candidate selection:** Character and personality, extracurricular participation, and geographical distribution are considered.
**Requirements:** Graduation from secondary school is required; GED is accepted. No specific distribution of secondary school units required. R.N. required of nursing program applicants. Conditional admission possible for applicants not meeting standard requirements. SAT or ACT is recommended. Campus visit and interview recommended. No off-campus interviews.
**Procedure:** Take SAT or ACT by January of 12th year. Visit college for interview by April 1 of 12th year. Notification of admission on rolling basis. Reply is required prior to beginning of semester. $100 tuition deposit, refundable until May 1. $200 room deposit, refundable until May 1. Freshmen accepted for terms other than fall.
**Special programs:** Admission may be deferred. Credit may be granted through CEEB Advanced Placement exams, CLEP general and subject exams, Regents College, ACT PEP, DANTES, and challenge exams, and military and life experience. Early entrance/early admission program. Concurrent enrollment program.
**Transfer students:** Transfer students accepted for terms other than fall. In fall 1993, 23% of all new students were transfers into all classes. 81 transfer applications were received, 72 were accepted. Application deadline is rolling for fall; rolling for spring. Minimum 2.0 GPA recommended. Lowest course grade accepted is "C." Maximum number of transferable credits is 45 semester hours from a two-year school and 90 semester hours from a four-year school. At least 30 semester hours must be completed at the college to receive degree.
**Admissions contact:** Mary G. Van Arsdale, M.A., Director of Admissions. 802 442-3171, extension 138.
**FINANCIAL AID. Available aid:** Pell grants, SEOG, state scholarships and grants, school scholarships and grants, and private scholarships and grants. PLUS, Stafford Loans (GSL), state loans, and SLS. Deferred payment plan. Four-month and 10-month installment plans.
**Financial aid statistics:** In 1993-94, 98% of all undergraduate applicants received aid; 98% of freshman applicants. Average amounts of aid awarded freshmen: Scholarships and grants, $3,545; loans, $2,715.
**Supporting data/closing dates:** FAFSA: Priority filing date is May 1. FAF: Priority filing date is May 1; accepted on rolling basis. Notification of awards on rolling basis.
**Financial aid contact:** Cathleen Seaton, Director of Financial Aid. 802 442-5427, extension 233.

# Trinity College

**Burlington, VT 05401 — 802 658-0337**

**1993-94 Costs.** Tuition: $10,470. Room: $2,946. Board: $2,124. Fees, books, misc. academic expenses (school's estimate): $802.
**Enrollment.** Undergraduates: 42 men, 453 women (full-time). Freshman class: 222 applicants, 201 accepted, 91 enrolled. Graduate enrollment: 12 men, 62 women.
**Test score averages/ranges.** Average SAT scores: 410 verbal, 420 math.
**Faculty.** 49 full-time; 82 part-time. 79% of faculty holds highest degree in specific field. Student/faculty ratio: 12 to 1.
**Selectivity rating.** Less competitive.

**PROFILE.** Trinity, founded in 1925, is a private, church-affiliated, arts and sciences college for women; qualified men admitted to the continuing education and Weekend College programs. Its 17-acre campus is located in Burlington, 90 miles from Montreal.

**Accreditation:** NEASC. Professionally accredited by the Council on Social Work Education.
**Religious orientation:** Trinity College is affiliated with the Roman Catholic Church (Sisters of Mercy); one semester of religion required.
**Library:** Collections totaling over 60,000 volumes, 366 periodical subscriptions, and 43,000 microform items.
**Athletic facilities:** Gymnasium, fitness center, aerobics room, weight room, tennis court.
**STUDENT BODY. Undergraduate profile:** 86% are state residents; 22% are transfers. 1% Asian-American, 1% Black, 1% Hispanic, 1% Native American, 96% White. Average age of undergraduates is 20.
**Freshman profile:** 1% of freshmen who took SAT scored 700 or over on math; 2% scored 600 or over on verbal, 3% scored 600 or over on math; 12% scored 500 or over on verbal, 21% scored 500 or over on math; 54% scored 400 or over on verbal, 64% scored 400 or over on math; 93% scored 300 or over on verbal, 91% scored 300 or over on math. 100% of accepted applicants took SAT. 92% of freshmen come from public schools.
**Undergraduate achievement:** 70% of fall 1992 freshmen returned for fall 1993 term. 68% of entering class graduated. 10% of students who completed a degree program went on to graduate study within one year.
**PROGRAMS OF STUDY. Degrees:** B.A., B.S.
**Majors:** Accounting, Biology, Business Administration, Chemistry, Communication, Comparative Cultural Studies, Early Childhood Education, Economics, Elementary Education, English, Environmental Science, French, History, Human Services, Mathematics, Medical Technology/Cytotechnology, Modern Languages, Philosophy, Psychology, Science/Math Elementary Education, Secondary Education, Social Work, Sociology/Criminal Justice, Spanish, Special Education, Special Studies, Teacher Licensure/Secondary Education.
**Distribution of degrees:** The majors with the highest enrollment are education, psychology, and business administration.
**Requirements:** General education requirement.
**Academic regulations:** Freshmen must maintain minimum 1.8 GPA; sophomores, 1.8 GPA; juniors, 2.0 GPA; seniors, 2.0 GPA.
**Special:** Minors offered in some majors and in art, computer programming, computer science, fine arts, gerontology, humanities/English, humanities/history, human resource development, music, and religious studies. Courses offered in geography and physics. Certificate programs in accounting, gerontology, human services, management, and small business administration. Associate's degrees offered. Self-designed majors. Double majors. Independent study. Pass/fail grading option. Internships. Preprofessional programs in law, medicine, veterinary science, and dentistry. 3-1 medical technology program with an approved hospital. Member of Consortium of Vermont Colleges. Teacher certification in early childhood, elementary, secondary, and special education. Certification in specific subject areas. Study abroad in England and in other European countries. ROTC at U of Vermont. AFROTC at St. Michael's Coll.
**Honors:** Honors program.
**Academic Assistance:** Remedial writing, math, and study skills.
**ADMISSIONS. Academic basis for candidate selection** (in order of priority): Secondary school record, standardized test scores, class rank, essay, school's recommendation.
**Nonacademic basis for candidate selection:** Character and personality, extracurricular participation, and particular talent or ability are important. Geographical distribution and alumni/ae relationship are considered.
**Requirements:** Graduation from secondary school is required; GED is accepted. 14 units and the following program of study are recommended: 4 units of English, 2 units of math, 2 units of science, 2 units of foreign language, 2 units of social studies, 2 units of history. Minimum 2.0 GPA required. Conditional admission possible for applicants not meeting standard requirements. SAT or ACT is required. Campus visit and interview recommended. No off-campus interviews.
**Procedure:** Take SAT or ACT by fall of 12th year. Visit college for interview by spring of 12th year. Notification of admission on rolling basis. $100 nonrefundable tuition deposit. $100 nonrefundable room deposit. Freshmen accepted for terms other than fall.
**Special programs:** Admission may be deferred one year. Credit and/or placement may be granted through CEEB Advanced Placement exams for scores of 3 or higher. Credit may be granted through CLEP general and subject exams, ACT PEP and DANTES exams, and military and life experience. Placement may be granted through challenge exams. Early entrance/early admission program.
**Transfer students:** Transfer students accepted for terms other than fall. In fall 1993, 22% of all new students were transfers into all classes. 45 transfer applications were received, 36 were accepted. Application deadline is August for fall; December for spring. Minimum 2.0 GPA required. Lowest course grade accepted is "C-." Maximum number of transferable credits is 64 semester hours from a two-year school and 90 semester hours from a four-year school. At least 30 semester hours must be completed at the college to receive degree.
**Admissions contact:** Pamela A. Chisolm, M.Ed., Director of Admissions and Financial Aid. 802 658-0337, extension 218.
**FINANCIAL AID. Available aid:** Pell grants, SEOG, school scholarships and grants, and academic merit scholarships. Perkins Loans (NDSL), PLUS, Stafford Loans (GSL), school loans, and SLS. Tuition Plan Inc., AMS, and Tuition Management Systems.
**Financial aid statistics:** 4% of aid is not need-based. In 1993-94, 82% of all undergraduate applicants received aid; 86% of freshman applicants. Average amounts of aid awarded freshmen: Scholarships and grants, $5,200; loans, $3,125.
**Supporting data/closing dates:** FAFSA/FFS: Priority filing date is March 1. Income tax forms: Priority filing date is March 1. Institutional application: Priority filing date is March 1. Notification of awards begins April 1.
**Financial aid contact:** Pamela Chisholm, M.Ed., Director of Financial Aid and Admissions. 802 658-0337, extension 529.

# University of Vermont

**Burlington, VT 05405-3596 — 802 656-3480**

**1993-94 Costs.** Tuition: $5,970 (state residents), $14,914 (out-of-state). Room: $2,868. Board: $1,868. Fees, books, misc. academic expenses (school's estimate): $965.
**Enrollment.** Undergraduates: 3,433 men, 3,822 women (full-time). Freshman class: 7,663 applicants, 6,008 accepted, 1,779 enrolled. Graduate enrollment: 545 men, 670 women.
**Test score averages/ranges.** Average SAT scores: 480 verbal, 550 math. Range of SAT scores of middle 50%: 440-500 verbal, 540-610 math.
**Faculty.** 864 full-time; 150 part-time. 87% of faculty holds highest degree in specific field. Student/faculty ratio: 15 to 1.
**Selectivity rating.** Competitive.

**PROFILE.** The University of Vermont, founded in 1791, is a public, comprehensive institution. Programs are offered through the Colleges of Agriculture and Life Sciences, Arts and Sciences, Education and Social Services, and Engineering and Mathematics; the Schools of Business Administration, Allied Health Sciences, Natural Resources, and Nursing; the Environmental Studies Program; and the Home Economics Program. Its 715-acre campus is located Burlington, 100 miles south of Montreal.

**Accreditation:** NEASC. Professionally accredited by the American Assembly of Collegiate Schools of Business, the American Dietetic Association, the American Home Economics Association, the American Medical Association (CAHEA), the American Physical Therapy Association, the American Psychological Association, the Council on Social

Work Education, the National Association of Schools of Music, the National Council for Accreditation of Teacher Education, the National League for Nursing.
**Religious orientation:** University of Vermont is nonsectarian; no religious requirements.
**Library:** Collections totaling over 1,260,804 volumes, 10,318 periodical subscriptions, and 1,219,804 microform items.
**Special facilities/museums:** Art and ethnography museum, chemistry/physics library, medical library, on-campus preschool, government research and world affairs centers, agricultural experiment station, horse farm, multinuclear magnetic resonance spectrometers, mass spectrometer.
**Athletic facilities:** Gymnasiums, basketball, racquetball, squash, tennis, and volleyball courts, dance studio, tracks, gymnastics and weight rooms, baseball, soccer, and softball fields, ice rink, field house, swimming pool, golf course, baseball and soccer stadiums.

**STUDENT BODY. Undergraduate profile:** 44% are state residents; 2% are transfers. 2% Asian-American, 1% Black, 1% Hispanic, 95% White, 1% Other. Average age of undergraduates is 21.
**Freshman profile:** 1% of freshmen who took SAT scored 700 or over on verbal, 3% scored 700 or over on math; 9% scored 600 or over on verbal, 31% scored 600 or over on math; 46% scored 500 or over on verbal, 76% scored 500 or over on math; 88% scored 400 or over on verbal, 91% scored 400 or over on math; 95% scored 300 or over on verbal, 94% scored 300 or over on math. 99% of accepted applicants took SAT; 1% took ACT. 70% of freshmen come from public schools.
**Undergraduate achievement:** 84% of fall 1992 freshmen returned for fall 1993 term. 60% of entering class graduated.
**Foreign students:** 192 students are from out of the country. Countries represented include Canada, China, India, Japan, Norway, and the United Kingdom; 45 in all.

**PROGRAMS OF STUDY. Degrees:** B.A., B.Mus., B.S.
**Majors:** Agricultural Economics, Agriculture/Life Sciences, Animal Science, Anthropology, Apparel/Textile Design, Art Education, Art History, Arts/Sciences, Asian Area Studies, Biochemical Science, Biological Science, Biology, Botany, Business Administration, Canadian Area Studies, Chemistry, Civil Engineering, Communication Sciences/Disorders, Community Forestry/Horticulture, Computer Science, Consumer Studies, Dairy Foods, Dietetics, Early Childhood/Pre-School Programs, Economics, Education, Education/Social Services, Electrical Engineering, Elementary Education, Elementary Education/Reading, Engineering, Engineering Management, English, European Area Studies, Fashion Merchandising, Forestry, French, Geography, Geology, German, Greek, History, Home Economics Education, Human Development Education, Human Development/Family Studies, Latin, Latin American Studies, Management Engineering, Mathematics, Mechanical Engineering, Medical Technology, Merchandising, Consumer Studies/Design, Microbiology, Music, Music Education, Natural Resources, Nutritional Science, Occupational/Extension Education, Philosophy, Physical Education, Physical Therapy, Physics, Plant/Soil Science, Political Science, Professional Nursing, Psychology, Recreation Management, Religion, Resource Economics, Russian, Russian/East European Studies, Secondary Education, Secondary Education/English, Secondary Education/Language, Secondary Education/Mathematics, Secondary Education/Science, Secondary Education/Social Science, Social Work, Sociology, Spanish, Statistics, Studio Art, Theatre, Urban Forestry/Landscape Horticulture, Wildlife/Fisheries Biology, Zoology.
**Distribution of degrees:** The majors with the highest enrollment are business administration, political science, and psychology.
**Academic regulations:** Freshmen must maintain minimum 1.67 GPA; sophomores, juniors, seniors, 2.0 GPA.
**Special:** Minors required only within the College of Arts and Sciences. Professional nursing major includes two-year and four-year programs. Associate's degrees offered. Self-designed majors. Double majors. Independent study. Internships. Cooperative education programs. Graduate school at which undergraduates may take graduate-level courses. Preprofessional programs in law, medicine, veterinary science, and dentistry. Member of Consortium of Vermont Colleges. Washington Semester and Sea Semester. Exchange program with Lincoln U. Teacher certification in early childhood, elementary, secondary, and vo-tech education. Certification in specific subject areas. Member of International Student Exchange Program (ISEP). Study abroad in Austria, Denmark, England, Finland, France, Italy, Japan, Norway, Sweden, and Russia. ROTC. AFROTC at St. Michael's Coll.
**Honors:** Phi Beta Kappa. Honors program. Honor societies.
**Academic Assistance:** Remedial reading, writing, math, and study skills. Nonremedial tutoring.

**STUDENT LIFE. Housing:** All freshmen and sophomores must live on campus. Coed dorms. 46% of students live in college housing.
**Social atmosphere:** The student newspaper reports "Some things have changed since the Vermont drinking age increased, but they have not changed as much as some would think." Popular campus events include the Red Square Affair, Oktoberfest, Winter Ball, and the NCAA hockey finals. The hockey team as well as the Student Association are among the most influential groups on campus. Favorite student gathering spots are the library, Billings Center, and numerous downtown bars.
**Services and counseling/handicapped student services:** Placement services. Health service. Day care. Counseling services for minority students. Birth control, personal, and psychological counseling. Career and academic guidance services. Physically disabled student services. Learning disabled services. Notetaking services. Tape recorders. Tutors. Reader services for the blind.
**Campus organizations:** Undergraduate student government. Student newspaper (Cynic, published once/week). Literary magazine. Yearbook. Radio station. Choir, orchestra, band, debating, drama groups, various athletic and outing clubs, environmental group, Volunteers in Action, BACCHUS, Disabled Student Union, Amnesty International, College Democrats, College Republicans, programming board, academic groups, 100 organizations in all. 14 fraternities, all with chapter houses; six sororities, all with chapter houses. 16% of men join a fraternity. 14% of women join a sorority.
**Religious organizations:** B'nai B'rith Hillel Foundation, Newman Center, Cooperative Christian Ministry, Ecumenical Center, Intervaristy Christian Fellowship, Campus Crusade for Christ, Bahai Club.
**Minority/foreign student organizations:** Allianza Latino, Asian-American Student Union, Black Student Union, Native American Student Union. International Club, Asian Cultural Exchange.

**ATHLETICS. Physical education requirements:** Two semesters of physical education required.
**Intercollegiate competition:** 10% of students participate. Alpine skiing (M,W), baseball (M), basketball (M,W), cross-country (M,W), diving (M,W), field hockey (W), golf (M), gymnastics (M,W), ice hockey (M), lacrosse (M,W), Nordic skiing (M,W), soccer (M,W), softball (W), swimming (M,W), tennis (M,W), track (indoor) (M,W), track (outdoor) (M,W), track and field (indoor) (M,W), track and field (outdoor) (M,W), volleyball (W). Member of ECAC, NCAA Division I, North Atlantic Conference.
**Intramural and club sports:** 70% of students participate. Intramural basketball, broomball, floor hockey, flag football, golf, ice hockey, racquetball, soccer, softball, squash, table tennis, tennis, triathlon, volleyball. Men's club cheerleading, crew, cycling, gymnastics, judo, karate, rugby, tae kwon do, ultimate frisbee, volleyball, wrestling. Women's club cheerleading, crew, cycling, figure skating, gymnastics, ice hockey, judo, karate, rugby, tae kwon do, ultimate frisbee.

**ADMISSIONS. Academic basis for candidate selection** (in order of priority): Secondary school record, class rank, standardized test scores, school's recommendation, essay.
**Nonacademic basis for candidate selection:** Alumni/ae relationship is important. Extracurricular participation, particular talent or ability, and geographical distribution are considered.
**Requirements:** Graduation from secondary school is required; GED is accepted. 16 units and the following program of study are required: 4 units of English, 3 units of math, 2 units of science including 1 unit of lab, 2 units of foreign language, 3 units of social studies. Additional electives strongly recommended; nonacademic electives may be counted. Qualified in-state applicants accepted first; out-of-state applicants then accepted on competitive basis. Trigonometry required of business, engineering, mathematics, and science program applicants; biology, chemistry, and physics required of physical therapy program applicants; physics and chemistry required of engineering and math program applicants; chemistry and biology required of professional nursing program applicants. Auditions required of music performance program applicants. SAT is required; ACT may be substituted. Campus visit and interview recommended. Off-campus interviews available with an alumni representative.
**Procedure:** Take SAT or ACT by December of 12th year. Application deadline is February 1. Acceptance notification on rolling basis for in-state applicants; by March 15 for out-of-state applicants. Reply is required by May 1. $225 tuition deposit, partially refundable until the first day of classes. $225 tuition deposit, $100 of which may be refunded in some cases. Freshmen accepted for terms other than fall.
**Special programs:** Admission may be deferred one year. Credit may be granted through CEEB Advanced Placement. Credit may be granted through CLEP general exams. Credit and/or placement may be granted through CLEP subject exams. Early decision program. Deadline for applying for early decision is November 1. Early entrance/early admission program.
**Transfer students:** Transfer students accepted for terms other than fall. In fall 1993, 2% of all new students were transfers into all classes. 959 transfer applications were received, 540 were accepted. Application deadline is April 1 for fall; November 1 for spring. Minimum 2.5 GPA recommended. Lowest course grade accepted is "C." Maximum number of transferable credits is 90 semester hours. At least 30 semester hours must be completed at the university to receive degree.
**Admissions contact:** Carol Cotman Hogan, Director of Admissions. 802 656-3370.

**FINANCIAL AID. Available aid:** Pell grants, SEOG, state grants, school scholarships and grants, private scholarships and grants, ROTC scholarships, academic merit scholarships, and athletic scholarships. Perkins Loans (NDSL), PLUS, Stafford Loans (GSL), NSL, Health Professions Loans, state loans, school loans, private loans, and SLS. Tuition Plan Inc., Knight Tuition Plans, and deferred payment plan.
**Financial aid statistics:** In 1993-94, 87% of all undergraduate applicants received aid; 75% of freshman applicants. Average amounts of aid awarded freshmen: Scholarships and grants, $3,400; loans, $3,700.
**Supporting data/closing dates:** FAFSA: Priority filing date is March 1. Income tax forms: Accepted on rolling basis. Notification of awards begins March 15.
**Financial aid contact:** Donald Honeman, M.Ed., Director of Financial Aid. 802 656-3156.

**STUDENT EMPLOYMENT.** College Work/Study Program. Institutional employment. Off-campus part-time employment opportunities rated "good."

**COMPUTER FACILITIES.** 115 IBM/IBM-compatible and Macintosh/Apple microcomputers. Students may access Digital, IBM minicomputer/mainframe systems, Internet. Residence halls may be equipped with stand-alone microcomputers. Computer languages and software packages include DW 4, Microsoft Word, Windows, WordPerfect. Computer facilities are available to all students.
**Fees:** None.
**Hours:** 24 hours for some; 8-12 hours/day for others.

**GRADUATE CAREER DATA.** Companies and businesses that hire graduates: Fortune 500 companies.

# Virginia

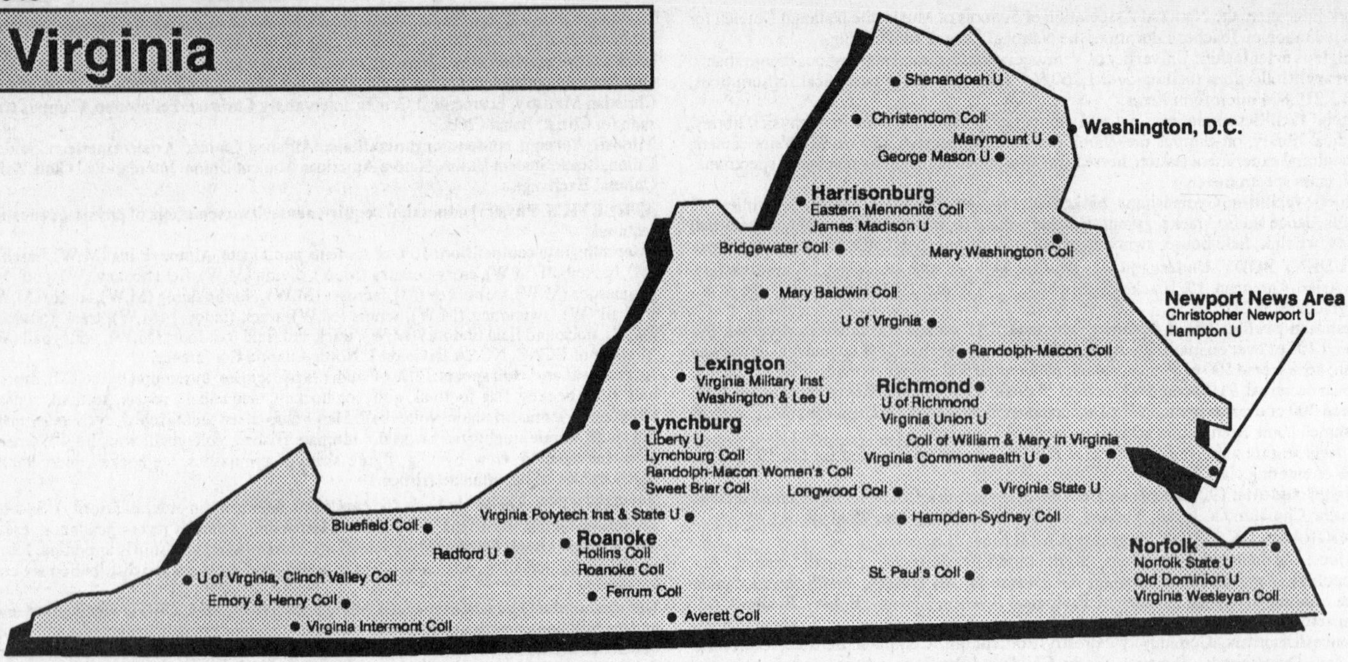


# Averett College

**Danville, VA 24541** **804 791-5600**

**1994-95 Costs.** Tuition: $9,925. Room & board: $4,135. Fees, books, misc. academic expenses (school's estimate): $650.
**Enrollment.** Undergraduates: 334 men, 443 women (full-time). Freshman class: 851 applicants, 745 accepted, 295 enrolled. Graduate enrollment: 446 men, 213 women.
**Test score averages/ranges.** Average SAT scores: 424 verbal, 469 math. Range of SAT scores of middle 50%: 400-450 verbal, 450-500 math.
**Faculty.** 55 full-time; 2 part-time. 70% of faculty holds doctoral degree. Student/faculty ratio: 12 to 1.
**Selectivity rating.** Less competitive.

**PROFILE.** Averett is a church-affiliated college. Founded in 1859 as the Union Female College, it adopted coeducation and began offering bachelor's degrees in 1969. Its 25-acre campus is located in Danville, 45 miles from Greensboro, NC.

**Accreditation:** SACS.
**Religious orientation:** Averett College is affiliated with the Baptist Church; one semester of religion required.
**Library:** Collections totaling over 126,450 volumes, 417 periodical subscriptions, and 29,130 microform items.
**Athletic facilities:** Gymnasium, tennis courts, equestrian center, soccer field, nearby community baseball, softball, and swimming facilities.
**STUDENT BODY. Undergraduate profile:** 76% are state residents; 45% are transfers. 5% Asian-American, 12% Black, 1% Hispanic, 1% Native American, 81% White.
**Freshman profile:** 2% of freshmen who took SAT scored 700 or over on verbal, 2% scored 700 or over on math; 8% scored 600 or over on verbal, 10% scored 600 or over on math; 29% scored 500 or over on verbal, 43% scored 500 or over on math; 68% scored 400 or over on verbal, 79% scored 400 or over on math; 96% scored 300 or over on verbal, 98% scored 300 or over on math. Majority of accepted applicants took SAT. 85% of freshmen come from public schools.
**Undergraduate achievement:** 60% of fall 1992 freshmen returned for fall 1993 term. 33% of entering class graduated. 30% of students who completed a degree program went on to graduate study within five years.
**Foreign students:** 90 students are from out of the country. Countries represented include the Bahamas, Finland, Korea, Middle Eastern countries, South American countries, and Sweden; 13 in all.

**PROGRAMS OF STUDY. Degrees:** B.A., B.Appl.Sci., B.Bus.Admin., B.S.
**Majors:** Accounting, Art, Aviation, Biology, Biology/Chemistry, Business Administration, Business Administration/Equestrian Studies, Chemistry, Church Ministries, Church Ministries/Music, Computer Science, Criminal Justice, Elementary Education, English, English/Drama/Speech, Environmental Science, Equestrian Studies, Finance, History, Journalism/Communications/English, Management/Psychology/Management Science, Marketing, Mathematics, Mathematics/Management, Medical Technology, Music, Physical Education, Political Science, Psychology, Radiologic Technology, Reading Education, Religion, Social Sciences, Sociology, Sports Management, Theatre Arts/Speech, Wellness/Sports Medicine.
**Distribution of degrees:** The majors with the highest enrollment are business administration, education, and aviation; art, theater arts, and music have the lowest.
**Requirements:** General education requirement.
**Academic regulations:** Freshmen must maintain minimum 1.8 GPA; sophomores, juniors, seniors, 2.0 GPA.
**Special:** Minors offered in most majors and in international affairs. Associate's degrees offered. Self-designed majors. Double majors. Independent study. Accelerated study. Pass/fail grading option. Internships. Cooperative education programs. Graduate school at which undergraduates may take graduate-level courses. Preprofessional programs in law, medicine, pharmacy, dentistry, and theology. Teacher certification in early childhood, elementary, and secondary education. Certification in specific subject areas. Study abroad in China, England (semester for horsemanship), and other western European countries.
**Honors:** Honors program. Honor societies.
**Academic Assistance:** Nonremedial tutoring.

**ADMISSIONS. Academic basis for candidate selection** (in order of priority): Secondary school record, class rank, standardized test scores, school's recommendation.
**Nonacademic basis for candidate selection:** Character and personality and particular talent or ability are important. Extracurricular participation is considered.
**Requirements:** Graduation from secondary school is required; GED is accepted. 17 units and the following program of study are recommended: 4 units of English, 3 units of math, 2 units of science including 1 unit of lab, 3 units of social studies, 2 units of history, 3 units of electives. Minimum combined SAT score of 800, rank in top three-fifths of secondary school class, and minimum 2.0 GPA recommended. Riding placement test required of equestrian studies program applicants. Aviation program applicants must pass a class II physical exam. Special admission programs for applicants not normally admissible and for older students. SAT is required; ACT may be substituted. Campus visit and interview recommended. No off-campus interviews.
**Procedure:** Take SAT or ACT by December of 12th year. Visit college for interview by April of 12th year. Suggest filing application by April 1. Application deadline is August 15. Notification of admission on rolling basis. Reply is required within three weeks of notification. $25 tuition deposit, refundable until May 1. $250 room deposit, refundable until May 1. Freshmen accepted for terms other than fall.
**Special programs:** Admission may be deferred two years. Placement may be granted through CEEB Advanced Placement exams for scores of 3 or higher. Credit and/or placement may be granted through CLEP general and subject exams. Credit may be granted through challenge exams and life experience. Early entrance/early admission program.
**Transfer students:** Transfer students accepted for terms other than fall. In fall 1993, 45% of all new students were transfers into all classes. 252 transfer applications were received, 213 were accepted. Application deadline is July 15 for fall; December 15 for spring. Minimum 2.0 GPA required. Lowest course grade accepted is "C." At least 30 semester hours must be completed at the college to receive degree.
**Admissions contact:** Gary Sherman, Dean of Enrollment Management. 804 791-5660, 800 AVE-RETT.

**FINANCIAL AID. Available aid:** Pell grants, SEOG, state scholarships and grants, school scholarships and grants, private scholarships and grants, academic merit scholarships, and aid for undergraduate foreign students. Perkins Loans (NDSL), PLUS, Stafford Loans (GSL), private loans, and SLS. Tuition Plan Inc., Knight Tuition Plans, AMS, and family tuition reduction.
**Financial aid statistics:** 38% of aid is not need-based. In 1993-94, 93% of all undergraduate applicants received aid. Average amounts of aid awarded freshmen: Scholarships and grants, $4,098; loans, $3,900.
**Supporting data/closing dates:** FAFSA/FAF/FFS: Priority filing date is April 1. School's own aid application: Priority filing date is April 1. Income tax forms: Priority filing date is April 1. Notification of awards on rolling basis.
**Financial aid contact:** Linda Shields, Director of Financial Aid. 804 791-5645.

# Bluefield College

**Bluefield, VA 24605** 703 326-3682

**1994-95 Costs.** Tuition: $7,150. Room: $1,500. Board: $2,600. Fees, books, misc. academic expenses (school's estimate): $300.
**Enrollment.** Undergraduates: 314 men, 339 women (full-time). Freshman class: 506 applicants, 472 accepted, 232 enrolled.
**Test score averages/ranges.** Average SAT scores: 377 verbal, 423 math. Average ACT scores: 21 composite.
**Faculty.** 47 full-time; 8 part-time. 57% of faculty holds highest degree in specific field. Student/faculty ratio: 16 to 1.
**Selectivity rating.** Competitive.

**PROFILE.** Bluefield, founded in 1922, is a church-affiliated, liberal arts college. Its 85-acre campus is located in Bluefield, 75 miles west of Roanoke.

**Accreditation:** SACS.
**Religious orientation:** Bluefield College is affiliated with the Southern Baptist Church; two semesters of religion required.
**Library:** Collections totaling over 42,000 volumes, 248 periodical subscriptions and 95 microform items.
**Athletic facilities:** Gymnasium, weight room, athletic fields, tennis and volleyball courts.
**STUDENT BODY. Undergraduate profile:** 95% are state residents. 1% Asian-American, 3% Black, 1% Hispanic, 95% White. Average age of undergraduates is 27.
**Freshman profile:** Majority of accepted applicants took SAT. 95% of freshmen come from public schools.
**Undergraduate achievement:** 64% of fall 1992 freshmen returned for fall 1993 term. 45% of entering class graduated.
**Foreign students:** Nine students are from out of the country. Countries represented include Canada and Japan; six in all.
**PROGRAMS OF STUDY. Degrees:** B.A., B.Gen.Studies, B.S.
**Majors:** Biology, Business Administration, Chemistry, Christian Ministry, Communication Arts, Computer Science, Criminal Justice, Elementary Education, English, Equitation, Fine Arts, General Studies, History, Interdisciplinary Studies, Management of Human Resources, Mathematics, Middle School Education, Music, Physical Education, Psychology, Religion/Philosophy, Secondary Education, Social Studies, Sports Medicine.
**Distribution of degrees:** The majors with the highest enrollment are business administration, education, and criminal justice; mathematics, equitation, and music have the lowest.
**Requirements:** General education requirement.
**Academic regulations:** Freshmen must maintain minimum 1.18 GPA; sophomores, 1.85 GPA; juniors, 1.99 GPA; seniors, 2.0 GPA.
**Special:** Minors offered in many majors and in accounting, art, computer information systems, drama, general business, health, physics, and sociology. Associate's degrees offered. Double majors. Dual degrees. Internships. Cooperative education programs. Bachelor's/M.B.A. program with Averett Coll. Member of Appalachian College Assessment Consortium for Southwest Virginia and Consortium for Teacher Education. Teacher certification in early childhood, elementary, and secondary education. Certification in specific subject areas. Study abroad possible in the United Kingdom.
**Honors:** Honors program. Honor societies.
**Academic Assistance:** Remedial reading, writing, math, and study skills.
**ADMISSIONS. Academic basis for candidate selection** (in order of priority): Secondary school record, class rank, school's recommendation, standardized test scores, essay.
**Nonacademic basis for candidate selection:** Character and personality are emphasized. Geographical distribution and alumni/ae relationship are important. Extracurricular participation and particular talent or ability are considered.
**Requirements:** Graduation from secondary school is required; GED is accepted. No specific distribution of secondary school units required. Minimum 2.0 GPA required; minimum 2.5 GPA recommended. Audition required of music program applicants. Conditional admission possible for applicants not meeting standard requirements. SAT is required; ACT may be substituted. PSAT is recommended. Campus visit and interview recommended. Off-campus interviews available with an admissions representative.
**Procedure:** Take SAT or ACT by April of 12th year. Application deadline is August 15. Notification of admission on rolling basis. $100 room deposit, refundable until May 1. Freshmen accepted for terms other than fall.
**Special programs:** Admission may be deferred two years. Credit and/or placement may be granted through CEEB Advanced Placement exams for scores of 3 or higher. Credit may be granted through CLEP general and subject exams, military and life experience. Placement may be granted through challenge exams. Concurrent enrollment program.
**Transfer students:** Transfer students accepted for terms other than fall. In fall 1993, 116 transfer applications were received, 103 were accepted. Application deadline is August 15 for fall; December 15 for spring. Minimum 2.0 GPA required. Lowest course grade accepted is "C." Maximum number of transferable credits is 68 semester hours. At least 24 semester hours must be completed at the college to receive degree.
**Admissions contact:** Nina Wilburn, M.B.A., Director of Enrollment Management. 703 326-4214, 800 872-0175.
**FINANCIAL AID. Available aid:** Pell grants, SEOG, state grants, school scholarships and grants, private scholarships and grants, academic merit scholarships, and athletic scholarships. PLUS, Stafford Loans (GSL), private loans, and SLS. AMS.
**Financial aid statistics:** 60% of aid is not need-based. In 1993-94, 91% of all undergraduate applicants received aid; 90% of freshman applicants. Average amounts of aid awarded freshmen: Scholarships and grants, $1,356; loans, $2,625.
**Supporting data/closing dates:** FAFSA: Priority filing date is March 10. FAF: Priority filing date is March 15. School's own aid application: Priority filing date is March 15. State aid form: Deadline is June 1. Income tax forms: Accepted on rolling basis. Notification of awards on rolling basis.
**Financial aid contact:** Nina Wilburn, M.B.A., Director of Enrollment Management. 703 326-4215.

# Bridgewater College

**Bridgewater, VA 22812** 703 828-2501

**1994-95 Costs.** Tuition: $11,265. Room & board: $4,725. Fees, books, misc. academic expenses (school's estimate): $560.
**Enrollment.** Undergraduates: 405 men, 476 women (full-time). Freshman class: 838 applicants, 671 accepted, 292 enrolled.
**Test score averages/ranges.** N/A.
**Faculty.** 62 full-time; 15 part-time. 67% of faculty holds doctoral degree. Student/faculty ratio: 13 to 1.
**Selectivity rating.** N/A.

**PROFILE.** Bridgewater, founded in 1880, is a church-affiliated, liberal arts college. Its 35-acre campus is located in Bridgewater, 20 miles from Staunton.

**Accreditation:** SACS. Professionally accredited by the Association of Collegiate Business Schools and Programs.
**Religious orientation:** Bridgewater College is affiliated with the Church of the Brethren; one semester of religion required.
**Library:** Collections totaling over 150,491 volumes, 553 periodical subscriptions, and 42,285 microform items.
**Special facilities/museums:** Museum of Shenandoah region and Brethren history.
**Athletic facilities:** Swimming pool, tennis courts, track, gymnasium, athletic fields.

**STUDENT BODY. Undergraduate profile:** 70% are state residents; 11% are transfers. .3% Asian-American, 2% Black, .6% Hispanic, 96% White, 1.1% Other. Average age of undergraduates is 20.
**Freshman profile:** 99% of accepted applicants took SAT; 1% took ACT. 92% of freshmen come from public schools.
**Undergraduate achievement:** 72% of fall 1992 freshmen returned for fall 1993 term. 52% of entering class graduated. 33% of students who completed a degree program went on to graduate study within five years.
**Foreign students:** 23 students are from out of the country. Countries represented include China, England, France, Germany, Japan, and Spain; 16 in all.

**PROGRAMS OF STUDY. Degrees:** B.A., B.Gen.Studies, B.S.
**Majors:** Art, Biology, Business Administration, Chemistry, Computer Science/Mathematics, Economics, Elementary Education, English, French, General Science, German, Health/Physical Education, Health Science, History, History/Political Science, Home Economics, International Studies, Mathematics, Medical Technology, Music, Philosophy/Religion, Physical Science, Physics, Physics/Mathematics, Political Science, Psychology, Sociology, Spanish.
**Distribution of degrees:** The majors with the highest enrollment are business administration, biology, and psychology; German, Spanish, and economics have the lowest.
**Requirements:** General education requirement.
**Academic regulations:** Freshmen must maintain minimum 1.6 GPA; sophomores, 1.7 GPA; juniors, 1.8 GPA; seniors, 1.9 GPA.
**Special:** Minors offered in most majors and in church music, communications, peace studies, social work, and theatre/speech. Courses offered in accounting, fashion merchandising, geography, interior design, linguistics, and nutrition/food science. Double majors. Independent study. Internships. Preprofessional programs in law, medicine, veterinary science, pharmacy, dentistry, theology, and medical technology. 3-2 engineering program with Pennsylvania State U. 3-2 forestry and environmental studies program with Duke U. Member of Shenandoah Valley Independent Colleges Library Consortium. Off-campus study possible during February interterm. Teacher certification in early childhood, elementary, and secondary education. Certification in specific subject areas. Exchange programs abroad in China (Dalian Foreign Languages Inst), Ecuador (U of Azuay), England (Cheltenham and Gloucester Coll of Higher Education), France (U of Nancy, U of Strasbourg), Germany (Phillips U), Greece (U of LaVerne), and Spain (U of Barcelona).
**Honors:** Honors program. Honor societies.
**Academic Assistance:** Remedial reading, writing, math, and study skills. Nonremedial tutoring.

**ADMISSIONS. Academic basis for candidate selection** (in order of priority): Secondary school record, class rank, school's recommendation, standardized test scores.
**Nonacademic basis for candidate selection:** Character and personality are emphasized. Extracurricular participation, particular talent or ability, and alumni/ae relationship are considered.
**Requirements:** Graduation from secondary school is required; GED is accepted. 16 units and the following program of study are required: 4 units of English, 2 units of math, 2 units of science, 2 units of foreign language, 2 units of social studies/history, 4 units of electives. Rank in top half of secondary school class recommended. Conditional admission possible for applicants not meeting standard requirements. SAT is required; ACT may be substituted. Campus visit and interview recommended. Off-campus interviews available with an admissions representative.
**Procedure:** Take SAT or ACT by January of 12th year. Suggest filing application by January 15. Application deadline is August 1. Notification of admission on rolling basis. Reply is required within 30 days of acceptance. $200 tuition deposit, refundable until May 1. Freshmen accepted for terms other than fall.
**Special programs:** Admission may be deferred one year. Credit and/or placement may be granted through CEEB Advanced Placement exams for scores of 3 or higher. Placement may be granted through challenge exams. Early entrance/early admission program.
**Transfer students:** Transfer students accepted for terms other than fall. In fall 1993, 11% of all new students were transfers into all classes. 95 transfer applications were received, 40 were accepted. Application deadline is rolling for fall; rolling for spring. Minimum 2.0 GPA required. Lowest course grade accepted is "C." Maximum number of transferable credits is 68 semester hours from a two-year school and 96 semester hours from a four-year school. At least 27 semester hours must be completed at the college to receive degree.

**Admissions contact:** Brian C. Hildebrand, M.A., M.Ed., Dean for Enrollment Management. 703 828-2501, extension 1400.

**FINANCIAL AID. Available aid:** Pell grants, SEOG, state scholarships and grants, school scholarships and grants, private scholarships and grants, academic merit scholarships, and aid for undergraduate foreign students. Perkins Loans (NDSL), PLUS, Stafford Loans (GSL), and SLS. AMS and Tuition Management Systems.
**Financial aid statistics:** 40% of aid is not need-based. In 1993-94, 98% of all undergraduate applicants received aid; 100% of freshman applicants. Average amounts of aid awarded freshmen: Scholarships and grants, $6,733; loans, $3,891.
**Supporting data/closing dates:** FAFSA: Priority filing date is March 15. State aid form: Deadline is July 31. Income tax forms: Deadline is May 1. Notification of awards on rolling basis.
**Financial aid contact:** J. Vern Fairchilds, Jr., Director of Financial Aids. 703 828-2501, extension 1444.

# Christendom College

**Front Royal, VA 22630** **703 636-2900**

**1993-94 Costs.** Tuition: $8,200. Room & board: $3,400. Fees, books, misc. academic expenses (school's estimate): $550.
**Enrollment.** Undergraduates: 57 men, 79 women (full-time). Freshman class: 65 applicants, 65 accepted, 44 enrolled.
**Test score averages/ranges.** Average SAT scores: 502 verbal, 530 math.
**Faculty.** 12 full-time; 2 part-time. 60% of faculty holds doctoral degree. Student/faculty ratio: 12 to 1.
**Selectivity rating.** Competitive.

**PROFILE.** Christendom College, founded in 1977, is a church-affiliated, liberal arts institution. Its 77-acre campus is located northeast of the town of Front Royal, 65 miles from Washington, D.C.

**Accreditation:** SACS.
**Religious orientation:** Christendom College is affiliated with the Roman Catholic Church; six semesters of theology required.
**Library:** Collections totaling over 36,742 volumes, 175 periodical subscriptions and 720 microform items.

**STUDENT BODY. Undergraduate profile:** 24% are state residents. 2% Asian-American, 5% Hispanic, 93% White. Average age of undergraduates is 20.
**Freshman profile:** Majority of accepted applicants took SAT.
**Undergraduate achievement:** 87% of fall 1991 freshmen returned for fall 1992 term. 31% of students who completed a degree program went on to graduate study.
**Foreign students:** Four students are from out of the country. Countries represented include Canada and Mexico.

**PROGRAMS OF STUDY. Degrees:** B.A.
**Majors:** English, History, Philosophy, Political Science, Theology.
**Requirements:** General education requirement.
**Special:** Minors offered. Associate's degrees offered. Double majors. Internships. Study abroad offered in Italy.

**ADMISSIONS. Academic basis for candidate selection** (in order of priority): Standardized test scores, essay, class rank, school's recommendation, secondary school record.
**Nonacademic basis for candidate selection:** Character and personality, extracurricular participation, particular talent or ability, geographical distribution, and alumni/ae relationship are considered.
**Requirements:** Graduation from secondary school is recommended; GED is accepted. No specific distribution of secondary school units required. Minimum combined SAT score of 950, rank in top half of secondary school class, and minimum 3.0 GPA recommended. SAT is required; ACT may be substituted. Campus visit and interview recommended. No off-campus interviews.
**Procedure:** Take SAT or ACT by June 1 of 12th year. Visit college for interview by May 1 of 12th year. Suggest filing application by April 1; no deadline. Notification of admission on rolling basis. Reply is required within 30 days of acceptance. $500 tuition deposit, refundable until July 1. Freshmen accepted for terms other than fall.
**Special programs:** Credit and/or placement may be granted through CEEB Advanced Placement exams for scores of 5 or higher. Placement may be granted through challenge exams. Early decision program. Deadline for applying for early decision is January 1. Early entrance/early admission program.
**Transfer students:** Transfer students accepted for terms other than fall. Application deadline is August 1 for fall; January 1 for spring. Lowest course grade accepted is "C." Maximum number of transferable credits is 90 semester hours. At least 30 semester hours must be completed at the college to receive degree.
**Admissions contact:** John Ciskanik, M.B.A., Director of Admissions. 800 877-5456.

**FINANCIAL AID. Available aid:** School scholarships and grants, private scholarships and grants, and academic merit scholarships. School loans and private loans. Family tuition reduction.
**Financial aid statistics:** Average amounts of aid awarded freshmen: Scholarships and grants, $1,600; loans, $2,631.
**Supporting data/closing dates:** FAFSA/FAF: Accepted on rolling basis; deadline is April 1. School's own aid application: Priority filing date is April 15; accepted on rolling basis. Notification of awards on rolling basis.
**Financial aid contact:** Alisa Polk, Financial Aid Officer. 800 877-5456.

# Christopher Newport University

**Newport News, VA 23606-2998** **804 594-7000**

**1994-95 Costs.** Tuition: $3,196 (state residents), $7,860 (out-of-state). Room & board: $4,750. Fees, books, misc. academic expenses (school's estimate): $440.
**Enrollment.** Undergraduates: 1,135 men, 1,775 women (full-time). Freshman class: 948 applicants, 768 accepted, 456 enrolled. Graduate enrollment: 33 men, 64 women.
**Test score averages/ranges.** Average SAT scores: 404 verbal, 442 math. Range of SAT scores of middle 50%: 400-449 verbal, 450-499 math.
**Faculty.** 165 full-time; 7 part-time. 80% of faculty holds highest degree in specific field. Student/faculty ratio: 20 to 1.
**Selectivity rating.** Competitive.

**PROFILE.** Christopher Newport, founded in 1961, is a comprehensive, public college. Programs are offered through the Schools of Business and Economics, Letters and Natural Science, and Social Science and Professional Studies. Its 75-acre campus is located in Newport News, midway between Williamsburg and Norfolk.

**Accreditation:** SACS. Professionally accredited by the American Bar Association, the Council on Social Work Education.
**Religious orientation:** Christopher Newport University is nonsectarian; no religious requirements.
**Library:** Collections totaling over 139,578 volumes, 1,367 periodical subscriptions, and 103,187 microform items.
**Special facilities/museums:** Art gallery, Japanese Tea House, greenhouse.
**Athletic facilities:** Gymnasiums, weight room, track, soccer field, tennis courts.

**STUDENT BODY. Undergraduate profile:** 92% are state residents; 42% are transfers. 2% Asian-American, 13% Black, 2% Hispanic, 1% Native American, 82% White. Average age of undergraduates is 23.
**Freshman profile:** 1% of freshmen who took SAT scored 700 or over on math; 2% scored 600 or over on verbal, 6% scored 600 or over on math; 12% scored 500 or over on verbal, 25% scored 500 or over on math; 52% scored 400 or over on verbal, 69% scored 400 or over on math; 92% scored 300 or over on verbal, 97% scored 300 or over on math. 96% of accepted applicants took SAT. 97% of freshmen come from public schools.
**Undergraduate achievement:** 71% of fall 1992 freshmen returned for fall 1993 term. 15% of students who completed a degree program went on to graduate study within one year.
**Foreign students:** 20 students are from out of the country. Eight countries represented in all.

**PROGRAMS OF STUDY. Degrees:** B.A., B.Mus., B.S., B.S.Bus.Admin.
**Majors:** Accounting, Applied Physics, Biology, Community Planning, Computer Science, Criminal Justice Administration, Economics, English, Finance, Fine/Performing Arts, History, Information Sciences, Interdisciplinary Studies, International Culture/Commerce, International Studies, Legal Studies, Leisure Studies/Physical Education, Management, Marketing, Mathematics, Modern Foreign Languages, Music Composition, Music History, Music Performance, Music Theory, Nursing, Philosophy, Physical Education, Physics/Microelectronics, Political Science, Psychology, Public Management, Real Estate, Social Work, Sociology, Spanish.
**Distribution of degrees:** The major with the highest enrollment is accounting; music, physics, and philosophy have the lowest.
**Requirements:** General education requirement.
**Academic regulations:** Freshmen must maintain minimum 1.5 GPA; sophomores, 1.8 GPA; juniors, 1.9 GPA; seniors, 2.0 GPA.
**Special:** Minors offered in some majors and in business administration, French, geography, German, gerontology, government, health, Latin American studies, professional writing, speech communication, and theatre arts. Courses in anthropology, astronomy, classical studies, communications, creative writing, geology, health professions, humanities, and speech. Self-designed majors. Double majors. Dual degrees. Independent study. Pass/fail grading option. Internships. Graduate school at which undergraduates may take graduate-level courses. Preprofessional programs in law, medicine, veterinary science, dentistry, and theology. B.S. engineering program with Old Dominion U. Forestry and environmental management programs with Duke U. Exchange programs with Hampton U, Old Dominion U, Thomas Nelson Comm Coll, and U of Virginia. Teacher certification in early childhood, elementary, and secondary education. Certification in specific subject areas. Study abroad in England, Japan, and Mexico. ROTC.
**Honors:** Honors program.
**Academic Assistance:** Remedial study skills. Nonremedial tutoring.

**STUDENT LIFE. Housing:** 10% of students live in college housing.
**Social atmosphere:** The editor of the student newspaper reports that the Terrace and Christopher's are popular on-campus hangouts, while off campus, students go to Chi Chi's, Red Baron, Mountain Jacks, and Darryl's. Basketball and soccer games, AKPsi and Gamma Phi Beta All Night Halloween Party, and other Greek-sponsored parties are special campus events. Greeks and the Minority Student Association have great influence over the student body.
**Services and counseling/handicapped student services:** Placement services. Career Resource Center, seminar series Counseling services for minority, veteran, and older students. Personal and psychological counseling. Career and academic guidance services. Physically disabled student services. Learning disabled services. Notetaking services. Tape recorders. Reader services for the blind.
**Campus organizations:** Undergraduate student government. Student newspaper (Captain's Log, published once/week). Literary magazine. Performing Artist Association, Blue Wave Dancers, Campus Activities Board, College Democrats, College Republicans, REAL Youth, BACCHUS, United Nations Society, equestrian club, volleyball club, social work club, academic, athletic, service, and special-interest groups, 49 organizations in all.

Five fraternities, no chapter houses; four sororities, no chapter houses. 7% of men join a fraternity. 6% of women join a sorority.
**Religious organizations:** Baptist Student Union, Intervarsity Christian Fellowship.
**Minority/foreign student organizations:** Minority Student Association. International Student Association.

**ATHLETICS. Physical education requirements:** One semester of physical education required.
**Intercollegiate competition:** 5% of students participate. Baseball (M), basketball (M,W), cheerleading (M,W), cross-country (M,W), golf (M), sailing (M,W), soccer (M), softball (W), tennis (M,W), track and field (indoor) (M,W), track and field (outdoor) (M,W), volleyball (W). Member of Dixie Intercollegiate Athletic Conference, Mason-Dixon Track Conference, NCAA Division III.
**Intramural and club sports:** 15% of students participate. Intramural aerobics, basketball, flag football, golf, road racing, rugby, skiing, softball, tennis, volleyball, weight lifting. Men's club equestrian sports, karate, tae kwon do, volleyball, water skiing. Women's club equestrian sports, karate, tae kwon do, volleyball, water skiing.

**ADMISSIONS. Academic basis for candidate selection** (in order of priority): Secondary school record, class rank, standardized test scores, essay, school's recommendation.
**Requirements:** Graduation from secondary school is required; GED is accepted. 23 units and the following program of study are recommended: 4 units of English, 3 units of math, 3 units of science, 3 units of foreign language, 3 units of social studies, 7 units of electives. Minimum SAT scores of 400 in both verbal and math, rank in top half of secondary school class, and minimum 2.0 GPA required. Audition required of music program applicants. R.N. required of nursing program applicants. College is designated as a Serviceperson's Opportunity College to serve the special educational needs of those in the service. Noncredit basic studies courses for students not normally admissible. SAT is required; ACT may be substituted. No off-campus interviews.
**Procedure:** Take SAT or ACT by December of 12th year. Suggest filing application by February 15. Application deadline is August 1. Notification of admission on rolling basis. $200 room deposit, refundable in full by June 1. Freshmen accepted for terms other than fall.
**Special programs:** Credit and/or placement may be granted through CEEB Advanced Placement exams. Credit and/or placement may be granted through CLEP general and subject exams. Credit and placement may be granted through DANTES and challenge exams, and military experience. Early entrance/early admission program. Concurrent enrollment program.
**Transfer students:** Transfer students accepted for terms other than fall. In fall 1993, 42% of all new students were transfers into all classes. 1,072 transfer applications were received, 940 were accepted. Application deadline is August 1 for fall; December 1 for spring. Minimum 2.0 GPA required. Lowest course grade accepted is "D." Maximum number of transferable credits is 66 semester hours from a two-year school and 92 semester hours from a four-year school. At least 30 semester hours must be completed at the university to receive degree.
**Admissions contact:** Keith F. McLoughland, Dean of Admissions. 804 594-7015.

**FINANCIAL AID. Available aid:** Pell grants, SEOG, state scholarships and grants, school scholarships, private scholarships, ROTC scholarships, and academic merit scholarships. Perkins Loans (NDSL), PLUS, Stafford Loans (GSL), and SLS. AMS.
**Financial aid statistics:** 26% of aid is not need-based. In 1993-94, 99% of all undergraduate applicants received aid; 99% of freshman applicants. Average amounts of aid awarded freshmen: Scholarships and grants, $2,015; loans, $2,200.
**Supporting data/closing dates:** FAFSA/FAF/FFS: Priority filing date is February 15. School's own aid application: Priority filing date is April 1. Notification of awards on rolling basis.
**Financial aid contact:** Sidney P. Dugas, Director of Financial Aid. 804 594-7170.

**STUDENT EMPLOYMENT.** College Work/Study Program. Institutional employment. 15% of full-time undergraduates work on campus during school year. Students may expect to earn an average of $2,200 during school year. Off-campus part-time employment opportunities rated "excellent."

**COMPUTER FACILITIES.** 235 IBM/IBM-compatible, Macintosh/Apple, and RISC-/UNIX-based microcomputers; 120 are networked. Students may access Digital, Hewlett-Packard, SUN minicomputer/mainframe systems, Internet. Client/LAN operating systems include Apple/Macintosh, DOS, UNIX/XENIX/AIX, LocalTalk/AppleTalk, Novell. Computer languages and software packages include BASIC, COBOL, dBASE, FORTRAN, IFPS, INGRES, Lotus 1-2-3, MicroCase, Microsoft Works, MINITAB, Pascal, SAS, SLAM, SPSS-X, WordPerfect. Computer facilities are available to all students.
**Fees:** $20 computer fee per course; included in tuition/fees.
**Hours:** 9 AM-10 PM (M-Th); 9 AM-3PM (Fr); noon-6 PM (Sa,Su).

**GRADUATE CAREER DATA.** Highest graduate school enrollments: Coll of William and Mary, Old Dominion U, Virginia Commonwealth U.

# The College of William and Mary in Virginia

**Williamsburg, VA 23185** **804 221-4000**

**1993-94 Costs.** Tuition: $4,414 (state residents), $12,604 (out-of-state). Room: $2,208. Board: $1,980. Fees, books, misc. academic expenses (school's estimate): $600.
**Enrollment.** Undergraduates: 2,404 men, 2,881 women (full-time). Freshman class: 7,222 applicants, 2,997 accepted, 1,215 enrolled. Graduate enrollment: 1,087 men, 1,223 women.
**Test score averages/ranges.** Average SAT scores: 583 verbal, 623 math. Range of SAT scores of middle 50%: 1170-1330 combined.
**Faculty.** 414 full-time; 157 part-time. 94% of faculty holds highest degree in specific field. Student/faculty ratio: 14 to 1.
**Selectivity rating.** Most competitive.

**PROFILE.** William and Mary, founded in 1693, is a public university. Programs are offered through the Faculty of Arts and Sciences and the Schools of Business Administration, Education, Law, and Marine Science. Its 1,200-acre campus, including a variety of colonial buildings, is located in Williamsburg, 15 miles northwest of Newport News.
**Accreditation:** SACS. Professionally accredited by the American Assembly of Collegiate Schools of Business, the American Bar Association, the American Psychological Association, the Association of American Law Schools, the National Council for Accreditation of Teacher Education.
**Religious orientation:** The College of William and Mary in Virginia is nonsectarian; no religious requirements.
**Library:** Collections totaling over 1,178,814 volumes, 10,253 periodical subscriptions, and 1,638,303 microform items.
**Special facilities/museums:** Art museum, language lab, greenhouse, herbarium, archaeological conservation lab, electron microscope, spectrometer, chromatograph, population ecology lab.
**Athletic facilities:** Gymnasiums, basketball, racquetball, squash, and tennis courts, track, weight and wrestling rooms, swimming pool, sauna, dance studio, field hockey, football, lacrosse, and soccer fields, stadium, recreational sports complex.

**STUDENT BODY. Undergraduate profile:** 70% are state residents. 6% Asian-American, 7% Black, 2% Hispanic, 84% White, 1% Other. Average age of undergraduates is 21.
**Freshman profile:** 100% of accepted applicants took SAT. 85% of freshmen come from public schools.
**Undergraduate achievement:** 95% of fall 1991 freshmen returned for fall 1992 term. 78% of entering class graduated. 29% of students who completed a degree program immediately went on to graduate study.
**Foreign students:** 120 students are from out of the country. Countries represented include Canada, Cyprus, El Salvador, Japan, Pakistan, and the United Kingdom; 33 in all.

**PROGRAMS OF STUDY. Degrees:** B.A., B.Bus.Admin., B.F.A., B.S.
**Majors:** American Studies, Anthropology, Biology, Business Administration, Chemistry, Classical Studies, Computer Science, Economics, English, Fine Arts, French, Geology, German, Government, Greek, History, Interdisciplinary, International Relations, International Studies, Mathematics, Music, Philosophy, Physical Education, Physics, Psychology, Public Policy, Religion, Sociology, Spanish, Theatre/Speech.
**Distribution of degrees:** The majors with the highest enrollment are English, government, and biology; music and German have the lowest.
**Requirements:** General education requirement.
**Academic regulations:** Freshmen must maintain minimum 1.0 GPA; sophomores, 1.3 GPA; juniors, 1.6 GPA; seniors, 1.8 GPA.
**Special:** Minors offered in most majors. Interdisciplinary concentrations offered in East Asian, Italian, Latin American, Russian/Soviet, and urban studies and in comparative literature, environmental science, and linguistics. Courses offered in Chinese, dance, geography, Japanese, and Portuguese. Self-designed majors. Double majors. Independent study. Pass/fail grading option. Internships. Graduate school at which undergraduates may take graduate-level courses. Preprofessional programs in medicine, veterinary science, dentistry, theology, engineering, forestry, physical therapy, and podiatry. 3-2 engineering programs with Case Western Reserve U, Columbia U, Cornell U, Rensselaer Polytech Inst, and Washington U. 3-2 forestry and environmental studies program with Duke U. Washington Semester. Medieval studies program with St. John's U (Minn). Teacher certification in elementary, secondary, and special education. Certification in specific subject areas. Exchange programs abroad in Australia (U of Adelaide), China (U of Beijing), France (U of Paul Valerie), and Spain (U of Madrid). Study abroad also in Denmark, England, Germany, Italy, the Netherlands, and Scotland. ROTC.
**Honors:** Phi Beta Kappa. Honors program. Honor societies.
**Academic Assistance:** Remedial writing, math, and study skills. Nonremedial tutoring.

**STUDENT LIFE. Housing:** All freshmen must live on campus unless living with family. Coed, women's, and men's dorms. Sorority and fraternity housing. 75% of students live in college housing.
**Social atmosphere:** According to the editor of the student newspaper, Greeks, who comprise around 40% of the student body, and Christian groups are among the socially influential groups on campus. Favorite events on campus are the Matoakafest (an end-of-the-year, day-long band bash for the Cancer Society), the Beaux Arts Ball, Homecoming, Derby Day, Anchor Splash, and the Superdance. On campus, students gather at the frats or the Campus Center for meals. Off-campus spots are Paul's Deli, The Green Leafe Cafe, and the Sunken Garden.
**Services and counseling/handicapped student services:** Placement services. Health service. Day care. Counseling services for minority and older students. Birth control, personal, and psychological counseling. Career and academic guidance services. Religious counseling. Physically disabled student services. Learning disabled services. Notetaking services. Tape recorders. Tutors. Reader services for the blind.
**Campus organizations:** Undergraduate student government. Student newspaper (Flat Hat, published once/week). Literary magazine. Yearbook. Radio station. Band, orchestra, chorus, choir, glee clubs, Mermettes, theatre, film series, debating, outing and ski clubs, tutoring groups, Circle K, Women's Forum, academic, political, professional, and special-interest groups. 16 fraternities, no chapter houses; 13 sororities, no chapter houses. 44% of men join a fraternity. 42% of women join a sorority.
**Religious organizations:** Baptist Student Union, Campus Ministries United, Campus Crusade for Christ, Canterbury Association, Catholic Student Association, Christian Science Organization, Fellowship of Christian Athletes, Hillel, Intervarsity Christian Fellowship, Latter-Day Saints Student Association, Lutheran Student Association, Maranatha Christian Fellowship, Wesley Student Fellowship, Westminster Fellowship, Young Life.
**Minority/foreign student organizations:** African-American student groups. International Circle, International Relations, Chinese, East Asian, Filipino, Indian, Iranian, Korean, Latin American, and Middle Eastern groups.

**ATHLETICS. Physical education requirements:** Four semesters of physical education required.
**Intercollegiate competition:** 10% of students participate. Baseball (M), basketball (M,W), cheerleading (M,W), cross-country (M,W), diving (M,W), fencing (M), field hockey (W), football (M), golf (M,W), gymnastics (M,W), lacrosse (W), soccer (M,W), swimming (M,W), tennis (M,W), track (indoor) (M,W), track (outdoor) (M,W), track and

field (indoor) (M,W), track and field (outdoor) (M,W), volleyball (W), wrestling (M). Member of Colonial Athletic Association, ECAC, NCAA Division I, NCAA Division I-AA for football, Yankee Conference for football.

**Intramural and club sports:** 80% of students participate. Intramural aerobics, basketball, billiards, bowling, flag football, floor hockey, golf, inner-tube water polo, racquetball, soccer, softball, squash, swimming, table tennis, tennis, volleyball, walleyball, weight lifting, wrestling. Men's club Alpine skiing, canoe/kayak, crew, cycling, horsemanship, ice hockey, lacrosse, martial arts, Nordic skiing, racquetball, rugby, sailing, softball, squash, ultimate frisbee, volleyball. Women's club Alpine skiing, canoe/kayak, crew, cycling, horsemanship, martial arts, Nordic skiing, racquetball, rugby, sailing, softball, squash, ultimate frisbee.

**ADMISSIONS. Academic basis for candidate selection** (in order of priority): Secondary school record, class rank, standardized test scores, essay, school's recommendation.

**Nonacademic basis for candidate selection:** Character and personality, extracurricular participation, particular talent or ability, and geographical distribution are important. Alumni/ae relationship is considered.

**Requirements:** Graduation from secondary school is recommended; GED is accepted. No specific distribution of secondary school units required. Conditional admission possible for applicants not meeting standard requirements. SAT or ACT is required. Campus visit recommended. Off-campus interviews available with an alumni representative.

**Procedure:** Take SAT or ACT by January of 12th year. Take ACH by January of 12th year. Visit college for interview by January of 12th year. Application deadline is January 15. Notification of admission by April 1. Reply is required by May 1. $150 nonrefundable tuition deposit. $100 nonrefundable room deposit. Freshmen accepted for terms other than fall.

**Special programs:** Admission may be deferred one year. Credit and/or placement may be granted through CEEB Advanced Placement exams for scores of 3 or higher. Placement may be granted through challenge exams. Early decision program. In fall 1992, 723 applied for early decision and 332 were accepted. Deadline for applying for early decision is November 1. Early entrance/early admission program. Concurrent enrollment program.

**Transfer students:** Transfer students accepted for terms other than fall. In fall 1992, 634 transfer applications were received, 234 were accepted. Application deadline is February 1 for fall; October 1 for spring. Minimum 3.0 GPA recommended. Lowest course grade accepted is "C." At least 60 semester hours must be completed at the college to receive degree.

**Admissions contact:** Virginia Carey, M.Ed., Dean of Admissions. 804 221-4223.

**FINANCIAL AID. Available aid:** Pell grants, SEOG, state scholarships and grants, school scholarships and grants, private scholarships and grants, ROTC scholarships, and athletic scholarships. Perkins Loans (NDSL), PLUS, Stafford Loans (GSL), and SLS. Tuition Plan Inc., Knight Tuition Plans, and AMS.

**Financial aid statistics:** 9% of aid is not need-based. In 1992-93, 80% of all undergraduate applicants received aid; 67% of freshman applicants. Average amounts of aid awarded freshmen: Scholarships and grants, $3,407; loans, $2,281.

**Supporting data/closing dates:** FAFSA/FAF/FFS: Priority filing date is February 15. Notification of awards begins April 1.

**Financial aid contact:** Edward P. Irish, M.P.A., Director of Financial Aid. 804 221-2420.

**STUDENT EMPLOYMENT.** College Work/Study Program. Institutional employment. 30% of full-time undergraduates work on campus during school year. Students may expect to earn an average of $720 during school year. Off-campus part-time employment opportunities rated "good."

**COMPUTER FACILITIES.** 350 IBM/IBM-compatible, Macintosh/Apple, and RISC-/UNIX-based microcomputers; all are networked. Students may access IBM minicomputer/mainframe systems, BITNET, Internet. Residence halls may be equipped with networked microcomputers, modems. Computer languages and software packages include APL, AppleWorks, BASIC, COBOL, dBASE, DrawPerfect, FORTRAN, LISP, Lotus 1-2-3, Modula 2, Paradox, Pascal, PL/1, Pro Windows, Prolog, Quattro, Reflex, SAS, SPSS-X, Star Trek, WordPerfect; 40 in all. Computer facilities are available to all students.

**Fees:** None.

**Hours:** 8 AM-midn.; 24 hours in some areas.

**GRADUATE CAREER DATA.** Graduate school percentages: 5% enter law school. 5% enter medical school. 1% enter graduate business programs. 16% enter graduate arts and sciences programs. Highest graduate school enrollments: American U, Coll of William and Mary, Duke U, George Washington U, Georgetown U, Medical Coll of Virginia, U of Pennsylvania, U of Richmond. 63% of graduates choose careers in business and industry. Companies and businesses that hire graduates: American Management, Big Six accounting firms, Continental Insurance, Sears.

**PROMINENT ALUMNI/AE.** Robert Gates, former director, CIA; Glenn Close, actress; Thomas Jefferson and James Monroe, U.S. Presidents; John Marshall, chief justice, U.S. Supreme Court.

# Eastern Mennonite College

**Harrisonburg, VA 22801 — 703 432-4000**

**1993-94 Costs.** Tuition: $9,100. Room & board: $3,600. Fees, books, misc. academic expenses (school's estimate): $600.

**Enrollment.** Undergraduates: 375 men, 528 women (full-time). Freshman class: 486 applicants, 420 accepted, 227 enrolled.

**Test score averages/ranges.** Average SAT scores: 482 verbal, 510 math. Range of SAT scores of middle 50%: 425-550 verbal, 450-600 math. Average ACT scores: 23 English, 21 math, 23 composite. Range of ACT scores of middle 50%: 21-27 English, 18-24 math.

**Faculty.** 68 full-time; 14 part-time. 55% of faculty holds doctoral degree. Student/faculty ratio: 13 to 1.

**Selectivity rating.** Less competitive.

**PROFILE.** Eastern Mennonite, founded in 1917, is a church-affiliated, liberal arts college. Its 117-acre campus is located in Harrisonburg, 60 miles from Charlottesville.

**Accreditation:** SACS. Professionally accredited by the American Dietetic Association, the Council on Social Work Education, the National Council for Accreditation of Teacher Education, the National League for Nursing.

**Religious orientation:** Eastern Mennonite College is affiliated with the Mennonite Church; 11 semester hours of religion/theology required.

**Library:** Collections totaling over 135,070 volumes, 1,070 periodical subscriptions, and 47,660 microform items.

**Special facilities/museums:** Natural history museum, language lab, planetarium, observatory.

**Athletic facilities:** Gymnasium, basketball, sand volleyball, and tennis courts, fitness trail, track, baseball, field hockey, soccer, and softball fields, weight room.

**STUDENT BODY. Undergraduate profile:** 35% are state residents; 24% are transfers. 2% Asian-American, 3% Black, 2% Hispanic, 92% White, 1% Other. Average age of undergraduates is 21.

**Freshman profile:** 3% of freshmen who took SAT scored 700 or over on verbal, 6% scored 700 or over on math; 17% scored 600 or over on verbal, 25% scored 600 or over on math; 42% scored 500 or over on verbal, 54% scored 500 or over on math; 81% scored 400 or over on verbal, 84% scored 400 or over on math; 98% scored 300 or over on verbal, 98% scored 300 or over on math. 10% of freshmen who took ACT scored 30 or over on English, 5% scored 30 or over on math, 5% scored 30 or over on composite; 34% scored 24 or over on English, 29% scored 24 or over on math, 49% scored 24 or over on composite; 80% scored 18 or over on English, 88% scored 18 or over on math, 93% scored 18 or over on composite; 90% scored 12 or over on English, 100% scored 12 or over on math, 100% scored 12 or over on composite. 82% of accepted applicants took SAT; 18% took ACT. 58% of freshmen come from public schools.

**Undergraduate achievement:** 77% of fall 1992 freshmen returned for fall 1993 term. 48% of entering class graduated. 14% of students who completed a degree program immediately went on to graduate study.

**Foreign students:** 32 students are from out of the country. Countries represented include Croatia, Ethiopia, Ghana, Japan, Switzerland, and Tanzania; 11 in all.

**PROGRAMS OF STUDY. Degrees:** B.A., B.S.

**Majors:** Accounting, Art, Biblical Studies/Theology, Biochemistry, Biology, Business Administration/Management, Camping/Recreation/Youth Ministries, Chemistry, Christian Ministries, Community Nutrition, Computer Information Systems, Computer Science, Congregational Leadership, Dietetics, Early Childhood Education, English, Food Service Administration, French, German, History, History/Social Science, International Agricultural Development, International Business, Liberal Arts, Mathematics, Medical Technology, Middle School Education, Music, Nursing, Physical Education, Psychology, Religion/Philosophy, Social Work, Sociology, Spanish, Special Education, Youth Ministry.

**Distribution of degrees:** The majors with the highest enrollment are business administration and nursing; art, chemistry, and Spanish have the lowest.

**Requirements:** General education requirement.

**Academic regulations:** Minimum 2.0 GPA must be maintained.

**Special:** Minors offered in many majors and in coaching, exercise science, family studies, journalism, missions, paralegal, peace and justice, physics, political science, socio-economic development, Teaching English as a Second Language, and theatre. One-year certificate program in Bible. Interdisciplinary studies. Courses offered in economics, geology, Greek, and philosophy. One term of off-campus study required. Associate's degrees offered. Double majors. Independent study. Pass/fail grading option. Internships. Graduate school at which undergraduates may take graduate-level courses. Preprofessional programs in law, medicine, veterinary science, and dentistry. 3-2 engineering program with Pennsylvania State U. Member of Christian College Coalition. Washington Semester. Teacher certification in early childhood, elementary, secondary, and special education. Certification in specific subject areas. Study abroad in Central American countries, England, France, Ivory Coast, Japan, Middle Eastern countries, the former Soviet Republics, and other countries.

**Honors:** Honors program.

**Academic Assistance:** Nonremedial tutoring.

**ADMISSIONS. Academic basis for candidate selection** (in order of priority): Secondary school record, standardized test scores, school's recommendation, class rank, essay.

**Requirements:** Graduation from secondary school is required; GED is accepted. 20 units and the following program of study are recommended: 4 units of English, 3 units of math, 2 units of science, 2 units of foreign language, 2 units of social studies, 1 unit of history, 6 units of electives. Minimum combined SAT score of 750 (composite ACT score of 17) and minimum 2.0 GPA recommended. SAT or ACT is required. Campus visit and interview recommended. Off-campus interviews available with an admissions representative.

**Procedure:** Take SAT or ACT by May of 12th year. Visit college for interview by June of 12th year. Suggest filing application by March 1. Application deadline is August 1. Notification of admission on rolling basis. Reply is required by May 1. $30 nonrefundable room deposit. Freshmen accepted for terms other than fall.

**Special programs:** Admission may be deferred three years. Credit may be granted through CEEB Advanced Placement for scores of 3 or higher. Credit and/or placement may be granted through CLEP general exams. Placement may be granted through CLEP subject exams. Credit may be granted through challenge exams. Early entrance/early admission program.

**Transfer students:** Transfer students accepted for terms other than fall. In fall 1993, 24% of all new students were transfers into all classes. 153 transfer applications were received, 105 were accepted. Application deadline is 30 days prior to beginning of term for fall; 30 days prior to beginning of term for spring. Minimum 2.0 GPA required. Lowest course grade accepted is "D." Maximum number of transferable credits is 98 semester hours. At least 30 semester hours must be completed at the college to receive degree.

**Admissions contact:** Ellen B. Miller, Director of Admissions. 703 432-4118.

**FINANCIAL AID. Available aid:** Pell grants, SEOG, Federal Nursing Student Scholarships, state scholarships and grants, school scholarships and grants, private scholarships and grants, academic merit scholarships, and aid for undergraduate foreign students. Per-

kins Loans (NDSL), PLUS, Stafford Loans (GSL), NSL, state loans, school loans, private loans, and SLS. AMS and Tuition Management Systems.
**Financial aid statistics:** 38% of aid is not need-based. In 1993-94, 99% of all undergraduate applicants received aid; 99% of freshman applicants. Average amounts of aid awarded freshmen: Scholarships and grants, $4,632; loans, $4,338.
**Supporting data/closing dates:** FAFSA: Priority filing date is April 15. School's own aid application: Priority filing date is April 15. State aid form: Priority filing date is July 31. Notification of awards begins February 15.
**Financial aid contact:** David E. Schrock, Director of Financial Aid. 703 432-4137.

## Emory & Henry College

**Emory, VA 24327-0947** **703 944-4121**

**1994-95 Costs.** Tuition: $8,578. Room: $1,920. Board: $2,488. Fees, books, misc. academic expenses (school's estimate): $1,322.
**Enrollment.** Undergraduates: 407 men, 402 women (full-time). Freshman class: 765 applicants, 646 accepted, 226 enrolled.
**Test score averages/ranges.** Average SAT scores: 443 verbal, 485 math. Range of SAT scores of middle 50%: 400-500 verbal, 425-525 math. Average ACT scores: 23 composite.
**Faculty.** 56 full-time; 8 part-time. 89% of faculty holds highest degree in specific field. Student/faculty ratio: 14 to 1.
**Selectivity rating.** Less competitive.

**PROFILE.** Emory & Henry, founded in 1838, is a church-affiliated, liberal arts college. Its 150-acre campus, a designated Historic Landmark, is located in the Appalachian foothills of Washington County.

**Accreditation:** SACS.
**Religious orientation:** Emory & Henry College is affiliated with the United Methodist Church; one semester of religion required.
**Library:** Collections totaling over 239,000 volumes, 1,000 periodical subscriptions, and 4,679 microform items.
**Special facilities/museums:** Language lab, capillary gas chromatograph, DNA vertical slab gel electrophoretic equipment, infrared spectrophotometer.
**Athletic facilities:** Gymnasiums, basketball, racquetball, tennis, and volleyball courts, baseball, football, and softball fields, golf course, swimming pool, billiards and weight rooms, track.

**STUDENT BODY. Undergraduate profile:** 82% are state residents; 24% are transfers. .5% Asian-American, 4% Black, .3% Hispanic, .2% Native American, 95% White. Average age of undergraduates is 20.
**Freshman profile:** 1% of freshmen who took SAT scored 700 or over on verbal, 1% scored 700 or over on math; 5% scored 600 or over on verbal, 10% scored 600 or over on math; 28% scored 500 or over on verbal, 45% scored 500 or over on math; 75% scored 400 or over on verbal, 89% scored 400 or over on math; 100% scored 300 or over on verbal, 100% scored 300 or over on math. 90% of accepted applicants took SAT; 10% took ACT. 90% of freshmen come from public schools.
**Undergraduate achievement:** 85% of fall 1992 freshmen returned for fall 1993 term. 79% of entering class graduated. 10% of students who completed a degree program immediately went on to graduate study.
**Foreign students:** Six students are from out of the country. Countries represented include African countries and Italy; four in all.

**PROGRAMS OF STUDY. Degrees:** B.A., B.S.
**Majors:** Art, Biology, Chemistry, Classical Studies, Computer Science, Economics/Business, English, French, Geography, German, History, Interdisciplinary English, Latin, Mass Communications, Mathematics, Music, Philosophy, Physical Education, Physics, Political Science, Psychology, Religion, Sociology, Spanish.
**Distribution of degrees:** The majors with the highest enrollment are economics/business, English, and education; art, philosophy, and classical studies have the lowest.
**Requirements:** General education requirement.
**Academic regulations:** Freshmen must maintain minimum 1.8 GPA; sophomores, 1.9 GPA; juniors, 2.0 GPA; seniors, 2.0 GPA.
**Special:** Minors offered in Appalachian studies, environmental studies, sports medicine, and women's studies. Self-designed majors. Double majors. Dual degrees. Independent study. Accelerated study. Pass/fail grading option. Internships. Preprofessional programs in law, medicine, veterinary science, dentistry, and theology. 2-2 pharmacy program with Medical Coll of Virginia. 3-1 medical technology program. 3-2 forestry and environmental studies program with Duke U. 3-2 engineering programs with North Carolina State U and Tulane U. Teacher certification in early childhood, elementary, and secondary education. Certification in specific subject areas. Exchange program abroad in England (U of Kent). Study abroad also in France, Germany, Italy, Middle Eastern countries, and Spanish-speaking countries.
**Honors:** Honors program.
**Academic Assistance:** Remedial writing, math, and study skills. Nonremedial tutoring.

**ADMISSIONS. Academic basis for candidate selection** (in order of priority): Secondary school record, standardized test scores, class rank, essay, school's recommendation.
**Nonacademic basis for candidate selection:** Character and personality are emphasized. Extracurricular participation and particular talent or ability are important. Alumni/ae relationship is considered.
**Requirements:** Graduation from secondary school is required; GED is accepted. 15 units and the following program of study are required: 4 units of English, 3 units of math, 2 units of lab science, 2 units of foreign language, 2 units of social studies. Rank in top half of secondary school class and minimum 3.0 GPA recommended. Conditional admission possible for applicants not meeting standard requirements. Program for applicants not normally admissible. SAT is required; ACT may be substituted. Campus visit and interview recommended. Off-campus interviews available with admissions and alumni representatives.
**Procedure:** Take SAT or ACT by December of 12th year. Suggest filing application by February 1; no deadline. Notification of admission on rolling basis. Reply is required by May 1. $150 tuition deposit, refundable until May 1. Freshmen accepted for terms other than fall.
**Special programs:** Admission may be deferred one year. Credit and/or placement may be granted through CEEB Advanced Placement exams for scores of 4 or higher. Early entrance/early admission program. Concurrent enrollment program.
**Transfer students:** Transfer students accepted for terms other than fall. In fall 1993, 24% of all new students were transfers into all classes. 132 transfer applications were received, 115 were accepted. Application deadline is August 1 for fall; December 1 for spring. Minimum 2.0 GPA required. Lowest course grade accepted is "C."
**Admissions contact:** Jean M. Luce, Ed.D., Dean of Admissions and Financial Aid. 703 944-4121, extension 3133.

**FINANCIAL AID. Available aid:** Pell grants, SEOG, state scholarships and grants, school scholarships and grants, private scholarships and grants, academic merit scholarships, and aid for undergraduate foreign students. Perkins Loans (NDSL), PLUS, Stafford Loans (GSL), school loans, and SLS. Knight Tuition Plans and AMS.
**Financial aid statistics:** 34% of aid is not need-based. In 1993-94, 93% of all undergraduate applicants received aid; 94% of freshman applicants. Average amounts of aid awarded freshmen: Scholarships and grants, $6,337; loans, $2,063.
**Supporting data/closing dates:** FAFSA: Priority filing date is February 15. School's own aid application: Priority filing date is February 15. all other required forms: Deadline is April 1. Notification of awards on rolling basis.
**Financial aid contact:** Deborah Jones, Director of Financial Aid. 703 944-4121, extension 3115.

## Ferrum College

**Ferrum, VA 24088** **703 365-2121**

**1994-95 Costs.** Tuition: $9,400. Room & board: $4,200. Fees, books, misc. academic expenses (school's estimate): $500.
**Enrollment.** Undergraduates: 642 men, 408 women (full-time). Freshman class: 1,339 applicants, 1,107 accepted, 336 enrolled.
**Test score averages/ranges.** Average SAT scores: 387 verbal, 433 math. Range of SAT scores of middle 50%: 330-430 verbal, 360-470 math.
**Faculty.** 77 full-time; 25 part-time. 63% of faculty holds doctoral degree. Student/faculty ratio: 14 to 1.
**Selectivity rating.** Less competitive.

**PROFILE.** Ferrum, founded in 1913, is a church-affiliated college. Its 880-acre campus is located in the foothills of the Blue Ridge Mountains of southwest Virginia.

**Accreditation:** SACS. Professionally accredited by the Council on Social Work Education, the National Recreation and Park Association.
**Religious orientation:** Ferrum College is affiliated with the United Methodist Church; two semesters of religion required.
**Library:** Collections totaling over 97,698 volumes, 525 periodical subscriptions, and 5,057 microform items.
**Special facilities/museums:** Blue Ridge Folklife Institute and Museum.
**Athletic facilities:** Gymnasium, swimming pool, baseball, football, intramural, soccer, and softball fields, tennis and volleyball courts, weight room, riding facilities, football stadium, student recreational facility.

**STUDENT BODY. Undergraduate profile:** 89% are state residents; 17% are transfers. 1.6% Asian-American, 11.5% Black, 1.6% Hispanic, .2% Native American, 85.1% White. Average age of undergraduates is 21.
**Freshman profile:** 1% of freshmen who took SAT scored 700 or over on math; 1% scored 600 or over on verbal, 4% scored 600 or over on math; 8% scored 500 or over on verbal, 22% scored 500 or over on math; 45% scored 400 or over on verbal, 64% scored 400 or over on math; 89% scored 300 or over on verbal, 94% scored 300 or over on math. 97% of accepted applicants took SAT. 93% of freshmen come from public schools.
**Undergraduate achievement:** 61% of fall 1992 freshmen returned for fall 1993 term. 18% of entering class graduated.
**Foreign students:** 14 students are from out of the country. Countries represented include Chile, Ecuador, Germany, India, Japan, and South Africa.

**PROGRAMS OF STUDY. Degrees:** B.A., B.S., B.Soc.Work.
**Majors:** Accounting, Agriculture, Art, Biology, Business, Business/Decision Support, Business Financial Management, Business Management, Business/Marketing, Chemistry, Computer Science, Drama, English, Environmental Science, Fine Arts, French, History, Information Systems, International Studies, Liberal Arts, Liberal Studies, Mathematics, Medical Technology, Outdoor Recreation, Philosophy, Physical Education, Political Science, Pre-Professional Science, Psychology, Recreation, Religion, Russian, Social Studies, Social Work, Spanish.
**Distribution of degrees:** The majors with the highest enrollment are social work and psychology; language and music have the lowest.
**Requirements:** General education requirement.
**Academic regulations:** Freshmen must maintain minimum 1.4 GPA; sophomores, 1.6 GPA; juniors, 1.8 GPA; seniors, 2.0 GPA.
**Special:** Minors offered in many majors and in criminal justice, economics, folk studies, journalism, and teacher education. Double majors. Independent study. Internships. Preprofessional programs in theology, professional, and science. Member of Appalachian College Association. Washington Semester. Teacher certification in elementary and secondary education. Certification in specific subject areas. Study abroad in England, France, Jamaica, and the U.S. Virgin Islands.
**Honors:** Honor societies.

**Academic Assistance:** Remedial reading, writing, math, and study skills. Nonremedial tutoring.

**STUDENT LIFE. Housing:** All unmarried students under age 21 must live on campus unless living near campus with relatives. Fifth year students and students over 21 may live off-campus. Coed, women's, and men's dorms. School-owned/operated apartments. On-campus married-student housing. 80% of students live in college housing.

**Social atmosphere:** Popular gathering spots include the Panther's Den, the Sale Theatre, and Sal's Pizza. The Student Activities Committee, the Student Government Association, and Hall Councils are influential campus groups. Popular Ferrum College events include the Folk Life Festival, Spring Fling, Homecoming, and sporting events. "We're in a very rural area. Sal's Pizza is our number one spot, but many types of entertainment are brought to the campus," reports the school newspaper.

**Services and counseling/handicapped student services:** Placement services. Health service. Counseling services for minority and veteran students. Birth control, personal, and psychological counseling. Career and academic guidance services. Religious counseling. Physically disabled student services. Learning disabled services. Notetaking services. Tape recorders. Tutors. Reader services for the blind.

**Campus organizations:** Undergraduate student government. Student newspaper (Iron Blade, published twice/month). Literary magazine. Yearbook. Radio station. Jack Tales Players, show band, gospel choir, firefighters club, social work club, Student Activities Committee, Bacchus, Russian club, Circle K, Alpha Mu Gamma, 12th Man, dance company, Peace Action Coalition, Chrysalis.

**Religious organizations:** Campus Crusade for Christ, Catholic Campus Ministry, Student Christian Fellowship, Catholic Peer Ministry, Kappa Delta Chi, Habitat for Humanity.

**Minority/foreign student organizations:** Black Student Union. Organization for World Understanding.

**ATHLETICS. Physical education requirements:** Two semesters of physical education required.

**Intercollegiate competition:** 23% of students participate. Baseball (M), basketball (M,W), cheerleading (M,W), football (M), golf (M), horsemanship (M,W), soccer (M,W), softball (W), tennis (M,W), volleyball (W). Member of Dixie Conference, NCAA Division III.

**Intramural and club sports:** 45% of students participate. Intramural basketball, bowling, fishing, football, softball, table tennis, volleyball.

**ADMISSIONS. Academic basis for candidate selection** (in order of priority): Secondary school record, school's recommendation, standardized test scores, essay, class rank.

**Nonacademic basis for candidate selection:** Character and personality, extracurricular participation, particular talent or ability, geographical distribution, and alumni/ae relationship are important.

**Requirements:** Graduation from secondary school is required; GED is accepted. 16 units and the following program of study are recommended: 4 units of English, 3 units of math, 1 unit of science, 3 units of social studies. Foreign language and 10 units of electives recommended. SAT is required; ACT may be substituted. Campus visit and interview recommended. Off-campus interviews available with an admissions representative.

**Procedure:** Take SAT or ACT by May of 12th year. Visit college for interview by April of 12th year. Suggest filing application by January. Application deadline is August. Notification of admission on rolling basis. Reply is required by May 1. $200 confirmation deposit, refundable until May 1. Freshmen accepted for terms other than fall.

**Special programs:** Admission may be deferred one year. Credit and/or placement may be granted through CEEB Advanced Placement exams for scores of 3 or higher. Credit and/or placement may be granted through CLEP general and subject exams.

**Transfer students:** Transfer students accepted for terms other than fall. In fall 1993, 17% of all new students were transfers into all classes. 209 transfer applications were received, 138 were accepted. Application deadline is August for fall; December for spring. Minimum 2.0 GPA recommended. Lowest course grade accepted is "C." Maximum number of transferable credits is 95 semester hours. At least 32 semester hours must be completed at the college to receive degree.

**Admissions contact:** Robert Bailey, Director of Admissions. 703 365-4290.

**FINANCIAL AID. Available aid:** Pell grants, SEOG, state scholarships and grants, school scholarships and grants, private scholarships and grants, academic merit scholarships, and aid for undergraduate foreign students. Perkins Loans (NDSL), PLUS, Stafford Loans (GSL), state loans, school loans, private loans, and SLS. Knight Tuition Plans, AMS, deferred payment plan, and family tuition reduction.

**Financial aid statistics:** 20% of aid is not need-based. In 1993-94, 92% of all freshman applicants received aid. Average amounts of aid awarded freshmen: Scholarships and grants, $3,800; loans, $2,500.

**Supporting data/closing dates:** FAFSA: Priority filing date is May 1. School's own aid application: Priority filing date is May 1; accepted on rolling basis. State aid form: Deadline is July 31. Notification of awards on rolling basis.

**Financial aid contact:** Judith Carter, Director of Financial Aid. 703 365-4282.

**STUDENT EMPLOYMENT.** College Work/Study Program. Institutional employment. 45% of full-time undergraduates work on campus during school year. Students may expect to earn an average of $1,200 during school year. Off-campus part-time employment opportunities rated "fair."

**COMPUTER FACILITIES.** 100 IBM/IBM-compatible and Macintosh/Apple microcomputers; 25 are networked. Students may access Internet. Computer languages and software packages include dBASE, Excel, Lotus 1-2-3, Pascal, WordPerfect, Works, most current computer programs. Computer facilities are available to all students.

**Fees:** Computer fee is included in tuition/fees.

**Hours:** 8 AM-9 PM.

**GRADUATE CAREER DATA.** Highest graduate school enrollments: James Madison U, U of Virginia, Virginia Commonwealth U, Virginia Polytech Inst and State Coll.

# George Mason University

**Fairfax, VA 22030** **703 993-1000**

**1993-94 Costs.** Tuition: $3,888 (state residents), $10,056 (out-of-state). Room: $3,271. Board: $1,651. Fees, books, misc. academic expenses (school's estimate): $580.

**Enrollment.** Undergraduates: 4,321 men, 5,205 women (full-time). Freshman class: 5,576 applicants, 4,366 accepted, 1,772 enrolled. Graduate enrollment: 3,303 men, 3,764 women.

**Test score averages/ranges.** Range of SAT scores of middle 50%: 450-540 verbal, 510-610 math.

**Faculty.** 660 full-time; 428 part-time. 95% of faculty holds highest degree in specific field. Student/faculty ratio: 17 to 1.

**Selectivity rating.** Less competitive.

**PROFILE.** George Mason, founded in 1957, is a public university. Programs are offered through the Colleges of Arts and Sciences and Professional Studies; the Division of Continuing Education; the Graduate School; and the Schools of Business Administration and Law. Its 677-acre campus is located in Fairfax, 18 miles from Washington, D.C.

**Accreditation:** SACS. Professionally accredited by the Accreditation Board for Engineering and Technology, the American Assembly of Collegiate Schools of Business, the American Bar Association, the American Psychological Association, the Council on Social Work Education, the National Association of Schools of Public Affairs and Administration, the National Council for Accreditation of Teacher Education, the National League for Nursing.

**Religious orientation:** George Mason University is nonsectarian; no religious requirements.

**Library:** Collections totaling over 580,200 volumes, 7,780 periodical subscriptions, and 140,429 microform items.

**Special facilities/museums:** Arts center, science and technology building.

**Athletic facilities:** Sports complex, tennis courts, tracks, intramural field.

**STUDENT BODY. Undergraduate profile:** 89% are state residents; 50% are transfers. 12% Asian-American, 7% Black, 4% Hispanic, 1% Native American, 73% White, 3% Other. Average age of undergraduates is 22.

**Freshman profile:** 82% of accepted applicants took SAT. 93% of freshmen come from public schools.

**Undergraduate achievement:** 74% of fall 1991 freshmen returned for fall 1992 term. 20% of entering class graduated. 23% of students who completed a degree program immediately went on to graduate study.

**Foreign students:** 380 students are from out of the country. Countries represented include China, India, Iran, Korea, Pakistan, and Taiwan; 83 in all.

**PROGRAMS OF STUDY. Degrees:** B.A., B.F.A., B.Indiv.Studies, B.Mus., B.S., B.S.Ed., B.S.Nurs.

**Majors:** Accounting, American Studies, Anthropology, Area Studies, Art, Biology, Business Administration, Chemistry, Classical Studies, Computer Science, Dance, Decision Sciences, Economics, Electronics Engineering, English, Finance, Fire Administration, French, Geography, Geology, German, Government/Politics, Health Education, History, Individualized Studies, International Studies, Law Enforcement, Management, Marketing, Mathematics, Medical Technology, Music, Nursing, Parks/Recreation/Leisure Studies, Philosophy, Physical Education, Physics, Psychology, Public Administration, Social Work, Sociology, Spanish, Speech Communication, Systems Engineering, Theatre, Urban Systems.

**Distribution of degrees:** The majors with the highest enrollment are business, English, and psychology; classics, fire administration, and German have the lowest.

**Requirements:** General education requirement.

**Academic regulations:** Freshmen must maintain minimum 1.8 GPA; sophomores, juniors, seniors, 2.0 GPA.

**Special:** Minors offered in linguistics, urban/suburban studies, and women's studies. Plan for Alternative General Education (PAGE) offers integrated introduction to the humanities, social sciences, and math and stresses writing, speaking, and computer skills. Self-designed majors. Double majors. Dual degrees. Independent study. Accelerated study. Pass/fail grading option. Internships. Cooperative education programs. Graduate school at which undergraduates may take graduate-level courses. Preprofessional programs in law, medicine, veterinary science, pharmacy, dentistry, theology, and teaching. Member of Consortium for Continuing Higher Education in Northern Virginia. Exchange program with Shenandoah U. Teacher certification in early childhood, elementary, secondary, special education, and bilingual/bicultural education. Certification in specific subject areas. Member of International Student Exchange Program (ISEP). Study abroad in Austria, Belgium, Canada, England, France, Germany, Hungary, Russia, Spain, and Sweden. ROTC. AFROTC at U of Maryland at College Park.

**Honors:** Honors program. Honor societies.

**Academic Assistance:** Remedial reading, writing, math, and study skills. Nonremedial tutoring.

**STUDENT LIFE. Housing:** Students may live on or off campus. Coed and women's dorms. 20% of students live in college housing.

**Social atmosphere:** Favorite gathering places include the Ratt, the pizza parlor, Student Union, Dharma CoffeeHouse, Planet Nova dance club, Fat Tuesday's raw bar, and Maggie's New York Style Pizza restaurant. Influential groups include Greeks, Campus Ministries, Student Government, Program Board, International Clubs, and various athletic groups. Popular events include Homecoming, Patriots Day, Mason Day, National Collegiate Alcohol Awareness Week, Hunger and Homeless Awareness Week, Rush Week, Greek Week, International Week, and basketball games. According to the student newspaper, GMU students have a wide range of places to go, including Old Towne Fairfax and Washingtown D.C. "Students take advantage of the free movies that are shown every weekend at the Lecture Hall. Different student organizations also hold parties and/or dances to which every student is invited."

**Services and counseling/handicapped student services:** Placement services. Health service. Women's center. Day care. Counseling services for minority, military, veteran, and older students. Birth control, personal, and psychological counseling. Career and academic guidance services. Religious counseling. Physically disabled student services. Learning disabled services. Notetaking services. Tape recorders. Tutors. Reader services for the blind.

**Campus organizations:** Undergraduate student government. Student newspaper (Broadside, published once/week). Literary magazine. Yearbook. Radio station. Choral ensembles, concert band, jazz ensemble, pep band, orchestra, Echoes of Joy, University Players, dance company, debating, forensics team, Amnesty International, Circle K, Habitat for Humanity, Women's Coalition, Society for Individual Liberty, Student Multicultural Coordinating Committee, academic, professional, special-interest, and volunteer groups, 212 organizations in all. 19 fraternities, one chapter house; 10 sororities, no chapter houses. 5% of men join a fraternity. 5% of women join a sorority.

**Religious organizations:** Advance for Christ, Bahai Club, Baptist Student Union, Campus Bible Study, Campus Crusade for Christ, Chinese Bible Study, Christian Fellowship, Jewish Student Association, Korean Christian Fellowship, Latter-Day Saints Student Association, Muslim Students Association.

**Minority/foreign student organizations:** Black Student Alliance, Black Law Students, National Society of Black Engineers, Society of Hispanic Engineers, Asian Student Union. International Student Association, Afghan, African, Arab, Chinese, Filipino, French, German, Greek, Iranian, Japanese, Korean, Latino, Lebanese, Pakistani, Russian, Spanish, Turkish, and Vietnamese groups.

**ATHLETICS. Physical education requirements:** None.

**Intercollegiate competition:** 1% of students participate. Baseball (M), basketball (M,W), cheerleading (M,W), cross-country (M,W), golf (M), lacrosse (W), soccer (M,W), softball (W), tennis (M,W), track (indoor) (M,W), track (outdoor) (M,W), track and field (indoor) (M,W), track and field (outdoor) (M,W), volleyball (M,W), wrestling (M). Member of CAA, ECAC, EIVA, IC4A, NCAA Division I.

**Intramural and club sports:** 10% of students participate. Intramural basketball, field goal kick, flag football, foul shooting, racquetball, sand volleyball, soccer, softball, swimming, table tennis, tennis, volleyball, weight lifting. Men's club crew/rowing, cycling, football, ice hockey, lacrosse, martial arts, racquetball, rugby, skiing, volleyball. Women's club crew/rowing, cycling, dance, ice hockey, lacrosse, martial arts, racquetball, skiing.

**ADMISSIONS. Academic basis for candidate selection** (in order of priority): Secondary school record, standardized test scores, school's recommendation, class rank, essay.

**Nonacademic basis for candidate selection:** Character and personality, extracurricular participation, particular talent or ability, geographical distribution, and alumni/ae relationship are considered.

**Requirements:** Graduation from secondary school is required; GED is accepted. 16 units and the following program of study are required: 4 units of English, 3 units of math, 1 unit of lab science, 2 units of foreign language, 3 units of social studies, 3 units of academic electives. Portfolio required of art program applicants. Audition required of music program applicants. Summer Transition and Retention Program for in-state applicants not normally admissible. SAT is required; ACT may be substituted. Campus visit recommended. Off-campus interviews available with an admissions representative.

**Procedure:** Take SAT or ACT by February of 12th year. Take ACH by January of 12th year. Suggest filing application by December 1. Application deadline is February 1. Notification of admission by April 1. Reply is required by May 1. $300 room deposit, refundable until June 1. Freshmen accepted for terms other than fall.

**Special programs:** Admission may be deferred one semester. Credit and/or placement may be granted through CEEB Advanced Placement exams for scores of 3 or higher. Credit and/or placement may be granted through CLEP subject exams. Credit and placement may be granted through DANTES and challenge exams. Early decision program. In fall 1992, 3,500 applied for early decision and 2,950 were accepted. Deadline for applying for early decision is December 30. Early entrance/early admission program. Concurrent enrollment program.

**Transfer students:** Transfer students accepted for terms other than fall. In fall 1992, 50% of all new students were transfers into all classes. 5,631 transfer applications were received, 4,235 were accepted. Application deadline is March 15 for fall; November 1 for spring. Minimum 2.0 GPA required. Lowest course grade accepted is "C." Maximum number of transferable credits is 60 semester hours from a two-year school and 90 semester hours from a four-year school. At least 30 semester hours must be completed at the university to receive degree.

**Admissions contact:** Patricia M. Riordan, Ed.D., Dean of Admissions. 703 993-2400.

**FINANCIAL AID. Available aid:** Pell grants, SEOG, Federal Nursing Student Scholarships, state scholarships and grants, school scholarships and grants, private scholarships and grants, ROTC scholarships, academic merit scholarships, and athletic scholarships. Perkins Loans (NDSL), PLUS, Stafford Loans (GSL), state loans, and school loans. AMS.

**Financial aid statistics:** In 1992-93, 80% of all freshman applicants received aid. Average amounts of aid awarded freshmen: Scholarships and grants, $3,110; loans, $3,181.

**Supporting data/closing dates:** FAFSA/FAF/FFS: Priority filing date is March 1; accepted on rolling basis. Notification of awards on rolling basis.

**Financial aid contact:** Jennifer Douglas, Director of Financial Aid. 703 993-4350.

**STUDENT EMPLOYMENT.** College Work/Study Program. Institutional employment. 5% of full-time undergraduates work on campus during school year. Students may expect to earn an average of $1,600 during school year. Off-campus part-time employment opportunities rated "good."

**COMPUTER FACILITIES.** 350 IBM/IBM-compatible, Macintosh/Apple, and RISC-/UNIX-based microcomputers; 300 are networked. Students may access Digital, Hewlett-Packard, IBM, SUN minicomputer/mainframe systems, BITNET, Internet. Residence halls may be equipped with stand-alone microcomputers. Client/LAN operating systems include Apple/Macintosh. Computer languages and software packages include Ada, Assembler, BASIC, C, COBOL, FORTRAN, KERMIT, Pascal, PL/1, SAS. Computer facilities are available to all students.

**Fees:** None.

**Hours:** 24 hours in some locations.

**GRADUATE CAREER DATA.** Highest graduate school enrollments: George Mason U. Companies and businesses that hire graduates: American Management Systems, Arthur Andersen, AT&T, Booze Allen & Hamit, EDS, General Services Administration, Hughes Aircraft, U.S. Department of Transportation.

# Hampden-Sydney College

**Hampden-Sydney, VA 23943 — 804 223-6000**

**1993-94 Costs.** Tuition: $12,576. Room: $1,670-$1,959. Board: $2,728. Fees, books, misc. academic expenses (school's estimate): $748.

**Enrollment.** 946 men (full-time). Freshman class: 817 applicants, 644 accepted, 307 enrolled.

**Test score averages/ranges.** Average SAT scores: 517 verbal, 564 math. Range of SAT scores of middle 50%: 460-570 verbal, 510-620 math.

**Faculty.** 60 full-time; 28 part-time. 87% of faculty holds doctoral degree. Student/faculty ratio: 13 to 1.

**Selectivity rating.** Competitive.

**PROFILE.** Hampden-Sydney, founded in 1776, is a private, liberal arts college for men. Its 566-acre campus, including Federal style building architecture, is located 70 miles southwest of Richmond.

**Accreditation:** SACS.

**Religious orientation:** Hampden-Sydney College is affiliated with the Presbyterian Church (Synod of the Virginias); One semester of religion or philosophy required.

**Library:** Collections totaling over 190,000 volumes, 798 periodical subscriptions, and 33,300 microform items.

**Special facilities/museums:** History museum, language lab, international communications center.

**Athletic facilities:** Gymnasiums, swimming pool, basketball, handball, racquetball, tennis, and volleyball courts, outdoor recreational facility, baseball, football, intramural, lacrosse, and soccer fields, weight room.

**STUDENT BODY. Undergraduate profile:** 53% are state residents; 3% are transfers. 1% Asian-American, 3% Black, 1% Hispanic, 94% White, 1% Other. Average age of undergraduates is 20.

**Freshman profile:** 1% of freshmen who took SAT scored 700 or over on verbal, 8% scored 700 or over on math; 17% scored 600 or over on verbal, 35% scored 600 or over on math; 58% scored 500 or over on verbal, 82% scored 500 or over on math; 95% scored 400 or over on verbal, 98% scored 400 or over on math; 100% scored 300 or over on verbal, 100% scored 300 or over on math. 92% of accepted applicants took SAT; 8% took ACT. 58% of freshmen come from public schools.

**Undergraduate achievement:** 78% of fall 1992 freshmen returned for fall 1993 term. 60% of entering class graduated. 20% of students who completed a degree program immediately went on to graduate study.

**Foreign students:** Six students are from out of the country. Countries represented include Australia, Canada, England, and Peru.

**PROGRAMS OF STUDY. Degrees:** B.A., B.S.

**Majors:** Biology, Biology/Chemistry, Biology/Physics, Chemistry, Chemistry/Physics, Classical Studies, Economics, Economics/Mathematics, English, French, German, Greek, History, Humanities, Latin, Latin/Greek, Management Economics, Mathematics, Mathematics/Computer Science, Mathematics/Natural Science, Philosophy, Physics, Political Science, Psychology, Religion, Religion/Philosophy, Spanish.

**Distribution of degrees:** The majors with the highest enrollment are economics, history, and biology; biology/chemistry, biology/physics, and chemistry/physics have the lowest.

**Requirements:** General education requirement.

**Academic regulations:** Freshmen must maintain minimum 1.5 GPA; sophomores, 1.85 GPA; juniors, 2.0 GPA; seniors, 2.0 GPA.

**Special:** Double majors. Dual degrees. Independent study. Internships. Preprofessional programs in law, medicine, and business. 3-2 programs in engineering with Georgia Tech and Virginia Polytech Inst. Washington Semester. Appalachian Semester (Kentucky). Cooperative exchange program with Longwood Coll for education, sociology, and anthropology. Junior/senior exchange with Hollins Coll, Mary Baldwin Coll, Randolph-Macon Coll, Randolph-Macon Woman's Coll, Sweet Briar Coll, and Washington and Lee U. Study abroad in England, Far East countries, France, Germany, Latin American countries, and Spain. ROTC at Longwood Coll.

**Honors:** Phi Beta Kappa. Honors program. Honor societies.

**Academic Assistance:** Remedial study skills. Nonremedial tutoring.

**ADMISSIONS. Academic basis for candidate selection** (in order of priority): Secondary school record, class rank, school's recommendation, standardized test scores, essay.

**Nonacademic basis for candidate selection:** Character and personality, extracurricular participation, and alumni/ae relationship are emphasized. Particular talent or ability is important. Geographical distribution is considered.

**Requirements:** Graduation from secondary school is required; GED is accepted. 16 units and the following program of study are required: 4 units of English, 3 units of math, 2 units of science including 1 unit of lab, 2 units of foreign language, 1 unit of social studies, 4 units of academic electives. Required math units should include two algebra and one plane geometry. Additional advanced math courses recommended. SAT or ACT is required. ACH recommended. Campus visit and interview recommended. No off-campus interviews.

**Procedure:** Take SAT or ACT by January of 12th year. Suggest filing application by fall. Application deadline is March 1. Acceptance notification usually between March 1 and April 15. Reply is required by May 1. $300 nonrefundable tuition deposit. Freshmen accepted for terms other than fall.

**Special programs:** Credit and/or placement may be granted through CEEB Advanced Placement exams for scores of 4 or higher. Early decision program. In fall 1993, 107 ap-

plied for early decision and 90 were accepted. Deadline for applying for early decision is November 15. Early entrance/early admission program.
**Transfer students:** Transfer students accepted for terms other than fall. In fall 1993, 3% of all new students were transfers into all classes. 29 transfer applications were received, 16 were accepted. Application deadline is July 1 for fall; December 1 for spring. Minimum 2.5 GPA required. Lowest course grade accepted is "C." Maximum number of transferable credits is 60 semester hours. At least 60 semester hours must be completed at the college to receive degree.
**Admissions contact:** Anita Garland, M.B.A., Director of Admissions. 804 223-6120.

**FINANCIAL AID. Available aid:** Pell grants, SEOG, state grants, school scholarships and grants, private scholarships and grants, ROTC scholarships, and academic merit scholarships. Virginia Tuition and College Scholarship Assistance Programs for Virginia residents. Perkins Loans (NDSL), PLUS, Stafford Loans (GSL), school loans, private loans, and SLS. EDVANTAGE. EXCEL. Knight Tuition Plans and AMS.
**Financial aid statistics:** 20% of aid is not need-based. In 1993-94, 98% of all undergraduate applicants received aid; 99% of freshman applicants. Average amounts of aid awarded freshmen: Scholarships and grants, $6,552; loans, $5,029.
**Supporting data/closing dates:** FAFSA/FAF: Deadline is March 1. State aid form: Deadline is July 31. Notification of awards begins March 15.
**Financial aid contact:** Sally Waters, Director of Financial Resource Counseling. 804 223-6119.

# Hampton University

**Hampton, VA 23368** 804 727-5000

**1994-95 Costs.** Tuition: $7,161. Room: $1,838. Board: $1,630. Fees, books, misc. academic expenses (school's estimate): $1,203.
**Enrollment.** Undergraduates: 1,808 men, 2,748 women (full-time). Freshman class: 7,178 applicants, 3,755 accepted, 1,433 enrolled. Graduate enrollment: 396.
**Test score averages/ranges.** Average SAT scores: 925 combined.
**Faculty.** 291 full-time; 99 part-time. 60% of faculty holds doctoral degree. Student/faculty ratio: 18 to 1.
**Selectivity rating.** Less competitive.

**PROFILE.** Hampton, founded in 1868, is a private university. Programs are offered through the Schools of Arts and Letters, Business, Education, Nursing, and Pure and Applied Sciences. Its 204-acre campus, including buildings listed with the National Register of Historic Places, is located within 40 miles of Jamestown, Yorktown, and Williamsburg.

**Accreditation:** SACS. Professionally accredited by the Accreditation Board for Engineering and Technology, the National Architecture Accrediting Board, the National Association of Schools of Music, the National Council for Accreditation of Teacher Education, the National League for Nursing.
**Religious orientation:** Hampton University is nonsectarian; no religious requirements.
**Library:** Collections totaling over 235,000 volumes, 1,200 periodical subscriptions, and 35,000 microform items.
**Special facilities/museums:** African, Native American, and oceanic museums, gallery, laboratory elementary school.
**Athletic facilities:** Gymnasium, swimming pools, tennis courts, athletic fields.

**STUDENT BODY. Undergraduate profile:** 50% are state residents. 90% Black, 9% White, 1% Other.
**Freshman profile:** Majority of accepted applicants took SAT.
**Undergraduate achievement:** 86% of fall 1992 freshmen returned for fall 1993 term. 60% of entering class graduated. 25% of students who completed a degree program immediately went on to graduate study.
**Foreign students:** 42 students are from out of the country.

**PROGRAMS OF STUDY. Degrees:** B.A., B.Arch., B.S., B.S.Nurs.
**Majors:** Accounting, Airway Science, Architecture, Art, Biology, Building Construction Technology, Business, Business Education, Chemical Engineering, Chemistry, Communication Disorders, Community Service Education, Computer Science, Early Childhood, Economics, Education, Electrical Engineering, Elementary Education, Engineering, English, Environmental Analysis, Finance, Health/Physical Education, History, Interior Design, Management, Marine Biology, Marketing, Mass Media Arts, Mathematics, Mechanical Engineering, Music, Music Education, Nursing, Physical Education, Physics, Political Science, Professional Tennis Management, Psychology, Recreation, Secondary Education, Sociology, Spanish, Special Education, Speech/Drama.
**Distribution of degrees:** The majors with the highest enrollment are accounting, biology, and psychology; special education and speech/drama have the lowest.
**Requirements:** General education requirement.
**Academic regulations:** Minimum 2.0 GPA must be maintained.
**Special:** Internships. Cooperative education programs. Graduate school at which undergraduates may take graduate-level courses. Preprofessional programs in law, medicine, veterinary science, pharmacy, and dentistry. Teacher certification in early childhood, elementary, secondary, and special education. Study abroad possible. ROTC and NROTC.
**Honors:** Phi Beta Kappa. Honors program. Honor societies.
**Academic Assistance:** Remedial reading, writing, math, and study skills. Nonremedial tutoring.

**STUDENT LIFE. Housing:** Students may live on or off campus. Coed, women's, and men's dorms. 50% of students live in college housing.
**Social atmosphere:** On campus, students gather at the student union and the library; off campus, Ogden Circle and Hampton Harbor are popular hangouts. The Student Government Association, the Student Christian Association, and the Greek community are among the groups that have a widespread influence on campus life. Popular annual events include Homecoming, the Black Family Conference, the Mass Media Arts Symposium, and Career Day. "The social and cultural atmosphere of the Hampton University community is one characterized by African-American unity. In addition, Hampton encourages academic as well as social development and the importance of reaching out to the community surrounding the campus."
**Services and counseling/handicapped student services:** Placement services. Health service. Personal counseling. Career and academic guidance services. Physically disabled student services. Learning disabled services. Tutors.
**Campus organizations:** Undergraduate student government. Student newspaper (Hampton Script, published once/two weeks). Yearbook. Radio station. Band, choir, orchestra, University Players, debating, athletic, departmental, service, and special-interest groups, 70 organizations in all. Five fraternities, no chapter houses; three sororities, no chapter houses.
**Religious organizations:** Student Christian Association.
**Minority/foreign student organizations:** International Student Club.

**ATHLETICS. Physical education requirements:** Two semesters of physical education required.
**Intercollegiate competition:** 3% of students participate. Basketball (M,W), cheerleading (M,W), cross-country (M,W), football (M), golf (M), softball (W), tennis (M), track (indoor) (M,W), track (outdoor) (M,W), track and field (indoor) (M,W), track and field (outdoor) (M,W), volleyball (W). Member of Central Intercollegiate Athletic Association, NCAA Division II.
**Intramural and club sports:** 1% of students participate. Intramural archery, basketball, bowling, flag football, softball, swimming, tennis.

**ADMISSIONS. Academic basis for candidate selection** (in order of priority): Secondary school record, standardized test scores, essay, school's recommendation, class rank.
**Nonacademic basis for candidate selection:** Character and personality, extracurricular participation, particular talent or ability, geographical distribution, and alumni/ae relationship are considered.
**Requirements:** Graduation from secondary school is recommended; GED is accepted. 17 units and the following program of study are required: 4 units of English, 3 units of math, 2 units of science, 2 units of history, 6 units of academic electives. Minimum combined SAT score of 800, rank in top half of secondary school class, and minimum 2.0 GPA required. Conditional admission possible for applicants not meeting standard requirements. SAT or ACT is required. Campus visit recommended. No off-campus interviews.
**Procedure:** Take SAT or ACT by September 15 of 12th year. Suggest filing application by September 1. Application deadline is March 15. Notification of admission on rolling basis. $600 tuition deposit, refundable until June 7. $100 room deposit, refundable until June 1. Freshmen accepted for terms other than fall.
**Special programs:** Admission may be deferred one year. Credit and/or placement may be granted through CEEB Advanced Placement exams for scores of 3 or higher. Credit and placement may be granted through military and life experience. Early decision program. Early entrance/early admission program. Concurrent enrollment program.
**Transfer students:** Transfer students accepted for terms other than fall. In fall 1993, 832 transfer applications were received, 292 were accepted. Application deadline is March 15 for fall; December 15 for spring. Minimum 2.3 GPA required. Lowest course grade accepted is "C." At least 30 semester hours must be completed at the university to receive degree.
**Admissions contact:** Dr. Ollie M. Bowman, Dean of Admissions. 800 624-3328, 804 727-5328.

**FINANCIAL AID. Available aid:** Pell grants, SEOG, state grants, school scholarships and grants, private scholarships and grants, ROTC scholarships, academic merit scholarships, athletic scholarships, and aid for undergraduate foreign students. Perkins Loans (NDSL), PLUS, Stafford Loans (GSL), NSL, state loans, private loans, and SLS. Tuition Plan Inc. and deferred payment plan.
**Supporting data/closing dates:** FAFSA/FAF: Priority filing date is March 31. School's own aid application: Priority filing date is March 31. State aid form: Accepted on rolling basis. Notification of awards on rolling basis.
**Financial aid contact:** Delores Davis, Director of Financial Aid. 800 624-3341, 804 727-5332.

**STUDENT EMPLOYMENT.** College Work/Study Program. Off-campus part-time employment opportunities rated "good."

**COMPUTER FACILITIES.** IBM/IBM-compatible microcomputers.
**Fees:** None.

**GRADUATE CAREER DATA.** Graduate school percentages: 3% enter law school. 1% enter medical school. 4% enter graduate business programs. 17% enter graduate arts and sciences programs.

**PROMINENT ALUMNI/AE.** Booker T. Washington, national leader and founder, Tuskegee Institute; Sarah Collins Fernandis; Susan La Flesche, first Native American woman to receive the degree of doctor of medicine.

# Hollins College

**Roanoke, VA 24020** 703 362-6000

**1994-95 Costs.** Tuition: $13,470. Room: $3,225. Board: $2,290. Fees, books, misc. academic expenses (school's estimate): $734.
**Enrollment.** 779 women (full-time). Freshman class: 602 applicants, 498 accepted, 215 enrolled. Graduate enrollment: 50 men, 138 women.
**Test score averages/ranges.** Average SAT scores: 505 verbal, 502 math. Range of SAT scores of middle 50%: 450-560 verbal, 440-550 math. Average ACT scores: 23 composite. Range of ACT scores of middle 50%: 20-25 composite.
**Faculty.** 78 full-time; 13 part-time. 90% of faculty holds highest degree in specific field. Student/faculty ratio: 9 to 1.
**Selectivity rating.** Competitive.

**PROFILE.** Hollins, founded in 1842, is a private, liberal arts college for women. Its 450-acre campus is located in the Roanoke Valley. The campus Quadrangle, which includes examples of Classical Revival architecture, is listed in the National Register of Historic Places.

**Accreditation:** SACS.
**Religious orientation:** Hollins College is nonsectarian; no religious requirements.
**Library:** Collections totaling over 146,000 volumes, 823 periodical subscriptions, and 193,293 microform items.
**Special facilities/museums:** Art museum, athletic complex, language labs, on-campus preschool, campus-wide computer network. Communications Research Institute. Sound spectrograph, nuclear magnetic resonance spectrometer, ultramicrotome, gas chromatograph, tissue culture and scanning electron microscope.
**Athletic facilities:** Gymnasiums, swimming pool, saunas, tennis courts, field hockey, lacrosse, and soccer fields, indoor riding facility, putting green, ropes course, aerobics, training, and weight rooms, fencing studio, riding trails, jogging course.

**STUDENT BODY. Undergraduate profile:** 34% are state residents; 9% are transfers. 1% Asian-American, 3% Black, 2% Hispanic, .5% Native American, 91% White, 2.5% Other. Average age of undergraduates is 20.
**Freshman profile:** 1% of freshmen who took SAT scored 700 or over on verbal, 1% scored 700 or over on math; 16% scored 600 or over on verbal, 13% scored 600 or over on math; 50% scored 500 or over on verbal, 50% scored 500 or over on math; 91% scored 400 or over on verbal, 88% scored 400 or over on math; 100% scored 300 or over on verbal, 94% scored 300 or over on math. 94% of accepted applicants took SAT; 33% took ACT. 73% of freshmen come from public schools.
**Undergraduate achievement:** 82% of fall 1992 freshmen returned for fall 1993 term. 68% of entering class graduated. 29% of students who completed a degree program immediately went on to graduate study.
**Foreign students:** 15 students are from out of the country. Countries represented include China, India, Japan, Norway, Panama, and Russia; 12 in all.

**PROGRAMS OF STUDY. Degrees:** B.A.
**Majors:** American Studies, Art, Art History, Art Studio, Biology, Chemistry, Classics, Communications Studies, Computational Sciences, Economics, English, French, German, History, Interdisciplinary Studies, Mathematics, Music, Philosophy, Physics, Political Science, Psychology, Religion, Sociology, Spanish, Theatre Arts.
**Distribution of degrees:** The majors with the highest enrollment are English, psychology, and economics; German, classical studies, and religion have the lowest.
**Requirements:** General education requirement.
**Academic regulations:** Freshmen must maintain minimum 1.8 GPA; sophomores, 1.9 GPA; juniors, 2.0 GPA; seniors, 2.0 GPA.
**Special:** Minors offered in most majors. Concentrations in creative writing, international relations, and Latin American studies. Majors focus on an idea, issue, or problem approached from the point of view of two or more disciplines. Field experience is an important part of many programs. Interdisciplinary programs offered in environmental, global, imagination, and women's studies, and Western traditions. "Pathways" program allows students in some majors to focus on a particular area of interest, combining academic course concentration with community service and internship. Four-week January period for individually-chosen special projects and career internships; all participate. Seminars. Undergraduate research program in natural sciences and math. Self-designed majors. Double majors. Dual degrees. Independent study. Accelerated study. Pass/fail grading option. Internships. Graduate school at which undergraduates may take graduate-level courses. Preprofessional programs in law, medicine, veterinary science, and dentistry. 3-2 engineering programs with Virginia Polytech Inst and Washington U. Six-year architecture program with Virginia Polytech Inst. Computer science program with Virginia Polytech Inst. Member of Seven College Exchange Consortium of Virginia schools, American Collegiate for East-West Cultural and Academic Exchange, and Consortium of Liberal Arts colleges offering study in Kobe, Japan. Washington Semester and UN Semester. Exchange programs with Hampden-Sydney Coll, Mary Baldwin Coll, Mills Coll, Randolph-Macon Coll, Randolph-Macon Women's Coll, Sweet Briar Coll, Washington and Lee U. Teacher certification in early childhood, elementary, and secondary education. Certification in specific subject areas. Exchange program abroad in Jamaica. Study abroad also possible in England, France, Germany, Greece, Japan, Mexico, and the former Soviet Republics.
**Honors:** Phi Beta Kappa. Honors program. Honor societies.
**Academic Assistance:** Nonremedial tutoring.

**ADMISSIONS. Academic basis for candidate selection** (in order of priority): Secondary school record, class rank, standardized test scores, school's recommendation, essay.
**Nonacademic basis for candidate selection:** Extracurricular participation and particular talent or ability are emphasized. Character and personality are important. Geographical distribution and alumni/ae relationship are considered.
**Requirements:** Graduation from secondary school is required; GED is accepted. 16 units and the following program of study are recommended: 4 units of English, 3 units of math, 3 units of science, 3 units of foreign language, 3 units of social studies. Minimum combined SAT score of 900, rank in top two-fifths of secondary school class, and minimum 3.0 GPA recommended. Letter of recommendation required. SAT is required; ACT may be substituted. ACH recommended. Campus visit and interview recommended. Off-campus interviews available with admissions and alumni representatives.
**Procedure:** Take SAT or ACT by January of 12th year. Take ACH by January of 12th year. Application deadline is February 15. Notification of admissions begins on February 1. Reply is required by May 1. $400 tuition deposit, refundable until May 1. Freshmen accepted for terms other than fall.
**Special programs:** Admission may be deferred one year. Credit may be granted through CEEB Advanced Placement for scores of 4 or higher. Early decision program. In fall 1993, 65 applied for early decision and 63 were accepted. Deadline for applying for early decision is December 1. Early entrance/early admission program.
**Transfer students:** Transfer students accepted for terms other than fall. In fall 1993, 9% of all new students were transfers into all classes. 65 transfer applications were received, 40 were accepted. Application deadline is July 1 for fall; December 1 for spring. Minimum 2.5 GPA recommended. Lowest course grade accepted is "C." Maximum number of transferable credits is 60 semester hours. At least 68 semester hours must be completed at the college to receive degree.
**Admissions contact:** Stuart Trinkle, Director of Admissions. 703 362-6401, 800 456-9595.

**FINANCIAL AID. Available aid:** Pell grants, SEOG, state grants, school scholarships and grants, private scholarships and grants, academic merit scholarships, and aid for undergraduate foreign students. Perkins Loans (NDSL), PLUS, Stafford Loans (GSL), private loans, and SLS. Tuition Plan Inc., Knight Tuition Plans, deferred payment plan, and guaranteed tuition.
**Financial aid statistics:** 47% of aid is not need-based. In 1993-94, 94% of all undergraduate applicants received aid; 100% of freshman applicants. Average amounts of aid awarded freshmen: Scholarships and grants, $9,500; loans, $4,000.
**Supporting data/closing dates:** FAFSA/FAF: Priority filing date is March 1. Income tax forms: Priority filing date is March 1; accepted on rolling basis. Notification of awards on rolling basis.
**Financial aid contact:** Laura Troy, M.S.Ed., Director of Financial Aid. 703 362-6332.

## James Madison University

**Harrisonburg, VA 22807 — 703 568-6211**

**1994-95 Costs.** Tuition: $3,900 (state residents), $7,994 (out-of-state). Room: $2,450. Board: $2,094. Fees, books, misc. academic expenses (school's estimate): $500.
**Enrollment.** Undergraduates: 4,243 men, 5,302 women (full-time). Freshman class: 11,512 applicants, 5,328 accepted, 2,082 enrolled. Graduate enrollment: 287 men, 524 women.
**Test score averages/ranges.** Average SAT scores: 521 verbal, 586 math.
**Faculty.** 508 full-time; 178 part-time. 81% of faculty holds highest degree in specific field. Student/faculty ratio: 18 to 1.
**Selectivity rating.** Highly competitive.

**PROFILE.** James Madison, founded in 1908, is a public university. Programs are offered through the Colleges of Letters and Sciences, Business, Education and Psychology, Fine Arts and Communication, and Health and Human Services and the Graduate School. Its 472-acre campus is located in Harrisonburg.

**Accreditation:** SACS. Professionally accredited by the American Assembly of Collegiate Schools of Business, the American Bar Association, the American Dietetic Association, the American Home Economics Association, the American Speech-Language-Hearing Association, the Council on Social Work Education, the National Association of Schools of Art and Design, the National Association of Schools of Music, the National Council for Accreditation of Teacher Education, the National League for Nursing.
**Religious orientation:** James Madison University is nonsectarian; three credit hours of philosophy, religion, or values required.
**Library:** Collections totaling over 344,017 volumes, 2,298 periodical subscriptions, and 1,209,913 microform items.
**Special facilities/museums:** Life science museum, language lab, development center, TV/film center, music and fine arts buildings, herbarium, university farm, planetarium.
**Athletic facilities:** Swimming pool, gymnasium, racquetball and tennis courts, weight rooms, track, artificial turf field, playing fields, golf practice range.

**STUDENT BODY. Undergraduate profile:** 73% are state residents; 18% are transfers. 3% Asian-American, 8% Black, 1% Hispanic, 88% White. Average age of undergraduates is 20.
**Freshman profile:** 1% of freshmen who took SAT scored 700 or over on verbal, 5% scored 700 or over on math; 12% scored 600 or over on verbal, 43% scored 600 or over on math; 59% scored 500 or over on verbal, 87% scored 500 or over on math; 94% scored 400 or over on verbal, 99% scored 400 or over on math; 100% scored 300 or over on verbal, 100% scored 300 or over on math. 100% of accepted applicants took SAT. 95% of freshmen come from public schools.
**Undergraduate achievement:** 91% of fall 1992 freshmen returned for fall 1993 term. 58% of entering class graduated. 16% of students who completed a degree program immediately went on to graduate study.
**Foreign students:** 69 students are from out of the country. Countries represented include Canada, India, Japan, Korea, Norway, and Sweden; 39 in all.

**PROGRAMS OF STUDY. Degrees:** B.A., B.Bus.Admin., B.F.A., B.Gen.Studies, B.Mus., B.S., B.S.Nurs., B.Soc.Work.
**Majors:** Accounting, Anthropology, Art, Art History, Biology, Business Economics, Chemistry, Computer Information Systems, Computer Science, Dance, Dietetics, Early Childhood Education, Economics, Elementary Education, English, Finance, General Special Education, Geography, Geology, Health Services, History, Hotel/Restaurant Management, Human Communication, Integrated Science and Technology, Interdisciplinary Social Science, International Affairs, International Business, Kinesiology, Living Sciences, Management, Marketing, Marketing Education, Mass Communication, Mathematics, Medical Technology, Middle School Education, Modern Foreign Language/French, Modern Foreign Language/German, Modern Foreign Language/Russian, Modern Foreign Language/Spanish, Music, Music Education, Nursing, Office Systems Management, Philosophy/Religion, Physics, Political Science, Production/Operations Management, Psychology, Public Administration, School Library Media Services, Social Work, Sociology, Speech Pathology, Theater, Trade/Industrial Education.
**Distribution of degrees:** The majors with the highest enrollment are psychology, communication, and English; dietetics, physics, and dance have the lowest.
**Requirements:** General education requirement.
**Academic regulations:** Minimum 2.0 GPA must be maintained.
**Special:** Minors offered in most majors and in many interdisciplinary areas. Double majors. Independent study. Accelerated study. Pass/fail grading option. Internships. Preprofessional programs in law, medicine, veterinary science, pharmacy, dentistry, and theology. Member of Valley of Virginia Consortium for Higher Education. Teacher certification in early childhood, elementary, secondary, and special education. Certification in specific subject areas. Exchange programs abroad in China (Zhengzhou U), Germany (European Business Sch), Hong Kong (Chinese U), and Russia (Herzen Inst, U of St. Petersburg). Study abroad also in England, France, Italy, Martinique, and Spain. ROTC.

**Honors:** Honors program. Honor societies.
**Academic Assistance:** Remedial reading and writing. Nonremedial tutoring.

**STUDENT LIFE. Housing:** All freshmen must live on campus. Coed, women's, and men's dorms. Sorority and fraternity housing. 49% of students live in college housing.
**Services and counseling/handicapped student services:** Placement services. Health service. Counseling services for minority and older students. Personal counseling. Career and academic guidance services. Physically disabled student services. Learning disabled services. Notetaking services. Tape recorders. Tutors. Reader services for the blind.
**Campus organizations:** Undergraduate student government. Student newspaper (Breeze, published biweekly). Literary magazine. Yearbook. Radio station. Advertising Association, Amnesty International, BACCHUS, Dance Theatre, Interior Design Club, Stratford Players, 215 organizations in all. 17 fraternities, 10 chapter houses; 12 sororities, eight chapter houses. 16% of men join a fraternity. 20% of women join a sorority.
**Religious organizations:** Bahai Association, Baptist Student Union, Canterbury, Hillel, campus ministry, other religious groups.
**Minority/foreign student organizations:** Black Student Alliance, Black Greek Caucus. International Students Club.

**ATHLETICS. Physical education requirements:** Two credit hours of physical education required; exemption for military service.
**Intercollegiate competition:** 5% of students participate. Archery (M,W), baseball (M), basketball (M,W), cheerleading (M,W), cross-country (M,W), diving (M,W), fencing (W), field hockey (W), football (M), golf (M,W), gymnastics (M,W), lacrosse (W), soccer (M,W), swimming (M,W), tennis (M,W), track (indoor) (M,W), track (outdoor) (M,W), track and field (indoor) (M,W), track and field (outdoor) (M,W), volleyball (W), wrestling (M). Member of Colonial Athletic Association, ECAC, NCAA Division I, NCAA Division I-AA for football, Yankee Conference for football.
**Intramural and club sports:** 65% of students participate. Intramural badminton, basketball, bowling, football, golf, lacrosse, pickleball, racquetball, rugby, soccer, softball, swimming, table tennis, tennis, volleyball, walleyball, water polo, wrestling. Men's club bowling, cycling, fencing, field hockey, lacrosse, martial arts, Nordic skiing, racquetball, rugby, volleyball, water polo. Women's club bowling, cycling, field hockey, martial arts, Nordic skiing, racquetball, rugby, softball, water polo.

**ADMISSIONS. Academic basis for candidate selection** (in order of priority): Secondary school record, class rank, standardized test scores, essay, school's recommendation.
**Nonacademic basis for candidate selection:** Character and personality, extracurricular participation, and particular talent or ability are emphasized. Geographical distribution and alumni/ae relationship are considered.
**Requirements:** Graduation from secondary school is required; GED is not accepted. 22 units and the following program of study are recommended: 4 units of English, 4 units of math, 4 units of science including 3 units of lab, 4 units of foreign language, 1 unit of social studies, 2 units of history. Minimum combined SAT score of 800 required of all applicants; rank in top half of secondary class recommended of in-state applicants and rank in top third of secondary school class recommended of out-of-state applicants. Audition required of dance, music, and theater program applicants. Supplemental applications and interviews required of nursing program applicants. Portfolio required of art program applicants. SAT is required. Campus visit recommended. No off-campus interviews.
**Procedure:** Take SAT by December of 12th year. Suggest filing application by December 1. Application deadline is January 15. Notification of admission by April 1. Reply is required by May 1. $250 tuition deposit, refundable until May 1. Freshmen accepted for fall terms only.
**Special programs:** Credit may be granted through CEEB Advanced Placement for scores of 3 or higher. Credit may be granted through military experience. Credit and placement may be granted through challenge exams. Early decision program. In fall 1993, 5,826 applied for early decision and 1,070 were accepted. Deadline for applying for early decision is December 1.
**Transfer students:** Transfer students accepted for terms other than fall. In fall 1993, 18% of all new students were transfers into all classes. 1,476 transfer applications were received, 830 were accepted. Application deadline is February 1 for fall; November 15 for spring. Minimum 2.0 GPA required. Lowest course grade accepted is "C-." Minimum number of transferable semester hours is the equivalent of one year of course work. At least 32 semester hours must be completed at the university to receive degree.
**Admissions contact:** Alan L. Cerveny, M.A., Director of Admissions. 703 568-6147.

**FINANCIAL AID. Available aid:** Pell grants, SEOG, Federal Nursing Student Scholarships, state scholarships and grants, school scholarships and grants, private scholarships and grants, ROTC scholarships, and athletic scholarships. Perkins Loans (NDSL), PLUS, Stafford Loans (GSL), NSL, state loans, private loans, and SLS. Tuition Plan Inc., Knight Tuition Plans, and AMS.
**Financial aid statistics:** In 1993-94, 35% of all undergraduate applicants received aid; 85% of freshman applicants. Average amounts of aid awarded freshmen: Scholarships and grants, $2,535; loans, $2,400.
**Supporting data/closing dates:** FAFSA/FFS: Priority filing date is February 15. Notification of awards begins April 15.
**Financial aid contact:** John H. Sellers, M.Ed., Director of Financial Aid and Student Employment. 703 568-6644.

**STUDENT EMPLOYMENT.** College Work/Study Program. Institutional employment. 20% of full-time undergraduates work on campus during school year. Students may expect to earn an average of $1,200 during school year. Off-campus part-time employment opportunities rated "good."

**COMPUTER FACILITIES.** 300 IBM/IBM-compatible and Macintosh/Apple microcomputers; 250 are networked. Students may access Digital, Hewlett-Packard minicomputer/mainframe systems, BITNET, Internet. Residence halls may be equipped with stand-alone microcomputers, networked microcomputers, networked terminals. Client/LAN operating systems include Apple/Macintosh, DOS. Computer languages and software packages include Ada, BASIC, C, COBOL, dBASE, FORTRAN, Lotus 1-2-3, MacDraw, MacWrite, Microsoft Word, Microsoft Works, Pascal, Ready-Set-Go!, SAS, SPSS-X, WordPerfect; 25 in all. Computer facilities are available to all students.
**Fees:** Computer fee is included in tuition/fees.
**Hours:** 8 AM-midn. (M-Th); 8 AM-5 PM (F); noon-6 PM (Sa); 1 PM-midn. (Su); one 24-hour lab.

**GRADUATE CAREER DATA.** Graduate school percentages: 2% enter law school. 2% enter graduate business programs. 3% enter graduate arts and sciences programs. Highest graduate school enrollments: Coll of William and Mary, George Mason U, James Madison U, Medical Coll of Virginia, U of Virginia, Wake Forest U. Companies and businesses that hire graduates: Arthur Andersen, Electronic Data Systems, Marriott.

**PROMINENT ALUMNI/AE.** J.G. Ferguson, president and CEO, American Safety Razor Co.; Sterling Baldwin, vice-president, Universal Leaf Tobacco Co.; Phoef Sutton, TV producer *(Bob)*; Charles Haley, football player, Dallas Cowboys; Gary Clark, football player, Phoenix Cardinals.

# Liberty University

**Lynchburg, VA 24506-8001** **804 582-2000**

**1993-94 Costs.** Tuition: $6,600. Room & board: $4,380. Fees, books, misc. academic expenses (school's estimate): $500.
**Enrollment.** Undergraduates: 2,182 men, 2,115 women (full-time). Graduate enrollment: 149 men, 49 women.
**Test score averages/ranges.** N/A.
**Faculty.** 156 full-time; 28 part-time. 57% of faculty holds highest degree in specific field. Student/faculty ratio: 24 to 1.
**Selectivity rating.** N/A.

**PROFILE.** Liberty, founded in 1971, is a church-affiliated university. Programs are offered through the College of Arts and Sciences and the Schools of Business and Government, Communications, Education, Life-Long Learning, and Religion. Its 5,300-acre campus is located in Lynchburg, in the Blue Ridge Mountains.
**Accreditation:** SACS.
**Religious orientation:** Liberty University is a nondenominational Christian school; 15 semester hours of religion required.
**Library:** Collections totaling over 190,405 volumes, 1,118 periodical subscriptions, and 32,440 microform items.
**Special facilities/museums:** Creation studies museum.
**Athletic facilities:** Gymnasiums, baseball, intramural, soccer, and softball fields, tennis courts, cross-country trails, track, weight and wrestling rooms, archery and pistol ranges.

**STUDENT BODY. Undergraduate profile:** 26% are state residents; 21% are transfers. 3% Asian-American, 6% Black, 2% Hispanic, 89% White. Average age of undergraduates is 21.
**Undergraduate achievement:** 28% of students who completed a degree program immediately went on to graduate study.
**Foreign students:** 119 students are from out of the country. Countries represented include the Bahamas, Canada, Korea, Nigeria, and Romania; 31 in all.

**PROGRAMS OF STUDY. Degrees:** B.A., B.S.
**Majors:** Accounting, Biblical Studies, Biology, Business, Chemistry, Church Ministries, Community Health Promotion, Computer Science, Drama, Economics, English, Exercise Science/Fitness Programming, General Studies, Government, Health Education, History, Home Economics, Human Ecology, Interdisciplinary Studies, Journalism, Mathematics, Missions/Cross-Cultural Studies, Modern Languages, Music, Musical Performance, Nursing, Pastoral Ministries, Philosophy, Physical Education, Psychology, Recreation, Sacred Music, Social Sciences, Speech Communication, Sport Management, Telecommunications.
**Distribution of degrees:** The majors with the highest enrollment are business, education, and psychology; philosophy and drama have the lowest.
**Requirements:** General education requirement.
**Academic regulations:** Freshmen must maintain minimum 1.5 GPA; sophomores, 1.65 GPA; juniors, 1.85 GPA; seniors, 2.0 GPA.
**Special:** Minors offered in most majors and in art, athletic training, aviation, Biblical Greek, coaching, counseling, French, German, personnel/human resources management, physics, school health education, Spanish, theology, and youth ministries. Associate's degrees offered. Self-designed majors. Double majors. Independent study. Internships. Cooperative education programs. Graduate school at which undergraduates may take graduate-level courses. Preprofessional programs in law, medicine, veterinary science, dentistry, and theology. Washington Semester. Teacher certification in early childhood, elementary, and secondary education. Certification in specific subject areas. Study abroad in Israel. ROTC.
**Honors:** Honors program. Honor societies.
**Academic Assistance:** Remedial reading, writing, math, and study skills. Nonremedial tutoring.

**STUDENT LIFE. Housing:** All unmarried students under age 22 must live on campus unless living with family. Women's and men's dorms. 61% of students live in college housing.
**Services and counseling/handicapped student services:** Placement services. Health service. Counseling services for veteran students. Personal and psychological counseling. Career and academic guidance services. Religious counseling. Physically disabled student services. Learning disabled services. Tutors.
**Campus organizations:** Undergraduate student government. Student newspaper (Liberty Champion, published once/week). Literary magazine. Yearbook. Radio and TV stations. Concert choir, marching band, touring drama group, traveling ensemble of musicians, Circle K, Young Americans for Freedom, Young Republicans, departmental and professional groups, 73 organizations in all.
**Religious organizations:** Christian Student Fellowship, Fellowship of Christian Athletes, Light Theological Society, Shepherds Club, Youthquest.
**Minority/foreign student organizations:** Black Student Fellowship.

**ATHLETICS. Physical education requirements:** Two semester hours of physical education required.
**Intercollegiate competition:** 8% of students participate. Baseball (M), basketball (M,W), cheerleading (M,W), cross-country (M,W), football (M), golf (M), soccer (M,W), softball (W), tennis (M), track (indoor) (M,W), track (outdoor) (M,W), track and field (indoor)

(M,W), track and field (outdoor) (M,W), volleyball (W), wrestling (M). Member of Big South, Colonial Athletic Conference for wrestling, ECAC, NCAA Division 1-AA for football, NCAA Division I.
**Intramural and club sports:** 25% of students participate. Intramural basketball, flag football, golf, soccer, softball, tennis, volleyball. Men's club ice hockey, lacrosse, weight lifting. Women's club weight lifting.
**ADMISSIONS. Academic basis for candidate selection** (in order of priority): Secondary school record, standardized test scores, class rank, essay, school's recommendation.
**Nonacademic basis for candidate selection:** Character and personality and particular talent or ability are emphasized. Extracurricular participation and alumni/ae relationship are considered.
**Requirements:** Graduation from secondary school is required; GED is accepted. 12 units and the following program of study are recommended: 4 units of English, 3 units of math, 2 units of science, 1 unit of foreign language, 1 unit of social studies, 1 unit of history. SAT is required; ACT may be substituted. Campus visit recommended.
**Procedure:** Take SAT or ACT by March of 12th year. Suggest filing application by May 1. Application deadline is August 15. Notification of admission on rolling basis. Reply is required within two weeks of acceptance. $250 nonrefundable tuition deposit. Freshmen accepted for terms other than fall.
**Special programs:** Admission may be deferred one year. Credit and/or placement may be granted through CEEB Advanced Placement exams for scores of 3 or higher. Credit and/or placement may be granted through CLEP general and subject exams. Credit and placement may be granted through ACT PEP, DANTES, and challenge exams, and military and life experience. Early entrance/early admission program. Concurrent enrollment program.
**Transfer students:** Transfer students accepted for terms other than fall. In fall 1993, 21% of all new students were transfers into all classes. 538 transfer applications were received, 534 were accepted. Application deadline is August 1 for fall; January 1 for spring. Minimum 2.0 GPA recommended. Lowest course grade accepted is "C." At least 32 semester hours must be completed at the university to receive degree.
**Admissions contact:** T. Randall Scott, M.B.A., Vice President for Recruitment. 804 582-2158, 800 522-6225.

**FINANCIAL AID. Available aid:** Pell grants, SEOG, state scholarships and grants, school scholarships and grants, private scholarships and grants, ROTC scholarships, academic merit scholarships, and athletic scholarships. PLUS, Stafford Loans (GSL), private loans, and SLS. Deferred payment plan. Installment payment plan.
**Financial aid statistics:** 50% of aid is not need-based. In 1993-94, 100% of all undergraduate applicants received aid. Average amounts of aid awarded freshmen: Scholarships and grants, $2,000; loans, $2,625.
**Supporting data/closing dates:** FAFSA: Priority filing date is April 15. School's own aid application: Accepted on rolling basis. Notification of awards on rolling basis.
**Financial aid contact:** William Kellaris, M.A., Director of Financial Aid. 804 582-2270.

**STUDENT EMPLOYMENT.** College Work/Study Program. Institutional employment. 23% of full-time undergraduates work on campus during school year. Students may expect to earn an average of $1,200 during school year. Off-campus part-time employment opportunities rated "good."

**COMPUTER FACILITIES.** 140 IBM/IBM-compatible and Macintosh/Apple microcomputers; 85 are networked. Students may access AT&T, Digital minicomputer/mainframe systems. Client/LAN operating systems include Apple/Macintosh. 14 major computer languages and software packages available. Computer facilities are available to all students.
**Fees:** $10-$80/course.
**Hours:** 8 AM-11 PM.

**GRADUATE CAREER DATA.** Graduate school percentages: 1% enter law school. 3% enter medical school. 3% enter graduate business programs. 10% enter graduate arts and sciences programs. 8% enter theological school/seminary. Highest graduate school enrollments: Liberty U, Lynchburg Coll, U of North Carolina, U of South Florida.

## Longwood College

**Farmville, VA 23909** — **804 395-2000**

**1994-95 Costs.** Tuition: $2,606 (state residents), $7,920 (out-of-state). Room & board: $3,814. Fees, books, misc. academic expenses (school's estimate): $2,140.
**Enrollment.** Undergraduates: 941 men, 1,937 women (full-time). Freshman class: 2,747 applicants, 1,870 accepted, 724 enrolled. Graduate enrollment: 69 men, 194 women.
**Test score averages/ranges.** Average SAT scores: 455 verbal, 497 math. Range of SAT scores of middle 50%: 410-490 verbal, 450-540 math.
**Faculty.** 153 full-time; 52 part-time. 80% of faculty holds doctoral degree. Student/faculty ratio: 14 to 1.
**Selectivity rating.** Less competitive.

**PROFILE.** Longwood, founded in 1839, is public college. Programs are offered through the Schools of Business and Economics, Education and Human Services, and Liberal Arts and Sciences. Its 50-acre campus and 100-acre recreational area are located in Farmville, 60 miles west of Richmond.

**Accreditation:** SACS. Professionally accredited by the Council on Social Work Education, the National Association of Schools of Music, the National Council for Accreditation of Teacher Education, the National Recreation and Park Association.
**Religious orientation:** Longwood College is nonsectarian; no religious requirements.
**Library:** Collections totaling over 294,225 volumes, 1,645 periodical subscriptions, and 549,936 microform items.
**Special facilities/museums:** Language lab, 100 acres of recreational area, small business development center, archaeology collection, flora collection, art gallery, on-campus preschool, radio station, television studio, electronic classroom.
**Athletic facilities:** Athletic complex, gymnasium, human performance and weight training labs, dance studio, swimming pool, natatorium, nine-hole golf course, basketball, tennis, and volleyball courts, baseball, soccer, and softball fields, gymnastics area.

**STUDENT BODY. Undergraduate profile:** 93% are state residents; 22% are transfers. 1% Asian-American, 8% Black, 1% Hispanic, 89% White, 1% Other. Average age of undergraduates is 21.
**Freshman profile:** 99% of accepted applicants took SAT; 1% took ACT. 92% of freshmen come from public schools.
**Undergraduate achievement:** 80% of fall 1992 freshmen returned for fall 1993 term. 45% of entering class graduated. 14% of students who completed a degree program immediately went on to graduate study.
**Foreign students:** 33 students are from out of the country. Countries represented include Barbados, China, the Czech Republic/Slovakia, Honduras, Japan, and South Africa; 12 in all.

**PROGRAMS OF STUDY. Degrees:** B.A., B.F.A., B.Gen.Studies, B.Mus., B.S., B.S.Bus.Admin.
**Majors:** Accounting, Anthropology, Art, Art Education, Art History, Biology, Business Administration, Chemistry, Computer Science, Economics, Elementary Education, English, Finance, Health/Physical Education, History, Liberal Studies, Management, Marketing, Mathematics, Modern Foreign Languages, Music, Music Education, Music Performance, Pathology/Audiology, Physical Education, Physics, Political Science, Pre-Engineering Physics, Psychology, Social Work, Sociology, Speech/Language Pathology/Audiology, Theatre, Therapeutic Recreation, Visual Arts/Performing Arts.
**Distribution of degrees:** The majors with the highest enrollment are business, education, and psychology; math and modern languages have the lowest.
**Requirements:** General education requirement.
**Academic regulations:** Freshmen must maintain minimum 1.31 GPA; sophomores, juniors, seniors, 2.0 GPA.
**Special:** Minors offered in many majors and in coaching, dance, geography, international studies, journalism, philosophy, and women's studies. Double majors. Dual degrees. Independent study. Accelerated study. Pass/fail grading option. Internships. Cooperative education programs. Graduate school at which undergraduates may take graduate-level courses. Preprofessional programs in law, medicine, veterinary science, pharmacy, and dentistry. 2-2 pre-medicine and allied health programs with Eastern Virginia Medical Sch, Medical Coll of Virginia, and U of Virginia. 2-2 and 3-2 programs in engineering with Georgia Tech, Old Dominion U, and U of Virginia. Five-year program in psychology/special education. Member of Southside Virginia Higher Education Consortium and Southside Virginia Business and Education Commission. Teacher certification in early childhood, elementary, secondary, and special education. Certification in specific subject areas. Exchange program abroad in Germany (U of Heidelberg). Study abroad also in Austria, Caribbean countries, England, France, Honduras, Spain, and Venezuela. ROTC.
**Honors:** Honors program. Honor societies.
**Academic Assistance:** Remedial reading, writing, math, and study skills. Nonremedial tutoring.

**STUDENT LIFE. Housing:** All unmarried students under age 23 and students with under 100 credits must live on campus unless living with family. Coed and women's dorms. Sorority and fraternity housing. 81% of students live in college housing.
**Social atmosphere:** The student newspaper reports, "Campus life is affected by the large number of student-run organizations on campus. Everyone is involved in something." On campus, students gather at the Student Union. Macado's, D.T. Bradleys, and Lancer Cafe are the most popular off-campus hangouts. All Greeks, the Baptist Student Union, residence life groups, and Giest (a leadership organization) have the most influence over student life. The Oktoberfest and Spring Weekend celebrations are the most popular campus events.
**Services and counseling/handicapped student services:** Placement services. Health service. Counseling services for minority, veteran, and older students. Birth control, personal, and psychological counseling. Career and academic guidance services. Physically disabled student services. Learning disabled services. Notetaking services. Tape recorders. Tutors. Reader services for the blind.
**Campus organizations:** Undergraduate student government. Student newspaper (Rotunda, published once/week). Literary magazine. Yearbook. Radio station. Choir, chorus, gospel choir, jazz, string, handbell, flute, and brass ensembles, Longwood Players, dance company, SOAR, goverance, Lancer Productions, student union, departmental, service, and special-interest groups, 110 organizations in all. Six fraternities, no chapter houses; nine sororities, no chapter houses. 19% of men join a fraternity. 23% of women join a sorority.
**Religious organizations:** Interreligious Council, Baptist Student Union, Campus Christian Fellowship, Chi Alpha, Catholic Student Association, Wesley Foundation.
**Minority/foreign student organizations:** Association of Black Students, LURE, NOW.

**ATHLETICS. Physical education requirements:** None.
**Intercollegiate competition:** 8% of students participate. Baseball (M), basketball (M,W), cheerleading (M,W), field hockey (W), golf (M,W), lacrosse (W), soccer (M), softball (W), tennis (M,W), wrestling (M). Member of NCAA Division II.
**Intramural and club sports:** 53% of students participate. Intramural badminton, baseball, basketball, billiards, bowling, football, golf, racquetball, soccer, superstars, softball, table tennis, tennis, volleyball, water polo. Men's club rugby. Women's club riding, soccer.

**ADMISSIONS. Academic basis for candidate selection** (in order of priority): Secondary school record, standardized test scores, class rank, essay, school's recommendation.
**Nonacademic basis for candidate selection:** Particular talent or ability is important. Extracurricular participation and alumni/ae relationship are considered.
**Requirements:** Graduation from secondary school is required; GED is accepted. 17 units and the following program of study are required: 4 units of English, 3 units of math, 3 units of science including 2 units of lab, 2 units of foreign language, 3 units of history, 2 units of academic electives. Minimum combined SAT score of 850, minimum 2.5 GPA, and rank in the top half of secondary school class required. Minimum combined SAT score of 900, minimum 3.0 GPA, and rank in top two-fifths of secondary school class recommended. Modern language program applicants should submit scores of corresponding achievement test. Audition required of music program applicants. Summer/Transition program

for minority students. SAT is required; ACT may be substituted. Campus visit recommended. Off-campus interviews available with an admissions representative.
**Procedure:** Take SAT or ACT by November of 12th year. Take ACH by November of 12th year. Suggest filing application by February 15. Application deadline is June 15. Notification of admission is sent on February 15, March 15, and April 1. Reply is required by May 1. $250 tuition deposit, refundable until May 1. Freshmen accepted for terms other than fall.
**Special programs:** Admission may be deferred two years. Credit and/or placement may be granted through CEEB Advanced Placement exams for scores of 3 or higher. Credit and/or placement may be granted through CLEP subject exams. Credit may be granted through DANTES exams. Credit and placement may be granted through challenge exams and military experience. Early decision program. Deadline for applying for early decision is November 15. Early entrance/early admission program. Concurrent enrollment program.
**Transfer students:** Transfer students accepted for terms other than fall. In fall 1993, 22% of all new students were transfers into all classes. 549 transfer applications were received, 352 were accepted. Application deadline is June 1 for fall; November 1 for spring. Minimum 2.2 GPA required. Lowest course grade accepted is "C." At least 30 semester hours must be completed at the college to receive degree.
**Admissions contact:** Robert J. Chonko, M.B.A., Director of Admissions and Enrollment Management. 804 395-2600.

**FINANCIAL AID. Available aid:** Pell grants, SEOG, state scholarships and grants, school scholarships and grants, private scholarships and grants, ROTC scholarships, academic merit scholarships, and athletic scholarships. Perkins Loans (NDSL), PLUS, Stafford Loans (GSL), state loans, school loans, private loans, and SLS. Tuition Plan Inc. Institutional payment plan.
**Financial aid statistics:** 24% of aid is not need-based. In 1993-94, 91% of all undergraduate applicants received aid; 86% of freshman applicants. Average amounts of aid awarded freshmen: Scholarships and grants, $1,492; loans, $2,566.
**Supporting data/closing dates:** FAFSA: Priority filing date is February 15. Notification of awards begins in April.
**Financial aid contact:** Lisa Turner, M.Ed., Director of Financial Aid. 804 395-2077.

**STUDENT EMPLOYMENT.** College Work/Study Program. Institutional employment. 33% of full-time undergraduates work on campus during school year. Students may expect to earn an average of $1,402 during school year. Off-campus part-time employment opportunities rated "good."

**COMPUTER FACILITIES.** 185 IBM/IBM-compatible, Macintosh/Apple, and RISC-/UNIX-based microcomputers; all are networked. Students may access Hewlett-Packard, IBM minicomputer/mainframe systems, BITNET, Internet, CompuServe. Residence halls may be equipped with networked microcomputers. Client/LAN operating systems include Apple/Macintosh, DOS, UNIX/XENIX/AIX, Microsoft. Computer languages and software packages include Assembler, BASIC, C, COBOL, dBASE, F(z), FORTH, FORTRAN, Harvard Graphics, Lotus 1-2-3, MacWrite, PageMaker, Pascal, PC Globe, SAS, SPSS-X, WordPerfect; 75 in all. Computer facilities are available to all students.
**Fees:** Computer fee is included in tuition/fees.
**Hours:** 8 AM-10 PM.

**GRADUATE CAREER DATA.** Graduate school percentages: 1% enter law school. 1% enter medical school. 1% enter dental school. 8% enter graduate business programs. 3% enter graduate arts and sciences programs. Highest graduate school enrollments: James Madison U, Longwood Coll, Medical Coll of Virginia, Old Dominion U, U of Tenneesse, Virginia Commonwealth U, U of Virginia. 25% of graduates choose careers in business and industry. Companies and businesses that hire graduates: Bell Atlantic, Crestar Mortgage Company, Leggetts Department Store, Life of Virginia, Sovran Bank, Virginia Auditor of Public Accounts, Virginia school systems, Virginia social services.

**PROMINENT ALUMNI/AE.** Camille Primm, president, Global Technology Center Inc.; Jerome Kersey, pro-basketball, Portland Trailblazers; John Todd, vice president for Equisitions and Business Development, Pizza Hut.

# Lynchburg College

**Lynchburg, VA 24501** **804 522-8100**

**1994-95 Costs.** Tuition: $12,450. Room & board: $5,400. Fees, books, misc. academic expenses (school's estimate): $450.
**Enrollment.** Undergraduates: 581 men, 943 women (full-time). Freshman class: 1,752 applicants, 1,500 accepted, 366 enrolled. Graduate enrollment: 151 men, 289 women.
**Test score averages/ranges.** Range of SAT scores of middle 50%: 390-470 verbal, 390-510 math.
**Faculty.** 125 full-time; 46 part-time. 62% of faculty holds doctoral degree. Student/faculty ratio: 12 to 1.
**Selectivity rating.** Less competitive.

**PROFILE.** Lynchburg, founded in 1903, is a church-affiliated, liberal arts college. Its 214-acre campus with colonial style architecture is located in Lynchburg, 100 miles west of Richmond.

**Accreditation:** SACS. Professionally accredited by the National League for Nursing.
**Religious orientation:** Lynchburg College is affiliated with the Disciples of Christ; no religious requirements.
**Library:** Collections totaling over 176,269 volumes, 772 periodical subscriptions, and 271,228 microform items.
**Special facilities/museums:** Art gallery, language labs, technical assistance center for preschool and handicapped children, arboretum, herbarium, greenhouse, center for advanced engineering.
**Athletic facilities:** Gymnasium, field house, basketball, racquetball, tennis, and volleyball courts, athletic fields, weight room, track, swimming pool.

**STUDENT BODY. Undergraduate profile:** 40% are state residents; 20% are transfers. 1% Asian-American, 9% Black, 1% Hispanic, 87% White, 2% Other. Average age of undergraduates is 19.
**Freshman profile:** 99% of accepted applicants took SAT. 75% of freshmen come from public schools.
**Undergraduate achievement:** 71% of fall 1992 freshmen returned for fall 1993 term. 55% of entering class graduated. 25% of students who completed a degree program immediately went on to graduate study.
**Foreign students:** 45 students are from out of the country. Countries represented include the Bahamas, Bermuda, India, Japan, and South Korea; 15 in all.

**PROGRAMS OF STUDY. Degrees:** B.A., B.S.
**Majors:** Accounting, American Studies, Art, Art/Psychology, Biology, Chemistry, Child Development, Communication, Computer Science, Economics, English, Environmental Science, European Literature, Foreign Language/Management, French, German, Health/Movement Science, Health Promotion, History, International Relations, Life Sciences, Management, Marketing, Mathematics, Music, Nursing, Philosophy, Philosophy/Political Science, Philosophy/Psychology, Philosophy/Religious Studies, Physics, Political Economy, Political Science, Psychobiology, Psychology, Psychology/Special Education, Public Service, Religious Studies, Religious Studies with other field, Social Sciences, Sociology, Sociology/Religious Studies, Spanish, Theatre Design/Technology, Theatre Performance, Theatre Production.
**Distribution of degrees:** The majors with the highest enrollment are child development, management, and psychology; religion, music, and philosophy have the lowest.
**Requirements:** General education requirement.
**Academic regulations:** Freshmen must maintain minimum 1.7 GPA; sophomores, 1.8 GPA; juniors, 1.9 GPA; seniors, 2.0 GPA.
**Special:** Double majors. Dual degrees. Independent study. Accelerated study. Pass/fail grading option. Internships. Graduate school at which undergraduates may take graduate-level courses. Preprofessional programs in law, medicine, veterinary science, pharmacy, dentistry, theology, optometry, and forestry. 3-1 medical technology program with Duke U. 3-2 engineering program with Georgia Tech and Old Dominion U. Member of Tri-College Consortium; cross-registration possible. Teacher certification in early childhood, elementary, secondary, and special education. Exchange programs abroad in Japan (Joshi Seigakuin Junior Coll) and South Korea (Han Nam U and Kijeon Women's Coll). Study abroad also in China, England, France, and Spain.
**Honors:** Honors program. Honor societies.
**Academic Assistance:** Remedial writing and study skills. Nonremedial tutoring.

**STUDENT LIFE. Housing:** All students, except seniors, must live on campus unless living with family. Coed and men's dorms. School-owned/operated apartments. Special education housing. 70% of students live in college housing.
**Social atmosphere:** West-Over Room and Gatsby's are hot spots for students. DuckFest and homecoming are popular social events.
**Services and counseling/handicapped student services:** Placement services. Health service. Counseling services for minority and older students. Personal and psychological counseling. Career and academic guidance services. Religious counseling. Learning disabled services.
**Campus organizations:** Undergraduate student government. Student newspaper (Critograph, published once/week). Literary magazine. Yearbook. TV station. Gospel ensemble, wind ensemble, concert choir, Hopwood Singers, dance company, theatre, Circle K, service organizations, Student Rescue Squad, Student Admissions Council, Student Activities Board, Cardinal Key, Gold Key, Earth Club, BACCHUS, departmental and special-interest groups, 60 organizations in all. Six fraternities, no chapter houses; three sororities, no chapter houses. 25% of men join a fraternity. 14% of women join a sorority.
**Religious organizations:** Intervarsity Christian Fellowship, Baptist Student Union, Catholic Student Association.
**Minority/foreign student organizations:** Alpha Kappa Alpha, Alpha Phi Alpha, UMOJA African Dance Group, Black Student Association. International Society, Korean Student Association.

**ATHLETICS. Physical education requirements:** One semester of physical education required.
**Intercollegiate competition:** 20% of students participate. Baseball (M), basketball (M,W), cross-country (M,W), field hockey (W), golf (M), horsemanship (M,W), lacrosse (M,W), soccer (M,W), softball (W), tennis (M,W), track (indoor) (M,W), track (outdoor) (M,W), track and field (indoor) (M,W), track and field (outdoor) (M,W), volleyball (W). Member of NCAA Division III, Old Dominion Athletic Conference.
**Intramural and club sports:** 50% of students participate. Intramural basketball, bowling, box lacrosse, flag football, racquetball, soccer, softball, street hockey, volleyball. Men's club swimming, water polo. Women's club swimming.

**ADMISSIONS. Academic basis for candidate selection** (in order of priority): Secondary school record, class rank, standardized test scores, school's recommendation, essay.
**Nonacademic basis for candidate selection:** Character and personality and extracurricular participation are important. Particular talent or ability and alumni/ae relationship are considered.
**Requirements:** Graduation from secondary school is required; GED is accepted. 15 units required and the following program of study recommended: 4 units of English, 3 units of math, 3 units of lab science, 3 units of foreign language, 3 units of social studies. SAT or ACT is required. Campus visit and interview recommended. Off-campus interviews available with an admissions representative.
**Procedure:** Take SAT or ACT by November of 12th year. Take ACH by summer of 12th year. Visit college for interview by January of 12th year. Priority admission filing date: November 15 to January 1. Notification of admission on rolling basis. Reply is required by date specified in letter of acceptance. $200 tuition deposit, refundable until May 1. Freshmen accepted for terms other than fall.
**Special programs:** Admission may be deferred one year. Placement may be granted through CEEB Advanced Placement exams for scores of 4 or higher. Credit may be granted through CLEP general and subject exams. Early entrance/early admission program. Concurrent enrollment program.
**Transfer students:** Transfer students accepted for terms other than fall. In fall 1993, 20% of all new students were transfers into all classes. 246 transfer applications were received, 183 were accepted. Application deadline is August 1 for fall; December 15 for spring.

Minimum 2.0 GPA required. Lowest course grade accepted is "C-." Maximum number of transferable credits is 88 semester hours. At least 48 semester hours must be completed at the college to receive degree.
**Admissions contact:** Deborah Hubble, Director of Admissions. 804 522-8300.

**FINANCIAL AID. Available aid:** Pell grants, SEOG, state grants, school scholarships and grants, and academic merit scholarships. Perkins Loans (NDSL), PLUS, Stafford Loans (GSL), private loans, and SLS. Knight Tuition Plans, AMS, and deferred payment plan.
**Financial aid statistics:** 52% of aid is not need-based. In 1993-94, 60% of all undergraduate applicants received aid; 65% of freshman applicants. Average amounts of aid awarded freshmen: Scholarships and grants, $3,000; loans, $3,000.
**Supporting data/closing dates:** FAFSA/FAF/FFS: Priority filing date is April 1. School's own aid application: Priority filing date is April 1. State aid form: Deadline is July 31. Income tax forms: Priority filing date is April 1. Notification of awards on rolling basis.
**Financial aid contact:** Linda Renschler, M.S., Director of Financial Aid. 804 522-8228.

**STUDENT EMPLOYMENT.** College Work/Study Program. Institutional employment. 34% of full-time undergraduates work on campus during school year. Students may expect to earn an average of $1,600 during school year. Off-campus part-time employment opportunities rated "fair."

**COMPUTER FACILITIES.** 230 IBM/IBM-compatible and Macintosh/Apple microcomputers. Residence halls may be equipped with networked terminals, modems. Computer languages and software packages include BASIC, COBOL, FORTRAN, Lotus 1-2-3, Pascal, WordPerfect. Computer facilities are available to all students.
**Fees:** None.

**GRADUATE CAREER DATA.** Graduate school percentages: 10% enter law school. 2% enter medical school. 75% enter graduate business programs. Highest graduate school enrollments: Lynchburg Coll, U of Richmond, U of Tennessee, U of Virginia, Virginia Tech. 44% of graduates choose careers in business and industry. Companies and businesses that hire graduates: Coopers & Lybrand, Babcock & Wilcox, Merrill Lynch.

**PROMINENT ALUMNI/AE.** Richard Thornton, Robert Frost's first American editor; Kim Hyul-Chul, former prime minister, Korea; Melinda Skinner, editor in chief, *American Criminal Law Review.*

## Mary Baldwin College

**Staunton, VA 24401 — 703 887-7000**

**1994-95 Costs.** Tuition: $11,200. Room & board: $7,400. Fees, books, misc. academic expenses (school's estimate): $300.
**Enrollment.** Undergraduates: 52 men, 774 women (full-time). Freshman class: 449 applicants, 411 accepted, 174 enrolled. Graduate enrollment: 9 men, 47 women.
**Test score averages/ranges.** Average SAT scores: 454 verbal, 461 math. Average ACT scores: 21 composite.
**Faculty.** 74 full-time; 40 part-time. 72% of faculty holds doctoral degree. Student/faculty ratio: 11 to 1.
**Selectivity rating.** Less competitive.

**PROFILE.** Mary Baldwin, founded in 1842, is a church-affiliated, liberal arts college for women. Its 54-acre campus is located in Staunton, 100 miles northwest of Richmond. The administration building, which dates from 1842, is listed with the National Register of Historic Places.

**Accreditation:** SACS.
**Religious orientation:** Mary Baldwin College is affiliated with the Presbyterian Church; no religious requirements.
**Library:** Collections totaling over 155,998 volumes, 677 periodical subscriptions, and 39,479 microform items.
**Special facilities/museums:** Audio-visual center, TV studio, communications lab, electron microscope, gas chromatoscope.
**Athletic facilities:** Gymnasium, aerobics and weight rooms, racquetball and tennis courts, swimming pool, dance studio, sauna, fencing salle, field hockey, lacrosse, soccer, and softball fields.

**STUDENT BODY. Undergraduate profile:** 60% are state residents; 23% are transfers. 2% Asian-American, 5% Black, 1% Hispanic, 89% White, 3% Other. Average age of undergraduates is 20.
**Freshman profile:** 1% of freshmen who took SAT scored 700 or over on verbal, 1% scored 700 or over on math; 10% scored 600 or over on verbal, 19% scored 600 or over on math; 50% scored 500 or over on verbal, 54% scored 500 or over on math; 85% scored 400 or over on verbal, 86% scored 400 or over on math; 100% scored 300 or over on verbal, 100% scored 300 or over on math. 95% of accepted applicants took SAT. 65% of freshmen come from public schools.
**Undergraduate achievement:** 80% of fall 1992 freshmen returned for fall 1993 term. 60% of entering class graduated. 20% of students who completed a degree program immediately went on to graduate study.
**Foreign students:** 30 students are from out of the country. Countries represented include Bulgaria, China, Japan, Korea, and Pakistan; 10 in all.

**PROGRAMS OF STUDY. Degrees:** B.A.
**Majors:** Art, Art/Communication, Art History, Arts Management, Asian Studies, Biology, Business Management, Chemistry, Communications, Economics, Education, English, French, Health Care Management, History, International Relations, Mathematics/Computer Science, Medical Technology, Philosophy/Religion, Political Science, Psychology, Sociology/Social Work, Spanish, Studio Art, Theatre.
**Distribution of degrees:** The majors with the highest enrollment are business, communications, and art.
**Requirements:** General education requirement.
**Academic regulations:** Freshmen must maintain minimum 1.5 GPA; sophomores, 1.75 GPA; juniors, 1.95 GPA; seniors, 2.0 GPA.
**Special:** Minors are offered in many majors and in business administration, computer information systems, health care administration, historic preservation, human resources management, human services, ministry, and women's studies. Self-designed majors. Double majors. Independent study. Accelerated study. Pass/fail grading option. Internships. Graduate school at which undergraduates may take graduate-level courses. Preprofessional programs in law, medicine, veterinary science, pharmacy, dentistry, and theology. 3-1 medical technology program. 3-2 engineering program with Washington U. 3-2 B.A./M.S.N. (nurse practitioner) nursing program with Vanderbilt U. 4-1 B.A./M.Ed. education program with U of Virginia. Sea Semester. Exchange programs with Hampden-Sydney Coll, Hollins Coll, Randolph-Macon Coll, Randolph-Macon Woman's Coll, Sweet Briar Coll, U of Richmond, and Washington and Lee U. Teacher certification in early childhood, elementary, and secondary education. Certification in specific subject areas. Study abroad in France or Spain encouraged for language majors. Study abroad also in England, Japan, Korea, and many other countries. ROTC at James Madison U.
**Honors:** Phi Beta Kappa. Honors program. Honor societies.
**Academic Assistance:** Remedial reading, writing, math, and study skills. Nonremedial tutoring.

**ADMISSIONS. Academic basis for candidate selection** (in order of priority): Secondary school record, standardized test scores, class rank, school's recommendation, essay.
**Nonacademic basis for candidate selection:** Character and personality are emphasized. Extracurricular participation and particular talent or ability are important. Alumni/ae relationship is considered.
**Requirements:** Graduation from secondary school is recommended; GED is accepted. 16 units and the following program of study are recommended: 4 units of English, 3 units of math, 1 unit of science, 2 units of foreign language, 3 units of social studies, 3 units of history. Conditional admission possible for applicants not meeting standard requirements. SAT or ACT is required. ACH recommended. Campus visit and interview recommended. Off-campus interviews available with an admissions representative.
**Procedure:** Application deadline is June 15. Notification of admission on rolling basis. Reply is required by May 1. $300 tuition deposit, refundable until May 1. Freshmen accepted for terms other than fall.
**Special programs:** Admission may be deferred one year. Credit may be granted through CEEB Advanced Placement for scores of 4 or higher. Early decision program. In fall 1993, 25 applied for early decision and 25 were accepted. Deadline for applying for early decision is November 15. Early entrance/early admission program.
**Transfer students:** Transfer students accepted for terms other than fall. In fall 1993, 23% of all new students were transfers into all classes. 99 transfer applications were received, 81 were accepted. Application deadline is June 15 for fall; November 15 for spring. Minimum 2.0 GPA required. Lowest course grade accepted is "C." At least 66 semester hours must be completed at the college to receive degree.
**Admissions contact:** Douglas E. Clark, M.A., Enrollment. 703 887-7019.

**FINANCIAL AID. Available aid:** Pell grants, SEOG, state scholarships and grants, school scholarships and grants, private scholarships and grants, academic merit scholarships, and aid for undergraduate foreign students. Perkins Loans (NDSL), PLUS, Stafford Loans (GSL), private loans, and SLS. Tuition Plan Inc., Knight Tuition Plans, AMS, and family tuition reduction.
**Financial aid statistics:** 20% of aid is not need-based. In 1993-94, 60% of all undergraduate applicants received aid; 75% of freshman applicants. Average amounts of aid awarded freshmen: Scholarships and grants, $3,000.
**Supporting data/closing dates:** FAFSA. Notification of awards on rolling basis.
**Financial aid contact:** Ellen Holtz, Director of Financial Aid. 703 887-7022.

## Mary Washington College

**Fredericksburg, VA 22401-5358 — 703 899-4100**

**1994-95 Costs.** Tuition: $2,026 (state residents), $6,490 (out-of-state). Room & board: $4,942. Fees, books, misc. academic expenses (school's estimate): $1,830.
**Enrollment.** Undergraduates: 1,069 men, 1,928 women (full-time). Freshman class: 4,350 applicants, 2,178 accepted, 756 enrolled. Graduate enrollment: 23 men, 35 women.
**Test score averages/ranges.** Range of SAT scores of middle 50%: 480-580 verbal, 520-620 math.
**Faculty.** 163 full-time; 59 part-time. 85% of faculty holds highest degree in specific field. Student/faculty ratio: 17 to 1.
**Selectivity rating.** Highly competitive.

**PROFILE.** Mary Washington is a public, liberal arts college. Founded in 1908, it adopted coeducation in 1970. Its 275-acre campus is located in Fredericksburg, 50 miles north of Richmond.

**Accreditation:** SACS. Professionally accredited by the National Association of Schools of Music.
**Religious orientation:** Mary Washington College is nonsectarian; no religious requirements.
**Library:** Collections totaling over 337,990 volumes, 1,390 periodical subscriptions, and 104,198 microform items.
**Special facilities/museums:** Galleries, center for historic preservation, language labs.
**Athletic facilities:** Indoor sports complex, gymnasiums, swimming pool, training and weight rooms, basketball, handball, racquetball, tennis, and volleyball courts, batting cage, cross country course, baseball, field hockey, lacrosse, soccer, and softball fields, track.

**STUDENT BODY. Undergraduate profile:** 70% are state residents; 17% are transfers. 3% Asian-American, 4% Black, 2% Hispanic, 1% Native American, 90% White. Average age of undergraduates is 20.

**Freshman profile:** 100% of accepted applicants took SAT. 83% of freshmen come from public schools.
**Undergraduate achievement:** 92% of fall 1992 freshmen returned for fall 1993 term. 65% of entering class graduated. 18% of students who completed a degree program went on to graduate study within one year.
**Foreign students:** 34 students are from out of the country. Countries represented include Germany, Japan, Korea, Spain, Venezuela, and the former Yugoslav Republics; 20 in all.

**PROGRAMS OF STUDY. Degrees:** B.A., B.Lib.Studies, B.S.
**Majors:** American Studies, Art, Biology, Business Administration, Chemistry, Classics, Computer Science, Dance, Drama, Economics, English, Environmental Earth Science, French, Geography, Geology, German, Historic Preservation, History, International Affairs, Latin, Liberal Studies, Mathematics, Music, Performing Arts, Philosophy, Physics, Political Science, Psychology, Religion, Sociology, Spanish.
**Distribution of degrees:** The majors with the highest enrollment are business administration, English, and psychology; music, performing arts/art history, and classics/physics have the lowest.
**Requirements:** General education requirement.
**Academic regulations:** Minimum 2.0 GPA must be maintained.
**Special:** Courses offered in anthropology, education, Italian, linguistics, library science, Russian, and statistics. Opportunities for undergraduate research projects with faculty members. Self-designed majors. Double majors. Independent study. Accelerated study. Pass/fail grading option. Internships. Cooperative education programs. Preprofessional programs in law, medicine, veterinary science, pharmacy, and dentistry. Teacher certification in early childhood, elementary, and secondary education. Junior year abroad in various countries.
**Honors:** Phi Beta Kappa. Honor societies.
**Academic Assistance:** Nonremedial tutoring.

**STUDENT LIFE. Housing:** Students may live on or off campus. Coed, women's, and men's dorms. Language houses. 75% of students live in college housing.
**Social atmosphere:** The student newspaper reports that MWC is "a very small, close campus where it is often necessary to make your own fun." Students spend free time in the Eagle's Nest, the Irish Brigade, Sammy T's, the Parthenon, Ruby Tuesday's, and Carlos O'Kelley's. Rugby games and formals are the most popular events during the year.
**Services and counseling/handicapped student services:** Placement services. Health service. Counseling services for minority, military, veteran, and older students. Birth control, personal, and psychological counseling. Career and academic guidance services. Learning disabled services.
**Campus organizations:** Undergraduate student government. Student newspaper (Bullet, published once/week). Literary magazine. Yearbook. Radio station. Art club, chorus, orchestra, concert band, debating, College Republicans, Young Democrats, Student Honor Council, community service group, departmental, professional, and special-interest groups, 85 organizations in all.
**Religious organizations:** Baptist Student Union, Campus Christian Community, Canterbury Association, Catholic Student Association, Hillel, Intervarsity Christian Fellowship.
**Minority/foreign student organizations:** Black Student Association, BOND, Voices of Praise, Women of Color, Hispanic and other multicultural groups. Asian Student Association, Citizens of the World.

**ATHLETICS. Physical education requirements:** Two semesters of physical education required.
**Intercollegiate competition:** 20% of students participate. Baseball (M), basketball (M,W), cheerleading (M,W), cross-country (M,W), diving (M,W), field hockey (W), horsemanship (M,W), lacrosse (M,W), soccer (M,W), softball (W), swimming (M,W), tennis (M,W), track (indoor) (M,W), track (outdoor) (M,W), track and field (indoor) (M,W), track and field (outdoor) (M,W), volleyball (W). Member of Capital Athletic Conference, Eastern College Athletic Conference, IHSA Region VII for equestrian sports, Mason-Dixon Conference for track and cross-country, NCAA Division III, Virginia Intercollegiate Soccer Association (men's), Virginia Intercollegiate Tennis Association (men's).
**Intramural and club sports:** 50% of students participate. Intramural aerobics, badminton, basketball, bowling, dance, flag football, indoor soccer, inner-tube water polo, soccer, softball, tennis, volleyball, weight lifting. Men's club crew, rugby, volleyball. Women's club crew, rugby, synchronized swimming.

**ADMISSIONS. Academic basis for candidate selection** (in order of priority): Secondary school record, class rank, standardized test scores, essay, school's recommendation.
**Nonacademic basis for candidate selection:** Extracurricular participation is emphasized. Particular talent or ability is important. Character and personality are considered.
**Requirements:** Graduation from secondary school is required; GED is accepted. 19 units and the following program of study are recommended: 4 units of English, 3 units of math, 3 units of science, 3 units of foreign language, 3 units of social studies, 3 units of electives. Preference given to in-state applicants, but out-of-state applicants are encouraged to apply. SAT is required. ACH recommended. Campus visit recommended. No off-campus interviews.
**Procedure:** Take SAT by January of 12th year. Take ACH by January of 12th year. Suggest filing application by January 15. Application deadline is February 1. Notification of admission by April 1. Reply is required by May 1. $500 tuition deposit, refundable until May 1. Freshmen accepted for terms other than fall.
**Special programs:** Admission may be deferred one year. Credit may be granted through CEEB Advanced Placement for scores of 3 or higher. Credit may be granted through CLEP subject exams. Early decision program. In fall 1993, 230 applied for early decision and 144 were accepted. Deadline for applying for early decision is November 1. Early entrance/early admission program.
**Transfer students:** Transfer students accepted for terms other than fall. In fall 1993, 17% of all new students were transfers into all classes. 563 transfer applications were received, 288 were accepted. Application deadline is March 1 for fall; November 1 for spring. Minimum 2.5 GPA recommended. Lowest course grade accepted is "C." Maximum number of transferable credits is 90 semester hours. At least 30 semester hours must be completed at the college to receive degree.
**Admissions contact:** Martin A. Wilder, Jr., Ed.D., Vice President for Admissions and Financial Aid. 703 899-4681.

**FINANCIAL AID. Available aid:** Pell grants, SEOG, state scholarships and grants, school scholarships, private scholarships, and academic merit scholarships. Perkins Loans (NDSL), PLUS, Stafford Loans (GSL), and SLS. Tuition Plan Inc., Knight Tuition Plans, and AMS.
**Financial aid statistics:** 37% of aid is not need-based. In 1993-94, 53% of all undergraduate applicants received aid; 53% of freshman applicants. Average amounts of aid awarded freshmen: Scholarships and grants, $1,800; loans, $2,500.
**Supporting data/closing dates:** FAFSA: Priority filing date is March 1. Income tax forms: Accepted on rolling basis. Notification of awards begins April 15.
**Financial aid contact:** Robert U. MacDonald, Director of Financial Aid. 703 899-4684.
**STUDENT EMPLOYMENT.** College Work/Study Program. Institutional employment. 20% of full-time undergraduates work on campus during school year. Students may expect to earn an average of $1,250 during school year. Off-campus part-time employment opportunities rated "good."
**COMPUTER FACILITIES.** 110 microcomputers. Students may access Prime mini-computer/mainframe systems. Computer languages and software packages include BASIC, COBOL, FORTRAN, FORTRAN 77, Pascal; numerous software packages. Computer facilities are available to all students.
**Fees:** None.
**GRADUATE CAREER DATA.** Highest graduate school enrollments: American U, Coll of William and Mary, George Washington U, U of Virginia. Companies and businesses that hire graduates: CIA, IBM, U.S. Defense Department, World Bank.
**PROMINENT ALUMNI/AE.** Hildy Park Cohen, TV producer; Frances D. Cook, ambassador; Deborah Scott McGuire, bank CEO and president.

# Marymount University

**Arlington, VA 22207-4299** **703 522-5600**

**1994-95 Costs.** Tuition: $11,390. Room & board: $5,280. Fees, books, misc. academic expenses (school's estimate): $600.
**Enrollment.** Undergraduates: 332 men, 997 women (full-time). Freshman class: 1,044 applicants, 830 accepted, 229 enrolled. Graduate enrollment: 627 men, 1,022 women.
**Test score averages/ranges.** Average SAT scores: 445 verbal, 459 math. Range of SAT scores of middle 50%: 360-470 verbal, 380-510 math.
**Faculty.** 115 full-time; 218 part-time. 76% of faculty holds doctoral degree. Student/faculty ratio: 14 to 1.
**Selectivity rating.** Less competitive.

**PROFILE.** Marymount, founded in 1950, is a church-affiliated university. Programs are offered through the Schools of Arts and Sciences, Business Administration, Education and Human Services, and Nursing. Its 17-acre campus is located in Arlington, five miles from Washington, D.C.

**Accreditation:** SACS. Professionally accredited by the American Assembly of Collegiate Schools of Business, the American Bar Association, the Foundation for Interior Design Education Research, the National Council for Accreditation of Teacher Education, the National League for Nursing.
**Religious orientation:** Marymount University is affiliated with the Roman Catholic Church (Religious of the Sacred Heart of Mary); no religious requirements.
**Library:** Collections totaling over 107,656 volumes, 1,097 periodical subscriptions, and 207,313 microform items.
**Special facilities/museums:** Learning resource center, audio-visual center and studio, elementary school, computer labs.
**Athletic facilities:** Gymnasium, swimming pool, basketball and tennis courts, hockey and soccer fields, exercise and weight rooms.
**STUDENT BODY. Undergraduate profile:** 56% are state residents; 54% are transfers. 9% Asian-American, 12% Black, 6% Hispanic, 73% White. Average age of undergraduates is 23.
**Freshman profile:** 1% of freshmen who took SAT scored 700 or over on math; 3% scored 600 or over on verbal, 8% scored 600 or over on math; 23% scored 500 or over on verbal, 36% scored 500 or over on math; 71% scored 400 or over on verbal, 79% scored 400 or over on math; 98% scored 300 or over on verbal, 100% scored 300 or over on math. Majority of accepted applicants took SAT.
**Undergraduate achievement:** 73% of fall 1991 freshmen returned for fall 1992 term. 36% of entering class graduated.
**Foreign students:** 337 students are from out of the country. Countries represented include Japan, Korea, Pakistan, Panama, Peru, and the Philipines; 85 in all.
**PROGRAMS OF STUDY. Degrees:** B.A., B.Bus.Admin., B.S., B.S.Nurs.
**Majors:** Accounting, Biology, Business Administration, Business Law, Communications, Computer Science, Economics, Elementary Education, English, Fashion Design, Fashion Merchandising, Finance, Graphic Design, Health Care Administration, Interior Design, International Business, Liberal Studies, Management, Management Science, Marketing, Mathematics, Nursing, Paralegal Studies, Personnel, Philosophy, Physical Fitness Management, Political Science, Psychology, Retail Management, Science.
**Distribution of degrees:** The majors with the highest enrollment are accounting, liberal studies, and interior design; business law, mathematics, and retail management have the lowest.
**Requirements:** General education requirement.
**Academic regulations:** Minimum 2.0 GPA must be maintained.
**Special:** Minors offered in most majors. Courses in business services, history, modern languages, natural science, speech and theatre arts. Mastery tutoring system. All seniors complete a 15-week internship program related to their major. Associate's degrees offered. Internships. Graduate school at which undergraduates may take graduate-level courses. Member of Washington D.C. Consortium and North Virginia Consortium. London Semester. Teacher certification in elementary and secondary education. Study abroad in England. ROTC at Georgetown U.
**Honors:** Honors program.

**Academic Assistance:** Nonremedial tutoring.

**STUDENT LIFE. Housing:** All students under age 21 must live on campus unless living with family. Coed and women's dorms. 31% of students live in college housing.
**Social atmosphere:** As reported by the student newspaper, George's and various night-spots in Georgetown are the popular gathering spots. Some of the influential groups on campus are sports teams, the Campus Ministry, S.E.A.R.C.H., and the Black Student Alliance. Favorite events of the year include the Snowball Winter Formal, the International Hat Party, Theater 18 one-act plays, Oktoberfest, and Springfest.
**Services and counseling/handicapped student services:** Placement services. Health service. Counseling services for military, veteran, and older students. Personal and psychological counseling. Career and academic guidance services. Religious counseling. Learning disabled services.
**Campus organizations:** Undergraduate student government. Student newspaper (Blue Banner, published once/month). Literary magazine. Yearbook. Vocal groups, theatre group, business club, College Republicans, Young Democrats, social organizations, community service groups, student-faculty councils.
**Religious organizations:** Campus Ministry.
**Minority/foreign student organizations:** International Club.

**ATHLETICS. Physical education requirements:** One semester of physical education required.
**Intercollegiate competition:** 15% of students participate. Basketball (M,W), cheerleading (W), golf (M), lacrosse (M), soccer (M,W), swimming (M,W), tennis (M,W), volleyball (W). Member of Capital Athletic Conference, NCAA Division III.
**Intramural and club sports:** 25% of students participate. Intramural basketball, football, soccer, softball, tennis, volleyball, water polo.

**ADMISSIONS. Academic basis for candidate selection** (in order of priority): Secondary school record, standardized test scores, school's recommendation, class rank.
**Nonacademic basis for candidate selection:** Character and personality and extracurricular participation are important. Alumni/ae relationship is considered.
**Requirements:** Graduation from secondary school is required; GED is accepted. 16 units and the following program of study are recommended: 4 units of English, 3 units of math, 2 units of science, 3 units of foreign language, 3 units of social studies, 1 unit of electives. Minimum combined SAT score of 810, rank in top half of secondary school class, and minimum 2.0 GPA required. 2 units of lab science recommended and R.N. required of nursing program applicants. Provisional admission possible for applicants not meeting standard requirements. SAT or ACT is required. Campus visit and interview recommended. Off-campus interviews available with an admissions representative.
**Procedure:** Take SAT or ACT by November 15 of 12th year. Suggest filing application by December. Notification of admission on rolling basis. Reply is required by May 1. $200 nonrefundable room deposit. Freshmen accepted for terms other than fall.
**Special programs:** Admission may be deferred one year. Credit and/or placement may be granted through CEEB Advanced Placement exams for scores of 3 or higher. Credit and/or placement may be granted through CLEP general and subject exams. Placement may be granted through challenge exams. Credit and placement may be granted through ACT PEP and DANTES exams, and military experience.
**Transfer students:** Transfer students accepted for terms other than fall. In fall 1992, 54% of all new students were transfers into all classes. 734 transfer applications were received, 676 were accepted. Application deadline is August for fall; December for spring. Minimum 2.0 GPA required. Lowest course grade accepted is "C." At least 36 semester hours must be completed at the university to receive degree.
**Admissions contact:** Charles Coe, M.A., Director of Admissions. 800 548-7638.

**FINANCIAL AID. Available aid:** Pell grants, SEOG, Federal Nursing Student Scholarships, state scholarships and grants, school scholarships and grants, private scholarships and grants, ROTC scholarships, and academic merit scholarships. Perkins Loans (NDSL), PLUS, Stafford Loans (GSL), NSL, state loans, private loans, and SLS. Tuition Plan Inc., AMS, deferred payment plan, and family tuition reduction.
**Financial aid statistics:** 54% of aid is not need-based. Average amounts of aid awarded freshmen: Scholarships and grants, $3,890; loans, $2,580.
**Supporting data/closing dates:** FAFSA/FAF/FFS: Priority filing date is March 1. School's own aid application: Priority filing date is March 1. Notification of awards begins March 15.
**Financial aid contact:** Debbie Raines, Director of Financial Aid. 703 284-1530.

**STUDENT EMPLOYMENT.** College Work/Study Program. Institutional employment. 42% of full-time undergraduates work on campus during school year. Students may expect to earn an average of $1,500 during school year. Off-campus part-time employment opportunities rated "excellent."

**COMPUTER FACILITIES.** 145 IBM/IBM-compatible and Macintosh/Apple microcomputers; all are networked. Residence halls may be equipped with stand-alone microcomputers. Computer languages and software packages include BASIC, C, COBOL, Pascal; other major word processing, spreadsheet, graphics, database, business software; 25 in all. Computer facilities are available to all students.
**Fees:** None.

# Norfolk State University

**Norfolk, VA 23504** **804 683-8600**

**1993-94 Costs.** Tuition: $1,355 (state residents), $2,995 (out-of-state). Room & board: $1,800. Fees, books, misc. academic expenses (school's estimate): $300.
**Enrollment.** Undergraduates: 2,663 men, 4,091 women (full-time). Freshman class: 4,291 applicants, 3,649 accepted, 1,534 enrolled. Graduate enrollment: 179 men, 717 women.
**Test score averages/ranges.** N/A.
**Faculty.** 399 full-time; 127 part-time. 56% of faculty holds doctoral degree. Student/faculty ratio: 22 to 1.
**Selectivity rating.** N/A.

**PROFILE.** Norfolk State, founded in 1935, is a public, historically black university. Programs are offered through the Schools of Arts and Letters, Business, Education, General and Continuing Education, Health-Related Professions and Sciences, Social Sciences, Social Work, and Technology. Its 110-acre campus is located in Norfolk, the center of the state's Tidewater region.

**Accreditation:** SACS. Professionally accredited by the American Assembly of Collegiate Schools of Business, the American Dietetic Association, the American Psychological Association, the Computing Sciences Accreditation Board, the Council on Social Work Education, the National Association of Schools of Music, the National Council for Accreditation of Teacher Education, the National League for Nursing.
**Religious orientation:** Norfolk State University is nonsectarian; no religious requirements.
**Library:** Collections totaling over 300,000 volumes, and 2,500 periodical subscriptions.
**Athletic facilities:** Basketball, racquetball, and tennis courts, baseball, football, and softball fields, gymnasiums, swimming pool.

**STUDENT BODY. Undergraduate profile:** 61% are state residents; 20% are transfers. 90% Black, 7% White, 3% Other. Average age of undergraduates is 26.
**Foreign students:** 127 students are from out of the country.

**PROGRAMS OF STUDY. Degrees:** B.A., B.Mus., B.S., B.Soc.Work.
**Majors:** Accounting, Administrative Systems Management, Biology, Building Construction Technology, Business, Business Education, Chemistry, Computer Science, Computer Technology, Consumer Service, Design Technology, Early Childhood Education, Economics, Electronic Technology, Electronics Engineering, English, Fine Arts, Foreign Languages, Health Education, Health Services Management, History, Home Economics, Hotel/Restaurant/Institutional Management, Industrial Electronics Technology, Interdisciplinary Studies, Journalism, Mass Communications, Mathematics, Medical Records Administration, Medical Technology, Mental Retardation, Music Media, Nursing, Personnel/Industrial Relations, Physical Education/Corrective Therapy, Physics, Political Science, Psychology, Public School Music, Recreation, Social Work, Sociology, Speech Pathology/Audiology, Vocational Industrial Education.
**Distribution of degrees:** The majors with the highest enrollment are business, mass communications, and computer science.
**Requirements:** General education requirement.
**Special:** Associate's degrees offered. Accelerated study. Cooperative education programs. Graduate school at which undergraduates may take graduate-level courses. 2-2 programs in 15 areas with Tidewater Community Coll. Member of Tidewater Consortium. Teacher certification in early childhood, elementary, secondary, and special education. ROTC and NROTC.
**Honors:** Honors program.
**Academic Assistance:** Nonremedial tutoring.

**STUDENT LIFE. Housing:** Students may live on or off campus. Women's and men's dorms. 23% of students live in college housing.
**Social atmosphere:** According to the editor of the school newspaper, "The social life at NSU is good because people from different walks of life are joined together in a good atmosphere both academically and socially." The most influential group on campus is the Student Government Association. Popular social events to attend are Homecoming Concerts, basketball games, and dances. On campus, students meet at the Student Union Building and the library. Off campus, they head for the Big Apple Club and MacDonald's.
**Services and counseling/handicapped student services:** Placement services. Health service. Personal counseling. Academic guidance services.
**Campus organizations:** Undergraduate student government. Student newspaper (Spartan Echo, published once/week). Yearbook. Radio station. Choir, sextet, bands, brass and saxophone ensembles, opera workshops, Norfolk State Players, debating, athletic, departmental, and special-interest groups. Eight fraternities, no chapter houses; seven sororities, no chapter houses.
**Minority/foreign student organizations:** NAACP.

**ATHLETICS. Physical education requirements:** One semester of physical education required.
**Intercollegiate competition:** 10% of students participate. Baseball (M), basketball (M,W), cheerleading (M,W), cross-country (M,W), football (M), softball (W), tennis (M), track (indoor) (M,W), track (outdoor) (M,W), track and field (indoor) (M,W), track and field (outdoor) (M,W), volleyball (W), wrestling (M). Member of Central Intercollegiate Athletic Association, NCAA Division II.
**Intramural and club sports:** 70% of students participate. Intramural basketball, football, softball, track and field, volleyball.

**ADMISSIONS. Academic basis for candidate selection** (in order of priority): Secondary school record, standardized test scores, school's recommendation, class rank.
**Nonacademic basis for candidate selection:** Character and personality, extracurricular participation, particular talent or ability, and alumni/ae relationship are considered.
**Requirements:** Graduation from secondary school is required; GED is accepted. No specific distribution of secondary school units required. 2 units of health/physical education and 7-9 units of electives recommended. 2 units of science required of nursing program applicants. 2 units of math (including algebra) required of computer science program applicants. Special services program for applicants not normally admissible. SAT or ACT is required. Campus visit and interview recommended. No off-campus interviews.
**Procedure:** Take SAT or ACT by January of 12th year. Notification of admission on rolling basis. No set date by which applicants must accept offer. Freshmen accepted for terms other than fall.
**Special programs:** Credit may be granted through CEEB Advanced Placement for scores of 3 or higher. Credit may be granted through CLEP subject exams. Placement may be granted through challenge exams.
**Transfer students:** Transfer students accepted for terms other than fall. In fall 1992, 20% of all new students were transfers into all classes. 1,054 transfer applications were received, 985 were accepted. Lowest course grade accepted is "D."
**Admissions contact:** Frank Cool, Director of Admissions. 804 683-8396.

**FINANCIAL AID. Available aid:** Pell grants, SEOG, state scholarships and grants, school scholarships, and ROTC scholarships. Perkins Loans (NDSL), Stafford Loans (GSL), and state loans. Tuition Plan Inc. and deferred payment plan.

**Financial aid statistics:** In 1992-93, 90% of all undergraduate applicants received aid; 85% of freshman applicants.
**Supporting data/closing dates:** FAFSA/FAF: Deadline is April 15.
**Financial aid contact:** Marty Miller, Director of Financial Aid. 804 683-8381.

**STUDENT EMPLOYMENT.** College Work/Study Program. Institutional employment. Off-campus part-time employment opportunities rated "good."

**COMPUTER FACILITIES.** 25 microcomputers. Students may access Digital minicomputer/mainframe systems.
**Fees:** None.

# Old Dominion University

**Norfolk, VA 23529-0050 804 683-3000**

**1994-95 Costs.** Tuition: $3,780 (state residents), $9,390 (out-of-state). Room & board: $4,500. Fees, books, misc. academic expenses (school's estimate): $487.
**Enrollment.** Undergraduates: 4,820 men, 4,805 women (full-time). Freshman class: 4,331 applicants, 3,562 accepted, 1,225 enrolled. Graduate enrollment: 2,407 men, 2,768 women.
**Test score averages/ranges.** Average SAT scores: 440 verbal, 494 math.
**Faculty.** 575 full-time. 78% of faculty holds doctoral degree. Student/faculty ratio: 18 to 1.
**Selectivity rating.** Less competitive.

**PROFILE.** Old Dominion is a private university. Founded in 1930 as a division of the College of William and Mary, it became an independent state university in 1962. Programs are offered through the Colleges of Arts and Sciences, Business and Public Administration, Education, Engineering and Technology, Health Sciences, and Sciences. Its 146-acre campus located in Norfolk reflects a Georgian architectural style.

**Accreditation:** SACS. Professionally accredited by the Accreditation Board for Engineering and Technology, the American Assembly of Collegiate Schools of Business, the American Dental Association, the American Medical Association (CAHEA), the American Physical Therapy Association, the National Association of Schools of Music, the National Council for Accreditation of Teacher Education, the National League for Nursing.
**Religious orientation:** Old Dominion University is nonsectarian; no religious requirements.
**Library:** Collections totaling over 513,379 volumes, 4,647 periodical subscriptions, and 953,058 microform items.
**Special facilities/museums:** Centers for urban research/service, economic education, and child study, planetarium, marine science research vessel, random wave pool.
**Athletic facilities:** Gymnasium, swimming pool, weight room, athletic fields, tennis courts.

**STUDENT BODY. Undergraduate profile:** 86% are state residents; 47% are transfers. 5% Asian-American, 11% Black, 1.5% Hispanic, .5% Native American, 82% White. Average age of undergraduates is 23.
**Freshman profile:** Majority of accepted applicants took SAT.
**Foreign students:** 1,000 students are from out of the country. Countries represented include Brazil, China, Cyprus, France, Japan, and Korea; 71 in all.

**PROGRAMS OF STUDY. Degrees:** B.A., B.F.A., B.Mus., B.S., B.S.Bus.Admin., B.S.Civil Eng., B.S.Commerce, B.S.Comp.Eng., B.S.Dent.Hyg., B.S.Elec.Eng., B.S.Elem.Ed., B.S.Eng.Tech., B.S.Env.Hlth., B.S.Hlth.Sci., B.S.Mech.Eng., B.S.Med.Tech., B.S.Nurs., B.S.Phys.Ed., B.S.Pub.Hlth., B.S.Sec.Ed., B.S.Spec.Ed.
**Majors:** Accounting, Art, Art Education, Biochemistry, Biology, Biology Education, Chemistry, Chemistry Education, Civil Engineering, Civil Engineering Technology, Communications Disorders, Computer Engineering, Computer Science, Criminal Justice, Dental Hygiene, Distributive Education, Economics, Electrical Engineering Technology, Elementary Education, Engineering/Electrical, Engineering Technology, English, English Education, Environmental Health, Financial Management, Fine Arts, French, French Education, Geography, Geology, German, Health Education, Health/Physical Education, Health Sciences, History, Human Services Counseling, Industrial Arts Education, Instrumental Music Education, Interdisciplinary Studies, International Business Management, Leisure Services, Library Science, Management, Management Information Systems, Marketing, Mathematics, Mathematics Education, Mechanical Engineering, Mechanical Engineering Technology, Medical Technology, Mental Retardation, Music, Music Performance/Composition, Nuclear Medicine Technology, Nursing, Occupational/Technical Studies, Operations Management, Orchestral Instrument, Organ, Philosophy, Physical Education, Physics, Physics Education, Political Science, Pre-Dentistry, Pre-Medicine, Pre-Pharmaceutical, Pre-Veterinary, Psychology, Recreation/Leisure Studies, Religious Studies, Russian, Russian Education, Social Sciences Education, Social Studies Education, Sociology, Spanish, Spanish Education, Special Education, Speech, Studio Art, Technical Operations, Theatre/Dance, Vocal Music Education, Voice.
**Distribution of degrees:** The majors with the highest enrollment are computer science, marketing, and management information systems.
**Requirements:** General education requirement.
**Academic regulations:** Minimum 2.00 GPA must be maintained.
**Special:** Minors offered in most majors. Self-designed majors. Double majors. Dual degrees. Independent study. Pass/fail grading option. Internships. Cooperative education programs. Graduate school at which undergraduates may take graduate-level courses. Preprofessional programs in law, medicine, veterinary science, and pharmacy. Five-year master's degree program in education. Dual engineering/arts and letters degree program. Joint medical school automatic admission program with Eastern Virginia Medical Sch. Cross-registration with Norfolk State U. Member of consortium with 20 different institutions. Teacher certification in early childhood, elementary, secondary, and special education. Study abroad in most countries, including England for student teaching. ROTC and NROTC.
**Honors:** Honors program.
**Academic Assistance:** Remedial reading, writing, math, and study skills. Nonremedial tutoring.

**STUDENT LIFE. Housing:** Students may live on or off campus. Coed dorms. School-owned/operated apartments. 13% of students live in college housing.
**Social atmosphere:** The managing editor of the student newspaper remarks, "The students at ODU are somewhat apathetic about getting into social and cultural life, events, and clubs." The college has a new Fine Arts Building and renovated Stables Theatre which provide a wide range of cultural activities. The most influential group on campus is the Student Activities Council which plans most school events. Students enjoy the Street Party (before exams), Oyster Bowl, and Main Street. On campus, students gather at the Webb Center and the Fine Arts Building. Off campus, they go to the 4400 Club, Friar Tuck's, Zeno's, Virginia Beach (the Strip, as well as the beach), Waterside Marketplace, the Naro Cinema, Town Point Park, and the Norfolk Zoo.
**Services and counseling/handicapped student services:** Placement services. Health service. Women's center. Counseling services for minority, military, veteran, and older students. Birth control, personal, and psychological counseling. Career and academic guidance services. Religious counseling. Physically disabled student services. Learning disabled services. Notetaking services.
**Campus organizations:** Undergraduate student government. Student newspaper (Mace and Crown, published biweekly). Literary magazine. Yearbook. Radio station. Choirs, service and special-interest groups, recreational sports groups, 180 organizations in all. 15 fraternities, three chapter houses; nine sororities, two chapter houses. 9% of men join a fraternity. 9% of women join a sorority.
**Religious organizations:** Bahai Club, Baptist Student Union, Canterbury Association, Catholic Campus Ministry, Hillel, Muslim Student Association, Student Christian Fellowship, other religious groups.
**Minority/foreign student organizations:** Students for Development of Black Culture, NAACP, Black Student Alliance, National Pan Hellenic Council, Caribbean Student Association. Greek and Indian associations, International Student Association, Korean-American Association, Vietnamese Student Organization.

**ATHLETICS. Physical education requirements:** None.
**Intercollegiate competition:** 2% of students participate. Baseball (M), basketball (M,W), cross-country (M,W), diving (M,W), field hockey (W), golf (M), lacrosse (W), sailing (M,W), soccer (M), swimming (M,W), tennis (M,W), wrestling (M). Member of Colonial Athletic Association, NCAA Division I, South Atlantic Field Hockey/Lacrosse Association.
**Intramural and club sports:** 60% of students participate. Intramural badminton, basketball, bowling, flag football, golf, ice hockey, inner-tube water polo, lacrosse, racquetball, rowing, rugby, soccer, softball, street hockey, table tennis, tennis, volleyball, water polo, wrestling. Men's club cheerleading. Women's club cheerleading.

**ADMISSIONS. Academic basis for candidate selection** (in order of priority): Secondary school record, standardized test scores, class rank, school's recommendation, essay.
**Nonacademic basis for candidate selection:** Character and personality are emphasized. Extracurricular participation is important. Particular talent or ability is considered.
**Requirements:** Graduation from secondary school is required; GED is accepted. 16 units and the following program of study are required: 4 units of English, 3 units of math, 3 units of science including 1 unit of lab, 2 units of foreign language, 3 units of social studies. Minimum combined SAT score of 850 (minimum scores of 400 in both verbal and math), rank in top half of secondary school class, and minimum 2.0 GPA recommended. Minimum SAT score of 500 math required of engineering program applicants. Portfolio required of art program applicants. Audition required of music program applicants. SAT is required; ACT may be substituted. Campus visit recommended. No off-campus interviews.
**Procedure:** Take SAT or ACT by November of 12th year. Notification of admission on rolling basis. Tuition due in full prior to first day of classes. $300 room deposit, $250 of which is refundable until May 1. Freshmen accepted for terms other than fall.
**Special programs:** Admission may be deferred. Credit and/or placement may be granted through CEEB Advanced Placement exams for scores of 3 or higher. Credit and/or placement may be granted through CLEP general and subject exams. Credit may be granted through DANTES exams and military experience. Placement may be granted through challenge exams. Concurrent enrollment program.
**Transfer students:** Transfer students accepted for terms other than fall. In fall 1993, 47% of all new students were transfers into all classes. 1,921 transfer applications were received, 1,838 were accepted. Application deadline is July 1 for fall; December 1 for spring. Minimum 2.0 GPA required. SAT/ACT scores required of transfer applicants with fewer than 24 credits and those who graduated from high school within the last two years. Lowest course grade accepted is "C." At least 30 semester hours must be completed at the university to receive degree.
**Admissions contact:** Patricia Cavendour, Director of Admissions. 804 683-3637.

**FINANCIAL AID. Available aid:** Pell grants, SEOG, state scholarships and grants, school scholarships and grants, private scholarships and grants, ROTC scholarships, academic merit scholarships, athletic scholarships, and aid for undergraduate foreign students. Perkins Loans (NDSL), PLUS, Stafford Loans (GSL), state loans, school loans, and private loans. Deferred payment plan. Major credit cards accepted.
**Financial aid statistics:** 61% of aid is not need-based. Average amounts of aid awarded freshmen: Scholarships and grants, $4,761; loans, $2,474.
**Supporting data/closing dates:** FAFSA/FAF: Priority filing date is March 1; deadline is May 1. School's own aid application: Priority filing date is March 1; deadline is May 1. Notification of awards on rolling basis.
**Financial aid contact:** Helga Greenfield, Director of Financial Aid. 804 683-3683.

**STUDENT EMPLOYMENT.** College Work/Study Program. Institutional employment. 45% of full-time undergraduates work on campus during school year. Students may expect to earn an average of $2,000 during school year. Off-campus part-time employment opportunities rated "excellent."

**COMPUTER FACILITIES.** 125 IBM/IBM-compatible, Macintosh/Apple, and RISC-/UNIX-based microcomputers; all are networked. Students may access IBM minicomputer/mainframe systems. Residence halls may be equipped with stand-alone microcomputers. Client/LAN operating systems include UNIX/XENIX/AIX, X-windows. Computer languages and software packages include BASIC, COBOL, dBASE, FORTRAN, Lotus

1-2-3; word processing packages. Some computers reserved for students enrolled in specific majors.
**Fees:** None.
**Hours:** 7 AM-midn.

**GRADUATE CAREER DATA.** Companies and businesses that hire graduates: Sovran Bank, NASA, IBM, Newport News Shipbuilding, AT&T, Texas Instruments, Internal Revenue Service, Blue Cross/Blue Shield.

**PROMINENT ALUMNI/AE.** Beth Polson, Emmy award-winning producer; Mills Godwin, former governor of Virginia; William Wiley, state treasurer, Virginia; Deborah Shelton, actress; Bill Howell, corporate director of public relations, IBM; L. Glenn Perry, former chief accountant, SEC's Enforcement Division.

# Radford University

**Radford, VA 24142** **703 831-5000**

**1993-94 Costs.** Tuition: $2,942 (state residents), $6,684 (out-of-state). Room & board: $4,110. Fees, books, misc. academic expenses (school's estimate): $500.
**Enrollment.** Undergraduates: 3,434 men, 4,562 women (full-time). Freshman class: 5,702 applicants, 4,894 accepted, 1,742 enrolled. Graduate enrollment: 270 men, 618 women.
**Test score averages/ranges.** Average SAT scores: 419 verbal, 455 math. Range of SAT scores of middle 50%: 400-499 verbal, 400-499 math. Average ACT scores: 22 composite. Range of ACT scores of middle 50%: 20-24 composite.
**Faculty.** 420 full-time; 119 part-time. 76% of faculty holds doctoral degree. Student/faculty ratio: 23 to 1.
**Selectivity rating.** Competitive.

**PROFILE.** Radford is a public, comprehensive university. Founded as a teachers college for women in 1910, it adopted coeducation in 1972. Its 154-acre campus is located in Radford, 40 miles southwest of Roanoke.

**Accreditation:** SACS. Professionally accredited by the American Assembly of Collegiate Schools of Business, the American Dietetic Association, the American Speech-Language-Hearing Association, the Computing Sciences Accreditation Board, the Council on Social Work Education, the National Association of Schools of Music, the National Council for Accreditation of Teacher Education, the National League for Nursing.
**Religious orientation:** Radford University is nonsectarian; one semester of religion required.
**Library:** Collections totaling over 284,778 volumes, 3,110 periodical subscriptions, and 1,214,264 microform items.
**Special facilities/museums:** On-campus preschool for elementary/early education student teachers. Language lab. Art gallery with sculpture garden, planetarium, and on-campus speech/hearing clinic.
**Athletic facilities:** Intramural fields, weight room, basketball, racquetball, and tennis courts, swimming pool.

**STUDENT BODY. Undergraduate profile:** 86% are state residents; 32% are transfers. 2.8% Asian-American, 3.3% Black, 1.6% Hispanic, .2% Native American, 92.1% White. Average age of undergraduates is 20.
**Freshman profile:** 1% of freshmen who took SAT scored 700 or over on verbal, 1% scored 700 or over on math; 2% scored 600 or over on verbal, 5% scored 600 or over on math; 14% scored 500 or over on verbal, 30% scored 500 or over on math; 63% scored 400 or over on verbal, 77% scored 400 or over on math; 99% scored 300 or over on verbal, 99% scored 300 or over on math. 99% of accepted applicants took SAT; 1% took ACT. 90% of freshmen come from public schools.
**Undergraduate achievement:** 75% of fall 1992 freshmen returned for fall 1993 term. 27% of entering class graduated. 20% of students who completed a degree program went on to graduate study within one year.
**Foreign students:** 164 students are from out of the country. Countries represented include China, Japan, Korea, Malaysia, Morocco, and the United Kingdom; 57 in all.

**PROGRAMS OF STUDY. Degrees:** B.A., B.Bus.Admin., B.F.A., B.Gen.Studies, B.Mus., B.S.
**Majors:** Accounting, Administrative Systems, Art, Biology, Business Administration, Chemistry, Child Development/Family Life, Communication Sciences/Disorders, Criminal Justice, Dance, Design, Early Education, Economics, English, Finance, Food/Nutrition, Foreign Languages, Geography, Geology, History, Human Development, Information Systems, Interdisciplinary Studies, Journalism, Liberal Studies, Management, Marketing, Mathematics, Medical Technology, Music, Music Therapy, Nursing, Philosophy/Religion, Physical Education, Physical Science, Political Science, Psychology, Recreation/Leisure Services, Social Science, Social Work, Sociology/Anthropology, Special Education, Speech, Statistics, Theatre.
**Distribution of degrees:** The majors with the highest enrollment are interdisciplinary studies, management, and marketing; music therapy, medical technology, and statistics have the lowest.
**Requirements:** General education requirement.
**Academic regulations:** Freshmen must maintain minimum 1.50 GPA; sophomores, 1.75 GPA; juniors, 2.00 GPA; seniors, 2.00 GPA.
**Special:** Minors offered in most majors; interdisciplinary minor in social gerontology. Liberal studies majors design own curricula. Design concentrations in environmental design, fashion design, fashion merchandising, and interior design. Music concentrations in business, composition, education, liberal arts, piano performance, and therapy. Physical education concentrations in teaching, general, sports medicine, commercial fitness, martial arts, and school health. Writing Across the Curriculum: oral communication program. Self-designed majors. Double majors. Dual degrees. Independent study. Pass/fail grading option. Internships. Graduate school at which undergraduates may take graduate-level courses. Preprofessional programs in law, medicine, veterinary science, pharmacy, dentistry, and physical therapy. Combined-degree program in pharmacy. Teacher certification in early childhood, elementary, secondary, and special education. Study abroad in Belgium, Bolivia, Brazil, Costa Rica, England, Germany, and Japan. ROTC. NROTC at Virginia Tech to nursing students only.
**Honors:** Phi Beta Kappa. Honors program.
**Academic Assistance:** Remedial study skills. Nonremedial tutoring.

**STUDENT LIFE. Housing:** All freshmen must live on campus unless living with family. Coed and women's dorms. Off-campus privately-owned housing. 36% of students live in college housing.
**Social atmosphere:** Favorite student gathering spots, according to the student newspaper, include the Busstop, Lucky's, Sackett's, BT's, Macade's, and Heth Hall. "The Halloween Bash at Radford attracts students from all over the state."
**Services and counseling/handicapped student services:** Health service. Counseling services for minority, military, veteran, and older students. Personal and psychological counseling. Career and academic guidance services. Physically disabled student services. Learning disabled services. Notetaking services. Tape recorders. Tutors. Reader services for the blind.
**Campus organizations:** Undergraduate student government. Student newspaper (Tartan, published once/week). Literary magazine. Yearbook. Radio and TV stations. Band, orchestra, concert committee, glee and choral clubs, choir, Cotillion, karate and photography clubs, Orchesis, Honor Council, Diversity Promotions Council, activity, departmental, service, and special-interest groups, 155 organizations in all. 13 fraternities, no chapter houses; 10 sororities, no chapter houses. 18% of men join a fraternity. 19% of women join a sorority.
**Religious organizations:** B'nai B'rith, Baptist Student Union, Campus Crusade for Christ, Catholic Student Association, Christian Student Fellowship, Hillel, Intervarsity Christian Fellowship, Latter-Day Saints, New Covenant Collegiate Fellowship, United Campus Chapel Fellowship, Wesley Foundation, Episcopal Fellowship.
**Minority/foreign student organizations:** Black Awareness Programming Board, Black Student Affairs Committee, NAACP, African American Heritage Association. International Club, International Student Affairs.

**ATHLETICS. Physical education requirements:** None.
**Intercollegiate competition:** 4% of students participate. Baseball (M), basketball (M,W), cross-country (M,W), field hockey (W), golf (M,W), gymnastics (M,W), lacrosse (M), soccer (M,W), softball (W), tennis (M,W), volleyball (W). Member of Big South Conference, NCAA Division I.
**Intramural and club sports:** 52% of students participate. Intramural basketball, flag football, football, inner-tube water polo, racquetball, soccer, softball, super hoops, tennis, volleyball. Men's club cheerleading, swimming. Women's club cheerleading, swimming.

**ADMISSIONS. Academic basis for candidate selection** (in order of priority): Secondary school record, standardized test scores, class rank, essay, school's recommendation.
**Nonacademic basis for candidate selection:** Character and personality, extracurricular participation, and particular talent or ability are considered.
**Requirements:** Graduation from secondary school is recommended; GED is accepted. 13 units and the following program of study are required: 4 units of English, 2 units of math, 2 units of lab science, 2 units of social studies, 1 unit of history. 2.0 minimum GPA required. Biology and chemistry recommended of nursing program applicants. Audition required of dance, music, and theatre program applicants for placement. Application to upper division (junior year) required of education, nursing, and B.B.A. program students. Portfolio required of art program applicants. SAT or ACT is required. Campus visit and interview recommended. No off-campus interviews.
**Procedure:** Take SAT or ACT by December of 12th year. Application deadline is April 1. Notification of admission on rolling basis. Reply is required by May 1. $200 room deposit, refundable until May 1. Freshmen accepted for terms other than fall.
**Special programs:** Credit and/or placement may be granted through CEEB Advanced Placement exams for scores of 3 or higher. Credit and/or placement may be granted through CLEP subject exams. Credit and placement may be granted through Regents College, DANTES, and challenge exams, and military experience. Early entrance/early admission program. Concurrent enrollment program.
**Transfer students:** Transfer students accepted for terms other than fall. In fall 1993, 32% of all new students were transfers into all classes. 1,774 transfer applications were received, 1,307 were accepted. Application deadline is June 1 for fall; December 1 for spring. Minimum 2.0 GPA required. Lowest course grade accepted is "C." At least 32 semester hours must be completed at the university to receive degree.
**Admissions contact:** Vernon L. Beitzel, M.S., Director of Admissions. 703 831-5371.

**FINANCIAL AID. Available aid:** Pell grants, SEOG, Federal Nursing Student Scholarships, state scholarships and grants, school scholarships and grants, private scholarships, ROTC scholarships, academic merit scholarships, and athletic scholarships. Perkins Loans (NDSL), PLUS, Stafford Loans (GSL), NSL, state loans, school loans, and SLS. Knight Tuition Plans and AMS.
**Financial aid statistics:** 36% of aid is not need-based. In 1993-94, 33% of all undergraduate applicants received aid; 33% of freshman applicants. Average amounts of aid awarded freshmen: Scholarships and grants, $2,512; loans, $3,523.
**Supporting data/closing dates:** FAFSA: Priority filing date is March 1. School's own aid application: Priority filing date is March 1. Notification of awards begins late April.
**Financial aid contact:** Herbert S. "Buddy" Johnston, M.S., Director of Financial Aid. 703 831-5408.

**STUDENT EMPLOYMENT.** College Work/Study Program. Institutional employment. 13% of full-time undergraduates work on campus during school year. Students may expect to earn an average of $1,275 during school year. Off-campus part-time employment opportunities rated "good."

**COMPUTER FACILITIES.** 260 IBM/IBM-compatible, Macintosh/Apple, and RISC-/UNIX-based microcomputers; 135 are networked. Students may access SUN minicomputer/mainframe systems. Residence halls may be equipped with stand-alone microcomputers. Numerous computer languages and software packages available. Computer facilities are available to all students.

**GRADUATE CAREER DATA.** Graduate school percentages: 2% enter law school. 5% enter graduate business programs. Highest graduate school enrollments: Duke U, U of Texas, U of Virginia. 45% of graduates choose careers in business and industry. Companies and businesses that hire graduates: auditor for public accounts, government agencies, health care facilities, school systems.

# Randolph-Macon College

**Ashland, VA 23005-5505** **804 752-7200**

**1994-95 Costs.** Tuition: $13,840. Room: $1,850. Board: $1,885. Fees, books, misc. academic expenses (school's estimate): $725.
**Enrollment.** Undergraduates: 549 men, 543 women (full-time). Freshman class: 1,771 applicants, 1,325 accepted, 306 enrolled.
**Test score averages/ranges.** Range of SAT scores of middle 50%: 430-520 verbal, 480-580 math.
**Faculty.** 96 full-time; 56 part-time. 82% of faculty holds highest degree in specific field. Student/faculty ratio: 11 to 1.
**Selectivity rating.** Competitive.

**PROFILE.** Randolph-Macon, founded in 1891, is a church-affiliated, liberal arts college. Its 111-acre campus, located in Ashland, includes three buildings registered on the National Register of Historic Buildings and one designated a National Historic Landmark.
**Accreditation:** SACS.
**Religious orientation:** Randolph-Macon College is affiliated with the United Methodist Church; two semesters of religion required.
**Library:** Collections totaling over 143,551 volumes, 889 periodical subscriptions, and 56,457 microform items.
**Special facilities/museums:** Language lab, learning center, observatory, electron microscopes, telescope.
**Athletic facilities:** Gymnasiums, tracks, baseball, field hockey, football, intramural, lacrosse, and soccer fields, basketball, tennis, and volleyball courts.
**STUDENT BODY. Undergraduate profile:** 45% are state residents; 10% are transfers. 2% Asian-American, 4% Black, 1% Hispanic, 91% White, 2% Foreign. Average age of undergraduates is 20.
**Freshman profile:** 1% of freshmen who took SAT scored 700 or over on verbal, 3% scored 700 or over on math; 10% scored 600 or over on verbal, 20% scored 600 or over on math; 35% scored 500 or over on verbal, 66% scored 500 or over on math; 90% scored 400 or over on verbal, 97% scored 400 or over on math; 100% scored 300 or over on verbal, 100% scored 300 or over on math. Majority of accepted applicants took SAT. 65% of freshmen come from public schools.
**Undergraduate achievement:** 85% of fall 1992 freshmen returned for fall 1993 term. 64% of entering class graduated. 28% of students who completed a degree program immediately went on to graduate study.
**Foreign students:** 22 students are from out of the country. Countries represented include Canada, China, Hong Kong, Japan, and Korea; 12 in all.
**PROGRAMS OF STUDY. Degrees:** B.A., B.S.
**Majors:** Art History, Arts Management, Biology, Business Economics, Chemistry, Classics, Computer/Information Sciences, Drama, Economics, English, Environmental Studies, French, German, Greek, History, International Relations, International Studies, Latin, Mathematics, Music, Philosophy, Physics, Political Science, Psychology, Religious Studies, Sociology, Spanish, Studio Art, Women's Studies.
**Distribution of degrees:** The majors with the highest enrollment are economics/business, psychology, and English; classics and philosophy have the lowest.
**Requirements:** General education requirement.
**Academic regulations:** Minimum 2.0 GPA required for graduation.
**Special:** Minors offered in all majors and in accounting, Asian studies, astrophysics, journalism, and elementary and secondary education. Courses offered in art, astronomy, drama, education, geology, music, and speech. Four-week January term with emphasis on internships, interdisciplinary study, and independent work. Transfer programs in health professions and travel study. Double majors. Dual degrees. Independent study. Accelerated study. Internships. Cooperative education programs. Preprofessional programs in law, medicine, veterinary science, pharmacy, dentistry, and theology. 3-2 forestry and environmental studies program with Duke U. 3-2 engineering programs with Washington U (St. Louis) and Columbia U. 4-1 master's program in accounting with Virginia Commonwealth U. Member of Virginia Seven College Consortium. Student exchange with Hampden-Sydney Coll, Hollins Coll, Mary Baldwin Coll, Randolph-Macon Woman's Coll, Sweet Briar Coll, and Washington and Lee U. Teacher certification in elementary and secondary education. Exchange program abroad in Japan (Nagoya Gakuin U). Study abroad also in England, France, Germany, Italy, Korea, and Spain. ROTC at U of Richmond.
**Honors:** Phi Beta Kappa. Honors program. Honor societies.
**Academic Assistance:** Remedial reading, writing, math, and study skills. Nonremedial tutoring.
**STUDENT LIFE. Housing:** Freshmen, sophomores, and juniors must live on campus unless living with family. Coed, women's, and men's dorms. Sorority and fraternity housing. Off-campus privately-owned housing. 80% of students live in college housing.
**Services and counseling/handicapped student services:** Placement services. Health service. Counseling services for minority, military, veteran, and older students. Birth control, personal, and psychological counseling. Career and academic guidance services. Religious counseling. Physically disabled student services. Learning disabled services.
**Campus organizations:** Undergraduate student government. Student newspaper (Yellow Jacket, published biweekly). Literary magazine. Yearbook. Concert choir, Drama Guild, Fine Arts Society, debating, literary society, business/economics and political science groups, German Club, Amnesty International, Habitat for Humanity, Hunger Task Force, 67 organizations in all. Seven fraternities, all with chapter houses; four sororities, all with chapter houses. 40% of men join a fraternity. 39% of women join a sorority.
**Religious organizations:** College Workship Council, Fellowship of Christian Athletes, Volunteers in Action Waging Peace, Christian Fellowship.
**Minority/foreign student organizations:** Multicultural Association, Black Student Union, Black Cultural Society. International Interest Group, Japanese Club.
**ATHLETICS. Physical education requirements:** Two semesters of physical education required.
**Intercollegiate competition:** 25% of students participate. Baseball (M), basketball (M,W), cross-country (M,W), field hockey (W), football (M), golf (M), lacrosse (M,W), soccer (M,W), tennis (M,W). Member of NCAA Division III, Old Dominion Athletic Conference.
**Intramural and club sports:** 70% of students participate. Intramural basketball, box lacrosse, flag football, frisbee golf, indoor soccer, powderpuff football, soccer, softball, volleyball.
**ADMISSIONS. Academic basis for candidate selection** (in order of priority): Secondary school record, class rank, standardized test scores, school's recommendation, essay.
**Nonacademic basis for candidate selection:** Character and personality, extracurricular participation, particular talent or ability, geographical distribution, and alumni/ae relationship are considered.
**Requirements:** Graduation from secondary school is required; GED is accepted. 16 units and the following program of study are required: 4 units of English, 3 units of math, 2 units of lab science, 2 units of foreign language, 1 unit of social studies, 2 units of history, 2 units of academic electives. Additional units recommended in foreign language, advanced math, lab sciences, European or world history, and civics. At least three-quarters of secondary school units must be in academic subjects. SAT is required; ACT may be substituted. ACH recommended. Campus visit and interview recommended. Off-campus interviews available with an admissions representative.
**Procedure:** Take SAT or ACT by January of 12th year. Take ACH by February of 12th year. Visit college for interview by March of 12th year. Application deadline is March 1. Notification of admission on rolling basis beginning in late January. Reply is required by May 1. $300 tuition deposit, refundable until May 1. Freshmen accepted for terms other than fall.
**Special programs:** Admission may be deferred one year. Credit and/or placement may be granted through CEEB Advanced Placement exams for scores of 4 or higher. Credit and/or placement may be granted through CLEP subject exams. Early decision program. In fall 1993, 36 applied for early decision and 26 were accepted. Deadline for applying for early decision is December 1. Early entrance/early admission program. Concurrent enrollment program.
**Transfer students:** Transfer students accepted for terms other than fall. In fall 1993, 10% of all new students were transfers into all classes. 134 transfer applications were received, 72 were accepted. Application deadline is March 1 for fall; January 1 for spring. Minimum 2.0 GPA required. Lowest course grade accepted is "C." Maximum number of transferable credits is 65 semester hours from a two-year school and 75 semester hours from a four-year school. At least 37 semester hours must be completed at the college to receive degree.
**Admissions contact:** John C. Conkright, M.A., Dean of Admissions. 804 752-7305.
**FINANCIAL AID. Available aid:** Pell grants, SEOG, state scholarships and grants, school scholarships and grants, private scholarships and grants, ROTC scholarships, and academic merit scholarships. One-third discount on tuition and fees for dependents of United Methodist ministers; one-half discount for candidates in church-related vocations. Perkins Loans (NDSL), PLUS, Stafford Loans (GSL), state loans, school loans, private loans, and SLS. Tuition Plan Inc., Knight Tuition Plans, deferred payment plan, and family tuition reduction.
**Financial aid statistics:** 24% of aid is not need-based. In 1993-94, 100% of all undergraduate applicants received aid. Average amounts of aid awarded freshmen: Scholarships and grants, $7,500; loans, $3,800.
**Supporting data/closing dates:** FAFSA/FAF: Priority filing date is February 1. School's own aid application: Priority filing date is March 1. Income tax forms: Priority filing date is March 1. Notification of awards begins April 1.
**Financial aid contact:** Mary Y. Neal, M.A., Director of Financial Aid. 804 752-7259.
**STUDENT EMPLOYMENT.** College Work/Study Program. Institutional employment. 29% of full-time undergraduates work on campus during school year. Students may expect to earn an average of $800 during school year. Off-campus part-time employment opportunities rated "excellent."
**COMPUTER FACILITIES.** 250 IBM/IBM-compatible, Macintosh/Apple, and RISC-/UNIX-based microcomputers; 90 are networked. Students may access Digital minicomputer/mainframe systems, BITNET, Internet. Client/LAN operating systems include Apple/Macintosh, DOS, X-windows, LocalTalk/AppleTalk, Novell. Computer languages and software packages include BASIC, C/C++, COBOL, FORTRAN, LISP, Paradox, Pascal, Quattro Pro, SPSS, WordPerfect. Computer facilities are available to all students.
**Hours:** 9 AM-midn. (M-F); noon-6 PM (Sa); 4 PM-midn. (Su).
**GRADUATE CAREER DATA.** Graduate school percentages: 3% enter law school. 3% enter medical school. 5% enter graduate business programs. 17% enter graduate arts and sciences programs. Highest graduate school enrollments: James Madison U, Medical Coll of Virginia, U of Richmond, U of Virginia, Coll of William & Mary. 63% of graduates choose careers in business and industry.
**PROMINENT ALUMNI/AE.** Hugh Scott, former senate minority leader; Jack Gibbons, science advisor to President Clinton; Porter Hardy, Jr., former congressman; J. Rives Childs, former ambassador, Ethiopia and Saudi Arabia; John Frazee, president, Sprint Co.

# Randolph-Macon Woman's College

**Lynchburg, VA 24503** **804 947-8000**

**1994-95 Costs.** Tuition: $13,970. Room & board: $6,110. Fees, books, misc. academic expenses (school's estimate): $490.
**Enrollment.** Undergraduates: 2 men, 653 women (full-time). Freshman class: 701 applicants, 621 accepted, 171 enrolled.
**Test score averages/ranges.** Average SAT scores: 502 verbal, 517 math. Range of SAT scores of middle 50%: 470-560 verbal, 470-570 math. Average ACT scores: 25 composite. Range of ACT scores of middle 50%: 21-28 composite.
**Faculty.** 66 full-time; 22 part-time. 95% of faculty holds highest degree in specific field. Student/faculty ratio: 9 to 1.
**Selectivity rating.** Competitive.

**PROFILE.** Randolph-Macon Woman's College, founded in 1891, is a church-affiliated, liberal arts college. Its 100-acre campus is located in a residential section of Lynchburg, 50 miles northeast of Roanoke.

**Accreditation:** SACS.
**Religious orientation:** Randolph-Macon Woman's College is affiliated with the United Methodist Church; no religious requirements.
**Library:** Collections totaling over 163,000 volumes, 828 periodical subscriptions and 340 microform items.
**Special facilities/museums:** American art museum, computer-equipped classrooms, language lab, science and math resource center, nursery school, nature preserves, observatory, electron microscope.
**Athletic facilities:** Swimming pool, aerobics, fencing, training, and weight rooms, gymnasium, tennis courts, dance studio, field hockey, lacrosse, and soccer fields; horseback riding facility.

**STUDENT BODY. Undergraduate profile:** 34% are state residents; 16% are transfers. 3% Asian-American, 5% Black, 2% Hispanic, 1% Native American, 84% White, 5% Other. Average age of undergraduates is 20.
**Freshman profile:** 2% of freshmen who took SAT scored 700 or over on verbal, 2% scored 700 or over on math; 17% scored 600 or over on verbal, 17% scored 600 or over on math; 49% scored 500 or over on verbal, 61% scored 500 or over on math; 93% scored 400 or over on verbal, 92% scored 400 or over on math; 100% scored 300 or over on verbal, 100% scored 300 or over on math. 8% of freshmen who took ACT scored 30 or over on composite; 56% scored 24 or over on composite; 98% scored 18 or over on composite; 100% scored 12 or over on composite. Majority of accepted applicants took SAT. 73% of freshmen come from public schools.
**Undergraduate achievement:** 78% of fall 1992 freshmen returned for fall 1993 term. 59% of entering class graduated. 30% of students who completed a degree program went on to graduate study within one year.
**Foreign students:** 21 students are from out of the country. Countries represented include European countries, India, Japan, and Latin American countries; 11 in all.

**PROGRAMS OF STUDY. Degrees:** A.B.
**Majors:** Art, Biology, Chemistry, Classics, Communication, Dance, Economics, Economics/Mathematics, English, French, German Studies, History, International Relations, Mathematics, Music, Philosophy, Physics, Political Economy, Politics, Psychology, Religion, Russian Studies, Sociology/Anthropology, Spanish, Theatre.
**Distribution of degrees:** The majors with the highest enrollment are politics, biology, and psychology.
**Requirements:** General education requirement.
**Academic regulations:** Minimum 2.0 GPA must be maintained.
**Special:** Minors offered in all majors and in computer science, economics/business administration, and women's studies. Courses offered in astronomy, education, and physical education. Interdepartmental studies. Self-designed majors. Double majors. Dual degrees. Independent study. Accelerated study. Pass/fail grading option. Internships. Cooperative education programs. Preprofessional programs in law, medicine, veterinary science, and dentistry. Dual-degree program in engineering with U of Virginia. 3-2 engineering programs with Duke U, Washington U, and Vanderbilt U. 3-2 nursing programs with John Hopkins U Sch of Nursing and Vanderbilt U Sch of Nursing. 3-2 master's degree program in public health with U of Rochester Sch of Medicine and Dentistry. 3-2 occupational therapy program with Washington U Sch of Medicine. Member of Tri-College Consortium. Washington Semester. Member of seven-college exchange with Hampden-Sydney Coll, Hollins Coll, Mary Baldwin Coll, Randolph-Macon Coll, Sweet Briar Coll, and Washington and Lee U. Teacher certification in elementary and secondary education. Exchange programs abroad in England (U of Reading), Greece (American Sch of Classical Studies), Italy (Intercollegiate Center for Classical Studies in Rome), and Japan (Kansai U of Foreign Studies). ROTC at Lynchburg Coll.
**Honors:** Phi Beta Kappa. Honors program. Honor societies.
**Academic Assistance:** Nonremedial tutoring.

**ADMISSIONS. Academic basis for candidate selection** (in order of priority): Secondary school record, school's recommendation, class rank, essay, standardized test scores.
**Nonacademic basis for candidate selection:** Extracurricular participation is emphasized. Character and personality are important. Particular talent or ability, geographical distribution, and alumni/ae relationship are considered.
**Requirements:** Graduation from secondary school is required; GED is not accepted. 16 units and the following program of study are recommended: 4 units of English, 3 units of math, 2 units of science, 3 units of foreign language, 2 units of history, 1 unit of electives. SAT or ACT is required. ACH recommended. Campus visit and interview recommended. Off-campus interviews available with admissions and alumni representatives.
**Procedure:** Take SAT or ACT by February of 12th year. Take ACH by May of 12th year. Visit college for interview by March 1 of 12th year. Suggest filing application by March 1; no deadline. Notification of admission on rolling basis beginning February 1. Reply is required by May 1. $300 tuition deposit, refundable until June 1. Freshmen accepted for terms other than fall.
**Special programs:** Admission may be deferred one year. Credit and/or placement may be granted through CEEB Advanced Placement exams for scores of 5 or higher. Placement may be granted through CLEP general exams, Regents College, ACT PEP, DANTES, and challenge exams, and military and life experience. Credit and/or placement may be granted through CLEP subject exams. Early decision program. In fall 1993, 48 applied for early decision and 47 were accepted. Deadline for applying for early decision is November 15. Early entrance/early admission program. Concurrent enrollment program.
**Transfer students:** Transfer students accepted for terms other than fall. In fall 1993, 16% of all new students were transfers into all classes. 74 transfer applications were received, 57 were accepted. Minimum 2.5 GPA recommended. Lowest course grade accepted is "C." Maximum number of transferable credits is 62 semester hours. At least 62 semester hours must be completed at the college to receive degree.
**Admissions contact:** Jean H. Stewart, Director of Admissions. 800 745-7692.

**FINANCIAL AID. Available aid:** Pell grants, SEOG, state scholarships and grants, school scholarships and grants, private scholarships and grants, academic merit scholarships, and aid for undergraduate foreign students. Perkins Loans (NDSL), PLUS, Stafford Loans (GSL), and SLS. Knight Tuition Plans.
**Financial aid statistics:** 26% of aid is not need-based. In 1993-94, 52% of all freshman applicants received aid. Average amounts of aid awarded freshmen: Scholarships and grants, $7,907; loans, $3,321.
**Supporting data/closing dates:** FAFSA: Accepted on rolling basis. School's own aid application: Priority filing date is March 1; accepted on rolling basis. Notification of awards on rolling basis.
**Financial aid contact:** Brantley R. Townes, Director of Financial Planning and Assistance. 804 947-8128.

# Roanoke College

**Salem, VA 24153** **703 375-2500**

**1994-95 Costs.** Tuition: $13,425. Room: $2,150. Board: $2,275. Fees, books, misc. academic expenses (school's estimate): $450.
**Enrollment.** Undergraduates: 579 men, 881 women (full-time). Freshman class: 2,227 applicants, 1,788 accepted, 437 enrolled.
**Test score averages/ranges.** Average SAT scores: 487 verbal, 532 math. Range of SAT scores of middle 50%: 430-540 verbal, 470-580 math.
**Faculty.** 100 full-time; 53 part-time. 85% of faculty holds doctoral degree. Student/faculty ratio: 14 to 1.
**Selectivity rating.** Competitive.

**PROFILE.** Roanoke, founded in 1842, is a church-affiliated, liberal arts college. The 68-acre campus, including several buildings registered as National Historic Landmarks, is located in Salem, five miles from Roanoke.

**Accreditation:** SACS. Professionally accredited by the Association of Collegiate Business Schools and Programs.
**Religious orientation:** Roanoke College is affiliated with the Evangelical Lutheran Church in America; no religious requirements.
**Library:** Collections totaling over 168,110 volumes, 935 periodical subscriptions, and 153,000 microform items.
**Special facilities/museums:** Fine arts center, community research center, language lab, church and society center.
**Athletic facilities:** Fitness center, gymnasium, badminton, basketball, racquetball, tennis, and volleyball courts, athletic fields, track.

**STUDENT BODY. Undergraduate profile:** 51% are state residents; 16% are transfers. 1% Asian-American, 2% Black, 1% Hispanic, 96% White. Average age of undergraduates is 20.
**Freshman profile:** 3% of freshmen who took SAT scored 700 or over on math; 9% scored 600 or over on verbal, 22% scored 600 or over on math; 43% scored 500 or over on verbal, 69% scored 500 or over on math; 89% scored 400 or over on verbal, 96% scored 400 or over on math; 100% scored 300 or over on verbal, 100% scored 300 or over on math. 90% of accepted applicants took SAT; 10% took ACT. 75% of freshmen come from public schools.
**Undergraduate achievement:** 75% of fall 1992 freshmen returned for fall 1993 term. 51% of entering class graduated.
**Foreign students:** 11 students are from out of the country. Countries represented include Bermuda, Brazil, China, El Salvador, England, and Japan; 10 in all.

**PROGRAMS OF STUDY. Degrees:** B.A., B.Bus.Admin., B.S.
**Majors:** Art, Biology, Business Administration, Chemistry, Computer Information Systems, Computer Science, Criminal Justice, English, Fine Arts, French, Health/Physical Education, History, International Relations, Mathematics, Medical Technology, Music, Philosophy, Philosophy/Religion, Physics, Political Science, Psychology, Sociology, Spanish, Theatre Arts.
**Distribution of degrees:** The majors with the highest enrollment are business administration, psychology, and English; physics, music, and medical technology have the lowest.
**Requirements:** General education requirement.
**Academic regulations:** Freshmen must maintain minimum 1.5 GPA; sophomores, 1.75 GPA; juniors, 2.0 GPA; seniors, 2.0 GPA.
**Special:** Minors offered in most majors and in American literature, American politics, anthropology, church music, coaching, English literature, European history, foreign politics, German, geography, health care administration, health care delivery, physical education, religion, theatre and criticism, theatre design, theatre performance, and U.S. history. Concentrations available in accounting, athletic training, communications, finance, human resource management, information analysis, marketing, social work, and urban studies. Double majors. Dual degrees. Independent study. Accelerated study. Pass/fail grading option. Internships. Preprofessional programs in law, medicine, veterinary science, pharmacy, dentistry, and theology. 3-2 engineering program with Virginia Tech U and Washington U. Washington Semester. Teacher certification in early childhood, elementary, and secondary education. Certification in specific subject areas. Exchange program abroad in England (Virginia at Oxford). Study abroad also in Australia, France, Germany, Italy, Japan, Luxembourg, and Spain.
**Honors:** Honors program. Honor societies.
**Academic Assistance:** Remedial study skills. Nonremedial tutoring.

**STUDENT LIFE. Housing:** Freshmen and sophomores not from local area must live on campus. Coed, women's, and men's dorms. Fraternity housing. 56% of students live in college housing.
**Social atmosphere:** Popular gathering spots for students include fraternity houses, the student center, Mac and Bob's, and Clancy's. Greeks, athletes, and the Baptist Student Union have a widespread influence on campus social life. The school year's most popular events include the Fall Ball, basketball, lacrosse, and soccer games, and student plays. According to the editor of the student newspaper, "There is not an abundance of things to do on campus, but there's more in town."

**Services and counseling/handicapped student services:** Placement services. Health service. Counseling services for older students. Personal and psychological counseling. Career and academic guidance services. Religious counseling. Physically disabled student services. Learning disabled services. Tutors. Reader services for the blind.

**Campus organizations:** Undergraduate student government. Student newspaper (Brackety-Ack, published once/week). Literary magazine. Yearbook. Program Board, Judicial Board, Model UN, choir, jazz and chamber ensembles, Interhall Council, resource development group, Panhellenic Council, Habitat for Humanity, Earthbound Environment Club, Amnesty International, 22 organizations in all. Four fraternities, three chapter houses; three sororities, no chapter houses. 30% of men join a fraternity. 30% of women join a sorority.

**Religious organizations:** Baptist Student Union, Catholic Student Organization, Fellowship of Christian Athletes, Campus Christian Fellowship, Peace and Justice Group.

**Minority/foreign student organizations:** Shades of Maroon.

**ATHLETICS. Physical education requirements:** Two semesters of physical education required.

**Intercollegiate competition:** 17% of students participate. Basketball (M,W), cross-country (M,W), field hockey (W), golf (M), lacrosse (M,W), soccer (M,W), tennis (M,W), track (indoor) (M,W), track (outdoor) (M,W), track and field (indoor) (M,W), track and field (outdoor) (M,W), volleyball (W). Member of NCAA Division III, Old Dominion Athletic Conference.

**Intramural and club sports:** 37% of students participate. Intramural basketball, floor hockey, golf, indoor soccer, inner-tube water polo, powderpuff football, racquetball, softball, speedball, tennis, volleyball.

**ADMISSIONS. Academic basis for candidate selection** (in order of priority): Secondary school record, standardized test scores, class rank, school's recommendation, essay.

**Nonacademic basis for candidate selection:** Character and personality and extracurricular participation are important. Particular talent or ability and alumni/ae relationship are considered.

**Requirements:** Graduation from secondary school is required; GED is accepted. 18 units and the following program of study are required: 4 units of English, 3 units of math, 2 units of science, 2 units of foreign language, 2 units of social studies, 3 units of electives. Portfolio required of art program applicants. Audition required of music program applicants. SAT is required; ACT may be substituted. ACH recommended. Campus visit and interview recommended. Off-campus interviews available with admissions and alumni representatives.

**Procedure:** Take SAT or ACT by January of 12th year. Take ACH by January of 12th year. Visit college for interview by March 1 of 12th year. Suggest filing application by January 1. Application deadline is March 1. Notification of admission by April 1. Reply is required by May 1. $500 tuition deposit, refundable until May 1. $250 room deposit, refundable until May 1. Freshmen accepted for terms other than fall.

**Special programs:** Admission may be deferred one year. Credit and/or placement may be granted through CEEB Advanced Placement exams for scores of 3 or higher. Credit and/or placement may be granted through CLEP general and subject exams. Early decision program. In fall 1993, 98 applied for early decision and 65 were accepted. Deadline for applying for early decision is November 15. Early entrance/early admission program.

**Transfer students:** Transfer students accepted for terms other than fall. In fall 1993, 16% of all new students were transfers into all classes. 264 transfer applications were received, 125 were accepted. Application deadline is August 1 for fall; December 1 for spring. Minimum 2.2 GPA required. Lowest course grade accepted is "C-." Maximum number of transferable credits is 18 courses. At least 18 courses must be completed at the college to receive degree.

**Admissions contact:** Michael C. Maxey, M.A., Vice President of Admissions Services. 703 375-2270.

**FINANCIAL AID. Available aid:** Pell grants, SEOG, state grants, school scholarships and grants, private scholarships and grants, and academic merit scholarships. Perkins Loans (NDSL), PLUS, Stafford Loans (GSL), school loans, and SLS. AMS. Manufacturers Hanover educational finance programs.

**Financial aid statistics:** In 1993-94, 100% of all undergraduate applicants received aid; 100% of freshman applicants. Average amounts of aid awarded freshmen: Scholarships and grants, $5,904; loans, $3,500.

**Supporting data/closing dates:** FAFSA: Priority filing date is March 1. Notification of awards on rolling basis.

**Financial aid contact:** Tommy Blair, Director of Financial Aid. 703 375-2235.

**STUDENT EMPLOYMENT.** College Work/Study Program. Institutional employment. 36% of full-time undergraduates work on campus during school year. Students may expect to earn an average of $1,500 during school year. Off-campus part-time employment opportunities rated "excellent."

**COMPUTER FACILITIES.** 85 IBM/IBM-compatible, Macintosh/Apple, and RISC-/UNIX-based microcomputers; 71 are networked. Students may access Digital minicomputer/mainframe systems, BITNET, Internet. Client/LAN operating systems include Apple/Macintosh, DOS, UNIX/XENIX/AIX, Windows NT, DEC, LocalTalk/AppleTalk. Computer languages and software packages include Ada, BASIC, C/C++, COBOL, Corel Draw, FORTRAN, LISP, Lotus 1-2-3, Mathmatica, MINITAB, PageMaker, Pascal, Paradox, Q&A, Quattro, SAS, SPSS, SimScript, Turbo Pascal, WordPerfect. Computer facilities are available to all students.

**Fees:** None.

**Hours:** 7 AM-2 AM.

**GRADUATE CAREER DATA.** Highest graduate school enrollments: Radford U, U of Virginia, Virginia Commonwealth U, Virginia Polytech Inst.

**PROMINENT ALUMNI/AE.** Henry Fowler, former Secretary of U.S. Treasury; Rick Boucher, congressman.

# Saint Paul's College

**Lawrenceville, VA 23868** **804 848-3111**

**1993-94 Costs.** Tuition: $5,006. Room & board: $3,650. Fees, books, misc. academic expenses (school's estimate): $1,715.

**Enrollment.** Undergraduates: 272 men, 384 women (full-time). Freshman class: 637 applicants, 465 accepted, 237 enrolled.

**Test score averages/ranges.** Average SAT scores: 303 verbal, 327 math.

**Faculty.** 37 full-time; 12 part-time. 37% of faculty holds doctoral degree. Student/faculty ratio: 13 to 1.

**Selectivity rating.** Less competitive.

**PROFILE.** Saint Paul's, founded in 1888, is a private, church-affiliated, multipurpose, historically black college. Its 75-acre campus is located in Lawrenceville, 60 miles south of Richmond.

**Accreditation:** SACS.

**Religious orientation:** Saint Paul's College is affiliated with the Episcopal Church; three semesters of religion/theology required.

**Library:** Collections totaling over 70,000 volumes, 225 periodical subscriptions, and 30,093 microform items.

**Special facilities/museums:** Language lab.

**Athletic facilities:** Gymnasium.

**STUDENT BODY. Undergraduate profile:** 73% are state residents; 8% are transfers. 95% Black, 4% White, 1% Other. Average age of undergraduates is 20.

**Undergraduate achievement:** 49% of fall 1991 freshmen returned for fall 1992 term. 16% of entering class graduated. 15% of students who completed a degree program immediately went on to graduate study.

**Foreign students:** Six students are from out of the country. Countries represented include Ghana, Liberia, Nigeria, and the West Indies.

**PROGRAMS OF STUDY. Degrees:** B.A., B.S., B.S.Ed.

**Majors:** Accounting, Biology, Business Administration, Business Education, Early Childhood Education, Elementary Education, English, General Office Procedures, General Science, General Studies, Management, Marketing, Mathematics, Political Science, Social Sciences, Sociology, Stenography.

**Distribution of degrees:** The majors with the highest enrollment are sociology, business administration, and political science; English, social sciences, and elementary education have the lowest.

**Requirements:** General education requirement.

**Academic regulations:** Minimum 2.0 GPA must be maintained.

**Special:** Minors offered in some majors and in chemistry, economics, and history. Independent study. Internships. Cooperative education programs. Preprofessional programs in theology. Washington Semester. Teacher certification in early childhood, elementary, and secondary education. Certification in specific subject areas. ROTC.

**Honors:** Honors program. Honor societies.

**Academic Assistance:** Remedial reading, writing, math, and study skills.

**ADMISSIONS. Academic basis for candidate selection** (in order of priority): Secondary school record, standardized test scores, class rank, school's recommendation, essay.

**Nonacademic basis for candidate selection:** Character and personality and extracurricular participation are emphasized. Alumni/ae relationship is important. Particular talent or ability is considered.

**Requirements:** Graduation from secondary school is required; GED is accepted. 16 units and the following program of study are required: 4 units of English, 2 units of math, 2 units of science, 2 units of social studies, 6 units of electives. Conditional admission possible for applicants not meeting standard requirements. SAT is required. Campus visit and interview recommended. Off-campus interviews available with an admissions representative.

**Procedure:** Notification of admission on rolling basis. Reply is required within 15 days of notification of admission. $2,723 nonrefundable tuition deposit. $50 refundable room deposit. Freshmen accepted for terms other than fall.

**Special programs:** Credit and/or placement may be granted through CEEB Advanced Placement exams for scores of 3 or higher. Credit and/or placement may be granted through CLEP general and subject exams. Credit may be granted through military experience. Placement may be granted through challenge exams. Concurrent enrollment program.

**Transfer students:** Transfer students accepted for terms other than fall. In fall 1992, 8% of all new students were transfers into all classes. 36 transfer applications were received, 36 were accepted. Application deadline is rolling for fall; rolling for spring. Lowest course grade accepted is "C." At least 30 semester hours must be completed at the college to receive degree.

**Admissions contact:** Larnell R. Parker, Vice-President for Enrollment and Records. 804 848-3984.

**FINANCIAL AID. Available aid:** Pell grants, SEOG, state grants, private scholarships and grants, ROTC scholarships, and athletic scholarships. Athletic and special ability scholarships. Virginia Tuition Assistance Grant Program. Some gift aid awarded on no-need basis. Perkins Loans (NDSL), PLUS, Stafford Loans (GSL), and SLS. Deferred payment plan and family tuition reduction.

**Financial aid statistics:** In 1992-93, 90% of all undergraduate applicants received aid; 85% of freshman applicants. Average amounts of aid awarded freshmen: Scholarships and grants, $2,000; loans, $2,000.

**Supporting data/closing dates:** FAFSA/FAF/FFS: Priority filing date is March 15. State aid form: Priority filing date is June 1; deadline is July 31. Income tax forms: Priority filing date is April 15. Notification of awards begins April 15.

## Shenandoah University

Winchester, VA 22601 703 665-4500

**1994-95 Costs.** Tuition: $10,700. Room & board: $4,300. Fees, books, misc. academic expenses (school's estimate): $550.
**Enrollment.** Undergraduates: 345 men, 524 women (full-time). Freshman class: 820 applicants, 616 accepted, 212 enrolled. Graduate enrollment: 169 men, 253 women.
**Test score averages/ranges.** Average SAT scores: 438 verbal, 477 math. Average ACT scores: 20 composite.
**Faculty.** 82 full-time; 102 part-time. 54% of faculty holds doctoral degree. Student/faculty ratio: 10 to 1.
**Selectivity rating.** Less competitive.

**PROFILE.** Shenandoah is a private, church-affiliated, comprehensive university. It was founded in 1875, adopted coeducation in 1930, and gained university status in 1991. Programs are offered in the Divisions of Allied Health, Arts and Sciences, Management, and Music. Its 70-acre campus is located in Winchester, 70 miles from Washington, D.C.

**Accreditation:** SACS. Professionally accredited by the National Association of Schools of Music, the National League for Nursing.
**Religious orientation:** Shenandoah University is affiliated with the United Methodist Church; one semester of religion required.
**Library:** Collections totaling over 104,024 volumes, 644 periodical subscriptions, and 47,871 microform items.
**Athletic facilities:** Gymnasium, soccer field.

**STUDENT BODY. Undergraduate profile:** 70% are state residents; 42% are transfers. 1% Asian-American, 5% Black, 1% Hispanic, 88% White, 5% International. Average age of undergraduates is 24.
**Freshman profile:** 2% of freshmen who took SAT scored 700 or over on math; 5% scored 600 or over on verbal, 16% scored 600 or over on math; 28% scored 500 or over on verbal, 43% scored 500 or over on math; 64% scored 400 or over on verbal, 76% scored 400 or over on math; 95% scored 300 or over on verbal, 99% scored 300 or over on math. 97% of accepted applicants took SAT; 3% took ACT.
**Undergraduate achievement:** 63% of fall 1992 freshmen returned for fall 1993 term. 26% of entering class graduated.
**Foreign students:** 57 students are from out of the country. Countries represented include Brazil, China, Japan, Korea, Russia, and Taiwan; 27 in all.

**PROGRAMS OF STUDY. Degrees:** B.A., B.Bus.Admin., B.F.A., B.Mus., B.Mus.Ther., B.S.
**Majors:** Accounting, American Studies, Art Studies, Arts Management, Biology, Chemistry, Church Music, Commercial Music, Composition, Computer Information Systems, Dance, Dance Education, English, Environmental Studies, Health Science, History, International Business, Jazz Studies, Management, Marketing, Mass Communications, Mathematics, Music Education, Music Theatre, Music Therapy, Nursing, Pedagogy, Performance, Physical Education, Piano Accompanying, Psychology, Religion, Respiratory Care, Theatre.
**Distribution of degrees:** The majors with the highest enrollment are psychology and music theatre; religion, church music, and music composition have the lowest.
**Requirements:** General education requirement.
**Academic regulations:** Freshmen must maintain minimum 1.75 GPA; sophomores, juniors, seniors, 2.0 GPA.
**Special:** Minors offered in several majors and in acting, business administration, costume design, French, political science, scenic/lighting design, and technical theatre. Certificate programs offered in business studies, church leadership, church music, elementary education, piano pedagogy, piano technology, and secondary education. Associate's degrees offered. Double majors. Dual degrees. Independent study. Internships. Cooperative education programs. Graduate school at which undergraduates may take graduate-level courses. Preprofessional programs in law. 2-3 physical therapy program and occupational therapy program. Member of Appalachian College Assessment Consortium. Teacher certification in elementary and secondary education. Certification in specific subject areas. Exchange programs abroad in Brazil (U Metodista De Sao Paulo, U Metodista De Piracicaba), China (Jiangxi Inst of Finance and Economics, Tianjin Normal U, Tianjin U of Finance and Economics), and Japan (Hirosaki Gakuin Coll).
**Honors:** Honors program. Honor societies.
**Academic Assistance:** Remedial math. Nonremedial tutoring.

**ADMISSIONS. Academic basis for candidate selection** (in order of priority): Secondary school record, standardized test scores, school's recommendation, class rank.
**Nonacademic basis for candidate selection:** Particular talent or ability is emphasized. Character and personality and extracurricular participation are important. Alumni/ae relationship is considered.
**Requirements:** Graduation from secondary school is required; GED is accepted. 15 units and the following program of study are recommended: 4 units of English, 3 units of math, 2 units of science including 1 unit of lab, 2 units of foreign language, 2 units of social studies, 2 units of electives. Minimum 2.5 GPA required. Audition required of music program applicants. Conditional admission possible for applicants not meeting standard requirements. SAT or ACT is required. Campus visit and interview recommended. Off-campus interviews available with an admissions representative.
**Procedure:** Take SAT or ACT by January of 12th year. Visit college for interview by March of 12th year. Suggest filing application by February 15; no deadline. Notification of admission on rolling basis. Reply is required within one month of acceptance. $200 nonrefundable tuition deposit. $100 nonrefundable room deposit. Freshmen accepted for terms other than fall.
**Special programs:** Admission may be deferred one year. Credit and/or placement may be granted through CEEB Advanced Placement exams for scores of 3 or higher. Credit may be granted through CLEP subject exams and challenge exams. Early entrance/early admission program. Concurrent enrollment program.
**Transfer students:** Transfer students accepted for terms other than fall. In fall 1993, 42% of all new students were transfers into all classes. 420 transfer applications were received, 402 were accepted. Minimum 2.0 GPA required. Lowest course grade accepted is "C." At least 30 semester hours must be completed at the university to receive degree.
**Admissions contact:** Patricia Coyle, M.S., M.B.A., Director of Admissions. 703 665-4581.

**FINANCIAL AID. Available aid:** Pell grants, SEOG, state scholarships and grants, school scholarships and grants, private scholarships and grants, and academic merit scholarships. Perkins Loans (NDSL), PLUS, Stafford Loans (GSL), NSL, state loans, school loans, and SLS. Deferred payment plan.
**Financial aid statistics:** 28% of aid is not need-based. In 1993-94, 100% of all undergraduate applicants received aid. Average amounts of aid awarded freshmen: Scholarships and grants, $4,000; loans, $2,625.
**Supporting data/closing dates:** FAFSA/FFS: Priority filing date is February 1; accepted on rolling basis. State aid form: Deadline is July 31. Income tax forms: Accepted on rolling basis. Shenandoah Application for Student Aid: Priority filing date is February 15; accepted on rolling basis. Notification of awards begins March 15.
**Financial aid contact:** Linda Thomas, Director of Financial Aid. 703 665-4538.

## Sweet Briar College

Sweet Briar, VA 24595 804 381-6100

**1993-94 Costs.** Tuition: $13,890. Room: $2,165. Board: $3,590. Fees, books, misc. academic expenses (school's estimate): $1,442.
**Enrollment.** Undergraduates: 2 men, 525 women (full-time). Freshman class: 462 applicants, 402 accepted, 136 enrolled.
**Test score averages/ranges.** Average SAT scores: 500 verbal, 510 math. Range of SAT scores of middle 50%: 450-550 verbal, 450-570 math. Average ACT scores: 24 composite. Range of ACT scores of middle 50%: 21-27 composite.
**Faculty.** 68 full-time; 38 part-time. 94% of faculty holds highest degree in specific field. Student/faculty ratio: 8 to 1.
**Selectivity rating.** Competitive.

**PROFILE.** Sweet Briar, founded in 1901, is a private, liberal arts college for women. The campus has retained a Georgian architectural style of the original campus buildings, designed by Ralph Adams Cram. Its 3,300-acre campus is located in Sweet Briar, 12 miles from Lynchburg.

**Accreditation:** SACS.
**Religious orientation:** Sweet Briar College is nonsectarian; no religious requirements.
**Library:** Collections totaling over 217,032 volumes, 1,127 periodical subscriptions, and 289,156 microform items.
**Special facilities/museums:** Art museum, college and local history museums, kindergarten/nursery school, riding center, electron microscope.
**Athletic facilities:** Gymnasium, swimming pool, tennis courts, athletic fields, dance studios, Nautilus and weight rooms, riding center, lake, fitness course, mountain bike and running trails.

**STUDENT BODY. Undergraduate profile:** 31% are state residents; 4% are transfers. 2% Asian-American, 4% Black, 2% Hispanic, 87% White, 5% Other. Average age of undergraduates is 19.
**Freshman profile:** 1% of freshmen who took SAT scored 700 or over on verbal, 1% scored 700 or over on math; 15% scored 600 or over on verbal, 11% scored 600 or over on math; 44% scored 500 or over on verbal, 51% scored 500 or over on math; 81% scored 400 or over on verbal, 83% scored 400 or over on math; 99% scored 300 or over on verbal, 100% scored 300 or over on math. Majority of accepted applicants took SAT. 69% of freshmen come from public schools.
**Undergraduate achievement:** 81% of fall 1992 freshmen returned for fall 1993 term. 65% of entering class graduated.
**Foreign students:** 31 students are from out of the country. Countries represented include Brazil, Canada, China, the Czech Republic/Slovakia, Japan, and Russia; 13 in all.

**PROGRAMS OF STUDY. Degrees:** B.A., B.S.
**Majors:** American History/Literature, Anthropology, Art History, Biochemistry, Biology, British Studies, Chemistry, Classical Civilization, Dance, Economics, Economics/Computer Science, English, English/Creative Writing, Environmental Studies, French, French Studies, German, German Studies, Government, Greek, Hispanic Studies, History, International Affairs, Italian Studies, Latin, Mathematical Physics, Mathematics, Mathematics/Computer Science, Mathematics/Economics, Modern Languages, Molecular Biology, Music, Philosophy, Physics, Political Economy, Pre-Engineering Studies, Psychology, Religion, Sociology, Spanish, Studio Art, Theatre Arts.
**Distribution of degrees:** The majors with the highest enrollment are psychology, English, and economics.
**Requirements:** General education requirement.
**Academic regulations:** Minimum 2.0 GPA must be maintained.
**Special:** Minors offered in most majors and in applied music and music history. Programs in arts management, Asian studies, business, European civilization, and public administration. Courses in computer math, education, film, journalism, management, and photography. Self-designed majors. Double majors. Independent study. Pass/fail grading option. Internships. Graduate school at which undergraduates may take graduate-level courses. Preprofessional programs in law, medicine, and engineering. 3-2 business programs with Georgia Tech and U of Virginia. 3-2 engineering programs with Columbia U, Georgia Tech, and Washington U. 3-2 occupational therapy program with Washington U. Member of Tri-College Consortium. Washington Semester. Environmental junior year semester-away programs. Member of Seven College Exchange Program. Teacher certification in early childhood, elementary, and secondary education. Exchange programs abroad in England (Royal Holloway Coll and New Bedford Coll at U of London) and Scotland (St. Andrew's U). Study abroad also in France, Germany, Italy, and Spain. ROTC at Lynchburg Coll.
**Honors:** Phi Beta Kappa. Honors program.

**Academic Assistance:** Remedial reading, writing, and math. Nonremedial tutoring.

**ADMISSIONS. Academic basis for candidate selection** (in order of priority): Secondary school record, school's recommendation, essay, class rank, standardized test scores.
**Nonacademic basis for candidate selection:** Character and personality are emphasized. Extracurricular participation is important. Particular talent or ability and alumni/ae relationship are considered.
**Requirements:** Graduation from secondary school is required; GED is accepted. 16 units and the following program of study are required: 4 units of English, 3 units of math, 2 units of science, 2 units of foreign language, 3 units of social studies, 1 unit of history, 1 unit of academic electives. Audition required of music program applicants. SAT or ACT is required. ACH recommended. Campus visit and interview recommended. Off-campus interviews available with admissions and alumni representatives.
**Procedure:** Take SAT or ACT by fall of 12th year. Take ACH by fall of 12th year. Visit college for interview by March 1 of 12th year. Application deadline is February 15. Notification of admission by April 1. Reply is required by May 1. $500 nonrefundable room deposit. Freshmen accepted for terms other than fall.
**Special programs:** Admission may be deferred one year. Credit and/or placement may be granted through CEEB Advanced Placement exams for scores of 4 or higher. Credit and placement may be granted through challenge exams. Early decision program. In fall 1993, 60 applied for early decision and 60 were accepted. Deadline for applying for early decision is November 15. Early entrance/early admission program.
**Transfer students:** Transfer students accepted for terms other than fall. In fall 1993, 4% of all new students were transfers into all classes. 24 transfer applications were received, 17 were accepted. Application deadline is August 1 for fall; January 1 for spring. Minimum 2.5 GPA recommended. Lowest course grade accepted is "C-." Maximum number of transferable credits is 60 semester hours. At least 60 semester hours must be completed at the college to receive degree.
**Admissions contact:** Nancy E. Church, Executive Director of Admissions and Financial Aid. 804 381-6142.

**FINANCIAL AID. Available aid:** Pell grants, SEOG, state scholarships and grants, school scholarships, and private scholarships and grants. Perkins Loans (NDSL), PLUS, Stafford Loans (GSL), state loans, school loans, and SLS. Knight Tuition Plans and AMS.
**Financial aid statistics:** 49% of aid is not need-based. In 1993-94, 94% of all undergraduate applicants received aid; 85% of freshman applicants. Average amounts of aid awarded freshmen: Scholarships and grants, $8,489; loans, $3,066.
**Supporting data/closing dates:** FAFSA: Priority filing date is March 1. Income tax forms: Priority filing date is March 1. Notification of awards begins February 15.
**Financial aid contact:** Robert A. Steckel, Director of Financial Aid. 804 381-6156.

# University of Richmond

**Richmond, VA 23173 — 804 289-8000**

**1994-95 Costs.** Tuition: $14,500. Room: $1,405. Board: $1,880. Fees, books, misc. academic expenses (school's estimate): $650.

**Enrollment.** Undergraduates: 1,449 men, 1,427 women (full-time). Freshman class: 5,892 applicants, 2,713 accepted, 759 enrolled. Graduate enrollment: 445 men, 417 women.

**Test score averages/ranges.** Range of SAT scores of middle 50%: 520-620 verbal, 590-690 math. Range of ACT scores of middle 50%: 26-30 composite.

**Faculty.** 265 full-time; 124 part-time. 92% of faculty holds doctoral degree. Student/faculty ratio: 12 to 1.

**Selectivity rating.** Highly competitive.

**PROFILE.** The University of Richmond, founded in 1830, is a church-affiliated, comprehensive institution. Programs are offered through the Richmond College, the Westhampton College, the E. Claiborne Robins School of Business, and the Jepson School of Leadership Studies. Its 350-acre campus is located six miles from downtown Richmond.

**Accreditation:** SACS. Professionally accredited by the American Assembly of Collegiate Schools of Business, the American Bar Association, the National Association of Schools of Music.
**Religious orientation:** University of Richmond is affiliated with the Baptist General Association of Virginia; no religious requirements.
**Library:** Collections totaling over 615,975 volumes, 7,341 periodical subscriptions, and 49,041 microform items.
**Special facilities/museums:** Art gallery, mineral museum, Virginia Baptist archives, language lab.
**Athletic facilities:** Gymnasiums, swimming pools, stadium, exercise and weight rooms; basketball, racquetball, squash, tennis courts; track; athletic, intramural fields.

**STUDENT BODY. Undergraduate profile:** 20% are state residents; 3% are transfers. 3% Asian-American, 3% Black, 1% Hispanic, 92% White, 1% Other. Average age of undergraduates is 20.
**Freshman profile:** 4% of freshmen who took SAT scored 700 or over on verbal, 20% scored 700 or over on math; 36% scored 600 or over on verbal, 73% scored 600 or over on math; 86% scored 500 or over on verbal, 97% scored 500 or over on math; 99% scored 400 or over on verbal, 100% scored 400 or over on math. 23% of freshmen who took ACT scored 30 or over on composite; 83% scored 24 or over on composite; 98% scored 18 or over on composite; 100% scored 12 or over on composite. 90% of accepted applicants took SAT; 22% took ACT. 72% of freshmen come from public schools.
**Undergraduate achievement:** 92% of fall 1992 freshmen returned for fall 1993 term. 79% of entering class graduated. 23% of students who completed a degree program immediately went on to graduate study.
**Foreign students:** 28 students are from out of the country. Countries represented include Brazil, Bulgaria, France, India, Japan, and the United Kingdom; 27 in all.

**PROGRAMS OF STUDY. Degrees:** B.A., B.Mus., B.S., B.S.Bus.Admin.
**Majors:** Accounting, American Studies, Art History, Biology, Business Administration, Business Economics, Chemistry, Classical Civilization, Classical Studies, Computer Science, Criminal Justice, Early Childhood Education, Economics, Elementary Education, English, Finance, French, German, Greek, Health, Health Education, History, Interdisciplinary Studies, International Business, International Studies, Journalism, Latin, Leadership Studies, Management Systems, Marketing, Mathematics, Middle Education, Music, Music Education, Music History, Music Performance, Music Theory, Philosophy, Physics, Political Science, Psychology, Religion, Secondary Education, Sociology, Spanish, Speech Communication, Sport Science, Sport Science Education, Studio Art, Theatre Arts, Urban Studies, Women's Studies.
**Distribution of degrees:** The majors with the highest enrollment are business, political science, and history; Greek, Latin, and middle education have the lowest.
**Requirements:** General education requirement.
**Academic regulations:** Freshmen must maintain minimum 1.5 GPA; sophomores, 1.7 GPA; juniors, 1.85 GPA; seniors, 2.0 GPA.
**Special:** Minors offered in many majors and in anthropology and sports management. Several concentrations available in international studies. Associate's degrees offered. Self-designed majors. Double majors. Dual degrees. Independent study. Accelerated study. Pass/fail grading option. Internships. Graduate school at which undergraduates may take graduate-level courses. Preprofessional programs in law, medicine, veterinary science, pharmacy, dentistry, optometry, and health. 3-2 forestry and environmental studies program with Duke U. Member of Southern Consortium. Washington Semester and Sea Semester. Teacher certification in early childhood, elementary, and secondary education. Certification in specific subject areas. Exchange programs abroad in England (U of Bath; U of Lancaster; Queen Mary, Westfield) and Japan (Saga U). Study abroad also in Austria, Costa Rica, France, Germany, Greece, Japan, Russia, Spain, Venezuela, and Zimbabwe. ROTC.
**Honors:** Phi Beta Kappa. Honors program. Honor societies.
**Academic Assistance:** Nonremedial tutoring.

**STUDENT LIFE. Housing:** Students may live on or off campus. Women's and men's dorms. School-owned/operated apartments. 92% of students live in college housing.
**Social atmosphere:** As reported by the student newspaper, the most influential group on campus is the Greeks. Popular campus events are Greekfest, Derby Days, Homecoming Weekend, the Snowball, and fraternity/sorority formals. Students like to gather at the Pier, Old and New Fraternity Rows, Barry's, Sharkey's, Darryl's, Potter's Pub, Penny Lane Pub, and the Stonewall Cafe.
**Services and counseling/handicapped student services:** Placement services. Health service. Women's center. Counseling services for minority and military students. Birth control, personal, and psychological counseling. Career and academic guidance services. Religious counseling. Learning disabled services.
**Campus organizations:** Undergraduate student government. Student newspaper (Collegian, published once/week). Literary magazine. Yearbook. Radio station. Choir, orchestra, pep band, University Players, debating, Amnesty International, BACCHUS, Circle K, Habitat for Humanity, College Republicans, Young Democrats, Word of Worth, Volunteer Action Council, Student Education Association, 175 organizations in all. 10 fraternities, no chapter houses; eight sororities, no chapter houses. 50% of men join a fraternity. 62% of women join a sorority.
**Religious organizations:** Baptist Student Union, Catholic Student Association, Campus Crusade for Christ, Episcopal Students' Fellowship, Fellowship of Christian Athletes, Lutheran Students Association, Greek Orthodox Students, Intervarsity Christian Fellowship, Jewish Student Association, Presbyterian Fellowship, United Methodist Student Fellowship, University Interfaith Council, Muslim League, Solon B. Cousins Society, Unitarian Universalist Student Community.
**Minority/foreign student organizations:** Multicultural Student Union, Race and Gender Issues Support Group, Asian Student Association, Community Through Diversity. International Club, Japanese Society.

**ATHLETICS. Physical education requirements:** Three semesters of physical education required.
**Intercollegiate competition:** 15% of students participate. Baseball (M), basketball (M,W), cheerleading (M,W), cross-country (M,W), diving (M,W), field hockey (W), football (M), golf (M), lacrosse (W), others (W), soccer (M), swimming (M,W), tennis (M,W), track and field (indoor) (M,W), track and field (outdoor) (M,W), water polo (M). Member of Colonial Athletic Association, ECAC, NCAA Division I, NCAA Division I-AA for football, Southern Water Polo League, Yankee Conference for football.
**Intramural and club sports:** 80% of students participate. Intramural aerobics, basketball, floor hockey, field hockey, fun runs, inner-tube water polo, racquetball, softball, squash, swimming, ultimate frisbee, volleyball, walleyball, water polo, wrestling. Men's club crew, fencing, lacrosse, martial arts, rugby. Women's club crew, fencing, lacrosse, martial arts, soccer, volleyball.

**ADMISSIONS. Academic basis for candidate selection** (in order of priority): Secondary school record, class rank, standardized test scores, school's recommendation, essay.
**Nonacademic basis for candidate selection:** Particular talent or ability is emphasized. Extracurricular participation is important. Geographical distribution and alumni/ae relationship are considered.
**Requirements:** Graduation from secondary school is required; GED is accepted. 16 units and the following program of study are required: 4 units of English, 3 units of math, 1 unit of lab science, 2 units of foreign language, 3 units of social studies, 1 unit of history. Audition and theory placement tests required of music program applicants. SAT is required; ACT may be substituted. ACH required. Campus visit recommended. No off-campus interviews.
**Procedure:** Take SAT or ACT by January of 12th year. Take ACH by January of 12th year. Application deadline is February 1. Notification of admission by April 1. Reply is required by May 1. $300 nonrefundable tuition deposit. $300 nonrefundable room deposit. Freshmen accepted for fall terms only.
**Special programs:** Admission may be deferred one year. Credit and/or placement may be granted through CEEB Advanced Placement exams for scores of 3 or higher. Credit and/or placement may be granted through CLEP subject exams. Credit and placement may be granted through challenge exams and military experience. Early decision program. In fall 1993, 184 applied for early decision and 90 were accepted. Deadline for applying for early

decision is November 1. Early entrance/early admission program. Concurrent enrollment program.
**Transfer students:** Transfer students accepted for terms other than fall. In fall 1993, 3% of all new students were transfers into all classes. 171 transfer applications were received, 40 were accepted. Application deadline is February 1 for fall; November 1 for spring. Minimum 2.0 GPA required. Lowest course grade accepted is "C." At least 60 semester hours must be completed at the university to receive degree.
**Admissions contact:** Pamela W. Spence, Dean of Admissions. 804 289-8640.

**FINANCIAL AID. Available aid:** Pell grants, SEOG, state scholarships and grants, school scholarships and grants, private scholarships and grants, ROTC scholarships, academic merit scholarships, athletic scholarships, and aid for undergraduate foreign students. Perkins Loans (NDSL), PLUS, Stafford Loans (GSL), private loans, and SLS. Tuition Plan Inc. and Knight Tuition Plans.
**Financial aid statistics:** 63% of aid is not need-based. In 1993-94, 24% of all undergraduate applicants received aid; 30% of freshman applicants. Average amounts of aid awarded freshmen: Scholarships and grants, $5,933; loans, $4,272.
**Supporting data/closing dates:** FAFSA: Priority filing date is February 15; deadline is February 25. School's own aid application: Priority filing date is February 15; accepted on rolling basis. Notification of awards begins April 1.
**Financial aid contact:** James Nolan, M.Ed., Director of Financial Aid. 804 289-8438.

**STUDENT EMPLOYMENT.** College Work/Study Program. Institutional employment. 25% of full-time undergraduates work on campus during school year. Students may expect to earn an average of $850 during school year. Off-campus part-time employment opportunities rated "good."

**COMPUTER FACILITIES.** 500 IBM/IBM-compatible, Macintosh/Apple, and RISC-/UNIX-based microcomputers. Students may access AT&T, Digital, IBM, SUN, UNISYS minicomputer/mainframe systems, BITNET, Internet. Residence halls may be equipped with stand-alone microcomputers. Client/LAN operating systems include Apple/Macintosh, DOS, UNIX/XENIX/AIX. Computer languages and software packages include BASIC, COBOL, Pascal, WordPerfect. Computer facilities are available to all students.
**Fees:** None.
**Hours:** 8 AM-1 AM; later during exams.

**GRADUATE CAREER DATA.** Graduate school percentages: 6% enter law school. 2% enter graduate business programs. 5% enter medical/dental school. 12% enter graduate arts and sciences programs. Highest graduate school enrollments: Coll of William and Mary, Columbia U, Duke U, Emory U, Johns Hopkins U, U of North Carolina, U of Richmond, U of Virginia, Virginia Commonwealth U (Medical Coll of Virginia). Companies and businesses that hire graduates: Coopers & Lybrand, Ernst & Young, KPMG Peat Marwick, Macy's, PepsiCo, Sovran Bank.

**PROMINENT ALUMNI/AE.** Mary Sue Terry, attorney general, Virginia; Dr. Carroll Williams, chairperson, biology department, Harvard U; E. Earl Hamner, Jr., writer/producer, *The Waltons*, Burbank Studios; E. Claiborne Robins, Sr., chairperson, A.H. Robins Co.; Dr. Douglas Lee, president, Stetson U; John Newman, New York Nets; Barry Redden, San Diego Chargers; Lonnie Shorr, comedian; Grant Shaud, actor, *Murphy Brown*.

# University of Virginia

**Charlottesville, VA 22906** **804 924-0311**

**1994-95 Costs.** Tuition: $3,724 (state residents), $12,212 (out-of-state). Room: $1,816. Board: $1,976. Fees, books, misc. academic expenses (school's estimate): $600.
**Enrollment.** Undergraduates: 5,417 men, 5,861 women (full-time). Freshman class: 15,849 applicants, 5,384 accepted, 2,678 enrolled. Graduate enrollment: 3,475 men, 2,841 women.
**Test score averages/ranges.** Average SAT scores: 572 verbal, 643 math. Range of SAT scores of middle 50%: 520-630 verbal, 590-710 math.
**Faculty.** 940 full-time; 148 part-time. 90% of faculty holds highest degree in specific field. Student/faculty ratio: 11 to 1.
**Selectivity rating.** Most competitive.

**PROFILE.** U Virginia, founded in 1819 by Thomas Jefferson, is a public university. Programs are offered through the College of Arts and Sciences and the Schools of Architecture, Commerce, Education, Engineering and Applied Science, and Nursing. Its 1,050-acre campus is located in Charlottesville, 70 miles northwest of Richmond. The original campus, designed by Jefferson, is considered a masterpiece of American architecture.

**Accreditation:** SACS. Professionally accredited by the Accreditation Board for Engineering and Technology, the American Assembly of Collegiate Schools of Business, the American Bar Association, the American Society of Landscape Architects, the American Speech-Language-Hearing Association, the Association of American Law Schools, the Liaison Committee on Medical Education, the National Association of Schools of Music, the National Council for Accreditation of Teacher Education, the National League for Nursing.
**Religious orientation:** University of Virginia is nonsectarian; no religious requirements.
**Library:** Collections totaling over 3,948,504 volumes, 44,349 periodical subscriptions, and 4,105,665 microform items.
**Special facilities/museums:** Art museum, center for studies in political economy, bureau of public administration, experimental farm, biological station, labs, observatory/planetarium, communications satellite for Russian TV reception, nuclear information center, nuclear reactor.
**Athletic facilities:** Gymnasiums, field house, stadium, basketball, handball, racquetball, tennis, and volleyball courts, arena, swimming pools, weight rooms, saunas, athletic fields, track.

**STUDENT BODY. Undergraduate profile:** 67% are state residents; 15% are transfers. 9% Asian-American, 12% Black, 1% Hispanic, 76% White, 2% Other. Average age of undergraduates is 19.
**Freshman profile:** 6% of freshmen who took SAT scored 700 or over on verbal, 29% scored 700 or over on math; 41% scored 600 or over on verbal, 73% scored 600 or over on math; 83% scored 500 or over on verbal, 94% scored 500 or over on math; 97% scored 400 or over on verbal, 99% scored 400 or over on math; 100% scored 300 or over on verbal, 100% scored 300 or over on math. 100% of accepted applicants took SAT. 79% of freshmen come from public schools.
**Undergraduate achievement:** 96% of fall 1992 freshmen returned for fall 1993 term. 80% of entering class graduated. 60% of students who completed a degree program went on to graduate study within 10 years.
**Foreign students:** 46 students are from out of the country. Countries represented include Canada, Malaysia, Pakistan, South Korea, and the United Kingdom; 28 in all.

**PROGRAMS OF STUDY. Degrees:** B.A., B.Arch.Hist., B.City Plan., B.S., B.S.Commerce, B.S.Ed., B.S.Eng., B.S.Nurs.
**Majors:** Aerospace Engineering, Afro-American Studies, Anthropology, Applied Mathematics, Architectural History, Architecture, Area Studies, Art, Astronomy, Biology, Chemical Engineering, Chemistry, City Planning, Civil Engineering, Classics, Commerce, Comparative Literature, Computer Science, Drama, Economics, Electrical Engineering, Engineering Science, English Language/Literature, Environmental Science, Foreign Affairs, French Language/Literature, German Language/Literature, Government, Health/Physical Education, History, Interdisciplinary Major, Italian, Mathematics, Mechanical Engineering, Music, Nursing, Philosophy, Physics, Psychology, Religious Studies, Rhetoric/Communication Studies, Slavic Languages/Literatures, Sociology, Spanish, Speech Pathology/Audiology, Systems Engineering.
**Distribution of degrees:** The majors with the highest enrollment are English, psychology, and history; Italian, architectural history, and comparative literature have the lowest.
**Academic regulations:** Minimum 1.8 GPA must be maintained.
**Special:** Minors offered in most majors. Concentrations offered in accounting, American studies, cognitive studies, finance, human resources management, management, management information systems, marketing, and women's studies. Self-designed majors. Double majors. Dual degrees. Independent study. Accelerated study. Pass/fail grading option. Internships. Graduate school at which undergraduates may take graduate-level courses. Preprofessional programs in law and medicine. Five-year B.A./M.T. education program. B.S./M.S. engineering program. Teacher certification in early childhood, elementary, secondary, and special education. Certification in specific subject areas. Study abroad in England, Italy, and many other countries. ROTC, NROTC, and AFROTC.
**Honors:** Phi Beta Kappa. Honors program.
**Academic Assistance:** Nonremedial tutoring.

**STUDENT LIFE. Housing:** All first-year students must live on campus. Coed dorms. Sorority and fraternity housing. On-campus married-student housing. Language houses. 51% of students live in college housing.
**Social atmosphere:** "Many separate groups have their own social/cultural life (Greeks, blacks, etc.) both on and off the Grounds. Many find their niche here where there can be pressure to conform. But there is a great deal of activity independent of this." Students gather at "The Corner, an area near the Grounds with many restaurants and bars, including Macadoo's, the Garrett, the Hardware Store, and the Mineshaft. The Lawn (which houses the top fourth-year students) also is popular."
**Services and counseling/handicapped student services:** Placement services. Health service. Women's center. Day care. Counseling services for minority, military, veteran, and older students. Birth control, personal, and psychological counseling. Career and academic guidance services. Physically disabled student services. Learning disabled services. Notetaking services. Tape recorders. Tutors. Reader services for the blind.
**Campus organizations:** Undergraduate student government. Student newspapers (Cavalier Daily; University Journal, published once/day). Literary magazine. Yearbook. Radio and TV stations. Band, orchestra, men's glee club, University Singers, pep band, film series, Virginia Players, legal environmental group, political and professional groups, professional fraternities, debating society, honor committee, student guide service, community service activities, 200 organizations in all. 39 fraternities, 33 chapter houses; 22 sororities, 18 chapter houses. 28% of men join a fraternity. 30% of women join a sorority.
**Religious organizations:** Hillel, Catholic Student Association, Cavalier Christian Fellowship, The Religion Club, Fellowship of Christian Athletes, several other religious groups.
**Minority/foreign student organizations:** Black Student Alliance, Black Engineering Society, Langston Hughes Literary Society, Black Voices, Black Student Service fraternities. Chinese Student Association, Iranian Student Organization, Korean Student Society, The Slavic Society, Vietnamese Student Association.

**ATHLETICS. Physical education requirements:** None.
**Intercollegiate competition:** 10% of students participate. Baseball (M), basketball (M,W), cheerleading (M,W), cross-country (M,W), diving (M,W), field hockey (W), football (M), golf (M), lacrosse (M,W), soccer (M,W), softball (W), swimming (M,W), tennis (M,W), track (outdoor) (M,W), track and field (indoor) (M,W), track and field (outdoor) (M,W), volleyball (W), wrestling (M). Member of Atlantic Coast Conference, NCAA Division I.
**Intramural and club sports:** 80% of students participate. Intramural badminton, basketball, billiards, bowling, field hockey, floor hockey, frisbee, golf, horseshoes, inner-tube water polo, lacrosse, racquetball, road races, softball, squash, swimming and diving, table tennis, tennis, touch football, volleyball, walleyball, wrestling. Men's club bowling, crew, cycling, fencing, floor hockey, golf, handball, lacrosse, martial arts, polo, racquetball, riding, rifle, rugby, sailing, skiing, soccer, squash, tennis, ultimate frisbee, volleyball, water polo, weight lifting. Women's club crew, cycling, dance, fencing, martial arts, polo, riding, rifle, rugby, sailing, skiing, soccer, tennis, ultimate frisbee, volleyball.

**ADMISSIONS. Academic basis for candidate selection** (in order of priority): Secondary school record, class rank, standardized test scores, essay, school's recommendation.
**Nonacademic basis for candidate selection:** Geographical distribution is emphasized. Character and personality, extracurricular participation, and alumni/ae relationship are important. Particular talent or ability is considered.
**Requirements:** Graduation from secondary school is recommended; GED is accepted. 16 units and the following program of study are required: 4 units of English, 4 units of math, 2

units of lab science, 2 units of foreign language, 1 unit of social studies. More competitive requirements for out-of-state applicants. Chemistry and physics required of engineering program applicants. SAT is required. ACH required. Campus visit recommended. No off-campus interviews.

**Procedure:** Take SAT by January of 12th year. Suggest filing application by December 1. Application deadline is January 2. Acceptance notification by first week of April. Reply is required by May 1. $250 tuition deposit, refundable until May 1. Freshmen accepted for fall terms only.

**Special programs:** Credit and/or placement may be granted through CEEB Advanced Placement exams for scores of 4 or higher. Early decision program. In fall 1993, 1,394 applied for early decision and 565 were accepted. Deadline for applying for early decision is November 1.

**Transfer students:** Transfer students accepted for terms other than fall. In fall 1993, 15% of all new students were transfers into all classes. 2,458 transfer applications were received, 723 were accepted. Application deadline is March 1 for fall; November 1 for spring. Lowest course grade accepted is "C." Maximum number of transferable credits is 66 semester hours. At least 54 semester hours must be completed at the university to receive degree.

**Admissions contact:** John A. Blackburn, M.S.Ed., Dean of Admissions. 804 982-3200.

**FINANCIAL AID. Available aid:** Pell grants, SEOG, state scholarships and grants, school scholarships and grants, private scholarships and grants, ROTC scholarships, academic merit scholarships, and athletic scholarships. Perkins Loans (NDSL), PLUS, Stafford Loans (GSL), NSL, and SLS.

**Financial aid statistics:** 5% of aid is not need-based. In 1993-94, 72% of all undergraduate applicants received aid; 68% of freshman applicants. Average amounts of aid awarded freshmen: Scholarships and grants, $5,345; loans, $3,400.

**Supporting data/closing dates:** FAFSA/FAF: Priority filing date is March 1. Income tax forms: Accepted on rolling basis. Notification of awards begins April 1.

**Financial aid contact:** Wayne Sparks, M.B.A., M.Ed., Director of Financial Aid. 804 924-3725.

**STUDENT EMPLOYMENT.** College Work/Study Program. Institutional employment. 18% of full-time undergraduates work on campus during school year. Students may expect to earn an average of $1,400 during school year. Off-campus part-time employment opportunities rated "fair."

**COMPUTER FACILITIES.** 800 IBM/IBM-compatible, Macintosh/Apple, and RISC-/UNIX-based microcomputers; 700 are networked. Students may access AT&T, Cray, Digital, IBM, SUN minicomputer/mainframe systems, Internet. Residence halls may be equipped with stand-alone microcomputers, networked microcomputers. Client/LAN operating systems include Apple/Macintosh, DOS, UNIX/XENIX/AIX, LocalTalk/AppleTalk, Novell. Computer languages and software packages include BASIC, C, FORTRAN, LISP, Mathematica, Pascal, PC SAS, Quattro Pro, SPSS, SuperPaint, WordPerfect. Computer facilities are available to all students.

**Fees:** None.

**Hours:** 24 hours for most computers.

**GRADUATE CAREER DATA.** Highest graduate school enrollments: Cornell U, Harvard U, New York U, Northwestern U, Stanford U, U of Virginia.

**PROMINENT ALUMNI/AE.** Edward M. Kennedy, U.S. senator; Charles Brown, retired chairperson and CEO, AT&T; Frank Batten, chairperson and CEO, Landmark Communications; S. Buford Scott, chairperson and CEO, Scott & Stringfellow.

## University of Virginia, Clinch Valley College

Wise, VA 24293-0016 703 328-0100

**1994-95 Costs.** Tuition: $2,988 (state residents), $6,826 (out-of-state). Room: $1,680. Board: $1,696. Fees, books, misc. academic expenses (school's estimate): $600.

**Enrollment.** Undergraduates: 564 men, 561 women (full-time). Freshman class: 689 applicants, 561 accepted, 250 enrolled.

**Test score averages/ranges.** Average SAT scores: 406 verbal, 449 math. Range of SAT scores of middle 50%: 400-499 verbal, 400-499 math.

**Faculty.** 58 full-time; 31 part-time. 70% of faculty holds doctoral degree. Student/faculty ratio: 18 to 1.

**Selectivity rating.** Less competitive.

**PROFILE.** U Virginia–Clinch Valley College, founded in 1954, is a public institution of arts and sciences. Its 350-acre campus is located in Wise, 60 miles northwest of Bristol.

**Accreditation:** SACS.

**Religious orientation:** University of Virginia, Clinch Valley College is nonsectarian; no religious requirements.

**Library:** Collections totaling over 140,000 volumes, 1,254 periodical subscriptions, and 51,295 microform items.

**Special facilities/museums:** Electron microscope, observatory.

**Athletic facilities:** Gymnasium, swimming pool, tennis courts, training and weight rooms, baseball, football practice, and intramural fields, track, cross-country course, batting cage.

**STUDENT BODY. Undergraduate profile:** 95% are state residents; 34% are transfers. 1% Asian-American, 3% Black, 1% Hispanic, 94% White, 1% Other. Average age of undergraduates is 22.

**Freshman profile:** Majority of accepted applicants took SAT. 99% of freshmen come from public schools.

**Undergraduate achievement:** 65% of fall 1992 freshmen returned for fall 1993 term. 7% of students who completed a degree program immediately went on to graduate study.

**Foreign students:** Four students are from out of the country. Countries represented include Canada, Finland, and Korea.

**PROGRAMS OF STUDY. Degrees:** B.A., B.S.

**Majors:** Accounting, Biology, Business Administration, Chemistry, College Major, Computer Information Systems, Economics, English, Environmental Science, Government, History, Mathematics, Medical Technology, Nursing, Psychology, Psychology/Sociology.

**Distribution of degrees:** The majors with the highest enrollment are business administration, social sciences, and history; environmental science and medical technology have the lowest.

**Requirements:** General education requirement.

**Academic regulations:** Minimum 2.0 GPA must be maintained.

**Special:** Minors offered in some majors and in art, business, computer science, foreign languages, international studies, library science, music, philosophy, political science, secondary education, and sociology. Self-designed majors. Double majors. Independent study. Accelerated study. Pass/fail grading option. Preprofessional programs in law, medicine, veterinary science, pharmacy, dentistry, physical therapy, and forestry. Member of Southwest Virginia Consortium for Continuing Higher Education. Teacher certification in early childhood, elementary, secondary, and special education. Certification in specific subject areas.

**Honors:** Honors program. Honor societies.

**Academic Assistance:** Remedial writing and math. Nonremedial tutoring.

**ADMISSIONS. Academic basis for candidate selection** (in order of priority): Secondary school record, class rank, standardized test scores, essay, school's recommendation.

**Nonacademic basis for candidate selection:** Extracurricular participation and particular talent or ability are emphasized. Character and personality are important. Alumni/ae relationship is considered.

**Requirements:** Graduation from secondary school is recommended; GED is accepted. 11 units and the following program of study are required: 4 units of English, 3 units of math, 2 units of science including 1 unit of lab, 1 unit of social studies, 1 unit of history. Two units of a single foreign language recommended. Minimum combined SAT score of 800 recommended. Rank in top half of secondary school class and minimum 2.3 GPA in a college preparatory curriculum required. R.N. required of nursing program applicants. Conditional admission possible for applicants not meeting standard requirements. SAT or ACT is required. Campus visit and interview recommended. No off-campus interviews.

**Procedure:** Take SAT or ACT by December of 12th year. Application deadline is August 1. Notification of admission on rolling basis. $100 room deposit, refundable until August 1. Freshmen accepted for terms other than fall.

**Special programs:** Credit and/or placement may be granted through CEEB Advanced Placement exams for scores of 4 or higher. Credit may be granted through challenge exams.

**Transfer students:** Transfer students accepted for terms other than fall. In fall 1993, 34% of all new students were transfers into all classes. 246 transfer applications were received, 228 were accepted. Application deadline is August 1 for fall; December 1 for spring. Minimum 2.0 GPA required. Lowest course grade accepted is "C." Maximum number of transferable credits is 66 semester hours from a two-year school and 94 semster hours from a four-year school. At least 30 semester hours must be completed at the college to receive degree.

**Admissions contact:** Doyle Bickers, M.Div., Director of Admissions/Financial Aid. 703 328-0102.

**FINANCIAL AID. Available aid:** Pell grants, SEOG, state scholarships and grants, school scholarships and grants, private scholarships and grants, academic merit scholarships, and athletic scholarships. Perkins Loans (NDSL), PLUS, Stafford Loans (GSL), and SLS. AMS.

**Financial aid statistics:** 12% of aid is not need-based. In 1993-94, 68% of all undergraduate applicants received aid; 72% of freshman applicants. Average amounts of aid awarded freshmen: Scholarships and grants, $2,612; loans, $1,365.

**Supporting data/closing dates:** FAFSA: Priority filing date is February 1. Notification of awards on rolling basis.

**Financial aid contact:** Rusty Necessary, Counselor. 703 328-0139.

## Virginia Commonwealth University

Richmond, VA 23284 800 841-3638

**1994-95 Costs.** Tuition: $3,747 (state residents), $10,304 (out-of-state). Room & board: $4,162. Fees, books, misc. academic expenses (school's estimate): $1,301.

**Enrollment.** Undergraduates: 4,277 men, 5,955 women (full-time). Freshman class: 4,963 applicants, 3,497 accepted, 1,567 enrolled. Graduate enrollment: 2,409 men, 4,116 women.

**Test score averages/ranges.** Average SAT scores: 485 verbal, 525 math. Range of SAT scores of middle 50%: 430-530 verbal, 470-570 math.

**Faculty.** 87% of faculty holds highest degree in specific field. Student/faculty ratio: 14 to 1.

**Selectivity rating.** Competitive.

**PROFILE.** Virginia Commonwealth, founded in 1838, is a public, multipurpose university. Programs are offered through the College of Humanities and Sciences and the Schools of Allied Health Professions, the Arts, Basic Health Sciences, Business, Community and Public Affairs, Dentistry, Education, Graduate Studies, Mass Communications, Medicine, Nursing, Pharmacy, and Social Work. Two campuses of 64 acres are both located in downtown Richmond.

**Accreditation:** SACS. Professionally accredited by the Foundation for Interior Design Education Research.

**Religious orientation:** Virginia Commonwealth University is nonsectarian; no religious requirements.

**Library:** Collections totaling over 898,000 volumes, 8,400 periodical subscriptions, and 28,754 microform items.

**Special facilities/museums:** Art museum.
**Athletic facilities:** Athletic field, gymnasiums, natatorium, tennis courts.

**STUDENT BODY. Undergraduate profile:** 94% are state residents; 52% are transfers. 5% Asian-American, 17% Black, 1% Hispanic, 1% Native American, 74% White, 2% Other. Average age of undergraduates is 22.
**Freshman profile:** 3% of freshmen who took SAT scored 700 or over on math; 10% scored 600 or over on verbal, 19% scored 600 or over on math; 40% scored 500 or over on verbal, 61% scored 500 or over on math; 90% scored 400 or over on verbal, 97% scored 400 or over on math; 100% scored 300 or over on verbal, 100% scored 300 or over on math. 93% of accepted applicants took SAT; 3% took ACT. 90% of freshmen come from public schools.
**Undergraduate achievement:** 77% of fall 1992 freshmen returned for fall 1993 term. 18% of entering class graduated.
**Foreign students:** 251 students are from out of the country. Countries represented include China, India, Korea, Kuwait, Russia, and Taiwan; 73 in all.

**PROGRAMS OF STUDY. Degrees:** B.A., B.F.A., B.Mus., B.Mus.Ed., B.S., B.S.Nurs., B.Soc.Work.
**Majors:** Accounting, Administration of Justice, Applied Music, Art Education, Art History/Appreciation, Biology, Business Administration/Management, Chemistry, Church Music, Clinical Radiation Sciences, Communication Arts/Design, Comparative/General Literature, Computer/Information Sciences, Crafts, Dance/Choreography, Dental Hygiene, Distributive Education, Economics, English, Fashion Design, Fashion Merchandising, French, German, Health Education, History, Information Systems, Interior Design, Marketing, Mass Communications, Mathematics, Medical Technology, Music Education, Music History/Literature, Music Theory/Composition, Nursing, Occupational Therapy, Operations Research, Painting/Printmaking, Pharmacy, Philosophy, Physical Education, Physical Therapy, Physics, Political Science, Psychology, Public Safety, Recreation, Recreation/Parks/Tourism, Rehabilitation Services, Religious Studies, Safety/Risk Administration, Science, Sculpture, Social Work, Sociology/Anthropology, Spanish, Special Education, Statistics, Theatre, Theatre Education, Urban Studies.
**Distribution of degrees:** The majors with the highest enrollment are psychology, nursing, and mass communications; science and health education have the lowest.
**Academic regulations:** Minimum 2.0 GPA must be maintained.
**Special:** Minors offered in College of Humanities and Sciences, School of Business, School of Community and Public Affairs, School of Social Work, and selected programs in School of the Arts. Associate's degrees offered. Self-designed majors. Double majors. Dual degrees. Accelerated study. Internships. Cooperative education programs. Preprofessional programs in law, medicine, veterinary science, pharmacy, dentistry, and optometry. 3-2 engineering programs with Auburn U, George Washington U, and Old Dominion U. Member of consortium with four other Virginia schools. Teacher certification in early childhood, elementary, secondary, and special education. Study abroad in African countries, Austria, France, Indonesia, Italy, Russia, Spain, and the United Kingdom. ROTC.
**Honors:** Phi Beta Kappa. Honors program. Honor societies.
**Academic Assistance:** Remedial writing, math, and study skills. Nonremedial tutoring.

**STUDENT LIFE. Housing:** Coed, women's, and men's dorms. School-owned/operated apartments. 19% of students live in college housing.
**Social atmosphere:** The editor of the school newspaper reports, "Richmond provides a host of cultural and art happenings. A large club and music scene has several nationally known bands performing. The climate provides many warm school months." Student Government exerts a strong influence on after-school activities. The Greeks are small, but growing. Students enjoy athletics, such as club sports (rugby) that dominate state region play, and basketball. Popular events are Greek Olympics, Bikini Contest (at Arnold's Restaurant), Black History Month, and dances. Students come down to the Library Tavern between research projects, and Shafer Court is popular for recreational sports. Monroe Park is a favorite nighttime gathering spot.
**Services and counseling/handicapped student services:** Placement services. Health service. Counseling services for minority, military, veteran, and older students. Birth control, personal, and psychological counseling. Career and academic guidance services. Physically disabled student services. Learning disabled services. Notetaking services. Tape recorders. Tutors. Reader services for the blind.
**Campus organizations:** Undergraduate student government. Student newspaper (Commonwealth Times, published biweekly). Literary magazine. Yearbook. Radio station. Drama group, music association, 170 organizations in all. 17 fraternities, seven chapter houses; 10 sororities, no chapter houses. 5% of men join a fraternity. 4% of women join a sorority.
**Religious organizations:** Bahai group, Baptist Student Union, Campus Crusade for Christ, Catholic Ministries, Christian Science Organization, Jewish Student Association.
**Minority/foreign student organizations:** Black Awakening Choir, black caucus, black leadership awareness group, Black Student Alliance, minority fraternities/sororities.

**ATHLETICS. Physical education requirements:** None.
**Intercollegiate competition:** 16% of students participate. Baseball (M), basketball (M,W), cheerleading (M,W), cross-country (M,W), field hockey (W), golf (M), soccer (M), tennis (M,W), track and field (indoor) (M,W), track and field (outdoor) (M,W), volleyball (W). Member of Colonial Conference, Metro Conference, NCAA Division I.
**Intramural and club sports:** 25% of students participate. Intramural basketball, flag football, soccer, softball, swimming, tennis, volleyball. Men's club fencing, gymnastics, karate/judo, kayaking, lacrosse, rugby, surfing. Women's club fencing, gymnastics, soccer.

**ADMISSIONS. Academic basis for candidate selection** (in order of priority): Secondary school record, class rank, standardized test scores, school's recommendation, essay.
**Nonacademic basis for candidate selection:** Particular talent or ability is emphasized. Extracurricular participation is considered.
**Requirements:** Graduation from secondary school is required; GED is accepted. 21 units and the following program of study are required: 4 units of English, 3 units of math, 2 units of science including 1 unit of lab, 3 units of social studies, 9 units of electives. Minimum combined SAT score of 800-1050 required depending on GPA and class rank; minimum 2.2 GPA required; rank in top half of secondary school class recommended. Portfolio required of visual arts program applicants. Audition required of performing arts program applicants. Interview and additional secondary school units required of some health science program applicants. Conditional admission possible for applicants not meeting standard requirements. Office of Academic Support for students not normally admissible. SAT is required; ACT may be substituted. Campus visit recommended. No off-campus interviews.
**Procedure:** Take SAT or ACT by January of 12th year. Visit college for interview by February 1 of 12th year. Suggest filing application by February 1. Application deadline is June 1. Notification of admission by April 1. Reply is required by May 1. $100 nonrefundable tuition deposit. $250 room deposit, refundable until June 30. Freshmen accepted for terms other than fall.
**Special programs:** Admission may be deferred one year. Credit and/or placement may be granted through CEEB Advanced Placement exams for scores of 3 or higher. Credit may be granted through CLEP general and subject exams, challenge exams, and military experience. Early decision program. In fall 1993, 143 applied for early decision and 42 were accepted. Deadline for applying for early decision is November 1. Early entrance/early admission program. Concurrent enrollment program.
**Transfer students:** Transfer students accepted for terms other than fall. In fall 1993, 52% of all new students were transfers into all classes. 3,466 transfer applications were received, 2,440 were accepted. Application deadline is June 1 for fall; December 1 for spring. Minimum 2.25 GPA recommended. Lowest course grade accepted is "C." At least 30 semester hours must be completed at the university to receive degree.
**Admissions contact:** Horace W. Wooldridge, Jr., M.Ed., Director of Admissions. 804 367-1222.

**FINANCIAL AID. Available aid:** Pell grants, SEOG, Federal Nursing Student Scholarships, state scholarships and grants, school scholarships, private scholarships, ROTC scholarships, academic merit scholarships, and athletic scholarships. Perkins Loans (NDSL), PLUS, Stafford Loans (GSL), NSL, Health Professions Loans, school loans, and SLS. Installment Payment Plan.
**Financial aid statistics:** 10% of aid is not need-based. In 1993-94, 70% of all undergraduate applicants received aid; 100% of freshman applicants. Average amounts of aid awarded freshmen: Scholarships and grants, $2,500; loans, $2,500.
**Supporting data/closing dates:** FAFSA: Priority filing date is April 15; deadline is November 1. Notification of awards begins June 10.
**Financial aid contact:** Charles R. Kinder, Ph.D., Director of Financial Aid. 804 367-0765.

**STUDENT EMPLOYMENT.** College Work/Study Program. Institutional employment. 20% of full-time undergraduates work on campus during school year. Students may expect to earn an average of $1,500 during school year. Off-campus part-time employment opportunities rated "good."

**COMPUTER FACILITIES.** 150 IBM/IBM-compatible and Macintosh/Apple microcomputers. Students may access Digital, IBM minicomputer/mainframe systems, BITNET, Internet. Residence halls may be equipped with modems. Client/LAN operating systems include Apple/Macintosh, DOS, Windows NT. Computer languages and software packages include BASIC, C, COBOL, FORTRAN 77, GKS, LISP, Pascal, Prolog, SAS; 17 in all. Computer facilities are available to all students.
**Fees:** None.

# Virginia Intermont College

**Bristol, VA 242014298** 703 669-6101

**1994-95 Costs.** Tuition: $9,150. Room & board: $4,250. Fees, books, misc. academic expenses (school's estimate): $600.
**Enrollment.** Undergraduates: 179 men, 390 women (full-time). Freshman class: 490 applicants, 441 accepted, 118 enrolled.
**Test score averages/ranges.** Average SAT scores: 409 verbal, 425 math. Range of SAT scores of middle 50%: 350-470 verbal, 370-470 math. Average ACT scores: 20 English, 19 math, 20 composite. Range of ACT scores of middle 50%: 17-23 English, 17-21 math.
**Faculty.** 36 full-time; 25 part-time. 56% of faculty holds highest degree in specific field. Student/faculty ratio: 12 to 1.
**Selectivity rating.** Less competitive.

**PROFILE.** Virginia Intermont is a church-affiliated college. Founded as a school for women in 1884, it became a four-year college and adopted coeducation in 1972. Its 16-acre campus is located in Bristol near the Tennessee state line, 100 miles southwest of Roanoke.

**Accreditation:** SACS. Professionally accredited by the American Bar Association, the Council on Social Work Education.
**Religious orientation:** Virginia Intermont College is affiliated with the Baptist General Association of Virginia; one semester of religion required.
**Library:** Collections totaling over 68,010 volumes, 327 periodical subscriptions, and 27,697 microform items.
**Special facilities/museums:** Museum/gallery, language lab, 129-acre riding center for equestrian program.
**Athletic facilities:** Gymnasium, tennis courts, baseball field.

**STUDENT BODY. Undergraduate profile:** 70% are state residents; 30% are transfers. 6% Black, 91% White, 3% Non-resident alien. Average age of undergraduates is 20.
**Freshman profile:** 2% of freshmen who took SAT scored 600 or over on verbal, 4% scored 600 or over on math; 20% scored 500 or over on verbal, 21% scored 500 or over on math; 51% scored 400 or over on verbal, 62% scored 400 or over on math; 84% scored 300 or over on verbal, 94% scored 300 or over on math. 3% of freshmen who took ACT scored 30 or over on English, 3% scored 30 or over on composite; 27% scored 24 or over on English, 17% scored 24 or over on math, 23% scored 24 or over on composite; 67% scored 18 or over on English, 64% scored 18 or over on math, 73% scored 18 or over on composite; 97% scored 12 or over on English, 97% scored 12 or over on math, 97% scored 12 or over on composite; 100% scored 6 or over on composite. 90% of accepted applicants took SAT; 10% took ACT.

**Undergraduate achievement:** 60% of fall 1992 freshmen returned for fall 1993 term. 30% of entering class graduated. 6% of students who completed a degree program immediately went on to graduate study.

**Foreign students:** 14 students are from out of the country. Countries represented include the Bahamas, Germany, Japan, and Spain; six in all.

**PROGRAMS OF STUDY. Degrees:** B.A., B.F.A., B.S., B.Soc.Work.

**Majors:** Art, Biology, Creative Writing, Dance, Early Childhood Education, English, History/Political Science, Horsemanship, Liberal/General Studies, Management, Medical Technology, Merchandising, Middle School Education, Office Administration, Paralegal Studies, Performing Arts, Photography, Physical Education, Psychology, Religion, Secondary Education, Social Work, Sports Management.

**Distribution of degrees:** The majors with the highest enrollment are horsemanship and paralegal studies; history/political science, early childhood education, and English have the lowest.

**Requirements:** General education requirement.

**Academic regulations:** Minimum 2.0 GPA must be maintained.

**Special:** Minors offered in many majors and in business administration, chemistry, dance, design, music, sociology, and theatre arts. Associate's degrees offered. Double majors. Independent study. Pass/fail grading option. Internships. Graduate school at which undergraduates may take graduate-level courses. Preprofessional programs in law, medicine, veterinary science, pharmacy, dentistry, theology, and optometry. 3-1 medical technology program with Holston Valley Hospital. Member of consortium with King Coll. Teacher certification in early childhood, elementary, and secondary education. Certification in specific subject areas. Study abroad in Germany.

**Honors:** Honor societies.

**Academic Assistance:** Nonremedial tutoring.

**ADMISSIONS. Academic basis for candidate selection** (in order of priority): Secondary school record, standardized test scores, class rank, essay, school's recommendation.

**Nonacademic basis for candidate selection:** Extracurricular participation is considered.

**Requirements:** Graduation from secondary school is required; GED is accepted. 16 units and the following program of study are required: 4 units of English, 2 units of math, 1 unit of lab science, 2 units of social studies, 6 units of electives. Minimum "C" average required. Specific programs require additional admissions forms. Conditional admission possible for applicants not meeting standard requirements. SAT or ACT is required. Campus visit and interview recommended. No off-campus interviews.

**Procedure:** Take SAT or ACT by December of 12th year. Visit college for interview by April of 12th year. Suggested filing admissions application between September and December of 12th year. Notification of admission on rolling basis. Reply is required by May 1. $250 tuition deposit, refundable until May 1. $250 room deposit, refundable until May 1. Freshmen accepted for terms other than fall.

**Special programs:** Admission may be deferred two years. Credit may be granted through CEEB Advanced Placement for scores of 4 or higher. Credit may be granted through CLEP general and subject exams, and life experience. Concurrent enrollment program.

**Transfer students:** Transfer students accepted for terms other than fall. In fall 1993, 30% of all new students were transfers into all classes. 135 transfer applications were received, 110 were accepted. Application deadline is rolling for fall; rolling for spring. Minimum 2.0 GPA required. Lowest course grade accepted is "C." At least 30 semester hours must be completed at the college to receive degree.

**Admissions contact:** R. Lawton Blandford, Jr., Dean of Admissions. 800 451-1VIC.

**FINANCIAL AID. Available aid:** Pell grants, SEOG, state grants, school scholarships and grants, private scholarships and grants, academic merit scholarships, and athletic scholarships. Perkins Loans (NDSL), PLUS, Stafford Loans (GSL), state loans, private loans, and SLS. AMS.

**Financial aid statistics:** 45% of aid is not need-based. In 1993-94, 78% of all undergraduate applicants received aid; 85% of freshman applicants. Average amounts of aid awarded freshmen: Loans, $2,625.

**Supporting data/closing dates:** FAFSA/FAF/FFS: Accepted on rolling basis. School's own aid application: Accepted on rolling basis. State aid form: Priority filing date is July 31; deadline is September 14. Notification of awards on rolling basis.

**Financial aid contact:** Cathy W. Ramsey, M.Ed., Director of Financial Planning. 800 451-1VIC.

## Virginia Military Institute

**Lexington, VA 24450** **703 464-7000**

**1993-94 Costs.** Tuition: $2,910 (state residents), $8,730 (out-of-state). Room & board: $3,690. Fees, books, misc. academic expenses (school's estimate): $2,620.

**Enrollment.** 1,191 men (full-time). Freshman class: 904 applicants, 683 accepted, 349 enrolled.

**Test score averages/ranges.** Average SAT scores: 484 verbal, 542 math. Range of SAT scores of middle 50%: 930-1110 combined. Average ACT scores: 22 composite. Range of ACT scores of middle 50%: 20-24 composite.

**Faculty.** 96 full-time; 20 part-time. 85% of faculty holds doctoral degree. Student/faculty ratio: 11 to 1.

**Selectivity rating.** Less competitive.

**PROFILE.** Virginia Military Institute, founded in 1839, is a public college for men. Its 134-acre campus is located in Lexington, 50 miles northeast of Roanoke.

**Accreditation:** SACS. Professionally accredited by the Accreditation Board for Engineering and Technology.

**Religious orientation:** Virginia Military Institute is nonsectarian; no religious requirements.

**Library:** Collections totaling over 237,631 volumes, and 1,019 periodical subscriptions.

**Special facilities/museums:** History museum, research library, observatory, nuclear reactor, robot.

**Athletic facilities:** Gymnasium, weight room, indoor and outdoor tracks, running trail, basketball, racquetball, and tennis courts, indoor and outdoor shooting ranges, football stadium, soccer and lacrosse fields.

**STUDENT BODY. Undergraduate profile:** 59% are state residents; 13% are transfers. 4.6% Asian-American, 7.3% Black, 1.3% Hispanic, .6% Native American, 83.6% White, 2.6% International. Average age of undergraduates is 20.

**Freshman profile:** 71% of freshmen come from public schools.

**Undergraduate achievement:** 78% of fall 1992 freshmen returned for fall 1993 term. 48% of entering class graduated. 11% of students who completed a degree program immediately went on to graduate study.

**Foreign students:** 29 students are from out of the country. Countries represented include Australia, Canada, China, Japan, and Thailand; nine in all.

**PROGRAMS OF STUDY. Degrees:** B.A., B.S.

**Majors:** Biology, Chemistry, Civil Engineering, Computer Science, Economics/Business, Electrical/Computer Engineering, English, History, International Studies, Mathematics, Mechanical Engineering, Modern Languages, Physics.

**Distribution of degrees:** The majors with the highest enrollment are history, economics/business, and civil engineering; physics, mathematics, and computer science have the lowest.

**Requirements:** General education requirement.

**Academic regulations:** Freshmen must maintain minimum 1.5 GPA; sophomores, 1.8 GPA; juniors, 2.0 GPA; seniors, 2.0 GPA.

**Special:** Minors offered in many majors and in fine arts, French, German, and Spanish. The purpose of VMI is to produce "citizen-soldiers," young men prepared to assume leadership roles in society and to aid the nation in times of national emergency. Degree program must be selected before entrance; major may be changed within degree program. Courses in aerospace studies, anthropology, astronomy, geology, library procedures, military science, naval science, physical education, philosophy, psychology, Russian, and speech. Summer Transition Program. Developmental reading course. Grades reduced in all courses for poor writing. All cadets must successfully complete ROTC courses in military science, naval science, or aerospace studies. If offered at graduation, commission in one of the armed forces must be accepted with the obligation for active duty. Double majors. Independent study. Study abroad in England, France, Germany, and Spain. ROTC, NROTC, and AFROTC.

**Honors:** Honors program. Honor societies.

**Academic Assistance:** Nonremedial tutoring.

**STUDENT LIFE. Housing:** All cadets must live on campus. Men's dorms. 100% of students live in college housing.

**Social atmosphere:** The student newspaper reports, "Since it's an all-male school, people tend to take off on weekends and go to the five female schools within an hour of VMI. There are a few dances and sporting events which are big. Cadets go to Mary Baldwin College, Hollins, University of Virginia, Virginia Tech, Randolph–Macon Women's College, University of Richmond, and the adventurous ones road trip to Georgetown. Cultural life is good. There is a yearly symposium on such subjects as the Constitution and U.S. history. Many poets come to speak, political leaders visit, and many movies are shown."

**Services and counseling/handicapped student services:** Placement services. Health service. Counseling services for military students. Personal counseling. Career and academic guidance services. Religious counseling.

**Campus organizations:** Undergraduate student government. Student newspaper (Cadet, published once/week). Literary magazine. Yearbook. Cadet Battery, Cadet Program Board, Cadet Ranger Platoon, Civil War Round Table, College Republicans, Society of Young Democrats, marching, dance, and pep bands, glee club, prelaw society, premed society, scientific and technical groups, theatre, debating, special-interest groups, 50 organizations in all.

**Religious organizations:** Baptist Student Union, Canterbury Club, Fellowship of Christian Athletes, Jewish Cadet Club, Methodist Student Movement, Newman Club, Westminster Fellowship.

**Minority/foreign student organizations:** Promaji (black student group). International Relations Club.

**ATHLETICS. Physical education requirements:** Four semesters of physical education required.

**Intercollegiate competition:** 36% of students participate. Baseball (M), basketball (M), cross-country (M), football (M), golf (M), lacrosse (M), riflery (M), soccer (M), swimming (M), tennis (M), track (outdoor) (M), track and field (M), track and field (indoor) (M), track and field (outdoor) (M), wrestling (M). Member of NCAA Division I, NCAA Division I-AA for football, Southern Conference.

**Intramural and club sports:** 54% of students participate. Intramural baseball, basketball, boxing, football, golf, handball, racquetball, soccer, swimming, tennis, weight lifting. Men's club boxing, fencing, rugby, water polo.

**ADMISSIONS. Academic basis for candidate selection** (in order of priority): Secondary school record, class rank, standardized test scores, school's recommendation, essay.

**Nonacademic basis for candidate selection:** Character and personality and extracurricular participation are emphasized. Particular talent or ability, geographical distribution, and alumni/ae relationship are considered.

**Requirements:** Graduation from secondary school is required; GED is not accepted. 16 units and the following program of study are required: 4 units of English, 4 units of math, 3 units of science. 3 units of foreign language, 4 units of social studies, and 2 units of electives are recommended. Rank in top half of secondary school class required; minimum 2.8 GPA and combined SAT score of 1050 recommended. SAT or ACT is required. Campus visit and interview recommended. No off-campus interviews.

**Procedure:** Take SAT or ACT by December of 12th year. Visit college for interview by April of 12th year. Suggest filing application by November 15. Application deadline is April 1. Notification of admission on rolling basis. Reply is required by May 1. $300 tuition deposit, refundable until May 1. Freshmen accepted for fall terms only.

**Special programs:** Credit and/or placement may be granted through CEEB Advanced Placement exams for scores of 4 or higher. Credit and placement may be granted through military experience. Early decision program. In fall 1993, 88 applied for early decision and 64 were accepted. Deadline for applying for early decision is November 15.

**Transfer students:** Transfer students accepted for fall term only. In fall 1993, 13% of all new students were transfers into all classes. 73 transfer applications were received, 40

were accepted. Application deadline is March 1. Minimum 2.0 GPA required. Lowest course grade accepted is "C." Maximum number of transferable credits is 68 semester hours. At least 75 semester hours must be completed at the institute to receive degree.
**Admissions contact:** Lt. Col. Daniel A. Troppoli, Director of Admissions. 703 464-7211, 800 767-4207.

**FINANCIAL AID. Available aid:** Pell grants, SEOG, state scholarships and grants, school scholarships and grants, private scholarships and grants, ROTC scholarships, academic merit scholarships, and athletic scholarships. Perkins Loans (NDSL), PLUS, Stafford Loans (GSL), and SLS. Tuition Plan Inc. and AMS.
**Financial aid statistics:** 60% of aid is not need-based. In 1993-94, 83% of all undergraduate applicants received aid; 85% of freshman applicants. Average amounts of aid awarded freshmen: Scholarships and grants, $4,825; loans, $4,625.
**Supporting data/closing dates:** FAFSA: Priority filing date is March 1. School's own aid application: Deadline is March 1. Income tax forms: Priority filing date is March 1; accepted on rolling basis. Notification of awards begins in April.
**Financial aid contact:** Lt. Col. Timothy Golden, M.A., Director of Financial Aid. 703 464-7208.

**STUDENT EMPLOYMENT.** College Work/Study Program. Institutional employment. 21% of full-time undergraduates work on campus during school year. Students may expect to earn an average of $870 during school year. Freshmen are discouraged from working during their first term. Off-campus part-time employment opportunities rated "poor."

**COMPUTER FACILITIES.** 250 IBM/IBM-compatible microcomputers; 200 are networked. Students may access Data General, Digital minicomputer/mainframe systems, BITNET, Internet, CompuServe. Client/LAN operating systems include DOS, UNIX/XENIX/AIX, Banyan, DEC. Computer languages and software packages include BASIC, C++, COBOL, FORTRAN, Lotus 1-2-3, Pascal, Pascaltext, Quattro, WordPerfect. Computer facilities are available to all students.
**Fees:** None.
**Hours:** 8 AM-1 AM.

**GRADUATE CAREER DATA.** Graduate school percentages: 1% enter law school. 9% enter graduate arts and sciences programs. 1% enter theological school/seminary. Highest graduate school enrollments: Medical Coll of Virginia, MIT, Mississippi State U, U of Richmond, U of Virginia, Virginia Polytech Inst, Washington and Lee U, U of West Virginia. 47% of graduates choose careers in business and industry. Companies and businesses that hire graduates: Burlington Industries, B&W Nuclear Technologies, Enterprise Leasing, Equitable, Ferguson Enterprises, J.A. Jones Construction Co., Kroger, Omni Services, Turner Corp., Union Camp Corp., West Vaco.

**PROMINENT ALUMNI/AE.** Gen. George C. Marshall, army chief of staff, secretary of state, Nobel Peace Prize winner; John DeButz, CEO, AT&T; Dabney W. Coleman, actor.

# Virginia Polytechnic Institute and State University

**Blacksburg, VA 24061-0202** **703 231-6000**

**1993-94 Costs.** Tuition: $3,300 (state residents), $9,168 (out-of-state). Room & board: $3,016. Fees, books, misc. academic expenses (school's estimate): $1,213.
**Enrollment.** Undergraduates: 10,792 men, 7,474 women (full-time). Freshman class: 17,031 applicants, 10,863 accepted, 3,844 enrolled. Graduate enrollment: 2,324 men, 1,208 women.
**Test score averages/ranges.** Range of SAT scores of middle 50%: 450-550 verbal, 520-650 math.
**Faculty.** 1,816 full-time; 697 part-time. 87% of faculty holds highest degree in specific field. Student/faculty ratio: 17 to 1.
**Selectivity rating.** More competitive.

**PROFILE.** Virginia Tech, founded in 1872, is a public, comprehensive university. Programs are offered through the Colleges of Agriculture and Life Sciences, Architecture and Urban Studies, Arts and Sciences, Business, Education, Engineering, Human Resources, and Veterinary Medicine and the Graduate School. Its 2,600-acre campus is located in Blacksburg, 31 miles west of Roanoke.

**Accreditation:** SACS. Professionally accredited by the Accreditation Board for Engineering and Technology, the American Assembly of Collegiate Schools of Business, the American Dietetic Association, the American Home Economics Association, the American Psychological Association, the American Society of Landscape Architects, the American Veterinary Medical Association, the National Council for Accreditation of Teacher Education, the Society of American Foresters.
**Religious orientation:** Virginia Polytechnic Institute and State University is nonsectarian; no religious requirements.
**Library:** Collections totaling over 1,789,975 volumes, 18,000 periodical subscriptions, and 5,296,475 microform items.
**Special facilities/museums:** Art gallery, day care center, digital music facilities, Black Cultural Center, television studio, on-campus preschool, anaerobic lab, CAD-CAM labs, wind tunnel, farms.
**Athletic facilities:** Gymnasium, swimming pool, field house, tennis pavilion, baseball and football stadiums, basketball coliseum, weight and wrestling rooms, handball and racquetball courts, golf course, athletic fields.

**STUDENT BODY. Undergraduate profile:** 75% are state residents; 16% are transfers. 7% Asian-American, 5% Black, 1% Hispanic, 86% White, 1% Other. Average age of undergraduates is 20.
**Freshman profile:** 1% of freshmen who took SAT scored 700 or over on verbal, 11% scored 700 or over on math; 11% scored 600 or over on verbal, 47% scored 600 or over on math; 52% scored 500 or over on verbal, 85% scored 500 or over on math; 93% scored 400 or over on verbal, 99% scored 400 or over on math; 99% scored 300 or over on verbal, 100% scored 300 or over on math. 99% of accepted applicants took SAT; 1% took ACT.
**Undergraduate achievement:** 88% of fall 1991 freshmen returned for fall 1992 term.
**Foreign students:** 158 students are from out of the country. Countries represented include Hong Kong, India, Indonesia, Pakistan, South Korea, and United Arab Emirates; 57 in all.

**PROGRAMS OF STUDY. Degrees:** B.A., B.Arch., B.Land.Arch., B.S.
**Majors:** Accounting, Aerospace Engineering, Agricultural Economics, Agricultural Education, Agricultural Engineering, Animal Science, Architecture, Art, Art History, Biochemistry, Biology, Building Construction, Business Education, Chemical Engineering, Chemistry, Civil Engineering, Clothing/Textiles, Communication Studies, Community Health, Computer Engineering, Computer Science, Crop/Soil Environmental Sciences, Dairy Science, Economics, Electrical Engineering, Engineering Science/Mechanics, English, Environmental Science, Family/Child Development, Finance, Food Science/Technology, French, Geography, Geology, Geophysics, German, History, Home Economics Education, Horticulture, Hotel/Restaurant/Institutional Management, Housing/Interior Design/Resource Management, Human Nutrition/Foods, Industrial/Systems Engineering, International Studies, Landscape Architecture, Liberal Arts/Sciences, Management, Management Science, Marketing, Marketing Education, Materials Science/Engineering, Mathematics, Mechanical Engineering, Mining/Minerals Engineering, Music, Ocean Engineering, Philosophy, Physical Education, Physics, Political Science, Poultry Science, Psychology, Public Administration, Sociology, Spanish, Statistics, Technology Education, Theatre Arts, Urban Affairs, Vocational Industrial/Health Occupations Education.
**Distribution of degrees:** The majors with the highest enrollment are electrical engineering, finance, and mechanical engineering; German, agricultural education, and poultry science have the lowest.
**Requirements:** General education requirement.
**Academic regulations:** Freshmen must maintain minimum 1.50 GPA; sophomores, 1.75 GPA; juniors, 2.00 GPA; seniors, 2.00 GPA.
**Special:** Minors offered in many College of Arts and Sciences majors and in some majors in other colleges. Architecture and landscape architecture are five-year programs. Interdisciplinary humanities courses. Corps of Cadets. Associate's degrees offered. Self-designed majors. Double majors. Dual degrees. Independent study. Accelerated study. Pass/fail grading option. Internships. Cooperative education programs. Graduate school at which undergraduates may take graduate-level courses. Preprofessional programs in law, medicine, veterinary science, pharmacy, dentistry, and physical therapy. Combined-degree programs in medicine, dentistry, veterinary medicine, law, and medical technology. Member of architecture consortium with California Polytech Inst, Miami U, Oxford U, and Polytech Inst. Washington, D.C. semester for architecture and urban studies. Teacher certification in early childhood, elementary, secondary, special education, and vo-tech education. Certification in specific subject areas. Member of International Student Exchange Program (ISEP). Study abroad in England, France, Italy, Mexico, Spain, and Switzerland. ROTC, NROTC, and AFROTC.
**Honors:** Phi Beta Kappa. Honors program. Honor societies.
**Academic Assistance:** Nonremedial tutoring.

**STUDENT LIFE. Housing:** All unmarried freshmen under age 21 must live on campus unless living with family. Members of the Corps of Cadets must live on campus. Coed, women's, and men's dorms. Sorority and fraternity housing. Housing for Corps of Cadets and athletes. 42% of students live in college housing.
**Social atmosphere:** "There really is something for everyone here," reports the student newspaper. "There are active religious groups, fraternities and sororities which provide ample opportunities to make friends and have fun; off-campus bars provide great music, atmosphere, and beverages. Also, individuals are always having parties throughout town, so weekends are always full of opportunities to have a good time. On campus, students can get together at our student center for study sessions or whatever. Off campus, some students enjoy fraternity parties. Others enjoy seeing bands at South Main Cafe, the Cellar, and Morgan's, or drinking imported beer and throwing darts at the Ton 80 Club." Spring block parties are very popular.
**Services and counseling/handicapped student services:** Placement services. Health service. Women's center. Counseling services for minority and military students. Birth control, personal, and psychological counseling. Career and academic guidance services. Physically disabled student services. Learning disabled services. Tape recorders. Tutors. Reader services for the blind.
**Campus organizations:** Undergraduate student government. Student newspaper (Collegiate Times, published twice/week). Literary magazine. Yearbook. Radio and TV stations. Cadet and civilian marching bands, jazz and pep bands, symphonic band, choral groups, debate and drama groups, departmental, professional, service, and special-interest groups, 400 organizations in all. 35 fraternities, 22 chapter houses; 16 sororities, 10 chapter houses. 15% of men join a fraternity. 20% of women join a sorority.
**Religious organizations:** Bahai Association, Baptist Student Union, Bibleway Pentecostal Fellowship, Chi Alpha Christian Fellowship, Chinese Bible Study Group, Christian Science Organization, Fellowship of Christian Athletes, Hillel.
**Minority/foreign student organizations:** Minority fraternities/sororities, Black Student Alliance, Black American Advisory Council, NAACP, National Society of Black Engineers, Black Organizations Council, Subcommittee on Minority Affairs, Gospel Experience. African, Chinese, Filipino, Greek, Hong Kong, Indian, Korean, Muslim, Turkish, and Vietnamese student groups, International Club.

**ATHLETICS. Physical education requirements:** None.
**Intercollegiate competition:** 3% of students participate. Baseball (M), basketball (M,W), cross-country (M,W), diving (M,W), football (M), golf (M), soccer (M,W), swimming (M,W), tennis (M,W), track (indoor) (M,W), track (outdoor) (M,W), track and field (indoor) (M,W), track and field (outdoor) (M,W), volleyball (W), wrestling (M). Member of Big East Football Conference, Metropolitan Athletic Conference, NCAA Division I.
**Intramural and club sports:** 50% of students participate. Intramural archery, badminton, basketball, flag football, golf, handball, horseshoes, racquetball, soccer, softball, squash, swimming, tennis, volleyball, walleyball, water polo, wrestling. Men's club archery, bowling, clay target shooting, crew, fencing, gymnastics, ice hockey, lacrosse, martial arts, rifle, rugby, scuba, softball, volleyball, water skiing. Women's club archery, bowling, clay target shooting, crew, fencing, field hockey, gymnastics, lacrosse, martial arts, rifle, rugby, scuba, soccer, softball, water skiing.

**ADMISSIONS. Academic basis for candidate selection** (in order of priority): Secondary school record, class rank, standardized test scores, school's recommendation, essay.

**Nonacademic basis for candidate selection:** Geographical distribution is important. Character and personality, extracurricular participation, particular talent or ability, and alumni/ae relationship are considered.
**Requirements:** Graduation from secondary school is required; GED is accepted. 18 units and the following program of study are required: 4 units of English, 3 units of math, 2 units of lab science, 1 unit of social studies, 1 unit of history, 7 units of electives including 3 units of academic electives. Lab science units must be in biology, chemistry, or physics. Four units of mathematics and three units of lab science required for engineering and science-related program applicants. Minimum 2.0 GPA required but must be higher to be competitive. Portfolio required of art program applicants. Audition required of music program applicants. SAT is required; ACT may be substituted. Campus visit recommended. No off-campus interviews.
**Procedure:** Take SAT or ACT by December of 12th year. Visit college for interview by March of 12th year. Suggest filing application by December 1. Application deadline is February 1. Notification of admission by April 15. Reply is required by May 1. $265 tuition deposit and $35 orientation fee required; refundable until May 1; half refundable before June 1. Freshmen accepted for terms other than fall.
**Special programs:** Admission may be deferred one year. Credit may be granted through CEEB Advanced Placement for scores of 3 or higher. Early decision program. In fall 1992, 1,600 applied for early decision and 800 were accepted. Deadline for applying for early decision is November 1. Early entrance/early admission program.
**Transfer students:** Transfer students accepted for terms other than fall. In fall 1992, 16% of all new students were transfers into all classes. 2,284 transfer applications were received, 1,199 were accepted. Application deadline is March 1 for fall; October 1 for spring. Minimum 2.0 GPA required. Lowest course grade accepted is "C." No more than half of credits required for graduation may be transferred. At least 30 semester hours must be completed at the university to receive degree.
**Admissions contact:** David R. Bousquet, M.Ed., Director of Admissions. 703 231-6267.

**FINANCIAL AID. Available aid:** Pell grants, SEOG, state scholarships and grants, school scholarships and grants, private scholarships and grants, ROTC scholarships, academic merit scholarships, and athletic scholarships. Perkins Loans (NDSL), PLUS, Stafford Loans (GSL), school loans, and SLS. Budget Tuition Plan. Credit card payments.
**Financial aid statistics:** 65% of aid is not need-based. In 1992-93, 52% of all undergraduate applicants received aid; 61% of freshman applicants. Average amounts of aid awarded freshmen: Scholarships and grants, $3,200; loans, $2,500.
**Supporting data/closing dates:** FAFSA/FAF/FFS: Deadline is February 15. Notification of awards begins March 15.
**Financial aid contact:** Anne Hahn Clarke, M.Ed., Director of Financial Aid. 703 231-5179.

**STUDENT EMPLOYMENT.** College Work/Study Program. Institutional employment. 30% of full-time undergraduates work on campus during school year. Students may expect to earn an average of $1,500 during school year. Off-campus part-time employment opportunities rated "fair."

**COMPUTER FACILITIES.** 15,000 IBM/IBM-compatible and Macintosh/Apple microcomputers. Students may access Digital, IBM minicomputer/mainframe systems, BITNET, Internet. Residence halls may be equipped with stand-alone microcomputers, networked microcomputers, networked terminals, modems. Computer languages and software packages include APL, Assembler, BASIC, C, COBOL, dBASE II, FORTRAN, ImSL, Lotus 1-2-3, MicroSpell, Pascal, PC-File III, PHIGS, PL/1, Quattro Pro, Readiwriter, REXX, SAS, SLAM, SN SuperCalc II, SPIDERS, SPSS-X, Volkswriter, WordPerfect; 150 in all. Some computer facilities are available to all students; individual departments and academic colleges have PC labs open to students. Access to university mainframe is restricted; special authorization required.
**Fees:** Computer fee is included in tuition/fees.

**GRADUATE CAREER DATA.** Highest graduate school enrollments: Medical Coll of Virginia, U of Virginia, Virginia Tech. Companies and businesses that hire graduates: IBM, DuPont, General Electric, Westinghouse.

**PROMINENT ALUMNI/AE.** Clifton C. Garvin, Jr., retired chairperson and CEO, Exxon; Christopher C. Kraft, Jr., former director, NASA Johnson Space Center; Willis S. White, Jr., chairperson and CEO, American Electric Power; Alexander F. Giacco, retired chairperson, president and CEO, Hercules, Inc.

# Virginia State University

**Petersburg, VA 23806** **804 524-5000**

**1993-94 Costs.** Tuition: $3,050 (state residents), $6,724 (out-of-state). Room & board: $4,704. Fees, books, misc. academic expenses (school's estimate): $400.
**Enrollment.** Undergraduates: 1,446 men, 1,984 women (full-time). Graduate enrollment: 187 men, 399 women.
**Test score averages/ranges.** N/A.
**Faculty.** 207 full-time; 60 part-time. 56% of faculty holds highest degree in specific field. Student/faculty ratio: 19 to 1.
**Selectivity rating.** N/A.

**PROFILE.** Virginia State, founded in 1882, is a public, comprehensive, historically black university. Programs are offered through the Schools of Agriculture, Business Administration, Education, Humanities and Social Sciences, and Natural Sciences. Its 216-acre campus is located in Petersburg, 25 miles south of Richmond.

**Accreditation:** SACS.
**Religious orientation:** Virginia State University is nonsectarian; no religious requirements.
**Library:** Collections totaling over 232,357 volumes, 1,220 periodical subscriptions, and 476,690 microform items.
**Athletic facilities:** Gymnasium, stadium, swimming pool, weight and wrestling rooms, tennis courts, baseball and softball fields.

**STUDENT BODY. Undergraduate profile:** 60% are state residents. 93% Black, 6% White, 1% Other.
**Foreign students:** 19 students are from out of the country. Countries represented include China, India, Kenya, Kuwait, and Nigeria.

**PROGRAMS OF STUDY. Degrees:** B.A., B.A.Soc.Work, B.F.A., B.Info.Sys., B.Mus., B.S.
**Majors:** Accounting, Agricultural Business/Economics, Agricultural Mechanization, Agriculture, Animal Science/Pre-Veterinary Medicine, Applied Music, Biology, Business Administration, Business Education/Office Management, Business Information Systems, Chemistry, Economics, Elementary Education, Engineering-Related Technologies, English, Environmental Science, Food Marketing/Food Industry, Foreign Languages, Geology, Health Education, History, Home Economics/Business, Home Economics Education, Hotel/Restaurant Management, Industrial Arts Education, Industrial Technology, International Studies, Management, Mathematics, Music Education, Physical Education, Physics, Plant/Soils/Water Science, Political Science, Psychology, Public Administration, Recreation Education, Social Welfare, Sociology, Special Education, Statistics, Vocational Industrial Education.
**Requirements:** General education requirement.
**Special:** Courses offered in drama, geography, journalism, non-Western studies, and speech. Double majors. Dual degrees. Internships. Preprofessional programs in law, medicine, theology, allied health fields, business, nursing, and physical therapy. 3-2 math/engineering program with Old Dominion U. Teacher certification in early childhood, elementary, secondary, and special education. ROTC.
**Honors:** Phi Beta Kappa. Honors program.

**STUDENT LIFE. Housing:** Women's and men's dorms. 54% of students live in college housing.
**Social atmosphere:** On campus, students frequent Foster Hall and Jones Dining Hall. Sororities and fraternities, Big Brothers/Big Sisters, New Generations Ministries, and the Trojan Cheerleaders are influential on student life. The CIAA basketball tournament and Homecoming are highlights of the school year.
**Services and counseling/handicapped student services:** Placement services. Health service. Counseling services for military and veteran students. Personal counseling. Career and academic guidance services. Religious counseling.
**Campus organizations:** Undergraduate student government. Student newspaper (Virginia Statesman, published once/two weeks). Yearbook. Radio station. Choir, dance band, concert and marching bands, ROTC band, orchestra, debating, drama club, Theatre Guild, Orchesis Dance Group, academic, service, and special-interest groups. Four fraternities, no chapter houses; four sororities, no chapter houses.
**Religious organizations:** Several religious groups.

**ATHLETICS. Physical education requirements:** Four semester hours of physical education required.
**Intercollegiate competition:** 15% of students participate. Baseball (M), basketball (M,W), cheerleading (W), cross-country (M,W), football (M), tennis (M), track and field (indoor) (M,W), track and field (outdoor) (M,W). Member of Central Intercollegiate Athletic Association, NCAA Division II.
**Intramural and club sports:** 10% of students participate. Intramural basketball, flag football, softball, volleyball.

**ADMISSIONS. Academic basis for candidate selection** (in order of priority): Secondary school record, standardized test scores, class rank, school's recommendation.
**Nonacademic basis for candidate selection:** Character and personality and geographical distribution are important. Extracurricular participation, particular talent or ability, and alumni/ae relationship are considered.
**Requirements:** Graduation from secondary school is required; GED is accepted. No specific distribution of secondary school units required. Minimum 2.0 GPA recommended. Qualifying exams required of music program applicants. SAT is required; ACT may be substituted. Campus visit recommended. No off-campus interviews.
**Procedure:** Take SAT or ACT by January of 12th year. Notification of admission on rolling basis. Reply is required by May 1 or within two weeks of acceptance. $150 refundable room deposit. Freshmen accepted for terms other than fall.
**Special programs:** Admission may be deferred one semester. Credit may be granted through CEEB Advanced Placement for scores of 3 or higher. Credit and/or placement may be granted through CLEP general and subject exams. Concurrent enrollment program.
**Transfer students:** Transfer students accepted for terms other than fall. Application deadline is May 1 for fall; October 1 for spring. Minimum 2.0 GPA recommended. Lowest course grade accepted is "C." At least 30 semester hours must be completed at the university to receive degree.
**Admissions contact:** Karen Winston, Interim Director of Admissions. 804 524-5902.

**FINANCIAL AID. Available aid:** Pell grants, SEOG, state scholarships and grants, school scholarships, private scholarships and grants, ROTC scholarships, academic merit scholarships, and athletic scholarships. Perkins Loans (NDSL), PLUS, state loans, and SLS.
**Supporting data/closing dates:** FAFSA/FAF/FFS: Priority filing date is March 30. School's own aid application: Priority filing date is March 30. Income tax forms: Priority filing date is March 30. Notification of awards begins April 1.
**Financial aid contact:** Henry Debose, Director of Financial Aid. 804 524-5990.

**STUDENT EMPLOYMENT.** College Work/Study Program. Institutional employment. 16% of full-time undergraduates work on campus during school year. Students may expect to earn an average of $1,650 during school year. Freshmen are discouraged from working during their first term. Off-campus part-time employment opportunities rated "good."

**COMPUTER FACILITIES.** 75 IBM/IBM-compatible and Macintosh/Apple microcomputers. Students may access IBM minicomputer/mainframe systems. Computer languages and software packages include BASIC, COBOL, dBASE II, DisplayWrite III, FORTRAN, Lotus 1-2-3, MUSIC, SPSS, WordPerfect. Computer facilities are available to all students.
**Fees:** None.
**Hours:** 8 AM-9 PM (M-F); 8 AM-5 PM (Sa).

# Virginia Union University

**Richmond, VA 23220** 804 257-5600

**1994-95 Costs.** Tuition: $7,384. Room & board: $3,494. Fees, books, misc. academic expenses (school's estimate): $1,458.
**Enrollment.** Undergraduates: 529 men, 619 women (full-time). Freshman class: 1,439 applicants, 1,397 accepted, 392 enrolled. Graduate enrollment: 118 men, 33 women.
**Test score averages/ranges.** Average SAT scores: 309 verbal, 341 math. Range of SAT scores of middle 50%: 300-399 verbal, 300-399 math.
**Faculty.** 78 full-time; 37 part-time. 41% of faculty holds doctoral degree. Student/faculty ratio: 16 to 1.
**Selectivity rating.** Noncompetitive.

**PROFILE.** Virginia Union, founded in 1865, is a church-affiliated, historically black university. Programs are offered through the College of Liberal Arts and Sciences and the Graduate School of Theology. Its 55-acre campus is located in Richmond.

**Accreditation:** CCA-ACICS, SACS.
**Religious orientation:** Virginia Union University is affiliated with the American Baptist Convention; one semester of religion required.
**Library:** Collections totaling over 140,524 volumes, 386 periodical subscriptions and 3 microform items.
**Special facilities/museums:** Museum of African art, language lab.

**STUDENT BODY. Undergraduate profile:** 52% are state residents; 12% are transfers. 1% Asian-American, 97% Black, 1% White, 1% Other. Average age of undergraduates is 21.
**Freshman profile:** 93% of accepted applicants took SAT. 99% of freshmen come from public schools.
**Foreign students:** Eight students are from out of the country. Countries represented include African countries.

**PROGRAMS OF STUDY. Degrees:** B.A., B.S.
**Majors:** Accounting, Biology, Biology Education, Business Administration, Chemistry, Chemistry Education, Early Childhood Education, Elementary Education, English, English Education, French, French Education, History Education, History/Political Science, Journalism, Mathematics, Mathematics Education, Music, Music Education, Philosophy/Religion, Psychology, Recreation, Social Work, Sociology, Special Education.
**Distribution of degrees:** The majors with the highest enrollment are business administration, history/political science, and accounting; chemistry education and French have the lowest.
**Requirements:** General education requirement.
**Academic regulations:** Minimum 2.0 GPA must be maintained.
**Special:** Minors offered in computer science, banking, pre-law, gerontology, and criminal justice. Dual degrees. Independent study. Internships. Preprofessional programs in law, medicine, pharmacy, dentistry, chemical research, journalism, library science, medical technology, scientific aid, and theology. 3-3 law program with St. John's U. 3-2 engineering programs with Howard U, U of Iowa, and U of Michigan. Member of Consortium of Central Virginia. Faculty and student exchange programs with Concordia Coll (Moorhead) and Fort Lewis Coll. ROTC.
**Honors:** Honors program.
**Academic Assistance:** Remedial reading and study skills. Nonremedial tutoring.

**STUDENT LIFE. Housing:** Coed, women's, and men's dorms. 55% of students live in college housing.
**Social atmosphere:** The Henderson Center is a favorite hang-out. The Student Government Association has widespread influence on campus life. Favorite on-campus events include basketball and football games, homecoming, Gold Bowl, and graduation.
**Services and counseling/handicapped student services:** Placement services. Health service. Testing service. Counseling services for older students. Birth control, personal, and psychological counseling. Career and academic guidance services.
**Campus organizations:** Undergraduate student government. Student newspaper (Informer, published once/month). Yearbook. Choir, band, University Players, athletic, departmental, and special-interest groups, 45 organizations in all. Four fraternities, all with chapter houses; four sororities, all with chapter houses. 40% of men join a fraternity. 40% of women join a sorority.
**Religious organizations:** Charisma Women's Association, Council of Religion, J.E. Jones Lyceum.

**ATHLETICS. Physical education requirements:** One semester of physical education required.
**Intercollegiate competition:** Basketball (M,W), cheerleading (M,W), cross-country (M,W), football (M), golf (M), softball (W), tennis (M), track and field (M,W), volleyball (W). Member of NCAA Division II.

**ADMISSIONS. Academic basis for candidate selection** (in order of priority): Secondary school record, standardized test scores, class rank, school's recommendation, essay.
**Nonacademic basis for candidate selection:** Character and personality, extracurricular participation, and particular talent or ability are important. Alumni/ae relationship is considered.
**Requirements:** Graduation from secondary school is required; GED is accepted. 16 units and the following program of study are required: 4 units of English, 3 units of math, 2 units of science, 2 units of foreign language, 2 units of social studies, 3 units of academic electives. Audition required of music program applicants. Conditional admission possible for applicants not meeting standard requirements. SAT is required; ACT may be substituted. Campus visit and interview recommended. Off-campus interviews available with an admissions representative.
**Procedure:** Take SAT or ACT by March of 12th year. Suggest filing application by March 1. Application deadline is August 15. Notification of admission on rolling basis. Reply is required within three weeks of notification. $25 nonrefundable tuition deposit. $25 room deposit, refundable until July 1. Freshmen accepted for terms other than fall.
**Special programs:** Admission may be deferred one year. Placement may be granted through ACT PEP exams. Early decision program. In fall 1991, 121 applied for early decision and 80 were accepted. Deadline for applying for early decision is January 31. Early entrance/early admission program. Concurrent enrollment program.
**Transfer students:** Transfer students accepted for terms other than fall. In fall 1991, 12% of all new students were transfers into all classes. 128 transfer applications were received, 110 were accepted. Application deadline is March 1 for fall; November 1 for spring. Minimum 2.0 GPA required. Lowest course grade accepted is "C." Maximum number of transferable credits is 60 semester hours. At least 30 semester hours must be completed at the university to receive degree.
**Admissions contact:** Gil M. Powell, B.A., Director of Admissions. 804 257-5881.

**FINANCIAL AID. Available aid:** Pell grants, SEOG, state grants, school scholarships, private scholarships, academic merit scholarships, and athletic scholarships. Perkins Loans (NDSL), PLUS, Stafford Loans (GSL), and SLS. Deferred payment plan.
**Financial aid statistics:** Average amounts of aid awarded freshmen: Scholarships and grants, $2,410; loans, $1,571.
**Supporting data/closing dates:** FAFSA/FAF/FFS: Priority filing date is May 15. State aid form: Priority filing date is July 31; deadline is December 1. Notification of awards on rolling basis.
**Financial aid contact:** Phennie Golatt, B.A., Director of Financial Aid. 804 257-5882.

**STUDENT EMPLOYMENT.** College Work/Study Program. Institutional employment. 31% of full-time undergraduates work on campus during school year. Students may expect to earn an average of $1,870 during school year. Off-campus part-time employment opportunities rated "fair."

**COMPUTER FACILITIES.** 124 IBM/IBM-compatible and Macintosh/Apple microcomputers; 51 are networked. Students may access Digital minicomputer/mainframe systems. Computer languages and software packages include BASIC Plus, COBOL, FORTRAN IV and 77, Lotus 1-2-3, SPSS, WordPerfect. Computer facilities are available to all students.
**Fees:** None.
**Hours:** 8:30 AM-4:30 PM.

**GRADUATE CAREER DATA.** 60% of graduates choose careers in business and industry. Companies and businesses that hire graduates: Federal government.

**PROMINENT ALUMNI/AE.** Henry Marsh, former mayor of Richmond; Charles Oakley, New York Knicks; L. Douglas Wilder, governor of Virginia; Roy West, mayor of Richmond.

# Virginia Wesleyan College

**Norfolk/Virginia Beach, VA 23502** 804 455-3200

**1993-94 Costs.** Tuition: $10,150. Room & board: $4,800. Fees, books, misc. academic expenses (school's estimate): $690.
**Enrollment.** Undergraduates: 456 men, 684 women (full-time). Freshman class: 1,463 applicants, 880 accepted, 288 enrolled.
**Test score averages/ranges.** Range of SAT scores of middle 50%: 460-600 verbal, 470-600 math.
**Faculty.** 73 full-time; 21 part-time. 85% of faculty holds highest degree in specific field. Student/faculty ratio: 16 to 1.
**Selectivity rating.** Competitive.

**PROFILE.** Virginia Wesleyan, founded in 1961, is a private, church-affiliated, liberal arts college. Its 300-acre campus is located in Norfolk.

**Accreditation:** SACS. Professionally accredited by the National Recreation and Park Association.
**Religious orientation:** Virginia Wesleyan College is affiliated with the United Methodist Church; no religious requirements.
**Library:** Collections totaling over 103,369 volumes, 569 periodical subscriptions, and 12,553 microform items.
**Special facilities/museums:** Greenhouse, language lab.
**Athletic facilities:** Gymnasium, weight rooms, tennis courts, baseball, field hockey, soccer, and softball fields.

**STUDENT BODY. Undergraduate profile:** 66% are state residents; 47% are transfers. 3% Asian-American, 6% Black, 3% Hispanic, .4% Native American, 87% White, .6% Other. Average age of undergraduates is 19.
**Freshman profile:** 5% of freshmen who took SAT scored 700 or over on verbal, 5% scored 700 or over on math; 31% scored 600 or over on verbal, 36% scored 600 or over on math; 66% scored 500 or over on verbal, 73% scored 500 or over on math; 100% scored 400 or over on verbal, 100% scored 400 or over on math. 99% of accepted applicants took SAT. 65% of freshmen come from public schools.
**Undergraduate achievement:** 85% of fall 1992 freshmen returned for fall 1993 term. 65% of entering class graduated. 25% of students who completed a degree program immediately went on to graduate study.
**Foreign students:** 44 students are from out of the country. Countries represented include China, Germany, Japan, Mexico, the Netherlands, and Spain; 23 in all.

**PROGRAMS OF STUDY. Degrees:** B.A.
**Majors:** Accounting, American Studies, Art, Art Education, Biology, Business, Chemistry, Communications, Computer Science/Mathematics, Education, Elementary Education, English, French, German, History, Human Services, International Studies, Journalism, Liberal Arts Management, Mathematics, Modern Foreign Languages, Music, Music Education, Philosophy, Philosophy/Religion, Political Science, Psychology, Recreation/Leisure Studies, Religion, Secondary Education, Social Ecology, Sociology/Anthropology, Spanish, Theatre Communication, Theatre/English, Western Cultural Heritage.
**Distribution of degrees:** The majors with the highest enrollment are business, communications, and education; mathematics, religious studies, and philosophy have the lowest.

**Requirements:** General education requirement.
**Academic regulations:** Minimum 2.0 GPA must be maintained.
**Special:** Self-designed majors. Double majors. Independent study. Pass/fail grading option. Internships. Preprofessional programs in law, medicine, veterinary science, pharmacy, dentistry, theology, and optometry. 2-2 program in business/accounting with Tidewater Comm Coll. Member of Tidewater Consortium; cross-registration with Old Dominion U, Norfolk State U, Tidewater Comm Coll, Coll of William and Mary. Teacher certification in elementary and secondary education. Certification in specific subject areas. Member of International Student Exchange Program (ISEP). Exchange programs abroad in Canada (U of Laval), France (U of Angers, U of Lyon, Schiller U), Germany (Schiller U), Mexico (U of Madero), and Spain (U of Salamanca, Schiller U).
**Honors:** Honors program. Honor societies.
**Academic Assistance:** Remedial writing, math, and study skills. Nonremedial tutoring.

**STUDENT LIFE. Housing:** All unmarried students under age 21 must live on campus unless living near campus with relatives. Coed and women's dorms. Sorority and fraternity housing. 60% of students live in college housing.
**Social atmosphere:** The student newspaper writes that the Central Tidewater area "provides many opportunities for entertainment and culture, from the nightclubs at the 'strips' to several museums and small theatres. The Greek organization is alive and thriving at VWC. The Christian fellowship groups are growing as well." The soccer, baseball, and softball seasons are popular with students, as are events such as Homecoming, the Fall Play, the Spring Art Show, Comedy Night, the Air Band Contest, and the Mr. Wesleyan Contest. Students like to gather in Virginia Beach and at nightclubs, malls, Daryl's, and Chi-Chi's.
**Services and counseling/handicapped student services:** Placement services. Health service. Counseling services for minority, military, veteran, and older students. Personal and psychological counseling. Career and academic guidance services. Religious counseling. Physically disabled student services. Learning disabled services. Notetaking services. Tape recorders. Tutors.
**Campus organizations:** Undergraduate student government. Student newspaper (Marlin Chronicle, published three times/semester). Literary magazine. Yearbook. Radio station. Student Activities Council, computer, psychology, political science, and surf clubs, recreation majors club, Student Education Association, chamber singers, Student Ecological Awareness League, Amnesty International, Gamer's club, Habitat for Humanity, College Republicans, Young Democrats, departmental and special-interest groups, 56 organizations in all. Three fraternities, all with chapter houses; three sororities, all with chapter houses. 15% of men join a fraternity. 10% of women join a sorority.
**Religious organizations:** Religious Life Council, Campus Catholic Ministry, Christian Fellowship Gaius (Christian performing arts), Hillel, Wings.
**Minority/foreign student organizations:** Minority Student Alliance, African American Society. International Awareness Council, UN Society.

**ATHLETICS. Physical education requirements:** None.
**Intercollegiate competition:** 3% of students participate. Baseball (M), basketball (M,W), cheerleading (M,W), field hockey (W), golf (M), lacrosse (M), soccer (M,W), softball (W), tennis (M,W). Member of NCAA Division III, Old Dominion Athletic Conference.
**Intramural and club sports:** 1% of students participate. Intramural badminton, basketball, flag football, indoor soccer, softball, tennis, volleyball.

**ADMISSIONS. Academic basis for candidate selection** (in order of priority): Secondary school record, standardized test scores, class rank, school's recommendation, essay.
**Nonacademic basis for candidate selection:** Character and personality, extracurricular participation, particular talent or ability, geographical distribution, and alumni/ae relationship are considered.
**Requirements:** Graduation from secondary school is required; GED is accepted. 16 units and the following program of study are recommended: 4 units of English, 3 units of math, 3 units of science including 2 units of lab, 2 units of foreign language, 2 units of social studies, 1 unit of history, 1 unit of electives. Minimum combined SAT score of 850, rank in top half of secondary school class, and minimum 2.75 GPA recommended. SAT is required; ACT may be substituted. PSAT is recommended. Campus visit and interview recommended. No off-campus interviews.
**Procedure:** Take SAT or ACT by November of 12th year. Visit college for interview by March of 12th year. Application deadline is March 1. Notification of admission by April 1. Reply is required by May 1. $300 nonrefundable tuition deposit. $200 nonrefundable room deposit. Freshmen accepted for terms other than fall.
**Special programs:** Admission may be deferred one year. Credit and/or placement may be granted through CEEB Advanced Placement exams for scores of 3 or higher. Credit and/or placement may be granted through CLEP general and subject exams. Placement may be granted through Regents College, ACT PEP, and challenge exams. Credit and placement may be granted through DANTES exams, and military and life experience. Early decision program. In fall 1993, 45 applied for early decision and 33 were accepted. Deadline for applying for early decision is December 1. Early entrance/early admission program. Concurrent enrollment program.
**Transfer students:** Transfer students accepted for terms other than fall. In fall 1993, 47% of all new students were transfers into all classes. 250 transfer applications were received, 200 were accepted. Application deadline is June 1 for fall; December 1 for spring. Minimum 2.0 GPA required. Lowest course grade accepted is "C." Maximum number of transferable credits is 64 semester hours. At least 30 semester hours must be completed at the college to receive degree.
**Admissions contact:** W. Steve Stocks, M.A., Vice President for Admission and Financial Aid. 804 455-3208.

**FINANCIAL AID. Available aid:** Pell grants, SEOG, state scholarships and grants, school scholarships and grants, private scholarships, and academic merit scholarships. Perkins Loans (NDSL), PLUS, Stafford Loans (GSL), and SLS. Knight Tuition Plans.
**Financial aid statistics:** 30% of aid is not need-based. In 1993-94, 90% of all undergraduate applicants received aid; 92% of freshman applicants. Average amounts of aid awarded freshmen: Scholarships and grants, $3,500; loans, $2,600.
**Supporting data/closing dates:** FAFSA/FAF: Priority filing date is March 1; accepted on rolling basis. Income tax forms: Accepted on rolling basis. Notification of awards begins March 15.
**Financial aid contact:** Eugenia F. Hickman, Director of Financial Aid. 804 455-3345.

**STUDENT EMPLOYMENT.** College Work/Study Program. 20% of full-time undergraduates work on campus during school year. Students may expect to earn an average of $1,500 during school year. Off-campus part-time employment opportunities rated "excellent."

**COMPUTER FACILITIES.** 30 IBM/IBM-compatible and Macintosh/Apple microcomputers; 10 are networked. Students may access Prime minicomputer/mainframe systems. Client/LAN operating systems include DOS. Computer languages and software packages include Assembler, COBOL, FORTRAN, LISP, Paradox, Pascal, Prolog, Quattro Pro, Reflex, Turbo BASIC, Turbo C, Turbo Pascal, WordPerfect. Computer facilities are available to all students.
**Fees:** Computer fee is included in tuition/fees.
**Hours:** 9 AM-midn.

**GRADUATE CAREER DATA.** Graduate school percentages: 10% enter law school. 7% enter medical school. 1% enter dental school. 10% enter graduate business programs. 8% enter graduate arts and sciences programs. 2% enter theological school/seminary. Highest graduate school enrollments: Medical Coll of Virginia, Old Dominion U, Coll of William and Mary. 50% of graduates choose careers in business and industry. Companies and businesses that hire graduates: NationsBank, Virginia Beach schools, WAVY TV.

**PROMINENT ALUMNI/AE.** Dr. Charles K. Barletta, dean of continuing education, American U in Cairo, Egypt; Martha "Lou" Mulford Greig, model and actress; Colon H. Whitehurst, general district court judge; Dr. Robert F. Saul, neuro-ophthalmologist.

# Washington and Lee University

**Lexington, VA 24450** **703 463-8400**

**1994-95 Costs.** Tuition: $13,750. Room & board: $4,620. Fees, books, misc. academic expenses (school's estimate): $815.
**Enrollment.** Undergraduates: 947 men, 636 women (full-time). Freshman class: 3,433 applicants, 986 accepted, 435 enrolled. Graduate enrollment: 216 men, 144 women.
**Test score averages/ranges.** Range of SAT scores of middle 50%: 564-644 verbal, 610-697 math. Range of ACT scores of middle 50%: 27-30 composite.
**Faculty.** 139 full-time. 95% of faculty holds doctoral degree. Student/faculty ratio: 11 to 1.
**Selectivity rating.** Most competitive.

**PROFILE.** Washington and Lee is a private university. Founded as an academy in 1749, it was a university for men until coeducation was adopted in 1985. Programs are offered through the College; the School of Commerce, Economics, and Politics; and the School of Law. Its 50-acre main campus is located in Lexington, approximately 50 miles north of Roanoke and Lynchburg.
**Accreditation:** SACS. Professionally accredited by the Accrediting Council on Education in Journalism and Mass Communication.
**Religious orientation:** Washington and Lee University is nonsectarian; no religious requirements.
**Library:** Collections totaling over 402,742 volumes, 1,492 periodical subscriptions, and 116,388 microform items.
**Special facilities/museums:** History and porcelain museums, performing arts center, communications and nuclear science labs, observatory, scanning electron microscope.
**Athletic facilities:** Gymnasiums, stadium, swimming pools, basketball, handball, racquetball, squash, and tennis courts, track, weight and wrestling rooms, baseball, football, lacrosse, practice, soccer fields, cross-country trail, sauna, pavilion.

**STUDENT BODY. Undergraduate profile:** 14% are state residents; 1% are transfers. 1% Asian-American, 3% Black, 1% Hispanic, 94% White, 1% Other. Average age of undergraduates is 20.
**Freshman profile:** 6% of freshmen who took SAT scored 700 or over on verbal, 22% scored 700 or over on math; 50% scored 600 or over on verbal, 81% scored 600 or over on math; 98% scored 500 or over on verbal, 99% scored 500 or over on math; 100% scored 400 or over on verbal, 100% scored 400 or over on math. 89% of accepted applicants took SAT; 11% took ACT. 64% of freshmen come from public schools.
**Undergraduate achievement:** 95% of fall 1992 freshmen returned for fall 1993 term. 85% of entering class graduated. 25% of students who completed a degree program immediately went on to graduate study.
**Foreign students:** 21 students are from out of the country. Countries represented include Germany, Greece, Hong Kong, Italy, Japan, and the former Soviet Republics; 16 in all.

**PROGRAMS OF STUDY. Degrees:** B.A., B.S.
**Majors:** Anthropology, Art, Biology, Business Administration, Business Administration/Accounting, Chemistry, Chemistry/Engineering, Classics, Cognitive Science, Commerce, Computer/Information Sciences, East Asian Studies, Economics, Engineering Physics, English, Environmental Studies, French, Geology, Geophysics, German, History, Interdisciplinary Studies, Journalism, Mathematics, Music, Natural Science/Mathematics, Neuroscience, Philosophy, Physics, Politics, Pre-Law, Pre-Medicine, Psychology, Public Policy, Religion, Romance Languages, Russian Studies, Sociology, Sociology/Anthropology, Spanish, Theatre.
**Distribution of degrees:** The majors with the highest enrollment are history, economics, and journalism; anthropology, computer/information sciences, and mathematics have the lowest.
**Requirements:** General education requirement.
**Academic regulations:** Freshmen must maintain minimum 1.5 GPA; sophomores, 1.6 GPA; juniors, 1.8 GPA; seniors, 1.9 GPA.
**Special:** Double majors. Independent study. Pass/fail grading option. Internships. Preprofessional programs in law, medicine, and engineering. 3-1 forestry and environmental studies program with Duke U. 3-2 and 4-2 engineering programs with Columbia U and Rensselaer Polytech Inst. Member of Interuniversity Consortium for Political and Social Research and seven-college consortium. Washington Semester. Exchange programs

abroad in Denmark (U of Copenhagen), Hong Kong (Chun Chi Coll of the Chinese U), and Japan (Kansai Gaidai, Rikkyo U). Study abroad also in England, France, the Galapagos Islands, Germany, Greece, Italy, Russia, Spain, and Taiwan.
**Honors:** Phi Beta Kappa. Honors program. Honor societies.
**Academic Assistance:** Nonremedial tutoring.

**STUDENT LIFE. Housing:** All freshmen must live on campus unless living with family. Coed dorms. Fraternity housing. School-owned/operated apartments. 79% of students live in college housing.
**Services and counseling/handicapped student services:** Placement services. Health service. Counseling services for minority and veteran students. Birth control, personal, and psychological counseling. Career and academic guidance services. Religious counseling. Learning disabled services.
**Campus organizations:** Undergraduate student government. Student newspaper (Ring-Tum Phi, published once/week). Literary magazine. Yearbook. Radio and TV stations. Brass and jazz ensembles, concert guild, glee clubs, orchestra, theatre, film societies, debating, Mock Convention, outing club, Amnesty International, professional and special-interest groups. 16 fraternities, all with chapter houses; four sororities, no chapter houses. 80% of men join a fraternity. 60% of women join a sorority.
**Religious organizations:** Fellowship of Christian Athletes, Intervarsity Christian Fellowship.
**Minority/foreign student organizations:** Minority Student Association. International Club.

**ATHLETICS. Physical education requirements:** Five terms of physical education required.
**Intercollegiate competition:** 37% of students participate. Baseball (M), basketball (M,W), cross-country (M,W), football (M), golf (M), lacrosse (M,W), soccer (M,W), swimming (M,W), tennis (M,W), track (indoor) (M,W), track (outdoor) (M,W), track and field (indoor) (M,W), track and field (outdoor) (M,W), volleyball (W), water polo (M), wrestling (M). Member of Eastern Water Polo Association, NCAA Division III, Old Dominion Athletic Conference.
**Intramural and club sports:** 75% of students participate. Intramural aerobics, basketball, bowling, box lacrosse, cross-country, golf, handball, racquetball, soccer, softball, squash, swimming, table tennis, tennis, touch football, track and field, tug-of-war, volleyball, wrestling. Men's club fencing, ice hockey, lacrosse, rugby, soccer, squash, volleyball. Women's club basketball, fencing, field hockey, softball.

**ADMISSIONS. Academic basis for candidate selection** (in order of priority): Secondary school record, class rank, school's recommendation, standardized test scores, essay.
**Nonacademic basis for candidate selection:** Character and personality are important. Extracurricular participation, particular talent or ability, geographical distribution, and alumni/ae relationship are considered.
**Requirements:** Graduation from secondary school is required; GED is not accepted. 16 units and the following program of study are required: 4 units of English, 3 units of math, 1 unit of lab science, 2 units of foreign language, 1 unit of social studies, 1 unit of history, 3 units of electives. Other subjects may be considered. SAT or ACT is required. ACH required. Campus visit and interview recommended. Off-campus interviews available with an alumni representative.
**Procedure:** Take SAT or ACT by January of 12th year. Take ACH by January of 12th year. Visit college for interview by February of 12th year. Application deadline is January 15. Notification of admission by April 1. Reply is required by May 1. $400 nonrefundable tuition deposit. $100 nonrefundable room deposit. Freshmen accepted for fall terms only.
**Special programs:** Admission may be deferred one year. Credit and/or placement may be granted through CEEB Advanced Placement exams. Placement may be granted through challenge exams. Early decision program. In fall 1993, 329 applied for early decision and 143 were accepted. Deadline for applying for early decision is December 1.
**Transfer students:** Transfer students accepted for terms other than fall. In fall 1993, 1% of all new students were transfers into all classes. 135 transfer applications were received, 16 were accepted. Application deadline is April 1 for fall; November 1 for spring. Minimum 2.0 GPA required. Lowest course grade accepted is "C." Maximum number of transferable credits is 87 semester hours. At least 60 semester hours must be completed at the university to receive degree.
**Admissions contact:** William M. Hartog, M.S.C., Dean of Admission and Financial Aid. 703 463-8710.

**FINANCIAL AID. Available aid:** Pell grants, SEOG, state scholarships and grants, school scholarships and grants, private scholarships and grants, academic merit scholarships, and aid for undergraduate foreign students. Perkins Loans (NDSL), PLUS, Stafford Loans (GSL), school loans, private loans, and SLS. Knight Tuition Plans.
**Financial aid statistics:** 28% of aid is not need-based. In 1993-94, 86% of all undergraduate applicants received aid; 78% of freshman applicants. Average amounts of aid awarded freshmen: Scholarships and grants, $6,580; loans, $2,275.
**Supporting data/closing dates:** FAFSA/FAF: Priority filing date is February 1. State aid form: Priority filing date is May 1. Income tax forms: Priority filing date is April 30. Notification of awards begins April 1.
**Financial aid contact:** John H. DeCourcy, M.A.T., Director of Financial Aid. 703 463-8715.

**STUDENT EMPLOYMENT.** College Work/Study Program. Institutional employment. 15% of full-time undergraduates work on campus during school year. Students may expect to earn an average of $1,150 during school year. Off-campus part-time employment opportunities rated "fair."

**COMPUTER FACILITIES.** 160 IBM/IBM-compatible, Macintosh/Apple, and RISC-/UNIX-based microcomputers; 120 are networked. Students may access Hewlett-Packard, Prime minicomputer/mainframe systems, Internet. Residence halls may be equipped with stand-alone microcomputers, networked terminals. Client/LAN operating systems include Apple/Macintosh. Computer languages and software packages include dBASE, Quattro, WordPerfect. Computer facilities are available to all students.
**Fees:** Computer fee is included in tuition/fees.
**Hours:** 24 hours.

**GRADUATE CAREER DATA.** Graduate school percentages: 7% enter law school. 4% enter medical school. 2% enter dental school. 2% enter graduate business programs. 8% enter graduate arts and sciences programs. 1% enter theological school/seminary. Highest graduate school enrollments: U of North Carolina at Chapel Hill, Vanderbilt U, U of Virginia, Wake Forest U. 40% of graduates choose careers in business and industry. Companies and businesses that hire graduates: Arthur Andersen, First Union Bank, The Hecht Co.

**PROMINENT ALUMNI/AE.** Lewis F. Powell, Jr., justice, U.S. Supreme Court; Roger Mudd, TV journalist; Tom Wolfe, author, *The Right Stuff;* Dr. Joseph Goldstein, 1985 Nobel Prize-winner, medicine; John Warner, U.S. senator.

# Washington

## Central Washington University

**Ellensburg, WA 98926** **509 963-1111**

**1994-95 Costs.** Tuition: $1,971 (state residents), $6,948 (out-of-state). Room & board: $3,415. Fees, books, misc. academic expenses (school's estimate): $669.

**Enrollment.** Undergraduates: 3,663 men, 3,648 women (full-time). Freshman class: 2,785 applicants, 2,011 accepted, 1,113 enrolled. Graduate enrollment: 119 men, 162 women.

**Test score averages/ranges.** N/A.

**Faculty.** 287 full-time; 98 part-time. 83% of faculty holds doctoral degree. Student/faculty ratio: 20 to 1.

**Selectivity rating.** Competitive.

**PROFILE.** Central Washington, founded in 1891, is a public university. Programs offered in the College of Letters, Arts, and Sciences; the Schools of Business and Economics and Professional Studies; and Special Programs. Its 350-acre campus is located in Ellensburg, 110 miles from Seattle.

**Accreditation:** NASC. Professionally accredited by the Accreditation Board for Engineering and Technology, the National Association of Schools of Music, the National Council for Accreditation of Teacher Education.

**Religious orientation:** Central Washington University is nonsectarian; no religious requirements.

**Library:** Collections totaling over 466,203 volumes, 2,276 periodical subscriptions, and 825,352 microform items.

**Special facilities/museums:** Language lab, environmental learning center, marine lab, primate lab, geographical information systems lab.

**Athletic facilities:** Gymnasium, swimming pool, field house, dance studio, training, weight, and wrestling rooms, baseball, football, and soccer fields, handball, racquetball, and tennis courts, track/field stadium.

**STUDENT BODY. Undergraduate profile:** 96% are state residents; 50% are transfers. 3% Asian-American, 2% Black, 3% Hispanic, 2% Native American, 90% White. Average age of undergraduates is 23.

**Freshman profile:** 2% of freshmen who took SAT scored 700 or over on verbal, 2% scored 700 or over on math; 8% scored 600 or over on verbal, 15% scored 600 or over on math; 27% scored 500 or over on verbal, 42% scored 500 or over on math; 84% scored 400 or over on verbal, 90% scored 400 or over on math; 100% scored 300 or over on verbal, 100% scored 300 or over on math. 3% of freshmen who took ACT scored 30 or over on composite; 24% scored 24 or over on composite; 95% scored 18 or over on composite; 98% scored 12 or over on composite; 100% scored 6 or over on composite.

**Undergraduate achievement:** 92% of fall 1992 freshmen returned for fall 1993 term. 49% of entering class graduated.

**Foreign students:** 154 students are from out of the country. Countries represented include China, Costa Rica, Italy, Japan, Korea, and Mexico; 38 in all.

**PROGRAMS OF STUDY. Degrees:** B.A., B.A.Ed., B.Mus., B.S.

**Majors:** Accounting, Administrative Office Management, Anthropology, Art, Bilingual Intercultural Major for Elementary Teaching, Bilingual/Language Arts, Biology, Business Administration, Business Education, Chemistry, Community Health Education, Computer Science, Construction Management, Drama, Early Childhood Education, Earth Science, Economics, Electronics Engineering Technology, Elementary Education, English, Family/Consumer Studies, Fashion Merchandising, Fitness/Sport Management, Flight Technology, Food Science/Nutrition, French, Geography, Geology, German, Gerontology, Graphic Design, History, Home Economics, Individual Studies, Industrial Education, Industrial Supervision, Industrial Technology, Language Arts, Law/Justice, Leisure Services, Loss Control Management, Manufacturing Engineering Technology, Marketing Education, Mass Communication, Mathematics, Mechanical Engineering Technology, Military Science, Music, Paramedic, Philosophy, Physical Education, Physics, Political Science, Primate Studies, Psychology, Public Relations, School Health Education, Science/Mathematics, Social Science, Social Services, Sociology, Spanish, Special Education, Speech Communication, Vocational-Technical Trade/Industrial Major.

**Distribution of degrees:** The majors with the highest enrollment are business, accounting, and education; paramedic, geology, and geography have the lowest.

**Requirements:** General education requirement.

**Academic regulations:** Minimum 2.0 GPA required for graduation.

**Special:** Minors offered in some majors and in art history, Asian studies, crafts, data processing, educational media, electronics/electricity, energy studies, engineering graphics, environmental studies, gifted education, Latin American studies, organizational communication, physical sciences, reading, and women's studies. Land studies program. Numerous certificate programs. Flight Officers/Flight Tech programs. Self-designed majors. Double majors. Dual degrees. Independent study. Pass/fail grading option. Internships. Cooperative education programs. Graduate school at which undergraduates may take graduate-level courses. Preprofessional programs in law, medicine, pharmacy, and dentistry. Physics engineering programs with U of Washington and Washington State U. Teacher certification in early childhood, elementary, secondary, and special education. Member of International Student Exchange Program (ISEP). ROTC and AFROTC.

**Honors:** Honors program.

**Academic Assistance:** Remedial reading, writing, and math. Nonremedial tutoring.

**STUDENT LIFE. Housing:** All freshmen under age 21 must live on campus. Coed dorms. School-owned/operated apartments. On-campus married-student housing. Quiet dorm. 61% of students live in college housing.

**Services and counseling/handicapped student services:** Placement services. Health service. Women's center. Day care. Counseling services for minority and veteran students. Birth control and personal counseling. Career guidance services. Physically disabled student services. Learning disabled services. Notetaking services. Reader services for the blind.

**Campus organizations:** Undergraduate student government. Student newspaper (Observer, published once/week). Radio and TV stations. Band, choirs, ensembles, drama group, Model UN, departmental, service, and special-interest groups, 100 organizations in all.

**Religious organizations:** Baptist Student Union, Campus Catholic Ministry, Christian Fellowship, CMA Salt Company, Lutheran Student Movement, Oasis, United Ministries in Higher Education.

**Minority/foreign student organizations:** MEChA, Aloha Club, Native American Council, Minority Student Association, Black Student Union. International Club, International Business Club, International Reading Club.

**ATHLETICS. Physical education requirements:** Two terms of physical education required.

**Intercollegiate competition:** 10% of students participate. Baseball (M), basketball (M,W), cheerleading (M,W), cross-country (M,W), diving (M,W), football (M), golf (M), soccer (M,W), softball (W), swimming (M,W), tennis (M,W), track and field (indoor) (M,W), track and field (outdoor) (M,W), volleyball (W), wrestling (M). Member of Columbia Football Association, NAIA.

**Intramural and club sports:** Intramural basketball, flag football, pickleball, racquetball, soccer, softball, tennis, volleyball. Men's club rugby. Women's club rugby.

**ADMISSIONS. Academic basis for candidate selection** (in order of priority): Secondary school record, standardized test scores, class rank, school's recommendation, essay.

**Nonacademic basis for candidate selection:** Character and personality and extracurricular participation are considered.

**Requirements:** Graduation from secondary school is required; GED is accepted. 15 units and the following program of study are required: 4 units of English, 3 units of math, 2 units of science including 1 unit of lab, 2 units of foreign language, 3 units of social studies, 1 unit of academic electives. University uses Eligibility Index based on test scores and GPA, with approximately one-third emphasis on test scores and two-thirds on GPA; index minimum is 13. Minimum 2.5 GPA required. Teachers Educational Test (TET) and minimum 3.0 GPA required of teaching applicants. EMT certification required of paramedic applicants. Academic Access Program for applicants not normally admissible. SAT or ACT is required. Campus visit recommended. Off-campus interviews available with an admissions representative.

**Procedure:** Take SAT or ACT by December of 12th year. Suggest filing application by March 1; no deadline. Notification of admission on rolling basis. Reply is required by May 1. $55 tuition deposit, refundable until July 1. $60 room deposit, refundable until July 1. Freshmen accepted in terms other than fall.

**Special programs:** Credit may be granted through CEEB Advanced Placement for scores of 3 or higher. Credit may be granted through Regents College, DANTES, and challenge exams and military experience. Early entrance/early admission program. Concurrent enrollment program.

**Transfer students:** Transfer students accepted for terms other than fall. In fall 1993, 50% of all new students were transfers into all classes. 2,455 transfer applications were received, 1,859 were accepted. Application deadline is March 1 for fall; October 1 for spring. Minimum 2.5 GPA required. Lowest course grade accepted is "C."

**Admissions contact:** William Swain, Director of Admissions and Academic Advising Services. 509 963-3001.

**FINANCIAL AID. Available aid:** Pell grants, SEOG, state scholarships and grants, school scholarships and grants, private scholarships, ROTC scholarships, academic merit scholarships, and aid for undergraduate foreign students. Perkins Loans (NDSL), PLUS, Stafford Loans (GSL), and school loans. Deferred payment plan for room and board.

**Financial aid statistics:** 8% of aid is not need-based. Average amounts of aid awarded freshmen: Scholarships and grants, $352; loans, $2,252.

**Supporting data/closing dates:** FAFSA/FAF: Priority filing date is March 15. Notification of awards on rolling basis.

**Financial aid contact:** Donna Croft, Financial Aid Director. 509 963-1611.

**STUDENT EMPLOYMENT.** College Work/Study Program. Institutional employment. 31% of full-time undergraduates work on campus during school year. Students may expect to earn an average of $1,825 during school year. Off-campus part-time employment opportunities rated "good."

**COMPUTER FACILITIES.** IBM/IBM-compatible and Macintosh/Apple microcomputers. Students may access Digital minicomputer/mainframe systems, BITNET. Residence halls may be equipped with stand-alone microcomputers, networked microcomputers. Computer languages and software packages include BASIC, C-Calc, COBOL, FORTRAN, MINITAB, Modula 2, Pascal, Powerhouse, SAS, SPSS. Computer facilities are available to all students.

**Fees:** $12 computer fee per quarter; included in tuition/fees.
**Hours:** 24 hours in some locations.

**GRADUATE CAREER DATA.** 75% of graduates choose careers in business and industry. Companies and businesses that hire graduates: Boeing, Ernst & Young, state and federal government, Weyerhaeuser.

**PROMINENT ALUMNI/AE.** Al Swift, U.S. congressman; Daniel Evans, state senator; Milton Colt, president, Horizon Air.

## City University

**Bellevue, WA 98004** — **206 643-2000**

**1994-95 Costs.** Tuition: $4,800. Housing: None. Fees, books, misc. academic expenses (school's estimate): $375.
**Enrollment.** Undergraduates: 98 men, 117 women (full-time). Graduate enrollment: 1,241 men, 1,376 women.
**Test score averages/ranges.** N/A.
**Faculty.** 29 full-time; 782 part-time. 35% of faculty holds doctoral degree. Student/faculty ratio: 15 to 1.
**Selectivity rating.** N/A.

**PROFILE.** City University, founded in 1973, is a private institution. Its 10-acre campus is located in Seattle.
**Accreditation:** NASC.
**Religious orientation:** City University is nonsectarian; no religious requirements.
**Library:** Collections totaling over 10,000 volumes, 350 periodical subscriptions, and 50,000 microform items.

**STUDENT BODY. Undergraduate profile:** 5% Asian-American, 5% Black, 2% Hispanic, 1% Native American, 82% White, 5% Other.
**Foreign students:** 28 students are from out of the country. Countries represented include China, Hong Kong, Indonesia, Japan, Taiwan, and Thailand; 22 in all.

**PROGRAMS OF STUDY. Degrees:** B.S.
**Majors:** Accounting, Aviation Management, Business Management, Computer Information Systems, Fire Command Administration, General Studies, Health Care Administration, Law Enforcement Administration, Legal Administration, Management, Telecommunications Management.
**Distribution of degrees:** The majors with the highest enrollment are accounting and management; aviation management, fire command administration, and law enforcement administration have the lowest.
**Requirements:** General education requirement.
**Academic regulations:** Minimum 2.0 GPA must be maintained.
**Special:** Associate's degrees offered. Self-designed majors. Double majors. Dual degrees. Independent study. Accelerated study. Pass/fail grading option. Internships. Cooperative education programs. Graduate school at which undergraduates may take graduate-level courses. Combined M.B.A/M.P.A. program. Teacher certification in early childhood, elementary, and secondary education. Certification in specific subject areas.
**Honors:** Honors program.

**ADMISSIONS.**
**Nonacademic basis for candidate selection:** Character and personality are important.
**Requirements:** Graduation from secondary school is recommended; GED is accepted. No specific distribution of secondary school units required. Open admissions policy. Campus visit and interview recommended. Off-campus interviews available with an admissions representative.
**Procedure:** Notification of admission on rolling basis. Freshmen accepted in terms other than fall.
**Special programs:** Credit may be granted through CEEB Advanced Placement for scores of 3 or higher. Credit may be granted through CLEP general and subject exams, Regents College, ACT PEP, DANTES, and challenge exams, and military and life experience.
**Transfer students:** Transfer students accepted for terms other than fall. Application deadline is rolling for fall; rolling for spring. Minimum 2.0 GPA required. Lowest course grade accepted is "C." Maximum number of transferable credits is 135 quarter hours. At least 45 quarter hours must be completed at the university to receive degree.
**Admissions contact:** Lisa Khatib, Director of Admissions. 800 422-4898.

**FINANCIAL AID. Available aid:** Pell grants, SEOG, state scholarships, school scholarships, private scholarships and grants, and academic merit scholarships. PLUS, Stafford Loans (GSL), private loans, and SLS.
**Financial aid statistics:** 30% of aid is not need-based. In 1993-94, 99% of all undergraduate applicants received aid; 99% of freshman applicants. Average amounts of aid awarded freshmen: Scholarships and grants, $1,800; loans, $2,625.
**Supporting data/closing dates:** FAFSA/FAF/FFS: Accepted on rolling basis. School's own aid application: Accepted on rolling basis. Notification of awards on rolling basis.
**Financial aid contact:** Caroline Caldwell, Director of Financial Aid. 800 426-5596.

## Cornish College of the Arts

**Seattle, WA 98102** — **206 323-1400**

**1994-95 Costs.** Tuition: $10,000. Housing: None. Fees, books, misc. academic expenses (school's estimate): $1,057-$1,857.
**Enrollment.** Undergraduates: 211 men, 274 women (full-time). Freshman class: 574 applicants, 407 accepted, 227 enrolled.
**Test score averages/ranges.** N/A.
**Faculty.** 27 full-time; 101 part-time. 56% of faculty holds highest degree in specific field. Student/faculty ratio: 7 to 1.
**Selectivity rating.** N/A.

**PROFILE.** The Cornish Institute, founded in 1914, is a private college of the arts. Its two-acre campus is located in downtown Seattle.
**Accreditation:** NASC.
**Religious orientation:** Cornish College of the Arts is nonsectarian; no religious requirements.
**Library:** Collections totaling over 12,000 volumes and 88 periodical subscriptions.
**Special facilities/museums:** Art galleries, extensive art studio space, theatres.

**STUDENT BODY. Undergraduate profile:** 69% are state residents. 4% Asian-American, 2% Black, 3% Hispanic, 2% Native American, 78% White, 11% Other. Average age of undergraduates is 25.
**Undergraduate achievement:** 70% of fall 1992 freshmen returned for fall 1993 term. 50% of entering class graduated.
**Foreign students:** 21 students are from out of the country. Countries represented include Canada, Japan, Scotland, Sweden, Thailand, and Venezuela; 12 in all.

**PROGRAMS OF STUDY. Degrees:** B.Appl.Arts, B.F.A., B.Mus.
**Majors:** Art, Dance, Design, Music, Performance Production, Theatre.
**Distribution of degrees:** The majors with the highest enrollment are art, design, and music; performance production has the lowest.
**Requirements:** General education requirement.
**Academic regulations:** Freshmen must maintain minimum 2.0 GPA; sophomores, 2.25 GPA; juniors, 2.5 GPA; seniors, 2.5 GPA.
**Special:** Independent study. Pass/fail grading option. Internships. Exchange program abroad in Scotland (Duncan of Jordanstone Coll of Art).
**Academic Assistance:** Remedial study skills. Nonremedial tutoring.

**ADMISSIONS. Academic basis for candidate selection** (in order of priority): Secondary school record, essay, school's recommendation, standardized test scores.
**Nonacademic basis for candidate selection:** Particular talent or ability is emphasized. Character and personality are important. Extracurricular participation is considered.
**Requirements:** Graduation from secondary school is required; GED is accepted. No specific distribution of secondary school units required. No specific distribution of secondary school units required. Minimum 2.0 GPA required. Portfolio required of art, design, and performance production program applicants. Audition required of music, dance, and theatre program applicants. SAT is required; ACT may be substituted. Campus visit and interview recommended. Off-campus interviews available with an admissions representative.
**Procedure:** Take SAT or ACT by June of 12th year. Visit college for interview by May 1 of 12th year. Suggest filing application by March 31. Application deadline is August 15. Notification of admission on rolling basis. Reply is required by August 15. $50 tuition deposit, refundable until May 1. Freshmen accepted in terms other than fall.
**Special programs:** Admission may be deferred one year. Credit and/or placement may be granted through CEEB Advanced Placement exams for scores of 3 or higher. Credit and/or placement may be granted through CLEP general and subject exams. Placement may be granted through challenge exams. Credit and placement may be granted through life experience. Early entrance/early admission program. Concurrent enrollment program.
**Transfer students:** Transfer students accepted for terms other than fall. Application deadline is August 15 for fall; December 15 for spring. Minimum 2.0 GPA required. Lowest course grade accepted is "C." Maximum number of transferable credits is 60 semester hours. At least 48 semester hours must be completed at the college to receive degree.
**Admissions contact:** Jane Buckman, M.F.A., Director of Admissions and Financial Aid. 206 323-1400, extension 205.

**FINANCIAL AID. Available aid:** Pell grants, SEOG, state grants, school scholarships and grants, private scholarships and grants, and academic merit scholarships. Perkins Loans (NDSL), PLUS, Stafford Loans (GSL), private loans, and SLS. AMS and deferred payment plan.
**Financial aid statistics:** In 1993-94, 90% of all undergraduate applicants received aid; 94% of freshman applicants. Average amounts of aid awarded freshmen: Scholarships and grants, $1,250; loans, $2,625.
**Supporting data/closing dates:** FAFSA/FAF/FFS: Priority filing date is February 28; accepted on rolling basis. School's own aid application: Priority filing date is March 31; accepted on rolling basis. Income tax forms: Priority filing date is March 31; accepted on rolling basis. Notification of awards begins April 1.
**Financial aid contact:** Jane Buckman, M.F.A., Director of Admissions and Financial Aid. 206 323-1400, extension 205.

## Eastern Washington University

**Cheney, WA 99004** — **509 359-6200**

**1993-94 Costs.** Tuition: $2,256 (state residents), $7,974 (out-of-state). Room: $1,590. Board: $2,028. Fees, books, misc. academic expenses (school's estimate): $807.
**Enrollment.** Undergraduates: 2,895 men, 3,666 women (full-time). Freshman class: 2,197 applicants, 1,862 accepted, 767 enrolled. Graduate enrollment: 287 men, 407 women.
**Test score averages/ranges.** Range of SAT scores of middle 50%: 350-470 verbal, 400-520 math. Range of ACT scores of middle 50%: 18-23 composite.
**Faculty.** 64% of faculty holds doctoral degree. Student/faculty ratio: 16 to 1.
**Selectivity rating.** Less competitive.

**PROFILE.** Eastern Washington, founded in 1882, is a public, multipurpose university. Its 335-acre campus is located in Cheney, 16 miles southwest of Spokane.

**Accreditation:** NASC. Professionally accredited by the American Assembly of Collegiate Schools of Business, the Council on Social Work Education, the National Association of Schools of Music, the National Council for Accreditation of Teacher Education, the National League for Nursing.

**Religious orientation:** Eastern Washington University is nonsectarian; no religious requirements.
**Library:** Collections totaling over 671,068 volumes, 3,569 periodical subscriptions, and 1,260,290 microform items.
**Special facilities/museums:** Anthropology museum, on-campus elementary school, education lab, primate research center, marine biology lab, ecological studies lab, wildlife refuge, planetarium.
**Athletic facilities:** Gymnasiums, basketball, racquetball, squash, and tennis courts, swimming pool, tracks, fitness center, dance studio, weight and wrestling rooms, baseball, football, soccer, and softball fields, field house, fitness trail.

**STUDENT BODY. Undergraduate profile:** 90% are state residents; 68% are transfers. 2.8% Asian-American, 2.1% Black, 2.7% Hispanic, 2% Native American, 81.1% White, 9.3% Other. Average age of undergraduates is 25.
**Freshman profile:** 1% of freshmen who took SAT scored 700 or over on verbal, 1% scored 700 or over on math; 3% scored 600 or over on verbal, 8% scored 600 or over on math; 15% scored 500 or over on verbal, 33% scored 500 or over on math; 50% scored 400 or over on verbal, 64% scored 400 or over on math; 78% scored 300 or over on verbal, 83% scored 300 or over on math. 84% of accepted applicants took SAT; 24% took ACT. 95% of freshmen come from public schools.
**Undergraduate achievement:** 76% of fall 1992 freshmen returned for fall 1993 term. 14% of students who completed a degree program immediately went on to graduate study.
**Foreign students:** 379 students are from out of the country. Countries represented include Canada, Hong Kong, Japan, Korea, Saudi Arabia, and Taiwan; 50 in all.

**PROGRAMS OF STUDY. Degrees:** B.A., B.A.Bus., B.A.Ed., B.Dent.Hyg., B.F.A., B.Mus., B.S., B.S.Nurs.
**Majors:** Accounting, Acting/Directing, Administrative Office Management, Anthropology, Applied Psychology, Art, Art History, Biochemistry, Biochemistry/Biotechnology, Biology, Botany, Broadcast Journalism, Business Administration, Business Education, Chemistry, Child Development, Communication Disorders, Communications Studies, Community Health Education, Computer Information Systems, Computer Science, Construction Technology, Corrections, Creative Writing, Criminal Justice, Dance, Decision Sciences, Dental Hygiene, Developmental Psychology, Earth Science, Economics, Electronics Technology, English, Environmental Biology, Exercise Science, Finance, French, General Studies, Geography, Geology, German, Government, Graphic Communication, Health Education, Health Services Administration, History, Human Resources Management, Humanities, Instrumental Performance, International Affairs, Journalism, Justice Administration, Labor Relations, Law Enforcement, Literary Studies, Management, Management Information Systems, Manufacturing Technology, Marketing, Marketing Education, Mathematics, Mathematics/Economics, Mechanical Engineering Technology, Medical Technology, Microbiology, Military Science, Music, Music Merchandising, Musical Theatre, Natural Sciences, News/Editorial, Nursing, Operations Management, Organizational/Mass Communications, Outdoor Recreation, Philosophy, Photographic Science, Physical Education, Physical Therapy, Physics, Piano Performance, Pre-Dentistry, Pre-Medicine, Pre-Pharmacy, Pre-Veterinary, Psychology, Public Administration, Radio/Television, Reading, Recreation Management, Social Science, Social Work, Sociology, Spanish, Special Education, Speech Communication, Sports Medicine/Athletic Training, Studio Art, Technical Communications, Technical Theatre, Technology, Technology Design, Technology Education, Theatre, Therapeutic Recreation, Urban/Regional Planning, Vocal Performance, Zoology.
**Requirements:** General education requirement.
**Academic regulations:** Minimum 2.0 GPA must be maintained.
**Special:** Minors offered in some majors and in aging studies, alcohol/drug studies, American Indian studies, area studies, black studies, early childhood education, English as a Second Language, environmental studies, gifted/talented education, handicapped learner in the regular classroom, library science/media, linguistics, religious studies, Russian, and women's studies. Self-designed majors. Double majors. Independent study. Pass/fail grading option. Internships. Graduate school at which undergraduates may take graduate-level courses. Preprofessional programs in law, medicine, veterinary science, pharmacy, and dentistry. Member of Intercollegiate Center for Nursing Education. Exchange programs offered. Teacher certification in early childhood, elementary, secondary, special education, and vo-tech education. Certification in specific subject areas. Exchange programs abroad in African countries, Australia, China, France, Ireland, Japan, Korea, Pakistan, Thailand, Ukraine, and the former Yugoslav Republics. ROTC.
**Honors:** Honors program. Honor societies.
**Academic Assistance:** Remedial reading, writing, math, and study skills. Nonremedial tutoring.

**STUDENT LIFE. Housing:** Students may live on or off campus. Coed dorms. Fraternity housing. School-owned/operated apartments. Off-campus privately-owned housing. On-campus married-student housing. 19% of students live in college housing.
**Social atmosphere:** The Pub and Pence Union Building are popular student gathering places. Favorite social events include homecoming and Club Vegas. There are many musical events and lots of skiing areas, according to the editor of the student newspaper.
**Services and counseling/handicapped student services:** Placement services. Health service. Women's center. Day care. Nontraditional student advisor. Counseling services for minority, military, veteran, and older students. Birth control, personal, and psychological counseling. Career and academic guidance services. Physically disabled student services. Learning disabled services. Notetaking services. Tape recorders. Tutors. Reader services for the blind.
**Campus organizations:** Undergraduate student government. Student newspaper (Easterner, published once/week). Literary magazine. Radio and TV stations. Choral groups, orchestra, band, jazz and dance groups, theatre, radio and TV groups, outdoor recreation groups, service and special-interest groups, 92 organizations in all. Six fraternities, two chapter houses; seven sororities, no chapter houses. 4% of men join a fraternity. 5% of women join a sorority.
**Religious organizations:** New Beginnings, Seventh-day Adventist group, His Life Catholic Organization, Campus Crusade for Christ, Baptist Student Ministries, Cayam, Intervarsity Christian Fellowship, Newman Club, Moslem group.
**Minority/foreign student organizations:** Black Student Union, MEChA, Native American Organization. International Student Association, Chinese, Taiwanese, Japanese, and Korean student groups.

**ATHLETICS. Physical education requirements:** None.
**Intercollegiate competition:** 3% of students participate. Basketball (M,W), cross-country (M,W), football (M), golf (M,W), tennis (M,W), track (indoor) (M,W), track (outdoor) (M,W), track and field (indoor) (M,W), track and field (outdoor) (M,W), volleyball (W). Member of Big Sky Athletic Conference, NCAA Division I, NCAA Division I-AA for football.
**Intramural and club sports:** 12% of students participate. Intramural basketball, bowling, football, golf, racquetball, soccer, swimming, tennis, triathlon, volleyball, water basketball.

**ADMISSIONS. Academic basis for candidate selection** (in order of priority): Secondary school record, standardized test scores.
**Nonacademic basis for candidate selection:** Particular talent or ability is considered.
**Requirements:** Graduation from secondary school is recommended; GED is accepted. 15 units and the following program of study are required: 4 units of English, 3 units of math, 2 units of science including 1 unit of lab, 2 units of foreign language, 3 units of social studies, 1 unit of elective in either academic subject or fine arts. Audition required of B.F.A. music program applicants. Alternative Admissions program for applicants not normally admissible. SAT or ACT is required. PSAT is recommended. Campus visit recommended. No off-campus interviews.
**Procedure:** Suggest filing application by February 15. Application deadline is July 1. Notification of admission on rolling basis. Reply is required by May 1. $80 room deposit, refundable in part until end of quarter. Freshmen accepted in terms other than fall.
**Special programs:** Credit and placement may be granted through challenge exams and military and life experience. Early entrance/early admission program. Concurrent enrollment program.
**Transfer students:** Transfer students accepted for terms other than fall. In fall 1993, 68% of all new students were transfers into all classes. 2,354 transfer applications were received, 2,019 were accepted. Application deadline is April 1 (priority), July 1 for fall; February 1 for spring. Minimum 2.0 GPA required. Lowest course grade accepted is "D." Maximum number of transferable credits is 90 quarter hours from a two-year school and 135 quarter hours from a four-year school. At least 45 quarter hours must be completed at the university to receive degree.
**Admissions contact:** Roger L. Pugh, Assistant Vice Provost for Enrollment Management. 509 359-2397.

**FINANCIAL AID. Available aid:** Pell grants, SEOG, state scholarships and grants, school scholarships and grants, private scholarships, ROTC scholarships, academic merit scholarships, athletic scholarships, and aid for undergraduate foreign students. Perkins Loans (NDSL), PLUS, Stafford Loans (GSL), school loans, and SLS.
**Financial aid statistics:** 15% of aid is not need-based. In 1993-94, 74% of all freshman applicants received aid.
**Supporting data/closing dates:** FAFSA: Priority filing date is February 15. Notification of awards begins April 1.
**Financial aid contact:** Susan Howe, Director of Financial Aid. 509 359-2314.

**STUDENT EMPLOYMENT.** College Work/Study Program. Institutional employment. 37% of full-time undergraduates work on campus during school year. Students may expect to earn an average of $1,050 during school year. Off-campus part-time employment opportunities rated "good."

**COMPUTER FACILITIES.** 1,000 IBM/IBM-compatible and Macintosh/Apple microcomputers; 125 are networked. Students may access Digital, SUN minicomputer/mainframe systems, Internet. Client/LAN operating systems include Apple/Macintosh, DOS, UNIX/XENIX/AIX, X-windows, DEC, LocalTalk/AppleTalk, Novell. Computer languages and software packages include BASIC, C, COBOL, FORTRAN, LISP, Pascal. Computer facilities are available to all students.
**Fees:** None.
**Hours:** 8 AM-12 midn.

**PROMINENT ALUMNI/AE.** Raul Cano, molecular biologist, DNA research; Thomas Hampson, opera singer; Tom Sneva, race car owner/driver.

# The Evergreen State College

**Olympia, WA 98505** **206 866-6000**

**1993-94 Costs.** Tuition: $2,352 (state residents), $8,070 (out-of-state). Room & board: $4,300. Fees, books, misc. academic expenses (school's estimate): $850.
**Enrollment.** Undergraduates: 1,366 men, 1,669 women (full-time). Freshman class: 1,801 applicants, 1,101 accepted, 348 enrolled. Graduate enrollment: 123 men, 151 women.
**Test score averages/ranges.** Average SAT scores: 521 verbal, 521 math. Range of SAT scores of middle 50%: 460-590 verbal, 460-580 math.
**Faculty.** 144 full-time; 33 part-time. 74% of faculty holds doctoral degree. Student/faculty ratio: 20 to 1.
**Selectivity rating.** Competitive.

**PROFILE.** Evergreen State, founded in 1967, is a public college. Its 1,000-acre campus is located on Puget Sound.

**Accreditation:** NASC.
**Religious orientation:** The Evergreen State College is nonsectarian; no religious requirements.
**Library:** Collections totaling over 261,000 volumes, 1,731 periodical subscriptions, and 130,000 microform items.
**Special facilities/museums:** Self-paced learning unit lab, art annex, media production center, graphics imaging lab, ship for marine studies, electron microscope.

**Athletic facilities:** Gymnasiums, swimming pool, diving well, sauna, badminton, basketball, handball, racquetball, tennis, and volleyball courts, dance studios, track, athletic fields, weight room, wellness center, rock climbing wall.

**STUDENT BODY. Undergraduate profile:** 76% are state residents; 58% are transfers. 5% Asian-American, 3% Black, 3% Hispanic, 3% Native American, 86% White. Average age of undergraduates is 22.

**Freshman profile:** 3% of freshmen who took SAT scored 700 or over on verbal, 4% scored 700 or over on math; 22% scored 600 or over on verbal, 23% scored 600 or over on math; 57% scored 500 or over on verbal, 61% scored 500 or over on math; 89% scored 400 or over on verbal, 88% scored 400 or over on math; 99% scored 300 or over on verbal, 99% scored 300 or over on math. Majority of accepted applicants took SAT. 95% of freshmen come from public schools.

**Undergraduate achievement:** 74% of fall 1992 freshmen returned for fall 1993 term. 55% of entering class graduated. 11% of students who completed a degree program immediately went on to graduate study.

**Foreign students:** 30 students are from out of the country. Countries represented include Canada and Japan; 16 in all.

**PROGRAMS OF STUDY. Degrees:** B.A., B.S.

**Majors:** Agricultural Sciences, American Studies, Anthropology, Biology, Business Administration, Chemistry, Communication, Community Service, Comparative Literature, Computer Science, Creative Writing, Ecology, Economics, Education, Energy Studies, Engineering, English, Environmental Studies, Film/Television Studies, Fine Arts, Geology, History, Human Development, Humanities, Literature, Marine Biology, Marine Science, Mathematics, Microbiology, Music, Native American Studies, Natural Science, Philosophy, Photography, Physical Sciences, Physics, Political Science, Pre-Law, Pre-Medicine, Psychology, Public Administration, Science, Social Sciences, Sociology, Theatre Arts/Drama, Urban Studies, Women's Studies, Zoology.

**Special:** Academic program enables students to enroll each quarter in a single, comprehensive program (Coordinated Studies) rather than several separate courses. Students' academic progress is monitored through faculty letters of evaluation. Foreign language program combines language study with cultural studies; French, Japanese, Russian, and Spanish have been offered. Self-designed majors. Independent study. Internships. Cooperative education programs. Graduate school at which undergraduates may take graduate-level courses. Preprofessional programs in law and medicine. 3-2 agriculture program with Washington State U. Teacher certification in elementary and secondary education. Certification in specific subject areas. Exchange program abroad in Japan (Kobe U, Myazaki U, and Hyogo Prefecture). Study abroad also in France, Latin America, the former Soviet Republics, and Spain.

**Academic Assistance:** Remedial reading, writing, math, and study skills. Nonremedial tutoring.

**STUDENT LIFE. Housing:** Students may live on or off campus. Coed dorms. Off-campus privately-owned housing. 33% of students live in college housing.

**Social atmosphere:** Popular gathering spots include The Housing Community Center, the East-Side Club, the Meadow, the CAB (College Activities Building), and the Coral Room. Influential student groups include the Carmilaa Society (vampire fan club), the Rape Response Coalition, the Native Student Alliance, the Happy Squad of Earth, and Tempo, the Evergreen Music Production Organization. Some of the most popular events of the year include a music festival held every spring, Disorientation Week, the Olympia Film Festival, the Northwest Lesbian/Gay Film Festival, and Super Saturday. The editor of the student newspaper reports, "Evergreen is full of hippies and northwest scenesters, and a lot of local bands. Creativity abounds. Chalking the campus is a popular activity. So is beer. Olympia is rich with micro-brews and espresso. It rains all winter. There is a large hippie contingent, with their big dogs, VW vans, the Grateful Dead. Evergreen is a great school. Mostly, we're here to learn. Academics are a very serious part of life at the college."

**Services and counseling/handicapped student services:** Placement services. Health service. Women's center. Day care. Counseling services for minority, military, veteran, and older students. Birth control, personal, and psychological counseling. Career and academic guidance services. Physically disabled student services. Learning disabled services. Tape recorders. Reader services for the blind.

**Campus organizations:** Undergraduate student government. Student newspaper (Cooper Point Journal, published once/week). Literary magazine. Radio station. Environmental resource center, political information center, peace center, Students with Challenges, lesbian/gay/bisexual center, PIRG.

**Religious organizations:** Campus Ministries, Inner Place.

**Minority/foreign student organizations:** Indian Center, Jewish Cultural Center, MEChA, UMOJA, Women of Color.

**ATHLETICS. Physical education requirements:** None.

**Intercollegiate competition:** 4% of students participate. Soccer (M,W), swimming (M,W). Member of NAIA, Northwest Collegiate Soccer Conference.

**Intramural and club sports:** 10% of students participate. Intramural basketball, boomerang, crew, mountaineering, pickleball, racquetball, river running, rugby, running, sailing, skiing, soccer, softball, swimming, table tennis, ultimate frisbee, volleyball, walleyball, weight lifting. Men's club basketball, martial arts, rugby, running, sailing, volleyball. Women's club basketball, martial arts, rugby, running, sailing, volleyball.

**ADMISSIONS. Academic basis for candidate selection** (in order of priority): Secondary school record, class rank, standardized test scores.

**Requirements:** Graduation from secondary school is recommended; GED is accepted. 16 units and the following program of study are required: 4 units of English, 3 units of math, 2 units of science including 1 unit of lab, 2 units of foreign language, 3 units of social studies, 1 unit of electives. Minimum 2.0 GPA required; rank in top half of secondary school class recommended. Conditional admission possible for applicants not meeting standard requirements. SAT or ACT is required. Campus visit recommended. No off-campus interviews.

**Procedure:** Take SAT or ACT by January 23 of 12th year. Application deadline is March 1. Notification of admission by April 1. Reply is required by June 11. $50 nonrefundable tuition deposit. $60 room deposit, refundable until July 15. Freshmen accepted for fall terms only.

**Special programs:** Credit may be granted through CEEB Advanced Placement for scores of 3 or higher. Credit may be granted through CLEP general and subject exams, ACT PEP and DANTES exams, and military and life experience.

**Transfer students:** Transfer students accepted for terms other than fall. In fall 1993, 58% of all new students were transfers into all classes. 1,403 transfer applications were received, 975 were accepted. Application deadline is March 1 for fall; December 1 for spring. Minimum 2.0 GPA required. Lowest course grade accepted is "C." Maximum number of transferable credits is 90 quarter hours from a two-year school and 135 quarter hours from a four-year school. At least 45 quarter hours must be completed at the college to receive degree.

**Admissions contact:** Doug Scrima, M.P.A., Asst. to the Dean for Admissions. 206 866-6000, extension 6170.

**FINANCIAL AID. Available aid:** Pell grants, SEOG, state scholarships and grants, school scholarships and grants, private scholarships, academic merit scholarships, and athletic scholarships. Perkins Loans (NDSL), PLUS, Stafford Loans (GSL), private loans, and SLS.

**Financial aid statistics:** Average amounts of aid awarded freshmen: Scholarships and grants, $2,233; loans, $2,240.

**Supporting data/closing dates:** FAFSA: Priority filing date is February 15. Notification of awards begins April 15.

**Financial aid contact:** Georgette Chun, M.P.A., Director of Financial Aid. 206 866-6000, extension 6205.

**STUDENT EMPLOYMENT.** College Work/Study Program. Institutional employment. 25% of full-time undergraduates work on campus during school year. Students may expect to earn an average of $1,545 during school year. Freshmen are discouraged from working during their first term. Off-campus part-time employment opportunities rated "fair."

**COMPUTER FACILITIES.** 139 IBM/IBM-compatible and Macintosh/Apple microcomputers; 124 are networked. Students may access AT&T, Digital, IBM minicomputer/mainframe systems, Internet. Computer languages and software packages include APL, BASIC, COBOL, Excel, FORTRAN, HyperCard, Kermit, LISP, Lotus 1-2-3, PageMaker, Pascal, Pixel Paint, PL/1, R:BASE, WordPerfect. Computer facilities are available to all students.

**Fees:** None.

**Hours:** 24 hours.

**GRADUATE CAREER DATA.** Graduate school percentages: 1% enter law school. 3% enter medical school. 6% enter graduate business programs. 4% enter graduate arts and sciences programs. Highest graduate school enrollments: Evergreen State Coll, U of Oregon, U of Washington. 13% of graduates choose careers in business and industry.

**PROMINENT ALUMNI/AE.** Matt Groening, writer/cartoonist/creator, ***The Simpsons;*** Linda Barry, writer; Joseph Dear, Fed Agency Director.

## Gonzaga University

**Spokane, WA 99258-0001** **509 328-4220**

**1993-94 Costs.** Tuition: $12,200. Room & board: $4,150. Fees, books, misc. academic expenses (school's estimate): $750.

**Enrollment.** Undergraduates: 1,207 men, 1,295 women (full-time). Freshman class: 2,171 applicants, 1,874 accepted, 625 enrolled. Graduate enrollment: 902 men, 935 women.

**Test score averages/ranges.** Average SAT scores: 488 verbal, 540 math. Range of SAT scores of middle 50%: 450-550 verbal, 500-599 math. Average ACT scores: 25 composite. Range of ACT scores of middle 50%: 23-27 composite.

**Faculty.** 216 full-time; 14 part-time. 76% of faculty holds doctoral degree. Student/faculty ratio: 14 to 1.

**Selectivity rating.** Competitive.

**PROFILE.** Gonzaga, founded in 1887, is a church-affiliated university. Programs are offered through the Colleges of Arts and Sciences; the Graduate School; and the Schools of Business Administration, Continuing Education, Education, Engineering, and Law. Its 83-acre campus is located in a residential area of Spokane.

**Accreditation:** NASC. Professionally accredited by the Accreditation Board for Engineering and Technology, the American Assembly of Collegiate Schools of Business, the National Council for Accreditation of Teacher Education, the National League for Nursing.

**Religious orientation:** Gonzaga University is affiliated with the Roman Catholic Church (Society of Jesus); three semesters of religion required.

**Library:** Collections totaling over 285,000 volumes, 2,400 periodical subscriptions, and 350,000 microform items.

**Special facilities/museums:** Language lab, TV production center, educational center, information and technology library, two electron microscopes.

**Athletic facilities:** Swimming pool, indoor track, basketball, racquetball, and volleyball courts, weight, crew, exercise, training, and weight rooms, baseball and playing fields.

**STUDENT BODY. Undergraduate profile:** 51% are state residents; 35% are transfers. 4% Asian-American, 1% Black, 3% Hispanic, 1% Native American, 81% White, 10% Other. Average age of undergraduates is 21.

**Freshman profile:** 1% of freshmen who took SAT scored 700 or over on verbal, 4% scored 700 or over on math; 12% scored 600 or over on verbal, 27% scored 600 or over on math; 45% scored 500 or over on verbal, 67% scored 500 or over on math; 86% scored 400 or over on verbal, 96% scored 400 or over on math; 100% scored 300 or over on verbal, 100% scored 300 or over on math. 65% of accepted applicants took SAT; 35% took ACT. 68% of freshmen come from public schools.

**Undergraduate achievement:** 82% of fall 1991 freshmen returned for fall 1992 term. 42% of entering class graduated.

**Foreign students:** 120 students are from out of the country. Countries represented include Canada, China, Ireland, Japan, Taiwan, and United Kingdom; 45 in all.

**PROGRAMS OF STUDY. Degrees:** B.A., B.Bus.Admin., B.Ed., B.Gen.Studies, B.S., B.S.Civil Eng., B.S.Elec.Eng., B.S.Mech.Eng., B.S.Nurs.

**Majors:** Accounting, Art, Biology, Broadcast Studies, Chemistry, Civil Engineering, Classical Civilization, Classics, Computer Science, Criminal Justice, Economics, Electrical Engineering, Elementary Education, English, Finance, French, German, Greek, History, Integrated Studies, International Business, Italian Studies, Journalism, Latin, Literary Studies, Management, Marketing, Mathematics, Mathematics/Computer Science, Mechanical Engineering, Music Education, Music Performance, Nursing, Operations Management, Philosophy, Physical Education, Physics, Political Science, Psychology, Public Relations, Religious Studies, Secondary Education, Sociology, Spanish, Special Education, Speech Communication, Theatre Arts.

**Distribution of degrees:** The majors with the highest enrollment are accounting, finance, and electrical engineering; Italian studies, international business, and Spanish have the lowest.

**Requirements:** General education requirement.

**Academic regulations:** Minimum 2.0 GPA must be maintained.

**Special:** Minors offered in most majors. Self-designed majors. Double majors. Dual degrees. Independent study. Accelerated study. Pass/fail grading option. Internships. Graduate school at which undergraduates may take graduate-level courses. Preprofessional programs in law, medicine, dentistry, and nursing. M.B.A./J.D. program. Five-year B.S.Eng./M.B.A. program. Program for master's degree in electrical engineering with Washington State U. 3-1 programs in medicine may be arranged. Member of Intercollegiate Consortium of Language Studies and Spokane Consortium for International Studies. Washington Semester. Teacher certification in early childhood, elementary, secondary, and special education. Certification in specific subject areas. Exchange program abroad in Japan (Sophia U). Study abroad also in England, France, Italy, and Spain. ROTC.

**Honors:** Honors program. Honor societies.

**Academic Assistance:** Remedial writing, math, and study skills.

**STUDENT LIFE. Housing:** All unmarried students under age 21 must live on campus unless living near campus with relatives. Coed, women's, and men's dorms. School-owned/operated apartments. 47% of students live in college housing.

**Social atmosphere:** The student newspaper reports that since the college is located in the center of Spokane, there is easy access to restaurants, movies, and shopping centers. Most influential groups on campus include the Knights and Spurs and the basketball and volleyball teams. Popular events include sports, the Charity Ball, and Spring Formal. On campus, students gather in the library, the Martin Center, or in dorm rooms to socialize. Thursday night is GU's night out, and students head for the Bulldog Tavern, Jack and Dan's, City Heights, and local skating rinks and lakes; off-campus parties are also popular.

**Services and counseling/handicapped student services:** Placement services. Health service. Counseling services for minority, military, and veteran students. Career and academic guidance services. Religious counseling. Physically disabled student services. Learning disabled services. Notetaking services. Reader services for the blind.

**Campus organizations:** Undergraduate student government. Student newspaper (Gonzaga Bulletin, published once/week). Literary magazine. Yearbook. Radio and TV stations. Brass ensemble, chamber singers, jazz band, pep band, business and political clubs, men's and women's service clubs, social dance club, 30 organizations in all.

**Religious organizations:** Campus Ministry, Students for Life, Pax Christi, Action Program.

**Minority/foreign student organizations:** Cultural Awareness Association. International Student Union.

**ATHLETICS. Physical education requirements:** None.

**Intercollegiate competition:** 6% of students participate. Baseball (M), basketball (M,W), crew (M,W), cross-country (M,W), golf (M), soccer (M,W), tennis (M,W), track (indoor) (M,W), track (outdoor) (M,W), track and field (indoor) (M,W), track and field (outdoor) (M,W), volleyball (W). Member of NCAA Division I, Northern Pacific 10 Conference, West Coast Conference.

**Intramural and club sports:** 88% of students participate. Intramural basketball, flag football, racquetball, softball, volleyball. Men's club Alpine skiing, cycling, ice hockey, lacrosse, racquetball, rugby. Women's club Alpine skiing, cycling, rugby.

**ADMISSIONS. Academic basis for candidate selection** (in order of priority): Secondary school record, standardized test scores, school's recommendation, essay, class rank.

**Nonacademic basis for candidate selection:** Character and personality are important. Extracurricular participation, particular talent or ability, and alumni/ae relationship are considered.

**Requirements:** Graduation from secondary school is required; GED is accepted. 17 units and the following program of study are required: 4 units of English, 3 units of math, 1 unit of science, 2 units of foreign language, 1 unit of social studies, 1 unit of history, 5 units of academic electives. Minimum SAT scores of 450 in both verbal and math and minimum 2.8 GPA required. R.N., A.D.N., or L.P.N. required of nursing program applicants. Conditional admission possible for applicants not meeting standard requirements. SAT is required; ACT may be substituted. Campus visit and interview recommended. Off-campus interviews available with admissions and alumni representatives.

**Procedure:** Take SAT or ACT by November of 12th year. Visit college for interview by May of 12th year. Suggest filing application by March 1. Application deadline is April 1. Notification of admission on rolling basis. Reply is required by May 1. $150 tuition deposit, refundable until May 1. $150 room deposit, refundable until June 1. Freshmen accepted in terms other than fall.

**Special programs:** Admission may be deferred one year. Credit and/or placement may be granted through CEEB Advanced Placement exams for scores of 3 or higher. Credit may be granted through CLEP subject exams, ACT PEP, DANTES, and challenge exams, and military experience. Concurrent enrollment program.

**Transfer students:** Transfer students accepted for terms other than fall. In fall 1992, 35% of all new students were transfers into all classes. 672 transfer applications were received, 539 were accepted. Application deadline is July 1 for fall; December 1 for spring. Minimum 2.5 GPA required. Lowest course grade accepted is "C." Maximum number of transferable semester hours is 64 from two-year schools; unlimited from four-year schools. Final 30 semester hours must be completed at the university to receive degree.

**Admissions contact:** Philip Ballinger, M.A., Dean of Admissions. 509 484-6484.

**FINANCIAL AID. Available aid:** Pell grants, SEOG, Federal Nursing Student Scholarships, state scholarships and grants, school scholarships and grants, private scholarships, ROTC scholarships, academic merit scholarships, and athletic scholarships. Perkins Loans (NDSL), PLUS, Stafford Loans (GSL), NSL, school loans, private loans, and SLS. Deferred payment plan and family tuition reduction.

**Financial aid statistics:** 34% of aid is not need-based. In 1992-93, 100% of all undergraduate applicants received aid. Average amounts of aid awarded freshmen: Scholarships and grants, $3,500; loans, $4,125.

**Supporting data/closing dates:** FAFSA/FAF: Priority filing date is February 1. Notification of awards begins April 1.

**Financial aid contact:** Bruce DeFrates, M.S., Director of Financial Aid. 509 328-4220, extension 3182.

**STUDENT EMPLOYMENT.** College Work/Study Program. Institutional employment. 22% of full-time undergraduates work on campus during school year. Students may expect to earn an average of $1,900 during school year. Off-campus part-time employment opportunities rated "excellent."

**COMPUTER FACILITIES.** 245 IBM/IBM-compatible and Macintosh/Apple microcomputers; 115 are networked. Students may access Digital minicomputer/mainframe systems. Residence halls may be equipped with stand-alone microcomputers. Computer languages and software packages include BASIC, C, COBOL, FORTRAN, LISP, Pascal; 24 in all. Computer facilities are available to all students.

**Fees:** None.

**Hours:** 24 hours.

**GRADUATE CAREER DATA.** Highest graduate school enrollments: Gonzaga U, U of Washington. Companies and businesses that hire graduates: Arthur Andersen, Boeing, Microsoft.

**PROMINENT ALUMNI/AE.** Thomas Foley, speaker of the U.S. House of Representatives; John Stockton, professional basketball player, Utah Jazz; Cornelia Davis, M.D., physician in Africa; Bing Crosby, entertainer, singer, actor.

## Heritage College

**Toppenish, WA 98948 509 865-2244**

**1993-94 Costs.** Tuition: $5,540. Housing: None.
**Enrollment.** Undergraduates: 88 men, 233 women (full-time). Graduate enrollment: 113 men, 308 women.
**Test score averages/ranges.** N/A.
**Faculty.** 34 full-time; 120 part-time. 55% of faculty holds doctoral degree. Student/faculty ratio: 10 to 1.
**Selectivity rating.** N/A.

**PROFILE.** Heritage, founded in 1982, is a private college. Its 12-acre campus is located in Toppenish, 20 miles from Yakima.

**Accreditation:** NASC.

**Religious orientation:** Heritage College is nonsectarian; no religious requirements.

**Library:** Collections totaling over 55,000 volumes, and 12,000 periodical subscriptions.

**STUDENT BODY. Undergraduate profile:** 18% are transfers. 1% Asian-American, 1% Black, 30% Hispanic, 20% Native American, 48% White. Average age of undergraduates is 35.

**Freshman profile:** 100% of freshmen come from public schools.

**Foreign students:** Five students are from out of the country. Countries represented include Japan and Mexico; three in all.

**PROGRAMS OF STUDY. Degrees:** B.A., B.A.Ed., B.S.

**Majors:** Administration, Computer Science, Elementary Education, English, English/Language Arts, Environmental Science, Interdisciplinary Studies, Management, Mathematics, Political Science, Psychology, Public Administration, Science, Social Studies, Sociology, Spanish.

**Requirements:** General education requirement.

**Academic regulations:** Minimum 2.0 GPA must be maintained.

**Special:** Minors offered in many majors and in accounting, art, biology, chemistry, economics, and history. Professional certificate programs available. Multicultural education built into curriculum. Associate's degrees offered. Independent study. Internships. Cooperative education programs. Graduate school at which undergraduates may take graduate-level courses. Preprofessional programs in law. Teacher certification in early childhood, elementary, secondary, and bilingual/bicultural education. Certification in specific subject areas. Study abroad possible.

**Academic Assistance:** Remedial reading, writing, math, and study skills. Nonremedial tutoring.

**ADMISSIONS. Academic basis for candidate selection** (in order of priority): Secondary school record.

**Nonacademic basis for candidate selection:** Character and personality and extracurricular participation are considered.

**Requirements:** Graduation from secondary school is required; GED is accepted. No specific distribution of secondary school units required. Academic Skills Center for placement testing and free tutoring for applicants not normally admissible. SAT or ACT is recommended. Campus visit and interview recommended. No off-campus interviews.

**Procedure:** Take SAT or ACT by January of 12th year. Application deadline is September 1. Notification of admission on rolling basis. Reply required by registration. Freshmen accepted in terms other than fall.

**Special programs:** Admission may be deferred two years. Credit may be granted through CEEB Advanced Placement for scores of 3 or higher. Credit may be granted through CLEP general and subject exams, Regents College, ACT PEP, DANTES, and challenge exams, and military and life experience. Early decision program. Early entrance/early admission program.

**Transfer students:** Transfer students accepted for terms other than fall. In fall 1993, 18% of all new students were transfers into all classes. Application deadline is September 1 for fall; January 10 for spring. Lowest course grade accepted is "C-." Maximum number of transferable credits is 60 semester credits. At least 28 semester hours must be completed at the college to receive degree.
**Admissions contact:** Winona Zack, Director of Admissions. 509 865-2244, extension 1605.
**FINANCIAL AID. Available aid:** Pell grants, SEOG, state grants, school scholarships, private scholarships and grants, and academic merit scholarships. Perkins Loans (NDSL), PLUS, Stafford Loans (GSL), NSL, state loans, school loans, and SLS. Deferred payment plan.
**Financial aid statistics:** In 1993-94, 90% of all undergraduate applicants received aid; 90% of freshman applicants. Average amounts of aid awarded freshmen: Scholarships and grants, $4,200; loans, $1,200.
**Supporting data/closing dates:** FAFSA/FAF/FFS: Accepted on rolling basis. School's own aid application: Accepted on rolling basis. State aid form: Accepted on rolling basis. Income tax forms: Accepted on rolling basis. Notification of awards on rolling basis.
**Financial aid contact:** Carla Lamka, M.Ed., Director of Financial Aid. 509 865-2244, extension 1412.

## Northwest College

**Kirkland, WA 98083-0579 — 206 822-8266**

**1994-95 Costs.** Tuition: $6,550. Room & board: $3,480. Fees, books, misc. academic expenses (school's estimate): $1,260.
**Enrollment.** Undergraduates: 339 men, 365 women (full-time). Freshman class: 309 applicants, 203 accepted, 167 enrolled.
**Test score averages/ranges.** Average SAT scores: 905 combined. Average ACT scores: 21 composite.
**Faculty.** 33 full-time; 27 part-time. 50% of faculty holds doctoral degree. Student/faculty ratio: 18 to 1.
**Selectivity rating.** Less competitive.

**PROFILE.** Northwest College, founded in 1934, is a private, church-affiliated, liberal arts college. Its 55-acre campus is located 10 miles from downtown Seattle.
**Accreditation:** AABC, NASC.
**Religious orientation:** Northwest College is affiliated with the Assemblies of God; 18 semester hours of religion required.
**Library:** Collections totaling over 92,500 volumes, 620 periodical subscriptions, and 17,200 microform items.
**Athletic facilities:** Gymnasium, soccer and softball fields, weight room.
**STUDENT BODY. Undergraduate profile:** 72% are state residents; 41% are transfers. 3.6% Asian-American, 1.1% Black, 2.5% Hispanic, 1.7% Native American, 91.1% White. Average age of undergraduates is 23.
**Freshman profile:** Majority of accepted applicants took SAT. 75% of freshmen come from public schools.
**Undergraduate achievement:** 65% of fall 1992 freshmen returned for fall 1993 term. 25% of entering class graduated.
**Foreign students:** 23 students are from out of the country. Countries represented include Canada, Hungary, Japan, Russia, Spain, and Zambia; six in all.
**PROGRAMS OF STUDY. Degrees:** B.A.
**Majors:** Behavioral Science, Biblical Literature, Business Management/Administration, Church Ministries, Church Music, Elementary Education, Interdisciplinary Studies, Religion/Philosophy, Secondary Education.
**Distribution of degrees:** The majors with the highest enrollment are behavioral science and Biblical literature; church music and religion/philosophy have the lowest.
**Requirements:** General education requirement.
**Academic regulations:** Freshmen must maintain minimum 1.7 GPA; sophomores, 1.8 GPA; juniors, 2.0 GPA; seniors, 2.0 GPA.
**Special:** Minors offered in biblical languages, business for church staff workers, Christian education, church music, communication/preaching, history, missions, New Testament Greek, pastoral care, pastoral ministries, and youth ministries. Associate's degrees offered. Self-designed majors. Double majors. Dual degrees. Independent study. Internships. Preprofessional programs in theology. Member of Christian College Coalition; special study programs available. Teacher certification in elementary and secondary education.
**Academic Assistance:** Remedial study skills. Nonremedial tutoring.
**ADMISSIONS. Academic basis for candidate selection** (in order of priority): School's recommendation, essay, secondary school record, standardized test scores, class rank.
**Nonacademic basis for candidate selection:** Character and personality are emphasized. Extracurricular participation and particular talent or ability are considered.
**Requirements:** Graduation from secondary school is required; GED is accepted. 16 units required and the following program of study recommended: 3 units of English, 2 units of math, 1 unit of science, 1 unit of foreign language, 1 unit of history, 8 units of electives. Rank in top half of secondary school class and minimum 2.0 GPA. Provisional admission possible for applicants not normally admissible. SAT or ACT is required. Campus visit and interview recommended. Off-campus interviews available with an admissions representative.
**Procedure:** Take SAT or ACT by November 1 of 12th year. Visit college for interview by spring of 12th year. Suggest filing application by November 15. Application deadline is August 1. Notification of admission on rolling basis. $25 tuition deposit, refundable until August 15. $90 room deposit, refundable until August 15. Freshmen accepted in terms other than fall.
**Special programs:** Admission may be deferred one year. Credit may be granted through CEEB Advanced Placement for scores of 3 or higher. Credit may be granted through CLEP general and subject exams, challenge exams, and military and life experience. Early decision program. In fall 1993, 22 applied for early decision and 22 were accepted. Deadline for applying for early decision is November 15.
**Transfer students:** Transfer students accepted for terms other than fall. In fall 1993, 41% of all new students were transfers into all classes. 271 transfer applications were received, 171 were accepted. Application deadline is August 1 for fall; December 15 for spring. Minimum 2.0 GPA required. Lowest course grade accepted is "C." Maximum number of transferable credits is 63 semester hours from a two-year school and 94 semester hours from a four-year school. At least 30 semester hours must be completed at the college to receive degree.
**Admissions contact:** Calvin L. White, Ph.D., Director of Enrollment Services. 800 6-NWEST-1.
**FINANCIAL AID. Available aid:** Pell grants, SEOG, state grants, school scholarships, private scholarships and grants, academic merit scholarships, athletic scholarships, and aid for undergraduate foreign students. Perkins Loans (NDSL), PLUS, Stafford Loans (GSL), state loans, private loans, and SLS. AMS, deferred payment plan, and family tuition reduction.
**Financial aid statistics:** In 1993-94, 79% of all undergraduate applicants received aid.
**Supporting data/closing dates:** FAFSA: Priority filing date is March 1. School's own aid application: Priority filing date is March 1. Notification of awards begins April 15.
**Financial aid contact:** Al Perry, Financial Planning Coordinator. 800 6-NWEST-1.

## Pacific Lutheran University

**Tacoma, WA 98447 — 206 531-6900**

**1994-95 Costs.** Tuition: $13,312. Room & board: $4,738. Fees, books, misc. academic expenses (school's estimate): $500.
**Enrollment.** Undergraduates: 1,076 men, 1,504 women (full-time). Freshman class: 1,385 applicants, 1,343 accepted, 500 enrolled. Graduate enrollment: 170 men, 297 women.
**Test score averages/ranges.** Average SAT scores: 464 verbal, 516 math. Range of SAT scores of middle 50%: 450-570 verbal, 500-630 math.
**Faculty.** 229 full-time; 90 part-time. 80% of faculty holds doctoral degree. Student/faculty ratio: 14 to 1.
**Selectivity rating.** Less competitive.

**PROFILE.** Pacific Lutheran, founded in 1890, is a church-affiliated university. Programs are offered through the College of Arts and Sciences and Schools of the Arts, Business Administration, Education, Nursing, and Physical Education. Its 130-acre campus is located in Tacoma.
**Accreditation:** NASC. Professionally accredited by the American Assembly of Collegiate Schools of Business, the Computing Sciences Accreditation Board, the Council on Social Work Education, the National Association of Schools of Music, the National Council for Accreditation of Teacher Education, the National League for Nursing.
**Religious orientation:** Pacific Lutheran University is affiliated with the Evangelical Lutheran Church in America; Eight semester hours of religious studies required.
**Library:** Collections totaling over 333,900 volumes, 2,110 periodical subscriptions, and 54,251 microform items.
**Special facilities/museums:** Language labs, center for human organization in changing environments, magnetometer, scanning electron microscope.
**Athletic facilities:** Gymnasiums, badminton, racquetball, squash, and tennis courts, swimming pool, fitness center, wrestling area, golf course, baseball, football, intramural, soccer, and softball fields, track.
**STUDENT BODY. Undergraduate profile:** 70% are state residents; 39% are transfers. 5% Asian-American, 2% Black, 2% Hispanic, 1% Native American, 82% White, 8% Foreign and Unknown. Average age of undergraduates is 22.
**Freshman profile:** 4% of freshmen who took SAT scored 700 or over on math; 7% scored 600 or over on verbal, 18% scored 600 or over on math; 30% scored 500 or over on verbal, 49% scored 500 or over on math; 67% scored 400 or over on verbal, 76% scored 400 or over on math; 84% scored 300 or over on verbal, 86% scored 300 or over on math. 88% of accepted applicants took SAT; 12% took ACT.
**Undergraduate achievement:** 80% of fall 1992 freshmen returned for fall 1993 term. 60% of entering class graduated. 10% of students who completed a degree program immediately went on to graduate study.
**Foreign students:** 148 students are from out of the country. Countries represented include Finland, Japan, Korea, Norway, Sweden, and Taiwan; 28 in all.
**PROGRAMS OF STUDY. Degrees:** B.A., B.A.Ed., B.A.Phys.Ed., B.A.Recr., B.Bus. Admin., B.F.A., B.Mus., B.Mus.Arts, B.Mus.Ed., B.S., B.S.Nurs., B.S.Phys.Ed.
**Majors:** Anthropology, Art, Art Teacher Education, Biological/Physical Sciences, Biology, Business Administration/Management, Chemistry, Chinese Studies, Church Music, Classics, Communication, Computer Engineering, Computer Science, Computer Teacher Education, Earth Sciences, Economics, Education, Electrical Engineering, Elementary Teacher Education, Engineering Science, English, English Teacher Education, English/Writing Concentration, Foreign Languages Teacher Education, French, German, Global Studies, Health Teacher Education, History, Honors, Individualized Major, Instrumental Performance, Language Arts, Legal Studies, Mathematics, Mathematics Teacher Education, Music, Music Teacher Education, Norwegian, Nursing, Philosophy, Physical Education, Physical Education Teaching/Coaching, Physics, Political Science, Psychology, Religion, Scandinavian Studies, Science Teacher Education, Secondary Teacher Education, Social Science Teaching, Social Sciences, Social Studies Teacher Education, Social Work, Sociology, Spanish, Special Education, Theatre.
**Distribution of degrees:** The majors with the highest enrollment are business, education, and nursing; physics and economics have the lowest.
**Requirements:** General education requirement.
**Academic regulations:** Minimum 2.0 GPA must be maintained.
**Special:** Minors offered in most majors. Programs in environmental studies and lay church staff worker. All undergraduate work includes at least one year in curriculum of College of Arts and Sciences. Students choosing a major in the College of Arts and

Sciences may enroll in a limited number of courses in other undergraduate schools of the university. Concentrations available in many majors. Double majors. Dual degrees. Independent study. Pass/fail grading option. Internships. Cooperative education programs. Graduate school at which undergraduates may take graduate-level courses. Preprofessional programs in law, medicine, veterinary science, pharmacy, dentistry, theology, optometry, and medical technology. 4-1 medical technology program. 3-2 engineering programs with Columbia U and Washington U. Exchange programs with Biola U, St. Olaf Coll, Whitworth Coll, and other schools. Teacher certification in elementary, secondary, and special education. Study abroad in 20 countries, including China, Mexico, Norway, Sweden, Taiwan. ROTC.
**Honors:** Honor societies.
**Academic Assistance:** Remedial reading, writing, math, and study skills. Nonremedial tutoring.

**STUDENT LIFE. Housing:** All freshmen, sophomores, and juniors under age 21 must live on campus unless living with family. Coed and women's dorms. On-campus married-student housing. 48% of students live in college housing.
**Social atmosphere:** The Cave and Marazano's restaurant are favorite hangouts. Football team, Younglife, and Rejoice are influential student groups. Homecoming, Songfest, and Grudge Match are popular social events. On-campus entertainment lacks but is getting better, according to the editor of the student newspaper. "We're getting more bands coming to campus."
**Services and counseling/handicapped student services:** Placement services. Health service. Women's center. Day care. Counseling services for minority, military, veteran, and older students. Personal and psychological counseling. Career and academic guidance services. Religious counseling. Physically disabled student services. Learning disabled services. Notetaking services. Tape recorders. Tutors. Reader services for the blind.
**Campus organizations:** Undergraduate student government. Student newspaper (Mast, published once/week). Literary magazine. Yearbook. Radio and TV stations. Drama organizations, debating, departmental, political, service, and special-interest groups, 65 organizations in all.
**Religious organizations:** Bible Fellowship, Campus Ministry, Fellowship of Christian Athletes, Intervarsity Christian Fellowship, Rejoice, Student Congregation, Young Life.
**Minority/foreign student organizations:** Kwanza, CAUSE. ANSA, International Student Organization, Malaysian Student Organization.

**ATHLETICS. Physical education requirements:** Four semester hours of physical education required.
**Intercollegiate competition:** 21% of students participate. Baseball (M), basketball (M,W), cross-country (M,W), football (M), golf (M), soccer (M,W), softball (W), swimming (M,W), tennis (M,W), track (outdoor) (M,W), track and field (outdoor) (M,W), volleyball (W), wrestling (M). Member of Columbia Football Association-Mount Rainier League, NAIA, Northwest Conference of Independent Colleges.
**Intramural and club sports:** 60% of students participate. Intramural badminton, basketball, bowling, flag football, golf, indoor soccer, racquetball, soccer, softball, squash, volleyball. Men's club Alpine skiing, crew, lacrosse, rugby, volleyball. Women's club Alpine skiing, crew.

**ADMISSIONS. Academic basis for candidate selection** (in order of priority): Secondary school record, standardized test scores, class rank, school's recommendation, essay.
**Nonacademic basis for candidate selection:** Character and personality, extracurricular participation, and particular talent or ability are considered.
**Requirements:** Graduation from secondary school is required; GED is accepted. 16 units and the following program of study are recommended: 4 units of English, 3 units of math, 2 units of lab science, 2 units of social studies, 3 units of electives. Minimum combined SAT score between 900 and 1000, rank in top half of secondary school class, and minimum 2.50 GPA recommended. Higher averages, successful completion of prerequisites, and separate applications required of business, education, and nursing program applicants. Portfolio required of art program applicants. Audition required of music program applicants. SAT is required; ACT may be substituted. Campus visit and interview recommended. Off-campus interviews available with admissions and alumni representatives.
**Procedure:** Take SAT or ACT by January of 12th year. Visit college for interview by February of 12th year. Suggest filing application by March 1. Application deadline is May 1. Notification of admission on rolling basis. Reply is required by May 1. $200 tuition deposit, refundable until May 15. Freshmen accepted in terms other than fall.
**Special programs:** Admission may be deferred two years. Credit and/or placement may be granted through CEEB Advanced Placement exams for scores of 3 or higher. Credit and/or placement may be granted through CLEP subject exams. Credit may be granted through DANTES exams. Credit and placement may be granted through challenge exams and life experience. Early decision program. Deadline for applying for early decision is November 15.
**Transfer students:** Transfer students accepted for terms other than fall. In fall 1993, 39% of all new students were transfers into all classes. 942 transfer applications were received, 625 were accepted. Application deadline is May 1 for fall; May 1 for spring. Minimum 2.5 GPA required. Lowest course grade accepted is "D." Maximum number of transferable credits is 64 semester hours. At least 32 semester hours must be completed at the university to receive degree.
**Admissions contact:** David Hawsey, M.B.A., Dean of Admissions and Enrollment Management. 800 274-6758.

**FINANCIAL AID. Available aid:** Pell grants, SEOG, Federal Nursing Student Scholarships, state scholarships and grants, school scholarships and grants, private scholarships and grants, ROTC scholarships, academic merit scholarships, athletic scholarships, and aid for undergraduate foreign students. Ministers' dependents grants. Perkins Loans (NDSL), PLUS, Stafford Loans (GSL), NSL, private loans, and SLS. Knight Tuition Plans. University Payment Plan.
**Financial aid statistics:** 20% of aid is not need-based. In 1993-94, 96% of all undergraduate applicants received aid; 93% of freshman applicants. Average amounts of aid awarded freshmen: Scholarships and grants, $5,441; loans, $4,170.
**Supporting data/closing dates:** FAFSA: Priority filing date is February 15. FAF: Priority filing date is March 1. Income tax forms: Accepted on rolling basis. Notification of awards begins April 1.
**Financial aid contact:** Kay Soltis, Director of Financial Aid. 206 535-7161.

**STUDENT EMPLOYMENT.** College Work/Study Program. Institutional employment. 50% of full-time undergraduates work on campus during school year. Students may expect to earn an average of $1,500 during school year. Off-campus part-time employment opportunities rated "excellent."

**COMPUTER FACILITIES.** 500 IBM/IBM-compatible, Macintosh/Apple, and RISC-/UNIX-based microcomputers; 100 are networked. Students may access Digital, SUN minicomputer/mainframe systems, BITNET, Internet. Client/LAN operating systems include Apple/Macintosh, DOS, UNIX/XENIX/AIX, DEC, LocalTalk/AppleTalk. Computer languages and software packages include Ada, BASIC, COBOL, dBASE, FORTRAN, Lotus 1-2-3, Microsoft Word, Pascal, SPSS. Computer facilities are available to all students. Residence hall students who own personal computers may access campus network.
**Fees:** None.
**Hours:** 16 hours/day (microcomputers); 24 hours (mainframe).

**GRADUATE CAREER DATA.** Graduate school percentages: 3% enter law school. 5% enter medical school. 1% enter dental school. 7% enter graduate business programs. 5% enter graduate arts and sciences programs. 3% enter theological school/seminary. Highest graduate school enrollments: U of Puget Sound, U of Washington. Companies and businesses that hire graduates: Boeing, Microsoft, Seafirst, Weyerhaeuser.

**PROMINENT ALUMNI/AE.** William Foege, M.D., director of Carter Center, former director of Centers for Disease Control; Dr. Roy Swarty, vice-president, American Medical Association.

# Saint Martin's College

**Lacey, WA 98503** | **206 491-4700**

**1993-94 Costs.** Tuition: $10,740. Room & board: $4,060-$4,860. Fees, books, misc. academic expenses (school's estimate): $630.
**Enrollment.** Undergraduates: 329 (full-time). Graduate enrollment: 127.
**Test score averages/ranges.** Average SAT scores: 426 verbal, 459 math. Average ACT scores: 23 composite.
**Faculty.** 50 full-time; 9 part-time. 55% of faculty holds doctoral degree. Student/faculty ratio: 12 to 1.
**Selectivity rating.** Noncompetitive.

**PROFILE.** Saint Martin's, founded in 1895, is a private, church-affiliated, liberal arts college. Its 480-acre campus is located in Lacey, three miles east of Olympia.
**Accreditation:** NASC. Professionally accredited by the Accreditation Board for Engineering and Technology, the National League for Nursing.
**Religious orientation:** Saint Martin's College is affiliated with the Roman Catholic Church; one semester of religion/theology required.
**Library:** Collections totaling over 85,000 volumes, 450 periodical subscriptions, and 18,000 microform items.
**Special facilities/museums:** Museum with Native American artifacts and contemporary Northwest art collections.
**Athletic facilities:** Largest indoor arena in southwest Washington, gymnasium, weight room, athletic fields, track, tennis courts.

**STUDENT BODY. Undergraduate profile:** 99% are state residents. 1% Asian-American, 3% Black, 2% Hispanic, 1% Native American, 90% White, 3% Other. Average age of undergraduates is 28.
**Freshman profile:** 5% of freshmen who took SAT scored 600 or over on verbal, 5% scored 600 or over on math; 42% scored 500 or over on verbal, 31% scored 500 or over on math; 100% scored 400 or over on verbal, 100% scored 400 or over on math.
**Undergraduate achievement:** 65% of fall 1991 freshmen returned for fall 1992 term. 45% of entering class graduated. 10% of students who completed a degree program went on to graduate study within one year.
**Foreign students:** 20 students are from out of the country. Countries represented include Canada, China, Japan, Jordan, Korea, and Saudi Arabia; 10 in all.

**PROGRAMS OF STUDY. Degrees:** B.A., B.S., B.S.Civil Eng., B.S.Nurs.
**Majors:** Accounting, Biology, Chemistry, Civil Engineering, Community Services, Computer Software Technology, Computers in Education, Criminal Justice, Economics, Elementary Education, English, Finance, History, Humane Studies, International Management, Management, Marketing, Mathematics, Mechanical Engineering, Nursing, Political Science, Psychology, Religious Studies, Social Studies, Special Education.
**Distribution of degrees:** The majors with the highest enrollment are education, psychology, and management; religious studies and finance have the lowest.
**Requirements:** General education requirement.
**Academic regulations:** Freshmen must maintain minimum 1.70 GPA; sophomores, 1.90 GPA; juniors, 2.0 GPA; seniors, 2.0 GPA.
**Special:** Concentrations offered in aviation maintenance management, aviation operations management, information systems management, and international marketing. Certificate programs offered in accounting, alcohol and substance abuse, computer science, educational staff counselor, management, and marketing. Courses offered in art, drama, English as a second language, and sociology. Associate's degrees offered. Double majors. Independent study. Pass/fail grading option. Internships. Graduate school at which undergraduates may take graduate-level courses. Preprofessional programs in law, medicine, veterinary science, pharmacy, dentistry, and optometry. Member of Independent Colleges of Washington and Washington Friends of Higher Education (all private colleges in Washington state). Member of Independent Colleges and Universities. Washington Semester. Teacher certification in elementary, secondary, and special education. ROTC at Seattle U.
**Honors:** Honors program. Honor societies.
**Academic Assistance:** Remedial writing and math. Nonremedial tutoring.

**ADMISSIONS. Academic basis for candidate selection** (in order of priority): Secondary school record, school's recommendation, class rank, standardized test scores, essay.

**Nonacademic basis for candidate selection:** Extracurricular participation is important. Character and personality, particular talent or ability, and alumni/ae relationship are considered.
**Requirements:** Graduation from secondary school is required; GED is accepted. 25 units and the following program of study is required: 4 units of English, 2 units of math, 1 unit of science, 1 unit of foreign language, 2 units of social studies, 2 units of history, 6 units of academic electives. Minimum 2.5 GPA required. Special admissions requirements for nursing program applicants. Minimum 3.0 GPA required of education program applicants. Conditional admission possible for applicants not meeting standard requirements. SAT or ACT is required. Campus visit and interview recommended. No off-campus interviews.
**Procedure:** Suggest filing application by March 1; no deadline. Notification of admission on rolling basis. No set date by which applicants must accept offer. $100 tuition deposit, refundable until May 1 for fall; December 15 for spring. $100 room deposit, refundable until May 1 for fall; December 15 for spring. Freshmen accepted in terms other than fall.
**Special programs:** Admission may be deferred two years. Credit may be granted through CEEB Advanced Placement for scores of 3 or higher. Credit may be granted through CLEP general and subject exams, DANTES exams, and military experience. Concurrent enrollment program.
**Transfer students:** Transfer students accepted for terms other than fall. Lowest course grade accepted is "C." Maximum number of transferable credits is 60 semester hours.
**Admissions contact:** Rob Kvidt, Director of Admissions. 206 438-4311.
**FINANCIAL AID. Available aid:** Pell grants, SEOG, state scholarships and grants, school scholarships and grants, private scholarships and grants, academic merit scholarships, and athletic scholarships. Perkins Loans (NDSL), PLUS, Stafford Loans (GSL), and SLS. Deferred payment plan.
**Financial aid statistics:** 17% of aid is not need-based. In 1992-93, 90% of all undergraduate applicants received aid; 84% of freshman applicants. Average amounts of aid awarded freshmen: Scholarships and grants, $7,400; loans, $2,000.
**Supporting data/closing dates:** FAFSA/FAF: Priority filing date is March 1. School's own aid application: Priority filing date is March 1. Notification of awards begins April 1.
**Financial aid contact:** Marianna Deeken, M.A., Director of Financial Aid. 206 438-4397.

# Seattle Pacific University

**Seattle, WA 98119** **206 281-2050**

**1993-94 Costs.** Tuition: $11,979. Room & board: $4,524. Fees, books, misc. academic expenses (school's estimate): $675.
**Enrollment.** Undergraduates: 653 men, 1,244 women (full-time). Freshman class: 1,183 applicants, 1,016 accepted, 411 enrolled. Graduate enrollment: 404 men, 761 women.
**Test score averages/ranges.** Average SAT scores: 479 verbal, 522 math.
**Faculty.** 145 full-time; 50 part-time. 79% of faculty holds doctoral degree. Student/faculty ratio: 15 to 1.
**Selectivity rating.** Competitive.

**PROFILE.** Seattle Pacific, founded in 1891, is a private, church-affiliated, comprehensive university. It was founded in 1891, adopted coeducation in 1910, and gained university status in 1977. Programs are offered through the Schools of Business and Economics, Education, Fine and Performing Arts, Health Sciences, Humanities, Natural and Mathematical Sciences, Physical Education and Athletics, Religion, and Social and Behavioral Sciences. Its 35-acre campus is located in downtown Seattle.

**Accreditation:** NASC. Professionally accredited by the Accreditation Board for Engineering and Technology, the American Dietetic Association, the National Association of Schools of Music, the National Council for Accreditation of Teacher Education, the National League for Nursing.
**Religious orientation:** Seattle Pacific University is affiliated with the Free Methodist Church; three terms of religion/theology required.
**Library:** Collections totaling over 170,000 volumes, 1,500 periodical subscriptions, and 380,000 microform items.
**Special facilities/museums:** Art gallery, language lab, instructional media center, performing arts theatre, science learning center, island campus used for seminars, summer workshops, and field work in botany and marine biology.
**Athletic facilities:** Gymnasiums, aerobics/fitness, training, and weight rooms, exercise science lab, athletic fields, canal for canoeing and crew.
**STUDENT BODY. Undergraduate profile:** 70% are state residents; 43% are transfers. 4% Asian-American, 1% Black, 2% Hispanic, 1% Native American, 79% White, 13% Other. Average age of undergraduates is 21.
**Freshman profile:** 1% of freshmen who took SAT scored 700 or over on verbal, 3% scored 700 or over on math; 9% scored 600 or over on verbal, 20% scored 600 or over on math; 38% scored 500 or over on verbal, 49% scored 500 or over on math; 77% scored 400 or over on verbal, 85% scored 400 or over on math; 97% scored 300 or over on verbal, 97% scored 300 or over on math. Majority of accepted applicants took SAT.
**Undergraduate achievement:** 72% of fall 1992 freshmen returned for fall 1993 term. 26% of entering class graduated. 10% of students who completed a degree program went on to graduate study within one and a half years.
**Foreign students:** Countries represented include Canada, Japan, Korea, Oman, Taiwan, and Thailand; 43 in all.
**PROGRAMS OF STUDY. Degrees:** B.A., B.S.
**Majors:** Accounting, Biblical Studies, Biology, Business Administration, Chemistry, Christian Education, Clothing/Textiles, Communication, Computer Science, Economics, Electrical Engineering, Engineering Science, English, European Studies, Exercise Science, Family Life Education/Consumer Sciences, Fine/Applied Arts, Foods/Nutrition, General Science, General Studies, History, Home Economics Education, Language Arts, Mathematics, Music Education, Music Performance, Nursing, Philosophy, Physical Education, Physics, Political Science, Psychology, Recreation/Sports Management, Religion, Social Science Education, Sociology, Special Education, Theatre, Theological Studies, Visual Arts.
**Distribution of degrees:** The majors with the highest enrollment are management, computer science, and nursing; religion, biblical studies, and food/nutrition have the lowest.
**Requirements:** General education requirement.
**Academic regulations:** Minimum 2.0 GPA must be maintained.
**Special:** Minors offered in most majors. Fields of specialization in cross-cultural ministries, French, geography, German, health education, interior design, journalism, linguistics, literature, Russian, social anthropology, Spanish, writing, and youth ministry or may be self-designed. Entrance exams in math and English; eight credits in courses with a writing emphasis required for graduation. Self-designed majors. Double majors. Independent study. Pass/fail grading option. Internships. Cooperative education programs. Graduate school at which undergraduates may take graduate-level courses. Preprofessional programs in law, medicine, dentistry, and theology. Member of Christian College Coalition and Christian College Consortium. American Studies Program (Washington, D.C.) and other off-campus study opportunities. Exchange programs with Asbury Coll, Bethel Coll, George Fox Coll, Gordon Coll, Greenville Coll, Houghton Coll, Malone Coll, Messiah Coll, Taylor U, Trinity Coll, Westmont Coll, and Wheaton Coll. Teacher certification in elementary, secondary, and special education. Exchange programs abroad in Korea (Han Nam U) and Spain (U of Salamanca). Study abroad also in Costa Rica, European countries, and Kenya. ROTC at Seattle U. AFROTC at U of Washington.
**Honors:** Honors program.
**Academic Assistance:** Remedial reading, writing, math, and study skills. Nonremedial tutoring.
**STUDENT LIFE. Housing:** All unmarried students under age 21, with less than 135 earned credits, and enrolled for nine or more credits must live on campus unless living with family. Coed and women's dorms. School-owned/operated apartments. On-campus married-student housing. 47% of students live in college housing.
**Social atmosphere:** According to the student newspaper, the university encourages a conservative lifestyle through such policies as a prohibition against dancing and the use of alcohol, so it is "pretty mellow." The Associated Students organization is one of the most socially influential groups on campus, as is Student Government. Popular events include the talent show, Homecoming, and the spring picnic. Students meet at the student union building and Gwinn Commons. Off campus, they frequent Dick's hamburger stand on Queen Anne Avenue and the Ship Canal.
**Services and counseling/handicapped student services:** Placement services. Health service. Counseling services for minority and older students. Personal and psychological counseling. Career and academic guidance services. Religious counseling. Physically disabled student services. Learning disabled services. Notetaking services. Reader services for the blind.
**Campus organizations:** Undergraduate student government. Student newspaper (Falcon, published once/week). Literary magazine. Yearbook. Concert and pep bands, orchestra, SPU Singers, drama productions, debating, forensics club, Centurions and Ambassador service clubs, departmental and special-interest groups.
**Religious organizations:** Campus Ministries.
**Minority/foreign student organizations:** Multiethnic student group. International Student Association.
**ATHLETICS. Physical education requirements:** None.
**Intercollegiate competition:** 8% of students participate. Basketball (M,W), cheerleading (M,W), crew (M,W), cross-country (M,W), gymnastics (W), soccer (M), track (indoor) (M), track and field (indoor) (M,W), track and field (outdoor) (M,W), volleyball (W). Member of NCAA Division II, Northwest Collegiate Soccer Conference, Pacific West Conference.
**Intramural and club sports:** 79% of students participate. Intramural badminton, basketball, cross-country, floor hockey, football, pickleball, softball, swimming, table tennis, tennis, volleyball, weight lifting, wrestling. Men's club cheerleading, rugby, volleyball. Women's club cheerleading, soccer.
**ADMISSIONS. Academic basis for candidate selection** (in order of priority): Secondary school record, standardized test scores, essay, school's recommendation, class rank.
**Nonacademic basis for candidate selection:** Character and personality and extracurricular participation are important. Particular talent or ability and alumni/ae relationship are considered.
**Requirements:** Graduation from secondary school is required; GED is accepted. 14 units and the following program of study are recommended: 4 units of English, 3 units of math, 2 units of science, 3 units of foreign language, 2 units of social studies. Minimum combined SAT score of 950 (composite ACT score of 20) and minimum 2.5 GPA recommended. Portfolios required of art scholarship applicants. Auditions required of music scholarship applicants. ACCESS program for applicants not meeting standard requirements. SAT or ACT is required. Campus visit and interview recommended. Off-campus interviews available with an admissions representative.
**Procedure:** Take SAT or ACT by February of 12th year. Suggest filing application by December 1. Application deadline is September 1. Notification of admission on rolling basis. Reply is required by May 1 or within 30 days of acceptance if accepted after May 1. $200 tuition deposit, refundable until June 1. $100 room deposit, refundable until June 1. Freshmen accepted in terms other than fall.
**Special programs:** Credit and/or placement may be granted through CEEB Advanced Placement exams for scores of 3 or higher. Credit and/or placement may be granted through CLEP general and subject exams. Credit and placement may be granted through ACT PEP, DANTES, and challenge exams, and military education. Early decision program. In fall 1993, 240 applied for early decision and 230 were accepted. Deadline for applying for early decision is December 1. Early entrance/early admission program. Concurrent enrollment program.
**Transfer students:** Transfer students accepted for terms other than fall. In fall 1993, 43% of all new students were transfers into all classes. 708 transfer applications were received, 576 were accepted. Application deadline is September 1 for fall; March 1 for spring. Minimum 2.5 GPA required. Lowest course grade accepted is "C." Maximum number of transferable credits is 90 quarter hours. At least 45 quarter hours must be completed at the university to receive degree.
**Admissions contact:** Janet Ward, M.P.A., Director of Admissions/Registrar. 206 281-2021, 800 366-3344.

**FINANCIAL AID. Available aid:** Pell grants, SEOG, state scholarships and grants, school scholarships and grants, private scholarships, ROTC scholarships, academic merit scholarships, and athletic scholarships. Black Achievers Scholarship. Perkins Loans (NDSL), PLUS, Stafford Loans (GSL), NSL, and SLS. Extended payment and installment plans.
**Financial aid statistics:** 13% of aid is not need-based. In 1993-94, 95% of all undergraduate applicants received aid; 98% of freshman applicants. Average amounts of aid awarded freshmen: Scholarships and grants, $6,658; loans, $3,384.
**Supporting data/closing dates:** FAFSA/FAF/FFS: Priority filing date is March 1. Notification of awards begins March 15.
**Financial aid contact:** Jeanne Rich, Director of Financial Aid/Student Employment. 206 281-2046, 800 366-3344.

**STUDENT EMPLOYMENT.** College Work/Study Program. Institutional employment. 15% of full-time undergraduates work on campus during school year. Students may expect to earn an average of $1,650 during school year. Off-campus part-time employment opportunities rated "excellent."

**COMPUTER FACILITIES.** 140 IBM/IBM-compatible and Macintosh/Apple microcomputers; 105 are networked. Students may access Digital minicomputer/mainframe systems, Internet. Client/LAN operating systems include Apple/Macintosh, DOS. Computer languages and software packages include dBASE, Lotus 1-2-3, WordPerfect. Computer use restricted to specific departments; most have fees.
**Fees:** None.
**Hours:** 8 AM-11 PM (M-Th); 8 AM-5 PM (F); 10 AM-5 PM (Sa).

# Seattle University

**Seattle, WA 98122 — 206 296-6000**

**1993-94 Costs.** Tuition: $12,150. Room: $2,850. Board: $1,200-$1,800. Fees, books, misc. academic expenses (school's estimate): $500.
**Enrollment.** Undergraduates: 1,099 men, 1,370 women (full-time). Freshman class: 1,386 applicants, 1,155 accepted, 454 enrolled. Graduate enrollment: 835 men, 836 women.
**Test score averages/ranges.** Average SAT scores: 462 verbal, 510 math. Range of SAT scores of middle 50%: 450-500 verbal, 475-525 math.
**Faculty.** 249 full-time; 167 part-time. 93% of faculty holds highest degree in specific field. Student/faculty ratio: 14 to 1.
**Selectivity rating.** Less competitive.

**PROFILE.** Seattle University, founded in 1891, is a private, church-affiliated, comprehensive institution. Programs are offered through the College of Arts and Sciences; the Schools of Business, Education, Nursing, and Science and Engineering; and the Graduate School. Its 56-acre campus is located in Seattle.

**Accreditation:** NASC. Professionally accredited by the Accreditation Board for Engineering and Technology, the American Assembly of Collegiate Schools of Business, the National Council for Accreditation of Teacher Education, the National League for Nursing.
**Religious orientation:** Seattle University is affiliated with the Roman Catholic Church (Society of Jesus); 10 quarter hours of religion required.
**Library:** Collections totaling over 198,000 volumes, 1,680 periodical subscriptions, and 183,500 microform items.
**Special facilities/museums:** Observatory, nuclear reactor.
**Athletic facilities:** Gymnasiums, basketball, handball, racquetball, squash, and tennis courts, weight room, swimming pools, athletic fields.

**STUDENT BODY. Undergraduate profile:** 69% are state residents; 12% are transfers. 15% Asian-American, 4% Black, 2% Hispanic, 1% Native American, 78% White. Average age of undergraduates is 22.
**Freshman profile:** 1% of freshmen who took SAT scored 700 or over on verbal, 3% scored 700 or over on math; 8% scored 600 or over on verbal, 22% scored 600 or over on math; 34% scored 500 or over on verbal, 53% scored 500 or over on math; 79% scored 400 or over on verbal, 93% scored 400 or over on math; 100% scored 300 or over on verbal, 100% scored 300 or over on math. 90% of accepted applicants took SAT; 10% took ACT. 52% of freshmen come from public schools.
**Undergraduate achievement:** 78% of fall 1991 freshmen returned for fall 1992 term. 45% of entering class graduated. 25% of students who completed a degree program went on to graduate study within five years.
**Foreign students:** 413 students are from out of the country. Countries represented include China, Indonesia, Japan, Korea, and Saudi Arabia; 61 in all.

**PROGRAMS OF STUDY. Degrees:** B.A., B.Crim.Just., B.Ed., B.Pub.Admin., B.S.
**Majors:** Accounting, Art, Biochemistry, Biology, Business, Business Economics, Chemistry, Civil Engineering, Clinical Chemistry, Communication Studies, Computer Science, Criminal Justice, Diagnostic Ultrasound, Drama, Economics, Electrical Engineering, English, Environmental Engineering, Finance, Fine Arts, French, General Science, German, History, Humanities, International Business, International Studies, Journalism, Liberal Studies, Management, Marketing, Mathematics, Mechanical Engineering, Medical Technology, Nursing, Philosophy, Physics, Political Science, Psychology, Public Administration, Sociology, Spanish, Theology/Religious Studies.
**Distribution of degrees:** The majors with the highest enrollment are business, psychology, and engineering; philosophy, sociology, and theology/religious studies have the lowest.
**Requirements:** General education requirement.
**Academic regulations:** Freshmen must maintain minimum 2.0 GPA; sophomores, 2.0 GPA; juniors, 2.25 GPA; seniors, 2.25 GPA.
**Special:** Minors offered in all arts and sciences areas. Alcohol studies program offered. Coeducational program beginning in ninth grade grants secondary school diploma and bachelor's degree in six years through Seattle U's Matteo Ricci College. Double majors. Independent study. Accelerated study. Pass/fail grading option. Internships. Graduate school at which undergraduates may take graduate-level courses. Preprofessional programs in law, medicine, veterinary science, and dentistry. Sea Semester. Teacher certification in early childhood, elementary, secondary, and special education. Certification in specific subject areas. Exchange programs abroad in France, Germany, Italy, Japan, Spain, Thailand, and Venezuela. ROTC. NROTC and AFROTC at U of Washington.
**Honors:** Honors program. Honor societies.
**Academic Assistance:** Remedial reading, writing, math, and study skills. Nonremedial tutoring.

**STUDENT LIFE. Housing:** All unmarried freshmen under age 21 must live on campus unless living with family. Coed dorms. 25% of students live in college housing.
**Social atmosphere:** According to the editor of the student newspaper, "Popular consensus is that cultural life at SU is 'culturally dead.' However, I think SU gets some popular speakers/lecturers, and activity on campus is fine." Popular events include men's and women's basketball games, and various dances at Campion Ballroom held throughout the year. On campus, students meet at the Student Union Building and Connolly Center. Off campus, they frequent the Comet Tavern.
**Services and counseling/handicapped student services:** Placement services. Health service. Women's center. Day care. Counseling services for minority, veteran, and older students. Personal and psychological counseling. Career and academic guidance services. Religious counseling. Physically disabled student services. Learning disabled services. Notetaking services. Tape recorders. Tutors. Reader services for the blind.
**Campus organizations:** Undergraduate student government. Student newspaper (Spectator, published once/week). Literary magazine. Yearbook. Associated Women Students, chorale, ensemble, debating, drama group, hiking, sailing, and ski clubs, political, service, and social groups.
**Religious organizations:** Campus Ministry.
**Minority/foreign student organizations:** Black Student Alliance, Pacific Islanders. International Student Center.

**ATHLETICS. Physical education requirements:** None.
**Intercollegiate competition:** 7% of students participate. Alpine skiing (M,W), basketball (M,W), cross-country (M,W), soccer (M,W), tennis (M,W). Member of NAIA, Northwest Collegiate Ski Association, Northwest Collegiate Soccer Conference.
**Intramural and club sports:** 40% of students participate. Intramural badminton, basketball, flag football, floor hockey, indoor soccer, racquetball, softball, swimming, table tennis, tennis, volleyball, walleyball. Men's club Alpine skiing, archery, cheerleading, crew, cycling, golf, hiking, riflery, sailing, table tennis, volleyball. Women's club Alpine skiing, archery, cheerleading, crew, cycling, golf, hiking, riflery, sailing, volleyball.

**ADMISSIONS. Academic basis for candidate selection** (in order of priority): Secondary school record, class rank, standardized test scores, school's recommendation, essay.
**Nonacademic basis for candidate selection:** Particular talent or ability is important. Character and personality, extracurricular participation, and alumni/ae relationship are considered.
**Requirements:** Graduation from secondary school is required; GED is accepted. 16 units and the following program of study are recommended: 4 units of English, 2 units of math, 1 unit of science, 2 units of foreign language, 2 units of social studies, 5 units of electives. More secondary school units recommended in each subject. Minimum combined SAT score of 850, rank in top half of secondary school class, and minimum 2.5 GPA required; minimum SAT score of 1000 and 3.0 GPA recommended. Minimum of 3 units of math, including trigonometry (preferred), and minimum of 2 units of lab science required of most applicants to School of Science and Engineering. Early Success Program for applicants not normally admissible. SAT or ACT is required. Campus visit recommended. Off-campus interviews available with an admissions representative.
**Procedure:** Take SAT or ACT by October of 12th year. Visit college for interview by February of 12th year. Suggest filing application by March 1. Application deadline is September 1. Notification of admission on rolling basis. Reply is required by June 1. $100 tuition deposit, refundable until May 1. $85 room deposit, refundable until June 1. Freshmen accepted in terms other than fall.
**Special programs:** Admission may be deferred one year. Placement may be granted through CEEB Advanced Placement exams. Credit and/or placement may be granted through CLEP subject exams. Credit and placement may be granted through challenge exams. Early decision program. In fall 1992, 2 applied for early decision and 2 were accepted. Deadline for applying for early decision is October 1. Early entrance/early admission program.
**Transfer students:** Transfer students accepted for terms other than fall. In fall 1992, 12% of all new students were transfers into all classes. 880 transfer applications were received, 709 were accepted. Application deadline is September 1 for fall; March 1 for spring. Minimum 2.5 GPA required. SAT/ACT scores and secondary school and college transcripts required of transfer applicants with fewer than 45 quarter hours. Lowest course grade accepted is "C." Maximum number of transferable credits is 90 quarter hours from a two-year school and 135 quarter hours from a four-year school. At least 45 quarter hours must be completed at the university to receive degree.
**Admissions contact:** Lee Gerig, M.S.Ed., Dean of Admission. 206 296-5800, 800 542-0833 (in-state), 800 426-7123 (out-of-state).

**FINANCIAL AID. Available aid:** Pell grants, SEOG, state scholarships and grants, school scholarships and grants, private scholarships and grants, ROTC scholarships, academic merit scholarships, athletic scholarships, and aid for undergraduate foreign students. Perkins Loans (NDSL), PLUS, Stafford Loans (GSL), NSL, private loans, and SLS. Deferred payment plan and family tuition reduction.
**Financial aid statistics:** 22% of aid is not need-based. In 1992-93, 98% of all undergraduate applicants received aid; 66% of freshman applicants. Average amounts of aid awarded freshmen: Scholarships and grants, $4,700; loans, $2,500.
**Supporting data/closing dates:** FAFSA/FAF/FFS: Priority filing date is February 1. Income tax forms: Accepted on rolling basis. Notification of awards begins February 15.
**Financial aid contact:** Jim White, Director of Financial Aid. 206 296-5850.

**STUDENT EMPLOYMENT.** College Work/Study Program. Institutional employment. 25% of full-time undergraduates work on campus during school year. Students may expect to earn an average of $2,200 during school year. Off-campus part-time employment opportunities rated "excellent."

**COMPUTER FACILITIES.** 250 IBM/IBM-compatible, Macintosh/Apple, and RISC-/UNIX-based microcomputers; 150 are networked. Students may access IBM minicomputer/mainframe systems. Residence halls may be equipped with stand-alone microcomputers, networked microcomputers. Computer facilities are available to all students. **Hours:** 6 AM-midn.

**GRADUATE CAREER DATA.** Highest graduate school enrollment: U of Washington.

## University of Puget Sound

**Tacoma, WA 98416** **206 756-3100**

**1994-95 Costs.** Tuition: $16,230. Room & board: $4,500. Fees, books, misc. academic expenses (school's estimate): $770.

**Enrollment.** Undergraduates: 1,132 men, 1,606 women (full-time). Freshman class: 4,044 applicants, 2,826 accepted, 688 enrolled. Graduate enrollment: 84 men, 231 women.

**Test score averages/ranges.** Average SAT scores: 520 verbal, 581 math. Range of SAT scores of middle 50%: 450-560 verbal, 510-630 math. Average ACT scores: 25 English, 25 math, 25 composite. Range of ACT scores of middle 50%: 23-27 English, 22-27 math.

**Faculty.** 202 full-time; 25 part-time. 86% of faculty holds highest degree in specific field. Student/faculty ratio: 13 to 1.

**Selectivity rating.** Highly competitive.

**PROFILE.** The University of Puget Sound is a private, church-affiliated university. Founded in 1888, it became a four-year college in 1913, and gained university status in 1960. Its 72-acre campus, with Tudor Gothic red brick buildings constructed during the 1950s and 1960s, is located in Tacoma, 35 miles from Seattle.

**Accreditation:** NASC. Professionally accredited by the American Bar Association, the American Physical Therapy Association, the Association of American Law Schools, the Committee on Allied Health Education and Accreditation, the National Association of Schools of Music, the National Council for Accreditation of Teacher Education.

**Religious orientation:** University of Puget Sound is nonsectarian; no religious requirements.

**Library:** Collections totaling over 345,533 volumes, 1,933 periodical subscriptions, and 146,320 microform items.

**Special facilities/museums:** Art gallery, natural history museum, transmission and scanning electron microscope, spectrophotometer, X-ray lab.

**Athletic facilities:** Gymnasium, field house, stadium, handball, racquetball, and tennis courts, track, weight room, baseball and intramural fields, swimming pool.

**STUDENT BODY. Undergraduate profile:** 46% are state residents; 26% are transfers. 9% Asian-American, 2% Black, 2% Hispanic, 1% Native American, 78% White, 8% Other. Average age of undergraduates is 20.

**Freshman profile:** 2% of freshmen who took SAT scored 700 or over on verbal, 10% scored 700 or over on math; 19% scored 600 or over on verbal, 45% scored 600 or over on math; 60% scored 500 or over on verbal, 84% scored 500 or over on math; 95% scored 400 or over on verbal, 98% scored 400 or over on math; 100% scored 300 or over on verbal, 100% scored 300 or over on math. 14% of freshmen who took ACT scored 30 or over on English, 14% scored 30 or over on math, 15% scored 30 or over on composite; 70% scored 24 or over on English, 63% scored 24 or over on math, 73% scored 24 or over on composite; 96% scored 18 or over on English, 97% scored 18 or over on math, 98% scored 18 or over on composite; 100% scored 12 or over on English, 100% scored 12 or over on math, 100% scored 12 or over on composite. 96% of accepted applicants took SAT; 41% took ACT. 83% of freshmen come from public schools.

**Undergraduate achievement:** 86% of fall 1992 freshmen returned for fall 1993 term. 55% of entering class graduated. 9% of students who completed a degree program immediately went on to graduate study.

**Foreign students:** 31 students are from out of the country. Countries represented include Canada, Germany, Hong Kong, Japan, Sri Lanka, and the United Kingdom; 16 in all.

**PROGRAMS OF STUDY. Degrees:** B.A., B.Mus., B.S.

**Majors:** Accounting, Art, Asian Studies, Biology, Business Administration, Chemistry, Church Music, Communication, Comparative Sociology, Computer Science, Computer Science/Business, Computer Science/Mathematics, Economics, Elective Studies in Business, English, Foreign Language/International Affairs, French, Geology, German, History, Mathematics, Music, Music Education, Music Performance, Natural Science, Occupational Therapy, Philosophy, Physical Education, Physics, Politics/Government, Psychology, Public Administration, Religion, Spanish, Theatre Arts.

**Distribution of degrees:** The majors with the highest enrollment are business administration, English, and psychology; public administration, Asian studies, and geology have the lowest.

**Requirements:** General education requirement.

**Academic regulations:** Minimum 2.0 GPA must be maintained.

**Special:** Minors offered in many majors and in Chinese, classics, Japanese, and women's studies. Business leadership and honors programs. Double majors. Dual degrees. Independent study. Pass/fail grading option. Internships. Cooperative education programs. Graduate school at which undergraduates may take graduate-level courses. Preprofessional programs in law, medicine, veterinary science, and dentistry. 3-2 engineering programs with Boston U, Columbia U, Duke U, U of Southern California, and Washington U (St. Louis). Washington Semester. Teacher certification in elementary and secondary education. Certification in specific subject areas. Exchange programs abroad in Germany (U of Passau), Scotland (U of Aberdeen), and Australia (Griffith U). Study abroad also in China, England, India, Japan, Malaysia, Singapore, South Korea, Spain, Thailand, and France. ROTC at Seattle U.

**Honors:** Phi Beta Kappa. Honors program. Honor societies.

**Academic Assistance:** Remedial math. Nonremedial tutoring.

**STUDENT LIFE. Housing:** Students may live on or off campus. Coed and women's dorms. Sorority and fraternity housing. School-owned/operated apartments. 57% of students live in college housing.

**Services and counseling/handicapped student services:** Placement services. Health service. Counseling services for minority students. Personal and psychological counseling. Career and academic guidance services. Religious counseling. Physically disabled student services. Learning disabled services. Tape recorders.

**Campus organizations:** Undergraduate student government. Student newspaper (The Trail, published once/week). Literary magazine. Yearbook. Radio station. Choral groups, orchestras, bands, chamber ensembles, Inside Theatre Productions, Model UN, Circle K, Earth Activists, Amnesty International, juggling club, academic and special-interest groups, 38 organizations in all. Six fraternities, all with chapter houses; six sororities, all with chapter houses. 33% of men join a fraternity. 33% of women join a sorority.

**Religious organizations:** Catholic Campus Ministry, Christian Science Organization, Fellowship of Christian Athletes, Intervarsity Christian Fellowship, Jewish Student Organization, Latter-Day Saints Association, Messenger Campus Fellowship, Wesley Christian Fellowship, Young Life Discipleship.

**Minority/foreign student organizations:** Black Student Union, Hui-O-Hawaii, CHISPA.

**ATHLETICS. Physical education requirements:** None.

**Intercollegiate competition:** 20% of students participate. Alpine skiing (M,W), baseball (M), basketball (M,W), cheerleading (M,W), crew (M,W), cross-country (M,W), diving (M,W), football (M), golf (M), softball (W), swimming (M,W), tennis (M,W), track (outdoor) (M,W), track and field (outdoor) (M,W), volleyball (W). Member of Columbia Football Association, NAIA, National Collegiate Ski Association, Northwest Collegiate Soccer Conference, United States Rowing Association.

**Intramural and club sports:** 40% of students participate. Intramural basketball, bowling, flag football, golf, pickleball, racquetball, soccer, softball, volleyball. Men's club lacrosse, sailing. Women's club lacrosse, sailing.

**ADMISSIONS. Academic basis for candidate selection** (in order of priority): Secondary school record, standardized test scores, school's recommendation, essay, class rank.

**Nonacademic basis for candidate selection:** Particular talent or ability is emphasized. Character and personality, geographical distribution, and alumni/ae relationship are important. Extracurricular participation is considered.

**Requirements:** Graduation from secondary school is required; GED is accepted. 16 units and the following program of study are recommended: 4 units of English, 3 units of math, 3 units of lab science, 2 units of foreign language, 3 units of social studies. Audition required of music program applicants. SAT is required; ACT may be substituted. Campus visit and interview recommended. Off-campus interviews available with an admissions representative.

**Procedure:** Take SAT or ACT by January of 12th year. Visit college for interview by February 15 of 12th year. Suggest filing application by February 15. Application deadline is March 1. Notification of admission on rolling basis. Reply is required by May 1. $100 tuition deposit, refundable until May 1. $200 room deposit, refundable until May 1. Freshmen accepted in terms other than fall.

**Special programs:** Admission may be deferred one year. Credit and/or placement may be granted through CEEB Advanced Placement exams for scores of 3 or higher. Early decision program. In fall 1993, 147 applied for early decision and 128 were accepted. Deadline for applying for early decision is November 15. Early entrance/early admission program. Concurrent enrollment program.

**Transfer students:** Transfer students accepted for terms other than fall. In fall 1993, 26% of all new students were transfers into all classes. 1,552 transfer applications were received, 1,190 were accepted. Application deadline is March 1 for fall; December 1 for spring. Minimum 2.5 GPA required. Lowest course grade accepted is "D." Maximum number of transferable credits is 64 semester hours. At least 64 semester hours must be completed at the university to receive degree.

**Admissions contact:** George H. Mills, Jr., Ph.D., Dean of Admissions. 206 756-3211.

**FINANCIAL AID. Available aid:** Pell grants, SEOG, state scholarships and grants, school scholarships and grants, private scholarships and grants, ROTC scholarships, academic merit scholarships, and athletic scholarships. Perkins Loans (NDSL), PLUS, Stafford Loans (GSL), school loans, private loans, and SLS. Deferred payment plan. Education Credit Corp., EXCEL, College Board Extra Credit.

**Financial aid statistics:** 35% of aid is not need-based. In 1993-94, 90% of all undergraduate applicants received aid; 90% of freshman applicants. Average amounts of aid awarded freshmen: Scholarships and grants, $6,800; loans, $3,440.

**Supporting data/closing dates:** FAFSA/FAF: Priority filing date is February 15. Notification of awards begins April 1.

**Financial aid contact:** Steven R. Thorndill, M.Ed., Director of Financial Aid and Scholarships. 206 756-3214.

**STUDENT EMPLOYMENT.** College Work/Study Program. Institutional employment. 33% of full-time undergraduates work on campus during school year. Students may expect to earn an average of $1,900 during school year. Off-campus part-time employment opportunities rated "excellent."

**COMPUTER FACILITIES.** 136 IBM/IBM-compatible and Macintosh/Apple microcomputers; 124 are networked. Students may access Digital minicomputer/mainframe systems, Internet. Client/LAN operating systems include Apple/Macintosh, DOS, LocalTalk/AppleTalk, Novell. Computer languages and software packages include BASIC, C, COBOL, Cricket Graph, dBASE III, EXCEL, FORTRAN, Lotus 1-2-3, MINITAB, Modula 2, PageMaker, Pascal, Prolog, SuperPaint, Word, WordPerfect, Works. Computer facilities are available to all students.

**GRADUATE CAREER DATA.** Graduate school percentages: 3% enter law school. 2% enter medical school. 1% enter dental school. 3% enter graduate business programs. 20% enter graduate arts and sciences programs. Highest graduate school enrollments: Seattle U, U of California, U of Chicago, U of Oregon, U of Puget Sound, U of Washington, U of Wisconsin, Washington State U, Western Washington U. 51% of graduates choose careers in business and industry. Companies and businesses that hire graduates: Boeing, Microsoft, Nordstrom, Weyerhaeuser, Hewlett-Packard, R.E.I., U.S. West Communications.

**PROMINENT ALUMNI/AE.** James Rawn, senior vice-president, Shearson Lehman Brothers; Judith Aaron, executive director, Carnegie Hall; Ronald Rau, senior physicist, Brookhaven National Laboratories; Jeff Smith, *The Frugal Gourmet*, PBS TV; Fredrick F. Holmes, researcher in cancer epidemiology; Richard Stolarski, research director, NASA's Goddard Space Institute.

# University of Washington

**Seattle, WA 98195** **206 543-2100**

**1993-94 Costs.** Tuition: $2,532 (state residents), $7,134 (out-of-state). Room & board: $4,086. Fees, books, misc. academic expenses (school's estimate): $687.
**Enrollment.** Undergraduates: 10,377 men, 10,337 women (full-time). Freshman class: 12,516 applicants, 6,969 accepted, 3,626 enrolled. Graduate enrollment: 4,842 men, 4,278 women.
**Test score averages/ranges.** Range of SAT scores of middle 50%: 420-540 verbal, 500-630 math. Range of ACT scores of middle 50%: 22-27 composite.
**Faculty.** 1,907 full-time; 665 part-time. 90% of faculty holds doctoral degree. Student/faculty ratio: 11 to 1.
**Selectivity rating.** More competitive.

**PROFILE.** The University of Washington, founded in 1861, is a public, comprehensive institution. Programs are offered through the Colleges of Architecture and Urban Planning; Arts and Sciences; Education; and Engineering, Forest Resources, and Ocean and Fishery Sciences; the Graduate Schools of Business, Library and Information Science, Public Affairs, and Public Health and Community Medicine; and the Schools of Business, Dentistry, Law, Medicine, Nursing, Pharmacy, and Social Work. Its 680-acre campus is located in a residential section of Seattle.

**Accreditation:** NASC. Numerous professional accreditations.
**Religious orientation:** University of Washington is nonsectarian; no religious requirements.
**Library:** Collections totaling over 4,800,000 volumes, 50,000 periodical subscriptions, and 5,300,000 microform items.
**Special facilities/museums:** Art gallery, anthropology and natural history museum, arboretum, closed-circuit TV studio.
**Athletic facilities:** Intramural activities center, waterfront activities center, golf driving range, practice climbing rock.

**STUDENT BODY. Undergraduate profile:** 90% are state residents; 33% are transfers. 19% Asian-American, 4% Black, 3% Hispanic, 1% Native American, 65% White, 8% Other. Average age of undergraduates is 21.
**Freshman profile:** 1% of freshmen who took SAT scored 700 or over on verbal, 7% scored 700 or over on math; 10% scored 600 or over on verbal, 38% scored 600 or over on math; 41% scored 500 or over on verbal, 75% scored 500 or over on math; 83% scored 400 or over on verbal, 97% scored 400 or over on math; 97% scored 300 or over on verbal, 100% scored 300 or over on math. 94% of accepted applicants took SAT; 19% took ACT.
**Undergraduate achievement:** 90% of fall 1991 freshmen returned for fall 1992 term. 30% of entering class graduated.
**Foreign students:** 644 students are from out of the country. Countries represented include Canada, China, Hong Kong, Japan, Korea, and Taiwan; 85 in all.

**PROGRAMS OF STUDY. Degrees:** B.A., B.Clin.Hlth.Serv., B.F.A., B.Mus., B.S.
**Majors:** Accounting, Aeronautics/Astronautics, Afro-American Studies, American Indian Studies, Anthropology, Architecture/Urban Planning, Art, Art History, Asian Languages/Literatures, Astronomy, Atmospheric Science, Biochemistry, Biology, Botany, Building Construction, Business Administration, Chemical Engineering, Chemistry, China Regional Studies, Civil Engineering, Classical Studies, Clinical Health Services, Communications, Comparative History of Ideas, Comparative Religion, Computer Engineering, Computer Science, Dance, Dental Hygiene, Drama, East Asian Studies, Economics, Electrical Engineering, Elementary Education, English, Environmental Health, Environmental Studies, Ethnic Studies, Fisheries, Forest Resource Management, French, General Studies, Geography, Geological Sciences, Germanics, Greek, History, Industrial Engineering, International Studies, Italian, Japan/Korea Regional Studies, Jewish Studies, Landscape Architecture, Latin, Linguistics, Logging Engineering, Mathematics, Mechanical Engineering, Medical Technology, Metallurgical/Ceramic Engineering, Microbiology/Immunology, Music, Near Eastern Languages/Literatures, Nuclear Engineering, Nursing, Occupational Therapy, Oceanography, Peace/Strategic Studies, Pharmacy, Philosophy, Physical Therapy, Physics, Political Science, Prosthetics/Orthotics, Psychology, Pulp/Paper Science, Russian/East European Studies, Scandinavian Languages/Literature, Secondary Education, Slavic Languages/Literatures, Social Welfare, Society/Justice, Sociology, South Asian Studies, Spanish, Speech Communication, Speech/Hearing Sciences, Statistics, Technical Communication, Women's Studies, Wood Science/Technology, Zoology.
**Distribution of degrees:** The majors with the highest enrollment are business administration, psychology, and English; Jewish studies has the lowest.
**Requirements:** General education requirement.
**Academic regulations:** Minimum 2.0 GPA must be maintained.
**Special:** Program offered in marine studies. Courses offered in biochemistry, genetics, geophysics, and many languages, including Bulgarian, Czech, Danish, Hindi, Korean, Polish, Romanian, Serbo-Croation, Thai, Tibetan, and Urdu. Self-designed majors. Double majors. Dual degrees. Independent study. Accelerated study. Pass/fail grading option. Internships. Cooperative education programs. Graduate school at which undergraduates may take graduate-level courses. Preprofessional programs in medicine and dentistry. Washington Semester. Teacher certification in elementary, secondary, special education, and bilingual/bicultural education. Study abroad in China, Denmark, Ecuador, Egypt, Finland, France, Germany, Iceland, Indonesia, Israel, Italy, Japan, Mexico, New Zealand, Norway, South Korea, the former Soviet Republics, Spain, Sweden, Taiwan, and the United Kingdom. ROTC, NROTC, and AFROTC.
**Honors:** Phi Beta Kappa. Honors program. Honor societies.
**Academic Assistance:** Remedial reading, writing, math, and study skills. Nonremedial tutoring.

**STUDENT LIFE. Housing:** Students may live on or off campus. Coed dorms. School-owned/operated apartments. Off-campus married-student housing. International, religious, language, and other special-interest houses. 15% of students live in college housing.
**Social atmosphere:** The student newspaper reports, "People find their niche within their major or with organizations they choose to be active in." On campus, students congregate at By George Cafe and the Husky Union Building. Gathering spots off campus include The Last Exit, the College Inn Pub, Allegro, Lox Stock and Bagel, and The Ram. Greeks and Student Government are influential groups on campus. "With a student population as large and diverse as ours, there is no single activity that binds us. However, there are ample social/entertainment/cultural/sports events available off campus."
**Services and counseling/handicapped student services:** Placement services. Health service. Women's center. Day care. Counseling services for minority, military, veteran, and older students. Birth control, personal, and psychological counseling. Career and academic guidance services. Physically disabled student services. Notetaking services. Tape recorders. Tutors. Reader services for the blind.
**Campus organizations:** Undergraduate student government. Student newspaper (Daily). Literary magazine. Yearbook. Radio station. Chorus and glee clubs, orchestra, band, opera workshop, madrigal singers, four theatres, Feminist Theory Colloquium, Circle K, Model UN, PIRG, Amnesty International, College Republicans, academic, social, and special-interest groups. 32 fraternities, all with chapter houses; 18 sororities, all with chapter houses. 18% of men join a fraternity. 16% of women join a sorority.
**Religious organizations:** Asian American Christian Fellowship, Bahai Association, B'nai B'rith Hillel, Baptist Student Union, Campus Crusade for Christ, Christian Student Association, Muslim Student Association, Newman Catholic Association, Student Buddhism Association, T.E.A.M. Calvary Fellowship, University Christian Union, Upper Room Bible Study.
**Minority/foreign student organizations:** Hui O Hawaii, MEChA, Native American Student Council. African, Chinese, Filipino, Indian, Israeli, Japanese, Khmer, Laotian, Norwegian, Scandinavian, Slavic, and Turkish groups.

**ATHLETICS. Physical education requirements:** None.
**Intercollegiate competition:** Baseball (M), basketball (M,W), crew (M,W), cross-country (M,W), football (M), golf (M,W), gymnastics (W), soccer (M), swimming (M,W), tennis (M,W), track and field (M,W), volleyball (W). Member of AAWU, NCAA Division I, NCAA Division I-A for football, Pacific 10 Conference.

**ADMISSIONS. Academic basis for candidate selection** (in order of priority): Secondary school record, standardized test scores, class rank.
**Nonacademic basis for candidate selection:** Extracurricular participation, particular talent or ability, and alumni/ae relationship are considered.
**Requirements:** Graduation from secondary school is recommended; GED is not accepted. 15 units and the following program of study are required: 4 units of English, 3 units of math, 2 units of science including 1 unit of lab, 2 units of foreign language, 3 units of social studies, 1 unit of electives including 1/2 unit of art. Minimum 2.0 GPA required. Auditions required of music, dance, and drama program applicants. SAT or ACT is required. No off-campus interviews.
**Procedure:** Take SAT or ACT by December of 12th year. Suggest filing application by February 1; no deadline. Notification of admission by March. Reply is required by May 1. $50 nonrefundable tuition deposit. $300 room deposit, refundable until July 15. Freshmen accepted in terms other than fall.
**Special programs:** Credit and/or placement may be granted through CEEB Advanced Placement exams for scores of 3 or higher. Credit and placement may be granted through challenge exams. Early entrance/early admission program. Concurrent enrollment program.
**Transfer students:** Transfer students accepted for terms other than fall. In fall 1992, 33% of all new students were transfers into all classes. 6,502 transfer applications were received, 2,794 were accepted. Application deadline is July 1 for fall; February 1 for spring. Minimum 2.0 GPA required. Lowest course grade accepted is "D." Maximum number of transferable credits is 135 quarter hours. At least 45 quarter hours must be completed at the university to receive degree.
**Admissions contact:** W.W. Washburn, Director of Admissions and Records. 206 543-9686.

**FINANCIAL AID. Available aid:** Pell grants, SEOG, Federal Nursing Student Scholarships, state scholarships and grants, school scholarships and grants, private scholarships, ROTC scholarships, academic merit scholarships, and athletic scholarships. Perkins Loans (NDSL), PLUS, Stafford Loans (GSL), NSL, Health Professions Loans, school loans, private loans, and SLS.
**Financial aid statistics:** In 1992-93, 36% of all undergraduate applicants received aid; 77% of freshman applicants. Average amounts of aid awarded freshmen: Scholarships and grants, $2,297; loans, $2,798.
**Supporting data/closing dates:** FAFSA/FAF: Priority filing date is February 28. Notification of awards on rolling basis.
**Financial aid contact:** Eric Godfrey, Director of Financial Aid. 206 543-6101.

**STUDENT EMPLOYMENT.** College Work/Study Program. Institutional employment. Off-campus part-time employment opportunities rated "good."

**COMPUTER FACILITIES.** 500 IBM/IBM-compatible, Macintosh/Apple, and RISC-/UNIX-based microcomputers; 400 are networked. Students may access Digital, IBM, Sequent minicomputer/mainframe systems, BITNET, Internet. Residence halls may be equipped with stand-alone microcomputers, networked terminals. Computer languages and software packages include APL, Assembly, BASIC, C, COBOL, FORTRAN, LISP, Pascal; data management, documentation/help, editing, file, formatting, graphics programs. Computer facilities are available to all students.
**Fees:** None.
**Hours:** 24 hours.

**GRADUATE CAREER DATA.** Companies and businesses that hire graduates: Boeing, Big Six accounting firms, Honeywell, Microsoft.

**PROMINENT ALUMNI/AE.** Bonnie Dunbar, astronaut; Edward Carlson, chairperson, United Airlines/Westin Hotels; Imogen Cunningham, photographer; John Fery, chairperson, Boise Cascade; Carolyn Dimmick, Washington State supreme court justice.

# Walla Walla College

**College Place, WA 99324** **509 527-2615**

**1994-95 Costs.** Tuition: $10,625. Room & board: $3,135. Fees, books, misc. academic expenses (school's estimate): $1,362.
**Enrollment.** Undergraduates: 807 men, 775 women (full-time). Freshman class: 620 accepted, 310 enrolled. Graduate enrollment: 32 men, 40 women.
**Test score averages/ranges.** Average ACT scores: 21 English, 20 math, 22 composite.
**Faculty.** 122 full-time; 52 part-time. 52% of faculty holds doctoral degree. Student/faculty ratio: 13 to 1.
**Selectivity rating.** Less competitive.

**PROFILE.** Walla Walla, founded in 1892, is a church-affiliated college. Its 55-acre campus is located in College Place, southwest of Spokane.

**Accreditation:** NASC. Professionally accredited by the Accreditation Board for Engineering and Technology, the Council on Social Work Education, the National Association of Schools of Music, the National League for Nursing.
**Religious orientation:** Walla Walla College is affiliated with the Seventh-day Adventist Church; 16 quarter hours of religion/theology required.
**Library:** Collections totaling over 207,000 volumes, 1,045 periodical subscriptions, and 22,000 microform items.
**Special facilities/museums:** Marine station.

**STUDENT BODY. Undergraduate profile:** 46% are state residents.
**Freshman profile:** 85% of accepted applicants took ACT.
**Undergraduate achievement:** 63% of fall 1992 freshmen returned for fall 1993 term.
**Foreign students:** 158 students are from out of the country. Countries represented include Canada, Japan, Korea, Mexico, Micronesia, and Palau; 34 in all.

**PROGRAMS OF STUDY. Degrees:** B.A., B.Mus., B.S., B.S.Bus.Admin., B.S.Eng., B.Soc.Work.
**Majors:** Art, Automotive Technology, Aviation Technology, Biblical Languages, Bioengineering, Biology, Biomedical Electronics Technology, Biophysics, Business Administration, Business Education, Chemistry, Computer Science, Computer Technology, Electronics Technology, Elementary Education, Engineering, English, French, German, Graphics Technology, Health, History, Humanities, Industrial Technology, Mass Communication, Mathematics, Medical Technology, Medical Technology/Clinical Chemistry, Music, Music Education, Music Performance, Nursing, Office Administration, Physical Education, Physics, Plant Maintenance Technology, Psychology, Religion, Social Work, Sociology, Spanish, Speech Communication, Technology Education, Theology.
**Requirements:** General education requirement.
**Special:** Minors offered in most majors and in aviation, broadcast media, economics, interior design, journalism, library science, and political science. Numerous certificate programs. Courses offered in anthropology, philosophy, and English as a Second Language. Comprehensive exams required for graduation; industrial technology majors must submit final project and/or report. Associate's degrees offered. Double majors. Dual degrees. Cooperative education programs. Preprofessional programs in law, medicine, veterinary science, pharmacy, dentistry, speech/language pathology, audiology, and physical therapy. Teacher certification in elementary and secondary education. Study abroad in Austria, Brazil, England, France, Greece, Italy, Singapore, Spain, and Taiwan.
**Honors:** Honors program.
**Academic Assistance:** Remedial reading, writing, math, and study skills. Nonremedial tutoring.

**STUDENT LIFE. Housing:** All unmarried students under age 22 who have less than 120 quarter hours must live on campus unless living with family. Women's and men's dorms. On-campus married-student housing. 75% of students live in college housing.
**Services and counseling/handicapped student services:** Placement services. Health service. Day care. Birth control and personal counseling. Career and academic guidance services. Religious counseling. Physically disabled student services. Learning disabled services. Notetaking services. Tape recorders. Reader services for the blind.
**Campus organizations:** Student newspaper (Collegian, published once/week). Yearbook. Radio station. Amnesty International, departmental groups.
**Minority/foreign student organizations:** International club, Canadian club.

**ATHLETICS. Physical education requirements:** Two terms of physical education required.

**ADMISSIONS. Academic basis for candidate selection** (in order of priority): Secondary school record, standardized test scores, school's recommendation, class rank.
**Nonacademic basis for candidate selection:** Character and personality are emphasized. Alumni/ae relationship is considered.
**Requirements:** Graduation from secondary school is required; GED is accepted. 10 units and the following program of study are required: 4 units of English, 2 units of math, 2 units of science, 2 units of history. 2 units of foreign language and additional units of mathematics, science, and history recommended. Minimum 2.0 GPA required. 3 units of math required of chemistry, computer science, engineering, math, and physics program applicants. Conditional admission possible for applicants not meeting standard requirements. SAT is recommended. ACT is required. PSAT is recommended. Campus visit and interview recommended. Off-campus interviews available with an admissions representative.
**Procedure:** Take ACT by spring of 12th year. Suggest filing application by spring. Application deadline is August 15. Notification of admission by September 15. Reply is required by September 20. $100 room deposit, refundable until August 1. Freshmen accepted in terms other than fall.
**Special programs:** Admission may be deferred. Credit may be granted through CEEB Advanced Placement for scores of 3 or higher. Credit may be granted through CLEP subject exams and challenge exams. Concurrent enrollment program.
**Transfer students:** Transfer students accepted for terms other than fall. In fall 1993, 148 transfer applications were received, 148 were accepted. Application deadline is August 15. Minimum 2.0 GPA required. Lowest course grade accepted is "D." Maximum number of transferable credits is 96 quarter hours from a two-year school and 156 quarter hours from a four-year school. At least 36 quarter hours must be completed at the college to receive degree. Applicant must be in residence at college a minimum three quarters to receive degree.
**Admissions contact:** Stephen Payne, M.Ed., Vice President for Admissions. 509 527-2327.

**FINANCIAL AID. Available aid:** Pell grants, SEOG, Federal Nursing Student Scholarships, state scholarships and grants, school scholarships and grants, private scholarships and grants, academic merit scholarships, and aid for undergraduate foreign students. Bureau of Indian Affairs grants. Canadian student grant. Perkins Loans (NDSL), PLUS, Stafford Loans (GSL), NSL, school loans, private loans, and SLS. Monthly payment plan (nine months).
**Financial aid statistics:** 30% of aid is not need-based. In 1993-94, 90% of all undergraduate applicants received aid; 70% of freshman applicants. Average amounts of aid awarded freshmen: Scholarships and grants, $3,915; loans, $3,750.
**Supporting data/closing dates:** FAFSA/FAF: Priority filing date is April 1. School's own aid application: Priority filing date is April 1. Income tax forms: Priority filing date is April 1. Notification of awards on rolling basis.
**Financial aid contact:** Cassie Ragenovich, Director of Financial Aid. 509 527-2815.

**STUDENT EMPLOYMENT.** College Work/Study Program. Institutional employment. 82% of full-time undergraduates work on campus during school year. Students may expect to earn an average of $1,650 during school year. Off-campus part-time employment opportunities rated "fair."

**COMPUTER FACILITIES.** 89 IBM/IBM-compatible and RISC-/UNIX-based microcomputers; all are networked. Students may access SUN minicomputer/mainframe systems, BITNET, Internet. Client/LAN operating systems include DOS, UNIX/XENIX/AIX, X-windows, Novell. 100 major computer languages and software packages available. Computer facilities are available to all students.
**Fees:** Computer fee is included in tuition/fees.
**Hours:** 6:30 AM-2 AM.

# Washington State University

**Pullman, WA 99164-1036** **509 335-3564**

**1994-95 Costs.** Tuition: $2,907 (state residents), $8,199 (out-of-state). Room & board: $3,832. Fees, books, misc. academic expenses (school's estimate): $800.
**Enrollment.** Undergraduates: 7,737 men, 6,708 women (full-time). Freshman class: 6,540 applicants, 5,839 accepted, 2,440 enrolled. Graduate enrollment: 1,711 men, 1,322 women.
**Test score averages/ranges.** Range of SAT scores of middle 50%: 370-480 verbal, 430-560 math.
**Faculty.** 965 full-time; 140 part-time. 77% of faculty holds doctoral degree. Student/faculty ratio: 17 to 1.
**Selectivity rating.** Less competitive.

**PROFILE.** Washington State, founded in 1890, is a public, comprehensive university. Programs are offered through the Colleges of Agriculture and Home Economics, Business and Economics, Education, Engineering and Architecture, Pharmacy, Sciences and Arts, and Veterinary Medicine and the Graduate School. Its 600-acre campus is located in Pullman, in southeastern Washington, 80 miles south of Spokane.

**Accreditation:** NASC. Professionally accredited by the Accreditation Board for Engineering and Technology, the American Assembly of Collegiate Schools of Business, the American Council for Construction Education, the American Council on Pharmaceutical Education, the American Dietetic Association, the American Psychological Association, the American Society of Landscape Architects, the American Speech-Language-Hearing Association, the American Veterinary Medical Association, the Foundation for Interior Design Education Research, the National Association of Schools of Music, the National Council for Accreditation of Teacher Education, the National League for Nursing, the National Recreation and Park Association, the Society of American Foresters.
**Religious orientation:** Washington State University is nonsectarian; no religious requirements.
**Library:** Collections totaling over 1,679,500 volumes, 23,356 periodical subscriptions, and 2,827,170 microform items.
**Special facilities/museums:** Art, natural history, and anthropology museums and special collections, performing arts center, mycological herbarium, energy research center, primate research center, observatory and planetarium, electron microscopy center, nuclear radiation center.
**Athletic facilities:** Gymnasiums, swimming pools, badminton, basketball, handball, racquetball, tennis, and volleyball courts, weight rooms, golf course, baseball, football, intramural, soccer and softball fields, climbing wall, and bowling alley.

**STUDENT BODY. Undergraduate profile:** 84% are state residents; 49% are transfers. 5% Asian-American, 2% Black, 2% Hispanic, 1% Native American, 81% White, 9% Other. Average age of undergraduates is 21.
**Freshman profile:** 3% of freshmen who took SAT scored 700 or over on math; 3% scored 600 or over on verbal, 17% scored 600 or over on math; 21% scored 500 or over on verbal, 50% scored 500 or over on math; 65% scored 400 or over on verbal, 82% scored 400 or over on math; 96% scored 300 or over on verbal, 98% scored 300 or over on math. Majority of accepted applicants took SAT.
**Undergraduate achievement:** 84% of fall 1992 freshmen returned for fall 1993 term.
**Foreign students:** 202 students are from out of the country. Countries represented include China, Hong Kong, Japan, Japan, Malaysia, and Taiwan; 88 in all.

**PROGRAMS OF STUDY. Degrees:** B.A., B.Arch., B.F.A., B.Lib.Arts, B.Mus., B.Pharm., B.S.
**Majors:** Agribusiness, Agricultural Economics, Agricultural Engineering, Agricultural Mechanization, Agricultural Molecular Genetics/Cell Biology, Agriculture, American Studies, Animal Science, Anthropology, Apparel/Merchandising/Textiles, Architectural

Studies, Architecture, Asian Studies, Biochemistry, Biology, Business Administration, Chemical Engineering, Chemistry, Child/Consumer/Family Studies, Civil Engineering, Communications, Comparative American Cultures, Computer Science, Construction Management, Criminal Justice, Crop Science, Economics, Education, Electrical Engineering, English, Entomology, Environmental Science, Fine Arts, Food Science/Human Nutrition, Foreign Languages/Literatures, Geology, History, Home Economics, Horticulture, Hotel/Restaurant Administration, Humanities, Interior Design, Landscape Architecture, Liberal Arts, Materials Science/Engineering, Mathematics, Mechanical Engineering, Microbiology, Music, Natural Resource Management, Pharmacy, Philosophy, Physical Education, Physics, Political Science, Psychology, Recreation/Leisure Studies, Social Sciences, Social Studies, Sociology, Soils, Speech/Hearing Sciences, Theatre Arts/Drama, Zoology.

**Distribution of degrees:** The majors with the highest enrollment are business administration, communications, and social sciences; American studies has the lowest.

**Requirements:** General education requirement.

**Academic regulations:** Minimum 2.0 GPA must be maintained.

**Special:** Minors offered in most majors. Students in College of Sciences and Arts may enroll in courses in any other college for which they satisfy prerequisites. Intensive American Language Center. Double majors. Dual degrees. Independent study. Accelerated study. Pass/fail grading option. Internships. Graduate school at which undergraduates may take graduate-level courses. Preprofessional programs in law, medicine, veterinary science, pharmacy, and dentistry. Member of Intercollegiate Center for Nursing Education. Teacher certification in early childhood, elementary, secondary, special education, vo-tech, and bilingual/bicultural education. Certification in specific subject areas. Member of International Student Exchange Program (ISEP). ROTC, NROTC, and AFROTC.

**Honors:** Phi Beta Kappa. Honors program.

**Academic Assistance:** Remedial writing, math, and study skills. Nonremedial tutoring.

**STUDENT LIFE. Housing:** All unmarried freshmen under age 20 must live on campus unless living with family. Coed, women's, and men's dorms. Sorority and fraternity housing. School-owned/operated apartments. Both on-campus and off-campus married-student housing. Special-interest housing. 44% of students live in college housing.

**Social atmosphere:** The student newspaper reports that popular student gathering spots include the Cong, the Campus Tavern, the Golden Goose, Rusty's, and the Old Post Office Theater. Favorite campus events include the Moscow Mardi Gras, Waterbust, the Apple Cup, Homecoming, and graduation. "There really aren't any major student forces. It's a real mix-and-match campus. If something 'big' happens, members of most groups are involved. Students enjoy partying to relieve stress. Intramural sports are big; three-fourths of the students participate. Outdoor recreation is popular."

**Services and counseling/handicapped student services:** Placement services. Health service. Women's center. Day care. Counseling services for minority, veteran, and older students. Birth control, personal, and psychological counseling. Career and academic guidance services. Physically disabled student services. Learning disabled services. Notetaking services. Tape recorders. Reader services for the blind.

**Campus organizations:** Undergraduate student government. Student newspaper (Evergreen, published once/day). Yearbook. Radio and TV stations. Choral group, Arnold Air Society, Circle K, Alpine Club, Amnesty International, College Republicans, academic, professional, and special-interest groups, 100 organizations in all. 25 fraternities, all with chapter houses; 14 sororities, all with chapter houses. 14% of men join a fraternity. 10% of women join a sorority.

**Religious organizations:** Bahai Club, Baptist Student Ministry, Campus Crusade for Christ, Faith Center Ministries, Intervaristy Christian Fellowship, Jewish Students, Living Faith, Maranatha, Navigators, Newman Association.

**Minority/foreign student organizations:** Black Women's Caucus, Native American Alliance. African, Chinese, Indian, Iraqi, Malaysian, Thai, and Vietnamese groups.

**ATHLETICS. Physical education requirements:** None.

**Intercollegiate competition:** 4% of students participate. Baseball (M), basketball (M,W), cheerleading (M,W), crew (W), cross-country (M,W), football (M), golf (M,W), soccer (W), swimming (W), tennis (M,W), track (indoor) (M,W), track (outdoor) (M,W), track and field (indoor) (M,W), track and field (outdoor) (M,W), volleyball (W). Member of NCAA Division I, Pacific 10 Conference.

**Intramural and club sports:** 75% of students participate. Intramural badminton, basketball, billiards, flag football, floor hockey, golf, inner-tube water polo, racquetball, soccer, softball, table tennis, tennis, track and field, volleyball, walleyball, water polo, wrestling. Men's club bowling, cheerleading, crew, handball, lacrosse, martial arts, Nordic skiing, rodeo, rugby, soccer. Women's club bowling, cheerleading, Nordic skiing, rodeo, rugby, softball.

**ADMISSIONS. Academic basis for candidate selection** (in order of priority): Secondary school record, standardized test scores, school's recommendation, essay.

**Nonacademic basis for candidate selection:** Character and personality, extracurricular participation, and particular talent or ability are important.

**Requirements:** Graduation from secondary school is required; GED is accepted. 15 units and the following program of study are required: 4 units of English, 3 units of math, 2 units of science including 1 unit of lab, 3 units of social studies/history, 2 units of foreign language, 1 unit of academic electives. Portfolio required of art program applicants. Audition required of music program applicants. Special application process for applicants not normally admissible. SAT or ACT is required. Campus visit recommended. No off-campus interviews.

**Procedure:** Take SAT or ACT by May of 12th year. Suggest filing application by May 1. Application deadline is August 1. Notification of admission on rolling basis. Reply is required by beginning of semester. $50 nonrefundable tuition deposit. $60 refundable room deposit. Freshmen accepted in terms other than fall.

**Special programs:** Credit and/or placement may be granted through CEEB Advanced Placement exams for scores of 3 or higher. Credit and/or placement may be granted through CLEP general and subject exams. Credit may be granted through DANTES exams and military experience. Placement may be granted through challenge exams. Early entrance/early admission program.

**Transfer students:** Transfer students accepted for terms other than fall. In fall 1993, 49% of all new students were transfers into all classes. 3,986 transfer applications were received, 3,164 were accepted. Application deadline is May 1 for fall; December 1 for spring. Minimum 2.0 GPA required. Lowest course grade accepted is "D." Maximum number of transferable credits is 60 semester hours from a two-year school and 90 semester hours from a four-year school. At least 30 semester hours must be completed at the university to receive degree.

**Admissions contact:** Terry Flynn, M.A., Director of Admissions. 509 335-5586.

**FINANCIAL AID. Available aid:** Pell grants, SEOG, Federal Nursing Student Scholarships, state scholarships and grants, school scholarships and grants, private scholarships and grants, ROTC scholarships, academic merit scholarships, and athletic scholarships. Perkins Loans (NDSL), PLUS, Stafford Loans (GSL), NSL, Health Professions Loans, state loans, and SLS.

**Financial aid statistics:** 23% of aid is not need-based. In 1993-94, 65% of all undergraduate applicants received aid; 37% of freshman applicants. Average amounts of aid awarded freshmen: Loans, $1,246.

**Supporting data/closing dates:** FAFSA: Priority filing date is March 1. Notification of awards on rolling basis.

**Financial aid contact:** Lola Finch, M.A., Director of Financial Aid. 509 335-9711.

**STUDENT EMPLOYMENT.** College Work/Study Program. Institutional employment. 9% of full-time undergraduates work on campus during school year. Students may expect to earn an average of $2,400 during school year. Off-campus part-time employment opportunities rated "good."

**COMPUTER FACILITIES.** 5,000 IBM/IBM-compatible and Macintosh/Apple microcomputers; 1,500 are networked. Students may access Digital, Hewlett-Packard, IBM, Sequent minicomputer/mainframe systems, BITNET, Internet. Residence halls may be equipped with stand-alone microcomputers, networked terminals, modems. Client/LAN operating systems include Apple/Macintosh. Computer languages and software packages include C, COBOL, dBASE, Excel, FORTRAN, Lotus 1-2-3, Natural, WordPerfect. Computer facilities are available to all students.

**Fees:** None.

**Hours:** 24 hours.

**GRADUATE CAREER DATA.** Highest graduate school enrollments: U of Washington, Washington State U.

**PROMINENT ALUMNI/AE.** Neva Abelson, co-developer of Rh factor infusions; Gary Larson, cartoonist, *The Far Side;* Edward R. Murrow, pioneering broadcast journalist.

## Western Washington University

**Bellingham, WA 98225-9009 — 206 650-3000**

**1994-95 Costs.** Tuition: $2,256 (state residents), $7,974 (out-of-state). Room & board: $4,140. Fees, books, misc. academic expenses (school's estimate): $789.

**Enrollment.** Undergraduates: 4,009 men, 4,900 women (full-time). Freshman class: 5,548 applicants, 3,563 accepted, 1,549 enrolled. Graduate enrollment: 297 men, 364 women.

**Test score averages/ranges.** Average SAT scores: 470 verbal, 520 math. Range of SAT scores of middle 50%: 410-520 verbal, 460-580 math.

**Faculty.** 405 full-time; 128 part-time. 82% of faculty holds doctoral degree. Student/faculty ratio: 21 to 1.

**Selectivity rating.** Less competitive.

**PROFILE.** Western Washington, founded in 1893, is a public, comprehensive university. Programs are offered through the Colleges of Arts and Sciences, Business and Economics, Environmental Studies, and Fine and Performing Arts; Fairhaven College; the Graduate School; and the School of Education. Its 190-acre campus is located in Bellingham, in the northwest corner of the state, 20 miles from Vancouver, British Columbia.

**Accreditation:** NASC. Professionally accredited by the American Assembly of Collegiate Schools of Business, the American Speech-Language-Hearing Association, the National Association of Schools of Music, the National Council for Accreditation of Teacher Education, the National Recreation and Park Association.

**Religious orientation:** Western Washington University is nonsectarian; no religious requirements.

**Library:** Collections totaling over 558,692 volumes, 5,644 periodical subscriptions, and 1,804,000 microform items.

**Special facilities/museums:** Outdoor art museum, planetarium, electronic music studio, air pollution lab, motor vehicle research lab, marine lab, wind tunnel, electron microscope, neutron generator lab.

**Athletic facilities:** Gymnasium, basketball, handball, racquetball, tennis, and volleyball courts, swimming pool, weight rooms, track, athletic fields, stadium.

**STUDENT BODY. Undergraduate profile:** 95% are state residents; 35% are transfers. 6.3% Asian-American, 1.4% Black, 2.3% Hispanic, 1.6% Native American, 82.6% White, 5.8% Other. Average age of undergraduates is 21.

**Freshman profile:** 2% of freshmen who took SAT scored 700 or over on math; 8% scored 600 or over on verbal, 17% scored 600 or over on math; 32% scored 500 or over on verbal, 55% scored 500 or over on math; 76% scored 400 or over on verbal, 88% scored 400 or over on math; 100% scored 300 or over on verbal, 100% scored 300 or over on math. 96% of accepted applicants took SAT; 4% took ACT. 90% of freshmen come from public schools.

**Undergraduate achievement:** 84% of fall 1992 freshmen returned for fall 1993 term. 31% of entering class graduated. 7% of students who completed a degree program immediately went on to graduate study.

**Foreign students:** 95 students are from out of the country. Countries represented include Canada, China, France, Germany, Japan, and Taiwan; 32 in all.

**PROGRAMS OF STUDY. Degrees:** B.A., B.A.Ed., B.F.A., B.Mus., B.S.

**Majors:** Accounting, Accounting/Computer Science, American Cultural Studies, Anthropology, Anthropology/Biology, Applied Environmental Geology, Applied Mathematics, Art, Biochemistry, Biology, Biology/Terrestrial Ecology, Business Administration, Business Administration/Computer Science, Canadian-American Studies,

Cellular/Molecular Biology/Biochemistry, Chemistry, Classical Studies, Communication, Community Health, Computer Science, East Asian Studies, Economics, Economics/Accounting, Economics/Environmental Studies, Economics/Mathematics, Economics/Political Science, Electronics Engineering Technology, Elementary Education, English, English/Writing Concentration, Environmental Education, Environmental Policy/Assessment, Environmental Studies, Environmental Studies/Biology, Environmental Studies/Economics, Environmental Studies/Journalism, Forest Biology, French, Geography, Geology, Geophysics, German, History, Human Services, Humanities, Industrial Design, Industrial Technology, Interdisciplinary Nutrition, Journalism, K-12 Education, Management, Manufacturing Engineering Technology, Marine Biology, Mathematics, Mathematics/Computer Science, Music, Philosophy, Physical Education/Exercise/Sport Science, Physics, Physics/Computer Science, Plastics Engineering Technology, Political Science, Political Science/Economics, Psychology, Recreation, Secondary Education, Sociology, Spanish, Special Education, Speech Pathology/Audiology, Student/Faculty-Designed Concentrations, Student/Faculty-Designed Major, Theatre Arts, Urban/Regional Planning, Visual Communication, Watershed Studies.
**Distribution of degrees:** The majors with the highest enrollment are business administration, psychology, and communication; philosophy, foreign languages, and theatre have the lowest.
**Requirements:** General education requirement.
**Academic regulations:** Minimum 2.0 GPA must be maintained.
**Special:** Minors offered in most majors. Programs in East Asian studies and museum training. Self-designed majors. Double majors. Independent study. Accelerated study. Pass/fail grading option. Internships. Graduate school at which undergraduates may take graduate-level courses. Preprofessional programs in law, medicine, veterinary science, pharmacy, dentistry, and optometry. 3-2 engineering program with U of Washington. 3-2 forest biology program with Washington State U. Member of National Student Exchange (NSE). Teacher certification in early childhood, elementary, secondary, special education, and vo-tech education. Certification in specific subject areas. Member of International Student Exchange Program (ISEP). Exchange programs abroad also in China (Beijing Foreign Studies U) and Japan (Asia U, Obirin U, Tsuda Coll). Study abroad also in Eastern European countries, England, France, Germany, Greece, Italy, and Mexico.
**Honors:** Honors program. Honor societies.
**Academic Assistance:** Nonremedial tutoring.

**STUDENT LIFE. Housing:** Students may live on or off campus. Coed dorms. School-owned/operated apartments. On-campus married-student housing. 32% of students live in college housing.
**Social atmosphere:** The student newspaper reports the atmosphere is "very fun." Outdoor sports are popular; the 'Rites of Spring' is a favorite event on campus. On campus, students meet at Red Square. Students frequent the numerous local taverns, coffee shops, parks, and bookstores. Influential groups on campus include religious organizations, abortion groups, and the Western Front newspaper.
**Services and counseling/handicapped student services:** Placement services. Health service. Women's center., Day care. Counseling services for minority, military, veteran, and older students. Birth control, personal, and psychological counseling. Career and academic guidance services. Physically disabled student services. Learning disabled services. Notetaking services. Tape recorders. Tutors. Reader services for the blind.
**Campus organizations:** Undergraduate student government. Student newspaper (Western Front, published twice/week). Literary magazine. Radio and TV stations. Bands, orchestras, choirs, debating, Lesbian/Gay/Bisexual Alliance, Outdoor Program, Summer Stock, recycling center, disabled student group, professional groups, 89 organizations in all.
**Religious organizations:** Baptist Student Ministries, Campus Crusade for Christ, Catholic Student Coalition, Hillel, Latter-Day Saints Student Association, Lutheran Student Movement.
**Minority/foreign student organizations:** Asia-Pacific Islander Student Union, Black Student Network, Chinese Student Association, Korean Student Association, MEChA, Native American Student Union, Vietnamese Student Association. International Student Club, Asian Student Union, Association of Korean Fraternity and Culture.

**ATHLETICS. Physical education requirements:** None.
**Intercollegiate competition:** 3% of students participate. Basketball (M,W), cheerleading (M,W), crew (M,W), cross-country (M,W), football (M), golf (M), soccer (M,W), softball (W), tennis (M,W), track and field (indoor) (M,W), track and field (outdoor) (M,W), volleyball (W). Member of Columbia Football Association, NAIA, Northwest Collegiate Soccer Conference.
**Intramural and club sports:** Intramural basketball, floor hockey, racquetball, soccer, softball, volleyball, wrestling. Men's club Alpine skiing, baseball, ice hockey, lacrosse, rugby, sailing, volleyball. Women's club Alpine skiing, lacrosse, rugby, sailing, softball.

**ADMISSIONS. Academic basis for candidate selection** (in order of priority): Secondary school record, standardized test scores, class rank, essay, school's recommendation.
**Nonacademic basis for candidate selection:** Extracurricular participation and particular talent or ability are emphasized. Character and personality are important. Geographical distribution is considered.
**Requirements:** Graduation from secondary school is required; GED is accepted. 15 units and the following program of study are required: 4 units of English, 3 units of math, 2 units of science including 1 unit of lab, 2 units of foreign language, 3 units of social studies, 1 unit of academic electives. Minimum 2.5 GPA required. Portfolio required of art program applicants. Audition required of music program applicants. SAT or ACT is required. Campus visit recommended. No off-campus interviews.
**Procedure:** Take SAT or ACT by January 1 of 12th year. Application deadline is March 1. Acceptance notification between January and April 15. Reply is required by May 1. $50 nonrefundable tuition deposit. $170 nonrefundable room deposit. Freshmen accepted in terms other than fall.
**Special programs:** Credit and/or placement may be granted through CEEB Advanced Placement exams for scores of 3 or higher. Credit may be granted through military experience. Credit and placement may be granted through challenge exams.
**Transfer students:** Transfer students accepted for terms other than fall. In fall 1993, 35% of all new students were transfers into all classes. 3,319 transfer applications were received, 1,958 were accepted. Application deadline is April 1 for fall; October 15 for winter; January 15 for spring. Minimum 2.0 GPA required. Lowest course grade accepted is "D-." Maximum number of transferable credits is 90 quarter hours. At least 45 quarter hours must be completed at the university to receive degree.
**Admissions contact:** Karen G. Copetas, M.S., Director of Admissions. 206 650-3440.

**FINANCIAL AID. Available aid:** Pell grants, SEOG, state scholarships and grants, school scholarships and grants, private scholarships and grants, academic merit scholarships, and athletic scholarships. Perkins Loans (NDSL), PLUS, Stafford Loans (GSL), school loans, private loans, and SLS. Installment plan.
**Financial aid statistics:** 57% of aid is not need-based. In 1993-94, 66% of all undergraduate applicants received aid.
**Supporting data/closing dates:** FAFSA: Priority filing date is February 28. Notification of awards begins April 1.
**Financial aid contact:** Kathy Sahlhoff, M.Ed., Director of Financial Aid. 206 650-3470.

**STUDENT EMPLOYMENT.** College Work/Study Program. Institutional employment. 25% of full-time undergraduates work on campus during school year. Students may expect to earn an average of $1,350 during school year. Freshmen are discouraged from working during their first term. Off-campus part-time employment opportunities rated "good."

**COMPUTER FACILITIES.** 500 IBM/IBM-compatible and Macintosh/Apple microcomputers; 40 are networked. Students may access Digital minicomputer/mainframe systems. Residence halls may be equipped with stand-alone microcomputers, networked terminals. Computer languages and software packages include Collegiate Writer, Excel, Microsoft Word, Microsoft Works, Quattro, WordPerfect; 40 in all. Computer facilities are available to all students.
**Fees:** None.
**Hours:** 9 AM-11 PM (M-F); noon-6 PM (Sa-Su).

**GRADUATE CAREER DATA.** Companies and businesses that hire graduates: Boeing, Microsoft, U.S. West.

# Whitman College

**Walla Walla, WA 99362** **509 527-5111**

**1994-95 Costs.** Tuition: $16,670. Room: $2,250. Board: $2,650. Fees, books, misc. academic expenses (school's estimate): $920.
**Enrollment.** Undergraduates: 570 men, 650 women (full-time). Freshman class: 1,727 applicants, 1,051 accepted, 359 enrolled.
**Test score averages/ranges.** Average SAT scores: 550 verbal, 600 math. Range of SAT scores of middle 50%: 500-610 verbal, 540-670 math. Average ACT scores: 27 composite.
**Faculty.** 100 full-time; 47 part-time. 93% of faculty holds highest degree in specific field. Student/faculty ratio: 11 to 1.
**Selectivity rating.** Highly competitive.

**PROFILE.** Whitman, founded in 1859, is a private, liberal arts college. Its 47-acre campus is located in Walla Walla, southwest of Spokane.

**Accreditation:** NASC.
**Religious orientation:** Whitman College is nonsectarian; no religious requirements.
**Library:** Collections totaling over 320,000 volumes, 1,950 periodical subscriptions, and 10,000 microform items.
**Special facilities/museums:** Art gallery, anthropology museum, planetarium, outdoor observatory, two electron microscopes.
**Athletic facilities:** Athletic center, stadium, gymnasiums, handball and squash courts, weight rooms, saunas, swimming pool.

**STUDENT BODY. Undergraduate profile:** 46% are state residents; 14% are transfers. 7% Asian-American, 2% Black, 3% Hispanic, 1% Native American, 83% White, 4% Other. Average age of undergraduates is 19.
**Freshman profile:** 8% of freshmen who took SAT scored 700 or over on verbal, 12% scored 700 or over on math; 32% scored 600 or over on verbal, 51% scored 600 or over on math; 76% scored 500 or over on verbal, 88% scored 500 or over on math; 97% scored 400 or over on verbal, 99% scored 400 or over on math; 100% scored 300 or over on verbal, 100% scored 300 or over on math. Majority of accepted applicants took SAT. 84% of freshmen come from public schools.
**Undergraduate achievement:** 95% of fall 1992 freshmen returned for fall 1993 term. 61% of entering class graduated. 78% of students who completed a degree program went on to graduate study within five years.
**Foreign students:** 47 students are from out of the country. Countries represented include China, France, Hong Kong, Japan, Korea, and Turkey; 27 in all.

**PROGRAMS OF STUDY. Degrees:** B.A.
**Majors:** Anthropology, Art, Biology, Chemistry, Dramatic Arts, Economics, English, Foreign Languages/Literatures, Geology, History, Mathematics, Mathematics/Computer Science, Music, Philosophy, Physics, Politics, Politics/Environmental Studies, Psychology, Sociology.
**Distribution of degrees:** The majors with the highest enrollment are history, politics, and English; foreign languages have the lowest.
**Requirements:** General education requirement.
**Academic regulations:** Sophomores must maintain minimum 2.0 GPA; juniors, 2.0 GPA; seniors, 2.0 GPA.
**Special:** Minors offered in all majors and in astronomy, Chinese, classics, computer science, education, environmental studies, gender studies, Japanese, physical education, religion, and world literature. Self-designed, combined, or interdepartmental major programs may be developed by students with unique interests, subject to faculty approval. Departments may also provide for an emphasis within the major. Comprehensive examinations required in major field. Double majors. Independent study. Pass/fail grading option. Internships. Preprofessional programs in law, medicine, and dentistry. 4-2 business program with U of Chicago. 3-2 engineering programs with Caltech, Columbia U, and Duke U. 3-2 forestry and environmental studies program with Duke U. 3-3 law program with Columbia U. Washington Semester. Philadelphia Center. Urban Studies Pro-

gram (Chicago). Teacher certification in elementary and secondary education. Study abroad in African countries, Australia, Belgium, China, Costa Rica, Denmark, France, Germany, Great Britain, Greece, Hong Kong, India, Iceland, Israel, Italy, Japan, Mexico, Poland, Scandinavian countries, Singapore, South American countries, Spain, Switzerland, Taiwan, and the former Yugoslav Republics. Whitman-in-China program allows recent graduates to spend one year teaching English in one of two Chinese universities.
**Honors:** Phi Beta Kappa. Honor societies.
**Academic Assistance:** Nonremedial tutoring.

**STUDENT LIFE. Housing:** All unmarried freshmen and sophomores under age 21 must live on campus. Coed and women's dorms. Fraternity housing. School-owned/operated apartments. Off-campus privately-owned housing. 59% of students live in college housing.
**Social atmosphere:** The most popular on-campus gathering spot is the student union. The Greek community has a considerable influence on campus social life. According to the editor of the student newspaper, Whitman is a "very intensely academic, small liberal arts college in a small conservative town. It's very isolated but also internally intimate."
**Services and counseling/handicapped student services:** Placement services. Health service. Women's center. Day care. Counseling services for minority and veteran students. Birth control, personal, and psychological counseling. Career and academic guidance services. Religious counseling. Physically disabled student services. Tape recorders. Tutors. Reader services for the blind.
**Campus organizations:** Undergraduate student government. Student newspaper (Pioneer, published once/week). Literary magazine. Yearbook. Radio station. Amnesty International, chamber music groups, orchestra choir, vocal ensemble, band, drama club, debating, student-faculty discussion groups, service clubs, outing programs, Women's Connection, Gay and Lesbian Association, student committees, departmental groups, 90 organizations in all. Five fraternities, all with chapter houses; six sororities, no chapter houses. 45% of men join a fraternity. 41% of women join a sorority.
**Religious organizations:** Catholic Student Organization, Christian Fellowship, Christian Science Organization, Jewish Interest Group, Latter-Day Saints Association, New Freedom Singers, Stephen Ministry.
**Minority/foreign student organizations:** Black Student Union, Chicano Student Group, Asian Club, Hawaiian Student Club, Multi-Ethnic Student Organization. International Students and Friends.

**ATHLETICS. Physical education requirements:** None.
**Intercollegiate competition:** 25% of students participate. Alpine skiing (M,W), baseball (M), basketball (M,W), cross-country (M,W), golf (M), soccer (M,W), swimming (M,W), tennis (M,W), track (outdoor) (M,W). Member of NAIA, Northwest Conference of Independent Colleges.
**Intramural and club sports:** 65% of students participate. Intramural basketball, football, frisbee, softball, tennis, volleyball. Men's club frisbee, lacrosse, rugby, water polo. Women's club lacrosse, rugby, softball, water polo.

**ADMISSIONS. Academic basis for candidate selection** (in order of priority): Secondary school record, class rank, essay, standardized test scores, school's recommendation.
**Nonacademic basis for candidate selection:** Extracurricular participation is emphasized. Character and personality, particular talent or ability, geographical distribution, and alumni/ae relationship are considered.
**Requirements:** Graduation from secondary school is required; GED is accepted. 18 units and the following program of study are recommended: 4 units of English, 4 units of math, 4 units of science including 2 units of lab, 2 units of foreign language, 1 unit of social studies, 1 unit of history, 2 units of electives. SAT is required; ACT may be substituted. Campus visit and interview recommended. Off-campus interviews available with an admissions representative.
**Procedure:** Take SAT or ACT by December of 12th year. Visit college for interview by February 15 of 12th year. Application deadline is February 15. Notification of admission by April 1. Reply is required by May 1. $300 nonrefundable tuition deposit. Freshmen accepted in terms other than fall.
**Special programs:** Admission may be deferred one year. Credit and/or placement may be granted through CEEB Advanced Placement exams for scores of 4 or higher. Credit and placement may be granted through challenge exams. Early decision program. In fall 1993, 93 applied for early decision and 93 were accepted. Deadline for applying for early decision is December 1. Early entrance/early admission program.
**Transfer students:** Transfer students accepted for terms other than fall. In fall 1993, 14% of all new students were transfers into all classes. 133 transfer applications were received, 90 were accepted. Application deadline is February 15 for fall; December 1 for spring. Minimum 2.5 GPA recommended. Lowest course grade accepted is "C-." Maximum number of transferable credits is 62 semester hours. At least 54 semester hours must be completed at the college to receive degree.
**Admissions contact:** Madeleine R. Eagon, Director of Admission. 509 527-5176.

**FINANCIAL AID. Available aid:** Pell grants, SEOG, state scholarships and grants, school scholarships and grants, private scholarships and grants, academic merit scholarships, and aid for undergraduate foreign students. Perkins Loans (NDSL), PLUS, Stafford Loans (GSL), school loans, private loans, and SLS. Knight Tuition Plans, AMS, and deferred payment plan.
**Financial aid statistics:** 38% of aid is not need-based. In 1993-94, 82% of all undergraduate applicants received aid; 89% of freshman applicants. Average amounts of aid awarded freshmen: Scholarships and grants, $8,757; loans, $3,300.
**Supporting data/closing dates:** FAFSA/FAF: Deadline is February 15. Notification of awards begins February 1.
**Financial aid contact:** Gene Adams, Director of Financial Aid. 509 527-5178.

**STUDENT EMPLOYMENT.** College Work/Study Program. Institutional employment. 47% of full-time undergraduates work on campus during school year. Students may expect to earn an average of $798 during school year. Off-campus part-time employment opportunities rated "good."

**COMPUTER FACILITIES.** 80 IBM/IBM-compatible and Macintosh/Apple microcomputers; all are networked. Students may access Digital, SUN minicomputer/mainframe systems, BITNET, Internet. Residence halls may be equipped with modems. Client/LAN operating systems include Apple/Macintosh, DOS, UNIX/XENIX/AIX, Windows NT, LocalTalk/AppleTalk, Microsoft. Computer languages and software packages include BASIC, C, COBOL, FORTRAN, DataTrieve, DECalc-Plus, e-mail, LISP, Macsyma, MINITAB, Modula 2, Pascal, SAS, SPSS-X, TRX. Computer facilities are available to all students.
**Fees:** None.
**Hours:** 8 AM-midn.

**GRADUATE CAREER DATA.** Graduate school percentages: 10% enter law school. 4% enter medical school. 2% enter dental school. 14% enter graduate business programs. 47% enter graduate arts and sciences programs. 1% enter theological school/seminary. Highest graduate school enrollments: Harvard U, Stanford U, U of Chicago, U of Washington. 24% of graduates choose careers in business and industry. Companies and businesses that hire graduates: Boeing, Microsoft, Seafirst.

**PROMINENT ALUMNI/AE.** William O. Douglas, former Justice, U.S. Supreme Court; Walter Brattain, Nobel Prize-winning physicist; Scotty Campbell, founder, Civil Service Agency; Margie Boule, TV anchor; Robert Graham, personal aide to Caspar Weinberger for disarmament talks; Dr. Willis Taylor, chair, Virginia Mason Cancer Commission.

# Whitworth College

**Spokane, WA 99251** **509 466-1000**

**1993-94 Costs.** Tuition: $11,840. Room & board: $4,300. Fees, books, misc. academic expenses (school's estimate): $625.
**Enrollment.** Undergraduates: 538 men, 732 women (full-time). Freshman class: 1,132 applicants, 941 accepted, 363 enrolled. Graduate enrollment: 128 men, 281 women.
**Test score averages/ranges.** Average SAT scores: 490 verbal, 544 math.
**Faculty.** 80 full-time; 15 part-time. 79% of faculty holds highest degree in specific field. Student/faculty ratio: 15 to 1.
**Selectivity rating.** More competitive.

**PROFILE.** Whitworth, founded in 1890, is a church-affiliated college. Its 200-acre campus is located seven miles from the center of Spokane.

**Accreditation:** NASC. Professionally accredited by the National Association of Schools of Music, the National Council for Accreditation of Teacher Education.
**Religious orientation:** Whitworth College is affiliated with the Presbyterian Church USA; one semester of religion required.
**Library:** Collections totaling over 135,373 volumes, 725 periodical subscriptions, and 58,000 microform items.
**Special facilities/museums:** Language lab.
**Athletic facilities:** Field house, gymnasium, aquatic center, baseball, football, intramural, soccer, and softball fields, track, cross-country course, tennis courts, Nautilus room.

**STUDENT BODY. Undergraduate profile:** 60% are state residents; 30% are transfers. 5% Asian-American, 1% Black, 2% Hispanic, 1% Native American, 91% White.
**Freshman profile:** 1% of freshmen who took SAT scored 700 or over on verbal, 2% scored 700 or over on math; 8% scored 600 or over on verbal, 22% scored 600 or over on math; 43% scored 500 or over on verbal, 62% scored 500 or over on math; 83% scored 400 or over on verbal, 92% scored 400 or over on math; 100% scored 300 or over on verbal, 100% scored 300 or over on math. 85% of accepted applicants took SAT; 15% took ACT. 90% of freshmen come from public schools.
**Undergraduate achievement:** 73% of fall 1992 freshmen returned for fall 1993 term.
**Foreign students:** 101 students are from out of the country. Countries represented include Canada, China, Japan, Kenya, South Korea, and Taiwan; 25 in all.

**PROGRAMS OF STUDY. Degrees:** B.A., B.S.
**Majors:** Accounting, American Studies, Art, Art Education, Art History, Art/Painting, Arts Administration, Biology, Business Management, Chemistry, Communications, Computer Science, Cross-Cultural Studies, Economics, Elementary Education, English, English Education, French, History, International Business, International Political Economics, International Studies, Journalism, Mathematics, Music, Music Education, Nursing, Peace Studies, Philosophy, Physical Education, Physics, Political Studies, Psychology, Religion, Secondary Education, Sociology, Spanish, Special Education, Speech Communication, Sports Medicine, Theatre Arts.
**Distribution of degrees:** The majors with the highest enrollment are education, business, and communications.
**Requirements:** General education requirement.
**Academic regulations:** Minimum 2.0 GPA must be maintained.
**Special:** Double majors. Dual degrees. Independent study. Pass/fail grading option. Internships. Cooperative education programs. Preprofessional programs in law, medicine, veterinary science, pharmacy, dentistry, theology, optometry, and nursing. 3-2 engineering programs with U of Southern California and Washington U. Teacher certification in elementary, secondary, and special education. Exchange programs abroad in China (Jilin Teachers Coll, Nanjing U), France (U of Provence), Germany (Academy of Music, Technical U), Japan (Hokuriku Gakuin Coll), Mexico (Iberoamericana U), and South Korea (Keimyung U, Soong Sil U). Study abroad also in Asian countries, Belize, Great Britain, Greece, Israel, and the former Soviet Republics. ROTC at Gonzaga U.
**Honors:** Honors program.
**Academic Assistance:** Remedial writing, math, and study skills. Nonremedial tutoring.

**STUDENT LIFE. Housing:** All freshmen and sophomores must live on campus unless living with family. Coed, women's, and men's dorms. Special-interest housing. 60% of students live in college housing.
**Social atmosphere:** According to the editor of the student newspaper, off-campus parties are all the rage, since Whitworth's Christian affiliation does not permit drinking and cohabitation on campus. Popular events include Homecoming, the Boat Cruise on Lake Couer d'Alene, Spring Formal, and The Weekend (spiritual retreat). Central American study tours are prevalent. Since no Greeks are allowed, the most influential groups are the male and female dorm residents, Habitat for Humanity, the Racism Awareness Project, and Amnesty International. Off campus, students enjoy going to the Loop, the HUB, The Big Dipper, Pleasant Blends (coffeehouse), Riverfront Park, The Onion, and Swackhammer's.

**Services and counseling/handicapped student services:** Placement services. Health service. Counseling services for minority, military, and older students. Birth control, personal, and psychological counseling. Career and academic guidance services. Religious counseling. Physically disabled student services. Learning disabled services. Notetaking services. Tape recorders. Reader services for the blind.
**Campus organizations:** Undergraduate student government. Student newspaper (Whitworthian, published once/week). Literary magazine. Yearbook. Radio station. Choir, vocal jazz, The Shepherds Bells, Chamber Singers, Circle K, Habitat for Humanity, 22 organizations in all.
**Religious organizations:** Young Life.

**ATHLETICS. Physical education requirements:** None.
**Intercollegiate competition:** 33% of students participate. Baseball (M), basketball (M,W), cheerleading (W), cross-country (M,W), diving (M,W), football (M), soccer (M,W), swimming (M,W), tennis (M,W), track (indoor) (M,W), track (outdoor) (M,W), track and field (indoor) (M,W), track and field (outdoor) (M,W), volleyball (W). Member of Columbia Football Association, Mt. Rainier Conference for football, NAIA, NCIC, Northwest Collegiate Soccer Conference.
**Intramural and club sports:** 40% of students participate. Intramural aerobics, badminton, basketball, billiards, flag football, floor hockey, inner-tube water polo, pickleball, soccer, softball, table tennis, tennis, volleyball. Men's club volleyball.

**ADMISSIONS. Academic basis for candidate selection** (in order of priority): Secondary school record, class rank, standardized test scores, school's recommendation, essay.
**Nonacademic basis for candidate selection:** Character and personality are emphasized. Extracurricular participation and particular talent or ability are considered.
**Requirements:** Graduation from secondary school is required; GED is accepted. 15 units and the following program of study are recommended: 4 units of English, 3 units of math, 3 units of science, 2 units of foreign language, 1 unit of social studies, 2 units of history. Minimum combined SAT score of 900, rank in top half of secondary school class, and minimum 2.75 GPA recommended. Conditional admission possible for applicants not meeting standard requirements. SAT or ACT is required. Campus visit and interview recommended. Off-campus interviews available with admissions and alumni representatives.
**Procedure:** Take SAT or ACT by May 1 of 12th year. Visit college for interview by May 1 of 12th year. Suggest filing application by November 30. Application deadline is March 15. Notification of admission on rolling basis. No set date by which applicants must accept offer. $150 tuition deposit, refundable until May 1. $70 room deposit, refundable until July 1. Freshmen accepted in terms other than fall.
**Special programs:** Admission may be deferred one year. Credit may be granted through CEEB Advanced Placement for scores of 3 or higher. Credit and/or placement may be granted through CLEP general and subject exams. Credit may be granted through military experience. Credit and placement may be granted through challenge exams. Early decision program. Deadline for applying for early decision is November 30. Early entrance/early admission program. Concurrent enrollment program.
**Transfer students:** Transfer students accepted for terms other than fall. In fall 1993, 30% of all new students were transfers into all classes. 329 transfer applications were received, 252 were accepted. Application deadline is September 1 for fall; February 1 for spring. Minimum 2.0 GPA recommended. Lowest course grade accepted is "C-." Maximum number of transferable credits is 98 semester hours. At least 32 semester hours must be completed at the college to receive degree.
**Admissions contact:** Kenneth P. Moyer, M.S., Director of Admissions. 509 466-3212.

**FINANCIAL AID. Available aid:** Pell grants, SEOG, state scholarships and grants, school scholarships and grants, private scholarships and grants, ROTC scholarships, academic merit scholarships, athletic scholarships, and aid for undergraduate foreign students. Perkins Loans (NDSL), PLUS, Stafford Loans (GSL), school loans, and SLS. Knight Tuition Plans. Campus-managed monthly payment plan.
**Financial aid statistics:** 10% of aid is not need-based. In 1993-94, 68% of all undergraduate applicants received aid; 67% of freshman applicants. Average amounts of aid awarded freshmen: Scholarships and grants, $5,917.
**Supporting data/closing dates:** FAFSA/FAF/FFS: Priority filing date is March 1. Notification of awards on rolling basis.
**Financial aid contact:** Wendy Olson, M.A., Director of Financial Aid. 509 466-3215.

**STUDENT EMPLOYMENT.** College Work/Study Program. Institutional employment. 80% of full-time undergraduates work on campus during school year. Students may expect to earn an average of $1,625 during school year. Off-campus part-time employment opportunities rated "good."

**COMPUTER FACILITIES.** 100 IBM/IBM-compatible and Macintosh/Apple microcomputers; 21 are networked. Students may access Digital minicomputer/mainframe systems. Computer languages and software packages include C, COBOL, FORTRAN, LISP, Microsoft Word, PageMaker, Pascal, Quattro Pro, SPSS, TextEditor, WordPerfect; database, spreadsheet, word processing programs. Computer facilities are available to all students.
**Fees:** $10 computer fee per semester.
**Hours:** 8 AM-11 PM (M-F); noon-6 PM (Sa); 2 PM-11 PM (Su).

**PROMINENT ALUMNI/AE.** Dorothea Teeter, missionary in Beirut, Presbyterian Church; Chaplain Major General Richard Carr, retired Chief of Chaplains, USAF; Alan Raul, Middle East bureau chief, NBC News; Dr. Richard Gray, dean, School of Journalism, Indiana U.

# West Virginia

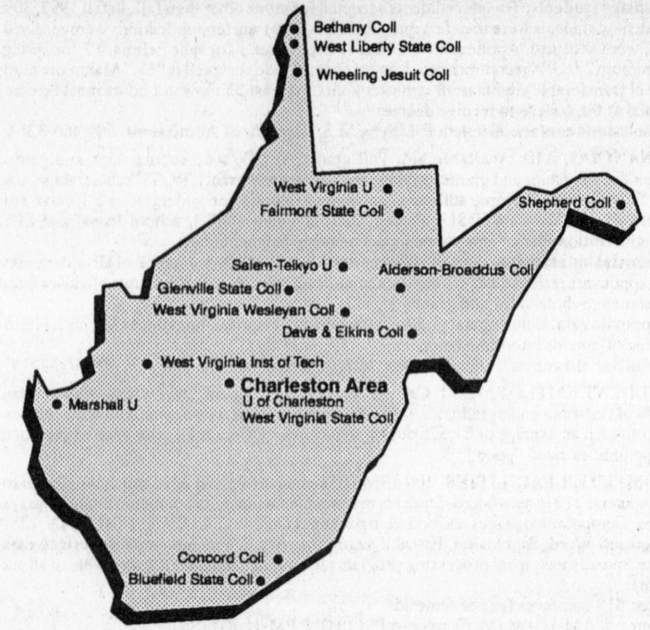


## Alderson-Broaddus College

**Philippi, WV 26416** **304 457-1700**

**1994-95 Costs.** Tuition: $10,468. Room & board: $3,380. Fees, books, misc. academic expenses (school's estimate): $592.

**Enrollment.** Undergraduates: 318 men, 418 women (full-time). Freshman class: 920 applicants, 598 accepted, 286 enrolled. Graduate enrollment: 13 men, 7 women.

**Test score averages/ranges.** Average SAT scores: 431 verbal, 465 math. Range of SAT scores of middle 50%: 360-470 verbal, 390-520 math. Average ACT scores: 21 English, 19 math, 20 composite. Range of ACT scores of middle 50%: 17-23 English, 16-21 math.

**Faculty.** 60 full-time; 17 part-time. 35% of faculty holds doctoral degree. Student/faculty ratio: 13 to 1.

**Selectivity rating.** Competitive.

**PROFILE.** Alderson-Broaddus, a church-affiliated, liberal arts college, was founded in 1871 as Broaddus College. In 1932 it merged with Alderson Junior College and adopted its present name. The 170-acre campus is located in Philippi, near the point of the first land battle of the Civil War.

**Accreditation:** NCACS. Professionally accredited by the American Medical Association (CAHEA), the National League for Nursing.
**Religious orientation:** Alderson-Broaddus College is affiliated with the American Baptist Churches, USA; one semester of religion required.
**Library:** Collections totaling over 101,000 volumes, 800 periodical subscriptions, and 7,791 microform items.
**Special facilities/museums:** Civil War historical collection.
**Athletic facilities:** Coliseum, swimming pool, weight room, athletic fields, basketball, handball, racquetball, and tennis courts.

**STUDENT BODY. Undergraduate profile:** 67% are state residents; 35% are transfers. 3% Asian-American, 4% Black, 1% Hispanic, 1% Native American, 91% White. Average age of undergraduates is 20.
**Freshman profile:** 7% of freshmen who took SAT scored 600 or over on verbal, 5% scored 600 or over on math; 20% scored 500 or over on verbal, 39% scored 500 or over on math; 63% scored 400 or over on verbal, 71% scored 400 or over on math; 94% scored 300 or over on verbal, 94% scored 300 or over on math. 40% of accepted applicants took SAT; 67% took ACT.
**Undergraduate achievement:** 90% of fall 1991 freshmen returned for fall 1992 term. 50% of entering class graduated.
**Foreign students:** Five students are from out of the country. Countries represented include Canada, China, India, Japan, and the United Kingdom.

**PROGRAMS OF STUDY. Degrees:** B.A., B.S.
**Majors:** Accounting, Applied Music, Biology, Broadcasting, Business Administration, Chemistry, Church Music, Computer Science, Creative Writing, Cytotechnology, Elementary Education, History, Literature, Management, Management Information Systems, Mathematics, Medical Sciences, Medical Technology, Music Education, Nursing, Physical Education, Political Science, Psychology, Radiologic Technology, Recreation/Leisure, Secondary Education, Sociology, Special Education, Speech Communication, Speech/Theatre, Sports Medicine, Technical/Business Writing.
**Distribution of degrees:** The majors with the highest enrollment are medical sciences, nursing, and music education; technical writing, management informations systems, and chemistry have the lowest.
**Requirements:** General education requirement.
**Academic regulations:** Minimum 2.0 GPA must be maintained.
**Special:** Minors offered in all majors. Associate's degrees offered. Self-designed majors. Double majors. Dual degrees. Independent study. Pass/fail grading option. Internships. Graduate school at which undergraduates may take graduate-level courses. Preprofessional programs in law, medicine, veterinary science, pharmacy, dentistry, theology, optometry, and physical therapy. 2-2 medical technology program with area hospitals. 3-1 radiography and cytotechnology programs with local hospitals. Appalachian Colleges Consortium, Appalachian Colleges Assessment Consortium, Mountain State Association. Teacher certification in elementary, secondary, and special education. Certification in specific subject areas. Study abroad in Austria. ROTC, NROTC, and AFROTC at Fairmont State Coll.
**Honors:** Honors program. Honor societies.
**Academic Assistance:** Remedial reading, writing, math, and study skills. Nonremedial tutoring.

**ADMISSIONS. Academic basis for candidate selection** (in order of priority): Secondary school record, standardized test scores, school's recommendation, class rank, essay.
**Nonacademic basis for candidate selection:** Character and personality and alumni/ae relationship are important. Extracurricular participation and particular talent or ability are considered.
**Requirements:** Graduation from secondary school is required; GED is accepted. 15 units and the following program of study are recommended: 4 units of English, 2 units of math, 2 units of science, 1 unit of foreign language, 2 units of social studies, 2 units of history, 2 units of electives. Minimum composite ACT score of 17 (combined SAT score of 800) and minimum 2.0 GPA required. 1 unit of biology and 1 unit of chemistry recommended of nursing and physician's assistant program applicants. Interview also required of physician's assistant program applicants. Audition required of music program applicants. Conditional admission possible for applicants not meeting standard requirements. SAT or ACT is required. Campus visit and interview recommended. Off-campus interviews available with an admissions representative.
**Procedure:** Take SAT or ACT by May of 12th year. Visit college for interview by March of 12th year. Suggest filing application by January 1. Application deadline is September 1. Notification of admission on rolling basis. Reply is required by September 1. $100 tuition deposit, refundable until May 1. Freshmen accepted for terms other than fall.
**Special programs:** Admission may be deferred one year. Credit and/or placement may be granted through CEEB Advanced Placement exams for scores of 4 or higher. Credit and/or placement may be granted through CLEP general and subject exams. Placement may be granted through challenge exams. Credit and placement may be granted through ACT PEP exams. Early decision program. Deadline for applying for early decision is October. Early entrance/early admission program. Concurrent enrollment program.
**Transfer students:** Transfer students accepted for terms other than fall. In fall 1992, 35% of all new students were transfers into all classes. Application deadline is September 1 for fall; January 21 for spring. Minimum 2.0 GPA required. Lowest course grade accepted is "C." Maximum number of transferable credits is 60 semester hours. At least 68 semester hours must be completed at the college to receive degree.
**Admissions contact:** Craig Gould, Director of Admissions. 304 457-1700, extension 256.

**FINANCIAL AID. Available aid:** Pell grants, SEOG, state scholarships and grants, school scholarships and grants, private scholarships and grants, ROTC scholarships, academic merit scholarships, athletic scholarships, and aid for undergraduate foreign students. Perkins Loans (NDSL), PLUS, Stafford Loans (GSL), NSL, Health Professions Loans, state loans, school loans, private loans, and SLS. AMS.
**Financial aid statistics:** 25% of aid is not need-based. In 1992-93, 95% of all undergraduate applicants received aid; 97% of freshman applicants. Average amounts of aid awarded freshmen: Scholarships and grants, $4,200; loans, $2,000.
**Supporting data/closing dates:** FAFSA/FAF/FFS: Priority filing date is March 1; deadline is June 1. State aid form: Accepted on rolling basis; deadline is March 1. Income tax forms: Accepted on rolling basis. Notification of awards on rolling basis.
**Financial aid contact:** Mamie Argo, Director of Financial Aid. 304 457-1700, extension 250.

## Bethany College

**Bethany, WV 26032** **304 829-7000**

**1993-94 Costs.** Tuition: $13,660. Room: $1,846. Board: $2,872. Fees, books, misc. academic expenses (school's estimate): $682.

**Enrollment.** Undergraduates: 351 men, 381 women (full-time). Freshman class: 764 applicants, 621 accepted, 243 enrolled.

**Test score averages/ranges.** Range of SAT scores of middle 50%: 430-500 verbal, 460-500 math. Range of ACT scores of middle 50%: 17-24 English, 22-29 math.

**Faculty.** 56 full-time; 13 part-time. 68% of faculty holds doctoral degree. Student/faculty ratio: 13 to 1.

**Selectivity rating.** Less competitive.

**PROFILE.** Bethany, founded in 1840, is a church-affiliated, liberal arts college. Its 300-acre campus is located in Bethany, 48 miles southwest of Pittsburgh, Pa.

**Accreditation:** NCACS. Professionally accredited by the Council on Social Work Education, the National Council for Accreditation of Teacher Education.
**Religious orientation:** Bethany College is affiliated with the Christian Church (Disciples of Christ); one semester of religion required.
**Library:** Collections totaling over 205,000 volumes, 600 periodical subscriptions, and 66,000 microform items.

**Special facilities/museums:** Language lab, economics lab, media center, elementary school training center, archives center, five computer labs, 1,300 acres of farm and timber land.
**Athletic facilities:** Field house, gymnasium, weight room, football, intramural, soccer, and softball fields, basketball, racquetball, and tennis courts, swimming pool, stadium, indoor track.

**STUDENT BODY. Undergraduate profile:** 31% are state residents; 13% are transfers. 2% Asian-American, 4% Black, 1% Hispanic, 91% White, 2% Other. Average age of undergraduates is 20.
**Freshman profile:** 30% of freshmen who took SAT scored 500 or over on verbal, 35% scored 500 or over on math; 85% scored 400 or over on verbal, 90% scored 400 or over on math; 100% scored 300 or over on verbal, 100% scored 300 or over on math. 10% of freshmen who took ACT scored 24 or over on English, 50% scored 24 or over on math; 85% scored 18 or over on English, 95% scored 18 or over on math; 100% scored 12 or over on English, 100% scored 12 or over on math. 70% of accepted applicants took SAT; 30% took ACT. 68% of freshmen come from public schools.
**Undergraduate achievement:** 76% of fall 1991 freshmen returned for fall 1992 term. 35% of students who completed a degree program went on to graduate study within five years.
**Foreign students:** 32 students are from out of the country. Countries represented include Canada, Germany, Greece, India, Spain, and Syria; 19 in all.

**PROGRAMS OF STUDY. Degrees:** B.A., B.S.
**Majors:** Accounting, Biology, Chemistry, Communication, Computer Science, Economics, Education, English, Fine Arts, French, German, History, Interdisciplinary Studies, Mathematics, Philosophy, Physical Education, Physics, Political Science, Psychology, Religious Studies, Social Work, Spanish.
**Distribution of degrees:** The majors with the highest enrollment are communication, economics, and psychology; philosophy and religious studies have the lowest.
**Academic regulations:** Minimum 2.0 GPA required for graduation.
**Special:** Minors offered in many majors. Bethany Plan combines classroom with experience-based learning, close student-faculty relations, and individualized study. Four practicums in non-classroom settings required for graduation. All seniors must complete a Senior Project and take Undergraduate Record Exams. Self-designed majors. Double majors. Dual degrees. Independent study. Accelerated study. Pass/fail grading option. Internships. Graduate school at which undergraduates may take graduate-level courses. Preprofessional programs in law, medicine, veterinary science, dentistry, theology, and engineering. 3-2 engineering programs with Columbia U, Case Western Reserve U, Georgia Tech, and Washington U. Member of consortium with East Central Colleges. Washington Semester and UN Semester. Teacher certification in early childhood, elementary, secondary, and special education. Exchange programs abroad in France (Sorbonne U) and Spain (Pomplona U). Study abroad also in England and Germany.
**Honors:** Honors program.
**Academic Assistance:** Remedial reading, writing, math, and study skills. Nonremedial tutoring.

**ADMISSIONS. Academic basis for candidate selection** (in order of priority): Secondary school record, class rank, school's recommendation, standardized test scores.
**Nonacademic basis for candidate selection:** Character and personality are emphasized. Extracurricular participation, particular talent or ability, geographical distribution, and alumni/ae relationship are important.
**Requirements:** Graduation from secondary school is required; GED is accepted. 15 units and the following program of study are required: 4 units of English, 3 units of math, 3 units of science, 2 units of foreign language, 3 units of social studies. Minimum combined SAT score between 950-1050 (composite ACT score between 22-25) and minimum 2.5 GPA recommended of out-of-state applicants. SAT or ACT is required. Campus visit and interview recommended. Off-campus interviews available with admissions and alumni representatives.
**Procedure:** Take SAT or ACT by June 1 of 12th year. Visit college for interview by May 1 of 12th year. Suggest filing application by April 1. Application deadline is August 1. Notification of admission on rolling basis. $100 tuition deposit, refundable until May 1. Freshmen accepted for terms other than fall.
**Special programs:** Admission may be deferred one year. Credit and/or placement may be granted through CEEB Advanced Placement exams for scores of 3 or higher. Credit and/or placement may be granted through CLEP general and subject exams. Credit and placement may be granted through DANTES exams and military experience. Early decision program. In fall 1992, 45 applied for early decision and 35 were accepted. Deadline for applying for early decision is December 15. Early entrance/early admission program.
**Transfer students:** Transfer students accepted for terms other than fall. In fall 1992, 13% of all new students were transfers into all classes. 78 transfer applications were received, 52 were accepted. Application deadline is August 1 for fall; January 1 for spring. Minimum 2.0 GPA required. Lowest course grade accepted is "C-." Maximum number of transferable credits is 90 semester hours. At least 32 semester hours must be completed at the college to receive degree.
**Admissions contact:** Gary R. Forney, M.A., Vice President for Enrollment Management/ Dean of Admissions. 800 922-7611.

**FINANCIAL AID. Available aid:** Pell grants, SEOG, state scholarships and grants, school scholarships and grants, private scholarships and grants, academic merit scholarships, and aid for undergraduate foreign students. Minority awareness scholarships. Christian Church (Disciples of Christ) awards. Perkins Loans (NDSL), PLUS, Stafford Loans (GSL), state loans, private loans, and SLS. Knight Tuition Plans, AMS, EFI Fund Management, and deferred payment plan.
**Financial aid statistics:** 52% of aid is not need-based. In 1992-93, 82% of all undergraduate applicants received aid; 78% of freshman applicants. Average amounts of aid awarded freshmen: Scholarships and grants, $9,650; loans, $1,950.
**Supporting data/closing dates:** FAFSA/FAF/FFS: Accepted on rolling basis. State aid form: Accepted on rolling basis. Income tax forms: Accepted on rolling basis. Notification of awards on rolling basis.
**Financial aid contact:** Theodore Bunnell, Director of Financial Aid. 304 829-7631.

# Bluefield State College

**Bluefield, WV 24701** — **304 327-4000**

**1994-95 Costs.** Tuition: $1,856 (state residents), $4,514 (out-of-state). Housing: None. Fees, books, misc. academic expenses (school's estimate): $500.
**Enrollment.** Undergraduates: 622 men, 841 women (full-time). Freshman class: 1,046 applicants, 832 accepted, 518 enrolled.
**Test score averages/ranges.** Average SAT scores: 380 verbal, 410 math. Range of SAT scores of middle 50%: 360-480 verbal, 390-450 math. Average ACT scores: 17 English, 18 math, 18 composite. Range of ACT scores of middle 50%: 14-18 English, 14-19 math.
**Faculty.** 91 full-time; 65 part-time. 20% of faculty holds doctoral degree. Student/faculty ratio: 16 to 1.
**Selectivity rating.** Less competitive.

**PROFILE.** Bluefield State, founded in 1895, is a public college. Programs are offered through the Divisions of Business, Continuing Education, Education, Engineering Technology, Health Services, Humanities and Social Sciences, and Natural Science. Its 100-acre campus is located one mile from downtown Bluefield.

**Accreditation:** NCACS. Professionally accredited by the Accreditation Board for Engineering and Technology, the National League for Nursing.
**Religious orientation:** Bluefield State College is nonsectarian; no religious requirements.
**Library:** Collections totaling over 108,490 volumes, 524 periodical subscriptions, and 242,251 microform items.
**Athletic facilities:** Swimming pool, gymnasium, tennis courts, fitness room, football field.

**STUDENT BODY. Undergraduate profile:** 90% are state residents; 37% are transfers. .5% Asian-American, 8.6% Black, .3% Hispanic, .3% Native American, 90.3% White. Average age of undergraduates is 26.
**Freshman profile:** 1% of freshmen who took ACT scored 30 or over on composite; 14% scored 24 or over on composite; 44% scored 18 or over on composite; 92% scored 12 or over on composite; 100% scored 6 or over on composite. 5% of accepted applicants took SAT; 95% took ACT. 98% of freshmen come from public schools.
**Undergraduate achievement:** 57% of fall 1992 freshmen returned for fall 1993 term. 25% of entering class graduated. 5% of students who completed a degree program immediately went on to graduate study.
**Foreign students:** 14 students are from out of the country. Countries represented include Canada, India, Japan, Jordan, Kuwait, and the Philippines; nine in all.

**PROGRAMS OF STUDY. Degrees:** B.A., B.S., B.S.Eng.Tech., B.S.Nurs.
**Majors:** Accountancy, Adolescent Education, Applied Science, Architectural Engineering Technology, Business Administration, Civil Engineering Technology, Computer Science, Criminal Justice Administration, Early/Middle Education, Education, Electrical Engineering Technology, Humanities, Mathematics, Middle/Adolescent Education, Mining Engineering Technology, Nursing, Regents Bachelor of Arts, Social Sciences.
**Distribution of degrees:** The majors with the highest enrollment are business administration, education, and criminal justice; mathematics has the lowest.
**Requirements:** General education requirement.
**Academic regulations:** Freshmen must maintain minimum 1.8 GPA; sophomores, 1.8 GPA; juniors, 1.9 GPA; seniors, 2.0 GPA.
**Special:** Minors offered in some majors and in art, biology, chemistry, international studies, physics, political science, psychology, sociology, and technical communications. Associate's degrees offered. Double majors. Independent study. Internships. Combined degree programs in computer science, engineering technology, and nursing. Teacher certification in early childhood, elementary, secondary, and special education. Certification in specific subject areas.
**Honors:** Honor societies.
**Academic Assistance:** Remedial reading, writing, math, and study skills. Nonremedial tutoring.

**STUDENT LIFE. Housing:** Commuter campus; no student housing.
**Social atmosphere:** Students gather at the student union and cafeteria on campus and at City Park and the Mercer Mall off campus. Influential campus groups include the Greeks, newspaper and yearbook staffs, and the Model United Nations. Popular annual events include Homecoming, Greek Week, athletic events, and concerts and plays.
**Services and counseling/handicapped student services:** Placement services. Health service. Counseling services for minority, veteran, and older students. Birth control and personal counseling. Career and academic guidance services. Physically disabled student services. Learning disabled services. Tutors.
**Campus organizations:** Undergraduate student government. Student newspaper (Bluefieldian, published twice/month). Yearbook. Gospel choir, jazz band, drama club, civil engineering technology club, criminal justice club, education association, physical education/recreation club, Society of Mining Engineering, Student Nurses Association, radiographers association, Rotaract, ski club, Young Republicans, Phi Beta Lambda, 35 organizations in all. Six fraternities, no chapter houses; four sororities, no chapter houses. 5% of men join a fraternity. 4% of women join a sorority.
**Religious organizations:** Christian Fellowship Organization.
**Minority/foreign student organizations:** Rainbow, Minorities On The Move. International Student Association.

**ATHLETICS. Physical education requirements:** Two credit hours of physical education required.
**Intercollegiate competition:** 3% of students participate. Baseball (M), basketball (M,W), cheerleading (W), cross-country (M,W), golf (M), softball (W), tennis (M,W). Member of NAIA, NCAA Division II, WVIAC.

**Intramural and club sports:** Intramural badminton, basketball, billiards, bowling, darts, flag football, golf, horseshoes, inner-tube water polo, racquetball, skiing, soccer, softball, swimming, table tennis, tennis, volleyball. Men's club softball.

**ADMISSIONS. Requirements:** Graduation from secondary school is recommended; GED is accepted. 17 units and the following program of study are required: 4 units of English, 2 units of math, 2 units of lab science, 3 units of social studies, 1 unit of history, 3 units of academic electives. Minimum composite ACT score of 17, rank in top half of secondary school class, and minimum 2.0 GPA recommended. Higher secondary school standards and minimum ACT score of 20 required of health science program applicants. Portfolio required of Regents Bachelor of Arts (R.B.A.) program applicants. PPST required of teacher education program applicants. R.N. required of nursing program applicants. Conditional admission possible for applicants not meeting standard requirements. SAT or ACT is required. Campus visit and interview recommended. Off-campus interviews available with an admissions representative.
**Procedure:** Take SAT or ACT by June 1 of 12th year. Suggest filing application by June 1. Notification of admission on rolling basis. Freshmen accepted for terms other than fall.
**Special programs:** Admission may be deferred. Credit and/or placement may be granted through CEEB Advanced Placement exams for scores of 5 or higher. Credit and/or placement may be granted through CLEP general and subject exams. Credit may be granted through life experience. Credit and placement may be granted through ACT PEP and DANTES exams, and military experience. Deadline for applying for early decision is December 15. Early entrance/early admission program. Concurrent enrollment program.
**Transfer students:** Transfer students accepted for terms other than fall. In fall 1993, 37% of all new students were transfers into all classes. 879 transfer applications were received, 796 were accepted. Application deadline is August 1 for fall; December 1 for spring. Minimum 2.0 GPA recommended. Lowest course grade accepted is "D." Maximum number of transferable credits is 72 semester hours from a two-year school and 96 semester hours from a four-year school. At least 32 semester hours must be completed at the college to receive degree.
**Admissions contact:** John C. Cardwell, M.A., Director of Admissions. 304 327-4065.

**FINANCIAL AID. Available aid:** Pell grants, SEOG, state scholarships and grants, school scholarships, private scholarships and grants, academic merit scholarships, and athletic scholarships. Perkins Loans (NDSL), PLUS, Stafford Loans (GSL), and SLS. School payment plan.
**Financial aid statistics:** 24% of aid is not need-based. In 1993-94, 70% of all undergraduate applicants received aid; 70% of freshman applicants. Average amounts of aid awarded freshmen: Scholarships and grants, $500.
**Supporting data/closing dates:** FAFSA: Priority filing date is March 1. School's own aid application: Priority filing date is March 1. State aid form: Priority filing date is March 1. Notification of awards begins June 1.
**Financial aid contact:** Audrey C. Clay, M.A., Director of Financial Aid. 304 327-4022.

**STUDENT EMPLOYMENT.** College Work/Study Program. Institutional employment. 16% of full-time undergraduates work on campus during school year. Students may expect to earn an average of $1,000 during school year. Off-campus part-time employment opportunities rated "fair."

**COMPUTER FACILITIES.** 300 IBM/IBM-compatible and Macintosh/Apple microcomputers; 150 are networked. Students may access Digital minicomputer/mainframe systems, Internet. Client/LAN operating systems include Apple/Macintosh, DOS, Windows NT, DEC. Computer languages and software packages include Ada, BASIC, C, COBOL, FORTRAN, Pascal; database, spreadsheet, statistical, word processing packages. Computer facilities are available to all students.
**Fees:** None.
**Hours:** 7 AM-midn.

**GRADUATE CAREER DATA.** Graduate school percentages: 1% enter law school. 1% enter medical school. 4% enter graduate business programs. 1% enter graduate arts and sciences programs. Highest graduate school enrollments: Radford U, West Virginia Coll of Graduate Studies, Virginia Polytechnic Inst and State U, West Virginia U. 55% of graduates choose careers in business and industry. Companies and businesses that hire graduates: Board of Education, hospitals.

**PROMINENT ALUMNI/AE.** Noel Taylor, mayor of Roanoke, Va.; Bernard Robertson, deputy assistant secretary for African affairs, U.S. Department of State.

# Concord College

**Athens, WV 24712** **304 384-3115**

**1993-94 Costs.** Tuition: $1,906 (state residents), $4,076 (out-of-state). Room & board: $3,096. Fees, books, misc. academic expenses (school's estimate): $500.
**Enrollment.** Undergraduates: 890 men, 1,236 women (full-time). Freshman class: 1,868 applicants, 1,825 accepted, 1,078 enrolled.
**Test score averages/ranges.** Average ACT scores: 20 English, 19 math, 20 composite. Range of ACT scores of middle 50%: 17-24 English, 16-22 math.
**Faculty.** 89 full-time; 64 part-time. 52% of faculty holds doctoral degree. Student/faculty ratio: 23 to 1.
**Selectivity rating.** Noncompetitive.

**PROFILE.** Concord, founded in 1872, is a public college. Programs are offered through the Divisions of Business and Economics; Education, Library Science, and Physical Education; Fine Arts; Languages and Literature; Natural Sciences; and Social Sciences. Its 123-acre campus is located in Athens, in the Appalachian Mountains.

**Accreditation:** NCACS. Professionally accredited by the Council on Social Work Education, the National Council for Accreditation of Teacher Education.
**Religious orientation:** Concord College is nonsectarian; no religious requirements.
**Library:** Collections totaling over 147,240 volumes, 525 periodical subscriptions, and 7,219 microform items.
**Athletic facilities:** Gymnasiums, swimming pool, athletic complex, stadium, baseball, football, and softball fields, racquetball and tennis courts, weight rooms.

**STUDENT BODY. Undergraduate profile:** 92% are state residents; 25% are transfers. 1% Asian-American, 4% Black, 1% Hispanic, 94% White. Average age of undergraduates is 23.
**Freshman profile:** 98% of accepted applicants took ACT. 98% of freshmen come from public schools.
**Undergraduate achievement:** 62% of fall 1992 freshmen returned for fall 1993 term. 41% of entering class graduated.
**Foreign students:** 57 students are from out of the country. Countries represented include Bulgaria, China, Japan, Korea, Kuwait, and Thailand; 12 in all.

**PROGRAMS OF STUDY. Degrees:** B.A., B.S., B.Soc.Work.
**Majors:** Accounting, Biology, Business Administration, Ceramics, Chemistry, Commercial Art/Advertising, Communications Art, Computer Information Systems, Computer Science, Education, English, Finance, Geography, History, Interdisciplinary Studies, Management, Marketing, Mathematics, Medical Technology, Office/Secretarial Administration, Political Science, Psychology, Small Business Management, Social Work, Sociology, Studio Art, Travel Industry Management.
**Distribution of degrees:** The majors with the highest enrollment are education, business administration, and travel industry management; chemistry, studio art, and medical technology have the lowest.
**Requirements:** General education requirement.
**Academic regulations:** Juniors must maintain minimum 2.0 GPA; seniors, 2.0 GPA.
**Special:** Minors offered in several majors and in Appalachian studies, dramatic arts, educational use of computers, music, philosophy, physics, secretarial science, speech/oral communications, and statistics. Associate's degrees offered. Self-designed majors. Double majors. Independent study. Pass/fail grading option. Internships. Preprofessional programs in law, medicine, veterinary science, pharmacy, dentistry, and optometry. 2-2 business administration program with Beckley Coll. 3-1 medical technology program; student complete programs at Duke U, the Medical Coll of South Carolina, and U of Virginia. Teacher certification in early childhood, elementary, secondary, and special education.
**Academic Assistance:** Remedial reading, writing, math, and study skills.

**STUDENT LIFE. Housing:** All unmarried students under 23 years old must live on campus unless living with family. Women's and men's dorms. Off-campus privately-owned housing. On-campus married-student housing. 47% of students live in college housing.
**Social atmosphere:** The Subway, Rockers, First & Ten, the Last Resort, and the Sweet Shop are popular gathering places for students. Greeks and the Baptist Student Union are influential student groups. Homecoming and sporting events are popular with Concord students. Since the campus is small, most social opportunities are located in the city of Princeton, notes the editor of the student newspaper.
**Services and counseling/handicapped student services:** Placement services. Health service. Day care. Counseling services for veteran students. Personal counseling. Career and academic guidance services. Learning disabled services.
**Campus organizations:** Undergraduate student government. Student newspaper (Concordian, published once/week). Literary magazine. Yearbook. Radio and TV stations. Conchords, jazz band, College Singers, Chamber Singers, choir, Lion Pride Dancers, geographers club, marketing and social work associations, accounting club, Center for Economic Action, 47 organizations in all. Six fraternities, no chapter houses; four sororities, no chapter houses. 25% of men join a fraternity. 25% of women join a sorority.
**Religious organizations:** Baptist Campus Ministry, Baptist Student Union, Newman Community.
**Minority/foreign student organizations:** International Student Organization.

**ATHLETICS. Physical education requirements:** One semester of physical education required.
**Intercollegiate competition:** 10% of students participate. Baseball (M), basketball (M,W), cheerleading (M,W), football (M), golf (M), softball (W), tennis (M,W), volleyball (W). Member of NAIA, NCAA Division II, West Virginia Intercollegiate Athletic Conference.
**Intramural and club sports:** 15% of students participate. Intramural basketball, bowling, flag football, golf, racquetball, soccer, softball, tennis, water polo.

**ADMISSIONS. Academic basis for candidate selection** (in order of priority): Secondary school record, standardized test scores, school's recommendation, essay, class rank.
**Requirements:** Graduation from secondary school is recommended; GED is accepted. 19 units and the following program of study are required: 4 units of English, 2 units of math, 2 units of lab science, 2 units of foreign language, 2 units of social studies, 1 unit of history, 6 units of academic electives. Minimum composite ACT score of 17 (combined SAT score of 700) and minimum 2.0 GPA required. Audition required of music program applicants. ACT is required; SAT may be substituted. Campus visit and interview recommended. No off-campus interviews.
**Procedure:** Take SAT or ACT by February of 12th year. Notification of admission on rolling basis. $50 room deposit, refundable until June 30. Freshmen accepted for terms other than fall.
**Special programs:** Admission may be deferred one year. Credit and/or placement may be granted through CEEB Advanced Placement exams for scores of 3 or higher. Credit and/or placement may be granted through CLEP general and subject exams. Credit and placement may be granted through ACT PEP, DANTES, and challenge exams, and military and life experience. Concurrent enrollment program.
**Transfer students:** Transfer students accepted for terms other than fall. In fall 1993, 25% of all new students were transfers into all classes. 371 transfer applications were received, 371 were accepted. Application deadline is rolling for fall; rolling for spring. Minimum 2.0 GPA recommended. Lowest course grade accepted is "C." Maximum number of transferable credits is 72 semester hours from a two-year school and 96 semester hours from a four-year school. At least 30 semester hours must be completed at the college to receive degree.
**Admissions contact:** L. Dale Dickens, B.F.A., Director of Admissions. 304 384-5249.

**FINANCIAL AID. Available aid:** Pell grants, SEOG, state scholarships and grants, school scholarships, private scholarships, academic merit scholarships, and athletic scholarships. Perkins Loans (NDSL), PLUS, Stafford Loans (GSL), and SLS. Deferred payment plan.

**Financial aid statistics:** 25% of aid is not need-based. In 1993-94, 64% of all undergraduate applicants received aid; 92% of freshman applicants. Average amounts of aid awarded freshmen: Scholarships and grants, $2,200; loans, $2,625.
**Supporting data/closing dates:** FAFSA/FFS: Priority filing date is April 15. State aid form: Priority filing date is March 1. Income tax forms: Accepted on rolling basis. Verification worksheet: Accepted on rolling basis. Notification of awards on rolling basis.
**Financial aid contact:** Patricia Harmon, Director of Student Financial Aid. 304 384-5358.

**STUDENT EMPLOYMENT.** College Work/Study Program. Institutional employment. 17% of full-time undergraduates work on campus during school year. Students may expect to earn an average of $1,800 during school year. Off-campus part-time employment opportunities rated "fair."

**COMPUTER FACILITIES.** 53 IBM/IBM-compatible and Macintosh/Apple microcomputers; 25 are networked. Students may access Digital minicomputer/mainframe systems, BITNET, Internet. Residence halls may be equipped with networked microcomputers, modems. Client/LAN operating systems include Novell. Computer languages and software packages include BASIC, COBOL, FORTRAN, ImSL, Oracle, Pascal, PL/1, SPSS, Turbo Pascal; 20 in all. Computer facilities are available to all students.
Fees: None.

**GRADUATE CAREER DATA.** Graduate school percentages: 2% enter law school. 2% enter medical school. 1% enter dental school. 7% enter graduate business programs. 3% enter graduate arts and sciences programs. Highest graduate school enrollments: Radford U, Virginia Polytech Inst and State U, Washington and Lee U, West Virginia Tech. 21% of graduates choose careers in business and industry. Companies and businesses that hire graduates: West Virginia public schools.

# Davis and Elkins College

**Elkins, WV 26241** **304 636-1900**

**1994-95 Costs.** Tuition: $9,400. Room & board: $4,450. Fees, books, misc. academic expenses (school's estimate): $530.
**Enrollment.** Undergraduates: 311 men, 443 women (full-time). Freshman class: 585 applicants, 501 accepted, 209 enrolled.
**Test score averages/ranges.** Average SAT scores: 399 verbal, 437 math. Range of SAT scores of middle 50%: 340-450 verbal, 360-500 math. Average ACT scores: 19 composite. Range of ACT scores of middle 50%: 17-22 composite.
**Faculty.** 58 full-time; 21 part-time. 62% of faculty holds doctoral degree. Student/faculty ratio: 14 to 1.
**Selectivity rating.** Less competitive.

**PROFILE.** Davis and Elkins, founded in 1904, is a church-affiliated, liberal arts college. Its 170-acre campus is located in Elkins, in the foothills of the Allegheny Mountains.

**Accreditation:** NCACS.
**Religious orientation:** Davis and Elkins College is affiliated with the Presbyterian Church USA; one semester of religion required.
**Library:** Collections totaling over 225,000 volumes and 700 periodical subscriptions.
**Special facilities/museums:** Art gallery, language lab, planetarium, and observatory.
**Athletic facilities:** Gymnasium, swimming pool, fitness center, cross-country course, tennis courts, baseball, field hockey, soccer, and softball fields, field house.

**STUDENT BODY. Undergraduate profile:** 50% are state residents; 28% are transfers. 2% Asian-American, 4% Black, 1% Hispanic, 1% Native American, 90% White, 2% Other. Average age of undergraduates is 22.
**Freshman profile:** 1% of freshmen who took SAT scored 700 or over on math; 2% scored 600 or over on verbal, 6% scored 600 or over on math; 12% scored 500 or over on verbal, 26% scored 500 or over on math; 46% scored 400 or over on verbal, 60% scored 400 or over on math; 89% scored 300 or over on verbal, 93% scored 300 or over on math. 10% of freshmen who took ACT scored 24 or over on composite; 70% scored 18 or over on composite; 100% scored 12 or over on composite. 50% of accepted applicants took SAT; 31% took ACT. 86% of freshmen come from public schools.
**Undergraduate achievement:** 65% of fall 1992 freshmen returned for fall 1993 term. 20% of entering class graduated.
**Foreign students:** 20 students are from out of the country. Countries represented include Canada, Colombia, Japan, Spain, Trinidad, and Turkey; 12 in all.

**PROGRAMS OF STUDY. Degrees:** B.A., B.S., B.S.Nurs.
**Majors:** Accounting, Art, Biology, Business Education, Chemistry, Communication, Computer Science, Economics, Elementary Education, English Composition, English Literary Studies, Environmental Science, Exercise Science, Fashion Merchandising, French, Health Care Administration, Health Education, History/Political Science, Journalism, Management, Marketing, Mathematics, Music, Nursing, Physical Education, Political Science, Psychology/Human Services, Recreation Management/Tourism, Religion/Philosophy, Secondary Education, Secretarial Science, Sociology/Anthropology, Spanish, Theatre Arts.
**Distribution of degrees:** The majors with the highest enrollment are management, education, and natural sciences; art, music, and religion/philosophy have the lowest.
**Requirements:** General education requirement.
**Academic regulations:** Minimum 2.0 GPA must be maintained.
**Special:** Minors offered in many majors and in Appalachian studies, business administration, fashion drawing/merchandising, German, health, human development, humanities, natural science, office administration, outdoor recreation, physics, real estate, social science, therapeutic recreation, and travel/tourism. Associate's degrees offered. Double majors. Independent study. Internships. Cooperative education programs. Graduate school at which undergraduates may take graduate-level courses. Preprofessional programs in law, medicine, pharmacy, dentistry, and theology. 3-2 forestry program with Duke U. 3-2 occupational therapy and engineering programs with Washington U. 3-2 engineering programs with West Virginia U and Washington U. Member of West Virginia Consortium of Colleges and Universities. Washington Semester. Teacher certification in elementary and secondary education. Certification in specific subject areas. European Study Program in cooperation with Central Coll; programs in Austria, England, France, Mexico, and Spain.
**Honors:** Honors program. Honor societies.
**Academic Assistance:** Remedial reading, writing, math, and study skills. Nonremedial tutoring.

**ADMISSIONS. Academic basis for candidate selection** (in order of priority): Secondary school record, class rank, standardized test scores, school's recommendation, essay.
**Nonacademic basis for candidate selection:** Extracurricular participation is considered.
**Requirements:** Graduation from secondary school is required; GED is accepted. 11 units and the following program of study are required: 4 units of English, 2 units of math, 2 units of science including 1 unit of lab, 3 units of social studies. Additional units in math and science recommended for science program applicants. Rank in top half of secondary school class and minimum 2.0 GPA required; students with minimum GPA must enter academic support program. Audition required of music program applicants. Conditional admission possible for applicants not meeting standard requirements. SAT or ACT is required. Campus visit and interview recommended. Off-campus interviews available with admissions and alumni representatives.
**Procedure:** Notification of admission on rolling basis. $100 tuition deposit, refundable until May 1. Freshmen accepted for terms other than fall.
**Special programs:** Admission may be deferred one year. Credit may be granted through CEEB Advanced Placement for scores of 3 or higher. Credit may be granted through DANTES exams, and military and life experience. Early decision program. Early entrance/early admission program. Concurrent enrollment program.
**Transfer students:** Transfer students accepted for terms other than fall. In fall 1993, 28% of all new students were transfers into all classes. 142 transfer applications were received, 134 were accepted. Application deadline is July 1 for fall; January 1 for spring. Minimum 2.0 GPA required. Lowest course grade accepted is "D." Maximum number of transferable credits is 90 semester hours. At least 28 semester hours must be completed at the college to receive degree.
**Admissions contact:** Kevin D. Chenoweth, Director of Admissions. 304 636-5850.

**FINANCIAL AID. Available aid:** Pell grants, SEOG, state grants, school scholarships and grants, private scholarships and grants, academic merit scholarships, and athletic scholarships. Perkins Loans (NDSL), PLUS, Stafford Loans (GSL), school loans, private loans, and SLS. AMS, Tuition Management Systems, and deferred payment plan.
**Financial aid statistics:** 13% of aid is not need-based. In 1993-94, 95% of all undergraduate applicants received aid; 95% of freshman applicants. Average amounts of aid awarded freshmen: Scholarships and grants, $2,000; loans, $3,000.
**Supporting data/closing dates:** FAFSA/FAF: Priority filing date is May 1; accepted on rolling basis. State aid form: Priority filing date is March 1. Income tax forms: Accepted on rolling basis. Notification of awards on rolling basis.
**Financial aid contact:** John Elza, Director of Financial Aid. 304 636-1900, extension 271.

# Fairmont State College

**Fairmont, WV 26554** **304 367-4000**

**1994-95 Costs.** Tuition: $1,800 (state residents), $4,400 (out-of-state). Room: $1,400. Board: $1,640. Fees, books, misc. academic expenses (school's estimate): $500.
**Enrollment.** Undergraduates: 1,982 men, 2,422 women (full-time). Freshman class: 1,997 applicants, 1,537 accepted, 1,500 enrolled.
**Test score averages/ranges.** Average ACT scores: 18 English, 18 math, 18 composite.
**Faculty.** 173 full-time; 243 part-time. 32% of faculty holds doctoral degree. Student/faculty ratio: 24 to 1.
**Selectivity rating.** Less competitive.

**PROFILE.** Fairmont State, founded in 1867, is a public college of the arts and sciences. Its 80-acre campus is located in Fairmont, 75 miles south of Pittsburgh.

**Accreditation:** NCACS. Professionally accredited by the National Council for Accreditation of Teacher Education, the National League for Nursing.
**Religious orientation:** Fairmont State College is nonsectarian; no religious requirements.
**Library:** Collections totaling over 215,000 volumes, 834 periodical subscriptions, and 31,559 microform items.
**Special facilities/museums:** On-campus one-room school house.
**Athletic facilities:** Gymnasiums, racquetball and tennis courts, weight room, athletic fields.

**STUDENT BODY. Undergraduate profile:** 94% are state residents; 10% are transfers. 4% Black, 95% White, 1% Other. Average age of undergraduates is 24.
**Freshman profile:** 2% of freshmen who took ACT scored 30 or over on English, 3% scored 30 or over on math, 2% scored 30 or over on composite; 10% scored 24 or over on English, 10% scored 24 or over on math, 10% scored 24 or over on composite; 52% scored 18 or over on English, 50% scored 18 or over on math, 49% scored 18 or over on composite; 87% scored 12 or over on English, 87% scored 12 or over on math, 87% scored 12 or over on composite; 97% scored 6 or over on English, 97% scored 6 or over on math, 97% scored 6 or over on composite. 8% of accepted applicants took SAT; 92% took ACT. 95% of freshmen come from public schools.
**Undergraduate achievement:** 60% of fall 1992 freshmen returned for fall 1993 term. 39% of entering class graduated. 5% of students who completed a degree program immediately went on to graduate study.
**Foreign students:** 53 students are from out of the country. Countries represented include Canada, India, Japan, the Netherlands, and Nigeria; 18 in all.

**PROGRAMS OF STUDY. Degrees:** B.A., B.A.Ed., B.Eng.Tech., B.S.
**Majors:** Accounting, Allied Health Administration, Art, Biology, Business Administration, Chemistry, Community Services, Computer Science, Criminal Justice, Economics, Education, Engineering Technology, English, French, General Business, Graphics/Fine Arts, Health Sciences, History, Home Economics, Interdisciplinary Studies, Mathematics,

Nursing, Occupational Health, Physical Education, Political Science, Psychology, Sociology, Speech Communication, Theatre.
**Distribution of degrees:** The majors with the highest enrollment are business, education, and engineering technology; English and history have the lowest.
**Requirements:** General education requirement.
**Special:** Minors offered in art, criminal justice, electronic data processing, German, graphics, library science, philosophy, physics, radio/television, communications, speech communication/theatre, and special education. Associate's degrees offered. Preprofessional programs in law, medicine, veterinary science, pharmacy, and dentistry. Teacher certification in early childhood, elementary, and special education. Certification in specific subject areas. ROTC.
**Honors:** Honors program. Honor societies.
**Academic Assistance:** Remedial reading, writing, math, and study skills. Nonremedial tutoring.

**STUDENT LIFE. Housing:** Students may live on or off campus. Women's and men's dorms. 8% of students live in college housing.
**Services and counseling/handicapped student services:** Placement services. Health service. Counseling services for minority, military, veteran, and older students. Personal and psychological counseling. Career and academic guidance services. Physically disabled student services. Learning disabled services. Tape recorders. Tutors. Reader services for the blind.
**Campus organizations:** Undergraduate student government. Student newspaper (Mound, published once/week). Yearbook. Concert and marching band, chorus, symphony orchestra, American Institute of Architects, American Society of Civil Engineers, Council for Exceptional Children, Engineering Technical Society, Graphics Communications Association, Student Nurses Association, Circle K, home economics club, political science association, Masquers Club, special-interest groups. Six fraternities, one chapter house; four sororities, no chapter houses. 10% of men join a fraternity. 10% of women join a sorority.
**Religious organizations:** Baptist Campus Ministry, Christian Student Union, Intervarsity Christian Fellowship.
**Minority/foreign student organizations:** Black Student Union. International Relations Club.

**ATHLETICS. Physical education requirements:** One semester of physical education required.
**Intercollegiate competition:** 30% of students participate. Baseball (M), basketball (M,W), cheerleading (M,W), cross-country (M,W), football (M), golf (M,W), swimming (M,W), volleyball (W). Member of NAIA, NCAA, WVIAC.
**Intramural and club sports:** 65% of students participate. Intramural archery, backgammon, badminton, basketball, billiards, bowling, flag football, foul shooting, golf, horseshoes, racquetball, shuffleboard, softball, spades, swimming and diving, table tennis, tennis, track and field, tug-of-war, turkey trot, volleyball, wrestling.

**ADMISSIONS. Academic basis for candidate selection** (in order of priority): Secondary school record, standardized test scores, class rank, school's recommendation, essay.
**Requirements:** Graduation from secondary school is required; GED is accepted. No specific distribution of secondary school units required. Foreign language recommended. Minimum composite ACT score of 19 and minimum 2.25 GPA required. ACT is required; SAT may be substituted. Campus visit and interview recommended. No off-campus interviews.
**Procedure:** Take SAT or ACT by June of 12th year. Application deadline is June 15. Notification of admission on rolling basis. No set date by which applicants must accept offer. $100 room deposit, refundable until June 15. Freshmen accepted for terms other than fall.
**Special programs:** Credit may be granted through CEEB Advanced Placement for scores of 3 or higher. Credit and/or placement may be granted through CLEP general and subject exams. Credit and placement may be granted through DANTES and challenge exams, and military experience. Concurrent enrollment program.
**Transfer students:** Transfer students accepted for terms other than fall. In fall 1993, 10% of all new students were transfers into all classes. 1,270 transfer applications were received, 1,140 were accepted. Application deadline is June 15 for fall; rolling for spring. Minimum 2.0 GPA required. Lowest course grade accepted is "D." Maximum number of transferable credits is 72 semester hours. At least 32 semester hours must be completed at the college to receive degree.
**Admissions contact:** John G. Conaway, Ed.D., Director of Admissions. 304 367-4141.

**FINANCIAL AID. Available aid:** Pell grants, SEOG, Federal Nursing Student Scholarships, state scholarships and grants, school scholarships, private scholarships, ROTC scholarships, academic merit scholarships, athletic scholarships, and aid for undergraduate foreign students. Perkins Loans (NDSL), Stafford Loans (GSL), NSL, and state loans.
**Financial aid statistics:** 15% of aid is not need-based. In 1993-94, 63% of all undergraduate applicants received aid; 60% of freshman applicants. Average amounts of aid awarded freshmen: Scholarships and grants, $450; loans, $500.
**Supporting data/closing dates:** FAFSA/FAF: Priority filing date is March 1. School's own aid application. Notification of awards begins June 15.
**Financial aid contact:** William D. Shaffer, M.A., Director of Financial Aid. 304 367-4213.

**STUDENT EMPLOYMENT.** College Work/Study Program. Institutional employment. 40% of full-time undergraduates work on campus during school year. Students may expect to earn an average of $500 during school year. Freshmen are discouraged from working during their first term. Off-campus part-time employment opportunities rated "good."

**COMPUTER FACILITIES.** 100 IBM/IBM-compatible and Macintosh/Apple microcomputers; 50 are networked. Students may access Digital minicomputer/mainframe systems. Computer languages and software packages include BASIC, COBOL, FORTRAN, Pascal. Computer facilities are available to all students.
**Fees:** None.
**Hours:** 8 AM-11 PM.

**GRADUATE CAREER DATA.** Highest graduate school enrollments: West Virginia U. 15% of graduates choose careers in business and industry.

# Glenville State College

**Glenville, WV 26351** **304 462-7361**

**1994-95 Costs.** Tuition: $1,730 (state residents), $3,944 (out-of-state). Room & board: $2,980. Fees, books, misc. academic expenses (school's estimate): $300.
**Enrollment.** Undergraduates: 832 men, 891 women (full-time). Freshman class: 1,244 applicants, 1,230 accepted, 553 enrolled.
**Test score averages/ranges.** Average ACT scores: 18 English, 18 math, 18 composite.
**Faculty.** 76 full-time; 74 part-time. 28% of faculty holds doctoral degree. Student/faculty ratio: 18 to 1.
**Selectivity rating.** Noncompetitive.

**PROFILE.** Glenville State, founded as a Normal school in 1872, is a public college. Its 170-acre campus is located in Glenville, between Charleston and Clarksburg.

**Accreditation:** NCACS. Professionally accredited by the National Council for Accreditation of Teacher Education, the National League for Nursing, the Society of American Foresters.
**Religious orientation:** Glenville State College is nonsectarian; no religious requirements.
**Library:** Collections totaling over 132,000 volumes, 68 periodical subscriptions, and 16,402 microform items.
**Athletic facilities:** Gymnasium, tennis courts, track, exercise and weight rooms, swimming pool.

**STUDENT BODY. Undergraduate profile:** 92% are state residents; 1% are transfers. 3% Asian-American, 4% Black, 1% Hispanic, 92% White. Average age of undergraduates is 27.
**Freshman profile:** 1% of accepted applicants took SAT; 99% took ACT. 99% of freshmen come from public schools.
**Undergraduate achievement:** 64% of fall 1992 freshmen returned for fall 1993 term. 28% of entering class graduated. 4% of students who completed a degree program immediately went on to graduate study.
**Foreign students:** 45 students are from out of the country. Countries represented include Canada, Ethiopia, Ireland, Japan, and Zambia; five in all.

**PROGRAMS OF STUDY. Degrees:** B.A., B.Bus.Admin., B.S., B.S.Nurs.
**Majors:** Art, Biological Science, Biology, Business, Business Administration, Chemistry, Criminal Justice, Early Childhood Education, Elementary Education, English, General Science, History, Interdisciplinary Studies, Learning Disabilities, Mathematics, Mental Retardation, Music, Nursing, Oral Communication, Physical Education, Safety Education, School Library Media, Secondary Education, Social Studies, Special Education, Sports Management.
**Distribution of degrees:** The majors with the highest enrollment are education, business administration, and nursing; chemistry, biology, and history have the lowest.
**Requirements:** General education requirement.
**Academic regulations:** Freshmen must maintain minimum 1.0 GPA; sophomores, 1.50 GPA; juniors, 1.75 GPA; seniors, 2.0 GPA.
**Special:** Associate's degrees offered. Self-designed majors. Double majors. Preprofessional programs in law, medicine, veterinary science, pharmacy, dentistry, and optometry. 2-2 programs in business administration, criminal justice, forest technology and surveying (biology and business). Teacher certification in early childhood, elementary, secondary, and special education. Certification in specific subject areas.
**Honors:** Honors program.
**Academic Assistance:** Remedial reading, writing, and math. Nonremedial tutoring.

**STUDENT LIFE. Housing:** All unmarried freshmen must live on campus unless living with family. Women's and men's dorms. Sorority housing. School-owned/operated apartments. Off-campus privately-owned housing. On-campus married-student housing. 66% of students live in college housing.
**Social atmosphere:** Students gather on campus at Heflin Student Center, Pickens Hall, and the Amphitheatre. Off-campus, students frequent the Derrick, the Campus Pub, and the Main Event. The Student Congress and the Pioneer Programming Board exert the most influence on campus social life. Students enjoy the annual Shai Concert, football games, the Multicultural Fair, and concerts by the Wheeling Symphony Orchestra. "We have a very diverse campus, and we are continually working on bettering relations between different groups. Most students are willing to get involved with activities–we're always trying new ideas," reports the editor of the student newspaper.
**Services and counseling/handicapped student services:** Placement services. Health service. Personal counseling. Academic guidance services.
**Campus organizations:** Undergraduate student government. Student newspaper (Mercury, published once/week). Literary magazine. Yearbook. Choir, several music ensembles, marching and jazz bands, Ohnimgohow Players, academic, professional, and social groups. One fraternity, no chapter house; two sororities, one chapter house. 1% of men join a fraternity. 3% of women join a sorority.
**Religious organizations:** Christian Fellowship Organization.

**ATHLETICS. Physical education requirements:** Two semesters of physical education required.
**Intercollegiate competition:** 15% of students participate. Basketball (M,W), cheerleading (M,W), cross-country (M,W), football (M), golf (M), track (indoor) (M,W), track and field (indoor) (M,W), track and field (outdoor) (M,W), volleyball (W). Member of NAIA, NCAA Division II, West Virginia Intercollegiate Athletic Conference.
**Intramural and club sports:** 20% of students participate. Intramural aerobics, badminton, basketball, billiards, bowling, golf, horseshoes, racquetball, punt-pass-kick, shuffleboard, softball, tennis, track, volleyball, weight lifting.

**ADMISSIONS. Academic basis for candidate selection** (in order of priority): Secondary school record, standardized test scores.
**Requirements:** Graduation from secondary school is required; GED is accepted. 21 units and the following program of study are required: 4 units of English, 2 units of math, 2 units

of lab science, 3 units of social studies, 8 units of electives. Minimum composite ACT score of 17 and minimum 2.0 GPA required. Conditional admission possible for applicants not meeting standard requirements. ACT is required; SAT may be substituted. Campus visit recommended. Off-campus interviews available with an admissions representative.

**Procedure:** Take SAT or ACT by October of 12th year. Notification of admission on rolling basis. No set date by which applicants must accept offer. $50 nonrefundable room deposit. Freshmen accepted for terms other than fall.

**Special programs:** Credit may be granted through CEEB Advanced Placement for scores of 3 or higher. Credit may be granted through CLEP general and subject exams, ACT PEP, DANTES, and challenge exams, and military experience. Early entrance/early admission program. Concurrent enrollment program.

**Transfer students:** Transfer students accepted for terms other than fall. In fall 1993, 1% of all new students were transfers into all classes. 144 transfer applications were received, 136 were accepted. Application deadline is rolling. Minimum 2.0 GPA required. Lowest course grade accepted is "D." Maximum number of transferable credits is 96 semester hours. At least 32 semester hours must be completed at the college to receive degree.

**Admissions contact:** Mack K. Samples, M.A., Dean of Records and Admissions. 304 462-4117.

**FINANCIAL AID. Available aid:** Pell grants, SEOG, state scholarships and grants, school scholarships, private scholarships and grants, academic merit scholarships, and athletic scholarships. Perkins Loans (NDSL), PLUS, Stafford Loans (GSL), school loans, private loans, and SLS. AMS.

**Financial aid statistics:** 11% of aid is not need-based. In 1993-94, 70% of all undergraduate applicants received aid; 81% of freshman applicants. Average amounts of aid awarded freshmen: Scholarships and grants, $1,721; loans, $1,813.

**Supporting data/closing dates:** FAFSA. Notification of awards on rolling basis.

**Financial aid contact:** August Kafer, Director of Financial Aid. 304 462-4103.

**STUDENT EMPLOYMENT.** College Work/Study Program. Institutional employment. 12% of full-time undergraduates work on campus during school year. Students may expect to earn an average of $962 during school year. Off-campus part-time employment opportunities rated "fair."

**COMPUTER FACILITIES.** 52 IBM/IBM-compatible microcomputers; 32 are networked. Students may access IBM minicomputer/mainframe systems. Client/LAN operating systems include Apple/Macintosh, Windows NT, Microsoft. Computer languages and software packages include BASIC, C, COBOL, dBASE, FORTRAN, Lotus 1-2-3, Pascal, PC-Write, PL/1, WordPerfect. Computer facilities are available to all students.

**Fees:** None.

**Hours:** 24 hours.

**GRADUATE CAREER DATA.** Graduate school percentages: 2% enter graduate arts and sciences programs. 4% enter theological school/seminary. Highest graduate school enrollments: Marshall U, Ohio U, West Virginia U. Companies and businesses that hire graduates: Public school systems.

**PROMINENT ALUMNI/AE.** Lloyd Elliot, president, National Geographic Society; Denzil Skinner, CEO, Hyatt Management Corp.; John P. Shock, medical science chairperson, U of Arkansas.

# Marshall University

**Huntington, WV 25755** **304 696-3170**

**1994-95 Costs.** Tuition: $1,882 (state residents), $5,144 (out-of-state). Room & board: $3,800. Fees, books, misc. academic expenses (school's estimate): $400.

**Enrollment.** Undergraduates: 4,726 men, 5,703 women (full-time). Freshman class: 4,481 applicants, 4,372 accepted, 2,129 enrolled. Graduate enrollment: 771 men, 1,921 women.

**Test score averages/ranges.** Average ACT scores: 20 English, 18 math, 20 composite.

**Faculty.** 371 full-time; 195 part-time. 69% of faculty holds doctoral degree. Student/faculty ratio: 23 to 1.

**Selectivity rating.** Noncompetitive.

**PROFILE.** Marshall, founded in 1837, is a public university. Programs are offered through the Colleges of Business, Education, Fine Arts, Liberal Arts, and Science; the Community College; the Graduate School; and the Schools of Medicine and Nursing. Its 75-acre campus is located in Huntington, 50 miles west of Charleston.

**Accreditation:** NCACS. Professionally accredited by the Accrediting Council on Education in Journalism and Mass Communication, the American Home Economics Association, the American Medical Association (CAHEA), the Liaison Committee on Medical Education, the National Association of Schools of Music, the National Council for Accreditation of Teacher Education, the National League for Nursing.

**Religious orientation:** Marshall University is nonsectarian; no religious requirements.

**Library:** Collections totaling over 401,195 volumes, 2,746 periodical subscriptions, and 181,498 microform items.

**Special facilities/museums:** Art gallery, audio-visual center, language lab, superconducting nuclear magnetic resonance spectrometer.

**Athletic facilities:** Gymnasiums, arena, tracks, basketball, racquetball, and tennis courts, stadium, natatorium, bowling lanes, weight rooms, baseball, football, and intramural fields, cross-country course, country club.

**STUDENT BODY. Undergraduate profile:** 87% are state residents; 6% are transfers. 1% Asian-American, 4% Black, 95% White. Average age of undergraduates is 22.

**Freshman profile:** Majority of accepted applicants took ACT.

**Undergraduate achievement:** 55% of fall 1991 freshmen returned for fall 1992 term.

**Foreign students:** 52 students are from out of the country. Countries represented include Iran, Lebanon, Malaysia, Nigeria, the Philippines, and the United Kingdom; 27 in all.

**PROGRAMS OF STUDY. Degrees:** B.A., B.Bus.Admin., B.F.A., B.S., B.S.M.T., B.S.Nurs., B.Soc.Work, Regents B.A.

**Majors:** Accounting, Adult Fitness, Advertising, Anthropology, Art, Athletic Training, Basic Humanities, Biology, Botany, Broadcasting, Business Education, Chemistry, Classical Languages, Community Development, Computer Information Systems, Computer Science, Corrections, Counseling/Rehabilitation, Criminal Justice, Cytotechnology, Dietetics, Early Childhood Education, Economics, Elementary Education, English, Fashion Merchandising, Finance/Business Law, Fine Arts, French, Geography, Geology, German, Health Education, History, Home Economics, Home Economics Education, International Affairs, Journalism, Management, Marketing, Marketing Education, Mathematics, Medical Technology, Music, Music Education, News/Editorial, Nursing, Parks/Leisure Services, Philosophy, Physical Education, Physics, Political Science, Psychology, Public Relations, Religious Studies, Safety Technology, School Library Media, Secondary Education, Social Work, Sociology, Spanish, Special Education, Speech, Speech Pathology/Audiology, Sports Communications, Sports Management/Marketing, Theatre/Dance, Zoology.

**Distribution of degrees:** The majors with the highest enrollment are elementary education, marketing, and secondary education; fashion merchandising and physics have the lowest.

**Requirements:** General education requirement.

**Special:** Associate's degrees offered. Double majors. Dual degrees. Independent study. Accelerated study. Pass/fail grading option. Internships. Cooperative education programs. Graduate school at which undergraduates may take graduate-level courses. Preprofessional programs in law, medicine, veterinary science, dentistry, and optometry. 3-1 cytotechnology and medical technology programs. 3-2 forestry and environmental management program with Duke U. Engineering, pharmacy, and physical therapy programs with West Virginia U. Physical therapy programs also with Wheeling Jesuit Coll and Wheeling U. Engineering program with West Virginia Tech. Member of Academic Common Market. Teacher certification in early childhood, elementary, secondary, and special education. Study abroad in Ecuador and Spain. ROTC.

**Honors:** Honors program.

**Academic Assistance:** Remedial reading, writing, math, and study skills. Nonremedial tutoring.

**STUDENT LIFE. Housing:** All unmarried students under age 21 must live on campus unless living near campus with relatives. Coed, women's, and men's dorms. Sorority and fraternity housing. School-owned/operated apartments. Off-campus privately-owned housing. Both on-campus and off-campus married-student housing. 89% of students live in college housing.

**Social atmosphere:** "Students here are, for the most part, 'responsible partiers' and are at MU to get a good education," reports the student newspaper. Popular events include Homecoming, the Southern Conference Basketball Tournament, Springfest, and week-long activities and concerts at an area park just before the pressure of finals. Greeks, Christian groups, and athletes exert some influence on campus social life. Favorite gathering spots include the Student Center cafeteria, Gumby's, Wiggin's, Marco's, Rubby's, and the Morrow Library.

**Services and counseling/handicapped student services:** Placement services. Health service. Women's center. Day care. Counseling services for minority, military, veteran, and older students. Birth control, personal, and psychological counseling. Career and academic guidance services. Physically disabled student services. Learning disabled program/services. Notetaking services. Reader services for the blind.

**Campus organizations:** Undergraduate student government. Student newspaper (Parthenon, published four times/week). Literary magazine. Yearbook. Radio and TV stations. Marching and concert bands, vocal jazz ensemble, jazz band, chamber choir and ensemble, chorus, Choral Union, wind ensemble, community orchestra, theatre, student alumni organization, Society of Professional Journalists, public relations society, Hall Advisory Council. 10 fraternities, six chapter houses; eight sororities, four chapter houses. 12% of men join a fraternity. 8% of women join a sorority.

**Religious organizations:** Campus Crusade for Christ, Students for Christ, Baptist Campus Ministry, Baptist Student Union, Canterbury Fellowship, Lutheran Student Movement, Newman Association, PROWL (Presbyterian group).

**Minority/foreign student organizations:** Black United Students. Chinese Student Association, International Club, Muslim Student Association.

**ATHLETICS. Physical education requirements:** None.

**Intercollegiate competition:** 3% of students participate. Baseball (M), basketball (M,W), cheerleading (M,W), cross-country (M,W), football (M), golf (M), soccer (M), softball (W), tennis (W), track (indoor) (M,W), track (outdoor) (M,W), track and field (indoor) (M,W), track and field (outdoor) (M,W), volleyball (W). Member of NCAA Division I, NCAA Division I-AA for football, Southern Conference.

**Intramural and club sports:** 60% of students participate. Intramural backgammon, badminton, basketball, beach volleyball, billiards, cross-country, darts, field goal kick, free throw, home run derby, horseshoes, Hula Hoop golf, indoor soccer, pickleball, racquetball, softball, swimming, tennis, track and field, tug-o-war, turkey trot, volleyball, walleyball, wrestling.

**ADMISSIONS. Academic basis for candidate selection** (in order of priority): Secondary school record, standardized test scores.

**Nonacademic basis for candidate selection:** Particular talent or ability is considered.

**Requirements:** Graduation from secondary school is required; GED is accepted. No specific distribution of secondary school units required. Minimum composite ACT score of 17 or minimum 2.0 GPA required. Minimum ACT score of 18 and separate application required of nursing program applicants. Audition required of music program applicants. Upward Bound program for applicants not normally admissible. ACT is required; SAT may be substituted. Campus visit recommended. No off-campus interviews.

**Procedure:** Notification of admission on rolling basis. No set date by which applicants must accept offer. $100 room deposit, refundable until June 30. Freshmen accepted for terms other than fall.

**Special programs:** Admission may be deferred one year. Credit and/or placement may be granted through CEEB Advanced Placement exams for scores of 4 or higher. Credit may be granted through CLEP general and subject exams, Regents College, ACT PEP, DANTES, and challenge exams, and military and life experience. Early entrance/early admission program. Concurrent enrollment program.

**Transfer students:** Transfer students accepted for terms other than fall. In fall 1992, 6% of all new students were transfers into all classes. 5,120 transfer applications were received,

827 were accepted. Application deadline is rolling for fall; rolling for spring. Minimum 2.0 GPA required. Maximum number of transferable credits is 72 from two-year schools; unlimited from four-year schools.
**Admissions contact:** James W. Harless, Ed.D., Director of Admissions. 304 696-3160.
**FINANCIAL AID. Available aid:** Pell grants, SEOG, state scholarships and grants, school scholarships and grants, private scholarships and grants, ROTC scholarships, academic merit scholarships, athletic scholarships, and aid for undergraduate foreign students. Perkins Loans (NDSL), PLUS, Stafford Loans (GSL), NSL, Health Professions Loans, state loans, school loans, and SLS.
**Financial aid statistics:** 25% of aid is not need-based.
**Supporting data/closing dates:** FAFSA/FAF/FFS: Priority filing date is February 1. School's own aid application: Priority filing date is February 1. State aid form: Priority filing date is March 1. Notification of awards on rolling basis.
**Financial aid contact:** Edgar Miller, Ed.D., Director of Financial Aid. 304 696-3162.
**STUDENT EMPLOYMENT.** College Work/Study Program. Institutional employment. 13% of full-time undergraduates work on campus during school year. Students may expect to earn an average of $1,400 during school year. Off-campus part-time employment opportunities rated "fair."
**COMPUTER FACILITIES.** 30 IBM/IBM-compatible microcomputers. Computer languages and software packages include Ada, C, COBOL, dBASE, FORTRAN, Lotus 1-2-3, Mimitab, Pascal, WordPerfect. Computer facilities available only to students enrolled in courses which require computers.
**Fees:** None.
**Hours:** 9 AM-9 PM (M-Th); 8:30 AM-4:30 PM (F); 7 PM (Sa); noon-5 PM (Su).

## Salem-Teikyo University

**Salem, WV 26426** 304 782-5011

**1994-95 Costs.** Tuition: $10,575. Room: $2,400. Board: $3,528. Fees, books, misc. academic expenses (school's estimate): $550.
**Enrollment.** Undergraduates: 471 men, 189 women (full-time). Freshman class: 418 applicants, 391 accepted, 136 enrolled. Graduate enrollment: 19 men, 32 women.
**Test score averages/ranges.** Average SAT scores: 906 combined. Average ACT scores: 22 composite.
**Faculty.** 46 full-time; 15 part-time. 29% of faculty holds doctoral degree. Student/faculty ratio: 12 to 1.
**Selectivity rating.** Less competitive.

**PROFILE.** Salem-Teikyo, founded in 1888, is a private, multipurpose university. Its 150-acre campus is located in Salem, 120 miles south of Pittsburgh.
**Accreditation:** NCACS.
**Religious orientation:** Salem-Teikyo University is nonsectarian; no religious requirements.
**Library:** Collections totaling over 10,000 volumes, 687 periodical subscriptions, and 211,558 microform items.
**Special facilities/museums:** Living museum of culture and crafts of West Virginia settlers, Fort New Salem.
**Athletic facilities:** Gymnasium, racquetball and tennis courts, fitness center, swimming pool, weight room.
**STUDENT BODY. Undergraduate profile:** 31% are state residents. 37% Asian-American, 10% Black, 44% White, 9% Other. Average age of undergraduates is 20.
**Freshman profile:** 256% of freshmen come from public schools.
**Undergraduate achievement:** 75% of fall 1991 freshmen returned for fall 1992 term. 40% of entering class graduated.
**Foreign students:** 274 students are from out of the country. Countries represented include Canada, the Czech Republic/Slovakia, India, Japan, Kuwait, and United Arab Emirates.
**PROGRAMS OF STUDY. Degrees:** B.A., B.English Lang., B.Equest.Ed., B.Japan Studies, B.S.
**Majors:** Accounting, Athletic Training, Aviation, Biology, Computer Science, Criminal Justice, Elementary Education, Engineering-Related Technologies, English as a Second Language, Equine Careers/Industry Management, Industrial Technology, Japanese Studies, Liberal Studies, Management, Marketing, Mathematics, Medical Technology, Outdoor Science, Physical Education, Radiologic Technology, Sports Broadcasting, Sports Medicine, Youth/Human Services.
**Distribution of degrees:** The majors with the highest enrollment are management, health professions, and aviation; computer science and biology have the lowest.
**Requirements:** General education requirement.
**Special:** Minors offered in some majors and in broadcast/telecommunications, industrial health/safety management, and technology studies. Aviation program with KCI, Inc., at Benedum Airport near Clarksburg. Associate's degrees offered. Double majors. Dual degrees. Internships. Graduate school at which undergraduates may take graduate-level courses. Member of Mountain State Association of Colleges and Appalachian Technical Education Consortium. Teacher certification in elementary, secondary, and special education. Exchange programs abroad in Japan (Teikyo U, Hachioji) the Netherlands (Teikyo Junior Coll), and Germany (Teikyo U Berlin Campus). ROTC at Fairmont State Coll. AFROTC at West Virginia U.
**Honors:** Honor societies.
**Academic Assistance:** Remedial reading, writing, math, and study skills. Nonremedial tutoring.
**ADMISSIONS. Academic basis for candidate selection** (in order of priority): Secondary school record, standardized test scores, class rank, essay, school's recommendation.
**Nonacademic basis for candidate selection:** Extracurricular participation is important. Character and personality and alumni/ae relationship are considered.
**Requirements:** Graduation from secondary school is required; GED is accepted. 16 units and the following program of study are recommended: 4 units of English, 3 units of math, 3 units of science, 2 units of foreign language, 2 units of social studies, 2 units of history. SAT or ACT is required. Campus visit and interview recommended. Off-campus interviews available with an admissions representative.
**Procedure:** Visit college for interview by August of 12th year. Notification of admission on rolling basis. $150 tuition deposit, refundable until two months prior to enrollment. $50 room deposit, refundable until two months prior to enrollment. Freshmen accepted for terms other than fall.
**Special programs:** Admission may be deferred one year. Credit and/or placement may be granted through CEEB Advanced Placement exams for scores of 3 or higher. Credit and/or placement may be granted through CLEP subject exams. Credit and placement may be granted through challenge exams. Concurrent enrollment program.
**Transfer students:** Transfer students accepted for terms other than fall. In fall 1992, 95 transfer applications were received, 59 were accepted. Minimum 2.5 GPA required. Lowest course grade accepted is "C." At least 32 credits must be completed at the university to receive degree.
**Admissions contact:** Paul Dauphinais, Ph.D, Director of Admissions. 800 283-4562.
**FINANCIAL AID. Available aid:** Pell grants, SEOG, state grants, private scholarships, academic merit scholarships, and athletic scholarships. Perkins Loans (NDSL), PLUS, Stafford Loans (GSL), and SLS. AMS.
**Financial aid statistics:** In 1992-93, 95% of all undergraduate applicants received aid; 92% of freshman applicants. Average amounts of aid awarded freshmen: Loans, $2,625.
**Supporting data/closing dates:** FAFSA/FAF/FFS. Income tax forms. Notification of awards on rolling basis.
**Financial aid contact:** Sue Ritter, Director of Financial Aid. 304 782-5205.

## Shepherd College

**Shepherdstown, WV 25443** 304 876-2511

**1993-94 Costs.** Tuition: $2,040 (state residents), $4,670 (out-of-state). Room & board: $3,500. Fees, books, misc. academic expenses (school's estimate): $800.
**Enrollment.** Undergraduates: 1,431 men, 2,134 women (full-time). Freshman class: 1,405 applicants, 1,100 accepted, 574 enrolled.
**Test score averages/ranges.** Average SAT scores: 550 verbal, 550 math. Range of SAT scores of middle 50%: 900-1060 combined. Average ACT scores: 22 composite. Range of ACT scores of middle 50%: 19-23 composite.
**Faculty.** 115 full-time; 141 part-time. 65% of faculty holds doctoral degree. Student/faculty ratio: 14 to 1.
**Selectivity rating.** Competitive.

**PROFILE.** Shepherd, founded in 1871, is a public college. Programs are offered through the Divisions of Business Administration; Creative Arts; Education; Health, Physical Education, Recreation, and Safety; Languages and Literature; Science and Mathematics; and Social Sciences. Its 165-acre campus is located in Shepherdstown, 65 miles from Washington, D.C.
**Accreditation:** NCACS. Professionally accredited by the Council on Social Work Education, the National Association of Schools of Music, the National Council for Accreditation of Teacher Education, the National League for Nursing.
**Religious orientation:** Shepherd College is nonsectarian; no religious requirements.
**Library:** Collections totaling over 255,336 volumes, 958 periodical subscriptions, and 47,285 microform items.
**Special facilities/museums:** Nursery school, elementary education lab, art galleries, theatres.
**Athletic facilities:** Basketball and tennis courts, swimming pool, track, football stadium, training and weight rooms, baseball, intramural, and softball fields, wellness center.
**STUDENT BODY. Undergraduate profile:** 70% are state residents; 31% are transfers. 3% Black, 1% Hispanic, 95% White, 1% Other. Average age of undergraduates is 21.
**Freshman profile:** 1% of freshmen who took SAT scored 700 or over on verbal, 1% scored 700 or over on math; 16% scored 600 or over on verbal, 16% scored 600 or over on math; 68% scored 500 or over on verbal, 68% scored 500 or over on math; 98% scored 400 or over on verbal, 98% scored 400 or over on math. 2% of freshmen who took ACT scored 30 or over on composite; 20% scored 24 or over on composite; 90% scored 18 or over on composite; 100% scored 12 or over on composite. 70% of accepted applicants took SAT; 60% took ACT. 70% of freshmen come from public schools.
**Undergraduate achievement:** 74% of fall 1992 freshmen returned for fall 1993 term. 69% of entering class graduated. 20% of students who completed a degree program immediately went on to graduate study.
**Foreign students:** Countries represented include Gambia, India, Japan, Spain, and Sweden.
**PROGRAMS OF STUDY. Degrees:** B.A., B.F.A., B.S., Regents B.A.
**Majors:** Accounting, Anthropology/Geography, Art, Art Education, Athletic Training, Biology, Biology Education, Business Administration, Business Education, Chemistry, Chemistry Education, Commerical Recreation Management, Communications, Computer Mathematics, Computer Programming/Information Systems, Consumer/Homemaking Education, Early Childhood Education, Economics, Elementary Education, English, English Education, Fashion Merchandising, Foods/Nutrition, French, General Science, General Science Education, Graphic Design, Health Education, History, Home Economics, Hotel/Motel/Restaurant Management, Language Arts Education, Library Science, Marketing, Mathematics, Mathematics Education, Music, Music Education, Music Pedagogy, Music Performance, Music Theory/Composition, Nursing, Office Technology, Painting, Photography, Physical Education, Physics, Political Science, Printmaking, Psychology, Radio Broadcasting, Recreation/Leisure Services, School Library Media, Secondary Education, Social Studies Education, Social Work, Sociology, Sport Management, Theatre.
**Distribution of degrees:** The majors with the highest enrollment are business, nursing, and elementry education; home economics, recreation, and health education have the lowest.
**Requirements:** General education requirement.

**Academic regulations:** Minimum 2.0 GPA must be maintained.
**Special:** Minors offered in most majors and in engineering. Associate's degrees offered. Double majors. Dual degrees. Pass/fail grading option. Internships. Cooperative education programs. Graduate school at which undergraduates may take graduate-level courses. Preprofessional programs in law, medicine, veterinary science, pharmacy, dentistry, and theology. 2-2 engineering programs with U of Maryland, U of Virginia, Virginia Polytech Inst and State U, and West Virginia U. Washington Semester. State legislative internships. Teacher certification in early childhood, elementary, and secondary education. Certification in specific subject areas. ROTC at Western Maryland Coll. AFROTC at U of Maryland at College Park.
**Honors:** Honors program. Honor societies.
**Academic Assistance:** Remedial reading, writing, math, and study skills. Nonremedial tutoring.

**STUDENT LIFE. Housing:** All unmarried students must live on campus unless living with family. Coed, women's, and men's dorms. Fraternity housing. 33% of students live in college housing.
**Services and counseling/handicapped student services:** Placement services. Health service. Student development center. Counseling services for minority, veteran, and older students. Personal and psychological counseling. Career and academic guidance services. Physically disabled student services. Tape recorders. Tutors. Reader services for the blind.
**Campus organizations:** Undergraduate student government. Student newspaper (Picket, published twice/month). Literary magazine. Yearbook. Radio station. Performing musical groups, debating, forensics, drama groups, Winter Carnival, Creative Arts Lecture Forum Series, academic and service groups, 70 organizations in all. Five fraternities, one chapter house; five sororities, no chapter houses. 20% of men join a fraternity. 20% of women join a sorority.
**Religious organizations:** Alpha Omega.
**Minority/foreign student organizations:** Minority Student Union, AHANA. Foreign Student Organization.

**ATHLETICS. Physical education requirements:** Two semesters of physical education required.
**Intercollegiate competition:** 15% of students participate. Baseball (M), basketball (M,W), cheerleading (M,W), cross-country (M,W), football (M), golf (M,W), soccer (M), softball (W), tennis (M,W), volleyball (W). Member of NAIA, NCAA Division II, West Virginia Intercollegiate Athletic Conference.
**Intramural and club sports:** 20% of students participate. Intramural archery, basketball, billiards, bowling, cross-country, football, golf, softball, tennis, volleyball, water polo.

**ADMISSIONS. Academic basis for candidate selection** (in order of priority): Secondary school record, standardized test scores, essay, school's recommendation.
**Nonacademic basis for candidate selection:** Character and personality, extracurricular participation, and particular talent or ability are important. Geographical distribution and alumni/ae relationship are considered.
**Requirements:** Graduation from secondary school is required; GED is accepted. 21 units and the following program of study are required: 4 units of English, 3 units of math, 3 units of science including 2 units of lab, 2 units of social studies, 1 unit of history, 6 units of electives. Additional units of foreign language recommended. Minimum combined SAT score of 1000 (composite ACT score of 21) and minimum "B" average required. Higher grades, test scores, additional application forms, and interviews required of engineering and nursing program applicants. Portfolio required of art program applicants. Audition required of music program applicants. ACT is required; SAT may be substituted. Campus visit and interview recommended. No off-campus interviews.
**Procedure:** Take SAT or ACT by December of 12th year. Visit college for interview by March of 12th year. Application deadline is February 1. Notification of admission by April 1. Reply is required by May 1. $100 tuition deposit, refundable until May 1. $150 room deposit, refundable until May 1. Freshmen accepted for terms other than fall.
**Special programs:** Admission may be deferred one year. Credit may be granted through CEEB Advanced Placement for scores of 3 or higher. Credit may be granted through CLEP general and subject exams, ACT PEP, DANTES, and challenge exams, and military and life experience. Early entrance/early admission program. Concurrent enrollment program.
**Transfer students:** Transfer students accepted for terms other than fall. In fall 1993, 31% of all new students were transfers into all classes. 760 transfer applications were received, 592 were accepted. Application deadline is March 15 for fall; November 1 for spring. Minimum 2.5 GPA required. Lowest course grade accepted is "D." Maximum number of transferable credits is 72 semester hours. At least 32 semester hours must be completed at the college to receive degree.
**Admissions contact:** Karl L. Wolf, M.B.A., Director of Admissions. 304 876-2511, extension 213.

**FINANCIAL AID. Available aid:** Pell grants, SEOG, Federal Nursing Student Scholarships, state scholarships and grants, school scholarships and grants, private scholarships and grants, ROTC scholarships, academic merit scholarships, and athletic scholarships. Perkins Loans (NDSL), PLUS, Stafford Loans (GSL), NSL, state loans, and SLS. AMS.
**Financial aid statistics:** In 1993-94, 39% of all undergraduate applicants received aid; 39% of freshman applicants. Average amounts of aid awarded freshmen: Scholarships and grants, $1,500.
**Supporting data/closing dates:** FAFSA/FAF/FFS: Deadline is March 1. School's own aid application: Deadline is March 1. State aid form: Deadline is March 1. Income tax forms: Deadline is March 1. Notification of awards begins April 1.
**Financial aid contact:** Clinton Davis, Interim Director of Financial Aid. 304 876-2511, extension 283.

**STUDENT EMPLOYMENT.** College Work/Study Program. Institutional employment. 15% of full-time undergraduates work on campus during school year. Students may expect to earn an average of $1,300 during school year. Freshmen are discouraged from working during their first term. Off-campus part-time employment opportunities rated "good."

**COMPUTER FACILITIES.** 200 IBM/IBM-compatible and Macintosh/Apple microcomputers; 100 are networked. Students may access Digital, IBM minicomputer/mainframe systems, Internet. Client/LAN operating systems include Apple/Macintosh, DOS, Windows NT, DEC, Novell. Computer languages and software packages include BASIC, COBOL, FORTRAN, Pascal, PL/1; 150 in all. Computer facilities are available to all students.
**Fees:** Computer fee is included in tuition/fees.
**Hours:** 7 AM-midn.

**GRADUATE CAREER DATA.** Graduate school percentages: 4% enter law school. 2% enter medical school. 1% enter dental school. 12% enter graduate business programs. 35% enter graduate arts and sciences programs. 1% enter theological school/seminary. Highest graduate school enrollments: George Washington U, U of Maryland,, U of Virginia, Virginia Polytech Inst and State U, West Virginia U. 40% of graduates choose careers in business and industry. Companies and businesses that hire graduates: IBM, Marriott, UNISYS, federal government agencies.

**PROMINENT ALUMNI/AE.** Mary Hendrix, medical research, U of Arizona and U of California medical schools; Stanley Ikenberry, president, U of Illinois; Michael Petrovich, assistant to former Presidents Carter and Reagan; Rae Ellen McKee, 1991 National Teacher of the Year.

# University of Charleston

**Charleston, WV 25304 — 304 357-4800**

**1993-94 Costs.** Tuition: $9,100. Room & board: $3,600. Fees, books, misc. academic expenses (school's estimate): $550.
**Enrollment.** Undergraduates: 246 men, 525 women (full-time). Freshman class: 640 applicants, 580 accepted, 199 enrolled. Graduate enrollment: 27 men, 25 women.
**Test score averages/ranges.** Average SAT scores: 443 verbal, 505 math. Range of SAT scores of middle 50%: 390-520 verbal, 450-480 math. Average ACT scores: 21 English, 19 math, 21 composite. Range of ACT scores of middle 50%: 18-24 English, 17-21 math.
**Faculty.** 72 full-time; 82 part-time. 60% of faculty holds highest degree in specific field. Student/faculty ratio: 11 to 1.
**Selectivity rating.** Competitive.

**PROFILE.** The University of Charleston, founded in 1888, is a private institution. Programs are offered through the Conservatory of Music and Fine Arts; the Colleges of Arts and Sciences, Business, and Health Sciences, and Lifelong Learning; the School of Art and Design; and the Graduate Center. Its 35-acre campus is located two miles from Charleston's business district.

**Accreditation:** NCACS. Professionally accredited by the American Medical Association (CAHEA), the National Athletic Trainers Association, the National Council for Accreditation of Teacher Education, the National League for Nursing.
**Religious orientation:** University of Charleston is nonsectarian; no religious requirements.
**Library:** Collections totaling over 118,857 volumes, 580 periodical subscriptions, and 91,416 microform items.
**Athletic facilities:** Gymnasiums, swimming pool, basketball, racquetball, and tennis courts, baseball, intramural, soccer, and softball fields, Nautilus and weight rooms, sports medicine clinic.

**STUDENT BODY. Undergraduate profile:** 79% are state residents; 49% are transfers. 2% Asian-American, 3% Black, 1% Hispanic, 1% Native American, 91% White, 2% Unknown. Average age of undergraduates is 23.
**Freshman profile:** 1% of freshmen who took ACT scored 30 or over on English, 1% scored 30 or over on math, 1% scored 30 or over on composite; 29% scored 24 or over on English, 13% scored 24 or over on math, 21% scored 24 or over on composite; 81% scored 18 or over on English, 73% scored 18 or over on math, 88% scored 18 or over on composite; 100% scored 12 or over on English, 100% scored 12 or over on math, 100% scored 12 or over on composite. 16% of accepted applicants took SAT; 71% took ACT.
**Undergraduate achievement:** 73% of fall 1992 freshmen returned for fall 1993 term. 52% of entering class graduated. 30% of students who completed a degree program immediately went on to graduate study.
**Foreign students:** 29 students are from out of the country. Countries represented include Australia, Canada, England, Ireland, Japan, and Trinidad; 17 in all.

**PROGRAMS OF STUDY. Degrees:** B.A., B.S., B.S.Nurs.
**Majors:** Accounting, Art, Art Education, Biology, Chemistry, Computer Information Systems, Elementary Education, English, Finance, General Studies, History/Area Studies, Interior Design, International Studies, Management, Marketing, Mass Communication, Mathematics, Music, Natural Science, Nursing, Physical Education, Political Science, Psychology, Radiologic Administration, Radiologic Technology, Religion/Philosophy, Respiratory Therapy, Secondary Education, Social Sciences, Special Education, Sports Medicine.
**Distribution of degrees:** The majors with the highest enrollment are nursing, radiation technology, and business; English, religion/philosophy, and social sciences have the lowest.
**Requirements:** General education requirement.
**Academic regulations:** Minimum 2.0 GPA must be maintained.
**Special:** Courses in German, Greek, Italian, journalism, physical science, and Spanish. Directed study program for superior juniors and seniors. Some departments offer special study courses with in-depth continuation of any course. Comprehensive exam in major field required for graduation. Associate's degrees offered. Double majors. Independent study. Pass/fail grading option. Internships. Cooperative education programs. Preprofessional programs in law, medicine, and dentistry. Washington Semester. Teacher certification in elementary and secondary education. Certification in specific subject areas. ROTC.
**Honors:** Honors program. Honor societies.
**Academic Assistance:** Remedial reading, writing, math, and study skills. Nonremedial tutoring.

**ADMISSIONS. Academic basis for candidate selection** (in order of priority): Secondary school record, standardized test scores, essay, school's recommendation, class rank.

**Nonacademic basis for candidate selection:** Character and personality and extracurricular participation are important. Particular talent or ability and alumni/ae relationship are considered.
**Requirements:** Graduation from secondary school is required; GED is accepted. 16 units and the following program of study are recommended: 4 units of English, 3 units of math, 3 units of science, 1 unit of foreign language, 3 units of social studies, 2 units of history. Minimum composite ACT score of 18 (combined SAT score of 800), rank in top half of secondary school class, and minimum 2.25 academic GPA recommended. Algebra and chemistry required of Division of Nursing program applicants. Audition required of music program applicants. Conditional admission possible for applicants not meeting standard requirements. SAT or ACT is required. Campus visit and interview recommended. Off-campus interviews available with an admissions representative.
**Procedure:** Suggest filing application by December 15; no deadline. Notification of admission on rolling basis. $100 tuition deposit, refundable until May 1. $100 room deposit, refundable until May 1. Freshmen accepted for terms other than fall.
**Special programs:** Admission may be deferred one year. Credit and/or placement may be granted through CEEB Advanced Placement exams for scores of 3 or higher. Credit may be granted through CLEP subject exams, DANTES and challenge exams, and military and life experience. Placement may be granted through ACT PEP exams. Early decision program. In fall 1993, 47 applied for early decision and 44 were accepted. Deadline for applying for early decision is December 15. Concurrent enrollment program.
**Transfer students:** Transfer students accepted for terms other than fall. In fall 1993, 49% of all new students were transfers into all classes. 356 transfer applications were received, 338 were accepted. Application deadline is rolling for fall; rolling for spring. Minimum 2.0 GPA required. Lowest course grade accepted is "C." Maximum number of transferable credits is 40 semester hours from a two-year school and 90 semester hours from a four-year school. At least 30 semester hours must be completed at the university to receive degree.
**Admissions contact:** Alan Liebrecht, Director of Admissions. 304 357-4750, 800 995-4682.
**FINANCIAL AID. Available aid:** Pell grants, SEOG, state scholarships and grants, school scholarships and grants, private scholarships and grants, ROTC scholarships, academic merit scholarships, and athletic scholarships. Perkins Loans (NDSL), PLUS, Stafford Loans (GSL), NSL, private loans, and SLS. AMS and Tuition Management Systems.
**Financial aid statistics:** 25% of aid is not need-based. Average amounts of aid awarded freshmen: Scholarships and grants, $3,950; loans, $4,500.
**Supporting data/closing dates:** FAFSA: Priority filing date is March 1. School's own aid application: Priority filing date is March 1. Income tax forms: Priority filing date is March 1. Notification of awards on rolling basis.
**Financial aid contact:** Janet M. Ruge, M.A., Director of Financial Aid. 304 357-4760.

# West Liberty State College

**West Liberty, WV 26074** **304 336-5000**

**1993-94 Costs.** Tuition: $1,650 (state residents), $3,800 (out-of-state). Room & board: $2,900. Fees, books, misc. academic expenses (school's estimate): $500.
**Enrollment.** Undergraduates: 1,042 men, 1,096 women (full-time). Freshman class: 1,164 applicants, 1,062 accepted, 478 enrolled.
**Test score averages/ranges.** Average ACT scores: 20 composite. Range of ACT scores of middle 50%: 19-26 composite.
**Faculty.** 131 full-time; 22 part-time. 34% of faculty holds doctoral degree. Student/faculty ratio: 18 to 1.
**Selectivity rating.** Less competitive.

**PROFILE.** West Liberty State, founded in 1837, is a public, multipurpose college. Its 290-acre campus is located in West Liberty, 10 miles from Wheeling.
**Accreditation:** NCACS. Professionally accredited by the American Dental Association, the American Medical Association (CAHEA), the National Association of Schools of Music.
**Religious orientation:** West Liberty State College is nonsectarian; no religious requirements.
**Library:** Collections totaling over 207,000 volumes, 800 periodical subscriptions, and 70,000 microform items.
**Special facilities/museums:** Book museums, language lab, medical technology and dental hygiene labs.
**Athletic facilities:** Field house, basketball, racquetball, and tennis courts, sauna, exercise, training, and weight rooms, tracks, athletic fields, football stadium, swimming pool.
**STUDENT BODY. Undergraduate profile:** 68% are state residents; 32% are transfers. 2% Black, 97% White, 1% Other. Average age of undergraduates is 20.
**Freshman profile:** 17% of accepted applicants took SAT; 83% took ACT. 90% of freshmen come from public schools.
**Undergraduate achievement:** 71% of fall 1992 freshmen returned for fall 1993 term. 31% of entering class graduated.
**Foreign students:** 21 students are from out of the country. Countries represented include Canada, Japan, and Suriname; seven in all.
**PROGRAMS OF STUDY. Degrees:** B.A., B.S., B.S.Nurs., Regents B.A.
**Majors:** Accounting, Administrative Mathematics, Administrative Science, Art, Art Education, Biology, Business Education, Chemistry, Communication, Criminal Justice, Data Processing, Dental Hygiene, Economics, Elementary Education, Energy Management, English, Fashion Marketing, Finance, General Business, Graphic Design, Health Education, History, Management, Marketing, Mathematics, Medical Technology, Middle School Education, Music Education, Nursing, Office Administration, Physical Education, Political Science/Government, Psychology, Safety Education, Science Exercise, Secondary Education, Social Science Education, Sociology, Spanish Education, Speech Education, Travel/Tourism.
**Distribution of degrees:** The majors with the highest enrollment are business, education, and criminal justice; chemistry, history, and mathematics have the lowest.
**Requirements:** General education requirement.
**Academic regulations:** Minimum 2.0 GPA must be maintained.
**Special:** Minor required of some majors for graduation. Minors offered in many majors and in business administration, computer information, French, geography, interdisciplinary pre-law, music, philosophy, religion, social work, and Spanish. Associate's degrees offered. Self-designed majors. Double majors. Independent study. Pass/fail grading option. Internships. Member of Four College Consortium. Teacher certification in early childhood, elementary, secondary, and special education. Certification in specific subject areas.
**Honors:** Honors program. Honor societies.
**Academic Assistance:** Remedial reading, writing, math, and study skills. Nonremedial tutoring.
**STUDENT LIFE. Housing:** Women's and men's dorms. Fraternity housing. School-owned/operated apartments. On-campus married-student housing. 57% of students live in college housing.
**Social atmosphere:** Groups with the most social influence on campus are the Greek organizations and sports groups. Popular events during the year include the annual Band Blast, Homecoming, Greek Week, and the basketball games. Students like to gather on campus at the Student Union and the Quad. Off campus, they head for Bubba's, The Swing Club, and bars near campus.
**Services and counseling/handicapped student services:** Placement services. Health service. Counseling services for minority students. Birth control, personal, and psychological counseling. Career and academic guidance services. Religious counseling. Physically disabled student services. Learning disabled services. Notetaking services. Tape recorders. Tutors. Reader services for the blind.
**Campus organizations:** Undergraduate student government. Student newspaper (Trumpet, once/week). Literary magazine. Radio and TV stations. Choral groups, marching band, orchestra, debating, Hilltop Players, Puppet Theatre, Hilltoppers 4-H Club, Panhellenic Council, Interfraternity Council, departmental groups, 45 organizations in all. Seven fraternities, no chapter houses; three sororities, no chapter houses. 18% of men join a fraternity. 16% of women join a sorority.
**Religious organizations:** Light on the Hill.
**Minority/foreign student organizations:** International Students' Organization.
**ATHLETICS. Physical education requirements:** Two semesters of physical education required.
**Intercollegiate competition:** 10% of students participate. Baseball (M), basketball (M,W), cheerleading (W), football (M), golf (M), softball (W), tennis (M,W), volleyball (W), wrestling (M). Member of NAIA, NCAA Division II, West Virginia Intercollegiate Athletic Conference.
**Intramural and club sports:** 30% of students participate. Intramural aerobics, basketball, billiards, flag football, racquetball, softball, tennis, volleyball.
**ADMISSIONS. Academic basis for candidate selection** (in order of priority): Secondary school record, standardized test scores, class rank.
**Requirements:** Graduation from secondary school is required; GED is accepted. 11 units and the following program of study are required: 4 units of English, 2 units of math, 2 units of lab science, 2 units of social studies, 1 unit of history. Minimum composite ACT score of 17 (combined SAT score of 680) and minimum 2.0 GPA required of out-of-state applicants. Interview and additional application required of dental hygiene program applicants. Audition required of music program applicants. ACT is required; SAT may be substituted. Campus visit and interview recommended. No off-campus interviews.
**Procedure:** Take SAT or ACT by April of 12th year. Visit college for interview by April of 12th year. Notification of admission on rolling basis. $50 room deposit, refundable until July 1. Freshmen accepted for terms other than fall.
**Special programs:** Admission may be deferred. Credit may be granted through CEEB Advanced Placement for scores of 3 or higher. Credit may be granted through CLEP general and subject exams, and challenge exams. Early entrance/early admission program. Concurrent enrollment program.
**Transfer students:** Transfer students accepted for terms other than fall. In fall 1993, 32% of all new students were transfers into all classes. 407 transfer applications were received, 367 were accepted. Application deadline is August 1 for fall; January 1 for spring. Minimum 2.0 GPA required. Lowest course grade accepted is "D." Maximum number of transferable credits is 72 semester hours from a two-year school and 92 semester hours from a four-year school. At least 36 semester hours must be completed at the college to receive degree.
**Admissions contact:** Paul B. Milam, M.A., Director of Admissions. 304 336-8076.
**FINANCIAL AID. Available aid:** Pell grants, SEOG, state scholarships and grants, school scholarships and grants, private scholarships and grants, academic merit scholarships, and athletic scholarships. Perkins Loans (NDSL), PLUS, Stafford Loans (GSL), NSL, and SLS. AMS and deferred payment plan. Credit card payment.
**Financial aid statistics:** 40% of aid is not need-based. In 1993, 80% of all undergraduate applicants received aid; 80% of freshman applicants. Average amounts of aid awarded freshmen: Scholarships and grants, $1,000; loans, $1,000.
**Supporting data/closing dates:** FAFSA: Priority filing date is March 1; accepted on rolling basis. School's own aid application: Priority filing date is March 1; accepted on rolling basis. State aid form: Priority filing date is March 1; accepted on rolling basis. Notification of awards on rolling basis.
**Financial aid contact:** Frank Harrar, M.S., Director of Financial Aid. 304 336-8016.
**STUDENT EMPLOYMENT.** College Work/Study Program. Institutional employment. 8% of full-time undergraduates work on campus during school year. Students may expect to earn an average of $1,000 during school year. Off-campus part-time employment opportunities rated "poor."
**COMPUTER FACILITIES.** 150 IBM/IBM-compatible, Macintosh/Apple, and RISC-/UNIX-based microcomputers; 25 are networked. Students may access Digital, IBM minicomputer/mainframe systems, BITNET, Internet. Client/LAN operating systems include Apple/Macintosh, DOS, UNIX/XENIX/AIX, Windows NT, DEC, LocalTalk/AppleTalk, Novell. Computer languages and software packages include Ada, Assembler, BASIC, C, COBOL, FORTRAN, LISP, Pascal, PL/1; 160 in all. Computer facilities are available to all students.

**Fees:** None.
**Hours:** 8 AM-midn. (M-F).

**GRADUATE CAREER DATA.** Highest graduate school enrollments: Marshall U, West Virginia U, Wheeling Jesuit Coll. 47% of graduates choose careers in business and industry. Companies and businesses that hire graduates: Aetna Insurance, EDS, U.S. Accounting Office.

**PROMINENT ALUMNI/AE.** Theresa Nagy, Ph.D., NASA senior scientist; Augusto Paglialunga, opera singer; Joe Niekro, baseball player, Minnesota Twins.

# West Virginia Institute of Technology

**Montgomery, WV 25136** **304 442-3071**

**1994-95 Costs.** Tuition: $1,998 (state residents), $4,472 (out-of-state). Room & board: $3,860. Fees, books, misc. academic expenses (school's estimate): $850.
**Enrollment.** Undergraduates: 1,514 men, 746 women (full-time). Freshman class: 1,638 applicants, 1,615 accepted, 617 enrolled. 22 men.
**Test score averages/ranges.** Average ACT scores: 20 English, 19 math, 20 composite.
**Faculty.** 146 full-time; 68 part-time. 45% of faculty holds doctoral degree. Student/faculty ratio: 14 to 1.
**Selectivity rating.** Noncompetitive.

**PROFILE.** West Virginia Institute of Technology, founded in 1895, is a public, multipurpose institution. Programs are offered through the Colleges of Arts and Sciences, Business and Economics, Engineering, and Technology and Applied Science. Its 112-acre campus is located in Montgomery, 28 miles southeast of Charleston.

**Accreditation:** NCACS. Professionally accredited by the Accreditation Board for Engineering and Technology, the American Dental Association, the National Council for Accreditation of Teacher Education.
**Religious orientation:** West Virginia Institute of Technology is nonsectarian; no religious requirements.
**Library:** Collections totaling over 153,167 volumes, 763 periodical subscriptions, and 398,053 microform items.
**Athletic facilities:** Swimming pool, weight room, tennis courts, gymnasiums, football field.

**STUDENT BODY. Undergraduate profile:** 93% are state residents; 21% are transfers. 2% Asian-American, 4% Black, 93% White, 1% Other. Average age of undergraduates is 22.
**Freshman profile:** 1% of freshmen who took ACT scored 30 or over on English, 2% scored 30 or over on math, 1% scored 30 or over on composite; 22% scored 24 or over on English, 19% scored 24 or over on math, 18% scored 24 or over on composite; 67% scored 18 or over on English, 58% scored 18 or over on math, 71% scored 18 or over on composite; 100% scored 12 or over on English, 100% scored 12 or over on math, 100% scored 12 or over on composite. Majority of accepted applicants took ACT. 95% of freshmen come from public schools.
**Undergraduate achievement:** 70% of fall 1992 freshmen returned for fall 1993 term. 5% of students who completed a degree program immediately went on to graduate study.
**Foreign students:** 73 students are from out of the country. Countries represented include Bangledesh, China, India, and Pakistan; 16 in all.

**PROGRAMS OF STUDY. Degrees:** B.A., B.Eng.Tech., B.Mech.Eng.Tech., B.S.
**Majors:** Accounting, Biology, Biology Education, Board of Regents, Business Education, Business Management, Business Management/Banking, Business Principles, Chemical Engineering, Chemistry, Chemistry Education, Civil Engineering, Computer Management/Data Processing, Computer Science, Electrical Engineering, Electronic Engineering Technology, Engineering Technology, General Science Education, Health Education, Health Services Administration, History/Government, Industrial Management, Industrial Relations/Human Resources, Industrial Technology, Industrial Technology Education, Language Arts Education, Mathematics, Mathematics Education, Mechanical Engineering, Music Education, Nursing, Physical Education, Physics, Physics Education, Printing Management, Public Service Administration, Safety Education, Social Studies Education, Vocational-Technical Education.
**Distribution of degrees:** The majors with the highest enrollment are engineering, business, and technology.
**Requirements:** General education requirement.
**Special:** Double majors. Dual degrees. Pass/fail grading option. Internships. Cooperative education programs. Graduate school at which undergraduates may take graduate-level courses. Preprofessional programs in medicine, pharmacy, dentistry, and engineering. Teacher certification in secondary and vo-tech education. ROTC.
**Honors:** Honor societies.
**Academic Assistance:** Remedial reading, writing, and math. Nonremedial tutoring.

**STUDENT LIFE. Housing:** All freshmen must live on campus unless living with family. Coed, women's, and men's dorms. Fraternity housing. 31% of students live in college housing.
**Services and counseling/handicapped student services:** Placement services. Counseling services for military, veteran, and older students. Birth control, personal, and psychological counseling. Career and academic guidance services. Religious counseling. Learning disabled services.
**Campus organizations:** Undergraduate student government. Student newspaper (Tech Collegian, published once/week). Yearbook. Appalachian Emphasis Week, bands and choirs, clubs for photography, radio, scuba, skiing, and canoe/kayaking, service organizations, Tech Players, women's association, 55 organizations in all. Eight fraternities, five chapter houses; four sororities, no chapter houses. 9% of men join a fraternity. 8% of women join a sorority.
**Religious organizations:** Christian Student Union, Campus Light Ministries, Tech United Ministries.
**Minority/foreign student organizations:** Black Student Guild. Chinese Student Association, International Students, Cultural Understanding Organization.

**ATHLETICS. Physical education requirements:** Two semesters of physical education required.
**Intercollegiate competition:** 10% of students participate. Baseball (M), basketball (M,W), cheerleading (M,W), football (M), softball (W), tennis (M,W), volleyball (W). Member of NAIA, NCAA II, West Virginia Intercollegiate Athletic Conference.
**Intramural and club sports:** 40% of students participate. Intramural basketball, flag football, softball, swimming, tennis, volleyball, water basketball, water polo. Men's club crew. Women's club crew.

**ADMISSIONS. Academic basis for candidate selection** (in order of priority): Secondary school record, standardized test scores, class rank, school's recommendation.
**Requirements:** Graduation from secondary school is required; GED is accepted. No specific distribution of secondary school units required. Minimum composite ACT score of 17 and minimum 2.0 GPA required. Minimum 3.0 GPA or minimum math ACT score of 21, and 2 units of algebra, 1 unit of plane geometry, and 1 unit of advanced math required of engineering program applicants. 1 unit of algebra, 1 unit of integrated geometry, and 1/2 unit of trigonometry recommended of engineering technology program applicants. 2 units of algebra and 1 unit of integrated geometry recommended of chemistry, math, and physics program applicants. 2 units of advanced math, 1 unit of chemistry plus 1 other lab science, and minimum composite ACT score of 20 required of nursing program applicants. 1 unit each of algebra and chemistry required of dental hygiene program applicants. Specific requirements for other programs vary. ACT is required; SAT may be substituted. Campus visit recommended. Off-campus interviews available with an admissions representative.
**Procedure:** Take SAT or ACT by April of 12th year. Notification of admission on rolling basis. $50 room deposit, refundable partially through the sixth week of semester. Freshmen accepted for terms other than fall.
**Special programs:** Credit may be granted through CEEB Advanced Placement for scores of 3 or higher. Credit may be granted through CLEP general and subject exams, ACT PEP and DANTES exams, and military and life experience. Early decision program. Early entrance/early admission program. Concurrent enrollment program.
**Transfer students:** Transfer students accepted for terms other than fall. In fall 1993, 21% of all new students were transfers into all classes. 411 transfer applications were received, 409 were accepted. Application deadline is August 1 for fall; December 15 for spring. Minimum 2.0 GPA required. Lowest course grade accepted is "D." At least 30 semester hours must be completed at the institute to receive degree.
**Admissions contact:** Robert P. Scholl, Jr., M.A., Director of Admissions. 304 442-3167.

**FINANCIAL AID. Available aid:** Pell grants, SEOG, state scholarships and grants, school scholarships and grants, private scholarships, ROTC scholarships, academic merit scholarships, and athletic scholarships. Perkins Loans (NDSL), PLUS, Stafford Loans (GSL), school loans, and SLS. AMS and Tuition Management Systems.
**Financial aid statistics:** 14% of aid is not need-based. In 1993-94, 84% of all undergraduate applicants received aid; 81% of freshman applicants. Average amounts of aid awarded freshmen: Scholarships and grants, $716; loans, $928.
**Supporting data/closing dates:** FAFSA/FAF/FFS: Priority filing date is January 2. School's own aid application: Priority filing date is January 2; accepted on rolling basis. State aid form: Priority filing date is January 2; deadline is March 1. Income tax forms: Priority filing date is March 1; accepted on rolling basis. Notification of awards on rolling basis.
**Financial aid contact:** Nina Morton, Director of Financial Aid. 304 442-3228.

**STUDENT EMPLOYMENT.** College Work/Study Program. Institutional employment. 16% of full-time undergraduates work on campus during school year. Students may expect to earn an average of $1,000 during school year. Off-campus part-time employment opportunities rated "fair."

**COMPUTER FACILITIES.** 625 IBM/IBM-compatible and Macintosh/Apple microcomputers; 150 are networked. Students may access Digital minicomputer/mainframe systems, Internet. Residence halls may be equipped with stand-alone microcomputers. Computer languages and software packages include BASIC, COBOL, FORTRAN, PL/1, Wylbur. Computer facilities are available to all students.
**Fees:** None.
**Hours:** 8 AM-10 PM.

**GRADUATE CAREER DATA.** Highest graduate school enrollments: Marshall U, West Viginia Graduate Sch, West Virginia Inst of Tech, West Virginia U. 47% of graduates choose careers in business and industry. Companies and businesses that hire graduates: Gannett, C&P Telephone, Dow Jones, Union Carbide.

# West Virginia State College

**Institute, WV 25112-1000** **304 766-3000**

**1993-94 Costs.** Tuition: $1,894 (state residents), $4,294 (out-of-state). Room & board: $3,150. Fees, books, misc. academic expenses (school's estimate): $570.
**Enrollment.** Undergraduates: 1,398 men, 1,439 women (full-time). Freshman class: 4,171 applicants, 3,779 accepted, 807 enrolled.
**Test score averages/ranges.** Average ACT scores: 16 English, 12 math, 13 composite.
**Faculty.** 139 full-time; 94 part-time. 24% of faculty holds doctoral degree. Student/faculty ratio: 21 to 1.
**Selectivity rating.** Less competitive.

**PROFILE.** West Virginia State, founded in 1891, is a public, multipurpose college. Programs are offered through the Divisions of Arts and Humanities, Business Administration and Economics, Natural Science and Mathematics, Professional Studies, and Social

Sciences. Its 85-acre campus is located in Institute, eight miles from downtown Charleston.

**Accreditation:** NCACS. Professionally accredited by the Accreditation Board for Engineering and Technology, the American Medical Association (CAHEA), the Council on Social Work Education, the National Council for Accreditation of Teacher Education.
**Religious orientation:** West Virginia State College is nonsectarian; no religious requirements.
**Library:** Collections totaling over 28,295 volumes, 630 periodical subscriptions, and 500,000 microform items.
**Special facilities/museums:** On-campus day-care center, art gallery, ROTC Hall of Fame, Sports Hall of Fame.
**Athletic facilities:** Football stadium, gymnasium, basketball and tennis courts, baseball and softball fields, bowling, weight room, swimming pool, track.

**STUDENT BODY. Undergraduate profile:** 96% are state residents; 7% are transfers. 1% Asian-American, 13% Black, 86% White. Average age of undergraduates is 26.
**Freshman profile:** 100% of accepted applicants took ACT. 99% of freshmen come from public schools.
**Foreign students:** 18 students are from out of the country. Countries represented include Iran, Jamaica, Jordan, and Lebanon.

**PROGRAMS OF STUDY. Degrees:** B.A., B.S.
**Majors:** Accounting, American Studies, Applied Mathematics, Architectural Industrial Technology, Art, Art Education, Biology, Biology Education, Board of Regents, Building Construction, Business Administration, Business Education, Business Principles Education, Chemistry, Chemistry Education, Communication, Computer Science, Computer Science Application, Corrections, Criminal Justice, Early Childhood Education, Economics, Education, Elementary Education, Elementary Education/Subject Specialization, English, English Education, Finance, General Science Education, Health Physics, History, Management, Marketing, Mathematics, Mathematics Education, Mental Retardation, Music Education, Nuclear Medicine, Physical Education, Political Science, Psychology, Recreation, Recreation Administration, Safety Education, Secondary Education, Secretarial, Social Studies Education, Social Work, Sociology, Therapeutic Recreation, Writing.
**Distribution of degrees:** The majors with the highest enrollment are business, education, and accounting; economics, history, and recreation have the lowest.
**Requirements:** General education requirement.
**Academic regulations:** Freshmen must maintain minimum 1.9 GPA; sophomores, juniors, seniors, 2.0 GPA.
**Special:** Minors offered in several majors and in French, music, safety management, security/loss prevention, and Spanish. Associate's degrees offered. Double majors. Independent study. Internships. Cooperative education programs. Graduate school at which undergraduates may take graduate-level courses. Preprofessional programs in law, veterinary science, pharmacy, dentistry, optometry, agriculture, forestry, history, government, engineering, and and nursing. Washington Semester. Teacher certification in early childhood, elementary, secondary, and special education. ROTC.
**Honors:** Honors program. Honor societies.
**Academic Assistance:** Remedial reading, writing, and math. Nonremedial tutoring.

**STUDENT LIFE. Housing:** All unmarried students under age 21 must live on campus unless living near campus with relatives. Women's and men's dorms. School-owned/operated apartments. On-campus married-student housing. 7% of students live in college housing.
**Social atmosphere:** The student newspaper reports, "Since the majority of students is made up of commuters, campus life is not as active as it is at most institutions. However, with the addition of Commuter Affairs and Commuter Activities, interest and attendance have increased." Influential groups on campus include the Student Government Association, the Residence Hall population, and the Greeks. Popular events include Homecoming, the Comedy Zone series, drama productions, and sporting events. Favorite on-campus hangouts are the College Union, Commuter's Lounge, Game Room, Snack Bar, and Pub; off campus, students gather at The Edge, Yancey's, Spanky's, and Crawdaddy's.
**Services and counseling/handicapped student services:** Placement services. Health service. Day care. Counseling services for military students. Birth control and personal counseling. Academic guidance services. Religious counseling. Physically disabled student services. Learning disabled services. Tutors.
**Campus organizations:** Undergraduate student government. Student newspaper (Yellow Jacket, published once/week). Literary magazine. Yearbook. TV station. College Players, jazz band, choir, departmental groups, May Week, College Ambassadors, Twelve Steps Anonymous, Women's Group, 46 organizations in all. Six fraternities, no chapter houses; three sororities, no chapter houses. 1% of men join a fraternity. 1% of women join a sorority.
**Religious organizations:** College Students for Christ, Fellowship of Christian Athletes.
**Minority/foreign student organizations:** Access Awareness Council, NAACP. International Student Organization.

**ATHLETICS. Physical education requirements:** One semester of physical education required.
**Intercollegiate competition:** 3% of students participate. Baseball (M), basketball (M,W), cheerleading (W), cross-country (M,W), football (M), softball (W), track and field (outdoor) (M,W). Member of NAIA, NCAA Division II, West Virginia Intercollegiate Athletic Conference.
**Intramural and club sports:** 13% of students participate. Intramural basketball, bowling, flag football, softball, swimming, tennis, volleyball. Men's club basketball, bowling, cheerleading, golf, soccer, swimming, tennis, weight lifting. Women's club basketball, bowling, golf, swimming, tennis, weight lifting.

**ADMISSIONS. Academic basis for candidate selection** (in order of priority): Secondary school record, standardized test scores, class rank, essay, school's recommendation.
**Nonacademic basis for candidate selection:** Particular talent or ability is emphasized. Character and personality are important. Extracurricular participation and alumni/ae relationship are considered.
**Requirements:** Graduation from secondary school is required; GED is accepted. 14 units and the following program of study are required: 4 units of English, 2 units of math, 2 units of science, 2 units of foreign language, 3 units of social studies, 1 unit of history. Minimum 2.0 GPA required. Minimum composite ACT score of 17 required of out-of-state applicants. ACT is required; SAT may be substituted. Campus visit recommended. No off-campus interviews.
**Procedure:** Take SAT or ACT by fall of 12th year. Suggest filing application by March 1. Application deadline is August 11. Notification of admission on rolling basis. $50 refundable room deposit. Freshmen accepted for terms other than fall.
**Special programs:** Admission may be deferred. Credit and/or placement may be granted through CEEB Advanced Placement exams and CLEP general and subject exams. Early decision program. Early entrance/early admission program. Concurrent enrollment program.
**Transfer students:** Transfer students accepted for terms other than fall. In fall 1993, 7% of all new students were transfers into all classes. 486 transfer applications were received, 486 were accepted. Application deadline is August 11 for fall; March 1 for spring. Minimum 2.0 GPA required. Lowest course grade accepted is "C." Maximum number of transferable credits is 72 semester hours. At least 30 semester hours must be completed at the college to receive degree.
**Admissions contact:** John L. Fuller, M.S., Director of Admissions. 304 766-3221.

**FINANCIAL AID. Available aid:** Pell grants, SEOG, state grants, school scholarships, private scholarships, ROTC scholarships, academic merit scholarships, and athletic scholarships. Perkins Loans (NDSL), PLUS, Stafford Loans (GSL), and SLS. Deferred payment plan.
**Supporting data/closing dates:** FAFSA/FAF/FFS: Priority filing date is March 1. School's own aid application: Priority filing date is March 1. Notification of awards on rolling basis.
**Financial aid contact:** Fred D. Black, Director of Financial Aid. 304 766-3131.

**STUDENT EMPLOYMENT.** College Work/Study Program. Institutional employment. Students may expect to earn an average of $1,300 during school year. Off-campus part-time employment opportunities rated "excellent."

**COMPUTER FACILITIES.** 400 IBM/IBM-compatible and Macintosh/Apple microcomputers. Residence halls may be equipped with stand-alone microcomputers, networked terminals. Computer languages and software packages include SAM, SQL, VAX BASIC. Computer facilities are available to all students.
**Fees:** None.

**PROMINENT ALUMNI/AE.** Dr. Perry Julian, arthritis and glaucoma researcher; Dr. Leon Sullivan, founder, Opportunities Industrialization Centers and leader of the anti-apartheid movement in the U.S.; Dr. Vincent Reed, vice president, *Washington Post*; Lou Myers, actor; Dr. L. Eudora Pettigrew, president, SUNY at Old Westbury.

## West Virginia University

**Morgantown, WV 26506-6710 — 304 293-0111**

**1993-94 Costs.** Tuition: $2,026 (state residents), $5,870 (out-of-state). Room: $2,198. Board: $1,958. Fees, books, misc. academic expenses (school's estimate): $400.
**Enrollment.** Undergraduates: 8,169 men, 6,802 women (full-time). Freshman class: 10,370 applicants, 8,386 accepted, 3,040 enrolled. Graduate enrollment: 2,934 men, 3,764 women.
**Test score averages/ranges.** Average SAT scores: 432 verbal, 489 math. Range of SAT scores of middle 50%: 380-470 verbal, 430-540 math. Average ACT scores: 22 English, 21 math, 22 composite. Range of ACT scores of middle 50%: 20-25 composite.
**Faculty.** 1,359 full-time; 184 part-time. 82% of faculty holds doctoral degree. Student/faculty ratio: 18 to 1.
**Selectivity rating.** Less competitive.

**PROFILE.** West Virginia University, founded in 1867, is a public, comprehensive institution. Programs are offered through the Colleges of Agriculture and Forestry, Arts and Sciences, Business and Economics, Creative Arts, Engineering, Human Resources and Education, and Mineral and Energy Resources and the Schools of Dentistry, Journalism, Medicine, Nursing, Pharmacy, Physical Education, and Social Work. Its two campuses totaling over 1,000 acres are located in Morgantown, 70 miles south of Pittsburgh.

**Accreditation:** NCACS. Numerous professional accreditations.
**Religious orientation:** West Virginia University is nonsectarian; no religious requirements.
**Library:** Collections totaling over 1,700,000 volumes, 9,000 periodical subscriptions, and 2,300,000 microform items.
**Special facilities/museums:** Art galleries, creative arts center, arboretum, herbarium, planetarium, concurrent engineering research center, discovery lab (for inventors), Appalachian hardwood center, small business development center, pharmacy museum, coal and energy museum, center for economic research, fluidization center, center for software development.
**Athletic facilities:** Stadium, indoor and outdoor coliseums, steam and weight rooms, tracks, natatorium with swimming and diving pools, badminton, basketball, racquetball, squash, tennis, and volleyball courts, golf cages, outdoor recreation center, bowling alley, athletic fields.

**STUDENT BODY. Undergraduate profile:** 50% are state residents; 20% are transfers. 2% Asian-American, 3% Black, 92% White, 3% International. Average age of undergraduates is 21.
**Freshman profile:** 1% of freshmen who took SAT scored 700 or over on math; 2% scored 600 or over on verbal, 10% scored 600 or over on math; 18% scored 500 or over on verbal, 44% scored 500 or over on math; 68% scored 400 or over on verbal, 88% scored 400 or over on math; 99% scored 300 or over on verbal, 100% scored 300 or over on math. 6% of freshmen who took ACT scored 30 or over on English, 3% scored 30 or over on math, 4% scored 30 or over on composite; 41% scored 24 or over on English, 26% scored 24 or over on math, 35% scored 24 or over on composite; 87% scored 18 or over on English, 82% scored 18 or over on math, 94% scored 18 or over on composite; 100% scored 12 or over

on English, 100% scored 12 or over on math, 100% scored 12 or over on composite. 50% of accepted applicants took SAT; 47% took ACT.
**Undergraduate achievement:** 76% of fall 1991 freshmen returned for fall 1992 term. 25% of entering class graduated. 5% of students who completed a degree program immediately went on to graduate study.
**Foreign students:** 360 students are from out of the country. Countries represented include Canada, China, India, Japan, Korea, and Taiwan; 81 in all.

**PROGRAMS OF STUDY. Degrees:** B.A., B.F.A., B.Mus., B.S. B.S.Bus.Admin., B.S.Elem.Ed., B.S.Journ., B.S.Nurs., B.S.Pharm., B.S.Sec.Ed., B.Soc.Work.
**Majors:** Accounting, Aerospace Engineering, Agricultural Education, Animal/Veterinary Sciences, Art, Biology, Business Administration, Business Management, Chemical Engineering, Chemistry, Civil Engineering, Communication Studies, Computer Engineering, Computer Science, Dental Hygiene, Economics, Electrical Engineering, Elementary Education, Engineering of Mines, English, Family Resources, Finance, Foreign Languages, Forest Resources Management, Geography, Geology, History, Industrial Engineering, Interdepartmental Studies, Journalism, Landscape Architecture, Marketing, Mathematics, Mechanical Engineering, Medical Technology, Mineral Processing Engineering, Music, Nursing, Petroleum Engineering, Pharmacy, Philosophy, Physical Education, Physical Therapy, Physics, Plant/Soil Science, Political Science, Psychology, Recreation/Parks Management, Resource Management, Secondary Education, Social Work, Sociology/Anthropology, Speech Pathology/Audiology, Sport/Exercise Studies, Statistics, Theatre, Visual Art, West Virginia Board of Regents Bachelor of Arts, Wildlife Resources, Wood Industries.
**Distribution of degrees:** The majors with the highest enrollment are business administration, journalism, and psychology; statistics, engineering of mines, and mineral processing engineering have the lowest.
**Requirements:** General education requirement.
**Academic regulations:** Minimum 2.0 GPA must be maintained.
**Special:** Minors offered; requirements and availability are established by the department offering the minor. Self-designed majors. Double majors. Dual degrees. Independent study. Accelerated study. Pass/fail grading option. Internships. Cooperative education programs. Graduate school at which undergraduates may take graduate-level courses. Preprofessional programs in law, medicine, and veterinary science. Member of Southern Regional Education Board. Washington Semester and Sea Semester. Teacher certification in early childhood, elementary, secondary, and special education. Certification in specific subject areas. Study abroad in Austria, Colombia, France, Mexico, Spain, and the United Kingdom. ROTC and AFROTC.
**Honors:** Phi Beta Kappa. Honors program. Honor societies.
**Academic Assistance:** Remedial reading, writing, math, and study skills. Nonremedial tutoring.

**STUDENT LIFE. Housing:** Freshmen are strongly encouraged to live on campus. Coed, women's, and men's dorms. Sorority and fraternity housing. School-owned/operated apartments. Off-campus privately-owned housing. Both on-campus and off-campus married-student housing. 23% of students live in college housing.
**Social atmosphere:** The Side Pocket Pub, Maximillian's, the Blue Moose Coffee Shop, the Student Union, and Mario's Back Door are popular student gathering-spots. Home football games, especially the "Backyard Brawl" with Pitt, are popular events, as are the Phi Kappa Psi Halloween Party, Sigma Chi Derby Days, and the annual Grant Street Block Party. "Morgantown is a small city with cosmopolitan appeal," reports the student newspaper. "Major musical acts from the Ramones to Alan Jackson have played here recently, while artists and actors are showcased in WVU's Creative Arts Center. Besides offering easy access to Washington, D.C. and Pittsburgh, Morgantown is minutes away from recreational lakes, parks, and wilderness."
**Services and counseling/handicapped student services:** Placement services. Health service. Women's center. Counseling services for minority, military, veteran, and older students. Birth control, personal, and psychological counseling. Career and academic guidance services. Physically disabled student services. Learning disabled services. Notetaking services. Tape recorders. Tutors. Reader services for the blind.
**Campus organizations:** Undergraduate student government. Student newspaper (Daily Athenaeum). Yearbook. Radio station. Choir, choral union, concert and marching bands, orchestra, women's glee club, ballet ensemble, theatre, craft shop, art guild, photography lab, forensics, debating, oratory, lecture series, film series, Circle K, service societies, Amnesty International, departmental, political, and special-interest groups, 200 organizations in all. 22 fraternities, 18 chapter houses; 13 sororities, nine chapter houses. 20% of men join a fraternity. 23% of women join a sorority.
**Religious organizations:** Alpha Omega Campus Ministry, Baptist Student Union, Campus Crusade for Christ, Campus Light Ministries, Canterbury Fellowship, Hillel House, Muslim Student Association, Newman Organization, World Christian Fellowship.
**Minority/foreign student organizations:** Black Unity Organization. African Student Association, Chinese Student Association, India Association, International Student Association, Japanese Club, Korean Student Association, other foreign student groups.

**ATHLETICS. Physical education requirements:** None.
**Intercollegiate competition:** 16% of students participate. Baseball (M), basketball (M,W), cheerleading (M,W), cross-country (M,W), diving (M,W), football (M), gymnastics (W), riflery (M,W), soccer (M), swimming (M,W), tennis (M,W), track (outdoor) (M,W), track and field (indoor) (M,W), track and field (outdoor) (M,W), volleyball (W), wrestling (M). Member of Atlantic 10 Conference, Big East Football Conference, NCAA Division I, NCAA Division I-A for football.
**Intramural and club sports:** 44% of students participate. Intramural badminton, basketball, bowling, broomball, flag football, golf, hockey, racquetball, rifle, soccer, softball, swimming and diving, table tennis, tennis, track and field, ultimate frisbee, volleyball, Wiffle ball, wrestling.

**ADMISSIONS. Academic basis for candidate selection** (in order of priority): Secondary school record, standardized test scores, school's recommendation.
**Nonacademic basis for candidate selection:** Character and personality, extracurricular participation, particular talent or ability, geographical distribution, and alumni/ae relationship are considered.
**Requirements:** Graduation from secondary school is required; GED is accepted. 18 units and the following program of study are required: 4 units of English, 2 units of math, 2 units of lab science, 2 units of social studies, 1 unit of history, 5 units of academic electives. 2 units of a foreign language strongly recommended. Recommended elective units may be selected from among fine arts, computer science, and typing. Listed units are general minimum requirements; some programs have higher requirements. Minimum combined SAT score of 770 (composite ACT score of 19) and minimum 2.0 GPA required of in-state applicants. Combined SAT score of 820 (composite ACT score of 20) and minimum 2.25 GPA required of out-of-state applicants. 3.5 units of mathematics required of computer science, engineering, and mineral and energy resources program applicants. Portfolio required of art program applicants. Audition required of music program applicants. Up to 5% of each freshman class may be admitted due to talents in a specific field; special consideration is given to the educationally disadvantaged. SAT or ACT is required. No off-campus interviews.
**Procedure:** Take SAT/ACT by spring of 11th year; submit score by January 15. Suggest filing application by March 1. Notification of admission on rolling basis. Reply is required by May 1. $75 tuition deposit, partially refundable until June 1. $225 room deposit, partially refundable until June 1. Freshmen accepted for terms other than fall.
**Special programs:** Admission may be deferred one year. Credit and/or placement may be granted through CEEB Advanced Placement exams. Credit and/or placement may be granted through CLEP general and subject exams. Credit may be granted through military and life experience. Credit and placement may be granted through challenge exams. Early entrance/early admission program. Concurrent enrollment program.
**Transfer students:** Transfer students accepted for terms other than fall. In fall 1992, 20% of all new students were transfers into all classes. 1,462 transfer applications were received, 1,192 were accepted. Application deadline is one month prior to registration for fall; one month prior to registration for spring. Minimum 2.0 GPA required. Maximum number of transferable credits is 72 semester hours. Final 30 semester hours must be completed at the university to receive degree.
**Admissions contact:** Glenn G. Carter, Ed.D., Dean of Admissions. 800 344-WVU1.

**FINANCIAL AID. Available aid:** Pell grants, SEOG, Federal Nursing Student Scholarships, state scholarships and grants, school scholarships, private scholarships and grants, ROTC scholarships, academic merit scholarships, and athletic scholarships. Performance grants (music, art, drama), Scholars Program (over 1800 scholarships given annually primarily based on academic achievement). Perkins Loans (NDSL), PLUS, Stafford Loans (GSL), NSL, Health Professions Loans, school loans, and SLS. AMS.
**Financial aid statistics:** 18% of aid is not need-based. In 1992-93, 81% of all undergraduate applicants received aid; 76% of freshman applicants. Average amounts of aid awarded freshmen: Scholarships and grants, $1,000; loans, $2,000.
**Supporting data/closing dates:** FAFSA: Priority filing date is February 1; deadline is March 1. School's own aid application: Priority filing date is March 1. Notification of awards begins mid-March.
**Financial aid contact:** Neil Bolyard, M.A., Director of Financial Aid. 304 293-5242.

**STUDENT EMPLOYMENT.** College Work/Study Program. Institutional employment. 16% of full-time undergraduates work on campus during school year. Students may expect to earn an average of $1,200 during school year. Off-campus part-time employment opportunities rated "excellent."

**COMPUTER FACILITIES.** IBM/IBM-compatible and Macintosh/Apple microcomputers. Students may access Digital, IBM minicomputer/mainframe systems, BITNET, Internet. Residence halls may be equipped with stand-alone microcomputers. Computer languages and software packages include Ada, ADABAS, BMDP, C, CICS, COBOL, FORTRAN, ImSL, Oracle, PL/1, SAS, Script, Spires, SPSS-X, Waterloo. Computer facilities are available to all students.
**Fees:** None.
**Hours:** 24 hours.

**GRADUATE CAREER DATA.** Graduate school percentages: 5% enter law school. 12% enter graduate business programs. 6% enter graduate arts and sciences programs. 58% of graduates choose careers in business and industry. Companies and businesses that hire graduates: General Electric, Union Carbide, Texas Instruments, Corning/Dow.

**PROMINENT ALUMNI/AE.** Joseph Antonini, president and CEO, K mart Corp.; Jayne Anne Phillips, writer; Vivien Woofter, Interior Design, U.S. Dept. of State; Jerry West, athlete and general manager of Los Angeles Lakers; David Selby, actor; Jon A. McBride, astronaut, Lyndon B. Johnson Space Center; Kathy Mattea, musician, Mercury Records; Charles Vest, president of MIT; Thomas R. Ferguson, Jr., Major General, U. S. Air Force.

# West Virginia Wesleyan College

**Buckhannon, WV 26201** **304 473-8000**

**1993-94 Costs.** Tuition: $13,400. Room & board: $3,500. Fees, books, misc. academic expenses (school's estimate): $450.
**Enrollment.** Undergraduates: 744 men, 765 women (full-time). Freshman class: 1,710 applicants, 1,395 accepted, 480 enrolled. Graduate enrollment: 54 men, 22 women.
**Test score averages/ranges.** Average SAT scores: 439 verbal, 489 math. Range of SAT scores of middle 50%: 370-500 verbal, 410-570 math. Average ACT scores: 23 composite. Range of ACT scores of middle 50%: 20-27 composite.
**Faculty.** 77 full-time; 55 part-time. 62% of faculty holds highest degree in specific field. Student/faculty ratio: 13 to 1.
**Selectivity rating.** Less competitive.

**PROFILE.** West Virginia Wesleyan, founded in 1890, is a church-affiliated college. Its 80-acre campus is located in Buckhannon, in north-central West Virginia.

**Accreditation:** NCACS. Professionally accredited by the National Association of Schools of Music, the National Council for Accreditation of Teacher Education, the National League for Nursing.
**Religious orientation:** West Virginia Wesleyan College is affiliated with the United Methodist Church; one semester of religion required.

**Library:** Collections totaling over 138,147 volumes, 642 periodical subscriptions, and 6,988 microform items.
**Special facilities/museums:** Art gallery, Lincoln collection, pipe organ, language lab, early education lab, aerobic exercise and rehabilitation equipment, herbarium, greenhouse, planetarium, atomic absorption spectrophotometer.
**Athletic facilities:** Gymnasiums, weight room, nautilus room, basketball, handball, racquetball, squash, tennis, volleyball, and walleyball courts, swimming pool, baseball, football, soccer, and softball fields.

**STUDENT BODY. Undergraduate profile:** 36% are state residents; 12% are transfers. 2% Asian-American, 5% Black, 90% White, 3% Other. Average age of undergraduates is 19.
**Freshman profile:** 4% of freshmen who took SAT scored 700 or over on math; 5% scored 600 or over on verbal, 15% scored 600 or over on math; 25% scored 500 or over on verbal, 46% scored 500 or over on math; 67% scored 400 or over on verbal, 82% scored 400 or over on math; 95% scored 300 or over on verbal, 97% scored 300 or over on math. 8% of freshmen who took ACT scored 30 or over on composite; 53% scored 24 or over on composite; 96% scored 18 or over on composite; 100% scored 12 or over on composite. 79% of accepted applicants took SAT; 40% took ACT. 85% of freshmen come from public schools.
**Undergraduate achievement:** 75% of fall 1992 freshmen returned for fall 1993 term. 41% of entering class graduated. 22% of students who completed a degree program immediately went on to graduate study.
**Foreign students:** 64 students are from out of the country. Countries represented include Bulgaria, England, Japan, Korea, and Norway; 22 in all.

**PROGRAMS OF STUDY. Degrees:** B.A., B.Mus.Ed., B.S., B.S.Nurs.
**Majors:** Adult Fitness, Art, Biology, Business, Chemistry, Christian Education, Computer Information Sciences, Computer Science, Dramatic Arts, Economics, Education, Elementary Education, Engineering Physics, English, Fashion Merchandising, Government, History, Human Ecology, International Studies, Mathematics, Music, Music Education, Nursing, Nutrition, Philosophy, Philosophy/Religion, Physical Education, Physics, Psychology, Public Relations, Rehabilitation Services, Secondary Education, Social Science, Sociology, Speech Communication, Speech/Dramatic Arts, Sports Medicine.
**Distribution of degrees:** The majors with the highest enrollment are business, government, and psychology; social science, physics, and philosophy/religion have the lowest.
**Requirements:** General education requirement.
**Academic regulations:** Freshmen must maintain minimum 1.75 GPA; sophomores, juniors, seniors, 2.0 GPA.
**Special:** Minors offered in several majors. Self-designed majors. Double majors. Independent study. Accelerated study. Pass/fail grading option. Internships. Preprofessional programs in law, medicine, veterinary science, pharmacy, dentistry, theology, optometry, and nursing. 4-1 aeronautical engineering program with NASA (Langley Research Center). 3-2 engineering program with U of Pennsylvania. 3-2 forestry and environmental science program with Duke U. Member of West Virginia Consortium of Independent Colleges and Universities. Washington Semester. Oak Ridge Science Semester (Tennessee). Exchange programs with other 4-1-4 colleges during January term. Teacher certification in early childhood, elementary, secondary, and special education. Certification in specific subject areas. Exchange programs abroad in Bulgaria and Korea. Study abroad also in other countries.
**Honors:** Honors program. Honor societies.
**Academic Assistance:** Remedial reading, writing, math, and study skills. Nonremedial tutoring.

**STUDENT LIFE. Housing:** All unmarried students under age 22 must live on campus unless living with family. Coed, women's, and men's dorms. Fraternity housing. School-owned/operated apartments. 80% of students live in college housing.
**Social atmosphere:** "On campus there are college–sponsored activities each weekend, but they are sparsely attended," reports the student newspaper. The local bars are popular gathering spots off campus. Greeks and the Community Council have an influence on campus social life. Homecoming, Greek Week, athletic events, and the Festival of Lessons and Carols are among the year's favorite events.
**Services and counseling/handicapped student services:** Placement services. Health service. Counseling services for minority and older students. Personal and psychological counseling. Career and academic guidance services. Religious counseling. Physically disabled student services. Learning disabled program/services. Notetaking services. Tape recorders. Tutors. Reader services for the blind.
**Campus organizations:** Undergraduate student government. Student newspaper (Pharos, published once/week). Literary magazine. Yearbook. Radio and TV stations. Choir, concert chorale, jazz ensemble, concert band, drama groups, forensics, debating, environmental club, volunteer projects, Lively Arts Science Board, Residence Hall Council, departmental and political groups, 75 organizations in all. Five fraternities, all with chapter houses; four sororities, no chapter houses. 26% of men join a fraternity. 26% of women join a sorority.
**Religious organizations:** Religious Life Council, Wesley Fellowship, Loveshine, Fellowship of Christian Athletes, Peace With Justice Committee.
**Minority/foreign student organizations:** Black Student Union. International Student Organization.

**ATHLETICS. Physical education requirements:** Four semester hours of physical education required.
**Intercollegiate competition:** 33% of students participate. Baseball (M), basketball (M,W), cheerleading (M,W), cross-country (M,W), football (M), golf (M), soccer (M,W), softball (W), swimming (M,W), tennis (M,W), track (outdoor) (M,W), track and field (outdoor) (M,W), volleyball (W). Member of NAIA, NCAA Division II, West Virginia Intercollegiate Athletic Conference.
**Intramural and club sports:** Intramural basketball, flag football, racquetball, softball, table tennis, tennis, volleyball. Men's club lacrosse.

**ADMISSIONS. Academic basis for candidate selection** (in order of priority): Secondary school record, class rank, standardized test scores, school's recommendation, essay.
**Nonacademic basis for candidate selection:** Character and personality, extracurricular participation, and particular talent or ability are important. Alumni/ae relationship is considered.
**Requirements:** Graduation from secondary school is required; GED is accepted. 14 units and the following program of study are required: 4 units of English, 2 units of math, 2 units of lab science, 2 units of social studies, 1 unit of history, 3 units of academic electives. Portfolio required of art program applicants. Audition required of music program applicants. SAT or ACT is required. Campus visit and interview recommended. Off-campus interviews available with an admissions representative.
**Procedure:** Take SAT or ACT by December of 12th year. Visit college for interview by June of 12th year. Suggest filing application by February 1. Application deadline is August 20. Notification of admission on rolling basis. $100 tuition deposit, refundable until May 31. Freshmen accepted for terms other than fall.
**Special programs:** Admission may be deferred one year. Credit may be granted through CEEB Advanced Placement for scores of 3 or higher. Credit may be granted through CLEP general and subject exams, ACT PEP, DANTES, and challenge exams, and military and life experience. Early entrance/early admission program. Concurrent enrollment program.
**Transfer students:** Transfer students accepted for terms other than fall. In fall 1993, 12% of all new students were transfers into all classes. Application deadline is August 20 for fall; January 15 for spring. Minimum 2.5 GPA recommended. Lowest course grade accepted is "D." Maximum number of transferable credits is 104 semester hours. At least 32 semester hours must be completed at the college to receive degree.
**Admissions contact:** Robert N. Skinner II, Director of Admission. 800 722-9933, 304 473-8510.

**FINANCIAL AID. Available aid:** Pell grants, SEOG, Federal Nursing Student Scholarships, state scholarships and grants, school scholarships and grants, private scholarships and grants, academic merit scholarships, athletic scholarships, and aid for undergraduate foreign students. Perkins Loans (NDSL), PLUS, Stafford Loans (GSL), NSL, school loans, private loans, and SLS. AMS.
**Financial aid statistics:** 54% of aid is not need-based. In 1993-94, 99% of all undergraduate applicants received aid; 99% of freshman applicants. Average amounts of aid awarded freshmen: Scholarships and grants, $7,392; loans, $3,141.
**Supporting data/closing dates:** FAFSA: Priority filing date is March 1; accepted on rolling basis. School's own aid application: Accepted on rolling basis. State aid form: Deadline is March 1. Notification of awards begins March 15.
**Financial aid contact:** Lana Golden, Director of Financial Aid. 800 343-2374, 304 473-8080.

**STUDENT EMPLOYMENT.** College Work/Study Program. Institutional employment. 5% of full-time undergraduates work on campus during school year. Students may expect to earn an average of $1,000 during school year. Off-campus part-time employment opportunities rated "poor."

**COMPUTER FACILITIES.** 170 IBM/IBM-compatible and Macintosh/Apple microcomputers; 100 are networked. Students may access Digital, Hewlett-Packard minicomputer/mainframe systems. Client/LAN operating systems include Apple/Macintosh, DOS, LocalTalk/AppleTalk, Novell. Computer languages and software packages include Ada, BASIC, C, COBOL, FORTRAN, GPSS, LISP, Prolog; 50 in all. Computer facilities are available to all students.
**Fees:** Computer fee is included in tuition/fees.
**Hours:** 7 AM-11 PM.

**GRADUATE CAREER DATA.** Graduate school percentages: 5% enter law school. 3% enter medical school. 2% enter dental school. 9% enter graduate business programs. 7% enter graduate arts and sciences programs. 1% enter theological school/seminary. Highest graduate school enrollments: Duke U, Marshall U, U of Maryland, U of North Carolina, U of Pittsburgh, U of Southern California, West Virginia U. 35% of graduates choose careers in business and industry. Companies and businesses that hire graduates: AT&T, Bell Research Labs, Citibank, Eddie Bauer, Ernst & Young, Martin Marietta, Mellon Bank, Price Waterhouse.

**PROMINENT ALUMNI/AE.** William Grimes, president, Univision; John D. Swan, prime minister, Bermuda; William Cummings, publisher, *Wall Street Journal* (Europe); James Walker, cardiovascular surgeon; John Shimrak, comptroller, Campbell Soup; Jack Sisson, comptroller, Dow Jones.

## Wheeling Jesuit College

**Wheeling, WV 26003** **304 243-2000**

**1994-95 Costs.** Tuition: $10,500. Room: $2,000. Board: $2,445. Fees, books, misc. academic expenses (school's estimate): $590.
**Enrollment.** Undergraduates: 419 men, 532 women (full-time). Freshman class: 903 applicants, 755 accepted, 213 enrolled. Graduate enrollment: 99 men, 65 women.
**Test score averages/ranges.** Range of SAT scores of middle 50%: 380-490 verbal, 410-520 math. Average ACT scores: 21 composite. Range of ACT scores of middle 50%: 19-24 composite.
**Faculty.** 70 full-time; 18 part-time. 66% of faculty holds doctoral degree. Student/faculty ratio: 13 to 1.
**Selectivity rating.** Less competitive.

**PROFILE.** Wheeling Jesuit, founded in 1954, is a church-affiliated college. Its 65-acre campus is located in a residential section of Wheeling, 60 miles south of Pittsburgh.

**Accreditation:** NCACS. Professionally accredited by the American Medical Association (CAHEA), the National League for Nursing.
**Religious orientation:** Wheeling Jesuit College is affiliated with the Roman Catholic Church (Society of Jesus); nine credits of religion required.

**Library:** Collections totaling over 126,000 volumes, 549 periodical subscriptions, and 84,000 microform items.
**Athletic facilities:** Aerobics room, field house, fitness center, performance gymnasium, racquetball and tennis courts, soccer and softball fields, swimming pool.
**STUDENT BODY. Undergraduate profile:** 43% are state residents; 17% are transfers. 1% Asian-American, 2% Black, 2% Hispanic, 91% White, 4% Foreign. Average age of undergraduates is 21.
**Freshman profile:** 1% of freshmen who took SAT scored 700 or over on math; 2% scored 600 or over on verbal, 11% scored 600 or over on math; 20% scored 500 or over on verbal, 39% scored 500 or over on math; 62% scored 400 or over on verbal, 79% scored 400 or over on math; 96% scored 300 or over on verbal, 97% scored 300 or over on math. 1% of freshmen who took ACT scored 30 or over on composite; 26% scored 24 or over on composite; 92% scored 18 or over on composite; 100% scored 12 or over on composite. 54% of accepted applicants took SAT; 69% took ACT. 63% of freshmen come from public schools.
**Undergraduate achievement:** 71% of fall 1992 freshmen returned for fall 1993 term. 57% of entering class graduated. 28% of students who completed a degree program immediately went on to graduate study.
**Foreign students:** 34 students are from out of the country. Countries represented include Belize, Canada, Honduras, Japan, Nepal, and Tobago/Trinidad; 19 in all.
**PROGRAMS OF STUDY. Degrees:** B.A., B.Lib.Arts, B.S., B.S.Bus.Admin., B.S.Nurs.
**Majors:** Accounting, Biology, Business Management, Chemistry, Computer Science, Criminal Justice, English Literature, French, General Science, History, Industrial Engineering, International Studies, Management, Marketing, Mathematics, Nuclear Medical Technology, Nursing, Philosophy, Physics, Political Economy/Philosophy, Political Science, Professional Writing, Psychology, Respiration Therapy, Romance Languages, Spanish, Teacher Preparation, Technology, Theology.
**Distribution of degrees:** The majors with the highest enrollment are psychology, marketing, and accounting; Spanish and romance languages have the lowest.
**Requirements:** General education requirement.
**Academic regulations:** Freshmen must maintain minimum 1.8 GPA; sophomores, juniors, seniors, 2.0 GPA.
**Special:** Minors offered in some majors and in business administration, economics, English, international business, peace studies, religious studies, and sociology. Self-designed majors. Double majors. Independent study. Pass/fail grading option. Internships. Graduate school at which undergraduates may take graduate-level courses. Preprofessional programs in law, medicine, veterinary science, pharmacy, dentistry, theology, optometry, engineering, and pre-physical therapy. 3-2 engineering program with Case Western Reserve U. Five-year B.A./M.B.A. program. Member of West Virginia Consortium in International Studies. Washington Semester. Member of Association of Jesuit Colleges and Universities; semester exchanges possible with 27 other association members. Teacher certification in secondary education. Certification in specific subject areas. Exchange program abroad in Italy (Loyola U Center of Liberal Arts). Study abroad also in Argentina, the Caribbean, Egypt, England, and Scotland.
**Honors:** Honors program. Honor societies.
**Academic Assistance:** Remedial reading, writing, math, and study skills. Nonremedial tutoring.
**ADMISSIONS. Academic basis for candidate selection** (in order of priority): Secondary school record, class rank, standardized test scores, school's recommendation.
**Nonacademic basis for candidate selection:** Character and personality and extracurricular participation are important. Particular talent or ability and alumni/ae relationship are considered.
**Requirements:** Graduation from secondary school is recommended; GED is accepted. 17 units and the following program of study are required: 4 units of English, 2 units of math, 1 unit of lab science, 2 units of social studies, 6 units of academic electives. Minimum combined SAT score of 850 (composite ACT score of 20), rank in top half of secondary school class, and minimum 2.0 GPA required. Conditional admission possible for applicants not meeting standard requirements. SAT or ACT is required. Campus visit and interview recommended. Off-campus interviews available with an admissions representative.
**Procedure:** Take SAT or ACT by March of 12th year. Visit college for interview by March of 12th year. Notification of admission on rolling basis. Reply is required by May 1. $100 nonrefundable tuition deposit. $100 room deposit, refundable until June 1. Freshmen accepted for terms other than fall.
**Special programs:** Admission may be deferred three terms. Credit and/or placement may be granted through CEEB Advanced Placement exams for scores of 4 or higher. Credit and/or placement may be granted through CLEP subject exams. Credit and placement may be granted through challenge exams, and military and life experience. Early entrance/early admission program.
**Transfer students:** Transfer students accepted for terms other than fall. In fall 1993, 17% of all new students were transfers into all classes. 147 transfer applications were received, 122 were accepted. Application deadline is July 15 for fall; December 15 for spring. Minimum 2.0 GPA required. Lowest course grade accepted is "C." Maximum number of transferable credits is 90 semester hours. At least 30 semester hours must be completed at the college to receive degree.
**Admissions contact:** Dennis Soberl, Director of Admissions. 304 243-2359, 800 624-6992.
**FINANCIAL AID. Available aid:** Pell grants, SEOG, Federal Nursing Student Scholarships, state scholarships and grants, school scholarships and grants, private grants, academic merit scholarships, and athletic scholarships. Perkins Loans (NDSL), PLUS, Stafford Loans (GSL), NSL, and SLS. Knight Tuition Plans, AMS, Tuition Management Systems, and deferred payment plan.
**Financial aid statistics:** 22% of aid is not need-based. In 1993-94, 90% of all undergraduate applicants received aid; 96% of freshman applicants. Average amounts of aid awarded freshmen: Scholarships and grants, $6,026; loans, $3,200.
**Supporting data/closing dates:** FAFSA/FAF/FFS: Priority filing date is March 1; accepted on rolling basis. Income tax forms: Priority filing date is March 1; accepted on rolling basis. Notification of awards on rolling basis.
**Financial aid contact:** Su Saunders, Director of Financial Aid. 304 243-2304.

# Wisconsin

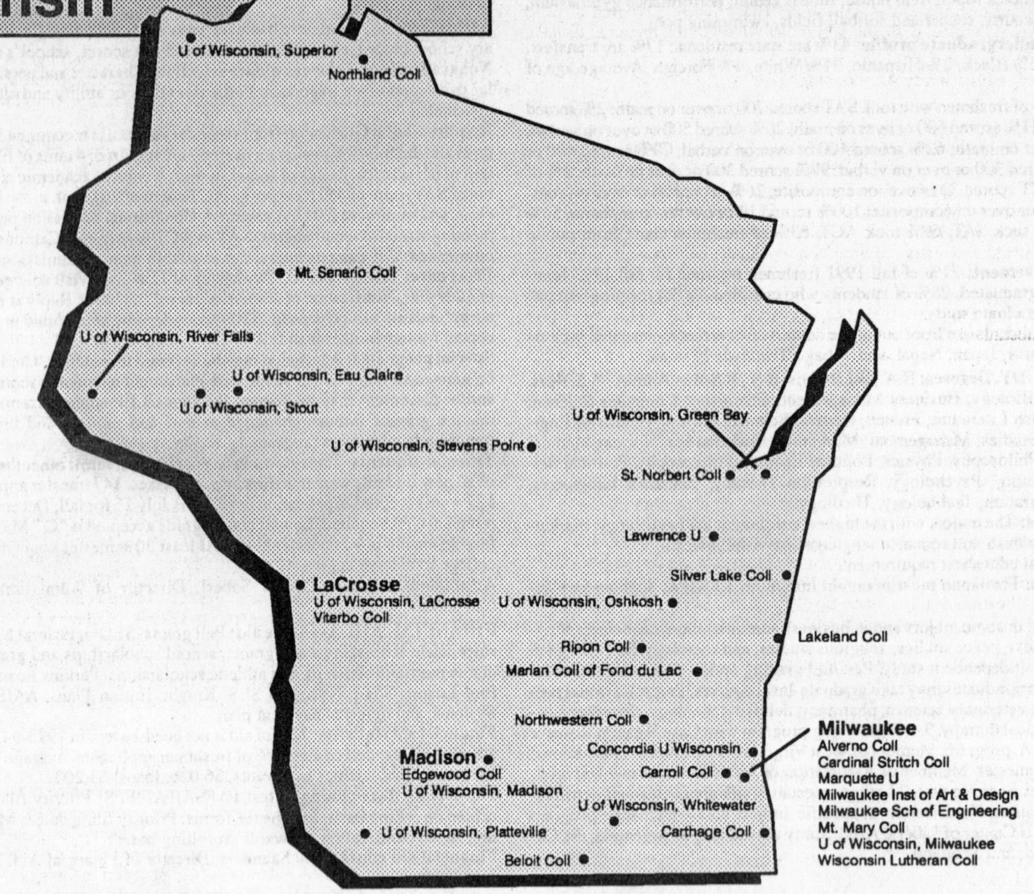


## Alverno College

**Milwaukee, WI 53234-3922** **414 382-6000**

**1994-95 Costs.** Tuition: $8,352. Room & board: $3,640. Fees, books, misc. academic expenses (school's estimate): $550.
**Enrollment.** 1,317 women (full-time). Freshman class: 670 applicants, 458 accepted, 231 enrolled.
**Test score averages/ranges.** Average ACT scores: 20 English, 19 math, 20 composite.
**Faculty.** 118 full-time; 97 part-time. 81% of faculty holds highest degree in specific field. Student/faculty ratio: 13 to 1.
**Selectivity rating.** Competitive.

**PROFILE.** Alverno, founded in 1887, is a church-affiliated, liberal arts college for women. Its 50-acre campus is located 12 miles from downtown Milwaukee.

**Accreditation:** NCACS. Professionally accredited by the American Medical Association (CAHEA), the National Association of Schools of Music, the National Council for Accreditation of Teacher Education, the National League for Nursing.
**Religious orientation:** Alverno College is affiliated with the Roman Catholic Church (School Sisters of St. Francis); no religious requirements.
**Library:** Collections totaling over 114,037 volumes, 1,541 periodical subscriptions, and 198,851 microform items.
**Special facilities/museums:** Art gallery, child development center, language lab, performing arts building with theatres, fitness center, air quality monitoring site for southeast Wisconsin.
**STUDENT BODY. Undergraduate profile:** 97% are state residents; 269% are transfers. 2% Asian-American, 15% Black, 5% Hispanic, 1% Native American, 75% White, 2% Other. Average age of undergraduates is 24.
**Freshman profile:** 5% of accepted applicants took SAT; 49% took ACT.
**Undergraduate achievement:** 90% of fall 1992 freshmen returned for fall 1993 term. 52% of entering class graduated. 7% of students who completed a degree program immediately went on to graduate study.
**Foreign students:** 16 students are from out of the country. Countries represented include Hong Kong, India, Japan, Poland, Somalia, and the Philippines; 11 in all.
**PROGRAMS OF STUDY. Degrees:** B.A., B.Mus., B.S., B.S.Ed., B.S.Nurs.
**Majors:** Art, Art Education, Art Therapy, Biology, Broad Field Science, Broad Field Social Studies, Business/Management, Chemistry, Communications, Education, Elementary Education, Engineering, English, History, Mathematics, Music, Music Education, Music in Culture, Music Performance, Music Therapy, Nuclear Medical Technology, Nursing, Philosophy, Professional Communication, Psychology, Religious Studies, Secondary Education, Social Sciences, Studio Art.
**Distribution of degrees:** The majors with the highest enrollment are business/management, professional communication, and nursing; nuclear medical technology, engineering, and philosophy have the lowest.
**Requirements:** General education requirement.
**Special:** Minors offered in many majors and in adult education, bilingual education, computer studies, creative arts, dance, early childhood education, global studies, informational studies, language arts, and theatre. Weekend College. Degree requirements in addition to major and minor include mastery of a range of liberal arts areas and ability in "competence areas" (communications, analysis, problem solving, valuing in decision-making, effective citizenship, and aesthetic response). Active performances (e.g., panels, simulations, media presentations, role-playing) are used as often as written work to assess student ability. Each student receives personal feedback and also assesses her own work. Career Development program begins first year. Double majors. Dual degrees. Internships. Preprofessional programs in law, medicine, veterinary science, and dentistry. 3-2 engineering program with Milwaukee Sch of Engineering. Art majors may take courses at Milwaukee Inst of Art and Design. Travelship program subsidizes off-campus and overseas learning experiences for credit. Teacher certification in early childhood, elementary, secondary, and bilingual/bicultural education. Certification in specific subject areas. Study abroad in England and Japan. ROTC at Marquette U.
**Honors:** Honor societies.
**Academic Assistance:** Remedial reading, writing, math, and study skills. Nonremedial tutoring.
**STUDENT LIFE. Housing:** Women's dorms. 11% of students live in college housing.
**Social atmosphere:** The student newspaper reports: "While Alverno prides itself on its serious academic foundation, the students also find time for an active social life. Having one of the highest percentages of minority students in the state means a rich multicultural environment." Circle K seems to be the most influential group on campus. Planned events include service projects, parties, dances, the 'I Wish It Was New Year's Eve' Party, Student Conference Day, and the Bowl-a-Thon fundraiser and party. Students like to gather at the student lounge, commons, residence halls, other local campuses, and in the city of Milwaukee.
**Services and counseling/handicapped student services:** Placement services. Health service. Day care. Counseling services for minority and older students. Personal counseling. Career and academic guidance services. Religious counseling. Physically disabled student services. Learning disabled services. Notetaking services. Tape recorders. Tutors. Reader services for the blind.
**Campus organizations:** Student newspaper (Alpha, published once/month). Literary magazine. Chamber singers, instrumental ensembles, women's chorus, Theatre Alverno, Guiding Lights, Artourage, Alchemist Club, Alverno Entrepreneurs, Management Association, College Republicans, Voices for Liberal Legislation, Student Activity Board, departmental, professional, and special-interest groups, 28 organizations in all.

**Religious organizations:** Ministry Committee, Spirituality Discussion Group, Campus Ministry.
**Minority/foreign student organizations:** Concerned Black Nurses, Women of Color Awareness Group, Black Alumnae, Hispanic Women of Alverno. International Cultures Interest Group.

**ATHLETICS. Physical education requirements:** None.

**ADMISSIONS. Academic basis for candidate selection** (in order of priority): Secondary school record, standardized test scores, class rank.
**Requirements:** Graduation from secondary school is recommended; GED is accepted. 17 units required and the following program of study recommended: 4 units of English, 3 units of math, 3 units of science, 2 units of foreign language, 3 units of social studies, 1 unit of history, 2 units of electives. Minimum composite ACT score of 19 and minimum 2.0 GPA recommended. Biology and chemistry required of music therapy program applicants. Biology, algebra, and chemistry required of nursing program applicants. Biology, chemistry, algebra, and geometry recommended of nuclear medical technology program applicants. Audition (or tape) and music theory exam required of music program applicants. Alternative admission program for applicants not normally admissible. ACT is required; SAT may be substituted. Campus visit and interview recommended. No off-campus interviews.
**Procedure:** Take SAT or ACT by April of 12th year. Visit college for interview by May of 12th year. Application deadline is August 1. Notification of admission on rolling basis. Reply is required by May 1. $50 tuition deposit, refundable until May 1. $100 room deposit, refundable until July 1. Freshmen accepted for terms other than fall.
**Special programs:** Admission may be deferred two years. Credit and/or placement may be granted through CEEB Advanced Placement exams for scores of 3 or higher. Credit and/or placement may be granted through CLEP general and subject exams. Credit and placement may be granted through ACT PEP and challenge exams and life experience. Early entrance/early admission program. Concurrent enrollment program.
**Transfer students:** Transfer students accepted for terms other than fall. In fall 1993, 269% of all new students were transfers into all classes. 494 transfer applications were received, 313 were accepted. Application deadline is August 1 for fall; January 1 for spring. Minimum 2.0 GPA required. Lowest course grade accepted is "C." Transfer requirements vary by program.
**Admissions contact:** Colleen K. Hayes, Director of Admissions. 414 382-6100.

**FINANCIAL AID. Available aid:** Pell grants, SEOG, state scholarships and grants, school scholarships and grants, and private scholarships and grants. Perkins Loans (NDSL), PLUS, Stafford Loans (GSL), NSL, and SLS. Deferred payment plan. Installment payment plan.
**Financial aid statistics:** In 1993-94, 79% of all undergraduate applicants received aid; 80% of freshman applicants. Average amounts of aid awarded freshmen: Scholarships and grants, $3,000; loans, $2,625.
**Supporting data/closing dates:** FAFSA: Priority filing date is March 1. Income tax forms: Priority filing date is March 1. College's verification form: Priority filing date is March 1. Notification of awards on rolling basis.
**Financial aid contact:** Robert Jacobson, M.S., Director of Student Financial Planning. 414 382-6046.

**STUDENT EMPLOYMENT.** College Work/Study Program. Institutional employment. 44% of full-time undergraduates work on campus during school year. Students may expect to earn an average of $1,200 during school year. Off-campus part-time employment opportunities rated "good."

**COMPUTER FACILITIES.** 82 IBM/IBM-compatible and Macintosh/Apple microcomputers; 32 are networked. Residence halls may be equipped with stand-alone microcomputers. Client/LAN operating systems include Apple/Macintosh, DOS, Novell. Computer languages and software packages include BASIC, COBOL, Pascal; database, graphics, spreadsheet, statistical, subject matter, word processing programs; Over 700 in all. Computer facilities are available to all students.
**Fees:** None.
**Hours:** 8 AM-10 PM.

**GRADUATE CAREER DATA.** Graduate school percentages: 1% enter medical school. 2% enter graduate business programs. 3% enter graduate arts and sciences programs. Highest graduate school enrollments: Marquette U, U of Wisconsin at Madison, U of Wisconsin at Milwaukee. 37% of graduates choose careers in business and industry. Companies and businesses that hire graduates: Archdiocese of Milwaukee schools, Arthur Andersen, Miller Brewing, Milwaukee public schools, St. Luke's Hospital, Wisconsin Bell.

**PROMINENT ALUMNI/AE.** Barbara Kluka, circuit court judge; Kathleen Gigl, vice president, Texas Woman's U; Sr. Joel Read, president, Alverno Coll.

8-29

# Beloit College

**Beloit, WI 53511** **608 363-2000**

**1994-95 Costs.** Tuition: $15,260. Room & board: $3,520. Fees, books, misc. academic expenses (school's estimate): $520.
**Enrollment.** Undergraduates: 485 men, 638 women (full-time). Freshman class: 1,230 applicants, 926 accepted, 284 enrolled. Graduate enrollment: 4 men, 1 woman.
**Test score averages/ranges.** Average SAT scores: 550 verbal, 580 math. Range of SAT scores of middle 50%: 490-610 verbal, 520-640 math. Average ACT scores: 26 composite. Range of ACT scores of middle 50%: 23-28 composite.
**Faculty.** 86 full-time; 50 part-time. 89% of faculty holds doctoral degree. Student/faculty ratio: 11 to 1.
**Selectivity rating.** Highly competitive.

**PROFILE.** Beloit, founded in 1846, is a private, liberal arts college. Programs are offered through the Divisions of Arts and Humanities, Natural Science and Mathematics, and Social Science. Its 65-acre campus is located in Beloit, 50 miles south of Madison.
**Accreditation:** NCACS.
**Religious orientation:** Beloit College is nonsectarian; no religious requirements.
**Library:** Collections totaling over 229,206 volumes, 928 periodical subscriptions, and 11,391 microform items.
**Special facilities/museums:** Art and anthropology museums, center for language study, social science research lab, archaeological field school, limnology lab, woodland wildlife refuge, prairie area, observatory with 22-inch telescope, two electron microscopes, superconducting NMR and ICAP spectrometer.
**Athletic facilities:** Gymnasium, stadium, basketball, handball, racquetball, tennis, and volleyball courts, tracks, baseball, football, intramural, soccer, and softball fields, natatorium, dance studio, arena, fitness center, batting and golf cages.

**STUDENT BODY. Undergraduate profile:** 22% are state residents; 12% are transfers. 3% Asian-American, 3% Black, 2% Hispanic, 82% White, 10% Other. Average age of undergraduates is 20.
**Freshman profile:** 2% of freshmen who took SAT scored 700 or over on verbal, 11% scored 700 or over on math; 31% scored 600 or over on verbal, 40% scored 600 or over on math; 74% scored 500 or over on verbal, 84% scored 500 or over on math; 97% scored 400 or over on verbal, 98% scored 400 or over on math; 100% scored 300 or over on verbal, 100% scored 300 or over on math. 62% of accepted applicants took SAT; 57% took ACT.
**Undergraduate achievement:** 97% of fall 1992 freshmen returned for fall 1993 term. 56% of entering class graduated. 31% of students who completed a degree program went on to graduate study within one year.
**Foreign students:** 123 students are from out of the country. Countries represented include the Bahamas, India, Indonesia, Japan, Malaysia, and Turkey; 40 in all.

**PROGRAMS OF STUDY. Degrees:** B.A., B.S.
**Majors:** Anthropology, Art Education, Art History, Behavioral Biology, Biochemistry, Biology, Business Administration, Chemistry, Classical Civilization, Classical Philology, Comparative Literature, Computer Science, Creative Writing, Economics, Economics/Management, English, Environmental Biology, French, Geology, Geology/Environmental Science, German, Government, History, Interdisciplinary Studies, International Relations, Literary Studies, Mathematical Biology, Mathematics, Medical Biology, Modern Languages/Literatures, Molecular Biology, Music, Music Education, Organismal Biology, Philosophy, Physics, Psychology, Religion, Russian, Science for Elementary Teaching, Sociology, Spanish, Studio Art, Theater Arts.
**Distribution of degrees:** The majors with the highest enrollment are economics/management and anthropology; economics, modern languages/literatures, and philosophy have the lowest.
**Requirements:** General education requirement.
**Academic regulations:** Minimum 2.0 GPA must be maintained.
**Special:** Minor or second major required for graduation. Minors offered in ancient Mediterranean, Asian, behavioral, environmental, European, health care, interdisciplinary, Latin American, museum, Russian, and women's studies, journalism, linguistics, performing and theater arts. Wilderness field program in biology and geology. Independently-funded research, business, and service projects. Summer intensive language programs in Chinese, Hungarian, Japanese, Russian, and Spanish. Self-designed majors. Double majors. Independent study. Pass/fail grading option. Internships. Graduate school at which undergraduates may take graduate-level courses. Preprofessional programs in law, medicine, dentistry, business, medical technology, and nursing. 2-2 nursing programs with Rush U Medical Center. 4-2 engineering program with Columbia U. Fifth-year M.A.T. program. 3-2 M.S.W. program with U of Chicago. 3-2 forestry and environmental studies program with Duke U. 3-2 engineering programs with Columbia U, Georgia Tech, Iowa State U, Northwestern U, Purdue U, Rensselaer Polytech Inst, U of Illinois, U of Michigan, and Washington U. Early admission to Medical Coll of Wisconsin and to M.B.A. program at U of Chicago. Member of Associated Colleges of the Midwest and Pew Midstates Science and Mathematics Consortium. Washington Semester. Argonne Science Semester and Newberry Library Program in the Humanities (Illinois). Urban Education Program and Urban Studies Program (Chicago). Other semester-away programs available. Teacher certification in elementary, secondary, and bilingual/bicultural education. Certification in specific subject areas. Exchange programs abroad in China (Fudan U), Hungary (Jozsef Eotvos Koll), Indonesia (Tas Satya Wacana U), Japan (Kansai Gaidai U), and over 25 universities in the former Soviet republics. Study abroad also in Costa Rica, Ecuador, England, France, Germany, India, Italy, Scotland, Thailand, Vietnam, the former Yugoslav republics, and Zimbabwe.
**Honors:** Phi Beta Kappa. Honor societies.
**Academic Assistance:** Nonremedial tutoring.

**STUDENT LIFE. Housing:** All freshmen, sophomores, and juniors must live on campus. Coed and women's dorms. Sorority and fraternity housing. Special-interest housing. 94% of students live in college housing.
**Social atmosphere:** The editor of the student newspaper reports: "Socially, Beloit township is devoid of entertainment, so the college works hard to create activities that provoke student participation." A large foreign student population creates an international flavor with the Cafe Belwah, the German House Koffestunde, and international dinners. Other influential groups include athletes, Greeks, the newspaper and C-House staffs, and the Arts Co-op. Hangouts off campus are the Coughy Haus ("a smoky bar with cheap beer"), Goodies and Sharkies (bars), and the Breeze Cafe. Among the popular social events are the Folk and Blues Weekend, Kon Tiki, Halloween, the Debutante's Ball, Homecoming, and Spring Day.
**Services and counseling/handicapped student services:** Placement services. Health service. Women's center. Day care. Counseling services for minority students. Birth control, personal, and psychological counseling. Career and academic guidance services. Physically disabled student services. Learning disabled services. Notetaking services. Tutors. Reader services for the blind.
**Campus organizations:** Undergraduate student government. Student newspaper (Roundtable, published once/week). Literary magazine. Yearbook. Radio and TV stations. Numerous musical and drama groups, College Bowl Team, conservation club, geology club, Kazoo Band, Science Fiction Society, Volunteer Connection, Amnesty International, Model UN, Young Democrats, Young Republicans, gay/lesbian/bisexual group, special-interest groups, 85 organizations in all. Four fraternities, all with chapter houses;

two sororities, all with chapter houses. 10% of men join a fraternity. 5% of women join a sorority.

**Religious organizations:** Chevrah, Quaker group, Hebrew club, Newman Center, Christian Fellowship, other religious groups.

**Minority/foreign student organizations:** Black Students United. International Club.

**ATHLETICS. Physical education requirements:** None.

**Intercollegiate competition:** 30% of students participate. Baseball (M), basketball (M,W), cross-country (M,W), diving (M,W), football (M), golf (M), soccer (M,W), softball (W), swimming (M,W), tennis (M,W), track (indoor) (M,W), track (outdoor) (M,W), track and field (indoor) (M,W), track and field (outdoor) (M,W), volleyball (W). Member of Midwest Athletics Conference for Women, Midwest Collegiate Athletic Conference, NCAA Division III.

**Intramural and club sports:** 50% of students participate. Intramural basketball, flag football, field hockey, racquetball, soccer, volleyball, walleyball. Men's club fencing, lacrosse, martial arts. Women's club fencing, lacrosse, martial arts.

**ADMISSIONS. Academic basis for candidate selection** (in order of priority): Secondary school record, standardized test scores, school's recommendation, essay, class rank.

**Nonacademic basis for candidate selection:** Character and personality, extracurricular participation, and particular talent or ability are important. Alumni/ae relationship is considered.

**Requirements:** Graduation from secondary school is required; GED is accepted. 16 units required and the following program of study recommended: 4 units of English, 3 units of math, 3 units of science, 2 units of foreign language, 3 units of social studies. Rank in top half of secondary school class recommended. EOP for applicants not normally admissible. Conditional admission possible for applicants not meeting standard requirements. SAT or ACT is required. Campus visit and interview recommended. Off-campus interviews available with admissions and alumni representatives.

**Procedure:** Take SAT or ACT by December of 12th year. Visit college for interview by March 15 of 12th year. Notification of admission on rolling basis. Reply is required by May 1. $100 nonrefundable tuition deposit. Freshmen accepted for terms other than fall.

**Special programs:** Admission may be deferred one year. Credit and/or placement may be granted through CEEB Advanced Placement exams for scores of 4 or higher. Credit and/or placement may be granted through CLEP subject exams. Early decision program. In fall 1993, 40 applied for early decision and 24 were accepted. Deadline for applying for early decision is December 15. Early entrance/early admission program. Concurrent enrollment program.

**Transfer students:** Transfer students accepted for terms other than fall. In fall 1993, 12% of all new students were transfers into all classes. 100 transfer applications were received, 66 were accepted. Application deadline is March 1 for fall; December 1 for spring. Minimum 2.5 GPA recommended. Both secondary school and college transcripts required of transfer applicants with fewer than one year of credits. Lowest course grade accepted is "C." Maximum number of transferable credits is 60 semester hours. At least 60 semester hours must be completed at the college to receive degree.

**Admissions contact:** Alan G. McIvor, M.A., Ed.Sp., Vice President for Enrollment Services. 608 363-2500.

**FINANCIAL AID. Available aid:** Pell grants, SEOG, state scholarships and grants, school scholarships and grants, private scholarships, academic merit scholarships, and aid for undergraduate foreign students. Perkins Loans (NDSL), PLUS, Stafford Loans (GSL), school loans, and SLS. Tuition Plan Inc., Knight Tuition Plans, AMS, Tuition Management Systems, deferred payment plan, family tuition reduction, and guaranteed tuition.

**Financial aid statistics:** 2% of aid is not need-based. In 1993-94, 99% of all undergraduate applicants received aid; 98% of freshman applicants. Average amounts of aid awarded freshmen: Scholarships and grants, $9,182; loans, $2,382.

**Supporting data/closing dates:** FAFSA: Priority filing date is April 1. School's own aid application: Accepted on rolling basis. Income tax forms: Priority filing date is April 1. Notification of awards on rolling basis.

**Financial aid contact:** Jane H. Hessian, Director of Financial Aid. 608 363-2663.

**STUDENT EMPLOYMENT.** College Work/Study Program. Institutional employment. 81% of full-time undergraduates work on campus during school year. Students may expect to earn an average of $1,050 during school year. Off-campus part-time employment opportunities rated "fair."

**COMPUTER FACILITIES.** 115 IBM/IBM-compatible and Macintosh/Apple microcomputers; 75 are networked. Students may access Digital, Hewlett-Packard, IBM minicomputer/mainframe systems, Internet. Residence halls may be equipped with stand-alone microcomputers, networked microcomputers, modems. Computer languages and software packages include Atlas Graphics, Atlas Pro, BASIC, C, COBOL, Cricket Graph, dBASE III, FORTRAN, JMP, KERMIT, Lotus 1-2-3, MacDraw, MacPaint, Microsoft Excel, Microsoft Word, Microsoft Works, MINITAB, Pascal, SAS, SPSS-PC+, Symphony, WordPerfect. Computer facilities are available to all students.

**Fees:** None.

**Hours:** 24 hours.

**GRADUATE CAREER DATA.** Graduate school percentages: 3% enter law school. 2% enter medical school. 2% enter graduate business programs. 18% enter graduate arts and sciences programs. 2% enter theological school/seminary. 23% of graduates choose careers in business and industry. Companies and businesses that hire graduates: Andersen Consulting, Peace Corps, U.S. government.

**PROMINENT ALUMNI/AE.** Robert Beebe, president, PepsiCo; Jameson Parker, TV actor; Robert Lee Morris, fashion designer; Robert Strong, former U.S. ambassador to Iraq; Robbin Fleming, former president, U of Michigan; Robert Nowinski, president, Patho-Genesis Corp.; Gene Banucci, president and CEO, Advanced Technology Materials; Dr. Alisan Goldfarb, assistant professor of surgery, Sloan-Kettering Institute.

# Cardinal Stritch College

**Milwaukee, WI 53217** **800 347-8822**

**1994-95 Costs.** Tuition: $8,000. Room: $590. Board: $1,210. Fees, books, misc. academic expenses (school's estimate): $549.

**Enrollment.** Undergraduates: 938 men, 1,465 women (full-time). Freshman class: 343 applicants, 272 accepted, 172 enrolled. Graduate enrollment: 742 men, 2,133 women.

**Test score averages/ranges.** Average ACT scores: 22 English, 22 math, 22 composite. Range of ACT scores of middle 50%: 22-24 English, 20-23 math.

**Faculty.** 74 full-time; 108 part-time. 53% of faculty holds highest degree in specific field. Student/faculty ratio: 16 to 1.

**Selectivity rating.** Less competitive.

**PROFILE.** Cardinal Stritch, founded in 1937, is a church-affiliated, liberal arts college. Its 40-acre campus is located in the Fox Point suburb, 10 miles from downtown Milwaukee.

**Accreditation:** NCACS. Professionally accredited by the National Council for Accreditation of Teacher Education, the National League for Nursing.

**Religious orientation:** Cardinal Stritch College is affiliated with the Roman Catholic Church; two semesters of theology required.

**Library:** Collections totaling over 113,734 volumes, 1,215 periodical subscriptions, and 87,849 microform items.

**Special facilities/museums:** Reading and learning center, children's center, art gallery.

**Athletic facilities:** Gymnasium, field house, track, training, weight, and wrestling rooms, soccer and softball fields, dance studio, tennis courts.

**STUDENT BODY. Undergraduate profile:** 93% are state residents; 42% are transfers. 1.7% Asian-American, 8.1% Black, 2.8% Hispanic, 1% Native American, 82.6% White, 3.8% Other. Average age of undergraduates is 30.

**Freshman profile:** 3% of freshmen who took ACT scored 30 or over on composite; 26% scored 24 or over on composite; 92% scored 18 or over on composite; 100% scored 12 or over on composite. Majority of accepted applicants took ACT. 75% of freshmen come from public schools.

**Undergraduate achievement:** 83% of fall 1992 freshmen returned for fall 1993 term. 52% of entering class graduated. 5% of students who completed a degree program immediately went on to graduate study.

**Foreign students:** 13 students are from out of the country. Countries represented include Canada, Kenya, the Philippines, Poland, Spain, and Taiwan.

**PROGRAMS OF STUDY. Degrees:** B.A., B.S.

**Majors:** Accounting, Art, Biology, Broad Fields English/Communication Arts, Business, Business Administration, Business Management, Chemistry, Computer Studies, Education, English, French, History, International Business, Interpersonal Communication, Mathematics, Mathematics/Computer Science, Nursing, Psychology, Public Communication, Religious Studies, Sociology, Spanish, Special Education, Theatre.

**Distribution of degrees:** The majors with the highest enrollment are business, education, and nursing; French and broad fields English/communication arts have the lowest.

**Requirements:** General education requirement.

**Academic regulations:** Minimum 2.0 GPA must be maintained.

**Special:** Minors offered in many majors. Associate's degrees offered. Double majors. Independent study. Accelerated study. Pass/fail grading option. Internships. Cooperative education programs. Graduate school at which undergraduates may take graduate-level courses. Preprofessional programs in law, medicine, veterinary science, dentistry, and theology. Teacher certification in early childhood, elementary, secondary, special education, and bilingual/bicultural education. Certification in specific subject areas. Study abroad in England, France, Mexico, and Spain.

**Honors:** Honor societies.

**Academic Assistance:** Remedial reading, writing, math, and study skills. Nonremedial tutoring.

**STUDENT LIFE. Housing:** Students may live on or off campus. Coed dorms. 13% of students live in college housing.

**Social atmosphere:** Students gather at the student union and at Kopp's Custard Stand. Popular events include soccer games, basketball games, and dances. According to the Chronicle, the campus has a friendly atmosphere. "Each person has his or her own culture and students respect each other."

**Services and counseling/handicapped student services:** Placement services. Health service. Counseling services for minority and older students. Career and academic guidance services. Religious counseling. Physically disabled student services. Learning disabled services.

**Campus organizations:** Undergraduate student government. Student newspaper (Chronicle, published four times/year). Yearbook. Art club, Genesian Players, Model UN, Student Activities Committee, Student Nurse Association, bowling club, business club, 16 organizations in all.

**Religious organizations:** Campus Ministry.

**Minority/foreign student organizations:** Organization for Minority Students.

**ATHLETICS. Physical education requirements:** None.

**Intercollegiate competition:** 5% of students participate. Baseball (M), basketball (M,W), soccer (M), softball (W), volleyball (W). Member of Lake Michigan Conference, NAIA, National Small College Athletic Association.

**Intramural and club sports:** 5% of students participate. Intramural basketball, pool, table tennis, volleyball.

**ADMISSIONS. Academic basis for candidate selection** (in order of priority): Secondary school record, standardized test scores, class rank, school's recommendation, essay.

**Nonacademic basis for candidate selection:** Extracurricular participation and particular talent or ability are important. Character and personality and alumni/ae relationship are considered.

**Requirements:** Graduation from secondary school is recommended; GED is accepted. 18 units and the following program of study are required: 4 units of English, 2 units of math, 2 units of science, 2 units of foreign language, 2 units of social studies, 1 unit of history, 5 units of electives. Minimum composite ACT score of 20, rank in top half of secondary school class, and minimum 2.0 GPA required. Conditional Acceptance Program (CAP) for applicants not normally admissible. ACT is required; SAT may be substituted. PSAT is recommended. Campus visit and interview recommended. Off-campus interviews available with an admissions representative.
**Procedure:** Take SAT or ACT by May of 12th year. Visit college for interview by May of 12th year. Suggest filing application by April 1. Application deadline is August 1. Notification of admission on rolling basis. Reply is required by August 30. $50 tuition deposit, refundable until August 1. $50 room deposit, refundable until June 15. Freshmen accepted for terms other than fall.
**Special programs:** Admission may be deferred one year. Credit and/or placement may be granted through CEEB Advanced Placement exams for scores of 4 or higher. Credit and/or placement may be granted through CLEP general and subject exams. Credit may be granted through military and life experience. Placement may be granted through challenge exams. Early entrance/early admission program.
**Transfer students:** Transfer students accepted for terms other than fall. In fall 1993, 42% of all new students were transfers into all classes. Application deadline is August 15 for fall; January 15 for spring. Minimum 2.0 GPA required. Lowest course grade accepted is "C-." Maximum number of transferable credits is 98 semester hours. At least 30 semester hours must be completed at the college to receive degree.
**Admissions contact:** Dave Wegener, Director of Admissions. 414 351-7504.

**FINANCIAL AID. Available aid:** Pell grants, SEOG, state scholarships and grants, school scholarships and grants, private scholarships and grants, academic merit scholarships, and athletic scholarships. Perkins Loans (NDSL), PLUS, Stafford Loans (GSL), and SLS. AMS, deferred payment plan, and family tuition reduction.
**Financial aid statistics:** 5% of aid is not need-based. In 1993-94, 100% of all undergraduate applicants received aid; 84% of freshman applicants. Average amounts of aid awarded freshmen: Scholarships and grants, $5,028; loans, $2,920.
**Supporting data/closing dates:** FAFSA: Priority filing date is April 1. School's own aid application: Priority filing date is April 1. Notification of awards on rolling basis.
**Financial aid contact:** Charles Carothers, Ph.D., Director of Financial Aid. 414 352-5400.

**STUDENT EMPLOYMENT.** College Work/Study Program. Institutional employment. 20% of full-time undergraduates work on campus during school year. Students may expect to earn an average of $1,000 during school year. Off-campus part-time employment opportunities rated "excellent."

**COMPUTER FACILITIES.** 60 IBM/IBM-compatible and Macintosh/Apple microcomputers; 20 are networked. Client/LAN operating systems include Apple/Macintosh, DOS. Computer languages and software packages include BASIC, COBOL, dBASE, Lotus 1-2-3, Microsoft Works, MINITAB, Pascal, WordPerfect; 20 in all. Computer facilities are available to all students.
**Fees:** Computer fee is included in tuition/fees.
**Hours:** 8 AM-9 PM (M-Th); 9 AM-4 PM (F-Su).

**GRADUATE CAREER DATA.** Graduate school percentages: 1% enter law school. 1% enter medical school. 10% enter graduate business programs. 5% enter graduate arts and sciences programs. 1% enter theological school/seminary. Highest graduate school enrollments: Cardinal Stritch Coll, Marquette U. 50% of graduates choose careers in business and industry.

**PROMINENT ALUMNI/AE.** Rosemary Hinkfuss, state representative, Wisconsin; Mickey Sadoff, president, Mothers Against Drunk Driving.

# Carroll College

**Waukesha, WI 53186** — **414 547-1211**

**1993-94 Costs.** Tuition: $11,680. Room: $1,870. Board: $1,830. Fees, books, misc. academic expenses (school's estimate): $510.
**Enrollment.** Undergraduates: 485 men, 872 women (full-time). Freshman class: 1,160 applicants, 991 accepted, 352 enrolled. Graduate enrollment: 12 men, 48 women.
**Test score averages/ranges.** N/A.
**Faculty.** 71 full-time; 55 part-time. 73% of faculty holds doctoral degree. Student/faculty ratio: 16 to 1.
**Selectivity rating.** Less competitive.

**PROFILE.** Carroll, founded in 1846, is a church-affiliated, liberal arts college. Its 45-acre campus is located in Waukesha, 15 miles from Milwaukee. The campus includes several 19th- and early 20th-century buildings, the oldest dating from 1885.

**Accreditation:** NCACS. Professionally accredited by the Council on Social Work Education, the National League for Nursing.
**Religious orientation:** Carroll College is affiliated with the United Presbyterian Church; one semester of religion required.
**Library:** Collections totaling over 181,600 volumes, 638 periodical subscriptions, and 16,987 microform items.
**Athletic facilities:** Field house, swimming pool, track, basketball, tennis, and volleyball courts, stadium, weight room, athletic fields.

**STUDENT BODY. Undergraduate profile:** 90% are state residents; 20% are transfers. 2% Asian-American, 5% Black, 3% Hispanic, 89% White, 1% Other. Average age of undergraduates is 21.
**Freshman profile:** 2% of freshmen who took ACT scored 30 or over on composite; 27% scored 24 or over on composite; 81% scored 18 or over on composite; 95% scored 12 or over on composite. 97% of accepted applicants took ACT. 70% of freshmen come from public schools.
**Undergraduate achievement:** 75% of fall 1992 freshmen returned for fall 1993 term. 54% of entering class graduated. 7% of students who completed a degree program went on to graduate study within one year.
**Foreign students:** 16 students are from out of the country. Countries represented include China, France, Honduras, India, Japan, and the United Kingdom; four in all.

**PROGRAMS OF STUDY. Degrees:** B.A., B.S., B.S.Med.Tech., B.S.Nurs.
**Majors:** Accounting, Art, Artificial Intelligence, Biology, Business Administration/Management, Chemistry, Communications, Computer Science/Physics, Criminal Justice, Early Childhood Education, Education, Elementary Education, English, Environmental Science, Fitness Management, French, Geography, German, History, International Relations, Journalism/Mass Communications, Kindergarten Education, Mathematics, Medical Technology, Music, Nursing, Philosophy, Physical Education, Physics, Political Science/Government, Psychology, Religion, Social Work, Sociology, Spanish, Speech Education, Theatre Arts, Theatre Education.
**Distribution of degrees:** The majors with the highest enrollment are business, nursing, and communications; artificial intelligence, computer science/physics, and German have the lowest.
**Requirements:** General education requirement.
**Academic regulations:** Minimum 2.0 GPA must be maintained.
**Special:** Minors offered in most majors and in coaching economics, health education, human services, and women's studies. Completion of two theme-related January terms required. Self-designed majors. Double majors. Dual degrees. Independent study. Accelerated study. Pass/fail grading option. Internships. Graduate school at which undergraduates may take graduate-level courses. Preprofessional programs in law, medicine, veterinary science, pharmacy, dentistry, and theology. Joint B.S.N. degree with Columbia Coll of Nursing/Columbia Hospital. 3-2 engineering/M.Tech program with Marquette U. Washington Semester and UN Semester. Teacher certification in early childhood, elementary, and secondary education. Exchange programs abroad in England (U of Nottingham) and France (U of Caen). Study abroad also in African countries, Australia, Bali, China, Egypt, South American countries, the former Soviet Republics, and Thailand.
**Honors:** Honors program. Honor societies.

**STUDENT LIFE. Housing:** All freshmen and sophomores must live on campus unless living with family. Coed and women's dorms. Fraternity housing. On-campus married-student housing. 58% of students live in college housing.
**Social atmosphere:** On campus, students gather at The PIT and in the main dining room. Off campus, students frequent The Club. Popular annual events include Homecoming and Spring Fling.
**Services and counseling/handicapped student services:** Placement services. Health service. Counseling services for minority students. Birth control and personal counseling. Career and academic guidance services. Religious counseling.
**Campus organizations:** Undergraduate student government. Student newspaper (Perspective, published bimonthly). Literary magazine. Yearbook. Radio station. Carroll Players, Alternate LifeStyle Organization, Commuter Organization, College Activities Board, Habitat for Humanity, Amnesty International, 59 organizations in all. Five fraternities, four chapter houses; four sororities, no chapter houses. 16% of men join a fraternity. 16% of women join a sorority.
**Religious organizations:** Intervarsity Christian Fellowship, Fellowship of Christian Athletes, nondenominational and interfaith groups, Catholic and Lutheran ministries.
**Minority/foreign student organizations:** Black Student Organization. Latin American Student Organization, International Student Organization.

**ATHLETICS. Physical education requirements:** One semester of physical education required.
**Intercollegiate competition:** 30% of students participate. Baseball (M), basketball (M,W), cheerleading (M,W), cross-country (M,W), diving (M,W), football (M), golf (M), soccer (M,W), softball (W), swimming (M,W), tennis (M,W), track (indoor) (M,W), track (outdoor) (M,W), track and field (indoor) (M,W), track and field (outdoor) (M,W), volleyball (W), wrestling (M). Member of MAC, MACW, NCAA Division III.
**Intramural and club sports:** 40% of students participate. Intramural badminton, basketball, flag football, floor hockey, inner-tube water polo, pickleball, softball, tennis, volleyball.

**ADMISSIONS. Academic basis for candidate selection** (in order of priority): Secondary school record, class rank, standardized test scores, school's recommendation, essay.
**Nonacademic basis for candidate selection:** Extracurricular participation is important. Character and personality and particular talent or ability are considered.
**Requirements:** Graduation from secondary school is required; GED is accepted. No specific distribution of secondary school units required. Minimum composite ACT score of 18 (combined SAT score of 850), rank in top half of secondary school class, and minimum 2.5 GPA recommended. College-preparatory curriculum recommended of all applicants. Audition required of music program applicants. Conditional admission possible for applicants not meeting standard requirements. ACT is required; SAT may be substituted. PSAT is recommended. Campus visit and interview recommended. Off-campus interviews available with an admissions representative.
**Procedure:** Take SAT or ACT by March 15 of 12th year. Take ACH by June 15 of 12th year. Visit college for interview by June 15 of 12th year. Application deadline is March 15. Notification of admission on rolling basis. Reply is required within 30 days of acceptance notification or financial aid determination. $200 nonrefundable tuition deposit. $100 room deposit, refundable until July 15. Freshmen accepted for terms other than fall.
**Special programs:** Admission may be deferred one year. Credit and/or placement may be granted through CEEB Advanced Placement exams for scores of 3 or higher. Credit and/or placement may be granted through CLEP general exams. Credit may be granted through CLEP subject exams, Regents College, ACT PEP, and DANTES exams. Credit and placement may be granted through challenge exams. Early entrance/early admission program. Concurrent enrollment program.
**Transfer students:** Transfer students accepted for terms other than fall. In fall 1993, 20% of all new students were transfers into all classes. 326 transfer applications were received, 251 were accepted. Application deadline is August 15 for fall; January 15 for spring. Minimum 2.0 GPA recommended. Lowest course grade accepted is "C." Maximum number of transferable credits is 64 semester hours. At least 32 semester hours must be completed at the college to receive degree.

**Admissions contact:** James Wiseman, Dean of Admission. 414 524-7220.

**FINANCIAL AID. Available aid:** Pell grants, SEOG, state scholarships and grants, school scholarships and grants, private scholarships and grants, academic merit scholarships, and aid for undergraduate foreign students. Perkins Loans (NDSL), PLUS, Stafford Loans (GSL), and SLS. Tuition Plan Inc., Tuition Management Systems, and deferred payment plan. College's 10-month payment plan.
**Financial aid statistics:** 34% of aid is not need-based. In 1993-94, 90% of all undergraduate applicants received aid; 90% of freshman applicants. Average amounts of aid awarded freshmen: Scholarships and grants, $8,200; loans, $2,590.
**Supporting data/closing dates:** FAFSA: Accepted on rolling basis. School's own aid application. Income tax forms: Accepted on rolling basis. Notification of awards on rolling basis.
**Financial aid contact:** Jane Lemke, Director of Student Financial Services. 414 524-7296.

**STUDENT EMPLOYMENT.** College Work/Study Program. Institutional employment. 41% of full-time undergraduates work on campus during school year. Students may expect to earn an average of $875 during school year. Off-campus part-time employment opportunities rated "good."

**COMPUTER FACILITIES.** 200 IBM/IBM-compatible and Macintosh/Apple microcomputers; 120 are networked. Students may access AT&T, SUN minicomputer/mainframe systems, Internet. Residence halls may be equipped with networked microcomputers. Computer languages and software packages include Ada, APL, BASIC, C, COBOL, FORTRAN, LISP, Pascal, Prolog; 25 in all. Computer facilities are available to all students.
**Fees:** None.
**Hours:** 24 hours.

**GRADUATE CAREER DATA.** Graduate school percentages: 1% enter law school. 1% enter medical school. 6% enter graduate arts and sciences programs. Highest graduate school enrollments: Northern Illinois U, U of Wisconsin at LaCrosse, U of Wisconsin at Madison. 30% of graduates choose careers in business and industry. Companies and businesses that hire graduates: GE Medical Systems, Northwestern Mutual Life Insurance.

**PROMINENT ALUMNI/AE.** Alfred Lunt, actor; Ricardo Diaz and Howard Fuller, public service.

# Carthage College

**Kenosha, WI 53140-1994 414 551-8500**

**1994-95 Costs.** Tuition: $13,125. Room & board: $3,775. Fees, books, misc. academic expenses (school's estimate): $500.
**Enrollment.** Undergraduates: 642 men, 763 women (full-time). Freshman class: 1,583 applicants, 1,427 accepted, 434 enrolled. Graduate enrollment: 13 men, 56 women.
**Test score averages/ranges.** Average SAT scores: 460 verbal, 520 math. Range of SAT scores of middle 50%: 390-540 verbal, 430-600 math. Average ACT scores: 22 English, 21 math, 22 composite. Range of ACT scores of middle 50%: 19-25 English, 18-25 math.
**Faculty.** 85 full-time; 50 part-time. 89% of faculty holds doctoral degree. Student/faculty ratio: 15 to 1.
**Selectivity rating.** Less competitive.

**PROFILE.** Carthage is a church-affiliated, liberal arts college. Founded in 1847 in Hillsboro, Ill., it moved to its present location in 1962. Its 72-acre campus is located beside Lake Michigan, 40 miles from Milwaukee and 60 miles from Chicago.

**Accreditation:** NCACS. Professionally accredited by the Council on Social Work Education, the National Association of Schools of Music.
**Religious orientation:** Carthage College is affiliated with the Evangelical Lutheran Church in America; two semesters of religion required.
**Library:** Collections totaling over 208,539 volumes, 1,081 periodical subscriptions, and 21,352 microform items.
**Special facilities/museums:** Language lab, civil war museum, science research lab.
**Athletic facilities:** Indoor and outdoor track, field house, tennis courts, natatorium.

**STUDENT BODY. Undergraduate profile:** 64% are state residents; 18% are transfers. 1% Asian-American, 6% Black, 2% Hispanic, 91% White. Average age of undergraduates is 18.
**Freshman profile:** 6% of freshmen who took ACT scored 30 or over on English, 4% scored 30 or over on math, 4% scored 30 or over on composite; 34% scored 24 or over on English, 31% scored 24 or over on math, 38% scored 24 or over on composite; 82% scored 18 or over on English, 80% scored 18 or over on math, 91% scored 18 or over on composite; 100% scored 12 or over on English, 100% scored 12 or over on math, 100% scored 12 or over on composite. 5% of accepted applicants took SAT; 95% took ACT. 80% of freshmen come from public schools.
**Undergraduate achievement:** 72% of fall 1992 freshmen returned for fall 1993 term. 50% of entering class graduated. 17% of students who completed a degree program went on to graduate study within one year.
**Foreign students:** 20 students are from out of the country. Countries represented include England, France, Germany, Japan, Namibia, and Spain; nine in all.

**PROGRAMS OF STUDY. Degrees:** B.A.
**Majors:** Accounting, Art, Athletic Training, Biology, Business Administration/Management, Chemistry, Cognitive Disabilities, Communication/Performing Arts, Criminal Justice, Economics, Elementary Education, English, French, Geography, German, Graphic Design, History, International Business, Learning Disabilities, Marketing Management/Research, Mathematics, Modern Languages, Music, Philosophy, Physical Education, Physics, Political Science/Government, Psychology, Recreation/Sports/Fitness Management, Religion, Social Sciences, Social Work, Sociology, Spanish.
**Distribution of degrees:** The majors with the highest enrollment are business administration, education, English, and psychology; mathematics and Spanish have the lowest.
**Requirements:** General education requirement.
**Academic regulations:** Minimum 2.0 GPA must be maintained.
**Special:** Minors offered in most majors and in computer studies and Japanese. Certificates offered in coaching and secondary education. Self-designed majors. Double majors. Dual degrees. Independent study. Internships. Preprofessional programs in law, medicine, veterinary science, pharmacy, dentistry, theology, and optometry. 3-1 and 4-1 medical technology programs with approved hospitals. 3-2 occupational therapy program with Washington U. 3-2 engineering programs with Case Western Reserve U, Washington U, and U of Wisconsin - Madison. Washington Semester. Teacher certification in elementary, secondary, and special education. Certification in specific subject areas. Study abroad in England, France, Italy, Japan, Spain, Wales, other European countries, and Mexico.
**Honors:** Honors program. Honor societies.
**Academic Assistance:** Remedial study skills. Nonremedial tutoring.

**STUDENT LIFE. Housing:** All unmarried students under age 21 must live on campus unless living near campus with relatives. Coed and women's dorms. 80% of students live in college housing.
**Social atmosphere:** Favorite gathering spots include Stars N Stripes restaurant, the Spot, Ron's Place, PT's, the View, WHO's, and Regency Mall. Greeks, along with the football, baseball, and basketball teams are among the groups with a significant influence on student life. Popular social events include Casino Night, Greek Week, May Madness, Winter Wonderland, Homecoming, Pals 'n Partner, skiing, body surfing, and ice skating.
**Services and counseling/handicapped student services:** Placement services. Health service. Personal and psychological counseling. Career and academic guidance services. Religious counseling. Physically disabled student services. Learning disabled services. Tutors.
**Campus organizations:** Undergraduate student government. Student newspaper (Arrow, published once/week). Literary magazine. Yearbook. Choir, cheerleading, band, theatre, Student Education Association, SADD, professional and services groups, 60 organizations in all. Eight fraternities, no chapter houses; four sororities, no chapter houses. 18% of men join a fraternity. 25% of women join a sorority.
**Religious organizations:** Campus Ministry Council, Living Hope, Christian Fellowship.
**Minority/foreign student organizations:** Black Student Union, Women of Color. International Friendship Society.

**ATHLETICS. Physical education requirements:** One semester of physical education required.
**Intercollegiate competition:** 30% of students participate. Baseball (M), basketball (M,W), cheerleading (W), cross-country (M,W), football (M), golf (M,W), softball (W), swimming (M,W), tennis (M,W), track (indoor) (M,W), track (outdoor) (M,W), track and field (indoor) (M,W), track and field (outdoor) (M,W), volleyball (W), wrestling (M). Member of College Conference of Illinois and Wisconsin, NCAA Division III.
**Intramural and club sports:** 50% of students participate. Intramural basketball, flag football, softball, swimming, table tennis, volleyball. Men's club ice hockey, soccer. Women's club soccer.

**ADMISSIONS. Academic basis for candidate selection** (in order of priority): Secondary school record, standardized test scores, class rank, school's recommendation, essay.
**Nonacademic basis for candidate selection:** Character and personality, extracurricular participation, and particular talent or ability are emphasized. Geographical distribution and alumni/ae relationship are considered.
**Requirements:** Graduation from secondary school is required; GED is accepted. 16 units and the following program of study are required: 4 units of English, 2 units of math, 2 units of science, 2 units of social studies, 4 units of academic electives. Minimum composite ACT score of 18, rank in top half of secondary school class, and minimum 2.0 GPA recommended. Portfolio required of art scholarship applicants. Admissions interview required of some applicants. Audition required of music scholarship applicants. Summer challenge program for applicants not normally admissible. ACT is required; SAT may be substituted. Campus visit and interview recommended. Off-campus interviews available with an admissions representative.
**Procedure:** Take SAT or ACT by October of 12th year. Visit college for interview by December of 12th year. Suggest filing application by December 1; no deadline. Notification of admission on rolling basis. Reply is required by May 1. $200 tuition deposit, refundable until May 1. Freshmen accepted for terms other than fall.
**Special programs:** Admission may be deferred two years. Credit may be granted through CEEB Advanced Placement for scores of 3 or higher. Credit may be granted through CLEP general and subject exams, DANTES exams, and military experience. Credit and placement may be granted through challenge exams. Early decision program. Deadline for applying for early decision is October 1. Early entrance/early admission program. Concurrent enrollment program.
**Transfer students:** Transfer students accepted for terms other than fall. In fall 1993, 18% of all new students were transfers into all classes. 188 transfer applications were received, 183 were accepted. Application deadline is rolling for fall; rolling for spring. Minimum 2.0 GPA required. Lowest course grade accepted is "C." Maximum number of transferable credits is 68 semester hours from a two-year school and 104 semester hours from a four-year school. At least 32 semester hours must be completed at the college to receive degree.
**Admissions contact:** Brenda A. Porter, Vice President for Enrollment. 414 551-6000.

**FINANCIAL AID. Available aid:** Pell grants, SEOG, state scholarships and grants, school scholarships and grants, private scholarships and grants, and academic merit scholarships. Perkins Loans (NDSL), PLUS, Stafford Loans (GSL), school loans, private loans, and SLS. Institutional payment plan.
**Financial aid statistics:** 12% of aid is not need-based. In 1993-94, 92% of all undergraduate applicants received aid; 83% of freshman applicants. Average amounts of aid awarded freshmen: Scholarships and grants, $7,600; loans, $2,512.
**Supporting data/closing dates:** FAFSA: Priority filing date is February 15; accepted on rolling basis. Notification of awards on rolling basis.
**Financial aid contact:** Steve Klein, M.A., Director of Financial Aid. 414 551-6001.

**STUDENT EMPLOYMENT.** College Work/Study Program. Institutional employment. 59% of full-time undergraduates work on campus during school year. Students may expect to earn an average of $1,000 during school year. Off-campus part-time employment opportunities rated "good."

**COMPUTER FACILITIES.** 70 IBM/IBM-compatible and Macintosh/Apple microcomputers; 63 are networked. Students may access Internet. Residence halls may be equipped with stand-alone microcomputers, networked microcomputers. Client/LAN operating systems include Apple/Macintosh, DOS, Windows NT, Banyan, LocalTalk/AppleTalk. Computer languages and software packages include Assembler, BASIC, COBOL, dBASE, FORTRAN, Lotus 1-2-3, MacPaint, Microsoft Word, Microsoft Works, Pascal, QuarkXPress, Quattro Pro, SPSS, SuperPaint, WordPerfect; 15 in all. Computer facilities are available to all students.
**Fees:** None.
**Hours:** 24 hours.

**GRADUATE CAREER DATA.** Graduate school percentages: 1% enter law school. 2% enter medical school. 2% enter graduate business programs. 11% enter graduate arts and sciences programs. 1% enter theological school/seminary. Highest graduate school enrollments: U of Illinois, Marquette U, National Louis U, U of Wisconsin. 44% of graduates choose careers in business and industry. Companies and businesses that hire graduates: Abbot Labs, Johnson Wax, Snap-On Tools, Western Publishing.

**PROMINENT ALUMNI/AE.** Alden Clausen, chairman and CEO (retired), Bank America; Masato Mizuno, president, Mizuno Corp.; Edward Smeds, president for customer service and operations, Kraft General Foods.

## Concordia University Wisconsin

**Mequon, WI 53097** **414 243-5700**

**1994-95 Costs.** Tuition: $9,300. Room & board: $3,400. Fees, books, misc. academic expenses (school's estimate): $525.
**Enrollment.** Undergraduates: 1,870 (full-time). Freshman class: 845 applicants, 690 accepted, 288 enrolled. Graduate enrollment: 150.
**Test score averages/ranges.** Average ACT scores: 22 composite. Range of ACT scores of middle 50%: 18-24 composite.
**Faculty.** 75 full-time; 60 part-time. 52% of faculty holds doctoral degree. Student/faculty ratio: 19 to 1.
**Selectivity rating.** Less competitive.

**PROFILE.** Concordia, founded in 1881, is a church-affiliated, liberal arts university. Its 126-acre campus is located in suburban Mequon, 15 miles from Milwaukee.

**Accreditation:** NCACS. Professionally accredited by the American Bar Association, the National League for Nursing.
**Religious orientation:** Concordia University Wisconsin is affiliated with the Lutheran Church–Missouri Synod; three semesters of theology required.
**Library:** Collections totaling over 80,000 volumes, 750 periodical subscriptions, and 7,000 microform items.
**Athletic facilities:** Gymnasium, stadium, field house, tracks, baseball, football, practice, soccer, and softball fields, basketball and tennis courts, training and weight rooms.

**STUDENT BODY. Undergraduate profile:** 85% are state residents; 28% are transfers. 1% Asian-American, 4% Black, 1% Hispanic, 1% Native American, 93% White. Average age of undergraduates is 21.
**Freshman profile:** Majority of accepted applicants took ACT. 66% of freshmen come from public schools.
**Undergraduate achievement:** 78% of fall 1992 freshmen returned for fall 1993 term. 45% of entering class graduated.
**Foreign students:** 93 students are from out of the country. Countries represented include China, India, Israel, Japan, Singapore, and Taiwan; 25 in all.

**PROGRAMS OF STUDY. Degrees:** B.A., B.S., B.S.Nurs.
**Majors:** Accounting, Athletic Training, Biology, Business, Business Education, Computer Engineering, Court Reporting, Early Childhood Education, Elementary Education, Engineering, English, History, Humanities, Individualized Major, Interior Design, Justice/Public Policy, Lay Ministry, Marketing, Mass Communications, Mathematics, Music, Natural Science/Mathematics, Nursing, Occupational Therapy, Paralegal, Parish Music, Pastoral Ministry, Physical Education, Psychology, Secondary Education, Social Science, Social Work, Sports Medicine, Theological Languages, Theology.
**Distribution of degrees:** The majors with the highest enrollment are business, education, and nursing; engineering and history have the lowest.
**Requirements:** General education requirement.
**Academic regulations:** Minimum 2.0 GPA must be maintained.
**Special:** Minors offered in some majors and in art, aviation science, church administration, coaching athletics, computer science, evangelism, older adults ministry, parish teaching, social ministry/visitation, Spanish, and youth ministry. Associate's degrees offered. Self-designed majors. Double majors. Dual degrees. Independent study. Pass/fail grading option. Internships. Preprofessional programs in law, medicine, theology, sports medicine, nursing, and seminary. 2-2 interior design and agribusiness programs. 3-2 engineering programs with Marquette U and U of Wisconsin at Milwaukee. Exchange programs with Cardinal Stritch Coll and Mount Mary Coll. Teacher certification in early childhood, elementary, and secondary education. Certification in specific subject areas. Study abroad in China, Germany, India, Israel, Mexico, and Taiwan. Global Education Program requires all students to travel abroad; cost is included in tuition.
**Honors:** Honor societies.
**Academic Assistance:** Remedial writing and math. Nonremedial tutoring.

**STUDENT LIFE. Housing:** Students may live on or off campus. Women's and men's dorms. 60% of students live in college housing.
**Social atmosphere:** The student newspaper reports: "Concordia is a very small campus with a high school atmosphere. Students who live in the dorms know each other well." Students tend to congregate at the cafeteria and the Miedleburg commuter lounge. Off-campus gathering spots include Attractions, Circle B. Grafton, and Judges. Student government, athletes, and the Student Activities Board are influential groups on campus. Homecoming, Pennyfest, and Springfest are popular events during the school year.
**Services and counseling/handicapped student services:** Placement services. Health service. Day care. Counseling services for minority students. Personal and psychological counseling. Career and academic guidance services. Religious counseling. Physically disabled student services. Tutors.
**Campus organizations:** Undergraduate student government. Student newspaper (Beacon, published once/month). Literary magazine. Yearbook. Radio station. Chorale, band, Kammerchor, Alleluia Ringers, drama groups, Student Life Board, business and recreational groups, 20 organizations in all.
**Religious organizations:** Spiritual Life Board, Sword.
**Minority/foreign student organizations:** Ebony, Minority Student Organization. Foreign Student Organization.

**ATHLETICS. Physical education requirements:** Two semesters of physical education required.
**Intercollegiate competition:** 25% of students participate. Baseball (M), basketball (M,W), cheerleading (M,W), cross-country (M,W), football (M), golf (M), soccer (M), softball (W), tennis (M,W), track (indoor) (M,W), track (outdoor) (M,W), track and field (indoor) (M,W), track and field (outdoor) (M,W), volleyball (W). Member of Illini-Badger-Hawkeye Football Conference, Lake Michigan Conference, NAIA.
**Intramural and club sports:** 50% of students participate. Intramural basketball, softball, tennis, track, volleyball. Men's club wrestling. Women's club soccer.

**ADMISSIONS. Academic basis for candidate selection** (in order of priority): Secondary school record, standardized test scores, class rank, school's recommendation, essay.
**Nonacademic basis for candidate selection:** Character and personality are important. Extracurricular participation, particular talent or ability, and alumni/ae relationship are considered.
**Requirements:** Graduation from secondary school is required; GED is accepted. 16 units and the following program of study are required: 3 units of English, 2 units of math, 2 units of science, 2 units of foreign language, 2 units of social studies, 5 units of academic electives. Minimum composite ACT score of 16, rank in top half of secondary school class, and minimum 2.25 GPA required. Developmental Program for students not normally admissible. ACT is required; SAT may be substituted. Campus visit and interview recommended. Off-campus interviews available with an admissions representative.
**Procedure:** Take SAT or ACT by September of 12th year. Visit college for interview by February of 12th year. Notification of admission on rolling basis. Reply is required by May 1. $100 nonrefundable tuition deposit. $160 nonrefundable room deposit. Freshmen accepted for terms other than fall.
**Special programs:** Credit and/or placement may be granted through CLEP general and subject exams. Concurrent enrollment program.
**Transfer students:** Transfer students accepted for terms other than fall. In fall 1993, 28% of all new students were transfers into all classes. 260 transfer applications were received, 202 were accepted. Application deadline is August 1 for fall; January 1 for spring. Minimum 2.0 GPA required. Lowest course grade accepted is "C." Maximum number of transferable credits is 90 semester hours. At least 36 semester hours must be completed at the university to receive degree.
**Admissions contact:** William H. Ebel, M.S., Director of Admissions. 414 243-4300.

**FINANCIAL AID. Available aid:** Pell grants, SEOG, state scholarships and grants, school scholarships and grants, private scholarships and grants, and academic merit scholarships. PLUS, Stafford Loans (GSL), and SLS. Tuition Management Systems.
**Financial aid statistics:** Average amounts of aid awarded freshmen: Scholarships and grants, $4,028; loans, $2,625.
**Supporting data/closing dates:** FAFSA: Priority filing date is May 1. School's own aid application: Priority filing date is May 1. Income tax forms: Priority filing date is May 1. Notification of awards on rolling basis.
**Financial aid contact:** Ed Schroeder, M.A., Director of Financial Aid. 414 243-4348.

**STUDENT EMPLOYMENT.** College Work/Study Program. Institutional employment. 25% of full-time undergraduates work on campus during school year. Students may expect to earn an average of $1,400 during school year. Off-campus part-time employment opportunities rated "good."

**COMPUTER FACILITIES.** 90 IBM/IBM-compatible and Macintosh/Apple microcomputers; 30 are networked. Computer languages and software packages include BASIC, C, FORTRAN, Pascal; communications, graphics, file management, spreadsheet, word processing programs; 25 in all. Computer facilities are available to all students.
**Fees:** Computer fee is included in tuition/fees.
**Hours:** 7 AM-11 PM.

**GRADUATE CAREER DATA.** Highest graduate school enrollments: Marquette U, U of Wisconsin at Milwaukee. 50% of graduates choose careers in business and industry.

## Edgewood College

**Madison, WI 53711** **608 257-4861**

**1994-95 Costs.** Tuition: $8,500. Room: $1,600. Board: $2,100. Fees, books, misc. academic expenses (school's estimate): $700.
**Enrollment.** Undergraduates: 225 men, 601 women (full-time). Freshman class: 375 applicants, 311 accepted, 143 enrolled. Graduate enrollment: 173 men, 214 women.
**Test score averages/ranges.** Average ACT scores: 21 composite. Range of ACT scores of middle 50%: 17-22 English, 16-21 math.
**Faculty.** 53 full-time; 59 part-time. 41% of faculty holds doctoral degree. Student/faculty ratio: 15 to 1.
**Selectivity rating.** Less competitive.

**PROFILE.** Edgewood, founded in 1927, is a church-affiliated college. Its 55-acre campus is located in a residential area of Madison.

**Accreditation:** NCACS. Professionally accredited by the American Assembly of Collegiate Schools of Business, the National Council for Accreditation of Teacher Education, the National League for Nursing.
**Religious orientation:** Edgewood College is affiliated with the Roman Catholic Church; no religious requirements.
**Library:** Collections totaling over 60,794 volumes, 470 periodical subscriptions, and 81,224 microform items.
**Special facilities/museums:** Nursery, elementary, and high schools for student teachers and psychology majors, satellite dish.
**Athletic facilities:** Gymnasium, tennis courts, baseball, soccer, and softball fields, golf course.

**STUDENT BODY. Undergraduate profile:** 85% are state residents; 50% are transfers. 3.8% Asian-American, 1.9% Black, .8% Hispanic, .2% Native American, 69.5% White, 23.8% Other. Average age of undergraduates is 25.
**Freshman profile:** 2% of accepted applicants took SAT; 96% took ACT. 75% of freshmen come from public schools.
**Undergraduate achievement:** 80% of fall 1992 freshmen returned for fall 1993 term. 16% of students who completed a degree program immediately went on to graduate study.
**Foreign students:** 65 students are from out of the country. Countries represented include Hong Kong, Indonesia, Japan, Korea, and Thailand; 28 in all.

**PROGRAMS OF STUDY. Degrees:** B.A., B.S.
**Majors:** Accounting, American Studies, Art, Art Therapy, Biology, Broad Field Social Studies, Business, Business/Computer Information Systems, Chemistry, Child Life, Childhood Education, Computer Information Systems, Criminal Justice, Cytotechnology, Economics, Elementary Education, English, French, History, Individualized Majors, International Relations, Medical Technology, Music, Natural Science/Mathematics, Nursing, Performing Arts, Psychology, Public Policy/Administration, Religious Studies, Sociology, Spanish.
**Distribution of degrees:** The majors with the highest enrollment are business, elementary education, and nursing; biology, art, and performing arts have the lowest.
**Requirements:** General education requirement.
**Academic regulations:** Minimum 2.0 GPA must be maintained.
**Special:** Minors in many majors and in communication arts, computer science, philosophy, political science, secondary education, and women's studies. Associate's degrees offered. Self-designed majors. Double majors. Dual degrees. Independent study. Pass/fail grading option. Internships. Preprofessional programs in law, medicine, veterinary science, pharmacy, dentistry, theology, engineering, and social work. Pre-engineering program with U of Wisconsin at Madison and Marquette U. Wisconsin Association of Independent Colleges. Exchange program with U of Wisconsin at Madison. Teacher certification in early childhood, elementary, secondary, and special education. Certification in specific subject areas. Exchange programs abroad in the Czech Republic/Slovakia (Masaryk U), France (Nantes Business Sch), and Finland (Alkio Opisto).
**Honors:** Honors program. Honor societies.
**Academic Assistance:** Remedial reading, writing, math, and study skills. Nonremedial tutoring.

**ADMISSIONS. Academic basis for candidate selection** (in order of priority): Secondary school record, standardized test scores, class rank, school's recommendation, essay.
**Nonacademic basis for candidate selection:** Extracurricular participation and particular talent or ability are considered.
**Requirements:** Graduation from secondary school is required; GED is accepted. 16 units and the following program of study are recommended: 4 units of English, 3 units of math, 2 units of science, 2 units of foreign language, 2 units of social studies, 3 units of electives. Minimum composite ACT score of 18, rank in top three-fifths of secondary school class, and minimum 2.0 GPA recommended. 1 unit each of algebra, geometry, biology, and chemistry and minimum 2.5 GPA in these areas recommended of nursing program applicants. Conditional admission possible for applicants not meeting standard requirements. ACT is required; SAT may be substituted. Campus visit and interview recommended. Off-campus interviews available with an admissions representative.
**Procedure:** Take SAT or ACT by June of 12th year. Visit college for interview by April 1 of 12th year. Suggest filing application by August 1; no deadline. Notification of admission on rolling basis. $100 tuition deposit, refundable until June 1. $100 room deposit, refundable until July 1. Freshmen accepted for terms other than fall.
**Special programs:** Admission may be deferred one semester. Credit and/or placement may be granted through CEEB Advanced Placement exams for scores of 3 or higher. Credit may be granted through CLEP general and subject exams, ACT PEP, DANTES, and challenge exams, and military and life experience. Concurrent enrollment program.
**Transfer students:** Transfer students accepted for terms other than fall. In fall 1993, 50% of all new students were transfers into all classes. 356 transfer applications were received, 246 were accepted. Application deadline is August 1 for fall; December 15 for spring. Minimum 2.0 GPA required. Lowest course grade accepted is "C." Maximum number of transferable credits is 60 semester hours from a two-year school and 88 semester hours from a four-year school. At least 32 semester hours must be completed at the college to receive degree.
**Admissions contact:** Kevin C. Kucera, B.S., Director of Admissions and Financial Aid. 800 444-4861.

**FINANCIAL AID. Available aid:** Pell grants, SEOG, state scholarships and grants, school scholarships and grants, private scholarships and grants, and academic merit scholarships. Perkins Loans (NDSL), PLUS, Stafford Loans (GSL), and SLS. Deferred payment plan.
**Financial aid statistics:** 25% of aid is not need-based. In 1993-94, 90% of all undergraduate applicants received aid; 90% of freshmen applicants. Average amounts of aid awarded freshmen: Scholarships and grants, $4,000; loans, $2,400.
**Supporting data/closing dates:** FAFSA: Accepted on rolling basis. FAF: Priority filing date is March 15; accepted on rolling basis. School's own aid application: Priority filing date is March 15. Income tax forms: Accepted on rolling basis. Notification of awards on rolling basis.

# Lakeland College

**Sheboygan, WI 53082-0359** 414 565-2111

**1994-95 Costs.** Tuition: $9,400. Room: $1,815. Board: $2,190. Fees, books, misc. academic expenses (school's estimate): $725.
**Enrollment.** Undergraduates: 358 men, 426 women (full-time). Freshman class: 421 applicants, 383 accepted, 180 enrolled. Graduate enrollment: 5 men, 20 women.
**Test score averages/ranges.** Average ACT scores: 20 English, 19 math, 20 composite. Range of ACT scores of middle 50%: 17-23 English, 17-22 math.
**Faculty.** 43 full-time; 122 part-time. 74% of faculty holds highest degree in specific field. Student/faculty ratio: 15 to 1.
**Selectivity rating.** Less competitive.

**PROFILE.** Lakeland, founded in 1862, is a church-affiliated, liberal arts college. Its 145-acre campus is located on the Sheboygan River, 60 miles north of Milwaukee.

**Accreditation:** NCACS.
**Religious orientation:** Lakeland College is affiliated with the United Church of Christ; one semester of religion required.
**Library:** Collections totaling over 62,274 volumes, 284 periodical subscriptions, and 26,664 microform items.
**Special facilities/museums:** Museum of college history.
**Athletic facilities:** Gymnasium, field house, baseball, football, practice, soccer, and softball fields, basketball, tennis, and volleyball courts, weight room, performance labs, saunas.

**STUDENT BODY. Undergraduate profile:** 90% are state residents; 30% are transfers. 1% Asian-American, 6% Black, 1% Hispanic, 1% Native American, 88% White, 3% Other.
**Freshman profile:** 4% of freshmen who took ACT scored 30 or over on English, 1% scored 30 or over on math, 2% scored 30 or over on composite; 21% scored 24 or over on English, 17% scored 24 or over on math, 18% scored 24 or over on composite; 72% scored 18 or over on English, 64% scored 18 or over on math, 78% scored 18 or over on composite; 100% scored 12 or over on English, 100% scored 12 or over on math, 100% scored 12 or over on composite. 14% of accepted applicants took SAT; 92% took ACT.
**Undergraduate achievement:** 65% of fall 1991 freshmen returned for fall 1992 term. 41% of entering class graduated. 5% of students who completed a degree program immediately went on to graduate study.
**Foreign students:** Seven students are from out of the country. Countries represented include Japan and Taiwan; four in all.

**PROGRAMS OF STUDY. Degrees:** B.A.
**Majors:** Accounting, Art, Biology, Broad Field Behavioral Science, Broad Field History, Business Administration, Chemistry, Church Administration, Computer/Information Sciences, Computer Science, Early Childhood Education, Economics, Elementary Education, Engineering, English Literature, Exercise Science/Sport Studies, Fine Arts Administration, German, History, Hospitality Management, International Business, Marketing, Mathematics, Medical Technology, Music, Philosophy, Pre-Dentistry, Pre-Law, Pre-Medicine, Pre-Ministry, Pre-Pharmacy, Psychology, Public Policy Administration, Religion, Research Analyst Administration, Secondary Education, Social Welfare, Sociology, Specialized Administration, Theatre, Writing.
**Distribution of degrees:** The majors with the highest enrollment are business administration, accounting, and computer science.
**Requirements:** General education requirement.
**Academic regulations:** Freshmen must maintain minimum 1.75 GPA; sophomores, juniors, seniors, 2.0 GPA.
**Special:** Minors offered in some majors and in anthropology, coaching, and Spanish. Double majors. Dual degrees. Internships. Preprofessional programs in law, medicine, veterinary science, pharmacy, dentistry, and theology. 2-3 pharmacy and engineering programs with U of Wisconsin at Madison. Washington Semester. Teacher certification in early childhood, elementary, and secondary education. Certification in specific subject areas. Exchange programs abroad in Germany (Gesamthochschule) and Japan.
**Honors:** Honors program.
**Academic Assistance:** Remedial reading, writing, math, and study skills.

**ADMISSIONS. Academic basis for candidate selection** (in order of priority): Standardized test scores, secondary school record, class rank, essay, school's recommendation.
**Nonacademic basis for candidate selection:** Character and personality, extracurricular participation, particular talent or ability, geographical distribution, and alumni/ae relationship are considered.
**Requirements:** Graduation from secondary school is required; GED is accepted. 16 units and the following program of study are recommended: 4 units of English, 2 units of math, 2 units of science, 2 units of foreign language, 2 units of social studies, 2 units of history, 2 units of electives. Minimum composite ACT score of 19, rank in top half of secondary school class, and minimum 2.0 GPA required. ACT is required; SAT may be substituted. Campus visit and interview recommended. Off-campus interviews available with an admissions representative.
**Procedure:** Take SAT or ACT by August 15 of 12th year. Visit college for interview by August 15 of 12th year. Application deadline is August 15. Notification of admission on rolling basis. Reply is required by August 15. $100 nonrefundable tuition deposit. Freshmen accepted for terms other than fall.
**Special programs:** Admission may be deferred one semester. Credit and/or placement may be granted through CEEB Advanced Placement exams for scores of 3 or higher. Credit may be granted through CLEP general exams. Credit and/or placement may be granted through CLEP subject exams. Placement may be granted through challenge exams. Credit and placement may be granted through DANTES exams.

**Transfer students:** Transfer students accepted for terms other than fall. In fall 1992, 30% of all new students were transfers into all classes. 142 transfer applications were received, 139 were accepted. Application deadline is August 15 for fall; January 15 for spring. Minimum 2.0 GPA required. Lowest course grade accepted is "C." Maximum number of transferable credits is 64 semester hours from a two-year school and 96 semester hours from a four-year school. At least 40 semester hours must be completed at the college to receive degree.
**Admissions contact:** Lyle Krueger, Vice President. 414 565-1217.

**FINANCIAL AID. Available aid:** Pell grants, SEOG, state scholarships and grants, school scholarships and grants, private scholarships, academic merit scholarships, and aid for undergraduate foreign students. Athletic grants. Perkins Loans (NDSL), PLUS, Stafford Loans (GSL), and SLS. Interest-free tuition payment plan.
**Financial aid statistics:** 12% of aid is not need-based. In 1992-93, 95% of all undergraduate applicants received aid; 93% of freshman applicants. Average amounts of aid awarded freshmen: Scholarships and grants, $3,500; loans, $2,453.
**Supporting data/closing dates:** FAFSA/FAF: Priority filing date is May 1; accepted on rolling basis. Income tax forms: Priority filing date is May 1; accepted on rolling basis. Notification of awards on rolling basis.
**Financial aid contact:** Don Seymour, Director of Financial Aid. 414 565-1297. 9-21

# Lawrence University

**Appleton, WI 54912** **414 832-7000**

**1994-95 Costs.** Tuition: $17,163. Room: $1,812. Board: $2,079. Fees, books, misc. academic expenses (school's estimate): $1,215.
**Enrollment.** Undergraduates: 548 men, 614 women (full-time). Freshman class: 1,243 applicants, 947 accepted, 325 enrolled.
**Test score averages/ranges.** Range of SAT scores of middle 50%: 480-630 verbal, 530-670 math. Range of ACT scores of middle 50%: 24-29 English, 23-27 math.
**Faculty.** 105 full-time; 24 part-time. 92% of faculty holds highest degree in specific field. Student/faculty ratio: 11 to 1.
**Selectivity rating.** Highly competitive.

**PROFILE.** Lawrence, founded in 1847, is a private, liberal arts university. Its 84-acre campus is located near downtown Appleton, 100 miles north of Milwaukee.

**Accreditation:** NCACS. Professionally accredited by the National Association of Schools of Music.
**Religious orientation:** Lawrence University is nonsectarian; no religious requirements.
**Library:** Collections totaling over 326,000 volumes, 1,297 periodical subscriptions, and 102,000 microform items.
**Special facilities/museums:** Art galleries, anthropology collection, 325-acre estate on Lake Michigan, electron microscope, laser physics lab, physics/computational graphics lab, nuclear magnetic resonance spectrometer.
**Athletic facilities:** Gymnasium, baseball and football stadiums, tracks, baseball, lacrosse, soccer, and softball fields, swimming pool, diving well, basketball, handball, racquetball, squash, and volleyball courts, batting cages, exercise, training, weight, and wrestling rooms, dance studio, saunas.

**STUDENT BODY. Undergraduate profile:** 44% are state residents; 5% are transfers. 3% Asian-American, 2% Black, 2% Hispanic, 1% Native American, 82% White, 10% Foreign. Average age of undergraduates is 20.
**Freshman profile:** 76% of accepted applicants took SAT; 69% took ACT. 80% of freshmen come from public schools.
**Undergraduate achievement:** 87% of fall 1992 freshmen returned for fall 1993 term. 65% of entering class graduated. 27% of students who completed a degree program immediately went on to graduate study.
**Foreign students:** 112 students are from out of the country. Countries represented include Bangladesh, China, India, Japan, the Netherlands, and Sweden; 46 in all.

**PROGRAMS OF STUDY. Degrees:** B.A., B.Mus.
**Majors:** Anthropology, Art History, Biology, Chemistry, Classics, Computer Science, East Asian Languages/Cultures, Economics, English, French, Geology, German, Government, History, Mathematics, Music, Music Education, Music Performance, Music Theory/Composition, Philosophy, Physics, Psychology, Religious Studies, Secondary Education, Slavic, Spanish, Studio Art, Theatre/Drama.
**Distribution of degrees:** The majors with the highest enrollment are government, biology, and English; East Asian language/culture, music theory/composition, and music education have the lowest.
**Requirements:** General education requirement.
**Academic regulations:** Freshmen must maintain minimum 1.83 GPA; sophomores, juniors, seniors, 2.00 GPA.
**Special:** Interdisciplinary majors in computer, environmental, and international studies and in linguistics, neuroscience, and public policy analysis. Music major offers professional curriculum. Over 600 tutorials or independent study programs each year. Approximately 90% of student body work individually with faculty members before graduation. Self-designed majors. Double majors. Dual degrees. Independent study. Pass/fail grading option. Internships. Preprofessional programs in law, medicine, and dentistry. 2-2 and 3-2 B.A./B.S.N. programs in allied health sciences and nursing with Rush Medical U. 3-2 B.A./B.S. engineering programs with Columbia U, U of Michigan, Rensselaer Polytech Inst, and Washington U. 3-2 B.A./M.A. social service administration program with U of Chicago. 3-2 B.A./M.S. environmental studies and forestry program with Duke U. Member of Associated Colleges of the Midwest. Washington Semester. Chicago Semester in the Arts. Newberry Library Program in the Humanities (Illinois). Oak Ridge Science Semester (Tennessee). Urban Studies Program (Chicago). Urban Education Program (Chicago). Other semester-away programs. Teacher certification in elementary and secondary education. Certification in specific subject areas. Study abroad in China, Costa Rica, the Czech Republic, Ecuador, England, France, Germany, India, Italy, Japan, Russia, Spain, and Zimbabwe.
**Honors:** Phi Beta Kappa. Honor societies.
**Academic Assistance:** Remedial writing, math, and study skills. Nonremedial tutoring.

**STUDENT LIFE. Housing:** All unmarried students under age 24 must live on campus unless living with family. Coed and women's dorms. Fraternity housing. School-owned/operated apartments. On-campus married-student housing. Theme houses. 97% of students live in college housing.
**Services and counseling/handicapped student services:** Health service. Counseling services for minority students. Personal and psychological counseling. Career and academic guidance services.
**Campus organizations:** Undergraduate student government. Student newspaper (Lawrentian, published once/week). Literary magazine. Yearbook. Radio station. Symphonic band, orchestra, wind and jazz ensembles, concert choir, chamber singers, opera theatre, brass choir, chorus, Artists Association, film society, Circle K, sailing and ski clubs, College Republicans, Young Democrats, outdoor recreation club, 120 organizations in all. Five fraternities, all with chapter houses; three sororities, no chapter houses. 42% of men join a fraternity. 24% of women join a sorority.
**Religious organizations:** Campus Crusade for Christ, Chavurah, Christian Fellowship, Christian Science Organization, Unitarian Universalist Fellowship.
**Minority/foreign student organizations:** Black Organization of Students. International student group, Asian cultural group, African theatre.

**ATHLETICS. Physical education requirements:** None.
**Intercollegiate competition:** 37% of students participate. Baseball (M), basketball (M,W), cross-country (M,W), diving (M,W), football (M), golf (M), ice hockey (M), soccer (M,W), softball (W), swimming (M,W), track (indoor) (M,W), track (outdoor) (M,W), track and field (indoor) (M,W), track and field (outdoor) (M,W), volleyball (W), wrestling (M). Member of Midwest Athletic Conference for Women, Midwest Collegiate Athletic Conference, NCAA Division III.
**Intramural and club sports:** 42% of students participate. Intramural badminton, basketball, bowling, broomball, cross-country, darts, flag football, frisbee golf, golf, handball, pool, racquetball, softball, squash, swimming, table tennis, tennis, track, volleyball, walleyball. Men's club cheerleading, crew, lacrosse. Women's club crew, lacrosse, rugby.

**ADMISSIONS. Academic basis for candidate selection** (in order of priority): Secondary school record, class rank, essay, standardized test scores, school's recommendation.
**Nonacademic basis for candidate selection:** Particular talent or ability is emphasized. Character and personality and alumni/ae relationship are important. Extracurricular participation and geographical distribution are considered.
**Requirements:** Graduation from secondary school is required; GED is not accepted. No specific distribution of secondary school units required. Audition required of music program applicants. SAT or ACT is required. Campus visit and interview recommended. Off-campus interviews available with admissions and alumni representatives.
**Procedure:** Take SAT or ACT by December of 12th year. Visit college for interview by February 1 of 12th year. Application deadline is February 1. Notification of admission by April 1. Reply is required by May 1. $200 nonrefundable tuition deposit. Freshmen accepted for fall terms only.
**Special programs:** Admission may be deferred one year. Credit and/or placement may be granted through CEEB Advanced Placement exams for scores of 4 or higher. Placement may be granted through challenge exams. Early decision program. In fall 1993, 87 applied for early decision and 74 were accepted. Deadline for applying for early decision is November 15 and January 1. Early entrance/early admission program. Concurrent enrollment program.
**Transfer students:** Transfer students accepted for terms other than fall. In fall 1993, 5% of all new students were transfers into all classes. 80 transfer applications were received, 52 were accepted. Application deadline is May 15 for fall; December 1 for winter; March 1 for spring. Minimum 2.75 GPA recommended. Lowest course grade accepted is "C." At least 18 courses must be completed at the university to receive degree.
**Admissions contact:** Steven T. Syverson, Dean of Admissions and Financial Aid. 414 832-6500.

**FINANCIAL AID. Available aid:** Pell grants, SEOG, state scholarships and grants, school scholarships and grants, private scholarships and grants, academic merit scholarships, and aid for undergraduate foreign students. Perkins Loans (NDSL), PLUS, Stafford Loans (GSL), school loans, private loans, and SLS. Knight Tuition Plans, AMS, Tuition Management Systems, and deferred payment plan.
**Financial aid statistics:** 10% of aid is not need-based. In 1993-94, 99% of all undergraduate applicants received aid; 84% of freshman applicants. Average amounts of aid awarded freshmen: Scholarships and grants, $11,258; loans, $3,025.
**Supporting data/closing dates:** FAFSA: Priority filing date is March 1. School's own aid application: Priority filing date is march 15. Income tax forms: Priority filing date is March 15. Notification of awards on rolling basis.
**Financial aid contact:** Debra Hintz, Director of Financial Aid. 414 832-6583.

**STUDENT EMPLOYMENT.** College Work/Study Program. Institutional employment. 50% of full-time undergraduates work on campus during school year. Students may expect to earn an average of $1,400 during school year. Off-campus part-time employment opportunities rated "good."

**COMPUTER FACILITIES.** 100 IBM/IBM-compatible and Macintosh/Apple microcomputers; 40 are networked. Students may access Digital minicomputer/mainframe systems, BITNET, Internet. Residence halls may be equipped with stand-alone microcomputers, networked terminals. Client/LAN operating systems include Apple/Macintosh, DOS, OS/2, UNIX/XENIX/AIX, DEC. Computer languages and software packages include BASIC, C, C++, COBOL, FORTRAN, LISP, Modula 2, Pascal, Prolog, SPSS; 50 in all. Computer facilities are available to all students.
**Fees:** Computer fee is included in tuition/fees.
**Hours:** 24 hours.

**GRADUATE CAREER DATA.** Graduate school percentages: 2% enter law school. 3% enter medical school. 1% enter dental school. 1% enter graduate business programs. 17% enter graduate arts and sciences programs. 1% enter theological school/seminary. Highest graduate school enrollments: U of Chicago, New England Conservatory of Music, Marquette U, Northwestern U, U of Wisconsin at Madison. 30% of graduates choose careers in business and industry. Companies and businesses that hire graduates: Andersen Consulting, Hewitt Associates, Kimberly-Clark.

**PROMINENT ALUMNI/AE.** David C. Mulford, former U.S. undersecretary for international affairs; Jeff Jones, actor; Colleen Dewhurst, actress; Anton Valukas, attorney; Dale Duesing, opera singer; Raymond H. Herzog, former CEO, 3M.

# Marian College of Fond du Lac

**Fond du Lac, WI 54935** **414 923-7600**

**1993-94 Costs.** Tuition: $8,500. Room & board: $3,750. Fees, books, misc. academic expenses (school's estimate): $700.

**Enrollment.** Undergraduates: 422 men, 744 women (full-time). Freshman class: 824 applicants, 670 accepted, 338 enrolled. Graduate enrollment: 176 men, 409 women.

**Test score averages/ranges.** Average ACT scores: 20 composite.

**Faculty.** 60 full-time; 27 part-time. 38% of faculty holds doctoral degree. Student/faculty ratio: 16 to 1.

**Selectivity rating.** Less competitive.

**PROFILE.** Marian College of Fond du Lac is a church-affiliated, liberal arts college. Founded in 1936, it adopted coeducation in 1962. Its 50-acre campus is located in Fond du Lac, 60 miles north of Milwaukee.

**Accreditation:** NCACS. Professionally accredited by the Council on Social Work Education, the National Council for Accreditation of Teacher Education, the National League for Nursing.
**Religious orientation:** Marian College of Fond du Lac is affiliated with the Roman Catholic Church; two semesters of religion required.
**Library:** Collections totaling over 95,000 volumes, 690 periodical subscriptions, and 5,629 microform items.
**Special facilities/museums:** On-campus child-care center, electron microscope.
**Athletic facilities:** Tennis courts, gymnasium, softball and baseball diamonds, soccer field.

**STUDENT BODY. Undergraduate profile:** 85% are state residents; 30% are transfers. 2% Asian-American, 2% Black, 1% Hispanic, 95% White.
**Freshman profile:** 1% of accepted applicants took SAT; 99% took ACT. 70% of freshmen come from public schools.
**Undergraduate achievement:** 73% of fall 1992 freshmen returned for fall 1993 term. 51% of entering class graduated. 10% of students who completed a degree program immediately went on to graduate study.
**Foreign students:** Eight students are from out of the country. Countries represented include Belize, Canada, El Salvador, England, and Macedonia.

**PROGRAMS OF STUDY. Degrees:** B.A., B.Bus.Admin., B.S., B.S.Bus.Admin., B.S.Nurs., B.S.Radiol.Tech.
**Majors:** Accounting, Administration of Justice, Art, Art Education, Biology, Business Education, Business Management, Chemistry, Communication, Cytotechnology, Early Childhood Education, Education, Elementary Education, English, History, Human Relations, Marketing, Marketing Education, Mathematics, Medical Technology, Music, Music Education, Nursing, Psychology, Radiologic Technology, Secondary Education, Social Studies, Social Work, Sports Management.
**Distribution of degrees:** The majors with the highest enrollment are nursing, business, and education; medical technology has the lowest.
**Requirements:** General education requirement.
**Academic regulations:** Minimum 2.0 GPA must be maintained.
**Special:** Minors offered in all majors and in athletic coaching. Self-designed majors. Double majors. Dual degrees. Independent study. Accelerated study. Internships. Cooperative education programs. Graduate school at which undergraduates may take graduate-level courses. Preprofessional programs in law, medicine, veterinary science, pharmacy, dentistry, and physical therapy. Combined degree programs in medical and radiologic technology. Teacher certification in early childhood, elementary, and secondary education. Study abroad in England (Harlexton Coll). ROTC.
**Honors:** Honor societies.
**Academic Assistance:** Remedial writing, math, and study skills. Nonremedial tutoring.

**STUDENT LIFE. Housing:** All freshmen and sophomores must live on campus. Coed dorms. School-owned/operated apartments. 60% of students live in college housing.
**Social atmosphere:** The most popular student gathering place is the College Commons. Highlights of the school year include Winterfest (a day-long series of snow and ice events) and the Sabre Show (a student musical variety show held in January).
**Services and counseling/handicapped student services:** Placement services. Health service. Day care. Counseling services for minority, military, veteran, and older students. Birth control, personal, and psychological counseling. Career and academic guidance services. Religious counseling. Physically disabled student services. Learning disabled services. Notetaking services. Tape recorders. Tutors. Reader services for the blind.
**Campus organizations:** Undergraduate student government. Student newspaper (Sabre, once/month). Literary magazine. Yearbook. Community orchestra, band, chorus, ensembles, Arts and Letters Society, departmental groups. Two fraternities, one chapter house; one sorority, no chapter house.
**Religious organizations:** Campus Ministry.
**Minority/foreign student organizations:** Minority Student Organization, Multi-Cultural Student Association.

**ATHLETICS. Physical education requirements:** None.
**Intercollegiate competition:** 1% of students participate. Basketball (W), cheerleading (M,W), cross-country (M,W), soccer (M), softball (W), volleyball (W). Member of NAIA.
**Intramural and club sports:** 2% of students participate. Men's club baseball, basketball.

**ADMISSIONS. Academic basis for candidate selection** (in order of priority): Secondary school record, standardized test scores, school's recommendation, class rank.
**Nonacademic basis for candidate selection:** Character and personality and particular talent or ability are emphasized. Extracurricular participation is important. Alumni/ae relationship is considered.
**Requirements:** Graduation from secondary school is required; GED is accepted. 16 units required and the following program of study recommended: 4 units of English, 2 units of math, 2 units of science, 2 units of foreign language, 2 units of social studies. Minimum composite ACT score of 18, rank in top half of secondary school class, and minimum 2.0 GPA required. 1 unit of chemistry required of nursing program applicants. Conditional admission possible for applicants not meeting standard requirements. ACT is required; SAT may be substituted. Campus visit and interview recommended. Off-campus interviews available with an admissions representative.
**Procedure:** Take SAT or ACT by June of 12th year. Visit college for interview by February of 12th year. Notification of admission on rolling basis. Reply is required by May 1. $100 tuition deposit, refundable until May 1. $100 room deposit, refundable until May 1. Freshmen accepted for terms other than fall.
**Special programs:** Admission may be deferred one year. Credit and/or placement may be granted through CEEB Advanced Placement exams and CLEP general and subject exams. Credit and placement may be granted through DANTES and challenge exams, and military and life experience. Early entrance/early admission program. Concurrent enrollment program.
**Transfer students:** Transfer students accepted for terms other than fall. In fall 1993, 30% of all new students were transfers into all classes. Application deadline is rolling for fall; rolling for spring. Minimum 2.0 GPA required. Lowest course grade accepted is "C." At least 32 semester hours must be completed at the college to receive degree.
**Admissions contact:** Carol A. Reichenberger, M.S.Ed., Vice President of Enrollment Services. 414 923-7650, 800 2MA-RIAN.

**FINANCIAL AID. Available aid:** Pell grants, SEOG, Federal Nursing Student Scholarships, state scholarships and grants, school scholarships and grants, private scholarships and grants, ROTC scholarships, academic merit scholarships, and aid for undergraduate foreign students. Perkins Loans (NDSL), PLUS, Stafford Loans (GSL), NSL, and SLS. Tuition Management Systems and family tuition reduction.
**Financial aid statistics:** 30% of aid is not need-based. In 1993-94, 80% of all undergraduate applicants received aid; 85% of freshman applicants. Average amounts of aid awarded freshmen: Scholarships and grants, $2,500; loans, $2,000.
**Supporting data/closing dates:** FAFSA/FAF/FFS: Priority filing date is March 1. School's own aid application: Priority filing date is March 1. Income tax forms. Notification of awards on rolling basis.

**STUDENT EMPLOYMENT.** College Work/Study Program. Institutional employment. Off-campus part-time employment opportunities rated "good."

**COMPUTER FACILITIES.** 80 IBM/IBM-compatible and Macintosh/Apple microcomputers. Computer languages and software packages include Lotus and WordPerfect. Computer facilities are available to all students.
**Fees:** Computer fee is included in tuition/fees.
**Hours:** 8 AM-10 PM (M-Sa); noon-10 PM (Su).

**GRADUATE CAREER DATA.** 30% of graduates choose careers in business and industry.

**PROMINENT ALUMNI/AE.** Anne Jones, director of nursing, Mayo Clinic, Rochester, Minn.

# Marquette University

**Milwaukee, WI 53233** **414 288-7302**

**1994-95 Costs.** Tuition: $11,610). Room & board: $4,800. Fees, books, misc. academic expenses (school's estimate): $750.

**Enrollment.** Undergraduates: 3,409 men, 3,620 women (full-time). Freshman class: 5,132 applicants, 4,600 accepted, 1,685 enrolled. Graduate enrollment: 1,722 men, 1,222 women.

**Test score averages/ranges.** Average SAT scores: 492 verbal, 561 math. Range of SAT scores of middle 50%: 440-540 verbal, 500-630 math. Average ACT scores: 25 English, 25 math, 25 composite. Range of ACT scores of middle 50%: 22-27 English, 22-28 math.

**Faculty.** 490 full-time; 201 part-time. 94% of faculty holds highest degree in specific field. Student/faculty ratio: 15 to 1.

**Selectivity rating.** Competitive.

**PROFILE.** Marquette, founded in 1881, is a church-affiliated university. Programs are offered through the Colleges of Arts and Sciences; Business Administration; Communication, Journalism, and Performing Arts; Engineering; and Nursing; the Graduate School; and the School of Education. Its 64-acre campus is located in downtown Milwaukee.

**Accreditation:** NCACS. Numerous professional accreditations.
**Religious orientation:** Marquette University is affiliated with the Roman Catholic Church (Society of Jesus); nine semester hours of theology required for most majors.
**Library:** Collections totaling over 971,791 volumes, 9,689 periodical subscriptions, and 362,178 microform items.
**Special facilities/museums:** Art museum, chromatography lab, electron microscope, lasers, oscilloscopes, spectrometers.
**Athletic facilities:** Athletic center, swimming pool, weight room, handball, racquetball, tennis, and volleyball courts.

**STUDENT BODY. Undergraduate profile:** 53% are state residents; 14% are transfers. 6% Asian-American, 5% Black, 4% Hispanic, 1% Native American, 84% White. Average age of undergraduates is 21.
**Freshman profile:** 1% of freshmen who took SAT scored 700 or over on verbal, 6% scored 700 or over on math; 9% scored 600 or over on verbal, 31% scored 600 or over on math; 41% scored 500 or over on verbal, 72% scored 500 or over on math; 86% scored 400 or over on verbal, 97% scored 400 or over on math; 99% scored 300 or over on verbal,

100% scored 300 or over on math. 9% of freshmen who took ACT scored 30 or over on English, 13% scored 30 or over on math, 11% scored 30 or over on composite; 65% scored 24 or over on English, 63% scored 24 or over on math, 70% scored 24 or over on composite; 98% scored 18 or over on English, 98% scored 18 or over on math, 100% scored 18 or over on composite; 100% scored 12 or over on English, 100% scored 12 or over on math. 55% of accepted applicants took SAT; 88% took ACT. 55% of freshmen come from public schools.

**Undergraduate achievement:** 85% of fall 1992 freshmen returned for fall 1993 term.

**Foreign students:** 136 students are from out of the country. Countries represented include India, Indonesia, Jordan, Kenya, Malaysia, and Singapore; 43 in all.

**PROGRAMS OF STUDY. Degrees:** B.A., B.S., B.S.Nurs.

**Majors:** Accounting, Advertising, Anthropology, Bilingual Education, Biochemistry/Molecular Biology, Biology, Biomedical Engineering, Broadcast/Electronic Communication, Business Administration, Business Economics, Chemistry, Civil/Environmental Engineering, Communication/Rhetorical Studies, Computational Mathematics, Computer Science, Criminology/Law, Dental Hygiene, Dramatic Arts, Economics, Electrical Engineering, Elementary Education, English, Finance, Foreign Languages/Literatures, French, German, History, Human Development, Human Resources Management, Industrial Engineering, Interdisciplinary Studies, International Affairs, International Business, Journalism, Latin, Law, Management Information Systems, Marketing, Mathematics, Mechanical Engineering, Medical Technology, Medicine, Molecular Biology, Nursing, Organizational Management, Philosophy, Physical Therapy, Physics, Political Science, Pre-Dentistry, Psychology, Public Relations, Secondary Education, Social Crime and Social Control, Social Philosophy, Social Work, Sociology, Spanish, Speech Pathology/Audiology, Statistics, Theatre Arts, Theology, Writing/English.

**Distribution of degrees:** The majors with the highest enrollment are mechanical engineering, accounting, and electrical engineering.

**Requirements:** General education requirement.

**Academic regulations:** Minimum 2.0 GPA must be maintained.

**Special:** Minors offered in all majors and in approximately 40 other fields. Associate's degrees offered. Self-designed majors. Double majors. Independent study. Accelerated study. Pass/fail grading option. Internships. Cooperative education programs. Graduate school at which undergraduates may take graduate-level courses. Preprofessional programs in law, medicine, dentistry, and physical therapy. Washington Semester. Teacher certification in elementary, secondary, and bilingual/bicultural education. Certification in specific subject areas. Exchange programs abroad in France, Germany, and Spain (U of Madrid). ROTC and NROTC. AFROTC at Milwaukee Sch of Engineering.

**Honors:** Phi Beta Kappa. Honors program. Honor societies.

**Academic Assistance:** Remedial writing and study skills. Nonremedial tutoring.

**STUDENT LIFE. Housing:** Freshmen and sophomores must live on campus unless living with family. Coed, women's, and men's dorms. School-owned/operated apartments. On-campus married-student housing. On-campus graduate student housing. 35% of students live in college housing.

**Services and counseling/handicapped student services:** Placement services. Health service. Day care. Counseling services for minority, military, and veteran students. Personal and psychological counseling. Career and academic guidance services. Religious counseling. Physically disabled student services. Learning disabled services. Notetaking services. Tape recorders. Tutors. Reader services for the blind.

**Campus organizations:** Undergraduate student government. Student newspaper (Tribune, published four times/week). Literary magazine. Yearbook. Radio and TV stations. Chess, criminology, and sports clubs, Habitat for Humanity, Knights of Columbus, College Republicans, College Democrats, Writers Ink, and numerous professional societies, 165 organizations in all. 10 fraternities, seven chapter houses; eight sororities, no chapter houses. 7% of men join a fraternity. 7% of women join a sorority.

**Religious organizations:** Campus Crusade for Christ, Campus Ministry, Baptist Student Union, Chi Alpha, Intervarsity Christian Fellowship.

**Minority/foreign student organizations:** Black Student Council, Latin American Student Association, American Indian Association, National Society of Black Engineers, Kappa Alpha Psi, Alpha Kappa Alpha, Asian-American Student Organization, Raices, Bayanihan International Association. International Student Association, African-Caribbean, Arab, Chinese, Indian, Korean, Malaysian, Palestinian, Singaporan, Turkish, Vietnamese, and other foreign student groups.

**ATHLETICS. Physical education requirements:** None.

**Intercollegiate competition:** 5% of students participate. Basketball (M,W), cross-country (M,W), golf (M), riflery (M,W), soccer (M,W), tennis (M,W), track (indoor) (M,W), track (outdoor) (M,W), track and field (indoor) (M,W), track and field (outdoor) (M,W), volleyball (W), wrestling (M). Member of Great Midwest Conference, NCAA Division I.

**Intramural and club sports:** 15% of students participate. Intramural badminton, basketball, football, golf, racquetball, soccer, softball, tennis, volleyball. Men's club baseball, cheerleading, crew, football, ice hockey, rugby, sailing, swimming, volleyball. Women's club cheerleading, crew, soccer, softball, swimming.

**ADMISSIONS. Academic basis for candidate selection** (in order of priority): Class rank, standardized test scores, secondary school record, school's recommendation.

**Requirements:** Graduation from secondary school is required; GED is accepted. 16 units and the following program of study are recommended: 4 units of English, 3 units of math, 2 units of science, 2 units of foreign language, 2 units of social studies, 3 units of electives. Minimum composite ACT score of 21 (combined SAT score of 800) and minimum 2.0 GPA required. Additional math and/or science required for business, engineering, and the health professions program applicants. EOP and Freshman Frontier Program for applicants not normally admissible. SAT or ACT is required. Campus visit and interview recommended. Off-campus interviews available with admissions and alumni representatives.

**Procedure:** Suggest filing application by fall; no deadline. Notification of admission on rolling basis. Reply is required by May 1. $100 nonrefundable tuition deposit. $100 nonrefundable room deposit. Freshmen accepted for terms other than fall.

**Special programs:** Credit and/or placement may be granted through CEEB Advanced Placement exams and CLEP subject exams. Credit and placement may be granted through challenge exams.

**Transfer students:** Transfer students accepted for terms other than fall. In fall 1993, 14% of all new students were transfers into all classes. 832 transfer applications were received, 655 were accepted. Application deadline is rolling for fall; rolling for spring. Minimum 2.0 GPA recommended. Lowest course grade accepted is "C." At least 30 semester hours must be completed at the university to receive degree.

**Admissions contact:** Raymond A. Brown, A.M., Dean of Admissions. 414 288-7302.

**FINANCIAL AID. Available aid:** Pell grants, SEOG, Federal Nursing Student Scholarships, state scholarships and grants, school scholarships and grants, private scholarships and grants, ROTC scholarships, academic merit scholarships, athletic scholarships, and aid for undergraduate foreign students. Perkins Loans (NDSL), PLUS, Stafford Loans (GSL), NSL, school loans, private loans, and SLS. Tuition Plan Inc., Knight Tuition Plans, AMS, EFI Fund Management, deferred payment plan, family tuition reduction, and guaranteed tuition.

**Financial aid statistics:** 20% of aid is not need-based. In 1993-94, 100% of all undergraduate applicants received aid. Average amounts of aid awarded freshmen: Scholarships and grants, $6,100; loans, $4,490.

**Supporting data/closing dates:** FAFSA: Accepted on rolling basis. Notification of awards on rolling basis.

**Financial aid contact:** Daniel L. Goyette, M.A., Director of Financial Aid. 414 288-7390.

**STUDENT EMPLOYMENT.** College Work/Study Program. Institutional employment. 33% of full-time undergraduates work on campus during school year. Students may expect to earn an average of $1,200 during school year. Off-campus part-time employment opportunities rated "excellent."

**COMPUTER FACILITIES.** 800 IBM/IBM-compatible and Macintosh/Apple microcomputers. Students may access Digital minicomputer/mainframe systems, Internet. Residence halls may be equipped with stand-alone microcomputers, networked terminals. Client/LAN operating systems include Apple/Macintosh, DOS, UNIX/XENIX/AIX. Computer languages and software packages include Ada, APL, BASIC, COBOL, FORTRAN, ImSL, MINITAB, Pascal, SAS, SPSS; 30 in all. Computer facilities are available to all students.

**Fees:** None.

**Hours:** 24 hours.

**GRADUATE CAREER DATA.** Graduate school percentages: 5% enter law school. 2% enter medical school. 1% enter dental school. 1% enter graduate business programs. 9% enter graduate arts and sciences programs. Highest graduate school enrollments: Marquette U, U of Wisconsin - Madison, U of Wisconsin - Milwaukee. Companies and businesses that hire graduates: Arthur Anderson, Northwestern Mutual Life, Price Waterhouse, Underwriters Labs.

**PROMINENT ALUMNI/AE.** Peter Bonerz, actor-director, films/TV; Edward A. Brennan, chairperson/CEO, Sears, Roebuck & Company; C.J. Smith, CEO, Izod Men's Wear; Frank C. DeGuire, dean, Marquette Law School; Rev. Jerome J. Hastrich, bishop, Diocese of Gallup, N. Mex.; James Keyes, CEO, Johnson Controls; Donald Schuenke, CEO, Northwestern Mutual Life Insurance.

# Milwaukee Institute of Art and Design

**Milwaukee, WI 53202** **414 276-7889**

**1993-94 Costs.** Tuition: $9,800. Housing: None. Fees, books, misc. academic expenses (school's estimate): $1,150.

**Enrollment.** Undergraduates: 251 men, 171 women (full-time). Freshman class: 438 applicants, 309 accepted, 149 enrolled.

**Test score averages/ranges.** N/A.

**Faculty.** 25 full-time; 57 part-time. 82% of faculty holds highest degree in specific field. Student/faculty ratio: 12 to 1.

**Selectivity rating.** N/A.

**PROFILE.** Millwaukee Institute of Art and Design, founded in 1974, is a private institution. Classes are held in buildings located in the Historic Third World District in downtown Milwaukee.

**Accreditation:** NCACS. Professionally accredited by the National Association of Schools of Art and Design.

**Religious orientation:** Milwaukee Institute of Art and Design is nonsectarian; no religious requirements.

**Library:** Collections totaling over 19,000 volumes, 52 periodical subscriptions, and 40,000 microform items.

**Special facilities/museums:** Art galleries, computer graphics lab, design center.

**STUDENT BODY. Undergraduate profile:** 84% are state residents; 20% are transfers. 3% Asian-American, 3% Black, 4% Hispanic, 1% Native American, 89% White. Average age of undergraduates is 21.

**Freshman profile:** 85% of freshmen come from public schools.

**Undergraduate achievement:** 85% of fall 1992 freshmen returned for fall 1993 term. 71% of entering class graduated. 4% of students who completed a degree program went on to graduate study within five years.

**Foreign students:** Two students are from out of the country.

**PROGRAMS OF STUDY. Degrees:** B.F.A.

**Majors:** Drawing, Graphic Design, Illustration, Industrial Design, Interior Design, Painting, Photography, Printmaking, Sculpture.

**Distribution of degrees:** The majors with the highest enrollment are graphic design, illustration, and industrial design; printmaking and sculpture have the lowest.

**Requirements:** General education requirement.

**Academic regulations:** Minimum 2.0 GPA must be maintained.

**Special:** Minors offered in all majors. All programs are studio-based. Double majors. Independent study. Internships. Cooperative education programs. Member of Alliance of Independent Colleges of Art and Design (AICAD); exchange possible. Semester away at AICAD studio (New York). Exchange program abroad in Japan (Osaka U of Arts).

**Academic Assistance:** Remedial writing.

**ADMISSIONS. Academic basis for candidate selection** (in order of priority): Secondary school record, class rank, school's recommendation, essay.
**Nonacademic basis for candidate selection:** Particular talent or ability is emphasized. Character and personality are important. Extracurricular participation is considered.
**Requirements:** Graduation from secondary school is required; GED is accepted. No specific distribution of secondary school units required. Portfolio required of all applicants; four years of art training recommended. Conditional admission possible for applicants not meeting standard requirements. SAT or ACT is recommended. Campus visit recommended. Off-campus interviews available with an admissions representative.
**Procedure:** Visit college for interview by March 1 of 12th year. Suggest filing application by March 1; no deadline. Notification of admission on rolling basis. Reply is required by May 1. $150 tuition deposit, refundable until May 1. Freshmen accepted for terms other than fall.
**Special programs:** Admission may be deferred one year. Credit and/or placement may be granted through CEEB Advanced Placement exams for scores of 4 or higher. Credit and placement may be granted through life experience. Concurrent enrollment program.
**Transfer students:** Transfer students accepted for terms other than fall. In fall 1992, 20% of all new students were transfers into all classes. 82 transfer applications were received, 63 were accepted. Application deadline is March 1 for fall; November 1 for spring. Minimum 2.0 GPA recommended. Lowest course grade accepted is "C." Maximum number of transferable credits is 90 semester hours. At least 30 semester hours must be completed at the institute to receive degree.
**Admissions contact:** Mary Strupp, Executive Director of Enrollment Services. 414 291-8070.

**FINANCIAL AID. Available aid:** Pell grants, SEOG, state scholarships and grants, school scholarships and grants, and private scholarships and grants. PLUS, Stafford Loans (GSL), private loans, and SLS. AMS and deferred payment plan.
**Financial aid statistics:** 23% of aid is not need-based. In 1993-94, 99% of all undergraduate applicants received aid; 100% of freshman applicants. Average amounts of aid awarded freshmen: Scholarships and grants, $2,365; loans, $4,420.
**Supporting data/closing dates:** FAFSA: Priority filing date is March 1; accepted on rolling basis. School's own aid application: Priority filing date is March 1; accepted on rolling basis. Notification of awards on rolling basis.
**Financial aid contact:** Robert Peiffer, Director of Financial Aid. 414 276-7889.

# Milwaukee School of Engineering

**Milwaukee, WI 53202-3109** **800 332-6763**

**1994-95 Costs.** Tuition: $11,505. Room & board: $3,255. Fees, books, misc. academic expenses (school's estimate): $1,000.
**Enrollment.** Undergraduates: 1,649 men, 274 women (full-time). Freshman class: 1,181 applicants, 1,069 accepted, 497 enrolled. Graduate enrollment: 353 men, 41 women.
**Test score averages/ranges.** Average ACT scores: 24 composite.
**Faculty.** 103 full-time; 150 part-time. 50% of faculty holds doctoral degree. Student/faculty ratio: 15 to 1.
**Selectivity rating.** More competitive.

**PROFILE.** The Milwaukee School of Engineering, founded in 1903, is a private school. Its eight-acre campus is located in downtown Milwaukee.

**Accreditation:** NCACS. Professionally accredited by the Accreditation Board for Engineering and Technology, the American Medical Association (CAHEA).
**Religious orientation:** Milwaukee School of Engineering is nonsectarian; no religious requirements.
**Library:** Collections totaling over 60,000 volumes, 675 periodical subscriptions, and 46,600 microform items.
**Special facilities/museums:** Center for business management, industrial robot, CAD/CAM system, fluid power institute, rapid prototyping lab, applied technology center.
**Athletic facilities:** Sports center, athletic field.

**STUDENT BODY. Undergraduate profile:** 77% are state residents; 24% are transfers. 4% Black, 2% Hispanic, 89% White, 5% Other. Average age of undergraduates is 21.
**Freshman profile:** 5% of freshmen who took SAT scored 700 or over on verbal, 9% scored 700 or over on math; 12% scored 600 or over on verbal, 37% scored 600 or over on math; 37% scored 500 or over on verbal, 77% scored 500 or over on math; 78% scored 400 or over on verbal, 97% scored 400 or over on math; 97% scored 300 or over on verbal, 100% scored 300 or over on math. 3% of freshmen who took ACT scored 30 or over on English, 14% scored 30 or over on math, 8% scored 30 or over on composite; 31% scored 24 or over on English, 54% scored 24 or over on math, 59% scored 24 or over on composite; 84% scored 18 or over on English, 83% scored 18 or over on math, 95% scored 18 or over on composite; 99% scored 12 or over on English, 97% scored 12 or over on math, 100% scored 12 or over on composite; 100% scored 6 or over on English, 100% scored 6 or over on math. Majority of accepted applicants took ACT.
**Undergraduate achievement:** 75% of fall 1992 freshmen returned for fall 1993 term. 29% of entering class graduated. 10% of students who completed a degree program immediately went on to graduate study.
**Foreign students:** 66 students are from out of the country. Countries represented include India, Indonesia, Pakistan, and Saudi Arabia; 27 in all.

**PROGRAMS OF STUDY. Degrees:** B.A., B.S.,
**Majors:** Architectural Engineering, Biomedical Engineering, Business/Computer Systems, Computer Engineering, Electrical Engineering, Electrical Engineering Technology, Industrial Engineering, Manufacturing Engineering Technology, Mechanical Engineering, Mechanical Engineering Technology, Technical Communication.
**Distribution of degrees:** The majors with the highest enrollment are electrical engineering, mechanical engineering, and architectural engineering; manufacturing engineering technology and biomedical engineering have the lowest.
**Requirements:** General education requirement.
**Academic regulations:** Freshmen must maintain minimum 1.7 GPA; sophomores, 1.8 GPA; juniors, 1.9 GPA; seniors, 2.0 GPA.
**Special:** Minors offered in business, management, management systems, and technical communications. Associate's degrees offered. Double majors. Dual degrees. Internships. Graduate school at which undergraduates may take graduate-level courses. 2-2 management systems program. Combined Ph.D. program in biomedical engineering with Medical Coll of Wisconsin. Five-year engineering program leads to B.S.Eng. and second bachelor's degree in either business or technical communication. Member of Consortium for Polytechnic Education. AFROTC. ROTC at Marquette U.
**Honors:** Honor societies.
**Academic Assistance:** Remedial writing, math, and study skills. Nonremedial tutoring.

**STUDENT LIFE. Housing:** All freshmen and sophomores under age 21 must live on campus unless living with family. Coed dorms. Fraternity housing. Off-campus privately-owned housing. 34% of students live in college housing.
**Social atmosphere:** According to the student newspaper, "MSOE's location in the heart of Milwaukee's cultural area gives students easy access to the many cultural activities in Milwaukee, including theatre, ballet, and opera. Fraternities and sororities have the most influence on student social life." Students gather at the science hall, student lounge, Rocky Rococo's, and Chapple's Pub.
**Services and counseling/handicapped student services:** Placement services. Health service. Counseling services for veteran and older students. Personal counseling. Career and academic guidance services. Physically disabled student services. Learning disabled services. Notetaking services. Tape recorders. Tutors. Reader services for the blind.
**Campus organizations:** Undergraduate student government. Student newspaper (Ingenium, published once/month). Literary magazine. Yearbook. Radio station. Pep band, choral group, American Heating, Refrigeration, and Air Conditioning Society, American Institute of Architects, management society, Society of Mechanical Engineers, Society of Women Engineers, 57 organizations in all. Five fraternities, two chapter houses; two sororities, no chapter houses. 10% of men join a fraternity. 5% of women join a sorority.
**Religious organizations:** Campus Crusade for Christ, Christian Science Organization, Intervarsity Christian Fellowship.
**Minority/foreign student organizations:** National Society of Black Engineers. Society of International Students, Vietnamese Student Organization.

**ATHLETICS. Physical education requirements:** None.
**Intercollegiate competition:** 9% of students participate. Baseball (M), basketball (M,W), cross-country (M,W), golf (M), ice hockey (M), soccer (M), softball (W), tennis (M,W), volleyball (W), wrestling (M). Member of IWCHA, Lake Michigan Conference, NAIA, NCAA Division III.
**Intramural and club sports:** 80% of students participate. Intramural basketball, flag football, softball, volleyball. Men's club Alpine skiing.

**ADMISSIONS. Academic basis for candidate selection** (in order of priority): Secondary school record, standardized test scores, essay, school's recommendation, class rank.
**Nonacademic basis for candidate selection:** Extracurricular participation is important. Character and personality, particular talent or ability, and alumni/ae relationship are considered.
**Requirements:** Graduation from secondary school is required; GED is accepted. 16 units and the following program of study are required: 4 units of English, 4 units of math, 2 units of science, 1 unit of social studies, 5 units of electives. Minimum composite ACT score of 21 and minimum 3.2 GPA recommended. Conditional admission possible for applicants not meeting standard requirements. Transition Track Program for applicants not meeting standard requirements. ACT is required; SAT may be substituted. Campus visit and interview recommended. Off-campus interviews available with an admissions representative.
**Procedure:** Suggest filing application by February 1. Application deadline is August 1. Notification of admission on rolling basis. Reply is required by May 1. $100 nonrefundable tuition deposit. $75 room deposit, refundable until July 1. Freshmen accepted for terms other than fall.
**Special programs:** Placement may be granted through CEEB Advanced Placement exams for scores of 4 or higher. Credit may be granted through CLEP general and subject exams. Credit and placement may be granted through challenge exams.
**Transfer students:** Transfer students accepted for terms other than fall. In fall 1992, 24% of all new students were transfers into all classes. 214 transfer applications were received, 184 were accepted. Application deadline is rolling for fall; rolling for spring. Minimum 2.0 GPA recommended. Lowest course grade accepted is "C." At least half of required quarter hours must be completed at the school in order to receive degree.
**Admissions contact:** Owen Smith, Dean of Admission. 414 277-7200, 800 332-6763.

**FINANCIAL AID. Available aid:** Pell grants, SEOG, state scholarships and grants, school scholarships and grants, private scholarships and grants, ROTC scholarships, academic merit scholarships, and aid for undergraduate foreign students. Perkins Loans (NDSL), PLUS, Stafford Loans (GSL), school loans, and SLS. School's own tuition plan.
**Financial aid statistics:** 41% of aid is not need-based. In 1993-94, 90% of all undergraduate applicants received aid; 90% of freshman applicants. Average amounts of aid awarded freshmen: Scholarships and grants, $4,000.
**Supporting data/closing dates:** FAFSA: Priority filing date is March 15. Notification of awards on rolling basis.
**Financial aid contact:** Sue Hebert, Director of Financial Aid. 800 332-6763.

**STUDENT EMPLOYMENT.** College Work/Study Program. Institutional employment. 19% of full-time undergraduates work on campus during school year. Students may expect to earn an average of $1,800 during school year. Freshmen are discouraged from working during their first term. Off-campus part-time employment opportunities rated "excellent."

**COMPUTER FACILITIES.** 350 IBM/IBM-compatible and Macintosh/Apple microcomputers; 275 are networked. Students may access Digital minicomputer/mainframe systems, Internet. Residence halls may be equipped with networked microcomputers, modems. Computer languages and software packages include Assembly, BASIC, C, CADKEY, COBOL, FORTRAN, Harvard Graphics, LISP, Pascal, Silos, SPICE, WordPerfect; 20 in all. Computer facilities are available to all students.

**Fees:** None.
**Hours:** 24 hours.

**GRADUATE CAREER DATA.** Graduate school percentages: 4% enter graduate business programs. Highest graduate school enrollments: Marquette U, Milwaukee Sch of Engineering, U of Iowa, U of Wisconsin at Milwaukee. 90% of graduates choose careers in business and industry. Companies and businesses that hire graduates: Andersen Consulting, Boeing, Commonwealth Edison, Compaq Computer, GE, Johnson Controls, Kimberly-Clark, Rockwell International.

**PROMINENT ALUMNI/AE.** Charles J. Tur, vice-president and general manager, Robotics International; Jerome L. Schnettler, president, Milwaukee Electric Tool Corp.; Dennis J. Woywood, vice-president for systems and advanced programs, RCA; Randy Cramp, president, Aptech, Inc.

## Mount Mary College

**Milwaukee, WI 53222** **414 258-4810**

**1994-95 Costs.** Tuition: $8,900. Room & board: $3,119. Fees, books, misc. academic expenses (school's estimate): $500.
**Enrollment.** 932 women (full-time). Freshman class: 235 applicants, 217 accepted, 121 enrolled. 114 women.
**Test score averages/ranges.** Average SAT scores: 510 verbal, 520 math. Average ACT scores: 20 composite. Range of ACT scores of middle 50%: 18-22 composite.
**Faculty.** 75 full-time; 78 part-time. 50% of faculty holds highest degree in specific field. Student/faculty ratio: 10 to 1.
**Selectivity rating.** Competitive.

**PROFILE.** Mount Mary, founded in 1913, is a private, church-affiliated, liberal arts college for women. Its 80-acre campus is located in Milwaukee, 77 miles east of Madison.

**Accreditation:** NCACS. Professionally accredited by the American Dietetic Association, the American Medical Association (CAHEA), the Council on Social Work Education, the Foundation for Interior Design Education Research, the National Council for Accreditation of Teacher Education.
**Religious orientation:** Mount Mary College is affiliated with the Roman Catholic Church (School Sisters of Notre Dame); two semesters of religion required.
**Library:** Collections totaling over 103,406 volumes, 818 periodical subscriptions, and 27,515 microform items.
**Special facilities/museums:** Art gallery, historic costume collection, language lab.
**Athletic facilities:** Gymnasium, swimming pool, weight room, basketball and volleyball courts, athletic field, fitness center.

**STUDENT BODY. Undergraduate profile:** 94% are state residents; 13% are transfers. 2% Asian-American, 6% Black, 2% Hispanic, 2% Native American, 87% White, 1% Other. Average age of undergraduates is 23.
**Freshman profile:** 15% of accepted applicants took SAT; 85% took ACT. 77% of freshmen come from public schools.
**Undergraduate achievement:** 77% of fall 1992 freshmen returned for fall 1993 term. 23% of entering class graduated. 6% of students who completed a degree program went on to graduate study within one year.
**Foreign students:** 14 students are from out of the country. Countries represented include Canada, Eastern European countries, Japan, Malaysia, the Philippines, and South American countries; 10 in all.

**PROGRAMS OF STUDY. Degrees:** B.A., B.S.
**Majors:** Accounting, Art, Art Therapy, Behavioral Science, Bilingual Education, Biology, Business, Business Administration, Business Education, Chemistry, Communications, Computer Science, Consumer Sciences, Dietetics, Early Childhood, Elementary/Middle Education, English, English/Communication Arts, Fashion, Fashion Merchandising, Food/Water Technology, French, German, Graphic Design, History, Hotel/Restaurant Management, Interior Design, Mathematics, Mathematics/Computer Science, Middle/Secondary Education, Music, Occupational Therapy, Philosophy, Pre-Dentistry, Pre-Law, Pre-Medicine, Pre-Veterinary, Public Relations, Social Work, Spanish, Teacher Education, Theology.
**Distribution of degrees:** The majors with the highest enrollment are occupational therapy, business administration, and teacher education; chemistry, German, and theology have the lowest.
**Requirements:** General education requirement.
**Academic regulations:** Minimum 2.0 GPA must be maintained.
**Special:** Minors offered in many majors and in fashion promotion, gerontology, journalism, political science, and religious studies. Peer counselors may receive academic credit. Self-designed majors. Double majors. Independent study. Pass/fail grading option. Internships. Graduate school at which undergraduates may take graduate-level courses. Preprofessional programs in law, medicine, veterinary science, and dentistry. Clinical dietician program includes internships in junior and senior years and in one summer session; qualifies student for membership in American Dietetics Association. Occupational therapy program includes four years at Mount Mary and nine months of clinical practice in teaching hospital; leads to B.S. degree and qualifies student to meet registration standards of American Occupational Therapy Association. 3-3 biology/dentistry program with Marquette U Dental School. Washington Semester. Exchange with Coll of Notre Dame of Maryland. Teacher certification in early childhood, elementary, secondary, and bilingual/bicultural education. Certification in specific subject areas. Study abroad possible.
**Honors:** Honors program. Honor societies.
**Academic Assistance:** Remedial reading, writing, math, and study skills.

**ADMISSIONS. Academic basis for candidate selection** (in order of priority): Secondary school record, class rank, standardized test scores, school's recommendation.
**Nonacademic basis for candidate selection:** Character and personality, extracurricular participation, particular talent or ability, geographical distribution, and alumni/ae relationship are considered.
**Requirements:** Graduation from secondary school is required; GED is accepted. 17 units and the following program of study are required: 3 units of English, 2 units of math, 2 units of science, 2 units of foreign language, 2 units of social studies, 2 units of history, 4 units of academic electives. Minimum composite ACT score of 18 (combined SAT score of 900), rank in top half of secondary school class, and minimum 2.3 GPA required. Conditional admission possible for applicants not meeting standard requirements. SAT or ACT is required. Campus visit and interview recommended. Off-campus interviews available with an admissions representative.
**Procedure:** Take SAT or ACT by July 1 of 12th year. Application deadline is August 15. Notification of admission on rolling basis. Reply is required by May 1. $100 tuition deposit, refundable until May 1. $50 nonrefundable room deposit. Freshmen accepted for terms other than fall.
**Special programs:** Admission may be deferred one year. Credit may be granted through CEEB Advanced Placement for scores of 3 or higher. Credit may be granted through CLEP general and subject exams, ACT PEP exams, and life experience. Credit and placement may be granted through challenge exams.
**Transfer students:** Transfer students accepted for terms other than fall. In fall 1993, 13% of all new students were transfers into all classes. 409 transfer applications were received, 323 were accepted. Application deadline is August 15 for fall; January 15 for spring. Minimum 2.0 GPA required. Lowest course grade accepted is "C." Maximum number of transferable credits is 60 semester hours from a two-year school and 96 semester hours from a four-year school. At least 32 semester hours must be completed at the college to receive degree.
**Admissions contact:** Mary Jane Reilly, Director of Admissions. 414 259-9220, 800 321-6265.

**FINANCIAL AID. Available aid:** Pell grants, SEOG, state scholarships and grants, school scholarships and grants, private scholarships, academic merit scholarships, and athletic scholarships. Perkins Loans (NDSL), PLUS, Stafford Loans (GSL), and SLS. Tuition Plan Inc., Knight Tuition Plans, AMS, and Tuition Management Systems.
**Financial aid statistics:** 2% of aid is not need-based. In 1993-94, 80% of all undergraduate applicants received aid; 97% of freshman applicants. Average amounts of aid awarded freshmen: Scholarships and grants, $3,160; loans, $2,625.
**Supporting data/closing dates:** FAFSA: Priority filing date is March 15. School's own aid application: Priority filing date is March 15. Notification of awards on rolling basis.
**Financial aid contact:** John Rdzak, M.S., Director of Financial Aid. 414 258-4810, extension 356.

## Mount Senario College

**Ladysmith, WI 54848** **715 532-5511**

**1994-95 Costs.** Tuition: $7,960. Room & board: $3,250. Fees, books, misc. academic expenses (school's estimate): $655.
**Enrollment.** Undergraduates: 254 men, 208 women (full-time). Freshman class: 288 applicants, 204 accepted, 96 enrolled.
**Test score averages/ranges.** Average ACT scores: 17 composite.
**Faculty.** 31 full-time; 15 part-time. 35% of faculty holds doctoral degree. Student/faculty ratio: 12 to 1.
**Selectivity rating.** Less competitive.

**PROFILE.** Mount Senario, founded in 1930, is a private, liberal arts college. Its 140-acre campus is located in Ladysmith, 65 miles north of Eau Claire.

**Accreditation:** NCACS.
**Religious orientation:** Mount Senario College is nonsectarian; one semester of religion required.
**Library:** Collections totaling over 48,508 volumes, 300 periodical subscriptions, and 11,500 microform items.
**Special facilities/museums:** Art gallery, fine arts center.
**Athletic facilities:** Gymnasium, basketball, tennis, and volleyball courts, weight room, baseball, football, soccer, and softball fields.

**STUDENT BODY. Undergraduate profile:** 87% are state residents. 11% Asian-American, 2% Black, 29% Native American, 58% White. Average age of undergraduates is 25.
**Freshman profile:** Majority of accepted applicants took ACT.
**Undergraduate achievement:** 61% of fall 1992 freshmen returned for fall 1993 term. 9% of entering class graduated.
**Foreign students:** 16 students are from out of the country. Countries represented include Hong Kong, Japan, Kenya, Turkey, and the former Yugoslav Republics.

**PROGRAMS OF STUDY. Degrees:** B.A., B.F.A., B.S.
**Majors:** Accounting, Art, Biology, Business, Criminal Justice, Criminal Justice/Political Science, Early Childhood Education, Elementary Education, Elementary Physical Education, English, History, History/Political Science, Mathematics, Music, Natural Science, Psychology, Recreation, Social Sciences, Social Work, Sociology/Criminal Justice, Technical Management.
**Distribution of degrees:** The majors with the highest enrollment are criminal justice, business, and education; art has the lowest.
**Requirements:** General education requirement.
**Academic regulations:** Minimum 2.5 GPA required for graduation.
**Special:** Minors offered in some majors and in American Indian studies, chemistry, choral music, coaching, computer science, ecology, and philosophy. Concentrations offered in art education, fine arts, language arts, science, and social science. Courses offered in economics, geography, and Ojibwe. Associate's degrees offered. Self-designed majors. Double majors. Dual degrees. Independent study. Internships. Cooperative education programs. Graduate school at which undergraduates may take graduate-level courses. Preprofessional programs in law. Combined forestry program with Michigan Tech U. HECUA semester-away study program. Teacher certification in early childhood, elementary, and secondary education.
**Academic Assistance:** Remedial reading, writing, math, and study skills.

**ADMISSIONS. Academic basis for candidate selection** (in order of priority): Standardized test scores, secondary school record, class rank, school's recommendation, essay.
**Nonacademic basis for candidate selection:** Character and personality, extracurricular participation, and particular talent or ability are emphasized.
**Requirements:** Graduation from secondary school is required; GED is accepted. No specific distribution of secondary school units required. Minimum composite ACT score of 15 and rank in top half of secondary school class required. Portfolio required of art program applicants. Audition required of music program applicants. Conditional admission possible for applicants not meeting standard requirements. ACT is required; SAT may be substituted. Campus visit and interview recommended. Off-campus interviews available with an admissions representative.
**Procedure:** Take SAT or ACT by April of 12th year. Visit college for interview by June of 12th year. Notification of admission on rolling basis. $100 refundable tuition deposit. Freshmen accepted for terms other than fall.
**Special programs:** Credit may be granted through CEEB Advanced Placement for scores of 3 or higher. Credit may be granted through DANTES exams and military and life experience. Concurrent enrollment program.
**Transfer students:** Transfer students accepted for terms other than fall. In fall 1993, 123 transfer applications were received, 90 were accepted. Application deadline is in July for fall; in December for spring. Minimum 2.0 GPA required. Lowest course grade accepted is "C." Maximum number of transferable credits is 97 semester hours. At least 32 semester hours must be completed at the college to receive degree.
**Admissions contact:** Dewey Floberg, B.S., Dean of Admissions. 715 532-5511, extension 233.

**FINANCIAL AID. Available aid:** Pell grants, SEOG, state scholarships, school scholarships and grants, and academic merit scholarships. PLUS, Stafford Loans (GSL), and SLS.
**Financial aid statistics:** 4% of aid is not need-based. In 1993-94, 92% of all undergraduate applicants received aid; 85% of freshman applicants. Average amounts of aid awarded freshmen: Scholarships and grants, $2,865; loans, $3,849.
**Supporting data/closing dates:** FAFSA. Notification of awards on rolling basis.
**Financial aid contact:** Vickie Hebard, Director of Financial Aid. 715 532-5511, extension 241.

# Northland College

**Ashland, WI 54806** 715 682-1699

**1993-94 Costs.** Tuition: $9,570. Room & board: $3,750. Fees, books, misc. academic expenses (school's estimate): $630.
**Enrollment.** Undergraduates: 381 men, 361 women (full-time). Freshman class: 905 applicants, 797 accepted, 204 enrolled.
**Test score averages/ranges.** Range of SAT scores of middle 50%: 440-550 verbal, 450-570 math. Range of ACT scores of middle 50%: 21-26 composite.
**Faculty.** 42 full-time; 10 part-time. 60% of faculty holds doctoral degree. Student/faculty ratio: 16 to 1.
**Selectivity rating.** Less competitive.

**PROFILE.** Northland, founded in 1892, is a private, liberal arts college. Its 65-acre campus is located in Ashland, 75 miles south of Duluth, Minn.

**Accreditation:** NCACS.
**Religious orientation:** Northland College is affiliated with the United Church of Christ; no religious requirements.
**Library:** Collections totaling over 83,000 volumes, 350 periodical subscriptions and 30 microform items.
**Special facilities/museums:** Native American museum, language lab, day care center, field stations in nearby national forest, observatory.
**Athletic facilities:** Gymnasium, swimming pool, ice rink, weight room, basketball, racquetball, and tennis courts, climbing wall, athletic field.

**STUDENT BODY. Undergraduate profile:** 38% are state residents; 25% are transfers. 2% Asian-American, 1% Black, 2% Hispanic, 5% Native American, 90% White. Average age of undergraduates is 21.
**Freshman profile:** 1% of freshmen who took SAT scored 700 or over on verbal, 3% scored 700 or over on math; 10% scored 600 or over on verbal, 19% scored 600 or over on math; 39% scored 500 or over on verbal, 52% scored 500 or over on math; 90% scored 400 or over on verbal, 90% scored 400 or over on math; 100% scored 300 or over on verbal, 99% scored 300 or over on math. 8% of freshmen who took ACT scored 30 or over on composite; 44% scored 24 or over on composite; 96% scored 18 or over on composite; 100% scored 12 or over on composite. 43% of accepted applicants took SAT; 45% took ACT.
**Undergraduate achievement:** 65% of fall 1991 freshmen returned for fall 1992 term. 42% of entering class graduated. 24% of students who completed a degree program went on to graduate study within one year.
**Foreign students:** 13 students are from out of the country. Countries represented include Canada, China, India, Japan, Mexico, and Nepal; eight in all.

**PROGRAMS OF STUDY. Degrees:** B.A., B.S.
**Majors:** Accounting, Biology, Business Administration, Chemistry, Computer Information Systems, Computer Science, Conflict/Peace Studies, Earth Science, Economics, Elementary Education, English, Environmental Studies, History, Management, Mathematics, Music, Outdoor Education, Psychology, Religions, Secondary Education, Sociology, Writing.
**Distribution of degrees:** The majors with the highest enrollment are biology, business administration, and environmental studies.
**Requirements:** General education requirement.
**Special:** Minors offered in coaching, French, Native American studies, philosophy, and political science. College program emphasizes environmental studies as a concern complementary to its concern for the liberal arts. Self-designed majors. Double majors. Dual degrees. Independent study. Accelerated study. Pass/fail grading option. Internships. Cooperative education programs. Preprofessional programs in law, medicine, veterinary science, pharmacy, dentistry, and theology. 2-2 engineering program with Michigan Tech U. 2-2 occupational therapy program with Washington U. 3-2 forestry and natural resources management programs with Michigan Tech U and U of Michigan at Ann Arbor. Member of Lake Superior Association of Colleges and Universities. Teacher certification in early childhood, elementary, and secondary education. Certification in specific subject areas. Exchange program abroad in Japan (Hagoromo Coll). Study abroad also in Greece, Italy, Japan, Kenya, Mexico, and the former Soviet Republics.
**Honors:** Honors program. Honor societies.
**Academic Assistance:** Remedial reading, writing, math, and study skills. Nonremedial tutoring.

**ADMISSIONS. Academic basis for candidate selection** (in order of priority): Secondary school record, standardized test scores, class rank, school's recommendation, essay.
**Nonacademic basis for candidate selection:** Character and personality, extracurricular participation, particular talent or ability, and geographical distribution are considered.
**Requirements:** Graduation from secondary school is required; GED is accepted. No specific distribution of secondary school units required. EOP and conditional admission possible for applicants not meeting standard requirements. 25 students admitted each year who show promise but have not achieved potential in secondary school. SAT or ACT is required. Campus visit and interview recommended. Off-campus interviews available with an admissions representative.
**Procedure:** Take SAT or ACT by December of 12th year. Visit college for interview by spring of 12th year. Notification of admission on rolling basis. Reply is required by May 1. $100 nonrefundable tuition deposit. $50 nonrefundable room deposit. Freshmen accepted for terms other than fall.
**Special programs:** Admission may be deferred two years. Credit and/or placement may be granted through CEEB Advanced Placement exams for scores of 3 or higher. Placement may be granted through CLEP general exams and life experience. Credit and/or placement may be granted through CLEP subject exams. Credit and placement may be granted through challenge exams and military experience. Early decision program. In fall 1992, 10 applied for early decision and 9 were accepted. Early entrance/early admission program. Concurrent enrollment program.
**Transfer students:** Transfer students accepted for terms other than fall. In fall 1992, 25% of all new students were transfers into all classes. 219 transfer applications were received, 195 were accepted. Application deadline is August 1 for fall; December 1 for spring. Minimum 2.0 GPA required. Lowest course grade accepted is "C." Maximum number of transferable credits is 65 semester hours. At least 30 semester hours must be completed at the college to receive degree.
**Admissions contact:** James L. Miller, Dean of Student Development and Enrollment. 715 682-1224.

**FINANCIAL AID. Available aid:** Pell grants, SEOG, state scholarships and grants, school scholarships and grants, private scholarships and grants, academic merit scholarships, athletic scholarships, and aid for undergraduate foreign students. Perkins Loans (NDSL), PLUS, Stafford Loans (GSL), and SLS. Tuition Plan Inc., AMS, and Tuition Management Systems.
**Financial aid statistics:** Average amounts of aid awarded freshmen: Scholarships and grants, $3,800; loans, $2,700.
**Supporting data/closing dates:** FAFSA/FAF/FFS: Priority filing date is May 1. School's own aid application: Priority filing date is May 1. Notification of awards on rolling basis.
**Financial aid contact:** Carol Shaddy, M.A., Director of Financial Aid. 715 682-1255.

# Northwestern College

**Watertown, WI 53094** 414 261-4352

**1994-95 Costs.** Tuition: $3,370. Room & board: $1,880. Fees, books, misc. academic expenses (school's estimate): $2,299.
**Enrollment.** 183 men (full-time). Freshman class: 46 applicants, 45 accepted, 37 enrolled.
**Test score averages/ranges.** Average ACT scores: 24 composite.
**Faculty.** 20 full-time; 2 part-time. Student/faculty ratio: 11 to 1.
**Selectivity rating.** Competitive.

**PROFILE.** Northwestern, founded in 1865, is a private, church-affiliated, theological college. Its 38-acre campus is located in Watertown, 50 miles west of Milwaukee.

**Accreditation:** NCACS.
**Religious orientation:** Northwestern College is affiliated with the Evangelical Lutheran (Wisconsin Synod); seven semesters of religion required.
**Library:** Collections totaling over 47,321 volumes and 256 periodical subscriptions.
**Athletic facilities:** Gymnasiums, weight and wrestling rooms, tennis courts, archery range, baseball, football, soccer, and softball fields, batting cage, cross-country track.

**STUDENT BODY. Undergraduate profile:** 48% are state residents; 5% are transfers. 1% Black, 99% White. Average age of undergraduates is 21.
**Freshman profile:** 11% of freshmen who took ACT scored 30 or over on composite; 54% scored 24 or over on composite; 100% scored 18 or over on composite. 94% of accepted applicants took ACT. 12% of freshmen come from public schools.
**Undergraduate achievement:** 70% of entering class graduated.
**Foreign students:** One student is from out of the country.

**PROGRAMS OF STUDY. Degrees:** B.A.
**Majors:** Pre-Theology.
**Academic regulations:** Freshmen must maintain minimum 1.75 GPA; sophomores, juniors, seniors, 2.00 GPA.
**Academic Assistance:** Remedial study skills. Nonremedial tutoring.

**ADMISSIONS. Academic basis for candidate selection** (in order of priority): Standardized test scores, school's recommendation, secondary school record, class rank.

**Nonacademic basis for candidate selection:** Character and personality are emphasized. Alumni/ae relationship is important. Extracurricular participation and particular talent or ability are considered.
**Requirements:** Graduation from secondary school is required; GED is accepted. No specific distribution of secondary school units required. Minimum composite ACT score of 18, rank in top two-thirds of secondary school class, and minimum 2.0 GPA required. ACT is required. Campus visit recommended. Off-campus interviews available with admissions and alumni representatives.
**Procedure:** Take ACT by April of 12th year. Suggest filing application by July 1; no deadline. Notification of admission on rolling basis. No set date by which applicants must accept offer. Freshmen accepted for terms other than fall.
**Special programs:** Admission may be deferred one year. Credit and placement may be granted through challenge exams.
**Transfer students:** Transfer students accepted for terms other than fall. In fall 1993, 5% of all new students were transfers into all classes. 16 transfer applications were received, 13 were accepted. Application deadline is August 1. Minimum 2.0 GPA required. Lowest course grade accepted is "C."
**Admissions contact:** John A. Braun, M.Div., M.A., Director of Admissions. 414 261-4352.
**FINANCIAL AID. Available aid:** Pell grants, SEOG, state scholarships and grants, school grants, private scholarships and grants, and academic merit scholarships. WELS College Grant, Salem Foundation grants, Aid Association for Lutherans grants. Perkins Loans (NDSL), PLUS, Stafford Loans (GSL), and SLS. Deferred payment plan. Monthly payment plan.
**Financial aid statistics:** 24% of aid is not need-based. In 1993-94, 97% of all undergraduate applicants received aid; 93% of freshman applicants. Average amounts of aid awarded freshmen: Scholarships and grants, $2,071; loans, $3,820.
**Supporting data/closing dates:** FAFSA: Priority filing date is May 1. School's own aid application: Priority filing date is May 1. Income tax forms: Priority filing date is May 1. Notification of awards begins June 25.
**Financial aid contact:** Wayne N. Zuleger, M.Ed., Director of Financial Aid. 414 261-4352.

8-23

# Ripon College

**Ripon, WI 54971** **414 748-8102**

**1994-95 Costs.** Tuition: $15,200. Room & board: $4,010. Fees, books, misc. academic expenses (school's estimate): $515.
**Enrollment.** Undergraduates: 360 men, 380 women (full-time). Freshman class: 585 applicants, 501 accepted, 213 enrolled.
**Test score averages/ranges.** Average SAT scores: 513 verbal, 557 math. Range of SAT scores of middle 50%: 470-580 verbal, 500-640 math. Average ACT scores: 24 composite. Range of ACT scores of middle 50%: 21-27 composite.
**Faculty.** 69 full-time; 27 part-time. 91% of faculty holds highest degree in specific field. Student/faculty ratio: 10 to 1.
**Selectivity rating.** Competitive.

**PROFILE.** Ripon, founded in 1851, is a private, liberal arts college. Its 250-acre campus is located in Ripon, 75 miles northwest of Milwaukee.

**Accreditation:** NCACS.
**Religious orientation:** Ripon College is nonsectarian; no religious requirements.
**Library:** Collections totaling over 150,000 volumes, 700 periodical subscriptions, and 30,000 microform items.
**Special facilities/museums:** Art gallery, language labs.
**Athletic facilities:** Gymnasium, physical education center, basketball, racquetball, and tennis courts, baseball, football, and soccer fields, aerobics, weight, and wrestling rooms, dance studio, swimming pool.
**STUDENT BODY. Undergraduate profile:** 53% are state residents; 10% are transfers. 3% Asian-American, 2% Black, 3% Hispanic, 1% Native American, 90% White, 1% Other. Average age of undergraduates is 20.
**Freshman profile:** 2% of freshmen who took SAT scored 700 or over on verbal, 8% scored 700 or over on math; 20% scored 600 or over on verbal, 42% scored 600 or over on math; 66% scored 500 or over on verbal, 76% scored 500 or over on math; 96% scored 400 or over on verbal, 94% scored 400 or over on math; 100% scored 300 or over on verbal, 98% scored 300 or over on math. 6% of freshmen who took ACT scored 30 or over on composite; 56% scored 24 or over on composite; 99% scored 18 or over on composite; 100% scored 12 or over on composite. 40% of accepted applicants took SAT; 60% took ACT. 60% of freshmen come from public schools.
**Undergraduate achievement:** 91% of fall 1992 freshmen returned for fall 1993 term. 68% of entering class graduated. 30% of students who completed a degree program immediately went on to graduate study.
**Foreign students:** 32 students are from out of the country. Countries represented include China, Germany, Japan, and Korea; 19 in all.
**PROGRAMS OF STUDY. Degrees:** B.A.
**Majors:** Anthropology, Art, Biology, Business Management, Chemistry, Chemistry/Biology, Computer Science, Drama, Economics, English, French, German, History, Latin American Studies, Mathematics, Mathematics/Computer Studies, Music, Philosophy, Physical Education, Physics, Politics/Government, Psychobiology, Psychology, Religion, Romance Languages, Sociology/Anthropology, Spanish, Speech Communication.
**Distribution of degrees:** The majors with the highest enrollment are English, history, and economics; drama, music, and speech communication have the lowest.
**Requirements:** General education requirement.
**Special:** Minors offered. Courses offered in Bible, black studies, East European affairs, education, history of science, Italian, leadership studies, and world literature. Self-designed majors. Double majors. Independent study. Accelerated study. Pass/fail grading option. Internships. Preprofessional programs in law, medicine, veterinary science, pharmacy, dentistry, theology, optometry, allied health, engineering, and nursing. 2-2 programs in nursing and allied health services with Rush U Medical Center. Medical technology program with St. Agnes Hospital; includes one-year internship after completion of bachelor's degree. 3-2 engineering programs with Rensselaer Polytech Inst and Washington U. 3-2 forestry and environmental studies program with Duke U. 3-2 social welfare program with U of Chicago. Member of Associated Colleges of the Midwest. Washington Semester. Argonne Science Semester (Illinois). Newberry Library Program in the Humanities (Illinois). Urban Studies Program (Chicago). Wilderness Field Station Program (Minnesota). Other semester-away programs. Teacher certification in elementary and secondary education. Certification in specific subject areas. Exchange programs abroad in England (Coll of Ripon and York St. John) and Germany (Bonn U). Study abroad also in Costa Rica, India, Japan, the former Soviet Republics, and Spain. ROTC.
**Honors:** Phi Beta Kappa. Honor societies.
**Academic Assistance:** Remedial study skills. Nonremedial tutoring.
**STUDENT LIFE. Housing:** All unmarried students must live on campus unless living with family. Coed, women's, and men's dorms. Sorority and fraternity housing. 96% of students live in college housing.
**Social atmosphere:** The student newspaper reports that the campus suffers from "lack of cultural life" and students tend to socialize in small gatherings. Students frequent the Bender's Pub, Roadhouse, Commons, Game Room, and the Pub. Merriman and SMAC are the most socially influential groups on campus. Popular social events include basketball games, Milwaukee Orchestra performances, Springfest, and Winterfest.
**Services and counseling/handicapped student services:** Placement services. Health service. Counseling services for minority and military students. Birth control, personal, and psychological counseling. Career and academic guidance services. Religious counseling. Learning disabled program/services.
**Campus organizations:** Undergraduate student government. Student newspaper (College Days, published once/week). Literary magazine. Yearbook. Radio station. Chamber Singers, Choral Union, Collegium Musicum, jazz ensemble, orchestra, symphonic wind ensemble, dance group, Readers Theatre, debating, forensics group, photo club, Republican Club, athletic, departmental, professional, and service groups, 45 organizations in all. Five fraternities, no chapter houses; three sororities, no chapter houses. 55% of men join a fraternity. 33% of women join a sorority.
**Religious organizations:** Christian Fellowship.
**Minority/foreign student organizations:** Black Student Union. International and multicultural clubs.
**ATHLETICS. Physical education requirements:** Two semesters of physical education required.
**Intercollegiate competition:** 35% of students participate. Baseball (M), basketball (M,W), cross-country (M,W), football (M), golf (M), soccer (M,W), softball (W), swimming (M,W), tennis (M,W), track and field (indoor) (M,W), track and field (outdoor) (M,W), volleyball (W), wrestling (W). Member of Midwest Athletic Conference, NCAA Division III.
**Intramural and club sports:** 60% of students participate. Intramural badminton, basketball, bowling, football, golf, soccer, softball, tennis, volleyball, water polo. Men's club ice hockey, lacrosse, rugby. Women's club lacrosse, rugby.
**ADMISSIONS. Academic basis for candidate selection** (in order of priority): Secondary school record, class rank, standardized test scores, school's recommendation, essay.
**Nonacademic basis for candidate selection:** Character and personality, extracurricular participation, and geographical distribution are important. Particular talent or ability and alumni/ae relationship are considered.
**Requirements:** Graduation from secondary school is required; GED is accepted. 15 units and the following program of study are required: 4 units of English, 3 units of math, 3 units of science including 2 units of lab, 3 units of social studies. Rank in top quarter of secondary school class recommended. SAT or ACT is required. Campus visit and interview recommended. Off-campus interviews available with admissions and alumni representatives.
**Procedure:** Take SAT or ACT by December of 12th year. Visit college for interview by March 1 of 12th year. Suggest filing application by December 1. Application deadline is March 15. Notification of admission on rolling basis. Reply is required by May 1. $100 nonrefundable tuition deposit. $100 room deposit, refundable until July 15. Freshmen accepted for terms other than fall.
**Special programs:** Admission may be deferred one year. Credit and/or placement may be granted through CEEB Advanced Placement exams for scores of 3 or higher. Credit and/or placement may be granted through CLEP general and subject exams. Placement may be granted through challenge exams. Early decision program. In fall 1993, 61 applied for early decision and 51 were accepted. Deadline for applying for early decision is December 1. Early entrance/early admission program.
**Transfer students:** Transfer students accepted for terms other than fall. In fall 1993, 10% of all new students were transfers into all classes. 46 transfer applications were received, 33 were accepted. Application deadline is June 15 for fall; December 15 for spring. Minimum 2.0 GPA required. Lowest course grade accepted is "C-." At least 32 semester hours must be completed at the college to receive degree.
**Admissions contact:** Paul Weeks, Dean of Admission. 800 94-RIPON.
**FINANCIAL AID. Available aid:** Pell grants, SEOG, state scholarships and grants, school scholarships and grants, private scholarships and grants, ROTC scholarships, academic merit scholarships, and aid for undergraduate foreign students. Perkins Loans (NDSL), PLUS, Stafford Loans (GSL), and SLS. Knight Tuition Plans and AMS.
**Financial aid statistics:** In 1993-94, 87% of all undergraduate applicants received aid; 90% of freshman applicants. Average amounts of aid awarded freshmen: Scholarships and grants, $9,666; loans, $2,814.
**Supporting data/closing dates:** FAFSA: Priority filing date is April 1. Income tax forms. Notification of awards on rolling basis.
**Financial aid contact:** Karri Verhelst, M.A., Director of Financial Aid. 800 94-RIPON.
**STUDENT EMPLOYMENT.** College Work/Study Program. Institutional employment. 47% of full-time undergraduates work on campus during school year. Students may expect to earn an average of $900 during school year. Off-campus part-time employment opportunities rated "good."
**COMPUTER FACILITIES.** 84 IBM/IBM-compatible and Macintosh/Apple microcomputers; 52 are networked. Students may access Digital minicomputer/mainframe sys-

tems, Internet. Residence halls may be equipped with networked terminals. Client/LAN operating systems include Apple/Macintosh. Computer languages and software packages include BASIC, C, FORTRAN, LISP, MacSpell, MINITAB, Pascal, SPSS; language processors, text processors, record management systems. Computer facilities are available to all students.
**Fees:** None.
**Hours:** 8 AM-midn.

**GRADUATE CAREER DATA.** Graduate school percentages: 5% enter law school. 14% enter medical or dental school. 2% enter graduate business programs. 22% enter graduate arts and sciences programs. Highest graduate school enrollments: Medical Coll of Wisconsin, Northwestern U, Rush Medical Coll, U of Wisconsin at Madison. 69% of graduates choose careers in business and industry. Companies and businesses that hire graduates: First Chicago Bank, IBM, Northwestern Mutual Life, Peace Corps.

**PROMINENT ALUMNI/AE.** Richard Threlkeld, chief correspondent, ABC News; Spencer Tracy and Harrison Ford, actors; Frances Lee McCain, actress; Gail Dobish, soprano, Metropolitan Opera; Al Jarreau, jazz vocalist; Joan Raymond, superintendent, Houston Public Schools.

# St. Norbert College

**DePere, WI 54115** **414 337-3005**

**1994-95 Costs.** Tuition: $12,215. Room: $2,390. Board: $2,205. Fees, books, misc. academic expenses (school's estimate): $500.
**Enrollment.** Undergraduates: 837 men, 1,109 women (full-time). Freshman class: 1,334 applicants, 1,243 accepted, 568 enrolled. Graduate enrollment: 3 men, 15 women.
**Test score averages/ranges.** Average SAT scores: 553 verbal, 614 math. Range of SAT scores of middle 50%: 460-615 verbal, 560-665 math. Average ACT scores: 24 English, 23 math, 24 composite. Range of ACT scores of middle 50%: 21-27 composite.
**Faculty.** 119 full-time; 32 part-time. 78% of faculty holds highest degree in specific field. Student/faculty ratio: 15 to 1.
**Selectivity rating.** Competitive.

**PROFILE.** St. Norbert, founded in 1898, is a private, church-affiliated, liberal arts college. Programs are offered through the Divisions of Humanities and Fine Arts, Natural Sciences, and Social Sciences. Its 72-acre campus is located in DePere, south of Green Bay.

**Accreditation:** NCACS.
**Religious orientation:** St. Norbert College is affiliated with the Roman Catholic Church (Order of St. Norbert); two semesters of religion required.
**Library:** Collections totaling over 167,562 volumes, 871 periodical subscriptions, and 24,304 microform items.
**Special facilities/museums:** Art gallery, language lab, nursery school, electron microscope.
**Athletic facilities:** Sports complex, sports center, stadium, athletic fields, tennis courts.

**STUDENT BODY. Undergraduate profile:** 71% are state residents; 10% are transfers. 1.7% Asian-American, .5% Black, .4% Hispanic, 1.7% Native American, 94.8% White, .9% Other. Average age of undergraduates is 20.
**Freshman profile:** 6% of freshmen who took ACT scored 30 or over on English, 6% scored 30 or over on math, 7% scored 30 or over on composite; 47% scored 24 or over on English, 41% scored 24 or over on math, 48% scored 24 or over on composite; 90% scored 18 or over on English, 91% scored 18 or over on math, 98% scored 18 or over on composite; 100% scored 12 or over on English, 100% scored 12 or over on math, 100% scored 12 or over on composite. 10% of accepted applicants took SAT; 90% took ACT. 60% of freshmen come from public schools.
**Undergraduate achievement:** 84% of fall 1992 freshmen returned for fall 1993 term. 71% of entering class graduated. 19% of students who completed a degree program went on to graduate study within one year.
**Foreign students:** 19 students are from out of the country. Countries represented include China, France, Germany, Japan, Spain, and the Ukraine; seven in all.

**PROGRAMS OF STUDY. Degrees:** B.A., B.Bus.Admin., B.Mus., B.S.
**Majors:** Accounting, Art, Art Education, Biology, Business Administration, Chemistry, Classical Languages, Communication Arts, Computer Information Systems, Computer Science, Computer Science/Mathematics, Economics, Elementary Education, English, Environmental Policy Studies, Environmental Science, French, German, Graphic Communications, History, Humanities/Fine Arts, International Business/Language Area Studies, International Economics, International Studies, Mathematics, Medical Technology, Music, Natural Science, Philosophy, Physics, Political Science, Pre-Engineering, Psychology, Religious Studies, Sociology/Anthropology, Spanish.
**Distribution of degrees:** The majors with the highest enrollment are business administration, communication, and elementary education; medical technology and French have the lowest.
**Requirements:** General education requirement.
**Academic regulations:** Freshmen must maintain minimum 1.75 GPA; sophomores, juniors, seniors, 2.0 GPA.
**Special:** Minors offered in many majors and in Japanese, leadership studies, liturgical studies, physical education, Russian area studies. Courses offered in geography. Self-designed majors. Double majors. Dual degrees. Independent study. Internships. Cooperative education programs. Preprofessional programs in law, medicine, veterinary science, pharmacy, dentistry, and optometry. 3-2 engineering program with Marquette U and U of Illinois at Urbana-Champaign. Member of Wisconsin Consortium for Foreign Studies and Higher Education Consortium for Urban Affairs. Washington Semester. City Arts and Urban Studies programs in Minneapolis. Teacher certification in early childhood, elementary, and secondary education. Certification in specific subject areas. Exchange programs abroad in China (Hunan Normal U), Germany (Westfalische Wilhelms U), Japan (Sofia U), and the Ukraine (Kharkov Polytech Inst). Study abroad also in Australia, Austria, Colombia, Ecuador, England, France, Ireland, Italy, Mexico, New Zealand, Norway, Scotland, and Spain. ROTC.
**Honors:** Honors program. Honor societies.
**Academic Assistance:** Remedial reading, writing, math, and study skills. Nonremedial tutoring.

**STUDENT LIFE. Housing:** All unmarried students under age 21 must live on campus unless living near campus with relatives. Coed and women's dorms. School-owned/operated apartments. Off-campus privately-owned housing. 85% of students live in college housing.
**Social atmosphere:** According to the student newspaper, "The campus is full of activities throughout the year. However, there is a need for more off-campus events in the cities of Green Bay and De Pere." Popular gathering spots are the Knight Klub, Abbey Bay, Nikki's, and Boodle's. Groups that have widespread influence on student social life are independents and the College Activities Board. Favorite events include Homecoming, the Winter Carnival, and school plays and concerts.
**Services and counseling/handicapped student services:** Placement services. Health service. Day care. Counseling services for minority, military, and older students. Birth control, personal, and psychological counseling. Career and academic guidance services. Religious counseling. Physically disabled student services. Learning disabled services. Notetaking services. Tape recorders. Tutors. Reader services for the blind.
**Campus organizations:** Undergraduate student government. Student newspaper (SNC Times, published once/week). Literary magazine. Yearbook. Radio and TV stations. Symphonic choir, brass ensemble, jazz, pep, and concert bands, Swinging Knights, debating, Commuter Student Association, Student Democrats, Young Republicans, Knights of Columbus, Leadership and Development, Amnesty International, College Activities Board, academic groups, 13 independent social organizations, 70 organizations in all. Six fraternities, no chapter houses; four sororities, no chapter houses. 11% of men join a fraternity. 3% of women join a sorority.
**Religious organizations:** Campus Ministries, Parish Council, outreach programs.
**Minority/foreign student organizations:** Committee for Student Diversity. Interact.

**ATHLETICS. Physical education requirements:** None.
**Intercollegiate competition:** 25% of students participate. Baseball (M), basketball (M,W), cross-country (M,W), football (M), golf (M), ice hockey (M), soccer (M,W), softball (W), tennis (M,W), track (indoor) (M,W), track and field (indoor) (M,W), track and field (outdoor) (M,W), volleyball (W). Member of Midwest Athletic Conference for Women, Midwest Collegiate Athletic Conference, NCAA Division III.
**Intramural and club sports:** 75% of students participate. Intramural basketball, racquetball, soccer, softball, tennis, touch football, volleyball. Men's club cheerleading, crew. Women's club cheerleading, crew.

**ADMISSIONS. Academic basis for candidate selection** (in order of priority): Secondary school record, class rank, standardized test scores, school's recommendation, essay.
**Nonacademic basis for candidate selection:** Extracurricular participation, particular talent or ability, and alumni/ae relationship are important. Character and personality are considered.
**Requirements:** Graduation from secondary school is required; GED is accepted. 16 units and the following program of study are recommended: 4 units of English, 3 units of math, 3 units of science, 3 units of foreign language, 2 units of social studies, 1 unit of history. Minimum combined SAT score of 900 (composite ACT score of 19), rank in top half of secondary school class, and minimum 2.5 GPA recommended. Conditional admission upon satisfactory completion of summer Academic Enhancemant Program for applicants not normally admissible. SAT or ACT is required. Campus visit and interview recommended. Off-campus interviews available with an admissions representative.
**Procedure:** Take SAT or ACT by January of 12th year. Suggest filing application by June 1. Notification of admission on rolling basis. Reply is required by May 1. $100 tuition deposit, refundable until May 1. $100 room deposit, refundable until May 1. Freshmen accepted for terms other than fall.
**Special programs:** Admission may be deferred one year. Credit and/or placement may be granted through CEEB Advanced Placement exams for scores of 3 or higher. Credit and/or placement may be granted through CLEP general and subject exams. Credit and placement may be granted through military experience. Concurrent enrollment program.
**Transfer students:** Transfer students accepted for terms other than fall. In fall 1993, 10% of all new students were transfers into all classes. Application deadline is August 1 for fall; January 1 for spring. Minimum 2.5 GPA required. Lowest course grade accepted is "C." At least 48 semester hours must be completed at the college to receive degree.
**Admissions contact:** Craig S. Wesley, Dean of Admission. 800 236-4878.

**FINANCIAL AID. Available aid:** Pell grants, SEOG, state scholarships and grants, school scholarships and grants, ROTC scholarships, and academic merit scholarships. Perkins Loans (NDSL), PLUS, Stafford Loans (GSL), and SLS. Tuition Plan Inc., Knight Tuition Plans, AMS, deferred payment plan, and guaranteed tuition.
**Financial aid statistics:** 14% of aid is not need-based. In 1993-94, 98% of all undergraduate applicants received aid; 98% of freshman applicants. Average amounts of aid awarded freshmen: Scholarships and grants, $6,445; loans, $2,649.
**Supporting data/closing dates:** FAFSA/FAF/FFS: Priority filing date is March 1. School's own aid application: Priority filing date is March 1. Income tax forms: Accepted on rolling basis. Notification of awards on rolling basis.
**Financial aid contact:** Jeff Zahn, Director of Financial Aid. 414 337-3071.

**STUDENT EMPLOYMENT.** College Work/Study Program. Institutional employment. 60% of full-time undergraduates work on campus during school year. Students may expect to earn an average of $1,100 during school year. Off-campus part-time employment opportunities rated "excellent."

**COMPUTER FACILITIES.** 90 IBM/IBM-compatible and Macintosh/Apple microcomputers; all are networked. Students may access Digital minicomputer/mainframe systems, BITNET, Internet. Client/LAN operating systems include Apple/Macintosh, DOS, UNIX/XENIX/AIX, DEC. Computer languages and software packages include BASIC, COBOL, FORTRAN, MINITAB, Pascal, SPSS-X, SORTEC; 75 in all. Computer facilities are available to all students.
**Fees:** None.
**Hours:** 8 AM-11 PM (M-Th); 8 AM-5 PM (F); 10 AM-5 PM (Sa); noon-11 PM (Su).

**GRADUATE CAREER DATA.** Graduate school percentages: 1% enter law school. 2% enter medical school. 2% enter graduate business programs. 6% enter graduate arts and sciences programs. Highest graduate school enrollments: Marquette U, U of Wisconsin at Madison, U of Wisconsin at Milwaukee. Companies and businesses that hire graduates: American Medical Security, Firstar Bank, Heritage Insurance, M&I Bank, Schneider National.

**PROMINENT ALUMNI/AE.** Stephen J. Cassidy, senior foreign editor, CNN; Jim Yuenger, foreign editor, Chicago Tribune; George Meyer, secretary, Washington Department of National Resources; Dr. Herbert J. Grover, former state superintendent (DPI), Wisconsin; Hon. Mary Mullarkey Korson, Colorado supreme court justice; Donald J. Schneider, president and CEO, Schneider National, Inc; Lieut. General Alfred J. Mallette, Deputy Director General of NATO Communications and Information Systems.

# Silver Lake College

**Manitowoc, WI 54220-9319 414 684-6691**

**1994-95 Costs.** Tuition: $8,660. Housing: None. Fees, books, misc. academic expenses (school's estimate): $500.

**Enrollment.** Undergraduates: 105 men, 284 women (full-time). Freshman class: 82 applicants, 75 accepted, 33 enrolled. Graduate enrollment: 46 men, 73 women.

**Test score averages/ranges.** Average ACT scores: 20 composite. Range of ACT scores of middle 50%: 16-20 composite.

**Faculty.** 48 full-time; 78 part-time. 25% of faculty holds doctoral degree. Student/faculty ratio: 9 to 1.

**Selectivity rating.** Less competitive.

**PROFILE.** Silver Lake is a private, church-affiliated, liberal arts college. Founded in 1869 as a Normal school, it became a four-year college in 1935. Its 30-acre campus is located in Manitowoc, 70 miles north of Milwaukee.

**Accreditation:** NCACS. Professionally accredited by the National Association of Schools of Music, the National Council for Accreditation of Teacher Education, the National League for Nursing.

**Religious orientation:** Silver Lake College is affiliated with the Roman Catholic Church; two semesters of religion required.

**Library:** Collections totaling over 63,692 volumes, 339 periodical subscriptions, and 1,931 microform items.

**Athletic facilities:** Off-campus softball diamonds, gymnasium, swimming pool, weight rooms, aerobic facilities.

**STUDENT BODY. Undergraduate profile:** 99% are state residents; 12% are transfers. .5% Asian-American, .2% Black, 1% Hispanic, 1% Native American, 97% White, .3% Foreign nationals.

**Freshman profile:** 74% of accepted applicants took ACT. 79% of freshmen come from public schools.

**Undergraduate achievement:** 69% of fall 1992 freshmen returned for fall 1993 term. 10% of entering class graduated. 20% of students who completed a degree program immediately went on to graduate study.

**PROGRAMS OF STUDY. Degrees:** A.B., B.A., B.Bus.Admin., B.Mus., B.S.

**Majors:** Accounting, Art Education, Biology, Business Administration, Early Childhood, Elementary Education, Emotional Disturbances, English, History, Human Resources Development, Learning Disabilities, Management, Mathematics, Mathematics/Computer Science, Mental Retardation, Music, Music Education, Psychology, Religious Studies, Social Sciences, Student-Designed Major, Studio Art.

**Distribution of degrees:** The majors with the highest enrollment are management and elementary education; English and social sciences have the lowest.

**Requirements:** General education requirement.

**Academic regulations:** Minimum 2.0 GPA must be maintained.

**Special:** Minors offered in some majors and in chemistry, church music, computer science, natural science, philosophy, and Spanish. Associate's degrees offered. Self-designed majors. Double majors. Dual degrees. Independent study. Accelerated study. Pass/fail grading option. Internships. Graduate school at which undergraduates may take graduate-level courses. Cooperative and Completion Programs with local technical college in manufacturing technology and police science. Teacher certification in early childhood, elementary, secondary, and special education. Certification in specific subject areas. Study abroad in several countries.

**Honors:** Honor societies.

**Academic Assistance:** Remedial study skills.

**ADMISSIONS. Academic basis for candidate selection** (in order of priority): Secondary school record, standardized test scores, school's recommendation, class rank, essay.

**Nonacademic basis for candidate selection:** Particular talent or ability is important. Character and personality, extracurricular participation, geographical distribution, and alumni/ae relationship are considered.

**Requirements:** Graduation from secondary school is required; GED is accepted. 16 units and the following program of study are required: 3 units of English, 2 units of math, 2 units of social studies, 8 units of electives. Minimum composite ACT score of 19 and minimum 2.0 GPA required. Audition required of music program applicants. Provisional admission possible for applicants not meeting standard requirements. ACT is required. Campus visit and interview recommended. Off-campus interviews available with an admissions representative.

**Procedure:** Notification of admission on rolling basis. Reply is required prior to entering term. $100 refundable tuition deposit. $50 refundable room deposit. Freshmen accepted for terms other than fall.

**Special programs:** Credit may be granted through CLEP general and subject exams, ACT PEP and DANTES exams, and military and life experience.

**Transfer students:** Transfer students accepted for terms other than fall. In fall 1993, 12% of all new students were transfers into all classes. 171 transfer applications were received, 145 were accepted. Minimum 2.0 GPA recommended. Lowest course grade accepted is "C." Maximum number of transferable credits is 98 semester hours. At least 30 semester hours must be completed at the college to receive degree.

**Admissions contact:** Sandra Schwartz, Director of Admissions. 414 684-5955.

**FINANCIAL AID. Available aid:** Pell grants, SEOG, state scholarships and grants, school scholarships and grants, private scholarships and grants, academic merit scholarships, and athletic scholarships. PLUS, Stafford Loans (GSL), and SLS. Monthly payment plan.

**Financial aid statistics:** In 1993-94, 100% of all undergraduate applicants received aid; 100% of freshman applicants. Average amounts of aid awarded freshmen: Scholarships and grants, $4,144; loans, $2,459.

**Supporting data/closing dates:** FAFSA/FAF: Priority filing date is April 15; accepted on rolling basis. Income tax forms: Priority filing date is April 15; accepted on rolling basis. Notification of awards on rolling basis.

**Financial aid contact:** Sr. Mary Beth Kornely, Director of Financial Aid. 414 684-6418.

# University of Wisconsin–Eau Claire

**Eau Claire, WI 54701 715 836-2637**

**1993-94 Costs.** Tuition: $2,188 (state residents), $6,680 (out-of-state). Room & board: $2,605. Fees, books, misc. academic expenses (school's estimate): $150.

**Enrollment.** Undergraduates: 3,395 men, 5,121 women (full-time). Freshman class: 5,729 applicants, 4,520 accepted, 1,957 enrolled. Graduate enrollment: 153 men, 412 women.

**Test score averages/ranges.** Average SAT scores: 460 verbal, 525 math. Range of SAT scores of middle 50%: 400-520 verbal, 460-580 math. Average ACT scores: 22 English, 22 math, 23 composite. Range of ACT scores of middle 50%: 20-25 English, 20-25 math.

**Faculty.** 479 full-time; 75 part-time. 64% of faculty holds doctoral degree. Student/faculty ratio: 18 to 1.

**Selectivity rating.** Less competitive.

**PROFILE.** U Wisconsin at Eau Claire is a public, comprehensive institution. Founded as a state Normal school in 1916, it gained university status in 1971. Programs are offered through the Schools of Arts and Sciences, Business, Education, Graduate Studies, and Nursing. Its 333-acre campus is located in Eau Claire, 95 miles east of Minneapolis-St. Paul.

**Accreditation:** NCACS. Professionally accredited by the Accrediting Council on Education in Journalism and Mass Communication, the American Assembly of Collegiate Schools of Business, the American Speech-Language-Hearing Association, the Council on Social Work Education, the National Association of Schools of Music, the National League for Nursing.

**Religious orientation:** University of Wisconsin–Eau Claire is nonsectarian; no religious requirements.

**Library:** Collections totaling over 541,501 volumes, 1,143 periodical subscriptions, and 1,327,899 microform items.

**Special facilities/museums:** Art gallery, human development center, bird museum, field station, planetarium.

**Athletic facilities:** Gymnasiums, weight rooms, track, basketball, racquetball, and tennis courts, swimming pool, athletic fields.

**STUDENT BODY. Undergraduate profile:** 84% are state residents; 19% are transfers. 1% Asian-American, 1% Black, 1% Hispanic, 1% Native American, 96% White. Average age of undergraduates is 22.

**Freshman profile:** 4% of freshmen who took SAT scored 700 or over on verbal, 6% scored 700 or over on math; 11% scored 600 or over on verbal, 23% scored 600 or over on math; 31% scored 500 or over on verbal, 62% scored 500 or over on math; 70% scored 400 or over on verbal, 88% scored 400 or over on math; 99% scored 300 or over on verbal, 100% scored 300 or over on math. 4% of freshmen who took ACT scored 30 or over on English, 4% scored 30 or over on math, 3% scored 30 or over on composite; 39% scored 24 or over on English, 35% scored 24 or over on math, 38% scored 24 or over on composite; 89% scored 18 or over on English, 90% scored 18 or over on math, 96% scored 18 or over on composite; 100% scored 12 or over on English, 100% scored 12 or over on math, 100% scored 12 or over on composite. 98% of accepted applicants took ACT. 93% of freshmen come from public schools.

**Undergraduate achievement:** 79% of fall 1992 freshmen returned for fall 1993 term. 13% of entering class graduated. 9% of students who completed a degree program immediately went on to graduate study.

**Foreign students:** 180 students are from out of the country. Countries represented include China, Japan, Malaysia, Mexico, Sweden, and the United Kingdom; 42 in all.

**PROGRAMS OF STUDY. Degrees:** B.A., B.Bus.Admin., B.F.A., B.Mus., B.Mus.Ed., B.S., B.S.Nurs., B.Soc.Work.

**Majors:** Accounting, Administrative Management, Art, Biochemistry/Molecular Biology, Biology, Business Administration, Business Education, Business/Finance, Chemistry, Chemistry/Business, Communication Arts, Communicative Disorders, Comparative Studies in Religion, Computer Science, Criminal Justice, Economics, Elementary Education, English, Environmental/Public Health, French, Geography, Geology, German, Health Care Administration, History, Journalism, Latin American Studies, Management, Management Information Systems, Marketing, Mathematics, Medical Technology, Music, Music Therapy, Nursing, Philosophy, Physical Education, Physical Sciences, Physics, Physics/Mathematics, Political Science, Psychology, Secretarial Administration, Social Studies, Social Work, Sociology, Spanish, Special Education, Theatre Arts.

**Distribution of degrees:** The majors with the highest enrollment are elementary education, nursing, and accounting; Latin American studies and physical science have the lowest.

**Requirements:** General education requirement.

**Academic regulations:** Minimum 2.0 GPA must be maintained.

**Special:** Minors offered in American Indian studies, anthropology, art history, coaching, family studies, general science, gerontology, language arts/teaching, language studies, library science, Scandinavian studies, Soviet studies, teaching English as a second language, telecommunications, women's studies, and writing. Training and topical minors. Double majors. Independent study. Pass/fail grading option. Internships. Cooperative education programs. Graduate school at which undergraduates may take graduate-level courses. Preprofessional programs in law, medicine, veterinary science, pharmacy, dentistry, theology, optometry, agriculture, architecture, chiropractic, engineering, forestry, mortuary science, occupational therapy, and physical therapy. Member of West Central Wisconsin Consortium. Member of National Student Exchange (NSE). Teacher certification in elementary, secondary, and special education. Exchange programs abroad in Austria, China, Denmark, England, France, Germany, Japan, Latvia, Mexico, Norway, Poland, the former Soviet Republics, Spain, Sweden, and other countries.
**Honors:** Honors program. Honor societies.
**Academic Assistance:** Remedial reading, writing, math, and study skills. Nonremedial tutoring.
**STUDENT LIFE. Housing:** All freshmen and sophomores must live on campus unless living with family. Coed, women's, and men's dorms. 34% of students live in college housing.
**Services and counseling/handicapped student services:** Placement services. Health service. Day care. Counseling services for minority and older students. Birth control, personal, and psychological counseling. Career and academic guidance services. Physically disabled student services. Learning disabled services. Tape recorders. Tutors. Reader services for the blind.
**Campus organizations:** Undergraduate student government. Student newspaper (Spectator, published twice/week). Literary magazine. Yearbook. Radio and TV stations. ACLU, Amnesty International, Circle K, College Republicans, Young Democrats, Hunger Project, bowling and martial arts groups, Orchesis, Students for Life, Toastmasters, 50 organizations in all. Four fraternities, no chapter houses; four sororities, no chapter houses. 1% of men join a fraternity. 1% of women join a sorority.
**Religious organizations:** Bahai Association, Alethia Campus Ministry, Campus Crusade for Christ, Chi Alpha, Ecumenical Religious Center, Fellowship of Christian Athletes, Intervarsity Christian Fellowship, Lutheran Collegians, Muslim Student Association, Navigators, Newman Student Association, Nurses Christian Fellowship, Student Fellowship, United Ministries.
**Minority/foreign student organizations:** Black Student League, Native American student group, Amigos de la Cultura Hispanica. International Student Association, Der Deutsche Verein, El Club Espanol, India Abroad Association, Japanese Culture Society, Le Salon Francais, Chinese, Hmong, and Scandinavian groups.
**ATHLETICS. Physical education requirements:** Two semester hours of physical education required.
**Intercollegiate competition:** 1% of students participate. Baseball (M), basketball (M,W), cheerleading (M,W), cross-country (M,W), diving (M,W), football (M), golf (M), gymnastics (W), ice hockey (M), soccer (W), softball (W), swimming (M,W), tennis (M,W), track and field (indoor) (M,W), track and field (outdoor) (M,W), volleyball (W), wrestling (M). Member of NCAA Division III, Northern Collegiate Hockey Association, Wisconsin State University Conference, Wisconsin Women's Intercollegiate Athletic Conference.
**Intramural and club sports:** 65% of students participate. Intramural Alpine skiing, basketball, body building, bowling, broomball, cycling, handball, Nautilus, Nordic skiing, racquetball, rugby, soccer, softball, swimming, touch football, tennis, volleyball, walleyball, water polo. Men's club Alpine skiing, bowling, handball, martial arts, racquetball, rugby, soccer, volleyball, water polo, weight lifting. Women's club Alpine skiing, bowling, martial arts, racquetball, rugby, volleyball, water polo, weight lifting.
**ADMISSIONS. Academic basis for candidate selection** (in order of priority): Secondary school record, class rank, standardized test scores, school's recommendation, essay.
**Nonacademic basis for candidate selection:** Extracurricular participation and particular talent or ability are considered.
**Requirements:** Graduation from secondary school is required; GED is accepted. 17 units and the following program of study are required: 4 units of English, 3 units of math, 3 units of science, 3 units of social studies, 4 units of electives including 2 units of academic electives. Minimum composite ACT score of 22 and rank in top half of secondary school class required. Audition required of music program applicants. EOP for applicants not normally admissible. Conditional admission possible for applicants not meeting standard requirements. ACT is required; SAT may be substituted. Campus visit recommended. No off-campus interviews.
**Supporting data/closing dates:** FAFSA: Priority filing date is April 15. Notification of awards on rolling basis.
**Financial aid contact:** Robert Sather, M.S., Director of Financial Aid. 715 836-3373.
**STUDENT EMPLOYMENT.** College Work/Study Program. Institutional employment. 20% of full-time undergraduates work on campus during school year. Students may expect to earn an average of $1,400 during school year. Off-campus part-time employment opportunities rated "good."
**COMPUTER FACILITIES.** 500 IBM/IBM-compatible and Macintosh/Apple microcomputers; 210 are networked. Students may access Digital, UNISYS minicomputer/mainframe systems, Internet. Residence halls may be equipped with stand-alone microcomputers, modems. Client/LAN operating systems include Apple/Macintosh, DOS, UNIX/XENIX/AIX, X-windows, LocalTalk/AppleTalk, Novell. Computer languages and software packages include C, COBOL, FORTRAN, Microsoft Word, PageMaker, SAS, SPSS, WordPerfect; 20 in all. Dorm microcomputer use restricted to residents.
**Fees:** None.
**Hours:** 7 AM-10 PM.
**GRADUATE CAREER DATA.** Graduate school percentages: 1% enter law school. 1% enter medical school. 2% enter graduate business programs. 3% enter graduate arts and sciences programs. Highest graduate school enrollments: U of Illinois, U of Iowa, U of Michigan, U of Minnesota, U of Wisconsin. 70% of graduates choose careers in business and industry. Companies and businesses that hire graduates: Arthur Andersen, Cargill, Johnson Controls, M&I Bank, NML, 3M, Wausau Insurance.
**PROMINENT ALUMNI/AE.** Leonard Haas, former chancellor, U of Wisconsin at Eau Claire; Richard Saykally, research chemist; Joan Reidy Heggen, former mayor, Tallahassee, Fla.

# University of Wisconsin–Green Bay

**Green Bay, WI 54311-7001 — 414 465-2293**

**1994-95 Costs.** Tuition: $2,209 (state residents), $6,880 (out-of-state). Room: $1,600. Board: $1,400. Fees, books, misc. academic expenses (school's estimate): $450.
**Enrollment.** Undergraduates: 1,520 men, 2,302 women (full-time). Freshman class: 2,409 applicants, 1,939 accepted, 758 enrolled. Graduate enrollment: 120 men, 115 women.
**Test score averages/ranges.** Average ACT scores: 22 English, 21 math, 22 composite. Range of ACT scores of middle 50%: 19-25 English, 18-24 math.
**Faculty.** 194 full-time; 62 part-time. 95% of faculty holds doctoral degree. Student/faculty ratio: 22 to 1.
**Selectivity rating.** Less competitive.

**PROFILE.** U Wisconsin at Green Bay, founded in 1968, is a public, comprehensive institution. Its 700-acre campus is located in Green Bay, north of Milwaukee.
**Accreditation:** NCACS. Professionally accredited by the American Dietetic Association, the Council on Social Work Education, the National Association of Schools of Music, the National League for Nursing.
**Religious orientation:** University of Wisconsin–Green Bay is nonsectarian; no religious requirements.
**Library:** Collections totaling over 330,000 volumes, 1,300 periodical subscriptions, and 700,000 microform items.
**Special facilities/museums:** Art gallery, natural history museum, arboretum, performing arts center.
**Athletic facilities:** Sports center, gymnasium, indoor swimming pool, athletic fields, nine-hole golf course, sailing facilities, cycling, Nordic skiing, and running trails, Nautilus and weight rooms, racquetball and tennis courts.
**STUDENT BODY. Undergraduate profile:** 97% are state residents; 30% are transfers. 1% Asian-American, 1% Black, 1% Hispanic, 2% Native American, 94% White, 1% Other. Average age of undergraduates is 22.
**Freshman profile:** 3% of freshmen who took ACT scored 30 or over on English, 3% scored 30 or over on math, 2% scored 30 or over on composite; 37% scored 24 or over on English, 27% scored 24 or over on math, 34% scored 24 or over on composite; 87% scored 18 or over on English, 82% scored 18 or over on math, 93% scored 18 or over on composite; 100% scored 12 or over on English, 100% scored 12 or over on math. 98% of accepted applicants took ACT. 85% of freshmen come from public schools.
**Undergraduate achievement:** 77% of fall 1992 freshmen returned for fall 1993 term. 11% of entering class graduated. 12% of students who completed a degree program immediately went on to graduate study.
**Foreign students:** 77 students are from out of the country. Countries represented include China, Germany, Hong Kong, Japan, Malaysia, and Mexico; 23 in all.
**PROGRAMS OF STUDY. Degrees:** B.A., B.Gen.Studies, B.Mus., B.S., B.S.Nurs., B.Soc.Work.
**Majors:** Accounting, Anthropology, Art, Biology, Business Administration, Chemistry, Communication Processes, Communications/Marketing, Dance, Earth Science, Economics, Elementary/Secondary Education, Environmental Planning, Finance, French Language/Literature, Geography, German Language/Literature, History, Human Adaptability, Human Biology, Human Development, Humanistic Studies, Information/Computing Science, Literature/Language, Management, Marketing, Mathematics, Media, Military Science, Music, Natural/Applied Science, Nonprofit Organization Management, Nursing, Nutritional Sciences, Philosophy, Photography, Physics, Political Science, Pre-Agriculture, Pre-Dentistry, Pre-Engineering, Pre-Journalism, Pre-Law, Pre-Medicine, Pre-Pharmacy, Pre-Veterinary Medicine, Psychology, Public/Environmental Administration, Regional Analysis, Science/Environmental Change, Social Change/Development, Social Services, Social Work, Sociology, Spanish Language/Literature, Theatre, Urban Studies, Women's Studies.
**Distribution of degrees:** The majors with the highest enrollment are business administration, human development, and psychology; philosophy, physics, and earth science have the lowest.
**Requirements:** General education requirement.
**Academic regulations:** Minimum 2.0 GPA must be maintained.
**Special:** Associate's degrees offered. Self-designed majors. Double majors. Independent study. Pass/fail grading option. Internships. Graduate school at which undergraduates may take graduate-level courses. Preprofessional programs in law, medicine, veterinary science, pharmacy, dentistry, theology, and optometry. 2-2 engineering and architecture programs with U of Wisconsin at Milwaukee. 2-2 physical therapy program with U of Wisconsin at LaCrosse. 2-2 occupational therapy program with U of Wisconsin at Madison. Pre-medicine, pre-dentistry, and veterinary medicine programs with U of Wisconsin at Madison. Pre-nursing program with Bellin Hospital. Pre-law programs with Hamline U, Marquette U, and U of Wisconsin at Madison. Pre-chiropractic program. Member of consortium with Bellin Coll of Nursing. Member of National Student Exchange (NSE). Teacher certification in early childhood, elementary, and secondary education. Certification in specific subject areas. Exchange programs abroad in France (Sorbonne) and Mexico (U of Yucatan). Study abroad also in China, Denmark, Germany, and Guatemala. ROTC.
**Academic Assistance:** Remedial reading, writing, math, and study skills. Nonremedial tutoring.
**STUDENT LIFE. Housing:** Students may live on or off campus. Coed dorms. School-owned/operated apartments. 20% of students live in college housing.
**Services and counseling/handicapped student services:** Placement services. Health service. Women's center. Day care. Counseling services for minority, military, veteran, and older students. Birth control, personal, and psychological counseling. Career and academic guidance services. Religious counseling. Physically disabled student services. Learning disabled services. Notetaking services. Tape recorders. Tutors. Reader services for the blind.

**Campus organizations:** Undergraduate student government. Student newspaper (Fourth Estate, published once/week). Literary magazine. Radio and TV stations. Music ensembles and clubs, theatre, dance concerts, foreign language clubs, environmental group, academic, athletic, and special-interest groups, 75 organizations in all. One fraternity, no chapter house; two sororities, no chapter houses. 1% of men join a fraternity. 1% of women join a sorority.
**Religious organizations:** Bahai Club, Christians in Action, Intervarsity Christian Fellowship, ecumenical center.
**Minority/foreign student organizations:** Black Student Union, American Indian Council, Hispanic group, Southeast Asian Students. International Club.
**ATHLETICS. Physical education requirements:** None.
**Intercollegiate competition:** 5% of students participate. Basketball (M,W), cross-country (M,W), diving (M,W), golf (M), Nordic skiing (M), soccer (M,W), softball (W), swimming (M,W), tennis (M,W), volleyball (W). Member of Mid-Continent Conference, NCAA Division I.
**Intramural and club sports:** 16% of students participate. Intramural basketball, football, softball, volleyball. Men's club cheerleading, sailing. Women's club cheerleading, sailing.
**ADMISSIONS. Academic basis for candidate selection** (in order of priority): Class rank, standardized test scores, secondary school record, school's recommendation, essay.
**Nonacademic basis for candidate selection:** Character and personality, extracurricular participation, and particular talent or ability are considered.
**Requirements:** Graduation from secondary school is required; GED is accepted. 17 units and the following program of study are required: 4 units of English, 3 units of math, 3 units of science including 1 unit of lab, 3 units of social studies, 4 units of electives including 2 units of academic electives. Rank in top half of secondary school class required; minimum composite ACT score of 23 recommended. R.N. required of nursing program applicants. EOP for applicants not normally admissible. Conditional admission possible for applicants not meeting standard requirements. ACT is required. Off-campus interviews available with an admissions representative.
**Procedure:** Take ACT by October of 12th year. Visit college for interview by December of 12th year. Suggest filing application by February 1; no deadline. Notification of admission on rolling basis. $75 room deposit, refundable until May 15. Freshmen accepted for terms other than fall.
**Special programs:** Admission may be deferred one year. Credit and/or placement may be granted through CEEB Advanced Placement exams for scores of 3 or higher. Credit may be granted through CLEP general and subject exams, ACT PEP and DANTES exams, and military and life experience. Credit and placement may be granted through challenge exams. Early entrance/early admission program. Concurrent enrollment program.
**Transfer students:** Transfer students accepted for terms other than fall. In fall 1993, 30% of all new students were transfers into all classes. 1,233 transfer applications were received, 1,046 were accepted. Priority application deadline is February 10 for fall; December 15 for spring. Minimum 2.0 GPA required. Lowest course grade accepted is "D." Maximum number of transferable credits is 88 semester hours. At least 36 semester hours must be completed at the university to receive degree.
**Admissions contact:** Myron Van de Ven, M.Ed., Director of Admissions. 414 465-2111.
**FINANCIAL AID. Available aid:** Pell grants, SEOG, state scholarships and grants, school scholarships, private scholarships and grants, academic merit scholarships, athletic scholarships, and aid for undergraduate foreign students. Talent incentive program. Perkins Loans (NDSL), PLUS, Stafford Loans (GSL), NSL, Health Professions Loans, and SLS. Partial payment plans.
**Financial aid statistics:** 15% of aid is not need-based. In 1993-94, 65% of all undergraduate applicants received aid; 60% of freshman applicants. Average amounts of aid awarded freshmen: Scholarships and grants, $3,343; loans, $1,200.
**Supporting data/closing dates:** FAFSA: Priority filing date is April 15; accepted on rolling basis. Notification of awards begins April 1.
**Financial aid contact:** Ron Ronnenberg, M.S., Director of Financial Aid. 414 465-2075.
**STUDENT EMPLOYMENT.** College Work/Study Program. Institutional employment. 20% of full-time undergraduates work on campus during school year. Students may expect to earn an average of $1,200 during school year. Off-campus part-time employment opportunities rated "good."
**COMPUTER FACILITIES.** 200 IBM/IBM-compatible and Macintosh/Apple microcomputers; 150 are networked. Students may access Digital minicomputer/mainframe systems, BITNET, Internet. Residence halls may be equipped with stand-alone microcomputers, networked terminals. Computer languages and software packages include BASIC, C, COBOL, dBASE, FORTRAN, LISP, Lotus 1-2-3, MINITAB, OPS-5, Pascal, TEXTRA, WordPerfect; 40 in all. Computer facilities are available to all students.
**GRADUATE CAREER DATA.** Graduate school percentages: 1% enter law school. 1% enter medical school. 5% enter graduate business programs. 2% enter graduate arts and sciences programs. Highest graduate school enrollments: U of Wisconsin system, Wisconsin Coll of Medicine. 49% of graduates choose careers in business and industry.
**PROMINENT ALUMNI/AE.** Robert Cowles, Wisconsin state senator; Janet Freedman, physician and president of Committee of Interns and Residents.

## University of Wisconsin–LaCrosse

**LaCrosse, WI 54601** **608 785-8000**

**1994-95 Costs.** Tuition: $2,217 (state residents), $6,665 (out-of-state). Room & board: $2,270. Fees, books, misc. academic expenses (school's estimate): $150.
**Enrollment.** Undergraduates: 3,182 men, 4,124 women (full-time). Freshman class: 4,868 applicants, 2,877 accepted. Graduate enrollment: 210 men, 436 women.
**Test score averages/ranges.** Average ACT scores: 22 composite. Range of ACT scores of middle 50%: 21-24 composite.
**Faculty.** 73% of faculty holds doctoral degree. Student/faculty ratio: 19 to 1.
**Selectivity rating.** Competitive.

**PROFILE.** U Wisconsin at LaCrosse, founded in 1906, is a public, comprehensive institution. Programs are offered through the Colleges of Arts, Letters, and Sciences; Business Administration; Education; and Health, Physical Education, and Recreation and the School of Health and Human Services. Its 119-acre campus is located in LaCrosse, northwest of Madison.

**Accreditation:** NCACS. Professionally accredited by the American Assembly of Collegiate Schools of Business, the American Physical Therapy Association, the Council on Social Work Education, the National Association of Schools of Music, the National Council for Accreditation of Teacher Education, the National Recreation and Park Association.
**Religious orientation:** University of Wisconsin–LaCrosse is nonsectarian; no religious requirements.
**Library:** Collections totaling over 529,520 volumes, 2,011 periodical subscriptions, and 902,461 microform items.
**Special facilities/museums:** Audio-visual center, greenhouse, planetarium.
**Athletic facilities:** Field house, tracks, basketball, racquetball, and tennis courts, swimming pool, football, rugby, soccer, and softball fields, gymnasiums, dance studio, weight room, stadium.
**STUDENT BODY. Undergraduate profile:** 85% are state residents; 16% are transfers. 1.4% Asian-American, 1.4% Black, 1% Hispanic, 1% Native American, 94% White, 1.2% Other. Average age of undergraduates is 21.
**Freshman profile:** 99% of accepted applicants took ACT. 90% of freshmen come from public schools.
**Undergraduate achievement:** 75% of fall 1992 freshmen returned for fall 1993 term. 6% of students who completed a degree program went on to graduate study within one year.
**Foreign students:** 45 students are from out of the country. Countries represented include England, France, Hong Kong, India, and the former Soviet Republics; 22 in all.
**PROGRAMS OF STUDY. Degrees:** B.A., B.S.
**Majors:** Accountancy, Archaeology, Art, Biology, Business Administration, Chemistry, Chemistry/Business, Community Health Education, Computer Science, Economics, Elementary Education, English, Finance, Finance/Risk/Insurance, French, French/Business, Geography, History, Marketing, Mass Communications, Mathematics, Mathematics/Statistics, Medical Technology, Microbiology, Military Science, Minority Studies, Music Education/Choral, Music Education/Instrumental, Music History, Music/Performance, Music Theory, Nuclear Medicine Technology, Physical Education, Physical Education/Athletic Training, Physical Education/Elementary Education, Physical Education/Fitness, Physical Education/Sports Management, Physical Therapy, Physics, Political Science, Psychology, Public Administration, Recreation/Parks Administration, Recreation Program Leadership, School Health Education, Science, Social Studies, Social Work, Sociology, Spanish, Spanish/Business, Speech, Theatre Arts, Therapeutic Recreation.
**Distribution of degrees:** The majors with the highest enrollment are elementary education, business administration, and physical education; math and foreign languages have the lowest.
**Requirements:** General education requirement.
**Academic regulations:** Freshmen must maintain minimum 1.6 GPA.
**Special:** Minors offered in most majors and in anthropology, creative/expository writing, early childhood education, earth science, English as a second language, general science, German, instructional media, interdisciplinary majors, international business, international studies, Latin American studies, photography, psychological foundations of education of exceptional children, special education, statistics, and women's studies. Double majors. Dual degrees. Independent study. Pass/fail grading option. Internships. Cooperative education programs. Graduate school at which undergraduates may take graduate-level courses. Preprofessional programs in law, medicine, veterinary science, pharmacy, dentistry, optometry, and chiropractic. Member of West Central Wisconsin Consortium. Teacher certification in early childhood, elementary, and secondary education. Certification in specific subject areas. Exchange programs abroad in African, Asian, and European countries. Study abroad also in China, Denmark, France, Germany, Mexico, the former Soviet Republics, Spain, and the United Kingdom. ROTC.
**Honors:** Honors program.
**Academic Assistance:** Remedial reading, writing, math, and study skills.
**STUDENT LIFE. Housing:** School recommends that all freshmen live on campus. Coed and women's dorms. 33% of students live in college housing.
**Services and counseling/handicapped student services:** Health service. Day care. Counseling services for minority, military, veteran, and older students. Birth control, personal, and psychological counseling. Career and academic guidance services. Religious counseling. Learning disabled services.
**Campus organizations:** Undergraduate student government. Student newspaper (Racquet, published once/week). Radio and TV stations. Men's chorus, women's glee club, Marching Chiefs, flags/color guard, advertising club, badminton and chess clubs, veterans club, Women's Studies Student Association, Handicapped Awareness Association, Amnesty International, special-interest groups, 100 organizations in all. Two fraternities, one chapter house; two sororities, no chapter houses. 1% of men join a fraternity. 2% of women join a sorority.
**Religious organizations:** Baptist Student Union, Christians Alive, Campus Crusade for Christ, Navigators, Latter-Day Saints Association, Lutheran Campus Center, Newman Club, United Campus Ministry, Intervarsity Christian Fellowship, Fellowship of Christian Athletes.
**Minority/foreign student organizations:** Black Student Unity, Native American Indian Council, Pan-American Club. International Student Association, Asian Association.
**ATHLETICS. Physical education requirements:** Two semesters of physical education required.
**Intercollegiate competition:** 8% of students participate. Baseball (M), basketball (M,W), cross-country (M,W), diving (M,W), football (M), gymnastics (W), soccer (W), softball (W), swimming (M,W), tennis (M,W), track and field (indoor) (M,W), track and field (outdoor) (M,W), volleyball (W), wrestling (M). Member of NCAA Division III, Wisconsin State University Conference, Wisconsin Women's Intercollegiate Athletic Conference.
**Intramural and club sports:** 45% of students participate. Intramural aerobics, basketball, flag football, floor hockey, racquetball, softball, tennis, volleyball. Men's club cheerleading, lacrosse, rugby, soccer, volleyball, weight lifting. Women's club cheerleading, weight lifting.

**ADMISSIONS. Academic basis for candidate selection** (in order of priority): Class rank, secondary school record, standardized test scores, school's recommendation, essay.
**Nonacademic basis for candidate selection:** Extracurricular participation and particular talent or ability are considered.
**Requirements:** Graduation from secondary school is required; GED is accepted. 16 units and the following program of study are required: 4 units of English, 2 units of math, 2 units of lab science, 3 units of social studies, 5 units of academic electives. Minimum composite ACT score of 23 or rank in top third of secondary school class. Interview required of physical therapy program applicants. Academic Summer Institute for applicants not normally admissible. ACT is required. Campus visit recommended. No off-campus interviews.
**Procedure:** Take ACT by October of 12th year. Suggest filing application by January 1; no deadline. Notification of admission on rolling basis. $100 nonrefundable tuition deposit. $75 room deposit, refundable until May 1. Freshmen accepted for terms other than fall.
**Special programs:** Credit and/or placement may be granted through CEEB Advanced Placement exams for scores of 3 or higher. Credit may be granted through CLEP general and subject exams and military experience. Credit and placement may be granted through challenge exams. Concurrent enrollment program.
**Transfer students:** Transfer students accepted for terms other than fall. In fall 1993, 16% of all new students were transfers into all classes. 861 transfer applications were received, 524 were accepted. Application deadline is rolling for fall; rolling for spring. Minimum 2.75 GPA required. Lowest course grade accepted is "D." Maximum number of transferable credits is 72 semester hours. At least 36 semester hours must be completed at the university to receive degree.
**Admissions contact:** Gale Grimslid, M.S., Director of Admissions. 608 785-8067.

**FINANCIAL AID. Available aid:** Pell grants, SEOG, state scholarships and grants, school scholarships and grants, academic merit scholarships, and aid for undergraduate foreign students. Perkins Loans (NDSL), PLUS, Stafford Loans (GSL), state loans, school loans, and SLS. Installment credit agreement.
**Financial aid statistics:** In 1993-94, 49% of all undergraduate applicants received aid; 52% of freshman applicants. Average amounts of aid awarded freshmen: Scholarships and grants, $300; loans, $2,040.
**Supporting data/closing dates:** FAFSA/FAF/FFS: Priority filing date is March 15. Income tax forms: Priority filing date is March 15. Notification of awards begins May 15.
**Financial aid contact:** A.C. Stadthaus, M.S., Director of Financial Aid. 608 785-8604.

**STUDENT EMPLOYMENT.** College Work/Study Program. Institutional employment. 25% of full-time undergraduates work on campus during school year. Students may expect to earn an average of $980 during school year. Freshmen are discouraged from working during their first term. Off-campus part-time employment opportunities rated "excellent."

**COMPUTER FACILITIES.** 300 IBM/IBM-compatible and Macintosh/Apple microcomputers; 275 are networked. Students may access Digital minicomputer/mainframe systems. Residence halls may be equipped with stand-alone microcomputers, networked terminals. Computer languages and software packages include Assembly, BASIC, COBOL, DECShell, LISP, Modula 2, PL/1; database management, statistical packages. Computer facilities are available to all students.
**Fees:** Computer fee is included in tuition/fees.
**Hours:** 24 hours for mainframes; lab hours vary.

**PROMINENT ALUMNI/AE.** Russel Cleary, president, G. Heileman Brewing; John Mwaura, ambassador to U.S. from Kenya; Timothy Nugent, originator of wheelchair basketball; Gayle Anderson, president, Golden Bank, Calif., first woman in U.S. to be appointed bank examiner of a state banking department.

9-5

# University of Wisconsin–Madison

**Madison, WI 53706** **608 262-1234**

**1993-94 Costs.** Tuition: $3,100 (state residents), $8,200 (out-of-state). Room & board: $3,850. Fees, books, misc. academic expenses (school's estimate): $1,875.
**Enrollment.** Undergraduates: 13,219 men, 13,419 women (full-time). Freshman class: 14,901 applicants, 10,932 accepted, 4,031 enrolled. Graduate enrollment: 6,580 men, 5,332 women.
**Test score averages/ranges.** Average SAT scores: 510 verbal, 610 math. Range of SAT scores of middle 50%: 460-590 verbal, 550-660 math. Average ACT scores: 26 composite. Range of ACT scores of middle 50%: 24-29 composite.
**Faculty.** 2,273 full-time; 95 part-time. 88% of faculty holds doctoral degree. Student/faculty ratio: 12 to 1.
**Selectivity rating.** Highly competitive.

**PROFILE.** U Wisconsin at Madison, founded in 1848, is a public, comprehensive institution. Programs are offered through the Colleges of Agricultural and Life Sciences, Engineering, and Letters and Science; the Schools of Business, Education, Family Resources and Consumer Sciences, Nursing, Pharmacy, and Veterinary Medicine; and the Graduate, Law, and Medical Schools. Its 911-acre campus is located in Madison, 77 miles west of Milwaukee.

**Accreditation:** NCACS. Numerous professional accreditations.
**Religious orientation:** University of Wisconsin–Madison is nonsectarian; no religious requirements.
**Library:** Collections totaling over 5,080,000 volumes, 51,000 periodical subscriptions, and 2,000,000 microform items.
**Special facilities/museums:** Art, physics, and geology museums, nuclear reactor, biotron, electron microscopes.
**Athletic facilities:** Gymnasiums, swimming pools, sports centers, tennis stadium.

**STUDENT BODY. Undergraduate profile:** 68% are state residents; 23% are transfers. 4% Asian-American, 3% Black, 3% Hispanic, 86% White, 4% Other. Average age of undergraduates is 21.
**Freshman profile:** 55% of accepted applicants took SAT; 65% took ACT. 70% of freshmen come from public schools.
**Undergraduate achievement:** 94% of fall 1992 freshmen returned for fall 1993 term. 77% of entering class graduated.
**Foreign students:** 962 students are from out of the country. Countries represented include China, Hong Kong, Indonesia, Korea, Malaysia, and Singapore; 66 in all.

**PROGRAMS OF STUDY. Degrees:** B.A., B.Bus.Admin., B.F.A., B.Mus., B.Nat.Sci., B.S.
**Majors:** Accounting, Actuarial Sciences, African Languages/Literature, Afro-American Studies, Agricultural Business Management, Agricultural Economics, Agricultural Education, Agricultural Engineering, Agricultural Journalism, Agricultural Mechanization/Management, Agronomy, Anthropology, Apparel Design, Applied Mathematics/Engineering/Physics, Art, Art Education, Art History, Asian Studies, Astronomy/Physics, Bacteriology, Behavior Science/Law, Biochemistry, Biological Aspects of Conservation, Botany, Cartography, Chemical Engineering, Chemistry, Chinese, Civil/Environmental Engineering, Classical Humanities, Classics, Communication Arts, Communicative Disorders, Comparative Literature, Computer Sciences, Computer Sciences/Statistics, Construction Administration, Consumer Science, Dairy Science, Dietetics, Economics, Electrical/Computer Engineering, Elementary Education, Engineering Mechanics, English, Entomology, Extension Education, Family/Consumer Communications, Family/Consumer Education, Finance/Investment/Banking, Food Science, Food Service Administration, Forest Science, French, Genetics, Geography, Geological Engineering, Geology/Geophysics, German, Greek, Hebrew/Semitic Studies, History, History of Culture, History of Science, Home Economics, Home Economics Education, Horticulture, Ibero-American Studies, Individual Major, Industrial Engineering, Information Systems Analysis/Design, Interior Design, International Relations, Italian, Japanese, Journalism/Mass Communication, Landscape Architecture, Latin, Linguistics, Management/Administration, Management/Personnel/Industrial Relations, Marketing, Mathematics, Meat/Animal Science, Mechanical Engineering, Medical Microbiology, Medical Science, Medical Technology, Metallurgical Engineering, Meteorology, Molecular Biology, Music, Nuclear Engineering, Nursing, Nutrition, Nutritional Sciences, Occupational Therapy, Pharmaceutical Sciences, Pharmacology/Toxicology, Philosophy, Physical Education, Physical Education/Dance, Physical Therapy, Physician Assistant, Physics, Plant Pathology, Polish, Political Science, Portuguese, Poultry Science, Psychology, Quantitative Analysis, Real Estate/Urban Land Economics, Recreation Resources Management, Rehabilitation Psychology, Related Arts, Retailing, Risk Management/Insurance, Rural Sociology, Russian, Scandinavian Studies, Secondary Education, Social Welfare, Social Work, Sociology, Soil Science, South Asian Studies, Spanish, Special Education, Statistics, Textile Science, Textiles/Clothing, Theatre/Drama, Transportation/Public Utilities, Wildlife Ecology, Women's Studies, Zoology.
**Distribution of degrees:** The majors with the highest enrollment are political science, mechanical engineering, and history; risk management/insurance, finance/investment/banking, and agricultural education have the lowest.
**Special:** Integrated liberal studies program. Medical Scholars Program offers 50 exceptional freshmen conditional admission to pre-med program. Self-designed majors. Double majors. Independent study. Pass/fail grading option. Internships. Cooperative education programs. Graduate school at which undergraduates may take graduate-level courses. Preprofessional programs in law, medicine, veterinary science, pharmacy, and dentistry. Member of Committee on Institutional Cooperation. Teacher certification in early childhood, elementary, secondary, special education, vo-tech, and bilingual/bicultural education. Study abroad in Brazil, Ecuador, France, Germany, Greece, Hungary, India, Israel, Italy, Japan, Mexico, Nepal, Peru, Russia, Scandinavian countries, Spain, Thailand, the United Kingdom, and other countries. ROTC, NROTC, and AFROTC.
**Honors:** Phi Beta Kappa. Honors program.
**Academic Assistance:** Remedial reading, writing, math, and study skills. Nonremedial tutoring.

**STUDENT LIFE. Housing:** Students may live on or off campus. Coed, women's, and men's dorms. Sorority and fraternity housing. School-owned/operated apartments. Off-campus privately-owned housing. Both on-campus and off-campus married-student housing. Unmarried-student graduate housing. 98% of students live in college housing.
**Services and counseling/handicapped student services:** Placement services. Health service. Day care. Counseling services for minority, military, veteran, and older students. Birth control, personal, and psychological counseling. Career and academic guidance services. Physically disabled student services. Learning disabled services. Notetaking services. Tape recorders. Tutors. Reader services for the blind.
**Campus organizations:** Undergraduate student government. Student newspapers (Badger Herald; Daily Cardinal). Literary magazine. Yearbook. Radio and TV stations. Numerous musical, special-interest, departmental, and professional committees and groups, 900 organizations in all. 34 fraternities, 26 chapter houses; 17 sororities, all with chapter houses. 14% of men join a fraternity. 14% of women join a sorority.
**Religious organizations:** 22 religious centers near or on campus.
**Minority/foreign student organizations:** 23 minority groups. 45 foreign student groups.

**ATHLETICS. Physical education requirements:** None.
**Intercollegiate competition:** 2% of students participate. Basketball (M,W), cheerleading (M,W), crew (M,W), cross-country (M,W), diving (M,W), football (M), golf (M,W), ice hockey (M), soccer (M,W), swimming (M,W), tennis (M,W), track (indoor) (M,W), track (outdoor) (M,W), track and field (indoor) (M,W), track and field (outdoor) (M,W), volleyball (W), wrestling (M). Member of Big 10 Conference, NCAA Division I, Western Collegiate Hockey Association.
**Intramural and club sports:** 10% of students participate. Intramural basketball, football, ice hockey, soccer, softball, tennis, volleyball. Men's club fencing, gymnastics, handball, lacrosse, racquetball, rugby, squash, volleyball, water polo. Women's club fencing, gymnastics, handball, racquetball, rugby, softball, squash, volleyball.

**ADMISSIONS. Academic basis for candidate selection** (in order of priority): Class rank, secondary school record, standardized test scores, school's recommendation, essay.

**Nonacademic basis for candidate selection:** Particular talent or ability and alumni/ae relationship are important. Character and personality, extracurricular participation, and geographical distribution are considered.
**Requirements:** Graduation from secondary school is required; GED is accepted. 17 units and the following program of study are required: 4 units of English, 3 units of math, 3 units of lab science, 2 units of foreign language, 3 units of social studies, 2 units of academic electives. Portfolio recommended of art program applicants. Audition required of music program applicants. Academic Advancement Program for applicants not normally admissible. ACT required of in-state applicants; out-of-state applicants may submit SAT or ACT. No off-campus interviews.
**Procedure:** Take SAT or ACT by October of 12th year. Application deadline is February 1. Notification of admission on rolling basis for some; April 1 for others. Reply is required by May 1. $100 nonrefundable tuition deposit. $150 nonrefundable room deposit. Freshmen accepted for terms other than fall.
**Special programs:** Credit and/or placement may be granted through CEEB Advanced Placement exams for scores of 3 or higher. Credit may be granted through CLEP general and subject exams. Credit and placement may be granted through challenge exams. Early entrance/early admission program. Concurrent enrollment program.
**Transfer students:** Transfer students accepted for terms other than fall. In fall 1993, 23% of all new students were transfers into all classes. 4,795 transfer applications were received, 2,108 were accepted. Application deadline is February 1 for some programs; March 1 for others for fall; November 15 for spring. Lowest course grade accepted is "C." At least 30 semester hours must be completed at the university to receive degree. and at least half of degree requirements.
**Admissions contact:** Millard Storey, M.A., Director of Admissions. 608 262-3961.

**FINANCIAL AID. Available aid:** Pell grants, SEOG, state scholarships and grants, school scholarships and grants, private scholarships and grants, ROTC scholarships, academic merit scholarships, and athletic scholarships. Perkins Loans (NDSL), PLUS, Stafford Loans (GSL), NSL, Health Professions Loans, state loans, school loans, private loans, and SLS.
**Financial aid statistics:** In 1993-94, 94% of all undergraduate applicants received aid; 56% of freshman applicants. Average amounts of aid awarded freshmen: Scholarships and grants, $2,902; loans, $2,841.
**Supporting data/closing dates:** School's own aid application: Priority filing date is March 1. Income tax forms: Priority filing date is March 1. Notification of awards on rolling basis.
**Financial aid contact:** Wallace Douma, Director of Financial Aid. 608 262-3060.

**STUDENT EMPLOYMENT.** College Work/Study Program. Institutional employment. 50% of full-time undergraduates work on campus during school year. Students may expect to earn an average of $1,500 during school year. Off-campus part-time employment opportunities rated "good."

**COMPUTER FACILITIES.** 2,800 IBM/IBM-compatible and Macintosh/Apple microcomputers. Residence halls may be equipped with stand-alone microcomputers, networked microcomputers, networked terminals, modems. Client/LAN operating systems include Apple/Macintosh, DOS, OS/2. Computer languages and software packages include BASIC, C, FORTRAN, Lotus 1-2-3, Microsoft Word, Pascal, WordStar. Computer facilities are available to all students.
**Fees:** $3 computer fee per hour.
**Hours:** 24 hours.

**PROMINENT ALUMNI/AE.** Daniel J. Travanti and Frederic March, actors; Edwin Newman, news commentator; A.C. Neilsen, founder, Neilsen Ratings Service; John Ringling, circus owner; Frank Lloyd Wright, architect; Joyce Carol Oates, novelist; Eudora Welty, author; Tommy Thompson, governor of Wisconsin; Dr. Karl Menninger, founder, Menninger Clinic; Charles Lindburgh, aviator; John Muir, naturalist.

# University of Wisconsin–Milwaukee

**Milwaukee, WI 53201-0749** **414 229-1122**

**1993-94 Costs.** Tuition: $2,725 (state residents), $8,721 (out-of-state). Room & board: $3,440. Fees, books, misc. academic expenses (school's estimate): $900.
**Enrollment.** Undergraduates: 5,738 men, 5,781 women (full-time). Freshman class: 5,141 applicants, 3,760 accepted, 1,930 enrolled. Graduate enrollment: 2,010 men, 2,668 women.
**Test score averages/ranges.** Average ACT scores: 21 English, 21 math, 22 composite. Range of ACT scores of middle 50%: 18-24 English, 18-24 math.
**Faculty.** 821 full-time; 421 part-time. 78% of faculty holds doctoral degree. Student/faculty ratio: 19 to 1.
**Selectivity rating.** Less competitive.

**PROFILE.** U Wisconsin at Milwaukee is a public, comprehensive institution. Founded as a state Normal school in 1885, it gained university status in 1956. Programs are offered through the Colleges of Engineering and Applied Science and Letters and Science; the Schools of Allied Health Professions, Architecture and Urban Planning, Business Administration, Education, Fine Arts, Library and Information Science, Nursing, and Social Welfare; and the Graduate School. Its 90-acre campus is located in a residential section two miles from downtown Milwaukee.

**Accreditation:** NCACS. Professionally accredited by the Accreditation Board for Engineering and Technology, the Accrediting Council on Education in Journalism and Mass Communication, the American Assembly of Collegiate Schools of Business, the American Library Association, the American Medical Association (CAHEA), the American Speech-Language-Hearing Association, the Council on Social Work Education, the National Architecture Accrediting Board, the National Association of Schools of Music, the National Council for Accreditation of Teacher Education, the National League for Nursing.
**Religious orientation:** University of Wisconsin–Milwaukee is nonsectarian; no religious requirements.
**Library:** Collections totaling over 3,700,000 volumes, 9,500 periodical subscriptions, and 1,300,000 microform items.
**Special facilities/museums:** Art and geology museums, childhood education center, foreign language resource center, Great Lakes research facility and environmental studies field station, planetarium.
**Athletic facilities:** Field house, gymnasium, swimming pool, weight room, basketball, racquetball, tennis, and volleyball courts, baseball and soccer fields.

**STUDENT BODY. Undergraduate profile:** 96% are state residents; 35% are transfers. 2% Asian-American, 8% Black, 3% Hispanic, 1% Native American, 85% White, 1% Other. Average age of undergraduates is 22.
**Freshman profile:** 2% of freshmen who took ACT scored 30 or over on English, 4% scored 30 or over on math, 3% scored 30 or over on composite; 29% scored 24 or over on English, 27% scored 24 or over on math, 30% scored 24 or over on composite; 80% scored 18 or over on English, 79% scored 18 or over on math, 87% scored 18 or over on composite; 99% scored 12 or over on English, 100% scored 12 or over on math, 100% scored 12 or over on composite; 100% scored 6 or over on English. 87% of accepted applicants took ACT.
**Undergraduate achievement:** 74% of fall 1992 freshmen returned for fall 1993 term. 11% of entering class graduated. 16% of students who completed a degree program went on to graduate study within one year.
**Foreign students:** 254 students are from out of the country. Countries represented include African, European, and Middle Eastern countries, Iceland, Mexico, and the former Soviet Republics; 74 in all.

**PROGRAMS OF STUDY. Degrees:** B.A., B.Bus.Admin., B.F.A., B.S., B.S.Appl.Sci., B.S.Eng., B.S.Nurs.
**Majors:** Accounting, Administrative Leadership and Supervision in Education, Afro-American Studies, Anthropology, Applied Mathematics/Physics, Architectural Studies, Architecture, Art, Art Education, Art History, Art History/Criticism, Biological Aspects of Conservation, Biological Sciences, Business Administration, Chemistry, Civil Engineering, Classics, Clinical Laboratory Science, Committee Interdisciplinary, Communication, Communication Sciences/Disorders, Community Education, Comparative Literature, Comparative Study of Religion, Computer Science, Criminal Justice, Cultural Foundations of Education, Curriculum/Instruction, Dance, Economics, Education, Educational Psychology, Educational Rehabilitation Counseling, Educational Studies, Electrical Engineering, Engineering, Engineering Sciences, English, Exceptional Education, Film, Finance, Foreign Language/Literature, French, Geography, Geological Science, Geosciences, German, Health Information Administration, Health Sciences, Hebrew Studies, History, Human Kinetics, Industrial Engineering, Industrial/Labor Relations, Industrial Relations, Inter-Arts, International Relations, Italian, Library/Information Studies, Linguistics, Management, Management Information Systems, Management Science, Marketing, Mass Communications, Materials Engineering, Mathematics, Mechanical Engineering, Medical Sciences, Medical Technology, Music, Music Education, Nursing, Occupational Therapy, Performing Arts, Philosophy, Physics, Political Science, Production Operations Management, Psychology, Public Administration, Real Estate/Urban Development, Recreation, Russian, Social Work, Sociology, Spanish, Theatre, Urban Education, Urban Planning, Urban Studies.
**Distribution of degrees:** The majors with the highest enrollment are business adminstration, education, and psychology.
**Requirements:** General education requirement.
**Academic regulations:** Minimum 2.0 GPA must be maintained.
**Special:** Minors offered in most majors. Interdisciplinary majors. Professional chemistry course. Urban emphasis option for economics, geography, history, political science, and sociology majors. College of Letters and Science offers two-year pre-professional preparation for Schools of Business Administration and Education. Joint degree programs with School of Business Administration and College of Engineering and Applied Science. Certificate of Junior Graduate in liberal studies after two years in College of Letters and Science. Ethnic, Native American, and women's studies programs. Self-designed majors. Double majors. Dual degrees. Independent study. Accelerated study. Internships. Cooperative education programs. Graduate school at which undergraduates may take graduate-level courses. Preprofessional programs in law, medicine, pharmacy, and optometry. Member of Consortium Nursing Program with U of Wisconsin at Parkside. Washington Semester. Metropolitan Arts Program. Teacher certification in early childhood, elementary, secondary, special education, and bilingual/bicultural education. Certification in specific subject areas. Study abroad in Denmark, England, France, Germany, Mexico, Poland, and Spain.
**Honors:** Phi Beta Kappa. Honors program. Honor societies.
**Academic Assistance:** Remedial reading, writing, math, and study skills. Nonremedial tutoring.

**STUDENT LIFE. Housing:** Students may live on or off campus. Coed dorms. 8% of students live in college housing.
**Social atmosphere:** Kalt's, BBC, Shank Hall, the Gasthaus, Harpo's, and numerous East Side establishments are favorite student haunts. The Student Association and UWM Programming are influential on campus life. Highlights of the year include Back to School Week and basketball games. "Since we are a commuter college, not much happens on campus," reports the editor of the school newspaper. "Most social activities happen at clubs and bars both near campus and downtown."
**Services and counseling/handicapped student services:** Placement services. Health service. Women's center. Day care. Learning skills center. Counseling services for minority, military, veteran, and older students. Birth control, personal, and psychological counseling. Career and academic guidance services. Physically disabled student services. Learning disabled services. Notetaking services. Tape recorders. Tutors. Reader services for the blind.
**Campus organizations:** Undergraduate student government. Student newspapers (UWM Post; Invictus). Literary magazine. Radio station. Choral groups, pep and concert bands, orchestra, dance group, drama and film groups, debating, community service clubs, athletic, departmental, political, professional, and special-interest groups, 215 or-

ganizations in all. Eight fraternities, two chapter houses; four sororities, no chapter houses. 1% of men join a fraternity.

**Religious organizations:** Bahai Club, Hillel Foundation, Baptist Student Union, Buddhist Studies and Meditation, Campus Crusade for Christ, Catholic Students Newman Group, Christian Advance, Christian Science Organization, Daystar Outreach, Deeper Roots Fellowship, Intervarsity Christian Fellowship, Latter-Day Saints Student Association, Lutheran Collegians, Orthodox Christian Fellowship.

**Minority/foreign student organizations:** American Indian Graduate Council, American Indian science society, Black Student Union/Invictus, Campus Satellite, NAACP, Cultural Arts Student Express, Hispanic Intellectuals of Milwaukee, LaColectiva. International Student Club, African, Chinese, Indian, Iranian, Korean, and Palestinian groups.

**ATHLETICS. Physical education requirements:** None.

**Intercollegiate competition:** 1% of students participate. Baseball (M), basketball (M,W), cross-country (M,W), diving (M,W), soccer (M,W), swimming (M,W), tennis (M,W), track and field (indoor) (M,W), track and field (outdoor) (M,W), volleyball (M,W). Member of Mid-Continent Conference, NCAA Division I.

**Intramural and club sports:** 10% of students participate. Intramural aerobics, basketball, bench press, curling, dance, flag football, floor hockey, free throw, frisbee, golf, horseback riding, indoor soccer, Nordic skiing, softball, tennis, volleyball, water aerobics.

**ADMISSIONS. Academic basis for candidate selection** (in order of priority): Class rank, standardized test scores, secondary school record, school's recommendation, essay.

**Requirements:** Graduation from secondary school is recommended; GED is accepted. 16 units and the following program of study are required: 4 units of English, 2 units of math, 2 units of science including 1 unit of lab, 3 units of social studies, 5 units of electives including 3 units of academic electives. Minimum ACT score of 21 (combined SAT score of 920) and rank in top half of secondary school class required. 4 units each of math and English and 1 unit each of chemistry and physics recommended of applicants to Coll of Engineering and Applied Science. Audition required of theatre and music program applicants. Appeal process for applicants not meeting standard requirements. ACT is required; SAT may be substituted. No off-campus interviews.

**Procedure:** Suggest filing application by June 30; no deadline. Notification of admission on rolling basis. $175 refundable room deposit. Freshmen accepted for terms other than fall.

**Special programs:** Admission may be deferred two years. Credit may be granted through CEEB Advanced Placement for scores of 3 or higher. Credit may be granted through CLEP general and subject exams and challenge exams. Early entrance/early admission program. Concurrent enrollment program.

**Transfer students:** Transfer students accepted for terms other than fall. In fall 1993, 35% of all new students were transfers into all classes. 3,100 transfer applications were received, 1,952 were accepted. Application deadline is August 3 for fall; December 15 for spring. Minimum 2.0 GPA required. Lowest course grade accepted is "D." Maximum number of transferable credits is 70 semester hours. At least 30 semester hours must be completed at the university to receive degree.

**Admissions contact:** Beth Weckmueller, Director of Admissions. 414 229-3800.

**FINANCIAL AID. Available aid:** Pell grants, SEOG, state scholarships and grants, school grants, private scholarships and grants, academic merit scholarships, and athletic scholarships. Perkins Loans (NDSL), PLUS, Stafford Loans (GSL), NSL, and SLS. Deferred payment plan.

**Financial aid statistics:** 13% of aid is not need-based. In 1993-94, 64% of all undergraduate applicants received aid; 48% of freshman applicants. Average amounts of aid awarded freshmen: Scholarships and grants, $2,700; loans, $2,548.

**Supporting data/closing dates:** FAFSA: Priority filing date is March 2; accepted on rolling basis. Notification of awards begins June 1.

**Financial aid contact:** Mary Roggeman, Director of Financial Aid. 414 229-4541.

**STUDENT EMPLOYMENT.** College Work/Study Program. Institutional employment. Off-campus part-time employment opportunities rated "good."

**COMPUTER FACILITIES.** 400 IBM/IBM-compatible and Macintosh/Apple microcomputers; 300 are networked. Students may access Digital minicomputer/mainframe systems, BITNET, Internet. Residence halls may be equipped with networked microcomputers. Computer facilities are available to all students.

**Fees:** None.

**GRADUATE CAREER DATA.** Highest graduate school enrollments: Marquette U, U of Wisconsin–Madison, U of Wisconsin–Milwaukee. 64% of graduates choose careers in business and industry. Companies and businesses that hire graduates: Allen Bradley, Andersen Consulting, Big Six accounting firms, M&I Bank, Northwestern Mutual Life Insurance, state of Wisconsin.

9-6

# University of Wisconsin–Oshkosh

**Oshkosh, WI 54901** **414 424-0202**

**1994-95 Costs.** Tuition: $2,100 (state residents), $6,500 (out-of-state). Room: $1,276. Board: $850. Fees, books, misc. academic expenses (school's estimate): $500.

**Enrollment.** Undergraduates: 3,357 men, 4,504 women (full-time). Freshman class: 4,800 applicants, 3,000 accepted, 1,517 enrolled. Graduate enrollment: 552 men, 702 women.

**Test score averages/ranges.** Average ACT scores: 21 English, 21 math, 21 composite. Range of ACT scores of middle 50%: 19-23 English, 19-23 math.

**Faculty.** 418 full-time; 117 part-time. 61% of faculty holds doctoral degree. Student/faculty ratio: 20 to 1.

**Selectivity rating.** Competitive.

**PROFILE.** U Wisconsin at Oshkosh is a public, comprehensive institution. Founded as a Normal school in 1871, it gained state university status in 1964 and its present status in 1971. Programs are offered through the Colleges of Business Administration, Education and Human Services, Letters and Science, and Nursing and the Graduate School. Its 192-acre campus is located in Oshkosh, 90 miles northwest of Milwaukee.

**Accreditation:** NCACS. Professionally accredited by the Accrediting Council on Education in Journalism and Mass Communication, the American Assembly of Collegiate Schools of Business, the Council on Social Work Education, the National Association of Schools of Music, the National Council for Accreditation of Teacher Education, the National League for Nursing.

**Religious orientation:** University of Wisconsin–Oshkosh is nonsectarian; no religious requirements.

**Library:** Collections totaling over 439,614 volumes, 1,787 periodical subscriptions, and 1,523,260 microform items.

**Special facilities/museums:** Art gallery, ceramics lab, electron microscope.

**Athletic facilities:** Gymnasium, field house, swimming pool, weight rooms, tracks, basketball, tennis, and volleyball courts, stadium, baseball, practice, soccer, and softball fields.

**STUDENT BODY. Undergraduate profile:** 96% are state residents; 8% are transfers. 2% Asian-American, 1% Black, 1% Hispanic, 1% Native American, 95% White. Average age of undergraduates is 23.

**Freshman profile:** 2% of freshmen who took ACT scored 30 or over on English, 2% scored 30 or over on math, 2% scored 30 or over on composite; 27% scored 24 or over on English, 22% scored 24 or over on math, 27% scored 24 or over on composite; 78% scored 18 or over on English, 79% scored 18 or over on math, 88% scored 18 or over on composite; 99% scored 12 or over on English, 100% scored 12 or over on math, 100% scored 12 or over on composite; 100% scored 6 or over on English. 88% of accepted applicants took ACT.

**Undergraduate achievement:** 73% of fall 1992 freshmen returned for fall 1993 term.

**Foreign students:** 90 students are from out of the country. Countries represented include Bangladesh, India, Japan, Malaysia, Pakistan, and Turkey; 26 in all.

**PROGRAMS OF STUDY. Degrees:** B.A., B.Art Ed., B.Bus.Admin., B.F.A., B.Lib.Studies, B.Mus., B.Mus.Ed., B.S., B.S.Nurs., B.Soc.Work.

**Majors:** Anthropology, Art, Art Education, Biology, Business Administration, Chemistry, Communicative Disorders, Computer Science, Criminal Justice, Economics, Elementary Education, English, Fine Arts, French, Geography, Geology, German, History, Human Services, Individually Planned Major, International Studies, Journalism, Mathematics, Medical Technology, Microbiology/Public Health, Music, Music Education, Music Therapy, Natural Science, Nursing, Philosophy, Physical Education, Physics, Political Science, Psychology, Radio/TV/Film, Religious Studies, Social Science, Social Work, Sociology, Spanish, Special Education, Speech, Urban/Regional Studies.

**Distribution of degrees:** The majors with the highest enrollment are elementary education and nursing; German, music therapy, and natural science have the lowest.

**Requirements:** General education requirement.

**Academic regulations:** Minimum 2.0 GPA must be maintained.

**Special:** Minors offered in many majors and in Afro-American studies, astronomy, athletic training, coaching, earth science, gerontology, health education, military science, operations research, public administration, reading, recreation, recreation therapy, and women's studies. Police administration training certificate program. Summer geology field study program in Canadian Rockies. Associate's degrees offered. Self-designed majors. Double majors. Dual degrees. Independent study. Pass/fail grading option. Internships. Preprofessional programs in law, medicine, veterinary science, pharmacy, dentistry, optometry, chiropractic, and physical therapy. Member of Urban Corridor Consortium. Teacher certification in early childhood, elementary, secondary, and special education. Study abroad in Mexico. ROTC.

**Honors:** Honors program. Honor societies.

**STUDENT LIFE. Housing:** All unmarried, nonveteran students with fewer than 60 credits must live on campus unless living with family. Coed and women's dorms. 38% of students live in college housing.

**Social atmosphere:** The Reeve Union Board, the Speakers Committee, and the United Students in Residence Halls are among the most influential groups on campus. Popular school-year events include Winter Carnival, Waterfest, and the individual hall olympics.

**Services and counseling/handicapped student services:** Placement services. Health service. Women's center. Day care. Testing service. Reading-study center with academic development services. Counseling services for minority, military, veteran, and older students. Birth control, personal, and psychological counseling. Career and academic guidance services. Religious counseling. Physically disabled student services. Learning disabled program/services. Notetaking services. Tape recorders. Tutors. Reader services for the blind.

**Campus organizations:** Undergraduate student government. Student newspaper (Advance Titan, published once/week). Radio and TV stations. Orchestra, percussion ensemble, concert band, jazz lab ensemble, choruses, choirs, opera theatre, drama group, public speaking and debating groups, veterans club, chess club, 125 organizations in all. Eight fraternities, no chapter houses; eight sororities, no chapter houses. 2% of men join a fraternity. 3% of women join a sorority.

**Religious organizations:** Christians in Action, Campus Crusade for Christ, Lutheran Student Movement.

**Minority/foreign student organizations:** Black Student Union, Native American and Hispanic groups. International Student Association, Asian Student Association, Hmong Lao Student Association.

**ATHLETICS. Physical education requirements:** Two semester hours of physical education required.

**Intercollegiate competition:** 6% of students participate. Baseball (M), basketball (M,W), cheerleading (M,W), cross-country (M,W), diving (M,W), football (M), gymnastics (W), soccer (M,W), softball (W), swimming (M,W), tennis (M,W), track and field (indoor) (M,W), track and field (outdoor) (M,W), volleyball (W), wrestling (M). Member of NCAA Division III, USGF, Wisconsin State University Conference, Wisconsin Women's Intercollegiate Athletic Conference.

**Intramural and club sports:** 30% of students participate. Intramural bowling, flag football, soccer, softball, swimming, tennis, track and field, volleyball, water basketball. Men's club bowling, lacrosse, volleyball. Women's club bowling.

**ADMISSIONS. Academic basis for candidate selection** (in order of priority): Class rank, secondary school record, standardized test scores.
**Nonacademic basis for candidate selection:** Particular talent or ability is considered.
**Requirements:** Graduation from secondary school is required; GED is accepted. No specific distribution of secondary school units required. Rank in top half of secondary school class or minimum composite ACT score of 23 required. Audition required of music program applicants. Project Success Program. ACT required of in-state applicants; out-of-state applicants may substitute SAT. Campus visit and interview recommended. No off-campus interviews.
**Procedure:** Take ACT by October of 12th year. Visit college for interview by December 1 of 12th year. Suggest filing application by December 1. Notification of admission on rolling basis. $100 tuition deposit, refundable until May 1. $75 room deposit, refundable until July 1. Freshmen accepted for terms other than fall.
**Special programs:** Admission may be deferred three semesters. Credit may be granted through CLEP general and subject exams. Concurrent enrollment program.
**Transfer students:** Transfer students accepted for terms other than fall. In fall 1993, 8% of all new students were transfers into all classes. Application deadline is rolling for fall; rolling for spring. Minimum 2.5 GPA recommended. Lowest course grade accepted is "D." Maximum number of transferable credits is 98 semester hours. At least 30 semester hours must be completed at the university to receive degree.
**Admissions contact:** August Helgerson, M.S., Director of Admissions. 414 424-0202.
**FINANCIAL AID. Available aid:** Pell grants, SEOG, Federal Nursing Student Scholarships, state scholarships and grants, school scholarships, private scholarships, ROTC scholarships, academic merit scholarships, and aid for undergraduate foreign students. Perkins Loans (NDSL), PLUS, Stafford Loans (GSL), NSL, and SLS. Institutional credit plan.
**Financial aid statistics:** 15% of aid is not need-based. In 1993-94, 85% of all undergraduate applicants received aid; 85% of freshman applicants. Average amounts of aid awarded freshmen: Scholarships and grants, $950; loans, $1,650.
**Supporting data/closing dates:** FAFSA: Priority filing date is March 15. Notification of awards on rolling basis.
**Financial aid contact:** Kenneth Cook, M.A., Director of Financial Aid. 414 424-3377.
**STUDENT EMPLOYMENT.** College Work/Study Program. Institutional employment. 30% of full-time undergraduates work on campus during school year. Students may expect to earn an average of $600 during school year. Off-campus part-time employment opportunities rated "excellent."
**COMPUTER FACILITIES.** 1,200 IBM/IBM-compatible and Macintosh/Apple microcomputers; 500 are networked. Students may access Digital, IBM minicomputer/mainframe systems, BITNET. Residence halls may be equipped with stand-alone microcomputers, modems. Computer languages and software packages include Ada, BASIC, C, COBOL, INGRES, LISP, MicroSim, MINITAB, Modula 2, NDB, SLAM II, SPICE, SPSS-X, SYMAP, Text DBMS; 17 in all. Computer facilities are available to all students.
**Fees:** None.
**Hours:** 8 AM-10 PM.
**PROMINENT ALUMNI/AE.** Warren Keading, senior scientist, Mobil Oil; Betty Gough, president, International Narcotics Control Board; Clark Byse, professor, Harvard Law School; John Gronouski, former U.S. Postmaster General, professor, U of Texas; June Dykstra, legislative aide, Republican staff director, U.S. Senate.

# University of Wisconsin–Platteville

**Platteville, WI 53818** **608 342-1491**

**1994-95 Costs.** Tuition: $1,900 (state residents), $6,614 (out-of-state). Room: $1,250. Board: $1,430. Fees, books, misc. academic expenses (school's estimate): $426.
**Enrollment.** Undergraduates: 3,014 men, 1,530 women (full-time). Freshman class: 2,330 applicants, 1,800 accepted, 879 enrolled. Graduate enrollment: 76 men, 149 women.
**Test score averages/ranges.** N/A.
**Faculty.** 250 full-time; 30 part-time. 65% of faculty holds doctoral degree. Student/faculty ratio: 20 to 1.
**Selectivity rating.** Competitive.

**PROFILE.** U Wisconsin at Platteville, founded in 1866, is a public, comprehensive institution. Programs are offered through the Colleges of Agriculture; Arts and Sciences; Business, Industry, and Communication; Education; and Engineering. Its 350-acre campus is located in Platteville, 65 miles southwest of Madison.

**Accreditation:** NCACS. Professionally accredited by the Accreditation Board for Engineering and Technology, the National Association of Schools of Music, the National Council for Accreditation of Teacher Education.
**Religious orientation:** University of Wisconsin–Platteville is nonsectarian; no religious requirements.
**Library:** Collections totaling over 254,000 volumes, 1,517 periodical subscriptions, and 683,000 microform items.
**Special facilities/museums:** Electron microscope.
**Athletic facilities:** Gymnasiums, field house, weight and wrestling rooms, swimming pool, stadium, track, basketball, racquetball, tennis, and volleyball courts, baseball, football, intramural, and soccer fields, golf course.
**STUDENT BODY. Undergraduate profile:** 93% are state residents; 14% are transfers. 1% Asian-American, 1% Black, 96% White, 2% Other. Average age of undergraduates is 22.
**Freshman profile:** 100% of accepted applicants took ACT. 90% of freshmen come from public schools.
**Undergraduate achievement:** 71% of fall 1992 freshmen returned for fall 1993 term. 52% of entering class graduated.
**Foreign students:** 60 students are from out of the country. 20 countries represented in all.
**PROGRAMS OF STUDY. Degrees:** B.A., B.S.
**Majors:** Accounting, Agribusiness, Agricultural Economics, Agricultural Education, Agricultural Engineering Technology, Animal Science, Biology, Broadcasting Technology Management, Business Administration, Chemistry, Civil Engineering, Comprehensive Business/Economics, Computer Science, Counselor Education, Criminal Justice, Economics, Electrical Engineering, Elementary Education, English, Fine Arts, General Engineering, General Science Comprehensive, Geography, German, History, Industrial Engineering, Industrial Technology Management, International Studies, Mathematics, Mechanical Engineering, Music, Philosophy, Physical Education, Physics, Political Science, Psychology, Reclamation, Secondary Education, Social Sciences, Soil/Crop Science, Spanish, Speech Communication, Technical Agriculture, Technical Communication Management, Technology Education.
**Distribution of degrees:** The majors with the highest enrollment are business administration and engineering; foreign languages and philosophy have the lowest.
**Requirements:** General education requirement.
**Academic regulations:** Freshmen must maintain minimum 1.85 GPA; sophomores, juniors, seniors, 2.0 GPA.
**Special:** Minors offered in most majors and in art, computer-integrated manufacturing, drafting/product design, electronics technology, geology, graphic arts, health education, horticulture, industrial power/control systems, industrial sales/service, journalism, materials/material processing, occupational safety, production/manufacturing management, radio/television broadcasting, theatre, and women's studies. Women's Studies Program may be selected as a minor, a certificate program, or an individually constructed major. Associate's degrees offered. Self-designed majors. Double majors. Pass/fail grading option. Cooperative education programs. Graduate school at which undergraduates may take graduate-level courses. Preprofessional programs in law, medicine, veterinary science, pharmacy, dentistry, theology, optometry, architecture, chiropractic, conservation, landscape architecture, medical technology, nursing, occupational therapy, osteopathy, physical therapy, physician's assistant, podiatry, and wildlife management. Member of College Consortium For International Studies. Exchange program with Westfield State Coll. Teacher certification in early childhood, elementary, secondary, and special education. Study abroad in China, Ecuador, England, France, Germany, Ireland, Italy, Mexico, Portugal, Spain, and Sweden.
**Honors:** Honors program. Honor societies.
**Academic Assistance:** Remedial reading, writing, math, and study skills. Nonremedial tutoring.

**STUDENT LIFE. Housing:** All unmarried students under age 21 must live on campus unless living near campus with relatives. Coed, women's, and men's dorms. Sorority and fraternity housing. Off-campus married-student housing. 45% of students live in college housing.
**Social atmosphere:** Students gather in the Student Center, which includes the popular Rendevous bar and grill. The Student Activities Board, Greeks, athletes, and Christian groups are influential on campus. The most popular events of the year are Homecoming, basketball games, the Pioneer Distinguished Lecturer presentation, and the lighting and whitewashing of the M, a giant letter M inscribed in a field outside Platteville. "Platteville is a small town, so students don't often go there for entertainment. Virtually all significant events are organized by the Student Activities Board or by the Greeks. In summer, we host a famous Shakespeare festival and the Chicago Bears' summer training camp," reports the student newspaper.
**Services and counseling/handicapped student services:** Placement services. Health service. Women's center. Day care. Counseling services for minority, veteran, and older students. Birth control, personal, and psychological counseling. Career and academic guidance services. Physically disabled student services. Learning disabled services. Notetaking services. Tape recorders. Tutors. Reader services for the blind.
**Campus organizations:** Undergraduate student government. Student newspaper (Exponent, published once/week). Literary magazine. Yearbook. Radio and TV stations. Orchestra, symphonic and marching bands, pep and varsity bands, ensembles, choir, madrigal singers, debating, Pioneer Players, Young Democrats, Young Republicans, flying club, agricultural judging teams, departmental and special-interest groups, 105 organizations in all. Six fraternities, all with chapter houses; three sororities, all with chapter houses. 10% of men join a fraternity. 10% of women join a sorority.
**Religious organizations:** Campus Bible Fellowship, Campus Crusade for Christ, Chi Alpha, Fellowship of Christian Athletes, Lutheran Church-Missouri Synod, Lutheran Collegians, Lutheran Student Movement, Newman Club.
**Minority/foreign student organizations:** Black Student Union, Native American Order. International Student Club, Hmong student group.

**ATHLETICS. Physical education requirements:** Two semesters of physical education required.
**Intercollegiate competition:** 20% of students participate. Baseball (M), basketball (M,W), cheerleading (M,W), cross-country (M,W), football (M), soccer (M,W), softball (W), track (indoor) (M,W), track (outdoor) (M,W), track and field (indoor) (M,W), track and field (outdoor) (M,W), volleyball (W), wrestling (M). Member of NCAA Division III, Wisconsin State University Conference, Wisconsin Women's Intercollegiate Athletic Conference.
**Intramural and club sports:** 40% of students participate. Intramural badminton, basketball, broomball, eightball, flag football, indoor soccer, softball, table tennis, tennis, volleyball, water polo, wrestling. Men's club ice hockey, rugby, volleyball.

**ADMISSIONS. Academic basis for candidate selection** (in order of priority): Secondary school record, class rank, standardized test scores, essay, school's recommendation.
**Nonacademic basis for candidate selection:** Extracurricular participation and particular talent or ability are considered.
**Requirements:** Graduation from secondary school is required; GED is accepted. 16 units and the following program of study are required: 4 units of English, 2 units of math, 2 units of science including 1 unit of lab, 3 units of social studies, 5 units of electives including 3 units of academic electives. Minimum composite ACT score of 22 and rank in top two-fifths of secondary school class required. Minimum composite ACT score of 24 or rank in top tenth of secondary school class required of elementary education program applicants. Conditional admission possible for applicants not meeting standard requirements. ACT is

required. Campus visit and interview recommended. Off-campus interviews available with an admissions representative.
**Procedure:** Take ACT by December of 12th year. Visit college for interview by December of 12th year. Suggest filing application by February 1; no deadline. Notification of admission on rolling basis. No set date by which applicants must accept offer. $100 room deposit, refundable until July 15. Freshmen accepted for terms other than fall.
**Special programs:** Admission may be deferred one semester. Credit may be granted through CEEB Advanced Placement. Credit and/or placement may be granted through CLEP subject exams. Credit may be granted through military experience. Credit and placement may be granted through DANTES exams.
**Transfer students:** Transfer students accepted for terms other than fall. In fall 1993, 14% of all new students were transfers into all classes. 532 transfer applications were received, 289 were accepted. Application deadline is February 1. Minimum 2.5 GPA required. Lowest course grade accepted is "D." At least 36 semester hours must be completed at the university to receive degree.
**Admissions contact:** Richard Schumacher, Ph.D., Dean, Enrollment Management Services. 608 342-1125.

**FINANCIAL AID. Available aid:** Pell grants, SEOG, state grants, school scholarships, and aid for undergraduate foreign students. Perkins Loans (NDSL), PLUS, and Stafford Loans (GSL). Partial payment plan.
**Financial aid statistics:** 10% of aid is not need-based. In 1993-94, 85% of all undergraduate applicants received aid; 80% of freshman applicants. Average amounts of aid awarded freshmen: Scholarships and grants, $800; loans, $1,200.
**Supporting data/closing dates:** FAFSA/FAF/FFS: Priority filing date is March 15. Notification of awards on rolling basis.
**Financial aid contact:** Liz Tucker, Director of Financial Aid. 608 342-1836.

**STUDENT EMPLOYMENT.** College Work/Study Program. Institutional employment. 25% of full-time undergraduates work on campus during school year. Students may expect to earn an average of $1,400 during school year. Off-campus part-time employment opportunities rated "good."

**COMPUTER FACILITIES.** 200 IBM/IBM-compatible and Macintosh/Apple microcomputers. Students may access Digital minicomputer/mainframe systems. Residence halls may be equipped with stand-alone microcomputers. Client/LAN operating systems include Apple/Macintosh, DOS, DEC, Novell. Computer languages and software packages include ACSL, ANSYS, C, COBOL, CPSS/II Automod, DT-3000, FORTRAN, I-G SPICE, JNET, LISP, MINITAB, NAG, Pascal, SAS, SimScript. Computer facilities are available to all students.
**Fees:** Computer fee is included in tuition/fees.

# University of Wisconsin–River Falls

**River Falls, WI 54022** **715 425-3911**

**1994-95 Costs.** Tuition: $2,200 (state residents), $6,600 (out-of-state). Room: $1,400. Board: $1,200. Fees, books, misc. academic expenses (school's estimate): $50.
**Enrollment.** Undergraduates: 2,050 men, 2,608 women (full-time). Freshman class: 2,563 applicants, 1,596 accepted, 846 enrolled. Graduate enrollment: 185 men, 235 women.
**Test score averages/ranges.** Average ACT scores: 22 English, 21 math, 22 composite.
**Faculty.** 295 full-time; 20 part-time. 69% of faculty holds doctoral degree. Student/faculty ratio: 17 to 1.
**Selectivity rating.** Competitive.

**PROFILE.** U Wisconsin at River Falls is a public, comprehensive institution. Founded as a state Normal school in 1874, it gained state university status in 1964 and its present status in 1971. Programs are offered through the Colleges of Agriculture, Arts and Sciences, and Education and the Graduate School. Its approximately 200-acre campus is located in River Falls, 29 miles east of Minneapolis-St. Paul.

**Accreditation:** NCACS. Professionally accredited by the Accrediting Council on Education in Journalism and Mass Communication, the American Society of Landscape Architects, the National Association of Schools of Music, the National Council for Accreditation of Teacher Education.
**Religious orientation:** University of Wisconsin–River Falls is nonsectarian; no religious requirements.
**Library:** Collections totaling over 217,000 volumes, 1,528 periodical subscriptions, and 471,438 microform items.
**Special facilities/museums:** Local history museum, 20-inch reflecting telescope, observatory, electron microscope, greenhouse, lab farms, educational technology center.
**Athletic facilities:** Gymnasium, swimming pool, tracks, weight room, basketball, tennis, and volleyball courts, ice rink, baseball, football, practice, and softball fields, climbing wall.

**STUDENT BODY. Undergraduate profile:** 52% are state residents; 28% are transfers. 1% Asian-American, 1% Black, 1% Hispanic, 1% Native American, 95% White, 1% Other. Average age of undergraduates is 21.
**Freshman profile:** Majority of accepted applicants took ACT. 93% of freshmen come from public schools.
**Undergraduate achievement:** 81% of fall 1992 freshmen returned for fall 1993 term. 8% of students who completed a degree program immediately went on to graduate study.
**Foreign students:** 35 students are from out of the country. Countries represented include China, Hong Kong, Hungary, Poland, and Taiwan; 20 in all.

**PROGRAMS OF STUDY. Degrees:** B.A., B.Earth Sci.Ed., B.F.A., B.Mus.Ed., B.S., B.Soc.Work.
**Majors:** Accounting, Agricultural Business, Agricultural Economics, Agricultural Education, Agricultural Engineering Technology, Agricultural Journalism, Agricultural Marketing, Agronomy, American Studies, Animal Science, Applied Computer Systems, Art, Art Education, Biology, Biotechnology, Business Administration, Chemistry, Communications Disorders, Conservation, Earth Science Education, Economics, Elementary Education, English, Farm Management, Food Science/Technology, French, General Agriculture, Geography, Geology, German, History, Horticulture, Journalism, Language Arts, Mathematics, Metropolitan Region Studies, Middle School Education, Music, Physical Education, Physics, Political Science, Psychology, Recreation, Science, Scientific Land Management, Secondary Education, Social Studies, Social Work, Sociology, Soil Science, Speech.
**Distribution of degrees:** The majors with the highest enrollment are business administration, elementary education, and agriculture.
**Requirements:** General education requirement.
**Academic regulations:** Minimum 2.0 GPA must be maintained.
**Special:** Minors offered in all majors and in ethnic studies, professional writing, theatre, and women's studies. Two- and three-year transfer programs in architecture, criminal justice, dentistry, engineering, forestry, home economics, law, medicine, mortuary science, music therapy, nursing, optometry, pharmacy, police science, and veterinary medicine. Self-designed majors. Double majors. Independent study. Pass/fail grading option. Internships. Cooperative education programs. Graduate school at which undergraduates may take graduate-level courses. Preprofessional programs in law, medicine, veterinary science, pharmacy, dentistry, optometry, chiropractic, engineering, and mortuary science. Member of West Central Wisconsin Consortium. Member of National Student Exchange (NSE). Teacher certification in early childhood, elementary, and secondary education. Certification in specific subject areas. Student teaching programs in Australia, England, Ireland, Scotland, and Wales. Study abroad also in Denmark, European countries, Israel, Japan, Korea, Mexico, the former Soviet Republics, and Taiwan.
**Honors:** Honors program. Honor societies.
**Academic Assistance:** Remedial reading, writing, math, and study skills. Nonremedial tutoring.

**STUDENT LIFE. Housing:** All freshmen and sophomores must live on campus unless living with family. Coed, women's, and men's dorms. Fraternity housing. 36% of students live in college housing.
**Social atmosphere:** The student newspaper reports, "Much of the social life is centered around River Falls taverns and University of Wisconsin at River Falls sporting events." Influential student groups include the Student Senate, athletes, the Intervarsity Christian Fellowship, and the Inter-Residential Hall Council. Students gather at the student center, Rodli Commons, and the library on campus and frequent local bars off campus. Spring Fling, Homecoming, and Winter Carnival highlight the school year.
**Services and counseling/handicapped student services:** Placement services. Health service. Women's center. Day care. Counseling services for minority, military, veteran, and older students. Birth control, personal, and psychological counseling. Career and academic guidance services. Physically disabled student services. Learning disabled program/services. Notetaking services. Tape recorders. Tutors. Reader services for the blind.
**Campus organizations:** Undergraduate student government. Student newspaper (Student Voice, published once/week). Literary magazine. Yearbook. Radio and TV stations. Symphonic and marching bands, brass ensemble, woodwind quintet, chorale, Chamber Singers, other musical groups, Masquers, Association of Women in Agriculture, Young Democrats, Young Republicans, leadership development club, professional, service, and special-interest groups, 120 organizations in all. Five fraternities, three chapter houses; four sororities, no chapter houses. 5% of men join a fraternity. 5% of women join a sorority.
**Religious organizations:** Campus Christian Fellowship, Campus Crusade for Christ, Ecumenical Campus Ministry, Fellowship of Christian Athletes, Intervarsity Christian Fellowship, Newman Center, UMHE Campus Ministry.
**Minority/foreign student organizations:** Black Student Coalition, African-American Alliance, Native American Council, Adelante, Hmong Student Association, ADEI-Hispanic. International Student Association.

**ATHLETICS. Physical education requirements:** Three semesters of physical education required.
**Intercollegiate competition:** 10% of students participate. Baseball (M), basketball (M,W), cross-country (M,W), football (M), gymnastics (W), ice hockey (M), rodeo (M), softball (W), swimming (M,W), tennis (M,W), track (indoor) (M,W), track (outdoor) (M,W), track and field (indoor) (M,W), track and field (outdoor) (M,W), volleyball (W), wrestling (M). Member of National Collegiate Gymnastics Association, NCAA Division III, NCHA, Wisconsin State University Conference, WWIAC.
**Intramural and club sports:** 40% of students participate. Intramural badminton, basketball, hockey, softball, touch football, volleyball. Men's club soccer. Women's club ice hockey, soccer.

**ADMISSIONS. Academic basis for candidate selection** (in order of priority): Class rank, standardized test scores, secondary school record, school's recommendation, essay.
**Nonacademic basis for candidate selection:** Particular talent or ability is important. Character and personality are considered.
**Requirements:** Graduation from secondary school is required; GED is accepted. 17 units and the following program of study are required: 4 units of English, 3 units of math, 3 units of science including 1 unit of lab, 3 units of social studies, 1 unit of history, 3 units of academic electives. Additional academic units recommended in all subjects except English. Minimum composite ACT score of 21 or rank in top two-fifths of secondary school class required. ACT is required. Campus visit and interview recommended. Off-campus interviews available with an admissions representative.
**Procedure:** Take ACT by fall of 12th year. Visit college for interview by winter of 12th year. Suggest filing application by January 1; no deadline. Notification of admission on rolling basis. $75 room deposit, refundable until June 15. Freshmen accepted for terms other than fall.
**Special programs:** Admission may be deferred one year. Credit may be granted through CLEP general and subject exams. Credit may be granted through military experience. Concurrent enrollment program.
**Transfer students:** Transfer students accepted for terms other than fall. In fall 1993, 28% of all new students were transfers into all classes. 701 transfer applications were received, 402 were accepted. Application deadline is January 1 for fall; July 1 for spring. Minimum 2.6 GPA required. Lowest course grade accepted is "C." Maximum number of transferable

credits is 72 quarter hours. At least 32 quarter hours must be completed at the university to receive degree.

**Admissions contact:** Alan Tuchtenhagen, M.S., Director of Admissions. 715 425-3500.

**FINANCIAL AID. Available aid:** Pell grants, SEOG, state scholarships and grants, school scholarships, private scholarships, academic merit scholarships, and aid for undergraduate foreign students. Black, Hispanic, and Native American scholarships. Perkins Loans (NDSL), PLUS, Stafford Loans (GSL), private loans, and SLS. Deferred payment plan.

**Financial aid statistics:** 5% of aid is not need-based. In 1993-94, 60% of all undergraduate applicants received aid; 60% of freshman applicants. Average amounts of aid awarded freshmen: Scholarships and grants, $500.

**Supporting data/closing dates:** FAFSA: Priority filing date is March 15. FAF/FFS: Priority filing date is March 15; accepted on rolling basis. School's own aid application: Priority filing date is March 15. Notification of awards begins May 15.

**Financial aid contact:** Terry Smith, M.S., Director of Financial Assistance. 715 425-3141.

**STUDENT EMPLOYMENT.** College Work/Study Program. Institutional employment. 40% of full-time undergraduates work on campus during school year. Students may expect to earn an average of $1,050 during school year. Off-campus part-time employment opportunities rated "good."

**COMPUTER FACILITIES.** IBM/IBM-compatible and Macintosh/Apple microcomputers. Residence halls may be equipped with stand-alone microcomputers, networked microcomputers. Computer languages and software packages include Assembler, BASIC, Bliss, C, COBOL, FORTRAN, INGRES, LISP, Pascal, Shazam, SPSS-X. Computer facilities are available to all students.

**Fees:** Computer fee is included in tuition/fees.

**Hours:** Over 80 hours/week.

**GRADUATE CAREER DATA.** Highest graduate school enrollments: Michigan State U, U of Minnesota at Minneapolis, U of Wisconsin at Madison. Companies and businesses that hire graduates: Cargill, Cenex/Land O'Lakes, Hormel, Norwest Banks, Pillsbury, Prudential, 3M.

**PROMINENT ALUMNI/AE.** Daniel Brandenstein, chief, NASA astronaut office; Bruce F. Ventro, U.S. congressman, Minnesota; William H. Hunt, retired chairperson of the board, Georgia Pacific; Daniel G. Dykstra, retired dean, Sch of Law, U of California at Davis.

# University of Wisconsin–Stevens Point

**Stevens Point, WI 54481** **715 346-0123**

**1993-94 Costs.** Tuition: $2,250 (state residents), $6,770 (out-of-state). Room & board: $3,030. Fees, books, misc. academic expenses (school's estimate): $300.

**Enrollment.** Undergraduates: 3,598 men, 3,770 women (full-time). Freshman class: 3,975 applicants, 2,440 accepted, 1,398 enrolled. Graduate enrollment: 139 men, 329 women.

**Test score averages/ranges.** Average ACT scores: 22 composite. Range of ACT scores of middle 50%: 22-23 composite.

**Faculty.** 392 full-time; 70 part-time. 76% of faculty holds doctoral degree. Student/faculty ratio: 19 to 1.

**Selectivity rating.** Competitive.

**PROFILE.** U Wisconsin at Stevens Point, founded in 1894, is a public, comprehensive institution. Programs are offered through the Colleges of Fine Arts, Letters and Science, Natural Resources, and Professional Studies and the Graduate School. Its 350-acre campus is located in Stevens Point, northwest of Milwaukee.

**Accreditation:** NCACS. Professionally accredited by the American Dietetic Association, the American Speech-Language-Hearing Association, the National Association of Schools of Art and Design, the National Association of Schools of Music, the Society of American Foresters.

**Religious orientation:** University of Wisconsin–Stevens Point is nonsectarian; no religious requirements.

**Library:** Collections totaling over 326,714 volumes, 2,003 periodical subscriptions, and 543,824 microform items.

**Special facilities/museums:** Art galleries, costume and goblet collections, museum of natural history, early childhood study institute, communicative disorders center, map center, observatory, planetarium, Foucault pendulum, nature preserve, environmental station, groundwater center, herbarium, aviary, wellness institute.

**Athletic facilities:** Gymnasiums, fitness center, weight rooms, aquatic center, baseball, football, and softball fields, ice arena, basketball, tennis, and volleyball courts, swimming pool, indoor and outdoor tracks, wrestling room.

**STUDENT BODY. Undergraduate profile:** 91% are state residents; 4% are transfers. 1% Asian-American, 1% Black, 1% Hispanic, 1% Native American, 93% White, 3% Other. Average age of undergraduates is 24.

**Freshman profile:** 2% of freshmen who took ACT scored 30 or over on composite; 31% scored 24 or over on composite; 90% scored 18 or over on composite; 100% scored 12 or over on composite. 97% of accepted applicants took ACT.

**Undergraduate achievement:** 76% of fall 1991 freshmen returned for fall 1992 term. 24% of entering class graduated.

**Foreign students:** 23 students are from out of the country. Countries represented include Indonesia, Japan, Korea, Malaysia, Singapore, and Taiwan.

**PROGRAMS OF STUDY. Degrees:** B.A., B.F.A., B.Mus., B.S.

**Majors:** Anthropology, Art, Art Education, Arts Management, Biology, Business Administration, Chemistry, Communication, Communicative Disorders, Computer Information Systems, Dance, Dietetics, Drama, Early Childhood Education, Economics, Elementary Education, English, Fashion Merchandising, Food Service Management, Forestry, French, Geography, German, Health Promotion/Physical Education, Health Promotion/Wellness, History, Home Economics Education, Individually Planned Major, Interior Design, International Studies, Managerial Accounting, Mathematics, Medical Technology, Music, Musical Theatre, Natural Science, Paper Science, Philosophy, Physics, Political Science, Psychology, Public Administration/Policy Analysis, Resource Management, Social Science, Sociology, Soil Science, Spanish, Theatre Arts, Water Resources, Wildlife.

**Distribution of degrees:** The majors with the highest enrollment are business administration, elementary education, and communication; physics, natural science, and philosophy have the lowest.

**Requirements:** General education requirement.

**Academic regulations:** Minimum 2.0 GPA must be maintained.

**Special:** Minors offered in most majors. Programs in captive wildlife management, child/family studies, and English as a Second Language. Associate's degrees offered. Self-designed majors. Double majors. Independent study. Pass/fail grading option. Internships. Cooperative education programs. Graduate school at which undergraduates may take graduate-level courses. Preprofessional programs in law, medicine, veterinary science, pharmacy, dentistry, optometry, chiropractice, engineering, forestry, mortuary science, nursing, occupational therapy, and physical therapy. Cooperative nursing program with U of Wisconsin at Eau Claire and St. Joseph's Hospital. Teacher certification in early childhood, elementary, secondary, and special education. Certification in specific subject areas. Study abroad in Australia, England, Germany, Poland, Spain, and Taiwan. ROTC.

**Honors:** Honors program. Honor societies.

**Academic Assistance:** Remedial reading, writing, math, and study skills.

**STUDENT LIFE. Housing:** All unmarried students under age 21 must live on campus unless living near campus with relatives. Coed, women's, and men's dorms. Sorority and fraternity housing. Off-campus privately-owned housing. 36% of students live in college housing.

**Social atmosphere:** The University Center and the Recreational Services center are favorite student hangouts on campus. Off campus, students head for The Square. Greeks, the Association for Community Tasks, and the University Activities Board influence campus life. Popular events include football, basketball, and hockey games, Homecoming, Arctic Fest (which includes rugby games), theatre presentations, and trivia contests hosted by the campus radio station. "UWSP is an enjoyable place offering many activities promoting academics and social well-being," reports the student newspaper.

**Services and counseling/handicapped student services:** Placement services. Health service. Women's center. Day care. Counseling services for minority, military, veteran, and older students. Birth control, personal, and psychological counseling. Career and academic guidance services. Religious counseling. Physically disabled student services. Learning disabled services. Notetaking services. Tape recorders. Tutors. Reader services for the blind.

**Campus organizations:** Undergraduate student government. Student newspaper (Pointer, published once/week). Yearbook. Radio and TV stations. American Chemical Society, American Advertising Federation, American Marketing Association, College Republicans, Young Democrats, Student Legal Society, Wildlife Society, Student Education Association, Amnesty International, judo and scuba clubs, 145 organizations in all. Three fraternities, all with chapter houses; four sororities, one chapter house. 2% of men join a fraternity. 2% of women join a sorority.

**Religious organizations:** Campus Crusade for Christ, Intervarsity Faith Fellowship, Lutheran Student Fellowship, Latter-Day Saints Student Association, Newman Catholic Student Community, United Ministries, Bahai Club, Lutheran Collegians, United Muslim Association.

**Minority/foreign student organizations:** EO/AA Office, Cultural Diversity Unit, Upward Bound, Native American Center, AIRO, United Brothers and Sisters. International Club, Club Koreana, Club Latino Americano, Permias/Indonesian Club, Southeast Asian-American Connection.

**ATHLETICS. Physical education requirements:** Four semesters of physical education required.

**Intercollegiate competition:** 9% of students participate. Baseball (M), basketball (M,W), cross-country (M,W), diving (M,W), football (M), golf (M), ice hockey (M), soccer (W), softball (W), swimming (M,W), tennis (W), track (indoor) (M,W), track (outdoor) (M,W), track and field (indoor) (M,W), track and field (outdoor) (M,W), volleyball (W), wrestling (M). Member of NCAA Division III, NCHA, Wisconsin State University Conference, Women's Wisconsin Intercollegiate Athletic Conference.

**Intramural and club sports:** 55% of students participate. Intramural archery, badminton, basketball, beach volleyball, flag football, floor hockey, inner-tube water polo, racquetball, soccer, softball, swimming, track, volleyball, wrestling. Men's club cheerleading, martial arts, rugby, soccer, volleyball. Women's club cheerleading.

**ADMISSIONS. Academic basis for candidate selection** (in order of priority): Class rank, standardized test scores.

**Nonacademic basis for candidate selection:** Particular talent or ability is considered.

**Requirements:** Graduation from secondary school is required; GED is accepted. 16 units and the following program of study are required: 4 units of English, 2 units of math, 2 units of lab science, 3 units of social studies, 5 units of electives. Minimum composite ACT score of 22 or rank in top half of secondary school class required. Minimum 2.5 GPA required of applicants to professional studies programs in School of Education and School of Communication Disorders and of applicants to Division of Business and Economics. ACT is required. Campus visit and interview recommended. No off-campus interviews.

**Procedure:** Take ACT by October of 12th year. Notification of admission on rolling basis. $100 tuition deposit, refundable until May 1. $125 room deposit, partially refundable until June 1. Freshmen accepted for terms other than fall.

**Special programs:** Admission may be deferred one semester. Credit and/or placement may be granted through CEEB Advanced Placement exams for scores of 3 or higher. Credit may be granted through CLEP general exams. Credit and/or placement may be granted through CLEP subject exams. Credit and placement may be granted through DANTES and challenge exams, and military and life experience. Concurrent enrollment program.

**Transfer students:** Transfer students accepted for terms other than fall. In fall 1992, 4% of all new students were transfers into all classes. 986 transfer applications were received, 468 were accepted. Application deadline is rolling for fall; rolling for spring. Minimum

2.75 GPA required. Lowest course grade accepted is "D." Maximum number of transferable credits is 72 semester hours. At least 30 semester hours must be completed at the university to receive degree.
**Admissions contact:** John Larsen, Ed.D., Director of Admissions. 715 346-2441.

**FINANCIAL AID. Available aid:** Pell grants, SEOG, state scholarships and grants, school scholarships, ROTC scholarships, and aid for undergraduate foreign students. Perkins Loans (NDSL), PLUS, Stafford Loans (GSL), and SLS. Deferred payment plan.
**Financial aid statistics:** 5% of aid is not need-based. In 1992-93, 86% of all undergraduate applicants received aid.
**Supporting data/closing dates:** FAFSA: Accepted on rolling basis. Notification of awards on rolling basis.
**Financial aid contact:** Phillip George, M.S., Director of Financial Aid. 715 346-4771.

**STUDENT EMPLOYMENT.** College Work/Study Program. Institutional employment. 38% of full-time undergraduates work on campus during school year. Students may expect to earn an average of $1,100 during school year. Off-campus part-time employment opportunities rated "excellent."

**COMPUTER FACILITIES.** 1,500 IBM/IBM-compatible microcomputers; all are networked. Residence halls may be equipped with stand-alone microcomputers, networked microcomputers. Computer languages and software packages include C, COBOL, FORTRAN, Pascal; 200 in all. Computer facilities are available to all students.
**Fees:** None.

**GRADUATE CAREER DATA.** Graduate school percentages: 1% enter law school. 1% enter medical school. 1% enter dental school. 1% enter theological school/seminary. Highest graduate school enrollments: U of Wisconsin at Madison, U of Wisconsin at Milwaukee, U of Wisconsin at Stevens Point. Companies and businesses that hire graduates: K mart, Prange Co., Sentry Insurance, U.S. Department of Agriculture.

**PROMINENT ALUMNI/AE.** Lawrence Eagleburger, former U.S. deputy secretary of state; William Bablitch, Wisconsin supreme court justice; Judy Goldsmith, former president, National Organization for Women; Terry Porter, point guard, Portland Trail Blazers; Dr. Arnold Gesell, author, child development specialist; Joseph D. Beck, U.S. congressman, Wisconsin.

# University of Wisconsin–Stout

**Menomonie, WI 54751** **715 232-1122**

**1994-95 Costs.** Tuition: $1,800 (state residents), $6,250 (out-of-state). Room & board: $2,650. Fees, books, misc. academic expenses (school's estimate): $765.
**Enrollment.** Undergraduates: 3,071 men, 2,890 women (full-time). Freshman class: 2,583 applicants, 1,966 accepted, 1,033 enrolled. Graduate enrollment: 254 men, 304 women.
**Test score averages/ranges.** Average ACT scores: 20 English, 20 math, 21 composite. Range of ACT scores of middle 50%: 18-22 English, 18-22 math.
**Faculty.** 330 full-time; 72 part-time. 75% of faculty holds highest degree in specific field. Student/faculty ratio: 20 to 1.
**Selectivity rating.** Less competitive.

**PROFILE.** U Wisconsin–Stout, founded in 1891, is a public, comprehensive institution. Programs are offered through the Graduate College and the Schools of Education and Human Services, Home Economics, Industry and Technology, and Liberal Studies. Its 118-acre campus is located in Menomonie, 60 miles east of Minneapolis-St. Paul.

**Accreditation:** NCACS. Professionally accredited by the American Dietetic Association, the National Association of Schools of Art and Design, the National Council for Accreditation of Teacher Education.
**Religious orientation:** University of Wisconsin–Stout is nonsectarian; no religious requirements.
**Library:** Collections totaling over 214,540 volumes, 1,516 periodical subscriptions, and 915,886 microform items.
**Special facilities/museums:** Audio-visual, photography, and other special labs, child and family study centers.
**Athletic facilities:** Field house, basketball, racquetball, tennis, and volleyball courts, swimming pool, gymnastics, weight, and wrestling rooms, tracks, baseball, football, and softball fields, hockey facility, fitness center, batting cages.

**STUDENT BODY. Undergraduate profile:** 74% are state residents; 32% are transfers. 3% Asian-American, 1% Black, 1% Hispanic, 95% White. Average age of undergraduates is 22.
**Freshman profile:** 1% of freshmen who took ACT scored 30 or over on English, 1% scored 30 or over on math; 17% scored 24 or over on English, 19% scored 24 or over on math, 16% scored 24 or over on composite; 71% scored 18 or over on English, 71% scored 18 or over on math, 79% scored 18 or over on composite; 96% scored 12 or over on English, 96% scored 12 or over on math, 96% scored 12 or over on composite; 98% scored 6 or over on English. 91% of accepted applicants took ACT.
**Undergraduate achievement:** 69% of fall 1992 freshmen returned for fall 1993 term.
**Foreign students:** 187 students are from out of the country. Countries represented include China, Indonesia, Japan, Korea, Mexico, and Taiwan; 35 in all.

**PROGRAMS OF STUDY. Degrees:** B.A., B.F.A., B.S.
**Majors:** Apparel Design/Manufacturing, Applied Mathematics, Art, Art Education, Construction, Dietetics, Early Childhood Education, Family/Consumer Educational Services, Food Systems/Technology, General Business Administration, Home Economics, Hospitality/Tourism Management, Human Development/Family Studies, Industrial Technology, Manufacturing Technology, Marketing Education, Psychology, Retail Merchandising, Technology Education, Vocational Rehabilitation, Vocational/Technical/Adult Education.
**Distribution of degrees:** The majors with the highest enrollment are industrial technology, hospitality/tourism management, and business administration; art education, home economics, and educational services have the lowest.
**Requirements:** General education requirement.
**Academic regulations:** Freshmen must maintain minimum 1.8 GPA; sophomores, 1.9 GPA; juniors, 2.0 GPA; seniors, 2.0 GPA.
**Special:** Minors offered in some majors. Double majors. Dual degrees. Independent study. Internships. Cooperative education programs. Graduate school at which undergraduates may take graduate-level courses. Member of West Central Wisconsin Consortium. Teacher certification in early childhood, elementary, secondary, special education, and vo-tech education. Certification in specific subject areas. Exchange programs abroad in England (American Coll, Middlesex U, West Surrey Coll of Art and Design), France (Ecole Nationale Superieure de Creation Industrielle), Germany (Fachhochschule), Mexico (Inst Tecnologico y de Estudios Superiories de Monterrey at Mazatlan), the Netherlands (Akademie Industriele Vormgeving), and Wales (North East Wales Inst of Higher Education). Study abroad also in China, Scotland, and Spain.
**Honors:** Honor societies.
**Academic Assistance:** Remedial reading, writing, math, and study skills. Nonremedial tutoring.

**STUDENT LIFE. Housing:** All unmarried, nonveteran freshmen and sophomores must live on campus when accommodations are available unless living with family. Coed dorms. Off-campus privately-owned housing. 35% of students live in college housing.
**Services and counseling/handicapped student services:** Placement services. Health service. Women's center. Day care. Counseling services for minority, veteran, and older students. Birth control, personal, and psychological counseling. Career and academic guidance services. Physically disabled student services. Learning disabled services. Notetaking services. Tape recorders. Tutors. Reader services for the blind.
**Campus organizations:** Undergraduate student government. Student newspaper (Stoutonia, published once/week). Literary magazine. Yearbook. Radio station. Concert band, choral groups, theatre, intercollegiate forensic contests, activity programming committees, athletic, departmental, political, service, and special-interest groups, 125 organizations in all. Seven fraternities, no chapter houses; four sororities, no chapter houses. 2% of men join a fraternity. 3% of women join a sorority.
**Religious organizations:** Campus Crusade for Christ, Campus Ministry, Chi Alpha Christian Fellowship, Intervarsity Christian Fellowship, Latter-Day Saints Student Association, The Ministry, United Ministry in Higher Education, WELS Lutheran Campus Ministry.
**Minority/foreign student organizations:** Black Student Union, Hmong club. Chinese Student Association, Malaysian Student Association, International Relations Club.

**ATHLETICS. Physical education requirements:** Two semesters of physical education required.
**Intercollegiate competition:** 8% of students participate. Baseball (M), basketball (M,W), cheerleading (M,W), cross-country (M,W), football (M), gymnastics (W), softball (W), tennis (M,W), track (indoor) (M,W), track (outdoor) (M,W), track and field (indoor) (M,W), track and field (outdoor) (M,W), volleyball (W), wrestling (M). Member of NCAA Division III, Wisconsin State University Conference, Wisconsin Women's Intercollegiate Athletic Conference.
**Intramural and club sports:** 60% of students participate. Intramural badminton, basketball, canoeing, cross-country, cycling, flag football, golf, hiking, hockey, martial arts, orienteering, racquetball, skating, skiing, soccer, softball, tennis, volleyball. Men's club bowling, ice hockey, martial arts, soccer, volleyball. Women's club bowling, martial arts, soccer.

**ADMISSIONS. Academic basis for candidate selection** (in order of priority): Class rank, standardized test scores.
**Requirements:** Graduation from secondary school is required; GED is accepted. 16 units and the following program of study are required: 4 units of English, 2 units of math, 2 units of science, 3 units of social studies, 5 units of academic electives. Minimum composite ACT score of 22 or rank in top half of secondary school class required. Conditional admission possible for applicants not meeting standard requirements. ACT is required. Campus visit recommended. No off-campus interviews.
**Procedure:** Take ACT by October of 12th year. Notification of admission on rolling basis. $100 room deposit, refundable until May 1. Freshmen accepted for terms other than fall.
**Special programs:** Admission may be deferred one year. Credit may be granted through CEEB Advanced Placement for scores of 3 or higher. Credit may be granted through CLEP subject exams, ACT PEP and challenge exams, and military experience. Concurrent enrollment program.
**Transfer students:** Transfer students accepted for terms other than fall. In fall 1993, 32% of all new students were transfers into all classes. 1,047 transfer applications were received, 871 were accepted. Minimum 2.0 GPA required. Lowest course grade accepted is "D." Maximum number of transferable credits is 72 semester hours. At least 32 semester hours must be completed at the university to receive degree.
**Admissions contact:** Charles Kell, M.S., Director of Admissions. 715 232-1411.

**FINANCIAL AID. Available aid:** Pell grants, SEOG, state scholarships and grants, school scholarships, private scholarships, and aid for undergraduate foreign students. Perkins Loans (NDSL), PLUS, Stafford Loans (GSL), school loans, private loans, and SLS. Minnesota SELF Loans. Partial payment plan.
**Financial aid statistics:** 33% of aid is not need-based. In 1993-94, 74% of all undergraduate applicants received aid; 52% of freshman applicants. Average amounts of aid awarded freshmen: Scholarships and grants, $965; loans, $2,285.
**Supporting data/closing dates:** FAFSA: Priority filing date is April 1. Notification of awards begins June 1.
**Financial aid contact:** Beth Resech, Assistant Director of Financial Aid. 715 232-1363.

**STUDENT EMPLOYMENT.** College Work/Study Program. Institutional employment. 43% of full-time undergraduates work on campus during school year. Students may expect to earn an average of $1,000 during school year. Off-campus part-time employment opportunities rated "fair."

**COMPUTER FACILITIES.** 800 IBM/IBM-compatible and Macintosh/Apple microcomputers; 150 are networked. Students may access Data General, Digital minicomputer/mainframe systems, BITNET, Internet. Residence halls may be equipped with stand-alone microcomputers, networked terminals. Computer languages and software packages in-

clude Ada, Assembler, AutoCAD, BASIC, COBOL, dBASE, FORTRAN, Lotus 1-2-3, MATLAB, MicroCAP, Pascal, Quattro, SPSS-X, WordPerfect, WordStar; 50 in all. Computer facilities are available to all students.
**Fees:** None.
**Hours:** 7:45 AM-11 PM (M-F); 9 AM-5 PM (Sa); 1 PM-11 PM (Su).

**GRADUATE CAREER DATA.** Highest graduate school enrollments: U of Minnesota, U of Wisconsin–Stout. 88% of graduates choose careers in business and industry. Companies and businesses that hire graduates: George Hormel, Radisson Hotels, Target Corp., 3M.

## University of Wisconsin–Superior

**Superior, WI 54880** **715 394-8101**

**1993-94 Costs.** Tuition: $2,100 (state residents), $6,000 (out-of-state). Room & board: $1,250-$1,100. Fees, books, misc. academic expenses (school's estimate): $600.
**Enrollment.** Undergraduates: 950 men, 1,000 women (full-time). Freshman class: 840 applicants, 680 accepted, 335 enrolled. Graduate enrollment: 200 men, 275 women.
**Test score averages/ranges.** Average ACT scores: 23 English, 19 math, 22 composite.
**Faculty.** 130 full-time; 20 part-time. 80% of faculty holds highest degree in specific field. Student/faculty ratio: 12 to 1.
**Selectivity rating.** Less competitive.

**PROFILE.** U Wisconsin at Superior is a public, comprehensive institution. Founded as a state Normal school in 1893, it gained state university status in 1964 and its present status in 1971. Its 230-acre campus is located in Superior, at the western tip of Lake Superior.

**Accreditation:** NCACS. Professionally accredited by the National Council for Accreditation of Teacher Education.
**Religious orientation:** University of Wisconsin–Superior is nonsectarian; no religious requirements.
**Library:** Collections totaling over 219,000 volumes.
**Special facilities/museums:** TV, radio, and film facilities, field stations at Pigeon Lake, Clam Lake, and Lake Superior.
**Athletic facilities:** Gymnasiums, weight room, swimming pool, track, arena, skating arena.

**STUDENT BODY. Undergraduate profile:** 62% are state residents; 9% are transfers. 1% Asian-American, 3% Black, 2% Hispanic, 3% Native American, 91% White. Average age of undergraduates is 21.
**Freshman profile:** 7% of freshmen who took ACT scored 30 or over on composite; 21% scored 24 or over on composite; 99% scored 18 or over on composite; 100% scored 12 or over on composite. 99% of accepted applicants took ACT. 90% of freshmen come from public schools.
**Undergraduate achievement:** 70% of fall 1992 freshmen returned for fall 1993 term.
**Foreign students:** 62 students are from out of the country. Countries represented include Canada, Hong Kong, Japan, and Sri Lanka; 15 in all.

**PROGRAMS OF STUDY. Degrees:** A.B., B.A., B.F.A., B.Mech.Eng., B.Mus., B.S., B.S.Nurs.
**Majors:** Accounting, Art, Art Therapy, Biology, Business, Business Administration, Business Education, Chemistry, Communication Arts, Computer Information Systems, Computer Mathematics, Computer Science, Drama, Economics, Education, Elementary Education, English, History, Individualized Majors, International Studies, Marketing, Mathematics, Medical Technology, Music, Music Education, Music Education/Elementary Education, Music/Performance, Nursing, Office Administration, Personnel Administration, Physical Education, Physics, Political Science, Political Science/Criminal Justice Emphasis, Psychology, Science, Secondary Education, Social Studies, Social Work, Sociology, Speech/Communicating Arts, Speech Education, Visual Arts, Visual Arts/Education, Visual Arts/Studio.
**Requirements:** General education requirement.
**Special:** Minors offered in aerospace studies, coaching, early childhood education, earth science, geology, health education, individually designed minors, journalism, learning disabilities, library science, police science, and women's studies. Associate's degrees offered. Self-designed majors. Double majors. Dual degrees. Independent study. Accelerated study. Pass/fail grading option. Internships. Cooperative education programs. Preprofessional programs in law, medicine, veterinary science, pharmacy, and dentistry. 2-2 maritime engineering program with Texas A&M U. 3-2 forestry program with Michigan Tech U. Cross-registration with Coll of St. Scholastica, Northland Coll, Texas A&M U, and U of Minnesota at Duluth. Teacher certification in early childhood, elementary, and secondary education. Certification in specific subject areas. Study abroad in Denmark, Norway, other European countries, and the former Soviet Republics. AFROTC.
**Honors:** Honors program.
**Academic Assistance:** Remedial reading, writing, math, and study skills. Nonremedial tutoring.

**STUDENT LIFE. Housing:** All unmarried students under age 21 must live on campus unless living near campus with relatives. Coed, women's, and men's dorms. 18% of students live in college housing.
**Social atmosphere:** According to the student newspaper, "UW Superior is a close-knit community. Everyone knows everyone." Athletics, especially hockey, football, and basketball, are popular with students. On campus, students frequent the Woodroom and the snackbar. Favorite off-campus spots include the Cove and Champion's Bar.
**Services and counseling/handicapped student services:** Placement services. Health service. Women's center. Day care. Counseling services for minority, military, veteran, and older students. Birth control, personal, and psychological counseling. Career and academic guidance services. Religious counseling. Physically disabled student services. Learning disabled services. Notetaking services. Tutors. Reader services for the blind.
**Campus organizations:** Undergraduate student government. Student newspaper (Promethean, published once/week). Concert and jazz bands, concert choir, opera workshop, drama groups, oratorio choruses, professional, departmental, service, and special-interest groups, 15 organizations in all. One fraternity, no chapter house. 1% of men join a fraternity.
**Religious organizations:** Ecumenical Coordinating Council, Intervarsity Christian Fellowship.
**Minority/foreign student organizations:** Black Student Union, Native American Student Association. International Student Association.

**ATHLETICS. Physical education requirements:** Two semesters of physical education required.
**Intercollegiate competition:** 58% of students participate. Baseball (M), basketball (M,W), cross-country (M,W), ice hockey (M), softball (W), track (indoor) (M,W), track (outdoor) (M,W), track and field (indoor) (M,W), track and field (outdoor) (M,W), volleyball (W). Member of NCAA Division III, Northern Collegiate Hockey Association, Wisconsin State University Conference, Wisconsin Women's Intercollegiate Athletic Conference.
**Intramural and club sports:** Intramural Alpine skiing, basketball, jogging, Nordic skiing, racquetball, skating, snow shoeing, softball, tennis, volleyball. Men's club curling, rifle, soccer. Women's club curling.

**ADMISSIONS. Academic basis for candidate selection** (in order of priority): Secondary school record, class rank, standardized test scores, school's recommendation, essay.
**Nonacademic basis for candidate selection:** Character and personality and particular talent or ability are considered.
**Requirements:** Graduation from secondary school is required; GED is accepted. 20 units and the following program of study are required: 4 units of English, 3 units of math, 3 units of lab science, 3 units of social studies, 4 units of electives. Minimum composite ACT score of 20 and rank in top half of secondary school class required. Audition required of music program applicants. ACT is required. Campus visit and interview recommended. Off-campus interviews available with an admissions representative.
**Procedure:** Take ACT by October of 12th year. Visit college for interview by April 1 of 12th year. Application deadline is May 1. Notification of admission on rolling basis. Reply is required by August 1. $75 room deposit, refundable until the first day of classes. Freshmen accepted for terms other than fall.
**Special programs:** Admission may be deferred two semesters. Credit may be granted through CEEB Advanced Placement for scores of 3 or higher. Credit may be granted through CLEP general exams, DANTES exams, and military experience. Credit and/or placement may be granted through CLEP subject exams. Credit and placement may be granted through challenge exams. Early entrance/early admission program. Concurrent enrollment program.
**Transfer students:** Transfer students accepted for terms other than fall. In fall 1993, 9% of all new students were transfers into all classes. 380 transfer applications were received, 290 were accepted. Application deadline is June 1 for fall; November 1 for spring. Minimum 2.3 GPA required. Lowest course grade accepted is "D." Maximum number of transferable credits is 72 semester hours. At least 32 semester hours must be completed at the university to receive degree.
**Admissions contact:** Jon Wojciechowski, M.A., Director of Admissions. 715 394-8230.

**FINANCIAL AID. Available aid:** Pell grants, SEOG, state scholarships and grants, school scholarships and grants, private scholarships, ROTC scholarships, academic merit scholarships, and aid for undergraduate foreign students. Perkins Loans (NDSL), PLUS, Stafford Loans (GSL), state loans, school loans, and SLS. Deferred payment plan. Partial payment plan.
**Financial aid statistics:** 10% of aid is not need-based. In 1993-94, 80% of all undergraduate applicants received aid; 80% of freshman applicants.
**Supporting data/closing dates:** FAFSA/FAF/FFS. Income tax forms. Notification of awards begins May.
**Financial aid contact:** Anne Podgorak, Director of Financial Aid. 715 394-8274.

**STUDENT EMPLOYMENT.** College Work/Study Program. Institutional employment. 21% of full-time undergraduates work on campus during school year. Students may expect to earn an average of $1,100 during school year. Off-campus part-time employment opportunities rated "excellent."

**COMPUTER FACILITIES.** 125 IBM/IBM-compatible and Macintosh/Apple microcomputers; all are networked. Students may access UNISYS minicomputer/mainframe systems. Computer languages and software packages include Bank Street Writer, BASIC, C, COBOL, FORTH, FORTRAN, Pascal, RPG. Computer facilities are available to all students.
**Fees:** Computer fee is included in tuition/fees.
**Hours:** 24 hours.

## University of Wisconsin–Whitewater

**Whitewater, WI 53190** **414 472-1234**

**1994-95 Costs.** Tuition: $2,124 (state residents), $6,525 (out-of-state). Room & board: $2,500.
**Enrollment.** Undergraduates: 3,635 men, 4,153 women (full-time). Freshman class: 4,400 applicants, 3,719 accepted, 1,846 enrolled. Graduate enrollment: 464 men, 779 women.
**Test score averages/ranges.** N/A.
**Faculty.** 347 full-time; 124 part-time. 69% of faculty holds doctoral degree. Student/faculty ratio: 21 to 1.
**Selectivity rating.** Competitive.

**PROFILE.** U Wisconsin at Whitewater, founded in 1868, is a public, comprehensive institution. Programs are offered through the Colleges of the Arts, Business and Economics, Education, and Letters and Sciences and the Graduate School. Its 385-acre campus is located in Whitewater, 45 miles southeast of Milwaukee.

**Accreditation:** NCACS. Professionally accredited by the American Assembly of Collegiate Schools of Business, the Council on Social Work Education, the National Association of Schools of Music, the National Council for Accreditation of Teacher Education.
**Religious orientation:** University of Wisconsin–Whitewater is nonsectarian; no religious requirements.
**Library:** Collections totaling over 348,238 volumes, 5,000 periodical subscriptions, and 1,042,684 microform items.
**Special facilities/museums:** Two electron microscopes.
**Athletic facilities:** Sports complex, gymnasium, swimming pool, track, stadium, jogging course, athletic fields, tennis courts.

**STUDENT BODY. Undergraduate profile:** 94% are state residents; 28% are transfers. 1% Asian-American, 4% Black, 1% Hispanic, 93% White, 1% Other. Average age of undergraduates is 22.
**Freshman profile:** 5% of accepted applicants took SAT; 95% took ACT. 80% of freshmen come from public schools.
**Undergraduate achievement:** 76% of fall 1992 freshmen returned for fall 1993 term. 48% of entering class graduated.
**Foreign students:** 181 students are from out of the country. Countries represented include Cameroon, Hong Kong, Malaysia, and Singapore; 33 in all.

**PROGRAMS OF STUDY. Degrees:** B.A., B.Bus.Admin., B.F.A., B.Mus., B.S., B.S.Ed.
**Majors:** Accounting, Adolescent Special Education, American Studies, Art, Art Education, Art History, Biology, Business Education, Business-Related Law, Chemistry, Communication, Communicative Disorders, Computer Systems, Distributive Education, Economics, Elementary Education, English, Finance/Business Law, French, General Business, Geography, German, Health/Physical Education/Recreation Education, History, International Studies, Journalism, Kindergarten/Primary Education, Management, Management Computer Systems, Marketing, Mathematics, Music, Music Education, Office Administration, Personnel/Human Relations, Physics, Political Science, Production/Operations Management, Psychology, Public Administration, Public Policy/Administration, Safety Education, Secondary Education, Secretarial, Social Welfare, Sociology, Spanish, Special Education, Speech, Theatre/Dance, Theatre Education.
**Distribution of degrees:** The majors with the highest enrollment are accounting, education, and marketing; German and art history have the lowest.
**Requirements:** General education requirement.
**Academic regulations:** Minimum 2.0 GPA must be maintained.
**Special:** Minors offered in most majors and in anthropology, business studies, coaching, computer science, criminal justice, dance, gerontology, health, library media, military science, philosophy, recreation/leisure studies, religious studies, and urban/area development. Courses offered in homemaking arts and Portuguese. Associate's degrees offered. Self-designed majors. Double majors. Dual degrees. Independent study. Pass/fail grading option. Internships. Graduate school at which undergraduates may take graduate-level courses. Preprofessional programs in law, medicine, veterinary science, pharmacy, dentistry, optometry, chiropractic, engineering, forestry, and medical technology. 2-3 engineering and pharmacy programs with U of Wisconsin at Madison. Teacher certification in early childhood, elementary, secondary, and special education. Certification in specific subject areas. Study abroad possible in many countries. ROTC.
**Honors:** Honors program. Honor societies.
**Academic Assistance:** Remedial reading, writing, math, and study skills. Nonremedial tutoring.

**STUDENT LIFE. Housing:** All unmarried students under age 21 must live on campus unless living near campus with relatives. Coed, women's, and men's dorms. Sorority and fraternity housing. Off-campus privately-owned housing. 40% of students live in college housing.
**Social atmosphere:** On campus, students gather at Down Under, the Warhawk Room, Monkey Island, and the Horicon Lounge. Off campus, students head for the bars. Athletes, minority groups, and Greeks are among the most prominent groups on campus. Highlights of the school year include athletic events, Homecoming, spring break, Halloween, and St. Patrick's Day.
**Services and counseling/handicapped student services:** Placement services. Health service. Women's center. Day care. Counseling services for minority, military, veteran, and older students. Personal and psychological counseling. Career and academic guidance services. Physically disabled student services. Learning disabled program/services. Notetaking services. Tape recorders. Tutors. Reader services for the blind.
**Campus organizations:** Undergraduate student government. Student newspaper (Royal Purple, published once/week). Radio and TV stations. Chamber Singers, Meistersingers, concert band, concert choir, Madrigalians, orchestra, stage band, small instrumental and vocal groups, Treble Clef, Warhawk Show Band, Orchesis Dance Group, theatres, children's entertainment companies, tenants union, 150 organizations in all. Seven fraternities, all with chapter houses; five sororities, all with chapter houses. 8% of men join a fraternity. 7% of women join a sorority.
**Religious organizations:** Campus Crusade for Christ, Catholic Student Association, Christian Science Organization, Christians in Action, Fellowship of Christian Athletes, Intervarsity Christian Fellowship, Lutheran Student Ministry, Navigators, Shalom Students, Share-A-Prayer Holy Spirit, The Light, Lutheran Collegiates, United Ministries.
**Minority/foreign student organizations:** Black Student Union, MEChA. International Club, Nigerian Student Union.

**ATHLETICS. Physical education requirements:** One semester of physical education required.
**Intercollegiate competition:** 15% of students participate. Baseball (M), basketball (M,W), cross-country (M,W), diving (M,W), football (M), gymnastics (W), soccer (M,W), softball (W), swimming (M,W), tennis (M,W), track (indoor) (M,W), track (outdoor) (M,W), track and field (indoor) (M,W), track and field (outdoor) (M,W), volleyball (W), wrestling (M). Member of NCAA Division III, Wisconsin State University Conference, Wisconsin Women's Intercollegiate Athletic Confrence.
**Intramural and club sports:** 50% of students participate. Intramural basketball, flag football, floor hockey, inner-tube water polo, sand volleyball, softball, tennis, volleyball. Men's club Alpine skiing, bowling, canoe/kayak, ice hockey, lacrosse, martial arts, Nordic skiing, rifle, rugby, volleyball. Women's club Alpine skiing, bowling, canoe/kayak, martial arts, Nordic skiing, rifle.

**ADMISSIONS. Academic basis for candidate selection** (in order of priority): Class rank, standardized test scores, secondary school record, school's recommendation.
**Nonacademic basis for candidate selection:** Character and personality, extracurricular participation, and particular talent or ability are considered.
**Requirements:** Graduation from secondary school is required; GED is accepted. 16 units and the following program of study are required: 4 units of English, 3 units of math, 2 units of science, 3 units of social studies, 4 units of academic electives. Rank in top half of secondary school class required; minimum composite ACT score of 20 recommended. Audition required of music program applicants. EOP for applicants not normally admissible. ACT is required; SAT may be substituted. Campus visit recommended. No off-campus interviews.
**Procedure:** Take SAT or ACT by October of 12th year. Suggest filing application by January 1; no deadline. Notification of admission on rolling basis. $125 room deposit, refundable until May 1. Freshmen accepted for terms other than fall.
**Special programs:** Credit may be granted through CEEB Advanced Placement for scores of 3 or higher. Credit and/or placement may be granted through CLEP general exams. Credit may be granted through CLEP subject exams and challenge exams.
**Transfer students:** Transfer students accepted for terms other than fall. In fall 1993, 28% of all new students were transfers into all classes. 990 transfer applications were received, 852 were accepted. Application deadline is rolling for fall; rolling for spring. Minimum 2.0 GPA required. Lowest course grade accepted is "D." Maximum number of transferable credits is 78 semester hours. At least 30 semester hours must be completed at the university to receive degree.
**Admissions contact:** I.A. Madsen, M.S., Director of Admissions. 414 472-1440.

**FINANCIAL AID. Available aid:** Pell grants, SEOG, state scholarships and grants, school scholarships, private scholarships, ROTC scholarships, academic merit scholarships, and aid for undergraduate foreign students. Perkins Loans (NDSL), PLUS, Stafford Loans (GSL), and state loans. Deferred payment plan.
**Financial aid statistics:** In 1993-94, 55% of all undergraduate applicants received aid.
**Supporting data/closing dates:** FAFSA/FAF/FFS: Priority filing date is March 15; accepted on rolling basis. Notification of awards on rolling basis.
**Financial aid contact:** Gerald Buhrow, M.S., Director of Financial Aid. 414 472-1130.

**STUDENT EMPLOYMENT.** College Work/Study Program. Institutional employment. 21% of full-time undergraduates work on campus during school year. Students may expect to earn an average of $900 during school year. Off-campus part-time employment opportunities rated "good."

**COMPUTER FACILITIES.** 600 IBM/IBM-compatible and Macintosh/Apple microcomputers; 255 are networked. Students may access Digital, IBM minicomputer/mainframe systems, Internet. Residence halls may be equipped with networked terminals. Computer languages and software packages include Ability, BASIC, BASK, COBOL, LISP, Lotus 1-2-3, Pascal, PC-Write, Quick C, SMART, Volkswriter, WordPerfect. Computer facilities are available to all students.
**Fees:** None.
**Hours:** 8 AM-midn.

**GRADUATE CAREER DATA.** 40% of graduates choose careers in business and industry.

# Viterbo College

**LaCrosse, WI 54601-4797** **608 791-0040**

**1994-95 Costs.** Tuition: $9,140. Room & board: $3,540. Fees, books, misc. academic expenses (school's estimate): $670.
**Enrollment.** Undergraduates: 257 men, 757 women (full-time). Freshman class: 625 applicants, 521 accepted, 270 enrolled. Graduate enrollment: 30 men, 84 women.
**Test score averages/ranges.** Range of ACT scores of middle 50%: 22-26 composite.
**Faculty.** 72 full-time; 46 part-time. 28% of faculty holds doctoral degree. Student/faculty ratio: 12 to 1.
**Selectivity rating.** Competitive.

**PROFILE.** Viterbo, founded in 1890, is a private, church-affiliated, multipurpose college. Its six-acre campus is located in LaCrosse, southeast of Minneapolis-St. Paul.

**Accreditation:** NCACS. Professionally accredited by the American Dietetic Association, the American Medical Association (CAHEA), the National Association of Schools of Music, the National Council for Accreditation of Teacher Education, the National League for Nursing.
**Religious orientation:** Viterbo College is affiliated with the Roman Catholic Church (Franciscan Sisters of Perpetual Adoration); two semesters of religion required.
**Library:** Collections totaling over 63,000 volumes, 689 periodical subscriptions and 29 microform items.
**Special facilities/museums:** Music museum, nursing center with labs and simulated medical records department.
**Athletic facilities:** Basketball, racquetball, tennis, volleyball, and walleyball courts, weight room, exercise bicycles.

**STUDENT BODY. Undergraduate profile:** 75% are state residents; 27% are transfers. 2% Asian-American, 2% Black, 1% Hispanic, 95% White. Average age of undergraduates is 23.
**Freshman profile:** 92% of accepted applicants took ACT. 73% of freshmen come from public schools.
**Undergraduate achievement:** 75% of fall 1992 freshmen returned for fall 1993 term. 33% of entering class graduated.
**Foreign students:** Eight students are from out of the country. Countries represented include Belize, Brazil, Colombia, India, Lebanon, and Zimbabwe; eight in all.

**PROGRAMS OF STUDY. Degrees:** B.A., B.Art, B.Art Ed., B.Lib.Studies, B.Mus., B.S., B.S.Ed., B.S.M.T., B.S.Nurs.

**Majors:** Accounting, Applied Music, Art, Art/Business, Art Education, Arts Administration, Biology, Business Administration, Business Education, Chamber Music, Chemistry, Church Music, Community/Medical Dietetics/Nutrition, Computer Information Systems/ Accounting, Computer Science, Education, Elementary Education, English, Health Care Administration, Interdepartmental Biology/Chemistry, Liberal Studies, Marketing, Ministry, Music, Music Education, Music/Theatre, Nursing, Psychology, Religious Study, Sociology, Theatre Arts.

**Distribution of degrees:** The majors with the highest enrollment are nursing, business, and fine arts; religious studies has the lowest.

**Requirements:** General education requirement.

**Academic regulations:** Minimum 2.0 GPA must be maintained.

**Special:** Minors offered in most majors and in communications, dance, French, history, journalism, management, math, philosophy, social research, Spanish, statistics, and women's studies. Double majors. Independent study. Pass/fail grading option. Internships. Cooperative education programs. Preprofessional programs in law, medicine, veterinary science, pharmacy, dentistry, optometry, and chiropractic. 3-1 and 4-1 medical technology programs. Cross-registration with U of Wisconsin at LaCrosse. Teacher certification in elementary and secondary education. Study abroad possible. ROTC at U of Wisconsin at LaCrosse.

**Honors:** Phi Beta Kappa.

**Academic Assistance:** Remedial reading, writing, math, and study skills. Nonremedial tutoring.

**ADMISSIONS. Academic basis for candidate selection** (in order of priority): Standardized test scores, class rank, secondary school record, school's recommendation, essay.

**Nonacademic basis for candidate selection:** Particular talent or ability is emphasized. Extracurricular participation is important. Character and personality and alumni/ae relationship are considered.

**Requirements:** Graduation from secondary school is required; GED is accepted. 16 units and the following program of study are required: 4 units of English, 2 units of math, 2 units of science, 2 units of social studies, 6 units of electives. Minimum composite ACT score of 20, rank in top half of secondary school class, and minimum 2.5 GPA recommended. Chemistry required of dietetics, medical technology, and nursing program applicants. Portfolio required of art program applicants. Audition required of music program applicants. Conditional admission possible for applicants not meeting standard requirements. ACT is required; SAT may be substituted. PSAT is recommended. ACH recommended. Campus visit recommended. Off-campus interviews available with admissions and alumni representatives.

**Procedure:** Take SAT or ACT by May of 12th year. Visit college for interview by June of 12th year. Suggest filing application by December 15. Application deadline is August 1. Notification of admission on rolling basis. Reply is required by May 1. $100 tuition deposit, refundable until May 1. $100 room deposit, refundable until May 1. Freshmen accepted for terms other than fall.

**Special programs:** Credit and/or placement may be granted through CEEB Advanced Placement exams for scores of 3 or higher. Credit may be granted through CLEP subject exams and military and life experience. Credit and placement may be granted through challenge exams. Early decision program. Early entrance/early admission program. Concurrent enrollment program.

**Transfer students:** Transfer students accepted for terms other than fall. In fall 1993, 27% of all new students were transfers into all classes. 144 transfer applications were received, 127 were accepted. Application deadline is August 1 for fall; December 1 for spring. Minimum 2.5 GPA required. Lowest course grade accepted is "C." Maximum number of transferable credits is 80 quarter hours. At least 48 quarter hours must be completed at the college to receive degree.

**Admissions contact:** Roland W. Nelson, Ph.D., Director of Admissions. 608 791-0420.

**FINANCIAL AID. Available aid:** Pell grants, SEOG, state scholarships and grants, school scholarships and grants, private scholarships and grants, ROTC scholarships, academic merit scholarships, and aid for undergraduate foreign students. Perkins Loans (NDSL), PLUS, Stafford Loans (GSL), NSL, state loans, private loans, and SLS. Tuition Plan Inc., Education Plan Inc., AMS, Tuition Management Systems, deferred payment plan, and family tuition reduction.

**Financial aid statistics:** In 1993-94, 91% of all undergraduate applicants received aid; 92% of freshman applicants. Average amounts of aid awarded freshmen: Scholarships and grants, $3,500; loans, $2,500.

**Supporting data/closing dates:** FAFSA/FAF/FFS: Priority filing date is March 1; accepted on rolling basis. Income tax forms: Priority filing date is March 1. Notification of awards on rolling basis.

**Financial aid contact:** Terry Norman, B.A., Director of Financial Aid. 608 791-0487.

# Wisconsin Lutheran College

**Milwaukee, WI 53226 414 774-8620**

**1994-95 Costs.** Tuition: $9,100. Room & board: $3,800. Fees, books, misc. academic expenses (school's estimate): $590.

**Enrollment.** Undergraduates: 105 men, 180 women (full-time). Freshman class: 144 applicants, 138 accepted, 85 enrolled.

**Test score averages/ranges.** Average ACT scores: 23 composite. Range of ACT scores of middle 50%: 20-24 composite.

**Faculty.** 31 full-time; 23 part-time. 42% of faculty holds doctoral degree. Student/faculty ratio: 10 to 1.

**Selectivity rating.** Less competitive.

**PROFILE.** Wisconsin Lutheran, founded in 1973, is a private, church-affiliated, liberal arts college. Its 12-acre campus is in Milwaukee.

**Accreditation:** NCACS.

**Religious orientation:** Wisconsin Lutheran College is affiliated with the Wisconsin Evangelical Lutheran Synod; one religion/theology course required each year.

**Library:** Collections totaling over 75,000 volumes, 300 periodical subscriptions, and 6,703 microform items.

**Athletic facilities:** Fitness center, gymnasium, training rooms, basketball, indoor soccer, tennis, and volleyball courts, batting cage, badminton and fencing areas.

**STUDENT BODY. Undergraduate profile:** 79% are state residents; 17% are transfers. 1% Asian-American, 3% Black, 1% Hispanic, 95% White.

**Freshman profile:** 26% of freshmen come from public schools.

**Undergraduate achievement:** 80% of fall 1992 freshmen returned for fall 1993 term. 31% of entering class graduated. 20% of students who completed a degree program immediately went on to graduate study.

**PROGRAMS OF STUDY. Degrees:** B.A., B.Bus.Admin., B.S.

**Majors:** Broad Field Social Sciences, Business Administration, Chemistry, Communication, Communicative Arts, Elementary Education, English, History, Mathematics, Music, Psychology, Theology.

**Distribution of degrees:** The majors with the highest enrollment are communication, psychology, and business administration; chemistry, music, and theology have the lowest.

**Requirements:** General education requirement.

**Academic regulations:** Freshmen must maintain minimum 1.75 GPA; sophomores, juniors, seniors, 2.0 GPA. Minimum 2.5 GPA in major required for graduation.

**Special:** Minors offered in several majors and in art, biology, computer information systems, philosophy, and Spanish. Double majors. Independent study. Internships. Preprofessional programs in law, medicine, veterinary science, pharmacy, and dentistry. Teacher certification in elementary and secondary education. Certification in specific subject areas.

**Academic Assistance:** Remedial writing and study skills.

**ADMISSIONS. Academic basis for candidate selection** (in order of priority): Secondary school record, standardized test scores, class rank, school's recommendation.

**Nonacademic basis for candidate selection:** Character and personality are important. Extracurricular participation and particular talent or ability are considered.

**Requirements:** Graduation from secondary school is recommended; GED is accepted. 20 units and the following program of study are recommended: 4 units of English, 3 units of math, 2 units of science, 2 units of foreign language, 2 units of social studies, 4 units of electives. Minimum composite ACT score of 20 (minimum combined SAT score of 930), rank in top half of secondary school class, and minimum 2.5 GPA required of applicants. Conditional admission possible for applicants not meeting standard requirements. ACT is required; SAT may be substituted. Campus visit recommended.

**Procedure:** Take SAT or ACT by December of 12th year. Visit college for interview by February of 12th year. Suggest filing application by March; no deadline. Notification of admission on rolling basis. No set date by which applicant must accept offer. $50 nonrefundable tuition deposit. $50 room deposit, refundable until July 15. Freshmen accepted for terms other than fall.

**Special programs:** Early entrance/early admission program. Concurrent enrollment program.

**Transfer students:** Transfer students accepted for terms other than fall. In fall 1993, 17% of all new students were transfers into all classes. 25 transfer applications were received, 25 were accepted. Lowest course grade accepted is "C."

**Admissions contact:** Joel P. Mischke, M.A., Director of Admissions. 414 774-8620, extension 12.

**FINANCIAL AID. Available aid:** Pell grants, SEOG, state scholarships and grants, school scholarships and grants, private scholarships and grants, academic merit scholarships, and aid for undergraduate foreign students. PLUS, Stafford Loans (GSL), and SLS. AMS and family tuition reduction.

**Financial aid statistics:** 15% of aid is not need-based. In 1993-94, 99% of all undergraduate applicants received aid; 99% of freshman applicants.

**Supporting data/closing dates:** FAFSA/FAF/FFS: Priority filing date is April 1. School's own aid application: Priority filing date is April 1. Income tax forms: Priority filing date is April 1.

**Financial aid contact:** Linda Loeffel, Director of Financial Aid. 414 774-8620, extension 42.

# Wyoming

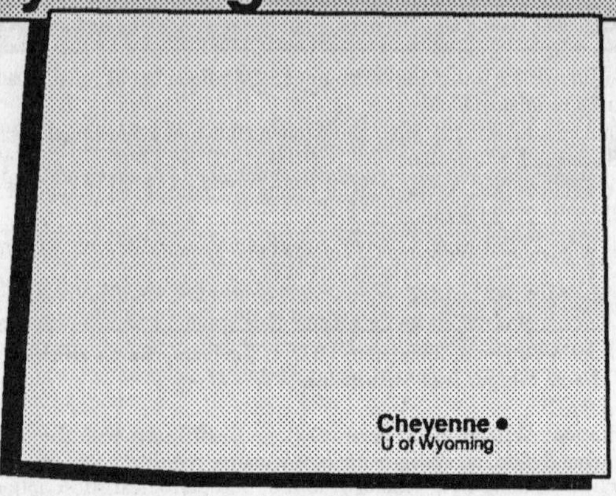


## University of Wyoming

**Laramie, WY 82071** **307 766-1121**

**1993-94 Costs.** Tuition: $1,648 (state residents), $5,182 (out-of-state). Room & board: $3,343. Fees, books, misc. academic expenses (school's estimate): $660.
**Enrollment.** Undergraduates: 3,945 men, 3,590 women (full-time). Freshman class: 2,029 applicants, 1,516 accepted, 1,240 enrolled. Graduate enrollment: 1,429 men, 1,560 women.
**Test score averages/ranges.** Average ACT scores: 22 English, 22 math, 23 composite. Range of ACT scores of middle 50%: 18-25 English, 18-25 math.
**Faculty.** 591 full-time; 157 part-time. 90% of faculty holds doctoral degree. Student/faculty ratio: 18 to 1.
**Selectivity rating.** Less competitive.

**PROFILE.** The University of Wyoming, founded in 1886, is a public, multipurpose institution. Programs are offered through the Colleges of Agriculture, Arts and Sciences, Commerce and Industry, Education, Engineering, Health Sciences, and Law and the Graduate School; an autonomous School of Religion is also located at the university. Its 785-acre campus is located in Laramie, in southeastern Wyoming, 50 miles west of Cheyenne.

**Accreditation:** NCACS. Professionally accredited by the Accreditation Board for Engineering and Technology, the American Assembly of Collegiate Schools of Business, the American Bar Association, the American Council on Pharmaceutical Education, the American Medical Association (CAHEA), the American Psychological Association, the American Speech-Language-Hearing Association, the Council on Social Work Education, the National Association of Schools of Music, the National Council for Accreditation of Teacher Education, the National League for Nursing.
**Religious orientation:** University of Wyoming is nonsectarian; no religious requirements.
**Library:** Collections totaling over 1,077,650 volumes, 11,347 periodical subscriptions, and 2,332,099 microform items.
**Special facilities/museums:** Art gallery, American studies, anthropology, geology, vertebrate, and wildlife research museums, language lab, on-campus elementary school, history research center, state veterinary lab, herbarium, Park Service research center, water resources research institute, planetarium, infrared telescope observatory, electron microscopes.
**Athletic facilities:** Gymnasium, weight room, swimming pool, basketball and racquetball courts, field house, tennis complex, baseball and softball fields.

**STUDENT BODY. Undergraduate profile:** 86% are state residents. 1% Asian-American, 1% Black, 3% Hispanic, 1% Native American, 85% White, 9% Other. Average age of undergraduates is 23.
**Freshman profile:** 4% of freshmen who took ACT scored 30 or over on English, 4% scored 30 or over on math, 4% scored 30 or over on composite; 36% scored 24 or over on English, 33% scored 24 or over on math, 36% scored 24 or over on composite; 72% scored 18 or over on English, 72% scored 18 or over on math, 79% scored 18 or over on composite; 87% scored 12 or over on English, 87% scored 12 or over on math, 86% scored 12 or over on composite. 28% of accepted applicants took SAT; 87% took ACT.
**Undergraduate achievement:** 71% of fall 1992 freshmen returned for fall 1993 term.
**Foreign students:** 185 students are from out of the country. Countries represented include Canada, China, Germany, India, Malaysia, and Norway; 44 in all.

**PROGRAMS OF STUDY. Degrees:** B.A., B.F.A., B.Mus., B.S., B.Soc.Work, B.Theatre/Dance.
**Majors:** Accounting, Administration of Justice, Agricultural Business, Agricultural Communications, Agroecology, American Studies, Animal Science, Anthropology, Applied Mathematics, Architectural Engineering, Art, Astronomy/Astrophysics, Biology, Botany, Broadcasting, Business Administration, Business Education, Chemical Engineering, Chemistry, Civil Engineering, Communication, Computer Science, Dental Hygiene, Distributive Education, Economics, Electrical Engineering, Elementary Education, Elementary/Special Education, English, English/Theatre, Farm/Ranch Management, Finance, Food Science, French, General Agriculture, Geography, Geology, Geophysics, German, Health Education, History, Home Economics, Humanities/Fine Arts, Industrial Arts Education, International Agriculture, International Studies, Journalism, Management, Management Information Systems, Marketing, Mathematics, Mechanical Engineering, Medical Technology, Molecular Biology, Music, Music Education, Music Performance, Music Theory/Composition, Natural Science/Mathematics, Nursing, Petroleum Engineering, Pharmacy, Philosophy, Physical Education, Physics, Political Economy, Political Science, Psychology, Range Management, Recreation/Park Administration, Russian, Secondary Education, Small Business Management, Social Science, Social Work, Sociology, Spanish, Special Education, Speech/Language/Hearing Sciences, Statistics, Theatre/Dance, Trades/Industrial Education, Vocational Agriculture, Vocational Homemaking, Wildlife/Fisheries/Biology Management, Women's Studies, Zoology/Physiology.
**Distribution of degrees:** The majors with the highest enrollment are elementary education, business administration, and psychology.
**Requirements:** General education requirement.
**Academic regulations:** Freshmen must maintain minimum 1.7 GPA; sophomores, 1.9 GPA; juniors, 2.0 GPA; seniors, 2.0 GPA.
**Special:** Minors offered in all academic disciplines. Interdisciplinary program in paleoenvironmental studies. Self-designed majors. Double majors. Dual degrees. Independent study. Accelerated study. Pass/fail grading option. Internships. Cooperative education programs. Graduate school at which undergraduates may take graduate-level courses. Preprofessional programs in law, medicine, veterinary science, dentistry, optometry, forestry, library science, occupational therapy, and physical therapy. Member of Western Interstate Commission for Higher Education (WICHE) and Public University Information Exchange. Washington Semester and UN Semester. Member of National Student Exchange (NSE). Teacher certification in early childhood, elementary, secondary, special education, and vo-tech education. Certification in specific subject areas. Member of International Student Exchange Program (ISEP). ROTC and AFROTC.
**Honors:** Phi Beta Kappa. Honors program. Honor societies.
**Academic Assistance:** Remedial reading, writing, math, and study skills. Nonremedial tutoring.

**STUDENT LIFE. Housing:** Students may live on or off campus. Coed dorms. Sorority and fraternity housing. School-owned/operated apartments. Off-campus privately-owned housing. On-campus married-student housing. 33% of students live in college housing.
**Services and counseling/handicapped student services:** Placement services. Health service. Women's center. Day care. Counseling services for minority and older students. Birth control, personal, and psychological counseling. Career and academic guidance services. Physically disabled student services. Learning disabled program/services. Notetaking services. Tape recorders. Tutors. Reader services for the blind.
**Campus organizations:** Undergraduate student government. Student newspaper (Branding Iron, published four times/week). Literary magazine. Radio and TV stations. Concert and marching bands, orchestra, ensembles, quartet, opera workshop, extemporaneous speaking, oratory, forum and panel discussions, debating, drama groups, departmental, political, professional, and special-interest groups, 128 organizations in all. 12 fraternities, 11 chapter houses; four sororities, all with chapter houses. 6% of men join a fraternity. 9% of women join a sorority.
**Religious organizations:** Baptist Student Union, Campus Christian Fellowship, Campus Ventures, Canterbury House, Catholic Student Organization, Christian Student Fellowship, Fellowship of Christian Athletes, Intervarsity Christian Fellowship, Lambda Delta Sigma, Latter-Day Saints Student Association, Lutheran Campus Center, Sigma Gamma Chi, University Common Ministry, Wesley Foundation.
**Minority/foreign student organizations:** Asian-American Student Association, Association of Black Student Leaders, Keepers of the Fire, MEChA. International Student Association, World Service Student Corps, Chinese, Indian, Muslim, and Norwegian groups.

**ATHLETICS. Physical education requirements:** Two semesters of physical education required.
**Intercollegiate competition:** 6% of students participate. Baseball (M), basketball (M,W), cheerleading (M,W), cross-country (M,W), diving (M,W), football (M), golf (M,W), riflery (M,W), swimming (M,W), track and field (indoor) (M,W), track and field (outdoor) (M,W), volleyball (W), wrestling (M). Member of NCAA Division I, NCAA Division I-A for football, Western Athletic Conference.
**Intramural and club sports:** 59% of students participate. Intramural badminton, basketball, bowling, flag football, golf, racquetball, soccer, softball, tennis, triathlon, volleyball, walleyball, water polo, wrestling. Men's club cycling, fencing, ice hockey, lacrosse, rodeo, rugby, skiing, soccer, trapshooting, ultimate frisbee, volleyball, water polo. Women's club cycling, fencing, rodeo, rugby, skiing, soccer, trapshooting, ultimate frisbee, volleyball.

**ADMISSIONS. Academic basis for candidate selection** (in order of priority): Secondary school record, standardized test scores, class rank, school's recommendation.
**Nonacademic basis for candidate selection:** Character and personality, extracurricular participation, particular talent or ability, geographical distribution, and alumni/ae relationship are considered.
**Requirements:** Graduation from secondary school is required; GED is accepted. 18 units and the following program of study are recommended: 4 units of English, 3 units of math, 3 units of science, 2 units of foreign language, 3 units of social studies, 3 units of electives. 1 unit each of speech, computer science, and art or music recommended. Minimum composite ACT score of 19 and minimum 2.5 GPA recommended of in-state applicants; minimum composite ACT score of 19 recommended and minimum 2.5 GPA required of out-of-state applicants. Conditional admission possible for applicants not meeting standard requirements. Special Admission for exceptionally talented applicants. ACT is required; SAT may be substituted. Campus visit and interview recommended. No off-campus interviews.
**Procedure:** Take SAT or ACT by fall of 12th year. Suggest filing application by March 1. Application deadline is August 10. Notification of admission on rolling basis. Reply is required by registration. $50 room deposit, refundable until August 1. Freshmen accepted for terms other than fall.
**Special programs:** Admission may be deferred one year. Credit may be granted through CEEB Advanced Placement for scores of 3 or higher. Credit may be granted through CLEP subject exams, and military and life experience. Credit and placement may be granted through challenge exams. Concurrent enrollment program.
**Transfer students:** Transfer students accepted for terms other than fall. In fall 1993, 1,468 transfer applications were received, 1,235 were accepted. Application deadline is August

10 for fall; 30 days prior to beginning of semester for spring. Minimum 2.3 GPA required. Lowest course grade accepted is "D." Maximum number of transferable semester hours is 70 from two-year schools; unlimited from four-year schools. At least 30 semester hours must be completed at the university to receive degree.

**Admissions contact:** Richard A. Davis, Ph.D., Director of Admissions. 307 766-5160, 800 342-5996.

**FINANCIAL AID. Available aid:** Pell grants, SEOG, school scholarships, private scholarships and grants, ROTC scholarships, academic merit scholarships, and athletic scholarships. Perkins Loans (NDSL), PLUS, Stafford Loans (GSL), school loans, and private loans.

**Financial aid statistics:** 49% of aid is not need-based. In 1993-94, 75% of all undergraduate applicants received aid; 79% of freshman applicants. Average amounts of aid awarded freshmen: Scholarships and grants, $1,200; loans, $1,665.

**Supporting data/closing dates:** FAFSA: Priority filing date is January 31; accepted on rolling basis. School's own aid application: Priority filing date is March 1; accepted on rolling basis. Notification of awards on rolling basis.

**Financial aid contact:** John Nutter, M.S., Director of Financial Aid. 307 766-2116.

**STUDENT EMPLOYMENT.** College Work/Study Program. Institutional employment. 20% of full-time undergraduates work on campus during school year. Students may expect to earn an average of $2,700 during school year. Off-campus part-time employment opportunities rated "good."

**COMPUTER FACILITIES.** 473 IBM/IBM-compatible and Macintosh/Apple microcomputers; all are networked. Students may access Digital, SUN minicomputer/mainframe systems, Internet. Residence halls may be equipped with stand-alone microcomputers, networked microcomputers, modems. Client/LAN operating systems include Apple/Macintosh, DOS, UNIX/XENIX/AIX, Novell. Computer languages and software packages include Ada, Assembler, BASIC, COBOL, dBASE, Lotus 1-2-3, MacPaint, MacWrite, Pascal, SAS, SPSS, WordPerfect; 25 in all. Computer facilities are available to all students.

**Fees:** Computer fee is included in tuition/fees.

**Hours:** 24 hours.

**PROMINENT ALUMNI/AE.** Alan K. Simpson, U.S. senator; Mike Sullivan, governor of Wyoming; Clifford P. Hansen, former governor of Wyoming and U.S. senator; Terry Buss, owner, L.A. Lakers; Curt Gowdy, TV sports commentator; W.E. Deming, management science expert; Dick Cheney, former U.S. secretary of defense.

# Canada

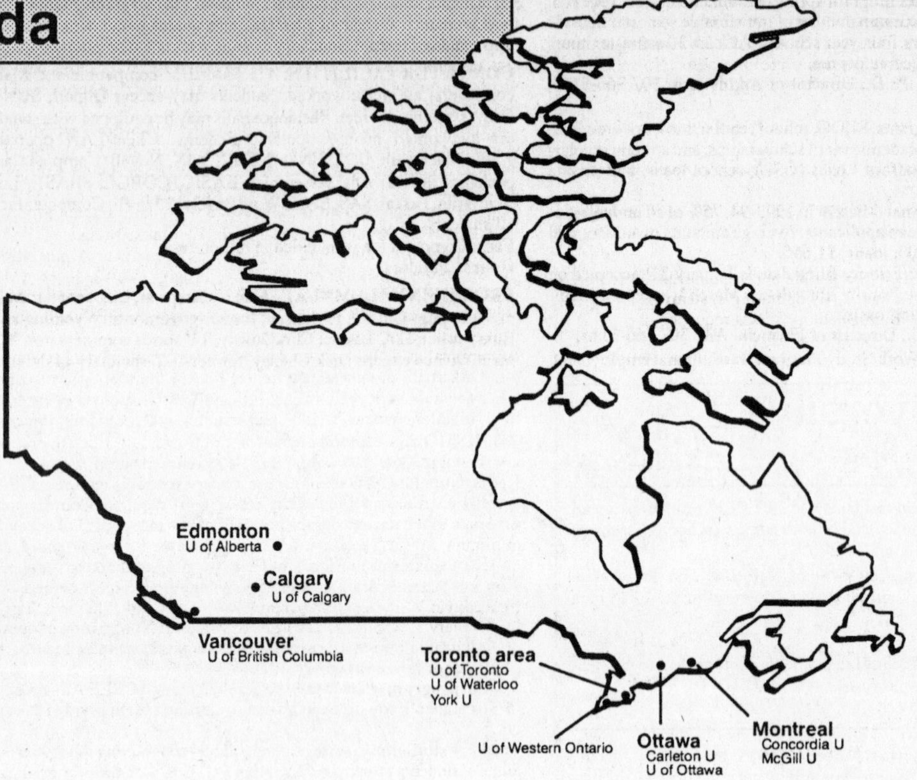


# Carleton University

**Ottawa, Ontario, CN K1S 5B6** **613 778-7400**

**1993-94 Costs.** Tuition and fees: $2,372-2,560 (Canadian residents), $7,985-12,815 (non-Canadians). Room & board: $4,723-$5,332. Fees, books, misc. academic expenses: $1,900. (Figures are in Canadian dollars; all figures are school's estimates.)
**Enrollment.** Undergraduates: 8,173 men, 6,826 women (full-time). Freshman class: 17,135 applicants, 11,778 accepted, 5,485 enrolled. Graduate enrollment: 1,390 men, 177 women.
**Test score averages/ranges.** N/A.
**Faculty.** 691 full-time; 59 part-time. 90% of faculty holds doctoral degree. Student/faculty ratio: 24 to 1.
**Selectivity rating.** N/A.

**PROFILE.** Carleton, founded in 1942, is a public university. Programs are offered by the Faculties of Arts, Social Sciences, Engineering, Science, and Graduate Studies and Research. Its 153-acre campus is located in downtown Ottawa between the Rideau River and the Rideau Canal.

**Accreditation:** Professionally accredited by the Association of Universities and Colleges of Canada.
**Religious orientation:** Carleton University is nonsectarian; no religious requirements.
**Library:** Collections totaling over 1,518,937 volumes, 12,903 periodical subscriptions, and 916,973 microform items.
**Special facilities/museums:** Art gallery, environmental labs, biology annex observatory.
**Athletic facilities:** Swimming pool, squash and tennis courts, gymnasiums, sports medicine clinic, weight training facilities, indoor jogging track, playing fields.

**STUDENT BODY. Undergraduate profile:** Average age of undergraduates is 20. Percentage of full-time undergraduates who are from the U.S.: 2%.
**Foreign students:** Countries represented include China, Hong Kong, Japan, Malaysia, Singapore, and the United Kingdom; 100 in all.

**PROGRAMS OF STUDY. Degrees:** B.A., B.Arch., B.Commerce, B.Comp.Sci., B.Eng., B.Indust.Design, B.Journ., B.Mus., B.Pub.Admin., B.S., B.Soc.Work.
**Majors:** Accounting, Aerospace Engineering, African Studies, Anthropology, Architecture, Art History, Asian Studies, Biochemistry, Biology, Biotechnology, Business, Canadian Studies, Central/East European/Russian Area Studies, Chemistry, Civil Engineering, Classical Civilization, Cognitive Science, Computer Hardware, Computer Mathematics, Computer Science, Computer Systems Engineering, Criminology/Criminal Justice, Directed Interdisciplinary Studies, Economics, Electrical Engineering, Engineering, English, English as a Second Language, English Language/Composition, Environmental Engineering, Environmental Science, Environmental Studies, Film Studies, Finance, Fine Arts, French, Geography, Geology, German, German Studies, Greek, History, Human Resources Management, Industrial Design, Information Systems, Integrated Science Studies, International Business, Italian, Journalism, Labor Studies, Latin, Law, Law Enforcement Studies, Linguistics, Management/Business Systems, Marketing, Mass Communication, Mathematics, Mechanical Engineering, Medieval Studies, Music, Operations Management, Operations Research, Philosophy, Physical Geography, Physics, Political Science, Population Studies, Psychology, Public Administration, Public Service Studies, Religion, Russian, Scientific Applications, Sociology, Software, Soviet/East European Studies, Spanish, Statistics, Teaching English as Second Language, Technology/Society/Environmental Studies, Theory of Computing, Urban Studies, Women's Studies.
**Distribution of degrees:** The majors with the highest enrollment are psychology, political science, and sociology/anthropology.
**Special:** Minor is required for some majors. Certificate in French translation. Self-designed majors. Double majors. Internships. Cooperative education programs. Graduate school at which undergraduates may take graduate-level courses. Study abroad in Belgium, Denmark, France, Germany, Hungary, Italy, Japan, the Netherlands, Poland, the former Soviet Republics, Spain, the United Kingdom, and the United States.

**STUDENT LIFE. Housing:** Students may live on or off campus. Coed, women's, and men's dorms. 11% of students live in college housing.
**Social atmosphere:** On campus, students gather at Rooster's & Mike's; students frequent the Duke of Somerset and the Royal Oak off campus. A wide variety of clubs influence student life. The most popular campus events are the Panda Game (the Carleton vs. U of Ottawa football game), the Superpub Halloween party, and the February Charity Ball. According to the student newspaper editor, campus life is quiet and "there's more to life off campus. Ottawa isn't a big happening city, but it's a nice town with some decent pubs."
**Services and counseling/handicapped student services:** Placement services. Health service. Women's center. Day care. Counseling services for older students. Birth control, personal, and psychological counseling. Career and academic guidance services. Physically disabled student services. Learning disabled services. Notetaking services. Reader services for the blind.
**Campus organizations:** Undergraduate student government. Student newspaper (Charlatan, published once/week). Radio station. Concerts, film series, lectures, readings by poets and novelists, Sock 'n' Buskin (theatre company).

**ATHLETICS. Physical education requirements:** None.
**Intercollegiate competition:** 2% of students participate. Basketball (M,W), fencing (M,W), field hockey (W), football (M), Nordic skiing (M,W), rugby (M), soccer (M,W), swimming (M,W), volleyball (W), water polo (M,W). Member of CIAU, Ontario Universities Athletic Association (OUAA), Ontario Women's Interuniversities Athletic Association (OWIAA), Ontario-Quebec Interuniversity Football Conference (OQIFC).
**Intramural and club sports:** 36% of students participate. Intramural ball hockey, basketball, broomball, fun run, ice hockey, inner-tube water polo, snow football, soccer, softball, squash, team handball, touch football, volleyball.

**ADMISSIONS. Academic basis for candidate selection** (in order of priority): Secondary school record, standardized test scores.
**Nonacademic basis for candidate selection:** Extracurricular participation and particular talent or ability are emphasized.
**Requirements:** Graduation from secondary school is required; GED is not accepted. 16 secondary school units required. Rank in top quarter of secondary school class and SAT or ACT required of U.S. applicants. Units in math and in two science subjects (biology, chemistry, or physics) required of science program applicants. Portfolio required of architecture and industrial design program applicants. "B-" average required of Pass program

applicants. "A" average required of honors program applicants. ACH required. Campus visit recommended. No off-campus interviews.
**Procedure:** Take SAT by April of 12th year. Take ACH by April of 12th year. $60 application fee (Canadian dollars). Notification of admission on rolling basis. No set date by which applicants must accept offer. $250 nonrefundable room deposit. Freshmen accepted for fall terms only.
**Special programs:** Admission may be deferred one year. Early entrance/early admission program. Concurrent enrollment program.
**Transfer students:** Transfer students accepted for fall term only. Lowest course grade accepted is "C."
**Admissions contact:** Victor Chapman, M.A., Director of Admissions. International Student Contact: Janyce Dale-Smithley. 613 788-3663.
**FINANCIAL AID.** Financial aid is not available to U.S. students.
**COMPUTER FACILITIES.** 350 IBM/IBM-compatible and Macintosh/Apple microcomputers. Students may access Internet. Client/LAN operating systems include DOS, OS/2, UNIX/XENIX/AIX. Students must be enrolled in courses requiring use.
**Fees:** None.
**Hours:** 24 hours.

# Concordia University

**Montreal, Quebec, CN H3G 1M8 — 514 848-2424**

**1994-95 Costs.** Tuition: $1,518 (Canadian residents); $7,307 (U.S. residents). Room: $1,700. Board: $1,800. Fees, books, misc. academic expenses (school's estimate): $1,025. (All figures are in Canadian dollars.)
**Enrollment.** Undergraduates: 5,942 men, 5,890 women (full-time). Freshman class: 11,770 applicants, 7,915 accepted, 4,643 enrolled. Graduate enrollment: 1,825 men, 1,445 women.
**Test score averages/ranges.** N/A.
**Faculty.** 850 full-time; 1,140 part-time. 73% of faculty holds doctoral degree. Student/faculty ratio: 17 to 1.
**Selectivity rating.** N/A.

**PROFILE.** Concordia, a public university, was founded in 1974 through the merger of Sir George Williams University and Loyola College. Programs are offered through the Faculties of Arts and Science, Commerce and Administration, Engineering and Computer Science, and Fine Arts. Its two campuses are located seven kilometers apart, in downtown and west-end Montreal.
**Accreditation:** Professionally accredited by the Associations of Universities and Colleges of Canada.
**Religious orientation:** Concordia University is nonsectarian; no religious requirements.
**Library:** Collections totaling over 1,500,000 volumes, 7,800 periodical subscriptions, and 75,000 microform items.
**Special facilities/museums:** Art museum.
**Athletic facilities:** Gymnasiums, badminton, basketball, and volleyball courts, ice rink, athletic fields, weight room, dance studio.
**STUDENT BODY. Undergraduate profile:** 7% are transfers. Average age of undergraduates is 25. In fall 1992, 3% of all freshmen came from the U.S.
**Undergraduate achievement:** 91% of fall 1992 freshmen returned for fall 1993 term.
**PROGRAMS OF STUDY. Degrees:** B.A., B.Admin., B.Commerce, B.Comp.Sci., B.Ed., B.Eng., B.F.A., B.S.
**Majors:** Accountancy, Actuarial Mathematics, Administration, Administrative Management, Analytical Chemistry, Anthropology, Applied Mathematics, Art Education, Art History, Biochemistry, Biology, Broadcast Journalism, Building Engineering, Canadian Studies, Ceramics, Chemistry, Child Studies, Cinema, Civil Engineering, Classical Philology, Classical Studies, Communication Studies, Computer Engineering, Computer Science, Contemporary Dance, Creative Writing, Decision Sciences, Design Art, Drama in Education, Drawing, Early Childhood Education, Ecology, Economics, Electrical Engineering, English/History, English Literature, English/Theatre, Exercise Science, Fibers, Film Animation, Film Production, Film Studies, Finance, French/English Translation, French Literature, French Studies, Geography, Geology, History, Individually Structured Program, Industrial Engineering, Integrative Music Studies, International Business, Interrelated Arts, Italian, Jazz Studies, Journalism, Judaic Studies, Leisure Studies, Library Studies, Linguistics, Marketing, Mathematics, Mechanical Engineering, Music Performance, Music Theory/Composition, Painting, Philosophy, Photography, Physics, Playwriting, Political Science, Printmaking, Psychology, Quebec Literature, Religion, Science/Human Affairs, Sculpture, Selected Music Studies, Sociology, Spanish, Teaching English as Second Language, Theatre, Theological Studies, Urban Studies, Western Society/Culture, Women's Studies.
**Distribution of degrees:** The majors with the highest enrollment are accountancy, economics, and political science; theological studies, classics, and women's studies have the lowest.
**Requirements:** General education requirement.
**Academic regulations:** Minimum 2.0 GPA must be maintained.
**Special:** Minors offered in many majors and in adult education, archaeology, business statistics, business studies, education, German, history of Quebec, Russian studies, transportation/distribution management, and women and the fine arts. Undergraduate certificate programs offered. Self-designed majors. Double majors. Dual degrees. Independent study. Accelerated study. Internships. Cooperative education programs. Five-year B.Eng./M.Eng. program in building engineering. Member of Conference des Universites du Quebec. Teacher certification in early childhood, elementary, and secondary education. Study abroad in England, France, Germany, and the U.S.
**Honors:** Honors program.
**Academic Assistance:** Nonremedial tutoring.
**STUDENT LIFE. Housing:** Students may live on or off campus; housing is limited. Coed dorms. School-owned/operated apartments. 2% of students live in college housing.
**Services and counseling/handicapped student services:** Placement services. Health service. Women's center. Day care. Remedial learning services. Counseling services for minority and older students. Birth control, personal, and psychological counseling. Career and academic guidance services. Religious counseling. Physically disabled student services. Learning disabled program/services. Notetaking services. Tape recorders. Tutors. Reader services for the blind.
**Campus organizations:** Undergraduate student government. Student newspapers (Link; Concordia). Literary magazine. Yearbook. Radio and TV stations. Choir, orchestra, jazz band, 75 organizations in all. Three fraternities, no chapter houses; two sororities, no chapter houses.
**Minority/foreign student organizations:** 16 ethnic student groups.
**ATHLETICS. Physical education requirements:** None.
**Intercollegiate competition:** 2% of students participate. Alpine skiing (M,W), basketball (M,W), football (M), ice hockey (M,W), rugby (M,W), soccer (M,W), volleyball (W), wrestling (M). Member of Canadian Inter-university Athletic Union, Ontario Universities Athletic Association, Ontario-Quebec Interuniversity Football Conference, Quebec Student Sports Federation.
**Intramural and club sports:** 25% of students participate. Intramural aerobics, badminton, basketball, broomball, dance, ice hockey, martial arts, soccer, softball, swimming, touch football, volleyball, weight lifting. Men's club cross-country, golf, outdoors, track/field, triathlon. Women's club cross-country, golf, outdoors, track/field, triathlon.
**ADMISSIONS. Academic basis for candidate selection** (in order of priority): Secondary school record, class rank, school's recommendation, essay.
**Requirements:** Graduation from secondary school is required; GED is not accepted. No specific distribution of secondary school units required. Courses presented should be appropriate to the desired degree program. Rank in top third of secondary school class and minimum 3.0 GPA required of U.S. applicants. Interview and audition or portfolio required of applicants to Faculty of Fine Arts programs and to some programs in Faculty of Arts and Science. Admissions interview required. No off-campus interviews.
**Procedure:** Visit college for interview by April 1 of 12th year. Suggest filing application by February 1. Application deadline is March 1. Notification of admission by June 1. $50 nonrefundable tuition deposit. $50 room deposit, refundable until August 15. Freshmen accepted for fall terms only.
**Special programs:** Credit may be granted through CEEB Advanced Placement for scores of 3 or higher. Early decision program. Deadline for applying for early decision is February 1.
**Transfer students:** Transfer students accepted for terms other than fall. In fall 1993, 7% of all new students were transfers into all classes. 867 transfer applications were received, 422 were accepted. Application deadline is March 1 for fall; November 1 for spring. Lowest course grade accepted is "C." Maximum number of transferable credits is 45 semester hours. Final 45 semester hours (60 for engineering) must be completed at the university to receive degree.
**Admissions contact:** Thomas Swift, Director of Admissions. International Student Contact: Cathy Hirst. 514 848-2668.
**FINANCIAL AID.** Financial aid not available to U.S. students. On-campus employment for U.S. undergraduates is available, however.
**COMPUTER FACILITIES.** 180 IBM/IBM-compatible microcomputers. Students may access CDC Cyber, Digital minicomputer/mainframe systems. Computer languages and software packages include Assembler, BASIC, COBOL, FORTRAN, Pascal. Computer facilities are available to all students.
**Fees:** None.
**Hours:** 24 hours.

# McGill University

**Montreal, Quebec, CN H3A 2T5 — 514 398-4455**

**1993-94 Costs.** Tuition: $1,515 (Canadian residents), $7,305 (U.S. residents). Room & board: $5,800. Fees, books, misc. academic expenses (school's estimate): $2,200. (All figures are in Canadian dollars.)
**Enrollment.** Undergraduates: 6,561 men, 7,918 women (full-time). Graduate enrollment: 6,797.
**Test score averages/ranges.** N/A.
**Faculty.** 1,400 full-time; 530 part-time. 85% of faculty holds doctoral degree. Student/faculty ratio: 17 to 1.
**Selectivity rating.** N/A.

**PROFILE.** McGill, founded in 1821, is a comprehensive, public university. Programs offered in ten faculties and ten schools. Classes are conducted in English, but a range of language and literature programs are offered in French. Its 80-acre main campus is situated in downtown Montreal, bounded on the north by Mount Royal, the city's largest public park.
**Accreditation:** Professionally accredited by the Associations of Universities and Colleges of Canada.
**Religious orientation:** McGill University is nonsectarian; no religious requirements.
**Library:** Collections totaling over 2,441,494 volumes, 17,509 periodical subscriptions, and 408,068 microform items.
**Special facilities/museums:** Natural sciences, physics, Canadiana museums, arboretum, herbarium, nature conservation and research center, tropical research institute, radiation lab with synchrocyclotron.
**Athletic facilities:** Stadiums, track, ice rink, gymnasiums, squash and tennis courts, gymnastics and weight training rooms, dance, fencing, and martial arts studios, swimming pools, playing fields, sports injury clinic.
**PROGRAMS OF STUDY. Degrees:** B.A., B.Arch., B.Commerce, B.Ed., B.Eng., B.Mus., B.S., B.Soc.Work, B.Theatre Arts, LL.B.
**Majors:** African Studies, Agricultural Economics, Agricultural Engineering, Anatomical Sciences, Animal Science, Anthropology, Art History, Biochemistry, Biology, Botanical Sciences, Canadian Studies, Chemical Engineering, Chemistry, Church Music Performance, Civil Engineering/Applied Mechanics, Classics, Classics/Linguistics, Communi-

ty Resource Development, Composition, Consumer Services, Crystallography, Dietetics, Early Music Performance, East Asian Studies, Economics, Economics/Accounting, Economics/Finance, Economics/Political Science, Education in the Arts, Electrical Engineering, Elementary Education, English, Environmental Biology, Food Science, Food Services Administration, French, French Canada Studies, General Agricultural Sciences, Geography, Geological Science, German, History, History/Political Science, Home Economics Education, Humanistic Studies, Industrial Relations, Italian, Jazz Performance, Jewish Studies, Labor/Management Relations, Latin American/Caribbean Studies, Linguistics, Management Information Systems, Mathematics, Mechanical Engineering, Meteorology, Microbiology, Microbiology/Immunology, Middle Eastern Studies, Mining/Metallurgical Engineering, Modern Languages, Music History, Music Theory, North American Studies, Nutrition, Performance, Philosophy, Physical Education, Physics, Physiology, Physiology/Physics, Plant Science, Political Science, Psychology, Religious Education, Religious Studies, Resource Conservation, Russian, School Music, Secondary Education, Sociology, Soil Science, Solid Earth Geophysics, Spanish, Teaching a Second Language, Vocational Education, Wildlife Resources, Zoological Sciences.

**Special:** Minors offered in many majors. Most faculties have several courses of study. Faculty program is a coherent selection of courses giving students concentration in recognized area; major program is more specialized and centered around specific discipline (can be interdisciplinary); honors program involves high degree of specialization and requires high academic standing. Double majors. Dual degrees. Independent study. Pass/fail grading option. Internships. Graduate school at which undergraduates may take graduate-level courses. Preprofessional programs in medicine and dentistry. Teacher certification in elementary, secondary, and special education. Exchange programs abroad in France, Switzerland, and the United States (California State U system, New England Board of Higher Education, SUNY system, U of California at Davis, U of New Mexico, and U of North Dakota). Interuniversity transfer agreements with other Quebec universities.

**Honors:** Honors program.

**Academic Assistance:** Nonremedial tutoring.

**STUDENT LIFE. Housing:** Students may live on or off campus. Coed and women's dorms. School-owned/operated apartments. Off-campus married-student housing.

**Services and counseling/handicapped student services:** Placement services. Health service. Women's center. Day care. Counseling services for minority and older students. Birth control, personal, and psychological counseling. Career and academic guidance services.

**Campus organizations:** Undergraduate student government. Student newspaper (McGill Daily). Literary magazine. Yearbook. Radio station. Chess and bridge clubs, outing club, music and theatre groups, political groups, science societies, 250 organizations in all. 13 fraternities, four chapter houses; four sororities, no chapter houses.

**Religious organizations:** Chinese Christian Fellowship, Christian Fellowship, Hillel, Network, Jewish Student Society.

**Minority/foreign student organizations:** 21 foreign student groups.

**ATHLETICS. Physical education requirements:** None.

**Intercollegiate competition:** 3% of students participate. Basketball (M,W), cross-country (M,W), football (M), ice hockey (M,W), soccer (M,W), swimming (M,W), volleyball (W). Member of CIAU, GPAC, Ontario Quebec Intercollegiate Football Conference (OQIFC), Ontario Women's Intercollegiate Athletic Association (OWIAA), Quebec Federation of Students' Sports (QSSF), Quebec University Athletic Association (QUAA).

**Intramural and club sports:** 65% of students participate. Intramural badminton, ball hockey, basketball, bowling, broomball, flag football, golf, ice hockey, inner-tube water polo, soccer, softball, squash, tennis, ultimate frisbee, volleyball. Men's club Alpine skiing, crew, fencing, indoor track/field, martial arts, Nordic skiing, rugby, sailing, squash, ultimate frisbee. Women's club Alpine skiing, cheerleading, crew, fencing, field hockey, ice hockey, indoor track/field, martial arts, Nordic skiing, rugby, sailing, ultimate frisbee.

**ADMISSIONS. Academic basis for candidate selection** (in order of priority): Secondary school record, standardized test scores, class rank, school's recommendation.

**Nonacademic basis for candidate selection:** Extracurricular participation and particular talent or ability are considered.

**Requirements:** Graduation from secondary school is required; GED is not accepted. No specific distribution of secondary school units required; college-preparatory academic program recommended. Minimum SAT scores of 550 in both verbal and math required of U.S. applicants. Three ACH required of U.S. applicants. Portfolio required of architecture program applicants; audition required of music program applicants; language tests required of English and/or French as a Second Language program applicants. No off-campus interviews.

**Procedure:** Take SAT or ACT by January of 12th year. Take ACH by January of 12th year. Reply is required within three weeks of acceptance. Freshmen accepted in terms other than fall.

**Special programs:** Admission may be deferred one year. Credit and/or placement may be granted through CEEB Advanced Placement exams for scores of 3 or higher.

**Transfer students:** Transfer students accepted for terms other than fall.

**Admissions contact:** Abbott Conway, Dean of Admissions. International Student Contact: Lawrence Lang. 514 398-3910.

**FINANCIAL AID. Available aid:** School scholarships and academic merit scholarships. School loans.

**Supporting data/closing dates:** FAFSA/FAF: Accepted on rolling basis. FFS: Accepted on rolling basis. School's own aid application: Accepted on rolling basis. State aid form: Deadline is June 30. Canadian aid form: Deadline is December 31. Notification of awards on rolling basis.

**Financial aid contact:** Judy Stymest, Director of Student Aid. 514 398-6013.

**COMPUTER FACILITIES.** Students may access IBM minicomputer/mainframe systems. Computer languages and software packages include ADINA, APL, Assembler, BASIC, BMDP, COBOL, FORTRAN, LISP, MINITAB, MINOS, MIX/360, Multiscale Pascal, PDP11, PL/1, PLOT1/PLOT2, RPG, SAS, Script, SPARSPAK, SPITBOL, SPSS-X, others.

**Fees:** None.

**Hours:** 24 hours.

**PROMINENT ALUMNI/AE.** Thomas Chang, professor, developer of first artificial cell; Elizabeth Monk, one of first two women to be admitted to Quebec Bar; Charles Drew, surgeon and pioneer in blood plasma research; Val Fitch, Nobel Prize winner, physics; William Shatner, actor; Leonard Cohen, poet, novelist, and songwriter; John Humphrey, author of draft of UN Declaration of Human Rights.

## University of Alberta

**Edmonton, Alberta, CN T6G 2M7 — 403 492-3111**

**1993-94 Costs.** Tuition: $2,338 (Canadian residents); $4,376 (U.S. residents). Room & board: $4,257. Fees, books, misc. academic expenses (school's estimate): $1,145. (All figures are in Canadian dollars.)

**Enrollment.** Undergraduates: 10,503 men, 12,244 women (full-time). Freshman class: 7,000 applicants, 4,800 accepted, 4,030 enrolled. Graduate enrollment: 2,437 men, 2,227 women.

**Test score averages/ranges.** N/A.

**Faculty.** 1,550 full-time; 200 part-time. 90% of faculty holds doctoral degree. Student/faculty ratio: 15 to 1.

**Selectivity rating.** N/A.

**PROFILE.** The University of Alberta, founded in 1906, is a comprehensive, public university. The Faculte Saint-Jean, which occupies a separate campus a few miles from the main campus, offers bilingual programs in the Faculties of Arts, Science, and Education. The 150-acre main campus, which borders the North Saskatchewan River, is located two miles southwest of Edmonton's business center.

**Accreditation:** Professionally accredited by the Associations of Universities and Colleges of Canada.

**Religious orientation:** University of Alberta is nonsectarian; no religious requirements.

**Library:** Collections totaling over 3,400,000 volumes, 21,000 periodical subscriptions, and 15,000 microform items.

**Special facilities/museums:** Nuclear reactor, sports medicine clinic, center for athletic training for the disabled, experimental farm, green houses, ranch, laser laboratories, forest reserve, meteorological station, physics lab.

**Athletic facilities:** Field house, ice arena, swimming pools, gymnasiums, dance, gymnastics, martial arts, weight, and wrestling rooms, aerobics, ballet, and fencing studios, basketball, racquetball, squash, tennis, and volleyball courts, soccer field, track, football stadium, athletic therapy clinic, training center for the physically disabled.

**STUDENT BODY. Undergraduate profile:** Average age of undergraduates is 24.

**Foreign students:** 2,754 students are from out of the country. Countries represented include China, England, Hong Kong, India, Malaysia, and the United States; 109 in all. 1% of full-time undergraduates are from the U.S.

**PROGRAMS OF STUDY. Degrees:** B.A., B.Commerce, B.Design, B.Ed., B.F.A., B.Mus., B.Phys.Ed., B.S.

**Majors:** Adult Education, Advertising Marketing, Agricultural Business Management, Agricultural Economics, Agricultural Food Business Management, Agriculture, Animal Science, Anthropology, Applied Mathematics, Art/Design, Biochemistry, Biological Sciences, Botany, Canadian Studies, Cell Biotechnology, Chemical Engineering, Chemistry, Civil Engineering, Classics, Clinical Chemistry, Comparative Literature, Computer Engineering, Computing Science, Conservation Biology, Consumer Studies, Criminology, Crop Science, Drama, Early Childhood Education, East Asian Languages/Literature, East Asian Studies, East European/Soviet Studies, Economics, Economics/Mathematics, Electrical Engineering, Elementary Education, Engineering Agrology, Engineering Physics, English, Entomology, Environmental Economics, Family Studies, Film Studies, Finance, Food Science, Foods/Nutrition, Forestry, Genetics, Geography, Geology, Geophysics, Germanic Languages, Hematology, Histopathology, History, Home Economics, Industrial Arts, Industrial Relations, Intercultural Education, Japan Studies, Land Remediation/Reclamation/Conservation, Legal Relations, Linguistics, Management Resources, Management Science, Managerial Economics, Marketing, Mathematical Physics, Mathematics, Mechanical Engineering, Medical Bacteriology, Medical Laboratory Sciences, Metallurgical Engineering, Meteorology, Microbiology, Mining Engineering, Music, Native Studies, Nursing, Occupational Therapy, Organization Theory/Behavior, Paleontology, Petroleum Engineering, Pharmacology, Pharmacy, Philosophy, Physical Education, Physical Geography, Physical Therapy, Physics, Physiology, Plant Protection, Plant Science, Political Science, Psychology, Recreation Administration, Religious Studies, Romance Languages, Rural Sociology, Secondary Education, Slavic Languages/Literatures, Sociology, Special Education, Statistics, Textiles/Clothing/Culture, Vocational Education, Wildlife/Rangeland Management, Women's Studies, Zoology.

**Distribution of degrees:** The majors with the highest enrollment are education, biological sciences, and psychology.

**Academic regulations:** Minimum 5.0 GPA must be maintained.

**Special:** Minors offered in all majors in Faculties of Arts, Science, and Education. Faculte Saint-Jean offers four bilingual degree programs (B.A., B.Ed., B.Sc., and B.Ed./B.Sc.); 75% of course work is in French. Double majors. Independent study. Accelerated study. Pass/fail grading option. Cooperative education programs. Graduate school at which undergraduates may take graduate-level courses. Preprofessional programs in law, medicine, veterinary science, pharmacy, dentistry, optometry, chiropractic, and occupational therapy. Five-year B.Sc./B.Ed. program. Five-year B.P.E./B.Ed. program. Four-year LL.B./M.B.A. program. Four-year LL.B/M.P.M. program. Four-year M.P.M./Ph.D. program. Teacher certification in early childhood, elementary, secondary, and special education. Certification in specific subject areas. Numerous exchange programs and other study-abroad opportunities possible.

**Honors:** Honors program.

**Academic Assistance:** Nonremedial tutoring.

**STUDENT LIFE. Housing:** Students may live on or off campus. Coed, women's, and men's dorms. School-owned/operated apartments. On-campus married-student housing.
**Social atmosphere:** Earl's, Room at the Top, the Power Plant, the Bronx, and the Ship are popular gathering-places for students. The Student's Union, Phi Gamma Delta, and university sports have a wide influence on student life. Popular events during the school year include Week of Welcome (orientation week), New Year's Eve Downtown, The Fringe, and the Street Performer's Festival. Social and cultural life at the university is diverse, ranging, for example, from "country music and two-stepping to moshing and dance techno. Often it'll even be the same people enjoying both types of music."
**Services and counseling/handicapped student services:** Placement services. Health service. Women's center. Day care. Counseling services for older students. Birth control, personal, and psychological counseling. Career and academic guidance services. Religious counseling. Physically disabled student services. Notetaking services. Reader services for the blind.
**Campus organizations:** Undergraduate student government. Student newspaper (Gateway, published twice/week). Radio station. Over 280 student clubs. 11 fraternities, no chapter houses; three sororities, no chapter houses.
**Religious organizations:** Chaplaincy for major denominations, numerous other religious groups.
**Minority/foreign student organizations:** Native student organization. Various foreign student groups.

**ATHLETICS. Physical education requirements:** None.
**Intercollegiate competition:** 14% of students participate. Basketball (M,W), field hockey (W), football (M), gymnastics (M,W), ice hockey (M), soccer (M,W), swimming (M,W), track (indoor) (M,W), track (outdoor) (M,W), track and field (indoor) (M,W), track and field (outdoor) (M,W), volleyball (M,W), wrestling (M). Member of Canada West Universities Athletic Association, Canadian Interuniversity Athletic Union, CIAU.
**Intramural and club sports:** 45% of students participate. Intramural Alpine skiing, badminton, basketball, bowling, curling, floor hockey, ice hockey, indoor track, Nordic skiing, soccer, table tennis, track, volleyball, walleyball, water polo. Men's club Alpine skiing, canoe/kayak, crew, fencing, martial arts, Nordic skiing, rugby, squash, ultimate frisbee. Women's club Alpine skiing, canoe/kayak, crew, fencing, martial arts, Nordic skiing, squash, ultimate frisbee.

**ADMISSIONS. Academic basis for candidate selection** (in order of priority): Secondary school record, class rank, standardized test scores, essay.
**Nonacademic basis for candidate selection:** Extracurricular participation is emphasized. Character and personality, particular talent or ability, and geographical distribution are important.
**Requirements:** Graduation from secondary school is recommended; GED is not accepted. No specific distribution of secondary school units required. Five grade 12 subjects or equivalent (including English) required of all applicants. Other course requirements vary with degree program. Minimum overall "C-" average required; applicants to limited-enrollment programs should possess an average well above minimum. Portfolio required of fine arts program applicants. Audition required of music program applicants and some fine arts program applicants. Questionnaires, reference letters, autobiography, and medical exam required for many programs. In quota programs (those with limited enrollment), enrollment of Canadians from outside Alberta limited to 10% and enrollment of non-Canadians limited to 5%. SAT or ACT recommended of U.S. applicants. Campus visit recommended. No off-campus interviews.
**Procedure:** Application deadline is May 1. Notification of admission on rolling basis. Reply is required within 15 days after notification of admission (for quota programs only). Admissions interview required for some majors. $50 nonrefundable tuition deposit. $150 room deposit, refundable until July 31. Freshmen accepted for fall terms only.
**Special programs:** Credit and/or placement may be granted through CEEB Advanced Placement exams for scores of 4 or higher. Early decision program. Deadline for applying for early decision is April 1.
**Transfer students:** Transfer students accepted for fall terms. Application deadline is May 1. Minimum 5.0 GPA (on a 9.0 scale) required; lowest courses grade accepted is 4.0 (on a 9.0 scale). Maximum number of transferable credits is 60 semester hours. At least 60 semester hours must be completed at the university to receive degree.
**Admissions contact:** Bonnie Neuman, M.A., Director of Admissions. 403 492-3113.

**FINANCIAL AID. Available aid:** School scholarships and grants and academic merit scholarships.
**Supporting data/closing dates:** School's own aid application: Deadline is June 1. Notification of awards begins August 15.
**Financial aid contact:** Ron Chilibeck, Director of Financial Aid. 403 492-3221.

**COMPUTER FACILITIES.** 525 IBM/IBM-compatible and Macintosh/Apple microcomputers. Students may access Digital, IBM minicomputer/mainframe systems, BITNET, Internet. Residence halls may be equipped with networked microcomputers. Client/LAN operating systems include Apple/Macintosh. Computer languages and software packages include all major languages and many software programs. Computer facilities are available to all students.
**Hours:** 24 hours.

# University of British Columbia

**Vancouver, BC, CN V6T 1Z1** **604 822-2211**

**1994-95 Costs.** Tuition: $5,250 (U.S. residents). Room & board: $6,080. Fees, books, misc. academic expenses (school's estimate): $925. (All figures are in Canadian dollars.)
**Enrollment.** Undergraduates: 19,439 men, 22,888 women (full-time). Graduate enrollment: 1,113 men, 507 women.
**Test score averages/ranges.** N/A.
**Faculty.** 1,880 full-time; 275 part-time. 70% of faculty holds highest degree in specific field. Student/faculty ratio: 18 to 1.
**Selectivity rating.** N/A.

**PROFILE.** The University of British Columbia, founded in 1915, is a public institution. Programs are offered through 12 faculties and nine schools. Its 1,000-acre campus is located in Vancouver. Most campus buildings have been constructed since 1945.

**Accreditation:** Professionally accredited by the Associations of Universities and Colleges of Canada.
**Religious orientation:** University of British Columbia is nonsectarian; no religious requirements.
**Library:** Collections totaling over 2,700,000 volumes, 35,000 periodical subscriptions, and 3,500,000 microform items. Second largest library in Canada, with extensive Asian and bio-medical collections.
**Special facilities/museums:** Fine arts gallery/center, Asian center, anthropology, geology, and zoology museums, herbarium, botanical and Japanese gardens, research forest, TRIUMF cyclotron (largest in the world).
**Athletic facilities:** Gymnasiums, basketball, squash, tennis, and volleyball courts, stadium, ice rinks, swimming pools, field hockey, football, intramural, rugby, and soccer fields, weight room, track.

**STUDENT BODY. Undergraduate profile:** Average age of undergraduates is 21. 97% of undergraduates are from Canada; 3% are from other countries.

**PROGRAMS OF STUDY. Degrees:** B.A., B.Appl.Sci., B.Arch., B.Commerce, B.Ed., B.F.A., B.Home Econ., B.Land.Arch., B.Med.Libr.Sci., B.Mus., B.Phys.Ed., B.S., B.S.Forestry, B.S.Nurs., B.Soc.Work, LL.B.
**Majors:** Agricultural Economics, Animal Science, Anthropology/Sociology, Architecture, Asian Studies, Astronomy, Biochemistry, Biology, Bioresource Engineering, Botany, Chemical Engineering, Chemistry, Civil Engineering, Classics, Commerce/Business Administration, Computer Science, Creative Writing, Dietetics, Economics, Education, Electrical Engineering, Engineering Physics, English, Family Science, Fine Arts, Food Science, Forest Harvesting, Forest Resource Management, Forest Science, French, Geography, Geological Engineering, Geological Sciences, Geophysics, Germanic Studies, Hispanic-Italian Studies, History, Home Economics, Human Nutrition, Landscape Architecture, Law, Linguistics, Mathematics, Mechanical Engineering, Medical Laboratory Science, Metallurgical Engineering, Microbiology, Mining/Mineral Process Engineering, Music, Nursing, Occupational Therapy, Oceanography, Pharmaceutical Sciences, Pharmacology, Philosophy, Physical Education/Recreation, Physical Geography, Physical Therapy, Physics, Physiology, Plant Science, Political Science, Pre-Veterinary Medicine, Psychology, Religious Studies, Slavonic Studies, Social Work, Soil Science, Statistics, Theatre, Wood Science/Industry, Zoology.
**Requirements:** General education requirement.
**Special:** University heads four Centres of Excellence, which are federally funded national networks of research. Three of the centres conduct research on bacterial diseases, protein engineering, and the genetic basis of human disease; the fourth studies international development. Double majors. Dual degrees. Independent study. Cooperative education programs. Preprofessional programs in law, medicine, and dentistry. Member of Open University Consortium of British Columbia with Simon Fraser U and U of Victoria; students combine home study and classroom-based courses from all member institutions toward a single degree. Exchange programs with Laval U (Quebec) and Washington State U. Teacher certification in elementary, secondary, and special education. Study abroad in Denmark, Japan, and the United States.
**Honors:** Honors program.

**STUDENT LIFE. Housing:** Coed, women's, and men's dorms. School-owned/operated apartments. On-campus married-student housing. International students are urged to apply for housing as early as possible. 24% of students live in college housing.
**Services and counseling/handicapped student services:** Placement services. Health service. Women's center. Day care. Counseling services for older students. Birth control, personal, and psychological counseling. Career and academic guidance services. Physically disabled student services. Notetaking services. Reader services for the blind.
**Campus organizations:** Undergraduate student government. Student newspaper (Ubyssey). Radio station. 175 registered organizations.
**Religious organizations:** University Religious Council.
**Minority/foreign student organizations:** International House.

**ATHLETICS. Physical education requirements:** None.
**Intercollegiate competition:** 3% of students participate. Alpine skiing (M,W), basketball (M,W), crew (M,W), cross-country (M,W), fencing (W), field hockey (W), football (M), golf (M,W), gymnastics (M,W), ice hockey (M), Nordic skiing (M,W), rugby (M,W), soccer (M,W), squash (M), swimming (M,W), tennis (M,W), track and field (indoor) (M,W), volleyball (M,W). Member of Canada West University Athletic Association, Canadian Interuniversity Athletic Union, National Collegiate Ski Association.
**Intramural and club sports:** 67% of students participate. Intramural archery, badminton, baseball, basketball, bowling, canoeing, cycling, fencing, golf, ice hockey, martial arts, skiing, soccer, softball, squash, tennis, volleyball, wrestling. Men's club canoeing, fencing, handball, racquetball, sailing, squash, water polo. Women's club handball, racquetball, sailing, soccer, water polo.

**ADMISSIONS. Academic basis for candidate selection** (in order of priority): Secondary school record, class rank, standardized test scores.
**Requirements:** Graduation from secondary school is required; GED is not accepted. 4 units (full years) of English, 3 units of mathematics, and 5 units of electives (3 in grade 12, 2 in grade 11) required of U.S. applicants. Minimum 2.5 GPA required of Canadian residents; minimum 3.4 GPA required of U.S. applicants. Requirements vary for admission to specific programs of study. Portfolio required of art program applicants. Audition required of music program applicants. SAT is recommended. Campus visit recommended. No off-campus interviews.
**Procedure:** Application deadline is April 30 (deadlines vary for specific programs of study). Notification of admission on rolling basis. $100 nonrefundable tuition deposit. Freshmen accepted for terms other than fall.
**Special programs:** Credit and/or placement may be granted through CEEB Advanced Placement exams for scores of 4 or higher. Early decision program. Early entrance/early admission program.
**Transfer students:** Transfer students from the U.S. accepted for fall term only. Application deadline is March 31. Minimum 3.5 GPA required. Lowest course grade accepted is

"D." Maximum number of transferable credits is 60 semester hours. At least 60 semester hours must be completed at the university to receive degree.
**Admissions contact:** Mary Cooney, Associate Registrar, Admissions. International Student Contact: Winnie Cheung, Director of International Student Centre. 604 822-3014.

**FINANCIAL AID. Available aid:** State scholarships, school scholarships and grants, private scholarships and grants, and academic merit scholarships. State loans, school loans, and private loans. Deferred payment plan.
**Supporting data/closing dates:** School's own aid application: Deadline is April 15.
**Financial aid contact:** Carol Gibson, Director of Awards and Financial Aid. 604 822-5111.

**STUDENT EMPLOYMENT.** Institutional employment available.

**COMPUTER FACILITIES.** IBM/IBM-compatible, Macintosh/Apple, and RISC-/UNIX-based microcomputers. Students may access IBM minicomputer/mainframe systems. Computer languages and software packages include major languages and database, graphics, numerical analysis, statistical, word processing programs. Computer facilities are available to all students.
**Fees:** None.
**Hours:** 24 hours.

**PROMINENT ALUMNI/AE.** Hon. Chief Justice Nathan Nemetz, former chancellor and chairperson of UBC's Board of Governors; Earle Birney, poet; Pierre Berton, author and historian; Judith Forst, opera singer; Joe Schlesinger, CBC broadcaster; Bjarni Tryggvason, astronaut; John Turner, former prime minister; Hon. J.V. Clyne, former chancellor, UBC.

## University of Calgary

**Calgary, Alberta, CN T2N 1N4 — 403 220-5110**

**1994-95 Costs.** Tuition: $2,390 (Canadian residents), $4,780 (U.S. residents). Room & board: $2,835-$4,210. Fees, books, misc. academic expenses (school's estimate): $2,223. (All figures are in Canadian dollars.)
**Enrollment.** Undergraduates: 16,208 (full-time). Freshman class: 2,527 enrolled. Graduate enrollment: 2,744.
**Test score averages/ranges.** N/A.
**Faculty.** 1,365 full-time; 1,131 part-time.
**Selectivity rating.** N/A.

**PROFILE.** The University of Calgary, founded in 1945, is a public university. Programs are offered through the Faculties of Continuing Education, Education, Engineering, Environmental Design, Fine Arts, General Studies, Graduate Studies, Humanities, Law, Management, Medicine, Nursing, Physical Education, Science, Social Sciences, and Social Welfare. Its 300-acre campus is located in the northwestern section of Calgary.

**Accreditation:** Professionally accredited by the Associations of Universities and Colleges of Canada.
**Religious orientation:** University of Calgary is nonsectarian; no religious requirements.
**Library:** Collections totaling over 1,900,000 volumes, 13,600 periodical subscriptions, and 2,600,000 microform items.
**Special facilities/museums:** Art museum, museum of ancient world coins.
**Athletic facilities:** Gymnasiums, swimming pool, ice rinks, basketball, racquetball, squash, tennis, and volleyball courts, speed skating oval, climbing wall, tracks, athletic fields, dance studio, combatives, gymnastics, and weight rooms.

**PROGRAMS OF STUDY. Degrees:** B.A., B.Commerce, B.Ed., B.F.A., B.Mus., B.Nurs., B.Phys.Ed., B.S., B.S.Eng., B.Soc.Work, LL.B.
**Majors:** Actuarial Science, Adolescent Studies, Ancient History/Archaeology, Ancient History/Civilization, Ancient/Medieval History, Anthropology, Applied Chemistry, Applied/Environmental Geology, Applied Mathematics, Applied Physics, Archaeology, Art, Art History, Astrophysics, Biochemistry, Biological Sciences, Biomechanics, Botany, Canadian Studies, Cellular/Molecular/Microbial Biology, Chemical Engineering, Chemical Physics, Chemistry, Civil Engineering, Classical/Early Christian Studies, Communications Studies, Computer Science, Development Studies, Drama, Early Childhood Education, Ecology, Economics, Electrical Engineering, Elementary Education, English, English/Latin, Exercise Physiology, French, French/Latin, Geography, Geology, Geophysics, German, Greek, Greek/Latin, History, Latin, Law/Society, Leisure/Tourism/Society, Linguistics, Management, Mechanical Engineering, Music, Nursing, Outdoor Pursuits, Peace/Conflict Studies, Philosophy, Physical Education, Physics, Political Science, Pre-Adolescent Studies, Psychology, Pure Mathematics, Rehabilitation Education, Religious Studies, Religious Studies/Applied Ethics, Russian, Science/Technology/Society, Secondary Education, Social Work, Sociology, Spanish, Statistics, Surveying Engineering, Urban Studies, Women's Studies, Zoology.
**Distribution of degrees:** The majors with the lowest enrollment are zoology, Russian, and Latin.
**Special:** Double majors. Dual degrees. Cooperative education programs. Graduate school at which undergraduates may take graduate-level courses. Preprofessional programs in law and medicine. Teacher certification in early childhood, elementary, and secondary education.
**Honors:** Honors program.

**STUDENT LIFE. Housing:** Students may live on or off campus. Coed dorms. School-owned/operated apartments. On-campus married-student housing.
**Services and counseling/handicapped student services:** Health service. Day care. Personal and psychological counseling. Career and academic guidance services. Physically disabled student services.
**Campus organizations:** Student newspaper (Gauntlet). Radio station.

**ATHLETICS. Physical education requirements:** None.
**Intercollegiate competition:** 4% of students participate. Basketball (M,W), cross-country (W), field hockey (W), football (M), gymnastics (M,W), ice hockey (M), soccer (M,W), swimming (M,W), track (indoor) (M,W), track and field (indoor) (M,W), volleyball (M,W), wrestling (M). Member of Canada West Universities Athletic Association, Canadian Interuniversity Athletic Union.
**Intramural and club sports:** 25% of students participate. Men's club crew, diving, rugby. Women's club crew, diving, lacrosse, rugby.

**ADMISSIONS. Requirements:** Graduation from secondary school is required; GED is not accepted. No specific distribution of secondary school units required. Education, engineering, law, management, medicine, nursing, physical education, and social work programs are quota faculties with limited enrollment; admission is competitive. Audition required of music program applicants. Conditional admission possible for applicants not meeting standard requirements. SAT and CEEB Achievement Tests required of U.S. applicants. No off-campus interviews.
**Procedure:** Freshmen accepted for fall terms only.
**Transfer students:** Transfer students accepted for fall term only.
**Admissions contact:** D.J. Hinton, Director of Admissions. 403 220-6645.

**FINANCIAL AID. Available aid:** School scholarships, private scholarships, and athletic scholarships.
**Financial aid contact:** J. Van Housen, Director of Financial Aid. 403 220-6925.

**COMPUTER FACILITIES.** 375 IBM/IBM-compatible and Macintosh/Apple microcomputers. Residence halls may be equipped with networked terminals.
**Fees:** None.

## University of Ottawa

**Ottawa, Ontario, CN K1N 6N5 — 613 564-3311**

**1994-95 Costs.** Tuition: $2,200-$2,400 (Canadian residents); $7,630-$12,320 (U.S. residents). Room: $2,242. Board: $2,000. Fees, books, misc. academic expenses: $600. (All figutres are in Canadian dollars; figures are school's estimates.)
**Enrollment.** Undergraduates: 6,155 men, 8,222 women (full-time). Freshman class: 23,707 applicants, 11,020 accepted, 4,791 enrolled. Graduate enrollment: 1,964 men, 1,738 women.
**Test score averages/ranges.** N/A.
**Faculty.** 1,066 full-time; 491 part-time. 85% of faculty holds doctoral degree. Student/faculty ratio: 13 to 1.
**Selectivity rating.** N/A.

**PROFILE.** The University of Ottawa, founded in 1848, is a public, comprehensive university. It is Canada's oldest officially bilingual university, with programs offered in both English and French. Programs are offered in the Faculties of Administration, Arts, Law, Education, Health Sciences, Engineering, Medicine, Science, and Social Sciences. Its 70-acre campus is located in Ottawa.

**Accreditation:** Professionally accredited by the Associations of Universities and Colleges of Canada.
**Religious orientation:** University of Ottawa is nonsectarian; no religious requirements.
**Library:** Collections totaling over 1,405,535 volumes, 11,161 periodical subscriptions, and 1,211,673 microform items.
**Special facilities/museums:** Language lab, TV studios, theater and concert hall.
**Athletic facilities:** Gymnasiums, swimming pool, dance studio, free weight and Nautilus rooms, climbing wall, basketball, racquetball, and squash courts, ice rink, arena, athletic field.

**STUDENT BODY. Undergraduate profile:** 99.1% Canada, .9% U.S./other countries. Average age of undergraduates is 22.
**Freshman profile:** 67% of freshmen come from public schools.

**PROGRAMS OF STUDY. Degrees:** B.A., B.A.Sci., B.Admin., B.Commerce, B.Ed., B.F.A., B.Mus., B.S., B.S.Kin., B.S.Med., B.S.Nurs., B.Soc.Sci., LL.B.
**Majors:** Biochemistry, Biology, Canadian Studies, Chemical Engineering, Chemistry, Civil Engineering, Classical Art/Archaeology, Classical Studies, Common Law, Communication, Computer Engineering, Computer Science, Criminology, Economics, Electrical Engineering, Elementary Education, English, Finance, Fine Arts, French, French Literature, Geography, Geology, History, Human Kinetics, Human Resources Management, Italian, Kinanthropology, Law/Business Administration, Leisure Studies, Linguistics, Management Sciences, Marketing, Mathematics, Mechanical Engineering, Medical Sciences, Medieval Study, Music, Nursing, Occupational Therapy, Philosophy, Physics, Physiotherapy, Political Science, Psychology, Public Policy/Public Management, Religious Studies, Secondary Education, Slavic Studies, Sociology, Spanish, Theatre, Theory/History of Art, Translation, Women's Studies.
**Distribution of degrees:** The majors with the lowest enrollment are Spanish and medical sciences.
**Special:** Minors offered in some majors and in accounting, international business, law, management, and management/information systems. University is bilingual, offering most programs in both English and French; students must demonstrate proficiency in their second official language prior to graduation. Double majors. Dual degrees. Accelerated study. Internships. Cooperative education programs. Graduate school at which undergraduates may take graduate-level courses. Combined LL.B./M.B.A. and B.Eng./M.B.A. programs. M.A./LL.B. International Affairs program with Carleton U. Exchange programs with St. Paul's U and Carleton U. Teacher certification in elementary and secondary education. Certification in specific subject areas. Study abroad in Denmark, England, France, and Spain.
**Honors:** Honors program.
**Academic Assistance:** Remedial writing and study skills.

**STUDENT LIFE. Housing:** Students may live on or off campus. Coed dorms. School-owned/operated apartments. On-campus married-student housing. 8% of students live in college housing.
**Services and counseling/handicapped student services:** Placement services. Health service. Women's center. Day care. Counseling services for minority and older students. Birth control, personal, and psychological counseling. Career and academic guidance services. Religious counseling. Physically disabled student services. Learning disabled program/services. Notetaking services. Tape recorders. Tutors. Reader services for the blind.

**Campus organizations:** Undergraduate student government. Student newspapers (Fulcrum; La Rotonde). Radio station. Student Federation, Francomite, Impro-Leagues, ski club, finance and entrepreneur clubs.
**Religious organizations:** Campus Ministry, Carrefour, Newman Gathering, Relais, Jewish Student Union/Hillel, Muslim Student Association.
**Minority/foreign student organizations:** Native Student Association. International Student Club, African, Arab, Chinese, Indian, Ismailian, Iranian, Lebanese, Ukrainian, and Vietnamese groups.

**ATHLETICS. Physical education requirements:** None.
**Intercollegiate competition:** 3% of students participate. Badminton (M,W), basketball (M,W), cross-country (M,W), fencing (M,W), football (M), ice hockey (M), swimming (M,W), volleyball (W), water polo (M). Member of Canadian Interuniversity Athletic Union (CIAU), OQIFC, OUAA, OWIAA.
**Intramural and club sports:** 25% of students participate. Intramural badminton, basketball, broomball, hockey, soccer, volleyball, water polo. Men's club Alpine skiing, crew, golf, indoor track, martial arts, Nordic skiing, soccer, tennis, volleyball. Women's club Alpine skiing, crew, figure skating, indoor track, martial arts, Nordic skiing, rugby, soccer, synchronized swimming, water polo.

**ADMISSIONS. Academic basis for candidate selection** (in order of priority): Secondary school record, standardized test scores, class rank.
**Requirements:** Graduation from secondary school is required; GED is accepted. Ontario Secondary School Diploma (or equivalent) required, including a minimum of six Ontario Academic Courses or equivalent from other provinces. Specific prerequisites such as biology, chemistry, and mathematics required for some degree programs. Strong "B" average required. SAT required of U.S. applicants; minimum scores of 500 in both verbal and math generally required. Advanced Placement course work recommended of U.S. applicants. Portfolio required of art program applicants. Audition required of music program applicants. U.S. applicants not satisfying normal admission requirements to first year science or engineering programs may be admitted to the pre-science year in the Faculty of Science and Engineering. Campus visit recommended. No off-campus interviews.
**Procedure:** Take SAT by November of 12th year. Suggest filing application by February 1. Application deadline is March 30. Notification of admission on rolling basis. Freshmen accepted for fall terms only.
**Special programs:** Early entrance/early admission program.
**Transfer students:** Transfer students accepted for fall term. Application deadline is April 30. Minimum 3.5 GPA required. Maximum number of transferable semester hours is two-thirds of number needed for degree. At least 30 semester hours must be completed at the university to receive degree.
**Admissions contact:** Andre Pierre Lepage, Director of Admissions. 613 564-3928.

**FINANCIAL AID.** Financial aid not available to U.S. students.

**STUDENT EMPLOYMENT.** Institutional employment available.

**COMPUTER FACILITIES.** 150 IBM/IBM-compatible, Macintosh/Apple, and RISC-/UNIX-based microcomputers. Students may access Digital, IBM, SUN minicomputer/mainframe systems, BITNET, Internet. Client/LAN operating systems include Apple/Macintosh, DOS, OS/2, UNIX/XENIX/AIX, X-windows, Novell. Computer languages and software packages include Ada, C, COBOL, CorelDRAW, dBASE III, FORTRAN, Lotus 1-2-3, MINITAB, PL/1, Quattro, SAS, SPSS, Tech & Latex, Turbo Pascal, WordPerfect, WP Presentation; 50 in all. Computer facilities are available to all students.
**Fees:** Computer fee is included in tuition/fees.
**Hours:** 24 hours.

# University of Toronto

**Toronto, Ontario, CN M5S 1A3 416 978-2190**

**1994-95 Costs.** Tuition: $2,025-$2,576 (Canadian residents); $7,639-$12,454 (U.S. residents). Room & board: $5,000. Fees, books, misc. academic expenses: $1,250. (All figures are in Canadian dollars; figures are school's estimates.)
**Enrollment.** Undergraduates: 15,462 men, 16,338 women (full-time). Graduate enrollment: 5,263 men, 5,515 women.
**Test score averages/ranges.** N/A.
**Faculty.** N/A.
**Selectivity rating.** N/A.

**PROFILE.** The University of Toronto, founded in 1827, is a public institution. Programs are offered in the Faculties and Schools of Applied Science and Engineering, Architecture, Basic Medical Sciences, Education, Forestry, Humanities, Landscape Architecture, Mathematical and Physical Sciences, Medicine, Music, Nursing, Pharmacy, Physical and Health Education, Rehabilitation Medicine, and Social Sciences. Its main campus is located in downtown Toronto.

**Accreditation:** Professionally accredited by the Associations of Universities and Colleges of Canada.
**Religious orientation:** University of Toronto is nonsectarian; no religious requirements.
**Athletic facilities:** Gymnasium, fencing salle, indoor track, swimming pools, badminton, basketball, squash, and tennis courts, gymnastics and weight rooms, stadium, sports medicine clinic, indoor golf, outdoor track, athletic fields.

**PROGRAMS OF STUDY. Degrees:** B.A., B.Appl.Sci., B.Arch., B.Commerce, B.Ed., B.Land.Arch., B.Phys./Hlth.Ed., B.S., B.S.Nurs., B.S.Occup.Ther., B.S.Pharm., B.S.Phys.Ther., LL.B., Mus.B.
**Majors:** Actuarial Science, African Studies, American Studies, Ancient Syria/Palestine, Animal Behavior, Anthropology, Applied Mathematics, Applied Physical Science, Architecture, Art/Art History, Art as Applied to Medicine, Assyriology, Astronomy, Biochemistry, Biochemistry/Chemistry, Biogeography, Biological Sciences, Biology, Biomedical Ethics, Botany, Canadian Studies, Cell/Molecular Biology, Celtic Studies, Chemical Engineering, Chemical Physics, Chemistry, Chemistry/Biochemistry, Chinese Language/Literature, Chinese Studies, Christianity/Culture, Cinema Studies, Civil Engineering, Classical Civilization, Classical Studies, Classics, Cognitive Science, Commerce/Finance, Computer Engineering, Computer Science, Computer Science for Data Management, Computer Science/Mathematics, Computer Science/Statistics, Cooperative Program in Administration, Cooperative Program in Arts Administration, Cooperative Program in Computer Science/Physics, Cooperative Program in International Development, Crime/Deviance, Criminology, Czech/Slovak Studies, Drama, East Asian Studies, Ecology/Environmental Biology, Economics, Education, Egyptology, Electrical Engineering, English, Environmental Chemistry, Environmental Management, Environmental Resource Management, Environmental Sciences, Environmental Studies, Ethics/Society/Law, Exceptionality in Human Learning, Fine Art, Fine Arts/Art History, Finnish, French, French Language/Linguistics, French Language/Literature, French Language/Literature/Translation, Geoarchaeology, Geography, Geology, Geology/Mineralogy, German, German Language/Literature, Greek, Greek/Roman History, Hebrew, Historical/Cultural Geography, History, History/Literature of Music, History of Art, History of Science/Technology, History/Philosophy of Science, Human Biology, Human/Computer Interaction, Humanities, Humanities/Psychoanalytic Thought, Hungarian Studies, Immunology, Industrial Engineering, Industrial Relations, International Development, International Relations, Italian, Japanese Language/Literature, Japanese Studies, Jewish Studies, Korean Studies, Labour/Management Relations, Landscape Architecture, Latin, Latin American Studies, Linguistics, Literary Studies, Logic, Materials Science, Mathematical Sciences, Mathematics, Mathematics/Statistics, Mechanical Engineering, Medieval Studies, Metallurgical Engineering/Materials Science, Microbiology, Middle East/Islamic Studies, Modern Languages/Literatures, Molecular Genetics/Molecular Biology, Molecular Plant Biology, Music, Music Composition, Music Education, Music History/Literature, Music Performance, Music Theory, Native Studies, Near Eastern Studies/Religious Studies, Neurosciences, Nursing, Nutritional Sciences, Occupational Therapy, Paleontology, Peace/Conflict Studies, Pharmacology, Philosophy, Philosophy Applied to Life Sciences, Physical Geography, Physical/Health Education, Physical Sciences, Physical Therapy, Physics, Physiology, Plant Pathology, Plant Population Biology/Evolution, Polish Language/Literature, Political Science, Population/Society, Portuguese, Psychology, Religion, Renaissance Studies, Russian/East European Studies, Russian Language/Literature, Science/Technology Studies, Semiotics, Slavic Languages, Slavic Languages/Literatures, Sociology, South Asian Studies, Spanish, Statistics, Studio Art, Surveying Science, Terrain/Environmental Earth Sciences, Theatre/Drama, Toxicology, Ukrainian Language/Literature, Urban/Economic Geography, Urban Studies, Victorian Studies, Women's Studies, Zoology.
**Special:** University has three campuses (St. George, Scarborough, and Erindale). Faculty of Arts and Science programs, with majors divided among the Divisions of Economics and Commerce, Humanities, Life Sciences, Basic Medical Sciences, Mathematical and Physical Sciences, and Social Sciences, are offered on all three campuses. Arts and science students belong to one of nine colleges on the three campuses. B.Arch., B.Ed., and B.Land.Arch. degrees are five-year programs. Graduate school at which undergraduates may take graduate-level courses.
**Academic Assistance:** Nonremedial tutoring.

**STUDENT LIFE. Housing:** Students may live on or off campus. Coed, women's, and men's dorms.
**Services and counseling/handicapped student services:** Health service. Birth control, personal, and psychological counseling. Career and academic guidance services. Physically disabled student services. Learning disabled services. Notetaking services. Reader services for the blind.
**Campus organizations:** Undergraduate student government. Student newspaper. Radio station. Musical groups, international folk dance club, theatre, film society, art shows, concerts and lectures, debating, language clubs, political associations, Amnesty International, Society for Creative Anachronism, special-interest groups, 200 organizations in all.
**Religious organizations:** Several religious groups.
**Minority/foreign student organizations:** Korean, Lithuanian, and other foreign student groups.

**ATHLETICS. Physical education requirements:** None.
**Intercollegiate competition:** 2% of students participate. Badminton (M,W), basketball (M,W), cheerleading (M,W), crew (M,W), cross-country (M,W), curling (M,W), fencing (M,W), field hockey (W), figure skating (W), football (M), golf (M), gymnastics (M,W), ice hockey (M,W), Nordic skiing (M,W), rugby (M), soccer (M,W), squash (M,W), swimming (M,W), tennis (M,W), track (indoor) (M,W), track and field (indoor) (M,W), volleyball (M,W), water polo (M,W), wrestling (M). Member of Canadian Interuniversity Athletic Union, Ontario Universities Athletic Association, Ontario Women's Interuniversity Athletic Association.
**Intramural and club sports:** 50% of students participate. Intramural ball hockey, basketball, broomball, curling, field hockey, football, ice hockey, indoor soccer, inner-tube water polo, lacrosse, rugby, soccer, softball, tennis, touch football, triathlon, ultimate frisbee, volleyball, water polo. Men's club boxing, karate, kendo, lacrosse. Women's club karate, kendo, rugby.

**ADMISSIONS. Academic basis for candidate selection** (in order of priority): Secondary school record, standardized test scores.
**Requirements:** Graduation from secondary school is required; GED is not accepted. No specific distribution of secondary school units required. Certificate of Proficiency in English Test (COPE), TOEFL (minimum score of 580), Michigan Test (minimum score of 90), or British Council English Language Testing required of foreign applicants. Minimum 3.0 GPA, minimum SAT scores of 550 on both math and verbal, and minimum score of 500 on three CEEB Achievement Tests required for admission to Faculty of Arts and Science. Applications reviewed on individual basis for admission to Faculty of Music; SAT and ACH scores considered. Minimum SAT scores of 550 on both math and verbal and three CEEB Achievement Tests required for admission to School of Physical and Health Education. All other divisions require 30 semester hours (45 quarter hours) from accredited institutions. Applicants with high GPA and two CEEB Advanced Placement exams may be considered. No off-campus interviews.
**Procedure:** Suggest filing application by March 1; no deadline. Freshmen accepted for fall terms only.
**Admissions contact:** Karel Swift, Associate University Registrar (Admissions and Awards). International Student Contact: Elizabeth Paterson. 416 978-2190.

**FINANCIAL AID.** Financial aid not available for U.S. undergraduates.

**PROMINENT ALUMNI/AE.** Mackenzie King and Lester Pearson, former Prime Ministers; Robertson Davies and Margaret Atwood, novelists; Northrop Frye, literary critic.

# University of Waterloo

Waterloo, Ontario, CN N2L 3G1 519 885-1211

**1994-95 Costs.** Tuition: $2,228 (Canadian residents), $8,404 (U.S. residents). Room: $2,744-$2,944. Board: $1,990-$2,790. Fees, books, misc. academic expenses (school's estimate): $985. (All figures are in Canadian dollars.)
**Enrollment.** Undergraduates: 9,030 men, 7,108 women (full-time). Freshman class: 20,810 applicants, 8,676 accepted, 3,354 enrolled. Graduate enrollment: 1,506 men, 704 women.
**Test score averages/ranges.** N/A.
**Faculty.** 833 full-time; 140 part-time. 90% of faculty holds doctoral degree. Student/faculty ratio: 19 to 1.
**Selectivity rating.** N/A.

**PROFILE.** The University of Waterloo, founded in 1957, is a public, comprehensive institution. Programs are offered in the Faculties of Arts, Engineering, Environmental Studies, Human Kinetics and Leisure Studies, Mathematics, and Science. Its 1,000-acre campus is located in the northwest section of the city of Waterloo, 60 miles from Toronto.

**Accreditation:** Professionally accredited by the Association of Universities and Colleges of Canada.
**Religious orientation:** University of Waterloo is nonsectarian; no religious requirements.
**Library:** Collections totaling over 2,800,000 volumes, 11,349 periodical subscriptions, and 1,000,000 microform items.
**Special facilities/museums:** Art gallery, games, biology, and optometry museums.
**Athletic facilities:** Gymnasiums, squash and tennis courts, swimming pool, fitness and weight rooms, ice arena, football stadium, field hockey, football, intramural, rugby, soccer, and softball fields.

**STUDENT BODY. Undergraduate profile:** Less than 1% of undergraduates are from the U.S.; 3% are from other foreign countries; 96% are from Canada.
**Foreign students:** 582 students are from out of the country. Countries represented include Germany, Hong Kong, Malaysia, Singapore, Sri Lanka, and Trinidad and Tobago; 43 in all.

**PROGRAMS OF STUDY. Degrees:** B.A., B.Appl.Sci., B.Arch., B.Env.Studies, B.Indep.Studies, B.Math., B.S.
**Majors:** Accountancy Studies, Actuarial Science, Anthropology, Applied Economics, Applied Mathematics, Applied Mathematics/Engineering Electives, Applied Mathematics/Physics Electives, Applied Statistics/Engineering Electives, Architecture, Arts Applied Studies/Arts Administration Specialization, Arts Applied Studies Cooperative Programs, Arts Applied Studies/French Teaching Specialization, Arts Applied Studies/International Trade Specialization, Arts Applied Studies/Management Studies Specialization, Arts Applied Studies/Personnel Studies Specialization, Biochemistry, Biochemistry/Teaching Option, Biology, Biology/Biotechnology, Biology/Business Economics, Biology/Chemistry, Biology/Environment/Resource Studies, Biology/Geography, Biology/Pre-Health Professions Option, Biology/Teaching Option, Canadian Studies, Chemical Engineering, Chemical Physics, Chemistry, Chemistry/Mathematics Option, Chemistry Teaching, Civil Engineering, Classical Studies, Classical Studies/Languages Option, Combinatorics/Optimization, Computer Engineering, Computer Science, Computer Science/Electrical Engineering Electives, Computer Science/Information Systems, Dance, Drama, Earth Sciences, Earth Sciences/Environmental Hydrogeology Option, Earth Sciences/Geography Option, Earth Sciences/Geology Option, Earth Sciences/Geophysics Option, Economics, Electrical Engineering, Engineering/Computer Engineering, Engineering/Environmental Engineering, Engineering/International Studies, Engineering/Management Sciences, Engineering Mathematics, Engineering/Physics, Engineering/Society/Technology/Values, Engineering/Statistics, Engineering/Water Resources, English, English/Literature Option, English/Rhetoric/Professional Writing Option, Environment/Resource Studies, Environment/Resource Studies/Business, Environmental Chemistry, Environmental Economics, Environmental Science, Fine Arts/Art History, Fine Arts/Film Studies, Fine Arts/Studio, French, French Studies, French Teaching, Geography, Geography/Business, Geography/Environmental Studies, Geological Engineering, German, Greek, Health Studies/Gerontology, Health Studies/Kinesiology, Health Studies/Pre-Health Professions, History, Independent Studies, International Studies, Kinesiology, Kinesiology/Ergonomics, Kinesiology/Health, Latin, Latin American Studies, Legal Studies, Liberal Science, Management Sciences, Management Studies, Mathematics, Mathematics/Business Administration, Mathematics/Chartered Accountancy, Mathematics/Management Accounting, Mathematics/Teaching, Mechanical Engineering, Medieval Studies, Middle East Studies, Music, Operations Research, Optometry, Peace/Conflict Studies, Personality/Religion, Personnel Studies, Philosophy, Physics, Physics Teaching, Political Science, Political Science/Administrative Studies, Psychology, Pure Mathematics, Recreation/Leisure Studies, Recreation/Leisure Studies/Business, Recreation/Leisure Studies/Therapeutic Studies, Recreation/Leisure Studies/Tourism, Recreation/Parks, Religious Studies, Russian, Russian/East European Area Studies, Science, Science/Business, Sexuality/Marriage/Family, Slavic Studies, Social Development Studies, Society/Technology/Values, Sociology, Spanish, Speech Communication, Statistics, Systems Design Engineering, Urban/Regional Planning, Women's Studies.
**Distribution of degrees:** The majors with the highest enrollment are mathematics, computer science, and English; drama, classical studies, and German have the lowest.
**Special:** Minors offered in many majors. Self-designed majors. Double majors. Dual degrees. Independent study. Accelerated study. Pass/fail grading option. Internships. Cooperative education programs. Graduate school at which undergraduates may take graduate-level courses. Preprofessional programs in optometry, accountancy, actuarial science, architecture, biology/health, engineering, French/teaching, health studies/health professions, kinesiology/health professions, management science, mathematics/teaching, science/teaching, and urban/regional planning. Five-year B.A./M.Acct. and B.Appl.Sci./M.Appl.Sci. programs. Cooperative teaching programs with Brock U (French), Queens U (science), and U of Western Ontario (math). Member of Association of Commonwealth Universities. Teacher certification in secondary education. Certification in specific subject areas. Study abroad programs offered in twenty countries.
**Honors:** Honors program.
**Academic Assistance:** Remedial reading, writing, math, and study skills.

**STUDENT LIFE. Housing:** Coed dorms. School-owned/operated apartments. On-campus married-student housing. 22% of students live in college housing.
**Social atmosphere:** According to the editor of the student newspaper, Waterloo offers "a wild time—close to Canada's biggest city, Toronto, and a great drawing place for alternative bands." Influential groups on campus include the Imprint staff, Jismo (a local band), the Engineering Society, the Math Society, and GLLOW (a gay/lesbian group). Some popular events at Waterloo are Homecoming, Canada Day party, Miss Oktoberfest pageant, Duck Appreciation Day, Grad Club sangria fests, and basketball games. On campus, students gather at Fed Hall, the Bombshelter, and the Imprint office. Off campus, they head for Huggy's (a local disco), Fistie's, Pogo's, and the Princess Cinema (a repertory theater).
**Services and counseling/handicapped student services:** Placement services. Health service. Women's center. Day care. Counseling services for minority, military, veteran, and older students. Birth control, personal, and psychological counseling. Career and academic guidance services. Religious counseling. Physically disabled student services. Learning disabled program/services. Notetaking services. Tape recorders. Tutors. Reader services for the blind.
**Campus organizations:** Undergraduate student government. Student newspaper (Imprint, published once/week). Yearbook. Legal Resources, Rainforest Action Group, Volunteer Placement Centre, Amateur Radio Club, Amnesty International, Chess Club, Entrepreneur Club, Fraternity-Sorority Awareness Club, House of Debates, Green Party, Progressive Conservative Club, Young Liberals, Students for Life, Peace Society, GLLOW, United Nations Club, Students of Objectivism, Warrior Band, other special-interest groups. Student Part-Time Employment Centre (SPEC) and Peer Assistance Links (PALS).
**Religious organizations:** Bahai Studies, Campus Crusade for Christ, Chinese Christian Fellowship, Huron Campus Ministry Fellowship, Jewish Student Association, Laymen's Evangelical Fellowship, Muslim Student Association, Student Christian Movement, Christian Fellowship.
**Minority/foreign student organizations:** Several minority student groups. International Student Board, Asian, Caribbean, Chinese, Indian, Ismailian, Korean, Pakistani, Palestinian, Polish, Slavic, Tamil, Ukrainian, and Vietnamese groups.

**ATHLETICS. Physical education requirements:** None.
**Intercollegiate competition:** 5% of students participate. Badminton (M,W), basketball (M,W), crew (M,W), cross-country (M,W), curling (M,W), field hockey (W), figure skating (W), football (M), golf (M), ice hockey (M), Nordic skiing (M,W), rugby (M), soccer (M,W), squash (M,W), swimming (M,W), tennis (M,W), track and field (indoor) (M,W), volleyball (M,W). Member of Canadian Interuniversity Athletic Union, Ontario Universities Athletic Association, Ontario Women's Intercollegiate Athletic Association.
**Intramural and club sports:** 80% of students participate. Intramural archery, badminton, ball hockey, basketball, broomball, curling, equestrian sports, fencing, fitness, floor hockey, ice hockey, ice skating, martial arts, rowing, skiing, sky diving, soccer, social dance, squash, swimming, table tennis, tennis, volleyball, water polo, weight training. Men's club archery, badminton, equestrian sports, fencing, martial arts, outers, rowing, sailing/windsurfing, sky diving, weight training. Women's club archery, badminton, equestrian sports, fencing, martial arts, outers, rowing, sailing/windsurfing, sky diving, weight training.

**ADMISSIONS. Academic basis for candidate selection** (in order of priority): Secondary school record, class rank, standardized test scores, school's recommendation, essay.
**Nonacademic basis for candidate selection:** Extracurricular participation is important. Particular talent or ability is considered.
**Requirements:** Graduation from secondary school is required; GED is not accepted. No specific distribution of secondary school units required. Ontario secondary school students must present Ontario Secondary School Diploma (OSSD) and a minimum of six Grade 13 or Ontario Academic Course credits. Minimum average of 60% in these courses required for consideration; higher averages may be required for admission to programs in which the number of applicants exceeds the spaces available. Rank in top tenth of secondary school class, and Advanced Placement exams in prerequisite subjects or first-year university standing in acceptable subjects from an accredited institution required of U.S. applicants. Specific course requirements vary according to program. SAT or ACT is recommended. Campus visit recommended. No off-campus interviews.
**Procedure:** Application deadline is May 1. Notification of admission on rolling basis. Reply is required by June 30. $152 nonrefundable room deposit. Freshmen accepted for fall terms only.
**Transfer students:** Transfer students from the U.S. accepted for fall term only. Application deadline is May 1. Lowest course grade accepted is "C-." Maximum number of transferable credits varies.
**Admissions contact:** Ken Lavigne, Director of Admissions. International Student Contact: Linda Kellar. 519 885-1211.

**FINANCIAL AID.** Financial aid is not available to U.S. students.

**STUDENT EMPLOYMENT.** Institutional employment. 10% of full-time undergraduates work on campus during school year. Undergraduates from the U.S. may not work off campus.

**COMPUTER FACILITIES.** Students may access Internet. Computer facilities available only to students enrolled in a computer course.
**Fees:** None.

# University of Western Ontario

London, Ontario, CN N6A 5B8 519 661-2111

**1994-95 Costs.** Tuition: $2,226 (Canadian residents), $8,403 (U.S. residents). Room & board: $5,168-$5,368. Fees, books, misc. academic expenses (school's estimate): $1,344. (All figures are in Canadian dollars.)
**Enrollment.** Undergraduates: 9,759 men, 10,372 women (full-time). Freshman class: 24,635 applicants, 14,372 accepted, 5,344 enrolled. Graduate enrollment: 1,646 men, 1,186 women.
**Test score averages/ranges.** N/A.
**Faculty.** 1,415 full-time.
**Selectivity rating.** N/A.

**PROFILE.** Western Ontario, founded in 1878, is a public, multipurpose university. Programs are offered in the Faculties of Applied Health Sciences, Arts, Dentistry, Education, Engineering Science, Graduate Studies, Law, Medicine, Music, Nursing, Part-time and Continuing Education, Physical Education, Science, and Social Science, the Graduate School of Journalism, and the Schools of Business Administration and Library and Information Science. Its 402-acre campus is located in London, 120 miles southwest of Toronto.

**Accreditation:** Professionally accredited by the Association of Universities and Colleges of Canada.
**Religious orientation:** University of Western Ontario is nonsectarian; no religious requirements.
**Library:** Collections totaling over 2,100,000 volumes, 17,300 periodical subscriptions, and 2,860,000 microform items.
**Special facilities/museums:** Indian archaeology museum, observatory, boundary-layer wind tunnel.
**Athletic facilities:** Gymnasiums, swimming pools, curling rink, ice rink, badminton, basketball, squash, tennis, and volleyball courts, gymnastics and weight rooms, stadium, field hockey, football, and soccer fields, track.

**STUDENT BODY. Undergraduate profile:** 95% Canada, 5% Other countries. Average age of undergraduates is 23.
**Foreign students:** Countries represented include England, Germany, Hong Kong, Japan, and Scotland; 46 in all.

**PROGRAMS OF STUDY. Degrees:** B.A., B.Ed., B.Eng.Sci., B.F.A., B.Mus., B.Musical Arts, B.S., B.S.Nurs., B.Soc.Work, LL.B.
**Majors:** Actuarial Science, Administrative/Commercial Studies, Anthropology, Anthropology/Linguistics, Applied Mathematics, Astronomy, Biochemistry, Biology, Biophysics, Business Administration, Cell Biology, Chemistry, Classical Studies, Computer Science, Ecology/Evolution, Economics, Engineering Science, English, English/Drama, Film, French, Genetics, Geography, Geography/Resources Conservation, Geography/Urban Development, Geology, Geophysics, German, Greek, History, History of Science, Home Economics, Latin, Mathematics, Microbiology/Immunology, Music Education, Music History, Music Performance, Music Theory/Composition, Nursing, Occupational Therapy, Pharmacology/Toxicology, Philosophy, Physical Education, Physical Therapy, Physics, Physiology, Plant Sciences, Political Science, Pre-Dentistry, Pre-Law, Pre-Medicine, Psychology, Russian, Sociology, Spanish, Statistical Sciences, Visual Arts, Western Literature/Civilization, Women's Studies, Zoology.
**Requirements:** General education requirement.
**Special:** Self-designed majors. Double majors. Dual degrees. Graduate school at which undergraduates may take graduate-level courses. Exchange program in nursing with U of Waterloo. Teacher certification in early childhood, elementary, secondary, and special education. Study abroad in Denmark, France, Germany, and Scotland.
**Honors:** Honors program.
**Academic Assistance:** Remedial writing, math, and study skills. Nonremedial tutoring.

**STUDENT LIFE. Housing:** Students may live on or off campus. Coed, women's, and men's dorms. School-owned/operated apartments. Both on-campus and off-campus married-student housing. 30% of students live in college housing.
**Social atmosphere:** The Spoke, The Wave, The Ceeps, and Joe Kool's are among the popular student gathering-spots. Fraternities and the Purple Spur are influential on campus social life. Highlights of the school year include football games and Thursday nights at The Ceeps. Campus life is "very much bar-oriented," reports the student newspaper, with "much live theatre and an impressive local music scene."
**Services and counseling/handicapped student services:** Placement services. Health service. Counseling services for older students. Birth control, personal, and psychological counseling. Career and academic guidance services. Religious counseling. Physically disabled student services. Learning disabled services. Notetaking services. Tape recorders.
**Campus organizations:** Undergraduate student government. Student newspaper (Gazette, published daily). Radio station. Choir, debating, political, service, and special-interest groups. 13 fraternities, no chapter houses; four sororities, no chapter houses. 6% of men join a fraternity. 2% of women join a sorority.
**Religious organizations:** Bahai group, Campus Crusade for Christ, Hillel, Muslim student group.
**Minority/foreign student organizations:** Native student group. African, Arab, Caribbean, Chinese, Filipino, Ismailian, Korean, Malaysian-Singaporan, Polish, Portuguese, Ukrainian, and Vietnamese groups.

**ATHLETICS. Physical education requirements:** None.
**Intercollegiate competition:** Badminton (M,W), basketball (M,W), crew (M,W), cross-country (M,W), curling (M,W), fencing (M,W), field hockey (W), figure skating (W), football (M), golf (M), gymnastics (M,W), ice hockey (M), Nordic skiing (M,W), rugby (M), soccer (M,W), squash (M,W), swimming (M,W), tennis (M,W), track (indoor) (M,W), track and field (indoor) (M,W), volleyball (M,W), water polo (M), wrestling (M). Member of Canadian Interuniversity Athletic Union (CIAU), Ontario Universities Athletic Association (OUAA), Ontario Women's Intercollegiate Athletic Association (OWIAA).
**Intramural and club sports:** Men's club Alpine skiing, baseball, basketball, cheerleading, cycling. Women's club baseball, basketball, cheerleading.

**ADMISSIONS. Academic basis for candidate selection** (in order of priority): Secondary school record, class rank, school's recommendation.
**Requirements:** Graduation from secondary school is required; GED is not accepted. No specific distribution of secondary school units required. Applicants who present Ontario Secondary School Diploma must have a minimum of six Ontario Academic Credits; applicants from Grade 13 must have a minimum of six approved Grade 13 credits. Graduation from an accredited secondary school and rank in top 15% of class required of U.S. applicants; 12th-year courses should be selected in accordance with first-year program requirements which vary. Audition and interview required of music program applicants. Campus visit and interview recommended. No off-campus interviews.
**Procedure:** Application deadline is June 1 for non-Canadians; July 1 for Canadians. Notification of admission on rolling basis. Freshmen accepted for fall terms only.
**Special programs:** Admission may be deferred one year. Concurrent enrollment program.
**Transfer students:** Transfer students accepted for terms other than fall. Application deadline is May 31 for summer; July 1 for fall; April 1 for spring. Lowest course grade accepted is "D." Maximum number of transferable credits is 10 courses. At least five senior courses in 15-course degree program or 10 in honors program must be completed at the university to receive degree.
**Admissions contact:** R.J. Tiffin, M.A., Director of Admissions. 519 661-2150. International Student Contact: International Student Office. 519 661-4073.

**FINANCIAL AID.** Financial aid is not available to U.S. students.

**STUDENT EMPLOYMENT.** U.S. students may work on campus for 5-20 hours/week (depending on course load) at $5-$6/hour.

**COMPUTER FACILITIES.** IBM/IBM-compatible and Macintosh/Apple microcomputers. Computer languages and software packages include Accent-R, Ada, BASIC, C, COBOL, DI-3000, FORTRAN, GK-2000, ImSL, LISP, MINITAB, Pascal, Prolog, SAS, SPSS.
**Fees:** None.
**Hours:** 24 hours.

**PROMINENT ALUMNI/AE.** Audrey McLaughlin, leader, National NDP Party; Silken Laumann, bronze medal-winner, '92 Olympics; Paul Beeston, CEO, Toronto Blue Jays.

# York University

North York, Ontario, CN M3J 1P3 416 736-2100

**1992-93 Costs.** Tuition: $2,026 (Canadian residents), $7,639 (U.S. residents). Room & board: $4,230. Fees, books, misc. academic expenses (school's estimate): $1,158. (All figures are in Canadian dollars.)
**Enrollment.** Undergraduates: 10,548 men, 14,787 women (full-time). Graduate enrollment: 1,995 men, 1,503 women.
**Test score averages/ranges.** N/A.
**Faculty.** 1,240 full-time; 2,293 part-time. 100% of faculty holds highest degree in specific field. Student/faculty ratio: 12 to 1.
**Selectivity rating.** N/A.

**PROFILE.** York, founded in 1959, is a public, comprehensive university. Programs are offered through Atkinson College; the Faculties of Administrative Studies, Arts, Education, Environmental Studies, Fine Arts, Graduate Studies, and Science; Glendon College; and Osgoode Hall Law School. Its 600-acre York campus and 85-acre Glendon College campus are both located in the city of North York, in the Toronto metropolitan area.

**Accreditation:** Professionally accredited by the Association of Universities and Colleges of Canada.
**Religious orientation:** York University is nonsectarian; no religious requirements.
**Library:** Collections totaling over 2,000,000 volumes, 19,000 periodical subscriptions, and 1,000,000 microform items.
**Special facilities/museums:** Several art galleries, observatory with 60 cm telescope.
**Athletic facilities:** Field house; track, multipurpose gymnasiums, squash and tennis courts, swimming pool, ice skating arena, playing fields.

**STUDENT BODY. Undergraduate profile:** Average age of undergraduates is 22.
**Foreign students:** 1,661 students are from out of the country. Countries represented include Hong Kong, India, Iran, Israel, the United Kingdom, and the United States.

**PROGRAMS OF STUDY. Degrees:** B.A., B.Admin.Studies, B.Bus.Admin., B.Ed., B.Env.Studies, B.F.A., B.S., B.S.Nurs., B.Soc.Work.
**Majors:** Accounting, African Studies, Anthropology, Applied Mathematics, Astronomy, Atmospheric Chemistry, Biology, Canadian Studies, Chemistry, Classical Studies, Classics, Communication Arts, Computer Science, Coordinated Business, Creative Writing, Cultural/Critical/Historical Studies, Dance, Early Childhood Education, Earth/Atmospheric Sciences, East Asian Studies, Economics, Economics/Business, English, Environmental Policy/Action, Film/Video, Finance, French Studies, Geography, German, Global Development, Greek, Health/Society, Hispanic Studies, History, Human Settlement/Population, Humanities, Individualized Studies, Intermediate/Senior Education, International Studies, Italian, Junior/Intermediate Education, Labour Studies, Languages, Latin, Latin American/Caribbean Studies, Law, Law/Society, Linguistics, Linguistics/Language Studies, Management Science, Marketing, Mass Communications, Mathematics, Mathematics for Commerce, Multidisciplinary Studies, Music, Nature/Technology/Society, Organizational Behavior/Industrial Relations, Peace/Justice, Philosophy, Physical Education, Physics, Policy, Political Science, Primary/Junior Education, Psychology, Public Policy/Administration, Rehabilitation Services, Religious Studies, Russian, Science/Technology/Culture and Society, Social/Political Thought, Sociology, Space/Communication Science, Spanish, Statistics, Theatre, Translation, Urban Studies, Visual Arts, Women's Studies.

**Distribution of degrees:** The majors with the highest enrollment are psychology and sociology; applied mathematics, communication arts, and Spanish have the lowest.
**Requirements:** General education requirement.
**Academic regulations:** Minimum 2.0 GPA must be maintained.
**Special:** Minors offered in many majors and in film/video studies, theatre production, theatre studies, visual arts/history. Bilingual liberal arts program offered through Glendon Coll. Self-designed majors. Double majors. Dual degrees. Independent study. Joint program with community colleges in early childhood education, rehabilitation services, and communication arts. Teacher certification in early childhood, elementary, secondary, special education, and bilingual/bicultural education. Study abroad in Denmark, England, France, Germany, Greece, Israel, Italy, Japan, and Sweden.
**Honors:** Honors program.
**Academic Assistance:** Remedial writing and math. Nonremedial tutoring.

**STUDENT LIFE. Housing:** Students may live on or off campus. Coed, women's, and men's dorms. School-owned/operated apartments. On-campus married-student housing. 10% of students live in college housing.
**Services and counseling/handicapped student services:** Placement services. Women's center. Day care. Birth control, personal, and psychological counseling. Career and academic guidance services. Religious counseling. Physically disabled student services. Learning disabled services. Notetaking services. Tape recorders. Reader services for the blind.
**Campus organizations:** Undergraduate student government. Student newspaper (Excalibur, published once/week). Radio and TV stations. York Against Apartheid, Students for Charity, Society for Creative Anachronism, Entrepreneur's Society, Le Cercle Francais, Royal Gaming Society, Greens, Hunger Action Resource Centre, Renaissance Stage Society, United Nations Forum, numerous academic, athletic, and special-interest groups, 137 organizations in all.
**Religious organizations:** Intervarsity Christian Fellowship, Navigators, Student Christian Movement, Bahai, Catholic, Chinese Christian, Christian Science, Indonesian Christian, Ismaili, Jewish, Latter-Day Saints, Lutheran, Moslem, and Orthodox Christian groups.
**Minority/foreign student organizations:** Numerous foreign student groups.

**ATHLETICS. Physical education requirements:** None.
**Intercollegiate competition:** Badminton (M,W), basketball (M,W), cross-country (M,W), field hockey (W), figure skating (W), football (M), golf (M), gymnastics (M,W), ice hockey (M,W), rugby (M), soccer (M,W), squash (M), swimming (M,W), tennis (M,W), track and field (indoor) (M,W), volleyball (M,W), water polo (M). Member of Canadian Interuniversity Athletic Association, Ontario Universities Athletic Association, Ontario Women's Interuniversity Athletic Association.
**Intramural and club sports:** Intramural badminton, basketball, broomball, cross-country, curling, flag football, hockey, inner-tube water polo, swimming, tennis, volleyball. Men's club fencing. Women's club fencing, synchronized swimming.

**ADMISSIONS. Nonacademic basis for candidate selection:** Particular talent or ability is important.
**Requirements:** Graduation from secondary school is required; GED is not accepted. No specific distribution of secondary school units required. Minimum combined SAT score of 1100 (composite ACT score of 24-26) and "B" average required of U.S. applicants. Supplementary application required of business administration and environmental studies program applicants. Portfolio required of art program applicants. Audition required of music program applicants. R.N. required of nursing program applicants. Applicants not meeting standard requirements may submit request for special review. Campus visit recommended. Interviews not available in the U.S.
**Procedure:** Suggest filing application by December 1. Application deadline is March 1. Notification of admission on rolling basis. Reply is required within three weeks of notification of admission. $75 (Canadian) refundable tuition deposit. $200 (Canadian) refundable room deposit. Freshmen accepted for fall terms only.
**Special programs:** Credit may be granted through CEEB Advanced Placement for scores of 4 or higher.
**Transfer students:** Transfer students from the U.S. accepted for fall terms only. Application deadline is March 1. Minimum 3.0 GPA required. Lowest course grade accepted is "C." Maximum number of transferable credits is 20 semester hours. At least 20 semester hours must be completed at the university to receive degree.
**Admissions contact:** Tom Myers, Director of Admissions. International Student contact: Clarke Hortzing. 416 736-5100.

**FINANCIAL AID.** No financial aid for U.S. undergraduates.

**STUDENT EMPLOYMENT.** College Work/Study Program. Institutional employment.

**COMPUTER FACILITIES.** 963 IBM/IBM-compatible, Macintosh/Apple, and RISC-/UNIX-based microcomputers. Students may access Internet. Computer languages and software packages include APL, BASIC, COBOL, FORTRAN, MINITAB, WordPerfect.
**Fees:** None.

**PROMINENT ALUMNI/AE.** Steve McLean, Canada's first astronaut; Jerome Ch'en, East Asian studies specialist.

# General Index

## Key to the General Index—

**Competitiveness:** 1 is Most competitive, 2 is Highly competitive, 3 is More competitive, 4 is Competitive, 5 is Less competitive, 6 is Noncompetitive.

**SAT/ACT range:** 1 is combined SAT of 1400 or more or composite ACT of 32 or more. 2 is combined SAT of between 1300 and 1400 or composite ACT of 30 or 31. 3 is combined SAT of between 1200 and 1299 or composite ACT of 28 or 29. 4 is combined SAT of between 1100 and 1199 or composite ACT of 26 or 27. 5 is combined SAT of between 1000 and 1099 or composite ACT of 24 or 25. 6 is combined SAT of between 900 and 999 or composite ACT of 22 or 23. 7 is combined SAT of between 800 and 899 or composite ACT of 20 or 21. 8 is combined SAT of between 700 and 799 or composite ACT of 18 or 19. 9 is combined SAT of less than 700 or composite ACT of less than 19.

**Tuition:** 1 is over $10,000; 2 is between $7,000 and $9,999; 3 is between $4,000 and $6,999; 4 is less than $4,000; 5 is no tuition for state residents; 6 is no tuition for any student.

**Enrollment:** 1 is over 20,000 students, 2 is between 12,000 and 19,999, 3 is between 4,000 and 11,999, 4 is less than 4,000.

**Religious affiliation:** AM is African Methodist Episcopal, AD is Adventist, AG is Assembly of God, B is Baptist, CC is Church of Christ, CM is Christian and Missionary Alliance, CS is Christian Science, CG is Church of God, CN is Church of the Nazarene, C is Congregational, DC is Disciples of Christ, EP is Episcopal, J is Jewish, L is Lutheran, MN is Mennonite, MT is Methodist, MV is Moravian, MM is Mormon, P is Presbyterian, Q is Quaker (Society of Friends), R is Reformed, RC is Roman Catholic, S is Swedenborgian, W is Wesleyan, OC is other Christian, ID is interdenominational, ND is nondenominational.

**Phi Beta Kappa:** (*) indicates participation in Phi Beta Kappa.

**Military training:** A is Army ROTC, AF is Air Force ROTC, N is Navy ROTC.

| | Selectivity | SAT/ACT | Tuition | Enrollment | Religious affiliation | Military training | Phi Beta Kappa |
|---|---|---|---|---|---|---|---|
| **Alabama** | | | | | | | |
| Alabama A&M U | 5 | 9 | 4 | 4 | | A | |
| Alabama St U | 6 | 9 | 4 | 3 | | A, AF | |
| Alabama, U of, Birmingham | 5 | 7 | 4 | 3 | | A, AF | |
| Alabama, U of, Huntsville | 5 | 6 | 4 | 4 | | A, AF | |
| Alabama, U of, Tuscaloosa | 5 | 6 | 4 | 2 | | A, AF | • |
| Auburn U | 4 | 5 | 4 | 2 | | A, AF, N | |
| Auburn U, Montgomery | N/A | N/A | 4 | 4 | | A, AF | |
| Birmingham-Southern Coll | 3 | 5 | 1 | 4 | MT | A, AF | • |
| Faulkner U | 5 | 9 | 3 | 4 | CC | | |
| Huntingdon Coll | 5 | 6 | 2 | 4 | MT | A, AF | |
| Jacksonville St U | 5 | 8 | 4 | 3 | | A | |
| Judson Coll | 5 | N/A | 3 | 4 | B | A | |
| Livingston U | 5 | 8 | 4 | 4 | | | |
| Mobile, U of | 4 | 7 | 3 | 4 | B | A, AF | |
| Montevallo, U of | 4 | 7 | 4 | 4 | | A, AF | |
| North Alabama, U of | 4 | 7 | 4 | 4 | | A | • |
| Oakwood Coll | 5 | 9 | 3 | 4 | AD | | |
| Samford U | 3 | 5 | 2 | 4 | B | A, AF | |
| South Alabama, U of | 5 | 6 | 4 | 3 | | A, AF | |
| Southeastern Bible Coll | 5 | 7 | 3 | 4 | ID | | |
| Spring Hill Coll | 4 | 5 | 1 | 4 | RC | A, AF | |
| Stillman Coll | 5 | 9 | 3 | 4 | P | A | |
| Talladega Coll | 5 | 9 | 3 | 4 | C | A | |
| Troy St U | 5 | 7 | 4 | 3 | | AF | |
| Tuskegee U | 5 | 7 | 3 | 4 | | A, AF | |
| **Alaska** | | | | | | | |
| Alaska Pacific U | 4 | 7 | 2 | 4 | MT | | |
| Alaska Southeast, U of, Juneau Campus | N/A | N/A | 4 | 4 | | | |
| Alaska, U of, Anchorage | N/A | N/A | 4 | 3 | | | |
| Alaska, U of, Fairbanks | 5 | 7 | 4 | 4 | | A | |
| Sheldon Jackson Coll | 6 | 7 | 2 | 4 | P | | |
| **Arizona** | | | | | | | |
| Arizona Coll of the Bible | 5 | N/A | 3 | 4 | ND | | |
| Arizona St U - Main Campus | 5 | 6 | 4 | 1 | | A, AF | • |
| Arizona, U of | 5 | 6 | 4 | 1 | | A, AF, N | • |
| DeVry Inst of Tech | N/A | N/A | 3 | 4 | | | |

| | Selectivity | SAT/ACT | Tuition | Enrollment | Religious affiliation | Military training | Phi Beta Kappa |
|---|---|---|---|---|---|---|---|
| Embry-Riddle Aeronautical U | 4 | 5 | 2 | 4 | | A, AF | • |
| Grand Canyon U | N/A | N/A | 2 | 4 | B | A, AF | |
| Northern Arizona U | 4 | 7 | 4 | 3 | | A, AF | |
| Prescott Coll | N/A | N/A | 2 | 4 | | | |
| Western International U | N/A | N/A | 3 | 4 | | | |
| **Arkansas** | | | | | | | |
| Arkansas St U | 6 | 7 | 4 | 3 | | A | |
| Arkansas Tech U | 6 | 8 | 4 | 4 | | | |
| Arkansas, U of, Fayetteville | 5 | 6 | 4 | 3 | | A, AF | • |
| Arkansas, U of, Little Rock | 5 | 8 | 4 | 3 | | A | |
| Arkansas, U of, Monticello | 5 | 9 | 4 | 4 | | | |
| Arkansas, U of, Pine Bluff | N/A | N/A | 4 | 4 | | A | |
| Central Arkansas, U of | 5 | 6 | 4 | 3 | | A | |
| Harding U | 3 | 5 | 3 | 4 | | A | |
| Henderson St U | 5 | 7 | 4 | 4 | | | |
| Hendrix Coll | 2 | 5 | 2 | 4 | MT | A | |
| John Brown U | 5 | 6 | 3 | 4 | ND | A | |
| Lyon Coll | 3 | 5 | 2 | 4 | P | | |
| Ouachita Baptist U | 5 | 6 | 3 | 4 | B | | |
| Ozarks, U of the | 6 | 7 | 3 | 4 | | A | |
| Southern Arkansas U - Magnolia | 5 | 7 | 4 | 4 | | | |
| Williams Baptist Coll | 5 | 8 | 4 | 4 | B | | |
| **California** | | | | | | | |
| Acad of Art Coll | N/A | N/A | 2 | 4 | | | |
| Art Center Coll of Design | 4 | 5 | 1 | 4 | | | |
| Azusa Pacific U | 5 | 6 | 1 | 4 | ND | A | |
| Biola U | 5 | 6 | 1 | 4 | ND | A, AF, N | |
| California Baptist Coll | 4 | 7 | 2 | 4 | B | A | |
| California Coll of Arts & Crafts | 5 | 6 | 1 | 4 | | | |
| California Inst of Tech | 1 | 1 | 1 | 4 | | A, AF | |
| California Inst of the Arts | N/A | N/A | 1 | 4 | | | |
| California Lutheran U | 5 | 6 | 1 | 4 | L | A, AF | |
| California Maritime Acad | 4 | 6 | 4 | 4 | | N | |
| California Polytechnic St U, San Luis Obispo | 4 | 5 | 5 | 2 | | A | |
| California St Polytechnic U, Pomona | 4 | 7 | 5 | 3 | | A | |
| California St U, Bakersfield | 4 | 7 | 5 | 4 | | | |
| California St U, Chico | 5 | 7 | 5 | 3 | | | • |
| California St U, Dominguez Hills | N/A | N/A | 5 | 3 | | A, AF | |
| California St U, Fresno | 4 | 7 | 5 | 2 | | A, AF | • |
| California St U, Fullerton | 5 | 7 | 5 | 2 | | A | |
| California St U, Hayward | N/A | N/A | 5 | 3 | | A, AF, N | |
| California St U, Long Beach | 5 | 7 | 5 | 2 | | A | • |
| California St U, Northridge | 5 | 7 | 5 | 2 | | A, AF | |
| California St U, Sacramento | 5 | 7 | 5 | 2 | | A, AF | • |
| California St U, San Bernardino | N/A | N/A | 5 | 3 | | A, AF | |
| California St U, Stanislaus | 4 | 7 | 5 | 4 | | | |
| California, U of, Berkeley | 2 | 3 | 5 | 1 | | A, AF, N | • |
| California, U of, Davis | 3 | 5 | 5 | 2 | | A | • |
| California, U of, Irvine | 4 | 5 | 5 | 2 | | A, AF, N | • |
| California, U of, Los Angeles | 3 | 4 | 5 | 1 | | A, AF, N | • |
| California, U of, Riverside | 5 | 6 | 5 | 3 | | A, AF | • |
| California, U of, San Diego | 3 | 4 | 5 | 2 | | | • |
| California, U of, Santa Barbara | 4 | 5 | 5 | 2 | | A | • |
| California, U of, Santa Cruz | 2 | 5 | 5 | 3 | | | • |
| Chapman U | 5 | 6 | 1 | 4 | DC | A, AF | |

| | Selectivity | SAT/ACT | Tuition | Enrollment | Religious affiliation | Military training | Phi Beta Kappa |
|---|---|---|---|---|---|---|---|
| Christian Heritage Coll | N/A | N/A | 2 | 4 | ND | A, AF, N | |
| Claremont McKenna Coll | 1 | 3 | 1 | 4 | | A, AF, N | • |
| Cogswell Polytechnical Coll | N/A | N/A | 3 | 4 | | | |
| Concordia U | 5 | 6 | 1 | 4 | L | | |
| DeVry Inst of Tech | N/A | N/A | 3 | 4 | | | |
| Dominican Coll of San Rafael | 5 | 7 | 1 | 4 | RC | AF | |
| Fresno Pacific Coll | 3 | 5 | 2 | 4 | MN | | |
| Golden Gate U | N/A | N/A | 3 | 4 | | AF | |
| Harvey Mudd Coll | 1 | 2 | 1 | 4 | | A, AF | |
| Holy Names Coll | 5 | 7 | 1 | 4 | RC | A, AF | |
| Humphreys Coll | N/A | N/A | 3 | 4 | | | |
| John F. Kennedy U | N/A | N/A | 2 | 4 | | | |
| Judaism, U of, Lee Coll | 3 | 4 | 1 | 4 | J | | |
| LaSierra U | 5 | 7 | 1 | 4 | AD | | |
| LaVerne, U of | 4 | 7 | 1 | 4 | | | |
| Loma Linda U | N/A | N/A | 1 | 4 | O | | |
| Loyola Marymount U | 4 | 5 | 1 | 4 | RC | A, AF, N | |
| Master's Coll | 5 | 6 | 2 | 4 | ND | | |
| Menlo Coll | 6 | 7 | 1 | 4 | | A | |
| Mills Coll | 3 | 5 | 1 | 4 | | | • |
| Mt St. Mary's Coll | 5 | 6 | 1 | 4 | RC | A, AF, N | |
| New Coll of California | N/A | N/A | 4 | 4 | | | |
| Northrop-Rice Aviation Inst of Tech | N/A | N/A | 2 | 4 | | | |
| Notre Dame, Coll of | 4 | 7 | 1 | 4 | RC | A, AF, N | |
| Occidental Coll | 2 | 4 | 1 | 4 | | A, AF | • |
| Otis Coll of Art & Design | 4 | 7 | 1 | 4 | | | |
| Pacific Christian Coll | 5 | 6 | 3 | 4 | CC | | |
| Pacific Union Coll | 5 | 7 | 1 | 4 | AD | | |
| Pacific, U of the | 5 | 6 | 1 | 4 | MT | AF | |
| Patten Coll | N/A | N/A | 3 | 4 | OC | | |
| Pepperdine U | 3 | 5 | 1 | 4 | CC | A, AF | |
| Pitzer Coll | 2 | 4 | 1 | 4 | | | • |
| Point Loma Nazarene Coll | 5 | 7 | 2 | 4 | CN | A, AF, N | |
| Pomona Coll | 1 | 2 | 1 | 4 | | | • |
| Redlands, U of | 3 | 5 | 1 | 4 | B | A, AF | • |
| Samuel Merritt Coll | 4 | 6 | 1 | 4 | | A, AF, N | |
| San Diego St U | 5 | 7 | 5 | 2 | | A, AF, N | • |
| San Diego, U of | 5 | 6 | 1 | 4 | RC | A, AF, N | |
| San Francisco Art Inst | N/A | N/A | 1 | 4 | | | |
| San Francisco Conservatory of Music | N/A | 5 | 1 | 4 | | | |
| San Francisco St U | 5 | 7 | 5 | 2 | | AF | • |
| San Francisco, U of | 5 | 6 | 1 | 4 | RC | A, AF | |
| San Jose St U | 6 | 7 | 5 | 2 | | A, AF, N | |
| Santa Clara U | 4 | 5 | 1 | 4 | RC | A, AF, N | • |
| Scripps Coll | 2 | 4 | 1 | 4 | | A, AF | • |
| Simpson Coll | N/A | N/A | 3 | 4 | CM | | |
| Sonoma St U | 5 | 6 | 4 | 3 | | | • |
| Southern California Coll | 4 | 7 | 2 | 4 | AG | | |
| Southern California Inst of Architecture | N/A | N/A | 1 | 4 | | | |
| Southern California, U of | 2 | 4 | 1 | 2 | | A, AF, N | • |
| St. Mary's Coll | 3 | 5 | 1 | 4 | RC | A, AF, N | |
| Stanford U | 1 | 2 | 1 | 3 | | A, AF, N | • |
| Thomas Aquinas Coll | 3 | 4 | 1 | 4 | RC | | |
| U.S. International U | 5 | 7 | 1 | 4 | | A | |
| West Coast U | N/A | N/A | 2 | 4 | | | |
| Westmont Coll | 4 | 5 | 1 | 4 | | A | |

| | Selectivity | SAT/ACT | Tuition | Enrollment | Religious affiliation | Military training | Phi Beta Kappa |
|---|---|---|---|---|---|---|---|
| Whittier Coll | 4 | 6 | 1 | 4 | | A, AF | |
| Woodbury U | 5 | 7 | 1 | 4 | | | |

## Colorado

| | Selectivity | SAT/ACT | Tuition | Enrollment | Religious affiliation | Military training | Phi Beta Kappa |
|---|---|---|---|---|---|---|---|
| Adams St Coll | 4 | 7 | 4 | 4 | | | |
| Colorado Christian U | 6 | 7 | 3 | 4 | ND | A, AF | |
| Colorado Coll | 2 | 4 | 1 | 4 | | A | • |
| Colorado Sch of Mines | 2 | 3 | 3 | 4 | | A, AF | |
| Colorado St U | 4 | 5 | 4 | 2 | | A, AF | • |
| Colorado Tech | 3 | 4 | 3 | 4 | | A | |
| Colorado, U of, Boulder | 4 | 5 | 4 | 2 | | A, AF, N | • |
| Colorado, U of, Colorado Springs | 5 | 6 | 4 | 4 | | A | |
| Colorado, U of, Denver | 4 | 6 | 4 | 4 | | A, AF | • |
| Denver, U of | 4 | 5 | 1 | 4 | ID | A, AF | • |
| Fort Lewis Coll | 4 | 7 | 4 | 4 | | | |
| Mesa St Coll | 6 | 8 | 4 | 4 | | | |
| Metropolitan St Coll of Denver | 5 | 7 | 4 | 3 | | A, AF | |
| Northern Colorado, U of | 5 | 6 | 4 | 3 | | A, AF | |
| Regis U | 5 | 6 | 1 | 4 | RC | A, AF | |
| Southern Colorado, U of | 6 | 7 | 4 | 4 | | | |
| U.S. Air Force Acad | 1 | 3 | 6 | 3 | | | |
| Western St Coll of Colorado | 5 | 7 | 4 | 4 | | | |

## Connecticut

| | Selectivity | SAT/ACT | Tuition | Enrollment | Religious affiliation | Military training | Phi Beta Kappa |
|---|---|---|---|---|---|---|---|
| Albertus Magnus Coll | 5 | 7 | 1 | 4 | RC | | |
| Bridgeport, U of | 5 | 6 | 1 | 4 | | A | |
| Central Connecticut St U | 5 | 7 | 4 | 3 | | A, AF | |
| Connecticut Coll | 2 | 3 | 1 | 4 | | | • |
| Connecticut, U of | 4 | 5 | 4 | 3 | | A, AF | • |
| Eastern Connecticut St U | 5 | 9 | 4 | 4 | | A, AF | |
| Fairfield U | 4 | 5 | 1 | 4 | RC | | |
| Hartford, U of | 5 | 6 | 1 | 4 | | A, AF | |
| New Haven, U of | 5 | 6 | 1 | 4 | | AF | |
| Quinnipiac Coll | 3 | 5 | 1 | 4 | | AF | |
| Southern Connecticut St U | 5 | 6 | 4 | 3 | | A, AF | |
| St. Joseph Coll | 4 | 7 | 1 | 4 | RC | A | |
| Teikyo Post U | N/A | N/A | 1 | 4 | | A | • |
| Trinity Coll | 2 | 4 | 1 | 4 | | A | • |
| U.S. Coast Guard Acad | 2 | 4 | 6 | 4 | | | |
| Wesleyan U | 2 | 3 | 1 | 4 | | A, AF, N | • |
| Yale U | 1 | 2 | 1 | 3 | | A, AF | • |

## Delaware

| | Selectivity | SAT/ACT | Tuition | Enrollment | Religious affiliation | Military training | Phi Beta Kappa |
|---|---|---|---|---|---|---|---|
| Delaware St Coll | N/A | N/A | 4 | 4 | | A, AF | |
| Delaware, U of | 4 | 5 | 4 | 2 | | A, AF | • |
| Goldey-Beacom Coll | 5 | 7 | 3 | 4 | | | |
| Wesley Coll | 5 | 7 | 2 | 4 | MT | | |
| Wilmington Coll | N/A | N/A | 3 | 4 | | A, AF | |

## District of Columbia

| | Selectivity | SAT/ACT | Tuition | Enrollment | Religious affiliation | Military training | Phi Beta Kappa |
|---|---|---|---|---|---|---|---|
| American U | 3 | 4 | 1 | 3 | MT | A, AF, N | |
| Catholic U of America | 4 | 5 | 1 | 4 | RC | A, AF, N | • |
| Corcoran Sch of Art | 4 | 6 | 1 | 4 | | | |
| District of Columbia, U of the | N/A | N/A | 4 | 4 | | A, AF, N | |
| Gallaudet U | N/A | N/A | 3 | 4 | | | |
| George Washington U | 3 | 4 | 1 | 3 | | A, AF, N | • |
| Georgetown U | 1 | 3 | 1 | 3 | RC | A, AF, N | • |
| Howard U | 5 | 7 | 2 | 3 | | A, AF | • |

| | Selectivity | SAT/ACT | Tuition | Enrollment | Religious affiliation | Military training | Phi Beta Kappa |
|---|---|---|---|---|---|---|---|
| Trinity Coll | 3 | 5 | 1 | 4 | RC | A, AF, N | • |
| **Florida** | | | | | | | |
| Barry U | 5 | 6 | 1 | 4 | RC | A, AF | |
| Bethune-Cookman Coll | 5 | 8 | 3 | 4 | MT | A, AF | |
| Central Florida, U of | 4 | 6 | 4 | 2 | | A, AF | |
| Eckerd Coll | 4 | 5 | 1 | 4 | P | A, AF | |
| Embry-Riddle Aeronautical U | 5 | 6 | 2 | 4 | | A, AF | • |
| Flagler Coll | 4 | 6 | 3 | 4 | | | |
| Florida A&M U | 5 | 7 | 4 | 3 | | A, AF, N | |
| Florida Atlantic U | 5 | 6 | 4 | 3 | | | |
| Florida Baptist Theological Coll | N/A | N/A | 4 | 4 | B | | |
| Florida Inst of Tech | 3 | 5 | 1 | 4 | | A | |
| Florida International U | 3 | 5 | 4 | 3 | | A, AF | |
| Florida Southern Coll | 4 | 5 | 2 | 4 | MT | A, AF | |
| Florida St U | 4 | 5 | 4 | 2 | | A, AF, N | • |
| Florida, U of | 2 | 4 | 4 | 1 | | A, AF, N | • |
| Jacksonville U | 5 | 6 | 2 | 4 | | A, N | |
| Lynn U | 5 | 6 | 1 | 4 | | | |
| Miami, U of | 4 | 5 | 1 | 3 | | A, AF | • |
| New Coll of the U of South Florida | 2 | 3 | 4 | 4 | | A, AF | |
| Nova Southeastern U | 5 | 6 | 2 | 4 | | | |
| Palm Beach Atlantic Coll | 4 | 6 | 2 | 4 | B | | |
| Ringling Sch of Art and Design | N/A | N/A | 1 | 4 | | | |
| Rollins Coll | 4 | 5 | 1 | 4 | | | |
| South Florida, U of | 4 | 5 | 4 | 1 | | A, AF | |
| Southeastern Coll of the Assemblies of God | N/A | N/A | 4 | 4 | AG | A | |
| St. Leo Coll | 5 | 7 | 2 | 4 | RC | A, AF | |
| St. Thomas U | 5 | 7 | 2 | 4 | RC | | |
| Stetson U | 4 | 5 | 1 | 4 | B | A | • |
| Tampa, U of | 5 | 7 | 1 | 4 | | A, AF | |
| Trinity C at Miami | 6 | 9 | 3 | 4 | | | |
| Warner Southern Coll | 5 | 8 | 3 | 4 | CG | | |
| Webber Coll | 5 | 7 | 3 | 4 | | | |
| West Florida, U of | 5 | 6 | 4 | 4 | | A | |
| **Georgia** | | | | | | | |
| Agnes Scott Coll | 3 | 5 | 1 | 4 | P | AF, N | • |
| Albany St Coll | 5 | N/A | 4 | 4 | | A | |
| American Coll for the Applied Arts | N/A | N/A | 2 | 4 | | | |
| Armstrong St Coll | N/A | N/A | 4 | 3 | | A, N | |
| Atlanta Coll of Art | 5 | 6 | 2 | 4 | | | |
| Augusta Coll | 5 | 6 | 4 | 4 | | A | • |
| Brenau U | 5 | 6 | 2 | 4 | | A | |
| Brewton-Parker Coll | 5 | 8 | 3 | 4 | | | |
| Clark Atlanta U | N/A | N/A | 1 | 4 | MT | A, AF, N | |
| Clayton St Coll | 5 | 8 | 4 | 4 | | | • |
| Columbus Coll | 6 | 7 | 4 | 4 | | A | |
| Covenant Coll | 4 | 5 | 2 | 4 | P | A | |
| DeVry Inst of Tech | N/A | N/A | 3 | 4 | | | |
| Emory U | 2 | 3 | 1 | 3 | MT | | • |
| Georgia Coll | 5 | 6 | 4 | 4 | | A | |
| Georgia Inst of Tech | 2 | 3 | 4 | 3 | | A, AF, N | |
| Georgia Southern U | 5 | 6 | 4 | 3 | | A | • |
| Georgia Southwestern Coll | 6 | 7 | 4 | 4 | | A | |
| Georgia St U | 4 | 6 | 4 | 3 | | A, AF, N | |
| Georgia, U of | 3 | 5 | 4 | 2 | | A, AF | • |

| | Selectivity | SAT/ACT | Tuition | Enrollment | Religious affiliation | Military training | Phi Beta Kappa |
|---|---|---|---|---|---|---|---|
| Kennesaw St Coll | 5 | 6 | 4 | 3 | | A | |
| LaGrange Coll | 5 | 8 | 2 | 4 | MT | | • |
| Life Coll | N/A | N/A | 1 | 4 | | | |
| Medical Coll of Georgia | N/A | N/A | 4 | 4 | | | |
| Mercer U | 4 | 5 | 1 | 4 | B | A | |
| Morehouse Coll | 3 | 5 | 3 | 4 | | A, AF, N | • |
| Morris Brown Coll | 6 | 8 | 3 | 4 | AM | A, AF, N | |
| North Georgia Coll | 5 | 6 | 4 | 4 | | A | • |
| Oglethorpe U | 2 | 4 | 1 | 4 | | A, AF | |
| Paine Coll | 5 | 9 | 3 | 4 | MT | A | |
| Piedmont Coll | 5 | 6 | 3 | 4 | C | | |
| Savannah Coll of Art & Design | 4 | 6 | 2 | 4 | | | |
| Savannah St Coll | 6 | 8 | 4 | 4 | | A, N | |
| Southern Coll of Tech | 5 | 6 | 4 | 4 | | A, AF, N | |
| Spelman Coll | 3 | 5 | 3 | 4 | | A, AF, N | |
| Toccoa Falls Coll | 5 | 7 | 3 | 4 | | | • |
| Valdosta St Coll | 5 | 7 | 4 | 3 | | AF | |
| Wesleyan Coll | 5 | 6 | 1 | 4 | MT | | |
| West Georgia Coll | 5 | 7 | 4 | 3 | | A | • |

## Hawaii

| | Selectivity | SAT/ACT | Tuition | Enrollment | Religious affiliation | Military training | Phi Beta Kappa |
|---|---|---|---|---|---|---|---|
| Brigham Young U, Hawaii Campus | 4 | 7 | 4 | 4 | MM | A, AF | |
| Chaminade U of Honolulu | 5 | 7 | 1 | 4 | RC | A, AF | |
| Hawaii Pacific U | 4 | 5 | 3 | 3 | | A, AF | |
| Hawaii, U of, Hilo | 4 | 7 | 4 | 4 | | | |
| Hawaii, U of, Manoa | 5 | 6 | 4 | 3 | | A, AF | • |

## Idaho

| | Selectivity | SAT/ACT | Tuition | Enrollment | Religious affiliation | Military training | Phi Beta Kappa |
|---|---|---|---|---|---|---|---|
| Albertson Coll | 4 | 5 | 1 | 4 | | | |
| Boise St U | 5 | 7 | 5 | 3 | | A | |
| Idaho St U | 5 | 7 | 5 | 3 | | | |
| Idaho, U of | 5 | 6 | 5 | 3 | | A, AF, N | |
| Lewis-Clark St Coll | N/A | N/A | 4 | 4 | | A | |

## Illinois

| | Selectivity | SAT/ACT | Tuition | Enrollment | Religious affiliation | Military training | Phi Beta Kappa |
|---|---|---|---|---|---|---|---|
| American Cons of Music | N/A | N/A | 3 | 4 | | | |
| Art Inst of Chicago, Sch of the | N/A | N/A | 1 | 4 | | | |
| Augustana Coll | 4 | 5 | 1 | 4 | L | | • |
| Aurora U | 5 | 7 | 1 | 4 | | A | |
| Barat Coll | 6 | 7 | 1 | 4 | RC | | |
| Blackburn Coll | 4 | 7 | 2 | 4 | P | | |
| Bradley U | 4 | 5 | 1 | 3 | | | |
| Chicago St U | 5 | 9 | 4 | 3 | | A, AF | • |
| Chicago, U of | 1 | 2 | 1 | 4 | | A, AF | • |
| Columbia Coll | N/A | N/A | 3 | 3 | | | |
| Concordia U | 5 | 6 | 2 | 4 | L | | |
| DePaul U | 4 | 5 | 1 | 3 | RC | A | |
| DeVry Inst of Tech (Addison) | N/A | N/A | 3 | 4 | | A | |
| DeVry Inst of Tech (Chicago) | N/A | N/A | 3 | 4 | | | |
| East-West U | N/A | N/A | 3 | 4 | | | |
| Eastern Illinois U | 5 | 6 | 4 | 3 | | A | |
| Elmhurst Coll | 4 | 7 | 2 | 4 | C | A, AF | |
| Eureka Coll | 5 | 6 | 1 | 4 | DC | | |
| Greenville Coll | 4 | 6 | 2 | 4 | MT | | |
| Illinois Benedictine Coll | 5 | 6 | 1 | 4 | RC | A, AF, N | |
| Illinois Coll | 5 | 6 | 2 | 4 | OC | | • |
| Illinois Inst of Tech | 3 | 5 | 1 | 4 | | A, AF, N | |
| Illinois St U | 5 | 6 | 4 | 2 | | A | |

| | Selectivity | SAT/ACT | Tuition | Enrollment | Religious affiliation | Military training | Phi Beta Kappa |
|---|---|---|---|---|---|---|---|
| Illinois Wesleyan U | 2 | 4 | 1 | 4 | | A | |
| Illinois, U of, Chicago | 4 | 7 | 4 | 2 | | A, AF, N | • |
| Illinois, U of, Urbana-Champaign | 2 | 4 | 4 | 1 | | A, AF, N | • |
| International Acad for Merchandising and Design | N/A | N/A | 2 | 4 | | | |
| Judson Coll | 4 | 7 | 2 | 4 | B | A | |
| Kendall Coll | 5 | 9 | 2 | 4 | | | • |
| Knox Coll | 3 | 5 | 1 | 4 | | | • |
| Lake Forest Coll | 3 | 5 | 1 | 4 | P | | • |
| Lewis U | 5 | 7 | 2 | 4 | RC | A, AF, N | |
| Loyola U, Chicago | 4 | 5 | 1 | 3 | RC | A, AF, N | |
| MacMurray Coll | 5 | 7 | 2 | 4 | MT | | |
| McKendree Coll | 4 | 7 | 2 | 4 | MT | AF | |
| Millikin U | 4 | 5 | 1 | 4 | P | | |
| Monmouth Coll | 5 | 6 | 1 | 4 | P | A | |
| Moody Bible Inst | 5 | 6 | 6 | 4 | | | |
| National-Louis U | 5 | 8 | 2 | 4 | | | |
| North Central Coll | 4 | 5 | 1 | 4 | MT | A, AF, N | |
| North Park Coll | 5 | 6 | 1 | 4 | EV | AF | • |
| Northeastern Illinois U | 5 | 9 | 4 | 3 | | A, AF | • |
| Northern Illinois U | 5 | 6 | 4 | 2 | | A, AF | |
| Northwestern U | 1 | 3 | 1 | 3 | | A, AF, N | • |
| Olivet Nazarene U | 5 | 6 | 2 | 4 | CN | A | |
| Parks Coll of St. Louis U | 5 | 6 | 2 | 4 | RC | A, AF, N | |
| Principia Coll | 4 | 5 | 1 | 4 | CS | | |
| Quincy U | 5 | 6 | 1 | 4 | RC | | |
| Rockford Coll | 4 | 7 | 1 | 4 | | A | • |
| Roosevelt U | 5 | 7 | 3 | 4 | | | |
| Rosary Coll | 5 | 6 | 1 | 4 | RC | | |
| Southern Illinois U, Carbondale | 4 | 6 | 4 | 2 | | A, AF | |
| Southern Illinois U, Edwardsville | 4 | 7 | 4 | 3 | | A, AF | |
| St. Francis, Coll of | 5 | 6 | 2 | 4 | RC | A | |
| St. Xavier U | 5 | 9 | 1 | 4 | RC | AF | |
| Trinity Christian Coll | 5 | 6 | 1 | 4 | | | |
| Trinity Coll | 5 | 6 | 1 | 4 | EV | | |
| VanderCook Coll of Music | 5 | 7 | 2 | 4 | | | |
| Western Illinois U | 4 | 7 | 4 | 3 | | A | |
| Wheaton Coll | 2 | 4 | 1 | 4 | ND | A | |

## Indiana

| | Selectivity | SAT/ACT | Tuition | Enrollment | Religious affiliation | Military training | Phi Beta Kappa |
|---|---|---|---|---|---|---|---|
| Anderson U | 4 | 7 | 1 | 4 | CG | | |
| Ball St U | 5 | 7 | 4 | 2 | | A | |
| Bethel Coll | 5 | 6 | 2 | 4 | OC | | |
| Butler U | 4 | 5 | 1 | 4 | | A, AF | |
| Calumet Coll of St. Joseph | 5 | 9 | 3 | 4 | RC | | |
| DePauw U | 3 | 4 | 1 | 4 | MT | A, AF | • |
| Earlham Coll | 4 | 5 | 1 | 4 | Q | | • |
| Evansville, U of | 4 | 5 | 1 | 4 | MT | | • |
| Franklin Coll | 5 | 6 | 1 | 4 | B | A | |
| Goshen Coll | 4 | 5 | 2 | 4 | MN | | |
| Grace Coll | 5 | 6 | 2 | 4 | CB | | |
| Hanover Coll | 4 | 5 | 2 | 4 | P | | |
| Huntington Coll | 5 | 6 | 2 | 4 | CB | | |
| Indiana Inst of Tech | 5 | 6 | 2 | 4 | | | |
| Indiana St U | 5 | 7 | 4 | 3 | | A, AF | |
| Indiana U Bloomington | 5 | 6 | 4 | 1 | | A, AF | • |
| Indiana U East | 6 | 8 | 4 | 4 | | | |

| | Selectivity | SAT/ACT | Tuition | Enrollment | Religious affiliation | Military training | Phi Beta Kappa |
|---|---|---|---|---|---|---|---|
| Indiana U Kokomo | 5 | 7 | 4 | 4 | | A | |
| Indiana U Northwest | N/A | N/A | 4 | 4 | | A | |
| Indiana U Purdue U, Indianapolis | 5 | 7 | 4 | 3 | | A, AF, N | |
| Indiana U South Bend | 5 | 6 | 4 | 4 | | A, AF, N | |
| Indiana U-Purdue U, Fort Wayne | 5 | 7 | 4 | 3 | | | • |
| Indianapolis, U of | 5 | 6 | 1 | 4 | MT | A | |
| Manchester Coll | 5 | 6 | 1 | 4 | CB | | |
| Marian Coll | 4 | 7 | 2 | 4 | RC | AF | |
| Notre Dame, U of | 1 | 3 | 1 | 3 | RC | A, AF, N | • |
| Oakland City Coll | 6 | 8 | 2 | 4 | B | | |
| Purdue U | 5 | 6 | 4 | 1 | | A, AF, N | • |
| Purdue U - North Central | 5 | 6 | 4 | 4 | | | |
| Purdue U, Calumet | 5 | 6 | 4 | 4 | | A | |
| Rose-Hulman Inst of Tech | 2 | 3 | 1 | 4 | | A, AF | |
| Southern Indiana, U of | 4 | 7 | 4 | 3 | | | |
| St. Francis C | 4 | 7 | 2 | 4 | RC | | |
| St. Joseph's Coll | 5 | 6 | 1 | 4 | RC | | |
| St. Mary's Coll | 4 | 5 | 1 | 4 | RC | A, AF, N | |
| St. Mary-of-the-Woods Coll | 5 | 6 | 1 | 4 | ID | A | |
| Taylor U | 2 | 4 | 1 | 4 | | A, AF, N | |
| Taylor U, Fort Wayne Campus | 5 | 6 | 2 | 4 | | | |
| Tri-State U | 5 | 6 | 2 | 4 | | | |
| Valparaiso U | 2 | 4 | 1 | 4 | L | | |
| Wabash Coll | 2 | 4 | 1 | 4 | | | • |

## Iowa

| | Selectivity | SAT/ACT | Tuition | Enrollment | Religious affiliation | Military training | Phi Beta Kappa |
|---|---|---|---|---|---|---|---|
| Briar Cliff Coll | 5 | 6 | 1 | 4 | RC | | |
| Buena Vista Coll | 4 | 5 | 1 | 4 | P | | |
| Central Coll | 4 | 5 | 1 | 4 | R | | |
| Clarke Coll | 5 | 6 | 1 | 4 | RC | | |
| Coe Coll | 4 | 5 | 1 | 4 | P | A | • |
| Cornell Coll | 4 | 5 | 1 | 4 | MT | | • |
| Dordt Coll | 5 | 6 | 2 | 4 | R | | |
| Drake U | 4 | 5 | 1 | 4 | | A, AF | • |
| Dubuque, U of | 5 | 6 | 1 | 4 | P | | |
| Faith Baptist Bible Coll & Sem | 5 | 8 | 3 | 4 | B | | |
| Graceland Coll | 5 | 6 | 2 | 4 | MM | | |
| Grand View Coll | 5 | 7 | 2 | 4 | L | A, AF | |
| Grinnell Coll | 2 | 3 | 1 | 4 | | | • |
| Iowa St U | 4 | 5 | 4 | 2 | | A, AF, N | • |
| Iowa Wesleyan Coll | 4 | 7 | 1 | 4 | MT | | |
| Iowa, U of | 4 | 5 | 4 | 2 | | A, AF | • |
| Loras Coll | 5 | 6 | 1 | 4 | RC | | |
| Luther Coll | 3 | 5 | 1 | 4 | L | | • |
| Maharishi International U | 5 | 7 | 1 | 4 | | | |
| Morningside Coll | 5 | 6 | 1 | 4 | MT | | |
| Mt Mercy Coll | 5 | 6 | 2 | 4 | RC | | • |
| Mt St. Clare Coll | 6 | 7 | 2 | 4 | RC | | • |
| Northern Iowa, U of | 5 | 6 | 4 | 3 | | A | |
| Northwestern Coll | 5 | 6 | 2 | 4 | R | | |
| Simpson Coll | 4 | 5 | 1 | 4 | MT | | |
| St. Ambrose U | 5 | 7 | 1 | 4 | RC | A, AF, N | • |
| Teikyo Marycrest U | 6 | 7 | 2 | 4 | | | |
| Teikyo Westmar U | 5 | 6 | 1 | 4 | | | |
| Vennard Coll | 5 | 8 | 3 | 4 | | | |
| Wartburg Coll | 4 | 5 | 1 | 4 | L | | |

| | Selectivity | SAT/ACT | Tuition | Enrollment | Religious affiliation | Military training | Phi Beta Kappa |
|---|---|---|---|---|---|---|---|
| William Penn Coll | 5 | 7 | 2 | 4 | Q | | |
| **Kansas** | | | | | | | |
| Baker U | 5 | 6 | 2 | 4 | MT | A, AF | |
| Benedictine Coll | 5 | 6 | 2 | 4 | RC | A | |
| Bethany Coll | 5 | 6 | 2 | 4 | | | |
| Bethel Coll | 5 | 6 | 2 | 4 | MN | | |
| Emporia St U | 6 | N/A | 4 | 4 | | A | |
| Fort Hays St U | 6 | 7 | 4 | 4 | | A | |
| Kansas Newman Coll | 5 | 7 | 2 | 4 | RC | | |
| Kansas St U | 5 | 6 | 4 | 2 | | A, AF | • |
| Kansas Wesleyan U | 5 | 7 | 2 | 4 | MT | | |
| Kansas, U of | 4 | 6 | 4 | 2 | | A, AF, N | • |
| Manhattan Christian Coll | 5 | 6 | 3 | 4 | OC | | |
| McPherson Coll | 4 | 7 | 2 | 4 | CB | | |
| MidAmerica Nazarene Coll | N/A | N/A | 3 | 4 | CN | A, AF | |
| Ottawa U | 4 | 7 | 2 | 4 | B | | |
| Pittsburg St U | 5 | 7 | 4 | 3 | | A | • |
| Southwestern Coll | 4 | 6 | 3 | 4 | MT | | |
| St. Mary Coll | 4 | 7 | 2 | 4 | RC | A | |
| Tabor Coll | 4 | 6 | 2 | 4 | MN | | |
| Washburn U of Topeka | 4 | 6 | 4 | 4 | | A, AF | |
| Wichita St U | 5 | 7 | 4 | 3 | | | • |
| **Kentucky** | | | | | | | |
| Alice Lloyd Coll | 6 | 7 | 5 | 4 | | | |
| Asbury Coll | 5 | 6 | 2 | 4 | ND | | |
| Bellarmine Coll | 5 | 6 | 2 | 4 | RC | A, AF | |
| Berea Coll | 4 | 6 | 6 | 4 | | | |
| Brescia Coll | 5 | 6 | 2 | 4 | RC | | |
| Campbellsville Coll | 4 | 7 | 3 | 4 | B | | |
| Centre Coll | 2 | 4 | 1 | 4 | | A | • |
| Cumberland Coll | 4 | 7 | 3 | 4 | B | A | |
| Eastern Kentucky U | 6 | 8 | 4 | 3 | | A, AF | • |
| Georgetown Coll | 5 | 6 | 2 | 4 | B | A, AF | |
| Kentucky Christian C | 4 | 7 | 3 | 4 | CC | | |
| Kentucky St U | N/A | N/A | 4 | 4 | | A, AF | |
| Kentucky Wesleyan Coll | 5 | 6 | 2 | 4 | MT | | |
| Kentucky, U of | 4 | 5 | 4 | 2 | | A, AF | • |
| Lindsey Wilson Coll | 5 | 8 | 3 | 4 | ND | | |
| Louisville, U of | 5 | 8 | 4 | 3 | | A, AF | |
| Midway Coll | 5 | 7 | 2 | 4 | DC | | • |
| Morehead St U | 5 | 7 | 4 | 3 | | A | |
| Murray St U | 5 | 6 | 4 | 3 | | A | • |
| Northern Kentucky U | 6 | 8 | 4 | 3 | | A, AF | |
| Pikeville Coll | 5 | 7 | 3 | 4 | P | | |
| Spalding U | 4 | 7 | 2 | 4 | | A, AF | |
| Thomas More Coll | 4 | 7 | 2 | 4 | RC | A, AF | |
| Transylvania U | 2 | 4 | 1 | 4 | DC | A, AF | |
| Union Coll | 5 | 7 | 2 | 4 | ND | A | |
| Western Kentucky U | 5 | 7 | 4 | 3 | | A, AF | |
| **Louisiana** | | | | | | | |
| Centenary Coll of Louisiana | 4 | 5 | 2 | 4 | MT | A | |
| Dillard U | 5 | 8 | 3 | 4 | ID | A, AF | |
| Grambling St U | 5 | 9 | 4 | 3 | | A, AF | • |
| Louisiana Coll | 4 | 7 | 3 | 4 | B | | |
| Louisiana St U & A&M Coll | 5 | 6 | 4 | 2 | | A, AF, N | • |

| | Selectivity | SAT/ACT | Tuition | Enrollment | Religious affiliation | Military training | Phi Beta Kappa |
|---|---|---|---|---|---|---|---|
| Louisiana St U, Shreveport | 6 | 7 | 4 | 4 | | A | |
| Louisiana Tech U | 5 | 6 | 4 | 3 | | A, AF | • |
| Loyola U | 4 | 5 | 1 | 4 | RC | A, AF, N | |
| McNeese St U | 6 | 8 | 4 | 3 | | A | |
| New Orleans, U of | 5 | 7 | 4 | 3 | | A, AF | |
| Nicholls St U | 6 | 8 | 4 | 3 | | | |
| Northeast Louisiana U | 6 | 8 | 4 | 3 | | A | |
| Northwestern St U of Louisiana | 5 | 8 | 4 | 3 | | A | |
| Our Lady of Holy Cross Coll | N/A | N/A | 3 | 4 | RC | A | |
| Southeastern Louisiana U | 6 | 8 | 4 | 3 | | A | |
| Southern U at New Orleans | N/A | N/A | 4 | 4 | | A | |
| St. Joseph Seminary Coll | 5 | 7 | 3 | 4 | RC | | |
| Tulane U | 2 | 4 | 1 | 3 | | A, AF, N | • |
| Xavier U of Louisiana | 4 | 7 | 3 | 4 | RC | A, AF, N | |

## Maine

| | Selectivity | SAT/ACT | Tuition | Enrollment | Religious affiliation | Military training | Phi Beta Kappa |
|---|---|---|---|---|---|---|---|
| Atlantic, Coll of the | 3 | 4 | 1 | 4 | | | |
| Bates Coll | 2 | 3 | 1 | 4 | | | • |
| Bowdoin Coll | 1 | 3 | 1 | 4 | | A, AF, N | • |
| Colby Coll | 2 | 3 | 1 | 4 | | A | • |
| Husson Coll | 5 | 7 | 2 | 4 | | A, N | |
| Maine Coll of Art | 5 | 6 | 1 | 4 | | | |
| Maine Maritime Acad | N/A | N/A | 4 | 4 | | N | |
| Maine, U of | 5 | N/A | 4 | 3 | | A, AF, N | • |
| Maine, U of, Augusta | 5 | 7 | 4 | 4 | | | |
| Maine, U of, Farmington | 5 | 6 | 4 | 4 | | | |
| Maine, U of, Fort Kent | 4 | 7 | 4 | 4 | | | |
| Maine, U of, Machias | 5 | 6 | 4 | 4 | | | |
| Maine, U of, Presque Isle | 5 | 7 | 4 | 4 | | | |
| New England, U of | 4 | 7 | 1 | 4 | | | |
| Southern Maine, U of | 5 | 6 | 4 | 3 | | A | |
| St. Joseph's Coll | 5 | 7 | 2 | 4 | RC | A | |
| Thomas Coll | 4 | 7 | 2 | 4 | | A | |
| Unity Coll | 5 | 6 | 2 | 4 | | A | |
| Westbrook Coll | 4 | 7 | 1 | 4 | | | |

## Maryland

| | Selectivity | SAT/ACT | Tuition | Enrollment | Religious affiliation | Military training | Phi Beta Kappa |
|---|---|---|---|---|---|---|---|
| Bowie St U | 5 | 8 | 4 | 4 | | A, AF | • |
| Capitol Coll | 5 | 7 | 2 | 4 | | A | |
| Coppin St Coll | 5 | 8 | 4 | 4 | | A | |
| Frostburg St U | 5 | 6 | 4 | 3 | | A | |
| Goucher Coll | 3 | 4 | 1 | 4 | | A | |
| Hood Coll | 4 | 5 | 1 | 4 | C | A | |
| Johns Hopkins U | 1 | 3 | 1 | 4 | | A, AF | • |
| Loyola Coll | 4 | 5 | 1 | 4 | RC | A, AF | |
| Maryland Institute, Coll of Art | N/A | N/A | 1 | 4 | | | |
| Maryland, U of, Baltimore County | 4 | 5 | 4 | 3 | | A, AF | |
| Maryland, U of, College Park | 4 | 5 | 4 | 2 | | AF | • |
| Maryland, U of, Eastern Shore | 5 | 8 | 4 | 4 | | A | |
| Morgan St U | 5 | 7 | 4 | 3 | | A | |
| Mt St. Mary's Coll | 5 | 6 | 1 | 4 | RC | A | |
| Notre Dame of Maryland, Coll of | 5 | 6 | 1 | 4 | RC | A | |
| Salisbury St U | 3 | 5 | 4 | 3 | | A | |
| St. John's Coll | 2 | 3 | 1 | 4 | | | |
| St. Mary's Coll of Maryland | 2 | 4 | 3 | 4 | | | |
| Towson St U | 5 | 6 | 4 | 3 | | A, AF | • |
| U.S. Naval Acad | 2 | 3 | 6 | 3 | | | • |

| | Selectivity | SAT/ACT | Tuition | Enrollment | Religious affiliation | Military training | Phi Beta Kappa |
|---|---|---|---|---|---|---|---|
| Washington Bible Coll | N/A | N/A | 3 | 4 | | | |
| Washington Coll | 5 | 6 | 1 | 4 | | | |
| Western Maryland Coll | 4 | 5 | 1 | 4 | | A, AF | • |

## Massachusetts

| | Selectivity | SAT/ACT | Tuition | Enrollment | Religious affiliation | Military training | Phi Beta Kappa |
|---|---|---|---|---|---|---|---|
| American International Coll | 5 | 7 | 2 | 4 | | A, AF | |
| Amherst Coll | 1 | 2 | 1 | 4 | | | • |
| Anna Maria Coll | 5 | 7 | 1 | 4 | RC | A, AF, N | |
| Assumption Coll | 5 | 6 | 1 | 4 | RC | A, AF, N | |
| Atlantic Union Coll | 5 | 7 | 1 | 4 | AD | | |
| Babson Coll | 3 | 5 | 1 | 4 | | A | |
| Bay Path Coll | 5 | 8 | 2 | 4 | | A | |
| Bentley Coll | 5 | 6 | 1 | 4 | | A, AF | |
| Berklee Coll of Music | N/A | N/A | 1 | 4 | | | |
| Boston Architectural Center | N/A | N/A | 4 | 4 | | | |
| Boston Coll | 2 | 3 | 1 | 3 | RC | A, AF, N | • |
| Boston Conservatory | 5 | 6 | 1 | 4 | | | |
| Boston U | 2 | 4 | 1 | 2 | | A, AF, N | • |
| Bradford Coll | N/A | N/A | 1 | 4 | | | |
| Brandeis U | 1 | 3 | 1 | 4 | | A, AF | • |
| Clark U | 4 | 5 | 1 | 4 | | A, AF | • |
| Curry Coll | 5 | 8 | 1 | 4 | | A | |
| Eastern Nazarene Coll | 5 | 6 | 2 | 4 | CN | | |
| Elms Coll | 4 | 7 | 1 | 4 | RC | A, AF | • |
| Emerson Coll | 4 | 5 | 1 | 4 | | | |
| Emmanuel Coll | N/A | N/A | 1 | 4 | RC | A | |
| Endicott Coll | 5 | 8 | 1 | 4 | | | |
| Fitchburg St Coll | 5 | 7 | 4 | 4 | | A | |
| Framingham St Coll | 5 | 6 | 4 | 4 | | A | |
| Gordon Coll | 4 | 5 | 1 | 4 | ND | AF | • |
| Hampshire Coll | N/A | N/A | 1 | 4 | | A | |
| Harvard U | 1 | 2 | 1 | 3 | | A, AF, N | • |
| Hellenic Coll | N/A | N/A | 3 | 4 | O | | |
| Holy Cross, Coll of the | 1 | 3 | 1 | 4 | RC | A, AF, N | • |
| Lasell Coll | 5 | 9 | 1 | 4 | | | |
| Lesley Coll | 5 | 7 | 1 | 4 | | | |
| Massachusetts Coll of Art | 4 | 6 | 4 | 4 | | | |
| Massachusetts Inst of Tech | 1 | 2 | 1 | 3 | | A, AF, N | • |
| Massachusetts Maritime Acad | N/A | N/A | 4 | 4 | | | |
| Massachusetts, U of, Amherst | 5 | 6 | 4 | 2 | | A, AF | • |
| Massachusetts, U of, Boston | 5 | 7 | 4 | 3 | | | |
| Massachusetts, U of, Dartmouth | 5 | 6 | 4 | 3 | | A | |
| Massachusetts, U of, Lowell | 5 | 6 | 4 | 3 | | A, AF | |
| Merrimack Coll | 5 | 6 | 1 | 4 | RC | AF | |
| Mount Holyoke Coll | 2 | 4 | 1 | 4 | | A, AF | • |
| Mt Ida Coll | N/A | N/A | 1 | 4 | | | |
| Museum of Fine Arts, Sch of the | N/A | N/A | 1 | 4 | | | |
| New England Conservatory of Music | N/A | N/A | 1 | 4 | | | |
| Nichols Coll | 6 | 7 | 2 | 4 | | A | |
| North Adams St Coll | 5 | 7 | 4 | 4 | | | |
| Northeastern U | 5 | 6 | 1 | 3 | | A, AF, N | |
| Pine Manor Coll | 6 | 8 | 1 | 4 | | | |
| Regis Coll | 5 | 7 | 1 | 4 | RC | | |
| Salem St Coll | 5 | 7 | 4 | 3 | | | |
| Simmons Coll | 5 | 6 | 1 | 4 | | A | |
| Simon's Rock Coll of Bard | 3 | 4 | 1 | 4 | | | |

| | Selectivity | SAT/ACT | Tuition | Enrollment | Religious affiliation | Military training | Phi Beta Kappa |
|---|---|---|---|---|---|---|---|
| Smith Coll | 2 | 4 | 1 | 4 | | A, AF | • |
| Springfield Coll | 4 | 6 | 1 | 4 | | A, AF | • |
| Stonehill Coll | 4 | 5 | 1 | 4 | RC | A | |
| Suffolk U | 5 | 6 | 1 | 4 | | | • |
| Tufts U | 2 | 3 | 1 | 3 | | A, AF, N | • |
| Wellesley Coll | 1 | 3 | 1 | 4 | | A, AF | • |
| Wentworth Inst of Tech | 5 | 7 | 2 | 4 | | A, AF | |
| Western New England Coll | 5 | 7 | 2 | 4 | | A, AF | |
| Westfield St Coll | 4 | 7 | 4 | 4 | | A, AF, N | |
| Wheaton Coll | 4 | 5 | 1 | 4 | | | • |
| Wheelock Coll | 5 | 7 | 1 | 4 | | | |
| Williams Coll | 1 | 2 | 1 | 4 | | | • |
| Worcester Polytechnic Inst | 2 | 4 | 1 | 4 | | A, AF, N | |
| **Michigan** | | | | | | | |
| Adrian Coll | 5 | 6 | 1 | 4 | MT | A | |
| Albion Coll | 4 | 5 | 1 | 4 | MT | | • |
| Alma Coll | 2 | 4 | 1 | 4 | P | A | • |
| Andrews U | 5 | 8 | 2 | 4 | AD | | |
| Aquinas Coll | 5 | 6 | 1 | 4 | RC | | |
| Baker Coll | N/A | N/A | 3 | 4 | | | |
| Baker Coll of Muskegon | N/A | N/A | 3 | 4 | | | |
| Calvin Coll | 4 | 5 | 1 | 4 | R | | |
| Center for Creative Studies - Coll of Art & Design | 5 | 7 | 1 | 4 | | | |
| Central Michigan U | 5 | 7 | 4 | 2 | | A | |
| Cleary Coll | N/A | N/A | 3 | 4 | | A, AF | |
| Concordia Coll | 5 | 7 | 1 | 4 | L | A, AF | |
| Detroit Mercy, U of | 5 | 6 | 1 | 4 | RC | A | |
| Eastern Michigan U | 5 | 7 | 4 | 2 | | A, AF, N | • |
| Ferris St U | 6 | 8 | 4 | 3 | | A | • |
| GMI Engineering & Management Inst | 2 | 4 | 1 | 4 | | | |
| Grand Rapids Baptist Coll & Sem | 5 | 6 | 3 | 4 | B | A | |
| Grand Valley St U | 5 | 6 | 4 | 3 | | | |
| Hillsdale Coll | 3 | 5 | 1 | 4 | | A, AF, N | |
| Hope Coll | 4 | 5 | 1 | 4 | R | | • |
| Kalamazoo Coll | 2 | 4 | 1 | 4 | | A | • |
| Kendall Coll of Art & Design | N/A | 8 | 2 | 4 | | | |
| Lake Superior St U | 5 | 7 | 4 | 4 | | | • |
| Lawrence Tech U | 5 | 6 | 3 | 4 | | | |
| Marygrove Coll | N/A | N/A | 2 | 4 | RC | | |
| Michigan Christian Coll | 5 | 6 | 3 | 4 | OC | | |
| Michigan St U | 5 | 6 | 4 | 1 | | A, AF | • |
| Michigan Tech U | 2 | 4 | 4 | 3 | | A, AF | |
| Michigan, U of, Ann Arbor | 2 | 4 | 3 | 1 | | A, AF, N | • |
| Michigan, U of, Dearborn | 5 | 6 | 4 | 4 | | A, AF, N | • |
| Michigan, U of, Flint | 5 | 6 | 4 | 4 | | | |
| Northern Michigan U | 5 | 7 | 4 | 3 | | A | |
| Northwood U, Midland Campus | N/A | N/A | 2 | 4 | | | |
| Oakland U | 5 | 6 | 4 | 3 | | | |
| Olivet Coll | 5 | 8 | 1 | 4 | C | | |
| Saginaw Valley St U | 5 | 8 | 4 | 4 | | A | |
| Siena Heights Coll | 6 | 7 | 2 | 4 | RC | | |
| Spring Arbor C | 5 | 7 | 2 | 4 | MT | | |
| St. Mary's Coll | 6 | 8 | 3 | 4 | RC | | |
| Wayne St U | 5 | 7 | 4 | 3 | | A, AF | |
| Western Michigan U | 5 | 6 | 4 | 2 | | A | |

| | Selectivity | SAT/ACT | Tuition | Enrollment | Religious affiliation | Military training | Phi Beta Kappa |
|---|---|---|---|---|---|---|---|
| William Tyndale Coll | 4 | 7 | 3 | 4 | ND | | |
| **Minnesota** | | | | | | | |
| Augsburg Coll | 5 | 7 | 1 | 4 | L | A, AF, N | • |
| Bemidji St U | 5 | 7 | 4 | 4 | | | |
| Carleton Coll | 2 | 3 | 1 | 4 | | | • |
| Concordia Coll, Moorhead | 4 | 5 | 1 | 4 | L | A, AF | |
| Concordia Coll, St. Paul | 5 | 7 | 1 | 4 | L | A, AF, N | |
| Crown Coll | 5 | 7 | 2 | 4 | CM | | |
| Dr. Martin Luther Coll | 5 | 6 | 4 | 4 | L | | |
| Gustavus Adolphus Coll | 3 | 5 | 1 | 4 | L | A | • |
| Hamline U | 4 | 5 | 1 | 4 | MT | AF | • |
| Macalester Coll | 2 | 3 | 1 | 4 | P | AF, N | • |
| Mankato St U | 5 | 7 | 4 | 3 | | A | |
| Minneapolis Coll of Art & Design | 5 | 7 | 1 | 4 | | | |
| Minnesota, U of, Duluth | 5 | 6 | 4 | 3 | | A, AF | |
| Minnesota, U of, Morris | 2 | 4 | 4 | 4 | | | |
| Minnesota, U of, Twin Cities | 4 | 6 | 4 | 1 | | A, AF, N | • |
| Moorhead St U | 5 | 6 | 4 | 3 | | A, AF | • |
| North Central Bible Coll | 6 | 7 | 3 | 4 | AG | | |
| Northwestern Coll | 4 | 7 | 1 | 4 | ND | AF | |
| Southwest St U | N/A | N/A | 4 | 4 | | | |
| St. Benedict, Coll of | 5 | 6 | 1 | 4 | RC | A | |
| St. Catherine, The Coll of | 5 | 6 | 1 | 4 | RC | A | • |
| St. Cloud St U | 5 | 8 | 4 | 3 | | A | • |
| St. John's U | 5 | 6 | 1 | 4 | RC | A | |
| St. Mary's Coll of Minnesota | 5 | 7 | 1 | 4 | RC | | |
| St. Olaf Coll | 3 | 4 | 1 | 4 | L | | • |
| St. Scholastica, Coll of | 5 | 6 | 1 | 4 | RC | AF | |
| St. Thomas, U of | 5 | 6 | 1 | 3 | RC | AF, N | |
| Winona St U | 4 | 6 | 4 | 3 | | | |
| **Mississippi** | | | | | | | |
| Alcorn St U | 5 | 8 | 4 | 4 | | A | |
| Belhaven Coll | 5 | 6 | 2 | 4 | P | A | • |
| Delta St U | 5 | 7 | 4 | 4 | | A, AF | |
| Jackson St U | 5 | 9 | 4 | 3 | | A | • |
| Millsaps Coll | 3 | 4 | 1 | 4 | MT | A | • |
| Mississippi Coll | 5 | 6 | 3 | 4 | B | A | |
| Mississippi St U | 5 | 6 | 4 | 3 | | A, AF | |
| Mississippi U for Women | 5 | 7 | 4 | 4 | | A, AF | |
| Mississippi Valley St U | 5 | 9 | 4 | 4 | | A, AF | |
| Mississippi, U of | 5 | 6 | 4 | 3 | | A, AF, N | |
| Rust Coll | 5 | 9 | 3 | 4 | MT | | |
| Southern Mississippi, U of | 5 | 7 | 4 | 3 | | A, AF | |
| Tougaloo Coll | 5 | 8 | 3 | 4 | C | A | |
| **Missouri** | | | | | | | |
| Avila Coll | 4 | 7 | 2 | 4 | RC | A | |
| Calvary Bible Coll | 6 | 8 | 4 | 4 | ND | | |
| Central Bible Coll | 5 | 7 | 4 | 4 | AG | | |
| Central Methodist Coll | 5 | 7 | 2 | 4 | MT | A | |
| Central Missouri St U | 5 | 7 | 4 | 3 | | A | |
| Columbia Coll | 5 | N/A | 2 | 4 | ID | A, AF, N | |
| Conception Seminary Coll | 5 | 6 | 3 | 4 | RC | | |
| Culver-Stockton Coll | 5 | 6 | 2 | 4 | DC | | |
| DeVry Inst of Tech | N/A | N/A | 3 | 4 | | | |
| Drury Coll | 4 | 5 | 2 | 4 | | | |

| | Selectivity | SAT/ACT | Tuition | Enrollment | Religious affiliation | Military training | Phi Beta Kappa |
|---|---|---|---|---|---|---|---|
| Evangel Coll | 6 | 7 | 3 | 4 | AG | A | |
| Fontbonne Coll | 5 | 6 | 2 | 4 | RC | A | |
| Hannibal-LaGrange Coll | 6 | 7 | 3 | 4 | B | | |
| Lincoln U | 6 | 8 | 4 | 4 | | A | |
| Lindenwood Coll | 4 | 6 | 2 | 4 | P | A | |
| Maryville U of St. Louis | 4 | 5 | 2 | 4 | | A | |
| Missouri Baptist Coll | 5 | 7 | 3 | 4 | B | A | |
| Missouri Southern St Coll | 4 | 7 | 4 | 4 | | A | |
| Missouri Valley Coll | 5 | 8 | 2 | 4 | ND | | |
| Missouri Western St Coll | 6 | 8 | 4 | 4 | | A | |
| Missouri, U of, Columbia | 3 | 5 | 4 | 2 | | A, AF, N | • |
| Missouri, U of, Kansas City | 4 | 5 | 4 | 4 | | A | |
| Missouri, U of, Rolla | 2 | 4 | 4 | 4 | | A, AF | |
| Missouri, U of, St. Louis | 5 | 6 | 4 | 3 | | A, AF | |
| Northeast Missouri St U | 2 | 4 | 4 | 3 | | A | |
| Northwest Missouri St U | 5 | 7 | 4 | 3 | | A | |
| Ozarks, Coll of the | 4 | 7 | 6 | 4 | P | A | |
| Park Coll | 5 | 7 | 4 | 4 | MM | A | |
| Rockhurst Coll | 4 | 5 | 2 | 4 | RC | A | |
| Southeast Missouri St U | 4 | 6 | 4 | 3 | | A, AF | |
| Southwest Baptist U | 5 | 6 | 2 | 4 | B | A | |
| Southwest Missouri St U | 5 | 6 | 4 | 2 | | A | |
| St. Louis Coll of Pharmacy | 4 | 5 | 2 | 4 | | | |
| St. Louis U | 4 | 5 | 1 | 3 | RC | A, AF | • |
| Stephens Coll | 5 | 7 | 1 | 4 | | A, AF, N | |
| Washington U | 2 | 3 | 1 | 3 | | A, AF | • |
| Webster U | 5 | 6 | 2 | 4 | | | |
| Westminster Coll | 4 | 5 | 1 | 4 | P | A, AF | |
| William Jewell Coll | 3 | 5 | 1 | 4 | B | | |
| William Woods U | 5 | 7 | 1 | 4 | DC | | |

## Montana

| | Selectivity | SAT/ACT | Tuition | Enrollment | Religious affiliation | Military training | Phi Beta Kappa |
|---|---|---|---|---|---|---|---|
| Carroll Coll | 5 | 6 | 2 | 4 | RC | | |
| Great Falls, Coll of | N/A | N/A | 3 | 4 | RC | | |
| Montana Coll of Mineral Science & Tech | 5 | 6 | 4 | 4 | | | |
| Montana St U | 5 | 6 | 4 | 3 | | A, AF | |
| Montana St U–Billings | 5 | 7 | 4 | 4 | | A | |
| Montana, U of | 4 | 6 | 4 | 3 | | A | |
| Northern Montana Coll | 5 | 8 | 4 | 4 | | | |
| Rocky Mountain Coll | 5 | 7 | 2 | 4 | | A | |

## Nebraska

| | Selectivity | SAT/ACT | Tuition | Enrollment | Religious affiliation | Military training | Phi Beta Kappa |
|---|---|---|---|---|---|---|---|
| Bellevue Coll | 6 | 8 | 4 | 4 | | A, AF | |
| Chadron St Coll | 5 | 7 | 4 | 4 | | | |
| Clarkson Coll | 4 | 7 | 3 | 4 | EP | A | |
| Concordia Coll | 5 | 6 | 2 | 4 | L | A, AF, N | |
| Creighton U | 4 | 5 | 1 | 4 | RC | A, AF | |
| Dana Coll | 5 | 6 | 2 | 4 | L | A | |
| Doane Coll | 5 | 6 | 2 | 4 | C | A, AF | |
| Hastings Coll | 5 | 6 | 2 | 4 | | | |
| Midland Lutheran Coll | 5 | 6 | 1 | 4 | L | | |
| Nebraska Wesleyan U | 5 | 6 | 2 | 4 | MT | A, AF | |
| Nebraska, U of, Kearney | 4 | 7 | 4 | 3 | | A | |
| Nebraska, U of, Lincoln | 5 | 6 | 4 | 2 | | A, AF, N | • |
| Nebraska, U of, Omaha | 5 | 7 | 4 | 3 | | A, AF | • |
| Peru St Coll | N/A | N/A | 4 | 4 | | A | |
| St. Mary, Coll of | 4 | 7 | 2 | 4 | RC | A, AF | |

| | Selectivity | SAT/ACT | Tuition | Enrollment | Religious affiliation | Military training | Phi Beta Kappa |
|---|---|---|---|---|---|---|---|
| Union Coll | N/A | N/A | 2 | 4 | AD | | |
| Wayne St Coll | 5 | 7 | 4 | 4 | | | |
| **Nevada** | | | | | | | |
| Nevada, U of, Las Vegas | 5 | N/A | 4 | 3 | | | |
| Nevada, U of, Reno | 5 | 7 | 4 | 3 | | A | • |
| Sierra Nevada Coll | N/A | N/A | 2 | 4 | | A | |
| **New Hampshire** | | | | | | | |
| Colby-Sawyer Coll | 5 | 7 | 1 | 4 | | A, AF | |
| Daniel Webster Coll | 5 | 6 | 1 | 4 | | A, AF, N | |
| Dartmouth Coll | 1 | 2 | 1 | 3 | | A | • |
| Franklin Pierce Coll | 5 | 7 | 1 | 4 | | AF | |
| Keene St Coll | 5 | 7 | 4 | 4 | | A, AF | |
| Lifelong Learning, Sch for | N/A | N/A | 4 | 4 | | | |
| New England Coll | 5 | 7 | 1 | 4 | | A, AF | |
| New Hampshire Coll | 5 | 7 | 1 | 4 | | A, AF | |
| New Hampshire, U of | 4 | 5 | 4 | 3 | | A, AF | • |
| Plymouth St Coll | 5 | 7 | 4 | 4 | | A | • |
| Rivier Coll | 5 | 7 | 1 | 4 | RC | AF | |
| St. Anselm Coll | 5 | 6 | 1 | 4 | RC | A, AF | |
| **New Jersey** | | | | | | | |
| Caldwell Coll | 5 | 6 | 2 | 4 | RC | A | |
| Centenary Coll | 5 | 8 | 1 | 4 | MT | | |
| Drew U | 2 | 4 | 1 | 4 | MT | | • |
| Fairleigh Dickinson U | 4 | 6 | 1 | 4 | | A, AF | |
| Felician Coll | 5 | 6 | 2 | 4 | RC | | |
| Georgian Court Coll | 4 | 7 | 2 | 4 | RC | | |
| Jersey City St Coll | 4 | 7 | 4 | 4 | | | |
| Kean Coll of New Jersey | 5 | 7 | 4 | 3 | | A, AF | |
| Monmouth Coll | 5 | 6 | 1 | 4 | | A | |
| Montclair St Coll | 4 | 6 | 4 | 3 | | A, AF | |
| New Jersey Inst of Tech | 4 | 5 | 3 | 4 | | AF | |
| Princeton U | 1 | 2 | 1 | 3 | | A, AF | • |
| Ramapo Coll of New Jersey | 4 | 6 | 4 | 4 | | | |
| Rider Coll | 5 | 6 | 1 | 4 | | A, AF | |
| Rowan Coll of New Jersey | 4 | 6 | 4 | 3 | | A | • |
| Rutgers U, Camden Coll of Arts & Sciences | 3 | 5 | 4 | 4 | | A, AF | |
| Rutgers U, Coll of Engineering | 2 | 4 | 4 | 4 | | A, AF | |
| Rutgers U, Coll of Nursing | 3 | 5 | 4 | 4 | | A, AF | |
| Rutgers U, Coll of Pharmacy | 2 | 4 | 4 | 4 | | A, AF | |
| Rutgers U, Cook Coll | 3 | 5 | 4 | 4 | | A, AF | |
| Rutgers U, Douglass Coll | 4 | 5 | 4 | 4 | | A, AF | • |
| Rutgers U, Livingston Coll | 4 | 5 | 4 | 4 | | A, AF | • |
| Rutgers U, Mason Gross Sch of the Arts | 3 | 5 | 4 | 4 | | A, AF | |
| Rutgers U, Newark Coll of Arts & Sciences | 4 | 6 | 4 | 4 | | A, AF | • |
| Rutgers U, Rutgers Coll | 2 | 4 | 4 | 3 | | A, AF | • |
| Seton Hall U | 5 | 6 | 1 | 3 | RC | A, AF | |
| St. Elizabeth, Coll of | 5 | 6 | 1 | 4 | RC | | |
| St. Peter's Coll | 5 | 6 | 2 | 4 | RC | A | |
| Stevens Inst of Tech | 2 | 4 | 1 | 4 | | A, AF | |
| Stockton Coll of New Jersey | 3 | 5 | 4 | 3 | | | |
| Thomas A. Edison St Coll | N/A | N/A | 4 | 3 | | | |
| Trenton St Coll | 2 | 4 | 4 | 3 | | A, AF | |
| Upsala Coll | 5 | 7 | 1 | 4 | L | | |
| Westminster Choir Coll, The Sch of Music of Rider Coll | 4 | 5 | 1 | 4 | | A, AF | |
| William Paterson Coll of New Jersey | 4 | 6 | 4 | 3 | | A | |

| | Selectivity | SAT/ACT | Tuition | Enrollment | Religious affiliation | Military training | Phi Beta Kappa |
|---|---|---|---|---|---|---|---|
| **New Mexico** | | | | | | | |
| Eastern New Mexico U | 6 | 7 | 4 | 4 | | A | |
| New Mexico Highlands U | 5 | 8 | 4 | 4 | | | |
| New Mexico Inst of Mining & Tech | 2 | 4 | 4 | 4 | | | |
| New Mexico St U | 6 | 7 | 4 | 3 | | A, AF | |
| New Mexico, U of | 5 | 6 | 4 | 2 | | A, AF | • |
| Santa Fe, Coll of | 5 | 6 | 1 | 4 | RC | | |
| Southwest, C of the | 5 | 8 | 4 | 4 | | | |
| St. John's Coll | 3 | 4 | 1 | 4 | | | |
| Western New Mexico U | 6 | 9 | 4 | 4 | | | • |
| **New York** | | | | | | | |
| Adelphi U | 5 | 6 | 1 | 4 | | A, AF | |
| Albany Coll of Pharmacy | 5 | 6 | 2 | 4 | | | |
| Alfred U | 4 | 5 | 1 | 4 | | A | |
| Audrey Cohen Coll | N/A | N/A | 2 | 4 | | | |
| Bard Coll | 2 | 3 | 1 | 4 | | | |
| Barnard Coll | 2 | 3 | 1 | 4 | | | • |
| Boricua Coll | N/A | N/A | 3 | 4 | | | |
| Canisius Coll | 3 | 5 | 2 | 4 | RC | A | |
| Cazenovia Coll | 5 | 8 | 2 | 4 | | | |
| Clarkson U | 2 | 4 | 1 | 4 | | A, AF | |
| Colgate U | 2 | 3 | 1 | 4 | | | • |
| Columbia U, Columbia Coll | 1 | 2 | 1 | 4 | | A, AF | • |
| Columbia U, Sch of Engineering and Applied Science | 1 | 2 | 1 | 4 | | | |
| Cooper Union | 1 | 2 | 6 | 4 | | | |
| Cornell U | 1 | 3 | 1 | 2 | | A, AF, N | • |
| CUNY, Baruch Coll | N/A | N/A | 4 | 3 | | | |
| CUNY, Brooklyn Coll | N/A | N/A | 4 | 3 | | | • |
| CUNY, City Coll | N/A | N/A | 4 | 3 | | | • |
| CUNY, Hunter Coll | N/A | N/A | 4 | 3 | | | • |
| CUNY, John Jay Coll of Criminal Justice | N/A | N/A | 4 | 3 | | | |
| CUNY, Queens Coll | N/A | N/A | 4 | 2 | | | • |
| CUNY, Staten Island, Coll of | 6 | N/A | 4 | 3 | | | |
| CUNY, York Coll | N/A | N/A | 4 | 4 | | | |
| D'Youville Coll | 5 | 6 | 2 | 4 | | A | |
| Daemen Coll | N/A | N/A | 2 | 4 | | A | |
| Dominican Coll of Blauvelt | N/A | N/A | 2 | 4 | | A | |
| Dowling Coll | 5 | 7 | 2 | 4 | | A, AF | |
| Elmira Coll | 5 | 6 | 1 | 4 | | A, AF | • |
| Eugene Lang Coll of the New Sch for Social Research | 4 | 5 | 1 | 4 | | | |
| Fashion Inst of Tech | 4 | 7 | 4 | 3 | | | |
| Five Towns Coll | 5 | 7 | 2 | 4 | | | |
| Fordham U | 4 | 5 | 1 | 3 | RC | A, AF, N | • |
| Hamilton Coll | 2 | 4 | 1 | 4 | | A | • |
| Hartwick Coll | 4 | 5 | 1 | 4 | | | |
| Hilbert Coll | 5 | 8 | 2 | 4 | | | |
| Hobart and William Smith Coll | 4 | 5 | 1 | 4 | | | • |
| Hofstra U | 3 | 5 | 1 | 3 | | A | • |
| Houghton Coll | 4 | 5 | 2 | 4 | W | A | |
| Insurance, Coll of | 3 | 5 | 1 | 4 | | | |
| Iona Coll | 5 | 7 | 2 | 4 | | A | • |
| Ithaca Coll | 4 | 5 | 1 | 3 | | A, AF | |
| Juilliard Sch | N/A | N/A | 1 | 4 | | | |
| Keuka Coll | 5 | 6 | 2 | 4 | B | A | |
| King's Coll | 5 | 6 | 2 | 4 | ND | | |

| | Selectivity | SAT/ACT | Tuition | Enrollment | Religious affiliation | Military training | Phi Beta Kappa |
|---|---|---|---|---|---|---|---|
| Laboratory Inst of Merchandising | N/A | N/A | 2 | 4 | | | |
| LeMoyne Coll | 4 | 5 | 1 | 4 | RC | A, AF | |
| Long Island U, Brooklyn Campus | N/A | N/A | 1 | 3 | | | • |
| Long Island U, C.W. Post Campus | 4 | 5 | 1 | 4 | | A, AF | |
| Long Island U, Southampton Campus | 5 | 6 | 1 | 4 | | A | |
| Manhattan Coll | 4 | 5 | 1 | 4 | RC | AF | • |
| Manhattan Sch of Music | N/A | N/A | 1 | 4 | | | |
| Manhattanville Coll | 4 | 5 | 1 | 4 | | | |
| Mannes Coll of Music | N/A | N/A | 1 | 4 | | | |
| Marist Coll | 4 | 5 | 1 | 4 | | | |
| Marymount Coll | 5 | 6 | 1 | 4 | | | |
| Medaille Coll | N/A | N/A | 2 | 4 | | A | |
| Mercy Coll | N/A | N/A | 2 | 3 | | A, AF | |
| Molloy Coll | 5 | 7 | 2 | 4 | RC | A, AF | • |
| Mt St. Mary Coll | 5 | 6 | 2 | 4 | | A | |
| Mt St. Vincent, Coll of | 5 | 7 | 1 | 4 | RC | AF | |
| Nazareth Coll of Rochester | 4 | 5 | 1 | 4 | | AF | |
| New Rochelle, Coll of | 4 | 7 | 1 | 4 | | | |
| New York Inst of Tech | 5 | 7 | 2 | 3 | | AF | |
| New York U | 2 | 4 | 1 | 2 | | A | • |
| Niagara U | 5 | 6 | 2 | 4 | | A | |
| Nyack Coll | 6 | 7 | 2 | 4 | CM | | |
| Pace U, New York City | 5 | N/A | 1 | 4 | | AF | |
| Pace U, Pleasantville/Briarcliff | 5 | N/A | 1 | 4 | | AF | |
| Pace U, White Plains | 5 | N/A | 1 | 4 | | AF | |
| Parsons Sch of Design | N/A | 6 | 1 | 4 | | | |
| Polytechnic U | 2 | 4 | 1 | 4 | | A, AF | |
| Pratt Inst | 5 | 6 | 1 | 4 | | A | |
| Rensselaer Polytechnic Inst | 2 | 4 | 1 | 3 | | A, AF, N | |
| Roberts Wesleyan Coll | 5 | 6 | 1 | 4 | MT | A, AF | • |
| Rochester Inst of Tech | 4 | 5 | 1 | 3 | | A, AF, N | |
| Rochester, U of | 2 | 4 | 1 | 3 | | A, AF, N | • |
| Russell Sage Coll | 5 | 6 | 1 | 4 | | A, AF, N | |
| Sarah Lawrence Coll | 2 | 4 | 1 | 4 | | | |
| Siena Coll | 3 | 5 | 1 | 4 | RC | A, AF | • |
| Skidmore Coll | 4 | 5 | 1 | 4 | | A, AF, N | • |
| St. Bonaventure U | 4 | 5 | 1 | 4 | RC | A | |
| St. Francis Coll | N/A | N/A | 3 | 4 | | A, AF | |
| St. John Fisher Coll | 5 | 6 | 2 | 4 | RC | A, AF | |
| St. John's U | 4 | 6 | 2 | 3 | RC | A | |
| St. Joseph's Coll (Brooklyn) | 5 | 7 | 2 | 4 | | | |
| St. Joseph's Coll (Patchogue) | 5 | 6 | 2 | 4 | | A, AF | |
| St. Lawrence U | 4 | 5 | 1 | 4 | | AF | • |
| St. Rose, The Coll of | 5 | 6 | 2 | 4 | ND | N | |
| St. Thomas Aquinas Coll | 5 | 7 | 2 | 4 | | AF | |
| SUNY at Albany | 3 | 4 | 4 | 3 | | A, AF, N | • |
| SUNY at Binghamton | 2 | 4 | 4 | 3 | | | • |
| SUNY at Buffalo | 4 | 5 | 4 | 2 | | A | • |
| SUNY at Stony Brook | 3 | 5 | 4 | 3 | | | • |
| SUNY Coll at Brockport | 4 | 6 | 4 | 3 | | A, AF, N | |
| SUNY Coll at Buffalo | N/A | N/A | 4 | 3 | | A | |
| SUNY Coll at Cortland | 4 | 6 | 4 | 3 | | A, AF | |
| SUNY Coll at Fredonia | 4 | 6 | 4 | 3 | | A | |
| SUNY Coll at Geneseo | 2 | 4 | 4 | 3 | | A, AF | |
| SUNY Coll at New Paltz | 3 | 5 | 4 | 3 | | | |
| SUNY Coll at Oneonta | 5 | 6 | 4 | 3 | | | |

| | Selectivity | SAT/ACT | Tuition | Enrollment | Religious affiliation | Military training | Phi Beta Kappa |
|---|---|---|---|---|---|---|---|
| SUNY Coll at Oswego | 3 | 5 | 2 | 3 | | A | • |
| SUNY Coll at Plattsburgh | 5 | 6 | 4 | 3 | | | |
| SUNY Coll at Potsdam | 4 | 5 | 4 | 4 | | A, AF | |
| SUNY Coll at Purchase | 4 | 6 | 4 | 4 | | | |
| SUNY Coll of Environmental Science & Forestry | 2 | 4 | 4 | 4 | | A, AF | • |
| SUNY Maritime Coll | 4 | 6 | 4 | 4 | | AF, N | |
| Syracuse U | 4 | 5 | 1 | 3 | | A, AF | • |
| U.S. Merchant Marine Acad | 2 | 4 | 6 | 4 | | | |
| U.S. Military Acad | 2 | 3 | 6 | 3 | | | • |
| Union Coll | 2 | 3 | 1 | 4 | | A, AF, N | • |
| Utica Coll of Syracuse U | 4 | 7 | 1 | 4 | | A, AF | • |
| Vassar Coll | 2 | 3 | 1 | 4 | | | • |
| Visual Arts, Sch of | 6 | 6 | 1 | 4 | | | |
| Wagner Coll | 5 | 6 | 1 | 4 | | A, AF | |
| Webb Inst of Naval Architecture | 1 | 2 | 6 | 4 | | | |
| Wells Coll | 4 | 5 | 1 | 4 | | A | • |
| Yeshiva U | 3 | 4 | 1 | 4 | | | |

## North Carolina

| | | | | | | | |
|---|---|---|---|---|---|---|---|
| Appalachian St U | 4 | 6 | 4 | 3 | | A | |
| Barber-Scotia Coll | 6 | 9 | 4 | 4 | P | A, AF | |
| Barton Coll | 5 | 7 | 2 | 4 | DC | | |
| Belmont Abbey Coll | 5 | 7 | 2 | 4 | RC | A, AF | |
| Bennett Coll | 5 | 8 | 3 | 4 | MT | A, AF | |
| Campbell U | 4 | 6 | 2 | 4 | B | A | |
| Catawba Coll | 5 | 6 | 2 | 4 | C | A | |
| Chowan Coll | 5 | 8 | 2 | 4 | | | |
| Davidson Coll | 1 | 3 | 1 | 4 | P | A | • |
| Duke U | 1 | 2 | 1 | 3 | MT | A, AF, N | • |
| East Carolina U | 5 | 6 | 4 | 2 | | A, AF | |
| Elon Coll | 5 | 6 | 2 | 4 | C | A | |
| Fayetteville St U | 6 | 7 | 4 | 4 | | AF | |
| Gardner-Webb Coll | 5 | 7 | 2 | 4 | | | |
| Greensboro Coll | 5 | 6 | 2 | 4 | MT | A, AF | |
| Guilford Coll | 4 | 5 | 1 | 4 | Q | A, AF | |
| High Point U | 5 | 7 | 2 | 4 | MT | A, AF | |
| Johnson C. Smith U | 5 | 8 | 3 | 4 | | A, AF | • |
| Lees-McRae Coll | 5 | 8 | 2 | 4 | P | | |
| Lenoir-Rhyne Coll | 5 | 6 | 1 | 4 | L | A | |
| Livingstone Coll | 5 | 9 | 3 | 4 | AM | A | |
| Mars Hill Coll | 5 | 7 | 2 | 4 | B | | |
| Meredith Coll | 5 | 6 | 3 | 4 | B | A, AF | |
| Methodist Coll | 5 | 7 | 2 | 4 | MT | A, AF | |
| Mt Olive Coll | 5 | 7 | 2 | 4 | B | | |
| North Carolina A&T St U | 5 | 7 | 4 | 3 | | A, AF | |
| North Carolina Sch of the Arts | 4 | 5 | 4 | 4 | | | |
| North Carolina St U | 3 | 5 | 4 | 2 | | A, AF, N | |
| North Carolina Wesleyan Coll | 5 | 7 | 2 | 4 | MT | | |
| North Carolina, U of, Asheville | 3 | 5 | 4 | 4 | | | |
| North Carolina, U of, Chapel Hill | 2 | 4 | 4 | 2 | | A, AF, N | • |
| North Carolina, U of, Charlotte | 5 | 6 | 4 | 3 | | A, AF | |
| North Carolina, U of, Greensboro | 5 | 6 | 4 | 3 | | A, AF | • |
| North Carolina, U of, Wilmington | 4 | 6 | 4 | 3 | | | |
| Pembroke St U | 5 | 7 | 4 | 4 | | A, AF | |
| Pfeiffer Coll | 5 | 7 | 2 | 4 | MT | A | |
| Queens Coll | 4 | 5 | 1 | 4 | P | A, AF | |

| | Selectivity | SAT/ACT | Tuition | Enrollment | Religious affiliation | Military training | Phi Beta Kappa |
|---|---|---|---|---|---|---|---|
| Salem Coll | 4 | 5 | 1 | 4 | MV | A | |
| St. Andrews Presbyterian Coll | 5 | 6 | 1 | 4 | P | | |
| Wake Forest U | 2 | 3 | 1 | 4 | B | A | • |
| Warren Wilson Coll | 4 | 5 | 1 | 4 | P | | |
| Western Carolina U | 5 | 7 | 4 | 3 | | A | |
| Wingate Coll | 5 | 7 | 2 | 4 | B | A, AF | |
| Winston-Salem St U | 5 | 8 | 4 | 4 | | A | • |
| **North Dakota** | | | | | | | |
| Dickinson St U | 6 | 8 | 4 | 4 | | | |
| Jamestown Coll | 5 | 6 | 2 | 4 | P | | |
| Mary, U of | 5 | 7 | 3 | 4 | RC | | |
| Minot St U | N/A | N/A | 4 | 4 | | | |
| North Dakota St U | 5 | 6 | 4 | 3 | | A, AF | |
| North Dakota, U of | 5 | 6 | 4 | 3 | | A | |
| Valley City St U | 6 | 7 | 4 | 4 | | | |
| **Ohio** | | | | | | | |
| Akron, The U of | 6 | 7 | 4 | 2 | | A, AF | |
| Antioch Coll of Antioch U | 4 | 5 | 1 | 4 | | | |
| Art Acad of Cincinnati | 5 | 9 | 2 | 4 | | A, AF, N | |
| Ashland U | 6 | 7 | 1 | 4 | CB | AF | |
| Baldwin-Wallace Coll | 5 | 6 | 1 | 4 | MT | A, AF | |
| Bluffton Coll | 5 | 6 | 2 | 4 | MN | | |
| Bowling Green St U | 5 | 6 | 4 | 2 | | A, AF | • |
| Capital U | 5 | 6 | 1 | 4 | L | A, AF, N | |
| Case Western Reserve U | 2 | 3 | 1 | 4 | | A, AF | • |
| Cedarville Coll | 4 | 5 | 3 | 4 | B | A, AF | |
| Central St U | N/A | N/A | 4 | 4 | | A, AF | |
| Cincinnati Bible Coll | N/A | N/A | 4 | 4 | ND | | |
| Cincinnati, U of | 5 | 6 | 4 | 3 | | A, AF | • |
| Cleveland Inst of Art | 5 | 7 | 1 | 4 | | | |
| Cleveland Inst of Music | N/A | N/A | 1 | 4 | | | |
| Columbus Coll of Art & Design | 5 | 7 | 2 | 4 | | | |
| Dayton, U of | 4 | 5 | 1 | 3 | RC | A, AF | |
| Defiance Coll | 5 | 7 | 1 | 4 | C | A | |
| Denison U | 4 | 5 | 1 | 4 | | | • |
| DeVry Inst of Tech | N/A | N/A | 3 | 4 | | A, AF | |
| Dyke Coll | N/A | N/A | 1 | 4 | | A | |
| Findlay, U of | 4 | 7 | 1 | 4 | CG | AF | |
| Franciscan U of Steubenville | 4 | 5 | 2 | 4 | RC | | |
| Franklin U | N/A | N/A | 3 | 4 | | A, AF | |
| Heidelberg Coll | 4 | 7 | 1 | 4 | C | A, AF | |
| Hiram Coll | 4 | 5 | 1 | 4 | DC | | • |
| John Carroll U | 5 | 6 | 1 | 4 | RC | A | |
| Kent St U | 5 | 7 | 4 | 2 | | A, AF | |
| Kenyon Coll | 2 | 4 | 1 | 4 | EP | | • |
| Lake Erie Coll | 5 | 6 | 2 | 4 | | | |
| Lourdes Coll | N/A | N/A | 3 | 4 | RC | | |
| Malone Coll | 4 | 7 | 2 | 4 | EV | | • |
| Marietta Coll | 3 | 5 | 1 | 4 | | | • |
| Miami U | 2 | 4 | 4 | 2 | | AF, N | • |
| Mt St. Joseph, Coll of | 5 | 7 | 2 | 4 | RC | A, AF | |
| Mt Union Coll | 4 | 5 | 1 | 4 | MT | A, AF | |
| Mt Vernon Nazarene Coll | 5 | 7 | 3 | 4 | CN | | |
| Muskingum Coll | 5 | 6 | 1 | 4 | P | A | • |
| Notre Dame Coll of Ohio | 4 | 7 | 2 | 4 | RC | | |

| | Selectivity | SAT/ACT | Tuition | Enrollment | Religious affiliation | Military training | Phi Beta Kappa |
|---|---|---|---|---|---|---|---|
| Oberlin Coll | 2 | 3 | 1 | 4 | | | • |
| Ohio Dominican Coll | N/A | N/A | 2 | 4 | RC | A, AF, N | |
| Ohio Northern U | 3 | 5 | 1 | 4 | MT | A, AF | |
| Ohio St U, Columbus | 5 | 6 | 4 | 1 | | A, AF, N | • |
| Ohio St U, Lima | 5 | 7 | 4 | 4 | | A, AF, N | |
| Ohio St U, Mansfield | 5 | 7 | 4 | 4 | | A, AF, N | |
| Ohio St U, Marion | 6 | 8 | 4 | 4 | | A, AF, N | |
| Ohio St U, Newark | 5 | 7 | 4 | 4 | | A, AF, N | |
| Ohio U | 4 | 5 | 4 | 2 | | A, AF | • |
| Ohio Wesleyan U | 3 | 4 | 1 | 4 | MT | AF | • |
| Otterbein Coll | 5 | 6 | 1 | 4 | MT | A, AF, N | |
| Pontifical Coll Josephinum | 6 | 8 | 3 | 4 | RC | | |
| Rio Grande, U of | 6 | 8 | 4 | 4 | | A | |
| Shawnee St U | N/A | N/A | 4 | 4 | | | |
| Tiffin U | 6 | 8 | 2 | 4 | | | |
| Toledo, The U of | 6 | 7 | 4 | 2 | | A, AF | • |
| Urbana U | 5 | 8 | 2 | 4 | S | AF | |
| Ursuline Coll | 5 | 7 | 2 | 4 | RC | A | |
| Walsh U | 5 | 7 | 2 | 4 | RC | | |
| Wilmington Coll | 5 | 7 | 1 | 4 | Q | | |
| Wittenberg U | 3 | 5 | 1 | 4 | L | A, AF | • |
| Wooster, The Coll of | 4 | 5 | 1 | 4 | P | | • |
| Wright St U | 5 | 7 | 4 | 3 | | A, AF | |
| Xavier U | 4 | 5 | 1 | 4 | RC | A, AF | |
| Youngstown St U | 5 | 7 | 4 | 3 | | A | |

## Oklahoma

| | Selectivity | SAT/ACT | Tuition | Enrollment | Religious affiliation | Military training | Phi Beta Kappa |
|---|---|---|---|---|---|---|---|
| Bartlesville Wesleyan Coll | 4 | 7 | 3 | 4 | W | | |
| Cameron U | 6 | 8 | 4 | 4 | | A | |
| Central Oklahoma, U of | 5 | 7 | 4 | 3 | | A | |
| East Central U | 4 | 7 | 4 | 4 | | A | • |
| Langston U | N/A | N/A | 4 | 4 | | A | |
| Northeastern St U | 5 | 6 | 4 | 3 | | A | |
| Northwestern Oklahoma St U | 6 | 8 | 4 | 4 | | | |
| Oklahoma Baptist U | 5 | 6 | 3 | 4 | B | | |
| Oklahoma Christian U of Science & Arts | 5 | 6 | 3 | 4 | CC | A, AF | |
| Oklahoma City U | 5 | 6 | 3 | 4 | MT | A, AF | |
| Oklahoma St U | 4 | 5 | 4 | 2 | | A, AF | • |
| Oklahoma, U of | 4 | 5 | 4 | 2 | | A, AF, N | • |
| Oral Roberts U | 4 | 7 | 2 | 4 | | A | |
| Panhandle St U | 5 | 8 | 4 | 4 | | | |
| Phillips U | 5 | 7 | 2 | 4 | DC | | |
| Science & Arts of Oklahoma, U of | N/A | N/A | 4 | 4 | | | |
| Southeastern Oklahoma St U | 5 | 7 | 4 | 4 | | | |
| Southern Nazarene U | 6 | 7 | 3 | 4 | CN | A, AF | • |
| Southwestern Oklahoma St U | 6 | 7 | 4 | 4 | | | |
| Tulsa, U of | 4 | 5 | 2 | 4 | P | A | • |

## Oregon

| | Selectivity | SAT/ACT | Tuition | Enrollment | Religious affiliation | Military training | Phi Beta Kappa |
|---|---|---|---|---|---|---|---|
| Bassist Coll | N/A | N/A | 2 | 4 | | | |
| Concordia Coll | 5 | 6 | 2 | 4 | L | | |
| Eastern Oregon St Coll | N/A | N/A | 4 | 4 | | | |
| George Fox Coll | 5 | 6 | 1 | 4 | Q | | |
| Lewis & Clark Coll | 3 | 4 | 1 | 4 | | | |
| Linfield Coll | 3 | 5 | 1 | 4 | B | AF | |
| Marylhurst Coll | N/A | N/A | 2 | 4 | RC | | |
| Multnomah Bible Coll & Biblical Seminary | N/A | N/A | 3 | 4 | ND | | |

| | Selectivity | SAT/ACT | Tuition | Enrollment | Religious affiliation | Military training | Phi Beta Kappa |
|---|---|---|---|---|---|---|---|
| Northwest Christian Coll | 5 | 7 | 2 | 4 | | A | |
| Oregon Inst of Tech | 5 | 7 | 4 | 4 | | | |
| Oregon, U of | 4 | 5 | 4 | 3 | | A | • |
| Pacific Northwest C of Art | 5 | 6 | 2 | 4 | | | |
| Pacific U | 4 | 5 | 1 | 4 | ND | A | |
| Portland St U | 6 | 7 | 4 | 3 | | A, AF | |
| Portland, U of | 4 | 5 | 1 | 4 | RC | A, AF | |
| Reed Coll | 2 | 3 | 1 | 4 | | A | • |
| Southern Oregon St Coll | 5 | 6 | 4 | 4 | | | |
| Warner Pacific Coll | 5 | 7 | 2 | 4 | CG | A, AF | |
| Western Baptist Coll | 4 | 7 | 2 | 4 | B | A, AF | |
| Western Oregon St Coll | 5 | 7 | 4 | 4 | | A, AF | • |
| Willamette U | 2 | 4 | 1 | 4 | MT | | |

## Pennsylvania

| | Selectivity | SAT/ACT | Tuition | Enrollment | Religious affiliation | Military training | Phi Beta Kappa |
|---|---|---|---|---|---|---|---|
| Acad of the New Church Coll | 5 | 6 | 4 | 4 | S | | |
| Albright Coll | 4 | 5 | 1 | 4 | MT | | |
| Allegheny Coll | 3 | 5 | 1 | 4 | MT | A | • |
| Allentown Coll of St. Francis de Sales | 5 | 6 | 2 | 4 | RC | A | |
| Alvernia Coll | 5 | 7 | 2 | 4 | RC | | |
| Arts, U of the | 5 | 7 | 1 | 4 | | | |
| Baptist Bible Coll & Theological Sem | 5 | 7 | 3 | 4 | B | A | |
| Beaver Coll | 5 | 6 | 1 | 4 | P | A | |
| Bloomsburg U of Pennsylvania | 4 | 6 | 4 | 3 | | A, AF | |
| Bryn Mawr Coll | 2 | 3 | 1 | 4 | | A, AF, N | |
| Bucknell U | 2 | 4 | 1 | 4 | | A | • |
| Cabrini Coll | 5 | 7 | 2 | 4 | RC | A | |
| California U of Pennsylvania | 4 | 7 | 4 | 3 | | A | |
| Carlow Coll | N/A | N/A | 2 | 4 | RC | A, AF, N | |
| Carnegie Mellon U | 2 | 3 | 1 | 3 | | A, AF, N | |
| Cedar Crest Coll | 5 | 6 | 1 | 4 | | A | |
| Chatham Coll | 5 | 6 | 1 | 4 | | A, AF, N | • |
| Chestnut Hill Coll | 5 | 6 | 1 | 4 | RC | A | |
| Cheyney U of Pennsylvania | N/A | N/A | 3 | 4 | | A | |
| Clarion U of Pennsylvania | 5 | 7 | 4 | 3 | | | |
| College Misericordia | 4 | 6 | 2 | 4 | RC | A, AF | |
| Delaware Valley Coll | 5 | 6 | 1 | 4 | | A | |
| Dickinson Coll | 3 | 4 | 1 | 4 | | A | • |
| Drexel U | 4 | 5 | 1 | 3 | | A, AF, N | |
| Duquesne U | 5 | 6 | 2 | 4 | RC | A, AF | • |
| East Stroudsburg U of Pennsylvania | 4 | 6 | 4 | 4 | | A, AF | |
| Eastern Coll | 5 | 6 | 1 | 4 | B | A, AF | |
| Edinboro U of Pennsylvania | N/A | N/A | 4 | 3 | | A | |
| Elizabethtown Coll | 4 | 5 | 1 | 4 | CB | | |
| Franklin & Marshall Coll | 2 | 4 | 1 | 4 | | | • |
| Gannon U | 5 | 6 | 1 | 4 | RC | A | |
| Geneva Coll | 5 | 6 | 2 | 4 | P | | |
| Gettysburg Coll | 2 | 4 | 1 | 4 | L | | • |
| Grove City Coll | 2 | 4 | 3 | 4 | P | | |
| Gwynedd-Mercy Coll | 4 | 6 | 1 | 4 | RC | A | |
| Hahnemann U, Sch of Health Sciences & Humanities | 5 | 8 | 2 | 4 | | | |
| Haverford Coll | 1 | 3 | 1 | 4 | | | • |
| Holy Family Coll | 4 | 6 | 2 | 4 | RC | | |
| Immaculata Coll | 5 | 6 | 1 | 4 | RC | | |
| Indiana U of Pennsylvania | 4 | 6 | 4 | 3 | | A | |
| Juniata Coll | 3 | 5 | 1 | 4 | | | |

| | Selectivity | SAT/ACT | Tuition | Enrollment | Religious affiliation | Military training | Phi Beta Kappa |
|---|---|---|---|---|---|---|---|
| King's Coll | 5 | 6 | 1 | 4 | RC | A, AF | |
| Kutztown U of Pennsylvania | 3 | 5 | 4 | 3 | | | |
| Lafayette Coll | 2 | 4 | 1 | 4 | P | A | • |
| Lancaster Bible Coll | 5 | 7 | 2 | 4 | ND | | |
| LaRoche Coll | 5 | 7 | 2 | 4 | RC | A, AF | |
| LaSalle U | 4 | 5 | 1 | 4 | RC | A, AF, N | |
| Lebanon Valley Coll | 5 | 6 | 1 | 4 | MT | A | |
| Lehigh U | 2 | 4 | 1 | 3 | | A, AF | • |
| Lock Haven U of Pennsylvania | 4 | 6 | 4 | 4 | | A | |
| Lycoming Coll | 5 | 6 | 1 | 4 | MT | A | |
| Mansfield U of Pennsylvania | 4 | 6 | 4 | 4 | | | |
| Marywood Coll | 5 | 6 | 1 | 4 | RC | AF | |
| Mercyhurst Coll | 5 | 6 | 2 | 4 | RC | A | |
| Messiah Coll | 3 | 5 | 1 | 4 | OC | | |
| Millersville U of Pennsylvania | 3 | 5 | 4 | 3 | | A | |
| Moore Coll of Art & Design | 5 | 7 | 1 | 4 | | | |
| Moravian Coll | 4 | 5 | 1 | 4 | MV | AF | |
| Mount Aloysius Coll | 5 | 8 | 2 | 4 | RC | | |
| Muhlenberg Coll | 4 | 5 | 1 | 4 | L | A | • |
| Pennsylvania St U | 3 | 5 | 3 | 1 | | A, AF, N | • |
| Pennsylvania St U, Erie, Behrend Coll | 5 | 6 | 3 | 4 | | | |
| Pennsylvania, U of | 1 | 3 | 1 | 3 | | A, AF, N | • |
| Philadelphia Coll of Bible | 4 | 6 | 3 | 4 | ND | | |
| Philadelphia Coll of Pharmacy & Science | 3 | 5 | 1 | 4 | | A | |
| Philadelphia Coll of Textiles & Science | 5 | 6 | 1 | 4 | | | |
| Pittsburgh, U of, Bradford | 5 | 6 | 3 | 4 | | A | |
| Pittsburgh, U of, Greensburg | 5 | 7 | 3 | 4 | | A, AF | |
| Pittsburgh, U of, Johnstown | 5 | 6 | 3 | 4 | | | |
| Pittsburgh, U of, Pittsburgh | 4 | 5 | 3 | 2 | | A, AF, N | • |
| Point Park Coll | 5 | 7 | 2 | 4 | | A, AF | |
| Robert Morris Coll | 5 | 7 | 3 | 4 | | A, AF | |
| Rosemont C | 4 | 5 | 1 | 4 | RC | | |
| Scranton, U of | 4 | 5 | 1 | 4 | RC | A, AF | |
| Seton Hill Coll | 4 | 6 | 1 | 4 | RC | A | |
| Shippensburg U of Pennsylvania | 4 | 6 | 4 | 3 | | A | |
| Slippery Rock U of Pennsylvania | 4 | 6 | 4 | 3 | | A | |
| St. Francis Coll | 5 | 6 | 1 | 4 | RC | A | |
| St. Joseph's U | 4 | 5 | 1 | 4 | RC | A, AF, N | |
| St. Vincent Coll | 5 | 6 | 1 | 4 | RC | AF | |
| Susquehanna U | 4 | 5 | 1 | 4 | L | A | |
| Swarthmore Coll | 1 | 2 | 1 | 4 | | N | • |
| Temple U | 4 | 6 | 3 | 2 | | A, AF, N | • |
| Thiel Coll | 5 | 7 | 1 | 4 | L | | |
| Ursinus Coll | 3 | 5 | 1 | 4 | C | | |
| Villanova U | 3 | 4 | 1 | 1 | RC | A, AF, N | • |
| Washington & Jefferson Coll | 4 | 5 | 1 | 4 | | A | • |
| Waynesburg Coll | N/A | N/A | 2 | 4 | P | | |
| West Chester U of Pennsylvania | 4 | 6 | 4 | 3 | | A, AF | |
| Westminster Coll | 5 | 6 | 1 | 4 | P | | |
| Widener U | 4 | 6 | 1 | 4 | | A, AF | |
| Wilson Coll | 5 | 6 | 1 | 4 | P | A | |
| York Coll of Pennsylvania | 4 | 5 | 3 | 4 | | | |

## Rhode Island

| | Selectivity | SAT/ACT | Tuition | Enrollment | Religious affiliation | Military training | Phi Beta Kappa |
|---|---|---|---|---|---|---|---|
| Brown U | 1 | 3 | 1 | 3 | | A | • |
| Bryant Coll | 5 | 6 | 1 | 4 | | A | |

| | Selectivity | SAT/ACT | Tuition | Enrollment | Religious affiliation | Military training | Phi Beta Kappa |
|---|---|---|---|---|---|---|---|
| Johnson & Wales U | 5 | 7 | 2 | 3 | | A | |
| Providence Coll | 4 | 5 | 1 | 4 | RC | A | |
| Rhode Island Coll | 4 | 7 | 4 | N/A | | A | • |
| Rhode Island Sch of Design | 3 | 5 | 1 | 4 | | | |
| Rhode Island, U of | 5 | 6 | 4 | 3 | | A | • |
| Roger Williams U | 4 | 7 | 1 | 4 | | A | |
| Salve Regina U | N/A | N/A | 1 | 4 | RC | A | |
| **South Carolina** | | | | | | | |
| Anderson Coll | 5 | 8 | 2 | 4 | B | A, AF | |
| Benedict Coll | 2 | 3 | 2 | 4 | B | A, AF | |
| Central Wesleyan C | 4 | 7 | 2 | 4 | W | A, AF | |
| Charleston, Coll of | 4 | 5 | 4 | 3 | | AF | |
| Citadel, The | 5 | 6 | 4 | 4 | | A, AF, N | |
| Clemson U | 3 | 5 | 4 | 3 | | A, AF | |
| Coastal Carolina U | 5 | 7 | 4 | 4 | | | • |
| Coker Coll | 5 | 6 | 2 | 4 | | | |
| Columbia Coll | 5 | 7 | 1 | 4 | MT | A, AF, N | |
| Columbia International U | 5 | 6 | 3 | 4 | ND | | |
| Converse Coll | 4 | 5 | 1 | 4 | | A | |
| Erskine Coll | 3 | 5 | 2 | 4 | P | | |
| Francis Marion U | N/A | N/A | 4 | 4 | | A | |
| Furman U | 2 | 4 | 1 | 4 | | A | • |
| Lander U | N/A | N/A | 4 | 4 | | A | |
| Limestone Coll | 5 | 8 | 2 | 4 | | | |
| Morris Coll | N/A | N/A | 3 | 4 | B | A | |
| Newberry C | 5 | 7 | 1 | 4 | L | A | |
| Presbyterian Coll | 2 | 4 | 1 | 4 | P | A | |
| South Carolina, U of (Columbia) | 5 | 6 | 4 | 2 | | A, AF, N | |
| South Carolina, U of, Aiken | 5 | 7 | 4 | 4 | | A | |
| South Carolina, U of, Spartanburg | 4 | 7 | 4 | 4 | | A | |
| Voorhees Coll | 5 | 9 | 4 | 4 | EP | A | |
| Winthrop U | 5 | 6 | 4 | 4 | | | |
| Wofford Coll | 3 | 5 | 1 | 4 | MT | A | • |
| **South Dakota** | | | | | | | |
| Augustana Coll | 5 | 6 | 1 | 4 | L | | |
| Black Hills St U | 6 | 8 | 4 | 4 | | A | |
| Dakota St U | 5 | 7 | 4 | 4 | | AF | • |
| Dakota Wesleyan U | 4 | 7 | 2 | 4 | MT | | |
| Mt Marty Coll | 5 | 7 | 3 | 4 | RC | A | |
| National Coll | 6 | 9 | 2 | 4 | | A | |
| Northern St U | 6 | 7 | 4 | 4 | | | |
| Oglala Lakota Coll | N/A | N/A | 3 | 4 | | | |
| Sioux Falls Coll | 4 | 7 | 2 | 4 | B | | |
| South Dakota Sch of Mines & Tech | 4 | 5 | 4 | 4 | | A | |
| South Dakota St U | 5 | 6 | 4 | 3 | | A, AF | |
| South Dakota, U of, Vermillion | 5 | 6 | 4 | 3 | | A | • |
| **Tennessee** | | | | | | | |
| Austin Peay St U | 5 | 7 | 4 | 3 | | A | |
| Belmont U | 5 | 6 | 2 | 4 | B | A, AF, N | |
| Bethel Coll | 6 | 8 | 3 | 4 | P | | |
| Bryan Coll | 5 | 6 | 2 | 4 | | | |
| Carson-Newman Coll | 5 | 6 | 2 | 4 | B | A | |
| Christian Brothers U | 5 | 6 | 2 | 4 | RC | A, AF, N | |
| Cumberland U | N/A | N/A | 3 | 4 | | | |
| David Lipscomb U | 5 | 6 | 3 | 4 | CC | A, AF, N | |

| | Selectivity | SAT/ACT | Tuition | Enrollment | Religious affiliation | Military training | Phi Beta Kappa |
|---|---|---|---|---|---|---|---|
| East Tennessee St U | 4 | 7 | 4 | 3 | | A | |
| Fisk U | N/A | N/A | 2 | N/A | | A, AF, N | • |
| Free Will Baptist Bible Coll | 5 | 8 | 4 | 4 | B | A, AF | |
| Freed-Hardeman U | 5 | 6 | 3 | 4 | CC | | |
| Johnson Bible Coll | 5 | 7 | 4 | 4 | OC | | |
| King Coll | 5 | 6 | 2 | 4 | P | A | |
| Lane Coll | 6 | 9 | 3 | 4 | MT | | |
| Lee Coll | N/A | N/A | 3 | 4 | CG | | |
| LeMoyne-Owen Coll | N/A | N/A | 3 | 4 | OC | A, AF, N | |
| Lincoln Memorial U | 5 | 6 | 3 | 4 | | | |
| Maryville Coll | 5 | 6 | 1 | 4 | P | | |
| Memphis Coll of Art | N/A | 8 | 2 | 4 | | | |
| Memphis, U of | 5 | 6 | 4 | 3 | | A, AF, N | • |
| Middle Tennessee St U | 5 | 7 | 4 | 2 | | A, AF | |
| Milligan Coll | 4 | 5 | 2 | 4 | ND | A | |
| Rhodes Coll | 2 | 4 | 1 | 4 | P | A, AF | • |
| South, U of the | 2 | 4 | 1 | 4 | EP | | • |
| Southern C of Seventh-day Adventists | 5 | 6 | 2 | 4 | AD | | |
| Tennessee St U | 5 | 7 | 4 | 3 | | A, AF, N | • |
| Tennessee Tech U | 5 | 6 | 4 | 3 | | A | |
| Tennessee Wesleyan Coll | 6 | 8 | 2 | 4 | MT | | |
| Tennessee, U of, Chattanooga | 5 | 6 | 4 | 3 | | A | • |
| Tennessee, U of, Knoxville | 5 | 6 | 4 | 2 | | A, AF | • |
| Tennessee, U of, Martin | 5 | 7 | 4 | 3 | | A | • |
| Trevecca Nazarene Coll | 6 | 8 | 3 | 4 | CN | A, AF, N | |
| Tusculum Coll | 5 | 8 | 2 | 4 | P | | |
| Union U | 5 | 6 | 3 | 4 | B | | |
| Vanderbilt U | 2 | 4 | 1 | 3 | | A, AF, N | • |

## Texas

| | Selectivity | SAT/ACT | Tuition | Enrollment | Religious affiliation | Military training | Phi Beta Kappa |
|---|---|---|---|---|---|---|---|
| Abilene Christian U | 5 | 7 | 2 | 4 | CC | A | |
| Angelo St U | 4 | 6 | 4 | 3 | | AF | |
| Austin Coll | 5 | 6 | 1 | 4 | P | | |
| Baylor U | 3 | 5 | 3 | 3 | B | AF | • |
| Concordia Lutheran Coll | 5 | 7 | 4 | 4 | L | A, AF | • |
| Dallas Baptist U | 5 | 6 | 3 | 4 | B | A, AF | |
| Dallas, U of | 2 | 4 | 1 | 4 | RC | A, AF | • |
| DeVry Inst of Tech | N/A | N/A | 3 | 4 | | | |
| East Texas Baptist U | 4 | 7 | 3 | 4 | B | A | |
| East Texas St U | 5 | 7 | 4 | 3 | | | • |
| Hardin-Simmons U | 5 | 6 | 3 | 4 | B | A | |
| Houston Baptist U | 5 | 6 | 2 | 4 | B | A, N | |
| Houston, U of | 4 | 5 | 4 | 2 | | A, N | • |
| Houston, U of, Downtown | N/A | N/A | 4 | 4 | | A, N | |
| Howard Payne U | 5 | 7 | 3 | 4 | B | A | |
| Huston-Tillotson Coll | 5 | 8 | 3 | 4 | | | |
| Incarnate Word Coll | 5 | 6 | 2 | 4 | RC | A | • |
| Jarvis Christian Coll | 6 | 9 | 4 | 4 | DC | | • |
| Lamar U | 5 | 8 | 4 | 3 | | A | |
| LeTourneau U | 4 | 5 | 2 | 4 | ND | | |
| Lubbock Christian U | 6 | 7 | 3 | 4 | CC | A, AF | |
| Mary Hardin-Baylor, U of | 6 | 7 | 3 | 4 | B | AF | |
| McMurry U | 4 | 7 | 3 | 4 | MT | A | |
| Midwestern St U | 4 | 7 | 4 | 4 | | | |
| North Texas, U of | 5 | 6 | 4 | 2 | | A, AF | |
| Northwood U - Texas Campus | 5 | 7 | 2 | 4 | | N | |

| | Selectivity | SAT/ACT | Tuition | Enrollment | Religious affiliation | Military training | Phi Beta Kappa |
|---|---|---|---|---|---|---|---|
| Our Lady of the Lake U | 6 | 7 | 2 | 4 | RC | A | |
| Prairie View A&M U | 5 | 8 | 4 | 3 | | A, N | |
| Rice U | 1 | 2 | 1 | 4 | | A, N | • |
| Sam Houston St U | 5 | 7 | 4 | 3 | | A | |
| Schreiner Coll | 4 | 7 | 2 | 4 | P | | |
| Southern Methodist U | 4 | 5 | 1 | 3 | MT | A, AF | • |
| Southwest Texas St U | 4 | 6 | 4 | 2 | | A, AF | |
| Southwestern Adventist Coll | 5 | 7 | 2 | 4 | AD | | |
| Southwestern Assemblies of God Coll | 6 | 7 | 4 | 4 | AG | | |
| Southwestern U | 2 | 4 | 1 | 4 | MT | | |
| St. Edward's U | 5 | 6 | 2 | 4 | RC | A, AF, N | |
| St. Mary's U | 5 | 6 | 2 | 4 | RC | A | |
| St. Thomas, U of | 3 | 5 | 2 | 4 | RC | A, N | |
| Stephen F. Austin St U | 5 | 7 | 4 | 3 | | A | • |
| Sul Ross St U | 6 | 9 | 4 | 4 | | | |
| Tarleton St U | 5 | 7 | 4 | 3 | | A | • |
| Texas A&M U - Kingsville | 5 | 9 | 4 | 3 | | A | |
| Texas A&M U, College Station | 3 | 5 | 4 | 1 | | A, AF, N | |
| Texas A&M U, Galveston | 5 | 6 | 4 | 4 | | N | |
| Texas Christian U | 4 | 5 | 2 | 3 | DC | A, AF | • |
| Texas Coll | N/A | N/A | 4 | 4 | OC | | |
| Texas Lutheran Coll | 5 | 6 | 2 | 4 | L | AF | |
| Texas Southern U | N/A | N/A | 4 | 3 | | | |
| Texas Tech U | 5 | 6 | 4 | 2 | | A, AF | • |
| Texas Wesleyan U | 4 | 7 | 3 | 4 | MT | A, AF | |
| Texas Woman's U | 5 | 7 | 4 | 4 | | A, AF | |
| Texas, U of, Arlington | 5 | 6 | 4 | 3 | | A, AF | |
| Texas, U of, Austin | 2 | 4 | 4 | 1 | | A, AF, N | • |
| Texas, U of, Dallas | 2 | 4 | 4 | 4 | | A, AF | |
| Texas, U of, El Paso | 5 | 8 | 4 | 3 | | A, AF | |
| Texas, U of, Permian Basin | 5 | 7 | 4 | 4 | | | |
| Texas, U of, San Antonio | 4 | 7 | 4 | 3 | | A, AF | |
| Trinity U | 2 | 3 | 1 | 4 | P | A, AF | • |
| Wayland Baptist U | 5 | 8 | 3 | 4 | B | | • |
| West Texas St U | N/A | N/A | 4 | 4 | | | |
| Wiley Coll | 6 | 8 | 3 | 4 | MT | | |
| **Utah** | | | | | | | |
| Brigham Young U | 2 | 4 | 4 | 1 | MM | A, AF | |
| Southern Utah U | 6 | 7 | 4 | 4 | | | |
| Utah St U | 5 | 6 | 4 | 2 | | A, AF | |
| Utah, U of | 5 | 6 | 4 | 2 | | A, AF, N | • |
| Weber St U | 6 | 8 | 4 | 3 | | A, AF, N | • |
| Westminster Coll of Salt Lake City | 5 | 6 | 2 | 4 | | A, AF, N | |
| **Vermont** | | | | | | | |
| Bennington Coll | 3 | 4 | 1 | 4 | | | |
| Burlington Coll | N/A | N/A | 2 | 4 | | | |
| Castleton St Coll | 5 | 7 | 4 | 4 | | | |
| Champlain Coll | 5 | 8 | 2 | 4 | | A, AF, N | |
| Goddard Coll | 5 | 6 | 1 | 4 | | | |
| Green Mountain Coll | 5 | 7 | 1 | 4 | | | • |
| Johnson St Coll | 5 | 6 | 4 | 4 | | | |
| Lyndon St Coll | 5 | 6 | 4 | 4 | | | |
| Marlboro Coll | 4 | 5 | 1 | 4 | | | |
| Middlebury Coll | 1 | 3 | 1 | 4 | | | • |
| Norwich U | 5 | 6 | 1 | 4 | | A, AF, N | |

| | Selectivity | SAT/ACT | Tuition | Enrollment | Religious affiliation | Military training | Phi Beta Kappa |
|---|---|---|---|---|---|---|---|
| Southern Vermont Coll | 4 | 7 | 2 | 4 | | | |
| St. Joseph, Coll of | 6 | 8 | 2 | 4 | RC | | |
| St. Michael's Coll | 4 | 5 | 1 | 4 | RC | A, AF | |
| Trinity Coll | 5 | 7 | 1 | 4 | RC | A, AF | |
| Vermont, U of | 4 | 5 | 3 | 3 | | A, AF | • |
| **Virginia** | | | | | | | |
| Averett Coll | 5 | 7 | 2 | 4 | B | | |
| Bluefield Coll | 4 | 7 | 2 | 4 | B | | |
| Bridgewater Coll | N/A | N/A | 1 | 4 | CB | | |
| Christendom Coll | 4 | 5 | 2 | 4 | RC | | |
| Christopher Newport U | 4 | 7 | 4 | 4 | | A | |
| Eastern Mennonite Coll | 5 | 6 | 2 | 4 | MN | | |
| Emory & Henry Coll | 5 | 6 | 2 | 4 | MT | | |
| Ferrum Coll | 5 | 7 | 2 | 4 | MT | | |
| George Mason U | 5 | 6 | 4 | 3 | | A, AF | |
| Hampden-Sydney Coll | 4 | 5 | 1 | 4 | P | A | • |
| Hampton U | 5 | 6 | 2 | 3 | | A, N | • |
| Hollins Coll | 4 | 5 | 1 | 4 | | | • |
| James Madison U | 2 | 4 | 4 | 3 | | A | |
| Liberty U | N/A | N/A | 3 | 3 | ND | A | |
| Longwood Coll | 5 | 6 | 4 | 4 | | A | |
| Lynchburg Coll | 5 | 7 | 1 | 4 | DC | | |
| Mary Baldwin Coll | 5 | 6 | 1 | 4 | P | A | • |
| Mary Washington Coll | 2 | 4 | 4 | 4 | | | • |
| Marymount U | 5 | 6 | 1 | 4 | RC | A | |
| Norfolk St U | N/A | N/A | 4 | 3 | | A, N | |
| Old Dominion U | 5 | 6 | 4 | 3 | | A, N | |
| Radford U | 4 | 7 | 4 | 3 | | A, N | • |
| Randolph-Macon Coll | 4 | 5 | 1 | 4 | MT | A | • |
| Randolph-Macon Woman's Coll | 4 | 5 | 1 | 4 | MT | A | • |
| Richmond, U of | 2 | 3 | 1 | 4 | B | A | • |
| Roanoke Coll | 4 | 5 | 1 | 4 | L | | |
| Shenandoah U | 5 | 6 | 1 | 4 | MT | | |
| St. Paul's Coll | 5 | 9 | 3 | 4 | EP | A | |
| Sweet Briar Coll | 4 | 5 | 1 | 4 | | A | • |
| Virginia Commonwealth U | 4 | 5 | 4 | 3 | | A | • |
| Virginia Intermont Coll | 5 | 7 | 2 | 4 | B | | |
| Virginia Military Inst | 5 | 6 | 4 | 4 | | A, AF, N | |
| Virginia Polytechnic Inst & St U | 3 | 5 | 4 | 2 | | A, AF, N | • |
| Virginia St U | N/A | N/A | 4 | 4 | | A | • |
| Virginia Union U | 6 | 9 | 4 | B | A | | |
| Virginia Wesleyan Coll | 4 | 5 | 1 | 4 | MT | | |
| Virginia, U of | 1 | 3 | 4 | 3 | | A, AF, N | • |
| Virginia, U of, Clinch Valley Coll | 5 | 7 | 4 | 4 | | | |
| Washington & Lee U | 1 | 3 | 1 | 4 | | | • |
| William & Mary, Coll of | 1 | 3 | 3 | 3 | | A | • |
| **Washington** | | | | | | | |
| Central Washington U | 4 | 7 | 4 | 3 | | A, AF | |
| City U | N/A | N/A | 3 | 4 | | | |
| Cornish Coll of the Arts | N/A | N/A | 1 | 4 | | | |
| Eastern Washington U | 5 | 7 | 4 | 3 | | A | |
| Evergreen St Coll | 4 | 5 | 4 | 4 | | | |
| Gonzaga U | 4 | 5 | 1 | 4 | RC | A | |
| Heritage Coll | N/A | N/A | 3 | 4 | | | |
| Northwest Coll | 5 | 6 | 3 | 4 | AG | | |

| | Selectivity | SAT/ACT | Tuition | Enrollment | Religious affiliation | Military training | Phi Beta Kappa |
|---|---|---|---|---|---|---|---|
| Pacific Lutheran U | 5 | 6 | 1 | 4 | L | A | |
| Puget Sound, U of | 2 | 4 | 1 | 4 | | A | • |
| Seattle Pacific U | 4 | 5 | 1 | 4 | MT | A, AF | |
| Seattle U | 5 | 6 | 1 | 4 | RC | A, AF, N | |
| St. Martin's Coll | 6 | 7 | 1 | 4 | RC | A | |
| Walla Walla Coll | 5 | 6 | 1 | 4 | AD | | |
| Washington St U | 5 | 6 | 4 | 2 | | A, AF, N | • |
| Washington, U of | 3 | 5 | 4 | 1 | | A, AF, N | • |
| Western Washington U | 5 | 6 | 4 | 3 | | | |
| Whitman Coll | 2 | 4 | 1 | 4 | | | • |
| Whitworth Coll | 3 | 5 | 1 | 4 | P | A | |
| **West Virginia** | | | | | | | |
| Alderson-Broaddus Coll | 4 | 7 | 1 | 4 | B | A, AF, N | |
| Bethany Coll | 5 | 6 | 1 | 4 | DC | | |
| Bluefield St Coll | 5 | 8 | 4 | 4 | | | |
| Charleston, U of | 4 | 7 | 2 | 4 | | A | |
| Concord Coll | 6 | 7 | 4 | 4 | | | |
| Davis & Elkins Coll | 5 | 7 | 2 | 4 | P | | |
| Fairmont St Coll | 5 | 8 | 4 | 3 | | A | |
| Glenville St Coll | 6 | 8 | 4 | 4 | | | |
| Marshall U | 6 | 7 | 4 | 3 | | A | |
| Salem-Teikyo U | 5 | 6 | 1 | 4 | | A, AF | |
| Shepherd Coll | 4 | 5 | 4 | 4 | | A, AF | |
| West Liberty St Coll | 5 | 7 | 4 | 4 | | | |
| West Virginia Inst of Tech | 6 | 7 | 4 | 4 | | A | |
| West Virginia St Coll | 5 | 9 | 4 | 4 | | A | |
| West Virginia U | 5 | 6 | 4 | 2 | | A, AF | • |
| West Virginia Wesleyan Coll | 5 | 6 | 1 | 4 | MT | | |
| Wheeling Jesuit Coll | 5 | 7 | 2 | 4 | RC | | |
| **Wisconsin** | | | | | | | |
| Alverno Coll | 4 | 7 | 2 | 4 | RC | A | |
| Beloit Coll | 2 | 4 | 1 | 4 | | | • |
| Cardinal Stritch Coll | 5 | 6 | 2 | 4 | RC | | |
| Carroll Coll | 5 | 7 | 1 | 4 | P | | |
| Carthage Coll | 5 | 6 | 1 | 4 | L | | |
| Concordia U Wisconsin | 5 | 6 | 2 | 4 | L | | |
| Edgewood Coll | 5 | 7 | 2 | 4 | RC | | |
| Lakeland Coll | 5 | 7 | 2 | 4 | C | | |
| Lawrence U | 2 | 4 | 1 | 4 | | | • |
| Marian Coll of Fond du Lac | 5 | 7 | 2 | 4 | RC | A | |
| Marquette U | 4 | 5 | 1 | 3 | RC | A, AF, N | • |
| Milwaukee Inst of Art & Design | N/A | N/A | 2 | 4 | | | |
| Milwaukee Sch of Engineering | 3 | 5 | 1 | 4 | | A, AF | |
| Mt Mary Coll | 4 | 7 | 2 | 4 | RC | | |
| Mt Senario Coll | 5 | 9 | 2 | 4 | | | |
| Northland Coll | 5 | 6 | 2 | 4 | C | | |
| Northwestern Coll | 4 | 5 | 4 | 4 | L | | |
| Ripon Coll | 4 | 5 | 1 | 4 | | A | • |
| Silver Lake Coll | 5 | 7 | 2 | 4 | RC | | |
| St. Norbert Coll | 4 | 5 | 1 | 4 | RC | A | |
| Viterbo Coll | 4 | 5 | 2 | 4 | RC | A | • |
| Wisconsin Lutheran Coll | 5 | 6 | 2 | 4 | L | | |
| Wisconsin, U of, Eau Claire | 5 | 6 | 4 | 3 | | | |
| Wisconsin, U of, Green Bay | 5 | 6 | 4 | 4 | | A | |
| Wisconsin, U of, LaCrosse | 4 | 6 | 4 | 3 | | A | |

| | Selectivity | SAT/ACT | Tuition | Enrollment | Religious affiliation | Military training | Phi Beta Kappa |
|---|---|---|---|---|---|---|---|
| Wisconsin, U of, Madison | 2 | 4 | 4 | 1 | | A, AF, N | • |
| Wisconsin, U of, Milwaukee | 5 | 6 | 4 | 3 | | | • |
| Wisconsin, U of, Oshkosh | 4 | 7 | 4 | 3 | | A | |
| Wisconsin, U of, Platteville | 4 | 5 | 4 | 3 | | | |
| Wisconsin, U of, River Falls | 4 | 6 | 4 | 3 | | | |
| Wisconsin, U of, Stevens Point | 4 | 6 | 4 | 3 | | A | |
| Wisconsin, U of, Stout | 5 | 7 | 4 | 3 | | | |
| Wisconsin, U of, Superior | 5 | 6 | 4 | 4 | | AF | |
| Wisconsin, U of, Whitewater | 4 | 7 | 4 | 3 | | A | |

## Wyoming

| | Selectivity | SAT/ACT | Tuition | Enrollment | Religious affiliation | Military training | Phi Beta Kappa |
|---|---|---|---|---|---|---|---|
| Wyoming, U of | 5 | 6 | 4 | 3 | | A, AF | • |

## Canada

| | Selectivity | SAT/ACT | Tuition | Enrollment | Religious affiliation | Military training | Phi Beta Kappa |
|---|---|---|---|---|---|---|---|
| Alberta, U of | N/A | N/A | 3 | 1 | | | |
| British Columbia, U of | N/A | N/A | 3 | 1 | | | |
| Calgary, U of | N/A | N/A | 3 | 2 | | | |
| Carleton U | N/A | N/A | 1 | 2 | | | |
| Concordia U | N/A | N/A | 2 | 3 | | | |
| McGill U | N/A | N/A | 2 | 2 | | | |
| Ottawa, U of | N/A | N/A | 1 | 2 | | | |
| Toronto, U of | N/A | N/A | 1 | 1 | | | |
| Waterloo, U of | N/A | N/A | 2 | 2 | | | |
| Western Ontario, U of | N/A | N/A | 2 | 1 | | | |
| York U | N/A | N/A | 2 | 1 | | | |

# Index of Colleges and Universities

## A



## B



## C

## D



## E



## F

## G



## H



## I



## J



## K



## L

## M



## N

# O



# P



# Q



# R



# S

# T

# U



# V



# W



# X



# Y